S0-AEU-787

Greek-English Lexicon

Oxford University Press, Amen House, London E.C.4

GLASGOW NEW YORK TORONTO MELBOURNE WELLINGTON
BOMBAY CALCUTTA MADRAS CAPE TOWN

Geoffrey Cumberlege, Publisher to the University

A
Greek-English Lexicon

COMPILED BY

HENRY GEORGE LIDDELL D.D.
1811–1898
Dean of Christ Church

AND

ROBERT SCOTT D.D.
1811–1887
Master of Balliol College; Dean of Rochester

A New Edition

Revised and Augmented throughout by

SIR HENRY STUART JONES D.LITT.
1867–1939
Fellow of the British Academy; Camden Professor of Ancient History
Fellow of Trinity and Brasenose Colleges

WITH THE ASSISTANCE OF

RODERICK McKENZIE M.A.
1887–1937
Fereday Fellow of St. John's College

AND WITH THE CO-OPERATION OF MANY SCHOLARS

Volume I: α—κώψ

OXFORD
AT THE CLARENDON PRESS

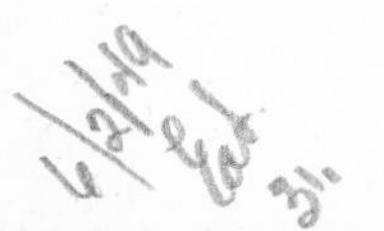

First edition published 1843
Second edition 1845
Third edition 1849
Fourth edition 1855
Fifth edition 1861
Sixth edition 1869
Seventh edition 1882
Reprinted 1885, 1890 (*twice*)
Eighth edition 1897
Reprinted 1901, 1908, 1922, 1928
New (ninth) edition completed 1940
Reprinted 1948

PRINTED IN GREAT BRITAIN
AT THE UNIVERSITY PRESS, OXFORD
BY CHARLES BATEY, PRINTER TO THE UNIVERSITY

PREFACE 1925

MORE than eighty years have passed since the first edition of the famous Lexicon upon which the present work is based was published by the Clarendon Press. Henry George Liddell and Robert Scott—the latter a Craven and Ireland Scholar—were both placed in the First Class in the Oxford list of 1833, both having been born in 1811. In 1835 Scott became a Fellow of Balliol and in the following year Liddell was elected to a Studentship of Christ Church. It appears that Mr. Talboys, an Oxford bookseller and publisher, first approached Scott with a proposal that a Greek-English Lexicon, based on that of Franz Passow, should be compiled, and that Scott made his acceptance conditional on the consent of Liddell to join in the work; at any rate, it was Talboys who first undertook the publication, which was taken over after his retirement by the Clarendon Press. There is, however, some ground for thinking that William Sewell, who had been an examiner in the Schools of 1833, suggested the idea to Liddell and Scott; and Liddell mentions in his correspondence the encouragement which the project received from Dean Gaisford.

The Lexicon of Passow, which the Oxford scholars took as the basis of their work, was itself founded upon that of Johann Gottlob Schneider, the editor of Theophrastus, the first edition of which had appeared in 1797–8. Passow had laid down, in his Essay on *Zweck, Anlage, und Ergänzung griechischer Wörterbücher*, published in 1812, the canons by which the lexicographer should be guided, amongst which the most important was the requirement that citations should be chronologically arranged in order to exhibit the history of each word and its uses. In obedience to this principle, Passow based his work on a special study of the Early Epic vocabulary, and the relatively full treatment of Homeric usage is a legacy bequeathed by him to Liddell and Scott which has persisted throughout the successive editions of their work. The first edition of his Lexicon appeared in 1819, and his expressed intention was to expand the work gradually by incorporating successively the results of special studies of Early Lyric Poetry, the Ionic Prose of Herodotus and Hippocrates, the Attic dramatists, and the Attic Prose writers: but little change was made in his second and third editions (1825 and 1827), and the fourth (1831), in which the Early Lyric poets and Herodotus received fuller recognition, was the first in which he felt himself at liberty to omit the name of Schneider from his title-page and also the last to appear in his lifetime. He died in 1833 in his forty-seventh year.

In the meantime two attempts had been made to adapt the *Thesaurus Linguae Graecae* of Henri Estienne to modern uses. The first of these was the result of the activities of Abraham Valpy, and was largely the work of E. H. Barker of Trinity College, Cambridge. It was completed in nine folio volumes, published in 1819–28, and reproduced the text of Stephanus' *Thesaurus*, interlarded with a mass of copious but ill-digested information. The first volume met with vigorous and not undeserved criticism on the part of Bishop Blomfield in an article in the *Quarterly Review* (vol. xxii, pp. 302 ff.) which is marred by a lavish display of *odium philologicum*. The editors, however, profited by the Bishop's strictures, and his prophecy that a work in which 139 columns were devoted to the word ἄγαλμα would run to fifty volumes and attain to completion in 1889 was signally falsified. The work labours under the serious disadvantage of retaining the etymological arrangement of Stephanus,[1] which forces the reader to make a laborious search for any compound or derived word.

This mistake was avoided by the compilers of the Paris *Thesaurus*, the publication of which was begun in 1831 by Firmin-Didot, and was placed under the general editorship of Karl Benedict Hase. This enterprise was also subjected to criticism in the *Quarterly Review* (vol. li, pp. 144 ff.) by J. R. Fishlake (the translator of Buttmann's *Lexilogus*) on the ground of its unwieldy bulk; but the association of the brothers Wilhelm and Ludwig Dindorf at an early stage of the work[2] enabled it to be carried through in thirty-four years, and its vast collections of material, though often ill-arranged and unevenly treated, were largely drawn upon by Liddell and Scott in their successive editions.

The first of these appeared in 1843; it was a quarto volume of 1,583 pages, priced at 42*s.*, and 6,000 copies were printed. A second, revised and enlarged, was called for in 1845, and the editors acknowledged their indebtedness to the German lexicon of Wilhelm Pape, which had appeared almost simultaneously with their own. In 1849 a third edition, corrected, but not substantially enlarged, was published, and six years later came the fourth, revised throughout. This marks a considerable advance on its predecessors, and much additional material was inserted; but the writers specially recognized were still chiefly those of the early classical period, including the Lyric poets, the authors of the Hippocratean writings, and the Attic orators. The editors now felt justified in omitting the name of Passow from their title-page. Eight thousand copies of this edition were printed, and the price was reduced to 30*s.* After another interval of six years the fifth edition, 'revised and augmented', appeared in 1861, and use was made of the greatly enlarged fifth edition of Passow, published by Valentin Rost and Friedrich Palm and completed in 1857, while the philological information was recast in the light of G. Curtius' *Griechische Etymologie* (1858). There were 10,000 copies of this edition, priced at 31*s.* 6*d.* The sixth is dated in 1869; it was again considerably augmented, the number of pages being increased from 1,644 to 1,865, and the verbal forms were more fully given with the aid of Veitch's *Greek Verbs, irregular and defective* (2nd ed., 1866). Of this edition 15,000 copies were printed, and the price was raised to 36*s.* Fourteen years later appeared a seventh edition, revised by Liddell, whose Preface is dated October 1882; the page was enlarged, and this made a reduction in the number to 1,776 possible. Bonitz's Index to Aristotle (1870) and Roehl's Index to *CIG* (1877) were largely drawn upon, and help was received from American scholars—Professors Drisler, Goodwin, and Gildersleeve—especially in regard to the particles and the technical terms of Attic law. This edition was stereotyped, and from time to time reprinted. Finally, in 1897, there was published an eighth edition, in which such corrections were made as could be inserted without altering the pagination. This made it impossible to take full account of such new sources as the Ἀθηναίων Πολιτεία, but there was a short list of Addenda, containing references to this work and to inscriptions published in the *Journal of Hellenic Studies*. Liddell appears to have been engaged for some years after the publication of the seventh edition on a lexicographical study of inscriptions; Sir William Thiselton-Dyer has kindly placed at my disposal two volumes of an interleaved edition of the abridged Lexicon in which his collections of material, largely drawn from the *Corpus Inscriptionum Atticarum* and Roehl's *Inscriptiones Graecae Antiquissimae*, are contained; but he seems to have laid the work aside in his later years, and he died in 1898, at the age of 87, a few months after the appearance of the eighth edition.

[1] In 1812 Passow himself had advocated the retention of Stephanus' arrangement; but he fortunately abandoned it in favour of the alphabetical principle.

[2] Their names appeared on the title-page of Part IV (containing β), which appeared concurrently with the second half of α.

Some five years later the Delegates of the Clarendon Press were invited to consider the revision of the Lexicon with a view to the incorporation of the rapidly growing material supplied by newly discovered texts on stone and papyrus, for which room might be found by the adoption of more compendious methods of reference; and a conference took place in March 1903, for which Ingram Bywater prepared a memorandum on the projected revision, advice being sought from Henry Jackson, Sir Richard Jebb, J. E. B. Mayor, and Arthur Sidgwick. The Delegates received the project favourably and it was hoped that Mr. Sidgwick might be able to act as editor. Contributions were invited in his name and a fair amount of material was collected, including a large number of notes and suggestions by Professor Leeper of Melbourne. Amongst other English and American scholars whose contributions were of considerable extent may be named the Rev. M. A. Bayfield and Prof. C. J. Goodwin, and particularly Mr. Herbert W. Greene, of whose services to the Lexicon more will be said presently. Mr. Sidgwick was, however, prevented by his duties as a teacher and afterwards by the failure of his health from commencing the work of revision.

In the meantime two more ambitious schemes had been initiated. At the second general assembly of the International Association of Academies, held in London in May 1904, Sir Richard Jebb submitted on behalf of the British Academy a scheme for the compilation of a new Thesaurus of Ancient Greek up to the early part of the seventh century A.D.; and after a discussion in which the difficulty and magnitude of the enterprise were emphasized[1] a Committee of Inquiry, consisting of Sir R. C. Jebb, Professors Diels, Gomperz, Heiberg, Krumbacher, Leo, and M. Perrot, with power to co-opt, was appointed to consider method, means, and preliminary questions in connexion with the proposal. In 1905 Prof. P. Kretschmer was added to the Committee, which drafted a memorandum on the question of establishing a periodical '*Archiv*' and an office for the collection of slips. At the close of the year Jebb, who had acted as Chairman, died, and was replaced in 1906 by Gomperz, while Bywater was added to the Committee, which, at a meeting held at Vienna in May, decided to constitute itself a permanent and independent body.

The difficulties of the project had been incisively stated by Diels in an article published in the *Neue Jahrbücher* for 1905,[2] in the course of which he wrote as follows:

> Any one who bears in mind the bulk of Greek literature, which is at least 10 times as great [as that of Latin], its dialectical variations, its incredible wealth of forms, the obstinate persistence of the classical speech for thousands of years down to the fall of Constantinople, or, if you will, until the present day: who knows, moreover, that the editions of almost all the Greek classics are entirely unsuited for the purposes of slipping, that for many important writers no critical editions whatever exist: and who considers the state of our collections of fragments and special Lexica, will see that at the present time all the bases upon which a Greek Thesaurus could be erected are lacking.
>
> But even if we were to assume that we possessed such editions and collections from Homer down to Nonnus, or (as Krumbacher proposed in London) down to Apostolius, and further that they had all been worked over, slipped, or excerpted by a gigantic staff of scholars, and that a great house had preserved and stored the thousands of boxes, whence would come the time, money, and power to sift these millions of slips and to bring Νοῦς into this Chaos? Since the proportion of Latin to Greek Literature is about 1 : 10, the office work of the Greek Thesaurus would occupy at least 100 scholars. At their head there would have to be a general editor, who, however, would be more of a general than an editor. And if this editorial cohort were really to perform its task punctually, and if the Association of Academies, which, as is well known, has not a penny of its own, were to raise the ten million marks necessary for the completion of (say) 120 volumes; and if scholars were to become so opulent that they could afford to purchase the *Thesaurus Graecus* for (say) 6,000 marks—how could one read and use such a monstrosity?

[1] Krumbacher was anxious to include Byzantine Greek in the ambit of the new Thesaurus.

[2] p. 692; Diels had already expressed his views in his *Elementum* (1899), p. ix sqq.

Diels's own solution was the compilation, not of one, but of ten Thesauri, representing the main branches of Greek Literature, Epic, Lyric, Tragic, Comic, Philosophical, Historical, Mathematical and Technical, Medical, Grammatical, and Jewish-Christian, each of which, he thought, would equal the Latin Thesaurus in bulk![1]

The majority of the members of the Committee, however, were still of the opinion that a foundation should be laid for the Thesaurus by the preparation of full slips for the whole of Greek literature on the method which had been adopted for the Latin Thesaurus, and made a recommendation in this sense to the third assembly of the International Association of Academies, held at Vienna in May 1907. The Association invited the British Academy (represented at Vienna by Bywater) to prepare a specimen for submission to the meeting which was to be held in 1910; but a Committee appointed by the Academy to consider this proposal, consisting of Bywater, H. Jackson, S. H. Butcher, and Sir F. Kenyon, reported in the following sense:

> They (the Committee) are not convinced that the *modus operandi* suggested for the projected Greek Thesaurus is the best possible. They think (*a*) that the Latin Thesaurus would not provide a proper scale and model; (*b*) that the mechanical slipping of Greek texts, besides being as is confessed a huge undertaking, would not serve as a satisfactory basis, inasmuch as it would give results difficult to manipulate and of questionable value. Rather, as recommended by M. Paul Meyer at the discussion in May 1904, they would suggest as a more promising plan that of the *New English Dictionary*.

In the face of this report, the British Academy felt that it was useless to proceed with the scheme, and it was tacitly dropped.

At about the date when the project of a *Thesaurus Graecus* was finally abandoned, a proposal was made by a group of Greek scholars for the preparation of a Lexicon of the Greek language—Ancient, Medieval, and Modern—the publication of which should commence in 1921 as a memorial of the Centenary of Greek independence. The Greek Government took the scheme under its patronage, and in November 1908 a Commission was appointed by royal decree, at the head of which was the veteran scholar Kontos, who was succeeded on his death by Hatzidakis. Krumbacher, in one of his latest articles in the *Byzantinische Zeitschrift*,[2] criticized the project, and advised the Greek scholars to confine themselves in the first instance to the Modern tongue; and though this recommendation was not, as it seems, formally adopted, the preliminary publications of the Commission consist mainly in a series of studies of the modern dialects, which appear as supplements to Ἀθηνᾶ, and it would appear that a Lexicon of Medieval and Modern Greek is contemplated in the first instance.

When it became clear that Mr. Sidgwick would be unable to carry out the revision of the Lexicon, the Delegates of the Clarendon Press invited me to undertake the work, which I did in the autumn of 1911, having been elected by Trinity College to a Research Fellowship which I continued to hold (except for a short period during the war) until my election to the Camden Professorship of Ancient History at the close of 1919. It was hoped at first that the preparation of a revised text might be completed in five years; but before the work had progressed very far it became clear that a more drastic revision than was suggested by a cursory examination would be necessary. Moreover, such large gaps (especially in technical subjects) remained to be filled if the new edition was to be adequate to the needs of modern scholarship—to say nothing of the large mass of new material awaiting incorporation—that the time allotted was evidently insufficient for more than a preliminary revision of Liddell and Scott's text, which would afterwards have to be worked up into a largely re-written Lexicon with the contributions of specialists and others whose help might be enlisted.

[1] A similar suggestion had been made more than half a century earlier by F. A. Wolf in his *Vorlesungen über die Altertumswissenschaft* i p. 187.

[2] xviii (1909), 708 ff.

Such assistance has been placed at my disposal with a generosity for which I cannot find words adequate to express my gratitude; nor would it be possible within the limits of this preface to enumerate all those who have supplied corrections of, or suggested improvements in, the text of the eighth edition. Mention, however, must be made of those who undertook special researches in aid of the revision.

Taking the more technical subjects first, the most laborious task was that of revising and amplifying the vocabulary of Medicine. It is interesting to recall the fact that many years ago the late Dr. Greenhill, of Trinity College, projected a Lexicon of Greek Medicine, for which he collected a certain amount of material in the shape of references arranged on slips and worked up a small portion of it in a series of articles in the *Medico-Chirurgical Journal.* He proposed to the Delegates that he should collaborate with M. Daremberg in preparing his Lexicon, but the suggestion did not meet with their approval, and Dr. Greenhill proceeded no further; his collection of slips passed after his death into the possession of the Royal College of Surgeons. It was clearly necessary that the field should be resurveyed, and I was fortunate enough to secure the services of Dr. E. T. Withington, who took up residence in Oxford and has worked untiringly on this difficult subject. He has read for lexicographical purposes the whole of the extant remains of Greek medical literature, and there is scarcely a page in the Lexicon which does not bear traces of his handiwork.[1]

For the subject of Botany, again, expert assistance was indispensable. Sir William Thiselton-Dyer, F.R.S., has for a long while been collecting material for a Glossary of Greek plants, and the publication of Max Wellmann's edition of Dioscorides, completed in 1914, has furnished a reliable critical text of the most important author in this branch of literature. Sir William Dyer has been most generous in placing the results of his study of Greek plant-names at my disposal, and his identifications are not likely to be disputed. A number of them had already been communicated to Sir Arthur Hort for use in his edition of Theophrastus' *Historia Plantarum.*[2]

The province of Greek Mathematics belongs in a special sense to Sir Thomas Heath, F.R.S., whose *History of Greek Mathematics* and editions of Euclid, Apollonius of Perga, Aristarchus of Samos, and Diophantus mark him out as the first authority in this subject. He has found leisure to contribute a large number of notes of the greatest value on Greek mathematical terms. To take an obvious instance, it will be seen that the eighth edition of Liddell and Scott recognizes the word ἀσύμπτωτος only in a Medical sense illustrated by a quotation (not quite accurately translated) from Hippocrates; Sir Thomas Heath has supplied the materials for a history of the use from which the modern *asymptote* is derived.

In the domain of Natural History Professor D'Arcy Thompson's help has enabled me to correct a number of mistakes made by previous lexicographers. His *Glossary of Greek Birds* has been in constant use, and his version of the *Historia Animalium* in the Oxford translations of Aristotle to a large extent supplies the want of a glossary of the Animal Kingdom.

In the field of Astronomy and Astrology I have to thank Mr. Edmund J. Webb for reading the *Almagest* of Ptolemy and other astronomical writings, and thereby greatly increasing the accuracy of the Lexicon in these matters. For the Astrological vocabulary a glossary was drafted by the Rev. C. T. Harley Walker, and the ground has also (as above mentioned) been worked over by Dr. Withington; but in this thorny subject difficulties frequently arise, for which Professor A. E. Housman, when appealed to, never fails to provide a solution.

[1] Dr. Withington has also found time to deal with the Alchemists and Astrologers, including the extensive collections of the *Catalogus Codicum Astrologorum.*

[2] Sir Arthur Hort has himself rendered aid in the difficult task of interpreting the Greek of Theophrastus.

Amongst technical writings must be classed those of the tacticians and military engineers. The first were studied for my purposes by the late Mr. C. D. Chambers; the latter group, whose works are often very difficult of interpretation, have been read (together with other authors) by Mr. F. W. Hall.

Besides these highly specialized branches of study, there were large tracts of literature which it was needful to explore, but which a single editor could not hope to cover unaided. In the matter of papyri, for example, he might be able to deal with the newly recovered literary texts such as the *Ἀθηναίων Πολιτεία*, Bacchylides, Herodas, Cercidas, and the recently found fragments of the Early Lyric poets and Callimachus, but the great mass of non-literary papyri, especially those concerned with the technique of law and administration in Ptolemaic and Roman Egypt, required to be dealt with by those specially versed in the new science of papyrology. The Ptolemaic papyri were therefore read, partly by Mr. Edgar Lobel (who dealt with the Petrie collection) and partly by Professor Jouguet of Lille, those of the Roman period by Professor Martin of Geneva. Mr. H. Idris Bell of the British Museum has supplied valuable notes on recent papyrological publications and on unedited documents in the British Museum Collection.[1] For the vocabulary of the Inscriptions little could be done by the editor except to revise the existing references to Boeckh's *Corpus Inscriptionum Graecarum*—no light task, seeing that so many of the stones have been re-examined and may be studied in improved texts—and to supplement these corrected citations by illustrations from collections such as those of Dittenberger[2] or Michel or the *Griechische Dialektinschriften*, with the aid of Herwerden's *Lexicon Suppletorium*, a work unfortunately marred by constant inaccuracy of reference, which it is charitable to ascribe to lack of the minute care required in lexicographical proof-reading. I was therefore compelled to invoke the aid of Mr. M. N. Tod, to whom I owe an incalculable debt for his services in this field. Mr. Tod has for several years read with an eye to the improvement of the Lexicon every epigraphical publication which has appeared, such for example as the later volumes of the *Inscriptiones Graecae*, Cagnat's *Inscriptiones Graecae ad res Romanas pertinentes*, the *Tituli Asiae Minoris*, and the special publications of the inscriptions of Delphi, Ephesus, Magnesia, Miletus, and Priene, and has excerpted the whole of the periodical literature in which inscriptions are to be found, so that it is hard to believe that any new material of real importance which has accrued since 1911 can have escaped his methodical scrutiny. I have also received help in epigraphical matters from Professor M. Cary and Miss C. A. Hutton.

Turning to Literature proper, it soon became clear that while the references to Plato and Aristotle needed careful revision and some amplification,[3] the terminology of the later schools of Philosophy had never been adequately treated by lexicographers. Neither Usener's *Epicurea* nor von Arnim's *Stoicorum Veterum Fragmenta* possesses an index; and Mr. (now Professor) J. L. Stocks generously undertook to remedy this defect, and to supply me with a vocabulary of the important technical terms of the Stoic and Epicurean schools (including in his survey of the latter such later works as the tracts or other remains of Philodemus, Polystratus, Demetrius Lacon, Diogenianus, and Diogenes of Oenoanda). Unfortunately his work was interrupted by the Great War, and on his return from service Mr. Stocks found himself unable to work up the material which he had collected within the

[1] The first part of Preisigke's *Wörterbuch der griechischen Papyrusurkunden* appeared after the sheets of Part I had been printed off, but has been used for Addenda.

[2] The appearance of a third edition of the *Sylloge Inscriptionum Graecarum*, completed in 1924, has necessitated the alteration of a large number of references. The pitfalls which beset the path of the lexicographer may be exemplified by the fact that on the first revision the word ἀπόπλωσις was illustrated by *SIG*²929.127, and this was altered by the concordance-table to *SIG*³685.127: fortunately it was discovered in time that the word had disappeared in the later text!

[3] Bonitz's *Index to Aristotle* and Ast's *Lexicon Platonicum* are no longer all-sufficing guides. Such words as μορυχώτερον (which should be read in Arist. *Metaph.* 987ᵃ10) and τεράμων (which there is reason to think once stood in the text of Pl. *Sph.* 221a, though it is not mentioned by Burnet) are addenda.

necessary limits of time. His notes on Stoic terminology were therefore transferred to Mr. A. C. Pearson, who carried the work a stage further, but found, after his appointment to the Regius Professorship of Greek at Cambridge, that he would not have time to complete it. Professor E. V. Arnold of Bangor, who is retiring from his post, hopes to find the leisure necessary for this much-needed work.

In dealing with the vocabulary of Epicurus and his school Mr. Stocks found that for an adequate treatment it would be necessary to obtain access to the transcripts of the fragments of the περὶ φύσεως and other writings made by Wilhelm Crönert and used by him in his revision of Passow's Lexicon, of which more will be said presently. Crönert (who had spent some time in England as a prisoner of war in 1917–19) very kindly acceded to a request which I made to him at the suggestion of von Wilamowitz-Moellendorff and generously placed his transcripts at the disposal of Mr. Stocks, who visited him in Germany and made full use of this valuable material.

The peculiar vocabulary of the later Platonists has not hitherto received the attention which it deserves in Lexica; it is worthy of note that even in the seventh edition (1883) Liddell and Scott stated that the word μετεμψύχωσις (which is absent from the Paris Thesaurus and appears in Rost and Palm with the note 'Clem.Al. (?)') 'seems to be of no authority', though in the eighth edition an example of its use is cited from Proclus' Commentary on the *Republic* of Plato. As a matter of fact, this word can be quoted from ten authors besides Proclus.[1] Professor Burnet, who in his edition of the *Phaedo* drew attention to some of these passages, added: 'Hippolytus, Clement and other Christian writers say μετενσωμάτωσις ("reincarnation") which is accurate but cumbrous'; but the implication that this word belongs to Patristic Greek is misleading. It is found in Plotinus and in later Platonists such as Hierocles and Proclus. Again, such a characteristic use as that of ἄτοπος in the philosophical sense of 'non-spatial' has escaped lexicographers. In dealing with this branch of literature I have received help from various scholars, notably Professor A. E. Taylor; and the late Mr. M. G. Davidson read the *Enneads* of Plotinus, the abstruse work of Damascius περὶ ἀρχῶν, and other treatises. The extant commentaries on the works of Aristotle of course belong to this school of thought, and Mr. W. D. Ross kindly undertook to supply notes on their vocabulary with the aid of the excellent indices of the Berlin edition and with the collaboration of certain of the Oxford translators;[2] the bulk of this work, however, fell upon his own shoulders.

Another branch of literature demanding special study was that of the magical and mystical writings—the *Corpus Hermeticum*, the magical papyri, the *Tabellae Defixionum*, and such like. This field was carefully worked over by Mr. Walter Scott, whose notes dealt very fully with the difficult words often found in these sources.

For the New Testament the intensive study of theologians has done great things in recent times, and the results of their labours are readily accessible; for the ordinary purposes of revision such Lexica as those of Ebeling and Zorell are generally sufficient; while for the illustration of Biblical usage from Hellenistic and later Greek we have a most valuable aid in Moulton and Milligan's *Vocabulary of the Greek Testament*, which (within its natural limits) may almost be regarded as a Lexicon of the κοινή as a whole. I owe a deep debt of gratitude to Professor Milligan for supplying advance proofs of the *Vocabulary*, the fifth part of which has just been published. Prof. A. H. McNeile and the Rev. A. Llewellyn Davies have advised me in matters relating to the LXX, Hexapla, etc.

Turning to post-classical Greek literature in general, help was received from various scholars (amongst whom may be named Mr. Ronald Burn and Mr. C. E. Freeman, who excerpted several of the less familiar writers), but such merits as the new edition may

[1] D. S. 10. 6, Gal. 4. 763, Alex. Aphr. *de An.* 27. 18, Porph. *Abst.* 4. 16, Herm. ap. Stob. 1. 49. 69 (tit.), Sallust. 20, Hieronym. *Ep.* 124. 4, *Theol. Ar.* 40, Serv. ad Verg. *Aen.* 3. 68, Sch. Iamb. *Protr.* 14.

[2] Two of these, Mr. Erwin Webster and Mr. Gibson, lost their lives in the Great War.

possess in virtue of largely increased illustration and more accurate interpretation of the ancient texts will in the main be due to the self-effacing and monumental labours of Mr. Herbert W. Greene, sometime Fellow of Magdalen. Amongst the materials placed at my disposal when I began my editorial work in 1911 were twenty-four volumes of notes compiled by Mr. Greene as contributions to the Lexicography of authors mainly (though not by any means entirely) of post-Alexandrian date, including Lucian, the Anthology, all the later Epic poets, the *Scriptores Erotici*, Aelian, Philostratus, and others. From that time onwards Mr. Greene has not ceased to read and excerpt the remains of later Greek literature, including the works of practically every non-technical writer of importance from Polybius to Procopius. The twenty-four volumes have grown to nearly eighty, and many of the notes which they contain are elaborate dissertations constituting an important contribution to Classical Scholarship. Valuable aid has also been received from Professor W. A. Goligher, who read the minor Greek historians, Mr. J. M. Edmonds, who supplied a vocabulary of the Greek Lyric poets, Mr. J. H. A. Hart, who is compiling an *index verborum* to Philo, Professor A. W. Mair and Mr. M. T. Smiley, whose notes on Callimachus have been of great use, and other scholars, such as Professors J. A. Platt, A. Souter, R. L. Dunbabin, and W. L. Lorimer, Mr. T. W. Allen, Mr. A. H. Smith, Mr. G. Middleton, and the late Mr. G. E. Underhill, to all of whom special thanks are due. The advice of Mr. Edgar Lobel has been constantly sought and freely given, especially in regard to the remains of Early Lyric poetry and the ancient lexicographers.

The procedure of revision was briefly as follows. At the outset the Clarendon Press supplied a paste-up of the eighth edition in columns, and the first step was to note in the margin the essential alterations of the text and the most important additions. After this had been done, a second paste-up in columns was made, and the marginalia of the first were fused with newly accumulated material and recast in a form suitable for publication; but it was found that the copy thus produced would present great difficulties to the printer, and that a clean copy based on the use of short sections of Liddell and Scott's text treated as a proof was required. When I became Camden Professor at the beginning of 1920 it became necessary to provide me with assistance in my editorial work, and Mr. R. McKenzie of Trinity College (now Fereday Fellow of St. John's College) was appointed Assistant-Editor by the Delegates of the Press. Apart from his arduous labour in putting my drafts into final shape and in arranging and working in a large mass of accumulated material, Mr. McKenzie has been able to render inestimable service to the Lexicon on the philological side. After careful consideration it was decided that etymological information should be reduced to a minimum. A glance at Boisacq's *Dictionnaire étymologique de la langue grecque* will show that the speculations of etymologists are rarely free from conjecture; and the progress of comparative philology since the days of G. Curtius (whose *Griechische Etymologie* was the main source drawn upon by Liddell and Scott) has brought about the clearance of much rubbish but little solid construction. Some assured results, however, have been attained, and the etymologies presented in the text have in almost every case been approved by Mr. McKenzie.

The space required for the incorporation of new material without an excessive increase in the bulk of the Lexicon has been saved partly by abbreviations and compendious methods of printing, partly by certain limitations of scope. Liddell and Scott, though they originally intended their work to be a Lexicon of Classical Greek,[1] admitted a number of words from Ecclesiastical and Byzantine writers, for many of which no reference was given except the symbols 'Eccl.' and 'Byz.' After due consideration it has been decided to exclude both Patristic and Byzantine literature from the purview of the present edition. It would

[1] This appears from letters written in 1877 by Dean Liddell to Mr. Falconer Madan (who kindly placed them at my disposal) with reference to J. E. B. Mayor's well-known articles on Greek Lexicography in the *Journal of Philology*.

have manifestly been impossible to include more than a small and haphazard selection of words and quotations from these literatures, which would therefore have had to be treated quite differently from the remains of Classical Greek, where (it may be hoped) sufficient illustration has been given of the vocabulary and usage of all writers of importance, accompanied by precise and easily verifiable references. There is, moreover, in preparation a Lexicon of Patristic Greek (including Christian poetry and inscriptions) under the editorship of Dr. Darwell Stone, which will, it is hoped, be printed when the publication of the present work is concluded.[1] For the Byzantine vocabulary we shall have to wait for the Modern Greek Lexicon to which allusion has already been made, but it will hardly be denied that some time-limit was called for, and this has been fixed roughly at A. D. 600 in order to include the historians and poets of the reign of Justinian, though such writers as the scholiasts, grammarians, and others who preserve the fragmentary remains of ancient scholarship must naturally be taken into account in their own province.

The present volume will not challenge comparison in scale with the revision of Passow's *Wörterbuch der griechischen Sprache* by Wilhelm Crönert, of which three parts, extending as far as *ἀνά*, appeared in 1912-14. This monument of Herculean toil will, if and when it is completed (a consummation for which all lovers of learning will devoutly pray), bulk about three times as large as Liddell and Scott; in fact, this estimate may be exceeded if Crönert is able to carry out the plan foreshadowed in the preface to his second part, where he looks forward to the gradual expansion of his work as it proceeds (after the manner of Passow) by means of a fuller treatment of post-Classical Greek. Crönert's work has been criticized by Kretschmer,[2] who regards it as too ambitious in scope and unlikely to be completed within a reasonable period of time, and would prefer a Lexicon on a somewhat smaller scale as a preliminary to the *Thesaurus Linguae Graecae* which must remain for a long while to come a pious aspiration. It may be hoped that the present work will do something to supply this need, and that it may be found to possess some compensating advantages denied to the larger Lexicon of Crönert, such as the provision of exact references for every word cited from an author and fuller and more representative quotations from the later literature, e.g. from such authors as Plotinus.[3]

My best thanks are due to those scholars who are generously devoting their time to the reading of the proof-sheets and the verification of references, especially to the authors originally read by them for the purposes of the Lexicon. Some of these have already been named, such as Sir W. Thiselton-Dyer, Professors D'Arcy Thompson, A. E. Taylor, A. C. Pearson, and J. L. Stocks, Mr. Herbert Greene, Mr. Tod, Dr. Withington, Mr. Ross, and Mr. F. W. Hall. Lieut.-Col. Farquharson's scrutiny of the quotations from Plato and Aristotle is producing important results; and Messrs. C. and G. M. Cookson, Mr. W. W. How, and the Rev. W. Evans are doing valuable work in maintaining the standard of accuracy. The Editor's task is naturally heavy, especially in view of the fact that the progress of scholarship tends to make the text originally drafted for the Press out of date or to bring fresh material to light. Such publications as Ulrich Wilcken's *Urkunden der*

[1] Christian authors are of course frequently cited as the source of classical quotations, and such treatises as those of Porphyry and Julian *Against the Christians* are reconstructed from Patristic writings.

[2] In *Glotta* vi pp. 300 ff.

[3] A comparison of the art. ἀμφίβιος in Crönert-Passow with that of the present work will illustrate the difference of method. Crönert, on the other hand, gives the lexicographical tradition of the ancient grammarians very fully. For this it would not have been possible to find room; nor, indeed, has it yet been thoroughly sifted and critically edited. The deaths of Wentzel, Leopold Cohn, and Egenolff, and the migration of Bethe and Reitzenstein to more succulent pastures, have brought the two great enterprises of the firm of Teubner—the *Corpus Grammaticorum Graecorum* and that of the ancient Lexica—to a premature end. De Stefani's edition of the *Etymologicum Gudianum* is, however, in course of appearing, and it is understood that Drachmann is editing the remains of the Glossary of 'Cyril' (see Pauly-Wissowa, *Realencyclopädie* xii 175).

Ptolemäerzeit furnish more accurate readings of Papyri and necessitate changes or deletions,[1] and I must place on record my gratitude to Professor Wilcken for kindly undertaking to verify and correct references to documents in the yet unpublished portions of his work,[2] as also to Mr. J. U. Powell for permitting me to use and refer to the proofs of his *Collectanea Alexandrina,* shortly about to appear. Professor J. Bidez and Mr. A. D. Knox kindly sent me advanced proofs of the editions of the *Epistles of Julian* and of Herodas in which they have collaborated. The care and accuracy shown by the Press readers have been altogether exceptional.

It has, I hope, been made abundantly clear that the new edition of Liddell and Scott's Lexicon is in reality the work of many hands, and represents a great sacrifice of leisure and an earnest devotion to Greek learning on the part of the present generation of scholars, and that not in this country alone. I would fain hope that in the world of science at least (which has, or should have, no frontiers) it may further in some small degree the restoration of the comity of nations.

H. Stuart Jones.

[1] For example, ἀντιπατάσσω was cited by me from *PPar.* 40, but the reference was deleted from the proof when it was found that in *UPZ* 12 Wilcken read ὠνηλάται ὄντες for ἀντιπατάσσοντες!

[2] This should cause little inconvenience to the user of the Lexicon, as Part I of *UPZ* contains concordance-tables for the whole work.

POSTSCRIPT 1940

THE Delegates of the Oxford University Press, in issuing the tenth and last part of the revised edition of Liddell and Scott's Greek Lexicon, wish to express their deep gratitude to all who have assisted in carrying this undertaking to a conclusion. They greatly regret that neither the Editor Sir Henry Stuart Jones, who died on 29 June 1939, nor the Assistant Editor Mr. Roderick McKenzie, who died on 24 June 1937, survived to see the work completed. McKenzie saw the main body of the work to its end, and himself wrote the long article on *ὡς*; Sir Henry was at work on the Addenda and Corrigenda up to within a fortnight of his death and had almost put them into shape. The work done by these two men could not be overrated. Sir Henry was the ideal Editor; his wide range of knowledge and his exact scholarship, his persistent devotion to his task even in periods of ill health, his tactful assiduity in consulting experts and his skill in co-ordinating their results, gave the work at once its consistency and its elasticity. McKenzie, to whom fell the arrangement, in their ultimate form, of most of the articles, provided a fine complement; his great knowledge of comparative philology, his laborious accuracy, and his tireless patience, gave his contribution inestimable value.

In the Preface published in 1925 Stuart Jones sketched the history of the work up to the publication of *ἀποβαίνω*, and recorded the signal services given by many scholars to the work in its formative stages. To that nothing need now be added. But Jones went on to thank the scholars who were 'generously devoting their time to the reading of proof-sheets and the verification of references'. It is important that the nature of this work should be understood. The procedure adopted, when work was resumed after the Four Years' War, was this: McKenzie wrote out Jones's corrections on a 'paste-up' of the previous edition. This was the 'copy'; and fresh material was to some extent incorporated in it from time to time. But as succeeding sections of the alphabet were revised and set up in type, proofs were sent to the volunteer helpers, whose labours, in the event, went far beyond mere verification; in their hands and the editors' the work was very largely recast. The method has obvious advantages, and the peculiar excellences of the revised lexicon owe much to its adoption. But inevitably it prolonged the process of gestation. The period of publication, 1925–40, was actually longer than the period of copy-writing, 1911–24, even although the earlier period was interrupted by the war, and in the later period there were two editors instead of one.

Of those who were named in the original Preface as having embarked on the labour of proof-reading, some are dead: notably Sir William T. Thiselton-Dyer, A. C. Pearson, and Herbert Greene.[1] Others have lived to see the work to its end. These, and not these alone, have more than doubled the debt of gratitude which, fifteen years ago, Jones could not 'find words adequate to express'.

Unhappily neither editor lived to prepare a final list of acknowledgements. McKenzie died suddenly in 1937. Jones, though he lived to see the end in sight, left no material for the brief 'epilogue' which it had been agreed he should furnish. It would be impossible now to produce a complete or balanced account of the labours of the proof-readers and verifiers without undertaking inquiries which the circumstances of the time make difficult. The list which follows does not attempt discrimination. Special mention must, however, be made of the prolonged and arduous labours of Mr. M. N. Tod of Oriel College on the inscriptions; of Lt.-Col. A. S. L. Farquharson of University College on Plato and Aristotle;

[1] Greene's notebooks (see the 1925 Preface, p. x) are in the Bodleian.

of Dr. E. T. Withington of Balliol College on the medical writers; of Sir D'Arcy Thompson of St. Andrews on natural history; and of the late Sir Thomas Heath on mathematics and astrology.

The proofs were read also, in whole or in part, by the following: Mr. P. V. M. Benecke of Magdalen College; Mr. F. H. Colson of St. John's College, Cambridge; Mr. Christopher Cookson of Magdalen College; Prof. E. S. Forster of Sheffield University; Mr. E. T. D. Jenkins of University College, Aberystwyth; Mr. Edgar Lobel of the Queen's College; Mr. W. L. Lorimer of St. Andrews; Prof. J. F. Mountford of Liverpool University; Mr. Maurice Platnauer of Brasenose College; Sir David Ross, Provost of Oriel College; Prof. A. E. Taylor of Edinburgh; and by the late F. W. Hall, A. E. Housman, A. C. Pearson, J. A. Smith, and J. L. Stocks. As press reader from the beginning of the work Mr. T. Bruce has made a special contribution to its accuracy.

The Addenda and Corrigenda issued with the several parts have been greatly enlarged, and are now consolidated in a single list. Of these, the proofs were read by Dr. H. Idris Bell of the British Museum, Prof. G. R. Driver of Magdalen College, and Prof. Paul Maas of Königsberg, as well as by some of those who have been named above.

The Addenda owe much to the reviews and private communications of Dr. Ernest Harrison of Trinity College, Cambridge; of Prof. Maas; of Prof. R. Pfeiffer of Munich (it is noted with pleasure that both Prof. Maas and Prof. Pfeiffer are now resident in Oxford); of Prof. K. Latte of Hamburg, of Prof. W. Schmid of Tübingen; of Herr Pfarrer P. Katz of Coblenz, and of many other scholars.

Both in the Addenda and in the main work the principle of anonymity has been applied to original contributions that appear first in the Lexicon, and it was the intention of the Editors that those who made them should be free at any later time to claim their own discoveries.

Miss Margaret Alford, who bears an honoured name, helped Sir Henry Stuart Jones in the compilation of the Addenda, and since his death, with the collaboration of Professor Maas in the final stages, has performed the laborious duty of preparing the Addenda for Part 10 and of correcting proofs of the whole.

It is impossible now, as it was impossible in 1925, to name all who have contributed to the improvement of the great lexicon. The sacrifice of leisure, and the devotion to Greek learning, of which Jones then wrote, have been nobly sustained by a generation of scholars, and the monument of unselfish industry is at last complete.

CLARENDON PRESS, OXFORD.
June, 1940.

The revised edition of Liddell and Scott was published in ten parts between 1925 and 1940. These comprise the text of the dictionary from page 1 to page 2042, and are continuous except that there is a break at the end of κ to permit the work to be conveniently bound in two volumes.

With each of Parts 2–9 were issued, on separate leaves, Aids to the Reader including *Addenda et Corrigenda* and other matter. These have been consolidated either (1) in the new *Addenda et Corrigenda* (pages 2043–2111) which are placed at the end of the text, or (2) in the preliminary leaves issued with Part 10 to supersede those issued with Part I. The original separate leaves are therefore of historical and bibliographical interest only, and many will think it well to discard them.

The preliminary leaves to Part 1 contained Sir Henry Stuart Jones's Preface of 1925, and various Aids to the Reader. Of these, the Preface has been reprinted with Part 10, and the Aids are superseded by the corrected or consolidated lists, which also are issued with Part 10.

Subscribers who have already bound Parts 1–5, and the preliminary leaves of Part 1, in one volume, are advised to detach the preliminary leaves from Part 10 and prefix them to Part 6, that is to their second volume. They will remember, when using the work, that they must turn to the second volume if they wish to consult the lists of Authors, &c. in their latest form.

Subscribers who have not yet bound are recommended (unless they are sticklers for bibliographical perfection) to discard the original preliminary leaves, and all odd leaves issued since, and to place the new preliminary at the beginning of the book.

AIDS TO THE READER

A. LISTS OF ABBREVIATIONS, ETC.

THE lists which follow are designed to make it easy for the reader to trace the quotations given in the Lexicon. The general list of abbreviations (V) gives references, where needed, to one or other of the lists (I–IV) in which the expansion will be found; but the abbreviated names of authors have not been inserted in List V unless their alphabetical position in List I is different from that of the full name (e.g. A. = Aeschylus). List V also contains the expansion of all abbreviations used without explanation in List I. The names of authors are in general printed in roman type, the titles of their works (given in alphabetical order under the author's name) in italics, which are also used for the titles of collections and periodical publications.

The list of authors (I) is not intended to furnish a bibliography of Greek Literature, but to indicate the editions which have been followed in respect of the form of reference, i.e. pagination, numeration of books, chapters, sections, lines, fragments, &c.; where the form adopted in the Lexicon differs from that of the edition cited (e.g. where the pagination of an earlier editor is used, but may be found in the margin of a later edition) the fact is stated. It will be understood that the reading adopted in the edition cited is not necessarily given (or referred to) in the Lexicon. For the convenience of readers a few editions of the fragments of individual authors have been named in the list, even when the remains of the author have been cited from the sources of the quotations. Where no abbreviation follows the author's name the full name is used in the Lexicon, and where no date is given it is to be understood that evidence to determine it is lacking. No attempt has in general been made to indicate which of the works attributed to an author are to be regarded as spurious.

In the description of the editions used 'OCT' is added to show that the work is one of the Oxford Classical Texts (*Scriptorum Classicorum Bibliotheca Oxoniensis*); similarly 'T.' indicates the smaller Teubner Series (*Bibliotheca Scriptorum Graecorum et Romanorum Teubneriana*), 'D.' the Didot editions, and 'Loeb' the Loeb Classical Library.

B. METHODS OF REFERENCE

Where the works of an author have been divided into recognized chapters and sections these are usually given, and the orators are (when possible) cited by speech and section; but references by page are given in accordance with custom to Aristotle (Bekker), the commentators on Aristotle (Berlin edition), Plato (Stephanus), Philo (Mangey), Plutarch's *Moralia* (Wyttenbach), Galen (Kühn, except for certain recently edited treatises), Athenaeus (Casaubon), Julian (Spanheim), and Themistius (Hardouin). Page-references to other authors are in general introduced by 'p.' and followed by the initial of the editor's name; if not, the facts are stated in List I. The symbol '*Fr.*' (= *Fragment*) is generally used where the remains of an author consist partly of complete works and partly of quotations; a simple number denotes a fragment drawn from one of the collections indicated in List I. Where supplementary or recent but uncompleted collections are quoted, the initial of the editor (e.g. 'D.' for Demiańczuk, 'J.' for Jacoby) is added to the number of the fragment. The annotations of ancient commentators are cited either by reference to the passage discussed or as substantive works: thus 'Ulp. ad D.' followed by reference to speech and section, but 'Did. *in D.*' cited by column and line of papyrus.

I. AUTHORS AND WORKS

Abydenus Historicus [Abyd.] ii A.D. (?)
Ed. C. Müller, *FHG* iv p. 279.
Aceratus Epigrammaticus [Acerat.]
v. *Anthologia Graeca.*
Acesander Historicus [Acesand.] iii or ii B.C.
Ed. C. Müller, *FHG* iv p. 285.
Achaeus Tragicus [Achae.] v B.C.
Ed. A. Nauck, *TGF* p. 746.
Achilles Tatius Astronomus [Ach.Tat.] iii A.D. (?)
Introductio in Aratum, ed. E. Maass, *Commentariorum in Aratum reliquiae*, Berlin 1898, p. 25. [*Intr.Arat.*]
Achilles Tatius Scriptor Eroticus [Ach.Tat.] iv A.D. (?)
Ed. R. Hercher, *Erotici* i p. 37.
Acusilaus Historicus [Acus.] v B.C.
Ed. F. Jacoby, *FGrH* i p. 47.
Adaeus Epigrammaticus i A.D.
v. *Anthologia Graeca.*
Adamantius Physiognomonicus [Adam.] iv A.D.
Ed. R. Förster, *Scriptores Physiognomonici*, Leipzig (T.) 1893, i p. 297.
Aelianus [Ael.] ii/iii A.D.
Ed. R. Hercher, Leipzig (T.) 1864–87.
Ep. = *Epistulae* (ed. R. Hercher, *Epistolographi*, p. 17)
Fr. = *Fragmenta*
NA = *De Natura Animalium* (excerpts in Ar.Byz.*Epit.*)
Tact. = *Tactica* (ed. H. Köchly & W. Rüstow, *Griechische Kriegsschriftsteller*, Leipzig 1855)
VH = *Varia Historia*
Aelius Dionysius Grammaticus [Ael.Dion.] ii A.D.
Ed. E. Schwabe, *Aelii Dionysii et Pausaniae Atticistarum Fragmenta*, Leipzig 1890.
Aemilianus Epigrammaticus [Aemil.] i A.D.
v. *Anthologia Graeca.*
Aeneas Gazaeus Rhetor [Aen.Gaz.] v/vi A.D.
Epistulae, ed. R. Hercher, *Epistolographi*, p. 24. [*Ep.*]
Theophrastus, ed. J. F. Boissonade, Paris 1836. [*Thphr.*]
Aeneas Tacticus [Aen.Tact.] iv B.C.
Ed. R. Schöne, Leipzig (T) 1911.
Aesara Philosophus [Aesar.]
Apud Stobaeum.
Aeschines Orator [Aeschin.] iv B.C.
Ed. F. Blass, Leipzig (T.) 1896.
Ep. = *Epistulae*
Aeschines Socraticus Philosophus [Aeschin.Socr.] iv B.C.
Ed. H. Dittmar, Berlin 1912.
Aeschrio Lyricus iv B.C.
Ed. T. Bergk, *PLG* ii p. 516.
Aeschylus Tragicus [A.] vi/v B.C.
Ed. A. Sidgwick, Oxford (OCT).
Scholia, ed. W. Dindorf in editione Aeschyli, Oxford 1851.
Scholia in Aeschyli Persas, ed. O. Dähnhardt, Leipzig (T.) 1894.
A. = *Agamemnon*
Ch. = *Choephori*
Eleg. = *Fragmenta Elegiaca*, ed. T. Bergk, *PLG* ii p. 240.
Eu. = *Eumenides*
Fr. = *Fragmenta*, ed. A. Nauck, *TGF* p. 3; new fragments, marked A, B, &c., ed. H. W. Smyth, *American Journal of Philology*, xli (1920) p. 101.
Pers. = *Persae*
Pr. = *Prometheus Vinctus*
Supp. = *Supplices*
Th. = *Septem contra Thebas*
Aeschylus Alexandrinus Tragicus [Aesch.Alex.] iii B.C.
Ed. A. Nauck, *TGF* p. 824.
Aesopus Fabularum Scriptor [Aesop.]
Ed. C. Halm, Leipzig (T.) 1889.
Prov. = *Proverbia*, ed. E. L. von Leutsch & F. G. Schneidewin, *Paroemiographi* ii p. 228.
Aethlius Historicus v B.C. (?)
Ed. C. Müller, *FHG* iv p. 287.
Aëtius Medicus [Aët.] vi A.D.
Editio Aldina, Venice 1534 (Lib. i–viii); Lib. vii 1–90, ed. J. Hirschberg, Leipzig 1899; Lib. ix, ed. S. Zervos, Ἀθηνᾶ xxiii (1911) p. 265; Lib. xi, ed. C. Daremberg & C. E. Ruelle, *Rufus*, Paris 1879, p. 85; Lib. xii, ed. G. A. Kostomiris, Paris 1892; Lib. xiii (parts), xv, ed. S. Zervos, Ἀθηνᾶ xviii (1906) p. 241, xxi (1909) p. 3; Lib. xvi, ed. S. Zervos, Leipzig 1901.
Africanus, Julius Historicus [Afric.] ii/iii A.D.
Cest. = Κεστοί in *POxy.* 412.
Agaclytus Historicus [Agaclyt.]
Ed. C. Müller, *FHG* iv p. 288.
Agatharchides Geographus [Agatharch.] ii B.C.
Ed. C. Müller, *GGM* i p. 111.
Fr.Hist. = *Fragmenta Historica*, ed. C. Müller, *FHG* iii p. 190.
Agathemerus Geographus [Agathem.] post Posidonium.
Ed. C. Müller, *GGM* ii p. 471.
Agathias Historicus et Epigrammaticus [Agath.] vi A.D.
Ed. L. Dindorf, *HGM* ii p. 132.
v. *Anthologia Graeca.*
Agathinus Medicus [Agathin.] i A.D.
Apud Oribasium.
Agatho Tragicus v B.C.
Ed. A. Nauck, *TGF* p. 763.
Agathocles Historicus [Agathocl.]
Ed. C. Müller, *FHG* iv p. 288.
Agis Epigrammaticus
v. *Anthologia Graeca.*
Aglaïas Elegiacus i A.D.
Ed. U. Cats Bussemaker, *Poetae Bucolici et Didactici*, p. 97, Paris (D.) 1850.
Albinus Philosophus [Alb.] ii A.D.
Introductio in Platonem, ed. C. F. Hermann, *Plato*, vol. vi, Leipzig (T.) 1892, p. 147. [*Intr.*]
Alcaeus Comicus [Alc.Com.] v/iv B.C.
Ed. T. Kock, *CAF* i p. 756; suppl. J. Demiańczuk, *Supp. Com.* p. 7.
Alcaeus Lyricus [Alc.] vii/vi B.C.
Ed. T. Bergk, *PLG* iii p. 147; suppl. E. Diehl, *Supp. Lyr.*[3] p. 10. [*Supp.*]
Alcaeus Messenius Epigrammaticus [Alc.Mess.] iii/ii B.C.
v. *Anthologia Graeca.*
Alcidamas Rhetor [Alcid.] iv B.C.
Ed. F. Blass, *Antipho*, Leipzig (T.) 1892, p. 183.
Od. = Ὀδυσσεύς.
Soph. = περὶ σοφιστῶν
Alcinous Philosophus [Alcin.]
Introductio in Platonem, ed. C. F. Hermann, *Plato*, Leipzig (T.) 1892, vol. vi, p. 152. [*Intr.*]
Alciphro Epistolographus [Alciphr.] iv A.D.
Ed. M. A. Schepers, Leipzig (T.) 1905. (Cited acc. to numeration of earlier edd.)
Alcmaeon Philosophus v B.C.
Ed. H. Diels, *Vorsokr.* i p. 131.
Alcman Lyricus [Alcm.] vii B.C.
Ed. T. Bergk, *PLG* iii p. 14.
Alexander Comicus [Alexand.Com.]
Ed. T. Kock, *CAF* iii p. 372.
Alexander Aetolus Elegiacus [Alex.Aet.] iii. B.C.
Ed. J. U. Powell, *Coll. Alex.* p. 121.
Alexander Aphrodisiensis Philosophus [Alex.Aphr.] iii A.D.
de An. = *de Anima liber*, ed. I. Bruns (*Supplementum Aristotelicum* ii *pars* i), Berlin 1887.
Fat. = *de Fato*, ed. I. Bruns (*Supplementum Aristotelicum* ii *pars* ii), Berlin 1892.
Febr. = *de febribus*, ed. J. L. Ideler, *Physici et Medici Graeci Minores*, Berlin 1841, i p. 81.
in APr. = *in Aristotelis Analyticorum Priorum librum I commentarium*, ed. M. Wallies (*Comm. in Arist. Graeca* ii *pars* i), Berlin 1883.
in Metaph. = *in Aristotelis Metaphysica commentaria*, ed. M. Hayduck (*Comm. in Arist. Graeca* i), Berlin 1891.
in Mete. = *in Aristotelis Meteorologicorum libros commentaria*, ed. M. Hayduck (*Comm. in Arist. Graeca* iii *pars* ii), Berlin 1899.
in SE = *in Aristotelis Sophisticos Elenchos commentarium*, ed. M. Wallies (*Comm. in Arist. Graeca* ii *pars* iii), Berlin 1898.
in Sens. = *in librum de sensu commentarium*, ed. P. Wendland (*Comm. in Arist. Graeca* iii *pars* i), Berlin 1901.
in Top. = *in Aristotelis Topicorum libros octo commentaria*, ed. M. Wallies (*Comm. in Arist. Graeca* ii *pars* ii), Berlin 1891.
Mixt. = *de Mixtione*, ed. I. Bruns (*Supplementum Aristotelicum* ii *pars* ii), Berlin 1892.

Pr. = *Problemata*, ed. J. L. Ideler, *Physici et Medici Graeci Minores*, Berlin 1841, i p. 3.
Pr. Anecd. = προβλήματα ἀνέκδοτα, ed. U. Cats Bussemaker, *Aristotelis Opera*, vol. iv (Paris (D.) 1857), p. 291.
Quaest. = *Quaestiones*, ed. I. Bruns (*Supplementum Aristotelicum* ii *pars* ii), Berlin 1892.

Alexander Ephesius Epicus [Alex.Eph.] i B.C.
Ed. J. A. F. A. Meineke, *Analecta Alexandrina*, Berlin 1843, p. 371.

Alexander Polyhistor Historicus [Alex.Polyh.] i B.C.
Ed. C. Müller, *FHG* iii p. 206.

Alexander Rhetor [Alex.] ii A.D.
De Figuris, ed. L. Spengel, *Rhet.* iii p. 7. [*Fig.*]
περὶ ῥητορικῶν ἀφορμῶν, ed. L. Spengel, op. cit., p. i. [*Rh.*]

Alexander Trallianus Medicus [Alex.Trall.] vi A.D.
Ed. T. Puschmann, Vienna 1878–9; Nachträge, ed. T. Puschmann, Berlin 1886.
Febr. = *de febribus*
Verm. = *epistula de vermibus*

Alexis Comicus [Alex.] iv B.C.
Ed. T. Kock, *CAF* ii p. 297.

Alpheus Epigrammaticus [Alph.] i A.D.
v. *Anthologia Graeca.*

Alypius Musicus [Alyp.] iii (iv?) A.D.
Ed. C. Jan, *Musici Scriptores Graeci*, Leipzig (T.) 1895, p. 367.

Amipsias Comicus [Amips.] v/iv B.C.
Ed. T. Kock, *CAF* i p. 670; suppl. J. Demiańczuk, *Supp. Com.* p. 7.

Ammianus Epigrammaticus [Ammian.] ii A.D.
v. *Anthologia Graeca.*

Ammianus Marcellinus Historicus [Amm.Marc.] iv A.D.
Ed. C. U. Clark, L. Traube, W. Heraeus, Berlin 1910–15.

Ammonius Epigrammaticus [Ammon.] v A.D. (?)
v. *Anthologia Graeca.*

Ammonius Grammaticus [Ammon.] i/ii A.D.
περὶ ὁμοίων καὶ διαφόρων λέξεων, ed. L. C. Valckenaer[2], Leipzig 1822. [*Diff.*]

Ammonius Philosophus [Ammon.] v A.D.
in APr. = *in Aristotelis Analyticorum Priorum librum I commentarium*, ed. M. Wallies (*Comm. in Arist. Graeca* iv *pars* vi), Berlin 1899.
in Cat. = *in Aristotelis Categorias commentarius*, ed. A. Busse (*Comm. in Arist. Graeca* iv *pars* iv), Berlin 1895.
in Int. = *in Aristotelis de Interpretatione commentarius*, ed. A. Busse (*Comm. in Arist. Graeca* iv *pars* v), Berlin 1897.
in Porph. = *in Porphyrii Isagogen sive V voces*, ed. A. Busse (*Comm. in Arist. Graeca* iv *pars* iii), Berlin 1891.

Amphis Comicus iv B.C.
Ed. T. Kock, *CAF* ii p. 236.

Anacharsis Epistolographus [Anach.] i B.C. (?)
Ed. R. Hercher, *Epistolographi*, p. 102.

Anacreon Lyricus [Anacr.] vi B.C.
Ed. T. Bergk, *PLG* iii p. 253.

Anacreontea [*Anacreont.*]
Ed. C. Preisendanz, Leipzig (T.) 1912; cited by T. Bergk's numeration, *PLG* iii p. 296.

Ananius Lyricus [Anan.] vi B.C.
Ed. T. Bergk, *PLG* ii p. 501.

Anaxagoras Philosophus [Anaxag.]. v B.C.
Ed. H. Diels, *Vorsokr.* i p. 375.

Anaxandrides Comicus [Anaxandr.] iv B.C.
Ed. T. Kock, *CAF* ii p. 135; suppl. J. Demiańczuk, *Supp. Com.* p. 7.

Anaxandrides Historicus [Anaxandr.Hist.] iii B.C. (?)
Ed. C. Müller, *FHG* iii p. 106 (perperam 'Alexandrides').

Anaxarchus Philosophus [Anaxarch.] iv B.C.
Ed. H. Diels, *Vorsokr.* ii p. 144.

Anaxilas Comicus [Anaxil.] iv B.C.
Ed. T. Kock, *CAF* ii p. 264.

Anaximander Historicus [Anaximand.Hist.] iv B.C.
Ed. F. Jacoby, *FGrH* i p. 159.

Anaximander Philosophus [Anaximand.] vi B.C.
Ed. H. Diels, *Vorsokr.* i p. 14.

Anaximenes Philosophus [Anaximen.] vi B.C.
Ed. H. Diels, *Vorsokr.* i p. 22.

Anaxippus Comicus [Anaxipp.] iv B.C.
Ed. T. Kock, *CAF* iii p. 296.

Andocides Orator [And.] v/iv B.C.
Ed. F. Blass[4] (C. Fuhr), Leipzig (T.) 1913.

Andromachus Poeta Medicus [Androm.] i A.D.
Apud Galenum.

Andron Historicus iv B.C.
Ed. F. Jacoby, *FGrH* i p. 161.

Andronicus Epigrammaticus [Andronic.]
v. *Anthologia Graeca.*

Andronicus Rhodius Philosophus [Andronic.Rhod.] i B.C.
De Passionibus, ed. X. Kreuttner, Heidelberg 1885; ed. K. Schuchardt, Darmstadt 1883; cited by page of F. W. A. Mullach, *FPG* iii p. 570.

Androtion Historicus [Androt.] iv B.C.
Ed. C. Müller, *FHG* i p. 371.

Anecdota Graeca e codd. MSS. Bibl. reg. Parisin., ed. L. Bachmann, Leipzig 1828–9. [*An.Bachm.*]

Anecdota Graeca ed. I. Bekker, 3 vols., Berlin 1814–21. [*AB*]

Anecdota Graeca e codd. MSS. Bibl. Oxon., ed. J. A. Cramer, 4 vols., Oxford 1835–7. [*An.Ox.*]

Anecdota Graeca e codd. MSS. Bibl. Reg. Parisiensis, ed. J. A. Cramer, 4 vols., Oxford 1839–41. [*An.Par.*]

Anecdota Graeca et Latina [*Anecd.Stud.*]
Ed. R. Schoell & G. Studemund, Leipzig 1886.

Anonymus vel **Anonymi** [Anon.]
Fig. = Anonymi *de Figuris*, ed. L. Spengel, *Rhet.* iii pp. 110, 171, 174.
Geog.Comp. = *GeographiaeExpositio Compendiaria*, ed. C. Müller, *GGM* ii p. 494.
in Cat. = *Anonymi in Aristotelis Categorias paraphrasis*, ed. M. Hayduck (*Comm. in Arist. Graeca* xxiii *pars* ii), Berlin 1883.
in EN = *Anonymi in Ethica Nicomachea commentaria*, ed. G. Heylbut (*Comm. in Arist. Graeca* xx), Berlin 1892.
in Prm. = *Anonymi Commentarius in Platonis Parmenidem*, ed. W. Kroll in *Rh. Mus.* xlvii (1892) 599.
in Rh. = *Anonymi in Artem Rhetoricam commentaria*, ed. H. Rabe (*Comm. in Arist. Graeca* xxi *pars* ii), Berlin 1896.
in SE = *in Sophisticos Elenchos paraphrasis*, ed. M. Hayduck (*Comm. in Arist. Graeca* xxiii *pars* iv), Berlin 1884.
in Tht. = *Anonymi Commentarius in Platonis Theaetetum*, ed. H. Diels & W. Schubart, *BKT* ii, Berlin 1905.
Incred. = Anonymus, περὶ ἀπίστων, ed. N. Festa (post Palaephatum (q. v.), p. 88), Leipzig (T.) 1902.
Trop. = Anonymi, περὶ τρόπων, ed. L. Spengel, *Rhet.* iii pp. 207, 227.

Anonymus Londnensis [Anon.Lond.] i A.D.
Anonymi Londinensis ex Aristotelis Iatricis Menoniis et aliis medicis eclogae, ed. H. Diels (*Supplementum Aristotelicum* iii *pars* i), Berlin 1893.

Anonymus Rhythmicus [Anon.Rhythm.]
Oxy. = *POxy.* 9.

Anonymus Vaticanus [Anon.Vat.]
Paradoxographus Vaticanus Rohdii, ed. O. Keller, *Rerum Naturalium Scriptores* i, Leipzig (T.) 1877, p. 106.

Antagoras Elegiacus [Antag.] iii B.C.
Ed. J. U. Powell, *Coll. Alex.* p. 120.

Antenor Historicus ii B.C. (?)
Ed. C. Müller, *FHG* iv p. 305.

Anthemius Paradoxographus [Anthem.] vi A.D.
Ed. A. Westermann, Παραδοξογράφοι, Brunswick-London 1839, p. 149.

Anthologia Graeca
(Names of epigrammatists, where found in codd., are added in brackets.)
Anthologia Palatina, Planudea, ed. F. Dübner, Paris (D.) 1864–72; ed. H. Stadtmüller, vols. i, ii (1), iii (1) (all published), Leipzig (T.) 1894–1906. [*AP*, *APl.*]
Appendix nova epigrammatum, ed. E. Cougny, Paris (D.) 1890. [*App.Anth.*]

Anticlides Historicus [Anticl.] iii B.C. (?)
Ed. C. Müller, *SRAM* p. 147.

Antidotus Comicus [Antid.] iv B.C.
Ed. T. Kock, *CAF* ii p. 410.

Antigonus Carystius Paradoxographus [Antig.] iii B.C.
Mirabilia, ed. O. Keller, *Rerum Naturalium Scriptores* i, Leipzig (T.) 1877, p. 1. [*Mir.*]

Antigonus Nicaeanus Astrologus [Antig.Nic.]
Apud Hephaestionem Astrologum.

Antimachus Colophonius Elegiacus et Epicus [Antim.] v/iv B.C.
Fragmenta Elegiaca, ed. T. Bergk, *PLG* ii p. 289. [*Eleg.*]
Fragmenta Epica, ed. G. Kinkel, *EGF* p. 273. [Antim.]; suppl. J. U. Powell, *Coll. Alex.* p. 249. [Antim.Col.]

Antiochus Atheniensis Astrologus [Antioch.Astr.] ii A.D.
Ed. A. Olivieri, *Cat. Cod. Astr.* i 108; ed. F. Boll, ib. vii 107.

Antiochus Epigrammaticus [Antioch.]
v. *Anthologia Graeca.*

Antiochus Historicus [Antioch.Hist.] v B.C.
Ed. C. Müller, *FHG* i p. 181.

Antipater Sidonius Epigrammaticus [Antip.Sid.] ii B.C.
v. *Anthologia Graeca.*

Antipater Tarsensis Stoicus [Antip.*Stoic.*] ii B.C.
Ed. H. von Arnim, *SVF* iii p. 244.

Antipater Thessalonicensis Epigrammaticus [Antip.Thess.] i B.C.
v. *Anthologia Graeca.*

Antiphanes Comicus [Antiph.] iv B.C.
Ed. T. Kock, *CAF* ii p. 12; suppl. J. Demiańczuk, *Supp. Com.* p. 8.

Antiphanes Macedo Epigrammaticus [Antiphan.] i A.D.
v. *Anthologia Graeca.*

Antiphanes Megalopolitanus Epigrammaticus [Antiphan.] i A.D.
v. *Anthologia Graeca.*

Antiphilus Epigrammaticus [Antiphil.] i A.D.
v. *Anthologia Graeca.*
Antipho Orator v B.C.
Ed. T. Thalheim, Leipzig (T.) 1914.
Antipho Sophista [Antipho Soph.] v B.C.
Ed. H. Diels, *Vorsokr.* ii p. 289.
Antipho Tragicus [Antipho Trag.] iv B.C.
Ed. A. Nauck, *TGF* p. 792.
Antisthenes Rhetor [Antisth.] iv B.C.
Ed. F. Blass (post Antiphontem), Leipzig (T.) 1892.
Aj. = Αἴας
Od. = Ὀδυσσεύς
Antistius Epigrammaticus [Antist.] i A.D.
v. *Anthologia Graeca.*
Antoninus Liberalis Mythographus [Ant.Lib.] ii A.D. (?)
Ed. E. Martini, *Mythographi Graeci* ii (1), Leipzig (T.) 1896.
Antonius Argivus Epigrammaticus [Anton.Arg.]
v. *Anthologia Graeca.*
Antonius Diogenes Scriptor Eroticus [Ant.Diog.] i or ii A.D.
Ed. R. Hercher, *Erotici* i p. 231.
Antyllus Medicus [Antyll.] ii A.D.
Apud Oribasium.
Anubion Poeta Astrologus [Anub.] i A.D.
Ed. H. Köchly (post Manethonem), Leipzig (T.) 1858.
Anyte Epigrammatica [Anyt.] iv/iii B.C.
v. *Anthologia Graeca.*
Aphthonius Rhetor [Aphth.] iv/v A.D.
Προγυμνάσματα, ed. L. Spengel, *Rhet.* ii p. 19. [*Prog.*]
Apion Grammaticus i A.D.
Ed. A. Ludwich in *Philol.* lxxiv (1917) p. 205, lxxv (1919) p. 9.
Apollinarius Epigrammaticus [Apollinar.] ii A.D. (?)
v. *Anthologia Graeca.*
Apollodorus Comicus [Apollod.Com.] iv/iii B.C.
Ed. T. Kock, *CAF* iii p. 288.
(Fragmenta utrum ad Apollodorum Carystium an ad Geloum pertineant incertum.)
Apollodorus Carystius Comicus [Apollod.Car.] iv/iii B.C.
Ed. T. Kock, *CAF* iii p. 280; suppl. J. Demiańczuk, *Supp. Com.* p. 8.
Apollodorus Gelous Comicus [Apollod.Gel.] iv/iii B.C.
Ed. T. Kock, *CAF* iii p. 278.
Apollodorus Mythographus [Apollod.] i A.D. (?)
Bibliotheca, ed. R. Wagner, *Mythographi Graeci* i, Leipzig (T.) 1894; cited without title.
Epitome, ed. R. Wagner, op. cit., p. 173. [*Epit.*]
Fragmenta Historica, ed. C. Müller, *FHG* i p. 428. [Hist.]
Apollodorus Damascenus Mechanicus [Apollod.] ii A.D.
Πολιορκητικά, Ed. R. Schneider, *Abhandlungen der Göttinger Gesellschaft der Wissenschaften* (*Phil.-hist. Klasse*), 1908. [*Poliorc.*] (Cited by Wescher's page, given in Schneider's margin.)
Apollodorus Lyricus [Apollod.Lyr.]
Ed. T. Bergk, *PLG* iii p. 378.
Apollodorus Seleuciensis Stoicus [Apollod.*Stoic.*] ii B.C.
Ed. H. von Arnim, *SVF* iii p. 259.
Apollonides Epigrammaticus [Apollonid.] i A.D.
v. *Anthologia Graeca.*
Apollonides Tragicus [Apollonid.Trag.]
Ed. A. Nauck, *TGF* p. 825.
Apollonius Biographus [Apollon.]
Vit.Aeschin. = *Vita Aeschinis*, ed. F. Blass (ante Aeschinem).
Apollonius Paradoxographus [Apollon.] ii B.C. (?)
Mirabilia, ed. O. Keller, *Rerum Naturalium Scriptores* i, Leipzig (T.) 1877, p. 43. [*Mir.*]
Apollonius Citiensis Medicus [Apollon.Cit.] i B.C.
Ed. H. Schöne, Leipzig 1896.
Apollonius Dyscolus Grammaticus [A.D.] ii A.D.
Ed. R. Schneider & G. Uhlig, Leipzig 1878–1910.
Adv. = *de Adverbiis*; cited by Schneider's page and line.
Conj. = *de Conjunctionibus*; cited by Schneider's page and line.
Pron. = *de Pronominibus*; cited by Schneider's page and line.
Synt. = *de Syntaxi*; cited by Bekker's page and line, given in Uhlig's margin.
Apollonius Pergaeus Geometra [Apollon.Perg.] iii/ii B.C.
Conica, ed. J. L. Heiberg, Leipzig (T.) 1891. [*Con.*]
Apollonius Medicus [Apollon.] i A.D.
Apud Galenum.
Apollonius Rhodius Epicus [A.R.] iii B.C.
Ed. R. C. Seaton, Oxford (OCT).
Apollonius Sophista [Apollon.] i/ii A.D.
Lexicon Homericum, ed. I. Bekker, Berlin 1833. [*Lex.*]
Apollonius Tyanensis Epistolographus [Ap.Ty.] i A.D.
Epistulae, ed. C. L. Kayser, *Philostratus* i p. 345. [*Ep.*]
Apollophanes Comicus [Apolloph.] v B.C.
Ed. T. Kock, *CAF* i p. 797; suppl. J. Demiańczuk, *Supp. Com.* p. 9.
Apollophanes Stoicus [Apolloph.*Stoic.*] iii B.C.
Ed. H. von Arnim, *SVF* i p. 90.
Apostolius Paroemiographus [Apostol.] xv A.D.
Ed. E. von Leutsch & F. G. Schneidewin, *Paroemiographi* ii p. 233.
Appianus Historicus [App.] ii A.D.
Ed. L. Mendelssohn & P. Viereck, Leipzig (T.) 1879–1905.
BC = *Bella Civilia*
Gall. = Κελτική
Hann. = Ἀννιβαϊκή
Hisp. = Ἰβηρική
Ill. = Ἰλλυρική
Ital. = Ἰταλική
Mac. = Μακεδονική
Mith. = Μιθριδάτειος
Praef. = *Praefatio*
Pun. = Λιβυκή
Reg. = Βασιλική
Sam. = Σαυνιτική
Sic. = Σικελική
Syr. = Συριακή
Apsines Rhetor [Aps.]
Rh. = *Ars Rhetorica*, ed. C. Hammer, in L. Spengel, *Rhet.* i² (2), Leipzig (T.) 1894, p. 217.
Apuleius Scriptor Botanicus [Apul.] iv A.D. (?)
Herbarium, Basel 1560. [*Herb.*]
Aquila Interpres Veteris Testamenti [Aq.] ii A.D.
Ed. F. Field, *Origenis Hexapla*, Oxford 1875; cf. Vetus Testamentum.
Arabius Epigrammaticus [Arab.] vi A.D.
v. *Anthologia Graeca.*
Araros Comicus [Arar.] v/iv B.C.
Ed. T. Kock, *CAF* ii p. 215.
Aratus Epicus [Arat.] iv/iii B.C.
Ed. E. Maass, Berlin 1893.
Scholia, ed. E. Maass, *Commentariorum in Aratum reliquiae*, Berlin 1898.
Arcadius Grammaticus [Arc.] iv A.D. (?)
Ed. E. H. Barker, Leipzig 1820; ed. M. Schmidt, Ἐπιτομὴ τῆς καθολικῆς προσῳδίας Ἡρωδιανοῦ, Jena 1860: cited by Barker's page, given in Schmidt's margin.
Arcesilaus Comicus [Arcesil.] v B.C.
Ed. J. Demiańczuk, *Supp. Com.* p. 10.
Archedicus Comicus [Arched.] iv/iii B.C.
Ed. T. Kock, *CAF* iii p. 276.
Archedemus Tarsensis Stoicus [Arched.*Stoic.*] iii B.C. (?)
Ed. H. von Arnim, *SVF* iii p. 262.
Archemachus Historicus [Archemach.]
Ed. C. Müller, *FHG* iv p. 314.
Archestratus Epicus [Archestr.] iv B.C.
Ed. P. Brandt, *Corpusculum poesis Epicae Graecae ludibundae* i p. 114, Leipzig (T.) 1888.
Archias (unus vel plures) Epigrammaticus [Arch.] i B.C.
v. *Anthologia Graeca.*
Archias Junior Epigrammaticus [Arch.Jun.]
v. *Anthologia Graeca.*
Archigenes Medicus [Archig.] ii A.D.
Apud Galenum, Aëtium, Oribasium.
Archilochus Lyricus [Archil.] vii B.C.
Ed. T. Bergk, *PLG* ii p. 383; suppl. E. Diehl, *Supp. Lyr.*³ p. 4. [*Supp.*]
Archimedes Geometra [Archim.] iii B.C.
Ed. J. L. Heiberg, ed. 2, Leipzig (T.) 1910–15.
Aequil. = περὶ ἰσορροπιῶν
Aren. = ψαμμίτης
Bov. = πρόβλημα βοεικόν
Circ. = κύκλου μέτρησις
Con.Sph. = περὶ κωνοειδέων καὶ σφαιροειδέων
Eratosth. = πρὸς Ἐρατοσθένην ἔφοδος
Fluit. = περὶ τῶν ὀχουμένων
Fr. = *Fragmenta*
Quadr. = τετραγωνισμὸς παραβολῆς
Sph.Cyl. = περὶ σφαίρας καὶ κυλίνδρου
Spir. = περὶ ἑλίκων
Stom. = στομάχιον
Archimelus Epigrammaticus [Archimel.] iii B.C.
v. *Anthologia Graeca.*
Archippus Comicus [Archipp.] v/iv B.C.
Ed. T. Kock, *CAF* i p. 679; suppl. J. Demiańczuk, *Supp. Com.* p. 10.
Archytas Amphissensis Epicus [Archyt.Amph.] iii B.C.
Ed. J. U. Powell, *Coll. Alex.* p. 23.
Archytas Tarentinus Philosophus [Archyt.] iv B.C.
Ed. H. Diels, *Vorsokr.* i p. 322.
Aretaeus Medicus [Aret.] ii A.D.
Ed. K. Hude, *CMG* ii, Leipzig 1923.
CA = ὀξέων νούσων θεραπευτικόν
CD = χρονίων νούσων θεραπευτικόν
SA = περὶ αἰτιῶν καὶ σημείων ὀξέων παθῶν
SD = περὶ αἰτιῶν καὶ σημείων χρονίων παθῶν
Arion Lyricus vi B.C.
Ed. T. Bergk, *PLG* iii p. 79.

Ariphron Lyricus iv B.C.
Ed. T. Bergk, *PLG* iii p. 595.
Aristaenetus Rhetor [Aristaenet.]
Ed. Hercher, *Epistolographi*, p. 133.
Aristagoras Comicus [Aristag.] v B.C.
Ed. T. Kock, *CAF* i p. 710.
Aristagoras Historicus [Aristag.Hist.] iv B.C.
Ed. C. Müller *FHG* ii p. 98.
Aristarchus Grammaticus [Aristarch.] iii/ii B.C.
Apud Scholia in Homerum.
Aristarchus Samius Astronomus [Aristarch.Sam.] iii B.C.
Ed. Sir T. L. Heath, Oxford 1913.
Aristarchus Tragicus [Aristarch.Trag.] v B.C.
Ed. A. Nauck, *TGF* p. 728.
Aristeas Epicus [Aristeas Epic.] vi B.C.
Ed. G. Kinkel, *EGF* p. 243.
Aristeas Judaeus ii B.C. (?)
Ed. P. Wendland, Leipzig (T.) 1900.
Aristias Tragicus v B.C.
Ed. A. Nauck, *TGF* p. 726.
Aristides Rhetor [Aristid.] 129–189 A.D.
Ed. S. Jebb, 2 vols., Oxford 1722–30; ed. W. Dindorf, 3 vols., Leipzig 1829; ed. B. Keil, vol. ii (all published), Berlin 1898.
Or. = *Orationes*, cited by speech and section, if from Keil; the rest cited without title by Jebb's vol. and page (given in margin of Dindorf).
Rh. = *τέχναι ῥητορικαί*, ed. L. Spengel, *Rhet.* ii p. 457; cited by Spengel's page.
Scholia, ed W. Dindorf, op. cit.; ed. W. Frommel, Frankfort 1826.
Aristides Milesius Historicus [Aristid.Mil.] ii B.C.
Ed. C. Müller, *FHG* iv p. 320.
Aristides Quintilianus Musicus [Aristid.Quint.] iii A.D. (?)
Ed. A. Jahn, Berlin 1882.
Aristippus Philosophus [Aristipp.] v/iv B.C.
Cited from sources; cf. F. W. A. Mullach, *FPG* ii p. 405.
Aristo Epigrammaticus i B.C. (?)
v. *Anthologia Graeca.*
Aristo Chius Stoicus [Aristo *Stoic.*] iii B.C.
Ed. H. von Arnim, *SVF* i p. 75.
Aristobulus Historicus [Aristobul.] iv B.C.
Ed. C. Müller, *SRAM* p. 94.
Aristocles Epigrammaticus [Aristocl.]
Apud Aelianum.
Aristocles Historicus [Aristocl.Hist.] i B.C./i A.D.
Ed. C. Müller, *FHG* iv p. 329.
Aristocles Philosophus [Aristocl.] ii A.D.
Apud Eusebium; cf. F. W. A. Mullach, *FPG* iii p. 206.
Aristodemus Historicus [Aristodem.] i B.C.
Ed. C. Müller, *FHG* iii p. 307.
Aristodicus Epigrammaticus [Aristodic.] iii or ii B.C.
v. *Anthologia Graeca.*
Aristomenes Comicus [Aristomen.] v/iv B.C.
Ed. T. Kock, *CAF* i p. 690.
Aristonous Lyricus iii B.C.
Ed. J. U. Powell, *Coll. Alex.* p. 162.
Aristonymus Comicus [Aristonym.] v/iv B.C.
Ed. T. Kock, *CAF* i p. 668.
Aristonymus Gnomologus [Aristonym.]
Apud Stobaeum.
Aristophanes Comicus [Ar.] v/iv B.C.
Ed. F. W. Hall & W. M. Geldart, Oxford (OCT); suppl. J. Demiańczuk, *Supp. Com.* p. 11.
Ach. = *Acharnenses*
Av. = *Aves*
Ec. = *Ecclesiazusae*
Eq. = *Equites*
Fr. = *Fragmenta*
Lys. = *Lysistrata*
Nu. = *Nubes*
Pax
Pl. = *Plutus*
Ra. = *Ranae*
Th. = *Thesmophoriazusae*
V. = *Vespae*
Scholia, ed. W. Dindorf in editione Aristophanis, Oxford 1835–8.
Aristophanes Boeotus Historicus [Aristoph.Boeot.] iv B.C.
Ed. C. Müller, *FHG* iv p. 337.
Aristophanes Byzantinus Philosophus [Ar.Byz.] iii/ii B.C.
Epit. = *Historiae Animalium Epitome subiunctis Aeliani Timothei aliorumque eclogis*, ed. Spyridon P. Lambros (*Supplementum Aristotelicum* i *pars* i), Berlin 1885.
Aristopho Comicus iv B.C.
Ed. T. Kock, *CAF* ii p. 276.
Aristoteles Philosophus [Arist.] iv B.C.
Ed. I. Bekker, Berlin 1831–70.
APo. = *Analytica Posteriora*
APr. = *Analytica Priora*
Ath. = Ἀθηναίων Πολιτεία, ed. Sir F. G. Kenyon, Oxford (OCT).
Aud. = *de Audibilibus*
Cael. = *de Caelo*
Cat. = *Categoriae*
Col. = *de Coloribus*
de An. = *de Anima*
Div.Somn. = *de Divinatione per Somnia*
EE = *Ethica Eudemia*
EN = *Ethica Nicomachea*
Ep. = *Epistulae, ed.* R. Hercher, *Epistolographi*, p. 170.
Fr. = *Fragmenta*, ed. V. Rose, Leipzig (T.) 1886.
GA = *de Generatione Animalium*
GC = *de Generatione et Corruptione*
HA = *Historia Animalium*
IA = *de Incessu Animalium*
Insomn. = *de Insomniis*
Int. = *de Interpretatione*
Juv. = *de Juventute*
LI = *de Lineis Insecabilibus*
Long. = *de Longaevitate*
MA = *de Motu Animalium*
MM = *Magna Moralia*
Mech. = *Mechanica*
Mem. = *de Memoria*
Metaph. = *Metaphysica*
Mete. = *Meteorologica*
Mir. = *Mirabilia*
Mu. = *de Mundo*
Oec. = *Oeconomica*
PA = *de Partibus Animalium*
Pepl. = *Peplus* (*Fr.* 640).
Ph. = *Physica*
Phgn. = *Physiognomonica*
Po. = *Poetica*
Pol. = *Politica*,
Pr. = *Problemata*
Resp. = *de Respiratione*
Rh. = *Rhetorica*
Rh.Al. = *Rhetorica ad Alexandrum*
SE = *Sophistici Elenchi*
Sens. = *de Sensu*
Somn.Vig. = *de Somno et Vigilia*
Spir. = *de Spiritu*
Top. = *Topica*
VV = *de Virtutibus et Vitiis*
Vent. = *de Ventis*
Xen. = *de Xenophane*
Aristoxenus Musicus [Aristox.] iv B.C.
Fragmenta Historica, ed. C. Müller, *FHG* ii p. 269. [*Fr.Hist.*]
Harmonica, ed. H. S. Macran, Oxford 1902. [*Harm.*] (Cited by Meibom's page, given in Macran's margin.)
Rhythmica, ed. R. Westphal, *Aristoxenos von Tarent Melik und Rhythmik*, vol. ii, Leipzig 1893. [*Rhyth.*]
Arius Didymus Doxographus [Ar.Did.] i B.C.
Ed. H. Diels, *Doxographi Graeci*, Berlin 1879, p. 447.
Arrianus Historicus [Arr.] ii A.D.
Alan. = *Expeditio contra Alanos*, ed. R. Hercher & A. Eberhard, *Arriani Scripta Minora*, Leipzig (T.) 1885.
An. = *Anabasis*, ed. A. G. Roos, Leipzig (T.) 1907.
Cyn. = *Cynegeticus*, ed. Hercher-Eberhard (v. supr.).
Epict. = *Epicteti Dissertationes*, ed. H. Schenkl, Leipzig (T.) 1894.
Fr. = *Fragmenta Historica*, ed. C. Müller, *FHG* iii p. 586.
Ind. = *Indica*, ed. Hercher-Eberhard (v. supr.).
Peripl.M.Eux. = *Periplus maris Euxini*, ed. Hercher-Eberhard (v. supr.).
Tact. = *Tactica*, ed. Hercher-Eberhard (v. supr.).
Artemidorus Daldianus Onirocriticus [Artem.] ii A.D.
Ed. R. Hercher, Leipzig 1864.
Artemidorus Tarsensis Epigrammaticus [Artemid.] i B.C.
v. *Anthologia Graeca.*
Artemo Epigrammaticus
v. *Anthologia Graeca.*
Artemones Historici
Ed. C. Müller, *FHG* iv p. 340.
Arusianus Messius Grammaticus [Arus.Mess.] iv/v A.D.
Ed. H. Keil, *Gramm. Lat.* vii p. 437.
Ascensio Isaiae [*Ascens.Is.*]
Ed. B. P. Grenfell and A. S. Hunt, *PAmh.* I. I.
Asclepiades Epigrammaticus [Asclep.] iii B.C.
v. *Anthologia Graeca.*
Asclepiades Junior Medicus [Asclep.Jun.] i/ii A.D.
Apud Galenum.
Asclepiades Myrleanus Historicus [Asclep.Myrl.] ii/i B.C.
Ed. C. Müller, *FHG* iii p. 298.
Asclepiades Prusensis Medicus [Asclep.] ii/i B.C.
Apud Galenum.
Asclepiades Tragilensis Historicus [Asclep.Tragil.] iv B.C.
Ed. F. Jacoby, *FGrH* i p. 166.
Asclepiodotus Tacticus [Ascl.] i B.C.
Ed. H. Köchly & W. Rüstow, *Griechische Kriegsschriftsteller*, Leipzig 1855; ed. W. A. Oldfather, v. Onosander. [*Tact.*]

Asclepius Philosophus [Ascl.] vi A.D.
in Metaph. = *in Aristotelis Metaphysicorum libros* A–Z *commentaria*, ed. M. Hayduck (*Comm. in Arist. Graeca* vi *pars* ii), Berlin 1888.

Asius Lyricus vii/vi B.C.
Ed. T. Bergk, *PLG* ii p. 406.

Aspasius Philosophus [Asp.] ca. 110 A.D.
in EN = *in Ethica Nicomachea commentaria*, ed. G. Heylbut (*Comm. in Arist. Graeca* xix *pars* i), Berlin 1889.

Astrampsychus Onirocriticus [Astramps.] ii A.D.
Onir. = *Onirocritica*, ed. N. Rigalt (post Artemidorum), Paris 1603.
Orac. = *Oracula*, ed. R. Hercher, Berlin 1863.

Astydamas Tragicus [Astyd.] iv B.C.
Ed. A. Nauck, *TGF* p. 777.
Fragmentum Elegiacum, ed. T. Bergk, *PLG* ii p. 326. [*Eleg.*]

Athanis Historicus iv B.C.
Ed. C. Müller, *FHG* ii p. 81.

Athenaeus Epigrammaticus [Ath.]
v. *Anthologia Graeca.*

Athenaeus Grammaticus [Ath.] ii/iii A.D.
Ed. G. Kaibel, 3 vols., Leipzig (T.) 1887–90.
Epit. = *Epitome*, ed. J. Schweighäuser, Strassburg 1801–7.

Athenaeus Mechanicus [Ath.Mech.]
Ed. C. Wescher, *Poliorcétique des Grecs*, Paris 1867 (page and line).

Athenaeus Medicus [Ath.Med.] i A.D.
Apud Oribasium.

Athenio Comicus iii B.C.
Ed. T. Kock, *CAF* iii p. 369.

Athenodorus Tarsensis Historicus [Athenodor.Tars.] i B.C.
Ed. C. Müller, *FHG* iii p. 485.

Atilius Fortunatianus Grammaticus Latinus [Atil.Fort.] iv A.D. (?)
Ed. H. Keil, *Gramm. Lat.* vi p. 278.

Attalus Grammaticus [Attal.] ii B.C.
Ed. E. Maass, *Commentariorum in Aratum reliquiae*, Berlin 1898, p. 3. [*in Arat.*]

Atticus Philosophus [Attic.] ii A.D.
Apud Eusebium.

Ausonius Poeta Latinus [Aus.] iv A.D.
Ed. R. Peiper, Leipzig (T.) 1886.
Ep. = *Epistulae*
Epigr. = *Epigrammata*
Idyll. = *Idyllia*

Autocrates Comicus [Autocr.] v/iv B.C.
Ed. T. Kock *CAF* i p. 806.

Autolycus Astronomus [Autol.] iv B.C.
Ed. F. Hultsch, Leipzig (T.) 1885.

Automedon Epigrammaticus [Autom.] i A.D.
v. *Anthologia Graeca.*

Axionicus Comicus [Axionic.] iv B.C.
Ed. T. Kock, *CAF* ii p. 411.

Axiopistus Poeta Ethicus [Axiop.] iv/iii B.C.
Ed. J. U. Powell, *Coll. Alex.* p. 219.

Babrius Fabularum Scriptor [Babr.] ii A.D.
Ed. O. Crusius, Leipzig (T.) 1897.

Bacchius Musicus [Bacch.]
Harm. = Εἰσαγωγὴ τέχνης μουσικῆς, ed. C. Jan, *Musici Scriptores Graeci*, Leipzig (T.) 1895, p. 292.

Bacchylides Lyricus [B.] v B.C.
Ed. Sir R. C. Jebb, Cambridge 1905.
Scolia, in *POxy.* 1361. [*Scol.Oxy.*]

Balbilla Lyrica [Balbill.] ii A.D.
v. *Epigrammata Graeca* in II.

Barbucallos Epigrammaticus [Barb.] vi A.D.
v. *Anthologia Graeca.*

Bassus, Lollius Epigrammaticus [Bass.] i A.D.
v. *Anthologia Graeca.*

Bato Comicus iii B.C.
Ed. T. Kock, *CAF* iii p. 326.

Bato Sinopensis Historicus [Bato Sinop.] ii B.C.
Ed. C. Müller, *FHG* iv p. 347.

Batrachomyomachia [Batr.]
Ed. T. W. Allen, *Homeri Opera* v, Oxford (OCT), p. 168.

Berosus Historicus [Beros.] iv/iii B.C.
Ed. C. Müller, *FHG* ii p. 495.

Besantinus Epigrammaticus [Besant.] ii A.D.
v. *Anthologia Graeca.*
Ara = *AP* 15.25.

Bianor Epigrammaticus i B.C./i A.D.
Idem qui et Statyllius Flaccus, q. v.
v. *Anthologia Graeca.*

Bias Lyricus vi B.C.
Ed. T. Bergk, *PLG* iii p. 199. [*Fr.Lyr.*]

Bion Bucolicus ii B.C.
Ed. U. von Wilamowitz-Möllendorff[2], *Bucolici Graeci*, Oxford (OCT).

Biotus Tragicus
Ed. A. Nauck, *TGF* p. 825.

Bito Mechanicus iii or ii B.C.
Ed. C. Wescher, *Poliorcétique des Grecs*, Paris 1867 (page and line).

Blaesus Comicus [Blaes.]
Ed. G. Kaibel, *CGF* p. 191.

Boeo sive **Boeus** Epicus ii B.C. (?)
Ed. J. U. Powell, *Coll. Alex.* p. 23.

Boethus Epigrammaticus [Boeth.] i A.D.
v. *Anthologia Graeca.*

Boethus Sidonius Stoicus [Boeth.*Stoic.*] ii B.C.
Ed. H. von Arnim, *SVF* iii p. 265.

Brutus Epistolographus [Brut.] i B.C.
Ep. = *Epistula*, ed. R. Hercher, *Epistolographi*, p. 177.

Butherus Philosophus [Buther.]
Apud Stobaeum.

Caelius Aurelianus Medicus [Cael.Aur.] v A.D.
Ed. C. Amman, Amsterdam 1709.
CP = *Celeres Passiones*
TP = *Tardae Passiones*

Callias Epigrammaticus [Call.]
v. *Anthologia Graeca.*

Callias Comicus [Call.Com.] v/iv B.C.
Ed. T. Kock, *CAF* i p. 693; suppl. J. Demiańczuk, *Supp. Com.* p. 27.

Callias Historicus [Call.Hist.] iv/iii B.C.
Ed. C. Müller, *FHG* ii p. 382.

Callicratidas Philosophus [Callicrat.]
Apud Stobaeum.

Callicter Epigrammaticus
Interdum scribitur Cillactor.
v. *Anthologia Graeca.*

Callimachus Epicus [Call.] iii B.C.
Ed. O. Schneider, 2 vols., Leipzig 1870–3; ed. A. W. Mair, London (Loeb) 1921; *Fragmenta nuper reperta*, ed. R. Pfeiffer, ed. major, Bonn 1923.
Aet. = *Aetia*
Ap. = *Hymnus in Apollinem*
Cer. = *Hymnus in Cererem*
Del. = *Hymnus in Delum*
Dian. = *Hymnus in Dianam*
Epigr. = *Epigrammata*
Fr. = *Fragmenta*
Fr.anon. = *Fragmenta anonyma*
Hec. = *Hecale*
Iamb. = *Iambi*
Jov. = *Hymnus in Jovem*
Lav.Pall. = *Lavacrum Palladis*
Sos. = *Sosibii Victoria*
Note.—*Aet.*, *Hec.*, *Iamb.* generally refer to Mair's edition; fragments cited from Pfeiffer's edition are distinguished by the initial 'P.'

Callinicus Rhetor [Callinic.Rh.] iii A.D.
Ed. H. Hinck (post Polemonem), Leipzig (T.) 1873.

Callinus Epicus [Callin.] vii B.C.
Ed. T. Bergk, *PLG* ii p. 3.

Callistratus Historicus [Callistr.Hist.] i B.C.
Ed. C. Müller, *FHG* iv p. 353.

Callistratus Sophista [Callistr.] iv A.D.
Ed. C. Schenkl & Aem. Reisch (post Philostratum Minorem), Leipzig (T.) 1902.
Stat. = *Statuarum descriptiones*

Callixinus Historicus [Callix.] iii B.C. (?)
Ed. C. Müller, *FHG* iii p. 55.

Candidus Historicus v A.D.
Ed. L. Dindorf, *HGM* i p. 441.

Cantharus Comicus [Canthar.] v B.C.
Ed. T. Kock, *CAF* i p. 764; suppl. J. Demiańczuk, *Supp. Com.* p. 28.

Carcinus Tragicus [Carc.] v B.C.
Ed. A. Nauck, *TGF* p. 797.

Carmen Aureum [*Carm.Aur.*]
Ed. E. Diehl, *Anthologia Lyrica* ii, Leipzig (T.) 1923, p. 186.

Carmina Popularia [*Carm.Pop.*]
Ed. T. Bergk, *PLG* iii p. 654.

Carneiscus Philosophus [Carneisc.] iv/iii B.C.
Ed. W. Crönert, *Kolotes und Menedemos*, Leipzig 1906, p. 69.

Carphyllides Epigrammaticus [Carph.]
v. *Anthologia Graeca.*

Carystius Historicus [Caryst.] ii B.C.
Ed. C. Müller, *FHG* iv p. 356.

Cassius Medicus [Cass.] iii A.D.
Προβλήματα, ed. J. L. Ideler, *Physici et Medici Graeci Minores*, Berlin 1841, i p. 144. [*Pr.*]

Cassius Felix Medicus [Cass.Fel.] iv A.D.
Ed. V. Rose, Leipzig (T.) 1879.

Castorio Lyricus iv/iii B.C.
Ed. T. Bergk, *PLG* iii p. 634.

Catalogus Codicum Astrologorum [*Cat.Cod.Astr.*]
Ed. F. Cumont et alii, Brussels 1898– ; cited by vol. and page.
Cebes Philosophus [Ceb.] i A.D.
Ed. K. Praechter, Leipzig (T.) 1893.
Celsus Medicus [Cels.] i A.D.
Ed. F. Marx, Leipzig 1915.
Celsus Philosophus [Cels.] ii A.D.
Apud Origenem.
Cephalio Historicus ii A.D.
Ed. C. Müller, *FHG* iii p. 625.
Cephisodorus Comicus [Cephisod.] v/iv B.C.
Ed. T. Kock, *CAF* i p. 800.
Cercidas Iambographus [Cerc.] iii B.C.
Ed. J. U. Powell, *Coll. Alex.* p. 201.
Cercopes [Cercop.]
Ed. T. W. Allen, *Homeri Opera* v, Oxford (OCT), p. 159.
Cerealius Epigrammaticus [Cereal.] i/ii A.D. (?)
v. *Anthologia Graeca.*
Certamen Homeri et Hesiodi [Certamen]
Ed. T. W. Allen, *Homeri Opera* v, Oxford (OCT), p. 225.
Chaeremon Historicus [Chaerem.Hist.] i A.D.
Ed. C. Müller, *FHG* iii p. 495.
Chaeremon Tragicus [Chaerem.] iv B.C.
Ed. A. Nauck, *TGF* p. 781.
Chamaeleon Grammaticus [Chamael.]
Apud Athenaeum.
Characteres Epistolici [*Epist.Charact.*]
Demetrii et Libanii qui feruntur τύποι ἐπιστολικοί *et* ἐπιστολιμαῖοι χαρακτῆρες, ed. V. Weichert, Leipzig (T.) 1910.
Charax Historicus ii A.D. (?)
Ed. C. Müller, *FHG* iii p. 636, iv p. 669.
Chares Historicus iv B.C.
Ed. C. Müller, *SRAM* p. 114.
Chares Iambographus [Chares Iamb.] iv/iii B.C.
Ed. J. U. Powell, *Coll. Alex.* p. 223.
Chares Tragicus [Chares Trag.]
Ed. A. Nauck, *TGF* p. 826.
Chariclides Comicus [Chariclid.]
Ed. T. Kock, *CAF* iii p. 393.
Charisius Grammaticus Latinus [Charis.] iv A.D.
Ed. H. Keil, *Gramm. Lat.* vol. i.
Charito Scriptor Eroticus ii A.D. (?)
Ed. R. Hercher, *Erotici* ii p. 3.
Charixenes Medicus [Charixen.] ii A.D.
Apud Galenum.
Charon Historicus v B.C.
Ed. C. Müller, *FHG* i p. 32, iv p. 627.
Charondas Philosophus [Charond.] (vii B.C.)
Apud Stobaeum.
Chilo Lyricus vi B.C.
Ed. T. Bergk, *PLG* iii p. 199.
Chio Epistolographus (iv B.C.)
Ed. R. Hercher, *Epistolographi*, p. 194.
Chionides Comicus [Chionid.] v B.C.
Ed. T. Kock, *CAF* i p. 4.
Choerilus Epicus [Choeril.] v B.C.
Ed. G. Kinkel, *EGF* p. 265.
Choerilus Tragicus [Choeril.Trag.] v B.C.
Ed. A. Nauck, *TGF* p. 719.
Choeroboscus Grammaticus [Choerob.] iv/v A.D.
περὶ ὀρθογραφίας, ed. Cramer, *An. Ox.* ii p. 167.
περὶ τρόπων, ed. L. Spengel, *Rhet.* iii p. 244. [Rh.]
Scholia in Hephaestionem, ed. W. Consbruch, post Hephaestionem, p. 177. [*in Heph.*]
Scholia in Theodosii Canones, ed. A. Hilgard, 2 vols., Leipzig 1889–94. [*in Theod.*]
Choricius Rhetor [Chor.] vi A.D.
Ed. J. F. Boissonade, Paris 1846.
Brum. = εἰς τὰ Ἰουστινιανοῦ Βρουμάλια, ed. R. Förster, *Ind. Lect. Vratisl.* 1891/2, Breslau 1891.
Lyd. = Λυδοί, ed. R. Förster, op. cit.
Milt. = Μιλτιάδης, ed. R. Förster, *Ind. Lect. Vratisl.* 1892/3, Breslau 1892.
Proc. = Ἐπιθαλάμιος εἰς Προκόπιον, ed. R. Förster, *Ind. Lect. Vratisl.* 1891/2, Breslau 1891.
Zach. = Ἐπιθαλάμιος εἰς Ζαχαρίαν, ed. R. Förster, op. cit.
Note.—Other orations cited from periodicals, *Hermes* xvii (1883), *Jahrb.* ix (1894), *Philol.* liv (1895), *Rev. Phil.* i (1877), *Rh. Mus.* xxxvii (1882), xlix (1894), or from Reiske's *Libanius*, vol. iv, pp. 512, 771.
Chrysippus Stoicus [Chrysipp.*Stoic.*] 281–208 B.C.
Ed. H. von Arnim, *SVF* ii and iii pp. 1–194.
Chrysippus Tyanensis Rei Coquinariae Scriptor [Chrysipp. Tyan.] i A.D.
Apud Athenaeum.
Cicero, M. Tullius Orator et Philosophus [Cic.] i B.C.
Acad. = *Academica*, ed. O. Plasberg, Leipzig (T.) 1922.
Att. = *Epistulae ad Atticum*, ed. L. C. Purser, Oxford (OCT).
Brut. = *Brutus*, ed. A. S. Wilkins, Oxford (OCT).
Fam. = *Epistulae ad Familiares*, ed. L. C. Purser, Oxford (OCT).
Fin. = *de Finibus*, ed. T. Schiche, Leipzig (T.) 1915.
ND = *de Natura Deorum*, ed. O. Plasberg, Leipzig (T.) 1917.
Off. = *de Officiis*, ed. C. Atzert, Leipzig (T.) 1923.
Orat. = *Orator*, ed. A. S. Wilkins, Oxford (OCT).
QF = *Epistulae ad Quintum Fratrem*, ed. L. C. Purser, Oxford (OCT).
Top. = *Topica*, ed. W. Friedrich, Leipzig (T.) 1893.
Tusc. = *Tusculanae Disputationes*, ed. M. Pohlenz, Leipzig (T.) 1918.
Cillactor, v. Callicter
Claudianus Epigrammaticus [Claudian.] iv/v A.D.
v. *Anthologia Graeca.*
Claudius Iolaus Historicus [Claud.Iol.]
Ed. C. Müller, *FHG* iv p. 362.
Cleaenetus Tragicus [Cleaenet.] iv B.C.
Ed. A. Nauck, *TGF* p. 807.
Cleanthes Stoicus [Cleanth.*Stoic.*] 331–233 B.C.
Ed. H. von Arnim, *SVF* i p. 103.
Poetical fragments, ed. J. U. Powell, *Coll. Alex.* p. 227.
Clearchus Comicus [Clearch.Com.] iv B.C.
Ed. T. Kock, *CAF* ii p. 408.
Clearchus Historicus [Clearch.] iv/iii B.C.
Ed. C. Müller, *FHG* ii p. 302.
Clemens Alexandrinus Theologus [Clem.Al.] ii/iii A.D.
Ed. O. Stählin, Leipzig 1905–9.
Paed. = *Paedagogus*
Protr. = *Protrepticus*
Strom. = *Stromateis*
Cleobulina Lyrica vi B.C.
Ed. T. Bergk, *PLG* ii p. 62.
Cleobulus Lyricus [Cleobul.] vi B.C.
Ed. T. Bergk, *PLG* iii p. 201.
Cleomedes Astronomus [Cleom.] ii A.D.
Ed. H. Ziegler, Leipzig (T.) 1891.
Cleon Siculus Lyricus [Cleon Sic.]
Ed. T. Bergk, *PLG* ii p. 363.
Cleonides Musicus [Cleonid.] ii A.D.
Harm. = *Introductio Harmonica*, ed. C. Jan, *Musici Scriptores Graeci*, Leipzig (T.) 1895, p. 179; ed. H. Menge, *Euclidis Opera* viii, Leipzig (T.) 1916, p. 186.
Cleopatra Medica
Apud Galenum.
Cleostratus Poeta Philosophus [Cleostrat.] iv/iii B.C. (?)
Ed. H. Diels, *PPF* p. 19.
Clidemus (vel **Clitodemus**) Historicus [Clidem. vel Clitodem.] iv B.C.
Ed. C. Müller, *FHG* i p. 359.
Clinias Philosophus [Clin.] iv B.C.
Apud Stobaeum.
Clitarchus Gnomologus [Clitarch.]
Sententiae, ed. A. Elter, *Index Lect. Hib.* ... Bonn 1892. [*Sent.*]
Clitarchus Historicus [Clitarch.] iv B.C.
Ed. C. Müller, *SRAM* p. 74.
Clitodemus, v. Clidemus
Clitomachus Philosophus [Clitom.] ii B.C.
Apud Stobaeum.
Clitopho Historicus
Ed. C. Müller, *FHG* iv p. 367.
Clytus Historicus iv/iii B.C.
Ed. C. Müller, *FHG* ii p. 333.
Codex Justinianus [*Cod.Just.*] iv/vi A.D.
Ed. P. Krüger, *Corpus Juris Civilis* ii^{9}, Berlin 1915.
Codex Theodosianus [*Cod.Theod.*] v A.D.
Ed. T. Mommsen & P. M. Meyer, Berlin 1895; ed. P. Krüger, Berlin 1923.
Colotes Philosophus [Colot.] iv/iii B.C.
In Platonis Euthydemum, *In Platonis Lysin*, ed. W. Crönert, *Kolotes und Menedemos*, Leipzig 1906. [*in Euthd.*, *in Ly.*]
Coluthus Epicus [Coluth.] v/vi A.D.
Ed. W. Weinberger (post Tryphiodorum), Leipzig (T.) 1896.
Comica Adespota [*Com.Adesp.*]
Ed. T. Kock, *CAF* iii p. 397; suppl. J. Demiańczuk, *Supp. Com.* p. 89, O. Schroeder, *Novae Comoediae fragmenta in papyris reperta exceptis Menandreis*, Bonn 1915.
Conon Historicus i B.C./i A.D.
Ed. F. Jacoby, *FGrH* i p. 190.
Corinna Lyrica [Corinn.] vi B.C.
Ed. T. Bergk, *PLG* iii p. 543; suppl. E. Diehl, *Supp. Lyr.*^{3} p. 48. [*Supp.*]
Cornelius Longus Epigrammaticus [Corn.Long.]
v. *Anthologia Graeca.*
Cornutus Philosophus [Corn.] i A.D.
de Natura Deorum, ed. C. Lang, Leipzig (T.) 1881. [*ND*]
Ars Rhetorica, ed. C. Hammer, in L. Spengel, *Rhet.* i^{2} (2), Leipzig (T.) 1894, p. 352. [*Rh.*]
Corpus Hermeticum [*Corp.Herm.*]
Hermetica, ed. W. Scott, Oxford 1924.

Crantor Philosophus Academicus iv/iii B.C.
Cited from sources; cf. F. W. A. Mullach, *FPG* iii p. 131.
Craterus Historicus [Crater.] iv/iii B.C.
Ed. C. Müller, *FHG* ii p. 617.
Crates Comicus [Crates Com.] v B.C.
Ed. T. Kock, *CAF* i p. 130; suppl. J. Demiańczuk, *Supp. Com.* p. 29.
Crates Historicus [Crates Hist.]
Ed. C. Müller, *FHG* iv p. 369.
Crates Thebanus Poeta Philosophus [Crates Theb.] iv B.C.
Ed. H. Diels, *PPF* p. 207.
Ep. = *Epistulae*, ed. R. Hercher, *Epistolographi*, p. 199.
Crateuas Botanicus ii/i B.C.
Fragmenta, ed. M. Wellmann (post Dioscoridem), vol. iii, p. 144. [*Fr.*]
Cratinus Comicus [Cratin.] v B.C.
Ed. T. Kock, *CAF* i p. 11; suppl. J. Demiańczuk, *Supp. Com.* p. 30.
Cratinus Junior Comicus [Cratin.Jun.] iv B.C.
Ed. T. Kock, *CAF* ii p. 289.
Cratippus Historicus [Cratipp.] v/iv B.C.
Ed. B. P. Grenfell et A. S. Hunt, post *Hellenica Oxyrhynchia*.
Creon Historicus
Ed. C. Müller, *FHG* iv p. 371.
Crinagoras Epigrammaticus [Crin.] i B.C./i A.D.
v. *Anthologia Graeca*.
Crinis Stoicus
Ed. H. von Arnim, *SVF* iii p. 268.
Critias Philosophus, Tragicus, Elegiacus [Critias] v B.C.
Ed. H. Diels, *Vorsokr.* ii p. 308.
Crito Comicus [Crito Com.] ii B.C.
Ed. T. Kock, *CAF* iii p. 354.
Crito Medicus i/ii A.D.
Apud Galenum.
Fragmenta Historica, ed. C. Müller, *FHG* iv p. 373. [Crito Hist.]
Crito Philosophus
Apud Stobaeum.
Crobylus Comicus [Crobyl.] iv B.C.
Ed. T. Kock, *CAF* iii p. 379.
Ctesias Historicus [Ctes.] v/iv B.C.
Ed. C. Müller (post Herodotum Dindorfii), Paris (D.) 1844.
Cydias Lyricus v B.C. (?)
Ed. T. Bergk, *PLG* iii p. 564.
Cyllenius Epigrammaticus [Cyllen.] i A.D. (?)
v. *Anthologia Graeca*.
Cypria [Cypr.]
Ed. T. W. Allen, *Homeri Opera* v, Oxford (OCT), p. 116.
Cyrilli Glossarium [Cyr.]
Ed. M. Schmidt (post Hesychium, vol. iv, p. 362), Jena 1862.
Cyrillus Epigrammaticus [Cyrill.] i A.D. (?)
v. *Anthologia Graeca*.
Cyrus, Flavius Epigrammaticus v A.D.
v. *Anthologia Graeca*.

Daimachus Historicus iii B.C.
Ed. C. Müller, *FHG* ii p. 440.
Damagetus Epigrammaticus [Damag.] iii B.C.
v. *Anthologia Graeca*.
Damascius Philosophus [Dam.] v/vi A.D.
Isid. = *Vita Isidori*, ed. Westermann, v. Diogenes Laertius.
Pr. = *de Principiis*, ed. C. A. Ruelle, Paris 1889.
Damianus Opticus [Damian.]
Opt. = *Optica*, ed. R. Schöne, Berlin 1897.
Damocharis Epigrammaticus [Damoch.] vi A.D.
v. *Anthologia Graeca*.
Damocrates Poeta Medicus [Damocr.] i A.D.
Apud Galenum.
Damocritus Historicus [Damocrit.] i B.C. or i A.D. (?)
Ed. C. Müller, *FHG* iv p. 377.
Damon Historicus
Ed. C. Müller, *FHG* iv p. 377.
Damostratus Epigrammaticus [Damostr.]
v. *Anthologia Graeca*.
Damoxenus Comicus [Damox.] iv/iii B.C.
Ed. T. Kock, *CAF* iii p. 348.
David Philosophus vi A.D.
in Porph. = *in Porphyrii Isagogen commentarium*, ed. A. Busse (*Comm. in Arist. Graeca* xviii *pars* ii), Berlin 1904.
Proll. = *Prolegomena Philosophiae*, ed. A. Busse (ibid.).
Deiochus Historicus [Deioch.]
Ed. C. Müller, *FHG* ii p. 17.
Demades Orator [Demad.] iv B.C.
Ed. F. Blass (v. Dinarchus).
Fr. = *Fragmenta*, ed. H. Sauppe, *Orat. Att.* ii p. 312.
Demetrius Astrologus [Demetr.]
Apud Palchum.
Demetrius Comicus Novae Comoediae [Demetr.Com.Nov.] iv/iii B.C.
Ed. T. Kock, *CAF* iii p. 357.
Demetrius Comicus Veteris Comoediae [Demetr.Com.Vet.] v/iv B.C.
Ed. T. Kock, *CAF* i p. 795.
Demetrius Apamensis Medicus [Demetr.Apam.]
Apud Caelium Aurelianum et Soranum.
Demetrius Lacon Philosophus [Demetr.Lac.]
Ed. W. Crönert, *Kolotes und Menedemos*, Leipzig 1906, p. 100; ed. V. de Falco, Naples 1923.
Demetrius Phalereus Rhetor [Demetr.] iv B.C.
Eloc. = *Demetrius on Style*, ed. W. Rhys Roberts, Cambridge 1902.
Demetrius Phalereus Historicus [Dem.Phal.] iv B.C.
Ed. C. Müller, *FHG* ii p. 362.
Demetrius Troezenius Poeta Philosophus [Demetr.Troez.] i B.C./i A.D. (?)
Ed. H. Diels, *PPF* p. 224.
Demochares Historicus [Democh.] iv/iii B.C.
Ed. C. Müller, *FHG* ii p. 445.
Democritus Epigrammaticus [Democr.]
v. *Anthologia Graeca*.
Democritus Philosophus [Democr.] v B.C.
Ed. H. Diels, *Vorsokr.* ii p. 10.
Pseudo-**Democritus** Alchemista [Ps.-Democr.]
Ed. M. Berthelot, *Collection des anciens alchimistes grecs*, p. 41.
Democritus Ephesius Historicus [Democr.Eph.]
Ed. C. Müller, *FHG* iv p. 383.
Demodocus Lyricus [Demod.] vi B.C.
Ed. T. Bergk, *PLG* ii p. 65.
Demon Historicus iv/iii B.C.
Ed. C. Müller, *FHG* i p. 378, iv pp. 626, 646.
Demonicus Comicus [Demonic.]
Ed. T. Kock, *CAF* iii p. 375.
Demophilus Gnomologus [Demoph.]
Sent. = *Sententiae*, ed. J. C. Orelli, *Opuscula Graecorum Veterum Sententiosa* i p. 37, Leipzig 1819; cf. H. Schenkl, *Wien. Stud.* viii (1886), p. 262.
Sim. = *Similitudines*, ed. F. W. A. Mullach, *FPG* i p. 485; cf. A. Elter, *Gnomica Homoeomata* v, Bonn 1900.
Demosthenes Orator [D.] 384–322 B.C.
Ed. F. Blass, Leipzig (T.) 1888–92; ed. S. H. Butcher & W. Rennie, Oxford (OCT).
Ep. = *Epistulae*
Prooem. = *Prooemia*
Demosthenes Bithynus Epicus [Dem.Bith.] iii B.C. (?)
Ed. J. U. Powell, *Coll. Alex.* p. 25.
Demosthenes Ophthalmicus Medicus [Dem.Ophth.] i A.D.
Apud Aëtium.
Dercylus Historicus [Dercyl.]
Ed. C. Müller, *FHG* iv p. 386.
Dexippus Historicus [Dexipp.] iii A.D.
Ed. L. Dindorf, *HGM* i p. 165.
Dexippus Philosophus [Dexipp.] iv A.D.
in Cat. = *in Aristotelis Categorias commentarium*, ed. A. Busse (*Comm. in Arist. Graeca* iv *pars* ii), Berlin 1888.
Diagoras Lyricus [Diagor.] v B.C.
Ed. T. Bergk, *PLG* iii p. 562.
Dialexeis [*Dialex.*] ca. 400 B.C.
Anonymi Δισσοὶ λόγοι, ed. H. Diels, *Vorsokr.* ii p. 334.
Dicaearchus Geographus [Dicaearch.] iv B.C.
Ed. C. Müller, *GGM* i p. 97.
Dicaearchus Historicus [Dicaearch.Hist.] iv B.C.
Ed. C. Müller, *FHG* ii p. 225.
Dicaeogenes Tragicus [Dicaeog.] iv B.C.
Ed. A. Nauck, *TGF* p. 775.
Didymus Grammaticus [Did.] i B.C.
in D. = *Commentary on Demosthenes*, ed. H. Diels & W. Schubart (*BKT* i), Berlin 1904; cited by col. and line.
Dieuches Medicus [Dieuch.]
Apud Oribasium.
Dieuchidas Historicus [Dieuchid.] iv B.C.
Ed. C. Müller, *FHG* iv p. 388.
Digesta [*Dig.*]
Ed. T. Mommsen & P. Krüger, *Corpus Juris Civilis* i[13], Berlin 1920.
Dinarchus Orator [Din.] iv/iii B.C.
Ed. (cum Demadis fragmentis) F. Blass, Leipzig (T.) 1888.
Fr. = *Fragmenta*, ed. H. Sauppe, *Orat. Att.* ii p. 321.
Dinias Historicus iii B.C.
Ed. C. Müller, *FHG* iii p. 24.
Dinolochus Comicus [Dinol.] v B.C.
Ed. G. Kaibel, *CGF* p. 149.
Dinon Historicus iv B.C.
Ed. C. Müller, *FHG* ii p. 88.
Dio Cassius Historicus [D.C.] ii/iii A.D.
Ed. U. P. Boissevain, Berlin 1895–1901; cited by the numeration of the earlier editions.
Dio Chrysostomus Sophista [D.Chr.] i/ii A.D.
Ed. Guy de Budé, Leipzig (T.) 1916, 1919.
Diocles Epigrammaticus [Diocl.] i A.D.
v. *Anthologia Graeca*.

Diocles Comicus [Diocl.Com.] v B.C.
Ed. T. Kock, *CAF* i p. 766; suppl. J. Demiańczuk, *Supp. Com.* p. 39.
Diocles Medicus [Diocl.*Fr.*]
Ed. M. Wellmann (*Fragmentsammlung der griechischen Ärzte* i p. 117), Berlin 1901.
Diodorus Comicus [Diod.Com.] iv B.C.
Ed. T. Kock, *CAF* ii p. 420.
Diodorus Epigrammaticus [Diod.] i B.C./i A.D.
Idem qui et Zonas, q.v.; v. *Anthologia Graeca.*
Diodorus Rhetor [Diod.Rh.]
Ed. H. Hinck (post Polemonem), Leipzig (T.) 1873, p. 51.
Diodorus Atheniensis Periegeta [Diod.Ath.] iv B.C.
Ed. C. Müller, *FHG* ii p. 353.
Diodorus Siculus Historicus [D.S.] i B.C.
Ed. I. Bekker, L. Dindorf, F. Vogel (C. Th. Fischer), Leipzig (T.) 1888–1906.
Diodorus Tarsensis Epigrammaticus [Diod.Tars.] i B.C./i A.D.
v. *Anthologia Graeca.*
Diogenes Apolloniates Philosophus [Diog.Apoll.] v B.C.
Ed. H. Diels, *Vorsokr.* i p. 416.
Diogenes Atheniensis Tragicus [Diog.Ath.]
Ed. A. Nauck, *TGF* p. 776.
Diogenes Babylonius Stoicus [Diog.Bab.*Stoic.*] ii B.C.
Ed. H. von Arnim, *SVF* iii p. 210.
Diogenes Cynicus Philosophus [Diog.] iv B.C.
Ep. = *Epistulae*, ed. R. Hercher, *Epistolographi*, p. 235; cf. F. W. A. Mullach, *FPG* ii p. 299.
Diogenes Laertius [D.L.] iii A.D. (?)
Diogenis Laertii de clarorum philosophorum vitis . . libri decem . . [ed.] C. G. Cobet: accedunt *Olympiodori, Ammonii, Iamblichi, Porphyrii et aliorum vitae Platonis, Aristotelis, Pythagorae, Plotini et Isidori,* Ant. Westermanno, et *Marini vita Procli* J. F. Boissonadio edentibus, Paris (D.) 1862.
Epigrammata: v. *Anthologia Graeca.*
Diogenes Oenoandensis Epicureus [Diog.Oen.] ii A.D.
Ed. Iohannes William, Leipzig (T.) 1907.
Diogenes Sinopensis Tragicus [Diog.Sinop.] iv B.C.
Ed. A. Nauck, *TGF* p. 807.
Diogenianus Paroemiographus [Diogenian.]
Ed. E. L. von Leutsch & F. G. Schneidewin, *Paroemiographi* i p. 177, ii p. 1.
Diogenianus Epicureus [Diogenian.Epicur.] ii B.C. (?)
Ed. Alfred Gercke, *Jahrbücher für klassische Philologie, Suppl.* xiv p. 748.
Diomedes Grammaticus [Diom.]
Ed. H. Keil, *Gramm. Lat.* i, Leipzig 1857, p. 299.
Dionysius Comicus [Dionys.Com.] iv B.C.
Ed. T. Kock, *CAF* ii p. 423.
Dionysius Epigrammaticus [Dionys.]
v. *Anthologia Graeca.*
Dionysius Rerum Naturalium Scriptor [Dionys.]
Av. = *de Avibus* (Paraphrasis Oppiani Ἰξευτικῶν), ed. F. S. Lehrs (post Oppianum, q.v.).
Dionysius Tragicus [Dionys.Trag.] iv B.C.
Ed. A. Nauck, *TGF* p. 793.
Dionysius Byzantius Geographus [Dion.Byz.] ii/iv A.D. (?)
de Bospori navigatione, ed. C. Wescher, Paris 1874; cited by section.
Dionysius Calliphontis filius Geographus [Dion.Calliph.] i B.C./i A.D.
Ed. C. Müller, *GGM* i p. 238.
Dionysius Chalcus Elegiacus [Dionys.Eleg.] v B.C.
Ed. T. Bergk, *PLG* ii p. 262.
Dionysius Halicarnassensis [D.H.] i B.C.
Antiquitates Romanae, ed. C. Jacoby, Leipzig (T.) 1885–1905; cited without title.
Opuscula, ed. H. Usener, L. Radermacher, Leipzig (T.) 1899, 1904.
Amm. 1, 2 = *Epistula ad Ammaeum* 1, 2
Comp. = *de Compositione Verborum*
Dem. = *de Demosthene*
Din. = *de Dinarcho*
Is. = *de Isaeo*
Isoc. = *de Isocrate*
Lys. = *de Lysia*
Orat.Vett. = *de Oratoribus Veteribus*
Pomp. = *Epistula ad Pompeium*
Rh. = *Ars Rhetorica*
Th. = *de Thucydide*
Vett.Cens. = *de Veterum Censura*, ed. J. Hudson, Oxford 1704.
Dionysius Heracleota Stoicus [Dionys.*Stoic.*] iii B.C.
Ed. H. von Arnim, *SVF* i p. 93.
Dionysius Minor Elegiacus [Dionys.Minor]
Ed. T. Bergk, *PLG* ii p. 324.
Dionysius Periegeta [D.P.]
Ed. G. Bernhardy (cum commentariis Eustathii), Leipzig 1828; cf. C. Müller, *GGM* ii p. 102.
Dionysius Samius Historicus [Dionys.Sam.] ii B.C. (?)
Ed. F. Jacoby, *FGrH* i p. 178.
Dionysius Thrax Grammaticus [D.T.] ii B.C.
Ed. G. Uhlig, Leipzig 1883; cited by Bekker's page, given in Uhlig's margin.
Scholia in Dionysium Thracem, ed. A. Hilgard, *Grammatici Graeci* i *pars* iii, Leipzig 1901.
Diophanes Epigrammaticus [Diophan.]
v. *Anthologia Graeca.*
Diophantus Mathematicus [Dioph.] iii A.D.
Ed. P. Tannery, Leipzig (T.) 1893, 1895.
Dioscorides Epigrammaticus [Diosc.] iii B.C.
v. *Anthologia Graeca.*
Dioscorides Historicus [Diosc.Hist.] iv B.C.
Ed. C. Müller, *FHG* ii p. 192.
Dioscorides (Dioscurides) Medicus [Dsc.] i A.D.
de Materia Medica, ed. M. Wellmann, Berlin 1906–14; cited without title.
Alex. = *Alexipharmaca*; *Ther.* = *Theriaca*; ed. K. Sprengel, *Dioscorides* (vols. xxv and xxvi of *Medici Graeci*, ed. C. G. Kühn), Leipzig 1829.
Eup. = περὶ Εὐποριστῶν, ed. Wellmann (v. supr.).
Dioscorides Glossator [Diosc.Gloss.]
Apud Galenum.
Diotimus Epigrammaticus [Diotim.] iii B.C. (?)
v. *Anthologia Graeca.*
Diotogenes Philosophus [Diotog.]
Apud Stobaeum.
Dioxippus Comicus [Diox.]
Ed. T. Kock, *CAF* iii p. 358.
Diphilus Comicus [Diph.] iv/iii B.C.
Ed. T. Kock, *CAF* ii p. 541; suppl. J. Demiańczuk, *Supp. Com.* p. 40.
Diphilus Siphnius Rerum Naturalium Scriptor [Diph.Siph.] iii B.C.
Apud Athenaeum.
Dius Philosophus
Apud Stobaeum.
Diyllus Historicus [Diyll.] iii B.C.
Ed. C. Müller, *FHG* ii p. 360, iii p. 198.
Donatus, Aelius Grammaticus Latinus [Donat.] iv A.D.
Ed. H. Keil, *Gramm. Lat.* iv p. 353.
Dorio Rerum Naturalium Scriptor i B.C.
Apud Athenaeum.
Dorotheus Astrologus [Doroth.] ii A.D.
Ed. H. Koechly (post Manethonem, q.v.); suppl. *Cat. Cod. Astr.*
Dosiadas Epigrammaticus [Dosiad.] iii B.C.
v. *Anthologia Graeca.*
Ara = *AP* 15. 26.
Dosiades Historicus [Dosiad.Hist.]
Ed. C. Müller, *FHG* iv p. 399.
Dositheus Grammaticus Latinus [Dosith.] iv A.D. (?)
Ed. H. Keil, *Gramm. Lat.* vii p. 363.
Dromo Comicus iv B.C.
Ed. T. Kock, *CAF* ii p. 419.
Duris Epigrammaticus iv/iii B.C.
v. *Anthologia Graeca.*
Duris Historicus iv/iii B.C.
Ed. C. Müller, *FHG* ii p. 466.

Ecphantides Comicus [Ecphantid.] v B.C.
Ed. T. Kock, *CAF* i p. 9.
Ecphantus Pythagoreus [Ecphant.]
Apud Stobaeum.
Elegiaca Alexandrina Adespota [*Eleg.Alex.Adesp.*]
Ed. J. U. Powell, *Coll. Alex.* p. 130.
Elias Philosophus vi A.D.
in Cat. = *in Aristotelis Categorias commentaria*, ed. A. Busse (*Comm. in Arist. Graeca* xviii *pars* i), Berlin 1900.
in Porph. = *in Porphyrii Isagogen commentaria* (ibid.).
Empedocles Poeta Philosophus [Emp.] v B.C.
Ed. H. Diels, *PPF* p. 74.
Sphaer. = *Sphaera*, ed. E. Maass, *Commentariorum in Aratum reliquiae*, pp. 154, 199.
Enoch Judaeus [1*Enoch*] ii/i B.C.
Ed. R. H. Charles, Oxford 1912.
Ephippus Comicus [Ephipp.] iv B.C.
Ed. T. Kock, *CAF* ii p. 250.
Ephorus Historicus [Ephor.] iv B.C.
Ed. C. Müller, *FHG* i p. 234, iv pp. 626, 641; suppl. F. Bilabel, *Die kleineren Historikerfragmente auf Papyrus*, Bonn 1923, p. 7.
Epica Alexandrina Adespota [*Epic.Alex.Adesp.*]
Ed. J. U. Powell, *Coll. Alex.* p. 71.
Epicharmus Comicus [Epich.] v B.C.
Ed. G. Kaibel, *CGF* p. 88.
Pseudepicharmea, v. Axiopistus.
Epicrates Comicus [Epicr.] iv B.C.
Ed. T. Kock, *CAF* ii p. 282.
Epictetus Philosophus [Epict.] i/ii A.D.
Ed. H. Schenkl, Leipzig (T.) 1894.
Ench. = *Enchiridion*
Fr. = *Fragmenta*
Gnom. = *Gnomologium*

Epicurus Philosophus [Epicur.] iv/iii B.C.
Ed. H. Usener, *Epicurea*, Leipzig 1887 (*Epistulae, Fragmenta, Sententiae*); ed. P. von der Mühll, Leipzig (T.) 1922 (*Epistulae, Sententiae, Gnomologium Vaticanum*).
Dial. 1413 = *Dialogus*, in *PHerc.* 1413 (ined.)
Ep. = *Epistulae*
Fr. = *Fragmenta*
Nat. = *De rerum natura*, partim ined. (cited by book [2, 11, 14, 15, or 28] and col. or *Fr.*: unnumbered books cited as *Nat.Herc.* followed by No. of papyrus and col. or *Fr.*: portions edited by Gomperz in *Wien. Stud.* i (1879) p. 27 cited by No. of line, followed by 'G.').
Sent. = *Sententiae* (κύριαι δόξαι)
Sent.Vat. = *Gnomologium Vaticanum*, ed. Wotke-Usener, *Wien. Stud.* X (1888) pp. 175–201 = Usener, *Kleine Schriften* i p. 297; ed. P. von der Mühll (v. supr.).
Note.—Unedited papyri are cited from transcripts furnished by W. Crönert.

Epigenes Comicus [Epig.] iv B.C.
Ed. T. Kock, *CAF* ii p. 416.

Epigoni
Ed. T. W. Allen, *Homeri Opera* v, Oxford (OCT), p. 115.

Epigonus Epigrammaticus [Epig.]
v. *Anthologia Graeca.*

Epilycus Comicus [Epil.] v/iv B.C. (?)
Ed. T. Kock, *CAF* i p. 803; suppl. J. Demiańczuk, *Supp. Com.* p. 40.

Epimenides Philosophus [Epimenid.] vi B.C.
Ed. H. Diels, *Vorsokr.* ii p. 185.

Epinicus Comicus [Epin.] ii B.C.
Ed. T. Kock, *CAF* iii p. 330.

Erasistratus Medicus [Erasistr.] iii B.C.
Apud Galenum.

Eratosthenes Epicus [Eratosth.] iii B.C.
Ed. J. U. Powell, *Coll. Alex.* p. 58.
Cat. = Καταστερισμοί, ed. A. Olivieri, *Mythographi Graeci* iii (1), Leipzig (T.) 1897.

Eratosthenes Scholasticus Epigrammaticus [Eratosth.] vi A.D.
v. *Anthologia Graeca.*

Erinna Lyrica [Erinn.]
Ed. T. Bergk, *PLG* iii p. 141.

Eriphus Comicus [Eriph.] iv B.C.
Ed. T. Kock, *CAF* ii p. 428.

Erotianus Grammaticus [Erot.] i A.D.
Ed. E. Nachmanson, Göteborg (Uppsala) 1918.

Erycius Epigrammaticus [Eryc.] i B.C.
v. *Anthologia Graeca.*

Etruscus Epigrammaticus [Etrusc.]
v. *Anthologia Graeca.*

Etymologicum Genuinum [*Et.Gen.*]
Ineditum; cf. R. Reitzenstein, *Geschichte der griechischen Etymologika*, Leipzig 1897, p. 1 ff.

Etymologicum Gudianum [*Et.Gud.*]
Ed. E. L. de Stefani, fasc. 1 (Α–Β), fasc. 2 (Β–Ζ), Leipzig 1909, 1920; ed. F. W. Sturz, Leipzig 1818.
z = Cod. Par. Suppl. Gr. 172.

Etymologicum Magnum [*EM*]
Ed. T. Gaisford, Oxford 1848.

Euangelus Comicus [Euang.]
Ed. T. Kock, *CAF* iii p. 376.

Eubulides Comicus [Eubulid.]
Ed. T. Kock, *CAF* ii p. 431.

Eubulus Comicus [Eub.] iv B.C.
Ed. T. Kock, *CAF* ii p. 164; suppl. J. Demiańczuk, *Supp. Com.* p. 40.

Euclides Geometra [Euc.] iii B.C.
Ed. J. L. Heiberg & H. Menge, Leipzig (T.) 1883–1916.
Elementa, cited without title
Dat. = *Data*
Fr. = *Fragmenta*
Opt. = *Optica*
Phaen. = *Phaenomena*
Sect.Can. = *Sectio Canonis*

Eucrates Historicus [Eucrat.]
Ed. C. Müller, *FHG* iv p. 407.

Eudemus Philosophus [Eudem.] iv B.C.
Cited from sources. Cf. F. W. A. Mullach, *FPG* iii p. 222; Spengel, *Eudemi Rhodii Fragmenta*, Berlin 1866.

Eudoxus Astronomus [Eudox.] iv B.C.
Ars = *Ars astronomica*, ed. F. Blass, Kiel 1887 (cited by col. and line).

Eudoxus Comicus [Eudox.Com.]
Ed. T. Kock, *CAF* iii p. 332.

Eugaeon Historicus v B.C.
Ed. C. Müller, *FHG* ii p. 16, iv p. 653 [fort. Euagon].

Eugenes Epigrammaticus
v. *Anthologia Graeca.*

Eumelus Epicus [Eumel.] viii B.C. (?)
Ed. G. Kinkel, *EGF* p. 185.

Eunapius Historicus [Eun.] iv/v A.D.
Hist. = *Fragmenta Historica*, ed. L. Dindorf, *HGM* i p. 205.
VS = *Vitae Sophistarum*, ed. J. F. Boissonade (post Philostratum, ed. Westermann), Paris (D.) 1849.

Eunicus Comicus [Eunic.] v B.C.
Ed. T. Kock, *CAF* i p. 781.

Euodus Epigrammaticus [Euod.]
v. *Anthologia Graeca.*

Euphorio Epicus [Euph.] iii B.C.
Ed. J. U. Powell, *Coll. Alex.* p. 28.
Fr.Hist. = *Fragmenta Historica*, ed. C. Müller, *FHG* iii p. 71.

Euphro Comicus iii B.C.
Ed. T. Kock, *CAF* iii p. 317.

Euphronius Lyricus [Euphron.] iii B.C.
Ed. J. U. Powell, *Coll. Alex.* p. 176.

Eupithius Epigrammaticus
v. *Anthologia Graeca.*

Eupolis Comicus [Eup.] v B.C.
Ed. T. Kock, *CAF* i p. 258; suppl. J. Demiańczuk, *Supp. Com.* p. 41.

Euripides Tragicus [E.] v B.C.
Ed. G. G. A. Murray, Oxford (OCT). Fragments, ed. A. Nauck, *TGF* p. 363, and H. von Arnim, *Supplementum Euripideum*, Bonn 1913 (titles of plays cited from this work are distinguished by an asterisk):
Alc. = *Alcestis*
Andr. = *Andromache*
**Antiop.* = *Antiope*
**Archel.* = *Archelaus*
Ba. = *Bacchae*
**Cret.* = *Cretes*
Cyc. = *Cyclops*
El. = *Electra*
Ep. = *Epistulae*, ed. R. Hercher, *Epistolographi*, p. 275.
Epigr. = *Epigrammata*, ed. T. Bergk, *PLG* ii p. 265.
Fr. = *Fragmenta*
HF = *Hercules Furens*
Hec. = *Hecuba*
Hel. = *Helena*
Heracl. = *Heraclidae*
Hipp. = *Hippolytus*
Hyps. = *Hypsipyle*, ed. A. S. Hunt, *Tragicorum Graecorum Fragmenta Papyracea*, Oxford (OCT).
IA = *Iphigenia Aulidensis*
IT = *Iphigenia Taurica*
Ion
Med. = *Medea*
**Melanipp.Capt.* = *Melanippe Captiva*
**Melanipp.Sap.* = *Melanippe Sapiens*
**Oen.* = *Oeneus*
Or. = *Orestes*
Ph. = *Phoenissae*
**Phaëth.* = *Phaëthon*
**Pirith.* = *Pirithous*
Rh. = *Rhesus*
**Sthen.* = *Stheneboea*
Supp. = *Supplices*
Tr. = *Troades*
Scholia in Euripidem, ed. W. Dindorf, 4 vols., Oxford 1863; ed. E. Schwarz, 2 vols., Berlin 1887, 1891.

Euryphamus Pythagoreus [Euryph.]
Apud Stobaeum; cf. F. W. A. Mullach, *FPG* ii p. 15.

Eusebius Historicus [Eus.Hist.] iii A.D.
Ed. L. Dindorf, *HGM* i p. 201.

Eusebius Caesariensis Scriptor Ecclesiasticus [Eus.] iv A.D.
DE = *Demonstratio Evangelica*, ed. I. A. Heikel, Leipzig 1913.
PE = *Praeparatio Evangelica*, ed. E. H. Gifford, Oxford 1903.

Eusebius Myndius Philosophus [Eus.Mynd.]
Ed. F. W. A. Mullach, *FPG* iii p. 7.

Eustathius Episcopus Thessalonicensis [Eust.] xii A.D.
Commentarii ad Homeri Iliadem et Odysseam, ad fidem exempli Romani [*editi*], 7 vols., Leipzig 1825–30.
See also Dionysius Periegeta.

Eustathius Epiphaniensis Historicus [Eust.Epiph.] v A.D.
Ed. L. Dindorf, *HGM* i p. 354.

Eustratius Philosophus [Eustr.] xi/xii A.D.
in APo. = *in Analyticorum Posteriorum librum secundum commentarium*, ed. M. Hayduck (*Comm. in Arist. Graeca* xxi *pars* i), Berlin 1907.
in EN = *in Ethica Nicomachea commentaria*, ed. G. Heylbut (*Comm. in Arist. Graeca* xx), Berlin 1892.

Euthycles Comicus [Euthycl.]
Ed. T. Kock, *CAF* i p. 805.

Eutocius Mathematicus [Eutoc.] vi A.D.
Commentarii in Archimedem et Apollonium Pergaeum (qq. v.).

Eutolmius Epigrammaticus [Eutolm.] vi A.D.
v. *Anthologia Graeca.*

Eutychianus Historicus [Eutych.] iv A.D.
Ed. L. Dindorf, *HGM* i p. 365.

Evenus Elegiacus [Even.] v B.C.
Ed. T. Bergk, *PLG* ii p. 269.

Ezekiel Poeta Judaeus [Ezek.] ii B.C.
Exag. = *Exagoge*, ed. K. Kuiper, *Mnemosyne* xxviii (1900) p. 237.

Favorinus Historicus [Favorin.] ii A.D.
Ed. C. Müller, *FHG* iii p. 577.
Favorinus Philosophus [Favorin.]
Apud Stobaeum.
Festus Grammaticus Latinus [Fest.] ii A.D.
Ed. W. M. Lindsay, Leipzig (T.) 1913.
Firmicus Maternus Astrologus [Firm.] iv A.D.
Ed. W. Kroll & F. Skutsch, Leipzig (T.) 1897, 1913.
Flaccus Epigrammaticus; v. Statyllius, Tullius
Fortunatianus Rhetor [Fortunat.*Rh.*] iv A.D. (?)
Ed. C. Halm, *Rhetores Latini Minores*, p. 79, Leipzig 1863.
Fronto, M. Cornelius Scriptor Latinus ii A.D.
Ep. = *Epistulae*, ed. S. A. Naber, Leipzig 1867; ed. C. R. Haines, London & New York (Loeb) 1919–20.

Gabrielius Epigrammaticus [Gabriel.] vi A.D.
v. *Anthologia Graeca.*
Gaetulicus, Cn. Lentulus Epigrammaticus [Gaet.] i A.D.
v. *Anthologia Graeca.*
Galenus Medicus [Gal.] ii A.D.
Ed. C. G. Kühn, Leipzig 1821–33 (cited by vol. and p.); ed. H. Diels et alii, *CMG* v 4 (2), 9 (1, 2), Leipzig 1918– (in progress): the following works (cited by title) are separately edited in the editions named:
Anim.Pass. = περὶ ψυχῆς παθῶν κτλ., ed. J. Marquardt, *Galeni Scripta Minora* i p. 1, Leipzig (T.) 1884.
Consuet. = περὶ ἐθῶν, ed. I. Müller, *Scripta Minora* (v. supr.) ii p. 9.
Inst.Log. = εἰσαγωγὴ διαλεκτική, ed. C. Kalbfleisch, Leipzig (T.) 1896.
Libr.Ord. = περὶ τῆς τάξεως τῶν ἰδίων βιβλίων, ed. I. Müller, *Scripta Minora* (v. supr.) ii p. 80.
Libr.Propr. = περὶ τῶν ἰδίων βιβλίων, ib. p. 91.
Med.Phil. = ὅτι ὁ ἄριστος ἰατρὸς καὶ φιλόσοφος, ib. p. 1.
Mixt. = περὶ κράσεων, ed. G. Helmreich, Leipzig (T.) 1904.
Nat.Fac. = περὶ φυσικῶν δυνάμεων, ed. G. Helmreich, *Scripta Minora* iii p. 101.
Opt.Doctr. = περὶ τῆς ἀρίστης διδασκαλίας, ed. J. Marquardt, ib. i p. 82.
Parv.Pil. = περὶ τοῦ διὰ τῆς σμικρᾶς σφαίρας γυμνασίου, ib. p. 93.
Phil.Hist. = φιλόσοφος ἱστορία, ed. H. Diels, *Doxographi Graeci*, Berlin 1879.
Protr. = προτρεπτικός, ed. J. Marquardt, *Scripta Minora* i p. 103.
Sect.Intr. = περὶ αἱρέσεων τοῖς εἰσαγομένοις, ed. G. Helmreich, ib. iii p. 1.
Subf.Emp. = *Subfiguratio Empirica*, ed. M. Bonnet, Bonn 1872.
Thras. = Θρασύβουλος, ed. G. Helmreich, *Scripta Minora* iii p. 33.
UP = *de Usu Partium*, ed. G. Helmreich, Leipzig (T.) 1907–9.
Vict.Att. = περὶ λεπτυνούσης διαίτης, ed. C. Kalbfleisch, *CMG* v (4), Leipzig 1923.
The work *De placitis Hippocratis et Platonis* (cited by vol. and p. of Kühn) has been re-edited by I. Müller, Leipzig 1874.
Gallus Epigrammaticus i B.C. (?)
v. *Anthologia Graeca.*
Gaudentius Musicus [Gaud.*Harm.*]
Ed. C. Jan, *Musici Scriptores Graeci*, Leipzig (T.) 1895, p. 327.
Gauradas Epigrammaticus
v. *Anthologia Graeca.*
Gellius, Aulus Grammaticus Latinus [Gell.] ii A.D.
Ed. C. Hosius, Leipzig (T.) 1903.
Geminus Astronomicus [Gem.] i B.C.
Ed. C. Manitius, Leipzig (T.) 1898.
Calend. = *Calendarium*, ed. C. Wachsmuth (post Lyd. *Ost.*, p. 181).
Geminus Epigrammaticus; v. Tullius Geminus.
Geoponica [*Gp.*]
Ed. H. Beckh, Leipzig (T.) 1895.
Germanicus Caesar Epigrammaticus [Germ.] i B.C./i A.D.
v. *Anthologia Graeca.*
Glaucus Atheniensis Epigrammaticus [Glauc.]
v. *Anthologia Graeca.*
Glaucus Nicopolitanus Epigrammaticus [Glauc.]
v. *Anthologia Graeca.*
Glossaria [*Gloss.*]
Ed. G. Loewe, G. Goetz & F. Schoell, *Corpus Glossariorum Latinorum*, Leipzig 1888–1924.
Gorgias Rhetor et Sophista [Gorg.] v B.C.
Ed. H. Diels, *Vorsokr.* ii p. 235.
Hel., *Pal.* = *Helena*, *Palamedes*, ed. F. Blass (post Antiphontem, q.v.).
Gorgon Historicus
Ed. C. Müller, *FHG* iv p. 410.
Gregorius Corinthius Grammaticus [Greg.Cor.] xii A.D.
Ed. G. H. Schaefer, Leipzig 1811.
Trop. = περὶ τρόπων, ed. L. Spengel, *Rhet.* iii p. 215.
Gregorius Cyprius Paroemiographus [Greg.Cypr.] xiii A.D.
Ed. E. L. von Leutsch & F. G. Schneidewin, *Paroemiographi* i p. 349, ii p. 53.

Hadrianus Rhetor [Hadr.Rh.] ii A.D.
Ed. H. Hinck (post Polemonem, p. 44), Leipzig (T.) 1873.
Hadrianus Imperator Epigrammaticus [Hadr.] ii A.D.
v. *Anthologia Graeca.*
Hanno Geographus translated iv B.C.
Peripl. = *Periplus*, ed. C. Müller, *GGM* i p. 1.
Harmodius Historicus [Harmod.]
Ed. C. Müller, *FHG* iv p. 411.
Harpocratio Grammaticus [Harp.] i or ii A.D.
Ed. W. Dindorf, Oxford 1853.
Harpocratio Medicus et Astrologus [Harp.Astr.] i A.D.
in *Cat. Cod. Astr.*
Hecataeus Abderita Historicus [Hecat.Abd.] iii B.C.
Ed. C. Müller, *FHG* ii p. 384.
Hecataeus Milesius Historicus [Hecat.] vi/v B.C.
Ed. F. Jacoby, *FGrH* i p. 1.
Hedyle Epigrammatica
Apud Athenaeum.
Hedylus Epigrammaticus [Hedyl.] iii B.C.
v. *Anthologia Graeca.*
Hegemon Comicus et Parodus [Hegem.] v B.C.
Ed. T. Kock, *CAF* i p. 700; ed. P. Brandt, *Corpusculum poesis epicae ludibundae* i p. 42, Leipzig (T.) 1888.
Hegesander Historicus [Hegesand.]
Ed. C. Müller, *FHG* iv p. 412.
Hegesianax Epicus [Hegesian.] ii B.C.
Ed. J. U. Powell, *Coll. Alex.* p. 8.
Hegesias Historicus
Ed. C. Müller, *SRAM* p. 138.
Hegesippus Comicus [Hegesipp.Com.] iii B.C.
Ed. T. Kock, *CAF* iii p. 312.
Hegesippus Epigrammaticus [Hegesipp.]
v. *Anthologia Graeca.*
Heliodorus Scriptor Eroticus [Hld.] iii A.D.
Ed. W. A. Hirschig, *Erotici*, p. 223, Paris (D.) 1856.
Heliodorus Medicus [Heliod.] i/ii A.D.
Apud Oribasium.
Heliodorus Periegeta [Heliod.Hist.]
Ed. C. Müller, *FHG* iv p. 425.
Heliodorus Philosophus [Heliod.]
in EN = *in Ethica Nicomachea paraphrasis*, ed. G. Heylbut (*Comm. in Arist. Graeca* xix *pars* ii), Berlin 1889.
Helladius Epigrammaticus [Hellad.] ii A.D. (?)
v. *Anthologia Graeca.*
Helladius [Hellad.]
Apud Photium (*Bibl.*, cod. 279).
Hellanicus Historicus [Hellanic.] v B.C.
Ed. F. Jacoby, *FGrH* i p. 104.
Hellenica Oxyrhynchia [*Hell.Oxy.*]
Cum Theopompi et Cratippi fragmentis, ed. B. P. Grenfell & A. S. Hunt, Oxford (OCT).
Hemerologium Florentinum [*Hemerolog.Flor.*]
= *Histoire de l'Acad. roy. des Inscr. et Belles-lettres avec Mém. de litt.*, Paris, t. xlvii, 1809, pp. 66–84.
Heniochus Comicus [Henioch.]
Ed. T. Kock, *CAF* ii p. 431.
Hephaestio Astrologus [Heph.Astr.] iv A.D.
in *Cat. Cod. Astr.*
Bk. i, ed. A. Engelbrecht, Vienna 1887.
Hephaestio Grammaticus [Heph.]
Hephaestionis Enchiridion cum commentariis veteribus, ed. M. Consbruch, Leipzig (T.) 1906; cited without title.
Poëm. = περὶ ποιημάτων, ed. M. Consbruch, ibid. p. 62.
Scholia, ibid. p. 79; ed. R. Westphal, *Scriptores Metrici Graeci* i p. 95, Leipzig (T.) 1866.
Heraclas Medicus [Heracl.]
Apud Oribasium.
Heraclides Comicus [Heraclid.Com.] iv B.C.
Ed. T. Kock, *CAF* ii p. 435.
Heraclides Historicus [Heraclid.]
Pol. = περὶ πολιτειῶν, ed. V. Rose, in Arist. *Fr.* pp. 370–86.
Heraclides Cumaeus Historicus [Heraclid.Cum.] iv B.C.
Ed. C. Müller, *FHG* ii p. 95.
Heraclides Lembus Historicus [Heraclid.Lemb.] ii B.C.
Ed. C. Müller, *FHG* iii p. 167.
Heraclides Ponticus Historicus [Heraclid.Pont.] iv B.C.
Ed. C. Müller, *FHG* ii p. 197; cf. O. Voss, *De Heraclidis Pontici vita et scriptis*, Rostock 1896.
Heraclides Sinopensis Epigrammaticus [Heraclid.Sinop.]
v. *Anthologia Graeca.*
Heraclides Tarentinus Medicus [Heraclid.] i B.C.
Apud Galenum.
Heraclitus [Heraclit.] i A.D. (?)
All. = *Allegoriae* = *Quaestiones Homericae*, ediderunt societatis philologae Bonnensis sodales, prolegomena scripsit F. Oelmann, Leipzig (T.) 1910.
Heraclitus Epigrammaticus [Heraclit.] iii B.C.
Anthologia Graeca.

Heraclitus Paradoxographus [Heraclit.]
Incred. = *de incredibilibus*, ed. N. Festa, *Mythographi Graeci* iii (2), Leipzig (T.) 1902.

Heraclitus Philosophus [Heraclit.] vi/v B.C.
Ed. H. Diels, *Vorsokr.* i p. 67.
Ep. = *Epistulae*, ed. R. Hercher, *Epistolographi*, p. 280.

Herillus Carthaginiensis Stoicus [Herill.*Stoic.*] iii B.C.
Ed. H. von Arnim, *SVF* i p. 91.

Hermes Trismegistus [Herm.]
Apud Stobaeum: see also *Corpus Hermeticum*.

Hermesianax Elegiacus [Hermesian.] iv/iii B.C.
Ed. J. U. Powell, *Coll. Alex.* p. 96.

Hermias Historicus [Herm.Hist.] iv B.C.
Ed. C. Müller, *FHG* ii p. 80.

Hermias Iambographus [Herm.Iamb.] iii B.C. (?)
Ed. J. U. Powell, *Coll. Alex.* p. 237.

Hermias Alexandrinus Philosophus [Herm.] v A.D.
in Phdr. = *in Platonis Phaedrum scholia*, ed. P. Couvreur, Paris 1901; cited by Ast's pages, given in Couvreur's margin.

Hermippus Comicus [Hermipp.] v B.C.
Ed. T. Kock, *CAF* i p. 224; suppl. J. Demiańczuk, *Supp. Com.* p. 53.
Iamb. = *Fragmenta Iamborum*, ed. T. Bergk, *PLG* ii p. 505.

Hermippus Historicus [Hermipp.Hist.] iii/ii B.C.
Ed. C. Müller, *FHG* iii p. 35.

Hermocles Lyricus [Hermocl.] iv/iii B.C.
Ed. J. U. Powell, *Coll. Alex.* p. 173.

Hermocreon Epigrammaticus [Hermocr.]
v. *Anthologia Graeca.*

Hermodorus Epigrammaticus [Hermod.]
v. *Anthologia Graeca.*

Hermogenes Rhetor [Hermog.] ii A.D.
Ed. H. Rabe, Leipzig (T.) 1913.
Id. = περὶ ἰδεῶν
Inv. = περὶ εὑρέσεως
Meth. = περὶ μεθόδου δεινότητος
Prog. = προγυμνάσματα
Stat. = περὶ τῶν στάσεων

Hermon vel **Hermonax** Epicus
Ed. J. U. Powell, *Coll. Alex.* p. 251.

Hero Mechanicus ii/i B.C. (?)
Ed. W. Schmidt, H. Schöne, J. L. Heiberg, Leipzig (T.) 1899–1914; *Belopoeica*, ed. R. Schneider, Metz 1907; spurious treatises (distd. by asterisk), ed. F. Hultsch, Berlin 1864.
Aut. = *Automatopoetica*
Bel. = *Belopoeica*
**Deff.* = *Definitiones*
Dioptr. = *Dioptra*
**Geep.* = *Liber Geeponicus*
**Geom.* = *Geometrica*
**Mens.* = *Mensurae*
Metr. = *Metrica*
Spir. = (*Spiritalia*) *Pneumatica*
**Stereom.* = *Stereometrica*

Herodas Mimographus [Herod.] iii B.C.
Ed. W. Headlam & A. D. Knox, Cambridge 1922.

Herodianus Grammaticus [Hdn.] ii A.D.
Hdn.Gr. = *Herodiani Technici reliquiae*, ed. A. Lentz, Leipzig 1867–70 (cited by vol. and p.).
Hdn.*Epim.* = *Partitiones*, ed. J. F. Boissonade, London 1819.
Hdn.*Philet.* = *Philetaerus*, ed. Pierson, with Moeris, q. v.
Hdn.*Vers.* = *de Versibus*, ed. W. Studemund, *Jahrbücher für klassische Philologie* xcv (1867) p. 618.

Herodianus Historicus [Hdn.] iii A.D.
Ed. K. Stavenhagen, Leipzig (T.) 1922.

Herodianus Rhetor [Hdn.]
Fig. = *de Figuris*, ed. L. Spengel, *Rhet.* iii p. 83.

Herodorus Historicus [Herodor.] v/iv B.C.
Ed. F. Jacoby, *FGrH* i p. 215.

Herodotus Historicus [Hdt.] v B.C.
Ed. C. Hude, Oxford (OCT).
Ps.-Hdt.*Vit.Hom.* = *Vita Homeri*, ed. T. W. Allen, *Homeri Opera* v, Oxford (OCT), p. 192.

Herodotus Medicus [Herod.Med.] i A.D.
Apud Oribasium.
Cf. R. Fuchs, *Rheinisches Museum* xlix (1894) p. 532, l (1895) p. 576, lviii (1903) p. 69, *Festschrift zu J. Vahlens 70. Geburtstag*, p. 147 sq.; M. Wellmann, *Hermes* xl (1905) p. 580, xlviii (1913) p. 141.

Herophilus Medicus [Herophil.] iii B.C.
Apud Galenum.

Hesiodus Epicus [Hes.]
Ed. A. Rzach, editio tertia, Leipzig (T.) 1913.
Fr. = *Fragmenta*
Op. = *Opera et Dies*
Sc. = *Scutum Herculis*
Th. = *Theogonia*

Hesychius Milesius Historicus [Hsch.Mil.] vi A.D.
Ed. C. Müller, *FHG* iv p. 143.

Hesychius Lexicographus [Hsch.] v A.D. (?)
Ed. M. Schmidt, Jena 1858–68.

Hicesius Medicus [Hices.] i B.C.
Apud Athenaeum.

Hierocles Facetiarum Scriptor [Hierocl.] iv A.D. (?)
Ed. A. Eberhard, *Philogelos: Hieroclis et Philagrii facetiae*, Berlin 1869. [*Facet.*]

Hierocles Historicus [Hierocl.Hist.] iii A.D. (?)
Ed. C. Müller, *FGH* iv p. 429.

Hierocles Platonicus Philosophus [Hierocl.] v A.D.
in CA = *in Carmen Aureum*, ed. F. W. A. Mullach, *FPG* i p. 408.
Prov. = *de providentia*, apud Photium; cited by Bekker's page.

Hierocles Stoicus Philosophus [Hierocl.] i/ii A.D.
Ed. H. v. Arnim, *BKT* iv (1906); cited by Arnim's page.

Hieronymus Cardianus Historicus [Hieronym.Hist.] iv/iii B.C.
Ed. C. Müller, *FHG* ii p. 450.

Himerius Sophista [Him.] iv A.D.
Ed. F. Dübner, Paris (D.) 1849 (post Philostratum, ed. Westermann).
Ecl. = *Eclogae*
Or. = *Orationes*

Hippagoras Historicus
Ed. C. Müller, *FHG* iv p. 430.

Hipparchus Astronomicus [Hipparch.] ii B.C.
Ed. C. Manitius, Leipzig (T.) 1894.

Hipparchus Comicus [Hipparch.Com.] iii B.C. (?)
Ed. T. Kock, *CAF* iii p. 272.

Hipparchus Philosophus Pythagoreus [Hipparch.]
Apud Stobaeum; cf. F. W. A. Mullach, *FPG* ii p. 16.

Hippias Eleus Historicus et Sophista v B.C.
Ed. F. Jacoby, *FGrH* i p. 156; ed. H. Diels, *Vorsokr.* ii p. 282.

Hippias Erythraeus Historicus [Hippias Erythr.]
Ed. C. Müller, *FHG* iv p. 431.

Hippiatrica [*Hippiatr.*]
Veterinariae Medicinae libri duo, ed. S. Grynaeus, Basel 1537; ed. E. Oder & C. Hoppe, Leipzig (T.) 1924.

Hippocrates Medicus [Hp.] v B.C.
Ed. E. Littré, 10 vols., Paris 1839–61; ed. H. Kuehlewein, vols. i–ii (all published), Leipzig 1894, 1902.
Acut. = περὶ διαίτης ὀξέων
Acut.(Sp.) = περὶ διαίτης ὀξέων (νόθα)
Aër. = περὶ ἀέρων ὑδάτων τόπων
Aff. = περὶ παθῶν
Alim. = περὶ τροφῆς
Anat. = περὶ ἀνατομῆς
Aph. = ἀφορισμοί
Art. = περὶ ἄρθρων ἐμβολῆς
de Arte = περὶ τέχνης
Carn. = περὶ σαρκῶν
Coac. = Κωακαὶ προγνώσιες
Cord. = περὶ καρδίης
Decent. = περὶ εὐσχημοσύνης
Dent. = περὶ ὀδοντοφυΐης
Dieb.Judic. = περὶ κρισίμων ἡμερέων
Ep. = ἐπιστολαί
Epid. = ἐπιδημίαι
Fist. = περὶ συρίγγων
Flat. = περὶ φυσῶν
Foet.Exsect. = περὶ ἐγκατατομῆς ἐμβρύου
Fract. = περὶ ἀγμῶν
Genit. = περὶ γονῆς
Gland. = περὶ ἀδένων
Haem. = περὶ αἱμορροΐδων
Hebd. = περὶ ἑβδομάδων, ed. W. H. Roscher, *Die Hippokratische Schrift von der Siebenzahl*, Paderborn 1913.
Hum. = περὶ χυμῶν
Insomn. = περὶ ἐνυπνίων
Int. = περὶ τῶν ἐντὸς παθῶν
Judic. = περὶ κρισίων
Jusj. = ὅρκος
Lex = νόμος
Liqu. = περὶ ὑγρῶν χρήσιος
Loc.Hom. = περὶ τόπων τῶν κατὰ ἄνθρωπον
Medic. = περὶ ἰητροῦ
Mochl. = μοχλικόν
Morb. = περὶ νούσων
Morb.Sacr. = περὶ ἱερῆς νούσου
Mul. = γυναικεῖα
Nat.Hom. = περὶ φύσιος ἀνθρώπου
Nat.Mul. = περὶ γυναικείης φύσιος
Nat.Puer. = περὶ φύσιος παιδίου
Oct. = περὶ ὀκταμήνου
Off. = κατ' ἰητρεῖον
Oss. = περὶ ὀστέων φύσιος
Praec. = παραγγελίαι
Prog. = προγνωστικόν
Prorrh. = προρρητικόν
Salubr. = περὶ διαίτης ὑγιεινῆς

Septim. = περὶ ἑπταμήνου
Septim.(Sp.) = περὶ ἑπταμήνου (second treatise)
Steril. = περὶ ἀφόρων
Superf. = περὶ ἐπικυήσιος
Ulc. = περὶ ἑλκῶν
VC = περὶ τῶν ἐν κεφαλῇ τρωμάτων
VM = περὶ ἀρχαίης ἰητρικῆς
Vict. = περὶ διαίτης
Vid.Ac. = περὶ ὄψιος
Virg. = περὶ παρθενίων

Hippodamus Pythagoreus [Hippod.]
Apud Stobaeum.

Hippolytus Scriptor Ecclesiasticus [Hippol.] iii A. D.
Haer. = *Refutatio Omnium Haeresium*, ed. P. Wendland, Leipzig 1916.

Hippon Philosophus v B. C.
Ed. H. Diels, *Vorsokr.* i p. 288.

Hipponax Iambographus [Hippon.] vi B. C.
Ed. T. Bergk, *PLG* ii p. 460.

Hippothoon Tragicus
Ed. A. Nauck, *TGF* p. 827.

Hippys Historicus v B. C. (?)
Ed. C. Müller, *FHG* ii p. 12.

Historiae Augustae Scriptores [*Hist.Aug.*]
Scriptores Historiae Augustae, ed. H. Peter², Leipzig (T.) 1884.

Homerus Epicus [Hom.]
Ed. D. B. Monro & T. W. Allen, Oxford (OCT).
Batr. = Batrachomyomachia (q.v.)
Il. = Ilias
Od. = Odyssea
} sine auctoris nomine laudantur.
Epigr. = *Epigrammata*, ed. D. B. Monro, Oxford 1896. [Hom. *Epigr.*]
Hymni, v. Hymni Homerici.
Scholia in Homeri Iliadem, ed. W. Dindorf, 4 vols., Oxford 1874; vols. v and vi, ed. E. Maass, Oxford 1887–8.
Scholia in Homeri Odysseam, ed. W. Dindorf, Oxford 1855.

Honestus Epigrammaticus [Honest.] i B. C. (?)
v. *Anthologia Graeca.*

Horapollo [Horap.] iv A. D. (?)
Hieroglyphica, ed. J. C. de Pauw, Utrecht 1727; ed. C. Leemans, Amsterdam 1835.

Hymni Homerici [*h.Hom.*]
Ed. T. W. Allen, *Homeri Opera* v, Oxford (OCT).
h.Ap. = *hymnus ad Apollinem*
h.Bacch. = *hymnus ad Bacchum*
h.Cer. = *hymnus ad Cererem*
h.Mart. = *hymnus ad Martem*
h.Merc. = *hymnus ad Mercurium*
h.Pan. = *hymnus ad Panem*
h.Ven. = *hymnus ad Venerem*

Hymni Magici [*Hymn.Mag.*]
Ed. G. Parthey, *Abh. Berl. Akad.* 1865, p. 109 sqq.; cf. C. Wessely, *Denkschr. Wien. Akad., philol.-hist. Kl.* xxxvi (2) (1888) p. 27: v. Orphica.

Hymnus ad Idaeos Dactylos [*Hymn.Id.Dact.*] iv B. C.
Ed. J. U. Powell, *Coll. Alex.* p. 171.

Hymnus ad Isim [*Hymn.Is.*]
IG 12(5).739.

Hymnus Curetum [*Hymn.Curet.*] iii B. C. (?)
Ed. J. U. Powell, *Coll. Alex.* p. 160.

Hyperides Orator [Hyp.] iv B. C.
Ed. F. G. Kenyon, Oxford (OCT)
Ath. = *adv. Athenogenem*
Dem. = *adv. Demosthenem*
Epit. = *Epitaphius*
Eux. = *pro Euxenippo*
Fr. = *Fragmenta*
Lyc. = *pro Lycophrone*
Phil. = *adv. Philippum*

Hypsicles Astronomus [Hypsicl.] ii B. C.
Ed. C. Manitius, Dresden 1888.

Iamblichus Philosophus [Iamb.] iv A. D.
Comm.Math. = *de communi mathematica scientia*, ed. N. Festa, Leipzig (T.) 1891.
in Nic. = *in Nicomachi arithmeticam introductionem*, ed. H. Pistelli, Leipzig (T.) 1894 (cited by page).
Myst. = *de Mysteriis*, ed. G. Parthey, Berlin 1857.
Protr. = *Protrepticus*, ed. H. Pistelli, Leipzig (T.) 1888.
VP = *de vita Pythagorica*, ed. A. Nauck, Leipzig 1884.

Iamblichus Scriptor Eroticus [Iamb.*Bab.*] ii A. D.
Ed. R. Hercher, *Erotici* i p. 217.

Ibycus Lyricus [Ibyc.] vi B. C.
Ed. T. Bergk, *PLG* iii p. 235.
Oxy. = *POxy.* 1790.

Idomeneus Historicus iii B. C.
Ed. C. Müller, *FHG* ii p. 489.

Ilias [Il.]
v. Homerus.

Ilias Parva [Il.Parv.]
Ed. T. W. Allen, *Homeri Opera* v, Oxford (OCT), p. 127.

Iliu Persis [Il.Pers.]
Ed. T. W. Allen, *Homeri Opera* v, Oxford (OCT), p. 137.

Ion Chius
Fragmenta Elegiaca, ed. T. Bergk, *PLG* ii p. 251. [Ion Eleg.]
Fragmenta Historica, ed. C. Müller, *FHG* ii p. 44. [Ion Hist.]
Fragmenta Lyrica, ed. T. Bergk, *PLG* ii p. 255. [Ion Lyr.]
Fragmenta Tragica, ed. A. Nauck, *TGF* p. 732. [Ion Trag.]

Iophon Tragicus v B. C.
Ed. A. Nauck, *TGF* p. 761.

Irenaeus Epigrammaticus [Iren.] vi A. D.
v. *Anthologia Graeca.*

Isaeus Orator [Is.] iv B. C.
Ed. T. Thalheim, Leipzig (T.) 1903.

Isidorus Tragicus [Isid.Trag.]
Ed. A. Nauck, *TGF* p. 829.

Isidorus Aegeates Epigrammaticus [Isid.Aeg.]
v. *Anthologia Graeca.*

Isidorus Characenus Geographus [Isid.Char.] i B. C./i A. D.
Ed. C. Müller, *GGM* i p. 244.

Isidorus Hispalensis Grammaticus [Isid.] vi/vii A. D.
Etym. = *Etymologiae*, ed. W. M. Lindsay, Oxford (OCT).

Isidorus Scholasticus Epigrammaticus [Isid.] vi A. D.
v. *Anthologia Graeca.*

Isigonus Paradoxographus [Isig.] ii/i B. C. (?)
Ed. C. Müller, *FHG* iv p. 435.

Isocrates Orator [Isoc.] v/iv B. C.
Ed. F. Blass, 2 vols., Leipzig (T.) 1889–98.
Ep. = *Epistulae*

Ister Historicus iii B. C.
Ed. C. Müller, *FHG* i p. 409.

Isyllus Lyricus [Isyll.] iii B. C.
Ed. J. U. Powell, *Coll. Alex.* p. 132 (= *IG* 4.950).

Joannes Alexandrinus Grammaticus [Jo.Alex. vel Jo.Gramm.] vi A. D.
Idem qui Philoponus (q.v.).
Compendium περὶ διαλέκτων, ed. O. Hoffmann, *Die griechischen Dialekte* ii, Göttingen 1893, p. 204. [Jo.Gramm.*Comp.*]
τονικὰ παραγγέλματα, ed. W. Dindorf, Leipzig 1825. [Jo.Alex.]

Joannes Diaconus Grammaticus [Jo.Diac.]
Ed. T. Gaisford, *Poetae Graeci Minores*, vol. iii, p. 448.

Joannes Gazaeus [Jo.Gaz.] vi A. D.
Ed. P. Friedländer, Leipzig–Berlin 1912.

Josephus Historicus [J.] i A. D.
Ed. S. A. Naber, Leipzig (T.) 1888–96.
AJ = *Antiquitates Judaicae*
Ap. = *contra Apionem*
BJ = *Bellum Judaicum*
Vit. = *Vita*

Juba, Rex Mauretaniae Historicus i B. C./i A. D.
Ed. C. Müller, *FHG* iii p. 465.

Julianus Imperator [Jul.] iv A. D.
Ed. F. C. Hertlein, Leipzig (T.) 1875–6.
ad Ath. = *Epistula ad Athenienses*
ad Them. = *Epistula ad Themistium*
Caes. = *Caesares*
Ep. = *Epistulae*, ed. J. Bidez & F. Cumont, Paris 1922.
Gal. = *contra Galilaeos*, ed. C. J. Neumann, Leipzig 1880.
Mis. = *Misopogon*
Or. = *Orationes*

Julianus Aegyptius Epigrammaticus [Jul. vel Jul.Aegypt.] vi A. D.
v. *Anthologia Graeca.*

Julianus Laodicensis Astrologus [Jul.Laod.] v/vi A. D.
v. *Catalogus Codicum Astrologorum.*

Juncus Philosophus [Junc.] ii A. D. (?)
Apud Stobaeum.

Justinianus Imperator [Just.] vi A. D.
Constitutio Δέδωκεν, ed. P. Krüger, *Corpus Juris Civilis* i¹³, Berlin 1920. [*Const.*Δέδωκεν]
Constitutio '*omnem*', ed. P. Krüger, op. cit. [*Const.omnem*]
Edicta, ed. R. Schoell et W. Kroll, *Corpus Juris Civilis* iii⁴, Berlin 1905. [*Edict.*]
Novellae, ed. R. Schoell et W. Kroll, op. cit. [*Nov.*]

Juvenalis, D. Junius Poeta Latinus [Juv.] i A. D.
Ed. S. G. Owen, Oxford (OCT) (post Persium).

Laco Epigrammaticus
v. *Anthologia Graeca.*

Lamprocles Lyricus [Lamprocl.] v B. C.
Ed. T. Bergk, *PLG* iii p. 554.

Lasus Lyricus vi B. C.
Ed. T. Bergk, *PLG* iii p. 376.

Leo Philosophus Epigrammaticus [Leo Phil.] v A. D.
v. *Anthologia Graeca.*

Leonidas Epigrammaticus [Leon.] iii B. C.
v. *Anthologia Graeca.*

Leonidas Medicus [Leonid.] i/ii A. D.
Apud Oribasium.
Leonidas Alexandrinus Epigrammaticus [Leon.] I A. D.
v. *Anthologia Graeca.*
Leontius Epigrammaticus [Leont.] vi A. D.
v. *Anthologia Graeca.*
Leontius Mathematicus [Leont. *in Arat.*] vii A. D.
Ed. E. Maass, *Commentariorum in Aratum reliquiae*, Berlin 1898, p. 559.
Lesbonax Grammaticus [Lesb.Gramm.] ii A. D.
Ed. R. Müller, Leipzig 1900.
Lesbonax Rhetor [Lesb.Rh.] ii A. D.
Ed. F. Kiehr, Leipzig 1907.
Leucippus Philosophus [Leucipp.] v B.C.
Ed. H. Diels, *Vorsokr.* ii p. 1.
Leucon Comicus v/iv B.C.
Ed. T. Kock, *CAF* i p. 703.
Lexicon Messanense [*Lex.Mess.*]
Ed. H. Rabe, *Rh. Mus.* xlvii (1892) p. 404; l (1895) p. 148.
Lexicon Rhetoricum [*Lex.Rhet.*]
Apud Aelium Dionysium et Eustathium.
Lexicon Rhetoricum Cantabrigiense [*Lex.Rhet.Cant.*]
Ed. M. H. E. Meier, Halle 1844; ed. E. O. Houtsma, Leyden 1870.
Lexicon Sabbaiticum [*Lex.Sabb.*]
Ed. A. Papadopulos-Kerameus, Petersburg 1892.
Lexicon de Spiritu [*Lex. de Spir.*]
Ed. L. C. Valckenaer (post Ammonium).
Lexicon Vindobonense [*Lex.Vind.*]
Ed. A. Nauck, Petersburg 1867.
Libanius Sophista [Lib.] iv A.D.
Ed. R. Foerster, Leipzig (T.) 1903–1923.
Arg.D. = *Argumenta Orationum Demosthenicarum* (viii p. 600)
Chr. = *Chriae* (viii p. 63)
Comp. = *Comparationes* (viii p. 334)
Conf. = *Confirmationes* (viii p. 138)
Decl. = *Declamationes* (v–vii)
Def.Leg. = *Defensio Legis* (viii p. 568)
Descr. = *Descriptiones* (viii p. 460)
Enc. = *Encomia* (viii p. 216)
Ep. = *Epistulae* (x, xi)
Eth. = *Ethopoeiae* (viii p. 372)
Fab. = *Fabulae* (viii p. 24)
Loc. = *Loci Communes* (viii p. 158)
Narr. = *Narrationes* (viii p. 33)
Or. = *Orationes* (i–iv)
Ref. = *Refutationes* (viii p. 123)
Sent. = *Sententiae* (viii p. 106)
Thes. = *Theses* (viii p. 550)
Vit. = *Vituperationes* (viii p. 282)
Licymnius Lyricus [Licymn.] iv B.C.
Ed. T. Bergk, *PLG* iii p. 598.
Limenius Lyricus [Limen.] ii B.C.
Ed. J. U. Powell, *Coll. Alex.* p. 149.
Linus Epicus
Apud Stobaeum.
Lollius Bassus Epigrammaticus [Loll.] i A.D.
v. *Anthologia Graeca*; cf. Bassus.
Longinus Rhetor [Longin.] (iii A.D.)
Ed. A. O. Prickard, Oxford (OCT); cited without title.
Fr. = *Fragmenta*, ed. C. Hammer in L. Spengel, *Rhet.* i^2 (2), Leipzig (T.) 1894, p. 213.
Proll.Heph. = *Prolegomena ad Hephaestionis Euchiridion*, ed. M. Consbruch (post Hephaestionem), Leipzig (T.) 1906, pp. 81 ff.
Rh. = *Ars Rhetorica*, ed. C. Hammer, op. cit., p. 179.
Longus Scriptor Eroticus iii A.D. (?)
Ed. R. Hercher, *Erotici* i p. 239.
Lucianus Sophista ii A.D.
Ed. C. Jacobitz, 3 vols., Leipzig (T.) 1896–7; ed. J. Sommerbrodt, 3 vols. [all published], Berlin 1886–99; ed. N. Nilén, Leipzig (T.) 1906–.
Scholia in Lucianum, ed. H. Rabe, Leipzig (T.) 1906.
Abd. = *Abdicatus*
Alex. = *Alexander*
Am. = *Amores*
Anach. = *Anacharsis*
Apol. = *Apologia*
Asin. = *Asinus*
Astr. = *de Astrologia*
Bacch. = *Bacchus*
Bis Acc. = *Bis Accusatus*
Cal. = *Calumniae non temere credendum*
Cat. = *Cataplus*
Charid. = *Charidemus*
Cont. = *Contemplantes*
Cyn. = *Cynicus*
DDeor. = *Dialogi Deorum*
DMar. = *Dialogi Marini*
DMeretr. = *Dialogi Meretricii*
DMort. = *Dialogi Mortuorum*
Dem.Enc. = *Demosthenis Encomium*
Demon. = *Demonax*
Deor.Conc. = *Deorum Concilium*
Dips. = *Dipsades*
Dom. = *de Domo*
Electr. = *Electrum*
Ep.Sat. = *Epistulae Saturnales*
Eun. = *Eunuchus*
Fug. = *Fugitivi*
Gall. = *Gallus*
Halc. = *Halcyon*
Harm. = *Harmonides*
Herc. = *Hercules*
Herm. = *Hermotimus*
Herod. = *Herodotus*
Hes. = *Hesiodus*
Hipp. = *Hippias*
Hist.Conscr. = *Quomodo historia conscribenda sit*
Icar. = *Icaromenippus*
Im. = *Imagines*
Ind. = *adversus Indoctum*
JConf. = *Juppiter Confutatus*
JTr. = *Juppiter Tragoedus*
Jud.Voc. = *Judicium Vocalium*
Laps. = *pro Lapsu inter Salutandum*
Lex. = *Lexiphanes*
Luct. = *de Luctu*
Macr. = *Macrobii*
Merc.Cond. = *de Mercede Conductis*
Musc.Enc. = *Muscae Encomium*
Nav. = *Navigium*
Nec. = *Necyomantia*
Ner. = *Nero*
Nigr. = *Nigrinus*
Ocyp. = *Ocypus*
Par. = *de Parasito*
Patr.Enc. = *Patriae Encomium*
Peregr. = *de Morte Peregrini*
Phal. 1, 2 = *Phalaris* 1, 2
Philopatr. = *Philopatris* [Ps.-Luc.]
Philops. = *Philopseudes*
Pisc. = *Piscator*
Pr.Im. = *pro Imaginibus*
ProMerc.Cond. = *pro Mercede Conductis*
Prom. = *Prometheus*
Prom.Es = *Prometheus es in verbis*
Pseudol. = *Pseudologista*
Rh.Pr. = *Rhetorum praeceptor*
Sacr. = *de Sacrificiis*
Salt. = *de Saltatione*
Sat. = *Saturnalia*
Scyth. = *Scytha*
Sol. = *Soloecista*
Somn. = *Somnium sive Vita Luciani*
Symp. = *Symposium*
Syr.D. = *de Syria Dea*
Tim. = *Timon*
Tox. = *Toxaris*
Trag. = *Tragodopodagra*
Tyr. = *Tyrannicida*
VH 1, 2 = *Verae Historiae* 1, 2
Vit.Auct. = *Vitarum Auctio*
Zeux. = *Zeuxis*
Lucillius Epigrammaticus [Lucill.] i A.D.
v. *Anthologia Graeca.*
LXX
v. Vetus Testamentum.
Lycophron Tragicus [Lyc.] iii B.C.
Ed. E. Scheer (cum scholiis), Berlin 1881–1908.
Fr. = *Fragmenta Tragica*, ed. A. Nauck, *TGF* p. 817.
Lycophronides Lyricus [Lycophronid.] iii B.C. (?)
Ed. T. Bergk, *PLG* iii p. 633.
Lycurgus Orator [Lycurg.] iv B.C.
Ed. F. Blass, Leipzig (T.) 1899.
Fragmenta, ed. H. Sauppe, *Orat. Att.* ii p. 258.
Lycus Historicus iv/iii B.C.
Ed. C. Müller, *FHG* ii p. 370.
Lydus, Joannes Laurentius Historicus [Lyd.] vi A.D.
de Magistratibus populi Romani, ed. R. Wünsch, Leipzig (T.) 1903. [*Mag.*]
de Mensibus, ed. R. Wünsch, Leipzig (T.) 1898. [*Mens.*]
de Ostentis, ed. C. Wachsmuth, Leipzig (T.) 1897. [*Ost.*]
Lynceus Comicus [Lync.]
Ed. T. Kock, *CAF* iii p. 274.
Cetera fragmenta apud Athenaeum.
Lyrica Adespota [*Lyr.Adesp.*]
Ed. T. Bergk, *PLG* iii p. 689.

Lyrica Alexandrina Adespota [*Lyr.Alex.Adesp.*]
Ed. J. U. Powell, *Coll. Alex.* p. 177.

Lysias Orator [Lys.] v B.C.
Ed. C. Hude, Oxford (OCT).
Fragmenta, ed. T. Thalheim, Leipzig (T.) 1901. [*Fr.*]; ed. H. Sauppe, *Orat. Att.* ii p. 170. [*Fr.* . . S.]

Lysimachides Historicus [Lysimachid.]
Ed. C. Müller, *FHG* iii p. 340.

Lysimachus Historicus [Lysim.] ii or i B.C.
Ed. C. Müller, *FHG* iii p. 334.

Lysippus Comicus [Lysipp.] v B.C.
Ed. T. Kock, *CAF* i p. 700.

Lysis Philosophus
Ep. = *Epistula*, v. Pythagorae et Pythagoreorum Epistulae.

Macarius Paroemiographus [Macar.] xv A.D.
Ed. E. L. von Leutsch & F. G. Schneidewin, *Paroemiographi* ii p. 135.

Macedonius Epigrammaticus [Maced.] i A.D. (?)
v. *Anthologia Graeca.*

Macedonius Lyricus [Maced.]
Paean, ed. J. U. Powell, *Coll. Alex.* p. 138. [*Pae.*]

Macedonius Thessalonicensis Epigrammaticus [Maced.] vi A.D.
v. *Anthologia Graeca.*

Macho Comicus iii B.C.
Ed. T. Kock, *CAF* iii p. 324.
Cetera fragmenta apud Athenaeum.

Macrobius Grammaticus [Macr.] iv/v A.D.
Exc. = *Excerpta Grammatica*, ed. H. Keil, *Gramm. Lat.* v p. 595.
Sat. = *Saturnalia*, ed. F. Eyssenhardt[2], Leipzig (T.) 1893.

Maecius Epigrammaticus [Maec.] i A.D. (?)
v. *Anthologia Graeca.*

Magnes Comicus [Magn.] v B.C.
Ed. T. Kock, *CAF* i p. 7; suppl. J. Demiańczuk, *Supp. Com.* p. 54.

Magnus Epigrammaticus iv A.D. (?)
v. *Anthologia Graeca.*

Magnus Historicus [Magnus Hist.] iv A.D.
Ed. L. Dindorf, *HGM* i p. 365.

Maiistas Epicus [Maiist.] iii B.C.
Ed. J. U. Powell, *Coll. Alex.* p. 68 (= *IG* 11(4).1299).

Malchus Historicus [Malch.] iv A.D.
Ed. L. Dindorf, *HGM* i p. 383.

Mamercus Elegiacus [Mamerc.]
Ed. T. Bergk, *PLG* ii p. 325.

Manetho Astrologus [Man.] iv A.D. (?)
Ed. H. Koechly (with Dorotheus and Anubion), Leipzig (T.) 1858.

Manetho Historicus [Man.Hist.] iii B.C.
Ed. C. Müller, *FHG* ii p. 511.

Mantissa Proverbiorum [*Mantiss.Prov.*]
Ed. E. L. von Leutsch & F. G. Schneidewin, *Paroemiographi* ii p. 745.

Marcellinus Biographus [Marcellin.] iv A.D. (?)
Vita Thucydidis, ed. H. Stuart Jones (ante Thucydidem), Oxford (OCT). [*Vit.Thuc.*]

Marcellinus Medicus [Marcellin.] ii A.D. (?)
Puls. = *de Pulsibus*, ed. H. Schöne, *Festschrift zur 49. Versammlung deutscher Philologen und Schulmänner*, Basel 1907.

Marcellus Sidetes Poeta Medicus [Marc.Sid.] ii A.D.
Ed. M. Schneider, *Commentationes philologae quibus O. Ribbeckio . . . congratulantur discipuli*, Leipzig 1888, p. 115.

Marcianus Geographus [Marcian.] iv/v A.D.
Ed. C. Müller, *GGM* i p. 515. [*Peripl.*]
Epit. = Artemidori Epitome, ed. C. Müller, ib. p. 574.

Marcus Antoninus Imperator [M.Ant.] ii A.D.
Ed. J. H. Leopold, Oxford (OCT).

Marcus Argentarius Epigrammaticus [Marc.Arg.] vi A.D.
v. *Anthologia Graeca.*

Margites
Ed. T. W. Allen, *Homeri Opera* v, Oxford (OCT), p. 152.

Maria Alchemista [Maria Alch.] ii A.D. (?)
Apud Olympiodorum et Zosimum.

Marianus Epigrammaticus [Marian.] v/vi A.D.
v. *Anthologia Graeca.*

Marinus Biographus [Marin.] v/vi A.D.
Procl. = *Vita Procli*, ed. J. F. Boissonade (post Cobeti Diogenem Laertium), Paris (D.) 1862.

Marius Victorinus Grammaticus Latinus [Mar.Vict.] iv A.D.
Ed. H. Keil, *Gramm. Lat.* vi p. 1.

Martialis Epigrammaticus Latinus [Mart.] i A.D.
Ed. W. M. Lindsay, Oxford (OCT).

Martianus Capella Grammaticus Latinus [Mart.Cap.] v A.D.
Ed. F. Eyssenhardt, Leipzig (T.) 1866.

Matro Parodius iv B.C.
Conv. = *Convivium*, ed. P. Brandt, *Corpusculum poesis epicae ludibundae* i, Leipzig (T.) 1888, p. 60.
Parod.Fr. = *Parodiarum Fragmenta*, op. cit. p. 91.

Maximus Astrologus [Max.] i B.C. (?)
Ed. A. Ludwich, Leipzig (T.) 1877.
Epit. = *Epitome*, ed. A. Ludwich, op. cit., p. 79.

Maximus Tyrius Sophista [Max.Tyr.] ii A.D.
Ed. H. Hobein, Leipzig (T.) 1910 (cited by the numeration of F. Dübner, post Theophrastum, Paris (D.) 1840).

Megasthenes Historicus [Megasth.] iv/iii B.C.
Ed. C. Müller, *FHG* ii p. 397.

Meges Medicus i A.D.
Apud Oribasium.

Melampus Scriptor de divinatione [Melamp.]
περὶ ἐλαιῶν τοῦ σώματος μαντικὴ πρὸς Πτολεμαῖον, ed. J. G. F. Franz, *Scriptores Physiognomiae Veteres*, Altenburg 1780.
περὶ παλμῶν, ed. H. Diels, *Abh. Berl.Akad.*, 1907; cf. *PRyl.* 1. 28.

Melanippides Lyricus [Melanipp.] v B.C.
Ed. T. Bergk, *PLG* iii p. 589.

Melanthius Historicus [Melanth.Hist.] iv B.C. (?)
Ed. C. Müller, *FHG* iv p. 444.

Melanthius Tragicus [Melanth.Trag.]
Ed. A. Nauck, *TGF* p. 760.

Meleager Epigrammaticus [Mel.] i B.C.
v. *Anthologia Graeca.*

Melinno Lyrica i A.D. (?)
Apud Stobaeum.

Melissa
Ep. = *Epistula*, v. Pythagorae et Pythagoreorum Epistulae.

Melissus Philosophus [Meliss.] v B.C.
Ed. H. Diels, *Vorsokr.* i p. 176.

Memnon Historicus [Memn.] i A.D.
Ed. C. Müller, *FHG* iii p. 525.

Menaechmus Historicus [Menaechm.] iii B.C.
Ed. C. Müller, *SRAM* p. 145.

Menander Comicus [Men.] iv/iii B.C.
Ed. T. Kock, *CAF* iii p. 3; suppl. J. Demiańczuk, *Supp. Com.* p. 54.
Menandrea, ed. A. Körte[2], Leipzig (T.) 1912:
Epit. = Ἐπιτρέποντες
Georg. = Γεωργός
Her. = Ἥρως
Inc. 1, 2 = *Fabula incerta* 1, 2
Kith. = Κιθαριστής
Kol. = Κόλαξ
Kon. = Κωνεαζόμεναι
Mis. = Μισούμεναι
Mon. = Μονόστιχοι, ed. A. Meineke, *Fragmenta Comicorum Graecorum* iv (1841) p. 340
Per. = Περινθία
Phasm. = Φάσμα
Pk. = Περικειρομένη
Sam. = Σαμία

Menander Rhetor [Men.Rh.] iii A.D.
Ed. L. Spengel, *Rhet.* iii p. 329.

Menander Ephesius Historicus [Men.Eph.]
Ed. C. Müller, *FHG* iv p. 445.

Menander Protector Historicus [Men.Prot.] vi A.D.
Ed. L. Dindorf, *HGM* ii p. 1.

Menecles Barcaeus Historicus [Menecl.] ii B.C.
Ed. C. Müller, *FHG* iv p. 448.

Menecrates Comicus [Menecr.]
Ed. J. Demiańczuk, *Supp. Com.* p. 63.

Menecrates Ephesius Poeta Philosophus [Menecr.Eph.] iv B.C.
Ed. H. Diels, *PPF* p. 171.

Menecrates Xanthius Historicus [Menecr.Xanth.] iv/iii B.C.
Ed. C. Müller, *FHG* ii p. 343.

Menemachus Medicus [Menemach.] i A.D.
Apud Oribasium.

Menesthenes Historicus [Menesth.]
Ed. C. Müller, *FHG* iv p. 451.

Menetor Historicus
Ed. C. Müller, *FHG* iv p. 452.

Menippus Epistolographus [Menipp.] iii B.C.
Epistulae, ed. R. Hercher, *Epistolographi*, p. 400. [*Ep.*]

Meno Medicus iv B.C.
Iatr. = *Iatrika*
v. Anonymus Londinensis.

Menodotus Samius Historicus [Menodot.] iii B.C. (?)
Ed. C. Müller, *FHG* iii p. 103.

Mesomedes Lyricus [Mesom.] ii A.D.
Ed. C. Jan, *Musici Scriptores Graeci*, Leipzig (T.) 1899, p. 454, *Suppl.* p. 46.
Mus. = *Hymnus in Musam*
Nem. = *Hymnus in Nemesin*
Sol. = *Hymnus in Solem*

Metagenes Comicus [Metag.] v B.C.
Ed. T. Kock, *CAF* i p. 704.

Metrodorus Epigrammaticus [Metrod.] iv A.D.
v. *Anthologia Graeca.*

Metrodorus Philosophus [Metrod.] iv/iii B.C.
Ed. A. Körte, *Jahrbücher für klassische Philologie, Suppl.* xvii p. 529, Leipzig 1890.

Metrodorus (*continued*)
Herc. 831 = Papyrus Herculanensis 831; ed. A. Körte, op. cit., pp. 571 ff.
Metrodorus Chius Philosophus [Metrod.Chius] v B.C.
Ed. H. Diels, *Vorsokr.* ii p. 140.
Metrodorus Scepsius Historicus [Metrod.Sceps.] i B.C.
Ed. C. Müller, *FHG* iii p. 203.
Michael Ephesius Philosophus [Mich.] xi/xii A.D.
in EN = *in Ethica Nicomachea commentarium*, ed. G. Heylbut (*Comm. in Arist. Graeca* xx), Berlin 1892; *in librum quintum Ethicorum Nicomacheorum commentarium*, ed. M. Hayduck (*Comm. in Arist. Graeca* xxii *pars* iii), Berlin 1901.
in PA = *in libros de Partibus Animalium, de Animalium Motione, de Animalium Incessu commentaria*, ed. M. Hayduck (*Comm. in Arist. Graeca* xxii *pars* ii), Berlin 1904.
in PN = *in Parva Naturalia commentaria*, ed. P. Wendland (*Comm. in Arist. Graeca* xxii *pars* i), Berlin 1903.
Michaelius Epigrammaticus vi A.D. (?)
v. *Anthologia Graeca.*
Mimnermus Lyricus [Mimn.] vi B.C.
Ed. T. Bergk, *PLG* ii p. 25.
Mimnermus Tragicus [Mimn.Trag.]
Ed. A. Nauck, *TGF* p. 829.
Minucianus Rhetor [Minuc.] ii A.D.
Ed. C. Hammer in L. Spengel, *Rhet.* i² (2), Leipzig (T.) 1894, p. 340.
Mithradates Epistolographus [Mithr.] (i B.C.)
Ed. R. Hercher, *Epistolographi*, p. 177.
Mnasalcas Epigrammaticus [Mnasalc.] iii B.C.
v. *Anthologia Graeca.*
Mnaseas Historicus iii/ii B.C.
Ed. C. Müller, *FHG* iii p. 149.
Mnesimachus Comicus [Mnesim.] iv B.C.
Ed. T. Kock, *CAF* ii p. 436.
Mnesitheus Atheniensis Medicus [Mnesith.Ath.] iii B.C.
Apud Oribasium.
Mnesitheus Cyzicenus Medicus [Mnesith.Cyz.]
Apud Oribasium; fortasse idem qui Atheniensis.
Moeris Grammaticus [Moer.] ii A.D.
Ed. J. Pierson, Leyden 1759.
Moero Epica iii B.C.
Ed. J. U. Powell, *Coll. Alex.* p. 21.
Molpis Historicus
Ed. C. Müller, *FHG* iv p. 453.
Moschio Gnomologus
Γνῶμαι, ed. H. Schenkl (post Epictetum), p. 481. [*Gnom.*]
Moschio Paradoxographus
Apud Athenaeum.
Moschio Tragicus [MoschioTrag.] iv B.C.
Ed. A. Nauck, *TGF* p. 812.
Moschus Bucolicus [Mosch.] ii B.C.
Ed. U. von Wilamowitz-Möllendorff², *Bucolici Graeci*, Oxford (OCT).
Moses Alchemista ii A.D. (?)
Ed. M. Berthelot, *Collection des anciens alchimistes grecs*, Paris 1888, p. 139.
Mucius Scaevola Epigrammaticus [Muc.Scaev.]
v. *Anthologia Graeca.*
Mundus Munatius Epigrammaticus [Mund.]
v. *Anthologia Graeca.*
Musaeus Epicus [Musae.] v/vi A.D.
Ed. A. Ludwich, Bonn 1912.
Musaeus Philosophus [Musae.]
Ed. H. Diels, *Vorsokr.* ii p. 179. [*Fr.* .. D.]
Musicius Epigrammaticus [Music.]
v. *Anthologia Graeca.*
Musonius Philosophus [Muson.] i A.D.
Ed. O. Hense, Leipzig (T.) 1905.
Ep. = *Epistula* in R. Hercher, *Epistolographi*, p. 401.
Myia
Ep. = *Epistula*, v. Pythagorae et Pythagoreorum Epistulae.
Myrinus Epigrammaticus [Myrin.]
v. *Anthologia Graeca.*
Myro Historicus
Ed. C. Müller, *FHG* iv p. 460.
Myrsilus Historicus [Myrsil.]
Ed. C. Müller, *FHG* iv p. 455.
Myrtilus Comicus [Myrtil.] v B.C.
Ed. T. Kock, *CAF* i p. 253.

Naumachius Epicus [Naumach.] ii A.D.
Apud Stobaeum.
Nausicrates Comicus [Nausicr.] iv B.C.
Ed. T. Kock, *CAF* ii p. 295; suppl. J. Demiańczuk, *Supp. Com.* p. 64.
Nausiphanes Philosophus [Nausiph.] iv/iii B.C.
Ed. H. Diels, *Vorsokr.* ii p. 155.
Neanthes Historicus [Neanth.] iii B.C.
Ed. C. Müller, *FHG* iii p. 2.
Nearchus Historicus [Nearch.]
Ed. C. Müller, *SRAM* p. 58.
Nechepso Astrologus [Nech.] ii B.C. (?)
Nechepsonis et Petosiridis fragmenta magica, ed. E. Riess (*Philologus* vi *Suppl.* (1891–3) pp. 325–94): etiam apud Vettium Valentem.
Neophron Tragicus [Neophr.] v B.C.
Ed. A. Nauck, *TGF* p. 729.
Neoptolemus Epicus [Neoptol.] iii/ii B.C.
Ed. J. U. Powell, *Coll. Alex.* p. 27.
Nepualius (Neptunalius, Neptunianus)
Ed. W. Gemoll, Striegau 1884; cf. *Rh. Mus.* xlviii (1893) 1, xlv (1890) 70.
Nessas Philosophus v B.C.
Ed. H. Diels, *Vorsokr.* ii p. 140.
Nestor Epigrammaticus iii A.D.
v. *Anthologia Graeca.*
Nicaenetus Epicus [Nicaenet.] ii B.C.
Ed. J. U. Powell, *Coll. Alex.* p. 1.
Nicander Epicus [Nic.] ii B.C.
Ed. O. Schneider, with scholia edited by H. Keil, Leipzig, 1856.
Alex. = *Alexipharmaca*
Ther. = *Theriaca*
Scholia vetera ed. H. Bianchi, *Stud. Ital.* xii (1904) p. 321.
Nicarchus Epigrammaticus [Nicarch.] i A.D.
v. *Anthologia Graeca.*
Nicias Epigrammaticus [Nic.] iii B.C.
v. *Anthologia Graeca.*
Nico Comicus
Ed. T. Kock, *CAF* iii p. 389.
Nicochares Comicus [Nicoch.] iv B.C.
Ed. T. Kock, *CAF* i p. 770; suppl. J. Demiańczuk, *Supp. Com.* p. 64.
Nicocles Historicus [Nicocl.]
Ed. C. Müller, *FHG* iv p. 464.
Nicodemus Epigrammaticus [Nicod.]
v. *Anthologia Graeca.*
Nicolaus Comicus [Nicol.Com.] iv B.C. (?)
Ed. T. Kock, *CAF* iii p. 383.
Nicolaus Rhetor [Nicol.]
Prog. = *Progymnasmata*, ed. J. Felten, Leipzig (T.) 1913.
Nicolaus Damascenus Historicus [Nic.Dam.] i B.C.
Ed. L. Dindorf, *HGM* i p. 1.
Vit.Caes. = *Vita Caesaris*
Nicomachus Comicus [Nicom.Com.]
Ed. T. Kock, *CAF* iii p. 386.
Nicomachus Tragicus [Nicom.Trag.]
Ed. A. Nauck, *TGF* p. 762.
Nicomachus Gerasenus Mathematicus [Nicom.] ii A.D.
Ar. = *Arithmetica Introductio*, ed. R. Hoche, Leipzig (T.) 1866.
Harm. = *Harmonicum Enchiridium*, ed. C. Jan, *Musici Scriptores Graeci*, Leipzig (T.) 1895, p. 237.
Exc. = *Excerpta*, ib., p. 266.
Nicopho Comicus v/iv B.C.
Ed. T. Kock, *CAF* i p. 775.
Nicostratus Comicus [Nicostr.Com.] iv B.C.
Ed. T. Kock, *CAF* ii p. 219; suppl. J. Demiańczuk, *Supp. Com.* p. 66.
Nicostratus Philosophus [Nicostr.]
Apud Stobaeum.
Niger, Sextius Medicus
Apud Plinium et Dioscoridem.
Nonius Marcellus Grammaticus Latinus iv A.D.
Ed. W. M. Lindsay, Leipzig (T.) 1903.
Nonnus Epicus [Nonn.] iv/v A.D. (?)
D. = *Dionysiaca*, ed. A. Ludwich, Leipzig (T.) 1909, 1911.
Nossis Epigrammatica [Noss.] iii B.C. (?)
v. *Anthologia Graeca.*
Nosti
Ed. T. W. Allen, *Homeri Opera* v, Oxford (OCT), p. 140.
Novum Testamentum
Ed. A. Souter, Oxford 1910.
Act.Ap. = Acts of the Apostles
Apoc. = Apocalypse
Ep.Col. = Epistle to the Colossians
1, 2 *Ep.Cor.* = 1st, 2nd Epistle to the Corinthians
Ep.Eph. = Epistle to the Ephesians
Ep.Gal. = Epistle to the Galatians
Ep.Hebr. = Epistle to the Hebrews
Ep.Jac. = Epistle of James
1, 2 *Ep.Jo.* = 1st, 2nd Epistle of John
Ep.Jud. = Epistle of Jude
1, 2 *Ep.Pet.* = 1st, 2nd Epistle of Peter
Ep.Phil. = Epistle to the Philippians
Ep.Philem. = Epistle to Philemon
Ep.Rom. = Epistle to the Romans
1, 2 *Ep.Thess.* = 1st, 2nd Epistle to the Thessalonians
1, 2 *Ep.Ti.* = 1st, 2nd Epistle to Timothy
Ep.Tit. = Epistle to Titus
Ev.Jo. = Gospel according to John
Ev.Luc. = Gospel according to Luke
Ev.Marc. = Gospel according to Mark
Ev.Matt. = Gospel according to Matthew

Numenius Apamensis Platonicus [Numen.] ii A.D.
Apud Eusebium: cf. F. W. A. Mullach, *FPG* iii p. 153.
Numenius Heracleota Poeta Didacticus [Numen.] iii B.C.
Apud Athenaeum.
Nymphis Historicus iii B.C.
Ed. C. Müller, *FHG* iii p. 12.
Nymphodorus Historicus [Nymphod.]
Ed. C. Müller, *FHG* ii p. 375.

Ocellus Lucanus Philosophus [Ocell.] i B.C. (?)
Ed. F. W. A. Mullach, *FPG* i p. 383.
Odyssea [Od.]
v. Homerus.
Oenomaus Philosophus [Oenom.] ii A.D.
Apud Eusebium.
Olympiodorus Alchemista [Olymp.Alch.] iv A.D. (?)
Ed. M. Berthelot, *Collection des anciens alchimistes grecs*, Paris 1888, p. 75.
Olympiodorus Historicus [Olymp.Hist.] v A.D.
Ed. L. Dindorf, *HGM* i p. 450.
Olympiodorus Philosophus [Olymp.] vi A.D.
in Alc. = *in Platonis Alcibiadem commentarii*, ed. F. Creuzer, Frankfurt 1820–25.
in Cat. = *in Categorias commentarium*, ed. A. Busse (*Comm. in Arist. Graeca* xii *pars* i), Berlin 1902.
in Grg. = *in Platonis Gorgiam commentaria*, ed. A. Jahn, in *Neue Jahrbücher für Philologie, Suppl.* xiv (1848) p. 104.
in Mete. = *in Aristotelis Meteora commentaria*, ed. W. Stüve (*Comm. in Arist. Graeca* xii *pars* ii), Berlin 1900.
in Phd. = *in Platonis Phaedonem commentaria*, ed. W. Norvin, Leipzig (T.) 1913.
in Phlb. = *in Platonis Philebum scholia*, ed. G. Stallbaum, in editione Philebi, Leipzig 1820.
Proll. = *Prolegomena*, ed. A. Busse (*Comm. in Arist. Graeca* xii *pars* i), Berlin 1902.
Vit.Pl. = *Vita Platonis*; v. Diogenes Laertius.
Onatas [Onat.]
Apud Stobaeum.
Onosander (Onasander) Tacticus [Onos.] i A.D.
Ed. W. A. Oldfather, *Aeneas Tacticus, Asclepiodotus, Onasander*, with an Engl. tr. by members of the Illinois Greek Club, Lond. &c. (Loeb) 1923.
Ophelio Comicus [Ophel.] iv B.C.
Ed. T. Kock, *CAF* ii p. 293.
Oppianus Anazarbensis Epicus [Opp.] ii/iii A.D.
H. = *Halieutica*, ed. F. S. Lehrs, in *Poetae Bucolici et Didactici*, &c., Paris (D.) 1851.
Oppianus Apamensis Epicus [Opp.] iii A.D.
C. = *Cynegetica*, ed. P. Boudreaux, Paris 1908.
(*Ix.* = *Ixeutica*, only in paraphrase; v. Dionysius.)
Scholia in Oppianum, ed. U. C. Bussemaker, Paris (D.) 1847.
Oracula Chaldaica [*Orac.Chald.*]
Thomae Stanleii Historia Philosophiae Orientalis, ed. J. Clericus, Amsterdam 1690.
Oribasius Medicus [Orib.] iv A.D.
Ed. U. C. Bussemaker & C. Daremberg, 6 vols., Paris 1851–76.
Eup. = *Euporista*
Fr. = *Fragmenta*
inc. = *liber incertus*
Syn. = *Synopsis*
Origenes Theologus iii A.D.
Ed. P. Koetschau, Leipzig 1899.
Cels. = *contra Celsum*
Orion Lexicographus v A.D.
Ed. F. W. Sturz (= *Etymologicum Magnum*, vol. iii), Leipzig 1820.
Orphica [Orph.]
Ed. E. Abel, Leipzig & Prague 1885.
A. = *Argonautica*
H. = *Hymni*
L. = *Lithica*
Fr. = *Fragmenta*, ed. O. Kern, Berlin 1922.

Paean Delphicus [*Pae.Delph.*] ii B.C.
Ed. J. U. Powell, *Coll. Alex.* p. 141.
Paean Erythraeus [*Pae.Erythr.*] iv B.C.
Ed. J. U. Powell, *Coll. Alex.* pp. 136, 140.
Palaephatus Paradoxographus [Palaeph.]
Ed. N. Festa, in *Mythographi Graeci* iii (2), Leipzig (T.) 1902.
Palchus Astrologus [Palch.] v or vi A.D.
in *Cat. Cod. Astr.*
Palladas Epigrammaticus [Pall.] vi A.D.
v. *Anthologia Graeca.*
Palladius Medicus [Pall.]
in Hp. = *in Hippocratem*, ed. F. R. Dietz, Königsberg 1834.
in Hp.Fract. = *in librum Hippocratis de fracturis*, ed. R. Charterius, *Hippocratis et Galeni Opera*, vol. xii, Paris 1679.
Pamphila Historica i A.D.
Ed. C. Müller *FHG* iii p. 520.
Pamphilus Epigrammaticus [Pamphil.]
v. *Anthologia Graeca.*
Pamphilus Medicus [Pamphil.]
Apud Galenum.
Pancrates Epicus [Pancrat.] ii A.D.
Apud Athenaeum.
Oxy. = *POxy.* 1085.
Pancrates Epigrammaticus [Pancrat.]
v. *Anthologia Graeca.*
Panyasis Epicus [Panyas.]
Ed. Kinkel, *EGF* p. 253; suppl. J. U. Powell, *Coll. Alex.* p. 248.
Pappus Mathematicus [Papp.] iii A.D. (?)
Ed. F. Hultsch, Berlin 1876–1878; cited by page.
Parmenides Poeta Philosophus [Parm.] vi/v B.C.
Ed. H. Diels, *PPF* p. 48.
Parmenio Epigrammaticus [Parmen.]
v. *Anthologia Graeca.*
Parmeno Epigrammaticus
v. *Anthologia Graeca.*
Parmeno Iambographus iii B.C. (?)
Ed. J. U. Powell, *Coll. Alex.* p. 237.
Parrhasius Elegiacus [Parrhas.] v/iv B.C.
Ed. T. Bergk, *PLG* ii p. 320.
Parthenius Mythographus [Parth.] i B.C.
Ed. E. Martini, *Mythographi Graeci* ii (1) *Suppl.*, Leipzig (T.) 1902.
Patrocles Thurius Tragicus [Patrocl.]
Ed. A. Nauck, *TGF* p. 830.
Paulus Aegineta Medicus [Paul.Aeg.] vii A.D.
Ed. J. L. Heiberg, *CMG* ix, Leipzig 1921–1924; Bk. vi ed. R. Briau, Paris 1855.
Paulus Alexandrinus Astrologus [Paul.Al.] iv A.D.
Ed. A. Schato, Wittenberg 1586 (cited by signature and page of quaternion, as: *G.* 3).
Paulus Silentiarius Epigrammaticus [Paul.Sil.] vi A.D.
v. *Anthologia Graeca.*
Pausanias Periegeta [Paus.] ii A.D.
Ed. H. Hitzig & H. Bluemner, Leipzig 1896–1910.
Pausanias Damascenus Historicus [Paus.Dam.] iv A.D. (?)
Ed. L. Dindorf, *HGM* i p. 154.
Pausanias Grammaticus [Paus.Gr.]
Ed. E. Schwabe; v. Aelius Dionysius.
Pediasimus [Pediasim.]
Ed. R. Wagner (post Apollodorum), *Mythographi Graeci* i, Leipzig (T.) 1894.
Pelagius Alchemista [Pelag.Alch.] iii A.D.
Ed. M. Berthelot, *Collection des anciens alchimistes grecs*, Paris 1888, p. 253.
Pempelus Philosophus [Pempel.]
Apud Stobaeum.
Perictione Philosophus [Perict.]
Apud Stobaeum.
Periplus Maris Rubri [*Peripl.M.Rubr.*] i A.D.
Ed. C. Müller, *GGM* i p. 257; ed. B. Fabricius, 2 Aufl., Leipzig 1883.
Persaeus Citieus Stoicus [Pers.*Stoic.*] iii B.C.
Ed. H. von Arnim, *SVF* i p. 96.
Fragmenta Historica, ed. C. Müller, *FHG* ii p. 623. [*Fr.Hist.*]
Perses Epigrammaticus [Pers.]
v. *Anthologia Graeca.*
Persius Poeta Latinus [Pers.] i A.D.
Ed. S. G. Owen², Oxford (OCT).
Petosiris Astrologus [Petos.]
Ed. E. Riess, v. Nechepso; etiam apud Vettium Valentem.
Petronius [Petron.]
Ed. F. Buecheler, Berlin 1862; ed. sextam curavit W. Heraeus, 1922.
Petrus Patricius Historicus [Petr.Patr.] vi A.D.
Ed. L. Dindorf, *HGM* i p. 425.
Phaedimus Epigrammaticus [Phaedim.] ii B.C.
v. *Anthologia Graeca.*
Phaënnus Epigrammaticus [Phaënn.] ii B.C. (?)
v. *Anthologia Graeca.*
Phaestus Epicus [Phaest.]
Ed. J. U. Powell, *Coll. Alex.* p. 28.
Phalaecus Epigrammaticus [Phal.] iii B.C.
v. *Anthologia Graeca.*
Phalaris Epistolographus [Phalar.] (vi B.C.)
Ep. = *Epistulae*, ed. R. Hercher, *Epistolographi*, p. 439.
Phanias Epigrammaticus [Phan.]
v. *Anthologia Graeca.*
Phanias Historicus [Phan.Hist.] iv/iii B.C.
Ed. C. Müller, *FHG* ii p. 293.
Phanocles Elegiacus [Phanocl.] iii B.C. (?)
Ed. J. U. Powell, *Coll. Alex.* p. 106.
Phanodemus Historicus [Phanod.] iv B.C.
Ed. C. Müller, *FHG* i p. 366.
Pherecrates Comicus [Pherecr.] v B.C.
Ed. T. Kock, *CAF* i p. 145; suppl. J. Demiańczuk, *Supp. Com.* p. 66.
Pherecydes Lerius Historicus [Pherecyd.] vi B.C.
Ed. F. Jacoby, *FGrH* i p. 58.

Pherecydes Syrius Philosophus [Pherecyd.Syr.] vi B.C.
Ed. H. Diels, *Vorsokr.* ii p. 198.
Philagrius Medicus [Philagr.] iii/iv A.D.
Apud Aëtium et Oribasium.
Philemo Comicus [Philem.] iv/iii B.C.
Ed. T. Kock, *CAF* ii p. 478; suppl. J. Demiańczuk, *Supp. Com.* p. 71.
Philemo Junior Comicus [Philem.Jun.] iii B.C. (?)
Ed. T. Kock, *CAF* ii p. 540.
Philetaerus Comicus [Philetaer.] v/iv B.C.
Ed. T. Kock, *CAF* ii p. 230; suppl. J. Demiańczuk, *Supp. Com.* p. 72.
Philetas (vel **Philitas**) Elegiacus [Philet.] iv/iii B.C.
Ed. J. U. Powell, *Coll. Alex.* p. 90.
Fragmenta glossarii, cited from sources.
Philippides Comicus [Philippid.] iv/iii B.C.
Ed. T. Kock, *CAF* iii p. 301.
Philippus Comicus [Philipp.Com.] iv B.C.
Ed. T. Kock, *CAF* ii p. 215.
Philippus Epigrammaticus [Phil.] i A.D.
v. *Anthologia Graeca.*
Philiscus Comicus [Philisc.Com.]
Ed. T. Kock, *CAF* ii p. 443.
Philiscus Tragicus [Philisc.Trag.]
Ed. A. Nauck, *TGF* p. 819.
Philistus Historicus [Philist.] v/iv B.C.
Ed. C. Müller, *FHG* i p. 185, iv pp. 625, 639.
Phillis Historicus
Ed. C. Müller, *FHG* iv p. 476.
Philo Epicus [Ph.Epic.]
Apud Eusebium.
Ed. A. Ludwich, *De Philonis carmine Graeco-Iudaico commentatio*, Königsberg 1900.
Philo Mechanicus [Ph.] iii/ii B.C.
Bel. = (*Belopoeica*) *Excerpte aus Philons Mechanik*, ed. H. Diels & E. Schramm, *Abh. Berl. Akad.* 1919, No. 12; cited by page and line of Wescher, given in margin.
Philo Byblius Historicus [Ph.Bybl.] i/ii A.D.
Ed. C. Müller, *FHG* iii p. 560.
Philo Byzantius Paradoxographus [Ph.Byz.]
Mir. = *de Septem Miraculis*, ed. R. Hercher (post Aelianum), Paris (D.) 1858.
Philo Judaeus [Ph.]
Ed. L. Cohn & P. Wendland (S. Reiter), Berlin 1896–1915.
Fr. = *Fragmenta*, ed. J. Rendel Harris, Cambridge 1886.
Philo Tarsensis Medicus [Ph.Tars.]
Apud Galenum.
Philochorus Historicus [Philoch.] iv B.C.
Ed. C. Müller, *FHG* i p. 385, iv p. 646.
Philocles Tragicus [Philocl.]
Ed. A. Nauck, *TGF* p. 759.
Philodamus Scarpheus Lyricus [Philod.Scarph.] iv B.C.
Ed. J. U. Powell, *Coll. Alex.* p. 165.
Philodemus Philosophus [Phld.] i B.C.
Acad.Ind. = *Academicorum Index*, ed. S. Mekler, Berlin 1902. [p. . . M.]
D. 1, 3 = περὶ θεῶν α', γ', ed. H. Diels, *Abhandlungen der Berliner Akademie*, 1916, 1917. [Col. or *Fr.*]
Herc. = *Herculanensia Volumina, Collectio altera*, Naples 1862–76, (i.e. partim inedita) (ex apographis W. Crönert). [No. of papyrus, Col. or *Fr.*]
Hom = περὶ τοῦ καθ' Ὅμηρον ἀγαθοῦ βασιλέως, ed. A. Olivieri, Leipzig (T.) 1909.
Ind.Sto. = *Stoicorum Index Herculanensis*, ed. D. Comparetti, *Riv. Fil.* iii (1875). [Col. or *Fr.*]
Ir. = *de Ira*, ed. C. Wilke, Leipzig (T.) 1914.
Lib. = περὶ παρρησίας, ed. A. Olivieri, Leipzig (T.) 1914.
Mort. = *de Morte*, ed. D. Bassi, *Papiri Ercolanesi*, Milan 1914. [Col.]
Mus. = *de Musica*, ed. J. Kemke, Leipzig (T.) 1884.
Oec. = περὶ οἰκονομίας, ed. C. Jensen, Leipzig (T.) 1906.
Piet. = *de Pietate*, ed. T. Gomperz, *Herkulanische Studien* ii, Leipzig 1866. [Col. or *Fr.*]
Po. = περὶ ποιημάτων, ed. A. Hausrath, *Jahrbücher für klassische Philologie, Suppl.* xvii (1889) p. 211; ed. T. Gomperz, *Philodem und die aesthetischen Schriften der Herkulanensischen Bibliothek, Sitzungsberichte der Wiener Akademie*, cxxiii (1891); ed. C. Jensen, *Philodemos über die Gedichte, fünftes Buch*, Berlin 1923. [No. of book (where known, otherwise No. of papyrus), Col. or *Fr.*]
Rh. = *Volumina Rhetorica*, ed. S. Sudhaus, 2 vols., Leipzig (T.) 1892, 1896, *Suppl.* 1895. [Cited by vol. and p.]
Sign. = περὶ σημείων καὶ σημειώσεων, ed. T. Gomperz, *Herkulanische Studien* i, Leipzig 1865. [Col. or *Fr.*]
Sto. = περὶ τῶν Στωικῶν, ed. W. Crönert, *Kolotes und Menedemos*, Leipzig 1906, pp. 53 sqq. [Col. or *Fr.*]
Vit. = περὶ κακιῶν ι', ed. C. Jensen, Leipzig (T.) 1911.
Philodemus Gadarensis Epigrammaticus [Phld.] i B.C.
Videtur idem fuisse ac philosophus.
v. *Anthologia Graeca.*

Philolaus Philosophus [Philol.] v/iv B.C.
Ed. H. Diels, *Vorsokr.* i p. 301.
Philomnestus Historicus [Philomnest.]
Ed. C. Müller, *FHG* iv p. 477.
Philonides Comicus [Philonid.] v B.C.
Ed. T. Kock, *CAF* i p. 254; suppl. J. Demiańczuk, *Supp. Com.* p. 73.
Philoponus, Joannes Philosophus [Phlp.] vi A.D.
Idem qui Joannes Alexandrinus, q.v.
in APo. = *in Aristotelis Analytica Posteriora commentaria*, ed. M. Wallies (*Comm. in Arist. Graeca* xiii *pars* iii), Berlin 1909.
in APr. = *in Aristotelis Analytica Priora commentaria*, ed. M. Wallies (*Comm. in Arist. Graeca* xiii *pars* ii), Berlin 1905.
in Cat. = *Philoponi* (*olim Ammonii*) *in Aristotelis Categorias commentarium*, ed. A. Busse (*Comm. in Arist. Graeca* xiii *pars* i), Berlin 1898.
in de An. = *in Aristotelis de Anima libros commentaria*, ed. M. Hayduck (*Comm. in Arist. Graeca* xv), Berlin 1897.
in GA = *Philoponi* (*Michaelis Ephesii*) *in libros de Generatione Animalium commentaria*, ed. M. Hayduck (*Comm. in Arist. Graeca* xiv *pars* iii), Berlin 1903.
in GC = *in Aristotelis libros de Generatione et Corruptione commentaria*, ed. Hieronymus Vitelli (*Comm. in Arist. Graeca* xiv *pars* ii), Berlin 1897.
in Mete. = *in Aristotelis Meteorologicorum librum primum commentarium*, ed. M. Hayduck (*Comm. in Arist. Graeca* xiv *pars* i), Berlin 1901.
in Ph. = *in Aristotelis Physica commentaria*, ed. Hieronymus Vitelli (*Comm. in Arist. Graeca* xvi, xvii), Berlin 1887–8.
Philostephanus Comicus [Philosteph.Com.]
Ed. T. Kock, *CAF* iii p. 393.
Philostephanus Historicus [Philosteph.Hist.]
Ed. C. Müller, *FHG* iii p. 28.
Philostratus Sophista [Philostr.] ii/iii A.D.
Ed. C. L. Kayser, Leipzig (T.) 1870, 1871.
Dial. = Διαλέξεις
Ep. = *Epistulae*
Her. = *Heroicus*
VA = *Vita Apollonii*
VS = *Vitae Sophistarum*
Gym. = *de gymnastica*, ed. J. Jüthner, Leipzig & Berlin 1909.
Im. = *Philostrati majoris imagines*, ed. O. Benndorf, C. Schenkl, Leipzig (T.) 1893.
Philostratus Junior Sophista [Philostr.Jun.] iii A.D.
Im. = *Imagines*, ed. C. Schenkl, Aemilius Reisch, Leipzig (T.) 1902.
Philoxenus Epigrammaticus [Philox.] iii B.C.
v. *Anthologia Graeca.*
Philoxenus Grammaticus [Philox.Gramm.] i B.C.
Ed. H. Funaioli, *Grammaticae Romanae Fragmenta*, vol. i, Leipzig (T.) 1907, p. 443.
Philoxenus Lyricus [Philox.] v/iv B.C.
Ed. T. Bergk, *PLG* iii p. 601.
Philumenus Medicus [Philum.] iii A.D.
Ven. = *de Venenatis Animalibus*, ed. M. Wellmann, Berlin 1908; etiam apud Oribasium et Aëtium.
Philyllius Comicus [Philyll.] v B.C.
Ed. T. Kock, *CAF* i p. 781; suppl. J. Demiańczuk, *Supp. Com.* p. 73.
Phintys Pythagoreus [Phint.]
Apud Stobaeum.
Phlegon Trallianus Paradoxographus [Phleg.] ii A.D.
Ed. O. Keller, *Rerum naturalium scriptores Graeci minores*, vol. i, Leipzig (T.) 1877.
Mir. = *Miracula*
Macr. = *Macrobii*
Olymp. = *Olympiades*
Fragmenta Historica, ed. C. Müller, *FHG* iii p. 602. [*Fr.Hist.*]
Phocylides Lyricus [Phoc.] vi B.C.
Ed. T. Bergk, *PLG* ii p. 68.
Phoebammon Rhetor [Phoeb.] v/vi A.D.
Fig. = *de Figuris*, ed. L. Spengel, *Rhet.* iii p. 41.
Phoenicides Comicus [Phoenicid.] iii B.C.
Ed. T. Kock, *CAF* iii p. 333.
Phoenix Iambographus [Phoen.] iii B.C.
Ed. J. U. Powell, *Coll. Alex.* p. 231.
Photius Lexicographus, etc. [Phot.] ix A.D.
Lexicon, ed. S. A. Naber, Leiden, 1864–65 (cited without title).
Der Anfang des Lexikons des Photios, ed. R. Reitzenstein, Leipzig & Berlin 1907 (cited thus: Phot. p. . . R.).
Bibl. = *Bibliotheca*, = J.-P. Migne, *Patrologia Graeca*, vol. ciii, Paris 1860 (cited by Bekker's pages).
Phrynichus Atticista [Phryn.] ii A.D.
Ed. W. G. Rutherford, London 1881.
PS = *Praeparatio Sophistica*, ed. I. de Borries, Leipzig (T.) 1911.
Phrynichus Comicus [Phryn.Com.] v B.C.
Ed. T. Kock, *CAF* i p. 369; suppl. J. Demiańczuk, *Supp. Com.* p. 74.

Phrynichus Tragicus [Phryn.Trag.] vi/v B.C.
Ed. A. Nauck, *TGF* p. 720.
Fragmenta Lyrica, ed. T. Bergk, *PLG* iii p. 561. [Phryn.Lyr.]
Phylarchus Historicus [Phylarch.] iii B.C.
Ed. C. Müller, *FHG* i p. 334; iv p. 645.
Phylotimus Medicus [Phylotim.]
Apud Athenaeum.
Pindarus Lyricus [Pi.] v B.C.
Ed. O. Schroeder, Leipzig 1900.
O., P., N., I. = *Olympian, Pythian, Nemean, Isthmian Odes; Fr.* = *Fragmenta.*
Dith.Oxy. = *Dithyrambi*, in *POxy.* 1604.
Pae., Parth. = *Paeanes, Parthenia*, ed. E. Diehl, *Supp. Lyr.*³ p. 52.
Scholia, ed. A. Boeckh, in editione Pindari, Berlin 1811–21; Scholia Vetera, ed. A. B. Drachmann, Leipzig (T.) 1903, 1910.
Pisander Epicus [Pisand.]
Ed. G. Kinkel, *EGF* i, Leipzig (T.) 1877, p. 248.
Pittacus Lyricus [Pittac.] vi B.C.
Ed. T. Bergk, *PLG* iii p. 198.
Placita Philosophorum [*Placit.*]
Ed. H. Diels, *Doxographi Graeci*, Berlin 1879, p. 273.
Plato Comicus [Pl.Com.] v/iv B.C.
Ed. T. Kock, *CAF* i p. 601; suppl. J. Demiańczuk, *Supp. Com.* p. 76.
Plato Philosophus [Pl.] v/iv B.C.
Ed. J. Burnet, Oxford (OCT).
*Alc.*1, 2 = *Alcibiades* 1, 2
Amat. = *Amatores*
Ap. = *Apologia*
Ax. = *Axiochus*
Chrm. = *Charmides*
Clit. = *Clitopho*
Cra. = *Cratylus*
Cri. = *Crito*
Criti. = *Critias*
Def. = *Definitiones*
Demod. = *Demodocus*
Ep. = *Epistulae*
Epigr. = *Epigrammata*, ed. T. Bergk, *PLG* ii p. 295
Epin. = *Epinomis*
Erx. = *Eryxias*
Euthd. = *Euthydemus*
Euthphr. = *Euthyphro*
Grg. = *Gorgias*
Hipparch. = *Hipparchus*
Hp.Ma., Mi. = *Hippias Major, Minor*
Ion
Just. = *De Justo*
La. = *Laches*
Lg. = *Leges*
Ly. = *Lysis*
Men. = *Meno*
Min. = *Minos*
Mx. = *Menexenus*
Phd. = *Phaedo*
Phdr. = *Phaedrus*
Phlb. = *Philebus*
Plt. = *Politicus*
Prm. = *Parmenides*
Prt. = *Protagoras*
R. = *Respublica*
Sis. = *Sisyphus*
Smp. = *Symposium*
Sph. = *Sophista*
Thg. = *Theages*
Tht. = *Theaetetus*
Ti. = *Timaeus*
Virt. = *De Virtute*
Scholia, ed. C. F. Hermann, *Platonis Dialogi*, vol. vi, Leipzig (T.) 1892.
Plato Junior Epigrammaticus [Pl.Jun.]
v. *Anthologia Graeca.*
Platonius Grammaticus [Platon.]
De Differentia Comoediarum, etc., ed. G. Kaibel, *CGF* p. 3. [*Diff. Com.*]
Plautus Comicus Latinus [Plaut.] iii/ii B.C.
Ed. W. M. Lindsay, Oxford (OCT).
Plinius Rerum Naturalium Scriptor [Plin.] i A.D.
HN = *Historia Naturalis*, ed. C. Mayhoff, 5 vols., Leipzig (T.) 1892–1909.
Plotinus Philosophus [Plot.] iii A.D.
Ed. R. Volkmann, Leipzig (T.) 1883–4.
Plutarchus Biographus et Philosophus [Plu.] i/ii A.D.
Moralia ed. G. N. Bernardakis, 7 vols., Leipzig (T.) 1888–96; cited by vol. (2) and page of Wyttenbach: *Vitae Parallelae*, ed. C. Sintenis, 5 vols., Leipzig (T.) 1881–65; ed. C. Lindskog & K. Ziegler, Leipzig (T.), i (1) (1914), i (2) (1914), iii (1) (1915).
Aem. = *Aemilius Paulus*
Ages. = *Agesilaus*
Agis
Alc. = *Alcibiades*
Alex. = *Alexander*
Ant. = *Antonius*
Arat. = *Aratus*
Arist. = *Aristides*
Art. = *Artoxerxes*
Brut. = *Brutus*
CG = *C. Gracchus*
Caes. = *Caesar*
Cam. = *Camillus*
Cat. Ma., Mi. = *Cato Major, Minor*
Cic. = *Cicero*
Cim. = *Cimon*
Cleom. = *Cleomenes*
Comp. = *Comparatio* [followed by two names]
Cor. = *Coriolanus*
Crass. = *Crassus*
Daed. = *de Daedalis Plataeensibus* (vol. vii, p. 43 B.)
Dem. = *Demosthenes*
Demetr. = *Demetrius*
Dio
Eum. = *Eumenes*
Fab. = *Fabius Maximus*
Flam. = *Flamininus*
Fr. = *Fragmenta* (vol. vii, pp. 1–149 B.); *Fr.inc.* = *Fragmenta incerta*, ib., pp. 150–2.
in Hes. = *Commentarii in Hesiodum* (vol. vii, p. 5 B.)
Lib. = *de Libidine et Aegritudine* (vol. vii, p. 1 B.)
Luc. = *Lucullus*
Lyc. = *Lycurgus*
Lys. = *Lysander*
Mar. = *Marius*
Marc. = *Marcellus*
Metr. = *de Metris* (vol. vii, p. 465 B.)
Nic. = *Nicias*
Nob. = *pro Nobilitate* (vol. vii, p. 194 B.)
Num. = *Numa*
Oth. = *Otho*
Pel. = *Pelopidas*
Per. = *Pericles*
Phil. = *Philopoemen*
Phoc. = *Phocion*
Pomp. = *Pompeius*
Prov. = *Proverbia* (ed. von E. L. Leutsch & F. G. Schneidewin, *Paroemiographi* i p. 321)
Publ. = *Publicola*
Pyrrh. = *Pyrrhus*
Rom. = *Romulus*
Sert. = *Sertorius*
Sol. = *Solon*
Strom. = Στρωματεῖς (vol. vii, p. 37 B.)
Sull. = *Sulla*
TG = *Tiberius Gracchus*
Them. = *Themistocles*
Thes. = *Theseus*
Tim. = *Timoleon*
Ps.-Plu.*Fluv.* = *de Fluviis* (vol. vii, p. 282 B.).
Ps.-Plu.*Vit.Hom.* = *Vita Homeri*, ed. T. W. Allen, *Homeri Opera* v, Oxford (OCT), p. 192.
Poeta *de herbis* [Poet. *de herb.*]
Ed. F. S. Lehrs, in *Poetae Bucolici et Didactici*, Paris (D.) 1851, p. 169 bis.
Polemo Historicus [Polem.Hist.] ii B.C.
Ed. C. Müller, *FHG* iii p. 108.
Polemo Physiognomonicus [Polem.*Phgn.*]
Ed. R. Förster, *Scriptores physiognomonici Graeci et Latini* i, Leipzig (T.) 1893, p. 427.
Polemo Sophista [Polem.] i/ii A.D.
Declamationes, ed. H. Hinck, Leipzig (T.) 1873.
Call. = *Callimachus*
Cyn. = *Cynegirus*
Poliochus Comicus [Polioch.]
Ed. T. Kock, *CAF* iii p. 390.
Pollianus Epigrammaticus [Poll.] ii A.D. (?)
v. *Anthologia Graeca.*
Pollux Grammaticus [Poll.] ii A.D
Bks. i–v ed. Bethe, Leipzig 1900: complete in W. Dindorf, Leipzig 1824.
Polus Philosophus
Apud Stobaeum.
Polyaenus Historicus [Polyaen.] ii A.D.
Ed. J. Melber, Leipzig (T.) 1887.
Polyaenus, Julius Epigrammaticus [Polyaen.] i B.C. (?)
v. *Anthologia Graeca.*
Polybius Historicus [Plb.] ii B.C.
Ed. T. Büttner-Wobst, Leipzig (T.) 1882–1905.
Fr. = *Fragmenta*

Polybius Sardianus Rhetor [Plb.Rh.]
Ed. L. Spengel, *Rhet.* iii p. 105.
Polycharmus Historicus [Polycharm.]
Ed. C. Müller, *FHG* iv p. 479.
Polyclitus Philosophus [Polyclit.] v/iv B.C.
Ed. H. Diels, *Vorsokr.* i p. 294.
Polycrates Historicus [Polycr.]
Ed. C. Müller, *FHG* iv p. 480.
Polystratus Epicureus [Polystr.] iii B.C.
Ed. C. Wilke, Leipzig (T.) 1905 (cited by page).
Polystratus Epigrammaticus [Polystr.]
v. *Anthologia Graeca.*
Polyzelus Comicus [Polyzel.] v/iv B.C.
Ed. T. Kock, *CAF* i p. 789; suppl. J. Demiańczuk, *Supp. Com.* p. 82.
Pompeius Epigrammaticus [Pomp.] i A.D.
v. *Anthologia Graeca.*
Pompeius Macer Tragicus [Pomp.Mac.]
Ed. A. Nauck, *TGF* p. 830.
Porphyrius Tyrius Philosophus [Porph.] iii A.D.
Abst. = *de Abstinentia*, ed. A. Nauck², *Porphyrii Opuscula*, Leipzig (T.) 1886.
ad Il. (Od.) = *Quaestionum Homericarum ad Iliadem (Odysseam) pertinentium reliquiae*, ed. H. Schrader, Leipzig 1880–82, 1890.
Antr. = *de Antro Nympharum*, ed. A. Nauck², *Porphyrii Opuscula*, Leipzig (T.) 1886.
Chr. = *adversus Christianos*, ed. A. von Harnack, *Abh. Berl. Akad.* 1916.
Fr.Hist. = *Fragmenta Historica*, ed. C. Müller, *FGH* iii p. 688.
Gaur. = *ad Gaurum* (πῶς ἐμψυχοῦται τὰ ἔμβρυα), ed. T. Kalbfleisch, *Abh. Berl. Akad.* 1895.
in Cat. = *in Aristotelis Categorias commentarium*, ed. A. Busse (*Comm. in Arist. Graeca* iv *pars* i p. 55), Berlin 1887.
in Harm. = *in Ptolemaei Harmonica*, ed. J. Wallis (post Ptolemaeum).
in Ptol. = *in Ptolemaei Tetrabiblon*, Basel 1559 (cited by page).
Intr. = *Isagoge sive quinque voces*, ed. A. Busse (*Comm. in Arist. Graeca* iv *pars* i p. 1), Berlin 1887.
Marc. = *ad Marcellam*, ed. A. Nauck², *Porphyrii Opuscula*, Leipzig (T.) 1886.
Plot. = *Vita Plotini*, ed. A. Westermann, v. Diogenes Laertius; ed. R. Volkmann, v. Plotinus.
Sent. = *Sententiae ad intelligibilia ducentes*, ed. B. Mommert, Leipzig (T.) 1907.
VP = *Vita Pythagorae*, ed. A. Nauck², *Porphyrii Opuscula*, Leipzig (T.) 1886.
Posidippus Comicus [Posidipp.] iii B.C.
Ed. T. Kock, *CAF* iii p. 335.
Posidippus Epigrammaticus [Posidipp.] iii B.C.
v. *Anthologia Graeca.*
Posidonius Historicus [Posidon.] ii/i B.C.
Ed. C. Müller, *FHG* iii p. 245.
Posidonius Medicus [Posidon.] iii/iv A.D.
Apud Aëtium.
Pratinas Lyricus et Tragicus [Pratin.] vi/v B.C.
Fragmenta Lyrica, ed. T. Bergk, *PLG* iii p. 557. [Lyr.]
Fragmenta Tragica, ed. A. Nauck, *TGF* p. 726. [Trag.]
Praxagoras Historicus [Praxag.] iv A.D.
Ed. L. Dindorf, *HGM* i p. 438.
Praxilla Lyrica [Praxill.] v B.C.
Ed. T. Bergk, *PLG* iii p. 566.
Priscianus Grammaticus [Priscian.] v/vi A.D.
Inst. = *Institutio*, ed. M. Hertz & H. Keil, *Gramm. Lat.*, vols. ii & iii, Leipzig 1855–9.
Priscianus Lydus Philosophus [Prisc.Lyd.] vi A.D.
Ed. I. Bywater (*Supplementum Aristotelicum* i *pars* ii), Berlin 1886.
Priscus Historicus [Prisc.] v A.D.
Ed. L. Dindorf, *HGM* i p. 275.
Proclus Philosophus [Procl.] v A.D.
ad Hes.*Op.* = ad Hesiodi *Opera et Dies*, ed. T. Gaisford, *Poetae Graeci Minores*, vol. iii, p. 9.
Chr. = *Chrestomathia*, ed. T. W. Allen, *Homeri Opera* v, Oxford (OCT), p. 99.
H. = *Hymni*, ed. E. Abel (post Orphica, p. 276).
Hyp. = *Hypotyposis astronomicarum positionum*, ed. C. Manitius, Leipzig (T.) 1909.
in Alc. = *in Platonis Alcibiadem*, ed. F. Creuzer, Frankfurt 1820.
in Cra. = *in Platonis Cratylum commentaria*, ed. G. Pasquali, Leipzig (T.) 1908.
in Euc. = *in primum Euclidis librum commentarius*, ed. G. Friedlein, Leipzig (T.) 1873.
in Prm. = *in Platonis Parmenidem commentarii*, ed. G. Stallbaum, Leipzig 1840.
in R. = *in Platonis Rempublicam commentarii*, ed. W. Kroll, 2 vols., Leipzig (T.) 1899, 1901.
in Ti. = *in Platonis Timaeum commentarii*, ed. E. Diehl, 3 vols., Leipzig (T.) 1903, 1904, 1906.
Inst. = *Institutio Theologica*, ed. F. Dübner, in F. Creuzer & G. Moser, *Plotinus*, pp. li–cxvii, Paris (D.) 1855.
Inst.Phys. = *Institutio Physica*, ed. A. Ritzenfeld, Leipzig (T.) 1912.
Par.Ptol. = *Paraphrasis Ptolemaei Tetrabiblou*, ed. L. Allatius, Basel 1554 (cited by page).
Theol.Plat. = περὶ τῆς κατὰ Πλάτωνα θεολογίας, ed. Aem. Portus, Hamburg 1618.
Procopius Caesariensis Historicus [Procop.] vi A.D.
Ed. J. Haury, Leipzig (T.) 1905–13.
Aed. = *de Aedificiis*
Arc. = *Historia Arcana*
Goth. = *de Bello Gothico*
Pers. = *de Bello Persico*
Vand. = *de Bello Vandalico*
Procopius Gazaeus Rhetor [Procop.Gaz.] v/vi A.D.
Ed. J. F. Boissonade, *Choricius*, Paris 1846, pp. 129–78.
Ecphr. = ἔκφρασις ὡρολογίου, ed. H. Diels, *Abh. Berl. Akad.* 1917, No. 7 (cited by Boissonade's page, given in margin).
Ep. = *Epistulae*, ed. R. Hercher, *Epistolographi*, p. 533.
Pan. = *Panegyricus in Anastasium*, ed. I. Bekker et B. G. Niebuhr, cum Dexippo et aliis, Bonn 1829 (cited by page); cf. C. Kemp, *Procopii Gazaei in Imp. Anastasium Panegyricus*, Bonn 1918.
Prodicus Philosophus [Prodic.] v B.C.
Ed. H. Diels, *Vorsokr.* ii p. 267.
Promathidas Historicus [Promathid.] i B.C.
Ed. C. Müller, *FHG* iii p. 201.
Protagoras Philosophus [Protag.] v B.C.
Ed. H. Diels, *Vorsokr.* ii p. 219.
Protagoridas Historicus [Protagorid.] ii B.C.
Ed. C. Müller, *FHG* iv p. 484.
Proxenus Historicus [Proxen.] iii B.C.
Ed. C. Müller, *FHG* ii p. 461.
Psalms of Solomon [*Psalm.Solom.*] i B.C.
Ed. H. E. Ryle & M. R. James, Cambridge 1891.
Pseudo-Callisthenes Historicus [Ps.-Callisth.]
Ed. C. Müller, *SRAM* p. 1 bis.
Pseudo-Phocylidea [Ps.-Phoc.] i A.D. (?)
Ed. T. Bergk, *PLG* ii p. 74.
Note.—The spurious works of other authors cited with the prefix 'Pseudo-' will be found under the names of the several authors.
Ptolemaeus Epigrammaticus [Ptol.]
v. *Anthologia Graeca.*
Ptolemaeus Mathematicus [Ptol.] ii A.D.
Ed. J. L. Heiberg, Leipzig (T.) 1898–1907; works included in this edition are marked with an asterisk.
**Alm.* = *Almagest* = *Syntaxis Mathematica*
**Anal.* = περὶ ἀναλήμματος
Calend. = *Calendarium*, ed. C. Wachsmuth, v. Lyd. *Ost.*
**Fr.* = *Fragmenta*
Geog. = *Geographia* (lib. i–iii, ed. C. Müller, C. T. Fischer, Paris 1883–1901; ed. F. A. Nobbe, Leipzig 1843–5).
Harm. = *Harmonica*, ed. J. Wallis, *Opera Mathematica* iii, Oxford 1699.
**Hyp.* = Ὑποθέσεις
**Inscr.Can.* = *Inscriptio Canobi*
Judic. = περὶ κριτηρίου, ed. J. Bullialdus, Paris 1663; ed. F. Hanow, Leipzig (Progr. Küstrin) 1870; cited by page of B., given in margin of H.
**Phas.* = Φάσεις
**Planisph.* = *Planisphaerium*
**Pseph.* = ψηφοφορία
Tetr. = *Tetrabiblos*, ed. J. Camerarius, Nürnberg 1535, cited by page of reprint, Basel 1553 (with Lat. transl. by P. Melanchthon).
Ps.-Ptol. *Centil.* = *Centiloquium* (καρπός), post *Tetrabiblon* editum.
Scholia in Ptolemaei Tetrabiblon, Basel 1559; v. Porphyrius.
Ptolemaeus Ascalonita [Ptol.Ascal.]
Ed. G. Heylbut, *Hermes* xxii (1887) p. 388.
Ptolemaeus Chennos [Ptol. Chenn.] c. 100 A.D.
Cited from sources; cf. A. Chatzis, *Der Philosoph und Grammatiker Ptolemaios Chennos*, Paderborn 1914.
Ptolemaeus Euergetes II Historicus [Ptol.Euerg.] ii B.C.
Ed. C. Müller, *FHG* iii p. 186.
Ptolemaeus Megalopolitanus Historicus [Ptol.Megalop.]
Ed. C. Müller, *FHG* iii p. 66.
Pyrgio Historicus
Ed. C. Müller, *FHG* iv p. 486.
Pythaenetus Historicus [Pythaen.]
Ed. C. Müller, *FHG* iv p. 487.
Pythagoras Philosophus [Pythag.] vi/v B.C.
Ed. H. Diels, *Vorsokr.* i p. 27, cf. p. 344.
Pythagorae et Pythagoreorum Epistulae [Pythag. *Ep.*]
Ed. R. Hercher, *Epistolographi*, p. 601. Cf. Melissa, Myia, Theano.
Pythocles Historicus [Pythocl.]
Ed. C. Müller, *FHG* iv p. 488.
Python Tragicus iv B.C.
Ed. A. Nauck, *TGF* p. 810.

Quintilianus Rhetor Latinus [Quint.] i A.D.
Ed. E. Bonnell, Leipzig (T.) 1884-9; ed. L. Radermacher, Leipzig (T.) 1907-.
Inst. = *Institutio Oratoria*
Quintus Smyrnaeus Epicus [Q.S.] iv A.D. (?)
Ed. A. Zimmermann, Leipzig (T.) 1891.

Rhetores Graeci [Rh.]
Ed. Ch. Walz, 9 vols., Stuttgart 1832-6.
Rhetorius Astrologus [Rhetor.] vi A.D.
in *Cat. Cod. Astr.*
Rhianus Epicus [Rhian.] iii B.C.
Ed. J. U. Powell, *Coll. Alex.* p. 9.
Rhinthon Comicus [Rhinth.] iii B.C.
Ed. G. Kaibel, *CGF* p. 183.
Rufinus Epigrammaticus [Rufin.]
v. *Anthologia Graeca.*
Rufus Medicus [Ruf.] ii A.D.
Ed. C. Daremberg & C. E. Ruelle, Paris 1879.
Anat. = ἀνατομή
Onom. = περὶ ὀνομασίας
Ren.Ves. = *de renum et vesicae affectionibus*
Sat.Gon. = *de satyriasmo et gonorrhoea*
Syn.Puls. = *synopsis de pulsibus*
Rufus Rhetor [Ruf.Rh.]
Ed. C. Hammer, in L. Spengel, *Rhet.* i² (2), p. 399.
Rutilius Lupus Rhetor [Rutil.]
Ed. C. Halm, *Rhetores Latini Minores*, Leipzig 1863, p. 3.

Sabinus, Tullius Epigrammaticus [Tull.Sab.] i A.D. (?)
v. *Anthologia Graeca.*
Sacerdos, Marius Plotius Grammaticus Latinus [Sacerd.] iii/iv A.D.
Ed. H. Keil, *Gramm. Lat.* vi p. 416.
Sallustius Philosophus [Sallust.] iv A.D.
Ed. F. W. A. Mullach, *FPG* iii p. 28.
Samus Epigrammaticus iii B.C.
v. *Anthologia Graeca.*
Sannyrio Comicus [Sannyr.] v B.C.
Ed. T. Kock, *CAF* i p. 793; suppl. J. Demiańczuk, *Supp. Com.* p. 83.
Sappho Lyrica [Sapph.] vii/vi B.C.
Ed. Th. Bergk, *PLG* iii p. 82.
Supp. = Papyrus fragments in E. Diehl, *Supp. Lyr.*³ p. 29.
Oxy. = Papyrus fragments in *POxy.*, cited by No. of Papyrus.
Satyrus Epigrammaticus [Satyr.] i B.C. (?)
v. *Anthologia Graeca.*
Satyrus Historicus [Satyr.] iii B.C.
Ed. C. Müller, *FHG* iii p. 159.
Vit.Eur. = *Vita Euripidis*, *POxy.* 1176.
Scamon Historicus
Ed. C. Müller, *FHG* iv p. 489.
Scholia
See under several authors.
Sciras Comicus iii B.C.
Ed. G. Kaibel, *CGF* p. 190.
Scolia [*Scol.*]
Ed. T. Bergk, *PLG* iii p. 643.
Scylax Geographus [Scyl.] iv B.C. (?)
Ed. C. Müller, *GGM* i p. 15.
Scymnus Geographus [Scymn.] ii B.C.
Ed. C. Müller, *GGM* i p. 196.
Scythinus Epigrammaticus [Scythin.]
v. *Anthologia Graeca.*
Scythinus Teius Poeta Philosophus [Scythin.] iv B.C.
Ed. H. Diels, *PPF* p. 169.
Secundus Gnomologus [Secund.] ii A.D.
Sent. = *Sententiae*, ed. F. W. A. Mullach, *FPG* i p. 512.
Seleucus Grammaticus et Historicus [Seleuc.]
Cited from sources; cf. C. Müller, *FHG* iii p. 500.
Seleucus Lyricus [Seleuc.Lyr.]
Ed. J. U. Powell, *Coll. Alex.* p. 176.
Semonides Iambographus [Semon.] vii/vi B.C. (?)
Ed. T. Bergk, *PLG* ii p. 441 (ubi perperam 'Simonides').
Semus Historicus
Ed. C. Müller, *FHG* iv p. 492.
Seneca, L. Annaeus i A.D.
QN = *Quaestiones Naturales*, ed. A. Gercke, Leipzig (T.) 1907.
Serapio Astrologus ii/i B.C. (?)
in *Cat. Cod. Astr.*
Serapio Epigrammaticus
v. *Anthologia Graeca.*
Serapio Tragicus
Ed. A. Nauck, *TGF* p. 831.
Serenus Geometra [Seren.] iv A.D.
Opuscula, ed. J. L. Heiberg, Leipzig (T.) 1896.
Sect.Con. = *Sectio Coni*
Sect.Cyl. = *Sectio Cylindri*
Serenus Gnomologus [Seren.]
Apud Stobaeum.

Servius Grammaticus Latinus [Serv.] iv A.D.
In Vergilii carmina commentarii, ed. G. Thilo & H. Hagen, Leipzig 1878-1902.
Severus Medicus [Sever.] iv A.D.
Clyst. = *de Clysteribus*, ed. F. R. Dietz, Königsberg 1836.
Severus Philosophus [Sever.] ii A.D.
Apud Eusebium.
Sextus Pythagoreus [Sext.]
Sent. = *Sententiae*, ed. A. Elter, Bonn 1891-2.
Sextus Empiricus Philosophus [S.E.] ii A.D.
Ed. H. Mutschmann, Leipzig (T.) 1912-; ed. I. Bekker, Berlin 1842.
M. = *adversus Mathematicos*
P. = Πυρρώνειοι ὑποτυπώσεις
Silenus Historicus [Silen.] iii/ii B.C.
Ed. C. Müller, *FHG* iii p. 100.
Simmias (vel **Simias**) Elegiacus [Simm.] iii B.C.
Ed. J. U. Powell, *Coll. Alex.* p. 109.
Simon Atheniensis
Eq. = *de forma et delectu equorum*, ed. F. Ruehl, *Xenophontis Scripta Minora*, p. 193, Leipzig (T.) 1912.
Simonides Lyricus [Simon.] vi/v B.C.
Ed. T. Bergk, *PLG* iii p. 382.
Simplicius Philosophus [Simp.] vi A.D.
in Cael. = *in Aristotelis de Caelo commentaria*, ed. J. L. Heiberg (*Comm. in Arist. Graeca* vii), Berlin 1894.
in Cat. = *in Aristotelis Categorias commentarium*, ed. C. Kalbfleisch (*Comm. in Arist. Graeca* viii), Berlin 1907.
in de An. = *in libros Aristotelis de Anima commentaria*, ed. M. Hayduck (*Comm. in Arist. Graeca* xi), Berlin 1882.
in Epict. = *in Epictetum commentaria*, ed. F. Dübner (post Theophrasti Characteras), Paris (D.) 1840.
in Ph. = *in Aristotelis Physica commentaria*, ed. H. Diels (*Comm. in Arist. Graeca* ix and x), Berlin 1882-95.
Simylus Comicus [Simyl.]
Ed. T. Kock, *CAF* ii p. 444.
Socrates Argivus Historicus [Socr.Arg.]
Ed. C. Müller, *FHG* iv p. 496.
Socrates Cous Historicus [Socr.Cous]
Ed. C. Müller, *FHG* iv p. 499.
Socrates Rhodius Historicus [Socr.Rhod.] i B.C.
Ed. C. Müller, *FHG* iii p. 326.
Socratis et Socraticorum Epistulae [Socr.*Ep.*] (v/iv B.C.)
Ed. R. Hercher, *Epistolographi*, p. 609.
Solon Lyricus [Sol.] vi B.C.
Ed. T. Bergk, *PLG* ii p. 34: new fragments cited apud Arist. *Ath.*
Sopater Comicus [Sopat.] iv B.C.
Ed. G. Kaibel, *CGF* p. 192.
Sopater Gnomologus [Sopat.] iv A.D.
Apud Phot. *Bibl.* cod. 161.
Sopater Rhetor [Sopat.Rh.] v A.D.
Ed. Ch. Walz, *Rhetores Graeci* (Stuttgart 1832-6) iv, v p. 1, viii p. 1.
Sophilus Comicus [Sophil.] iv B.C. (?)
Ed. T. Kock, *CAF* ii p. 444.
Sophocles Tragicus [S.] v B.C.
Tragoediae, ed. A. C. Pearson, Oxford (OCT).
Aj. = *Ajax*
Ant. = *Antigone*
El. = *Electra*
Eleg. = *Elegiae*, ed. T. Bergk, *PLG* ii p. 243.
Fr. = *Fragmenta*, ed. A. C. Pearson, Cambridge 1917.
OC = *Oedipus Coloneus*
OT = *Oedipus Tyrannus*
Ph. = *Philoctetes*
Tr. = *Trachiniae*
Sophonias Philosophus [Sophon.] xiv A.D.
in de An. = *in libros Aristotelis de Anima paraphrasis*, ed. M. Hayduck (*Comm. in Arist. Graeca* xxiii *pars* i), Berlin 1883.
Sophron Comicus [Sophr.] v B.C.
Ed. G. Kaibel, *CGF* i p. 152; suppl. J. Demiańczuk, *Supp. Com.* p. 125.
Soranus Medicus [Sor.] ii A.D.
Ed. V. Rose, Leipzig (T.) 1882.
Fasc. = *de fasciis*, ed. R. Charterius, *Opera Hippocratis et Galeni*, vol. xii, p. 505, Paris 1679 (cited by vol. and p.).
Fract. = *de signis fracturarum*, ed. J. L. Ideler, *Physici et Medici Graeci Minores* i p. 248, Berlin 1841.
Sosibius Historicus [Sosib.] iii B.C.
Ed. C. Müller, *FHG* ii p. 625.
Sosicrates Comicus [Sosicr.]
Ed. T. Kock, *CAF* iii p. 391.
Sosicrates Historicus [Sosicr.Hist.]
Ed. C. Müller, *FHG* iv p. 500.
Sosicrates Rhodius Historicus [Sosicr.Rhod.]
Ed. C. Müller, *FHG* iv p. 501.
Sosipater Comicus [Sosip.] iii B.C. (?)
Ed. T. Kock, *CAF* iii p. 314.
Sosiphanes Tragicus [Sosiph.] ii B.C.
Ed. A. Nauck, *TGF* p. 819.

Sositheus Tragicus [Sosith.]
Ed. A. Nauck, *TGF* p. 821.
Sostratus Historicus [Sostrat.]
Ed. C. Müller, *FHG* iv p. 504; ed. F. Jacoby, *FGrH* i p. 186.
Sosylus Historicus [Sosyl.] iii/ii B.C.
Ed. F. Bilabel, *Die kleineren Historikerfragmente auf Papyrus*, Bonn 1923, p. 29.
Sotades Comicus [Sotad.Com.]
Ed. T. Kock, *CAF* ii p. 447; suppl. J. Demiańczuk, *Supp. Com.* p. 83.
Sotades Lyricus [Sotad.] iii B.C.
Ed. J. U. Powell, *Coll. Alex.* p. 238.
Sotion Paradoxographus i/ii A.D.
Ed. A. Westermann, Παραδοξογράφοι, Brunswick–London 1839, p. 183 (cited by page).
Speusippus Philosophus [Speus.] iv B.C.
Cited from sources; cf. F. W. A. Mullach, *FPG* iii p. 75.
Sphaerus Historicus [Sphaer.Hist.]
Ed. C. Müller, *FHG* iii p. 20.
Sphaerus Stoicus [Sphaer.*Stoic.*] iii B.C.
Ed. H. von Arnim, *SVF* i p. 139.
Stadiasmus sive **Periplus Maris Magni** [*Stad.*] i B.C./i A.D.
Ed. C. Müller, *GGM* i p. 427.
Staphylus Historicus [Staphyl.]
Ed. C. Müller, *FHG* iv p. 505.
Statyllius Flaccus Epigrammaticus [Stat.Flacc.] i B.C./i A.D.
Idem qui Bianor, q.v.
Stephanus Comicus [Steph.Com.] iv/iii B.C.
Ed. T. Kock, *CAF* iii p. 360.
Stephanus Medicus [Steph.] vii A.D.
in Gal., *in Hp.* = *in Galenum*, *in Hippocratem*, ed. F. R. Dietz, Königsberg 1834.
Stephanus Philosophus [Steph.] vii A.D.
in Int. = *in librum Aristotelis de Interpretatione commentarium*, ed. M. Hayduck (*Comm. in Arist. Graeca* xviii *pars* iii), Berlin 1885.
in Rh. = *in Artem Rhetoricam commentaria*, ed. H. Rabe (*Comm. in Arist. Graeca* xxi *pars* ii), Berlin 1896.
Stephanus Byzantius [St.Byz.] v A.D. (?)
Ed. A. Meineke, vol. i (all published), Berlin 1849.
Stesichorus Lyricus [Stesich.] vii/vi B.C.
Ed. T. Bergk, *PLG* iii p. 205.
Stesimbrotus Historicus [Stesimbr.] v B.C.
Ed. C. Müller, *FHG* ii p. 52.
Sthenidas Philosophus [Sthenid.]
Apud Stobaeum.
Stobaeus, Joannes [Stob.] v A.D.
Ed. C. Wachsmuth & O. Hense, 5 vols., Berlin 1884–1912.
App. = *Appendix* to the ed. of T. Gaisford, vol. iv, Oxford 1822.
Scholia, ed. A. H. L. Heeren, *Stobaeus*, Göttingen 1792–1801.
Stoicorum Veterum Fragmenta [*Stoic.*]
Ed. H. von Arnim, Leipzig 1903 (cited by vol. and page).
Strabo Geographus [Str.] i B.C./i A.D.
Ed. G. Kramer, Berlin 1844–52.
Chr. = *Chrestomathiae* (cited by bk. and section as given in C. Müller, *GGM* ii p. 529).
Strato Comicus [Strato Com.] iii B.C. (?)
Ed. T. Kock, *CAF* iii p. 361.
Strato Epigrammaticus [Strat.] ii A.D.
v. *Anthologia Graeca.*
Strattis Comicus [Stratt.] v B.C.
Ed. T. Kock, *CAF* i p. 711; suppl. J. Demiańczuk, *Supp. Com.* p. 84.
Suetonius Grammaticus et Historicus Latinus [Suet.] ii A.D.
Ed. M. Ihm, Leipzig (T.) 1908.
περὶ βλασφημιῶν, ed. E. Miller, *Mélanges de littérature grecque*, Paris 1868, p. 413.
Suidas Lexicographus [Suid.] x A.D.
Ed. G. Bernhardy, Halle 1853.
Sulpicius Maximus Epicus [Sulp.Max.] i A.D.
IG 14. 2012.
Susario Comicus [Sus.] vi B.C.
Ed. T. Kock, *CAF* i p. 3.
Symmachus Interpres Veteris Testamenti [Sm.] ii/iii A.D.
Ed. F. Field, *Origenis Hexapla*, Oxford 1875.
Synesius Alchemista [Syn.Alch.] iv A.D.
Ed. M. Berthelot, *Collection des anciens alchimistes grecs*, Paris 1888, p. 75.
Syrianus Philosophus et Rhetor [Syrian.] v A.D.
in Hermog. = *in Hermogenem commentaria*, ed. H. Rabe, Leipzig (T.) 1892–3.
in Metaph. = *in Metaphysica commentaria*, ed. W. Kroll (*Comm. in Arist. Graeca* vi *pars* i), Berlin 1902.

Teleclides Comicus [Telecl.] v B.C.
Ed. T. Kock, *CAF* i p. 209; suppl. J. Demiańczuk, *Supp. Com.* p. 86.
Teles Philosophus iii B.C.
Ed. O. Hense[2], Tübingen 1909.
Telesilla Lyrica [Telesill.] vi/v B.C. (?)
Ed. T. Bergk, *PLG* iii p. 380.
Telestes Lyricus [Telest.] iv B.C.
Ed. T. Bergk, *PLG* iii p. 627.
Terentianus Maurus Grammaticus Latinus [Ter.Maur.] ii A.D.
Ed. H. Keil, *Gramm. Lat.* vol. vi p. 313.
Terentius Scaurus Grammaticus Latinus [Ter.Scaur.] ii A.D.
Ed. H. Keil, *Gramm. Lat.* vii p. 1.
Terpander Lyricus [Terp.] vii B.C.
Ed. T. Bergk, *PLG* iii p. 7.
Teucer Babylonius Astrologus i A.D. (?)
Ed. F. Boll, *Sphaera*, Leipzig 1903, pp. 6, 31.
Teucer Cyzicenus Historicus
Ed. C. Müller, *FHG* iv p. 508.
Thales Philosophus [Thal.] vi B.C.
Ed. H. Diels, *Vorsokr.* i p. 1; *fragmentum lyricum*, ed. T. Bergk, *PLG* iii p. 200.
Thallus, Antonius Epigrammaticus i B.C./i A.D.
v. *Anthologia Graeca.*
Theaetetus Epigrammaticus [Theaet.] iii B.C.
v. *Anthologia Graeca.*
Theagenes Historicus [Theagen.]
Ed. C. Müller, *FHG* iv p. 509.
Theages Philosophus [Theag.]
Apud Stobaeum.
Theano
Ep. = *Epistulae*, v. Pythagorae et Pythagoreorum Epistulae.
Thebaïs
Ed. T. W. Allen, *Homeri Opera* v, Oxford (OCT), p. 112.
Themiso Historicus [Themiso Hist.]
Ed. C. Müller, *FHG* iv p. 511.
Themiso Medicus i B.C.
Apud Galenum.
Themistius Sophista [Them.] iv A.D.
in APo. = *Aristotelis Analyticorum Posteriorum paraphrasis*, ed. M. Wallies (*Comm. in Arist. Graeca* v *pars* i), Berlin 1900.
in APr. = *in Aristotelis Analyticorum Priorum librum I paraphrasis*, ed. M. Wallies (*Comm. in Arist. Graeca* xxiii *pars* iii), Berlin 1884.
in de An. = *in libros Aristotelis de Anima paraphrasis*, ed. R. Heinze (*Comm. in Arist. Graeca* v *pars* iii), Berlin 1899.
in Ph. = *in Aristotelis Physica paraphrasis*, ed. H. Schenkl (*Comm. in Arist. Graeca* v *pars* ii), Berlin 1900.
in PN = *Themistii* (*Sophoniae*) *in Parva Naturalia commentarium*, ed. P. Wendland (*Comm. in Arist. Graeca* v *pars* vi), Berlin 1903.
Or. = *Orationes*, ed. W. Dindorf, Leipzig 1832; cited by page of Hardouin.
Themistocles Epistolographus [Themist.] v B.C.
Ep. = *Epistulae*, ed. R. Hercher, *Epistolographi*, p. 741.
Theocles Lyricus [Theocl.] iv/iii B.C.
Ed. J. U. Powell, *Coll. Alex.* p. 173.
Theocritus Poeta Bucolicus [Theoc.] iii B.C.
Ed. U. von Wilamowitz-Möllendorff[2], *Bucolici Graeci*, Oxford (OCT).
Beren. = *Coma Berenices*
Ep. = *Epigrammata*
Scholia, ed. C. Wendel, Leipzig (T.) 1914.
Theodectes Tragicus [Theodect.] iv B.C.
Ed. A. Nauck, *TGF* p. 801.
Theodoridas Epigrammaticus [Theodorid.] iii B.C.
v. *Anthologia Graeca.*
Theodorus Epigrammaticus [Theod.]
v. *Anthologia Graeca*
Theodosius Alexandrinus Grammaticus [Theodos.] iv A.D. (?)
Can. = *Canones*, ed. A. Hilgard, in *Grammatici Graeci*, *pars* iv, vol. i, Leipzig 1889.
Spuria, ed. C. W. Göttling, Leipzig 1822. [Theodos.Gr.]
Theodotion Interpres Veteris Testamenti [Thd.] ii A.D. (?)
F. Field, *Origenis Hexapla*, Oxford 1875.
Theognetus Comicus [Theognet.]
Ed. T. Kock, *CAF* iii p. 364.
Theognis Elegiacus [Thgn.] vi B.C.
Ed. T. Bergk, *PLG* ii p. 117.
Theognis Tragicus [Thgn.Trag.] v/iv B.C.
Ed. A. Nauck, *TGF* p. 769.
Theognis Rhodius Historicus [Thgn.Hist.]
Ed. C. Müller, *FHG* iv p. 514.
Theognostus Grammaticus [Theognost.] ix A.D.
Can. = *Canones*, ed. J. A. Cramer, *An. Ox.*, vol. ii.
Theologumena Arithmeticae [*Theol.Ar.*]
[Iamblichus], *Theologumena Arithmeticae*, ed. V. de Falco, Leipzig (T.) 1922; cited by Ast's pages (in margin).
Theolytus Epicus [Theolyt.]
Ed. J. U. Powell, *Coll. Alex.* p. 9.
Theon Epigrammaticus
v. *Anthologia Graeca.*
Theon Rhetor i/ii A.D. (?)
Prog. = *Progymnasmata*, ed. L. Spengel, *Rhet.* ii p. 59.

Theon Gymnasiarcha Medicus [Theon Gymn.]
Apud Galenum
Theon Smyrnaeus Philosophus [Theo Sm.] ii A.D.
Ed. E. Hiller, Leipzig (T.) 1878.
in Ptol. = *in Ptolemaeum*, ed. Halma, *Œuvres de Ptolémée*, tom. v, Paris 1821.
Theophanes Epigrammaticus [Theoph.]
v. *Anthologia Graeca.*
Theophilus Comicus [Theophil.]
Ed. T. Kock, *CAF* ii p. 473.
Theophrastus Philosophus [Thphr.] iv/iii B.C.
Ed. F. Wimmer, Leipzig (T.) 1854–62; *HP*, *Od.*, *Sign.*, ed. Sir Arthur Hort, London and New York (Loeb) 1916.
CP = *de Causis Plantarum*
Char. = *Characteres*, ed. H. Diels, Oxford (OCT).
Fr. = *Fragmenta*
HP = *Historia Plantarum*
Ign. = *de Igne*
Lap. = *de Lapidibus*
Lass. = *de Lassitudine*
Metaph. = *Metaphysica*, ed. H. Usener, Bonn 1890.
Od. = *de Odoribus*
Sens. = *de Sensu*
Sign. = *de Signis Tempestatum*
Sud. = *de Sudore*
Vent. = *de Ventis*
Vert. = *de Vertigine*
Theopompus Comicus [Theopomp.Com.] v B.C.
Ed. T. Kock, *CAF* i p. 733; suppl. J. Demiańczuk, *Supp. Com.* p. 86.
Theopompus Historicus [Theopomp.Hist.] iv B.C.
Ed. B. P. Grenfell & A. S. Hunt, v. *Hellenica Oxyrhynchia.*
Theopompus Colophonius Epicus [Theopomp.Coloph.]
Ed. J. U. Powell, *Coll. Alex.* p. 28.
Thespis Tragicus vi/v B.C.
Ed. A. Nauck, *TGF* p. 832.
Thomas Epigrammaticus [Thom.] vi A.D.
v. *Anthologia Graeca.*
Thomas Magister Grammaticus [Thom.Mag.] xiii/xiv A.D.
Ed. F. Ritschl, Halle 1832.
Thrasymachus [Thrasym.] iv B.C.
Ed. H. Diels, *Vorsokr.* ii p. 276.
Thucydides Historicus [Th.] v B.C.
Ed. H. Stuart Jones, Oxford (OCT).
Thugenides Comicus [Thugen.]
Ed. T. Kock, *CAF* iii p. 377; suppl. J. Demiańczuk, *Supp. Com.* p. 87.
Thyillus Epigrammaticus [Thyill.] i B.C.
v. *Anthologia Graeca.*
Thymocles Epigrammaticus [Thymocl.]
v. *Anthologia Graeca.*
Tiberius Rhetor [Tib.]
Fig. = *de Figuris*, ed. L. Spengel, *Rhet.* iii p. 59.
Tiberius Illustrius Epigrammaticus [Tib.Ill.] i A.D. (?)
v. *Anthologia Graeca.*
Timaeus Grammaticus [Tim.]
Lex. = *Lexicon Platonicum*, ed. C. F. Hermann, *Platonis Dialogi*, vol. vi, Leipzig (T.) 1892.
Timaeus Historicus [Timae.] iv/iii B.C.
Ed. C. Müller, *FHG* i p. 193, iv pp. 625, 640.
Timaeus Locrus Philosophus [Ti.Locr.]
Ed. C. F. Hermann, post Platonis Timaeum, Leipzig (T.) 1852.
Timagenes Historicus [Timag.] i B.C.
Ed. C. Müller, *FHG* iii p. 317.
Timo Phliasius Poeta Philosophus iii B.C.
Ed. H. Diels, *PPF* p. 173.
Timocles Comicus [Timocl.] iv B.C.
Ed. T. Kock, *CAF* ii p. 451; suppl. J. Demiańczuk, *Supp. Com.* p. 88.
Timocreon Lyricus [Timocr.] v. B.C.
Ed. T. Bergk, *PLG* iii p. 536.
Timostratus Comicus [Timostr.] ii B.C.
Ed. T. Kock, *CAF* iii p. 355.
Timotheus Comicus [Tim.Com.] iv/iii B.C. (?)
Ed. T. Kock, *CAF* ii p. 450.
Timotheus Lyricus [Tim.] v/iv B.C.
Ed. U. von Wilamowitz-Möllendorff, Leipzig 1903.
Fr. = *Fragmenta*
Pers. = *Persae*
Timotheus Gazaeus Philosophus [Tim.Gaz.]
v. Aristophanes Byzantinus, Philosophus.
Titanomachia [Titanomach.]
Ed. T. W. Allen, *Homeri Opera* v, Oxford (OCT), p. 110.
Tragica Adespota [*Trag.Adesp.*]
Ed. A. Nauck, *TGF* p. 837.
Trophilus [Trophil.]
Apud Stobaeum.
Tryphiodorus Epicus [Tryph.]
Ed. W. Weinberger, v. Coluthus.
Trypho Grammaticus i B.C.
Fr. = *Fragmenta*, ed. A. von Velsen, Berlin 1853.
Pass. = Excerpta περὶ παθῶν, ed. R. Schneider, Progr. Gymn. Duisburg, Leipzig 1895.
Trop. = περὶ τρόπων, ed. L. Spengel, *Rhet.* iii p. 189.
Tullius Flaccus Epigrammaticus [Tull.Flacc.]
v. *Anthologia Graeca.*
Tullius Geminus Epigrammaticus [Tull.Gem.]
v. *Anthologia Graeca.*
Tullius Laurea Epigrammaticus. [Tull.Laur.] i B.C.
v. *Anthologia Graeca.*
Tullius Sabinus, v. Sabinus.
Tymnes Epigrammaticus [Tymn.]
v. *Anthologia Graeca.*
Tyrtaeus Elegiacus [Tyrt.] vii B.C.
Ed. T. Bergk, *PLG* ii p. 8.
Tzetzes, Joannes Grammaticus [Tz.] xii A.D.
ad Hes.*Op.* = ad Hesiodi *Opera et Dies*, ed. T. Gaisford, *Poetae Graeci Minores*, vol. iii.
ad Lyc. = ad Lycophronem, ed. E. Scheer, v. Lycophron.
Diff. Poet. = περὶ διαφορᾶς ποιητῶν, ed. G. Kaibel, *CGF* p. 34.
H. = *Historiarum variarum chiliades*, ed. T. Kiessling, Leipzig 1826.
Proll.Com. = *Prolegomena de Comoedia Graeca*, ed. G. Kaibel, *CGF* p. 17.
Trag.Poes. = *De Tragica Poesi*, ed. G. Kaibel, op. cit., p. 43.

Ulpianus Grammaticus [Ulp.] iii A.D.
Commentary on Demosthenes, ed. H. Wolf, Basel 1572.
Uranius Historicus [Uran.] i B.C. (?)
Ed. C. Müller, *FHG* iv p. 523.

Varro, M. Terentius Historicus et Grammaticus Latinus i B.C.
LL = *de Lingua Latina*, ed. G. Goetz & F. Schoell, Leipzig 1910.
RR = *Res Rusticae*, ed. G. Goetz, Leipzig (T.) 1912.
Sat.Men. = *Saturae Menippeae*, ed. F. Buecheler, post Petronium (q.v.)
Velius Longus Grammaticus Latinus [Vel.Long.] ii A.D.
Ed. H. Keil, *Gramm. Lat.* vii p. 37.
Vettius Valens Astrologus [Vett.Val.] ii A.D.
Ed. W. Kroll, Berlin 1908 (cited by page and line).
Vetus Testamentum Graece redditum [LXX]
Ed. H. B. Swete, ed. 3, Cambridge 1901.
A. Versiones ab Origene collectae
Ed. F. Field, *Origenis Hexapla*, Oxford 1875.
Al. = ἄλλοι
Aq. = Aquila (q.v.)
Heb. = Ἑβραῖος
Quint. = Quinta
Sext. = Sexta
Sm. = Symmachus (q.v.)
Thd. = Theodotion (q.v.)
B. Libri singuli his siglis notantur:—
Am. = *Amos*
Ba. = *Baruch*
Bel
Ca. = *Canticles*
1, 2 *Ch.* = 1, 2 *Chronicles*
Da. = *Daniel*
De. = *Deuteronomy*
Ec. = *Ecclesiastes*
Ep.Je. = *Epistle of Jeremiah*
Es. = *Esther*
1, 2 *Es.* = 1, 2 *Esdras*
Ex. = *Exodus*
Ez. = *Ezekiel*
Ge. = *Genesis*
Hb. = *Habakkuk*
Hg. = *Haggai*
Ho. = *Hosea*
Is. = *Isaiah*
Jb = *Job*
Jd. = *Judges*
Je. = *Jeremiah*
Jl. = *Joel*
Jn. = *Jonah*
Jo. = *Joshua*
Ju. = *Judith*
1–4 *Ki.* = 1–4 *Kings*
La. = *Lamentations*
Le. = *Leviticus*
Ma. = *Malachi*
1–4 *Ma.* = 1–4 *Maccabees*
Mi. = *Micah*
Na. = *Nahum*
Ne. = *Nehemiah*
Nu. = *Numbers*
Ob. = *Obadiah*
Pr. = *Proverbs*
Prec.Man. = *Prayer of Manasses*

Vetus Testamentum (*continued*)
Ps. = *Psalms*
Ru. = *Ruth*
Si. = *Ecclesiasticus* (*Siracides*)
Su. = *Susanna*
To. = *Tobit*
Wi. = *Wisdom of Solomon*
Za. = *Zechariah*
Ze. = *Zephaniah*
Vita Philonidis Epicurei [*Vit.Philonid.*]
= *PHerc.* 1044, ed. W. Crönert, *Berl. Sitzb.* xli (1900); cited by page of offprint (942–959 = 1–18).
Vitae Homeri [*Vit.Hom.*]
Ed. T. W. Allen, *Homeri Opera*, Oxford (OCT), v p. 245.
Vitruvius Scriptor de Architectura Latinus [Vitr.] i B.C.
Ed. F. Krohn, Leipzig (T.) 1912.

Xanthus Historicus [Xanth.] v B.C.
Ed. C. Müller *FHG* i p. 36, iv pp. 623, 628.
Xenagoras Historicus [Xenag.]
Ed. C. Müller, *FHG* iv p. 526.
Xenarchus Comicus [Xenarch.] iv B.C.
Ed. T. Kock, *CAF* ii p. 467.
Xeno Comicus
Ed. T. Kock, *CAF* iii p. 390.
Xenocles Tragicus [Xenocl.] v B.C.
Ed. A. Nauck, *TGF* p. 770.
Xenocrates Medicus (apud Oribasium) [Xenocr.] i A.D.
Ed. J. L. Ideler, *Physici et Medici Graeci Minores* i p. 121, Berlin 1841.
Xenophanes Poeta Philosophus [Xenoph.] vi B.C.
Ed. H. Diels, *PPF* p. 20.
Xenophon Historicus [X.] v/iv B.C.
Ed. E. C. Marchant, Oxford (OCT).
Ages. = *Agesilaus*
An. = *Anabasis*
Ap. = *Apologia Socratis*
Ath. = *Respublica Atheniensium*
Cyn. = *Cynegeticus*
Cyr. = *Institutio Cyri* (*Cyropaedia*)
Ep. = *Epistulae*, ed. R. Hercher, *Epistolographi*, p. 788.
Eq. = *de Equitandi ratione*
Eq.Mag. = *de Equitum magistro*
HG = *Historia Graeca* (*Hellenica*)
Hier. = *Hiero*
Lac. = *Respublica Lacedaemoniorum*
Mem. = *Memorabilia*
Oec. = *Oeconomicus*
Smp. = *Symposium*
Vect. = *de Vectigalibus*
Xenophon Ephesius Scriptor Eroticus [X.Eph.] ii A.D. (?)
Ed. R. Hercher, *Erotici* i p. 327.

Zaleucus [Zaleuc.] (vii B.C.)
Apud Stobaeum.
Zelotus Epigrammaticus [Zelot.]
v. *Anthologia Graeca.*
Zeno Citieus Stoicus [Zeno *Stoic.*] iv/iii B.C.
Ed. H. von Arnim, *SVF* i p. 1.
Zeno Eleaticus Philosophus [Zeno Eleat.] v B.C.
Ed. H. Diels, *Vorsokr.* i p. 165.
Zeno Tarsensis Stoicus [Zeno Tars.*Stoic.*] iii/ii B.C.
Ed. H. von Arnim, *SVF* iii p. 209.
Zenobius Paroemiographus [Zen.] ii A.D.
Ed. E. L. von Leutsch & F. G. Schneidewin, *Paroemiographi* i p. 1.
Zenodotus Grammaticus [Zenod.] iv/iii B.C.
Apud Scholia in Homerum.
Zonaeus Rhetor [Zonae.]
Fig. = *de Figuris*, ed. L. Spengel, *Rhet.* iii p. 161.
Zonaras Lexicographus [Zonar.]
Ed. J. A. H. Tittmann, Leipzig 1808.
Zonas Epigrammaticus [Zon.] i B.C./i A.D.
Idem qui et Diodorus Sardianus, q. v.
Zopyrus Historicus [Zopyr.Hist.]
Ed. C. Müller, *FHG* iv p. 531.
Zopyrus Medicus [Zopyr.] i A.D.
Apud Oribasium.
Zosimus Alchemista [Zos.Alch.] iii/iv A.D.
Ed. M. Berthelot, *Collection des anciens alchimistes grecs*, Paris 1888, p. 107.
Zosimus Epigrammaticus [Zos.]
v. *Anthologia Graeca.*
Zosimus Historicus [Zos.] v A.D.
Ed. L. Mendelssohn, Leipzig 1887.

I. AUTHORS AND WORKS (ADDITIONAL)

[**Adamantius**]
Vent. = περὶ ἀνέμων, ed. V. Rose, *Anecdota Graeca et Graeco-Latina* i, Berlin 1864, pp. 29–48; cited by page.
[**Aeschines** Orator]
Scholia, ed. F. Schultz in editione orationum, Leipzig 1865.
[**Aeschrio**]
Ed. E. Diehl, *Anth. Lyr.* i² (3) p. 101.
[**Aeschylus**]
Ed. G. Murray, Oxford (OCT) 1937.
[**Aesopus**]
Ed. A. Chambry, Paris 1925.
[**Aëtius**]
Lib. i–iv, ed. A. Olivieri, *CMG* viii 1, Leipzig & Berlin 1935.
[**Africanus**]
Jules Africain, *Fragments des Cestes*, ed. J.-R. Vieillefond, Paris 1932. [Afric. *Cest.* p.... V.]
[**Agatharchides**]
Fr.Hist., ed. F. Jacoby, *FGrH* ii p. 205.
[**Alcaeus** Lyricus]
Ed. E. Diehl, *Anth. Lyr.* i² (4) p. 86; ed. E. Lobel, Oxford 1927.
[**Alcmaeon**]
Ed. H. Diels & W. Kranz, *Vorsokr.*⁵ i p. 210.
[**Alcman**]
Ed. E. Diehl, *Anth. Lyr.* ii p. 7.
[**Anacreon**]
Ed. E. Diehl, *Anth. Lyr.* i² (4) p. 160.
[**Anaxagoras**]
Ed. H. Diels & W. Kranz, *Vorsokr.*⁵ ii p. 5.
[**Anaxarchus**]
Ed. H. Diels & W. Kranz, *Vorsokr.*⁵ ii p. 235.
[**Anaximander**]
Ed. H. Diels & W. Kranz, *Vorsokr.*⁵ i p. 81.
[**Anaximenes**]
Ed. H. Diels & W. Kranz, *Vorsokr.*⁵ i p. 90.
[**Anonymus**]
Vit.Arist. etc., v. Diogenes Laertius.
Anonymus Argentinensis [Anon. Argent.]
Ed. B. Keil, Strassburg 1902.
Anonymus Bellermannianus [Anon.Bellerm.]
Anonymi scriptio de musica, Bacchii senioris introductio artis musicae, ed. [J.] F. Bellermann, Berlin 1841.
For '**Anonymus Londnensis**' read '**Anonymus Londinensis**'
[**Anticlides**]
Ed. F. Jacoby, *FGrH* ii p. 799.
[**Antimachus Colophonius**]
Ed. B. Wyss, Berlin (Weidmann) 1936.
Fragmenta Elegiaca, ed. E. Diehl, *Anth. Lyr.* i² (1) p. 100.
[**Antipho Sophista**]
Ed. H. Diels & W. Kranz, *Vorsokr.*⁵ ii p. 334.
[**Aphthonius**]
Progymnasmata, ed. H. Rabe, Leipzig (T.) 1926.
[**Apollonius Rhodius**]
Fr. = *Fragmenta*, ed. J. U. Powell, *Coll. Alex.* p. 4.
Scholia in A.R. vetera, rec. C. Wendel, Berlin (Weidmann) 1935.
Appendix Proverbiorum [*App.Prov.*]
Ed. E. L. v. Leutsch & F. G. Schneidewin, *Paroemiographi* i pp. 379–467.
[**Apuleius** Scriptor Botanicus], after 'Basel 1560' add '; *Pseudo-Apulei Platonici Herbarius*, ed. E. Howald & H. E. Sigerist in *Corpus Medicorum Latinorum* iv, Leipzig & Berlin 1927 [*Herb.*]'
[**Archilochus**]
Ed. E. Diehl, *Anth. Lyr.* i² (3) p. 3.
[**Archytas Tarentinus**]
Ed. H. Diels & W. Kranz, *Vorsokr.*⁵ i p. 421.
[**Arion**]
Ed. E. Diehl, *Anth. Lyr.* ii p. 5.
[**Ariphron**]
Ed. E. Diehl, *Anth. Lyr.* ii p. 130.
[**Aristides** Rhetor], for 'cited by Spengel's page' read 'ed. W. Schmid, Leipzig (T.) 1926; cited by Spengel's page, given in the margin of Schmid'
[**Aristobulus**]
Ed. F. Jacoby, *FGrH* ii p. 769.
[**Aristodemus**]
Ed. F. Jacoby, *FGrH* i p. 186, ii p. 493 (= *FHG* v p. 1).

[**Arrianus**], for '*Epict*.... 1894' read '*Epict*...ed. 2, 1916' and add '*Fr.*, ed. F. Jacoby, *FGrH* ii p. 837.'
Scripta minora et fragmenta, ed. A. G. Roos, Leipzig (T.) 1928.
[**Asius**] for 'p. 406' read 'p. 23' and add '; ed. E. Diehl, *Anth. Lyr.* i² (1) p. 22'; add '*Fr.Ep.* = *Fragmenta Epica*, ed. G. Kinkel, *EGF* p. 202.'
[**Athenaeus** Mechanicus], substitute: 'Ed. R. Schneider, *Abhandlungen der Gesellschaft der Wissenschaften zu Göttingen* (Phil.-hist. Klasse), N. F. XII (1912), No. 5: cited by Wescher's page, given in Schneider's margin.'

[**Bacchylides**]
Ed. B. Snell, Leipzig (T.) 1934.
[**Bias**]
Ed. E. Diehl, *Anth. Lyr.* ii p. 191.
[**Bito**]
Ed. A. Rehm & E. Schramm, *Abhandlungen der Bayerischen Akademie der Wissenschaften, Philosophisch-historische Abteilung*, Neue Folge 2, 1929.

[**Callinus**], for 'Epicus' read 'Elegiacus' and add '; ed. E. Diehl, *Anth.Lyr.* i² (1) p. 3'
[**Carmen Aureum**], for 'ii' read 'i' and add '; i² (2), p. 87'
[**Castorio**]
Ed. E. Diehl, *Anth. Lyr.* i² (3) p. 67.
[**Cephalio**]
Ed. F. Jacoby, *FGrH* ii p. 436.
[**Cercidas**]
Ed. A. D. Knox, London (Loeb, after Theophrastus, *Characters*) 1929.
[**Charax**]
Ed. F. Jacoby, *FGrH* ii p. 482.
[**Chares**]
Ed. F. Jacoby, *FGrH* ii p. 657.
[**Charisius**]
Ed. C. Barwick, Leipzig (T.) 1925.
[**Chilo**]
Ed. E. Diehl, *Anth. Lyr.* ii p. 191.
[**Choricius**]
Ed. R. Foerster & E. Richtsteig, Leipzig (T.) 1929.
[**Cleobulina**]
Ed. E. Diehl, *Anth. Lyr.* i² (1) p. 130.
[**Cleobulus**]
Ed. E. Diehl, *Anth. Lyr.* i² (1) p. 130, ii p. 192.
[**Cleon Siculus**]
Ed. E. Diehl, *Anth.Lyr.* i² (1) p. 128.
[**Clitarchus**]
Ed. F. Jacoby, *FGrH* ii p. 741.
Columella, L. Junius Scriptor rei rusticae Latinus [Colum.] i A.D.
Ed. J. G. Schneider, Leipzig 1794; *lib. de arboribus, rei rust. lib. x, xi*, ed. V. Lundström, Uppsala 1897–1906.
[**Corinna**]
Ed. E. Diehl, *Anth. Lyr.* i² (4) p. 193.
[**Critias**]
Ed. H. Diels & W. Kranz, *Vorsokr.*⁵ ii p. 371.
[**Cydias**]
Ed. E. Diehl, *Anth. Lyr.* ii p. 127.
Cyranides (Βίβλοι κυρανίδες sive κοιρανίδες) [Cyran.] i or ii A.D.
Ed. C. E. Ruelle in F. de Mély, *Les lapidaires de l'antiquité et du moyen âge*, tome ii, *Les lapidaires grecs*, Paris 1898–9; cited by page.

[**Daimachus**]
Ed. F. Jacoby, *FGrH* ii p. 15.
[**Demades**]
Fr., sometimes cited from Blass.
[**Demetrius Phalereus** Historicus]
Ed. F. Jacoby, *FGrH* ii p. 956.
Demetrius Scepsius ii B.C.
Cited from Strabo & Athenaeus.
[**Demochares**]
Ed. F. Jacoby, *FGrH* ii p. 133.
[**Democritus** Philosophus]
Ed. H. Diels & W. Kranz, *Vorsokr.*⁵ ii p. 81.
[Pseudo-**Democritus**], add '; cf. H. Diels & W. Kranz, *Vorsokr.*⁵ ii p. 218'
Symp. Ant. = περὶ συμπαθειῶν καὶ ἀντιπαθειῶν, una cum Nepualio (q.v.).
[**Demodocus**]
Ed. E. Diehl, *Anth. Lyr.* i² (1) p. 62.
[**Demophilus**, *Sim.*], for '1900' read '1904'
[**Demosthenes**]
Fr. = *Fragmenta*, ed. H. Sauppe, *Orat. Att.* ii p. 250.
[**Demosthenes Ophthalmicus**], cited also from Simon Januensis, *Clavis Sanationis*, Venice 1510.
[**Dexippus** Historicus]
Ed. F. Jacoby, *FGrH* ii p. 452.
[**Diagoras**]
Ed. E. Diehl, *Anth. Lyr.* ii p. 126.
[**Dialexeis**]
Ed. H. Diels & W. Kranz, *Vorsokr.*⁵ ii p. 416.
[**Diocles** Medicus] add 'prob. iv, perh. iv/iii, B.C.'
[**Dionysius Halicarnassensis**]
Vett. Cens. (Hudson ii pp. 122–7) = περὶ μιμήσεως B (Usener-Radermacher ii pp. 202. 18–214. 2).
[**Dionysius Minor**]
Ed. E. Diehl, *Anth. Lyr.* i² (1) p. 112.
[**Diyllus**]
Ed. F. Jacoby, *FGrH* ii p. 130.
[**Dositheus**]
Ed. J. Tolkiehn, Leipzig 1913.
[**Duris** Historicus]
Ed. F. Jacoby, *FGrH* ii p. 136.

[**Empedocles**, *Sphaer.*], for 'pp. 154, 199' read 'p. 154'
[**Ephorus**]
Ed. F. Jacoby, *FGrH* ii p. 37.
[**Epictetus**], for '1894' read 'ed. 2, 1916' and after '*Gnomologium*' add '*Sent.* = *Gnom. D* (*Sententiae Codicis Vaticani* 1144).'
[**Epicurus**]
Epicuri et Epicureorum scripta in Herculanensibus Papyris servata, ed. A. Vogliano, Berolini 1928.
[**Erinna**]
Ed. E. Diehl, *Anth. Lyr.* i² (4) p. 207.
[**Euclides**]
Catoptr. = *Catoptrica* (vii p. 286 Heiberg).
[**Eusebius** Historicus]
Ed. F. Jacoby, *FGrH* ii p. 480.
[**Eutychianus**], for 'p. 365' read 'p. 369' and add '; ed. F. Jacoby, *FGrH* ii p. 954'
[**Evenus**]
Ed. E. Diehl, *Anth. Lyr.* i² (1) p. 92.
Excerpta Barocciana [Exc. Barocc.]
Ed. A. Nauck post *Lexicon Vindobonense*.

Favorinus Philosophus
Exil. = περὶ φυγῆς in *PVat.* 11 (v. List III).

[**Galenus**], for '*CMG*..(in progress): the' substitute: '*CMG* v 4 (1) = Kühn v 1–148; v 4 (2) = Kühn vi 1–831; v 9 (1) = Kühn xv 1–223, 418–919, xix 182–221; v 9 (2) = Kühn xvi 489–840, vii 643–665, xviii (2) 1–317; v 10 (1) = Kühn xvii 4–302; v 10 (2) = Kühn xvii 480–791; ed. R. Charterius (with Hippocrates) 13 vols., Paris 1639, reprinted 1679. The': and after '*Subf. Emp.*...1872' add '; ed. Karl Deichgräber, *Die griechische Empirikerschule, Sammlung der Fragmente und Darstellung der Lehre*, Berlin 1930: cited by Bonnet's page, given in Deichgräber's margin': and after '*Vict.Att.*... Leipzig 1923.' add; '*in Pl.Ti.* = *Fragments du commentaire de Galien sur le Timée de Platon*,..par le dʳ Ch. Daremberg, Paris–Leipzig 1848; *in Platonis Timaeum commentarii fragmenta*, ed. H. O. Schroeder, *CMG* suppl. i, 1934.'
Gnomologium Vaticanum [*Gnomol. Vat.*].
L. Sternbach, *De Gnomologio Vaticano inedito* in *Wiener Studien*, vols. ix, x, xi.
[**Gorgias**]
Ed. H. Diels & W. Kranz, *Vorsokr.*⁵ ii p. 271.

[**Hemerologium Florentinum**]
Ed. W. Kubitschek, *Die Kalenderbücher von Florenz, Rom und Leiden*, in *Wiener Denkschr.*, 1915 (Bd. 57) Abh. 3.
[**Heraclitus**]
Ed. H. Diels & W. Kranz, *Vorsokr.*⁵ i p. 139.
[**Hero**]
Bel., ed. H. Diels & E. Schramm, *Abh.Berl.Akad.* (1918), No. 2; cited by page and line of Wescher, given in margin.
Herodes Atticus Historicus
Pol. = περὶ πολιτείας, ed. E. Drerup, *Studien zur Geschichte und Kultur des Altertums*, Band II, Heft i, Paderborn 1908.
[**Hippocrates**]
Jusj., *Lex*, *de Arte*, *Medic.*, *Decent.*, *Praec.*, *VM*, *Aër.*, *Alim.*, *Liqu.*, *Flat.*, ed. I. L. Heiberg, *CMG* i 1, Leipzig & Berlin 1927.
[**Hippon**]
Ed. H. Diels & W. Kranz, *Vorsokr.*⁵ i p. 385.
[**Hipponax**]
Ed. E. Diehl, *Anth. Lyr.* i² (3) p. 74.
[**Homerus**]
Fr. = *Fragmenta*, ed. T. W. Allen, *Homeri Opera* v, Oxford (OCT), p. 147.
Sch.D, ed. J. Barnes in editione Homeri, Cambridge 1711.
Sch.Gen. = *Les scolies genevoises de l'Iliade*, ed. J. Nicole, Paris 1891.

[**Iamblichus**]
VP, ed. L. Deubner, Leipzig (T.) 1937.

[Iamblichus Scriptor Eroticus], for 'Ed. R. Hercher, *Erotici* i p. 217.' read 'Ed. W. A. Hirschig, *Erotici Scriptores*, Paris (D.) 1856, p. 515.'
[Ibycus]
Ed. E. Diehl, *Anth. Lyr.* ii p. 48.
[Ion Chius], add 'v B.C.'
Fragmenta Elegiaca et Lyrica, ed. E. Diehl, *Anth. Lyr.* i² (1) p. 83.
[Isaeus]. Fragments cited by the numbering of *Orat.Att.* ii pp. 228 ff. (Baiter-Sauppe).
[Ister], for '409' read '418'

[Josephus], add '; ed. B. Niese, 7 vols., Berlin 1887–95'

[Lamprocles]
Ed. E. Diehl, *Anth. Lyr.* ii p. 123.
[Lasus]
Ed. E. Diehl, *Anth. Lyr.* ii p. 60.
[Leucippus]
Ed. H. Diels & W. Kranz, *Vorsokr.*⁵ ii p. 70.
[Licymnius]
Ed. E. Diehl, *Anth. Lyr.* ii p. 131.
[Longus]
Ed. G. Dalmeyda, Paris (*Collection des Universités de France, Assn. Guillaume Budé*) 1934.
[Lucianus], add '[Luc.]'; also, after 'Scholia ... 1906' add '; other scholia in the Bipontine Edition, Zweibrücken 1789–1793'
Epigr. = *Epigrammata.*
[Lycophronides]
Ed. E. Diehl, *Anth. Lyr.* ii p. 157.
[Lynceus], for 'Cetera... Athenaeum.' read 'Prose writings cited from Athenaeus.'
[Lyrica Adespota]
Ed. E. Diehl, *Anth. Lyr.* i² (1) p. 138; (3) pp. 68, 118; (4) p. 214; ii p. 157.

[Mamercus]
Ed. E. Diehl, *Anth. Lyr.* i² (1) p. 113.
Marcellus Empiricus Medicus Latinus [Marcell. Emp.] iv A.D.
Ed. M. Niedermann in *Corpus Medicor. Lat.* v, Leipzig 1916.
[Martianus Capella]
Ed. A. Dick, Leipzig (T.) 1925.
Mela, Pomponius Geographus Latinus i A.D.
Ed. C. Frick, Leipzig (T.) 1880 (cited by Bk. and short section).
[Melanippides]
Ed. E. Diehl, *Anth. Lyr.* ii p. 153.
[Melissus]
Ed. H. Diels & W. Kranz, *Vorsokr.*⁵ i p. 258.
[Menander]
Reliquiae in papyris et membranis vetustissimis servatae. Tertium ed. A. Koerte, Leipzig (T.) 1938.
Arg. Men. *Oxy.* = Arguments of plays by Menander in *POxy* 1235.
Menecrates: two or more of the name wrote epigrams v. *Anthologia Graeca.*
[Mesomedes]
Ed. U. v. Wilamowitz-Moellendorff, *Griechische Verskunst*, Berlin 1921, pp. 595–607; poems are cited from this edition by No. and line, with 'W.-M.'
[Metrodorus Chius]
Ed. H. Diels & W. Kranz, *Vorsokr.*⁵ ii p. 231.
[Mimnermus]
Ed. E. Diehl, *Anth. Lyr.* i² (1) p. 50.
[Musaeus Philosophus]
Ed. H. Diels & W. Kranz, *Vorsokr.*⁵ i p. 20.

[Nausiphanes]
Ed. H. Diels & W. Kranz, *Vorsokr.*⁵ ii p. 246.
[Nessas]
Ed. H. Diels & W. Kranz, *Vorsokr.*⁵ ii p. 230.
[Nicolaus]
Prog., sts. cited from L. Spengel, *Rhetores Graeci* iii pp. 447–98; sts. from. Ch. Walz, *Rhetores Graeci* ii pp. 565–684, al.

[Ocellus Lucanus]
Ed. R. Harder, Berlin 1926.
[Olympiodorus]
in Grg. = *in Platonis Gorgiam commentaria*, ed. W. Norvin, Leipzig (T.) 1936.
[Oribasius]
Ed. J. Raeder, *CMG* vi, Leipzig & Berlin 1926–1933.
Collectionum medicarum reliquiae vi 1, 2, cited without title.
Syn., *Eup.* vi 3.

[Palladius]
Febr. = *de febribus*, ed. J. L. Ideler, *Physici et Medici Graeci minores*, Berlin 1841, i p 107.
Palladius Episcopus Helenopolitanus iv–v A.D.
περὶ τῶν τῆς Ἰνδίας ἐθνῶν καὶ τῶν Βραχμάνων ap. Pseudo-Callisthenem.
[Pappus]
Commentaires de Pappus et de Théon d'Alexandrie sur l'Almageste, texte établi et annoté par A. Rome. I. *Pappus*, Rome 1931 (= Studi e Testi 54, Biblioteca Apostolica Vaticana).
[Parrhasius]
Ed. E. Diehl, *Anth. Lyr.* i² (1) p. 111.
[Paulus Alexandrinus], for 'page' read 'leaf'
[Perictione], for 'Philosophus' read 'Philosopha'
Periplus Maris Euxini [*Peripl.M.Eux.*]
Ed. C. Müller, *GGM* i p. 402 + *FHG* v *pars* i p. 174.
[Periplus Maris Rubri] Ed. H. Frisk, Göteborg 1927.
[Pherecydes Syrius]
Ed. H. Diels & W. Kranz, *Vorsokr.*⁵ i p. 43.
Philicus Lyricus [Philic.], identified with Philiscus. Apud Hephaestionem.
[Philo Mechanicus], before '1919, No. 12' insert '1918, No. 16,' and for 'Wescher' read 'Thévenot'
[Philo Judaeus], add 'i A.D.' and 'cited by vol. and page of Mangey, given in margin of Cohn-Wendland (Ph. 2. 264–9 M. = V 67–8 + I 209–16 C.-W.; Ph. 2. 437–44 M. = V 324–35 C.-W.; Ph. 2. 492. 10–497. 8 M. = VI 89. 11–97. 3 C.-W.). References containing higher numbers than 2. 600 will be found in T. Mangey's edition, London 1742, not in that of Cohn and Wendland'.
Fragments (*Fr.*) cited by page of Rendel Harris.
[Philodemus Philosophus], add 'Sts. cited by page of Vogliano (p. .. V.), cf. [Epicurus].' Also for 'D. 1, 3 .. 1916, 1917' read 'D. 1, 3 .. 1915, 1916' and for '*Oec.* .. 1906' read '*Oec.* .. 1907'
[Philolaus]
Ed. H. Diels et W. Kranz, *Vorsokr.*⁵ i p. 398.
[Philoxenus Lyricus]
Ed. E. Diehl, *Anth. Lyr.* i² (3) p. 133.
[Phocylides]
Ed. E. Diehl, *Anth. Lyr.* i² (1) p. 58.
[Phoenix], add: 'Gerhard *Phoinx* = G. A. Gerhard, *Phoinix von Kolophon*, Leipzig & Berlin 1909.'
[Phoronis]
Ed. G. Kinkel, *EGF* p. 209.
[Pindarus], add at end ', 1927' and for 'Dith.Oxy.' read 'Dith.'
Ed. C. M. Bowra, Oxford (OCT) 1935; tertium ed. O. Schroeder, Leipzig (T.) 1930.
[Pittacus]
Ed. E. Diehl, *Anth. Lyr.* ii p. 191.
[Plutarchus]
Moralia, vol. i ed. W. R. Paton and I. Wegehaupt, Leipzig (T.) 1925; vol. ii ed. W. Nachstädt, W. Sieveking, J. B. Titchener, 1935; vol. iii ed. W. R. Paton, M. Pohlenz, W. Sieveking, 1929; vol. iv ed. C. Hubert, 1938.
in Arat. = *quaestiones de Arati signis* (vol. vii p. 102 B.).
Ps.-Plu. *Vit.Hom.* (vol. vii p. 329 B.).
[Plutarchus, *Vitae Parallelae*] for 'iii (1) (1915)' read 'ii (1) (1932), ii (2) (1935), iii (1) (1915), iii (2) (1926), iv (1935)'
[Polyclitus]
Ed. H. Diels & W. Kranz, *Vorsokr.*⁵ i p. 391.
[Polystratus Epicureus], add 'Sts. cited by page of Vogliano (p. .. V.), cf. [Epicurus].'
[Porphyrius], after '*in Harm.* .. Ptolemaeum)' add '; Porphyrios' *Kommentar zur Harmonielehre des Ptolemaios*, ed. I. Düring, Göteborg 1932'
Ep.Aneb. = *Porphyrii epistola ad Anebonem Aegyptium, a Thoma Galeo partim refícta* (Iamb.*Myst.*, ed. Parthey, pp. xxix–xlv).
Hist.Phil. = *Historiae Philosophicae Fragmenta*, ed. A. Nauck², *Porphyrii Opuscula*, Leipzig (T.) 1886.
Possis Historicus
Ed. C. Müller, *FHG* iv p. 483.
[Pratinas]
Fragmenta Lyrica, ed. E. Diehl, *Anth. Lyr.* ii p. 124.
[Praxilla]
Ed. E. Diehl, *Anth. Lyr.* ii p. 129.
[Proclus], for '*Par.Ptol.* .. Basel 1554' read '*Par.Ptol.* .. Lugd. Batav. 1635'. Add:
Phil.Chald. = *Eclogae e Proclo de Philosophia Chaldaica*, ed. A. Jahn, Halle 1891.
Sacr. = περὶ τῆς καθ' Ἕλληνας ἱερατικῆς τέχνης, ed. J. Bidez in *Catalogue des manuscrits alchimiques grecs* vi (1928) pp. 148–51.
[Prodicus]
Ed. H. Diels & W. Kranz, *Vorsokr.*⁵ ii p. 308.
[Protagoras]
Ed. H. Diels & W. Kranz, *Vorsokr.*⁵ ii p. 253.
Pseudo-Asconius Scholiasta [Ps.-Ascon. *in Verr.*]
= *Ciceronis Orationum Scholiastae*, ed. T. Stangl, vol. ii (*commentarios continens*), Vienna–Leipzig 1912.
[Pseudo-Callisthenes]
Ed. W. Kroll, vol. i, Berlin 1926.
[Pseudo-Phocylidea]
Ed. E. Diehl, *Anth. Lyr.* i² (2) p. 96.
[Ptolemaeus Chennos]
Sts. cited by page of A. Westermann, Μυθογράφοι, Brunswick 1843.

[**Ptolemaeus** Mathematicus]
Geog., for 'i–iii' read 'i–v'
Harm., ed. Ingemar Düring, *Die Harmonielehre des Klaudios Ptolemaios*, Göteborg 1930.

[**Pythagoras**]
Ed. H. Diels & W. Kranz, *Vorsokr.*[5] i p. 96, cf. p. 446.
Pyth.Sim. = *Pythagoreorum Similitudines*, ed. F. W. A. Mullach, *FPG* i pp. 485–509.

Romanus Sophista [Roman.] vi A.D.
περὶ ἀνειμένου, ed. W. Camphausen, Leipzig (T.) 1922.

Rufinianus, Julius Rhetor [Rufin.]
Fig. = *de Figuris*, ed. C. Halm, *Rhetores Latini Minores*, Leipzig 1863, p. 38.

[**Rufus**]
Fr. = *Fragmenta*
Interrog. = *Interrogationes*
Oss. = *de ossibus*
Podagr. = *de podagra*

[**Sallustius**]
Ed. A. D. Nock, Cambridge 1926.

[**Sappho**]
Ed. E. Diehl, *Anth. Lyr.* i² (4) p. 3; ed. E. Lobel, Oxford 1925.

[**Scolia**]
Ed. E. Diehl, *Anth. Lyr.* ii pp. 60, 181.

Scribonius Largus Medicus [Scrib. Larg.]
Ed. G. Helmreich, Leipzig (T.) 1887.

[**Semonides**]
Ed. E. Diehl, *Anth. Lyr.* i² (3) p. 50.

[**Simon Atheniensis**]
Ed. J. Soukup, Innsbruck 1911 (*Commentationes Aenipontanae*, ed. E. Kalinka, No. VI).

[**Simonides**]
Ed. E. Diehl, *Anth. Lyr.* ii p. 61, i² (1) p. 138, (3) pp. 62, 63.

Solinus, C. Julius Geographus Latinus [Solin.] iii A.D. (?)
Ed. T. Mommsen², Berlin 1895.

[**Solon**]
Ed. E. Diehl, *Anth. Lyr.* i² (1) p. 23.

[**Sophocles**]
Ichn. = Ἰχνευταί (= *Fr.* 314).
Scholia Vetera, ed. P. N. Papageorgiu, Leipzig (T.) 1888.
Scholia, ed. W. Dindorf, Oxonii 1852.

[**Soranus**]
Gynaeciorum libri iv, de signis fracturarum, de fasciis, vita Hippocratis secundum Soranum, ed. J. Ilberg, *CMG* iv, Lips. et Berol. 1927 [*Gynaecia* cited by Rose's numeration].

[**Stesichorus**]
Ed. E. Diehl, *Anth. Lyr.* ii p. 39.

[**Suetonius**]
Gramm. = *de Grammaticis et Rhetoribus deperditorum librorum reliquiae*, ed. C. L. Roth, Leipzig (T.) 1893.

[**Suidas**]
Ed. Ada Adler, Leipzig 1928–38.

Synesius iv/v A.D.
Ed. J.-P. Migne, *Patrologiae Cursus Completus, Series Graeca*, vol. 66, Paris 1859.
Calv. = *Calvitii Encomium* col. 1167.
Insomn. = *De Insomniis* col. 1281.
Ep. = *Epistulae*, ed. R. Hercher, *Epistolographi*, p. 638.

[**Telesilla**]
Ed. E. Diehl, *Anth. Lyr.* ii p. 61.

[**Telestes**]
Ed. E. Diehl, *Anth. Lyr.* ii p. 155.

[**Terpander**]
Ed. E. Diehl, *Anth. Lyr.* ii p. 3.

[**Teucer Babylonius**], for 'pp. 6' read 'pp. 16'

[**Thales**]
Ed. H. Diels & W. Kranz, *Vorsokr.*[5] i p. 67.

[**Theocritus**]
Adon. = εἰς νεκρὸν Ἄδωνιν.

[**Theognis**]
Ed. E. Diehl, *Anth. Lyr.* i² (2) p. 3.

Theon Alexandrinus Mathematicus [Theon Al.] iv A.D.
in Ptol. = *in Ptolemaeum*, ed. A. Rome, *Commentaires de Pappus et de Théon d'Alexandrie sur l'Almageste. II. Théon d'Alexandrie* (= Studi e Testi 72); ed. L'Abbé Halma, *Œuvres de Ptolémée*, tom. v, Paris 1821.

[**Theon Smyrnaeus**], delete '*in Ptol.*..Paris 1821'. **N.B.** In references, for 'Theo Sm. *in Ptol.*' read 'Theon Al. *in Ptol.*'

[**Thucydides**]
Scholia, ed. C. Hude, Leipzig (T.) 1927.

[**Timocreon**]
Ed. E. Diehl, *Anth. Lyr.* ii p. 120.

[**Tyrtaeus**]
Ed. E. Diehl, *Anth. Lyr.* i² (1) p. 6.

[**Vetus Testamentum Graece redditum**] under 'A.' add 'Syr. = ὁ Σύρος'; also add 'L. Lütkemann & A. Rahlfs, Hexaplarische Randnoten zu Isaias 1–16, aus einer Sinai-Handschrift (*Gött. Nachr.* 1915. Beiheft). NOTE.—Words cited from this are followed by "(L.-R.)".'

[**Xenocrates**]
Lap. = Λιθογνώμων, *cuius fragmenta collegit* M. Wellmann in *Quellen und Studien zur Geschichte der Naturwissenschaften und der Medizin*, ed. P. Diepgen und J. Ruska, Band 4, Heft 4, pp. 86 [426] sqq. (Berlin 1935).

[**Zeno Eleaticus**]
Ed. H. Diels & W. Kranz, *Vorsokr.*[5] i p. 247.

II. EPIGRAPHICAL PUBLICATIONS

Anatolian Studies = *Anatolian Studies presented to Sir W. M. Ramsay*, Manchester 1923.

Arangio-Ruiz et Olivieri *Inscr. Gr.* = V. Arangio-Ruiz et A. Olivieri, *Inscriptiones Graecae Siciliae et infimae Italiae ad ius pertinentes*, Milan 1925.

BMus.Inscr. = *Ancient Greek Inscriptions in the British Museum*, Oxford 1874–1916.

Baillet *Inscr. des tombeaux des rois* = J. Baillet, *Inscriptions grecques et latines des tombeaux des rois à Thèbes*, Le Caire 1920–23.

Benndorf-Niemann *Reisen in Lykien* = O. Benndorf & G. Niemann, *Reisen in Lykien und Karien*, Vienna 1884.

Buckler *Anat. Studies* = *Anatolian Studies presented to W. H. Buckler*, ed. W. M. Calder & J. Keil, Manchester 1939.

CIG = A. Boeckh, *Corpus Inscriptionum Graecarum*, Berlin 1828–77.

CIJud. = *Corpus Inscriptionum Iudaicarum*, ed. J.-B. Frey: vol. i (Europe), Rome 1936.

CIL = *Corpus Inscriptionum Latinarum*, Berlin 1862–.

Chron.Lind. = *Chronicle of Lindos*, ed. Chr. Blinkenberg, *Die Lindische Tempelchronik*, Bonn 1915; ed. F. Jacoby, *FGrH* ii p. 1005.

Corinth = *Corinth, results of excavations conducted by the American School of Classical Studies at Athens*, Cambridge, Massachusetts 1929–; vol. viii Part i, *Greek Inscriptions*, ed. B. D. Meritt, 1931.

Cumont *Fouilles de Doura-Europos* = F. Cumont, *Fouilles de Doura-Europos* (1922–3), Paris 1926.

Dain *Inscr. du Louvre* = A. Dain, *Inscriptions grecques du musée du Louvre: Les textes inédits*, Paris 1933.

*Delph.*3(1),(2),.. = *Fouilles de Delphes*, tome iii: *Épigraphie*. Paris 1909–. (École française d'Athènes.)

Demitsas Μακεδ. = M. G. Demitsas, Ἡ Μακεδονία κτλ., vol. i (all published), Athens 1896.

Dessau *ILS* = H. Dessau, *Inscriptiones Latinae Selectae*, Berlin 1892–1916.

Dura[1], *Dura*[2],.. = *The Excavations at Dura-Europos. Preliminary Report of First* (*Second*..) *Season of Work*, ed. P. V. C. Bauer, M. I. Rostovtzeff, A. R. Bellinger, and others, Yale University Press 1929–.

Durrbach *Choix d'inscrr. de Délos* = F. Durrbach, *Choix d'inscriptions de Délos*, Paris 1921.

Edict.Diocl. = *Edictum Diocletiani*, ed. T. Mommsen & H. Blümner, *Der Maximaltarif des Diocletian*, Berlin 1893; suppl. *CIL* iii pp. 1926 ff., 2208 ff., 2328[57] ff.: cited where possible by Mommsen's chaps. & lines, recently found portions by place of discovery (*Aeg.* = Aegira; *Clit.* = Clitor; *Delph.* = Delphi; *Troez.* = Troezen); *Geronthr.* = *IG*5(1)1115; *Gyth.* = 5(1)1148.

Eph.Epigr. = *Ephemeris Epigraphica, Corporis Inscriptionum Latinarum Supplementum*, Berlin 1872–.

*Ephes.*2,3,... = *Forschungen in Ephesos, veröffentlicht vom Oesterreichischen Archaeologischen Institute*..Bde. 2, 3, Vienna 1912, 1923; 4(1), 1932; 4(2), Baden bei Wien 1937.

Epigr.Gr. = G. Kaibel, *Epigrammata Graeca ex lapidibus conlecta*, Berlin 1878.

Foed.Delph.Pell. = *Foedus inter Delphos et Pellanenses*, ed. B.

Haussoullier, *Traité entre Delphes et Pellana*, Paris 1917; *Schwyzer* (q.v.) No. 328[a].

GDI = *Sammlung der griechischen Dialekt-Inschriften*, ed. H. Collitz et alii, Göttingen 1884–1915.

Gerasa = *Gerasa, City of the Decapolis*, ed. C. H. Kraeling, New Haven, Connecticut, 1938.

Haussoullier *Milet* = B. Haussoullier, *Études sur l'histoire de Milet et du Didymeion*, Paris 1902.

Heuzey-Daumet *Mission Arch. de Macédoine* = L. Heuzey et H. Daumet, *Mission Archéologique de Macédoine*, Paris 1876.

Histria = V. Pârvan, *Histria*, Part iv, Bucarest 1916; Part vii, Bucarest 1923.

IG = *Inscriptiones Graecae.*

vol. i = *Inscriptiones Atticae anno Euclidis vetustiores*, ed. A. Kirchhoff, 1873: *Supplementa, indices* 1877, 1887, 1891 [= *Corpus Inscriptionum Atticarum*, vol. i *et* vol. iv *pars* i fasc. i–iii].

*IG*1² = *IG* vol. i ed. minor, ed. F. Hiller von Gaertringen, 1924.

vol. ii = *Inscriptiones Atticae aetatis quae est inter Euclidis annum et Augusti tempora*, ed. U. Koehler [5 parts, 1877, 1883, 1888, 1893 (*indices* by J. Kirchner), 1895 (*supplementa*) = *Corpus Inscriptionum Atticarum*, vol. ii *partes* i–iv et vol. iv *pars* ii].

vol. iii = *Inscriptiones Atticae aetatis Romanae*, ed. W. Dittenberger, *pars* i 1878, *pars* ii 1882, *pars* iii (v. *Tab. Defix.*) 1897 [= *Corpus Inscriptionum Atticarum*, vol. iii *partes* i, ii, *et Appendix*].

*IG*2² = *Voluminum* ii *et* iii *editio minor*, ed. J. Kirchner, *pars* i fasc. i 1913, fasc. ii 1916; *pars* ii fasc. i (1370–1695) 1927, fasc. ii (1696–2788) 1931; *pars* iii fasc. i (2789–5219) 1935.

vol. iv = *Inscriptiones Argolidis*, ed. M. Fraenkel, 1902 [= *Corpus Inscriptionum Graecarum Peloponnesi et insularum vicinarum*, vol. i].

*IG*4² = *Voluminis* iv *editio minor*, fasc. i = *Inscriptiones Epidauri*, ed. F. Hiller von Gaertringen, 1929.

vol. v fasc. i = *Inscriptiones Laconiae et Messeniae*, ed. W. Kolbe, 1913; fasc. ii = *Inscriptiones Arcadiae*, ed. F. Hiller von Gaertringen, 1913.

vol. vii = *Inscriptiones Megaridis et Boeotiae*, ed. W. Dittenberger, 1892 [= *Corpus Inscriptionum Graecarum Graeciae Septentrionalis*, vol. i].

vol. ix *pars* i = *Inscriptiones Phocidis, Locridis, Aetoliae, Acarnaniae, insularum maris Ionii*, ed. W. Dittenberger, 1897 [= *Corpus Inscriptionum Graecarum Graeciae Septentrionalis*, vol. iii *pars* i]; *pars* ii = *Inscriptiones Thessaliae*, ed. O. Kern, 1908.

*IG*9² = Voluminis ix *partis* i *editio minor*, fasc. i = *Inscriptiones Aetoliae*, ed. G. Klaffenbach, 1932.

vol. xi = *Inscriptiones Deli*: fasc. ii, ed. F. Dürrbach, 1912; fasc. 3 cited as *Inscr. Délos* (q.v.); fasc. iv, ed. P. Roussel, 1914.

vol. xii = *Inscriptiones insularum maris Aegaei praeter Delum*: fasc. i, *Inscriptiones Rhodi, Chalces, Carpathi cum Saro, Casi*, ed. F. Hiller von Gaertringen, 1895.

fasc. ii, *Inscriptiones Lesbi, Nesi, Tenedi*, ed. W. Paton, 1899.

fasc. iii, *Inscriptiones Symes, Teutlussae, Teli, Nisyri, Astypalaeae, Anaphes, Therae et Therasiae, Pholegandri, Meli, Cimoli*, ed. F. Hiller von Gaertringen, 1898; *Supplementa*, ed. F. Hiller von Gaertringen 1904.

fasc. v, *Inscriptiones Cycladum*: *pars* i, *Inscriptiones Cycladum praeter Tenum*, ed. F. Hiller von Gaertringen, 1903; *pars* ii, *Inscriptiones Teni insulae*, ed. F. Hiller von Gaertringen, 1909.

fasc. vii, *Inscriptiones Amorgi et insularum vicinarum*, ed. J. Delamarre, 1908.

fasc. viii, *Inscriptiones insularum maris Thracici*, ed. C. Fredrich, 1909.

fasc. ix, *Inscriptiones Euboeae*, ed. E. Ziebarth, 1915.

vol. xiv = *Inscriptiones Siciliae et Italiae additis Galliae Hispaniae Britanniae Germaniae inscriptionibus*, ed. G. Kaibel, 1890.

IGRom. = *Inscriptiones Graecae ad res Romanas pertinentes*, ed. R. Cagnat et alii, Paris, vol. i 1911, iii 1906, iv 1927.

IPE = *Inscriptiones orae septentrionalis Ponti Euxini*, ed. B. Latyshev, Petersburg 1885–1901: 1² = vol. i, second edition, 1916.

Inscr. Cos = *The Inscriptions of Cos*, ed. W. R. Paton & E. L. Hicks, Oxford 1891.

Inscr. Cret. = *Inscriptiones Creticae opera et consilio Friderici Halbherr collectae.* I. *Tituli Cretae mediae praeter Gortynios. Curavit Margarita Guarducci.* Rome 1935.

Inscr. Cypr. = Cyprian Inscriptions in O. Hoffmann, *Die griechischen Dialekte*, vol. i, Göttingen 1891.

Inscr. Délos = Nos. 290–371, 372–509, ed. F. Durrbach, Paris 1926, 1929 (*Acad. des Inscriptions et Belles-Lettres*). [The numeration is continued from *IG*11(2).] Nos. 1400–96 [an interval is left after the nos. of *IG*11(4)] ed. F. Durrbach & P. Roussel, 1935. Nos. 1497–2879 (2 pts.) ed. P. Roussel & M. Launey, 1937.

Inscr. gr. et lat. de la Syrie = *Inscriptions grecques et latines de la Syrie*; I. Commagène et Cyrrhestique, ed. L. Jalabert & R. Mouterde, Paris 1929.

Inscr. Magn. = *Die Inschriften von Magnesia am Maeander*, ed. O. Kern, Berlin 1900.

Inscr. Mus. Alex. = E. Breccia, *Iscrizioni greche e latine* (*Catal. gen. des antiq. égypt. du musée d'Alexandrie*, 57), 1911.

Inscr. Olymp. = *Olympia: die Ergebnisse der... Ausgrabung: Textband* v, *Die Inschriften*, ed. W. Dittenberger & K. Purgold, Berlin 1896.

Inscr. Perg. = *Die Inschriften von Pergamon* (in *Altertümer von Pergamon* viii), ed. M. Fraenkel, Berlin 1890–1895.

Inscr. Prien. = *Die Inschriften von Priene*, ed. F. Hiller von Gaertringen, Berlin 1906.

Keil-Premerstein *Erster* (*zweiter, dritter*) *Bericht* = J. Keil & A. von Premerstein, *Bericht über eine* (*eine zweite, eine dritte*) *Reise in Lydien* (*Denkschriften der Wiener Akademie, phil.-hist. Klasse*, LIII, 2. *Abh.*, LIV, 2. *Abh.*, LVII, 1. *Abh.*), Vienna 1908, 1911, 1914.

LF, LW = Philippe Le Bas, W. H. Waddington & P. Foucart, *Voyage Archéologique en Grèce et en Asie Mineure*, Paris 1847–70.

Leg. Gort. = *Leges Gortynensium* (*GDI* 4991, *Schwyzer* 179).

Leg. Sacr. = *Leges Graecorum Sacrae*, ed. J. de Prott & L. Ziehen, Leipzig fasc. i 1896, fasc. ii (1) 1906.

MacDowell *Stamped Objects from Seleucia* = R. H. MacDowell, *Stamped & Inscribed Objects from Seleucia on the Tigris* (Univ. of Michigan Studies, Humanistic Series, vol. xxxvi), Ann Arbor 1935.

Maiuri *Nuova Silloge* = A. Maiuri, *Nuova Silloge Epigrafica di Rodi e Cos*, Firenze 1925.

MAMA = *Monumenta Asiae Minoris Antiqua*, vol. i, ed. W. M. Calder, Manchester–London 1928 (Publications of the American Society for Archaeological Research in Asia Minor); vol. iii, ed. J. Keil & A. Wilhelm, 1931; vol. iv, ed. W. H. Buckler, W. M. Calder, W. K. C. Guthrie, 1933; vol. v, ed. C. W. M. Cox & A. Cameron, 1937; vol. vi, ed. W. H. Buckler & W. M. Calder, 1939 (iii–vi Manchester).

Marm. Par. = *Marmor Parium* (*IG*12(5).444) ed. F. Jacoby, *Das Marmor Parium*, Berlin 1904, and *FGrH* ii p. 992.

Mél. Bidez = *Mélanges Bidez* (*Annuaire de l'Institut de philologie et d'histoire orientales*, tome ii), Brussels 1934.

Mél. Glotz = *Mélanges Gustave Glotz*, Paris 1932.

Mél. Navarre = *Mélanges offerts à M. Octave Navarre par ses élèves et ses amis*, Toulouse 1935.

Michel = C. Michel, *Recueil d'inscriptions grecques*, Brussels 1900: Supplements i, ii, Brussels 1912, 1927.

Milet = *Milet. Ergebnisse der Ausgrabungen und Untersuchungen seit dem Jahre 1899*, herausg. von Theodor Wiegand (*Königliche Museen zu Berlin*), 1906–. *Milet*3 = *Milet* Bd. 1 Heft iii; for other parts Band and Heft are given.

*Milet*6,7 = *Sechster* (*siebenter*) *vorläufiger Bericht über die in Milet und Didyma unternommenen Ausgrabungen*, *Abh. Berl. Akad.* 1908 Anhang I, 1911 Anh. I.

Mon. Anc. Gr. = *Monumenti Ancyrani versio Graeca* (*Res Gestae Divi Augusti*, ed. E. Diehl³, Bonn 1918).

Mon. Piot = *Monuments et mémoires publiés par la fondation Piot*, Paris 1894–.

Mueller-Bees = N. Mueller & N. A. Bees, *Die Inschriften der jüdischen Katakombe am Monteverde zu Rom*, Leipzig 1919.

Myres *Cesnola Coll.* = J. L. Myres, *Handbook of the Cesnola Collection of Antiquities from Cyprus*, New York 1914.

Naukratis = *Naukratis*, Pt. i by [Sir] W. M. Flinders Petrie, London 1886, Pt. ii by E. A. Gardner, 1888 (*Egypt Exploration Fund, Memoirs* iii, vi).

OGI = *Orientis Graeci Inscriptiones Selectae*, ed. W. Dittenberger, Leipzig 1903–5.

Pelekides *Thessalonica* = S. Pelekides, *Ἀπὸ τὴν πολιτεία καὶ τὴν κοινωνία τῆς ἀρχαίας Θεσσαλονίκης*, Salonika 1934.

Petersen-Luschan *Reisen in Lykien* = E. Petersen & F. von Luschan, *Reisen in Lykien, Milyas und Kibyratis*, Vienna 1889.

Princeton Exp. Inscr. = *Publications of the Princeton University Archaeological Expeditions to Syria in 1904–5 and 1909*: Division III, *Greek and Latin Inscriptions*, Leyden, Section A by E. Littmann, D. Magie, & D. R. Stuart, 1921; Section B by W. K. Prentice, 1922.

Puchstein *Epigr. Gr.* = O. Puchstein, *Epigrammata Graeca in Aegypto reperta*, Strassburg 1880.

Ramsay *Cities and Bishoprics* = [Sir] W. M. Ramsay, *Cities and Bishoprics of Phrygia*, Oxford 1895–7.

Ramsay *Studies in Eastern Rom. Prov.* = *Studies in the History and Art of the Eastern Provinces of the Roman Empire*, ed. [Sir] W. M. Ramsay, Aberdeen 1906.

Robert *Collection Froehner* = *Collection Froehner* (Bibliothèque nationale. Département des médailles et des antiques), i. *Inscriptions grecques*, ed. L. Robert, Paris 1936.

Robert *Ét. Anat.* = L. Robert, *Études Anatoliennes*, Paris 1937 (*Études orientales publiées par l'institut français d'archéologie de Stamboul* No. v).

Roussel *Cultes Égyptiens* = P. Roussel, *Les Cultes égyptiens à Délos*, Nancy 1916.

Ruppel *T. von Dakke* = W. Ruppel, *Der Tempel von Dakke*, vol. 3, Cairo 1930 (*Service des Antiquités d'Égypte*).
Rüsch = E. Rüsch, *Grammatik der delphischen Inschriften* i, Berlin 1914 (*Epigraphischer Anhang*, pp. 312–31).
SIG = *Sylloge Inscriptionum Graecarum*, ed. W. Dittenberger, editio tertia, Leipzig 1915–24. (*SIG*² = editio altera, 1898–1901.)
*Sardis*7(1) = *Sardis, Publications of the American Society for the Excavation of Sardis*, Vol. vii, *Greek and Latin Inscriptions*, Part I, by W. H. Buckler and D. M. Robinson, Leyden 1932.
Schwyzer = E. Schwyzer, *Dialectorum Graecarum Exempla epigraphica potiora*, Leipzig 1923.
Stud.Pont. = *Studia Pontica*, Brussels 1903–: vol. iii *Recueil des inscriptions grecques et latines du Pont et de l'Arménie*, publ. par J. G. C. Anderson, F. Cumont, H. Grégoire, fasc. i (1910).
Supp.Epigr. = *Supplementum Epigraphicum Graecum*, adjuvantibus P. Roussel, A. Salač, M. N. Tod, E. Ziebarth, ed. J. J. E. Hondius, Leyden 1923–.
Swoboda *Denkmäler* = *Denkmäler aus Lykaonien, Pamphylien und Isaurien*, herausgegeben von H. Swoboda, J. Keil, und F. Knoll, Brünn etc., 1935.
TAM = *Tituli Asiae Minoris*, vol. ii fasc. i, ed. E. Kalinka, Vienna 1920; fasc. ii, 1930.
Tab.Defix. = *Defixionum Tabellae in Attica regione repertae*, ed. R. Wuensch (*IG*3 *pars* iii).
Tab.Defix.Aud. = *Defixionum Tabellae quotquot innotuerunt*, ed. A. Audollent, Paris 1904.
Tab.Heracl. = *Tabulae Heracleenses* (*IG*14.645, *Schwyzer* 62–3).
Test.Epict. = *Testamentum Epictetae* (*IG*12(3).330, *Michel* 1001, *Schwyzer* 227); cited by col. and line.
Wiegand Mnemos. = *Mnemosynon Theodor Wiegand dargebracht*, Munich 1938.
Wood *Ephesus* = J. T. Wood, *Discoveries at Ephesus*, London 1877.

III. PAPYROLOGICAL PUBLICATIONS

BGU = *Berliner griechische Urkunden* (*Ägyptische Urkunden aus den Königlichen Museen zu Berlin*), Berlin 1895–.
BKT = *Berliner Klassikertexte, herausgegeben von der Generalverwaltung der Kgl. Museen zu Berlin*, Berlin 1904–.
Berichtigungsl. = *Berichtigungsliste der griechischen Papyrusurkunden aus Ägypten*: I. F. Preisigke, Hefte 1 & 2, Strassburg 1913; Hefte 3 & 4, Berlin & Leipzig 1922; II. F. Bilabel, Heidelberg 1931, 1933.
Bilabel 'Οψαρτ. = F. Bilabel, 'Οψαρτυτικά *und Verwandtes* (*Sitzungsberichte d. Heidelberger Akademie der Wissenschaften, Phil.-hist. Kl.* 1919, 23. *Abh.*), Heidelberg 1920.
CPHerm. = *Corpus Papyrorum Hermopolitanorum* i, ed. C. Wessely (*Studien zur Paläogr. u. Papyruskunde* v), Leipzig 1905.
CPR = *Corpus Papyrorum Raineri Archiducis Austriae*, vol. i, *Griechische Texte*, ed. C. Wessely, Wien 1895; cf. *PRain.*(*NS*).
Διηγήσεις = Διηγήσεις *di poemi di Callimaco in un papiro di Tebtynis*, a cura di M. Norsa e G. Vitelli, Firenze 1934: cited by column and line; ed. A. Vogliano *PUniv.Milan.* i. 18.
Frisk *Bankakten* = *Bankakten aus dem Faijûm nebst anderen Berliner Papyri*, ed. H. Frisk (*Göteborgs Kungl. Vetenskaps- och Vitterhets-Samhälles Handlingar, femte följden, Ser.A. Band 2 No. 2*), Göteborg 1931.
Herc. (following an author's name) = Herculaneum papyri, cited by No. of papyrus and column or fragment from *Herculanensium Voluminum quae supersunt, Collectio altera*, Naples 1862–76, D. Bassi, *Herculanensium Voluminum, Collectio tertia*, fasc. i, Milan 1914, and other publications; 'Epicureus *Herc.*...p...V.' refers to *Epicuri et Epicureorum scripta...*, ed. A. Vogliano (v. I (Add.) s.v. Epicurus).
Kapsomenakis = S. G. Kapsomenakis, *Voruntersuchungen zu einer Grammatik der Papyri der nachchristlichen Zeit*, Munich 1938.
Meyer *Ostr.* = Ostraca in *P.Meyer* (q.v.).
Mitteis *Chr.*, Wilcken *Chr.* = L. Mitteis & U. Wilcken, *Grundzüge und Chrestomathie der Papyruskunde*, Leipzig & Berlin 1912.
Möller *Pap.Berl.Mus.* = S. Möller, *Griechische Papyri aus dem Berliner Museum*, Göteborg 1929.
Ostr. = U. Wilcken, *Griechische Ostraka aus Ägypten und Nubien*, Leipzig & Berlin 1899.
Ostr.Bodl. = J. G. Tait, *Greek Ostraca in the Bodleian Library and other collections*, I, London 1930 (cited by No. of part and No. of ostracon).
Ostr.Mich. = L. Amundsen, *Greek Ostraca in the University of Michigan Collection*, Part I, Texts (= University of Michigan Studies, Humanistic Series, vol. xxxiv), Ann Arbor 1935.
Ostr.Strassb. = *Griechische und griechisch-demotische Ostraka der Universitäts- und Landesbibliothek zu Strassburg*, ed. P. Viereck, Berlin 1923.
Ostr.Wilbour = C. Préaux, *Les ostraca grecs de la Collection Charles-Edwin Wilbour au Musée de Brooklyn*, New York 1935.
PAberd. = *Catalogue of Greek & Latin papyri & ostraca in the possession of the University of Aberdeen*, ed. E. G. Turner (*Aberdeen Univ. Studies* No. 116), 1939.
PAlex. = *Papyrus ptolémaïques du Musée d'Alexandrie*, ed. G. Botti, *Bull.Soc.Alex.* First Series No. 2 (1899) p. 65.
PAmh. = *Amherst Papyri*, ed. B. P. Grenfell & A. S. Hunt, 2 vols., London 1900–1; cited by No. of vol., papyrus, and line.
PAntin. = *the Antinoe Papyrus* of Theocritus in *Two Theocritus Papyri*, ed. A. S. Hunt & J. Johnson, London 1930.
PAvrom. = *Parchments of the Parthian period from Avroman in Kurdistan*, ed. E. H. Minns, *JHS* xxxv (1915) p. 22.
PBaden = F. Bilabel, *Veröffentlichungen aus den badischen Papyrus-Sammlungen*, Heft 2 and Heft 4, *Griechische Papyri*, Heidelberg 1923, 1924.
PBasel = *Papyrusurkunden der öffentlichen Bibliothek der Universität zu Basel*, I. *Urkunden in griechischer Sprache*, ed. E. Rabel (*Abh. Gött. Gesellsch.* Neue Folge, vol. xvi, No. 3), Berlin 1917.
PBerl.Leihg. = *Berliner Leihgabe griechischer Papyri*, herausgegeben vom griechischen Seminar der Universität Uppsala durch T. Kalén, Uppsala 1932.
PBerol. = Berlin Papyri, cited by inventory No. (*PBerol.* 6926, 7927ᵛ = B. Lavagnini, *Eroticorum Graecorum Fragmenta Papyracea*, Leipzig (T.) 1922, pp. 1ff., 21ff.).
PBouriant = *Les papyrus Bouriant*, ed. P. Collart, Paris 1926.
PBremen = U. Wilcken, *Die Bremer Papyri* (*Abhandlungen der Preussischen Akademie der Wissenschaften*, 1936, Phil.-hist. Klasse No. 2), Berlin 1936.
PCair. = Cairo Papyri cited by catalogue No. from B. P. Grenfell & A. S. Hunt, *Greek Papyri, Catalogue général des Antiquités égyptiennes du Musée du Caire*, vol. x, Nos. 10001–10869, Oxford 1903.
PCair.Preis. = F. Preisigke, *Griechische Urkunden des ägyptischen Museums zu Kairo* (*Schriften der wissenschaftlichen Gesellschaft zu Strassburg*, Heft 8), Strassburg 1911.
PCair.Zen. = C. C. Edgar, *Zenon Papyri*, 4 vols. (*Catal. gén. des Antiq. égypt. du Musée du Caire*, 79) 1925–31: digits indicating 59(000) omitted in refs., thus 2 = 59002.
PCornell = *Greek Papyri in the Library of Cornell University*, ed. W. L. Westermann & C. J. Kraemer, New York 1926.
PEdgar = C. C. Edgar, *Selected papyri from the archives of Zenon*, *Annales du Service des Antiquités de l'Égypte*, Nos. 1–10 in vol. xviii (1918) pp. 159–82; Nos. 11–21, ib. pp. 224–44; Nos. 22–36, vol. xix (1920) pp. 13–36; Nos. 37–48, ib. pp. 81–104; Nos. 49–54, vol. xx (1920) pp. 19–40; Nos. 55–64, ib. pp. 181–206; Nos. 65–6, vol. xxi (1921) pp. 89–109; Nos. 67–72, vol. xxii (1922) pp. 209–31; Nos. 73–76, vol. xxiii (1923) pp. 73–98; Nos. 77–88, ib. pp. 187–209; Nos. 89–104, vol. xxiv (1924) pp. 17–52.
PEleph. = *Elephantine Papyri*, ed. O. Rubensohn, *Ägyptische Urkunden aus den Kgl. Museen zu Berlin: Griechische Urkunden*: Sonderheft, Berlin 1907.
PEnteux. = *Publications de la Société royale égyptienne de Papyrologie, Textes et Documents*, i, 'Εντεύξεις.., ed. O. Guéraud, Cairo 1931–2.
PFay. = B. P. Grenfell, A. S. Hunt, D. G. Hogarth, *Fayûm Towns and their Papyri*, London 1900.
PFlor. = *Papiri Fiorentini, documenti pubblici e privati dell'età romana e bizantina*: I ed. G. Vitelli, Milano 1906; II ed. D. Comparetti, 1908–11; III ed. G. Vitelli, 1915.
PFrankf. = H. Lewald, *Griechische Papyri aus dem Besitz des rechtswissenschaftlichen Seminars der Universität Frankfurt* (*Sitzungsberichte der Heidelberger Akademie der Wissenschaften, Phil.-hist. Kl.* 1920, 14. *Abh.*).
PFreib. = *Mitteilungen aus der Freiburger Papyrussammlung*, in *Sitzungsberichte der Heidelberger Akademie der Wissenschaften, Phil.-hist. Klasse*, 1914, 2. *Abh.*, 1916, 10. *Abh.*
PGand } *PSorb.* } = *Quelques papyrus des collections de Gand et de Paris*, ed. M. Hombert, *Revue belge de Philologie et d'Histoire* iv (1925), 633–76: republished in *Sammelb.* iii.
PGen. = *Les papyrus de Genève* transcrits et publiés par Jules Nicole, Geneva 1896, 1900.
PGiss. = *Griechische Papyri im Museum des oberhessischen Geschichtsvereins zu Giessen*, Bd. I, Hefte 1–3, ed. O. Eger, E. Kornemann, P. M. Meyer, Leipzig etc. 1910–12.
PGnom. = *Der Gnomon des Idios Logos* (*BGU* v (1) 1210) ed. W. Schubart 1919.
PGoodsp. = E. J. Goodspeed, *A group of Greek papyrus texts* (*Class. Phil.* i, 1906, p. 167).
PGoodsp.Cair. = E. J. Goodspeed, *Greek papyri from the Cairo*

Museum.. (*Decennial publications of the University of Chicago*, 1st series, vol. v p. 3), Chicago 1904.

PGot. = H. Frisk, *Papyrus grecs de la Bibl. Municipale de Gothembourg*, Göteborg 1929.

PGrad. = G. Plaumann, *Griechische Papyri der Sammlung Gradenwitz* (*Sitzungsberichte der Heidelberger Akademie der Wissenschaften*, 1914, 15. *Abh.*).

PGrenf. 1. = B. P. Grenfell, *An Alexandrian erotic fragment and other Greek papyri chiefly Ptolemaic*, Oxford 1896.
2. = B. P. Grenfell & A. S. Hunt, *New Classical Fragments and other Greek and Latin papyri*, 1897.

PGurob = *Greek papyri from Gurob*, ed. J. G. Smyly (Royal Irish Academy, Cunningham Memoirs, No. 12, Dublin–London 1921).

PHal. = Halle Papyri = *Dikaiomata: Auszüge aus alexandrinischen Gesetzen und Verordnungen in einem Papyrus des Philologischen Seminars der Universität Halle, mit einem Anhang.. herausgegeben von der Graeca Halensis*.., Berlin 1913.

PHamb. = P. M. Meyer, *Griechische Papyrusurkunden der Hamburger Stadtbibliothek* (*Staats- und Universitätsbibliothek* 1924), Bd. 1, Leipzig etc. 1911–24.

PHarris = *The Rendel Harris Papyri*, ed. J. Enoch Powell, Cambridge 1936.

PHaw. = *The Hawara Papyri*, ed. [Sir] W. M. Flinders Petrie, *Hawara, Biahmu, and Arsinoe*, 1889: in part re-edited by J. G. Milne, *Arch. Pap.* v (1913) p. 378: *PHaw.* 80 and 81 re-edited by U. Wilcken in *Genethliakon für C. Robert*, Berlin 1910, p. 191.

PHeid. = *Veröffentlichungen aus der Heidelberger Papyrussammlung* (vol. i = A. Deissmann, *Die Septuaginta-Papyri und andere altchristliche Texte*, 1905; vol. iii (1) = C. H. Becker, *Papyri Schott-Reinhardt*, i, 1906).

PHib. = *Hibeh Papyri*, Part I, ed. B. P. Grenfell & A. S. Hunt, London 1906.

PHolm. = *Papyrus Graecus Holmiensis*, ed. O. Lagercrantz, Uppsala 1913.

PIand. = *Papyri Iandanae: cum discipulis edidit* Carolus Kalbfleisch, Leipzig & Berlin 1912–.

PJena = *Jenaer Papyrus-Urkunden*, ed. F. Zucker & F. Schneider, Jena 1926.

PKaran. = E. J. Goodspeed, *Papyri from Karanis* (*Univ. of Chicago: Studies in Classical Philology*, vol. iii), Chicago 1902.

PKlein.Form. = *Stud.Pal.* (q.v.) iii, viii.

PLeid. = C. Leemans, *Papyri Graeci musei antiquarii publici Lugduni-Batavi*, tom. i Leiden 1843; tom. ii 1885.

PLeid.U. = *Somnium Nectanebi*, ed. B. Lavagnini, *Eroticorum Graecorum Fragmenta Papyracea*, Leipzig (T.) 1922, p. 37 := *UPZ* 81.

PLeid.V., v. *PMag.Leid.V.*
" *W.*, v. " " *W.*

PLeid.X. = chemical papyrus in *PLeid.* (q.v.) vol. ii: reprinted in M. Berthelot, *Archéologie et Histoire des Sciences* (Paris 1906), pp. 269–306 (= *Comptes rendus des séances de l'Acad. des Sciences*, tom. xlix): cited by Berthelot's sections.

PLille = *Institut papyrologique de l'université de Lille: Papyrus grecs* publiés sous la direction de Pierre Jouguet.., Paris 1907–28.

PLips. = L. Mitteis, *Griechische Urkunden der Papyrussammlung zu Leipzig*, vol. i, 1906.

PLit.Lond. = H. J. M. Milne, *Catalogue of the Literary Papyri in the British Museum*, London 1927.

PLond. = *Greek papyri in the British Museum*, vols. i and ii ed. F. G. Kenyon, vol. iii ed. F. G. Kenyon & H. I. Bell, vols. iv and v ed. H. I. Bell, London 1893–; unpublished papyri (*PLond. ined.*) are cited by inventory No.

PLond. 1821, ed. H. I. Bell & W. E. Crum, *Aegyptus* vi (1925) pp. 177–226.

*PLond.*1912–29 = H. I. Bell, *Jews and Christians in Egypt*, London 1924.

PMag. = *Papyri Graecae Magicae*, herausgegeben und übersetzt von K. Preisendanz, 2 vols., Leipzig & Berlin 1928, 1931.

PMag.Berol. = G. Parthey, *Zwei griechische Zauberpapyri des Berliner Museums*, *Abh. Berl. Akad.* 1865 pp. 109–80; cf. W. Kroll, *Philol.* liv (1895) p. 564 (= *PMag.* 1, 2).

PMag.Leid.V. = *Papyrus magica musei Lugdunensis Batavi*, ed. A. Dieterich, *Jahrb. f. kl. Phil.*, Suppl. xvi (1888) pp. 793–818; cited by column and line (= *PMag.* 12).

PMag.Leid.W. = Leiden magical papyrus *W.*, ed. A. Dieterich, *Abraxas* (*Festschrift.. Hermann Usener..* Bonn), Leipzig 1891; cited by page and line of the papyrus, as in Leemans' edition (= *PMag.* 13, cited by column and line).

PMag.Lond. = *PLond.*1.46, 121, etc.

*PMag.Par.*1,2 = C. Wessely, *Wiener Denkschr.* xxxvi (2) (1888) pp. 44–126, pp. 139–148; partly in A. Dieterich, *Eine Mithrasliturgie*, Leipzig 1903, pp. 1ff., and A. Deissmann, *Light from the Ancient East*, London 1919, pp. 258 ff. (= *PMag.*4, 3).

PMag.Rain. = C. Wessely, *Wiener Denkschr.* xlii (2) (1893) p. 65.

PMagd. = *Papyrus de Magdola*, rééd... par Jean Lesquier, Paris 1912 (*PLille* II 2–4); republished in *PEnteux.*

PMasp. = Jean Maspéro, *Papyrus grecs d'époque byzantine*, in *Catalogue général des antiquités égyptiennes du Musée du Caire*, I (Nos. 67001–67124) 1911, II (Nos. 67125–67278) 1913, III (Nos. 67279–67359) 1916. Digits indicating 67(000) omitted in refs., thus: 2 = 67002.

PMed.Lond. = *London Medical Papyrus*, No. 155, ed. C. Kalbfleisch in *Papyri graecae Musei Britannici et Musei Berolinensis*, Rostock 1902.

PMed.Strassb. = *Papyri Argentoratenses Graecae*, ed. C. Kalbfleisch, *Index lectionum in Academia Rostochiensi* 1901.

PMerton = H. Idris Bell & C. H. Roberts, *Catalogue of the Greek papyri in the collection of Wilfred Merton*, London, vol. i 1939.

PMeyer = P. M. Meyer, *Griechische Texte aus Ägypten*: 1. *Papyri des neutestamentlichen Seminars der Universität Berlin*; 2. *Ostraka der Sammlung Deissmann*, Berlin (Leipzig) 1916.

PMich. = *University of Michigan papyri*, published in *Trans. Am. Ph. Ass.* liii (1922) p. 134.

*PMich.*iii = *Michigan Papyri* vol. iii: Miscellaneous Papyri, edited by J. G. Winter (= University of Michigan Studies, Humanistic Series, vol. xl), Ann Arbor 1936.

PMich.Teb. = *Michigan Papyri* vol. ii: Papyri from Tebtunis, in two volumes, Part I, ed. A. E. R. Boak (= University of Michigan Studies, Humanistic Series, vol. xxviii), Ann Arbor 1933.

PMich.Zen. = *Zenon papyri in the University of Michigan collection*, ed. C. C. Edgar (= University of Michigan Studies, Humanistic Series, vol. xxiv), Ann Arbor 1931.

PMilan. = *Papiri Milanesi*, ed. A. Calderini (Pubbl. di 'Aegyptus', S. Scient., vol. i), Parte i, Collezione Jacovelli-Vita, Milano, Università Cattolica del Sacro Cuore, 1928.

PMilan.R.Univ. = *PUniv.Milan.* (q.v.).

*PMilan.*17 = Commentario ad Antimaco da Colofone, ed. A. Vogliano, *PUniv.Milan.* i. 17.

PMonac. = A. Heisenberg & L. Wenger, *Byzantinische Papyri* (*Veröffentlichungen aus der Papyrus-Sammlung der K. Hof- und Staatsbibliothek zu München* I), Leipzig 1914.

POsl. = *Papyri Osloenses*, ed. S. Eitrem, Oslo 1925–.

POxy. = *Oxyrhynchus Papyri*, ed. B. P. Grenfell & A. S. Hunt, London 1898–.

PPar. = W. Brunet de Presle, *Notices et extraits des papyrus grecs du musée du Louvre et de la bibliothèque impériale* xviii (2), Paris 1865.

PPar.Wess. = C. Wessely, *Die Pariser Papyri des Fundes von El Faijûm* (*Wiener Denkschr.* xxxvii (2) (1889) pp. 97 ff.).

PPetr. = *The Flinders Petrie Papyri*.., Pt. 1, ed. J. P. Mahaffy (Royal Irish Academy, Cunningham Memoirs, No. 8); Pt. 2, ed. J. P. Mahaffy (ibid., No. 9); Pt. 3, ed. J. P. Mahaffy & J. G. Smyly (ibid., No. 11), Dublin 1891–1905.

PPrincet. = *Papyri in the Princeton University Collections*, vol. I ed. A. C. Johnson and H. B. van Hoesen (= Johns Hopkins University Studies in Archaeology No. 10), Baltimore 1931; vol. II ed. E. H. Kase (= Princeton University Studies in Papyrology No. 1), Princeton 1936.

PRain. (*NS*) = *Mitteilungen aus der Papyrussammlung der Nationalbibliothek in Wien* (*Papyrus Erzherzog Rainer*). Neue Serie I i (1932), ed. H. Gerstinger; I ii (1939), ed. H. Oellacher; cf. *CPR.*

PRein. = *Papyrus grecs et démotiques*.., ed. Théodore Reinach, Paris 1905.

PRev.Laws = B. P. Grenfell, *Revenue Laws of Ptolemy Philadelphus*, Oxford 1896.

PRoss.-Georg. = *Papyri Russischer und Georgischer Sammlungen*, herausgegeben von Gregor Zereteli, bearbeitet von G. Zereteli, O. Krüger, P. Jernstedt, Tiflis 1925–35.

PRyl. = *Catalogue of the Greek papyri in the John Rylands Library at Manchester*, vol. i 1911, ed. A. S. Hunt; vol. ii 1915, ed. A. S. Hunt, J. de M. Johnson, V. Martin; vol. iii 1938, ed. C. H. Roberts.

PSI = *Papiri greci e latini* (*Pubblicazioni della Società italiana per la ricerca dei papiri greci e latini in Egitto*), Firenze 1912–; cited by No. of vol., papyrus, and line.

PSorb. (i.e. Papyri in the Sorbonne), v. *PGand.*

PStrassb. = F. Preisigke, *Griechische Papyrus der kaiserlichen Universitäts- und Landesbibliothek zu Strassburg*, 2 vols., Strassburg (afterwards Leipzig) 1906–20.

PTaur. = V. A. Peyron, *Papyri graeci regii Taurinensis musei Aegyptii*, Turin 1826–7.

PTeb. = *Tebtunis Papyri*, ed. B. P. Grenfell, A. S. Hunt, J. G. Smyly, E. J. Goodspeed, London & New York, vol. i 1902, vol. ii 1907, vol. iii pt. i 1933, pt. 2 (ed. A. S. Hunt, J. G. Smyly, C. C. Edgar; London & Univ. of California Press) 1938.

PThead. = *Papyrus de Théadelphie*, éd. par Pierre Jouguet, Paris 1911.

PTheb.Bank = U. Wilcken, *Aktenstücke aus der Kgl. Bank zu Theben* (*Abh. Berl. Akad.* 1886).

PUniv.Giss. = H. Kling and others, *Mitteilungen aus der Papyrussammlung der Giessener Universitätsbibliothek*, 1924–.

PUniv.Milan. = A. Vogliano, *Papiri della R. Università di Milano*, vol. i, Milan 1937.

PVarsov. = G. Manteuffel, *Papyri Varsovienses*, Warsaw 1935.

PVat. 11 = *Il Papiro Vaticano Greco* 11 (1. Φαβωρίνου περὶ φυγῆς; 2. *Registri Fondiari della Marmarica*), ed. M. Norsa & G. Vitelli, Città del Vaticano, Biblioteca Apostolica Vaticana 1931. (*Studi e Testi* 53.)

PWarren = *The Warren Papyri*, ed. A. S. Hunt, cited from *Studi in onore di S. Riccobono* ii, Palermo 1932, pp. 521–5, and *Aegyptus* xiii (1933) pp. 241–6.
PWürzb. = *Mitteilungen aus der Würzburger Papyrussammlung*, von Ulrich Wilcken (*Abhandlungen der Preussischen Akademie der Wissenschaften*, 1933, Phil.-hist. Klasse No. 6), Berlin 1934.
PZen.Col. = *Zenon papyri: business papers of the 3rd century B.C.*, ed. W. L. Westermann and E. S. Hasenoehrl, New York, vol. i (*Columbia Papyri, Greek Series*, vol. iii) 1934.
Raccolta Lumbroso = *Raccolta di Scritti in onore di G. Lumbroso*, Milan 1925.
Sammelb. = *Sammelbuch griechischer Urkunden aus Ägypten* (both inscriptions and papyri), Bde. i, ii ed. F. Preisigke, Strassburg (later Berlin & Leipzig) 1913–22; Bd. iii (6001–7269) ed. F. Bilabel, Berlin & Leipzig 1926–7; Bd. iv (7270–7514), Bd. v Heft 1 (7515–7654) ed. F. Bilabel, Heidelberg 1931, 1934.
Stud.Pal. = C. Wessely, *Studien zur Paläographie und Papyruskunde*, Leipzig 1901–.
Studi Riccobono, v. *PWarren*.
Theb.Ostr. = *Theban Ostraca*. Pt. iii: *Greek texts*, by J. G. Milne, Toronto (Oxford) 1913.
Thunell *Sitologenpapyri* = K. Thunell, *Sitologen-Papyri aus d. Berliner Museum*, Uppsala 1924; republished in *PBerl. Leihg.*
UPZ = U. Wilcken, *Urkunden der Ptolemäerzeit*: I. *Papyri aus Unterägypten*, Berlin & Leipzig 1922; II. *Papyri aus Oberägypten*, 1935–.
Wilcken *Chr.*, v. Mitteis *Chr.*

IV. PERIODICALS

NOTE.—(*a*) Periodicals are cited by No. of vol. except where otherwise stated. (*b*) References to periodicals (unless otherwise explained in the context) are to inscriptions published therein.

AEM = *Archäologisch-epigraphische Mittheilungen aus Oesterreich-Ungarn*, 1877–97.
AJA = *American Journal of Archaeology*, second series, 1897–.
AJP = *American Journal of Philology*, 1880–.
Abh.Berl.Akad. = *Abhandlungen der Preussischen Akademie der Wissenschaften* (Berlin), earlier *der Koeniglichen Akademie der Wissenschaften zu Berlin* (cited by Jahrgang).
Aegyptus, Milan 1920–.
Aevum = *Aevum, rassegna di scienze storiche*, etc. (Università Cattolica del Sacro Cuore), Milan 1927–.
Africa Italiana = *Africa Italiana, collezione di monografie*, Rome 1925–.
Africa Italiana Riv. = *Africa Italiana, rivista di storia e d'arte*, Bergamo 1927–.
Albania = *Albania: revue d'archéologie, d'histoire, d'art et des sciences appliquées en Albanie et dans les Balkans*, i, ii, Milan etc., iii–, Paris 1925–.
Ann.Épigr. = *L'Année épigraphique*, published in *Revue Archéologique* (cited by year).
Annales du Service = *Annales du Service des Antiquités de l'Égypte*, 1899–.
Annuario = *Annuario della regia Scuola Archeologica di Atene*, 1914–.
Arch.Anz. = *Archäologischer Anzeiger*, in *Jahrb.* (q.v.).
'Αρχ.Δελτ. = 'Αρχαιολογικὸν Δελτίον, 1915– (cited by year).
'Αρχ.'Εφ. = 'Αρχαιολογικὴ 'Εφημερίς, 1910– (cited by year).
Arch.Pap. = *Archiv für Papyrusforschung*, 1900–.
Arch.f.Religionswiss. = *Archiv für Religionswissenschaft*, Freiburg im Breisgau 1898–.
Atene e Roma, 1898–.
Ath.Mitt. = *Mitteilungen des deutschen archäologischen Instituts, Athenische Abteilung*, 1876–.
'Αθηνᾶ, 1889–.
Atti Acc. Napoli = *Atti della Reale Accademia di Archeologia ecc., Napoli, Nuova Serie*, 1910–.
Ausonia = *Ausonia, Rivista della Società italiana di archeologia e storia dell'arte*, 1906–.
BCH = *Bulletin de Correspondance Hellénique*, 1877–.
BpW = *Berliner philologische Wochenschrift*, 1881–1920. Cf. *Phil. Wochenschr.*
BSA = *Annual of the British School at Athens*, 1895–.
Berl.Sitzb. = *Sitzungsberichte* (*Monatsberichte* before 1882) *der Preussischen Akademie der Wissenschaften* (Berlin) (cited by year).
Bull.Comm.Arch.Com. = *Bullettino della Commissione Archeologica Comunale di Roma*, Rome 1872–.
Bull.Inst.Arch.Bulg. = *Bulletin de l'Institut archéologique bulgare*, Sophia 1921–.
Bull.Inst.Ég. = *Bulletin de l'institut égyptien*, cinquième série, Cairo 1907–18.
Bull.Inst.Franç. = *Bulletin de l'Institut Français d'Archéologie Orientale*, Le Caire 1901–.
Bull.Soc.Alex. = *Bulletin de la Société Archéologique d'Alexandrie*, Alexandria. First Series 1898–1902 (Nos. 1–5); Nouv. Série (vol. i, No. 6–) 1904– (cited by volume).
Byz.-neugr.Jahrb. = *Byzantinisch-neugriechische Jahrbücher*, 1920–.
Βυζάντιον = Βυζάντιον, *Revue internationale des études byzantines*, Paris 1924–.
CQ = *Classical Quarterly*, 1907–.
CR = *Classical Review*, 1887–.
CRAcad.Inscr. = *Comptes rendus de l'Académie des Inscriptions et Belles-Lettres* (cited by year).
Clara Rhodos = *Clara Rhodos, studi e materiali pubbl. a cura dell'Istituto storico-archeologico di Rodi*, Rhodes 1928–.
Class.Phil. = *Classical Philology*, Chicago 1906–.
Dacia = *Dacia: recherches et découvertes archéologiques en Roumanie, publ. sous la dir. de* V. Pârvan, Bucarest 1927–.
Docum. ant. dell'Africa Italiana = *Documenti antichi dell'Africa Italiana*, Bergamo 1932–.
'Ελληνικά = 'Ελληνικά, ἱστορικὸν περιοδικὸν δημοσίευμα, Athens 1928–.
Eos, Commentarii Societatis Philologae Polonorum, Lwów 1894–.
'Εφ.'Αρχ. = 'Εφημερὶς 'Αρχαιολογική, περίοδος τρίτη, 1883–1909 (cited by year).
'Ηπειρωτικὰ χρονικά, 1926–.
Eranos = *Eranos: Acta philologica Suecana*, 1906–.
Ét.de Pap. = *Société royale égyptienne de papyrologie: Études de Papyrologie*, Le Caire 1932–.
Glotta, 1907–.
Gött.gel.Anz. = *Göttingische gelehrte Anzeigen* (cited by year).
Gött.Nachr. = *Nachrichten der Gesellschaft der Wissenschaften zu Göttingen* (cited by year).
Harv.Theol.Rev. = *Harvard Theological Review*, 1908–.
Hermes, 1866–.
Hesperia = *Hesperia: Journal of the American School of Classical Studies at Athens*, Cambridge, Mass. 1932–.
Historia = *Historia, studi storici per l'antichità classica*, 1–9, Milan & Rome 1927–35.
Istros = *Istros: revue roumaine d'archéologie et d'histoire ancienne*, Bucarest 1934–.
Izv.Arch.Comm. = Извѣстія археологической Комиссіи русской академіи наукъ (Reports of the Archaeological Commission of the Russian Academy of Sciences), Petrograd 1901–18.
JEA = *Journal of Egyptian Archaeology*, 1914–.
JHS = *Journal of Hellenic Studies*, 1880–.
JRS = *Journal of Roman Studies*, 1911–.
Jahrb. = *Jahrbuch des (kaiserlich) deutschen archäologischen Instituts*, 1886– (contains *Arch. Anz.*).
Jahresh. = *Jahreshefte des österreichischen archäologischen Institutes*, 1898–; *Beibl.* = *Beiblatt.*
Klio = *Klio, Beiträge zur alten Geschichte*, 1901–.
L'Ant.Cl. = *L'Antiquité Classique*, Louvain 1932–.
Leipz.Stud. = *Leipziger Studien zur klassischen Philologie*, 1878–95.
Liv.Ann. = *Liverpool Annals of Archaeology and Anthropology*, 1908–.
Mél. de l'éc. fr. de Rome = *Mélanges d'archéologie et d'histoire: École française de Rome*, Paris & Rome 1881–.
Mélanges Beyrouth = *Mélanges de l'Université Saint-Joseph, Beyrouth (Liban)*, Beyrouth 1906–.
Mém.Inst.Franç. = *Mémoires publiés par les membres de l'Institut français d'archéologie orientale du Caire*, Le Caire 1902–.
Mnemos. = *Mnemosyne*, 1852–.
Mon.Ant. = *Monumenti antichi pubblicati per cura della Reale Accademia dei Lincei*, 1890–.
Μουσ.Σμυρν. = Μουσεῖον [Σμυρναῖον] καὶ βιβλιοθήκη τῆς Εὐαγγελικῆς Σχολῆς, Smyrna 1875–86 (cited by year).
Mus.Belg. = *Musée Belge*, 1897–.
Not.Scav. = *Notizie degli Scavi*, Serie v, 1904–.
Notiz.Arch. = *Notiziario Archeologico del Ministero delle Colonie*, Milan–Rome 1915–.
Papers of Amer. School at Athens = *Papers of the American School of Classical Studies at Athens*, Boston 1882 (publ. 1885)–1897.
Phil.Wochenschr. = *Philologische Wochenschrift* (incorporating *Berliner philologische Wochenschrift* and *Wochenschrift für klassische Philologie*), 1921–.
Philol. = *Philologus*, 1841–.
Πολέμων = Πολέμων, ἐπιστημονικὸν ἀρχαιολογικὸν περιοδικόν, Athens 1929 (only vol. i published, but there are offprints from vol. ii).

Πρακτικὰ ᾽Ακ.᾽Αθ. = Πρακτικὰ τῆς ᾽Ακαδημίας ᾽Αθηνῶν, 1926–.
QDAP = *Quarterly of the Department of Antiquities in Palestine*, London 1931–.
Recueil de Travaux = *Recueil de Travaux relatifs à la philologie et à l'archéologie égyptiennes et assyriennes*, 1870–.
Rend. Pont. Accad. Arch. = *Rendiconti della Pontificia Accademia Romana di Archeologia*, 1921/2–.
Rev.Arch. = *Revue Archéologique* (cited by year).
Rev.Bibl. = *Revue Biblique internationale*, Paris 1892–.
Rev.Épigr. = *Revue Épigraphique*, 2 vols., 1913–14 (all published).
Rev.Ét.Gr. = *Revue des Études grecques*, 1888–.
Rev.Hist.Rel. = *Revue de l'histoire des religions*, Paris 1880–.
Rev.Phil. = *Revue de Philologie*, Nouv. Série 1877–1926, Troisième Sér. 1927–.
Rh.Mus. = *Rheinisches Museum*, Neue Folge, Frankfurt 1842–1920.
Riv.Fil. = *Rivista di Filologia*, 1873–.
Riv.Ist.Arch. = *Rivista del R. Istituto d'Archeologia e Storia dell'Arte*, Rome 1929–.
Röm.Mitt. = *Mitteilungen des deutschen archäologischen Instituts, Römische Abteilung*, 1886–.
Sitzb.Heidelb.Akad. = *Heidelberg. Akademie der Wissenschaften. Sitzungsberichte* (*phil.-hist. Klasse*) 1910– (cited by year).
Sokrates = *Sokrates*, Neue Folge, Berlin 1913–24.
Stud.Ital. = *Studi italiani di filologia classica*, nuova serie i–, Florence 1920–.
Syria, Paris 1920–.
Trans.Am.Phil.Ass. = *Transactions of the American Philological Association*, 1869–.
Univ. of Eg. Fac. Bull. = *Université Égyptienne, Faculty of Arts Bulletin*, Cairo 1933–.
WkP = *Wochenschrift für klassische Philologie*, 1884–1920. Cf. *Phil. Wochenschr.*
Wien.Sitzb. = *Sitzungsberichte der* (*Kaiserlichen*) *Akademie der Wissenschaften in Wien, Philosophisch-historische Klasse*, 1849–.
Wien.Stud. = *Wiener Studien*, 1879–.
Wiener Denkschr. = *Denkschriften der Akademie der Wissenschaften in Wien, Phil.-hist. Klasse*, 1850– (cited by year).
Yale Class. Studies = *Yale Classical Studies*, 1928–.
Zeitschr.d.Savigny-Stiftung = *Zeitschrift der Savigny-Stiftung für Rechtsgeschichte, romanistische Abteilung*, 1880–.

V. GENERAL LIST OF ABBREVIATIONS

NOTE.—This list contains:

(1) Abbreviations used in the Lexicon or in Lists I–IV, but not explained in those lists.

(2) Abbreviations explained in List I but out of their alphabetical order. For all names of authors List I is to be consulted; the note 'v. I' has been added only to names of works cited without an author's name.

(3) All abbreviations explained in Lists II–IV, with references to those lists.

It does not contain titles of works given in List I under the author's name or under Anonymus.

A. = Aeschylus
AB = *Anecdota Graeca*, v. I
A.D. = Apollonius Dyscolus
AEM, v. IV
AJA, v. IV
AJP, v. IV
AP, APl., v. *Anthologia Graeca*
A.R. = Apollonius Rhodius
Abh.Berl.Akad., v. IV.
abs. = absolute, absolutely
acc. = accusative
acc. to = according to
Act. = Active
Act.Ap. = *Acts of the Apostles*
ad loc. = ad locum
Adj. = Adjective
Adv., Advbs. = Adverb, Adverbs
Aeol. = Aeolic
Aesch.Alex. = Aeschylus Alexandrinus
afterwds. = afterwards
Agath. = Agathias
Al. = ἄλλοι, v. Vetus Testamentum
al. = alibi (i.e. elsewhere in the same author)
Alc. = Alcaeus
Alcm. = Alcman
Alex. = Alexis, *when followed directly by a number, otherwise* = Alexander
Amm.Marc. = Ammianus Marcellinus
An.Ox.,Par. = *Anecdota Oxoniensia, Parisiensia*, v. I
anap. = anapaests
Anat. = in Anatomy
Anatolian Studies, v. II
And. = Andocides
Anecd.Stud. = *Anecdota Graeca et Latina*, ed. R. Schoell & G. Studemund, v. I
Ann.Épigr., v. IV
Annales du Service, v. IV
Annuario, v. IV
Ant.Diog. = Antonius Diogenes
Ant.Lib. = Antoninus Liberalis
Antip. = Antipater
Antiph. = Antiphanes
aor. = aorist
ap. = apud (quoted in)
Ap.Ty. = Apollonius Tyanensis
Apoc. = *Apocalypse*
Apollon. = Apollonius
App. = Appianus
App.Anth., v. *Anthologia Graeca*
Appellat. = Appellative
apptly. = apparently
Ar. = Aristophanes
Ar.Byz. = Aristophanes Byzantinus
Ar.Did. = Arius Didymus
Arc. = Arcadius *or* Arcadian dialect
Arch. = Archias
Arch.Anz., v. IV
᾽Αρχ.Δελτ., v. IV
᾽Αρχ.᾽Εφ., v. IV
Arch.Pap., v. IV
Archit. = in Architecture
Arg. = Argive *or* Argument
Arist. = Aristoteles
Aristoph. = Aristophanes (the Homeric critic)
Arm. = Armenian
Art. = Article
Ascl. = Asclepiodotus *or* Asclepius
Asclep. = Asclepiades
Asp. = Aspasius
Astrol. = in Astrology
Aten. e Roma, v. IV
Ath. = Athenaeus
Ath.Mitt., v. IV
᾽Αθηνᾶ, v. IV
Att. = Attic dialect
augm. = augment
Aus. = Ausonius
Ausonia, v. IV
Avest. = Avestan

B. = Bacchylides
BCH, v. IV
BGU, v. III
BKT, v. III
BMus.Inscr., v. II
BpW, v. IV
BSA, v. IV
Bacch. = Bacchius
Benndorf-Niemann *Reisen in Lykien*, v. II
Berl.Sitzb., v. IV
Bgk. = Bergk
Bilabel *᾽Οψαρτ.*, v. III
Blomf. = Blomfield
Boeot. = Boeotian dialect
Buttm. = Philipp Buttmann
Byz. = Byzantine

CAF = T. Kock, *Comicorum Atticorum Fragmenta*, 3 vols., Leipzig 1880–8
CGF = G. Kaibel, *Comicorum Graecorum Fragmenta*, vol. i fasc. i (all published), Berlin 1899
CIA, v. *IG* in II
CIG, v. II
CIL, v. II
CMG = *Corpus Medicorum Graecorum*, Leipzig 1908–
CPHerm., v. III
CPR, v. III
CQ, v. IV
CR, v. IV
CRAcad.Inscr., v. IV
c. gen. pers., etc. = cum genitivo personae, etc.
ca. = circa
Call. = Callimachus
Call.Com. = Callias Comicus
Call.Hist. = Callias Historicus
Callin. = Callinus
Carm. = *Carmen, Carmina*, v. I
Cerc. = Cercidas
Cercop. = Cercopes, v. I
Certamen, v. I
cf. = confer, conferatur
Chron.Lind., v. II
cj. = conjecture, conjectured by
Cleobul. = Cleobulus
Cod. = *Codex*, v. I
cod., codd. = codex, codices
cogn. = cognate
coll. *or* collect. = collective
Coll.Alex. = J. U. Powell, *Collectanea Alexandrina*, Oxford 1925
collat. = collateral
Com. = Comedy, Comic, in the language of the Comic writers
Com.Adesp., v. I
Comm.in Arist.Graeca = *Commentaria in Aristotelem Graeca*
Comp. = Comparative
compd. = compound
compos. = composition
Const.Δέδωκεν, v. Justinianus
Const.omnem, v. Justinianus
Conj. = Conjunction
conj. = conjunctive
constr. = construction
contr. = contracted, contraction
copul. = copulative
Corc. = Corcyra, Corcyraean
Corp.Herm., v. I
correl. = correlative
Cret. = Cretan
Cypr. = Cypria (v. I) *or* Cyprian dialect

D. = Demosthenes
D.C. = Dio Cassius
D.Chr. = Dio Chrysostomus
D.H. = Dionysius Halicarnassensis
D.L. = Diogenes Laertius
D.P. = Dionysius Periegeta
D.S. = Diodorus Siculus
D.T. = Dionysius Thrax
Dam. = Damascius
dat. = dative
Decr. = Decretum
defect. = defective
*Delph.*3(1), (2), v. II
Dem.Bith. = Demosthenes Bithynus
Dem.Ophth. = Demosthenes, Ophthalmicorum Scriptor
Dem.Phal. = Demetrius Phalereus, Historicus
demonstr. = demonstrative
Dep. = Deponent Verb
deriv. = derived, derivation, derivative
Desiderat. = Desiderative
difft. = different
Dig. = *Digesta*, v. I
Dim. = Diminutive
Din. = Dinarchus
Dind. = Dindorf (W. *or* L.)
Diog. = Diogenes
Dion.Byz. = Dionysius Byzantius
Dioph. = Diophantus
dissim. = dissimilated
dist., distd., distn. = distinct, distinguished, distinction
disyll. = disyllable
Docum. = Documentum
Dor. = Doric
downwds. = downwards
Dsc. = Dioscorides Medicus
dub., dub. l., dub. sens. = dubious, dubia lectio, dubio sensu

E. = Euripides
EGF = G. Kinkel, *Epicorum Graecorum Fragmenta* i (all published), Leipzig (T.) 1877
EM = *Etymologicum Magnum*
e.g. = exempli gratia
Ecphant. = Ecphantus

ed. = edited by
edd. = editors
Edict.Diocl., v. II
Eleg.Alex.Adesp., v. I
ellipt. = elliptically
Elmsl. = Elmsley
elsewh. = elsewhere
enclit. = enclitic
Ep. = Epice, in the Epic dialect
Ep. = *Epistula*, rarely *Epigram*
Ep.Col., etc. = Epistle to the Colossians, etc., v. Novum Testamentum
'Εφ.'Αρχ., v. IV
Eph.Epigr., v. II
*Ephes.*2, v. II
Epic. = Epicus
Epic.Alex.Adesp., v. I
Epid. = Epidaurus
Epig. = Epigenes *or* Epigonus
Epigoni, v. I
Epigr. = Epigram
Epigr.Gr., v. II
Epin. = Epinicus
Epist.Charact. = *Charactères Epistolici*, v. I
Epistolographi = R. Hercher, *Epistolographi Graeci*, Paris (D.) 1873
epith. = epithet
equiv. = equivalent
Eranos, v. IV
Erotici = R. Hercher, *Erotici Scriptores Graeci*, Leipzig (T.) 1858–9
esp. = especially
Et.Gen. = *Etymologicum Genuinum*
Et.Gud. = *Etymologicum Gudianum*
etc. = et cetera (i.e. in other authors)
etym. = etymology, etymologically
Eub. = Eubulus
Euc. = Euclides
Eup. = Eupolis
Euph. = Euphorio
euph. *or* euphon. = euphonic
euphem. = euphemistic, euphemistically
Eust. = Eustathius
Eustr. = Eustratius
Ev.Jo., etc. = Gospel according to John, etc., v. Novum Testamentum
exc. = except
exclam. = exclamation
expl., expld. = explanation, explained

FGrH = F. Jacoby, *Fragmente der griechischen Historiker*, Berlin 1923–
FHG = C. Müller, *Fragmenta Historicorum Graecorum*, 5 vols., Paris (D.) 1841–70
FPG = F. W. A. Mullach, *Fragmenta Philosophorum Graecorum*, 3 vols., Paris (D.) 1860–81
f.l. = falsa lectio
fem. = feminine
fin. = sub finem
Foed. = Foedus
Foed.Delph.Pell., v. II
folld. = followed
foreg. = foregoing
fort. = fortasse
Fr. = Fragment
fr. = from
freq. = frequent, frequently
Frequentat. = Frequentative Verb
fut. = future

GDI, v. II
GGM = C. Müller, *Geographici Graeci Minores*, Paris (D.) 1855–61
Gal. = Galenus
gen. *or* genit. = genitive
Geom. = in Geometry
Germ. = German
Gloss. = *Glossaria*, v. I
Glotta, v. IV
Goth. = Gothic
Gött.gel.Anz., v. IV
Gött.Nachr., v. IV.
Gp. = *Geoponica*, v. I
Gr. = Greek
Gramm. = Grammarians, in the language of the Grammarians
Gramm.Lat. = H. Keil, *Grammatici Latini*, Leipzig 1855–80

HGM = L. Dindorf, *Historici Graeci Minores*, Leipzig (T.) 1870–1
h.Ap., etc. = *Hymnus ad Apollinem*, etc., v. sq.
h.Hom. = *hymni Homerici*
Halic. = Halicarnassus
Haussoullier *Milet*, v. II
Hdn. = Herodianus
Hdt. = Herodotus
Heb. = 'Εβραῖος, v. Vetus Testamentum
Hebr. = Hebrew
Hell.Oxy. = *Hellenica Oxyrhynchia*, v. I
Hemerolog.Flor., v. I
Heracl. = Heraclas
Herc., v. III
Herm. = Hermann, Hermes, *or* Hermias
Hermes, v. IV
Herod. = Herodas
Herod.Med. = Herodotus Medicus
Hes. = Hesiodus
heterocl. = heteroclite
heterog. = heterogeneous
hex. = hexameters
Hippiatr., v. I
Hist.Aug. = *Historiae Augustae Scriptores*, v. I
Hld. = Heliodorus, Scriptor Eroticus
Hp. = Hippocrates
Hsch. = Hesychius
Hymn. = *Hymnus*, *Hymni*, v. I
hyperdor. = hyperdorian

I.-E., I.-Eur. = Indo-European
IG, v. II
IGRom., v. II
IPE, v. II
i.e. = id est
ib. = ibidem (i.e. in the same work)
ibid. = ibidem (i.e. in the same passage)
Icel. = Icelandic
Id. = Idem
Il. = Iliad
imper. = imperative
impers. = impersonal
impf. = imperfect
inc.loc. = incerto loco
ind. *or* indic. = indicative
indecl. = indeclinable
indef. = indefinite
inf. = infinitive
init. = ad initium
Inscr. = Inscription
Inscr.Cos, *Cypr.*, etc., v. II
insep. = inseparable
instr. = instrumental
intens. = intensive
interp. *or* interpol. = interpolated
interpr. = interpreted, interpretation
interrog. = interrogative
intr. = intransitive
Ion. = Ionic
irreg. = irregular
Is. = Isaeus
Iterat. = Iterative
Izv.Arch.Comm., v. IV

J. = Josephus
JHS, v. IV
JRS, v. IV
Jahrb., v. IV
Jahresh., v. IV
Jo. = Joannes
Jusj. = Jusjurandum

Keil-Premerstein, v. II
Klio, v. IV

LF, *LW*, v. II
l. = lege
l. c., ll. cc. = loco citato, locis citatis
Lacon. = Laconian
Lat. = Latin
Leg.Gort., v. II
Leg.Sacr., v. II
leg. = legendum
Leipz.Stud., v. IV
lengthd. = lengthened
Leon. = Leonidas (two epigrammatists)
Leonid. = Leonidas Medicus
Lett. = Lettish
Lex = Lex (law)
Lex. = Lexicon, v. I
lit. = literally, literal
Lit.Crit. = in Literary Criticism
Lith. = Lithuanian
Liv.Ann., v. IV
Lob. = C. A. Lobeck
loc. = locative
Lyc. = Lycophron
Lyr. = Lyricus, Lyric poetry
Lyr.Adesp., v. I
Lyr.Alex.Adesp., v. I
Lys. = Lysias
Lysim. = Lysimachus

M.Ant. = Marcus Antoninus, v. Marcus
ME., MHG., etc. = Middle English, Middle High German, etc.
Magn. = Magnes
Man. = Manetho
Mantiss.Prov., v. I
Mar.Vict. = Marius Victorinus
Marc.Arg. = Marcus Argentarius
Marc.Sid. = Marcellus Sidetes
Margites, v. I
Marm.Par., v. II
masc. = masculine
Math. = in Mathematics
Med. = Medium, Middle
Medic. = in medical writers
Megar. = Megarian
Megalop. = Megalopolis
Mein. = Meineke
Mel. = Meleager
Meliss. = Melissus
Men. = Menander
Mess. = Messenian
metaph. = metaphorically, metaphorical
metaplast. = metaplastice
metath. = metathesis
metr. = metrically
metri gr. = metri gratia
Michel, v. II
*Milet.*3, 6, 7, v. II
Mitteis *Chr.*, v. III
Mnemos., v. IV
Mod. = modern
Moer. = Moeris
Mon.Anc.Gr., v. II
Mon.Ant., v. IV
Mosch. = Moschus
Μουσ.Σμυρν., v. IV
Mus.Belg., v. IV
Music. = in musical writers

NT = Novum Testamentum
n. pr. = nomen proprium
neg. = negative
neut. *or* n. = neuter
Nic. = Nicander *or* Nicias
Nic.Dam. = Nicolaus Damascenus
nom. = nominative
Nosti, v. I
Not.Scav., v. IV

OE. = Old English
OGI, v. II
OHG. = Old High German
OIr. = Old Irish
Od. = Odyssey
oft. = often
opp. = opposed to
opt. = optative
Orac. = Oraculum
Orat.Att. = J. G. Baiter and H. Sauppe, *Oratores Attici*, Zurich 1839–50
orat. obliq. = oratio obliqua
Oratt. = Oratores Attici
Orchom. = Orchomenos
orig. = originally
Osc. = Oscan
Ostr., v. III
Ostr.Strassb., v. III
Oxy. = *POxy.*, q. v. (III)
oxyt. = oxytone

PAlex. and other abbrevs. beginning with *P*, v. III
PLG = T. Bergk, *Poetae Lyrici Graeci*[4], Leipzig 1882 (reprint 1914–15)
PPF = H. Diels, *Poetarum Philosophorum Fragmenta*, Berlin 1901
Pall. = Palladius *or* Palladas
Pamph. = Pamphylian
Pap. = Papyrus
paratrag. = paratragoedia
Parm. = Parmenides
Parmen. = Parmenio
parod. = parody
Paroemiographi = E. L. von Leutsch & F. G. Schneidewin, *Corpus Paroemiographorum Graecorum*, Göttingen 1839–51
parox. = paroxytone
part. = participle
partit. = partitive
Pass. = Passive
Patron. = Patronymic
pecul. = peculiar
perh. = perhaps
Peripl.M.Rubr., v. I
perispom. = perispomenon
pers., person. = person, personal
Petersen-Luschan *Reisen in Lykien*, v. II
pf. *or* perf. = perfect
Ph. = Philo
Phan. = Phanias
Phil. = Philippus Epigrammaticus
Phil.Wochenschr., v. IV
Philet. = Philetas
Philipp.Com. = Philippus Comicus
Philol. = Philolaus
Philol., v. IV
Philonid. = Philonides; for *Vit. Philonid.* v. infr.
Philos. = in Philosophy
Phld. = Philodemus Philosophus
Phlp. = Philoponus
Phoen. = Phoenix
Pi. = Pindarus
pl. = plural
Pl. = Plato
Placit., v. I
Plb. = Polybius
Plin. = Pliny
plpf. = pluperfect
Poet. = Poeta, poetical
Pors. = Porson
post-Hom. = post-Homeric
pr. n. = proper name
Prep. = Preposition
pres. = present
Prisc. = Priscus Historicus
Prisc.Lyd. = Priscianus Lydus
Priscian.*Inst.* = Priscianus Grammaticus, *Institutio*

priv. = privative
prob. = probable, probably
prob. for = probably to be read instead of
prob. l. = probable reading
Pron. = Pronoun
prop. = properly
proparox. = proparoxytone
properisp. = properispomenon
prov. = proverbially, proverbial

Q.S. = Quintus Smyrnaeus
q. v., qq. v. = quod vide, quae vide
qn. = question
Quint. = Quintilianus *or* Quinta Versio (v. Vetus Testamentum)

radic. = radical
Ramsay *Cities and Bishoprics*, v. II
Recueil de Travaux, v. IV
reflex. = reflexive
regul. = regular, regularly
relat. = relative
rest. = restoration
Rev.Arch., v. IV
Rev.Épigr., v. IV
Rev.Ét.Gr., v. IV
Rev.Phil., v. IV
Rh. = Rhetores Graeci, ed. Walz
Rh.Mus., v. IV
Rhet. = Rhetorical, Rhetoric
Rhet. = L. Spengel, *Rhetores Graeci*, 3 vols., Leipzig (T.) 1853–6: i pars ii, iterum ed. C. Hammer 1894
Riv.Fil., v. IV
Roussel *Cultes Égyptiens*, v. II
Ruf. = Rufus
Rufin. = Rufinus
Ruhnk. = Ruhnken
Rüsch, v. II

S. = Sophocles
S.E. = Sextus Empiricus

SIG, v. II
SRAM = C. Müller, *Scriptores Rerum Alexandri Magni*, Paris (D., post Arrianum) 1846
SVF = H. von Arnim, *Stoicorum Veterum Fragmenta*, Leipzig 1903
s. v. = sub voce
s. v. l. = si vera lectio
Sammelb., v. III
sc. = scilicet
Sch. = Scholia; see under several authors
Schneid. = Schneider
Schw. = Schweighäuser
Schwyzer, v. II
Scol. = *Scolia*
sens.obsc. = sensu obsceno
Sext. = Sextus Philosophus *or* Sexta Versio (v. Vetus Testamentum)
sg. = singular
shd. = should
shortd. = shortened
signf. = signification
Skt. = Sanskrit
Slav. = Slavonic
Sm. = Symmachus
sq., sqq. = sequens, sequentia
St.Byz. = Stephanus Byzantius
Stad. = *Stadiasmus*, v. I
Stoic. = *SVF*, q. v.
Str. = Strabo
strengthd. = strengthened
sts. = sometimes
Stud.Ital. = *Studi italiani di filologia classica*, 1893–
Stud.Pal., v. III
Stud.Pont., v. II
sub. = subaudi
subj. = subjunctive
Subst. = Substantive
Sup. = Superlative

Supp.Com. = J.Demiańczuk, *Supplementum Comicum*, Cracow 1912
Supp.Epigr., v. II
Supp.Lyr. = E. Diehl, *Supplementum Lyricum*³, Bonn 1917
suppl. = supplement
Surg. = in Surgery
susp., susp. l. = suspected, suspecta lectio
syll. = syllable
sync. = syncopated
Syngr. = Syngrapha
synon. = synonymous
Syrac. = Syracuse, Syracusan

TAM, v. II
TGF = A. Nauck, *Tragicorum Graecorum Fragmenta*², Leipzig 1889
t.t. = technical term
Tab.Defix., v. II
Tab.Defix.Aud., v. II
Tab.Heracl., v. II
Tarent. = Tarentum, Tarentine
termin. = termination
Test. = Testimonium
Test.Epict., v. II
Th. = Thucydides
Thd. = Theodotion
Theb.Ostr., v. III
Thebaïs, v. I
Them. = Themistius
Themist. = Themistocles
Theo Sm. = Theon Smyrnaeus
Theoc. = Theocritus
Theod. = Theodorus
Theol.Ar., v. I
Thess. = Thessalian
Thgn. = Theognis
Thphr. = Theophrastus
Ti.Locr. = Timaeus Locrus
Tim. = Timotheus Lyricus

Tim.Com. = Timotheus Comicus
Tim.Gaz. = Timotheus Gazaeus
Tim.*Lex.* = Timaeus Grammaticus
tit. = titulus
Titanomach. = Titanomachia, v. I
tm. = tmesis
Trag. = Tragic, Tragedy, in the language of the Tragic writers
Trag.Adesp., v. I
trans. = transitive
trisyll. = trisyllable
Tryph. = Tryphiodorus
Tull.Sab. = Sabinus (q. v.), Tullius
Tyrrhen. = Tyrrhenian

UPZ, v. III
Umbr. = Umbrian
usu. = usually

v. = vide; *also* voce *or* vocem
v.h.v. = vide hanc vocem
v. l., vv. ll. = varia lectio, variae lectiones
Ved. = Vedic
verb. Adj. = verbal Adjective
Vit.Philonid. = *VitaPhilonidisEpicurei*, v. I
voc. = voce, vocem; *also* vocative
Vorsokr. = H. Diels, *Fragmente der Vorsokratiker*⁴, Berlin 1922

WkP, v. IV
Wien.Stud., v. IV
Wiener Denkschr., v. IV
Wilcken *Chr.*, v. III

X. = Xenophon
X.Eph. = Xenophon Ephesius
Xenoph. = Xenophanes

Zeitschr.d.Savigny-Stiftung, v. IV
Zen. = Zenobius
Zon. = Zonas

V. GENERAL LIST OF ABBREVIATIONS (ADDENDA ET CORRIGENDA)

Anon. *Intr. Arat.* = Anonymi *Introductio in Aratum* in *Commentariorum in A. reliquiae*, v. I s.v. Aratus.
Anth.Lyr. = E. Diehl, *Anthologia Lyrica Graeca*, Leipzig (T.) 1925, ed. 2, vol. i 1936.
App. Prov. = *Appendix Proverbiorum*, v. I (Add.).
Arg. Men., v. I (Add.) s.v. Menander.

Ind. Lect. Rost. = *Index Lectionum in Academia Rostochiensi.*
s.v. *Orat. Att.*, for '1839' read '1845'
Pyth. or Pythag. = Pythagoras, Pythagorean.
[*Vit.*], for 'Anon. *Vit.Arist.*' and some other references containing *Vit.*, see Diogenes Laertius.
*Vorsokr.*⁵ = 5th edition, re-edited by Kranz, 1934

VI. SIGNS, ETC.

*, to denote words not actually extant.

=, equal *or* equivalent to, the same as.

( ) Between these brackets stand the Etymological remarks.

[ ] Between these brackets stand the Prosodial remarks.

The Hyphen has for the most part been used without regard to etymology, to represent that group of letters which is common to two or more consecutive words.

A

A — ἄβαρις

A α, ἄλφα (q.v.), *τό*, indecl., first letter of the Gr. alphabet: as Numeral, *α′ = εἷς* and *πρῶτος*, but *͵α* = 1,000.

ἀ–, as insep. Prefix in compos.: I. *α στερητικόν* (Sch.Od. 3.279, etc., cf. Eust.985.16), expressing *want* or *absence* (cf. Arist. *Metaph.*$1022^{b}32$), as *σοφός* wise, *ἄσοφος* *un*wise: for *n̥*, the weak form of the negative *ne*, commonly used in the formation of adjs. and advbs., very rarely in that of vbs. and substs., cf. *ἀδώτης, ἀτιμάω, ἀτίω.* Before a vowel it usu. appears as *ἀν–* (exc. where *ϝ* or *spiritus asper* has been lost, as *ἄ-οινος, ἄ-υπνος*, when it sts. coalesces with the following vowel, as *ἀργός = ἀ-ϝεργός*): the forms *ἀνάεδνος, ἀν-άελπτος* are probably misspelt for *ἀν-έϝεδνος, –έϝελπτος.* Adjs. formed with it freq. take gen., esp. in Trag., cf. *ἀλαμπὲς ἡλίου, = ἄνευ λάμψεως ἡλίου*, S.*Tr.*691. [*ᾰ*, exc. in adjs. which begin with three short syllables, which have *ᾱ* in Ep., and freq. also in Lyr., Trag., and Com.; *ἀθάνατος* invariably has *ᾱθ.*] II. *α ἀθροιστικόν* (Eust. 641.61; *τὸ ἄλφα σημαίνει πολλαχοῦ τὸ ὁμοῦ* Pl.*Cra.*405c), properly *ἁ–* since it represents *sm̥-* (cf. *ἅμα, εἷς = sems*), and so in *ἁπλόος, ἁθρόος*: but freq. *ἀ–* by dissimilation from following aspirate, as *ἄ-λοχος*, and hence by analogy in *ἄ-κοιτις*, etc., q.v.: sts. in the form *ὀ–*, as in *ὄπατρος, ὀγάστριος, ὄζυξ.* [*ᾰ*.] III. *α ἐπιτατικόν* (Eust. 641.61), strengthening the force of compds., as *ἀ-τενής*; prob. identical in etymology with II, from which it is distinguished by Gramm., who sts. confuse it with I; v. *ἀδάκρυτος.* [*ᾰ*.]

ἀ– as a prothetic vowel, usually before a double consonant, as *ἀ-βληχρός, ἀ-σπαίρω*; sts. before a single consonant, as *ἀ-μέλγω*; before a vowel where *ϝ* is lost, as *ἀ-ϝείδω.* [*ᾰ*.]

ἆ, exclamation expressing pity, envy, contempt, etc., in Hom. always *ἆ δειλέ, ἆ δειλώ, ἆ δειλοί*, Il.11.441, 17.443, Od.20.351, cf. Thgn.351, Theoc.*Ep.*6; also in Lyr., Archil.135, and Trag., A.*Ag.* 1087, etc.; in reproofs or warnings, *ἆ, μηδαμῶς* . . S.*Ph.*1300, cf. *OT*1147, E.*Hel.*445, etc.:—freq. with adj., *ἆ μάκαρ* Thgn.1013, Choeril.1; *ἆ τάλας* Semon.7.76, cf. B.15.30; *ἆ τρισευδαίμων* Id.3. 10; rarely alone, Ar.*Ra.*759; sts. doubled, *ἆ ἆ* A.*Pr.*114,566, Ar. *V.*1379.—Rare in Prose, Pl.*Hp.Ma.*295a (Euclus ap.Sch. ad loc. is said to have used it = *νῦν*).

ἃ ἅ or **ἃ ἃ,** to express laughter, *ha ha*, E.*Cyc.*157, Pl.Com.16 (prob. l.), etc.; *ἃ ἃ δασυνθὲν γέλωτα δηλοῖ* Hsch., Phot., Eust.855.19.

ἄα· *σύστημα ὕδατος*, Hsch., Phot., cf. *Et.Gud.* II. v. *ἄας.*

ἀάατος, *ον*, (*ἀάω*) in Il. ⏑ – – ⏑, *not to be injured, inviolable, νῦν μοι ὄμοσσον ἀ. Στυγὸς ὕδωρ* 14.271. II. in Od. ⏑ – ⏑ ⏑, *ἄεθλος ἀ. ἐκτετέλεσται* 22.5, cf. 21.9, prob. *unimpeachable*, i.e. *decisive.* III. later, *invincible, κάρτος ἀάᾰτος* A.R.2.77. (*ἀάϝατος*, cf. sq., Hsch.)

ἀάβακτοι· *ἀβλαβεῖς*, Hsch.; cf. **ἀάβηκτον·** *μέλαν, ἀβλαβές*, *Et. Gud.* (*–βυκτον* Cyr.)

ἀᾱγής, *ές*, *unbroken, hard*, Od.11.575, Theoc.24.123, etc. (*ἀϝαγής*, cf. *ἄγνυμι.*) [First *α* short ll. cc., long A.R.3.1251, Q.S.6.596.]

ἄαδα· *ἔνδεια* (Lacon.), Hsch. **ἀαδεῖν·** *ὀχλεῖν, ἀπορεῖν*, *Et.Gud.*, cf. Hsch., Phot.p.3R. (prob. for *ἀ-ϝαδεῖν*, cf. *ἀαδής*). **ἀαδένη** (*ἀαδέν Et.Gud.*, Cyr.)· *ὑεία κόπρος*, Hsch. **ἀαδής,** *ές*, (for *ἀ-ϝαδής*) *unpleasant*, cj. for *ἀδαής* in Thgn.296.

ἀάζω, *breathe with the mouth wide open*, Arist.*Pr.*$964^{a}11$. (Onomatopoeic word, for *ἀᾶζω*, make the sound *aha!*)

ἄαθι· *αὐτόθι*, Cyr.

ἀάκατος· *τριακάς* (Cypr.), *Et.Gud.* **ἀακίδωτος,** *ον*, (*ἀκίς*) *barbless*, Cyr. **ἄακτος,** *ον*, = *ἀαγής*, Hsch., *Et.Gud.* **ἀάλιον·** *ἄτακτον*, Apollon.*Lex.*, cf. Hsch.: *ἀ.·* *ἄπληκτον*, *Et.Gud.* **ἀανές** (*ἄνω*)· *οὐ τελεσθησόμενον*, Hsch.:—also **ἀάνης·** *χρήσιμος*, Id., *Et.Gud.*

ἄανθα, *ἡ*, a kind of *ear-ring*, Alcm.120, Ar.*Fr.*926.

ἀάπλετος, *ον*, lengthd. Ep. for *ἄπλετος*, v.l. in Q.S.1.675.

ἄαπτος, *ον*, (*ἅπτομαι*) *not to be touched, resistless, invincible, χεῖρες* Hom. (mostly in Il., as 1.567), Hes.*Op.*148; *κῆτος ἄ.* Opp.*H.*5.629. (Ar.Byz. read *ἄεπτος* (q.v.) in Hom.; cf. *ἀπτοεπής.*)

ἄᾱς, *to-morrow* or *the day after to-morrow*, gen. of *ἄα*, = *ἠώς*, read by Zenod. for *ἠοῦς* in Il.8.470 (cf. Sch.Ven.); as Adv. in Boeot., Hsch.; cf. *ἀές.*

ἀασι-φόρος· *βλάβην φέρων*, Hsch., *Et.Gud.*, cf. *EM*1.49. **–φρονία,** *ἡ*, *folly*, Phot.p.4R. **–φροσύνη, –φρων,** v. *ἀεσι–.*

ἀάσκει· *βλάπτει*, Hsch.

ἀασμός, *ὁ*, (*ἀάζω*) *breathing out, expiration*, Arist.*Pr.*$964^{a}18$.

ἀάσπετος, ἀάσχετος, v. sub *ἄσπετος, ἄσχετος.*

ἀάστονα· *ἀνεύφραντα*, Hsch.

ἀατήρ, *ῆρος*, *ὁ*, *dishonourer*, *ἀλλοτρίων λεχέων* Man.4.56 s.v.l.

ἄᾰτος, contr. **ἆτος,** *ον*, (*ἄω*) *insatiate*, c. gen., *ἄατος πολέμοιο* Hes. *Th.*714; *Ἄρης ἆτος πολέμοιο* Il.5.388; *μάχης ἆτόν περ ἐόντα* 22. 218: abs., *ἄατος ὕβρις* A.R.1.459. [First syll. short in Hes., long in A.R.]

ἄᾱτος, *ον*, = *ἄητος* (q.v.), Q.S.1.217.

ἀάτυλον· *ἀβλαβές*, Hsch.

ἀάω, Ep. Verb (twice in Trag., v. infr.), used by Hom. in aor. Act. *ἄᾰσα* (*ᾱᾶσαν* Od.10.68, later *ἄᾰσε* prob. in Matro *Conv.*29) contr. *ἆσα*, Med. *ἀᾰσάμην* (*ἀᾶσατο*, v.l. *ἀάσσατο*, Il.9.537) contr. *ἀσάμην*, Pass. *ἀάσθην*: pres. only in 3 sg. Med. *ἀᾶται* Il.19.91:—*hurt, damage*, always in reference to the mind, *mislead, infatuate*, of the effects of wine, sleep, divine judgements, etc., *ἄασάν μ' ἕταροί τε κακοὶ πρὸς τοῖσί τε ὕπνος* Od.10.68; *ἆσέ με δαίμονος αἶσα κακὴ καὶ* . . *οἶνος* 11.61; *φρένας ἄασε οἴνῳ* 21.297; of love, *θαλερὴ δέ μιν ἄασε Κύπρις* Epic. ap.Parth.21.2; inf. *ἆσαι* A.*Fr.*417; part. *ἄσας* S.*Fr.*628:—Med., *Ἄτη ἣ πάντας ἀᾶται* Il.19.91:—Pass., *Ἄτης, ᾗ πρῶτον ἀάσθην* Il. 19.136, cf. Hes.*Op.*283, *h.Cer.*258. II. Intr. in aor. Med., *to be infatuated, act foolishly*, *ἀασάμην* Il.9.116, etc.; *ἀάσατο δὲ μέγα θυμῷ* ib.537, 11.340; *καὶ γὰρ δή νύ ποτε Ζεὺς ἄσατο* 19.95, Aristarch., v.l. *Ζῆν' ἄσατο* (sc. *Ἄτη*), cf. Sch.Ven. ad loc.; *εἴ τί περ ἀασάμην* A.R.1.1333; *ἀασάμην* . . *ἄτην* 2.623. (*ἀϝάω*, cf. *ἀτάω.*)

ἄβα· *τρόχος, ἡ βοή*, Hsch. **ἀβάγητρον·** *λεπτόν*, Hsch., cf. *ἀβαήρ.* **ἄβαγνα·** *ῥόδα ἀμάραντα* (Maced.), Hsch. **ἀβάδιστος,** *ον*, *untrodden*, *πόντος* Sch.Opp.*H.*2.526. **ἄβαζος·** *ἥσυχος*, Suid. **ἀβαήρ·** *ὁ λεπτός*, Suid. **ἀβάθ·** *διδάσκαλος* (Cypr.), Hsch. **ἀβάθματα·** *στρέμματα*, Hsch.

ἀβᾰθής, *ές*, (*βάθος*) *not deep*, *φάλαγξ* Arr.*Tact.*5.6; *in single rank*, *ἡ ἐφ' ἑνὸς ἀ. τάξις* ib.17.5, *ἕλκεα* Aret.*SA*1.9, Gal.11.127. 2. Geom., *without depth*, *ἐπιφάνεια* S.E.*P.*3.43, cf. Simp.*in Ph.*572.25.

ἄβαθρος, *ον*, *without foundation*, Cyr.

ἀβαίνω· *στένω, οἰμώζω*, Cyr.

ἀβᾰκέω, (*ἀβακής*) *to be speechless*, only in aor., *οἱ δ' ἀβάκησαν πάντες said nothing, took no heed*, Od.4.249.

ἀβακηνούς· *τοὺς γυναικὶ μὴ ὁμιλήσαντας*, Phot., *AB*323.

ἀβᾰκής, *ές*, (*βάζω*) *speechless*: hence, *calm, gentle*, *ἀβάκην* (Aeol. acc.) *τὰν φρέν' ἔχω* Sapph.72. Adv. *–κέως, εὕδοντι* Poet.ap.*EM*2.57: —also **ἀβακήμων** Hsch., **ἄβαξ** *Lex.Rhet.*ap.Eust.1494.64.

ἀβάκητον· *ἀνεπίφθονον*, Hsch., Phot.

ἀβᾰκίζομαι, = *ἀβακέω*, Anacr.74.

ἀβάκιον, *τό*, = *ἄβαξ* I.1a, Lys.*Fr.*50, Alex.15.3, Plb.5.26.13. b. = *ἄβαξ* I.1b, Plu.*Cat.Mi.*90. 2. = *ἄβαξ* I.2, Poll.10.150. 3. pl., *slabs* (?) in theatre, Suid. s.v. *ἄβαξι.*

ἀβᾰκίσκος, *ὁ*, Dim. of *ἄβαξ*, *small stone for inlaying*, in mosaic work, Moschio ap.Ath.5.207c.

ἀβακλή· *ἅμαξα*, Cyr.

ἀβακοειδής, *ές*, *like an ἄβαξ*, Sch.Theoc.4.61.

ἄβακτον· *τὸν μὴ μακαριστόν* (Dor.), Phot., *AB*323; cf. *σαβάκτης.*

ἀβάκχευτος, *ον*, *uninitiated in Bacchic orgies*, E.*Ba.*472: generally, *joyless*, Id.*Or.*319:—in late Prose, Luc.*Lap.*3, Jul.*Or.*7.221d.

ἀβακχίωτος, *ον*, *having no part in Bacchus, undrinkable*, *ὄμβρος*, i.e. salt spray, Tim.*Pers.*72.

ἄβᾰλε [*ᾱβ*], properly *ἆ βάλε*, expressing a wish, *O that* . . *!* c. indic., Call.*Fr.*455; c. inf., *AP*7.699, *IPE*1^{2}.519 (Chersonesus); cf. *βάλε.*

ἀβαμβάκευτος, *ον*, *not seasoned*, of food, Pyrgion ap.Ath.4.143e.

ἄβαξ [*ᾰ*], *ἄκος*, *ὁ*, *slab, board*: 1. *reckoning-board*, used for counting votes, Arist.*Ath.*69.1. b. *board* sprinkled with sand or dust for drawing geometrical diagrams, S.E.*M.*9.282, Iamb.*Protr.* 34 (pl.), *VP*5.22. 2. *dice-board*, Caryst.3. 3. *sideboard*, Ammon.*Diff.*1. 4. *trencher, plate*, Cratin.86, cf. *BCH*29.510 (Delos, iii B.C.). II. in Lat. form *abacus*, *slab* on capital of column, Vitr.3.5.5. 2. *marble wall-slab*, Id.7.3.10. III. v. *ἀβακής.*

ἀβάπτιστος, *ον*, (*βαπτίζω*) *not to be dipped, that will not sink*, *ἀ. ἄλμας*, of a net, Pi.*P.*2.80; *ναῦς EM*811.26; *τρύπανον* trepan *with a guard, to stop it from going too deep*, Gal.10.447. II. *not drenched with liquor*, Plu.2.686b.

ἄβαπτος, *ον*, (*βάπτω*) of iron, *not tempered*, Hsch., Suid.

ἀβαρβάριστος, *ον*, *without barbarisms*, *Lex.Vind.*294. Adv. *–τως EM*331.37. **ἀβάρβαρος,** f.l. for *ἀβόρβορος*, q.v.

ἀβαρής, *ές*, (*βάρος*) *without weight*, Arist.*Cael.*$277^{b}19$; *ἀβαρῆ εἶναι ἀέρα καὶ πῦρ* Zeno *Stoic.*1.27, cf. Chrysipp.*Stoic.*2.143, Plot. 6.9.9, etc.; *light*, *γῆ AP*7.461 (Mel.): metaph., *ἀ. χρῆμα* a *light* matter, *Com.Adesp.*158; *παρρησία* . . *μαλακὴ καὶ ἀ.* Plu.2.59c; of the pulse, Archig.ap.Gal.8.651. II. *not offensive*, *ὀσμαί* Aret.*CA*2.3; of persons, *not burdensome*, *ἀ. ἑαυτὸν τηρεῖν, παρέχειν*, 2*Ep.Cor.*11.9, *CIG*5361.15 (Berenice). Adv. *–ρῶς without giving offence*, Simp.*in Epict.*p.85 D.; *without taking offence*, ib.p.88 D.

ἄβαρις, (*βᾶρις*) *having no boat, landsman*, Hsch. **ἀβαριστάν·** *γυναικιζομένην* (Cypr.), Id. **ἀβαρκνᾷ·** *κομᾷ* (Maced.), but **ἄβαρ-**

κνα· λιμός, Id. **ἀβαρλεῖται·** ταράσσεται, κροτεῖ, Id. **ἀβάρνου·** στένε, Id. **ἀβαρταί,** = πτηναί (Cypr.), Id. **ἀβαρύ,** = ὀρίγανον (Maced.), Id. **ἀβάς·** εὐήθης; also = ἱερὰ νόσος (Tarent.), Id. **ἀβάσαι·** ἀριστῆσαι, καὶ ἀρθῆναι, Id.

ἀβασάνιστος, ον, *not tortured,* ἀ. θνήσκειν J.*BJ*1.32.3, cf. Plu.2.275c; κημοῖς ὑπερῴαν ἀ. Ael.*NA*13.9. Adv. -τως *without pain,* βλέπειν τὸν ἥλιον ib.10.14. 2. *untried, unexamined,* ἀ. τι ἐᾶσαι Antipho 1.13; ἀπολιπεῖν Plb.4.75.3; παραλείπειν Plu.2.59c. Adv. -τως *without due examination,* Th.1.20, Plu.2.28b.

ἀβασίλευτος, ον, *not ruled by a king,* Th.2.80, X.*HG*5.2.17: generally, *free from rule,* Plu.2.1125d, Artem.1.8.

ἀβασκάνιστος, ον, *free from malice,* perh. to be read for ἀβασάν–, Plu.2.755d.

ἀβάσκᾰνος, ον, (βασκαίνω) *free from envy,* Teles p.56.1 H.; τὸ ἀ. Ph.1.252; *unprejudiced,* μάρτυς J.*BJ*1.9.4. Adv. -νως M.Ant.1.16.

ἀβάσκαντος, ον, *secure against enchantments, free from harm, CIG*5053,5119 (Nubia), *Cat.Cod.Astr.*7.234; esp. of children, *BGU* 8.11, al., *POxy.*300 (i A.D.):—in act. sense, *acting as a charm* or *protection against witchcraft,* ἀ. ἀνθρώποις καὶ ζῴοις v.l. in Dsc.3.91. Adv. -τως, ὑγιαίνειν *POxy.*292 (i A.D.), cf. *AP*11.267. II. Act., *not harming, PMag.Leid.W.*18.7.

ἀβάστακτος, ον, (βαστάζω) *not to be borne* or *carried,* Plu.*Ant.*16; *not removable,* σημεῖον *IGRom.*4.446 (Perg.). Adv. -τως Hsch.

ἄβαστον· ἄβατον, Hsch.

ἀβατόομαι, Pass., *to be made desert,* Lxx *Je.*29.20(21).

ἄβᾰτος, ον, also η, ον Pi.*N.*3.21:—*untrodden,* ἐρημία A.*Pr.*2 codd.; *impassable,* of mountains, Hdt.4.25, 7.176, S.*OT*719, etc.: ἀβάτου τῆς Ἑλλάδος οὔσης διὰ τὸν πόλεμον Isoc.3.33; of a river, *not fordable,* X.*An.*5.6.9; ἅλς Pi. l. c.; ὕλη Str.5.4.5; εἶναι εἰς ἄβατον to be made *desolate,* Lxx *Je.*29.17, al.: metaph., *inaccessible,* τὸ πόρσω σοφοῖς ἄ. κἀσόφοις Pi.*O.*3.44; οἰκίαι ἄ. τοῖς ἔχουσι μηδὲ ἕν Aristopho 3; ἀ. ποιεῖν τὰς τραπέζας Anaxipp.3; [τὸ ἀγαθὸν] ἐν ἀβάτοις ὑπεριδρυμένον Procl. *in Alc.*p.319C. 2. of holy places, *not to be trodden,* S.*OC*167,675; ἕρπει πλοῦτος.. ἐς τἄβατα καὶ πρὸς βέβηλα Id.*Fr.*88.7, cf. Porph.*Abst.* 4.11; ἄ. ἱερόν Pl.*La.*183b; ἀβατώτατος ὁ τόπος (sc. οἱ τάφοι) Arist. *Pr.*924^{a}5: metaph., *pure, chaste,* ψυχή Pl.*Phdr.*245a. b. as Subst., ἄβατον, τό, *adytum,* Theopomp.Hist.313, *IG*4.952 (Epidaur.), etc.; = *bidental,* Διὸς καταιβάτου ἄ. ib.2.1659b. 3. metaph., φύσις ἄ. οἴκτῳ Ph.2.53. 4. of a horse, *not ridden,* Luc.*Zeux.*6; of female animals, Id.*Lex.*19. 5. ἄβατον, τό, a plant eaten pickled, Gal.6.623. II. Act., ἄ. πόνος a plague *that hinders walking,* i.e. gout, Luc.*Ocyp.*36; ὑποδήματα Phot., Suid. s. v. ἀναξυρίδας.

ἀβᾰφής, ές, = ἄβαπτος, v. sub ἀναφής:—also **-ος,** ον, *Gloss.*

ἄβδελον· ταπεινόν, Hsch.

ἀβδέλυκτος, ον, (βδελύσσω) *not to be abominated,* A.*Fr.*137.

Ἀβδηρίτης [ῑ], ου, ὁ, *a man of Abdera* in Thrace, the *Gothamite* of antiquity, prov. of simpletons, D.17.23:—Adj. **Ἀβδηριτικός,** ή, όν, *like an Abderite,* i.e. *stupid,* Cic.*Att.*7.7.4, Luc.*Hist.Conscr.*2.

ἄβδης, ὁ, said by Hsch. to mean *scourge* in Hippon.98.

ἀβέβαιος, ον, *unreliable,* of remedies, Hp.*Aph.*2.27; ἀβεβαιότατον ὧν κεκτήμεθα (sc. πλοῦτος) Alex.281, cf. Men.128; ὀφθαλμὸς ἀ. *unsteady,* Arist.*HA*492^{a}12: metaph., τύχη Democr.176, cf. Plb. 15.34.2; αἰτία Epicur.*Ep.*3,p.65U.; φιλία Arist.*EE*1236^{b}19; τὸ ἀ. = ἀβεβαιότης, Hierocl. *in CA*2p.422 M., Heraclit.*Ep.*7; ἐξ ἀβεβαίου from *an insecure position,* Arr.*An.*1.15.2. 2. of persons, *unstable, fickle,* D.58.63, Arist.*EN*1172^{a}9. Adv. -ως Men.*Georg.Fr.*2.

ἀβεβαιότης, ητος, ἡ, *instability,* τῆς τύχης Plb.30.10.1; of persons, D.S.14.9, cf. Ph.1.276.

ἀβέβηλος, ον, *sacred, inviolable,* Plu.*Brut.*20, cf. *Cam.*30; of persons, *pure, Inscr.Prien.*113.67.

ἄβεις· ἔχεις, Hsch. **ἀβέλιος,** i.e. ἀϝέλιος, Cret. for ἥλιος, ἥλιος, Hsch.

ἄβελλον· ταπεινόν, Hsch.

ἀβελτέρειος, α, ον, lengthd. for **ἀβέλτερος,** as ἡμετέρειος for ἡμέτερος, Hdn.Gr.1.137; prob. (for -ίου) in Anaxandr.12 (Dind.).

ἀβελτερεύομαι, *play the fool,* Epicur.*Nat.*89G.

ἀβελτερία, ἡ, *silliness, fatuity,* Pl.*Tht.*174c, *Smp.*198d, D.19.98, Arist.*Pol.*1315^{a}3, etc.; ἀ. καὶ νωθρότης Id.*Rh.*1390^{b}30; pl., Phld. *Lib.*p.41O.

ἀβελτεροκόκκυξ, υγος, ὁ, *silly fellow,* Pl.Com.64.

ἀβέλτερος, ον, (α, ον Pl.*Phlb.*48c) *silly, stupid,* Ar.*Nu.*1201, Antiph. 324, Pl.*R.*409c, etc.; δόξαι Polystr.p.29W.; πρός τι Anaxandr.21; ἀ. τι παθεῖν D.19.338: c. inf., ἀ. ἀντιτείνειν Hierocl. *in CA*10p.434M.: irreg. Comp. ἀβελτερέστερος (s.v.l.) Gal.18(2).337: Sup. -ώτατος Ar.*Ra.*989; of Margites, Hyp.*Lyc.*7. Adv. -ρως Polystr. l. c., Plu. 2.127e. (Comic formation, cf. βέλτερος.)

ἀβέρβηλον· πολύ, ἐπαχθές, μέγα, βαρύ, ἀχάριστον, μάταιον, Hsch., cf. -λος· ἀκατάστατος, Suid.; cf. ἀβύρβηλος.

ἀβηδών, i.e. ἀϝηδών, for ἀηδών (prob. Lacon.), Hsch. **ἀβήρ,** i.e. ἀϝήρ, Lacon. word for οἴκημα στοὰς ἔχον, Id.; cf. αὐήρ. **ἀβήρει·** ᾄδει, **ἀβηροῦσιν·** ᾄδουσιν, Id. **ἀβής·** ἀναίσχυντος, ἀνόσιος, Id. **ἀβήσσει·** ἐπινοεῖ, Id.

ἀβίαστος, ον, (βιάζομαι) *unforced, without force* or *violence,* Pl.*Ti.* 61a; τὸ ἀ. φυλάξει *shall maintain order, PThead.*19.21. 2. *unstrained, unaffected,* χάρις D.H.*Dem.*38. 3. *not liable to compulsion,* ἀ. τὸ ἀπαθεῖ Porph.ap.Eus.*PE*5.10. 4. *irresistible,* Sch.Opp.*H.* 2.8. 5. Adv. -τως Arist.*MA*703^{a}22, Aët.9.28, Simp. *in Epict.* p.117D.

ἀβίβαστος, ον, = ἄβατος, *POxy.*1380.115, *Gloss.*

ἀβίβλης, ου, ὁ, *without books,* Tz.*H.*6.407,475.

ἄβιδα· ἀνδρεῖον, Hsch.

ἄβιν· ἐλάτην, οἱ δὲ πεύκην, Hsch. **ἀβίολη·** σπέρμα ἐμφερές.., Id.

ἄβιος, ον (A), = ἀβίωτος, βίος *AP*7.715 (Leon.). 2. *not to be survived,* αἰσχύνη Pl.*Lg.*873c. II. *without a living, starving,* Luc.*D.Mort.*15.3, Man.4.113, Vett.Val.46.12; ἄτεκνος καὶ ἄ. καὶ προώλης, an imprecatory form in *CIG*3915.46 (Hierapolis). III. perh. *having no fixed subsistence, nomad,* Ἱππημολγῶν γλακτοφάγων ἀβίων τε Il.13.6 (various expl. in Nic.Dam.p.145 D.); but prob. Ἀβίων, pr. n., cf. Arr.*An.*4.1.1, Str.7.3.2, etc.; Ἄ. Σαυρομάται *Mus. Belg.*16.70 (Attic, ii A.D.).

ἄβιος, ον (B), (α intensive) *wealthy,* Antipho Soph.43.

ἀβίοτος, ον, *making life unliveable,* κατακονὰ ἀ. βίου, ἀ. βίου τύχα E.*Hipp.*821,868; βίοτος *AP*9.574 (v.l. κοὐ βίοτον).

ἀβίυκτον (-ηκ- cod.)· ἐφ' οὗ οὐκ ἐγένετο βοὴ ἀπολλυμένου, Hsch. (For ἀϝίυκτον, cf. ἰύζω.)

ἀβιωτοποιός, όν, *making life insupportable,* Sch.E.*Hipp.*821.

ἀβίωτος, ον, (βιόω) *not to be lived, insupportable,* ἀ. πεποίηκε τὸν βίον Ar.*Pl.*969; ἀ. ζῶμεν βίον Philem.93.7, cf. 90.7, Boeth.*Stoic.*3. 266; ἀ. χρόνον βιοτεῦσαι E.*Alc.*242; ἀ. φέτ' ἔσεσθαι τὸν βίον αὐτῷ D.21.131; ἀ. ἡγουμένων τὸ καταγνωσθῆναι Phld.*Mort.*35:—ἀβίωτόν [ἐστι] *life is intolerable,* Pl.*R.*407a; ἀ. ζῆν Id.*Lg.*926b; ἀ. ἡμῖν E.*Ion* 670. Adv. ἀβιώτως, ἔχειν Plu.*Dio*6; αἰσχρῶς καὶ ἀ. διατεθῆναι Id. *Sol.*7. II. ἀβίωτον, τό, = κώνειον, Ps.-Dsc.4.78.

ἀβλάβ-εια, ἡ, *freedom from harm,* σαρκός Plu.2.1090b; for A.*Ag.* 1024 v. εὐλάβεια. II. Act., *harmlessness,* Cic.*Tusc.*3.8.16. **-ής,** ές, *without harm,* i.e., I. Pass., *unharmed, unhurt,* Sapph. *Supp.*1.1, Pi.*O.*13.27, *P.*8.54, A.*Th.*68, X.*Cyr.*4.1.3, Pl.*R.*342b, etc.; ζῶσαν ἀβλαβεῖ βίῳ S.*El.*650. Adv. ἀβλαβῶς, Ion. -έως, *safely,* ζώειν Thgn.1154; ἔχειν Dexipp.p.148 D., cf. Arr.*An.*6.19.2: Sup. -έστατα X.*Eq.*6.1:—*securely,* ἐδήσατο σάνδαλα *h.Merc.*83. II. Act., *not harming, harmless, innocent,* ξυνουσία A.*Eu.*285; ἡδοναί Pl.*R.*357b, etc.; ἀ. σπασμοί *doing no serious injury,* Hp.*Epid.*1.6; τὸ πρὸς ἀνθρώπους ἀ. Phld.*Piet.*65: c. gen., ἀ. τῶν πλησίον Porph.*Sent.*32: c. dat., Eus.Mynd.1. Adv. -ῶς, c. dat., *without harm to,* τῇ γαστρί Metrod.41. 2. *averting* or *preventing harm,* ὕδωρ Theoc.24. 98:—in Pl.*Lg.*953b we have the act. and pass. senses conjoined, ἀ. τοῦ δρᾶσαί τε καὶ παθεῖν. 3. in treaties, *without violating the terms,* ἀβλαβῶς σπονδαῖς ἐμμένειν, coupled with δικαίως and ἀδόλως, Th.5.18 and 47: so in Adj., ξύμμαχοι πιστοὶ.. καὶ ἀ. *IG*1. 33. **-ία,** ἡ, poet. for ἀβλάβεια II, ἀβλαβίῃσι νόοιο *h.Merc.*393; Ἀβλαβίαι personified, *SIG*1014.67 (Erythrae); sg. in later Prose, Phld.*Piet.*28.

ἀβλαβύνιον· σειρὰ πλεκομένη παρ' Αἰγυπτίοις ἐκ βύβλων ⟨πρὸς⟩ κάθαρσιν οὖσα, Hsch. **ἀβλαδέως·** ἡδέως, Id. (cf. βλαδαρός). **ἀβλάξ·** λαμπρῶς (Cypr.), Id.

ἄβλαπτος, ον, = ἀβλαβής II, Nic.*Th.*488. Adv. -τως Orph.*H.*64. 10.

ἄβλαροι· ξύλα, Hsch. **ἄβλας·** ἀσύνετος, Hsch. (ἀβλής Cyr.).

ἀβλαστ-έω, *not to run to leaf,* Thphr.*CP*1.20.5. II. *not to germinate,* of seeds, Id.*Ign.*44. **-ος,** ον, *not growing out,* of fibre, Id.*HP*1.2.5:—also **-ής,** ές, *not growing,* ib.2.2.8; of seeds, *not germinating,* 8.11.7; of places, *unfruitful,* ἐδάφη *CP*2.4.1; τόποι *Gp.* 9.9.4 (Comp.): metaph., ἀ. πρὸς ἀρετήν Plu.2.38c; πλοῦτος ἄ. Them. *Or.*18.221d. **-ητος,** ον, *not striking from cuttings,* v.l. Thphr. *CP*1.3.2.

ἄβλαυτος, ον, (βλαύτη) *unslippered,* Opp.*C.*4.369, Philostr.Jun. *Im.*5.

ἀβλεμής, ές, (βλεμεαίνω) *feeble,* Nic.*Al.*82; in Lit. Crit. [τὸ πρᾶγμα] ἀβλεμὲς προσπίπτει falls *flat,* Longin.29.1. Adv. ἀβλεμέως, πίνων drinking *intemperately,* Panyas.13.8.

ἀβλεννής, ές, (βλέννα) without *mucus,* Apollon.*Lex.*51.32 (glossed by ἄχυμος); as name of fish, = βελόνη II, Diph.Siph.ap.Ath.8.355f.

ἀβλεπτ-έω, *overlook, disregard,* τὸ πρέπον Plb.30.6.4, Anon.ap. Suid.; Pass., τὰ -ηθέντα Hp.*Decent.*13. **-ῆ·** τὸν ἀβλεπτεῦντα, Hsch. **-ημα,** τό, *mistake, oversight,* Plb.*Fr.*90, Arr.*Epict. Fr.*12. **-ος,** ον, = ἀτέκμαρτος, Sch.Opp.*H.*1.773. 2. Astrol., = ἀσύνδετος, Firm.2.23.7.

ἀβλέφᾰρος, ον, *without eyebrows, AP*11.66 (Antiphil.).

ἀβλεψία, ἡ, *blindness,* metaph., Suet.*Claud.*39, Hierocl. *in CA*25 p.477M.: c. gen., *failure to see,* Polystr.p.31W. II. *invisibility, PMag.Leid.W.*7.5.

ἄβληρα, i.e. ἄϝληρα, for αὔληρα, εὔληρα (q.v.), Hsch.

ἀβλής, ῆτος, ὁ, ἡ, (βάλλω) *not thrown* or *shot,* ἰὸν ἀβλῆτα an arrow *not yet used,* Il.4.117; cf. A.R.3.279.

ἀβλήτηρες· μάρτυρες, Hsch.

ἄβλητος, ον, *not hit* (by missiles), opp. ἀνούτατος, Il.4.540.

ἀβληχής, ές, (βληχή) *without bleatings,* ἐπαύλιον *AP*9.149 (Antip.).

ἀβληχρής, ές, gen. έος, = ἀβληχρός, *mild, soothing,* Nic.*Th.* 885.

ἀβληχρός, ά, όν, (α euphon., βληχρός, q.v.):—*weak, feeble,* of Aphrodite's hand, Il.5.337; τείχεα 8.178; θάνατος an *easy* death in ripe old age, opp. a *violent* one, Od.11.135, 23.282; πόνος Epicur. *Sent.Vat.*4; κῶμα A.R.2.205; πυρετός Procop.*Pers.*2.22.

ἀβλοπές· ἀβλαβές, Hsch. **ἀβλοπία,** ἡ, Cret. = ἀβλάβεια, *GDI* 4986 (Gortyn), 5125 (Oaxos), cf. Hsch.

ἀβοαί· εὐχαί, Hsch.

ἀβοᾱτί, -ατος, Dor. for ἀβοητί, -ητος.

ἀβοηθ-ησία, ἡ, *helplessness*, Lxx *Si.*51.10. **–ητος**, ον, *admitting of no help, without remedy, incurable*, of disease, Hp.*Acut.* (*Sp.*)33; πάθος Plu.2.454d; of wounds, Plb.1.81.5, etc.; *fatal*, of poisons, Thphr.*HP*9.16.6; ἀ. ἔχειν τὴν ἐπικουρίαν, *unserviceable, useless*, D.S.20.42; νὺξ ἀ. Gal.19.481. Adv. –τως Dsc.*Ther.*12, Gal. 5.122. II. of persons, *helpless*, Lxx *Ps.*87(88).6, Plu.*Arat.*2, Epict.*Ench.*24; γυνὴ χήρα καὶ ἀ. *BGU*970.8 (ii A.D.). III. Act., *unhelpful*, ἀφιλανθρωπία –ήτους ποιεῖ Phld.*Oec.*p.68J.

ἀβοηθί, Adv. *without assistance*, prob. in Euph.54.2.

ἀβοητί, Dor. –ᾱτί, Adv. (βοάω) *without summons*, Pi.*N.*8.9.

ἀβόητος, Dor. –ᾱτος, ον, (βοάω) *not loudly lamented*, *Epigr.Gr.* 240 (Smyrna). 2. *not noised abroad*, [κλέος] οὐκ ἀ. *IG*2.4174.

ἀβολαία (–βαλ– cod.)· συγγραφή, ὁμολογία, Hsch. **ἀβολεῖς**· περιβολαί (Sicel.), Hsch.

ἀβολέω, later Ep. for ἀντιβολέω, *meet*, A.R.3.1145; Ep. aor. ἀβόλησαν Id.2.770, Call.*Fr.*455.

ἀβολ-ητύς, ύος, ἡ, *a meeting*, Ion. word, Antim.[108]. **–ήτωρ**, ορος, ὁ, *one who meets*, Id.58.

ἀβόλλα, ἡ, = Lat. *abolla, thick woollen cloak*, *Peripl.M.Rubr.*6, *CPR*1.27 (ii A.D.).

ἄβολος, ον, (βολή) *that has not shed his foal-teeth*, of a young horse, S.*Fr.*408, Pl.*Lg.*834c, Stratt.52, Arist.*HA*576^{b}15, *IG*2.978: also of an old horse, *that no longer sheds them*, *AB*322. 2. ἄβολα, τά, *an unlucky throw* of the dice, Poll.7.204.

ἀβόρβορος, ον, *without filth*, ψαλὶς οὐκ ἀ. S.*Fr.*367 (–βάρβ– codd.).

Ἀβοριγῖνες, οἱ, = Lat. *aborigines*, D.H.1.9, al.

ἄβορος, ον, *greedy*, Hdn.Gr.ap.Sch.Il.8.178.

ἀβοσκ-ής, ές, (βόσκω) *unfed, fasting*, Nic.*Th.*124. **–ητος**, ον, *pastureless*, ὄρη Babr.45.10, cf. Eust.307.27.

ἄβοστοι· οἱ αἴτησιν ὑπὸ Λακώνων, Hsch.

ἄβοτος, ον, (βόσκω) *without pasture*, Hsch.

ἀβουκόλητος, ον, (βουκολέω) *untended*: metaph., *unheeded*, ἀ. τοῦτ' ἐμῷ φρονήματι A.*Supp.*929.

ἀβουλ-εί, Adv. *inconsiderately*, Suid.:—also –ί, Ph.1.124.

ἀβούλευτος, ον, *ill-advised, inconsiderate*. Adv. –τως Lxx 1*Ma.* 5.67.

ἀβουλ-έω, *to be unwilling*, Pl.*R.*437c: c. acc. inf., Id.*Ep.*347a:—c. acc., *dislike, object to*, D.C.55.9. II. *not to will*, οὐ γὰρ –ῶν ἐνεργεῖ *without willing*, Plot.6.8.13, cf. ib.21. **–ητος**, ον, (βούλομαι) *involuntary*, Pl.*Lg.*733d, Ph.1.561; ἀ. καρδίας κίνησις, ἔκκρισις Gal.2.610, Aët.13.56. Adv. –τως Asclep.Cypr.ap.Porph.*Abst.*4.15, Plu.2.631c, S.E.*P.*1.19. II. *not according to one's wish* or *will*, τὰ ἀ. Zeno*Stoic.*1.53; τύχη Phld.*Mort.*33, cf. Ph.2.392, Plu.2. 599b. **–ία**, ἡ, *ill-advisedness, thoughtlessness*, Pi.*O.*10.41, Hdt.7. 210, Antipho4.2.6, Men.16.9D., etc.; ἐπαρθέντες ἀβουλίῃ Hdt.7.9. γ'; ἐξ ἀ. πεσεῖν, ἀβουλίᾳ πεσεῖν S.*El.*398,429: pl., A.*Th.*750, Hdt. 8.57. 2. *irresolution*, Th.5.75; *indecision*, Democr.119. **–ος**, ον, *inconsiderate, ill-advised*, S.*Ant.*1026, Men.*Pk.*382, *Anacreont.*12. 4; τέκνοισι Ζῆν' ἄβουλον *taking no thought* for them, *unfeeling*, S.*Tr.* 140, cf. *El.*546, E.*Heracl.*152: Comp., Th.1.120.7: Sup., Plu.*Dio*43. Adv. –ως Hdt.3.71; οὐκ ἀ. Pherecr.143.6; ἀ. καὶ ἀθέως Antipho 1. 23: Sup. ἀβουλότατα Hdt.7.9.β', Plb.*Fr.*92.

ἀβουσκολεῖ· θορυβεῖ, Hsch.

ἀβούτης, ου, ὁ, (βοῦς) *without oxen*, i.e. *poor*, Hes.*Op.*451.

ἄβουτον· τὴν οὐλίαν (Arg.), Hsch.

ἅβρα, ἡ, *favourite slave*, Men.64.3, al., Lxx *Ge.*24.61, *Ex.*2.5, al., Plu.*Caes.*10, Aristaen.1.22, Luc.*Tox.*14. (Prob. Semitic; written by some Gramm. ἄβρα, cf. *AB*322.)

ἀβράβεσθαι· ἀβρύνεσθαι, Hsch.

ἀβραμίδιον, τό, Dim. of sq., Xenocr.78.

ἀβρᾱμίς, or **ἄβραμις**, ιδος, ἡ (also **ἀβραβίς**, *PLond.ined.*2184 (iii A.D.)), kind of *mullet*, salted in Egypt, Ath.7.312b, *PLond.ined.* 2143 (ii A.D.), Opp.*H.*1.244.

ἀβραμύας, ὁ, *throw at dice*, Hsch. **ἀβράνας**, Celtic word = κερκοπίθηκος, Id. **ἀβρανίδας**· κροκευτούς (Lacon.), Id.

ἄβραχος, ον, prob. = ἄβροχος, *not steeped*, στροβίλια *PMag.Berol.* 1.245.

ἄβρεκτος, ον, = ἄβροχος, Hp.*Aff.*52, Plu.2.381c, Mosch.2.114.

ἀβρεμής· ἀβλεπτής (Cypr.), Hsch.

ἀβρίζομαι, Med. or Pass., = ἀβρύνομαι, Hsch. (in Lacon. form –ίδδ–).

ἀβρῑθής, ές, *of no weight*, βάρος μὲν οὐκ ἀβριθές E.*Supp.*1125.

ἄβρικτος, ον, (βρίζω) *wakeful*, Hsch., Suid.:—**ἀβρίξ**, Adv., Hsch.

ἀβρινά· κεκαθαρμένα, Hsch. **ἀβριστήν**· μαστιγίαν, Id.

ἀβρο-βάτης, ου, ὁ, *softly* or *delicately stepping*, A.*Pers.*1072; Subst. in B.3.48. **–βιος**, ον, *living delicately, effeminate*, Ἴωνες B.17.2, cf. Plu.*Demetr.*2 (Sup.), D.P.968, Alciphr.1.12. **–βόστρυχος**, ον, = ἀβροκόμης, Tz.*H.*1.230. **–γοος**, ον, *wailing womanishly*, A.*Pers.*541. **–δαις**, ὁ, ἡ, *luxurious*, ἀβρόδαιτι τραπέζῃ Archestr. *Fr.*61.1. **–δίαιτα**, ἡ, *luxurious living*, a faulty compd., *AB*322, Suid., Ael.*VH*12.24 (in lemmate). **–δίαιτος**, ον, *living delicately*, ἀβροδιαίτων Λυδῶν ὄχλος A.*Pers.*41, cf. Epigr.ap.Clearch.4: τὸ ἀ. *effeminacy*, Th.1.6, Ath.12.513c; ἀ. βίος, *luxurious*, Diog.Oen.23. Adv. –τως Ph.1.324. **–είμων**, ον, (εἷμα) *softly clad*, *Com.Adesp.* 1275. **–καρπον**, = ἀβρότονον, Hsch.

ἀβρο-κόμης, ου, ὁ, *with luxuriant foliage*, φοῖνιξ E.*Ion*920, *IT* 1099. II. *with delicate hair*, Orph.*H.*56.2, Nonn.*D.*13.91, al.; (with play on both meanings) *AP*12.256 (Mel.):—also **–κομος**, ον, Nonn.*D.*13.456, Man.2.446.

ἀβρομία· σκοτεία, Hsch.

ἀβρόμιος, ον, *without Bacchus*, *AP*6.291 (Antip.).

ἀβρομίτρης, ου, ὁ, *with dainty girdle*, Hsch.

ἄβρομος, ον, (α collect.) *joining in a shout*, Il.13.41; taken by Aristarch. to mean *noisy* (α intens.). 2. (α priv.) *noiseless*, κῦμα A.R.4.153. II. v. ἄβρωμος.

ἀβροπάρθενοι χοροί, *consisting of delicate maidens*, *Lyr.Alex.Adesp.* 22.

ἀβρο-πέδῑλος, ον, *soft-sandalled*, Ἔρως *AP*12.158 (Mel.). **–πενθής**, ές, v. ἀκροπενθής. **–πέτηλος**, ον, *with soft leaves*, Jo.Gaz.*Ecphr.* 2.2. **–πηνος**, ον, (πήνη) *of delicate texture*, Lyc.863. **–πλουτος**, ον, *richly luxuriant*, χαίτη E.*IT*1148.

ἁβρός, ά, όν, poet. also ός, όν:—*graceful, delicate, pretty*, παρθένος Hes.*Fr.*218; παῖς, Ἔρως Anacr.17,65; ἅβραι Χάριτες Sapph.60; esp. of the body, σῶμα, πούς, etc., Pi.*O.*6.55, E.*Tr.*506; neut. pl., ἁβρὰ παρηίδος *Ph.*1486; of women, A.*Fr.*313, S.*Tr.*523; ἁ. ἄθυρμα, of a pet dog, *IG*14.1647 (Lipara): of things, *splendid*, στέφανος, κῦδος, πλοῦτος Pi.*I.*8.65, *O.*5.7, *P.*3.110: of style, *graceful, pretty*, λόγος Hermog.*Id.*2.5; freq. with a notion of disparagement, *dainty, luxurious*; hence, ἁβρὰ παθεῖν live *delicately*, Sol.24.4, Thgn.474; a common epithet of Asiatics, Hdt.1.71, etc.; Ἰώνων ἁβρὸς.. ὄχλος Antiph. 91; Ἀγάθυρσοι –ότατοι ἀνδρῶν Hdt.4.104. Adv. ἁβρῶς, ψάλλειν Anacr.17; ὑμνεῖν Stesich.37; βαίνειν step *delicately*, Sapph.5, E.*Med.* 831: neut. sg. as Adv., ἁβρὸν βαίνοντες E.*Med.*1164; neut. pl., ἁβρὰ γελᾶν *Anacreont.*41.3, 42.5: Comp. ἁβροτέρως, ἔχειν Hld.1.17.—Chiefly poet., never in old Ep.; rare in early Prose, X.*Smp.*4.44, Pl.*Smp.*204c, Clearch.4. [ᾰ by nature, cf. E.*Med.*1164, *Tr.*820.]

ἁβροσία, ἡ, = ἁβροσύνη, Sch.E.*Or.*349.

ἁβροσταγής, ές, (στάζω) *dropping rich unguents*, μέτωπον Anon. ap.Suid. s.v. ἁβρός.

ἁβροσύνη, ἡ, = ἁβρότης, Sapph.79, E.*Or.*349, Xenoph.3.1 (pl.).

ἁβρόσφυρος, ον, *with delicate ankles*, Ναΐδες *Lyr.Alex.Adesp.*3.3.

ἀβροτάζω, *miss*, c. gen., only in aor. 1 subj., μήπως ἀβροτάξομεν (Ep. for –ωμεν) ἀλλήλοιϊν Il.10.65:—Subst. **ἀβρόταξις**, εως, ἡ, *error*, Hsch., Eust.789.52: Adj. **ἀβροτήμων**, ον, *erring*, in Hsch., *AB*322. (For ἀμβροτάζω, cf. ἀμβροτ-εῖν, ἁμαρτ-εῖν.)

ἁβρότης, ητος, ἡ, *splendour, luxury*, δόμους ἁβρότατος houses *of luxury*, i.e. *luxurious*, Pi.*P.*11.34, cf. B.*Fr.*26; τῇ Μήδων στολῇ καὶ ἁβρότητι X.*Cyr.*8.8.15, cf. Pl.*Alc.*1.122c, E.*Ba.*968; οὐκ ἐν ἁβρότητι κεῖσαι thou art not in a position *to be fastidious*, Id.*IA*1343; also, ἁβρότατος ἔπι in *the freshness of youth*, Pi.*P.*8.89. II. of style, *sweetness, charm*, Hermog.*Id.*1.12.

ἁβρότῑμος, ον, *delicate and costly*, προκαλύμματα A.*Ag.*690 (lyr.).

ἀβροτίνη, ἡ, = ἁμαρτωλή, Hsch.; cf. ἀβροτάζω.

ἀβροτόν-ινος, η, ον, *made of* ἀβρότονον, ἔλαιον Dsc.1.50. **–ίτης** οἶνος wine *prepared with* ἀβρότονον, Dsc.5.52.

ἀβρότονον or **ἀβρ–**, τό, *wormwood*, *Artemisia arborescens*, Thphr. *HP*6.7.3, Nic.*Th.*92, etc.; ἀ. ἄρρεν, *southernwood*, *Artemisia fragrans*, Gal.11.804; ἀ. θῆλυ, *lavender cotton*, *Santolina Chamaecyparissus*, Dsc.3.24; written ἀβούτονον Ps.-Dsc. l.c.

ἄβροτος, ον, also η, ον, = ἄμβροτος (q. v.), *holy*, in Hom. only once, νὺξ ἀβρότη Il.14.78; ἀβρότη alone, = νύξ, Eust. ad loc. II. *without men, deserted of men*, ἄβροτον εἰς ἐρημίαν v.l. for ἄβατον A.*Pr.*2, as quoted by Sch.Ven.Il.14.78.

ἀβροχαίτης, ου, ὁ, = ἀβροκόμης, *Anacreont.*41.8.

ἀβροχ-έω, *not to be inundated*, *BGU*973.14, *PFay.*33 (ii A.D.), etc. **–ία**, ἡ, *want of rain, drought*, Men.Eph.ap.J.*AJ*8.13.2, Heph.*Astr.*1.23, S.E.*M.*9.203. 2. in Egypt, *failure of the inundation* of the Nile, *OGI*56.15 (pl., iii B.C.), cf. *CPHerm.*119 ii 22 (iii A.D.). **–ικός**, ή, όν, = ἄβροχος, *PFlor.*286.23 (vi A.D.). **–ιστος**, ον, = foreg., *PGoodsp.*15.22 (iv A.D.). **–ος**, ον, (βρέχω) *unwetted, unmoistened*, Aeschin.2.21, Nic.*Th.*339, Sotion p.183W.; κατὰ πόντον ἄ. ἀΐσσεις Mosch.2.143 (v.l. ἄτρομος): c. gen., ἅλμης Nonn.*D.*1.75. Adv. –χως *without getting wet*, Lib.*Or.*11.217. 2. *wanting rain, waterless*, πεδία E.*Hel.*1485; Ἀρκαδίη Call.*Jov.*19. 3. *not inundated*, *PHib.*1.85 (iii B.C.), *BGU*455 (i A.D.), etc.

ἀβροχίτων [ῐ], ωνος, ὁ, ἡ, *in soft tunic, softly clad*, *AP*9.538; epith. of Dionysus, *Inscr.Cos*5.11; εὐνὰς ἀβροχίτωνας beds *with soft coverings*, A.*Pers.*543.

ἄβρυνα (ἄβρ– Hsch.), τά, *mulberries* (Cypr.), Parth.ap.Ath.2. 51f, cf. *AB*224.

ἁβρ-υντής, οῦ, ὁ, *coxcomb, fop*, Adam.1.23. **–ύνω**, (ἁβρός) *make delicate, treat delicately*, μὴ γυναικὸς ἐν τρόποις ἐμὲ ἄβρυνε A.*Ag.* 919; *deck out*, εἰς γάμον ἁβρῦναί τινα *AP*6.281 (Leon.):—Med. or Pass., *live delicately*; hence, *wax wanton, give oneself airs*, ἁβρύνεται γὰρ πᾶς τις εὖ πράσσων πλέον A.*Ag.*1205, cf. S.*OC*1339; ἐκαλλυνόμην τε καὶ ἡβρυνόμην ἄν Pl.*Ap.*20c: c. dat. rei, *pride, plume oneself on* a thing, οὐχ ἁβρύνομαι τῷδ' E.*IA*858; ἡβρύνετο τῷ βραδέως διαπράττειν X.*Ages.*9.2; οἷς ὁ τῶν γυναικῶν ἁβρύνεται βίος Clearch.9.

ἄβρυστος· ἡ ἄβροστος ἢ ὁ βιβρωσκόμενος, Hsch. **ἀβρυτός**, = βρύσσος, Id.

ἄβρωμα, τό, *a woman's garment*, Hsch.

ἄβρωμος, ον, *free from smell*, Diph.Siph.ap.Ath.8.355b, Xenocr. 9, Dsc.1.16, Aët.9.1. (ἄβρομος is a common v.l.)

Ἅβρων, ωνος, ὁ, *Abron*, an Argive, proverbial for luxurious living, Ἅβρωνος βίος Suid., Zen.1.4.

ἀ-βρώς, ῶτος, ὁ, ἡ, *not devoured*; hence, *not bitten* by mosquitoes, *AP*9.764 (Paul. Sil.). **–βρωσία**, ἡ, *want of food, fasting*, Poll.

6.39. **-βρωτος**, ον, (βιβρώσκω) *uneatable, not good for food*, κρέα Ctes.*Fr.*57.26, cf. Arist.*HA*618^{a}1, Phanias Hist.34, Thphr.*HP*3.12. 2; ὀστᾶ Men.129. 2. *not eaten*, Nic.*Fr.*74.44; οὐθὲν ἄ. περιλείποντες Porph.*Abst.*2.27:—of wood, *not eaten* by worms, Thphr.*HP* 5.1.2. II. of persons, *without eating*, S.*Fr.*967; ἄ., ἄποτος Charito 6.3.

Ἄβῡδος, ἡ, *Abydos*, on the Asiatic side of the Hellespont:—**Ἀβυδόθεν**, Adv. *from Abydos*, Il.4.500; **Ἀβυδόθι**, *at Abydos*, 17. 584:—Adj. **Ἀβυδηνός**, ή, όν, *of* or *from Abydos*, Ath.13.572e, etc.: prov., Ἀ. ἐπιφόρημα a dessert *of Abydos*, i.e. *something unpleasant*, variously expl., Zen.1.1, etc.; μὴ εἰκῇ τὴν Ἄβυδον (sc. πατεῖν) Paus.Gr.*Fr.*2: **Ἀβυδοκόμης** (Ἀβυδηνοκώμης or -κόμος Zen. 1.1), ου, ὁ, = ὁ ἐπὶ τῷ συκοφαντεῖν κομῶν, Ar.*Fr.*733.

ἀβύθητος, ον, = sq., Sch.Opp.*H.*2.216.

ἄβυθος, ον, = ἄβυσσος, εἴς τινα ἄ. φλυαρίαν Pl.*Prm.*130d (sed leg. εἴς τινα βυθὸν φλυαρίας).

ἀβύρ-βηλος, = ἀβέρ-, Hsch., Phot., Suid.; -**βητος**, *EM*4.52.

ἀβύρσευτος, ον, *untanned*, Sch.Il.2.527.

ἀβυρτ-άκη [ᾰκ], ἡ, *sour sauce of leeks, cress, and pomegranate-seeds*, Pherecr.181, Theopomp.Com.17, Alex.141.13, Nymphod.19, Polyaen.4.3.32. **-ἀκοποιός**, όν, *making* ἀβυρτάκη, Demetr. Com.Nov.1.5. **-ἀκώδης**, ες, *like* ἀβυρτάκη, Hsch. s.v. νεοδάρτης.

ἄβυσσος, ον, *bottomless, unfathomed*, πηγαί Hdt.2.28; ἄτης ἄβυσσον πέλαγος A.*Supp.*470; χάσματα E.*Ph.*1605; λίμνη Ar.*Ra.*137: generally, *unfathomable, boundless*, πλοῦτος A.*Th.*948; ἀργύριον Ar. *Lys.*174; φρένα Δίαν καθορᾶν, ὄψιν ἄβυσσον A.*Supp.*1058. II. ἡ ἄ. *the great deep*, Lxx *Ge.*1.2, etc.: *the abyss, underworld*, *Ev. Luc.*8.31, *Ep.Rom.*10.7, *Apoc.*9.1, etc.; *the infinite void*, *PMag.Par.* 1.1120, cf. *PMag.Lond.*121.261.

ἀβῶ· ἐπινοῶ, Cyr.; fut. ἀβήσω, Id.: **ἀβώ**, v. ἀβώρ.

ἀβωλόκοπος, ον, *not hoed*, Poll.1.246.

ἄβωλος, ον, *not mixed with clods of earth*, πυρός, etc., *PTeb.*370. 13 (ii A.D.), etc.

ἀβώρ, i.e. ἀϝώρ, Lacon. for ἠώς, and **ἀβώ** = πρωΐ, Hsch.

ἄβως or **ἀβῶς**, (βοή) *speechless*, Hsch., *EM*4.54. (Ion. form.)

ἀγ, apoc. form of ἀνά before κ, γ, χ, v. ἀνά init.

ἀγα-, intensive prefix, *very*, as ἀγα-κλεής, etc., cf. ἄγαν. (Prob. for *mga*, reduced form of μέγα.)

ἄγᾱ, Dor. for ἄγη.

ἀγάασθαι, **ἀγάασθε**, Ep. forms from ἄγαμαι, Od.

ἀγάζηλοι· μεγαλόζηλοι, οἱ δὲ φθονεροί, *EM*5.29.

ἀγάζω, (ἄγαν) *exalt overmuch*, τὰ θεῶν μηδὲν -ειν A.*Supp.*1061, cf. S.*Fr.*968. II. Med., *honour, adore*: λοιβαῖσιν Pi.*N.*11.6, cf. Orph.*A.*64.

ἀγαθάγγελος, *bringing good tidings*, trans. of Persian Οἰβάρας, Nic.Dam.p.53.14 D.

ἀγαθαίνω, = -ύνω, Simp. *in Epict.*p.70 D.

ἀγαθείκελος, ον, *like the good*, Hdn.*Epim.*187.

ἀγαθίδιον, τό, Dim. of ἀγαθίς, Paul.Aeg.2.57, Hsch. s.v. τολύπη.

ἀγαθικός, ή, όν, = ἀγαθός, Epich.99.

ἀγᾰθίς, ίδος (ῐ Hdn.Gr.2.18), ἡ, *ball of thread*, Pherecyd.148 J., Aen.Tact.31.19, Orib.*Fr.*57, etc.; ἀγαθῶν ἀγαθίδες, prov., *quantities* of goods, *Com.Adesp.*827. II. = σησαμίς, Hsch., Eust.1366.33.

ἀγαθο-γονία, ἡ, *production of good*, Iamb. *in Nic.*82.22. **-δαιμονέω**, Astrol., *occupy the house of* ἀγαθοδαίμων III, Vett.Val.62.20, Paul.Al.*O.*3: **-δαιμονητικός**, ή, όν, *belonging thereto*, Jul.Laod. in *Cat.Cod.Astr.*5.184. **-δαιμονισταί**, οἱ, *guests who drink only to the* ἀγαθὸς δαίμων (cf. δαίμων): hence, *moderate drinkers*, Arist. *EE*1233^{b}3.: **-δαιμονιασταί**, a club of such drinkers, *IG*12(1).161 (Rhodes). **-δαίμων**, ονος, ὁ, *the good Genius*, less correct for ἀγαθὸς δαίμων, A.D.*Adv.*60.15, *PMag.Leid.W.*17.25. II. *an Egyptian serpent*, *Hist.Aug.Elag.*28, Philum.*Ven.*29. III. Astrol., *propitious region* (east of μεσουράνημα), Vett.Val.135. 32. **-δοσία**, ἡ, (δόσις) *the giving of good*, Alex.Aphr. *in Metaph.* 707.19. **-δότης**, ου, ὁ, *the giver of good*, Diotog.ap.Stob.4. 7.62. Adv. -δότως Eustr. *in EN*387.11. **-ειδής**, ές, *like good, seeming good*, opp. ἀγαθός, Pl.*R.*509a, etc. II. *having the form of good*, Plot.1.7.1, al., Jul.*Or.*4.135a, Procl.*Inst.*25: Comp., Iamb.*Protr.*4: Sup., Marin.*Procl.*27. **-εργασία**, ἡ, = ἀγαθοεργία, Procop.*Aed.*1.7. **-εργέω**, *do good* or *well*, 1*Ep.Ti.*6. 18: contr. **-ουργέω**, *Act.Ap.*14.17. **-εργία**, Ion. -ίη, contr. **-ουργία**, ἡ, *good deed, service*, Hdt.3.154,160, Jul.*Or.*4.135d. 2. *beneficence*, Procl. *in Cra.*pp.13,90 P. **-εργός** (contr. **-ουργός**, Plu.2.1015e, Procl.*Inst.*122), όν, *doing good*, Jul.*Or.*4.144d, Dam. *Isid.*296, Procl. *in Alc.*p.54 C.:—οἱ Ἀ., at Sparta, *Commissioners sent on foreign service*, Hdt.1.67. **-θέλεια**, ἡ, *desire of good*, Anon.ap.Suid. **-θελής**, ές, *benevolent*, Antigonus ap.Heph.*Astr.* 2.18, *Gloss.* **-λογέω**, *use fair words*, Eust.378.30. **-ποιέω**, *do good*, *Ev.Marc.*3.4, S.E.*M.*11.70, Aesop.66. 2. ἀ. τινά *do good to*, *Ev.Luc.*6.33: c. dupl. acc., Lxx *Nu.*10.32, Aristeas 242: τινί Lxx 2*Ma.*1.2. 3. *make good*, τι Plot.6.7.22; τὰ κακά *Corp.Herm.* 9.4. 4. Astrol., *make favourable*, Vett.Val.203.32: Pass., Jul.Laod. in *Cat.Cod.Astr.*5(1).185. b. *exert beneficent influence*, Procl. *Par.Ptol.*292. II. *do well, act rightly*, 1*Ep.Pet.*2.15. **-ποίησις**, ἡ, *well-doing*, Eustr. *in EN*17.25. **-ποιΐα**, ἡ, = foreg., 1*Ep. Pet.*4.19, al. II. *propitious influence*, Vett.Val.164.17, Ptol.*Tetr.* 38. **-ποιός**, όν, *beneficent*, Lxx *Si.*42.14, Plu.2.368b, Porph.*Marc.* 17; of the King of Persia, Men.Prot.p.16 D.: c. gen., -ποιὲ τῆς οἰκουμένης *PMag.Lond.*122.16. II. Astrol., *exerting beneficent influence*, Ptol.*Tetr.*19, Artem.4.59, *PMag.Lond.*46.48, etc. III. *creating the Good*, Dam.*Pr.*33.

ἀγᾰθός [ᾰγ], ή, όν, Lacon. **ἀγασός** Ar.*Lys.*1301, Cypr. **ἀζαθός** *GDI*57:—*good*: I. of persons, 1. *well-born, gentle*, opp. κακός, δειλός, οἷά τε τοῖς ἀγαθοῖσι παραδρώωσι χέρηες Od.15. 324, cf. Il.1.275; ἀφνειός τ' ἀ. τε Il.13.664, cf. Od.18.276; πατρὸς δ' εἴμ' ἀγαθοῖο, θεὰ δέ με γείνατο μήτηρ Il.21.109, cf. Od.4.611; κακὸς ἐξ ἀ. Thgn.190, cf. 57 sq.; πραῢς ἀστοῖς, οὐ φθονέων ἀγαθοῖς Pi.*P.* 3.71, cf. 2.96, 4.285; τίς ἂν εὔπατρις ὧδε βλάστοι; οὐδεὶς τῶν ἀ. κτλ. S.*El.*1082; οἵ τ' ἀ. πρὸς τῶν ἀγενῶν κατανικῶνται Id.*Fr.*84; τοὺς εὐγενεῖς γὰρ κἀγαθοὺς.. φιλεῖ Ἄρης ἐναίρειν ib.649, cf. E.*Alc.*600, al.: ἀγαθοὶ καὶ ἐξ ἀγαθῶν Pl.*Phdr.*274a:—in political sense, *aristocrats*, esp. in the phrase καλοὶ κἀγαθοί (v. sub καλοκἀγαθός). 2. *brave, valiant*, since courage was attributed to Chiefs and Nobles, Il.1.131, al.; τῷ κ' ἀγαθὸς μὲν ἔπεφν', ἀγαθὸν δέ κεν ἐξενάριξεν 21.280; cf. Hdt.5.109, etc. 3. *good, capable*, in reference to ability, ἀ. βασιλεύς Il.3.179; ἰητήρ 2.732; θεράπων 16.165, 17.388; πύκτης Xenoph.2.15; ἰητρός Hp.*Prog.*1; προβατογνώμων A.*Ag* 795; ἄρχοντες Democr.266: freq. with qualifying words, ἀ. ἐν ὑσμίνῃ Il.13. 314; βοὴν ἀ. 2.408,563, al.; πύξ Od.11.300; βίην Il.6.478; γνώμην S.*OT*687; πᾶσαν ἀρετήν Pl.*Lg.*899b, cf. *Alc.*1.124e; τέχνην Id.*Prt.*323b; τὰ πολέμια, τὰ πολιτικά, Hdt.9.122, Pl.*Grg.*516b, etc.: more rarely c. dat., ἀ. πολέμῳ X.*Oec.*4.15: with Preps., ἄνδρες ἀ. περὶ τὸ πλῆθος Lys.13.2; εἴς τι Pl.*Alc.*1.125a; πρός τι Id.*R.*407e: c. inf., ἀ. μάχεσθαι Hdt.1.136; ἱππεύεσθαι 1.79; ἀ. ἱστάναι *good at weighing*, Pl.*Prt.*356b. 4. *good*, in moral sense, first in Thgn.438, cf. Heraclit.104, S.*El.*1082, X.*Mem.*1.7.1, Pl.*Ap.*41d, etc.; ψυχῆς ἀγαθῆς πατρὶς ὁ ξύμπας κόσμος Democr.247: freq. with other Adjs., ὁ πιστὸς κἀ. S.*Tr.*541; δικαίων κἀ. ib.1050:—ironical, τὸν ἀ. Κρέοντα Id.*Ant.*31. 5. ὦ 'γαθέ, *my good friend*, as a term of gentle remonstrance, Pl.*Prt.*311a, etc. 6. ἀ. δαίμων, v. sub δαίμων; ἀ. τύχη, v. sub τύχη; ἀ. θεός = Lat. *bona dea*, Plu.*Caes.*9, *Cic.*19. II. of things, 1. *good, serviceable*, Ἰθάκη.. ἀ. κουροτρόφος Od.9.27, etc.; ἀ. τοῖς τοκεῦσι, τῇ πόλει X.*Cyn.*13.17: c. gen., εἴ τι οἶδα πυρετοῦ ἀ. *good for* it, Id. *Mem.*3.8.3; ἑλκῶν Thphr.*HP*9.11.1. 2. of outward circumstances, αἰδὼς οὐκ ἀ. κεχρημένῳ ἀνδρὶ παρεῖναι Od.17.347; εἰπεῖν εἰς ἀγαθόν *to good purpose*, Il.9.102; ὁ δὲ πείσεται εἰς ἀ. περ *for his own good end*, 11.789; οὐκ ἀγαθὸν πολυκοιρανίη 2.204:—ἀγαθόν [ἐστι], c. inf., *it is good* to do so and so, Il.7.282, 24.130, Od.3.196, etc. 3. *morally good*, πρῆξις Democr.177; ἔργα Emp.112.2, cf. *Ep.Rom.*2.7, etc. 4. ἀγαθόν, τό, *good, blessing, benefit*, of persons or things, ὦ μέγα ἀ. σὺ τοῖς φίλοις X.*Cyr.*5.3.20; φίλον, ὃ μέγιστον ἀ. εἶναί φασι Id.*Mem.*2.4.2, cf. Ar.*Ra.*74, etc.; as term of endearment for a baby, *blessing!, treasure!*, Men.*Sam.*28:—ἀγαθόν τινα δεδρακέναι, πεποιηκέναι confer *a benefit* on.., Th.3.68, Lys.13.92; ἐπ' ἀγαθῷ τινος for one's *good*, Th.5.27, X.*Cyr.*7.4.3; ἐπ' ἀ. τοῖς πολίταις Ar.*Ra.*1487; οὐκ ἐπ' ἀ. *for no good end*, Th.1.131; ἐπ' οὐδενὶ ἀ. τῆς Ἑλλάδος X.*HG*5.2.35:—in pl., ἡ ἐπ' ἀγαθοῖς γεναμένη (sic) καταπορὰ *PFlor.*21.10 (iii A.D.):—τὸ ἀ. or τἀ., *the good*, Epich.171.5, cf. Pl.*R.*506b, 508e, Arist.*Metaph.*1091^{a}31, etc.:—in pl., ἀγαθά, τά, *goods of fortune, treasures, wealth*, Hdt.2.172, Lys.13. 91, X.*Mem.*1.2.63, etc.; ἀγαθὰ πράττειν *fare well*, Ar.*Av.*1706; also, *good things, dainties*, Thgn.1000, Ar.*Ach.*873, etc.: *good qualities*, τοῖς ἀ., οἷς ἔχομεν ἐν τῇ ψυχῇ Isoc.8.32, cf. Democr.37; *good points*, of a horse, εἰ τἆλλα πάντα ἀ. ἔχοι, κακόπους δ' εἴη X.*Eq.* 1.2. III. Comp. and Sup. are usu. supplied from other stems, viz. Comp. ἀμείνων, ἀρείων, βελτίων, κρείσσων (κάρρων), λωΐων (λῴων), Ep. βέλτερος, λωΐτερος, φέρτερος:—Sup. ἄριστος, βέλτιστος, κράτιστος, λωΐστος (λῷστος), Ep. βέλτατος, κάρτιστος, φέρτατος, φέριστος:—later, reg. Comp. ἀγαθώτερος Lxx *Jd.*11.25, 15.2, D.S.8*Fr.*12, Plot. 5.5.9, Diod.Rh.p.53.9 H.: Sup. ἀγαθώτατος D.S.16.85, Hld.5.15, etc. (-ότατος *POxy.*1757.26 (ii A.D.)). IV. Adv. usually εὖ, q.v.: ἀγαθῶς Hp.*Off.*9, Arist.*Rh.*1388^{b}6, Lxx 1*Ki.*20.7. (Etym. dub. (ὅτι ἄγει ἡμᾶς ἐπὶ τὸν ὀρθὸν βίον *Stoic.* 3.49); perh. cognate with ἄγαμαι, hence *admirable*.)

ἀγάθοσμον· τήλινον (sc. ἔλαιον), *EM*5.34, Hsch. (prob. l.).

ἀγαθοσύμβουλος, *benesuasor*, *Gloss.*

ἀγαθότης, ητος, ἡ, *goodness*, Lxx *Wi.*1.1, Ph.1.50, Alex.Aphr. *in Metaph.*695.37, Plot.4.8.6, Sallust.3, etc.; as a form of address, ἡ σὴ ἀ. Jul.*Ep.*12,86.

ἀγαθοτυχέω, Astrol., *occupy the house of* ἀγαθὴ τύχη, Vett.Val.83. 20; ἀγ. πρός.. *Cat.Cod.Astr.*1.118.

ἀγαθουργέω, **-ουργία**, **-ουργός**, v. ἀγαθοεργ-.

ἀγαθο-φανής, ές, *appearing good, hypocritical*, Democr.82. **-φόρος**, ον, *bearing good tidings*, *PMag.Par.*1.3166; -φόρον, τό, *Cat. Cod.Astr.*2.170. **-φρων**, ον, gen. -ονος, (φρήν) *well-disposed*, Ptol. *Tetr.*163.

ἀγαθόω, *do good to* one, τινί or τινά Lxx 1*Ki.*25.31, *Si.*49.9. 2. *make good*, Numen.ap.Eus.*PE*11.22 (Pass.).

ἀγάθ-υνσις, ἡ, *making good*, Eustr. *in EN*276.32. **-ύνω**, first and freq. in Lxx: I. *honour, magnify*, 3*Ki.*1.47, *Ps.*50(51). 18: *adorn*, τὴν κεφαλήν 4*Ki.*9.30. 2. *cheer*, ἀγαθυνάτω σε ἡ καρδία *Ec.*11.9:—Pass., *to be of good cheer, rejoice greatly*, 2*Ki.*13.28, *Da.*6.23, al. II. *make good*, Alex.Aphr. *in Metaph.*707.11, al., Procl.*Inst.*13,122: Pass., Simp. *in Epict.*p.6 D., al. b. Astrol., *make beneficent*, in Pass., Doroth. in *Cat.Cod.Astr.*2.196, Jul.Laod.ib. 4.24. III. *do good to*, τινά Heliod. *in EN*86.41. IV. *do good, do well*, Lxx *Ps.*35(36).3; τινί (v.l. τινά) to one, ib.124(125).4.

ἀγάθωμα, τό, *embodiment of the good,* Procl. *in Prm.*p.863S.

ἀγαθωσύνη, ἡ, *goodness, kindness,* Lxx *Jd.*9.16, al., *Ep.Rom.*15.14, *Ep.Eph.*5.9.

ἀγαίομαι, Ep. and Ion. for ἄγαμαι, only pres. and impf.: I. in bad sense (cf. ἄγη II), 1. c. acc. rei, *to be indignant at,* ἀγαιομένου κακὰ ἔργα Od.20.16: *look on with jealousy* or *envy,* οὐδ' ἀγαίομαι θεῶν ἔργα Archil.25. 2. c. dat. pers., *to be wroth* or *indignant with,* τῷ.. Ζεὺς αὐτὸς ἀγαίεται Hes.*Op.*333; ἀγαιόμενοί τε καὶ φθονέοντες αὐτῇ Hdt.8.69 (cf. Sch.Od.20.16). II. in good sense, *admire,* τι Opp.*H.*4.138; abs. in part., A.R.1.899, 3.1016; οἴνῳ ἀγαιομένη κούρῳ Διός Orph.*Fr.*204; ἀγαίετο θυμός Hes.*Fr.*81.4.

ἀγαῖος, α, ον (A), *enviable,* Hsch., *AB*334, *EM*8.50.

ἀγαῖος, α, ον (B), (ἄγω) *leading the procession,* μόσχος, dub. in *SIG*²438.203 (Delphi).

ἀγα-κλεής, ές, voc. -κλεές Il.17.716, al.: Ep. gen. ἀγακλῆος Il.16.738, nom. pl. ἀγακληεῖς Man.3.324: shortened acc. sing. ἀγακλέα Pi.*P.*9.106, *I.*1.34; dat. ἀγακλέϊ *APl.*5.377; acc. pl. ἀγακλέας Antim.*Eleg.*2:—*very glorious, famous,* in Il. always of men, as 16.738, 23.529; later of places and things, ναός, Δᾶλος, B.15.12, Pi.*Pae.*4.12; παιάν ib.5.48.—Ep. and Lyr. word (not in Od.), exc. in Adv. ἀγακλεῶς, Hp.*Praec.*12. **-κλειτός,** ή, όν, = foreg., of men, Il.2.564, Hes.*Th.*1016, etc. 2. of things, ἀ. ἑκατόμβη Od.3.59; πάθος S.*Tr.*854 (lyr.). **-κλυμένη,** poet. fem. = sq., Antim.*Eleg.*4. **-κλυτός,** όν, = -κλειτός, Il.6.426, Hes.*Th.*945, etc. 2. of things, ἀ. δώματα Od.3.388, 7.3, 46. **-κτιμένη,** poet. fem. = εὐκτιμένη, *well-built* or *placed,* πόλις Pi.*P.*5.81.

ἀγαλακτία, ἡ, *want of milk,* Autocr.3.

ἀγάλακτος [γᾰ], ον, (α priv., γάλα) *giving no milk,* Hp.*Nat.Puer.*30, cf. Call.*Ap.*52. 2. *getting no milk,* A.*Ag.*718. 3. νομαὶ ἀγάλακτοι pastures *bad for milch cattle,* Gal.6.346. II. (α collect.) = ὁμογάλακτος, Hsch.; also **ἀγαλακτοσύνη,** = συγγένεια, Id.

ἀγάλαξ, ακτος, ὁ, ἡ, = foreg. I, only in pl. ἀγάλακτες, Call.*Ap.*52. II. = foreg. II, Hsch., Suid.

ἀγαλλί-ᾱμα, τό, *transport of joy,* Lxx *Ps.*31(32).7, etc. **-ᾱσις,** εως, ἡ, *great joy, exultation,* Lxx *Jb.*8.21, al., *Ev.Luc.*1.14, 44, 1*Enoch* 5.9, Ps.-Callisth.2.22. **-άω,** late form of ἀγάλλομαι, *rejoice exceedingly, Apoc.*19.7 (v.l. ἀγαλλιώμεθα); ἠγαλλίασα *Ev.Luc.*1.47, cf. *POxy.*1592.4 (iii/iv A.D.):—more common as Dep. ἀγαλλιάομαι, Lxx *Is.*12.6, al.: fut. -άσομαι *Ps.*5.11: aor. ἠγαλλιασάμην *Ps.*15(16).2, *Ev.Jo.*8.56; ἠγαλλιάσθην ib.5.35.—This family of words seems also to have been used *in malam partem,* **ἀγαλλιάζει·** λοιδορεῖται, **ἀγάλλιος·** λοίδορος, **ἀγαλμός·** λοιδορία, Hsch., cf. *EM*7.8.

ἀγαλλίς, ίδος, ἡ, *dwarf iris, Iris attica, h.Cer.*7, 426:—also **ἀγαλλιάς,** ἡ, Nic.*Fr.*74.31.

ἀγάλλω [ᾰ], Pi.*O.*1.86b, Ar.*Th.*128, etc.: fut. ἀγᾰλῶ Ar.*Pax* 399, Theopomp.Com.47: aor. ἤγηλα D.C.44.48, etc., subj. ἀγήλω Hermipp.8, inf. ἀγῆλαι E.*Med.*1027:—Pass., only pres. and impf. in early writers: aor. 1 inf. ἀγαλθῆναι D.C.51.20:—*glorify, exalt,* Pi. l. c., *N.*5.43: esp. *pay honour to* a god, ἄγαλλε Φοῖβον Ar.*Th.*128, cf. Pl.*Lg.*931a; ἀ. τινὰ θυσίαισι Ar.*Pax* l. c.; φέρε νῦν, ἀγήλω τοὺς θεούς Hermipp. l. c.; θεοὺς καρποῖς Xenocr.ap.Porph.*Abst.*4.22:—*adorn,* γαμηλίους εὐνάς E. l. c.:—Med. in act. sense, εὔιον ἀγαλλόμεναι θεόν E.*Ba.*157:—Pass., *glory, exult in* a thing, c. part., τεύχεα δ' Ἕκτωρ.. ἔχων ὤμοισιν ἀγάλλεται Il.17.473; νικῶν Archil.66.4; ἣν ἕκαστος πατρίδα ἔχων.. ἀ. Th.4.95; but mostly c. dat., ἵπποισιν καὶ ὄχεσφιν ἀγαλλόμενος Il.12.114; πτερύγεσσι 2.462; νῆες.. ἀ. Διὸς οὔρῳ Od.5.176; Μοῦσαι.. ἀ. ὀπὶ καλῇ Hes.*Th.*68; ἀσπίδι Archil.6; ἑορταῖς E.*Tr.*452: in Prose, τῷ οὐνόματι ἠγάλλοντο Hdt.1.143, cf. Th.2.44, Pl.*Tht.*176b; ἀλλοτρίοις πτεροῖς ἀ. *strut* in borrowed plumes, Luc.*Ap.*4; ἐπί τινι Th.3.82, X.*Cyr.*8.4.11; διὰ τἄλλα καὶ ὅτι.. D.C.66.2: c. acc., *AP*7.378 (Apollonid.): abs., Hdt.4.64, 9.109, Hp.*Art.*35, E.*Ba.*1197.

ἄγαλμα, ατος, τό, acc. to Hsch. πᾶν ἐφ' ᾧ τις ἀγάλλεται, *glory, delight, honour,* Il.4.144, etc.; κεφάλαισιν ἀνδρῶν ἀγάλματα (sc. λόφοι) Alc.15; χώρας ἄ., of an ode, Pi.*N.*3.13, cf. 8.16; of children, τέκνον δόμων ἄ. A.*Ag.*208; εὐκλείας τέκνοις ἄ. conversely, of a father, S.*Ant.*704; Καδμείας νύμφας ἄ., addressed to Bacchus, ib.1115; ματέρος ἄ. φόνιον, of slain sons, E.*Supp.*371; ἀγάλματ' ἀγορᾶς *mere ornaments* of the agora, Id.*El.*388, cf. Metagen.10.3; rare in Prose, Pl.*Ti.*37c. 2. *pleasing gift,* esp. for the gods, ἄ. θεῶν Od.8.509, of a bull adorned for sacrifice, ib.3.438; of a tripod, Hdt.5.60, al.; generally, = ἀνάθημα, *IG*1.373^{12a}, etc.; Χάρης εἰμὶ.. ἄ. τοῦ Ἀπόλλωνος *GDI*5507 (Miletus); ἀνθηκεν ἄ. Simon.155; so, Ἑκάτης ἄ... κύων, because sacred to her, E.*Fr.*968, = Ar.*Fr.*594a; ἄ. Ἀΐδα, of a tombstone, Pi.*N.*10.67. 3. *statue in honour of a god,* Hdt.1.131, 2.42, 46, Lys.6.15 (pl.):—τὸ τοῦ Διὸς ἄ., opp. εἰκόνες of men, Isoc.9.57, cf. *Michel*545 (Phrygia, ii B.C.), etc.; as an object of worship, A.*Th.*258, *Eu.*55, S.*OT*1379, Pl.*Phdr.*251a:—*sculpture,* μήτε ἄ. μήτε γραφή Arist.*Pol.*1336^{b}15. 4. *statue* (more general than ἀνδριάς, q.v.), Pl.*Men.*97d, etc.:—also, *portrait, picture,* ἐξαλειφθεῖσ' ὡς ἄ. E.*Hel.*262. 5. generally, *image,* τῶν ἀιδίων θεῶν Pl.*Ti.*37c; νεφέλης E.*Hel.*705; μητρός *Trag.Adesp.*126; Ἄρεως Polemo *Call.*52:—expressed by painting or words, Pl.*Smp.*216e, cf. *R.*517d; *hieroglyphic sign,* Plot.5.8.6.

ἀγαλμ-ατίας, ου, ὁ, *like a statue, beautiful as one,* Philostr.*VS*2.25.6. **-άτιον,** τό, Dim. of ἄγαλμα, *IG*4.1588 (Attic, fr. Aegina, v B.C.), Theopomp.Com.47, Polycharm.5, Plu.*Lyc.*25, etc. **-ατίτης,** ὁ, = λιθοκόλλα, Hsch.

ἀγαλματο-γλύφος, ὁ, = *sculptor,* Vett.Val.4.12, *Rev.Ét.Gr.*19.265 (Aphrodisias). **-ποιέω,** *make statues,* Poll.7.108: Pass., *have a statue made of oneself,* Steph. *in Rh.*280.10. **-ποιητικός,** όν, ή, *of* or *for statuary,* Jul.*Gal.*235c: -κή, ἡ, *sculpture,* [Gal.]14.686. **-ποιΐα,** ἡ, *sculptor's art,* Philostr.*VS*1.11.2, Porph.*Abst.*2.49. **-ποιικός,** = -ποιητικός, Poll.1.13: -ποϊκόν, τό, *sculptor's fee, IG*1.324. **-ποιός,** ὁ, *sculptor,* Hdt.2.46, Pl.*Prt.*311c, etc.; γραφεῖς ἢ ἀ. Arist.*Pol.*1340^{a}38.

ἀγαλματ-ουργία, ἡ, = ἀγαλματοποιΐα, Max.Tyr.33.3. **-ουργικός,** ή, όν, = ἀγαλματοποιικός, ibid. **-ουργός,** όν, = ἀγαλματοποιός, Poll.1.12.

ἀγαλματο-φορέω, *carry an image in one's mind, bear impressed upon one's mind,* Ph.1.16, al.; Pass., 2.136. **-φόρος,** ον, *carrying an image in one's mind,* Hsch. **-φώρας,** ὁ, *temple-robber, Jahresh.*2.197 (Elis, iv B.C.).

ἀγαλματ-όω, *make into an image,* Lyc.845. **-ώδης,** ες, *like a statue,* f.l. in Gal.*UP*11.13.

ἀγαλμητόν· ἀσθενές, Hsch. **ἀγαλμός,** v. ἀγαλλιάω.

ἀγαλμο-ειδής, ές, f.l. for ἀγλαο-, q.v. **-τῠπεύς,** έως, *maker of statues,* Man.4.569.

ἀγάλοχον, τό, *eagle-wood, Aquilaria malaccensis,* Dsc.1.22, etc.

ἄγαλσις, ἡ, *rejoicing, EM*9.52.

ἄγᾰμαι [ᾰ], 2 pl. ἄγασθε Od.5.129, Ep. ἀγάασθε ib.119; Ep. inf. ἀγάασθαι 16.203: impf. ἠγάμην Pl.*R.*367e, X.*Smp.*8.8, Ep. 2 pl. ἠγάασθε Od.5.122: fut. Ep. ἀγάσσομαι Od.4.181; later, ἀγασθήσομαι Them.*Or.*27.335d, Themist.*Ep.*8: aor. ἠγασάμην Hom., D.18.204, Plu.*Fab.*18, etc.; Ep. ἠγάσσατο or ἀγάσσατο Il.3.181, 224; after Hom. the pass. ἠγάσθην prevails, Hes.*Fr.*93.2, Sol.33, etc. (Perh. cognate with ἀγα-, q.v.) [ἄγᾰμαι, but ἠγᾱασθε metri grat., Od. l. c.] I. abs., *wonder,* μνηστῆρες δ'.. ὑπερφιάλως ἀγάσαντο Od.18.71, etc.; c. part., Ὀδυσῆος ἀγασσάμεθ' εἶδος ἰδόντες Il.3.224. 2. more freq. c. acc., *admire* a person or thing, τὸν δ' ὁ γέρων ἠγάσσατο Il.3.181; ὥς σέ, γύναι, ἄγαμαι Od.6.168; μῦθον ἄ. Il.8.29; τὸ προορᾶν ἄ. σευ Hdt.9.79; ὑμέων ἀγάμεθα τὴν προνοίην Id.8.144; οὐκ ἄγαμαι ταῦτ' ἀνδρὸς ἀριστέως E.*IA*28; ταῦτα ἀγασθεὶς X.*Cyr.*2.3.19, cf. Isoc.4.84, etc.: c. acc. pers. et gen. rei, *admire* one *for* a thing, Pl.*R.*426d, X.*Cyr.*2.3.21. 3. c. gen., *wonder at,* freq. in Com., ἄγαμαι δὲ λόγων Ar.*Av.*1744; ἄ. κεραμέως αἴθωνος Eup.21D.; ἄ. σοῦ στόματος, ὡς.. Phryn.Com.10:—also in Prose, X.*Mem.*2.6.33, Pl.*Euthd.*276d, etc. 4. c. gen. pers., foll. by part., *wonder at* one's doing, ἄ. Ἐρασίνου οὐ προδιδόντος Hdt.6.76.β'; ἀ. αὐτοῦ εἰπόντος Pl.*R.*329d, etc.; ἄ. τινος ὅτι,.. διότι.., Id.*Hp.Ma.*291e, X.*Mem.*4.2.9, etc. 5. c. dat., *to be delighted with* a person or thing, Hdt.4.75, Pl.*Smp.*179c, X.*Cyr.*2.4.9; later, ἐπί τινι, D.*Ep.*2.11, Menetor Hist.1, Phalar.*Ep.*79. II. in bad sense, *feel envy, bear a grudge,* c. dat. pers., εἰ μή οἱ ἀγάσσατο Φοῖβος Ἀπόλλων Il.17.71; ἀγασσάμενοι [μοι] περὶ νίκης 23.639; with inf. added, *to be jealous* of one *that..,* σχέτλιοί ἐστε, θεοί,.. οἵ τε θεαῖς ἀγάασθε παρ' ἀνδράσιν εὐνάζεσθαι Od.5.119, 23.211; foll. by a relat., ἔφασκε Ποσειδάων' ἀγάσεσθαι ἡμῖν, οὕνεκα.. 8.565:—Pass. aor. ἠγάσθην Hes.*Fr.*93.2, dub. in E.*HF*845. 2. c. acc., *to be jealous of, angry at* a thing, ἀγασσάμενοι κακὰ ἔργα Od.2.67; of Gods, 4.181, cf. 23.64. Cf. ἀγαίομαι.

Ἀγαμέμνων, ονος, ὁ, *Agamemnon,* Hom., etc.: Ἀγαμέμνονος δαίς, of a fatal feast, Eust.1507.60:—also epith. of Zeus at Sparta, Staphylus Hist.10, Eust.168.10.—Adj. **Ἀγᾰμεμνόνεος,** έα, εον, Hom., also -όνειος, εία, ειον, and -όνιος, ία, ιον, Pi., A.: Patron. **-ονίδης,** ου, ὁ, *Agamemnon's son,* Orestes, Od.1.30, S.*El.*182.

ἀγᾰμένως, Adv. part. pres. of ἄγαμαι, *with admiration* or *respect,* ἀ. λέγειν Arist.*Rh.*1408^{a}18; ἀ. τὸν λόγον ἀπεδέξατο Pl.*Phd.*89a.

ἀγάμ-ετος, ον, = ἄγαμος, S.*Fr.*970:—also -ητος, ον, *Com.Adesp.*315. **-ία,** ἡ, *single estate, celibacy,* Plu.2.491e. **-ίου δίκη** action against a bachelor *for not marrying,* Plu.*Lys.*30, cf. Poll.3.48; ἀγαμίου ζημία AristoStoic.1.89. **-ος,** ον, *unmarried, single,* prop. of the man, whether bachelor or widower (ἄνανδρος being used of the woman), Il.3.40, X.*Smp.*9.7, etc.; ζῶ δὲ Τίμωνος βίον, ἄγαμον, ἄδουλον Phryn.Com.18:—of the woman, A.*Supp.*143, S.*OT*1502, E.*Or.*205. Adv. -ως Sch. ad loc. II. γάμος ἄ. *marriage that is no marriage, fatal marriage,* S.*OT*1214, E.*Hel.*690.

ἄγαν, Adv. *very much,* chiefly Aeol. Dor. and Trag., not in Hom., rare in Ion., as Hdt.2.173, Hp.*Art.*4, al., Democr.222; freq. in bad sense, *too much*:—prov., μηδὲν ἄ. Pi.*Fr.*216 (attributed to Chilo by Arist.*Rh.*1389^{b}4); μηδὲν ἄ. σπεύδειν Thgn.335:—with Verbs, ἄ. διαστρέψαι Hp.*Fract.*8; ἄ. ἐλευθεροστομεῖς A.*Pr.*182; ἄ. τι ποιεῖν Pl.*R.*563e:—with Adjs. either preceding or following, ἄ. κοῦφος Hp.*Art.*4; ἄ. βαρύς A.*Pers.*515; πιθανὸς ἄ. Id.*Ag.*485; with Sup., ἄ. ἀγριωτάτους *far* the most savage, Ael.*NA*1.38, cf. 8.13:—with Adv., ὑπερθύμως ἄ. A.*Eu.*824; ἄ. οὕτω S.*Ph.*598; ὠμῶς ἄ. X.*Vect.*5.6:—with a Subst., ἡ ἄ. χρημάτων συναγωγή Democr.222; ἡ ἄ. σιγή S.*Ant.*1251; ἡ ἄ. ἐλευθερία Pl.*R.*564a; without Art., εἰς ἄ. δουλείαν ib. (Cf. ἀγα-.) [ἀγᾱν Thgn.219, Orac.ap.Hdt.4.157, A.*Eu.*121, etc.; in late poets, ἀγᾰν *AP*5.215.6 (Agath.), 10.51 (Pall.), cf. Eust.1433 fin.]

ἄγανα· σαγήνην (Cypr.), Hsch. (Prob. ἀγάνα.)

ἀγᾰνακτ-έω, properly in physical sense, *feel a violent irritation,* of the effects of cold on the body, Hp.*Liqu.*2, cf. Heliod.ap.Orib.46.7.8; of wine, *ferment,* Plu.2.734e; so metaph., ζεῖ τε καὶ ἀ., of the soul, Pl.*Phdr.*251c. II. metaph., *to be displeased, vexed,* μηδ' ἀγανάκτει Ar.*V.*287; esp. *show outward signs of grief,* κλάων καὶ ἀ.

Pl.*Phd.*117d; τὰ σπλάγχν' ἀγανακτεῖ Ar.*Ra.*1006, etc.; ἀ. ἐνθυμούμενος.. And.4.18:—foll. by a relat., ἀ. ὅτι.. Antipho 4.2.1, Lys. 3.3; ἀ. εἰ.., ἐάν.. And.1.139, Pl.*La.*194a. 2. c. dat. rei, *to be vexed at* a thing, θανάτῳ Pl.*Phd.*63b, etc.; c. acc. neut., ib.64a; ἀ. ταῦτα, ὅτι.. Id.*Euthphr.*4d; ἀ. ἐπί τινι Lys.1.1, Isoc.16.49, etc.; ὑπέρ τινος Pl.*Euthd.*283e, etc.; περί τινος Id.*Ep.*349d; διά τι Id. *Phd.*63c; πρός τι Epict.*Ench.*4, M.Ant.7.66; and sts. c. gen. rei, *AB*334. 3. *to be vexed at* or *with* a person, τινί X.*HG*5.3.11; πρός τινα Plu.*Cam.*28, Diog.Oen.68; κατά τινος Luc.*Tim.*18:—c. part., *to be angry at*, ἀ. ἀποθνῄσκοντας Pl.*Phd.*62e, cf. 67d. III. Med. in act. sense, aor. part. -ησάμενος Luc.*Somn.*4; prob. in Palaeph.40; ἠγανάκτηνται τῷ πράγματι Hyp.*Fr.*70. **-ησις**, εως, ἡ, *physical pain and irritation*, ἀ. περὶ τὰ οὖλα, of the irritation caused by teething, Pl.*Phdr.*251c. II. *vexation*, ἀγανάκτησιν ἔχει Th.2.41, cf. 2*Ep.Cor.*7.11, Plot.4.4.19:—of God, *wrath*, Porph. *Marc.*7, Jul.*Gal.*171e. **-ητέον**, *one must complain*, Plot.4.8.7. **-ητικός**, ή, όν, *apt to be vexed, irritable, peevish*, Pl.*R.*604e, 605a (v.l. ἀγανακτικός). **-ητός**, ή, όν, *vexatious*, Pl.*Grg.* 511b. **-ικός**, ή, όν, = ἀγανακτητικός (q.v.), Luc.*Pisc.*14. Adv. -κῶς M.Ant.11.13.

ἀγάνεται· πραγματεύεται, χρῆται, Hsch. **ἀγάνημαι**· ἀσχάλλω, ἀγανακτῶ, Id. **ἀγανίδα**· ἀτρέμας, Id. (fort. -ηδά).

ἀγάννα· ἅμαξα ἱερά· καὶ ἡ ἐν οὐρανῷ ἄρκτος, *Et.Gud.*, cf. Hsch.

ἀγάννῐφος, ον, *much snowed on, snow-capt*, Ὄλυμπος Il.1.420; ἄκρα Epich.130.

ἀγᾰνοβλέφαρος, ον, *mild-eyed*, Πειθώ Ibyc.5, cf. *AP*9.604 (Nossis).

ἀγᾰνόμματος, ον, *mild-eyed*, *Lyr.Alex.Adesp.*20.

ἀγᾱνόρειος, ἀγᾱνορία, Dor. for ἀγην-.

ἀγᾰνός, ή, όν (ἀγᾱνοῖσιν is corrupt in *Il.Parv.*6), poet. Adj. *mild, gentle*, of persons or their words and acts, ἀ. καὶ ἤπιος ἔστω σκηπτοῦχος βασιλεύς Od.2.230, 5.8; ἀ. ἐπέεσσιν Il.2.164, 180, etc.; μύθοις ἀ. Od.15.53; εὐχωλῇς Il.9.499, Od.13.357; δώροισι Il.9.113; Ἀτθίς Sapph.*Supp.*25.15; λόγοις Pi.*P.*4.101; ὀφρύι ib.9.38; Trag. only in A.*Ag.*101; αὐλῶν ἀγαναὶ φωναί Mnesim.4.56. 2. in Hom. freq. of the shafts of Apollo and Artemis, as *bringing an easy death*, ἀλλ' ὅτε γηράσκωσι.., Ἀπόλλων Ἀρτέμιδι ξὺν οἷς ἀγανοῖς βελέεσσιν ἐποιχόμενος κατέπεφνεν Od.15.411, cf. 3.280, Il.24.759, etc.: Sup. ἀγανώτατος Hes.*Th.*408, Pi.*Fr.*149, Them.*Or.*20.234a. Adv. -νῶς Anacr.51.1, E.*IA*601: Comp. ἀγανώτερον, βλέπειν Ar. *Lys.*886.—Poet. and late Prose, Them. l.c.

ἄγᾰνος, ον, (ἄγνυμι) *broken*, ξύλον ἄ. sticks *broken for firewood*, S.*Fr.*231.

ἀγανο-φροσύνη, ἡ, *gentleness, kindliness*, Il.24.772, Od.11. 202. **-φρων**, ον, gen. ονος, poet. Adj. *gentle of mood*, Il.20.467, Cratin.238; Ἡσυχία Ar.*Av.*1321.

ἀγανῶπις, ιδος, ἡ, (ὤψ) *mild-eyed*, Marcell.Sid.80, cf. Hsch.

ἀγάνωτος, ον, (γᾰνόω) *not enamelled* or *lacquered*, Posidon.Medic. ap.Paul.Aeg.7.20, Zos.Alch.p.220B.

ἀγάομαι, Ep. collat. form of ἄγαμαι, only part. ἀγώμενος, *admiring*, Hes.*Th.*619; and opt. ἀγήσα⟨ι⟩το Alc.14:—ἄγασθε is the right reading in Od.5.129.

ἀγαπάζω, Ep. and Lyr. form of ἀγαπάω, Hom.; Dor. 3 pl. -οντι Pi.*I.* 4(5).54; Ep. impf. ἀγάπαζον A.R.4.1291:—also in Med., Hom.; Dor. impf. ἀγαπάζοντο Pi.*P.*4.241:—Pass., Diotog.ap.Stob.4.7.62:—only in pres. and impf., exc. aor. act. ἀγαπάξαι Callicrat.ap.Stob.4. 28.18:—*treat with affection, receive with outward signs of love*, ὡς δὲ πατὴρ ὃν παῖδα.. ἀγαπάζει, ἐλθόντ' ἐξ ἀπίης γαίης δεκάτῳ ἐνιαυτῷ Od.16.17; νεμεσσητὸν δέ κεν εἴη ἀθάνατον θεὸν ὧδε βροτοὺς ἀγαπαζέμεν ἄντην Il.24.464; νέκυν E.*Ph.*1327:—Med. in abs. sense, *show signs of love, caress*, κύνεον ἀγαπαζόμενοι κεφαλήν τε καὶ ὤμους Od. 21.224: c. acc., like Act., Pi.*P.* l.c.; τινὰ δώροις A.R.4.416. 2. *welcome, receive gratefully*, τιμαὶ καλλίνικον χάρμ' ἀγαπάζοντι Pi.*I.* l.c.

ἀγαπάω (Dor. -έω Archyt.ap.Stob.3.1.110), Ep. aor. ἀγάπησα Od.23.214: pf. ἠγάπηκα Isoc.15.147, etc. I. *greet with affection* (cf. foreg.), once in Hom., Od. l.c.:—in Trag. only *show affection for* the dead, ὅτ' ἠγάπα νεκρούς E.*Supp.*764, cf. *Hel.*937:—Pass., *to be regarded with affection*, ξένων εὐεργεσίαις ἀγαπᾶται Pi.*I.*5(6).70:—generally, *love*, ὥσπερ.. οἱ ποιηταὶ τὰ αὑτῶν ποιήματα καὶ οἱ πατέρες τοὺς παῖδας ἀγαπῶσι Pl.*R.*330c, cf. *Lg.*928a; ὡς λύκοι ἄρν' ἀγαπῶσ' Poet.ap.*Phdr.*241d; ἀ. τοὺς ἐπαινέτας ib.257e; ἐπιστήμην, τὰ χρήματα, etc., Id.*Phlb.*62d, al.; τούτους ἀγαπᾷ καὶ περὶ αὑτὸν ἔχει D.2.19; ὁ μέγιστον ἀγαπῶν δι' ἐλάχιστ' ὀργίζεται Men.659; esp. of children, αὐτὸν ἐτιθηνούμην ἀγαπῶσα Id.*Sam.*32, etc.:—Pass., Pl.*Plt.*301d, etc.; ὑπὸ τῶν θεῶν ἠγαπῆσθαι D.61.9; ὑπὸ τοῦ Φθᾶ *OGI*90.4 (Rosetta, ii B.C.); so in Lxx of the love of God for man and of man for God, *Is.*41.8, *De.*11.1, al., cf. *Ev.Jo.*3.21, *Ep.Rom.*8.28:—as dist. fr. φιλέω (q.v.) implying regard rather than affection, but the two are interchanged, cf. X.*Mem.*2.7.9 and 12; φιλεῖσθαι defined as ἀγαπᾶσθαι αὐτὸν δι' αὑτόν Arist.*Rh.*$1371^{a}21$:—seldom of sexual love, for ἐράω, Arist.*Fr.*76, Luc.*J.Tr.*2; ἀ. ἑταίραν Anaxil.22.1 (but ἀ. ἑταίρας *to be fond of* them, X.*Mem.*1.5.4; ἐρωτικὴν μέμψιν ἡ ἀγαπωμένη λύει dub. in Democr.271):—of brotherly love, *Ev.Matt.*5.43, al. 2. *persuade, entreat*, Lxx 2*Ch.*18.2. 3. *caress, pet*, Plu.*Per.*1. II. of things, *to be fond of, prize, desire*, Pl.*Lys.*215a,b, etc.; τὰ χρήματα *R.* 330c; μᾶλλον τὸ σκότος ἢ τὸ φῶς *Ev.Jo.*3.19; *prefer*, τὰ Φιλίππου δῶρα ἀντὶ τῶν κοινῇ τοῖς Ἕλλησι συμφερόντων D.18.109:—Pass., λιθίδια τὰ ἀγαπώμενα *highly prized, precious stones*, Pl.*Phd.*110d. III. *to be well pleased, contented*, once in Hom., οὐκ ἀγαπᾷς ὃ ἕκηλος.. μεθ' ἡμῖν δαίνυσαι; Od.21.289; freq. in Att., ἀγαπᾶν ὅτι..Th.6.36; more commonly, ἀ. εἰ.. *to be well content* if.., Lys.12.11, Pl.*R.*450a, al.; ἐὰν.. ib.330b, cf. Ar.*V.*684, Pl.*Grg.*483c, al. 2. c. part., ἀ. τιμώμενος Pl.*R.*475b, cf. Isoc.12.8, Antiph.169: c. inf., οὐκ ἀ. τῶν ἴσων τυγχάνειν τοῖς ἄλλοις Isoc.18.50, cf. D.55.19, Hdn.2.15.4, Alciphr. 3.61, Luc.*D.Mort.*12.4, etc. 3. c. dat. rei, *to be contented with*, ἀ. τοῖς ὑπάρχουσιν ἀγαθοῖς Lys.2.21; τοῖς πεπραγμένοις D.1.14. 4. c. acc. rei, *tolerate, put up with*, μηκέτι τὴν ἐλευθερίαν ἀ. Isoc. 4.140; τὰ παρόντα D.6.15; τὸ δίκαιον Pl.*R.*359a (Pass.), cf. Arist. *Rh.*$1398^{a}23$. 5. rarely c. gen., ἵνα.. τῆς ἀξίας ἀγαπῶσιν *may be content with* the proper price, Alex.125.7. 6. abs., *to be content*, ἀγαπήσαντες Lycurg.73, cf. Luc.*Nec.*17. 7. c. inf., *to be fond* of doing, *wont* to do, like φιλέω, τοὺς Λυκίους ἀγαπῶντας τὸ τρίχωμα φορεῖν Arist.*Oec.*$1348^{a}29$, cf. Lxx *Ho.*12.7.

ἀγάπ-η, ἡ, *love*, Lxx *Je.*2.2, *Ca.*2.7, al.; ἀ. καὶ μῖσος *Ec.*9.1; dub. l. in *PBerol.*9859 (ii B.C.), Phld.*Lib.*p.52 O.; of the love of husband and wife, Sch.Ptol.*Tetr.*52. 2. esp. *love* of God for man and of man for God, Lxx *Wi.*3.9, Aristeas 229; φόβος καὶ ἀ. Ph.1. 283, cf. *Ep.Rom.*5.8, 2*Ep.Cor.*5.14, *Ev.Luc.*11.42, al.:—also *brotherly love, charity*, 1*Ep.Cor.*13.1, al. II. in pl., *love-feast*, 2*Ep.Pet.* 2.13, *Ep.Jud.*12. III. *alms, charity*, *PGen.*14 (iv/v A.D.). IV. ἀγάπη θεῶν, title of Isis, *POxy.*1380.109 (ii A.D.). **-ημα**, τό, *darling*, of a person, Crates Theb.*Fr.*12, cf. Suet.*Gramm.*3, *Epigr. Gr.*1023 (Talmis):—generally, *delight*; of a dainty dish, λίχνων ἀνδρῶν ἀ. Axionic.4.6; φίλον ὥραισιν ἀ. *Lyr.Alex.Adesp.*24. **-ήνωρ**, ορος, ὁ, = ἠνορέην ἀγαπῶν, *loving manliness, manly*, epith. of heroes, Il.8.114, etc. **-ησις**, εως, ἡ, *affection*, Arist.*Metaph.*$980^{a}22$, Pl. *Def.*413b, Clearch.39, Lxx *Ho.*11.12, al., Aristeas 44, Phld.*Lib.*p. 38 O., Plu.*Per.*24, etc. **-ησμός**, ὁ, = foreg., Men.453. **-ητέος**, α, ον, *to be loved, desired*, Pl.*R.*358a. **-ητικός**, ή, όν, *affectionate*, Plu.*Sol.*7; περὶ τὰ τέκνα M.Ant.1.13, etc. Adv. -κῶς Ph.2.216, Sch.E.*Ph.*309. **-ητός**, ή, όν, Dor. **-ᾱτός**, ά, όν, *that wherewith one must be content* (cf. ἀγαπάω III), hence of only children, μοῦνος ἐὼν ἀ. Od.2.365; Ἑκτορίδην ἀ. Il.6.401, cf. Od.4.817, Sapph. 85, Ar.*Th.*761, Pl.*Alc.*1.131e; Νικήρατος.. ὁ τοῦ Νικίου ἀ. παῖς D.21. 165, cf. Arist.*Pol.*$1262^{b}23$, *EE*$1233^{b}2$; αὕτη μονογενὴς αὐτῷ ἀγαπητή Lxx *Jd.*11.34, cf. *To.*3.10, *Ev.Marc.*12.6 (but cf. also 11.2), etc.; ἀγαπητός· μονογενής, Hsch.:—so of things, Arist.*Rh.*$1365^{b}16$; δαπίδιον ἐν ἀ. Hipparch.Com.1; προβάτιον Men.319.3. 2. *to be acquiesced in* (as the least in a choice of evils), And.3.22, J.*BJ*5.10.3:—hence, ἀγαπητόν [ἐστι] *one must be content*, εἰ.., ἐάν.. Pl.*Prt.*328b, X.*Oec.* 8.16, D.18.220, Arist.*Metaph.*$1076^{a}15$, etc.; c. inf., *EN*$1171^{a}20$. II. of things, *desirable*, ἤθη X.*Mem.*3.10.5; βίος Pl.*Phlb.*61e (Sup.). 2. of persons, *beloved*, ἀδελφὲ ἀγαπητέ Lxx *To.*3.10: in letters, as a term of address, *Ep.Rom.*12.19, cf. *PGrenf.*2.73, etc. III. Adv. -τῶς *gladly, contentedly*, Pl.*Lg.*735d, D.19.219, etc. 2. *just enough to content one, barely, scarcely*, Pl.*Lys.*218c; ἀ. σωθῆναι Lys. 6.45, cf. Diph.89.2, etc.

ἀγαπώντως, = ἀγαπητῶς, Pl.*Lg.*735d, Numen.ap.Eus.*PE*14.5.

ἀγᾰρῐκόν, τό, name for various *tree-fungi*, Dsc.3.1, etc.: ἀ. ἄρρεν, *Boletus Agaricum*; ἀ. θῆλυ, *Agaricus dryinus*; ἀ. μέλαν, *fly-agaric*, *Amanita muscaria*, l.c. [ᾰγ Damocr.ap.Gal.14.96 (iamb.): ᾱγ Androm.ap.Gal.14.39 (hex.).]

ἀγαρράπτει· τε· ἔφθορεν, Hsch.

ἄγαρρις, ἡ, (ἀγείρω) *meeting*, *IG*14.759.12 (Naples), Hsch.

ἀγάρροος, ον, contr. -ρρους, ουν, (ῥέω) *strong-flowing*, Ἑλλήσποντος Il.2.845, 12.30; πόντος *h.Cer.*34; Τίγρις *AP*7.747 (Lib.), cf. Q.S. 10.174.

ἀγάς· ἡ πτῶσις τοῦ ἀστραγάλου, Hsch.

ἀγασθενής, ές, (σθένος) *very strong*, Opp.*C.*2.3, *Epigr.Gr.*1052 (Stratonicea):—in Il. only as pr. n. Ἀγασθένης.

ἄγασις, ἡ, *rejoicing*, *EM*9.52; *envy*, Hsch. (ἄγασσις cod.).

ἄγασμα, τό, (ἄγαμαι) *object of adoration*, S.*Fr.*971 (pl.).

ἀγάστονος, ον, *much groaning*, of the sea, Od.12.97, *h.Ap.*94: *loud-wailing, lamentable*, A.*Th.*99, cf. *AP*14.123; πόνος Naum.ap. Stob.4.22.32.

ἀγαστός, ή, όν, (ἄγαμαι) later form of Hom. ἀγητός, *admirable*, A.*Fr.*268; οὐκέτι μοι βίος ἀ. E.*Hec.*168; ἐκεῖνο δὲ κρίνω τοῦ ἀνδρὸς ἀ. X.*HG*2.3.56, cf. *An.*1.9.24, Plu.*Aem.*22, Procop.*Aed.*1.4. Adv. -τῶς, prob. in S.*Ichn.*243, cf. X.*Ages.*1.24. (Pure Att. θαυμαστός.)

ἀγάστωρ, ορος, ὁ, ἡ, (α copul., γαστήρ, cf. ἀδελφός) *from the same womb*: pl., *twins*, Hsch.: generally, *near kinsman*, Lyc.264.

ἀγασυλλίς, ίδος, ἡ, the plant which produces ἀμμωνιακόν, *Ferula marmarica*, Dsc.3.84.

ἀγάσυρτος, ὁ, '*swept and garnished*' (σύρω), epith. given to Pittacus by Alc.37B, cf. D.L.1.81.

ἀγᾱτός, ή, όν, = ἀγαστός, v.l. in *h.Ap.*515, (ἀγᾱ-) Theoc.1.126.

ἀγαυός, ή, όν, in Hom. almost always of kings or heroes, *illustrious, noble*, κήρυκες Il.3.268; Περσεφόνεια Od.11.213; πομπῆες *noble* guides, 13.71, cf. Pi.*P.*4.72; once in Trag., Πέρσαις ἀγαυοῖς A.*Pers.*986 (lyr.): Sup. -ότατος Od.15.229. 2. of things, *brilliant, glorious*, δῶρον *h.Merc.*442; θρόος Pi.*Pae.*9.36; esp. of stars, Arat.71, al., Man.2.14 (Sup.):—in late Prose, Hierocl. *in CA* 4 p.425 M. (Perh. α intens., γαίω, cf. Hdn.Gr.2.166.)

ἀγαυρ-ίᾱμα, τό, *insolence*, Lxx *Ba.*4.34, Hsch., *AB*325. **-ιάομαι**, *to be insolent*, Lxx *Jb.*3.14: Act., *EM*6.38.

ἀγαύρισμα, τό, kind of wrestling, Eust.1444.8.

ἀγαυρός, ά, όν, = γαῦρος with α euphon., *stately, proud*, ταῦρος Hes.

*Th.*832; δένδρον Nic.*Th.*832 (Sup.). Adv. Sup. -ότατα Hdt.7.57.β'. 2. Ion., euphem. for a beggar, *EM*6.30, Suid.

ἀγάφθεγκτος, ον, (φθέγγομαι) *loud-sounding*, ἀοιδαί Pi.*O.*6.91.

ἀγάω, = ἀγάζομαι, Alcm.121.

ἄγγᾰρα, τά, *daily stages of the* ἄγγαροι, *EM*7.17.

ἀγγᾰρ-εία, ἡ, *impressment for the public service*, *OGI*665.21 (pl.), cf. Arr.*Epict.*4.1.79; in pl. = *cursus publicus*, *SIG*880.53 (Pizus, iii A. D.). **-ευτής**, οῦ, ὁ, *one who impresses*, Hsch. s. v. ἀγγαρεύεται. II. *impressed workman, labourer*, *PSI*200.2 (vi A. D.); ὁ ἐπικείμενος τῶν ἀ. *PLand.*24.1 (vi A. D.). **-εύω**, *press* one *to serve as an* ἄγγαρος, generally, *press into service*, *Ev.Matt.*5.41, 27.32, *OGI* 665.24; κτήνη, πλοῖα *PTeb.*5.182, 252 (ii B. C.), cf. *PPetr.*2 p.64 (iii B. C.):—Pass., *to be pressed into service*, Men.440: metaph., *to be constrained*, Procop.*Arc.*13. **-ήιος**, ὁ, Ion. form of ἄγγαρος, Hdt.3.126. II. Subst. **-ήιον**, τό, *posting-system*, Id. 8.98.

ἄγγᾰρος, ὁ, in Persia, *mounted courier*, for carrying royal dispatches, Hdt.3.126, X.*Cyr.*8.6.17, Theopomp.Hist.106, etc. 2. term of abuse (= φορτηγός), ἄ. ὄλεθρος Men.2D., cf. Lib.*Or.*1.129. II. as Adj., ἄ. πῦρ the *courier* flame, of beacon fires, A.*Ag.* 282; ἄ. ἡμίονοι *posting-mules*, Lib.*Or.*18.143. (Assyr. *agarru*, 'hired labourer'.)

ἀγγαροφορέω, *bear as an* ἄγγαρος, Procop.*Arc.*30, *Aed.*2.4; generally, 'toil and moil', Men.10D.

ἄγγατος· τὸ εἰς ἀναδενδράδα ξύλον, Hsch.

ἀγγείδιον, τό, Dim. of ἀγγεῖον, Thphr.*HP*9.6.4, Hero*Spir.*1.6, Democr.ap.Gal.13.41 (prob. l.), *BGU*590.8 (ii A. D.). II. *gall-bladder*, Ruf.*Anat.*30.

ἀγγειο-λογέω, *take up a vein and operate upon it*, c. acc., interp. in Sor.1.85, cf. Paul.Aeg.6.5:—hence Subst. **-λογία**, ἡ, Antyll. or Heliod.ap.Orib.45.18.32, Aët.7.95.

ἀγγεῖον, Ion. **-ήιον**, τό, *vessel* for holding liquid or dry substances (τοῦτο.. ξηροῖς καὶ ὑγροῖς.. ἐργασθέν, ἀγγεῖον δὴ μιᾷ κλήσει προσφθεγγόμεθα Pl.*Plt.*287e); of metal, ἀργύρεα ἀ. silver *jars* or *vases* for water, Hdt.1.188; ἀργυρᾶ καὶ χαλκᾶ ἀ. Plu.2.695b; ἐν ἀ. χαλκῷ *mortar*, Thphr.*Lap.*60; ξύλινα ἀ. *tubs*, Hdt.4.2; *vessels* for holding money, in a treasury, Id.2.121.β'; for masons' use, Th.4.4; ὀστράκινα ἀ. Hp.*Mul.*2.193, Lxx *La.*4.2; *pails* or *buckets* used by firemen, Plu.*Rom.*20; *sacks* of leather, θύλακοι καὶ ἄλλα ἀ. X.*An.* 6.4.23; τὰς ῥαφὰς τῶν ἀ. Plu.*Lys.*16; for corn, Lxx *Ge.*42.25; for wine, Lxx 1*Ki.*25.18; for bread, 1*Ki.*9.7; *box* for petitions, *PTaur.* 1ii6 (ii B. C.), etc. 2. *receptacle, reservoir*, X.*Oec.*9.2, Pl.*Lg.* 845e; *bed* of the sea, Pl.*Criti.*111a. 3. *coffin, sarcophagus*, *IG* 12(2).494 (Lesbos), *BSA*17.227 (Pamphyl.), etc. II. of the human or animal body, *vessel, cavity*, Hp.*Morb.*4.37, Arist.*HA*521^{b}6, *PA*680^{b}33; of the veins, Id.*HA*511^{b}17, al.; the lungs, Id.*GA*787^{b}3; the female breast, Id.*PA*692^{a}12; *afterbirth*, Sor.2.57; of plants, *capsule*, Thphr.*HP*1.11.1:—later, *the body* itself, M.Ant.3.3, cf. Secund. *Sent.*7.

ἀγγειοτομία, ἡ, *section of a vein*, Paul.Aeg.6.31.

ἀγγειώδης, ες, *like a vessel, hollow*, Arist.*PA*671^{a}23, Eudem.*Fr.* 44, M.Ant.10.38.

ἀγγελία, Ion. and Ep. **-ίη**, ἡ, (ἄγγελος) *message, tidings*, as well the substance as the conveyance thereof, Il.18.17, Od.2.30, etc.; ἀ. λέγουσα τάδε Hdt.2.114; ἀγγελίην φάτο, ἀπόφασθε, ἀπέειπε, Il.18.17, 9.422, 7.416; φέρειν 15.174; πέμπειν Hdt.2.114; ἐσπέμπειν 3.69; τὰς ἀ. ἐσφέρειν 1.114, 3.77:—ἐμὴ ἀ. *a report of* me, *concerning* me, Il.19.337; ἀ. τινός *a message about* a person or thing, ἀγγελίην πατρὸς φέρει ἐρχομένοιο *news of* thy father's coming, Od.1. 408; ἀνέρος αἴθονος ἀ. S.*Aj.*222; ἀ. τῆς Χίου ἀφικνεῖται Th.8.15; ἦλθε ἀ. τῶν πόλεων ὅτι ἀφεστᾶσι Id.1.61: ἀ. ἦλθον ἐκ τῶν πολεμίων X.*Cyr.*6.2.14; with Verbs of motion, ἀγγελίην ἐλθεῖν Il.11. 140: Ep. in gen., τευ ἀγγελίης.. ἤλυθες Il.13.252; ἀγγελίης οἴχνεσκε 15.640; ἤλυθε σεῦ ἕνεκ' ἀγγελίης (i. e. ἀγγελίης σοῦ ἕνεκα) 3.206; ἀγγελίης πωλεῖται Hes.*Th.*781:—wrongly expl. by Sch.Il., Apollon.*Lex.* as a masc. Subst. ἀγγελίης. 2. *announcement, proclamation*, Pi.*P.*2.4: *command, order*, *h.Cer.*448, Pi.*O.*3.28, cf. Od.5.150, 7.263. 3. 'Α. personified as daughter of Hermes, Pi. *O.*8.82. II. *messenger*, Ἶρις ἀ. v. l. Hes.*Th.*781.

ἀγγελια-φορέω, *bear messages*, Sch.A.*Pr.*969. **-φόρος**, Ion. **ἀγγεληφ-**, ον, *messenger*, Hdt.1.120, Arist.*Mu.*398^{a}31, Luc. *Sacr.*8, etc.: esp. *Persian chamberlain*, Hdt.3.118.

ἀγγελικός, ή, όν, *of* or *for a messenger*, ῥῆσις Phryn.*PS* p.45B. b. *conveying information*, πάθος, of sensation, Gal.19. 378. 2. *angelic*, τάξις, νοῦς Procl.*in Ti.*1.341, 3.126D.; γένος Hierocl.*in CA*2 p.423M. Adv. -κῶς Procl.*in Ti.*3.192D.: opp. δαιμονίως, Id.*in Cra.*p.71P. II. ἀ. ὄρχησις Sicilian pantomimic dance at banquets, Ath.14.629e, cf. Poll.4.103, and v. ἄγγελος II; perh. from Ἄγγελος a name of Hecate, cf. Ath. l. c., Poll. l. c., Hsch.

ἀγγελιώτης, ου, ὁ, *messenger*, *h.Merc.*296, Call.*Jov.*68, *Hec.*1.1.6, Nonn.*D.*13.36: fem. **ἀγγελιῶτις**, ιδος, Call.*Del.*216.

ἀγγέλλω, (ἄγγελος): impf. ἀγγέλλεσκον Hsch.: Ep. and Ion. fut. ἀγγελέω Il.9.617, Hdt., Att. ἀγγελῶ, Dor. -ίω (ἀν-) *Tab.Heracl.*1.118: aor. 1 ἤγγειλα Hom., Att.: pf. ἤγγελκα Plb.35.4.2, (κατ-) Lys.25.30, (εἰσ-) Lycurg.1, (περι-) D.21.4:—**Med.** (v. infra): aor. ἠγγειλάμην (ἐπ-) Hdt.6.35, Pl.*Grg.*458d:—**Pass.**, fut. ἀγγελθήσομαι (ἀπ-) D.19. 324, later ἀγγελήσομαι (ἀν-) Lxx *Ps.*21(22).30: aor. ἠγγέλθην Hdt., Att.: pf. ἤγγελμαι A.*Ch.*774, Th.8.97: plpf. ἄγγελτο v. l. in Hdt. 7.37:—aor. 2 Pass. ἠγγέλην is found *IG*1.27b (ἐπ-), E.*IT*932, and became usual in Hellenistic Gk., cf. Lxx *Jo.*2.2 (ἀπ-), Plu.*Ant.*68, Hdn.3.7.1, etc.: aor. 2 Act. ἤγγελον is rare even in late writers, as (παρ-) App.*BC*1.121 without impf. as v. l., though in *AP*7.614 (Agath.) ἀγγελέτην is required by the metre:—*bear a message*, ὦρτο δὲ Ἶρις.. ἀγγελέουσα Il.8.409; τινί Od.4.24, 15.458: c. inf., οἵ κε.. κείνοις ἀγγείλωσι.. οἰκόνδε νέεσθαι *may bring* them *word* to return home, 16.350, cf. *EM*6.52: c. acc. inf., κήρυκες δ'.. ἀγγελλόντων.. γέροντας λέξασθαι Il.8.517. 2. c. acc. rei, *announce, report*, ἐσθλά Il.10.448; φάος ἠοῦς Od.13.94; Ποσειδάωνι πάντα τάδε Il. 15.159:—in Prose, μή τι νεώτερον ἀγγέλλεις; Pl.*Prt.*310b; prov., οὐ πόλεμον ἀγγέλλεις 'that's good news', Id.*Phdr.*242b; ἀγγέλλωμεν ἐς πόλιν τάδε; E.*Or.*1539; πρὸς τίν' ἀγγεῖλαί με χρὴ λόγους; Id.*Supp.* 399. 3. c. acc. pers., *bring news of*.., εἴ κέ μιν ἀγγείλαιμι Od.14.120; later, ἀ. περί τινος S.*El.*1111:—dependent clauses are added with a Conj., ἤγγειλ' ὅττι ῥά οἱ πόσις ἔκτοθι μίμνε Il.22.439; ἀ. ὡς.. E.*IT*704, D.18.169; ὁθούνεκα.. S.*El.*47:—also in part., ἢ καὶ θανόντ' ἤγγειλαν; ib.1452; Κῦρον ἐπιστρατεύοντα.. ἤγγειλεν X.*An.*2.3.19, cf. *Cyr.*6.2.15; with ὡς, πατέρα τὸν σὸν ἀγγελῶν ὡς οὐκέτ' ὄντα S.*OT*955; ἤγγειλας ὡς τεθνηκότα Id.*El.*1341. II. Med., only pres., Τεύκρῳ ἀγγέλλομαι εἶναι φίλος *I announce myself* to him as a friend, Id.*Aj.*1376. III. Pass., *to be reported of*, ἐπὶ τὸ πλεῖον Th.6.34: c. part., ζῶν ἢ θανὼν ἀγγέλλεται S.*Tr.*73, cf. E. *Hec.*591, Th.3.16, X.*HG*4.3.13: c. inf., ἤγγελται ἡ μάχη ἰσχυρὰ γεγονέναι Pl.*Chrm.*153b, cf. X.*Cyr.*5.3.30:—ἠγγέλθη τοῖς στρατηγοῖς, ὅτι φεύγοιεν that.., Id.*HG*1.1.27:—ἐπὶ τοῖς ἠγγελμένοις Th.8.97. (ἀπ-αγγέλλω is more common in Oratt.)

ἄγγελμα, τό, *message, tidings*, E.*Or.*876, Th.7.74, etc.

ἄγγελος, ὁ, ἡ, *messenger, envoy*, Il.2.26, etc.; δι' ἀγγέλων ὁμιλέειν τινί Hdt.5.92.ζ', cf. *SIG*229.25 (Erythrae):—prov., Ἀράβιος ἄ., of a loquacious person, Men.32. 2. generally, *one that announces* or *tells*, e. g. of birds of augury, Il.24.292, 296; Μουσῶν ἄγγελος, of a poet, Thgn.769; ἄγγελε ἔαρος.. χελιδοῖ Simon.74; ἄ. ἄφθογγος, of a beacon, Thgn.549; of the nightingale, ὄρνις.. Διὸς ἄ. S.*El.*149: c. gen. rei, ἄ. κακῶν ἐμῶν Id.*Ant.*277; ἄγγελον γλῶσσαν λόγων E.*Supp.*203; αἴσθησις ἡμῖν ἄ. Plot.5.3.3; neut. pl., ἄγγελα νίκης Nonn.*D.*34.226. 3. *angel*, Lxx *Ge.*28.12, al., *Ev.Matt.*1. 24, al., Ph.2.604, etc. 4. in later philos., *semi-divine being*, ἡλιακοὶ ἄ. Jul.*Or.*4.141b, cf. Iamb.*Myst.*2.6, Procl. *in R.*2.243K.; ἄ. καὶ ἀρχάγγελοι *Theol.Ar.*43.10, cf. Dam.*Pr.*183, al.: also in mystical and magical writings, Herm.ap.Stob.1.49.45, *PMag.Lond.*46.121, etc. II. title of Artemis at Syracuse, Hsch.

ἀγγέλτειρα, ἡ, fem., = foreg., prob. in Orph.*H.*78.3.

ἀγγελτικός, ή, όν, *premonitory*: c. gen., τεράστια συμφορᾶς ἀ. Heracl.*Alleg.*42; τοῦ μέλλοντος Porph.*Abst.*3.3: ἀ. ζῴδια Jul.Laod. in *Cat.Cod.Astr.*5(1).192.

ἀγγέριος· ἄγγελος, Hsch. **ἀγγεράκομον**· σταφυλήν, Id.

ἀγγοθήκη, ἡ, *receptacle for vessels*, Ath.5.210c, cf. ἐγγυθήκη.

ἀγγοπήνια· τὰ τῶν μελισσῶν κηρία, Hsch., Suid. **ἀγγόρπη**· ᾧ τοὺς ἐλέφαντας τύπτουσι σιδήρῳ, Hsch.

ἄγγος, εος, τό, *vessel* to hold liquids, e.g. wine, Od.16.13, cf. 2. 289; milk, Il.16.643; *vat* for the vintage, Hes.*Op.*613; *pitcher*, Hdt. 5.12, E.*El.*55; *bucket, pail*, Hdt.4.62; *wine-bowl*, E.*IT*953, 960. II. for dry substances, *cradle*, Hdt.1.113, E.*Ion*32, 1337; *casket*, S.*Tr.* 622; *cinerary urn*, Id.*El.*1118, 1205; *coffin*, *CIG*3573 (Assos). III. of parts of the body, e.g. *womb*, Hp.*Epid.*6.5.11, v. Gal. ad loc.; τρόφιμον ἄ. *stomach*, Tim.*Pers.*73. IV. *shell* of the κάραβος, Opp. *H.*2.406. V. *cell* of a honey-comb, *AP*9.226 (Zonas).

ἄγγουρος, kind of *cake* or *tart*, Hsch. **ἀγγριάς**· τοὺς ἐρεθισμούς· οἱ δὲ τὰς ἀνίας, Orion ap.*EM*6.49, cf. Hsch. **ἀγγρίζειν**· ὑφαιρεῖσθαι (cf. ἀγρέω), ἐρεθίζειν, Hsch., *EM*7.28. **ἀγγρίς**· ὀδύνη, Suid. **ἀγγρισμός**, *irritatio*, *Gloss.* **ἀγγριστής**, *irritator*, ib.

ἄγγων, ωνος, ὁ, *Frankish javelin*, Agath.2.5.

ἄγδην, Adv. (ἄγω) *by carrying*, ἄγδην σύρειν Luc.*Lex.*10.

ἄγε, ἄγετε, imper. of ἄγω, used as Adv., *come on!* freq. in Hom., who mostly strengthens it, εἰ δ' ἄγε, νῦν δ' ἄγε, ἄγε δή, ἀλλ' ἄγε, in Att. freq. ἄγε νύν Ar.*Eq.*1011, etc.; before 1 and 2 pers. pl., ἄγε δὴ τραπείομεν Il.3.441; ἄγε δὴ στέωμεν 11.348; ἄγε τάμνετε Od.3.332; ἀλλ' ἄγε, Πέρσαι, φροντίδα θώμεθα A.*Pers.*140; ἄγε δὴ καὶ χορὸν ἄψωμεν Id.*Eu.*307; rarely before 1 sg., ἄγε δὴ.. ἀριθμήσω Od.13.215; before 3 pl., ἀλλ' ἄγε, κήρυκες.. λαὸν.. ἀγειρόντων Il.2.437; in Prose, ἄγε τοίνυν.. σκοπῶμεν X.*Cyr.*5.5.15; foll. by ὅπως c. fut., Ar.*Ec.*149; abs., E.*Cyc.*590:—also, ἄγετε,.. λύσασθε A.*Ch.*803; ἄγετε with 1 pl., Il.2.139, Od.1.76, Ar.*Lys.*665; with 1 sg., Od.22.139: cf. ἄγι.

ἀγέγωνος, ον, *speechless*, πέτρα Epigr. in *AEM*6.6 (Callatis).

ἄγεθλον, τό, (ἄγω) *sacrificial victim*, *GDI*1266 (Pamphyl.).

ἄγει, Dor. = ἄγρει, *An.Ox.*1.71.

ἄγειος, ον, (γῆ) *landless*, corrupt in A.*Supp.*858.

ἀγείρᾰτος, ον, poet. for ἀγέραστος, Hdn.Gr.2.269.

ἀγείρω, Aeol. **ἀγέρρω** *EM*8.13: fut. ἀγερῶ *IG*5(1).1447.16 (Messene, ii B. C.): aor. 1 ἤγειρα, Ep. ἄγειρα Od.14.285:—**Med.**, aor. 1 ἠγειράμην A.R.4.1335, (συν-) Od.14.323, Ael.*VH*4.14:—**Pass.**, aor. 1 ἠγέρθην Hom.: pf. ἀγήγερμαι App.*BC*2.134: plpf. ἀγήγερτο Id.*Mith.*108, Ep. 3 pl. ἀγηγέρατο Il.4.211, App.*Hisp.*40.—Hom. has shortened pres. ἀγέρεσθαι (al. ἀγερέσθαι) Od.2.385 (also in later Ep., A.R.3.895, etc., cf. *IG*14.1389 i 35), aor. 2 ἀγέροντο Il.18.245, part. ἀγρόμενος 2.481, etc.:—*gather together*, λαὸν ἀγείρων Il.4.377, etc.; ἐνθάδ' ἀπὸ.. πολίων ἤγειρα ἕκαστον 17.222; so in Att., τὸν ἐς Θήβας στόλον S.*OC*1306, Th.1.9; τὸ Ἑλλάδος στράτευμα S.*El.*695;

στρατιάν X.An.3.2.13, cf. App.Mith.84; εἰς μίαν οἴκησιν ἀ. κοινωνούς Pl.R.369c:—Pass., *gather, assemble*, Il.2.52, Od.2.8, etc.; ἀγρόμενοι σύες *herded* swine, Od.16.3; θυμὸς ἐνὶ στήθεσσιν ἀγέρθη, ἐς φρένα θυμὸς ἀγέρθη Il.4.152, 22.475 (cf. ἐγείρω). II. of things, *collect, gather*, δημόθεν ἄλφιτα.. καὶ αἴθοπα οἶνον ἀγείρας Od.19.197; πολὺν βίοτον καὶ χρυσὸν ἀγείρων 3.301; πολλὰ δ' ἄγειρα χρήματα 14.285:—so in Med., ἀγειρόμενοι κατὰ δῆμον 13.14. 2. *collect by begging*, ὡς ἂν πύρνα κατὰ μνηστῆρας ἀγείροι 17.362, cf. Hdt.1.61; ἀφ' ὧν ἀγείρει καὶ προσαιτεῖ D.8.26:—abs., *collect money* for the gods, Νύμφαις ἀ. A.Fr.168, cf. Hdt.4.35, Pl.R.381d, SIG1015.26 (Halicarnassus); esp. for Cybele, Luc.Alex.13, cf. μητραγύρτης:—abs., *go about begging*, Philostr.VA5.7, Man.6.299, Max.Tyr.19.3, etc. 3. *put things together, accumulate arguments*, as in a speech, A.Ch.638. 4. ὀφρύας εἰς ἓν ἀ. *frown*, AP5.299 (Paul. Sil.).—Rare in good Prose.

ἀγείσωτος, ον, *without cornice*, EM8.55.

ἀγείτης· ὑβριστής, Hsch., EM8.51. (Perh. f.l. for ἀλείτης.)

ἀγείτων, ον, gen. ονος, *neighbourless*, πάγος A.Pr.272; οἶκος φίλων ἀ. E.El.1130; ἄφιλος καὶ ἀ. Plu.2.423e.

ἀγελάζομαι, Pass., *to be gregarious, flock*, Arist.HA597^{b}7, 610^{b}2, Nic.Dam.p.151D.; ἐς τὴν ἤπειρον Men.Prot.p.49D.:—Act., ἀγελάσαι· κομίσαι, Hsch.

ἀγελαιοκομικός, ή, όν, (κομέω) *pertaining to cattle-breeding*; ἡ ἀγελαιοκομικὴ (sc. τέχνη) *the art of breeding and keeping cattle*, Pl.Plt.275e sq., 299d.

ἀγελαῖος, α, ον, (ἀγέλη) *belonging to a herd*, in Hom. always with βοῦς, Il.11.729, Od.10.410, al., cf. S.Aj.175; βοσκήματα E.Ba.677; αἱ ἀ. τῶν ἵππων, i.e. brood-mares, X.Eq.5.8. II. *in herds* or *shoals, gregarious*, ἰχθύες Hdt.2.93; ἀγελαῖα, τά, *gregarious animals*, Pl.Plt.264d; opp. μοναδικά, σποραδικά, Arist.HA487^{b}34, Pol.1256^{a}23; πολιτικὸν ὁ ἄνθρωπος ζῷον πάσης μελίττης καὶ παντὸς ἀ. ζῴου μᾶλλον ib.1253^{a}8. 2. *of the common herd*, ἀ. ἄνθρωποι, opp. ἄρχοντες, Pl.Plt.268a; hence, *common, ordinary*, ἀ. ἰσχάδες Eup.374; ἄρτοι Pl.Com.76; κεραμίδες SIG^{2}587.209, cf. Ath.Mitt.22.182 (Lebad.):—σοφισταί Isoc.12.18, νῆσοι Philostr.Im.2.17; proparox. in this sense, Eust.1752.63.

ἀγελαιο-τροφία, ἡ, *keeping of herds*, Pl.Plt.261e. **-τροφικός**, ή, όν, *of* or *fit for* ἀγελαιοτροφία: ἡ -κή, = foreg., Pl.Plt.267b. **-τρόφος**, ον, *keeping herds*, Max.Tyr.26.6, al.

ἀγελαιών, ῶνος, ὁ, *a place for herds* (τὰ ἀγελαῖα), *pasture*, Suid.

ἀγέλαοι, οἱ, *members of an* ἀγέλη II, GDI4952 (Dreros).

ἀγελ-αρχέω, *lead a herd* or *company*, Ph.1.679: c. gen., 1.658, Plu.Galb.17. **-άρχης**, ου, ὁ, (ἄρχω) *leader of a flock* or *herd*, Procl.in Cra.p.38P.; ἀ. ταῦρος Luc.Am.22: generally, *leader, captain*, Plu.Rom.6; τῶν φιλοσοφίας ἐραστῶν Procl.in Prm.p.526S.:—also **-αρχος**, ὁ, dub. l. in Ph.2.144. **-αρχία**, ἡ, IGRom.3.648 (Idebessus, ii A.D.):—Adj. **-αρχικός**, prob. l. for -ιανός, ibid.

ἀγέλασμα, ατος, τό, *gathering, crowd*, νούσων Procl.H.7.44.

ἀγελ-αστέω, *to be* ἀγέλαστος, Heraclit.Ep.7.2,9. **-αστί**, Adv. *without laughter*, Pl.Euthd.278e, Thphr.Fr.124, Plu.2.727a.

ἀγελαστικός, ή, όν, *gregarious, social*, Ph.2.202, Max.Tyr.21.7.

ἀγέλαστος, ον, (γελάω) *not laughing, grave, gloomy*, h.Cer.200; ἀ. πρόσωπα βιαζόμενοι A.Ag.794; of the orator Crassus, Lucil.ap.Cic.Fin.5.30, cf. Vett.Val.75.11: metaph., Σίβυλλα ἀγέλαστα φθεγγομένη Heraclit.92; ἀ. φρήν A.Fr.290; βίος Phryn.Com.18; ἀ. πέτρα, stone at Eleusis on which Demeter sat, SIG^{2}587.183, Apollod.1.5.1. II. Pass., *not to be laughed at, not trifling*, ξυμφοραί A.Ch.30, v.l. Od.8.307.

ἀγελάτης, Dor. **-άτας**, ου, ὁ, chief of an ἀγέλη II, Heraclid.Pol.15. II. = ἔφηβος, Hsch. (cod. ἀγελάστους), cf. GDI5142 (Oaxos).

ἀγελείη, ἡ, Ep. epith. of Athena, = ἄγουσα λείαν, *driver of spoil, the forager*, Il.6.269, etc., cf. Hes.Sc.197. II. ἀγελεία, ἡ, mystical name of *Seven*, Theol.Ar.42.30.

ἀγέλ-η, ἡ, (ἄγω) *herd*, of horses, Il.19.281; elsewhere in Hom. always of oxen and kine, Il.11.678, etc., cf. βουνόμος:—also, *any herd* or *company*, συῶν ἀ. Hes.Sc.168; ἀ. παρθένων Pi.Fr.112; μαινάδων E.Ba.1022; πτηνῶν ἀγέλαι S.Aj.168, E.Ion106; *shoal* of fish, Opp.H.3.639: metaph., πόνων ἀγέλαι E.HF1276:—also in Pl.R.451c, Arist.HA570^{a}27, etc., but rare in early Prose. II. in Crete and at Sparta, *bands* in which boys were trained, Ephor.64, Plu.Lyc.16, Heraclid.Pol.15, GDI4952 (Dreros), etc.; νέων ἀ. Epigr.Gr.223.8 (Miletus); ἀϊθέων ib.239 (Smyrna). III. = ἀστρικαὶ σφαῖραι Theol.Ar.43.6. **-ηδόν**, Adv. (ἀγέλη) *in herds* or *companies*, Il.16.160, Hdt.2.93, AP9.24 (Leon.), etc.:—also **-ηδά**, Arat.965, 1079. **-ηθεν**, Adv. (ἀγέλη) *from a herd*, A.R.1.356, 406. **-ηΐς**, ίδος, ἡ, pecul. fem. of ἀγελαῖος, Numen.ap.Ath.7.327b. II. = ἀγελείη, Corn.ND20. **-ηκόμος**, ον, *keeping herds*, Nonn.D.47.208. **-ήτης**, ου, ὁ, *belonging to a herd*, βοῦς Suid.; cf. ἀγελάτης. **-ητρόφος**, ὁ, *horse-keeper*, Poll.1.181 (v.l. ἀγελο-). **-ηφι**, Ep. dat. of ἀγέλη, Il.2.480. **-ίζει**· ἀθροίζει, *gregat*, Gloss. **-ικός**, ή, όν, *of the flock*, πρόβατα Sammelb.4322.9 (i A.D.). **-ισμός**, ὁ, gloss on ἀγελαῖος, Sch.Opp.C.1.240.

ἀγέλοιος, ον, *not laughable*, οὐκ ἀγέλοιον *no bad joke*, Henioch.4.6. Adv. -ως Arg.1 Ar.Ra.

ἄγελος, ου, ὁ, = ἀγέλη III, Theol.Ar.43.6.

ἀγέμιστος, ον, *not put on board ship*, στέμφυλα, PAvrom.1^{b}34 (i B.C.).

ἄγεν, Ep. for ἐάγησαν, v. sub ἄγνυμι, Il.4.214.

ἀγενεᾱλόγητος, ον, *of unrecorded descent*, Ep.Heb.7.3.

ἀγένεια, ἡ, (ἀγενής) *low birth*, Arist.Pol.1317^{b}40.

ἀγένειος, ον, (γένειον) *beardless, boyish*; ἀγένειόν τι εἰρηκέναι to speak *like a boy*, Luc.J.Tr.29; τὸ ἀ. Id.Eun.9. Adv. -είως, ἔχειν Philostr.VS1.8.1. II. ἀγένειοι, οἱ, *boys* within the age to enter for certain prizes at the games, Pi.O.8.54, 9.89, cf. Ar.Eq.1373, Lys.21.4, Pl.Lg.833c, IG2.965, al., Paus.6.6.3. III. (γενεά) *childless*, GDI1891.29 (Delph.), Hsch.

ἀγεν-ής, ές, (γενέσθαι) *unborn, uncreated*, Pl.Ti.27c. II. *of no family, ignoble*, opp. ἀγαθός, S.Fr.84, cf. POxy.33^{v}5.5 (ii A.D.); of things, οὐκ ἀγενεῖς στίχοι Sch.Od.11.568; cf. AB336, St.Byz. s.v. Ἀνακτορεία. III. *childless*, Is.2.10, cf. Harp. (ἄπαις codd.). **-ησία**, ἡ, *uncreatedness*, τοῦ κόσμου Simp.in Cael.139.24. **-ητος**, ον, (γενέσθαι) *uncreated, unoriginated*, Parm.8.3, Heraclit.50; of the elements, Emp.7; ἀρχή Pl.Phdr.245d, cf. Arist.Cael.281^{b}26, al. Adv. -τως Plu.2.1015b (prob.), Syr.in Metaph.146.1, Dam.Pr.409. II. *not having happened*, Gorg.Pal.23; τὸ γὰρ φανθὲν τίς ἂν δύναιτ' ἂν ἀγένητον ποιεῖν; S.Tr.743; ἅπαντα τὰ πρῶτον ἦλθ' ἅπαξ Id.Fr.860; ἀγένητα ποιεῖν, ἅσσ' ἂν ᾖ πεπραγμένα Agatho5; αἰτίαι ἀ. *groundless* charges, Aeschin.3.225; διαβολαί Alciphr.3.58; ὕπνοι ἀ. *baseless* dreams, Phld.D.1.22; ὧν οὐδὲν.. ἀ. was *left undone*, Isoc.20.8. III. translator's error for Lat. *infectus, dyed*, Edict.Diocl.24.13.

ἀγένν-εια (in Mss. often ἀγένεια or ἀγεννία), ἡ, *meanness, baseness*, Arist.Virt.Vit.1251^{b}16, Plb.30.9.1, al., Phld.Herc.1457.4. II. *sordidness*, opp. πολυτέλεια, D.S.33.7. **-ής**, ές, (γέννα) = ἀγενής II (q.v.), *low-born*, Hdt.1.134 (Comp.), Pl.Prt.319d, etc.; οἱ ἀ., opp. οἱ γενναῖοι, Arist.Pol.1296^{b}22, etc.; of a cock, Pl.Tht.164c, Men.223.13. 2. of things, *sordid*, Hdt.5.6, Pl.Grg.465b, 513d, al.; βωμολοχεύματ' Ar.Pax748; οὐδὲν ἀ. Dem.21.152. Adv. -νῶς E.IA1458, Pl.Com.46.6.—In Pl. mostly with neg., οὐκ ἀ. Chrm.158c, etc. **-ησία**, ἡ, *uncreatedness*, opp. γένεσις, τῆς ὕλης Herm.ap.Stob.1.11.2. **-ητος**, ον, (γεννάω) *unbegotten, unborn*, ἀ. τότ' ᾖ S.OC973: *unoriginated*, Pl.Ti.52a. Adv., ἀναιτίως καὶ ἀ. Plu.2.1015b codd. 2. *non-existent*, αἰτία Aret.SD2.11. II. = ἀγεννής, *low-born, mean*, S.Tr.61. III. Act., *not productive*, Thphr.CP6.10.1. Adv. -τως *without leaving issue*, Epigr.Gr.333a (Perg.). **-ία**, v. sub ἀγέννεια. **-ίζω**, *act like an* ἀγεννής, Teles p.6.4H.

ἀγέομαι, Dor. for ἡγέομαι: τὰ ἀγημενα *custom, prescription*, Orac.ap.D.43.66.

ἀγέραστος, ον, (γέρας) *without a gift of honour, unrecompensed*, Il.1.119, Hes.Th.395; ἀ. τύμβος, ὄνομα E.Hec.115, Ba.1378; ἀπελθεῖν ἀ. Luc.Tyr.3: c. gen., θυέων ἀ. A.R.3.65:—cf. ἀγείρᾰτος.

ἀγέρδα (ἀγέραα cod.)· ἄπιος, ὄγχνη, Hsch.

ἀγερέθω, v. sub ἠγερέθομαι.

ἄγερθεν, Dor. and Ep. 3 pl. aor. 1 Pass. of ἀγείρω.

ἀγερ-μός, ὁ, *collection of money for the service of the gods* (cf. ἀγείρω II.2), SIG1015.27 (Halicarnassus), D.H.2.19 (with v.l. ἀγυρμός), Ath.8.360d, Poll.3.111. II. *the call-to-arms* of the Greeks against Troy, Arist.Po.1451^{a}27. III. metaph., *collection*, of wisdom and experience, Ael.VH4.20. **-μοσύνη**, ἡ, = ἄγερσις, Opp.C.4.251. **-σῐκύβηλις** [ῠ], ὁ, *mendicant priest*, Cratin.62. (From κύβηλις II, not Κυβέλη.) **-σις**, εως, ἡ, *gathering, mustering*, στρατιῆς Hdt.7.5,48. II. = πανήγυρις, SIG^{2}660.3 (Miletus, iii B.C., pl.). **-της**, Dor. **-τας**, ὁ, *collector of dues*, IG14.423i35 (Tauromenium).

ἀγερωπεῖ (-ύπτει cod.)· ἐφορᾷ, ἀσπαστὸν ἡγεῖται, Hsch., cf. Et.Gud., EM8.29. **ἀγερώσσει**· ἀγρυπνεῖ, Hsch., Et.Gud.

ἀγερ-ωχία, ἡ, *arrogance*, Plb.10.35.8, D.Chr.32.9; in good sense, *high-heartedness*, Ps.-Callisth.3.25. II. *revelry*, Lxx Wi.2.9; pl., *feats of mastery*, Philostr.VA2.28. **-ωχος** [ᾰ], ον, poet. Adj. (used also in late Prose, v. infr.), in Hom. always in good sense, *high-minded, lordly*, Τρῶες, Ῥόδιοι, Μυσοί, Il.3.36, 2.654, 10.430, cf. Alcm.122, B.5.35; βάτραχοι Batr.145; once of a single man, viz. Periclymenus, Od.11.286, Hes.Fr.14; of *noble* actions, ἀ. ἔργματα Pi.N.6.34; νίκη O.10(11).79; πλούτου στεφάνωμ' ἀ. *lordly* crown of wealth, P.1.50; *high-spirited*, Philostr.Im.2.2, al.; ἀγέρωχα σκιρτᾶν ib.32; -ότερα γυμνάσια Id.Gym.46. II. later in bad sense, *arrogant*, Archil.154, Alc.120, Com.Adesp.162, Lxx 3Ma.1.25; ἀ. ὄνος Luc.Asin.40; of things, φυτόν Anacreont.53.42. Adv. -χως AP9.745 (Anyte), Plb.2.8.7: Comp. -ότερον Id.18.34.3.

Ἀγεσίλαος, Ἀγεσίλας, v. sub Ἀγησίλαος.

ἀγεσίφρων· τὰς ὀφρῦς ἐπαίρων, Hsch. (fort. -οφρύων).

ἀγέστρατος, ὁ, ἡ, *host-leading*, Ἀθήνη Hes.Th.925; ἦχος, αὐλός, Nonn.D.26.15, 28.28.

ἀγέτης, ἀγέτις, Dor. for ἡγ-.

ἀγετοί· θαυμαστοί, ἔνδοξοι, Hsch. **ἀγέτρια**· μαῖα (Tarent.), Id. (perh. for ἀγρέτρια, cf. ἀγρέω). **ἀγευστί**, gloss on ἀπαστί, Id.

ἀγευστία, ἡ, *fasting*, Sch.Ar.Nu.621.

ἄγευστος, ον, (γεύομαι) Act., *not tasting* or *having tasted*, πλακοῦντος Pl.Com.113; ἰχθύων Luc.Sat.28: metaph., οἶσι κακῶν ἄ. αἰών S.Ant.583; ἐλευθερίας ἄ. Pl.R.576a; τῶν τερπνῶν X.Mem.2.1.23; τοῦ καλοῦ Arist.EN1179^{b}15; τῶν ἀγαθῶν Phld.Ir.p.60W.; προβλήματα ἀμφιβολίας καὶ ζητήσεως ἄ. Alex.Aphr.Pr.Praef.:—abs., *without eating*, ἄποτοι καὶ ἄ. Luc.Tim.18. II. Pass., *tasteless*, Arist.de An.422^{a}30. 2. *untasted*, Plu.2.731d, Porph.Abst.2.27.

ἀγεωμέτρητος, ον, of persons, *ignorant of geometry*, Arist.APo.77^{b}13; ἀ. μηδεὶς εἰσίτω, Inscr. on Plato's door, Elias in Cat.118.18, cf. Phlp.in de An.117.29. Adv. -τως Anon.in SE29.35. 2. of problems, *not geometrical*, Arist.*APo.*77b17. II. *not measured* or *surveyed*, prob. in *PTeb.*87.84 (ii B.C.).

ἀγεωργ-ησία, ἡ, *bad husbandry*, Thphr.*CP*2.15.1. **-ητος**, ον, *uncultivated*, Thphr.*CP*1.16.2, *PPar.*63.6 (ii B.C.), *SIG*685.73 (Magn. Mae., ii B.C.), D.S.2.36, Ph.1.564, etc. **-ίου** δικάζεσθαι bring an action *for neglect of tillage*, Phryn.*PS* p.33 B.

ἄγη, Dor. **ἄγα** [ᾰγ], ἡ, (ἄγαμαι) *wonder, amazement*, Hom. only in phrase ἄγη μ' ἔχει Il.21.221, Od.3.227, 16.243: glossed by τιμή, σεβασμός, Hsch. II. *envy, malice*, φθόνῳ καὶ ἄγῃ χρεώμενος Hdt.6.61; of the gods, *jealousy*, μή τις ἄγα θεόθεν κνεφάσῃ A.*Ag.* 131: pl. ἄγαις, = ζηλώσεσιν, Id.*Fr.*85.

ἀγή (A), Dor. **ἀγά** [ᾱγ], ἡ, (ἄγνυμι) *breakage*: 1. *fragment, splinter*, ἀγαῖσι κωπῶν A.*Pers.*425; πρὸς ἁρμάτων τ' ἀγαῖσι E.*Supp.* 693. 2. κύματος ἀγή *place where* the wave *breaks, beach*, A.R.1.554, Numen.ap.Ath.7.305a. 3. *curve, bending*, ὄφιος, ποταμοῦ, Arat.668, 729 (v.l.):—hence Böckh cj. ἀγάν (for ἄγαν) Pi.*P.*2.82, in the sense of *crooked arts, deceit*. 4. *wound*, Hsch.

ἀγή (B), ἡ, (ἄγω) = ἀγωγή, ξύλων *Michel* 1359.17 (Chios).

ἄγη, Ep. for ἐάγη, v. sub ἄγνυμι.

ἀγηθής, ές, *joyless*, cj. in S.*Tr.*869.

ἀγηλᾰτ-έω, *drive out one accursed* or *polluted*, esp. *one guilty of sacrilege and murder*, Hdt.5.72, S.*OT*402, Arist.*Ath.*20.3:—also **-ίζω**, *EM*10.34.

ἀγήλατος, ον, (ἄγος, ἐλαύνω) *driving out a curse*, ἀ. μάστιξ, i.e. lightning *which consumes and so purifies*, Lyc.436.

ἄγημα, τό, (from ἄγω, or perh. Dor. for ἥγημα; Boeot. **ἄγειμα**, *BCH*18.534 (Thisbe)) *anything led, division, corps* of an army, of the Lacedaemonians, X.*Lac.*11.9, 13.6: in the Macedonian army, *the Guard*, Plb.5.65.2, Arr.*An.*1.1.11; τῶν ἱππέων τὸ ἄ. ib.4.24.1; τῶν πεζῶν τὸ ἄ. 2.8.3; τῶν ἐλεφάντων Phylarch.1: in the armies of the Ptolemies, etc., *PPetr.*3p.22 (iii B.C.), Plu.*Eum.*7, App.*Syr.*32, cf. Ael.Dion.*Fr.*8; βασιλικὸν ἄ. Plb.5.82.4. II. name of a district in the Heracleopolite nome, *PHib.*101.3, *PTeb.*3.38.4.

ἀγηνόρειος, Dor. **ἀγᾱνόρ-**, α, ον, = ἀγήνωρ, A.*Pers.*1026.

ἀγην-ορέω [ᾰ], *to be valiant*, Nonn.*D.*12.206, 37.338, al. **-ορία**, ἡ, *manliness, courage*, of men, Il.22.457; *arrogance, pride*, in pl., 9.700; sg., Nonn.*D.*42.384, *AP*10.75.7 (Pall.), etc.; of a lion, Il. 12.46. **-ωρ**, Dor. **ἀγάνωρ**, ορος, ὁ, ἡ, (ἀγα-, ἀνήρ) poet. Adj. *manly, heroic*, θυμός Il.2.276, 12.300; κραδίη καὶ θυμὸς ἀ. 9.635, etc.; βίῃ καὶ ἀγήνορι θυμῷ εἴξας, of a lion, 24.42: freq. with collat. notion of *headstrong, arrogant*, of Achilles, 9.699; Thersites, 2.276; the suitors, Od.1.106, 144, al.; the Titans, Hes.*Th.*641, cf. *Op.*7; the Seven against Thebes, A.*Th.*124 (lyr.). 2. of animals and things, *stately, magnificent*, ἵππος Pi.*O.*9.23; *lavish*, μισθός *P.*3.55; πλοῦτος ib.10.18; κόμπος *I.*1.43.

ἀγήοχα, pf. of ἄγω.

ἀγήραντος, ον, = sq., Simon.100.4, E.*Epigr.*2.1.

ἀγήραος, ον, Att. contr. **ἀγήρως**, ων (of which Hom. uses nom. dual ἀγήρω (v. infr.), nom. sg. and acc. pl. ἀγήρως Od.5.218, al.); acc. sg. ἀγήρων *h.Cer.*242; ἀγήρω Hes.*Th.*949, Jul.*Or.*4.142b: nom. pl. ἀγήρῳ Hes.*Th.*277; dat. ἀγήρῳς Ar.*Av.*689:—*ageless, undecaying*, ἀθάνατος καὶ ἀγήρως ἤματα πάντα Il.8.539; σὺ δ' ἀθάνατος καὶ ἀ. Od.5.218; ἀγήρω τ' ἀθανάτω τε Il.12.323, cf. Hes.*Th.*949; ἀπήμαντος καὶ ἀ. ib.955; ἄνοσοι καὶ ἀ. Pi.*Fr.*143; ἀ. χρόνῳ δυνάστας S.*Ant.*608 (lyr.). 2. of things, once in Hom., of the aegis, Il.2.447; κῦδος ἀ. Pi.*P.*2.52; χάριν τ' ἀγήρων ἕξομεν E.*Supp.*1178: in Prose, τὸν ἀγήρων ἔπαινον Th.2.43; ἀθάνατον καὶ ἀ. πάθος Pl.*Phlb.*15d, etc.

ἀγηρασία, ἡ, *eternal youth*, Sch.Il.11.1.

ἀγήρατον, τό, *pot-marjoram, Origanum Onites*, Dsc.4.58. 2. = θύμβρα, Ps.-Dsc.3.37.

ἀγήρᾱτος (A), ον, *ageless*, κλέος E.*IA*567 (lyr.), *IG*14.1930.3: also in Prose, Lys.2.79, X.*Mem.*4.3.13, Pl.*Ax.*370d, Arist.*Cael.* 270b2, Gal.12.201. [Later -ᾰτος, *Epigr.Gr.*35a (Athens), *IG*14.1188, Orac.ap.Ps.-Callisth.1.33.]

ἀγήρατος (B), ὁ, *stone* used by shoemakers to polish women's shoes, Gal.12.201, Asclep.ap.Aët.8.43.

ἀγής [ᾱ], ές, *guilty, accursed*, dub. in Hippon.11. II. in good sense, *pure, holy*, of the sun, ἀγέα κύκλον Emp.47.

Ἀγήσανδρος, ὁ, epith. of Pluto, = Ἀγησίλαος, Hsch.

ἀγησί-λᾱος [ᾱγ], ου, ὁ, *leader of the people*, epith. of Hades, A.*Fr.* 406; Ion. ἡγησίλεως *AP*7.545 (Hegesipp.); Ep. ἡγεσίλαος Nic.*Fr.* 74.72; poet. also ἀγεσίλας, α, Call.*Lav.Pall.*130, *Epigr.Gr.*195 (Oaxos):—the form ἀγεσίλαος, cited in *EM*8.32 (misquoting Call. *Lav.Pall.* l.c.), etc., is corrupt. II. pr. n., esp. of the well-known Spartan king, Ἀγησίλαος X.*HG*3.3.4, etc.; Ἡγησίλεως Id.*Vect.*3.7, D.19.290, cf. Hdt.7.204, 8.131; Ἀγησίλας, α, Paus.8.18.8. **-χορος**, ον, *leading the chorus* or *dance*, προοίμια Pi.*P.* 1.4: fem. -χόρα, as pr. n., Alcm.23.77.

ἀγητός, ή, όν, (ἀγάομαι) *admirable, wonderful*, φυὴν καὶ εἶδος ἀγητὸν Ἕκτορος Il.22.370; elsewh. in Hom. of persons, c. acc. rei, δέμας καὶ εἶδος ἀ. 24.376; εἶδος ἀγητοί *wonderful* in form only, as a reproach, Il.5.787, 8.228; εἶδος ἀγητή *h.Ap.*198: later c. dat. rei, χρήμασιν ἀ. Sol.5.3:—of things, ῥόδων ἀ. ἔρνος *Anacreont.*53.36.

Ἀγήτωρ, ὁ, *Leader*, epith. of Zeus at Sparta, X.*Lac.*13.2.

ἄγι, -ιτε, = ἄγε, ἄγετε, Alc.*Supp.*7.4, 10, Sapph.*Supp.*19.6: perh. ἄγ' ἴτε, from which sg. was formed.

ἁγι-άζω, = ἁγίζω, Lxx *Ge.*2.3, al., Ph.2.238:—Pass., ἁγιασθήτω τὸ ὄνομά σου *Ev.Matt.*6.9. **-ασμα**, ατος, τό, = ἁγιαστήριον, Lxx *Am.* 7.13, al. II. *holiness*, ib. *Ps.*92(93).5. **-ασμός**, οῦ, ὁ, *consecration, sanctification*, Lxx *Jd.*17.3, al., 1*Ep.Thess.*4.7. **-αστήριον**, τό, *holy place, sanctuary*, Lxx *Le.*12.4, al. **-αστία**, ἡ, v.l. for ἁγιστεία, Lxx 4*Ma.*7.9. **-αφόρος**, ον, = ἱεραφόρος, *IG*3.162.

ἀγίγαρτος, ον, of grapes, etc., *without seed* or *stone*, Thphr.*CP* 5.5.1, Aët.9.30.

ἁγίζω, (ἅγιος) *hallow, make sacred*, esp. by burning a sacrifice, θεῷ βούθυτον ἑστίαν ἁγίζων S.*OC*1495 (lyr.); πόπανα ἥγιζεν ἐς σάκταν (for ἐς βωμόν) Ar.*Pl.*681:—Pass., βωμοὶ πατρὶ ἁγισθέντες Pi.*O.*3.19; θύματα ἐπὶ καθαρῷ πυρὶ -όμενα D.H.1.38:—Med., = ἅζομαι, Alcm.123.

ἀγῑνέω, lengthd. Ep. and Ion. (also later Dor., v. sub fin.) form of ἄγω, mostly used in pres. and impf. (with or without augm. in Hom.); inf. pres. ἀγινέμεναι Od.20.213: impf. ἀγίνεσκον Od.17.294 (ἠγίνεσκον Arat.111): fut. ἀγινήσω *h.Ap.*57, 249, al.:—*lead, bring*, νύμφας.. ἠγίνεον ἀνὰ ἄστυ Il.18.493; μῆλον ἀ. Od.14.105; ἀ. αἶγας μνηστήρεσσι 22.198; ἀγίνεον ἄσπετον ὕλην Il.24.784; freq. of offerings, dedications, etc., δῶρα ἀγίνεον Hdt.3.89, cf. 93, 97, etc., Hp.*Ep.*27, Herod. 4.87, Call.*Iamb.*1.251, *AP*6.75 (Paul. Sil.); πλοῦτον ἀ. εἰς ἀρετήν Crates Theb.10.8; ληιάδας ἀ. *lead captive*, A.R.1.613; ἄνθεα τοσσάπερ ὧραι ποικίλ' ἀγινεῦσι Call.*Ap.*82; τέτρατον ἦμαρ ἀ., of the moon, Arat.792; *keep, observe*, παιγνίην Herod.3.55:—Med., *cause to be brought*, ἐς τὸ ἱρὸν ἀγινεόμενος γυναῖκας Hdt.7.33:—Pass., Arr.*Ind.* 32.7; αἴκα τὰ πάθεα τᾶς ψυχᾶς ἐς τὸ μέτριον ἀγινῆται Hippod.ap.Stob. 4.1.94.

ἁγιο-λόγος, ον, *speaking holy things*, dub. in 1*Enoch*1.2. **-ποιέω**, *sanctify*, Phot.

ἅγιος [ᾰ], α, ον, *devoted to the gods*: I. in good sense, *sacred, holy*: 1. of things, esp. temples, Ἀφροδίτης ἱρὸν ἅ. Hdt. 2.41; ἱρὸν Ἡρακλέος ἅ. ib.44, cf. Pl.*Criti.*116c, X.*HG*3.2.19; θηρίον Antiph.147.7; νηὸν ἐπὶ τῷ χάσματι Ἥρης ἅ. ἐστήσατο Luc.*Syr.D.*13: generally, θυσίαι, ξυμβόλαια, Isoc.10.63, Pl.*Lg.*729e (Sup.); μητρός.. ἐστι πατρὶς ἁγιώτερον Id.*Cri.*51a; ὅρκος ἅ. Arist.*Mir.*834b11; ἅ., τό, *temple*, *OGI*56.59 (Canopus), Lxx *Ex.*26.33, al., cf. *Ep.Heb.*9.2; τὸ ἅ. τῶν ἁγίων *Holy of Holies*, Lxx l. c.; τὰ ἅ. τῶν ἁ. 3*Ki.*8.6, etc., cf. *Ep.Heb.*9.3. 2. of persons, *holy, pure*, Ar.*Av.*522 (anap.); λαὸς ἅ. Κυρίῳ Lxx *De.*7.6, al.; οἱ ἅ. *the Saints*, 1*Ep.Cor.*6.1, al.; πνεῦμα ἅ. *the Holy Spirit*, *Ev.Matt.*3.11, al. Adv. ἁγίως καὶ σεμνῶς ἔχειν Isoc. 11.25. II. in bad sense, *accursed, execrable*, Cratin.373, Eust. 1356.59.—Never in Hom., Hes., or Trag. (who use ἁγνός); rare in Att. (v. supr.). (Possibly cognate with Skt. *yájati* 'sacrifice'.)

ἁγιότης, ητος, ἡ, = ἁγιωσύνη, Lxx 2*Ma.*15.2, *Ep.Heb.*12.10. II. as title, *PGiss.*55.5 (vi A.D.).

ἁγ-ισμός, οῦ, ὁ, = ἐναγισμός, *offering to the dead*, D.S.4.39. **-ιστεία**, ἡ, *ritual, service*, τῶν θεῶν, in pl., Isoc.11.28, cf. Pl.*Ax.*371d, Arist. *Cael.*268a14; later in sg., Str.9.3.7, J.*Ap.*1.7, Plu.*Rom.*22, Jul.*Or.* 5.178d. **-ίστευμα**, τό, *sanctuary*, Procop.*Aed.*1.4. **-ιστεύω**, *perform sacred rites*, Pl.*Lg.*759d: c. acc., ἱερουργίαν D.H.1.40:—Pass., ὅσα ἄλλα -εύεται Ph.2.231. 2. *to be holy, live purely*, ὅστις.. βιοτὰν ἁ. καὶ θιασεύεται ψυχάν E.*Ba.*74; *to be sacred*, Paus.6.20.2, cf. 8.13.1. II. Act., *purify*, φόνου χεῖρας Orac.ap.Paus.10.6.7. 2. *deem holy*:—Pass., of places, Str.9.3.1, D.H.1.40. **-ιστήριον**, τό, = περιρραντήριον, *Inscr.Perg.*255.9 (pl.). **-ιστός**, ή, όν, *hallowed*, *Et.Gud.* s.v. ἁγιστεία. **-ιστύς**, ύος, ἡ, *ceremony*, Call.*Aet.*1.1.3.

ἁγιώδως, Adv. *in sacred manner*: Sup. -έστατα dub. in Ph.1.675.

ἁγιωσύνη, ἡ, *holiness, sanctity*, Lxx 2*Ma.*3.12, *Ep.Rom.*1.4, etc. II. as title, *PMeyer*24.2 (vi A.D.).

ἀγκ-, Poet. abbrev. for ἀνακ- in compds. of ἀνά.

ἀγκάζομαι, (ἀγκάς) Ep., *lift up in the arms*, νεκρὸν ἀπὸ χθονὸς ἀγκάζοντο Il.17.722; λίθον ἀγκάσσασθαι Call.*Hec.*21.1, cf. Nonn.*D.*7.318.

ἀγκᾰθεν, Adv. *in the arms*, ἄ. λαβεῖν τι A.*Eu.*80. 2. *resting on the elbows*, A.*Ag.*3; also expl. as contr. for ἀνέκαθεν, = ἄνωθεν, *on the top*, cf. Sch. ad l. c., Hsch., *AB*337.

ἀγκάλη [ᾰ], ἡ, *bent arm*, mostly in pl., ἐν ἀγκάλαις A.*Ag.*723, *Supp.*481, E.*Alc.*351, al.; prov., ἐν ταῖς ἀ. περιφέρειν τινά X.*Cyr.*7.5.50; without ἐν, ἀγκάλαις ἔχειν, περιφέρειν, E.*IT*289, *Or.*464; ἐπ' ἀγκάλαις λαβεῖν Id.*Ion*761, cf. *IT*1250; ἐς ἀ. *Ion*1598; πρὸς ἀγκάλαις πεσεῖν ib.962; ὑπ' ἀγκάλαις σταθείς Id.*Andr.*747: rarely in sg., Corinn.19 (s.v.l.); φέρειν ἐν τῇ ἀ. Hdt.6.61, cf. X. l.c., Timocl.7. 4. 2. *bend of knee*, Cael.Aur.*TP*5.1.2. II. metaph., *anything closely enfolding*, κυμάτων ἐν ἀγκάλαις Archil.23; πετραία ἀ. A.*Pr.* 1019; πόντιαι ἀ. Id.*Ch.*587, cf. E.*Or.*1378; πελαγίοις ἐν ἀ. Nausicr. 1.3; of the air, γῆν.. ἔχονθ' ὑγραῖς ἐν ἀ. E.*Fr.*941. III. *bundle, sheaf*, *BGU*1180 (i B.C.), *PLond.*1.131r396 (i A.D.), *POxy.*935.19 (iii A.D.).

ἀγκᾰλῐδ-αγωγέω, *carry a bundle*, Paus.Gr.*Fr.*90. **-ᾰγωγός**, όν, *carrying an armful* or *bundle*, of beasts of burden; **ἀγκαλιδη-φόρος**, **-φορέω** being used of men, Poll.2.139, 7.109.

ἀγκαλίδη, ἡ, = ἀγκαλίς, ἐν ἀγκαλίδησι γυναικός *Stud.Pont.*3.6 (Amisus).

ἀγκᾰλ-ίζομαι, *embrace*, ὅστις κακὸν ἀγκαλίζεται Semon.7.77; εἰς τρυφερὰς ἠγκαλίσασθε χέρας *AP*12.122 (Mel.), cf. Man.1.45; χεροῖν εἴδωλον ἠγκαλισμένος Lyc.142: ἀγκαλιζόμενος in pass. sense, Aesop. 366. **-ῖναι**, αἱ, = ἀγκάλαι (Arg.), Hsch. **-ίς**, ἡ, in pl., = ἀγκάλαι, *arms*, Ep. dat. pl. ἀγκαλίδεσσιν Il.18.555, 22.503; ὑπ' ἀγκαλίσιν *IG* 9(1).882.13 (Corcyra). 2. *armful*, Ar.*Fr.*418, Nicostr.24, Ister 54 (s.v.l.), Ph.5.147C., Plu.*Rom.*8. II. = δρέπανον, Maced. word, J.*AJ*5.1.2, Hsch. **-ισμα**, ατος, τό, *that which is embraced* or *taken in the arms*, Luc.*Am.*14; hence, *darling*, Lyc.308. II. *embrace*, metaph., ἀ. κλυσιδρομάδος αὔρας Tim.*Pers.*91. **-ισμός**, ὁ, *making* into bundles, *POxy*.1631.9 (iii A.D.). **-ος**, ὁ, *armful, bundle*, *h.Merc*.82.

ἀγκαλπίς· κρημνός. οἱ δὲ βόθρον, Hsch.

ἀγκάς [ᾰς], Adv. *into* or *in the arms*, ἔχε δ' ἀ. ἄκοιτιν Il.14.353, cf. Theoc.8.55, A.R.1.276; ἀ. ἔμαρπτε Il.14.346; ἀ. ἐλάζετο θυγατέρα ἣν 5.371; τρόπιν ἀ. ἑλὼν νεός Od.7.252; ἀ. δ' ἀλλήλων λαβέτην (of wrestlers) Il.23.711.

ἀγκή, ἡ, = ἀγκάλη, Hsch.; metapl. dat. pl. ἀγκάσιν Opp.*H*.2.315.

ἀγκηθής· ἀβλαβής, Hsch. **ἀγκής**· ἀντηχής, Hsch.

ἀγκιστρ-εία, ἡ, *angling*, Pl.*Lg*.823d. **-ευτικός**, ή, όν, *of* or *for angling*: τὸ -κόν, *angling*, Pl.*Sph*.220d; -κὴ τέχνη Gal.*Thras*. 30. **-εύω**, *angle for, entice*, τινά Aristaenet.1.5:—Med., Ph.1.344: metaph., ψυχάς 2.265; ἀπόλαυσιν 1.304. **-ιον**, τό, Dim. of ἄγκιστρον, Theoc.21.57, Bito51.1.

ἀγκιστρό-δετος, ον, *with a hook bound to it*, δόναξ *AP*6.27 (Theaet.). **-ειδής**, ές, *hook-shaped, barbed, Placit*.1.3.18, etc. Adv. -δῶς Erot. s. v. ἠγκίστρευται.

ἄγκιστρον, τό, (ἄγκος) *fish-hook*, Od.4.369, Hdt.2.70, etc.; *hook of a spindle*, Pl.*R*.616c; *surgical instrument*, Philum.*Ven*.2.6, Cael. Aur.*TP*5.1; generally, *hook*, D.C.60.35.

ἀγκιστρόομαι, Pass., *to be furnished with barbs*, Plu.*Crass*.25. II. *to be caught by a hook*, ἠγκιστρωμένος πόθῳ Lyc.67.

ἀγκιστρο-πώλης, ου, ὁ, *seller of fish-hooks*, Poll.7.198. **-φάγος**, ον, (φαγεῖν) *biting the hook*, Arist.*HA*621b1.

ἀγκιστρ-ώδης, ες, = ἀγκιστροειδής, Plb.34.3.5, D.S.5.34, Str.1.2. 16. **-ωτός**, ή, όν, *barbed*, βέλος Plb.6.23.10; ἐμβόλια Ph.*Bel*.95.45.

ἀγκλάριον, τό, perh. Dor. for ἀνακλήριον, *reapportionment*, *CIG* 2562.13 (Hierapytna).

ἀγκλίνω, and **ἄγκλιμα**, τό, poet. for ἀνακλ-.

ἀγκλόν· σκολιόν, Hsch.

ἄγκοινα, ἡ, (ἀγκον-yᾰ, cf. ἀγκών) poet. for ἀγκάλη, only in pl., Ζηνὸς.. ἐν ἀγκοίνῃσιν ἰαύεις Il.14.213, cf. Od.11.261, Hes.*Fr*.245, A.R. 2.954. 2. metaph., *anything enfolding*, ἐν χθονὸς ἀγκοίναις *AP*9.398 (Jul. Aegypt.), cf. Opp.*H*.3.34. II. *halyard*, *IG*2.794b20, al., prob. in Alc.18.9.

ἀγκοινίζω, = ἀγκαλίζω, dub. l. in Poll.3.155. **ἀγκόλαι**· ἀγκῶνες, Hsch.

ἀγκομιδά, v. ἀνακομιδή.

ἀγκονίω, v. l. for ἐγκ-, Ar.*Lys*.1311, as if from ἀνακονίω, = ἐγκονέω.

ἀγκοπτήρ· σφῦρα, Hsch.

ἄγκος, εος, τό, properly, *bend, hollow*: hence, *mountain glen*, Il. 20.490, Od.4.337, Hes.*Op*.389, Hdt.6.74, Theoc.8.33, etc.; Trag. only E.*Ba*.1051. (Cf. Skt. *áñcati* 'bend', Lat. *ancus, uncus*, etc.)

ἀγκοτύλη, ἡ, a game, Hsch. **ἀγκταλιάζει**· ἄγχει, Hsch. **ἄγκτειρα**, ἡ, fem. of sq., ποιναί *Orac.Chald*.265.

ἀγκτήρ, ῆρος, ὁ, (ἄγχω) *instrument for closing wounds*, Cels.5.26, Plu.2.468c, Heliod.ap.Orib.44.10.4, Gal.1.385. 2. part of the throat, Poll.2.134, Hsch. 3. in pl., *bonds*, Procl.*in Euc*.20.25F.: metaph., τῆς ὕλης Id.*in R*.2.150K., prob. *in Alc*.p.41C. 4. *bandage*, Heliod.ap.Orib.48.28.5. **ἀγκτηριάζω**, *bind with an* ἀγκτήρ, Crito ap.Gal.13.878.

ἀγκυλένδετος, ον, *bound with thongs*, [Ἄρης] ἀ., i.e. javelin, Tim. *Pers*.23.

ἀγκῠλέομαι, *hurl like a javelin*, Ἔρως κεραυνὸν ἠγκυλημένος Satyr.1.

ἀγκύλ-η [ῠ], ἡ, (ἄγκος) properly, like ἀγκάλη, *bend of the arm* or *wrist*, ἀπ' ἀγκύλης ἱέναι, a phrase descriptive of the way in which the cottabus was thrown, B.*Fr*.13.2, cf. Hsch.; ἀπ' ἀγκύλης ἵησι λάταγας Cratin.273; wrongly expl. as *cup*, Ath.11.782d. 2. *bend of the knee, ham*, Philostr.*Im*.2.6, Sch.Il.23.726. 3. *joint bent and stiffened by disease*, Hp.*Liqu*.6, cf. Poll.4.196. II. *loop, noose*, πλεκτὰς ἀγκύλας E.*IT*1408; in the leash of a hound, X.*Cyn*.6.1; in bandages, Gal.18(1).790; in torsion-engines, Hero *Bel*.83.1. 2. *thong of a javelin*, by which it was hurled, Str.4.4.3; hence, *the javelin* itself, E.*Or*.1476, cf. Plu.*Phil*.6; δι' ἀγκυλῶν ἱππόται Them. *Or*.21.256d. 3. *bow-string*, ἀ. χρυσόστροφοι S.*OT*203. 4. ἀγκύλη τῆς ἐμβάδος sandal-*thong*, Alex.31. 5. *curtain-ring, hook*, Lxx *Ex*.38.18(36.34), al.; *hook* for a door, *IG*11(2).165.11, al. (Delos, iii B.C.). 6. *sides of the* κεραία, Poll.1.91. **-ητός**, ή, όν, verb. Adj. of ἀγκυλέομαι, *thrown from the bent arm*, of the cottabus, A.*Fr*.179. II. Subst., ἀγκυλητόν, τό, *javelin*, Id.*Fr*.16, *IG*2. 733*B*17. **-ιδωτός**, όν, *having a loop for a handle* (ἀγκύλη II), Hp.ap.Gal.19.69. **-ίζομαι**, in wrestling, *clasp the adversary's neck*, dub. l. in Poll.1.176. **-ιον**, τό, Dim. of ἀγκύλη, *loop* in noose, Heracl.ap.Orib.48.2.1; *link of a chain*, *AB*329, Suid. 2. = ἀγκύλωσις, Antyll.ap.Orib.45.15.1. II. τὰ ἀγκύλια, = Lat. *ancilia*, Plu. *Num*.13. **-ίς**, ίδος, ἡ, *hook, barb*, Opp.*C*.1.155.

ἀγκύλλω, *bend back*, Aret.*SA*1.6, cf. Hsch.

ἀγκῠλο-βλέφαρον, τό, *adhesion of the eyelids*, Cels.7.7. **-γλωσσον** πάθος, τό, *contraction of the tongue*, Orib.45.15 tit., Paul.Aeg.6. 29; and **-γλωσσος**, ὁ, *one who suffers from it*, Aët.8.38. **-γλώχιν**, ινος, ὁ, of a cock, *with hooked spurs*, Babr.17.3. **-δειρος**, ον, *crook-necked*, Opp.*H*.4.630.

ἀγκῠλόδους, οντος, ὁ, ἡ, *crook-toothed*, of a scimitar, Q.S.6.218; ἀ. χαλινοί, of anchors, Nonn.*D*.3.50. II. *barbed*, *AP*6.176 (Maced.).

ἀγκυλοειδής, ές, *winding*, τόποι, Suid. s. v. ἄγκη.

ἀγκυλο-κοπέω, *hamstring*, dub. in *PLond*.2.415.15. **-κυκλος**, ον, *curved in spires*, of a dragon's tail, Nonn.*D*.35.217. **-κωλος**, ον, *crook-limbed*, Κᾶρες Archestr.*Fr*.41 B. **-μαχία**, ἡ, *contest with javelin*, *IPE*1².435 (Chersonesus). **-μήτης** (Boeot. **ἀγκουλομείτας** Corinn.*Supp*.1.13), ὁ, (μῆτις) *crooked of counsel*, epith. of Κρόνος, Il.2.205, Od.21.415, al., Hes.*Th*.18, etc.; of Prometheus, ib. 546, *Op*.48. **-μητις**, ιος, ὁ, ἡ, = foreg., Nonn.*D*.21.255. **-πους**, ὁ, ἡ, πουν, τό, gen. ποδος, *with bent legs*, δίφρος, = Lat. *sella curulis*, Plu.*Mar*.5.

ἀγκύλος [ῠ], η, ον, (ἄγκος) *crooked, curved*, τόξα Il.5.209, Od.21. 264, etc.; ἅρμα Il.6.39; κάλαμος Theoc.21.47; of the eagle, ἀγκύλον κάρα *beaked*, Pi.*P*.1.8; ἀ. ἐκ τῶν ὀδόντων Ant.Lib.22.6; of greedy fingers, *hooked*, Ar.*Eq*.205; of the movement of a snake, ἀ. ἕρπων D.P.123. II. metaph., 1. of style, *intricate*, Luc.*Bis Acc*. 21; ἐριστικὸς καὶ ἀ. τὴν γλῶσσαν *catchy*, Alciphr.3.64; in good sense, *terse*, D.H.*Th*.25 (Comp.). Adv. -λως ib.31; *intricately*, Procl.*in Prm*. p.525 S., Dam.*Pr*.187. 2. *wily, crafty*, Lyc.344; -ώτεραι ἐνέδραι Archig.ap.Orib.8.2.24.

ἀγκῠλό-τοξος, ον, *with crooked bow*, Παίονες Il.2.848, 10.428; Μήδειοι Pi.*P*.1.78. **-χείλης**, ου, ὁ, (χεῖλος) *with hooked beak*, αἰετός Od.19.538, *AP*6.229 (Crin.); αἰγυπιοί Il.16.428, Hes.*Sc*.405, Batr. 294. (Perh. -χήλης shd. always be read.) **-χήλης**, ου, ὁ, (χηλή) *with crooked claws*, v. l. in *Batr*.294, Ar.*Eq*.197, cf. Sch. (-χείλης codd.).

ἀγκυλ-όω, *crook, bend*, τὴν χεῖρα, as in throwing the cottabus, Pl.Com.47:—Pass., ὄνυχας ἠγκυλωμένος *with crooked* claws, Ar.*Av*. 1180. **-ωμα**, τό, *loop*, Gal.18(1).798. **-ωσις**, ἡ, as medic. term, *tongue-tie*, Antyll.ap.Orib.46.16.4; *stiffening of joints*, Paul. Aeg.4.55; *adhesion of the eyelids*, Gal.14.772. **-ωτός**, ή, όν, of javelins, *furnished with a thong*, στοχάσματα E.*Ba*.1205.

ἄγκῡρα, ἡ, *anchor*, Alc.18.9 (v. ἄγκοινα), Thgn.459; ἄ. βάλλεσθαι, καθιέναι, μεθιέναι, ἀφιέναι to cast *anchor*, Pi.*I*.6(5).13, Hdt.7.36, A.*Ch*. 662, X.*An*.3.5.10; ἄ. αἴρειν, αἴρεσθαι to weigh *anchor*, Plu.*Pomp*.50, 80; ἀνέλοιο *AP*10.1 (Leon.); τὰς νέας ἔχειν ἐπ' ἀγκυρέων Hdt.6.12; ὁρμίζειν Th.7.59; ἐπ' ἀγκυρέων ὁρμεῖν ride at *anchor*, Hdt.7.188; νηῦς μιῆς ἐπ' ἀγκύρης [οὐκ ἀσφ]αλὴς ὁρμεῦσα Herod.1.41; ἐπ' ἀγκύρας ἀποσαλεύειν D.50.22, cf. E.*Hel*.1071; prov., ἀγαθαὶ πέλοντ'.. δύ' ἄγκυραι 'tis good to have 'two strings to your bow', Pi.*O*.6.101; ἐπὶ δυοῖν ἀγκύραιν ὁρμεῖν αὐτοὺς ἐᾶτε D.56.44, cf. Plu.*Sol*.19; ἄ. δ' ἥ μου τὰς τύχας ὤχει μόνη E.*Hel*.277; ἐπὶ τῆς αὐτῆς (sc. ἀγκύρας) ὁρμεῖν τοῖς πολλοῖς, i.e. 'to be in the same boat' with the many, D.18.281; εἰσὶ μητρὶ παῖδες ἄγκυραι βίου S.*Fr*.685; οἴκων ἄ., of a son, E.*Hec*.80; ἱερὰ ἄ., last hope, Luc.*J.Tr*.51. II. *pruning-hook*, Thphr.*CP* 3.2.2. III. = αἰδοῖον, Epich.191.

ἀγκῡρηβόλιον, τό, = ἀγκυροβ-, Democr.148.

ἀγκῡρίζω, fut. Att. ιῶ, (ἄγκυρα) in wrestling, *hook* with the leg, *trip*, διαλαβὼν ἀγκυρίσας Ar.*Eq*.262; ἀγκυρίσας ἔρρηξεν Eup.262.

ἀγκύριον, τό, Dim. of ἄγκυρα, Ph.*Bel*.100.34, Plu.2.604d, Arr. *Epict.Fr*.30, Demoph.*Sim*.45, Luc.*Cat*.1. II. **ἀγκύρια** (sc. πείσματα), τά, *anchor-cables*, D.S.14.73.

ἄγκυρ-ις· βοτάνη τις, Hsch. **-ισμα**, τό, *hook*, in wrestling, Schol.Ar.*Eq*.262, Hsch. **-ίτης** λίθος *anchor-stone*, Hsch. s. v. μασχάλην. **-ίττει**· μεταμέλεται (Cret.), Hsch.

ἀγκῡρο-βολέω, *secure by throwing an anchor*: *hook fast in, fasten securely*, ἠγκυροβόληται Hp.*Dent*.18. **-βόλιον**, τό, *anchorage*, Str.3.4.7 (pl.), Plu.2.507b. **-ειδής**, ές, *anchor-shaped*, Dsc.3. 158, Gal.2.766. Adv. -ειδῶς Erot. s. v. ῥυβδοειδέα τρόπον. **-μαχος**, ὁ, a kind of ship, Isid. *Etym*. 19.1.16, *Gloss*. **-μήλη**, ἡ, *hooked probe*, Hp.ap.Erot., cf. Gal.19.69.

ἀγκῡρουχία, ἡ, (ἔχω) *a holding by the anchor*, ἐν ἀγκυρουχίαις A.*Supp*.766.

ἀγκῡρωτός, ή, όν, *bent like an anchor*, δοκίδες Ph.*Bel*.85.36.

ἀγκωβόλος· ἁλιεύς, Hsch.

ἀγκών, ῶνος, ὁ, *bend of the arm*, hence, *elbow*, ὀρθωθεὶς δ' ἐπ' ἀγκῶνος Il.10.80; ἧ, καὶ ἐπ' ἀγκῶνος κεφαλὴν σχέθεν Od.14.494; ἀγκῶνα τυχὼν μέσον Il.5.582, cf. 20.479; ἀγκῶνι νύττειν to nudge, Od.14.485, cf. Pl.*Riv*.132b; κροτεῖν τοῖς ἀγκῶσιν τὰς πλευράς D.54.9; prov., ἀγκῶνι ἀπομύττεσθαι Bion ap.D.L.4.46; ἐπ' ἀγκῶνος δειπνεῖν, of the attitude at meals, Luc.*Lex*.6. 2. *arm*, Νίκας ἐν ἀγκώνεσσι πίτνειν Pi.*N*.5.42; ἐς δ' ὑγρὸν ἀγκῶνα.. προσπτύσσεται S.*Ant*.1237, etc. 3. *bend* in animals' legs, X.*Cyn*.4.1. II. *any nook* or *bend*, as the *angle* of a wall, ἀγκὼν τείχεος Il.16.702, cf. Hdt.1.180; *bend, bay* of a river, Id.2.99; ἑσπέροι ἀγκῶνες S.*Aj*.805; *headlands which form a bay*, Str.12.8.19; ἀγκῶνες κιθάρας *ribs which support the horns* of the cithara, Semus 1, Hsch.; *ends* of stomach-bow, Hero *Bel*.78.4; *arms* of torsion-engine, Ph.*Bel*.53.40, al., Hero *Bel*.81.9; *cross-bar* of same, Bito 49.12; *arm* of throne or chair, Lxx 2*Ch*.9.18, Cael.Aur. *TP*2.1; perh. *clamp*, *PPetr*.3p.144. 2. kind of *vase*, Artem.1.74, cf. *Sammelb*.4292. III. prov., γλυκὺς ἀ. used κατ' ἀντίφρασιν of a difficulty, Pl.*Phdr*.257d, Clearch.6; expl. by Sch.Pl. l. c., Zen.2. 92, Ath.12.516a, from *a long bend* or *reach* in the Nile; but apptly. = παραγκάλισμα, *thing to be embraced, treasure*, Pl.Com.178; also = ἀβρότονον, Dsc.3.24. (For the Root v. ἄγκος.)

ἀγκών-η, ἡ, = ἄγκοινα, Sch.D.T.191.37 H. **-ίζω**, *recline at table*, *Gloss*. II. Med., *pursue a sinuous course*, hence metaph., *use circumlocutions*, *Com.Adesp*.14.8 D. **-ιον**, τό, *elbow*, Gal.4. 452. **-ίσκιον**, τό, Dim. of ἀγκών, Hero *Spir*.1.42. **-ίσκος**, ὁ, = foreg., Hero *Spir*.1.42, Lxx *Ex*.26.17. **-ισμός**, οῦ, ὁ, *a bending, reach*, of an estuary, Eust.1712.29.

ἀγκωνό-δεσμος, *cubital*, *Gloss*. **-ειδής**, ές, *curve-shaped, curved*, Bito 58.9 (v. l.). **-φόρος**, ὁ, *bearer of an* ἀγκών II. 2, *IG*3.1280.

ἀγλαέθειρος, ον, *bright-haired*, *h.Pan.*5.

ἀγλα-ΐα, Ion. **-ΐη**, ἡ, (ἀγλαός) *splendour, beauty*, κῦδός τε καὶ ἀ. καὶ ὄνειαρ Od.15.78; ἀγλαΐηφι πεποιθώς Il.6.510; of Penelope, Od.18.180; *splendour, magnificence*, S.*El.*211; ὡρῶν Jul.*Or.*4.148d; in bad sense, *pomp, show*, [κύνας] ἀγλαΐης ἕνεκεν κομέουσιν Od.17.310; in pl., *vanities*, 17.244, E.*El.*175. **2.** *joy, triumph*, Pi.*O.*13.14, etc.; pl., *festivities, merriment*, Hes.*Sc.*272,285. **3.** *adornment*, of a horse's *mane*, colours of oyster's *shell*, etc., X.*Eq.*5.8, Ael.*NA*10.13, cf. A.R.4.1191. **4.** pr. n., Ἀγλαΐα, one of the Graces, who presided over victory in the games, Hes.*Th.*945, cf. B.3.6.—Mostly poet. **-ΐζω**, Hp.*Mul.*2.188, Ael., v. infr.: fut. Att. ἀγλαϊῶ (ἐπ-) Ar.*Ec.*575: aor. ἠγλάϊσα (Dor. ἀγλ-) Theoc.*Ep.*1.4, etc., (ἐπ-) Ar.*Fr.*682:—Pass., v. infr.:—*make splendid, glorify*, B.3.22, etc.; ἀθανάταις ἠγλάϊσεν χάρισιν *IG*12(3).1190.10 (Melos); θυσίαις τέμενος Isyll.28, cf. Plu.2.965c, Ael.*NA*8.28. **2.** *give as an honour*, σοί, Βάκχε, τάνδε μοῦσαν ἀγλαΐζομεν *Carm.Pop.*8, cf. Theoc. l. c. **II.** Ep. and Lyr. only Med. and Pass., *adorn oneself with* a thing, *take delight in*, σέ φημι διαμπερὲς ἀγλαϊεῖσθαι (sc. ἵπποις) Il.10.331 (the only form in Hom., even of compds.); ὅστις τοιούτοις θυμὸν ἀγλαΐζεται Semon.7.70; ἀ. μουσικᾶς ἐν ἀώτῳ Pi.*O.*1.14; Com., ἐλαίῳ ῥάφανος ἠγλαϊσμένη Ephipp.3.6 (cf. Eub.150). **III.** intr., ἀγλαΐζει· θάλλει, Hsch., cf. Antiph.301 codd.—Never in Trag. or Att. Prose. **-ϊσμα**, τό, *ornament, honour*, A.*Ag.*1312; of a child, μητρὸς ἀ. E.*Hel.*11, cf. 282; of the hair of Orestes placed on his father's tomb, A.*Ch.*193, S.*El.*908, cf. E.*El.*325; of a sarcophagus, *IG*12(8).600 (Thasos).—Poet. and late Prose; ἀ. φυτῶν, of the rose, Ach.Tat.2.1. **-ϊσμός**, ὁ, *adorning, ornament*, ῥημάτων Pl.*Ax.*369d. **-ϊστός**, ή, όν, *adorned*, Hsch.

ἀγλαό-βοτρυς, υ, gen. υος, *with splendid bunches*, Nonn.*D.*18.4. **-γυιος**, ον, *beautiful-limbed*, Ἥβα Pi.*N.*7.4. **-δενδρος**, ον, *with beautiful trees*, Pi.*O.*9.20. **-δωρος**, ον, *bestowing splendid gifts*, Δημήτηρ *h.Cer.*54,192,492. **-εργός**, όν, (ἔργον) *ennobled by works*, Max.68. **-θηλές**· ἁπαλόν, Hsch. **-θρονος**, ον, *with splendid throne, bright-throned*, Μοῖσαι Pi.*O.*13.96, cf. *N.*10.1, B.16.124. **-θυμος**, ον, *noble-hearted*, *AP*15.40.25 (Cometas). **-καρπος**, ον, (καρπός A) *bearing beautiful* or *goodly fruit*, of fruit-trees, ῥοιαί Od.7.115, 11.589; Σικελία Pi.*Fr.*106; εἰρήνη Epigr.ap.*SIG*274 (Delph., iv B.C.): of Demeter and the Nymphs, *givers of the fruits of the earth*, *h.Cer.*4,23. **II.** (καρπός B) *with fair wrists*, of Thetis, Pi.*N.*3.56 (v.l. ἀγλαόκολπος). **-κοιτος**· πάνυ τίμιος, Phot., Suid. **-κουρος**, ον, *rich in fair youths*, Κόρινθος Pi.*O.*13.5. **-κωμος**, ον, *giving splendour to the feast*, φωνή Pi.*O.*3.6. **-μειδής**, ές, *brightly smiling*, Ἔρως Eurytus (*PLG*3.639). **-μητία**· ἡ μεγάλη βουλή, *EM*11.30. **-μητις**, ιος, ὁ, ἡ, *of rare wisdom*, Tryph.183, Procl.*H.*5.10. **-μορφέω**, in Pass., *to be endowed with beauteous form*, -ουμένους τοὺς ἀστέρας ἱστάς *PLeid.W.*4.16. **-μορφος**, ον, *of beauteous form*, *AP*9.524, Orph.*H.*14.5, al. **-παις**, ὁ, ἡ, *rich in fair children*, Opp.*H.*2.41, *Epigr.Gr.*896 (Syria). **-πεπλος**, ον, *beautifully veiled*, Q.S.11.240. **-πηχυς**, υ, gen. εος, *with beautiful arms*, Nonn.*D.*32.80. **-πιστος**, ον, *splendidly faithful*, Hsch. **-ποιέω**, *make famous*, Hermap.ap.Amm.Marc.17.4.19.

ἀγλαός [ᾰγλᾰ-], ή, όν, also ός, όν Thgn.985, E.*Andr.*135:—*splendid, shining, bright*, epith. of beautiful objects, ἀ. ὕδωρ Il.2.307, etc.; γυῖα 19.385, cf. B.16.103; μηρία Hes.*Op.*337; ἥβης ἀ. ἄνθος Tyrt.10.28, cf. Thgn. l. c., B.5.154; then generally, *splendid, beautiful*, ἄποινα Il.1.23; δῶρα ib.213, etc.; ἔργα Od.10.223; ἄλσος Il.2.506, cf. Pi.*N.*4.20, Simon.13, etc.; *noble, glorious*, ἀγλαόν [ἐστιν] ἀνδρὶ μάχεσθαι γῆς πέρι Callin.1.6. **II.** of men, either *beautiful* or *famous, noble*, Il.2.736,826, Hes.*Sc.*37, Pi.*O.*14.7, B.16.2, etc.: c. dat. rei, *famous for* a thing, κέρᾳ ἀγλαός, sarcastically, Il.11.385.—Ep. and Lyr. word, twice in Trag. (lyr.) ἀγλαὰς Θήβας S.*OT*152; Νηρῆδος ἀγλαὸν ἕδραν E. l.c.; also in later poetry, as Theoc.28.3. Adv. ἀγλαῶς Ar.*Lys.*640. (Perh. containing base γελα- in reduced form.)

ἀγλαό-τῑμος, ον, *splendidly honoured*, Orph.*H.*12.8, al. **-τρίαινᾰ** [ῐ], ὁ, acc. -αινᾶν, *he of the bright trident*, epith. of Poseidon, Pi.*O.*1.40. **-φαντον**, τό, = ἀγλαοφῶτις, *Cat.Cod.Astr.*8(3).154, 164. **-φεγγής**, ές, *splendidly shining*, Max.189. **-φημος**, ον, *of splendid fame*, Orph.*H.*31.4; Dor. **-φᾱμος**, pr. n. of Thracian mystic, Iamb.*VP*28.146, etc. **-φοιτος**, ον, *one who 'walks in beauty'*, Max.403. **-φορτος**, ον, *proud of one's burden*, Nonn.*D.*7.253. **-φωνος**, ον, *with a splendid voice*, Procl.3.2. **-φῶτις**, ιδος, ἡ, *peony*, = γλυκυσίδη, Dsc.3.140, Plin.*HN*24.160, Ael.*NA*14.24. **-χαρτος**, ον, *rejoicing in beauty*, *IG*12(1).783 (Rhodes).

ἀγλαρόν· μωρόν, Hsch. **ἀγλασινόν**· καλόν, Id. **ἀγλαυκόν**· ἀλυκόν, Id.

ἄγλαυρος, ον, = ἀγλαός, Nic.*Th.*62,441. **II.** Ἄγλαυρος, ἡ, daughter of Cecrops, worshipped on the Acropolis at Athens, Hdt.8.53.β′, Paus.1.18.2.

ἀγλαφόρε· ἄσιτε (Cret.), Hsch.

ἀγλαφύρως, Adv. *without polish, inelegantly*, Hegesand.22, cf. Eust.1295.15.

ἀγλαώψ, ῶπος, ὁ, ἡ, *bright-eyed, beaming*, πεύκη S.*OT*214 (lyr.).

ἀγλευκής, ές, (γλεῦκος) *not sweet, sour*, X.*Hier.*1.21 (Comp.), cf. Rhinth.28; opp. γλυκύς, Arist.*Pr.*877^{b}25; οἶνος Luc.*Lex.*6; heterocl. acc. ἀγλευκῆν, θάλασσαν Nic.*Al.*171: metaph., of persons, *sour, crabbed*, Epich.140; of the style of Thuc., *harsh*, Hermog.*Id.*2.12, cf. [Longin.]*Rh.*p.195 H.

ἀγλευ⟨κι⟩τάς· ἄρτος ἄναλος, Hsch.

ἀγλίδια· σκόροδα, Hsch., *EM*11.41 (leg. ἀγλίθια).

ἀγλίη, ἡ, f. l. for αἰγίς, Gal.19.69.

ἀγλιθάριον, τό, Dim. of ἄγλις, Ruf.ap.Orib.8.39.10.

ἀγλῖς, gen. ἄγλιθος (ἀγλῖθος Choerob. *in Theod.*p.327 H., ἀγλῖθες Nic.*Th.*874), ἡ:—*clove* of garlic, Antyll.ap.Orib.8.16.3; = ῥάξ, Dsc.2.152; mostly pl., *head* of garlic (cf. κεφαλή), made up of separate cloves, Ar.*Ach.*763, *V.*680, Hp.*Mul.*2.133, Call.*Fr.*140.

ἄγλισχρος, ον, *not sticky*, Hp.*Prorrh.*1.117, Thphr.*CP*6.11.16.

ἀγλίτης· οἰκέτης, *EM*11.45, *AB*338, cf. **ἀγλεῖτις**· οἰκέτις, prob. in Hsch.

ἄγλυ, Scyth. word = *swan*, Hsch.

ἀγλῠκής, ές, = ἀγλευκής, Thphr.*CP*6.14.12 and 18.8.

ἄγλῠφος, ον, *unhewn*, Sch.S.*OC*101.

ἀγλῶν· ἀγλαός, Hsch. **ἀγλωσσεῖν**· δυσφημεῖν, Id.

ἀγλωσσία, Att. **-ττία**, η, *want of eloquence*, E.*Fr.*56, Antipho Soph.97.

ἄγλωσσος, Att. **-ττος**, ον, *without tongue*, of the crocodile, Arist.*PA*690^{b}23, cf. Eub.107.1; of a flute, *without reed*, Poll.2.108. Adv. -τως Id.6.145. **II.** *lacking in eloquence*, Pi.*N.*8.24, Ar.*Fr.*734, D.Chr.12.55; *dumb*, *AP*7.191 (Arch.). **2.** = βάρβαρος, οὔθ' Ἑλλὰς οὔτ' ἄ. S.*Tr.*1060.

ἀγλ-ῶστα· ἔντριμμα γυναικεῖον, Hsch. **-ωστῖναι**· γογγυλίδες, Id.

ἄγμα, τό, (ἄγνυμι) *fragment*, Plu.*Phil.*6; *fracture*, Pall. *in Hp.*12.271 C. **II.** = κλέμμα, Hsch. **III.** *nasalized g*, Ion ap.Prisc.*Inst.*1.39.

ἀγμείονες· βουβῶνες, Hsch. **ἀγμή**· ἑστία, Id. **ἀγμηρόν**· ἥσυχον, Id. **ἀγμικόν**· ἄκρατον, Id.

ἀγμός, ὁ, (ἄγνυμι) *fracture* of a bone, περὶ ἀγμῶν, title of treatise by Hp., etc. **II.** *broken cliff, crag*, E.*IT*263; pl., Id.*Ba.*1094, Nic.*Al.*391, St.Byz. s.v. Ὀαξός.

ἀγναῖος· καθαρός, Hsch. **ἀγναιώτης**· ἐπὶ πολὺ κεκαυμένος, Id. **ἀγνάκορος**, ὁ, = ἀνάγυρος, Sch.Nic.*Th.*71 (fort. -κοπος). **ἀ-γνα⟨μ⟩πτοπόλεμος**, ον, *inflexible in war*, Hsch.

ἄγναμπτος, ον, *unbending, inflexible, inexorable*, Ἔρωτες B.8.73, Orph.*L.*27; τὸ πρὸς ἡδονὰς ἄ. Plu.*Cat.Mi.*11, cf. *APl.*4.278 (Paul. Sil.); cf. ἄκναμπτος.

ἄγναπτος, ον, of cloth, *not fulled* or *carded*, hence, *new*, χλαῖνα Pl. Com.18 D., cf. Plu.2.691d. **II.** *not cleansed, unwashed*, ib.169c.

ἄγνᾰφος, ον, (γνάπτω) = foreg., *Ev.Matt.*9.16, *Marc.*2.21, *PLond.*2.193^{v}22 (ii A.D.).

ἁγν-εία, ἡ, *purity, chastity*, λόγων ἔργων τε S.*OT*864 (lyr.), coupled with καθαρότης Hp.*Morb.Sacr.*1, cf. 1*Ep.Tim.*4.12; τῶν θεῶν Antipho 2.1.10; ἁγνείη δ' ἐστὶ φρονεῖν ὅσια *App.Anth.*4.18. **II.** *strict observance of religious duties*, Pl.*Lg.*909e (pl.), etc.; in pl., *purifications, ceremonies*, Isoc.11.21, J.*BJ* *prooem.*10, *BGU*1198.12, etc. **-ευμα**, τό, *chastity*, E.*Tr.*501. **-ευτήριον**, τό, *place of purification*, Chaerem.Hist.4, cf. *AB*267; *sacristy*, *POxy.*840.8. **-ευτικός**, ή, όν, *inclined to chastity*, opp. ἀφροδισιαστικός, Arist.*HA*488^{b}5. **II.** Act., *purificatory*, τὸ ἁ. *sin-offering*, Ph.2.206; ἁ. ἡμέρα *BGU*993 (ii B.C.). **-εύτρια**, ἡ, *female purifier*, *Gloss.* **-εύω**, pf. ἥγνευκα D. l. citand., *consider as part of purity, make it a point of religion*, c. inf., ἁγνεύουσι ἔμψυχον μηδὲν κτείνειν Hdt.1.140: abs., *to be pure*, ὄρνιθος ὄρνις πῶς ἂν ἁγνεύοι φαγών; A.*Supp.*226, cf. Lys.6.51, Pl.*Lg.*837c, Alex.15.6: c. acc. rei, χεῖρας ἁ. E.*IT*1227; *keep oneself pure from*, τινός D.22.78, Phld.*Sto.Herc.*339.15, Luc.*Am.*5; also in Med., γυναικός *GDI*3636.43 (Cos). **2.** *perform religious ceremonies, officiate*, *BGU*1201.6 (ii B.C.), cf. 149.8 (ii/iii A.D.). **3.** Med., *purify*, τὸν νοῦν Phld.*Sto.Herc.*339.20. **II.** Act., = ἁγνίζω, *purify*, πόλιν Antipho 2.3.11:—Pass., *SIG*978 (Cnidus): c. gen., *purify from*, ὁ παντὸς ἁγνεύων, of Epicurus, Phld.*Lib.*p.26 O.

ἀγνέω, Dor. = ἄγω, pf. ἀγνηκώς, *GDI*1413 (Aetol.), cf. Hsch.

ἁγνεών, ῶνος, ὁ, *place of purity*, κατ' ἀντίφρασιν, for *a brothel*, Clearch.6.

ἁγνιασμός, ὁ, = ἁγνισμός, v.l. in Lxx *Nu.*8.7.

ἁγνίζω, fut. ιῶ (ἀφ-) Lxx *Nu.*8.6: pf. ἥγνικα 1*Ep.Pet.*1.22: (ἁγνός):—*wash off, cleanse away*, esp. by water (τὸ πῦρ καθαίρει.. τὸ ὕδωρ ἁγνίζει Plu.2.263e), λύμαθ' ἁγνίσας ἐμὰ S.*Aj.*655; τινὰ πηγαῖς E.*IT*1039. **2.** *cleanse, purify*, χέρας σὰς ἁγνίσας μιάσματος E.*HF*1324, cf. Diph.126.1, Lxx *Ex.*19.10:—Med., *purify oneself*, ib. *Jo.*3.5, Plu.2.1105b:—Pass., ἁγνίσθητι *Act.Ap.*21.24; ἀπὸ οἴνου Lxx *Nu.*6.3 (Pass.). **3.** esp. ἁ. τὸν θανόντα *purify* the dead *by fire*, S.*Ant.*545:—Pass., σῶμαθ' ἡγνίσθη πυρί E.*Supp.*1211. **4.** *sacrifice*, E.*Fr.*314, *IT*705 (Pass.). **5.** *hallow, consecrate*, Aristonous 1.17 (Pass.). **6.** *burn up, consume*, S.*Fr.*116; ἐπαστράψας αἰθὴρ ἥγνισε ..ἱστορίαν *AP*7.49 (Bianor).

ἅγνινος, η, ον, *made of* ἄγνος, Plu.2.693f.

ἁγν-ισμα, τό, *purification, expiation*, ματρῷον ἅ. φόνου, of Orestes, A.*Eu.*326 (lyr.), cf. Lxx *Nu.*19.9. **-ισμός**, ὁ, *purification, expiation*, ἁ. ποιεῖσθαι D.H.3.22; τοῖς ἁ. τοῖς πρὸ τῶν Θεσμοφορίων *SIG*1219.19 (Gambreion); τῷ ὕδατι τοῦ ἁ. Lxx *Nu.*6.5. **-ιστέος**, α, ον, *to be purified*, E.*IT*1199. **-ιστήριον**, τό, *instrument of purification*, Hero *Spir.*2.32. **-ιστής**, οῦ, ὁ, *purifier*, *Gloss.* **-ιστικός**, ή, όν, = ἁγνευτικός II, Eust.43.6. **-ίτης** [ῑ], ου, ὁ, *purifier*, θεοὶ ἁ. Poll.1.24; πάγος Lyc.135. **II.** *one who requires purification*, Hsch., *AB*338, v.l. in Il.24.480 (Sch. T.).

ἁγνοδικεῖς· οἱ θεοί, Phot., *AB*338, Hsch. (-δοχεῖς). **ἀγνόδικος**· ἀγνοοῦσα τὸ δίκαιον, Hsch. (cod. -μος), Phot., *AB*338.

ἀγνο-έω, Ep. ἀγνοι-, 3 sg. subj. ἀγνοιῇσι Od.24.218: impf. ἠγνόουν Isoc.7.21, etc.: fut. ἀγνοήσω B.*Fr.*12, Isoc.12.251, D.32.10,

54.31: aor. ἠγνόησα A.*Eu.*134, Th.2.49, etc.; Ep. ἠγνοίησα Il.2.807, Hes.*Th.*551, Ep. contr. 3 sg. ἀγνώσασκε Od.23.95: pf. ἠγνόηκα Pl. *Sph.*221d, Alex.20.4:—Pass., fut. (of med. form) ἀγνοήσομαι D. 18.249; ἀγνοηθήσομαι v.l. in Luc.*J.Tr.*5: aor. ἠγνοήθην, v. infr.: pf. ἠγνόημαι Isoc.15.171, Pl.*Lg.*797a. (This Verb implies a form ἄγνοος, = ἀγνώς II):—*not to perceive* or *recognize*; Hom., almost always in aor., ἄνδρ' ἀγνοιήσασ' ὑλάει Od.20.15, cf. Th. l. c., Pl.*Phdr.* 228a; mostly with neg., οὐκ ἠγνοίησεν *he perceived* or *knew well*, Il. 2.807, etc.; μηδὲν ἀγνόει E.*Andr.*899.—Mostly c. acc., *to be ignorant of*, Hdt.4.156, S.*Tr.*78; πάντα Pl.*Smp.*216d; ἑαυτοὺς ἀ. *forget* their former selves, D.10.74; τὴν πόλιν ἀ. *not to discern* the temper of the city, Id.19.231; τὸν ξένον Philostr.*VA*2.26; *fail to understand*, τὸ ῥῆμα *Ev.Marc.*9.32; περί τινος Pl.*Phdr.*277d: c. gen. pers. and rel. clause, ἀγνοοῦντες ἀλλήλων ὅ τι λέγομεν Id.*Grg.*517c: dependent clauses in part., τίς..ἀ. τὸν ἐκεῖθεν πόλεμον δεῦρο ἥξοντα; D.1. 15: with Conj., οὐδεὶς ἀ. ὅτι.. Id.21.156, etc.; ἀγνοῶν εἰ.. X.*An.*6. 5.12:—Pass., *not to be known, recognized*, Pl.*Euthphr.*4a, *Hp.Ma.* 294d, etc.; ἀγνοούμενα ὅπῃ..ἀγαθὰ ἐστι Id.*R.*506a; ἠγνοῆσθαι ξύμπασιν ὅτι..Id.*Lg.*797a; ὑπελάμβανον ἀγνοήσεσθαι D.18.249; καιρὸν οὐ παρεθέντα οὐδ' ἀγνοηθέντα ib.303, cf. Isoc.15.171; τὰ ἠγνοημένα *unknown parts*, Arr.*An.*7.1.4. II. abs., *go wrong, make a false step*, first in Hp.*Art.*46, Antipho 5.44 (dub. l.), Isoc.8.39; part. ἀγνοῶν *ignorantly, by mistake*, X.*An.*7.3.38, Arist.*EN*1110ᵇ27; ἀγνοήσαντες And.4.5: in moral sense, *to be ignorant of what is right, act amiss*, Plb.5.11.5, cf. *Ep.Heb.*5.2:—Med., *fail to recognize*, Gal.14. 630. **-ημα**, τό, *fault of ignorance, oversight*, ψυχῆς Gorg.*Hel.* 19, ἀ. ἕτερον προσαγνοεῖν Thphr.*HP*9.4.8, cf. D.S.1.1, Hipparch. 1.3.11, Lxx *To.*3.3, *Ep.Heb.*9.7; in pl., opp. ἁμαρτήματα, *PTeb.*5.3 (ii B.C.). II. *ignorance*, περί τινος Str.7.2.4. III. *object of* ἄγνοια, Dam.*Pr.*7. **-ηματίζω**, *fail to observe*, Aq.*Ps.*118(119). 10. **-ησις**, ἡ, *ignorance*, Phld.*D.*1.7. **-ητέον**, with neg., οὐκ ἀ. *one must not fail to remark*, Dsc.*Praef.*7, Ph.1.11, al. **-ητικός**, ή, όν, *mistaken*, τὰ ἀ. πράττειν Arist.*EE*1246ᵃ48. **-ητός**, ή, όν, *ignored*; τὸ -όν, *the object of ignorance*, Dam.*Pr.*6.

ἄγνοια, ἡ, (v. γιγνώσκω) *want of perception, ignorance*, ἀγνοίᾳ A. *Ag.*1596; ἀγνοίας ὕπο *Supp.*499; ἣν ὑπ' ἀγνοίας ὁρᾷς whom seeing you *pretend not to know*, S.*Tr.*419; ἀγνοίᾳ ἐξαμαρτάνειν X.*Cyr.*3. 1.38, cf. Th.8.92, Ar.*Av.*577, D.9.64, etc.; opp. ἐπιστήμη, Pl.*Tht.* 199d, Arist.*APr.*66ᵇ26; ἀ. κενότης ἐστὶ τῆς περὶ ψυχὴν ἕξεως Pl.*R.* 585b; δι' ἄγνοιαν πράττειν, opp. ἀγνοῶν, Arist.*EN*1110ᵇ25: in Logic, ἡ τοῦ ἐλέγχου ἄ. *ignoratio elenchi, ignorance* of the conditions of a valid proof, Arist.*SE*168ᵃ18, al. II. *mistaken conduct, a mistake*, D.18.133, *Ep.*2.19, Plb.27.2.2. [In Poets sts. ἀγνοίᾱ, S.*Tr.*350, *Ph.*129; old Att., acc. to Ael. Dion.*Fr.*11, cf. Moer.191; Ion. ἀγνοίη Phot.]

ἀγνοιῆσι, etc., v. ἀγνοέω.

ἀγνό-κοκκος, ὁ, = οἰσόκαρπος, Gal.14.552, Eust.834.36.

ἀγνοούντως, Adv. of ἀγνοέω, *ignorantly*, Arist.*Top.*114ᵇ10.

ἁγνο-πολέομαι, *to be purified by sacrifices*, Phot. **-πόλος**, ον, (*qᵘel-*, cf. τελέω) *making pure*, Δημήτηρ Orph.*H.*18.12, *A.* 38. **-ρυτος**, ον, *pure-flowing*, ποταμός A.*Pr.*434 (lyr.).

ἁγνός, ή, όν, (cf. ἅγιος) *pure, chaste, holy*, Hom. (only in Od.), etc.: I. of places and things dedicated to gods, *hallowed*, ἑορτή Od.21.259; of frankincense, ἁγνὴ ὀδμή Xenoph.1.7; ἄλσος *h.Merc.*187; τέμενος Pi.*P.*4.204; ὕδωρ Id.*I.*6(5).74; πυρὸς ἁγνόταται παγαί Id.*P.*1.21; αἰθήρ A.*Pr.*282; φάος, λουτρόν, S.*El.*86, *Ant.*1201; θύματα Id.*Tr.*287, cf. Th.1.126, D.H.1.38; of food, Jul.*Or.*6.192c (Comp.); χρηστήρια E.*Ion*243, etc.; ἐν ἁγνῷ on *holy* ground, A.*Supp.* 223, but χῶρον οὐχ ἁ. πατεῖν a spot not *lawful* to tread on, S.*OC* 37. 2. of divine persons, *chaste, pure*, Hom., mostly of Artemis, χρυσόθρονος Ἄ. ἁ. Od.5.123, 18.202, etc.; also ἁ. Περσεφόνεια 11. 386, cf. *h.Cer.*337; of Demeter, *h.Cer.*203,439; Χάριτες Sapph.65; ἁ. θεαί, Demeter and Persephone, *IG*14.204, 431; Apollo, Pi.*P.*9.64; Zeus, A.*Supp.*653, S.*Ph.*1289: of the attributes of gods, θεῶν σέβας S.*OT*830. II. after Hom., of persons, *undefiled, chaste*, of maidens, Alc.55, Pi.*P.*4.103, A.*Fr.*242; ἁ. αὐδά, of a maiden's voice, *Ag.*245; of Hippolytus, E.*Hipp.*102: c. gen., λέχους ἁ. δέμας ib.1003; γάμων ἁ. Pl.*Lg.*840d, cf. Men.*Epit.*223; ἁ. ἀπ' ἀνδρὸς συνουσίας Jusj. ap.D.59.78. 2. *pure from blood, guiltless*, ἁγνοὶ τοὐπὶ τήνδε τὴν κόρην S.*Ant.*889; ἁ. χεῖρας E.*Or.*1604; μητροκτόνος.. τόθ' ἁ. ὤν Id.*El.*975, cf. *IA*940; ὅθ' ἁ. ἦν when he had been *purified*, S.*Tr.* 258: c. gen., ἁγνὰς χεῖρας αἵματος E.*Hipp.*316; φόνου Pl.*Lg.*759c; Δάματρος ἀκτὰς δέμας ἁ. ἴσχειν *pure* from food, E.*Hipp.*138. 3. generally, *pure, upright*, ἀέθλων ἁ. κρίσις Pi.*O.*3.21; ψυχῆς φιλία ἁ. X.*Smp.*8.15, etc. III. Adv. ἁγνῶς καὶ καθαρῶς *h.Ap.*121, Hes. *Op.*337; ἁ. ἔχειν X.*Mem.*3.8.10.

ἄγνος, ἡ, Att. ὁ, = λύγος, *chaste-tree*, the branches of which were strewed by matrons on their beds at the Thesmophoria, *Vitex Agnus-castus*, *h.Merc.*410, Chionid.2, cf. *Trag.Adesp.*396, Pl.*Phdr.* 230b, Hp.*Intern.*30, Arist.*HA*627ᵃ9, Nic.*Th.*71, Dsc.1.103. (Associated with the notion of chastity from the likeness of its name to ἁγνός.) II. ἄγνος, ὁ, name of *a fish*, = καλλιώνυμος. Diph.Siph. ap.Ath.8.356a (sine acc. cod., ἁγνός Kaib.). III. a kind of *bird*, Sch.Pl.*Phdr.* l. c., Suid.

ἁγνό-στομος, ον, *with pure mouth*, Tz.*H.*6.33. **-σύνη**, ἡ, = ἁγνότης, *Eranos*13.87 (loc. incert.), Phld.*D.*3*Fr.*76. **-τελής**, ές, *worshipped in holy rites*, Θέμις Orph.*A.*551.

ἁγνότης, ητος, ἡ, (ἁγνός) *purity, chastity, integrity*, *IG*4.588.15 (Argos, ii A.D.), *2Ep.Cor.*6.5.

ἄγνῡμι, 3 dual ἄγνῡτον Hom., v. infr.: fut. ἄξω (κατ-) Il.8.403: aor. 1 ἔαξα Hom., (κατ-) Ar.*V.*1436, etc., ἦξα Il.23.392, (κατ-) Hp.*Epid.*5. 26; imper. ἆξον Il.6.306; part. ἄξας 16.371, E.*Hel.*1598 (κατ-εάξαντες Lys.3.42 codd., perh. to distinguish it from aor. 1 of ἄγω); inf. ἆξαι Il.21.178:—**Pass.**, pres., v. infr.: aor. 2 ἐάγην (ᾰ, exc. ἐᾱγη Il.11. 559) Hom., etc.; Ep. 3 sing. ἄγη Il.3.367, 3 pl. ἄγεν 4.214: pf. Act. (in pass. sense) ἔᾱγα Hes.*Op.*534, Q.S.1.204; Ion. ἔηγα (κατ-) Hdt.7. 224, Hp.*Fract.*24: pf. Pass. κατ-έαγμαι Luc.*Tim.*10: (ϝ, cf. καυάξαις; ᾱ by nature, ἆξον (Hdn.Gr.2.14), ἆξαι on analogy of contr. forms of κατα-ϝάγνυμι):—*break, shiver*, εἴσω δ' ἀσπίδ' ἔαξε Il.7.270; ἦξε θεὰ ζυγόν 23.392; ἵπποι ἄξαντ' ἐν πρώτῳ ῥυμῷ λίπον ἅρματα 16.371; νῆας.. ἔαξαν κύματα Od.3.298; πρό τε κύματ' ἔαξεν *broke* the waves, 5.385; ἄγνυντον ὕλην *crashed through* it, of wild boars, Il.12.148; ἄγνυσι κεραυνόν *APl.*4.250:—Pass., with pf. ἔᾱγα, *to be broken, shivered*, ἐν χείρεσσιν ἄγη ξίφος Il.3.367, cf. 16.801; ἐν καυλῷ ἐάγη δολιχὸν δόρυ 13.162; πάταγος... ἀγνυμενάων (sc. of the trees) 16.769; νηῶν θ' ἅμα ἀγνυμενάων Od.10.123; τοῦ [ὀϊστοῦ] δ' ἐξελκομένοιο πάλιν ἄγεν ὀξέες ὄγκοι Il.4.214; ποταμὸς περὶ καμπὰς πολλὰς ἀγνύμενος *with a broken*, i.e. *winding, course*, Hdt.1.185: metaph., ἄγνυτο ἠχώ the sound *spread around*, Hes.*Sc.*279,348; κέλαδος ἀγνύμενος διὰ στομάτων, of the notes of song, *Lyr.Adesp.*93.—Act. never in Prose, Pass. once in Hdt., κατάγνυμι being in general use.

ἄγνυον, τό, doubtful word, perh. *water-wheel*, *PLond.*3.1177.149.

ἀγνύς, ῦθος (on the accent v. Hdn.Gr.2.763), ἡ, *loom-weight*, in pl., Plu.2.156b, cf. Poll.7.36.

ἀγνώδης, ες, f.l. for ἀκανθώδης, Thphr.*HP*3.18.4.

ἀγνωμονεύω, f.l. for -έω, Plu.2.484b (Pass.).

ἀγνωμ-ονέω, *to be* ἀγνώμων, *act without right feeling*, X.*HG*1.7.33; coupled with ἀδικεῖν, Zeno*Stoic.*1.69; ἀ. εἴς τινα *to act unfeelingly* or *unfairly towards* one, D.18.94, Men.*Sam.*292; πρός τινα Apollod. Com.7.6: with a neut. Adj., μή νυν τὰ θνητὰ θνητὸς ὢν ἀγνωμόνει *Trag. Adesp.*112: abs., *disregard a summons, be contumacious*, *PStrassb.*41. 16 (iii A.D.); ἀ. περί τινα, περί τι, Plu.*Alc.*19, *Cam.*28: c. acc., *treat unfairly*, τὴν πόλιν Him.*Or.*2.31:—Pass., *to be so treated*, Plu.2.484b; ἀγνωμονηθεὶς Id.*Cam.*18; ὑπὸ τοῦ πατρός *POxy.*237ᵛ40 (ii A.D.). 2. *act ill-advisedly*, Aq.1*Ki.*13.13. **-οσύνη**, ἡ, *want of acquaintance with* a thing, Pl.*Tht.*199d. 2. *want of sense, folly*, Thgn.896, Democr.175; *senseless pride, arrogance*, Hdt.2.172, E.*Ba.*885 (lyr.); πρὸς ἀ. τραπέσθαι Hdt.4.93; ἀγνωμοσύνῃ χρᾶσθαι Id.5.83; ὑπ' ἀγνωμοσύνης Id.9.3. 3. *want of feeling, unkindness*, D.18.252; θεῶν ἀ. S.*Tr.*1266 (dub.); ἀ. τύχης, Lat. *iniquitas fortunae*, D.18.207. 4. in pl., *misunderstandings*, X.*An.*2.5.6. **-ων**, ον, gen. ονος, (γνώμη) *ill-judging, senseless*, Thgn.1260 codd. (s. v. l.), Pi.*O.*8.60, Pl.*Phdr.* 275b; ὥσπερ κυνίδιον τοῖς εἴκουσιν ἀ. Phld.*Lib.*p.10O.; opp. μετὰ λογισμοῦ πράττειν, Men.617; *inconsiderate*, τὸ ἄ. καὶ θυμοειδές Hp.*Aër.* 16. Adv. -όνως *senselessly*, X.*HG*6.3.11, etc.; ἀ. ἔχειν D.2.26. 2. *headstrong, reckless*, (in Comp.) Hdt.9.41: Sup., X.*Mem.*1.2.26. 3. *unfeeling, hard-hearted*, Φοίβῳ τε κἀμοὶ μὴ γένησθ' ἀγνώμονες S.*OC*86; of judges, X.*Mem.*2.8.5; joined with ἀχάριστος, Id.*Cyr.*8.3.49, cf. *Mem.*2.10.3, D.21.97; esp. *ignoring one's debts*, Ulp.ad D.2.26, Jul. *Or.*3.117e (Comp.); ἀ. περὶ τὰς ἀποδόσεις Luc.*Herm.*10. 4. *unknowing, in ignorance*, ἀ. πλανᾶσθαι Hp.*Vict.*1.6. II. of things, *senseless, brute*, Aeschin.3.244; also φρονοῦσαν θνητὰ κοὐκ ἀγνώμονα (neut. pl.) S.*Tr.*473. 2. *cruel*, πρᾶγμα ἀ. πάσχειν Parth. 17.5. III. of horses, *without the teeth that tell the age* (γνώμονες) Poll.1.182. [ᾰγν- only in Man.5.338.]

ἀγνώριστος, ον, *unascertained, unknown*, Thphr.*HP*1.2.3, cf. Poll. 5.150, Hierocl.*Facet.*150; *not recognized*, Steph.*in Hp.*1.61 D.

ἀγνώς, ῶτος, ὁ, ἡ, (γνῶ-ναι): I. Pass., *unknown*, mostly of persons, ἀγνῶτες ἀλλήλοις Od.5.79; ἀγνὼς πρὸς ἀγνῶτ' εἶπε A.*Ch.*677, cf. *Supp.*993, S.*Ph.*1008; ἀ. πατρί *clam patre*, E.*Ion*14: in Prose, ἀ. τοῖς ἐν τῇ νηΐ Th.1.137, cf. Pl.*R.*375e, etc. b. of things, *obscure, unintelligible*, ἀ. φωνὴ βάρβαρος A.*Ag.*1051, cf. S.*Ant.*1001; ἀ. δόκησις *dark, vague* suspicion, Id.*OT*681. 2. *obscure, ignoble*, ἀ. ἀκλεής E.*IA*18; οὐκ ἀ. νίκαν a victory not *unknown to fame*, Pi.*I.*2. 12; ἀ. διὰ νεότητα Jul.*Or.*3.116b. II. Act., *ignorant*, S.*OT*1133; ἀ. τί δύναται.. X.*Oec.*20.13. III. c. gen., where the sense fluctuates between Pass. and Act., [χθὼν] οὐκ ἀ. θηρῶν Pi.*P.*9.58, cf. *I.*2.30; ἀγνῶτες ἀλλήλων Th.3.53; ὁ ἀ. τῶν λόγων Arist.*SE*178ᵃ26.

ἀγνωσία, ἡ, *ignorance*, Hp.*VM*9, Demetr.Lac.*Herc.*1055.15; συμφορᾶς ἀ. E.*Med.*1204; κέρδος ἐν κακοῖς ἀ. Id.*Fr.*205; διὰ τὴν ἀλλήλων ἀ. Th.8.66; opp. γνῶσις, Pl.*Sph.*267b: c. gen., θεοῦ Lxx *Wi.*13.1, 1*Ep.Cor.*15.34. 2. *lack of acquaintance*, Luc.*Tim.*42. II. *being unknown, obscurity*, Pl.*Mx.*238d.

ἀγνώσσω, = ἀγνοέω, pres. only, mostly poet., Simm.1.13, Musae. 249, D.P.173, Coluth.8, Nonn.*D.*1.425, etc.; in late Prose, Luc.*Ep. Sat.*25.

ἀγνωστί, Adv. *secretly, unperceived*, Ps.-Callisth.3.19.

ἄγνωστος, ον, *unknown*, τινί Od.2.175; *unheard of, forgotten*, Mimn. 5.7; ἄ. ἐς γῆν E.*IT*94; *unfamiliar*, Arist.*Top.*149ᵃ5 (Comp.). 2. *not to be known*, ἄγνωστόν τινα τεύχειν Od.13.191; πάντεσσι ib.397; ἀγνωστότατοι γλῶσσαν *most unintelligible* in tongue, Th.3.94. 3. *not an object of knowledge, unknowable*, ἄλογα καὶ ἄ. Pl.*Tht.*202b; ἡ ὕλη ἄ. καθ' αὑτήν Arist.*Metaph.*1036ᵃ9; in Comp., *harder to know*, ib. 995ᵃ2. Adv. -τως Procl.*in Alc.*p.52C. 4. as the name of a divinity at Athens, νὴ τὸν Ἄγνωστον Ps.-Luc.*Philopatr.*9, cf. *Act.Ap.*17. 23; in pl., θεῶν.. ὀνομαζομένων ἀ. Paus.1.1.4. II. Act., *not knowing, ignorant of*, ψευδέων Pi.*O.*6.67 (v.l. ἄγνωτον), cf. Luc.*Halc.*3. Adv. -τως *inconsiderately*, Phld.*Lib.*p.29O.

ἀγνωτίδιον, τό, = μύλλος, Dorio ap.Ath.3.118d.

ἄγνωτος, ον, = ἄγνωστος, γνωτὰ κοὐκ ἄ. μοι S.*OT*58; ἄγνωτα τοῖς θεωμένοις Ar.*Ra.*926.

ἀγξηραίνω, v. ἀναξηραίνω.

ἄγξις, ἡ, (ἄγχω) *throttling*, *EM*194.50, *Gloss.*

ἀγόγγυστος, ον, *not murmuring*, in Adv. -τως, Sor.1.88.

ἀγοήτευτος, ον, *not to be bewitched* or *beguiled*, Plot.4.4.44. II. Act., *without guile*. Adv. -τως Cic.*Att.*12.3.1.

ἀγόμφιος, ον, *without grinders*, ἀ. αἰών *toothless* age, Diocl.Com. 14.

ἀγόνᾰτος, ον, (γόνυ) *without a knee*, Arist.*IA*709^{a}3. II. of plants, *without knots* or *joints*, Id.*Fr.*195, Thphr.*HP*4.8.7.

ἀγον-έω, *to be unfruitful*, Thphr.*HP*9.18.3, Ph.2.402: metaph., ψυχῇ ἀ. τινῶν ib.435. -ία, ἡ, *sterility*, Arist.*GA*746^{b}20, Dsc.2.179, Plu.*Rom.*24 (pl.); opp. εὐγονία, Iamb.*Comm.Math.*15. -ος, ον, (γονή): I. Pass., *unborn*, Il.3.40 (which Augustus translated *childless*, Suet.*Oct.*65), E.*Ph.*1598, Eub.107.11. 2. γόνος ἄ. *no longer a son*, of a horse that mounts his dam, Opp.*C.*1.260. II. Act., *unfruitful*, *sterile*, of animals both male and female, Hp.*Aph.*5.59, *Art.*41 (Comp.), Arist.*GA*726^{a}3 (Comp.), etc.; γαστήρ Ael.*NA*15.9; τόκοισι ἀ. travail *without issue*, *bringing no children to the birth*, S.*OT* 27: metaph., ἄ. ποιητής Plu.2.348b. b. of flowers, *sterile*, or seeds, *infertile*, Thphr.*HP*1.13.4, 1.11.1; ὁμίχλη νεφέλη ἄ., i.e. not producing water, Arist.*Mete.*346^{b}35, cf. Ar.Did.p.451.33 D. c. metaph., ἄ. ἡμέρα, ἔτος a day or year *unlucky for begetting children*, Hp. *Epid.*2.6.8 and 10 (of *odd* days and years); τὸ ἄ. τῆς ὕλης Plot.3.6.19, cf.6.3.8. d. Astrol., *impeding generation*, ζῴδιον Vett.Val.10.11. 2. c. gen., *not productive of*, σοφίας Pl.*Tht.*150c, cf. 157c; γῆ θηρίων ἄ. *Mx.*237d. III. *childless*, γένος E.*HF*888, Hld.4.12. IV. **ἄγονον**, τό, = μυρσίνη ἀγρία, Ps.-Dsc.4.144; **ἄγονος**, = ἄγνος, Id.1.103, Sch.Nic.*Th.*71.

ἄγοος, ον, *unmourned*, A.*Th.*1068 (lyr.).

ἀγορά [ἄγ], ᾶς, Ion. **ἀγορή**, ῆς, ἡ, (ἀγείρω):—*assembly*, esp. *of the People*, opp. the Council of Chiefs, Il.2.93, Od.2.69, etc.; τοῖσιν δ' οὔτ' ἀγοραὶ βουληφόροι (sc. Κυκλώπεσσι) Od.9.112; ὀρθῶν ἑσταότων ἀ. γένετ' οὐδέ τις ἔτλη ἕζεσθαι Il.18.246; ἀ. Πυλάτιδες, of the *Amphictyonic Council* at Pylae, S.*Tr.*638, cf. Ion Eleg.1.3; μακάρων ἀ. Pi.*I.* 8(7).29, cf. *AB*210; ἀγορήνδε καλέσσασθαι, κηρύσσειν, Il.1.54, 2.51; ἀγορὴν ποιήσασθαι, θέσθαι, Il.8.489, Od.9.171; εἰς ἀ. ἰέναι, ἀγέρεσθαι, 8.12, Il.18.245; ἀγορήνδε καθέζεσθαι Od.1.372.—Not common in Prose, ἀγορὰν συνάγειν, συλλέγειν X.*An.*5.7.3; ποιῆσαι Aeschin.3.27; ἀγορὰς ποιεῖσθαι Hyp.*Fr.*150: of the assembly in Attic demes, D.44.36, *IG*2.585, al.; ἀ. συνέδριον φυλετῶν καὶ δημοτῶν *AB*327: in late Prose, ἀ. δικῶν προθεῖναι, καταστήσασθαι, = Lat. *conventus agere*, Luc.*Bis Acc.* 4,12: *meeting for games*, Pi.*N.*3.14: metaph., μυρμήκων ἀ. Luc. *Icar.*19: prov., θεῶν ἀ. 'Babel', Suid., etc. II. *place of assembly*, τοὺς δ' εὗρ' εἰν ἀγορῇ Il.7.382; ἵνα σφ' ἀ. τε θέμις τε 11.807, cf. Od.6.266; pl., Od.8.16; οὔτε.. εἰς ἀ. ἔρχεται οὔτε δίκας Thgn. 268. 2. *market-place*, perh. not earlier than *Hom.Epigr.* 14.5 πολλὰ μὲν εἰν ἀγορῇ πωλεύμενα, πολλὰ δ' ἀγυιαῖς; freq. in later authors, πρυμνοῖς ἀγορᾶς ἔπι Pi.*P.*5.93; θεοὶ.. ἀγορᾶς ἐπίσκοποι A.*Th.* 272; μέσῃ Τραχινίων ἀ. S.*Tr.*424; ἀγορᾷ οὐδὲ ἄστει δέχεσθαι Th.6. 44; ὀλιγάκις.. ἀγορᾶς χραίνων κύκλον E.*Or.*919; οἱ ἐκ τῆς ἀ. *market* people, X.*An.*1.2.18; ἐξ ἀγορᾶς εἶ Ar.*Eq.*181, etc.; εἰς ἀ. ἐμβάλλειν to go into *the forum*, i.e. be a citizen, Lycurg.5; ἐν τῇ ἀ. ἐργάζεσθαι to trade in *the market*, D.57.31; εἰς τὴν ἀ. χειροτονεῖν (opp. ἐπὶ τὸν πόλεμον) 'for *the market*', Id.4.26; the Roman *Forum*, D.H.5.48. III. *business of the* ἀγορά: 1. *public speaking, gift of speaking*, mostly in pl., ἔσχ' ἀγοράων withheld him *from speaking*, Il.2.275; οἱ δ' ἀγορὰς ἀγόρευον ib.788, cf. Od.4.818; ᾠδὴν ἀντ' ἀγορῆς θέμενος Sol.1. 2. *market*, ἀγορὰν παρασκευάζειν Th.7.40, X. *HG*3.4.11; ἀ. παρέχειν Th.6.44, etc.; ἄγειν X.*An.*5.7.33, etc.; opp. ἀγορᾷ χρῆσθαι to have *supplies*, ib.7.6.24; τῆς ἀ. εἴργεσθαι Th.1.67, Plu.*Per.*29; ἀ. ἐλευθέρα, i.e. καθαρὰ τῶν ὠνίων πάντων, Arist.*Pol.* 1331^{a}31, cf. X.*Cyr.*1.2.3; opp. ἀ. ἀναγκαία Arist.*Pol.*1331^{b}11; generally, *provisions*, *supplies*, *PPetr.*3p.131 (iii B.C.), *PSI*4.354 (iii B.C.), al.; in pl., Nic.Dam.p.6.17 D.; ἀγορὰς περικόπτειν cut off *supplies*, D.H.10.43. b. *market*, *sale*, ἀ. τῶν βιβλίων, τῶν παρθένων, Luc. *Ind.*19, Ael.*VH*4.1, cf. Nicoch.7. IV. as a mark of time, ἀ. πλήθουσα *the forenoon*, when the market-place was full, ἀγορῆς πληθυούσης Hdt.4.181; πληθούσης ἀγορᾶς X.*Mem.*1.1.10, cf. *SIG*695.38 (Magn. Mae.); περὶ or ἀμφὶ ἀ. πλήθουσαν X.*An.*2.1.7, 1.8.1; ἐν ἀ. πληθούσῃ Pl.*Grg.*469d, cf. Th.8.92; also ἀγορῆς πληθώρῃ Hdt.2.173, 7.223; poet., ἐν ἀ. πλήθοντος ὄχλου Pi.*P.*4.85; πρὶν ἀ. πεπληθέναι Pherecr.29: ἀγορῆς διάλυσις *the time just after mid-day*, when they went home from market, Hdt.3.104, cf. X.*Oec.*12.1. V. *market-day*, = Lat. *nundinae*, D.H.7.58.

ἀγοράζω [ἄγ], fut. άσω Ar.*Lys.*633, ἀγορῶ Lxx *Ne.*10.31: aor. ἠγόρασα X.*HG*7.2.18, D.21.149, etc.: pf. ἠγόρακα Arist.*Oec.*1352^{b}7, Plb.6.17.4:—Med., aor. ἠγορασάμην D.50.55: pf. ἠγόρασμαι (v. infr.):—Pass., aor. ἠγοράσθην Id.59.46: pf. ἠγόρασμαι Is.8.23, Men. 828:—*frequent the* ἀγορά, αἱ γυναῖκες ἀ. καὶ καπηλεύουσι Hdt.2.35, 4.164, cf. Arist.*Ph.*196^{a}5, *Com.Adesp.*710; *occupy the market-place*, Th.6.51. 2. *buy in the market*, πωλεῖν ἀ. Ar.*Ach.*625; ἐπιτήδεια ἀ. X.*An.*1.5.10; generally, *buy*, Ar.*Pl.*984, etc.; *farm* taxes or state-contracts, ὠνὴν ἀ. *PRev.Laws*41.22, al.; τὸν Σαίτην ἀγοράσας ib.60.23:—Med., *buy for oneself*, X.*An.*1.3.14:—Pass., διά τινος ἀ. D. 50.25: pf. Pass. in med. sense, ἀντὶ τοῦ ἠγοράσθαι αὐτοῖς τὸν οἶνον Id. 35.19. 3. *haunt the* ἀγορά, Corinn.34, Pi.*Fr.*103; οὐδ' ἀγοράσει γ' ἀγένειος οὐδεὶς ἐν ἀγορᾷ nor shall any boy *lounge in the* ἀγορά, Ar.*Eq.*1373. [-ᾱζω (i.e. -ᾴζω) in sense 1, Hdn.Gr.2.14.]

ἀγοραῖος [ἄγ], ον, (fem. -αία epith. of Artemis and Athena, v. infr.):—*in*, *of*, or *belonging to the* ἀγορά, Ζεὺς Ἀ. as *guardian of popular assemblies*, Hdt.5.46, A.*Eu.*973 (lyr.), E.*Heracl.*70; Ἑρμῆς Ἀ. as *patron of traffic*, Ar.*Eq.*297, cf. *IPE*1^2.128 (Olbia), *IG*12(8).67 (Thasos), Paus.1.15.1; Ἄρτεμις Ἀ. at Olympia, Id.5.15.4; Ἀθηνᾶ Ἀ. at Sparta, Id.3.11.9; generally, θεοὶ ἀ. A.*Ag.*90. 2. of things, τὰ ἀ. *details of market-business*, Pl.*R.*425c. II. *frequenting the market*, ὁ ἀ. ὄχλος X.*HG*6.2.23; δήμου εἶδος Arist.*Pol.*1291^{b}19, etc.; τὸ ἀ. πλῆθος.. τὸ περὶ τὰς πράσεις καὶ τὰς ὠνὰς καὶ τὰς ἐμπορίας καὶ καπηλείας διατρῖβον ib.1291^{a}4:—ἀγοραῖοι (with or without ἄνθρωποι), οἱ, *those who frequented the* ἀγορά, Hdt.1.93, 2.141; opp. ἔμποροι, X. *Vect.*3.13, but = *traders* (i.e. *sutlers*), Ael.*Tact.*2.2:—hence, *the common sort*, *low fellows*, Ar.*Ra.*1015, Pl.*Prt.*347c, Thphr.*Char.*6.2; of agitators, *Act.Ap.*17.5, Plu.*Aem.*38: Comp., *the baser sort*, Ptol. Euerg.1. Adv. -αίως, λέγειν D.H.*Rh.*10.11. 2. of things, *vulgar*, σκώμματα Ar.*Pax*750; τοὺς νοῦς ἀ. ἧττον.. ποιῶ Id.*Fr.*471; ἀ. φιλία (opp. ἐλευθέριος) Arist.*EN*1162^{b}26; *common*, ἄρτοι Lync.ap.Ath.3. 109d. III. generally, *proper to the* ἀγορά, *skilled in*, *suited for forensic speaking*, Plu.*Per.*11, al.:—ἀγοραῖος (sc. ἡμέρα) *court-day*, *assize*, τὰς ἀ. ποιεῖσθαι Str.13.4.12; ἄγειν τὴν ἀ. Epist.Galb.ap.J.*AJ*14. 10.21, cf. *Act.Ap.*19.38, *IGRom.*4.790. Adv. -ως *in forensic style*, Plu. *CG*4, *Ant.*24. 2. ἀγοραῖος, ὁ, = *tabellio*, *notary*, Aristid.*Or.*50(26). 94, *Edict.Diocl.*7.41, *Gloss.*; also, *pleader*, *advocate*, in pl., Philostr.*VA* 6.36. b. ἀγοραῖος, ἡ, *market-day*, *IGRom.*4.1381 (Lydia). (The distn. ἀγόραιος *vulgar*, ἀγοραῖος *public speaker*, drawn by Ammon., etc., is prob. fictitious.)

ἀγορᾱ-νομέω, *to be* ἀγορανόμος, Alex.247, *IG*12(3).170 (Astypalaea); τῆς πόλεως *POxy.*910.2 (ii A.D.); at Rome, *to be aedile*, D.H. 10.48, Plu.*Caes.*5, App.*BC*2.1, etc.: pf. -ηκα D.C.52.32. -**νομία**, ἡ, *office of* ἀγορανόμος, Arist.*Pol.*1331^{b}9, *IG*4.203 (Corinth), *PGrenf.*1. 10.7 (ii B.C.), etc. II. = Lat. *aedilitas*, Plb.10.4.1, D.H.5.18, App. *Pun.*112. -**νομικός**, ή, όν, *of* or *for the* ἀγορανόμος or *his office*, ἀ. ἄττα Pl.*R.*425d; νόμιμα Arist.*Pol.*1264^{a}31; νόμος *Milet.*3.145 (200 B.C.); τιμαί *CIG*1716 (Delph.); στέφανος *POxy.*1252^{v}17 (iii A.D.). II. = Lat. *aedilicius*, ἀρχαιρέσια Plu.*Pomp.*53; ἐξουσία D.H.6.95. -**νόμιον**, τό, *court* or *office of the* ἀγορανόμος, Pl.*Lg.*917e, *IG*2.192c11, 12(3).170, *PHib.*29.3 (iii B.C.), *AP*11.17 (Nicarch.). -**νόμιος**, ον, *of* or *in the forum*, περίπατος *IGRom.*4.504 (Perg.). -**νόμος**, ὁ, *clerk of the market*, who regulated buying and selling, Hp.*Epid.*4.24, Ar.*Ach.*723, al., Lys.22.16, Arist.*Pol.*1299^{b}17, *IG*2.192c12, etc. 2. *public notary*, *PGrenf.*2.23^{a}ii 2 (ii B.C.), *POxy.*99.2 (i A.D.), etc. II. = Lat. *aedilis*, D.H.7.14, *IG*14.719, etc.

ἀγοράομαι, almost always in Ep. forms, pres. ἀγοράασθε, impf. ἠγοράασθε, ἠγορόωντο (cf. Hdt.6.11), aor. 1 only 3 sing. ἀγορήσατο (v. infr.): 2 sg. impf. ἠγορῶ S.*Tr.*601; inf. ἀγορᾶσθαι Thgn.159:—*meet in assembly*, *sit in debate*, οἱ δὲ θεοὶ πὰρ Ζηνὶ καθήμενοι ἠγορόωντο Il.4.1. II. *speak in the assembly*, *harangue*, ὅ σφιν ἐϋφρονέων ἀγορήσατο Il.1.73, 9.95, cf. Od.7.185, Hdt. l. c.; παισὶν ἐοικότες ἀγοράασθε Il.2.337. 2. generally, *speak*, *utter*, εὐχωλαί.. ἃς.. κενεαυχέες ἠγοράασθε 8.230, μήποτε.. ἀγορᾶσθαι ἔπος μέγα Thgn. l. c.: c. dat., *speak*, *talk with*, ἕως σὺ.. ἠγορῶ ξέναις S. l. c. [ᾱγ- only in Il.2.337, metri grat.; otherwise ἀγ-.]

ἀγορ-ᾱσείω, Desid. of ἀγοράζω, *wish to buy*, Sch.Ar.*Ra.*1068. -**ᾰσία**, ἡ, *purchase*, Telecl.51, Hyp.*Fr.*70, *Inscr.Magn.*116.20 (ii A.D.), D.L. 2.78 (pl.), etc. -**ᾰσις**, εως, ἡ, = foreg., Pl.*Sph.*219d (pl.), cf. *Leg. Sacr.*2.69 (-ασσις, Tanagra), *PRyl.*2.45.5 (iii A.D.). -**ασμα**, τό, *that which is bought* or *sold*: mostly in pl., *wares*, *merchandise*, Aeschin. 3.223, D.34.9, etc., cf. Alex.168. -**ασμός**, ὁ, *purchasing*, Phint. ap.Stob.4.23.61^a, Vett.Val.180.11, al. II. *purchase*, Lxx *Ge.*42. 19, al., *OGI*669.20 (Egypt, i A.D.) (pl.); freq. of auctions, ποιεῖσθαί τινος τὸν ἀ. *BGU*1128.9 (14 B.C.). -**αστής**, οῦ, ὁ, *the slave who had to buy* provisions for the house, *purveyor*, X.*Mem.*1.5.2:—generally, *purchaser*, μέτριος ἀ. Men.500, cf. Arist.*Oec.*1352^{b}6, Dinon12, Ael.*VH*12.1, *POxy.*298.48 (i A.D.). -**αστικός**, ή, όν, *of* or *for traffic*, *commercial*, Pl.*Cra.*408a; ἡ -κή (sc. τέχνη) *traffic*, *commerce*, Id.*Sph.*223c; τὸ ἀ. δίκαιον *right of purchase*, *POxy.*1268.16 (iii A.D.), 1475.14 (iii A.D.). -**αστός**, ή, όν, *bought*, *paid for*, *PPetr.*3p.243 (iii B.C.), *BGU*802 iv 8 (i A.D.); δούλη *POxy.*95.14 (i A.D.), cf. Porph.Hist.20. -**άστρια**, ἡ, fem. of ἀγοραστής, *BGU* 907.11 (ii A.D.), *PThead.*1.11 (iv A.D.). -**ατρός**, ὁ, = πυλαγόρας, *IG*2^2.1132.6, *Klio*14.287 (Delph., iii B.C.). -**ατυπεῖς**· ἄγαν θορυβεῖς, Hsch. -**ᾶχος**, ἡ, female official at Sparta, *IG*5(1).589.

ἀγόρ-ευσις, ἡ, *speech*, *oration*, *EM*13.51. -**ευτήριον**, τό, *place for speaking*, *IG*14.742 (Naples, i/ii A.D.). -**ευτής**, οῦ, ὁ, *speaker*, *POxy.* 1590.1 (iv A.D.). -**εύω** (ἀγορά), impf. ἠγόρευον, Ep. ἀγόρευον Il.1.385: fut. -εύσω Hom., Alciphr.3.52, Philostr.*VA*4.45: aor. -ευσα Hom., D.H.1.65, Luc.*Pisc.*15: pf. -ευκα Lib.*Or.*37.4: 1 aor. Pass. -εύθην (προσ-) Str.3.3.5: in compds. these tenses and pf. Pass. -ευμαι are found in early Prose and Att. Inscrr., the simple vb. only in pres. and impf.:—*speak in the assembly*, *harangue*, freq. in Ep., ἀγορὰς ἀ. Il.2.788; ἐν Ἀργείοις ἔπεα πτερόεντ' ἀ. 23.535; ὡς Ἕκτωρ ἀγόρευε 8.542; τοῖσιν ἀ. *address* them, 1.571, al.; πρὸς ἀλλήλους ἔπεα 24.142; ὀνειδίζων ἀ. Od.18. 380: in Att., of the crier's proclamation in the Ecclesia, τίς ἀγορεύειν βούλεται; who wishes *to address the house?* Ar.*Ach.*45, D.18.170, etc.; ἀ. ὡς... Il.1.109: c. inf., μή τι φόβονδ' ἀγόρευε *counsel* me not to flight, Il.5.252; ἀ. μὴ στρατεύεσθαι Hdt.7.10.α'. 2. generally, *speak*, *say*, τοιαῦτα πρὸς ἀλλήλους ἀγόρευον Il.5.274; κακόν τι ἀ. τινά Od.18.15;

κακῶς ἀ. τινά Arist.*Fr.*417; ἀ. ὡς.., ὅτι.., Hdt.3.156, Ar.*Pl.*102; οὐκ ἠγόρευον; *did I* not *say so?* Id.*Ach.*41, cf. S.*OC*838; *tell of, mention,* τι Od.2.318, 16.263, al.; ὑπὲρ τοῦ Διὸς ἀγορεύων *speaking* of Zeus, Pl.*Lg.*776e: metaph., δέρμα θηρὸς ἀ. χειρῶν ἔργον *tells a tale of ..* Theoc.25.175. **3.** *proclaim,* Il.1.385; πέμπων κήρυκα ἠγόρευέ σφι τάδε Hdt.6.97:—Pass., ὁ πολίτης..κακὸς ἀγορευέσθω Pl.*Lg.*917d:—aor. Med., ἀγορεύσασθαι ὡς..*to have* it *proclaimed* that.., Hdt.9.26:—ὁ νόμος ἀ. the law *declares,* Antipho3.3.7, Lys.9.9, Arist.*Rh.*1354^{a}22; ἀ. μὴ ποιεῖν Ar.*Ra.*628; οὔνομα..ἤδ' ἀ. στήλη *IG*2.2753. **4.** Pass., *to be delivered,* λόγον καλὸν ἐπὶ τοῖς..θαπτομένοις -εσθαι Th. 2.35.

ἀγορ-ηγός, sc. ναῦς, ἡ, *ship which conveys provisions, EM*13.52. **-ῆθεν,** Adv. *from the assembly* or *market,* Il.2.264, al. **-ήιος,** = ἀγοραῖος, θεοί *IG*12(3).452 (Thera). **-ήνδε,** Adv. *to the assembly* or *market,* Il.1.54. **-ητής,** οῦ, ὁ, *speaker,* Ep. word, chiefly used of Nestor, λιγὺς Πυλίων ἀ. Il.1.248, al., cf. Ar.*Nu.*1057, Timo30.1. **II.** = ἀγορανόμος, or perh. *public auctioneer, OGI*262.20 (pl., Baetocaece). **-ητύς,** ύος, ἡ, *eloquence,* Od.8.168.—Ep. word. **-ῆφι,** Adv. *in the assembly,* Hes.*Th.*89.

ἄγορος, ὁ, = ἀγορά, used only by E. in lyr., generally in pl., as *IT* 1096, *El.*723, *Andr.*1037; sg. only *HF*412 ἄγορον ἁλίσας φίλων.

ἀγορρίον· ἐκκλησία, and **ἀγορρίς·** ἀγορά, ἄθροισις, Hsch.

ἀγός [ᾰ], οῦ, ὁ, (ἄγω) *leader, chief,* c. gen., Il.4.265, al., cf. Pi.*N.* 1.51, A.*Supp.*248, 904 (lyr.), E.*Rh.*29 (lyr.), *AP*9.219 (Diod.).

ἄγος (A), [ᾰ], εος, τό, *any matter of religious awe:* **1.** *pollution, guilt,* ἐν τῷ ἄγεϊ ἐνέχεσθαι Hdt.6.56; ἄ. ἐκθύσασθαι 6.91; ἄ... κεκτήσεται θεῶν A.*Th.*1022; ἄ. αἱμάτων ἀρέσθαι Id.*Eu.*168, cf. *AP* 7.268 (Plato); ἄ. φυλάσσεσθαι A.*Supp.*375; φεύγειν S.*Ant.*256; ὅθεν τὸ ἄ. συνέβη τοῖς Συβαρίταις Arist.*Pol.*1303^{a}30; ἄ. ἀφοσιώσασθαι Plu.*Cam.*18: in concrete sense, the *person* or *thing accursed,* S.*OT* 1426; ἄ. ἐλαύνειν, = ἀγηλατεῖν, Th.1.126. **2.** *expiation, sacrifice,* S.*Ant.*775, *Fr.*689, prob. so in A.*Ch.*155. **3.** ἄγεα· τεμένεα, and ἀγέεσσι· τεμένεσι, Hsch.; ἄγη· τὰ μυστήρια, *AB*212. (ἅγος (= τὸ καθαρόν, σέβασμα) postulated by Gramm. (cf. ἅγιος ἐκ τοῦ ἅγος γέγονεν *Et. Gud.*) is not found, unless ἄγος 3 be a dialectic form.)

ἄγος (B), εος, τό, (ἄγνυμι) *fragment,* Hsch., *EM*418.2.

ἀγοσταί, ἀγοστέω, variants for ἀκ- in Gramm., as *AB*213.

ἀγοστός, ὁ, *flat of the hand,* Hom. only in Il., in the phrase ὁ δ' ἐν κονίῃσι πεσὼν ἕλε γαῖαν ἀγοστῷ 11.425, al.; χειρὸς ἀ. A.R.3.120. **II.** *arm,* = ἀγκάλη, Theoc.17.129, *AP*7.464 (Antip.); pl., ib.5.254.15 (Paul. Sil.): metaph., ['Ακαδημείας] ἐν ἀγοστῷ Simon. 150. **III.** *dirt, filth,* Sch.Il.6.506. (Perh. cognate with Skt. *hástas* 'hand'.)

ἄγουρος, ὁ, *youth,* Thracian word, Eust.1788.56.

ἄγρα, Ion. **ἄγρη,** ἡ, *hunting, the chase,* (never in Il.), ἄγρην ἐφέπειν Od.12.330; χαίρουσι δέ τ' ἀνέρες ἄγρῃ 22.306; ἐς ἄγρας ἰέναι E.*Supp.* 885; ἄ. ἀνθρώπων Pl.*Lg.*823e; ἁλιαδᾶν ἔχων ἀΰπνους ἄγρας S.*Aj.* 880 (lyr.). **2.** *way of catching,* Pi.*N.*3.81, Hdt.2.70. **II.** *quarry, prey,* Hes.*Th.*442; ἄγραν ὤλεσα A.*Eu.*148 (lyr.); εὔκερως ἄ. S.*Aj.* 64, cf. 407 (pl.); Μελέαγρε, μελέαν γάρ ποτ' ἀγρεύεις ἄ. E.*Fr.*517; *game,* Hdt.1.73, etc.; of fish, *draught, take, Ev.Luc.*5.9: metaph., δορὸς ἄγρα A.*Th.*322 (lyr.). **III.** Ἄγρα, ἡ, title of Artemis at Athens, Pl.*Phdr.*229c; τὰ ἐν Ἄγρας (sc. μυστήρια) Paus.Gr.*Fr.*13; τὰ πρὸς Ἄγραν *IG*2.315; μήτηρ ἐν Ἄγρας ib.273:—also **Ἄγραι,** αἱ, the precinct of Artemis Agra, Paus.1.19.6, St. Byz., *AB*334, etc. (With ἄγρα : ἄγρια cf. θήρα : θηρία.)

ἄγρᾰδε, Adv., poet. form of ἀγρόνδε, Call.*Fr.*26.

ἀγραῖος, α, ον, (ἄγρα) *of the chase,* epith. of Apollo, Paus.1.41.6; of Artemis, Paus.Gr.*Fr.*13; δαίμονες Opp.*H.*3.27.

ἀγραμμ-ᾰτία, ἡ, *illiteracy,* Ph.1.502, Ael.*VH*8.6: pl., Phld.*Vit.* p.41 J. **-ᾰτος,** ον, *illiterate,* X.*Mem.*4.2.20, Damox.2.12, Epicur. *Fr.*236, *AP*11.154 (Lucill.), cf. S.E.*M.*1.99; *unable to read* or *write,* Pl.*Ti.*23a. Adv. -τως Ph.1.195, Arr.*Epict.*2.9.10. **II.** = ἄγραπτος, ἔθη Pl.*Plt.*295a. **III.** of animals, *unable to utter articulate sounds,* Arist.*HA*488^{a}33. **2.** of sounds, *inarticulate,* Id.*Int.*16^{a}29, D.L.3.107; *incapable of being written,* Porph.*Abst.*3.3, cf. Eustr.*in APo.*102.19; ᾠδὴ ἀ. *song without words,* Phld.*Po.*2*Fr.*47.22. **-ος,** ον, *not on the line,* ἄγραμμα ἀφεῖται, of a throw of the dice, *counting nothing,* Hsch.

ἀγράνδις, = ἀγρόνδε, Dor. Adv. in Theognost.*Can.*163.33.

ἄγραπτος, ον, *unwritten,* ἄ. θεῶν νόμιμα S.*Ant.*454. **II.** ἄ. δίκη action *cancelled* in consequence of a special plea, Poll.8.57.

ἀγρ-αυλέω, *live in the open, out of doors,* Arist.*Mir.*831^{a}29, Parth. 29.1, Plu.*Num.*4, Str.4.4.3; of shepherds, *Ev.Luc.*2.8. **-αυλής,** ές, *in the fields, out of doors,* κοίτη Nic.*Th.*78. **-αυλία,** ἡ, *service in the field,* D.H.6.44 (pl.), D.S.16.15 (pl.), etc. **-αυλος,** ον, (ἀγρός, αὐλή) *dwelling in the field,* of shepherds, Il.18.162, Hes.*Th.*26, A.R.4.317, Megasth.40; epith. of Pan, *AP*6.179 (Arch.); ἄ. ἀνήρ *a boor,* ib. 11.60 (Paul. Sil.). **2.** of oxen, βοὸς ἀγραύλοιο Il.10.155, Od.12. 253; θήρ S.*Ant.*349 (lyr.), E.*Ba.*1188 (lyr.), etc. **3.** of things, *rustic,* πύλαι Id.*El.*342.

ἀγραφ-ής, ές, = ἄγραφος, δάνειον *BGU*895.31 (ii A.D.). **-ίου** γραφή an action against state-debtors, *who had got their debts cancelled* without paying, D.58.51, Arist.*Ath.*59.3, Lycurg.*Fr.*6, Poll. 8.54. **-ος,** ον, *unwritten,* μνήμη Th.2.43; ἄ. διαθῆκαι *nuncupatory* wills, Plu.*Cor.*9; ἄ. κληρονόμος Luc.*Tox.*23; ἄγραφα λέγειν to speak *without book,* Plu.*Dem.*8. Adv. -φως, κατὰ μνήμης σῴζεσθαι Procl. *in Prm.*p.553 S. **II.** ἄ. δίκαιον, *moral* or *equitable justice,* Arist. *EN*1162^{b}22; ἄ. νόμοι or νόμιμα *unwritten laws:* **1.** *laws of nature,* τοῖς ἀ. νομίμοις καὶ τοῖς ἀνθρωπίνοις ἤθεσι D.18.275, cf. Arist. *EN*1180^{b}1. **2.** *laws of custom,* Th.2.37; ἄ. νόμιμα Pl.*Lg.*793a, cf. Arist.*Rh.*1373^{b}5; ἄγραφα, τά, ib.1368^{b}9; ἄ. ἀδίκημα a crime *not recognized by law,* Hsch. **3.** *religious traditions,* as of the Eumolpidae, Lys.6.10. **III.** *not registered,* ἄ. πόλεις (in a treaty) Th.1.40; ἄ. γάμοι *without written contract, CPR*18.30 (ii A.D. Adv. -ως ibid., *POxy.*267.19 (i A.D.)); ἄ. συνουσίαι *not written down,* Phlp.*in Ph.*513.30; συναλλαγματογραφίαι *PTeb.*1.140; ἄγραφα καὶ ἄστατα neither *catalogued* nor weighed, *IG*2.652*B*2; hence ἄγραφα, τά, *sundries, PTeb.*112.104 (ii B.C.), al. **2.** ἄ. μέταλλα mines *not registered,* but worked clandestinely, Suid. s.v. **IV.** *without inscription, IG* 2.754, al.—Prose word.

ἄγρει, v. sub ἀγρέω II.

ἀγρεῖος, α, ον, (ἀγρός) *of the field* or *country,* πλάτανος *AP*6.35 (Leon.). **2.** *clownish, boorish,* Ar.*Nu.*655, *Th.*160.

ἀγρειοσύνη, ἡ, *clownishness:* or *a rude, vagrant life, AP*6.51.

ἀγρεῖφνα, ἡ, *harrow, AP*6.297 (Phanias); cf. ἀγρίφη.

ἀγρέμιον, τό, = ἄγρα II, *AP*6.224 (Theodorid.).

ἀγρεμών, όνος, ὁ, *hunter, EM*13.56; also glossed by κάμαξ, λαμπάς, δόρυ, Hsch.; = ἐπιμήνιος, A.*Fr.*141.

ἀγρεσία, Ion. -ίη, ἡ, = ἄγρα I, *AP*6.13 (Leon.).

ἀγρεταί, αἱ, (fem. pl. of ἀγρετός 'chosen', cf. ἀγρέω) priestesses of Athena at Cos, *B.Mus.Inscr.*968*A,* Hsch.

ἀγρετεύω, *hold office of* ἀγρέτας, *IG*5(1).1346 (Laconia, ii A.D.).

ἀγρετήματα· τὰ ἀγορευόμενα τῶν παρθένων (Lacon.), Hsch.

ἀγρέτης, ου, Dor. **-τας,** ὁ, = ἡγεμών, Hsch.; prob. for ἀγρόται, A. *Pers.*1002 Toup. **II.** **Ἀγρέτης,** ὁ, perh. from ἀγρός, *god of the fields,* title of Apollo at Chios, *GDI*5666.

ἄγρ-ευμα, τό, in pl., = τὰ ἐπὶ τῆς ἀγροικίας κτήματα, Sol.ap.*AB* 340. **II.** *that which is taken in hunting, prey,* E.*Ba.*1241: metaph., X.*Mem.*3.11.7; ἄ. ἀνθέων E.*Fr.*754. **2.** *means of catching,* ἄ. θηρός A.*Ch.*998; ἐντὸς..μορσίμων ἀ., of the *net* thrown over Agamemnon, Id.*Ag.*1048, cf. *Eu.*460. **-εύς,** έως, ὁ, *hunter,* epith. of Aristaeus, Pi.*P.*9.65; of Apollo, A.*Fr.*200, Herod.3.34; of Bacchus, E.*Ba.*1192 (lyr.); of Poseidon, Luc.*Pisc.*47; of Pan, Apollod.ap.Hsch. **II.** of an arrow, *AP*6.75 (Paul. Sil.). **III.** a kind of bird, Ael.*NA*8.24. (From ἀγρός, cf. οἰκεύς : οἶκος; the reference to hunting is secondary.) **-εύσιμος,** η, ον, *easy to catch,* Sch.S.*Ph.*863. **-ευσις,** εως, ἡ, *catching,* Hsch. **-ευτεῖ·** ὑβρίζει, Hsch. **-ευτήρ,** ῆρος, ὁ, = sq., Theoc.21.6, Call.*Dian.*218, *AP*7.578 (Agath.). **II.** as Adj., ἀ. κύνες Opp.*C.*3.456; ἀγρευτῆρι λίνῳ, i.e. with *fishing*-net, Man.5.279. **-ευτής,** οῦ, ὁ, *hunter,* epith. of Apollo as slayer of Python, S.*OC*1091 (lyr.), *PFlor.*297.19 (vi A.D.): metaph., of sleep, ἀ. πτηνοῦ φάσματος *AP*12.125 (Mel.). **II.** Adj., κύνες ἀ. *hounds,* Sol.23; ἀ. κάλαμοι a fowler's *trap of reeds, AP*7.171 (Mnasalc.), cf. 6.109 (Antip.). **-ευτικός,** ή, όν, *of* or *skilled in hunting,* ἀγρευτικόν [ἐστι] *useful for ensnaring* an enemy, X.*Eq.Mag.*4.12; ἀ. λίνος Sch.E.*Ba.*611. Adv. -κῶς Poll.5.9. **-ευτίς,** ίδος, ἡ, fem. of ἀγρευτής, prob. l. in Sch.Ar.*V.*367. **-ευτός,** όν, *caught,* Opp.*H.* 3.541. **-εύω,** fut. εύσω Call.*Dian.*85: aor. ἤγρευσα E.*Ba.*1204:—**Med.,** v. infr.:—**Pass.,** aor. ἠγρεύθην *AP,* v. infr.: (ἀγρεύς):—*take by hunting* or *fishing, catch,* ἰχθῦς Hdt.2.95, cf. X.*Cyn.*12.6; ἄγραν ἠγρευκότες E.*Ba.*434; of war, φιλεῖ..ἄνδρας..ἀγρεύειν νέους S.*Fr.* 554:—also in Med., θύματ' ἠγρεύσασθε *ye caught* or *chose your* victim, E.*IT*1163; τί μοι ξίφος ἐκ χερὸς ἠγρεύσω; why *didst thou snatch..?* Id.*Andr.*842:—Pass., X.*An.*5.3.8, cf. Sphaer.*Stoic.*1.142; ἀγρευθεὶς ἤγρευσε *AP*9.94 (Isid.), 12.113 (Mel.). **2.** metaph., *hunt after, thirst for,* αἷμα E.*Ba.*138; σὰν (sc. Ἀρετᾶς) ἀ. δύναμιν Arist.*Fr.*675.11; ὕπνον *AP*7.196 (Mel.), cf. 12.125 (Mel.); but ἀγρεύειν τινὰ λόγῳ *to catch* by his words, *Ev.Marc.*12.13.

ἀγρέω, = αἱρέω, *take, seize,* freq. in Aeolic Inscrr. as *IG*12(2).6.33 (Pass., Lesbos); ἄγρει δ' οἶνον ἐρυθρόν Archil.4.3; τρόμος παῖσαν ἄγρει Sapph.2.14, cf. Thgn.294; ἀγρεῖ πόλιν *captures,* A.*Ag.*126 (lyr.); of fishing, *AP*6.304 (Phanias); in prescriptions, ἄγρει, *take!* Nic.*Th.*534, al. **II.** Hom. only in imper. ἄγρει, prop. *take it!,* hence, *come on!* ἄγρει μάν οἱ ἔπορσον Ἀθηναίην Il.5.765, cf. A.R.1.487; pl., ἀγρεῖτε (ἄγρειτε *An.Ox.*1.71) Od.20.149. Cf. ἄργειτε.

ἄγρηθεν, Adv. *from the chase,* A.R.2.938. **ἀγρήθετο·** ἠθέλησεν, Hsch.

ἀγρηνόν, τό, *net,* Hsch.:—also, *net-like woollen robe* worn by Bacchanals and soothsayers, Id., Poll.4.116.

ἀγρία, ἡ, = ἄγρα II, *BGU*1123.9 (Aug.).

ἀγρίαζε· ἄγριος ἴσθι, Hsch.

ἀγριαίνω, fut. ανῶ Pl.*R.*501e: aor. ἠγρίᾱνα D.C.44.47, Ael.*VH*2. 13:—**Pass.,** D.H.9.32, Plu.*Ant.*58: fut. ἀγριανθήσομαι Lxx *Da.*11.11: aor. ἠγριάνθην D.S.24.1.—In Att. the Pass. was supplied by ἀγριόω (q.v.), which was rare in Act.; but the compd. Pass. ἐξαγριαίνομαι occurs in Pl.*R.*336d, and the Act. ἐξαγριόω in Hdt 6.123, E.*Ph.*876, Pl.*Lg.*935a. **1.** intr., *to be* or *become wild, to be angered, provoked,* Pl.*R.*493b, etc.; τινί *with* one, Id.*Smp.*173d; πρός τινα Porph.*Abst.* 3.12; of animals, Arist.*HA*608^{b}31; of rivers and the like, *chafe,* πρὸς τὴν πλήμμυραν..ἀγριαίνων ὁ ποταμός Plu.*Caes.*38:—Pass., D.S. l.c.; of sores, *to be angry* or *inflamed,* Aret.*SD*2.11, cf. Antyll.ap. Orib.10.13.2. **II.** causal, *make angry, provoke,* D.C.44.47; of love, *irritate,* Ach.Tat.2.7:—Pass., *to be angered,* Plu. l.c., Hierocl. *in CA*10p.434 M.; ὑπὸ τῶν δημαγωγῶν D.H. l.c.

ἀγρι-άνθρωπος, ου, ὁ, *wild man, savage,* Ps.-Callisth.3.28. **-απιος,** -ιδος, = ἀγριο-αππίδιον, *Gloss.*

ἀγριάς, άδος, ἡ, = fem. of ἄγριος, *wild,* A.R.1.28; νῆσσαι Arat.

918; αἶγες Call.*Aet.*3.1.13; ἄμπελον ἀ. *AP*9.561 (Phil.), cf. Numen. ap.Ath.371c. II. **Ἀγριάδες**, αἱ, *Nymphs*, Hsch.

ἀγριαχράς, ἡ, *wild pear*, Zopyr.ap.Orib.14.61.1.

ἀγριάω, *to be savage*, Opp.*C.*2.49, in Ep. form ἀγριόωντα.

ἀγρίδιον, τό, Dim. of ἀγρός, *Sammelb.*5230.29 (i A.D.), Arr.*Epict.* 1.10.9, al., M.Ant.4.3.

ἀγρι-ελαία, ἡ, *wild olive*, Hp.*Mul.*2.112, Dsc.1.105, etc. **-ελάϊνος**, *of wild olive*, ξύλα *IG*7.3073.189 (Lebad.). **-έλαιος**, ον, = foreg., σκυτάλη *AP*9.237 (Erycius). II. as Subst., = ἀγριελαία, Theoc. 7.18, Thphr.*HP*2.2.5, *Ep.Rom.*11.17, etc.

ἀγρ-ιεύς· ἀγροῖκος, Hsch. **-ιεύω**, *catch by hunting* or *fishing*, *PRyl.*98ᵃ7 (ii A.D.). **-ίζω**, *inflame, irritate*, in Pass., dub. l. in Hp.*Mul.*2.154; Act., Sm.*Pr.*15.18; cf. ἀγγρίζω.

ἀγρικός, ή, όν, = ἄγριος, πήγανον *POxy.*1675.4 (iii A.D.).

ἀγριμαῖος, α, ον, *wild*; τὰ ἀ. *game*, Ptol.Euerg.6, *PLond.*3.1159.73 (ii A.D.).

ἀγριμέλισσα, ἡ, *wasp*, metaph. of Hegesias, Hsch.; cf. ἀγριομέλιττα.

ἄγρινοι· ἀγρονόμοι, Hsch.

ἀγριο-απίδιον, τό, *wild pear tree*, *Gp.*8.37.3. **-βάλανος**, ἡ, *evergreen oak, Quercus pseudo-coccifera*, Aq.Thd.*Is.*44.14. **-βουλος**, ον, *wild of purpose*, Adam.1.18. **-δαίτης**, ου, ὁ, *eating wild fruits*, Orac.ap.Paus.8.42.6.

ἀγριόεις, εσσα, εν, = ἄγριος, Nic.*Al.*604. 2. *maddening*, ὀπώρη ib.30.

ἀγριό-θῡμος, ον, *wild of temper*, Orph.*H.*12.4. **-κάναβος**, ὁ, *hemp-mallow, Althaea cannabina*, Hsch. **-κάρδαμον**, τό, = ἰβηρίς, Gal.13.353. **-καρδον**, τό, = ἄκανθα Αἰγυπτία, *AB*1096. **-κάρυον**, τό, *cob-nut*, Hsch. **-κινάρα**, = ἄκανθα λευκή, Ps.-Dsc.3.12; = *carduus*, *Gloss.* **-κοκκύμηλον**, τό, = προῦμνον, Gal.6.619. **-κολοκύντη**, = τολύπη 3, Phot. **-κρόμμυον**, τό, = βολβός, Sch.Ar.*Pl.* 283. **-κύμῑνον**, τό, *wild cumin*, Sch.Nic.*Th.*709. **-λάχᾰνα**, ων, τά, *wild pot-herbs*, Sch.Theoc.4.52. **-λειχήν**, ὁ, = ἄγριος λειχήν (3), Hsch. s.v. ἀγριοψωρία.

ἀγρίολον, τό, = ἱπποσέλινον Dsc.3.67.

ἀγριο-μᾰλάχη, ἡ, = ἀλθαία, Sch.Nic.*Th.*89. **-μέλιττα**, ἡ, *wasp*, *Gloss.* **-μορφος**, ον, f.l. for συαγρ-, Orph.*A.*979. **-μῡρίκη** [ῐ], ἡ, *tamarisk*, Lxx *Je.*17.6; Adj. **-μυρίκινος**, ξύλα *PHamb.*12.19 (iii A.D., ἀγρο- Pap.). **-μύρμηξ**, *weevil*, *Gloss.* **-νους**, ουν, *fierce*, *IG*12(7).115 (Amorgos). **-πήγανον**, τό, *Syrian rue*, Hsch., Aët.1. 295, al. **-πηγός**, ὁ, (πήγνυμι) = ἁμαξουργός, ἀγρίων ξύλων ἐργάτης, Sch.Ar.*Eq.*464. **-ποιέω**, *to make wild*, Sch.A.*Pers.*613. **-ποιός**, όν, *poet of savagery*, of Aeschylus in Ar.*Ra.*837. II. *making savage*, Sch.Nic.*Al.*30. **-πρασον**· *serpyllum* (sic), *Gloss.*

ἀγριορίγᾰνος, ὁ, *marjoram, Origanum viride*, Dsc.3.29.

ἀγριόρροδον, τό, = *saliuncula* (i.e. Κελτικὴ νάρδος), *Gloss.*

ἄγριος, α, ον, Od.9.119; also ος, ον (not in Trag. or Com.) Il.19.88, Phoc.3.6, Pl.*Lg.*824a, Theoc.22.36: Comp. -ώτερος Th.6.60: Sup. -ώτατος Pl.*R.*564a (ἀγρός): *living in the fields, wild, savage.* I. of animals, opp. τιθασός, ἥμερος, *wild*, βάλλειν ἄγρια πάντα Il.5.52; αἶξ, σῦς, 3.24, 9.539; even of flies, ἄ. φῦλα, μυίας 19.30; ἵπποι, ὄνοι, etc., Hdt.7.86, etc.; ἄ. τέρας, of a bull, E.*Hipp.*1214; ἄ. θηρία X.*An.* 1.2.7; of men, *living in a wild state*, Hdt.4.191. 2. of trees, opp. ἥμερος, *wild*, Pi.*Fr.*46, Hdt.4.21, etc.; μητρὸς ἀγρίας ἄπο ποτόν of the *wild* vine, A.*Pers.*614, cf. Arist.*Pr.*896ᵃ8; ἄ. ἔλαιον S.*Tr.*1197; ὕλη Id.*OT*476, etc.; μέλι *Ev.Matt.*3.4. 3. of countries, *wild, uncultivated*, Pl.*Phd.*113b, *Lg.*905b. II. mostly of men, beasts, etc.: 1. in moral sense, *savage, fierce*, Il.8.96, Od.1.199, etc., cf. Ar.*Nu.*567; δεσπότης Pl.*R.*329c; ἄ. καὶ ἀπαίδευτος Id.*Grg.*510b; ἄγριε παῖ καὶ στυγνέ Theoc.23.19, cf. 2.54; ἄ. κυβευτής a *passionate* gambler, Men.965; esp. of παιδερασταί, Ar.*Nu.*349 (cf. Sch. ad loc.), Aeschin.1.52, Aen.Gaz.*Thphr.* p.14 B. 2. of temper, *wild, fierce*, θυμός, χόλος, Il.9.629, 4.23; λέων δ' ὥς, ἄγρια οἶδεν 24.41; ἄ. πτόλεμος, μῶλος, 17.737,398; ἄγριος ἄτη 19.88; ἄ. ὁδοί *cruel* ways or counsels, S.*Ant.*1274; ὀργή *OT*344 (Sup.); ἀγριώτατα ἤθεα Hdt.4. 106; ἔρωτες Pl.*Phd.*81a; φιλία Id.*Lg.*837b, cf. *R.*572b, etc.; τὸ ἀ. *savageness*, Id.*Cra.*394e; ἐς τὸ -ώτερον *to harsher measures*, Th. l.c. 3. of things, circumstances, etc., *cruel, harsh*, δεσμά A.*Pr.* 177; νὺξ -ωτέρη *wild, stormy*, Hdt.8.13; δουλεία Pl.*R.*564a; σύντασις ἀ. a *violent* strain, Id.*Phlb.*46d; ἄ. βάρος, of strong, hot wine, Ar.*Fr.*351. b. ἀ. νόσος, prob., *malignant*, S.*Ph.*173,265; ἄ. ἕλκος Bion 1.16. III. Adv. -ίως, *savagely*, A.*Eu.*972, Ar.*V.*705; ἄγρια δερκομένω, παίσδων, Hes.*Sc.*236, Mosch.1.11. [ᾰ Hom.; ᾰ in trim., ᾰ in lyr. A. and S.; ᾱ E.; ῑ metri grat., where the ult. is long, Il.22.313 (nisi leg. ἀγρίοο).]

ἀγριο-σέλῑνον, τό, = ἀγρίολον, Dsc.3.67. **-σίκυον**, τό, *squirting cucumber*, Hippiatr.22. **-σταφίδες** and **-σταφύλιες** (sic), *wild grapes*, Hsch. **-σταφυλίτης** οἶνος wine *made therefrom*, Dsc.5. 6. **-σῡκῆ**, ἡ, *wild fig*, Horap.2.77.

ἀγριό-της, ητος, ἡ, *savageness, wildness*, of animals, opp. ἡμερότης, X.*Mem.*2.2.7, cf. Isoc.12.163, Arist.*HA*588ᵃ21; of plants, Thphr.*HP* 3.2.4; of untilled ground, ἀ. γῆς *Gp.*7.1.4; of diet, Hp.*VM*7 (as v.l. for θηριότητα), *Aër.*23. II. of men, in moral sense, *fierceness, cruelty*, Pl.*Smp.*197d, al., D.26.26 (pl.). **-φαγρος**, ὁ, *wild* φάγρος, Opp.*H.* 1.140. **-φανής**, ές, *appearing wild*, Corn.*ND*27. **-φυλλον**, τό, = πευκέδανος, Ps.-Dsc.3.78. **-φυτα**, τά, *wild herbs*, Sch.Nic.*Al.* 429. **-φωνος**, ον, *with rough voice* or *tongue*, like βαρβαρόφωνος, Od.8.294; Δᾶτις *App.Anth.*3.74.22. **-χοιρος**, ὁ, *wild swine*, Sch. Ar.*Pl.*304. **-ψωρία**, ἡ, (ψώρα) *inveterate itch*, Hsch.

ἀγριόω, aor. ἠγρίωσα E.*Or.*616, the act. tenses being mostly supplied by ἀγριαίνω, (ἄγριος):—*make wild* or *savage, provoke*, ἡ τῇ τεκούσῃ σ' ἠγρίωσε *against* thy mother, E. l.c. II. mostly in Pass., ἀγριοῦμαι Hp.*Aër.*4: impf. ἠγριούμην E.*El.*1031 codd.: aor. ἠγριώθην Plu.*Per.* 34: pf. ἠγρίωμαι S.*Ph.*1321, E.*IT*348, Ar.*Ra.*897:—*grow wild*; in pf. *to be wild*, properly of plants, countries, etc., νῆσος ἠγριωμένη τῇ ὕλῃ Thphr.*HP*5.8.2, cf. *CP*5.3.6; of men, *to be unkempt*, ὡς ἠγρίωσαι διὰ μακρᾶς ἀλουσίας E.*Or.*226, cf. 387. 2. in moral sense, *to be savage, cruel* ἠγρίωσαι S.*Ph.* l.c., cf. E.*El.* l.c., etc.; γλῶσσα. . ἠγρίωται, of Aeschylus, Ar. l.c.: metaph., ἠγριωμένον πέλαγος an *angry* sea, Plu.*Pyrrh.*15. 3. Medic., *become malignant*, of wounds, Hp. l.c.

Ἀγριππιασταί, οἱ, *worshippers of Agrippa*, guild at Sparta, *IG*5(1). 374.8.

ἄγριππος, ὁ, Lacon. name for the *wild olive*, Suid., etc.; prov., ἀκαρπότερος ἀγρίππου Zen.1.60; in Hsch. **ἄγριφος.**

ἀγρίς, ἡ, *Valonia oak*, opp. ἡμερίς, *EM*429.17.

ἀγρίτης, ου, ὁ, *countryman*, St. Byz. s.v. ἀγρός.

ἀγρίφη [ῐ], ἡ, *harrow, rake*, Hdn.Gr.1.345, Hsch.; cf. ἀγρεῖφνα.

ἀγριώδης, ες, *of wild nature*, Str.3.3.8.

Ἀγριώνιος, ὁ, epith. of Dionysus, transferred to Antony, Plu.*Ant.* 24. **Ἀγριώνια**, τά, festival in honour of Dionysus, Id.2.291a, 299f, etc.

ἀγριωπός, όν, *wild-looking*, ὄμμα E.*HF*990, cf. *Ba.*542; τὸ ἀ. τοῦ προσώπου Plu.*Mar.*14, cf. Corn.*ND*6.

ἀγρο-βόας, ὁ, *rudely shouting*, Cratin.374. **-βότης**, ου, Dor. **-ας**, α, ὁ, *feeding in the field, dwelling in the country*, S.*Ph.*214 (lyr.), E.*Cyc.*54 (lyr.). **-γείτων**, ονος, ὁ, *country neighbour*, Plu.*Cat. Ma.*25, *POxy.*1106.2 (vi A.D.); ἀ. τινός *having a field adjoining* his, J.*AJ*8.13.8. **-δίαιτος**, ον, *living in the country*, *Gloss.* **-δότης**, ου, ὁ, (ἄγρα) *giver of game*, δαίμονες *AP*6.27 (Theaet.).

ἀγρό-θεν, Adv. *from the country*, Od.13.268, 15.428, Epich.161, E.*Or.*866, Luc.*Macr.*22: also **-θε**, *AP*7.398 (Antip.). **-θι**, Adv. *in the country*, Call.*Cer.*136, Poll.9.12.

ἀγροικ-εύομαι, *to be stupid*, Phld.*Mus.*p.95 K., cf. *EM*14.2, Hsch. s.v. ἀγροιτιᾷ. **-ηρός**, ά, όν, *boorish*, ἀ. φύσις Anon.ap.St.Byz. s.v. ἀγρός. **-ία**, ἡ, *rusticity, boorishness*, Pl.*Grg.*461c, *R.*560d, al.; cf. Arist.*EN*1108ᵃ26. II. *the country*, Herod.1.2, *Inscr.Magn.* 8, *SIG*344.100 (Teos), Muson.*Fr.*11 p.60 H., Plu.2.519a, Longus 1.13, Aristid.*Or.*47(23).45; pl., Plu.2.311b. III. in pl., *country-houses*, D.S.20.8, Nymphod.12, M.Ant.4.3. **-ίζομαι**, *to be rude and boorish*, Pl.*Tht.*146a, Plu.*Sull.*6: aor. ἠγροικισάμην Aristid. 1.491 J. **-ικός**, ή, όν, *rustic*, Cephalio 6, Ath.11.477a, Sch. Nic.*Th.*78; ἀνδράποδα Just.*Nov.*7.6. Adv. -κῶς Alciphr.3.70.

ἀγροικοπυρρώνειος, ὁ, *rude, coarse Pyrrhonist*, Gal.8.711.

ἄγροικος, ον, (ἀγρός, οἰκέω) *dwelling in the fields*, ζῷα, opp. ὄρεια, Arist.*HA*488ᵇ2; esp. of men, *countryman, rustic*, Ar.*Nu.*47; in Attica, οἱ ἄ., = γεωμόροι (q.v.), Arist.*Ath.*13.2, D.H.2.8: mostly with the collat. sense of *boorish, rude*, Ar.*Nu.*628,646, etc., cf. Thphr. *Char.*4; μέλος -ότερον Ar.*Ach.*674; ἄ. σοφία Pl.*Phdr.*229e, cf. Isoc.5. 82 (Comp.), Arist.*EN*1128ᵃ9; of fortune, Apollod.Car.5.14; ἄ. Δημοσθένης, of Dinarchus, D.H.*Din.*8. Adv. -κως Ar.*V.*1320: Comp. -οτέρως Pl.*R.*361e, X.*Mem.*3.13.1; -ότερον Pl.*Phdr.*260d. II. *rustic*, βίος Ar.*Nu.*43. 2. of fruits, *common*, opp. γενναῖος, ὀπώρα Pl.*Lg.*844d. (ἀγροῖκος *dwelling in the country*, ἄγροικος *boorish*, acc. to Ammon.*Diff.*5, but this is very doubtful.)—Not found in early Ep. or Trag.

ἀγροικόσοφος, ον, *with rude mother-wit*, Ph.1.448; in bad sense, ib.577.

ἀγροικώδης, ες, *clownish, rude*, Sch.Il.23.476, Aristid.Quint.2.6.

ἀγροιώτης, ου, ὁ, = ἀγρότης 1, Hom. always in nom. pl., ἀνέρες ἀγροιῶται Il.11.549; βουκόλοι ἀ. Od.11.293; λαοὶ ἀ. Il.11.676; νήπιοι ἀ. Od.21.85; ποιμένας ἀ. Hes.*Sc.*39; sg., Ar.*Th.*58:—fem. **ἀγροιῶτις**, ἡ, (perh. as Adj., cf. II) Sapph.70. II. as Adj., *rustic*, Πρίηπος *AP*6.22 (Zon.), ὕλη 7.411 (Diosc.); *wild*, Numen.ap.Ath.371c.

ἀγρο-κήπιον, τό, Dim. of sq., Str.12.3.11. **-κηπος**, ὁ, *field kept as garden*, *IG*3.60*B*1.26. **-κόμος**, ὁ, *land-steward*, J.*AJ*5.9.2.

ἀγρ-ολέτειρα, ἡ, *waster of land*, Hsch.; epith. of Artemis, Suid.

ἀγρολικός, ή, όν, prob. by mistake for ἀρβυλικός (q.v.), *IG*11(2). 199*B*19 (Delos, iii B.C.).

ἀγρομενής, ές, *dwelling in the country*, Call.*Fr.anon.*142 (nisi leg. -μανής).

ἀγρόνδε, Adv., (ἀγρός) *to the country*, Od.15.370.

ἀγρονόμης, ου, Dor. **-ας**, = sq., μοῦσα *AP*7.196 (Mel.).

ἀγρο-νόμος, ον, (νέμομαι) *haunting the country*, Νύμφαι Od.6.106; θῆρες A.*Ag.*142 (lyr.), cf. Hp.*Vict.*2.49; βοτῆρες *Epic.Oxy.*1015. 7. 2. Subst. **ἀγρονόμος**, ὁ, (νέμω) a magistrate in charge of the country districts, Pl.*Lg.*760b, al., cf. Arist.*Pol.*1321ᵇ30. II. **ἀγρόνομος**, ον, *affording open pasturage*, πλάκες, αὐλαί, S.*OT*1103, *Ant.*785 (both lyr.); ὕλη Opp.*H.*1.27. **-πόνος**, ὁ, *tiller of the soil*, *Gloss.*

ἀγρός, οῦ, ὁ, *field*, mostly in pl., *fields, lands*, Il.23.832, Od.4.757, Pi.*P.*4.149, etc.; opp. κῆποι, Theopomp.Hist.89; sg., *farm*, Od.24. 205; also in pl., X.*HG*2.4.1:—*tilled land*, opp. fallow, ἀγρὸς καὶ ἀργός, Ἀθηνᾶ 20.167 (Erythrae). 2. *country*, opp. town, Od.17. 182, E.*Supp.*884, etc.; ἀγρὸν τὰν πόλιν ποιεῖς Epich.169; ἀγρῷ *in the country*, Od.11.188; ἐπ' ἀγροῦ *in the country*, 1.190, 22.47; ἐπ' ἀγροῦ νόσφι πόληος 1.185; in pl., κατὰ πτόλιν ἠὲ κατ' ἀγρούς 17.18; ἐν οἴκοις ἢ 'ν ἀγροῖς S.*OT*112; ἐπ' ἀγρῶν ib.1049; ἀγροῖσι Id.*El.*313; τὸν ἐξ ἀγρῶν Id.*OT*1051; τὰ ἐξ ἀγρῶν Th.2.13, cf. 14; κατ' ἀγρούς Cratin. 318, Pl.*Lg.*881c; οἰκεῖν ἐν ἀγρῷ Ar.*Fr.*387.2; τὰ ἐν ἀγρῷ γιγνόμενα *fruits*, X.*Mem*.2.9.4, cf. *An*.5.3.9:—prov., οὐδὲν ἐξ ἀγροῦ λέγεις, ἀγροῦ πλέως, i.e. boorish, Suid., Hsch.—Rare in later Greek, *Ev.Marc.* 15.21, *PAmh*.2.134.5, *POxy*.967. [ᾰ by nature, so always in Com., exc. Ar.*Av*.579, Philem.116; ἀγρόθεν in Alc.Com.19 is paratrag.] (Cf. Skt. *ájras* 'plain', prob. fr. *aj* 'drive' (cf. ἄγω), i.e. *pasture.*)

ἀγροτέκτων, ὁ, = ἔποψ, Al.*Le*.11.19.

ἀγρό-τερος, α, ον, (ἀγρός; properly opp. ὀρέσ-τερος) poet. for ἄγριος. in Hom. always of *wild* animals, ἡμίονοι, σύες, αἶγες, Il.2.852, 12.146, Od.17.295; ἀγροτέρης ἐλάφοιο Hes.*Sc*.407; φὴρ ἀ. Pi.*P*.3.4: abs., ἀγρότεροι Theoc.8.58; ἀ. καὶ νέποδες *AP*6.11 (Satyr.). 2. of *countrymen*, *AP*9.244 (Apollonid.), *APl*.4.235 (Id.). 3. of plants, *wild*, *AP*9.384.8, cf. Nic.*Th*.711, Coluth.111. II. (ἄγρα) *fond of the chase, huntress*, of the nymph Cyrene, Pi.*P*.9.6: metaph., μέριμνα ἀ. Id.*O*.2.60. 2. pr. n. Ἀγροτέρα, Artemis *the huntress*, Il.21.471, X.*Cyn*.6.13; worshipped at Agra in Attica, *IG*2.467, Paus.1.19.6; at Sparta and elsewhere, X.*HG*4.2.20, Ar.*Eq*.660, etc. **-τήρ** [ᾰ], ῆρος, ὁ, = ἀγρότης, E.*El*.463 (lyr.):—fem. **ἀγρότειρα**, as Adj., *rustic*, ib.168 (lyr.). **-της**, ου, ὁ, (ἀγρός) poet. word, *countryman, rustic*, ἀ. ἀνήρ E.*Or*.1270, cf. *App.Anth*.4.20; πάροινος ἀ. ib.5.57. II. (ἄγρα) *hunter*, οἰωνοί . . οἷσί τε τέκνα ἀγρόται ἐξείλοντο Od.16.218, cf. Alcm.23.8; ἀγρότα Πάν, to whom δίκτυα ἀπ' ἀγρεσίης are offered, *AP*6.13 (Leon.):—fem. **ἀγρότις**, νύμφη A.R.2.509; ἀ. κούρα, i.e. Artemis, *AP*6.111 (Antip.); ἀ. αἰγανέη ib.57 (Paul. Sil.). III. for A.*Pers*.1002 v. ἀγρέτης.

ἀγροῦαι· ἀγροῖκοι, Hsch.

ἄγροφον· ὀρεινόν, Hp.ap.Gal.19.69, Suid.

ἀγροφύλαξ [ῠ], ὁ, *guardian of the country*, *APl*.4.243 (Antist.), *PRein*.48 (ii A.D.), *PLond*.403.11 (iv A.D.).

ἄγρυκτος, ον, (ἀ- priv., γρύζω) *not to be spoken of*, ἄγρυκτα παθεῖν Pherecr.157. **ἀγρυξία**, ἡ, *dead silence*, Pi.*Fr*.229.

ἀγρυπν-έω, pf. ἠγρύπνηκα Hp.*Progn*.2:—*lie awake, pass sleepless nights*, Thgn.471, Hp. l. c., Pl.*Lg*.695a, etc.; opp. καθεύδω, X.*Cyr*. 8.3.42; ἀγρυπνεῖν τὴν νύκτα *to pass a sleepless* night, Id.*HG*7.2.19, Men.113; οἱ -οῦντες *sufferers from insomnia*, Dsc.4.64. 2. metaph., *to be watchful*, Lxx *Wi*.6.15, *Ev.Marc*.13.33, *Ep.Eph*.6.18; ὑπὲρ τῶν ψυχῶν *Ep.Heb*.13.17; ἐπὶ τὰ κακά Lxx *Da*.9.14: c. inf., μηθέν σε ἐνοχλήσειν *PGrenf*.2.14*a*3. 3. c. acc., *lie awake and think of*, τινά *PMag.Par*.1.2966. **-ητέον**, *one must watch*, Eust.168.16. **-ητήρ**, ῆρος, ὁ, *watcher*, Man.1.81. **-ητής**, *excubitor*, *Gloss*. **-ητικός**, ή, όν, *wakeful*, D.S.33.21, Plu.*Cam*.27. II. *producing wakefulness*, *PLond*.1.96, *PMag.Par*.1.2943, Gal.10.930:—**-ητικόν**, τό, *spell for this purpose*, *PMag.Lond*.121.374, *PMag.Leid.V*.11.26. **-ία**, Ion. -ίη, ἡ, *sleeplessness, wakefulness*, Hp.*Aph*.2.3, al., Pl.*Cri*.43b, etc.; in pl., Hp.*Acut*.42; ἀγρυπνίῃσιν εἴχετο Hdt.3.129, cf. *IG*4.952.50 (Epid.), Ar.*Lys*.27, Pl.*R*.460d. II. *time of watching*, Pl.*Ax*.368b; οἱ τῆς ἀ. ἄρχοντες Just.*Nov*.13*Pr*. III. of poetry, *product of sleepless nights*, Call.*Epigr*.29.4. [ῑ in Opp.*C*.3.511.] **-ος**, ον, *wakeful*, Hp.*Epid*.1.18, Pl.*R*.404a, Arist.*Pol*.1314^{b}35, etc.: metaph., Ζηνὸς ἄ. βέλος A.*Pr*.360; ἠιόνες *AP*7.278 (Arch.):—τὸ ἄ. *vigilance*, Hp.*Aër*.24, Plu.2.355b. Adv. -νως *OGI* 194.23 (Egypt, i B.C.). II. Act., *banishing sleep, keeping awake*, νοήσεις Arist.*Pr*.917^{b}1; μέριμναι *APl*.4.211 (Stat. Flacc.). [ἀγρῠπνος E.*Rh*.2 (lyr.), ἀγρῦπνος Theoc.24.106.] **-ώδης**, ες, *making sleepless*, Hp.*Prorrh*.1.10 as v.l.

ἄγρωμα, τό, perh. = *right of hunting*, *Annuario*3.195 (Gortyn).

ἄγρωσσα, ἡ, *huntress*, epith. of a hound, Simon.130.

ἀγρώσσω, Ep. for ἀγρεύω, only in pres., *catch*, ἀγρώσσων ἰχθῦς Od.5.53; freq. in Opp., *H*.3.339,543, al., cf. Call.*Ap*.60, Lyc.598, etc.: abs., *go hunting*, Opp.*C*.1.129:—Pass., Id.*H*.3.415, 4.565.

ἀγρ-ώστης, ου, ὁ, = ἀγρότης, Subst. and Adj., S.*Fr*.94, E.*HF*377 (lyr.), *Rh*.287, *AP*6.37, Call.*Hec*.1.1.13, v.l. in Theoc.25.48. 2. *wild*, κήρυκες Babr.115.2. II. *hunter*, A.R.4.175. 2. a kind of *spider*, Nic.*Th*.734. **-ωστῖνος**, Syrac. for ἄγροικος, name of play by Epich.; ἀγρωστῖναι· νύμφαι ὄρειοι, Hsch. **-ωστις**, ιδος, Thphr. *HP*1.6.10, and εως, Arist.*HA*552^{a}15, *PTeb*.104.26 (ii B.C.), ἡ, acc. ἄγρωστιν Plb.34.10.3, Str.4.1.7:—*dog's-tooth grass, Cynodon Dactylon*, Od.6.90; εἰλιτενὴς ἄ. Theoc.13.42, cf. Aeschrio 6, D.S. 1.43, Dsc.4.29. 2. ἀ. μελιηδής Id.*Ch*.639... 2. ἄ. ἐν Κιλικίᾳ *Hordeum marinum*, Dsc.4.32; ἄ. ἐν Παρνασσῷ *grass of Parnassus, Parnassia palustris*, ib.31. **-ωστήρ**, ῆρος, ὁ, = -ώστης, S.*Ichn*.33:—also **-ώστωρ**, ορος, ὁ, Nic.*Al*.473. **-ώτηρ**, ὁ, fem. **ἀγρώτειρα**, = ἀγρότης, St. Byz. s. v. ἀγρός. **-ώτης**, ου, ὁ, *of the field, wild*, θῆρες E.*Ba*.564 (lyr.), *Rh*.266.

ἄγ-υια, ᾶς, ἡ, *street, highway*, chiefly in pl., Il.5.642; σκιόωντό τε πᾶσαι ἀ. Od.2.388, etc.; of the paths of the sea, 11.12; ἀγυιαῖς *in the streets*, Hom.*Epigr*.14.5, cf. Pi.*P*.2.58, B.3.16, S.*OC*715, *Ant*.1136, E.*Ba*.87 (all lyr.): esp. in the phrase κνισᾶν ἀγυιάς Ar.*Eq*.1320, *Av*.1233, D.21.51:—rare in Prose, X.*Cyr*.2.4.3, *PPetr*.3p.7 (iii B.C.), Lxx 3*Ma*.1.20, etc.; ἐν ἀγυιᾷ, of documents executed *in public* by a notary, *POxy*.722.12 (i A.D.), etc. 2. *collection of streets, city*, Pi.*O*.9.34, *N*.7.92; πολύπυρος ἀ. *Hymn.Is*.2. (Quasi-participial form from ἄγω, cf. ἄρπυια.) [ἀγυιᾶν Il.20.254 (Aristarch.), cf. Pi.*N*.7.92 codd. vett.; ἄγυια Ion. and old Att. acc. to Hdn.Gr.2.613, Eust.1631.29; ἀγυιά, incorrectly, *EM*14.21, etc.; ἀγυιάν freq. in codd., e. g. Pi.*O*.9.34, X. l. c.] **-υιαῖος**, α, ον, *with streets or highways*, γῆ S.*Fr*.202. **-υιάτης**, ου, ὁ, = Ἀγυιεύς, voc. Ἀγυιᾶτα, A.*Ag*.1081. 2. in pl., *inhabitants of an* ἄγυια, *IG*9(2).241 (Phars.), cf. ἀγυιῆται· κωμῆται, Hsch., *EM*15.31. **-υιᾶτις**, ιδος, ἡ, fem. from foreg., *neighbour*, Pi.*P*.11.1. II. Adj. -άτιδες, θεραπεῖαι worship *of Apollo Agyieus*, E.*Ion*186 (lyr.).

Ἀγυι-εύς, έως, ὁ, a name of Apollo, as *guardian of the streets and highways*, E.*Ph*.631, Orac.ap.D.21.52, *IG*3.159, al. 2. *pointed pillar, set up as his statue* or *altar* at the street-door, Ar.*V*.875, Pherecr.87, Dieuchid.2; Ἀγυιεὺς βωμός S.*Fr*.370. **-ηος**, ὁ, sc. μήν, name of month at Argos, *Mnemos*.44.221 (iii B.C.).

ἀγυιό-πεζα Κουρῆτις, ἡ, mystical name for Pythagorean triad, Nicom.ap.Phot.*Bibl*.143B. **-πλαστέω**, (πλάσσω) *to build in streets* or *rows*, Lyc.601.

ἄγυιος, ον, *without limbs, weak in limb*, Hp.*Mul*.1.25.

ἀγυμν-ασία, ἡ, (γυμνάζω) *want of exercise* or *training*, Ar.*Ra*.1088, Arist.*EN*1114^{a}24. **-αστία**, ἡ, = foreg., Porph.*Abst*.1.35. **-αστος**, ον, *unexercised, untrained*, ἵπποι X.*Cyr*.8.1.38, cf. Arist.*Pr*.888^{a}23; ἀ. τοῖς σώμασιν Plu.*Arat*.47: metaph., *undisciplined*, φαντασίαι *Stoic*.2.39. 2. *unpractised*, τινός in a thing, E.*Ba*.491, X.*Cyr*.1.6.29, Pl., etc.; also εἴς or πρός τι Pl.*Lg*.731b,816a; περί τι Plu.2.802d, Gal.8.608; ἐν λόγοις Phld.*Rh*.1.189 S.: c. inf., Muson.*Fr*.6p.23 H. 3. *unharassed*, S.*Tr*.1083; οὐδ' ἀγύμναστον πλάνοις E.*Hel*.533; πόνοις οὐκ ἀγύμναστος φρένας Id.*Fr*.344. II. Adv. ἀγυμνάστως, ἔχειν πρός τι X.*Mem*.2.1.6.

ἀγύναιξ, ὁ, (γυνή) *wifeless*, S.*Fr*.4:—also **ἀγύναικος**, Phryn.Com. 19; **ἀγύναιος**, Lxx *Jb*.24.21, *PGnom*.79 (ii A.D.), D.C.56.1, Porph. *Abst*.4.17, Man.1.173; **ἀγύνης**, Poll.3.48; **ἄγυνος**, Ar.*Fr*.735.

ἀγυρ-εῖ· συναγκροτεῖ, Hsch. **-ίζειν**· συνάγειν, ἀγυρτάζειν, Id.

ἄγῡρ-ις [ᾰ], ιος, ἡ, Aeol. for ἀγορά, *gathering, crowd*, ἀνδρῶν ἄγυριν Od.3.31; ἐν νεκύων ἀγύρει Il.16.661; ἐν νηῶν ἀ. 24.141; also in E.*IA*753 (lyr.); παμπληθὴς ἄ. Orac.ap.Phleg.*Macr*.4. 2. *gathering* of herbs, Orph.*L*.416. **-ισμός**, ὁ, *collection*, Suid. **-μα**, ατος, τό, *anything collected*, *AB*327. **-μός**, ὁ, = ἄγυρις, ἀγρίων ζῴων Babr.102.5, cf. *AB*331; = ἀγερμός (which is a v.l.), D.H.2.19, cf. *EM* 8.7. **-τάζω**, (ἀγύρτης) *collect by begging*, χρήματα Od.19.284. **-τεία**, ἡ, *begging, imposture*, Them.*Or*.5.70b; μαγγανεῖαι καὶ ἀ. Just.*Nov*.22.15. **-τευτής**, οῦ, ὁ, = ἀγύρτης, Tz.*H*.13c.475 tit. **-τεύω**, *live by begging as a vagabond*, ἀπὸ μουσικῆς καὶ μαντικῆς Str.7*Fr*.18, cf. Sch.Luc.*Alex*.13. **-τήρ**, ῆρος, ὁ, = sq., Man. 4.221. **-της**, ου, ὁ, (ἀγείρω) prop. *collector*, esp. *begging priest* of Cybele, Μητρὸς ἀ. *AP*6.218 (Al.); Γάλλοις ἀ. Babr.141.1:—then, 2. *vagabond*, E.*Rh*.503,715, cf. Lysipp.6, Clearch.5; δόλιος ἀ., of Tiresias, S.*OT*388; ἀ. καὶ μάντεις Pl.*R*.364b. II. a throw of the dice, Eub.57.5. (On the accent cf. Hdn.Gr.1.77.) **-τικός**, ή, όν, *vagabond*, μάντις Plu.*Lyc*.9; *juggling*, πίνακες Id.*Comp.Aristid.Cat*.3; τὸ ἀ. γένος Id.2.407c; τὸ ἀ. *jugglery*, Str. 10.3.23. Adv. -κῶς Hierocl.*in CA*26p.479M. **-τός**, ή, όν, *got by begging*, Hsch. **-τρια**, ἡ, fem. of ἀγυρτήρ, A.*Ag*.1273.

ἄγυψος, ον, *not clarified by gypsum*, οἶνος Alex.Trall.1.13.

ἀγχ-, Poet. abbrev. for ἀναχ- in compds. of ἀνά with words beginning with χ.

ἀγχάζω, Poet. for ἀναχάζω 1. 2, *retire*, S.*Fr*.973.

ἄγχαρμον· ἀνωφερῆ τὴν αἰχμήν, Hsch.

ἄγχαυρος, ον, (ἄγχι, αὔριον) *near the morning*, νύξ A.R.4.111.

ἀγχέ-μᾰχος, ον, *fighting hand to hand*, Il.13.5, Hes.*Sc*.25; τὰ ἀ. ὅπλα καλούμενα X.*Cyr*.1.2.13, cf. Arr.*Ind*.24.4; τεύχεσιν ἀ. *APl*.4.173 (Jul. Aegypt.). **-μωλία**, ἡ, (μῶλος, cf. ἀμφι-μωλέω) prob. = ἀγχιστεία, *GDI*4972 (Gortyn).

ἀγχήρης, ες, *neighbouring*, S.*Fr*.7, Orph.*A*.1072.

ἄγχῐ, Poet. Adv. of place, *near*, Il.5.185, Od.3.449, etc.:—freq. c. gen., which sts. precedes, Ἕκτορος ἄ. Il.8.117, cf. Od.4.370; but usu. follows, ἄ. νεῶν Il.10.161, etc.; ἄ. πελαγίας ἁλός A.*Pers*.467; ἄ. πλευμόνων Id.*Ch*.639; ἄ. γῆς S.*OC*399. 2. of Time, ἄ. γὰρ ἀμέρα Sapph.*Supp*.19.7. II. of resemblance, *like*, c. dat., Pi. *N*.6.9.—For Comp. and Sup. v. ἄσσον, ἄγχιστος.

ἀγχί-ᾰλος, ον, also η, ον *h.Ap*.32, Androm.ap.Gal.14.42: (ἅλς):—poet. word, *near the sea*, of cities, Il.2.640; Ἐπίδαυρος Androm. l. c.; Κίρρας μυχοί B.4.14; of islands, *sea-girt*, as Peparethos, Lemnos, Salamis, *h.Ap*. l. c., A.*Pers*.887 (lyr.), S.*Aj*.135 (lyr.), *AP*9.288 (Gemin.); of the fountain Arethusa, ἀ. ὕδατα E.*IA*169 (lyr.), cf. A.R.2.160. **-βᾰθής**, ές, *deep inshore*, θάλασσα Od.5.413, cf. Pl.*Criti*.111a; τὰ ἀ. Arist.*Pr*.935^{a}2, cf. Ph.*Bel*.95.20, Parth.26.2, Plu.2.667c; ἀκταί Arist.*HA*548^{b}28; λιμήν Str.17.1.6, cf. 5.2.5, Dion.Byz.6, al. 2. of persons, *standing deep in water*, Nonn. *D*.10.166. **-βασίη**, = ἀμφισβήτησις, Heraclit.122. **-βᾰτέω**, *stand by*, Hsch. II. Ion. for ἀμφισβητέω, Suid. **-βάτης**, ου, ὁ, *one that comes near*, Hsch. **-βιον**· μέγα· ἐγγὺς βοῆς, ἢ ἐπὶ τοῦ στενάξαι, Hsch., cf. *EM*15.36. **-βλώς**· ἄρτι παρών, Hsch., *EM*15.37. **-γᾰμος**, ον, *near marriage*, Parth.*Fr*.22, Nonn.*D*.5.572. **-γείτων**, ον, gen. ονος, *neighbouring*, A.*Pers*.886 (lyr.). **-γῠος**, ον, (γύης) *neighbouring*, A.R.1.1222, D.P.215. II. *near land*, Nonn.*D*.3.44. **-δίαι**· ἐν θαλάσσῃ δίαι, Hsch. **-δομος**, ον, *dwelling near*, Νύμφαι B.12.89; μέλαθρα Coluth.247.

ἀγχίζω, Cret. aor. inf. ἀγχίξαι· ἐγγίσαι, Hsch.

ἀγχι-θάλασσος, Att. -ττος, ον, *near the sea*, Poll.9.17. **-θεος**, ον, *near the gods*, i.e. akin to them, *godlike*, Od.5.35: as Subst., *demigod*, *IG*3.947, Luc.*Syr.D*.31. **-θῠρέω**, *to be at the door, be close at hand*, Eust.1133.61. **-θῠρος**, ον, *next door*, γείτονες Thgn.302, *IG*14.1389ii3; ἀ. ναίοισα Theoc.2.71; generally, *neighbouring*, Men.Prot.p.54D., al. 2. *near the door*, of a statue, *Epigr.Gr*.906 (Gortyn). **-κέλευθος**, ον, *whose way is hard by*, Nonn.*D*.40.328; mostly = *near*, 5.476. **-κρημνος**, ον, *near the cliffs* or *coast*, Αἴγυπτος Pi.*Fr*.82. **-κρηνος**, ον, *from a neighbouring spring*, ὕδωρ *Arch.Anz*.26.333 (Panticapaeum).

ἀγχιλά· ἁλμυρά, θαλάσσια, ἄβρωτα, Hsch.

ἀγχι-λεχής, ές, *close to the bed*, Antim.66. **-λωψ**, ωπος, ὁ, *swelling which obstructs the lachrymal duct*, Gal.19.438. **-μαστρον·** ἀμφίεσμα, Hsch. **-μᾰχητής**, οῦ, ὁ, = ἀγχέμαχος, only in pl., Il.2.604, etc. **-μᾰχος**, ον, = ἀγχέμαχος, *EM*14.53, *AB*332. **-μολέω**, *come nigh*, Nonn.*D*.25.426. **-μολος**, ον, (μολεῖν) *coming near*; Ep. word, mostly used in neut. as Adv., *near, close at hand*, ἀγχίμολον δέ οἱ ἦλθε Il.4.529, cf. Od.8.300, etc., Hes.*Sc*.325; ἐξ ἀγχιμόλοιο ἰδών Il.24.352; ἀγχίμολον δὲ μετ' αὐτόν *close* behind him, Od.17.336: c. gen., ἔθεν ἀγχίμολοι cj. in Theoc.25.203.

ἄγχιμος, ον, (ἄγχι) = πλησίος, E.*Fr*.867.

ἀγχί-μουσος, ον, dub. in *Anacreont*.56.31. **-νεφής**, ές, *near the clouds*, σκόπελος *AP*6.219.14 (Antip.), Nonn.*D*.3.208, al.:—late Prose, ὄρη Men.Prot.p.48 D. **-νοια**, ἡ, (νοέω) *ready wit, sagacity, shrewdness*, Pl.*Chrm*.160a, Arist.*EN*1142^{b}6, *APo*.89^{b}10, Zeno *Stoic*. 1.56, Onos.*Praef*.9, D.S.1.65, etc.; ἀ. αὐλική Plb.15.34.4. **-νοος**, ον, contr. **-νους**, ουν, *ready of wit, shrewd*, Od.13.332, Pl.*Lg*.747b, *Stoic*.2.39, etc.; πρὸς τὰ συμβαίνοντα Arist.*HA*587^{a}12: Comp., Ptol. *Tetr*.57, S.E.*P*.2.41: Sup., ib.42. Adv. -νόως Aen.Tact.11.10; -νως Id.24.11, Arist.*VV*1250^{a}33, Andronic.Rhod.p.575 M.: Sup. -νούστατα Phlp.*in Ph*.483.1. **-πλοος**, ον, contr. **-πλους**, ουν, *near by sea*, πόρος *direct* voyage, E.*IT*1325. **-πολις**, poet. **-πτολις**, *near the city, dwelling hard by*, Παλλάς A.*Th*.501; Ἄρης S.*Ant*.970 (lyr.). **II.** *neighbouring*, of a city, Nonn.*D*.11.36. **-πορος**, ον, *passing near, always near*, κόλακες *AP*10.64 (Agath.); simply, *neighbouring*, Nonn.*D*.5.38, al. **-πους**, ὁ, ἡ, πουν, τό, *near with the foot, near*, Lyc.318.

ἀγχίρροος, ον, *flowing near*, A.R.2.367.

ἀγχίσπορος, ον, *near of kin*, οἱ θεῶν ἀγχίσποροι, οἱ Ζηνὸς ἐγγύς A.*Fr*.162; φύσιν αἰθέρος οὖσαν ἀ. Ph.2.374.

ἀγχιστ-εία, ἡ, (ἄγχιστος) *close kinship*, ἡ τοῦ γένους ἀ. Pl.*Lg*. 924d; ἀ. ὑπάρχει τινὶ πρός τινα Arist.*Rh*.1385^{a}3. **2.** *rights of kin, right of inheritance*, Ar.*Av*.1661; προτέροις τοῖς ἄρρεσι τῶν θηλειῶν τὴν ἀ. πεποίηκε Is.7.20; νόθῳ μηδὲ νόθῃ εἶναι ἀ. Id.6.47, Lex ap.D.43.51; παῖς ἀ. πρότεροι ὄντες τινός Is.7.44, cf. D.44.2. **3.** *exclusion by descent*, Lxx *Ne*.13.29. **-εῖα**, τά, = foreg., γένους κατ' ἀ. S.*Ant*.174. **-εύς**, έως, ὁ, mostly in pl. ἀγχιστεῖς, *next of kin*, of nations, Hdt.5.80:—*heir-at-law*, Lxx *Ru*.3.9 (with v.l. **-ευτής**, ib.4.1), Hierocl. *in CA*5 p.428 M.; συγγενὴς ἀ. Luc.*Tim*. 51. **-ευτικός**, ή, όν, *of the* ἀγχιστεύς, Asp. *in EN*77.14. **-εύω**, *to be next* or *near*, γῇ ἀγχιστεύουσα.. πόντῳ E.*Tr*.224 (lyr.). **II.** *to be next of kin, heir-at-law*, τινί Is.11.11: metaph., ἀ. ἀγοραίης ἐργασίης Hp.*Praec*.8. **2.** c. acc., ἀ. τινά *do a kinsman's office* to a woman, i.e. *marry* her, Lxx *Ru*.3.13, 4.4; also κληρονομίαν ἀ. *enter upon*.., *Nu*.36.8. **3.** Pass., *to be excluded by descent*, ἀπὸ τῆς ἱερατείας 2*Es*.2.62, *Ne*.7.64. **-ήρ**, ῆρος, ὁ, *one who brings near*, πάθους S.*Tr*.256. **-ικός**, ή, όν, *belonging to the* ἀγχιστεία, Ammon.*Diff*.5. **-ίνδην**, Adv. *within the near kin*, γαμεῖν Poll.6.175, Lex ap.Hsch. **-ῖνος**, η, ον, Ep. Adj. *close, crowded, in heaps*, αἱ μέν τ' ἀ. ἐπ' ἀλλήλῃσι κέχυνται Il.5.141; τοὶ δ' ἀ. ἔπιπτον νεκροί 17.361, cf. Od.22.118. **-ος**, ον, Arc. **ἄσιστος** (v. sub fin.), Sup. of ἄγχι, *nearest*: as Adj. not in Ep.; *nearest* in place, A.*Ag*.256 (lyr.), S.*OT*919; γένει ἀ. πατρός E.*Tr*.48; τὸν ἄ. S.*El*.1105; *ever nigh*, Pi.*P*.9.64. **II.** Hom. has only neut. as Adv., ἄγχιστον *nearest*, Od.5.280; more commonly pl., ἄγχιστα ἐῴκει was *most nearly* like, Il.2.58, 14.474; ἄ. ἐοικώς Od.13.80; ἄ. ἐΐσκω 6.152, cf. Pi.*I*.2.10: freq. c. gen., Διὸς ἄ. *next to* Zeus, A.*Supp*.1035 (lyr.); ἄ. τοῦ βωμοῦ Hdt.9.81; ἄ. οἰκεῖν τινος Id.1.134, al., cf. Hp.*Mul*.2.181:—οἱ ἄ. those *next of kin*, Hdt.5.79; ἃ. ἦν αὐτῷ γένους Luc.*Cat*.17; also τοὶ 's ἄσιστα πόθικες *IG*5(2).159.17 (Tegea), cf. *Jahresh*.1.197 (Elis). **2.** *nearest to what is right*, 'for choice', Hp.*Art*.14, cf. *Acut*.57. **III.** of Time, *most lately, but now*, ἄ...πόλεμος δέδηεν Il.20.18; ὁ ἄ. ἀποθανών he who died *last*, Hdt.2.143; τὰ ἄ. *most recently*, Antipho 2.1.6.

ἀγχί-στροφος, ον, *turning closely, quick-swooping*, ἰκτῖνος Thgn. 1261. **2.** *quick-changing, changeable*, ἀγχίστροφα βουλεύεσθαι Hdt.7.13; ἀ. μεταβολή *sudden* change, Th.2.53; ἀστάθμητον πρᾶγμα εὐτυχία καὶ ἀ. D.H.4.23:—Rhet., τὸ ἀ. *rapidity of transition*, Longin. 27.3; ἁρμονία ἀ. περὶ τὰς πτώσεις a style *flexible* in the use of the cases, D.H.*Comp*.22. Adv. -φως Longin.22.1. **-τελής**, ές, *near its wane*, σελήνη Nonn.*D*.40.314. **-τέρμων**, ον, gen. ονος, (τέρμα) *near the border, neighbouring*, S.*Fr*.384, E.*Rh*.426; τινός Theodect.17, Lyc.1130.—Poet. (Dithyrambic acc. to Poll.6.113) and in X.*Hier*.10.7. **-τόκος**, ον, *near the birth*, ὠδῖνες pangs *of child-birth*, Pi.*Fr*.88.2, Nonn.*D*.24.197; of a woman, *AP*7.462 (Dionys.); νύμφαι Nonn.*D*.8.12. **-φανής**, ές, *appearing close at hand*, Nonn.*D*.2.97, al. **-φρων**, ονος, = ἀγχίνους, Ptol.*Tetr*. 160. **-φυτος**, ον, *growing hard by*, Nonn.*D*.3.152, 12.279.

ἀγχίων, ον, Comp. of ἄγχι, *nearer*, *EM*14.47.

ἀγχοάδην· ἀμβολάδην, Hsch.

ἀγχό-θεν, Adv. *from near at hand*, Hdt.4.31, Luc.*Syr.D*.28. **-θι**, Poet. Adv. *near*, δειρῆς Il.14.412, cf. Od.13.103, A.R.1.37, etc.: abs., Theoc.22.40, *IG*9(2).645 (Thessal.).

ἀγχ-όμορος, ον, *neighbouring*, c. gen., dub. in Theoc.25.203.

ἀγχον-άω, (ἀγχόνη) *strangle*, Man.1.317, Suid. **-η**, ἡ, (ἄγχω) *strangling, hanging*, ἀγχόνης..τέρματα A.*Eu*.746; ἔργα κρείσσον' ἀγχόνης deeds too bad for *hanging*, S.*OT*1374; τάδ' ἀγχόνης πέλας 'tis nigh as bad as *hanging*, E.*Heracl*.246; ταῦτ' οὐχὶ.. ἀγχόνης ἔστ' ἄξια; Id.*Ba*.246; ταῦτα..οὐκ ἀ.; Ar.*Ach*.125; οἱ δ' ἀγχόνην ἥψαντο Semon.1.18: rare in Prose, ἀ. καὶ λύπη Aeschin.2.38:—in pl., ἐν ἀγχόναις θάνατον λαβεῖν E.*Hel*.200, cf. ib.299, *HF*154; αἱ ἀ. μάλιστα τοῖς νέοις Arist.*Pr*.954^{b}35. **II.** = μανδραγόρα, Ps.-Dsc. 4.75. **-ίζω**, *strangle*, Sch.E.*Hipp*.780 (Pass.). **-ιος**, α, ον, *fit for strangling*, βρόχος E.*Hel*.686; δεσμός Nonn.*D*.21.31, 34.229. **-ιστής**, ὁ, *hangman*, *Gloss*.

ἀγχόσε, Adv. *coming near*, A.D.*Adv*.194.17.

ἀγχοτάτω, Adv., Sup. of ἀγχοῦ, *nearest, next*, c. gen., *h.Ap*.18, Hdt.2.169, E.*Fr*.620; ἀ. τινός, of likeness, Hdt.7.64 (v.l. -ότατα), 80, al.; τινί ib.91; οἱ ἀ. προσήκοντες the *nearest* of kin, 4.73.

ἀγχότερος, α, ον, Comp. of ἀγχοῦ, *nearer*, c. gen., Hdt.7.175. Adv. -οτέρω App.*BC*1.57.

ἀγχοῦ, = ἄγχι, *near*, freq. in Hom., usu. in phrase ἀγχοῦ δ' ἱσταμένη (or -ος) Il.2.172, al.; στεῦται δ' Ὀδυσῆος ἀκοῦσαι ἀ. Od.17.526, cf. 19.271; ἀ. καθῆσθαι Archil.*Supp*.3.3, cf. S.*Tr*.962: twice c. gen., Il.24.709, Od.6.5: c. dat., Pi.*N*.9.40, Hdt.3.85: in late Prose, λόγοι ἀ. τούτων Philostr.*VA*6.16.

ἀγχούρης· πένης, Hsch.

ἄγχουρος (A), ον, (ἄγχι, οὖρος Ion. for ὅρος) *neighbouring*, *AP*9.235 (Crin.); *bordering on*, τινί Orph.*A*.124; τινός Lyc.418.

ἄγχουρος (B), ὁ, *gold*, from the name of the son of Midas, *AP*15.25.7 codd. (Besant.), cf. Plu.2.306f.

ἀγχοῦρος, *dawn*, Call.*Hec*.1.4.10; Cypr. acc. to Hsch.

ἄγχουσα, ἡ, *alkanet*, *Anchusa tinctoria*, Thphr.*HP*7.8.3, Dsc.4.23; cf. ἔγχουσα.

ἀγχουσίζομαι, Med., *rouge*, Hsch.

ἄγχραν· μύωπα (Locr.), Hsch. **ἀγχράνασθαι** (for ἀναχρ-), *anoint* or *wash oneself*, Id.

ἀγχύνωψ, ωπος, ὁ, = φοῖνιξ, Dsc.4.43.

ἄγχω, fut. ἄγξω Ar.*Ec*.638, Luc.*D.Mort*.22.1: aor. 1 inf. ἄγξαι v.l. for ἄξαι Lxx 4*Ma*.9.17, (ἀπ-) Ar.*Pax*796:—Med. and Pass. (v. infr.) only in pres.:—*squeeze*, esp. the throat, ἄγχε μιν ἱμὰς ὑπὸ δειρήν Il.3.371; *embrace*, μὴ θέλουσαν *Anacreont*.57.22, cf. Herod.1.18; *hug*, in wrestling, Id.2.12, Luc.*Anach*.1, Paus.8.40.2, Philostr.*Im*. 1.6 (Pass.); *strangle, throttle*, τοὺς πατέρας ἦγχον νύκτωρ Ar.*V*.1039, cf. *Ec*.638, 640; τὸν Κέρβερον ἀπῆξας ἄγχων Id.*Ra*.468, cf. *Av*.1575; κἂν ταῦρον ἄγχοις Id.*Lys*.81, cf. Crates Com.29, D.54.20, Theoc.5.106, *APl*.4.90; ἐν χαλινῷ τὰς σιαγόνας ἄ. Lxx *Ps*.31(32).9: metaph., of pressing creditors, Ar.*Eq*.775, Luc.*Symp*.32; ψυχὴ ὑπὸ τοῦ σώματος ἀγχομένη *Corp.Herm*.10.24, cf. 7.3; of a guilty conscience, τοῦτο.. ἄγχει, σιωπᾶν ποιεῖ D.19.208:—Med., *strangle oneself*, Hp.*Morb*.2.68:—Pass., Pi.*N*.1.46, D.47.59, Theoc.7.125; *to be drowned*, Hp.*Virg*.1.—Not in Trag.

ἀγχώμᾰλος, ον, (ὁμαλός) *nearly equal*, ἀγχώμαλοι ἐν χειροτονίᾳ Th. 3.49; ἀ. μάχη a *doubtful* battle, Id.4.134; τὴν νίκην ἐν ἀγχωμάλῳ καταλιπόντες J.*BJ*6.2.6; τὸ πλῆθος οὐκ ἀ. Plu.*Caes*.42, cf. D.H.5.14:—neut. pl. as Adv., ἀγχώμαλα ναυμαχεῖν, Lat. *aequo Marte pugnare*, Th.7.71; ἀ. σφισι ἐγένετο Luc.*Herm*.12. Adv. -άλως Id.*VH* 2.37, App.*Praef*.11.

ἄγω [ᾰ], impf. ἦγον, Ep. and Ion. ἄγεσκον Hdt.1.148, A.R.1.849: fut. ἄξω Il.1.139, etc.: thematic aor. imper. ἄξετε Il.3.105, inf. ἀξέμεναι, -έμεν, Il.23.50, 111: aor. 2 ἤγαγον Il.6.291, etc., opt. ἀγαγοίην Sapph.159: aor. 1 ἦξα rare, ἦξε Tim.*Pers*.165, part. ἄξας Batr. 119, inf. ἄξαι Antipho 5.46: pf. ἦχα *SIG*1 (Abu Simbel, vii/vi B.C.), Plb.3.111.3, (προ-) D.19.18, (συν-) X.*Mem*.4.2.8; ἀγήγοχα *OGI*219.15 (Sigeum, iii B.C.), etc., Dor. συν-αγάγοχα *Test.Epict*.3.12; ἀγήοχα Lxx *To*.12.3, J.*BJ*1.30.1, Alex.*Fig*.1.11, etc. (also in compds., (εἰσ-) Ps.-Philipp.ap.D.18.39, (κατ-) Decr.ib.73); ἀγείοχα *PTeb*.5.193 (ii B.C.), etc.; ἀγέωχα (δι-) *CIG*4897*d* (Philae, i B.C.), *PTeb*.5.198 (ii B.C.), etc.: plpf. ἀγηόχει Plb.30.4.17:—**Med.**, fut. ἄξομαι Hom., Hdt., Trag.: them. aor. 1 ἄξοντο Il.8.545, imper. ἄξεσθε ib.505: also ἀξάμην (ἐσ-) Hdt.5.34, (προεσ-) 1.190, 8.20: aor. 2 ἠγαγόμην Hom., etc., 2 sg. ἀγάγαο *GDI*5088.8 (Cret.):—**Pass.**, fut. ἀχθήσομαι Pl.*Hp.Ma*.292a, (προσ-) Th.4.87, etc.; ἄξομαι in pass. sense, A.*Ag*.1632, Pl.*R*.458d, (προσ-) Th.4.115, etc.: aor. 1 ἤχθην X.*An*.6.3.10, Ion. ἄχθην Hdt.6.30, part. ἀχθείς Hippon. 9: pf. ἦγμαι Hdt.2.158, D.13.15; also in med. sense, v. infr. B.2. **I.** *lead, carry, fetch, bring*, of living creatures, φέρω being used of things, δῶκε δ' ἄγειν ἑτάροισι..γυναῖκα, καὶ τρίποδα..φέρειν Il.23.512; βοῦν δ' ἀγέτην κεράων by the horns, Od.3.439; ἄ. εἰς or πρὸς τόπον, poet. also c. acc. loci, νόστοι δ' ἐκ πολέμων ἀπόνους (sc. ἄνδρας)..ἄγον οἴκους A.*Pers*.863 (lyr.); Ἅιδας..ἄγει τὰν Ἀχέροντος ἀκτάν S.*Ant*.811 (lyr.); ἄ. τινά τινι Od.14.386; ἵππους ὑφ' ἅρματ' ἄ. 3.476, cf. A.*Pr*.465. **b.** part. ἄγων *taking*, στῆσε δ' ἄγων Il.2.558, cf. Od.1.130, S.*OC*1342, etc. **2.** *take with one*, ἑταίρους Od.10.405, cf. S.*OC*832, etc.; τι Il.15.531, Hdt.1.70; of a wife, A.*Pr*.559 (lyr.) (more usu. Med., q.v.). **3.** *carry off* as captives or booty, Il.1.367, 9.594, A.*Th*.340, etc.; ἄχθη ἀγόμενος παρὰ βασιλέα Hdt.6.30; ἀγόμενος, i.e. δοῦλος, Archil.155, cf. E.*Tr*.140, Pl.*Lg*.914e; Δίκην ἄγειν *to lead* Justice *forcibly away*, Hes.*Op*.220; ἡ ἐπιθυμία ἄγει Arist.*EN*1147^a 34; of a fowler, φῦλον ὀρνίθων ἀμφιβαλὼν ἄγει S.*Ant*.343: esp. in phrase ἄ. καὶ φέρειν *harry, ravage* a country, first in Il.5.484 οἷόν κ' ἠὲ φέροιεν Ἀχαιοὶ ἤ κεν ἄγοιεν, cf. 23.512 sq.; freq. in Hdt. and Att. Prose:—in Pass., ἀγόμεθα, φερόμεθα E.*Tr*.1310, cf. Ar.*Nu*.241: more rarely reversed, φέρουσί τε καὶ ἄγουσι Hdt.1.88; ἔφερε καὶ ἦγε πάντας Id.3.39: c. acc. loci, φέρων καὶ ἄγων τὴν Βιθυνίδα X.*HG*3.2.2; ἦγον καὶ ἔκαον τὴν Β. ib.5; ἄ. alone, *ravage*, *IG*9(1).333 (Locr., v B.C.):—but φέρειν καὶ ἄγειν sts. means simply *bear and carry, bring together*, Pl.*Phdr*.279c; τὴν ποίησιν φέρειν τε καὶ ἄγειν, i.e. *bring* it into the state, Id.Lg.817a, cf. X.Cyr.3.3.2. **4.** ἄ. εἰς δίκην or δικαστήριον, ἐπὶ τοὺς δικαστάς *to carry* one before a court of justice, freq. in Att., πρὸς τὴν δίκην ἄ. E.Fr.1049; ὑπ' ἐπίγνωσιν ἀχθῆναι PTeb.28.11 (ii B.C.); simply ἄγειν Pl.Grg.527a, etc.; ἐπὶ θανάτῳ ἄ. X.An.1.6.10, etc.:—Pass., ἐπὶ βασιλεῖς ἀχθήσεσθε Ev.Matt.10.18, cf. PTeb.331.16 (ii A.D.); φόνου ἄγεσθαι Plu.2.309e. **b.** Pass., *to be confiscated*, τὰ κτήνη ἀχθήσεται πρὸς τὰ ἐκφόρια (to meet the rent) PTeb.27.75 (ii B.C.). **5.** of ships, *carry* as cargo, *import*, [οἶνον] νῆες ἄγουσι Il.9.72, etc.; ἵνα οἱ σὺν φόρτον ἄγοιμι (i.e. σύν οἱ) Od.14.296. **6.** *draw on, bring on*, πῆμα τόδ' ἤγαγον Οὐρανίωνες Il.24.547; Ἰλίῳ φθοράν A.Ag.406 (lyr.); τερμίαν ἁμέραν S.Ant.1330 (lyr.); ὕπνον Id.Ph.638; χαράν E.Fr.174; δάκρυ Id.Alc.1081. **7.** *bear up*, φελλοὶ δ' ὥς, ἄγουσι δίκτυον A.Ch.506. **8.** *carry far and wide, spread abroad*, κλέος Od.5.311. **9.** Medic., *remove*, φλέγμα Hp. Nat.Hom.6, cf. Aph.4.2; ἕλμινθα Dsc.1.16. **II.** *lead towards* a point, *lead on*, τὸν δ' ἄγε μοῖρα κακὴ θανάτοιο τέλοσδε Il.13.602; κῆρες ἄγον θανάτοιο 2.834; οἷ μ' ἀτιμίας ἄγεις S.El.1035: also c. inf., ἄγει θανεῖν *leads* to death, E.Hec.43: c. acc. cogn., ἄγομαι τάνδ' ἑτοίμαν ὁδόν S.Ant.877 (lyr.); ὁδὸς ἄγει the road *leads*, Heraclit.71, S.OT734, Tab.Heracl.1.16, etc.: metaph., *tend*, ἐπὶ τὸ ἄκρον Pl.Lg.701e. **2.** *lead, guide*, esp. in war, λαόν Il.10.79; ἄ. στρατιάν, ναῦς, etc., Th.7.12, 8.59, etc., cf. X.An.4.8.12; hence abs., *march*, θᾶσσον ὁ Νικίας ἦγε Th.7.81, cf. X.HG4.2.19, etc.: simply, *go*, ἄγωμεν Ev.Marc.1.38; of the gods, etc., *guide*, Pi., Hdt., etc.; ἐπ' ἀρετήν E.Fr.672; διὰ πόνων ἄγειν τινά Id.IT988. **3.** *manage*, νόῳ πλοῦτον Pi.P.6.47; πολιτείαν Th.1.127; τὴν σοφίαν *conduct* philosophical inquiry, Pl.Tht.172b; of reasoning, ἀγαγεῖν τοὺς λόγους Arist.APr.47^{a}21; εἰς τὸ ἀδύνατον ἄ. ib.27^{a}15 (v.l. ἀπάγοντας):—Pass., *to be led, guided*, λογισμῷ Pl.R.431c; ἡγούμενος τῶν ἡδονῶν ἀλλ' οὐκ ἀγόμενος ὑπ' αὐτῶν Isoc.9.45. **4.** *refer, attribute*, τι εἰς ἐθελοκάκησιν Plb.27.15.13; τι ἐς Διόνυσον Luc.Syr.D.33. **5.** *bring up, train, educate*, ἀγόμενοις ὀρθῶς Pl.Lg.782d; ἤχθη τὴν λεγομένην ἀγωγήν Plu.Ages.1; of animals, *train*, X.Mem.4.1.3. **6.** *reduce*, ἐς βραχὺ τὴν ἀρχήν Hp. VM1; ἐς τὸ ἥμισυ Id.Mul.1.78; of propositions, εἰς ῥᾳδιεστέραν κατασκευήν Papp.1076.6. **III.** *draw out* in length, τεῖχος ἄ. *to draw a line of* wall, Th.6.99; μέλαθρον εἰς ὀρόφους AP9.649 (Maced.); ὄγμον ἄ. Theoc.10.2; ἄ. γραμμάς *to draw* lines, Arist.Top.101^{a}16; ἤχθωσαν κάθετοι *let* perpendiculars *be drawn*, Mete.373^{a}11; ἄ. ἐπίπεδον *describe* a plane, Archim.Sph.1.7, etc.:—Pass., ἦκται ἡ διῶρυξ Hdt.2.158, cf. Th.6.100; κόλπου ἀγομένου τῆς γῆς, i.e. when the land forms a bight, Hdt.4.99. **IV.** *hold, celebrate*, Ἀπατούρια, ὀρτήν, Hdt.1.147, 183 (more usu. ἀνάγειν); freq. in Att., ἄ. ἀγῶνα IG1.53.33; θυσίαν, θεωρίαν Isoc.19.10; κρεουργὸν ἦμαρ εὐθύμως ἄγειν A.Ag.1592; γάμους Men.Sam.336, cf. Lxx To.11.19 (Pass.); ἐκκλησίαν Plu.Aem.30:—Pass., ἀγοραῖοι ἄγονται Act.Ap.19.38. **2.** *keep, observe* a date, ἄ. τὴν ἡμέραν ταύτην πάντα τὸν χρόνον Th.5.54, cf. Men.521; κατὰ σελήνην τὰς ἡμέρας Ar.Nu.626; *reckon*, τοὺς ἐνιαυτοὺς καθ' ἥλιον Gem.8.6. **3.** *keep, observe*, ὀρθὰν ἄγεις ἐφημοσύναν Pi.P.6.20; σπονδὰς ἄ. πρός τινας Th.6.7; εἰρήνην Pl.R.465b, etc.: c. acc., as periphr. for a neut. Verb, σχολὴν ἄγειν, = σχολάζειν, E.Med.1238, Pl.R.376d; ἡσυχίαν ἄ., = ἡσυχάζειν, X.An.3.1.14; ἄ. ἀπαστίαν Ar.Nu.621; κρύψιν ἄ., of stars betw. setting and rising, Autol.2.9; *keep up, sustain, maintain*, νεῖκος Pi.P.9.31; γέλωτ' ἄγειν *to keep* laughing, S.Aj.382; ἄ. κτύπον E.Or.182 (lyr.); with predicate, *maintain*, ἐλευθέραν ἦγε τὴν Ἑλλάδα D.9.36. **4.** of Time, *pass*, ἀπήμαντον ἄγων βίοτον Pi.O.8.87; ποίας ἡμέρας δοκεῖς μ' ἄγειν; S.El.266; ὁ βίος οὑμὸς ἑσπέραν ἄγει Alex.228, cf. ὥραν ἄγειν *to be ripe*, τῆς γαστρὸς ὥραν ἀγούσης Philostr.VA2.14; ὥραν ἦγε θανάτου Chor.p.38B.; τῆς ἡλικίας ἄγον τὸ ἄνθος Id.p.53B.; τέταρτον ἔτος ἄγων καὶ τριακοστόν Gal.Lib.Propr.1. **5.** of beliefs, *hold*, αἵρεσιν Plb.27.15.14. **V.** *hold account, treat*, ἄ. ἀρετὰν οὐκ αἴσχιον φυᾶς Pi.I.7(6).22; ἐν τιμῇ ἄγειν or ἄγεσθαι, ἐν οὐδεμιῇ μοίρῃ ἄ., περὶ πλείστου ἄ., Hdt.1.134, 2.172, 9.7, etc.; θεοὺς ἄ. *to believe in*, A.Supp.924; διὰ τιμῆς ἄ. τινά, etc., Luc. Prom.Es4, etc.; τὸ πρᾶγμ' ἄ. . . ὡς παρ' οὐδέν S.Ant.34; τὴν Ἀφροδίτην πρόσθ' ἄ. τοῦ Βακχίου E.Ba.225; τιμιώτερον ἄ. τινά Th.8.81; εὐεργεσίας εἰς ἀχαριστίαν καὶ προπηλακισμὸν ἄ. D.18.316:—with Adverbs, δυσφόρως τοὔνειδος ἦγον S.OT784; ἐντίμως ἄ. Pl.R.528c, etc.:—Pass., ἠγόμην δ' ἀνὴρ ἀστῶν μέγιστος S.OT775. **VI.** *draw down* in the scale, hence, *weigh*, ἄ. μνᾶν, τριακοσίους δαρεικούς, etc., *weigh* a mina, 300 darics, etc., D.22.76, 24.129, cf. Philippid.9.4, etc.; ἄ. πλέον Arist.Pr.931^{b}15; ἄ. σταθμόν Plu.2.96b. **VII.** on ἄγε, ἄγετε, v. s. vocc.

B. Med. ἄγομαι, *carry away for oneself*, χρυσόν τε καὶ ἄργυρον οἴκαδ' ἄγεσθαι Od.10.35; *take with one*, 6.58, E.Heracl.808, etc.; of a ship's cargo, D.35.20; *take to oneself*, δῶρον Theoc.1.9, cf. 11; *take upon oneself*, ἄγεσθαι ἐς χεῖρας Hdt.1.126, 4.79. **2.** ἄγεσθαι γυναῖκα *take to oneself* a wife, Od.14.211; γυναῖκα ἄ. ἐς τὰ οἰκία Hdt.1.59, etc.; ἄγεσθαί τινα ἐς δῶμα Hes.Th.410; simply ἄ. *marry*, Hdt.2.47, etc.: pf. Pass. ἦγμαι is used in this med. sense, J.AJ14.12.1; of the father, *bring home* a wife *for his son*, Od.4.10, Hdt.1.34; of a brother, Od.15.238; of friends of the bridegroom and bride, Od.6.28, Hes.Sc.274: later in Pass. of the wife, PGnom.138 (ii A.D.). **3.** like Act., *bring*; διὰ στόμα ἄγεσθαι μῦθον *bring* through the mouth, i.e. *utter*, Il.14.91.

ἀγωγαῖος, ον, (ἀγωγή) *fit for leading by*, of a dog's collar or *leash*, AP6.35 (Leon.).

ἀγωγεῖον, τό, *pander's house*, Poll.9.48 (perh. f.l. for ἀσωτ-).

ἀγωγεύς, έως, ὁ, *haulier*, Hdt.2.175. **2.** *escort, guide*, Milet.3.152.16 (Methymna, ii B.C.). **3.** *prosecutor* (cf. ἄγω I. 4), Suid. **II.** *leading-rein, leash*, S.Fr.974, Stratt.52, X.Eq.6.5. **III.** epith. of Zeus, *guide, director*, Anecd.Stud.1.265.

ἀγωγή, ἡ, (ἄγω) *carrying away*, Hdt.6.85, etc.; *freight, carriage*, πρὸς τὰς ἀγωγάς . . χρῆσθαι ὑποζυγίοις Pl.R.370e, cf. X.Lac.7.5, PLond.3.948.2 (iii A.D.). **b.** intr., τὴν ἀ. διὰ τάχους ἐποιεῖτο pursued his *voyage*, Th.4.29 (v.l.); *movement*, Pl.R.604b; ἀ. ἐπί τι *tendency* towards . ., Hp.Epid.1.1. **2.** *bringing to* or *in*, ὑμῶν ἡ ἐς τοὺς ὀλίγους ἀ. your *bringing* us *before* the council, Th.5.85. **3.** *forcible seizure, carrying off, abduction*, A.Ag.1263, S.OC662; ἀγωγὴν ποιήσασθαι PTeb.39.22 (ii B.C.), cf. 48.22. **4.** ὕδατος ἀγωγαί *aqueducts*, IG12(5).872 (Tenos), cf. D.H.3.67. **5.** *load*, Ostr.1168; *weight*, AB333. **6.** *winding up* of engine, Ph.Bel.57.13 (pl.). **7.** *drawing* of lines, Procl. in Euc.pp.284, 376 F. **8.** *evoking*, πνευμάτων Iamb.Myst.3.6 (pl.). **b.** *spell for bringing* a person, usu. *love-charm*, PMag.Par.1.1390. **II.** *leading, guidance*, ἵππου X.Eq.6.4; ἡ τοῦ νόμου, τοῦ λογισμοῦ ἀ. Pl.Lg.645a, cf. Plt.274b. **2.** *leading* of an army, Id. Lg.746e (pl.); ἀ. στραταρχίας *conduct* of an expedition, Vett.Val.339.29; ἡ ἀ. τῶν πραγμάτων Plb.3.8.5. **3.** *direction, training*, παιδεία μέν ἐσθ' ἡ παίδων ὁλκή τε καὶ ἀ. πρὸς τὸν ὑπὸ τοῦ νόμου λόγον ὀρθὸν εἰρημένον Pl.Lg.659d, cf. 819a; ἀ. ὀρθῆς τυχεῖν πρὸς ἀρετήν Arist.EN1179^{b}31; διὰ τὸ ἦθος καὶ τὴν ἀ. Id.Pol.1292^{b}14, cf. Cleanth.Stoic.1.107: in pl., *systems of education*, Chrysipp. Stoic.3.173; esp. of the public education of the Spartan youth, Λακωνικὴ ἀ. Plb.1.32.1; Ἀγησίλαος ἤχθη τὴν λεγομένην ἀγωγὴν ἐν Λακεδαίμονι Plu.Ages.1; ἀ. στοιχειώδης elementary *course*, Apollon.Perg.Con.1 Praef.:—also of plants, *culture*, Thphr.HP1.3.2; of diseases, *treatment*, Gal.12.414, 15.436. **4.** *way* of life, *conduct*, Archyt.ap.Stob.2.31.120 (pl.), PTeb.24.57 (ii B.C.), OGI223.15 (Erythrae, iii B.C.), Lxx 2Ma.6.8, 2Ep.Tim.3.10, M.Ant.1.6. **5.** *keeping, observance*, ἡμερῶν Aristox.Rhyth.2.37; μηνῶν Gem.8.48. **6.** generally, *method, construction* (of a law), Arist.Rh.1375^{b}12; *style*, D.H.Isoc.20, al.; ἡ ἀ. τῶν διαλέκτων Str.14.1.41. **7.** *method of proof*, esp. of syllogistic reasoning, λόγοι τὰς ἀγωγὰς ὑγιεῖς ἔχοντες Chrysipp.Stoic.2.84, cf. Simp. in Ph.759.14; *line of argument*, Plu.2.106b. **8.** *school* of philosophers, Phld.Sto.Herc.339.12, Acad.Ind.p.68 M., S.E.P.1.145, etc. **9.** Milit., *manœuvre, movement*, Ascl.Tact.12.7 and 10; *order of march*, ib.11.8, cf. Ael.Tact.39.1. **10.** in Law, = Lat. *actio*, Cod.Just.4.24.1, al. **III.** *tempo*, in music, Pl.R.400c (pl.), Aristox.Harm. p.34 M., Aristid.Quint.1.19; *sequence*, of a melody, Aristox.Harm. p.29 M.; musical *style*, Str.14.1.41, Plu.2.1141c.

ἀγωγικά, τά, *expenses of transport*, Cod.Just.10.30.4.

ἀγώγιμος, ον, of things, *capable of being carried*, τρισσῶν ἁμαξῶν . . ἀ. βάρος *enough to load*, E.Cyc.385; τὰ ἀ. *things portable, wares*, Pl. Prt.313c, X.An.5.1.16, etc.; ἄλλο δὲ μηδὲν ἀ. ἄγεσθαι ἐν τῷ πλοίῳ D.35.20. **II.** of persons, *liable to seizure*, X.HG7.3.11, cf. D.23.11, Plu.Sol.13, BGU1116.27 (13 B.C.):—also of things, D.H.5.69. **2.** *easily led, pliable*, Plu.Alc.6. **III.** Act., ἀγώγιμον, τό, *love-charm, philtre*, Plu.2.1093d, cf. PMag.Lond.121.295: pl., PMag.Par.1.2231.

ἀγώγιον, τό, *load of a wagon*, X.Cyr.6.1.54, PPetr.3 p.101 (iii B.C.), PLond.3.1166.13 (i A.D.). **II.** *carriage* of such a load, PPetr. l. c.

ἀγωγός, όν, *leading, guiding*, and as Subst., *guide*, Hdt.3.26; *escort*, Th.2.12, cf. 4.78; ἀ. ὕδατος *aqueduct*, Mon.Anc.Gr.19.5 (pl.); without ὕδατος, Just.Nov.128.16 (pl.): c. gen., δύναμις ἀνθρώπων ἀ. power *of leading* men, Plu.Lyc.5. **II.** *leading towards*, ἐπί τι Pl.R.525a, Phld.D.3.12; εἰς . . Plu.Per.1. **III.** *drawing, attracting*, δύναμις ἀ. τινος, of the magnet, Dsc.5.130. **2.** *drawing forth, eliciting*, χοαὶ νεκρῶν ἀγωγοί E.Hec.536; δακρύων ἀ. Id.Tr.1131; γυναικείων Hp.Aph.5.28; ἐμμήνων Dsc.1.16. **3.** abs., *attractive*, Plu.Crass.7; τὸ ἀ. *attractiveness*, Id.2.25b.

ἀγωίλιον, τό, = ἀωίλιον, PSI4.423.6, al. (iii B.C.).

ἀγών [ᾰ], ῶνος, ὁ, Aeol. **ἄγωνος**, ου, ὁ, Alc.121 (also E.ap.Sch.Il. Oxy.1087.60); Elean dat. pl. ἀγώνοιρ GDI1172.26: (ἄγω):—*gathering, assembly*, ἵζανεν εὐρὺν ἀ. Il.23.258; λῦτο δ' ἀ. 24.1, cf. Od.8.200; νεῶν ἐν ἀγῶνι Il.15.428, cf. Eust.1335.57: esp. *assembly met to see games*, freq. in Il.23; Ὑπερβορέων ἀ. Pi.P.10.30; κοινοὺς ἀ. θέντες A. Ag.845. **2.** *place of contest, lists, course*, βήτην ἐς μέσσον ἀ. Il.23.685, cf. 531, Od.8.260, Hes.Sc.312, Pi.P.9.114, and esp. Th.5.50: prov., ἔξω ἀγῶνος out of the *lists* or course, i.e. *beside the mark*, Pi.P.1.44, Luc.Anach.21: pl., κατ' ἀγῶνας Od.8.259. **II.** *assembly* of the Greeks *at the national games*, ὁ ἐν Ὀλυμπίῃ ἀ. Hdt.6.127; ὁ Ὀλυμπικὸς ἀ. Ar.Pl.583; Ἑλλάδος πρόσχημ' ἀ. S.El.682, cf. 699:—hence, *contest for a prize* at the games, ἀ. γυμνικός, ἱππικός, μουσικός, Hdt.2.91, Pl.Lg.658a, Ar.Pl.1163, cf. Th.3.104; οἱ τῶν λαμπάδων ἀ. Arist.Ath.57.1; ἀ. τῶν ἀνδρῶν *contest* in which the chorus was composed of men, opp. to παίδων or ἀγενείων (q.v.), D.21.18, etc.; ἀ. στεφανηφόρος or στεφανίτης *contest* where the prize is a crown, Hdt.5.102, Arist.Rh.1357^{a}19; ἀ. χάλκεος, where it is a shield of brass, Pi.N.10.22; ἀ. θεματικός IG14.739 (Naples); ἀργυρίτης δωρίτης Plu.2.820d:—hence many phrases, ἀγῶνα καταστῆσαι establish *a contest*, Isoc.4.1; τιθέναι Hdt.5.8; ποιεῖν Th.3.104; οὐ λόγων τοὺς ἀ. προθήσοντες Id.3.67; προηγόρευέ τε ἀγῶνας καὶ ἆθλα προυτίθει X. Cyr.8.2.26; προκαλούμενος ἑαυτὸν εἰς ἀ. Id.Mem.2.3.17; τοὺς ἀ. νικᾶν ib.3.7.1; ἐν τοῖς ἀγῶσι Isoc.15.301; of contests in general, εἰς ἀ. λόγων ἀφικέσθαι τινί Pl.Prt.335a; πρὸς τίν' ἀγῶνας τιθέμεσθ' ἀρετῆς; E. Ion863 (lyr.); ἀ. σοφίας Ar.Ra.883. **III.** generally, *struggle*, πολλοὺς ἀ. ἐξιών, of Hercules, S.Tr.159; ξιφηφόρος ἀ. A.Ch.584; εἰς ἀ. τῷδε συμπεσὼν μάχης S. Tr.20, etc.; ὁ Φίλιππος, πρὸς ὃν ἦν ἡμῖν ὁ ἀ. D.18.67; ποιέειν ἢ παθεῖν πρόκειται ἀ. Hdt.7.11; ἀληθείην ἀσκέειν ἀ.

μέγιστος ib.209 : pl., πραγμάτων ἀγῶνας κεκτημένων Epicur.*Sent.*21 ; ἄπορος ἀ. Lys.7.2 ; ὅπλων ἔκειτ' ἀ. πέρι S.*Aj.*936 ; and without περί, τῶν Ἀχιλλείων ὅπλων ἀ. ib.1240 ; ψυχῆς ἀ. τὸν προκείμενον πέρι *struggle* for life and death, E.*Or.*847, cf. *Ph.*1330 ; πολλοὺς ἀ. δραμέονται περὶ σφέων αὐτῶν Hdt.8.102 ; λόγων γὰρ οὐ.. ἀγών, ἀλλὰ σῆς ψυχῆς πέρι S.*El.*1492, cf. infr. 5. **2.** *battle, action*, Th.2.89, etc. **3.** *action at law, trial*, Antipho6.21, etc., cf. A.*Eu.*677, 744 ; εἰς ἀγῶνα καθιστάναι ἀνθρώπους Pl.*Ap.*24c, *R.*494e ; περὶ τῆς ψυχῆς εἰς ἀγῶνα καταστῆσαί τινα X.*Lac.*8.4. **4.** *speech* delivered in court or before an assembly or ruler, πρεσβευτικοὶ ἀ. Plb.9.32.4; τοὺς ἐπιφανεστάτους εἰρηκότος ἀ. τούς τε δικανικοὺς καὶ τοὺς δημηγορικοὺς D.H.*Amm.*1.3, cf. *OGI*567 (Attalia, ii A.D.); ἀ. ἐσχηματισμένοι D.H.*Rh.*8.1, al. **b.** Rhet., *main argument* of a speech (opp. προοίμιον, ἐπίλογος), in pl., Syr. *in Hermog.*2.111, 170R., cf. *Proll.Hermog.*ap. Rh.4.12W. **5.** metaph., οὐ λόγων ἔθ' ἀγών now is not *the time for* words, E.*Ph.*588 ; οὐχ ἕδρας ἀ. 'tis no *time for* sitting still, Id.*Or.*1291 ; ἀ. πρόφασιν οὐ δέχεται *the crisis* admits no dallying, Ar.*Fr.*331, cf. Pl.*Cra.*421d, *Lg.*751d ; μέγας ὁ ἀ...τὸ χρηστὸν ἢ κακὸν γενέσθαι *the issue* is great..., Id.*R.*608b, cf. E.*Med.*235 ; οὐ περί τινος ὁ ἀ. *the question* is not about.., Th.3.44. **6.** *mental struggle, anxiety*, Th.7.71, Plb.4.56.4, *Ep.Col.*2.1 : in pl., τρόμοι καὶ ἀ. Plu. *Sol.*7. **b.** of speakers, *vehemence, power*, Longin.15.1, cf. 26. 3. **IV.** personified, Ἀγών, *divinity of the contest*, Paus.5.26.3.

ἀγων-άρχης, ου, ὁ, *judge of a contest*, S.*Aj.*572. **II.** (ἀγών = assembly) Boeotian magistrate, *IG*7.1817 (Thespiae), cf. Sch.Il. 24.1. **-ία**, ἡ, *contest, struggle for victory*, ἀγῶν διὰ πάσης ἀγωνίης ἔχων Hdt.2.91 ; πολεμίων ἀ. E.*Hec.*314, cf. *Tr.*1003 ; esp. in games, Pi.*O.*2.52, *P.*5.113 :—also in Prose, ἐν δημοτικῇ ἀ. X.*Cyr.*2.3.15 ; ἅπασαν ἀ. ἐκτεῖναι [D.]60.30, etc. **2.** *gymnastic exercise*, Hp.*Art.*11, Pl.*Men.*94b, *Lg.*765c, etc. : generally, *exercise*, Id.*Grg.*456d sq., *R.*618b. **3.** of the mind, *agony, anguish*, ἐν φόβῳ καὶ πολλῇ ἀ. D.18.33, cf. Men.534.12 (pl.), Arist.*Pr.*869^{b}6 ; ἐν τοῖς τῆς ψυχῆς φόβοις, ἐλπίσιν, ἀγωνίαις Id.*Spir.*483^{a}5 ; cf. Chrysipp.*Stoic.*2.248, al., Phld.*Ir.*p.56 W. (pl.), Nic.Dam.*Vit.Caes.*9. **-ιάτης** [ᾰτ], ου, ὁ, *nervous person*, D.L.2.131. **-ιάω**, inf. -ιᾶν Pl.*Prt.*333e, part. -ιῶν Id.*Chrm.*162c, Isoc.4.91 : impf. ἠγωνίων Plb.1.10.6, etc. : fut. -άσω [ᾱ] Porph.*Abst.*1.54 : aor. ἠγωνίασα Timocl.22.5, Phld.*Oec.*p.41 J., D.S. 14.60 : pf. ἠγωνίακα (ὑπερ-) [D.]61.28 :—*contend eagerly, struggle*, D.21.61 ; πρὸς ἀλλήλους Isoc. l. c. **II.** *to be distressed* or *anxious, be in an agony*, τετραχύνθαι τε καὶ ἀ. Pl.*Prt.*333e ; ἀγωνιῶντα καὶ τεθορυβημένον Id.*Lys.*210e, cf. Arist.*Pr.*869^{b}8, Men.*Her.*2, *PPetr.*3 p.151 ; περί τινος Arist.*Rh.*1367^{a}15 : c. acc., Plb.1.20.6, al. ; ἐπί τινι Plu.*Caes.*46 ; ἀ. μή.. Plb.3.9.2, etc. ; ἀ. εἴ τι πείσεται Nic.Dam.*Vit. Caes.*9. **-ίζομαι**, fut. -ιοῦμαι E.*Heracl.*992, etc. (in pass. sense, v. infr. B) ; -ίσομαι only in late writers, as Porph.*Abst.*1.31 ; -ισθήσομαι Aristid.1.504 J. : aor. ἠγωνισάμην E.*Supp.*427, etc. : pf. ἠγώνισμαι (in act. sense) Id.*Ion*939, Ar.*V.*993, Isoc.18.31 (Pass., v. infr. B) : aor. ἠγωνίσθην in pass. sense, infr. B : act. form ἀγωνίσας *IG*4. 429 (Sicyon) :—

A. *contend for a prize*, esp. in the public games, Hdt.2.160, al. ; πρός τινα Pl.*R.*579c, al. ; περί τινος *about* a thing, Hdt.8.26; Ὀλυμπίασιν Pl.*Hp.Mi.*364a ; περὶ πρωτείων D.18.66 ; ὑπὲρ τῆς ἐλευθερίας Id.18.177 : freq. c. acc. cogn., ἀ. στάδιον Hdt.5.22 ; τῶν ἀγώνων, οὓς περὶ τῆς ψυχῆς ἠγωνίζεσθε D.18.262 ; ἀγῶνα..τόνδ' ἠγώνισω thou *didst provoke* this contest, E.*Supp.*427, cf. *Ion*939 ; ἠγωνίζου τι ἡμῖν; Pl.*Ion* 530a : metaph., τὰ τῆς ψυχῆς Ὀλύμπια Porph.*Abst.* l. c. **2.** *fight*, Hdt.1.76,82, al. ; περὶ τῶν ἁπάντων Th.6.16 ; πρός τινα Id.1.36, cf. 8.27 : c. acc. cogn., μῶν τι κεδνὸν -ίζετο ; E.*Heracl.*795 ; [μάχην] -ίσαντο E.*Supp.*637. **3.** *contend for the prize on the stage*, of the rhapsode, Hdt.5.67 ; of the playwright, Ar.*Ach.*140,419; of the actor, D.19.246, cf. 250, Arist.*Po.*1451^{a}8 ; of the choragus, D. 21.66 : c. acc., δράματα *IG*12(7).226 (Amorgos) : generally, *contend for victory*, καλῶς..ἠγώνισαι Pl.*Smp.*194a, cf. *Mx.*235d ; *argue*, ὅλῳ τῷ πράγματι about the question as a whole, *Hp.Mi.*369c ; esp. *argue sophistically*, opp. διαλέγομαι, *Tht.*167e. **4.** of public speaking, X.*Mem.*3.7.4 ; ἀ. πρὸς ἀπόδειξιν Arist.*Fr.*133 (Theodect. ap.Rh.6.19W.). **II.** *contend in court*, as law-term, Antipho 5.7 : c. acc. cogn., ἀ. δίκην, γραφήν *fight* a cause *to the last*, Lys.3.20, D.23.100 ; ἀ. ψευδομαρτυριῶν (sc. γραφήν) Id.24.131 ; ἀ. ἀγῶνα And. 1.20, Lys.7.39 ; ἀ. φόνον *fight against* a charge of murder, E.*Andr.*336 ; αὐτοῖς ἀ. τοῖς πράγμασιν *grapple with* the facts of the case, Arist. *Rh.*1404^{a}5. **III.** generally, *struggle, exert oneself*, c. inf., Th. 4.87 ; εὖ ἀ. Lys.20.22, cf. Plu.*Phoc.*37.

B. Pass., *to be decided by contest, brought to issue*, mostly in pf., πολλοὶ ἀγῶνες ἀγωνίδαται Hdt.9.26 ; τὰ ἠγωνισμένα *points at issue*, E.*Supp.*465, D.24.145 : rarely in pres., ὁ ἀγωνιζόμενος νόμος the law *on trial*, D.24.28 ; or aor., δεινὸς..κίνδυνος ὑπὲρ τῆς..ἐλευθερίας ἠγωνίσθη Lys.2.34 ; ἠγωνίσθη λαμπρῶς (impers.) Plu.*Sert.*21 : fut. Med. in pass. sense, ἀγωνιεῖται καὶ κριθήσεται τὸ πρᾶγμα *shall be brought to issue* and determined, D.21.7. **-ικός**, ή, όν, v.l. for ἀγωνιστικός, D.H.*Rh.*6.6. **-ιος** (A), ον, *of* or *belonging to the contest*, ἄεθλος ἀ. *its* prize, Pi.*I.*5(4).7 ; εὖχος Id.*O.*10(11).63 ; πούς Simon.29 :— epith. of Hermes as *president of games*, Pi.*I.*1.60, cf. *IG*5(1).658 ; of Zeus as *decider of the contest*, S.*Tr.*26 :—ἀ. θεοί, in A.*Ag.*513, *Supp.*189,242, Pl.*Lg.*783a, either gods *in assembly*, or the gods *who presided over the great games* (Zeus, Poseidon, Apollo, and Hermes), = ἀγοραῖοι θ., Eust.1335.58. **2.** ἀγωνίῳ σχολᾷ S. *Aj.*194, either *pause from battle*, or *strenuous rest* (oxymoron, cf. Sch.).

ἀ-γώνιος (B), ον, *without angle*, ἀ. σχῆμα ὁ κύκλος Arist.*Metaph.* 1020^{a}35, cf. Thphr.*HP*3.14.2.

ἀγών-ῐσις, ἡ, *a contending for a prize*, Th.5.50. **-ισμα**, τό, *contest, conflict* : in pl., *deeds done in battle, brave deeds*, Hdt.8.76 ; *feats* of horsemanship, X.*Eq.Mag.*3.5 ; ἀ. κατὰ τὰ ἆθλα *CIG* 2741. **2.** in sg., *feat, achievement*, ἀ. τινος *a feather in* his *cap*, Th.8.12, cf. 17 : c. inf., Id.7.59,86 ; ξυνέσεως ἀ. *prize* of sagacity, Id.3.82 ; ἀρᾶς ἀ. *issue* of the curse, E.*Ph.*1355. **II.** ἀ. ποιεῖσθαί τι make it *an object to strive for*, Hdt.1.140 ; οὐ μικρὸν τὸ ἀ. προστάττεις Luc.*Im.*12. **III.** *that with which one contends, declamation*, ἀ. ἐς τὸ παραχρῆμα Th.1.22 ; of plays, Arist.*Po.*1451^{b}37. **IV.** in Law, *plea*, Antipho 5.36, Lys.13.77. **-ισμός**, ὁ, *rivalry*, Th.7.70. **-ιστέον**, *one must contend*, X.*Cyr.*1.6.9, D.9.70. **-ιστήριος**, α, ον, also ος, ον (Poll.4.89), = ἀγωνιστικός, κύβηλις Anaxipp.6.6. **II. -ιστήριον**, τό, *place of assembly*, Aristid.1.108 J. **-ιστής**, οῦ, ὁ, *combatant*, ἀ. πικροί E.*Ion* 1257 :—esp. *competitor* in the games, Hdt.2.160, 5.22 ; generally, opp. κριτής, Isoc.2.13, Th.3.37, etc. :—as Adj., ἀ. ἵπποι *racehorses*, Plu.*Them.*25. **2.** *pleader, debater*, Pl.*Phdr.*269d, *Tht.* 164c. **3.** *actor*, Arist.*Pr.*918^{b}28 ; θεωροῖς εἴτ' ἀγωνισταῖς Achae.3 ; ἀ. τραγικῶν παθῶν Timae.119. **II.** *master* in any art or science, Isoc.15.201,204 ; ἄκρος ἀ. [τῆς γεωμετρίας] [D.]61.44. **III.** c. gen., *one who struggles for* a thing, *champion*, ἀ. τῆς ἀρετῆς, ἀληθείας, Aeschin.3.180 (pl.), Plu.2.16c. **-ιστικός**, ή, όν, *fit for contest*, esp. in the games, δύναμις ἀ. Arist.*Rh.*1360^{b}22 ; ἀ. σώματος ἀρετή ib.1361^{b}21 ; ἡ -κή the art *of combat* or *contest*, Pl.*Sph.*225a sq. ; τὸ ἀ. ib.219c,e. **2.** *fit for contest* in speaking, ἀ. λέξις *debating* style, Arist.*Rh.*1413^{b}9 ; *contentious*, λόγοι Id.*SE*165^{b}11, al. ; ἀ. διατριβαί Id.*Top.*157^{a}23 : Comp. -ώτεραι, προτάσεις Alex.Aphr.*in Top.*522.27. **3.** *masterly, striking*, ἀ. προρρήματα Hp.*Art.*58 ; ἀ. τι ἔχουσα having in it something *glorious*, ib.70 ; πράξεις Men.Rh. p.384 S. **b.** Rhet., *striking, impressive*, Longin.23.1 ; -κόν, τό, Id.22.3 : Sup. -ώτατος ἑαυτοῦ, of Plato, Them.*Or.*34 p.448 D. **4.** Medic., '*heroic*', i. e. *copious*, πόσεις Philagr.ap.Orib.5.19. Adv. -κῶς Herod.ib.5.30.31, Gal.15.499 ; and so of '*heroic*' measures generally, -κῶς θεραπεύειν 18(1).61. **II.** of persons, *contentious, eager for applause*, Pl.*Men.*75c, Phld.*Oec.*p.65 J. **III.** Adv. -κῶς *contentiously*, Arist.*Top.*164^{b}15 ; ἀ. ἔχειν to be *disposed to fight*, Plu. *Sull.*16 : Comp., ἐπιστολὰς -ώτερον τοῦ δέοντος ἐπέστελλε Philostr. *VS*2.33.3. **2.** *dramatically*, ᾄδειν Arist.*Pr.*918^{b}21 ; opp. καταστατικῶς, Aps.p.266 H.

ἀγωνο-δίκης, ου, ὁ, *judge of the contest*, Hsch. **-θεσία**, ἡ, *office of* ἀγωνοθέτης, *direction* or *exhibition of games*, *IG*2.379 (iii B.C.), Nic.Dam.*Vit.Caes.*9, Plu.*Ages.*21, etc. : pl., prob. in Phld.*Rh.*2. 27 S. **-θετέω**, *exhibit games*, *GDI*1842 (Delph.), etc. ; ἀ. Πύθια, Ὀλύμπια *AP*12.255 (Strat.) ; μίμοις ἀ. Plu.2.621c : metaph., Th.3. 38. **2.** c. acc., ἀ. τινάς *embroil* them, Plb.9.34.3 ; ἀ. στάσιν, πόλεμον, etc., *stir up* faction, war, etc., Plu.*Cat.Mi.*45, J.*AJ*17.3.1. **II.** *preside at the games*, D.9.32, cf. Pl.*Smp.*184a. **-θετήρ**, ῆρος, ὁ, = sq., *IG*14.502 (Catana). **-θέτης**, ου, ὁ, *judge of the contests, president of the games*, or (later) *exhibitor of games*, Hdt.6.127, And.4.26, Decr. ap.D.18.84, *IG*2.314 (iii B.C.), etc. **2.** generally, *judge*, X.*An.* 3.1.21 ; πολιτικῆς ἀρετῆς Aeschin.3.180. **-θετικός**, ή, όν, *of* or *for the direction of the games*, χρήματα *CIG*2742 (Aphrodisias), *IG*5(1). 550 (Sparta) :—of a person, *CIG*6824 (Constantinople). **-θέτις**, ιδος, fem. of ἀγωνοθέτης, *IGRom.*4.1225 (Thyatira), 1238. **-θήκη**, ἡ, = ἀγωνοθεσία, S.*Fr.*975, criticized as irreg. by Poll.3.141. **-λογία**, ἡ, (λέγω) *laborious discussion*, Gal.1.79.

ἄ-γωνος, ον, = ἀγώνιος, *without angle*, Thphr.*HP*7.6.2 (Comp.).

ἄγωνος, ὁ, Aeol. and Elean for ἀγών, q. v.

ἀγωνότριψ, ιβος, ὁ, *frequenting declamations*, Phld.*Rh.*2.85 S.

ἀδαγμός, ὁ, v. sub ὀδαγμός ; cf. ἀδακτῶ.

ἄδᾳδος, ον, (δαΐς, δᾴς) *without resin*, Thphr.*HP*5.1.5.

ἀδᾳδούχητος, ον, (δᾳδουχέω) *not lighted by torches* : of marriage, *clandestine*, Apion ap.Eust.622.42.

ἀδᾱ-ημονία, Ep. -ίη, ἡ, *ignorance, unskilfulness in* doing, c. inf., Od.24.244 (v.l. **ἀδαημοσύνη**). **-ήμων**, ον, *unknowing, ignorant*, c. gen., μάχης ἀδαήμονι φωτί Il.5.634 ; κακῶν ἀδαήμονες Od.12.208 ; ἀ. τῶν ἱρῶν τῶν ἐν Ἐλευσῖνι Hdt.8.65, cf. Matro*Parod.Fr.*6, Hierocl.*in CA*4 p.425 M. : abs., Ps.-Phoc.86. **-ής**, ές, (*δάω, δαῆναι) = foreg., c. gen. pers., Hdt.9.46 : c. gen. rei, τῆς θυσίης, τῶν χρησμῶν, Id.2.49, 5.90, cf. X.*Cyr.*1.6.43 ; βουνομίας -έστερος Pi.*Pae.*4.27 ; ὕπν' ὀδύνας ἀ. S.*Ph.*827 (lyr.) : c. inf., *unknowing how to*.., ἀ. δ' ἔχειν μυρίον ἄχθος (sc. κῆρ) ib.1167 (lyr.) ; οὐκ ἀ. *APl.*4.84 : abs., ἀ. κόρη, of a virgin, Paus.Dam.p.160 D. **II.** *dark*, Parm.8.59. **-ητος**, ον, *unknown*, Hes.*Th.*655, *Hymn.Is.*157.

ἀδαίδαλτος, ον, *not carved, plain*, Orph.*A.*403.

ἀδαίετος, ον, (δαίω B) *undivided*, A.R.3.1033.

ἀδάϊκτος, ον, *undestroyed*, Q.S.1.196, 11.165.

ἀδάϊος, ον, Dor. for ἀδήϊος, Hsch.

ἀδαῖος, ον, (ἄδην) *producing surfeit*, Sophr.137.

ἄδαιτος, ον, (δαίνυμαι) *of which none might eat*, θυσία A.*Ag.*151.

ἀδαίτρευτος, ον, *for which nothing has been slain*, δεῖπνον Nonn. *D.*17.51, 40.419.

ἄδαιτρος, ον, (δαίω B) *undivided*, Hsch.

ἄδακρ-ῠς, υ, gen. υος, *tearless*, αἰών Pi.*O.*2.66, E.*Alc.*1047, Clearch. 8 ; ὑπὸ τροφῷ ἄ., of a healthy child, Theoc.24.31. **II.** = ἀδάκρυτος II, E.*Med.*861 (lyr.) : *costing no tears*, πόλεμος D.S.15.72 ; μάχη Plu.*Ages.*33. **-ῡτί**, Adv. *tearlessly, without tears*, Isoc.14.47, Ph.

2.67, Plu.*Caes.*7, etc. **-ῦτος**, ον, *without tears*: I. Act., *tearless*, ἀ. καὶ ἀπήμων Il.1.415, cf. Od.24.61; ἀδακρύτω ἔχεν ὄσσε 4.186; ἀστένακτος κἀ. S.*Tr.*1200; εὐνάζειν ἀ. βλεφάρων πόθον *so that they weep not*, ib.106 (lyr.):—Medic., ἀ. ὀφθαλμὸς *abnormally dry*, Aët. 7.91. 2. c. gen., *not weeping for*, τινός *Epigr.Gr.*241 a 13. II. Pass., *unwept*, S.*Ant.*881 (lyr.). 2. *costing no tears*, τρόπαια Plu. *Tim.*37.

ἀδακτῶ· κνήθομαι, Hsch.

ἀδαλές· ὑγιές, Hsch. [ᾰ, if from δαλέομαι, Dor. for δηλ-.]

ἀδαμάντῖνος, η, ον, *adamantine, of steel*, Pi.*P.*4.224, A.*Pr.*6,64, Aeschin.3.84; ἀ. κερκίδες, of the Μοῖραι, *Lyr.Adesp.*ap.Stob.1.5.11; αἱμασιή Eus.Mynd.*Fr.*63. 2. metaph., *hard as adamant*, οὐδεὶς ἂν γένοιτο.. οὕτως ἀ., ὃς ἂν.. Pl.*R.*360b; σιδηροῖς καὶ ἀ. λόγοις Id.*Grg.* 509a; δεσμοὶ Metrod.*Herc.*831.12; οὐκ ἀ. ἐστίν, of a girl, Theoc.3.39. Adv. -νως Pl.*R.*618e.

ἀδᾰμαντό-δετος, ον, *iron-bound*, λῦμαι A.*Pr.*148,426 (lyr.). **-πέδῖλος**, ον, *on a base of adamant*, κίονες Pi.*Fr.*88.5.

ἀδάμ-ας, αντος, ὁ, (δαμάω):—first in Hes. (in Hom. only as pr. n.), properly, *unconquerable*: I. Subst., *adamant*, i.e. the hardest metal, prob. *steel*, χλωρός, πολιός, Hes.*Sc.*231, *Th.*161: metaph., ἀδάμαντος ἔχον κρατερόφρονα θυμόν *Op.*147; of anything *fixed, unalterable*, ἔπος ἐρέω ἀδάμαντι πελάσσας Orac.ap.Hdt.7.141; ἀδάμαντος δῆσεν ἅλοις fixed them with nails *of adamant*, i.e. inevitably, Pi.*P.* 4.71, cf. *APl.*4.167 (Antip. Sid.); τὸν ἐν Ἅιδα κινήσαις ἀδάμαντα Theoc.2.34. 2. *diamond*, Thphr.*Lap.*19, Paus.8.18.6, *Peripl. M.Rubr.*56; prob. so meant in Pl.*Ti.*59b, *Plt.*303e, cf. Plin.*NH*37. 55. 3. metaph., ὁ πόνος ἀδάμαντος, of love, Alex.245.13. II. Adj., *unbreakable*, ἀνακτίτης Orph.*L.*192. **-αστί**, Adv. *unconquerably*, Suid. **-αστος**, ον, (δαμάω) *unsubdued, inflexible*, of Hades, Il.9.158, cf. Phld.*D.*1.18: later in the proper sense, *untamed, unbroken*, πῶλος X.*Eq.*1.1, cf. Corn.*ND*20; ἀ. πᾶσιν Timo 9.1. **-ᾰτος**, ον, = ἀδάμαστος, *unconquered*, A.*Ch.*54, *Th.*233, S.*OT*205, etc.: of females, *unwedded*, S.*Aj.*450; *untamed*, μόσχος ἀ. πέσημα δίκε E. *Ph.*640.—Trag. word, always in lyr. (exc. S.*Aj.* l.c.); restored by Elmsl. for ἀδάμαντος or -αστος of codd. **-άτωρ**, ἡ, epith. of Hecate, *PMag.Par.*1.2717. **-νεῖς** (cod. -αῖς)· ἀκολασταίνεις (cod. -αις), Hsch. **-νής**, ές, and **-νος**, ον, = ἀδάμαστος, Id. **-ος**, ον, = ἀδάμαστος, Ion Lyr.9.

ἅδᾱν, Aeol. for ἅδην, Alcm.76.

ἀδάνειστος, ον, *not pledged as security*, ἄλλου δανείου *BGU*741 (ii A.D.).

ἀδαξάω, or -έω, ἀδαξῆσαι, ἀδάξομαι, v. sub ὀδάξω.

ἀδάπᾰνος, ον, *without expense, costing nothing*, γλυκέα κἀδάπανα Ar.*Pax* 593, cf. Teles p.7.8 H., D.S.10*Fr.*12. Adv. ἀδαπάνως, τέρψαι φρένα E.*Or.*1176, cf. Phld.*Rh.*2.133 S. (prob.). II. of persons, *not spending*, ἀ. χρημάτων εἰς τὸ δέον Arist.*VV*1251^{b}7; ἀ. καταστῆσαι τὸ κοινόν *Michel* 1007.33 (Teos), cf. *Inscr.Prien.*111.133 (i B.C.).

ἄδαπτον· γυμνόν, ἄδερμον, Hsch.

ἀδάρκη, ἡ, or **ἀδάρκης**, ὁ, *salt efflorescence on the herbage of marshes*, Dsc.5.119, Damocr.ap.Gal.13.105: **ἄδαρκος**, ὁ, Gal.12.370; Dim. **ἀδάρκιον**, τό, ibid.

ἄδαρτος, ον, (δέρω) *unflayed*: *not cudgelled*, Hsch., *Gloss.*

ἄδασμος, ον, *tribute-free*, A.*Fr.*63.

ἄδαστος, ον, (δάσασθαι) *undivided*, S.*Aj.*54; also **ἄδατος**, Hsch.

ἀδαυῶς· ἐγρηγόρως, Hsch.

ἀδαχέω, *scratch*, Ar.*Fr.*410.

ἄδδαυον (i.e. ἄζαυον)· ξηρόν (Lacon.), Hsch.

ἄδδιξ, ῖχος, ἡ, *measure of four* χοίνικες, Ar.*Fr.*709.

ἄδε, v. sub ἁνδάνω.

ἀδεαλτόω (sic), (ἀ-, δάλτος, = δέλτος) *erase, deface*, στάλαν *Michel* 1334 (Elis).

ἀδεής (A), Ep. **ἀδειής**, ές: voc. ἀδεές [ᾰ, i.e. ἀδϝεές]:—*fearless*, εἴ περ ἀδειής τ' ἐστί, of Hector, Il.7.117; κύον ἀδεές 8.423, Od.19. 91: c. gen., ἀ. θανάτου Pl.*R.*386b, cf. Arist.*EN*1115^{a}33; ἐν θαλάττῃ καὶ ἐν νόσοις ἀ. ὁ ἀνδρεῖος 1115^{b}1. 2. *without anxiety, secure*, τὸ ἀ. *security*, Th.3.37; ἀ. δέος δεδιέναι to fear *where no fear is*, Pl. *Smp.*198a. II. *causing no fear, not formidable*, πρὸς ἐχθροὺς Th.1.36 (Comp.); οὐ γὰρ ἀδεὲς τοῦθ' ὑπολαμβάνω D.16.22. III. most common in Adv. ἀδεῶς *without fear* or *scruple, confidently*, Hdt.3.65, 9.109; ἀ. τινὰ ὠφελοῦμεν Th.2.40; ἀ. περί τινος ἀποφαίνεσθαι Pl.*La.*186d; ἀ. πολιτεύεσθαι Lys.24.25; ἀ. *bibit* Cic.*Att.*13. 52: Comp. -έστερον Th.4.92. 2. *with impunity*, μηνύειν Id.6. 27.

ἀδε-ής (B), ές, (δέομαι) *not in want*, τινός Max.Tyr.5.1, al. **-ητος**, ον, (δέομαι) *not wanting a thing*, Antipho Soph. 10. II. *inexorable*, Ptol.*Tetr.*159; cf. ἀδεύητος.

ἄδεια (A), ἡ, (ἀδεής A) *freedom from fear*, Th.7.29; esp. *safe conduct, amnesty, indemnity*, ἀδείην διδόναι Hdt.2.121.ζ'; τοῖς ἄλλοις ἄ. ἐδώκατε οἰκεῖν τὴν σφετέραν Antipho 5.77; ἐν ἀ. εἶναι Hdt.8.120; ἐν ἀ. οὐ ποιεῖσθαι τὸ λέγειν to hold it not *safe*, Id.9.42; τὸ σῶμά τινος εἰς ἄ. καθιστάναι Lys.2.15; τῶν σωμάτων ἄ. ποιεῖν Th.3.58; πολλὴν ἄ. αὐτοῖς ἐψηφισμένοι ἔσεσθε ποιεῖν ὅτι ἂν βούλωνται Lys.22. 19; ἄ. τινι παρασκευάσαι Id.16.13, cf. D.13.17; παρέχειν Id.21.210; opp. ἄ. εὑρίσκεσθαι And.1.34, D.24.47; λαμβάνειν Id.18.286; ἀδείας τυγχάνειν 5.6; τοῦ μὴ πάσχειν ἄδειαν ἤγετε 19.149; μετὰ πάσης ἀδείας 18.305; μετ' ἀ. 22.25:—also γῆς ἄ. a *secure* dwelling-place, S.*OC*447:—*licence* to bring forward proposals or make charges, D.24.45, Plu.*Per.*31, etc. 2. Lit. Crit., *licence*, ἄ. ποιητική A.D. *Pron.*38.3, al., Him.*Or.*1.1; κωμική A.D.*Pron.*69.19.

ἄδεια (B), ἡ, (δέομαι) *abundance, plenty*, Teles p.44.1 H.; κρεῶν Sch.Ar.*Nu.*386.

Ἀδειγάνες, οἱ, *name of certain Seleucian magistrates* in Plb.5.54. 10; prob. an Eastern word.

ἀδειγμάτιστος, ον, *without a sample*, or perh. *without an official stamp*, *PHib.*98.17 (iii B.C.), *PSI*4.358.5 (iii B.C.).

ἀδειής, ές, Ep. for ἀδεής (A).

ἄδεικτος, ον, *not shown, invisible*, of God, Ph.1.197,618.

ἄδειλος, ον, *fearless*, Ps.-Callisth.1.6.

ἀδείμαντος, ον, (δειμαίνω) *fearless, dauntless*, Pi.*N.*10.17, etc.; ἦλθ' ἀ. ποδί E.*Rh.*697: c. gen., ἐμαυτῆς ἀ. *without fear for* myself, A.*Pers.*162. Adv. -τως Id.*Ch.*771. 2. *where no fear is*, οἰκία Luc.*Philops.*31.

ἄδειμος, ον, (δεῖμα) *fearless*, Hsch., Suid.

ἀδεῖν, Aeol. ἀδ-, v. sub ἁνδάνω.

ἄδειος· ἀκάθαρτος (Cypr.), Hsch.

ἄδειπνος, ον, *without the evening meal, supperless*, Hp.*Aph.*5.41, X.*An.*4.5.21, etc.

ἀδεισία, ἡ, = ἀφοβία, *EM*16.56.

ἀδεισι-βόας, ὁ, *not fearing the battle-cry*, B.5.155, 10.61. **-δαιμονία**, ἡ, *freedom from superstition*, Hp.*Decent.*5. **-δαίμων**, ον, *without superstition*, Adv. -μόνως D.S.38.7: Comp. -έστερον Sor.1. 80. **-θεος**, ον, *impious*, λογισμοί Orac.ap.Jul.*Ep.*88; ἄνδρες Procl.*H.*3.12.

ἀδέκαστος, ον, (δεκάζω) *unbribed, impartial*, Arist.*EN*1109^{b}8, Plu. *Cim.*10, Ael.*NA*17.16; διάνοια D.H.*Th.*34, etc. Adv. -τως, ἔχουσα φιλοσοφία Philostr.*VA*8.7.3, cf. Gal.11.417, Max.Tyr.6.6: Comp. -ότερον Luc.*Hist.Conscr.*47.

ἀδεκάτευτος, ον, *tithe-free*, Ar.*Eq.*301, *OGI*229.101 (Smyrna, iii B.C.).

ἄδεκτος, ον, (δέχομαι) *not receptive*, Thphr.*Metaph.*9: c. gen., *not capable of*, τῆς εὐδαιμονίας Hippod.ap.Stob.4.39.26; τοῦ μοιχεύειν Phld. *D.*3*Fr.*78; μεταβολῆς Plu.2.1025c, cf. Plot.3.6.13, Herm.ap.Stob. 3.11.31, Procl.*in Prm.*p.842 S., etc. II. Pass., *incomprehensible*, dub. l. in Ph.1.486. 2. *unacceptable*, δῶρα Zos.1.58.

ἀδέλεσχος, v. ἀδόλ-.

ἀδελφεά, -εή, **ἀδελφεός**, -ειός, v. sub ἀδελφή, ἀδελφός.

ἀδελφεοκτόνος, ον, Ion. for ἀδελφοκτόνος.

ἀδελφ-ή, ἡ, fem. of ἀδελφός, *sister*, Trag., E.*Fr.*866, etc.; ὁμοπατρία ἀ. Men.*Grg.*12, cf. *PTeb.*320.5 (ii A.D.): Ion. **-εή**, Hdt.2. 56, al.; Ep. -ειή, Q.S.1.30; Dor. **-εά**, Pi.*N.*7.4, and in lyr. passages of Trag., S.*OT*160, *OC*535. 2. *kinswoman*, Lxx *Jb.*42.11. 3. term of endearment, *Ca.*4.9, *To.*5.21; applied to a wife, *POxy.*744.1 (i B.C.), etc.:—as a title, Βερενίκη ἡ ἀ. καὶ γυνὴ αὐτοῦ (of a cousin) *OGI*60.3 (iii B.C.):—*sister* (as a fellow Christian), *Ep.Rom.*16.1, etc. **-ιδέος**, contr. **-οῦς**, ὁ, *nephew*, Alcm.56A, etc.; usu. *brother's son*, Hdt.1.65, 6.94, al., Th.2.101, etc.; also, *sister's son*, Hdt.4.147, Str.10.5.6, etc.:—also **-ιδός**, *beloved one*, Lxx *Ca.*2.3, al. **-ιδῆ**, ἡ, Att. contr. for ἀδελφιδέη, *a brother's* or *sister's daughter, a niece*, Ar.*Nu.*47, Lys.3.6, Hp.*Epid.*6.2.19, etc. **-ιδῆς**, ὁ, and **-ίδισσα** (sic), ἡ, = foreg., *IGRom.*4.621 (Temenothyrae). **-ίδιον**, τό, Dim. of ἀδελφός, Ar.*Ra.*60, *PPar.*39.6 (ii B.C.). **-ίζω**, *adopt as a brother, call brother*, Hecat.8 J., Apolloph.4, Isoc.19.30:—Pass., *to be very like*, Hp.*Acut.*9, etc.; τινί Id.*Fract.*31, *Art.*45. **-ικός**, ή, όν, *brotherly* or *sisterly*, φιλία Arist.*EN*1161^{a}6; ἔρις Just.*Nov.*18.7; ἡ ὑμετέρα ἀ. παίδευσις *POxy.*1165.2 (vi A.D.). Adv. -κῶς Lxx 4*Ma.* 13.9, Ps.-Callisth.3.20. **-ιξις**, ἡ, *brotherhood, close connexion*, Hp. *Art.*57. **-ιον**, τό, Dim. of ἀδελφός, Keil-Premerstein *Zweiter Bericht* 215 (Lydia, ii A.D.), *POxy.*1300.4 (v A.D.). **-ίς**, ἡ, kind of *date*, Plin.*HN*13.45, *Gloss.* **-οδότης**, ου, ὁ, *bestowing brothers*, ἀστήρ Vett.Val.123.21. **-όθεν**, *germanitus*, *Gloss.*

ἀδελφο-κτόνος, ον, *murdering a brother* or *sister*, Hdt.3.65 (in Ion. form ἀδελφεοκτ-), Nic.Dam.p.142 D., Plu.2.256f, Ph.1.148. **-κτονέω**, *to be murderer of a brother* or *sister*, J.*BJ*2.11.4, Vett.Val.74. 28. **-κτονία**, ἡ, *murder of a brother* or *sister*, J.*BJ*1.31.2, Ph. 1.210, al. **-μιξία**, ἡ, *marriage of brother and sister*, Tz.*H.*1. 590. **-παις**, παιδος, ὁ, ἡ, *brother's* or *sister's child*, D.H.4.64 (Cod. Vat.), cf. Just.*Nov.*127.1. **-ποιός**, όν, *adopting as a brother*, *EM* 255.1. **-πρεπῶς**, Adv. *as befits a brother*, Lxx 4*Ma.*10.12.

ἀδελφός [ᾰ], (ἀ- copul., δελφύς, Arist.*HA*510^{b}13; cf. ἀγάστωρ) properly, *son of the same mother*: I. as Subst., ἀδελφός, ὁ, voc. ἄδελφε; Ep., Ion., and Lyr. ἀδελφεός (gen. -ειοῦ in Hom. is for -εόο), Cret. ἀδελφιός, ἀδευφιός, *Leg.Gort.*2.21, *Mon.Ant.*18.319:—*brother*, Hom., etc.; ἀδελφοί *brother and sister*, E.*El.*536; so of the Ptolemies, θεοὶ ἀδελφοί Herod.1.30, *OGI*50.2 (iii B.C.), etc.; ἀπ' ἀμφοτέρων ἀδελφεός Hdt.7.97: prov., χαλεποὶ πόλεμοι ἀδελφῶν E.*Fr.*975: metaph., ἀ. γέγονα σειρήνων Lxx *Jb.*30.29. 2. *kinsman*, ib.*Ge.*13.8, al.; *tribesman*, *Ex.*2.11, al. 3. *colleague, associate*, *PTeb.*1.12, *IG*12 (9).906.19 (Chalcis); *member of a college*, ib.14.956. 4. term of address, used by kings, *OGI*138.3 (Philae), J.*AJ*13.2.2, etc.; generally, Lxx *Ju.*7.30; esp. in letters, *PPar.*48 (ii B.C.), etc.:—as a term of affection, applicable by wife to husband, Lxx *To.*10.12, *PLond.*1.42.1 (ii B.C.), etc. 5. *brother* (as a fellow Christian), *Ev.Matt.*12.50, *Act.Ap.*9.30, al.; of other religious communities, e.g. Serapeum, *PPar.*42.1 (ii B.C.), cf. *PTaur.*1.1.20. 6. metaph., of things, *fellow*, ἀνὴρ τῷ ἀ. προσκολληθήσεται, of Leviathan's scales, Lxx *Jb.*41.8. II. Adj., ἀδελφός, ή, όν, *brotherly* or *sisterly*, A.*Th.* 811, etc.; φύσιν ἀ. ἔχοντες, of Hephaistos and Athena, Pl.*Criti.* 109c. 2. generally, of anything double, *twin, in pairs*, X.*Mem.*

2.3.19:—also, *akin, cognate*, μαθήματα Archyt.1; ἀ. νόμοις Pl.*Lg.* 683a: mostly c. gen., ἀδελφὰ τῶνδε S.*Ant.*192; ἡ δὲ μωρία μάλιστ' ἀ. τῆς πονηρίας ἔφυ Id.*Fr.*925; freq. in Pl., *Phd.*108b, *Cra.*418e, al., cf. Hyp.*Epit.*35: c. dat., ἀδελφὰ τούτοισι S.*OC*1262, cf. Pl.*Smp.*210b.

ἀδελφότης, ητος, ἡ, *brotherhood*, Lxx 1*Ma.*12.10, Vett.Val.2.28, D.Chr.38.15: metaph., of men and animals, Iamb.*VP*24.108. II. *the brotherhood*, 1*Ep.Pet.*2.17, 5.9. III. as form of address, ἡ σὴ ἀ. *PGrenf.*2.89, *PAmh.*2.156; χάριν ἀπονέμομεν τῇ ἀ. τοῦ Καίσαρος Men.Prot.p.16 D.

ἀδέμνιος, ον, *unwedded to* any one, τινός Opp.*C.*3.358.

ἄδενδρος, ον, *without trees*, Plb.3.55.9, D.H.1.37:—poet. **ἀδένδρεος**, Opp.*C.*4.337.

ἀδενοειδής, ές, (ἀδήν) *glandular*, Herophil.ap.Gal.*UP*14.11:— **ἀδενώδη** φύματα Plu.2.664f, cf. Gal.*UP*14.13, Sor.1.12.

ἀδέξιος, ον, *left-handed, awkward*, Arr.*Epict.*4.2.2, Luc.*Merc.Cond.* 14, *Sat.*4: c. inf., Steph. *in Rh.*283.13.

ἀδερκ-ής, ές, *unseen, invisible*, *AP*11.372 (Agath.). **-τος**, ον, (δέρκομαι) *not seeing*, ἀδέρκτων ὀμμάτων τητώμενος *so that they see not*, S.*OC*1200. Adv. -τως *without looking*, ib.130.

ἀδέρματος, ον, *without skin*, Sch.Pi.*P.*4.398, cf. S.*Fr.*336. **ἄδερμος**, ον, = foreg., Hsch. s. v. ἄδαπτον.

ἀδέσμ-ευτος, ον, = sq., Sch.E.*Hec.*550. **-ιος**, ον, = sq., Nonn.*D.* 15.138. **-ος**, ον, *unfettered, unbound*, ἄ. φυλακή, Lat. *libera custodia, 'parole'*, Th.3.34, D.H.1.83, etc.; βαλλάντια ἄ. *open* purses, Plu.2.503c; δεσμὸν ἄδεσμον φυλλάδος, of suppliant's wreath, E. *Supp.*32; *unbandaged*, Gal.18(2).505.

ἀδέσποτος, ον, *without master* or *owner*, ἀρετὴ ἀ. Pl.*R.*617e; τὸ παρ' ἡμᾶς ἀ. Epicur.*Ep.*3p.65U.: of property, *POxy.*1188.15 (13 A.D.), cf. Str.17.1.12: of freedmen, Myro Hist.2; οἰκήσεις Arist.*EN*1161^{a}7, cf. E.*Hyps.Fr.*1.11; ἀ. καὶ αὐτοκρατεῖς, of the gods, Plu.2.426c; ἀ. βίος Sallust.21. II. of rumours or writings, *anonymous*, Cic. *Fam.*15.17.3, D.H.11.50, Plu.*Cic.*15, etc. Adv. -τως J.*Ap.*1.16, Sch.Ar.*Ra.*1400. III. *ungovernable*, λύπη Democr.290.

ἄδετος, ον, (δέω) *unbound, loose*, Hp.*Art.*44; *not clamped together*, λίθοι *IG*7.3074 (Lebad.). 2. *free*, D.24.169, Aristaenet.1.20. 3. *unshod*, Philostr.*Ep.*37.

ἀδετοχίτων, gloss on ἀμιτροχίτων, *EM*83.53.

ἀδεύητος, ον, Ep. form of ἀδέητος, Hsch.: **ἀδεύητον**· χαλεπόν, ἢ οὗ οὐκ ἄν τις ἔτι δεηθείη, *EM*17.4.

ἀδευκής, ές, Hom. only in Od., ὀλέθρῳ ἀδευκέϊ 4.489; ἀδευκέα πότμον 10.245; φῆμιν ἀδευκέα 6.273, cf. A.R.2.267, etc. (Expl. by Scholl. either (cf. δεῦκος, q. v.) *not sweet*, i. e. *bitter, cruel*, or (cf. δεύκει) *unexpected*, cf. Apollon. *Lex.*, Hsch.:—ἀ. φωνή expl. as *not imitative*, opp. πολυδευκής, Ael.*NA*5.38.)

ἀδέψητος, ον, (δεψέω) *untanned*, βοέη Od.20.2,142, cf. A.R.3.206, *AP*6.298 (Leon.).

ἀδέω [ᾰ], *to be sated with*, c. dat., only in aor. and pf., μὴ ξεῖνος .. δείπνῳ ἀδήσειε lest he *should be sated with* the repast, *feel loathing at* it, Od.1.134 (v.l. ἀηδήσειε); καμάτῳ ἀδηκότες ἠδὲ καὶ ὕπνῳ *sated with* toil and sleep, Il.10.98, cf. 312, 399, 471, Od.12.281; cf. ἄδην.

ἀδῆ· οὐρανός (Maced.), Hsch.

ἀδήϊος, contr. **ἄδῃος**, Dor. **ἀδάϊος**, ον, *unmolested, unravaged*, ἄδῃον .. σπαρτῶν ἀπ' ἀνδρῶν S.*OC*1533: of persons, *not harmed*, A.R. 4.647.

ἄδηκε, v. ἁνδάνω.

ἄδηκτος, ον, (δάκνω) *not gnawed* or *worm-eaten*, Hes.*Op.*420 (Sup.); *not bitten*, Dsc.2.60, al. 2. metaph., *unmolested*, Phld. *D.*3*Fr.*81, Plu.2.864c. Adv. -τως ib.448a. 3. *unaffected, untouched*, by love, anger, etc., in Adv. -τως, Phld.*Mort.*34, Plu.*Pomp.* 2, M.Ant.11.18, Eun.*VS*p.495 B. II. Act., *not biting* or *pungent*, Hp.*Mul.*1.11, Dsc.1.30: Comp. -ότερος *less stimulating*, Aret. *CA*1.10.

ἀδηλ-έω, (ἄδηλος) *to be in the dark about* a thing, *understand not*, σκοπὸς προσήκεις ὧν ἀδηλοῦμεν φράσαι S.*OC*35:—Pass., *to be obscure*, Ph.2.42, al., S.E.*M.*11.233, cf. 7.393; *fail to appear*, ἐπιμήνια -εύμενα Hp.*Mul.*1.2. **-ητος**, ον, (δηλέομαι) *unhurt*, A.R.2.709; *invulnerable*, Nonn.*D.*47.617. II. Act., *not hurting*, δεσμός ib.41. 199. **-ία**, ἡ, = ἀδηλότης, A.D.*Pron.*25.18, v.l. in Corn.*ND*13; ἀ. τοῦ μέλλοντος Iamb.*Myst.*10.4, cf. *AP*10.96 (Pall.). **-οποιέω**, *make unseen*, Sm.*Jb.*9.5, Ps.-Alex.Aphr.*in SE*124.3. **-οποιός**, όν, *making unseen*, Sch.Il.2.455; φάρμακα Sch.E.*Med.*1201. **-ος**, ον, *unseen, invisible*, of a fish, ποιεῖν ἑαυτὸν ἄ. Arist.*HA*620^{b}31; ἄ. χιτών, of the hyaloid membrane of the eye, [Gal.]14.712; *unknown, obscure*, Hes.*Op.*6; τὸν ἄ. ἄνδρα .. ἰχνεύειν S.*OT*475; ἐὰν δὲ .. ἄ. ὁ κτείνας ᾖ Pl.*Lg.*874a; of troops, ἀ. τοῖς πολεμίοις X.*Cyr.*6.3.13; εἰς τὸ ἄ. ἀποκρύπτειν Id.*Eq.Mag.*5.7. II. mostly of things, ἀ. θάνατοι death *by an unknown hand*, S.*OT*496; ἄ. ἔχθρα *secret* enmity, Th. 8.108; ῥεῖ πᾶν ἄδηλον melts all *to nothing*, S.*Tr.*698; *inscrutable*, E.*Or.*1318. b. neut., ἄδηλόν [ἐστι] εἰ .. *it is uncertain* whether .., Pl.*Phdr.*232e, al.; ἄ. μή .. Id.*Phd.*91d: abs., ἄ. ὄν Th.1.2; ἐν ἀδήλῳ εἶναι Antipho 5.6; ἐν ἀδηλοτέρῳ εἶναι X.*HG*7.5.8; ἐξ ἀδήλου ἔρχεται [σελήνη] S.*Fr.*871.5; also ἄ. agreeing with the subject (like δίκαιός εἰμι), παῖδες ἄ. ὁποτέρων, = ἄδηλον ὁποτέρων παῖδές εἰσιν, Lys. 1.33; ἀδήλοις .. πῶς ἀποβήσεται, = ἃ ἄ. ἐστι πῶς ἀ., Arist.*EN*1112^{b}9, cf. X.*Mem.*1.1.6. 2. *not evident to sense*, ὄψις τῶν ἀ. τὰ φαινόμενα Anaxag.21a, cf. Epicur.*Ep.*1p.6U.; opp. φανερόν, Phld.*Sign.*6, al.; opp. ἐναργές, ib.14, cf. Diog.Oen.8. 3. *unintelligible*, φωνή 1*Ep. Cor.*14.8. 4. *unproved*, *Stoic.*2.89. III. Adv. -λως *secretly*, Th.1.92, etc.: Sup. -ότατα Id.7.50. **-ότης**, ητος, ἡ, *uncertainty*, Protag.4, Plb.5.2.3, Ph.1.277, Corn.*ND*13, etc. **-όφλεβος**, ον, *with inconspicuous veins*, Arist.*GA*727^{a}24, *PA*667^{a}31. **-όω**, *render invisible*:—Pass., *to be obliterated*, *Tab.Heracl.*1.57.

ἄδημα, τό, = ψήφισμα, Hsch. (cod. ἀδήμας).

ἀδημιούργητος, ον, *not fashioned*, ἀ. πρὸς ἀνάστασιν *not made for* getting up again, of a fallen elephant, D.S.3.27.

ἀδημοκράτητος, ον, *not democratic*, D.C.43.45.

ἀδημονέω, *to be sorely troubled* or *dismayed, be in anguish*, Hp.*Virg.* 1; ἀδημονῶν τε καὶ ἀπορῶν Pl.*Tht.*175d, cf. D.19.197; ἀδημονῆσαι τὰς ψυχάς X.*HG*4.4.3: c. dat. rei, ἀδημονεῖ τῇ ἀτοπίᾳ τοῦ πάθους Pl.*Phdr.* 251d; ὑπό τινος *to be puzzled* by .., Epicur.*Nat.*11.8; ἐπί τινι D.H. 3.70; χάριν τινός *POxy.*298.45 (i A.D.). (Eust., 833.15, derives it from ἀδήμων, which is found only as v.l. in Hp.*Epid.*1.18 (cf. Gal.17 (1).177), and is itself of doubtful derivation.) [ἄδ- Nic.*Fr.*16.]

ἀδημονία, ἡ, *trouble, distress*, Epicur.*Fr.*483, *AP*12.226 (Strat.), Plu.*Num.*4: pl., Ph.2.541.

ἄδημος, ον, = ἀπόδημος, S.*Fr.*639.

ἀδημοσύνη, ἡ, rarer form for ἀδημονία, Democr.212, X.ap.*AB*80.

ἀδήμων, ον, gen. ονος, *sore-troubled*, v. sub ἀδημονέω.

ἄδην, Ep. and Ion. **ἄδην**, Adv. *to one's fill*, ἔδμεναι ἄ. Il.5.203, al.; ἐμπιμπλάμενοι σίτων ἄ. Pl.*Plt.*272c; πιοῦσ' ἄ. χορεύω *Anacreont.*14. 30. 2. c. gen., οἵ μιν ἄ. ἐλόωσι .. πολέμοιο will drive him *to satiety* of war, Il.13.315; Τρῶας ἄ. ἐλάσαι πολέμοιο 19.423; ἔτι μέν φημι ἄ. ἐλάαν κακότητος Od.5.290; ἄ. ἔλειξεν αἵματος licked *his fill* of blood, A.*Ag.*828; καὶ τούτων μὲν ἄ. Pl.*Euthphr.*11e, cf. *R.*341c, etc.; ἄ. ἔχειν τινός to have *enough of* a thing, be *weary of* it, Id.*Chrm.*153d, cf. E.*Ion*975; τοῦ φαγεῖν Arist.*Pr.*950^{a}15; ἄ. ἔχουσιν οἱ λόγοι Pl.*R.* 541b: c. part., ἄ. εἶχον κτείνοντες Hdt.9.39. 3. *unceasingly*, A.R.2.82, cf. 4.1216. 4. = ἅλις, ἄ. ἐγένοντο μύκητες Call.*Fr.*47. [ᾰ, except in the phrase ἔδμεναι ἄδην; v. sub ἀδέω.] (From sə-δην, cf. Lat. *să-tis*.)

ἀδήν (ἀδ- Hdn.Gr.2.922), ένος, ἡ, *gland*, Hp.*Art.*11; later, ὁ, Gal. *UP*3.9, al., Alex.Aphr.*Pr.*2.12, Hdn.Gr. l.c. (ŋguen, cf. Lat. *inguen*.)

ἀδηνής, ές, (δῆνος) *ignorant, inexperienced*, Semon.7.53, cj. for ἀληνής, but expl. as '*without malice prepense*' by Hsch., *EM*17.11: so in Adv. -έως *without malice*, διὰ τῆς πόλεως ἀ. γεγωνέοντες *GDI* 5653 (Chios):—hence -εια, ἡ, *ignorance*, Hsch. (-είη).

ἄδηρις, ιος, ὁ, ἡ, *without strife*, *AP*7.440 (Leon.), Epigr. in *Rev.Phil.* 19.178 (Egypt).

ἀδήριτος, ον, *without strife* or *battle*, Il.17.42. 2. *uncontested, undisputed*, Plb.1.2.3, Orph.*A.*846. Adv. -τως Plb.3.93.1, D.S.4.14, Plu.*Caes.*3. II. *not to be striven against, unconquerable*, ἀνάγκης σθένος A.*Pr.*105.

Ἅιδης or **ᾅδης**, ου, ὁ, Att.; Ep. **Ἀΐδης**, αο and εω; Dor. **Ἀΐδας**, α, used by Trag., in lyr. and anap.: gen. Ἄϊδος, dat. Ἄϊδι, Hom., Trag., v. infr.: (perh. ἀ- priv., ἰδεῖν):—in Hom. only as pr. n. *Hades*, Ζεὺς καὶ ἐγώ, τρίτατος δ' Ἀΐδης Il.15.188, cf. Hes.*Th.*455:—εἰν Ἀΐδαο δόμοισι in the *nether* world, Od.4.834; freq. εἰν, εἰς Ἀΐδαο (sc. δόμοις, δόμους), as Il.22.389, 21.48; εἰν Ἄϊδος Il.24.593; Trag. and Att. ἐν Ἅιδου, εἰς Ἅιδου (sc. οἴκῳ, οἶκον), S.*Aj.*865, Ar.*Ra.*69, etc.; Ἄϊδόσδε, Adv. *to the nether world*, Il.7.330, etc.; παρ' Ἅιδῃ, παρ' Ἅιδην, *OT*972, *OC* 1552:—hence, 2. *place of departed spirits*, first in Il.23.244 εἰσόκεν αὐτὸς .. Ἄϊδι κεύθωμαι; ἐπὶ τὸν ᾅδην Luc.*Cat.*14; εἰς ἀΐδην *AP*11.23; ἐν τῷ ᾅδῃ *Ev.Luc.*16.23. II. after Hom., *the grave, death*, ἀΐδαν λαγχάνειν, δέξασθαι, Pi.*P.*5.96, *I.*6(5).15; ᾅδης πόντιος *death* by sea, A.*Ag.*667, cf. E.*Alc.*13, *Hipp.*1047; ᾅδου πύλη, Astrol., region below the Horoscope, Vett.Val.179.13. 2. gen. ᾅδου with nouns in adjectival sense, *devilish*, θύουσαν ᾅ. μητέρ' A.*Ag.*1235; ᾅ. μάγειρος E.*Cyc.*397; *fatal, deadly*, δίκτυον, ξίφη ᾅ., A.*Ag.*1115, E.*Or.*1399. [ᾰ Hom. in all forms exc. ἄϊδος before vowels; ᾱ̈ίδης Semon.7.117, prob. in S.*OC*1689.]

ἀδήσω, v. sub ἁνδάνω.

ἀδη-φαγέω [ᾰδ], *to be greedy*, Hermipp.84; of horses, S.*Fr.*976, Isoc.6.55. **-φαγία**, ἡ, *gluttony*, Call.*Dian.*160: pl., Arist.*Fr.*144, Opp.*H.*2.218:—personified, Ἀδηφαγίας ἱερόν Polem.Hist.39. **-φάγος**, ον, (ἄδην) *gluttonous, greedy*, ἀνήρ Theoc.22.115; τὴν ἀ. νόσον S. *Ph.*313; ἀ. λύχνος, of a lamp *that burns much oil*, Alc.Com.21. 2. metaph., *devouring much money, costly*, τριήρεις Lys.*Fr.*39, cf. Philist.58; of racehorses, Pherecr.197, Ar.*Fr.*736.

ἀδῄωτος, ον, *not ravaged*, X.*HG*3.1.5.

ἀδιά-βᾰτος, ον, *not to be passed*, ποταμός, νάπη, X.*An.*2.1.11, *HG*5. 4.44; ὄρη Them.*Or.*16.206d. II. Act., *not striding, closed*, σκέλη *AB*343. **-βεβαίωτος**, ον, *unconfirmed*, Ptol.*Geog.*2.1. **-βίβαστος**, ον, Gramm., *intransitive*, A.D.*Synt.*286.6. **-βλητος**, ον, *not listening to calumny*, ἡ τῶν ἀγαθῶν φιλία ἀ. ἐστι Arist.*EN*1157^a 21; ἀνύποπτος καὶ ἀ. Plu.*Brut.*8. II. *unexceptionable*, φιλοπονία ἕξις ἀ. πρὸς πόνον Pl.*Def.*412c; τοῖς βίοις ἀ. Plu.2.4b; τὰ πρὸς τοὺς ἄλλους ἀ. App.*Samn.*4.4. Adv. -τως Just.*Nov.*137.2. **-βολος**, ον, = foreg. 1, *Stoic.*3.153. II. Pass., *unexceptionable*, *Mon.Ant.* 23.60 (Seleucia in Cilicia). **-γλυπτος**, ον, *not to be cut through*, *AB*344. **-γλυφος**, ον, *not hollowed out*, ὦτα Adam.2.29. **-γνωστος**, ον, *indistinguishable*, D.S.1.30; ἀ. τῷ χρώματι τοῦ ἐδάφους Antig.*Mir.*25(29); *hard to distinguish* or *understand*, ὀνόματα Aristid. Quint.1.5.

ἀδι-άγωγος, ον, *impossible to live with*, Ph.2.268; συνουσία 1.118.

ἀδιά-δοχος, ον, *without successor, perpetual*, βουλή Sch.Aeschin. 3.2. **-δραστος**, ον, *inevitable*, Zeno *Stoic.*1.27, Ael.*Fr.*210. **-ζευκτος**, ον, *not disjoined, inseparable*, Corn.*ND*14, Iamb. *in Nic.*pp.15,

107 P. ; ἕνωσις Procl. *in Prm.*p.521 S. ; *indistinguishable*, Phld.*D.*1.19. **-θετος,** ον, *not disposed* or *set in order*, Sch.Ar.*Nu.*1370, etc. ; στίχοι ἀ. Sch.Il.22.487. **2.** *having made no will, intestate*, Plu.*Cat.Ma.*9, D.Chr.54.4, *POxy.*105.6 (ii A.D.), al. **b.** *not disposed of by will*, *PGrenf.*1.17 (ii B.C.), *Sammelb.*4638.5.

ἀδιαίρετος, ον, *undivided*, Arist.*Pol.*1265^{b}4 ; χώρα *SIG*141.10 (Corc. Nigr.), cf. *BGU*1119.9 (i B.C.), etc. **2.** *indivisible*, like ἀμερής, Arist.*Ph.*231^{b}3, al. ; Comp., *less divisible*, *Metaph.*1052^{a}21. Adv. -τως Phryn.146 (interp.). **II.** Act., *not having divided* joint property, ἀδελφοί Sor.2.1.

ἀδιαίτητος· ἀλλότριος, ἀήθης, Phot., Suid., *AB*341.

ἀδια-κίνητος, ον, *unmoved*, Phld.*Rh.*1.366 S. **-κλειστος,** ον, *not shut off*, τοῦ οὐρανοῦ τὸ -τον J.*BJ*5.5.4.

ἀδιᾱκόνητος, ον, *not executed*, ἐκλιπεῖν ἀ. τὴν ἐπιστολήν J.*AJ*19.1.1.

ἀδιακόντιστος, ον, *which no dart can pierce*, δέρμα prob. in Ael.*VH* 13.15 (interpol., codd. -κόνιστος, which Hsch. explains ἀναίσθητος, ἄτρωτος).

ἀδιά-κοπος, ον, *unbroken, uninterrupted*, χάρακες Aristeas 139 ; συνέχεια Herod.ap.Orib.7.8.4 ; λόγος Ph.1.81, cf. Porph.*Plot.*8. Adv. -πως Hero *Def.*37, Ulp. ad D.18.308, Steph. *in Hp.*1.149 D. **-κόρευτος,** ον, *undeflowered, virginal*, Sor.1.10. **-κόσμητος,** ον, *not set in order*, D.H.3.10 ; οὐσία *Stoic.*2.189, cf. Ph.2.505 ; of lands, *not disposed of, unassigned*, J.*AJ*5.1.23. **-κρισία,** ἡ, *want of discernment*, Suid. s.v. ἀκρισία. **-κρῐτος,** ον, *undistinguishable, mixed*, Hp.*Coac.*570 ; αἷμα Arist.*Somn.*458^{a}21 (Comp.) ; *not discriminated*, Dam.*Pr.*35. Adv. -τως *without distinction, in common*, Ph.*Fr.*105 H., Hierocl. *in CA*12 p.446 M., Iamb.*Myst.*4.1, Just.*Nov.* 89.7. **b.** *promiscuous*, ἐπιμιξίαι D.H.19.1. **2.** *unintelligible*, Plb.15.12.9. **3.** *undecided*, Luc.*J.Tr.*25, *OGI*509.8 (Aphrodisias). **4.** Act., *not making due distinctions*, τὸ -τον Ph.2.664. **5.** Adv. -τως *without examination*, *POxy.*715.36 (ii A.D.). **-κωλύτως,** Adv. *without hindrance*, Herm.ap.Stob.1.49.68, *BGU*1048.19 (i A.D.). **-λειπτος,** ον, *unintermitting, incessant*, Ti. Locr.98e, *Ep.Rom.*9.2, Hierocl.p.19.55 A., Plu.2.121e, M.Ant.6.15. Adv. -τως Metrod.*Herc.*831.8, Polem.Hist.30, Plb.9.3.8, Posidon.25, Lxx 1 *Ma.*12.11, *Ep.Rom.*1.9, *PLond.*3.1166.6 (i A.D.). **-λεκτος,** ον, *without conversation*, βίος *solitary* life, Phryn.Com.18. **-ληπτεύω,** *to be lacking in comprehension, confused in mind*, Phld.*Rh.*2.184 S. **-ληπτος,** ον, *indistinct, confused*, λόγος Metrod.*Herc.*831.11, cf. 13 ; ἄδηλα καὶ ἀ. Phld.*Rh.*2.44 S. :—also of persons, *confused in mind*, ib.47 S., Id.*Po.*1676.3. Adv. -τως, opp. διειλημμένως, Id. *Mus.*p.32 K., al. **-ληψία,** *confusion, obscurity*, διανοημάτων Phld. *Rh.*2.190 S. : pl., ib.1.7 S. :—of persons, *failure to distinguish*, τινός ib.1.43 S. : abs., ib.1.204 S.

ἀδιάλλακτος, ον, *irreconcilable*, τὰ πρὸς ὑμᾶς ἀ. ὑπάρχει my relation to you *admits no reconciliation*, D.*Ep.*2.21, cf. 24.8, D.Chr.38.17, etc. Adv. -τως, ἔχειν πρός τινα D.H.6.56, cf. Plu.*Brut.*45.

ἀδια-λόγιστος, ον, *unreasoning* : c. gen., τοῦ συμφέροντος Phld.*Lib.* p.60 O. **-λῠτος,** ον, *undissolved* : *indissoluble*, Pl.*Phd.*80b ; ἕνωσις Ph.2.635 ; σύμβασις Hierocl.p.17.23 A. :—*indestructible*, Epicur.*Fr.* 356 (nisi Hermarcho tribuendum) ; στερεὰ καὶ ἀ. Id.*Nat.*14.2. **II.** *irreconcilable*. Adv. -τως, πολεμεῖν πρός τινα Plb.18.37.4. **III.** -τον, τό, = ἡλιοτρόπιον, Ps.-Dsc.4.190. **-λώβητον·** ἀβλαβές, Hsch.

ἀδι-αμάρτητος, ον, *infallible*, Gem.17.24, cf. Gal.19.595.

ἀδια-μέριστος, ον, = ἀδιαίρετος, Sch.A.R.3.1033. **-μόρφωτος,** ον, *not fully formed*, Sor.1.101 ; σάρξ Sch.Orib.22.5.3. **-νέμητος,** ον, *not to be divided*, Longin.22.3. **2.** *undivided*, Timae. 77. **-νοησία,** ἡ, *inconceivability*, Phld.*Sign.*38. **-νοητεύομαι,** *speak unintelligibly*, Sch.Ar.*Av.*1377. **-νόητος,** ον, *unintelligible*, -ητα σκώπτειν Did.ap.Sch.Ar.*V.*1309. Adv. -τως D.H. *Rh.*9.16. **2.** *inconceivable*, Pl.*Sph.*238c, Epicur.*Fr.*606, cf. *Ep.* 2 p.43 U., Phld.*Sign.*12, al., Arr.*Epict.*2.20.18, S.E.*M.*8.389. **II.** Act., *not understanding, silly*, Arist.*Fr.*90 ; *unreflecting*, Phld.*Ir.* p.23 W. ; τὸ ἀ. τοῦ πλήθους Id.*Rh.*2.40 S. Adv. -τως Pl.*Hp.Ma.* 301c.

ἀδίαντος, ον, (διαίνω) *unwetted*, ἀδιάντοισι παρειαῖς Simon.37.3 ; ἀ. ἐξ ἁλός B.16.122 ; *not bathed in sweat*, σθένος Pi.*N.*7.72. **II.** as Subst., ἀδίαντος, ὁ, *maidenhair, Adiantum Capillus-Veneris*, Orph. *A.*915 : **ἀδίαντον,** τό, Theoc.13.41 ; ἀ. [τὸ μέλαν] Thphr.*HP*7.10.5: pl., Plu.2.614b. **2.** ἀ. τὸ λευκόν, = τριχομανές, Thphr.*HP*7.14.1, Dsc.4.135.

ἀδιά-ξεστος, ον, *unpolished*, Gal.*UP*11.13. **-πάτητος,** ον, *untrodden*, πυρός *POxy.*1259.15 (iii A.D.). **-παυστος,** ον, *not to be stilled, incessant, violent*, Plb.4.39.10, Phalar.*Ep.*67.3. Adv. -τως Plb.1.57.1, Antyll.ap.Orib.4.11.14. **-πεπτος,** ον, *undigested*, Sch. Nic.*Al.*66. **-πλαστος,** ον, *as yet unformed*, Pl.*Ti.*91d, cf. Suid. s.v. φρῦνος. **-πνευστέω,** *not to evaporate*, [Gal.]10.528. **-πνευστία,** ἡ, *want of perspiration* or *suppressed perspiration*, Gal.10.763, Alex. Trall.*Febr.*1. **-πνευστος,** ον, (διαπνέω) *not ventilated*, Gal.10.745 ; *air-tight*, Asclep.ap.eund.13.159. **II.** Act., *without drawing breath*, Iamb.*VP*31.188. **-πόνητος,** ον, *undigested*, κρέα Ath.9. 402d. **-πόρευτος,** ον, *that cannot be traversed*, Simp. *in Cat.*470. 2. **-πταιστος,** ον, = ἀδιάπτωτος, Iamb.*Protr.*21.κδʹ, cf. Hierocl. *Prov.*p.463 B. **-πτωσία,** ἡ, *infallibility*, Hp.*Ep.*17, Iamb.*Protr.* 21.κʹ. **-πτωτος,** ον, *infallible*, Hp.*Decent.*12, S.E.*M.*7.110 ; ἀρχὴ ἀ. τῇ πόλει *PRyl.*77.46 (ii A.D.). Adv. -τως Plb.6.26.4, cf. *Stoic.*3.69 ; *unerringly*, of archers, Hld.9.18. **2.** *faultless*, of writers, Longin. 33.5 ; τὸ ἀ. *perfection* of style, Id.36.4 ; φράσις Diog.Bab.*Stoic.*3. 214 ; προφορά D.T.629.12. **3.** Gramm., *not using cases at random*, A.D.*Pron.*109.23. **b.** *uninflected*, *EM*643.47.

ἀδί-αρθρος, ον, faulty form for sq., Thphr.*HP*3.10.5 (Comp.). **-άρθρωτος,** ον, *not jointed* or *articulated*, Arist.*HA*579^{a}24, al. **II.** *confused*, λόγος Arr.*Epict.*1.17.1, Plu.2.378c. **2.** *not distinctly conceived, unanalysed*, Phld.*D.*1.24 (Comp.) ; δόξα Alex.Aphr. *in Metaph.*26.22. **3.** of literary style, *disjointed*, ἀ. ἐν σχήμασι Hermog.*Id.*2.11. **III.** *unorganized*, Arr.*Epict.*4.8.10. **IV.** Adv. -τως *without distinction*, Gal.16.240, cf. Alex.Aphr. *in Metaph.* 61.4, Plot.3.8.9.

ἀδια-ρίπιστος, ον, *not scattered by the winds*, Hsch. s.v. ἄκροτον. **-ρρευστος,** ον, *non-deliquescent*, φάρμακον Gal.12.840. **-ρρηκτος,** ον, *not torn in pieces*, gloss on ἄρρηκτος, *EM*149.12. **-ρροια,** ἡ, *constipation*, Hp.ap.Erot.48. **-σειστος,** ον, *not shaken about*, Gal.19. 81 ; gloss on ἀτίνακτος, Sch.Opp.*H.*4.415. **-σκέδαστος,** ον, *not scattered*, Sch.Ar.*Th.*1027. **-σκέπτως,** Adv. *inconsiderately*, Aen.Tact. 29.12 (prob. l.). **-σκευος,** ον, *unequipt*, ἵππος Anon.ap.Suid. **-σκοπος,** ον, *not perspicuous*, Sch.A.*Ch.*816. **-σπαστος,** ον, *not torn asunder, uninterrupted, unbroken*, X.*Ages.*1.4, Plb.1.34.5 ; *inseparable*, Dam.*Pr.*418, cf. Olymp.Alch.p.77 B. Adv. -τως Steph. *in Hp.* 1.65 D., Hsch. **-σταλτος,** ον, *not clearly unfolded*, Sch.Od.19. 560. **-στασία,** ἡ, *continuity*, Iamb. *in Nic.*p.57 P. **-στᾰτος,** ον, *continuous*, Antipho Soph.24 ; ἀγάπησις Andronic.Rhod. p.513 M. Adv. -τως *without intermission*, Ph.1.342,501, etc. **b.** *without distinctions* or *intervals*, Plot.3.7.2, Dam.*Pr.*105,370. **2.** Gramm., of ι in diphthongs, *inseparable*, not forming a distinct syllable, A.D.*Pron.*86.21. Adv. -τως, σύλληψις συμφώνων μετὰ φωνήεντος . . ἀ. λεγομένη Sch.D.T.p.48 H. **II.** *without extension* or *dimension*, Plu.2.601c, Plot.1.5.7, Alex.Aphr. *in Top.*31.18. Adv. -τως Procl. *in Prm.*p.543 S., *Inst.*176. **-στικτος,** ον, *undistinguished, unvarying*, Ph.2.297. Adv., *Gloss.* **-στολος,** ον, Gramm., *not distinguished*, A.D.*Pron.*11.26. Adv. -λως, λ[έγο]ντας Phld.*Rh.*1.53 S., cf. Phoeb.*Fig.*1.3, Porph.*Abst.*2.37. **-στομος,** ον, (διὰ στόμα) *not currently named*, *PPar.*5.15 (ii B.C.), al. **-στρέπτως,** Adv. *without turning, continuously*, Hp.*Fract.*19. **-στροφος,** ον, *incapable of turning* : metaph., *rigid, inexorable*, νόμος Orph.*H.*64.9 ; *incontrovertible*, προλήψεις Procl.*Hyp.*5.20 ; of remedies, *infallible*, Aët.3.91,109 ; Gramm., *strictly accurate*, S.E.*M.*1.187. **II.** *not distorted*, Arist.*Pr.*958^{a}12 ; κανών Plu.2.780b ; θώρηξ Aret.*SD*1.12. Adv. -φως Gal.18(2).334. **2.** metaph., *not perverted*, of persons, Ph.*Fr.*14 H., Lxx 3 *Ma.*3.3 ; ζῷα S.E.*P.*3.194. Adv. -φως *in the absence of perversion*, i. e. *by natural instinct*, Demetr.Lac.*Herc.*1012. 70 ; *straightforwardly*, ἀ. καὶ ἀπανούργως S.E.*M.*2.77. **b.** of judgements, etc., *unperverted*, κρίσεις D.H.*Th.*55 ; λόγοι, ἔννοιαι, Procl. *in Alc.*p.4 C., *Theol.Pl.*1.17. **III.** Adv. -φως *without molestation*, ἀ. καὶ ἀταράχως μεῖναι ἐν τοῖς ἰδίοις *PLond.*5.1674 (vi A.D.) ; ἀφίεσθαι ἀζημίως καὶ ἀ. *Cod.Just.*9.47.26.7. **-σφαλτος,** ον, *free from error*, μέθοδοι Hero *Geep.*164. Adv. -τως Ps.-Dioph.p.xxi H. **-σχιστος,** ον, *not cloven*, Arist.*HA*532^{b}13. **-σωστος,** ον, *not preserved*, βιβλίον Ptol.*Tetr.*47. **-τακτος,** ον, *disorganized*, ὄχλοι, πόλις, Artapan.ap.Alex.Polyh.14, D.H.3.10. Adv. -τως Simp. *in Cat.* 379.26. **2.** *unclassified*, πρόσοδοι *BCH*6.14 (Delos, ii B.C.). **-τμητος,** ον, *not cut in pieces*, Aen.Tact.32.1. **-τρεπτος,** ον, *not to be turned aside*, c. gen., γνώμης Sch.Luc.*Herm.*53. **II.** *headstrong*, Lxx *Si.*26.10. Adv. -τως Lxx v. l. ibid., Jul.*Or.*6. 197b. **-τρεψία,** ἡ, *shamelessness*, Caligula ap.Suet.*Calig.* 29. **-τύπωτος,** ον, *unshapen*, D.S.1.10, Ocell.2.3, Ph.2.317, al. ; ψυχή 1.50.

ἀδίαυλος, ον, *with no way back, without return*, of the nether world, E.*Fr.*868 ; Φερσεφόνας ἀδίαυλον ὑπὸ . . δόμον *Epigr.Gr.*244.9 (Cyzicus).

ἀδιά-φθαρτος, ον, = ἀδιάφθορος I, Pl.*Ap.*34b, *Lg.*951c, Ph.1. 408. **II.** = sq. II, Epicur.*Fr.*267, Gal.2.27. **-φθορος,** ον, *not affected by decay*, Antyll.ap.Orib.46.22.3 ; *uncorrupted, chaste*, Pl.*Phdr.*252d ; ἀπ' ὀρθῆς . . καὶ ἀδιαφθόρου τῆς ψυχῆς D.18.298, cf. Men. 984, D.S.1.59, Plu.2.5e. Adv. -ρως, ἐρᾶσθαι Aeschin.1.137. **2.** of judges, *incorruptible*, Pl.*Lg.*768b ; of witnesses, Arist.*Rh.*1376^a 17 ; of magistrates, Id.*Pol.*1286^{a}39 (Comp.), cf. *IG*2.240^{b}13. Sup. Adv. -ώτατα Pl. l. c. **II.** *imperishable*, Pl.*Phd.*106e. **-φορέω,** *to be indifferent*, κατά τι S.E.*P.*1.191 ; πρός τι M.Ant.11.16 ; ἀδιαφορεῖ impers., ἐάν . . ἐάν . . Ph.2.243 : c. inf., A.D.*Pron.*45.22. **2.** Gramm., *not to agree*, in case, gender, etc., ib.68.15, al. **II.** ἀ. τινός *not to differ from*, Ph.1.414. **III.** personal, *bring about no change*, Gal.1.194. **IV.** Math., *to be negligible*, Procl.*Hyp.* 3.31 ; ἀ. πρὸς αἴσθησιν *not to differ* appreciably, ib.3.15. **V.** of persons, *to be neglected, uncared for*, *PLond.*2.144 (i A.D.). **-φορητικός,** ή, όν, *like indifference* : τὸ ἀ. = ἀδιαφορία, Arr.*Epict.*2.1. 14. **-φόρητος,** ον, *not evaporating* or *perspiring*, Alex.Trall.2. **II.** *showing no difference*, Iamb. *in Nic.*p.76 P. **-φορία,** ἡ, *indifference*, Stoic, of the moral agent, Aristo *Stoic.*1.83, Chrysipp.ib.3.9, cf. Cic. *Acad.Pr.*2.42.130, S.E.*P.*1.152 ; *absence of difference*, Syr. *in Metaph.* 122.1, cf. sq. **II.** *neglect*, Hierocl. *in CA*7 p.430 M. **III.** *equivalence of signification*, Eust.150.25. **-φορος,** ον, *not different*, Arist.*Rh.*1373^{a}33 ; τοῖς ὁμοίοις καὶ ἀ. Id.*Cael.*310^{b}5 ; *indistinguishable*, ὅμοιον καὶ ἀ. Epicur.*Nat.*15 G. **2.** in Logic, ἀδιάφορα, τά, *individual objects*, as having no logical *differentia*, ἀ. ὧν ἀδιαίρετον τὸ εἶδος Arist. *Metaph.*1016^{a}18 ; ἀ. εἴδει *Top.*121^{b}15 ; κατὰ τὸ εἶδος ib.103^{a}11. **3.** *undiscriminating*, ὀνομασία Epicur.*Nat.*14.10. **II.** *indifferent* ;

in Stoic philosophy, τὰ ἀ. things *neither good nor bad*, Zeno *Stoic.* 1.47,48, cf. Cic.*Fin.*3.16.53, Epict.*Ench.*32, etc., cf. S.E.*P.*3.177 sq.: Sup., Phld.*Rh.*1.129 S. Adv. -φως, ἔχειν to be *indifferent*, of the moral agent, Aristo *Stoic.*1.79. **III.** in metre, *common*, Heph.4, cf. Sch.Pi.p.15 Böckh. **IV.** of persons, *making no distinction*, πρὸς πάντα ξένον καὶ δημότην Dicaearch.1.14. **2.** *steadfast, unwearying*, Ant.Lib.41.2. **V.** Math., *negligible*, πρός τι Procl.*Hyp.*4.61; ἀ. πρὸς αἴσθησιν *not differing* sensibly, Aristarch.Sam.4. Adv., Hipparch.3.5.7. **VI.** Adv. -φως *without discrimination*, D.H.*Dem.* 56, S.E.*P.*3.225. **-φρακτος**, ον, *with no divisions* or *joints*, Thphr. *HP*1.5.3, 8.5.2. Adv. -τως ib.6.5.3. **-χῠτος**, ον, (διαχέω) *not softened by cooking*, Thphr.*CP*4.12.2; *not dissolved*, Dsc.5.79. **II.** *not diffuse* or *extravagant*, of persons, Hp.*Decent.*3:—of style, Longin.34.3. **-χώρητος**, ον, *without evacuation*, κοιλίη Hp.*Acut.* (*Sp.*)38; *not passing through the bowels*, Sor.1.125. **-χώριστος**, ον, *unseparated, undistinguished*, *EM*538.34, Suid. Adv. -τως Hsch. s.v. ἀδιασπάστως. **-ψευστος**, ον, *not deceitful*, D.S.5.37; of καταληπτικὴ φαντασία, Sphaer.*Stoic.*1.141, cf. M.Ant.4.49, Iamb. *Protr.*21. Adv. -τως S.E.*M.*7.191, Ruf.*Fr.*68.10.

ἀδίδακτος, ον, *untaught, ignorant*, Ps.-Phoc.89: c. gen., ἀ. ἐρώτων *AP*5.121 (Diod.), cf. Hp.*Alim.*39. **2.** *unpractised, untrained*, of a chorus, D.21.17. **II.** *untaught*, τοῖς ἀφ' αὑτοῦ καὶ ἀ. πάθεσι Plu.2.968c, cf. Luc.*Hist.Conscr.*34; *that cannot be taught*, Philostr.*VA*5.36. **2.** ἀ. δρᾶμα *not yet acted* (v. διδάσκω III) Ath.6.270a. **III.** Adv. -τως *without teaching*, Phld.*Rh.* 2.93 S., Juba 32, Plu.2.673f; οὐκ ἀ. οὐδὲ αὐτοφυῶς Ph.*Fr.*70 H.

ἀδι-έγγυος, ον, *not covered by security*, μέρος τῆς ὠνῆς *PRev.Laws* 17.3 (iii B.C.). **-έκβατος**, ον, = sq., ἕρκος Sch.Opp.*H.*4.117. **-έκδῠτος**, ον, *not to be escaped*, Apollon.*Lex.* s.v. νήδυμος. **-έξακτος**, ον, *not carried through, undone*, μηδὲν ἀ. ἀπολείποντες *OGI*335.34 (Perg.). **-εξέργαστος**, ον, *not wrought out*, τόπος Isoc.5.109. **-εξέταστος**, ον, *that will not stand examination*, λόγοι Lxx *Si.*21.18. **-εξήγητος**, ον, *indescribable*, πλῆθος Ph.1.407, prob. in *IG*5(1).1359 (Messenia, i B.C.):—*inexhaustible*, ταῖς ἡμετέραις ἐπιβολαῖς Dam.*Pr.*178. **-εξίτητος**, ον, (διέξειμι) *that cannot be exhausted, infinite in extent* or *duration*, Arist.*Ph.*207^{b}29, cf. Alex.Aphr.*in Top.* 86.27, Plot.2.4.7, al.; αἰών Ph.1.554. **2.** *with no outlet*, ἄγυια Orib.9.20.3. **-εξόδευτος**, ον, *having no outlet*, λαβύρινθος Eust. 1688.37, cf. Sch.E.*Or.*25. **-έξοδος**, ον, *that cannot be gone through*, τὸ ἄπειρον Arist.*Ph.*204^{a}14. **2.** *having no outlet*, of places, App.*Mith.*100, Plu.2.957d. **II.** Act., *unable to get out*, *AP* 11.395 (Nicarch.), cf. Plu.2.679b, Ocell.1.15. **-έργαστος**, ον, *not wrought out, unfinished*, Isoc.12.268, Poll.6.143. Adv. -τως ib.144. **-ερεύνητος**, ον, *inscrutable*, Pl.*Ti.*25d. **2.** *uninvestigated*, Ph.1.470, etc. **II.** of persons, *not searched*, Plu.*Dio* 19. **-ευκρίνητος**, ον, *obscure, lacking in order*, of style, Hermog. *Id.*2.11; ὕλη Heraclit.*All.*48. **-εχής**, ές, = ἀζηχής, Sch.Opp.*H.* 3.129. **-ήγητος**, ον, *indescribable*, X.*Cyr.*8.7.22, D.17.29, Cic.*Att.* 13.9.1. Adv. -τως *PMag.Lond.*125.13. **II.** *not related*, Hld. 5.16. **-ήθητος**, ον, *not filtered* or *strained*, πτισάνη ἀ. gruel *with the meal in it*, Hp.*Acut.*7.

ἀδῐκαίαρχος, ον, = ἄδικος ἄρχων Cic.*Att.*2.12 (with play on the name of the historian Dicaearchus).

ἀδῐκαιοδότητος, ον, *where no justice can be got*, Σικελία D.S.39. 20.

ἀδίκαστος, ον, *without judgement given*, Pl.*Ti.*51c; δίκη *IG*12(2). 530 (Eresos); *undecided*, Luc.*Bis Acc.*23. Adv. -τως *without judgement*, Aesop.223.

ἀδίκευσις, εως, ἡ, *wrongdoing*, = ἐνέργεια κατ' ἀδικίαν, *Stoic.*3. 25.

ἀδῐκέω, Aeol. -ήω Sapph.1.20, Dor. -ίω *Tab.Heracl.*1.138: Ion. impf. ἠδίκεον or -ευν Hdt.1.121:—**Pass.**, fut. in med. form ἀδικήσομαι E.*IA*1436, Th.5.56, etc.; also ἀδικηθήσομαι Apollod.1.9.23, etc.:—*to be* ἄδικος, *do wrong* (defined by Arist.*Rh.*1368^{b}6 τὸ βλάπτειν ἑκόντα παρὰ τὸν νόμον, cf. ἀδίκημα), τῶν ἀδικησάντων τίσις ἔσσεται *those who have sinned*, *h.Cer.*367; freq. in Hdt. and Att.; τἀδικεῖν *wrongdoing*, S.*Ant.*1059; τὸ μὴ ἀδικεῖν *righteous dealing*, A.*Eu.*85,749:—in legal phrase, *do wrong in the eye of the law*, the particular case being added in part., as Σωκράτης ἀ... ποιῶν.. καὶ διδάσκων Pl.*Ap.*19b, cf. X.*Mem.*1.1.1: c. acc. cogn., ἀδικίαν, ἀδικήματα, etc., Pl.*R.*344c, 409a, cf. Arist.*Rh.*1389^{b}7; also ἀ. οὐδὲν ἄξιον δεσμοῦ Hdt.3.145; ἀ. πολλά, μεγάλα, etc., Pl.*Smp.*188a, al.; οὐδέν, μηδὲν ἀ. ib., al.:—ἀ. περὶ τὰ μυστήρια D.21.175, cf. *IG*2.811^{c}154; ἀ. εἰς πόλιν, κτῆμα, Lib. *Or.*15.39, 31.7:—in games or contests, *play foul*, Ar.*Nu.*25, Arist. *EN*1123^{b}32. **b.** in pres., *to be in the wrong*, εἰ μὴ ἀδικῶ γε *if I am* not *mistaken*, Pl.*Chrm.*156a. **II.** trans. c. acc. pers., *wrong, injure*, Archil.*Supp.*2.13, Sapph.1.20, Epich.286, Hdt.1.112, etc.:—*ruin*, of a girl, Men.*Georg.*30: c. dupl. acc., *wrong* one *in* a thing, Ar. *Pl.*460; ἃ πολλοὺς ὑμῶν ἠδίκηκεν D.21.129; μείζον' ἢ ἐλάττονα ἀ. τινά 20.124; ἀ. ἀδικίαν περί τινας Pl.*Lg.*854e:—Pass., *to be wronged, injured*, μὴ δῆτ' ἀδικηθῶ S.*OC*174; ἀ. εἴς τι E.*Med.*265; μέγιστα ἀ. Aeschin.3.84; οὔτ' ἀδικεῖ οὔτ' ἀδικεῖται Pl.*Smp.*196b, etc.; pres. ἀδικεῖται, -ούμενος used for the pf. ἠδίκηται, -ημένος (v. supr. I), Antipho 4.4.9, Pl.*R.*359a: c. acc., *to be defrauded of*, μισθὸν ἀδικίας v.l. in 2*Ep.Pet.*2.13. **2.** *harm, injure*, ἀ. γῆν Th.2.71, etc.; ἵππον X.*Eq.*6.3; esp. in Medical sense, ἄνθρωπον Hp.*Nat.Hom.*9; νεφρούς Diph.Siph.ap.Ath.2.62f; τέμνειν καὶ θλᾶν καὶ ὁπωσοῦν ἄλλως ἀ. Gal. *UP*13.8, cf. Archig.ap.Philum.*Ven.*14.

ἀδίκη, ἡ, = ἀκαλήφη, Ps.-Dsc.4.93.

ἀδίκ-ημα, ατος, τό, (ἀδικέω) *wrong done*, Hdt.1.2,100, etc.: properly, *intentional wrong*, opp. ἁμάρτημα and ἀτύχημα, Arist.*EN* 1135^{b}20 sq., *Rh.*1374^{b}8; ἀ. ὥρισται τῷ ἑκουσίῳ Id.*EN*1135^{a}19: c. gen., *wrong done to*.., ἀ. τῶν νόμων D.21.225: also ἀ. πρός τινα Arist.*Rh.*1373^{b}21; ἀ. εἴς τι D.37.58; περί τι Plu.2.159c:—ἐν ἀδικήματι θέσθαι to consider as *a wrong*, Th.1.35; ἀ. θεῖναί τι D.14.37; ψηφίζεσθαί τι ἐν ἀ. εἶναι Hyp.*Eux.*26. **2.** *error of judgement*, dub. in Plb.9.26^{a}.7. **II.** *that which is got by wrong, ill-gotten goods*, Pl.*R.*365e, *Lg.*906d. **-ητέον**, *one ought to do wrong*, Pl.*R.*365e; φαμὲν ἑκόντας ἀ. εἶναι Id.*Cri.*49a. **-ητής**, ὁ, *wronger, injurer*, Eust. 756.58. **-ητικός**, ή, όν, *disposed to do wrong*, Plu.2.562d. Adv. -κῶς Stoic.ap.Stob.2.7.11^{m}. **-ήω**, v. ἀδικέω. **-ία**, Ion. -ίη, ἡ, *wrongdoing, injustice*, ἀδικίης ἄρχειν Hdt.1.130, cf. 4.1, E.*Or.*26, Pl.*Grg.*477c, al.; τύχῃ μᾶλλον ἢ ἀδικίᾳ Antipho 6.1; '*foul*' in racing, Anon.*in SE*30.15. **II.** *wrongful act, offence*, Hdt.6.136; καταγνόντες αὐτῶν ἀδικίαν And.1.3:—in pl., Pl.*Phd.*82a, etc. **-ιον**, τό, = ἀδίκημα, Hdt.5.89, cf. *IG*7.235 (pl.) (Orop.); esp. -ίου γραφή suit for *malversation*, Arist.*Ath.*54.2, cf. Plu.*Per.*32; also, *damage*, *PTaur.*4.15 (iii B.C.), cf. *PPar.*14.44 (iii B.C.).

ἀδῐκο-δοξέω, *seek fame by unworthy means*, D.S.31.6. **-δοξία**, ἡ, *evil design*, Plb.22.17.7, *Fr.*95. **-κρισία**, ἡ, *unjust judgement*, Heph.Astr.3.34. **-μαχέω**, *fight unfairly*, esp. in the law-courts, Alciphr.3.29; dub. in Poll.3.154. **-μᾰχία**, ἡ, *unfair fighting*, Arist.*SE*171^{b}23, cf. Ascl.*in Metaph.*243.9. **-μαχος**, ον, of horses, *obstinate*, X.ap.*AB*344 (perh. fr. *Cyr.*2.2.26). **-μήχᾰνος**, ον, *plotting injustice*, Ar.*Fr.*697. **-πήμων**, ον, *unjustly harming*, *AB* 343. **-πρᾱγέω**, = ἀδικέω, *act wrongly*, Plu.2.501a, Ph.2. 329. **-πράγημα**, τό, *wrong action*, Stoic.ap.Stob.2.7.11^{e}, Phld. *Piet.*19 G. **-πρᾱγής**, Ion. -πρηγής, ές, *acting wrongly*, Perict.ap. Stob.4.28.19.

ἄδῐκος, ον, (δίκη) of persons, *wrongdoing, unrighteous, unjust*: ἄνθρωποι Hes.*Op.*260: Comp. -ώτερος ib.272; δίκαν ἐξ ἀδίκων ἀπαιτῶ A.*Ch.*398 (lyr.): Sup. -ώτατος S.*Tr.*1011 (lyr.): ἄ. εἴς τι *unjust in* a thing, ἔς τινα *towards* a person, Hdt.2.119; εἰς χρήματα X. *Cyr.*8.8.6; περί τινα ib.27; ἄ. [ἐν τῷ ἀστραγαλίζειν] one who *plays unfairly*, Pl.*Alc.*1.110b: c. inf., *so unjust as to*.., *Ep.Heb.*6.10. **2.** ἄ. ἵπποι *obstinate, unmanageable*, X.*Cyr.*2.2.26; ἄ. γνάθος the *hard* mouth of a horse, Id.*Eq.*3.5. **II.** of things, *unjust, unrighteous*, ἔργα Hes.*Op.*334, Hdt.1.5; ἔργματα Thgn.380, Sol.13.12; ἄδικα φρονέειν Thgn.395; ἄ. λόγος freq. in Ar.*Nu.*; ἄρχειν χειρῶν ἀ. begin *an assault*, Antipho 4.2.1, Lys.4.11, cf. X.*Cyr.*1.5.13, D.47.39; τὸ δίκαιον καὶ τὸ ἄ., τὰ δίκαια καὶ τὰ ἄ. right and *wrong*, Pl.*Grg.*460a, etc.; πλοῦτος ἄ. *ill-gotten, unrighteous*, Isoc.1.38; ζυγὸν ἄ. Lxx *Am.*8.5; νομὴ ἄ. οὐδὲν ἰσχύει *PTeb.*286.7 (ii A.D.); ἡ ἄ... συναγωγὴ ἀνδρὸς καὶ γυναικός the *unrighteous* union, Pl.*Tht.*150a; ἄ. δίκη *vexatious* suit, Cratin.19 D. **2.** of the punishment of wrongdoing, Ζεὺς νέμων ἄδικα κακοῖς A.*Supp.*404 (lyr.), cf. E.*Or.*647. **III.** ἄ. ἡμέρα, i.e. ἄνευ δικῶν, a day *on which the courts were shut*, Luc.*Lex.*9: δίκαιος ἄ. *who has not appeared in court*, Archipp.46. **IV.** Adv. -κως Sol.13.7, A.*Ag.*1546; τοὺς ἀ. θνῄσκοντας S.*El.*113 (anap.); εἴτε ὧν δὴ δικαίως εἴτε ἀ. *jure an injuria*, Hdt.6.137; δικαίως καὶ ἀ. Pl. *Lg.*743b; οὐκ ἀ. not *without reason*, *h.Merc.*316, Simon.89.3, Pl.*Phd.* 72a.

ἀδῐκό-τροπος, ον, *of unjust disposition*, Crates Com.*Fr.inc.*7 M. **-χειρ**, χειρος, ὁ, ἡ, *with unrighteous hand*, S.*Fr.*977. **-χρήματος**, ον, *with ill-gotten wealth*, Crates Com.42.

ἀδῐνός [ᾰ], ή, όν, radic. sense, *close, thick*: hence in Hom., **1.** *crowded, thronging*, ἁ. κῆρ, like πυκιναὶ φρένες, in physical sense, Il.16.481, Od.19.516; of bees, flies, sheep, Il.2.87,469, Od.1. 92. **2.** *vehement, loud*, of sounds, ἁ. γόος Il.18.316; Σειρῆνες ἁ. the *loud-voiced* Sirens, Od.23.326. Adv. -νῶς *frequently*, or *loudly, vehemently*, ἁ. ἀνενείκατο Il.19.314: neut. as Adv., ἁδινὸν γοόωσα Od.4.721; ἁ. μυκώμεναι 10.413: pl., ἁδινὰ στεναχίζων Il. 23.225; κλαῖ' ἁ. 24.510: Comp. ἁδινώτερον Od.16.216:—rare in Lyr. and Trag., ἁ. δάκος *a deep* bite, Pi.*P.*2.53; ἁ. δάκρυα *thick-falling* tears, S.*Tr.*848 (lyr.); βίοτος ἁ. *abundant*, Tim.*Pers.*29; and freq. in A.R., ἁ. ὕπνος, κῶμα *abundant, deep* sleep, 3.616,748; ἁ. εὐνή *frequent* wedded joys, 3.1206. (Aristarch. wrote ἀδ-, cf. ἁδρός.)

ἄδιξις, ἡ, *agreement* (Tarent.), Hsch. (ϝαδ-, cf. Hsch. s.v. γάδιξις.)

ἀδι-όδευτος, ον, *not to be travelled through*, δυσχωρίαι Them.*Or.*16. 206d, cf. Charito 7.3. **-οικησία**, ἡ, *want of management*, Vett.Val. 240.15. **-οίκητος**, ον, *unarranged*, D.24.28, cf. *IG*5(2).433 (Megalopolis, ii B.C.); *undigested*, Gal.19.217, *Hippiatr.*31:—of property, = ἐκτὸς μισθώσεως, *PPetr.*3p.198 (iii B.C.). **-οπος**, ον, *without commander*, of a ship, A.*Fr.*269. **-όρᾱτος**, ον, *not to be seen through*, Poll.5.150. **-οργάνωτος**, ον, *unorganized*, Iamb.*VP*17. 73. **-όρθωτος**, ον, *not corrected, not set right*, D.4.36:—of books, *unrevised*, Cic.*Att.*13.21a.1. **II.** *irremediable*, ὁρμή D.S.37.3; δουλεία App.*BC*3.90, cf. D.L.5.66; ἀδιόρθωτα ἀδικεῖν D.H.6.20. Adv. -τως D.S.29.25. **-οριστία**, ἡ, *indefiniteness*, Nicom.ap.Phot.*Bibl.* p.143 B. **-όριστος**, ον, in Logic, *indesignate*, Arist.*APr.*26^{b}23; *undefined*, ἀ. ἀπολέλοιπε τὴν ἀρετὴν τοῦ ποιητοῦ Phld.*Po.*1425.1, al.; *indefinite*, ἄδηλον καὶ ἀ. Arist.*PA*639^{a}22, cf. Dam.*Pr.*37, al. Adv. -τως Arist.*Ph.*184^{b}11, al.; *vaguely, loosely*, Anon.*in SE*62.31.

ἀδιούνιος ταῦρος· ὁ Ἀπόλλων ὑπὸ τῶν Κρητῶν, *AB*344, Phot.

ἀδιπλ-ασίαστος, ον, *not doubled*, of letters, Eust.781.15. Adv. -τως Id.870.63. **-αστος**, = foreg., Eust.763.25. **-ωτος**, ον, = foreg., Id.185.34.

ἄδις· ὡς Ἀπίων, ἀθρόοι· καὶ ἐσχάρα, Hsch. **ἄδισκον**· κυκεῶνα (Maced.), Id.

ἀδίστακτος, ον, *undoubted, undisputed*, *PTeb.*124.26 (ii B.C., written -αστος), Phld.*Mus.*p.80 K. Adv. -τως *AP*12.151, Sch.A.R.2.62, Ptol.*Geog.*1.4. **II.** Act., *undoubting*: hence, *instinctive*, v. l. for ἀδίδακτος I (q.v.), Pall.*in Hp.*2.127 D. Adv. -τως *unhesitatingly*, Phld.*Rh.*1.133 S., Syr.*in Metaph.*73.18, Procl.*in Prm.*p.756 S.

ἀδίστονον· οἰκτρὸν στένοντα, Hsch., *EM*18.30.

ἀδιύλιστος, ον, (διυλίζω) *not strained* or *filtered*, Gal.13.285.

ἀδίχαστος, ον, (δῐχάζω) *not to be cut in two*, Nicom.*Ar.*1.9.

ἀδιψ-έω, *to be free from thirst*, Hp.*Coac.*599. **-ος**, ον, *not thirsty, not suffering from thirst*, Hp.*Epid.*3.17.ιϛ', E.*Cyc.*574, Arist.*PA*669a34, Clearch.74. Adv. -ψως Hp.*Epid.*3.13. **II.** Act., *quenching thirst*, Hp.*Acut.*15 (Sup.),59, Diph.Siph.ap.Ath.2.69f. **2.** *not causing thirst*, Xenocr.34. **III. ἄδιψον**, τό, = γλυκυρρίζα, Dsc.3.5; *adipsos*, a kind of *date*, gathered unripe, Plin.*HN*12.103.

ἀδίωκτος, ον, *not to be eliminated, irremovable*, Syn.Alch.p.63 B.

ἀδιώμοτος, ον, *not feeling bound by an oath*, Procop.*Arc.*5.

ἀδμαίνειν· ὑγιαίνειν, ζῆν, Hsch. **ἀδμενίδες**, αἱ, = δοῦλαι, *EM*18.32. **ἀδμεύειν**, = ἀδμαίνειν, *EM*18.31, Suid. **ἀδμηλοῖ**· ἀφανίζει, Hsch.

ἀδμ-ής, ῆτος, ὁ, ἡ, poet. for ἀδάματος, (Hom. only in Od.), of maidens, *unwedded*, παρθένος ἀδμής 6.109,228; ἀδμῆτας ἀδελφάς S.*OC*1056 (lyr.). **2.** of animals, *unbroken*, ἡμίονοι.. ἀδμῆτες Od.4.637. **3.** c. gen., ἀδμᾶτες νούσων *unsubdued by*.., B.*Fr.*19. **-ῆτις**, ιδος, ἡ, v.l. for ἀδμήτη in Il.23.655:—*virgin*, Benndorf-Niemann *Reise in Lykien* p.77. **-ητος**, η, ον, poet. for ἀδάματος, in Hom. only in fem. and of cattle, *unbroken*, βοῦν ἦνιν.. ἀδμήτην, ἣν οὔ πω ὑπὸ ζυγὸν ἤγαγεν ἀνήρ Il.10.293, Od.3.383; ἵππον.. ἑξέτε' ἀδμήτην Il.23.266; ἡμίονον ib.655. **2.** *unwedded*, of maidens, παρθένῳ ἀδμήτῃ *h.Ven.*82, cf. 133, A.*Supp.*149; of Artemis, τὰν αἰὲν ἀδμήταν S.*El.*1239 (lyr.); of Atalanta, τῆς πρόσθεν ἀ. Id.*OC*1321.

ἀδμολίη, ἡ, *uncertainty*, Call.*Fr.*338 (-μωλ- Suid.). **ἀδμωλεί**· χωρὶς δόλου ἢ δουλείας, Suid. **ἀδμωλή**, ἡ, = ἄγνοια, Hdn.Gr.1.324, cf. Hsch. **ἀδμωλῶ**· ἀκηδιῶ, Suid.:—also **ἀδμωλεῖν**· ἀγνοεῖν ἢ ἀγνωμονεῖν ἢ ἀκηδιᾶν, *EM*18.33.

ἄδμωνες or **ἄδμωες**, οἱ, a kind of *sea-fish*, Opp.*H.*3.371,380.

ἀδνός, Cret. for ἁγνός, Hsch.

Ἀιδοβάτης, ου, ὁ, *one who has gone to the nether world*, prob. l. for ἀγδαβάται, A.*Pers.*924 (lyr.).

ἀιδόθεν, Adv. *from the nether world*, Hermesian.7.3.

ἀδοιάστως, (δοιάζω) *without doubt*, Anacr.95. [οἱ l. c.]

ἀδοκεῖ· ἀδοκήτως διακείμενος, Hsch.

ἀδόκητος, ον, *unexpected*, Hes. (v. infr.); τὰν ἀ. χάριν S.*OC*249 (lyr.); τὰ δοκηθέντ' οὐκ ἐτελέσθη, τῶν δ' ἀ. πόρον ηὗρε θεός E.*Med.*1418 (also in *Alc.*, *Ba.*, *Andr.*, *Hel.*, ad fin.); ξυμφορὰ ἀ. Th.7.29, etc.; τὸ ἀ. *surprise*, Id.4.36, al. **II.** ἀδόκητον καὶ δοκέοντα either *inglorious and glorious*, or *unexpecting and expectant*, Pi.*N.*7.31, cf. *Trag.Adesp.*482 (lyr.):—*unexpecting*, Memn.28.2, cf. Nonn.*D.*31.209. **III.** Adv. -τως Th.4.17, Phld.*Ir.*p.49 W.; ἀδόκητα, as Adv., Hes.*Fr.*79, E.*Ph.*311; ἀπὸ τοῦ ἀδοκήτου Th.6.47; ἐκ τοῦ ἀ. D.H.3.64.

ἀδοκία· ἀπροσδοκία, Hsch.

ἀδοκίμ-αστος, ον, *not approved*, Lys.14.8, 15.11, Aeschin.3.15, etc.; πρᾶγμα D.H.11.57; τὸ ἀ. Onos.*Praef.*7. **-ος**, ον, *not legal tender, not current*, of coin, Pl.*Lg.*742a; *not approved*, of horses, Arist.*Ath.*49.1. **2.** *unsatisfactory, unconvincing*, of a statement, Ph.*Bel.*76.47, Alex.Aphr.*in Top.*576.14. **3.** *disreputable*, λακίσματ' ἀδόκιμ' ὀλβίοις ἔχειν E.*Tr.*497; μοῦσα Pl.*Lg.*829d, cf. D.25.36, *Ep.Rom.*1.28. Adv. -μως Poll.5.160. **4.** of persons, Pl.*R.*618b; *discredited, reprobate*, X.*Lac.*3.3, 2*Ep.Tim.*3.8, etc.

ἀδο-λεσχέω [ᾰ], *talk idly, prate*, Eup.353, Pl.*Phd.*70c, X.*Oec.*11.3, etc.; ἱκανῶς ἡμῖν ἠδολεσχήσθω ἐπὶ τοῦ πάροντος Epicur.*Nat.*28.13. **II.** generally, *talk*, Lxx *Ps.*68(69).12. **III.** *meditate*, ib.*Ge.*24.63, *Ps.*118(119).15, al. **-λέσχης**, ου, ὁ, *prater, idle talker*, esp. of reputed sophists: Σωκράτην, τὸν πτωχὸν ἀ. Eup.352, cf. Ar.*Nu.*1485; ἢ Πρόδικος ἢ τῶν ἀ. εἷς γέ τις Id.*Fr.*490; ἀ. τις σοφιστής Pl.*Plt.*299b, cf. *Tht.*195b, *R.*488e: generally, *talker, babbler*, Thphr.*Char.*3.2, Arist.*EN*1117b35, etc. **II.** in good sense, *subtle reasoner*, Pl.*Cra.*401b. [ᾱ- in Eup. and Ar. ll. c.; cf. ἀδέω, λέσχη.] **-λεσχία** [ᾰ], ἡ, *prating, garrulity*, Ar.*Nu.*1480, Isoc.13.8, Pl.*Tht.*195c, Arist.*Rh.*1390a9, Thphr.*Char.*3: pl., Simp.*in Ph.*1141.8. **II.** *keenness, subtlety*, Pl.*Phdr.*269e. **III.** *conversation, talk*, Lxx 4*Ki.*9.11, *Ps.*54(55).2. **-λεσχικός** [ᾰ], ἡ, όν, *prating*, τὸ -κόν *garrulity*, Pl.*Sph.*225d, Procl.*in Prm.*p.501 S. **-λεσχος** [ᾰ], ον, = ἀδολέσχης, Cic.*Att.*16.11.2, *IG*14.1746 (ἀδελ- lapis); ἀ. καὶ λάλος Alciphr.3.66; τὸ ἀ. S.E.*M.*1.141: Comp. -ότερος Gal.5.315: Sup. -ότατος Plu.2.509a. Adv. -χως Phld.*Ir.*p.17 W., *Rh.*1.212 S. (Comp.).

ἀδολίευτος, ον, = sq., ἤθη Sch.Ar.*Pl.*1158. **II.** *not concealed*, ἄγκιστρον Sch.Opp.*H.*3.532.

ἄδολος, ον, *guileless, honest*, σοφία Pi.*O.*7.53; in Att. esp. of treaties, ἄ. εἰρήνα Ar.*Lys.*169; σπονδαὶ ἄ. καὶ ἀβλαβεῖς Th.5.18. Adv., freq. in the phrase ἀδόλως καὶ δικαίως *without fraud* or covin, Th.5.23, cf. *IG*1.42e; ἁπλόως καὶ ἀ. *GDI*5024 (Gort.): generally, πλουτεῖν ἀδόλως *Scol.*8; ἀδολώτερον λέγεσθαι, opp. πιστότερον, Antipho 3.3.4:—also, *genuinely, truly*, τεθνάκην ἀ. θέλω Sapph.*Supp.*23.1, cf. Theoc.29.32. **II.** *unadulterated, genuine*, χρίματος ἀδόλοισι παρηγορίαις A.*Ag.*95; στύραξ Dsc.1.66; χρυσός Eupolem.ap.Alex.Polyh.18; ἀργύριον Poll.3.86; σῖτος, πυρός, *PHib.*1.85, *PGrenf.*1.18; ἀ. ἀπὸ παντός ib.2.29.14: metaph., αὔραις ἀδόλοις *pure*, E.*Supp.*1029 (lyr.); τὸ λογικὸν ἄ. γάλα 1*Ep.Pet.*2.2. **2.** *unpretentious*, Plu.*Pel.*3.

ἄδον, Ep. for ἕαδον, aor. 2 of ἁνδάνω.

ἀδόνητος, ον, (δονέω) *unshaken*, *AP*5.267 (Paul. Sil.).

ἀδονίς, ἡ, poet. for ἀηδονίς, Mosch.3.46.

ἀδοξάζω, incorrectly formed, = ἀδοξέω II, Anon. *in Rh.*105.15 (Pass.).

ἀδόξαστος, ον, *unexpected*, S.*Fr.*223. **2.** *not matter of opinion*, i.e. *certain*, Pl.*Phd.*84a. **II.** Stoic, *free from* δόξα, *not opining*, Aristo *Stoic.*1.78, Pers.ib.102; *refusing to form opinions*, Timo ap. Aristocl.ap.Eus.*PE*14.18. Adv. -τως, opp. δογματικῶς, S.E.*P.*1.15, etc.

ἀδοξ-έω, *to be held in no esteem, be in ill repute*, ἀδοξοῦντες, opp. οἱ δοκοῦντες, E.*Hec.*294, cf. D.19.103; opp. εὐδοκιμεῖν, Arist.*Rh.*1372b22. **II.** trans., *hold in no esteem, in contempt*, τινά J.*BJ* 1.26.2, al., cf. Plu.*Luc.*14:—hence in Pass., αἱ βαναυσικαὶ [τέχναι].. ἀδοξοῦνται πρὸς τῶν πόλεων X.*Oec.*4.2. **-ημα**, ατος, τό, *disgrace*, Plu.2.977e. **-ία**, ἡ, *ill repute*, Hp.*Lex*1, Th.1.76, Pl.*Phd.*82c, D.1.11, Phld.*Lib.*p.4 O., etc.; *obscurity*, Plu.*Agis*2. **II.** *contempt*, App.*Syr.*41. **-οποίητος**, ον, *not forming notions, unreasoning*, Plb.6.5.8. **-ος**, ον, *without* δόξα, *inglorious*, πόλεμος D.5.5; *disreputable*, τέχνη X.*Smp.*4.56. **2.** *obscure, ignoble*, πόλεις Isoc.12.253; ἀνώνυμοι καὶ ἄ. D.8.66, cf. Arist.*Rh.*1384b31; of eunuchs, *despised*, X.*Cyr.*7.5.61. Adv. -ξως Plu.*Thes.*35. **II.** = παράδοξος, *unexpected*, S.*Fr.*71; *improbable*, opp. ἔνδοξος, Arist.*Top.*159a39, etc.; τὰ -ότατα λέγειν ib.159a19.

ἄδορος, ον, (δέρω) = ἀνέκδαρτος, Suid. **II.** as Subst., ἄδορος, ὁ, = κώρυκος, *skin*, Antim.64.

ἄδορπος, ον, *without food, fasting*, Pi.*Pae.*6.128, Lyc.638.

ἀδορῠφόρητος, ον, *without body-guard*, Arist.*Pol.*1315b28.

ἄδος (A), ὁ or τό, *satiety, loathing*, τάμνων δένδρεα μακρά, ἄδος τέ μιν ἵκετο θυμόν Il.11.88. (Cf. ἄδην.)

ἄδος (B), ὁ, *decree*, *SIG*45 (Halic.), *IG*12(8).263.8 (Thasos); cf. Hsch. s. v. ἄδημα. (Cf. ἀδεῖν, ἁνδάνω.)

ἆδος, ἀδοσύνη, Dor. for ἦδος, ἡδοσύνη.

ἄδοτος, ον, *without gifts*, *h.Merc.*573.

ἀδουλαγώγητος, ον, *not enslaved*, ψυχή Vett.Val.220.20.

ἀδούλ-ευτος, ον, *one who has never been a slave*, Is.*Fr.*138, Arr.*Epict.*2.10.1. **-έω**, *have no slaves*, Str.15.1.59. **-ία**, ἡ, *being without slaves*, Arist.*Pol.*1323a6. **-ος**, ον, *unattended by slaves*, ἄδουλα δώμαθ' ἑστίας E.*Andr.*593: c. gen., τῶν τοιούτων ἄδουλος *unattended by*.., Ael.*NA*6.10. **2.** *having no slaves, too poor to keep a slave*, Phryn.Com.18, Plu.2.831b. **II.** *impatient of slavery*, ἀδουλότερος τῶν λεόντων Ph.2.451. **-ωτος**, ον, *unenslaved, unsubdued*, Pers.*Stoic.*1.99, D.S.1.53; ὑπό τινων Procl. *in Alc.*p.95 C.; ἀδούλωτοι ἡδονῇ Crates Theb.5.

ἀδούπητος, ον, *noiseless*, *AP*5.293.8 (Agath.).

ἀδουσιασάμενοι· ὁμολογησάμενοι, and **ἀδούσιον**· ἀρεστόν, σύμφωνον, Hsch.

Ἀιδοφοίτης, ου, ὁ, = *frequenting Hades*, Ar.*Fr.*149.4,6.

ἀδραία, Maced. for αἰθρία, Hsch. **ἀδρᾰκής**, ές, = ἀδερκής, Id.

ἀδράν-εια, or -ία, ἡ, *listlessness, weakness*, Hdn.2.10.8, Just.*Nov.*102.3: Ep. **ἀδρανίη**, A.R.2.200, Call.*Fr.*520, *AP*6.296 (Leon.), etc. **II.** *non-efficiency*, τοῦ μὴ ὄντος Simp. *in Cael.*136.30. [δρᾰ.] **-εος**, η, ον, = ἀδρανής, *AP*9.135. **-έω**, *to be weak*, of starlight, Arat.471, cf. Opp.*H.*1.296, Nonn.*D.*32.280. **-ής**, ές, (δραίνω) *impotent, feeble*, *AP*9.359 (Posidipp.), Plu.2.373d, etc.; τὸ -έστατον ταῖς χερσίν Lxx *Wi.*13.19; τὴν χεῖρα ἀ. Philostr.*VA*3.39; -έστατοι ζῴων Babr.25.3; *non-efficient*, i.e. *unreal*, Simp. *in Ph.*533.19, 815.24; of nations, Arr.*Epict.*3.7.13: Comp., *less efficacious*, Dsc.3.110. **2.** *deprived of its strength, useless*, of iron, Plu.*Lyc.*9, *Lys.*17. **-ίζομαι**, = ἀδρανέω, Sch.Arat.471, *Gloss.*

Ἀδράστεια, Ion. **Ἀδρήστεια**, ἡ, (ἀ- priv., διδράσκω) title of Nemesis, A.*Pr.*936, cf. Pl.*R.*451a, etc. **2.** fabulous plant, Ps.-Plu.*Fluv.*18.13.

ἄδραστος, Ion. **ἄδρηστος**, ον, *not running away, not inclined to do so*, of slaves, Hdt.4.142, *PLond.*2.251.14 (iv A.D.): metaph., χαλκός D.Chr.37.10.—In Il. only as pr. n.

ἄδρᾱτος, ον, (δράω) *not done*, Hermipp.3 D. (ἄδραστα, Hsch., Phot.).

ἀδράφαξυς or **ἀδράφαξυς**, ἡ, v. ἀτράφαξυς.

ἀδρέπᾰνος, ον, *untouched by sickle*, S.*Fr.*978.

ἀδρεπήβολος, ον, (ἁδρός) τὸ περὶ τὰς νοήσεις ἀ. the *power of forming great* conceptions, Longin.8.1:—in bad sense, *ambitious*, Vett. Val.43.2.

ἄδρεπτος, ον, *unplucked*, A.*Supp.*663 (lyr.).

ἁδρέω, *to be full-grown, matured*, πυροὶ ἡδρηκότες Dsc.2.85:—Pass. forms ἁδρεῖτο, ἁδρώμενον (-ούμενον), Hsch.

Ἀδρίας, ου, Ion. **Ἀδρίης**, εω, ὁ, *the Adriatic*, Hdt.5.9, etc.:—Adj. **Ἀδρι-ᾱνός**, ή, όν, A.*Fr.*71, also **-ηνός**, κῦμα τᾶς Ἀδριηνᾶς ἀκτᾶς E.*Hipp.*736 (lyr.): later, **-ακός**, νέκταρ, of Italian wine, called *Adriatic* because imported through Corcyra, *AP*6.257 (Antiphil.): **-ᾰνικός**, ἀλεκτορίδες Arist.*GA*749b29: **-ᾱτικός**, ὄρνιθες Chrysipp. Tyan.ap.Ath.7.285d:—also fem. **-άς**, ἀδὸς, ἅλμη D.P.92.

ἀδρῖμυς, υ, *not tart* or *pungent*, Luc.*Trag.*323.

ἁδρό-βωλος, ον, *in large pieces* or *masses*, of bdellium, Dsc.1.67. **-γραφία**, ἡ, *forcible writing*, Phld.*Rh.*1.165 S. (dub.). **-κέφαλος**, ον, *with large head*, Sor.2.63, Paul.Aeg.6.74; sens. obsc., Hierocl.

*Facet.*251. -μερής, ές, *of coarse, large grains*, opp. λεπτομερής, D.S.5.26, Gal.8.336 (Sup.); *coarse*, of wine, Dsc.5.6: Comp. -έστεροι, ὄγκοι Ph.1.493. Adv. -ῶς Herasap.Gal.13.1045.

Ἀδρόμιος, sc. μήν, month at Halos, *IG*9(2).109*a*6.

ἀδρόμισθος, ον, *with large prizes*, ἀγῶνες Scymn.353.

ἄδρομος, ον, *that will not gallop*, ἵπποι *Hippiatr.*105.

ἀδρόομαι, Pass., (ἁδρός) *grow stout*, Myro Hist.1.

ἁδροπόρος, ον, *with large pores*, Cass.*Pr.*48.

ἁδρός, ά, όν, *thick, stout, bulky*: I. of things, χιόνα ἁ. πίπτουσαν ἰδεῖν falling *thick*, Hdt.4.31; τῶν ἀνθράκων οἱ ἁδρότατοι the *most solid*, Hp.*Mul.*2.133; κίονες ἁ. *large*, D.S.3.47; τοὺς ἁδροτάτους τῶν λέμβων Id.20.85:—*strong, violent*, πόλεμος Ar.*Ra.*1099; τὰ ἁδρότατα τῶν.. συμβάντων *Hell.Oxy.*4.1; ῥεύματα *full, swollen*, Arist.*Pr.*949^{b}5; of raindrops, Id.*Mu.*394^{a}31 (Comp.); δῆγμα D.S.1.35; δωρεάς τε καὶ τιμὰς ἁ. δοῦναι *in abundance*, Id.19.86; κοιλότης *severe* deficiency, Phld.*Oec.*p.71 J.:—of style, *powerful*, Longin.40.4 (Comp.), cf. Phld.*Rh.*1.182 S.; ἁ. νοήματα dub. in D.H.*Comp.*4; ἀπειλή Phld. *Hom.*p.35 O.; τὸ ἁ. *the grand style*, opp. τὸ ἰσχνόν, Ps.-Plu.*Vit.Hom.* 72. Adv., Comp. ἁδροτέρως, διαιτᾶν live *more freely*, Hp.*Aph.*1.7; ἁ. φαρμακεύειν ib.4.9; neut. as Adv., ἁδρὸν γελάσαι laugh *loud*, Antiph. 144; ἁδρότερον πιεῖν drink *more deeply*, Diph.5. II. of persons, *fine, well-grown*, ἐπεὰν τὸ παιδίον ἁ. γένηται Hdt.4.180; τῷ παιδί, ἐπὴν ἁ. ἔῃ Hp.*Genit.*2; τῶν παίδων ὅσοι ἁ. Pl.*R.*466e; οἱ -ότεροι *the best-grown, the stronger*, Isoc.12.110; οἱ ἁ. *chiefs, princes*, Lxx 4*Ki.*10.6; also ἁ. τὴν ψυχήν Democh.3; ἡ κατὰ ψυχὴν ἁ. ὑπεροχή Procl.*in Alc.*p.94 C. 2. of animals, *fine, fat*, χοῖρος X.*Oec.*17.10; λύκος Babr.101; freq. in Com. of flesh, fish, etc., Antiph.20.5, 26.21, Alex. 170, etc. 3. of fruit or corn, *full-grown, ripe*, ὅκως εἴη καρπὸς ἁ. Hdt.1.17, cf. Arist.*Metaph.*1017^{b}8. b. ἁ. ῥίζα, = ἀριστολοχεία στρογγύλη, Ps.-Dsc.3.4. c. of an egg, *ready to be laid*, Arist. *HA*559^{b}11 (Comp.).—First in Hdt., never in Trag., rare in Att.; but the derivs. ἁδροτής, ἁδροσύνη occur in Ep. and ἁδρύνω in Trag.

ἀδροσία, ἡ, (δρόσος) *want of dew*, J.*AJ*2.5.5, Vett.Val.145.13: poet. -ίη *POxy.*1796.18 (sg. and pl.).

ἁδροσύνη, ἡ, (ἁδρός) = ἁδροτής, of ears of corn, Hes.*Op.*473.

ἁδρόσφαιρος, ον, *in large balls*, μαλάβαθρον *Peripl.M.Rubr.*65.

ἁδροτής, ῆτος, ἡ, *vigour, strength*, Epicur.*Ep.*1 p.31 U.; of plants, Thphr.*HP*7.4.11: metaph. of sound, *loudness*, Amarant.ap.Ath. 10.415a; of style or expression, *force*, Aristid.Quint.2.9. II. *abundance*, 2*Ep.Cor.*8.20. (In Hom. v.l. for ἀνδροτής, q.v.)

ἁδρό-χωροι· οἱ ἁδρὰς ἔχοντες χώρας, Hsch. -χωρον, τό, *full*, χῶρον, a wine-measure, *Ostr.*1600.

ἁδρόω, v. ἀδρόομαι.

ἄδρυα, τά, = ἀκρόδρυα, Ath.3.83a; Sicilian word, Hsch. II. *upright pieces* of a plough, Id. III. (ἀ- copul.) *canoes made of hollowed tree-trunks, dug-outs* (Cypr.), Id.

ἀδρυάς, άδος, ἡ, (ἀ- copul., δρῦς) = Ἁμαδρυάς, in pl., Prop.1.20.12, *AP*9.664 (Paul. Sil.).

ἀδρύμακτον· καθαρόν, Hsch.; cf. δρυμάττω.

ἅδρ-υνσις, εως, ἡ, *coming to maturity*, Arist.*Metaph.*1065^{b}20, *Ph.*201^{a}19, Thphr.*CP*2.12.1:—written -υσις, Simp. *in Epict.* p.32 D. -ύνω, (ἁδρός) *ripen, mature*, S.*Fr.*979, X.*Mem.*4.3.8; ἁδρῦναι καὶ πέψαι τὸν καρπόν Thphr.*HP*3.1.3:—Pass., *grow ripe, ripen, come to maturity*, of fruit or corn, Hdt.1.193, Arist.*Ph.*230^{b}2; of embrya, Hp.*Septim.*1, *Oct.*12, cf. Arist.*HA*565^{b}13; of nestlings, 619^{b}30.

ἄδρυπτος, ον, (δρύπτω) *not scratching* or *tearing*, Nonn.*D.*11.137.

ἀδρύφακτος, ον, *unfenced*, ἀτείχιστος, ἀφύλακτος, ἄνευ δικαστηρίου, Hsch.: metaph., ἄπονος καὶ ἀταλαίπωρος, *AB*345.

ἀδρώδης, = φύτευμα, Ps.-Dsc.4.128.

ἀδυβόας, etc., Dor. for ἡδυ-.

ἀδῠνᾰμ-έω, *to want power, be incapable*, Lxx *Si.Prol.*, Simp. *in Cael.* 139.24: c. inf., *PLond.*2.361^{r}8 (i A.D.). -ία, Ion. -ίη, ἡ, *want of strength, debility*, Hp.*VM*10: pl., ib.19, Plu.2.791d; of medicine, *want of strength*, Thphr.*HP*9.18.4. 2. generally, *inability, incapacity*, Hdt.8.111, Arist.*Metaph.*1019^{b}15, etc.; ἡ τοῦ λέγειν ἀ. Antipho 5.2, cf. Pl.*Lg.*646b, etc.: pl., Lxx 3*Ma.*2.13: c. gen., ἀ. τοῦ ἀδικεῖν *for* wrongdoing, Pl.*R.*359b; τῶν πραγμάτων *for* political action, Arist.*Pol.*1314^{a}23; [ψυχῆς] *Stoic.*3.23: c. inf., Pl.*R.*532b. 3. *poverty, lack of resources*, X.*Oec.*20.22, D.19.186. -ος, ον, *weak*, of wine, Dsc.5.6:—*without potency*, Procl.*Inst.*80,149: -μον, τό, *absence of potency*, Olymp. *in Phd.*p.40 N.:—Astrol., of planets, Ptol. *Tetr.*53.

ἀδῠνᾰσία, ἡ, = ἀδυναμία, Hdt.3.79, 7.172, Th.8.8: c. gen., ἀ. τοῦ λέγειν Id.7.8:—also **ἀδυναστία**, v.l. for -ασία in D.H.*Dem.*26, cf. *Gloss.* (**ἀδύναστος**, ib.), and **ἀδυνατία**, Dinol.9.

ἀδῠναστί, Adv. *impotently*, Suid.

ἀδῠνᾰτ-έω, of persons, *to be* ἀδύνατος, *lack strength*, Epich.266, Arist.*Somn.*454^{a}27: c. inf., *to be unable* to do, Hp. *de Arte* 7, Pl.*R.* 366d, X.*Mem.*1.2.23, Arist.*EN*1165^{b}22, *Pol.*1287^{b}17, etc. II. of things, *to be impossible*, Lxx *Jb.*10.13, Phld.*Ir.*p.98 W., *Ev.Matt.*17. 20, *Ev.Luc.*1.37, Ps.-Callisth.3.26. -ος, ον, I. of persons, *unable* to do a thing, c. inf., Hdt.3.138, Epich.272, E.*HF*56, etc.; ἀ. εἰπεῖν Arist.*Rh.*1379^{a}2; ἀ. ὥστε.. Onos.1.13: Comp., τὸν δυνατώτερον τοῦ -ωτέρου [πλέον ἔχειν] Pl.*Grg.*483d: Sup. -ώτατος, λέγειν Eup.95. 2. abs., *without strength, powerless, weakly*, Hdt.5. 9, E.*Ion*596, *Andr.*746; οἱ ἀ. men *disabled for service*, whether as *invalids* or *paupers*, Lys.24 tit., Arist.*Ath.*49.4; ἐν τοῖς ἀ. μισθοφορεῖν Aeschin.1.103; ἀ. σώματι Lys.2.73; ἀ. χρήμασι *poor*, Th.7.28; εἴς τι Pl.*Hp.Mi.*366b; οἱ -ώτατοι persons *of no importance*, Phld.*Herc.* 1457.8; of ships, *disabled*, Hdt.6.16; τὸ ἀ. *want of strength*, Pl. *Hp.Ma.*296a; τὰ ἀ. *disabilities*, D.18.108. II. of things, *impossible*, E.*Or.*665, *Hel.*1043; ἐλπίδες *unrealizable*, Democr.58; τὸ ἀ. Arist.*Cael.*280^{b}12; ἡ εἰς τὸ ἀ. ἀπαγωγή *reductio ad impossibile*, *APr.*29^{b}5; ὁ διὰ τοῦ ἀ. συλλογισμός, ἡ διὰ τοῦ ἀ. δεῖξις, ib.34^{b}30, 45^{a}35; ἀδύνατα βούλομαι Lync.1.12:—ἀδύνατόν [ἐστι] c. inf., Hdt.1.32, al.; ἀδύνατά [ἐστι] Pi.*P.*2.81, Hdt.1.91, 6.106, Th.1.59; ἀ. ὑμῖν ὥστε.. Pl.*Prt.*338c; ὑμέας καταλελάβηκε ἀ. τι βοηθέειν Hdt.9.60; τὰ ἀ. καρτερεῖν E.*IA*1370; τολμᾶν ἀδύνατα Id.*Hel.*811; ἀδυνάτων ἐρᾶν Id.*HF*318, cf. Luc.*D.Deor.*8, etc.; prov., ἀδύνατα θηρᾷς Macar.1.26: Comp. -ώτερον, ἔτι.. εἰ οἷόν τε.. Pl.*Tht.*192b, cf. *Prm.*138d: Sup., ὃ δὴ πάντων -ώτατον Id.*Phlb.*15b. III. Adv. -τως *without power* or *skill, feebly*, ἀμύνεσθαι Antipho 4.3.3, cf. 3.3.4 (Comp.), Lys.12. 3:—ἀ. ἔχειν to be *unwell*, Pl.*Ax.*364b; to be *unable*, c. inf., Arist. *Rh.Al.*1435^{a}16; ἀ. ἔχει it is *impossible*, Epicur.*Ep.*2 p.49 U.; ἀ. λέγεται it is an *impossible* story, Phld.*Rh.*2.122 S.—Rare in poetry: Trag. only in E.

ἀδυνατόω, *debilitate*, in Pass., Erot. s.v. κατηπορήθη.

ἀδυσκόλως, Adv. *without complaint*, prob. in *Vit.Philonid.*p.13 C.

ἀδυσώπητος, ον, *not to be put out of countenance, inexorable*, Μοῖραι *JHS*32.274 (Pamphyl.), cf. Ph.2.543, Plu.2.64f. Adv. -τως, ἐνοχλεῖν ib.534b.

ἄδῠτος, ον, (δύω) *not to be entered*, θησαυρός Pi.*P.*11.4; ἄ. ἐστιν ὁ τόπος Str.14.1.44. 2. *never setting*, of stars, Sch.Arat.632. II. mostly as Subst. (masc. in *h.Merc.*247, neut. in Hdt.5.72, E.*Ion*938), *innermost sanctuary* or *shrine*, Il.5.448,512, *h.Ap.*443; εὐώδεος ἐξ ἀ. Pi.*O.*7.32: metaph., ἐκ τοῦ ἀ. τῆς βίβλου Pl.*Tht.*162a; ἄ. θαλάσσης Opp.*H.*1.49, cf. *Hymn.Is.*152.

ᾄδω, Att. contr. for ἀείδω, q.v. **ἀδῶ**· ἀρέσκω, Hsch.

ἀδώμητος, ον, (δωμάω) *unbuilt*, Nonn.*D.*17.40.

ἀδών [ᾱ], όνος, ἡ, Dor. for ἀηδών, Mosch.3.9; cf. ἀδονίς.

Ἄδων [ᾰ], ωνος, ὁ, = Ἄδωνις, *AP*6.275 (Nossis), Theoc.15.149.

Ἀδων-αία, ἡ, epith. of Aphrodite, Orph.*A.*30; cf. Ἀδωνιάς. -άρια, τά, kind of *shoes* (prob. with play on ἀ- priv., Lat. *donarium, worthless gifts*), Procop.Gaz.*Ep.*146. -ειος, α, ον, *of Adonis*, κῆποι Suid. -ηίς· χελιδόνιον (prob. for -ώς), ἡ θριδακίνη, Hsch. -ια, τά, *mourning for Adonis*, Cratin.15, Pherecr.170:—hence Ἀδωνιάζουσαι (from -ιάζω, *keep the Adonia*), title of Theoc. 15. -ιακός, ή, όν, *of* or *for Adonis*, κῆπος Arr.*Epict.*4.8.36. -ιάς, άδος, ἡ, = Ἀδωναία, Nonn.*D.*33.25. -ιασμός, οῦ, ὁ, *mourning for Adonis*, Ar.*Lys.*389. -ιος, ὁ, rare form of Ἄδωνις, Plu.2. 756c. II. as Adj., ος, ον, *of Adonis*:—hence Ἀδώνιον, τό, *a statue of him* borne in the Adonia, Suid. 2. (sub. μέτρον) a kind of *verse*, consisting of a dactyl and spondee, Sacerd.p.516 K. 3. = Ἄδωνις III, Plin.*HN*21.60. -ις [ᾰ], ιδος (also ιος Pherecr.198), ὁ, *Adonis*, ὦ τὸν Ἄδωνιν Sapph.63; Ἀδώνι' ἄγομεν καὶ τὸν Ἄ. κλάομεν Pherecr.170; ὤδωνις, i.e. ὁ Ἄ., Theoc.3.47:—hence, generally, *favourite, darling*, δεῖ Ἀδώνιδας αὐτοὺς ἀκούειν Luc.*Merc.Cond.*35, cf. Alciphr.1.39, *AP*5.112 (Marc.Arg.). 2. Ἀδώνιδος κῆποι cuttings planted in pots *for the Adonia*, Pl.*Phdr.*276b, Thphr.*HP*6.7.3, cf. Theoc.15.113: prov., of *any short-lived pleasure*, Sch.Pl. l. c. 3. αὐλὴ Ἀδώνιδος, at Rome, garden on the Palatine, Philostr.*VA*7. 32. II. kind of *flying-fish*, = ἐξώκοιτος, Clearch.73, Opp.*H.* 1.157, etc. III. *Adonis-flower, Anemone fulgens*, Aus.*Idyll.*6. 11. -ίσιος, sc. μήν, month at Seleucia, *Hemerolog.Flor.* -ιών, sc. μήν, month at Iasos, *JHS*9.342.

ἀδώρ-ητος, ον, = ἄδωρος, *h.Merc.*168; πρός τινος E.*Hec.*42; ἀ. λίθος of the philosopher's stone, Zos.Alch.p.114 B.: c. gen., πάντων ἀγαθῶν ἀ. *not endowed with*, Epicur.*Fr.*364. -ία, ἡ, *incorruptibility*, Poll.8.11.

ἀδωρο-δόκητος, ον, *incorruptible*, Aeschin.3.82, etc. Adv. -τως D.18.250, 19.4, *IG*2.114*A*5, Onos.1.8, D.S.39.20. -δοκία, ἡ, = ἀδωρία, D.C.*Fr.*40.1. -δόκος, ον, *incorruptible*, *AP*9.779. II. = ἀνάεδνος (q.v.), ὑμέναιοι Nonn.*D.*4.33, 34.176. -ληπτος, ον, = foreg., Hsch., Sch.Th.2.65.

ἄδωρος, ον, *taking no gifts, incorruptible*, c. gen., -ότατος χρημάτων Th.2.65. Adv. -ως Poll.8.11: Sup., D.C.72.10. b. *receiving no gifts*, Max.Tyr.11.8. 2. *unpaid*, πρέσβευσις *IG*7.2712 (Acraephia). II. *giving no gifts*, c. gen., ἄ. τινος *not giving* it, Pl.*Smp.* 197d; ἀ. ἐλαφαβολίαις by hunting *from which no gifts were offered*, S.*Aj.*177 (lyr.); *miserly*, Aret.*SD*1.5. III. ἄδωρα δῶρα gifts *that are no gifts*, like βίος ἀβίωτος, S.*Aj.*665.

ἀδωσι-δικία, ἡ, *failure to give satisfaction*, *PLond.*2.357.7 (14 B.C.). -δικος, ον, ib.354.6 (10 B.C.).

ἀδώτης, ου, ὁ, *non-giver*, coined as antithesis of δώτης, Hes.*Op.* 355. (Irregularly formed, cf. α I.)

ἄεδν-ος, ον, *undowered*, Hsch. II. (α III) = πολύφερνος, Id. -ωτος, ον, (ἑδνόω) *not accompanied by bridal gifts*, ἁλφή Lyc. 549.

ἀέθλ-ευμα, -εύω, -έω, -ητήρ, -ητής, etc., Ep. and Ion. for ἀθλ-.

ἀέθλιον, Ep. and Ion. for ἆθλον, *prize*, Il.9.124, Od.8.108, *APl.*5. 374, *AP*9.637 (Damoch.). II. = ἆθλος, *contest*, Od.24.169, Call. *Del.*187.

ἀέθλιος, α, ον, *gaining the prize*, or *running for it*, ἵππος καλὴ καὶ ἀεθλίη a *race*-horse, Thgn.257; ἵππος ἀέθλιος Call.*Del.*113:—contr. ἆθλιος (q.v.) only in a restricted sense.

ἀεθλοθέτης, ου, ὁ, = ἀθλοθέτης, *IG*3.1171.

ἄεθλον, τό, **ἄεθλος**, ὁ, Ep. and Ion. for ἆθλον, ἆθλος.

ἀεθλο-νῑκία, ἡ, *victory in the games*, Pi.*N*.3.7. **-σύνη**, ἡ, *contest, struggle*, *AP*5.293.18(Agath.). **-φορέω**, *win prize*, ἐκ διαύλου Call.*Sos*.42. **-φόρος**, ον, Ep. and Lyr. for ἀθλοφόρος.

ἀεί, Adv. *ever, always*, Hom., etc.; with other specifications of time, ἐμμενὲς αἰεί Od.21.69; συνεχὲς αἰ. 9.74; ἀ. καθ' ἡμέραν, καθ' ἡμέραν ἀ., ἀ. καὶ καθ' ἡμέραν, ἀ. κατ' ἐνιαυτόν, ἀ. διὰ βίου, etc., Pl.*Phd*. 75d, etc.; ἀ. πανταχοῦ D.21.197, cf. Ar.*Eq*.568; διὰ παντὸς ἀ. *Pax* 397; ἐνδελεχῶς ἀ. Men.521; δεῦρ' ἀεί *until now*, E.*Or*.1663, Pl.*Lg*. 811c; αἰεί κοτε, ποτε *from of old*, Hdt.1.58, Th.6.82; αἰ. δήποτε 1.13; cf. εἰσαεί:—with the Art., ὁ ἀ. χρόνος *eternity*, Hdt.1.54, Pl.*Phd*. 103e, etc.; οἱ ἀ. ὄντες the *immortals*, X.*Cyr*.1.6.46, etc.:—but ὁ αἰ. βασιλεύων the king *for the time being*, Hdt.2.98; οἱ ἀ. δικάζοντες D. 21.223; ὁ αἰ. ἐντὸς γιγνόμενος *every one* as he got inside, Th.4.68; τὸν ἀ. προστυχόντα D.21.131; τοῖσι τούτων αἰ. ἐκγόνοισι to their descendants *for ever*, Hdt.1.105, cf. 3.83, etc.; in A.*Pr*.937, θῶπτε τὸν κρατοῦντ' ἀ., ἀεί is postponed metri gr.—Dialectic forms (cf. Hdn.Gr.1.497, *Et.Gud.z*): **1. αἰεί**, Ep., Ion., Poet., and Early Att. (cf. Marcellin.*Vit.Thuc*.52); found (beside ἀεί) in Att. Inscrr. to 361 B.C. **2. ἀεί** [ᾰ three times in Hom., ᾱ Att.] normal in Att. Inscrr. from 361 B.C. **3. αἰέν**, Il.1.290,al. (ἀεν is v.l. in Il.11. 827), Pi.*N*.6.3, Sophr.90, A.*Pr*.428, *Ag*.891, S.*Aj*.682. **4.** Dor. **αἰές**, Ar.*Lys*.1266, Bion *Fr*.1.1; also **ἀές**, *Tab.Heracl*.1.134. **5.** Aeol. **αἶ(ν)**, **ἄι(ν)**, Hdn.Gr.l.c.; cf. *IG*9(2).461 (ἄιν, Thess.), *SIG*58 (Milet.), and v. αἰπάρθενος, ἀείδασμος. **6. αἰέ**, Hdn.Gr.l.c. **7. ἀέ**, Pi.*P*.9.88, Pisand.11(ἀέ); cf. ἀέ-ναος. **8.** Boeot. **ἡί**, Hdn. Gr.l.c. **9.** Tarent. **αἰή**, ibid. **II.** τὸ ἀ. *eternity*, τὸ ἀ. τοῦτο οὐκ αἰώνιόν ἐστιν ἀλλὰ χρονικόν Procl.*Inst*.198. The statement of Harp. that ἀεί = ἕως in Att. is based on misinterpretation of such phrases as ἐς τόνδε αἰ. τὸν πόλεμον Th.1.18. (αἰϝεί *Epigr.Gr*.742, *GDI*60.31 (Cypr.), *IG*9(1).334.4 (Locr.), cf. Lat. *aevum*.)

ἀει-βλαστής, ές, *ever-budding*, Thphr.*CP*1.11.6. **-βλάστησις**, εως, ἡ, *perpetual budding*, ibid. **-βλύων**· ἐπιρρέων, Hsch. **-βολος**, ον, (βάλλω) *continually thrown*, σφαῖρα *AP*6.282(Theod.). **-βρύης**, ές, (βρύω) *ever-sprouting*, Nic.*Th*.848. **-γενεσία**, ἡ, *perpetual generation*, Jul.*Or*.6.185c, al., Iamb.ap.Stob.1.49.38, Procl.*in Cra*. p.24 P., etc. **-γενέτης**, only in Ep. form **αἰειγενέτης**, ου, ὁ, epith. of the gods, *everlasting*, used by Hom. only at the end of a line, θεῶν αἰειγενετάων Il.2.400, cf. 3.296. **-γενής**, ές, *eternal*, Hp.*Virg*.1, Pl.*Lg*.773e, *Smp*.206e, X.*Smp*.8.1; θεοί Antag.1.2. **2.** *everlasting*, opp. ἀΐδιος, Plu.2.374d. **-γένητος**, ον, *eternally generated*, ψυχή Dam.*Pr*.410. **II.** = ἀειγενής, θεοί Procl.*in Ti*.3. 311 D. **-γεννητής**, οῦ, ὁ, *perpetual producer*, epith. of Apollo (τῷ τὸν αὐτὸν ἀεὶ γίγνεσθαι καὶ ἀεὶ γεννᾶν), Macr.*Sat*.1.17.35. **-γλεῦκος**, τό, *unfermented wine*, Plin.*HN*14.83. **-γνητος**, ον, = ἀειγενέτης, Orph.*A*.15. **-δάκρυτος**, *ever-lamented*, μνήμη *IG*2.3552b. **-δασμος**, ον, *subject to a perpetual charge*, γῆ *GDI*5661 (Chios, written ἀιδ-); δασμὸς ἀ., Ἀθηνᾶ 20.169 (Chios).

ἀ-ειδέλιος, ον, = sq., *EM*21.33, Hsch. **-είδελος**, ον, (*ϝείδω) *unseen, dark*, Hes.*Fr*.112; *obscure*, Opp.*H*.1.86, etc. **II.** *not to be looked on, dazzling*, Nic.*Th*.20. **-ειδής**, ές, (εἶδος) *formless*, Arist.*Cael*.306^{b}17; *indistinct*, ὀσμαί Thphr.*Od*.1; f.l. for ἀιδής, Pl. *Phd*.79a. **2.** *unsightly*, χροιά a *bad* complexion, Hp.*Nat.Mul*. 41. **-ειδία**, ἡ, (ἀειδής 2) *deformity*, J.*BJ*7.5.5.

ἀειδίνητος [ῑ], ον, *ever-revolving*, ἄτρακτος, σφαῖρα, *AP*6.289 (Leon.), Nonn.*D*.6.87.

ἀείδιος, ον, Adj. from ἀεί, *everlasting*, Hsch.

ἀει-δουλεία or **-δουλία**, ἡ, *perpetual slavery*, Poll.3.80, Hdn.*Epim*. 221. **-δράστεια**, ἡ, etym. of Ἀδράστεια, Corn.*ND*13.

ἀείδω, Ion. and poet. form used by Hom., Pi., and sometimes in Trag. and Com. (even in trim., A.*Ag*.16, E.*Fr*.188; in tetram., Cratin. 305), also in Ion. Prose; contr. ᾄδω (also Anacr.45, Theoc.), Trag., Pl., etc.: impf. ἤειδον Od., Ep. ἄειδον Il., etc.; Trag. and Att. ᾖδον E.*Alc*.761, Th.2.21: fut. ἀείσομαι Od.22.352, Thgn.943, but ᾄσομαι *h.Hom*.6.2, 32.19, Thgn.243, and always in Att. (ᾄσεις, ᾄσουσιν in Ar. *Pax*1297, Pl.*Lg*.666d are corrupt); rarely in act. form ἀείσω, Sapph. 11, Thgn.4, Ar.*Lys*.1243 (Lacon.), and late Poets, as Nonn.*D*.13.47 (in E.*HF*681 ἀείδω is restored by Elmsl.); still more rarely ᾄσω, Babr. 12.13, Men.Rh.p.381S., Him.*Or*.1.6; Dor. ἀσεῦμαι Theoc.3.38, ᾀσῶ Id.1.145: aor. ἤεισα Call.*Ep*.23.4, Opp.*C*.3.1, Ep. ἄεισα [ᾰ] Od.21. 411; ἄεισον E.*Tr*.513(lyr.); ἀείσατε Ar.*Th*.115(lyr.); ᾖσα Ar.*Nu*. 1371, Pl.*Ti*.21b:—Med., aor. ἀεισάμην (in act. sense) *PMag.Lond*. 47.43, imper. ἀείσεο *h.Hom*.17.1 (nisi leg. ἀείδεο):—**Pass.**, ἀείδομαι Pi., Hdt.: poet. impf. ἀείδετο Pi.: aor. ᾔσθην, v. infr. II.1: pf. ᾖσμαι Pl.Com.69.11. (ἀϝείδω, cf. αὐδή, ὑδέω.) [ᾰ: but ᾱ metri gr. Od. 17.519, *h.Hom*.12.1, 27.1, *Il.Parv*.1, Thgn.4, Theoc.7.41, etc.]:—*sing*, Il.1.604, etc.: hence of all kinds of vocal sounds, *crow* as cocks, Pl.*Smp*.223c; *hoot* as owls, Arat.1000; *croak* as frogs, Arist. *Mir*.835^{b}3, Thphr.*Sign*.3.5, etc.; οἱ τέττιγες χαμόθεν ᾄσονται Stes. ap.Arist.*Rh*.1412^{a}23:—of other sounds, *twang*, of the bow-string, Od.21.411; *whistle*, of the wind through a tree, Mosch.*Fr*.1.8; *ring*, of a stone when struck, Theoc.7.26:—prov., πρὶν νενικηκέναι ᾄδειν '*to crow* too soon', Pl.*Tht*.164c.—Constr.:—ἀ. τινί *sing to* one, Od.22.346; also, *vie with* one *in singing*, Theoc.8.6; ᾆ. πρὸς αὐλὸν ἢ λύραν *sing* to.., Arist.*Pr*.918^{a}23; ὑπ' αὐλοῖς Plu.2. 41c:—ἀείσας.. χαίρειν Δημοκλέα, poet. for εἰπών, *Epigr.Gr*.237.7 (Smyrna). **II.** trans., **1.** c. acc. rei, *sing of, chant*, μῆνιν ἄειδε Il.1.1; παιήονα 1.473; κλέα ἀνδρῶν, νόστον, 9.189, Od.1.326; τὸν Βοιώτιον νόμον S.*Fr*.966: c. gen. (sc. μέλος), *sing* an air of..., Φρυνίχου Ar.*V*.269, cf. 1225: abs., ἀ. ἀμφί τινος *to sing* in one's praise, Od.8.266; ἀμφί τινα Terp.2, cf. E.*Tr*.513; εἴς τινα Ar.*Lys*. 1243: later, simply = καλεῖν, Ael.*NA*3.28:—Pass., of songs, *to be sung*, Hdt.4.35; τὰ λεχθέντα καὶ ᾀσθέντα Pl.*Lys*.205e; ᾆσμα καλῶς ᾀσθέν, opp. λόγος καλῶς ῥηθείς, X.*Cyr*.3.3.55; ᾄδεται λόγος the story *runs*, Ph.1.189. **2.** of persons, places, etc., *sing, praise, celebrate*, B.6.6, etc.:—Pass., ἀείδεται θρέψαισ' ἥρωας *is celebrated* as the nurse of heroes, Pi.*P*.8.25, cf. 5.24. **3.** Pass., *to be filled with song*, ἀείδετο πᾶν τέμενος.. θαλίαις Pi.*O*.10(11).76.

ἀει-εστώ, ἡ, *eternal being*, Antipho Soph.22. **-ζωής**, ές, *ever-living*, Dam.*Pr*.161. **-ζωΐα**, ἡ, *everlasting life*, ibid. **-ζωος**, ον, Trag. contr. **-ζως**, ων, *ever-living, everlasting*, πῦρ ἀείζωον Heraclit. 30, Nic.*Al*.174; ἀείζως γενεά S.*Fr*.740; ἀείζων πένθος ib.741; ἀείζως θεός *CIG*4598 (Palaest.), *BGU*1247 (ii A.D.); οἱ ἀείζωοι *the immortals*, Call.*Iamb*.1.265; ἀειζώου ψυχᾶς Melanipp.6, *IG*14.2241 (Italy): metaph., ἄχθος ἀείζων A.*Supp*.988:—dist. fr. ἀΐδιος, *Corp.Herm*. 8.2. **II.** *evergreen*, πόα A.*Fr*.28, 29, cf. *Gp*.2.18.1: esp. **-ζωον**, τό, *houseleek, Sempervivum*, Thphr.*HP*1.10.4, Dsc.4.88; ἀ. μέγα *S. arboreum*, ἀ. μικρόν *S. tectorum*, ib.89; ἀ. λεπτόφυλλον *stone-crop, Sedum stellatum*, Ps.-Dsc.4.90. **-ζωτος**, ον, prob. *ever-girded, aye ready*, *EM*22.20, sine expl. **-ζώων**, ουσα, ον, *ever-living*, κεραυνός Cleanth.*Stoic*.1.122; ἱερά Call.*Del*.314. **-θαλής**, ές, *evergreen*, *AP*7.195 (Mel.), 12.256 (Mel.); δένδρα Chor.p.87 B.: metaph., *ever-blooming*, Χάριτες Orph.*H*.60.5; νέος (of Γάμος personified) Men.Rh.p.404S.; τὸ ἀ. τῶν φύλλων Dsc.4.88. **-θανής**, ές, *ever-dying, ever fearing death*, Man.1.166. **-θερής**, ές, (θέρω) *always warming*, Eratosth.16.8. **II.** *where it is always summer*, Μερόη Nonn.*D*.17.396.

ἀειθέσσω· ἀληθεύω, Cyr.

ἀεί-θουρος, ον, *ever-warlike*, Opp.*C*.2.189. **-θρύλητος**, ον, *ever talked of, celebrated*, Lyd.*Mag*.3.51. **-καρπος**, ον, *ever fruit-bearing*, Thphr.*CP*1.22.4.

ἀ-εικέλιος, α, ον, Od.4.244, also ος, ον 19.341; poet. form of ἀεικής, 13.402, Il.14.84; contr. **αἰκέλιος** Thgn.1344, E.*Andr*.131 (lyr.):—of things, words, and actions; more rarely of persons, Od.6.242. Adv. -ίως Od.8.231, 16.109, B.3.45. **-εικής**, ές, (Att. αἰκής, q.v.) *unseemly, shameful*, ἀεικέα λοιγὸν ἀμύνειν Il.1.456, al.; ἀεικέα [εἵματα] ἕσσαι Od.24.250; δεσμός A.*Pr*.97, cf. 525; ἀεικεῖ σὺν στολᾷ S.*El*.191 (lyr.); -έστερα ἔπεα Hdt.7.13; οὐδὲν ἀ. παρέχεσθαι cause no *inconvenience*, Id.3.24; ἀεικέα μισθόν (v.l. ἀνεικέα, q.v.) *meagre*, Il.12.435; so οὐ.. ἀεικέα.. ἄποινα 24.594. Adv. ἀεικῶς Hsch.; Ion. -έως Simon.13; ἀεικές as Adv., Od.17.216. **2.** οὐδὲν ἀεικές ἐστι, c. inf., it is nothing *strange* that.., Hdt.3.33, 6.98, A.*Pr*.1042. **3.** *injurious, deadly*, ἰός Opp.*H*.2.422. **-εικία**, Ion. **-ίη** (Att. αἰκία, q.v.) [ῐ, whence in codd. often written -είη], ἡ, *outrage, injury*, πᾶσαν ἀεικίην ἄπεχε χροΐ (from Hector's body) Il.24.19: pl., μή τίς μοι ἀεικίας ἐνὶ οἴκῳ φαινέτω Od.20.308; ἀεικίῃ περιέπειν τινά Hdt.1.73, 115; ἀπαθὴς τῆς ἀ. Id.3.160. **-εικίζω** (Att. αἰκίζω, q.v.), fut. -ιῶ Il. (v. infr.), later Ep. also ἀεικίσσω Q.S.10.401: Ep. aor. ἀείκισσα Il.16.545:—**Med.**, Ep. aor. ἀεικισσάμην ib.559, 22.404:—**Pass.**, Ep. aor. inf. ἀεικισθήμεναι Od.18.222:—*treat unseemly, injure*, Hom. ll. cc.; οὐ γὰρ ἐγώ σ' ἔκπαγλον ἀεικιῶ *I will do* thee no great *dishonour*, Il.22.256, cf. 24.22 and 54, etc.:—Med. in act. sense, Il. ll. cc.

ἀει-κῑνησία, ἡ, *perpetual motion*, *Inscr.Perg*.333, [Gal.]19.376, Syr. *in Metaph*.37.13, Procl.*in Prm*.p.874S. **-κίνητος**, ον, *in perpetual motion*, Pl.*Phdr*.245c, Philol.21, Ruf.*Anat*.27, Aen.Gaz.*Thphr*. p.46B. Adv. -τως Arist.*Mu*.400^{b}31.

ἀείκιον· τὴν αἰκίαν, *EM*21.38.

ἀείκλαυτος, ον, *filled with perpetual lamentation*, μέλαθρα prob. in Hymn.ap.Hippol.*Haer*.4.36.

ἀει-κορσώσασθαι· κεῖραι κεφαλήν, Hsch. **-κόρσωτοι**· ἄκαρποι, Id.

ἀεί-κωμος, ον, *continually revelling*, Man.4.301. **-λάλος**, ον, *ever-babbling*, *AP*5.177 (Mel.). **-λαμπής**, ές, gloss on Ὄλυμπος, *ever-shining*, Stob.1.22.2.

ἀείλη· πνοή, Hsch.; cf. ἀέλλη.

ἀείλλω, *wheedle, cajole*, *EM*21.40, Hsch.; cf. ἀελλεῖ.

ἀει-λογέω, *to be always talking*, Hsch.; condemned by Phryn.*PS* p.35 B. **-λογία**, ἡ, *continual talking*:—as Att. law-term, τὴν ἀ. προτείνεσθαι or παρέχειν to court *continual inquiry* into one's conduct, D.19.2, 57.27.

ἄειλος, ον, (εἵλη) *unsunned*, πεδία A.*Fr*.334.

ἀεί-μαργος, ον, *ever-greedy*, Opp.*H*.2.213. **-μεριστός**, όν, *infinitely divisible*, Dam.*Pr*.178. **-μετάβλητος**, ον, *ever-changing*, ib. 405. **-μεταβόλος**, ον, = foreg., Procl.*in Ti*.1.125 D. **-μνημόνευτος**, ον, *ever-remembered*, J.*AJ*17.6.2, Ps.-Callisth.1.30. **-μνήμων**, ον, gen. ονος, *ever-remembering, of good memory*, Arist.*Phgn*.808^{a} 37. **-μνηστος**, ον, *had in everlasting remembrance*, ἔργον A.*Pers*. 760; τάφος S.*Aj*.1166, E.*IA*1531 (lyr.), etc.; μετ' ἀ. μαρτυρίου Th. 1.33; τρόπαια Lys.2.20: Comp., Id.26.4; ἅπασι ἀ. ἡ ἁμαρτία Antipho 5.79; ἀρετή Isoc.9.4; χάριτες *PLips*.35.22 (iv A.D.). Adv. -τως Aeschin.2.180, *PLond*.3.854.12 (i A.D.). **-νάης**, ές, = sq., Nic.*Fr*. 78, in Ep. dat. pl. ἀειναέεσσι. **-ναος**, ον, = ἀέναος, q.v. **-ναῦται**, ῶν, οἱ, board of magistrates at Chalcis, *IG*12(9).909 (ἀε-), 923 (iii B.C.); also at Miletus, Plu.2.298c. (Cf. ναῦος; wrongly expl. by Plu. l.c. as *meeting on board ship*.)

ἀεινεφεῖς· τυφλώσεις, Hsch., cf. *EM*21.41.

ἀείνως, ων, Att. contr. for ἀείναος, v. ἀέναος.

ἀει-πᾰθής, ές, *perpetually passive*, φύσις Crito ap.Stob.3.3.64, cf. Philol.21. **-πάθεια**· ἡ, *perpetual passivity*, Gal.1.317. **-παλής**, ές, *always beating*, καρδία *Hippiatr*.7. **-πάρθενος**, ἡ, *ever a virgin*,

Sapph.96 (in Aeol. form ἄϊπ–); of the Vestals, αἱ ἱέρειαι αἱ ἀειπ. D.C. 56.5, cf. 59.3. 2. in Pythag. language, of the number 7 (as being neither factor nor multiple of any number up to 10), Ph.1.46; of the Sabbath, ib.497. **–πλᾰνος**, ον, *ever-wandering*, χέλεα γρηός Call.*Fr.anon.*2.

ἄειρον (ἐρῶ)· ἄρρητον, Hsch., *EM*21.43: also = ἀθώπευτον, ib.:— but **ἄειρος**, ον, (εἴρω) = ἄπειρος, Hsch., Suid.

ἀεί-ροος, ον, contr. **-ρους**, ουν, = sq., Aristeas 116, Suid. **–ρῦτος**, ον, *ever-flowing*, κρήνη S.*OC*469.

ἀείρω, Ep., Ion., and poet.; **αἴρω** (once in Hom., v. infr.), Att. and Trag. (exc. A.*Th.*759, *Pers.*660, both lyr.); Aeol. **ἀέρρω**, Alc.78: impf. ἤειρον (συν–) Il.10.499, Hdt.2.125, Ep. ἄειρον Il.19.386, Att. and Trag. ἦρον: fut. ἀρῶ [ᾱ], contr. for ἀερῶ (which is not found), A. *Pers.*795, E.*Heracl.*322, *Tr.*1148, prob. in Luc.*Hist.Conscr.*14: aor. 1 ἤειρα (συν–) Il.24.590, (παρ–) Archil.94, Herod.9.13, Ep. ἄειρα Il.23.730; Aeol. imper. ἀέρρατε Sapph.91; subj. ἀέρσῃ Panyas.13.13; part. ἀείρας S.*Ant.*418; also ἄηρα *IG*12(3).449 (Thera); ἦρα Hdt. 9.59, A.*Ag.*47, Th.6.18, etc., 3 pl. ἤροσαν Lxx*Jo.*3.14, opt. ἄραις Herod.5.71, inf. ἆραι Call.*Cer.*35, part. ἄρας Th.2.12, etc., Cret. ἤραντας *GDI*5015 (Gort.) [ᾱ– in all moods]: pf. ἦρκα D.25.52, (ἀπ–) Th.8.100, plpf. ἤρκεσαν (ἀπ–) D.19.150:—**Med. ἀείρομαι** (ἀπ–) Il. 21.563, S.*Tr.*216 (lyr.); **αἴρομαι** E.*El.*360, Th.4.60: fut. ἀροῦμαι [ᾰ] E.*Hel.*1597: aor. 1 imper. ἀείραο A.R.4.746, inf. ἀείρασθαι (ἀντ–) Hdt.7.212, part. –άμενος Il.23.856, *IG*4.952.112 (Epid.); also ἠρά-μην [ᾱ– in all moods] Il.14.510, Od.4.107, E.*Heracl.*986, Ar. *Ra.*525, Pl.*R.*374e, etc., Dor. ἄρατο B.2.5: pf. ἦρμαι S.*El.*54:— **Pass.**, E.*Alc.*450 (lyr.), Hp.*Mul.*2.174: fut. ἀρθήσομαι Ar.*Ach.*565: aor. ἠέρθην A.R.4.1651, (παρ–) Il.16.341, Ep. ἀέρθην Od.19.540, 3 pl. ἄερθεν Il.8.74, subj. ἀερθῶ E.*Andr.*848 (lyr.), part. ἀερθείς Od.8.375, Pi.*N.*7.75, A.*Ag.*1525 (lyr.), Hp.*Mul.*1.1, etc.; also ἤρθην Simon.111, A.*Th.*214 (lyr.), Th.4.42, etc., part. ἀρθείς Il.13.63, (ἐπ–) Hdt.1.90, etc.: pf. ἤερμαι A.R.2.171: Ep. plpf. 3 sg. ἄωρτο (for ἤορτο) Il.3.272, Theoc.24.43, ἕωρτο Hsch. [ἀείρω has ᾰ, exc. in late poetry, as Opp. *C.*1.347.] (ἀείρω = ἀ-ϝερ-yω, cf. ἀνειρομέναι Alcm.23.63; αἴρω (once in Hom., Il.17.724 in part. αἴροντας) may = ϝαρ-yω for ϝr̥-yω from the reduced form of the root, but is more probably an analogical formation arising from the contracted forms. Fut. ἀροῦμαι [ᾰ] and aor. ἀρόμην, ἤρετο, etc., inf. ἀρέσθαι [ᾰ], belong to ἄρνυμαι, q.v.; ἠράτο may have displaced ἤρετο in Hom., cf. Eust. ad Il.3.373. The sense *attach* found in compds. συν–, παρ-αείρω is prob. derived from the use v.1.)

I. Act., *lift, raise up*, νέκυν Il.17.724; ὑψόσ' ἀείρας [κυνέην] 10.465; πίνακας παρέθηκεν ἀείρας Od.1.141; Εὐμάστας με ἄηρεν ἀπὸ χθονός *IG*12(3).449, inscr. on a stone (Thera); ἀπὸ γῆς αἴ. Pl.*Ti.*90a; ἱστία στεῖλαν ἀείραντες furled by *brailing them up*, Od.3.11; but ἀ. ἱστία *hoist* sail, A.R.2.1229; αἴ. κεραίας D.S.13.12; εὔμαριν ἀ. A.*Pers.* 660; κοῦφον αἴ. βῆμα *walk lightly, trip*, E.*Tr.*342; αἴ. σκέλη, of a horse, X.*Eq.*10.15, cf. Arist.*IA*710ᵇ20; ὀρθὸν αἴ. τὸ κάρα A.*Ch.*496; ὀφθαλμὸν ἄρας S.*Tr.*795; ἄρασα μύξας, of a deer, Id.*Fr.*89; ὀφρῦς αἴροντα Diph.85; αἴ. σημεῖον *make* a signal, X.*Cyr.*7.1.23; αἴ. μηχανήν, in the theatre, Antiph.191.15; so ἐπὶ τὰς μηχανὰς καταφεύγουσι θεοὺς αἴροντες Pl.*Cra.*425d; τεῖχος ἱκανὸν αἴ. Th.1.90, cf. 2.75:—freq. in part., ἄρας ἔπαισε he *raised* [them] and struck, S.*OT* 1270; ἡ βουλὴ ἄρασα τὴν ἀφ' ἱερὰς ἀφῆκεν Plu.*Cor.*32, cf. 1*Ep.Cor.* 6.15:—Pass., ἐς αἰθέρα δῖαν ἀέρθη Od.19.540, cf. Il.8.74; ὑψόσ' ἀερθείς Od.12.432; ἔμπνους ἀρθείς Antipho 2.1.9; φρυκτοὶ ἤροντο Th.2.94, cf. Aen.Tact.26.14; *mount up*, X.*HG*5.2.5; ἄνω ἀρθῆναι, of the sun, *to be high* in heaven, Hp.*Aër.*6; *to be seized, snatched up*, Ar.*Ach.*565. 2. *take up*, in various uses: *draw* water, Ar.*Ra.* 1339; *gather* food, S.*Ph.*707; *pluck* herbs, *PMag.Par.*1.287, al. 3. *take up and carry* or *bring*, ἐκ βελέων Σαρπηδόνα δῖον ἀείρας Il.16.678; νόσφιν ἀειράσας 24.583; ἄχθος ἀ. *convey*, of ships, Od.3.312; μῆλα ἐξ Ἰθάκης ἄειραν νηυσὶ *carried* them *off*, 21.18; μή μοι οἶνον ἄειρε *bring* me not wine, Il.6.264. 4. *take up and bear*, as a burden, μόρον A.*Pers.*547; ἆθλον S.*Tr.*80; ἄλγος A.R.4.65. b. *wear* clothes, Lxx 1*Ki.*2.28, al. 5. of armies or fleets, τὰς ναῦς αἴ. *get* the ships *under sail*, Th.1.52; esp. intr., *get under way, set out*, ἆραι τῷ στρατῷ Id.2.12: abs., ib.23:—Pass., ἀερθῆναι Hdt.9.52; ἀερθέντες ἐκ.. 1.165; ἀ. εἰς.. 1.170; ἐφ' ἡμετέρᾳ γᾷ ἀρθείς S.*Ant.*111 (lyr.); but ἀερθείς *carried too far*, Pi.*N.*7.75. 6. *raise, levy*, λεκτὸν ἀροῦμεν στόλον A. *Pers.*795. 7. *rear* a child, τοῖς τοκεῦσί σ' ἤειρα Herod.9.13. II. *raise up, exalt*, ἀπὸ σμικροῦ δ' ἂν ἄρειας μέγαν A.*Ch.*262, cf. 791; ὄλβον ὃν Δαρεῖος ἦρεν Id.*Pers.*164:—esp. of pride and passion, *exalt, excite*, ὑψοῦ αἴ. θυμόν *grow excited*, S.*OT*914; αἴ. θάρσος *pluck up* courage, E.*IA*1598:—Pass., *to be raised, increased*, ἡ δύναμις ἤρετο Th.1.118; ἤρετο τὸ ὕψος τοῦ τείχους μέγα Id.2.75; ἤρθη μέγας *rose* to greatness, D.2.8; οὐκ ἤρθη νοῦν ἐς ἀτασθαλίην Simon.111; ἀρθῆναι φόβῳ, δείμασι, A.*Th.*214, E.*Hec.*69: abs., ἀείρομαι S.*Tr.*216 (lyr.), cf. Ar.*Ec.* 1180. 2. *raise by words*, hence, *praise, extol*, E.*Heracl.*322, etc.; αἴ. λόγῳ *to exaggerate*, D.21.71. III. *lift and take away, remove*, ἀπό με τιμὰν ἦραν A.*Eu.*847; τινὰ ἐκ τῆς πόλεως Pl.*R.*578e; generally, *take away, put an end to*, κακά E.*El.*942; τραπέζας αἴ. *clear away* dinner, Men.273; ἀρθέντος τοῦ αἰτίου Arist.*Pr.*920ᵇ11; *deny* (opp. τίθημι *posit*), S.E.*P.*1.10; Delph. and Locr. pf. Pass. part. ἀρμένος *cancelled, null and void*, ὠνὰ ἀ. καὶ ἄκυρος *GDI*1746 (Delph.); ἀτελὴς καὶ ἀ. *IG*9(1).374 (Naupactus). 2. *make away with, destroy*, *Ev.Matt.*24.39; ἆρον, ἆρον *away with him! Ev.Jo.*19.15; ἐκ τῶν ζώντων αἴ. *Tab.Defix.Aud.*1.18. IV. Med., *lift, take up for oneself* or *what is one's own*, [πέπλων] ἕν' ἀειραμένη Il.6.293; hence, *carry off, win*, πάντας ἀειράμενος πελέκεας 23.856; ἄρατο νίκαν B.2.5; ἠρμένοι νίκην Str.3.2.13. 2. ὄγκον ἄρασθαι *to be puffed up*, S.*Aj.* 129; θαυμαστὸν ὄγκον ἀράμενοι τοῦ μύθου Pl.*Plt.*277b. 3. *raise, lift*, τύπωμα ἠρμένοι χεροῖν S.*El.*54; κανοῦν αἴ. Ar.*Av.*850; βοῦς *IG*2².1028.28, cf. Thphr.*Char.*27.5; ῥόθιον *raise* a surging cheer, Ar.*Eq.* 546; Σαμόσατα ἀράμενος μετέθηκεν Luc.*Hist.Conscr.*24; ἀείρεσθαι τὰ ἱστία *hoist* sail, Hdt.8.56, cf. 94. 4. *raise, stir up*, νεῖκος ἀειράμενος Thgn.90, cf. E.*Heracl.*986, 991; *begin, undertake*, πόλεμον A. *Supp.*342, Hdt.7.132, Th.4.60, D.5.5 (Pass., πόλεμος αἴρεται Ar.*Av.* 1188); κίνδυνον Antipho 5.63; φυγὴν αἴρεσθαι *take to* flight, A.*Pers.* 481, E.*Rh.*54. 5. *take upon oneself, undergo*, πόνον S.*Ant.*907; πένθος Id.*OT*1225; βάρος E.*Cyc.*473. 6. abs., βαρὺς ἀ. slow to *undertake anything*, Hdt.4.150. 7. *take away, remove*, E.*IT*1201; hence, *kill* or *destroy*, D.H.4.4, J.*AJ*19.1.3; πόλιν D.H.6.23. V. Pass., *to be suspended, hang*, [μάχαιρα] πὰρ ξίφεος μέγα κουλεὸν αἰὲν ἄωρτο Il.3.272, 19.253. 2. Medic., *to be swollen*, [σπλὴν] ἀερθείς Hp.*Mul.*1.61; μαζοὶ ἀείρονται ib.2.174.

ἀείς, part. of ἄημι.

ἀείσε, late form for ἀεί, Steph. *in Hp.*1.129 D., al.

ἀει-σιτία, Ion. –ίη, ἡ, *privilege of an* ἀείσιτος, Hp.*Ep.*27. **–σῖτος**, ον, *always fed*: *perpetual guest*, Epich.34; at Athens, of those maintained at public cost in the Prytaneum (in form ἀΐσ–), *IG*2².678.42, 3.1019, al.

ἀείσκωψ, a kind of *owl* (cf. σκώψ), so called (acc. to Arist.) from not being migratory, perh. *Ephialtes scops*, Arist.*HA*617ᵇ32. (Pl. –σκῶπες, but ἀείσκωπες Eust.1524.6.)

ἄεισμα, τό, poet. and Ion. for ᾆσμα, Hdt.2.79, Eup.139, Call.*Ep.* 29.1.

ἀείστροφος, ον, *ever-turning*, Tz.*H.*10.568.

ἀείτας, α, ὁ, Boeot. for ἀετός, Lyc.461. II. v. sub ἀΐτας.

ἀειτελής, ές, *ever-perfect*, θεός Alcin.*Intr.*10.

ἄειτον· ταχύ, Hsch., *EM*21.42; cf. ἄελλον.

ἀει-φᾰνής, ές, *always above the horizon*, of stars, Nearch.ap.Arr. *Ind.*25.6, cf. Cleom.1.5. 2. *ever-shining*, πῦρ, of the sun, D.P. 583; λύχνος Nonn.*D.*27.320. **–φεγγής**, ές, *ever-shining*, *Corp. Herm.*18.14. **–φόρος**, ον, = ἀειθαλής, dub. in S.*Fr.*580. **–φρουρος**, ον, *ever-watching*, i.e. *everlasting*, τῷ ἀ. μελιλώτῳ Cratin.98.7; οἴκησις ἀ., of the grave, S.*Ant.*892; πόνοι Opp.*H.*4.189. **–φῠγία**, ἡ, *exile for life*, φευγέτω ἀειφυγίαν Pl.*Lg.*877c, *IG*1.9, *SIG*194 (Amphipolis, iv B. C.); ἀειφυγίᾳ ζημιοῦν τινά D.21.43, etc. **–φύλακτος**, ον, gloss on ἀείφρουρος, Sch.Opp.*H.*4.189. **–φυλλία**, ἡ, *being non-deciduous*, Thphr.*CP*2.17.2. **–φυλλος**, ον, *not deciduous*, Arist. *GA*783ᵇ10, Thphr.*CP*1.10.7. **–χλωρος**, ον, *always green*, Euph. 133; used of κάππαρις, Dsc.2.173. **–χρόνιος**, ον, *everlasting*, *AP* 12.229 (Strat.). **–χρυσον**, τό, = ἀείζωον μέγα, Ps.-Dsc.4.88.

ἀεκαζόμενος, η, ον, particip. form, = ἀέκων, πόλλ' ἀ. Od.13.277, cf. *h.Cer.*30, Od.18.135. **ἀέκασσα**· ἄκουσα, Hsch. **ἀέκαστι**, Adv., etym. of ἀέκητι, A.D.*Conj.*233.26, *EM*19.33.

ἀεκήλιος, ον, for ἀεικέλιος, Il.18.77. (Derived from ἀ- priv., ἕκηλος by Hdn.Gr.2.106.)

ἀέκητι, Ep. Adv. *against one's will*, c. gen., ἀ. σέθεν Od.3.213, 16.94; θεῶν ἀ., ἀ. θεῶν, Il.12.8, Od.4.504.

ἀεκούσιος, ον (also α, ον Luc.*Syr.D.*18), Ion. and Ep. (also in anap., S.*Tr.*1263); Att. contr. **ἀκούσιος** [ᾱ], ον, also in Democr. 240:—*against the will, constrained*, of acts or their consequences, καὶ τῷ οὔ κως ἀεκ. ἐγίνετο τὸ ποιεύμενον Hdt.2.162; τλήσομαι.. ἀεκούσια πολλὰ βίαια Thgn.1343; ἐς ἀ. ἀνάγκας πίπτειν Th.3.82; πόνοι Democr. l.c.; often in Att. of *involuntary* offences, ἀ. φόνος Antipho 3.2.6; πράκτορες τῶν ἀκουσίων ib., cf. Pl.*Lg.*733d, 864a, Arist.*EN*1109ᵇ35, al.; τὰ μὲν ἀ. ἁπλῆ, τὰ δὲ ἑκούσια διπλῆ *IG*1.1. Adv. –ίως D.21.43, Sever.ap.Eus.*PE*13.17. II. of persons, only in Adv. ἀκουσίως *involuntarily*, Th.2.8, Pl.*Ti.*62c; ἀ. ἀποθανεῖν, opp. ἑκουσίως ἀποκτείνειν, Antipho 1.5; ἀ. τινὶ ἀφῖχθαι to have come *as an unwelcome* guest, Th.3.31.

ἀέκων, Ep. and Ion.; Att. and Trag. contr. **ἄκων** [ᾱ], ουσα, ον (uncontr. form also in *IG*1.61 (law of Draco), A.*Supp.*39 (anap.), sts. found in codd. of Hdt., as 4.120, 164):—*involuntary, constrained*, of persons, ἀέκοντος ἐμεῖο Il.1.310; ἑκὼν ἀέκοντί γε θυμῷ 4.43; πόλλ' ἀέκων 11.557; opp. βουλόμενος, Hp.*VC*11; τὼ δ' οὐκ ἀέκοντε πετέσθην (v.l. ἄκοντε) Il.5.366, Od.3.484; κάρτα ἀ. Hdt.9.111; ἀέκουσι (v.l. ἀεκούσια) δάκρυα παραρρεῖ Hp.*Epid.*1.19: contr. first in *h.Cer.*413; ἄκοντος Διός *invito Jove*, A.*Pr.*771; repeated, ἄκοντά σ' ἄκων προσπασσαλεύσω ib.19, cf. 671; ἀ. ἀκούει οὓς ἑκὼν εἶπεν λόγους S.*Fr.*929, cf. *Ant.*276; μηδένα τῶνδ' ἀέκοντα μένειν κατέρυκε Thgn.467. Adv. ἀκόντως *unwillingly*, ὁμολογεῖν Pl.*Prt.*333b, cf. *Hp.Mi.*374d; οὐκ ἀ. ἀλλὰ προθύμως ἐπείσθησαν X.*HG*4.8.5. II. Poet., like ἀκούσιος, of acts or their consequences, *involuntary*, κακὰ ἑκόντα κοὐκ ἄ. S.*OT* 1230; ἔργων ἀ. Id.*OC*240 (lyr.), cf. 977.

ἀέλικτος, ον, v.l. for τριέλικτος, Orac.ap.Hdt.6.77.

ἀέλιοι and **αἰέλιοι**, οἱ, *brothers-in-law*, whose wives are sisters, Hsch. (αἴλιοι), Eust.648.45, *EM*31.24; cf. εἰλίονες.

ἀέλιος, ὁ, Dor. for ἠέλιος, ἥλιος. [ᾱ, but ᾰ S.*Tr.*835.]

ἄελλα, Ep. **ἀέλλη**, ης, Aeol. **αὔελλα** Alc.125 (αὐεοῦλλαι cod. Hsch.), ἡ, *stormy wind, whirlwind*, ἀργαλέων ἀνέμων ἀτάλαντοι ἀέλλῃ Il.13.795; ἀέλλαι παντοίων ἀνέμων Od.5.292, 304; of dust, ὕψι δ' ἀέλλη σκίδνατο Il.16.374, cf. 13.334; in late Prose, Olymp. *in Mete.*13. 18. 2. metaph., of any *whirling motion*, ὠκυδρόμοις ἀ., of an animal, E.*Ba.*873; ἄστρων ὑπ' ἀέλλαισι Id.*Hel.*1498.—Cf. ἀελλη.

ἀελλαῖος, α, ον, *storm-swift*, πελειάς S.*OC*1081 (lyr.). **ἀελλάς**, άδος, ἡ, = foreg., ἵπποι S.*OT*466 (lyr.); φωναί Id.*Fr.*688.

ἀελλεῖ· φιλεῖ, κολακεύει, Hsch.; but **ἀελλῶν**· στρέφων, ὀπτῶν, ποικίλ⟨λ⟩ων, Id. **ἀέλλεται**· πνεῖ, *EM*20.1.

ἀελλήεις, εσσα, εν, = ἀελλαῖος, Nonn.*D*.5.322, al.

ἀελλής κονίσαλος *eddying* dust, Il.3.13. (Perh. rather ἀελλῆς, contr. for -ήεις.)

ἀελλησιθύμοις (prob. -μυθοις)· ἀνυποστάτοις μετὰ παρρησίας, Hsch., *AB*348.

ἀελλο-δρόμας, α, *storm-swift*, πῶλος B.5.39. **-θριξ**, τριχος, ὁ, ἡ, *with hair floating in the wind*, S.*Fr*.292.

ἀελλο-μάχος, ον, *struggling with the storm*, *AP*7.586 (Jul. Aeg.). **-πος**, ποδος, ὁ, ἡ, for ἀελλόπους (like ἀρτίπος, Οἰδίπος, etc.):—*storm-footed, storm-swift*, Il.8.409, etc. (never in Od.); Ἅρπυια Euph.113; dat. pl. ἀελλοπόδεσσιν *h.Ven*.217: pl. ἀελλόποδες, -πόδων, Simon.7, Pi.*N*.1.6, etc.: once in Trag., E.*Hel*.1314.—Later **ἀελλοπόδης**, ου, of the hare, Opp.*C*.1.413.

ἄελλον· ταχύ, *EM*20.7.

ἀελλός, ὁ, a bird, Hsch.

Ἀελλώ, όος, contr. οῦς, ἡ, (ἄελλα) *Storm-swift*, name of a Harpy, Hes.*Th*.267.

ἀελλώδης, ες, *storm-like, stormy*, Sch.Il.3.13, cf. Hsch.

ἀέλον· ἕωλον (Cret.), Hsch. **ἀελπάρεα**· δεινά, Id.

ἀελπ-ής, ές, *unhoped for*, γαῖαν ἀελπέα δῶκεν ἰδέσθαι Od.5.408. **-τέω**, *have no hope, despair*, only in part., ἀελπτέοντες σόον εἶναι Il.7.310; ἀ. τοὺς Ἕλληνας ὑπερβαλέεσθαι Hdt.7.168. **-τία**, ἡ, *an unlooked for event*, ἐξ ἀελπτίης *unexpectedly*, Archil.54; *unexpected stroke*, Pi.*P*.12.31 [where ῑ]. **-τος**, ον, *unhoped for, unexpected*, *h.Cer*.219, Hes.*Fr*.96.57, B.3.29; ἐξ ἀέλπτου *beyond hope, unexpectedly*, in good sense, Hdt.1.111; ἐξ ἀέλπτων S.*Aj*.715 (lyr.); in bad sense, A.*Supp*.357,987 (prob. l.); πῆμ' ἄ., ἄ. κακόν, Id.*Pers*.265,1006; εἴπερ ὄψομαι τὰν ἄ. ἁμέραν E.*Supp*.784; ἄελπτα γὰρ λέγεις Id.*Hel*.585. 2. *beyond hope, despaired of*, Archil.74, Hp.*Art*.42. II. Act., *hopeless, desperate*, *h.Ap*.91, A.*Supp*.907. III. Adv. -τως *beyond all hope*, in good sense, A.*Pers*.261, S.*El*.1263: neut. pl. as Adv., ἀ. φανεὶς E.*Ph*.311. [ᾰ Hes. l.c.]

ἄεμμα, τό, Ep. for ἅμμα, *bow-string* or *bow*, Call.*Dian*.10, *Ap*.33.

ἀέμπεδον· βέβαιον, Hsch.

ἀε-ναής, ές, = sq., κελάδημα *IPE*1².519 (Chersonesus, ii A.D.). **-νάος** [ᾱ-], ον, (νάω A) ἀέναος Hdt., αἰέναος *IG*5(1).1119 (Geronthrae, iv B.C.); contr. **ἀείνως** Ar.*Ra*.146, gen. pl. ἀείνων Cratin.20D.: Trag. only in lyr.:—*ever-flowing*, κρήνης τ' ἀενάου καὶ ἀπορρύτου Hes.*Op*.595; ἀ. λίμνη, ποταμός, Hdt.1.93,145, cf. Simon.120; ποταμοὶ A.*Supp*.553, E.*Ion*1083, cf. 118; Ἀχέρων Theoc.15.102; ἀενάου πυρός Pi.*P*.1.6, cf. Call.*Ap*.83; βόρβορον καὶ σκῶρ ἀείνων Ar. l.c.; ἀέναοι νεφέλαι Id.*Nu*.275:—generally, *everlasting*, ἀρετᾶς..κόσμον ἀέναόν τε κλέος Simon.4.9; ἀ. τιμά, of Zeus, Pi.*O*.14.12; ἀ. κράτος E.*Or*.1299 (lyr.); ἀενάοις ἐν τραπέζαις, of public hospitality, Pi.*N*.11.8; γλῶτταν καλῶν λόγων ἀείνων Cratin. l.c.:—also in Prose, κλέος Heraclit.29; τροφή X.*Ages*.1.20; ἀεναώτερον...τὸν ὄλβον παρέχειν Id.*Cyr*.4.2.44; ἀέναον οὐσίαν πορίσαι Pl.*Lg*.966e; ἀ. ποταμῶν ἀμήχανα μεγέθη Id.*Phd*.111d, cf. Arist.*Mete*.349^{b}9; θῖνες Lxx *Ba*.5.7; ἀένναοι τῶν θεῶν πρόσοδοι Procl.*Inst*.152. Adv. ἀενάως Arist.*Oec*.1346^{b}15. **-νάων**, ουσα, ον, = foreg., Od.13.109, Hes.*Op*.550, Antim.59.3.

ἀέντιον· Αἰγύπτιον σμυρνίον, Hsch.

ἀεξί-βιος, ον, *increasing while one lives* (?), πένθος *IG*14.2123. **-γυιος**, ον, *strengthening the limbs*, ἄεθλα Pi.*N*.4.73. **-κερως**, ων, gen. ω, *growing horns*, κριός *IG*14.1301. **-νοος**, ον, contr. **-νους**, ουν, *strengthening the mind*, Procl.*H*.3.16, Nonn.*D*.14.119. **-τοκος**, ον, *nourishing the fruit of the womb*, ib.5.614, al. **-τροφος**, ον, *fostering growth*, Orph.*H*.51.18. **-φυλλος**, ον, *nourishing leaves, leafy*, ἀκταί A.*Ag*.697. **-φυτος**, ον, *nourishing plants*, Ἠώς *AP*9.363.5 (Mel.), cf. Nonn.*D*.7.304, al.

ἀέξω, poet. form of αὔξω (αὐξάνω), once in Hdt., twice in Trag.(lyr.); in early writers only in pres. and unaugm. impf.: in later Poets fut. ἀεξήσω Nonn.*D*.12.24, aor. ἠέξησα ib.8.104, *IG*4.787 (Troezen, iv A.D.): fut. Med. ἀεξήσομαι A.R.3.837: aor. Pass. ἀεξήθην *AP*9.631 (Agath.): plpf. ἠέξητο (ἀν-) Nonn.*D*.4.427: (ἀϝέξω, cf. Lat. *augeo*, Skt. *vakṣáyati*, etc.):—*increase, foster*, ἀνδρὶ δὲ κεκμηῶτι μένος μέγα οἶνος ἀέξει Il.6.261; θυμὸν ἀ. Il.17.226; πένθος ἀ. *cherish* woe, Od.17.489; υἱὸν ἀ. *rear* him *to man's estate*, 13.360; ἔργον ἀέξουσι.. θεοί they *bless* the work, 15.372. 2. *exalt, glorify*, αὐτούς τ' ἀέξοι καὶ πόλιν Pi.*O*.8.88; τὸ πλῆθος ἀ. Hdt.3.80; *spread, diffuse*, [ἀγγελίαν] μῦθος ἀέξει S.*Aj*.226. 3. ἀ. βούταν φόνον E.*Hipp*.537. II. Pass., *increase, grow*, Τηλέμαχος δὲ νέον μὲν ἀέξετο *was waxing tall*, Od.22.426; καλὰ μὲν ἠέξευ Call.*Jov*.55; οὐ..ποτ' ἀέξετο κῦμά γ' ἐν αὐτῷ no wave *rose high* thereon, Od.10.93; χόλος ..ἀνδρῶν ἐν στήθεσσιν ἠΰτε καπνὸς ἀ. *rises high*, Il.18.110; τόδε ἔργον ἀ. it *prospers*, Od.14.66; ἀέξετο ἱερὸν ἦμαρ *was getting on to noon*, Il.8.66; μηνὸς -ομένοιο Hes.*Op*.773; μῆτις ἀ. Emp.106; κέρδος ἀ. A.*Ch*.825 (cod. M), cf. *Supp*.856 (prob.). III. intr., = Pass., Q.S.1.116.

ἄεπτος, ον, (ἕπομαι) v.l. for ἀέλπτοις in A.*Ag*.141 (Sch. Med. τοῖς ἕπεσθαι τοῖς γονεῦσι μὴ δυναμένοις). II. (ἔπος), = ἄρρητος, v.l. for ἄαπτος, q.v.

ἀεργ-ηλός, ή, όν, = ἀεργός, A.R.4.1186; ὕπνος *Lyr.Adesp*.92:—also **-ής**, ές, Nic.*Fr*.72.4. **-ία**, Ion. **-ίη** [ῐ], ἡ, *a not-working, idleness*, Od.24.251, Hes.*Op*.311, Bion *Fr*.14.6 (ubi vulg. ἀεργείᾳ). 2. of a field, *a lying fallow* or *waste*, Orac.ap.Aeschin.3.108; of the bowels, *sluggishness*, Aret.*SD*1.15. **-ός**, όν, *not working, idle*, Il.9.320, Od.19.27, Hes.*Op*.303, Theoc.28.15, etc.; opp. ἐνεργός, Hp.*de Arte* 11: c. gen., *not working out, not doing*, ἔργων αἰσχρῶν ἀπαθὴς καὶ ἀ. Thgn.1177:—of things, *inert*, Aret.*SD*1.9. Adv. -γῶς *PFlor*.295.5 (vi A.D.). II. Act., *debilitating*, μάλκαι Nic.*Th*.381 codd.—Att. **ἀργός**, q.v.

ἀέργυγον· καθέδραν, οἱ δὲ τάγηνα, Hsch.

ἀέρδην, Adv. *lifting up*, A.*Ag*.234 (Att. ἄρδην).

ἀερέθομαι, see under Ion. form ἠερ-.

ἀερήιον· ἀμέτρητον, πολὺ ἀερῶδες, Hsch.

Ἀερία, ας, Ion. **Ἠερίη**, ης, ἡ, old name of Egypt, prob. from ἀήρ, *the misty land*, A.*Supp*.75, cf. A.R.4.267; also of Crete, Plin.*HN* 4.58. II. name of plant, *PMag.Par*.1.2360.

ἀερίδες· μέλισσαι, Hsch.

ἀερ-ίζω, (ἀήρ) *to be like air*, Secund.*Sent*.4; hence, 1. *to be thin as air*, Dsc.1.68.6. 2. *to be light blue* (or perh. *grey, cloudy*), of μολύβδαινα, Id.5.85; of cataract, Dem.Ophth.ap.Aët.7.53; of a kind of jasper, Plin.*HN*37.115, *PMag.Leid.V*.6.28. II. '*tread on air*', of boxers, Philostr.*Gym*.50. **-ικόν**, τό, *tax on lights*, Procop.*Arc*.21. **-ῐνος**, η, ον, *aerial, like air*, Arist.*Metaph*.1049^{a}26, cf. *de An*.435^{a}12. 2. *light blue* (or *grey*), στολή Lxx *Es*.8.15; ἐσθής Poll.4.119; κολλύριον Gal.12.780. 3. of the planet Jupiter, ὁ λεγόμενος Ζεὺς ἀ. Ps.-Callisth.1.4.

ἀερίοικος, ον, *dwelling in air*, Eub.139 (mock heroic).

ἀέριος [ᾰ], α, ον, also ος, ον; Ion. **ἠέριος**, η, ον (q.v.): (ἀήρ):—*misty*, σκότον E.*Ph*.1534. II. *in the air, high in air*, κρότον ποδῶν Id.*Tr*.546; *of the air, aerial*, opp. χθόνιος, Id.*Fr*.27; πῦρ Hp.*Vict*.1.10; αἰτίαι ἀ., title of work by Democr.; opp. ὑπόγειος, *PMag.Lond*.121.893; ἀ. φύσις Arist.*Mu*.392^{b}14; ζῷα ib.398^{b}33; γένος Pl.*Epin*.984e; τὰ ἀ. Luc.*Prom.Es* 6. Adv. -ως Iamb.*Myst*.1.9. III. *wide as air, infinite*, ἄμμου μέγεθος ἀ. D.S.1.33, cf. 5.42. b. *indefinite, vain, futile*, Phld.*Vit*.p.9 J., *Ir*.p.79 W.; ἐπιζήτησις Id.*Sign*.21.

ἀέριπον· οὐ περιειργόμενον (i.e. ἄερκτον), Hsch.

ἀερίτης λίθος, kind of *precious stone*, Ps.-Callisth.3.22.

ἀερῖτις, ἡ, = ἀναγαλλὶς ἡ κυανῆ, Ps.-Dsc.2.178.

ἄερκτος, ον, (ἔργω, εἴργω) *unfenced, open*, Lys.7.28.

ἀερο-βαθής, ές, in neut. pl. -βαθῆ, τά, *depths of air*, 1 *Enoch* 17.3. **-βᾰτέω**, *walk the air*, of Socrates, Ar.*Nu*.225,1503, Pl.*Ap*.19c: aor. part. ἀεροβατήσας Ps.-Luc.*Philopatr*.12. II. *to be unduly puffed up*, Procop.*Arc*.13, cf. *Pers*.1.25. **-βάτης**, ου, ὁ, *one who walks the air*, Poet.ap.Plu.2.952f. **-βατικός**, ή, όν, *traversing air*, ζῷα prob. in Ath.3.99b. **-δονέομαι**, *to be whirled through air*, Sch.A.*Pr*.128. **-δόνητος**, ον, *air-tossed, soaring*, Ar.*Av*.1385. **-δρομέω**, *traverse the air*, Luc.*VH*1.10. **-δρόμος**, ον, *traversing the air*, *PMag.Par*.1.1359,1375. **-ειδής** [ᾰ], Ep. and Ion. **ἠεροειδής**, ές, *like the sky* or *air*, Pl.*Ti*.78c, Arist.*GC* 330^{b}24, etc.:—*cloudy* in colour, Id.*Col*.794^{a}4, cf. 797^{a}7, *BGU*1207.6 (i B.C.).—For the Homeric usage of the word v. ἠεροειδής.

ἀερόεις, = ἠερόεις (q.v.), Τάρταρος *Tab.Defix*.108.3 (iii B.C.), cf. Hsch.

ἀερό-θεν, Adv. *out of the air, from on high*, Eust.1239.10. **-κόρδακες**, οἱ, and **-κώνωπες**, οἱ, fabulous creatures in Luc.*VH*1.16. **-λέσχης**, ου, ὁ, *man of big empty words*, Hsch. **-μαντεία**, ἡ, *divination by air*, Varr.ap.Serv.ad Virg.*Aen*.3.359. **-μαντις**, ὁ, *air-diviner*, Id.ap.Isid.*Etym*.8.9.13. **-μᾰχία**, ἡ, *air-battle*, Luc.*VH*1.18. **-μελι**, ιτος, τό, *oak-manna*, Amynt.ap.Ath.11.500d, cf. Gal.6.739. **-μετρέω**, *measure the air*; hence, *lose oneself in vague speculation*, X.*Oec*.11.3. **-μέτρητος**, ον, gloss on ἠεροειδής, Heracleon ap.*EM*421.49. **-μῑγής**, ές, *compounded of air*, Cleom.2.1, al., Corn.*ND*19, D.L.7.145, etc. **-μυθέω**, = μετεωρολογέω, περὶ σελήνης Ph.1.457:—from **-μυθος**, Id.2.268. **-νηχής**, ές, (νήχομαι) *floating in air*, οἰωνοί Ar.*Nu*.337. **-νομέω**, *to move in air*, Hld.10.30. **-νομικός**, ή, όν, *living in the air*, ζῷον prob. in Ath.3.99b.

ἀερόομαι, *turn into air*, Heraclit.*All*.22. 2. *evaporate*, Gal.5.523.

ἀερο-πετής, ές, (πίπτω) *fallen from the sky*, Ph.Bybl.ap.Eus.*PE* 1.10, cf. Plb.36.10.2. **-πέτης**, ες, (πέτομαι) *flying in air*, σφὴξ Horap.2.24, *PMag.Lond*.121.554. **-πλᾰνος**, ον, *wandering in air*, Hsch. s.v. ἠεροφοῖτις. **-πορέω**, *traverse the air*, Ph.2.116, 300. **-πόρος**, ον, *traversing the air*, Pl.*Ti*.40a, Ph.1.35, al. **-ριφής**, ές, *hurled through the air*, *PMag.Par*.1.2508. **-σκοπία**, ἡ, *divination by observing the heavens*, 1*Enoch* 8.3, cf. Sch.Il.1.62 (as f.l. for ἱερο-). **-τεμις**, etym. of Ἄρτεμις, Porph.ap.Eus.*PE*3.11, Lyd.*Mens*.2.2. **-τόμα**· τὰ πετεινά, Cyr. **-τονος**, ον, *driven by air*, καταπάλτης Ph.*Bel*.77.13. **-φόβος**, ον, *afraid of the air*, Cael.Aur.*CP*3.12.108. **-φοίτητος**, ον, = sq., ἄνεμος *Hymn.Mag*.4.1; φοῖνιξ *PMag.Lond*.46.242. **-φοιτος**, ον, *roaming in air*, A.*Fr*.282:—also **-φοίτας**, ὁ, ἀστήρ Ion Eleg.10. **-φόρητος**, ον, *upborne by air*, Eub.104. **-φυής**, ές, *springing from air*, ῥίζωμα (i.e. γῆ), Secund.*Sent*.15. **-χροος**, **-ους**, = ἀέρινος 2, Dsc.5.75.

ἀέροψ, οπος, ὁ, Boeot. name for the bird μέροψ (q.v.), Sch.Ar.*Av*.1354.

ἀέρρω, Aeol. for ἀείρω, *lift, raise*, Sapph.91; *take away*, νόον Alc.78.

ἀερσί-λοφος, ον, *high-crested*, A.R.2.1060; of places, Nonn.*D*.2.684, al. **-μαχος**, ον, *rousing the fight*, B.12.67. **-νοος**, ον, contr. **-νους**, ουν, *increasing intelligence*, Οὐρανίη Nonn.*D*.33.67. II. *cheering*, οἶνος prob. l. Ion Eleg.9; Βάκχος Orph.*Fr*.280.9. **-πέτης**, ες, (πέτομαι) = ἀερσιπότης, Q.S.3.211. **-πόδης**, ου, ὁ, = ἀερσίπους, Nonn.*D*.10.401. **-πόρος**, ον, *going on high*, Nonn.*D*.1.285. **-πότης**, ου, ὁ, (ποτάομαι) *high-soaring*, Hes.*Sc.*316, *AP*5.298 (Agath.). **-πότητος**, ον, = foreg., ἀράχνης Hes.*Op.*777; ἀτμός Nonn.*D.*2.483. **-πους**, ὁ, ἡ, πουν, τό, *high-stepping*, ἵπποι ἀερσίποδες Il.18.532; contr. ἀρσίποδες *h.Ven.*211, *AP*7.717. **-φρων**, ονος, *uplifting*, *cheering the heart*, Διόνυσος *Ath.Mitt.*17.273 (Athens), cf. *EM*20.47.

ἀερτάζω, lengthd. Ep. form of ἀείρω, *lift up*, Call.*Fr.*19, etc.: impf. ἠέρταζον *AP*9.12 (Leon.), A.R.1.738, etc.: irreg. opt. ἀερτάζειε Nonn.*D.*43.99 :—also (from *ἀερτάω) aor. 1 ἠέρτησε *AP*6.223 (Antip.): pf. Pass. ἠέρτημαι ib.5.229 (Paul. Sil.), Opp.*C.*2.99.

ἀερώδης, ες, *like air*, of the soul, Epicur.*Fr.*314; Astrol., of signs, *connected with the air*, Vett.Val.7.26; *light of texture*, Sch.E.*Or.* 1431. **2.** = ἀέρινος 2, τὴν χρόαν Dsc.5.152 (dub.). **3.** τὸ ἀ. *the airy nature*, *Placit.*2.11.2, al., cf. Arist.*Mu.*395ᵃ20. **II.** *full of air*, Id.*PA*669ᵇ2.

ἀέρωσις, ἡ, *rarefaction*, αἵματος Gal.10.742.

ἀές, Dor. for ἀεί. **ἄες**, Boeot. = ἄας (q.v.), Hsch.

ἄεσα, v. ἀέσκω.

ἀεσίμαινα· ἡ τοῖς πνεύμασι τῶν ἀνέμων μαινομένη, θαλάσσης δὲ τὸ ἐπίθετον, Hsch. **ἄεσις**· πόνος, βλάβη, Hsch., *EM*20.48.

ἀεσι-φροσύνη, ἡ, *folly*, in pl., Od.15.470, Hes.*Th.*502. **-φρων**, ον, gen. ονος, = φρεσὶν ἀασθείς, *damaged in mind*, *witless*, *silly*, Il.20.183, Od.21.302, Hes.*Op.*335 (more correctly ἀασίφρων Apollon.*Lex.*, Phot.).

ἀέσκω, Hdn.Gr.1.436, *EM*20.11: impf. Med. ἀέσκοντο Hsch.: aor. 1 ἄεσα, ἀέσαμεν, contr. ἄσαμεν, ἄεσαν, inf. ἀέσαι :—*sleep*, Od.19.342, 3.151, 490, 15.40, A.R.4.884. (Etym. dub., but νύκτα ἀ. has been expl. as *pass*, *spend* the night, cf. Skt. *vásati*.) [ᾱ metri gr. or by contraction, ᾰ otherwise.]

ἀέτειος [ᾱ], ον, (ἀετός) *of the eagle*, πτερόν Suid.

ἀετής, ές, v. sub αὐετής.

ἀετιδεύς [ᾱ], έως, ὁ, *eaglet*, Ael.*Fr.*128, Aesop.5.

ἀετίτης [ῑ] λίθος, ὁ, *eagle-stone*, said to be found in the eagle's nest, Ael.*NA*1.35, Philostr.*VA*2.14, Dsc.5.160.

ἄετμα· φλόξ, οἱ δὲ τὸ πνεῦμα, *EM*20.10; Hsch. gives **ἀετμόν** in the latter sense.

ἀετογενής, ές, prob. *bearing a mark in the shape of an eagle*, ἵππος *Hippiatr.*115.

ἀετός, Ep., Lyr., Ion., and early Att. **αἰετός** (v. fin.), οῦ, ὁ, *eagle*, as a bird of omen, αἰ. τελειότατον πετεηνῶν Il.8.247, cf. 12.201, Od.2.146 (cf. II): favourite of Zeus, ὅστε σοὶ αὐτῷ φίλτατος οἰωνῶν Il.24.310, cf. Pi.*P.*1.6; Διὸς.. πτηνὸς κύων, δαφοινὸς αἰ. A.*Pr.*1022, cf. *Ag.*136; ὁ σκηπτροβάμων αἰ., κύων Διός S.*Fr.*885 :—prov., αἰετὸς ἐν ποτανοῖς Pi.*N.*3.80; αἰετὸς ἐν νεφέλαισι, of a thing quite out of reach, Ar.*Av.*987; ἀετὸν κάνθαρος μαιεύσομαι (v. μαιεύομαι):—the diff. kinds are distinguished by specific names, Arist.*HA*618ᵇ18 sqq. **2.** *eagle as a standard*, of the Persians, X.*Cyr.*7.1.4; of the Romans, Plu.*Mar.*23, etc. **3.** the constellation *Aquila*, Arat.591, Ptol.*Tetr.* 27, etc. **II.** *omen*, Theoc.26.31. **III.** *eagle-ray*, *Myliobatis aquila*, Arist.*HA*540ᵇ18. **IV.** in Architecture, *gable*, *pediment* (from its resemblance to outspread wings, Gal.18(1).519), Ar.*Av.* 1110, ubi v. Sch., *IG*1.322 ii 80, cf. Pi.*O.*13.21, *Fr.*53, E.*Fr.*764; ὑπὸ τὸν αὐτὸν ἀετὸν ὑπελθεῖν *come under the same roof*, *IG*14.644 (Bruttii, iii B.C.). **V.** name of *bandage*, Sor.*Fasc.*12.508 C. **VI.** *temporal vein* (Magna Graecia), Philistion ap.Ruf.*Onom.*201. **VII.** *iron part of spoke of wheel*, Poll.1.145, Hsch. **VIII.** Astrol. and Magic, fabulous plant growing in Libya, Pamphil.ap.Gal.11.798, *Cat.Cod.Astr.*7.222. (αἰετός in early Att. Inscrr., *IG*1.322 ii 80, 2.1054.39; αἰητός Arat.522, v.l. in Pi.*P.*4.4; αἰβετός (i.e. αἰϝετός) Hsch.) [ᾱ always.]

ἀετοφόρος, ὁ, *standard-bearer*, = Lat. *aquilifer*, Plu.*Caes.*52.

ἀετώδης [ᾱ], ες, *eagle-like*, ἀθληταί Philostr.*Gym.*37, cf. Ael.*NA* 4.27; -δες βλέπειν *see as clearly as an eagle*, Luc.*Icar.*14.

ἀέτωμα [ᾱ], τό, = ἀετός IV, *gable*, οἴκου Hp.*Art.*43; ἱεροῦ *IG*2².1271.6., cf. Timae.50, J.*AJ*3.6.4: **αἴτωμα** (sic) *IG*3.162.

ἀετώνυχον, τό, = λιθόσπερμον, Dsc.3.141; = κῆμος, Ps.-Dsc.4.133: cf. **ἀετόνυχες**· βοτάνη, Hsch.

ἀετώσιος, ον, apptly. = ἐτώσιος, Ibyc.51, cf. Hsch., *EM*20.13.

ἀέτωσις [ᾱ], εως, ἡ, *arched roof* of χελώνη, Ath.Mech.13.3.

ἀεφανέων· λαμπρῶν, Hsch.

ἀέχεια, ἡ, *non-possession*, *privation*, Chrysipp.*Stoic.*2.51 (pl.).

ἀεχῆνες· πένητες, Hsch.

ἀέχοντο· ὥρμων, Hsch.

ἀϝάταται, v. ἀτάω.

ἀϝλανέως, = ἀδόλως, *GDI*1156 (Elis, v B.C.); cf. ἀλανές.

ἄζα, ἡ, *heat*, ἠελίου Opp.*C.*1.134, cf. 3.324. **2.** *dryness*, of the skin, χροός Nic.*Th.*304. **3.** metaph., *unsatisfied desire*, Call. in *PGen.*97 ii 7. **II.** *dirt*, *mould*, σάκος πεπαλαγμένον ἄζῃ Od.22.184. **2.** *dry sediment*, Sch.Theoc.5.109. (Cf. Lat. *areo*.)

ἀζαές (cod. -ζαλές)· πολύπνουν, καὶ ὀλιγόπνουν, Hsch. **ἀζαθός**, Cypr. = ἀγαθός, ἰ(ν) τύχᾳ ἀζαθᾷ *Inscr.Cypr.*134 H., cf. 137. **ἀζαΐα**· φθονερά, Hsch.

ἀζαίνω, (ἄζω) *dry*, *parch up*, aor. subj. ἀζήνῃ, -ήνῃσι Nic.*Th.*205, and v.l. in 368 :—Pass., ἀζαίνεται (as v.l. for αὐαίνεται) ib.339: aor. ἀζάνθη Hsch.

ἀζαλαί· νέαι καὶ ἁπαλαί, Hsch.

ἀζᾰλέος, α, ον, *dry*, *parched*, οὖρος Il.20.491; ὕλη Od.9.234, etc.; βῶν ἀζαλέην *dry* bull's-hide, Il.7.239; ἀ. γῆρας *withered*, *sapless*, *IG* 14.1389 i 12, Plu.2.789c. **2.** metaph., *harsh*, *cruel*, *AP*5.237 (Maced.). **II.** Act., *parching*, *scorching*, Σείριος Hes.*Sc.*153, cf. A.R.4.679; of love, μανίαι Ibyc.1.9; of thirst, Nic.*Th.*339.—Poet. word. **III.** **ἀζαλέα**, ἡ, = ψίλωθρον, *Gloss.*

ἀζάλη· νήνεμος, Hsch. **ἀζάλιον**· ξηρόν, ἢ ἄγαν ζέον, Phot.p.38 R.

Ἀζᾶνες, οἱ, title of play by Achaeus. **Ἀζανία**, ἡ, *land of* Ζάν or Ζεύς, i.e. Arcadia, St.Byz. **ἀζανίτης**, ὁ, horse-medicine, *Hippiatr.* 129.

ἀζάνω, = ἀζαίνω, *h.Ven.*270 (Pass.).

ἀζάπα· πτισάνη, Hsch. **ἀζατά**, ἡ, *drought*, *Inscr.Cypr.*59 H. **ἀζάτη**· ἐλευθερία, Hsch. (Cf. Zend *āzāta* 'free'.) **ἀζαυτός**· παλαιότης, καὶ κόνις, Id. **ἀζαχής**, ές, = σκληρός, χαλεπός: also = ἀδιάλειπτος (cf. ἀζηχής), Id. **ἀζειvoί** (cod. ἀζην-)· κύκνοι ταῖς πτέρυξιν ἀπολαμβάνοντες ἀέρα, Id. **ἀζείρει**· ξηραίνει, Id. (ἀζήρει Suid.). **ἀζειρός**, όν, (ζειρά) *not embroidered*, Hsch., *EM*22.56, Suid. **ἀζένα**· πώγωνα (Phryg.), Hsch. **ἄζενον**· γενειῶντα, Id. **ἀζέσιμοι**· ἀζειvoί, Id. **ἀζέσιος**, v. Ἀζόσιος. **ἄζεστος**, ον, (ζέω) *not coming to the boil*, Hp.*Morb.*3.17. **ἄζετον**· ἄπιστον (Sicel), Hsch. **ἀζετόω**, *detect*, in Pass., *GDI*2034 (Delph., ii A.D.).

ἄζευκτος, ον, *unyoked*, D.H.2.31; ἄ. γάμου Sch.Ar.*Lys.*217: abs. in same sense, Sch.A.R.4.897.

ἀζεχής, ές, = ἀζαχής (cf. ἀζηχής), Hsch.

ἀζηλία, ἡ, *simplicity* of style, *freedom from mannerisms*, v.l. in Plu.*Lyc.*21.

ἀζηλοπραγμόνως, Adv. *without jealousy*, *ungrudgingly*, *PLips.* 119ᵛ ii 5 (iii A.D.).

ἄζηλος, ον, *unenvied*, *unenviable*, *dreary*, γῆρας Semon.1.11; φρουρά A.*Pr.*143; θέα S.*El.*1455; βίος Id.*Tr.*284; ἔργον *sorry* deed, ib. 745; ἄζηλα πέλει all are *in ill plight*, Orac.ap.Hdt.7.140; πλοῦτος Plu. *Lyc.*10; ζῆλος ἀζήλων *not deserving of envy*, Phld.*Oec.*p.66 J. **II.** Act., *not envious*, Menetor ap.Ath.13.594c.

ἀζηλο-τύπητος, ον, *not likely to arouse jealousy*, Cic.*Att.*13.19.4; *not exposed to jealousy*, γῆρας Plu.2.787d. **-τῠπος**, ον, *free from envy*, Plu.*Comp.Lyc.Num.*3.

ἀζήλωτος, ον, *not to be envied*, Pl.*Grg.*469b: neut. pl. as Adv., -ωτα φιληθείς *AP*12.105 (Asclep.). Adv. -τως Poll.5.160. **2.** *not imitated*, ἀ. παραλιπεῖν τι J.*BJ*7.8.1.

ἀζήμιος, ον, *free from further payment*, Hdt.6.92. **2.** *without loss*, *scot-free*, ἄπιθι ἀ. Id.1.212; ἀβλαβῆ παρεχέτω καὶ ἀζήμιον Pl.*Lg.* 865c; *unpunished*, E.*Med.*1050, Ar.*Ra.*408, Antipho 3.3.10, etc.; ὑπὸ θεῶν Pl.*R.*366a; *not liable to penalty*, ναῦς *IG*1.40; *not deserving punishment*, S.*El.*1102, etc.: c. gen., ἀσεβημάτων ἀ. Plb.2.60.5. Adv. -ίως *with impunity*, Philem.94.5: also, *without fraud*, *honestly*, J.*AJ* 15.4.4; ἐκδικεῖν *Cod.Just.*1.2.17. **II.** Act., *harmless*, of sour looks, Th.2.37; οὐκ ἀ. J.*AJ*15.5.1, cf. Ph.1.428, 2.246.

ἀζημίωτος, ον, *immune from penalties*, Secund.*Sent.*10.

ἄζηρις, ἡ, *chariot-pole*, Hsch. (ἀζηλίς Poll.1.143).

Ἀζησία, ἡ, a name of Demeter, S.*Fr.*981, cf. Ἀζοσία.

ἀζῆται· οἱ ἐγγύτατοι τοῦ βασιλέως, Hsch.

ἀζήτητος, ον, *unexamined*, *untried*, Aeschin.3.22, Aristox.*Fr.Hist.* 15; *outside the scope of inquiry*, Thphr.*Metaph.*10. Adv. -τως, ἔχειν τῶν θείων Ph.1.96; τῆς αἰτίας Hierocl.*in CA*10 p.437 M.

ἀζητός· σεβαστός, Suid.

ἀζηχής, ές, (prob. for ἀ-δια(σ)εχής, *continuous*, cf. ἀζαχής, ἀζεχής) *unceasing*, ὀδύνη Il.15.25; ὀρυμαγδός 17.741: neut. as Adv., ἀζηχὲς φαγέμεν καὶ πιέμεν Od.18.3; [ὄϊες] ἀ. μεμακυῖαι Il.4.435. **II.** (ἄζα, cf. ἀζαλέος) *hard*, *seasoned*, κορύνη A.R.2.99; θυμός v.l. Il.15.25.

ἀζηώρα· ταχέα, πυκνά, Hsch. **ἀζόκροτος**, v. αἰζ-.

ἄζομαι, only pres. and impf.; Act. only in part. ἄζοντα S.*OC* 134 :—*stand in awe of*, esp. gods and one's parents, ἁζόμενοι.. Ἀπόλλωνα Il.1.21; μήτ' οὖν μητέρ' ἐμὴν ἄζευ Od.17.401; followed by inf., χερσὶ δ' ἀνίπτοισιν Διὶ λείβειν.. ἄζομαι Il.6.267; ξείνους οὐχ ἅζεο.. ἐσθέμεναι Od.9.478; ἅ. μή Il.14.261; τίς δή κεν.. ἅζοιτ' ἀθανάτους; Thgn.748, cf. Alcm.54: used by A. in lyr., τίς οὖν τάδ' οὐχ ἅζεται; *Eu.* 389; Παλλάδος δ' ὑπὸ πτεροῖς ὄντας ἅζεται πατήρ (sc. Ζεύς) *respects*.., ib.1002; ἅζονται γὰρ ὁμαίμους Id.*Supp.*652; πλόκαμον οὐδάμ' ἅζεται ib.884 (all lyr.); θανεῖν οὐχ ἅζομαι *I fear* not to die.., E.*Or.* 1116. **2.** abs. in part., *reverently*, *in holy fear*, Od.9.200; ἀμφί σοι ἁζόμενος S.*OT*155. **3.** *to be angry*, E.*Fr.*348. (Cf. ἅγιος.)

ἄζον· μέλαν, ὑψηλόν, Hsch. **ἄζοξ**· ὕλη, Id.

ἄζος, ὁ, contr. from ἄοζος, *a servant*, Gloss.ap.Ath.6.267c.

ἀζός, η, ον, *dry*, v.l. in Sch.Theoc.5.109.

Ἀζόσιος, ὁ, (sc. μήν) month at Epidaurus, *IG*4.1485.20, al. (Ἀζέσιος ib.51) :—**Ἀζόσιοι** θεοί (= Δαμία and Αὐξησία), ib.1539.4; **Ἀζοσία**, ἡ, ib.1062.12.

ἀζῠγής, ές, *not paired*, μόριον ἀ. ἑτέρῳ Gal.*UP*15.2, cf. 5.14.

ἄζῠγος, ον, *unwedded*, κοίτη Luc.*Am.*44. **2.** = foreg., φλέψ the *vena azygos*, Gal.15.529: in pl., *not a pair*, σανδάλια Str.6.1.8.

ἄζῡμος, ον, *without process of fermentation*, Pl.*Ti.*74d:—of bread, *unleavened*, ἄρτος Hp.*Vict.*3.79, Trypho *Fr.*117; ἄρτους ἀ., ἄζυμα λάγανα, Lxx *Ex.*29.2, *Le.*2.4: abs., ἄζυμα, τά, *Ex.*12.15; τὰ ἄ. *the feast of unleavened cakes*, *Ev.Marc.*14.1; ἡ ἑορτὴ τῶν ἀ. Lxx 2*Ch.*8.13, al., *Ev.Luc.*22.1.

ἄζυξ, ῠγος, ὁ, ἡ, τό, (ζεύγνυμι) *unyoked*, *unpaired*, Archil.157; δάμαλις D.H.1.40; *unmarried*, E.*Ba.*694; of Pallas, Id.*Tr.*536 (lyr.): c. gen., ἄ. λέκτρων, γάμων, εὐνῆς, Id.*Hipp.*546 (lyr.), *IA*805, *Med.* 673. **II.** *isolated*, ἄ. ὥσπερ ἐν πεττοῖς Arist.*Pol.*1253ᵃ7, cf. *AP*9.482.26 (Agath.); *single*, αὐλοί, opp. σύριγγες, Nonn.*D.*3.76: in pl., ἄζυγα *vowels*, opp. σύζυγα, ib.4.262.

ἄζω, v. sub ἄζομαι.

ἄζω (A), *dry up, parch,* ὁπότε χρόα Σείριος ἄζει Hes.*Sc.*397, cf. *Op.* 587, Alc.39.8, Nic.*Th.*779 :—Pass., [αἴγειρος] ἀζομένη κεῖται lies *drying,* Il.4.487.

ἄζω (B), *cry* ἆ, *groan, sigh,* S.*Fr.*980 ; so perh. in Med., εἴ τις.. ἄζηται κραδίην ἀκαχήμενος Hes.*Th.*99. **2.** *breathe hard,* Nicoch. 19. (Perh. ἄζω (from the sound *ha!*) in this sense.)

ἀζωΐα, ἡ, *absence of life,* Porph.*Sent.*21,23, Procl.*in Prm.*p.646 S., Olymp.*in Grg.*p.356 J.

ἀζωλεῖ· ἀγανακτεῖ, Hsch.

ἀζωνικός, ή, όν, = sq., τάξις Procl.*in Ti.*3.127 D., Dam.*Pr.*131. Adv. **-κῶς** ibid.

ἄζωνος, ον, *confined to no zone* or *region,* opp. *local* deities, Serv. ad Virg.*Aen.*12.118, cf. Dam.*Pr.*96, al. (with secondary sense *not wearing a zone as a girdle*).

ἄζωος, ον, (ζωή) *without life,* Porph.*Sent.*20, Procl.*Inst.*188. **II.** (ζῷον) *without maggots,* of seeds, Thphr.*CP*4.15.3.

ἄζωπες· αἱ ξηραὶ ἐκ τῆς θεωρίας, Hsch. **ἄζωρος·** ὁ εὔκρατος οἶνος, Id. **ἄζως,** ων, = ἄζωος 1, Plot.3.4.1, 3.6.6, Syr.*in Metaph.*48.16, Procl.*in Prm.*p.543 S.

ἄζωστος, ον, (ζώννυμι) *ungirt,* from haste, Hes.*Op.*345, Call.*Fr.* 225 ; *not girded,* Pl.*Lg.*954a ; *unarmed, SIG*527.140 (Dreros, iii B.C.), Hsch.

ἀζῶτες· οἱ μὴ εἰς τὰ συνεστῶτα παρόντες, Hsch.

ἄζωτος, ον, = ἄζωστος, *EM*22.21. **II. ἄζωτον·** ἀβίωτον, Hsch.

ἀηδ-έω, *feel disgust at,* δείπνῳ ἀηδήσειεν v.l. for ἀδήσειεν in Od.1. 134, cf. **ἀηδῆσαι·** κοπιάσαι, καμεῖν, Hsch., cf. *EM*23.26. **-ής,** ές, (ἦδος) *distasteful, nauseous,* of food, drugs, etc., Hp.*VM*10 (Comp.), *Acut.*23, Pl.*Lg.*660a, etc. **2.** generally, *unpleasant,* οὐδέν οἱ ἀηδέστερον ἔσεσθαι Hdt.7.101, cf. Pl.*Lg.*893a, al.: freq. in Pl. of narration, ἀηδές or οὐκ ἀηδές ἐστι, *Ap.*33c, 41b, *Phd.*84d : Comp., Hdt. l. c. : Sup. **-έστατος** Pl.*Lg.*663c, *Phdr.*240b. **II.** of persons, *disagreeable, odious,* ἀπογηράσκων ἀ. γίγνεται Alex.278, cf. D.47.28, Arist. *EN*1108ᵃ30, Thphr.*Char.*20.1 ; τινί to one, Pl.*Phd.*91b, Phld.*Ir.* p.51 W. **III.** Adv. **-δῶς** *unpleasantly,* ζῆν Pl.*Prt.*351b ; ἀ. ἔχειν τινί to be *on bad terms with* one, D.20.142, cf. 37.11 ; ἀ. διακεῖσθαι, διατεθῆναι, πρός τινα, Lys.16.2, Isoc.12.19. **2.** *without pleasure to oneself, unwillingly,* πίνειν, ἀκούειν, X.*Cyr.*1.2.11, Isoc.12.62 ; οὐκ ἀ. Pl.*Prt.*335c. **-ία,** ἡ, *nauseousness,* of drugs, Hp.*Acut.*23. **2.** *unpleasantness,* opp. ἡδονή, Phld.*Rh.* 1.163 S. : pl., Id.*Oec.*p.64 J. **II.** mostly of persons, *unpleasantness, odiousness,* D.21.153, Aeschin.3. 72, Thphr.*Char.*20.1 ; τὴν σὴν ἀ. your *odious presence,* Aeschin.3. 164. **2.** *disgust, dislike,* Pl.*Phdr.*240d, *Lg.*802d, etc. : pl., ἀ. καὶ βαρύτητες τῶν ἄλλων Isoc.12.31. **-ίζω,** *disgust,* τὴν γεῦσιν S.E. *P.*1.92 :—Pass., *to be disgusted,* Anon.*in Rh.*194.32 ; τινι Alex.Aphr. *Pr.*2.15 ; ἐπί τινι *PLond.*1.42 (ii B.C.). **-ισμός,** ὁ, *disgust,* opp. ἡδονή, S.E.*P.*1.87.

ἀηδονία, ἡ, *absence of pleasure,* D.L.2.89,90.

ἀηδ-ονιδεύς, έως, ὁ, *young nightingale,* pl. **-ῆες** Theoc.15.121 (prob.). **-όνιον,** τό, Dim. of ἀηδών, prob.l. in D.Chr.66.11. **-όνιος,** ον, *of a nightingale,* γόος, νόμος ἀ., A.*Fr.*291, Ar.*Ra.*684. **2.** of sleep, *light,* Nicoch.4 D., cf. Nonn.*D.*5.411. **-ονίς,** ίδος, ἡ, = ἀηδών, *nightingale,* E.*Rh.*550 (lyr.), Call.*Lav.Pall.*94, Theoc.8.38 ; Μουσάων ἀηδονίς, of a poet, *AP*7.414 (Noss.) ; of a girl, *IG*14.1942.

ἀήδονος, ον, = ἀνήδονος, δαίμων Sch.E.*Hec.*685, cf. *Gloss.*

ἀηδοποιός, όν, *quarrelsome, Gloss.*

ἀηδ-ώ, = sq., gen. ἀηδοῦς S.*Aj.*628 (lyr.), voc. ἀηδοῖ Ar.*Av.*679 (lyr.) : nom. pl. ἄηδοι Sapph.*Oxy.*1787.6.7. (Mytil. acc. to Sch.S. l. c.) **-ών,** όνος, ἡ (ὁ, v. infr.), (ἀείδω) *songstress,* i. e. *the nightingale,* Hes.*Op.*203, etc. ; Πανδαρέου κούρη, χλωρηὶς ἀ., i. e. *living in the greenwood,* Od.19.518 ; χλωραύχην ἀ. Simon.73 :—metaph., of a *poet,* B.3.98, cf. E.*Fr.*588 (lyr.), *AP*7.44 (Ion), Hermesian.7.49 ; also of the poet's song, τεαὶ ἀηδόνες thy *strains,* Call.*Ep.*2.5 ; ζωούσας ἔλιπες γὰρ ἀηδόνας *IG*14.2012. **2.** metaph., *cicada, AP*7.190 (Anyte). **II.** *mouthpiece* of a flute, E.*Fr.*556 ; the *flute* itself, ib.931. **2.** metaph., of *shuttle, AP*6.174 (Antip. Sid.).—Masc., only Ion l. c. ; Ἀττικὸς ἀνὴρ τὸν αἶγα λέγει ὥσπερ καὶ τὸν ἀηδόνα Eust.376.24.

ἀήθ-εια, Ion. **-ίη** [ῑ metri gr.], ἡ, (ἀήθης) *unaccustomedness, novelty* of a situation, Batr.72, Pl.*Ti.*18c ; ἀ. τινος *inexperience of* a thing, Th.4.55 ; ὑπὸ ἀηθείας from *inexperience,* Pl.*Tht.*175d ; δι' ἀήθειαν (cod. ἀλήθ-) Aen.Tact.38.3. **-έσσω,** *to be unaccustomed,* c. gen., once in Hom., ἀήθεσσον γὰρ ἔτ' αὐτῶν Il.10.493 ; ἀηθέσσουσα δύης A.R.4. 38 ; λυγμοὶ ἀηθέσσοντες Nic.*Al.*378 :—for A.R.1.1171 v. sq. **-έω,** *to be unaccustomed,* Hsch. : impf. ἀήθεον prob. l. A.R.1.1171 (codd. ἀήθεσον). **-ης,** ες, (ἦθος) *unwonted, strange,* ὄψις A.*Supp.*567 ; δώματα v. l. in S.*Fr.*583.10. Adv. **-θως** *unexpectedly,* Th.4.17. **II.** *unused to* a thing, c. gen., μάχης Th.4.34, cf. Pl.*Tht.*146b, al. ; ἀ. τοῦ κατακούειν, τοῦ προπηλακίζεσθαι, D.1.23, 21.72. **b.** *strange in manner, unlike oneself,* prob. f.l. for ἀγηθής in S.*Tr.*869. **2.** *without character,* τραγῳδία Arist.*Po.*1450ᵃ25, cf. 1460ᵃ11. **-ία,** ἡ, = ἀήθεια, E.*Hel.*418. **-ίζομαι,** *to be unaccustomed to* a thing, Posidon.26.

ἄημα, τό, *blast, wind,* A.*Ag.*1418, *Eu.*905, S.*Aj.*674, Call.*Aet.*3. 1.36.

ἄημι, 3 sg. ἄησι Hes.*Op.*516, A.*Fr.*178 A., 3 dual ἄητον Il.9.5, 3 pl. ἀεισι Hes.*Th.*875 ; imper. 3 sg. ἀήτω A.R.4.768 ; inf. ἀῆναι Od.3. 183, Ep. ἀήμεναι ib.176 ; part. ἀείς, ἀέντος, etc., Emp.84.4, Il.5.526, al.: impf. 3 sg. ἄη Od.12.325, 14.458 :—**Pass.,** 3 sg. ἄηται, impf. ἄητο, part. ἀήμενος, v. infr. (ἄϝημι, cf. Skt. *vāti* 'blows', Lith. *vėjas* 'wind') :—Ep. Verb, prop. *breathe hard* ; hence, *blow,* of winds, τώ τε Θρῄκηθεν ἄητον Il.9.5, cf. Od.3.176,183, etc. ; οἵ τε νέφεα.. διασκιδνᾶσιν ἀέντες Il.5.526 ; ἀνέμων.. μένος ὑγρὸν ἀέντων Od.19.440, cf. Hes.*Th.*869,875 :—Pass., *to be beaten by the wind,* ὑόμενος καὶ ἀήμενος Od.6.131 ; of sound, *to be carried by the wind,* A.R.2.81 : more freq. metaph., *toss, wave to and fro,* of the mind in doubt or fear, δίχα θυμὸς ἄητο Il.21.386 ; περὶ παίδων θυμὸς ἄηται A.R.3.688 :—also μαρτύρια ἄηται ἐπ' ἀνθρώπους *are wafted to and fro,* Pi.*I.*4(3).9 ; περί τ' ἀμφί τε κάλλος ἄητο beauty *breathed* all about her, *h.Cer.*276 ; ἀπὸ κρῆθεν τοῖον ἄητο Hes.*Sc.*8, cf. *Fr.*245. **II.** Act., *breathe,* διὰ πνευμόνων ὕπνον A.*Fr.*178 A.

ἀήρ, ἀέρος, Hom. ἀήρ, ἠέρος ; Ion. nom. **ἠήρ** Hp.*Aër.*6, al., Aret. *CA*2.3 ; Aeol. **αὐήρ** Sch.Pi.*P.*2.52 ; Dor. **ἀβήρ** (i.e. ἀϝήρ) Hsch. :—fem. in Hom. and Hes. (exc. *Op.*549), Anaxag.ap.Thphr.*Sens.*30 ; from Hdt. downwds. masc. (Il.5.776, 8.50, *h.Cer.*383 cannot be quoted for the masc. usage, since there πουλύς and βαθύς need not be masc.) :—in Hom. and Hes. always *mist, haze,* not (as Aristarch.) *lower air* (opp. αἰθήρ, q. v.) ; [ἐλάτη] μακροτάτη πεφυυῖα δι' ἠέρος αἰθέρ' ἵκανεν Il.14.288, cf. Anaxag.1, Ar.*Nu.*264 sq. ; περὶ δ' ἠέρα πουλὺν ἔχευεν Il.5.776, cf. 3.381, 8.50 ; ἠέρα μὲν σκέδασεν καὶ ἀπῶσεν ὁμίχλην 17.649 ; τρὶς δ' ἠέρα τύψε βαθεῖαν 20.446 ; rare in Prose, Hp. l.c. **2.** later, generally, *air,* Anaxim.1, Emp.17.18, S.*El.*87, Ar. *Av.*187,694, etc. ; πρὸς τὸν ἀέρα διατρίβειν in *the open air,* Ar.*Nu.*198, cf. Teles p.11.3 H., Luc.*Anach.*24 ; τὸν ἀέρ' ἕλκειν καθαρόν Philyll.20, cf. Philem.119 ; ἔσπασας τὸν ἀ. τὸν κοινόν Men.531.7 ; ἀέρα δέρειν 1 *Ep. Cor.*9.26 ; εἰς ἀέρα λαλεῖν ib.14.9 :—in pl., Pl.*Phd.*98c,d ; *climates,* Hp.*Aër.*tit., cf. Men.Rh.p.383 S. ; of mephitic *exhalations,* Str.5. 4.5. **3.** personified, ὦ δέσποτ' ἄναξ ἀμέτρητ' Ἀ. Ar.*Nu.*264 ; Ἀ. ὃν ἄν τις ὀνομάσειε καὶ Δία Philem.91.4, cf. Diph.126.6. **II.** *hot-air room* in baths, Gal.11.14. **2.** *volume,* Hero *Stereom.*57, al. **III.** a pigment, *sky-blue* or *grey,* Id.*Aut.*28.3. [ᾱ, except in Arist.*Fr.* 642, Ps.-Phoc.[108].]

ἄησις, εως, ἡ, (ἄημι) = ἄημα, *blowing,* E.*Rh.*417, cf. *Fr.*781.46.

ἀήσσητος, Att. **ἀήττητος,** ον, *unconquered, not beaten,* Th.6.70, Lys.33.7, D.18.247, *AP*7.741 (Crin.), etc. ; esp. of the Stoic sage, Zeno *Stoic.*1.53, etc. **2.** *unconquerable,* Pl.*R.*375b, Phld.*D.*3 *Fr.*88b.

ἀήσυλος, = αἴσυλος, *wicked,* ἔργα Il.5.876.

ἀήσυρος, ον, (ἄημι) *light as air,* μύρμηκες A.*Pr.*452 ; ἀ. γόνυ κάμψει Call.*Fr.anon.*3 ; γυῖα Orph.*Fr.*18 ; *springing lightly,* πόρτις Tryph. 360 ; *blowing softly,* Βορέας A.R.2.1101.

ἀητέομαι, *fly,* Arat.523 (with play on αἰητός). **ἀήτη,** ἡ, = sq., Hes.*Op.*645,675.

ἀήτης, ου, ὁ, (ἄω, ἄημι) *blast, gale,* ἀνέμοιο, Ζεφύροιο, ἀνέμων ἀῆται, Il.15.626, Od.4.567, Hes.*Op.*621 : abs., *wind,* Tim.*Pers.*117, Theoc. 2.38.—Poet. word, οἱ ποιηταὶ τὰ πνεύματα ἀήτας καλοῦσι Pl.*Cra.* 410b.

ἀητόρρους, ουν, *creating* ἀῆται, coined by Pl.*Cra.*410b.

ἄητος (A), ὁ, = αἰετός, the constellation *Aquila,* Arat.315.

ἄητος (B), ον, only in phrase θάρσος ἄητον Il.21.395 (= θάρσος ἄατον Q.S.1.217) ; also **ἄητοι·** ἀκόρεστοι, ἄπληστοι, and **ἀήτους·** μεγάλας (A.*Fr.*3), Hsch. **ἄητος** (C)· ὁ ἀκατάπαυστος, Hdn.Gr.1.220 ; perh. *insatiate* (ἄω) ; cf. αἴητος.

ἄηχος, ον, *without sound,* φωνή Aret.*SD*1.11, Sch.E.*Ph.*960.

ἀθᾰλάμευτος, ον, *unwedded,* ἡλικίη *Epigr.Gr.*372.32 (Cotiaeum).

ἀθᾰλάσσ-ευτος, ον, = ἀθαλάσσωτος, Poll.1.121. **-ία,** ἡ, *ignorance of the sea,* v.l. for sq. in Secund.*Sent.*16. **-ος,** Att. **-ττος,** ον, *without sea, far from it, inland,* Men.462.9. **2.** = ἀθαλάσσωτος, βασιλεὺς Max.Tyr.1.3 ; ἔμπορος Secund.*Sent.*16. **II.** *not mixed with sea-water,* οἶνος Democr.ap.Gal.14.134, Zopyr.ap.Orib.14.61.1, cf. Sor.1.95. **-ωτος,** Att. **-ττωτος,** ον, (θαλασσόω) *unused to the sea, a land-lubber,* Ar.*Ra.*204, Agath.1 *Praef.*

ἄθαλδον· ἐτύγχανον, τινὲς δὲ ἀθάδανον, Hsch.

ἀθαλής or **ἀθαλλής,** ές, of the laurel, *not verdant, withered,* Plu. *Pomp.*31, Orac.ap.Ath.12.524b.

ἀθαλπής, ές, *without warmth,* Nonn.*D.*37.151, 40.286, etc. Adv. **-πέως** Hp.*Acut.*29.

ἀθαμβ-ής, ές, *fearless, unabashed,* ἔρος, ὕβρις, σῶμα, Ibyc.1.9, B.14. 58, Phryn.Trag.2 ; σκότου Plu.*Lyc.*16. **-ητος,** ον, *free from alarms, PMag.Par.*1.1064. **-ία,** Ion. **-ίη,** ἡ, *imperturbability,* Democr.215. **-ος,** ον, *imperturbable,* Id.216.

Ἀθάνα, Ἀθᾶναι, Ἀθᾱναία, Dor. for Ἀθην-, v. Ἀθήνη.

ἀθᾰνᾰσία, ἡ, *immortality,* Pl.*Phdr.*246a, Arist.*EN*1111ᵇ22, Epicur. *Ep.*3 p.60 U., etc. ; ὁ δὲ λιμός ἐστιν ἀθανασίας φάρμακον Antiph.86. 6. **II.** *elixir* or *antidote,* ἀ. Μιθριδάτου Gal.14.148, cf. 13. 203. **2.** = ἀμβροσία, Luc.*D.Deor.*4.5.

ἀθᾰνᾰτ-ίζω, *make immortal,* τὴν φύσιν Arist.*Fr.*645, cf. Ph.2. 255, al. :—Pass., *to become* or *be immortal,* Plb.6.54.2, Ph.1.32, 37, al. **2.** *regard as immortal,* ψυχάς J.*AJ*18.1.5. **II.** abs., *hold oneself immortal,* Γέται οἱ ἀθανατίζοντες Hdt.4.93 sq., cf. 94 ; ἐφ' ὅσον ἐνδέχεται ἀ. *put off the mortal,* Arist.*EN*1177ᵇ33, cf. Philostr.*VA*8. 7. **-ισμός,** ὁ, *gift of immortality,* ὁ διὰ τῆς δόξης ἀ. D.S.1.1. **-ος,** ον, also η, ον (so regularly in sense I. 1, poet. and Isoc.9.16) :—*undying, immortal,* Hom., etc. ; ἀ. πρόσωπον, of Aphrodite, Sapph.1.14 :—hence ἀθάνατοι, οἱ, *the Immortals,* Hom., Pi.*Pae.*6.50, etc. ; ἀθάναται ἅλιαι, i. e. the sea goddesses, Od.24.47 : Comp. **-ώτερος** Pl.*Phd.* 99c. **2.** *of immortal fame,* Tyrt.12.32. **II.** of things, etc., *everlasting, perpetual,* ἀ. κακόν Od.12.118 ; χάρις Hdt.7.178 ; ἀρετή, ἀρχά, S.*Ph.*1420, *OT*905 (lyr.) ; κλέος, μνήμη, B.12.65, Lys.2.81 ; συκοφάντης Hyp.*Lyc.*2 ; ἀ. ὁ θάνατος 'death *that cannot die*', Amph.8 ; of Nisus' purple locks, ἀ. θρίξ *on which life depended,* A.*Ch.*619. **III.**

οἱ ἀ. *the immortals*, a body of Persian troops in which vacancies were filled up by successors already appointed, Hdt.7.83,211; so ἀ. ἀνήρ one whose successor in case of death is appointed (as we say, *the king never dies*), ib.31; of a *standing* army, D.C.52.27. **2.** *maintained at a constant figure*, πρόβατα *PSI*4.377.5 (iii B.C.), *PThead.*30.6 (iii A.D.); αἶγες *PStrassb.*30.6 (iii A.D.); διὰ τὸ ἀθάνατον (sc. τὸ παιδίον) αὐτὴν ἐπιδεδέχθαι τροφεύειν *BGU*1106.25 (Aug.). **IV.** = λυχνὶς στεφανωματική, Ps.-Dsc.3.100. **V.** Adv. ἀθανάτως, εὕδειν *AP*9.570 (Philod.). [ᾰθ- always in the Adj. and all derivs., v. sub ἀ- 1 fin.] **-όω**, *make immortal*, Tz.*H*.6.740.

ἀθᾰνής, ές, *undying*, ψυχή Max.Tyr.16.2.

ἄθαπτος, ον, *unburied*, Il.22.386, Moschio Trag.6.32, etc.; ἄθαπτον ὠθεῖν, βάλλειν, ἐᾶν τινά, S.*Aj.*1307,1333, *Ant.*205. **II.** *unworthy of burial*, *AP*9.498.

ἀθαράπευτος, v. ἀθεράπ-.

ἀθάρη (not ἀθάρα, Moer.184, cf. Hdn.Gr.1.340), ἡ, *gruel* or *porridge*, Ar.*Pl.*673, Pherecr.108.3, Crates 9, Nicoph.15, Anaxandr.41.42. [ᾰθᾱρη ll. cc.: cf. ἀθήρα.]

ἀθαρής· ἄφθορος, of women, Hsch. **ἀθάριοι·** αἱ μὴ διαπεπαρθενευμέναι, τινὲς δέ, μὴ δεδεμέναι ἄρθρῳ, Id. **ἀθαρσέω**, *to be discouraged*, Procop.*Vand.*2.11 (s.v.l.).

ἀθαρσής, ές, *discouraged, downhearted*, Plu.*Cic.*35, Max.Tyr.25.4, Doroth. in *Cat.Cod.Astr.*2.195: τὸ ἀ. *want of courage*, Plu.*Nic.*4. Adv. -σῶς Id.*Pomp.*60, 2.150c (Comp.).

ἀθᾰρώδης, ες, *like* ἀθάρη, of the brain, Ruf.*Anat.*3.

ἀθαυμ-αστία, ἡ, *absence of wonder*, Str.1.3.21: c. gen., 1.3.16. **-αστος**, ον, *not wondering at* anything, πρός τι Zeno *Stoic.*1.57, M.Ant.1.15. Adv. -τως S.*Fr.*982; also **ἀθαυμαστί** Suid. **II.** *not wondered at* or *admired*, Luc.*Am.*13.

ἀθεάμων [ᾱμ], ον, gen. ονος, *not beholding*, καλλέων τοσούτων Men.Rh.p.383 S. Adv. -όνως, i.q. ἀνεπιστημόνως, ἀπείρως, Poll.4.10:—also Subst. -οσύνη, ἡ, ib.9.

ἀθέᾱτος, ον, *unseen, invisible*, Luc.*Nav.*44, Plu.2.575b, Ael.*NA* 8.7. **2.** *that may not be seen, secret*, Ps.-Phoc.100, Plu.*Num.*9, Luc.*D.Mar.*14.2; τὰ ἀ. J.*AJ*14.16.3, etc. **II.** Act., *not seeing, blind to*, τινός X.*Mem.*2.1.31, Arist.*Mu.*391ᵃ25, Plu.2.7c, Max.Tyr.3.10. Adv. -τως Poll.4.10.

ἀθεησίη, ἡ, Ion. Subst. *want of sight, blindness*, Aret.*CD*1.4.

ἀθεεί, Adv., (θεός) *without the aid of God*, mostly with neg., οὐκ ἀθεεί Od.18.353, Philostr.*VS*1.21.2, D.C.59.12, Plot.4.3.16, Nonn.*D*.7.178, etc.

ἀθεΐα, ἡ, = ἀθεότης, Ael.*Fr.*39, Sm.*Ho.*4.15, Sallust.18 (pl.), Hierocl. *in CA*1 p.418 M.; v.l. for ἀθεσία, Lxx 1*Ma.*16.17.

ἀθείαστος, ον, *uninspired*, οὐκ ἀ. Plu.*Cor.*33.

ἀθειρής, ές, Ep. for ἀθερής, prob. in Thgn.733; also, = ἀκριβής, *EM* 24.58. Adv. ἀθειρέως ibid.

ἀθελβάζω, *filter*, Hsch., who also has **ἀθελβεῖ·** ἕλκει.

ἀθελγ-ής, ές, *unappeased*, Nonn.*D*.33.200. **II.** Act., *having no power to soothe*, 12.261, al. **-ία**, ἡ, *implacability*, *BGU*1024 (iv/v A.D.).

ἀθέλγω, = ἀμέλγω, Hsch.:—Pass., ἀθέλγεται *is drawn off* or *pressed out*, Hp.*Hum.*1 (expl. by Gal. ad loc. διηθεῖται, διεκλύεται).—For **ἄθελξις** v. ἄλθεξις.

ἀθέλδω, *filter*, in Pass., Diocl.Com.7.

ἀθέλ-εος, ον, (θέλω) = sq., dub. l. A.*Supp.*862 (lyr.). **-ητος**, ον, *unwilling*, Hsch. Adv. -τως Aspas.ap.Ath.5.219d.

ἀθέλιμνος· κακός, Suid., cf. Hsch.

ἄθελκτος, ον, *implacable*, A.*Supp.*1055, Lyc.1335.

ἀθελξίνοος, ον, *not beguiling* or *seductive*, Μοῦσαι Auson.*Ep.*12.26.

ἀθεμείλιος, ον, *without foundation*, Ep. word implied by Hsch. **ἀθέμηλος·** οὐδὲν οὐκ ἔχουσα οὐδὲ θεμέλιον, and **ἀθεμίλιος·** ἀκροσφαλής, ψεύστης.

ἀθεμελίωτος, ον, = foreg., Hsch.; ἀ. οἰκία, of a ship, Secund.*Sent.*17.

ἄθεμ-ις, ιτος, ὁ, ἡ, *lawless*, Pi.*P.*3.32, 4.109, E.*Ion* 1093 (lyr.): Comp. -ίστερος Opp.*H*.1.756. **-ιστέω**, *do lawless deeds*, Hsch. **-ιστία**, ἡ, *lawlessness*, App.*BC*2.77 (pl.). **-ίστιος**, ον, *lawless, godless*, ἀνήρ Od.18.141; freq. in phrase ἀθεμίστια εἰδώς versed in *wickedness*, 9.428, etc.; ἀ. ἔργα Xenoph.12, Man.2.301. **-ιστος** or **ἀθέμιτος**, ον, (the former in Poetry, the latter more correct in Prose) = foreg., Il.9.63; of the Cyclopes, Od.9.106; ἀθεμιστότεροι X.*Cyr.*8.8.5. Adv. -ίστως Phaënnis ap.Paus.10.15.3; -ίτως App.*Pun.*53. **II.** of things, *unlawful*, freq. in neut., ἀθέμιτα ἔρδειν Hdt.7.33; ποιεῖν X.*Mem.*1.1.9; εὔχεσθαι Id.*Cyr.*1.6.6; -ιστα δρᾶν S.*Fr.*742 (dub.), Din.*Fr.*89.4 S.; κείνοις δ' οὐκ ἀθέμιστον *IG*14.1389 ii 29:—ἀ. εἰδωλολατρείαι 1*Ep.Pet.*4.3: c. dat., αἷς [θεαῖς] ἀ. νεκρὰ σώματα *PTaur.*1 ii 22 (ii B.C.).

ἀθεμιτο-γαμία, ἡ, *unlawful marriage*, Just.*Nov.*154.1:—Adj. -γαμος, ον, *Cat.Cod.Astr.*8(4).196 (Rhetor.). **-μιξία**, ἡ, = foreg., Tz. ad Lyc.1143. **-ποιός**, όν, *infanda faciens*, *Gloss.*

ἀθεμιτ-ουργία, ἡ, *doing of unlawful deeds*, *Cat.Cod.Astr.*2.178:—Adj. -ουργός, -ον, Hld.8.9.

ἀθεμιτο-φαγέω, *eat unlawful meats*, Vett.Val.184.6. **-φάγος**, ον, Ptol.*Tetr.*159.

ἄθεος (A), ον, *without God, denying the gods*, esp. those recognized by the state, Pl.*Ap.*26c, etc.: applied to Diagoras, Cic.*ND*1.23.63; παράδειγμα ἄ., opp. θεῖον, Pl.*Tht.*176e. **2.** generally, *godless, ungodly*, Pi.*P.*4.162, A.*Eu.*151, S.*Tr.*1036: Comp. -ώτερος Lys.6.32: Sup. -ώτατος X.*An.*2.5.39. **3.** *abandoned of the gods*, S.*OT*661; μανίαι B.10.109. **4.** *not derived from* the name of *a god*, ὀνόματα Clearch.63. **II.** Adv. -ως *by the anger of heaven* (cf. 1. 3), ἀ. ἐφθαρμένη S.*OT*254, cf. *El.*1181: Sup. -ώτατα *in most unholy wise*, ib.124 (lyr.).

ἄθεος (B), ον, *without vision*, τινός Plot.5.3.17 (s.v.l.; ἀθέ(ατ)ος Volkmann). **2.** *unseen*, Sch.Opp.*H*.1.10.

ἀθεότης, ητος, ἡ, *godlessness*, Pl.*Plt.*308e: in pl., Id.*Lg.*967c. **II.** *atheism*, Ph.1.360,368, etc., Plu.2.165c. **2.** *neglect of the gods of the state*, D.C.67.14.

ἀθεραπ-εία, ἡ, = sq., *neglect of medical care*, Antipho 4.3.5. **-ευσία**, ἡ, *want of attendance*, c. gen., *neglect of* a thing, θεῶν ἀθεραπευσίαι Pl.*R.*443a; σώματος Thphr.*Char.*19.1, cf. Plb.3.60.3 (pl.). **-ευτος**, ον, *uncared for*, of things, X.*Mem.*2.4.3; of persons, D.H.3.22; of faults, *neglected, not treated*, Phld.*Lib.*p.39 O.; τὸ ἀ. *neglect of one's personal appearance*, Luc.*Pisc.*12. **II.** *incurable*, πάθος *PGnom.*205 (ii A.D., in form ἀθαράπ-), cf. Luc.*Ocyp.*27, [Gal.]14.689; ταραχή Phld.*D*.1.15. Adv. -τως Ph.2.404. **III.** *not prepared* or *cured*, στέαρ Dsc.2.76.16.

ἀθερηΐς, ΐδος, ἡ, *prickly*, Nic.*Th.*849.

ἀθερής, ές, *reckless, impious*, Hsch., *EM*25.1; cf. sq.

ἀθερίζω, Hom. (only pres. and impf.): aor. 1 ἀθέριξα A.R.2.477, 488:—Med., aor. 1 ἀθερίσσατο D.P.997:—*make light of*, c. acc. pers., οὔποτέ μ' οἵ γ' ἀθέριζον Il.1.261; οὔ..τιν' ἀναίνομαι οὐδ' ἀ. Od.8.212, cf. Man.6.217: abs., Od.23.174: also c. gen., A.R. ll. cc.

ἀθερίνη [ῐ], ἡ, kind of *smelt*, *Atherina hepsetus*, Arist.*HA*570ᵇ15, Call.*Fr.*38, Dorio ap.Ath.7.285a, etc.:—also **ἀθερῖνος**, ὁ, Arist.*HA* 610ᵇ6.

ἀθέριστος, ον, = ἀφρόντιστος, Zonar. **2.** Act., χαλκὸς ἀ., i.e. ὁ ἀθερίζων καὶ οὐδενὸς ἔχων λόγον, A.*Fr.*128 (cod. -ιτον). **II.** (θερίζω) *not reaped*, Thphr.*HP*8.11.4, *PTeb.*72.372 (ii B.C.), *PFay.*112.13 (i A.D.).

ἀθέρμ-αντος, ον, *not heated*; ἑστία A.*Ch.*629, either a *cold* hearth, or (as Sch.) a household *not heated by strife* or *passion*. **-ος**, ον, *without warmth*; τὸ ἄ. Pl.*Phd.*106a.

ἀθερολόγιον, τό, *surgical instrument for extracting splinters*, Heliod.(?) ap.Orib.46.11.30; cf. ἐθειρολόγος.

ἀθερώδης, ες, (ἀθήρ) *bearded like ears of corn*, Thphr.*HP*7.11.2. **2.** = ἀθαρώδης, [Gal.]19.440.

ἀθέρωμα, τό, v. ἀθηρ-.

ἀθεσία, ἡ, *faithlessness, fickleness*, Plb.2.32.8, Lxx *Je.*20.8, al., *IPE*1².352.16 (Chersonesus, i B.C.), D.S.18.32: pl., ἀ. εἰς αὐτούς Plb.4.29.4.

ἀθεσμία, ἡ, *lawlessness*, *EM*25.7.

ἀθέσμιος, ον, *unlawful*, Suid.

ἀθεσμό-βιος, ον, *living a lawless life, lawless*, -βια φρονεῦντες Hp.*Ep.*17. **-λεκτρος**, ον, *joined in lawless love*, Lyc.1143.

ἄθεσμος, ον, = ἀθέσμιος, Lxx 3*Ma.*5.12, Ph.2.165, J.*BJ*7.8.1, Plu.*Caes.*10. Adv. -μως Lxx 3*Ma.*6.26 (v.l.), Hsch.

ἀθεσμοφάγος, ον, *eating unlawful meats*, Man.4.564.

ἄθεστος, ον, (θέσσασθαι) *not to be entreated, inexorable*, of the Erinyes, Hsch.

ἀθέσφᾰτος, ον, *beyond even a god's power to express, unutterable*: or *not according to a god's utterance, unblest, portentous, awful*, ὄμβρος, θάλασσα, νύξ, Il.3.4, Od.7.273, 11.373; *vast*, ἀ. οἶνος, σῖτος, Od.11.61, 13.244; βόες 20.211; of great beauty, ὕμνος Hes.*Op.*662; φρὴν ἱερὴ καὶ ἀ. Emp.134.4.—Once in Trag., ἀ. θέα E.*IA*232 (lyr.).

ἀθετ-έω, (ἄθετος) *set at naught* a treaty, promise, etc., πίστιν Plb.8.36.5; θυσίαν Lxx 1*Ki.*2.17; διαθήκην *Ep.Gal.*3.15; θεόν 1*Ep.Thess.*4.8; σύμφωνον *OGI*444.18 (Ilium); *deny, disprove*, τἀληθές Phld.*Rh.*1.5 S., cf. *Sign.*37 (Pass.):—Pass., *to be struck off a register*, *PTeb.*74.29 (ii B.C.); *to be rejected*, of a petition, *POxy.*1120.8 (iii A.D.):—Astrol., *cancel, render ineffectual*, Vett.Val.115.3, cf. 105.8 (Pass.). **2.** c. dat., *refuse one's assent*, τοῖς ὑπὸ Τιμαίου εἰρημένοις Plb.12.14.6. **3.** *deal treacherously with, break faith with*, τινά Plb.9.36.10, Lxx *Is.*1.2, *Ev.Marc.*6.26; εἴς τινα Lxx 3*Ki.*12.19; ἐν Ἰσραήλ 4*Ki.*1.1: abs., *IG*12(5).129 (Paros). **II.** Gramm., *reject as spurious*, D.H.*Din.*9, D.L.7.34, etc. **III.** abs., *to be unsuitable, unfit*, Diph.1 D. **-ημα**, τό, *a breach of faith, transgression*, D.H.4.27 (v.l.), Lxx 3*Ki.*8.50 (pl.); *cancellation, annulment* of grant, *PTeb.*124.9. **-ήσιμος**, ον, *to be cancelled*, *BGU*1028.17 (ii A.D.). **-ησις**, ἡ, *a setting aside, abolition*, ἁμαρτίας *Ep.Heb.*9.26, cf. S.E.*M*.8.142; '*annulling*' of a deed, *PLond.*2.142.24 (i A.D.). **II.** *rejection* (of a spurious passage), A.D.*Synt.*5.8, D.L.3.66; generally, *rejection*, opp. ἐποχή, Cic.*Att.*6.9.3. **III.** *breach of faith*, Vett.Val.191.24 (pl.). **-ητέον**, *one must set aside*, Plb.3.29.2. **-ητος**, ον, *cancelled*, ἡμισφαίριον Heph.Astr.2.11. **-ος**, ον, (τίθημι) *without position* or *place*, μονὰς οὐσία ἄ., στιγμὴ δὲ οὐσία θετός Arist.*APo.*87ᵃ36, cf. *Metaph.*1016ᵇ25, 1084ᵇ27, Dam.*Pr.*22. **2.** *not in its place*, i.e. lying about, πλίνθος, λίθος, *IG*1.322 i 10,22. **3.** *not adopted*, Posidipp.39, Anon.Rhythm.*Oxy.*9 iv 16. **II.** *wasted, useless*, χρόνος Plb.18.9.10; *unfit, to be rejected*, πρός τι D.S.11.15: c. dat., ῥευματισμοῖς, σπληνικοῖς, Dsc.1.128, 2.70.6; of persons, *incompetent*, *PAmh.*2.64.12 (ii A.D.). Adv. -τως, = ἀθέσμως, *lawlessly, despotically*, A.*Pr.*150 (lyr.); *unsuitably*, ἔχειν πρός τι Plu.2.715b, Philum.*Ven.*2.3.

ἀθεωρ-ησία, ἡ, *want of observation*, D.S.1.37. **-ητί**, Adv. *without examination*, Hdn.Gr.2.934, Suid. **-ητος**, ον, *not seen, not to be seen*, Antipho Soph.67, D.S.2.35, Arist.*Mu.*399ᵇ22; ἄγνωστος καὶ ἀ. Procl. *in Prm.*p.799 S. **2.** *not scientifically considered*, διαφοραί Aristox.*Harm.*p.35 M.; τὸ ἀ. M.Ant.1.9 (prob.); οὐκ ἀ. *not without* considered meaning, J.BJ5.5.4. II. Act., not having observed, not conversant with, τῶν ὑπαρχόντων Arist.GC316^{a}8; πολιτικῶν πραγμάτων Phld.Rh.2.107 S.; unable to perceive, τῶν ἐναργειῶν Diogenian. Epicur. 3.25: abs., ἀ. ἐν λόγοις Plu.2.405a, cf. Gell.1.9. Adv. -τως Plu. Num.18. 2. non-intellectual, ἀρετή Hecatoap.D.L.7.90.

ἀθήητος, ον, Ion. for ἀθέατος, that may not be beheld, Nonn.D.5.305, al.; unseen, ib.2.6.

ἀθήλαστος, ον, (θηλή) not having suckled, EM739.44.

ἀθηλής, ές, = foreg., μαζοί Nonn.D.48.365, cf. Tryph.34.

ἄθηλος, ον, unsuckled, Ar.Lys.881; just weaned, Semon.5.

ἀθήλυντος, ον, not womanish, Ptol.Tetr.69; Pythag., of odd numbers, Theol.Ar.53.20.

ἄθηλυς, υ, = foreg., Plu.2.285c, Comp.Lyc.Num.3.

Ἀθῆναι, Dor. **Ἀθᾶναι**, ῶν, αἱ, the city of Athens (for the pl. cf. Θῆβαι, Μυκῆναι), Hom., etc.; (sg. Ἀθήνη Od.7.80, IG1.373^{107}):—Ἀθῆναι generally, = Ἀττική, of the whole country, Hdt.9.17. II. Advbs., **Ἀθήν-αζε**, to Athens, IG1.27a, Th.4.46, X.Ath.1.16: **-ηθεν**, from Athens, Lys.13.25, etc.; poet. **-όθεν**, AP7.369 (Antip.): **-ησιν**, at Athens, IG1.59, D.18.66, etc.

Ἀθήναια, τά, older name of the Παναθήναια, Paus.8.2.1: ephebic festival, IG3.1147.

Ἀθην-αΐζω, to be wise as Athena, Eust.1742.2. **-αϊκός**, ή, όν, pertaining to Athena, Dam.Pr.90, Procl.in Alc.p.43 C. Adv. -κῶς Id.Theol.Plat.5.33.

Ἀθήν-αιον, τό, (Ἀθηνᾶ) the temple of Athena, Hdt.5.95, etc. II. lecture-hall at Rome, D.C.73.17. **-αῖος**, α, ον, Athenian, Il.2.551, etc. II. Dor. **Ἀθαναῖος**, sc. μήν, month in Locris, IG9(1).385. **-αιότης**, τητος, ἡ, quality of being Athenian, Gal.19.431.

Ἀθήνη, ἡ, Athene, Il.1.194, etc.; Παλλὰς Ἀ. ib.400, etc.:—also **Ἀθηναίη**, Παλλὰς Ἀ. ib.221,200, etc.:—Att. **Ἀθηναία**, A.Eu.288, Ar.Eq.763, Pax 271; Ἀ. Πολιάς Av.828, cf. X.An.7.3.39, and earlier Attic Inscrr.: contr. **Ἀθηνᾶ**, which in cent. iv superseded the fuller form: Dor. **Ἀθάνα** (this form and Ἀθηναία are the only ones used in Trag.); Ἀθαναία IG1.373^{105}, Theoc.15.80: Aeol. **Ἀθανάα** [νᾰ], Alc.9, Theoc.28.1 (also in some Attic Inscrr., as IG1.351; Ἀθηνάα ib.373^{120}). 2. Ἀθηνᾶς ψῆφος casting vote, from that of A. given for Orestes, Philostr.VS2.3. 3. = Ἀθῆναι, q.v. 4. Pythag. name for 7 (cf. ἀειπάρθενος), TheoSm.p.103 H. 5. name of a plaster, Orib.Fr.88.

Ἀθηνιάω, long to be at Athens, Luc.Pseudol.24.

ἀθήρ, έρος, ὁ, awn, πυραμίνους ἀ. Hes.Fr.117; εἴσδυσις οὐδ' ἀθέρι prob. l. in Lyr.Adesp.2 B, cf. X.Oec.18.1, Arist.HA595^{b}27:—in pl., chaff, Luc.Anach.31; χωρὶς δείσης καὶ ἀθέρος POxy.988 (iii A.D.). II. barb of a weapon, A.Fr.154, Hp.Epid.5.49, Plu.Cat.Mi.70. III. spine or prickle of a fish, prob. in Ath.7.303d.

ἀθήρα or **ἀθήρη**, ἡ, = ἀθάρη, Hellanic.192, Sophr.77, PTeb.131 (100 B.C.), Dsc.2.92, Eust.1675.60.—Egyptian, acc. to Plin.HN22.121.

ἀθήρ-ᾱτος, ον, not caught, or not to be caught, Opp.C.1.514, Ael. NA1.4, Longus 2.4; τὰ ἀ. ἐκθηρᾶσθαι Max.Tyr.6.3. **-ευτος**, ον, not hunted, X.Cyr.1.4.16.

ἀθηρηλοιγός, ὁ, (ἀθήρ) consumer of chaff, i.e. winnowing-fan, Od.11.128, 23.275.

ἀθηρία, ἡ, want of game, Ael.NA8.2. 2. immunity from being hunted, ib.14.1. 3. want of experience in hunting, ib.12.7.

ἀθηρόβρωτος, ον, (ἀθήρ) devouring chaff, ἀ. ὄργανον, i.e. a winnowing-fan, S.Fr.454.

ἀθηρόλοον· ἀθηρηλοιγόν, Hsch.

ἀθηροπώλης, ὁ, seller of ἀθάρη, POxy.1432.6 (iii A.D.).

ἄθηρος, ον, without wild beasts or game, χώρη Hdt.4.185; τὸ ἄθηρον ταῖς λίμναις ἔνεστι, = ἀθηρία 2, Plu.2.981c; ἄ. ἡμέρα a blank day, A.Fr.241. II. repelling noxious animals, κλάδος Gp.10.32, etc.

ἀθηρ-ώδης, ες, = ἀθερώδης, Hsch. s.v. ἔτνος. **-ωμα**, ατος, τό, tumour full of gruel-like matter (ἀθήρη), Gal.10.985, Heliod.ap.Orib.45.5 tit. **-ωμάτιον**, τό, Dim. of foreg., ibid.1.

ἀθησαύριστος, ον, not hoarded, not fit for hoarding, Pl.Lg.844d; of food, not fit for preserving, not keeping well, Thphr.HP6.4.11. II. Act., not hoarding, prodigal, Poll.3.117.

ἀθήτευτος, ον, not serving for hire, Hsch.

ἀθίγγανος· ὁ μὴ θέλων τινὶ προσεγγίσαι, EM25.28.

ἀθῐγής, ές, (θιγεῖν) untouched, Theopomp.Hist.76; of a virgin, Epigr.Gr.521 (Thessalonica). 2. intangible, S.E.M.9.281. II. Act., not having touched, νεκροῦ Porph.ap.Eus.PE5.10.

ἄθικτος, ον, untouched: mostly c. gen., untouched by a thing, ἀκτῖνος ἄ. S.Tr.686; ἄ. ἡγητῆρος Id.OC1521, etc.; κερδῶν ἄθικτον βουλευτήριον untouched by gain, i.e. incorruptible, A.Eu.704, cf. Plu.Cim.10: c. dat., νόσοις ἄ. A.Supp.561; ἄ. ὑπὸ τοῦ χρόνου Plu. Per.13. 2. chaste, virgin, κόραι Ion Trag.11; εὐνή E.Hel.795, cf. Arar.14; ἄ. ἄμματα παρθενίης Epigr.Gr.248.8 (Phryg.); ἄ. εἰς Κυθηρίην σφρηγίς Herod.1.55: of substances, ἄ. θεῖον, virgin sulphur, Ps.-Democr.Alch.p.45 B. 3. not to be touched, holy, τὸν ἄ. γᾶς ὀμφαλόν, of Delphi, S.OT897; ἄ. οὐδ' οἰκητὸς [ὁ χῶρος] Id. OC39; ἄθικτα holy things, A.Ag.371, S.OT891. 4. not to be touched, abominable, EM25.10. II. Act., not touching, c. gen., Call.Dian.201.

ἀθίλοι· κόγχου θαλασσίας εἶδος, Hsch.

ἄθλαστος, ον, which cannot be crushed or dinted, Arist.Mete.385^{a}15, 386^{a}18. 2. unbruised, of olives, Gp.9.29; **ἄθλαστον**, τό, of a food-stuff (?), PFay.333 (ii A.D.).

ἀθλ-εύω, Ep. and Ion. **ἀεθλεύω**: fut. -εύσω A.Pr.95 (anap.), Q.S. 4.113, Nonn.D.37.557:—contend for a prize, abs., ἀεθλεύειν προκαλίζετο Il.4.389, cf. 23.274,737, Hes.Th.435; once in Hdt.5.22: contr. ἀθλ-, once in Hom., ἀθλεύων πρὸ ἄνακτος struggling or suffering for him, Il.24.734; once in Pl., ἐν ἀγῶνι ἀ. Lg.873e; but Trag. always use ἀθλέω, exc. A. l. c. **-έω**, Ion. impf. ἀέθλεον Hdt.1.67, 7.212: aor. ἤθλησα (v. infr.): pf. ἤθληκα Plu.Demetr.5:—Med., aor. ἐνηθλησάμην AP7.117 (Zenod.):—Pass., pf. κατήθλημαι Suid.: (ἆθλος, ἆθλον):—commoner form of foreg., used by Hom. only in aor. part., Λαομέδοντι.. ἀθλήσαντε having contended with him, Il.7.453; πολλά περ ἀθλήσαντα having gone through many struggles, 15.30; contend in battle, Hdt.7.212; πρός τινα 1.67; ἀ. ἄθλους, ἀ. κατὰ τὴν ἀγωνίαν Pl.Ti.19c and b, cf. Lg.830a; ἤθλησα κινδυνεύματα have engaged in perilous struggles, S.OC564; φαῦλον ἀθλήσας πόνον E.Supp. 317; ἀ. τῷ σώματι Aeschin.2.147. II. to be an athlete, contend in games, Simon.149, CIG2810b (Aphrodisias). III. hold games, ἐπ' Ἀρχεμόρῳ B.8.12. **-ημα**, τό, contest, struggle, Pl.Lg.833c, etc.: pl., athletic exercises, Arist.Pr.956^{b}26, Phld.Mus.p.69 K. II. implement of labour, Theoc.21.9. **-ησις**, ἡ, contest, combat, esp. of athletes, Plb.5.64.6, SIG1073.24 (Olympia), IG14.1102: pl., Phld.Mus.p.14 K.; κατὰ τὴν ἄ. 'in the athletic world', CPHerm. 119^{v}iii 13 (iii A.D.); training, practice, D.S.3.33. 2. generally, struggle, trial, ἄ. ὑπομένειν Ep.Heb.10.32. **-ητέον**, one must practise athletics, Hermog.Prog.11. 2. glossed by ἀσκητέον, Erot. **-ητήρ**, ῆρος, ὁ, = ἀθλητής, Od.8.164, IG3.1171.3, POxy. 1015.8 (poet.). **-ητής**, contr. from ἀεθλητής, οῦ, ὁ:—combatant, champion; esp. in games, Pi.N.5.49, 10.51 (in form ἀεθλ-), cf. Pl.R. 410b, IG4.1508^{B} (Epid.), etc.: of Christian martyrs, Epist.Gall.ap. Jul.454d, cf. JRS 10.53. 2. as Adj., ἀ. ἵππος a race-horse, Lys.19.63, Pl.Prm.137a. II. c. gen. rei, practised in, master of, πολέμου Pl.R.543b; τῶν καλῶν ἔργων D.25.97; βδελυρίας Theopomp.Hist.217; τῶν ἔργων (sc. τῶν πολεμικῶν) Arist.Pol.1321^{a}26; τῆς ἀληθινῆς λέξεως D.H.Dem.18; πάσης ἀρετῆς D.S.9.1; οἵους ἡ γῆ τοὺς ἑαυτῆς ἀ. ἀποτελεῖ Philostr.Im.2.24. **-ητικός**, ή, όν, of or for an athlete, athletic, ἕξις Arist.Pol.1338^{b}10; ἐνεργεῖαι prob. in Phld. Mus.p.14 K.; ἀ. ἀγῶνες Plu.2.724f; στέφανος PRyl.153.25 (ii A.D.). Adv. -κῶς Plu.2.192c, Aët.16.34.

ἄθλητος, ον, = ἄθλαστος, dub. l. Hierocl.p.25.3 A.

ἀθλῐβής, ές, not pressed or hurt, Nonn.D.9.31; not pressed out, ἰκμάδες 22.27. II. Act., not pressing, ib.37.220.

ἄθλιβος, ον, = ἀθλιβής I, Gal.13.686.

ἀθλιό-ομαι, to be made miserable, Tz.H.3.364. **-ποιός**, όν, creating misery, Olymp.in Alc.p.224 C.

ἄθλιος, α, ον, also ος, ον E.Alc.1038, etc., Att. contr. from ἀέθλιος: (ἄεθλον, ἆθλον):—lit. winning the prize or running for it (this sense only in Ep. form ἀέθλιος, q.v.). II. metaph., struggling, unhappy, wretched, miserable (this sense only in Att. form ἄθλιος), freq. of persons, A.Th.922, etc.: Comp. -ιώτερος S.OT815,1204: Sup. -ιώτατος E.Ph.1679:—also of states of life, ἄ. γάμοι A.Th.779; βίος, τύχη, E.Heracl.878, Hec.425:—of that which causes wretchedness, ἆρ' ἄθλιον τοὔνειδος; S.OC753, cf. El.1140; πρόσοψις E.Or.952. Adv., τὸν ἀθλίως θανόντα S.Ant.26, cf. E.HF707, etc. 2. in moral sense, pitiful, wretched, Lys.32.13, D.10.43; τίς οὕτως ἄ. ὅστις ...; Id.21.66; καὶ γὰρ ἂν ἄ. ἦν, εἰ.. ib.191. 3. without any moral sense, wretched, sorry, θηρσὶν ἄθλιον βοράν E.Ph.1603; ἄ. ζωγράφος Plu.2.6f. Adv. -ίως καὶ κακῶς with wretched success, D.18.145; ζῆν ἀ. Philem.203.

ἀθλιότης, ητος, ἡ, suffering, wretchedness, Pl.R.545a, Clearch.25, Plu.2.112b, etc. 2. degradation, ἀ. βαθεῖα Phld.Rh.1.206 S.

ἄθλιπτος, ον, (θλίβω) = ἀθλιβής, Gal.9.373: metaph., not oppressed, βίος PSI1.65.4 (vi A.D.). Adv. -τως without pressure or crushing, Gal.18(2).794, Aët.9.28: metaph., ἐκπονεῖν Simp.in Epict.p.46 D.

ἀθλο-θεσία, ἡ, office of ἀθλοθέτης IG2^{2}.1368.131 (Athens, ii A.D.):—also **-θετία**, ἡ, Ar.Fr.739a. **-θετέω**, (τίθημι) offer a prize, offer rewards, Lxx 4 Ma.17.12; τισί Clearch.18. II. preside over, direct, metaph., τὸν Ῥωμαϊκὸν ὄλεθρον Eun.Hist.p.264 D., cf. Hld.7.12. **-θετήρ**, ῆρος, ὁ, = sq., IG5(1).456 (Sparta), 14.1815. **-θέτης**, ου, ὁ, one who awards the prize, the judge or steward in the games, Pl. Lg.764d, Arist.EN1095^{b}1, IG1.188, etc.

ἆθλον, τό, Att. contr. from Ep., Ion., Lyr. **ἄεθλον** (which alone is used by Hom. and Hdt., mostly also by Pi., once by S.Tr.506 (lyr.)):—prize of contest, Il.23.413,620, etc., Pi.O.9.108, al., A.Supp. 1033, E.Hel.43; τῶν Ἀθήνηθεν ἄ., inscr. on Attic prize amphorae, CIG776, etc.; ἀ. μουσικῆς IG2.814; in Prose, ἆθλα ἀρετῆς Th.2.46; ἁμαρτημάτων Lys.1.47. Phrases: ἄεθλα κεῖται or πρόκειται prizes are offered, Hdt.8.26, 9.101; ἆθλα προφαίνειν, προτιθέναι offer prizes, X.Cyr.2.1.23, Hier.9.4; τιθέναι Pl.Lg.834c; ἆθλα λαμβάνειν, φέρεσθαι to win prizes, Pl.R.613c, Ion 530a, etc.; ἆθλον νίκης λαμβάνειν as the prize, Arist.Pol.1296^{a}30, cf. Th.6.80; ἆ. ποιεῖσθαι τὰ κοινά Th.3.82; τὰ ἆθλα ὑπὲρ ὧν ἐστιν ὁ πόλεμος D.2.28; ἆθλα πολέμου Id. 4.5; τῆς ἀρετῆς Id.20.107; βέλτιον τοῖς δούλοις ἆ. προκεῖσθαι τὴν ἐλευθερίαν Arist.Pol.1330^{a}33. II. = ἆθλος, contest, only in pl., ζώννυνταί τε νέοι καὶ ἐπεντύνονται ἄεθλα Od.24.89, cf. Xenoph.2.5, Pi.O. 1.3: metaph., conflict, struggle, πολλῶν ἔλεξεν δυσοίστων πόνων ἆθλα S.Ph.508; ἄεθλ' ἀγώνων Id.Tr.506:—this usage is censured by Luc. Sol.2. III. in pl., place of combat, Pl.Lg.868a, 935b. IV. Astrol., = κλῆρος (q.v.), Manil.3.162.

ἆθλος, ὁ, contr. from Ep. and Ion. **ἄεθλος**, which alone is used by Hom. (except in Od.8.160), and mostly by Hdt. and Pi.:—contest either in war or sport, esp. *contest for a prize*, Hom.; νικῶν τοιῷδ' ἐπ' ἀέθλῳ (for the arms of Achilles) Od.11.548; ἄεθλος πρόκειται *a task* is set one, Hdt.1.126; ἐμοὶ μὲν οὗτος ἄ. ὑποκείσεται Pi.*O.*1.84; ἄεθλον προτιθέναι to set it, Hdt.7.197; ἆθλοι Πυθικοί, Δελφικοί, S.*El.*49,682; *toil*, Pi.*P.*4.165; of the labours of Heracles, D.S.4.11, etc.: metaph., *conflict, struggle, ordeal*, Alc.33, A.*Pr.*702,752, S.*Ant.*856. **II.** = ἆθλον 1, Theoc.8.11 sqq.—On the proper difference of ἆθλον and ἆθλος v. ἆθλον II. (For ἄϝεθλος, ἄϝεθλον, as in *IG*5(2).75.)

ἀθλοσύνη, ἡ, = ἆθλος, *AP*6.54 (Paul. Sil.).

ἀθλοφόρος, ον, Ep. and Lyr. **ἀεθλ-**, *bearing away the prize, victorious*, ἵππος Il.9.124, 22.22, Ibyc.2, cf. *Inscr.Olymp.*166; ἄνδρες Pi. *O.*7.7, cf. Hdt.1.31, etc.; of martyrs, *JRS*10.47. **II.** *prize-giving*, ἀγῶνες *IG*7.530.3 (Tanagra). **III.** ἀθλοφόρος, ἡ, title of priestess at Alexandria, ἀ. Βερενίκης *OGI*90.5 (Canopus), *PTeb.*176 (circ. 200 B.C.), etc.

ἄθολ-ος, ον, *not turbid, clear*, Luc.*Hist.Conscr.*51: Sup., Olymp. *in Mete.*271.22. **-ωτος**, ον, *untroubled*, of water, Hes.*Op.*595; of *pure* air, Luc.*Trag.*62: metaph., λόγος Them.*Or.*19.232d; ἀ. τὴν αἰδῶ φυλάττειν Just.*Nov.*78.2.1.

ἄθορος, ον, (θορεῖν) of male animals, *veneris expers*, Ant.Lib.13.7.

ἀθορύβ-ητος, ον, *undisturbed*: τὸ -ητότατον *tranquillity* of mind, X.*Ages.*6.7. **-ος**, ον, *without uproar*, Pl.*Lg.*640c; *unperturbed*, Polystr.p.29 W., prob. l. in Metrod.*Fr.*48 K.: Comp., Anon.*in SE* 15.19. Adv. -βως E.*Or.*630, Epicur.*Fr.*489, J.*BJ*2.12.6, Hierocl. *in CA*12 p.447 M. **II.** *not causing confusion*, Ascl.*Tact.*12.10 (Comp.).

ἄθουρος, prob. f.l. for ἄθορος, *EM*25.12.

ἀθραγένη, ἡ, *smoke-wood, Clematis Vitalba*, Thphr.*HP*5.9.6.

ἄθρακτος, ον, (θράσσω) = ἀτάρακτος, Hsch.

ἀθράνευτος, ον, expl. by ἄστρωτος, prob. *uncushioned*, E.*Fr.*569, *AB*352.

ἀθράσυντος, ον, = ἄτολμος, Sch.A.*Ch.*629.

ἄθραυστος, ον, *unbroken*, E.*Hec.*17, *IG*2.1054d14, Melinno ap.Stob. 3.7.12; of persons, Plb.2.22.5; μέρος τῆς δυνάμεως D.S.19.30. Adv. -τως *without breakage*, κάμπτειν *Gp.*10.19.2, etc. **2.** *unbreakable*, Arist.*Mete.*385a14; *indestructible*, ἄτομος *Placit.*1.3.18.

ἄθρεπτος, ον, *ill-nourished, underfed*, Ar.Byz.*Epit.*2.9.8; f.l. for ἄτρεπτος, *AP*5.177 (Mel.).

ἀθρέω (not ἀθρέω, Hdn.Gr.2.83): aor. opt. ἀθρήσειε, inf. ἀθρῆσαι, Il. 12.391, S.*OT*1305 (lyr.): aor. Med. ἀθρήσασθαι Timo 5.5:—*gaze at, observe*, ἵνα μή τις Ἀχαιῶν βλήμενον ἀθρήσειε Il. l.c., cf. 14.334; οὐδέ πῃ ἀθρῆσαι δυνάμην (sc. Σκύλλην) Od.12.232, cf. 19.478, E.*Hec.*679, *El.* 827; [οἱ μεθύοντες] ἀθρεῖν τὰ πόρρω οὐ δύνανται Arist.*Pr.*872a19. **b.** *inspect*, ἱερά *IG*12(1).694 (Rhodes). **2.** abs. or with a Prep., *look earnestly, gaze*, ὅτ' ἐς πεδίον τὸ Τρωϊκὸν ἀθρήσειε Il.10.11; ἄθρει *observe, watch*, A.*Fr.*226; δεῦρ' ἄθρησον *look* hither, E.*Hipp.*300; λεύσσετ', ἀθρήσατε Id.*Andr.*1228; οὐ γὰρ ἴδοις ἂν ἀθρῶν *by observing*, S.*OC* 252; ἄθρει πᾶς κύκλῳ σκοπῶν Ar.*Av.*1196. **II.** later, of the mind, *look upon, observe*, θέλων ἄθρησον *view* kindly, Pi.*P.*2.70; πολλὰ πυθέσθαι, πολλὰ δ' ἀθρῆσαι S.*OT*1305, cf. *OC*1032; ἄθρησον αὐτό E.*Ba.* 1281; ἐς τοῦδ' ἀθρήσας θάνατον ἡγείσθω θεούς ib.1326, etc.:—foll. by interrog. or rel. clause, καὶ ταῦτ' ἄθρησον, εἰ.. *consider* this also, whether..., S.*Ant.*1077, cf. 1216: imper. freq. in Pl., as τόδε τοίνυν ἄθρει, πότερον.. *R.*394e; ἄθρει μὴ οὐ.. *Grg.*495b; ἄθρει ὅτι.. *R.* 583b; also ἀθρῶ *Prm.*144d, ἀθρῶν *Ti.*91e. **2.** abs., ἄθρησον *consider*, E.*IA*1415. **III.** *perceive*, ἢ δοῦπον νέον οὔασιν ἠέ τιν' αὐγὴν ἀ. Nic.*Th.*165.

ἀθρήματα, τά, *wedding-gifts*, Hsch.

ἀθρήνητος, ον, *unlamented*, gloss on νώνυμνος, Eust.928.63.

ἀθρηνί, Adv., (θρῆνος) *without mourning*, Hdn.*Epim.*255, Suid.

ἀθρητέον, *one must consider*, E.*Hipp.*379, X.*Smp.*8.39, Max.Tyr. 7.9.

ἀθρίγγωτος, ον, *without coping*, gloss on ἀγείσωτος, *EM*8.56.

ἄθριξ, τρῖχος, ὁ, ἡ, *without hair*, Matro *Fr.*4, Alex.Aphr.*Pr.*1.6.

ἀθρῑπήδεστος, ον, *not worm-eaten*, Thphr.*HP*5.1.2 (codd. ἀθριπηδέστατον); δέλτος Them.*Or.*23.293b.

ἀθροίζω, Att. **ἁθροίζω**: aor. ἤθροισα E.*Ph.*495, etc.: pf. ἤθροικα Plu. *Caes.*20:—Pass., aor. ἠθροίσθην: pf. ἤθροισμαι: plpf. ἤθροιστο A.*Pers.* 414:—quadrisyll. ἀθροΐζω Archil.60,104, *APl.*4.308 (Eugen.); prob. in E.*IA*267 (lyr.), Ar.*Av.*253: (ἀθρόος):—*gather together, collect, muster*, ἀ. λαόν, etc., S.*OT*144, etc.; τὸ βαρβαρικὸν καὶ τὸ Ἑλληνικόν X. *An.*1.2.1; Τροίαν ἀ. *gather* the Trojans *together*, E.*Hec.*1139; πνεῦμ' ἄθροισον *collect* breath, Id.*Ph.*851, cf. Arist.*GA*738b7; περιπλοκὰς λόγων ἀθροίσας *having strung together*, E.*Ph.*495: abs., *hoard* treasure, Arist.*Pol.*1314b10:—Med., *gather for oneself, collect round one*, E. *Heracl.*122, X.*Cyr.*3.1.19:—Pass., *to be gathered* or *crowded together*, εὖτε πρὸς ἄεθλα δῆμος ἠθροΐζετο Archil.104, cf. 60; ἐς τὴν ἀγορὴν ἀ. Hdt.5.101; ἁθροισθέντες *having rallied*, Th.1.50; τὸ δὲ.. ξύμπαν ἠθροίσθη δισχίλιοι but the whole *amounted collectively to*.., Id.5.6; ἐνταῦθα ἠθροίζοντο *they mustered in force* there, Id.6.44, etc.; *form a society*, Pl.*Prt.*322b; ἀθροισθέντες *having formed a party*, Arist.*Pol.*1304b33: of things, περὶ πολλῶν ἀθροισθέντων *taken in the aggregate*, Pl.*Tht.* 157b. **2.** in Pass. of the mind, ἀθροίζεσθαι εἰς ἑαυτὸν *collect* oneself, Pl.*Phd.*83a, cf. 67c; φόβος ἤθροισται fear *has gathered strength*, X.*Cyr.*5.2.34.

ἄθροισις, Att. **ἅθρ-**, εως, ἡ, *gathering, collecting*, στρατοῦ E.*Hec.* 314; χρημάτων Th.6.26; αἱ τῶν νεφῶν ἀ. Arist.*Mete.*340a31; λόγων Porph.*Abst.*1.29; κατ' ἄθροισιν λέγειν *collectively*, Hermog.*Id.*1.4.

ἄθροισμα, τό, *that which is gathered, a gathering*, ἀστῶν E.*Or.*874, cf. Lxx 1*Ma.*3.13; κυνῶν D.S.34.2.30. **2.** *process of aggregation*, Pl.*Tht.*157b; *aggregate*, τέχνη ἀ. καταλήψεων Chrysipp.*Stoic.*2.23; ψυχὴ ἐννοιῶν καὶ προλήψεων ἀ. ib.2.228, cf. Gal.1.67; *compound*, Max. Tyr.40.5. **II.** in Epicur. philos., *assemblage of atoms*, Epicur. *Fr.*59, al.; esp. of the *human organism*, Id.*Ep.*1 p.19 U., al.

ἀθροισμός, ὁ, = ἄθροισις, Thphr.*CP*1.10.7, cf. Epicur.*Ep.*2 p.38 U., *Nat.*14.4, S.E.*P.*3.188; μισθοφόρων Max.Tyr.6.7; *condensation*, Thphr.*CP*5.2.1. **ἀθροιστέον**, *one must collect*, X.*Lac.*7.4.

ἀθροιστικός, ή, όν, *given to accumulation*, χρημάτων, Procl.*Par. Ptol.*246. **II.** Gramm., *collective*, ὀνόματα A.D.*Synt.*42.24; *copulative*, σύνδεσμοι Id.*Conj.*230.20, al.

ἀθροοποσία, ἡ, *copious drinking*, Herod.ap.Orib.5.30.23.

ἀθρόος, α, ον, (ος, ον D.19.228, Arist.*PA*675b21, etc.), **ἀθρόος** in Hom. acc. to Aristarch.ap.Sch.Ven.Il.14.38 and Att. (also sometimes **ἄθρους**, ουν, as Ar.*Fr.*633, Hyp.*Eux.*33, D.27.35), poet. acc. pl. ἀθρόας *h.Merc.*106; dat. pl. ἀθροῖσιν *Epigr.Gr.*1034.26 (Callipolis):—but in later writers the spir. lenis prevailed: (ἀ- II, θρόος):—*in crowds, heaps*, or *masses, crowded together*, Hom. only in pl., as Il.2.439, al.; ἁθρόοι.. ἅπαντες Od.3.34, etc.: sg. first in Pi.*P.*2.35; ἀθρόοι, of soldiers, *in close order*, Hdt.6.112, X.*An.*1.10.13, etc.; opp. ἀσύντακτοι, Id.*Cyr.*8.1.46; *in column*, ib.5.3.36; πολλαὶ κῶμαι ἀ. *close together*, Id.*An.*7.3.9. **II.** *together, in a body*, ἀθρόα πάντ' ἀπέτεισε he paid for all *at once*, Od.1.43; ἀ. πόλις the citizens *as a whole*, opp. καθ' ἕκαστον, Th.2.60, cf. 1.141; ἀ. δύναμις Id.2.39; ἀ. ἣν αὐτῷ τὸ στράτευμα was *assembled*, X.*Cyr.*3.3.22; τὸ ἀ. their *assembled force*, ib.4.2.20, cf. *An.*5.2.1; ἀθρόῳ στόματι with *one* voice, E.*Ba.*725; ἀ. δάκρυ *one flood of* tears, Id.*HF*489; ἀ. λόγος *a flood of* words, Pl.*R.* 344d; ἀθρόους κρίνειν to condemn *all by a single vote*, Id.*Ap.*32b; πολλοὺς ἀ. ὑμῶν D.21.131; ἄθρους ὤφθη was seen *with all his forces*, Plu. *Them.*12, cf. Id.*Sull.*12; ἀ. λεγόμενον used in a *collective* sense, opp. κατὰ μέρος, Pl.*Tht.*182a; ἀθρόας γινομένης μεταβολῆς taking place *all at once*, Arist.*Ph.*186a15; opp. ἐκ προσαγωγῆς, Id.*Pol.*1308b16; κατήριπεν ἀ. he fell *all at once*, Theoc.13.50, cf. 25.252; ἀθρόαι πέντε νύκτες five *whole* nights, Pi.*P.*4.130; κατάστασις ἀθρόα καὶ αἰσθητή Arist. *Rh.*1369b34; κάθαρσις ἀ., opp. κατ' ὀλίγον, Id.*HA*582b7; καταπιεῖν ἀθρόους τεμαχίτας *at a gulp*, Eub.9, cf. Plu.2.650c, etc.; ἀθρόον ἐκκαγχάζειν *burst out* laughing, Arist.*EN*1150b11, cf. Hp.*Ep.*17. **2.** *continuous*, κίνησις Plot.3.7.8, cf. ib.1 (Comp.). **3.** *sudden*, ἔφοδος Malch.p.412 D.; τῷ ἀ. μὴ καταπλαγῆναι Men.Prot.p.68 D.:—this sense may perh. be found in Plu.*Them.* l.c., *Sull.* l.c. **4.** ἀθρόον, τό, = ἄθροισμα II, Epicur.*Ep.*1 p.16 U., *Fr.*314, Zeno Sidon.ap. Phld.*Herc.*1005.7. **III.** *complete, overwhelming*, ἀ. κακότης Pi.*P.* 2.35; *continuous, incessant*, πνεῦμα Arist.*Mete.*367a30; *concentrated*, of noise, D.H.*Comp.*22, etc. **IV.** Adv. ἀθρόον *all at once*; ἄθρουν *in one payment*, *PPetr.*2 p.27, cf. D.27.35; *generally*, εἰρῆσθαι Aret. *SA*1.6:—regul. Adv. ἀθρόως X.*Smp.*2.25, Arist.*HA*533b10, etc.; ἀ. λέγειν to speak *collectively* or *generally*, Aristid.*Rh.*2.547 S. **2.** *suddenly*, ἀετὸς ἀ. φανείς Hsch.Mil.4.11, cf. 19 (perh. also in Arist.*HA* l.c.). **V.** Comp. ἀθροώτερος Th.6.34, etc.; ἀθρουστέρα Phylotim. ap.Ath.3.79b: Sup. ἀθρούστατος Plu.*Caes.*20.

ἄθροος, ον, *noiseless*, Hdn.Gr.1.126.

ἀθροότης, ητος, ἡ, (ἀθρόος) *a being massed together, collectivity*, κατὰ -ότητα, opp. κατὰ μέρη, Epicur.*Ep.*2 p.49 U.

ἄθρυπτος, ον, (θρύπτω) *unbroken, imperishable*, Plu.2.1055b; *tough*, of flesh, Herophil.ap.Gal.4.596. **II.** *not enervated*, *Carm.Aur.* 35; of language, *not affected*, λέξις ἀφελὴς καὶ ἄ. Plu.*Lyc.*21:—of a person, ἄ. εἰς γέλωτα *never breaking* into laughter, Id.*Per.*5; ὦτα ἄθρυπτα κολακείᾳ Id.2.38b. Adv. -τως Id.*Fab.*3.

ἀθρυψία, ἡ, *a simple way of life*, Plu.2.609c.

ἀθῡμ-έω, *to be disheartened, despond*, ἐς νόσον πεσὼν ἀθυμεῖς A.*Pr.* 474; οἴμ' ὡς ἀθυμῶ S.*Aj.*587; ἀ. τινι *at* or *for* a thing, Id.*El.*769, etc.; ἐπί τινι Isoc.4.3; εἴς τι Pl.*Sph.*264b; πρὸς τὴν παροῦσαν ὄψιν Th.2.88; τὴν τελευτήν Id.5.91; τοῦτο, ὡς.. X.*Oec.*8.21; ἕνεκά τινος Id.*An.*5. 4.19:—*to be sore afraid* lest, ἀθυμῶ δ' εἰ φανήσομαι S.*Tr.*666; δεινῶς ἀθυμῶ μὴ βλέπων ὁ μάντις ᾖ Id.*OT*747. **-ητέον**, *one must lose heart*, X.*An.*3.2.23; οὐκ ἀ. τοῖς παροῦσι πράγμασιν D.4.2. **-ία**, Ion. -ίη, ἡ, *lack of spirit*, Hp.*Aër.*16; *faintheartedness, despondency*, Hdt.1.37, E.*HF*552; εἰς ἀ. καθιστάναι or ἐμβάλλειν τινά Pl.*Lg.*731a, Aeschin.3.177; ἀ. παρέχειν τινί X.*Cyr.*4.1.8; εἰς ἀ. καταστῆναι Lys.12.3; ἐν πάσῃ ἀ. εἶναι X.*HG*6.2.24; ἀθυμίαν ἔχειν S.*Ant.*237; ἀ. ἐμπίπτει τινί X.*Mem.*3.12.6: pl., ἀ. ἢ φόβοι Arist.*Pr.*954a23.

ἀθυμί-αστος, ον, *unconsecrated*, Procl.ad Hes.*Op.*746. **-ᾱτος**, ον, *which cannot exhale*, Arist.*Mete.*385a18.

ἄθῡμος, ον, *fainthearted, spiritless*, once in Hom., ἀσκελέες καὶ ἄ. Od.10.463; κακὸς καὶ ἄ. Hdt.7.11; οὐ τοῖς ἀ. ἡ τύχη ξυλλαμβάνει S.*Fr.* 927, cf. *OT*319; of nations, opp. ἔνθυμος, Arist.*Pol.*1327b28: Comp. -ότερος Men.405.2; ἄ. εἶναι πρός τι to have *little heart* for it, X.*An.*1. 4.9. Adv. ἀθύμως, ἔχειν πρός τι Id.*HG*4.5.4, cf. Isoc.3.58; ἀθύμως διάγειν X.*Cyr.*3.1.24; ἀθύμως πονεῖν to work *without spirit*, Id.*Oec.* 21.5; ὁδοὺς ἀ. τιθέντες *discouraging* their marches, A.*Eu.*770. **2.** *without anger* or *passion*, Pl.*R.*411b, *Lg.*888a.

ἀθυμόω, *dishearten*, τινά Phld.*Lib.*p.7 O.

ἀθυρεύεσθαι, παίζειν, μιγνύειν, σκιρτᾶν, Hsch.

ἄθυρ-μα, τό, (ἀθύρω) *plaything, toy*, Il.15.363, *h.Merc.*40: in pl., *beautiful objects, adornments*, Od.18.323, Sapph.*Supp.*20a.9; *delight, joy*, Ἀπολλώνιον ἄ., of a choral ode, Pi.*P.*5.23; ἀθύρματα Μουσᾶν, i.e. songs, B.*Fr.*33, cf. 8.87; ἀρηΐων ἀ. *pastimes* of Ares, i.e. battle, 17. 57; ἁβρὸν ἄ., of a pet dog, *IG*14.1647, cf. 12(5).677.10 (Syros):—rare in Trag. and Com., E.*Fr.*272, Cratin.145, *Com.Adesp.*839,

Alcid.ap.Arist.*Rh*.1406ᵃ9, ᵇ13; of a court-jester, ἄ. τοῦ βασιλέως J.*AJ*12.4.9, cf. Philostr.*VS*1.8.3. **-μάτιον**, τό, Dim. of foreg., Philox.3.23; *pet*, Luc.*D.Mar*.1.5.

ἀθῠρο-γλωττία, ἡ, *impudent loquacity*, Plb.8.10.1. **-γλωττος**, ον, *one that cannot keep his mouth shut, ceaseless babbler*, E.*Or*. 903 (-γλωσσος). **-νόμος**, ον, *making game of the laws*, Hsch.

ἄθῠρος, ον, (θύρα) *without door*, βούστασις *IG*11(2).287*A*161 (Delos, iii B.C.); οἶκος ib.2².1322 (iii/ii B.C.); νεώς Menodot.1; οἰκίαι Nic. Dam.p.148 D., cf. Plu.2.503c, Hdn.8.1.5, etc. II. metaph., *open, unchecked*, Adam.2.60; ῥῆτραι Nic.*Al*.132; γλῶττα Ph.1.678.

ἀθῠρο-στομία, ἡ, = ἀθυρογλωττία, Plu.2.11c, *AP*5.251 (Paul. Sil.). **-στομος**, ον, = ἀθυρόγλωττος, ἀ. Ἀχώ *ever-babbling* Echo, S.*Ph*.188 (lyr.).

ἄθυρσις, ἡ, *sport, festivity*, B.12.93.

ἄθυρσος, ον, *without thyrsus*, E.*Or*.1492 (lyr.).

ἀθύρω [ῠ], Ep. word, only pres. and impf., rare in Prose (v. infr.):—*play, sport*, of children, Il.15.364, Hp.*Ep*.17; νέος μὲν οὖν.. ἦλατ' ἀθύρων E.*Ion* 53; τάχ' ἂν πρὸς ἀγκάλαισι..πηδῶν ἀθύροι Id.*Fr*. 323; σφαίρῃ A.R.4.950; of dancing, Pl.*Lg*.796b; playing on an instrument, κατὰ πηκτίδων *Anacreont*.41.11: c. acc. cogn., μοῦσαν ἀθύρων *singing sportive* songs, *h.Hom*.19.15:—Med., simply, *sing*, *h.Merc*.485. 2. metaph., ἀ. περὶ τὰ θειότατα τῶν πραγμάτων Procl. *in Prm*.p.863 S. II. c. acc., παῖς ἐὼν ἄθυρε μεγάλα ἔργα (of Achilles) *he did* them *in play*, Pi.*N*.3.44; ἔργα φωτῶν ἀ. *play* the deeds of men, of the comic Muse, *AP*9.505.8, cf. Him.*Or*.17.7. 2. *sing of*, ἀρετάν Pi.*I*.4(3).39. 3. *mock at*, Nonn.*D*.45.244.

ἀθύρωτος [ῠ], ον, = ἄθυρος, στόμα Ar.*Ra*.838 (v.l.), cf. Phryn. Com.82, *JHS*41.195 (Delos, ii B.C.).

ἀθύσσει· μιγνύει, ῥαπίζει, Hsch.

ἄθυστος, ον, = sq., ἱρά Semon.7.56.

ἄθῦτος, ον, *not offered*, i.e. *omitted*, ἱερά Lys.26.6. 2. *not successfully offered*, ἱερά Aeschin.3.131, 152: metaph., ἄ. παλλακῶν σπέρματα, of illegitimate children, Pl.*Lg*.841d, cf. Suid. s.v. ἄθυτοι γάμοι. 3. *not fit to be offered*, Lxx *Le*.19.7, cf. Philostr.*VA*8. 7.10. 4. of a god, *to whom no sacrifice is offered*, D.H.8.25. 5. *not fit for sacrifice*, opp. θύσιμος, Lib.*Decl*.13.63. 6. = ἄπυρος, Hsch. II. Act., *without sacrificing*, ἄθυτος ἀπελθεῖν X.*HG*3.2.22.

ἀθώητος· ἀζημίωτος, Hsch.

ἀθῷος, ον, (θωή, Ion. θωιή):—*scot-free*, E.*Ba*.672, etc.; ἐγὼ μὲν ἀ. ἅπασι D.18.125; ἀθῴους καθιστάναι τινάς to secure their *immunity*, Id.3.11; ἀθῷον ἀφιέναι Test.ap.eund.21.107; ἀ. ἀπαλλάττειν or -εσθαι to get off *scot-free*, Pl.*Sph*.254d, Lys.6.4; ἀπέρχεσθαι Archipp. 40; διαφυγεῖν Men.130. 2. c. gen., *free from* a thing, πληγῶν Ar. *Nu*.1413; ἀ. ἀδικημάτων *unpunished for* offences, Lycurg.79, cf. D.S.14.76. 3. *unharmed by*, ἀθῷος τῆς Φιλίππου..δυναστείας D.18.270. II. *not deserving punishment, guiltless*, ἀ. ὁ κτείνων Democr.257; ἀ. χερσί Lxx *Ps*.23(24).4; ἀ. ἀπὸ τοῦ αἵματος *Ev.Matt*. 27.24. III. Act., *causing no harm, harmless*, κίνδυνος D.*Prooem*. 26. (ἀθῷος distinguished by Gramm. from Ἄθωος, *of Mt. Athos*, A.*Ag*.285, cf. Hdn.Gr.1.128.)

ἀθῳόω, (ἀθῷος) *to hold guiltless*, ἀθῷον ἀθῳοῦν τινά Lxx *Na*.1.3, cf. Iamb.*Bab*.223; τινά τινος Ps.-Callisth.1.7:—fut. Pass. ἀθῳωθήσομαι Lxx *Pr*.6.29, al. 2. *avenge*, ἀπό τινος ib.*Je*.15.15. (Written ἀθο- before ω in codd. of Lxx.)

ἀθώπευτος, ον, *unflattered, without flattery*, τῆς ἐμῆς γλώσσης *from* my tongue, E.*Andr*.459. 2. *not open to flattery*, δίκαι Lyc.1399, cf. Nic.Dam.p.144 D. II. Act., *not flattering*, Telesp.44.8 H.; hence, *rough, rude*, θήρ *AP*6.168 (Paul. Sil.); συρίγματα, of the Python, *Pae.Delph*.20; ἀδροσίη *POxy*.1796.17. III. Adv. -τως *without flattery*, Them.*Or*.15.193d.

ἀθωράκιστος [ᾰκ], ον, *without breastplate* or *body-armour*, X.*Cyr*. 4.2.31, Plu.*Aem*.19.

ἀθώρηκτος, ον, = foreg., Nonn.*D*.35.162. II. *not drunken* (v. θωρήσσω II), Hp.*Steril*.220.

Ἄθως [ᾰ], ω, ὁ, acc. Ἄθω Aeschin.3.132, Theoc.7.77, etc., but in earlier writers Ἄθων, Hdt.6.44, 7.22, Th.5.3: Ep. gen. Ἀθόω Il. 14.229; later gen. Ἄθωος Str.*Fr*.33:—*mount Athos*, Ἄθως σκιάζει νῶτα Λημνίας βοός (prov. of those whose influence is felt at a distance, from the shadow cast by Athos) S.*Fr*.776.

ἀθῴωσις, ἡ, *acquittal*, Ctes.*Fr*.29.61.

αἰ, Dor. and Aeol. for εἰ, *if*, Epich.55, 170, before a vowel αἰκ Id. 21, Sophr.25:—in Hom. only αἴ κε or κεν, *if only, so that*, always c. subj., exc. in or. obliq., as Il.7.387; Dor. αἴκα Epich.35, Theoc. 1.4, al. II. αἶ γάρ (with accent), Ep. for εἰ γάρ, *O that! would that!* c. opt., Il.7.132, al., cf. Hdt.1.27; once c. inf., αἶ γάρ..παῖδά τ' ἐμὴν ἐχέμεν καὶ ἐμὸς γαμβρὸς καλέεσθαι Od.7.311.—Cf. αἴθε.

αἴ or **αἶ** (authorities vary, cf. Hdn.Gr.1.496, Tz. ad Lyc.31), interj. of astonishment or grief:—αἶ τάλαν Ar.*Pl*.706, cf. *Mim.Oxy*.413.73: c. acc., αἶ τὸν Ἄδωνιν Bion 1.32; freq. doubled αἰαῖ (Hdn.Gr.2.933), Thgn.1341, B.5.153, A.*Th*.787, Alciphr.*Fr*.4: c. gen., αἰαῖ τόλμας E. *Hipp*.814 (lyr.), cf. A.*Ch*.1007, Alciphr.3.67, etc.: c. acc., αἰαῖ Ἄδωνιν Ar.*Lys*.393, cf. Bion 1.28; αἰαῖ πέτρον ἐκεῖνον *AP*7.554 (Phil.), cf. 9.424 (Duris Elait.). [ᾱῑᾱῑ generally, sometimes αἰαῖ, as A.*Th*. l.c.]

αἰ, v. ἀεί.

αἶα (A), ἡ, Ep. form used for γαῖα metri gr., φυσίζοος αἶα Il.3.243, etc., cf. Emp.27, *Scol*.12, A.R.1.580, *Tab.Defix*.7; also in Trag., chiefly in lyr., A.*Pers*.59, S.*El*.95, also in trim., E.*Andr*.51: never in pl. II. Αἶα, ἡ, orig. name of Colchis, S.*Fr*.914: also part of Thessaly, ib.915.

αἶα (B)· ὑπὸ Κυρηναίων τηθὶς καὶ μαῖα, καὶ ἀδελφὴ Κρήτης· καὶ φυτόν τι. ἔτι δὲ ὁ καρπὸς αὐτῷ ὁμώνυμος, *EM*27.24. (Possibly cogn. with Lat. *avia*.)

αἶα (C), = ὄα, Ael.Dion.*Fr*.16.

αἴαγμα, τό, *wail*, E.*Alc*.873 (lyr.), etc.: **αἰαγμός**, οῦ, ὁ, Eust.1164.8.

αἰάζω, fut. -άξω E.*HF*1053 (cj. Herm.): aor. part. αἰάξας *Epigr. Gr*.233 (Chios):—*cry* αἰαῖ, *wail*, S.*Aj*.904, etc., Luc.*Salt*.45: c. acc. cogn., αὐδάν E.*IT*227, cf. Timo 66: c. acc., *bewail*, A.*Pers*.922, E.*Or*. 80, *AP*7.476 (Mel.), etc. 2. *groan*, ἐκπνεῖν καὶ αἰ. Arist.*HA* 536ᵇ22, cf. *GA*788ᵃ22.

αἰαῖ, v. sub αἶ.

αἰακίς, ἡ, = κύλιξ, Timach.ap.Ath.11.782f; **αἰακίξ**, Hsch., Suid.

αἰακτός, ή, όν, (αἰάζω) *lamentable*, πήματα A.*Th*.846 (lyr.), cf. Ar. *Ach*.1195 (paratrag.); *lamented*, θυγάτηρ *Epigr.Gr*.205 (Halic.). II. *wailing, miserable*, A.*Pers*.932, 1068 (both lyr.).

αἰᾱνής, Ion. αἰηνής, ές, poet. word, δεῖπνον αἰηνές Archil.38; αἰανῆς κόρος, κέντρον, λιμός, Pi.*P*.1.83, 4.236, *I*.1.49: also in Trag. (not E.), Νυκτὸς αἰανῆ τέκνα A.*Eu*.416; νυκτὸς αἰ. κύκλος S.*Aj*.672; αἰ. νόσος A.*Eu*.479, 942 (lyr.); αἰ. βάγματα Id.*Pers*.636 (lyr.); αἰ. πάνδυρτον αὐδάν ib.941 (lyr.); Πέλοπος..ἱππεία, ὡς ἔμολες αἰ. τᾷδε γᾷ S.*El*.506; of Time, εἰς τὸν αἰ. χρόνον A.*Eu*.572, *IG*9(1).886.2 (Corcyra); *eternal*, θεός Lyc.928. Adv. αἰανῶς *for ever*, A.*Eu*.672:— **αἰανός**, Hsch., Suid. s.v. λευκὴ ἡμέρα, and v.l. in A.*Eu*.416, 479, S.*Aj*.672, *El*.506, is dub. (Prob. fr. αἰεί, *everlasting, perpetual*, hence in bad sense, *wearisome, persistent*.)

Αἰάντειος, α, ον, *of Ajax*: τὸ Αἰ. *his tomb*, Philostr.*VA*4.13; τὰ Αἰ. (sc. ἱερά) *festivals in his honour*, Hsch.: prov., Αἰ. γέλως, of *insane* laughter, Zen.1.43. [Penult. short Pi.*O*.9.112.]

Αἰαντίδης, ου, ὁ, *son of Ajax*, patron.: hence, *one of the tribe* Αἰαντίς in Attica, [D.]60.31.

αἰαντόν· ἁμαρτία, Hsch.

Αἴᾱς, αντος, ὁ, *Ajax*, masc. pr. n., borne by two heroes, the Greater, son of Telamon, the Less, son of Oïleus, Hom.:—nom. Αἴας Alcm.68; voc. Αἶαν Pi.*Fr*.184, Aeol. Αἶαν Alc.48 A: pl. Αἴαντες, of tragedies named after Ajax, Arist.*Po*.1455ᵇ34. (S. derives it fancifully from αἰαῖ, *Aj*.430.)

αἰαστής, οῦ, ὁ, 'the mourner', of the plant ὑάκινθος, Nic.*Fr*.74. 32. **αἰαφοί**· αὐτοὶ ἀκούοντες, Hsch. **αἴαψ**· ματαίως, Id. (i.e. μάψ). **αἴαψος**· ὁ ποικίλος, Suid. **αἰβάνη**· θύρα, Hsch. (αἰβάλη Suid.).

αἰβετός, i.e. αἰϝετός, ὁ, dial. form of ἀετός, Hsch.

αἰβοῖ, *faugh!* exclam. of disgust, Ar.*Ach*.189, *V*.37; αἰβοιβοῖ, of laughter, Id.*Pax* 1066.

αἴγαγρος, ὁ and ἡ, *the wild goat*, Babr.102.8, Opp.*C*.1.71.

Αἰγᾶθεν, Dor. for Αἰγῆθεν, Adv. *from* Αἰγαί (an island off Euboea), Pi.*N*.5.37.

Αἰγαῖος, α, ον, *Aegean*, πέλαγος A.*Ag*.659; ὄρος Αἰ. *mount Ida* in Crete, Hes.*Th*.484:—title of Poseidon, Pherecyd.115. II. Αἰγαῖος (sc. πόντος), ὁ, *the Aegean*, Pl.*Eleg*.9.1, Arist.*Mete*.354ᵃ14, etc.

Αἰγαίων, ωνος, ὁ, *Aegaeon*, the name given by men to the hundred-armed son of Uranus and Gaia, called by gods Βριάρεως (q.v.), Il.1. 404. II. *the Aegaean sea*, πόντιόν τ' Αἰγαίων' E.*Alc*.595 (lyr.).

αἰγᾰνέη, ἡ, *hunting-spear, javelin*, Il.2.774, Od.4.626, *AP*6.57 (Paul. Sil.).

αἰγάριον, τό, Dim. of αἴξ, *Gloss*.

ἀΐγδην, Adv., (ἀΐσσω) *rushing swiftly, impetuously*, A.R.2.826.

αἰγέα, αἰγέη, ἡ, v. sub αἴγεος.

Αἰγεῖον, τό, *temple of Aegeus*, Din.*Fr*.3.1.

αἴγειος, α, ον, *of a goat*, αἴγειον κνῇ τυρόν Il.11.639, Hp.*Nat.Mul*. 38; ἀσκῷ ἐν αἰγείῳ in a *goat's* skin, Il.3.247; αἰγείη κυνέη a helmet *of goatskin*, Od.24.231; γάλα αἰ. Arist.*HA*522ᵃ23; κρέα αἰ. Hp.*Acut*. (*Sp*.)49.

αἰγείρινος, ον, *of the poplar*, Orib.*Syn*.5.16, Alex.Trall.8.1. **αἰγειρῖται** μύκητες mushrooms *produced from stump of poplar*, *Gp*.12. 41.1.

αἴγειρος, ἡ, *black poplar, Populus nigra*, μακεδνή, μακρή, Od.7.106, 10.510, cf. Il.4.482, S.*Fr*.23, etc.; αἰ. ὑδατοτρεφέες Od.17.208, cf. 9. 141, 5.64, 239, E.*Hipp*.210 (lyr.); named among ἄκαρπα in Arist.*Mu*. 401ᵃ4; καρποφόρος *Mir*.835ᵇ2: prov., αἰγείρου θέα, of a seat in the theatre which had no view of the stage, Cratin.339.

αἰγειροφόρος, ον, *poplar-bearing*, Max.Tyr.29.7.

αἰγειρών, ῶνος, ὁ, *poplar-grove*, Str.16.4.14.

αἰγελάτης [ᾰ], ου, ὁ, (ἐλαύνω) *goatherd*, Plu.*Pomp*.4, *APl*.4.229.

αἴγεος, α, ον, = αἴγειος, Od.9.196; διφθέραι Hdt.5.58. II. Subst., αἰγέη (sc. δορά), ἡ, *a goat's skin*, Hdt.4.189; τὴν αἰγέαν J.*AJ*1.18.6, cf. Lxx *Nu*.31.20; contr. αἰγῆ Hdn.Gr.1.310.

αἴγερος, ἡ, = αἴγειρος, *Com.Adesp*.1276.

αἰγ-ήκης, ες, *made of goatskin*, τύμπανον Procl.*Theol.Plat*.4.16 (nisi leg. αἰνήχης). **-ιάζω**, *to talk of goats*, Eup.2.

αἰγιάλ-ειος, α, ον, *frequenting the shore*, Aët.2.141, Ath.Med.ap. Orib.*Inc*.23.8. **-εύς**, ῆος, ὁ, = foreg., Nic.*Th*.786, Numen.ap.Ath.7. 313e:—pr. n., of the inhabitants of north coast of Peloponnese, Hdt. 5.68, 7.94; of the Argives, Theoc.25.174. **-ικός**, ή, όν, *for coastwise traffic*, sc. πλοῖα prob. l. in *PCair.Preis*.33.6 (iv A.D.). **-ίτης**, ου, ὁ, fem. **-ῖτις**, ιδος, ψῆφοι Str.4.1.7; Πάν *AP*10.10 (Arch. Jun.); γῆ *POxy*.918 (ii A.D.)

αἰγιᾰλός, ὁ, *sea-shore, beach*, Il.4.422, Od.22.385, Hdt.7.59, al., Th. 1.7 (pl.), X.*An*.6.4.4, Thphr.*HP*7.13.8 (pl.), etc.; distinguished from ἀκτή, Arist.*HA*547^{a}10; also in E. (lyr.), *IT*425, *IA*210; αἰγιαλὸν ἔνδον τρέφει *a whole beach of voting-pebbles*, Ar.*V*.110: prov., αἰγιαλῷ λαλεῖς, of deaf persons, Suid., Zen.1.38. (Prob. connected with αἰγίς II, αἴξ IV.)

αἰγιαλοφύλαξ, ὁ, *warden of the shore*, *PRyl*.81.3 (ii A.D.).

αἰγιαλ-ώδης, ες, *frequenting the shore*, ζῷα Arist.*HA*488^{b}7. **-ώτης**, ὁ, *dweller on the shore*, Sch.Opp.*H*.3.375.

αἰγιάς, άδος, ἡ, = αἰγίς IV, Hsch.

αἰγι-βάτης [ᾰ], ου, ὁ, *goat-mounting*, epith. of he-goats, etc., Pi. *Fr*.201; of Pan, Theoc.*Ep*.5.6, *AP*6.31. **-βοσις**, εως, ἡ, *goat-pasture*, *AP*9.318 (Leon.). **-βότης**, ου, ὁ, *browsed by goats*, σκόπελος *AP*6.334 (Leon.). **-βοτος**, ον, = foreg., Ἰθάκη Od.4.606, cf. 13.246, *AP*9.219 (Diod.). II. **-βότος**, ον, *feeding goats*, Πάν Nonn.*D*.1.368, al.

αἰγίδιον, τό, Dim. of αἴξ, *kid*, Pherecr.25, Antiph.20.4, *IG*11(2).287*A*55 (Delos, iii B.C.), *PTeb*.404.9 (iii A.D.). II. *eye-salve*, Aët.7.103.

αἰγίζω, (αἰγίς) *rend asunder*, S.*Fr*.984.

αἰγίθαλλος or **αἰγίθᾰλος**, ὁ, *titmouse* (of various species), *parus*, Ar.*Av*.888, Alc.Com.3, cf. Arist.*HA*592^{b}17, 616^{b}3: prov., αἰγιθάλου τολμηρότερος, Apostol.1.76.

αἴγιθος, also **αἰγίοθος**, ὁ, an unknown bird, possibly *linnet*, Arist.*HA*609^{a}31, 616^{b}10, Call.*Fr*.321, Ael.*NA*5.48, etc.

αἰγίκερας, = αἰγόκερας, Hsch.

αἰγί-κνημος, ον, *goat-shanked*, *AP*6.167 (Agath.). **-κορεῖς**, έων, οἱ, *goatherds*; name of one of the four Ionic tribes in Attica (cf. Hdt.5.66, who makes Αἰγικόρης son of Ion), E.*Ion*1581, Plu.*Sol*.23; also at Cyzicus, *IGRom*.4.144, cf. **Αἰγικορὶς** φυλή *Ath.Mitt*.9.27. (Expl. as *goatherds*, but this is doubtful.)

αἰγικός, ή, όν, = αἴγειος, *PGrenf*.2.51.15 (ii A.D.). 2. **-κόν**, τό, = ἄγρωστις, Ps.-Dsc.4.29.

αἰγιλάδην, = αἰγίλωψ I, dub. l. in Ps.-Dsc.4.137.

αἰγίλιψ [γῐ], ἴπος, ὁ, ἡ, (expl. by Gramm. from αἴξ, λείπω, cf. Sch. Il.9.15) *destitute even of goats*, hence, *steep*, *sheer*, πέτρη Il.9.15, al. (not in Od.), A.*Supp* 794 (lyr.), Lyc.1325; also in form **αἰγίλιπος**, Hsch. (Perh. cognate with Lith.*lipti* 'climb'.)

αἰγίλος, ἡ, *a herb of which goats are fond*, = αἰγίλωψ I, Theoc.5.128, Babr.3.4.

αἰγιλωπικός, ή, όν, *for the treatment of* αἰγίλωψ III, καυτήρια Paul. Aeg.6.22.

αἰγιλώπιον, τό, = αἰγίλωψ III, Dsc.3.137.

αἰγίλωψ [ῐ], ωπος, poet. οπος Nic.*Th*.857, ὁ, *haver-grass*, *Aegilops ovata*, Thphr.*CP*5.15.5, Ph.*Bel*.89.3, Dsc.4.137. II. *Turkey oak*, *Quercus Cerris*, Thphr.*HP*3.8.2. III. *ulcer in the eye*, *lachrymal fistula*, Cels.7.7, Dsc.4.70, Gal.*UP*10.10. IV. a bulbous plant, Plin.*HN*19.95.

Αἰγῖν-α, ης, ἡ, *Aegina*, Il., etc.:—hence **-ήτης**, ου, ὁ, fem. **-ῆτις**, ιδος, *an Aeginetan*, ib., etc. **-αῖος**, α, ον, *Aeginetan*, Cratin.165, al.; ὀβολὸς Αἰ., δραχμὴ Αἰ., etc., Th.5.47, etc.:—also **-ητικός**, ή, όν, Luc.*Tim*.57; ἔργα statues *of the Aeginetan School*, Paus.1.42.5.

αἰγίνη, ἡ, = περικλύμενον, Ps.-Dsc.4.14.

αἰγῑ-νομεύς, έως, ὁ, *goatherd*, *AP*9.318 (Leon.). **-νόμος**, ον, (νέμω) *feeding goats*: Subst., *goatherd*, *AP*6.221 (Leon.), cf. 9.744 (Leon.). II. αἰγίνομος, ον, Pass., *browsed by goats*, βοτάνη ib.217 (Muc. Scaev.).

αἴγινος (A), ὁ, = κώνειον, Ps.-Dsc.4.78.

αἴγινος (B), = αἰγικός, *PFay*.222 (iii A.D.); δέρματα *PLond*.2.236.6 (iv A.D.).

αἰγίοθος, ὁ, v. sub αἴγιθος.

αἰγιόνομοι· ζῷα οὕτω καλούμενα, Hsch.

αἰγίοχος, ον, (ϝέχω = veho) *aegis-bearing*, epith. of Zeus, Il.2.375, al., Alc.85, Emp.142, etc.

Αἰγί-πᾶν, ᾶνος, ὁ, *goat-Pan*, *goat-footed Pan*, Eratosth.*Catast*.27, Plu.2.311b. **-πλαγκτος**, ον, *wandered over by goats*:—pr. n., ὄρος Αἰγίπλαγκτον, a mountain near Megara, A.*Ag*.303. **-πόδης**, ου, ὁ, *goat-footed*, *h.Hom*.19.2,37; voc. αἰγιπόδη Πάν *AP*6.57 (Paul. Sil.). **-πους**, ποδος, ὁ, ἡ, πουν, τό, = foreg., Hdt.4.25.

αἰγίποψ· ἀετός (Maced.), *EM*28.19.

αἰγίπῡρος, ὁ, *rest-harrow*, *Ononis antiquorum*, Thphr.*HP*2.8.3, Theoc.4.25; αἰγίπυρον, τό, *IG*14.2508 (Nemausus).

αἰγίς, ίδος, ἡ, (αἴξ, cf. νεβρίς): I. *goatskin*, worn as a dress, Hdt.4.189, E.*Cyc*.360 (lyr.); hence, 2. esp. the skin shield of Zeus, Il.5.738, al.; lent by him to Athena, 2.447, al.; to Apollo, 15.318, al.; later, with fringe of snakes and Gorgon's head, the *aegis* of Athena, A.*Eu*.404, etc. 3. dress worn by priestess of Athena, Lycurg.*Fr*.23. 4. ornament worn on the breast, Poll.5.100. 5. *cuirass* (Lacon.), Nymphod.22. II. *rushing storm*, *hurricane*, terrible as the shaken aegis, A.*Ch*.593 (lyr.), Pherecr.117, Aristid.1.487 J., Lib.*Or*.18.268. III. *heart-wood* of the Corsican pine, Thphr.*HP*3.9.3; in Arcadia also that of the silver-fir, ib.8; cf. Ἐφ. Ἀρχ.1895.59 (Eleusis). IV. *speck in the eye*, Hp.*Coac*.214, *Prorrh*.2.20.

αἰγίσκος, ὁ, Dim. of αἴξ, *IG*11(2).287*A*19 (Delos, iii B.C.).

αἰγλάεις, contr. **αἰγλᾶς**, Dor. for αἰγλήεις.

αἰγλάζω, *to beam brightly*, Man.4.264.

αἴγλη, ἡ, *the light of the sun* or *moon*, Od.4.45, etc.:—of the radiance of Olympus, λευκὴ αἴ. 6.45, cf. S.*Ant*.610 (lyr.); εἰς αἴγλαν μολεῖν to come to *daylight*, i.e. to be born, Pi.*N*.1.35; φοιβὰν ὑπαὶ χειμῶνος αἴ., of *sunshine* on edge of storm-cloud, B.12.140; of *dream light* in sleep, S.*Ph*.831 (lyr.). 2. generally, *radiance*, *gleam*, ἀπὸ χαλκοῦ αἴ. Il.2.458; τὰς πυρφόρους Ἀρτέμιδος αἴ. the *gleam* of her torches, S.*OT*207 (lyr.); μέλαιναν αἴ., of dying embers, E.*Tr*.549 (lyr.). 3. metaph., *splendour*, *glory*, αἴ. ποδῶν, of swiftness, Pi.*O*.13.36; διόσδοτος αἴ. Id.*P*.8.96. II. of shining objects, as a *bracelet*, S.*Fr*.594; *fetter*, Epich.20.

αἰγλήεις, εσσα, εν, *dazzling*, *radiant*, in Hom. always αἰγλήεντος Ὀλύμπου Il.1.532, Od.20.103; Κλάρος αἰγλήεσσα *h.Ap*.40; πῶλοι αἰ. *h.Hom*.32.9: neut. as Adv., αἰγλῆεν στίλβουσι ib.31.11:—Dor. **αἰγλάεις**, contr. **αἰγλᾶς**, κῶας αἰγλᾶεν.. θυσάνῳ Pi.*P*.4.231; αἰγλᾶντα κόσμον ib.2.10; αἰγλᾶντα σώματα E.*Andr*.285 (lyr.).

αἰγλήτης, Dor. **-άτας**, ου, ὁ, *the radiant one*, epith. of Apollo, A.R.4.1716, *IG*12(3).259 (Anaphe), 412 (Thera).

αἰγλο-βολέω, Astrol., = ἀκτινοβολέω, Man.4.188. **-φανής**, ές, *radiant*, *AP*12.5 (Strat.).

αἰγο-βάτης, ου, ὁ, = αἰγιβάτης, *AP*12.41 (Mel.). **-βόλος**, ὁ, *goat-slayer*, title of Dionysus, Paus.9.8.1. **-βοσκός**, οῦ, ὁ, *goatherd*, Aesop.12b, *Gloss*. **-δίωξ**, ωκος, *pursuing goats*, Hdn.Gr.1.46. **-δορος**, ον, (δορά) *of goatskin*, Opp.*H*.5.356. **-θήλας**, ὁ, *goatsucker*, *nightjar*, or *fern-owl*, *Caprimulgus europaeus*, Arist.*HA*618^{b}2, Ael.*NA*3.39. **-θηρικός**, ή, όν, *belonging to ibex-hunting*, σοφία ib.14.16. **-κερας**, ατος, τό, = τῆλις, Hp.*Int*.30, Dsc.2.102, Gal.12.426. **-κερεύς**, έως, Ion. ῆος, ὁ, = -κερως II, Arat.386, Q.S.1.356. **-κεριανός**, ὁ, *born under Capricorn*, *Cat.Cod.Astr*.8(4).191 (Rhetor.). **-κερως**, gen. -κερω, dat. -κερῳ Man.1.106; acc. -κερων *Placit*.5.18.6, Luc.*Astr*.7; later gen. -κέρωτος Jul.*Or*.4.156a: (κέρας):—*goat-horned*, *APl*.4.234 (Phld.). II. Subst., *Capricorn*, Gem.*Calend*.7, Eudox.ap.Hipparch.1.2.20, Arat.286, *Placit*.l.c., Luc. l.c., *IG*14.1307.

αἰγοκέφᾰλος, ὁ, perh. *horned owl*, *Strix otus*, Arist.*HA*506^{a}17.

αἰγ-όλεθρος, ὁ, *goat's-bane*, *Rhododendron ponticum*, Antig.*Mir*.17, Plin.*HN*21.74.

αἰγο-μελής, ές, *goat-limbed*, Orph.*H*.11.5. **-μορον**, τό, = κώνειον, Ps.-Dsc.4.78. **-νομεύς**, έως, Ion. ῆος, ὁ, = αἰγινομεύς, *goatherd*, Nic.*Al*.39. **-νόμια**· αἰπόλια, Hsch. **-νόμιον**, τό, *herd of goats*, Id. s.v. αἰγοπόλιον, etc. **-νόμος**, ον, = αἰγινόμος, *AP*7.397 (Eryc.).

αἰγ-όνυξ, υχος, ὁ, ἡ, = αἰγῶνυξ, *APl*.4.258.

αἰγό-πλαστος, ον, *goat-shaped*, Ps.-Emp.*Sphaer*.140. **-πόδης**, ου, ὁ, = αἰγιπόδης, *APl*.1.15. **-πρόσωπος**, ον, *goat-faced*, Hdt.2.46; *stamped with a goat's face*, Aët.7.101. **-στασις**, ἡ, *goat-pen*, *Gloss*. **-τρῐχέω**, *have goat's hair*, Str.17.2.3. **-τριψ**, ῖβος, ὁ, ἡ, (τρίβω) *trodden by goats*, ἀτραποί D.H.20.11. **-φάγος**, ον, *goat-eating*, epith. of Zeus, Nic.*Fr*.99; of Hera at Sparta, Paus.3.15.7.

αἰγ-όφθαλμος, ὁ, *goat's-eye*, a precious stone, Plin.*HN*37.187.

αἰγῠπιός, ὁ, *vulture*, αἰ. γαμψώνυχες ἀγκυλοχεῖλαι Il.16.428, cf. 17.460, Od.16.217, Hes.*Sc*.405, Hdt.3.76, S.*Aj*.169, Arist.*HA*610^{a}1, etc.:—αἰγυπιοὶ γῦπές τε Nic.*Th*.406, cf. Ael.*NA*2.46. (Both words seem to be generic terms, but αἰ. is an older word chiefly found in poetry.)

αἰγυπτάριον, τό, name of eye-salve, Aët.7.101.

Αἰγύπτειος, α, ον, = Αἰγύπτιος, prob. in A.*Supp*.817 (lyr.).

αἰγύπτης· σύντης, ὁ καλοβότης, Hsch.

Αἰγυπτι-άζω, *to be like an Egyptian*, i.e. *to be sly and crafty*, Cratin.378, cf. Ar.*Th*.922. 2. *speak Egyptian*, Luc.*Philops*.31. II. *to be like Egypt*, i.e. *be under water*, Philostr.*Im*.2.14. **-ακός**, ή, όν, *of* or *for the Egyptians*, Ath.4.150c, etc.: Αἰγυπτιακά, τά, title of works by Hellanicus and others, Id.15.679f, etc.; by Manetho, J.*Ap*.1.14. **-ασμός**, ὁ, *imitation of the Egyptians*, Eust. ad D.P.391.

Αἰγύπτιος, α, ον, *Egyptian*, Hom., etc.: Adv. -ίως *in Egyptian style*, D.C.48.30. 2. **αἰγυπτία**, ἡ, name of an ointment, Gal.13.643, etc. [In Hom. Αἰγυπτίη, Αἰγυπτίων, etc., are trisyll., Od.4.83, etc.]

Αἰγυπτιόω, *to make like an Egyptian*, i.e. *swarthy*, χρόαν *Com. Adesp*.9, Hsch.

Αἰγυπτιστί, Adv. *in the Egyptian tongue*, Hdt.2.46, J.*Ap*.1.14. II. *in Egyptian fashion*, i.e. *craftily*, Theoc.15.48.

Αἰγυπτιώδης, ες, *Egyptian-like*, Cratin.Jun.2.

Αἰγυπτογενής, ές, *of Egyptian race*, A.*Pers*.35.

Αἴγυπτος, ὁ, *the river Nile*, Od.4.477, al. 2. *King Aegyptus*, A.*Supp*.9, etc. II. ἡ, *Egypt*, Od.17.448, etc.; Αἴγυπτόνδε *to Egypt*, ib.426.

αἰγωγαίαν· ὀφθαλμός, Hsch.

αἰγωλιός or **αἰγώλιος**, ὁ, a small kind of *owl*, perh. *Strix flammea*, Arist.*HA*592^{b}11, 609^{a}27, Ant.Lib.19.3; f.l. αἰτώλιος, Arist.*HA*563^{a}31.

αἰγών, ῶνος, ὁ, = μάνδρα, *Gloss*. II. **Αἰγών**, name of a month at Alexandria, Ptol.*Alm*.10.9.

αἰγῶνυξ, ῠχος, ὁ, ἡ, (ὄνυξ) *goat-hoofed*, *AP*6.35 (Leon.).

αἰγωπόμματος, ον, = sq., Phlp.*in GA*212.8.

αἰγωπός, όν, *goat-eyed*, of persons, Arist.*GA*779^{b}1; also, *like those of a goat*, of eyes, ib., cf. *HA*492^{a}3.

αἰδάας· δεσπότης, Hsch.

αἰδάνης· διατρίβων (Tarent.), Hsch.

Ἀΐδας, Dor. for Ἀΐδης, Ἅιδης, freq. in lyr. passages of Trag.

αἰδ-έομαι, and poet. **αἴδομαι** Hom., etc., Ep. imper. αἰδεῖο Il.24.503, Od.9.269; part. αἰδόμενος Hom. and Trag. (lyr.); imper. αἴδεο Il.21.74: impf. ᾐδοῦντο A.*Pers*.810, etc., αἰδέοντο Pi.*P*.9.41, poet. αἴδετο Il.21.468, *APl*.4.106: fut. αἰδέσομαι Il.22.124, Att., Ep. αἰδέσσομαι Od.14.388; αἰδεσθήσομαι D.C.45.44, Gal.1.62, (ἐπ-) E.*IA*

900: aor. Med. ᾐδεσάμην, Ep. αἰδ- Od.21.28, Att. (v. sub fin.), Ep. imper. αἴδεσσαι Il.9.640; aor. Pass. ᾐδέσθην Hom., etc., and in Prose, Ep. 3 pl. αἴδεσθεν Il.7.93: pf. ᾔδεσμαι (v. sub fin.): Act. only in καταιδέω, q. v.:—*to be ashamed*, c. inf., αἴδεσθεν μὲν ἀνήνασθαι δεῖσαν δ' ὑποδέχθαι Il.7.93; αἰδέομαι δὲ μίσγεσθ' ἀθανάτοισι 24.90; αἰ. γὰρ γυμνοῦσθαι Od.6.221: less freq. c. part., αἴδεσαι μὲν πατέρα προλείπων S.*Aj.*506, cf. Plu.*Aem.*35: c. dat., μὴ αἰδοῦ τῷ εὐκόλῳ Philostr.*Ep.* 19: abs., αἰδεσθεὶς *from a sense of shame*, Il.17.95. 2. mostly c. acc., *stand in awe of, fear*, esp. in moral sense, αἰδεῖο θεούς Il.24. 503, Od.9.269; Τρῶας Il.6.442, cf. Od.2.65, etc.; ἀλλήλους αἰδεῖσθε *show a sense of regard* one for another, Il.5.530; οὐδὲ θεῶν ὄπιν αἰδέσατο Od.21.28; αἴδεσσαι μέλαθρον *respect* the house, Il.9.640; freq. of respect for suppliants, Il.22.124, cf. Hdt.7.141; ἐχθρὸν ὧδ' αἰδεῖ νέκυν; S.*Aj.*1356; τόνδ' ὅρκον αἰδεσθεὶς Id.*OT*647, cf. 1426:—in Pi. *P.*4.173 αἰδεσθέντες ἀλκάν *regarding* their reputation for valour, i.e. from *self-respect*, cf. ἑωυτὸν μάλιστα αἰδεῖσθαι Democr.264: abs., τὸ αἰδεῖσθαι *self-respect*, Id.179; in Prose, Δία αἰδεσθέντες Hdt.9.7.α'; φοβοῦμαί γε.. τοὺς μοχθηρούς (οὐ γὰρ δήποτε εἴποιμ' ἂν ὥς γε αἰδοῦμαι) Pl.*Lg.*886a, cf. *Euthphr.*12b, *Phdr.*254e; later αἰ. ἐπί τινι D.H.6.92; ὑπὲρ τῆς ἀνθρωπίνης φύσεως *have compassion upon, show mercy*, Plu. *Cim.*2. II. *respect* another's *misfortune, feel regard for* him, μηδέ τί μ' αἰδόμενος.. μηδ' ἐλεαίρων Od.3.96 (cf. I. 2); αἰ. τὴν τῶν μηδὲν ἀδικούντων εὐσέβειαν Antipho 2.4.11; esp. 2. as Att. law-term, *to be reconciled to* a person, of kinsmen who allow a homicide to return from exile, Lex ap.D.43.57; ἐὰν ἑλών τις ἀκουσίου φόνου.. αἰδέσηταί καὶ ἀφῇ D.37.59, cf. 38.22; αἰδούμενος Pl.*Lg.*877a; ᾐδεσμένος D.23.77. 3. of the homicide, *obtain forgiveness*, D.23.72 codd. **-έσιμος**, ον, *exciting shame* or *respect, venerable*, M.Ant.1.9 (Sup.), Aristid.2.99 J. (Sup.), Hierocl. *in CA*13 p.448 M. (Comp.): c. dat., Aristid.*Or.*37(2).6; as honorary title, *PFlor.*15.6 (vi A.D.); τοῦ προσώπου τὸ αἰ. Luc.*Nigr.*26; *holy*, Paus.3.5.6. Adv. -μως *reverently*, Ael.*NA*2.25. **-εσιμότης**, ἡ, as title, *Your Reverence, Your Worship*, *POxy.*125 (vi A.D.), al. **-εσις**, ἡ, *forgiveness* (cf. αἰδέομαι II. 2), Arist.*Ath.*57.3, cf. D.21.43. **-εστέον**, *one must reverence*, Eust.1434.35. **-εστικός**, ή, όν, *modest, shamefaced*, τὸ αἰ. Sch.E. *Hipp.*345. **-εστός**, ή, όν, *revered, venerable*, Plu.2.67b.

ἀΐδηλος [ῐ], Dor. **ἀΐδαλος**, ον, (ἀ- priv., ϝιδεῖν) *making unseen, annihilating, destructive*: in Hom., as epith. of Ares and Athena, Il.5. 897,880; πῦρ ἀ. 2.455, al., Emp.109; ἠελίοιο ἔργ' ἀΐδηλα Parm.10. 3; ἀΐδαλος τύχα *Epigr.Gr.*240.5 (Smyrna); ἄτη Opp.*H.*2.487; πότμος ib.1.150. Adv. -λως, = ὀλεθρίως, Il.21.220. II. Pass., *unseen, unknown, obscure*, v.l. in Il.2.318, cf. Hes.*Op.*756, A.R.1.102, al.; *unforeseen*, ib.298; *formless*, 4.681; *unsubstantial*, φρίκη Nic. *Th.*727; as epith. of Hades, *dark, gloomy*, S.*Aj.*608 (lyr.).

αἰδη-μονικός, ή, όν, *modest*, τὸ αἰ. Sch.E.*Hipp.*78. **-μοσύνη**, ἡ, *modesty*, *Stoic.*3.64, *IG*14.1637.

αἰδήμων, ον, gen. ονος, *bashful, modest*, Arist.*EN*1108ᵃ32, etc.: Comp. -έστερος X.*Lac.*2.10: Sup. αἰδημονέστατος Id.*An.*1.9.5. Adv. -μόνως Id.*Smp.*4.58, Arr.*Epict.*3.18.6, *PGen.*1.9. II. in bad sense, *ignominious, shameful*, θωή Max.576.

ἀϊδής, ές, (ἀ- priv., ϝιδεῖν) *unseen*, Hes.*Sc.*477, Pl.*Phd.*79a, al.; *secret*, γλῶσσα B.12.209. II. Act., *blind*, *IG*4.951.125 (Epid.), dub. in Thgn.1310.

'Αΐδης, ὁ, poet. for Ἅιδης; v. sub ᾅδης.

αἰδήσιμος, ον, poet. for αἰδέσιμος, Orph.*A.*1346.

ἀΐδιος [ᾱῐδ], ον, also η, ον Orph.*H.*10.21, al., (ἀεί):—*everlasting, eternal*, *h.Hom.*29.3, Hes.*Sc.*310; freq. in Prose, χρόνος Antipho 1. 21; ἔχθρα Th.4.20; οἴκησις, of a tomb, X.*Ages.*11.16; ἡ ἀ. οὐσία *eternity*, Pl.*Ti.*37e; ἀ. στρατηγία, ἀρχή, βασιλεία, *perpetual*.., Arist. *Pol.*1285ᵃ7, 1317ᵇ41, 1301ᵇ27; ἀ. βασιλεῖς, γέροντες, ib.1284ᵇ33, 1306ᵃ17; τὰ ἀ., opp. τὰ γενητά and φθαρτά, Id.*Metaph.*1069ᵃ32, *EN* 1139ᵇ23, al.; ἐς ἀΐδιον *for ever*, Th.4.63; *ad infinitum*, Arist.*PA* 640ᵃ6; ἐξ ἀϊδίου Plot.2.1.3: Comp. -ώτερος Arist.*Cael.*284ᵃ17:—ἀ. is dist. fr. αἰώνιος as *everlasting* from *timeless*, Olymp. *in Mete.*146.16; but dist. fr. ἀείζωος as *eternal* (without beginning or end) from *ever-living*, *Corp.Herm.*8.2. Adv. -ίως Sm.*Mi.*7.18, Iamb.*Comm.Math.* 1, Hierocl. *in CA*1 p.419 M.

ἀϊδιότης, ητος, ἡ, *eternity*, Arist.*Cael.*284ᵃ1, *Ph.*252ᵇ3, Ph.1.3, al., Plot.3.7.5, Procl.*Inst.*55, etc.

ἀϊδνός, ή, όν, (ἀ- priv., ϝιδεῖν) poet. word, = ἀϊδής, *unseen, obscure*, Hes.*Th.*860, A.*Fr.*451 A; λιγνύς A.R.1.389; Νύξ *Lyr.Adesp.*92:—later **ἀϊδνήεις**, εσσα, εν, καπνός Euph.139: **ἀϊδνής**, ές, πηλός Call.*Fr. anon.*220 (as v.l.), cf. Opp.*H.*4.245 (perh. -νῆς, contr. fr. -νήεις).

αἰδοιϊκός, ή, όν, *of* or *belonging to the* αἰδοῖα, Antyll.ap.Orib.50.5.3, Paul.Aeg.3.59.

αἰδοιολείκτης, ὁ, = *cunnilingus*, Hsch. s. v. σκερός.

αἰδοῖον, τό, freq. in pl. αἰδοῖα, τά, *privy parts, pudenda*, both of men and women, Il.13.568, Hes.*Op.*733, Heraclit.15, Tyrt.10.25, Hp. *Aër.*9, Pl.*Ti.*91b, etc.: sg., Hdt.2.30,48, etc., freq. in Arist., *HA* 493ᵃ25, al. II. αἰ. θαλάσσιον, a sea animal, perh. *pennatula*, Nic.*Fr.*139, cf. Arist.*HA*532ᵇ23.

αἰδοῖος, α, ον, (αἰδώς) *having a claim to regard, reverence*, or *compassion* (cf. αἰδώς), in Hom., Hes. only of persons, sts. of gods, θεῶν γένος Hes.*Th.*44, cf. *Op.*257, Il.18.394; more freq. of human beings, as kings, Il.4.402, members of family, esp. wife, 21.460, servants, ταμίη Od.1.139, women generally, παρθένος Il.2.514; then of the helpless or those needing protection, guests, Od.9.271, suppliants, 7.165: abs., αἰδοίοισιν ἔδωκα 15.373: Comp. -ότερος καὶ φίλτερος 11. 360 (later -έστερος D.P.172):—after Hom. of things, ξείνων αἰ. λιμένες Emp.112.3: Sup. -ότατον, γέρας Pi.*P.*5.18; but -έστατος.. χρυσός *O.*3.42, cf. Alcm.74A. Adv. -ως, ἀπέπεμπον, of a guest, Od. 19.243. II. Act., *bashful, shamefaced*, κακὸς δ' αἰ. ἀλήτης Od.17. 578. 2. *showing reverence* or *compassion*, πνεῦμα A.*Supp.*28 (anap.); Ζεὺς Αἰ. the god *of mercy*, ib.192. 3. *claiming compassion*, λόγοι ib.455.—Poet.: used by Pl. in quotations.

αἰδοιώδης, ες, *like the* αἰδοῖα, Arist.*HA*541ᵇ8, Thphr.*HP*3.7.4, 8.2.1.

αἴδομαι, poet. for αἰδέομαι.

''Αϊδος, Ep. gen. of an obsol. nom. ''Αϊς, v. ᾅδης. II. ''Αιδος, ου, = ᾅδης, Antim.ap.Sch.Il.*Oxy.*1087.43.

αἰδοσύνη, ἡ, = αἰδημοσύνη, *AB*354, Phot.

αἰδοφοίτης, = ᾀδοφοίτης, Hsch.

αἰδόφρων, ον, gen. ονος, (φρήν) *regardful of mind, compassionate*, S.*OC*237 (lyr.); *respectful*, πρός τινα E.*Alc.*659.

ἀϊδρείη, Ep. and Ion. -ίη [ῐη], ἡ, *want of knowledge, ignorance*, Od. 12.41, Hdt.6.69; also in pl., Od.10.231, 11.272.

ἀϊδρήεις, εσσα, εν, = sq., Nic.*Al.*415.

ἄϊδρις, ι, gen. ιος and εος, poet. Adj. *unknowing, ignorant*, Il.3. 219, Pi.*P.*2.37; often c. gen., Od.10.282, Hes.*Sc.*410, A.*Ag.*1105, etc.; also **ἄιδρος**, ον, Alc.*Oxy.*1789*Fr.*6, Ion Trag.34.

ἀϊδροδίκης [δῐ], ου, Dor. **-δίκας**, α, ὁ, *lawless*, θῆρας Pi.*N.*1.63, cf. S.*Fr.*985.

ἀΐδρυτος or (more freq.) **ἀνίδρυτος**, ον, *unsettled, unstable*, δρόμοι ἀν. E.*IT*971; χρόνοι *irregular*, Ruf.*Interrog.*12; ἄοικοι καὶ ἀν. Plu.*TG* 9; νῆσος ἀν. *floating*, D.H.1.15; τὸ ἀν. τῆς γνώμης, τῆς οὐσίας, Ph.2. 112, Dam.*Pr.*413. II. *with no fixed abode*, Τίμων ἦν ἀ. τις Ar. *Lys.*809 (lyr.); ἄσπειστος, ἀν. D.25.52; οἰκοῦσιν φεύγοντες, ἀ. κακὸν ἄλλοις Cratin.209 (expl. by ὃ οὐκ ἄν τις αὑτῷ ἱδρύσαιτο *EM*42.10).

ἀΐδυλος· θρασύς, Hsch.:—**αἰδύλος**, *EM*30.19.

αἰδώ, ἡ, = αἰδώς, Philet.9.

'Αϊδωνεύς, έως (έος *AP*7.480 (Leon.)), ὁ, lengthd. poet. form of Ἅιδης, twice in Hom., Il.5.190, 20.61, cf. Hes.*Th.*913, A.*Pers.*650 (lyr.); prob. scanned Αἰδωνεύς S.*OC*1560 (lyr.): gen. and dat. 'Αϊδονῆος, -ῆι in later poets, Q.S.6.490, Nonn.*D.*30.172; Αἰδωνῆος Mosch. 4.86:—hence **'Αιδωναία**, ἡ, epith. of Hecate, *PMag.Par.*1.2855.

ἀϊδώνια· θανάσιμα, Hsch., *EM*30.20. **αἰδῷος**, = αἰδοῖος, *EM*29.25.

αἰδώς, όος, contr. οῦς, ἡ (late nom. pl. αἰδοί Sch.E.*Hipp.*386), as a moral feeling, *reverence, awe, respect* for the feeling or opinion of others or for one's own conscience, and so *shame, self-respect* (in full ἑαυτοῦ αἰδώς Hierocl. *in CA*9 p.433 M.), *sense of honour*, αἰδῶ θέσθ' ἐνὶ θυμῷ Il.15.561; ἴσχε γὰρ αἰ. καὶ δέος ib.657, cf. Sapph.28, Democr. 179, etc.; αἰ. σωφροσύνης πλεῖστον μετέχει, αἰσχύνης δὲ εὐψυχία Th. 1.84, cf. E.*Supp.*911, Arist.*EN*1108ᵃ32, etc.; αἰδοῖ μειλιχίῃ Od.8. 172; so ἀλλά με κωλύει αἴδως Alc.55 (Sapphus est versus); ἅμα κιθῶνι ἐκδυομένῳ συνεκδύεται καὶ τὴν αἰδῶ γυνή Hdt.1.8; δακρύων πένθιμον αἰδῶ tears of grief and *shame*, A.*Supp.*579; αἰ. τίς μ' ἔχει Pl. *Sph.*217d; αἰ. καὶ δίκη Id.*Prt.*322c; αἰδοῦς ἐμπίπλασθαι X.*Cyr.*1.4.4; *sobriety, moderation*, Pi.*O.*13.115; αἰδῶ λαβεῖν S.*Aj.*345. 2. *regard for others, respect, reverence*, αἰδοῦς οὐδεμιῆς ἔτυχον Thgn.1266, cf. E.*Heracl.*460; αἰ. τοκέων *respect for* them, Pi.*P.*4.218; τὴν ἐμὴν αἰδῶ *respect* for me, A.*Pers.*699; *regard* for friends, αἰδοῦς ἀχαλκεύτοισιν ἔζευκται πέδαις E.*Fr.*595; esp. *regard for the helpless, compassion*, αἰδοῦς κῦρσαι S.*OC*247; *forgiveness*, Antipho 1.26, Pl.*Lg.* 867e (cf. αἰδέομαι II. 2). II. *that which causes shame* or *respect*, and so, 1. *shame, scandal*, αἰδώς, 'Αργεῖοι, κάκ' ἐλέγχεα Il.5.787, etc.; αἰδώς, ὦ Λύκιοι· πόσε φεύγετε; 16.422; αἰδὼς μὲν νῦν ἧδε.. 17. 336. 2. = τὰ αἰδοῖα, Il.2.262, Arat.493, D.H.7.72. 3. *dignity, majesty*, αἰ. καὶ χάρις *h.Cer.*214. III. Αἰδώς personified, *Reverence*, Pi.*O.*7.44; *Mercy*, Ζηνὶ σύνθακος θρόνων Αἰ. S.*OC*1268, cf. Paus. 1.17.1; παρθένος Αἰδοῦς Δίκη λέγεται Pl.*Lg.*943e.

αἰδῶσσα· αἴθουσα, Hsch. **ἀϊδώτατον**· τειχίονα, Id.

αἰεί, Ion. and poet. for ἀεί, q.v. (For compds. omitted here v. sub ἀει-.)

αἰει-γενέτης, ὁ, poet. for ἀειγενέτης, Il.2.400, Od.2.432, al. **-γενής**, ές, = foreg., Opp.*C.*2.397.

αἰέλιοι, v. ἀέλιοι. **αἰέλουρος**, v. αἴλουρος. **αἰέν**, v. ἀεί.

αἰεν-αοιδός, όν, *ever-singing*, Μοῦσα Alcm.1. **-υπνος**, ον, *giving eternal sleep*, epith. of Death, S.*OC*1578 (lyr.).

αἰές, Dor. for αἰέν, αἰεί.

αἰετηδόν, Adv. *like an eagle*, Apollon.*Lex.*68, Sch.Il.18.410.

αἰετιαῖος, α, ον, (ἀετός IV) *belonging to* or *placed in the pediment*, *IG*1.322 ii 73.

αἰέτιον χάριν ἐκτείσω, prov. of those who repay benefits quickly, Apostol.1.78.

αἰετόεις, εσσα, εν, *of eagle-kind*, Opp.*C.*3.117.

αἰετός, ὁ, v. sub ἀετός.

αἰζήεις, εσσα, εν, late form of αἰζηός, Theopomp.Col.ap.Ath.4. 183b; Dor. neut. αἰζᾶεν Hsch.

αἰζήϊος, ὁ, lengthd. form of αἰζηός, Il.17.520, Od.12.83, Hes.*Sc.*408.

ἀΐζηλος, ον, = ἀΐδηλος, *unseen*, τὸν μὲν ἀΐζηλον θῆκεν θεός v.l. (prob. Aristarch.) in Il.2.318.

αἰζηός, lengthd. **αἰζήϊος** (q.v.), ὁ, *in full bodily strength, vigorous*; in Hom. as Adj., ἀνέρι.. αἰζηῷ τε κρατερῷ τε Il.16.716, cf. 23.432; of a *stout, lusty* slave, τεσσερακονταέτης αἰ. Hes.*Op.*441, cf. *Th.*863:—freq. as Subst., Il.2.660, Od.12.440, Call.*Jov.*70, A.R.4.268, Nic.*Al.* 176, etc.; κταμένοις ἐπ' αἰζηοῖσι καυχᾶσθαι μέγα Cratin.95.

αἰζόκροτος· ξηρασία, Hsch., *EM*31.55: for ἀζο- (cf. ἄζα), Eust. 648.46.

αἰηνής, Ion. for αἰᾱνής, q.v.

αἶητος, prob. = ἄητος (q.v.), πέλωρ, of Hephaestus, Il.18.410.

αἰητός, ὁ, Dor. for ἀετός, αἰετός.

αἰθᾰλέος (better -άλεος, cf. *EM*262.4), α, ον, (αἰθάλη) *smoky*, A.R. 4.777. II. of ants, = αἰθαλόεις II.2, Nic.*Th.*750.

αἰθάλη, ἡ, (αἴθω) = αἴθαλος, esp. *soot*, Hp.*Mul.*1.91, Lxx *Ex.*9.8, Dsc.5.75, v.l. in Luc.*D.Deor.*15.1. II. *sublimed vapour*, Zos. Alch.p.250B., al.

ἀϊθᾰλής [ᾰῐ-], ές, = ἀειθαλής, Orph.*H.*8.13.

αἰθαλ-ίδας· τὰ ἐν τῷ σίτῳ γινόμενα, ἢ τοὺς ἐν τῷ ὕδατι σταλαγμοὺς τοῦ ἐλαίου, Hsch. **-ίων**, ωνος, prob. = αἰθαλόεις II.2, τέττιγες Theoc.7.138. **-όεις**, όεσσα, όεν, contr. **αἰθᾰλοῦς**, οῦσσα, οῦν : (αἴθαλος) :—poet. Adj. *smoky, sooty*, μέλαθρον Il.2.415, cf. Theoc.13. 13; κόνις αἰ. *black* ashes *that are burnt out*, Il.18.23, Od.24.316. II. *burning, blazing*, κεραυνός Hes.*Th.*72, cf. E.*Ph.*183 (lyr.); φλόξ A. *Pr.*992. 2. *burnt-coloured*, i.e. *dark-brown*, Σάϊς Nic.*Th.*566; ῥώξ ib.716.

αἰθᾰλοκομπία, ἡ, *empty boasting*, that is nothing but smoke, Sch. Ar.*Eq.*696.

αἴθᾰλ-ος, ὁ, *smoky flame, thick smoke*, Hp.*Mul.*1.91 (as v.l. for αἰθάλη), E.*Hec.*911 (lyr.), Semus 20, Lyc.55, etc. 2. grape grown in Egypt, Plin.*HN* 14.74. II. as Adj., αἴθαλος, ον, = αἰθαλόεις II.2, Nic.*Th.*659. **-όω**, *to soil with soot* or *smoke*, E.*El.*1140:— Pass., *burn to soot*, Dsc.1.66; poet., *to be laid waste by fire*, Lyc. 141. **-ώδης**, ες, *sooty, black*, Arist.*Mu.*395ᵃ26, Gal.9.470. **-ωσις**, εως, ἡ, in pl., *clouds of sooty smoke*, Max.Tyr.41.4 (pl.). **-ωτός**, ή, όν, *burnt to ashes*, Lyc.338.

αἰθε, Ep. for εἴθε, as αἰ for εἰ, in Hom. αἴθ' ὄφελες Il.1.415, al.

ἀϊθεος, Dor. for ἠΐθεος.

αἰθερεμβᾰτέω, *to walk in ether*, *APl.*4.328.

αἰθεριβόσκας, ὁ, *feeding on ether*, Cerc.1.3.

αἰθέριος, α, ον, also ος, ον E.*Fr.*839.10, Arist.*Mu.*392ᵃ31 :—*of* αἰθήρ or *the upper air*, hence, 1. *high in air, on high*, A.*Pr.*158 (anap.), *Th.*81, S.*OC*1082, etc.; αἰθερία ἀνέπτα flew up *into the air*, E.*Med.* 440, cf. *Andr.*830; αἰ. γῆ, of the moon, Pythag.ap.Simp.*in Cael.*511. 26: epith. of Zeus, Arist.*Mu.*401ᵃ17. 2. *ethereal, heavenly*, φύσις Parm.10.1; οἱ αἰ. Hierocl.*in CA*27p.484M.; γονή E.*Fr.* l.c. Adv. -ίως Iamb.*Myst.*1.9.—Trag. only in lyr.

αἰθερίτης λίθος, a precious stone, Ps.-Callisth.1.4 (as v.l. for ἀέρινος).

αἰθεριώδης, ες, = αἰθερώδης, φύσις Heraclit.*All.*36.

αἰθερο-βᾰτέω, = αἰθερεμβατέω, of birds, Ph.1.506: metaph. of men, 2.242, al., cf. Ps.-Luc.*Philopatr.*25. **-δρόμος**, ον, *ether-skimming*, οἰωνοί Cines.ap.Ar.*Av.*1393; ὧραι *IG*12(5).891 (Tenos, perh. by Aratus), cf. 9(1).881.7 (Corcyra). **-ειδής**, ές, = αἰθερώδης, Plu.2.430e. **-λαμπής**, ές, *shining in ether*, οὐρανός Man. 4.29. **-λόγος**, ον, *talking of ether and the like*, of Thales, Anaximen. ap.D.L.2.4: hence **-λογέω**, ib.2.5, cf. 8.50. **-ναία**, etym. of Ἀθηνᾶ, Corn.*ND*20. **-νόμος**, ον, (νέμομαι) = αἰθεροβόσκας, Hsch. **-νωμάω**, *to rule the sky*, Man.4.25.

αἰθερόομαι, *to be high in air*, Sch.Opp.*H.*1.201. **αἰθερόπλαγκτος**, ον, *roaming in ether*, Orph.*H.*6.1.

αἰθερώδης, ες, *like ether*, Plu.2.432f, Gal.*UP*10.4.

Αἴθη, v. αἰθός III.

αἰθήεις, εσσα, εν, (αἴθω) = αἰθαλόεις II.2, Nic.*Al.*394.

αἰθήρ, έρος, in Hom. always ἡ; in Hes. and Att. Prose always ὁ; in Lyr. and Trag. mostly ὁ, as always in A., but ἡ Pi.*O.*1.6, B.8.35, S.*OT*867, and freq. in E.: (αἴθω):—in Hom., *ether, the heaven* (wrongly distinguished by Aristarch. from ἀήρ (q.v.) as *upper* from lower *air*); δι' ἠέρος αἰθέρ' ἵκανεν Il.14.288; [Ζεὺς] αἰθέρι ναίων 2.412, Hes.*Op.*18; νόμοι δι' αἰθέρα τεκνωθέντες S.*OT*867; αἰθὴρ μὲν ψυχὰς ὑπεδέξατο σώματα δὲ χθών *IG*1.442, cf. E.*Supp.*533; of the *sky*, both cloudless, νήνεμος αἰ. Il.8.556, and clouded, ἐν αἰθέρι καὶ νεφέλῃσι 15. 192, cf. 16.365; freq. in Trag., etc., A.*Pr.*1044, 1088, *Pers.*365, E. *Ba.*150; αἰ. ζοφερός, ἀχλυόεις, A.R.3.1265, 4.927; of the fumes of the Cyclops' mouth, E.*Cyc.*410. 2. *air*, Emp.100.5. 3. fifth element, Pl.*Epin.*981c, 984b, Arist.*Cael.*270ᵇ22; but equivalent to πῦρ, Anaxag.1, 15. b. = πῦρ τεχνικόν, Chrysipp.*Stoic.*2. 168, cf. Arist.*Mu.*392ᵃ5. 4. the divine element in the human soul, Philostr.*VA*3.34, cf. 42. II. *clime, region*, E.*Alc.*594 (lyr.).

αἰθής, ές, *burning*: αἰ. πέπλος the robe of Nessus, prov. of those who stir up στάσις, Cratin.88, cf. Zen.1.33. (Perh. rather αἰθῆς, contr. for -ήεις.)

αἴθινος, η, ον, *burning*, Hsch.; = αἴθοψ, καπνός *EM*33.11.

Αἰθιοπίζω, *to speak* or *be like an Ethiopian*, Hld.10.39.

Αἰθίοψ, οπος, ὁ, fem. **Αἰθιοπίς**, ίδος, ἡ (Αἰθίοψ as fem., A.*Fr.*328, 329): pl. Αἰθιοπῆες Il.1.423, whence nom. Αἰθιοπεύς Call.*Del.*208: (αἴθω, ὤψ):—properly, *Burnt-face*, i.e. *Ethiopian, negro*, Hom., etc.; prov., Αἰθίοπα σμήχειν 'to wash a blackamoor white', Luc.*Ind.* 28. 2. *a fish*, Agatharch.109. II. Adj., *Ethiopian*, Αἰθιοπὶς γλῶσσα Hdt.3.19; γῆ A.*Fr.*300, E.*Fr.*228.4: Subst. Αἰθιοπίς, ἡ, title of Epic poem in the Homeric cycle; also name of a plant, *silver sage, Salvia argentea*, Dsc.4.104:—also **Αἰθιόπιος**, α, ον, E.*Fr.*349: **Αἰθιοπικός**, ή, όν, Hdt., etc.; Αἰ. κύμινον, = ἄμι, Hp.*Morb.*3.17, Dsc. 3.62:—Subst. **Αἰθιοπία**, ἡ, Hdt., etc. 2. *red-brown*, *AP*7.196 (Mel.), cf. Ach.Tat.4.5.

αἰθόλιξ, ικος, ἡ, *pustule, pimple*, Hp.*Liqu.*6:—Adj. **-κώδης** Gal. 19.71.

αἶθος, ὁ, *burning heat, fire*, E.*Rh.*990, cf. *Supp.*208 codd. (but cf. αἶθρος):—later also **αἶθος**, εος, τό, A.R.3.1304, Orph.*L.*174.

αἰθός, ή, όν, *burnt*, Ar.*Th.*246. II. *shining*, ἀσπίς Pi.*P.*8.46; *red-brown*, ἀράχναι B.*Fr.*3.6, cf. Call.*Dian.*69, Nic.*Th.*288. III. pr. n. Αἴθη, name of a *bay* horse, Il.23.295.

αἴθουσα (sc. στοά), ἡ, properly part. of αἴθω (q.v.), in the Homeric house, *portico, verandah, to catch the sun*, δόμον.. ξεστῇς αἰθούσῃσι τετυγμένον Il.6.243, cf. 20.11, A.R.3.39, 237: in Od. esp. of a *loggia* leading from αὐλή to πρόδομος, 3.399, al.; αἰ. ἐρίδουπος, echoing to the tramp of horses, 15.146. 2. = κώνειον, Ps.-Dsc.4.78. (αἴθουσσα Hdn.Gr.2.919, v.l. in Hom., which may point to αἰθοῦσσα = αἰθόεσσα.)

αἴθοψ, οπος, (αἰθός, ὤψ) *fiery-looking*, in Hom. as epith. of metal, *flashing*, αἴθοπι χαλκῷ Il.4.495, etc.; and of wine, *sparkling* (or *'fiery'*, cf. Epigr.ap.Luc.*Dips.*6), αἴθοπα οἶνον 4.259, etc.; once of smoke, *mixed with flame* (cf. αἴθαλος), Od.10.152; αἰ. φλογμός, λαμπάς, E. *Supp.*1019, *Ba.*594 (both lyr.). 2. *black*, Opp.*H.*1.133, etc.; αἴθοπι κισσῷ *App.Anth.*3.166 (Procl.). II. metaph., *fiery, keen*, λιμός Hes.*Op.*363; μῶμος Tim.*Pers.*223; δίψη Nonn.*D.*15.7; βασκανίη *AP*5.217 (Agath.).

αἴθρανος, ὁ, *foot-warmer*, Suid., Eust.1571.25 (-κος codd.).

αἰθρεῖ· χειμάζει, Hsch., Suid.

αἴθρη, ἡ, Hom. and Ar. ll. cc.: later **αἴθρα**, Antiph.52.14, etc.:— *clear sky*, ποίησον δ' αἴθρην Il.17.646; ἀλλὰ μάλ' αἴθρη πέπταται ἀνέφελος Od.6.44, cf. Ar.*Av.*778 (lyr.), Lyc.700, *AP*6.179 (Arch.), etc. II. *air*, as an element, *Orac.Chald.*169.

αἰθρη-γενής, ές, (γενέσθαι) *born in clear sky*, Βορέας Il.15.171. **-γενέτης**, Od.5.296. **-εις**, εσσα, εν, = αἴθριος, Pherenic.ap.Sch.Pi.*O.* 3.28, Opp.*C.*4.73.

αἰθρ-ία, Ion. -ίη, ἡ, = αἴθρη, first in Sol.13.22, then in Ion. Prose, Com., X., and Arist.: ἐξ αἰθρίης καὶ νηνεμίης Hdt.7.188; ἐξ αἰθρίας ἀστράψω Cratin.53, cf. Hdt.3.86, X.*HG*7.1.31; αἰθρίας οὔσης *in clear weather*, Arist.*Mete.*342ᵃ12; αἰθρίης or -ίας abs., Hdt.7.37, Ar.*Nu.* 371; τῆς αἰθρίας Arist.*Pr.*939ᵇ15. 2. esp. *the clear cold air* of night, Hdt.2.68, cf. Hp.*Aër.*8. [ῐ in penult. exc. in dact. and anap., Sol. l.c., Ar. l.c.] **-ιάζω**, *clear the sky*, ἀέρα Arist.*Pr.*941ᵃ4:—also = αἰθριάω, in pf. part. Pass. ἠθριασμένα Hp.*Morb.*3.17. **-ίασις**, *exposure to air*, Olymp.Alch.p.87B. **-ιάω**, *expose to the air, cool*, αἰθριήσας Hp.*Morb.*3.17; cf. αἰθριάζω. II. intr., *clear up*, of the sky, ὡς δ' ᾐθρίασε Babr.45.9.

αἰθρίδιον, τό, Dim. of αἴθριον, *PRyl.*312 (i A.D.).

αἰθρινός, ή, όν, = πρωϊνός, Hsch.

αἰθριο-κοιτέω, *sleep in the open air*, Theoc.8.78, Antyll.ap.Orib.9. 3.8. **-ποιέω**, *clear the sky*, Gloss.

αἴθριος, ον, *clear, bright*, of weather, αἰθρίου ἐόντος τοῦ ἠέρος Hdt. 2.25; αἰ. πάγος *clear* frost, S.*Fr.*149; f.l. in *Ant.*357. 2. epith. of Ζεύς, Heraclit.120, Theoc.4.43, cf. Arist.*Mu.*401ᵃ17, Thphr.*CP*5. 12.2; of winds *which cause a clear sky*, *h.Ap.*433, Arist.*Mete.*364ᵇ 29; esp. of the North wind, ib.358ᵇ1. II. *kept in the open air*, στέφη Cratin.22. III. **αἴθριον**, τό, adaptation of Lat. *atrium* to a Greek sense, J.*AJ*3.6.2, Luc.*Anach.*2, *POxy.*268.22 (i A.D.), etc.

αἰθρο-βάτης, ου, ὁ, *walking through ether*, of Abaris, Porph.*VP* 29. II. *rope-dancer*, Man.4.278. **-βολέω**, Astrol., = ἀκτινοβολέω (q.v.), c. acc., ib.224. **-δόνητος**, ον, *whirling through ether*, ib. 298. **-πλᾰνής**, ές, *wandering in ether*, ἀστήρ *a planet*, ib.586. **-πολεύω**, *roam through air*, Id.2.383:—also **-πολέω**, Max.483.

αἶθρος, ὁ, *the clear chill air* of morn, Od.14.318, cf. Alc.*Supp.*4. 14. II. = αἴθριον, *PLond.*3.1023.20 (v/vi A.D.).

αἰθρότοκος, ον, *born of air*, Man.4.339.

αἴθυγμα, ατος, τό, (αἰθύσσω) *gleam, glamour*, ὅπλων Onos.28 (pl.); πυρός D.Chr.80.5, cf. Plu.2.966b: metaph., *spark*, αἰ. εὐνοίας, δόξης, Plb.4.35.7 (pl.), 20.5.4; μήτ' ἴχνος μήτ' αἰ. Phld.*Sign.*29; μηδενὸς εἰς τοὐναντίον μηδ' ἕως αἰθύγματος ἀνθέλκοντος ib.18.

αἴθυια, ἡ, diving-bird, prob. *shearwater*, Od.5.337, cf. Arist.*HA* 542ᵇ17, Call.*Del.*12, *AP*7.285 (Glauc.); ἰχθυβόλοι ib.6.23 (Zon.):— epith. of Athena, as protecting ships, Paus.1.5.3. II. metaph., *ship*, Lyc.230.

αἰθυιόθρεπτος, ον, *feeding with sea-birds*, Lyc.237.

αἰθυκτήρ, ῆρος, ὁ, *rushing violently*, of pigs, Opp.*C.*2.332; φύσαλοι αἰ. Id.*H.*1.368.

αἰθύσσω (usu. in pres., impf. ᾔθυσσον Hsch., κατ-αίθυσσον Pi.*P.* 4.83): aor. παρ-αίθυξα Id.*O.*10(11).73, A.R.2.1253: (akin to αἴθω):— *set in rapid motion, stir up, kindle*, S.*Fr.*542, cf. Nonn.*D.*1.187, al.; κτύπον, νόον, ib.38.382, 48.689:—Pass., *quiver*, of leaves, Sapph.4, cf. Nonn.*D.*1.31. II. intr., Arat.1034.

αἴθω, only pres. and impf., *light up, kindle*, Hdt.4.145, A.*Ag.*1435; θεοῖς ἱερά S.*Ph.*1033; λαμπάδας E.*Rh.*95; δάφναν Theoc.2.24, etc.; πυρά E.*Rh.*41, 78, 823: metaph., σέλας ὄμμασιν αἴθει *AP*12.93 (Rhian.); χόλον αἶθες ib.5.299 (Paul. Sil.). 2. rarely intr., *burn, blaze*, Pi.*O.*7.48; λαμπτῆρες οὐκέτ' ᾖθον S.*Aj.*286. 3. Pass., **αἴθομαι**, *burn, blaze*, Hom. always in part., πυρὸς μένος αἰθομένοιο Il. 6.182, cf. 8.563; αἰ. δαλός 13.320; δαΐδες Od.7.101, cf. Pi.*O.*1.1, *Pae.* 6.97, E.*Hipp.*1279, etc.; after Hom. in other moods, αἴθεται κάλλιστα [τὰ ὀστέα] Hdt.4.61; αἰθέσθω δὲ πῦρ E.*IA*1470; δώματ' αἴθεσθαι δοκῶν Id.*Ba.*624, cf. X.*An.*6.3.19: metaph., ἔρωτι αἴθεσθαι X.*Cyr.*5.1. 16, cf. *AP*12.83 (Mel.); αἴθετο.. ἔρως (Ep. impf.) *burnt fiercely*, A.R. 3.296. (Cf. Lat. *aestas, aestus*: the weak form of the root appears in ἰθαίνεσθαι, cf. Skt. *inddhé* 'kindles'.)

αἴθων, ωνος, ὁ, ἡ, (αἴθω) *fiery, burning*, κεραυνός Pi.*O.*10(11).83; of *fiery* smoke, *P.*1.23. II. of burnished metal, *flashing, glitter-*

ing, σίδηρος Il.4.485, Od.1.184, S.*Aj*.147 (lyr.); χαλκός B.12.50; λέβητες, τρίποδες, Il.9.123, 24.233. III. of animals or birds, ἵπποι Il. 2.839; αἰετός 15.690; βόες Od.18.372; ἀλώπηξ Pi.*O*.11(10).20; δορά, of a boar, B.5.124; prob. of colour, *red-brown, tawny*, since *sleek, shining*, or *fiery, fierce* do not suit all cases (but αἴ. θῆρες *fierce*, Pl.*R*. 559d); pr. n. of horse, Il.8.185. IV. metaph. of men, *hot, fiery*, S.*Aj*.221 (lyr.), 1088, Hermipp.46; αἴθων λῆμα *fiery* in spirit, A.*Th*. 448; λιμὸς αἴθων prob. in Hes.*Op*.363, Epigr.ap.Aeschin.3.184, Call. *Cer*.68. (The forms αἴθονα, αἴθονος have been corrupted into αἴθοπα, αἴθοπος, Hes.*Op*. l.c., S.*Aj*.221.)

αἰθωπός, όν, *fiery*, Man.4.166.

αἰκάλη, ἡ, = ἀπάτη, Zonar.

αἰκάλλω, only pres. and impf., (αἰκάλος) *flatter, wheedle, fondle*, properly of dogs (cf. Phryn.*PSp*.36 B.), c. acc., E.*Andr*.630, cf. Pl.Com. 21 D.; τὸν δεσπότην ᾔκαλλε Ar.*Eq*.48; τὰ μὲν λόγι' αἰκάλλει με *flatter, please* me, ib.211; αἰκάλλει καρδίαν ἐμὴν *it cheers* my heart, Id.*Th*.869; τοὺς περὶ τὴν αὐλὴν Plb.5.36.1, cf. Axiop.3.4, Philostr.*VA*5.42:— Pass., ὑπό τινων Plb.15.25.31:—of a fox, σεσηρὸς αἰκάλλουσα *wagging the tail fawningly*, Babr.50.14.—Trag., Com., and later Prose.

αἰκάλος, ὁ, *flatterer*, Hsch.

αἴκε, αἴκεν, poet. and Dor. for ἐάν.

αἰκείη, Ion., = αἰκία, Herod.2.41.

αἰκέλιος, ον, poet. for ἀεικέλιος, Thgn.1344, E.*Andr*.131 (lyr.).

ἀϊκή [ᾱῐ], ἡ, (ἀΐσσω) *rapid motion, flight*, τόξων ἀϊκαί Il.15.709; ἐρετμῶν Opp.*H*.4.651.

ἀϊκής [ῐ], ές, poet. for ἀεικής. Adv. ἀϊκῶς Il.22.336:—in Trag. **αἰκής**, ές, αἰκὲς πῆμα A.*Pr*.472; θανάτους αἰκεῖς S.*El*.206 (lyr.). Adv. αἰκῶς S.*El*.102, 216 (both lyr.), Pl.Com.225.

αἰκ-ία, ἡ, Att. for Ion. ἀεικίη (q.v.), *insulting treatment, outrage*, A. *Pr*.179, S.*El*.515 (lyr.), *OC*748, etc. 2. *torture*, Plb.1.80.8, cf.24.9. 13: pl., *torments*, A.*Pr*.93, S.*El*.486 (lyr.), And.1.138, etc. 3. in Prose usu. law-term, *assault*, αἰκίας δίκη Pl.*R*.425d, 464e; ἣν ὁ τῆς βλάβης ὑμῖν νόμος πάλαι, ἣν ὁ τῆς αἰ., ἣν ὁ τῆς ὕβρεως D.21.35, cf. Lys.*Fr*.44, etc. 4. generally, *suffering*, Th.7.75. [Prob. misspelt for –εια (which is freq. v.l.); – – – in Poets.] **–ίζω**, aor. ᾔκισα Herod.2.46: pf. αἴκικα· ὕβρικα, Hsch.:—*maltreat*, τινά S.*Aj*. 403, *Tr*.839; σῶμα Tim.*Pers*.189; of a storm, *mar, spoil*, πᾶσαν αἰκίζων φόβην ὕλης S.*Ant*.419:—Pass., *to be tortured*, rarely in pres. in A.*Pr*. 169, Pl.*Ax*.372a: pf. ᾔκισμαι D.S.18.47, Polyaen.8.6: more freq. in aor. 1, πρὸς κυνῶν ἐδεστὸν αἰκισθέντα S.*Ant*.206; ἐδέθη καὶ ᾐκίσθη Lys.6.27; τὰ σφέτερα αὐτῶν σώματα αἰκισθέντες And.1.138, cf. Isoc. 4.154; εἰς τὸ σῶμα αἰκισθῆναι πληγαῖς Arist.*Pol*.1311^{b}24. II. more freq. in Med. **αἰκίζομαι**, A.*Pr*.197, Isoc.4.123: impf. ᾐκιζόμην S.*Aj*. 300: fut. αἰκίσομαι *AP*12.80 (Mel.), Att. –ιοῦμαι (κατ–) E.*Andr*.829: aor. ᾐκισάμην S.*Aj*.111, *OT*1153, Isoc.5.103, X.*An*.3.4.5: pf. ᾔκισμαι E.*Med*.1130, plpf. ᾔκιστο Plu.*Caes*.29:—in same sense as Act., ll. cc.; *damage*, τὰ χωρία D.43.72: c. dupl. acc. pers. et rei, αἰκίζεσθαί τινα τὰ ἔσχατα X.*An*.3.1.18; αἰκίσασθαί τινας πᾶσαν αἰκίαν Plb. 24.9.13. **–ισμα**, ατος, τό, *outrage, torture*, A.*Pr*.989, Lys.6.26:— in pl. -ίσματα νεκρῶν *mutilated* corpses, E.*Ph*.1529. **–ισμός**, ὁ, = foreg., D.8.51, Ctes.*Fr*.29.58, etc.; πόλεως Lxx 2*Ma*.8.17. 2. Medic., *discomfort*, Antyll.ap.Orib.6.23.13; *wrench, shock*, αἰ. αἰφνίδιος Apollon.Cit.1. **–ιστικός**, ή, όν, *prone to outrage*, only in Adv. –κῶς Sch.Il.22.336, Poll.8.75, etc. **–ίστρια**, ἡ (as if from a masc. αἰκιστής), *she who tortures*, Suid.

αἶκλοι· αἱ γωνίαι τοῦ βέλους, Hsch.

αἶκλον or **ἄϊκλον**, τό, *the evening meal* at Sparta, Epich.37, Alcm. 71, Polem.Hist.86, cf. Ath.4.139b:—also **αἶκνον**, Hsch., Suid.

ἀϊκτήρ [ᾱ], ῆρος, ὁ, (ἀΐσσω) *swift-rushing, darting*, σκορπίος Opp. *H*.1.171; ἀστέρες Nonn.*D*.2.192.

ἄϊκτος, ον, (ἱκνέομαι) *unapproachable*, καὶ ὄψει καὶ ψαύσει Hp.*Vict*. 1.10 (sed leg. ἄθικτος), Hsch.

αἴλινον, τό, = λίνον, Ps.-Dsc.2.103.

αἴλῐνος, ὁ, *cry of anguish, dirge*, αἴλινον αἴλινον εἰπέ A.*Ag*.121 (lyr.), cf. S.*Aj*.627 (lyr.), E.*Or*.1395; of an *epitaph*, *AP*6.348 (Diod.); said to be from αἶ Λίνον *ah me for Linos!* cf. Paus.9.29.8. 2. Adj., αἴλινος, ον, *mournful, plaintive*, αἰλίνοις κακοῖς E.*Hel*.171; βρέφος αἴ. *unhappy*, *IG*14.1502: neut. pl. αἴλινα as Adv., Call.*Ap*.20, Mosch.3.1: hence **αἰλινέω** *sing a dirge*, cj. in Dosiad.*Ara*15.

αἶλος, v. ἄλλος.

αἰλούριος, ὁ, ῥίζα τις, Hsch., *EM*34.9.

αἰλουρίς, ἡ, fem. of αἴλουρος 1, *Gloss*.

αἰλουρο-βοσκός, ὁ, *keeper of sacred cats*, *PSI*4.440.2 (iii B.C.). **–πρόσωπος**, ον, *cat-faced*, θεός *PMag.Par*.2.4.13 (ἐλ–).

αἴλουρος, Arist.*HA*540^{a}10, *Phgn*.811^{b}9, or **αἰέλουρος**, ὁ, ἡ, Hdt. and Comici ll. cc., S.*Ichn*.296:—*cat, Felis domesticus*, Hdt.2.66, Ar. *Ach*.879, Anaxandr.39.12, Timocl.1, Lxx *Ep.Je*.22, Plu.2.144c. II. = ἀναγαλλὶς ἡ κυανῆ, Ps.-Dsc.2.178; also αἰλούρου ὀφθαλμός, ὁ, ibid.

αἰλουροτάφος, ου, ὁ, *burier of cats*, Wilcken *Chr*.385 ii 25 (iii B.C.).

αἰλουρόφθαλμος, ον, *with cat-like eyes*, Heph.Astr.1.1.

αἷμα, ατος, τό, *blood*, Il.1.303, etc.; φόνος αἵματος 16.162; ψυχῆς ἄκρατον αἷμα S.*El*.786: in pl., *streams of blood*, A.*Ag*.1293, S.*Ant*. 121, E.*El*.1172, *Alc*.496. 2. of *anything like blood*, Βακχίου Tim. *Fr*.7; αἷ. σταφυλῆς Lxx *Si*.39.26, cf. *App.Anth*.3.266 (Procl.). b. *dye* obtained from ἄγχουσα, *alkanet*, *PHolm*.15.25, *PLeid.X*.99. 3. 3. with collat. meaning of *spirit, courage*, οὐκ ἔχων αἷμα *pale, spiritless*, Aeschin.3.160; τοὺς αἷμα φάσκοντας τὴν ψυχὴν Arist.*de An*. 405^{b}4. II. *bloodshed, murder*, A.*Ch*.520, S.*OT*101; ὅμαιμον αἷ. a kinsman's *murder*, A.*Supp*.449; εἴργασται μητρῷον αἷ. E.*Or*. 285, cf. 406; αἷ. πράττειν ib.1139; αἷμα συγγενὲς κτείνας S.*Fr*.799.3; αἷμα τραγοκτόνον shedding of goat's *blood*, E.*Ba*.139; ἐφ' αἵματι φεύγειν to avoid trial for *murder* by going into exile, *SIG*58 (Milet., v B.C.), D.21.105; αἷμα συγγενὲς φεύγων E.*Supp*.148: pl. in this sense, A.*Ch*.66, 650, freq. in E., never in S.; αἵματα σύγγονα brothers' *corpses*, E.*Ph*.1502:—concrete, νεακόνητον αἷ. keen-edged *death*, i.e. a sword, S.*El*.1394 (expl. by μάχαιρα, Hsch.). III. *blood relationship, kin*, αἷ. τε καὶ γένος Od.8.583; αἵματός εἰς ἀγαθοῖο 4.611; οἵ σῆς ἐξ αἵματός εἰσι γενέθλης Il.19.111; τὸ αἷ. τινος his *blood* or *origin*, Pi.*N*.11.34; αἷ. ἐμφύλιον incestuous *kinship*, S.*OT*1406; τοὺς πρὸς αἵματος Id.*Aj*.1305, cf. Arist.*Pol*.1262^{a}11; μητρὸς τῆς ἐμῆς ἐν αἵματι *akin* to her *by blood*, A.*Eu*.606, cf. *Th*.141; ἀφ' αἵματος ὑμετέρου S.*OC*245. 2. concrete, of a person, ὦ Διὸς . . αἷμα *IG*14.1003.1, cf. 1389 ii 4, etc.

αἱμαγμός, οῦ, ὁ, *bloodshed*, in pl., Vett.Val.3.4, al.

αἱμαγωγός, όν, (ἄγω) *drawing off blood*, Sor.1.71: –γόν, τό, = γλυκυσίδη, Ps.-Dsc.3.140.

αἱμακουρίαι, ῶν, αἱ, (κορέννυμι) Boeot. for ἐναγίσματα, *offerings of blood* made to the dead, Pi.*O*.1.90, B.7.5 (prob. l.):—sg. in Plu.*Arist*. 21 (v.l. αἱμο–).

αἱμακ-τικός, ή, όν, *making bloody*, Sch.S.*Ant*.1003. **–τός**, ή, όν, *mingled with blood, of blood*, E.*IT*645 (lyr.).

αἱμαλ-έος, α, ον, *blood-red*, Tryph.70; *bloodstained*, *AP*6.129 (Leon.), Nonn.*D*.5.14. **–ώδης**, v.l. for αἱματ–, Hp.*Epid*.4.29 (Erot.).

αἱμαλωπιάω, *have the appearance of clotted blood*, Dsc.2.77.

αἱμάλωψ, ωπος, ὁ, *mass of blood*: *bloodshot place*, Hp.*Coac*.542, *Nat.Puer*.13, *POxy*.1088 i 3 (i A.D.); *blood-clot*, Aret.*SA*2.9. II. as Adj., *looking like clotted blood*, χυμός Id.*SD*2.1.

αἵμαξις, εως, ἡ, *letting of blood*, Aret.*CA*1.6.

αἱμάρροια, ἡ, = αἱμόρρ–, and **αἱμαροϊκός**, = αἱμορρ–, *BGU*1026 xxii 15 B (iv/v A.D.).

αἱμάς, άδος, ἡ, *gush, stream of blood*, S.*Ph*.695 (lyr.).

αἱμᾰσιά, ἡ, *wall* of dry stones, αἱμασιάς τε λέγειν to lay *walls*, Od.18.359; αἱ. λέξοντες 24.224, cf. Hdt.2.69, Theoc.7.22; αἱ. ἐγγεγλυμμένη τύποισι Hdt.2.138: of the walls of a city or fortress, Id.1. 180, 191, Th.4.43; αἱ. περιοικοδομῆσαι D.55.11; ἐφ' αἱμασιῇσιν ἥμενος Theoc.1.47, cf. *IG*12(3).248 (Anaphe).

αἱμᾰσιολογέω, *lay walls*, Theopomp.Com.73.

αἱμᾰσιώδης, ες, *like a* αἱμασιά, Pl.*Lg*.681a.

αἱμάσσω, Att. –ττω, D.H.2.74: fut. –άξω (v. infr.): aor. ᾕμαξα (v. infr.):—**Pass.**, aor. ᾑμάχθην E.*El*.574, αἱμάχθην S.*Aj*.909 (lyr.), part. A.*Pers*.595: pf. ᾕμαγμαι *SIG*1171 (Lebena):—*make bloody, stain with blood*, πεδίον Pi.*I*.8(7).50, cf. A.*Ag*.1589; ἑστίας θεῶν Id. *Th*.275; βωμόν Theoc.*Ep*.1, cf. Philostr.*VA*1.1; λίθους D.H. l.c.; κρᾶτ' ἐμὸν τόδ' αὐτίκα πέτρᾳ . . αἱμάξω πεσών S.*Ph*.1002; πότερος ἄρα πότερον αἱμάξει; *shall bring to a bloody end*, E.*Ph*.1289; πέσεα δάϊα . . αἱμάξετον ib.1299; αἱμάξεις . . τὰς καλλιφθόγγους ᾠδάς Id.*Ion* 168: abs., τοῖς μὲν οὐχ ᾕμασσεν βέλος *drew* no *blood*, Id.*Ba*.761; οἰκέτη πλευράν Lxx *Si*.42.5:—Med., ᾑμάξαντο βραχίονας *AP*7.10:—Pass., *become bloody*, Hp.*Mul*.1.91; ᾑμαγμέναι σάρκες *SIG*1171:—*to be slain*, αὐτόχειρ αἱμάσσεται S.*Ant*.1175. 2. Medic., *draw blood*, as by cupping, Aret.*CA*1.4. II. intr., *to be bloody, blood-red*, Nic.*Al*.480, Opp.*H*.2.618.

αἱματάω, *to be bloodthirsty*, dub. l. Alcm.68.

αἱμᾰτεκχυσία, ἡ, *shedding of blood*, *Ep.Heb*.9.22.

αἱμάτη, ἡ, = λεκάνη, Theognost.*Can*.5.32.

αἱμᾰτηρός, ά, όν (ός, όν E.*Or*.962):—*bloodstained*, χεῖρες S.*Ant*. 975 (lyr.); ξίφος E.*Ph*.625; ὄμμα *bloodshot*, Id.*IA*381; φλὸξ αἱματηρὰ κἀπὸ . . δρυός, i.e. ἀφ' αἵματος καὶ δρυός, *fed by the blood of the victim* and the wood, S.*Tr*.766: esp. *bloody, murderous*, πνεῦμα A.*Eu*. 137; τεῦχος Id.*Ag*.815; θηγάναι Id.*Eu*.859; ὀμμάτων διαφθοραί S.*OC* 552; στόνος *caused by the blood-reeking wound*, Id.*Ph*.694 (lyr.). II. *of blood*, μένος A.*Ag*.1067; σταγόνες gouts *of blood*, E.*Ph*.1415; αἱ. ῥοῦς Hp.*Coac*.502; αἱ. φλέβες *conveying blood*, Philostr.*VA*8.7.

αἱμᾰτηφόρος, ον, *bringing blood*: *bloody*, μόρος A.*Th*.419 (lyr.).

αἱμᾰτία, ἡ, *blood-broth*, eaten at Sparta, Poll.6.57.

αἱμᾰτίζω, *stain with blood*, αἱματίσαι πέδον γᾶς A.*Supp*.662. II. of insects, *draw blood, sting*, Arist.*HA*532^{a}13.

αἱμᾰτικός, ή, όν, *of the blood*, θερμότης Arist.*PA*697^{a}29; ὑγρότης Id.*GA*777^{a}7; τροφή, ὕλη, Id.*PA*652^{a}21, 665^{b}6; χυμός Gal.13. 332. II. = ἔναιμος, of animals *which have blood*, opp. ἄναιμος, Arist.*PA*665^{b}5, cf. *HA*489^{a}25; τὸ ἧπαρ –κώτατον *PA*673^{b}27.

αἱμάτῐνος, η, ον, *of blood, bloody*, στιγμή Arist.*HA*561^{a}11; δάκρυα Sch.E.*Hec*.241. 2. *red*, of glass, Plin.*HN*36.198.

αἱμάτιον, τό, Dim. of αἷμα, *a little blood*, Arr.*Epict*.1.9.33, Heliod.(?) ap.Orib.46.11.9, M.Ant.5.4. II. *blood-sauce*, a kind of γάρον, *Gp*.20.46.6. III. *black-pudding*, *SIG*1002.11 (Milet.), 1025.53 (Cos), Hsch.

αἱμᾰτίς, ίδος, ἡ, *blood-red cloak* (?), Arist.*Col*.797^{a}6: perh. f.l. for sq.

αἱμᾰτίτης [ῑτ], ου, ὁ, *blood-like*, λίθος αἱ. *haematite*, a red iron-ore, Dsc.5.126, cf. Athenod.Tars.4; εἰλεὸς αἱ., a disease, Hp.*Int*.46:— fem., αἱματῖτις φλέψ a vein *as conductor of blood*, Id.*Morb.Sacr*.15; αἱ. χορδή a *black*-pudding, Sophil.5; λίθος (cf. supr.), Thphr.*Lap*.37.

αἱμᾰτο-δεκτικός, ή, όν, = sq., ἀγγεῖον Sch.Ar.*Th*.754. **–δόχος**, ον, *holding blood*, Sch.Od.3.444. **–ειδής**, ές, *like blood, blood-red*, D.S.17.10.

αἱμᾰτόεις, όεσσα, όεν, contr. **αἱματοῦς**, οῦσσα (S.*OT*1279 cj.), οῦν, = αἱματηρός, Il.5.82. 2. *blood-red*, or *of blood*, ψιάδες, σμῶδιξ, 16.

459, 2.267. 3. *suffused with blood, flushed*, ῥέθος S.*Ant.*528; of the petals of a rose, *AP*6.154 (Leon.). 4. *bloody, murderous*, πόλεμος, etc., Il.9.650, etc.; ἔρις A.*Ag.*698 (lyr.); βλαχαί Id.*Th.* 348 (lyr.).

αἱμᾰτο-λοιχός, όν, (λείχω) *licking blood*: ἔρως αἱ. thirst *for blood*, A.*Ag.*1478 (lyr.). **-ποιέω**, *to make into blood*, Pall. *in Hp.*2.74 D. **-ποιητικός**, ή, όν, *blood-making*, δύναμις τοῦ ἥπατος Gal.16.506:—also **-ποιός**, 7.213, Sch.E.*Hec.*90. **-ποσία** or **αἱμο-ποσία**, ἡ, *drinking of blood*, Porph.ap.Stob.1.49.53. **-ποτέω**, *drink blood*, Sch.Ar.*Eq.*198. **-πώτης**, ου, ὁ, *blood-drinker, blood-sucker*, Ar.*Eq.* 198:—fem. **-πῶτις**, ιδος, Man.4.616. **-ρρόφος**, ον, *blood-drinking*, A.*Eu.*193, Archipp.4 D.; τίσις S.*Fr.*743. **-ρρῦτος**, ον, *blood-streaming*, αἱ. ῥανίδες a shower *of blood*, E.*IA* 1515 (lyr.). **-σπόδητος**, ον, *splashed with blood*, S.*Fr.*817. **-στᾰγής**, ές, (στάζω) *blood-dripping, reeking with blood*, φόνος A.*Ag.*1309, cf. *Pers.*816, E.*Supp.*812 (lyr.), Ar.*Ra.*471.

αἱμᾰτουργός, ή, ον, *murderous*, Ἄρεος δύναμις Porph.ap.Eus.*PE*3.11.

αἱμᾰτο-φλοιβοστάσιες, αἱ, corrupt word, Hp.*Epid.*6.7.2, cf. Gal.19.71. **-φυρτος**, ον, *blood-stained*, βέλη *AP*5.179 (Mel.); φόνος Phleg.*Mir.*3. **-χᾰρής**, ές, *delighting in blood*, Suid.

αἱμᾰτ-όω, *make bloody, stain with blood*, αἱμάτου θεᾶς βωμόν E.*Andr.*260; διὰ παρῆδος ὄνυχα.. αἱματοῦτε Id.*Supp.*77:—Pass., μηδὲν αἱματώμεθα A.*Ag.*1656; κρᾶτας αἱματούμενοι E.*Ph.*1149; ᾑματωμένη χεῖρας Id.*Ba.*1135, cf. Ar.*Ra.*476, Th.7.84, X.*Cyr.*1.4.10, etc. 2. *slay*, aor. αἱματῶσαι S.*Fr.*987. II. *turn into blood*, τὴν τροφήν Gal.8.379:—Pass., Ruf.*Ren.Ves.*5.2, Gal.17(2).692. **-ώδης**, ες, *looking like blood*, διαχωρήματα Hp.*Prog.*11; φάρυγξ Th.2.49, cf. Arist.*Mete.*342^{a}36, Thphr.*HP*6.4.6, etc. 2. *of the nature of blood, bloody*, ὑγρότης Arist.*GA*726^{b}32, cf. *PA*665^{b}7 (Comp.), al.; διαχώρησις Diocl.*Fr.*147. **-ωπός**, όν, *bloody to behold, blood-stained*, κόραι, of the Furies, E.*Or.*256; δεργμάτων διαφθοραί Id.*Ph.*870. **-ωσις**, εως, ἡ, *changing into blood*, Gal.6.256, 8.350. **-ώψ**, ῶπος, ὁ, ἡ, = αἱματωπός, E.*HF*933 (cj. Pors.).

αἱμηπότης, ὁ, Ion. for αἱμοπότης, A.D.*Adv.*189.10.

αἱμηρός, ά, όν, = αἱματηρός, Man.1.338, of women, cf. Androm.ap. Gal.14.33, St. Byz. s.v. Ἐπίδαυρος; πρόσωπον αἱ. *flushed* with anger, Phld.*Ir.*p.5 W.

αἱμίθεος, Aeol. for ἡμί–, Alc.*Supp.*8.13. **αἱμίονος**, Aeol. for ἡμί–, Sapph.*Supp.*20.14. **αἴμισυς**, Aeol. for ἥμισυς, q.v.

αἰμνίον, τό, *basin for blood*, v.l. for ἀμνίον, Od.3.444.

αἱμο-βᾰρής, ές, *heavy with blood*, Opp.*H.*2.603. **-βαφής**, -ές, *bathed in blood*, S.*Aj.*219 (anap.), Nonn.*D.*2.52; τελαμῶνες Sor.1.28. **-βόρος**, ον, *blood-sucking*, of certain insects, Arist.*HA*596^{b}13; γαστέρας αἱ., of serpents, *greedy of blood*, Theoc.24.18; ἔχιδνα *IG*4.620.4 (Argos); λύκος βλέπων -βόρον Alciphr.3.21. **-βότος**, ον, *feeding on blood*, Orac.ap.Porph.*Plot.*22. **-δαιτέω**, *to revel in blood*, Thphr.ap.Porph.*Abst.*2.8. **-διψος**, ον, *bloodthirsty*, Luc.*Ocyp.*97. **-δόχος**, ον, = αἱματοδόχος, *EM*84.41, Suid. s.v. αἰμνίον. **-δωρον**, τό, *herb-bane, Orobanche cruenta*, Thphr.*HP*8.8.5, Plin.*HN*19.176 (prob.). **-ειδής**, ές, = αἱματοειδής, Ph.2.244. **-κέρχνον**, τό, *cough with bloodspitting*, Hp.*Epid.*4.37. **-πότης**, = αἱματοπώτης, Vett.Val.78.6, Hsch. s.v. ἠεροπότης:—fem. **-πότις**, ἡ, epith. of Hecate, *PMag.Par.*1.2864: of the Moon, *Hymn.Mag.*5.53. **-πτυϊκός**, ή, όν, *spitting blood*, Charixenes ap.Gal.13.50, Cael.Aur.*TP*3.2.25, etc. **-πτυον**, τό, *bloodstained sputum*, Gal.14.444. **-πώτης**, ου, ὁ, = αἱματοπώτης, Lyc.1403. **-ροος**, ον, poet. for αἱμόρροος, Nic.*Th.*318. **-ρρᾰγέω**, *have a haemorrhage, bleed violently*, ἐκ ῥινῶν Hp.*Acut.*67; αἱμορραγεῖ πλῆθος *there is a violent haemorrhage*, Id.*Aph.*4.27, cf. Sostrat.1, Zopyr.Hist.3:—impers. αἱμορραγεῖ Hp.*Aph.* 4.74; τούτοισιν αἱ. διὰ ῥινῶν Id.*Epid.*1.12. **-ρρᾰγής**, ές, *bleeding violently*, S.*Ph.*825. **-ρρᾰγία**, ἡ, *haemorrhage*, Hp.*Art.*69, *Aph.*7.21; any *violent bleeding*, ib.5.16; *nose-bleeding*, Gal.17(1).50, etc. **-ρρᾰγικός**, ή, όν, *liable to* αἱμορραγία, Hp.*Prorrh.*1.135, etc. Adv. -κῶς, τελευτᾶν Gal.8.304. **-ρραγώδης**, ες, = foreg., σημεῖα symptoms *of haemorrhage*, Hp.*Prorrh.*1.130, Ruf.*Ren.Ves.*9.2. **-ρραντος**, ον, (ῥαίνω) *blood-sprinkled*, θυσίαι E.*Alc.*134 (anap.), cf. *IT*225 (lyr.). **-ρροέω**, *to lose blood*, Hp.*Coac.*86, 110, Aristobul.32, etc.; *to have a* αἱμόρροια, Lxx *Le.*15.33, *Ev.Matt.*9.20. **-ρροια**, ἡ, *discharge of blood, bloody flux*, Hp.*Coac.*292, 301; αἱ. ἐκ ῥινῶν v.l. Id.*Aër.*4. **-ρροϊδοκαύστης**, ου, ὁ, *forceps for applying caustics*, Paul.Aeg.6.79. **-ρροϊκός**, ή, όν, *belonging to* αἱμόρροια, *indicating* or *causing it*, Hp.*Aph.*5.24, cf. *Coac.*300, etc. **-ρροΐς**, ΐδος, ἡ, mostly in pl., αἱμορροΐδες (sc. φλέβες) veins *liable to discharge blood*, esp. *haemorrhoids, piles*, Hp.*Aph.*3.30, etc. II. kind of *shell-fish*, perh. *Aporrhais pes-pelicani*, Arist.*HA*530^{a}19. III. female of αἱμόρροος II, Plin.*HN*20.210; poet., αἱμορροῒς θήλεια Nic.*Th.*315. **-ρροος**, ον, contr. **-ρρους**, ουν, *flowing with blood*, τρώματα Hp.*Art.*69; αἱ. φλέβες veins so large *as to cause a haemorrhage* if wounded, Id.*Fract.*11, ubi v. Gal. 2. *suffering from haemorrhoids*, Hp.*Epid.*4.7. II. as Subst., a serpent, whose bite makes *blood flow* from all parts of the body, Philum.*Ven.*21, Nic.*Th.*282; cf. αἱμορροΐς III. **-ρρώδης**, ες, = αἱμορραγώδης, Hp.*Coac.*306. **-ρρυής**, ές, = αἱμόρρυτος, Phryn.*PSp.*26 B. **-ρρῠσις**, εως, ἡ, = αἱμόρροια, Poll.4.186. **-ρρῦτος**, ον, (ῥέω) *dripping blood*, A.*Fr.*230:—poet. **-ρυτος**, νόσος *IG*12(5).310 (Paros). **-ρυγχιάω**, (ῥύγχος) *have a bloody snout*, Hermipp.80 (better taken as Subst. **-ίας**, ου, ὁ, reading -ίαν for -ιᾶν).

αἱμός, ὁ, = δρυμός, A.*Fr.*9 (pl.).

αἱμο-σάτης, ὁ, a Samian earth used in burnishing gold, interp. in Dsc.5.154. **-στᾰγής**, ές, = αἱματοσταγής, E.*Fr.*384. **-στασις**, εως, ἡ, *styptic*, Androm.ap.Gal.13.76: = σύμφυτον, prob. in Ps.-Dsc.4.9. **-στᾰφίς**, ίδος, ἡ, = ῥοδοδάφνη, Dsc.4.81. **-φᾰνής**, ές, *bloodshot*, of the eye, Aët.7.22. **-φόβος**, ον, *afraid of blood*, i.e. of bleeding, Gal.10.627. **-φόρυκτος**, ον, (φορύσσω) *defiled with blood*, κρέα Od.20.348; ῥεύματα Heraclit.*All.*42. **-φυρτος**, ον, = αἱματόφυρτος, Plb.15.14.2, Posidon.8. **-χᾰρής**, ές, = αἱματοχαρής, *Sammelb.*5829.4, Sch.E.*Hec.*24, *Or.*1563, Suid. s.v. αἱμωπούς. **-χροώδης**, ες, *blood-coloured*, Hp.*Epid.*4.52.

αἱμόω, = αἱματόω, in Pass., Hsch.

αἱμυλία, ἡ, (αἱμύλος) *wheedling*, αἱ. καὶ χάρις Plu.*Num.*8, prob. in Phld.*Rh.*2.77 S.

αἱμύλιος, ον, = αἱμύλος, Od.1.56, *h.Merc.*317, Hes.*Th.*890, Thgn.704; in good sense, *Eranos* 13.87.

αἱμῠλο-μήτης, ου, ὁ, *of winning wiles*, *h.Merc.*13. **-πλόκος**, ον, *weaving wiles*, Cratin.379a.

αἱμύλος [ῠ], η, ον, also ος, ον *AP*7.643 (Crin.):—*wheedling, wily*, mostly of words, αἱμύλα κωτίλλουσα Hes.*Op.*374; μῦθος Pi.*N.*8.33, cf. Ar.*Eq.*687; also αἱ. μηχαναί A.*Pr.*208; μὴ κλωπὸς αἰνεῖ φωτὸς αἱμύλον δόρυ E.*Rh.*709; of persons, τὸν αἱμυλώτατον S.*Aj.*389 (lyr.), cf. Pl.*Phdr.*237b, Lyc.1124; of foxes, Ar.*Lys.*1268 (lyr.).

αἱμῠλόφρων, ον, gen. ονος, (φρήν) *wily-minded*, Cratin.379b.

αἱμ-ωδέω (more correct than αἱμωδιάω acc. to Phryn.*PSp.*14 B.), *to be set on edge*, of the teeth, Hp.*Hum.*9, Cratin.3 D., cf. Orion 617.30. **-ώδης**, ες, *bloody, blood-red*, Luc.*D.Syr.*8. II. *having the teeth set on edge*, Gal.14.523. **-ωδία**, ἡ, *sensation of having the teeth set on edge*, caused by acid food or vomit, Hp.*Morb.*2.16, Arist.*Pr.*863^{b}11, Dsc.*Eup.*1.72 (pl.), Archig.ap.Gal.8.86. **-ωδιασμός**, ὁ, = foreg., Hsch. s.v. γομφιασμός. **-ωδιάω**, *have the teeth set on edge*, Hp.*Morb.*2.55, Diocl.*Fr.*43, Arist.*Pr.*886^{b}12, Lxx *Ez.*18.4 (Cod. A): c. acc., αἱ. τοὺς ὀδόντας Hp.*Morb.*2.73: metaph. of one *whose mouth waters*, ᾑμωδία Timocl.11.7. (In this group of words the termination may be connected with ὀδών.)

αἵμων, ονος, ὁ, dub. sens., perh. *eager*, Σκαμάνδριον αἵμονα θήρης Il.5.49; expl. by Gramm. as = δαίμων, for δαήμων, *skilful*, cf. *EM*251.13. II. (αἷμα) *bloody*, E.*Hec.*90, dub. l. in A.*Supp.*847 (lyr.).

αἱμώνιος, ον, *blood-red*, σῦκα Ath.3.76b.

αἱμωπός, όν, = αἱματωπός, *AP*6.35 (Leon.), S.E.*P.*1.44, Paul.Aeg.3.41; *flushed*, Ph.2.585.

αἰνᾰρέτης, ου, ὁ, (αἰνός) *terribly brave*, voc. -έτη (v.l. -έτα) Il.16.31.

Αἰνείας, ου, ὁ, *Aeneas*, Ep. gen. Αἰνείᾱο, but in Il.5.534 Αἰνείω:—also **Αἰνέας**, Il.13.541 (disyll.), cf. S.*Fr.*373.1, etc.

αἰν-ελένη, *Helen the direful* (cf. Αἰνόπαρις), *Epic.Alex.Adesp.*2.11. **-επίκουρος**· ἐπὶ κακῷ βοηθῶν, Hsch. **-έσιμοι**· καθήκοντες, Id.

αἴνεσις, εως, ἡ, *praise*, Lxx *Ps.*72(73).28 (pl.), al., *Ep.Heb.*13.15.

αἰνετ-ήριος, α, ον, *laudatory*, Hdn.*Epim.*34. **-ής**, οῦ, ὁ, *one that praises*, opp. μωμητής, dub. in Hp.*de Arte* 8. **-ός**, ή, όν, *praiseworthy*, dub. in Antim.25 codd., Arist.*Rh.*1402^{b}11, *AP*7.429 (Alc.), Lxx *Le.*19.24.

αἰνέω (cf. αἴνημι, αἰνίζομαι), impf. ᾔνουν E.*Hec.*1154, Ion. αἴνεον Hdt.3.73: fut. αἰνήσω Od.16.380, Thgn.1080, Pi.*N.*1.72; in Att. Poets always αἰνέσω, as in Pi.*N.*7.63, Semon.7.112: aor. ᾔνησα Hom., opt. αἰνήσειε Simon.57.1; Dor. αἴνησα Pi.*P.*3.13; in Att. always ᾔνεσα, Ion. αἴνεσα Hdt.5.113; pf. ᾔνεκα (ἐπ–) Isoc.12.207:—**Med.**, fut. αἰνέσομαι (only in compds. ἐπ–, παρ–):—**Pass.**, aor. part. αἰνεθείς Hdt.5.102: pf. ᾔνημαι (ἐπ–) Hp.*Acut.*51, Isoc.12.233.—Poet. and Ion. Verb, very rare in good Att. Prose (Pl.*R.*404d, *Lg.*952c), ἐπαινέω being used instead:—properly, *tell, speak of*, A.*Ag.*98, 1482 (both lyr.), *Ch.*192; σε κρηγύην αἰνεῖ *reports of* you as honest, Herod.4.47. II. usu. *praise, approve*, opp. νεικέω, ψέγω, Il.10.249, Thgn.612, etc.; ἀνδρὸς ὃν οὐδ' αἰνεῖν τοῖσι κακοῖσι θέμις Arist.*Fr.*673:—Pass., ὑπὸ Σιμωνίδεω αἰνεθείς Hdt.5.102; ἐπ' ἔργμασιν ἐσθλοῖς Theoc.16.15. b. esp. in religious sense, *glorify* God, Lxx 1*Ch.*16.4, *Ev.Luc.*2.13, *PMag.Par.*1.1146, al.:—also c. dat., τῷ κυρίῳ, τῷ θεῷ, Lxx 1*Ch.*16.36, *Apoc.*19.5. 2. *approve, advise, recommend*, Od.16.380, 403: c. inf., *recommend* to do a thing, euphem. for κελεύω, A.*Ch.*555, 715: c. part., αἰνεῖν ἰόντα *to commend* one's going, Id.*Pers.*643:—ὦ δεινὸν αἶνον αἰνέσας *giver of* dire *counsel*, S.*Ph.*1380:—c. acc. rei, *to be content with, acquiesce in*, γάμον Pi.*P.*3.13, cf. *N.*1.72, A.*Eu.*469, *Supp.*902, 1070 (lyr.), E.*Med.*1157; θῆσσαν τράπεζαν αἰνέσαι Id.*Alc.*2. 3. *praise*, with collateral sense, *decline courteously*, νῆ' ὀλίγην αἰνεῖν, μεγάλῃ δ' ἐνὶ φορτία θέσθαι Hes.*Op.*643 (cf. Plu.2.22f), cf. S.*Fr.*109; but, *thank*, cj. in E.*Supp.*388. 4. abs., *approve*, ὁ δᾶμος αἰνεῖ *IG*9(1).119 (Locr.). III. *to promise* or *vow*, τινί τι or τινὶ ποιεῖν τι, S.*Ph.*1398, E.*Alc.*12.

αἴνη, ἡ, = αἶνος, *praise, fame*, ἐν αἴνῃ ἐών Hdt.3.74, 8.112.

αἰνήθεστος· οὐκ εὐλιτάνευτος, Hsch.; cf. θέσσασθαι.

αἴνημι, Aeol. for αἰνέω, Hes.*Op.*683.

αἴνησις, = αἴνεσις, Ph.2.245.

αἰνητός, ή, όν, = αἰνετός, *IG*4.1607 (Cleonae), Pi.*N.*8.39; αἰνητὸν πάντεσσιν ἐπιχθονίοις [Arist.]*Pepl.*14; παράκοιτις *IG*14.1363; στέμμα *Epigr.Gr.*247, al.

αἴνιγμα, ατος, τό, *dark saying, riddle*, Pi.*Fr.*177, A.*Pr.*610, etc., cf. Lxx *De.*28.37: freq. in pl., ἐξ αἰνιγμάτων *in riddles, darkly*, A.*Ag.*1112, 1183; δι' αἰνιγμάτων Aeschin.3.121 (v.l.), etc.; ἐν αἰνίγματι 1*Ep.Cor.*13.12; αἱ. προβάλλειν, ξυντιθέναι, πλέκειν *to make* a riddle, Pl.*Chrm.*162b, *Ap.*27a, Plu.2.988a; opp. διειπεῖν, εἰδέναι, S.*OT* 393, 1525; μαθεῖν E.*Ph.*48. II. *taunt*, Aristaenet.1.27. III. *ambush* (Theban), Palaeph.4.

αἰνιγμ-ατίας, ου, ὁ, = αἰνιγματιστής, D.S.5.31. **-ατικός**, ή, όν, = -ώδης. Adv. -ῶς *in riddles, darkly*, Sch.E.*Hipp*.337. **-ατιστής**, οῦ, ὁ, *one who speaks riddles*, Lxx *Nu*.21.27. **-ατοποιός**, όν, *propounding riddles*, Eust.1074.60. **-ατώδης**, ες, *riddling, dark*, A.*Supp*.464; ῥηματίσκια, of the Heracliteans, Pl.*Tht*.180a; χρησμός D.S.32.10; of persons, Max.Tyr.38.4. Adv. -δῶς Arist.*Rh*.1441b22, Pl.*Chrm*.164e (Comp.), etc.

αἰνιγμός, ὁ, *riddle*, mostly like αἴνιγμα in pl., δι' αἰνιγμῶν ἐρεῖν Ar.*Ra*.61, cf. Pl.*Ti*.72b, Aeschin.3.121; ἐν αἰνιγμοῖσι σημαίνειν τι E.*Rh*.754; ἐν αἰ. λαλεῖν Anaxil.22.23: sg., Callisth.ap.Ath.10.452a.

αἰνίζομαι, Dep. only pres., = αἰνέω, Il.13.374, Od.8.487:—Act. αἰνίζω in *AP*11.341 (Pall.).

αἰνικ-τήρ, ῆρος, ὁ, *one who speaks darkly*, αἰ. θεσφάτων S.*Fr*.771. **-τήριος**, ον, known from the Adv. -ίως *in riddles*, A.*Pr*.949. **-τής**, οῦ, ὁ, = αἰνικτήρ, of Heraclitus, Timo 43. **-τός**, ή, όν, *expressed in riddles, riddling*, S.*OT*439.

αἴνιξις, ἡ, *use of dark sayings*, δι' αἰνίξεως λέγεσθαι Plot.6.8.19.

αἰνίσσομαι, Att. **-ττομαι**: fut. -ίξομαι: aor. ᾐνιξάμην: (αἶνος):—*speak darkly* or *in riddles*, μῶν ᾐνιξάμην; S.*Aj*.1158; λόγοισι κρυπτοῖσιν αἰ. E.*Ion*430; γνωρίμως αἰνίξομαι so as to be understood, Id.*El*.946: c. acc. cogn., λόγον.. αἰνίξατο Pi.*P*.8.40; αἰνίσσεσθαι ἔπεα *to speak riddling* verses, Hdt.5.56: c. acc. rei, *hint* a thing, *intimate, shadow forth*, Pl.*Ap*.21b, *Tht*.152c; τὸ δίκαιον ὃ εἴη *R*.332b; ὅτι.. *Phd*.69c; αἰ. εἰς.. *to refer as in a riddle to, to hint at*, εἰς Κλέωνα τοῦτ' αἰνίττεται Ar.*Pax*47; τὴν Κυλλήνην.. εἰς τὴν χεῖρ' ὀρθῶς ᾐνίξατο *used the riddling word* Cyllene (cf. κυλλός).., Id.*Eq*.1085; so ᾐνίξαθ' ὁ Βάκις τοῦτο πρὸς τὸν ἀέρα Id.*Av*.970; αἰνιττόμενος εἰς ἐμέ Aeschin.2.108; αἰ. ὡς.. Ps.-Plu.*Vit.Hom*.4:—αἰ. τὸν ὠκεανόν *form guesses about* it, Arist.*Mete*.347a6. **II.** Act. in late Prose, Philostr.*VA*6.11. **III.** Pass., *to be spoken darkly*, aor. ᾐνίχθην Pl.*Grg*.495b: pf. ᾔνιγμαι Thgn.681, Ar.*Eq*.196, Arist.*Rh*.1405b4.

αἰνο-βάκχευτος, ον, *raging direfully*, Lyc.792. **-βίας**, Ion. **-βίης**, ὁ, *terribly strong*, *AP*7.226 (Anacr.). **-γᾰμος**, ον, *fatally wedded*, E.*Hel*.1120 (lyr.), Orph.*A*.867, Man.3.148. **-γένεθλος**, ον, *born to ill luck*, Man.1.145. **-γένειος**, ου, *with dreadful jaws*, Call.*Del*.92. **-γίγας**, αντος, ὁ, *terrible giant*, Nonn.*D*.4.447. **-γόνος**, *child of praise*, Ph.Epic.ap.Eus.*PE*9.20. **-δακρυς**, ὁ, = foreg., *IG*12(7).115 (Amorgos). **-δότειραι** Ἐρινύες *giving terrible gifts*, Orph.*A*.352. **-δρυπτος**, ον, *terribly scarred*, term of abuse for a slave, Theoc.15.27 (v.l. αἰνόθρυπτε). **-δρυφής**, ές, *sadly torn*, in sign of mourning, Antim.[107].

αἰνόθεν, Adv. from αἰνός, only in the phrase αἰνόθεν αἰνῶς *horror of horrors*, Il.7.97.

αἰνο-λαμπής, ές, *horrid-gleaming*, A.*Ag*.389 (lyr.). **-λεκτρος**, ον, *fatally wedded*, ib.713 (lyr.), Lyc.820. **II.** *with a frightful bed*, of the cave of Echidna, Id.1354.

αἰν-ολέτης, ου, ὁ, *dire destroyer*, Orph.*A*.426.

αἰνο-λεχής, ές, = αἰνόλεκτρος, Orph.*A*.878. **-λέων**, οντος, ὁ, *dreadful lion*, Theoc.25.168. **-λῖνος**, ον, *unfortunate in life's thread* (i.e. dying young), *AP*7.527 (Theod.). **-λόγος**, ὁ, *terrible speaker*, *POxy*.465 (Astrol.). **-λῦκος**, ὁ, *a horrible wolf*, *AP*7.550 (Leon.). **-μᾰνής**, ές, *raving horribly*, Man.5.185, Nonn.*D*.20.152, etc. **-μορος**, ον, *doomed to a sad end*, Il.22.481, Od.9.53, Theoc.30.1; *come to a dreadful end*, A.*Th*.904 (lyr.). **II.** *of terrible doom*, ζόφος *h.Merc*.257; *deadly*, ὕδρος Q.S.9.395; σμύραιναι Marcell.Sid.14. **-πᾰθής**, ές, *suffering dire ills*, Od.18.201, A.R.4.1078, *AP*7.167 (Diosc. or Hecat.); πατρίς Anacr.36. **-πᾰρις**, ιδος, ὁ, like Δύσπαρις, *direful Paris, Paris the author of ill*, Alcm.40, E.*Hec*.945 (lyr.). **-πᾰτηρ**, ερος, ὁ, *unhappy father*, A.*Ch*.315. **-πέλωρος**, ον, *monstrous and terrible*, δάκος Opp.*H*.5.303. **-πλήξ**, ῆγος, ὁ, ἡ, *with dire sting*, ἔχιδνα Nic.*Th*.517. **-ποιέω**, *sing praises*, Aq.*Ps*.80(81).2, al. **-ποτμος**, ον, = αἰνόμορος, Orph.*A*.1016.

αἶνος, ὁ, (αἰνέω) poet. and Ion. word, *tale, story*, Il.23.652, Od.14.508, A.*Supp*.534 (lyr.); αἰνεῖν αἶνον to tell *a tale*, Id.*Ag*.1483 (lyr.), S.*Ph*.1380: esp. *story with moral, fable*, Hes.*Op*.202, Archil.86,89; ἄκουε δὴ τὸν αἶνον Call.*Iamb*.1.211: generally, *saying, proverb*, παλαιὸς αἶ. E.*Fr*.508, cf. Theoc.14.43; *riddle*, *Carm.Pop*.34. **II.** = Att. ἔπαινος, *praise*, Il.23.795, Od.21.110, Pi.*N*.1.6; ἐπιτύμβιος αἶ. A.*Ag*.1547, cf. 780, S.*OC*707 (all lyr.); ἄξιος αἴνου μεγάλου Hdt.7.107 (v.l. ἐπαίνου), cf. Lxx *Ps*.8.2, al., *Ev.Luc*.18.43. **III.** *decree, resolution*, τῶν Ἀχαιῶν *IG*4.926 (Epid.); κατ' αἶνον, opp. κατὰ ψήφισμα, *SIG*672.15 (Delph.), cf. *EM*36.16.

αἰνός, ή, όν, poet., = δεινός, *dread, horrible*, freq. in Hom., of feelings, ἄχος, χόλος, τρόμος, κάματος, ὀϊζύς, Il.4.169, 22.94, 7.215, 10.312, Od.15.342; of states and actions, as δηϊοτής, πόλεμος, μόρος, Il.5.409, Od.8.519 (Sup.), Il.18.465; of persons, *dread, terrible*, esp. of Zeus, αἰνότατε Κρονίδη Il.4.25, etc.; σύ γ' αἰνοτάτη, of Pallas, 8.423; of monsters or animals, πέλωρα Od.10.219; ὄφις Hes.*Fr*.14; λῖς Theoc.25.252. **II.** Adv. -νῶς *terribly*, i.e. *strangely, exceedingly*, Il.10.38; ἔοικέ τινι 3.158, Od.1.208; φιλέεσκε 1.264; ἐπὶ γόνυ κέκλιται A.*Pers*.930 (lyr.); φεύγειν τι Hdt.4.76; with Adj., αἰ. κακός *terribly* bad, Od.17.24; αἰ. πικρός Hdt.4.52; τῆς Σκυθικῆς αἰ. ἀξύλου ἐούσης ib.61:—neut. pl. αἰνά as Adv., Il.1.414: Sup. -ότατον 13.52.

ἄϊνος [ῐ], ον, (ἴς) *without fibres* or *veins*, Thphr.*HP*1.5.3, 8.3.1.

αἰνο-τάλᾱς, αντος, ὁ, *most miserable*, Antim.[106] = Call.*Fr*.506. **-τίταν**, ὁ, *fearful Titan*, Hdn.Gr.1.13. **-τλητος**, ον, *terrible to bear*, ἀνίη Max.224. **-τόκεια**, ἡ, *unhappy in being a mother*, Mosch.4.27. **-τόκος**, ον, *unhappy in being a parent*, Opp.*H*.5.526, *IG*14.1858:—but **αἰνότοκος**· ὁ ἐπὶ κακῷ τεχθείς, Hsch. **-τύραννος**, ὁ, *dreadful tyrant*, *APl*.5.350. **-φρων**, gloss on ἀγανόφρων, Apollon.*Lex*. **-φυτα**, τά, *plants of praise*, Ph.Epic.ap.Eus.*PE* 9.20.

αἴνυμαι, poet. Verb, only in pres. and impf. without augm.:—*take*, αἴνυτο τεύχε' ἀπ' ὤμων Il.11.580, 13.550; ἀπὸ πασσάλου αἴνυτο τόξον Od.21.53; χεῖρας αἰνύμεναι *taking hold of*, 22.500: c. gen. partit., τυρῶν αἰνυμένους 9.225: metaph., ἀλλά μ' Ὀδυσσῆος πόθος αἴνυται a longing *seizes* me for him, 14.144, cf. Hes.*Sc*.41; *enjoy, feed on*, καρπόν Simon.5.17. (Root αἰ-, as in ἐξ-αι-τος.)

αἴνω, aor. inf. ἦναι Hp.ap.Gal.19.103 (glossed by κόψαι), Phot.:—*sift, winnow*, Pherecr.183, cf. Hdn.Gr.2.930; v. ἀνέω. (Possibly for ϝαν-yω, cf. *vannus*.)

αἴξ, αἰγός, ὁ, ἡ: dat. pl. αἴγεσιν Il.10.486, αἴγεσσιν Choerob. *in Theod*.323; also Boeot. ἦγυς, = αἰγοις, *IG*7.3171:—*goat*, mostly fem., μηκάδας αἶγας Od.9.124; λεύκας αἶγος Sapph.7 (s.v.l.), cf. Ar.*Nu*.71, Pl.*Lg*.639a, etc., but masc. in Od.14.106,530; also τῶν αἰγῶν τῶν τραγῶν Hdt.3.112:—once in Trag., S.*Fr*.793 (anap.). **2.** αἶξ ἄγριος wild *goat*, prob. *ibex* (cf. αἴγαγρος), ἰονθάς Od.14.50; ἴξαλος Il.4.105; αἶγες ὀρεσκῷοι Od.9.155; ἀγρόтεραι 17.295:—proverbs, αἶξ οὐρανία in Com. as a source of mysterious and suspected wealth, in allusion to the horn of Amalthea, Cratin.244; οὐράνιον αἶγα πλουτοφόρον *Com.Adesp*.8; αἶξ τὴν μάχαιραν (sc. ηὗρε), of those who 'ask for trouble', Zen.1.27; αἶξ οὔπω τέτοκεν 'don't count your chickens before they are hatched', 1.42; αἶξ Σκυρία· ἐπὶ τῶν τὰς εὐεργεσίας ἀνατρεπόντων· ἀνατρέπει γὰρ τὸ ἀγγεῖον ἀμελχθεῖσα Diogenian.2.33; αἶξ ἐς θάλασσαν· ἀτενὲς ὁρᾷς, ἐπὶ τῶν φιληδούντων 3.8; κἂν αἶξ δάκῃ ἄνδρα πονηρόν 5.87; οὐ δύναμαι τὴν αἶγα φέρειν, ἐπί μοι θέτε τὸν βοῦν Plu.2.830a; ἐλεύθεραι αἶγες ἀρότρων· ἐπὶ τῶν βάρους τινὸς ἀπηλλαγμένων Zen.3.69; κατ' αἶγας ἀγρίας, = ἐς κόρακας, Hsch., Diogenian.5.49; νοῦσος, αἶγας ἐς ἀγριάδας τὴν ἀποπεμπόμεθα Call.*Aet*.3.1.13; αἰγῶν ὀνόματα, of worthless objects, Suid. **3.** *the star Capella*, Arat.157. **II.** a water-bird, apparently of the *goose* kind, Arist.*HA* 593b23. **III.** *fiery meteor*, Arist.*Mete*.341b3. **IV.** in pl., *waves*, Artem.2.12. (Att. αἶξ, acc. to Hdn.Gr.1.937.)

ἄϊξ, ἄϊκος [ᾰῐ], ἡ, (ἀΐσσω) = ἀϊκή, ἀνέμων ἄϊκες A.R.4.820.

ἀΐξασκε, Ion. and Ep. aor. of ἀΐσσω, Il.

αἰξωνεύομαι, Dep., *to be slanderous*, like the people of the Attic deme *Aexone*, Harp. s.v. Αἰξωνή.

αἰολάομαι, Pass., (αἰόλος) *to be restless*, Hp.*Mul*.2.174b (with vv.ll.).

αἰόλειος· ὁ ποικίλος, *EM*33.32.

Αἰολεύς, έως, ὁ, *Aeolian*; pl. Αἰολέες Hdt.1.28, Att. Αἰολεῖς or -ῆς Th.7.57:—hence Adj. **Αἰολικός**, ή, όν, *of* or *like the Aeolians*, Theoc.1.56 (v.l.); of the Aeolic dialect, A.D.*Adv*.193.15, al.: Comp. -ώτερον 194.8; of Aeolic metre, Heph.7.5. Adv. -κῶς S.E.*M*.1.78:—**Αἰόλιος**, α, ον, *in the Aeolian mode*, νόμος Plu.2.1132d:—fem. **Αἰολίς**, ίδος, Hes.*Op*.636, Hdt., etc.; of the Aeolian mode, Pratin.5; of the Aeolic dialect, A.D.*Adv*.155.11: Subst., Αἰολίς, ἡ, Id.*Synt*.309.25: poet. fem. **Αἰοληΐς**, Pi.*O*.1.102.

αἰολέω, = ποικίλλω, Pl.*Cra*.409a.

αἰόλησις, εως, ἡ, *rapid motion*, Sch.Pi.*P*.4.412.

αἰολίας, ου, ὁ, *a speckled fish*, Epich.44, Pl.Com.173.13; as Adj., αἰολίην κορακῖνον Numen.ap.Ath.7.308e.

αἰολίδας· ποικίλους, ταχεῖς, Hsch.

αἰολ-ίζω, = αἰόλλω: metaph., *trick out with false words*, μηδ' αἰόλιζε ταῦτα S.*Fr*.912. **II.** (Αἰολεύς) *compose in the Aeolian mode*, αἰ. τῷ μέλει Pratin.*Fr*.5; *speak Aeolic*, Dicaearch.3.2, Str.8.1.2, Plu.*Cim*.1; αἰολίζεται τὰ Ἀλκαίου ποιήματα A.D.*Synt*.279.52. **III.** = ἀολλίζω, Menecl.8, cf. Hsch. **-ισμα**, τό, *varied tones*, λύρας S.*Ichn*.319. **-ιστί**, *in the Aeolic dialect*, Str.8.1.2.

αἰόλλω, only pres., *to shift rapidly to and fro*, ὡς δ' ὅτε γαστέρ' ἀνὴρ.. αἰόλλῃ Od.20.27. **II.** *variegate*, Nic.*Th*.155:—Pass., *shift colour*, ὄμφακες αἰόλλονται Hes.*Sc*.399.

αἰολό-βουλος, ον, *wily*, Opp.*C*.3.449, al. **-βρόντης**, ου, ὁ, *wielder of the flashing thunderbolt*, Ζεὺς αἰ. Pi.*O*.9.42. **-δακρυς**, *with glistening tears*, Nonn.*D*.26.79, 43.365. **-δείκτης**, ου, ὁ, *showing himself in various forms*, of Phoebus; voc. αἰολόδεικτα, cj. for -δικτε, Orph.*H*.8.12. **-δειρος**, ον, *with sheeny neck*, Ibyc.8, cf. Opp.*C*.2.317, Nonn.*D*.12.76, al. **-δωρος**, ον, *bestowing various gifts*, Epimenid.19. **-θώρηξ**, ηκος, ὁ, *with glancing breastplate*, Il.4.489, *Hymn.Mag*.2(2).16. **-μητις**, ιος, ὁ, ἡ, *full of various wiles*, like αἰολόβουλος, Hes.*Th*.511, A.*Supp*.1036 (lyr.); also **-μήτης**, ου, ὁ, Hes.*Fr*.7 (s.v.l.). **-μίτρης**, ου, ὁ, *with glittering girdle*, Il.5.707. **II.** *with variegated mitre* or *turban*, Theoc.17.19. **-μολπος**, ον, *of varied strain*, σῦριγξ Nonn.*D*.40.223. **-μορφος**, ον, *of changeful form*, Orph.*H*.4.7, etc. **-νωτος**, ον, *with spangled back*, Opp.*H*.1.125. **-πεπλος**, ον, *with spangled robe*, Nonn.*D*.7.173. **-πους**, = στικτόπους, Sch.Opp.*C*.1.306. **-πρυμνος**, ον, *with gleaming stern*, νῆες B.1.4. **-πτέρυξ**, υγος, ὁ, ἡ, *quick-fluttering*, Telest.1.12 (dub.). **-πωλος**, ον, *with quick-moving steeds*, Il.3.185, *h.Ven*.137, Theoc.22.34.

αἰόλος, η, ον, (ος, ον Arist.*Pr*., v. infr.) *quick-moving, nimble*, πόδας αἰόλος ἵππος Il.19.404; αἰόλαι εὐλαί *wriggling* worms, 22.509; σφῆκες μέσον αἰ. 12.167; ὄφις ib.208; οἶστρος Od.22.300, cf. Achae.48. **2.** as epith. of armour, *glittering*, τεύχεα Il.5.295; σάκος 7.222, 16.107; κνώδων S.*Aj*.1025:—generally, *changeful of hue, sheeny*, δράκων Id.*Tr*.11; αἰόλα νύξ *star-spangled* night, ib.94 (lyr.); αἰ. πυρὸς κάσις smoke *flushed by* fire-light, A.*Th*.494; κύων αἰ. *speckled*, Call.*Dian*.91, etc.; αἰόλα σάρξ *discoloured*, S.*Ph*.1157 (lyr.); ὀφθαλμοί Adam.1.8, cf. 11. **II.** metaph., **1.** *chequered*, αἰόλ' ἀνθρώπων κακά A.*Supp*.328;

changeful, ἰαχή E.*Ion*499 (lyr.); χορεία Ar.*Ra.*248 (lyr.); νόμος Telest.2; αἰόλα φωνέων Theoc.16.44; αἰόλοι ἡμέραι *changeable* days, Arist.*Pr.*941ᵇ24. 2. *shifty, slippery*, ἔπος Sol.11.7; ψεῦδος Pi.*N.* 8.25; κέρδεσσι B.14.57; μηχάνημα λυγκὸς αἰολώτερον *Trag.Adesp.* 349.—Chiefly poet.

B. proparox. Αἴολος, ου, ὁ, the lord of the winds, properly *the Rapid* or *the Changeable*, Od., etc. 2. name of a kind of σκάρος, Nic.Thyat.ap.Ath.7.320c. 3. Pythag., = 4, or ἐνιαυτός, *Theol. Ar.*22.

αἰολό-στομος, ον, *shifting in speech*, of an oracle, A.*Pr.*661. **-φοιτος**, v. l. for -φυλος, *subject to changeful madness*, Sch.Opp.*H.*2. 420. **-φῦλος**, ον, *of divers kinds*, Opp.*H.*1.617. **-φωνος**, ον, *with changeful notes*, ἀηδών Opp.*H.*1.728. **-χαίτης**, ου, ὁ, *with parti-coloured hair*, Eust.1645.5. **-χρως**, ωτος, ὁ, ἡ, *spangled*, νύξ Critias 19.4 D.

αἰον-άω, *moisten, foment*, Hp.*Nat.Mul.*44: fut. αἰονήσω *BKT*3. 20: aor. 1 ᾐόνησα A.*Fr.*425:—Med., Lyc.1425. **-ημα**, ατος, τό, *fomentation*, D.C.55.17, *EM*348.27. **-ησις**, εως, ἡ, *fomenting*, Hp.*Liqu.*1, Poll.4.180, Gal.10.781.

αἶος, = αἰών, Stes. in Cod.Bodl.Auct.T.11(11)f.90.

αἰπάρθενος, v. ἀειπάρθενος.

αἰπεινής, ές, = sq., *Epigr.Gr.*1069 (ἐπ- lapis) (Syria).

αἰπεινός, ή, όν, (αἰπύς) poet. Adj. *high, lofty*, of cities on heights, Ἴλιον Il.9.419, al., cf. A.*Fr.*284, S.*Tr.*858 (lyr.), *Ph.*1000; αἰθήρ B. 8.34; of Delphi, μαντεῖα E.*Ion*739; of mountain-tops, κάρηνα Il.2. 869, Od.6.123. II. metaph., 1. αἰ. λόγοι *hasty, wicked* words, Pi.*N.*5.32. 2. *hard to reach*, σοφίαι μὲν αἰ. Id.*O.*9.108.

αἰπήεις, εσσα, εν, = foreg., Il.21.87, A.R.2.721, *AP*7.273 (Leon.).

αἰπολ-έω, only in pres. and impf., *tend goats*, Eup.13, Theoc.8.85; ᾐπόλει ταῖς αἰξίν Lys.*Fr.*25:—Pass., ἄνευ βοτῆρος αἰπολούμεναι a flock *tended* by no herdsman, A.*Eu.*196. **-ή**, sine expl., Suid. **-ικός**, ή, όν, *of* or *for goatherds*, θάημα Theoc.1.56; τρύπανον Call.*Fr.*412; σύριγγες *AP*12.128 (Mel.), cf. 9.217 (Muc. Scaev.). **-ιον**, τό, *herd of goats*, αἰπόλι' αἰγῶν Il.11.679, al., cf. Hdt.1.126, S.*Aj.*375 (lyr.), Lxx *Pr.*24.66(30.31). II. *goat-pasture*, *AP*9.101 (Alph.). **-ος**, ὁ, *goatherd*, αἰπόλος αἰγῶν Od.20.173, cf. Hdt.2.46, Pl.*Lg.*639a, Lxx *Am.*7.14. II. αἰπόλος· κάπηλος (Cypr.), Hsch.

αἶπος, εος, τό, (αἰπύς) *height, steep*, A.*Ag.*285,309, etc.; πρὸς αἶπος ὁδοιπορῆσαι, ἰέναι to toil up-*hill*, Hp.*Morb.*2.51,70; πρὸς αἶπος ἔρχεται, metaph. of a difficult task, E.*Alc.*500: hence αἶ. (v. l. ἄπος) ἐκβαλὼν ὁδοῦ, i.e. the *weariness* of the ascent (expl. by Hsch. as κάματος), Id. *Ph.*851 (unless ἐκβαλών = 'forgetting').

αἰπός, ή, όν, *high, lofty*, of cities, Il.13.625, al.; αἰπὰ ῥέεθρα streams *falling sheer down*, Il.8.369, Hes.*Oxy.*1358.2.23: αἰπόν, τό, dub. in *Ath.Mitt.*31.138 (Athens).

αἰπύ-δμητος, ον, (δέμω) *high-built*, Coluth.235, Nonn.*D.*4.13. **-κερως**, ων, gen. ω, = ὑψίκερως, *EM*37.38, Suid. **-λοφος**, ον, *high-crested*, Nonn.*D.*2.379, etc. **-μήτης**, ου, ὁ, *with high thoughts*, Θέμιδος αἰπυμῆτα παῖ A.*Pr.*18. **-νοος**, ον, = foreg., of Osiris, *Hymn.Is.*19. **-νωτος**, ον, *on a high mountain-ridge*, of Dodona, A.*Pr.*830. **-πλάνής**, ές, *high-roaming*, Man.4.249.

αἰπύς, εῖα, ύ, Ep. and Lyr. Adj., rare in Trag., *high and steep*, in Hom. mostly of cities on rocky heights, esp. of Troy, Od.3.485, al.; of hills, Il.2.603; later of the sky, αἰθήρ B.3.36; οὐρανός S.*Aj.*845; *on high*, ποδῶν αἰ. λωή Hes.*Th.*682; ἁψαμένη βρόχον αἰπὺν *hanging high*, Od.11.278. 2. metaph., *sheer, utter*, αἰ. ὄλεθρος freq. in Hom., death being regarded as *the plunge from a high precipice*; φόνος αἰ. Od.4.843; θάνατος Pi.*O.*10(11).42; σκότος *utter* darkness, Id. *Fr.*228; of passions, etc., αἰ. χόλος *towering* wrath, Il.15.223; δόλος αἰ. *h.Merc.*66, Hes.*Th.*589; αἰπυτάτη σοφίη *AP*11.354 (Agath.); *arduous*, πόνος Il.11.601, 16.651; αἰπύ οἱ ἐσσεῖται 'twill be *hard work* for him, 13.317.

αἶρα, ἡ, *hammer*, αἰράων ἔργα *smith's* work, Call.*Fr.*129. 2. = ἀξίνη, Hsch. II. *darnel, Lolium temulentum*, Thphr.*HP* 1.5.2: in pl., Ar.*Fr.*412, Pherecr.188, Arist.*Somn.*456ᵇ30, Herod. 6.100, etc.

αἱρέσια, τά, prob. *dues paid on discharge of cargoes*, *IG*11(2).203 *A*30 (Delos, iii B.C.), al.

αἱρεσι-αρχέω, Astrol., *dominate the 'condition'*, Rhetor. in *Cat.Cod. Astr.*1.146. **-άρχης**, ου, ὁ, *leader of a school*, S.E.*P.*3.245; esp. of a medical school, *IG*14.1759, Gal.6.372; *heresiarch*, Just.*Nov.* 42.1.1 (pl.). II. Astrol., *dominating the 'condition'* (cf. αἵρεσις B. II. 4), Paul.Al.*R.*3.

αἱρέσιμος, ον, *that can be taken*, X.*Cyr.*5.2.4.

αἱρεσιομάχος, ον, *fighting for a sect*, Ph.2.84.

αἵρεσις, εως, ἡ, *taking*, esp. of a town, Hdt.4.1, etc.; ἡ βασιλέος αἷ. *the taking by* the king, Id.9.3; ἐλπίζων ταχίστην -σιν ἔσεσθαι Th. 2.75; αἷ. δυνάμεως *acquisition* of power, Pl.*Grg.*513a:—generally, *taking, receiving*, ἐπιγενημάτων *PTeb.*27.66 (ii B.C.).

B. (αἱρέομαι) *choice*, αἵρεσιν τ' ἐμοὶ δίδου A.*Pr.*779; τῶνδε.. αἵρεσιν παρδίδωμι Pi.*N.*10.82; foll. by relat., αἷ. διδόναι ὁκοτέρην.., εἰ.., etc., Hdt.1.11, cf. D.22.19; αἷ. προτιθέναι, προβάλλειν, Pl.*Tht.*196c, *Sph.*245b; εἰ νέμοι τις αἵρεσιν S.*Aj.*265; αἵρεσιν λαβεῖν D.36.11; ποιεῖσθαι Isoc.7.19; αἷ. γίγνεταί τινι Th.2.61; οὐκ ἔχει αἵρεσιν it admits no *choice*, Plu.2.708b. 2. *choice, election* of magistrates, Th.8.89, cf. Arist.*Pol.*1266ᵃ26, al.; αἱρέσει, opp. κλήρῳ, 1300ᵃ19, etc. 3. *inclination, choice*, πρός τινα Philipp.ap.D.18.166, Plb.2.61.9, etc., cf. *IG*2.591*b*; opp. φυγή, Epicur.*Ep.*3p.62U.; περὶ αἱρέσεων καὶ φυγῶν, title of treatise by Epicurus. II. *purpose, course of action* or *thought*, like προαίρεσις, Pl.*Phdr.*256c; ἡ αἷ. τῆς πρεσβείας Aeschin. 2.11; αἷ. Ἑλληνική *the study* of Greek literature, Plb.39.1.3:—*conduct*, *PTeb.*28.10 (ii B.C.). 2. *system of philosophic principles*, or *those who profess such principles, sect, school*, Plb.5.93.8, D.S.2.29, Polystr.p.20W., D.H.*Amm.*1.7, *Comp.*2, al., cf. Cic.*Fam.*15.16.3; κατὰ τῶν αἷ., title of treatise by Antipater of Tarsus; περὶ αἱρέσεων, title of Menippean satire by Varro, cf. *Fr.*164; αἵρεσις πρὸς Γοργιππίδην, title of work by Chrysippus, D.L.7.191; esp. *religious party* or *sect*, of the Essenes, J.*BJ*2.8.1; the Sadducees and Pharisees, *Act.Ap.*5.17, 15.5, 26.5; the Christians, ib.24.5,14, 28.22, generally, *faction, party*, App.*BC*5.2. 3. *corps* of epheboi, *OGI* 176 (Egypt). 4. Astrol., *'condition'*, Ptol.*Tetr.*21; ἡ ἡμερινὴ αἷ. Vett.Val.1.13. III. *proposed condition, proposal*, D.H.3. 10. 2. *commission*, ἡ ἐπὶ τοὺς νέους αἷ. Pl.*Ax.*367a; *embassy, mission*, *IG*4.937 (Epid.). 3. *freewill offering*, opp. *vow*, Lxx *Le.*22.18, al. 4. *bid* at auction, τὴν ἀμείνονα αἷ. διδόντι παραδοθῆναι *POxy.*716.22 (ii A.D.), cf. 1630.8 (iii A.D.).

αἱρεσιώτης, ου, ὁ, *member of a sect*, Porph.*Abst.*4.11 (v.l. αἱρετισταῖς):—fem. **-ῶτις**, πολιτεία Suid.

αἱρετ-έος, α, ον, *to be chosen*, ὠφελήματα, opp. αἱρετὰ ἀγαθά, Chrysipp.*Stoic.*3.22,61, al. II. αἱρετέον, *one must choose*, Pl.*Grg.* 499e, Phld.*Rh.*1.287S., etc. **-ής**, ὁ, (αἱρέω) *searcher of archives*, αἱ. ἡγεμονικῆς βιβλιοθήκης *POxy.*1654.7 (ii A.D.). II. (αἱρέομαι) *one who chooses*, ἀγαθῶν Vett.Val.55.17. 2. Astrol., = αἱρετιστής 4, Sch.Ptol.*Tetr.*96. **-ίζω**, fut. -ιῶ Lxx *Ge.*30.20, *choose*, τινά Com.ap.Phot.p.54 R., cf. Hp.*Ep.*17, Lxx *Ge.* l. c., Babr. 61.5; ᾑρέτικα ἐν αὐτῷ εἶναί μου υἱόν 1*Ch.*28.6; ᾑρέτικέ σε οἰκοδομῆσαι ib.10; αἱρετίσας πατήρ *adoptive* father, *IPE*2.299 (Panticap.): abs., αἱρετίσαντος τοῦ θεοῦ *IG*3.74:—Med., Lxx *Ps.*118(119).30, al., Aesop.53, Ctes.*Fr.*29.9. **-ικός**, ή, όν, (αἱρέω) *able to choose*, Pl.*Def.* 412a; *due to choice*, οἰκείωσις Hierocl.p.41.5A., Anon. *in Tht.*7. 40. 2. *factious*, *Ep.Tit.*3.10. 3. Astrol., *belonging to the 'condition'*, Paul.Al.*Q.*2. 4. Adv. -κῶς *from choice*, D.L.7.126, Hierocl. p.41.7 A. **-ίς**, ίδος, ἡ, *one who chooses*, Lxx *Wi.*8.4. **-ιστής**, οῦ, ὁ, *one who chooses*, τινός Plb.22.6.11. 2. *partisan*, τῶν τρόπων τινός Philem.131, cf. Plb.1.79.9, etc.; *founder of a philosophical school*, D.L.9.6; τῶν λόγων *Vit.Philonid.*p.12C. 3. *sectarian*, J.*BJ*2.8.2, Iamb.*Protr.*21.κα'. 4. Astrol., *belonging to the 'condition'*, Jul.Laod. in *Cat.Cod.Astr.*5(1).183. **-ός**, ή, όν, *that may be taken* or *conquered*, δόλῳ Hdt.4.201; *to be understood*, Pl.*Phd.* 81b. II. (αἱρέομαι) *to be chosen, eligible*, opp. φευκτός, Pl.*Phlb.* 21d sq., Arist.*EN*1097ᵃ32, etc.: freq. in Comp. or Sup., Hdt.1.126, 156, al.; ζόης πονηρᾶς θάνατος αἱρετώτερος A.*Fr.*401. 2. *chosen, elected*, esp. opp. κληρωτός, Isoc.12.154, Pl.*Lg.*759b, Arist.*Pol.*1294ᵇ 9, cf. Pl.*Lg.*915c, Aeschin.3.13; αἱ. βασιλῆς Pl.*Mx.*238d; τυραννίς Arist.*Pol.*1285ᵃ31:—αἱ. ἄνδρες *commissioners*, Plu.*Lyc.*26; οἱ αἱ. X. *An.*1.3.21: = Lat. *optiones*, Lyd.*Mag.*1.46. 3. *that may be chosen*, opp. αἱρετέος (q.v.), Chrysipp.*Stoic.*3.22.

αἱρέω, impf. ᾕρεον Il.24.579, Ion. αἵρεον Hdt.6.31, but contr. ᾕρει even in Il.17.463, ᾕρευν Hes.*Sc.*302: fut. αἱρήσω Il.9.28, etc.: aor. 1 ᾕρησα late (ἀν-) Q.S.4.40, etc.: pf. ᾕρηκα A.*Ag.*267, Th.1.61, etc., Ion. ἀραίρηκα or αἵρηκα (ἀν-) Hdt.5.102: plpf. ἀραιρήκεε 3.39:—**Med.**, fut. αἱρήσομαι Il.10.235, etc.: aor. 1 ᾑρησάμην Plb.38.13.7 s. v. l., Gal.19.53, etc.: pf. in med. sense ᾕρημαι Ar.*Av.*1577, X.*An.*5.6.12, D.2.15, etc.: 3 pl. plpf. ᾕρηντο Th.1.62:—**Pass.**, fut. αἱρεθήσομαι Hdt. 2.13, Pl.*Mx.*234b; rarely αἱρήσομαι Id.*Prt.*338c: aor. ᾑρέθην and pf. ᾕρημαι D.20.146, al.; pf. part. ἀραιρημένος Hdt.4.66: plqf. ᾕρητο X. *An.*3.2.1, ἀραίρητο Hdt.1.191, etc.—From √ἑλ-: fut. ἑλῶ only late (δι-) *Test.Epict.*6.18, (ἀν-) D.H.11.18, (καθ-) *APl.*4.334 (Antiphil.): aor. 1 εἷλα (ἀν-) *Act.Ap.*2.23, (ἀν-) *Epigr.Gr.*314.24 (Smyrna): elsewh. aor. 2 εἷλον Il.10.561, etc., Ep. ἕλον 17.321, Ion. ἕλεσκε 24.752:—**Med.**, fut. ἑλοῦμαι D.H.4.75, (ἀφ-) Timostr.5, (δι-) D.H.4.60, (ἐξ-) Alciphr.1.9: aor. 1 εἱλάμην *Epigr.Gr.*314.5 (Smyrna), (ἀφ-) v.l. in Ath.12.546a, (δι-) *AP*9.56 (Phil.): elsewh. aor. 2 εἱλόμην Il.16.139, etc., 2 sg. ἥλεο Sapph.*Oxy.*1787.6.3:—Cret. forms αἰλεθῆ *Leg.Gort.* 2.21, ἀν-αιληθαι ib.7.10, al.:—the etym. is doubtful, and ἀγρέω (q.v.) prob. has a difft. root.

A. Act., *take with the hand, grasp, seize*, αἱ. τι ἐν χερσίν Od.4.66; αἱ. τινὰ χειρός *to take* one by the hand, Il.1.323; κόμης τινά ib.197; μ' ἑλὼν ἐπὶ μάστακα χερσίν Od.23.76: part. ἑλών adverbially, κατακτεῖναί μ' ἑλὼν S.*Ant.*497; ἄξω ἑλών Il.1.139, cf. Pi.*O.*7.1; but ἔνθεν ἑλὼν *having taken up* [the song], Od.8.500. 2. *take away*, ἀπ' ἀπήνης ᾕρεον ἄποινα Il.24.579. II. *take, get into one's power*, νῆας ib.13.42; esp. *take* a city, 2.37, S.*Ph.*347, etc.; *overpower, kill*, Il.4.457, etc.; ἕλοιμί κεν ἤ κε ἁλοίην 22.253:—freq. of passions, etc., *come upon, seize*, χόλος Il.18.322; ἵμερος 3.446; ὕπνος 10.193; λήθη 2.34, etc.: c. dupl. acc., τὸν δ' ἄτη φρένας εἷλε 16.805; of disease, Pl.*Tht.*142b. 2. *catch, take*, ζωὸν ἑλεῖν Il.21.102; *take in hunting*, Hes.*Sc.*302, Hdt. 1.36, etc.; *overtake*, in a race, Il.23.345; *get into one's power, entrap*, S.*OC*764, etc.; in good sense, *win over*, X.*Mem.*2.3.16, cf. 3.11.11, Pl.*Ly.*205e, etc. b. c. part., *catch, detect* one doing a thing, S. *Ant.*385,655; ἐπ' αὐτοφώρῳ ἑλεῖν E.*Ion*1214; φῶρα ἐπὶ κλοπῇ ἑλεῖν Pl.*Lg.*874b. 3. generally, *win, gain*, κῦδος Il.17.321; στεφάνους Pi.*P.*3.74, etc.; esp. in games, Ἴσθμι' ἑλὼν πύξ Simon.158; with double sense, *overcome* and *win*, ἑλέτην δίφρον τε καὶ ἀνέρε Il.11.328; ἕλεν Οἰνομάου βίαν παρθένον τε σύνευνον Pi.*O.*1.88, cf. S.*Tr.*353:—Pass., ἀγὼν ᾑρέθη the fight *was won*, S.*OC*1148. b. generally, *get, obtain*, Pl.*R.*359a, *Ti.*64b, etc. 4. as law-term, *convict*, τινά τινος Ar.*Nu.*591, Is.9.36, Aeschin.3.156; εἷλέ σ' ἡ Δίκη E.

Heracl.941, cf. *Supp.*608: c. part., αἱ. τινὰ κλέπτοντα *to convict* of theft, Ar.*Eq.*829, Pl.*Lg.*941d; ᾑρῆσθαι κλοπεύς (sc. ὤν) S.*Ant.*493, cf. 406. b. αἱ. δίκην, γραφήν *get a verdict for conviction*, Antipho 2.1.5, etc.; also ἑλεῖν τινα *obtain a conviction against* one, Is.7.13; ἑλεῖν τὰ διαμαρτυρηθέντα *convict* the evidence of falsehood, Isoc.18.15. c. abs., *get a conviction*, οἱ ἑλόντες, opp. οἱ ἑαλωκότες, D.21.11; δολίοις εἷλε Κύπρις λόγοις Aphrodite *won her cause*.., E.*Andr.*289, cf. Pl.*Lg.*762b, etc. d. of a thing or circumstances which *convict*, τοῦτ' ἔστιν ὃ ἐμὲ αἱρεῖ Id.*Ap.*28a. 5. ὁ λόγος αἱρέει reason or the reason of the thing *proves*, Hdt.2.33: c. acc. pers., reason *persuades* one, i.e. it *seems good* to one, Id.1.132, 7.41; ὡς ἐμὴ γνώμη αἱ. Hdt.2.43; ὅπῃ ὁ λόγος αἱ. βέλτιστ' ἂν ἔχειν Pl.*R.*604c, cf. *Lg.*663d: c. inf., *R.*440b; ὁ αἱρῶν λόγος Chrysipp.*Stoic.*3.92; αἱρεῖ alone, *proves*, Plu.2.651b. b. τὸ αἱροῦν the sum *due*, *PRyl.*167.25 (i A.D.); τὰ αἱροῦντα [τάλαντα] *PGrenf.*2.23.14 (ii B.C.), *PRyl.*88.19 (ii A.D.). III. *grasp with the mind, understand*, Pl.*Phlb.*17e, 20d, *Plt.*282d.

B. Med., with pf. ᾕρημαι (v. supr.), *take for oneself*, ἔγχος ἑλέσθαι *take one's* spear, Il.16.140, etc.; ἐκ γαίας λίθον A.*Fr.*199; δόρπον, δεῖπνον *take one's* supper, Il.7.370, 2.399; πιέειν δ' οὐκ εἶχεν ἑλέσθαι Od.11.584; Τρωσὶν.. ὅρκον ἑλ. *obtain* it from.., Il.22.119; and so in most senses of the Act., with the reflexive force added. II. *take to oneself, choose*, ἕταρον Il.10.235, cf. 9.139, Od.16.149, etc.; *prefer*, τι πρό τινος Hdt.1.87; τι ἀντί τινος X.*An.*1.7.3, D.2.15; τί τινος S.*Ph.*1101, cf. Theoc.11.49. b. c. inf., *prefer* to do, Hdt.1.11, etc.; ἑλέσθαι μᾶλλον τεθνάναι X.*Mem.*1.2.16, cf. Pl.*Ap.*38e; μᾶλλον ἂν ἕλοιτό μ' ἢ τοὺς πάντας Ἀργείους λαβεῖν S.*Ph.*47: without μᾶλλον, Pi.*N.*10.59, Lys.2.62. c. αἱ. εἰ.. *to be content* if.., *AP* 12.68 (Mel.). 2. αἱ. τά τινων *take* another's part, *join* their *party*, Th.3.63, etc.; αἱ. γνώμην *to adopt* an opinion, Hdt.4.137. 3. *choose by vote, elect* to an office, αἱ. τινὰ δικαστήν, στρατηγόν, etc., Id.1.96, Eup.117, etc.; τινὰς ἀριστίνδην· Lex ap.D.43.57; αἱ. τινὰ ἐπ' ἀρχήν Pl.*Men.*90b; αἱ. τινὰ ἄρχειν Id.*Ap.*28e, cf. Il.2.127.

C. Pass., *to be taken*, Hdt.1.185, 191, 9.102; more commonly ἁλίσκομαι. 2. v. supr. A. II. 3. II. Pass. to med. sense, *to be chosen*, in pf. ᾕρημαι A.*Ag.*1209, etc.; Ion. ἀραίρημαι Hdt.7.118, 172, 173, al.; στρατηγεῖν ᾑρημένος X.*Mem.*3.2.1; ἐπ' ἀρχῆς ᾑρῆσθαι ib.3.3.2; ἐπὶ τὴν τῶν παίδων ἀρχήν Pl.*Lg.*809a; τοῦ ἔτους.. ᾑρημένοι *elected* for the year.., *IGRom.*3.1422 (Bithyn.):—aor. ᾑρέθην is always so used, A.*Th.*505, Ar.*Av.*799, Th.7.31, etc.; pres. rarely, αἱροῦνται πρεσβευταὶ *are chosen*, Arist.*Pol.*1299a19, cf. And.4.16.

αἱρησιτείχης, ους, ὁ, *taker of cities*, name of play by Diphilus.

αἴρινος, η, ον, *of darnel*, ἄλευρον Dsc.2.112, Archig.ap.Orib.8.46.3; ἄλητα Aret.*CA*2.6.

αἰρο-λογέω, *clear of darnel*, in Pass., *IG*5(2).514.15 (Lycosura, ii B.C.). **-πινον**, τό, *sieve* (ἐν ᾧ πυροὶ σήθονται ὑπὲρ τοῦ τὰς αἴρας διελθεῖν), Ar.*Fr.*480.

ἄϊρος, ὁ, only in phrase Ἶρος ἄϊρος *Irus, unhappy Irus*, Od. 18.73.

αἴρω, v. ἀείρω.

αἰρώδης, ες, *apt to be infested with darnel*, πυρός Thphr.*HP*8.4.6.

Αἶσα, ἡ, like Μοῖρα, the divinity *who dispenses to every one his lot* or *destiny*, ἅσσα οἱ Αἶ. γιγνομένῳ ἐπένησε Il.20.127, cf. Od.7.197; Αἶ. φασγανουργός A.*Ch.*648 (lyr.). II. as Appellat., 1. *decree, dispensation* of a god, τετιμῆσθαι Διὸς αἴσῃ Il.9.608; ὑπὲρ Διὸς αἶσαν 17.321, cf. 6.487; δαίμονος αἶσα κακή Od.11.61; τεὰν κατ' αἶσαν thanks to the *destiny decreed* by thee, Pi.*N.*3.16; θεοῦ αἶσα E.*Andr.*1203 (lyr.):—κατ' αἶσαν *fitly, duly*, Il.10.445, etc.; κατ' αἶσαν, οὐδ' ὑπὲρ αἶσαν Il.6.333, cf. B.9.32; ἐν αἴσᾳ A.*Supp.*545 (lyr.); opp. παρ' αἶσαν Pi.*P.*8.13. 2. *one's lot, destiny*, οὐ γάρ οἱ τῇδ' αἶσα.. ὀλέσθαι, ἀλλ' ἔτι οἱ μοῖρ' ἐστί.. Od.5.113: c. inf., ἔτι γάρ νύ μοι αἶσα βιῶναι 14.359, cf. 13.306, al.; κακῇ αἴσῃ.. ἐλόμην by ill *luck*, Il.5.209; ἀσφαλεῖ σὺν αἴσᾳ B.12.66; τὸν αἶσ' ἄπλατος ἴσχει S.*Aj.*256 (lyr.), cf. *AP*7.624 (Diod.). 3. generally, *share in* a thing, ληΐδος, ἐλπίδος, αἶ., Od.5.40, 19.84; χθονός Pi.*P.*9.56; at a common meal (Argive), Hegesand.31; τῶ Διὸς τῶ Ϝοίνω αἶ. *Inscr.Cypr.*148; λαχεῖν αἶ. *IG*5(2).40 (Tegea); for the prov. ἐν καρὸς αἴσῃ v.s. κάρ.—Ep., Lyr., and Trag., but only in lyr. in S. and E.

αἴσακος, ὁ, *branch of myrtle* or *laurel*, handed by one to another at table as a challenge to sing, Plu.2.615b, Hsch. II. = ἐριθακός, *EM*38.49.

αἰσάλων, ωνος, ὁ, a kind of hawk, prob. *merlin, Falco aesalon*, Arist.*HA*609b8, Plin.*HN*10.205:—**αἰσάρων**, Hsch.

αἰσθ-άνομαι (cf. αἴσθομαι), Ion. 3 pl. opt. αἰσθανοίατο Ar.*Pax* 209: impf. ᾐσθανόμην: fut. αἰσθήσομαι S.*Ph.*75, etc.; later αἰσθανθήσομαι Lxx *Is.*49.26; αἰσθηθήσομαι ib.33.11: aor. 2 ᾐσθόμην: pf. ᾔσθημαι: later, aor. 1 ᾐσθησάμην Sch.Arat.418; ᾐσθήθην Lxx *Jb.*40.18: (cf. ἀΐω):—*perceive, apprehend by the senses*, Alcmaeon 1a, Hdt.3.87, Democr.11, etc.; τῇ ὄψει, τῇ ἀφῇ, τῇ ἀκοῇ Hp.*Off.*1; αἰ. τῇ ἀκοῇ, τῇ ὀσμῇ, Th.6.17, X.*Mem.*3.11.8; *see*, S.*Ph.*75, etc.; *hear*, βοήν Id.*Aj.*1318, cf. *Ph.*252; οὐκ εἶδον αὐτόν, ᾐσθόμην δ' ἔτ' ὄντα νιν ib.445; τινὸς ὑποστενούσης αἰ. Id.*El.*79; βοῆς E.*Hipp.*603, etc. 2. of mental perception, *perceive, understand*, τῇ γνώμῃ αἰσθέσθαι Hp.*Off.*1; τὸ πραχθέν Lys.9.4, cf. Th.3.36, etc.:—*hear, learn*, v. infr. II: abs., αἰσθάνει *you are right*, E.*Or.*752; ᾔσθημαι, in parenthesis, Id.*Hipp.*1403. II. Construct. in both senses, c. gen., *take notice of, have perception of*, τῶν κακῶν E.*Tr.*638 s. v. l.; rarely περί τινος Th.1.70; αἰ. ὑπό τινος *learn* from one, Id.5.2; διά τινος Pl.*Tht.*184e, al.: c. acc., S.*El.*89, *Ph.*252, E.*Hel.*653, 764, etc.:—freq. with part. agreeing with subject, αἰσθάνομαι κάμνων Th.2.51; αἰσθώμεθα γελοῖοι ὄντες Pl.*Thg.*122c; agreeing with object, τυράννους ἐκπεσόντας ᾐσθόμην A.*Pr.*957, cf. Th.1.47, etc.; ἤδη τινῶν ᾐσθόμην ἀχθομένων Lys.16.20, cf. Pl.*Ap.*22c; ᾐσθόμην τεχνωμένου Ar.*V.*176: less freq. c. acc. et inf., Th.6.59; αἰ. ὅτι.. Id.5.2, Pl.*Ap.*21e, etc.; ᾔσθετο ὅτι τὸ στράτευμα ἦν.. X.*An.*1.2.21; αἰ. ὡς.. ib.3.1.40, etc.; οὕνεκα.. S.*El.*1477:—abs., αἰσθανόμενος *having full possession of one's faculties*, τῇ ἡλικίᾳ Th.5.26; *sensible, of keen perception*, καὶ μετρίως αἰσθανομένῳ φανερόν X.*Mem.*4.1.1, cf. Th.1.71, Pl.*R.*360d.—The Pass. is supplied by αἴσθησιν παρέχω, cf. αἴσθησις I. III. *display feeling*, Arist.*Po.*1454b37. **-ημα**, ατος, τό, *object of sensation*, Arist.*APo.*99b37, *Metaph.*1010b32, Plot.4.3.25 and 29; τὸ νοεῖν γέγονεν αἰσθήμασι μόνοις Phld.*D.*1.13, etc. II. *sense* or *perception of* a thing, κακῶν E.*IA*1243. **-ησίη**, ἡ, = sq., Aret.*SD*1.1. **-ησις**, εως, ἡ, *sense-perception, sensation*, Philol.13, Archyt.1, Arist.*APo.*99b35; τοῦ σώματος ἡ αἴ. Hp.*VM*9; πρὸς αἴσθησιν *perceptibly*, Ptol.*Alm.*1.10, etc.: in pl., *the senses*, Democr.9, al.; δι' ἑπτὰ σχημάτων αἱ αἰ. Hp.*Vict.*1.23, cf. Pl.*Tht.*156b, etc.: in sg. of the several senses, ἡ τοῦ ὁρᾶν αἴ. Id.*R.*507e; ἀπ' ὄψεως ἤ τινος ἄλλης αἰ. Id.*Phlb.*39b; *organ* or *seat of sensation*, X.*Mem.*1.4.6; πάσας τὰς αἰ. ἐν τῇ κεφαλῇ εἶναι Arist.*Fr.*95, cf. *Pr.*958b16; αἴ. πημάτων *perception, sense of*.., E.*El.*290; esp. of *pain*, Vett.Val.113.10, al.; also of the mind, *perception, knowledge* of a thing, ἐν αἰ. γενέσθαι τινός Plu.*Luc.*11, etc.; αἴ. ἔχειν τινός, = αἰσθάνεσθαί τινος, have *a perception of* a thing, Pl.*Ap.*40c; περὶ ὑμῶν *Tht.*192b; πᾶσαν αἴσθησιν αἰσθάνεσθαι *Phdr.*240d; λαμβάνειν Isoc.1.47; ἐν αἰ. εἶναι Plot.4.7.15:—also of things, αἴσθησιν ἔχειν give *a perception*, i.e. become *perceptible*, serving as Pass. to αἰσθάνομαι, Th.2.61; more freq. αἴσθησιν παρέχειν Id.3.22, X.*An.*4.6.13, etc.; αἴ. ποιῆσαί τινι Antipho 5.44, cf. D.10.7; αἴ. παρέχειν τινός furnish *the means of observing*, Th.2.50; αἴ. ἐγένετο περί τινος D.48.16. II. in object. sense, *impressions of sense*, Arist.*Metaph.*980a22; *stage-effects*, *Po.*1454b16; αἰσθήσεις θεῶν *visible appearances* of the gods, Pl.*Phd.*111b. 2. *display of feeling*, Arist.*Rh.*1386a32 (v.l.). 3. in hunting, *scent*, X.*Cyn.*3.5 (pl.).—Confined to Prose in early writers, exc. E. l.c., Antiph.196.5. **-ητήριον**, τό, *organ of sense*, Hp.*Vict.*4.86, Arist.*de An.*421b32, etc.; τὰ αἰ., opp. ἡ διάνοια, Epicur.*Ep.*1p.12U.; ἐπὰν ᾖ καθαρὰ τἀσθητήρια Macho 2; τὰ αἰ. *the faculties*, Lxx 4*Ma.*2.22, cf. *Ep.Heb.*5.14. **-ητής**, οῦ, ὁ, *one who perceives*, Pl.*Tht.*160d. **-ητικός**, ή, όν, *of* or *for sense-perception, sensitive, perceptive*, Pl.*Ti.*67a, etc.; ζῷα -κώτερα Thphr.*Sens.*29; αἰ. ἀναθυμίασις, of the soul, Zeno *Stoic.*1.39; τὸ αἰ. [τῆς ψυχῆς] Diog.Oen.*Fr.*39; ζωὴ αἰ. Arist.*EN*1098a2; *quick*, γραῦς Alex.65. Adv. αἰσθητικῶς, ἔχειν to be *quick of perception*, Arist.*EE*1230b37; κινεῖσθαι Arr.*Epict.*1.14.7, S.E.*M.*7.356; αἰ. ἔχειν ἑαυτοῦ, c. part., to be *conscious* of oneself doing, Ael.*VH*14.23; αἰ. γιγνώσκειν Procl.*in Prm.*p.754S. II. of things, *perceptible*, Plu.2.90b. **-ητός**, ή, όν, and ός, όν Pl.*Men.*76d; *sensible, perceptible*, opp. νοητός, Id.*Plt.*285e, etc.; τὸ αἰ. *object of sensation* or *perception*, Id.*Ti.*37b, Arist. *de An.*431b22, cf. *Metaph.*999b4. Adv. -τῶς Id.*Col.*793b27, Posidon.95, Plu.2.953c; in act. sense, Ascl.*in Metaph.*277.13.

αἴσθομαι, sometimes in good Mss. as v.l. for αἰσθάνομαι, as Th.5.26, Isoc.3.5, Pl.*R.*608a.

ἀΐσθω, (ἄημι) Ep. Verb, *breathe out*, θυμὸν ἄϊσθε *he was giving up* the ghost, Il.20.403, cf. 16.468.

αἰσιμία, ἡ, *due apportionment*, αἰσιμίαις πλούτου A.*Eu.*996.

αἰσιμνάτας, v. αἰσυμνήτης.

αἴσιμος, ον, also η, ον Od.23.14: (αἶσα):—Ep. Adj. *appointed by the will of the gods, destined*, αἴ. ἦμαρ the *fatal* day of death, Il.8.72, Bacis ap.Hdt.9.43, etc.; αἴσιμόν ἐστι Il.21.291. II. *agreeable to the decree of fate, meet, fitting*, αἴσιμα εἰπεῖν Od.22.46; αἴσιμα εἰδώς, opp. αἴσυλα ῥέζειν, 2.231; φρένας αἰσίμη *right*-minded, 23.14; αἴσιμα πίνειν to drink *in decent measure*, 21.294.

αἰσιμῶ, *expend*, Suid. **αἰσ⟨ιμ⟩ώματα**, *expenses*, Hsch.

αἰσιομήτης, ὁ, *of right counsel*, Zonar.

αἰσιόομαι, Med., *take as a good omen, think lucky*, Plu.2.774c, App.*BC*5.97: c. inf., *Mith.*20.

αἰσιοποιέω, *secundo*, and Pass., *prosperabitur*, Gloss.

αἴσιος, ον, also α, ον Pi.*N.*9.18, E.*Ion*421: (αἶσα):—poet. Adj. *auspicious, opportune*, ὁδοιπόρος Il.24.376, cf. A.*Ag.*104 (lyr.), S.*OC*34; ἡμέρα E. l. c.; αἴ. ἐν φιλότητι *IG*14.2068.9:—freq. of omens, αἰσία ὄρνις Pi. l. c., cf. S.*OT*52; ἀετός X.*Cyr.*2.4.19; ἄνεμος App.*Mith.*29; ὥρα Id.*Syr.*58 (Comp.). Adv. -ίως E.*Ion*410, Timae.114. II. *meet, right*, αἴσιος ὁλκή, Lat. *justum pondus*, Nic.*Th.*93; αἴ. ἐμβολή Just.*Edict.*13.4.1.

αἶσις, ἡ, = κεῦσις, Hdn.*Epim.*37. **ἀϊσόμενος**· φραξάμενος, Hsch. **ἀΐσονες**· φραγμοί, Id.

ἄϊσος, ον, = ἄνισος, *unlike, unequal*, Pi.*I.*7(6).43.

ἀΐσσω, Hom., Hdt.; in Pi. and Trag. contr. **ᾄσσω**; Att. **ᾄττω**, or **ἄττω** (without ι subscr.) in Mss. of Pl., etc.: impf. ἤϊσσον Il.18.506, Ion. ἀΐσσεσκον (παρ-) A.R.2.276, Att. ᾖσσον A.*Pr.*676, E.*Ph.*1382: fut. ἀΐξω (ὑπ-) Il.21.126, Att. ᾄξω E.*Hec.*1106 (lyr.), Ar.*Nu.*1299: aor. ἤϊξα Hom., B.12.144, (δι-) Hdt.4.134; Dor. ᾆξα B.9.23 (prob.); Att. and Trag. ᾖξα A.*Pr.*837, S.*OC*890, etc., part. ᾄξαντες Is.4.10; Ion. ἀΐξασκον Il.23.369:—**Med.**, aor. ἀΐξασθαι Il.22.195:—**Pass.**, Hom.: aor. ἠΐχθην, ἀΐχθην Il. (v. infr.).—Trag. use the uncontr. forms in lyr., S.*OC*1499, *Tr.*843, E.*Tr.*156, 1086, *Supp.*962; once in trim., E.*Hec.*31. Poet., chiefly Ep., Verb, rarely found in Prose:—of rapid motion, *shoot, dart, glance*, as light, αὐγὴ Il.18.212, etc.; νόος 15.80; διά μου κεφαλῆς ᾄσσουσ' ὀδύναι E.*Hipp.*

1351:—of one *darting upon* his enemy, ἀΐσσειν ἔγχει, φασγάνῳ, ἵπποις, Il.11.484, 5.81, 17.460, etc.; τοῖσιν (sc. σκήπτροισιν) 18.506; of the *rapid flight* of birds, 23.868, etc.; ἤϊξεν πέτεσθαι 21.247; of ghosts *gliding about*, τοὶ δὲ σκιαὶ ἀΐσσουσιν Od.10.495; of javelins, Il. 5.657; of a tree, *shoot up*, Pi.*N*.8.40; of veins, etc., in the body, Hp.*Epid*.2.4.1, cf. *Morb*.4.54: c. acc. cogn., ἦξαν δράμημα E.*Ph*. 1379; κέλευθον A.*Pr*.837: once in aor. Med., ἀντίον ἀΐξασθαι Il.22. 195: also in Pass., [ἔγχος] ὦσεν..ἐτώσιον ἀϊχθῆναι Il.5.854; ἐς οὐρανὸν ἀϊχθήτην 24.97; ἐκ χειρῶν ἡνία ἠΐχθησαν *slipped* from his hands, 16.404; ἀμφὶ δὲ χαῖται ὤμοις ἀΐσσονται 6.510; κόμη δι' αὔρας..ᾄσσεται S.*OC*1261; *shoot forth*, of limbs, Emp.29:—Act., *to be driven*, πνευμάτων ὑπὸ δυσχίμων ἀΐσσω E.*Supp*.962. 2. later, *turn eagerly to* a thing, *be eager after*, εἴς τι Id.*Ion* 328; ἐπὶ τά τινος ᾄξαντες *making onslaught on* his property, Is.4.10; πρὸς τὰ πολιτικὰ ᾄ. Pl.*Alc*.1.118b, cf. Phld. *Mus*.p.12K., Plu.2.87d: c. inf., εἰπεῖν Pl.*Lg*.709a. II. trans., αὔραν.. ἀΐσσων *putting* the air *in motion* (with a fan), E.*Or*.1430; ἦξεν χέρα S.*Aj*.40. [ᾱ in Hom., save in the compd. ὑπαΐξει Il.21. 126, cf. A.R.3.1302; ᾰ Lyr., Trag. (exc. E.*Tr*.1086), Arat.334.]

ἀϊστί, Adv. of sq., Suid.

ἄϊστος, ον, (ἰδεῖν) :—poet. Adj. *unseen*, καί κέ μ' ἄ. ἀπ' αἰθέρος ἔμβαλε πόντῳ Il.14.258; κεῖνον μὲν ἄ. ἐποίησαν περὶ πάντων Od.1.235; οἴχετ' ἄ., ἄπυστος ib.242; ὤλετ' ἄκλαυτος, ἄϊστος A.*Eu*.565; βωμοὶ δ' ἄϊστοι Id.*Pers*.811; ἐν ἀΐστοις τελέθων Id.*Ag*.466; ἀποτρέψειεν ἄϊστον ὕβριν (prolept.) Id.*Supp*.881; ἄ. ἀείραο A.R.4.746. Adv. ἀΐστως, θυμὸν ὄλεσσαν *utterly*, Man.3.263, cf. 28. II. Act., *unconscious of*, ἄτας ἐμᾶς ἄϊστος E.*Tr*.1314, cf. 1321.

ἀϊστοσύνη, ἡ, = ἀπώλεια, *EM*43.21; = *coniventia*, Gloss.

ἀϊστόω: fut. -ώσω Hdt.3.69: aor. ἠΐστωσα ib.127, contr. ἠστ- (v. infr.):—Med., aor. ἀϊστώσαντο Orph.*A*.473:—poet. Verb, not in Il., used by Hdt., and once in Pl., *make unseen, make away with, destroy*, ὥς ἔμ' ἀϊστώσειαν Od.20.79; πῦρ..ἀΐστωσεν ὕλαν Pi.*P*.3.37; ἀϊστώσας γένος τὸ πᾶν A.*Pr*.234, cf. Pl.*Prt*.321a; πατρίδ' ἤστωσας δόρει S.*Aj*.515; κόρον ἀϊστώσας πυρί Id.*Fr*.536; τὰ πρὶν δὲ πελώρια ..ἀϊστοῖ A.*Pr*.151; ἀϊστώσει μιν Hdt.3.69; δύο ἡμέων ἠΐστωσε ib. 127:—Pass., οἱ δ' ἅμ' ἀϊστώθησαν ἀολλέες Od.10.259.

ἀΐστωρ, ορος, ὁ, ἡ, *unknowing, unaware*, ἀΐστωρ ὢν αὐτός Pl.*Lg*. 845b: c. gen., μάχης E.*Andr*.682.

αἰσωτήριος, ον, *destructive*, Lyc.71.

αἰσῠητήρ, ῆρος, ὁ, v.l. for αἰσυμνητήρ (q.v.), Il.24.347, expl. as ἐντρεχής, νεανίας, or νομεύς (Nic.); cf. pr. n. Αἰσυήτης in Il.

αἰσῠλοεργός, όν, = αἴσυλα ῥέζων, *ill-doing*, Max.368; read by Aristarch. in Il.5.403 for ὀβριμοεργός, cf. Clem.Al.*Protr*.2.33.

αἴσῠλος, ον, *unseemly, evil, godless*, αἴσυλα ῥέζων Il.5.403 (cf. αἴσιμος); μυθήσασθαι 20.202; οἶδε *h.Merc*.164, cf. *AP*7.624 (Diod.).

αἰσυμν-άω, Dor. **αἰσιμνάω**, *rule over*, αἰσυμνᾷ χθονός E.*Med*.19; *preside over*, μολπῶν *SIG*57.1 (Miletus); generally, *rule*, οὐ δίκαια αἰ. Call.*Iamb*.1.162. 2. *hold office of* αἰσυμνήτης (q.v.), *GDI*3053 (Chalcedon), 5632 (Teos); at Naxos, *IG*12(9).223 (Eretria, iii B.C.). **-ητεία**, ἡ, *office of* αἰσυμνήτης II.1, = αἱρετὴ τυραννίς, Arist. *Pol*.1285b25, cf. D.L.1.100. **-ητήρ**, ῆρος, ὁ, *ruler, prince*, κούρῳ αἰ. Il.24.347 (v.l.). **-ήτης**, ου, ὁ, Dor. **αἰσιμνάτας**, *judge, umpire* at games, Od.8.258. 2. *overseer, bailiff*, Theoc.25.48. II. *ruler chosen* by the people, *elective monarch*, Arist.*Pol*.1285a31, 1295a 14, Arg.S.*OT*; compared with the Roman *dictator*, D.H.5.73. 2. title of magistrates in Greek cities, *IG*7.15 (Megara), *GDI*3045 (Chalcedon). 3. epith. of Dionysus in Achaia, Paus.7.21.6:— fem. **αἰσυμνῆτις**, ιδος, Suid. **-ητύς**, ύος, ἡ, *office of* αἰσυμνήτης, *Milet*.7.17. **-ιον**, τό, *council-chamber* at Megara, Paus.1.43.3.

αἰσχεο-κερδής, ές, = αἰσχροκερδής, Man.4.314; **-μυθος**, ον, **-ρήμων**, ονος, and **-φημος**, ον, *talking shameful things*, ib.57,445,592.

αἶσχος, εος, τό, *shame, disgrace*, Hom. (freq. in pl., as Il.3.242), Hes.*Op*.211, Sol.3, A.*Supp*.1008, etc. 2. in pl., *disgraceful deeds*, Od.1.229. II. *ugliness, deformity*, of mind or body, Pl.*Smp*. 201a, X.*Cyr*.2.2.29, etc.; αἶ. περὶ τὴν κάτηξιν Hp.*Art*.14; αἶ. ὀνόματος Arist.*Rh*.1405b8.

αἰσχόω, = αἰσχύνω, censured by Hdn.Gr.2.933, citing Eup.142; dub. in *Epigr.Gr*.336.

αἰσχρήμων, ον, gen. ονος, *shameful, base*, *APl*.1.15* (dub.); ἀσχήμων Porson.

αἰσχρό-γελως, ωτος, ὁ, ἡ, *shamefully ridiculous*, Man.4.283. **-διδάκτης**, ου, ὁ, *teacher of shameful things*, Man.4.307. **-επέω**, *use foul language*, Ephipp.23: c. acc., τὰς τέχνας Hp.*de Arte*1. **-επής**, ές, *foul-mouthed*, prob. in Ael.*Fr*.80. **-εργέω**, v. αἰσχρουργέω. **-κέρδεια**, ἡ, *sordid love of gain, base covetousness*, Hp.*Decent*.2, S.*Ant*. 1056, Lys.12.19, Pl.*Lg*.754e, Thphr.*Char*.30. **-κερδέω**, *to be sordid, greedy of gain*, Hyp.*Fr*.223. **-κερδής**, ές, *sordidly greedy of gain*, Hdt.1.187, E.*Andr*.451, And.4.32 (Sup.), cf. Pl.*R*.408c, Arist.*EN*1122a8, etc. Adv. **-δῶς** 1*Ep.Pet*.5.2. **-κερδία**, = αἰσχροκέρδεια, Diph.99, cf. Hdn.Gr.2.453. **-λογέω**, = αἰσχροεπέω, Pl. *R*.395e, Bryson ap.Arist.*Rh*.1405b10. **-λογία**, ἡ, *foul language, obscenity*, X.*Lac*.5.6, Arist.*EN*1128a23. 2. *abuse*, Plb.8.11.8, cf. *POxy*.410.77, *Ep.Col*.3.8, Phld.*Rh*.1.176S., etc. **-λόγος**, ον, *foul-mouthed*, and Adv. **-γως**, Poll.6.123, 8.80,81. **-λοιχός**, ὁ, *fellator*, Eust.518.52, Phot. s.v. λαπτώμενος. **-μητις**, ιος, ὁ, ἡ, *fostering* or *forming base designs*, A.*Ag*.222 (lyr.). **-μῡθέω**, = αἰσχροεπέω, of a delirious woman, Hp.*Epid*.3.17.ια'. **-πᾰθής**, ές, *submitting to foul usage*, Ph.2.268. **-ποιέω**, *act filthily*, Ath.8.342c; = λεσβιάζω, Sch.Ar.*Ra*.1308. II. trans., *degrade, dishonour*, τὰς τέχνας v.l. in Hp.*de Arte*1. **-ποιΐα**, ἡ, euphem. for *fellatio*, Sch.Ar.*Nub*.296. **-ποιός**, όν, *doing foully*, E.*Med*.1346; euphem. for *fellator*, Macho ap.Ath.13.582d. **-πρᾱγέω**, = αἰσχροποιέω, Arist.*EN*1120a15. **-πρεπής**, ές, *of hideous appearance*, Sch.E. *Hipp*.75; f.l. for -επής, Ael.*Fr*.80. **-πρόσωπος**, ον, *of hideous countenance*, Suid. s.v. Φιλοκλῆς. **-ρρημονέω**, = αἰσχροεπέω, Charond. ap.Stob.4.2.24. **-ρρημοσύνη**, ἡ, = αἰσχρολογία, D.*Ep*.4.11, Phld. *Rh*.1.175S., Oenom.ap.Eus.*PE*5.32 (pl.). **-ρρήμων**, ον, = αἰσχρολόγος, Poll.8.80. Adv. -μόνως ib.81.

αἰσχρός, ά, όν, also ός, όν *APl*.4.151: (αἶσχος):—in Hom., *causing shame, dishonouring, reproachful*, νείκεσσεν..αἰσχροῖς ἐπέεσσιν Il.3. 38, etc. Adv. αἰσχρῶς, ἐνένισπεν 23.473. II. opp. καλός: 1. of outward appearance, *ugly, ill-favoured*, of Thersites, Il.2.216, cf. *h.Ap*.197, Hdt.1.196 (Comp.), etc.; *deformed*, Hp.*Art*.14 (Sup.); αἰσχρῶς χωλός *with an ugly* lameness, ib.63: but commonly, 2. in moral sense, *shameful, base*, Hdt.3.155, A.*Th*.685, etc.; αἰσχροῖς γὰρ αἰσχρὰ πράγματ' ἐκδιδάσκεται S.*El*.621; αἰσχρόν [ἐστι], c. inf., Il.2.298, S.*Aj*.473, etc.; αἰσχρόν, εἰ πύθοιτό τις ib.1159; ἐν αἰσχρῷ θέσθαι τι E.*Hec*.806; ἐπ' αἰσχροῖς *on the ground of base actions*, S. *Fr*.188, E.*Hipp*.511:—τὸ αἰ. as Subst., *dishonour*, S.*Ph*.476; τὸ ἐμὸν αἰ. my *disgrace*, And.2.9; τὸ καλὸν καὶ τὸ αἰ. virtue and *vice*, Arist.*Rh*. 1366a24, etc. Adv., *shamefully*, S.*El*.989, Pl.*Smp*.183d, etc.: Sup. αἴσχιστα A.*Pr*.959, S.*OT*367. 3. *ill-suited*, αἰ. ὁ καιρός D.18.178; αἰ. πρός τι *awkward* at it, X.*Mem*.3.8.7; αἰσχρὸν καὶ ἄτεχνον Hp. *Fract*.30. III. Regul. Comp. and Sup. -ότερος, -ότατος are late, Phld.*Rh*.2.58S. (prob.), Ath.13.587b: elsewh. αἰσχίων, αἴσχιστος (formed from a Root **αἰσχο**-), Il.21.437, 2.216; double Sup. αἰσχιστότατος Olymp.*in Alc*.p.124C. Adv., Sup. αἰσχίστως Mnasalc.ap. Ath.4.163a, Man.1.21.

αἰσχροσεμνία, ἡ, *avoidance of obscenity*, Aus.*Idyll*.13.

αἰσχρότης, ητος, ἡ, *ugliness, deformity*, Pl.*Grg*.525a. II. *filthy conduct*, *Ep.Eph*.5.4; euphem. for *fellatio*, Sch.Ar.*Ra*.1308:—

αἰσχροσύνη, ἡ, Tz.*H*.11.229.

αἰσχρ-ουργέω, contr. for αἰσχροεργέω, *act obscenely*, esp. = *masturbari*, S.E.*P*.3.206:—Pass., τὰ -ούμενα D.L.*Prooem*.5. **-ουργία**, ἡ, *shameless conduct*, E.*Ba*.1062: pl., D.Chr.4.102. II. *obscenity*, Aeschin.2.99, cf. Plu.2.1044b. **-ουργός**, όν, *obscene*, Gal.12.249. Adv., Sup., D.C.79.3.

Αἰσχύλειος, α, ον, *of* or *like Aeschylus*, Sch.Il.19.87.

αἰσχυνετάι (-υντάδην Meinek.)· κατ' αἰσχύνην, Hsch.

αἰσχύν-η [ῡ], ἡ, *shame, dishonour*, ἐς αἰσχύνην φέρει Hdt.1.10, cf. 3.133; αἰσχύνην φέρει, ἔχει, S.*Tr*.66, E.*Andr*.244, etc.; αἰ. περιίσταταί με, συμβαίνει μοι, D.3.8, 18.85; αἰσχύνῃ πίπτειν S.*Tr*.597; περιπίπτειν X.*HG*7.3.9; αἰσχύνην περιάπτειν τῇ πόλει Pl.*Ap*.35a; αἰ. προσβάλλειν τινί Id.*Lg*.878c; ἐν αἰ. ποιεῖν τὴν πόλιν D.18.136; ἡ τῶν πραγμάτων αἰ. 1.27. 2. αἰ. γυναικῶν *dishonouring* of women, Isoc.4.114 (pl.), 12.259 (pl.); γράφεσθαί τινα γένους αἰσχύνης for *dishonour done* to his race, Pl.*Lg*.919e. 3. concrete, of a person, αἰ. φίλοις, πάτρᾳ, Thgn.1272, A.*Pers*.774; ἄνθρωπος αἰ. τῆς πόλεως γεγονώς Aeschin.3.241; of a decree, ib.105. II. *shame for* an ill deed, personified in A.*Th*.409; Αἰσχύνην οὐ νομίσασα θεόν *AP*7.450 (Diosc.). 2. like αἰδώς, *sense of shame, honour*, πᾶσαν αἰ. ἀφεὶς S.*Ph*.120; ἡ γὰρ αἰ. ⟨πάρος⟩ τοῦ ζῆν..νομίζεται E.*Heracl*. 200; δι' αἰσχύνης ἔχειν τι *to be ashamed of*, Id.*IT*683; αἰσχύνην ἔχειν τινός *for* a thing, S.*El*.616; αἰ. ἐπί τινι Pl.*Smp*.178d; ὑπέρ τινος D.4.10; joined with δέος, S.*Aj*.1079; with ἔλεος and αἰδώς, Antipho 1.27:—rare in pl., πτήσσουσαν αἰσχύνῃσιν S.*Fr*.659.9; ἐν αἰσχύναις ἔχω I hold it *a shameful thing*, E.*Supp*.164. III. later = αἰδοῖον, Sch.Ar.*Eq*.365; cf. τὴν τοῦ σώματος αἰ. Alcid.ap.Arist.*Rh*. 1406a29. **-ομένη**, ἡ, *sensitive plant, Mimosa asperata*, Apollod. ap.Plin.*HN*24.167. **-ομένως**, Adv. *modestly, shamefacedly*, D.H. 7.50. **-τέον**, *one must be ashamed*, X.*Cyr*.4.2.40. **-τηλία**, ἡ, *bashfulness*, Plu.2.66c. **-τηλός**, ή, όν, *bashful, modest*, Pl.*Chrm*. 160e, Arist.*EN*1128b20; τὸ αἰ. *modesty*, Pl.*Chrm*.158c. Adv. -λῶς Id.*Lg*.665e. II. of things, *shameful*, Arist.*Rh*.1384b18. **-τήρ**, ῆρος, ὁ, *dishonourer*, of Aegisthus, A.*Ch*.998. **-τηρός**, ά, όν, = αἰσχυντηλός, in Comp., Pl.*Grg*.487b. **-τικός**, ή, όν, *provocative of shame*, Arist.*Rh*.1384a9. **-τός**, ή, όν, *shameful*, Ps.-Phoc. 189.

αἰσχύνω [ῡ]: Ion. impf. αἰσχύνεσκε (κατ-) Q.S.14.531: fut. -ῠνῶ E. *Hipp*.719, Ion. -υνέω Hdt.9.53: aor. ᾔσχῡνα Il.23.571, Lys.1.4, etc.: pf. ᾔσχυγκα D.C.58.16:—Pass., fut. αἰσχῠνοῦμαι A.*Ag*.856, Ar.*Fr*. 200, Pl.*Ti*.49d, etc., rarely αἰσχυνθήσομαι (v. sub fin.): aor. ᾐσχύνθην Hdt. and Att., poet. inf. αἰσχυνθήμεν Pi.*N*.9.27: pf. ᾔσχυμμαι (v.infr.B.1):—*make ugly, disfigure*, πρόσωπον, κόμην, Il.18.24,27, cf. S.*Ant*.529; αἰ. τὸν ἵππον *give* the horse *a bad form*, X.*Eq*.1.12. 2. mostly in moral sense, *dishonour, tarnish*, μηδὲ γένος πατέρων αἰσχυνέμεν Il.6.209, cf. 23.571; τὴν Σπάρτην Hdt.9.53; ξενίαν τράπεζαν A.*Ag*.401; τοὺς πρὸς αἵματος S.*Aj*.1305; τοὺς πατέρας Pl.*Mx*. 246d. b. esp. *dishonour* a woman, E.*El*.44, cf. Plu.*Marc*.19, etc.; εὐνὴν A.*Ag*.1626; εἰς τὸ σῶμα αἰ. Arist.*Pol*.1311b7; abs., *Foed. Delph.Pell*.2A12. 3. *disdain*, ἐπιχώρια Pi.*P*.3.22.

B. Pass., *to be dishonoured*, νέκυς ᾐσχυμμένος, of Patroclus, Il. 18.180. II. *to be ashamed, feel shame*, abs., Od.7.305, 18.12, Hdt.1.10, E.*Hipp*.1291. 2. more commonly, *to be ashamed at* a thing, c. acc. rei, αἰσχυνόμενοι φάτιν ἀνδρῶν Od.21.323; τὴν δυσγένειαν τὴν ἐμὴν αἰ. S.*OT*1079: c. dat. rei, Ar.*Nu*.992, Lys.3.9, D.4. 42, etc.; αἰ. ἐπί τινι X.*Mem*.2.2.8; ἔν τινι Th.2.43; ὑπέρ τινος Lys.14. 39; περί τινος 33.6, etc. b. c. part., *to be ashamed at* doing a thing (which one does), A.*Pr*.642 (v.l.), S.*Ant*.540, Ar.*Fr*.200, Pl.*Grg*.

494e, etc. c. c. inf., *to be ashamed to* do a thing (and therefore not to do it), Hdt.1.82, A.*Ag.*856, *Ch.*917, Pl.*R.*414e, *Phdr.*257d, etc.; though this condition must not be pressed absolutely, cf. *Ap.* 22b. d. foll. by relat. clause, αἰσχύνεσθαι εἰ.. *to be ashamed* that.., S.*El.*254, And.4.42; ἐάν.. X.*Oec.*21.4; μή.. Pl.*Tht.*183e, cf. Macho ap.Ath.13.579f; ὅτι.. Lys.2.23. 3. c. acc. pers., *to feel shame before* one, E.*Ion*934,1074, Pherecr.23.6, Pl.*Smp.*216b; τοὺς γέροντας (at Sparta) Aeschin.1.180; ὅστις γὰρ αὐτὸς αὑτὸν οὐκ αἰσχύνεται, πῶς τόν γε μηδὲν εἰδότ' αἰσχυνθήσεται; Philem.229, cf. Gal. 5.26: c. acc. et inf., E.*Hel.*415; ᾐσχύνθημεν θεοὺς.. προδοῦναι αὐτόν X.*An.*2.3.22; αἰσχύνομαι ὑμᾶς λέγειν D.40.48; αἰ. πρός τινα Arist.*Rh.* 1383b12.

Αἰσώπειος, α, ον, *of Aesop*, λόγοι D.L.5.80, Theon *Prog.*1, etc.; ἀθύρματα Him.*Or.*20.1; κύων Plu.2.157b; αἷμα, prov. of an indelible stain, Zen.1.47.

Αἰσωποποίητος, ον, *made by Aesop*, Quint.*Inst.*5.11 (prob.).

ἀΐτας [ῑ], ὁ, Dor. word for *a beloved youth*, answering to εἰσπνήλας or εἴσπνηλος (the lover), Ar.*Fr.*738 (fort. Eratosth.), Theoc.12.14 (αἴτης, said to be a Thessalian word), cj. in 23.63; generally, *lover*, Χρύσας (sc. Ἀθανᾶς) δ' ἀΐτας Dosiad.*Ara* 5, cf. Lyc.461:—fem. **ἀΐτις** Hdn.Gr.1.105, 2.296, cf. Alcm.125.

αἴτε, Dor. and Aeol. for εἴτε.

αἰτ-έω (Aeol. **αἴτημι** Pi.*Fr.*155, Theoc.28.5), Ion. impf. αἴτεον Hdt.: fut. αἰτήσω: aor. ᾔτησα: pf. ᾔτηκα 1*Ep.Jo.*5.15: plpf. ᾐτήκει Arr.*An.*6.15.5: pf. Pass. ᾔτημαι, etc.:—*ask, beg*, abs., Od.18.49, A.*Supp.*341. 2. mostly c. acc. rei, *ask for, demand*, Il.5.358, Od.17.365, etc.; ὁδὸν αἰ. *ask leave* to depart, Od.10.17; αἰ. τινί τι *to ask* something for one, 20.74, Hdt.5.17: c. acc. pers. et rei, *ask* a person *for* a thing, Il.22.295, Od.2.387, Hdt.3.1, etc.; δίκας αἰ. τινὰ φόνου *to demand* satisfaction from one for.., Hdt.8.114; αἰ. τι πρός τινος Thgn.556; παρά τινος X.*An.*1.3.16; τὰ αἰτήματα ἃ ᾐτήκαμεν παρ' αὐτοῦ 1*Ep.Jo.*5.15. 3. c. acc. pers. et inf., *ask* one *to* do, Od.3.173, S.*OC*1334, *Ant.*65, etc.; αἰ. παρά τινος δοῦναι Pl.*Erx.* 398e. 4. c. acc. only, *beg of*, D.L.6.49. 5. in Logic, *postulate, assume*, Arist.*APr.*41b9 (Pass.), *Top.*163a6, etc. II. Med., *ask for one's own use, claim*, Λύσανδρον ἄρχοντα Lys.12.59; freq. almost = the Act., and with the same construct., first in Hdt.1.90 (παρ-), 9. 34, A.*Pr.*822, etc.; αἰτεῖσθαί τινα ὅπως.. Antipho 1.12 codd.; πάλαισμα μήποτε λῦσαι θεὸν αἰτοῦμαι S.*OT*880; freq. abs. in part., αἰτουμένῳ μοι δὸς A.*Ch.*480, cf. 2, *Th.*260, S.*Ph.*63; αἰτουμένη που τεύξεται Id.*Ant.*778; αἰτησάμενος ἐχρήσατο Lys.19.27; οὐ πῦρ γὰρ αἰτῶν, οὐδὲ λοπάδ' αἰτούμενος Men.476; αἰτεῖσθαι ὑπέρ τινος *to beg* for one, Lys. 14.22. III. Pass., of persons, *have a thing begged of* one, αἰτηθέντες χρήματα Hdt.8.111, cf. Th.2.97, etc.; αἰτεύμενος Theoc.14.63: c. inf., *to be asked to* do a thing, Pi.*I.*8(7).5. 2. of things, *to be asked*, τὸ αἰτεόμενον Hdt.8.112; ἵπποι ᾐτημένοι *borrowed* horses, Lys. 24.12. **-ημα**, ατος, τό, *request, demand*, Pl.*R.*566b, Lxx 1*Ki.*1.17, *Ev.Luc.*23.24, *PFlor.*296.16 (vi A.D.). II. in Logic and Math., *postulate, assumption*, Arist.*APo.*76b23, Plu.*Demetr.*3, Luc.*Herm.* 74. **-ηματικός**, ή, όν, *disposed to ask*, Artem.4.2. **-ηματώδης**, ες, *question-begging*, Plu.2.694f. **-ήσιμος**, ον, *obtained by petition*, *Ath.Mitt.*44.25 (Samos, iii B.C.). **-ησις**, εως, ἡ, *request, demand*, Hdt.7.32, Antipho 5.4, *POxy.*1024.20 (ii A.D.); ἡ ἐρώτησις ἀποκρίσεώς ἐστιν αἴ. Arist.*Int.*20b22. **-ητέον**, verb. Adj. *one must ask*, X.*Eq.Mag.*5.11. **-ητής**, οῦ, ὁ, *one that asks, petitioner*, *POxy.* 788 (i B.C.), D.C.*Fr.*66.2. **-ητικός**, ή, όν, *fond of asking*, τινός Arist.*EN*1120a33. Adv. αἰτητικῶς, ἔχειν πρός τινα D.L.6.31. **-ητός**, όν, verb. Adj. *asked for*, ἀρχὴν δωρητόν, οὐκ αἰτητόν freely given, not *asked for*, S.*OT*384.

αἰτί-α, ἡ, *responsibility*, mostly in bad sense, *guilt, blame*, or the imputation thereof, i.e. *accusation*, first in Pi.*O.*1.35 and Hdt., v. infr. (Hom. uses αἴτιος):—Phrases: αἰτίαν ἔχειν bear *responsibility for*, τινός A.*Eu.*579, S.*Ant.*1312; but usu. *to be accused*, τινός *of* a crime, φόνου Hdt.5.70: c. inf., Ar.*V.*506; foll. by ὡς.., Pl.*Ap.*38c; by ὡς c. part., Id.*Phdr.*249d; ὑπό τινος *by* some one, A.*Eu.*99, Pl. *R.*565b; reversely, αἰτία ἔχει τινά Hdt.5.70,71; αἰ. φεύγειν τινός S.*Ph.*1404; ἐν αἰτίᾳ εἶναι or γίγνεσθαι, Hp.*Art.*67, X.*Mem.*2.8.6; αἰτίαν ὑπέχειν lie under *a charge*, Pl.*Ap.*33b, X.*Cyr.*6.3.16; ὑπομεῖναι Aeschin.3.139; φέρεσθαι Th.2.60; λαβεῖν ἀπό τινος ib.18; αἰτίαις ἐνέχεσθαι Pl.*Cri.*52a; αἰτίαις περιπίπτειν Lys.7.1; εἰς αἰτίαν ἐμπίπτειν Pl.*Tht.*150a; αἰτίας τυγχάνειν D.*Ep.*2.2; ἐκτὸς αἰτίας κυρεῖν A. *Pr.*332; ἐν αἰτίῃ ἔχειν hold one *guilty*, Hdt.5.106; δι' αἰτίας ἔχειν Th. 2.60, etc.; ἐν αἰτίᾳ βάλλειν S.*OT*656; τὴν αἰτίαν ἐπιφέρειν τινί impute *the fault* to one, Hdt.1.26; αἰτίαν νέμειν τινί S.*Aj.*28; ἐπάγειν D.18.283; προσβάλλειν τινί Antipho 3.2.4; ἀνατιθέναι, προστιθέναι, Hp.*VM*21, Ar.*Pax*640, etc.; ἀπολύειν τινὰ τῆς αἰτίης to acquit of *guilt*, Hdt.9.88, etc. 2. in forensic oratory, *invective* without proof (opp. ἔλεγχος), D.22.23, cf. 18.15. 3. in good sense, εἰ.. εὖ πράξαιμεν, αἰτία θεοῦ *the credit* is his, A.*Th.*4; δι' ὅντινα αἰτίαν ἔχουσιν Ἀθηναῖοι βελτίους γεγονέναι *are reputed* to have become better, Pl.*Grg.*503b, cf. *Alc.*1.119a, Arist.*Metaph.*984b19; ὧν.. πέρι αἰτίαν ἔχεις διαφέρειν in which you *are reputed* to excel, Pl.*Tht.*169a; οἱ.. ἔχουσι ταύτην τὴν αἰ. who have this *reputation*, Id.*R.*435e, cf. And. 2.12; αἰτίαν λαμβάνειν Pl.*Lg.*624a. 4. *expostulation*, μὴ ἐπ' ἔχθρᾳ τὸ πλέον ἢ αἰτίᾳ Th.1.69. II. *cause*, δι' ἣν αἰτίην ἐπολέμησαν Hdt.*Prooem.*, cf. Democr.83, Pl.*Ti.*68e, *Phd.*97a sq., etc.; on the four causes of Arist. v. *Ph.*194b16, *Metaph.*983a26:—αἰ. τοῦ γενέσθαι or γεγονέναι Pl.*Phd.*97a; τοῦ μεγίστου ἀγαθοῦ τῇ πόλει αἰτία ἡ κοινωνία Id.*R.*464b:—dat. αἰτίᾳ *for the sake of*, κοινοῦ τινος ἀγαθοῦ Th.4.87, cf. D.H.8.29:—αἴτιον (cf. αἴτιος II. 2) is used like αἰτία in the sense of *cause*, not in that of *accusation*. III. *occasion, motive*, αἰτίαν ῥοαῖσι Μοισᾶν ἐνέβαλε gave them *a theme* for song, Pi.*N.*7.11; αἰτίαν παρέχειν Luc.*Tyr.*13. IV. *head, category* under which a thing comes, D.23.75. V. *case in dispute*, ἡ αἰ. τοῦ ἀνθρώπου μετὰ τῆς γυναικός *Ev.Matt.*19.10. **-άζομαι**, only in Pass., *to be accused*, ἡ πόλις αἰτιάζεται X.*HG*1.6.5, cf. 12, Anon.*Oxy.*1012*Fr.*14; ᾐτιάζετό τινος *of* a thing, D.C.38.10. **-ᾱμα**, ατος, τό, *charge, accusation*, λαβεῖν ἐπ' αἰτιάματί τινα A.*Pr.*196, cf. 257, Th.5.72. **-άομαι**, used by Hom. only in Ep. forms, 3 pl. αἰτιόωνται, opt. αἰτιόῳο, -ῷτο, inf. αἰτιάασθαι, impf. ᾐτιάασθε, -όωντο: Aeol. impf. 2 sg. αἰτίαο *Lyr. Adesp.*66: fut. -άσομαι Ar.*Nub.*1433, Pl.*Phd.*85d: aor. ᾐτιᾱσάμην E.*Fr.*254, Th.1.120, etc., Ion. -ησάμενος Hdt.4.94, -ήσασθαι Hp.*de Arte* 4: pf. ᾐτίᾱμαι D.19.215, Ion. -ίημαι Hp.*Ep.*17 (also in pass. sense, and aor. ᾐτιάθην always so, v. infr. I. 1): (αἰτία):—*accuse, censure*, c. acc. pers., τάχα κεν καὶ ἀναίτιον αἰτιόῳτο Il.11.654, cf. Od. 20.135; ἀναίτιον αἰτιάασθαι Il.13.775; θεοὺς βροτοὶ αἰτιόωνται Od. 1.32, cf. E.*Fr.*254; καί μ' ᾐτιάασθε ἕκαστος Il.16.202, cf. S.*OT*608, Lys.7.38, etc.; αἰ. ὡς μιαρούς Pl.*R.*562d; αἰ. τινά τινος *to accuse* of a thing, Hdt.5.27, Pl.*R.*619c, D.21.104, etc.: c. inf., αἰ. τινὰ ποιεῖν τι *accuse* one of doing, Hdt.5.27, Pl.*Criti.*120c, X.*Mem.*1. 1.2; οὐ τὰ ὑμέτερα αἰτιασόμεθα μὴ οὐχ ἕτοιμα εἶναι Pl.*La.*189c; αἰ. τινὰ ὡς... or ὅτι.., Th.1.120, X.*An.*3.1.7; αἰ. τινὰ περί τινος X.*HG*1.7.6: c. acc. cogn., αἰ. αἰτίαν κατά τινος *bring a charge* against one, Antipho 6.27:—Pass., *to be accused*, aor. I ᾐτιάθην (always) Th.6.53, 8.68, X.*HG*2.1.32: pf. ᾐτίαμαι Th.3.61: fut. αἰτιαθήσομαι D.C.37.56. b. in good sense, *give* one *the credit* of being, σὲ τίς αἰτιᾶται νομοθέτην ἀγαθὸν γεγονέναι; Pl.*R.*599e, cf. 379c, *Cra.*396d. 2. c. acc. rei, *lay to* one's *charge, impute*, τοῦτο αἰ. X.*Cyr.*3.1.39; ταῦτα D.19.215: c. dupl. acc., τί ταῦτα τοὺς Λάκωνας αἰτιώμεθα; Ar.*Ach.*514. 3. *injure*, ὁπλήν *Hippiatr.*105. II. *allege as the cause*, οὐ τὸ αἴτιον αἰ. not *to allege* the real cause, Pl.*R.* 329b; τίνα ἔχεις αἰτιάσασθαι.. τούτου κύριον; ib.508a; φωνάς τε.. καὶ ἄλλα μυρία αἰ. Id.*Phd.*98e; τἀναίτια Id.*Ti.*88a; ὧν τὴν πενίαν αἰτιάσαιτ' ἄν τις D.18.263; τὴν δίνην Arist.*Cael.*295a32; τὸ αὐτόματον Id. *Ph.*196a25. 2. c. inf., *allege*, τὸν λόγον αἰ. δυσχερῆ εἶναι Pl.*Prt.* 333d, cf. *Men.*93d; αἰ. τι αἴτιον εἶναι *Phlb.*22d, *Grg.*518d; ἰλίγγους ἐκ φιλοσοφίας ἐγγίγνεσθαι *allege by way of accusation* that.., Id.*R.* 407c; τῆς ἱερᾶς χώρας ᾐτιᾶτο εἶναι *he alleged* that it was part of.., D. 18.150, cf. 37.12. (Late in Act., *POxy.*1032.51 (ii A.D.).) **-ᾱσις**, εως, ἡ, *complaint, accusation*, Antipho 5.25, Arist.*Po.*1455b31, *PFlor.* 311.4 (v A.D.). **-ᾱτέον**, verb. Adj. *one must accuse, blame*, X.*Cyr.* 7.1.11, Str.1.2.30. II. *one must allege as the cause*, Pl.*R.*379c, *Ti.*57c, 87b, Arist.*Mete.*339a32. **-ᾱτικός**, ή, όν, *causal*, Sch.Il. 23.627. 2. Astrol., *noxious*, τόπος Vett.Val.208.10. II. ἡ αἰ. (sc. πτῶσις) *accusative case*, indicating the thing caused by the vb., *Stoic.*2.59, D.T.636.6, A.D.*Pron.*11.9, etc. Adv. **-κῶς** *in the accusative*, Sch.E.*Ph.*470. **-ᾱτός**, ή, όν, verb. Adj. *produced by a cause, effected*, Arist.*APo.*76a20; τὸ αἰ. *effect*, opp. τὸ αἴτιον *cause*, ib.98a36, Plot.6.2.3: Comp. -ότερος Eustr.*in APo.*40.28.

αἰτίζω, Ep. form of αἰτέω (not in Il., once in Ar.); only pres. (exc. aor. part. αἰτίσσας in *AP*10.66 (Agath.)), *ask, beg*, c. acc. rei, σῖτον.. αἰτίζων κατὰ δῆμον Od.17.558, cf. 222; ἡνίκ' ἂν αἰτίζητ' ἄρτον Ar. *Pax* 120 (hex.); generally, *ask*, φέρειν τέκος ὅσσ' ἐθελημὸς αἰτίζεις Call.*Dian.*32. 2. c. acc. pers., *beg of*, αἰτίζειν.. πάντας ἐποιχόμενον μνηστῆρας Od.17.346. 3. abs., *beg*, αἰτίζων βόσκειν ἣν γαστέρα ib.228, cf. 4.651.

αἰτιο-λογέω, *inquire into causes, reason, account for*, ὑπὲρ τῶν μετεώρων Epicur.*Ep.*1 p.31 U., cf. Diocl.*Fr.*112, Plot.6.7.3, Plu.2.689b; τὸ ζητούμενον Aenesid.ap.S.E.*P.*1.181, cf. Demetr.Lac.1012.68:—Pass., ἐκ τοῦ συνδέσμου ᾐτιολογημένον ἐστὶν the conjunction indicates that *the cause resides in*.., A.D.*Conj.*235.9. **-λογητέον**, verb. Adj. *one must investigate causes*, Epicur.*Ep.*1 p.29 U. **-λογία**, ἡ, *a giving the cause* of a thing, Democr.118, Aenesid.ap.S.E.*P.*1.181, Phld.*D.*1.10, A.D.*Conj.*231.16; ἡ ⟨περὶ⟩ τῶν μετεώρων αἰ. Epicur. *Ep.*2 p.42 U. **-λογικός**, ή, όν, *ready at giving the cause, inquiring into causes*, αἰτιολογικώτατος, of Aristotle, D.L.5.32; *causal*, τρόπος Epicur.*Nat.*144 G.:—Subst., τὸ -κόν *investigation of causes*, Str.2. 3.8. 2. Gramm., *causal*, σύνδεσμοι, σύνταξις, etc., A.D.*Conj.* 231.4, al., *Adv.*200.2. Adv. **-κῶς** Id.*Synt.*320.3.

αἴτι-ος, α, ον, more rarely ος, ον Ar.*Pl.*547: (v. αἰτία):—*culpable, responsible*, ἐπεὶ οὔ τί μοι αἴτιοί εἰσιν Il.1.153, cf. B.10.34, Hdt.7.214: Comp. αἰτιώτερος Th.4.20: Sup., τοὺς αἰτιωτάτους *the most guilty*, Hdt.6.50; αἰ. τινος Id.3.52. 2. Subst., αἴτιος, ὁ, *the accused, the culprit*, A.*Ch.*70, etc.; οἱ αἴ. τοῦ πατρός *they who have sinned against* my father, ib.273:—c. gen. rei, οἱ αἴ. τοῦ φόνου ib.117, cf. S.*Ph.*590, Hdt.4.200. II. *responsible for*, c. gen. rei, Hdt.1.1, etc.; αἴτιός τινός τινι being *the cause of* a thing *to* a person, Lys.13.57, cf. D.23. 54, Isoc.8.100: c. inf., αἴ. τὸν ἠέρα ξηρὸν εἶναι Hdt.2.26; τοῦ μὴ φαλακροῦσθαι Id.3.12, etc.; αἴ. θανεῖν S.*Ant.*1173; αἴ. πεμφθῆναι ἄγγελον Antipho 5.23, cf. Lys.13.82; αἴτιος τὸ σὲ ἀποκρίνασθαι Pl.*La.*190e: Comp., τοῦ.. ἐλευθέραν εἶναι.. αἰτιώτερον D.24.5, cf. 51.21: Sup. αἰτιώτατος, ἐν τῷ στενῷ ναυμαχῆσαι *mainly instrumental in causing* the sea-fight, Th.1.74; αἰ. τοῦ μὴ ἀποθανεῖν D.20.42; -ώτατόν τι καὶ τελέως δραστικόν Phld.*D.*1.23. 2. αἴτιον, τό, *cause*, Hp.*VM*6 (pl.), 21, Hdt.7.125, E.*IA*939, Th.4.26, etc.; τί ποτ' οὖν ἐστι τὸ αἴτιον τό.. μηδένα εἰπεῖν; D.8.56; freq. in Philos., τὸ δ' αἴ. τούτου εἶναι ὅτι.. Pl.*Phd.*110e, etc. **-ώδης**, ες, *resembling a cause, quasi-causal*, *Stoic.*2.119 (in Adv. -δῶς, sed leg. -ῶδες); *causal*, οὐσία

Plot.6.8.14; στοιχεῖα Simp.*inPh.*17.25; τὸ αἰτιῶδες *formal*, as opp. to τὸ ὑλικόν, M.Ant.4.21, etc.; πρότασις αἰ. *giving the cause of* the conclusion, Anon.*inSE*3.36. Adv. -δῶς *causally*, Dam.*Pr.* 106. II. Gramm., *causal*, ἀξίωμα Chrysipp.*Stoic.*2.70; σύνδεσμοι A.D.*Synt.*245.13, al. -ωμα, τό, = αἰτίαμα, *PFay.*111 (I A.D.), *Act.Ap.*25.7. -ώνυμος, ον, (ὄνομα) *named from a fault*, πάθος Sch.S.*Aj.*205. -ωσις, ἡ, = αἰτίασις, Eust.1422.21.

Αἰτναῖος, α, ον, *of* or *belonging to Etna* (Αἴτνη), Pi.*P.*3.69, *O.*6.96, A.*Pr.*367, etc.; *Sicilian*, πῶλος S.*OC*312; of a beetle, A.*Fr.*233, Ar.*Pax*73, S.*Ichn.*300. II. αἰτναῖος, ὁ, *sea-fish*, Opp.*H.*1.512.

αἰτρία, for αἰθρία, barbarism in Ar.*Th.*1001.

ἀΐττεσθαι· δικάζειν ἢ δικάζεσθαι, Hsch. (Fort. ἄττεσθαι· διάζειν ἢ διάζεσθαι.) **ἄϊτυρον**· ὕαλον, Id.

Αἰτωλάρχης, ὁ, *president of Aetolian League*, Phleg.*Mir.*2.

Αἰτωλία, ἡ, *Aetolia*, Th.3.96, etc.:—hence **Αἰτωλοί**, οἱ, *Aetolians*, Il.2.638, etc.: fem. **Αἰτωλίς**, χώρη Hdt.6.127: Adj. **Αἰτωλικός**, ή, όν, Th.4.30, etc.

αἰτώλιος, v. sub αἰγωλιός.

αἴφνης, Adv. *suddenly*, E.*IA*1581, Hp.*Int.*39 (**αἰφνηδίς**, Hdn. Gr.1.512; -δόν, Id.*Epim.*270). (Prob. cognate with αἶψα rather than with ἄφαρ, ἄφνω.)

αἰφνίδιος, ον, *unforeseen, sudden*, A.*Pr.*680, Th.2.61, Arist.*EN* 1117^{a}18; ἀφικνοῦνται αἰφνίδιοι τοῖς Χίοις Th.8.14. Adv. -ίως Id.2.53; also -ιον Plu.*Num.*15. **αἰφνιδιοτυχής**, ές, *profiting by strokes of good fortune*, Vett.Val.18.16.

αἰχμάεις, **αἰχμᾶτάς**, Dor. for αἰχμήεις, αἰχμητής.

αἰχμάζω, Ep. fut. -άσσω, *throw the spear*, αἰχμὰς αἰχμάσσουσι Il.4.324; ἔνδον αἰχμάζειν *play the warrior* at home, A.*Pers.*756; αἰχμάσαι τάδε *to perform* these *feats of arms*, S.*Tr.*355; '*trail a pike*', Men.*Sam.*284. II. *arm with the spear*, πρὸς Ἀτρείδαισιν ᾔχμασας χέρα S.*Aj.*97: metaph. of general's speech, ἀ. τὴν διάνοιαν Onos.1.13. III. *wound*, Nonn.*D.*35.178 s.v.l.

αἰχμᾰλ-ωσία, ἡ, *captivity*, D.S.20.61, Lxx *Am.*1.15, al., Plu.*Them.*31. II. *body of captives*, D.S.17.70, Lxx *Nu.*31.12, al. -ωτεύω, = sq., Lxx *Ge.*34.29, al., *Ep.Eph.*4.8; *capture*, πλοῦτον Ps.-Callisth.3.20. -ωτίζω, *take prisoner*, D.S.14.37, Lxx 4*Ki.*24.14, al.:—more freq. in Med., αἰχμαλωτίζομαι J.*BJ*4.8.1: fut. -ίσομαι ib.2.4: aor. ᾐχμαλωτισάμην ib.1.22.1, D.S.13.24: pf. ᾐχμαλώτισμαι J.*BJ*4.9.8 (with v.l. -σάμενοι); also in pass. sense, *SIG*763 (Cyzicus). -ωτικός, ή, όν, *of* or *for a prisoner*, E.*Tr.*871. -ωτίς, ίδος, ἡ, *captive*, S.*Aj.*1228, E.*Tr.*28, Lxx *Ge.*31.26. 2. Adj. fem. of αἰχμάλωτος, τὰς αἰχμαλωτίδας χέρας S.*Aj.*71. -ωτισμός, ὁ, = αἰχμαλωσία, Sch.Ar.*Nu.*186. -ωτιστής, *captivator*, *Gloss.* -ωτος, ον, *taken by the spear, captive, prisoner*, Pi.*Fr.*223, Hdt.6.79,134; freq. of women, A.*Ag.*1440, S.*Tr.*417:—αἰχμάλωτοι *prisoners of war*, And.4.22, Th.3.70; αἰ. λαμβάνειν, ἄγειν take *prisoner*, X.*Cyr.*3.1.37, 4.4.1; αἰ. γίγνεσθαι to be *taken*, ib.3.1.7; of things, αἰ. χρήματα A.*Eu.*400, cf. *Ag.*334, D.19.139; νῆες X.*HG* 2.3.8, *IG*2.789; τὰ αἰ. *booty*, X.*HG*4.1.26, *An.*4.1.13; αἰχμάλωτον, τό, = ἀνδράποδον, D.S.13.57. II. = αἰχμαλωτικός, δουλοσύνη αἰ. *such as awaits a captive*, Hdt.9.76; εὐνά A.*Th.*364 (lyr.); τύχη D.S.27.6, Lib.*Or.*59.157. III. αἰχμάλωτος, ὁ, name of plasters, Aët.15.20.

αἰχμ-ή, ἡ, (Aeol. αἶχμα *AB*1095) *point of a spear*, πάροιθε δὲ λάμπετο δουρὸς αἰ. χαλκείη Il.6.320; αἰ. ἔγχεος 16.315. 2. generally, *point*, of arrows, τοξουλκὸς αἰ. A.*Pers.*239; ἀγκίστρου, κεράων, Opp.*H.* 1.216, *C.*2.451. II. *spear*, Il.12.45, etc.; δαμασίμβροτος αἰ. Pi.*O.* 9.79; πρὸς τὴν αἰχμὴν ἐτράπετο took to his *spear*, Hdt.3.78; αἰχμῇ εἷλε *with the spear*, i.e. in war, Id.5.94; otherwise rare in Prose, X.*Cyr.* 4.6.4. b. metaph. of the trident of Poseidon, A.*Pr.*925. 2. *body of spear-bearers*, Pi.*O.*7.19, E.*Heracl.*276. 3. *war, battle*, κακῶς ἡ αἰ. ἑστήκεε the *war* went ill, Hdt.7.152; παρμένοντας αἰχμᾷ standing their ground in *battle*, Pi.*P.*8.40; θηρῶν *with* wild beasts, E.*HF*158. 4. metaph. of plague, *sharpness*, βρωτῆρας αἰ. A.*Eu.* 803. III. *warlike spirit*, αἰ. νέων θάλλει Terp.6; θρέψε δ' αἰχμὰν Ἀμφιτρύωνος Pi.*N.*10.13; γυναικὸς αἰ. a woman's *temper*, A.*Ag.*483 (lyr.), cf. *Ch.*630 (lyr.; but perh. = *rule*, cf. *Pr.*406). (Cf. Lith. *jiešmas* 'spit'.) -ήεις, Dor. -άεις, εσσα, εν, *armed with the spear*, A.*Pers.* 137; *pointed*, σίδηρος Opp.*C.*3.321. -ητά [ᾰ], ὁ, Ep. collat. form of αἰχμητής, Il.5.197. -ητήρ, ῆρος, ὁ, = αἰχμητής, Opp.*C.*3.211, Q.S.8.85, Nonn.*D.*28.122; as Adj., αἰ. γάμος *prize of the spear*, ib.42. 501. -ητήριος, α, ον, *warlike*, Lyc.454. -ητής, οῦ, Dor. -ατάς, ᾶ, ὁ, (αἰχμή) poet., *spearman, warrior*, esp. opp. to archers, Il.2.543, Od.2.19, al., Archil.119, cj. in Alcm.68, etc. II. In Pi. as Adj., 1. *pointed* (or *spear-wielding*), αἰ. κεραυνὸς *P.*1.5. 2. *warlike*, αἰ. θυμός *N.*9.37:—fem. **αἴχμητις** (sic), *EM*595.39.

αἰχμό-δετος, ον, (δέω) *bound in war*, = αἰχμάλωτος, S.*Fr.*47 (fort. -όλετος, cf. *EM*41.3). -φόρος, ον, *spearman*, Hdt.1.103, 215. 2. esp., like δορυφόρος, of *body-guards*, Id.1.8, 7.40, B.10.89.

αἶψα (Boeot. ἦψα prob. in Corinn.*BKT*5(2).36), Adv. *quick, forthwith, on a sudden*, freq. in Hom. (also αἶψα μάλα, αἶψα δ' ἔπειτα, Il.4.70, Od.15.193), cf. Sapph.1.13, Thgn.663, Sol.2, Pi.*P.*4.133, Emp.35.14, A.*Supp.*481.—Poet., exc. in *Mon.Ant.*18.322 (Gortyn).

αἰψηροκέλευθος, ον, *swift-speeding*, epith. of Boreas, Hes.*Th.*379, Poet.ap.Apollod.3.4.4.

αἰψηρός, ά, όν, (αἶψα) *quick, speedy, sudden*, αἰψηρὸς δὲ κόρος κρυεροῖο γόοιο satiety in grief *comes soon*, Od.4.103; λῦσεν δ' ἀγορὴν αἰψηρήν he dismissed the assembly *in haste*, Il.19.276, Od.2.257; Ζεφύρου αἰ. πνοαί Pi.*Parth.*2.17; πούς Lyc.515. Adv. -ῶς Aristarch. ap.Apollon.*Lex.* s.v. αἶψα.—Not in Trag.

ἀΐω (A), Ep. and Lyr. word, freq. used by Trag. in lyr., cf. Hermipp.47.7 (anap.); once only in dialogue (S.*OC*304): only pres. and impf. (aor. ἐπ-ήϊσα Hdt.9.93):—*perceive* by the ear, *hear*, c. acc. rei, οὐκ ἀΐεις ἅ τέ φησι; Il.15.130, cf. 248; Νέστωρ δὲ πρῶτος κτύπον ἄϊε 10.532, cf. 21.388, Pi.*Pae.*6.8, A.*Ag.*55, *Supp.*59, E.*Med.*148, etc.: c. gen. rei, Sapph.1.6, S.*OC*304, *Ph.*1410: c. gen. pers., ἀΐει μου.. βασιλεύς A.*Pers.*633:—also, *perceive* by the eye, *see*, Od. 18.11, S.*OC*181:—generally, *perceive*, οὐκ ἀΐεις ὡς Τρῶες.. ἥαται ἄγχι νεῶν; Il.10.160. 2. c. gen., *listen to, give ear to*, δίκης Hes. *Op.*213 (dub. l.); *obey*, A.*Pers.*874, Ar.*Nu.*1166. (Cf. Skt. *ávis* 'clear', Lat. *au-dio*.) [Hom. uses ᾰ always in pres., ἄϊω; so A. *Pers.*633, S.*Ph.*1410; but ἀΐεις, ἀΐων A.*Supp.*59 (prob.), S.*OC*181, 304: impf. ἄϊε Il.10.532, 21.388 (as always in Trag.), but ἄϊεν Il.11. 463, ἄϊον 18.222:—ι is always short, except ἄϊε in Hes.*Op.*213 (dub. l.), and perh. ἀϊόντεσσι Od.1.352.]

ἀΐω (B), [ᾰ], = ἄημι, *breathe*, (dub.) once in impf., ἐπεὶ φίλον ἄϊον ἦτορ when *I was breathing out* my life, Il.15.252.

ἀϊών [ᾰ], Dor. for ἠϊών.

αἰών, ῶνος, ὁ, Ion. and Ep. also ἡ, as in Pi.*P.*4.186, E.*Ph.*1484: apocop. acc. αἰῶ, like Ποσειδῶ, restored by Ahrens (from *AB*363) in A.*Ch.*350: (properly αἰϝών, cf. *aevum*, v. αἰεί):—*period of existence* (τὸ τέλος τὸ περιέχον τὸν τῆς ἑκάστου ζωῆς χρόνον.. αἰὼν ἑκάστου κέκληται Arist.*Cael.*279^{a}25): I. *lifetime, life*, ψυχή τε καὶ αἰών Il.16.453; ἐκ δ' αἰ. πέφαται Il.19.27; μηδέ τοι αἰ. φθινέτω Od.5.160; λείπει τινά Il.5.685; ἀπ' αἰῶνος νέος ὤλεο (Zenod. νέον) 24.725; τελευτᾶν τὸν αἰῶνα Hdt.1.32, etc.; αἰῶνος στερεῖν τινά A.*Pr.*862; αἰῶνα διοιχνεῖν Id.*Eu.*315; συνδιατρίβειν Cratin.1; αἰ. Αἰακιδᾶν, periphr. for *the Aeacidae*, S.*Aj.*645 s.v.l.; ἀπέπνευσεν αἰῶνα E.*Fr.*801; ἐμὸν κατ' αἰῶνα A.*Th.*219. 2. *age, generation*, αἰ. ἐς τρίτον ib.744; ὁ μέλλων αἰών *posterity*, D.18.199, cf. Pl.*Ax.*370c. 3. *one's life, destiny, lot*, S.*Tr.*34, E.*Andr.*1215, *Fr.*30, etc. II. *long space of time, age*, αἰὼν γίγνεται '*tis an age*, Men.536.5; esp. with Preps., ἀπ' αἰῶνος *of old*, Hes.*Th.*609, *Ev.Luc.*1.70; οἱ ἀπὸ τοῦ αἰ. Ῥωμαῖοι D.C. 63.20; δι' αἰῶνος *perpetually*, A.*Ch.*26, *Eu.*563; *all one's life long*, S. *El.*1024; δι' αἰῶνος μακροῦ, ἀπαύστου, A.*Supp.*582, 574; τὸν δι' αἰ. χρόνον *for ever*, Id.*Ag.*554; εἰς ἅπαντα τὸν αἰ. Lycurg.106, Isoc.10. 62; εἰς τὸν αἰ. Lxx *Ge.*3.23, al., D.S.21.17, *Ev.Jo.*8.35, Ps.-Luc. *Philopatr.*17; εἰς αἰῶνα αἰῶνος Lxx *Ps.*131(132).14; ἐξ αἰῶνος καὶ ἕως αἰῶνος ib.*Je.*7.7; ἐπ' αἰ. ib.*Ex.*15.18; ἕως αἰῶνος ib.1*Ki.*1.22, al.:—without a Prep., τὸν ἅπαντα αἰ. Arist.*Cael.*279^{a}22; τὸν αἰῶνα Lycurg. 62, Epicur.*Ep.*1 p.8 U.; *eternity*, opp. χρόνος, Pl.*Ti.*37d, cf. Metrod. *Fr.*37, Ph.1.496, 619, Plot.3.7.5, etc.; τοὺς ὑπὲρ τοῦ αἰῶνος φόβους Epicur.*Sent.*20. 2. *space of time* clearly defined and marked out, *epoch, age*, ὁ αἰὼν οὗτος this present *world*, opp. ὁ μέλλων, *Ev. Matt.*13.22, cf. *Ep.Rom.*12.2; ὁ νῦν αἰ. 1*Ep.Tim.*6.17, 2*Ep.Tim.*4. 10:—hence in pl., *the ages*, i.e. *eternity*, Phld.*D.*3 *Fr.*84; εἰς πάντας τοὺς αἰ. Lxx *To.*13.4; εἰς τοὺς αἰ. ib.*Si.*45.24, al., *Ep.Rom.*1.25, etc.; εἰς τοὺς αἰ. τῶν αἰώνων Lxx 4*Ma.*18.24, *Ep.Phil.*4.20, etc.; ἀπὸ τῶν αἰ., πρὸ τῶν αἰ., *Ep.Eph.*3.9, 1*Cor.*2.7; τὰ τέλη τῶν αἰ. ib.10.11. 3. Αἰών, ὁ, personified, Αἰὼν Χρόνου παῖς E.*Heracl.*900 (lyr.), cf. *Corp. Herm.*11, etc.; as title of various divine beings, Dam.*Pr.*151, al.; esp. = Persian Zervan, Suid. s.v. Ἡραΐσκος. 4. Pythag., = 10, *Theol.Ar.*59.

B. *spinal marrow* (perh. regarded as seat of *life*), *h.Merc.*42, 119, Pi.*Fr.*111, Hp.*Epid.*7.122; perh. also Il.19.27.

αἰωνίζω, *to be eternal*, Phot., Suid.; *to be eternalized*, Dam.*Pr.*105.

αἰώνιος, ον, also α, ον Pl.*Ti.*37d, *Ep.Heb.*9.12:—*lasting for an age* (αἰών II), *perpetual, eternal* (but dist. fr. ἀΐδιος, Plot.3.7.3), μέθη Pl.*R.* 363d; ἀνώλεθρον.. ἀλλ' οὐκ αἰώνιον Id.*Lg.*904a, cf. Epicur.*Sent.*28; αἰ. κατὰ ψυχὴν ὄχλησις Id.*Nat.*131 G.; κακά, δεινά, Phld.*Herc.*1251. 18, *D.*1.13; αἰ. ἀμοιβαῖς βασανισθησόμενοι ib.19; τοῦ αἰ. θεοῦ *Ep.Rom.* 16.26, Ti.Locr.96c; οὐ χρονίη μοῦνον.. ἀλλ' αἰωνίη Aret.*CA*1.5; αἰ. διαθήκη, νόμιμον, πρόσταγμα, Lxx *Ge.*9.16, *Ex.*27.21, *To.*1.6; ζωή *Ev.Matt.*25.46, Porph.*Abst.*4.20; κόλασις *Ev.Matt.* l.c., Olymp.*in Grg.*p.278 J.; πρὸ χρόνων αἰ. 2*Ep.Tim.*1.9: opp. πρόσκαιρος, 2*Ep.Cor.* 4.18. 2. *holding an office or title for life, perpetual*, γυμνασίαρχος *CPHerm.*62. 3. = Lat. *saecularis*, Phleg.*Macr.*4. 4. Adv. -ίως *eternally*, νοῦς ἀκίνητος αἰ. πάντα ὤν Procl.*Inst.*172, cf. Simp.*in Epict.*p.77 D.; *perpetually*, μισεῖν Sch.E.*Alc.*338. 5. αἰώνιον, τό, = ἀείζωον τὸ μέγα, Ps.-Dsc.4.88.

αἰωνιότης, ἡ, *perpetuitas*, *Gloss.*

αἰώνισμα, τό, *perpetual memorial*, *Ostr.*1148.

αἰωνό-βιος, ον, *immortal*, title of Egyptian kings, Πτολεμαῖος *OGI*90.4 (Rosetta, ii B.C.), *PMag.Par.*1.154; of God, *PMag.Lond.* 46.176, 482. -πολοκράτωρ, ορος, ὁ, *eternal ruler of the heavens*, *PMag.Berol.*1.201.

αἰωνόφθαλμος, ον, *seeing with eternal eyes*, *PMag.Lond.*46.465.

αἰώρα, ἡ, (ἀείρω) *swing, hammock, chariot on springs*, Pl.*Lg.* 789d. 2. *noose, halter*, S.*OT*1264 (in the form ἐώρα). II. *oscillatory movement, see-saw, pulsation*, Pl.*Phd.*111e, D.H.3.47, etc. 2. Medic., *passive exercise*, Plu.2.793b, Antyll.ap.Orib.6. 23, Sor.1.125: pl., *IG*4.955 (Epid., ii A.D.). III. metaph., αἰ. ψυχῆς *fluctuation* of mind, Metrod.*Herc.*831.8 (cf. Epicur.*Fr.*434).

αἰωρ-έω: fut. Pass. -ηθήσομαι D.C.41.1, (ἀπ-) Hp.*Fract.*14, but -ήσομαι Aristid.2.289 J.: aor. ᾐωρήθην (v. infr.): pf. ᾐώρημαι Opp. *H.*3.532: (ἀείρω):—*lift up, raise*, ὑγρὸν νῶτον αἰωρεῖ, of the eagle *raising* his back and feathers, Pi.*P.*1.9; *swing* as in a hammock, αἰ. [γυναῖκα] ἐπὶ κλίνης φερομένην Hp.*Mul.*1.68, cf. Aret.*CA*1.4; τοὺς ὄφεις.. ὑπὲρ τῆς κεφαλῆς αἰωρῶν D.18.260. 2. *hang*, τινὰ ἐκ τοῦ ἀτράκτου Luc.*J.Conf.*4 :—metaph., ᾐώρει.. ἐλπίς, ὅτι τὸν χάρακα αἱρήσουσι *excited* them *to think* that.., App.*BC*2.81, cf. Plu.*Brut.* 37.—Never in good Att. II. more freq. in Pass., *to be hung, hang*, δέρματα περὶ τοὺς ὤμους αἰωρεύμενα Hdt.7.92 ; αἰωρουμένων τῶν ὀστῶν *being raised, lifted*, Pl.*Phd.*98d ; αἷμα ᾐωρεῖτο *spouted up*, Bion 1.25 ; ὁ ἥλιος ὑπὸ πνευμάτων αἰωρεῖται *is tossed, carried to and fro*, Diog.Oen.*Fr.*8. 2. *swing, float in air*, Pl.*La.*184a ; *hover*, of birds, Arist.*Mir.*836ᵃ12 ; of a dream, S.*El.*1390 (lyr.) ; *oscillate*, Pl. *Phd.*112b ; of an army, αἰωρουμένης στρατιᾶς περὶ Μεσοποταμίαν Plu. *Ant.*28. b. *take passive exercise*, Gal.*Thras.*23. 3. metaph., *to be in suspense*, ἐν κινδύνῳ *to hang* in doubt and danger, Th.7.77 ; αἰ. ἐν ἄλλοις *depend* upon.., Pl.*Mx.*248a ; αἰωρηθεὶς ὑπὲρ μεγάλων *playing for a* high *stake*, Hdt.8.100 ; αἰ. τὴν ψυχήν X.*Cyn.*4.4 ; τὸ μὴ -ούμενον τῆς ψυχῆς Epicur.*Nat.*22G. 4. Pass., *to be held in suspense, threatened*, ἀπαιδίας πρὸς τιμωρίαν -ουμένης Chor.p.71.3B. -ημα, ατος, τό, *that which is hung up* or *hovers*, Lyc.1080. 2. *hanging cord, halter*, E.*Hel.*353 (lyr.) ; *hanging slings* or *chains*, Id.*Or.*984 (lyr.). -ησις, εως, ἡ, *oscillatory movement*, esp. Medic., of *passive exercise*, Pl.*Ti.*89a, cf. Gal.10.710 ; αἰ. δι' ὀχημάτων Poll.10. 51. -ητέον, *one must take passive exercise*, Sor.1.109 ; ἐν φορείῳ Herod.Med.ap.Aët.9.13. -ητός, όν, *hanging*, *AP*5.203 (Mel.).

ἀκᾶ, Dor. Adv. = ἀκήν, *softly, gently*, Pi.*P.*4.156 ; cf. ἦκα.

Ἀκᾰδήμεια (the form is protected by metre in Alex.25,94, cf. Ar. *Nu.*1005, Epicr.11.11, St. Byz. s.v. Ἑκαδήμεια, Ath.10.419d), freq. written -ία, ἡ, *Academy*, a gymnasium in the suburbs of Athens, named from the hero Academus, ἐν δρόμοισιν Ἀκαδήμου θεοῦ Eup.32, cf. Pl.*Ly.*203a, etc., where Plato taught : hence, *the Platonic school of philosophy*, Ἀκ. παλαιά, μέση, νεωτέρα Phld.*Acad.Ind.*p.77M. : prov., **Ἀκαδημίηθεν** ἥκεις, of a philosopher, Apostol.2.1 :—hence Adj. **Ἀκαδημεικός**, ή, όν, *Academic, of the school of Plato*, Phld. *Acad.Ind.*p.18M. : also **Ἀκαδημαϊκός**, Plu.2.1077c, Ath.11.509a, Luc.*Pisc.*43, Timo35 codd., etc. ; **Ἀκαδημιακός**, D.L.4.67, etc. ; **Ἀκαδημικός**, Cic.*Att.*13.12.3 and 16.1 ; **Ἀκαδήμιος**, Philostr.*VA* 7.2 s.v.l.

ἀκᾰθαίρετος, ον, (καθαιρέω) *not to be put down*, Ph.1.39, al. ; *not weakened*, Sor.1.21.

ἀκᾰθαρ-σία, ἡ, *uncleanness, foulness*, of a wound or sore, Hp. *Fract.*31, cf. Pl.*Ti.*72c (pl.) ; ἀγγείων Hp.*Epid.*6.31. b. *dirt, filth*, *BGU*1117.27 (13 B.C.), etc. 2. in moral sense, *depravity*, D.21. 119. 3. *ceremonial impurity*, Lxx *Le.*15.3, al. -τίζομαι, *to be ceremonially unclean*, v.l. ib.14.36. -τος, ον, (καθαίρω) *uncleansed, foul*, ἀήρ Hp.*Aër.*6 ; of the body, Arist.*Pr.*883ᵇ27 ; ἕλκος Hp.*Fract.* 27 ; of a woman, *quae menstrua non habet*, Demad.*Fr.*4, Luc.*Lex.*19 ; of ceremonial impurity, Lxx *Le.*12.2, al., *IG*3.74.3. b. *unpurified*, Pl.*Lg.*866a, 868a. 2. *morally unclean, impure*, Pl.*Phd.*81b, D.19.199, etc. ; ἀκάθαρτε *thou beast !* Bato5 ; = μανιώδης, Achae.30 ; ἀ. πνεῦμα Lxx *Za.*13.2, *Ev.Matt.*12.43, cf. *PMag.Par.*1.1238. Adv. ἀκαθάρτως, ἔχειν Pl.*Ti.*92b. 3. of things, *not purged away, unpurged*, S.*OT*256, Pl.*Lg.*854b. b. *unpruned*, Thphr.*CP*1.15.1. c. *ceremonially unclean*, of food, Lxx *Le.*5.2, al., *Act.Ap.*10.14. d. *not sifted, containing impurities*, *PPetr.*2p.8 (iii B.C.). II. Act., *not fit for cleansing*, [φάρμακα] ἑλκέων ἀκαθαρτότερα Aret.*CD*1.8.

ἀκᾰθεκτέομαι, Pass., *to be unoccupied*, διάστημα -ούμενον ὑπὸ σώματος *Stoic.*2.163.

ἀκάθεκτος, ον, *ungovernable*, Ps.-Phoc.193, Plu.*Nic.*8. Adv. -τως, λυττᾶν Ph.2.48 ; μαργαίνειν Sch.Opp.*H.*1.38.

ἀκαθήκουσα διαθήκη, = Lat. *inofficiosum testamentum*, Just.*Nov.* 38.3 (pl.), cf. *Gloss.*

ἀκᾰθ-οσίωτος, ον, *unpurified*, Phot., Suid. -υπερτέρητος, ον, *unsurpassed*, Ptol.*Tetr.*157. -υστέρητος, ον, *lacking nothing*, βίος Vett.Val.67.18, cf. Ps.-Callisth.2.11. Adv. -τως *without delay*, *BGU* 1126.11 (i B.C.).

ἄκαινα, ης, ἡ, (ἀκή A, ἀκίς) *spike, prick, goad*, A.R.3.1323, *AP*6. 41 (Agath.). II. *ten-foot rod* used as a measure, ἄκαιναν ἀμφότερον κέντρον τε βοῶν καὶ μέτρον ἀρούρης Call.*Fr.*214, cf. Sch.A.R. l.c. 2. *square measure of 100 ft.*, in Egypt, Hero*Def.*130, cf. Sch. A.R. l.c., *POxy.*669.41 (? iii A.D.) ; in Bithynia, *BCH*27.318 :—also **ἄκαινον**, τό, Olymp.*in Metaph.*43.1.

ἀκαινοτόμητος, ον, = *inlibatus*, *Gloss.* ; *free from innovations*, Just. *Nov.*61.1.4.

ἀκαιρ-εύομαι, *behave unseasonably*, Ph.2.166,280. -έω, *to be without an opportunity*, opp. εὐκαιρέω, D.S.10.7 :—Med., impf. ἠκαιρεῖσθε *Ep.Phil.*4.10. 2. *talk nonsense*, Astramps.*Orac.*74. 9. -ία, ἡ, *unfitness of times*, opp. ἐπικαιρία, Democr.26ᵉ (pl.) ; opp. εὐκαιρία, Pl.*Phd.*272a ; opp. ἐγκαιρία, Id.*Plt.*305d ; *time of trouble*, Lib.*Or.*59.38. 2. of bad seasons, *unseasonableness*, ἐνιαυτῶν πολλῶν ἀ. Pl.*Lg.*709a (pl.) ; τῶν πνευμάτων Arist.*Pr.*941ᵇ25 (pl.). 3. *impropriety*, Pl.*Smp.*182a. 4. *bad taste* in writing, D.H.*Dem.* 7, al. 5. opp. καιρός, *want of opportunity*, τὴν ἀκαιρίαν τὴν ἐκείνου καιρὸν ὑμέτερον νομίσαντες D.1.24 ; *want of time*, Plu.2.130e. II. of persons, *tactlessness*, Thphr.*Char.*12. -ιμος, η, ον, *ill-timed* : prov., ὅ τι κ' ἐπ' ἀκαιρίμαν γλῶσσαν ἔλθῃ *quicquid in buccam venerit*, *Lyr.Adesp.*86A. -ιος, ον, poet. for ἄκαιρος, ἀ. ἥκεις, of untimely death, *IG*14.1363.11. Adv. -ίως *unseasonably*, *BGU*846.14 (ii A.D.).

ἀκαιρό-γελως, ωτος, *given to unseemly laughter*, Archig. (or Posidon.) ap.Aët.6.8. -λογέω, *prate unseasonably*, Sch.Pl. *Grg.*469a. -λογία, ἡ, Hsch. s.v. βαττολογία ; prob. in D.H. *Lys.*4. -λόγος, ον, *unseasonable prater*, Ph.2.268, Eust.208. 38. -παρρησία, ἡ, *ill-timed freedom of speech*, Eust.1069. 10. -παρρησιαστής, οῦ, ὁ, *one who employs ill-timed freedom of speech*, Id.1857.2.

ἄκαιρος, ον, *ill-timed, unseasonable*, ἐς ἄκαιρα πονεῖν Thgn.919 ; οὐκ ἄκαιρα λέγειν A.*Pr.*1036 ; ἀ. κένωσις Hp.*VM*10 ; προθυμία Th.5. 65 ; ἐλευθερία Pl.*R.*569c ; ἔπαινος Id.*Phdr.*240e ; ῥαθυμία D.18.46 ; γέλως Men.*Mon.*88. Adv. -ρως A.*Ag.*808, *Ch.*624 (both lyr.), Hp. *Acut.*17, al. : Comp. -οτέρως Id.*Epid.*1.19 : neut. pl. as Adv., ἄκαιρ' ἀπώλλυτο E.*Hel.*1081. II. of persons, *importunate, troublesome*, Thphr.*Char.*12 ; ἀ. καὶ λάλος Alciphr.3.62. 2. c. inf., *ill-suited* to do a thing, X.*Eq.Mag.*7.6 (Comp.). III. ἄκαιρον, τό, = μυρσίνη ἀγρία, Dsc.4.144.

ἀκακαλίς, ίδος, ἡ, *gall of the Oriental tamarisk*, Dsc.1.89. 2. = νάρκισσος, Eumach.ap.Ath.15.681e. 3. = ἄρκευθος, Ps.-Dsc.1.75.

ἀκᾰκέμφατος· κακῆς φήμης ἀπηλλαγμένος, *in no ill repute*, Hsch.

ἀκάκης, Dor. **ἀκάκας** [ᾰκᾰ], ὁ, poet. form of ἄκακος, A.*Pers.*855 (lyr.) ; epith. of Hades, *IG*7.117.3 (Megara).

ἀκᾰκήσιος, ὁ, epith. of Hermes in Arcadia, = sq., Call.*Dian.*143, Paus.8.36.10.

ἀκάκητᾰ [ᾰκᾰ], Ep. form, = ἄκακος, *guileless, gracious*, epith. of Hermes, Il.16.185, Od.24.10, Hes.*Fr.*23 ; of Prometheus, Id.*Th.* 614 ; of the poet's father, Orph.*L.*151. (Acc. ἀκακήτην in later poetry, *IPE*1².436 (Chersonesus, ii A.D.) ; ἀκάκητος Suid.)

ἀκακία (A), ἡ, *shittah tree, Acacia arabica*, Dsc.1.101, Aret.*CD*2. 6. II. = *Genista acanthoclada*, Dsc. l.c.

ἀκᾰκία (B), ἡ, (ἄκακος) *guilelessness*, D.59.81, Arist.*Rh.*1389ᵇ9, Lxx *Jb.*2.3, etc.

ἀκάκιστος, ον, *not violent, gentle*, of remedies, Cass.Fel.76.

ἀκᾰκο-ήθευτος, ον, = sq., Eust.404.8. -ήθης, ες, *guileless*, Phot. ; Medic., *benign*, μυρμηκιά Heliod.ap.Orib.45.14.44. Adv. -θως Iamb.*Protr.*21.ιθ'. -παθέω, *to be free from suffering*, *EM* 85.12. Adv. -παθήτως Apollon.*Mir.*35.

ἄκᾰκ-ος, ον, *unknowing of ill, guileless*, A.*Pers.*663 (lyr.), Pl.*Ti.* 91d, *Ep.Rom.*16.18. 2. *innocent, simple* (cf. εὐήθης), D.47.46, 82 ; ἀ. ἀνθρώπων τρόπος Anaxil.33. Adv. -κως D.47.50. II. *unharmed*, Sapph.149. 2. *unadulterated*, *POxy.*142 (vi A.D.). -ούργητος, ον, *uncorrupted*, Harp. s.v. διασείστους ; *undamaged*, φορτία σῶα καὶ ἀ. *PLond.*3.948.8 (iii A.D.). -ούργως, Adv., used to expl. εὐήθως, Sch.D.19.167. -υντος, ον, = sq., αἰτίας Hierocl.*in CA*1p.418M., cf. 3p.424M. Adv. -τως Id.*Prov.*p.462B. -ωτος, ον, *unharmed*, Ph.1.490, D.C.77.15 ; ἀ. εὐχῇ *IG*14.2012*A*39 (Sulp.Max.). Astrol., *subject to no malignant influence, not 'afflicted'*, Vett.Val.111.24. II. *unsubdued*, M.Ant.5.18.

ἀκᾰλανθίς, ίδος, ἡ, = ἀκανθίς, Ar.*Pax*1079, Ant.Lib.9.3 ; epith. of Artemis, Ar.*Av.*872 (Lacon. **ἀκκαλανσίρ** (sic), Hsch. ; **ἀκάλανθος**, *AB*370 ; **ἀκαλάνθεια**, *EM*44.26).

ἀκᾰλαρ-ρείτης, ου, ὁ, (ἀκαλός, ῥέω) *soft-flowing*, epith. of Ocean, Il.7.422, Od.19.434. -ροος, ον, = foreg., Orph.*A.*1187.

ἀκᾰλήφη (ἀκαλύφη Thphr.*HP*7.7.2 codd.), ἡ, *stinging-nettle*, Dsc.4.93, etc. : metaph., ἀπὸ τῆς ὀργῆς τὴν ἀ. ἀφελέσθαι Ar.*V.*884, cf. Anon.ap.Chrysipp.*Stoic.*3.178. II. *sea-anemone*, so called from its stinging properties, Eup.60, Pherecr.24, Ar.*Lys.*549 (cf. Sch.), Arist.*HA*531ᵃ31, 588ᵇ20, Plu.2.670d.

ἀκαλλ-ής, ές, *without charms*, γυνή Hp.*Ep.*15 ; σῶμα Luc.*Hist. Conscr.*48 ; γῆ αὐχμηρὰ καὶ ἀ. (v.l. ἀκαμής) Id.*Prom.*14 ; [ὕλη] ἀ. καὶ αἰσχρά Procl. *in Alc.*p.326C. : Comp., Olymp. *in Grg.* p.243J. -ιέρητος, ον, *not accepted* by gods, *ill-omened*, ἱερά Aeschin. 3.131,152. -ώπιστος, ον, *unadorned*, Heraclit.92, Ph.1.1, Luc. *Pisc.*12, Gal.*Protr.*10, Max.Tyr.29.7.

ἀκᾰλός, ή, όν, (ἀκᾶ, ἀκήν) *peaceful, still*, ἀκαλὰ προρέων, of a river, Hes.*Fr.*218 ; ἄκαλα κλόνει Sapph.*Supp.*19, cf. Hsch., Eust.1009. 30, *EM*44.29. Adv. -λῶς Eust.1871.54. **ἀκάλως**, Adv., (καλός) *unwell*, ἐὰν οὐκ ἀ. ἔχῃς, χαίρω *POxy.*1676.22 (iii A.D.).

ἀκάλυπτος, ον, *uncovered, unveiled*, S.*OT*1427, Arist.*HA*489ᵇ5, 1*Enoch*9.5 ; ἐν ἀκαλύπτῳ.. βίῳ, of one who has no house over his head, Men.404. Adv. -τως Lxx 3*Ma.*4.6.

ἀκᾰλῠφής, ές, = foreg., S.*Ph.*1327, Arist.*de An.*422ᵃ1 :—-ος, ον, Hippobot.ap.D.L.8.72.

ἀκᾰμαντο-λόγχας, α, ὁ, *unwearied at the spear*, Pi.*I.*7(6).10. -μάχας, α, ὁ, *unwearied in fight*, Id.*P.*4.171. -πους, ὁ, ἡ, πουν, τό, gen. ποδος, *untiring of foot*, ἵππος Id.*O.*3.3 ; βροντή, ἀπήνη, ib.4.1, 5.3. -ρόας, α, ὁ, *of untiring stream*, Ἀλφεός B.5.180. -χάρμας, α, ὁ, *unwearied in fight*, Pi.*Fr.*184, in voc. ἀκαμαντοχάρμαν Αἶαν.

ἀκάμας [ᾰκᾰ], αντος, ὁ, (κάμνω) *untiring*, ἠέλιος, Σπερχειός, etc., Il.18.239, 16.176, al. (not in Od.) ; ἵπποι Pi.*O.*1.87 ; Νότος, Βορέας S.*Tr.*112 (lyr.) ; χρόνος Critias18 ; πόνοι *unceasing*, Arist.*Fr.*675 ; νόος Them.*Or.*6.79c.

ἀκάμᾰτος, ον, also η, ον Hes.*Th.*747, B.5.25, S.*Ant.*339 :—*without sense of toil*, hence, 1. *untiring, unresting*, in Hom. always epith. of fire, Il.5.4, Od.20.123, al. ; ἄνεμοι Emp.111.3 ; σθένος A. *Pers.*901 ; ἅλς B.l.c. ; ἀ. γῆ earth *that never rests* from tillage, or *inexhaustible*, S. l.c. :—neut. ἀκάματα as Adv., Id.*El.*164 (lyr.). 2. *not tired*, χείρ Hp.*Fract.*3 ; ὄμματα B.18.20. 3. metaph., δόξα 12. 178 ; πρόνοια *Stoic.*1.125. II. Act., *not tiring*, Aret.*CD*2.13. Adv. -τως, in Comp., *less painfully*, Hp.*Mul.*1.1 :—also -τεί Hsch. s.v. ἀκμητί. [ᾰκᾰμᾰτος S.*El.*164 ; but first syll. long in dactylic verse.]

ἀκάμμυστος, ον, *without winking*, Hsch. s.v. ἀσκαρδάμυκτος.

ἄκαμνος, ον, *unwearied*, prob. f.l. for ἀκάμας, *PMag.Berol.*2.91.

ἀκαμπ-ής, ές, = ἄκαμπτος, Thphr.*HP*3.10.4, Orph.*A.*173, etc. : metaph., θυμός ib.999, cf. Ph.1.528, Plu.2.959f. -ία, Ion. -ίη, ἡ, = ἀκαμψία, Hp.*Art.*55. **-ίας**· ὁ εὐθὴς δρόμος, ἡ δρομεύς, Hsch., cf. Suid. **-ιος,** ον, = ἀκαμπής, S.*Fr.*988 :— neut. **-ιον,** τό, in chariot- or horse-racing, *straight course*, *IG*2.966*A*43, *Delph.*3(2).38, al., cf. *EM*45.3. **-τόπους,** ὁ, ἡ, *with unbending foot*, ἐλέφαντες Nonn.*D.*15.148. **-τος,** ον, *unbent, rigid*, Hp.*Fract.*2 (Sup.), Pl.*Ti.*74b (Comp.), etc.; τὸ ἄ. *the part that will not bend*, Arist.*HA*493^{b}29. 2. metaph., *unbending, unflinching*, βουλαί Pi.*P.*4.72; ψυχὰν ἄ. Id.*I.*4(3).53; ἀ. μένει A.*Ch.*455 (lyr.); τὸ πρὸς τοὺς πόνους, τὸ εἰς ἐπιείκειαν ἄ., Plu.*Lyc.*11, *Cat.Mi.*4. 3. *from which there is no return*, χῶρος ἐνέρων *AP*7.467 (Antip.); τρίβος *IG*12(7).449 (Amorgos).

ἀκαμψία, ἡ, *inflexibility*, Arist.*PA*654^{a}24.

ἄκαν, ανος, ὁ, = *thistle*, only in Lxx 4*Ki.*14.9.

ἄκανθ-α [ᾰκ], ης, ἡ, (ἀκή A) *thorn, prickle*, Arist.*PA*655^{a}19, Thphr.*HP*6.1.3: hence, 1. *any thorny* or *prickly plant* (in Od.5.328 (pl.) prob. *Eryngium campestre*), S.*Fr.*718, Eub.107.19, Theoc.1.132, etc.: prov., οὐ γὰρ ἄκανθαι no *thistles*, i.e. 'an easy job', Ar.*Fr.*272, 483:—special kinds: ἄ. Ἀραβική *smaller milk-thistle, Notobasis syriaca*, Dsc.3.13; ἄ. βασιλική *fish-thistle, Cnicus Acarna*, Thphr.*CP* 1.10.5; ἄ. Ἰνδική, = *Balsamodendron Mukul*, Id.*HP*9.1.2; ἄ. λευκή *Acacia albida*, ib.4.2.8; = ἄ. βασιλική, Dsc.3.12; ἄ. λευκὴ τρίοζος, = *Euphorbia antiquorum*, Thphr.*HP*4.4.12; ἄ. ἀκανώδης (prob.) *corn-thistle, Carduus arvensis*, ib.10.6. 2. of other plants, e.g. *Spanish broom, Spartium junceum*, Str.3.5.10:— = ἀκακία, ἄ. Αἰγυπτία, Thphr.*HP*9.1.2, cf. *POxy.*1188.10 (13 A.D.), etc.; ἄ. μέλαινα *Acacia arabica*, Thphr.*HP*4.2.8, cf. Hdt.2.96, Thd.*Is.*41.19; ἄ. διψάς, = *Acacia tortilis*, Thphr.*HP*4.7.1. 3. central flowering-bud of χαμαιλέων λευκός, ib.9.12.1, Dsc.3.8. 4. = ἄκανθος, Ps.-Dsc.3.17. 5. in pl., *prickles* or *spines* of the hedgehog and of certain fish, Ion Trag.38, Arist.*HA*530^{b}8. 6. *backbone* or *spine* of fish, A.*Fr.*275, Ar.*V.*969, Alex.110.11, al.; of serpents, Hdt.2.75, Theoc.24.32, A.R.4.150; of men, Hdt.4.72, Hp.*Art.*14, E.*El.*492, Arist.*PA* 654^{a}26, Gal.2.451, etc.; improperly used of mammalia, acc. to Arist.*APo.*98^{a}22; of *the spinous processes of the vertebrae*, Gal.2.758; χονδρώδεις ἄ. false ribs, Ruf.*Oss.*25. 7. metaph. in pl., *thorny* questions, Luc.*Hes.*5, Ath.3.97d. **-έα,** ἡ, = ἄκανθα Αἰγυπτία, *PLond.*2.214.13 (iii A.D.). **-ές**· ἀκανθῶδες, Hsch. **-εών,** ῶνος, ὁ, *thorny brake*, = *spinetum*, *Gloss.* **-ήεις,** εσσα, εν, *thorny, prickly*, Nic.*Th.*638. **-ηλή,** sine expl., Hdn.*Epim.*227. **-ηρός,** ά, όν, *with spines*, of certain fish, Arist.*HA*621^{b}16 (Comp.). **-ίας,** ου, ὁ, *prickly thing*, and so, 1. kind of *shark*, prob. *Squalus acanthias* L., Arist.*HA*565^{a}29, 621^{b}17. 2. kind of *grasshopper*, Ael.*NA*10.44. 3. = ἀσφάραγος, Poll.1.247, 6.54. **-ικός,** ή, όν, *spinous*, τὰ -κά Thphr.*HP*6.1.3, al.; φύσις ib.4.6. **-ινος,** η, ον, *of thorns*, στέφανος *Ev.Marc.*15.17, *Jo.*19.5. 2. metaph., *thorny*, ἐν ἀ. ἀταρποῖς *Anacreont.*53.12. II. *of shittah-wood*, ἱστός Hdt.2.96; ξύλα *PLond.*3.1177.191 (ii A.D.); τὰ ἀ. cloths *made of* ἀκάνθιον 2, Str.3.5.10. 2. ἀ. πάππος *thistle-down*, Dsc.4.81. **-ιον,** τό, Dim. of ἄκανθα, Arist.*HA*516^{b}19, Hp.*Mul.*1.36, *PStrassb.*29.37 (iii A.D.). 2. *cotton-thistle, Onopordum illyricum*, Dsc.3.16. **-ίς,** ίδος, ἡ, a bird, *goldfinch, Fringilla carduelis*, or *linnet*, *Fr. linaria*, Arist.*HA*616^{b}31, Theoc.7.141. II. = ἠριγέρων, Call.ap.Plin.*HN*25.168: = ἄκανθα Ἀραβική, Ps.-Dsc.3.13: = ἀκάνθιον, ib.16. III. = κανθός, Gal.17(1).666. **-ίων,** ονος, ὁ, *hedgehog*, Gal.12.423.

ἀκανθο-βάτης, ου, ὁ, *walking among thorns*, nickname of grammarians, *AP*11.322 (Antiphan.):—fem. **-βάτις,** ιδος, ib.7.198 (Leon.). **-βόλος,** ον, (βάλλω) *prickly*, χαίτη (of the plant ἔχις) Nic.*Th.*542; ῥόδον Id.*Fr.*74.9. II. Subst. ἀ., ὁ, *surgical instrument for extracting a bone*, prob. f.l. for sq., Paul.Aeg.6.32. **-λάβος,** ὁ, *instrument for extracting thorns*, ibid.:—also **-λαβίς,** ἡ, *Gloss.* **-λόγος,** ον, *gathering thorns*, nickname of quibblers (cf. ἄκανθα 7), *AP*11.20 (Antip. Thess.), 347 (Phil.). **-νωτος,** ον, *prickle-backed*, Hsch.

ἀκανθόομαι, Pass., (ἄκανθα) *become prickly*, Thphr.*HP*7.6.2.

ἀκανθοπλήξ, ῆγος, ὁ, ἡ, *wounded by the prickle* of a fish (cf. τρυγών), Ὀδυσσεὺς ἀ., name of play of Sophocles.

ἄκανθος, ὁ, *bearsfoot, Acanthus mollis*, a plant imitated in Corinthian capitals, Arist.*Fr.*269 (prob.), cf. *IG*4.1484.243 (Epid.); ὑγρὸς ἄ. Theoc.1.55; ἄ. ἀγρία *Acanthus spinosus*, Dsc.3.17. II. *Acanthus*, = ἀκακία, Virg.*G.*2.119.

ἀκανθο-στεφής, ές, of a fish, *prickle-backed*, Arist.*Fr.*295. **-φάγος** [ᾰ], ον, *feeding on thistles*, Arist.*HA*592^{b}30. **-φορέω,** *bear thorns*, Dsc.3.18. **-φόρος,** ον, *producing thorns*, Thphr.*HP*3.18.2. 2. *prickly*, ἐχῖνος Nonn.*D.*13.421. **-φυέω,** *produce thorns*, (v.l. for -φορέω) Dsc.3.18. **-φυλλος,** ον, *with spinous leaves*, cj. in Thphr.*HP*1.10.4. **-χοιρος,** ὁ, *hedgehog*, Hsch. s.v. ἐχῖνος, Suid. s.v. χοιρογρύλλιος.

ἀκανθ-υλλίς, ίδος, ἡ, Dim. of ἀκανθίς (in form), prob. *goldfinch*, Eub.123 (dub.), Arist.*HA*593^{a}13, 616^{a}5, cf. *Edict.Diocl.*4.34. 2. = ἀσφάραγος, Apul.*Herb.*84. **-ώδης,** ες, *full of thorns, thorny*, χῶρος Hdt.1.126; τὸ ῥόδον Arist.*Pr.*907^{a}22, cf. Thphr.*HP*1.5.3, etc. 2. *prickly*, γλῶττα Arist.*HA*503^{a}2; τρίχες ib.490^{b}28; of the vertebrae, *spinous*, ib.516^{b}20: Comp., ib.516^{b}22. 3. metaph., λόγοι ἀ. *thorny* arguments, Luc.*D.Mort.*10.8; ἀ. βίος Suid. **-ών,** ῶνος, ὁ, = ἀκανθεών, *PFlor.*50.72 (iii A.D.), Hdn.Gr.1.29.

ἀκᾰνίζω, (ἄκανος) *to be thistle-headed*, Thphr.*HP*6.4.8.

ἀκανικός, ή, όν, *thistle-like*, Thphr.*HP*4.6.10.

ἀκάνιον, τό, Dim. of ἄκανος, Hsch.

ἄκᾰνος, ὁ, (ἀκή A, ἀκίς) *pine-thistle, Atractylis gummifera*, Thphr.*HP*1.10.6, al. 2. *thistle-head*, ib.6.4.3.

ἀκᾰνώδης, ες, *thistle-headed*; τὸ τῶν ἀ. γένος Thphr.*HP*1.10.6, cf. 6.4.3.

ἀκαπήλευτος, ον, = sq., Suid.

ἀκάπηλος, ον, *free from tricks of trade*, βίος Str.11.8.7.

ἀκάπν-ιστος, ον, *unsmoked*, μέλι ἀ. honey *taken without smoking the bees*, Str.9.1.23. **-ος,** ον, *without smoke, free from it*, σκέπη Hp.*Acut.*65; *not smoking, making no smoke*, πῦρ Thphr.*Ign.*71; θυσία ἄ. an offering but *no burnt offering*, Luc.*Am.*4; so a poem is called Καλλιόπης ἄ. θύος *AP*6.321 (Leon.):—ἄκαπνα γὰρ αἰὲν ἀοιδοὶ θύομεν we sacrifice *without a fire of our own*, i.e. live at others' expense, Call.*Fr.*53P. II. = ἀκάπνιστος, Plin.*HN*11.45. III. ἄκαπνον, τό, = σάμψουχον, Ps.-Dsc.3.39. **-ωτος,** ον, *free from vapour*, E.*Fr.*781.54 (dub.).

ἄκαρα· τὰ σκέλη (Cret.), Hsch., *EM*45.16.

ἀκαρᾱδόκητος, ον, *unexpected*, Eust.1127.62.

ἀκάρδιος, ον, *wanting the heart*, Polyaen.8.23.33, Plu.*Caes.*63: metaph., *spiritless, cowardly*, Chrysipp.*Stoic.*2.247, 249; *heartless, weak*, Lxx *Je.*5.21; ἄφωνος καὶ ἀ. Procl.*in Cra.*p.41P. II. of wood, *without heart* or *pith, solid*, Thphr.*HP*3.12.1.

ἀκάρηνος, ον, *headless*, *APl.*4.116 (Euod.), *Epigr.Gr.*1013 (Memnon).

ἀκᾰρής, ές, (κείρω) properly of hair, *too short to be cut*, hence generally, *small, tiny*, ἀκαρῆ τινα ἐνθυμήματα D.H.*Isoc.*20; ἐν ἀκαρεῖ χρόνῳ *Com.Adesp.*370 (and codd. in Ar.*Pl.*244). II. metaph., *within a hair's breadth of, all but*, στρουθὶς ἀκαρὴς νὴ Δί' εἶ Alex.144; ἀ. παραπόλωλας Men.835; ἀ. δέω φάσκειν Id.*Pk.*166; κατέπεσον ἀ. τῷ δέει *Com.Adesp.*581. III. freq. of Time, esp. neut. ἀκαρές, *moment*, ἐν ἀκαρεῖ χρόνου Ar.*Pl.*244 (ap.*EM*), Alciphr.3.56, Luc.*Tim.*3 (also ἐν ἀ. τοῦ χρόνου ib.23); ἐν ἀ. alone, Id.*Asin.*37, Plot.5.5.7; also ἀκαρῆ διαλιπών (sc. χρόνον) having waited *a moment*, Ar.*Nu.*496; ἀκαρὲς ὥρας *in a moment*, Plu.*Ant.*28; ἡμέρας μιᾶς ἀ. Id.2.938a; ἐπ' ἀκαρές Aret.*SD*2.2. 2. neut. pl. ἀκαρῆ, usu. with negs., not *a bit*, not *at all*, οὐκ ἀπολαύεις πλὴν τοῦθ' ὃ φέρεις ἀκαρῆ not *a bit*, not *at all*, Ar.*V.*701; οὐδ' ἀκαρῆ ib.541 (lyr.), D.50.56; ἀκαρῆ παντελῶς (v.l. ἀκαρεῖ) Xenarch.7.15; παρ' ἀκαρῆ within *a hair's breadth*, Pl.*Ax.*366c, Phld.*Rh.*2.28S. IV. τὸ ἀ. *ring on the little finger*, Poll.5.100, Hsch. V. Adv. ἀκαρῶς Sch.Ar.*Pl.*244 (-έως Hsch.); **ἀκαρεί,** *instantly*, Plu.*Sert.*16.

ἀκαρί, τό, kind of *mite*, bred in wax, Arist.*HA*557^{b}8.

ἀκαριαῖος, α, ον, (ἀκαρής) *momentary, brief*, πλοῦς D.56.30, cf. Arist.*HA*590^{a}3, Phld.*Ir.*p.80W., etc.; τὸ ἀ. S.E.*P.*3.79; of a locus, ἀ. τόπος Aristox.*Harm.*p.55M. Adv. -ως Alciphr.1.39 (cj.).

ἀκαρνάν, ὁ, a fish, prob. = λάβραξ (cf. **ἀκάρναξ**· λάβραξ, Hsch.), Ath.8.356b.

ἀκαρπ-έω, *bear no fruit*, Thphr.*HP*3.3.4, etc. **-ία,** ἡ, *unfruitfulness, barrenness*, A.*Eu.*801, Hp.*Vict.*4.90, Arist.*Mir.*842^{a}22. **-ιστος,** ον, *where nothing is to be reaped, unfruitful*, of the sea, E.*Ph.*210 (lyr.). **-ος,** ον, *without fruit, barren*, E.*Fr.*898.8, Pl.*Ti.*91c; ἄ. ξύλον, = ἀκακία, Lxx *Is.*41.19: c. gen., λίμνη ἄ. ἰχθύων Paus.5.7.3. 2. metaph., *fruitless, unprofitable*, πόνος B.*Fr.*7.5; λόγοι Pl.*Phdr.*277a; τὰ ἄ. Arist.*EN*1125^{a}11. Adv. -πως S.*OT*254. II. Act., *making barren*, A.*Eu.*942, cf. Max.Tyr.5.4. **-ωτος,** ον, *not made fruitful, uncultivated*, Thphr.*CP*3.13.3. 2. metaph., χρησμὸς ἀ. *unfulfilled* oracle, A.*Eu.*714; νίκας ἀκάρπωτον χάριν because of some victory *which yielded her no tribute*, S.*Aj.*176.

ἀκαρτέρητος, ον, *insupportable*, κακόν Chrysipp.*Stoic.*3.131. Adv. -τως [Gal.]19.694. II. Act., *lacking in endurance*, Vett.Val.222.12.

ἀκαρτέω, = ἀκρατέω, γλώσσης Call.*Aet.*3.1.8.

ἄκαρτος, ον, (κείρω) *unshaven*, πώγωνες Ath.5.211e; ἀνθρωπάρια Ps.-Callisth.3.8.

ἀκαρφής, ές, (κάρφω) *not dried* or *withered*, Nic.*Fr.*70.9.

ἄκασκᾰ, Adv., (ἀκή B) *gently*, ἄ. προβῶντες Cratin.126; but ἀκασκᾷ Pi.*Fr.*28.

ἀκασκαῖος, α, ον, (ἀκή B) *gentle*, ἄγαλμα πλούτου A.*Ag.*741 (lyr.).

ἄκαστος, ὁ, = σφένδαμνος, Hsch.

ἀκάτα, corrupt in A.*Ag.*985; Ahrens' emend. (ψαμμὶς ἀκτά for ψαμμιὰς ἀκάτα) would suit the metre.

ἀκατά-βλητος, ον, *irrefragable*, λόγος Ar.*Nu.*1229. II. *not to be thrown down*, πύργοι Sch.E.*Hec.*1. **-βολέω,** *default* in payment, *GDI*1804 (Delph., ii B.C.). **-βολος,** ον, *unpaid, outstanding*, of arrears of taxation, *IG*5(1).1433 (Messene).

ἀκατ-αγγείωτος, ον, *not supplied with blood vessels*, δέρμα Antyll.(?) ap.Orib.45.17.8. **-άγγελτος,** ον, *unproclaimed*, πόλεμος D.H.1.58, Plu.*Num.*12, cf. App.*Hisp.*11.

ἀκατάγνωστος, ον, *not to be condemned*, Lxx 2*Ma.*4.47, *Ep.Tit.*2.8, *CIG*1971 (Thessalonica), *IG*14.2139; σύμβιος Keil-Premerstein *Zweiter Bericht* 225 (iii A.D.). Adv. -τως *unexceptionably*, λογιστεύσας *IG*5(2).152 (Tegea, iii A.D.), cf. *POxy.*140.15 (vi A.D.).

ἀκαταγώνιστος, ον, *unconquerable*, D.S.17.26, Olymp.Hist.p.451 D., Procl.*in Cra.*p.112P.; epith. of the Stoic sage, *Stoic.*1.53.

ἀκατα-δίκαστος, ον, *indemnatus*, *Gloss.* **-δούλωτος,** ον, *not enslaved*, Sch.E.*Hec.*420, 754. **-θύμιος,** ον, *disagreeable*, interp. in Artem.2.48, cf. Just.*Nov.*53.3.1, Eust.149.28, etc.

ἀκαταιτίᾱτος, ον, *not to be accused*, J.*BJ*4.3.10, al.; *not to be accused, blameless*, ib.2.14.8.

ἀκατα-κάλυπτος, ον, *uncovered*, Lxx *Le.*13.45 (v.l.), Plb.15.27.2, 1*Ep.Cor.*11.5, 13; ἀκαθαρσία Ph.1.72. **-καυστος,** ον, *not burnt*, Apollon.*Mir.*36:—also **-καυτος,** Dsc.5.102. **-κλαστος,** ον, *not* *to be broken, stubborn,* Sch.Od.10.329. **–κόσμητος,** ον, *unarranged,* Plu.2.424a. **–κράτητος,** ον, gloss on ἀάσχετος, *EM*1.31. **–κρῖτος,** ον, *uncondemned, Act.Ap.*16.37, 22.25.

ἀκάτακτος, ον, *not to be broken,* Arist.*Mete.*385^{a}14; *unbroken,* Phld.*Mort.*39.

ἀκατά-ληκτος, ον, *incessant,* γένεσις Ocell.4.2, cf. Arr.*Epict.*1.17.3, Procl.*inPrm.*p.873S., etc. Adv. –τως Agathin.ap.Orib.10.7.26. II. *acatalectic,* in prosody, Heph.4, Aristid.Quint.1.23. **–ληπτέω,** *not to understand,* S.E.*P.*1.201,al. **–ληπτος,** ον, *that cannot be reached* or *touched,* Arist.*Pr.*921^{b}23; τί ἐστι φίλος; ἄνθρωπος ἀ. Secund.*Sent.*11. Adv. –τως Sch.Il.17.75. II. *not to be conquered,* J.*BJ*3.7.7; *defying suppression,* τὸ ἀ. τῆς γοητείας Vett. Val.238.25. 2. Philos., *incomprehensible,* Phld.*Acad.Ind.*p.91 M., M.Ant.7.54, S.E.*M.*7.432; *that cannot be grasped,* πλῆθος, of the stars, Chrysipp.*Stoic.*2.168. 3. *not comprehending* or *attaining conviction,* φαντασία (opp. καταληπτική, q.v.) Chrysipp.*Stoic.*2.40, al.: c. gen., ἀ. τῶν ὁμοειδῶν Phld.*Herc.*1457.12. Adv. –τως, ἔχειν περί τινος Ph.1.78; prob. l. in Arr.*Epict.*2.23.46:—hence **ἀκαταληψία,** ἡ, *inability to comprehend* or *attain conviction,* Sceptic term, attrib. to Stoics by Galen, *Stoic.*1.17, but to Arcesilaus by Cic.*Att.* 13.19.3, Numen.ap.Eus.*PE*14.7, S.E.*P.*1.1.

ἀκατάλλακτος, ον, *irreconcilable,* Zaleuc.ap.Stob.4.2.19, D.S.12.20. Adv. –τως, πολεμεῖν D.11.4; διακεῖσθαι πρός τινα Plb.11.29.13; ἔχειν Ph.1.507; μισεῖν ib.479.

ἀκαταλληλ-ία, ἡ, *failure to conform with rules, inaccurate designation, PGnom.*138 (ii A.D.). II. Gramm., *false concord,* A.D.*Synt.* 167.1. **–ος,** ον, *not fitting together, incongruous,* τόποι Plb.6.42.3, cf. Arist.*Mu.*397^{b}31, Arr.*Epict.*2.11.8; *unsuitable,* Ruf.*Fr.*62; *inconsequent,* Phld.*Po.*1676.8:—esp. Gramm., *ungrammatical,* ἐνθύμημα D.H.*Dem.*27; *lacking in concord,* A.D.*Synt.*30.5,al. Adv. –ως *ungrammatically,* λόγος –ως συντεταγμένος Diog.Bab.*Stoic.*3.214; –ως κείμενα A.D.*Synt.*89.18; generally, *incongruously,* Porph.*Abst.*2.40:—also in Law, *not in conformity with regulations,* χρηματίζειν, πρᾶξαι, *PGnom.*117,106 (ii A.D.).

Ἀκάταλλος, ὁ, sc. μήν, month at Zelea, *SIG*279.23.

ἀκατά-λῦτος, ον, *indissoluble, perpetual,* κράτος, ζωή, D.H.10.31, *Ep.Heb.*7.16; βάσανος Lxx 4*Ma.*10.11; *unimpaired, Jahresh.*14 *Beibl.*135 (Cyme). **–μάθητος,** ον, *not learnt* or *known,* Hp.*Acut.* 7, 51, Plot.3.9.3. **–μακτος,** ον, *not softened by kneading,* Sch.Ar. *Lys.*656. **–μαρτύρητος,** Astrol., *not aspected by, not configurate with,* Vett.Val.117.8. **–μάχητος,** ον, *unconquerable,* Lxx *Wi.*5.19, M.Ant.8.48, Men.Prot.p.4D., Ps.-Callisth.2.11. **–μέμπτως,** Adv. *unexceptionably, IG*12(7).231 (Amorgos). **–μέτρητος,** ον, *unmeasured,* Eratosth.ap.Str.2.1.21, Nicom.*Ar.*1.17. **–μικτος,** ον, *not to be met with, rare, Gloss.*

ἀκατ-ανάγκαστος, ον, *not compulsory,* Diogenian.Epicur.3.61, Porph.ap.Eus.*PE*5.10.

ἀκατα-νέμητος, ον, *not pastured, PTeb.*66.75 (ii B.C.). **–νόητος,** ον, *inconceivable,* Ps.-Luc.*Philopatr.*13, Hsch.s.v. δύσληπτα, gloss on ἀθέσφατος, Sch.Opp.*H.*4.520. Adv. –τως Suid.s.v. Νουμᾶς. **–ξεστος,** ον, *not hewn, smooth, IG*1.322, 7.3074 (Lebad.). **–πάλαιστος,** ον, *unconquerable in wrestling,* Sch.Pi.*N.*4.153, *Gloss.* **–πάτητος,** ον, v.l. for ἀκατάποτος (q.v.). **–παυστος,** ον, *not to be set at rest, incessant,* Plb.4.17.4, D.S.11.67, etc.; *that cannot cease from,* τινός 2*Ep.Pet.*2.14. Adv. –τως Sch.A.R.1.1001. II. *not to be checked, irresistible, PMag.Par.*1.2364. **–πληκτος,** ον, *undaunted,* Epicur.*Fr.* 37, D.H.1.81, App.*BC*2.142. Adv. –τως Phld.*Mort.*39, D.H.1.57, App.*BC*1.110. **–πληξία,** ἡ, *imperturbability,* as the highest good, Nausiph.3; –πληξίαν ἔχειν πρὸς τὰ δεινά Phld.*D.*3*Fr.*81. **–πόνητος,** ον, *inexhaustible,* Philol.21, *Theol.Ar.*15. **–ποτος,** ον, *not to be swallowed,* Lxx *Jb.*20.18. **–πράϋντος,** ον, *unappeasable,* Sch. S.*Tr.*999, *Gloss.* **–πτόητος,** ον, *not to be scared,* Sch.Il.3.63. **–πτωτος,** ον, *not liable to fall,* Eustr.*inEN*311.18. **–σβεστος,** ον, *unslaked,* τίτανος Gal.12.471; *unquenchable,* ἐλλύχνια Apollon.*Mir.*36. **–σειστος,** ον, *not to be shaken,* Hsch. **–σήμαντος,** ον, *unsealed, unwritten,* ἀ. [ἔνταλμα] a commission *by word of mouth,* Hdn.3.11.9. **–σκεύαστος,** ον, *not properly prepared,* φάρμακον Thphr.*HP*9.16.6; *unwrought, unformed,* γῆ Lxx *Ge.*1.2; ἡ ἀ. *chaos,* 1*Enoch*21.1; *unpolished, unartificial,* ἁπλᾶ καὶ μονοειδῆ καὶ ἀ. Ps.-Plu.*Vit.Hom.*218. Adv. –τως D.H.*Is.*15. **–σκευος,** ον, *lacking equipment,* πλοῖα *PEdgar*8.4 (iii B.C.); of savage tribes, Theagen.17. II. in Lit. Crit., *without artifice* or *elaboration,* Phld.*Rh.*1.8S., D.H.*Th.*27, Philostr.*VA*6.11; epith. of orator, Plu. 2.835b. Adv. –ως Plb.6.4.7. III. *uncivilized,* βίος D.S.5.39. IV. *disordered,* v.l. for ἀπαρασκ., Aeschin.3.163. **–σκήνωτος,** ον, *unsuitable for encampment,* τόπος Onos.10.17. **–σκοπος,** ον, gloss on ἀνώϊστος, Sch.Opp.*C.*4.101. **–σόφιστος,** ον, *not to be put down by fallacies,* Ap.Ty.*Ep.*44. **–στᾰσία,** ἡ, *instability, anarchy, confusion, Stoic.*3.99, Plb.1.70.1, Nic.Dam.*Vit.Caes.*28, etc.: pl., Lxx *Pr.*26.28, D.H.6.31, 2*Ep.Cor.*6.5. II. *unsteadiness,* τοῦ σώματος Chrysipp.*Stoic.*3.121; ἀ. καὶ μανία Plb.7.4.8: pl., Man. 5.57. **–στᾰτέω,** *to be unstable,* Arr.*Epict.*2.1.12, Heph.Astr. 1.1:—Pass., Lxx *To.*1.15. **–στᾰτος,** ον, (καθίστημι) *unstable, unsettled,* καιροί Hp.*Aph.*3.8; πνεῦμα D.19.136, cf. Arist.*Pr.*941^{b}29; *disorderly,* ὁρμαί *Stoic.*3.166; πολιτεία D.H.6.74:—of men, *fickle,* Plb.7.4.6; of fevers, *irregular,* Hp.*Acut.*(*Sp.*)20. Adv. –ως, ἔχειν Isoc.21.7. II. *not making any deposit,* οὖρον Hp.*Prorrh.*1.32.

ἀκατ-αστέριστος, ον, *not arranged in constellations,* οὐρανός Ach. Tat.*Intr.Arat.*40.

ἀκατα-στόχαστος, *not conjectural,* πράγματα Phld.*Rh.*2.274S. (dub.), cf. Suid. **–στρεπτος,** ον, *not to be overthrown,* Sch.Pi.*O.*2.146. **–στροφος,** ον, *never-ending,* Favor.ap.Stob.4.15.29; of a literary period, *without conclusion,* D.H.*Comp.*22. Adv. –φως *incessantly,* Chrysipp.*Stoic.*2.273. **–σχαστος,** ον, *without scarification,* Herod.in *Rh.Mus.*58.92. **–σχεσία,** ἡ, *ungovernableness,* Ptol.*Tetr.*170. **–σχετος,** ον, (κατέχω) *not to be checked,* ὁρμή Hipparch.ap.Stob.4.44.81, cf. Onos.1.3; δάκρυα D.S.17.38; of persons, *uncontrollable,* Phld.*Piet.*86, Apollon.*Mir.*40, Plu.*Mar.*44. Adv. –τως D.S.17.34, Plu.*Cam.*37. **–τακτος,** ον, *not reduced to order,* Procl.*inPrm.*p.560S.; *abstract,* Ps.-Alex.Aphr.*inSE*38.13. II. *unclassified,* of sources of income, *BCH*6.14 (Delos, ii B.C.). **–τρητος,** ον, *not pierced,* ὀστοῦν Gal.*UP*9.13. **–τριπτος,** ον, *inexhaustible,* Plb.3.89.9; *not wearing out,* Gal.*UP*1.15.

ἀκατ-αύγαστος, ον, *not illuminated,* Steph.*inHp.*2.295D.

ἀκατά-φθορος, *unharmed, safe, SIG*700.32 (ii B.C.). **–φόρητος,** ον, *not to be borne,* Hsch. s.v. ἀνάρσιος. **–φρόνητος,** ον, *not to be despised,* X.*Ages.*6.8, J.*AJ*9.11.2, Plu.2.483a, etc. Adv. –ως *without negligence, PLond.*1.113(4).15 (vi A.D.). **–χρημάτιστος,** *not encumbered with debt, PTeb.*318.1 (ii A.D.), *PFlor.*28b, *Sammelb.* 364 (Alexandria), etc. **–χρηστος,** ον, *unused,* Eust.812.52, *Gloss.* **–χώριστος,** ον, *undigested,* ὕλη Arist.*Pr.*949^{b}3. II. *unregistered, Sammelb.*5232.33. **–ψευστος,** ον, *not fabulous,* θηρία Hdt.4.191; *not belied,* διάληψις *Ath.Mitt.*33.380 (Pergam.).

ἀκάτειος, ον, prop. *belonging to an* ἄκατος, q.v.; esp. ἀ. ἱστός *foremast, IG*2.793, etc.; ἀ. κεραία yard belonging thereto, ib., cf. Poll. 1.91. II. Subst. ἀκάτειον, τό, (sc. ἱστίον) *small sail,* opp. τὰ μεγάλα ἱστία, X.*HG*6.2.27, Epicr.10 (with play on ἄκατος II), cf. Luc.*Lex.*15, *J.Tr.*46, *Hist.Conscr.*45; ἄρασθαι τὸ ἀ., i.e. *take to flight,* prob. l. for ἀκάτιον in Epicur.*Fr.*163, cf. Ar.*Lys.*64.

ἀκατ-έργαστος, ον, *not cultivated,* γῆ *PTeb.*61^{b}32 (ii B.C.); *not worked up,* Longin.15.5; of bread, *not thoroughly baked,* Gal.6.484. II. *undigested,* τροφή Arist.*PA*650^{a}15, Diocl.*Fr.*43, etc.; *indigestible,* Xenocr.112, Gal.6.484. **–εύναστος,** ον, *not put to bed, waking,* Hsch., Suid., Phot. **–ηγόρητος,** ον, *not accused, PTeb.* 5.47 (ii B.C.), *Sammelb.*343 (Alexandria), D.S.11.46, J.*AJ*17.11.3, *BGU*183.8 (i A.D.); *blameless,* Phalar.*Ep.*10. **–ήχητος,** ον, *not encompassed by sound,* Suid.

ἀκάτιον [ᾰκᾰ], τό, Dim. of ἄκατος, *light boat,* used by pirates, Th. 1.29, 4.67, Plb.1.73.2, etc. II. sort of *woman's shoe,* Ar.*Fr.* 739b, Hsch. III. *dwarf, Com.Adesp.*923.

ἀκατίς, ίδος, *millepede,* Steph.*inHp.*1.154D.

ἀκατ-ονόμαστος, ον, *nameless,* ποιότης Epicur.*Fr.*314, cf. D.H. *Comp.*21, Archig.ap.Gal.8.592; θεός Ph.1.630, al. **–όπτευτος,** ον, *not in aspect with,* Paul.Al.*O.*2. **–οπτος,** ον, *unobserved,* Hld.6.14.

ἄκᾰτος [ᾰκ], ἡ (rarely ὁ, as Hdt.7.186):—*light vessel, boat,* Thgn. 458, Pi.*P.*11.40, Hdt. l.c., Th.7.25, etc.; used in the mysteries, *IG* 1.225*c*:—generally, *ship,* E.*Hec.*446, *Or.*342. II. *boat-shaped cup,* Theopomp.Com.3 (= Telest.6), Antiph.4.

ἀκατούλωτος, ον, *not scarred over,* Herod.Med.ap.Orib.10.11.3, Philum.*Ven.*10, Ruf.*Fr.*118.

ἀκάττῡτος, ον, *not stitched,* i.e. *new,* of shoes, Teles p.40H.

ἄκαυλος, ον, *without stalk,* Dsc.1.8.2. II. of a feather, *without shaft* or *stalk,* Arist.*PA*682^{b}18. III. Subst. ἄκαυλον, τό, = φυλλῖτις, Ps.-Dsc.3.107.

ἄκαυστ-ος, ον, (καίω) *unburnt,* Hp.*Haem.*2, X.*An.*3.5.13. 2. *incombustible,* Arist.*Mete.*387^{a}18, Thphr.*Lap.*4; *unquenchable* (v.l. for ἄσβεστος), πῦρ Lxx *Jb.*20.26. **–όω,** *make fireproof,* Zos.Alch. p.166B. **–ωσις,** ἡ, Id.p.217B.

ἀκαυτ-ηρίαστος, ον, *not branded,* of horses, Str.5.1.9. **–ος,** ον, = ἄκαυστος, Gal.12.212.

ἀκάχημαι, ἀκαχήσω, ἀκάχησα, etc., v. ἀχέω.

ἀκᾰχίζω [ᾰκ], only pres., *trouble, grieve,* τινά Od.16.432:—Med., μὴ . . λίην ἀκαχίζεο θυμῷ *be* not *troubled,* Il.6.486: c. part., μή τι θανὼν ἀκαχίζευ Od.11.486.

ἀκαχμένος, η, ον, Epic part. (cf. ἀκή A), *sharp-edged,* ἀ. ὀξέϊ χαλκῷ Il.15.482, Od.1.99, al.; πέλεκυν . . ἀμφοτέρωθεν ἀ. 5.235; φάσγανον 22.80. II. *armed,* c. dat., γένος σκυλάκων κυνόδουσιν ἀ. Opp.*C.* 1.476, cf. 3.252.

ἀκαχύνω, = ἀχέω, inf. –έμεν Antim.80. **ἀκεᾶνες·** ἰχθύες (Ambrac.), Hsch.

ἀκέᾰνος, ὁ, kind of leguminous vegetable, Pherecr.188, cf. Ael. Dion.*Fr.*28.

ἀκέαστος, ον, = ἄκλαστος, Hsch.

ἀκειόμενος, v. sub ἀκέομαι.

ἀκεῖον· τὸ φάρμακον, Hsch., *EM*46.19.

ἀκειρεκόμης, Dor. –ας, ὁ, = ἀκερσεκόμης, of Apollo, Pi.*P.*3.14, *I.*1.7, Philostr.*Ep.*16; of Asclepius, *IG*3.171; of Avars, *APl.*4.72.

ἀκέλευθος, ον, *pathless,* Hsch.

ἀκέλευμνον· οὐ βεβηκῶς ἀσφαλῶς, οἱ δὲ τὸν σκληρὸν σίδηρον, Hsch.

ἀκέλευστος, ον, *unbidden,* A.*Ag.*731 (lyr.), S.*Aj.*1284, E.*El.*71, Pl.*Lg.*953d. Adv. –ως Suid. s.v. ἀπαγγέλτως.

ἀκέλλεα(ν)· ἔκλεψαν (Tarent.), Hsch.

ἀκέλῡφος, ον, *without husk* or *capsule,* of fruits, Thphr.*CP*1.17.8.

ἀκενό-δοξος, ον, *without vain conceit,* M.Ant.1.16. Adv. –ως Sch. Od.3.411:—hence **–δοξία,** ἡ, Zonar. **–σπουδος,** ον, *shunning vain pursuits,* Antip.Tars.*Stoic.*3.254, Cic.*Fam.*15.17.4, M.Ant.1.6.

ἀκέντ-ητος, ον, *needing no spur,* Pi.*O.*1.21, *AP*5.202 (Asclep.), Ael.*NA*15.24. 2. metaph., *unpricked,* by love, Chor.*Zach.*5. II.

flawless, of crystals, Plin.*HN*37.28. **-ριστος**, ον, = foreg. 1, Hsch., *EM*432.11. **-ρος**, ον, *stingless*, κηφῆνες Pl.*R.*552c, 564b; *without spur*, of a cock, Clyt.1; *without thorns*, βάτος Ph.2.91. 2. *not responding to the spur*, of horses, *Hippiatr.*105: metaph., of style, *pointless*, Longin.21.2. II. *not occupying a cardinal point*, Man. 5.108, Vett.Val.89.30. **-ρότης**, ἡ, *absence from a cardinal point*, Demoph.ap.Jul.Laod. in *Cat.Cod.Astr.*5(1).189 (pl.).

ἀκέομαι [ᾰ], Ion. imper. ἀκέο (for ἀκέεο) Hdt.3.40; Ep. part. ἀκειόμενος Il.16.29, Od.14.383, Pi.*P.*9.104: fut. ἀκέσομαι D.C.38.19, Ep. ἀκέσσομαι Musae.199, Att. ἀκοῦμαι (ἐξ-) Men.863: aor. ἠκεσάμην, Ep. imper. ἄκεσσαι, etc.:—**Pass.**, v. sub fin.: I. trans., *heal, cure*, c. acc. of thing healed, ἕλκος ἄκεσσαι Il.16.523; ἕλκε' ἀκειόμενοι 16.29; ψώρην ἀκέσασθαι Hdt.4.90; of part healed, τὰ ἔσω ἀσκοῖσιν Hp.*Mochl.*25; ἄχος S.*Tr.*1035; βλέφαρον ἀκέσαιο τυφλόν E.*Hec.*1067; τὸν Λητώ τε καὶ Ἄρτεμις..ἀκέοντο Il.5.448, cf. 402: c. gen. morbi, νούσου..μ' ἀκέσω βαρυαλγέος *Epigr.Gr.*803 (Delos), cf. Paus.8.18.8. 2. *stanch, quench*, πίον τ' ἀκέοντό τε δίψαν Il.22.2, cf. Pi.*P.*9.104. 3. generally, *mend, repair*, νῆας ἀκειόμενος Od.14.383; freq. of tailors or cobblers, Luc.*Fug.*33, *Nec.*17; of a spider *mending* its web, Arist. *HA*623ᵃ18. 4. metaph., *make amends for, repair*, ἁμαρτάδα Hdt.1.167; τὰ ἐπιφερόμενα Id.3.16, cf. E.*Med.*199; μήνιμα Antipho 4.3.7; ἀδίκημα Pl.*R.*364c; ἀπορίας X.*Mem.*2.7.1. II. intr. or abs., *apply a remedy, make amends*, ἀλλ' ἀκεώμεθα θᾶσσον· ἀκεσταί τοι φρένες ἐσθλῶν Il.13.115; ἀλλ' ἀκέσασθε, φίλοι Od.10.69, cf. S.*Ant.*1027, Hdt.3.40, Pl.*Phlb.*30b. III. Act., Hp.*Loc.Hom.* 10; ἀκέεται in pass. sense, Aret.*CA*1.1; ἀκεομένου τοῦ κακοῦ Id.*SD* 1.6: aor. ἀκεσθῆναι Paus.2.27.3.

ἀκεόντως, Adv. *noiselessly*, Hsch. **ἄκερα**· ἔνδυμά τι πολυτελές, Id.

ἀκεραι-όομαι, Pass., *to be* ἀκέραιος, Eust.277.16. **-ος**, ον (fem. -αία Sch.Ar.*Pl.*593), Prose word (used by E., v. infr.) for poet. ἀκήρατος, *pure, unmixed*, ὕδωρ Arist.*HA*605ᵃ15; οἶνος Dsc.5.6; ἀργύριον Poll.3.86, etc.; *untouched*, γῆ, νομή, Pl.*Criti.*111b, Arist.*HA* 575ᵇ3; *unalloyed*, ἡδοναί Epicur.*Sent.*12. 2. of persons, *pure in blood*, E.*Ph.*943. II. *unharmed, unravaged*, ἀ. ἀπολαμβάνειν τὴν πόλιν Hdt.3.146; γῆ Th.2.18; χώρα D.1.28; δύναμις, of an army, *in full force*, Th.3.3; of troops, *fresh*, X.*An.*6.5.9, Plb.1.40.12, etc.; of property, *untouched*, οὐσία D.44.23; ἐάν τι ἀσινὲς καὶ ἀ. *IG*3.1418*f*; of a person, Persae.*Stoic.*1.99. 2. metaph., *pure, inviolate*, ἀκέραιον ὡς σῴσαιμι Μενέλεῳ λέχος E.*Hel.*48; [τέχνη] ἀβλαβὴς καὶ ἀ. Pl. *R.*342b; *complete, perfect*, φαντασίαι Phld.*D.*3.8; ἐλπίς Plb.6.9.3; ὁρμαί Id.1.45.2. 3. of persons, *uncontaminated, guileless*, E.*Or.*922; *incorruptible*, κριτής D.H.7.4: c. gen., ἀ. κακῶν ἠθῶν Pl.*R.*409a, cf. Men.*Epit.*489; *unprejudiced, with an open mind*, Plb.21.31.12. 4. ἐξ ἀκεραίου *anew*, Id.23.4.10; *while matters are undecided*, Id.6.24.9; ἀκέραιον ἐᾶν leave *alone*, Id.2.2.10; εἰς -ον ἀποκαθιστάναι, = Lat. *in integrum restituere*, *IG*14.951. Adv. -ως, of payment, *in full*, Cic. *Att.*15.21.2; *unreservedly*, Phld.*Lib.* p.57 O. **-οσύνη**, ἡ, *guilelessness, innocence*, Suid. **-ότης**, ητος, ἡ, *freshness*, of troops, Plb. 3.73.6, 6.40.9. 2. *integrity*, Just.*Edict.*7.8 *Intr.* **-οφανής**, v. ἀκραιφνής.

ἀκέραστος, ον, *unmixed, pure*, τόλμης ἀνδρείας Pl.*Plt.*310d. Adv. ἀκεράστως, πνέων, gloss on ἀκραής, Sch.Od.2.421. II. of vowel-sounds, *not coalescing*, D.H.*Comp.*22.

ἀκέρᾰτος, ον, (κέρας) *without horns*, Pl.*Plt.*265c sq., Arist.*HA* 501ᵃ14, al.

ἀκέραυν-ος, ον, = sq., of Capaneus, A.*Fr.*17. **-ωτος**, ον, *not struck by lightning*, Luc.*J.Tr.*25.

ἀκέρδ-εια, ἡ, *want of gain, loss*, Pi.*O.*1.53:—also -ία Procop.*Arc.* 13. **-ής**, ές, *bringing no gain, unprofitable*, χάρις S.*OC*1484, cf. Pl.*Cra.*417d, D.H.6.9, *AP*9.649 (Maced.). Adv. -δῶς *without profit*, Arist.*Pol.*1309ᵃ13, Plu.2.27d. II. *not greedy of gain*, φιλοτιμία Id.*Arist.*1. Adv. -ῶς Id.2.483e.

ἀκέρκιστος, ον, (κερκίζω) *unwoven*, *AP*7.472 (Leon.).

ἄκερκος, ον, *tailless*, Arist.*PA*689ᵇ6.

ἀκερμ-ατία, ἡ, (κέρμα) *want of money*, Ar.*Fr.*15 (unless as Verb -ιᾶν). **-ία**, ἡ, = foreg., Lyd.*Mag.*3.14.

ἄκερος, ον, = ἄκερως, Arist.*HA*499ᵇ16.

ἀκερσεκόμης (ἀκερσι- in Nonn. ll. cc. infr.), ου, ὁ, (Dor. voc. -κόμα Pi.*Pae.*9.45: dat. pl. -κόμοισιν Nonn.*D.*14.232), (κείρω, κόμη) *with unshorn hair*, i.e. *ever-young* (for Greek youths wore long hair till they reached manhood), of Phoebus, Il.20.39, *h.Ap.*134, etc. 2. *long-haired*, Nonn.*D.*10.29, al.; cf. ἀκειρεκόμης.

ἀκερσίλα· μυρσίνη (Sicel), Hsch. **ἀκερχές**· ἀπενθές, Id.

ἄκερχνος, ον, *without hoarseness*, Aret.*CA*1.10. II. Act., *curing hoarseness*, Id.*CD*1.8.

ἄκερως, ων, gen. ω, = ἀκέρατος, Pl.*Plt.*265b, Ael.*NA*2.53, Max.Tyr. 17.5.

ἀκερωσύνη, dub. in Suid. s.v. ἀκεραιοσύνη.

ἀκέρωτος, ον, (κέρας) *not horned*, *AP*6.258 (Adaeus).

ἀκεσ-ίας· ἰατρός, Phot. **-ίμβροτος** [ᾰ], ον, *healing mortals*, of Asclepius, Orph.*L.*8; ἀ. ἄνθος Poet. *de herb.*146. **-ιμος**, ον, (ἀκέομαι) *wholesome, healing*, Plu.2.956f. **-ιος**, ον, *healing*, epith. of Apollo, Paus.6.24.6. **-ίπονον**· θεραπευτικόν, Suid., Phot. **-ις**, εως, ἡ, *healing, cure*, Hdt.4.90,109, Hierocl. *in CA*25 p.477 M.; τὸν εὑράμενον παυσινόσους ἀκέσεις *IG*3.900. 2. *mending, repair*, θυρᾶν *IG*4.1484 (Epid.); μηχανώματος *GDI*2502.62 (Delph.). II. name of *plaster*, Asclep.ap.Gal.13.442. **-μα**, τό, *remedy*, Il.15. 394 (v.l.), Pi.*P.*5.64, A.*Pr.*482, *IG*14.1750. **-μιος**, ον, *curable*, Hsch. **-μός**, ὁ, = ἄκεσις, Call.*Fr.anon.*227.

ἀκεσσί-νοσος, ον, *healing disease*, cj. in *AP*9.516 (Crin.). **-πονος**, ον, *assuaging pain* or *toil*, Nonn.*D.*7.86.

ἀκεσ-τήρ, ῆρος, ὁ, *healer*: Adj., ἀ. χαλινός rein *that tames the steed*, S.*OC*714 (lyr.). **-τήριον**, τό, *tailor's shop*, Lib.*Or.*11.254. **-τήριος**, ον, *medicinal, healing*, metaph., κακῶν φάρμακον App.*Pun.* 88. **-τής**, οῦ, ὁ, = ἀκεστήρ, Lyc.1052: Phrygian acc. to Sch.Ven. Il.22.2, Eust.1254.2, *EM*51.7. 2. ἀκεσταὶ ἱματίων ῥαγέντων *menders* of torn clothes, X.*Cyr.*1.6.16 (v.l. ἠπηταί), cf. Alciphr.3. 27. **-τίδες**, αἱ, *bars* in sublimating furnaces, Dsc.5.74. **-τικός**, ή, όν, *fitted for healing* or *mending*: ἡ -κή (sc. τέχνη) Democr.154, Pl.*Plt.*281b, Ael.*NA*6.57, Gal.*Thras.*30. **-τορία**, ἡ, *the healing art*, A.R.2.512, *APl.*4.272 (Leont.), Max.314. **-τορίς**, ίδος, ἡ, fem. of ἀκέστωρ, Hp.*Flat.*1. **-τός**, ή, όν, *curable*, Hp.*Art.*58; πρᾶγμα Antipho 5.91: metaph., ἀκεσταὶ φρένες ἐσθλῶν the hearts of the noble *admit treatment*, Il.13.115. **-τρα**, ἡ, *darning-needle*, Luc. *D.Mort.*4.1, *PLips.*28.6. **-τρια**, ἡ, *sempstress*, Antip.Tars.*Stoic.* 3.254, Luc.*Rh.Pr.*24; ἀ., ἡ, title of play by Antiphanes: in pl., title of mime by Sophron. **-τρίς**, ίδος, ἡ, fem. of ἀκεστήρ, *midwife*, Hp.*Carn.*19. **-τρον**, τό, *remedy*, S.*Ichn.*317, *Fr.*480. **-τωρ**, ορος, ὁ, *healer, saviour*, Φοῖβος E.*Andr.*900. **-φορία**, ἡ, *healing, salvation*, *AP*9.349 (Leon.), Max.167. **-φόρος**, ον, *bringing cure, healing*, c. gen. rei, E.*Ion*1005, Astyd.Trag.6. **-ώδῠνος**, ον, *allaying pain*, Paetus ap.Hp.*Ep.*2, *AP*9.815, *IG*14.1015, Men.Rh.p.443 S.

ἀκεύει· τηρεῖ (Cypr.), Hsch., dub. in *Leg.Gort.*2.17.

ἀκέφᾰλος, ον, *headless*: οἱ ἀ., fabulous creatures in Libya, Hdt.4. 191; ἀ. ταῦροι J.*BJ*4.8.4. 2. *without beginning*, λόγος, μῦθος, Pl.*Phdr.*264c, *Lg.*752a; *without peroration*, μῦθος Luc.*Scyth.*9; of verses *which lack the first mora*, Heph.6.2, al., cf. Ath.14.632d. Adv. -λως, ἐμβάλλειν τοῖς πράγμασι Hermog.*Inv.*2.7. 3. αἵρεσις ἀ. sect *with no known head*, Suid.; ἀ., οἱ, Just.*Nov.*109 *Praef.* II. = ἄτιμος, Artem.1.35; cf. Lat. *capite deminutus*.

ἀκέω (A), v. ἀκέομαι sub fin. **ἀκέω** (B), *to be silent* (cf. sq.), only opt. pres. ἀκέοις A.R.1.765.

ἀκέων, ουσα, participial form, *softly, silently*, fem. ἀκέουσα Il.1.565, Od.11.142: dual. ἀκέοντε 14.195; also indecl., ἀκέων δαίνυσθε 21.89, cf. *h.Ap.*404; Ἀθηναίη ἀκέων ἦν Il.4.22, 8.459.

ἀκή (A), ἡ, (cf. ἀκίς) *point*, Hsch., Suid. **ἀκή** (B), ἡ, (cf. ἀκᾶ) *silence*, ἀκὴν ἔχεν Mosch.2.18; ἀκὴν ἦγες Hsch. **ἀκή** (C), ἡ, (cf. ἀκέομαι) *healing*, Hp.*Mochl.*21, cf. *Hum.*1.

ἀκηδ-εια, ἡ, (κῆδος) *carelessness, indifference*, in pl., Emp.136, A.R.2.219: sg., 3.260, Diog.Oen.24. II. in pl., *anguish*, A.R. 3.298 (Sch. πολυκηδείαισι). **-εστος**, ον, *uncared for*, Il.6.60; esp. *unburied*, *AP*7.686 (Pall.); *unkempt*, κάρηνον Nonn.*D.*10. 272. Adv. -τως *without care for others, ruthlessly*, Il.22.465, 24.417, cf. *AP*9.375. **-ευτος**, ον, *unburied*, Plu.*Per.*28, J.*AJ*6.14.8. **-έω**, fut. -ήσω cj. in S.*Ant.*414, cf. Q.S.10.29: aor. -ησα 12.376, ἀκήδεσα Il.14.427: (ἀκηδής):—*take no care for, no heed of*, c. gen., οὔ τίς εὖ ἀκήδεσεν Il. l.c.; οὐ μέν μευ ζώοντος ἀκήδεις, ἀλλὰ θανόντος 23.70; σαυτοῦ δ' ἀκήδει δυστυχοῦντος (imper.) A.*Pr.*508, cf. Mosch.4.81, Onos.33.3. 2. abs., *grow weary*, Q.S.10.16. (See also ἀφειδέω.) **-ής**, ές, I. Pass., *uncared for*: esp. *unburied*, ὄφρα μὲν Ἕκτωρ κεῖται ἀ. Il.24.554; ἢ αὔτως κεῖται ἀ. Od.20.130; σώματ' ἀκηδέα κεῖται Od.24.187, cf. 6.26, 19.18. Adv. -ῶς Suid. II. Act., *without care* or *sorrow*, Il.24.526, Hes.*Th.*489, *AP*11.42 (Crin.). 2. *careless, heedless*, τὸν δὲ γυναῖκες ἀκηδέες οὐ κομέουσιν Od.17.319, cf. Il.21.123: c. gen., *taking no thought for*, φίλων S.*Fr.* 208.10; παίδων Pl.*Lg.*913c. III. (κήδω *harm*) *harmless*, Opp.*H.* 1.611, 2.648, cf. Epic.ap.Suid. **-ία**, Ion. -ίη, ἡ, = ἀκήδεια: *indifference, torpor, apathy*, Hp.*Gland.*12, Cic.*Att.*12.45. 2. *weariness, exhaustion*, Luc.*Herm.*77, D.C.*Fr.*73; πνεύματος Lxx *Is.*61.3. 3. c. gen., *neglect, disregard*, τῆς παραφορῆς Aret.*CA*1.1. **-ιαστής**, Hsch. and Suid. s.v. ἀσηκόρος. **-ιάω**, *to be careless*, Zos.Alch. p.133 B. 2. *to be exhausted, weary*, Lxx *Ps.*60(61).2, etc.

ἀκήλητος, ον, *proof against enchantment*, Od.10.329 (dub. vers.), Pl.*Phdr.*259b; μανίας ἄνθος S.*Tr.*999 (lyr.); of the Dioscuri, Theoc. 22.169; ἀ. τὸ ἀπαθές Porph.ap.Eus.*PE*5.10.

ἀκηλίδωτος [ῐ], ον, *spotless*, ἔσοπτρον, ἐσθής, πέδιλα, Lxx *Wi.*7.26, Ph.1.156, Porph.*Abst.*2.46: metaph., βίος, ἀρετή, Lxx *Wi.*4.9, Ph.2. 235; σωτηρία Steph. *in Hp.*2.238 D.

ἄκημα, τό, = ἄκεσμα, *cure, relief*, ὀδυνάων Il.15.394 codd., Max.142.

ἀκήμων· ἐκκεχυμένος, Hsch.

ἀκήν (cf. ἀκή B), acc. form as Adv., *softly, silently*, Hom. mostly in phrase ἀκὴν ἐγένοντο σιωπῇ Il.3.95, al.; also οἱ δ' ἄλλοι ἀκὴν ἴσαν 4.429.

ἀκήνιον· ἥσυχον, *EM*48.1.

ἀκήπευτος, ον, *not in a garden, wild*, γογγυλίδες Posidon.29, cf. Gal.12.509.

ἀκηρ-ασία, ἡ, *purity*, Hsch. (ἀκηρεσία in Ms.). **-άσιος**, ον, Ep. form of ἀκήρατος, *untouched*, ἀ. λειμῶνες *meadows not yet grazed* or *mown*, *h.Merc.*72; γυίων ἄνθος ἀ. *pure, fresh*, *AP*12.93 (Rhian.); σκῆπτρα ἀ. *inviolate*, *Epigr.Gr.*907 (Sinope). II. (κεράννυμι) *unmixed*, οἶνος Od.9.205. **-ᾰτος**, ον, (κηραίνω) *undefiled, pure*, ὕδωρ Il.24.303; *inviolate*, χεῦμα, ὄμβρος, S.*OC*471, 690 (lyr.); χρυσός *pure* gold, Archil.*Supp.*4, Alcm.23.54, Hdt.7.10.α', Simon.64, cf. Pl. *R.*503a, *Plt.*303e; φλόξ Secund.*Sent.*5; *untouched, unhurt*, οἶκος καὶ κλῆρος, κτήματα, Il.15.498, Od.17.532; ἀπαρτίη Hippon.26; σκάφος A.*Ag.*661; ἀνίαι *strong* reins, Pi.*P.*5.32; πλόκοι *unshorn* locks, E. *Ion*1266; λειμών *unmown* meadow, Id.*Hipp.*73; ἀ. ἐμπόριον *virgin* market, Hdt.4.152; ἀ. φιλία X.*Hier.*3.4; ἐπιστήμη, ἤθη, Pl.*Phdr.*247d,

*Lg.*735c; ἀ. φάρμακα spells *that have all their power*, A.R.4.157. 2. of persons, *undefiled*, a virgin, E.*Tr.*675, Pl.*Lg.*84cd; ἀ. λέχος E. *Or.*575: c. dat., ἀκήρατος ἄλγεσι, τύχαις *untouched by* woes, etc., *Hipp.*1113, *HF*1314: c. gen., ἀ. κακῶν *without taint* of ill, *Hipp.*949; ἀ. ὠδίνων *free from* throes of child-birth, A.R.1.974, etc.: poet. Sup. ἀκηρότατος *AP*12.249 (Strat.). II. (κεράννυμι) *unmixed*, ποτόν A.*Pers.*614.

ἀκήριος (A), ον, *unharmed by the* Κῆρες; generally, *unharmed*, Od. 12.98, 23.328, *h.Merc.*530, Nic.*Th.*190, Call.*Ap.*41, A.R.3.466; ψυχαὶ ἀκήριοι, = ἀθάνατοι, *free from power of the Fates*, Ps.-Phoc.99. II. *having no* κήρ, i.e. *with no fortune attached to them*, ἡμέραι Hes.*Op.* 823. III. *harmless*, πάμπαν δ' ἄμωμος οὔτις οὐδ' ἀ. Semon.4, cf. Nic.*Th.*771.

ἀκήριος (B), ον, (κῆρ) *without heart*, i.e., I. *lifeless*, Hom. (not in Od.), ἀκήριον αἶψα τίθησι Il.11.392. cf. 21.466. II. *heartless, spiritless*, σέ που δέος ἴσχει ἀκήριον ib.5.812, cf. 13.224; ἥμενοι αὖθι ἕκαστοι ἀκήριοι 7.100; ἀκήριον ἠύτ' ὄνειρον A.R.2.197.

ἄκηρος (sc. ἔμπλαστρος), ἡ, name of *a plaster*, Gal.13.759.

ἀκηρ-υκτεί and **-υκτί**, Adv. *without flag of truce*, ἐπιμείγνυσθαι Th. 2.1; πολεμεῖν D.C.50.7. **-υκτος**, ον, *unannounced, unproclaimed*, ἀ. πόλεμος *sudden* war, Hdt.5.81; also a war *in which no herald was admitted, truceless*, X.*An.*3.3.5, Pl.*Lg.*626a, Aeschin.2.33; ἦν γὰρ ἄσπονδος καὶ ἀ. ὑμῖν πρὸς τοὺς θεατὰς πόλεμος D.18.262; ἀ. ἔχθρα Plu. *Per.*30. 2. *without flag of truce*, τὸ ἀ. τῆς ὁδοῦ App.*Mith.*104. Adv. -τως, ἐφοίτων Th.1.146; cf. foreg. II. *not proclaimed victor by heralds, inglorious*, E.*Heracl.*89, Aeschin.3.230. III. *with no tidings, not heard of*, S.*Tr.*45, Nonn.*D.*9.249. 2. *unheralded*, ἔρωτες ib.48.653.

ἀκήρωτος, ον, (κηρόω) *unwaxed*, Luc.*Icar.*3, Polyaen.2.20.

ἀκῆσκος· τάλαρος, Hsch. **ἀκητόν**· κράτιστον, Id.

ἀκηχέδαται, ἀκηχέμενος, v. sub ἀχέω.

ἀκηχεδών, όνος, ὁ, = λύπη, Hsch. (pl.), cf. *EM*48.2.

ἀκιβδήλευτος, ον, = sq., Ph.1.565, etc.

ἀκίβδηλος, ον, *unadulterated, genuine*, Pl.*Lg.*916d, Arist.*Ath.*51. 1; χρυσός Hierocl. *in CA Praef.*p.417 M. 2. metaph., of men, *guileless, honest*, Hdt.9.7.α'. Adv. -λως Isoc.1.7.

ἀκίδιον, τό, Dim. of ἀκίς, *small barb*, *BCH*29.572.

ἀκιδνός [ᾰ], ή, όν, Ep. and Ion., *weak, feeble*, Hom. only in Od., always in Comp., εἶδος ἀκιδνότερος 8.169, cf. 5.217, 18.130, cf. Nic. *Th.*224; later in Posit., δμωαί Man.2.178: Sup. -ότατον, βέλεμνον Nonn.*D.*7.270; *insipid*, ἔδεσμα Archestr.*Fr.*38 B. (s.v.l., καὶ κεδνόν Meineke, Brandt).—Ep. word, also in Hp., ἰατρός *Praec.*8: δύναμις *Nat.Puer.*30.

ἀκιδοειδής, ές, *barb-like*, of quadrilateral with re-entrant angle, Procl. *in Euc.*p.165 F. **ἀκιδόω**, (ἀκίς) *furnish with barb* or *point*, in Pass., βέλη ἠκιδωμένα *IG*2.807. **ἀκιδρός**· ἀσθενής, Cyr. **ἀκιδρωπάζω**· ἀμβλυωπῶ, Hsch.

ἀκῐδ-ώδης, ες, *pointed*, Thphr.*HP*4.12.2. **-ωτός**, ή, όν, = foreg., Paul.Aeg.6.88, Poll.1.97, 10.133, Hsch. II. **-ωτός**, ὁ, = παρωνυχία, Ps.-Dsc.4.54: **-ωτόν**, τό, = σέλινον ἄγριον, Id.2.175; = ποτίρριον, Dsc.3.15.

ἀκίθαρις, ι, *without the harp*, A.*Supp.*681 (lyr.).

ἄκῑκυς, υος, ὁ, ἡ, *powerless, feeble*, Od.9.515, 21.131, Theoc.*Ep.* 11. II. *weakening*, νοῦσος Orph.*L.*22.—Ep. word, also in A. *Pr.*548 (lyr.), and Ion. Prose, cf. Hp.*Morb.*4.43 (in sense 1).

ἀκίναγμα [ᾰκῐ], τό, = τίναγμα, χειρῶν ἠδὲ ποδῶν *Lyr.Adesp.*30 B (= Call.*Fr.anon.*68):—also **ἀκιναγμός**, ὁ, Hsch.

ἀκινάκης, ου, ὁ, Persian word, *short straight sword*, Hdt. (v. infr.), cf. X.*An.*1.2.27 (also acc. -άκεα Hdt.3.118; pl. -άκεας v.l. ib.128); ἀ. ἐπίχρυσος, a Persian *sword* kept in the Parthenon, *IG*1.170.17, cf. 2.646.11; νὴ τὸν ἀκινάκην, a Scythian oath, Luc.*Tox.*38, cf. *J.Tr.*42. [*acinaces* in Hor.*Od.*1.27.5.]

ἀκινδῡν-ί, Adv. of sq., *without danger*, Suid. **-ος**, ον, *free from danger*, σιγᾶς ἀ. γέρας Simon.66; βίος Id.36, cf. E.*IA*17, Th.1.124; πυρετοί Hp.*Aph.*7.63; ἀρεταὶ ἀ. virtues *that court no danger*, i.e. *cheap, easy* virtues, Pi.*O.*6.9, cf. Th.3.40; ἀ. εἶναί τινι τὸν ἀγῶνα Hyp. *Lyc.*8: c. gen., *guaranteed against risk*, ἀ. παντὸς κινδύνου *IG*12(7).67 (Amorgos), *PTeb.*105.18 (ii B.C.). II. Adv. -νως E.*Rh.* 588, Antipho 2.4.7, etc.; ἡ ἀ. δουλεία Th.6.80; τὸ ἀ. ἀπελθεῖν αὐτούς their departure *without danger* to us, Id.7.68: Comp. ἀκινδυνότερον *with less danger*, Pl.*Phd.*85d: Sup. ἀκινδυνότατα, ζῆν X.*Mem.*2.8. 6. **-ότης**, ητος, ἡ, *freedom from danger*, Gal.9.491. **-ώδης**, ες, *of no dangerous appearance*, f.l. in Hp.*Art.*65 (Comp.).

ἀκιν-ήεις, εσσα, εν, = ἀκίνητος, Nic.*Al.*436. **-ησία**, ἡ, *absence of motion*, Arist.*Ph.*202^{a}5, al.; *stagnancy*, Hp.*Vict.*2.37; *incapacity to move*, Thphr.*Fr.*11; *failure of mobility*, Epicur.*Nat.*908.6; *pause, intermission*, of the pulse, Gal.8.510, Aret.*CA*2.3. **-ητέω**, *to be at rest* or *immovable*, Hp.*Mul.*1.11, cf. *Stoic.*2.161, Antyll.(?) ap.Orib.8.6.9, S.E.*M.*7.188; of bones, as opp. joints, Gal.19. 460. **-ητί** or **-τεί**, Adv. *immovably*, Poll.3.89, 9.115. **-ητίζω**, = ἀκινητέω, Arist.*HA*537^{b}7, *Stoic.*2.161. **-ητίνδᾰ**, Adv., ἀ. παίζειν play the game 'who stirs first', Poll.9.110. **-ητος**, ον, also η, ον Pi.*O.*9.33, *IG*14.1389 ii 14:—*unmoved, motionless*, Parm.8, Emp.17, etc.; of Delos, Orac.ap.Hdt.6.98, cf. Pi.*P.*4.57; ἐξ ἀκινήτου ποδός *without stirring* a step, S.*Tr.*875; τὰς κινήσεις ἀκίνητος Pl.*Ti.* 40b; τὸ πρῶτον κινοῦν ἀκίνητον αὐτό Arist.*Metaph.*1012^{b}31; ὕλη ἀ. Stoic.ap.Plu.2.1054a; ἄστρα ἀ. *fixed* stars, Poll.4.156. 2. *idle, sluggish*, ἐπ' ἀκινήτοισι καθίζειν to sit in *idleness*, Hes.*Op.*750 (where others, to sit *on graves*, v. infr. II. 2); ἀ. φρένες a *sluggish* soul, Ar.*Ra.* 899; of the Boeotians, Alex.237; χώρα ἀ. *untilled*, Plu.2.38c. 3. *unmoved, unaltered*, ἀ. νόμιμα Th.1.71, etc.; τοὺς νόμους ἐᾶν ἀ. Arist. *Pol.*1269^{a}9, cf. Pl.*Lg.*736d, cf. X.*Lac.*14.1. II. *immovable, hard to move*, Pl.*Sph.*249a, Luc.*Im.*1 (in Comp.). Adv. -τως, ἔχειν Isoc.13.12, cf. Pl.*Euthphr.*11d. b. of property, *realty*, Olymp. Hist.p.458 D., *Cod.Just.*1.11.10.1, al. 2. *not to be stirred, inviolate*, τάφος Hdt.1.187: esp. prov. of sacred things, κινεῖν τὰ ἀκίνητα Id.6.134, cf. Pl.*Tht.*181a:—hence, *that must be kept secret*, τἀκίνητ' ἔπη S.*OC*624; τἀκίνητα φράσαι Id.*Ant.*1060. 3. of persons, etc., *not to be shaken, steadfast*, ib.1027; νοῦς ἀκίνητος πειθοῖ Pl.*Ti.*51e; ἕξις ἀ. ὑπὸ φόβου Id.*Def.*412a; πρὸς τὸ θεῖον Plu.2.165b. 4. *unalterable*, κοινότητες Phld.*Sign.*25. 5. c. gen., *inseparable from*, *PMag.Berol.*1.80, 165. III. Adv. -τως, v. supr. II. 1.

ἀκίνινος, ον, *made of* ἄκινος, στέφανοι Ath.15.680d. **ἄκῐνος**, ὁ, *wild basil, Calamintha graveolens*, Dsc.3.43:—also **ἄκονος**, ib.

ἄκιος, ον, (κίς) *not worm-eaten*, Sup. ἀκιώτατος Hes.*Op.*435.

ἀκιρίς· λύχνος, Hsch.

ἀκῐρός, όν (Aeol. **ἄκῐρος**, α, ον), *weak*, sc. γυνή, Theoc.28.15; πτέρυγες Nic.*Al.*559; v.l. Hes.*Op.*435 (Sup.), cf. *EM*48.50. Adv. ἀκιρῶς· εὐλαβῶς, ἀτρέμας, Hsch. II. ἀκιρός· ὁ βορρᾶς, Id.

ἀκίς, ίδος, ἡ, (cf. ἀκή A) *pointed object*; hence, *needle*, Hp.*Int.* 41; *splinter*, Id.*Epid.*5.46; πετροτόμος ἀ., of a chisel, *APl.*4.221 (Theaet.). 2. *barb* of an arrow or hook, βελῶν Plu.*Demetr.*20; ἀγκίστρου *AP*6.5 (Phil.). 3. *arrow, dart*, Ar.*Pax*443, Mnesim.7, Opp.*H.*5.151. 4. metaph., ἔρως.. ἡ φρενῶν ἀ. Tim.Com.2; πόθων ἀκίδες *stings* of desire, *AP*12.76 (Mel.): in pl., *sharp, acute pains*, Aret.*SD*2.4. II. surgical *bandage*, Gal.18(1).823.

ἀκίσκλη, ης, ἡ, *chisel*, *BGU*1028.13 (ii A.D.).

ἀκίχητος [ῐ], ον, *not to be reached, unattainable*, ἀκίχητα διώκων Il. 17.75; μεταθεῖν Ael.*NA*4.52; *not to be overtaken, swift*, ἀκίχητος ἀΐσσειν Nonn.*D.*45.236, cf. Tryph.333. II. *not to be reached by prayer, inexorable*, ἦθεα A.*Pr.*186.

ἀκίων, ονος, ὁ, ἡ, *not supported by pillars*, Hsch., *AB*391.

ἄκκαθεν· ἄναλθεν, Hsch. **ἀκκαῖον**· εὐκαταφρόνητον, Id.

ἀκκ-ίζομαι, Dep. (Act. only Ael.*Ep.*9), fut. ἀκκιοῦμαι Men.*Epit.* 309:—*affect indifference*, Pi.*Fr.*203 (cj.). 2. *affect ignorance, dissemble*, οἶσθα, ἀλλ' ἀκκίζει Pl.*Grg.*497a, Cic.*Att.*2.19.5, Luc.*Merc. Cond.*14, Jul.*Or.*7.223b; τὰ κοινὰ ταυτὶ ἀκκιοῦμαι *I will dissemble* and talk commonplaces, Men. l.c. 3. esp. of women, *to be prudish, affect to be shocked*, Philippid.5, cf. Ael. l.c., Alciphr.1.39. **-ισμός**, ὁ, *prudery*, Philem.4.14, Luc.*Am.*4, Philostr.*Ep.*35, Hld.6.4. **-ιστικός**, ή, όν, *disposed to be coy*, Eust.1727.28.

ἀκκιπήσιος, ὁ, Lat. *acipenser, sturgeon*, Apion ap.Ath.7.294f.

ἀκκόρ, Lacon. for ἀσκός, Hsch. **ἀκκός**· παράμωρος, λέγεται δὲ παιδίοις ὡς μωροῖς, Id.

ἀκκώ, ἡ, *bogey*, that nurses used to frighten children with, Plu. 2.1040b: acc. to others, *vain woman*, Zen.1.53.

ἀκλάδας· ἀμπέλους ἀκλαδεύτους (Aeol.), Hsch.

ἄκλαστος, ον, *unbroken*, Thphr.*CP*1.15.17, *AP*9.322 (Leon.), Phld.*D.*1.17: metaph., of motion, *continuous* in space, ἡ κύκλῳ φορὰ μήκει ἄ. Arist.*Cael.*288^{a}25; *unbent*, of a vein, Gal.5.659.

ἀκλαυστεί or **-τί, ἀκλαυτεί** or **-τί**, (κλαίω) Adv. of sq., *without weeping*, Call.*Dian.*267, A.D.*Adv.*133.19, Sor.1.79, Longus 1.5.

ἄκλαυτος or **ἄκλαυστος** (the latter form has less Ms. authority), ον: (κλαίω): I. Pass., *unwept*, esp. *without funeral lamentation*, Il.22.386, Od.11.54, Sol.21; ὤλετ' ἄκλαυτος, ἄϊστος A.*Eu.*565: c. gen., φίλων ἄκλαυτος S.*Ant.*847:—in E.*Andr.*1235 Thetis says, ἐγὼ γάρ, ἣν ἄκλαυτα χρῆν τίκτειν τέκνα.., i.e. children *not liable to death*. II. Act., *unweeping, tearless*, οὐδέ σέ φημι δὴν ἄκλαυτον ἔσεσθαι Od.4.494, cf. A.*Th.*696, E.*Alc.*173:—in S.*El.*912, = χαίρων, *with impunity*.

ἀκλεής, ές: acc. -εᾶ *Epigr.Gr.*850, -εῆ D.H.*Isoc.*5, Ep. ἀκλεᾶ Od. 4.728: dat. -εῖ Nonn.D.31.42:—Ep. **ἀκλειής**, A.R.3.932, Call.*Fr. anon.*365: nom. pl. ἀκλεέες (vulg. ἀκληεῖς) Il.12.318: (κλέος):—*without fame, inglorious*, Hom. ll. cc., Pi.*O.*12.15, Hdt.*prooem.*, E. *Hipp.*1028, Pl.*La.*179d, etc. Adv. ἀκλεῶς Hdt.5.77, Antipho 1.21; Ep. ἀκλειῶς Il.22.304: Comp. ἀκλεέστερον Jul.*Or.*1.28a: neut. as Adv., ἀκλεὲς αὔτως Il.7.100. 2. *ignominious*, ἀκλεεστάτῳ ὀλέθρῳ ἀπόλλυσθαι Lys.13.45.

ἀκλεΐα, Ion. -ῐη, ἡ, *ingloriousness*, *AP*9.80 (Leon.).

ἀκλειής, ές, Ep. for ἀκλεής.

ἄκλειστος, ον, Ion. **ἀκλήϊστος** Call.*Hec.*2, Att. contr. **ἄκληστος** E.*Andr.*593, Th.2.93: (κλείω):—*not closed* or *fastened*, ll. cc., X.*Cyr.* 7.5.25, Nic.Dam.p.72 D., etc.

ἄκλεπτος, ον, *not stealing, not deceiving*, S.*Fr.*690.

ἀκληδονίστως, gloss on ἀκλειῶς, *EM*49.11.

ἀκλήης, ές, v. sub ἀκλεής.

ἀκληΐδας· ἄζυγας, Hsch.

ἀκλήϊστος, ον, v. ἄκλειστος.

ἀκληρ-εί· χωρὶς κλήρου, Zonar. **-έω**, *to be unfortunate*, Teles p.26 H., D.S.3.13, al.: pf. ἠκλήρηκα Plb.1.7.4, D.S.27.16. **-ημα**, ατος, τό, *loss, mishap*, Dicaearch.1.25 (pl.), Teles p.25 H., Agatharch.24, M.Ant.10.33, etc. **-ία**, ἡ, *misfortune*, S.*Fr.*989, Antiph. 14, Plb.22.8.9, etc. **-ονόμητος**, ον, *without heirs*, *Berl.Sitzb.*1880. 649 (Anisa, i B.C.), *BGU*868.12 (ii A.D.), Eust.533.32:—also **-όνομος**, ον, *PLond.*3.905.12 (ii A.D.). **-ος**, ον, *without lot* or *portion, poor, needy*, Od.11.490, etc.: c. gen., *without lot* or *share in*, A.*Eu.*353, Is.3.32, etc. II. *unallotted, without owner*, *h.Ven.*123, E. *Tr.*32. **-ούχητος**, ον, *not having received a lot*, *OGI*229.102

(Smyrna). **-ωτεί** or **-ωτί,** Adv. *without casting lots,* Lys.16.16, Arist.*Ath.*30.5, *CIG*2880 (Miletus). **-ωτος,** ον, *without lot* or *portion in* a thing, c. gen., χώρας ἀκλάρωτος Pi.*O.*7.59. 2. *without casting lots,* D.C.*Fr.*62. II. *not distributed in lots,* Plu.2.231e.

ἄκληστος, v. sub ἄκλειστος.

ἀκλητ-ί, Adv. *uncalled, unbidden,* Com.ap.Zen.2.46 [where ῐ]. **-ος,** ον, *uncalled, unbidden,* Asius 1, A.*Pr.*1024, *Ch.*838, S.*Aj.* 289, Th.1.118, Pl.*Smp.*174b, Arist.*EN*1171ᵇ21.

ἀκλῑνής, ές, *bending to neither side, unswerving,* Pl.*Phd.*109a; πρὸς τὸ δίκαιον Nic.Dam.p.144 D.; *impartial,* ἀκοαί *POxy.*904.9 (v A.D.); *regular,* ἀκλινέων καλάμων *AP*10.11 (Satyr.), etc.: Math., *without inclination,* of a perpendicular, Procl.*in Euc.*p.132 F.; *horizontal,* of a plane, Papp.1048.2, Hero *Dioptr.*19: Music., *fixed,* of notes in scale, Alyp.4: Medic., *persistent,* πυρετοί Herod.ap.Orib.6.20.24. Adv. -νῶς Ph.2.669; Ion. -νέως *AP*5.54 (Diosc.). 2. metaph., *steadfast, steady,* φιλία ib.12.158 (Mel.); ὁμολογία *Ep.Heb.*10.23; ψυχή Luc.*Dem.Enc.*33; *unmoved, tranquil,* Nonn.*D.*35.11, al.

ἀκλῐσία, ἡ, *indeclinability,* A.D.*Pron.*12.4, etc.

ἄκλῐτος, ον, Gramm., *indeclinable,* D.T.641.23, A.D.*Synt.*30.10; Ael. Dion. wrote περὶ ἀκλίτων ῥημάτων. Adv. ἀκλίτως, ἔχειν Eust. 162.32. 2. Math., = ἀκλινής, Procl.*in Euc.*p.290 F. 3. *stable,* Iamb.*Myst.*1.15.

ἀκλόνητος, ον, *unshaken, unmoved,* Suid., Phot.

ἄκλονος, ον, of the pulse, *steady, regular,* Gal.9.347; of a limb, *free from jars,* 17(1).513; of a rider, *with a firm seat,* Palaeph.52.

ἀκλοπ-εία, ἡ, *honest administration, BCH*32.204 (Alabanda). **-ος,** ον, *not guilty of peculation, Cat.Cod.Astr.*1.100 (v A.D.). II. *not furtively concealed,* ἄγκιστρον Opp.*H.*3.532.

ἀκλῠδώνιστος, ον, *not lashed by waves*; generally, *sheltered from,* λιμὴν ἀ. τῶν πνευμάτων Plb.10.10.4.

ἄκλυστος, ον, = foreg., Zeno *Stoic.*1.56, Lyc.736, Plu.*Mar.*15, Nonn.*D.*39.8, al.; λιμὴν ἄ. D.S.3.44; γῆ, *free from inundation,* Max. Tyr.414: fem., Αὖλιν ἀκλύσταν E.*IA*121.

ἄκλῠτος, ον, (κλύω) *unheard, IG*14.1389 ii 32; opp. κλυτός, Plu.2. 722e (nisi leg. ἄκλυστος).

ἄκλων, ὁ, ἡ, *without branches,* Thphr.*HP*6.6.2.

ἄκλωστος, ον, (κλώθω) *unspun,* στήμονες Pl.Com.221.

ἄκμα· νηστεία, ἔνδεια, Hsch.; cf. ἄκμηνος.

ἀκμάδιον, τό, kind of *surgical instrument, Hermes* 38.281 (s. v. l.); *conical crucible,* Ps.-Mos.Alch.p.39 B.

ἀκμ-άζω, (ἀκμή) *to be in full bloom, at the prime*: I. of persons, Hdt.2.134, Pl.*Prt.*335e; ἀ. σώματι, ῥώμῃ, X.*Mem.*4.4.23, Pl.*Plt.*310d, etc.; of cities and states, Hdt.3.57, 5.28; ἀ. τὸ σῶμα ἀπὸ τῶν λ' ἐτῶν μέχρι τῶν ε' καὶ λ' Arist.*Rh.*1390ᵇ9; = τὰ τῶν νέων πράττειν Hyp.*Fr.* 122. 2. *flourish, abound in* a thing, πλούτῳ Hdt.1.29; παρασκευῇ πάσῃ Th.1.1; νεότητι Id.2.20; ναυσὶ καὶ χρήμασι Aeschin.3.163. 3. c. inf., *to be strong enough* to do, X.*An.*3.1.25. II. of things, ἀ. ὁ πυρετός, ἡ νόσος *is at its height,* Hp.*Aph.*2.29, *Epid.*1.25, Th.2.49; τοῦ πάθους ἀκμάζοντος Phld.*Lib.*p.31 O.; ἀ. ὁ πόλεμος Th.3.3; of corn, *to be ripe,* Id.2.19. 2. ἡνίκα.. ἀκμάζοι [ὁ θυμός] when passion *is at its height,* Pl.*Ti.*70d; ἀκμάζουσα ῥώμη Antipho 4.3.3; ἀκμάζει πάντα ἐπιμελείας δεόμενα require *the utmost* care, X.*Cyr.*4.2.40. 3. impers., c. inf., ἀκμάζει βρετέων ἔχεσθαι *'tis time to*.., A.*Th.*97 (lyr.); νῦν γὰρ ἀ. Πειθὼ.. ξυγκαταβῆναι now *'tis time* for her to.., Id.*Ch.* 726. **-αῖος,** α, ον, Aeol. **ἄκμαος** Jo.Gramm.*Comp.*2.14; *in full bloom, at prime, vigorous,* πῶλοι A.*Eu.*405; ἥβη Id.*Th.*11; ἀκμαῖος φύσιν *in the prime of* strength, Id.*Pers.*441; ἀ. τὴν ὀργὴν Luc.*Tim.*3; κάλλει ἀκμαία *Epigr.Gr.*127; τὸ ἀκμαιότατον D.H.5.22; ἀκμαίων λέσχῃ at Chalcis, Plu.2.298d:—ἀ. πρὸς ἔρωτα *AP*7.221, cf. Luc.*D.Deor.*8.2, Ael.*NA*15.10. Adv. ἀκμαίως, ἔχειν κατὰ τὴν ἡλικίαν Plb.31.29.7: Comp. -ότερον *more vigorously,* Gal.4.525:—of things, *at the height,* ὁ ἀκμαιότατος καιρὸς τῆς ἡμέρας, i.e. noon, Plb.3.102.1; τὸ ἀ. τοῦ χειμῶνος Arr.*An.*4.7.1, etc. 2. Rhet., *belonging to the supreme effort, culmination of oratory,* ἔννοιαι, λόγος, Hermog.*Id.*1.7, *Inv.*4.4: Comp., *Id.*1.10. II. *in time, in season,* ἀ. καιρὸς *PTeb.*24.56 (ii B.C., Sup.); ἀ. ἡμέραι the *seasonable* days, Ath.5.180c, cf. *AP*10.2 (Antip. Sid.): neut. pl. as Adv., ἀκμαῖ' ἂν μόλοι S.*Aj.*921 (cj.). **-αστής,** οῦ, ὁ, = foreg. I.1, Hdn.1.17.11; ἀκμασταί, οἱ, gymnastic club at Thyatira, *IGRom.*4.1234, al. **-αστικός,** ή, όν, = ἀκμαῖος, Hp. *Sept.*28; ἀ. πυρετός Gal.10.615, of a continuous fever; ἀ. πρόσωπα persons *in their prime, Cat.Cod.Astr.*2.173. 2. = ἀκμαῖος I.2, σχήματα Hermog.*Id.*1.10.

ἀκμή, ἡ, (cf. ἀκή A) *point, edge*: prov., ἐπὶ ξυροῦ ἀκμῆς on the razor's *edge* (v. sub ξυρόν); ἀ. φασγάνου, ὅπλων, Pi.*P.*9.81, Plb.15.16.3 (pl.); ὀδόντων Pi.*N.*4.63, etc.; λόγχης ἀκμή E.*Supp.*318; κερκίδων ἀκμαί S.*Ant.*976; ἀμφιδέξιοι ἀ. both *hands,* Id.*OT*1243; ποδοῖν ἀ. *feet,* ib.1034; ἔμπυροι ἀκμαί *pointed* flames, E.*Ph.*1255, cf. πυρὸς ἀκμαί Epicr.6 codd. II. *highest* or *culminating point* of anything, *flower, prime, zenith,* esp. of man's age, ἀκμὴ ἥβης S.*OT*741; ἐν τῇδε τοῦ κάλλους ἀκμῇ Cratin.195; σώματός τε καὶ φρονήσεως Pl.*R.*461a; μέτριος χρόνος ἀκμῆς 460e; ὀξυτάτη δρόμου ἀ. ibid.; ἀ. βίου X.*Cyr.*7.2.20, etc.; ἐν ταύταις ταῖς ἀ. Isoc.7.37; ἐν ἀκμῇ εἶναι, of corn, to be *ripe,* Th.4.2; ἀκμὴν ἔχειν τῆς ἄνθης Pl.*Phdr.*230b; τοσοῦτον τῆς ἀ. ὑστερῶν Isoc. *Ep.*6.4; τῆς ἀ. λήγειν begin to decline, Pl.*Smp.*219a:—in various relations, ἀ. ἦρος spring-*prime,* Pi.*P.*4.64; ἀ. θέρους *mid*-summer, X. *HG*5.3.19; βραχεῖα ἀ. πληρώματος Th.7.14; ἀ. τοῦ ναυτικοῦ *flower* of their navy, Id.8.46; ἀ. τῆς δόξης Id.2.42; ἡ ἀ. τῆς Σπάρτης, τῶν νέων Demad.12; ἀ. νούσου *crisis* of disease, Hp.*Acut.*38:—generally, *strength, vigour,* ἐν χερὸς ἀκμᾷ Pi.*O.*2.63, cf. A.*Pers.*1060; ἀ. ποδῶν *swiftness,* Pi.*I.*8(7).41, cf. A.*Eu.*370; φρενῶν Pi.*N.*3.39; συμπεσεῖν ἀκμᾷ βαρύς cj. Id.*I.*4(3).51:—periphr. like βία, ἀκμὴ Θησειδᾶν S.*OC* 1066. 2. Rhet., ἀκμὴ λόγου *supreme effort, culmination, climax,* Hermog.*Inv.*4.4, *Id.*1.10; pl., ib.11, cf. Philostr.*VS*1.25.7. III. of Time, like καιρός, *the time,* i.e. *best, most fitting time,* freq. in Trag., ἡνίκ' ἂν δὴ πρὸς γάμων ἥκητ' ἀκμάς S.*OT*1492; ἔργων, λόγων, ἕδρας ἀκμή *time* for doing, speaking, sitting still, Id.*El.*22, *Ph.*12, *Aj.*811: c. inf., κοὐκέτ' ἦν μέλλειν ἀ. A.*Pers.*407, cf. *Ag.*1353; ἀπηλλάχθαι δ' ἀ. S.*El.*1338; σοί.. ἀ. φιλοσοφεῖν Isoc.1.3; ὁ καιρὸς ἔστ' ἐπ' αὐτῆς τῆς ἀκμῆς Ar.*Pl.*256; ἐπ' ἀκμῆς εἶναι, c. inf., to be on *point* of doing, E.*Hel.* 897; εἰς ἀκμὴν ἐλθὼν φίλοις *in the nick of time,* E.*HF*532; ἐπ' αὐτὴν ἥκει τὴν ἀκμήν it is come to *the critical time,* D.4.41; ἀκμὴν εἴληφεν have reached a *critical moment,* Isoc.*Ep.*1.1, cf. Plu.*Sol.*12,15, 2. 656f. IV. *eruption* on face, Cass.*Pr.*13, Aët.7.110, 8.13 (f.l. ἀκνάς, whence mod. *acne*). **ἄκμη,** v. ἄκμηνος.

ἀκμήν, acc. of ἀκμή, used as Adv., *as yet, still,* A.*Fr.*451 G, Men. in *Cod.Vat.Gr.*122; un-Attic acc. to Phryn.100, but cf. Hyp.*Fr.*116; τὰ σκευοφόρα... ἀκμὴν διέβαινε were *just* crossing the river, X.*An.*4.3. 26, cf. Plb.1.13.12, Theoc.4.60, *AP*7.141 (Antiphil.), Phld.*Ir.*p.29 W., *Ev.Matt.*15.16, etc.; νέος ἀ. Theoc.25.164; strengthd., ἀκμὴν ἔτι Plb.14.4.9, 15.6.6; ἔτι ἀ. Sor.1.26. II. = ἀκμαίως, Cratin. in *Cod.Vat.Gr.*122: perh., = *much, OGI*201.13 (Nubia).

ἀκμηνός, ή, όν, (ἀκμή) *full-grown,* θάμνος ἐλαίης Od.23.191; νυμφῶν ἃς ἀκμηνὰς καλοῦσιν Paus.5.15.6, cf. Jul.Laod. in *Cat.Cod.Astr.* 5(1).189.

ἄκμηνος, ον, *fasting from* food, four times in Il.19.163,207,320, 346 (expl. by Sch. fr. Aeol. **ἄκμη,** = ἀσιτία); also in Lyc.672; σίτων Nic.*Th.*116; δόρποιο Call.*Fr.anon.*4.

ἀκμής, ῆτος, ὁ, ἡ, also as neut., Paus.6.15.5: (κάμνω):—*untiring, unwearied,* Il.11.802, 15.697, S.*Ant.*353; πύλαι ἀ. Ὀλύμπου *AP*9.526 (Alph.):—also in late Prose, D.H.9.14, Paus. l. c., Plu.*Cim.*13, Onos.22.1.

ἀκμητεί and **-τί,** Adv. *without toil, easily,* J.*BJ*1.16.2, Lib.*Or.*59.71.

ἄκμητος, ον, Lyr. **-ατος** S.*Ant.*609 Jebb, = ἀκμής, *unwearied,* ποσὶν *h.Ap.*520, Onos.10.5. II. *not causing pain,* Nic.*Th.*737.

ἀκμοθέτης, ου, ὁ, (τίθημι) *anvil-block,* Poll.10.147. **-θετον,** τό, = foreg., Il.18.410, Od.8.274.

ἀκμόνιον, τό, Dim. of sq., Aesop.413.

ἄκμων, ονος, ὁ, orig. prob. *meteoric stone, thunderbolt* (v. sub fin.), χάλκεος ἄ. οὐρανόθεν κατιών Hes.*Th.*722, cf. 724. II. *anvil,* Il.18.476, Od.8.274, Hdt.1.68: metaph., πρὸς ἄκμονι χάλκευε γλῶσσαν Pi.*P.*1.86; λόγχης ἄκμονες *very anvils* to bear blows (cf. Sch. ad loc.), A.*Pers.*51; ὑπομένειν πληγὰς ἄκμων Aristopho 4; Τιρύνθιος ἄ., i.e. Hercules, Call.*Dian.*146 (expl. by Sch. ὁ μὴ καμὼν ἐπὶ τοῖς ἄθλοις). 2. *pestle* (Cyprian), Hsch. 3. *head* of a battering-ram, Apollod.*Poliorc.*161.4. III. kind of *eagle,* Hsch. IV. kind of *wolf,* Opp.*C.*3.326. V. Pythag., = 6, *Theol.Ar.*37. (Cf. Skt. *áśman-* 'sling-stone', etc.)

ἄκναμπτος, ἄκναπτος, ἀκνάφος, = ἄγν-.

ἄκνημος, ον, (κνήμη) *without calf,* of the leg, Plu.2.520c.

ἀκνησ-μος, ον, *without irritation* or *itching,* Hp.*Off.*18. **-τις,** ιος, ἡ, *spine* or *backbone* of animals, Od.10.161 (nisi leg. κατὰ κνῆστιν), A.R.4.1403; also τὸ μέσον τῆς ὀσφύος Poll.2.179. II. *stinging-nettle,* = ἀκαλήφη, Nic.*Th.*52 (other expl. ap. Sch. ad loc.). **-τον,** τό, = χαμελαία, Dsc.4.171.

ἄκνῑσος, ον, (κνῖσα) *without fat of sacrifices,* βωμός *AP*10.7 (Arch.); βωμοῖσι παρ' ἀκνίσοισι cj. Cobet in Luc.*J.Tr.*6. 2. *lacking in fats,* τροφή Thphr.*CP*2.4.6, cf. Plu.2.123b. 3. *without savoury odour,* Hp.*Morb.*2.54; ἔλαιον *not greasy,* Aret.*CA*1.6. Adv. -ως *without being smoked* or *burnt,* Gal.14.266.

ἀκνίσωτος [ῑ], ον, *without steam of sacrifice,* A.*Fr.*292.

ἀκο-άζη· ἀκούεις, Hsch. **-αστῆρες,** οἱ, board of officials at Metapontum, Id.

ἀκοή, ἡ, Ep. **ἀκουή**: (ἀκοϝ, cf. ἀκούω):—*hearing, sound heard,* ἕκαθεν δέ τε γίγνετ' ἀ. Il.16.634. 2. *thing heard, tidings,* μετὰ πατρὸς ἀκουὴν ἱκέσθαι, βῆναι, Od.2.308, 4.701; κατὰ τὴν Σόλωνος ἀκοήν according to Solon's *story,* Pl.*Ti.*21a; *report,* Pi.*P.*1.84,90; ἀ. σοφοῖς *thing* for wise men *to listen to,* ib.9.78; ἀκοῇ ἱστορεῖν, παραλαβεῖν τι *by hearsay,* Hdt.2.29,148; ἐπίστασθαι Antipho 5.67, Th. 4.126; ἐξ ἀκοῆς λέγειν Pl.*Phd.*61d; τὰς ἀ. τῶν προγεγενημένων *traditions,* Th.1.20; ἀκοαί.. λόγων Id.1.73; ἀκοὴν μαρτυρεῖν, προσάγειν, give, bring *hearsay evidence,* D.57.4; βαρὺν.. ἀκοῆς ψόφον *AP*6.220 (Diosc.); ἐκ γὰρ ἀκουῆς οἰκτίρω σε ib.7.220 (Agath.). II. *sense of hearing,* Hdt.1.38, etc.; joined with ὄψις, Pl.*Phd.*65b, etc.; οἷς ὦτα μέν ἐστιν, ἀκοαὶ δὲ οὐκ ἔνεισιν Ph.1.474. 2. *act of hearing,* ἐς ἀκοὰν ἐμήν to my *hearing,* my *ear,* A.*Pr.*689; γᾶρυν ἀραρεῖν ἀκοαῖσι Simon. 41; ὀξεῖαν ἀ... λόγοις διδοὺς S.*El.*30; ἀκοῇ κλύειν Id.*Ph.*1412; ἀκοαῖς δέχεσθαι, εἰς ἀκοὰς.. ἥκειν, E.*IT*1496, *Ph.*1480; δι' ἀκοῆς αἰσθάνεσθαι Pl.*Lg.*900a; ἀκοὴν ὑπειπών demanding *a hearing,* E.*HF*962; τοῖς ἀκροάμασι τὰς ἀ. ἀνατεθεικώς Plb.24.5.9. 3. *ear,* ὀππάτεσσι δ' οὐδὲν ὄρημ', ἐπιρρόμβεισι δ' ἄκουαι Sapph.2.12, cf. A.R.4.17; ἀπεσθίει μου τὴν ἀ. Hermipp.52, cf. Pherecr.199; δυσὶν ἀκοαῖς κρίνειν with two *ears,* Arist.*Pol.*1287ᵇ27, cf. *Pr.*960ᵃ30, Call.*Fr.*106.5. III. *hearing, listening to,* ἀκοῆς ἄξιος Pl. *Tht.*142d; εἰς ἀκοὴν φωνῆς within *hearing* of.., D.S.19.41. IV. *obedience,* ἀ. ὑπὲρ θυσίαν ἀγαθή Lxx 1*Ki.*15.22. V. in pl., place where *supernatural voices are heard, IG*4. 955.10 (Epid.), Marin.*Procl.*32; αἱ ἀ. τοῦ θεοῦ Aristid.*Or.*47(23).13.

ἀκοΐδιον, τό, Dim. of ἀκοή II.3, *Gloss.* **ἀκοιλάντως,** Adv. *without deficiency, in full, PLond.*3.954.18 (iii A.D.), al.

ἀκοίλιος, ον, *without ducts*, Hp.*Loc.Hom.*4, Gal.5.617. 2. *without stomach*, Gal.5.384.

ἄκοιλος, ον, *not hollow*, Arist.*HA* 515^{a}31, Gal.4.900.

ἀκοίμητος, ον, *sleepless, unresting*, of sea, A.*Pr.*139; Νύμφαι Theoc.13.44; πῦρ Plu.*Cam.*20, Ael.*NA* 11.3; φέγγος Lxx *Wi.*7.10; ἀ. καὶ ἀπαραλόγιστος Arr.*Epict.*1.14.12, etc.; ἀ. δάκρυσι *IG*9(2).317.4 (Tricca). Adv. -τως, ἔχει πρὸς τὰ θεῖα Ph.*Fr.*101 H.

ἀκοίμιστος, ον, dub. in D.S.38/39.17; gloss on ἀκατεύναστος, Phot.

ἀκοινονόητος, ον, *lacking in 'savoir-faire'* (Lat. *sensus communis*), Cic.*Att.*6.3.7, cf. Gell.12.12, Juv.7.218. Adv. -τως Cic.*Att.*6.1.7 codd.

ἄκοινος, ον, *not common*, Them.*Or.*11.142a.

ἀκοιν-ωνησία, ἡ, *non-existence of community* of property, Arist.*Pol.*1236^{b}22. II. *unsociableness*, Stob.2.7.25. III. *lack of community, incompatibility*, Dam.*Pr.*221,423. **-ώνητος**, ον, *not shared with*, γάμοις ἀκοινώνητον εὐνάν bed *not shared in common with* other wives, E.*Andr.*470. 2. *not to be communicated*, ὄνομα Lxx *Wi.*14.21; *not to be shared, incommunicable*, Ph.2.201; τὸ ἴδιον καὶ ἀ. Alex.Aphr.*Pr.*2.72. II. Act., *having no share of* or *in*, c. gen., νόμων Pl.*Lg.*914c, cf. *Inscr.Prien.*114, D.S.20.15; τὸ ἀ. τῶν ἄρθρων absence of anything in common with the article, A.D.*Synt.*49.12: also c. dat., τὸ τοῖς κακοῖς -ότερον Arist.*Top.*117^{b}31: abs., *unsocial*, Pl.*Lg.*774a; *inhuman*, Cic.*Att.*6.3.7. Adv. -τως cj. ib.6.1.7, Jul.*Ep.*89.292d. **-ωνία**, ἡ, *unsociableness*, Pl.*Ep.*318e.

ἀκοίτης, ου, ὁ, (ἀ- copul., κοίτη, cf. Pl.*Cra.*405d) *bedfellow, husband*, Il.15.91, Od.5.120, Pi.*N.*5.28, S.*Tr.*525, E.*El.*166 (lyr.):—fem. **ἄκοιτις**, ιος, ἡ, *wife*, Il.3.138, B.5.169, A.*Pers.*684, etc.—Poet. words.

ἄκοιτος, ον, *unresting*, of Argus, B.18.23.

ἀκολάκ-ευτος, ον, *not liable to flattery*, οὐσία, τροφή, Pl.*Lg.*729a, Them.*Or.*6.97b; *not pampered*, σώματα Max.Tyr.23.1. II. Act., *not flattering*, λόγοι Id.31.6; θεραπεία Jul.*Or.*2.86b; ψῆφος Them.*Or.*2.27b. Adv. -τως Cic.*Att.*13.51.1, Ph.1.449. **-ος**, ον, = foreg. II, ψήφισμα D.L.2.141.

ἀκολᾰσ-ία, ἡ, *licentiousness, intemperance*, opp. σωφροσύνη, Hecat.144, Antipho 4.1.6, Th.3.37, Pl.*Grg.*505b, cf. Arist.*EN* 1107^{b}6, etc.: pl., Lys.16.11, Pl.*Lg.*884. **-ταίνω**, fut. -ᾰνῶ Ar.*Av.*1227, *to be licentious*, Ar. l. c., Mnesim.4.19, Pl.*R.*555d, etc. **-τασμα**, τό, = ἀκολάστημα, restored by Dobree in Ar.*Lys.*398 (ἀκόλαστ' ᾄσματα codd.); ἀκολαστάσματα is prob. l. for -άματα in Anaxandr.73, Alciphr.1.38. **-τημα**, ατος, τό, *act of* ἀκολασία, Plu.*Crass.*32, M.Ant.11.20, Muson.*Fr.*4p.14 H. **-τία**, ἡ, v.l. for ἀκολασία, Alex.36.6. **-τος**, ον, *undisciplined, unbridled*, δῆμος Hdt.3.81; ὄχλος E.*Hec.*607; στράτευμα X.*An.*2.6.10, cf. Ar.*Nu.*1348, Pl.*Prt.*341e, etc. 2. esp. *incontinent, licentious*, S.*Fr.*744; opp. σώφρων, Pl.*Grg.*507c, Arist.*EN* 1117^{b}32, al.; περί τι Id.*HA* 572^{a}12; πρός τι 582^{a}26. Adv. ἀκολάστως, ἔχειν Pl.*Grg.*493c: Comp. -οτέρως, ἔχειν πρός τι X.*Mem.*2.1.1, cf. Aen.Tact.26.2, dub. in Vett.Val.153.32, 271.12 (leg. ἀκοπιάστως). II. *unpunished*, c. gen., App.*Ill.*17.

ἀκολλ-ητί, Adv. of sq., *without adhering*, Herm.ap.Stob.1.49.68. **-ητος**, ον, *not cemented* or *glued*, λίθοι *BCH* 35.43 (Delos); *not adhering*, δέρμα σώμασι Gal.11.125; *not united, healed up*, of wounds, Id.18(2).802. 2. *incapable of being compacted*, D.H.*Comp.*22. **-ος**, ον, *without glue, not adhesive*, Thphr.*CP*6.10.3.

ἀκολλύβιστος, ον, *without premium on exchange*, ἀργύριον *IG* 12(5).817 (Tenos, ii B.C.).

ἀκολόβωτος, ον, *not curtailed*, Eust.727.39.

ἀκολος, ου, ἡ, *bit, morsel*, Od.17.222, *AP*9.563 (Leon.), cf. 6.176 (Maced.), J.*BJ*5.10.3; Boeot. for ἔνθεσις, Stratt.47.7. (Perh. Phryg., cf. Inscr. Phryg. in *Jahresh.*8 *Beibl.*95 βεκος ακκαλος τι.)

ἀκολουθ-έω, *follow* one, *go after* or *with* him, freq. of soldiers and slaves:—mostly c. dat. pers., Ar.*Pl.*19, etc.; ἀ. τῷ ἡγουμένῳ Pl.*R.*474c; with Preps., ἀ. μετά τινος Th.7.57, Pl.*La.*187e, Lys.2.27, etc.; τοῖς σώμασι μετ' ἐκείνων ἠκολούθουν, ταῖς δ' εὐνοίαις μεθ' ὑμῶν ἦσαν Isoc.14.15; ἀ. σύν τινι X.*An.*7.5.3; κατόπιν τινός Ar.*Pl.*13: rarely c. acc., Men.558: abs., Pl.*Plt.*277e, Thphr.*Char.*18.8, etc.; ἀ. ἐφ' ἁρπαγήν, of soldiers, Th.2.98; ἀκολουθῶν, ὁ, as Subst., = ἀκόλουθος I, Men.*Adul.Fr.*1. 2. of stars, *follow* in the diurnal rotation, Autol.2.2. II. metaph., *follow, be guided by*, τῇ γνώμῃ τινός Th.3.38; τοῖς πράγμασιν, τοῖς τοῦ πολέμου καιροῖς, D.4.39, 24.95; *obey*, τοῖς νόμοις And.4.19: c. acc. neut., ἀ. ἅπαντα *PLille* 1.26. 2. *follow the thread* of a discourse, Pl.*Phd.*107b, etc. 3. of things, *follow upon, to be consequent upon, consistent with*, εὐλογία.. εὐηθείᾳ ἀ. Id.*R.*400e, cf. 398d; *follow analogy of*, Arist.*HA* 499^{a}10, al. b. abs., *to be consequent*, ὡς γένους ὄντος τοῦ ἀεὶ ἀκολουθοῦντος *Top.*128^{b}4; as species to individual, *GA* 768^{b}13. 4. abs., ἀκολουθεῖ *it follows*, Id.*Cat.*14^{a}31.—Not in Trag.: first in Hippon.55, with ᾱ (s.v.l.), elsewhere ᾰ; takes place of ἕπομαι in later Greek. **-ησις**, εως, ἡ, *following*, Arist.*Rh.*1410^{a}4. 2. *sequence in argument*, with reference to the *fallacia consequentis*, Id.*APr.*52^{b}29, *SE* 181^{a}23. II. *obedience, conformity*, Pl.*Def.*412b. **-ητέον**, *one must follow*, abs., X.*Oec.*21.7; τῷ λόγῳ Pl.*R.*400d. **-ητικός**, ή, όν, *disposed to follow*, ταῖς ἐπιθυμίαις, τοῖς πάθεσι, Arist.*Rh.*1389^{a}5, *EN* 1095^{a}4; τῷ αἱροῦντι λόγῳ Chrysipp.*Stoic.*3.93; τῷ ἄρχοντι *Stoic.*3.158. 2. *capable of following*, πόδες (in metre, opp. ἡγεμονικοί) Clearch.68. 3. *expressing consequence*, σύνδεσμος v.l. in Sch.D.T.p.62 H. **-ία**, ἡ, *following, attendance*, S.*Fr.*990, Pl.*Alc.*1.122c:—ἀ. πρὸς τὸ κενούμενον *filling up* a vacuum, Erasistr.(?)ap.Gal.*Nat.Fac.*1.16. 2. *sequence, succession*, τάξις καὶ ἀ. Chrysipp.*Stoic.*2.266, al.; *succession* of philosophers, D.L.2.47; κατ' ἀκολουθίαν in *regular succession*, Hdn.7.5.2: Lit.Crit., *natural sequence* of words, D.H.*Comp.*22, cf. Longin.22.1; *sequence* of argument, Phlp.*in Ph.*707.3; in rhythm, *orderly sequence*, D.H.*Comp.*25: Gramm., *agreement*, Id.*Amm.*2.2; *analogy*, A.D.*Pron.*2.24, al. II. *retinue, train*, D.S.27.6. III. *conformity with*, τοῖς πράγμασι Pl.*Cra.*437c; φύσεως *Stoic.*3.4; κατ' ἀκολουθίαν τῶν ἐτῶν *in conformity with* his age, *POxy.*1202.20 (iii A.D.): abs., *consistency, coherence*, Phld.*Sign.*37 (sg. and pl.). 2. *obedience*, τοῖς θεοῖς M.Ant.3.9. IV. in Logic, *consequence*, Ph.2.497, Chrysipp.*Stoic.*2.68, al.; ἐξ ἀκολουθίας Phld.*Ir.*p.90 W. **-ίσκος**, ὁ, Dim. of ἀκόλουθος, *foot-boy*, Ptol.Euerg.6. **-ος**, ον, (ἀ- copul., κέλευθος, cf. Pl.*Cra.*405d) *following, attending on*, mostly as Subst., *follower, attendant*, *IG*1.1, Ar.*Av.*73; ὅτοισι παῖς ἀ. ἔστιν Eup.159.3; freq. in Att. Prose, Antipho 2.1.4, Th.6.28, 7.75, Pl.*Smp.*203c, etc.; οἱ ἀ. *camp-followers*, X.*Cyr.*5.2.36: fem., Plu.*Caes.*10: metaph., Δίκα Εὐνομίας ἀ. B.14.55. 2. *following after*, c. gen., πλάτα.. Νηρῄδων ἀ. S.*OC*719 (lyr.). 3. *following, consequent upon, in conformity with*, c. gen., τἀκόλουθα τῶν ῥακῶν Ar.*Ach.*438, cf. Pl.*Phd.*111c: mostly c. dat., Id.*Lg.*716c, *Ti.*88d; ἀκόλουθα τούτοις πράττειν D.18.257; ἀ. τοῖς εἰρημένοις ἐστὶ τὸ διῃρῆσθαι Arist.*Pol.*1321^{b}3; *consistent*, οὐδὲν ἀ. αὑτῷ λέγει Demetr.*Eloc.*153; of persons, *conforming*, τῇ ὑμετέρᾳ βουλήσει *PTeb.*44.34 (ii B.C.): abs., *correspondent*, Lys.21.10; τἆλλα πάντα τὰ ἀ. Hyp.*Eux.*25; λόγους πράξεις ἀ. Epicur.*Sent.*25; *consistent with one another*, X.*An.*2.4.19. Adv. -θως *in accordance with*, τοῖς νόμοις D.44.67; ἀ. τῇ φύσει ζῆν Chrysipp.*Stoic.*3.4, cf. Phld.*Piet.*100, D.S.4.17: abs., *consistently*, Metrod.*Fr.*17, Aristid.2.28 J., Plot.4.3.20. 4. *in accordance with nature*, Zeno *Stoic.*1.55. 5. Gramm., *analogical*, A.D.*Pron.*11.21, al. Adv. -θως *analogically*, Id.*Synt.*159.6. 6. in Logic, *consequent*, περὶ ἀκολούθων, title of work by Chrysipp., *Stoic.*2.5, cf. 69; τοῦτο γὰρ ἀ. that *follows*, Phld.*Ir.*p.84 W.—Used once by S. l. c.; otherwise only in Com. and Prose.

ἀκολουτέω, for ἀκολουθέω, barbarism in Ar.*Th.*1198.

ἄκολπος, ον, *without sinus genitalis*, of the pipe-fish, Ael.*NA* 15.16.

ἀκόλυμβος, ον, *unable to swim*, Batr.158, Str.6.2.9, Plu.2.599b.

ἀκομιστ-ία, Ep. -ίη [ῐ], ἡ, *lack of tending* or *care*, Od.21.284, Them.*Or.*22.274a, Max.Tyr.34.2. **-ος**, ον, *slovenly*, S.*Ichn.*143; *untended*, D.L.5.5, Nonn.*D.*40.174, al.

ἀκόμμωτος, ον, *unpainted*; metaph., *without meretricious ornament*, ὕμνος Them.*Or.*18.218b.

ἄκομος, ον, (κόμη) *without hair, bald*, Luc.*VH* 1.23; of trees, *leafless*, Poll.1.236.

ἀκόμπαστος, ον, *unboastful*, A.*Th.*538, E.*Fr.*872:—**ἄκομπος**, A.*Th.*554, S.*Fr.*210.

ἀκόμψευτος, ον, *unadorned*, of style, D.H.*Comp.*22.

ἄκομψος, ον, *unadorned*, Archil.158, cf. Jul.*Caes.*317c; ἐγὼ δ' ἄκομψος '*rude* I am *in speech*', E.*Hipp.*986, cf. M.Ant.6.30, Chor. in *Jahrb.*9.176; οὐκ ἄ. Phlp.*in Ph.*528.19. Adv. -ψως Plu.2.4f.

ἀκονάω, (ἀκόνη) *sharpen*, μαχαίρας Ar.*Fr.*684; λόγχην X.*Cyr.*6.2.33:—Med., ἀκονᾶσθαι μαχαίρας Id.*HG*7.5.20:—Pass., Arist.*Pr.*886^{b}10, Phld.*Sign.*34. 2. metaph., *spur, goad on*, D.25.46; *provoke*, γλῶσσαν ἠκονημένος *Trag.Adesp.*423, cf. X.*Oec.*21.3, Ph.1.469, al., Chor. in *Jahrb.*9.184; θυμὸν ἐπ' ἐλπίδι τινὸς ἀ. Demad.17:—Pass., Ph.2.178, al.

ἄκονδος (leg. ἄκοννος)· ἄχαρις κονδάς (leg. κόννος), γὰρ ἡ χάρις, Hsch.

ἀκόνδῠλος, ον, *without knuckles*:—*without blows*, Luc.*Char.*2.

ἀκόν-η [ᾰ], ἡ, *whetstone, hone*, λιθίνη Chilo 1, Hermipp.46, etc. 2. metaph., δόξαν ἔχω ἀκόνας λιγυρᾶς ἐπὶ γλώσσᾳ I feel the shrill note of a *whetstone* on my tongue, i. e. am roused to song, Pi.*O.*6.82; of persons, e. g. a trainer, ἀνδράσιν ἀεθληταῖσιν Ναξίαν ἀκόναν Pi.*I.*6(5).73; of Ἔρως, *AP* 12.18 (Alph.), cf. Plu.2.838e. 3. part of tragus of ear, Poll.2.86. (Cf. Skt. *áśan-* 'stone'.) **-ησις**, εως, ἡ, *sharpening*, Hsch. and Suid. s.v. βρυγμός. **-ητής**, οῦ, ὁ, *one who sharpens*, σπάθης *Edict.Diocl.*7.33, cf. Hdn.Gr.1.73. **-ητί**· ἄνευ πόνου, *EM* 50.29. **-ητός**, ή, όν, = θηκτός, Sch.Opp.*H.*2.354. **-ήτως**· ἀκοπιάστως, Hsch.

ἀκονίας, ου, ὁ, *a fish*, Numen.ap.Ath.17.326a (s.v.l.).

ἀκονίᾱτος, ον, (κονιάω) *unplastered, not whitewashed*, Thphr.*HP* 8.11.1, cf. Gal.13.356 (nisi leg. ἀκώνητος).

ἀκόνιον, τό, in Medicine, specific for eyes, prob. powdered *by rubbing on an* ἀκόνη, Dsc.1.98.

ἀκονῑτί or **-εί** (*SIG* 36*B* (Olympia, v B.C.), D.19.77), Adv. of ἀκόνιτος, *without the dust of the arena*, i.e. *without struggle, without effort*, usu. of the conqueror, Th.4.73, X.*Ag.*6.3; of the loser, εἰ ταῦτα προεῖτο ἀ. D.18.200.

ἀκονιτικός, ή, όν, *made of* ἀκόνιτον, X.*Cyn.*11.2.

ἀκόνῑτον, τό, *leopard's bane, Aconitum Anthora*, Theopomp.Hist.177a, Thphr.*HP*9.16.4, Dsc.4.76, Gal.11.820:—also **-ῑτος**, ἡ, dub. l. in Nic.*Al.*42, cf. *AP* 11.123 (Hedyl.), Euph.142. II. *wolf's bane, Aconitum Napellus*, Dsc.4.77.

ἀκόνῑτος, ον, (κονίω) *without dust, combat* or *struggle*, Q.S.4.319. II. f.l. for ἀκώνητος, Dsc.1.7; for κωνικός, Arist.*GA* 739^{b}12.

ἄκονος, v. ἄκινος.

ἀκοντί, Adv. of ἄκων, *unwillingly*, Plu.*Fab.*5, Suid.

ἀκοντ-ίας, ου, ὁ, (ἄκων) *quick-darting serpent* (cf. ἀκοντίλος), Nic.*Th.*491, Philum.*Ven.*26, Luc.*Dips.*3. II. *meteor*, in pl., Plin.*HN*2.89. III. a plant, Hsch., *EM* 50.53. **-ίζω**, Att. fut.

-ιῶ, (ἄκων) *hurl a javelin*, τινός *at* one, Αἴαντος.. ἀκόντισε φαίδιμος Ἕκτωρ Il.14.402, cf. 8.118; also Αἴας.. ἐφ' Ἕκτορι.. ἵετ' ἀκοντίσσαι 16.359; ἀ. ἐς or καθ' ὅμιλον, Od.22.263, Il.4.490; ἔς τινας Th. 7.40; εἰς τὸ φῶς ἐκ τοῦ σκότους X.*An.*7.4.18: c. dat., of the weapon, ἦ καὶ ἀκόντισε δουρί Il.5.533; ἀ. δουρὶ φαεινῷ ib.611, al.; αἰχμαῖς Pi.*I.*1.24: also c. acc., ἀκόντισαν ὀξέα δοῦρα Od.22.265; ἀκοντίζουσι θαμειὰς αἰχμὰς ἐκ χειρῶν Il.12.44, cf. 14.422: abs., *use the javelin*, τοξεύειν καὶ ἀ. Hdt.4.114, cf. Hp.*Aër.*17, Th.3.23, etc.:—Pass., κῶλα.. ἐς πλευρὰ καὶ πρὸς ἧπαρ ἠκοντίζετο E.*IT*1370; ἀ. ἀπὸ τῶν ἵππων ὀρθός Pl.*Men.*93d. 2. after Hom., *hit* or *strike with javelin*, or simply *aim at*, ἀ. τὸν σῦν Hdt.1.43, etc.:—Pass., *to be hit* or *wounded*, E.*Ba.*1098, Antipho3.1.1, X.*HG*4.5.13. 3. *hurl, throw*, ἑαυτούς, i.e. *leap overboard*, Ach.Tat.5.7; *jettison* cargo, Id. 3.2: metaph., τινὰς εἰς ἄπειρον χρόνον Olymp.Alch.p.75B. 4. *shoot forth rays*, of moon, E.*Ion*1155:—Med., *flash*, Arist.*Mu.* 392^{b}3. 5. metaph., μῦθον Nonn.*D.*34.299; μερίμνας ἀνέμοισιν ib.12.258. II. intr., *dart* or *pierce*, metaph., of curses, εἴσω γῆς E.*Or.*1241. -ίλος, ὁ, = ἀκοντίας, Hsch., *EM*50.52. -ιον, τό, Dim. of ἄκων (A), *javelin*, *h.Merc.*460, Hdt.1.34, Aen.Tact.29.6,8, al. 2. in pl., *javelin-exercise*, Pl.*Lg.*794c; also in sg., X.*Eq.Mag.* 1.21,25. -ισία, ἡ, = sq., *SIG*1060 (Tralles). -ισις, εως, ἡ, *throwing the javelin*, X.*An.*1.9.5, Ascl.*Tact.*1.3. -ισμα, ατος, τό, *distance thrown with javelin*, ἐντὸς ἀκοντίσματος within *dart's throw*, X.*HG*4.4.16. II. *dart, javelin*, Str.4.6.7 (pl.), Plu.*Alex.*43, Arr.*Tact.*9.1. III. in pl., = the concrete ἀκοντισταί, Plu.*Pyrrh.* 21. -ισμός, ὁ, = ἀκόντισις, X.*Eq.Mag.*3.6, Str.11.5.1, Arr.*An.*1. 2.6; as a contest, *OGI*339 (Sestos); *emission* of liquids, [Gal.]19. 456, Sch.Il.17.297. 2. ἀκοντισμοὶ ἀστέρων, of *shooting* stars, Ptol. *Tetr.*102. -ιστήρ, ῆρος, ὁ, = -ιστής, E.*Ph.*142. II. as Adj., *darting, hurtling*, τρίαινα Opp.*H.*5.535: metaph., μαζοὶ ἀ. ἐρώτων Nonn. *D.*7.264:—also in pass. sense, θύρσος, λᾶας, 24.134, 30.230; ἀκοντιστῆρες μόλυβοι, prob. *bullets*, Keil-Premerstein *Dritter Bericht* p. 89. -ιστήριον, τό, *engine for hurling projectiles*, τὰ τῶν μεγάλων λίθων ἀ. Agath.3.5. -ιστής, οῦ, ὁ, *darter, javelin-man*, Il.16.328, Od.18.262, Hdt.8.90, A.*Pers.*52, Th.3.97, Theoc.17.55, etc. -ιστικός, ή, όν, *skilled in throwing the dart*, X.*Cyr.*7.5.63: Sup., ib.6.2. 4; -κά, τά, *art of throwing the dart*, Pl.*Thg.*126b; -κή, ἡ, Ael.*Tact. Praef.*, Arr.*Tact.Praef.* Adv. -κῶς Poll.3.151. -ιστύς, ύος, ἡ, = ἀκόντισις, *game of the dart*, ἀκοντιστὺν ἐσδύσεαι Il.23.622.

ἀκοντο-βόλος, ον, *dart-throwing*, A.R.2.1000: as Subst. in pl., Agath.3.20. -**δόκος**, ον, *receiving* (i.e. *hit by*) *the dart*, Simon. 106. -**φόρος**, ον, *bearing darts*, of persons or things, Nonn.*D.*20. 148, al.

ἀκόντως, Adv. of ἄκων (B), v. ἀέκων.

ἀκοός, όν, = ἀκουστικός, Pl.Com.226.

ἀκοπ-ητί, Adv. of ἄκοπος, f.l. for ἀκονιτί, Lib.*Decl.*29.6. -ία, ἡ, (ἄκοπος) *freedom from fatigue*, Cic.*Fam.*16.18.1. -ίαστος, ον, (κοπιάω) *not wearying*, ὁδός Arist.*Mu.*391^{a}12 (v.l. -ατος). II. *untiring, unwearied*, φῶς ἡλίου Herm.ap.Stob.1.49.44. Adv. -άστως Sch.S.*Aj.*852. -ίατος, ον, = foreg., πρόνοια *Stoic.*1.125, cf. *IG* 2.630*b*, Vett.Val.263.17, *PMag.Par.*1.1127; ἀ. πίστεις proofs which a writer *never tires of* repeating, Phld.*Mus.*p.40 K. Adv. -τως, ἀπολαύειν Id.*Piet.*15, Lxx *Wi.*16.20. -ος, ον, *unwearied*, Pl.*Lg.* 789d. Adv. -πως, διαπονεῖν Hp.*Vict.*3.70: Comp., ἡγούμενος -ωτέρως ἔσεσθαι τοῖς στρατιώταις prob. in *Hell.Oxy.*17.2. 2. *free from trouble*, Amips.28. 3. *unbruised*, of fruit, etc., *PHib.*49.9 (Sup., iii B.C.). II. Act., *not wearying*, ὄχησις Pl.*Ti.*89a; of a horse, *easy*, X.*Eq.*1.6 (Comp.); τοῖς τετράποσιν ἄκοπον τὸ ἑστάναι Arist.*PA*689^{b}17. 2. *removing weariness, refreshing*, Hp.*Aph.* 2.48, *Acut.*66, Pl.*Phdr.*227a, Agathin.ap.Orib.10.7.21 (Comp.):— ἄκοπον (sc. φάρμακον), τό, *application* (of various kinds) *for relief* of pain, etc., Dsc.1.1, Gal.13.1005, Luc.*Alex.*22, etc., cf. Antyll.ap. Orib.10.29; in Asclep.ap.Gal.13.343 also ἄκοπος, ἡ. 3. = ἀνάγυρος, Dsc.3.150, Sch.Nic.*Th.*71. III. (from κόπτω) *not worm-eaten*, Arist.*Pr.*909^{a}19. Adv. -πως, ἔχειν Thphr.*CP*4.16.2. 2. *not broken* or *ground*, whole, πέπερι Alex.Aphr.*Pr.*1.67; *not moth-eaten*, ἱμάτια Thphr.*HP*4.4.2. 3. *uncut*, χόρτος *PFlor.*232.11 (iii A.D.).

ἀκόπρ-ιστος, ον, (κοπρίζω) *not manured*, Thphr.*CP*4.12.3. -ος, ον, *with little excrement in the bowels*, Hp.*Acut.*62. II. = foreg., Thphr.*HP*8.6.4. -ώδης, ες, *producing little excrement*, of food, Hp.*Acut.*57 (Comp.).

ἀκοράζεσθαι· ἀκροᾶσθαι, Hsch. (i.e. ἀκοϝάζεσθαι). **ἀκοραῖος**· βλαβερός, ἀνωφελής, Id.

ἀκόρ-εστος, ον, (κορέννυμι) = ἀκόρητος, *insatiate*, αὐάτα *Lyr.Adesp.* 123, Trag. in lyr. passages, A.*Ag.*1002, E.*Heracl.*927: c. gen., αἰχμᾶς ἀ. A.*Pers.*998, cf. Eus.Mynd.1. Adv. -τως, ὀπυίεσθαι *AP*10.56 (Pall.), cf. Eun.*VSp.*456B.; ἀ. ὕδατος ἔχειν *Gp.*15.9.2, cf. Them.*Or.* 24.304d. 2. of things, *unceasing*, οἰζύς A.*Ag.*756; οἰμωγά S.*El.* 123; νείκη E.*Med.*638: Sup., γόοις A.*Pers.*545. II. Act., *not causing surfeit*, Id.*Ag.*1331; φιλία X.*Smp.*8.15 (Comp.). -ετος, ον, used in Trag. (metri gr.) for ἀκόρεστος, A.*Ag.*1117,1143, S.*El.* 122. -ής, ές, = ἀκόρεστος, οἰμωγῆς Them.*Or.*7.90d, cf. Hsch. (cod. ἀγκ-): Sup. -έστατος, of a person, S.*OC*120 (lyr.). -ητος, ον, *insatiate, unsated*, c. gen., πολέμου, μάχης, ἀπειλάων, Il.12.335, 20. 2, 14.479 (not in Od.), cf. Hes.*Sc.*346; προκάδων *h.Ven.*71. II. (κόρις) *undisturbed by bugs*, Ar.*Nu.*44 (wrongly expl. by Sch. and Phot.p.63 R. as *unswept*). -ία, ἡ, *not eating to satiety, moderation in eating*, Hp.*Epid.*6.4.18. II. ἀ. ποτοῦ *insatiable desire* of drink, Aret.*CD*2.2.

ἀκορίτης [ῑ] οἶνος, ὁ, *wine flavoured with* ἄκορον, Dsc.5.63.

ἄκορνα, ἡ, *fish thistle*, *Cnicus Acarna*, Thphr.*HP*1.10.6, 6.4.6.

ἀκορνοί· ἀττέλεβοι, Hsch.; cf. ὀκορνός.

ἄκορον, τό, *yellow flag*, *Iris Pseudacorus*, Dsc.1.2, Gal.11.819:—f.l. for ἄκκιρον, κόρκορον, Plin.*HN*15.27, 25.144, for ἄκαιρον, Dsc.4.144.

ἄκορος, ον, = ἀκόρεστος: *untiring, ceaseless*, εἰρεσία Pi.*P.*4.202.

ἀκορραί· ἄκανθαι, Hsch. **ἀκόρσωτον**· ἀκτένιστον, ἄκαρτον, ἀξύλιστον, Id.

ἀκόρῠφ-ος, ον, (κορυφή) *without top, without beginning*, D.H.*Comp.* 22. II. = sq., Hsch. -**ωτος**, ον, *not to be summed, countless*, Id. s.v. ἄκριτα.

ἄκος, εος, τό, (ἀκέομαι) *cure, remedy*, c. gen. rei, κακῶν Od.22.481, etc.; νυμφικῶν ἑδωλίων A.*Ch.*71; κύβους.. τερπνὸν ἀργίας ἄ. S.*Fr.* 479.4; κακὸν κακῷ διδοὺς ἄ. Id.*Aj.*363: abs., ἄ. εὑρεῖν Il.9.250; δίζησθαι, ἐξευρεῖν, ἐκπονεῖν, λαβεῖν, Hdt.1.94, 4.187, A.*Supp.*367, E.*Ba.* 327; ἄκη ποιεῖσθαι, c. dat., Pl.*Lg.*910a: in medical sense, Hp.*Acut.*1; by a medical metaph., ἄ. ἐντέμνειν, τέμνειν, A.*Ag.*17, E.*Andr.*121; ἄ. τομαῖον A.*Ch.*539: ἄ. [ἐστι], c. inf., ἄ. γὰρ οὐδὲν τόνδε θρηνεῖσθαι *it boots* not to.., Id.*Pr.*43. 2. *means of obtaining* a thing, c. gen., σωτηρίας E.*Hel.*1055.

ἀκοσκίνευτος, ον, *unwinnowed*, *PPetr.*3p.218 (iii B.C.).

ἀκοσμ-έω, *to be disorderly, offend*, οἱ ἀκοσμοῦντες S.*Ant.*730, *Ph.* 387, Lys.14.13, D.24.92, Hyp.*Fr.*14, Arist.*Ath.*3.6; ἀ. περί τι *offend* in a point, Pl.*Lg.*764b. -**ήεις**, εσσα, εν, = ἄκοσμος, Nic.*Al.* 175. -**ητος**, ον, (κοσμέω) *unarranged*, Pl.*Grg.*506e, *Prt.*321c. Adv. -τως Id.*Lg.*781b. b. *not organized as a* κόσμος, ὕλη Plot.4.3. 9; σύγχυσις Dam.*Pr.*205. 2. of style, *unadorned*, D.H.*Th.*23, etc. 3. *unfurnished with*, χρήμασιν X.*Oec.*11.9. -**ία**, ἡ, *disorder*, Pl.*Grg.*508a, Ael.*Tact.*41.2; *extravagance, excess*, λόγων E.*IA*317:—in moral sense, *disorderliness* (with play on κόσμος II. 1), S.*Fr.*846: in pl., Pl.*Smp.*188b; αἱ ἀ. τοῦ πλήθους Phld.*Hom.* p.34 O. 2. *absence of* κόσμος, *chaos*, Dam.*Pr.*205. II. *abeyance of* κόσμοι, in Crete (κόσμος III), Arist.*Pol.*1272^{b}8. -**ιος**, ον, = ἀκοσμήεις, Sch.Nic.*Al.*175. -**ος**, ον, *disorderly*, φυγή A.*Pers.* 470; ἄ. καὶ ταραχώδης νυκτομαχία Plu.*Mar.*20:—in Hom. once, ἔπεα ἄκοσμά τε πολλά τε ᾔδη Il.2.213. Adv. -μως Hdt.7.220, A.*Pers.*374, etc. II. κόσμος ἄ. a world *that is no world*, *AP*7.561 (Jul.), but in 9.323 (Antip.) of an *inappropriate* ornament.

ἀκοστ-άω or -έω, (cf. sq.) only aor. part., ἵππος ἀκοστήσας ἐπὶ φάτνῃ horse *well-fed* at rack and manger, Il.6.506, 15.263; cf. ἀγοστέω. -**ή**, ἡ, *barley*, Nic.*Al.*106. (Cypr. acc. to Hsch., but Thess. for *grain* of all kinds acc. to Sch.Il.6.506.)

ἀκόστιλα· ἐλάχιστα, Hsch.

ἄκοτος, ον, *free from anger, cheerful*, Pi.*Pae.*1.3, cf. Hsch.

ἀκουάζομαι, *hear, listen to*, c. gen., ἀοιδοῦ Od.9.7, cf. 13.9; δαιτὸς ἀκουάζεσθον *ye are bidden to* the feast, like καλεῖσθαι, Il.4.343: Medic., of auscultation, ἀ. πρὸς τὰ πλευρά Hp.*Morb.*2.61:—Act., *h.Merc.*423.

ἀκουή, ἡ, Ep. for ἀκοή (q.v.).

ἀκουόντως, Adv. *as one that listens*, i.e. *with deference*, λέγειν Sch. Il.*Oxy.*1085.72.

ἀκούρευτος, ον, (κουρεύω) *unshaven, unshorn*, *EM*120.28, *Gloss.*

ἄκουρος, ον, (κοῦρος) *childless, without male heir*, Od.7.64. II. (κουρά) *unshaven*, Ar.*V.*476, Lyc.976, Str.10.3.6.

ἀκουσείω [ᾰ], Desiderat. of ἀκούω, *long to hear*, S.*Fr.*991; and in Hsch. the order of words requires ἀκουσείων for ἀκουστιῶν.

ἀκουσ-ία [ᾰκ], ἡ, *involuntary action*, S.*Fr.*746. -**ιάζομαι** [ᾱκ], in aor. 1 Pass., *sin through ignorance*, Lxx *Nu.*15.28.

ἀκουσί-θεος [ᾰ], ον, *heard of God*, *AP*6.249 (Antip. Thess.). -**μος** [ᾰ], η, ον, *fit to be heard*, S.*Fr.*745.

ἀκούσι-ος [ᾱ], ον, Att. contr. for ἀεκούσιος. -**ότης** [ᾱ], ητος, ἡ, = ἀκουσία, Hsch. s.v. ἀέκητι, al.

ἄκου-σις [ᾰ], εως, ἡ, *hearing*, Arist. *de An.*426^{a}1, al., Phld.*Rh.*2. 90S. 2. in pl., = ἀκουσμάτια, Plot.4.1.12. -**σμα**, ατος, τό, *thing heard*, such as music, ἥδιστον ἄ. X.*Mem.*2.1.31, Men.660; ἀ. καὶ δράματα Arist.*Pol.*1336^{b}2, cf. *EN*1174^{b}28, Posidon.23, Plu.*Crass.*33. 2. *rumour, report*, S.*OC*518 (lyr.), Jul.*Or.*3.110d. 3. *oral instruction*, in the Pythag. school, Iamb.*VP*18.82. -**σματικός**, ή, όν, lit. *eager to hear*: οἱ ἀ. *probationers* in the school of Pythagoras, Iamb.*VP* 18.81, etc. -**σμάτιον**, τό, Dim. of ἄκουσμα, Ps.-Luc.*Philopatr.* 18. -**στέον**, *one must hear* or *hearken to*, c. gen. pers., E.*IA* 1010, X.*Smp.*3.9, etc. (also in pl. ἀκουστέα, Hdt.3.61; τῶν κρατούντων ἐστὶ πάντ' ἀκουστέα S.*El.*340): c. acc. rei, Pl.*R.*386a: abs., S.*OT* 1170. b. *one must understand*, τι διττῶς Str.9.5.12, cf. Gal. 15.484, Olymp. *in Mete.*337.14; *one must interpret*, ὀνείρους Artem. 1.3. -**στήριον**, τό, *lecture-hall*, Gal.*Libr.Propr.*2, Them.*Or.*2. 26c. 2. *assembly of hearers, audience*, Porph.*Plot.*15. -**στής**, οῦ, ὁ, *hearer, listener*, Men.988; τῶν ἀλλοτρίων κακῶν D.H.*Dem.* 45. 2. *auditor, disciple*, Scymn.20, Agathem.1.1, Phld.*Rh.*1. 95S., D.H.*Isoc.*1, etc. -**στικός**, ή, όν, *of* or *for hearing*, πάθος Epicur.*Ep.*1p.13U.; αἴσθησις ἀ. Plu.2.37f; δύναμις ἀ. Arr.*Epict.* 2.23.2; πόρος ἀ. orifice *of ear*, Gal.10.455; τὸ ἀ. *faculty of hearing*, Arist.*de An.*426^{a}7. 2. *ready to hear*, c. gen., Id.*EN*1103^{a}3, Arr. *Epict.*3.1.13. Adv. -κῶς Phld.*Mus.*p.107K., S.E.*M.*7.355. 3. = ἀκουσματικός, Gell.1.9. 4. = sq., Sch.E.*Or.*1281. -**στός**, ή, όν, *heard, audible*, *h.Merc.*512, Hp.*Insomn.*86, Pl.*Ti.*33c, Phld.*Herc.* 698.20, etc.; opp. θεατός, Isoc.2.49. II. *that should be heard*, with neg., δεινόν, οὐκ ἀ. S.*OT*1312, cf. E.*Andr.*1084. -**τίζω**, *make to hear*, τινά τι or τινος Lxx *Ps.*50(51).8, *Si.*45.5.

ἀκούω: Ep. impf. ἄκουον Il.12.442: fut. ἀκούσομαι (Act. ἀκούσω first in Hyp.*Epit.*34 s. v. l., then in Lyc.378,686, D.H.5.57, *Ev.Matt.*12.19, etc.: aor. ἤκουσα, Ep. ἄκουσα Il.24.223: pf. ἀκήκοα, Lacon. ἄκουκα Plu.*Lyc.*20, *Ages.*21; ἤκουκα is a late form, *POxy.*237 vii 23 (ii A.D.); later Ion. ἀκήκουκα Herod.5.49: plpf. ἀκηκόειν Hdt.2.52, 7.208; ἠκηκόειν X.*Oec.*15.7; old Att. ἠκηκόη Ar.*V.*800, *Pax*616, Pl.*Cra.*384b:—rare in **Med.**, pres. (v. infr. II. 2): Ep. impf. ἀκούετο Il.4.331: aor. ἠκουσάμην Mosch.3.119:—**Pass.**, fut. ἀκουσθήσομαι Pl.*R.*507d: aor. ἠκούσθην Th.3.38, Luc.*Somn.*5: pf. ἤκουσμαι D.H.*Rh.*11.10, Ps.-Luc.*Philopatr.*4; ἀκήκουσμαι is dub. in Luc.*Hist. Conscr.*49: plpf. ἤκουστο Anon.ap.Demetr.*Eloc.*217, (παρ-) J.*AJ*17.10.10. (ἀ-κοϝ-, cf. κοέω):—*hear*, Hom., etc.: prop. c. acc. of thing heard, gen. of person from whom it is heard, ταῦτα Καλυψοῦς ἤκουσα Od.12.389, cf. S.*OT*43, etc.; gen. pers. freq. omitted, πάντ' ἀκήκοας λόγον Id.*Aj.*480, etc.; or the acc. rei, ἄκουε τοῦ θανόντος Id.*El.*792, cf. 793:—also c. gen. rei, φθογγῆς, κτύπου, *hear it*, Od.12.198 (as v. l.), 21.237; λόγων S.*OC*1187; once in Hom. in Med., ἀκούετο λαὸς ἀϋτῆς Il.4.331. b. c. gen. objecti, *hear of, hear tell of*, ἀ. πατρός Od.4.114: freq. c. part., τεθνηῶτος (sc. πατρός) ἀκούσῃς 1.289, etc.; but εἰ.. πατρὸς νόστον ἀ. ib.287; ἀ. περί τινος Od.19.270, cf. E.*IT*964, Isoc.5.72, Pl.*R.*358d,e; τι περί τινος X.*An.*7.7.30. c. in Prose the pers. from whom thing is heard freq. takes Prep., ἀ. τι ἀπό, ἐκ, παρά, πρός τινος, first in Il.6.524, cf. Hdt.3.62, S.*OT*7,95, Th.1.125. d. less freq. c. dupl. gen. pers. et rei, *hear of* a thing *from* a person, as Od.17.115, D.18.9. e. with part. or inf. added, as εἰ πτώσσοντας ὑφ' Ἕκτορι πάντας ἀκούσαι *should he hear* that all are now crouching under Hector, Il.7.129, cf. Hdt.7.10.θ', X.*Cyr.*2.4.12, D.3.9; ἀ. αὐτὸν ὄλβιον εἶναι *to hear* [*generally*] that he is happy, Il.24.543, cf. X.*An.*2.5.13, etc.:—also ἀ. τινὰ ὅτι or ὡς, Ἀτρεΐδην ἀκούετε ὡς.. Od.3.193; τὸν Δαίδαλον οὐκ ἀκήκοας, ὅτι..; X.*Mem.*4.2.33; ἀ. οὕνεκα S.*OC*33. f. c. gen. et part., to express *what one actually hears* from a person, ταῦτ'.. ἤκουον σαφῶς Ὀδυσσέως λέγοντος S.*Ph.*595; ἀ. τινὸς λέγοντος, διαλεγομένου, Pl.*Prt.*320b, X.*Mem.*2.4.1: rarely c. acc. et part., S.*Ph.*614. 2. *know by hearsay*, ἔξοιδ' ἀκούων S.*OT*105: pres. is used like a pf., νῆσός τις Συρίη κικλήσκεται, εἴ που ἀκούεις Od.15.403, cf. 3.193; in Prose, Pl.*Grg.*503c, Luc.*Gall.*13. 3. abs., *hearken, give ear*, esp. in proclamations, ἀκούετε λεῴ *oyez! oyez!* Susar.1, etc.: for S.*OT*1386 v. πηγή 2. 4. οἱ ἀκούοντες *readers of a book*, Plb.1.13.6, al. II. *listen to, give ear to*, c. gen., Il.1.381, etc.: metaph., Φωκυλίδου οὐκ ἀκούεις; Pl.*R.*407a: rarely c. dat., ἀ. ἀνέρι κηδομένῳ Il.16.515 (in S.*El.*227 τίνι is Eth. dat.): with gen. of part. after dat., ὅττι οἱ ὦκ' ἤκουσε.. θεὸς εὐξαμένοιο ib.531. 2. *obey*, βασιλῆος, θεοῦ, Il.19.256, Od.7.11:—Med., Λεωφίλου δ' ἀκούεται [πάντα] Archil.64. 3. *hear and understand*, κλύοντες οὐκ ἤκουον A.*Pr.*448, cf. *Ch.*5, Ar.*Ra.*1173; τὸ μὴ πάντας πάντων ἀκούειν S.E.*M.*1.37. 4. *to be a pupil of*, c. gen., D.L.9.21. III. after Hom., serving as Pass. to λέγειν, *hear oneself called, be called*, like Lat. *audire*, εἴπερ ὄρθ' ἀκούεις, Ζεῦ S.*OT*903 (cf. A.*Ag.*161); freq. with εὖ and κακῶς, κακῶς ἀ. ὑπό τινος *to be ill spoken of by* one; πρός τινος Hdt.7.16.α'; περί τινος for a thing, Id.6.86.α'; ἀμείνον, ἄριστα ἀ., Hdt.2.173, 8.93, cf. S.*Ph.*1313, Antipho 5.75, etc. 2. with nom. of subject, ἀκούειν κακός, καλός, S.*OC*988, Pl.*Ly.*207a; νῦν κόλακες καὶ θεοῖς ἐχθροὶ... ἀκούουσι D.18.46, etc.; ἔχαιρε ἀκούων Αἰετὸς ὁ Πύρρος Ael.*NA*7.45; later in Pass. in this sense, Nonn.*D.*21.220, al. 3. c. inf., ἤκουον εἶναι πρῶτοι *were said* to be first, Hdt.3.131; also ἀκούσομαι μὲν ὡς ἔφυν οἴκτου πλέως S.*Ph.*1074. 4. c. acc. rei, ἀ. κακά *have* evil *spoken of* one, Ar.*Th.*388, cf. S.*Ph.*607; ἀ. λόγον ἐσλόν Pi.*I.*5(4).13; φήμας.. κακὰς ἤκουσεν E.*Hel.*615. 5. οὕτως ἀ. *hear it* so *said*, i.e. *at first hearing*, ὡς οὕτω γ' ἀκοῦσαι Pl.*Euthphr.*3b; ὥς γε οὑτωσὶ ἀκοῦσαι Id.*Ly.*216a. IV. *understand, take* in a certain sense, Jul.*Or.*4.147a; esp. in Scholl., as Sch.E.*Or.*333; τι ἐπί τινος Sch.E.*Hipp.*73. V. Astrol., *aspect mutually*, of signs equidistant from an equinoctial sign, Doroth.189, Heph. Astr.2.2; also, = ὑπακούειν (q. v.), Id.1.9.

ἄκρα, Ion. **ἄκρη**, ἡ, (fem. of ἄκρος) *highest* or *farthest point*: 1. *headland, cape*, Il.4.425, 14.36, Od.9.285, S.*Tr.*788, Pl.*Criti.*111a: metaph., ἄκρην πενίης οὐχ ὑπερεδράμομεν Thgn.619, cf. A.*Eu.*562; κάμπτειν Men.4. 2. *hill-top, height*, Od.8.508, *Hymn.Is.*72 (pl.). 3. of a wave, *crest*, οὐ γὰρ ὑπερθεῖν κύματος ἄκραν δυνάμεσθα E.*Fr.*230. 4. Hom. only in phrase κατ' ἄκρης, νῦν ὤλετο πᾶσα κατ' ἄκρης Ἴλιος αἰπεινὴ *from top to bottom*, i.e. *utterly*, Il.13.772; κατ' ἄ. Ἴλιον ἑλέειν 15.557, cf. 24.728, Hdt.6.18, Th.4.112; κατ' ἄ. ἐξαιρεῖν Pl.*Lg.*909b; γῆν πατρῴαν.. πρῆσαι κατ' ἄ. *utterly*, S.*Ant.*201: metaph., κατ' ἄ. ὡς πορθούμεθα how *utterly*..! A.*Ch.*691, cf. S.*OC*1242, E.*IA*778; but ἔλασεν μέγα κῦμα κατ' ἄ. *from above*, Od.5.313. 5. *citadel* built on a *steep* rock overhanging a town (usu. ἀκρόπολις), X.*An.*7.1.20, Hyp.*Lyc.Fr.*3, Luc.*BisAcc.*13. 6. *end, extremity*, Arist.*HA*512ᵃ6, 518ᵃ9: Math., of lines, Papp.682.14; of *the extremes* in a proportion, Id.70.6, Euc.6.16, etc.

ἀκράαντος [κρᾱ], ον, (κραιαίνω) = ἄκραντος, Il.2.138, Od.2.202.

ἀκραγής, ές, (κράζω) *not barking*, ἀκραγεῖς κύνες, of gryphons, A.*Pr.*803. Hsch. expl. ἀκραγές by δυσχερές, σκληρόν, ὀξύχολον, cf. ἄκραγγες (leg. ἀκραγές)· ἀκρόχολον *AB*369.

ἀκράδαντος, ον, (κραδαίνομαι) *unshaken*, Ph.2.136, etc. Adv. -τως 1.352, Nicom.*Harm.*4.

ἀκραής, ές, (ἄκρος, ἄημι) *blowing strongly*, of winds, Od.2.421, 14.253, Hes.*Op.*594; *si ἀκραὲς erit* if a *brisk breeze* spring up, Cic.*Att.*10.17.9. Adv. **ἀκραεί**, πλεῖν sail *with fresh breeze*, Arr.*Ind.*24.1.

ἀκραίνει· ἀκρατεῖ, Hsch.: **ἀκραινές**· ἀκρατές (cod. -ῶς· ἐγκρ-), Id.

ἀκραῖος, α, ον, = ἄκρος, Opp.*H.*2.395, *Tab.Defix.*18; ἀκραῖα, τά, *extremities*, Gal.7.416: Ion. ἄκρεα, τά, Hp.*Epid.*1.18, *Fract.*16, *Art.*30. II. *dwelling on heights*, epith. of Hera, E.*Med.*1379, Apollod.1.9.28; Aphrodite, Paus.1.1.3, 2.32.6; gods whose temples were ἐν ἀκροπόλει, Poll.9.40.

ἀκραιπᾰλ-ος, ον, *relieved of drunken nausea*, Arist.*Pr.*873ᵇ11. 2. of wines, *not producing nausea*, Ath.1.32d. 3. of herbs, *counteracting nausea*, Dsc.1.26. **-ωτος**, ον, = foreg. 3, Orib.*Eup.*1.12.5.

ἀκραιφνής, ές, derived by Sch.Th.1.52, etc., from ἀκεραιο-φανής, = ἀκέραιος, *unmixed, pure*, κόρης ἀ. αἷμα E.*Hec.*537; ὕδωρ Ar.*Fr.*32: metaph., ἀρετή J.*AJProoem.*4; πενία ἀ. *sheer, utter* poverty, *AP*6.191 (Corn. Long.). Adv. -νῶς Ph.1.100; *honestly*, Hld.2.30: Sup. -έστατον (but may be Adj.) Ph.2.319. II. *untouched, inviolate*, E.*Alc.*1052; in Att. Prose only Th.1.19,52; freq. later, as D.H.6.14, Procop.*Aed.*1.10, al.; *innocent*, ψυχή Ph.1.515:—of troops, *fresh*, J.*AJ*18.10.7. 2. c. gen., *untouched by*.., ἀ. τῶν κατηπειλημένων S.*OC*1147; κόρους ἀκραιφνεῖς μυρρίνης *free from*.., Lysipp.9.

ἀκραιφνότης, τητος, ἡ, *purity*, Anon. *in Prm.*(*Rh.Mus.*47.614).

ἀκραμύλα· κοχλίας, Hsch.

ἄκραντος, ον, poet. Adj. (in Hom. ἀκράαντος, q. v.), *unfulfilled, fruitless, idle*, ἔπεα, ἐλπίδες, Pi.*O.*1.86, *P.*3.23; τέχναι A.*Ag.*249:—neut. pl. as Adv., *in vain*, Pi.*O.*2.87; ἄκραντα βάζω A.*Ch.*882; οὐδ' ἄκρανθ' ὡρμήσαμεν E.*Ba.*435, cf. 1231; ἄκραντ' ὀδύρῃ *Supp.*770. 2. *ineffectual*, νύξ A.*Ch.*65.

ἀκραξόνιον, τό, (ἄξων) *end of the axle*, Poll.1.145, Sch.A.R.1.752.

ἀκρᾱσία (A), Ion. **-ησίη**, ἡ, (ἄκρᾱτος) *bad mixture, ill temperature*, opp. εὐκρασία, ἀ. ἀέρος an *unwholesome* climate, Thphr.*CP*3.2.5; διὰ τὴν ἀκρησίην, of meats, Hp.*VM*7; χυμῶν ἀκρησίαι ib.18.

ἀκρᾰσ-ία (B), Ion. **-σίη**, = ἀκράτεια, Archil.*Supp.*2.10, Democr.234, D.2.18, X.*Mem.*4.5.6, Isoc.15.221 (pl.), Arist.*EN*1145ᵃ16, Men.544, *Ev.Matt.*23.25, etc.; βρώσιος *Dialex.*1.3. **-ίων**, ωνος, ὁ, *incontinent person*, Cerc.4.1.

ἀκράσπεδος, ον, *without fringes*: metaph., of words, *without the article*, Plu.2.1010d (cj. Madvig).

ἀκρατάριον, τό, Dim. of ἄκρατον, = *mericulum, Gloss.*

ἀκράτ-εια [κρᾰ], ἡ, (ἀκρατής) *want of power, debility*, νεύρων Hp.*Aph.*5.16, *Liqu.*1. II. *incontinence, want of self-control*, opp. ἐγκράτεια, Pl.*R.*461b, *Lg.*734b, etc.; ἀ. ἡδονῶν τε καὶ ἐπιθυμιῶν ib.886a, etc., cf. Ph.2.406. **-εύομαι**, *to be incontinent*, Arist.*EN*1145ᵇ22; τῶν ἀκρασιῶν ἣν οἱ μελαγχολικοὶ -εύονται 1152ᵃ28: censured by Phryn.406, who quotes however Men.989:—Act. is cj. in Plu.ap. Stob.3.6.53. **-ευτικός**, ή, όν, *arising from incontinence*, ἀδικήματα Arist.*Rh.*1391ᵃ19. **-έω**, *to be* ἀκρατής, Hp.*Mul.*1.25, Poll.2.154; Ep. part. -έοντι λογισμῷ Man.4.548. **-ής**, ές, (κράτος) *powerless, impotent*, γῆρας S.*OC*1236; παιδία Hp.*Aër.*10; of paralysed limbs, *IG*4.951.22 (Epid.), Aret.*SD*1.7. 2. in Law, *invalid*, πρῆσις *GDI*5653 (Chios), cf. *IG*12(8).267.12 (Thasos). II. c. gen. rei, *not having power* or *command over* a thing, γλώσσης A.*Pr.*884; φωνῆς, παντὸς τοῦ σώματος, ἑωυτοῦ, Hp.*Morb.*1.3, *Art.*48, *Morb.*2.6; ὀργῆς Th.3.84; θυμοῦ Pl.*Lg.*869a; ἀ. τῶν χειρῶν, of persons *with their hands tied*, D.H.1.38; *intemperate in the use of* a thing, ἀφροδισίων, οἴνου, X.*Mem.*1.2.2, *Oec.*12.11; ἀ. κέρδους, τιμῆς *intemperate in pursuit of* them, Arist.*EN*1147ᵇ33; with Preps., ἀ. πρὸς τὸν οἶνον Id.*HA*594ᵃ10; περὶ τὰ πόματα Id.*PA*691ᵃ3: c. inf., ἀ. εἴργεσθαί τινος *unable to* refrain from.., Pl.*Sph.*252c. Adv. -τῶς, Ion. -τέως, διακεῖσθαι Hp.*Acut.*(*Sp.*)55. 2. abs. in moral sense, *without command over* oneself or one's passions, *incontinent*, Arist.*EN*1145ᵇ11; ἀ. στόμα Ar.*Ra.*838; νηδὺς Aristias 3. Adv. ἀκρατῶς, ἔχειν πρός τι Pl.*Lg.*710a. 3. of things, *uncontrolled, immoderate*, δαπάνη *AP*9.367 (Luc.); οὖρον.. ἀκρατές *incontinence* of urine, Aret.*SA*1.6; cf. ἀκρᾶτί. **-ησία**, ἡ, *want of control, incontinence*, σπέρματος Sor.2.47. **-ητος**, ον, *unsubdued*, Arist.*Mete.*384ᵃ33: *uncontrollable*, ἐπιθυμία Hdn.1.8.2. Adv. -τως Orib.*Syn.*7.47.3; ἐπτόηνται Iamb.*VP*20.94. **-ί**, Adv. = ἀκρατῶς, τὰ οὖρα ἐκχέειν Aret.*SD*1.7.

ἀκρᾰτία, Ion. **-τίη**, = ἀκράτεια, Pl.*Grg.*525a, dub. in Hp.*Coac.*166. **ἀκρᾱτία**, ἡ (sic), for ἀκρασία, *absence of mixture*, Dam.*Pr.*155 (s. v. l.).

ἀκρᾱτ-ίζομαι, (ἄκρᾱτος) *drink neat wine*; hence, *breakfast*, because this consisted of *bread dipped in wine* (Ath.1.11c sq.), Ar.*Pl.*295, ubi v. Sch., Canthar.8: c. acc., ἀ. κοκκύμηλα *to breakfast on* plums, Ar.*Fr.*607; μικρόν Aristomen.14: metaph., c. gen., ἀμιγοῦς ἠκρατίσω σοφίας Ph.2.166:—later in Act. -ίζω, fut. -ιῶ, *entertain at breakfast*, τοὺς ἐφήβους *Inscr.Prien.*113.41: metaph., ποτιζέτω καὶ ἀκρατιζέτω ψυχάς Ph.1.103. **-ισμα**, ατος, τό, *a breakfast*, ἕως ἀκρατίσματος ὥρας Arist.*HA*564ᵃ20, cf. *Inscr.Prien.*113.54, Ath.1.11d, Plu.2.726c. **-ισμός**, ὁ, *breakfasting*, Ath.1.11d, v.l. in Theoc.1.51 (ap.Sch.). **-ιστος**, ον, Theoc.1.51 codd. πρὶν ἢ ἀκράτιστον ἐπὶ ξηροῖσι καθίξῃ *having made a* dry *breakfast*, i.e. none at all; vv.ll. ἀκρατισμόν (Sch.), ἀνάριστον *dinnerless*.

ἀκρᾱτο-κώθων, ωνος, ὁ, *a hard toper*, Hyp.*Dem.Fr.*(a), Ath.6.246a. **-ποσία**, Ion. ἀκρητοποσίη, ἡ, *drinking of neat wine*, Hdt.6.84, Hp.*Aph.*6.31, Satyr.1, Plu.*Alex.*70. **-ποτέω**, *drink neat wine*, Arist.*Pr.*871ᵃ28. **-πότης**, ου, Ion. ἀκρητοπότης, εω, ὁ, (πίνω) *drinker of neat wine*, Hdt.6.84, Ael.*VH*2.41; personified as name of hero, Polem.Hist.40. **-πώλιον**· *meritorium, Gloss.*

ἄκρᾱτος, Ion. **ἄκρητος**, ον: (κεράννυμι): 1. of liquids, *unmixed, neat*, esp. of wine, Od.24.73; ἄκρητοι σπονδαί drink-offerings *of pure wine*, Il.2.341, 4.159; οἶνος πάνυ ἄ. very *strong*, X.*An.*4.5.27; οἶνος ἄκρητος wine *without water*, Hdt.1.207, etc.; ἄκρατος (without οἶνος) Ar.*Eq.*105, etc.; ὁ πολὺς ἄ. ὀλίγ' ἀναγκάζει φρονεῖν

Men.779, cf. Call.*Ep.*43, Phoen.3.3; ἄκρατον, τό, Arist.*Po.*1461ᵃ15; γάλα Od.9.297; αἷμα A.*Ch.*578, etc. (without αἷμα Hp.*Epid.*1.26.α′); χυμός Hp.*VM*14; ὑποχωρήσιες Id.*Aph.*7.6; διάρροια Th.2.49. Adv. -τως Hp.*Prorrh.*2.24 (-κρίτως Littré). 2. of any objects, ἄ. σώματα *pure, simple* bodies, Pl.*Ti.*57c; ἄ. χρῶμα Hp.*Acut.*42; ἄ. μέλαν *pure* black, Thphr.*Col.*26; ἄ. νύξ Ael.*Fr.*262, cf. *NA*12.33; ἄ. σκότος Plu. *Nic.*21; ἄ. σκιά Id.2.932b. 3. of qualities, *pure, absolute*, ἄ. νοῦς X.*Cyr.*8.7.20; πῶς.. ἡ ἄ. δικαιοσύνη πρὸς ἀδικίαν τὴν ἄ. ἔχει Pl.*R.*545a, cf. 491e. Adv. -τως *Lg.*731d. 4. of conditions or states, *pure, untempered, absolute*, ἐλευθερία, ἡδονή, *R.*562d, *Lg.*793a; ὀλιγαρχία Arist.*Pol.*1273ᵇ37, etc.; παρρησία Demad.18; νόμων ἀποτομία *POxy.*237 vii 40 (ii A.D.); ἄ. νόμος *absolute* law, Pl.*Lg.*723a; ἄ. ψεῦδος *sheer* lie, Id.*R.*382c. Adv. ἀκράτως *absolutely, entirely*, ἀ. μέλας, λευκός, Ael. *NA*16.11, Luc.*D.Mar.*1.3. 5. of persons, *intemperate, violent*, ἄ. ὀργήν A.*Pr.*678; of sleep, ἄ. ἐλθέ come *with all thy power*, E.*Cyc.*602. 6. of feelings, ἄ. ὀργή Alcid.ap.Arist.*Rh.*1406ᵃ10; ἵμερος S.*Fr.*941; ἄ. καῦμα *AP*9.71 (Antiphil.); φόβος *EM*621.13; τὸ τῆς δεισιδαιμονίας ἄ. J.*BJ*2.9.3, etc. II. Comp. ἀκρατέστερος, Ion. ἀκρητ- (as if fr. ἀκρατής) Hp.*VM*5, Hyp.*Dem.Fr.*(6), Arist.*Pr.*871ᵃ16, Thphr. *Od.*24: Sup. ἀκρατέστατος Pl.*Phlb.*53a: but ἀκρατότερος Plu.2.677c.

ἀκρᾱτόστομος, ον, gloss on ἀθυρόγλωσσος, Sch.E.*Or.*903.

ἀκρᾱτότης, Ion. -ητότης, ητος, ἡ, *unmixed state*, οἴνου, μέλιτος Hp. *Acut.*56.

ἀκρᾱτο-φόρος, ὁ, and **-φόρον**, τό, *vessel for pure wine*, elsewh. ψυκτήρ, Cic.*Fin.*3.4.15, Poll.6.99, 10.70, J.*BJ*5.13.6.

ἀκρᾱτόφρων, ονος, *lacking in self-control*, gloss on χαλίφρων, Sch. Od.19.530.

ἀκράτωρ [ᾰ], ορος, ὁ, = ἀκρατής 1, S.*Ph.*486, Ph.1.116, al. II. = ἀκρατής II, ἀ. ἑαυτοῦ Pl.*R.*579c, *Criti.*121a; γαστέρων Theopomp. Hist.39, cf. Ph.2.357, Ael.*Fr.*90.

ἀκρᾱ-χολέω, *to be passionate*, only in pres. part., Pl.*Lg.*731d. **-χολία**, Ion. **ἀκρηχολίη**, ἡ, *passionateness, burst of passion*, Hp.*Epid.*7.11: later **ἀκροχολία**, Sopat.ap.Stob.4.5.56, Plu.2.454b. **-χολος** [ρᾱ], ον, *quick to anger, irascible*, Ar.*Eq.*41, Pl.*R.*411c, Phld.*Lib.* p.44 O., etc.; κύων ἀ. *ill-tempered* dog, Ar.*Fr.*594a; μέλισσα Epin. 1.7: Sup., ἀχέρδου τῆς ἀκραχολωτάτης, of a *spinous* pear, Pherecr. 164:—also **ἀκρόχολος**, ον, Arist.*EN*1126ᵃ18, Ph.2.268, Plu.2.604b, etc. II. generally, *in passionate distress*, Theoc.24.61. (ἀκρᾱ- is confirmed by metre of Com., Ion. form ἀκρη-, and etym. (shortened fr. ἀκρατ-); ἀκρο- is freq. v.l. in codd. of early authors, as Pl. l.c.)

ἄκρεα, v. ἀκραῖος. II. **ἀκρέα**, ἡ, *girl* (Maced.), Hsch.

ἀκρελεφάντινος, ον, (ἄκρος, ἐλέφας) *with extremities of ivory*, ἱερόν (i.e. statue) *IGRom.*3.800 (Syllium).

ἀκρεμονικός, ή, όν, *branching*, Thphr.*HP*4.6.8.

ἀκρεμών, όνος, ὁ (for the accent v. Hdn.Gr.1.33, -έμων in most codd.): (ἄκρος):—*bough, branch*, Thphr.*HP*1.1.9; οἱ ἀ. τῶν κλάδων Ael.*NA*4.38, cf. Simon.183, E.*Cyc.*455, Theoc.16.96, A.R.2.1101.

ἀκρ-εσπέριος, ον, = sq., *IG*12(7).123 (Amorgos). **-έσπερος**, ον, *on edge of evening* (ἄκρος II), hence, *at nightfall*, Nic.*Th.*25 (cf. Sch.), *AP*7.633 (Crin.); τὴν ἀκρέσπερον [νύκτα] Arist.*HA*619ᵇ21, as cited by Ath.8.353b (ἀρχέσπερον codd. Ath., ἄχρις ἑσπερίου codd. Arist.):—neut. ἀκρέσπερον as Adv., Theoc.24.77; but, *on approach of evening*, Hp.*Epid.*7.23. **-εῶτις**, ἡ, Pythagorean word = ἑβδομάς, *Theol.Ar.*ap.Phot.p.144B. **-ήβης**, ου, ὁ, *youth in his prime*, *AP* 6.71 (Paul. Sil.), 12.124 (Artemo). **-ηβος**, ον, *in earliest youth*, Theoc.8.93.

ἀκρήδεμνος, ον, *without head-band*, Opp.*C.*1.497, Nonn.*D.*2.95.

ἀκρηθής· ἄψεκτος, Hsch. **ἀκρήμορον**· ἀστεργές, Id. **ἀκρήπεδος**· ἡ ἀγαθή (sc. γῆ), Id. **ἀκρήμης**, (κράζω) *dumb with astonishment*, Id. **ἀκρηστής**· δοῦλος, Id.; cf. ἄκριστιν. **ἀκρῆστις**· ῥάχις, καὶ ἄκρα, Id. **ἀκρηστόλουχος**· δοῦλος, Id.

ἄκρητος, ἀκρητο-ποσίη, -πότης, v. sub ἀκρατ-.

ἀκρητόχολος, ον, *accompanied by bilious vomiting*, of fever, Hp. *Fract.*43, *Art.*19. **ἀκρηχολία**, v. ἀκραχ-.

ἀκρία, ἡ, *goddess of the citadel*, epith. of Athena, Hsch. **ἀκρίαι**· τὰ ἄκρα τῶν ὀρῶν, Id.

ἄκρια, τά, = ἄκρα, ἄκρια ῥινός Opp.*C.*2.552. **ἀκριάω**, *adjoin*, of land, *GDI*4999 (Gortyn, dub.).

ἀκρῑβ-άζω, = ἀκριβόω, Aq.Thd.*Pr.*8.27, cf. Ps.-Callisth.3.20:—Pass., *to be proud*, Lxx *Si.*46.15; censured by Poll.5.152. **-ασμα**, τό, *commandment*, Aq.*De.*6.17. **-ασμός**, ὁ, *commandment*, Lxx 3*Ki.*11.34: pl., ἀ. καρδίας *searchings* of heart, ib.*Jd.*5.15 (cod. A); *portion, gift*, Aq.*Ge.*47.22. **-αστής**, οῦ, ὁ, *lawgiver*, Id.*Is.*33.22; *inquirer*, Id.*Jd.*5.14. **-εια**, ἡ, *exactness, precision*, Hp.*VM* 12, Th.1.22, etc.; τῶν πραχθέντων Antipho4.3.1, cf. Lys.17.6:—freq. with Preps. in adv. sense, δι' ἀκριβείας *with minuteness* or *precision*, Pl.*Tht.*184c, *Ti.*23d, etc.; διὰ πάσης ἀ. *Lg.*876c; εἰς τὴν ἀ. φιλοσοφεῖν *Grg.*487c; εἰς ἀ. Arist.*Pol.*1331ᵃ2; πρὸς τὴν ἀ. Pl.*Lg.*769d, cf. Arist.*Resp.*478ᵇ1:—ἡ ἀ. τοῦ ναυτικοῦ its *efficiency, rigid discipline*, Th.7.13; ἀ. νόμων *strictness, severity*, Isoc.7.40; περὶ τὸ διάφορον *strictness* in money matters, Plb.31.27.11: pl., *niceties*, Pl.*R.*504e, Is. 7.16. 2. *parsimony, frugality*, Plu.*Per.*16; ὕδωρ δι' ἀκριβείας ἐστί τινι is *scarce*, Pl.*Lg.*844b. **-εύω**, *use accurately*, τὴν ἀντωνυμίαν Did.ap.Sch.Pi.*N.*4.3:—in Med., S.E.*M.*1.71:—Pass., ἐὰν μὴ ἀκριβεύσωμαι ὑφ' ὑμῶν unless *I receive precise instructions* from you, *PAmh.*2.154.7 (vi A.D.). **-ής**, ές, *exact, accurate, precise*, E.*El.*367, etc.; σημεῖον Th.1.10; δίαιτα Hp.*Aph.*1.4; τριταῖος *returning precisely* at its time, Id.*Epid.*1.24; γαλήνη *complete* calm, Jul. *Or.*1.25c. II. of persons, *precise, strict*, δικασταί Th.3.46; ἐπίσκοποι Pl.*Lg.*762d; δεινὸς καὶ ἀ. Lys.7.12; ἀ. τοῖς ὄμμασι *sharp-sighted*, Theoc.22.194; of arguments, Ar.*Nu.*130; ἀ. μουσική E. *Supp.*906, etc.; τὸ ἀ., = ἀκρίβεια, Hp.*VM*9; τὸ πάνυ ἀ. Th.6.18: freq. in Adv. -βῶς *to a nicety, precisely*, ἀ. εἰδέναι, ἐπίστασθαι, καθορᾶν, μαθεῖν, etc., Hdt.7.32, etc.; ἀ. οἶσθα A.*Pr.*330; opp. ἁπλῶς, Isoc.5.46; opp. τύπῳ (*in outline, roughly*), Arist.*EN*1104ᵃ2: Comp. -έστερον Pl.*R.*436c, *Act.Ap.*18.26: Sup. -έστατα Pl.*R.*484c; ἀ. καὶ μόλις *with greatest difficulty*, Plu.*Alex.*16:—also οὐκ εἰς ἀκριβὲς ἦλθες *at the right moment*, E.*Tr.*901. 2. *in the strict sense of the word*, ὁ ἀ. ἰατρός Pl.*R.*342d; ὁ τῷ ἀ. λόγῳ ἰατρός ib.341c. b. *pure-bred, genuine*, Κόλχος Eun.*Hist.*p.263 D. c. Astron., *true*, opp. φαινόμενος, Procl. *Hyp.*4.31. 3. *parsimonious, stingy*, ἀ. τοὺς τρόπους Men.235. Adv. -βῶς, διαιτᾶσθαι And.4.32.—Rare exc. in Att., mostly Prose. (The sense points to ἄκρος as the first part of the word, but -ῑβης remains dub.)

ἀκρῑβο-δίκαιος, ον, *precise as to one's rights*, ἀ. ἐπὶ τὸ χεῖρον of one who strains the law, Arist.*EN*1138ᵃ1; but in good sense, Ph.1.672, al. **-λογέομαι**, *to be exact* or *precise* in language, investigation, etc., abs., Pl.*R.*340e, *Cra.*415a: c. acc. rei, *weigh accurately*, Id.*R.*403d; ταυτὶ πάνθ' ὑπὲρ τῆς ἀληθείας ἀκριβολογοῦμαι D.18.21; ἐμοῦ περὶ τούτων ἀκριβολογουμένου ib.240:—later in Act., D.H.*Dem.*26, Alex.Aphr. *in Metaph.*479.15. **-λογητέον**, *one must require precision*, Arist.*Rh.*1404ᵃ37, Antyll.ap.Orib.45.16.4. **-λογία**, ἡ, *exactness, precision* in speech, investigation, etc., Arist.*Rh.*1361ᵇ34, *Metaph.*995ᵃ15; περί τι Ph.1.251. 2. *niggardliness*, Arist.*EN* 1122ᵇ8. **-λόγος**, ον, *precise in argument*, in pl., Timo 25.2. **-ψηφία**, ἡ, *accurate computation*, Hero *Mens.*27.

ἀκρῑβ-όω, fut. -ώσω, *make exact* or *accurate*, E.*Hipp.*469; ἀ. τάδε *to be perfect in* bearing these hardships, X.*Cyr.*2.3.13; *arrange precisely*, Ar.*Ec.*274:—Pass., *to be exact* or *perfect*, Ar.*Ra.*1483; ἠκριβῶσθαι πρὸς πᾶσαν ἀρετήν Arist.*Pol.*1279ᵇ1.—Later in Med., J.*AJ*17.2.2, Eust.1799.33, etc. 2. *investigate accurately, understand thoroughly*, οἱ τάδ' ἠκριβωκότες E.*Hec.*1192, cf. X.*Cyr.*2.2.9; τοὔνομά μου σὺ ἀκριβοῖς; *are you sure of..?* Pl.*Chrm.*156a; *inquire carefully of*, τὸν χρόνον *Ev.Matt.*2.7:—Pass., Vett.Val.265.3. 3. *describe accurately*, τι Phld.*Lib.*p.47 O. 4. abs., *to be exact*, ἡ φύσις οὐκ ἀκριβοῖ Arist.*GA*778ᵃ6; [ὁ ἄνθρωπος] κατὰ τὴν ἁφὴν διαφερόντως ἀκριβοῖ Id.*de An.*421ᵃ22; ἀ. περί τι *GA*780ᵇ26. **-ωμα**, τό, *exact knowledge*, τὸ κατὰ μέρος ἀ. Epicur.*Ep.*1 p.3 U.; *precise account*, τινός ib.p.4 U. 2. *consummate display of execution*, in music, Phld. *Mus.*p.90 K. (pl.). **-ωσις**, ἡ, *exact observance*, νόμου J.*AJ*17.2.4 (v.l. ἐξακρ-). **-ωτέον**, *one must examine* or *describe accurately*, Ph.1.357, al., Aët.16.65.

ἀκρίδιον, τό, Dim. of ἀκρίς, in metaph. sense, *spikelet*, Dsc.2.94.

ἀκρῐδο-θήρα, ἡ, *locust-trap*, Theoc.1.52, Longus 1.10 (v.l. -θήκη *cage*). **-φάγος**, ον, *locust-eater*, D.S.3.29, cf. Str.16.4.12.

ἀκρι⟨δ⟩ώδης, ες, *like locusts*, Hsch. s.v. ὀκορνούς.

ἀκρίζω, (ἄκρος) *go on tiptoe*, E.*Fr.*570. 2. = τὰ ἄκρα ἐσθίειν, Sch.Il.21.12.

ἄκρῑθος, ον, (κριθή) *not mixed with barley*, πυρός *POxy.*101 (ii A.D.), 1124.11 (i A.D.).

ἀκρίνας· γωνίας, καὶ καθαρός, ἀγνός, Hsch. **ἀκρινόμος**, ὁ, *forest-warden* (Lacon.), Id. **ἄκριον**· ποῖον (leg. βίον), Id.

ἄκρις, ιος, ἡ, (ἄκρος) Ep.Noun, *hill-top, mountain peak*, Hom. only in Od., always in pl., ἄκριες ἠνεμόεσσαι windy *mountain tops*, Od. 9.400, cf. *h.Cer.*382; δι' ἄκριας through *hill-country*, Od.10.281:—sg., Περγαμίης ὑπὲρ ἄκριος *Epigr.Gr.*1035.8 (Pergam.).

ἀκρίς, ίδος, ἡ, *grasshopper, locust, cricket*, Il.21.12, Ar.*Ach.*1116, Arist.*HA*555ᵇ18, Thphr.*Fr.*174.3, Theoc.7.41, Lxx *Ex.*10.4, etc.:—sg., in collective sense, Men.Prot.p.108 D.; πολλὴ ἀ. Heph.Astr. 1.21.

ἀκρῐσία, ἡ, (ἄκριτος) *want of distinctness and order, confusion*, X. *HG*7.5.27; ἀ. καὶ ταραχή Epicur.*Sent.*22. II. *want of judgement, bad judgement* or *choice*, Plb.2.35.3, *AP*7.629 (Antip.); περὶ τῶν φίλων Luc.*Tim.*8. III. *undecided character* of a disease, *not coming to a crisis*, Hp.*Epid.*1.8: pl., ἠέρος ἀ. *unsettled* climate, *POxy.*1796.22.

ἄκριστιν· κλέπτρια, ἀλετρίδα (Phryg.), Hsch. **ἀκρίστιος**, ον, *on top of the mast*, Id. **ἄκριστοι**· ἄκρα ὀρῶν, Id.

ἀκρίσχιον, τό, *end of the hip*, Heliod.ap.Orib.48.55.1, *SIG*1025.53 (Cos).

ἀκριταγών· πολύγωνον, Hsch.

ἀκρῐτί [τῑ], Adv. of ἄκριτος, Lys.*Fr.*88: **-τεί**, Aq.*Je.*17.11.

ἀκρῐτο-βάται· ἀρχή τις παρὰ Ἐφεσίοις τῆς Ἀρτέμιδος θυσιῶν, Hsch. **-βουλος**, ον, *indiscreet of counsel*, Man.4.530. **-δακρυς**, υ, *shedding floods of tears*, Τάνταλος *AP*5.235 (Paul. Sil.). **-μῡθέω**, *babble*, Eust.349.17. **-μῡθία**, ἡ, *babbling*, Id.1878.4. **-μῡθος**, ον, *confusedly babbling*, Il.2.246, Ph.1.111. II. ὄνειροι ἀ. *hard of discernment*, Od.19.560.

ἄκρῐτος, ον, (κρίνω) *undistinguishable, confused*, ἄκριτα πόλλ' ἀγορεύειν Od.8.505; τύμβος ἄ. one *common undistinguished* grave, Il. 7.337; ἄ. πάγος *confused* mass, Hp.*Sept.*6, cf. Pl.*Grg.*465d, Philostr. *Gym.*26; ἄ. ἔρις καὶ ταραχή D.18.18; ἄ. καιροί Demad.34. 2. *continual, unceasing*, μῦθοι Il.2.796; ἄχεα 3.412: neut. as Adv., πενθήμεναι ἄκριτον αἰεί Od.18.174, 19.120; δηρὸν καὶ ἄ. *h.Merc.*126; ὄρος ἄ. *continuous chain of* mountains, *AP*6.225 (Nicaen.). 3. after Hom. in poets, *countless*, ἄστρων ὄχλος Critias 19; μυρία φῦλα καὶ ἄ. Opp.*H.*1.80; ἄ. πλήθει Babr.33.3. II. *undecided, doubtful*, νείκεα, ἄεθλος, Il.14.205, Hes.*Sc.*311; ἄ. τελευταί *which cannot be* *predicted*, B.9.45; ἀκρίτων ὄντων while the issue *is doubtful*, Th.4.20; *uncertain*, of weather-signs, Ὠρίων Arist.*Mete*.361^{b}31; πυρετὸς ἄ. fever *that will not come to a crisis*, Hp.*Acut*.(*Sp*.)17. Adv. -τως Id. *Epid*.1.3; τὸ ἀκρίτως ξυνεχὲς τῆς ἁμίλλης *without decisive issue*, Th.7.71: neut. pl. as Adv., ἄκριτα δηρινθέντες Euph.94.3. 2. *unjudged, untried*, of persons and things, ἀκρίτους κτείνειν, ἀποκτεῖναι *without trial*, Hdt.3.80, Th.2.67, cf. Lys.19.7, D.17.3; ἄ. ἀποθανεῖν Antipho 5.48, cf. Th.8.48, etc.; πρᾶγμα ἄ. cause *not yet tried*, Isoc.19.2, cf. Pl.*Ti*.51c:—also, *subject to no judge*, πρύτανις A.*Supp*.371. Adv. ἀκρίτως, ἀποκτείνειν D.H.11.43, cf. Conon 28.1, Lxx 1*Ma*.2.37. III. Act., *not giving judgement*, Hdt.8.124; *not capable of judging*, Parm.6.7, Plb.3.19.9, cf. Luc.*Am*.37; ἄκριτα μηχανώμενοι engaged in *rash* attempts, E.*Andr*.549; κατ' ἄκριτον *recklessly*, Phld.*Ir*.p.69 W. Adv. -τως *rashly, indiscreetly*, Plb.2.7.2, Epict.*Gnom*.65; *indiscriminately*, ἐκφέρειν Procl.*in Prm*.p.553 S. 2. *not exercising judgement, undiscriminating*, of fate, *AP*7.439 (Theodorid.), cf. 5.283 (Rufin.); ἄκριτε δαῖμον, of death, *Epigr.Gr*.204.3 (Cnid.).

ἀκρῐτό-φυλλος, ον, *of undistinguishable*, i.e. *closely blending, leafage*, ὄρος Il.2.868. **-φυρτος**, ον, *undistinguishably mixed*, A.*Th*.360. **-φωνος**, ον, gloss on βαρβαρόφωνος, Apollon.*Lex*., Hsch. **-χειρος**, ον, *with countless hands*, Emp.60.

ἀκρο-άζομαι, = ἀκροάομαι, Epich.109, f.l. in Men.150. **-ᾱμα**, ατος, τό, *anything heard*, esp. *with pleasure, piece read, recited, played* or *sung*, X.*Smp*.2.2, *Hier*.1.14; ἀ. καὶ δράματα Arist.*EN*1173^{b}18; ἀ. καὶ πότοι Plb.31.25.4. II. pl. for concrete, *lecturers, singers*, or *players*, esp. during meals, Phylarch.62, *BCH*30.272 (Delph.), Plb.4.20.10, 16.21.12; so in Lat., *acroama* Cic.*Sest*.54.116, etc. **-ᾱματικός**, ή, όν, *designed for hearing only*, αἱ ἀ. διδασκαλίαι the *esoteric* doctrines of philosophers, delivered orally, Plu.*Alex*.7. 2. c. gen., *capable of attending to*, Asp.*in EN*27.14. **-άομαι** [ᾰ Ar.*Ra*.315], fut. -άσομαι [ᾱ] Pl.*Ap*.37d, etc.: aor. ἠκροασάμην Ar. l. c., etc.: pf. ἠκρόαμαι Arist.*HA*537^{b}3: 2 sg. plpf. ἠκρόασο Antiph.93 (ἠκροᾶσο, ἠκροῶ, wrongly, *AB*98): aor. ἠκροάθην (in pass. sense) J.*AJ*17.5.2, Aristid.1.30 J.:—*hearken, listen to*: c. gen. pers., Antipho 5.4, Pl.*Grg*.499b: c. acc. rei, Th.6.89, etc.: c. gen. rei, Th. 2.21, 6.17: c. gen. pers. et acc. rei, Pl.*Hp.Ma*.285d. 2. abs., *listen*, Hp.*Int*.35, Ar.*Lys*.503, Pherecr.154, Lys.19.3; ὁ ἀκροώμενος *hearer*, Eup.94.7; esp. of *those who hear lectures*, X.*Smp*.3.6; also, *reader*, Philostr.*VA*5.14: c. gen., ἀνὴρ Ἀριστοτέλους ἠκροαμένος Str. 13.1.54, cf. Plu.*Caes*.3. II. *attend to, obey*, τινός Th.3.27, cf. Lys.20.9, Pl.*Grg*.488c: abs., ἐνδοιαστῶς ἀ. Th.6.10. **-ᾱσις**, εως, ἡ, *hearing, hearkening* or *listening to*, Antipho 5.4, Th.1.21,22, etc.; ἀ. ποιεῖσθαί τινος, = ἀκροᾶσθαι, And.1.9; κλέπτειν τὴν ἀ. ὑμῶν to cheat you into *hearing*, Aeschin.3.35. 2. *obedience*, τῶν ἐν ἀρχῇ Th.2.37. II. *thing listened to, recitation, lecture*, Hp. *Praec*.12, Plb.32.2.5, *IG*2.466, etc.:—φυσικὴ ἀ., title of work by Arist. III. = ἀκροατήριον, Plu.2.58c. **-ᾱτέον**, *one must give heed to*, τῶν κρειττόνων Ar.*Av*.1228. **-ᾱτήριον**, τό, *place of audience*, *Act.Ap*.25.23; *lecture-room*, Ph.1.528 (pl.), Plu.2.45f, etc. II. *audience*, Id.*Cat.Ma*.22. **-ᾱτής**, οῦ, ὁ, *hearer*, of persons who come to hear a public speaker, Th.3.38, Pl.*R*.536c, D.18.7, Men.286, etc.; *disciple, pupil*, Arist.*Pol*.1274^{a}29, cf. *EN* 1095^{a}2. II. *reader*, Plu.*Thes*.1, *Lys*.12. **-ᾱτικός**, ή, όν, *of* or *for hearing*; μισθὸς ἀ. *lecturer's* fee, Luc.*Enc.Dem*.25. Adv. -κῶς ἔχειν to be *fond of hearing*, Ph.1.215. 2. = ἀκροαματικός, λόγοι Arist.*Fr*.662, Iamb.*Protr*.21.

ἀκροαπής, *unable to articulate*, γλῶσσα dub. l. in Gal.19.73; cf. ἄκροπις.

ἀκρο-βάζειν· ἄκροις τοῖς ποσὶν ἐπιβαίνειν, Hsch. **-βαμονέω**, = ἀκροβατέω, *Hippiatr*.117. **-βαρέω**, *become top-heavy, lose balance by being overloaded at the extremity*, Apollod.*Poliorc*.164.3, 166.10. **-βασις**, ἡ, *foot* of table, *BCH*29.541 (Delos). **-βᾰτέω**, *walk on tiptoe, strut*, of ostriches, D.S.2.50; of haughty people, Ph. 2.404. II. *climb aloft*, Polyaen.4.3.23. III. c. acc., ἀτραπόν *AP*9.13b. **-βάτης**, ὁ, *acrobat*, *Inscr.Magn*.119; τῆς Ἀρτέμιδος *B.Mus.Inscr*.4.481*.459 (Ephesus). **-βᾰτικός**, ή, όν, *fit for mounting*, Vitr.10.1. **-βᾰτος**, ον, *walking on tiptoe*, ἴχνεσιν ἀκροβάτοισιν Nonn.*D*.47.235. **-βᾰφής**, ές, *tinged at point* or *slightly*, *AP*6.66 (Paul. Sil.); *wetting feet* or *tip* of garment *only*, Nonn. *D*.1.65, 48.339. **-βελής**, ές, *with point at end*, *AP*6.62 (Phil.).

ἀκρ-οβελίς, ίδος, ἡ, (ὀβελός) *point of dart*, Archipp.10. II. = εἶδος ἀκοντίου, Suid.

ἀκρο-βηματίζω, = ἀκροβατέω, Hsch., Sch.Il.13.158. **-βλαστος**, ον, *with terminal growth*, Thphr.*HP*1.14.2. **-βολέω**, *throw*, καλαύροπα *AP*6.106 (Zon.). II. Astrol., = ἀκτινοβολέω, Man.4.354. **-βόλη**, ἡ, *skirmish*, *POxy*.1873.3 (v A.D.). II. in pl., αἱ τοῦ ἡλίου βολαί, Hsch. **-βολής**, ές, *skilful in hitting*, dub. l. in *APl*.4.213 (Mel. or Strat.). **-βολία**, ἡ, *slinging, skirmishing*, App.*BC*1.84, al. **-βολίζομαι**: aor. ἠκροβολισάμην Hdt. 8.64, Th.3.73:—*throw from afar, fight with missiles*, as opp. to close combat, *skirmish*, πρός τινα Th.4.34: abs., Id.3.73, X.*Cyr*.8.8.22: metaph., ἀ. ἔπεσι Hdt.8.64, cf. Ph.1.134:—Act. only *AP*7.546, Hsch. **-βόλισις**, εως, ἡ, *skirmishing*, X.*An*.3.4.18, *Cyr*.6.2.15 (pl.). **-βόλισμα**, ατος, τό, = foreg., App.*Pun*.36 (pl.). **-βολισμός**, οῦ, ὁ, = ἀκροβόλισις, Th.7.25, X.*HG*1.3.14, Aen.Tact.39.6, etc.; *discharge of weapons by light-armed troops*, Arr.*Tact*.15.4, 37.1. **-βολιστής**, οῦ, ὁ, = -βόλος II, X.*Cyr*.6.1.28. II. *mounted bowman* or *javelineer*, Ascl.*Tact*.7.1, Ael.*Tact*.2.13, Arr.*Tact*. 4.5. **-βολιστικός**, ή, όν, *used as missiles*. -κά, τά, sc. ὅπλα, Ael. *Tact*.17. **-βολος**, ον, Pass., *struck from afar*, A.*Th*.158. II. **-βόλος**, ὁ, *one who throws from afar, skirmisher*, *IG*5(1).1426.10 (Messene, iv/iii B.C.), Hsch., Suid. **-βύθιον**, τό, *headland*, Dion. Byz.30. **-βυστέω**, *to be uncircumcised*, Aq.Sm.Thd.*Le*.19.23 (nisi leg. -ιῶ, fut. of -βυστίζω). **-βυστία**, ἡ, *foreskin*, Lxx *Ge*.17.11, al., Ph.*Fr*.49 H., *Act.Ap*.11.3. II. *state of having the foreskin, uncircumcision*, *Ep.Rom*.2.25, etc. 2. collect., *the uncircumcised*, ib.2.26, 3.30, etc. (Prob. from ἄκρος and a Semitic root, cf. Bab. *buštu* 'pudenda', Heb. *bōsheth* 'shame': wrongly derived from ἄκρος, βύω by *EM*53.48.) **-βυστος**, ον, *uncircumcised*, Aq.*Ex*. 6.12, etc. **-γείσιον**, τό, *top of cornice*, *IG*2^{2}.463. **-γένειος**, ον, *with prominent chin*, Arist.*Phgn*.812^{b}24. **-γωνιαῖος**, α, ον, *at the extreme angle*, ἀ. λίθος *corner foundation*-stone, Lxx *Is*.28.16, *Ep. Eph*.2.20. **-δάκτυλον**· *pollex*, *Gloss*. **-δετος**, ον, *bound at end* or *top*, *AP*6.5 (Phil.). **-δίκαιος**, ον, = ἀκριβοδίκαιος, v.l. in Stob.2.7.25, Phot.

ἀκρό-δρυα, τά, prop. *fruits grown on upper branches of trees*, esp. *hard-shelled fruits*, opp. ὀπώρα, Hp.*Aff*.61, Arist.*HA*606^{b}2, cf. *Gp*. 10.74.2, Ath.2.52a; also, *fruits* generally, Glaucides ap.eund.3.81a, Arist.*Pr*.930^{b}26, *PPetr*.3p.196 (iii B.C.), *PAvrom*.1 A 13 (i B.C.), Plu.*Alex*.23; μάζῃ καὶ τοῖς ἀ. ἀρκούμενοι Epicur.*Fr*.466. 2. *trees which produce such fruits*, Pl.*Criti*.115b, X.*Oec*.19.12, Thphr.*CP*6. 11.2; φυτὰ ἀκροδρύων D.53.15:—*fruit-trees* in general (incl. vine and olive), Thphr.*HP*4.4.11. (Sg. in *AP*9.555 (Crin.), Ath.2.49e; cf. ἀκρόδρυον· πλῆρες μέτρον (Tarent.), Hsch.) **-ζεστος**, ον, (ζέω) *boiled* or *heated slightly*, Dsc.2.120. **-ζύγια**, τά, = ζεύγλη, Hsch., Poll.1.253. **-ζυμος**, ον, *slightly leavened*, Archig.ap.Gal.13.173, Isid.*Etym*.20.2.15. **-ζώνη**· *instita*, *Gloss*. **-θάλυπτος**, ον, *burnt at end*, Hsch.

ἀκρόθεν, Adv. *from the end* or *top*, Arist.*Phgn*.811^{a}29, Nic.*Th*. 337.

ἀκρόθι, Adv. *at the end*, c. gen., νυκτός Arat.308.

ἀκρο-θῐγής, ές, *touching on surface, touching the lips*, φίλημα *AP* 12.68 (Mel.): metaph., ἀ. περὶ τὰς πράξεις Vett.Val.40.1. Adv. ἀκροθιγῶς, ἐμβάπτειν *just* dip in, *so that it is hardly wetted*, Dsc.2.83: metaph., ἀ. εἴρηται Marin.*Procl*.26, cf. Vett.Val.271.11, Men.Rh. p.417 S. **-θῑνιάζομαι**, *take the spoils, pick out for oneself*, E.*HF* 476, cf. Dionys.Trag.1:—Act. in Hsch. **-θίνιον** [θῐ], τό, E.*Ph*. 282, Th.1.132, Pl.*Lg*.946b; mostly pl. -θίνια or -θῖνα, Pi.*N*.7.41, al.: sg. -θις, ἡ, acc. -θινα *GDI*2561 D 47 Rüsch (Delph., iv B.C.): (ἄκρος, θίς):—*topmost* or *best part of heap*; hence, *firstfruits of the field, booty*, etc., offered to the gods, Simon.109, Hdt.1.86,90, al., Pi. l. c., etc.; ἀ. τῆς Μαραθῶνι μάχης *Michel*1117 (Delph.); ἀκρόθινα πολέμου, in Pi.*O*.2.4, of the Olympic games, *as founded from spoils taken in war*, cf. ib.10(11).57.—Properly neut. Adj., A.*Eu*.834 ἀκροθίνια θύη offerings *of firstfruits*. Post-Hom., rare in early Prose. **-θώραξ**, ᾶκος, ὁ, ἡ, (θωρήσσω II) *slightly drunk*, = ἡμιμέθυσος, Hsch., cf. Arist. *Pr*.871^{a}9, Plu.2.656c; πεπωκότ' ἤδη τ' ἀκροθώρακ' ὄντα Diph.46: Ion. -θώρηξ Hp.ap.Erot. s. v. θωρῆξαι. 2. *well drunken*, Ph.1. 390. **-καρπος**, ον, *fruiting at top*, φοῖνιξ Thphr.*HP*1.14.2, al. **-κελαινιάω**, only used in Ep. part. ἀκροκελαινιόων *growing black on surface*, of swollen stream, Il.21.249; cf. Nonn.*D*.18. 156. **-κέραια**, τά, (κέρας) *ends of sail-yards* (cf. κέρας VIII), Poll. 1.91:—also -κερα, Sch.A.R.1.566; ἀκρόκεροι κάλοι Phot. s. v. ἡνιόχους. **-κιόνιον**, τό, (κίων) *capital of a pillar*, Ph.2.147. **-κλαδος**, ὁ, gloss on ὄζος ἀκρότατος, Sch.Il.2.312. **-κνέφαιος**, ον, *at beginning of night, in twilight*, Hes.*Op*.567:—also **-κνεφής**, ές, of *morning twilight*, Luc.*Lex*.11, Id.*Rh.Pr*.17; cf. **ἀκρόκνεφα**· πρὸς ὄρθρον, Hsch. **-κόμης**, ὁ, = sq., Poll.2.28. **-κομος**, ον, (κόμη) *with hair on crown*, epith. of Thracians, who either tied up their hair in a top-knot, or shaved all their head except crown, Il.4.533, Archil. *Supp*.1.4; *with hair at tip*, of goat's chin, Plb.34.10.9. II. *with leafy crown*, E.*Ph*.1516; esp. of palms, D.S.2.53, D.P.1010; ἀ. κυπάρισσοι *tapering* cypresses, Theoc.22.41. **-κονδύλιον**· *articulare*, *Gloss*. **-κόρινθος**, ὁ, *citadel of Corinth*, E.*Fr*.1084, X.*HG*4. 4.4. **-κόρυμβοι**, πόδες, *extremities of* the feet, Poet.*de herb*.177:—also **-κόρυμβα**· τὰ ἀκροστόλια τῶν νεῶν, Hsch. **-κῡματόω**, (κῦμα) *float on topmost waves*, bombastic word ridiculed by Luc.*Lex*. 15. **-κώλιον**, τό, mostly pl., *extremities of body*, esp. of animals, *snout, ears, trotters*, Hp.*Vict*.3.75, Pherecr.108.14, Telecl.48, Ar.*Fr*. 4, Archipp.11, Arist.*Pr*.935^{b}38, etc.: sg., Antiph.126, Alex.118, Eub.7. **-λειον**, τό, (λεία) = ἀκροθίνιον, Suid. **-λῐθος**, ον, *with ends made of stone*; ξόανον ἀ. statue *with head, arms, and legs marble, rest wood*, *AP*12.40; ἄγαλμα *IG*4.558 (Argos). **-λῖνος**, ον, *at the edge of the net*, Opp.*C*.4.383. **-λῐπᾰρος** [λῐ], ον, *fat on the surface*, Alex.192. **-λογέω**, *gather at top*, στάχυας *AP*9.89 (Phil.). **-λοφία**, ἡ, *mountain ridge, hilly country*, Aen.Tact.15. 6 (pl.), Plb.2.27.5, Str.15.1.29 (pl.). **-λοφίτης** [ῐ], ου, ὁ, *mountaineer*, *AP*6.221 (Leon.). **-λοφος**, ον, *high-crested, peaked*, πρῶνες Opp.*C*.1.418; πέτραι *AP*12.185 (Strat.):—Subst., *mountain crest*, Plu.*Publ*.22. **-λῦτέω** ζώνην, *play with the ends* of a belt, *as if untying it*, *AP*5.252 (Iren.). **-μαλλος**, ον, *very woolly*, Str.4. 4.3. **-μᾰνής**, ές, *on the verge of madness, somewhat mad* (cf. ἀκράχολος, ἀκροθώραξ), οὐ φρενήρης ἀ. τε Hdt.5.42. **-μάσθιον**, τό, *teat*, *Gloss*. **-μέθῠσος**, ον, = ἀκροθώραξ, Sch.Ar.*Ach*.1132, *V*.1190. **-μέλας**, αινα, αν, *black at top*, πτερόν *PMag.Par*.1.800. 10. **-μέτωπος**, dub. l. perh. for εὐρυ-, Nonn.*D*.26.310. **-μόλυβδος**, ον, *leaded at edge*, λίνον *AP*6.5 (Phil.); δίκτυον ib.30 (Maced.). **-μύλη**· ἡ γουνὶς μύλων ἢ μύλος αὐτός, Hsch.

ἀκρ-ομφάλιον, τό, *middle of navel*, Poll.2.169:—also **-όμφαλον**, τό, Ruf.*Onom.*98.

ἄκρον, ου, τό, (neut. of ἄκρος) like ἄκρα, *highest* or *farthest point*: 1. *mountain top, peak*, Γάργαρον ἄκρον Ἴδης Il.14.292; ἄκρον ὑπερβαλέειν Od.11.597; τὰ ἄκρα *heights*, Hdt.6.100, Pl.*Criti.*110e, etc. b. ἄκρα νάων ships' *tops*, Alc.*Supp.*12.9. 2. *headland, cape*, Σούνιον ἄκρον Ἀθηνέων Od.3.278. 3. *end, extremity*, τὰ ἄ. τῆς θαλάσσης, [τοῦ ἀέρος], Pl.*Phd.*109d, e; ἄκρα χειρῶν *hands*, Luc.*Im.*6; ἐξ ἄκρων at *the end*, Ar.*Fr.*29; ἐξ ἄκρου *Com.Adesp.*398; ἐπ' ἄκροις Pl.*Sph.*220d:—*border, frontier*, Plb.1.42.2. II. metaph., *highest pitch, height*, πανδοξίας ἄκρον Pi.*N.*1.11; εἰς ἄκρον ἀνδρείας ἱκέσθαι to *highest pitch*, Simon.58; εἰς ἄκρον ἀδύς *exceedingly*, Theoc.14.61; ἐπ' ἄκρον ἀφικέσθαι, ἐλθεῖν, Pl.*Plt.*268e, *Ti.*20a; πρὸς ἄκρῳ γενέσθαι Id.*Phdr.*247b; ἄκρον ἔχων σοφίης *Epigr.Gr.*442 (Nabataea); ἄκρον ἐρώτων εἰδότος, ἄκρα μάχας *AP*7.448 (Leon.):—ἄκρα, τά, *heights, highest point*, οὗτοι ποθ' ἥξει (sic) τῶν ἄκρων ἄνευ πόνου S.*Fr.*397; ἄκρα φέρεσθαι win *prize*, Theoc.12.31; ἄκρα φέρουσ' ἀρετῆς ὑμῖν *Epigr.Gr.*224.2 (Samos). 2. of persons, Ἄργεος ἄκρα Πελασγοί *pride* of Argos, Theoc.15.142. III. δρυὸς ἄκρα, = ἀκρόδρυα, ib.112. IV. in Logic of Arist. τὰ ἄκρα are *major and minor terms* of syllogism, opp. to μέσον or middle, *APr.*25^{b}36, al. V. *extremes* in a proportion, Id.*EN*1133^{b}2.

ἀκρό-νηον· τὸ τῆς νεὼς ἄκρον, Suid. **-νιφής**, ές, *snow-capped*, πάγος *Pae.Delph.*16. **-νῠχῶς**, Adv., (νύσσω) *touching at the edge*, συμβάλλοντα βλέφαρα Gal.14.701. **-νύκτιος**, ον, = sq., Ἄρης Man.5.177. **-νυκτος**, ον, lit. *rising at sunset*: hence, *in opposition*, Ζεύς Vett.Val.168.13; ἀ. σχηματισμοί, προηγήσεις, Ptol.*Alm.*10.6, *Tetr.*78:—as Subst., -νυκτος, ἡ, with or without φάσις, *opposition*, Ptol.*Alm.*10.7, *Tetr.*77. (Freq. written ἀκρων-.) **-νυξ**, -νυχος (Hdn.Gr.2.743), = ἀκρονυχία, *nightfall*, S.ap.Phot.p.68 R.

ἀκρ-ονῠχί [ῑ], Adv. *with tip of nail*, for ἀκρωνυχί, *AP*12.126 (Cod. Pal. ἀκρονυχῆ, from an Adj. -νυχής; but cf. αὐτονυχί).

ἀκρο-νῠχία, ἡ, *nightfall*, Suid., Tz. ad Hes.*Op.*565. **-νῠχος** (A), ον, *at nightfall*, ἄνεμοι Arist.*Mete.*367^{b}26; ἀνατολαί Thphr.*Sign.*2; φάσεις Procl.*Hyp.*5.66; σφάζων ἀκρόνυχος Theoc.*Beren.*3, cf. Nic.*Th.*761:—neut. as Adv., Arist.*Pr.*942^{a}23. (Written ἀκρώνυχος in *PHib.*27 (iii B.C.).)

ἀκρ-όνῠχος (B), ον, = ἀκρώνυχος, *AP*6.103 (Phil.), Q.S.8.157.

ἀκρο-ξιφίς, ἡ, *sword-point*, Lyd.*Mag.*1.8. **-ουλος**, ον, = ἄκρουλος, ib.1.23. **-πᾰγής**, ές, *fastened at the extremity*, Jo.Gaz.1.111. **-παθος**, ον, f. l. for ἀκρόπλοος, q. v. **-παστος**, ον, (πάσσω) *sprinkled on the surface*: *slightly salted*, Sopat.13, Xenocr.76. **-πᾰχής**, ές, *thick at the end*, Moer.346. **-πενθής**, ές, f. l. for ἁβρο-, A.*Pers.*135 (lyr.). **-πηλος**, ον, *muddy on the surface*, Plb.3.55.2.

ἄκροπις, *unable to articulate*, γλῶσσα Hp.*Epid.*7.43,46, cf. Gal.19.73 (dub., v. l. ἀκροαπίς).

ἀκρό-πλοος, ον, contr. **-πλους**, ουν, *swimming at the top, skimming the surface*, φλέβια Hp.*Morb.*1.14, cf. Plu.2.591e; *buoyant*, ὑστέρη Aret.*SA*2.11; restored for ἀκρόπαθος in Hp.*Prorrh.*2.11:—*superficial*, Id.*Ep.*18 (Democr.). **-ποδητί** or **-ιτί** [τῐ], Adv., (πούς) *on tiptoe*, Luc.*Prom.*1, *D.Mar.*14.3, al. **-πόδιον**, τό, Dim. of ἀκρόπους, Sor.1.101, Ptol.*Alm.*7.5. **-πολεύω**, *traverse the top*, Man.4.79.

ἀκρό-πολις, poet. **ἀκρό-πτολις**, εως, ἡ, *upper* or *higher city*; hence, *citadel, castle*, ἐς ἀκρόπολιν Od.8.494 (in Il. only *divisim*, ἄκρη πόλις, v. ἄκρος I. 1), cf. Pi.*O.*7.49, A.*Th.*240, Hdt.1.84, etc.; as seat of tyranny, Ph.1.401,417. 2. esp. the *Acropolis* of Athens, *IG*1.58, al., And.1.76 (cf. Hdt.1.60, 8.51); which served as treasury, Th.2.13; hence ἀνενεχθῆναι εἰς ἀκρόπολιν, γεγράφθαι ἐν ἀκροπόλει to be entered as a state-debtor, D.58.19,48; freq. without Art., as And.l.c., D.ll.cc.; at Erythrae, *IG*1.11. II. metaph., ἀ. καὶ πύργος ἐὼν δήμῳ, of a person, Thgn.233; ἀ. Ἑλλάνων, of Corinth, Simon.137; γῆν Δελφίδ' ..Φωκέων ἀκρόπτολιν E.*Or.*1094; *stronghold*, τῆς ψυχῆς, τοῦ σώματος, Pl.*R.*560b, Arist.*PA*670^{a}26, cf. Pl.*Ti.*70a; Pythag., of *seven*, *Theol.Ar.*44. **-πόλος**, ον, (πολέω) *high-ranging, lofty*, ἐπ' ἀκροπόλοισιν ὄρεσσιν Il.5.523, cf. Od.19.205. II. Subst., **ἀκροπόλοι**, οἱ, *arctic* and *antarctic circles*, Olymp. *in Mete.*183.30. **-πόρος**, ον, *boring through, piercing with the point*, ὀβελοί Od.3.463. 2. proparox., ἀκρόπορος, ον, Pass., *with opening at end*, σῦριγξ Nonn.*D.*2.2. II. (πορεύομαι) *going on high*, ib.46.136. **-πόρφυρος**, ον, *with purple edge*, χιτῶνες Lyd.*Mag.*1.17. **-ποσθία**, Ion. -ίη, ἡ, *tip of foreskin*, Hp.*Aph.*6.19, Arist.*HA*493^{a}29:— **-πόσθιον**, τό, Poll.2.171, Ruf.*Onom.*102, Hsch. **-πότης**, ἡ, *a hard drinker*, Nonn.*D.*14.108. **-πουδίς**, Adv. = ἀκροποδητί, Hdn.Gr.1.512. **-πους**, ὁ, *extremity of leg*, i. e. *foot*, Ptol.*Alm.*7.5, al., Pall. *in Hp.Fract.*12.285 C.: pl., *PMag.Leid.W.*18.37; *trotters*, Aret.*CA*1.10. **-πρῳρον**, τό, *end of ship's prow*, Str.2.3.4. **-πτερον**, τό, *quill*, *AP*6.229 (Crin.); ἀκρόπτερα φωτῶν *flanking* men of a hunting-party, Opp.*C.*4.127. **-πτολις**, ἡ, poet. for ἀκρόπολις, q. v. **-πτυξ**, χος, perh. *cloth, napkin*, Hierocl.*Facet.*71. **-πῦρος**, ον, *exceedingly hot*, κρύσταλλος Olymp.Alch.p.76 B. **-ρρίνιον**, τό, (ῥίς) *tip of the nose*, Poll.2.80. **-ρρύμιον**, τό, *fore-end of a pole*, Id.1.146.

ἄκρος, α, ον, (on the Root v. ἀκή A) *at the farthest point* or *end*, hence either *topmost, outermost*, or *inmost*. 1. *highest, topmost*, ἀκροτάτῃ κορυφῇ Il.1.499, al.; ἐν πόλει ἄκρῃ, = ἐν ἀκροπόλει, Il.6.88, cf. 257; ἄκρῳ Ὀλύμπῳ 13.523; ἀνὰ Γαργάρῳ ἄκρῳ 14.352; λάψοντες ..μέλαν ὕδωρ ἄκρον *at its surface*, 16.162; ἄκρον ῥινόν *surface of* skin, Od.22.278; ἐπ' ἄκρων ὀρέων on mountain *tops*, S.*OT*1106: Sup. ἀκρότατος, ὔσδος Sapph.93.2; ὀρόφοισι Orac.ap.Hdt.7.140. 2. *outermost*, πεδίον ἐπ' ἄκρον to the *farthest edge* of the plain, S.*Ant.*1197; κατ' ἄκρας σπιλάδος from the *surface* of a stone, Id.*Tr.*678; esp. of *extremities* of body, ἄ. χείρ, πόδες, ὦμος, *end* of hand, *ends* of feet, *tip* of shoulder, Il.5.336, 16.640, 17.599; ἄκρων χειρῶν καὶ ποδῶν Hdt.1.119, cf. Th.2.49, Pl.*La.*183b, *Ti.*76e; but τὸ ἄ. τῆς χειρός, τοῦ ποδός, *thumb, great toe*, Lxx *Ex.*29.20, *Le.*18.22; γλῶσσαν ἄκραν S.*Aj.*238; πίτυν ἄκρας τῆς κόμης καθέλκων by the *top* of the crown, Cratin.296:—ἐπ' ἄκρων [δακτύλων] on *tiptoe*, S.*Aj.*1230, ubi v. Sch.; comically, ἐπ' ἄκρων πυγιδίων on *tip-tail*, Ar.*Ach.*638; ἐν ἄκροισι βὰς ποσί E.*Ion*1166; παρ' ἄκρας τρίχας *Or.*128; ἀκροτάτοις χείλεσι *Epigr.Gr.*547.8:—οὐκ ἀπ' ἄκρας φρενός not from the *outside of* the heart, i. e. from the inmost heart, A.*Ag.*805, cf. E.*Hec.*242; ἄκροισι λαίφους κρασπέδοις with *mere edges of* sail, i. e. under *close-reefed* sails, Id.*Med.*524, cf. Ar.*Ra.*999. b. Geom., of the *extremity* of a line, ἡ ἐπ' ἄκραν τὴν ἀπολημφθεῖσαν ἀγομένη Apollon.Perg.*Con.*4.8: Math., of *extremes* in a proportion, Pl.*Ti.*36a, etc.; εἰς ἄκρον καὶ μέσον λόγον τέμνειν cut in *extreme* and mean ratio, Euc.6.30, cf. 5*Def.*17. c. in Tactics, ἄκροι, οἱ, *flank men*, Ascl.*Tact.*1.3, cf. 7.6. 3. *inmost*, μυελός E.*Hipp.*255. II. of Time, ἄκρᾳ σὺν ἑσπέρᾳ on the *edge* of evening, i. e. at *nightfall*, Pi.*P.*11.10, cf. ἄκρῃ νυκτί Arat.775; ἄκρου τοῦ ἔαρος at *beginning* of spring, *IPE*1^2.352.29 (Cherson., ii B.C.); but usu. denoting completeness, ἄκρου τοῦ θέρεος at *mid*-summer, Hp.*Aph.*3.18; χειμῶνος ἄκρῳ Theoc.11.37; ἄκρας νυκτός at *dead* of night, S.*Aj.*285. III. of Degree, *highest* in its kind, *consummate*, 1. of persons, Hdt.5.112, 6.122; τοξότης ἄ. A.*Ag.*628; θεσφάτων γνώμων ἄ. ib.1130; μάντις S.*El.*1499; ἰατροί Phld.*Lib.*p.67 O.; οἱ πάντῃ ἄ., οἱ ἀκρότατοι Pl.*Tht.*148c; of any extremes, opp. τὰ μεταξύ, τοῖς ἄ. τὰ ἄ. ἀποδιδόναι Id.*R.*478e, cf. *Phd.*90a; of classes in a state, Arist.*Pol.*1296^{b}39: in moral sense, both good and bad, ἐπιδικάζονται οἱ ἄ. τῆς μέσης χώρας Id.*EN*1107^{b}31; αἱ ἄ. [διαθέσεις] ib.1108^{b}14, cf. ἄκρον II. 1:—c. acc. modi, ψυχὴν οὐκ ἄ. not *strong* of mind, Hdt.5.124; ἄ. τὰ πολέμια 7.111; ἄ. ὀργήν *quick* to anger, *passionate*, 1.73; Εὐρώπη ἀρετὴν ἄκρη 7.5: c. gen., οἱ ἄ. τῆς ποιήσεως Pl.*Tht.*152e; ἄ. εἰς φιλοσοφίαν *R.*499c; περὶ ὁπλομαχίαν *Lg.*833e. 2. of things, *highest, extreme*, συμφορά Alex.222.4 (cj. Dobree); νηστεία Diph.54: Sup., Pl.*Phlb.*45a. IV. as Subst., v. ἄκρα, ἄκρον. V. neut. as Adv., *on the top* or *surface*, ἄκρον ἐπὶ ῥηγμῖνος Il.20.229; ἄκρα δ' ἐπ' αὐτᾶς βαθμῖδος *AP*7.428.3 (Mel.). 2. reg. Adv. ἄκρως, ἀνεστάλθαι to be turned up *at the point*, Hp.*Mochl.*24. b. *utterly, perfectly*, Pl.*R.*543a, Hegesand.4; μόνος ἄκρως Euphro 1.5; σχῆμα ἄ. στρογγύλον *absolutely* round, Hero *Def.*76. c. *skilfully*, Phld.*Lib.*p.27 O.

ἀκρο-σᾰπής, ές, (σήπομαι) *slightly 'high'*, Hp.*Alim.*41. **-σίδηρος**, ον, *pointed* or *tipped with iron*, *AP*6.95 (Antiphil.). **-σκιρία**, ἡ, *hill-copse*, *Tab.Heracl.*1.65,71; cf. σκῦρος. **-σοφος**, ον, *high in wisdom*, Pi.*O.*11(10).19, *Lyr.Adesp.*93, D.H.*Dem.*51. **-σπάθια**, τά, gloss on ὑποχόνδρια, Suid. **-σπελλος**, ὁ, = αἰγίλωψ, Ps.-Dsc.4.137.

ἄκροσσος, ον, *without fringes*, λέντια *Gp.*20.22.

ἀκρο-στήθιον, τό, *lower end of breast-bone*, Arist.*Phgn.*810^{b}17. **-στιχίς**, ίδος, ἡ, *acrostic*, D.H.4.62, Cic.*Div.*2.54.111:—also **-στιχα**, τά, *AP*9.385 tit. **-στόλιον**, τό, *terminal ornament* of ship (cf. ἄφλαστον), crowning either the stern-post, Ptol.*Alm.*8.1; or more commonly, the stem-post, Callix.1, Plu.*Demetr.*43; taken as trophy, Str.3.4.3, D.S.18.75, Plu.*Alc.*32, App.*Mith.*25, Polyaen.4.6.9. **-στόμιον**, τό, *edge of the lips*, D.H.*Comp.*14. II. = ἀκροφύσιον, Eust.1153.38. **-σφᾰλής**, ές, (σφάλλω) *apt to trip, unsteady*, Plu.2.713b; ἀ. πρὸς ὑγίειαν *precarious* in health, Pl.*R.*404b; ἀ. οὐσίαι *insecure*, Phld.*Oec.*p.47 J.; ψυχὴ ἐν εὐτυχίᾳ ἀ. Max.Tyr.5.2. Adv. -ῶς, διακεῖσθαι Phld.*Oec.*p.49 J.; ἔχειν Plu.2.682d. II. Act., *apt to throw down, slippery, dangerous*, Plb.9.19.7. **-σφυρα**, τά, sort of *woman's shoes*, Hsch.:—also **-σφύρια**, τά, Herod.7.60, Poll.7.94. **-σχῐδής**, ές, *cloven at the end*, Thphr.*HP*3.11.1. **-τελεύτιον**, τό, *fag-end* of anything, esp. of verse or poem, Th.2.17, Phryn.Com.86: generally, τοῦ γήρως *Vit.Philonid.*p.8 C.:—*burden, chorus*, D.C.63.10. **-τελής**, ές, *pointed*, γένειον Hp.*Ep.*23 (Democr.). **-τενής**, ές, *stretching high*, Nonn.*D.*7.310.

ἀκρότης, ητος, ἡ, (ἄκρος) *highest pitch*, Hp.*VM*22. II. *extreme*, opp. μεσότης, Arist.*EN*1107^{a}8; ἀμφοτέρας παθεῖν τὰς ἀ. Diog.Oen.*Fr.*38: metaph., *excellence, perfection*, ἡ ἀνυπέρεκτος ἀ. Phld.*D.*3.5, cf. D.H.*Dem.*2, etc.; *summit*, Procl.*Inst.*147.

ἀκρότητος, ον, *not beaten down*, Hld.9.8. II. *not struck together* or *in unison*, μέλη πάραυλα κἀκρότητα κύμβαλα *Trag.Adesp.*93 = *Com.Adesp.*1254, cf. Phot. s. v. οὐκ ἀποψάλακτος.

ἀκρο-τομέω, *lop off* corn *by the ear*, X.*Oec.*18.2, cf. *PLond.*2.163.21 (i A.D.); *saw off at end* σφῆνας Ph.*Bel.*67.21:—Pass., -τομηθεὶς τράχηλον Man.4.51: metaph., τῶν εὐγενεστάτων ἀνδρῶν ἀ. τὴν πατρίδα J.*BJ*2.10.1. **-τομία**· *rupes*, *Gloss.* **-τομος**, ον, (τέμνω) *cut off sharp, abrupt*, of precipice, Plb.9.27.4, Ph.1.82; ἡ ἀ. (sc. πέτρα) Lxx *Ps.*113(114).8, cf. *Jb.*28.9, *De.*8.15: of a stone, *sharp*, Thd.*Ex.*4.25; *smooth*, J.*AJ*8.3.2; of ends *sawn off*, τὰ τῶν σφηνῶν -τομα Ph.*Bel.*67.23. **-τονος**, ον, *strained to the utmost, muscular*, Metrod.Sceps.14.

ἄκροτον· ἀδιαρρίπιστον, Hsch.

ἄκρουλος, ον, *curled at the tip*, τρίχες Arist.*Phgn.*812^{b}33.

ἀκροῦν· ὄρους κορυφή, and **ἀκρουνοί**· ὅροι (Maced.), Hsch.

ἄκρουρα· οὐραί, Hsch.

ἀκρουρᾰνία, ἡ, *heaven's citadel*, Luc.*Lex.*15.

ἀκρουροβόρη, ἡ, *swallowing the tip of her tail*, metaph. of the Moon, *Tab.Defix.Aud.*41^{A}7 (Megara, i/ii A.D.).

ἄκρουρον· ἄκρατον, Hsch.

ἄκρουστος· *impercussus*, *Gloss.*

ἀκρουχέω, (ἄκρον, ἔχω) *haunt the heights*, S.*Fr.*309.

ἀκρο-φᾰής, ές, = ἀκροφανής, Nonn.*D.*4.130, Jo.Gaz.1.331. **-φᾰληριάω**, *shine* or *be white at top*, only in Ep. part. ἀκροφαληριόωσα Nonn.*D.*2.462. **-φᾰνής**, ές, *just showing at the edge* or *tip*, Nonn. *D.*14.138, al.; of an island, *Peripl.M.Rubr.*42. **-φῠής**, ές, *grown high up on a tree*, Thphr.*HP*9.5.1. **-φύλαξ**, ἄκος, ὁ, *governor of a citadel*, Plb.5.50.10, *BCH*33.23 (Pontus, ii B.C.), *IG*3.3906. **-φυλλον**, τό, = βήχιον, Ps.-Dsc.3.112. **-φυλλος**, ον, *with leaves in a terminal crown*, Thphr.*HP*1.14.2. **-φύσιον**, τό, (φῦσα) *snout* or *pipe of pair of bellows*, S.*Fr.*992, Th.4.100; ῥήματα.. ἐπιδεικνύναι πάντ' ἀπ' ἀκροφυσίων fresh from *the bellows* (as we say, 'from the anvil'), Ar.*Fr.*699. II. *comet's tail*, D.C.78.30. **-χάλιξ**, ὁ, ἡ, = ἀκροθώραξ, A.R.4.432, D.P.948. **-χᾰνής**, ές, *yawning at top*, δέρμα *AP*6.57 (Paul. Sil.). **-χειρας**· τοὺς ὀξύχειρας, ἢ ἀνδρ(οφ)όνους, *EM*53.37, cf. Hsch.

ἀκροχειρ-ία, Ion. **-ίη**, ἡ, = -ισμός, Hp.*Vict.*2.64. **-ίζω**, *take hold of*, Aristaenet.1.4. II. more freq. in Med., *struggle at arm's length*, opp. συμπλέκεσθαι, *spar*, ἀ. τινι Pl.*Alc.*1.107e, cf. Arist.*EN* 1111ᵃ15, Posidon.24, Philostr.*Gym.*36. **-ιον**, τό, = ἀκρόχειρον, Sor.1.84. **-ίς**· τὸ ἄκρον τῆς χειρός, Suid. **-ισις**, εως, ἡ, = sq., Hp.*Vict.*3.78:—also **-ιξις**, v.l. ibid. and 2.64. **-ισμός**, ὁ, *wrestling with hands*, Luc.*Lex.*5, Gal.6.324: in pl., Hp.*Vict.*3.78. **-ον**, τό, = ἄκρα χείρ *hand*, Ptol.*Alm.*7.5, al., Gal.*UP*2.2; τὰ τῶν ἀγαλμάτων ἀ. *SIG*²754.6, cf. *Hymn.Id.Dact.*13.

ἀκρο-χέριον· *armilla*, Prisc.*Inst.*5.15. **-χερσίτης**, ου, ὁ, nickname of wrestler who broke his opponent's fingers, Paus.6.4.1. **-χηνίσκοι**, οἱ, *extremities of* ζεῦγλαι in chariot, Poll.1.146. **-χλιᾰρος** [ῐ], ον, *just warm*, *lukewarm*, Hp.*Acut.*58:—also **-χλίερος**, *Nat.Mul.*53, *Mul.*2.201. Adv. -χλιάρως *Mul.*2.204. **-χολέω**, **-χολία**, **-χολος**, v. sub ἀκραχ-. **χορδών**, όνος, ἡ, (χορδή) *wart with a thin neck*, Hp.*Aph.*3.26, Plu.*Fab.*1, Dsc.2.64, etc.; distinguished from μυρμήκια, τά, Paul.Aeg.4.15 (also **-δάνη** *Gloss.*, **-δόνη** Erot., Dim. **-δόνιον**) *Gloss.*: hence **-χορδονώδης**, ες, *troubled with warts*, D.C.*Fr.*47. **-χωλος**· ὁ πρὸς ὀλίγον χωλεύων, Suid. **-ψῑλος**, ον, *bare* or *smooth at top*, αἰδοῖον Hp.*Epid.*4.31. **-ψωλος**, ον, ψωλός *only at the end*, Suid. s.v. ψωλός.

ἄκρυπτος, ον, *unhidden*, E.*Andr.*834, Aen.Tact.39.6. Adv. -τως Phryn.*PS*p.11 B.

ἀκρύσταλλος, ον, *free from ice*, χώρη Hdt.2.22.

ἀκρῶα· σπλάγχνα, ἔντερα, Hsch.

ἀκρ-ωβέλια· τὰ ἄκρα τοῦ ὀβελίσκου, Hsch. (cod. -σβ-). **-ωλένιον**, τό, *elbow* of a net, i.e. *outer angle* of mesh, X.*Cyn.*2.6, Poll.5.29. **-ωμία**, ἡ, *point of the shoulder*, *acromion process*, Hp.*Art.*14: in a horse, *withers*, X.*Eq.*1.11, cf. Arist.*HA*498ᵇ30:— **-ώμιον**, τό, Hp.*Art.*16, *Mochl.*5, Arist.*HA*606ᵃ16: **-ωμίς**, ἡ, Alciphr.*Fr.*5.4.

ἄκρων, ονος, ὁ, = ἀκροκώλιον, *Hippiatr.*7:—Dim. **ἀκρωνάριον**, ib. 64, 129, cf. Sch.Luc.*Lex.*6.

ἀκρωνία, ἡ, prob. = ἀκρωτηριασμός, A.*Eu.*188; but expl. as ἄθροισμα by Hdn.Gr.1.294 ap.Sch. (reading κακῶν ἀ.), cf. *AB*372.

ἀκρωνῠχ-ία, ἡ, (ὄνυξ) *tip of the nail*; hence, *ridge* or *top of a mountain*, = ἀκρώρεια, X.*An.*3.4.37, *HG*4.6.7, Plu.*Eum.*11. **-ος**, ον, (ὄνυξ) *with nails*, *claws*, *hoofs*, etc., χερὸς ἀκρώνυχα *tips of fingers*, *AP*12.82; ἴχνος ἀ. traces *of one walking on his toes*, Plu.2.317e, cf. 325b:—**ἀκρῶνυξ**, Suid.

ἀκρώρ-εια, ἡ, (ὄρος) *mountain ridge*, X.*HG*7.2.10, Theoc.25.31, Hp.*Ep.*10, Timae.94, Plb.24.6.5. **-εῖται**, οἱ, *inhabitants of mountain ridges*, Hdn.Gr.2.869.

ἀκρωρία, ἡ, (ὥρα) *daybreak*, Thphr.*Sign.*21.42.

ἀκρώσσει· ἀκροᾶται, ἑκὼν οὐχ ὑπακούει, προσποιεῖται, Hsch.

ἀκρωτερῆσαι· κόψαι ἢ ἀχρειῶσαι, Hsch.

ἀκρωτηρι-άζω, *cut off* ἀκρωτήρια, of ships, τὰς πρῴρας ἠκρωτηρίασαν *cut the beaks off* the prows, Hdt.3.59:—so in Med., τὰς τριήρεις ἀκρωτηριασάμενος X.*HG.*6.2.36:—Pass., Ath.12.535d. 2. of persons, *cut off hands and feet*, *mutilate*, Plb.5.54.10, etc.; ῥῖνα, πρόσωπον, Clearch. 8, Plu.*Alc.*18; χεῖρας σὺν αὐτοῖς τοῖς βραχίοσιν D.S.34.8; ὄργανον, of circumcision, Ph.2.211; μηδὲν ἀκρωτηριάσῃς ἐνθάδε, Inscr. on statue, *CIG*6855:—so in Med., μέλη Lxx 4*Ma.*18.20: metaph., ἠκρωτηριασμένοι τὰς πατρίδας D.18.296; ἀ. τὴν ἀρετήν τινος Max.Tyr. 5.8. 3. Medic., *amputate*, Heliod.ap.Orib.45.14.4. 4. metaph., *mutilate*, *maim*, τῇ συγκοπῇ τὸ μέγεθος Longin.39.4; πρᾶγμα *POxy.*237 vi 7 (ii A.D.); θείαν φύσιν Heraclit.*All.*26. II. intr., *form a promontory*, *jut out like one*, Plb.4.43.2, Str.2.1.40. **-ασις**· *truncatio*, *mutilatio*, *Gloss.* **-ασμα**, τό, *mutilation*, Hsch. s.v. τομία, Sch.A.R.4.477. **-ασμός**, ὁ, *amputation*, Dsc.*Ther.Praef.*, Heliod.ap.Orib.47.14tit., Philum.*Ven.*7.7, Leonid. ap.Aët.16.49.

ἀκρωτήριον, τό, (ἄκρος) *topmost* or *prominent part*, ἀ. τοῦ οὔρεος mountain *peak*, Hdt.7.217, cf. Pi.*O.*9.7; of a cup, *projecting part*, Arist.*Metaph.*1024ᵃ25. 2. *cape*, *promontory*, Hdt.4.43, Th.1.30. II. *end* or *extremity* of anything, ἀ. νεὸς *ornament of* ship's *stern-* or *stem-post*, Hdt.8.121, cf. X.*HG*2.3.8, Polyaen.5.41, *Michel* 1116 (Delph.); ἀκρωτήρια πρύμνης *h.Hom.*33.10. 2. in pl., *extremities of body*, *hands and feet*, *fingers and toes*, Hp.*Aph.*7.1, *Acut.* 59, Th.2.49, Lys.6.26; τὰ ἀ. τῆς Νίκης her *wings*, D.24.121, cf. *IG*2.652 *A*23: sg., Arist.*GA*772ᵇ36. 3. in temples, etc., statues or ornaments placed on the angles of a pediment, Pl.*Criti.*116d, *SIG*80 (Olymp.), *IG*4.1484.102 (Epid.); generally, *pediment*, Plu.*Caes.*63.

ἀκρωτηριώδης, ες, *like an* ἀκρωτήριον, Sch.rec.A.*Pr.*726.

ἀκτάζω, (ἀκτή A) *banquet on the shore*, *enjoy oneself*, Plu.2.668b, in prov. σήμερον ἀκτάσωμεν, cf. Hsch. s.v. ἀκτή. II. = ἀκταίνω, *EM*54.39:—**ἀκταΐζω**, Hsch.

ἀκταία, ας, ἡ, *a Persian state robe*, Democr.Ephes.1. II. *marble mortar*, Clearch.65; cf. ἀκτίτης. III. *baneberry*, *Actaea spicata*, Plin.*HN*27.43.

ἀκταινόω, *lift up*, *raise*, only aor. -ῶσαι Anacr.137, Pl.*Lg.*672c, Pl.Com.180, cf. 19. (Derived fr. ἀκτῆ by Phryn.*PS*p.38 B.)

ἀκταίνω, = foreg., ἀκταίνειν στάσιν (γρ. βάσιν) *keep* my stature *erect*, A.*Eu.*36: metaph., ἀ. μένος *Trag.Adesp.*147; cf. ὑποακταίνομαι.

ἀκταῖος, α, ον, (ἀκτή A) *on the shore* or *coast*, epith. of cities in Aeolis, Th.4.52: Ἀκταία (sc. γῆ), ἡ, old name of Attica, = ἀκτή (A) I.2, Call. *Fr.*348, Paus.1.2.6. 2. *dwelling on the coast*, *belonging thereto*, ἰχθύες Hp.*Aff.*52; θεοί Orph.*A.*342; βάτραχοι Babr.25.6.

ἀκτέα (ἀκταία f.l. in Luc.*Trag.*71), contr. **ἀκτῆ**, ἡ, *elder-tree*, *Sambucus nigra*, Emp.93, B.8.34, Hp.*Nat.Mul.*2 (ἀκτῆ), *Mul.*1.34 (ἀκτέα), Thphr.*HP*3.13.4, Dsc.4.173. 2. ἀ. ἕλειος, = χαμαιάκτη, *deadwort*, *Sambucus Ebulus*, ibid.

ἀκτέᾰνος, ον, *without property*, *poor*, *BCH*15.430 (Stratonicea), Man.4.114, *AP*7.353 (Antip.).

ἀκτέῐνος, (ἀκτέα) *made of elder*, perh. to be read in Simon.155.6, Thphr.*HP*5.3.3.

ἀκτένιστος, ον, *uncombed*, κόμη S.*OC*1261, Sch.A.R.1.60.

ἄκτενος· ὀριός, ἀξίνης κροῦσμα, Hsch.

ἀκτέον, (ἄγω) *one must lead*, Pl.*R.*467e, etc.; *one must treat*, τινὰς τρυφερώτερον Sor.2.9; *one must bring*, εἰς ὑπόμνησιν Apollon.Cit. 3. 2. εἰρήνην ἀκτέον *one must keep* peace, And.3.40, D.8.5. II. *one must go*, *march*, X.*HG*6.4.5. III. Adj., **ἀκτέος**, α, ον, *to be drawn*, γραμμαί Gal.16.406; *to be led away*, ἐπὶ τὸ κολασθῆναι D.23 *Arg.*2.3.

ἀκτέος, ὁ, = ἀκτέα, Thphr.*HP*3.4.2.

ἀκτερ-έϊστος, ον, *unhallowed by funeral rites*, *AP*7.564. **-ής**, ές, = foreg., prob. in Hsch. **-ιστος**, ον, = foreg., S.*Ant.*1071, Lyc.1155.

ἀκτεροί· ἄταφοι, αἱ κράνιοι ῥάβδοι, Hsch.

ἀκτή (A), ἡ, *headland*, *foreland*, *promontory*, ἀ. προὔχουσα Od.24.82; ἀ. προβλῆτες 5.405, 10.89; opp. λιμήν, Il.12.284; often with epithets, denoting high rugged coast, τρηχεῖα, ὑψηλή, Od.5.425, Il.2.395; τρηχέα Hdt.7.33; στυφλοί A.*Pers.*303; ἀμφίκλυστος S.*Tr.*752; στόνῳ βρέμουσι δ' ἀντιπλῆγες ἀκταί Id.*Ant.*592:—usu. of sea-coast, χλωρὰ ἀ. ib.1132; ἀκταὶ ἔναλοι Tim.*Pers.*109; but also of *rugged banks* or *strand* of rivers, Ἑλώρου, Νείλου, Pi.*N.*9.40, *I.*2.42; Σιμόεντος A.*Ag.*697; Ἀχέροντος S.*Ant.*813.—Rare in early Prose, X.*An.* 6.2.1, Lycurg.17. 2. generally, *tract of land running out into the sea*, ἀ. διφάσιαι of the north and south coasts of Asia Minor, Hdt.4.38; of Africa, as jutting out from Asia, 4.41, cf. 177; of Cape Sepias, 7.183, al.; of Mt. Athos, Th.4.109; of Italy, Arist.*Pol.*1329ᵇ11; of the peninsula of the Piraeus, Hyp.*Fr.*185, Arist.*Ath.*42.3, Lycurg. 17 (also of Attica in general, E.*Hel.*1673, cf. Str.9.1.3); of the coast of Argolis, Plb.5.91.8, D.S.12.43: pl., ἀκτὰς τῆσδε γῆς S.*Fr.* 24. II. generally, *edge*, χώματος ἀ. of a sepulchral mound, A. *Ch.*722; βώμιος ἀ. of an altar, S.*OT*182 (lyr.). (As there is no trace of ϝ, the word is more probably connected with $\sqrt{ak}$ 'pointed' than with ϝάγ-νυμι.)

ἀκτή (B), ἡ, poet. word for *corn*, Δημήτερος ἀκτή Il.13.322, 21.76, cf. E.*Hipp.*138 (lyr.), Epin.1.9; μυληφάτου ἀλφίτου ἀ. Od.2.355, cf. 14.429, Il.11.631:—in Hes. of *corn* generally, ὡσεὶ Δημήτερος ἀ., of standing crop, *Sc.*290, of unthreshed corn, *Op.*597, 805; of seed, οὐ σπόρον ὀλκοῖσιν Δηοῦς ἐνιβάλλομαι ἀ. A.R.3.413. (The connexion with ἄγνυμι is doubtful.)

ἀκτῆ, contr. for ἀκτέα, q.v.

ἀκτημ-οσύνη, ἡ, *poverty*, Crates Theb.ap.Epiph.*Haer.*3.2, Poll.3.111, 6.197. **-ων**, ον, gen. ονος, *without property*, *poor*, χρυσοῖο *in* gold, Il.9.126: abs., ἀ. πενίη Theoc.16.33; cf. Plu.*Sol.*14, Demoph. *Sent.*16, Alex.Aphr.*Pr.*1.89.

ἀκτήν, ῆνος, = ἀκτήμων, *EM*55.11.

ἀκτηρίς, ίδος, ἡ, *staff*, Achae.21. 2. *bar of wood* supporting chariot-pole, Poll.10.157.

ἄκτητος, ον, *not worth getting*, Pl.*Hp.Mi.*374e. II. *unobtainable*, prob. in Phld.*Herc.*1251.4.

ἀκτινείδωλον, τό, *ray-image*, *visual impression*, Hestiaeus ap. *Placit.*4.13.5.

ἀκτίνη, ἡ, = βούνιον, Ps.-Dsc.4.123.

ἀκτῑνηδόν, Adv. *like a ray*, Luc.*Salt.*18.

ἀκτῑνο-βολέω, *emit rays*, φέγγος ἀ. Ph.1.638:—Pass., *receive the rays of the sun*, Isid.Char.ap.Ath.3.94a. II. Astrol., of a planet, *aspect from the left* (opp. ἐφοράω, q.v.), Heph.Astr.1.16, Porph.*Intr.* p.189:—Pass., Vett.Val.116.22. **-βολία**, ἡ, *shooting of rays*, Plu. 2.781a. II. Astrol., *aspecting from the left*, Thessal. in *Cat. Cod.Astr.*8(3).138, Porph.*Intr.*p.189:—also **ἀκτινηβολίη**, Man.1.322. **-βόλος**, ον, *sending forth rays*, δέσποτα *Sammelb.*4127 (Talmis). **-γρᾰφία**, ἡ, *treatise on radiation* (by Democritus), D.L. 9.48. **-ειδής**, ές, = ἀκτινώδης, στέφανοι Ph.2.559; τρίχες Horap. 1.17. Adv. -δῶς Gal.19.171, Steph. *in Hp.*1.144 D., al. **-κράτωρ**, *lord of the sun's rays*, *PMag.Berol.*1.200.

ἄκτῑνος, η, ον, (ἀκτῆ) *of elder-wood*, Thphr.*HP*5.3.3; cf. ἀκτέϊνος.

ἀκτῑνο-φόρος, ον, *bearing rays*, *Gloss.*:—as Subst., *rayed shellfish*, Xenocr.85. **-χαῖτις**, ἡ, *with rays for hair*, *PMag.Par.*1.2286.

ἀκτιν-ώδης, ες, *like rays*, Philostr.*VA*3.46. **–ωτός**, ή, όν, *decorated with rays*, Ph.2.560; φιάλη *Michel*815 (Delos, iv B.C.); of cog-wheels, *toothed*, Hero *Spir.*2.32.

ἄκτιον, τό, = ἀκτή (A), Ael.*NA*13.28. II. = βούνιον, Dsc.4.123.

ἄκτιος, ον, (ἀκτή A) *of the sea-shore*, of Pan as god of the coast, Theoc.5.14; of Apollo, A.R.1.404.

ἀκτίς (nom. **ἀκτίν** Hdn.Gr.2.511), [ῐ], ῖνος, ἡ, *ray, beam*: Hom. only dat. pl., ἀκτῖσιν Od.5.479, 19.441, ἀκτίνεσσιν 11.16, Il.10.547; Ἠελίοιο ἀκτῖνες Mimn.11.6, cf. Emp.84, Ar.*Av.*1009, Arist.*Mete.*374ᵇ4, etc.; sg., S.*Tr.*685, cf. ἀνὰ μέσσαν ἀκτῖνα, i.e. from south, S.*OC*1247; ἀκτῖνες μέσαι *noonday*, E.*Ion*1136; τὰ πρὸς ἀκτῖνα ἔθνη peoples of the *East*, Philostr.*VA*2.2:—of lightning, ἀκτῖνες στεροπᾶς ἀπορηγνύμεναι Pi.*P.*4.198; ὦ Διὸς ἀκτίς, παῖσον S.*Tr.*1086; πυρός Sopat.13, Pl.*Ti.*78d; of the eyes, ἀκτῖνας προσώπου, Pi.*Fr.*123, cf. Ar.*V.*1032; visual *rays*, Hipparch.ap.*Placit.*4.13.9. 2. metaph., *brightness, splendour, glory*, ἀ. ἀγώνων, καλῶν ἐργμάτων, Pi.*P.*11.48, *I.*4(3).42; ἀκτῖνες ὄλβου *splendid* fortunes, Id.*P.*4.255. 3. *ray shot from the left by planet to planet* (opp. ὄψις, q.v.), Heph.Astr.1.16, Porph.*Intr.*p.189; τὴν ἀ. ἐπιφέρων Vett.Val.136.19, cf. Ptol.*Tetr.*126. II. *spoke* of a wheel, *AP*9.418 (Antip.).

ἄκτιστον· *inconditum*, *Gloss.*: ἀποίητον, Hsch.

ἀκτίτης [ῐ], ου, ὁ, (ἀκτή A) *dweller on coast*, *AP*6.304 (Phan.). II. ἀ. λίθος stone *from the Piraeus* (cf. ἀκτή (A) I.2), *IG*2.1054.16, al.; *from the Argolid*, S.*Fr.*68.

ἄκτῑτος, ον, poet. for ἄκτιστος, *untilled*, *h.Ven.*123.

ἄκτῠπος, ον, *noiseless*, Eust.964.60. Adv. ἀκτυπί Adam.2.41.

ἄκτωρ, ορος, ὁ, (ἄγω) *leader*, A.*Pers.*557, *Eu.*399: as pr. n., Il., etc. II. *leash*, = ἀγωγεύς, Hsch.

ἀκτ-ωρέω and **–ωρία**, from **–ωρός**, ὁ, *coastguard*, Hsch.

ἀκῠβέρνητος, ον, *without steersman*, Ph.1.219, Plu.*Caes.*28, Luc.*J.Tr.*46: metaph., θυμός Ph.*Fr.*110 H., cf. 1.696; ἀμέλεια Onos.33.2.

ἀκύβευτος, ον, *risking nothing upon a die, cautious*, M.Ant.1.8.

ἀκυητήριον (sc. φάρμακον), τό, *drug to prevent conception*, Hsch.

ἀκύθηρος, ον, (Κυθήρη) like ἀναφρόδιτος, *without charms*, Cic.*Fam.*7.32.2; τὸ ἀ. Eun.*VS*p.457.14 B.

ἄκῡθος, ον, (cf. *EM*55.15) *unfruitful*, ὄϊες, opp. ὕπαρνοι, Call.*h.Ap.*52: c. gen., τόκων Id.*Iamb.*1.242 (dub.). [ῡ in *Iamb.* s.v.l.]

ἀκυθῶν· ἀγρυπνῶν, Hsch.

ἀκύκητος, ον, *untroubled*, διάνοιαι Phld.*D.*1.17.

ἀκύκλιος, ον, *one who has not gone the round* of studies, opp. ἐγκύκλιος, Pl.Com.227. **ἀκύκλωτος**, ον, *not surrounded*, Tz.*H.*8.596. **ἀκυλαῖον**, τό, = ἄκυλος, Orac.ap.Eus.*PE*4.20. **ἀκυλεής**· ἀετός, Hsch.

ἀκύλιστος, ον, *not to be rolled about*: metaph., κραδίη ἀ. an *undaunted* heart, Timo 16. II. of Protagoras, οὐκ ἀ. not *without volubility* or *versatility*, Id.5.

ἄκῠλος, ὁ (ἡ, Theoc.5.94), the *acorn* of *Quercus Ilex*, given to swine with βάλανος, Od.10.242, Pherecr.186, Arist.*HA*595ᵃ29, cf. Amphis 38, Thphr.*HP*3.16.3:—used in games, Poll.9.103. II. *ornament* or *jewel in form of acorn*, *IG*2.767*b*11:—neut., ἄκυλον, τό, Ἐφ. Ἀρχ.1895.70.

ἀκυλωτός, ή, όν, *with acorn-shaped ornament*, φιάλαι Ἐφ. Ἀρχ.1903.146 (dub.).

ἀκύμ-αντος [ῠ], ον, *not washed by waves*, ψαμάθοις ἐπ' ἀκυμάντοις on sands *washed by no waves*, i.e. those of the stadium, E.*Hipp.*235, cf. 229; πλοῦς Them.*Or.*18.221b (Comp.); προσοχὴ σκάφους Iamb.*VP*3.16. II. *waveless, calm*, πέλαγος Luc.*D.Marin.*5.1; θάλαττα Max.Tyr.31.5. III. Act., *not raising waves*, ἐρετμοί, αὖραι, Nonn.*D.*2.14, 3.36. **–ατος** [ῠ], ον, = foreg. II, πορθμός *Trag.Adesp.*336. **–ος**, ον, = foreg., τόπος Arist.*Pr.*931ᵇ31: metaph., ἀ. βίοτος E.*HF*698; ψυχή Plu.2.1090b; ἄφοβον καὶ ἀ. Epicur.*Fr.*413. **–ων** (A), [ῠ], ον, gen. ονος, (κῦμα) = ἀκύμαντος, Pi.*Fr.*235, A.*Ag.*566; θάλασσα Ar.*Fr.*708; ἀ. πομπὰ σιγώντων ἀνέμων E.*Fr.*773.39 (Pap.); γαλήνη Ph.1.680; ἀήρ Plu.2.722e; οὐρανός prob. in Plot.5.1.2: metaph., βίος Plu.2.8a. **–ων** (B), [ῡ], ον, gen. ονος, (κυέω) *without fruit, barren*, of women, E.*Andr.*158; of the earth, Moschio Trag.8.

ἄκυνον (fort. ἄκυον)· ἄτοκον, Hsch. **ἀκυντόν**· ἀπρόσιτον, Id. **ἄκυον**· ἀτόκιον, Id. **ἄκυπρον** (Κύπρις)· ἀμιγῆ, παρθένιον, Id. **ἀκύρβιστος**, ον, prob. *without patches* or *insertions*, *BCH*35.43 (Delos).

ἀκύρής, ές, = ἀτυχής: hence **ἀκύρημα**· ἀτύχημα, and **ἄκυρμα**, τό, Hsch., *EM*55.5.

ἀκῡρία λέξεως, *impropriety* of language, Hermog.*Meth.*3.

ἀκυρόεντα· ἀνάρμοστα, ἄκυρα, Hsch.

ἀκυρο-λέκτητος, ον, *incorrectly used*, Eust.569.6 (ubi male ἀκυριο–). **–λεξία**, ἡ, = ἀκυρολογία, Suid. s.v. αὐθέντης, Eust.1770. **–λογέω**, *speak incorrectly*, Ph.1.216, *Lex.Vind.*3.19. **–λόγητος**, ον, Astrol., *not dominant*, ἀστέρες Vett.Val.203.7. **–λογία**, ἡ, *incorrect phraseology*, D.H.*Lys.*4 (nisi leg. ἀκαιρο–, q.v.). **ἄκυρον**, τό, = ἄλισμα, Ps.-Dsc.3.152.

ἄκῡρος, ον, *without authority*, opp. κύριος, hence, I. of laws, sentences, etc., *invalid, unratified, obsolete*, ψήφισμα And.1.8; δίκη Pl.*Lg.*954e; συνθῆκαι Lys.18.15; ἄκυρον ποιεῖν, καταστῆσαι set *aside*, Pl.*Prt.*356d, Is.1.21, etc.; νόμοις ἀ. χρωμένη *not enforcing* the laws, Th.3.37. Adv. **–ως** Simp. *in Ph.*168.10. II. of persons, *having no right* or *power*, ἀ. ποιεῖν τινά X.*HG*5.3.24; καθιστάναι Lys.9.19; τινός *over* a thing, Pl.*Tht.*169e; ἀ. πάντων..γενήσεσθε D.19.2: c. inf., Pl.*Lg.*929e. 2. of things, ἀκυροτέρα κρίσις *less trustworthy* decision, Pl.*Tht.*178d; ἀ. ἀμφορεύς voting urn *into which neutral votes were thrown*, Sch.Ar.*Eq.*1150, Poll.8.123; τὰ ἀκυρότερα *less important* parts of nature, Arist.*GA*778ᵃ1; of bodily members, *unimportant*, ἀ. μόριον Gal.16.540, cf. 18(1).33 (Comp.); *impotent*, Arist.*GA*772ᵇ28. III. of words and phrases, *used in improper sense*, Cic.*Fam.*16.17.1 (Comp.), Phlp. *in Ph.*717.12. Adv. **–ρως** Str.12.3.23, Phld.*Rh.*1.161 S., Hermog.*Meth.*3, cf. Dam.*Pr.*7, 306.

ἀκυρότης, τητος, ἡ, *improper, illegitimate use*, οὐσίας Dam.*Pr.*306.

ἀκῡρόω, *cancel, set aside*, ψήφισμα, δόγμα, Din.1.63, D.S.16.24; ὀφειλήματα *SIG*742.30 (Pass., Ephesus), cf. Str.8.4.10 (Pass.), D.H.2.72, *BGU*1053 ii 14 (i B.C.). 2. *set at naught, treat as of no effect*, Lxx 1*Es.*6.32; λόγον θεοῦ *Ev.Matt.*15.6, cf. J.*AJ*18.8.8. b. *reject, deny the validity of*, Phld.*Sign.*30. 3. metaph., *render powerless*, τῷ λογισμῷ τὸν τῶν παθῶν οἶστρον Lxx 4*Ma.*2.3. **–ωσία**, ἡ, *declaration of invalidity*, *BGU*944.20 (iv/v A.D.), *Gloss.* **–ωσις**, εως, ἡ, *cancelling*, D.H.8.21; συγγραφῶν Phld.*Rh.*1.276 S., cf. *BGU*1282.35 (i A.D.), *POxy.*266.107.5 (ii A.D.). **–ωτος**, ον, verb. Adj., *unconfirmed*, E.*Ion*801, *PRyl.*427 *Fr.*14.

ἄκῠτος, ον, (κύω) = ἄτοκος, *EM*54.52, Hsch.

ἀκχαλίβαρ· κράββατος (Lacon.), Hsch. **ἀκχημονικά**· καὶ κακοπαθήεντα, Id.

ἀκχός· ὠμός, Hsch.

ἀκωδώνιστος, ον, *not tested*, Ar.*Lys.*485.

ἀκωκή [ᾰ], ἡ, (ἀκή A) *point* (Att. ἀκίς), δουρός, βέλεος, ἔγχεος, Il.10.373, 13.251, 22.327, cf. Od.19.453, Theoc.22.195; of horns, quills, claws, teeth, Opp.*C.*2.166,604, 4.185, *H.*5.327:—also in late Prose, Arr.*Tact.*4.9 (pl.), Luc.*D.Mort.*27.4. 2. scorpion's *sting*, Orph.*L.*622; snake's *fangs*, ib.126 (pl.).

ἀκώλιστος, ον, *not divided into clauses* (κῶλα), D.H.*Comp.*23.

ἄκωλος, ον, *without limbs, mutilated*, Paus.1.24.3. II. *ill-jointed*, and so, *moving slowly*, gloss on ἄωροι πόδες, Sch.Od.12.89.

ἀκώλῡτος, ον, *unhindered*, Luc.*Tim.*18; τύχη, of death, *Epigr.Gr.*149.8 (Rhenea), etc. Adv. **–τως** Pl.*Cra.*415d, Chrysipp.*Stoic.*2.269, Str.17.1.25, *Act.Ap.*28.31, etc.; γλῶσσα ἀ. ῥέουσα Procop.*Ep.*46; also ἀκωλυτί [Democr.] in Fabr.*Bibl.*4.338.

ἀκώμαστος, ον, *without revelry*, of persons, Lib.*Decl.*28.24.

ἀκωμῴδητος, ον, *not ridiculed*. Adv. **–τως** Luc.*VH*1.2.

ἄκων (A), [ᾰ], οντος, ὁ, (ἀκή A) *javelin, dart*, smaller and lighter than ἔγχος, Il.15.709, Od.14.531, al., Pi.*P.*9.20, E.*Ph.*1402, etc.; in later Prose, Eratosth.*Cat.*33, Aristid.*Or.*26(14).84, Artem.1.57, Ant.Lib.41.5.

ἄκων (B), [ᾱ], ἄκουσα, ἆκον, Att. contr. for ἀέκων, q.v.

ἀκώνητος, ον, *unpitched*, Dsc.1.7. **ἄκωνος**, ον, *without conical top*, πῖλος J.*AJ*3.7.3. **ἀκώπητος**, ον, *not having oars*: *unequipt*, *AB*373, Hsch. **ἄκωπος**, ον, *without oars*, *AP*9.88 (Phil.).

ἄλαβα, *ink*, Hsch., who also has **ἀλάβη**· λιγνύς, σποδός, καρκίνος, ὑπὸ δὲ Κυπρίων μαρίλη, and ἀ.· ἄνθρακες.

ἀλᾰβ-αρχέω, *to be* ἀλαβάρχης, J.*AJ*20.5.2. **–άρχης**, v. Ἀραβάρχης. **–αρχία** [ᾰλ], ἡ, *office* of ἀλαβάρχης, J.*AJ*20.7.3; also ἐξ ἀλαβαρχείης *AP*11.383 (Pall.).

ἀλᾰβάστιον, τό, Dim. of ἀλάβαστος, Eub.100. **ἀλαβαστῖτις**, v. ἀλαβαστρίτης. **ἀλᾰβαστοθήκη**, ἡ, *case for alabaster ornaments*, Ἐφ. Ἀρχ.1903.443, D.19.237: generally, *small box* or *casket*, Ar.*Fr.*548 (–στρο–), *PLond.*2.12 (–στρο–).

ἀλάβαστος [ᾰλᾰ–] or **–στρος**, ὁ (ἡ, v.l. in *Ev.Marc.*14.3), *globular vase without handles for holding perfumes*, often made of alabaster, Hdt.3.20, Ar.*Ach.*1053, Crates Com.15.6, Alex.62,143, etc. (ἀλάβαστος (or –ον) is the earlier Att. form, *SIG*102, cf. Ael.Dion.*Fr.*31, Men.990: Dor. acc. pl. ἀλαβάστρως Call.*Lav.Pall.*15):—neut. **ἀλάβαστρον** *IG*2.745*B*4, 11(2).161*B*9 (Delos, iii B.C.), Lxx 4*Ki.*21.13 (cod. A), v.l. in *Ev.Marc.*14.3: pl. ἀλάβαστρα or –τα Theoc.15.114, *AP*9.153 (Agath.).

ἀλᾰβ-αστρίνη (sc. λιθοτομία), ἡ, *alabaster quarry*, *PThead.*54. **–άστρινος**, η, ον, *of alabaster*, ἔργα *PRyl.*92.1 (ii/iii A.D.). **–άστριον**, τό, *alabaster quarry*, *PThead.*36.3 (iv A.D.). **–αστρίτης** (sc. λίθος), ου, ὁ, *calcareous alabaster*, Thphr.*Lap.*65, cf. Str.12.8.14, Zos.Alch.p.113 B.:—also **–αστῖτις**, ιδος, ἡ, πέτρα Callix.1. **–αστροειδής**, *like alabaster*, Zos.Alch.p.111 B. Adv. **–δῶς**, στίλβουσα Dsc.4.76. **–αστρος**, v. ἀλάβαστος. **–αστροφόρος**, ον, *carrying vases*, A.*Fr.*409. **–αστρών**, ῶνος, ὁ, *alabaster quarry*, *Sammelb.*4639 (iii A.D.).

ἀλάβη, v. sub ἄλαβα.

ἀλάβης or **ἀλλάβης**, ητος, ἡ, a Nile fish, Str.17.2.4, Ath.7.312b, *Gp.*20.7.1, *POxy.*1857.2 (vi A.D.); in Plin.*HN*5.51 *alabetes.*

ἀλάβητοι· θόρυβοι, and **ἀλαβυτῶ**· θορυβῶ, Hsch.

ἀλαβώδης, ες, *sooty, murky*, πύργος Antim.Col.1.5, cf. Hsch.

ἅλαδε [ᾰλ], Adv., (ἅλς) *to* or *into the sea*, Il.1.308, Epicur.*Fr.*194, etc.; εἰς ἅλαδε Od.10.351. II. ἅλαδε μύσται, name of the second day of the Eleusinian mysteries, 16th Boedromion, Polyaen.3.11.2, cf. *IG*1.53*a*35, 2.385*d*20.

ἀλάδρομος [ᾰλ], ὁ, dithyrambic word coined by Ar.*Av.*1396, prob. from ἅλς (B), *race over the sea.*

ἄλαζα· αἰσχρά, Hsch.

ἀλαζ-ονεία, ἡ, *false pretension, imposture*, Pl.*Grg.*525a, D.22.47, etc., cf. Arist.*EN*1127ᵃ13, Thphr.*Char.*23; ὑπ' ἀλαζονείας Ar.*Ra.*919: in pl., Id.*Eq.*290,903, Isoc.12.20; *boastfulness*, Procop.*Pers.*1.11: metaph., ἀ. χορδῶν their *over-readiness* to sound, opp. ἐξάρνησις, Pl.*R.*531b. [That penult. is long appears from Ar. ll.cc., Men.737.] **–όνευμα**, ατος, τό, *imposture, piece of humbug*, Aeschin.3.

238, cf. Aristid.27(16).29: in pl., *quackeries*, Ar.*Ach*.87, Aeschin.1.178. **–ονεύομαι**, fut. -εύσομαι D.36.41: (ἀλαζών):—*make false pretensions, brag*, Ar.*Ra*.280, Lys.*Fr*.73; of the Sophists, X.*Mem*.1.7.5, etc.; περί τινος Eup.146b, Isoc.12.74; ἐπί τινι Aristipp.ap.D.L.2.73. 2. *feign*, Pl.*Hp.Mi*.371a; τὰ ἤθη ἀ. Arist.*Oec*.1344ᵃ19. **–ονίας**, ου, ὁ, *boaster, braggart*, Hdn.*Epim*.183. **–ονικός**, ή, όν, *disposed to make false pretensions, boastful, braggart*, Hp.*Medic*.4, X.*Mem*.1.2.5, Phld.*Rh*.2.149S. (Sup.); -κόν, τό, Arist.*EN*1127ᵇ29. Adv. -κῶς Plu.*Mar*.9: Comp. -ώτερον Apollon.Cit.3: Sup. -ώτατα Men.Prot.p.118D. **–ονοχαυνοφλυᾶρος**, ὁ, *swaggering empty babbler*, Archestr.*Fr*.59.12B. **–οσύνη**, ἡ, = ἀλαζονεία, Aq.*Je*.49.16(29.17). **–ών** [ᾰλ], όνος, ὁ, ἡ, (ἄλη) prop. *wanderer about country, vagrant*, Alc.Com.31. II. *charlatan, quack*, esp. of Sophists, Cratin.380, Ar.*Nu*.102, Pl.*Chrm*.173c, al. 2. *braggart, boaster*, X.*Cyr*.2.2.12, Arist.*EN*1127ᵃ21; title of play by Men. 3. Adj., *boastful, pretentious*, Hdt.6.12; ἀ. λόγοι Pl.*R*.560c: Comp. -έστερος Suid. s.v. εἴρων: Sup., ἡδονὴ ἀλαζονίστατον *most shameless*, Pl.*Phlb*.65c. Adv. Sup. -έστατα, δρῶν Ael.*NA*4.29.

ἀλάθεια, ἀλᾱθής, Dor. for ἀλήθ–. **ἀλᾱθείς**, v. sub ἀλάομαι.

ἀλάθητος [λᾱ], ον, gloss on ἄληστος, Suid.: coupled with ἄλαστος, Sch.E.*Hec*.685. 2. *not escaping detection*, Astramps.*Orac*.13.1.

ἀλαίνω [ᾰλ], = ἀλάομαι, *wander about*, A.*Ag*.82, E.*Tr*.1084, *El*.204, 589, *Cyc*.79: c. acc., ἀ. πόδα δύστηνον Id.*Ph*.1536.—Always in lyr., exc. *Or*.532.

ἀλαιός, όν, f.l. for ἀλεός, q.v. **ἀλακάτα**, ἡ, Dor. for ἠλακάτη:—Dim. **ἀλακάτιον**, τό, *POxy*.1740.8 (iii/iv A.D.).

ἀλάκητον· ἀψόφητον, Hsch. **ἀλακῶσαι**· ἀθροῖσαι, and συνάγεσθαι, Id. **ἀλαλά**, Dor. for ἀλαλή, q.v.

ἀλᾰλ-ᾱγή, ἡ, *shouting*, S.*Tr*.206. **–αγμα**, ατος, τό, = sq., Call.*Fr*.310, *Psalm.Solom*.17.8, Plu.*Mar*.45. **–αγμός**, ὁ, = ἀλαλαγή, Hdt.8.37, Plu.2.564b, Arr.*An*.5.10.4, Onos.29.1. II. generally, *loud noise*, τυμπάνων, αὐλοῦ, E.*Cyc*.65, *Hel*.1352 (lyr.). **–αγξ**· πλάνη, Hsch. **–άζω**, fut. -άξομαι v.l. in E.*Ba*.593, -άξω Lxx *Ez*.27.30: aor. ἠλάλαξα E.*HF*981, X. (v. infr.), poet. ἀλάλαξα Pi.*O*.7.37:—Med., S.*Fr*.534, Arr.*An*.5.10.3: (formed from the cry ἀλαλαί):—*raise the war-cry*, τῷ Ἐνυαλίῳ ἠλάλαξαν (as v.l. for ἠλέλιξαν) X.*An*.5.2.14, cf.6.5.27; Med., Arr. l.c.: c. acc. cogn., νίκην ἀλαλάζειν *shout the shout of* victory, S.*Ant*.133. 2. generally, *cry, shout aloud*, Pi. l.c., E.*El*.855; esp. in orgiastic rites, A.*Fr*.57; of Bacchus and Bacchae, E.*Ba*.593 (in Med.), 1133, etc.; ὠλόλυξαν αἱ γυναῖκες, ἠλάλαξαν δὲ οἱ ἄνδρες Hld.3.5. 3. rarely of a cry of pain or grief, ἠλάλαζε δυσθνῄσκων φόνῳ E.*El*.843, Lxx *Je*.4.8, al., *Ev.Marc*.5.38, Plu.*Luc* 28. II. rarely also of other sounds than the voice, *sound loudly*, ψαλμὸς δ' ἀλαλάζει A.*Fr*.57; κύμβαλον ἀλαλάζον 1*Ep.Cor*.13.1.—Poet. word, used by X. and in late Prose.

ἀλᾰλαί or **ἀλαλαλαί** [ᾰλ], exclam. of joy, in formula ἀλαλαὶ ἰὴ παιών Ar.*Av*.1763, *Lys*.1291. **ἀλαλάξιος**, *god of the war-cry*, epith. of Ares, Corn.*ND*21; of Zeus, Call.*Aet*.3.1.60.

ἀλᾰλᾱτός, ὁ, Dor. for ἀλαλητός.

ἀλᾰλάω, (ἄλαλος) *make dumb*, in Pass., Aq.*Ps*.38(39).3; but **ἀλαλόω**, Pass., ib.30(31).19.

ἀλαλή [ᾰλ], Dor. **ἀλαλά**, ἡ, (ἀλαλαί) *loud cry*, μανίαι τ' ἀλαλαί τ' ὀρινομένων Pi.*Fr*.208; ἀλαλαὶ αἱαγμάτων (v.l. ἀλαλαγαί) E.*Ph*.337:—esp. *war-cry*, Pi.*N*.3.60; *battle*, Id.*I*.7(6).10: comically, ἀ. "μύρου χεῖτε" Phoen.3.3:—Ἀλαλά personified, κλῦθ', Ἀλαλά, πολέμου θύγατερ, Pi.*Fr*.78, cf. Plu.2.349c.

ἀλάλημαι [ᾰλᾰ], pf. of ἀλάομαι, only in pres. sense (part. ἀλαλήμενος with accent of pres., Od.14.122), *wander, roam about*, like a beggar, Hom. mostly in Od., 2.370, 15.10, etc.; of seamen, μαψιδίως ἀλάλησθε 3.72, cf. 313; of a departed spirit, ἀ. ἀν' εὐρυπυλὲς Ἄϊδος δῶ Il.23.74; of things, μυρία λυγρὰ κατ' ἀνθρώπους ἀλάληται Hes.*Op*.100:—once Trag., in plpf., ἀλάλητο E.*Andr*.306 (lyr.).

ἀλάλητος [λᾰ], ον, *unspeakable, unutterable*, v.l. in Thgn.422, cf. *AP*5.3 (Phld.), *Ep.Rom*.8.26. Adv. -τως, as expl. of ἀλόγως, Eust.723.30. II. ἀλάλητα· ξύλα ποταμόκλυστα, γομφώδη, Hsch.

ἀλᾰλητός, Dor. -ᾱτός, οῦ, ὁ, (ἀλαλαί) *shout of victory*, Il.16.78; *war-cry, battle-shout*, Hes.*Th*.686, Pi.*P*.1.72. 2. generally, *loud shouting*, Il.2.149; *halloo*, in hunting, Nic.Dam.p.6D. 3. rarely, *cry of woe* or *wailing*, Il.21.10; com., τῶν δὲ πλακούντων.. ἦν ἀ. Telecl.1.13. II. rarely of other sounds, *loud noise*, αὐλῶν *AP*6.51.

ἀλαλία, ἡ, = πονηρία, ἀταξία, S.*Fr*.232.

ἄλαλκε [ᾰλα], 3 sg. aor. 2 (also 2 imper., Thgn.13), Il.23.185, Hes.*Th*.527, Pi.*N*.4.60 (augm. ἤλαλκε Hsch.); subj. (v. infr.); opt. ἀλάλκοις, -κοι, -κοιεν, Od.13.319, Il.21.138, 22.196; inf. ἀλαλκέμεναι Il.17.153, ἀλαλκεῖν (ἀλαλκέμεν Ar.Byz.) 19.30, *AP*7.8 (Antip.); part. ἀλαλκών Il.9.605, *AP*9.374:—*ward, keep off*, τί τινι something from a person, Il.19.30, etc.; less freq. τί τινος 21.539; ἀ. τί τινι κρατός Od.10.288.—Hence A.R.2.235 formed fut. ἀλαλκήσουσιν, Q.S.7.267 pres. ἀλάλκουσιν. (Cf. ἀλέξω.)

Ἀλαλκ-ομενηΐς, ΐδος, epith. of Athena, Il.4.8, 5.908: either from Boeot. town Alalcomenae or (as Aristarch.) from ἀλαλκεῖν, *Protectress*:—also **–ομένη** *BCH* 1.82 (Chios): masc. **–ομενεύς**, έως, of Zeus, *EM*56.10. **–ομένιος** or **–ειος**, ὁ, Boeot. month, answering to the Att. Μαιμακτηριών, *IG*7.2227, al., Plu.*Arist*.21. **–τήριον**, τό, (ἄλαλκε) *remedy*, Zonar.

ἄλᾰλος, ον, *speechless, dumb*, prob. in A.*Fr*.60, Lxx *Ps*.37(38).13, *Ev.Marc*.9.17, etc.; κείμεσθα ἄ. *IG*14.1627: Comp. -ώτερος Sch.Pi.*N*.8.41.

ἀλάλυγξ [ᾰλᾰ], υγγος, ἡ, = λυγμός, *gulping, choking*, Nic.*Al*.18, cf. *AB*374.

ἀλαλύκτημαι [ᾰλᾰ], *to be in anguish, sore distressed*, pf. formed by redupl. from ἀλυκτέω, οὐδέ μοι ἦτορ ἔμπεδον, ἀλλ' ἀ. Il.10.94.

ἀλαλύσθαι· φοβεῖσθαι, (ἀ)λύειν, Hsch. **ἀλαμπάν**· τὸν ἥλιον, Id.

ἀλάμπ-ετος, ον, (λάμπω) *without light, darksome*, h.*Hom*.32.5; of the nether world, S.*OC*1662 (v.l. ἀλύπητον), cf. *Epigr.Gr*.264.5 (dub.); ἀ. οὖδας Ἀΐδεω ib.149.3 (Rhenea), cf.ib.241.5 (Smyrna); σκότος (metaph. of Heraclitus) *AP*9.540. **–ής**, ές, = foreg., νύξ Simon.37.8; *dull, not bright*, ὄψιες v.l. in Hp.*Prog*.2, πῦρ D.S.3.48; of colour, Arist.*Col*.793ᵃ12; of sound, Orib.50.51.2; ἀ. ἡλίου *out of* sun's *light*, S.*Tr*.691; ὑπόγαιον J.*BJ*1.3.3; ἀλαμπέας Ἄϊδος εὐνάς *Epigr.Gr*.431 (Antioch.). 2. metaph., *obscure*, ἀρετὴν.. ἀμαυρὰν καὶ ἀ. Plu.*Phoc*.1, cf. B.12.175. **–ία**, ἡ, Pythag. name for *one*, *Theol.Ar*.6.

ἀλανές· ἀληθές, Hsch. Adv. **ἀλανέως**· ὁλοσχερῶς (Tarent.), Id.; ἀϝλανέως, dub. sens., *GDI*1156.4 (Elis). **ἄλαξ**, v. ἄλξ.

ἀλάομαι [ᾰλ], Ep. 3 pl. ἀλόωνται, imper. ἀλόω (v. infr.), used by Hom. mostly in contr. forms ἀλᾶσθε, ἀλώμενος, impf. ἠλώμην, Ep. ἀλᾶτο: fut. ἀλήσομαι (ἀπ–) Hes.*Sc*.409 (v.l. ἀπαλήσατο): Ep. aor. ἀλήθην Od.14.120, 362, Dor. part. ἀλᾱθείς A.*Supp*.870: pf. ἀλάλημαι (q.v.): (ἄλη):—*wander, roam*, οἷά τε ληιστῆρες.. τοί τ' ἀλόωνται ψυχὰς παρθέμενοι Od.3.73; ὅδε τις δύστηνος ἀλώμενος ἐνθάδ' ἱκάνει 6.206; μὴ πάθωμέν τι ἀλώμενοι Hdt.4.97; αἰσχρῶς ἀλῶμαι A.*Eu*.98; ἄσιτος νηλίπους τ' ἀ. S.*OC*349: esp. *to be outcast, banished*, ib.444, Th.2.102, Lys.6.30, D.19.310; ἐκ σέθεν by thee, S.*OC*1363:—freq. with Preps., ἀνὰ στρατὸν οἶοι ἀλᾶσθε Il.10.141; κὰπ πεδίον.. οἶος ἀλᾶτο 6.201; πολλὰ βροτῶν ἐπὶ ἄστε' ἀλώμενος Od.15.492; γῆς ἐπ' ἐσχάτοις ὅροις A.*Pr*.666; ἐπὶ ξένης χώρας S.*Tr*.300, cf. Isoc.4.168; οὕτω νῦν.. ἀλόω κατὰ πόντον Od.5.377, cf. A.*Supp*.870; νομάδεσσι γὰρ ἐν Σκύθαις ἀλᾶται Ar.*Av*.942: c. acc. loci, ἀ. γῆν *wander over* the land, S.*OC*1686; πορθμοὺς ἀ. μυρίους E.*Hel*.532; οὔρεα Theoc.13.66. 2. c. gen., *wander away from, miss* a thing, εὐφροσύνας ἀλᾶται Pi.*O*.1.58; ψυχὴν ἀλᾶται τῆς πάροιθ' εὐπραξίας E.*Tr*.640. II. metaph., *wander in mind, be perplexed*, S.*Aj*.23.

ἀλᾰός [ᾰλ], όν, *not seeing, blind* (Cypr. for τυφλός, *AB*1095), Od.8.195, etc. (not in Il., Trag. only in lyr.); τὸ φωτῶν ἀ. γένος A.*Pr*.549, ἀλαοί, opp. δεδορκότες, *the dead*, Id.*Eu*.322; of eyes, S.*OC*149, 244, E.*Ph*.1531; ἕλκος ἀ. *blinding* wound, i.e. *blindness*, S.*Ant*.974; ἐπ' ὀφθαλμῶν ἀ. νέφος A.R.2.259. II. *invisible imperceptible*, φθίσις ἀλαή prob. l. in Hp.*Loc.Hom*.10 (codd. ἄλλη, Gal. ἀλαΐα). (If from ἀ- priv., λάω A (q.v.), the accent is exceptional, but cf. Hdn.Gr.1.112.) [ἀλᾰος Od. l.c., etc.; but μάντιος ἀλαοῦ init. vers. Od.10.493, 12.267.]

ἀλᾰο-σκοπιά, Ion. -ιή, ἡ, *blind man's watch*, i.e. *careless watch*, Il.10.515, 13.10, Od.8.285, Hes.*Th*.466. **–τόκος**, ον, *bringing forth young blind*, Suid. **ἀλᾰόω**, *blind*, ὀφθαλμοῦ ἀλαῶσαι *blind* him *of* his eye, Od.1.69, 9.516: c. acc., *AP*7.601 (Jul.).

ἀλᾰπ-αδνός, ή, όν, (ἀλαπάζω) *easily exhausted*, i.e. *powerless, feeble*, στίχες, σθένος, μῦθος, etc., Il.4.330, Od.18.373, h.*Merc*.334, cf. Hes.*Op*.437: Comp., ἀλαπαδνότεροι γὰρ ἔσεσθε Il.4.305. (ἀ- euph., cf. λαπαδνός.) **–αδνοσύνη**, ἡ, *feebleness*, Q.S.7.12. **–άζω** [ᾰλ], Ep. impf. ἀλάπαζον Il.11.503: fut. -άξω 2.367, A.*Ag*.130 (anap.): Ep. aor. ἀλάπαξα Il.11.750, Thgn.951:—Pass., Il.24.245:—*empty, drain, exhaust*, Od.17.424; ἀ. πόλιν *sack, plunder*, Il.2.367; of men, *overpower, destroy*, 5.166, 11.503, al.: metaph., [οἶνος] ἐκ κραδίης ἀνίας ἀνδρῶν ἀ. Panyas.14. (ἀ- euph., cf. λαπάσσω.)

ἄλαρα· Ποντικὰ κάρυα, Hsch., *EM*57.53; also, *butt of spear-shaft*, Hsch., and **ἀλαρία**, ἡ, tree which furnished shafts for spears, *EM*57.54. **ἀλαρῦναι**· ῥυπᾶναι, Hsch.

ἅλας, ἅτος, τό, = ἅλς, *salt*, Arist.*Mir*.844ᵇ16, Lycon ap.Hdn.Gr.2.716, Lxx *Le*.2.13, al., *Ep.Col*.4.6, Gal.14.327; ἅ. ἀμμωνιακόν *POxy*.1222.2 (iv A.D.).

ἀλασταίνω· δυσπαθέω, Hsch.:—Pass., *EM*58.3 (codd. ἀλαιστάνομαι). **ἀλαστέω**, *to be full of wrath* or (more prob.) *to be distraught*, ἠλάστεον δὲ θεοί (as trisyll.) Il.15.21; ᾤμωξεν.. καὶ ἀλαστήσας ἔπος ηὔδα 12.163, cf. Call.*Del*.239, Musae.202, etc., cf. Gal.*Lex*. s.v. ἀλάστορες. (Only impf. and aor. part. in earlier Ep.; fut. -ήσω Q.S.5.584.)

ἀλαστ-ορία, ἡ, *vengeance of heaven*, J.*AJ*17.1.1. **–ορος**, ον, *under influence of an* ἀλάστωρ, A.*Fr*.294: *crying for vengeance*, ἀλαστόροισιν ὀμμάτων κύκλοις S.*Ant*.974 (lyr.). II. epith. of Zeus, *avenging*, Pherecyd.175J.

ἄλαστος, ον, (cf. ἄληστος): (ἀ- priv., λαθεῖν, λήθομαι):—*not to be forgotten, insufferable*, πένθος, ἄχος, Il.24.105, Od.4.108, Hes.*Th*.467, cf. Alcm.23, A.*Pers*.990; ἔπαθον ἄλαστα S.*OC*538: Sup. -ότατον, πῆμα *IG*12(5).64 (Naxos); neut. as Adv., ἄλαστον ὀδύρομαι I wail *inconsolably*, Od.14.174, cf. B.3.34. 2. of persons, as in Il.22.261, where Achilles calls Hector ἄλαστε *thou whom I will never forget nor forgive!*; *accursed wretch*, S.*OC*1482; πατρὸς.. ἄ. αἷμα ib.1672, cf. *Mim.Oxy*.413.60.—Poet. and late Prose, Demoph.*Sent*.13: used by Trag. only in lyr.

ἀλάστωρ, ορος, ὁ, ἡ, *avenging spirit* or *deity*, with or without δαίμων, freq. Trag., A.*Pers*.354, *Ag*.1501, 1508, cf. Men.8D.; ἀ. θυμός S.*OC*788; ἐξ ἀλαστόρων νοσεῖν Id.*Tr*.1235; ἀλάστορας ἔχειν Hp.*Morb.Sacr*.1; ἀ. Πελοπιδῶν, prov. of utter ruin, Xenarch.1.3; generally, βουκόλων ἀ. herdsmen's *scourge*, of Nemean lion, S.*Tr*.1092: fem., of the Sphinx, Nicoch.18; Ζεὺς Ἀ. Orph.*H*.73. II. Pass., *he who does deeds which merit vengeance, wretch*, A.*Eu*.236, S.*Aj*.374; μιαροὶ.. καὶ κόλακες καὶ ἀ. D.18.296; βάρβαρόν τε. . καὶ ἀ. τὸν Φίλιππον ἀποκαλῶν Id. 19.305; ἄνθρωπ' ἀλάστωρ Bato 2.5, cf. Men.7 D., *Pk*.408; Διονύσιος ἀπάσης Σικελίας ἀ. Clearch.10. (Connected with ἀλάομαι by Chrysipp.*Stoic*.2.47.)

ἀλάτας, ἀλᾱτεία, Dor. for ἀλήτης, ἀλητεία.

ἁλ-ατίζω, *sprinkle with salt*, [Gal.]14.576, Anon.*in Rh*.14.2.30 (Pass.). **-ατικόν,** *salarium*, Gloss. **-άτινος,** η, ον, (ἅλας) *made of salt*, Alex.Trall.12. **-άτιον,** τό, Dim. of ἅλας, Aesop.322b, Aët. 3.109.

ἅλατο, Dor. 3 sg. aor. 1 of ἅλλομαι.

ἁλᾰτοπωλία, ἡ, *right of vending salt*, Arist.*Oec*.1346^{b}21, *PFlor*.16. 33.

ἀλατρίας· ἁμαρτωλίας, Hsch. **ἀλαυρίδας·** σχίζας, Id.

ἀλα-ῶπις, ιδος, ἡ, pecul. fem. of sq., Emp.49. **-ωπός,** ον, lit. *blind-eyed*; hence, *dark*, ὀμίχλη Nonn.*D*.25.282. **-ωτύς,** ύος, ἡ, (ἀλαόω) *blinding*, ὀφθαλμοῦ Od.9.503.

ἀλβάριος, ὁ, *plasterer*, *IG*14.2271.

ἀλγᾷ· κρύπτει, Hsch. **ἀλγάς·** ἀλγηδόνας, Id. **ἀλγείη·** ἀρρωστία (Lacon.), Id.

ἀλγεινός, ή, όν, *painful, grievous*, A.*Pr*.199,240, S.*OT*1530, E.*Med*. 1037; τὰ μέλλοντα ἀ. Th.2.39, cf. ib.43 (Comp.). Adv. -νῶς S.*Ant*. 436, Pl.*Grg*.476c. II. rare in pass. sense, *feeling pain, suffering*, S.*OC*1664.—Comp. and Sup. in common use ἀλγίων, ἄλγιστος (q. v.), but ἀλγεινότερος, -ότατος, Th.2.43, Pl.*Grg*.477d, *Smp*.218a, Arist. *Pr*.890^{a}37, and v.l. Isoc.14.48. Hom. form ἀλεγεινός, q.v.

ἀλγεόθυμος· ἀνώδυνος τῇ ψυχῇ, Hsch.

ἀλγεσί-δωρος, ον, *bringing pain*, Ἔρως Sapph.125; Ἔρις Opp.*H*. 2.668. **-θῡμος,** ον, *grieving the heart*, Orph.*H*.65, cf. *PMag.Lond*. 121.355.

ἀλγ-έω, fut. -ήσω Od.12.27, (ἄλγος) *feel bodily pain, suffer*, ἀλγήσας *smarting with pain*, Il.2.269, etc.; *suffer, be ill*, Hdt.4.68; more fully, ἀλγήσας ὀδύνῃσι Il.12.206: suffering part in acc., ἄλγησον ἧπαρ A.*Eu*. 135; τὰς γνάθους ἀλγήσετε Ar.*Pax*237; τὸν δάκτυλον Pl.*R*.462d; τὰ ὄμματα ib.515e. 2. *suffer hardship*, ἢ ἁλὸς ἢ ἐπὶ γῆς ἀλγήσετε Od. l. c. II. *feel pain of mind, grieve*, ἀ. ψυχήν, φρένα, Hdt.3.43, E.*Or*.608, etc.; ἀ. τινί *to be pained at* a thing, Hdt.3.120, S.*OC*744, etc.; ἐπ' ἐξειργασμένοις Id.*Aj*.377, etc.; διά τι Hdt.4.68; περί τι or τινος, Th.2.65, E.*Andr*.240: c. gen., ἀλγεῖν χρὴ τύχης παλιγκότου A.*Ag*.571, cf. E.*Hec*.1256: c. acc., ἀλγῶ μὲν ἔργα A.*Ch*.1016; πρᾶξιν ἣν ἤλγησ' ἐγώ S.*Aj*.790: c. part., ἤλγησ' ἀκούσας Hdt.3.50, A.*Pers*. 844; ἀλγῶ κλύων S.*Ph*.86; ὁρῶν Eup.117.2: abs., τὸ ἀλγοῦν, opp. τὸ ἡδόμενον, Epicur.*Sent*.4. III. Pass., ὑποχόνδριον -ούμενον Hp. *Coac*.273; τὸν ἀλγούμενον ὀδόντα Dsc.*Eup*.1.66. **-ηδών,** όνος, ἡ, *pain, suffering*, of body, Hdt.5.18, Hp.*Coac*.394, E.*Med*.24; ὀδύνη τις ἢ ἀ. Pl.*R*.413b: pl., *Prt*.354b. II. of mind, *pain, grief*, S.*OC*514, E.*Med*.56, Metrod.7: pl., Phld.*D*.1.16, etc. III. *cause of pain*, ἀλγηδόνες ὀμμάτων αἱ Περσίδες Alex.ap.Plu.*Alex*.21.—Not in A., once in S. **-ημα,** τό, *pain felt* or *caused, suffering*, S. *Ph*.340, Hp.*VM*6, E.*Fr*.507, Plu.*Sull*.26, Plot.6.1.19; οὐκ ἔστι λύπης ἄ. μεῖζον Men.667. **-ηρός,** ά, όν, *painful*, Lxx *Je*.10.19, al. **-ησις,** εως, ἡ, *sense of pain*, S.*Ph*.792, Ar.*Th*.147: in later Prose, Iamb.*Protr*.21.κζ'; νεύρων Vett.Val.38.13. **-ητέον,** *one must grieve*, περί τινος Agath.1.13. **-ῑνόεις,** εσσα, εν, *painful, grievous*, Hes.*Th*.214,226, Mimn.11, Xenoph.2.4, A.R.4.64: in pass. sense, κρόταφος, τένων, Q.S.11.45,57. **-ίων,** ον, **ἄλγιστος,** η, ον, irreg. Comp. and Sup. of ἀλγεινός, formed fr. Subst. ἄλγος (cf. καλλίων, αἰσχίων):—*more* or *most painful, grievous*, or *distressing*:—of Comp., Hom. has only neut. ἄλγιον, in signf. *so much the worse*, τῷ δ' ἄλγιον, αἴ κ' ἐθέλῃσιν. . ἄμμι μάχεσθαι Il.18.278, cf. 306, Od.4.292: Sup. only in Il.23.655 ἥτ' ἀλγίστη δαμάσασθαι (of a mule).—Both are common in Trag., as ἀλγίων A.*Pr*.934, S.*Ant*.64; ἄλγιστος Id.*OT* 675, etc. [-ῖον Hom., -ῑον Trag.]

ἄλγος, εος, τό, (Cypr., = ὀδύνη, *AB*1095) *pain* of body, Il.5.394, S. *Ph*.734,1379; ἀ. καρδίης, ποδῶν, κεφαλᾶς, Hp.*Epid*.7.20, X.*Cyn*.3.3, *IG*4.953.52 (Epid.); in Hom. mostly in pl., *sufferings*, ἄλγεα τεύχει Il.1.110; ἄ. πάσχων 2.667, cf. Alc.95. 2. *pain* of mind, *grief*, freq. in pl., Il.1.2, 2.39, al.: sg., ἄλγος ἱκάνει θυμόν Il.3.97, cf. Od. 2.41, etc.; τὴν δ' ἅμα χάρμα καὶ ἄ. ἕλε φρένα 19.471; ἄ. ἀεικέλιον 14. 32; τὰ κύντατ' ἄλγη κακῶν E.*Supp*.807; ὑπ' ἄλγους *from pain*, A.*Eu*. 183; αἰσχύνας ἐμὰς ὑπ' ἀλγέων *from grief for* my shame, E.*Hel*.201; ἄ. καρδίας Lxx *Si*.26.6. II. later, *anything that causes pain*, Bion 2.11, *AP*9.390 (Menecr.), 5.166 (Asclep.); τοῦ ἄ. θιγεῖν Aret.*SD*2.9.

ἀλγ-υνσις, εως, ἡ, *causing of pain*, Phlp.*in de An*.17.33; δι' ἀλγύνσεως, opp. δι' ἡδύνσεως, Olymp.*in Grg*.p.531 J. **-υντήρ,** ῆρος, ὁ, *causing pain*, τινῶν Orac.ap.Zos.1.57. **-ύνω** [ῡ], Ion. impf. ἀλγύνεσκε Q.S.4.416: fut. -υνῶ S.*OT*332, etc.: aor. ἤλγυνα Id.*Tr*.458, etc.:—Pass., with fut. Med. ἀλγυνοῦμαι (in pass. sense) Id.*Ant*.230, E.*Med*.622: aor. ἠλγύνθην, v. infr.—Rare exc. in Trag., Eup.90 (paratrag.), Democr.223, X.*Ap*.8, and later Prose, as Plu.2.82c:—*pain, grieve, distress*, τινά A.*Ch*.746, etc.:—Pass., *feel, suffer pain, be grieved* or *distressed* at a thing, τινί S.*Ant*.468; νόσοις X. l. c.; ἐπί τινι E.*Tr*.172; τι S.*Ph*.1021; εἰσιδοῦσά τ' ἠλγύνθην κέαρ A.*Pr*.247.

ἀλδαίνω, only pres. and impf., exc. Ep. aor. 3 sg. ἤλδᾰνε (v. infr.), ἀλδήσασκε Orph.*L*.370:—causal of ἀλδήσκω, *make to grow, nourish, strengthen*, μέλε' ἤλδανε ποιμένι λαῶν *she filled out* his limbs, Od.18.70, 24.368, cf. A.*Th*.12; θυμὸν ἀλδαίνουσαν ἐν εὐφροσύναις Id.*Pr*.539; *increase, multiply*, ὃς οὐκ ἐάσει γλῶσσαν. . ἀλδαίνειν κακά Id.*Th*.557:—Pass., Aglaïas 12.

ἄλδετα· ἄτμητα, Hsch. (leg. ἄλαστα· ἄτλητα).

ἄλδ-η, ἡ, *growth*, Hdn.Gr.1.311. **-ήεις,** εσσα, εν, *waxing, increasing*, Max.533. **-ήμιος,** *causing growth*, epith. of Zeus, Method.ap.*EM*58.20. **-ήσκω,** *grow*, λήιου ἀλδήσκοντος Il.23.599, cf. Democr.ap.Gal.14.101. II. trans. = ἀλδαίνω, Theoc.17.78, *Epigr.Gr*.511 (Epirus). **-ισκάνω,** = ἀλδήσκω, Hdn.Gr.2. 716. **-ομαι,** v. ἀλδαίνω.

ἀλέα (A), [ᾰλ], Ion. **ἀλέη,** ἡ, (ἄλη, ἀλέομαι) *avoiding, escape*, ἐγγύθι μοι θάνατος. . οὐδ' ἀλέη Il.22.301 (not in Od.); οὐκ ἔστιν ἀ. οὐδὲ σκέπη Hp.*Aër*.19: c. gen., *shelter from* a thing, ὑετοῦ Hes.*Op*.545.—Ep. and Ion. word.

ἀλέα (B), [ᾰλ], Ion. **ἀλέη,** ἡ, contr. ἀλῆ Androm.ap. Gal.14.33, cj. in Babr.18.11:—*warmth, heat*, of fire, Od.17.23 (not in Il.), Jul.*Mis*.341c; generally, *warmth*, or *warm spot*, ἐν ἀλέῃ γενέσθαι Hp.*VM*16, cf. Diocl.*Fr*.141; ἐσενεγκὼν ἐς ἀ. Hp.*Aër*.8; χρέεσθαι περιπάτοις ἐν ἀ. Id.*Vict*.3.68; ἐν ἀ. κατακείμενος Ar.*Ec*.541; ἀλέας καὶ ψύχους *in heat* and cold, Pl.*Erx*.401d, cf. Arist.*EN*1148^{a}8; πνῖγος καὶ ἀ. Id.*Metaph*.1026^{b}34; ἐν ταῖς ἀ. in the *hot season*, Id.*Pr*.939^{b}9: later, *animal, bodily heat*, Plu.2.131d, Ael.*NA*3.20, Aristid.*Or*.48 (24).22; generally, *source of warmth*, τὸ ἔριον ἡμῖν κόσμος καὶ ἀ. Porph.*Abst*.1.21, etc.: in pl., *fomentations*, Alex.Trall.*Febr*.3.

ἀλεάζω (A), *to be warm*, Arist.*Pr*.863^{b}22, *Resp*.472^{b}4; trans., = θερμαίνω, Gal.19.73, Hsch.

ἀλεάζω (B)· κρύπτειν, ἢ προβάλλειν, καὶ εἴργειν, ἀφανίζειν, and -άζων· δικαζόμενος, Hsch. **ἀλεάζω·** ἀθροίζω, Id.; cf. ἀλής, ἁλία.

ἀλεαί, αἱ, = ἁλαί, *Inscr.Prien*.111 (i B. C.): sg., *SIG*827*D* iii 24 (Delph., ii A. D.).

ἀλε-αίνω, aor. -ᾱνα Ael.*VH*9.30, (ἀλέα B) *warm, make warm*, Hp. *Epid*.5.57, *Mul*.2.124:—Pass., Archil.ap.Plu.2.954f, etc. II. intr., *grow warm, be warm*, Ar.*Ec*.540, Arist.*PA*656^{a}22, *Pr*.885^{b}27; ἀ. πρὸς τὸ πῦρ καθημένη Men.832. **-αντικός,** ή, όν, *fit for warming*, S.E.*P*.3.179.

ἀλέαντος, ον, *not ground*, σίνηπι Phlp.*in GA*15.12.

ἄλεαρ· ἀλεωρίαν ἢ πολυωρίαν, Hsch.

ἀλέασθαι, ἀλέασθε, v. ἀλέομαι. **ἀλέατα,** v. ἀλείατα.

ἀλεβεβᾶν· ἐρευνᾶν, Hsch.

ἀλεγεινός, ή, όν, Ep. for ἀλγεινός, *causing pain, grievous*, αἰχμή, μάχη, Il.5.658, 18.248; εἰρεσίη Od.10.78; μεριμνάματα Pi.*Fr*.277: c. inf., *troublesome*, ἵπποι ἀλεγεινοὶ δαμήμεναι Il.10.402: neut. as Adv. -εινὸν ἀλαστήσασα Call.*Del*.239. Regul. Adv. -νῶς Q.S.3.557.

ἀλεγίζω, Ep. Verb, used only in pres. and impf.: (ἀλέγω):—*trouble oneself about* a thing, *care for, mind, heed*, in Hom. (only in Il.) always with neg., c. gen., τῶν οὔτι μετατρέπῃ οὐδ' ἀλεγίζεις Il.1. 160, al.; τῶν μὲν ἄρ' οὐκ ἀλέγιζε πατήρ 11.80, cf. Hes.*Th*.171: abs., ὁ δ' ἀφήμενος οὐκ ἀλεγίζει οὐδ' ὅθεται Il.15.106; in late Ep. c. acc., ἐγὼ δέ μιν οὐκ ἀλεγίζω Q.S.2.428; rare without neg., ὃς τρία μὲν τίκτει, δύο δ' ἐκλέπει, ἓν δ' ἀλεγίζει Musae.*Fr*.3 D.; ἡρώων ἀ. *IG*14.1389 i 42:—Pass., οὐκ ἀλεγιζόμενος f.l. in *AP*5.17 (Rufin.).—Poet. word, found in Aret.*CA*1.4.

ἀλεγύνω, Ep. Verb, Hom. only pres. and impf.: aor. ἀλέγῡνα A.R. 1.394, Med. ἀλεγύνατο Emp.137.4: (ἀλέγω):—*heed, care for*, Hom. (only Od.) always c. acc. δαῖτα or δαῖτας, ἄλλας δ' ἀλεγύνετε δαῖτας *find* your meals elsewhere, 1.374; δαῖτ' ἀλέγυνον, of invited guests, 13.23; but δαῖτας ἐΐσας. . ἀλεγύνειν *prepare* a meal *for guests*, 11. 186; δολοφροσύνην ἀλεγύνων *h.Merc*.361; ἀγλαΐας ἀλέγυνε ib.476.

ἀλέγω, Ep. and Lyr., once in A. (lyr.), only pres., *have a care, mind, heed*, usu. neg.: 1. abs., οὐκ ἀ. *have* no *care*, Il.11.389, Od. 17.390; κύνες οὐκ ἀλέγουσαι Od.19.154: without neg., Λιταὶ ἀλέγουσι κιοῦσαι walk *with good heed*, Il.9.504. II. with a case, 1. c. gen., *heed, care for*, οὐδ' ἀλλήλων ἀλέγουσιν Od.9.115; οὐ γὰρ Κύκλωπες Διὸς. . ἀλέγουσιν ib.275, cf. Simon.37.10; βωμῶν ἀλέγοντες οὐδέν A.*Supp*.752; μακάρων οὐκ ἀλέγοντα θεῶν Call.*Aet*.3.1.65: without neg., ψυχῆς ἀ. ὕπερ A.R.2.634. 2. less freq. c. acc., *regard, respect*, θεῶν ὄπιν οὐκ ἀλέγοντες Il.16.388, Hes.*Op*.251; οἰωνούς R.A. 1.145: without neg., νηῶν ὅπλα. . ἀλέγουσιν *take care of*, Od.6.268, cf. Pi.*O*.11(10).15, *I*.8(7).51. III. *count among*, Λύκαισον ἐν καμοῦσιν Alcm.32, cf. Pi.*O*.2.78 (Pass.); ἐν ἀθανάτοις ἀ. *IG*14.1389 ii 6. (Commonly deriv. from ἀ- copul., λέγω, *count with*, cf. III.)

ἄλεε· φύλασσε, Hsch. **ἀλεεῖ·** ἀδικεῖ, Id.

ἀλεεινός, ή, όν, (ἀλέα B) *lying open to the sun, warm, hot*, χώρη Hdt.2.25; νῆσοι Hp.*Vict*.2.37 (Comp.); opp. ψυχεινός, X.*Cyn*.10.6; χιτών Id.*Smp*.4.38; freq. in Arist., ἄνεμος, ὕδωρ, *Mete*.358^{a}30 (Sup.), *HA*503^{a}13 (Comp.). Adv. -νῶς Poll.5.111.

ἀλεείνω [ᾰ], Ep., only pres. and impf. (exc. aor. ἀλεεῖναι Man.6. 736): (ἀλέα A, ἄλη):—*avoid, shun*, mostly c. acc. rei, θυμὸν ὀπίζομαι ἠδ' ἀλεείνω Od.13.148, al.; κῆρ' ἀλεείνοντες Hes.*Fr*.96.83; ὁ δὲ κερδοσύνῃ ἀλέεινε *evaded* [my question], Od.4.251: less freq. c. acc. pers., ἀλέεινε δ' ὑφορβόν 16.477, cf. *h.Merc*.239 codd.: c. inf., κτεῖναι μέν ῥ' ἀλέεινε Il.6.167; ἀλεξέμεναι ἀλέεινε 13.356, cf. Antim.53:—also in Luc.*Dem.Enc*.23. II. intr., *shrink*, ἂψ τ' ἀλέεινεν A.R.3.650.

ἀλεεύς, v. ἁλιεύς. **ἀλέη,** v. ἀλέα.

ἀλεής, ές, like ἀλεεινός, *in the warmth*, ὕπνος S.*Ph*.859 (lyr.) (codd., Sch.; ἀδεής cj. Reiske).

ἄλεθρα (cod. -αιθ-)· ἄλευρα, Hsch.

ἀλεία, ἡ, (ἄλη) *wandering about*, *AB*376, Hsch.

ἁλεία, ἡ, = ἁλιεία, v.l. in Arist.*Oec*.1346^{b}20, cf. Hdn.3.1.5, etc. II. = ἀλεά (cf. ἀλεαί), *SIG*826*E* iv 28 (Delph., ii A. D.).

ἀλείαντος, ον, (λεαίνω) *unmasticated*, τροφή Arist.*PA*674^{b}28.

ἀλείατα, τά, (ἀλέω A) *wheat-groats, coarse wheaten meal*, Od.20. 108:—**ἀλέατα,** *Milet*.3 p.163 No.31 (vi B. C.). [-ει- metri gr.]

ἄλειμμ-α, ατος, τό, (ἀλείφω) *anything used for anointing, unguent,* *fat, oil*, Pl.*Ti.*50e, Antiph.154, Arist.*Pr.*884b37, etc.: pl., Hices.ap. Ath.15.689c, Diocl.*Fr.*141. **-άτιον**, τό, Dim. of foreg., Diog.ap. D.L.6.52. **-ατώδης**, ες, *unctuous*, Hp.*Steril.*235.

ἀλεῖν· οἰκεῖν, Hsch. (fort. νάειν). **ἀλεινόν**· ἀσθενές, λεπτόν, Id. **ἀλέϊον** ὕδωρ· ἀθροιστὸν καὶ συλλεκτόν, Id. **ἀλέϊος**· πένης, Id. (i.e. Ἀλήιος).

ἀλειπ-τέον, *one must anoint*, Sor.2.16, Gal.6.229, *Gp.*16.4.1. **-τήρ**, ῆρος, ὁ, = ἀλείπτης, Man.4.178. **-τήριον**, τό, *place for anointing* in gymnasia, or in Roman Thermae, used also as *sudatory*, Alex.101, Thphr.*Ign.*13, *IG*5(1).1390.108 (Andania, i B.C.), *CIG* 2782.25, al., Herod.Med.ap.Orib.10.10.1. II. *paint-brush* (Cypr.), Hsch. (-πήριον cod.). III. *unguent*, Erot. s.v. καμμάρω. **-της**, ου, ὁ, *anointer*: hence (cf. ἀλείφω I) *trainer* in gymnasia, Arist.*EN* 1106b1, Plb.27.7.1, *Sammelb.*4224.7 (i B.C.), Plu.2.133b. 2. metaph., οἱ ἀθληταὶ τῆς ἀρετῆς μὴ ψεύσαντες τοὺς ἀλείπτας νόμους Ph. 2.409; *teacher*, τῶν πολιτικῶν Plu.*Per.*4; τῆς κακίας S.E.*M.*1. 298. 3. Lat. *aliptes, bath-attendant*, Juv.6.422. **-τικός**, ή, όν, *of* or *for the* ἀλείπτης, *trained under him*, Plu.2.619a:—ἁ -κά (sc. τέχνα) *art of training*, Ti.Locr.104a; ἁ. συγγράμματα, treatises thereon, Iamb.*VP*5.25; ἁ. ἐπιμέλεια, kind of *massage*, Sor.2.38. Adv. -κῶς *like an* ἀλείπτης, Sch.Ar.*Eq.*492.

ἀλειπτός όν, *anointed, smeared*, Hdn.Gr.2.472: ἀλειπτά, τά, *ointments*, Hp.*Liqu.*7.

ἄλειπτος ον, (λείπω) *not left behind, unconquered*, πυθαύλης, περιοδονίκης, *IG*14.737,1102, cf. D.Chr.28.9, *PLond.*3.1178.54 (ii A.D.). Adv. -τως *perfectly*, Porph. *in Cat.*124.2.

ἀλείπ-τρια, ἡ, fem. of ἀλείπτης, Lys.*Fr.*88 S.; title of plays by Amphis, Antiph., etc. **-τρον**, f.l. for ἐξάλειπτρον, q.v.

ἀλείς, εἶσα, έν, v. εἴλω.

ἄλεισον [ᾰ], τό, *cup, goblet*, = δέπας (Ath.11.783a), χρύσειον Il.11. 774, Od.3.50, al.; περιστείχοντος ἀλείσου Call.*Aet.*1.1.13:—masc. **ἄλεισος** Ar.*Fr.*623. II. *hip-socket*, Marsyas ap.Ath.11.479c.

ἀλειτεία, ἡ, = ἀλίτημα, Suid.

ἀλείτης, ου, ὁ, *sinner*, of Paris and suitors of Penelope, Il.3.28, Od.20.121:—ἀλείτης τινός *sinner against* one, A.R.1.1338:—fem. **ἀλεῖτις** Hdn.Gr.2.67; cf. ἀλιταίνω, ἀλοιτός.

ἀλειτ-ουργησία, ἡ, *exemption from* λειτουργίαι, late word for Att. ἀτέλεια, Str.13.1.27, *IGRom.*4.295 (Pergam.), *POxy.*1.140.10 (ii/iii A.D.), *Sammelb.*4224.15 (i B.C.), etc.; censured as εὐτελές by Poll.8.156:—also **-ουργία**, ἡ, Benndorf-Niemann *Reise in Lykien* p.78 (Sidyma). **-ούργητος**, ον, *free from* λειτουργίαι, ἁ. πασᾶν τᾶν λειτουργιᾶν Decr.Byz.ap.D.18.91; πάσης ὑπουργίας Megasth.ap. D.S.2.40, cf. Din.*Fr.*89.5, *IG*2[2].682.17, *POxy.*62v (iii A.D.); ἁ. καὶ ἀνεπίσταθμος *IG*7.2413 (Thebes): metaph., ἡ θεία φύσις ἁ. διατηρείσθω Epicur.*Ep.*2 p.42 U.

ἄλειφα, τό, collat. form of sq., v.l. in Hes.*Th.*553, cf. *SIG*57.34 (Milet., vi/v B.C.), A.*Ag.*322, Call.*Fr.*12, Q.S.14.265.

ἄλειφαρ, ατος, τό, (ἀλείφω) *unguent, anointing-oil, oil, fat*, used in funeral sacrifices, Il.23.170, Od.3.408, etc.; ἄλειφαρ ἀπὸ κέδρου, ἀπὸ σιλλικυπρίων, *oil* of cedar, etc., Hdt.2.87,94; ἄ. ῥόδινον Hp.*Mul.*1. 74. II. *pitch* or *resin*, to seal wine-jars, Theoc.7.147.—Cf. foreg.

ἀλειφάς, άδος, ἡ, *blotting out, erasure*, πρᾶσιν καθαρὰν ἀπὸ ἀλειφάδος καὶ ἐπιγραφῆς *PRyl.*163.17 (ii A.D.).

ἀλειφᾰτίτης ἄρτος, ὁ, bread *baked with oil*, Epich.52.

ἀλειφεύς, ὁ, = ἀλείπτης, *Inscr.Prien.*313.716.

ἀλείφιον· ᾧ χρῶνται οἱ ἀλεῖπται, Hsch.

ἀλειφόβιος, ον, *one that lives by anointing*, contemptuous word for ἀλείπτης, Ar.*Fr.*740. 2. generally, *poor*, Ph.2.537, Hsch.

ἀλείφω, Hdt.3.8, etc.: fut. -ψω Lxx *Ex.*40.15, (ἐξ-) E.*IA*1486, Pl.*R.*386c: aor. ἤλειψα Hom., Att., Ep. ἄλειψα Od.12.177: pf. ἀλήλιφα (ἀπ-) D.52.29:—**Med.**, fut. -ψομαι Th.4.68: aor. ἠλειψάμην Att., Ep. ἀλ- Il.14.171:—**Pass.**, fut. ἀλειφθήσομαι (ἐξ-) D.25.73: aor. 1 ἠλείφθην Hp.*Morb.*4.54, Pl.*Ly.*217c, etc.: aor. 2 ἐξ-ηλίφην v.l. in Pl.*Phdr.*258b, (ἀπ-) D.C.55.3: pf. ἀλήλιμμαι Th.4.68, (ἐξ-, ὑπ-) D.25.70, X.*Oec.*10.6 (-ει- is freq. found in pf. forms in codd.): (ἀ- euph., λιπ-, cf. λίπος):—*anoint the skin with oil*, as was done after bathing, Act. referring to another, Med. to oneself, λοῦσαι κέλετ' ἀμφί τ' ἀλεῖψαι Il.24.582; Hom. elsewh. always adds λίπα or λίπ' ἐλαίῳ (v. sub λίπα), πάντα λοέσσατο καὶ λίπ' ἄλειψεν Od.6.227; λοεσσαμένω καὶ ἀλειψαμένω λίπ' ἐλαίῳ Il.10.577, cf. 14.171, 18.350: later of *anointing for gymnastic exercises*, λίπα μετὰ τοῦ γυμνάζεσθαι ἠλείψαντο Th.1.6; generally, λίπα ἀλείφεσθαι Id.4.68; βακκάρι ῥῖνας Hippon.41; of *anointing* the sick, Men.*Georg.*60, cf. *Ep.Jac.*5. 14. 2. *supply oil* for gymnasts, ἀλειφούσης τῆς πόλεως *CIG* (add.) 1957g (Maced.); ἁ. πανήγυριν, ἔθνη, *Inscr.Magn.*163, *OGI*533.47 (Ancyra); οἱ -όμενοι *youths undergoing gymnastic training*, ib. 339.72 (Sestos), etc.; οἱ ἁ. ἐν τῷ γυμνασίῳ ib.764.5 (Pergam.), al.; ἀλείφεσθαι παρά τινι *to attend* a *gymnastic school*, Arr.*Epict.*1.2. 26. 3. *polish*, τράπεζαν Diph.74; δακτύλιον Thphr.*Char.*21; ἀγάλματα Artem.2.33. 4. metaph., *prepare as if for gymnastics, encourage, stimulate, instigate*, Demad.17, Pl.ap.D.L.4.6; ἐπὶ τὴν πολιτικὴν ἀγωνίαν Phld.*Rh.*2.59 S.; τινὰ ἐπὶ τὸν Κλώδιον App.*BC*2. 16, cf. Plu.*Them.*3; τινὰ κατά τινος Ph.1.549; τινὰ ἐπὶ φαρμακείαν App.*Mac.*11.7:—Pass., τοὺς -ομένους ἐπί τι Phld.*Rh.*2.158 S. II. *daub, plaster, besmear*, οὔατα ἀλεῖψαι *stop up* ears, Od.12.47,177,200; ἁ. αἵματι Hdt.3.8; μίλτῳ X.*Oec.*10.5; ψιμυθίῳ Pl.*Ly.*217d; κυανῷ Paus.5.11.5.

ἄλειψις, εως, ἡ, *anointing*, Hp.*Hum.*10, Arist.*GA*785a30, Thphr. *Sud.*39, etc.: pl., Perict.ap.Stob.4.28.19. 2. *method* or *custom of anointing*, Hdt.3.22. 3. *polishing*, ἀνδριάντων *BGU*362 vii 14 (iii A.D.).

ἀλείωτος, ον, *not ground*, Gal.14.47.

ἀλεκινός· δυνατός, Cyr., Suid. (cf. ἀλικῖνος).

ἀλεκτόρ-ειος, ον, (ἀλέκτωρ) *of a fowl*, κόπρος Aët.2.118. **-ιδεύς**, έως, ὁ, *chicken*, Ael.*NA*7.47. **-ιον**, τό, *poultry-yard*, *IGRom.* 4.921 (Cibyra). **-ίς** [ῐ], ίδος, ἡ, fem. of ἀλέκτωρ, *hen*, Hp.*Int.* 27, *Nat.Puer.*29 (pl.), Epich.152,172, Hecat.58 (pl.):—used by Trag. and Com. acc. to Phryn.207 as generic name, cf. Arist.*HA*544a32, 614b10, Diocl.*Fr.*141, Herod.6.100, etc.; Ἀδριαναὶ ἁ., a small kind, Arist.*HA*558b16. II. = θρὶξ ἡ ἀπὸ τῆς κεφαλῆς τρεφομένη, Hsch., cf. *EM*59.24. **-ίσκος**, ὁ, Dim. of ἀλέκτωρ, *cockerel*, Babr.5.1, Aesop.341.12: as ornament, ἁ. χαλκοῦς Roussel *Cultes Égyptiens* 230 (Delos). **-ον**, ου, τό, = ἀλέκτωρ, *PLond.*3.1259.25 (iv A.D.). **-οφωνία**, ἡ, *cock-crow*, i.e. third watch of night, Str.7 *Fr.*35, *Ev.Marc.*13.35.

ἄλεκτος, ον, *not to be told, indescribable*, Hp.*Ep.*13, Pherecr.157, Plb.30.22.12, App.*Hann.*40.

ἄλεκτρος, ον, *unwedded*, S.*Ant.*917, Heraclit.*All.*44; ἄλεκτρ', ἄνυμφα γάμων ἁμιλλήματα marriage *that is no marriage*, i.e. unhallowed marriage, S.*El.*492; ἄ. ζόα E.*Tr.*254 (lyr.); ἄλεκτρα γηράσκουσαν, as Adv., S.*El.*962.

ἀλεκτρύαινα, ἡ, fem. of ἀλεκτρυών, coined by Ar.*Nu.*666.

ἀλεκτρυ-όνειος, ον, *of a fowl*, κρέα Hp.*Int.*9. **-όνιον**, τό, Dim. of ἀλεκτρυών, Ephipp.15.8. **-ονίς**, = ἀλεκτορίς, Sch.Ar. *Nu.*226 (Suid. ἀλεκτορίς), cf. Gal.12.285. **-ονοπώλης**, ου, ὁ, *poulterer*, Poll.7.136. **-ονοτρόφος**, ὁ, *cock-feeder*, Aeschin.Socr. 14:—also **-οτρόφος** (sic), ὁ, *IG*5(1).771 (Sparta). **-ονώδης**, ες, *like a cock*, πρὸς ἡδονάς, prob. for -υώδης, Eun.*Hist.*p.266 D. **-οπώλιον**, τό, *poultry-market*, Phryn.Com.13. **-ών** [ᾰ], όνος, ὁ, *cock*, Thgn.864, etc., cf. Arist.*HA*536a28, etc.; ἤδη ἁ. ᾀδόντων at *cock-crow*, Pl.*Smp.*223c. 2. ἁ. Νομάς or Νομαδικός *guinea-fowl*, Luc. *Nav.*23. II. ἡ, *hen*, Ar.*Nu.*663, *Fr.*185, Pl.Com.19.20, Theopomp.Com.9, etc.

ἀλέκτωρ (A), [ᾰ], ορος, ὁ, poet. form of ἀλεκτρυών, *cock*, ἕως ἐβόησεν ἁ. Batr.192, cf. Pi.*O.*12.14, Simon.80 B, A.*Ag.*1671, *Eu.*861, Herod.4.12, etc.; later Prose, Arist.*Fr.*347, *PTeb.*140 (i B.C.), Lxx *Pr.*24.66 (30.31), *Ev.Matt.*26.34, al., *IG*3.77: metaph., of a trumpeter, κοινὸς Ἀθηναίων ἁ. Demad.*Fr.*4; of a flute, Ion Trag.39. 2. ἀλέκτορος λόφος *yellow rattle, Rhinanthus major*, Plin.*HN*27.40. II. *husband, consort*, Tz. *in Lyc.*1094, and so perh. in B.4.8, S.*Fr.*851. (Perh., like ἀκοίτης, ἄλοχος, from ἀ- copul., λέκτρον.)

ἀλέκτωρ (B), ορος, ἡ, (ἀ- priv., λέγω) = ἄλεκτρος, Ath.3.98b.

ἀλέκω [ᾰ], = ἀλέξω, *ward off*, ἀλέκοις πενίην, prob. for ἀλέγοις, *AP* 6.245 (Diod.):—for fut. ἀλέξω, etc., v. sub ἀλέξω.

ἀλέλαιον, τό, *salt in oil*, [Gal.]14.386.

ἀλέματος, ἀλεμάτως, Dor for ἠλεμ-.

ἄλεν and **ἀλέν**, v. εἴλω.

ἀλεξαίθριος, ον, *screening from chill air*, S.*Fr.*117.

Ἀλεξανδρ-ίζω, *to be on Alexander's side*, Apolloph.ap.Phylarch. 46. **-ιστής**, οῦ, ὁ, *partisan of Alexander*, Chares ap.Plu.*Alex.*24.

Ἀλεξανδροκόλαξ, ακος, ὁ, *flatterer of Alexander*, Chares ap.Ath.12. 538f.

ἀλέξανδρος, ον, *defending men*, πόλεμος Epigr.ap.D.S.11.14: fem., epith. of Hera, Menaechm.3. II. freq. as pr. n., esp. of Paris in Il., cf. A.*Ag.*61,363.

Ἀλεξανδρώδης, ες, *Alexander-like*, Men.924.

ἀλεξ-ἄνέμας [ᾰ], α, ὁ, *averting wind*, applied to Empedocles, Porph.*VP*29. **-άνεμος**, ον, = foreg., Od.14.529, Ph.1.666, Alciphr. 3.41:—also **-ήνεμος**, ον, Eust.1767.43. **-ημα**, ατος, τό, *defence, guard, help*, A.*Pr.*479: c. gen., *remedy for*, ὀδύνης Hp.*Mul.*2.212; *protection* against, κρύους καὶ θάλπους Gal.*UP*12.3; ὑπονοίας Longin. 17.2; ἁ. πρός τι D.H.7.13, Paus.10.18.3. **-ήνωρ**, ορος, ὁ, *aiding man*, as name of physician, Paus.2.11.6 (in Dor. form -άνωρ). **-ησις**, εως, ἡ, *keeping off, defence*, πρὸς ἁ. τραπέσθαι Hdt.9.18. 2. *helping, assistance*, Hp.*Ep.*16. **-ήτειρα**, ἡ, *AP*9.764 (Paul. Sil.), Nonn.*D.*25.529: fem. of **-ητήρ**, ῆρος, ὁ, *one who keeps off*, ἁ. μάχης *stemmer* of battle, Il.20.396; λοιμοῦ ἁ. *a protector from* plague, A.R.2.519; κακῶν *IG*14.1003.25:—rare in Prose, ταῖς πατρίσιν ἀλεξητῆρες εἶναι X.*Oec.*4.3. II. as Adj., θυμὸς ἁ. Opp.*H.*4. 42. **-ητήριος**, α, ον, *able to keep off, defend*, or *help*, esp. as epith. of gods, Ζεὺς ἁ. A.*Th.*8; ξύλον ἁ. club *for defence*, E.*HF*470. 2. ἀλεξητήριον (sc. φάρμακον), τό, *remedy, medicine*, Hp.*Acut.*54; *protection*, X.*Eq.*5.6; ἁ. τῆς δηλήσεως *charm against*.., Thphr.*HP*7.13. 4; ἁ. νούσων Nic.*Th.*7, *IG*9(1).881.3 (Corcyra); ὄρη ἁ. ὑετῶν Aristid. *Or.*48(1).11. **-ητικός**, ή, όν, *preventive*, ἀγαθά Alex.Aphr. *de An.* 162.16. **-ήτωρ**, ορος, ὁ, = ἀλεξητήρ, Ζεῦ ἀλεξῆτορ S.*OC*143, cf. Apollod.Hist.30.

ἀλεξι-άρη [ᾱρ], ἡ, (ἀρή, Ἄρης) *she that guards from death and ruin*, Hes.*Op.*464; ἁ. ῥάμνος wand *that served as amulet*, Nic.*Th.*861:—masc. **ἀλεξιάρης** Hsch. **-βέλεμνος**, ον, *keeping off darts*, *AP*6.81 (Paul. Sil.). **-γάμος**, ον, *shunning marriage*, Βάκχαι Nonn.*D.* 40.541. **-κάκος**, ον, *keeping off ill* or *mischief*, μῆτις Il.10.20, cf. Hes.*Op.*123 (as v.l.), Ar.*V.*1043, Paus.8.41.8; ῥάμνος Euph.137; τὸ ἁ. τῆς ἐπιστήμης Hierocl. *in CA*12 p.447 M.: c. gen., δίψης ἁ. *AP*6. 170 (Thyill.): epith. of Heracles, Luc.*Alex.*4, etc.; of Hermes, Ar. *Pax*422; ὠλεξίκακε *save the mark!* Ar.*Nu.*1372; of Zeus, *Tab.Defix. Aud.*26.2 (Crete, iv/iii B.C.), Plu.2.1076b. **-κηπος**, ὁ, title of work on gardening by Nestor, *Gp.*12.16.1, 12.17.16. **-λογος**, ον, *promoting* or *supporting discourse*, γράμματα dub. in Critias 2.10, cf. *AB* 382. -μβροτος, ον, *protecting mortals*, λόγχη Pi.*N.*8.30; ἀ. πομπαί sacred processions *which shield men from ill*, Id.*P.*5.91. -μορος, ον, *warding off death*, τρισσοὶ ἀ., i.e. Apollo, Artemis, Athena, S.*OT* 164.

ἀλέξιον, τό, = ἀλεξητήριον, Nic.*Th.*702 (v.l. ἀλέξιμον, cf. Phot.), 805, *Al.*4. **ἀλεξίπονος**, ον, *warding off pain*, S.(?)*Eleg.*7, *Carm. Pop.*47.10; σοφία Maced.*Pae.*10. **ἄλεξις**, εως, ἡ, *help*, *EM* 59. 23. II. Κῷοι ἄλεξιν τὸν Ἡρακλέα νομίζουσιν Aristid.1.34 J.

ἀλεξι-φάρμᾰκος, *acting as antidote*, μανίης *against* it, Hp.*Ep.* 10. II. ἀλεξιφάρμακον, τό, *antidote*, Thphr.*HP* 9.15.7; Ἀλεξιφάρμακα, title of poem by Nic. 2. *charm, spell*, Ἐφέσια τοῖς γαμοῦσιν.. λέγων ἀ. Men.371. 3. generally, *remedy*, τινός *against* a thing, Pl.*Lg.*957d, cf. Muson.*Fr.*17 p.91 H. -χορος, ον, *helping* or *favouring the chorus*, ἀοιδαί *IG* 3.171^c 17.

ἀλέξω [ᾰ], Ep. inf. ἀλεξέμεναι, -έμεν Hom., v. infr.: fut. ἀλεξήσω Il.9.251: aor. opt. ἀλεξήσειε Od.3.346:—Med., fut. ἀλεξήσομαι Hdt. 8.81,108.—Besides these tenses (formed as if from ἀλεξέω), we find others formed from **ἀλέκω**, fut. ἀλέξω, aor. ἤλεξα (v. sub ἀπ-αλέξω):—Med., fut. ἀλέξομαι S.*OT* 171,539, X.*An.*7.7.3: aor. ἀλέξασθαι Il., Hp.*Salubr.*1, Hdt.7.207, X.*An.*1.3.6, al.:—for aor. 2 ἄλαλκε, ἀλκαθεῖν, v. sub vocc. (Cf. Skt. *rákṣati* 'protect'):—*ward off, turn aside*, constructed like ἀμύνω:—c. acc. rei, Ζεὺς τό γ' ἀλεξήσειε Od.3.346: c. acc. rei et dat. pers., Δαναοῖσιν ἀλεξήσειν κακὸν ἦμαρ *will ward* it *off from* them, Il.9.251, cf. 20.315; ἀλλήλοις.. ἀλεξέμεναι φόνον αἰπύν 17.365, etc.: c. dat. pers. only, *assist, defend*, ἀλεξέμεν ἀλλήλοισιν Il. 3.9, cf. 5.779, al., X.*Cyr.*4.3.2: abs., *lend aid*, Il.1.590:—Med., ἀλέξασθαι *keep off from oneself*, κύνας ἠδὲ καὶ ἄνδρας Il.13.475, cf. Hdt.7. 207; ἀλέξεσθαι περί τινι or τινος, A.R.4.551,1488: abs., *defend oneself*, Il.11.348, 15.565, Archil.66, Hdt.1.211, 2.63, al., Hp. l.c., S. *OT* 539, X.*Cyr.*1.5.13: c. dat. instrum., οὐδ' ἔνι φροντίδος ἔγχος, ᾧ τις ἀλέξεται S.*OT* 171. 2. in Med., also, *recompense, requite*, τοὺς εὖ καὶ κακῶς ποιοῦντας ἀλεξόμενος X.*An.*1.9.11.—Not in A. or E. (exc. ἀπ-).

ἀλέομαι [ᾰλ], contr. **ἀλεῦμαι** Thgn.575, pres. part. ἀλευόμενοι Hes. *Op.*535 (v.l.), ἀλευμένη Semon.7.61: impf. ἀλέοντο (ἐξ-) Il.18.586:—chiefly used by Hom. in aor. ἀλευάμην, v. infr.; inf. ἀλέασθαι, -εύασθαι, Hes.*Op.*734, 505; subj. ἀλεύεται Od.14.400; part. ἀλευάμενος 9. 277, Thgn.400. (Perh. from same Root as ἄλη, ἀλάομαι: ἀλεϝ- as aor. shows):—*avoid, shun*, c. acc. rei, ἔγχεα δ' ἀλλήλων ἀλεώμεθα Il. 6.226, cf. 13.184; ἐμὸν ἔγχος ἄλευαι 22.285; ἀλεύατο κῆρα μέλαιναν 3.360; Διὸς δ' ἀλεώμεθα μῆνιν 5.34; ὄφρα τὸ κῆτος.. ἀλέαιτο 20.147; κακὸν.. τό κεν οὔτις.. ἀλέαιτο Od.20.368; μύθους μὲν ὑπερφιάλους ἀλέασθε 4.774: rarely c. acc. pers., θεοὺς ἢ δειδίμεν ἢ ἀλέασθαι 9.274: c. inf., *avoid* doing, λίθου δ' ἀλέασθαι ἐπαυρεῖν Il.23.340; ἀλεύεται (Ep. subj.) ἠπεροπεύειν Od.14.400. 2. abs., *flee for one's life*, τὸν μὲν ἀλευάμενον τὸν δὲ κτάμενον Il.5.28; οὔτε.. φυγέειν δύνατ' οὔτ' ἀλέασθαι 13.436; μή πως.. ἀλέηται Od.4.396.

ἀλεός, όν, = ἀλεεινός, Hsch. II. = ἠλεός, Hdn.Gr.2.909, *EM* 59.45.

ἀλεόσσω· ματαΐζω, Hsch.; cf. ἀλεώσσω.

ἀλεότης, ητος, ἡ, (ἀλής) *assemblage*, Hp.ap.Gal.19.75.

ἀλεόφρων, ον, gen. ονος, = Homer's φρένας ἠλεός, Hsch., *EM* 59. 45.

ἀλεπαδνόν· ἄζευκτον, Hsch. **ἀλέπεσσι**· στέατι, Id.

ἀλεπίδωτος, ον, *without scales*, σελάχη Arist.*PA* 697^a 7: to be read for ἄλεπος, Ael.*NA* 12.27, and prob. for ἀλέπιδος, Ph.2.352.

ἀλέπιστος, ον, *not scaled, unscaled*, Archestr.*Fr.*45.8 B. II. *unpeeled*, καρπός *Gp.*10.11.1; of flax, *not scutched*, Sch.Ar.*Lys.* 737.

ἀλέρα, dub. in Hdn.Gr.1.260. **ἀλέρον**· κόπρον, Hsch.

ἄλ-εσις, εως, ἡ, (ἀλέω) *grinding*, *Gp.*2.32.1. -εσμα, ατος, τό, *anything ground*, ἐλαιῶν *EM* 216.22. -εσμός, ὁ, *grinding*, J.*AJ* 3.10.5. -εσούριος, ὁ, a fish, = καλλιώνυμος, *EM* 59.52; also a shell-fish, Hsch. -εστέον, *one must grind*, Dsc.5.88: pl. -τέα Poll.1.226. -εστρον, τό, *cost of grinding*, *POxy.*739.6 (i A.D.).

ἀλέ-της, ου, ὁ, *grinder*, ὄνος *GDI* 4992 (Gortyn, v B.C.), cf. X.*An.* 1.5.5. -τικός, ἡ, όν, *for grinding*, [μηχανή] *PRyl.*321.5 (ii A.D.). -τός, ὁ, *grinding*, Plu.*Ant.*45; cf. ἀλητός. -τρεύω, fut. -εύσω, Lyc.159, strengthd. from ἀλέω, *grind*, Od.7.104, Hes.*Fr.* 264, A.R.4.1095, Babr.129. -τρίβᾰνος [ῑ], ὁ, (τρίβω) (Asiatic for δοῖδυξ, acc. to Crat.Mall.ap.Sch.Ar. l.c.), *pestle*, Ar.*Pax* 259, al. -τρίς, ίδος, ἡ, *female slave who grinds corn*, γυνὴ ἀλετρίς Od. 20.105, cf. *Lyr.Adesp.*21, Call.*Del.*242, Ph.2.102, Zos.3.22. 2. at Athens, *one of the noble maidens who prepared meal* for offering-cakes, Ar.*Lys.*643, Eust.1885.9. -τροπόδιον, τό, i.e. ἀλεκτρο-, late name for the *constellation Orion*, interp. in Anon.*II Intr.Arat.*p.116 Maass. -τών, ῶνος, ὁ, = ἀλέτης, ἀ. ὄνος *upper millstone*, Alex. 13; also ἀλετών alone, Dieuchid.7.

ἀλετώρια· ἀσεβῆ, πονηρά, ἀθέμιστα, ἁμαρτήματα, Hsch.

ἀλεύκαντος, ον, *not growing white*, τρίχες *Cat.Cod.Astr.*8(3).157, cf. *Gloss.*

ἀλεύρειν· ἀφεστάναι, Hsch.

ἀλεύρινος, ον, *made of* ἄλευρον, ἄρτος, σταῖς, Dieuch.ap.Orib.4.5. 1,5.

ἀλευρίτης ἄρτος, ὁ, bread *of wheaten flour* (ἄλευρα), Diph.Siph.ap. Ath.3.115c, Philistion ib.d; πυροί Ath.Med.ap.Orib.1.2.2.

ἀλευροδοῦντες, οἱ, kind of *wheaten cakes*, dub. in Anticl.20.

ἀλευρό-κλεψ, ὁ, *flour-thief*, Hdn.Gr.1.246. -μαντεῖον, τό, *divination from flour*, Oenom.ap.Eus.*PE* 5.25. -μαντις, εως, ὁ, *one that divines from flour*, Hsch.; epith. of Apollo, Phot.

ἄλευρον (A), [ᾰ], τό, mostly in pl. **ἄλευρα**, (ἀλέω A) = ἀλείατα, *wheat-meal* (opp. ἄλφιτα *barley-meal*), Hdt.7.119; ἐκ μὲν τῶν κριθῶν ἄλφιτα σκευαζόμενοι, ἐκ δὲ τῶν πυρῶν ἄλευρα Pl.*R.*372b, cf. *Epin.*975b, X.*An.*1.5.6, Arist.*Pr.*863^b 2: in sg., Ar.*Fr.*50, Sotad.Com.1.24, Arist.*Pr.*927^a 11, Theoc.14.7. 2. generally, *meal*, ἄ. κρίθινον Dsc. 1.72; τήλινον 3.40, cf. 2.102; made from dried sorbs, 1.120.

ἄλευρον (B)· τάφος (Cypr.), Hsch.

ἀλευρο-ποιέω, *make into flour*, *POxy.*1454.9 (ii A.D.), *EM* 62. 54. -ποιία, ἡ, Eust.1835.42.

ἄλευρος, ἡ, = ἄλευρον, *Et.Gud.z.*

ἀλευρόττησις, εως, ἡ, (cf. δια-ττάω) *flour-sieve*, Poll.6.74, *AB* 382. II. *flour sifted, fine flour*, Suid.

ἀλευρώδης, ες, *like flour*, Gal.12.212; ἄρτος Lyc.(?)ap.Orib.9. 26.8.

ἄλευστος, ον, (λεύσσω) *unseen*, Hsch.

ἀλεύω, used rarely by Trag. in lyr. passages as Act. of ἀλεύομαι (v. ἀλέομαι), *remove, keep far away*, imper. ἄλευ' ἃ Δᾶ A.*Pr.*567: fut. ἀλεύσω S.*Fr.*993: aor. imper., ἄλευσον ἀνδρῶν ὕβριν A.*Supp.*528, cf. *Th.*141; ἰὼ θεοί.. κακὸν ἀλεύσατε ib.87.

ἀλεφάτισον· ἄλειψον, Hsch.

ἀλέω (A), [ᾰ]: impf. ἤλουν Pherecr.10.1: aor. ἤλεσα Id.183, Hp.*Fist.* 7, *Steril.*230, etc.; Ep. ἄλεσσα (κατ-) Od.20.109: pf. ἀλήλεκα *AP* 11. 251 (Nicarch.):—Pass., pf. ἀλήλεσμαι Hp.ap.Gal.19.76, Hdt.7.23; ἀλήλεμαι Th.4.26, Amph.9: aor. ἠλέσθην Dsc.1.120:—*grind, bruise*, Hom. only in compd. κατ-αλέω, q.v.; ἤλουν τὰ σιτία Pherecr. l.c.; βίος ἀληλεμένος *civilized* life, in which one uses *ground* corn and not raw fruits, Amph. l.c.; ἄλει, μύλα, ἄλει *grind*, mill, *grind!* *Carm. Pop.*43: metaph., ὀψὲ θεῶν ἀλέουσι μύλαι, ἀλέουσι δὲ λεπτά Poet.ap. S.E.*M.*1.287.

***ἀλέω** (B), only in Med. ἀλέομαι, q.v.

ἀλεωρή, Att. -ρά, ἡ, (ἀλέομαι) *escape*, Il.24.216; ἀ. τινα εὑρέσθαι Hdt.9.6. 2. *place of shelter*, Opp.*H.*1.790. 3. c. gen., *defence* or *shelter from*, δηΐων ἀνδρῶν ἀ., of palisade, Il.12.57; of breastplate, 15.533; σκευὴν βελέων ἀ. (mock heroic) Ar.*V.*615; τὴν περὶ τὸ σῶμα ἀ. Arist.*PA* 687^a 29; of an animal's shell, etc., ib.679^b 28, cf. *HA* 488^b 10; τῆς περὶ τοὺς ἱέρακας ἕνεκα ἀ. ib.613^b 11; ἀ. παρέχειν, ποιεῖν, Hp. *Praec.*7, D.S.3.34.

ἀλ⟨ε⟩ώσσω· μωραίνω, Hsch.

ἄλη [ᾰ], ἡ, *wandering* or *roaming* without home or hope of rest, Od.10.464, E.*Or.*56 (pl.); θεία ἄ., as etym. of ἀλήθεια, Pl.*Cra.*421b; in later Prose, Plu.*Mar.*45, Hld.7.6 (pl.), etc.; in pl., of the blood in fever, Hp.*Flat.*8. 2. *wandering of mind, distraction*, E.*Med.* 1285. II. Act., πνοαὶ βροτῶν ἄλαι winds *that keep* men *wandering*, A.*Ag.*194.

ἀλή, ἡ, only pl. ἀλαί *salt-works*, ἀλαὶ τῶν ὀρυκτῶν ἁλῶν Str.12.3. 39; Ἄλυς.. ὠνόμασται ἀπὸ τῶν ἀλῶν ἃς παραρρεῖ Id.12.3.12; ἀλάς, ἀλαῖς shd. be read for ἄλλας, ἄλλαις D.H.3.41, cf. 2.55, *PRyl.*92.22 (iii A.D.).

ἀληγός, όν, *carrying salt*, Plu.2.685e.

ἀληδόν· ἀθρόως, ἐξαίφνης, Hsch.

ἀληθάργητος, ον, *free from lethargy, energetic*, εὐεργέτης *CIG* 2804 (Aphrod.); γυνή *JRS* 2.92 (Antioch. Pisid.), cf. Hsch. s.v. ἀλήστων.

ἀλήθ-εια [ᾰλ], ἡ, Dor. **ἀλάθεια** (also ἀλαθείᾱ B.12.204); ἀλάθεα Alc.57, Theoc.29.1 is neut. pl. of ἀλᾱθής; Ep. (and Early Att. acc. to Hdn.Gr.2.454) **ἀληθείᾱ**; Ion. **ἀληθείη**: I. *truth*, opp. *lie* or *mere appearance*: 1. in Hom. only opp. *a lie*, freq. in phrase ἀληθείην καταλέξαι Il.24.407, al.; ἀ. ἀποειπεῖν 23.361; παιδὸς πᾶσαν ἀ. μυθεῖσθαι to tell whole *truth* about the lad, Od.11.507; ἀλάθει' ἀτρεκής Pi.*N.*5.17, cf. B. l.c.; prov., οἶνος καὶ ἀ. '*in vino veritas*', Alc. l.c., etc.; ἁπλᾶ γάρ ἐστι τῆς ἀ. ἔπη A.*Fr.*176, cf. E.*Ph.*469; χρᾶσθαι τῇ ἀ. Hdt.1.116; εἰπεῖν τὴν ἀ. Id.6.69; ἡ ἀ. περί τινος Th.4.122, S. *Tr.*91; ἀ. ἔχειν to be *true*, Arist.*Pol.*1281^a 42: pl., ταῖς ἀ. χρῆσθαι Isoc.9.5; τὰς ἀ. λέγειν Men.87,925; τὰς ἀ. ἀκοῦσαι τῶν γενομένων Alcid.*Od.*13:—Ἀλήθεια or περὶ Ἀληθείας, title of works by Protag., Pl.*Tht.*161c, *Cra.*391c; by Antipho Soph., *POxy.*1364, cf. Hermog. *Id.*2.11, etc. 2. after Hom. also *truth, reality*, opp. *appearance*, σὺν ἀλαθείᾳ καλῶν B.3.96; ἡ ἀ. τῶν πραχθέντων Antipho 2.4.1; τῶν ἔργων ἡ ἀ. Th.2.41; μιμήματα ἀληθείας Pl.*Plt.*300c:—in adverb. usages, τῇ ἀ. *in very truth*, Th.4.120, etc.; ταῖς ἀ. Isoc.15.283, cf. Philem.130, Plb.10.40.5, Babr.75.20; rarely (without the Art.) ἀληθείᾳ Pl.*Prt.*343d:—with Preps., ἐν τῇ ἀ. Pl.*La.*183d; ἐπὶ τῆς ἀληθείας καὶ τοῦ πράγματος *in truth and reality*, D.21.72; ἐπ' ἀληθείᾳ *for the sake of truth*, A.*Supp.*628, Ar.*Pl.*891; also, *according to truth and nature*, Theoc.7.44:—μετ' ἀληθείας X.*Mem.*2.1.27, D.2.4:—κατὰ τὴν ἀ. Isoc.1.2.46, etc.; κατ' ἀλήθειαν Arist.*Pol.*1278^b 33, etc.:—ξὺν ἀληθείᾳ A.*Ag.*1567:—πρὸς ἀλήθειαν D.S.5.67, etc. 3. *real war*, opp. *exercise* or *parade*, Plb.10.20.4, al.; ἐπ' αὐτῆς τῆς ἀ. Id.1.21. 3. 4. *true event, realization* of dream or omen, Hdt.3.64, Damon ap.Sch.Ar.*Pl.*1003. II. of persons, *truthfulness, sincerity*, Hdt. 1.55; ἀλαθείᾳ φρενῶν A.*Ag.*1550, cf. Pl.*R.*331c, Arist.*EN* 1108^a 20. III. Ἀ. personified, Emp.1, Parm.1.29, etc. IV. *symbol of truth, jewel* worn by Egyptian high-priest, D.S.1.48,75, Ael. *VH* 14.34: of the Thummim, Lxx *Le.*8.8. -ευσις, εως, ἡ, *possession of truth*, S.E.*M.*7.394. -ευτής, οῦ, ὁ, *truth-speaking person*, ἀ. λόγων Max.Tyr.21.6. -ευτικός, ή, όν, *truthful, frank, candid*, Arist.*EN* 1127^a 24, al.; τὸ ἀ. Hierocl.*in CA* 2 p.422 M. Adv. -κῶς Eust.385.6, etc. -εύω, fut. -εύσω X.*Mem.*1.1.5, al.:—*speak truth*,

A. *Th.*562, Hp.*Prog.*15, Pl.*R.*589c; περί τι Id.*Tht.*202b: with neut. Adj., ἀ. πάντα *speak truth* in all things, Batr.14; πολλὰ ἀ. X.*An.*4.4.15; τὰς δέκα ἡμέρας ἠλήθευσε he *rightly foretold*.., ib.5.6.18; ἀ. τοὺς ἐπαίνους *prove* their praises *true*, Luc.*Ind.*20; τοὔνομα 'make good', Them.*Or.*1.4c. 2. of things, *to be, prove true*, σημεῖα Hp.*Prog.*25:—Pass., *to be fulfilled*, of conditions, ἐπὶ τούτοις -ομένοις X.*Cyr.*4.6.10, freq. in Arist.:—Act. of reasoners, *arrive at truth*, Id.*Metaph.*1062ᵃ25:—Pass., ὁ λόγος -εύεται *is in accordance with truth*, *Top.*132ᵇ4, al.; ἀληθεύεσθαι κατά τινος *to be truly predicated of* .., ib.132ᵃ31, al.: fut. Med. in same sense, *EN*1100ᵃ35, al. -ής [ᾰ], Dor. **ἀλᾱθής**, ές, (λήθω, = λανθάνω: ἀληθὲς τὸ μὴ λήθῃ ὑποπῖπτον *EM*62.51):—*unconcealed*, so *true, real*, opp. *false, apparent*: I. Hom., opp. ψευδής, in phrases ἀληθέα μυθήσασθαι, εἰπεῖν, ἀγορεύειν, ἀληθὲς ἐνισπεῖν, Il.6.382, Od.13.254, 3.254,247, al.; in Hdt. and Att. τὸ ἀληθές, by Trag. crasis τἀληθές, Ion. τὠληθές (Hdt.6.68, 69), or τὰ ἀληθῆ, by crasis τἀληθῆ, etc.; ἀληθεῖ λόγῳ χρᾶσθαι Hdt.1.14, etc.; οἱ ἀληθεῖ λόγῳ βασιλέες 1.120; ἀληθεστάτη πρόφασις Th.1.23. 2. of persons, etc., *truthful, honest* (not in Hom., v. infr.), ἀ. νόος Pi.*O.*2.92; κατήγορος A.*Th.*439; κριτής Th.3.56; οἶνος ἀ. '*in vino veritas*', Pl.*Smp.*217e; ὁ μέσος ἀ. τις Arist.*EN*1108ᵃ20. 3. of oracles, *true, unerring*, ἀλαθέα μαντίων θῶκον Pi.*P.*11.6, cf. S.*Ph.*993, E.*Ion* 1537; of dreams, A.*Th.*710. II. of qualities or events, *true, real*, φίλος E.*Or.*424; ἀ. τὸ πραχθέν Antipho 1.6; *genuine*, ἀ. εἶναι δεῖ τὸ σεμνόν, οὐ κενόν Men.596. 2. *realizing itself, coming to fulfilment*, ἀρά A.*Th.*944. III. Adv. ἀληθῶς, Ion. -θέως, *truly*, Simon.5.1, Hdt.1.11, al., A.*Supp.*315, etc. b. *actually, in reality*, γένος τόδε Ζηνός ἐστιν ἀ. ib.585; ἀ. οὐδὲν ἐξῃκασμένα Id.*Ag.*1244, cf. Th.1.22, etc.; τὴν ἀ. μουσικήν (sc. οὖσαν) Antiph.209.6:—ὡς ἀ. *in the true way, really*, E.*Or.*739, Pl.*Phd.*63a, etc.; ἡ μὲν γὰρ ὡς ἀ. μήτηρ D.21.149: Comp. -εστέρως Pl.*R.*347e, -έστερον Antipho 3.3.4: Sup. -έστατα X.*Mem.*4.8.1. 2. neut. as Adv., proparox. ἄληθες; *indeed? really?* ironically, S.*OT* 350, *Ant.*758, E.*Cyc.*241, Ar.*Ra.*840, *Av.*174. 3. τὸ ἀληθές *truly*, Ion. τὠληθές Herod.7.70. B. *not forgetting, careful*, γυνὴ χερνῆτις ἀ. Il.12.433, cf. Nonn.*D.*24.233:—the sense *honest* is post-Hom. -ίζω, *dye with genuine purple*, *PHolm.*18.6. II. Med. -ίζομαι, = ἀληθεύω, Hdt.1.136, 3.72, Plu.2.230b, Alciphr.3.39, 59. -ικός, ή, όν, = ἀληθινός, Ps.-Callisth.1.4.

ἀληθινο-λογέω, *speak truly*, Phld.*Rh.*1.286, 2.158S. (Pass.). -λογία, ἡ, *speaking truth*, Pl.ap.Poll.2.124, Plb.12.26ᴰ.1.

ἀληθινόν· τὸ κοπανιστήριον, Hsch.

ἀληθινό-πινος (-πειν- Pap.), ον, *with genuine patina*, ἐνώτια *CPR* 22.6 (ii A.D.). -πόρφυρος, ον, *of genuine purple*, *POxy.*114 (ii/iii A.D.).

ἀληθινός, ή, όν, *agreeable to truth*: 1. of persons, *truthful, trusty*, στράτευμα, φίλοι, X.*An.*1.9.17, D.9.12, cf. Posidipp.26. Adv. -νῶς, φιλεῖν X.*Smp.*9.5: Sup. -ώτατα Plb.39.37. 2. of things, *true, genuine*, Pl.*R.*499c, Arist.*EN*1107ᵃ31 (Comp.); esp. of purple, πορφυρίς X.*Oec.*10.3, cf. *Edict.Diocl.*24.6; ἰχθύς Amph.26; πέλαγος Men.65; λόγος Id.*Sam.*114; τὰ ἀ. *real objects*, opp. τὰ γεγραμμένα, Arist.*Pol.*1281ᵇ12; of persons, ἐς ἀ. ἄνδρ' ἀποβῆναι to turn out a *genuine* man, Theoc.13.15: Astron., *true* (opp. φαινόμενος *apparent*), of risings and settings, Autol.1 *Def.*1, al. II. Adv. -νῶς *truly, really*, opp. γλίσχρως, Isoc.5.142; ζῶντα ἀ. *really* alive, Pl.*Ti.*19b; ἀ. γεγάμηκεν; Antiph.221. 2. *honestly, straightforwardly*, *OGI* 223.17 (Erythrae).

Ἀληθιών, ῶνος, sc. μήν, month at Iasos, *Leipz.Stud.*7.397.

ἀληθο-επής, ές, = ἀψευδής, Hsch. -μαντις, εως ὁ, ἡ, *prophet of truth*, A.*Ag.*1241, Ph.2.176. -μῡθέω, *speak truth*, Democr.225. -μῡθος, ον, *speaking truth*, Id.44.

ἀληθ-ορκέω, *swear truly*, Chrysipp.*Stoic.*2.63. -οσύνη, ἡ, poet. for ἀλήθεια, Thgn.1226. -ότης, ητος, ἡ, = ἀλήθεια, Ph.1.111, S.E.*M.*8.472. -ουργής, ές, *acting truly*, Heraclit.*All.* 67 (Comp.).

ἀλήθω [ᾰ], = Att. ἀλέω (A), mostly pres. (and impf., Lxx *Nu.*11.8), Hp.*Vict.*1.20, Thphr.*CP*4.12.13, D.S.3.13, *AP*11.154 (Lucill.), *POxy.*908.26 (ii A.D.); prob. in Herod.2.20 (sens. obsc.): aor. part. Pass. ἀλησθέν *Gp.*9.19.7.

Ἀλήιον πεδίον, τό, (ἄλη) lit. *land of wandering*, in Lycia or Cilicia, κὰπ πεδίον τὸ Ἀλήιον οἶος ἀλᾶτο.. πάτον ἀνθρώπων ἀλεείνων (with play on ἀλᾶτο, ἀλεείνων) Il.6.201, cf. Hdt.6.95.

ἀλήϊον, τό, v. ἀλήσιον. **ἀλήιος**, ον, (λήιον) *without cornlands, poor in lands*, or (ληΐς) *without booty*, opp. πολυλήιος, Il.9.125, 267. **ἀληίς**· ἄκλοπος, ἀπόρθητος, Hsch. **ἄληκτος** (A), ον, (λήγω) *unceasing*, πένθος *IG*14.2126.6; δίψα Ph.1.381, al.; *interminable*, βυβλίον Demetr.Lac.*Herc.*1061.7. Adv. ἀλήκτως Ph.2.420; ἀ. ἔχειν τινός Eun.*VSp.*458.26B. **ἄληκτος** (B), ον, = ἄδαστος, Eust.64.40; cf. ἀλλ-. **ἀλήλεκα**, -λεμαι or -λεσμαι, v. ἀλέω (A). **ἀλήλῖφα**, -λιμμαι, v. ἀλείφω. **ἄλημα** [ᾰλ], ατος, τό, (ἀλέω A) *fine meal*: metaph., of a *fine-witted, wily knave*, as Ulysses, S.*Aj.*381, 390 (lyr.), cf. *Ant.*320 (v.l.). II. (ἀλάομαι), = ὁδοιπορία, Hsch. **ἀλήμεναι, ἀλῆναι**, v. εἴλω.

ἀλημ-οσύνη, ἡ, (ἄλη) *wandering about*, Man.4.34, D.P.716: in pl., A.R.2.1260 codd., Man.6.226. -ων [ᾰ], ονος, ὁ, ἡ, (ἀλάομαι) *wanderer, rover*, ἀλήμονες ἄνδρες Od.19.74; of planets, *AP*9.25 (Leon.): abs., Od.17.376.—Ep. word.

ἀλημώτων· ἀφυλάκτων, Hsch. (leg. ἀλήμπτων· εὐφυλάκτων).

ἀληνής· μαινόμενος, Hsch.; prob. l. in Semon.7.44.

ἄληνον ἔλαιον, *oil of almonds*, Aët.7.69.

ἀλήπεδον, τό, = Ἀλήιον πεδίον, Lyc.681.

ἀλήπορον· λευκὸν τὸ ἄνθος, Hsch.

ἄληπτος, ον, *not to be laid hold of, hard to catch*, Plu.*Sert.*16, Poll.5.169, etc.; ἄ. τοῖς ἐχθροῖς J.*AJ*5.8.11: in Comp. ἀληπτότερος Th.1.37, 82,143. II. *incomprehensible*, Phld.*Mus.*p.54K., Plu.*Nic.*11, al. III. in Stoic philos., ἄληπτα, τά, things *not to be made matter of choice*, opp. ληπτά, *Stoic.*3.34.

ἀλήπτωρ· ἱερεύς, Hsch.

ἀλής, ές, Ion., = Att. ἀθρόος, *thronged, crowded, in a mass*, πολλὰ ἁλέα Hp.*Mul.*1.5, cf. Hdt.1.133; ὡς ἁλέες εἴησαν οἱ Ἕλληνες Hdt.9.15, cf. 7.104, al.: sg. with collective nouns, ἁ. γενομένη πᾶσα ἡ Ἑλλάς 7.157; ἁ. ἐὼν ὁ στρατός ib.236; ἁ. τροφή, αἷμα, Hp.*Vict.*2.45, *Morb.*2.4. Adv. -έως prob. in Hp.*Mul.*1.36: neut. pl. as Adv., ἐκχέουσιν τὸ οὖρον ἁλέα Aret.*SD*2.2. [ᾰ, Call.*Fr.*86; ἁλέα λέσχην is v.l. Hes.*Op.* 493.] (*sm-*ϝαλής, cf. ϝαλῆναι.)

ἀλησθύω or -ίω, = ἀλυσθαίνω, Hp.*Mul.*2.124 codd. **ἀλήσθω**· γῆ σπορίμη, κτηνοτρόφος, Hsch.

ἀλησία, ἡ, = ἀσυλία, *EM*62.41: in pl., *truce*, Hsch. **ἀλήσιον**, τό, (ἀλέω A) *meal*, Hsch.: Lacon. ἀλήϊον *IG*5(1).1316 (Thalamae, v B.C.).

ἄλησις, εως, ἡ, (ἀλάομαι) = ἄλη, of the course of the sun, Arat. 319. II. (ἀλέω A) *grinding*, *Gp.*9.19.7.

ἀλησμόνητος, ον, *unforgotten*, *IG*3.3446.

ἀλήστευτος, ον, *unpillaged*, J.*AJ*18.9.4, Arr.*Epict.*4.1.93.

ἄληστος, ον, = ἄλαστος (q.v.); *unforgettable*, κακά Ph.1.320. II. Act., *unforgetting*, μνήμη Id.1.619, al.

ἀλητ-εία, Dor. **ἀλᾱτεία**, ἡ, *wandering, roaming*; δυσπλάνοις ἀλατείαις A.*Pr.*900 (lyr.); ἀλατείᾳ βιότου ταλαίφρων E.*Hel.*523 (lyr.), cf. 934; in later Prose, Vett.Val.4.18, prob. in Ph.1.658. -εύω, Dor. ἀλατ-, fut. -σω E.*Herad.*515:—*wander, roam*, mostly of beggars, Od. 17.501, al., *AP*9.12 (Leon.); of hunters, Od.12.330; of exiles, E. l. c., *Hipp.*1048, Phalar.*Ep.*95; θνητὸν βίον ἀ. Ph.1.463. -ήρ, ῆρος, ὁ, name of a *dance* in Ithaca and at Sicyon, Aristox.Hist.*Fr.* 50. -ης [ᾰ], ου, Dor. **ἀλάτας**, α, ὁ; voc. ἀλῆτα S.*OC*1096, Dor. ἀλᾶτα ib.165: (ἀλάομαι):—*wanderer, vagabond*, Hom. only in Od., always of beggars (17.420, al.); in Trag. also of exiles, A.*Ag.*1282, *Ch.*1042, S.*OC*50,746, E.*Heracl.*224, *Supp.*280 (lyr.):—τὸν μακρῶν ἀλάταν πόνων *one who has wandered* in long labour, S.*Aj.*888. 2. as Adj., *vagrant, roving*, πόδ' ἀλάταν E.*El.*139 (anap.); βίος ἀλήτης Hdt.3.52; in later Prose, ἄνδρες D.Chr.1.9:—so also fem. **ἀλῆτις**, ιδος, D.P.490 (as v.l.); name of song in honour of Erigone, Ath.14. 618e, Poll.4.55, Hsch. s. v.; cf. ἐώρα II. -ικός, ή, όν, *appropriate to a wanderer*, D.Chr.7.1.

ἀλητοειδής, ές, *like meal, meal-coloured*, Hp.*Coac.*590.

ἄλητον, τό, *meal*, Hp.*Art.*36, Philotim.ap.Orib.4.10.1; ἀ. κριθῆς Aret.*CA*1.1: pl., Sophr.39; ἀλήτων κἀλφίτων Rhinth.3.

ἀλητός (A), ὁ, poet. for ἀλετός, εἰς ἀ. ἐπράθη was sold *to grind* in the mill, Babr.29.1.

ἀλητός (B), ή, όν, Adj. *ground*, Archig.ap.Orib.8.1.33.

ἀλητύς, ύος, ἡ, Ion. for ἄλη, Call.*Fr.*277, Man.3.379.

ἀλήτωρ, ορος, ὁ, = ἱερεύς, Hsch. **ἄλθα**· θερμασία (i. e. ἁλέα) ἢ θεραπεία, Id.

ἀλθαία, ἡ, *marsh mallow*, *Althaea officinalis*, Thphr.*HP*9.15.5, Aret.*CA*1.6. 2. = δενδρομαλάχη, Gal.12.67. 3. = ὠκιμοειδές, Ps.-Dsc.4.28. (For **ἀλθαιᾶτις**, ἡ, *EM*63.12, ἀλθαία τις should be read.)

ἀλθ-αίνω, *heal*, Lyc.582, Timae.15: fut. ἀλθήσω Nic.*Th.*587: aor. ἤλθησα ib.496, *Al.*112: aor. 2 inf. ἀλθεῖν· ὑγιάζειν Hp.ap.Gal.19.76: —Pass., *become whole and sound*, pres., ἐπὴν τὸ ἕλκος ἀλθαίνηται Hp.*Morb.*2.33: Ep. impf. or aor. ἄλθετο χείρ Il.5.417; ἀλθομένη Q.S.9. 475 (nisi leg. ἀλδομένη): fut. ἀλθήσομαι (ἀπ-) Il.8.405: aor. ἀλθεσθῆναι (συν-) Hp.*Art.*14:—later aor. Med. ἠλθησάμην Poet. *de herb.* 44. -εῖναι· χαλεπῆναι, Hsch. -εξις, εως, ἡ, *healing, cure*, Hp.*Fract.*10, *Art.*34, cf. Aret.*CA*2.2:—fut. Med. **ἀλθέξομαι** (as if from *ἀλθέσσω) = ἀλθήσομαι, *SD*2.8. -εστήρια, τά, *remedies*, Nic.*Th.*493. -εύς, έως, ὁ, *healer, physician*, Hsch. -ήεις, εσσα, εν, *healing, wholesome*, Nic.*Th.*84,645. -ήσκω or **ἀλθίσκω**, = ἀλθαίνω, Hp.*Morb.*2.36. -ίσκον, τό, = ἀλθαία, Ps.-Dsc.3. 146. -ος, εος, τό, *healing, medicine*, *EM*63.10, Hsch.

ἁλία (A), Ion. -ίη [ᾱλ], ἡ, *assembly of people*, in Dor. states, answering to Att. ἐκκλησία, at Sparta, ἁ. συλλέγειν Hdt.7.134; at Byz., Decr.ap.D.18.90; at Corcyra, *IG*9(1).682; in Sicily and Magna Graecia, *IG*14.952 (Agrigentum), 612 (Rhegium), *Tab.Heracl.*1.118, 2.10; at Epidamnus and Tarentum, Arist.*Pol.*1301ᵇ23 (prob. cj. for ἡλιαία). II. generally, *meeting, assembly*, ἁλίην ποιεῖσθαι Hdt. 5.29,79; of the Persians, 1.125.

ἁλία (B), [ᾰλ], ἡ, (ἅλς) *salt-cellar*, Archipp.13, Stratt.14; ἁλίην τρυπᾶν clear out *the salt-cellar*, mark of extreme poverty, Ap.Ty.*Ep.* 7, cf. Call.*Ep.*48.1.

ἁλιάδης, ου, ὁ, (ἅλς) *seaman*, S.*Aj.*880 (lyr.). II. **Ἁλιάδαι**, οἱ, Dor. for Ἡλ-, religious association at Rhodes, *IG*12(1).155.

ἁλιαδίτης, ὁ, title of posting-official, = γραμματηφόρος τοῦ ὀξέως δρόμου, *PFlor.*39.16 (iv A.D.).

ἁλι-άετος, poet. -αίετος, ὁ, *sea-eagle*, prob. *osprey*, E.*Fr.*636, Ar.*Av.*891, Arist.*HA*619ᵃ4. -āής, ές, (ἄημι) *blowing seaward*, Od. 4.361.

ἁλιαία, ἡ, = ἁλία (A), *IG*4.479 (Nemea), 497 (Mycenae); ἁ. τελεία *Mnemos.*44.221 (Argos, iii B.C.); at Epidamnus, Arist.*Pol.*1301ᵇ 23 (ἡλιαία codd.).

Ἁλιαῖος, sc. μήν, month at Dreros, *SIG*527.108.

ἁλι-ανθής, ές, prop. *sea-blooming*, hence = ἁλιπόρφυρος, *bright purple*, *AP*5.227 (Paul. Sil.), 7.705 (Antip.), cj. in Orph.*A*.586.

ἁλιαρός, όν, (ἅλς) *salted*, Eust.1506.61.

ἁλιάς, άδος, ἡ, (ἅλς) *of* or *belonging to sea*: ἁλιάς (sc. κύμβα), ἡ, *fishing-boat* or *bark*, Arist.*HA*533ᵇ20, Moschio ap.Ath.5.208f, D.S.3.21.

ἅλιας, = ἅλις, Hippon.101. **ἀλιάς**· πρασιάς, πλινθείας, Hsch.

ἁλίασμα, τό, (ἁλία A) *decree*, βουλᾶς *IG*14.256 (Gela).

ἁλίασσις, ἡ, either *assembly* (cf. ἁλία A), or for ἀλ-λίασσις, = ἀναλίασσις, *withdrawal* (cf. λιάζομαι), *IG*4.554 (Argos, v B.C.).

ἁλιαστάς, ὁ, *member of the* ἁλία, at Tegea, *IG*5(2).6.24 (iv B.C.).

ἀλίαστος, ον, (λιάζομαι) *not to be turned aside, unabating*, μάχη, ὅμαδος, γόος, Il.14.57, 12.471, 24.760; πόλεμον δ' ἀ. ἔγειρε 20.31; ἀ. ἀνίη Hes.*Th*.611: neut. as Adv., μηδ' ἀλίαστον ὀδύρεο Il.24.549, cf. φρὴν ἀλίαστος φρίσσει E.*Hec*.85. 2. = πολύς, κῦμα A.R.1.1326, acc. to Sch., cf. *EM*63.33. II. of persons, *undaunted*, E.*Or*. 1479.—Ep. word, used twice by E. in lyr.

ἀλῐβάνωτος [ᾰν], ον, *not honoured with incense*, Pl.Com.113.

ἁλίβαπτος, ον, *dipped in sea, drowned therein*, Nic.*Al*.618 [where ἁλῐ- metri gr.]. II. *a purple bird*, Alcm.126, Alc.122 (cod. Hsch. ἀλί-).

ἄλιβας, αντος, ὁ, *dead body, corpse*, ἔνεροι καὶ ἄλιβαντες Pl.*R*. 387c, cf. *IPE* 1².519 (Cherson.). 2. *dead river*, i.e. *Styx*, S.*Fr*. 790 (cf. 994). 3. *dead wine*, i.e. *vinegar*, Hippon.102; ἔβηξαν οἶον (v.l. οἶνον) ἄλιβαντα (or ἀλίβ-, i.e. οἱ ἀλίβ-) πίνοντες Call.*Fr*. 88; cf. *EM*63.52. (Ancient Gramm. derived the word fr. ἀ- priv., λιβάς and gave it the meaning *dry, withered*, cf. Did.ap.Sch.Ar.*Ra*. 186, Corn.*ND*35, Plu.2.736a; the quantity of the first α is dub.)

ἀλίβατος, ον, Dor. for ἠλίβατος.

ἁλιβᾰφής, ές, = ἁλίβαπτος, πολύδονα σώμαθ' ἁλιβαφῆ restored in A.*Pers*.275 (lyr.) for ἁλίδονα σώματα πολυβαφῆ.

ἀλιβδύω [ῠ], expl. by Gramm. as Aeol. for *ἁλιδύω, *sink* or *submerge in the sea*, νῆας ἀλιβδύουσι Call.*Fr*.269: *hide*, aor. ἀλιβδύσασα Lyc.351, cf. *EM*63.13, Hsch.

ἁλί-βρεκτος, ον, *washed by the sea*, *AP*7.501 (Pers.), Nonn.*D*.1. 96. **-βρομος**, ον, *murmuring like the sea*, ib.43.385. **-βροχος**, ον, = ἁλίβρεκτος, A.R.2.731. **-βρωτος**, ον, *swallowed by the sea*, Lyc. 760:—also **ἁλι-βρώς**, Id.443. **-γδουπος**, ον, poet. for ἁλίδουπος, Opp.*H*.5.423, Nonn.*D*.1.266. **-γείτων**, ον, gen. ονος, *near the sea*, Hom.*Epigr*.4.6, Nonn.*D*.42.17. **-γενής**, ές, *sea-born*, of Aphrodite, Plu.2.685f.

ἀλίγκιος [ᾰ], ον, *resembling, like*, ἀ. ἀστέρι καλῷ Il.6.401; ἀ. ἀθανάτοισιν Od.8.174; εἴδεα πᾶσιν ἀ., of paintings, Emp.23.5; σοὶ φυὰν ἀ. B.5.168; ὀνειράτων ἀ. μορφαῖσι A.*Pr*.449; ἀ. ἡρώεσσιν *IG*14.1356, cf. Arat.462, A.R.4.966, etc.:—but compd. ἐναλίγκιος is more freq.

ἀλιγύγλωσσος, ον, *with no clear voice*, Timo 5.

ἁλιδῑνής, ές, *sea-tossed*, D.P.908. **ἁλιδίως**· ἱκανῶς, μετρίως, Hsch.

ἁλι-δνοφεῖ· ἁλουργεῖ, Hsch. **-δονος**, ον, = ἁλιδινής, σώματα A.*Pers*.275; cf. ἁλιβαφής. **-δουπος**, ον, *sea-resounding*, of Poseidon, Orph.*H*.17.4. **-δρομος**, ον, *running over the sea*, Nonn. *D*.43.281. **-δροσος**, ον, dub. in *Lyr.Adesp.Oxy*.219.11.

ἁλιεία, ἡ, *fishing*, Arist.*Pol*.1256ᵃ36, *Oec*.1346ᵇ20, Str.11.2.4 (pl.); later ἁλεία (q.v.).

Ἁλιεῖα, τά, Dor. for Ἡλιεῖα, *festival of the Sun*, at Rhodes, *Com. Adesp*. (perh. Lysipp.) 336, cf. *SIG*1067.

ἁλι-ειδής, ές, *sea-coloured*, κίχλαι Numen.ap.Ath.7.305c. **-εινὴ** ἐρέα *sea-blue* wool, *Edict.Diocl*.21.2. **-ειος**, α, ον, *fisher's*, τέχνη Alcid.*Od*.12. **-εργής**, ές, *working in sea, fishing*, Opp.*H*.4.635:—also **-εργός**, όν, Nonn.*D*.40.306. II. = ἁλουργής, *purple*, *EM*63.45. **-ερκής**, ές, *sea-fenced, sea-girt*, of Aegina, Pi.*O*.8.25; of the Isthmus, Id.*I*.1.9; ἁ. ὄχθαι Id.*P*.1.18.

ἀλιετρόν· ἁμαρτωλόν, Hsch.

ἁλί-ευμα, ατος, τό, *draught of fish*, Str.11.2.4. **-εύς** (later written ἁλεεύς Lxx *Is*.19.8, *Ev.Matt*.4.18, *PFlor*.127.15), ὁ, gen. έως, Ion. ῆος, and contr. ἁλιῶς Pherecr.200: acc. pl. ἁλιέας Antiph.190.17, Alex.155.1; gen. ἁλιέων Id.76.5: (ἅλς, ἅλιος A):—*one who has to do with the sea*, and so, 1. *fisher*, Od.12.251, 22.384, Hdt.3. 42, S.*Fr*.115, Pl.*Ion* 539e, etc.: ἀνὴρ ἁ. Hes.*Sc*.214. 2. *seaman, sailor*, Od.24.419; ἐρέτας ἁλιῆας rowers *on the sea*, 16.349; as Adj., ἁλιεὺς στρατός Opp.H.5.121. 3. a fish, = βάτραχος, Arist.*HA* 620ᵇ12, Plu.2.978d, Paus.3.21.5. **-ευτής**, οῦ, ὁ, = foreg. 1, metaph., Πιερίδων Cerc.4.8. **-ευτικός**, ή, όν, *of* or *for fishing*, ἁ. πλοῖον *fishing*-boat, X.*An*.7.1.20; ἁ. κάλαμος *fishing*-rod, Arist.*PA*693ᵃ23; ἁ. βίος *fisher's* life, Id.*Pol*.1256ᵇ2:—ἡ -κή (with or without τέχνη) *art of fishing*, Pl.*Ion* 538d, *Sph*.220b; Ἁλιευτικά, τά, title of poem by Opp. on this subject; ἁλιευτικόν, τό, *the fishing population*, Arist. *Pol*.1291ᵇ22. **-εύω**, (ἅλς) *fish*, *Ev.Jo*.21.3; *to be a fisher*, Plu. *Ant*.29; *fish for, catch*, σπάρους dub. l. in Epich.54; λίθους Luc.*Pisc*. 47: abs., Luc.*Herm*.65, etc.: metaph. of avenger, ἁλιεύειν τινάς Lxx *Je*.16.16. II. only Med. occurs in Att., Pl.Com.44; Ἁλιευομένη, title of play by Antiph.:—also later, Posidon.68.

ἄλιζα· ἡ λεύκη τῶν δένδρων, i.e. *abele* (Maced.), Hsch.

ἁλίζω (A), [ᾰ]: aor. ἥλῐσα E.*HF*412, Hdt.1.77, (συν-) X.*Cyr*.1.4. 14:—Pass., aor. ἡλίσθην Emp.41, Hp. (v. infr.), Hdt.1.79: Ion. pf. part. ἁλισμένος Hdt.4.118, 7.172 (but ἡλ- Scriptor Ionicus ap. Stob.3.28.21): (ἀλής):—*gather together, assemble*, of military forces, Hdt.1.77, 80, al.; *collect*, of fragments, ib.119, etc.; ἁ. εἰς ἕν E.*Heracl*. 403:—Pass., *meet together*, Hdt.1.63, 79, 7.172; *to be massed into a globe*, Emp. l.c.; *collect*, αἷμα ἁλισθέν Hp.*Int*.47, cf. *Morb*.1.15; of moisture, etc., Arist.*Pr*.869ᵃ17, cf. 936ᵇ32; of rapid breathing, πνεῦμα ἁλίζεται Hp.*Coac*.333.—Not in A. or S.; rare in Prose, Act. in Pl.*Cra*.409a, App.*Fr*.1.4; Pass., X.*An*.2.4.3, 6.3.3, Arist.*Pr*.936ᵇ 32: generally, compd. συναλίζω more freq.

ἁλίζω (B), [ᾰ], (ἅλς) *salt*, Pass., *to be salted*, Arist.*HA*570ᵃ1, *Pr*. 927ᵃ36, Lxx *Le*.2.13:—Pass., *Ev.Matt*.5.13, Ph.*Bel*.86.29. II. *supply with salt* or *salt food*, Arist.*HA*574ᵃ9, al.:—Pass., of sheep, ib.596ᵃ24.

ἁλί-ζωνος, ον, *sea-girt*, Call.*Sos*.24, *AP*7.218 (Antip.Sid.). **-ζωος**, ον, *living on* or *in the sea*, *AP*7.654 (Leon.), Pancrat.ap.Ath.7.321f.

ἁλίη· κάπρος (Maced.), Hsch. **ἁλίη**, ἡ, Ion. for ἁλία.

ἁλι-ηγής, ές, (ἄγνυμι) *broken on by the sea*, πέτρα Opp.*H*.3. 460. **-ήμαθον**· παρὰ τὸν ἅλα καὶ τὴν ἄμαθον, Hsch. **-ήρης**, ες, (ἐρέσσω) *sweeping the sea*, κώπη E.*Hec*.455 (lyr.). **-ήτωρ**, ορος, ὁ, poet. for ἁλιεύς 1, Hom.*Epigr*.16.1. **-ηχής**, ές, *resounding like the sea*, Musae.26.

ἁλίθιος, Dor. for ἠλίθιος.

ἁλιθοκόλλητος, ον, *not cemented*, οἶκοι Antyll.ap.Orib.9.13.5.

ἄλῐθος, ον, *without stones, not stony*, of lands, X.*An*.6.4.5. II. *without a stone* set in it, of a ring, Poll.7.179. III. *free from the stone*, as disease, Aret.*CD*2.3.

ἁλι-κάκαβον, τό, *winter-cherry*, *Physalis Alkekengi*, Dsc.4.71, cf. *BGU*1120.37 (i B.C.):—also **ἁλικάκκαβα**, Hsch. 2. = στρύχνον ὑπνωτικόν, Dsc.4.72. 3. = δορύκνιον, Crateuas ap.Dsc.4.74.

Ἁλικαρνασσός, Ion. **-νησσός**, ἡ, *Halicarnassus*, Hdt.1.144, etc.:—Adj. **Ἁλικαρνασσεύς**, έως, Ion. **-νησσεύς**, έος, ὁ, *Halicarnassian*, Hdt. l.c., *SIG*45.2 (-σσ- expressed by Ͳ), etc.:—fem. **-νασσίς**, ίδος, ἡ, Aristodem.1.5. **Ἁλικαρνασσόθεν**, Adv. *from Halicarnassus*, Luc.*Dom*.20.

ἁλικία, ἡ, Dor. for ἡλικία. **ἁλικίανες** (leg. -κρατες)· θαλασσομιγεῖς, Hsch. **ἀλικινός**· δυνατός, Id. (cf. ἀλεκινός).

ἁλίκλυστος, ον, *sea-washed, sea-beaten*, of coast, S.*Aj*.1219 (lyr.); ἁ. πὰρ χθονὶ Πειραέως *IG*3.1344; ἁ. δέμας *AP*9.228 (Apollonid.). 2. *high-surging*, πόντος Orph.*A*.333.

ἀλίκμητος, ον, *not winnowed*, ἄχυρα Aq. Sm. Thd.*Is*.30.24.

ἁλικνήμῑς, ῖδος, ὁ, ἡ, ἀπήνη ἁ. *sea-borne* car, Nonn.*D*.43.199. **ἁλίκος**, α, ον, Dor. for ἡλίκος. **ἁλικός**, v. ἁλυκός:—hence **ἁλική**, ἡ, *salt-tax*, *PSI*4.388.1 (iii B.C.), *PTeb*.482 (ii B.C.): **ἁλικά**, τά, *charges for salt*, *PPetr*.3 p.106 (iii B.C.).

ἁλί-κρᾱς, ᾶτος, ὁ, ἡ, *mixed with salt water*, Ael.Dion.*Fr*. 32. **-κρείων**, οντος, ὁ, *lord of the sea*, Eust.57.27. **-κρήπῑς**, ῖδος, ὁ, ἡ, *at the sea's edge*, Nonn.*D*.1.289. **-κρόκᾰλος**, ον, *shingly, pebbly*, Orph.*A*.335. **-κτῠπος**, ον, *sea-smitten*, of ships, S.*Ant*. 953 (lyr.), cf. *AP*6.23, Nonn.*D*.31.113; also ἁ. κῦμα *roaring on the sea*, E.*Hipp*.754 (lyr.). **-κύμων** [ῠ], ον, *surrounded by sea-waves*, *AP*9.429 (Crin.).

ἀλικύρκης, ὁ, a made dish, Hsch.

ἁλιμέδων, οντος, ὁ, = ποντομέδων, Ar.*Th*.323.

ἀλιμενία, ἡ, *want of harbours*, Hyp.*Fr*.156, Poll.1.101.

ἀλίμενος [ῐ], ον, *harbourless*, A.*Supp*.768, E.*Hel*.1211, Th.4.8, etc. 2. metaph., *shelterless, inhospitable*, ὄρεα, ἄντλος, E.*Hel*. 1132, *Hec*.1025; ἀλίμενον αἰθέρος αὔλακα Ar.*Av*.1400; καρδία E.*Cyc*. 349.

ἀλῐμενότης, ἡ, = ἀλιμενία, X.*HG*4.8.7, *Peripl.M.Eux*.37.

ἀλιμενώτης τόπος· μὴ ἔχων λιμένα, Suid., cf. Hsch.

ἀλίμικτος, v. ἀλίσμηκτος.

ἁλιμοκτόνον, = ποταμογείτων, Ps.-Dsc.4.100.

ἅλῐμος, ον, (ἅλς) *of* or *belonging to the sea*, ὄτοβος *Trag.Adesp*.247; τὰ ἅ. *seaside*, Lxx *Je*.17.6. II. as Subst., ἅλιμον, τό, *tree purslane*, *Atriplex Halimus*, Antiph.160, Thphr.*HP*4.16.5, Dsc.1.91 (ἅλιμος, ὁ, Ps.-Dsc. ibid.). (Sts. written ἄλιμον, cf. *AB*376.)

ἄλῑμος, ον, *banishing hunger*, τροφή, a food said to be prepared from asphodel and mallows, Herodor.1 J., Hermipp.Hist.1.8, cf. Plu.2. 157d, Porph.*Abst*.4.20.

ἁλῐ-μυρήεις, εσσα, εν, (μύρω) *flowing into the sea*, ποταμοί Il.21.190, Od.5.460, cf. A.R.2.936; cf. sq. **-μυρής**, ές, = foreg., Orph.*A*. 344. 2. *salt-surging*, πόντος *Epigr.Gr*.256 (Cyprus); *of the flowing sea*, ἀφρός *APl*.4.180 (Democr.). II. = ἁλίκλυστος, πέτρη, αἰγιαλοί, A.R.1.913, Phanocl.1.17. **-ναιέτης**, ου, *dwelling in the sea*, δελφῖνες B.16.97.

ἄλινδα, mythical plant, Ps.-Plu.*Fluv*.14.2.

ἀλινδ-έω, later **ἀλίνδω** [ᾰ], (pres. only in Pass.): aor. ἤλῖσα (ἐξ-) Ar.*Nu*.32, and pf. ἤλῖκα (ἐξ-) ib.33 (the simple forms only in Hsch., Suid.):—*make to roll*. II. Pass., mostly in part., *rolling in the dust*, like a horse, ἀλινδούμενος Plu.2.396e; ἀλινδόμενοι ψαμάθοισι Nic.*Th*.156; ἀλινδηθείς ib.204; ἠλινδημένος *rolled over, overturned*, Din.*Fr*.10; *to be twirled*, Call.*Iamb*.1.113. 2. generally, *roam about*, ἄλλην ἐξ ἄλλης εἰς χθόν' ἀλινδόμενος *AP*7.736 (Leon.); ἠλινδημένος ἐν αὐλαῖς σατραπικαῖς *having grovelled*, Plu.*Agis* 3; *frequent*, περὶ τὴν Ἀκαδημίαν ἀ. Alciphr.3.14; of money-lenders, οἱ περὶ τὰς ψήφους -ούμενοι ib.1.26. 3. sens. obsc., μετά τινος Herod.5. 30. **-ήθρα**, ἡ, *place for horses to roll in*, Phryn.*PS*p.5 B.: metaph., ἀλινδῆθραι ἐπῶν, of Euripides' tragedies, Ar.*Ra*.904. **-ησις**, εως, ἡ, *rolling in dust*, exercise in which wrestlers rolled on the ground, Hp. *Vict*.2.64, 3.68, Ruf.ap.Orib.*Inc*.2.11.

ἀλινδόν· δρόμον, Hsch.

ἁλῐ-νήκτειρα, ἡ, (νήχω) fem. as if fr. *ἁλινηκτήρ, *swimming in the sea*, *AP*6.190 (Gaet.). [ῑ metri gr.] **-νηχής**, ές, = foreg., ib. 10.9; *of swimmers*, τέχνη ib.6.29 (Jul.).

ἀλιννόν· ἀμυδρόν (Cret.), Hsch. **ἀλινοί·** ἐπαφρόδιτοι, Id.

ἅλῐνος, η, ον, (ἅλς) *of salt,* χόνδροι Hdt.4.185; τοῖχοι ib.; οἰκίαι Str. 16.3.3. **ἄλῐνος,** ον, (λίνον) *without net,* ἄ. θήρα game *not caught with net, AP*9.244 (Apollonid.). **ἄλινσις,** εως, ἡ, = ἄλειψις, τοῦ ἐργαστηρίου *IG*4.1484.39 (Epid.). **ἄλιντος·** ἅμιλλα, Hsch. **ἀλίνω,** (ἀλέω A) = λεπτύνω, *pound,* S.*Fr.*995. II. ἀλινεῖν (leg. ἀλίνειν)· ἀλείφειν, and ἀλῖναι· ἐπαλεῖψαι, Hsch. (cf. ἄλινσις, Lat. *lino*).

ἄλιξ, Dor. for ἧλιξ. **ἄλιξ,** ἴκος, ὁ, *groats of rice-wheat* (ζέα), Chrysipp.Tyan.ap.Ath.14.647d, cf. Plin.*HN*18.112. II. = Lat. *hallec, fish-sauce,* Dsc.4.148, *Gp.*20.46.2. **ἀλίξαντος,** ον, *worn by sea,* χοιράδες *AP*6.89 (Maec.); τύμβος *IG*9(1).878 (Corcyr.); ἁ. μόρος death *by being dashed on the beach, AP.*7.404 (Zon.).

ἁλιονείκης (sic) = ἀλειονίκης, ὁ, *victor in the* 'Αλιεῖα at Rhodes, *PLond.*3.1178.67 (ii A.D.), *Rev.Arch.*1915 ii 200 (Trajana Augusta).

ἅλιος (A), α, ον, also ος, ον S.*Aj.*357, E.*Heracl.*82(lyr.): (ἅλς):— *of the sea,* of sea-gods, nymphs, etc., θυγάτηρ ἁλίοιο γέροντος, i.e. of Nereus, Il.1.556, Hes.*Th.*1003, cf. Od.4.365, al.; θεαὶ ἅ. *sea-goddesses,* Nereids, Il.18.432; of Apollo, Arist.*Mir.*840ᵃ20; ἅ. ψάμαθοι *sea*-sand, Od.3.38; ἅ. πρών A. (only in lyr.) *Pers.*131,879; κῦμα Id. *Supp.*14; πρύμναι, πλάτα, νηῦς, Pi.*O.*9.72, S.*OC*716, Orph.*A.*236.

ἅλιος (B), α, ον: (perh. cf. ἠλίθιος):—mostly of things, *fruitless, idle,* ἔπος, μῦθος, Il.18.324, 5.715; πόνος 4.26; βέλος 5.18; ὅρκιον 4.158; in Od. only with ὁδός 2.273,318; of a person, Il.10.324: neut. as Adv., *in vain,* 13.505, cf. 4.179, S.*OC*1469: reg. Adv. -ίως Id.*Ph.* 840.—Ep. word, used by S. in lyr.

ἅλιος (C), ὁ, Dor. for ἥλιος. II. (ἁλίζω), Pythag. name for *nine, Theol.Ar.*57.

ἁλιοτρεφής, ές, *feeding in the sea, sea-reared,* φῶκαι Od.4.442.

'Αλιοτρόπιος, sc. μήν, month at Epidamnus, *Inscr.Magn.*46.

ἁλιόω, poet. Verb, only fut. ἁλιώσω, aor. ἠλίωσα, Ep. ἀλίωσα: fut. Med. in act. sense, Max.582, in pass. sense, Id.512: (ἅλιος B):— *make fruitless, disappoint,* Διὸς νόον.. ἁλιῶσαι Od.5.104; οὐδ' ἀλίωσε βέλος nor *did he hurl* the spear *in vain,* Il.16.737; οὐχ ἠλίωσε τοὔπος *spake* not word *in vain,* S.*Tr.*258. 2. *destroy,* τὸ μέν τις οὐ.. ἁλιώσει Id.*OC*704.

ἀλίπαντος, ον, *without grease,* Paul.Aeg.4.4.

ἀλῑπᾰρής, ές, *not fit for a suppliant,* ἀ. θρίξ dub. l. in S.*El.*451; expl. by Sch. as αὐχμηρά, from ἀ- priv., λιπαρός.

ἁλί-παστος, ον, *sprinkled with salt,* Aristomen.6, Eub.7.10, Archestr.*Fr.*57.4 B. **-πεδον,** τό, *plain by the sea, sandy plain,* Thphr.*HP*7.15.2, Aristid.*Or.*17(15).16; of a plain in Attica near Piraeus, X.*HG*2.4.30. (ἀλ- Ar.*Fr.*233, acc. to Harp.)

ἀλῐπής, ές, (λίπος) *without fat, meagre, poor,* Hices.ap.Ath.7.315d; *without fatty substance,* Thphr.*HP*9.1.3, Str.4.4.1, Dsc.1.26: Medic., *not thick and fatty,* of lotions as opp. to salves, Gal.13.843; of perfumes, Thphr.*Od.*15 (Sup.); of bones, Gal.4.550; of persons, *skinny,* Aret.*CA*2.7. II. (λείπω, λιπεῖν) *unfailing,* προχοαί Poet.ap. Porph.*Antr.*8 (*PLG*3.684).

ἁλί-πλαγκτος, ον, *sea-roaming,* ὦ Πάν, Πὰν ἁλίπλαγκτε.. φάνηθι S.*Aj.*695; Τρίτων *AP*6.65 (Paul. Sil.); ἔχις *IG*2.1660. **-πλᾰνής,** ές, *sea-wandering,* νῆες *AP*11.390 (Lucill.). **-πλᾰνία,** ἡ, *wandering voyage, AP*6.38 (Phil.). **-πλᾰνος,** ον, = ἁλιπλανής, Opp. *C.*4.258. **-πλεύμων,** ονος, ὁ, = πλεύμων II, Marcell.Sid.27. **-πληκτος,** Dor. **-πλακτος,** ον, *sea-beaten,* of islands, Pi.*P.*4.14, v.l. in S. *Aj.*597 (lyr.). **-πλήξ,** ῆγος, ὁ, ἡ, = foreg., Call.*Del.*11, *AP*6.193 (Stat. Flacc.). **-πλοος,** ον, contr. **-πλους,** ουν, *covered with water,* τείχεα Il.12.26. II. later Act., *sailing on the sea,* ναῦς Arion 1.17, cf. Apollod.Hist.209: as Subst., *seaman, fisher,* A.R.3.1329, Call.*Del.*15. 2. in form **ἁλίπλωος,** ἰχθύες Babr.61.4. **-πνοος,** ον, *redolent of sea,* ὀδμή Musae.265. **-πόρος,** ον, *through which the sea flows,* διασφάξ Luc.*Trag.*24. **-πόρφῠρος,** ον, *of sea-purple, of true purple dye,* ἠλάκατα, φάρεα, Od.6.53, 13.108; οἶδμα Arion 1.18 codd.; ὄρνις Alcm.26.4; Νηρηΐδες Him.*Or.*16.2.

ἄλιππα, τό, Aeol., = ἄλειμμα, *EM*64.40.

ἁλιπτοίητος, ον, *driven by fear across the sea,* Nonn.*D.*8.58, cf. 13. 119; perh. Act. in meaning, 'Ενυώ 39.85.

ἀλίρ· ὀξύβαφον, Hsch.

ἁλιρ-ρᾱγής, ές, (ῥήγνυμι) *against which the tide breaks,* σκόπελος *AP*7.383 (Phil.). **-ραίστης,** ὁ, (ῥαίω) *ravening in the sea,* δράκων Nic.*Th.*828. **-ραντος,** ον, (ῥαίνω) *sea-surging,* πόντος *AP*9.333 (Mnas.) (s.v.l.); *washed by sea,* ἀκταί 14.72. **-ρηκτος,** ον, = ἁλιρραγής, δειράδες *AP*7.278 (Arch.). **-ρόθιος,** α, ον, *sea-beaten,* κόνις *AP*7.6 (Antip. Sid.); f.l. ib.624 (Diod., leg. ἀλὶ ῥοθίῃ). II. *roaring,* θάλασσα Orph.*A.*1296. **-ροθος,** ον, = foreg.; ἁ. πόροι pathways *of the roaring sea,* A.*Pers.*367, cf. S.*Aj.*412 (lyr.); ἁ. ἀκτή E.*Hipp.*1205, Mosch.2.132. **-ροιζος,** ον, = ἁλιρρόθιος, Nonn.*D.*13. 322, etc. **-ρῦτος,** ον, *washed by the sea, AP*12.55 (Artemo). II. ἁ. ἄλσος *surging sea's* domain, A.*Supp.*868 (lyr.).

ἅλις [ᾰ], Adv. *in crowds, in plenty,* hence, in a modified sense, *sufficiently, enough*: 1. Hom. mostly with Verbs, ἅ. πεποτήαται [μέλισσαι] Il.2.90; περὶ δὲ Τρῳαὶ ἅ. ἦσαν 3.384; κόπρος ἅ. κέχυτο Od. 17.298; ἅ. δέ οἱ ἦσαν ἄρουραι Il.14.122:—sts. *just enough, in moderation,* εἰ δ' ἅ. ἔλθοι Κύπρις E.*Med.*630; ἔφερε κακὸν ἅ. Id.*Alc.*907. 2. in Ep. freq. closely attached to Noun, χαλκόν τε χρυσόν τε ἅ. bronze and gold *in abundance,* Od.16.231, cf. Il.22.340; νῆα ἅ. χρυσοῦ καὶ χαλκοῦ νηησάσθω 9.137; ἅ. χέραδος 21.319; ἅ. δ' εὐῶδες ἔλαιον Od. 2.339:—rare in Trag. and Com., ἅ. βίοτον εὗρον E.*Med.*1107; λύπας ἅ. ἔχων (Elmsl. λύπης) Id.*Hel.*589; ἅ. ἐλαδίῳ διείς prob. in Sotad.Com.1.27; freq. in Alex. poetry, ἔχω οὐδ' ἅ. ὄξος Theoc.10. 13; ἅ. ὄλβος Call.*Jov.*84; ἄρτους ἅ. κατέθηκεν Id.*Hec.*35; ἵδρῷ ἅ. A.R.2.87:—rare with Adj., ἅ. ἦσθ' ἀνάρσιος A.*Ag.*511. 3. ἅλις (sc. ἐστί) *'tis enough,* ἢ οὐχ ἅ. ὅττι..; is't not *enough* that..? Il. 5.349; ἢ οὐχ ἅ. ὡς..; 17.450, Od.2.312; ἅ. ἵν' ἐξήκεις δακρύων S.*OT* 1515: abs., ἅλις *enough!* Id.*Aj.*1402:—in Trag. c. acc. et inf., 'Αργείοισι Καδμείους ἅ. ἐς χεῖρας ἐλθεῖν A.*Th.*679: c. dat., ἅ. δὲ κλάειν τοὐμὸν ἦν ἐμοὶ κακόν E.*Alc.*1041. 4. like an Adj., as predicate, ἅ. γὰρ ἡ παροῦσα συμφορά ib.673, cf. *IT*1008, S.*Tr.*332. 5. ἅλις (sc. εἰμί) c. part., ἅ. νοσοῦσ' ἐγώ *enough* that I suffer, Id.*OT* 1061; ἅ. ἐγὼ δυστυχῶν *Trag.Adesp.*76. 6. c. gen. rei, *enough of* a thing, ἅ. ἔχειν τῆς βορῆς Hdt.1.119, cf. 9.27; πημονῆς ἅ. γ' ὑπάρχει A.*Ag.*1656, cf. 1659; ἅ. [ἐστὶ] λελεγμένων Id.*Eu.*675; ἅ. λόγων S.*OC*1016; ἅ. ἀφύης μοι Ar.*Fr.*506; to conclude an argument, καὶ τούτων μὲν ἅ. Pl.*Plt.*287a; καὶ περὶ μὲν τούτων ἅ. Arist.*EN* 1096ᵃ3, etc.—Cf. ἅλιας. (ϝαλ-, cf. γάλι· ἱκανόν, Hsch.; cf. ἀλής.)

ἁλίς, ίδος, ἡ, (ἅλς) = ἁλμυρίς, Eust.706.56.

ἀλίσβη, ἡ, = ἀπάτη, Hsch.

ἀλισγ-έω, *pollute,* Lxx *Da.*1.8, al. **-ημα,** ατος, τό, *pollution, Act.Ap.*15.20.

ἀλισθένειν· ἀσθενεῖν, Hsch.

ἁλίσκομαι [ᾰλ], defect. Pass., Act. supplied by αἱρέω (ἁλίσκω Aq. *Ps.*21(22).14, cf. ἐλέφας μῦν οὐχ ἁλίσκει Zen.3.67): impf. ἡλισκόμην (never ἑαλ-) Hdt., etc.: fut. ἁλώσομαι Hdt., etc., later ἁλωθήσομαι Lxx *Ez.*21.24(19) cod. A: aor. (the only tense used by Hom.) ἥλων Od.22.230, always in Hdt., and sometimes in codd. of Att., as Pl. *Hp.Ma.*286a, Hyp.*Eux.*15, cf. X.*An.*4.4.21, but the common Att. form was ἑάλων *IG*2.38, etc., cf. Thom.Mag.146 [ᾱ, Ar.*V.*355, later ᾰ *AP*7.114 (D.L.), 11.155 (Lucill.); ᾰ in other moods, exc. part. ἁλόντε Il.5.487, inf., v. infr.]; subj. ἁλῶ, ῷς, ῷ A.*Th.*257, E.*Hipp.* 420, Ar.*Ach.*662, *V.*898, etc., Ion. ἁλώω Il.11.405, ἁλώῃ 14.81, Hdt. 4.127; opt. ἁλοίην Il.22.253, Antipho 5.59, etc., Ep. 3 sg. ἁλῴη (v.l. ἁλοίη, which is to be preferred) Il.17.506, Od.15.300; inf. ἁλῶναι [ᾰ] Il.21.281, [ᾱ] Hippon.74 s.v.l., Ep. ἁλώμεναι Il.21.495; part. ἁλούς Il.2.374, etc.; later, inf. ἁλωθῆναι v.l. in Lxx *Ez.*40.1, D.S.21.6: pf. ἥλωκα Hdt.1.83, Antiph.204.7, Xenarch.7.17, Hyp.*Phil.*11, D. 21.105; part. ἁλωκότα Pi.*P.*3.57; ἑάλωκα [ᾱλ] A.*Ag.*30, Hdt. 1. 191,209 codd., and Att., as Th.3.29, Pl.*Ap.*38d, D.19.179: plpf. ἡλώκειν Hdt.1.84, X.*An.*5.2.8.: (ϝαλ-, cf. ϝαλίσκηται *IG*9(2). 1226 (Thess.), ϝαλόντοις ib.5(2).351.7 (Stymphalus)):—*to be taken, conquered, fall into an enemy's hand,* of persons and places, Il.2.374, etc.; ἁλώσεται (sc. ὁ Κρέων) S.*OC*1065; ἁλίσκεσθαι εἰς πολεμίους *to fall into the hands of* the enemy, Pl.*R.*468a, *IG*12(7).5 (Amorg.); ἐν τοιαύταις ξυμφοραῖς Pl.*Cri.*43c. 2. *to be caught, seized,* of persons and things, θανάτῳ ἁλῶναι *to be seized* by death, *die,* Il.21.281, Od.5.312; without θανάτῳ, Il.12.172, Od.18.265, etc.; ἄνδρ' ἐκ θανάτου κομίσαι ἤδη ἁλωκότα (sc. νόσῳ) Pi.*P.*3.57; γράμματα ἑάλωσαν εἰς 'Αθήνας letters *were seized and taken* to Athens, X.*HG*1.1.23; τοῖς αὐτῶν πτεροῖς ἁλισκόμεσθα, of eagle, i.e. by a feathered arrow, A.*Fr.*139:—*to be taken* or *caught* in hunting, Il.5.487, X.*An.*5.3. 10:—ἁ. ἀπάταις, μανίᾳ, S.*El.*125, *Aj.*216; ὑπ' ἔρωτος Pl.*Phdr.*252c; ὑπὸ νοσήματος τεταρταίου Hp.*Nat.Hom.*15; νοσήματι Arist.*Pr.*954ᵃ 35, etc.; μιᾷ νίκῃ ἁλίσκονται by one victory *they are ruined,* Th.1. 121: abs., *to be overcome,* A.*Eu.*67, S.*Aj.*648. 3. in good sense, *to be won, achieved,* S.*OT*542, E.*Alc.*786, X.*Cyn.*12.21. 4. c. gen., *succumb to,* τῆς ὥρας, τοῦ κάλλους, Ael.*VH*12.52, Ps.-Luc. *Charid.*9; κόρης Philostr.*Her.*8.2, prob. in Eun.*Hist.*p.238 D. 5. *to be established* by argument, *proved,* Phld.*Sign.*29,33. II. c. part., *to be caught* or *detected* doing a thing, οὔτε σὺ ἁλώσεαι ἀδικέων Hdt.1.112; ἐπιβουλεύων ἐμοὶ.. ἑάλωκε ib.209; ἐὰν ἁλῷς ἔτι τοῦτο πράττων Pl.*Ap.*29c; with Subst. or Adj., οὐ γὰρ δὴ φονεὺς ἁλώσομαι S.*OT*576; μοιχὸς γὰρ ἦν τύχῃς ἁλούς Ar.*Nu.*1079; ἁ. ἐν κακοῖσι S. *Ant.*496. 2. freq. as law-term, *to be convicted and condemned,* λιποταξίου γραφὴν ἡλωκέναι D.21.105, cf. Antipho 2.2.9, 2.3.6; ἁ. μιᾷ ψήφῳ And.4.9:—c. gen. criminis, ἁλῶναι ψευδομαρτυριῶν, ἀστρατείας, ἀσεβείας, etc. (sc. γραφήν), v. sub vocc.; ἁ. θανάτου *to be convicted of* a capital crime, Plu.2.552d; ἁλοῦσα δίκη *conviction,* Pl.*Lg.* 937d; of false evidence, ὁπόσων ἂν μαρτυρίαι ἁλῶσιν ibid.

ἄλισμα, τό, *water-plantain, Alisma Plantago,* Dsc.3.152.

ἁλι-σμᾰρᾰγος, ον, *sea-resounding,* Nonn.*D.*39.362. **-σμηκτος,** ον, *washed by the sea,* Lyc.994: Hsch. has ἁλίσμηκτα (cod. ἁλισίμικτα)· ἠλισμένα, Suid. ἁλίμικτον· πεπασμένον. **-σμός,** ὁ, *sprinkling with salt,* Sor.1.82; = *salsura, Gloss.* **-σπαρτος,** ον, *sown* or *sprinkled with salt,* Eust.1827.61, Hsch., *EM*65.12. **-στέφανος,** ον, *sea-crowned, sea-girt,* πτολίεθρον *h.Ap.*410; νῆσος Alex. Lychn.ap.St.Byz. s.v. Ταπροβάνη, Nonn.*D.*40.521. **-στεφής,** ές, = foreg., Θάσος *Epigr.Gr.*208.16, cf. Orph.*A.*145, 186.

ἀλιστία· ἀναπέπληστα, Hsch.

ἁλίστονος, ον, *sea-resounding,* ῥαχίαι A.*Pr.*712. II. *groaning on the sea,* of fishers, Opp.*H.*4.149.

ἄλιστος, v. ἄλλιστος.

ἁλιστός [ᾰ], ή, όν, (ἁλίζω) *salted, pickled,* Str.4.4.3, Orib.*Fr.*58, Aët.9.38, *AP*9.377 (Pall.).

ἀλίστρα, ἡ, = ἀλινδήθρα, Poll.1.183, cf. Hsch. (cod. -τρία).

ἁλίστρεπτος, ον, *sea-tossed,* ναῦς *AP*9.84 (Antiphan.).

ἁλίσχοινος, ον, ὁ, = ὀλόσχοινος, Aët.2.214 (codd. -σχινος).

ἀλῐταίνω [ᾰλ], Ep. Verb, used by A. in lyr., chiefly in aor. 2 Act. and Med.:—**Act.,** aor. 2 ἤλῐτον Il.9.375, Thgn.1170, A.*Eu.*269; subj. ἀλίτῃ Ps.-Phoc.208; opt. ἀλίτοιμι A.*Pr.*533; part. ἀλιτών *Eu.*316 (cj. Auratus): later Ep. aor. 1 ἀλίτησα Orph.*A.*644:—**Med.,** ἀλιταίνεται Hes.*Op.*330: aor. ἀλίτοντο, ἀλίτωμαι, ἀλιτέσθαι Hom., v. infr.: participial form ἀλιτήμενος :—*sin* or *offend against*, c. acc. pers., ἐκ γὰρ δή μ' ἀπάτησε καὶ ἤλιτεν Il.9.375; ὅτις σφ' ἀλίτηται ὀμόσσας 19.265; Ἀθηναίην ἀλίτοντο Od.5.108; ἀθανάτους ἀλιτέσθαι 4.378, cf. Hes.*Sc.*80, Thgn. l. c.; ἀλιταίνητ' ὀρφανὰ τέκνα Hes.*Op.*330, cf. A.*Eu.*269, Ps.-Phoc. l. c. 2. c. acc. rei, *transgress*, Διὸς δ' ἀλίτωμαι ἐφετμάς Il.24.570; ὅρκον, σπονδάς, A.R.4.388, Opp.*H.*5.563. 3. c. gen., *stray from*, ἀλίτησεν ἀταρποῦ Orph. l. c., cf. Call.*Dian.* 255. 4. ἀλιτήμενος as Adj., = ἀλιτρός, θεοῖς ἀ. *sinful* in the eyes of gods, Od.4.807.

ἀλιτάνευτος, ον, *inexorable*, *PMag.Par.*1.1176, *Gloss.*; cf. ἀλλ–. Adv. -ως *AB*374, *EM*57.30.

ἀλῐ-τενής, ές, *projecting into the sea*, πέτρα D.S.3.44, Longus 2.12; ἄκρα, χερρόνησος, Str.8.2.3, 7.3.19, cf. Posidon.66, Arr.*Ind.*21.9, Eun.*Hist.*p.241 D.; *ambulatio* ἁ. walk *by the shore*, Cic.*Att.*14.13.1. II. of ships, *of light draught*, Callix.1, Plu.*Them.*14. III. of the sea, *shallow*, Plb.4.39.3, App.*BC*2.84. **-τέρμων**, ον, gen. ονος, *bounded by sea*, *AP*9.672.

ἀλίτ-ημα, ατος, τό, *sin*, *offence*, *AP*5.277 (Agath.), 9.643 (Id.) (both pl.). **-ήμερος**, ον, *missing the right day*, *untimely born*, like ἠλιτόμηνος, cj. Guyet in Hes.*Sc.*91 (for ἀλιτήμενον), cf. *EM*428.10. **-ημοσύνη**, ἡ, = ἀλίτημα, Orph.*A.*1318 (pl.). **-ήμων**, ον, gen. ονος, (ἀλιτεῖν) = sq., Il.24.157,186, Call.*Dian.*123, A.R.4.1057. **-ήριος**, ον, (ἀλιτεῖν) *sinning* or *offending against*, c. gen., τῶν ἀλιτηρίων..τῶν τῆς θεοῦ Ar.*Eq.*445; ἐναγεῖς καὶ ἀ. τῆς θεοῦ Th.1.126; but κοινὸν ἀλιτήριον τῶν ὀλωλότων..ἁπάντων common *plague* of all, D.18.159; ἀλιτήριος Ἑλλάδος Aeschin.3.157, cf. Din.1.77. 2. abs., *guilty*, D.19.197, Lys.13.79, And.1.130; Πρωταγόρας..ἀλιτήριος (i.e. ὁ ἀ.) Eup.146b, cf. 96, Men.563. II. = ἀλάστωρ, *avenging spirit*, Antipho 4.1.4, 4.2.8. **-ηριώδης**, ες, *abominable*, *accursed*, οἶστρος Pl.*Lg.*854b; στάσις Id.*R.*470d; γνώμη D.C.44.1. **-ηρός**, όν, = ἀλιτήριος: κἀξ ἀλιτηροῦ φρενός is prob. f.l. for καλιτηρίου in S.*OC*371.

ἀλίτης, ου, ὁ, = ἀλείτης, Apollon.*Lex.*22.28, Orion 32.

ἁλίτης [ῑ], ου, ὁ, *salted*, ἄρτος Ludw.*Anecd.*175; = θαλάσσιος, Hdn.*Epim.*181; = ἁλιευτής, *Et.Gud.z.*

ἀλιτό-καρπον· ματαιότεκνον, Hsch. **-μηνος** [ᾱ], ον, = ἠλιτόμηνος, Suid., etc.; Pythag., = ὀκτάς, *Theol.Ar.*55.

ἀλιτό-ξενος [ᾰ], ον, *sinning against one's friend*, Pi.*O.*10(11).6. **-φροσύνη**, ἡ, *wicked mind*, *AP*7.648.10 (Leon.).

ἀλιτραί· οἱ ἄδικα δικάζοντες, Hsch.

ἀλιτραίνω, Ep. for ἀλιταίνω (when required by metre), abs., *sin*, *offend*, ὅστις ἀλιτραίνει or ὅς κεν ἀλιτραίνῃ Hes.*Op.*243 (cf. Aeschin.2.158, 3.134); ἢν μὲν ἀλιτραίνῃς *AP*9.763 (Jul.); οὐδὲν ἀ. Tryph.269.

ἁλῐτρεφής, ές, *sea-bred*, Q.S.3.272, Nonn.*D.*24.114.

ἀλῐτρέω, = ἀλιταίνω (q. v.), A.*Eu.*316 codd.

ἀλῐτρία, ἡ, *sinfulness*, *mischief*, S.*Fr.*48, Ar.*Ach.*907; but **ἀλίτρια**· ἡ ἁμαρτωλός, *Et.Gud.z.*

ἀλῐτρό-βιος, ον, *living wickedly*, Nonn.*D.*12.72. **-νοος**, ον, *wicked-minded*, Maiist.56, Orac.ap.Eus.*PE*14.20, *Epigr.Gr.*1052 (Stratonicea).

ἀλῐτρός, όν, = ἀλιτηρός, *sinful*, *wicked*, Il.8.361, Thgn.377, Sol.13.27; also in late Prose, *PPar.*63.95 (ii B.C.): neut. pl., ἀλιτρά, τά, *sins*, Pi.*O.*2.59: as Subst., δαίμοσιν ἀλιτρός *sinner against* the gods, Il.23.595, cf. Theoc.10.17, Call.*Ap.*2, etc.; *knave*, Od.5.182; fem., ἀλιτρῆς ἀλώπεκος Semon.7.7.

ἀλῐτροσύνη, ἡ, = ἀλιτρία, A.R.4.699 (pl.), *IG*14.1389 ii 19, *AP*7.574 (Agath.), etc.

ἁλί-τροφος, ον, *sea-nurtured*, φῦλα, i.e. fishes, Opp.*H.*1.76, cf. Nonn.*D.*5.182, al. **-τροχος**, ον, *rushing through the sea*, Ibyc.50, in metapl. acc. sing. ἁλίτροχα. **-τρῦτος**, ον, *sea-beaten*, *sea-worn*, γέρων Theoc.1.45; κύμβη *AP*7.294 (Tull. Laur.). **-τῦπος**, ον, *sea-beaten*, ἁ. βάρη griefs *for sea-tossed corpses*, A.*Pers.*946 (lyr.): as Subst., *seaman*, *fisherman*, E.*Or.*373. **-τῦρος**, ὁ, *salted cheese*, v.l. in *AP*9.412 (Phld.).

ἀλίφατα· ἄλφιτα ἢ ἄλευρα, Hsch.

ἁλι-φθερόω, *shipwreck*, and metaph., *ruin*, Sophr.35:—ἀλιφθερῶσαι· ἀφανίσαι, Hsch. **-φθορία**, ἡ, *disaster at sea*, *shipwreck*, *AP*9.41 (Theon). **-φθόρος**, ον, *destroying on sea*: as Subst., *pirate*, *AP*7.654 (Leon.). **-φιλεῖς**· πτωχοί, Hsch. **-φλοιος**, ὁ, ἡ, *sea-bark oak*, *Quercus Pseudosuber*, Thphr.*HP*3.8.5, Sch.Theoc.9.20 (**ἁλίφαλος**· δρῦς, Hsch., is f.l.). **-φροσύνη**, ἡ, = ἱκανὴ φρόνησις (from ἅλις, φρήν), Hsch.:—Adj. **ἀλίφρονες**, Naumach.ap.Stob.4.31.76.

ἁλιχευτρίς, ίδος, ἡ, dub. sens., *PFay.*331 (ii A.D.).

ἁλί-χλαινος, ον, *purple-clad*, Nonn.*D.*20.105.

ἅλιψ or **ἄλιψ**· πέτρα, Hsch.; cf. αἰγίλιψ, ἠλίβατος.

ἀλκάζω, *put forth strength* or *prowess*, *EM*56.11, 66.10:—Med., ἠλκάζοντο· ἠμύνοντο, Hsch. **ἀλκᾰθεῖν**, poet. aor. (accented as pres. by Gramm., Phot.p.76 R., *AB*383), *assist*, A.*Fr.*411, S.*Fr.*996.

ἀλκαία, ἡ, *tail*, esp. of lion, Ael.*NA*5.39, Sch.A.R.4.1614; generally, Com. ib. cit., Call.*Fr.*317, Opp.*H.*5.264. II. *vervain mallow*, *Malva moschata*, Dsc.3.147:—also **ἀλκαῖον**, τό, Hsch.

Ἀλκαϊκός, ή, όν, *used by Alcaeus*, μέτρον Trypho *Trop.*3.

ἀλκαῖος, α, ον, (ἀλκή) *strong*, *mighty*, δόρυ E.*Hel.*1152 (lyr.).

ἄλκαρ, τό, only nom. and acc.:—*safeguard*, *defence*, οὐδέ τί σε Τρώεσσιν ὀΐομαι ἄ. ἔσεσθαι Il.5.644; ἄ. Ἀχαιῶν 11.823; σᾶς δάμαρτος ἄ. E.*Tr.*590 (lyr.): c. gen. obj., γήραος ἄ. *defence against* old age, *h.Ap.*193; ἴδεος, ὑετοῦ ἄ., Call.*Fr.*124, A.R.2.1074: abs., *remedy*, Aret.*CA*1.1.—Ep. and Lyr. word, cf. Pi.*P.*10.52, Ps.-Phoc.128. Cf. ἀλέξω.

ἀλκᾶς, v. ἀλκήεις. **ἄλκασμα**, τό, in pl., *deeds of prowess*, S.*Ichn.*247.

ἀλκή, ἡ, (cf. ἀλέξω) *strength* as displayed in action, *prowess*, *courage*, poet. word (also in Hdt., Th., and later Prose, Ti.Locr.103b, Arist.*EN*1115^{b}4, *Pol.*1338^{a}20, etc.), in Hom. joined with σθένος Il.17.212, Od.22.237; with μένος Il.9.706; with ἠνορέη Od.24.509; ἐπιειμένοι ἀλκήν Il.8.262; φρεσὶν εἱμένος ἀλκήν 20.381; δύεσθαι ἀλκήν 9.231:—later, χερὸς ἀλκᾷ Pi.*O.*10(11).100; θηρία ἐς ἀλκὴν ἄλκιμα Hdt.3.110: generally, *force*, *might*, συνῆψαν ἀλκήν E.*Supp.*683; κατ' ἀλκήν, opp. κατὰ σύνεσιν, Arr.*Tact.*12.11: in pl., *feats of strength*, *bold deeds*, Pi.*N.*7.12, B.10.126, E.*Rh.*933, Hierocl.p.33.61 A. II. *strength to avert danger*, *defence*, *help*, Διὸς ἀ. Il.15.490, cf. 8.140; οὐδέ τις ἀ. Od.12.120, 22.305; ποῦ τις ἀ.; A.*Pr.*546; ἀ. βελέων S.*Ph.*1151; δορός E.*Ph.*1098: also ἀ. τινος *defence* or *aid against* thing, Hes.*Op.*201, Pi.*N.*7.96, S.*OT*218; ἀλκὴν ποιεῖσθαι give *aid*, *OC*459; ἀ. τιθέναι make a *defence*, ib.1524; ἐς or πρὸς ἀ. τρέπεσθαι turn *and resist*, stand on *one's guard*, Hdt.2.45, 3.78, Th.2.84; στρέψας πρὸς ἀ. E.*Andr.*1149; ἐς ἀ. ἐλθεῖν Id.*Ph.*421; ἀλκῆς μεμνῆσθαι Hdt.9.70; ἐν οἷς ἐστιν ἀ. where they can *defend themselves*, Arist.*EN* l.c. III. *battle*, *fight*, A.*Th.*498,569,878 codd., E.*Med.*264.

ἄλκη, ἡ, *elk*, Paus.5.12.1.

ἀλκήεις, εσσα, εν, Dor. contr. **ἀλκᾶς**, ᾶντος, *valiant*, *courageous*, *h.Hom.*28.3, Pi.*O.*9.72, *P.*5.71, A.R.1.71; of patients, Aret.*CA*1.10, al.; *strong*, ὀϊστοί *AP*6.277 (Damag.); πίστις Man.4.48: Sup., Poet.ap.Parth.21.3.

ἀλκηστής, οῦ, ὁ, = foreg., συνόδοντες Opp.*H.*1.170.

ἀλκί [ῐ], metapl. poet. dat. of ἀλκή, *might*, *strength*: λέων ὣς ἀλκὶ πεποιθώς Il.5.299, cf. Od.6.130, Thgn.949; of Hector, Il.18.158, cf. Nonn.*D.*39.34, etc.

ἀλκιβιάδειον, τό, = ἔχιον, Dsc.4.27: = ἄγχουσα, ib.24, Gal.13.149.

ἀλκιβιάδες, αἱ, sort of *shoes* (from Ἀλκιβιάδης), Ath.12.534c, Poll.7.89.

ἀλκίβιος, ἡ, = ἔχις, *Cretan bugloss*, *Echium parviflorum*, used as an antidote to snake-bite, Sch.Nic.*Th.*541. (Ἀλκιβίου is pr. n. in Nic. l.c.)

ἀλκίμαχος, η, ον, *bravely fighting*, or *defender in fight*, of Athena, *AP*6.124 (Heges.).

ἀλκῐμόβρῑθος, ον, *mighty in weight*, *PMag.Par.*1.1364.

ἄλκῐμος, ον, also η, ον S.*Aj.*401: (ἀλκή):—*stout*, *brave*, of men and things, Τρῶες, ἔγχος, δοῦρε, Il.11.483, 3.338, Od.22.125; ἦτορ Callin.1.10; θυμός Tyrt.10.17; νέκυς Pi.*Pae.*6.98; δράκων Epich.60: Comp. -ώτερος Hdt.1.79,103, Arist.*HA*607^{a}11, etc.: Sup. -ώτατος E.*Ph.*743, Plb.6.5.9; ἄ. τὰ πολεμικά Hdt.3.4; ἐς ἀλκὴν ἄλκιμα ib.110; ἄ. μάχη E.*Heracl.*683:—prov., πάλαι ποτ' ἦσαν ἄλκιμοι Μιλήσιοι 'times are changed', Anacr.85, Ar.*Pl.*1002, Philostr.*VS*1.22.4:—less common in Prose, Pl.*R.*614b (with play on Ἀλκίνου), Arist.*HA*628^{b}6. II. *fortifying*, ὕδωρ Plu.2.669b s. v.l.; *giving succour*, *PMag.Leid.W.*14.10.

ἀλκίφρων, ον, gen. ονος, (φρήν) *stout-hearted*, λαός A.*Pers.*92 (lyr.).

ἀλκμαῖος· νεανίσκος, Hsch.

Ἀλκμανικός, ή, όν, *used by Alcman*, σχῆμα Hdn.*Fig.*p.101 S., Lesb.Gramm.5.

ἀλκμαρές· ἰσχυρόν, Hsch.

ἀλκ-τήρ, ῆρος, ὁ, *one who wards off*, *protector from* a thing, c. gen., ἀρῆς, κυνῶν καὶ ἀνδρῶν, Il.18.100, Od.14.531; νούσων Pi.*P.*3.7. **-τήριος**, ον, *helping*, *healing*, ὕδωρ Nonn.*D.*45.348:—neut. **-τήριον**, τό, *remedy*, *antidote*, τινός *against* a thing, Nic.*Th.*528, etc.; so prob. E.*Fr.*697 (cod. ἀρκτήρια).

ἀλκυόνειον (-ιον Dsc.5.118), τό, *bastard-sponge*, a zoophite, so called because like *the halcyon's nest*, Hp.*Mul.*1.106, Antyll.ap.Orib.10.21.2.

ἀλκυόνειος, α, ον, *of the* ἀλκυών, ἀ. ἡμέραι, = ἀλκυονίδες, Arist.*HA*542^{b}6, cf. Ael.*NA*1.36.

ἀλκυονίς, ίδος, ἡ, = ἀλκυών, A.R.1.1085, *Epigr.Gr.*205 (Halicarn.), 241.8 (Smyrna). II. Adj. **ἀλκῠονίδες**, αἱ, with or without ἡμέραι, *winter days during which the halcyon builds, and the sea is calm*, hence prov. of undisturbed tranquillity, Ar.*Av.*1594, cf. Arist.*HA*542^{b}15, Philoch.180, Luc.*Halc.*2, Suid.; placed in spring by Ps.-Democr.ap.Gem.*Calend.*9: sg. in Alciphr.1.1.

ἀλκυών, όνος, ἡ, mythical bird, identified with the *kingfisher*, *Alcedo ispida*, Il.9.563, Alcm.26, Simon.12, Ar.*Av.*251, Arist.*HA*542^{b}4, Theoc.7.57. (Freq. written ἁλ– by false etymology from ἅλς, κυέω: **ἀλκυδών** Hdn.Gr.2.285.)

ἀλλά, Conj., orig. neut. pl. of ἄλλος, *otherwise*: used adversatively to limit or oppose words, sentences, or clauses, stronger than δέ: I. in simple oppositions, *but*, 1. after neg. clauses, οὐ κακός, ἀλλ' ἀγαθός Thgn.212; οὐδὲ μὲν Ἕκτωρ μίμνεν, ἀλλ'..ἐφορμᾶται Il.15.690, etc. b. after a simple neg., ἢ παραφρονεῖς; οὔκ, ἀλλ' ὕπνος μ' ἔχει Ar.*V.*9, etc. c. freq. after οὐ μόνον, μὴ μόνον, with or without καί, οὐ μόνον ἅπαξ, ἀ. πολλάκις Pl.*Phdr.*228a, cf. Th.3.59, X.*Mem.*1.4.13, etc.; without μόνον, οὐχ ἑσπέρας, ἀλλὰ καὶ μεσημβρίας E.*Fr.*1006: also after οὐχ (or μὴ) ὅτι, οὐχ (or μὴ) ὅπως, either, *not only.. but..*, μὴ ὅτι ἰδιώτην τινά, ἀλλὰ τὸν μέγαν βασιλέα Pl.*Ap.*40d; μὴ ὅτι τὰ τῷ σώματι, ἀλλὰ καὶ κατὰ τὴν ψυχὴν Id.*Smp.*207e; or, *not only not .. but..*, οὐχ ὅπως κωλυταὶ..γενήσεσθε, ἀλλὰ καὶ..περιόψεσθε Th.1.35; οὐχ ὅτι ὠργίζοντο, ἀλλ' ἐζήλουν D.19.265; the neg. form is ἀλλ' οὐδέ, μὴ ὅτι ὑπὲρ ἄλλου, ἀλλ' οὐδὲ ὑπὲρ ἐμαυτοῦ δίκην εἴρηκα Is.10.1, etc. 2. in the apodosis of hypothetical sentences, *still, at least*, εἴπερ γάρ τε.. ἀλλά τε Il.1.82, etc.: in Prose, esp. ἀλλ' οὖν..γε or ἀλλά...γε, εἰ καὶ σμικρά, ἀ. οὖν ἴση γε ἡ χάρις Hdt.3.140; εἰ μή (sc. δρῶ), ἀλλ' ἀκούω γε, Pl.*Grg.*470d, cf. Isoc.3.15, al.; εἰ μηδέν ἐστι τελευτήσαντι, ἀλλ' οὖν τοῦτόν γε τὸν χρόνον ἧττον ἀηδὴς ἔσομαι Pl.*Phd.*91b (in later Gk. ἀλλά γε may be in juxtaposition, εἰ ἄλλοις οὐκ εἰμὶ ἀπόστολος, ἀλλά γε ὑμῖν εἰμί 1*Ep.Cor.*9.2, and ἀ. γε δή is found with vv.ll. in Pl.*Phdr.*262a); εἰ καὶ μετέχουσι .. ἀλλ' οὐ .. Arist.*Pol.*1282ᵃ11:—less freq. after Conjunctions of Time, as ἐπεὶ δή Od.14.151; ἐπεί S.*OC*241. b. after Hom., ἀ. is used elliptically, esp. with Advbs. of Time, ὦ θεοὶ πατρῷοι, συγγένεσθέ γ' ἀ. νῦν (sc. εἰ μὴ πρότερον, ἀ. νῦν γε) S.*El.*411, cf. *Ant.*552, E.*Heracl.*565; ἀ. τῷ χρόνῳ Id.*Med.*912; ἐὰν οὖν ἀ. νῦν γ' ἔτι, i.e. ἐὰν οὖν [μὴ ἄλλοτε], ἀ. νῦν γε.. if then now *at least* ye still.., D.3.33, cf. Lys.10.15:—without an Adv. of Time, *at least*, ἡ δ' ἀ. πρός σε μικρὸν εἰπάτω μόνον Ar.*Pax* 660, cf. S.*OC*1276, E.*HF* 331. 3. sts. = ἀλλ' ἤ (q.v.), *except, but*, οὔτι μοι αἴτιος ἄλλος, ἀ... τοκῆε no one else, *but*..., Od.8.312; οὐδέ τις ἄλλη φαίνετο γαιάων, ἀ. οὐρανὸς ἠδὲ θάλασσα 12.404; ἔπαισεν οὔτις ἀ. ἐγώ S.*OT*1331; ἡδέα ..οὐκ ἔστιν ἀ. τούτοις Arist.*EN*1176ᵃ22, cf. 1152ᵇ30: cf. reverse process in our word *but* = *be out, except*:—sts. with force of ἤ after comparatives, τάφον, οὐκ ἐν ᾧ κεῖνται μᾶλλον, ἀ. ἐν ᾧ ἡ δόξα κτλ. not that in which they are lying, *but* far more..., Th.2.43; οὐχ ὅπλων τὸ πλέον, ἀ. δαπάνης Id.1.83. 4. with neg. after an affirmative word or clause, to be rendered simply by *not*, ἀγαθῶν, ἀ. οὐχὶ κακῶν αἴτιον Lys.14.16; τῶν σπουδαίων, ἀ. μὴ τῶν φαύλων Isoc.1.2; ἐκεῖθεν, ἀ. οὐκ ἐνθένδε ἡρπάσθη Pl.*Phdr.*229d:—after a question, τί δεῖ ἐμβαλεῖν λόγον περὶ τούτου, ἀ. οὐχὶ προειπεῖν; X.*Cyr.*2.2.19, cf. Isoc.15.229, etc. b. without neg., μικρὸς μὲν ἔην δέμας, ἀ. μαχητής Il.5.801. II. to oppose whole sentences, *but, yet*: 1. freq. in transitions, as Il.1.135, 140, etc.; ἀ. καὶ ὥς.. 1.116; ἀ. οὐδ' ὥς.. Od.1.6:—after Hom. in answers and objections, *nay but..., well but...*, freq. with negs., esp. in making and answering objections, Ar.*Ach.*402, 407; also in affirmative answers, Pl.*Prt.*330b, *Grg.*449a, etc.:—repeated in a succession of questions or objections, πότερον ᾔτουν σέ τι..; ἀ. ἀπῄτουν; ἀ. περὶ παιδικῶν μαχόμενος; ἀ. μεθύων ἐπαρῴνησα; X.*An.*5.8.4, cf. Pl.*Thg.*123e, Isoc.17.47; ἀ. μήν..., answered by ἀ., Arist.*Pol.*1287ᵃ23:—in vehement answers Pl. often uses νὴ τοὺς θεοὺς ἀ..., μὰ Δί' ἀ..., *Grg.*481c, *Phlb.*36a, cf. *Alc.*1.110b, c:—at beginning of speech, to introduce a general objection, Od.4.472, cf. X.*Smp.*1, Men.*Georg.*22. 2. with imper. or subj., to remonstrate, encourage, persuade, etc., freq. in Hom., ἀ. ἄγε, ἴθι, Il.1.210, 11.611; ἀ. ἴομεν 6.526; ἀ. πίθεσθε 1.259; after voc., ὦ Φίντις, ἀ. ζεῦξον Pi.*O.*6.22, cf. Tyrt.10.15, etc.; answered by a second ἀ., ἀ. περιμένετε. ἀ. περιμενοῦμεν Pl.*R.*327b; ἀλλ' ἕρπεθ' ὡς τάχιστα S.*OC*1643, cf. *Ant.*1029, etc. 3. to break off a subject abruptly, ἀ. τά γε Ζεὺς οἶδεν Od.15.523; ἀ. ταῦτα μὲν τί δεῖ λέγειν; S.*Ph.*11, cf. *Tr.*467, etc. 4. in resuming an address after parenthesis, Pi.*O.*2.12, 4.7. 5. in elliptical phrases, οὐ μὴν ἀ., οὐ μέντοι ἀ.. *it is not* [*so*], *but*.., ὁ ἵππος πίπτει καὶ μικροῦ αὐτὸν ἐξετραχήλισεν· οὐ μὴν [ἐξετραχήλισεν] ἀ. ἐπέμεινεν ὁ Κῦρος it did not however [throw him], *but*..., X.*Cyr.*1.4.8; οὐ μέντοι ἀ. Pl.*Smp.*173b; οὐ γὰρ ἀ. Ar.*Ra.*58, 498:—after δέ, ὑμεῖς δέ μ' ἀ. παιδὶ συμφονεύσατε E.*Hec.*391. III. when joined with other Particles, each retains proper force, as, 1. ἀλλ' ἄρα, used by Hom. in transitions, Il.6.418, 12.320, etc.; later, to introduce an objection, Pl.*Ap.*25a; in questions, ἀλλ' ἆρα..; Id.*R.*381b. 2. ἀλλ' οὖν, concessive, *at all events*, Ar.*Ra.*1298; τοὺς πρώτους χρόνους ἀ. οὖν προσεποιοῦνθ' ὑμῖν εἶναι φίλοι Aeschin.3.86; *well then*, Pl.*Prt.*310a; *but then, however*, with γε following, Hdt.3.140, S.*Ant.*84, E.*Cyc.*652, Isoc.3.18, etc.; ἀλλ' οὖν γε in apodosi, v. supr. I. 2. 3. ἀλλὰ γάρ, freq. with words between, *but really, certainly*, as ἀλλὰ γὰρ Κρέοντα λεύσσω.., παύσω γόους, but this is irreg. for ἀλλά, Κρέοντα γὰρ λεύσσω, παύσω γόους, E.*Ph.*1308, cf. S.*Ant.*148; for the reg. order cf. S.*Ph.*81, E.*Heracl.*480, *Med.*1067; freq. elliptical, the Verb being understood, Hdt.8.8, A.*Pr.*941, S.*Ant.*155: in Hom. only with negs., ἀλλ' οὐ γάρ Il.7.242, Od.14.355, al., cf. S.*OT*1409; ἀ. γὰρ δή, ἀ. γάρ τοι, S.*Aj.*167, *Ph.*81. 4. ἀ. εἰ.. *quid si..?* Il.16.559. 5. ἀ. ἤ in questions, chiefly of surprise or remonstrance, A.*Ch.*220, S.*El.*879, Ar.*Ach.*1111; ἀλλ' ἦ, τὸ λεγόμενον, κατόπιν ἑορτῆς ἥκομεν; Pl.*Grg.*447a, cf. *Prt.*309c. 6. ἀ. followed by strengthening Particle, ἀλλ' ἤτοι μὲν ταῦτα θεῶν ἐν γούνασι κεῖται Il.17.514; esp. c. imper., 1.211, al.; ἀλλά τοι Od.15.518, A.*Pers.*795, etc.; ἀ. μέντοι, with or without γε, Pl.*Smp.*214e, *Hp.Ma.*287d, al.; ἀ. μήν, v. μήν; ἀ. δή, mostly with words between, S.*Aj.*1271, *OC*586, Isoc.4.109, etc.; without intervening words, Pl.*Ap.*37c, al.; ἀ. δῆτα Id.*Hp.Ma.*285c; ἀ. μὲν δὴ καὶ αὐτὸς Id.*Tht.*143b, cf. S.*El.*103. IV. = *et quidem*, Olymp. *in Mete.*1.13, al.

ἀλλάγ-δην, Adv. *alternately*, Doroth.65, Hdn.Gr.1.508. **-ή** [ᾰγ], ἡ (ἀλλάσσω) *change*, A.*Ag.*482, etc.; ἀλλαγᾷ βίου S.*OT*1206; ἡ κατὰ τόπον ἀ. Arist.*Spir.*485ᵃ22; ἀ. θεῶν Plu.2.166d. II. *exchange, barter, buying and selling*, Pl.*R.*371b, Arist.*EN*1133ᵃ19, *Pol.*1257ᵃ13; pl., διὰ τὰς ἀ. *for purposes of exchange*, ib.1280ᵃ35. 2. *agio*, whether premium or discount, *Peripl.M.Rubr.*49, *PEleph.*14.10 (iii B.C.), *PTeb.*99.2 (ii B.C.), *BGU*1194.17 (i B.C.), etc. III. later, *change of post-horses, stage*, Eust.531.21, cf. *POxy.*1863.5, etc. **-μα**, ατος, τό, *that which is given* or *taken in exchange*, καινῆς διαίτης Hp.*VM*3. 2. *reward, price* of a thing, *AP*12.132 (Mel.), Lxx *De.*23.18(19). 3. *change, vicissitude*, Lxx *Si.*2.4. **-μός**, ὁ, = foreg., Man.4.189.

ἀλλάθαρον· ἁλμυρόν (Cret.), Hsch.

ἀλλαθεάς, ἄδος, ἡ, at Delphi, *funeral ceremony*, in pl., τὰ ἐς τὰν ταφὰν καὶ ἀ. *GDI*1796, cf. 1731, 1775.

ἀλλακ-τέον, *one must change*, Plu.2.53b, Sor.2.11. **-τικός**, ή, όν, *of* or *for exchange*: ἡ -κή or τὸ -κόν *the business of exchange*, Pl.*Sph.*223c; κοινωνία ἀ. Arist.*EN*1132ᵇ31. Adv. -κῶς *in exchange*, Sch.E.*Hec.*1159. **-τός**, ή, όν, *equivalent*, πρός τι Phld.*Oec.*pp.47, 55 J.: -τόν, τό, = ἀνάφορον, Arg. Ar.*Ra.*

ἀλλαμπᾶν· τὸν ἥλιον, οἱ δὲ ἐπιχειρίδιον (leg. -χωρ-) δαίμονα, Hsch.

ἀλλανής (-ῆς cod.)· ἀσφαλής (Lacon.), Id.

ἀλλάντιον, τό, in later Gk., Dim. of ἀλλᾶς, Moer.12.

ἀλλαντο-ειδής, ές, *sausage-shaped*, ἀ. ὑμήν the *allantoid* membrane of the foetus, Gal.*UP*15.5, Aët.16.2. **-ποιός**, ὁ, *maker of sausages*, Hsch.Mil.7 A 3, D.L.2.60. **-πωλέω**, *deal in sausages*, Ar.*Eq.*1242. **-πώλης**, ου, ὁ, *sausage-seller*, Ar.*Eq.*143, al., Procop.*Pers.*1.26 (pl.).

ἀλλάξ, Adv. = ἐνηλλαγμένως, Hsch.

ἀλλάξιμα (sc. ἱμάτια), *changes of raiment*, *POxy.*1728.2 (iii A.D.), *Gloss.*

ἄλλαξις, εως, ἡ, *exchange, barter*, Arist.*MM*1194ᵃ24.

ἀλλᾶς, ᾶντος, ὁ, *force-meat, sausage* or *black-pudding*, Hippon.48, Ar.*Eq.*161, Crates Com.17, etc.

ἀλλάσσω, later Att. -ττω Pl.*Prm.*139a: impf. ἤλλαττον Men.*Epit.*466: fut. -άξω Thgn.21: aor. ἤλλαξα E.*Alc.*661: pf. ἤλλᾰχα (ἀπ-) X.*Mem.*3.13.6, (δι-) Dionys.Com.2.10:—**Med.**, fut. ἀλλάξομαι Luc.*Tyr.*7, (ἀντ-) E.*Hel.*1088: aor. ἠλλαξάμην Id.*El.*103, Antipho 5.79, Th.8.82, etc.: pf. (in med. sense) ἤλλαγμαι (ἐν-) S.*Aj.*208:—**Pass.**, fut. ἀλλαχθήσομαι Trag. and Com., (ἀπ-) E.*Med.*878, Ar.*Av.*940; ἀλλαγήσομαι in early Prose, (ἀπ-) Hdt.2.120, (ἐξαπ-) Th.4.28: aor. ἠλλάχθην and ἠλλάγην, former more freq. in S. and E., latter in Prose: pf. ἤλλαγμαι Antiph.176, *AP*9.67, al.: plpf. ἤλλακτο Hdt.2.26. (More common in compds., esp. in later Gk.): (ἄλλος):—*make other than it is, change, alter*, τόπον Parm.8.41; μορφήν Emp.137; χροιάν E.*Med.*1168; ἤλλαττε χρώματ' Men.*Epit.*466; τὸ ἑαυτοῦ εἶδος εἰς πολλὰς μορφάς Pl.*R.*380d; χώραν Id.*Prm.*139a. II. ἀ. τί τινος *give in exchange, barter* one thing *for* another, τῆς σῆς λατρείας τὴν ἐμὴν δυσπραξίαν.. οὐκ ἂν ἀλλάξαιμ' ἐγώ A.*Pr.*967; τι ἀντί τινος E.*Alc.*661:—Med., τὴν παραυτίκα ἐλπίδα.. οὐδενὸς ἂν ἠλλάξαντο Th.8.82. 2. *repay, requite*, φόνον φονεῦσιν E.*El.*89. 3. *leave, quit*, οὐράνιον φῶς S.*Ant.*944, cf. E.*IT*193. 4. Med., ἔξω τρίβου ἀλλάσσεσθαι ἴχνος *move one's position*, Id.*El.*103. III. *take* one thing *in exchange for* another, κάκιον τοὐσθλοῦ παρεόντος Thgn.21; πόνῳ πόνον ἀ. *to exchange* one suffering *with* another (nisi leg. πόνου), *Trag.Adesp.*7.3; ἠλλαττόμεσθ' ἂν δάκρυα δόντες χρυσίον *should take in exchange*, Philem.73: ἀ. θνητὸν εἶδος *assume* it, E.*Ba.*53, cf. 1331:—more freq. in Med., τί τινος one thing *for* another, εὐδαιμονίας κακοδαιμονίαν Antipho 5.79, cf. Pl.*Lg.*733b; τὰ οἰκήϊα κακὰ ἀλλάξασθαι τοῖσι πλησίοισι *exchange* them with them, Hdt.7.152: hence, *buy*, τι ἀντ' ἀργυρίου Pl.*R.*371c; διά τινος ὠνῆς ἢ καὶ πράσεως ἀλλάττεσθαί τί τινι Id.*Lg.*915d, e; τοῦ παντὸς ἀ. *prize above* all things, Ph.*Bel.*56.30. 2. *take a new position*, i.e. *go to* a place, ἀ. Ἅιδα θαλάμους E.*Hec.*483; πόλιν ἐκ πόλεως Pl.*Plt.*289e. IV. abs., *have dealings*, as buyer or seller, in Med., πρός τινα Pl.*Lg.*915e. 2. *alternate*, Emp.17.6; σκῆπτρ' ἔχειν ἐνιαυτὸν ἀλλάσσοντε to enjoy power *in turn*, E.*Ph.*74, cf. Pl.*Ti.*42c:—Pass., ἀρεταί.. ἀλλασσόμεναι *in turns*, Pi.*N.*11.38, cf. Arist.*Pr.*940ᵃ15. V. Pass., *to be reconciled*, S.*Fr.*997.

ἀλλαττόλογος, ον, *complicated*, μῦθος *POxy.*1381.180 (ii A.D.).

ἀλλαχ-ῆ, Delph. -χᾷ *GDI*2085, Adv., (ἄλλος) *elsewhere, in another place*, ἄλλος ἀ. one *here*, another *there*, X.*An.*7.3.47; ἄλλοτε ἀ. now *here*, now *there*, Id.*Mem.*1.4.12; = ἄλλοσε, ἀπιὼν ἀ. Ar.*Av.*1020, cf. *PLips.*104 (i B.C.). **-όθεν**, Adv. *from another place*, Lxx 4*Ma.*1.7, *Ev.Jo.*10.1, Plu.2.1129e; *from another source*, δηλοῦσθαι Antipho 3.4.3. **-όθι**, Adv. *elsewhere*, A.D.*Synt.*333.26, Plu.2.20d, *AP*9.378 (Pall.), Jul.*Or.*1.5c. **-όσε**, Adv. *elsewhither*, v.l. in X.*Cyr.*7.4.7, Simp. *in Ph.*1164.38. **-οῦ**, Adv. *elsewhere*, S.*OC*43, X.*HG*2.3.20; ἄγωμεν ἀ. *Ev.Marc.*1.38, cf. Arr.*Epict.*3.26.4.—These forms are censured by Moer.11 as less Att. than ἄλλοθεν, ἄλλοθι, ἄλλοσε.

ἄλλεγον, ἀλλέξαι, v. sub ἀναλέγω.

ἀλλεπαλληλία, ἡ, *accumulation*, Eust.12.3. **ἀλλεπάλληλος**, ον, *one upon another, successive*, ῥανίδες *EM*702.20; νῆσσαι Sch.Arat.982; *cumulative*, σύνθεσις (as in συν-ομ-ήλικες) *EM*291.37; τὸ ἀ. *accumulation*, Paus.6.39.4; *alternating, varying*, δρόμοι Vett.Val.331.22; *constantly changing*, ἀποτελέσματα 243.29. Adv. -ως *in varied style*, 272.23:—also, *in layers*, of stones, Arg.E.*Ph.*:—perh. to be written divisim ἀλλ' ἐπ., Alciphr.*Fr.*6.11.

ἄλλῃ, Dor. ἄλλᾳ or ἀλλᾷ (as A.D.*Adv.*175.13), Delph. and Megar. ἄλλει *GDI*1830, 3052 (Chalcedon), Adv., properly dat. fem. of ἄλλος: I. of Place, 1. *elsewhere*, Il.13.49, S.*Ph.*23, etc.; τῇ ἄ. Hdt.2.36, 4.28: c. gen. loci, ἄλλος ἄ. τῆς πόλεως one *in one part of* the city, one *in another*, Th.2.4; ἄ. τῆς κεφαλῆς Hp.*VC*8; ἄλλοτε ἄ. X.*HG*1.5.20; ἄ. καὶ ἄ. *here and there*, prob. l. Id.*An.*5.2.29. 2. *to another place, elsewhither*, Il.5.187, Od.18.288; ἔρχεται ἄ., i.e. *is lost* Il.1.120; ἄλλοι ἄ. Hdt.1.46, cf. 7.25; οὔτ' ἐπὶ θήρην ἰοῦσαι οὔτ' ἄ. οὐδαμῇ Id.4.114. II. of Manner, *otherwise*, Il.15.51, etc.; τῇ τε ἄ. πολλαχῇ καὶ.. Hdt.6.21; ἄ. γέ πῃ Pl.*Smp.*189c; ἄ. πως X.*Cyr.*1.1.1.

ἀλλ' ἤ, = ἀλλά I. 3, *except, but*, after negs., esp. οὐδείς or μηδείς, which are often joined with ἄλλος or ἕτερος, as οὐδεὶς ἀλλ' ἢ ἐκείνη no one *except* her, Hdt.9.109, cf. Th.3.71, al.; μηδὲν ἄλλο δοκεῖν εἶναι ἀληθὲς ἀλλ' ἢ τὸ σωματοειδές Pl.*Phd.*81b, cf. *R.*429b, etc.; ἀργύριον μὲν οὐκ ἔχω ἀλλ' ἢ μικρόν τι X.*An*.7.7.53 :—after questions implying a neg., Pl.*Phdr*.258e :—in Ar.*Ach*.1111,1112 ἀλλ' ἤ (bis) is prob. l. for ἀλλ' ἦ (bis). (This form seems to arise from a confusion of οὐδὲν ἄλλο ἤ *other than, except*, cf. Hdt.1.49, 9.8, ἄλλο γε ἢ ὅτι.. *except* that.., and οὐδὲν ἄλλο..ἀλλά.)

ἀλλ' ἦ, in questions, v. ἀλλά III. 5.

ἀλληγορ-έω, (ἀγορεύω) *interpret allegorically*, Ἕλληνες Κρόνον ἀλληγοροῦσι τὸν χρόνον Plu.2.363d, cf. 996b, Heraclit.*All*.1 :—Pass., *to be spoken allegorically*, *Ep.Gal*.4.24 ; ἀλληγορεῖται ὁ Ἀπόλλων εἰς τὸν Ἥλιον, Sch.S.*Aj*.186. 2. abs., *speak figuratively* or *metaphorically*, Demetr.*Eloc*.151,285 ; *speak allegorically*, J.*AJProoem*. 4. **-ητής**, οῦ, ὁ, *allegorical expounder*, Eust.123.32. **-ία**, ἡ, *allegory, veiled language*, Cic.*Att*.2.20.3(pl.) :—*allegorical exposition* of mythical legends, Plu.2.19e ; κατ' ἀλληγορίαν Longin.9.7. II. *figurative, metaphorical language*, Demetr.*Eloc*.99, Cic.*Orat*.27.94, Quint.*Inst*.8.6.44 ; χρῆσθαι μεταφοραῖς ἢ -γορίαις Phld.*Rh*.1.174S., cf. 164S. **-ικός**, ή, όν, *figurative*, Demetr.*Eloc*.282 ; ἀ. στόμφος Longin.32.7. Adv. -κῶς Cleanth.*Stoic*.1.118, Demetr.*Eloc*.243. **-ος**, ον, *allegorical*, *Et.Gud*.515.42. Adv. -ως *allegorically*, Anon. (fort. Tz.) ap.Sch.A.*Pr*.428.

ἄλληκτος (A), ον, poet. for ἄληκτος (A), *unceasing, ceaseless*, νότος Od.12.325 ; ὀδύναι S.*Tr*.985 (lyr.) ; *implacable*, θυμὸς Il.9.636 : neut. as Adv., ἄλληκτον, ἄλληκτα, Man.3.252,206.—So Ἀλληκτώ is restored for Ἀληκτώ (the Fury) in Luc.*Trag*.6.

ἄλληκτος (B), ον, = ἄληκτος (B), *AB*202 :—Adv. -τί, Hsch.

ἀλληλ-ανάδοχος, ον, *giving mutual security*, *PLond*.3.994.7 (vi A.D.), *PHamb*.23.7 (vi A.D.). **-ανεμία**, ἡ, *constant change of wind*, ἀ. ἐπισφαλὴς ταῖς βοτάναις Lyd.*Ost*.31.

ἀλληλάξαι· ἀλλήλους ἐλάσαι, Hsch.

ἀλληλ-εγγύη, ἡ, *mutual security*, ἐξ -ύης *PFlor*.368.10 (i A.D.), *POxy*.918ii 15 (ii A.D.), etc. ; τὸ τῆς ἀ. δίκαιον *PCair*.67126.18. **-έγγυοι**, α, *mutual sureties*, *BGU*1001 (i B.C.), 1106.41 (i B.C.) : sg., Hsch. Adv. -ως Just.*Edict*.9.3, *Nov*.99.

ἀλληλίζω, *lie together*, sens. obsc., *AB*383 :—also ἀλληλίζειν· ἄλλως καὶ ἄλλως λέγειν, and ἀλληλίζεσθαι· τὸ ἀλλήλους ἐπιχειρῆσαι, Hsch.

ἀλληλο-βόρος, ον, in pl., *devouring one another*, Hsch. s.v. ἀλληλοδωδόται. **-γραφία**, ἡ, *writing of amoebaean poems*, Eust. 55.39.

ἀλληλ-οδωδόται, *devouring one another*, dub. in Hsch.

ἀλληλο-κληρονομία, ἡ, *mutual inheritance*, Suid. s.v. ῥευξωρία. **-κτονέω**, *slay each other*, Hp.*Ep*.17, Arist.*Fr*.344, Ph.2. 38. **-κτονία**, ἡ, *mutual slaughter*, D.H.1.87, Ph.2.567. **-κτόνος**, ον, of things, *producing mutual slaughter*, δαῖτες Moschio Trag.6 ; ζῆλος D.H.2.24. **-μανδάτορες**, οἱ, *mandatories of each other*, *PHamb*.23.7 (vi A.D.). **-μαχία**, ἡ, *mutual fight*, Sch.Il.3. 443. **-μισέω**, *hate one another*, *PMag.Lond*.46.108. **-πάθεια**, ἡ, Astrol., *subjection to mutual influence*, Vett.Val.5.13. **-τυπέω**, *impinge mutually*, Alex.Aphr.*in Metaph*.36.22. **-τυπία**, ἡ, *mutual impact*, of atoms, *Placit*.1.12.6 : pl., Ph.2.489.

ἀλληλ-ουχέω, *hold together*, intr., Ph.1.464, 2.417 :—Pass., Nicom. *Ar*.1.2 ; -ούμενος κόσμος Iamb.*in Nic*.p.7.13P., cf. Simp.*in Ph*.711.16, Syrian.*in Metaph*.150.1, Dam.*Pr*.206. **-ουχία**, ἡ, *holding together, conjunction*, Longin.36.4 ; *coherence*, Epicur.*Nat*.2.993.5 ; *continuity*, opp. παράθεσις, *Theol.Ar*.4 ; τάξις καὶ ἀ. Procl.*Inst*.97, cf. Dam.*Pr*. 85 ; κόσμου Iamb.*Protr*.21.ιζ' ; *close texture, consistency*, Gal.14.12 ; κτηδόνων Dsc.5.127 ; *mutual support*, of words in composition, D.H. *Comp*.23. **-ουχοι**, α, *holding together*, ἄτομοι Epicur.*Ep*.2 p.44 U. ; φύσεις Id.*Nat*.2.9 ; ἐγκεντρίσεις Jul.*Ep*.180.

ἀλληλο-φαγέω, *eat one another*, Arist.*HA*591ᵃ17. **-φαγία**, ἡ, *an eating one another*, Hdt.3.25, Pl.*Epin*.975a, Athenio 1, etc. **-φάγοι**, α, *eating each other*, Arist.*HA*593ᵇ27, Orac.ap.Paus.8.42.6 ; ἡ ἀ. ἀνομία S.E.*M*.2.32 ; ἀ. δίκαι Telecl.2. **-φθονία**, ἡ, *mutual envy*, D.H.4.26. **-φθορία**, ἡ, *mutual slaughter*, Pl.*Prt*.321a (pl.), D.H.5.66 (pl.). **-φθόρος**, ον, *destroying one another*, Max.Tyr. 41.5. **-φιλέω**, *love one another*, *PMag.Lond*.46.107. **-φιλοι**, α, *fond of each other*, *Gp*.20.6.1. **-φονία**, Dor. ἀλλᾱλ-, ἡ, *mutual slaughter*, Pi.*O*.2.42, Philipp.Perg. in *IG*4.1153 (Epid.), Them. *Or*.6.74b, Herm.ap.Stob.1.49.44. **-φόνοι**, Dor. ἀλλᾱλ-, α, *murdering one another*, λόγχαι Pi.*Fr*.163 ; χεῖρες, μανίαι, A.*Th*.931, *Ag*.1576 ; ἀδελφοί X.*Hier*.3.8. **-φυής**, ές, in pl., *grown out of one another*, f.l. for ὁλοφυής, *Placit*.5.19.5.

ἀλλήλων, Aeol. and Dor. **ἀλλάλων**, gen. pl., dual ἀλλήλοιν, Ep. ἀλλήλοιϊν Il.10.65, fem. -αιν X.*Mem*.2.3.18 codd. : dat. ἀλλήλοις, αις, οις, dual ἀλλήλοιν : acc. ἀλλήλους, ας, α, dual ἀλλήλω (fem.) X.*Mem*. 2.3.18, cf. Lxx *Ge*.15.10, al. : the dual is rare in Prose : sg., κεράμῳ ἁρμόττοντι πρὸς ἄλληλον *IG*2.1054.59 : (redupl. from ἄλλος) :—*of one another, to one another, one another* ; hence, *mutually, reciprocally*, used of all three persons, Il.4.62, Od.1.209, etc. : freq. with Preps., ἐν ἀλλήλοισι among *one another*, Pi.*P*.4.223, etc. ; τούτω.. ἐν ἀλλήλαισι A.*Pers*.188 ; πρὸς ἀλλήλους, εἰς ἄλληλα, Id.*Pr*.491,1086 ; ἐπί, πρὸς ἀλλήλοις, Od.22.389, A.*Pers*.506, *Ag*.654 ; ἐξ ἀλλήλων X.*Mem*. 4.4.23 ; κύκλῳ καὶ ἐξ ἀλλήλων δεικνυσθαι Arist.*APr*.57ᵇ18 ; παρ' ἀλλήλους, -α, Pl.*Grg*.472c, *Phdr*.264b ; ἡ δι' ἀλλήλων δεῖξις *reciprocal* proof, Arist.*APr*.59ᵃ32, cf. D.L.9.89, etc. ; μετ' ἀλλήλων Arist.*Pr*. 953ᵇ32 ; πρὸς αὑτὰ καὶ πρὸς ἄλληλα Pl.*Grg*.451c ; ὑπ' ἀλλήλων A.*Th*. 821. (Wrongly interpreted by Gramm. as = ἑαυτούς, -ῶν, Il.12.105, Th.2.70, E.*Fr*.1124.)

ἄλλην, acc. fem. of ἄλλος, used (sc. ὁδόν) as Adv., *elsewhither*, ἄ. καὶ ἄ. διώκειν X.*Cyr*.4.1.15, cf. Aen.Tact.26.3 : also of Time, ἄ. καὶ ἄ. ἀποβλέπειν εἰς τινα *again and again*, Pl.*Euthd*.273b.

ἄλλην· λάχανον (Ital.), Hsch.

ἀλλήναλλος, ον, *this way and that, irregular*, κίνησις Theo Sm. p.151 H. Adv. -ως Eustr.*in APo*.149.29.

ἀλλῆσαι· ἀναστρέψαι, Hsch. (fort. ἀλλῦσαι).

ἄλλιξ, ῖκος, ἡ, *man's upper garment*, Euph.144, Call.*Fr*.149 ; *purple cloak* (Thessal.), *EM*68.33.

ἄλλιστος, ον, Ep. for ἄλιστος, (λίσσομαι) *inexorable*, Ἅιδης *AP*7. 643 (Crin.), *IG*14.1909.3.

ἀλλιτάνευτος, Ep. for ἀλιτάνευτος, *inexorable*, *AP*7.483.

ἄλλῐτος, ον, = foreg., αἶσα *Epic.Alex.Adesp*.6.5 ; ἄλλιτα κωκύοντες shrieking *unanswered prayers*, *App.Anth*.4.54.7.

ἀλλο-γενής, ές, *of another race*, *OGI*598, Lxx *Ge*.17.27, al., *Ev.Luc*. 17.18, Agath.4.5, Ps.-Callisth.3.26. **-γλωσσία**, ἡ, *use of a strange tongue, difference of tongue*, J.*AJ*1.5.1. **-γλωσσος**, ον, *using a strange tongue*, Hdt.2.154, *SIG*1.4 (Abu Simbel, vi B.C.), *IG*12(3). 328.20 (Thera, iii B.C.), Lxx *Ba*.4.15. **-γνοέω**, (γνο-, γνῶναι) *take one for another*, ἀλλογνώσας Κροῖσον Hdt.1.85. II. *to be deranged*, Hp.ap.Gal.19.75. **-γνώμων**, ονος, *fickle*, Ptol.*Tetr*.183 ; *holding strange opinions*, Agath.4.26. **-γνώς**, ῶτος, ὁ, ἡ, *unknown, strange*, Emp.126. **-γνωτος**, ον, = foreg., δῆμος Od.2. 366. **-δαπός**, ή, όν, (perh. ἀλλοδ-, cf. Lat. *aliud*, -απος = -$n̥q^u$os, cf. Lat. *long-inquus*) *belonging to another people* or *land, foreign*, Il. 16.550, Od.17.485, Sapph.92, Pi.*N*.1.22, A.*Th*.1082, X.*Cyr*.8.7. 14, etc. ; ἐν ἀλλοδαπῇ *in foreign parts*, *Sammelb*.4284.7 (iii A.D.) :—later **-δαπής**, ές, *EM*68.2, cf. Ps.-Callisth.2.21. **-δημία**, Dor. **-δαμία**, ἡ, = ἀποδημία, *stay in foreign land*, Hp.*Int*.48 ; ἐν ἀλλοδημίᾳ *abroad*, Pl.*Lg*.954e ; καταστρέφειν ἐπ' ἀλλοδημί⟨ας⟩ Phld.*Mort*.26 : pl., Iamb.*VP*35.252. II. concrete, *foreign people*, στείχειν ἐπ' ἀλλοδαμίαν B.17.37, cf. Poll.9.21. **-δημος**, ον, *foreign*, Id.3.54. **-δοξέω**, *mistake one thing for another*, Pl.*Tht*.189d, 190cd. **-δοξία**, ἡ, *mistaking of one thing for another*, ib.189b. II. *revolutionary spirit*, D.C.79.5. **-δοξος**, ον, *holding a different opinion, belonging to a different school*, Phld.*Herc*.19.2. **-εθνής**, ές, *of foreign nation*, D.S.2.37, Nic.Dam.p.94 D., J.*AJ*15.11.5 ; *with foreign foe*, πόλεμος D.H.5.5, cf. Lxx 3*Ma*.4.6. **-εθνία**, ἡ, *difference of nation*, Str.12. 1.2. **-ειδής**, ές, *of different form*, τοὔνεκ' ἄρ' ἀλλοειδέα (trisyll., but perh. ἀλλοϝιδέα) φαινέσκετο πάντα ἄνακτι Od.13.194, cf. Plu. *Strom*.2, Plot.6.8.18. Adv. -δῶς, f.l. for στυλοειδῶς, Epicur.*Ep*.2 p.47 U.

ἄλλοθεν, Adv. *from another place*, ἄ. ἄλλος one *from one place*, another *from another*, Il.2.75, etc., cf. Alc.86, Emp.23, Thgn.518, A. *Ag*.92,595, etc. ; ἄ. εἰλήλουθε he came *from abroad*, Od.3.318 ; ποθεν ἄλλοθεν 7.52 ; in Att., ἄ. ὁθενοῦν or ὁποθενοῦν *from* what *other place* soever, Pl.*Lg*.738c, *Grg*.512a ; οὐδαμόθεν ἄ. Id.*Phlb*.3ca : c. gen. loci, ἄ. τῶν Ἑλλήνων Id.*Lg*.707e.

ἄλλοθι, Adv. *elsewhere, in another place*, esp. *in a strange* or *foreign land*, Od.14.130, al. (not in Il.) : c. gen., ἄ. γαίης *in another* or *strange* land, Od.2.131 ; but ἄ. πάτρης *elsewhere than* in one's native land, i.e. *away from* home, 17.318 ; ἄ. που or πῃ somewhere *else*, Pl.*Phd*. 91e (v.l.), *Sph*.243b ; ἄ. οὐδαμοῦ, πολλαχοῦ, X.*Mem*.1.4.8, Pl.*Smp*. 209e ; ἄ. ἐν οἷς.., as if ἐν ἄλλοις ἔργοις, Id.*La*.181e ; ἄ. καὶ ἄ. *to different points* (cf. ἄλλος II.3), Arist.*Mete*.376ᵇ11. II. *in other ways, from other causes*, Th.1.16 ; ἄ. οὐδαμοῦ in no *other way*, Pl.*Prt*.324e, *Smp*.184e, etc. III. with Verbs of motion, Antipho 1.4, X.*HG* 2.2.2, D.34.37.

ἀλλό-θροος, ον, contr. **-θρους**, ουν (as always in Trag.) *speaking a strange tongue*, ἐπ' ἀλλοθρόους ἀνθρώπους, κατ' ἀλλοθρόους ἀνθρ., Od. 1.183, 3.302, 15.453 : generally, *foreign*, στρατός Hdt.1.78 ; Αἴγυπτος Id.3.11 ; πόλις A.*Ag*.1200 ; *strange, alien*, γνώμη S.*Tr*.844.—Not in Att. Prose.

ἀλλοινία, ἡ, *drinking several wines, mixing liquors*, Plu.2.661c (pl.).

ἀλλοιό-μορος, ον, *unfortunate*, *PMag.Par*.1.1409. **-μορφος**, ον, *strangely formed*, ἄνθρωπος Hanno *Peripl*.7 ; θεωρία Onos.10. 28. **-προσωπέω**, *to be separated from another planet by a distance differing from that between their two domiciles*, Vett.Val.65.8.

ἀλλοῖος, α, ον, (ἄλλος) *of another sort* or *kind, different*, Il.4.258, 5.638 (v.l.), Od.16.181, etc. ; ἄλλοτε ἀλλοῖος Pi.*I*.4(3).5, cf. *P*.3. 104, Diog.Apoll.2 : prov., ἢν πολλὰ βάλλῃς, ἄλλοτ' ἀλλοῖον βαλεῖς 'every bullet has its billet', *Com.Adesp*.448 ; ἀλλοῖα φρονεῖν Emp. 108 ; ἀλλοῖόν τι, euphem. for κακόν τι, *other than good*, Hdt.5.40 ; εἴ τι γένοιτο ἀ. Arcesil.ap.D.L.4.44 ; ἂν..[ὁ λόγος] ἀλλοιότερος φανῇ D. *Prooem*.32.4, cf. Alex.Aphr.*Pr*.1.99 :—foll. by ἤ.., Hdt.2.35, Pl.*Ap*. 20c, etc. ; or by gen., Id.*Lg*.836b :—Comp. ἀλλοιότερος Hdt.7.212, Th.4.106, D.l.c., Arist.*Cael*.280ᵃ12 ; ἀλλοιέστερος Epich.186, cf. Sch.Od.2.190. 2. *containing* or *subject to diversity*, Porph.*Sent*. 20,21. II. Adv. -ως *otherwise*, Pl.*Ly*.212d : Comp. -ότερον X. *Mem*.4.8.2 ; -οτέρως *worse*, Charis.80.17.

ἀλλοιό-στροφος, ον, *of irregular strophes*, i.e. not consisting of alternate strophe and antistrophe, Heph.*Poëm*.5. **-σχήμων**, ον, *of varying form*, κόσμοι Epicur.*Fr*.82, cf. S.E.*M*.7.206. **-της**, ητος, ἡ, *difference, alteration*, Hp.*Flat*.2, Pl.*Ti*.82b. **-τροπέω**, *change colour*, Hp.*Int*.37 :—Med. -έομαι *vary*, Gal.19.75. **-τροπος**, prob. l. for ἀλλότροπος, Linus ap.Stob.1.10.5 ; gloss on αἰλότροπος, Hsch. **-φανής**, ές, gloss on ἀλλοίους, Hsch. ; on ἀείδελον, *EM*21. 28. **-χροος**, ον, contr. **-χρους**, ουν, (χρόα) *of varying colour*, S.E. *M*.7.206.

ἀλλοι-όω, (ἀλλοῖος) *change, alter*, φύσιν Hp.*Praec*.9 ; τροφὴν ἐς τὸ γάλα Id.*Gland.*16, Pl.*R.*381a, etc. 2. *represent as* ἀλλοῖος (q.v.), Plot.3.6.3. II. Pass., fut. -ωθήσομαι Gal.*UP*8.6, etc., but -ώσομαι ib.10.1:—*become different, be changed*, Hp.*Vict.*1.4, etc.; ἀλλοιοῦσθαι τὴν γνώμην Th.2.59; τῇ ὄψει X.*Cyn.*9.4; ἀλλοίωσιν ἀλλοιοῦσθαι *undergo an alteration*, Pl.*Tht.*181d; rare in Poetry, ὅλοιντ' ἰδοῦσαι τούσδ' ἂν ἠλλοιωμένους E.*Supp.*944. 2. *to be estranged*, D.C.37.11. 3. *to be changed for the worse*, X.*Cyr.*3.3.9, Euphro 10, Lxx *La.*4.1. 4. *to be confused in mind*, ὑπὸ τῆς μέθης Plb. 8.27.5. 5. *disguise oneself*, Lxx 3*Ki.*14.2. -ώδης, ες, *strange, altered in appearance*, τὰς ὄψιας Aret.*SD*1.6; *strange in manner*, Vett. Val.18.5. -ωμα, ατος, τό, = -ωσις Damox.2. -ωπός, όν, *of different shapes*, Emp.21. -ωσις, εως, ἡ, *difference*, Pl.*R.*454c; *alteration*, Arist.*Ph.*226a26, Aristox.*Harm.*p.74 M.: pl., Thphr.*CP* 4.5.5; cf. ἀλλοιόω II.1. 2. *confusion of mind*, Plb.3.81.5. 3. Gramm., *varied construction*, Ps.-Plu.*Vit.Hom.*41,48. -ωτικός, ή, όν, *transformative*, Arist.*Sens.*441b21, *Ph.*257a24; δύναμις, of digestion, Gal.*UP*4.7; *alterative*, φάρμακον ὅτι περ ἂν ἀ. ᾖ τῆς φύσεως Id.11.380. -ωτός, ή, όν, *subject to change*, Arist.*Ph.*201a12, cf. *Placit.*1.9.2, etc.

ἀλλο-κοτία, ἡ, *absurdity*, Simp.*in Ph.*1142.31, *in Epict.*p.72 D. **-κοτος**, ον, *of unusual nature* or *form, strange, portentous*, Hp.*Fract.*1, Ar.*V.*71, Crates Com.43, etc.; ἀ. πρᾶγμα *unwelcome, against the grain*, Th.3.49; ἀ. ὄνομα *strange, uncouth* word, Pl.*Tht.*182a: c. gen., ἀλλοκότῳ γνώμᾳ τῶν πάρος with purpose *utterly different from...*, S.*Ph.* 1191; of persons, Pl.*Euthd.*306e, etc.: Comp. and Sup. -ώτερος, -ώτατος Pl.Com.28. Adv. -τως Pherecr.201, Pl.*Ly.*216a (v.l.). (κότος = ὀργή, i.e. *temper*, Phryn.*PSp.*23 B.)

ἅλλομαι, *h.Cer.*175, etc.: impf. ἡλλόμην X.*Cyr.*1.4.11, etc.: fut. ἁλοῦμαι (ὑπερ-) X.*Eq.*8.4, Dor. ἁλεῦμαι Theoc.3.25, 5.144: aor. 1 ἡλάμην Batr.225, E.*Ion* 1402, Ar.*Ra.*243, no subj. or opt., part. ἁλάμενος [1st syll. long] *Av.*1395, inf. ἅλασθαι Ael.*Ep.*16, (καθ-) v.l. Luc. *D.Mort.*14.5: aor. 2 ἡλόμην, rare in ind., v.l. X.*HG*4.4.11, (ἐξ-) S.*OT*1311, (ἐν-) v.l. A.*Pers.*516, subj. ἅληται [ᾰ] Il.21.536, opt. ἁλοίμην X.*Mem.*1.3.9 (cf. εἰσ-), inf. ἁλέσθαι Opp.*C.*1.83, etc., part. ἁλόμενος [ᾰ] A.*Eu.*368 (lyr.), X.*An.*4.2.17, etc.; to aor. 2 also belong Ep. 2 and 3 sg. ἆλσο, ἆλτο, subj. ἅλεται Il.11.192, part. ἄλμενος only in compds., but ἅλμενος Opp.*H.*5.666: (*sal-*, cf. Lat. *sal-io*):—*spring, leap*, prop. of living beings, μή.. ἐς τεῖχος ἅληται Il.21.536; ἐπεί κ'.. εἰς ἵππους ἅλεται 11.192; εἰς ἅλα ἆλτο 1.532 (but ἥλατο πόντον Call.*Dian.*195); ἐξ ὀχέων.. ἆλτο χαμᾶζε Il.6.103; ἆλτο κατ' Οὐλύμπου 18.616:—ἅλλεσθαι ἐπί τινι *leap upon* or *against*, 21.174, Od.22.80; ἐπὶ στίχας Il.20.353: c. inf., ἆλτο θέειν, πέτεσθαι, *h.Cer.* 389, *Ap.*448: abs., of horse, X.*Eq.*8.4. 2. c. acc., *leap over*, βόθρον Ael.*NA*6.6; τάφρον Opp.*C.*1.83. 3. of things, ἆλτο ὀϊστός Il.4.125; of sound, ἀπὸ λείων ἠχὼ ἀλλομένη Pl.*Phdr.*255c; of parts of body, *twitch, quiver, throb*, ἅλλεται ὀφθαλμός Theoc.3.37, cf. Arist. *HA*604a27, *PRyl.*1.28.

ἀλλο-μορφέω, *disguise oneself*, Ps.-Callisth.1.3; *change one's shape*, Sm.*Ez.*31.15. **-μορφος**, ον, *of strange shape*, τέρατα, σώματα Hp.*Morb.*4.93.

ἀλλόμος· τυφλός, Hsch.; i.e. ἀλαό[λαο]ς.

ἀλλο-πάθεια, ἡ, *subjection to external influences*, D.S.26.1. **-παθής**, ές, properly, *subject to external influence*, hence in Gramm. of Pronouns, *non-reflexive*, A.D.*Pron.*44.17, *Synt.*175.13, *EM*496. 45. 2. Adv. -θῶς, of Verbs, *transitively*, Eust.920.27. **-πειρίους**· ἀλλοφύλους, Hsch. **-πίας**, Ep. -ίης, ὁ, a fish, Numen.ap.Ath. 7.326a. **-ποιός**, ά, όν, *producing otherness*, Procl.*in Prm.* p.569 S. **-πολία**, ἡ, = ἀλλοδημία, *Leg.Gort.*6.47: hence **-πολιᾶται**, οἱ, *GDI*4954 (Cret.). **-πρόσαλλος**, ὁ, i.e. ἄλλοτε πρὸς ἄλλον, *leaning first to one side, then to the other, fickle*, epith. of Ares, Il.5.831,889, cf. Eun.*VS* p.496 B.; πλοῦτος *AP*15.12, cf. 1.34 (Agath.); τὸ ἀ. *respect of persons*, *Corp.Herm.*18.14. 2. simply, *transferred*, ἀ. ἀρωγή, coupled with ἑτεραλκέα νίκην, Tryph.565; *deceitful*, Nonn.*D.*46.4, al.; *changeful, successive*, of waves, etc. (cf. ἀλλεπάλληλος), ib.3.24, al., cf. Man.5.68.

ἄλλος, η, ο, Cypr. **αἶλος** *Inscr.Cypr.*135 H. (Idalion): (from ἀλyος, cf. Lat. *alius*):—*another*, i.e. *one besides* what has been mentioned, either Adj. or Pron.: when Adj., its Subst. is either in the same case, or in gen., Ζεῦ ἄλλοι τε θεοί Il.6.476; θεῶν ἄ. 16.446:—ἄ. μέν.. ἄ. δέ.. *one.. another...*, more rarely *the one.. the other..* (of *two* persons, etc.), Il.22.493, etc.; τὰ μέν.. ἄλλα δέ.. Il.6.147, and Att.; ἕτερον μέν.. ἄλλον δέ.. Il.9.313; ἄλλο μέν.. ἑτέρου δέ.. Hdt.1.32; θάτερον.. τὸ δ' ἄλλο E.*IT*962. II. with τις, *any other*, οὐδέ τις ἄ. ἔγνω ἀλλ' ἄρα Κασσάνδρη Il.24.697; ἄ. τις Hdt. 3.85; οὐδεὶς ἄ. no *other*, ibid.; ἄλλα πολλά Il.9.639; πολλὰ καὶ ἄλλα Th.3.56; for εἴ τις ἄλλος Id.6.32, etc., and εἴ τις καὶ ἄ. X.*An.*1.4. 15, etc., v. εἰ. 2. freq. with another of its own cases or derived Adverbs, ἄ. ἄλλα λέγει *one man* says *one thing, one another*, X.*An.*2.1.15; ἄ. ἄλλῳ ἔλεγεν Pl.*Smp.*220c; ἄ. ἄλλῃ ἐτράπετο X.*An.* 4.8.19; v. ἄλλοθεν, ἄλλοσε, ἄλλοτε; also with Verb in pl., παραλαμβάνων ἄ. ἄλλον ἐπ' ἄλλου, τὸν δ' ἐπ' ἄλλου χρείᾳ.. ἐθέμεθα πόλιν ὄνομα Pl.*R.*369c, cf. X.*Cyr.*2.1.4, etc.: pl., ἄλλοι when the several parties are pl., λείπουσι τὸν λόφον.. ἄλλοι ἄλλοθεν X.*An.*1.10. 13. 3. ἄ. καὶ ἄ., *one and then another, one or two*, X.*An.*1.5. 12; ἄλλο καὶ ἄλλο *one thing after another*, Id.*Cyr.*4.1.15; πρὸς ἄλλῳ καὶ ἄλλῳ σημείῳ to *different* points, Euc.1.7. 4. repeated for emphasis, ἄ. ἄ. τρόπος *quite another* sort, E.*Ph.*132. 5. οὐδ' ἄ. for οὐδέτερος, Theoc.6.45. 6. with Art., ὁ ἄλλος, *the rest, all besides*; in pl., οἱ ἄλλοι (Ion. contr. ὦλλοι) *all the others, the rest*, freq. from Hom. downwards (ἄλλοι in same signf., Il.2.1); τὰ ἄλλα, contr. τἆλλα, *all else*, τἆλλα πλὴν ὁ χρυσός *Scol.*1 (Pytherm.); in Att. freq. as Adv., *for the rest*, esp. in amendments to decrees, τὰ μὲν ἄλλα καθάπερ ὁ δεῖνα κτλ. *IG*1.27a70, etc.: of Time, = τὸν ἄλλον χρόνον, X.*HG*3.2.2; ὁ ἄ. χρόνος, = ὁ λοιπὸς χρόνος, of the future, Lys. 14.4 (but also of the past, D.20.16); τῇ ἄλλῃ ἡμέρᾳ, τῷ ἄλλῳ ἔτει, *next* day, *next* year, X.*HG*1.1.13, 1.2.1; οἵ τε ἄλλοι καί.. *all others* and *especially..*, γυναῖκας ἄλλας τε πολλὰς καὶ δὴ καὶ βασιλέος θυγατέρα Hdt.1.1, etc.; ἄλλα τε δὴ εἶπε, καί.. Pl.*Tht.*142c; (v. ἄλλως I):—τὸ ἄλλο is much less freq. than τὰ ἄλλα. 7. with Numerals, *yet, still, further*, τρίτον ἄ. γένος Hes.*Op.*143; πέμπτος ποταμὸς ἄ. *yet* a fifth river, Hdt.4.54, cf. A.*Th.*486, S.*Ant.*1295, etc. 8. in enumerations, *as well, besides*, ἅμα τῇγε καὶ ἀμφίπολοι κίον ἄλλαι with her their mistress came attendants *also*, Od.6.84; μήτηρ ἠδὲ πατὴρ ἠδ' ἄλλοι πάντες ἑταῖροι 9.367; οὐ γὰρ ἦν χόρτος οὐδὲ ἄ. δένδρον οὐδέν there was no grass nor any tree *at all*, X.*An.*1.5.5; πολιτῶν καὶ τῶν ἄλλων ξένων Pl.*Grg.*473d; προσοφλὼν οὐ τὴν ἐπωβελίαν μόνον ἀλλὰ καὶ ἄλλην ὕβριν *besides*, Aeschin.1.163:—pleonastic, παρ' ἀγγέλων ἄλλων ἀκούειν S.*OT*7, cf. X.*Cyr.*1.6.2; ἰδὼν ἐς πλησίον ἄλλον Il.4. 81; γυναικῶν τῶν ἄλλων μία E.*Med.*945; μόνη τῶν ἄλλων ἐπιστημῶν Pl.*Chrm.*166e; with Comp., freq. in Hom., οὔτις σεῖο νεώτερος ἄ. Ἀχαιῶν Il.15.569, cf. 22.106, al.; with Sup., ὀϊζυρώτατος ἄλλων Od. 5.105. III. less freq., = ἀλλοῖος, *of other sort, different*, Il.13.64, 21.22; ἄ. γέγονεν Pl.*Phdr.*241a. 2. in this sense, c. gen., ἄλλα τῶν δικαίων *other than* just, X.*Mem.*4.4.25:—followed by ἤ.., with preceding neg., οὐδὲ ἄλλο..., οὐδὲν ἄλλο (or ἄλλο οὐδέν).., ἤ.. nothing *else* than.., Hdt.1.49, 7.168, Th.4.14; οὐδὲν ἄλλο γ' ἢ πτήξας A.*Pers.*209; ὃ μηδὲν ἄλλο ἢ διανοεῖταί τις which one *only* thinks, Pl. *Tht.*195e:—more freq. in questions, τίς ἄλλος ἢ 'γώ..; A.*Pr.*440; τί δ' ἄλλο γ' ἢ πόνοι..; Id.*Th.*852: ellipt., τί ἄλλο (sc. πάσχω) ἢ ἱπποκένταυρος γίγνομαι; X.*Cyr.*4.3.20; τί ἄλλο (sc. ἐποίησαν) ἢ ἐπεβούλευσαν; Th.3.39:—followed by πλήν, S.*Aj.*125, Ar.*Ach.*39; by Preps., πρό.. Hdt.3.85; ἀντί.. A.*Pr.*467; παρά.. Pl.*Phd.*80b, etc.: with neg., sts. followed by ἀλλά, Il.18.403, 21.275:—see also ἄλλο τι. 3. *other than what is, untrue, unreal*, Od.4.348. 4. *other than right, wrong, bad*, ἄλλου τινὸς ἡττῆσθαι yield to some *unworthy* motive, D. 21.218, cf. Plu.2.187d, etc.; cf. ἄλλως.

ἄλλος, Aeol., = ἠλέος, dub. in Sapph.110.

ἄλλοσε, Adv. *elsewhither*, Od.23.184; ἄλλος ἄ. A.*Pers.*359; ἄ... ὄμμα θατέρᾳ δὲ νοῦν ἔχοντα S.*Tr.*272; *to foreign lands*, ἄ. ἐκπέμπειν to export, X.*HG*6.1.11; ἄ. οὐδαμόσε *to* no *other place*, Pl.*Cri.*52b; ἄ. πολλαχόσε *to* many *other places*, Id.*Mx.*241e; ποῖ ἄ.; *to what other place?* Id.*Phd.*82a; ἄ. ποι *to* some *other place*, Id.*Tht.*202e: c. gen., ἄ. ποι τῆς Σικελίας *to* some *other part* of Sicily, Th.7.51; ἄ. τοῦ σώματος Pl.*Lg.*841a:—by attraction, = ἀλλαχοῦ, ἄλλοσε ὅποι ἂν ἀφίκῃ Id. *Cri.*45b.

ἄλλοτε, Aeol. **ἄλλοτα** Alc.47, Dor. **ἄλλοκα** Theoc.1.37, Adv. *at another time*, freq. repeated, ἄ. μέν.. ἄ. δέ.. *at one time... at another..*, Il.23.368, etc.; also ὁτὲ μέν.., ἄ. δέ.. Il.11.65; ἄ. μέν..., ἄ. δ' αὖτε Od.16.209, Hes.*Fr.*14; τότ' ἄλλος, ἄλλοθ' ἅτερος S.*El.*739; ποτὲ μὲν κακόν, ἄ. ἐπ' ἐσθλὸν ἕρπει Id.*Ant.*367; ἄ. μέν.., τότε δέ X.*An.*4.1.17: sts. the former ἄλλοτε is omitted, φοιτῶν ἐναργὴς ταῦρος, ἄ. αἰόλος δράκων S.*Tr.*11; κεῖμαι δ' ἐπ' ἀκταῖς, ἄ. ἐν πόντου σάλῳ E.*Hec.*28; ἄ. μέν.. ἐν πυμάτῳ S.*OC*1674:—ἄ. καὶ ἄ. *now and then*, X.*An.*2.4.26:—freq. with ἄλλος, etc., πρὸς ἄλλοτ' ἄλλον *sometimes* to this man, *sometimes* that, A.*Pr.*278, etc.; ἄλλως ἄ. *Th.*1077.

ἀλλοτέρμων, ονος, (τέρμα) *foreign*, γῆ Ezek.*Exag.*58.

ἀλλότης, τητος, ἡ, *otherness*, Simp. *in Ph.*862.13.

ἄλλο τι, *anything else*, in interrog. sentences, mostly foll. by ἤ, ἤ σοι ἄλλο τι φαίνεται.. ἢ λόγος; Pl.*Phdr.*258a, cf. *Phd.*64c:—hence freq. (esp. in Pl.) elliptical, implying an affirm. answer, ἄλλο τι ἢ πεινήσουσι; (i.e. ἄλλο τι πείσονται ἢ πεινήσουσι;) *will* they *not* be starved? Hdt.2.14, cf. 1.109; ἄλλο τι ἢ ἠρέμα ἐπανασκεψόμεθα; *shall we not* calmly reconsider? (i.e. let us do so) Pl.*Tht.*154e, cf. *Phd.* 70c, *Meno* 82d, *Grg.*481c, etc.; ἄλλο τι ἢ καταγελάφης ἄν; Id.*Alc.*1. 116d:—with other words interposed, σκόπει εἰ ἄλλο τι λέγεις ἢ τόδε Id.*Smp.*200d, cf. *Phd.*106a, *Sph.*228a, etc.:—ἄλλο τι πλήν..; Id.*Sph.* 228a:—but often ἄλλο τι with or without οὖν stands alone, ἄλλο τι οὖν.. ἔλεγες; *did not* you say? Id.*Grg.*495c, cf. 470b, *Phd.*79b, *Tht.* 165e, *R.*337c, etc. 2. rarely without a question, ἀπόγνοια τοῦ ἄλλο τι ἢ κρατεῖν τῆς γῆς Th.3.85.

ἀλλοτριάζω, *to be ill-disposed*, Plb.15.22.1: c. gen., *towards..*, τοῦ βασιλέως ib.25.34.

ἀλλοτριό-γνωμος, ον, *thinking of other things, absent*, Cratin. 154. **-επίσκοπος**, ὁ, *busybody in other men's matters*, 1*Ep.Pet.* 4.15. **-λογέω**, *speak irrelevantly*, Aristox.*Harm.*p.32 M., Str.1.4. 1. **-λογία**, ἡ, *unorthodox views*, Phld.*Acad.Ind.*p.67 M. **-μορφοδίαιτος**, ον, *ever changing in form*, epith. of nature, Orph.*H.*10. 23. **-νομέω**, *assign* things *to their wrong place*, opp. διανέμειν ἐπὶ τὰ αὐτῶν ἕκαστα, Pl.*Tht.*195a. II. *adopt foreign customs*, D.C.52.36. **-πραγέω**, *meddle with other folk's business*: *excite commotions*, Plb.5.41.8; opp. αὐτοπραγέω, Procl. *in R.*2.149 K. **-πραγία**, ἡ, *meddling with other folk's business*, Plu.2.57d, Procl. *in R.*1.216 K. **-πραγμονέω**, = -πραγέω, Simp. *in Epict.*pp. 51,113 D. **-πραγμοσύνη**, ἡ, *meddlesomeness*, Pl.*R.*444b, Procl. *in Alc.*p.14 C. **-πράγμων**, ον, *meddlesome*, *AB*81.

ἀλλότριος, Aeol. **ἀλλότερρος** *EM*529.24, α, ον, (ἄλλος) *of* or *belonging to another*, βίοτος, νηῦς, ἄχεα, Od.1.160, 9.535, Il.20.298; γυνή *another man's* wife, A.*Ag.*448 (lyr.); ἀλλοτρίων χαρίσασθαι to be bountiful *of what is another's*, Od.17.452 ; γναθμοῖσι γελοίων ἀλλοτρίοισιν with faces *unlike their own*, of a *forced, unnatural* laugh, ib.20.347 ; ἀ. ὄμμασιν εἷρπον by the help of *another's* eyes, S.*OC* 146 (lyr.) ; οὐκ ἀ. ἄτην not *inflicted by other hands*, Id.*Ant.*1259 ; but ἀ. φόνος murder *of a stranger* (cf. II. 1), Pl.*Euthphr.*4b : prov., ἀ. ἀμᾶν θέρος reap *where one has not sown*, Ar.*Eq.*392, cf. Hes.*Th.*599 ; ἀλλοτριωτάτοις τοῖς σώμασιν χρῆσθαι deal with one's body *as if it belonged to another*, Th.1.70 ; τὰ ἀλλότρια, contr. τἀλλότρια, *what belongs to others, not one's own*, τἀ. ἀποστερεῖν, δειπνεῖν, X.*Ages.*4.1, Theopomp. Com.34. **II.** opp. οἰκεῖος, *foreign, strange*, 1. of persons, ἀ. φώς *stranger*, Od.18.219, cf. Ar.*Ra.*481 ; almost = *enemy*, Il.5.214, Od.16.102 ; οὐδέ τις ἀλλοτρίων no *stranger*, Hdt.3.155 ; εἴτε ἀ. εἴτε οἰκεῖος ὁ τεθνεώς Pl.*Euthphr.*4b ; ἀ. τῆς πόλεως Lys.28.6 ; οὐδείς ἐστί μοι ἀ., ἂν ᾖ χρηστός Men.602 ; ἀλλοτριώτερος τῶν παίδων *less near* than thy children, Hdt.3.119 ; ἀλλοτριώτερος, opp. οἰκειότερος, Arist.*EN* 1162^{a}3 : c. dat., ἀλλότριοι ὑμῖν ὄντες Isoc.14.51. **b.** *hostile, unfavourably disposed*, c. gen., ἀ. Ῥωμαίων Plb.28.4.4 ; -ώτατος μοναρχίας D.S.16.65 ; ἀλλότρια φρονῶν τοῦ βασιλέως Plb.36.15.7, cf. *OGI*90.19 (Rosetta). **c.** *disinclined*, πρὸς τὰς κακοπαθείας Plb.36.15.2. **2.** of things, *alien, strange*, τροφή Pl.*R.*491d (Comp.), etc. ; εἴ τι πρότερον γέγονεν ἀ. *estrangement*, Decr.ap.D.18.185 ; ἡ ἀ. *alien country, enemy's country*, Lys.2.6, Isoc.10.50, cf. Hdt.8.73 : c. gen., *alien from*, ἐπιτηδεύματα δημοκρατίας ἀ. Lys.31.34 ; οὐδὲν ἀ. ποιῶν τοῦ τρόπου Decr.ap.D.18.182. **b.** Medic., *abnormal*, Sor.2.5, Gal.14.780 ; ἀ. σάρκες *superfluous* fat, Pl.*R.*556d. **c.** *foreign to the purpose*, λόγοι Arist.*EE*1218^{b}23 : Comp., Id.*EN*1159^{b}24 : Sup., Id. *Cat.*15^{b}29, cf. Polystr.p.17 W. **d.** Astrol., = ἀπόστροφος, *POxy.* 464.16. **III.** Adv. ἀλλοτρίως, διακεῖσθαι πρὸς ἀλλήλας to be *unfavourably* disposed towards . ., Lys.33.1, cf. Isoc.12.159 ; ἀ. ἔχειν πρός . . Id.5.80 : Comp. -ιώτερον *less favourably*, D.18.9. **2.** *strangely, marvellously*, *Epigr.Gr.*989.2. **3.** *in a manner foreign to*, c. gen., Pers.*Stoic.*1.100. [-ŏτρ- only in Men.557 s. v. l.]

ἀλλοτριότης, ητος, ἡ, *derivativeness*, opp. οἰκειότης, *Plt.*261a ; *estrangement*, Arist.*Pol.*1311^{b}15 ; τινὸς πρός τινα Pl.*Ep.*318d, cf. Decr.ap.D.18.165, Plb.38.12.3. **2.** *unattractiveness*, of style, Phld. *Po.*994.6,37. **II.** *qualitative difference*, Epicur.*Nat.*11.12.

ἀλλοτριο-φᾰγέω, *eat another's bread*, Eust.1404.9. **-φαγία**, ἡ, ib.13. **-φάγος**, ον, *eating another's bread*, S.*Fr.*329, Eust.1404.13. **-φρονέω**, *to be estranged, ill-disposed*, D.S.17.4. **-χρως**, ωτος, ὁ, ἡ, *changing colour*, *AP*11.7 (Nic.). **-χωρος**, ον, *of strange land*, J.*AJ*3.12.3, 8.7.5.

ἀλλοτριόω, *estrange from* : c. gen., *deprive*, τῶν σωμάτων τὴν πόλιν οὐκ ἀλλοτριοῦντες Th.3.65 ; τοὺς ἠλλοτριωκότας ἑαυτοὺς ἀπὸ τῆς λητουργίας those who have *withdrawn* themselves from . . , D.51.17. **2.** c. dat. pers., *make hostile to* another, τὴν χώραν τοῖς πολεμίοις X.*Cyr.*6.1.16 :—Pass., *become estranged, be made enemy*, τινί Th.8.73 ; πρὸς τὴν αἵρεσιν *Vit.Philonid.*p.12 C. ; πρός τι *to be prejudiced* against thing, D.H.*Th.*27 ; ἀπό τινος *disguise oneself from*, Lxx *Ge.* 42.7 ; πρὸς τὰ καίοντα *to be inaccessible* to cautery, Antyll.ap.Orib.10.22.4. **3.** *to be unnatural, have a strange taste*, τροφὴν -ιοῦσαν ἔκπτυε Phld.*Lib.*p.9 O. **4.** Pass., *to be alienated from one's natural condition*, Pl.*Ti.*64e. **5.** Pass., also of things, *to be alienated, fall into other hands*, ἀλλοτριοῦται ἡ ἀρχή Hdt.1.120, cf. D.18.88.

ἀλλοτρίωσις, εως, ἡ, *estrangement*, Phld.*D.*3*Fr.*1 ; *aversion*, πρὸς πόνον Gal.5.459 ; τινὸς *from* one, App.*BC*5.78 ; τινὸς εἴς τινα 3.13 ; opp. οἰκείωσις, Porph.*Abst.*3.19 ; τῆς ξυμμαχίας οὐχ ὁμοία ἡ ἀ. Th.1.35 :—Medic., *loss of substance, mortification*, Aët.13.3.

ἀλλο-τροπῆσαι· μεταθεῖναι, Hsch. **-τροπος**, ον, *strange*, φαντασίαι Linus ap.Stob.1.10.5 ; ᾄσματα Iamb.*VP*25.114. Adv. -τρόπως Sch.E.*Hec.*299. **-τύπωτος**, ον, *differently formed*, Man.4.75. **-φᾰνής**, ές, *appearing otherwise*, Nonn.*D.*14.156, Jo.Gaz.2.225, etc. **-φασ(σ)ις**· θόρυβος ταραχώδης, Hsch., *AB*386. **-φάσσω**, *to be delirious*, Hp.*Prog.*20, al., cf. Gal.18(2).249, prob. l. in Aret.*SA*2.4.—Ionic word, cf. Xenocrit.ap.Erot.*Fr.*1, Eust.1324.10. **-φᾰτος**, ον, (v. φόνος) *slain by others*, *AB*386, Hsch. **II.** (φαίνομαι) = ἀλλοφανής, Nic.*Th.*148. **-φέρμονες**· ἀλλαχοῦ τραφέντες, Hsch.

ἄλλοφος, ον, Ep. for ἄλοφος, *without a crest*, Il.10.258, *AP*6.163 (Mel.).

ἀλλο-φρήτωρ, ορος, ὁ, *one of another* φρατρία, *IG*14.759 (Naples). **-φρονέω**, (ἀλλόφρων) Ep. and Ion., *think of other things, give no heed*, ἀλλ' ἥμην ἀλλοφρονέων Od.10.374 ; of one in a swoon, *to be senseless*, κὰδ δ' ἀλλοφρονέοντα . . εἷσαν Il.23.698 ; κεῖτ' ἀλλοφρονέων Theoc.22.129, cf. Arist.*Metaph.*1009^{b}30 ; ὑπὸ τούτων ἀλλοφρονῆσαι *were seized with frenzy* by reason of the thunder, etc., Hdt.5.85 ; ἀλύει καὶ ἀ. ὑπὸ τῆς ὀδύνης Hp.*Morb.*2.16, cf. *Mul.*1.41. **II.** *to be of another mind, have other views*, v.l. in Hdt.7.205. **-φροσύνη**, ἡ, *absence* or *derangement of mind*, Poll.8.163. **-φρων**, ονος, ὁ, ἡ, *thinking differently*, Man.4.563. **-φυής**, ές, *changed in shape*, Nonn.*D.*4.419, al. **2.** *of strange, abnormal shape*, ib.2.148, al. **-φῡλέω**, *adopt foreign customs* or *religions*, Lxx 4*Ma.*18.5. **-φῡλία**, ἡ, *foreign matter*, Epicur.*Ep.*2 p.48 U. **-φῡλισμός**, ὁ, *adoption of foreign customs*, Lxx 2*Ma.*4.13. **-φῡλος**, ον, (φυλή) *of another tribe, foreign*, Hp.*Aër.*12 ; freq. in Lxx of Philistines, *Jd.*14.1, al. ; in Egypt, *settled in another nome*, *BGU*419.2 (iii A.D.) ; ἐς ἀλλόφυλον . . χθόνα A.*Eu.*851 ; ἄνθρωποι Th.1.102, Pl.*Lg.*629d ; ζῷα *alien to man, wild*, D.S.3.18, Porph.*Abst.*1.10 ; πόλεμος ἀ. war *with foreigners*, Plu.*Cam.*23 ; opp. ὁμόφυλος, Epicur.*Sent.*39 ; ἀ. πρός τι Dam.*Pr.* 308 ; μᾶζαν ἐπ' ἀ. *alien, not one's own*, Eup.159.12. **-φωνία**, ἡ, *confusion of tongues*, J.*AJ*1.4.3. **-φωνος**, ον, *speaking a foreign tongue*, Lxx *Ez.*3.6, Hsch. s.v. ἀλλόθροος. **-χροέω**, *to change colour*, Arist.*Pr.*880^{a}25, Them.*Or.*4.56a, 19.228c. **-χροια**, ἡ, *change of colour*, Adam.2.36. **-χροος**, ον, contr. -χρους, ουν, *changed in colour*, E.*Hipp.*174 (lyr.) :—also -χρως, ωτος, ὁ, ἡ, *looking strange* or *foreign*, Id.*Ph.*138, *Andr.*879.

ἄλλῠδις, Adv., (ἄλλος) Ep. for ἄλλοσε, *elsewhither*, in Hom. only with ἄλλος, ἄ. ἄλλος one *hither*, another *thither*, Il.11.486, Od.5.71, cf. A.R.2.980, etc. ; τρέπεται χρὼς ἄ. ἄλλῃ his colour changes *now one way, now another*, Il.13.279 ; imitated from Hom. by Eup.159.11 ; later by itself, *AP*15.24.1 (Simm.).

ἀλλύεσκε, ἀλλύουσα [ῡ], Ep. for ἀνέλυε, ἀναλύουσα.

ἄλλυι, Aeol., = ἄλλῃ, Hdn.Gr.1.507, prob. in Alc.89 :—also **ἀλλῦς** (dub.), *AB*1316.

ἀλλύτας, v. sub ἀναλύτης.

ἄλλῠτος, ον, = ἄλυτος, Μοιράων νῆμα Phanocl.2.

ἀλλώνιος, Aeol., = ἀλλοῖος, Sch.D.T.p.542 H., Eust.1214.28.

ἄλλως, Dor. ἀλλῶς, A.D.*Adv.*175.13, Adv. of ἄλλος, *otherwise*, Il. 19.401, etc. : freq. with other Advbs., ἄ. πως *in* some *other way*, ἄ. οὐδαμῶς *in* no *other wise*, Pl.*R.*343b, 526a, etc. ; πως ἄ. X.*Mem.*2.6.39 ; ἄ. καὶ ἄ. Hierocl. *in CA*23 p.468 M. **2.** καὶ ἄλλως and *besides* (cf. ἄλλος II. 8), ἀγήνωρ ἐστὶ καὶ ἄλλως Il.9.699 ; a woman is described as very tall καὶ ἄ. εὐειδής Hdt.1.60, etc. ; ἀρίστου καὶ ἄ. φρονιμωτάτου Pl.*Phd.*118 :—so ἄ. δέ . . Hdt.6.105, Ar.*Av.*1476 ; ἄλλως τε S.*OT*1114, Hdt.8.142. **b.** *at all events, any how*, εἴ πέρ γε καὶ ἄ. ἐθέλει . . Hdt.7.16.γ' ; ἄλλως alone, εἰ ἄ. βούλοιτο Id.8.30 ; ἐπείπερ ἄλλως . . εἰς Ἄργος κίεις A.*Ch.*680. **3.** freq. in phrase ἄλλως τε καί . . *both otherwise and* . . , i. e. *especially, above all*, A.*Eu.*473, Th.1.70, etc. ; strengthd., ἄ. τε πάντως καί . . A.*Pr.* 636, *Eu.*726 ; freq. followed by ἤν, εἰ, ἐπειδή, *especially* if . . , Hp.*VC* 21, Th.1.81, 2.3 ; by part., Id.4.104, 7.80 :—without καί, ἄ. τε ἐάν X.*Mem.*1.2.59 ; ἄλλως τε ἐπειδή Isoc.2.51, Pl.*Men.*85e, etc. **II.** *otherwise than* something implied, *differently*, τοῦτ' οὐκ ἔστιν ἄ. εἶπαι to deny it, Hdt.6.124 ; οὐκ ἄ. λέγω I say no *otherwise*, i. e. I say *so*, E. *Hec.*302 : hence, **2.** *far otherwise*, i. e. *better*, οὐδέ κεν ἄλλως οὐδὲ θεὸς τεύξειε Od.8.176, cf. Il.14.53. **3.** more freq., *otherwise than should be, at random, without aim* or *purpose*, Od.14.124, Hdt.3.16, 4.77, etc. :—*in vain*, Il.23.144 ; freq. in Trag. and Com., ἀλλ' ἄ. πονεῖ S.*OT*1151, cf. 333, E.*Med.*1030, Ar.*Eq.*11 ; with Subst., εἴδωλον ἄ. *mere* image, S.*Ph.*947 ; ἀριθμὸν ἄ. E.*Tr.*476 ; παρὰ καιρὸν ἄ. Id.*IA* 800 ; ἀριθμός, πρόβατ' ἄ. Ar.*Nu.*1203 ; ὄχλος ἄ. καὶ βασκανία D.19.24, cf. Th.8.78 ; τὴν ἄ., sc. ἄγουσαν ὁδόν, *in vain*, λέγειν D.3.21 ; ψηφίζεσθαι 19.181, cf. Philem.51, etc. ; also, *in no particular way*, i. e. *concerning indifferent matters*, οἱ ἀγῶνες οὐδέποτε τὴν ἄ., ἀλλ' ἀεὶ τὴν περὶ αὐτοῦ Pl.*Tht.*172e ; τὴν ἄ. θεωρεῖν Pl.*Lg.*650a ; τήν γε ἄλλως *otherwise*, i. e. *generally*, D.C.38.24, 42.50 :—*for nothing*, Hdt.3.139 : —*otherwise than right, wrongly*, D.*Ep.*1.12, etc.

ἅλμα, τό, (ἅλλομαι) *spring, leap*, poet. for Prose πήδημα, Od.8.103, 128 ; ἅ. πέτρας, πετραῖον *leap* or *fall from* rock, E.*HF*1148, *Ion* 1268 ; κρημνῶν ἅ. *Epigr.Gr.*225 (Ephesus) ; οἰκεῖον . . ἅ. ἐπὶ ξίφος E.*Hel.*96 ; κυνῆς ἅ. *the leap* of the lot from the helmet, S.*Aj.*1287 ; κοῦφον ἅλμα ποδῶν Ἀχιλῆ E.*El.*439 ; *track* of a comet, Arist.*Mete.*343^{b}23. **2.** *jumping*, as an athletic contest, Simon.153 :—in pl., *jumping-ground*, τῶν ἁ. τὴν σκάψιν καὶ ὁμάλιξιν *BCH*23.566 (Delph., iii B.C.). **II.** Medic., *pulsation, palpitation*, of the embryo, Hp.*Alim.*42 ; of the heart, Id.*Cord.*4 ; f.l. in Pl.*Ti.*70d.

ἄλμα, τό, (ἀλδω) = ἄλσος, Lyc.319, Epic.ap.Did. ad D.13.32.

ἁλμ-αία, ἡ, = ἅλμη, *brine*, Ar.*Fr.*706, Nic.*Fr.*70.18 : in pl., Dsc.2.174. **-αιοπώλης**· *salgamarius* (sic), *Gloss.* **-άς**, άδος, ἡ, *salted, steeped in brine*, ἐλάα Ar.*Fr.*141 : Subst., *salted olive*, ἐς τὰς ἁ. (sc. ἐλάας) Hermipp.81, cf. Eup.255, Ar.*Fr.*393, Apollon.ap.Gal.12.999. **-ατίας**, ου, ὁ, *person of tripping gait*, Adam.2.52. **-ατισταί**· *salitores*, *Gloss.* **-ατύραι**· τὰ παραθαλάσσια χωρία, Hsch. **-άω**, *become mildewed*, cj. in Thphr.*HP*7.5.4, 8.10.1, *CP*6.10.5. **-εῖον**· ἀνδρεῖον, Hsch. **-ευσις**, εως, ἡ, *pickling*, Dsc.3.77 (pl.). **-ευτής**, οῦ, ὁ, *seller of pickled fruit*, Id.1.29. **-εύω**, (ἅλμη) *steep in brine, pickle*, Id.2.111 (Pass.). **-η**, ἡ, (ἅλς) *sea-water, brine*, Od.5.53, Pi.*P.*2.80, etc. ; *spray that has dried on the skin*, Od.6.219 ; *salt incrustation* on soil, Hdt.2.12, Thphr.*CP*6.10.4. **2.** after Hom., *brine*, i.e. *the sea*, Arion l.3, Pi.*P.*4.39, A.*Pers.*397, Tim.*Pers.*96, etc. **3.** *salt-water, brine* used for pickling, Hdt.2.77, Ar.*V.*1515, *Fr.*416 ; ἡ Θασία ἅ. Cratin.6 ; ἐν ἅλμῃ ἕψειν [τὸν ἰχθύν] Antiph.222, cf. Eub.44 ; καταπνίγειν Sotad.Com.1.21, etc. : prov., πρὶν τοὺς ἰχθῦς ἑλεῖν σὺ τὴν ἅλμην κυκᾷς 'first catch your hare, then cook it', Phot. s.v. πρίν. **II.** *saltness*, esp. as a bad quality in soil, X.*Oec.*20.12, cf. Thphr.*CP*6.10.4. **2.** *salt soil*, *PLond.*2.267.95, al. (i/ii A.D.). **-ήεις**, εσσα, εν, *salt, briny*, πόρος ἁ., i.e. *the sea*, A.*Supp.* 844 (lyr.) codd. (-ιόεις Herm.). **-ια**, τά, *salted provisions*, Men. 462.5. **-ίζομαι**, *to be made salt*, ὑπὸ θαλάσσης Sch.Il.2.538, cf. Zos.Alch.p.248 B.

ἁλμο-ποσία, ἡ, *drinking of brine*, Afric.*Cest.*2 (pl.). **-πότις**, ιδος, ἡ, *drinking brine*, Menipp.ap.Ath.1.32e.

ἁλμῡρίδιον, τό, Dim. of ἁλμυρίς I. 3a, Plin.*HN*19.142.

ἁλμῡρίζω, *to be saltish*, Arist.*HA*613^{a}3 ; πρὸς τὴν γεῦσιν Dsc.2.129.

ἁλμῡρίς, ίδος, ἡ, *anything salt*, and so, 1. *salt humour*, Hp. *Epid.*3.13 ; *salt scum*, Arist.*Mete.*357^{b}4. **2.** *salt soil* or *land*, Thphr.*CP*2.5.4, Lxx *Jb.*39.6, *PPetr.*3 p.237, etc. ; in Attica, = ἁλίπεδον, *IG*2.1059, Hsch. : pl., Ἁλμυρίδες, Ar.*Fr.*132. **3.** kind of κράμβη, *Brassica cretica*, Eudem.ap.Ath.9.369e, *POxy*.736.73 (i B.C.): pl., Diocl.*Fr*.138, Plu.2.801a. b. = ἅλιμον, Aët.1.21. II. *saltness*, D.S.3.39. **ἁλμυρῖτις** γῆ, = foreg. I. 2, Zopyr.ap.Orib. 14.62.1.

ἁλμῠρόγεως, ων, (γῆ) *with salt soil*, πεδιάς Ph.2.111.

ἁλμῠρ-ός, ά, όν, (ἅλμη) *salt, briny*, Hom. only in Od., and always in phrase ἁ. ὕδωρ *salt sea*-water, 4.511, etc.; πόντος Hes.*Th*.107, Alc.26; θάλασσα Sapph.*Supp*.25.10; καθ' ἁ. ἅλα Epich.53, E.*Tr*.76; βένθεα Pi.*O*.7.57; ποταμός, of the Hellespont, Hdt.7.35. 2. in Prose, of taste, *salt*, γίνεται τὸ στόμα ἁ. Hp.*Acut*.(*Sp*.)44; ὄψα ἁ. X.*Cyr*.6.2.31, cf. Hp.*Vict*.1.56; αἷμα Pl.*Ti*.84a s.v.l.; of drinking-water, *brackish*, Th.4.26; of soil, Thphr.*CP*6.10.1, Lxx *Je*.17.6; opp. μωρός (insipid), *Com.Adesp*.596. 3. metaph., *bitter, distasteful*, γειτόνημα Alcm.116, cf. Pl.*Lg*.705a; ἀκοή *Phdr*.243d; λόγοι Ath.3.121e; ἁλμυρὰ κλαίειν weep *bitterly*, Theoc.23.34; ἁλμυρὸν καταπτύσαι Cerc.19.37. b. *piquant*, ἁ. καὶ δριμύ Plu.2.685e. **-ότης**, ητος, ἡ, *saltness*, Arist.*Mete*.356^{b}4. **-όω**, *make salt*, θάλασσαν Olymp.*in Mete*.152.9. **-ώδης**, ες, *saltish*, ῥεῦμα Hp.*Epid*.1.26.ϛ'; πτύαλον Id.*Coac*.238, cf. X.*Oec*.20.12 (Comp.); of soil, *impregnated with salt*, Thphr.*HP*8.7.6; *hoary*, χνοῦς Id.*CP*.6.10.7.

ἀλξ· πῆχυς (Athaman.), Hsch. (cod. ἄλαξ). **ἄλξεων**· τειχέων, Id. **ἀλξίας**· πράξεις, καὶ ἐκλήψεις, Id.

ἀλοατός, ὁ, *threshing-floor*, X.*Oec*.18.5 (v.l. -ητός).

ἀλοάω, Ep. **ἀλοιάω** Theoc.10.48: Ep. impf. ἀλοία Il.9.568: fut. -ήσω Lxx *Je*.5.17, Dor. ἀλοιησέω Tyrt. in *Berl.Sitzb*.1918.728: aor. ἠλόησα Ar.*Ra*.149, Herod.2.34 (ἀλοιήσῃ ib.51), part. ἀλοάσας [ᾱσ] Pherecr.65; Ep. ἠλοίησα (ἀπ-) Il.4.522, (συν-) Theoc.22.128:— **Pass.**, fut. -ηθήσομαι Lxx *Je*.28(51).33: aor. ἠλοήθην Thphr.*CP*4.6.5, Plb.10.12.9, Plu.2.327a: pf. ἠλόημαι Thphr.*CP*4.12.9 (Cod.Urb.):— poet. aor. part. ἀλοίσας (as if from ἀλοίω, cf. Eust.775.8, Hdn.*Epim*. 277) dub. l. in Epigr.ap.D.L.7.31; ἀλοϝάω dub. in *Glotta* 4.202 (archaic Apulian vase):—*tread, thresh*, Pl.*Thg*.124a, X.*Oec*.18.2, Lxx *De*.25.4. 2. *thresh, smite*, γῆν χερσὶν ἀλοία Il.9.568, cf. Epigr. l. c.; μηρόν Plu.*TG*2; *cudgel, thrash*, *Glotta* l. c., S.*Fr*.20 (dub.), Ar. *Ra*.149, Herod.2.34; ῥοπάλῳ τινά Babr.98.15. 3. *crush, smash*, σκεύη Id.129.16; *destroy*, πόλεις Lxx *Je*.5.17. II. *drive round and round*, like cattle treading out corn, Ar.*Th*.2 (acc. to Sch.).

ἄλοβος, ον, *with lobe wanting*, of livers of victims, ἄ. ἱερά X.*HG*3.4.15, Plu.*Ages*.9, Arr.*An*.7.18.4.

ἀλογεύομαι, *speak casually*, Cic.*Att*.6.4.3.

ἀλόγευτος, ον, *not collected*, *PLond*.2.354.22 (i B.C.).

ἀλογ-έω, *pay no regard to* thing, εἰ δέ μοι οὐκ ἐπέεσσ' ἐπιπείσεται, ἀλλ' ἀλογήσει Il.15.162: c. gen., δίκης Democr.174; πάσης συμβουλίης Hdt.3.125; τῶν ἐντολέων Id.8.46: abs., ib.116: c. acc., Procop. *Pers*.1.4, al.; *insult*, *PTeb*.138 (ii B.C.):—Pass., *to feel slighted*, Cic. *Att*.12.3.3. 2. *to be unreasonable*, Phld.*Ir*.p.34 W. II. Pass., *to be disregarded*, D.L.1.32; *commit an indiscretion, be misled*, διά τινος *miscalculate*, Plb.8.36.4, cf. 28.9.8. 2. *to be out of one's senses*, Luc.*Ocyp*.143; ἠλογημένη 'nonplussed', Alciphr.2.1; ἠ. ψυχή Hierocl.*in CA*12 p.446 M. 3. Gramm., *to be irregularly formed*, A.D.*Adv*.162.18, al., *EM*405.34, etc. **-ημα**, ατος, τό, *miscalculation, error*, Plb.12.20.2: in pl., 9.16.5, al. **-ητέον**, *one must take no heed of*, τινός Ph.1.312. **-ητος**, ον, gloss on ἀλόγιστος, Sch.E.*Or*.1156. **-ί**, = ἀλογιστί, Lib.*Decl*.16.31 (s. v.l.). **-ία**, Ion. -ίη, ἡ, *want of respect* or *regard*, ἀλογίην εἶχον τοῦ χρηστηρίου took *no heed* of it, Hdt.4.150; ἐν ἀλογίῃ ἔχειν καὶ ποιεῖσθαί τι 6.75, 7.226:—in 2.141 ἐν ἀλογίῃσι ἔχειν παραχρησάμενον τῶν Αἰγυπτίων, gen. is anacoluthon (as if ἀλογίην ἔχειν τῶν Αἰγ.); ἀλογίης ἐγκυρῆσαι to be *disregarded*, 7.208 codd.:—this sense is Ion. and late Prose, ἐν ἀλογίᾳ ποιεῖσθαί τι Procop.*Pers*.1.2, al. 2. Att., *want of reason, absurdity*, opp. λόγος, Pl.*Tht*.207c, cf. 199d, *Phd*.67e, D.23.168; πολλὴ ἀ. τῆς διανοίας Th.5.111; concrete, *the irrational part of the soul*, Porph.*Abst*.1.42. 3. *confusion, disorder*, Plb.15.14.2; τύχη ἐν ἀλογίᾳ κειμένη Plot.6.8.17:—*speechlessness, amazement*, Plb. 36.7.4. 4. *indecision, doubt*, Paus.7.17.6. 5. Rhythm., *irrationality*, relation of time-elements which cannot be expressed by a simple ratio, Aristox.*Rhyth*.2.20. **-ίζομαι**, Dep., *to be irrational*, Eust.1656.43, etc.:—Act. only as f.l. for ἀλογέω, Procop. *Goth*.4.20. **-ίου** δίκη prosecution of a public official *for not having his accounts passed*, Eup.349.

ἀλογίστ-ευτος, ον, *unheeded, unprovided for*, τῇ προνοίᾳ Hierocl. *Prov*.p.466 B. **-έω**, *lose one's senses, rave*, Plu.2.656d, Longin.10.3, Vett.Val.130.30. **-ί**, Adv. *thoughtlessly*, Harp., *AB*380. **-ία**, Ion. -ίη, ἡ, *thoughtlessness*, Democr.289, Plb.5.15.3, Chrysipp.*Stoic*. 3.129, Phld.*Ir*.p.93 W., Plu.2.466c. **-ος**, ον, *inconsiderate, thoughtless*, τόλμα Th.3.82; ὀργή Men.574; of persons, Phld.*Ir*.p.97 W. Adv. -τως *thoughtlessly*, Lys.7.12, Isoc.2.29; δαπανᾶν ἀ. βίον Men. 623, etc. 2. *irrational*, Pl.*Ap*.37c; opp. λογιστικός, *R*.439d, al.; *foolish, unthinking*, Phld.*Ir*.p.97 W.; πλοῦτος ἀ. προσλαβὼν ἐξουσίαν Men.665; τὸ ἀ. *unreason*, i.e. *chance*, Th.5.99. Adv. -τως Id.3.45, Pl.*Prt*.324b, al. II. *incalculable*, S.*OC*1675 (lyr.); *indefinite, indeterminate*, φορά Procl.*in Prm*.p.547 S. 2. *not to be accounted, vile*, E.*Or*.1156, Men.75.

ἀλογο-γράφητος, ον, *undescribed*, Eust.888.49. **-ειδής**, ές, = ἀλογώδης, *irrational*, ἀ. τὴν ψυχήν Dam.*Pr*.401. **-θέτητος**, ον, *of which no account is given*, *Gloss*. **-μυῖα**, ἡ, *horse-fly*, Anon.*in Rh*. 125.10.

ἀλογόομαι, *to be rendered irrational*, Plot.5.3.10 (prob. l.); [φύσις] ἠλογωμένη *non-rational*, Procl.*in Prm*.p.617 S.

ἀλογο-πάθεια, *irrational affection*, Plot.4.4.28 (pl.). **-πρεπῶς**, *unreasonably*, Eustr.*in EN*275.8.

ἄλογος, ον, *without* λόγος, hence, I. *speechless*, Pl.*Lg*.696e. Adv. -ως *without speech*, S.*OC*131, Isoc.3.9:—ἄ. ἡμέρα, = Lat. *dies nefastus, on which no business may be done*, Luc.*Lex*.9. b. *lacking in eloquence*, Lxx *Ex*.6.12. 2. *inexpressive*, Pl.*Tht*.203a; *unutterable*, = ἄρρητος, S.*Fr*.262. II. *unreasoning*, ἡδονή, ὄχλος, etc., Pl.*R*.591c, *Ti*.42d, etc.; τὰ ἄλογα *brutes, animals*, Democr.164, Pl.*Prt*.321b, X.*Hier*.7.3; esp. in late Greek, ἄλογον, τό, = *horse*, *POxy*. 138.29 (610 A.D.), *PGen*.14 (late). 2. *not according to reason, irrational*, ἄ. δόξα, opp. ἡ μετὰ λόγου δ., Pl.*Tht*.201c; ἀλόγῳ πάθει τὴν ἄ. συνασκεῖν αἴσθησιν, *instinctive* feeling, in appreciating works of art, D.H.*Lys*.11; ἄ. πάθος Id.*Comp*.23. 3. *contrary to reason, absurd*, Th.6.85, Pl.*Tht*.203d; *unaccountable, unintelligible*, Lys.26.19; *unfit, unsuited to its end*, Th.1.32; *groundless*, Plb.3.15.9; ἀηδία *PRyl*.144.15 (38 A.D.). Adv. most freq. in this sense, Pl.*R*. 439d, etc.; οὐκ ἀ. οὐδ' ἀκαίρως Isoc.15.10: Sup. -ώτατα Phld.*Ir*. p.44 W. III. *without reckoning*: 1. *not reckoned upon, unexpected*, Th.6.46 (Comp.). 2. *not counted, null and void*, ἡμέραι Lxx *Nu*.6.12. 3. Act., *not having paid one's reckoning*, of an ἐρανιστής, *EM*70.31. IV. of magnitudes, *incommensurable*, περὶ ἀλόγων γραμμῶν, title of work by Democr., cf. Arist.*APo*. 76^{b}9, *LI*968^{b}18, Euc.10.*Def*.10, etc. 2. in Rhythm, *irrational*, of feet or syllables whose time-relations cannot be expressed by a simple ratio, χορεῖος Aristox.*Rhyth*.2.20; ἄλογοι, sc. συλλαβαί, D.H. *Comp*.20:—in Music, ἄ. διαστήματα Plu.2.1145d:—of the pulse, *unrhythmical*, Herophil. ap.Ruf.*Syn.Puls*.4.3.

ἀλογχεῖν· Ἀλόγχους μιμεῖσθαι, ὅ ἐστι ἔθνος Θρᾳκῶν, Hsch.

ἄλογχος (A), ον, *without lances* or *weapons*, ἄ. ἀνθέων στρατός Chaerem.10. II. of a spear, *without a head*, Hsch., *EM*70.36.

ἄλογχος (B), ον, (λογχή, = λῆξις) *unlucky*, opp. εὔλογχος (q. v.), sc. ἡμέρα, prob. l. in Democr.ap.Gem.*Calend*.8.

ἀλογώδης, ες, *irrational*, v.l. Arist.*Spir*.481^{b}27 (Comp.); τὰ -έστερα ψυχῶν γένη Procl.*in Cra*.p.69 P.

ἀλόη, ἡ, *bitter aloes, Aloe vera*, Dsc.3.22, Plu.2.141f, etc. 2. = ἀγάλλοχον, Lxx *Ca*.4.15 (in Heb. form **ἀλώθ**), *Ev.Jo*.19.39. 3. ἀ. γαλλική, = γεντιανή, Ps.-Dsc.3.3. 4. ἀ. ἡπατῖτις, *hepatic aloes, Aloe Perryi*, *Gp*.6.6.2.

ἀλοηδάριον, τό, *purgative prepared from aloes*, Aët.3.100, al.

ἀλό-ησις, εως, ἡ, (ἀλοάω) *threshing*, *Gloss*.:—**ἀλοίησις**, *EM*74. 22. **-ησμός** (written -ωεισ-), ὁ, *threshing*, *PLond*.1.113(3).8 (vi A.D.), *BGU*840 (vi A.D.). **-ητέα**, *one must thresh*, Poll.1. 226. **-ητής**, οῦ, ὁ, *thresher*, *PLond*.1.131^{r}619 (i A.D.). **-ητός**, ὁ, *threshing*, Ael.*NA*6.43; *threshing-time*, Lxx *Le*.26.5, *BGU*1031.11 (ii A.D.): perh. *payment for threshing*, *PTeb*.48.17 (ii B.C.). **-ητρα**, τά, *payment for threshing*, *PFlor*.379.18 (ii A.D.), prob. in *BGU*698.27 (ii A.D.).

ἁλόθεν, Adv., (ἅλς) *from the sea*, ἐξ ἁλόθεν Il.21.335.

ἁλοθήκη, ἡ, *salt-box*, Hdn.Gr.2.418.

ἄλοι· πηλοί, Hsch. **ἀλοιάω**, Ep. for ἀλοάω.

ἀλοιδόρ-ητος, ον, *unreviled*, Plu.2.757a. 2. *irreproachable*, *IG*14.2139, 12(7).395 (Amorgos), Plu.2.89a. II. *not reviling*: neut. pl. as Adv., ἄκομπ' ἀλοιδόρητα διαβεβλημένοι S.*Fr*.210.8. **-ος**, ον, = foreg. II, A.*Ag*.412.

ἀλοιητήρ, ῆρος, ὁ, (ἀλοιάω) *thresher, grinder*, as Adj., σίδηρος Nonn. *D*.17.237; ἀ. ὀδόντες *grinders*, *AP*11.379 (Agath.): metaph., λιμός Orac.ap.Jul.*Mis*.370a.

ἀλοιμός, οῦ, ὁ, *polishing* or *plastering*, of wall-decoration, S.*Fr*.69, cf. *IG*2^{2}.463.85.

ἀλοιτ-εύειν· ἀλιτήριος εἶναι, *EM*69.52. **-ήεσσαν**· κοινήν, ἄνανδρον, Hsch.

ἀλοιτηρός, v. sub ἀλιτηρός.

ἀλοίτης, ου, ὁ, = ἀλείτης, *avenger*, Emp.10:—fem. **Ἀλοῖτις**, ιδος, ἡ, of Athena, Lyc.936: but ἀλοῖτις, ἡ, = γεντιανή, Ps.-Dsc.3.3; = μανδραγόρα ἄρρεν, Id.4.75. **ἀλοιτός**, ὁ, (ἀλιτεῖν) = ἀλείτης, Lyc. 136: fem. ἀλοιταί· κοιναί, ἁμαρτωλαί, ποιναί (cf. ἀλοίτης), Hsch.

ἀλοιφ-αῖος, α, ον, *for anointing*, Lyc.579. **-άω**, *daub with pitch*, κιβωτόν Aq.*Ge*.6.14. **-εῖον**, τό, *anointing-room*, Eust.764.14. **-ή**, ἡ, (ἀλείφω) *anything with which one can smear* or *anoint*; esp. *hog's lard, grease*, either in carcase, Il.9.208, or when melted for use, 17. 390. 2. *unguent*, Od.6.220, 18.179. 3. *paint, varnish*, etc., Pl.*Criti*.116b, cf. *IG*2^{2}.463.85, Lxx *Mi*.7.11, etc.; νεώς Polyaen. 5.34. II. *anointing, laying on* of unguents or paint, ἀ. μύρων Pl.*Alc*.1.122c. III. *erasure*, Lxx *Ex*.17.14, Plu.2.611a.

ἀλοίω, v. sub ἀλοάω.

ἀλοκίζω, (ἄλοξ) prop. *trace furrows*: hence, *write, draw*, with play on words, Ar.*V*.850:—Pass., pf. part. ἠλοκισμένος *scratched, torn*, Lyc.119, 381.

ἄλοξ, οκος, ἡ, = αὖλαξ (q. v.).

ἀλοπεύει, v. ἀλωπ-.

ἁλο-πήγιον, τό, *salt-works, salt-pit*, Str.7.4.7, al., Plu.*Rom*. 25 (pl.). **-πηγός**, όν, *one who prepares salt*, Nic.*Al*.519.

ἀλόπιστος, ον, *not barked* or *peeled*, Thphr.*HP*5.1.2.

ἄλοπος, ον, (λέπω) *not scutched*, ἀμοργίς Ar.*Lys*.736: neut. pl., ἄλοπα, τά, *PTeb*.120.16 (i B.C.).

ἁλο-πώλης, ου, ὁ, *dealer in salt*, *PTeb*.1.120, *PFay*.23.12 (ii A.D.), etc.:—fem. **-πῶλις**, *IG*2.3932. **-πώλια**, τά, *salt-stores*, *BGU*9 (iii A.D.).

ἀλορόα· ἄρουρα, καὶ γεωργία παρὰ θάλασσαν, Hsch.

ἆλος, Dor. for ἧλος.

ἁλοσ-άνθινος, η, ον, *prepared with efflorescence of salt*, οἶνος Dsc.5.76 tit. **-ανθον**, τό, *efflorescence of salt*, Gal.12.374. **-άχνη**, ἡ, lit. *sea-foam*, a zoophyte of the class ἀλκυόνεια, Arist.*HA*616a20, Thphr.*Od*.35.

Ἁλοσύδνη, ἡ, epith. of Thetis, Il.20.207; νέποδες καλῆς ἁλοσύδνης, of seals, Od.4.404 (expl. by Gramm. as 'child of the sea'); of Nereids, A.R.4.1599; cf. ὑδατοσύδνη. (Perh. containing the root of ὕδωρ.)

ἁλο-τρίβανος, (τρίβω) *pestle to pound salt*, Eust.183.10. **-τριψ**, ῖβος, ὁ, = foreg., *AP*6.306 (Aristo). **-τροφέω**, *feed with salt*, Sch.Il.13.493.

ἄλουα· κῆποι (Cypr.), Hsch.

ἁλούργ-ημα, ατος, τό, *purple clothing*, Vett.Val.263.16, Lib.*Decl*.12.27 (pl.). **-ής**, ές, (ἅλς, ἔργον) lit. *wrought in* or *by the sea*, always in sense *sea-purple*, i.e. *genuine purple dye*, opp. imitations, ἐμβαίνονθ' ἁλουργέσιν on *cloths of purple*, A.*Ag*.946; μίτρα ἁ. Pherecr.100; στρώμαθ' ἁ. Anaxandr.41.7; γῆ Pl.*Phd*.110c; τὸ ἁ. Arist.*Col*.792a7:—less freq. **ἁλουργός**, όν (also ά, όν Phylarch.41), ἔρια Pl.*R*.429d; χιτωνίσκος *IG*2.754.12,14, etc. (but χ. ἁλουργής ib.21); στολαί Phylarch. l.c.; στρωμναί Plu.*Lyc*.12, *AB*81:—also **ἁλουργοῦς**, οῦν, *IG*2.757, v.l. in Arist.*Sens*.442a24, Ion. **ἁλοργοῦς** *GDI*5702.23 (Samos). **-ία**, Ion. **ἁλοργίη**, ἡ, *purple-dyeing*, *GDI*5633 (Teos). **2.** *purple clothing*, Philostr.*VA*4.21. **-ίδιον**, τό, Dim. of ἁλουργίς, Antiph.310 (also attrib. to Ar., *Fr*.741: vv. ll. ἁλουργαῖον, ἁλουργιαῖον). **-ικός**, ή, όν, = ἁλουργής, *AB*379, Phot. **-ίς**, ίδος, ἡ, *purple robe*, Ar.*Eq*.967, *IG*2.754, Chamaeleon ap.Ath.9.374a. **II.** as Adj., ἐσθὴς ἁ. f. l. in Luc.*Nav*.22.

ἁλουργο-πώλης, ου, ὁ, *dealer in purple*, Arist.*Mech*.849b34. **-πωλική** (τέχνη), ἡ, *trade of an* ἁλουργοπώλης, Is.*Fr*.38.

ἁλουργός, όν, v. sub ἁλουργής.

ἀλουσία, ἡ, *being unwashed*, Hp.*de Arte*5; ἠγρίωσαι διὰ μακρᾶς ἀλουσίας E.*Or*.226, cf. Alex.197: pl., ἀλουσίῃσι.. συμπεπτωκώς Hdt.3.52, cf. Hp.*Morb*.2.71.

ἀλουτ-έω, *go without bathing*, Hp.*Salubr*.4, al., Arr.*Epict*.3.22.73, etc. **-ία**, ἡ, = ἀλουσία, Eup.251. **-ιάω**, Sch.Ar.*Nu*.442. **-ος** (ἄλουστος *Gloss*.), ον, *unwashen*, Hdt.2.64, Semon.7.5, E.*El*.1107, Ar.*Av*.1554.

ἁλοφόρος, ὁ, *one who conveys salt*, *Jahresh*.7 *Beibl*.44, cf. ib.18 *Beibl*.287 (Ephesus, i B.C.).

ἄλοφος, v. ἄλλοφος.

ἀλόχευτος, ον, *born not in the natural way*, of Athena, Coluth.183. **2.** *unborn*, Nonn.*D*.8.27. **II.** *without birth-pangs*, αὖλαξ κόσμου ib.24.269, cf. 41.53.

ἄλοχος [ᾰ], ου, ἡ, (ἀ- copul., λέχος) poet., *partner of one's bed, wife*, Il.1.114, Od.3.403, al., A.*Pers*.63, S.*OT*181, E.*Fr*.543, etc., cf. Arist.*Pol*.1253b7; ἄλοχον εἰς δόμους ἄγειν Theodect.13. **2.** *leman, concubine*, Il.9.336, Od.4.623. **II.** (ἀ- priv.) *unwedded*, ἄ. οὖσα τὴν λοχείαν εἴληχε, of Artemis, Pl.*Tht*.149b, cf. Porph. ad Il.11.155.

ἀλόω, Ep. imper. of ἀλάομαι, Od.5.377.

ἄλπνιστος, η, ον, Sup. of ἄλπνος (only in compd. ἔπαλπνος, q.v.), *sweetest, loveliest*, Pi.*I*.5(4).12; cf. **ἀλπαλέον** (cod. -αῖον)· ἀγαπητόν, Hsch. (Cf. ἔλπω (ϝέλπω), Lat. *volup*.)

ἅλς (A), ἁλός [ᾰ], ὁ: dat. pl. ἅλασιν (v. infr.):—*salt*, πάσσε δ' ἁλὸς θείοιο Il.9.214, cf. Od.17.455; ἁλὸς μέταλλον a *salt*-mine, Hdt.4.185; ἁλὸς χόνδροι lumps of *rock-salt*, ib.181: sg. also Ar.*Ach*.835, Philyll.28, Axionic.8: more freq. in pl., Od.11.123, Hdt.4.53, al., etc.:—prov. phrases: οὐ σύ γ' ἂν.. σῷ ἐπιστάτῃ οὐδ' ἅλα δοίης Od.17.455; φῄς μοι πάντα δόμεν· τάχα δ'.. οὐδ' ἅλα δοίης Theoc.27.61; ἅλας συναναλῶσαι, i.e. to be bound by ties of hospitality, Arist.*EN*1156b27; τῶν ἁλῶν συγκατεδηδοκέναι μέδιμνον to have eaten a bushel of *salt* together, i.e. to be old friends, *Com.Adesp*.176; οἱ περὶ ἅλα καὶ κύαμον, of friends, Plu.2.684e, cf. Arist.*EE*1238a3; ὅρκον μέγαν, ἅλας τε καὶ τράπεζαν Archil.96; ποῦ ἅλες; ποῦ τράπεζαι; D.19.189; τοὺς ἅλας παραβαίνειν ib.191; τοὺς τῆς πόλεως ἅλας περὶ πλείονος ποιήσασθαι τῆς ξενικῆς τραπέζης Aeschin.3.224; ἁλῶν δὲ φόρτος ἔνθεν ἦλθεν, ἔνθ' ἔβη 'light come, light go', Zen.2.20; ἅλασιν ὕει, of great abundance, Suid. **2.** in pl. of medical preparations, Dsc.5.109. **II.** *brine*, Call.*Fr*.50. **III.** ἅ. ἀμμωνιακός *rock-salt*, *PLond*.1.78.90. **2.** ἅ. Ἰνδικός *sugar*, Archig.ap.Paul.Aeg.2.53. **IV.** ἅλες, οἱ, metaph., like Lat. *sales, wit*, possible but unlikely in Pl.*Smp*.177b, *Ep.Col*.4.6; certain in Plu.2.854c; ἅλες called "χάριτες" ib.685a. (Cf. sq.)

ἅλς (B), ἁλός [ᾰ], ἡ (ἁλὸς πολιοῖο Il.20.229), *sea* (generally of shallow water near shore), εἰς ἅλα δῖαν Il.1.141; χεῖρας νιψάμενος πολιῆς ἁλός *in sea-water*, Od.2.261; ἢ ἁλὸς ἢ ἐπὶ γῆς 12.27: sts. pleonast. πόντος ἁλός Il.21.59, Thgn.10; ἁλὸς πελάγη or πέλαγος, Od.5.335, *h.Ap*.73, E.*Tr*.88; πελαγίαν ἅλα A.*Pers*.427; παρ' ἁλμυρὰν ἅλα E.*Ba*.17; in pl. (with a pun on ἅλς A), Ar.*Ach*.760.—Poet. word: nom. only Emp.56. (Cf. Lat. *sal*: both masc. and fem. are from the same root.)

ἀλσείαν· πορείαν, Hsch.

Ἄλσειος, ὁ, sc. μήν, month at Cos, *SIG*1023.25.

ἀλσηίς, ἡ, (ἄλσος) *of the grove*, νύμφαι A.R.1.1066.

ἀλσίνη, ἡ, *lich-wort, Parietaria lusitanica*, Thphr.*HP*9.13.3, Dsc.4.86.

ἅλσις, εως, ἡ, (ἅλλομαι) *leaping*, Hp.*Morb.Sacr*.17, Arist.*EN*1174a31, Antyll.ap.Orib.6.31.5, etc.

ἄλσις, εως, ἡ, (ἀλδαίνω) *growth*, Did. ad D.13.32, Apollon.*Lex*. s.v. ἀλδαίνει, etc.

ἆλσο, v. sub ἅλλομαι.

ἀλσο-κομέω, *to be keeper of a grove* or *precinct*:—also **-κομία**, ἡ; **-κομικός**, ή, όν, (**-κομική**, ἡ, sc. τέχνη). Adv. -κῶς Poll.7.141:—**-κόμος**, ὁ, ib. 140. **-ποιία**, ἡ, *planting of groves*, ibid.

ἄλσος, εος, τό, *grove*, Il.20.8, Od.10.350: pl., Phanocl.1.3, Theoc.1.117, etc. **II.** esp. *sacred grove*, Od.6.291, Hes.*Sc*.99, Hdt.5.119, Pl.*Lg*.761c, etc.:—hence, *any hallowed precinct*, even without trees, Il.2.506, Sch.Pi.*O*.3.31, cf. B.3.19, S.*Ant*.844; Μαραθώνιον ἄ., of the field of battle, viewed as a holy place, A.*Eleg*.4: metaph., πόντιον ἄ. the ocean-*plain*, B.16.85, A.*Pers*.111. (Perh. for ἄλτ-ιος (cf. Ἄλτις), i.e. *alq-ios*, cf. Goth. *alhs* 'temple'.)

ἀλσ-ώδης, ες, *woodland*, κρῆναι E.*IA*141 (lyr.); τόποι Nic.Thyat. ap.Ath.11.503c, Dsc.4.86. **II.** *growing in woods*, of plants, Thphr.*HP*3.2.4, Lxx 4*Ki*.16.4, Hecat.Abd.ap.J.*Ap*.1.22, Plu.2.648c. **-ωμα**, τό, = ἄλσος, Aq. 4*Ki*.23.4. **-ών**, ῶνος, ὁ, = foreg., ib.17.16.

ἀλτεῖ· ἀπορεῖ, Hsch. (leg. ἀλύει). **ἀλτηρεία**· ἀφὴ τῆς χειρός, Id.

ἁλ-τῆρες, ων, οἱ (sg., Philostr.*Gym*.55), (ἅλλομαι) *weights held in the hand* to give an impetus *in leaping*, Crates Com.11, Arist.*IA*705a16, *Pr*.881b5, etc. **-τηρία**, ἡ, *use of* ἁλτῆρες, Artemid.1.57. **-τηροβολία**, ἡ, = foreg., Iamb.*VP*21.97. **-τικός**, ή, όν, *good at leaping*, X.*Cyr*.8.4.20; τὰ ἁ. μόρια parts *used in leaping*, Arist.*PA*683b3; ἁ. ὄρχησις, of the Salii, Plu.*Num*.13.

Ἄλτις, ιος, ἡ, *sacred precinct of Zeus at Olympia*, Pi.*O*.10(11).50, X.*HG*7.4.29, etc.: Elean for ἄλσος, Paus.5.10.1.

ἄλτο· πολύ, ἐλαφρόν, Hsch. **ἀλτὸς** καὶ **ἀλτρός**· μισθός, Id. **ἄλυγος**· ἄνευ μάστιγος, Id. **ἀλύδαινος**· ὁ κακὸς ἄνεμος, Suid. **ἀλύδοιμος**, ον, = πικρός, Sophr.139. **ἀλύζα**· ἄλυπον, Hsch. **ἀλύζω**, fut. ἀλύξω, = ἀλύω, Gal.19.76. **ἀλύη**, ἡ, *socket for* ἐχέτλη, q.v., Eratosth.ap.*EM*173.24; dub. l. Phld.*Mort*. p.318 M. **ἁλυκᾶτος**, η, ον, *pickled*, κεστρεῖς Xenocr.149.

ἁλυκεία, ἡ, *salting*, Ptol.*Tetr*.181.

ἀλύκη [ῠ], ἡ, = ἄλυσις, ἀλυσμός, Hp.*Aph*.7.56, al.

ἁλῠκ-ίς, ίδος, ἡ, (ἅλς) *salt-spring*, Str.4.1.6. **II.** *saltness*, Plu.2.897a. **-ός**, ή, όν, *salt*, Hp.*Acut*.42, *Aër*.1, Ar.*Lys*.403, Lxx *Ge*.14.3; *brackish*, Thphr.*HP*4.3.5. **-όσμυρνα**, ἡ, a kind of *myrrh*, *Hippiatr*.52. **-ότης**, ητος, ἡ, *saltness*, Arist.*Fr*.217, Thphr.*CP*2.5.4, Mnesith.ap.Ath.3.92b. **-ρός**, ά, όν, *lukewarm*, Epic.ap.*EM*71.31, Nic.*Al*.386 (Comp.); cf. ἀλυκτρόν.

ἀλυκτάζω, (v. ἀλύω) only impf., *wander distraught*, B.10.93; *to be distressed*, Hdt.9.70:—also **ἀλυκτέω**, *to be in distress, anguish*, Hp.*Mul*.1.5, cf. Erot., *EM*71.38, Hsch., Suid.: aor. part. ἀλυκτήσας in act. sense, = θορυβήσας, Hsch., *EM*71.39; cf. ἀλαλύκτημαι.

ἀλυκτέω· ὑλακτέω (Cret.), Hsch., cf. *EM*71.33.

ἀλυκτοπέδαι, αἱ, *bonds*, in pl., Hes.*Th*.521, A.R.2.1249: sg., *AP*5.229 (Paul. Sil.), etc. (ἀλυκτο- prob. = *unbreakable*, cf. Skt. *rujáti* 'break', but taken by late Poets as = ἀλυτο- *indissoluble*, cf. Paul. Sil. l.c., *AP*9.641 (Agath.), Nonn.*D*.21.56.)

ἀλυκτός, όν, *to be shunned*, φόνοι *Epigr.Gr*.793 (Phryg.):—wrongly expl. by ἄφυκτος, Suid., Zonar.

ἀλυκτοσύνη, ἡ, = ἔκκλισις, Suid. **2.** = ἀκοσμία, Hsch.

ἀλυκτρόν· εὔδινον, Hsch. **ἀλύνει**· φύει, Id.

ἁλῠκώδης, ες, *like salt, saltish*, γλῶσσα Hp.*Acut*.(*Sp*.)2; φλοιός Thphr.*HP*9.11.2 (ubi ἁλικώδης).

ἀλύμαντος [ῡ], ον, *unhurt, unimpaired*, Plu.2.5e, Porph.ap.Eus.*PE*11.28.

ἄλυξις, εως, ἡ, (ἀλύσκω) *escape*, A.*Ag*.1299, Q.S.12.212.

ἀλῡπ-έω, *to be free from pain*, imper. ἀλύπει *IG*14.1030, etc.; prob. l. in Phld.*Rh*.1.373 S. **-ητος**, ον, *not pained* or *grieved*, S.*Tr*.168. **II.** Act., *not causing pain*, S.*OC*1662 (but v. sub ἀλάμπετος): so Adv. -τως Pl.*Lg*.958e. **-ία**, ἡ, *freedom from pain* or *grief*, Antipho Soph.ap.Plu.2.833c, Pl.*Ax*.371d, Men.549, Arist.*Rh*.1365b13, Epicur.*Fr*.120, Sotad.5.10, etc. **II.** *digestibility*, Thphr.*HP*2.4.2. **-ιάς**, ἡ, = sq. III, Paul.Aeg.7.4, Alex.Trall.1.15. **-ος**, ον, *without pain*, freq. in Trag. (not A.), E.*IA*163, etc.: c. gen., ἄ. γήρως *without pains* of age, S.*OC*1519; ἄ. ἄτης *El*.1002; βίος E.*Ba*.1004; ἀρχή S.*OT*593; τὸ ἄ. Pl.*R*.585a: Comp. -ότερος ib.581e: Sup. -ότατος *Lg*.848e. Adv. ἀλύπως, ζῆν, διατελεῖν live *free from pain and sorrow*, Id.*Prt*.358b, *Phlb*.43d, cf. Men.549; ἀποθανεῖν Id.14: Sup. ἀλυπότατα Lys.24.10. **II.** Act., *causing no pain* or *grief*, Hp.*Art*.39 (Sup.), Pl.*Plt*.272a, etc.; ἄ. οἶνος *harmless*, Hermipp.82.5, cf. E.*Ba*.423; ἄ. ἄνθος ἀνίας *setting free from the pain* of sorrow of wine, S.*Fr*.172; ἀλυπότατος κλιντήρ, of a hospice, *Epigr.Gr*.450 (Batanaea); σωλῆνες -ότατοι μετὰ ἁλῶν *cause least pain*, i.e. *are least indigestible*, Xenocr.57, cf. Mnesith.ap.Ath.3.92c; πεσσὸς -ότατος Aët.16.36. Adv. ἀλύπως, τοῖς ἄλλοις ζῆν live *without offence* to others, Isoc.12.5. **III.** ἄλυπον, τό, *herb terrible, Globularia Alypum*, Plin.*HN*27.22, Dsc.4.178.

ἄλῡρος, ον, *without the lyre, unaccompanied by it*, ὕμνοι ἄ., i.e. *wild* dirges (accompanied by flute, not lyre), E.*Alc*.447; ἄ. ἔλεγος *Hel*.185; μέλος Poet.ap.Arist.*Rh*.1408a7; Ἅιδος μοῖρ' ἄ., of death, S.*OC*1223 (lyr.); ἄ. φθόγγοι *sad* talk, Alexis 162.6 (anap.); ἄ. μαθήματα ποιητῶν Pl.*Lg*.810b.

ἄλυς, υος, ὁ, (ἀλύω) *agitation*, Hp.*Ep*.1, Gal.9.613; χειρῶν Adam.2.21. **II.** *ennui, boredom*, Zeno *Stoic*.1.58, Plu.*Eum*.11, Diog. Oen.*Fr*.24; ἄ. ναυτιώδης Plu.*Pyrrh*.13.

ἁλῠσηδόν, Adv. *in chains*, Man.4.486.

ἀλυσθαίνω, (ἀλύω) = ἀδημονέω, Nic.*Th*.427, *EM*70.45, prob. in Hp.*Morb*.2.54,58,67; cf. ἀλυσταίνω.

ἀλυσθένεια, ἡ, = ἀσθένεια, *EM*70.45.

ἀλῠσίδετος, ον, *bound with chains*, Hsch.

ἀλῠσίδιον or -είδιον, τό, Dim. of ἅλυσις, Hero *Spir.*1.38, Ph.2.152, *POxy.*496.3 (ii A.D.), *AB*380.

ἀλῠσιδωτός, ή, όν, *wrought in chain fashion*, ἁ. θώραξ Plb.6.23.15 (pl.), D.S.5.30, etc.; opp. λινοθώραξ, σταδίος θώραξ, Str.3.3.6, Sch. A.R.3.1226.

ἀλῠσιον, τό, Dim. of sq., Men.258, Philippid.33, *PHib.*1.121.3 (iii B.C.), *PMeyer* 22.6 (iii/iv A.D.).

ἅλῠσις (on the breathing v. Hdn.Gr.1.539), εως, ἡ, *chain*, χαλκέῃ ἁλύσι δεδεμένη ἄγκυρα Hdt.9.74, cf. Th.2.76, etc.; ἐν ἁλύσει μιᾷ δεδεμένους D.Chr.30.17, cf. *Ep.Eph.*6.20; πέτραν ἁλύσεσι χρυσέαισι φερομέναν E.*Or.*982:—as a woman's ornament, Ar.*Fr.*320.12, Nicostr. 33; σφραγῖδε.. ἁλύσεις χρυσᾶς ἔχουσαι *IG*2.652*B*35. 2. collectively, *chains, bondage*, Plb.21.3.3. 3. *link* in chain armour, Arr. *Tact.*3.5.

ἄλῠσις, εως, ἡ, (ἀλύω) *distress, anguish*, Dsc.5.2; gloss on ἀλυσμός, Gal.19.75.

ἀλῡσι-τέλεια, ἡ, *damage, prejudice*, Plb.4.47.1. **-τελής**, ές, *unprofitable*, Pl.*Cra.*417d, X.*Oec.*14.5, Polystr.p.18 W.; of a person, ἀ. τῇ πόλει Bato 2.9: Sup. -έστατος Aeschin.1.105. Adv. -λῶς X. *Mem.*1.7.2, Hierocl.*in CA* 12 p.447 M., etc. II. Medic., *unfavourable*, of symptoms, Hp.*Prog.*14.

ἀλυσκάζω, strengthd. for ἀλύσκω (from which it borrows obl. tenses); irreg. opt. ἀλυσκάζειε Nonn.*D.*42.135, al.:—*shun, avoid*, c. acc., ὕβριν ἀλυσκάζειν Od.17.581: abs., *skulk*, Il.5.253, 6.443, Orph.*A.*437; dub. in Hes.*Fr.*96.94.—Ep. word, used by Cratin. 137. **ἀλύσκω**, Od.22.363: fut. ἀλύξω Il.10.371, A.*Pers.*94, S.*Ant.* 488, etc.; ἀλύξομαι v.l. in Hes.*Op.*363: aor. ἤλυξα, poet. ἄλυξα, v. infr.:—**Med.** in compd. ἐξαλύσκω.—Ep. Verb used by A. and S., both in lyr. and dialogue (also in late Prose, Philostr.*Her.*7):—*flee from, shun*, c. acc., Il.10.371, Od.12.335, Hes. l.c., Pi.*P.*8.16, A. *Pr.*587, etc.: rarely c. gen., S.*Ant.*488, *El.*627: abs., *escape*, ὅθεν οὔπως ἦεν ἀλύξαι Od.22.460; προτὶ ἄστυ ἀλύξαι Il.10.348; ἄλυξεν ἐν Γερήνῳ *he escaped* by staying in Gerenus, Hes.*Fr.*16. II. = ἀλύω, *wander restlessly*, A.R.4.57.

ἀλυσμ-ός, ὁ, (ἀλύω) *anguish, disquiet*: esp. *tossing about*, of sick persons, Hp.*Prog.*3, al. **-ώδης**, ες, *uneasy, troubled*, Hp.*Coac.*296.

ἀλυσπαθείῃ· κακοπαθείᾳ, Hsch. (leg. δυσπ-).

ἄλυσσον, τό, (λύσσα) *madwort*, *Farsetia clypeata*, Dsc.3.91 (ἀλύσσιον Ps.-Dsc. l.c.), cf. Plu.2.648a. 2. *Galen's madwort, Sideritis romana*, Ruf.*Fr.*76.10; cf. sq.

ἄλυσσος, ον, *curing madness*, βοτάνη (= foreg. 2) Asclep.ap.Gal. 14.168; πηγὴ ἄ. well (in Arcadia) *curing hydrophobia*, Paus.8.19.3.

ἀλύσσω, fut. -ξω, v. infr., (ἀλύω) *to be uneasy, restless*, pres. only Il. 22.70 ἀ. περὶ θυμῷ: fut., ἀλύξει τε καὶ ῥίψει ἑαυτὴν *will be restless*.., Hp. *Mul.*1.2: plpf. Pass., κραδίη ἀλάλυκτο φόβῳ *was disquieted*, Q.S.14.24.

ἀλυστ-άζω· ἀλύω, Hsch., *EM*71.54. **-αίνω**· ἀλυσθαίνω, Hsch., *EM*70.46 (-ιαιν-). **-ινόν**· δεινόν, Hsch., *EM*70.46 (-τηνόν). **-ον**· [σ]τρυβλίον, Hsch. **-ονέω**, = ἀλυσθαίνω, dub. in Cerc.19.89.

ἀλυτ-αρχέω, *hold office of* ἀλυτάρχης, *Inscr.Olymp.*468, *BCH*28.82 (Tralles). **-άρχης**, ὁ, *chief of police at* Olympic games, Luc.*Herm.* 40, *Inscr.Olymp.*240; ἀ. τῶν μεγάλων Ὀλυμπίων *BCH*28.81 (Tralles), cf. *Cod.Theod.*15.9.2 (Antioch.). **-αρχία**, ἡ, *office of* ἀλυτάρχης, *Cod.Just.*1 36.1; cf. ἀλύτης.

ἀλύταται· παρατηρεῖ, Hsch.

ἀλύτης, ου, ὁ, *police-officer* at Olympic games (and elsewhere), *Inscr.Olymp.*483, *EM*72.14.

ἀλυτίς, ἡ, = *pediculus*, Apul.*Herb.*81.

ἄλυτον· χλιαρόν, Hsch. (cf. ἀλυκρός, ἀλυκτρόν).

ἄλῠτος, ον, poet. ἄλλυτος Phanocl.2.1, *AP*6.30 (Maced.), *not to be loosed* or *broken, indissoluble*, πέδαι, δεσμοί, Il.13.37, Od.8.275, A.*Pr.* 55; ἀδάμας *AP*12.93 (Rhian.); Μοιράων νῆμα Phanocl. l.c., cf. *Epigr. Gr.*520 (Thessalonica); πτολέμοιο πεῖραρ Il.13.360; κύκλος (of the wheel of the ἴϋγξ) Pi.*P.*4.215; *irremediable*, S.*El.*230 (lyr.): of substances, *insoluble*, Arist.*Mete.*384ᵇ7. Adv. -τως Pl.*Ti.*60c. 2. of arguments or evidence, *not to be confuted, irrefutable*, Arist.*Rh.*1357ᵇ 17, 1403ᵃ14; συλλογισμός Arist.*APr.*70ᵃ29. II. *undissolved*, Pl. *Ti.*60e.

ἄλυτρον, τό, perh. for ἄλοιτρον = ἀλόητρον, *threshing implement*, *PAmh.*2.143.14 (iv A.D.).

ἀλύτρωτος, ον, *not redeemed*, Sm.*Le.*25.23.

ἀλυχή, ἡ, = ἀλυσμός, Gal.19.76, cf. Hsch., who also has **ἄλυχα**· ἀδημονία; cf. ἀλύκη.

ἄλῠχνος, ον, *without lamp* or *light*, E.*Fr.*411, D.L.1.81.

ἀλύω, Att. ἁλύω acc. to Suid., cf. Eust.1636.28, Aeol. ἀλυίω *EM* 254.16; only pres. and impf.; Poet. (rare in Com.) and late Prose:—*to be deeply stirred, excited*: 1. from grief, *to be distraught, beside oneself*, ἡ δ' ἀλύουσ' ἀπεβήσετο Il.5.352; δινεύεσκ' ἀλύων παρὰ θῖνα 24. 12; ἀλύων *in mad passion*, Od.9.398; ἐᾶτέ μ' ὧδ' ἀλύειν S.*El.*135; τί χρῆμ' ἀλύω; E.*Or.*277, etc. 2. from perplexity or despair, *to be at a loss, perplexed*, ἀλύει δ' ἐπὶ παντὶ S.*Ph.*174; ἀλύοντα χειμερίῳ λύπᾳ ib.1194; ἐν πόνοις ἀλύουσαν Id.*OT*695; οἱ μὲν εὐποροῦμεν οἱ δ' ἀλύομεν *are at our wit's end*, Alex.116.13; ἄλλως ἀλύει *is wasting her pains*, Men.*Epit.*342; ψυχὴ ἀ. διὰ τὴν ἀπορίαν Plu.*Brut.*15. 3. *to be weary, ennuyé*, ἐπὶ τῶν συμποσίων Metrod.*Herc.*831.13, cf. Plu.2. 965a, Ael.*VH*14.12. 4. *to be fretful, restless*, Hp.*Epid.*1.26.α', Men.*Epit.Fr.*4, Gal.18(1).167. 5. *struggle, kick*, τῶν σκελῶν ἀλυόντων Hld.10.30. 6. from joy or exultation (rarely), *to be beside oneself*, Od.18.333, A.*Th.*391, cf. Jac.*AP*p.760. II. later, *wander, roam about*, Plb.26,1.1, Luc.*DMar.*13.1, Plu.*TG*21; *lounge idly*, Babr.9.[11]. III. trans., μετὰ φρεσὶν ἄχθος ἀλύει Opp.*H.* 4.195. [ῠ Hom., except at the end of the verse, Od.9.398, as A.R. 3.866; ἀλῡοντες in 4th foot, Emp.145, Opp.*H.*4.195; ῡ always in Trag.]

ἄλφα, τό, indecl. (pl. τὰ ἄ. Arist.*Metaph.*1087ᵃ8), v. A α init.; cf. Aen.Tact.31.18, Callias ap.Ath.10.453d, Pl.*Cra.*431e; ἐπίσταται δ' οὐδ' ἄλφα συλλαβὴν γνῶναι Herod.3.22. 2. T-*square*, Eustr. *in EN*74.2. 3. Phoenician for βοὸς κεφαλή, Hsch. 4. metaph., τὸ ἄλφα καὶ τὸ ὦ the *first* and last, *Apoc.*1.8, al.

ἀλφάβητος, ὁ, *alphabet*, *AB*181, Sch.D.T.p.320 H.

ἀλφαδεῖ· εὑρίσκει, καὶ ἀλφαίνει, and **ἀλφαίει**· τὸ αὐτὸ δηλοῖ, Hsch.

ἀλφάδιον· ἐχθρόν, Hsch. 2. Dim. of ἄλφα, *carpenter's square*, Eustr.*in EN*322.18.

ἀλφάνω [ᾰν] (**ἀλφαίνω** *EM*72.39, Aët.13.133), Hom. only in aor. 2 ἦλφον, cf. *IG*1.53*a*15, Plu.2.668c: pres., E.*Med.*297, *Fr.*326 (nowhere else in Trag.), Ar.*Fr.*324, Eup.258, Men.362:—*bring in, yield, fetch*, ἵνα μοι βίοτον πολὺν ἄλφοι Od.17.250; ὁ δ' ὑμῖν μυρίον ὦνον ἄλφοι 15.452, cf. 20.383; ἑκατόμβοιον δέ τοι ἦλφον Il.21.79; ὁπόσην ἂν ἄλφῃ μίσθωσιν τὸ τέμενος *IG*1. c., cf. Plu. l.c.: metaph., φθόνον ἀλφάνειν *to incur* envy, E.*Med.*297. II. = ἐναλλάσσω, *change*, Aët. l.c. (cf. Skt. *arghás* 'price').

ἀλφάριον, τό, Dim. of ἄλφα, *plumb-line, level*, Theo Sm.*in Ptol.* p.228 H.

ἀλφεσίβοιος, α, ον, *bringing in oxen*, παρθένοι ἀ. maidens *who yield their parents many oxen as presents from their suitors*, i.e. *much-courted*, Il.18.593, *h.Ven.*119; ὕδωρ ἀ., of the Nile, water *that yields fat oxen* (by enriching pastures), A.*Supp.*855 (lyr.); Πειρήνης ἀ. ὕδωρ Alex.Aet.3.8: pr. n. **Ἀλφεσίβοια** used at beginning of trim., S. *Fr.*880.

ἀλφ-ή, ἡ, *produce, gain*, Lyc.549, 1394. **-ησις**, εως, ἡ, *Gloss.* **-ηστής**, οῦ, ὁ, Hom. only in Od., in phrase ἀνέρες ἀλφησταί, lit. *earners* (ἀλφάνω), i.e. *enterprising* men, Od.1.349, cf. Hes. *Op.*82; esp. of *traders* or *seafarers*, Od.13.261, *h.Ap.*458; ἑκὰς ἀνδρῶν ἀλφηστάων, of the Phaeacians, Od.6.8.—Ep. word, twice in Trag. (lyr.), A.*Th.*770, S.*Ph.*709. II. kind of *fish* that went in pairs, *Labrus cinaedus*, Epich.44, Numen.ap.Ath.7.320e: metaph., of *lewd men*, Sophr.63. **-ηστικός**, ὁ, = ἀλφηστής II, Arist.*Fr.*307, Diocl. *Fr.*135.

ἄλφῐ, τό, poet. indecl. abbrev. of ἄλφιτον, ἄλφι καὶ ὕδωρ *h.Cer.*208, cf. Str.8.5.3, *EM*769.39.

ἀλφινία, ἡ, = λεύκη (Perrhaeb.), Hsch.

ἀλφίσκω, f.l. in Od.22.57 ap.*EM*758.47.

ἀλφῐτ-ᾰμοιβός, ὁ, *dealer in* ἄλφιτα, Ar.*Av.*491, al. **-εία**, ἡ, *preparing of* ἄλφιτα, Hyp.*Fr.*225 (ἀλφίτια codd. Poll.), Poll.7. 18. **-εῖον**, τό, *mill for grinding* ἄλφιτα, Poll.3.78, 7.19, *AB* 261. **-εύς**, έως, ὁ, *barley-miller*, Hyp.*Fr.*224. **-εύω**, *grind barley*, Hippon.46. **-ηδόν**, Adv. *like* ἄλφιτα, Dsc.*Eup.*2.51. II. of fractures, *where bone is comminuted*, Gal.10.424, Paul.Aeg. 6.89. **-ηρός**, ά, όν, *of* or *belonging to* ἄλφιτα, ἀγγεῖον ἀ. *meal*-tub, Antiph.63 (-τήριον Poll.10.179). 2. ἀλφιτηρὸν ἐργαλεῖα κινεῦσι 'a living wage for the worker', Herod.7.73. **-ισμός**, ὁ, *mixing with barley-groats*, οἴνου *BCH*6.26 (Delos, ii B.C.).

ἀλφῐτο-ειδής, ές, *like* ἄλφιτα, Poet. *de herb.*77. **-μαντις**, εως, ὁ, ἡ, *one that divines from barley-meal*, Iamb.*Myst.*3.17, Phryn.*PS* p.91 B., Poll.7.188, Hsch.

ἄλφῐτον, τό, *barley-groats*, sg. in Hom. only in phrase ἀλφίτου ἀκτῇ Il.11.631, Od.2.355, 14.429, and Medic., Gal.6.507: elsewh. in pl. ἄλφιτα, opp. ἀλείατα, q.v., ἄ. μυελὸν ἀνδρῶν Od.2.290, al., Hdt.7. 119, freq. in Att.; used to sprinkle over roast meat, Il.18.560, cf. Od. 14.77; esp. over sacrificial victims, Od.14.429: ἐπ' ἀλφίτου πίνειν to drink wine with *barley-groats* in it, Epin.1:—of this was made a kind of *barley-water*, πιεῖν ἄλφιτα Hp.*Epid.*5.10; also, *poultices*, Dsc.4.87: also used as *hair-powder* by κανηφόροι, Hermipp.26. II. generally, *meal, groats*, ἄ. πύρινα Hp.*Acut.*(*Sp.*)53; ἄ. φακῶν καὶ ὀρόβων Id. *Int.*23; even λίθοιο ἄλφιτα Orph.*L.*212. III. metaph., *one's daily bread*, 'bread and cheese', Ar.*Pl.*219, *Nu.*106, etc.

ἀλφῐτο-ποιέω, Suid. s. v. τηλία. **-ποιία**, ἡ, = ἀλφιτεία, X.*Mem.* 2.7.6. **-ποιός**, ὁ, ἡ, *preparer of* ἄλφιτα, Oenom.ap.Eus.*PE*5. 34. **-πώλης**, ου, ὁ, *seller of* ἄλφιτα, Nicoph.19:—fem. **-πωλις**, D.L.6.9, 7.168; as Adj., ἀ. στοά *flour*-market at Athens, Ar.*Ec.* 682. **-πωλήτρια**, ἡ, pecul. fem. of ἀλφιτοπώλης, Poll.6.37. **-πωλικός**, ή, όν, *of the meal-sellers*, πλατεῖα *AB*275. **-σῑτέω**, *eat barley-bread*, X.*Cyr.*6.2.28. **-σκόπος**, ὁ, = ἀλφιτόμαντις, Hsch. (-σκόπαι cod.). **-φάγος** [ᾰ], ον, *eating barley-bread*, Ael.*NA* 17.31. **-χρως**, ωτος, ὁ, ἡ, *of the colour of barley-meal*, κεφαλὴ ἀ. *powdered*, i.e. *mangy* head, Ar.*Fr.*533.

Ἀλφῐτώ, οῦς, ἡ, *bugbear* with which nurses frightened children, Chrysipp.*Stoic.*3.77.

Ἀλφιῷος, ὁ, sc. μήν, name of month at Elis, *GDI*1168.

ἀλφο-ειδής, ές, = ἀλφώδης, Philum.*Ven.*23.2. **-πρόσωπος**, ον, *white-faced*, a. d **-ρυγχος**, ον, *with white snout*, *Hippiatr.*13.

ἀλφός, ὁ, *dull-white leprosy*, esp. on the face, Hes.*Fr.*29, Thphr. *Char.*19.2, Lxx *Le.*13.39, etc.: pl. in Hp.*Aph.*3.20, Pl.*Ti.*85a. (Cf. Lat. *albus*.)

ἀλφώδης, ες, *leprous*, Gal.6.243, Vett.Val.13.2.

ἀλχηρῆς ὕπνος· ἀηδής, οὐκ ἔχων χαράς, Hsch.

Ἀλῶα or **Ἁλῷα**, ων, τά, (ἅλως) festival of Demeter as inventress of agriculture, *harvest-home*, *IG*2.834*b* ii 8, D.59.116, Philoch.161, Luc.

*D.Meretr.*7.4. **ἀλωαῖος**, α, ον, (ἅλως) *belonging to the threshing-floor*: Ἀλωαίη, epith. of Demeter, Orph.*H.*41.5. **Ἀλωάς**, άδος, or **Ἀλωΐς**, ίδος, ἡ, = Ἀλωαία, Theoc.7.155.

ἀλώβητος, ον, *unblemished*, φύσις Ph.1.451; *intact*, ἀ. καὶ ἀκέραιος Them.*Or.*3.43c, cf. Zos.2.5; *sound* in limb, Gal.13.1026.

ἀλώδης, ες, *like salt*, Plu.2.627f. **ἀλωεινός**, ή, όν, (ἅλως) *of* or *used in a threshing-floor*, ἵπποι *AP*9.301 (Secund.). **ἀλωεύς**, έως, Ep. ῆος, ὁ, *one who works in an* ἀλωή, *husbandman*, A.R.3.1401, Arat. 1045, etc.: in Hom. only as pr. n.

ἀλωή [ᾰ], Dor. **ἀλωά**, ἡ, (ἀλέω A, cf. Att. ἅλως) poet.: I. *threshing-floor*, ἱερὰς κατ' ἀλωάς Il.5.499; μεγάλην κατ' ἀλωήν, ἐϋκτιμένῃ ἐν ἀλωῇ, 13.588, 20.496, cf. Hes.*Op.*597. II. more commonly, *any prepared ground* (cf. Sch.Od.1.193), *garden, orchard, vineyard*, etc., Il.5.90, Od.6.293, etc.: Ποσειδάωνος ἀ., i.e. sea, Opp. *H.*1.797. III. *halo*, of sun or moon, Arat.811,875.

Ἀλωιάς, ἡ, *of the threshing-floor*, Δηώ Nonn.*D.*30.68.

ἀλώιος, α, ον, = ἀλωεινός, Nic.*Th.*113. **Ἀλωΐς**, v. Ἀλωάς.

ἀλωίτης [ῑ], ου, ὁ, = ἀλωεύς, dub. l. *AP*6.98 (Zon.).

ἄλωμα, τό, Boeot. = ἀνάλωμα, *SIG*1185 (Tanagra), *IG*7.2426 (Thebes).

ἀλώμεναι, Ep. for ἁλῶναι, v. sub ἁλίσκομαι.

ἅλων, ωνος, ἡ, = ἅλως (usu. in sense I), rare in nom., Thphr.*Sign.* 31 (pl., in sense II. 1), Lxx *Ho.*9.2, *BGU*651.5 (ii A.D.); more freq. in oblique cases, *BCH*39.55 (Arcad., iv B.C., in sense of *plantation* (?)), *PLille*13.3, Arist.*Vent.*973ᵃ14, Lxx *Ge.*50.10, etc.

ἀλωνάκη· ἀνάλωμα (Chalcis), Hsch.

ἀλωνεύομαι, *work on a threshing-floor*, App.*Mac.*13.

ἀλώνης, ου, ὁ, *contractor for salt-works*, *Inscr.Prien.*111.

ἁλώνητος, ον, *bought with salt*, ἁ. δουλάρια worthless slaves from Thrace, because Thracians *sold men for salt*, Zen.2.12.

ἀλων-ία, ἡ, = ἅλως, *threshing-floor*, Ath.12.524a, *CPR*73.20 (ii A.D.), Sch.Nic.*Th.*541:—written **ἀλωνεία**, ἡ, Sch.Il.5.499, *BGU* 663 (iii A.D.). II. *grain on threshing-floor*, *PRyl.*442.4 (iii A.D.), *POxy.*1107.3 (v/vi A.D.). III. = ἅλως II. 2, Sch.Nic. *Th.*166. **-ίζω**· ἀλωνεύομαι, Hsch. **-ικός**, ή, όν, *for a threshing-floor*, ὑποζύγια prob. in *PStrassb.*93.5 (ii B.C.); κόσκινον *Edict.Diocl.* 15.56. **-ιον**, τό, Dim. of ἅλων, *Gp.*12.2.2, Hdn.Gr.2.763, *Gloss.*

ἀλωνο-ειδής, ές, *shaped like a threshing-floor*, χώρα Hero *Mens.* 56. **-τρῐβέω**, = ἀλωνεύομαι, Suid. s. v. ἀλωνία. II. *beat on a threshing-floor*, Longus 3.29. **-φυλακία**, ἡ, *office of guard of a threshing-floor*, *PRyl.*90.39 (iii A.D.). **-φύλαξ**, ακος, ὁ, *guard of a threshing-floor*, *POxy.*1465.8 (i B.C.).

ἀλωόφυτος, ον, *grown in a vineyard*, οἶνος Nonn.*D.*13.267.

ἀλωπέκ-ειος, α, ον, Ion. **-εος**, η, ον, *of a fox*, στέαρ Gal.14.331; λίπος Philum.ap.Orib.45.29.36. II. ἀλωπεκέη, Att. contr. -κῆ (sc. δορά), *fox-skin*, Hdt.7.75: prov., ὅπου ἡ λεοντῆ μὴ ἐφικνεῖται, προσραπτέον ἐκεῖ τὴν ἀλωπεκῆν Plu.*Lys.*7. **-εως**, ὁ, name of a vine, and of the wine made therefrom, Hsch.; cf. ἀλωπεκίς III. **-ία**, ἡ, disease, like *mange in foxes*, in which hair falls off, dub. in S.*Fr.*419, cf. Gal.12.381: pl., *bald patches* on the head, Arist.*Pr.*893ᵇ38. II. *fox-earth*, Hsch., *EM*75.6. **-ίας**, ου, ὁ, *branded with a fox*, Luc. *Pisc.*47. II. *thresher shark*, Lat. *Squalus vulpes*, Arist.*Fr.*310, Mnesim.4.49, Diph.Siph.ap.Ath.8.356c. **-ίασις**, εως, ἡ, = ἀλωπεκία I, Gal.6.244. **-ιδεύς**, έως, ὁ, *fox-cub*, Ar.*Pax*1067, Ael.*NA* 7.47. 2. = ἀλωπεκίς, *Epic.Alex.Adesp.*2.9. **-ίζω**, *play the fox*, οὐκ ἔστιν ἀλωπεκίζειν Ar.*V.*1241; ἄλλοις ἀλωπέκιζε τοῖς ἀπειρήτοις Babr.95.64: prov., ἀ. πρὸς ἑτέραν ἀλώπεκα 'Greek meets Greek', Zen.1.70. II. trans., *overreach*, Hsch. **-ιον**, τό, Dim. of ἀλώπηξ, *little fox*, Ar.*Eq.*1076,1079. **-ίς**, ίδος, ἡ, *mongrel between fox and dog*, = κυναλώπηξ, X.*Cyn.*3.1. II. *fox-skin cap*, X.*An.* 7.4.4. III. kind of *grape*, so-called from its colour, Plin.*HN* 14.42. **-οειδής**, ές, *like fox*, Gal.4.604. **-ουρος**, ὁ, *beard-grass, Polypogon monspeliensis*, Thphr.*HP*7.11.2. **-ώδης**, ες, *fox-like, sly*, Hsch., *EM*75.5.

ἀλωπεύει (cod. ἀλοπ-)· ἀνιχνεύει, Hsch.; cf. ἀλωπός.

ἀλώπηξ [ᾰ], εκος (also ἀλώπηκος Anan.5), ἡ; dat. pl., ἀλώπεξι Lxx 3*Ki.*21.10, Ep. ἀλωπήκεσσι Opp.*C.*1.433:—*fox, Canis vulpes* (smaller Egyptian species Arist.*HA*606ᵃ24, *C. niloticus*), Archil.86.2, 89.5, Semon.7.7, Hdt.2.67, etc.: of sly persons, ἀλώπεκος ἴχνεσι βαίνειν Sol.11.5; μῆτιν ἀ. *a very fox* for craft, Pi.*I.*4(3).65: prov., τὴν . . Ἀρχιλόχου ἀλώπεκα ἑλκτέον ἐξόπισθεν we must trail Archilochus' *fox-skin* behind, i.e. deceive by false appearances, Pl.*R.*365c; πολλῆς αὐτῆς τῆς ἀ. ἐπιχέαντες Eun.*Hist.*p.249 D.; ἡ ἀ. τὸν βοῦν ἐλαύνει 'sleight masters might', Diogenian.2.73; πεινῶσαν ἀ. ὕπνος ἐπέρχεται 'qui dort dîne', Id.7.91; ἡ κέρκος τῇ ἀλώπεκι μαρτυρεῖ 'ex pede Herculem', Id.5.15; ἀλλ' οὐκ αὖθις ἀ. (sc. πάγαις ἁλώσεται) 'a burnt child dreads the fire', Id.2.15. II. a large *bat, Sciurus* or *Pteromys volans*, Arist.*HA*490ᵃ7. III. = ἀλωπεκίας II, ib.566ᵃ 31. IV. in pl., *muscles of the loins, psoas-muscles*, Clearch.92, Ruf.*Onom.*189. V. = ἀλωπεκία I, *mange*, Herod.7.72, Call.*Dian.* 79: in pl., *bald patches*, Hp.*Aff.*35. VI. kind of *dance*, dub. in S.*Fr.*419 (prob. in sense V), cf. Hsch. s. v. ὄρχησις.

ἀλωπός, ὁ, = ἀλώπηξ, Hdn.Gr.1.189:—fem. **ἀλωπά**, ἡ, Hsch. II. as Adj., = ἀλωπεκώδης, S.*Fr.*263. **ἀλωπόχροος**, ον, contr. **-χρους**, ουν, *fox-coloured*, f. l. for ἀλφιτόχρους, *AB*381, Eust.1968.39.

ἁλωρῆται, οἱ, *watchers of salt*, Suid., *EM*74.28.

ἅλως [ᾰ], ἡ, gen. ἅλω Hp.*VM*13, X.*Oec.*18.8, ἅλωος *AP*6.258 (Adaeus); dat. ἅλῳ Arist.*Ph.*198ᵇ22; acc. ἅλω A.*Th.*489, *IG*2.834*b* ii 21, ἅλων Nic.*Th.*166, ἅλωα Call.*Fr.*51: pl., nom. ἅλῳ Arist.*Mete.* 344ᵇ2, ἅλωες Ach.Tat.*Intr.Arat.*32, ἅλως D.42.6, Thphr.*Sign.*22; acc. ἅλως Arist.*Mir.*835ᵇ9, etc.: (v. sub ἀλέω A):—*threshing-floor*, Hp. l.c., X. l.c., etc.; *grain on the floor*, *PRyl.*122.10 (ii A.D.):—hence, from round shape, II. *disk* of sun or moon, or shield, A. l.c.: later, *halo*, Arist.*Mete.*344ᵇ2, Epicur.*Ep.*2 p.51 U., Gal.5.640, etc. 2. *serpent's coil*, Nic.*Th.*166. 3. *bird's nest*, Ael.*NA* 3.16. 4. *ciliary body of the eye*, Poll.2.71. 5 *circular piazza* at Delphi, *GDI*2101, 2642.

ἁλ-ώσῐμος, ον, (ἁλῶναι) *easy to take* or *conquer*, of places and persons, Hdt.3.153, E.*Hel.*1622, Th.4.9: metaph., *easily beguiled*, X. *Mem.*3.11.11. 2. of the mind, *easy to apprehend*, S.*Ph.*863 (lyr.). 3. *capable of solution*, ἀπόκρισις Aristid.2.275 J. II. (ἅλωσις) *of* or *belonging to capture* or *conquest*, παιὰν ἁ. song of triumph *on taking city*, A.*Th.*635; βάξις ἁ. tidings *of capture*, *Ag.*10. **-ωσις**, εως, Ion. ιος, ἡ, *capture*, Pi.*O.*10(11).42, Hdt.1.5, 3.156, A.*Ag.*589, etc.; δαΐων ἅ. *conquest* by enemy, Id.*Th.*119: *means of conquest*, S. *Ph.*61. 2. *taking, catching* of birds and fish, Arist.*HA*593ᵃ20, 600ᵃ3 (pl.); ἑαλωκότες ἰσχυρὰν ἅλωσιν taken *without power to escape*, Plu.*Num.*15. II. law-term, *conviction*, Pl.*Lg.*920a, D.C.*Fr.*97.3.

ἅλωσος, dub. sens., Hdn.Gr.1.213.

ἄλωστοι· ἄρραφοι, Hsch.

Ἀλώτια, τά, festival at Tegea, Paus.8.47.4.

ἁλωτός, ή, όν, *liable to capture* or *conquest*, Th.6.77, Philostr.*Im.*1. 4; ἡδονῇ ἁλωτὸν ἄνθρωπος Ph.2.381. 2. *captured*, Philostr.*VA* 2.10. II. *attainable*, S.*OT*111, Men.132.

ἀλώφητος, ον, (λωφάω) *unremitting*, Plu.*Fab.*23, *AP*5.254.12 (Paul. Sil.).

ἀλωφούς· λευκούς, Hsch.

ἀμ, for ἀνά, before words beginning with β, π, φ, μ, e.g. ἂμ βωμοῖσι, ἂμ μέσον, ἂμ πεδίον, ἂμ πέλαγος, ἂμ φυτά; also compds., as ἀμπαύω:—mostly Dor., as in Pi., but also in Hom., sts. in Trag.

ἅμᾰ [ᾰμ], Dor. **ἁμᾶ**, q.v.: (v. sub fin.): A. Adv. *at once, at the same time*, mostly of Time, freq. added to τε . . καί, ἅμ' οἰμωγή τε καὶ εὐχωλή Il.8.64; ἅ. τ' ὠκύμορος καὶ ὀϊζυρός 1.417; σέ θ' ἅ. κλαίω καὶ ἐμέ 24.773; σαυτόν θ' ἅ. κἀμέ S.*Ph.*772, cf. 119; ἄνους τε καὶ γέρων ἅ. *Ant.*281:—with καί only, ἅ. πρόσσω καὶ ὀπίσσω Il.3.109; with τε . . τε, χειρῶν τε βίης θ' ἅ. ἔργον ἔφαινον Hes.*Th.*677. 2. ἅ. μέν . . ἅ. δέ . ., *partly . . partly . .*, Pl.*Phd.*115d, X.*HG*3.1.3:—ἅ. τε . . καὶ ἅ. Pl. *Grg.*497a; ἅμ' ἡδέως ἔμοιγε κἀλγεινῶς ἅμα S.*Ant.*436. 3. in Prose ἅ. δέ . . καί . ., ἅ. τε . . καί . ., ἅ. . . καί . . may often be translated by *no sooner . . than . .*, ἅ. δὲ ταῦτα ἔλεγε καὶ ἀπεδείκνυε Hdt.1.112; ταῦτά τε ἅμα ἠγόρευε καὶ πέμπει 8.5; ἅ. ἀκηκόαμέν τε καὶ τριηράρχους καθίσταμεν D.4.36; ἅ. διαλλάττονται καὶ τῆς ἔχθρας ἐπιλανθάνονται Isoc.4.157. b. ἅ. μῦθος ἔην, τετέλεστο δὲ ἔργον 'no sooner said than done', Il.19.242; ἅ. ἔπος τε καὶ ἔργον ἐμήδετο *h.Merc.*46; ταῦτα εἶπε καὶ ἅ. ἔπος τε καὶ ἔργον ἐποίεε Hdt.3.134, cf. 9.92: prov., ἅμ' ἔπος ἅμ' ἔργον Diogenian.1.36. c. with part. and finite Verb in same sense, βρίζων ἅ. . . ἐξήμελξας εὐτραφὲς γάλα A.*Ch.*897; ἅ. εἰπὼν ἀνέστη *as soon as* he had done speaking, he stood up, X.*An.*3.1.47; τῆς ἀγγελίας ἅ. ῥηθείσης ἐπεβοήθουν *as soon as* news was brought they assisted, Th.2.5; ἅ. γιγνόμενοι λαμβάνομεν Pl.*Phd.*76c; ἡμῖν ἅ. ἀναπαυομένοις ὁ παῖς ἀναγνώσεται *Tht.*143b. 4. ἅ. μέν . . ἔτι δέ . . X.*Cyr.*1.4.3; ἅ. μέν . . πρὸς δέ . . Hdt.8.51. II. *together, at once, both*, without direct ref. to time, ἅ. πάντες or πάντες ἅ. Il.1.495, al.; ἅ. ἄμφω *h.Cer.*15; ἅ. κρατερὸς καὶ ἀμύμων Od.3.111, etc.: of Place, Arist.*Metaph.*1028ᵇ27. III. with σύν or μετά, E.*Ion*717, Pl.*Criti.*110a. IV. abs. with Verb, *at one and the same time*, αἱ πᾶσαι [νῆες] ἅ. ἐγίγνοντο ἐν ἑνὶ θέρει σ' καὶ ν' Th.3.17, cf. οὐχ ἅ. ἡ κτῆσις παραγίγνεται D.23.113.

B. Prep. with dat. (freq. with part. added), *at the same time with, together with*, ἅμ' ἠοῖ φαινομένηφι *at* dawn, Il.9.682, al.; ἅ. ἕῳ, ἅ. ἕῳ γιγνομένῃ, Th.1.48, 4.32; ἅμ' ἠελίῳ ἀνιόντι or καταδύντι *at* sunrise or sunset, Il.18.136, 210, al.; ἅμ' ἡμέρῃ διαφωσκούσῃ Hdt.3.86, al.; ἅμ' ἡμέρᾳ E.*El.*78, Th.2.94, etc., Att.; ἅμ' ἦρι ἀρχομένῳ or ἅ. ἦρι *at* beginning of spring, Th.5.20, 2.2, etc.; ἅ. κήδεϊ κεκάρθαι τὰς κεφαλάς *during the time of . .*, Hdt.2.36; ἅ. τειχισμῷ Th.7.20; ἅμα τῷ διαυγάζειν Plb.3.104.5 (without Art. ἅμα εὑρεθῆναι Ps.-Plu.*Fluv.*23. 2). 2. generally, *together with*, ἅ. τινὶ στείχειν Il.16.257; ὀπάσσαι 24.461, al.; Ἑλένην καὶ κτήμαθ' ἅμ' αὐτῇ 3.458; ἅ. πνοιῇς ἀνέμοιο *keeping pace with* the wind, Od.1.98; repeated, ἅμ' αὐτῷ . . ἅμ' ἕποντο 11.371; οἱ ἅ. Θάλητι Hdt.6.138, cf. Th.7.57. II. rarely c. gen., Herod.4.95, *POxy.*903 (iv A.D.), Pythag.*Sim.*28, Olymp.Hist. p.453 D.; dub. in Thphr.*Char.*6.9.

C. Conj., *as soon as*, ἅ. ἂν ἡβήσῃ τις τῶν ὀρφανῶν Pl.*Lg.*928c, cf. Lex ap.D.46.20; ἅ. κα διεξέλθῃ ὁ χρόνος *GDI*2160 (Delph., ii B.C.). (Root *sm̥-*, cf. A a II.)

ἁμᾶ, Dor. for ἅμα, Pi.*O.*3.21, *IG*5(1), Ar.*Lys.*1318, Call.*Lav.Pall.* 75, Theoc.9.4. (ἁμᾶ Hdn.Gr.1.489; ἁμᾷ Thphr.*Metaph.*6, al. (cod. opt.).)

ἀμαδέον, τό, kind of *fig*, Cretan, Hermonax ap.Ath.3.76f.

ἀμάδις, Adv. = ἅμα, Theognost.*Can.*163.22; in form ἀμάδιος, *Et. Gen.*

ἀμάδρυα· κοκκύμηλα (Sicyon.), Phot.p.85 R., Hsch.

Ἀμαδρυάδες, αἱ, (δρῦς) Nymphs whose life depended on that of trees to which they were attached, Pl.*Epigr.*14, Pherenicus ap.Ath. 3.78b: sg., Ἀμαδρυάς A.R.2.477, Ant.Lib.30.4.

ἀμαζακάραν· πολεμεῖν (Persian), Hsch.

ἀμαζανίδες· μηλέαι, Hsch.

Ἀμαζονομαχία, ἡ, *battle with Amazons*, Sch.Il.2.219.

Ἀμαζών, όνος, ἡ, mostly pl., *the Amazons*, Il.3.189, etc.; ὁ τῶν Ἀ. τροχίσκος, a famous remedy, Asclep.ap.Gal.12.152, etc.:—also **Ἀμαζονίδες,** αἱ, Pi.*O.*13.87, Call.*Dian.*237. II. epith. of Artemis, Paus.4.31.8:—Adj. **Ἀμαζ-ονικός,** ή, όν, Plu.*Pomp.*35, Paus. 1.41.7:—**-κά,** τά, title of Epic by Onasus, Sch.A.R.1.1236, Sch. Theoc.13.46:—also **-όνιος,** ον, Nonn.*D.*37.17; epith. of Apollo in Laconia, Paus.3.25.3. (Commonly derived from μαζός, from the fable that they got rid of the right breast, that it might not interfere with the use of the bow.) III. (ἀ- priv., μᾶζα) *poor, starveling*, ἄνδρες Call.*Fr.*523.

ἀμᾰθ-αίνω, (ἀμαθής) *to be untaught, ignorant*, only pres.; abs., Pl.*R.*535e, Ph.1.498, Aristid.34(50).44, Plot.4.4.24; ἀ. τι or εἴς τι *to be ignorant in* a thing, Pl.*Lg.*689c,d. **-εί,** Adv. of ἀμαθής, Suid.

ἀμαθεῖν· θερίζειν, Hsch. **ἀμαθηΐς,** suggested for ψαμαθηΐς (v. ἄμαθος) by Sch.Nic.*Th.*887.

ἀμαθ-ής, ές, (μαθεῖν) *ignorant, stupid*, Hdt.1.33, Democr.169, etc.; ἔθνεα ἀμαθέστατα Hdt.4.46; ἀνὴρ πένης, εἰ καὶ γένοιτο μὴ ἀ. E. *Supp.*421, al., Ar.*Nu.*135; ἀ. καὶ βδελυρός Id.*Eq.*193; ἀμαθεστάτους πάντων ἀνθρώπων And.2.2; ἀ. τὴν [ἐκείνων] ἀμαθίαν Pl.*Ap.*22e; opp. δεξιός, Th.3.82; of animals, such as wild boars, *unmanageable*, θυμώδη καὶ ἀ. Arist.*HA*488^{b}14: c. gen. rei, *without knowledge of* a thing, *unlearned in* it, -έστερος τοῦ καλοῦ E.*Or.*417; λῃστείας Th. 4.41, cf. 3.37; ἀ. περί τινος Pl.*Erx.*394e; τι *La.*194d; πρός τι *Lg.* 679d. Adv. **-θῶς** *ignorantly, through ignorance*, ἥμαρτον E.*Ph.*874: Comp. -έστερον, τῶν νόμων ὑπεροψίας παιδεύεσθαι to be educated *with too little learning* to despise the laws, Th.1.84; -έστερόν πως εἰπὲ καὶ σαφέστερον *less learnedly*, Ar.*Ra.*1445. b. of moral defects, *unfeeling, inhuman*, ἀ. τις εἶ θεός E.*HF*347. 2. of things, ἀ. παρρησία *boorish* freedom of speech, E.*Or.*905; ἀ. ῥώμη *brute* force, Id.*Fr.*732; ἀ. δύναμις Plu.*Demetr.*42; ἀ. φρόνημα *barbarous* pride, E.*Heracl.*459. II. *not heard of, unknown*, ἀ. ἔρρει E.*Ion*916. Adv. ἀμαθῶς, χωρῆσαι, of events, to take *an unforeseen course*, Th.1.140. **-ητος,** ον, = ἀμαθής, Phryn.Com.8; ἀ. γραμμάτων Procop.*Arc.*6. **-ία,** ἡ, *ignorance, stupidity*, Heraclit.95, 109, Hp.*Art.*67 (v.l. -είην), S.*Fr.*924, E.*Ph.*584, etc.; opp. δεξιότης, Th.3.37; ἀ. τινός Democr.83, X.*Mem.*4.2.22; περὶ τὰ μέγιστα Pl. *Lg.*688c. 2. *boorishness, lack of culture*, X.*Ath.*1.5, E.*Cyc.*173, Isoc.15.248. 3. *wilful blindness, sin*, *IG*4.951.39 (Epid.), cf. E. *Ba.*490. 4. *discourtesy*, Id.*Med.*224; *perversity*, Id.*HF*1254.

ἀμᾰθῖτις, ιδος, ἡ, (ἄμαθος) *dwelling in sand*, ἀ. κόγχοι *sand*-snails, Epich.42. **ἄμᾰθος** [ἄμ], ἡ, Ep. form of ἄμμος, *sand*, Il.5.587, A.R.4.1239, etc.: pl., *links, dunes* by the sea, *h.Ap.*439; generally, *sandy soil*, Nic.*Th.*262. (Dist. by Gramm., e.g. Sch.Il.9.384, from ψάμμος (q.v.) as *dust* from sea-sand, but prob. wrongly:—ἄμ- is for ἄμ-, i.e. σάμ-, cf. *sand*.)

ἀμᾰθύνω, (ἄμαθος) Ep., only pres., impf., and (in Q.S.14.645) aor.:—*level with the dust, utterly destroy*, πόλιν Il.9.593; [ἄνδρα] μέγα φωνοῦντα A.*Eu.*937 (lyr.); ἀ. ἐν φλογὶ σάρκα Theoc.2.26:—Pass., Q.S.2.334. 2. *scatter like sand*, *h.Merc.*140.

ἀμᾰθώδης, ες, *sandy*, ποταμός Str.8.3.14.

ἀμαίευτος, ον, *not yet delivered*, Nonn.*D.*1.5; γαστήρ 41.133. II. *without aid of midwife*, λοχείη Opp.*C.*1.40.

ἀμαιμάκετος, η, ον, also ος, ον Hes.*Sc.*207:—*irresistible*, old Ep. word, also in Lyr. and Trag. (lyr.); of Chimaera, Il.6.179, 16.329; of fire vomited by her, Hes.*Th.*319; of fire generally, S.*OT*177; θάλασσα, πόντος, Hes.*Sc.*207, Pi.*P.*1.14; of ship's mast, proof against any strain, Od.14.311; of the trident, Pi.*I.*8(7).37; ἀ. μένος, κινηθμός, *P.*3.33, 4.208; νεῖκος *stubborn*, B.10.64; of the Furies, S.*OC*127; ἀ. βυθοῖς in *unfathomable* depths, *IG*3.900. [Usu. derived fr. ἀ- intens., μαιμάω, i.e. *furious*; but apptly. connected with ἄμαχος by Poets.]

ἀμάκιον· ἄβαξ (Lacon.), Hsch.

ἀμάκις· ἅπαξ (Cret.), Hsch. (-κι- = -q^ui-, cf. ἀμάτις, πολλάκις).

ἀμακρῶτις, = ἀμπελόπρασον, Ps.-Dsc.2.150.

ἄμαλα· τὴν ναῦν ἀπὸ τοῦ ἀμᾶν τὴν ἅλα, Hsch. (A.*Fr.*214); ἀμάδα· τὴν ναῦν, *EM*75.22: hence ἐπ' ἄμαλα restored by Herm., A.*Supp.* 842,847, where ἐπαμίδα cod. Med.

ἀμαλακ-ία, ἡ, v.l. for sq., Lyd.*Mens.*4.71. **-ιστία,** ἡ, *incapability of being softened, hardness*, etym. of Ἀμάλθεια, D.S.4.35. **-τος,** ον, (μαλάσσω) *that cannot be softened, intractable*, of materials, Arist. *Mete.*385^{a}13; ἄτηκτα καὶ ἀ. 388^{b}25. 2. *unmitigated*, τὸ ψυχρόν Plu.2.953e: metaph. of expression, *harsh*, Longin.15.5. II. *unfeeling*, Sch.S.*Aj.*776.

ἀμᾰλάπτω, = ἀμαλδύνω, *destroy, efface*, aor. ἠμάλαψα S.*Fr.*465, Lyc.34:—Pass., ἀμαλαπτομέναν prob. in A.*Pr.*899 (Weil).

ἀμαλαυρεῖ· μαραίνει, Hsch.

ἀμαλδύνω, (ἀμαλός) Ep. (not in Od.) and Ion. word, properly, *soften, mitigate*, ἐλπωρὴ ἀμαλδύνει κακότητα Q.S.1.73, cf. 13.401; but in early Ep. *crush, destroy*, τεῖχος ἀμαλδῦναι Il.12.18; *bring low*, συμφορὰ ἐσθλὸν ἀμαλδύνει B.13.3; *put an end to*, τὴν διὰ τοῦ ὀμφαλοῦ πνοήν Hp.*Nat.Puer.*17; *use up, squander*, χρήματα Theoc.16.59; *weaken*, ὀφθαλμούς *Cat.Cod.Astr.*2.174:—Pass., ὥς κεν .. τεῖχος ἀμαλδύνηται Il.7.463; ἀμαλδυνθήσομαι Ar.*Pax*380; ὄμματα .. ἀ. Hp.*Mul.* 2.201; ἀ. ἡ δίοδος τῆς γονῆς Id.*Genit.*2; ἀμαλδυνθεῖσα χρόνῳ περικαλλέα μορφήν *AP*6.18 (Jul.); *neglect, waste*, Democr.202. 2. metaph., *conceal, disguise*, εἶδος *h.Cer.*94, cf. A.R.1.834; *efface*, στίβον Id.4.112.

ἀμάλη [ᾰμᾰ], ἡ, = ἄμαλλα, Semus 19, Philostr.Jun.*Im.*10.

ἀμαλητόμος, ον, (τέμνω) *reaper*, Opp.*C.*1.522.

ἀμάλθακτος, ον, (μαλθάσσω) *unmitigated*, Aret.*CA*2.11; *inexorable*, φρένες *AP*5.233 (Paul. Sil.); ἐπιθυμία Olymp. *in Alc.*p.66C.

Ἀμάλθ-εια, Ion. **-είη** or **-ίη,** ἡ, goat *Amaltheia*, which suckled Zeus, Call.*Fr.*49: from her horn flowed whatever its possessor wished, hence κέρας Ἀμαλθείας horn *of plenty*, Anacr.8, Phoc.7, Ar. *Fr.*39D.; applied to parks, etc., Duris 41, D.S.3.68, etc.; title of book, Gell.*Praef.*6:—also **-εῖον,** τό, country-house of Atticus in Epirus, Cic.*Att.*1.16, cf. 18.

ἀμαλθεύω, = τρέφω, S.*Fr.*95; cf. foreg.

ἀμαλίζω· πνίγω, in impf., Hsch.

Ἀμάλιος, ὁ, sc. μήν, month at Delphi, *GDI*1694, al.

ἀμαλκιεῖν· τὸ μὴ ῥιγοῦν, *EM*76.5.

ἄμαλλ-α [ᾰμ], ἡ, (ἀμάω A) *bundle of ears of corn, sheaf*, S.*Fr.*607, Plu. *Publ.*8. 2. poet. for *corn*, Q.S.11.156,171, etc. **-εῖον,** τό, *sheaf-band*, Call.Com.3D. **-εύω,** *bind into sheaves* or *bundles*, *EM*76.6. **-ιον,** τό, = ἀμαλλεῖον, Hsch., Eust.1162.29.

ἀμαλλο-δετήρ, ῆρος, ὁ, (δέω) *binder of sheaves*, Il.18.553, Aret.*SD* 2.13. **-δέτης,** ου, ὁ, = foreg., Theoc.10.44, *AP*10.16 (Theaet.).

ἄμαλλος (A), ον, *without fleece* or *nap*, Eust.1057.12.

ἄμαλλος (B)· πέρδιξ (Polyrrhenian), Hsch.:—also **ἄμαλλοι·** φυτὰ σικύων ἢ τῶν ὁμοίων, Id.

ἀμαλλο-τόκεια, ἡ, *producer of sheaves*, Jo.Gaz.2.31; pecul. fem. of, **-τόκος,** ον, *sheaf-producing*, Nonn.*D.*7.84; πεδία *Hymn.Is.* 3. **-φόρος,** ον, *bringing sheaves*, Euph.103, Porph.*Abst.*2.19; of Demeter, Nonn.*D.*17.153, Eust.1162.27; cf. ἀμιλλοφόρος.

ἀμα-λογεῖ (prob. for ὁμο-)· *effutat*, *Gloss.* **-λογία·** ἀβδηριτισμός, *Gloss.*, v.l. for ὁμολογία in Alciphr.2.3. **-λόγος·** φλύαρος, *Gloss.*

ἀμᾰλ-ός [ᾰμ], ή, όν, *soft, weak*, in Hom. of young animals, Il.22. 310, Od.20.14; γέρων E.*Heracl.*75; παῖς Call.*Fr.*49P.: irreg. Comp. -έστερος, ὄψις -εστέρα Adam.2.2. (Perh. cognate with Skt. *mṛdús* 'soft', Lat. *mollis*.) **-όω·** ἀμαλδύνω, Hsch.

Ἀμαλώιος, ὁ, sc. μήν, month at Cyme in Aeolis, *BCH*12.362.

ἀμαλῶς, Adv. = ὁμαλῶς (in the sense of ὁμοίως), v.l. in Hp.*Morb.* 1.8, 2.8, *Int.*30, cf. Gal.19.76.

ἀμάμαξυς [ᾰμᾰ], ἡ, gen. υος or (in Sapph.) υδος, *vine trained on two poles*, Epich.24, Sapph.150, Matro *Conv.*114.

ἀμᾰμηλίς, ίδος, ἡ, = ἐπιμηλίς, *medlar, Mespilus germanica*, Hp. *Mul.*1.44, Aristomen.11, cf. Ath.14.650c.

ἀμαμιθάδες, αἱ, *mince-meat*, Phot.p.86R. **ἀμαμίξαι·** ἀποπνῖξαι, Hsch. (Cf. ἀμαλίζω, ἀμμιάξαι.) **ἀμάναν·** ἄμαξαν, Id. **ἀμανδαλοῖ·** ἀφανίζει, Id. **ἀμάνδᾰλος,** = ἀφανής, as if ἀμάλδανος fr. ἀμαλδύνω, Alc.123.

ἀμᾱνῖται [ᾰμ], ῶν, οἱ, '*champignons*', a kind of fungus, Nic.*Fr.*79, Gal.6.656, Eust.290.3, etc. **ἀμάνορες·** δοθιῆνες (Elean), Hsch.

ἀμάντευτος, ον, *not to be foretold* or *conjectured*, τύχη Max.Tyr.11. 6. 2. *lacking in oracles*, Philostr.*Im.*1.4. 3. Act., *not divining*, τοῦ μέλλοντος Charito 2.2: hence, of dogs with bad noses, Poll. 5.63. **ἄμαντις,** ι, *not divining*, ἄ. μαντική Oenom.ap.Eus.*PE*5.21.

ἅμαξα [ᾰ], Att. **ἅμαξα,** ἡ, (v. ἄξων) prop. *frame-work*, '*châssis*' of a four-wheeled wagon (ἀπήνη), opp. πείρινς (body), Il.24.263 sqq., cf. Od.6.37, al.:—also, of the whole *wagon*, ib.260, cf. Hes.*Op.*453, Hdt.1.31, Th.1.93, etc.; of the *wagons* of the Scythians, Hdt.4.114, 121; βοῦς ὑφ' ἁμάξης *draught*-oxen, X.*An.*6.4.22,25. 2. c. gen., *wagon-load*, πετρῶν, σίτου, X.*An.*4.7.10, *Cyr.*2.4.18; ἐλλεβόρου Pl. *Euthd.*299b; τρισσῶν ἁμαξῶν βάρος E.*Cyc.*385, cf. 473. 3. prov., ἡ ἅμαξα τὸν βοῦν (sc. ἕλκει) 'the cart before the horse', Luc.*D.Mort.* 6.2; ἐξ ἁμάξης ὑβρίζειν, of abusive ribaldry, such as was allowed to the women as they were taken *in wagons* to the Eleusinian mysteries, Sch.D.18.122, cf. Ar.*Pl.*1014, Men.396; βοᾷς .. ὥσπερ ἐξ ἁμάξης D.l.c. II. *carriage of a plough*, Hes.*Op.*426,453. III. = Ἄρκτος, *the Great Bear*, Il.18.487, Od.5.273, Call.*Iamb.*1.119, etc. IV. metaph., of a *ship*, A.*Fr.*451B. V. = ἁμαξιτός, *AP* 7.479 (Theodorid.).

ἁμαξ-αία, = ἅμαξα, A.D.*Adv.*160.6, Hdn.Gr.1.281. **-αῖος,** α, ον, *of* or *like a wagon*, ἅ. ἄρκτος (cf. ἅμαξα III), Arat.93, cf. Nonn.*D.*1.251.

ἁμαξακάρινον (?-κάρριον)· ἅμαξα, Hsch.

ἁμαξ-άρχης, ου, ὁ, prob. *official of the imperial transport service*, *BCH*33.67 (Caesarea Cappad.). **-εία,** ἡ, *loading of wagons*, Suid.; *haulage* (in form -ήα), *IG*4.823 (Troezen). **-εύς,** έως, ὁ, *wagoner*, D. Chr.64.23: βοῦς ἁ. *draught*-ox, Plu.*Dio*.38, Philostr.*Gym.*43. **-εύω,** *traverse with a wagon*:—Pass., *to be traversed by wagon-roads*, of country, Hdt.2.108. 2. metaph., ἁ. βίοτον *drag on a weary life*, *AP*9.574. II. intr., *to be a wagoner*, Plu.*Eum.*1; *travel in a wagon*, *AP*7.478 (Leon.); *live in wagons*, of Scythians, Philostr. *VA*7.26. **-ηγός,** ὁ, = Βοώτης, Eust.1535.29. **-ηδόνια,** τά, *axle-pins*, Sch.E.*Hipp.*1235. **-ηλατέω,** *drive a wagon*, Hsch. s.v. ἀμπρεύειν. **-ηλάτης,** ου, ὁ, *wagoner*, *Ostr.Strassb.*671 (ii A.D.): written **-ολάτης** ib.738. **-ήλᾰτος,** ον, *traversed by wagons*: ἡ ἁ. (sc. ὁδός) *carriage-road*, Aen.Tact.16.14, Poll.9.37, cf. Str.6.3.7. **-ήποδες,** οἱ, *axle-blocks*, Poll.1.253, cf. Ath.Mech.16.9: sg., -ήπους *IG*2. 834c. **-ήρης,** ες, (*ἄρω) *of* or *on a carriage*, θρόνος, = δίφρος, A.*Ag.* 1054; τρίβος *high*-road, E.*Or.*1251. **-ιαῖος,** α, ον, *large enough to load a wagon*, λίθος X.*HG*2.4.27, Arist.*Mir.*838^{b}1, D.55.20, Diph. 38, cf. *IG*2^2.463.45, Ἐφ.Ἀρχ.1895.59: metaph., ἁ. ῥῆμα of big words, *Com.Adesp.*836; ἁ. χρήματα money *in cart-loads*, ib.835. **-ικός,** ή, όν, *for wagon*, Thphr.*HP*5.7.6. **-ιον,** τό, = sq., Arist.*MA*701^{b}4, Plu.*Dio*9. **-ίς,** ίδος, ἡ, Dim. of ἅμαξα, *little wagon*, Hdt.3.113; *go-cart*, as child's toy, or *cake* of that shape, Ar.*Nu.*864. 2. = ἀμάμαξυς, Hsch. **-ίτης** [ῑ], ου, ὁ, *of* or *for wagon*, φόρτος *AP*

9.306 (Antiphil.). **-ῖτις**, ἡ, = ἄγρωστις, Ps.-Dsc.4.29. **-ῑτός**, όν, Ep. and Lyr. ἀμ-, (ἅμαξα, εἶμι *ibo*) *traversed by wagons*, ἁ. ὁδός *carriage-road, high-road, highway*, Pi.*N*.6.54, X.*An*.1.2.21; without ὁδός, as Subst., Il.22.146, *h.Cer*.177, Thgn.599, Hdt.7.200, *IG*4.926 (Epid.), *Tab.Heracl*.1.60; ἐν τριπλαῖς ἁ. in a place where three *ways* meet, S.*OT*716, etc. 2. metaph., πειθοῦς ἁ. Emp.133; μακρά μοι νεῖσθαι κατ' ἀμαξιτόν Pi.*P*.4.247.

ἁμαξό-βιος, ον, *living in wagons*, as nomad tribes do, Porph.*Abst*. 3.15. **-ειδῶς**, Adv. *like a wagon*, Eust.1156.15.

ἁμάξοικος, ον, *dwelling in a wagon*, Str.7.3.2, 11.2.1.

ἁμαξο-κῠλιστής, οῦ, ὁ, (κυλίνδω) *down-roller* (i.e. *destroyer*) *of wagons*: in pl., name of a Megarian family, Plu.2.304e. **-πηγέω**, *build wagons*, Nic.Dam.p.28D., Poll.7.115. **-πηγία**, ἡ, *wagon-building*, Thphr.*HP*5.7.6. **-πηγός**, όν, *cartwright*, *PLond.ined*. 2383A (ii B.C.), Plu.*Per*.12. **-πληθής**, ές, (πλῆθος) *large enough to fill a wagon*, λᾶας E.*Ph*.1158; λίθος Aen.Tact.32.5; ὄστρεια Luc. *VH*1.41. **-ποδες**, οἱ, = ἁμαξήποδες, Vitr.10.14.1. **-ποιός**, ὁ, = -πηγός (quod fort. leg.), Heraclid.*Pol*.36. **-τροχιά**, ἡ, (τροχός) *track of a wain* or *car*, Call.Com.10.

ἁμαξ-ουργία, ἡ, = ἁμαξοπηγία, Thphr.*HP*3.10.1. **-ουργός**, όν, = ἁμαξοπηγός, ἐξ ἁμαξουργοῦ λέγειν talk *cartwrights'* slang, Ar.*Eq*. 464.

ἁμαξοφόρητος, ον, *carried in wagons*, οἶκος, of the Scythians, Pi. *Fr*.104.

ἆμαρ, ατος, τό, Dor. for ἦμαρ.

ἀμάρα [ᾰμᾰ], Ion. **ἀμάρη**, ἡ, *trench, conduit, channel*, for watering meadows, χερσὶ μάκελλαν ἔχων, ἀμάρης ἐξ ἔχματα βάλλων Il.21.259; κρηναῖαι ἀμάραι A.R.3.1392; βάλλεις εἰς ἀμάραν με Theoc.27.53, cf. Sapph.151, Call.*Cer*.30, *PFlor*.50.106. 2. *hollow* of ear, *EM*77. 23 (pl.).

ἀμᾱράκινος, η, ον, *made of amaracus*, μύρον Antiph.106; ἔλαιον *Edict.Diocl.Delph*.16. **ἀμᾱρακόεις**, εσσα, εν, *like amaracus*, Nic. *Th*.503.

ἀμάρᾰκον [ᾰμᾰ], τό, and **ἀμάρᾰκος**, ὁ, *marjoram, Origanum Majorana*, Pherecr.131.3 (gender uncertain); masc. in Chaerem.14.16; Thphr. has both, *HP*6.1.1 (-ος), 1.9.4 (-ον), cf. Nic.*Th*.575, *APl*.4. 188 (Nicias). II. = σάμψουχον, Dsc.3.39, Gal.11.823.

ἀμαρανθίς, ἡ, = ὠκιμοειδές, Ps.-Dsc.4.28.

ἀμᾰράντινος, η, ον, *of amaranth*, i.e. *unfading*, στέφανος Philostr. *Her*.19.14. 2. *unfading, imperishable*, στέφανος 1*Ep.Pet*.5.4.

ἀμάραντος [ᾰμᾰ], ον, (μαραίνω) *unfading*, λειμών Luc.*Dom*.9: metaph., σοφία Lxx *Wi*.6.12; κληρονομία 1*Ep.Pet*.1.4, cf. *CIG*2942c (Tralles); πνεῦμα prob. in *IPE*2.286 (Panticapaeum): neut. pl. as Adv., Philostr.*Im*.1.9. II. Subst. ἀμάραντον, τό (but in Lat. *amarantus*), *never-fading flower*, *IG*14.607e (Carales), Poll.1.229; = ἑλίχρυσον, Dsc.4.57; = κενταύρειον μικρόν, Ps.-Dsc.3.7; = χρυσοκόμη, Id.4.55.

ἀμαράσαι· αἱ σῦς, οἱ δὲ κύνες, Hsch.; cf. μαράσαι. **ἄμαργος**, ον, = ἄπληστος, Id. s.v. ἄβαρτος. **ἀμαρεῖν**· ἀκολουθεῖν, πείθεσθαι, ἁμαρτάνειν, Id.

ἀμάρ-ευμα, ατος, τό, *foul water carried off by drain* (ἀθροίσματα βορβόρου), Hsch. **-εύω**, (ἀμάρα) *flow off*, Aristaenet.1.17.

ἀμαρήιος, ον, *from a conduit*, ὕδωρ Nonn.*D*.47.183.

ἀμαρησκαπτήρ, ῆρος, ὁ, *digger of trenches*, Man.4.252.

ἀμαρθρῖτις, ιδος, ἡ, *gout in all limbs at once*, Cael.Aur.*TP*5.2.

Ἀμάριος, fem. **Ἀμαρία**, epith. of Zeus and Athena in Achaea, *SIG*490 (Orchomenus in Arcadia, iii B.C.), cf. *Sammelb*.357 (Egypt):—Ἀμάριον, τό, precinct at Aegium in which the Achaean League met, prob. l. in Str.8.7.3 and 5 (but Ὁμάριον Plb.5.93.10, hence Ἀμάριος prob. = Ὁμάριος, Ὁμαγύριος (cf. ἁμαρεῖν, ἁμαρτῇ), and is not connected with ἀμάρα = ἡμέρα).

ἁμαρτάνω [ᾰμ.. ᾰν]: fut. ἁμαρτήσομαι Od.9.512, Th.4.55, etc.; later -ήσω *Ev.Matt*.18.21, D.C.59.20, Gal.7.653, (δι-) Hp.*Praec*.9, (ἐξ-) Id.*Acut*.(*Sp*.)13: aor. 2 ἥμαρτον Thgn., Pi., Att.; Ep. ἤμβροτον, but only ind.; Aeol. 3 sg. ἄμβροτε Sapph.*Supp*.1.5, inf. ἀμβρότην *IG*12(2).1.15 (Mytilene); opt. ἁμάρτοιν (for ἁμάρτοιμι) Cratin.55 (dub.): aor. 1 ἡμάρτησα Emp.115.4 (dub.), *AP*7.339 (Pall. or Luc.), D.S.2.14: pf. ἡμάρτηκα Hdt.9.79, Ar.*Pl*.961, etc., Att.:—Pass., aor. ἡμαρτήθην Th.2.65, X.*Vect*.4.37: pf. ἡμάρτημαι S.*OC*439, Antipho 5.77, etc.: plpf. ἡμάρτητο Th.7.18, Lys.31.20:—*miss the mark*, esp. of spear thrown, abs., Il.5.287, etc.; ἔρριψεν, οὐδ' ἥμαρτε A. *Fr*.80: c. gen., φωτὸς ἁ. Il.10.372; also τῶν μεγάλων ψυχῶν ἱεὶς οὐκ ἂν ἁμάρτοις S.*Aj*.155; ἁ. τῆς ὁδοῦ *miss* road, Ar.*Pl*.961; τοῦ σκοποῦ Antipho 3.4.5. 2. generally, *fail of one's purpose, go wrong*, abs., Od.21.155, A.*Ag*.1194, etc.: c. gen., οὔ τι νοήματος ἤμβροτεν ἐσθλοῦ Od.7.292; μύθων ἡμάρτανε *failed of good* speech, 11.511; γνώμης, ἐλπίδων, βουλήσεως ἁ., Hdt.1.207, E.*Med*.498, Th. 1.33,92; ἁ. τοῦ χρησμοῦ *mistake* it, Hdt.1.71: c. acc., ἁ. τὸ ἀληθές Hdt.7.139 (codd., τἀληθέος Schäfer). 3. *fail of having, be deprived of*, mostly c. gen., χειρῶν ἐξ Ὀδυσῆος ἁμαρτήσεσθαι ὀπωπῆς *that I should lose* my sight by Ulysses' hands, Od.9.512; τοῦ βυσίου θ' ἥμαρτε A.*Ag*.535; ἁ. πιστῆς ἀλόχου E.*Alc*.879, cf. 144:—once with neut. Adj., οὐ γὰρ εἰκὸς.. ἐμὲ ὑμῶν ἁμαρτεῖν τοῦτό γ' 'tis not seemly *that I should ask* this of you *in vain*, S.*Ph*.231:—rare in Prose, ἡμάρτομεν τῆς Βοιωτίης Hdt.9.7.β', cf. Th.7.50; δυοῖν κακοῖν οὐκ ἦν ἁμαρτεῖν (i.e. either one or the other) And.1.20, cf. S.*El*. 1320:—so μηδὲ δυοῖν φθάσαι ἁμάρτωσιν, ἢ..ἢ.. *fail* to be beforehand in one of two things, Th.1.33. 4. rarely, *fail to do, neglect*, φίλων ἡμάρτανε δώρων Il.24.68; ξυμμαχίας ἁμαρτών A.*Ag*.213. II. abs., *do wrong, err, sin*, Il.9.501, Semon.7.111, A.*Pr*.262, S.*El*.1207, etc.; ἄκοντες ἡμαρτάνομεν Pl.*R*.336e, cf. 340e, etc.:—c. part., ἥμαρτε χρηστὰ μωμένη S.*Tr*.1136; πρόθυμος ὢν ἥμαρτες E.*Or*.1630, cf. Antipho 2.2.1: c. dat. rei, ἁ. ῥήματι Pl.*Grg*.489b; ἐν λόγοις Id.*R*.396a; τοιαῦθ' ἁμαρτάνουσιν ἐν λόγοις ἔπη S.*Aj*.1096:—with cognate acc., ἁμαρτίαν ἁ. S.*Ph*.1249, E.*Hipp*.320: with neut. Adj. or Pron., αὐτὸς ἐγὼ τόδε γ' ἤμβροτον I *erred* in this, Od.22.154; πόλλ' ἁμαρτών A. *Supp*.915; ἀνθρώπινα X.*Cyr*.3.1.40: in Prose more freq. ἁ. περί τινος or τι *do wrong in* a matter, Pl.*Lg*.891e, *Phdr*.242e; ἐπί τινι Antipho 5.91 (codd.); ἁ. εἴς τινα *sin* against.., Hdt.1.138, S.*OC*968; ἐπὶ τὴν ἔλλειψιν, ἐπὶ τὸ πλεῖον, Arist.*EN*1126ᵇ1, 1118ᵇ16; περί τινα Antipho 3.2.7; τινί Lxx *Jd*.10.10. 2. Pass., ἡμαρτήθη ὁ ἐς Σικελίαν πλοῦς Th.2.65, etc.: in pf. part., τἀμὰ δ' ἡμαρτημένα my plans *are frustrate*, S.*OT*621; τῶν περὶ τὰ τοιαῦτα ἐς τὰ θεῖα ἁμαρτανομένων Pl.*Lg*.759c; ἀπειρίᾳ αὐτὸ μᾶλλον ἢ ἀδικίᾳ ἡμαρτῆσθαι Antipho 5. 5:—τὰ ἡμαρτημένα, τὰ ἁμαρτηθέντα, S.*OC*439,1269, X.*An*.5.8. 20. 3. ἁμαρτανόμενος, as Adj., *wrong, mistaken*, Pl.*Phlb*.37d, al.; αἱ ἡμαρτημέναι πολιτεῖαι Id.*R*.449a, Arist.*Pol*.1275ᵇ1, 1301ᵃ36; and of persons, ἡμαρτημένοι *mistaken*, Id.*EN*1125ᵃ19.

ἁμαρτάς, άδος, ἡ, Ion. and later Gk. for ἁμαρτία, Hdt.1.91,119, al., Hp.*Acut*.39, A.*Fr*.451C, S.*Fr*.999, Phld.*Sto*.339.15, Eus.Mynd.*Fr*. 31, Olymp. *in Mete*.146.7; copyist's *error*, Str.13.1.54; *sin*, in religious sense, J.*AJ*3.9.3, al.

ἁμαρτέω, = ὁμαρτέω, *attend, accompany*, c. dat., B.17.46, E.*Fr*.682, prob. l. in Herod.4.95.

ἁμαρτῇ or **ἁμαρτῆ** (-τῇ Aristarch.) [ᾰμ], Adv. *together, at same time, at once*, Il.5.656, Od.22.81, Sol.33.4. **ἁμαρτήδην**, Adv. = foreg., Sch.Il.21.162, Hsch.

ἁμάρτ-ημα, ατος, τό, *failure, fault*, S.*Ant*.1261 (lyr.); freq. in Att. Prose, Antipho 3.3.8, Th.2.65, etc.; midway between ἀδίκημα and ἀτύχημα, Arist.*EN*1135ᵇ18, *Rh*.1374ᵇ7; *sinful action*, opp. κατόρθωμα, Zeno *Stoic*.1.54, cf. *PTeb*.5.3, etc.; τὸ περὶ τὴν τέχνην λεγόμενον ἁ. Pl.*Plt*.296b, cf. *Ap*.22d; εἴς τινα Id.*Lg*.729e; περὶ τὸ σῶμα Id.*Grg*.479a. **-ημον** (sic, prob. neut. of Adj. -ήμων *sinful*), Pl. (Com.?) ap.Phot.p.88R. **-ητικός**, ή, όν, *prone to err*, Arist.*EN* 1104ᵇ33; περὶ τοὺς πλησίον M.Ant.11.18. **-ία**, ἡ, *a failure, fault*, τῶνδ' ἁ. δόμων A.*Ag*.1197, etc.; οὐ τῇ ἑαυτοῦ ἁμαρτίᾳ χρῆσθαι Antipho 4.3.4; ἁ. δόξης *error* of judgement, Th.1.32. 2. in Philos. and Religion, *guilt, sin*, Pl.*Lg*.660c, al., Arist.*EN*1148ᵃ3, al., Lxx *Ge*.18.20, al., *Ev.Jo*.8.46, al.

ἁμαρτί-γαμος, ον, *failing of marriage*, Nonn.*D*.48.94. **-νοος**, ον, *erring in mind, distraught*, Hes.*Th*.511, Sol.22.2, A.*Supp*.542 (lyr.), Rhian.1.1.

ἁμάρτιον, τό, = ἁμάρτημα, in pl., A.*Pers*.676, *Ag*.537.

ἁμαρτο-επής, ές, (ἔπος) *erring in words, speaking at random*, Il.13. 824; οἶνος ἁ. wine *that makes men talk at random*, Poet.ap.Clem.Al. *Paed*.2.2.28. **-λόγος**, ον, *speaking faultily*, Ath.4.165b.

ἀμαρτ-ύρητος [ῠ], ον, *needing no witness*, E.*HF*290, Antiph.311. Adv. **-τί** *without witnesses*, *POxy*.1852.10 (vi A.D.). **-ῠρος**, ον, *without witness, unattested*, Th.2.41, D.20.149, *PFlor*.59.13 (iii A.D.); ἀμαρτύρων εὐντων Herod.2.85; ἁ. οὐδὲν ἀείδω Call.*Fr*.442; *unsupported by evidence*, δίκη Procop.*Arc*.16, etc. Adv. -ρως Antipho Soph.93ᵇ, D.30.21, cf. Sch.Il.*Oxy*.21.203. **-υς**, υ, = foreg., Agatho ap.Phot.p.87R.

ἁμαρτωλ-ή, ἡ, = ἁμαρτία, Thgn.327, Rhian.1.12; ἁ. διαίτης Aret. *CD*1.6. **-ία**, ἡ, = foreg., Hp.*Epid*.2.1.8, Eup.199, Ar.*Pax*415. **-ός**, όν, *erroneous*, ἁμαρτωλότερον Arist.*EN*1109ᵃ33; *erring*, ἐν πᾶσιν Plu. 2.25c. 2. *of bad character*, δοῦλοι Phld.*Ir*.p.73W.: c. gen., *sinning against*, θεῶν *Michel*547.31 (Telmessus):—ἁμαρτωλὴ γέρων, barbarism in Ar.*Th*.1111. Adv. -ῶς Eup.24D. II. Subst. ἁμαρτωλός, ὁ, *sinner*, Lxx *Ge*.13.13, al., *Ev.Luc*.18.13, al.

ἀμᾰρυγή [Att. ῠ, Ep. ῡ], ἡ, *sparkling, twinkling, glancing*, of objects in motion, as of the eye, *h.Merc*.45; of stars, A.R.2.42; of the sun, Procop.*Vand*.2.14; of any quick motion, ἵππων ἁ. Ar.*Av*.925:—also **ἀμάρυγξ**, γγος, ἡ, Hdn.Gr.2.743: **ἀμάρυξις**, εως, ἡ, Sch.A.R. 3.1018.

ἀμαρυγκυσία· βοστρυχία, Hsch.

ἀμάρυγμα, Aeol. **-υχμα**, ατος, τό, *sparkle, twinkle*, ἁ. λάμπρον προσώπω *flashing, radiant glance*, Sapph.*Supp*.5.18, cf. A.R.3.288; of changing colour, and light, *AP*5.258 (Paul. Sil.); διδύμης ἁ. χροιῆς, of gems, Tryph.71, etc.; of any quick, light motion, Χαρίτων ἀμαρύγματ' ἔχουσα with *the flashing steps* of Graces, Hes.*Fr*.21,94; of wrestling, ἁ. πάλας B.8.36; ἁ. χείλεος *quivering* of the lip, Theoc. 23.7: metaph., τῶν πισύρων ἀρετῶν ἀμαρύγματα *AP*7.343.

ἀμαρύκαρ· ἀπ' ἀρχῆς, Hsch. **ἀμαρύς**· ἄπλετος, πολύς, Id.

ἀμᾰρύσσω [ᾰμ], Ep., only pres. and impf., *sparkle, twinkle, glance*, of the eye, ἐκ δέ οἱ ὄσσων πῦρ ἀμάρυσσεν Hes.*Th*.827; πυκνόν or πύκν' ἀμαρύσσων *darting quick glances*, *h.Merc*.278; φολίδων στικτοῖσι τύποις ἀμάρυσσεν ὀφίτης Nonn.*D*.18.79:—Med., of light, colour, etc., A.R. 4.178,1146; ἀμαρύσσεται ἄνθεσι λειμών *AP*9.668 (Marian.), cf. Nonn. *D*.5.77, al. II. Act., *shoot forth, dart*, πῦρ *h.Merc*.415, Q.S.8. 29. 2. *dazzle*, Nonn.*D*.5.485.

ἀμαρύττα· τοὺς ὀφθαλμούς, Hsch.

ἀμάσητος, ον, (μασάομαι) *unchewed*, Lxx *Jb*.20.18, Archig.ap. Orib.8.46.11, Philum.*Ven*.3.3.

ἀμαστίγωτος, ον, *unscourged*, Ach.Tat.5.18, Procop.*Arc*.17.

ἀμάστικτος, ον, = foreg., Sch.Pi.*O*.1.32.

ἀμάστρευτος, ον, (μαστρός) *unexamined*, *IG*5(2).357.38 (Stymphalus, iii B.C.).

ἀμασῡκάς, εἶδος, ἡ, = sq., Hsch.

ἀμάσῡκον, τό, with or without μῆλον, *fruit-tree flowering at the same time as the fig*, Paus.Gr.*Fr*.42.

ἀμάτα, Adv., (perh. ἀ- priv., μάτην) = ἀδόλως, *SIG*421*A*5,26 (Aetolia, iii B.C.): but perh. ἅματα, cf. ἦμαρ.

ἀμᾰταιότης, ητος, ἡ, = ἕξις ἀναφέρουσα τὰς φαντασίας ἐπὶ τὸν ὀρθὸν λόγον, *Stoic*.2.39.

ἀματίζει· ἀναφυρᾷ, Hsch. **ἀμάτις**· ἅπαξ (Tarent.), Id.; cf. ἀμάκις.

ἀμα-τροχάω, (τρέχω) *run together, run along with*, only Ep. part. ἀματροχόων (al. ἅμα τρ.) Od.15.451:—also **-έω**, Hsch. **-τροχιά**, ἡ, *driving side by side*, ἀματροχιὰς ἀλεείνων Il.23.422; of stars, *common motion*, -τροχιῇ πεφόρηται Man.4.108. 2. by error for ἁρματροχιά, *track of wheels*, Call.*Fr*.135, Nic.*Th*.263, *Hippiatr*.87.

ἀμάτωρ, Dor. for ἀμήτωρ.

ἀμαυρ-ία [ἄμ]· *caligo*, *Gloss*., cf. *PMag.Rain*.1.38. **-ίσκω**, = ἀμαυρόω, Democr.177. **-όβῐος**, ον, *living in darkness*, ἄνδρες Ar.*Av*.685. **-ός** [ἄμ], ά, όν (ός, όν Pl.Com.1 D.), *dark*, i.e., 1. *hardly seen, dim, faint*, εἴδωλον ἀ. *shadowy* spectre, Od.4.824; νέκυες Sapph.68; ἴχνος *faint* footstep, of an old man, E.*HF*124, cf. X.*Cyn*.6.21; of the sun, ἀχλυώδης καὶ ἀμαυρότερος *obscure, glimmering*, Arist.*Mete*.367ᵃ21; of a comet's tail, ib.343ᵇ12, cf. Theoc.22.21. 2. *having no light*, νύξ Luc.*Am*.32; ὄψις X.*Cyn*.5.26:—hence, *blind, sightless*, of man, S.*OC*1018; ἕπεο..ἀμαυρῷ κώλῳ ib.182; ψαύσας ἀμαυραῖς χερσίν ib.1639; ἀμαυρά or ἀμαυρῶς βλέπειν *dimly*, Hp.*Acut*.(*Sp*.)55, *AP*12.254 (Strat.), cf. *IG*14.2111. 3. of sound, *dim, faint*, Arist.*Aud*.802ᵃ19. II. metaph., 1. *dim, faint, uncertain*, κληδών A.*Ch*.853; σθένος E.*HF*231; δόξα, ἡδοναί, ἐλπίς, Plu.*Lyc*.4, 2.125c, Arr.ap.Suid.; ζῷα -ότερα creatures *of obscure kind*, Arist.*HA*608ᵃ11; ἔντομαὶ -ότεραι *less conspicuous* notches, Thphr.*HP*6.2.5, cf. 6.7.1. 2. *obscure, mean, unknown*, -οτέρη γενεή Hes.*Op*.284; τυχηρὸν..τιθεῖσ' ἀμαυρόν A.*Ag*.466, cf. E.*Andr*.204; ἀ. ἀσθενής τε Pl.Com. l. c. Adv. -ρῶς *obscurely*, opp. ἀκριβῶς, Arist.*Cael*.279ᵃ29. 3. *gloomy, troubled*, φρήν A.*Ag*.546, *Ch*.157. III. Act., *enfeebling* (or perh. *baffling, obscure*), νοῦσος *AP*7.78 (Dionys.): Subst. ἀμαυρά, ἡ (sc. τελετή), = ἀμαύρωσις I. 3, *PMag.Leid.W*.6.21. **-ότης**, ητος, ἡ, *dimness*, αἰσθήσεων Gal.11.282; *obscurity*, Epist.Maximini ap.Eus.*HE*9.7, cf. Eust.1585.47. **-οφᾰνής**, (φαίνομαι) *dimly gleaming*, of the moon, *Stoic*.2.198. **-όω**, Sol. and X., v. infr.: fut. -ώσω Simon.4.5: aor. ἀμαύρωσα Pi.*P*.12.13, ἠμαύρωσα *AP*9.24, Plb.6.15.7, etc.: pf. ἠμαύρωκα Str.8.1.1:—**Med.**, aor. opt. ἀμαυρώσαιτο Aristaenet.1.16:—**Pass.**, Philist. ap.Phot.p.88 R.: pf. ἠμαύρωμαι Plu.*Per*.11: aor. ἀμαυρώθην (without augm.) Hdt.9.10:—*make dim, faint*, or *obscure*, ἡ σελήνη ἀ. τὰ ἴχνη X.*Cyn*.5.4; ἄστρα ἠμαύρωσε ἥλιος *AP*9.24 (Leon.):—Pass., *become dark* or *dim*, ὁ ἥλιος ἀμαυρώθη Hdt. l. c.; ὄμμα -ούμενον Hp.*Prorrh*.1.46; φορτί' ἀμαυρωθείη *perished utterly*, Hes.*Op*.693; τὸ θερμὸν μικρὸν ὂν ἐν μεγάλοις ἀ. Arist.*PA*667ᵃ19. 2. *render invisible*, *PMag.Berol*.1.102. 3. *blind*, ὄμματα *Tab.Defix.Aud*.241.13 (Carthage, ii/iii A.D.), etc. II. metaph. in same sense, εὐνομία..ὕβριν ἀ. Sol.4.35; ἐντάφιον..οὔτ' εὐρὼς οὔτ'..ἀμαυρώσει χρόνος Simon.4.5, cf. Call.*Iamb*.1.429; χρόνος δ' ἀμαυροῖ πάντα S.*Fr*.954, cf. Str. l. c.; τίς ἄρα σὰν..ἀμαυροῖ ζόαν; E.*Hipp*.816; πολλοί γε..τῷ θράσει τὰς συμφορὰς ζητοῦσ' ἀμαυροῦν Id.*Fr*.416; ἀ. δόξαν Plb.20.4.3; τὰς ἄλλας κακίας Plu.*Crass*.2; οἶκον -ώσας ὤλετο *IG*12(7).107 (Amorgos); *deface* a tomb, ib.12(9).1129.22 (Chalcis):—*weaken, impair*, πόνος πόνον ἀ. Hp.*Aph*.2.46, cf. *Aër*.23, Aret.*CD*2.6; ἡ νεαρὴ [τροφὴ] ἠμαύρωσε τὴν παλαιήν ib.13:—Pass., Thphr.*HP*9.14.3; ἡ ἡδονὴ -οῦται Arist.*EN*1175ᵃ10; ἠμαυρωμένος τὸ ἀξίωμα, τῇ δόξῃ, Plu.*Per*.11, *Cor*.31; *to be dazzled*, περὶ τὸν χρυσόν Onos.1.8. **-ωμα**, ατος, τό, *obscuration*, of sun, Plu.*Caes*.69. 2. *dimness* of sight, Mnesith.ap.Orib.4.4.2. **-ωσις**, εως, ἡ, *darkening*, ὀμμάτων ἀ. *becoming dull* of sight, Hp.*Coac*.221: later, *complete hindrance to sight without any visible cause*, Gal.14.776. 2. *dulling*, as of mind in old age, Arist.*de An*.408ᵇ20, cf. Diog.Oen.*Fr*.70 (pl.). 3. *spell which renders invisible*, *PMag.Berol*.1.222ᵃ,247. II. *lowering, detraction*, Plu.2.149a. III. = κώνειον, Ps.-Dsc.4.78. IV. Astrol., name for eighth τόπος of the δωδεκάωρος, *Cat.Cod.Astr*.8(4).161.

ἀμάχαιρος, ον, *without knife*, Pherecr.82.

ἀμᾰχ-εί, Adv. of ἄμαχος, *without stroke of sword, without resistance*, Th.1.143, X.*An*.1.7.9, etc.: *without question, undoubtedly*, prob. f. l. for ἀμελεί, Plu.2.433c:—written ἀμαχί, Phot.p.88 R. **-ετος**, ον, poet. for ἀμάχητος, A.*Th*.85 (lyr.), S.*Fr*.813. **-ητί**, Adv. of sq., *without battle, without stroke of sword*, Il.21.437, Hdt.1.174 (freq. written -τεί in codd., X.*Cyr*.4.2.28, etc.). **-ητος**, ον, *not to be fought with, unconquerable*, S.*Ph*.198 (lyr.). II. *not having fought, not having been in battle*, X.*Cyr*.6.4.14; ἀ. ὄλεθρος destruction *without fighting*, Lys.*Fr*.71. **-ος**, ον, *without battle*: hence, I. *with whom no one fights, unconquerable*, of persons, Hdt.5.3, A.*Pers*.856 (lyr.), Ar.*Lys*.253,1014 (lyr.); χεῖρες Pi.*I*.6(5).41; δύναμις Pl.*Mx*.240d, Isoc.5.139: c. inf., πολύποδες..πᾶν ὅτι οὖν φαγεῖν ἄ. Ael.*VH*1.1, etc.: of places, *impregnable*, Hdt.1.84: of things, *irresistible*, κακόν Pi.*P*.2.76; κῦμα θαλάσσης A.*Pers*.90: of feelings, ἄλγος Id.*Ag*.733; φθόνος E.*Rh*.456; ἄ. πρᾶγμα, of a woman whose beauty is *irresistible*, X.*Cyr*.6.1.36; ἄ. φιλοφροσύνη Plu.2.667d; ἄ. κάλλος Aristaenet.1.24; ἄ. τρυφή Ael.*NA*16.23:—ἄμαχόν [ἐστι] c. inf., like ἀμήχανον, 'tis *impossible* to do.., Pi.*O*.13.13. Adv. -ως *irresistibly*, Luc.*Merc.Cond*.3; *incontestably*, S.E.*M*.8.266. II. Act., *not having fought, taking no part in the battle*, X.*Cyr*.4.1.16; ἄ. διάγειν to remain *without fighting*, Id.*HG*4.4.9: ἄμαχον, τό, *non-combatants*, Ael.*Tact*.2.2, cf. D.C.53.12; ἄ. νίκη *gained without fighting*, Eun.*VS* p.472 B. 2. *disinclined to fight, not contentious*, 1*Ep.Ti*.3.3, *Ep.Tit*.3.2, cf. *Inscr.Cos* 325; ἄ. ἐβίωσα *Epigr.Gr*.387.6 (Apamea Cibotus).

ἀμαχητηρία· εἶδος ἀκάνθης, Hsch.

ἀμάω (A), Od.9.135, etc.; Ep. pres. part. ἀμάων A.R.3.1187, dat. pl. ἀμώντεσσι Theoc.10.16: impf. ἤμων Il.18.551: fut. ἀμήσω Hes.*Op*.480, Hdt.6.28: aor. ἤμησα Hes.*Th*.181, A.*Ag*.1044, Ep. ἄμησα (δι-) Il.3.359:—**Med.**, Hes.*Op*.778, E.*Fr*.419: fut. ἀμήσομαι S.*Fr*.625 (v. infr. 3), A.R.1.688:—**Pass.**, aor. part. ἀμηθείς Nic.*Al*.216: pf. ἤμημαι (ἐξ-) S.*Aj*.1179. Simple Verb takes augm. in Hom., but not compds., v. Il.3.359, 24.165, Od.5.482. [Hom. has ᾱ in simple Verb, ᾰ in compds., Trag. always ᾰ; later, ᾱ Theoc.10.16,50, A.R.1.1183, etc., ᾰ Theoc.11.73, Call.*Cer*.137, etc.]:—orig., *reap corn*, abs., ἤμων ὀξείας δρεπάνας ἐν χερσὶν ἔχοντες Il.18.551; γυμνὸν ἀμάειν Hes.*Op*.392; θερίζειν καὶ ἀ. *PHib*.1.47.12 (iii B.C.); ἤμενος ἀμήσεις Hes.*Op*.480: metaph., ἤμησαν καλῶς they *reaped* abundantly, A.*Ag*.1044: c. acc., μάλα κεν βαθὺ λήϊον..εἰς ὥρας ἀμῷεν Od.9.135, cf. Thgn.107; ὡς ἀμήσων τὸν σῖτον Hdt.6.28, cf. 4.199; τἀλλότριον ἀμῶν θέρος Ar.*Eq*.392. b. metaph., ἐλευθερίαν ἀμώμεθα Plu.2.210b. 2. generally, *cut*, λαχνήεντ' ὄροφον λειμωνόθεν ἀμήσαντες Il.24.451; θαλλὸν ἀμάσας Theoc.11.73:—Med., σχοῖνον ἀμησάμενος *AP*4.1.26 (Mel.); στάχυν ἀμήσονται A.R.1.688, cf. Call.*Di*.164; ἀμῶνται Q.S.14.199. 3. *mow down* in battle, A.R.3.1187,1382, *AP*9.362.25: fut. Med. ἀμάσεται is cited from S.(*Fr*.625) in this sense by Hsch.

ἀμάω (B), mostly Ep. in Med., *draw, gather* (cf. ἐξ-, ἐπ-, κατ-αμάομαι), ταλάροισιν ἀμησάμενοι [γάλα] Od.9.247, cf. A.R.3.859; ἀλλότριον κάματον σφετέρην ἐς γαστέρ' ἀμῶνται Hes.*Th*.599; ἀμήσατο γαῖαν ἀμφ' αὐτοῖς A.R.1.1305: metaph., ἀρετήν Jul.*Or*.5.169b:—Act., χερσὶν ἀμήσας κρατὸς ὕπερθε κόνιν, of a mourner, *pouring* dust on his head, *AP*7.241 (Antip.).—Poet. and later Prose. (Cf. Lith. *sémti* 'draw (water)'.)

ἀμβ-, Ep. Ion., and poet. for ἀναβ- at the beginning of words. Only the most important of such forms will be found in their place: for the rest v. sub ἀναβ-.

ἀμβαδέως, Adv. *thoughtlessly*, Hsch.

ἀμβαδόν, = ἀναβαδόν, Opp.*C*.3.500.

ἄμβαξ, ακος, = ἄμβη, Orib.49.24.2.

ἄμβαρ, αρος, τό, *ambergris*, Aët.16.130,142.

ἄμβᾰσε, Dor. for ἀνέβησε: **ἄμβᾰσις, ἀμβάτης, ἄμβᾰτος**, poet. for ἀναβ-: **ἀμβᾶτε**, Dor. for ἀναβῆτε.

ἀμβές· δύσκολον, ἢ ἀβλαβές, Hsch.

ἄμβη, ἡ, Ion. for ἄμβων, *raised edge* or *protuberance*, Hp.*Art*.7, cf. 80, Gal.18(1).340; *rim* of felloe of wheel, Democr.29.

ἄμβιξ, ῐκος, ὁ, *spouted cup*, Ath.11.480d:—also **ὄμβῐκος**, ὁ, Posidon.25, *CIG*3071.7 (Teos), Hsch., etc. 2. *cap of still*, Dsc.5.95. 3. *alembic*, Zos.Alch.p.141 B.

ἀμβλακ-εῖν, -ημα, -ίσκω, older and Dor. forms of ἀμπλ-.

ἀμβλήδην, Adv., poet. for ἀναβλήδην (q. v.):—*with sudden bursts*, ἀ. γοόωσα Il.22.476.

ἀμβλίσκω, Pl.*Tht*.149d: **ἀμβλισκάνω**, Max.Tyr.16.4, Poll.3.49; cf. ἀμβλύσκω:—also **ἀμβλόω** J.*Ap*.2.24, **ἀμβλώω** Max.172, -ώεσθαι 197, and in comp. ἐξ-αμβλόω (q. v.): fut. ἀμβλώσω *Gp*.14.14, (ἐξ-) Ael.*NA*13.27: aor. ἤμβλωσα Hp.*Mul*.1.25, Ael.*VH*13.6, (ἐξ-) Pl.*Tht*.150e: pf. (ἐξ-)ήμβλωκα, (ἐξ-)ήμβλωμαι, Ar.*Nu*.137,139: (ἀμβλύς):—*cause to miscarry*, S.*Fr*.132, Pl.*Tht*.149d. 2. of the woman, *bring on miscarriage*, Muson.*Fr*.15A p.77 H., Plu.*Lyc*.3, Ael.*VH*13.6. 3. intr., *miscarry*, Procop.*Pers*.2.22. II. **ἀμβλόω**, usu. in Pass. **ἀμβλόομαι**, *to be abortive*, κἂν..τὸ γινόμενον ἀμβλωθῇ Arist.*GA*773ᵃ1: also of eyes of vines, ἀμβλοῦνται *they go 'blind'*, Thphr.*HP*4.14.6; rare in Act., Ph.2.580: metaph., ἀμβλώσαντες καὶ ἐπιφράξαντες ἀργὸν τὸ μεγαλοφυὲς κατέλιπον 1.637.

ἀμβλουχία, ἡ, = ἄμβλωσις, S.*Fr*.1000.

ἀμβλῠ-γώνιος, ον, *obtuse-angled*, τρίγωνα Euc.1.28, al.; κωνοειδές, κῶνος, Archim.*Con.Sph.Praef*.: Subst. -γώνιον, τό, *obtuse angle*, Plb.34.6.7. **-δερκής**, ές, *dull of sight*, Nicom.Trag.ap.Phot.p.89 R. **-ηκοΐα**, ἡ, *hardness of hearing*, Alex.Aphr.*in Top*.327.15.

ἄμβλ-υνσις, εως, ἡ, *blunting, dulling*, νοήσεων Phlp.*in de An*.164.10. **-υντέον**, *one must deaden, counteract*, Dsc.*Ther.Praef*. **-υντήρ**, ῆρος, ὁ, *causing dimness of sight*, in pl., Poet.*de herb*.65. **-υντικός**, ή, όν, *apt to dull*, ὄψεως Diph.Siph.ap.Ath.2.64b, cf. Dsc.1.69, Antyll.ap.Orib.10.24. **-ύνω** [ῠ], fut. -ῠνῶ (ἀπ-) A.*Th*.715: aor. ἤμβλῠνα *AP*6.67 (Jul.):—**Pass.**, fut. -υνθήσομαι (ἀπ-) A.*Pr*.866, but -υνοῦμαι (in pass. sense) Hp.*Aph*.1.9: aor. ἠμβλύνθην Lxx *Ge*.27.1, *AP*6.65 (Paul. Sil.), etc.: pf. ἤμβλυμμαι, 3 sg. ἤμβλυνται S.E.*M*.7.183, pl. -υνται (ἀπ-) Hom.*Epigr*.12; ἀπήμβλυνται is 3 sg. in Herod.*Fr*.10.4:—*blunt, dull, take the edge off*, properly of a sharp instrument, and metaph., *make dim, dull*, μερίμνας Emp.2, cf. 110.7; τὸ ψυχρὸν..τοὺς χυμοὺς ἀ. Arist.*Sens*.443ᵇ15; ὄμματος αὐγὴν ἀμβλύνας *AP*6.67 (Jul.); τὸ ἄλγος Aret.*CA*1.10; ἄκρατον *take away strength of* wine, Plu.2.656a; οὐ γὰρ ἀοιδὰς ἀμβλύνειν αἰὼν..δύναται *AP*7.225; θυμὸν ἀ. Phld.*Mus*.p.76 K. II. Pass., *become blunt* or *dull, lose edge*, of the teeth, Arist.*PA*661ᵇ22, cf. *GA*789ᵃ9; of eyesight, ἠμβλύνθησαν οἱ ὀφθαλμοὶ τοῦ ὁρᾶν Lxx *Ge*.27.1. 2. *become obtuse*, γωνία Papp.118.6. 3. metaph., ὀργὴ γέροντος ὥστε μαλθακὴ κοπὶς..ἀμβλύνεται S.*Fr*.894, cf. Pl.*R*.490b; of an oracle, *lose its edge or force*, A.*Th*.844; ἡ νοῦσος ἀμβλυνεῖται Hp.*Aph*.1.9; of the mind, *to be disheartened*, Th.2.87: c. gen., ἀμβλύνεσθαι ἐρωῆς Opp.*H*.2.338.

ἀμβλυό-εις, εσσα, εν, *dull, dark*, ὀμίχλη Man.4.156. **-χρους**, ουν, *faint*, ἥλιος Lyd.*Ost*.9[c] (vv. ll. ἀμβλυώχρους, -ωχρος).

ἀμβλ-ύς, εῖα, ύ, *blunt, dulled, with edge* or *point taken off*, properly of a sharp instrument, opp. ὀξύς, Pl.*Ly*.215e, *Tht*.165d; ἀ. γωνία *obtuse* angle, Id.*Ti*.55a; ἀμβλεῖα, ἡ, sc. γωνία, Arist.*Mech*.855[a]10, etc.; ἀ. πλευρά side *adjacent to such angle*, Hero *Geom*.12.35, etc. 2. of light, *dim, faint*, ὄρθρος Ion ap.Phot.p.89 R. 3. metaph., *dim, faint*, of sight, ἀμβλὺ ὁρᾶν, -ύτερον βλέπειν, Pl.*Tht*.174e, Arist.*PA* 656[b]36, al.; of hearing, τῆς ἀκοῆς οὔσης -υτέρας αἰσθήσεως ἢ τῆς ὄψεως *Pr*.886[b]32; of the feelings or mind, ἀμβλυτέρᾳ τῇ ὀργῇ *less keen*, Th. 3.38; ἀμβλύτερον ποιεῖν τι *less vigorous*, Id.2.65. Adv. ἀμβλέως Archig.ap.Orib.8.2: Comp., v. supr. b. *dull, monotonous*, τὠμβλὺ τῆς ζόης Herod.3.52. c. of persons, in A.*Eu*.238, of Orestes purified, *having lost the edge* of guilt: mostly, *dull, spiritless, having lost keenness of feeling*, E.*Fr*.821; ἀμβλύτερος τὴν φύσιν *duller*, X.*Mem*.3.9.3; ἀ. εἴς, περί, or πρός τι *dull* or *sluggish* in a thing, Plu. *Cat.Ma*.24, *Alc*.30, D.S.11.43 (Comp.): abs., Th.2.40. Adv., Comp. -υτέρως J.*AJ*19.2.5. II. Act., *making dull, darkening*, of a cloud, *AP*7.367 (Antip.). **-ύσκω**, dub. form of ἀμβλίσκω, S.*Fr*.132, Procop. *Arc*.17, *Hippiatr*.15. **-υσμός**, ὁ, = ἀμβλωσμός, Pall. *in Hp*.2. 5 D. **-υστονέω**, v. ἀναβλ-. **-ύτης**, ητος, ἡ, *bluntness* of teeth, Arist.*GA*789[a]11; *dullness*, τῆς διανοίας, τῆς ὄψεως, Plu.2.42c, 1110d; *sluggishness*, Aret.*CA*1.5 (pl.), cf. Plu.*Galb*.18; σπερμάτων, of seeds which *fail to germinate*, Max.Tyr.16.4. 2. *obtuseness*, σχήματος Them.*in Ph*.173.7.

ἀμβλυ-φαέω, = ἀμβλυώσσω, S.*Fr*.647. **-χειλής**, ές, *with rounded rim*, of cupping-glass, Antyll.ap.Orib.7.16.15. **-ωγμός**, ὁ, (ἀμβλυώσσω) *dull* or *dim sight*, Hp.*Prog*.24. **-ωπέω**, *to be dim-sighted*, Hp.*Prog*.7, X.*Cyn*.5.27 codd., Men.908, Lxx 3*Ki*.12.24, Sor.1.82, Plu.2.53f, etc.; un-Attic acc. to Harp., etc. **-ωπής**, ές, in Comp. -έστερον Suid. II. Act., *weakening sight*, Dsc.2.141. **-ωπία**, ἡ, *dim-sightedness*, Hp.*Aph*.3.33 (pl.), Pl.*Hp.Mi*.374d, etc. **-ωπισμός**, ὁ, = ἀμβλυωγμός, Archig. or Posidon.ap.Aët.6.7. **-ωπός**, όν, *dim-sighted*, E.*Fr*.1096, Arist.*Fr*.588 (Comp.), *Epigr.Gr*.459 (Trachonitis); of stars, *dim*, ἀμβλυωπότερα Hp.*Morb.Sacr*.13. II. Act., = ἀμβλυωπής II, Dsc.2.107. **-ωσμός**, ὁ, v.l. for -ωγμός in Hp.*Prorrh*.1.18. **-ώσσω**, Att. -ττω, only in pres.: (ἀμβλύς):—*to be short-sighted, have weak sight*, Hp.*Prorrh*.2.42, etc., Pl.*R*.508c, al., *Hp.Mi*.374d; ἀ. πρὸς τὸ φῶς *to be dazzled* by it, Luc. *Cont*.1, cf. Jul.*Or*.5.163a; ἀ. τὰ τηλικαῦτα Luc.*Tim*.27; τὸ τοῦ γήρως ἀμβλυῶττον Plu.2.13e.

ἀμβλ-ωθρίδιον, τό, I. (sc. παιδίον) *abortive child*, ἀ. καὶ ἐκτρώματα Ph.1.59, cf. Hsch., Harp. II. Act. (sc. φάρμακον), *drug to cause abortion*, Poll.2.7.—Prop. neut. from **ἀμβλωθρίδιος**, ον, *causing abortion*, Aret.*CA*2.11:—also **ἀμβλώθριον**, τό, Sch.Ar.*Nu*. 137 (s.v.l.). **-ωμα**, ατος, τό, (ἀμβλίσκω) *abortion*, Antipho Soph. 148, Aret.*CA*1.6. **-ῶνες**· χαλβάνη, Διονύσιος, Hsch. **-ωπής**, ές, *abortive*, of the flowers of the vine, Thphr.*CP*3.15.2. **-ωπός**, όν, = foreg., *bedimmed, dark*, βίος A.*Eu*.955; ἀχλύς Critias 6, cf. Pl.Com.23 D. **-ώσιμος**, ον, *belonging to abortion*, Max.275. **-ωσις**, εως, ἡ, *abortion*, Lys.*Fr*.8; ἄμβλωσιν ποιεῖσθαι Arist.*Pol*.1335[b]25; ἄ. γίγνεται τοῦ κυήματος Id.*GA*773[a]1, cf. Ph.2.319, Procop.*Arc*.10 (pl.). II. *abortion of* buds in vines and trees, Thphr.*CP*5.9. 13. **-ώσκω**, = ἀμβλίσκω I. 2. **-ωσμός**, οῦ, ὁ, = ἄμβλωμα, Aret.*CD*2.11, Man.4.413. **-ώσσω**, = ἀμβλυώσσω, Nic.*Th*.33. 2. = ἀμβλίσκω, Hsch. **-ωτήριον**, τό, *instrument for causing abortion*, Orib.*Inc*.6.19 (Gal. or Ruf.). **-ωτικός**, ή, όν, *producing abortion*, φάρμακα Gal.17(1).799. **-ώψ**, ῶπος, ὁ, ἡ, = ἀμβλωπός, αὐγαί E.*Rh*. 737, cf. S.*Fr*.1001, Ion Trag.ap.Phot.p.89 R., Pl.Com.23 D.

ἀμβόαμα, ἀμβοάω, poet. for ἀναβόαμα, ἀναβοάω.

ἀμβοειδής, ές, *like an* ἄμβων, *protuberant*, Heliod.ap.Orib.49.8.7.

ἀμβολά, ἡ, poet. for ἀναβολή. **ἄμβολα**, τά, *middle of ship's yard*, Poll.1.91.

ἀμβολ-άδην [ᾰδ], Adv., poet. for ἀναβολάδην: (ἀναβολή):—*bubbling up*, ὡς δὲ λέβης ζεῖ ἔνδον..πάντοθεν ἀ. Il.21.364, cf. Hdt.4.181: metaph., *by jets*, i.e. *capriciously*, *AP*10.70 (Maced.). II. *like an* ἀναβολή or *prelude*, *h.Merc*.426, Pi.*N*.10.31. **-αδίς**, Adv., poet. for ἀναβολαδίς, either *in turns*, or *with uplifted arms*, τετυπόντες Call. *Dian*.61. **-άς**, άδος, ἡ, for ἀναβολάς, ἀ. γῆ earth *thrown up*, X.*Cyr*. 7.5.12.

ἀμβολι-εργός, όν, poet. for ἀναβολ-, (ἀναβάλλω B. II) *putting off work, dilatory*, ἀνήρ Hes.*Op*.413; τινός or ἔν τινι in a thing, Plu.2. 548d, 118c. **-η**, ἡ, poet. for ἀναβολή, *delay*, A.R.3.144: c. gen., 4.396, Nonn.*D*.38.12, al. **-μος**, ον, = ἀναβ-, *surging up*, ἅλμα Tim. *Pers*.74. II. *adjourned*, ἁλιαία *Mnemos*.44.221 (Argos, iii B.C.).

Ἀμβολογήρα, ἡ, *she that puts off old age, youth-prolonging*, Spartan title of Aphrodite, Paus.3.18.1. **ἄμβος**· ἡ ἐπίγειος πλάστη, Hsch.

Ἀμβούλιος, (perh. connected with βουλή) title of Zeus, Athena, and the Dioscuri at Sparta, Paus.3.13.4.

Ἀμβρακίδες, αἱ, *Ambracian women's shoes*, Poll.7.94.

ἀμβρίζειν· θεραπεύειν ἐν τοῖς ἱεροῖς, Hsch.

ἀμβροσί-α, Ion. -ίη, ἡ, *immortality*, rare in general sense, σώματος ἀ. *Epigr.Gr*.338 (Cyzicus); usu. *elixir of life*, as used by gods for food, Od.5.93, etc.; as perfume, 4.445; as unguent, Il.14.170, cf. 16.680; as pasture for horses, 5.777; coupled with νέκταρ (q.v.), the two distinguished as food and drink, Od.5.93 (later reversed, ἀ. being drunk, Sapph.51, Ar.*Eq*.1095, Anaxandr.57), cf. Pi.*O*.1.62, *P*.9.63, Arist.*Metaph*.1000[a]12, A.R.4.871, Theoc.15.108; βολβοφακῆ δ' ἴσον ἀμβροσίῃ ψύχους κρυοέντος Chrysipp.*Stoic*.3.178; allegorically expl. as vapour, Democr.25. 2. in religious rites, *mixture of water, oil, and various fruits*, Anticl.13. 3. Medic., name for antidote, Zopyr.ap.Cels.5.23, Gal.14.149; also of an external emollient, Aët.14.2. 4. *ambrose, Ambrosia maritima*, Dsc.3.114. b. Corinthian, = κρίνον, Nic.*Fr*.126. c. = ἀείζωον μέγα, Dsc.4. 88. d. vine whose grapes were eaten, Plin.*HN*14.40. B. Ἀμβροσία, ἡ, *a festival* of Bacchus, *EM*564.13. **-οδμος**, ον, *smelling of ambrosia*, Philox.2.43. **-ος**, α, ον, also ος, ον E.*Med*.983 (lyr.):—*immortal, divine*, rarely of persons, νύμφη *h.Merc*.230:—in Ep., epith. of everything *belonging to gods*, as hair, Il.1.529, etc.; robes, sandals, etc., 5.338, 21.507, 24.341, al.; anointing oil, 14.172, 23. 187; voice and song, *h.Hom*.27.18, Hes.*Th*.69; fodder and mangers of horses, Il.5.369, 8.434; of night and sleep, as *divine* gifts, Od. 4.429, etc.; ὕδωρ Hom.*Epigr*.1.4; κρῆναι E.*Hipp*.748:—of things *divinely excellent* or *beautiful*, κάλλος Od.18.193; of verses, Pi.*P*.4. 299; Ἀφροδίτας ἀ. φιλοτάτων Id.*N*.8.1. **-ώδης**, ες, *ambrosial, fragrant*, φυτά *Corp.Herm*.18.11 (Sup.).

ἀμβρότιγνον· ἄκοιρον, Hsch. **ἀμβροτίξας**· ἀπαρξάμενος, Id.

ἀμβροτόπωλος, ον, *with immortal steeds*, Παλλάς E.*Tr*.536.

ἄμβροτος, ον, also η, ον Pi.*Fr*.75.17, Tim.*Fr*.7: (v. βροτός):—poet. Adj. *immortal, divine*, of persons as well as things, θεὸς ἄ. Il. 20.358, Od.24.445, Pi.*N*.10.7; θεά A.*Eu*.259 (lyr.); ἄμβροτε Φάμα, of an oracle, S.*OT*158 (lyr.). 2. epith. of all *belonging to the gods*, αἷμα Il.5.339; ἵπποι 16.381; τεύχεα 17.194, κρήδεμνον Od.5. 347; ἱστός 10.222; νύξ 11.330:—also Pythag., = *five*, *Theol.Ar*.32.

ἄμβρυττοι, kind of *shell-fish* (cf. βρύττοι), Hsch. **ἀμβρυχαί**· αἱ τῶν χειρῶν ἐμβολαί, Id.

ἄμβυξ, ῦκος, ὁ, perh. = ἄμβιξ, Hdn.Gr.1.44, al.

ἄμβων, ωνος, ὁ, Att. for Ion. **ἄμβη**, acc. to Gal.18(1).340, but Rhodian acc. to Bacchius ap.Apollon.Cit.1.7:—*crest* of a hill, A.*Fr*. 103; ἐπ' οὔρεος ἀμβώνεσσιν Call.*Aet*.3.1.34. 2. *rim* or *edge* of a cup (esp. of one that curves inwards), Eup.52, Ephipp.3.16, Critias 34 D., Plu.*Lyc*.9. b. (from similarity of shape), *rim of joint-socket*, Gal.*UP*1.15, al., cf. 18(1).340. 3. = γυναικεῖον αἰδοῖον, Eust.1539.33 (so perh. in Eup. l. c.). 4. in Cos, *steps, rungs* of ladder, Apollon.Cit.1.7. 5. *pulpit*, title of poem by Paul. Sil., cf. *JHS*28.195 (Aspendus).

ἀμβώσας, Ion. for ἀναβοήσας, v. sub ἀναβοάω.

ἀμέ or **ἀμέ**, Dor. for ἡμᾶς, Ar.*Ach*.759, *Lys*.95, Decr.Byz.ap.D. 18.90.

ἀμέγαρτος, ον, poet. Adj., (ἀ- priv., μεγαίρω) *unenviable*: 1. mostly of things or conditions, *sad, melancholy*, πόνος Il.2.420; ἀνέμων..ἀϋτμή Od.11.400; μάχη Hes.*Th*.666; ἀμέγαρτα κακῶν E. *Hec*.192; πάθος Ar.*Th*.1049 (lyr.), cf. A.*Pr*.403. 2. *undesirable*, κρέα *AP*11.60 (Paul. Sil.); ἄγρη, of fish which follow a wreck, Opp. *H*.4.412. 3. of persons, *unhappy, miserable*, ἀμέγαρτε συβῶτα *wretched* swineherd! Od.17.219; ἀμεγάρτων φῦλ' ἀνθρώπων *h.Merc*. 542; ἀ. ποίμνα A.*Supp*.642 (lyr.).

ἀμεγέθης, ες, *without magnitude, unextended*, Arist.*Metaph*.1075[b] 29, Plot.6.5.12, etc. Adv. -θῶς *non-spatially*, Syrian.*in Metaph*. 85.15; *non-quantitatively*, Porph.*Sent*.34. 2. *lacking in size*, σύγκριμα τῶν μαστῶν Sor.1.88: metaph., *without dignity*, σύνθεσις D.H.*Comp*.18, Longin.34.4; of writers, 40.2.

ἀμέθεκτος, ον, *imparticipable*, Alex.Aphr.*in Metaph*.637.12, Simp.*in de An*.218.5, Procl.*Inst*.23, al.; αἰτίαι Chrysipp.(?) *Stoic*.2.308. Adv. -τως Ascl.*in Metaph*.115.36.

ἀμέθελκτος, ον, *free from distraction*, dub. in Ph.2.427. Adv. -τως Id.1.559.

ἀμεθεξία, ἡ, *non-participation*, τινός Corn.*ND*35, Procl.*in Prm*. p.559 S.

ἀμεθίστατος, ον, incorrect for ἀμετάστατος, *PAmh*.2.85.

ἀμεθόδευτος, ον, *not to be cajoled, led astray*, κριτής Herm.ap.Stob.1. 49.44. 2. *unscientific*, ἰατρός Alex.Trall.*Febr*.5.

ἀμέθοδος, ον, *not in logical* (i.e. *syllogistic*) *form*, λόγοι Chrysipp. *Stoic*.2.83, cf. Phld.*Rh*.1.132 S. Adv. -ως, περαίνειν Chrysipp.*Stoic*. 2.87. 2. *without plan* or *system*, Longin.2.2, S.E.*P*.2.21; esp. Medic., *non-'methodic'*, αἵρεσις Gal.10.51. Adv. -ως, δημιουργῆσαι Phld.*Rh*.1.127 S., cf. S.E.*M*.8.300, Alex.Aphr.*in Metaph*.50.7.

ἀμέθυσον, τό, = ἀμέθυστος II. 1, Dsc.1.123 (s.v.l.). II. = ἀμέθυστος II. 2, Thphr.*Lap*.30, Hld.5.13; ἀμέθυσος, ἡ, v.l. in J.*AJ*3.7.5; cf. Hsch.

ἀμεθύστινος, η, ον, *of amethyst*, βωμοί Luc.*VH*2.11.

ἀμέθυστος, ον, (μεθύω) *not drunken, without drunkenness*, Plu.2. 464c: Comp., *Gp*.7.34.2. II. *not intoxicating*, perh. so used in Nonn.*D*.19.133: as Subst., ἀμέθυστον, τό, *remedy against drunkenness*, Archig.ap.Gal.12.572, Dsc.*Eup*.1.24; also ἀμέθυστος, ἡ, Plu. 2.15b, Ath.1.34c:—hence, such things as were supposed to act as remedies, viz., 1. kind of *herb*, Plu.2.647b; = σέλινον ἄγριον, Ps.-Dsc.2.175. 2. *amethyst*, Lxx *Ex*.28.19, *Apoc*.21.20, D.P. 1122, *AP*5.204, 9.748 (Pl. Jun.):—also **ἀμέθυστον**, τό, *IG*11(2). 287 *B*22 (Delos, iii B.C.). 3. **ἀμέθυστον**, τό, kind of *grape*, Colum.3.2.24.

ἀμεῖ, Delph., = ἅμα, *GDI*2561 *D*47.

ἀμείβοντες, οἱ, v. sq. A. II.

ἀμείβω [ᾰ], Il., Trag.: Ep. impf. ἄμειβον Il.14.381: fut. -ψω A.*Pr*. 23: aor. ἤμειψα, Ep. ἄμειψα [ᾰ] *h.Cer*.275, A.R.3.280; Dor. ἀμ-[ᾰ] Pi.*P*.5.38; Trag.:—Med., impf. ἠμειβόμην, Ep. ἀμ- Il.3.171, etc.: fut. ἀμείψομαι E.*Supp*.517: aor. ἠμειψάμην, Ep. and Ion. ἀμ- Il.4.403, Hdt.1.37, al.:—Pass., fut. ἀμειφθήσεται Hsch.: aor. ἠμείφθην AP7.589 (Agath.), 638 (Crin.), etc. (in med. sense, Pi.P.4.102, Theoc.7.27): pf. ἤμειπται Gal.1.210: Ep. plpf. ἄμειπτο Nonn.D.44.241.—Verb and compds. are almost exclus. poet. and Ion., but used once or twice in Pl. and X., and late Prose.

A. Act., *change, exchange*, (not Od.), ἔντε' ἄμειβεν Il.17.192, etc.: τί τινος, as γόνυ γουνὸς ἀμείβων *changing* one knee for other, i.e. walking slowly, ib.11.547, etc.:—so either, 1. *give in exchange*, ὃς πρὸς Τυδεΐδην Διομήδεα τεύχε' ἄμειβε χρύσεα χαλκείων ib. 6.235: c. acc., δάμαρτ' ἀμείψας E.Alc.46: or more freq., 2. *take in exchange*, τι ἀντί τινος Pi.P.4.17, E.Hel.1382; πόσιν ἀντὶ σᾶς ἀμεῖψαι ψυχᾶς *redeem* at that price, Id.Alc.462, etc.; μορφὴν ἀ. ἐκ θεοῦ βροτησίαν Id.Ba.4; ἀ. τὰν ἐμὰν [φυλακάν] Id.Rh.527; τιμὰν πρὸς ἀνθρώπων ἀμείψω Ibyc.24, cf. A.Ch.1019 (anap.) (prob.). 3. in Att. often of Place, *change* it, so *pass, cross*, πορθμόν, πόρον, Id.Pers. 69, E.IA144, etc.:—hence, b. either *pass out of* a house, *leave* it, ἀ. στέγας, δώματα, S.Ph.1262, E.El.750; or *pass into, enter* it, ἀ. θύρας Hdt.5.72, cf. A.Ch.571: generally, πόλιν ἐκ πόλεως ἀ. Pl.Sph. 224b, cf. Prm.138d; v. infr. B.II.2. 4. *change, alter*, χρῶτα βαφῇ A.Pers.317; χροιᾶς ἄνθος Id.Pr.23; ἐς κακοχυμίην ἤμειψε τὰ σπλάγχνα Aret.SD2.13: abs., πολλὰ ἀ. *change* colour, Jul.Caes. 309a; so Med., χροιῆς ἄνθος ἀμειβομένης Sol.27.6. 5. causal, *make* others *change*, τεύχε' ἄμειβον Il.14.381; *pass on, hand on from one to another*, τέκνα..διαδοχαῖς ἀμείβουσαι χεροῖν E.Hec.1159. b. *shift, dislodge*, κακὸν κακῷ Aret.SD2.1. 6. rarely like Med. B.I.3, *repay, return*, ἀ. χάριν A.Ag.729, cf. Ch.793. II. intr. in part., ἀμείβοντες, οἱ, *the interchangers*, i.e. *rafters that meet and cross each other*, Il.23.712, cf. Theo Sm.p.122 H., Nonn.D.37.588; ἐν ἀμείβοντι, = ἀμοιβάδις, Pi.N.11.42:—so prob. ἀμείβει καινὸν ἐκ καινῶν τόδε *succeeds*, E.Or.1503.

B. Med., *change one with another, do in turn* or *alternately*, abs., ἀμειβόμενοι φυλακὰς ἔχον Il.9.471; ἄειδον ἀμειβόμεναι ὀπὶ καλῇ 1.604; ὀρχείσθην..ἀμειβομένω Od.8.379; ἀμειβόμενοι κατὰ οἴκους at every house *in turn*, 1.375, 2.140; ἄρουραι ἀμειβόμεναι *ploughed and fallow in turn*, Pi.N.6.9; so ἀμειβόμεναι ὁπλαῖς *alternating, crosswise*, of the motion of the legs in horses or oxen, Id.P.4.226; ἄλλα ἄλλοθεν ἀμείβεται now *comes* one thing, now another *in turn*, E.Hipp.1108; ἀμείβεται μιάσματα Id.Med.1267: c. part., θρῴσκων ἄλλοτ' ἐπ' ἄλλον ἀμείβεται leaps *in turn*.., Il.15.684:—ἀ. στενότητι *vary* in narrowness, X.Cyn.9.14. 2. of dialogue, ἀμείβεσθαι ἐπέεσσι *answer one another*, Od.3.148, etc.; in part., ἀμειβόμενος προσέειπε, προσηύδα, Il.3.437, 17.33; ἀ. πρός τινα Hdt.8.60 codd.; πρός τι ib.58, E.Tr.903: c. acc. pers. et dat. rei, ἀ. τινα μύθῳ, μύθοις, Od. 12.278, 2.83; ἀ. τινα alone, *answer* one, *reply to* him, Il.1.172, etc.; τὸν λόγοις ἀμείφθη Pi.P.4.102, cf. Theoc.7.27; ἀμείβετο τοῖσδε in these words, Hdt.1.35, al.:—later c. acc. rei, τούτοις ἀμείβου..εὐμαθές τι A.Eu.442; ἔπος πρὸς ἔπος 586; μὴ σφριγῶντ' ἀμείψῃ μῦθον E.Supp.478; ταῦτα ἀμείψατο Hdt.1.37: c. dupl. acc., ταῦτα τοὺς φίλους ἀμείψατο Id.2.173, cf.3.52, A.Supp.195; ἔν μ' ἄμειψαι μοῦνον S.OC991; τὸν δὲ..μῆτιν..ἀμείβετο *gave* him counsel *in reply*, Pi.P. 9.39:—also late Prose, Luc.Alex.19. 3. *repay, requite*, c. acc. pers. et dat. rei, δώροισιν ἀ. τινα Od.24.285; χρηστοῖσι Hdt.1.41, cf. 4.97; ὁμοίοις D.20.6; ἀμείβομαί σε τῷ φυγεῖν τὴν οἰκίαν Com. Adesp.371: c. acc. pers. only, τὸν ἄδικον ἀ. S.Fr.12; τοὺς μὲν ἐκόλαζε, τοὺς δὲ ἠμείβετο D.C.74.8: c. acc. et dat. rei, ἀ. εὐεργεσίας χάρισιν X.Mem.4.3.15: c. acc. rei only, χάριν φιλότητος S.El.134; βροτῶν ἀσυνεσίας E.Ph.1727; τὴν προϋπαρχὴν Arist.EN1165^{a}5: rarely c. dat. pers., πολλοῖσι γὰρ κέρδη πονηρὰ ζημίαν ἠμείψατο E.Cyc.312: rarely also c. gen. rei compensatae, ἀ. τινα τῆς δικαιοσύνης Luc.Somn. 15:—mostly, *return good for good*; but also, *bad for good*, φθόνον ἀμειβόμενον τὰ καλὰ ἔργα Pi.P.7.17; *bad for bad*, ἀμείψεται φόνον φόνος E.El.1093; κακὸν κακῷ Aret.SD2.13. 4. *purchase*, λύχνον Lib. Or.45.10. II. *get in exchange*, [οὗτοι] νιν (sc. Καρθαίαν) Βαβυλῶνος ἀμείψομαι Pi.Pae.4.16; θητικοῦ ἀντὶ τέλους ἱππάδ' ἀμειψάμενος Epigr. ap. Arist. Ath.7.4; λῷος φρένας τῶν νῦν παρουσῶν S.Tr. 737. 2. like Act., *change* a place, *pass* either *out* or *in*, ψυχὴ.. ἀμείψεται ἕρκος ὀδόντων Il.9.409; and reversely of things swallowed, φάρμακα..ἀ. ἕρκ. ὀδ. Od.10.328; ἀμειβόμεναι μέγαν οὐδὸν.., ἡ μὲν ἔσω.., ἡ δὲ θύραζε Hes.Th.749; πατρίδ' ἀμειψάμενος Sol.2; ποταμὸν Simon.94; πρόθυρα A.Ch.965; πύλας E.Alc.752; γῆν οὐρανοῦ ἀ. *change* earth for heaven, Plu.2.607e; ὑπὲρ οὐδὸν ἀμειβόμενον Theoc. 2.104; ἄλλην ἐξ ἄλλης πόλεως ἀμειβόμενος Pl.Ap.37d; ἕτερα δ' ἕτερος ἀμείβεται πήματα *passes through* them, E.Or.979. 3. *exchange*, τὶ πρὸς νόμισμα Plu.Aem.23. III. *surpass, outdo*, μελισσᾶν πόνον Pi.P.6.54. IV. χεροῖν πίτυλον, ὃς αἰὲν δι' Ἀχέροντ' ἀ. θεωρίδα *convoys, accompanies* it, A.Th.856.

ἀμειβώ, οῦς, ἡ, = ἀμοιβή, Eust.1471.30.

ἀμειδ-ής, ές, *not smiling, gloomy*, Plu.2.477e, Orph.A.1079, Opp.C.2.459. **-ητος**, ον, = foreg., Lxx Wi.17.4; νύξ A.R.2.908; βέρεθρον Orph.A.975; Τάρταρος IG14.769 (Naples). **-ίᾱτος**, ον, = foreg., D.Chr.4.92 (v.l. -ίαστος).

ἀμειλέοις· ἀθλίοις, Hsch.

ἀμείλ-ικτος, ον, (μειλίσσω) *unsoftened, harsh, cruel*, of words, Il. 11.137, 21.98; ἀρά Max.Tyr.12.6; of fetters, Hes.Th.659; μίτοι, of the thread of Clotho, IG12(7).301 (Amorgos); τὸ ἀ. Hierocl. in CA 13 p.448 M. II. of persons, = sq., A.R.3.337, Mosch.4.26. Adv. -τως, ἔχειν τινί Ph.2.298, cf. Syrian. in Metaph.42.3; μοίρας ἀτυχούσης ἀμειλίκτως, of *pitiless* fate, App.BC4.54. **-ῐχος**, ον, *implacable, relentless*, Ἀΐδης Il.9.158; ἦτορ ib.572; βία Sol.32; στρατός (of rain), κότος, Pi.P.6.12, 8.8:—a form **ἀμειλίχιος** occurs in Adv. -ίως Epigr.Gr.313 (Smyrna). II. of things, *unmitigated*, πόνοι A.Ch.623; ἀμείλιχα σάρκες ἔχουσιν IG14.2461 (Massilia).

ἀμείνασις· ἡ δύοσμον (Perga), EM83.50, cf. Hsch.

ἀμείνων, ον, gen. ονος, irreg. Comp. of ἀγαθός, *better*: I. of persons, *stouter, stronger, braver*, freq. Hom., etc.: μέγ' ἀ. Il.22. 158; πολλὸν ἀ. Hes.Op.19: c. acc. vel inf., ἀμείνων παντοίας ἀρετάς, ἠμὲν πόδας ἠδὲ μάχεσθαι Il.15.641, cf. Hes.Op.445, A.Pr.337, etc.; οἱ ἀμείνονες *the better sort*, Pl.Lg.627a. II. of things, ὀμίχλην νυκτὸς ἀμείνω Il.3.11; esp. from Hom. downwds., ἄμεινόν [ἐστι] *'tis better*, either c. inf., ἐπεὶ πείθεσθαι ἄ. Il.1.274, cf. S.El.1238, etc.; or ἄμεινόν ἐστι or γίγνεταί τινι c. part., εἴ σφι ἄμεινον γίγνεται τιμωρέουσι *if it is good* for them to assist, Hdt.7.169, cf. Th.1.118, 6.9: abs., εἴ τό γ' ἄ. Il.1.116; βουλοίμην..εἴ τι ἄ. καὶ ὑμῖν καὶ ἐμοί Pl.Ap.19a; freq. with neg., οὐ γὰρ ἄ. 'twere *better* not, Hes.Op.750, Hdt.1. 187; εἰρήσεται γάρ, εἴτ' ἄ. εἴτε μή D.21.198. 2. neut. as Adv., ἄ. πρήσσειν to fare *better*, Hdt.4.156 sq., etc.; συνήνεικεν Ἀθηναίοις ἐπὶ τὸ ἄ. Decr.ap.And.1.77, cf. Orac.ap.D.43.86; τὰ ἀμείνω φρονέειν choose the *better part*, Hdt.7.145; τοῖσι τὰ ἀ. ἑάνδανε Id.9.19. III. Adv. ἀμεινόνως Ar.Fr.340. IV. new Comp. ἀμεινότερος, α, ον, formed from ἀμείνων, Mimn.14.9, Poet.ap.Phld. Rh.2.61 S.

ἀμειξία, ἡ, *interruption of communications*, PLond.2.301.20, PTeb.72.45 (ii B.C.); cf. ἀμιξία.

ἀμειπτικός, ή, όν, *of* or *for exchange*, τράπεζα IG5(1).18 (Sparta, i A.D.); -κή, ἡ, *business of exchange*, OGI484 (Pergam.). II. *in requital*, χάρις Sch.Pi.P.2.33.

ἀμείρω, = ἀμέρδω, *bereave*, c. gen. rei, Pi.P.6.26.

ἀμεῖς· εὑρήσεις, Hsch.

ἀμειψι-κοσμίη, ἡ, = μετακόσμησις, Democr.138. **-ρρυσμέω**, (ῥυσμός = ῥυθμός) *change form*, Id.139. **-ρρυσμία**, ἡ, *change of form*, περὶ -ιῶν, title of work by Democr.ap.D.L.9.47.

ἄμειψις, εως, ἡ, (ἀμείβω) *exchange, interchange*, Plb.10.1.5; ἐν ἀμείψει τῶν τάξεων Plu.Arist.16; ὀνομάτων Anon. in SE46.25: *succession*, τῶν γενῶν Plu.Sull.7; *change*, τῆς χρόας Id.2.978d. II. *requiting, repaying*, [τῶν εὐεργετημάτων] Inscr.Prien.105.18. 2. *repartee*, Plu.2.803c.

ἀμείψιχρον· μεταβάλλοντα.., Hsch. (fort. -χρουν *changing colour*).

ἀμείωτος, ον, *not to be diminished*, σιτωνία Ph.2.66; *incapable of diminution*, ἀναυξὲς καὶ ἀ. Simp. in Cael.109.22. Adv. -τως Olymp. in Alc.p.111 C.

ἀμέλαθρος, ον, *houseless*, Man.4.113.

ἀμέλατον· τὸ ἴσον, Hsch.

ἀμέλγω [ᾰ], fut. -ξω Theoc.23.25, *milk*, with acc. of animals milked, μῆλα..ὅσσ' ἤμελγε Od.9.238; ἤμελγεν ὄϊς καὶ μηκάδας αἶγας ib. 244; βόας Theoc.4.3: metaph., ἀμέλγεις τοὺς ξένους *you drain* them *of all they have*, Ar.Eq.326: prov., ἀ. τὸν τράγον, of wasted labour, Plb.33.21.1, Luc.Demon.28:—Med., ἀ. χροὸς αἷμα Nic.Al.506: metaph., ἐκ Σαπφοῦς τόδ' ἀμελγόμενος μέλι τοι φέρω Lyr.Adesp. 62. 2. *suck up* moisture, of the sun, Nonn.D.2.500. II. c. acc., of milk, ἀ. γάλα Hdt.4.2:—Pass., ὄϊες..ἀμελγόμεναι γάλα λευκόν *milch*-ewes, Il.4.434; γάλα πολὺ ἀ. Arist.HA523^{a}7, cf. 522^{a}15; νέκταρ ἀμέλγονται Ion Eleg.1:—Med., *let suck*, Opp.C.1.437. 2. metaph., *squeeze out like milk, press out*, ἐκ βοτρύων ξανθὸν ἄμελξε γάνος AP9.645 (Maced.); δάκρυ ἠλέκτροιο D.P.293. III. *drink*, αὐτὸ λαβὼν ποτὶ χεῖλος ἀμέλξω Theoc.23.25, cf. Bion 1.48, Nonn.D. 12.321:—Med., ib.12.320, al. (ἀ- euph., cf. *mulgeo, milk*.)

ἀμέλδειν· τήκειν, Hsch.

ἀμέλει, properly imper. of ἀμελέω (cf. ἀμέλησον Luc.DMort.5.2), *never mind, do not trouble yourself*, esp. to begin an answer, Ar.Nu. 877, Lib.Decl.20.18:—hence, II. as Adv., *doubtless, by all means, of course*, Ar.Ach.368, Nu.488, al., Pl.Phd.82a, al., X.Mem.1.4.7, Men.Sam.8; freq. ironically, as Ar.Ra.532; freq. in Thphr.Char. to introduce a subject, 13.1, al., or a further point, 2.9, al. 2. *for instance*, Thphr.Char.6.3, Luc.DDeor.25.1, etc. 3. *at any rate*, Luc. Nigr.26, Gp.10.2.3. 4. *and indeed*, Phld.Ir.p.16 W., Str.1.2.34, D.H.Rh.2.2, J.AJ7.4.1; *and so*, Polyaen.2.22.3, 7.6.4. 5. *actually*, to give emphasis, Agath.2.3, al. **ἀμέλεια**, ἡ, *indifference, negligence*, Th.1.122, 5.38, etc.; θεῶν *towards* the gods, Pl.Lg. 905b, cf. ib.903a: also in pl., *negligences*, Id.R.443a, Arist.Rh.1370^a 15.

ἀμελεϊστί, prob. f.l. for ἀμελλητί, Suid.

ἀμελετ-ησία, ἡ, *want of practice, negligence*, Pl.Tht.153b; μνήμης Id.Phdr.275a, cf. Eus.Mynd.Fr.33, Ph.1.548, etc. **-ητος**, ον, *unpractised, unprepared*, περί τινος Pl.Smp.172a: c. inf., ἀ. ἐν ταῖς ἡδοναῖς καρτερεῖν Id.Lg.635c, cf. Procop.Goth.1.9; τινός, πρός τι, Luc.Cont.7, Tox.29, Arist.SE175^{a}26: abs. of horses, *untrained*, X. Eq.Mag.1.19, al. Adv. -τως, ἔχειν τινός Jul.Or.1.2d. Adv. -τως, ἔχειν to be *unprepared*, Pl.Smp.173c.

ἀμελ-έω [ᾰ], aor. ἠμέλησα, Ep. ἀμ- Il., v. infr.: pf. ἠμέληκα X. Cyr.1.6.43: (ἀμελής):—*have no care for, be neglectful of*, in Hom. always c. neg. (not in Od.), οὐδ' ὡς Μενελάου ἐφημοσύνης ἀμέλησεν Il.17.697; οὐκ ἀμέλησε κασιγνήτοιο πεσόντος 8.330; οὐκ ἀμέλησε Πατρόκλοιο πεσόντος *he lost* not *sight* of Patroclus [in order to *plunder* him], 17.9:—after Hom., with and without neg., εἰ τούτων ἀμελήσει Hdt.2.121.γ', cf. Ar.Nu.989, Th.3.40, Pl.Lg.900b, al.; δόξης ἀμελῆσαι D.18.227; ἀμελήσας ὑμῶν 21.167; (τούτῳ is f.l. for τούτου in Lycurg.15); οὐκ ἐμοῦ τοῦ νομοθέτου ἀμελήσων ἀλλ' εἰς τὸν Κρόνον αὐτόν Luc.Sat.10. 2. abs., *to be careless, negligent*, Hes.Op.400, freq. in Att., Isoc.9.78, etc.; τὸ μὴ ἀμελεῖν μάθε A.*Eu*.86; πῶς ἐπὶ τοῖς φθιμένοις ἀμελεῖν καλόν; S.*El*.237. 3. c. acc. rei, Hdt.7.163: c. acc. pers. et part., *overlook*: hence, *allow, suffer*, παῖδας ἐκτεκνούμενος λάθρᾳ θνήσκοντας ἀμελεῖ *lets* them die, E.*Ion* 439: c. gen., τοῦ ὀργίζεσθαι X.*Mem*.2.3.9. 4. c. inf., *neglect* to do, Hdt.2.66, Pl. *Phd*.98d, *Lg*.944d, al. II. Pass., *to be slighted, overlooked*, E.*IA* 1094, Th.1.68; ἐκφεύγει τἀμελούμενον S.*OT* 111; οὐδ' ἐκεῖνά μοι ἀμελεῖται X.*Oec*.12.2; οἱ ἠμελημένοι ἄνθρωποι Th.2.49. III. pf. part. Pass. in med. sense, *careless*, Max.Tyr.8.7, 21.9. Adv. ἠμελημένως *carelessly*, X.*An*.1.7.19. IV. ἀμέλει, v. sub voc. -ής (A), [ᾰ], ές, (μέλει) *careless, negligent*, Ar.*Lys*.882, X.*Mem*.2.6.19; φιλοπότης τε κἀμελής Eup.208; ἀργὸς.. καὶ ἀ. Pl.*R*.421d, etc. Adv. -λῶς *carelessly*, Th.6.100: Comp. -έστερον Id.2.11; -εστέρως Aen.Tact. 26.8. 2. c. gen., *careless of*.., Pl.*Sph*.225d, etc.; περί τινα Isoc. 19.32. Adv., ἐάν τις γονέων -έστερον ἔχῃ τοῦ δέοντος Pl.*Lg*.932a; ἀμελῶς ἔχειν πρός τι X.*Oec*.2.7; περὶ θεούς Id.*Cyr*.1.2.7. 3. c. inf., οὐκ ἀ. ποιεῖν not *negligent* in doing, Plu.2.64f. II. Pass., *uncared for, unheeded*, οὐδενὶ τούτων ἀ. X.*HG*6.5.41, cf. D.50.15; οὐκ ἀμελὲς γεγένηταί μοι, c. inf., I have taken *pains* to.., Luc.*Dips*.9. ής (B), ές, (μέλος) *unmelodious*, φωνή Poll.2.117. -ητέον, *one must neglect*, τινός Isoc.9.7: also in pl., ἀμελητέα ἐστί τινος Arr.*An*.1.24.1. II. ἀμελητέος, α, ον, *to be neglected*, Luc.*Tim*.9, Arr.*An*.1.7.4. -ητής, οῦ, ὁ, *one who neglects*, Gal.3.827. -ητικός, ή, όν, *carelessly written*, ἦτα, of a musical note, Alyp.1, al., Gaud.*Harm*.23. -ητος, ον, *not to be cared for, unworthy of care*, πόλλ' ἀμέλητα μέλει Thgn.422. Adv. **ἀμελητί** *heedlessly*, Luc.*Tim*.12. -ία, ἡ, poet. for ἀμέλεια, E.*IA* 850, *Fr*.187:—also in Inscrr. and Papyri, *OGI*383 (Nimrud Dagh), *PTeb*.61^{a}176 (ii B.C.). -ίου δίκη action for *negligence*, Hsch.

ἀμελκ-τέον, *one must milk*, *Gp*.18.3.9. -τήρ, ῆρος, ὁ, *milking-pail*, Hsch. s. v. ἀρακτήρ. -τός, όν, *milked*, or *to be milked*, Hdn. Gr.2.901.

ἀμέλλ-ητος, ον, *without delay* or *hesitation*, Luc.*Nigr*.27. Adv. -τως Plb.16.34.12, al.:—also -ητί Ph.1.172, J.*AJ*19.6.3, Them. *Or*.16.208c, Iamb.*VP*3.14.

ἄμελξις, εως, ἡ, (ἀμέλγω) *milking*, Pi.*Fr*.106, Lxx *Jb*.20.17.

ἀμελῴδητος, ον, *unmelodic*, διαστήματα Aristox.*Harm*.p.25 M.

ἄμεμπτος, ον, *blameless, without reproach*, E.*IA*1158, *Cyc*.342; ἀμέμπτους ὑμᾶς ἐδείξατε D.18.216; ἄ. χρόνου in regard of time, A.*Pers*. 692; ἄ. τἄλλα Men.521; πρός τι A.*Supp*.629 (dub.); ἄ. ὑπὸ τῶν φίλων X.*Ag*.6.8; ἄ. ἐκείνῃ *without blame* to her, Plu.*Sull*.35: Comp. -ότερος *less blameworthy*, Plu.*Ages*.5. 2. of things, *perfect in its kind*, δεῖπνον X.*Smp*.2.2; δίκη Pl.*Lg*.945d; ἄ. πάντα ἔχειν X.*Mem*.3.10.2. Adv. -τως *irreproachably*, A.*Supp*.269, S.*Ph*.1465, X.*Cyr*.7.3.10, *Stoic*.3.64. II. Act., *not blaming, well content*, ἄμεμπτόν τινα ποιεῖν or ποιεῖσθαι, X.*Cyr*.4.5.52, 8.4.28. Adv. -τως, δέχεσθαί τινα ib.4.2.37.

ἀμεμφ-ής, ές, mostly in pass. sense, = ἄμεμπτος 1, *IG*12(3).1075 (Melos), Pi.*O*.6.46, A.*Pers*.168, *Supp*.581; in epitaph, Εὔκλειαν ἀ. Ἀρχ. Ἐφ.1910.66 (Piraeus):—poet. and late Prose, Plu.*Cim*.2, Jul. *Or*.2.99a. II. Act., = ἄμεμπτος II, Plu.2.610e; ἀ. τῶν ἀμελειῶν Id.*Aem*.3. Adv. -φῶς, Ion. -φέως Orph.*H*.43.11. -ία, ἡ, *freedom from blame*, διαλλακτῆρι δ' οὐκ ἀ. φίλοις mediator has no *freedom from blame* on the part of his friends, A.*Th*.909; ἀμεμφίας χάριν for *avoidance of censure*, S.*Fr*.283. (ἀμεμφεία shd. perh. be written in both passages.)

ἀμεμψι-μοίρητος, ον, *unexceptionable*, *OGI*323 (Pergam.), *PPar*. 63.8 (ii B.C.). Adv. -τως *without cause of complaint*, *BGU*251 (i A.D.). -μοιρος, ον, *not complaining of one's lot*, Teles p.56.2 H., M.Ant.5.5.

ἄμεναι [ᾰ], Ep. pres. inf. from ἄω (q.v.), Il.21.70.

ἀμενην-ός [ᾰ], όν, also ή, όν Opp.*H*.2.58: (ἀ- priv., μένος):—poet. Adj., in Hom. chiefly of ghosts or shades, *fleeting*, νεκύων ἀ. κάρηνα Od.10.521, al.; of dreams, 19.562; of one wounded, ἀ. ἔα χαλκοῖο τυπῇσι Il.5.887; Πυγμαῖοι Hes.*Oxy*.1358.18; rare in Trag. (alw. lyr.), ἀ. ἀνήρ, of Ajax, S.*Aj*.890; νεκύων ἀ. ἄγαλμα E.*Tr*.193. 2. of men in general, *fleeting, feeble*, φῦλ' ἀ. ἀνθρώπων *h.Cer*.352; σκιοειδέα φῦλ' ἀ. Ar.*Av*.686. 3. in physical sense, *feeble, weak*, ἰσχνοῖσι καὶ ἀμενηνοῖσι Hp.*Prorrh*.2.30; ἀ. φωνή Arist.*Pr*.899^{a}30; οἱ ἄκεντροι σφῆκες .. ἀμενηνότεροι Id.*HA*628^{b}4, cf. Ti.Locr.100c; ὕδωρ -ότατον πάντων Arr.*Ind*.6.3; ἀ. κλῆμα, φύλλον, Thphr.*CP*3.14.5, *HP*3.9.1; σπερμάτιον 4.12.2 (Comp.); πῦρ Ph.2.564; *faint, shadowy*, ὄναρ Them.*Or*.21.263c:—neut. as Adv., *feebly, faintly*, ἀμενηνὸν φθέγγεσθαι Arist.*Pr*.899^{a}31; ὁρᾶν Philostr.*Jun.Im*.17; ἀμενηνὰ φαείνειν Arat.905. Regul. Adv. -νῶς Agathem.ap.Gal.8.938. II. (as if from ἀ- priv., μένω) *not permanent*, κατηγορίαι Simp.*in Ph*.832. 12. -όω, *weaken, deaden the force of*, ἀμενήνωσεν δέ οἱ αἰχμήν Il.13. 562.

ἀμενής, ές, = ἀμενηνός, E.*Supp*.1116 (lyr.).

ἀμενητά· ὑμένα, Hsch. **ἀμενητί**, Adv. *without remaining*, Suid.

ἀμένητος, ον, = ἀμενηνός, Hdn.Gr.2.684.

ἀμενθήριστος, ον, *not careful*, Timo 59 (codd. ἀπενθ–).

ἀμεργόν· ἡ εἱμαρμένη (Cret.), Hsch.

ἀμέργω [ᾰ], fut. -ξω (v. infr.), *pluck* or *pull*, ἄνθε' ἀμέργοισαν παῖδα Sapph.121; πετάλων ἄπο.. χερὶ καρπὸν ἀμέρξων E.*HF*397 (lyr.), cf. A.R.1.882; ἀ. τὰς ἐλάας *Com.Adesp*.437 (*squeeze out* juice, acc. to Eust.318.11):—Med., ἀμερξάμεναι.. δρυὸς ἄγρια φύλλα Theoc.26.3, cf. A.R.4.1144, Nic.*Th*.864, etc.

ἀμέρδω [ᾰ], fut. -σω Orph.*L*.169: aor. ἤμερσα, poet. ἄμ- (v. infr.):—**Pass.**, aor. ἠμέρθην (v. infr.).—Ep., rarely in Trag., never in Att. Prose:—*deprive, bereave* one *of* something properly belonging to one, c. acc. pers. et gen. rei, ὀφθαλμῶν μὲν ἄμερσε Od.8.64 (v.l.); εὖτ' ἂν δὴ Κύκνον γλυκερῆς αἰῶνος ἀμέρσῃς Hes.*Sc*.331, cf. Simon.117; εἰ μὴ στάσις.. σ' ἄμερσε πάτρας Pi.*O*.12.16: also c. dupl. acc. pers. et rei, τιμὴν ἤμερσεν Ὀλύμπια δώματ' ἔχοντας *h.Cer*.312: also c. acc. et dat., ὀφθαλμῶν σέλας ἤμερσε βροτοῖσιν Man.6.550:—Pass., *to be bereft of*, φίλης αἰῶνος ἀμερθῇς Il.22.58; οὐδέ τι δαιτὸς ἀμέρδεαι Od.21.290; τὸ ἧπαρ τῆς ἐκροῆς ἀμερθέν Aret.*CA*2.6, cf. Hierocl.*in CA*24 p.470 M.: rarely c. acc. rei, ἂν.. καρπὸν ἀμερθῶσι Thphr.*HP*9.8.2. 2. c. acc. pers. only, *bereave of natural rights*, τὸν ὁμοῖον ἀμέρσαι Il.16.53; ὄσσε δ' ἄμερδεν αὐγὴ χαλκείη *blinded* the eyes, ib.13.340, cf. Hes.*Th*.698; ἔντεα πατρὸς καλά, τὰ.. καπνὸς ἀμέρδει *robs of their lustre, tarnishes*, Od.19.18. 3. Act. in pass. sense, *lose*, βίον E.*Hec*.1029 (lyr.). II. later, = ἀμέργω, *pluck*, λειμώνιον ἄνθος ἀμέρσας (cj. Scalig.) *AP*7.657 (Leon.). (ἀ- euph., cf. μέρδει.)

ἀμέρ-εια, ἡ, *being without parts*, Porph.*Sent*.34, Procl.*Inst*.86, al., Dam.*Pr*.60; τοῦ νοῦ Hero *Def*.136.25. -ής, ές, *without parts, indivisible*, Pl.*Tht*.205e, *Prm*.138a, Arist.*Ph*.231^{b}3, etc.; τὸ ἀ. Hp. *Virg*.1; introduced into Latin by Cic., Plu.*Cic*.40. Adv. -ρῶς Alex. Aphr.*in Metaph*.714.25; ἀ. καὶ ἀδιαστάτως Porph.*Sent*.33. 2. τὰ ἀ. in Logic, *summa genera*, Arist.*APo*.100^{b}2. 3. *impartial*, κρίσεις Luc.*Cal*.8. -ιαῖος, α, ον, *momentary*, φρόνησις Chrysipp.*Stoic*.3.50.

ἀμεριμν-έω, *to be care-free*, Iamb.*VP*5.21. (ἀμεριμνάω, only Moer. 79.) -ία, ἡ, *freedom from care*, Plu.2.830a, Secund.*Sent*.8^b; ἀ. τῆς δεσποτείας Hdn.2.4.6. 2. as law-term, *guarantee, release*, *IG*14.956; τινός *PLips*.59; *receipt*, Just.*Nov*.128. II. personified, Σεβαστῶν Ἀ., = *Securitas Augustorum*, *CIG*2778 (Aphrodisias). -ικός, ή, όν, = ἀμέριμνος 1, c. gen. obj., ἐμοῦ *PFay*.130 (iii A.D.). -ος, ον, *free from care, unconcerned*, Men.1083; βίος *AP*9.359 (Posidipp. or Pl.Com.); ἀ. ὕπνον εὕδεις *Eranos* 13.87. Adv. -νως Vett.Val.355.6, Hdn.4.5.7, *IG*14.1839: Comp. -ότερον, ἔχειν *PLips*.105 (i A.D.). II. Pass., *uncared for*, S.*Aj*.1207. III. οἰνοχοεῖ κρήνης ἐξ ἀμεριμνοτέρης, either *causing less care*, i.e. *more easily attained*, of the fount of inspiration, or possibly *less celebrated*, *AP*11.24 (Antip.). IV. ἀμέριμνον, τό, = ἀείζωον μέγα, Plin.*HN* 25.160.

ἀμέριστος, ον, *undivided, indivisible*, Pl.*Tht*.205c, *Ti*.35a, Dam.ap. Simp.*in Ph*.625.4, Procl.*Theol.Plat*.1.4: Comp., Id.*Inst*.62. Adv. -τως Iamb.*Myst*.1.9, Jul.*Or*.4.157a, Syrian.*in Metaph*.107.6. II. Astrol., in act. sense, *not imparting*, ἀστέρες ἀ. τῶν ἰδίων ἀγαθῶν Vett.Val.64.3.

ἀμέρμερα· πολλά (Lacon.), Hsch.

ἀμερμηρεί, Adv. *carelessly*, Suid., Eust.1416.10.

ἀμερνός· ἄπειρος, Hsch.

ἀμερο-κοίτης, -κοιτος, Dor. for ἡμερό–.

ἀμερσί-γάμος, ον, *robbing of wedlock*, Nonn.*D*.7.226. -νη, ἡ, = ἑλξίνη, Dsc.4.39. -νοος, ον, *depriving of mind, maddening*, Nonn.*D*.1.388, prob. in Ps.-Dsc.4.78. **ἄμερσις**, εως, ἡ, *deprivation*, Eust.1585.46. **ἀμερσίφρων**, ον, = ἀμερσίνοος, Hsch.

ἀμερφές· αἰσχρόν, Hsch. **ἀμέσαι**· ἀμαυρῶσαι, Id. (leg. ἀμέρσαι).

ἀμεσολάβητος, ον, *not seized by the middle*, i.e. *not thrown*, of a victorious wrestler, *BCH*16.445 (Phaselis), *LW*3.363 (Mylasa): metaph., φῶς ἀ. παρέχων, of the sun, Jul.*Or*.4.153c.

ἄμεσος, ον, *immediate*: ἄμεσα καὶ ἀναπόδεικτα, of propositions *that cannot be proved syllogistically by means of a middle term*, Arist.*APr*. 68^{b}30, *APo*.72^{b}19, etc.; τὰ ἄ. τῶν ἐναντίων *direct* opposites, Plot.6.3. 20. Adv. ἀμέσως *immediately*, Olymp.*in Phlb*.p.256 S., Alex.Aphr.*in Metaph*.162.19, Procl.*Inst*.30, dub. in Phld.*Herc*.1251.3. **ἀμεσότης**, ητος, ἡ, *immediacy*, Eustr.*in APo*.176.4. **ἀμέσω**· ὠμοπλάται, Hsch. (cf. Lat. *umerus*, Goth. *ams*–).

ἀμετά-βᾰτος, ον, *not changing place, stationary*, ἥλιος Cleom.2.1; οὐρανός Simp.*in Ph*.611.5. Adv. -τως *without transition*, ἀκινήτως καὶ ἀ. Procl.*Inst*.52, cf. Simp.*in Ph*.1162.6. 2. Gramm., *intransitive*, ῥῆμα A.D.*Pron*.44.12, al. Adv. -τως *intransitively*, Sch.Ar.*Pl*. 158. II. Pass., *incapable of being traversed*, i.e. *unextended*, Epicur. *Ep*.1 p.18 U. -βλησία, ἡ, *unchangeableness*, Arist.*Ph*.230^{a}10, Thphr.*CP*6.19.3. -βλητος, ον, hyperdor. -ατος Philol.21, *unchangeable*, κόσμος l.c., cf. Arist.*Metaph*.1019^{a}27; ἄτομα καὶ ἀ. Epicur.*Ep*.1 p.7 U.; ἀ. εἰς ἄλλα Ti.Locr.98c. 2. *unchanged*, J.*AJ* 15.7.5; τὸ ἀμετάβλητον Plu.2.1011a: Gramm., *not inflected*, A.D. *Synt*.322.26; of food, *not transformed* by digestion, Gal.6.575, cf. Thphr.*CP*6.10.2. Adv. -τως Iamb.*Protr*.21.κϛʹ, Hierocl. *in CA* 1 p.420 M.; and -τί, gloss on ἀσπερχές, Sch.Il.16.61. -βολος, ον, = foreg., Plu.*Mar*.42. 2. Music, *without modulation*, σύστημα Aristid.Quint.1.8, Bacch.*Harm*.74; ἁρμονία Plu.2.437d -γνωστος, ον, *unalterable, implacable*, μῖσος J.*AJ*16.10.1. 2. *not to be repented of*, ἡδονή Max.Tyr.1.4. -δόξαστος, ον, *unshakeable in one's convictions*, Phld.*Herc*.1003. Adv. -τως ibid. -δοσία, ἡ, *the habit of not giving, avarice*, Sch.Od.17.407. -δοτος, ον, *not imparting, sharing*, τινός Sch.E.*Hipp*.145: abs., *niggardly*, βίος Nic.Dam.p.144^b 28 D.; of persons, opp. κοινωνητικοί, Epict.*Sent*.6. Adv. -ως, ζῆν live *without giving to any one*, Plu.2.525d. II. Pass., *not imparted, secret*, ὑφήγησις Vett.Val.331.6, cf. *PMag.Par*.1.256. -θετος, ον, *unalterable, immutable*, κατάληψις, of knowledge, Zeno *Stoic*.1.20; of fate, Chrysipp.ib.2.264, cf. Plb.30.17.2; ἀκίνητα καὶ ἀ. *OGI*331 (Pergam.), etc. Adv. -τως, διακεῖσθαι D.S.1.83, cf. Ascl.*in Metaph*. 22.6. 2. Gramm., *not inflected*, A.D.*Synt*.322.1. -κίνητος, ον, *not to be moved from place to place, immovable*, Pl.*Ep*.343a, Arist. *Ph*.212^{a}15; of persons, D.H.8.74. Adv. -τως, ἔχειν stand *unmoved*,

Arist.*EN*1105ᵃ33, cf. Jul.*Mis.*348d, al. **-κλαστος,** ον, *not to be broken, inflexible*, τὸ ἀ. τῆς γνώμης X.*Ep.*1.2. **-κλητος,** ον, *irrevocable, uncontrollable*, ὁρμή Plb.36.15.7; ὀργή Hld.2.10 (v.l. -βλητος). **-κλιτος,** ον, *inflexible, steadfast*, Sch.A.*Th.*312, cf. ib.*Pr.*34. **-ληπτος,** ον, *not to be substituted*, A.D.*Pron.*8.19, 46.28.

ἀμετ-άλλακτος, ον, *unchanging*, J.*AJ*18.1.6, Dam.*Pr.*370.

ἀμετα-μέλητος, ον, *not to be repented of* or *regretted*, ἡδονή Pl.*Ti.* 59d; τὸ πεπραγμένον αὐτοῖς ἀ. γίγνεται Id.*Lg.*866e; ἀμεταμέλητον ἐστί τί τινι one has *nothing to repent of*, Plb.21.11.11. 2. *having no opportunity of repentance*, Just.*Nov.*129.3. II. of persons, *unrepentant, feeling no remorse*, ἀ. ἀνίατος Arist.*EN*1150ᵃ22, 1166ᵃ29. Adv. -τως Them.*Or.*19.231a, *Inscr.Prien.*114. **-μίσθωτος,** ον, *not sublet*, *PTeb.*372 (ii A.D.). **-νόητος,** ον, = ἀμεταμέλητος I, Luc.*Abd.*11, Plot.6.7.26, Vett.Val.263.16, al. II. Act., *unrepentant*, *Ep.Rom.*2.5, Arr.*Epict.Fr.*25. Adv. -τως *PStrassb.*29 (iii A.D.). **-πειστος,** ον, *not to be moved by persuasion, inexorable*, Arist.*APo.*72ᵇ3; ἀ. ὑπὸ λόγου Id.*Top.*130ᵇ16; of necessity, Id. *Metaph.*1015ᵃ32. Adv. -τως Epicur.*Fr.*222, Phld.*Herc.*1003. II. of things, *unchangeable, steadfast*, συμμαχία D.S.37.20. **-πλαστος,** ον, *not to be remoulded* or *altered*, Diog.ap.Stob.*App.*p.42G. **-ποίητος,** ον, *indigestible*, Xenocr.42. **-πταιστος,** ον, *infallible*, πρόρρησις Gal.17(1).863. **-πτωσία,** ἡ, *unchangeableness*, Arr.*Epict.*3.2.8, Hierocl.p.48.7A. **-πτωτος,** ον, *unchanging, unchangeable*, λόγοι μόνιμοι καὶ ἀ. Pl.*Ti.*29b; ἐπιστήμη Arist.*Top.*139ᵇ33; ἡ ἀρετή Id.*MM* 1209ᵇ13, *Stoic.*1.50, etc.; κατάληψις ἀ. ὑπὸ λόγου Zenoib.1.20; πίστεις Phld.*Rh.*1.378S. (Sup.). b. *not losing its power*, of medicine, Gal.12.422. II. of persons, Plu.2.659f. Adv. -τως Id.*Dio* 14, cf. Phld.*Rh.*1.158S., Polystr.p.29W. **-στατος,** ον, *unchangeable, unchanging*, ἴτω ἀ. μέχρι θανάτου Pl.*R.*361c; of ideas, ib.378e; τὸ ἀμετάστατον *uniformity*, Plu.2.135b. Adv. -τως Procl.*in Ti.*3.22D., etc. **-στρεπτος,** ον, *not to be diverted*, Max.Tyr.11.5, cf. *POxy.* 705.62. Adv. **-στρεπτί** [ῑ] or -εί *without turning round, straight forward*, φεύγειν X.*Smp.*4.50, Pl.*Lg.*854c, cf. *R.*620e, Ph.1.517, M.Ant.8.5 (v.l. -τρεπτί), etc. **-στροφος,** ον, *not to be turned round, unalterable*, Pl.*R.*620e, *Lg.*960c. **-τρεπτος,** ον, = foreg., Plu.*Thes.*17, Iamb.*Myst.*6.6, Herm.ap.Stob.1.4.7ᵇ. Adv. -τως, gloss on ἀσκελές, Sch.Od.4.543; also **-τρεπτί** v.l. in M.Ant.8.5. **-τρεψία,** ἡ, = sq., Ptol.*Tetr.*16. **-τροπία,** ἡ, *immovableness*, Sch.A.R. 4.1082. **-τροπος,** ον, = ἀμετάτρεπτος, Orph.*H.*59.17; δόγμα Μοιρῶν *IG*12(7).393 (Amorgos). **-φόρητος,** ον, *irremovable*, Phlp.*in Cat.*32.21. **-φραστος,** ον, *untranslatable*, Phot. s.v. πύππαξ, Sch.Il.9.607, Hsch. s.v. θρίττε. **-χείριστος,** ον, *not hanselled, new*, Ar.*Fr.*710. II. *difficult to handle, intractable*, *Gloss.*, Hsch.

ἀμετέναι· ἀποδοῦναι, Hsch.

ἀμέτ-οιστος, ον, *which cannot be alienated* or *secularized*, πρόσοδοι *OGI*332.19 (Pergam.). **-ουσίαστον·** ἀμέτοχον, Hsch. **-οχος,** ον, *having no share of, free from*, ἐγκλημάτων interp. in Th.1.39; ἀγαθῶν Epicur.*Fr.*364; ἀρετῆς, κακίας *Stoic.*3.90, cf. S.E.*M.*7.93; Αἰὼν μεταβολῆς ἀ. *SIG*1125.11 (Eleusis), cf. Ph.1.17, Hierocl.p.33.7A., Alex. Aphr.*in Metaph.*644.12, Dsc.5.87; ἀ. ὕλης οὐσία Plot.3.5.2; πολλὰ ἑνὸς ἀ. Procl.*in Prm.*p.559S.; without gen., Phld.*Ir.*p.63W.

ἀμετρ-ητος, ον, also η, ον Pi.*I.*1.37:—*immeasurable, immense*, πένθος, πόνος, Od.19.512, 23.249; ἅλς Pi. l.c.; ἀήρ Ar.*Nu.*264; ταραχαί Phld.*Herc.*1251.18; *inexhaustible*, στόμα Μούσης *AP*7.75 (Antip.), cf. Pyth.*Sim.*1. Adv. -τως, χρῆσθαι τῇ τιμῇ J.*AJ*11.6.12. 2. *unnumbered, countless*, ἐρετμοί E.*El.*433. 3. *not measured*, πλευρόν Str.2.1.23, cf. 29. **-ί,** Adv. of ἄμετρος, μέτρῳ ὕδωρ πίνοντες, ἀ. δὲ μᾶζαν ἔδοντες Zen.5.19. **-ία,** ἡ, *excess, disproportion*, opp. συμμετρία, Pl.*Ti.*87d, cf. *R.*486d, Heraclit.*All.*8, Alex.Aphr.*Pr.*1. 112, etc. b. *want of moderation*, Arist.*VV*1251ᵇ15. 2. *infinity, countless number*, κακῶν Pl.*Ax.*367a (in pl.). **-ιος,** α, ον, *unreasonable*, οὐκ ἀ. *Inscr.Prien.*113.32.

ἀμετρο-βαθής, ές, *immensely deep*, Opp.*H.*1.85. **-βιος,** ον, *of immensely long life*, ἐλέφαντες Man.1.53; κόρακες prob. l. in Epigr. ap. Philostr.*Her.*19.17. **-δικος,** ον, *breaking bounds of justice*, διχοστασίαι B.10.68. **-επής,** ές, *unbridled of tongue*, Il.2.212, Ph. 1.616. **-επία,** ἡ, *garrulity*, in pl., Gal.18(1).253. **-κᾰκος,** ον, *immeasurably bad*, Eun.*Hist.*p.255D. **-παθής,** ές, *excessive in emotion*, Alcin.*Intr.*30. **-πότης,** ου, ὁ, *drinking to excess*, *AP* 9.644 (Agath.), Zen.5.19.

ἄμετρος, ον, *without* or *beyond measure, immense*, κακόν Simon. 37.16 codd.; opp. μετρητός, Pl.*Lg.*820c. Adv. -τρως Id.*Phd.*86c, etc.: neut. pl. as Adv., Babr.11.10. 2. *immoderate*, in moral sense, Pl.*Lg.*690e, etc. Adv. -τρως X.*Cyr.*1.6.34. 3. *neverceasing*, τέττιγες Simon.174. 4. *disproportionate*, Pl.*Ti.*87e: Sup. -ότατος *most unequal*, Cleom.1.7. II. *without metre, prosaic*, opp. ἔμμετρος, Arist.*Po.*1451ᵇ1, D.H.*Comp.*3, etc. Adv. -τρως *unmetrically*, Critias 4; *not in metre*, Poll.1.19. III. ἄμετρος, = βάτος, Dsc.4.37.

ἀμεύομαι, Dor. = ἀμείβομαι, only fut. and aor. 1, *surpass, outstrip*, ἀμεύσασθ' ἀντίους Pi.*P.*1.45; ἀμεύσεσθε Τίσανδρον Id.*Fr.*23. 2. *pass over*, ὕδατα Euph.119. II. *purchase* (?), *GDI*4964 (Gortyn).

ἀμευσιεπής, ές, *surpassing words*, φροντίς Pi.*Fr.*24.

ἀμεύσιμος, ον, (ἀμεύομαι) *passable*, A.R.4.297.

ἀμευσίπορος, ον, *path-shifting*, τρίοδος Pi.*P.*11.38.

ἄμη, ἡ, *shovel*, Ar.*Av.*1145, *Pax* 426, X.*Cyr.*6.2.34; *hod*, *IG*1.225e, cf. Suid. 2. *water-bucket, pail*, ἄμαις καὶ σκάφαις ἀρύσασθαι, prov. of great abundance, Plu.2.963c. 3. *spade*, *Gp.*2.23.5. 4. Ion. for ἄμης, Silen.ap.Ath.14.644f. 5. *hobble* for young goats, Hsch.

ἀμῆ, Adv., (properly ἀμῇ, dat. fem. of ἀμός = τὶς) *in a certain way*, Hp.ap.Gal.19.78: elsewh. in the phrase ἀμῇ γέ πῃ *somehow or other*, Ar.*Ach.*608, Pl.*Prt.*331d, *R.*474c, etc.

ἀμήκωα· δεινά (Tarent.), Hsch.

ἀμήν, Hebr. Adv. *verily, of a truth, so be it*, Lxx 1*Ch.*16.36; at beginning of sentence, *Ev.Matt.*5.18, al.; doubled, *Ev.Jo.*1.51, al.; τὸ ἀ. 1*Ep.Cor.*14.16.

ἀμήνας· ἐκπιάξας, ἀμύξας, Hp.ap.Gal.19.78.

ἄμηνις, ιος, ὁ, ἡ, = sq., J.*AJ*19.4.6.

ἀμήνῑτος, ον, (μηνίω) *not angry*, Hdt.9.94; βάξις A.*Supp.*975; χειμὼν Ἀχαιῶν οὐκ ἀμήνιτος θεοῖς Id.*Ag.*649. Adv. -τως ib.1036.

ἀμήν-ῡτος, ον, *not denounced*, Hld.8.13, cf. Theognost.*Can.*83. Adv. **-υτί** *unannounced, without warning*, Steph. *in Hp.*1.100 D., al., prob. in A.D.*Adv.*161.8.

ἄμηροι, = ὅμηροι, *EM*83.19, Hsch.; cf. Ἀμάριος. **ἄμηρον·** νέον, *EM*83.18. **ἀμήρυος,** v.l. for sq. ap.Sch.A.R.2.221.

ἀμήρῠτος, ον, *not to be wound up*, i.e. *tedious*, γῆρας A.R.2.221; λόγοι *Com.Adesp.*837; μάθησις Phld.*Herc.*873.8; ἥλιοι Anon.ap. Stob.3.28.21.

ἄμης, ητος, ὁ, kind of *milk cake*, Ar.*Pl.*999, Antiph.89, Men.491, Clearch.65, Ph.1.390. II. kind of *oven*, Dieuch.ap.Orib.4.5.2.

ἀμ-ητήρ [ᾰ, but ᾱ metri gr.], ῆρος, ὁ, (ἀμάω A) *reaper*, Il.11.67, Theoc.7.29: Adj., ἀμητῆρι τύπῳ in form *like a sickle*, Nonn.*D.*26. 302:—fem. **-ήτειρα** *EM*83.2. **-ητήριον,** τό, *sickle*, Max.Tyr.30. 7. **-ητής,** ὁ, *reaper*, Porph.ad Il.19.222. **-ητικός,** ή, όν, *of* or *for reaping*, δρέπανον ἀ. *reaping*-hook, Ael.*HA*17.37.

ἀμητίσκος, ὁ, Dim. of ἄμης, Telecl.1.12, cf. Pherecr.130.7 codd. Ath. **ἄμητος** [ᾰ], ὁ, (ἀμάω A) *reaping, harvesting*, Il.19.223. 2. *harvest, harvest-time*, Hes.*Op.*384, 575, Hdt.2.14, 4.42, Hp.*Epid.*6.8.19, Thphr.*HP*3.4.4, A.R.3.418, etc. II. *crop, harvest gathered in*, or *field when reaped*, D.P.194, Arat.1097: with another Subst., ληΐοιο ἀμήτοιο Opp.*C.*1.527: metaph., of a beard, *AP*11.368 (Jul.). (Gramm. distinguish ἄμητος (I) from ἀμητός (II), the latter being regarded as Adj. (sc. σῖτος), cf. Hdn.Gr.1.220, but Ammon. reverses the distinction.) **ἀμητρίς,** ίδος, ἡ, fem. of ἀμητήρ, dub. l. in Poll.1.122.

ἀμητύς, ύος, ἡ = ἄμητος I, *Hymn.Is.*85.

ἀμήτωρ, ορος, *motherless*, Hdt.4.154, E.*Ion* 109, Id.ap.Phot.p.91R.; of Melchizedek, *Ep.Hebr.*7.3: of the number 7, Hierocl. *in CA*20 p.465M., cf. Ph.1.24; but ἡ μονὰς ἀ. Gal.9.934. II. *that is no mother, unmotherly*, μήτηρ ἀμήτωρ S.*El.*1154; of dam mounted by her foal, Opp.*C.*1.261; *childless*, *Epigr.Gr.*365 (Cotiaeum).

ἀμηχαν-άω, = sq., Opp.*H.*3.328, *AP*9.591, etc., in Ep. forms ἀμηχανόωσιν, -όων. **-έω,** fut. -ήσω Th.7.48: impf. ἠμηχάνουν Pl.Com. 45:—*to be* ἀμήχανος, *to be at a loss for*, or *in want of*, χρήματος οὐδενός Hdt.1.35, cf. A.R.4.692; ἀ. περί τινος *about* thing, E.*IT*734: c. acc., τέρμα A.*Ag.*1177, etc.; ταῦτα E.*Heracl.*492: c. dat., ἀ. θεσφάτοισι A.*Ag.*1113:—freq. foll. by relative clause, ἀ. πότερον.. ἢ.. S.*Ph.* 337; ἀ. ὅπᾳ τράπωμαι, ὅποι τράποιντο, A.*Ag.*1530, *Pers.*458: abs., A. *Supp.*379, S.*El.*1174, E.*Andr.*983, Epicur.*Fr.*203, etc. 2. c. inf., *not to know how* to do, ὅσσαν συμβαλεῖν ἀμηχανῶ Neophr. 1; χρόνος.. ὃν λανθάνειν ἀ. *know not how* to escape, Antiph.254. 3. ἀμηχανῶν βιοτεύειν live *without the necessaries of life*, X.*Cyr.*2.1.19; *to be reduced to great straits*, τὰ μὲν ἀπορεῖν, τὰ δ' ἔτι ἀμηχανήσειν Th.7. 48. 4. *to be at a loss, amazed, perplexed*, ἀ. κιόντων *at* their coming, A.R.4.692; so prob. ἀ. κακότητι 2.410. **-ής,** ές, poet. for ἀμήχανος, *h.Merc.*447, in gen. pl. -έων (but perh. fem. of -ος). **-ητος,** ον, = ἀμήχανος II, X.ap.Suid., f.l. in J.*AJ*1.19.8. **-ία,** Ion. -ίη, ἡ, *want of means* or *resources, helplessness*, ἀμηχανίη δ' ἔχε θυμόν Od.9.295; πενίην μητέρ' ἀμηχανίης Thgn.385, cf. 619 (pl.), Alc.92, Hdt.8.111, etc.; ὑπ' ἀμηχανίας Ar.*Av.*475. II. of things, *hardship, trouble*, χειμῶνος ἀμηχανίη Hes.*Op.*496.

ἀμηχᾰνο-εργός, όν, *unfit for work*, Hes.*Fr.*198. **-ποιέομαι,** *go awkwardly to work*, μηχανοποιέοντα ἀ. Hp.*Fract.*30.

ἀμήχᾰνος, Dor. **ἀμάχανος,** ον, *without means* or *resources, helpless*, Od.19.363; πενία ἀ. B.1.61; πόριμον αὐτῷ τῇ πόλει δ' ἀ. Ar.*Ra.*1429; ἀ. καὶ ἄτεχνος Pl.*Plt.*274c; of animals, opp. εὐμήχανος, Arist.*HA* 614ᵇ34: hence, 2. *incapable, awkward*, ἀφραδέες καὶ ἀ. *h.Ap.* 192, cf. Theoc.1.85; τὸν ἀ. ὀρθοῦν A.*Th.*227; ἀ. γυνή E.*Hipp.*643; ἀ. εἴς τι *awkward at* thing, Id.*Med.*408. Adv., ἀμηχάνως ἔχειν, = ἀμηχανεῖν, A.*Ch.*407, E., etc. 3. c. inf., *at a loss how to* do, *unable to* do, τὸ δὲ βίᾳ πολιτῶν δρᾶν ἔφυν ἀ. S.*Ant.*79; -ώτατος ὅ τι χρὴ λέγειν πορίσασθαι [D.]60.12, etc. II. more freq. in pass. sense, *allowing of no means*: 1. *impracticable, unmanageable*, c. inf., ἀμήχανός ἐσσι πιθέσθαι Il.13.726. b. of things, *hard, impossible*, τοῦτό μ' ἄνωγας ἀμήχανον ἄλλο τελέσσαι ib.14.262; τοῦτο δ' ἀ. εὑρεῖν Pi.*O.*7.25, cf. Hdt.1.48; ὁδὸς ἀ. εἰσελθεῖν road *hard* or *impossible* to enter on, X.*An.*1.2.21; ἀ. ἐστὶ γενέσθαι Emp.12, cf. Hdt. 1.48, 204, S.*Ant.*175, etc.: abs., ἀμήχανα *impossibilities*, ἀμηχάνων ἐρᾶν ib.90, cf. 92; δεινὸς.. εὑρεῖν κἀξ ἀ. πόρον A.*Pr.*59, cf. Ar.*Eq.*759: Sup., Them. *in Ph.*91.12. 2. *against whom* or *which nothing can be done, irresistible*, freq. in Hom. of Zeus, Hera, Achilles; ἀ. ἐσσι, ἀ. ἔπλευ, Il.10.167, 16.29; Ἔρος.. ἀ. ὄρπετον Sapph.40. b. of things, ἀ. ἔργα mischief *without help* or *remedy*, Il.8.130; δόλος Hes.*Th.* 589; κήδεα Archil.66; δύαι A.*Eu.*561 (lyr.); ἄλγος, νόσοι, S.*El.*140 (lyr.), *Ant.*363 (lyr.); συμφορά Simon.5.11, cf. E.*Med.*392; κακόν ib.447: Comp. -ώτερα, ἀγλαΐα Them.*Or.*4.51c. c. esp. of dreams, *inexplicable, not to be interpreted*, Od.19.560. 3. *extraordinary*, *enormous*, ποταμῶν ἀ. μεγέθη Pl.*Phd.*111d ; ἡδοναί Id.*Phlb.*46e ; ἀμήχανον εὐδαιμονίας *an inconceivable amount* of happiness, Id.*Ap.*41c : freq. c. acc., ἀ. τὸ μέγεθος, τὸ κάλλος, τὸ πλῆθος, etc., i.e. *inconceivable* in point of size, etc., Id.*R.*584b, 615a, X.*Cyr.*7.5.38 : c. dat., ἀ. πλήθει τε καὶ ἀτοπίᾳ Pl.*Phdr.*229d (nisi leg. ἀμηχάνων πλήθη τε καὶ ἀτοπίαι, where ἀ. = *monsters*) : abs., *infinitely great*, δύναμις Plot.5.3.16. b. freq. in Pl. with οἷος, ὅσος, ἀμήχανον ὅσον χρόνον *Phd* 95c ; ἀμηχάνῳ ὅσῳ πλέονι by *it is impossible to say* how much more, *R.*588a ; ἀμήχανόν τι οἷον *Chrm.*155d. Adv., ἀμηχάνως ὡς εὖ *R.*527e ; ἀ. γε ὡς σφόδρα *Phdr.*263d.

ἀμηῷος, ον, *with the dawn*, Orph.*A.*484.

ἄμι (ἄμμι Eudem.ap.Gal.14.185), -εως (or -ιος *PTeb.*, v. infr.), τό, *ajowan*, *Carum copticum*, *PTeb.*55.5 (ii B.C.), Plin.*HN*20.163, Dsc. 3.62, etc. 2. ἄ. ἄγριον, = δρακοντία μεγάλη, Ps.-Dsc.2.166.

ἀμία (A), ἡ, kind of *tunny*, which ascends rivers, perh. *bonito*, Sotad.Com.1.26, Archipp.20, Arist.*HA*506^{b}13, *Fr.*308 :—also **ἀμίας**, ου, ὁ, Matro*Conv.*61 :—gender indeterminate, Epich.59, cf. 124, Arist. *HA*488^{a}7, al.

ἀμία (B)· φυλακία, Hsch.

ἀμίαντος, ον, *undefiled, pure*, ὕδωρ Thgn.447 ; φάος Pi.*Fr.*142 ; αἰθήρ B.3.86 ; A.*Pers.*578 calls the sea ἡ ἀμίαντος ; ἀ. τοῦ ἀνοσίου πέρι *free from stain* of ungodliness, Pl.*Lg.*777d ; περὶ τῶν ὁσιωτάτων Epicur.*Nat.*15.34 ; γάμοι οἱ ἀ. *Epigr.Gr.*204.13 (Cnidos), cf. *Ep.Hebr.* 13.4 ; τόπος Lxx 2*Ma.*15.34 ; κληρονομία 1*Ep.Pet.*1.4. 2. *not to be defiled*, D.H.2.75. II. ὁ ἀ. λίθος *asbestos*, Arist.*Fr.*495, Dsc. 5.138, Plin.*HN*36.139.

ἀμίας, ου, ὁ, v. ἀμία (A).

ἀμῐγής, ές, (μίγνυμι) *unmixed, pure*, ἡδοναί Arist.*EN*1173^{a}23 ; ἀ. καὶ καθαρός, of νοῦς, Id.*Metaph.*989^{b}15 ; τὰ ἐλάχιστα καὶ ἀ. πέρατα τῶν μηκῶν, of geometrical points, Epicur.*Ep.*1 p.17 U. : c. gen., εἰλικρινῶς Ἕλληνες καὶ ἀ. βαρβάρων Pl.*Mx.*245d ; ἀ. πρὸς ἄλληλα Id.*Plt.*265e ; ἀ. τινί Aret.*CD*2.3, Jul.*Or.*2.70b. Adv. -γῶς Iamb.*Myst.*1.9, Herm. ap.Stob.1.49.68 ; also -γί Hdn.*Epim.*254. II. *virgin*, Sch.E. *Or.*108. III. ἀ. βίβλοι rolls *containing a single author*, opp. συμμιγεῖς, Tz.*Proll.Ar.*

ἀμιδάναι· κρύψαι, Hsch.

ἀμίδιον, τό, Dim. of ἀμίς, Aeschin.Socr.43, S.E.*M.*1.234.

ἀμιέρα· ἀμμώδη, ἔρημα, Hsch. **ἀμιερεῖ**· δείξει, Id.

ἄμιθα, kind of *cake*, perh. = ἄμης, Anacr.139, *PHamb.*90.18 (iii A.D.).

ἀμίθιος· μωλῶν, Hsch.

ἀμιθρέω, ἀμιθρός, Ep. and Ion. metath. for ἀριθμέω, ἀριθμός, Nicoch.5 D., Call.*Cer.*86, *Fr.*339, Phoen.1.9, Herod.6.6, Simon.228.

ἀμικτίσας· αἰτήσας, χωρισάμενος, Hsch.

ἀμικτομίαινον, = ἄγνος, Ps.-Dsc.1.103.

ἄμικτος, ον, *unmingled, that will not mingle*, Emp.35.8 ; ἄ. βοή cries *that will not blend* or *harmonize*, A.*Ag.*321 ; ὡς ἄμικτον ἀνθρώποις ἐρᾶν λεόντων Babr.98.19. Adv. -τως, Sup. -τότατα Pl.*Phlb.*59c. II. *unmixed, pure*, βίος, ἡδονή, ib.50e, 61b :—ἀ. τινι *unmixed with* a thing, Id.*Plt.*310d ; ἄμικτα κατὰ στίχον, of poems, *uniform* in metre e.g. of the Epic hexameter, Heph.*Poëm.*2. III. of persons, *not mingling with others, unsociable, savage*, of Centaurs and Cyclopes, S.*Tr.*1095, E.*Cyc.*429 ; δράκαινα Anaxil.223 ; τὸ ἄ., = ἀμιξία II, Hp. *Aër.*23 ; ἄ. πατήρ *morose*, E.*Fr.*500 ; φίλοις ἄ. καὶ πάσῃ πόλει ib.425 ; of laws and customs, ἄ. νόμιμα τοῖς ἄλλοις Th.1.77 ; πρὸς ἀλλήλω Pl. *Sph.*254d ; ἄ. τινα ἑαυτοῖς καταστῆσαι *refuse to admit* him *to* their *society*, D.25.63. b. *not mixing the breed*, Pl.*Plt.*276a ; ἄ. θυραίῳ ἀνδρὸς *not having intercourse with*.., Phint.ap.Stob.4.23.61. 2. of places, *uncivilized*, ἄ. αἶα *inhospitable* land, E.*IT*402 ; τόπος Isoc. 9.67. (Better written ἄμεικτος.)

ἅμιλλα, ης, ἡ, *contest for superiority, conflict*, τῶν νεῶν ἅμιλλαν.. ἰδέσθαι Hdt.7.44 ; ἅ. ἵππων *horse-race*, ib.196, cf. Pi.*O.*5.6, *I.*5(4).6 ; ῥιμφαρμάτοις ἁμίλλαις *in racing* of swift chariots, S.*OC*1063, cf. *El.* 861 ; ἅ. ἀγαθῶν ἀνδρῶν *contest* of brave men, D.20.108 ; μειρακίων Ar. *Eq.*556 ; χορῶν Pl.*Lg.*834e ; of boat-*races*, *IG*2^{2}.1028.20, Pl.Com. 183. 2. c. gen. rei, ἰσχύος *trial* of strength, Pi.*N.*9.12 (pl.) ; πτερύγων ἁμίλλαις A.*Pr.*129 ; ποδοῖν, λόγων, φρονήματος, E.*IA*212, *Med.* 546, *Andr.*214 ; ἀρετῆς Pl.*Lg.*731b : c. gen. obj., ἅ. λέκτρων *contest for* marriage, E.*Hipp.*1141 ; ἔρωτος Gorg.*Hel.*5 : abs., *eager desire*, Herod.6.68 (s.v.l.) :—also ἅ. περί τινος Isoc.10.15 ; freq. in Poets with Adj., ἅ. φιλόπλουτος, πολύτεκνος *striving after* wealth or children, E. *IT*411, *Med.*557 : with gen. in adjectival sense, ἅ. αἵματος, = αἱματόεσσα, Id.*Hel.*1155 :—phrases : ἅμιλλαν τιθέναι, προτιθέναι propose *contest*, Id.*Andr.*1020, *Med.* l.c. ; ἅ. ποιεῖσθαι *contend* eagerly, ὅκως.. Hdt.8.10 ; ἅ. ἐποιοῦντο they had a *race*, Th.6.32 ; ἅ. ποιεῖσθαι πρὸς ἀλλήλους Pl.*Lg.*830d ; εἰς ἅ. ἔρχεσθαι, ἐξελθεῖν, E.*Tr.*621, *Hec.*226 ; πρὸς ἅ. ἐλθεῖν Id.*Med.*1083 ; ἅ. γίγνεται ὅπως..*struggle* arises, Th.8.6.

ἀμίλλακαν· οἶνον (Theban), Hsch.

ἁμιλλ-άομαι : fut. -ήσομαι Ar.*Pax*950, Pl.*R.*349c : aor. ἡμιλλήθην E. (v. infr.), Th.6.31 ; later ἡμιλλησάμην Plu.*Arat.*3, Luc.*Par.*51, Aristid.1.127, 149 J., etc. : pf. ἡμίλλημαι E. (v. infr. II. 1) :—*compete, vie, contend*, Ar. l.c., etc. ; πρὸς ἀλλήλους Th. l.c. : c. dat. pers., Hdt.4. 71, E.*Andr.*127, etc. ; πρός τινα Id.*HF*960 : c. dat. rei, *contend in* or *with* a thing, ἁμιλληθεὶς λόγῳ Id.*Supp.*195, cf. *HF*1255 ; βίᾳ *Hipp.*426 ; ἵπποις, τόξοις, etc., And.4.27, Pl.*R.*328a, cf. *Lg.*834a ; περί τινος *about* or *for* a thing, Luc.*Charid.*20 ; περί τινι Pi.*N.*10.31 ; ἐπί or πρός τι, Pl.*Lg.*830e, 968b ; ὑπέρ τινος Plb.5.86.8 : ἁ. ὡς..or ὅπως.., Pl.*R.* 349c, X.*HG*7.2.14 : c. acc. cogn., ἁ. στάδιον Pl.*Lg.*833a. 2. in pass. sense, πόλλ' ἁμιλληθέντα *made subjects of contest*, E.*Fr.*812. 2. II. without idea of rivalry, *strive, hasten eagerly*, ἐπὶ τὸ ἄκρον X.*An.*3.4.44 ; πρός τι to obtain a thing, Pl.*R.*490a, Arist.*EN*1162^{b}8, al. ; δεῦρ' ἁμιλλᾶται ποδί E.*Or.*456 ; σὲ τὴν ὄρεγμα δεινὸν ἡμιλλημένην Id.*Hel.*546 : metaph., c. acc. cogn., ποῖον ἁμιλλαθῶ γόον ; how shall I groan loud enough? ib.165 ; τόνδ' ἁμιλλῶμαι λόγον *Hec.*271. III. Hsch. has Act., ἁμιλλᾶν· ἐρίζειν, καὶ εἰς τάχος γράφειν. -**ημα**, ατος, τό, *conflict, struggle*, S.*El.*493 ; καθ' ἁμιλλάματα πρᾶτος *CIG* 5149*b* (Cyrene). -**ητέον**, *one must vie*, πρός τι Isoc.7.73 ; Socr.*Ep.* 31 ; τινί Isoc.*Ep.*7.7. -**ητήρ**, ῆρος, *racing*, τρόχους ἁμιλλητῆρας ἡλίου S.*Ant.*1065. -**ητήριος**, α, ον, *of contest*, ἵππος Philostr.*VA* 2.11, *Gym.*26 ; ἅρμα Aristid.*Or.*37(2).15 ; ἀγῶνες Men.Prot.p.1 D. :— τὸ ἁ. *place of contest*, Suid. -**ητικός**, ή, όν, *of* or *for contest*, Pl.*Sph.* 225a.

ἅμιλλος, ὁ, = ἅμιλλα, Doroth.ap.Phot.p.92 R. **ἁμιλλοφόρος**, Ar.*Fr.*42 D., perh. f.l. for -ότερος (cf. **ἀμιλλότεροι**· ἐπὶ πλέον ἐρίζοντες, Hsch.) ; sed potius leg. ἁμαλλοφόρος.

ἀμίλλυκα· δρέπανον (Elean), Hsch.

ἀμίλτωτος, ον, *not painted red*, λύχνος *PMag.Par.*1.2372, *PMag. Berol.*1.377, etc.

ἀμῑμητόβιοι, οἱ, *the 'Inimitables'*, name of club, Plu.*Ant.*28.

ἀμίμητος [ῑ], ον, *inimitable*, χάριτες *AP*5.107 (Crin.) ; τινί *in* thing, Plu.*Per.*13, etc. Adv. -τως, *of inferior imitation*, opp. μιμητικῶς, Arist.*Po.*1460^{b}32 ; *superlatively*, Plu.*Nic.*1. II. *not imitated*, Id.2.53d.

ἀμιναῖος or **ἀμμιναῖος** οἶνος, an Italian wine, Dsc.5.19, *Gp.*4.1.3 ; made from the grape of that name, Gal.12.922 :—hence **ἀμμινίζοντες** οἶνοι *Gp.*8.22.1.

ἀμῖξαι· οὐρῆσαι ἢ ἠχῆσαι ἢ ὀμίξαι, Hsch., *EM*83.36.

ἀμιξία, Ion. -ίη, ἡ, *a being* ἄμικτος, and so, I. *purity*, Thphr. *CP*4.16.2. II. of persons, *want of intercourse*, ἀλλήλων Th. 1.3 ; πρὸς ἅπαντας Luc.*Tim.*42 ; *unsociableness*, Isoc.6.67 ; ἀμιξίῃ χρημάτων *want of* commercial *dealings*, Hdt.2.136 ; cf. ἀμειξία. 2. *abstinence from sexual intercourse*, Aristaenet.2.3.

ἄμιξος, ον, = ἄμικτος, πυρὸς *PLond.*2.256(a)11.

ἄμιππος, ον, *keeping up with horses*, i.e. *fleet as horse*, S.*Ant.* 985 (lyr.). II. ἅμιπποι, οἱ, *infantry mixed with cavalry*, Th.5. 57, X.*HG*7.5.23 (cj.), Arist.*Ath.*49.1, cf. Aristarch.ad Hdt.1.215 in *PAmh.*2.12. 2. *pair of horses* ridden by a postillion, Suid.

ἀμίς, ίδος, ἡ, *chamber-pot*, Hp.*Loc.Hom.*47, Ar.*V.*935, *Th.*633, etc., f.l. in A.*Supp.*842 ; prov., σιτία εἰς ἀμίδα μὴ ἐμβάλλειν 'cast not pearls before swine', Plu.2.12f ; ἐς τὴν ἀμίδα ἐνουρεῖν 'to be suitably treated' (in contempt), Luc.*Merc.Cond.*4. (ἀμ- Ar.*Fr.*41 D.)

ἀμίσαλλος, ον, *unsociable*, expl. as = ἀμίσγαλλος, γέροντες Epic. ap.*Et.Gen.*

ἀμίσαρος· ἀκόρεστος, Hsch.

ἀμισγής, ές, poet. for ἀμιγής, Nic.*Al.*195.

ἀμῑσής, ές, *not hateful, agreeable*, Ph.2.70, Plu.2.10a : Comp. -έστερος *less troublesome*, X.*Eq.*8.9. Adv. -σῶς Ph.2.57.

ἀμισθ-ί, Adv. of ἄμισθος, *without reward* or *hire*, Archil.41, E.*Tr.* 409, D.24.99 ; *rent-free*, *SIG*344 (Teos) ; χρημάτων καὶ δόξης ἀ. *without reward* of money or honour, Plu.*Arist.*3 ; ἀ. ἐπαινεθέντες *only paid with* praise, Brut.*Ep.*38 ; ἀ. θεάσασθαι *without paying*, Plu.*CG* 12. [ῐ Archil. l.c.] -**ία**, ἡ, *non-receipt of pay*, App.*Hann.*17 ; of *free teaching*, Olymp.*in Alc.*p.140 C. -**ος**, ον, *without hire* or *pay*, opp. ἔμμισθος : hence, 1. Pass., *unpaid, unhired*, ἀοιδή A. *Ag.*979, cf. S.*Fr.*829, etc. ; λύπη, ἄ. ξυνέμπορος A.*Ch.*733. Adv. -θως, Cret. -τως *GDI*5125 (Oaxos). 2. Act., *without paying*, Luc.*DMeretr.*12.1. -**ωτος**, ον, *not let, bringing no return*, οἶκος D. 30.6, cf. *BCH*35.14 (Delos). II. *unhired*, D.S.18.21.

ἀμιστύλλευτος, ον, = sq., metaph., θεοί Dam.*Pr.*182 ; **κραδίη** Procl. *H.*7.11.

ἀμίστυλλος, ον, *not cut into small pieces*, Call.*Aet.Fr.*7.35 P.

ἄμισχος, ον, *without stalk*, Thphr.*HP*1.10.7, 3.7.5.

ἄμιτρα· μικρά (Cret.), Hsch.

ἄμιτρος, ον, *without head-band* or *girdle*, παῖδες ἄ. girls *who have not yet put on the woman's girdle*, i.e. *unmarriageable*, Call.*Dian.*14.

ἀμιτροχίτωνες, οἱ, *wearing no* μίτρη (q.v.) *with the* χιτών, epith. of Lycian warriors, Il.16.419 ; of women, Nonn.*D.*48.507.

ἀμίτρωτος, ον, *not bound with a head-band*, Nonn.*D.*35.220.

ἀμιχθαλόεις, εσσα, εν, = ἄμικτος III, *inhospitable*, epith. of Lemnos in Il.24.753, *h.Ap.*36 : otherwise expl. as *smoky*, from the volcano Mosychlos, cf. ὀμίχλη. (Cypr. acc. to Sch. Il. l.c.)

ἀμμ-, poet. for ἀναμ-, e.g. **ἄμμιγα, ἀμμίγνυμι**, = ἀναμ-, Tim. *Pers.*37, B.*Fr.*16, etc.

ἅμμα, ατος, τό, (ἅπτω) *anything tied* or *made to tie* : hence, 1. *knot*, Hp.*Fist.*4 ; ἅ. λύειν, ἀπάπτειν Hdt.4.98 ; ἅ. ποιεῖσθαι X.*Eq.* 5.1. 2. *noose, halter*, E.*Hipp.*781. 3. *cord*, Id.*Ba.*696, cf. Hp.*Steril.*244, etc. ; ἅ. παρθενίας maiden *girdle*, *AP*7.182 (Mel.), cf. 164 (Antip.), imitated in *Epigr.Gr.*248.8 (Philomelium). 4. *link* of chain, Them.*Or.*2.32d. 5. in pl., *clinches* in wrestling, Gal. 6.143, cf. Plu.*Fab.*23 ; of the *wrestler's arms*, Id.*Alc.*2. 6. *measure of length* (like our *chain*), = 40 πήχεις, Hero *Geom.*23.14, al., *POxy.*669 (iii A.D.). II. *that which kindles*, Ph.2.504.

ἀμμά, ἡ, *mother*, *EM*84.24 ; *foster-mother, nurse*, *SIG*^{2}868 (Calymna) :—also **ἀμμάς**, ἡ, *EM*84.26, *BGU*449 (iii A.D.) ; epith. of Rhea and Demeter, Hsch.

ἀμμαλλῆς· ἀνοστία, Hsch. **'Αμμαλῶ**· ἑορτὴ ἀγομένη Διί, Id. **ἀμμαμηθάδης**, = ἀμαμινθάδες (q.v.), Id. **ἀμμάξαι**· αἰωρῆσαι καὶ κρεμάσαι, ἢ ἀποπηδῆξαι, Id.

ἀμματ-ίζω, (ἅμμα) *tie, bind*, in Pass., Orib.49.21.4 (prob. Heliod.),

Heliod.ib.48.28.4, Apollod.*Poliorc.*180.13. **-ιον**, τό, Dim. of ἅμμα 1.1, Gal.14.794. **-ισμός**, ὁ, *tieing, knotting*, Heliod.ap.Orib. 48.43.1, cf. 48.28.5.

ἀμμεδαπάν· τὴν ἐγχώριον, Hsch.

ἀμμεμίξεται, ἀμμένω, poet. for ἀναμεμίξεται, ἀναμένω. **ἄμμες**, Aeol. and Ep. for ἡμεῖς: acc. ἄμμε: gen. ἀμμέων: dat. ἄμμι(ν) Hom., etc.; ἄμμεσιν, Alc.100. **ἀμμέσον**, poet. for ἀνὰ μέσον, Hes. **ἀμμέτερος** and **ἄμμος**, = ἡμέτερος, Alc.105 A, B.

ἄμμι, v. ἄμι. II. v. ἄμμες.

ἀμμία, Ion. -ίη, ἡ, *mother* or *nurse*, Herod.1.7, *EM*84.26.

ἀμμιάξαι· ἀποπνίξαι, Hsch.

ἄμμινος, η, ον, = ψάμμινος, *sandy*, νῆσοι *Peripl.M.Rubr.*4.

ἀμμιρός· πεπληρωμένος, Hsch. **ἀμμισκόμιστον**· συγκομιστὸν ἄρτον, Id. **ἀμμίτης** (sc. λίθος), ὁ, also **ἀμμῖτις**, ἡ, *sandstone*, Plin. *HN*37.168.

ἀμμο-βάτης, ὁ, = ἀμμοδύτης, Ael.*NA*6.51. **-γειος**, α, ον, *in sandy soil*, ἀγκυροβόλια *Peripl.M.Rubr.*24. **-δρομος**, ὁ, *sandy place for racing*, *AB*208. **-δύτης**, ὁ, *sand-burrower*, a kind of *serpent*, Philum.*Ven.*22.1.; διψάς Str.17.1.21. **-δύτωρ**, ορος, (prob. for -δυόνας codd.) *burrowing in sand*, πάγουρος *AP*6.196 (Stat. Flacc.). [ῠ, but cf. χηραμοδύτης, σισυρνοδύτης.] **-κονία**, ἡ, *sand mixed with lime, cement*, Str.5.4.6, cf. *Gp.*2.27.4. **-κοπρηγὸν** πλοῖον ship *carrying sand and manure*, *Sammelb.*423. **-νιτρον**, τό, *potash mixed with sand*, fused together to produce glass, Plin.*HN*36.194. **-πλῠσία**, ἡ, *sand-washing* for gold, Zos.Alch. p.240 B. **-πλυτα**, τά, *results of such washing*, Anon.Alch.p.37 B.

ἀμμορία (A), Ion. -ίη, ἡ, poet. for ἀμορία (not in use), Ζεὺς οἶδε μοῖράν τ' ἀμμορίην τ' ἀνθρώπων what is man's fate and *what is not*, or their good fortune and their *bad*, Od.20.76, cf. *AP*9.284 (Crin.).

ἀμμορία (B), Ion. -ίη, ἡ, = ὁμορία, Epigr.ap.D.7.40.

ἄμμορος, ον, poet. for ἄμοιρος (q. v.), *without share of, without lot in*, c. gen., ἄμμορος.. λοετρῶν Ὠκεανοῖο Il.18.489, Od.5.275; καλῶν Pi.*O.*1.84; τέκνων S.*Ph.*182 (lyr.); τέκνων ἄ. *bereft of* children, E. *Hec.*421; οὐκ ἄ. ἀμφὶ πάλᾳ κυναγέτας Pi.*N.*6.14; ἄ. ἐσθλῆς ἐλπίδος *IG* 14.1942.11. 2. later, simply, *free from, without*, ἄ. κακότητος Q.S.1.430. II. abs., *ill-fated*, Il.6.408, 24.773. (ἀ- priv., *smor-*, cf. κάσμορος.)

ἄμμος (A), or **ἄμμος** (cf. ὕφ-αμμος), ἡ, *sand*, Pl.*Phd.*110a, etc. II. *sandy ground, racecourse*, X.*Mem.*3.3.6. (Related to ἄμαθος as ψάμμος to ψάμαθος.)

ἄμμος (B), Aeol. = ἀμός (A), q. v.

ἀμμο-σκοπία, ἡ, *divination by sand*, title of Orphic work, prob. in Suid. s. v. Ὀρφεύς. **-τροφος**, ον, *growing in sand*, *AP*4.1.20 (Mel.).

Ἀμμούς, epith. of Zeus, Arist.*Fr.*530.

ἀμμο-φᾰνής, ές, *sandy*, χθών *Epigr.Gr.*430 (Egypt). **-χρῦσος**, ὁ, gem resembling *sand veined with gold*, Plin.*HN*37.188. **-χωσία**, ἡ, *sand-bath*, Herod.Med.ap.Orib.10.8 tit., Antyll.ap.Aët.3.9. **-χωστος**, ον, *sanded up* or *over*, Eust.690.5.

ἀμμωδέω, suggested as error for αἱμωδέω, Hermog.*Meth.*3.

ἀμμώδης, ες, *sandy, gravelly*, Arist.*HA*547^b^14, 569^a^29, Thphr. *CP*2.4.1, D.S.17.50, etc.; οὖρον Hp.*Coac.*478.

Ἄμμων, ωνος, ὁ, the Libyan *Zeus*, Ζεὺς Ἄ. Pi.*P.*4.16: said to be Egyptian, Hdt.2.42; Ἄμμωνος (κέρας), = κορωνόπους, Ps.-Dsc.2.130, etc.:—fem. Adj. **Ἀμμωνίς**, ίδος, *Libyan*, Ἀ. ἕδρα seat *of Ammon*, i. e. Libya, E.*Alc.*114, *El.*734: Subst. Ἀ., ἡ, name of state-trireme, Din.*Fr.*14.2:—also **Ἀμμωνιάς**, άδος, Phot. s. v. Πάραλος: **Ἀμμωνιακός**, ή, όν, ἀπάτη *AP*7.687 (Pall.), esp. Ἀ. ἅλας kind of *rock-salt*, Dinon15, cf. Dsc.5.109, *Gp.*6.6.1, *PMag.Lond.*46.397:—**-κή**, ἡ, *Ferula marmarica*, Ps.-Dsc.3.84:—**-κόν**, τό, *gum-ammoniacum*, Dsc.3.48.

ἀμμωχεῖν· ἀργεῖν, Hsch.

ἄμνᾱμος, ὁ, *descendant*, Lyc.144, 872, etc.:—also **ἀμνάμων** (A), ονος, ὁ, Poll.3.19, cf. *EM*84.43.

ἀμνάμων (B), Dor. for ἀμνήμων.

ἀμνάς, άδος, ἡ, fem. of ἀμνός, *lamb*, Lxx *Ge.*21.28, al., J.*AJ*7.7.3.

ἀμνάσει, ἀμνάσειε, Dor. for ἀναμνήσ-. **ἀμναστέω, ἄμναστος**, Dor. for ἀμνηστ-.

ἀμνεῖος, α, ον, *of lamb*, ἀ. χλαῖνα *lambskin* cloak, Theoc.24.62:—also **ἀμναῖος**, *PRev.Laws*97.7 (iii B. C.). II. **ἀμνειός** or **ἄμνιος** (sc. χιτών, ὑμήν), ὁ, *inner membrane* surrounding the foetus, Sor.1.58, Gal.*UP*15.4: also in neut. form **ἀμνεῖον**, τό, *Hippiatr.*14; cf. ἀμνίον. **ἀμνεύς**, έως, ὁ, *south-east wind*, Arist.*Vent.*973^b^7.

ἀμνή, Dor. **ἀμνά**, ἡ, fem. of ἀμνός, *ewe-lamb*, *GDI*3639 (Cos), 4990.11 (Gortyn), Orph.*A.*319.

ἀμνημόνευτος, ον, *unmentioned*, Plb.2.35.4, Plu.*Cam.*29; τὸ μετὰ τὴν ζωὴν ἀ. Phld.*Mort.*36; *impossible to be remembered*, Gal.8.856; ἐξ ἀ. χρόνου *POxy.*1915 (vi A. D.); *unheeded*, E.*IT*1419. II. Act., = ἀμνήμων, *unmindful*, D.L.1.86, Numen.ap.Eus.*PE*14.7.

ἀμνημονέω, A.*Eu.*24, etc.: fut. -ήσω Isoc.12.253: aor. ἠμνημόνησα Id.5.72, X.*Smp.*8.1, etc.:—*to be unmindful*, abs., A. l. c., E.*Or.*216: c. acc., *forget*, D.6.12, 7.19, Aeschin.3.221: also c. gen., D.18.285: freq. in sense, *make no mention of*, E.*IT*361, Th.3.40, Lys.31.25; ἀ. τι περί τινος Th.5.18; Pass., Max.Tyr.8.5:—dependent clauses either in partic., ἀμνημονεῖς σαυτὸν δρῶντα; *do you forget* your doing? Pl. *Tht.*207d; or in relative clause with ὅτι.., Id.*R.*474d. **ἀμνημοσύνη**, ἡ, *forgetfulness*, E.*Ion*1100 (lyr.).

ἀμνημοῦντες· ἀθυμοῦντες, Phot.p.93 R. (-ύονες Hsch.).

ἀμνήμων, Dor. **ἀμνάμων**, ον, gen. ονος, *unmindful, forgetful*, Pi.*I.*7(6).17, S.*Fr.*920, Pl.*Ti.*88b; τινός *of* a person or thing, θεῶν A.*Th.* 606, cf. E.*HF*1397, Antipho 2.1.7; *unmindful of kindness, ungrateful*, Arist.*EN*1167^b^27. 2. Pass., *forgotten, not mentioned*, E.*Ph.* 64. II. Ἀμνήμονες, οἱ, council of 60 at Cnidus, Plu.2.292a.

ἀμνησία, ἡ, = λήθη, *forgetfulness*, Lxx *Wi.*14.26, *Si.*11.25. 2. *decree of amnesty*, *POxy.*1668.18 (iii A. D.).

ἀμνησι-κᾰκέω, *forgive and forget, bestow amnesty on*, τινός Nic. Dam.*Vit.Caes.*29:—Pass., *enjoy an amnesty*, D.S.18.56. **-κάκητος**, ον, *not maliciously remembered*, ἀμνησικάκητον ποιεῖσθαι τὴν ἁμαρτίαν Plb.39.7.5. **-κᾰκία**, ἡ, *forgivingness*, Lxx 3*Ma.*3.21. **-κᾰκος**, ον, *forgiving*, Nic.Dam.p.110 D. Adv. -κως D.S.31.8.

ἀμνήστευτος, ἡ, *unwooed*; *not sought in lawful wedlock* (but as concubine), E.*Fr.*815: neut. pl. as Adv., *without honourable wooing*, Ps.-Phoc.198.

ἀμνηστ-έω, Dor. **ἀμναστέω**, = ἀμνημονέω, only pres., *to be unmindful, forget*, S.*El.*482 (lyr.), Arat.847:—Pass., *to be forgotten*, Th.1.20. **-ία**, Ion. -ίη, ἡ, *forgetfulness*, εἶναι ἐν ἀ. Pl.*Mx.*239e; ἀ. ἔχειν τινός Heraclit.*Ep.*2, cf. Lxx *Wi.*19.4, Plu.2.612d, etc. 2. esp. *amnesty*, τῶν προγεγενημένων ἐγκλημάτων *SIG*633.36 (Milet., ii B. C.), cf. Str.7.2.1, Nic.Dam.*Vit.Caes.*28, Ph.2.75, Plu.*Cic.*42, *Ant.*14. II. *failure to mention* thing, *passing* it *over* Corn.*Rh.* p.371 H. **-ος**, ον, *forgotten*, Theoc.16.42, Lyc.1230. 2. Act., *forgetful*, Phryn.*PS*p.20 B.

Ἀμνιάς, ἡ, epith. of Eileithyia, Ruf.*Onom.*229; cf. sq.

ἀμνίον (not so well ἄμνιον), τό, *bowl in which the blood of victims was caught*, Od.3.444. 2. *inner membrane round the foetus*, Emp.71; cf. ἀμνειός. II. Dim. of ἀμνός, Hermipp.3 (Ἄμνιος as pr. n. wrongly *Et.Gen.*).

ἀμνίς, ίδος, ἡ, = ἀμνή, Theoc.5.3.

ἀμνόα· πρόβατον, οἱ δὲ ἀμνός, Hsch.

ἀμνο-κόπος· ποιμήν, Hsch. **-κῶν**, ὁ, (κοέω) *sheep-minded*, i. e. *simpleton*, Ar.*Eq.*264.

ἀμνός, ὁ, *lamb*, S.*Fr.*751, Ar.*Av.*1559; ἀμνοὶ τοὺς τρόπους *lambs* in temper, Id.*Pax*935: metaph., ὁ ἀ. τοῦ θεοῦ *Ev.Jo.*1.36: fem. (cf. ἀμνή, ἀμνίς), Theoc.5.144, 149, *AP*5.205.—Oblique cases usu. formed from ἀρήν, q. v. (For ἀβνός, i. e. *ag^u^nos*, cf. Lat. *agnus*.)

ἀμνοφόρος, ον, f. l. for μαννοφόρος, Theoc.11.41.

ἀμογ-ητί, Adv. of sq., *without toil* or *effort*, Il.11.637, Call.*Dian.* 25, D.H.*Dem.*8, Luc.*Nav.*21, Plot.6.2.21, etc. **-ητος**, ον, (μογέω) *untiring*, *h.Hom.*8.3. **-ῳ**· ἀκοπιάστῳ, Hsch.

ἀμόθεν, Ion. **ἀμόθεν**, Adv.: (ἀμός):—*from some place or other*, τῶν ἀμόθεν γε, θεά,.. εἰπὲ καὶ ἡμῖν Od.1.10; ἀ. γέ ποθεν *from some quarter or other*, Pl.*Grg.*492d, *Lg.*798b; ἀ. alone, Opp.*C.*1.401.

ἀμόθι (cf. ἅμα), *together, in common*, Decr.Laced.ap.Th.5.77 (codd. ἀμοθεί, expl. by Hdn.Gr.2.464 as *without strife*, cf. μόθος).

ἀμοῖ, Adv., (ἀμός B) *somewhither*, ἀμοιγέποι *AB*204.

ἀμοιβ-άδιος, α, ον, = ἀμοιβαῖος, Opp.*C.*4.349, Q.S.5.65, *AP*12.238 (Strat.). **-ᾰδίς**, Adv., (ἀμοιβή) *by turns, alternately*, ἀ. ἄλλοθεν ἄλλος one after another, Theoc.1.34; ἀ. ἀνέρος ἀνὴρ ἑζόμενος A.R.4.199, cf. Nonn.*D.*24.227:—also **-αδόν**, Parm.1.19, A.R.2.1226, Ti. Locr.68e, Them.*Or.*17.215b, Agath.2.21. II. *in turn, again*, *Epigr.Gr.*998.9. **-άζω**, *exchange*, τὰς ἐμπορίας Men.Prot. p.22 D. **-αῖος**, ον, also α, ον, *giving like for like, retributive*, δεῖπνα Pi.*O.*1.39; *retributive*, νέμεσις, φόνος, *AP*10.123 (Aesop.), Opp.*C.*2.485. Adv. -ως *alternately*, Luc.*Am.*9. II. *interchanging, reciprocal*, Emp.30.3; ἀ. βιβλία *interchanged* letters, Hdt.6.4; ἀ. χάρις *exchange of* favours, A.R.3.82 (but ἀ. εὐνή *ambiguous* (half-human, half-animal), 2.1241):—τὰ ἀ. *dialogue* in Trag., Pl.*R.*394b; of the responsion of choric odes, Plu.*Pomp.*48; ἀ. ἀοιδά Theoc.8.31, cf. Il. 1.604; *answering as in dialogue*, Sch.Ar.*Pl.*253, 487. **-άς**, άδος, ἡ, pecul. fem. of foreg., χλαῖναν.. ἥ οἱ παρεκέσκετ' ἀμοιβάς which lay beside him *as change of raiment*, Od.14.521; *in succession*, μάχαιρα Nonn.*D.*28.135. **-εύς**, έως, ὁ, *exchanger*, γηπέδων Lyc. 617. **-ή**, ἡ, (ἀμείβω) *requital, recompense*, Hom. only in Od.; σοὶ δ' ἄξιον ἔστιν ἀμοιβῆς Od.1.318; ἄλλοισι δίδου χαρίεσσαν ἀ... ἑκατόμβης 3.58; εὖ ἔρδοντι κακὴν ἀπέδωκας ἀ. Thgn.1263, cf. E.*Or.* 467; γλυκεῖαν μόχθων ἀ. Pi.*N.*5.48; ἀγαναῖς ἀ. τινὰ τίνεσθαι to requite him *by like return*, Id.*P.*2.24; χαρίεσσα ἀμοιϝά *GDI*3119c (Corinth); οἵας ἀ. ἐξ Ἰάσονος κυρεῖ E.*Med.*23; ἀμοιβαὶ τῶν θυσιῶν Pl.*Smp.*202e; *retribution*, ἔργων ἀντ' ἀδίκων χαλεπὴν ἐπέθηκεν ἀ. Hes.*Op.*334: pl., αἰωνίαις ἀ. βασανισθησόμενοι Phld.*D.*1.19. 2. *repayment, compensation*, τείσουσι βοῶν ἐπιεικέ' ἀ. Od.12.382. 3. *that which is given in exchange*, τῷ σκυτοτόμῳ ἀντὶ τῶν ὑποδημάτων ἀ. γίνεται κατ' ἀξίαν Arist.*EN*1163^b^35; τὴν ἀ. ποιητέον κατὰ τὴν προαίρεσιν 1164^b^1; δέκα μνῶν ἀ. Plu.*Lyc.*9. 4. *answer*, ἀσχήμων ἐν τῇ ἀ. Hdt.7.160. II. *change, exchange*, τὰς ἀ. ποιεῖσθαι Str.11.4.4; of money, Plu.*Luc.*2. III. *change, alternation*, κακῶν E.*El.*1147; ἑορτῶν Pl.*Lg.*653d. 2. *transformation*, D.L.9.8. **-ήδην**, A.R.2.1071, Orph.*L.*691. **-ηδίς**, Adv., (ἀμοιβή) *alternately, in succession*, Il.18.506, Od.18.310, *h.Cer.*326. **-ηδόν**, Hp.*Ep.*17; read by Aristarch. in Il.18.506. **-ιμαῖος**, α, ον, in neut. sg., *requital, reward*, *IGRom.*4.1348 (Lydia). **-ός**, ὁ, *one who exchanges*, ἀμοιβοί *soldiers that relieve others*, Il.13.793. II. Adj. *in requital* or *exchange for*, νέκυν νεκρῶν ἀ. ἀντιδοὺς S.*Ant.*1067; ἀ. ἑῆς θρέψε διδασκαλίης *AP*7.341 (Procl.). 2. *alternating*, κληῖδες, of Day and Night, Parm.1.14.

ἀμοιμός, = ἀμοιβός, Theognost.*Can.*65.2.

ἄμοινα, ἡ, dub. sens., *IG*5(2).4.22 (Tegea, iv B. C.).

ἄμοιος· κακός (Sicel), Hsch.; cf. σμοῖος.

ἀμοιρ-έω, *have no lot* or *share in*, ὑγροῦ *Placit.*1.3.1, cf. Phld.*Rh.*1.

45 S., Ph.2.9, Plu.*Alex*.23, etc.; *get no benefit from*, c. gen., Jul.Laod. in *Cat.Cod.Astr*.4.104: also in Pass., c. gen., Steph. *in Hp*.1.222 D. **–ημα**, τό, *loss*, *want*, Hsch. (cod. ἀμύρ–). **–ία**, ἡ, = foreg., Ael.*NA*6.65. **–ος**, ον, (cf. ἄμμορος) *without lot* or *share in* thing, τινός A.*Th*.733, *Eu*.353, etc.; mostly of those *bereft of* some good, τῶν καλῶν καὶ ἀγαθῶν ἄ. Pl.*Smp*.202d; τῆς τοῦ θείου συνουσίας Id.*Phd*. 83e; τῆς ἀρετῆς Arist.*EN*$1102^{b}12$:—rarely, *freed from* some evil, ἄ. ὕβρεως, μεταβολῆς, Pl.*Smp*.181c, *Plt*.269e; τοῦ γήρως Isoc.9.71. 2. abs., *portionless*, E.*Ph*.610, Pl.*Smp*.197d:—of things, ἄχωρα καὶ ἄ. *Tab. Defix*.96.18, 97.30. 3. *exempt from fate*, *Trag.Adesp*.248. II. c. gen. pers., τῶν κάτωθεν θεῶν *having no portion with* them, S.*Ant*. 1071.

ἀμοίχευτος, ον, *not born in adultery*, παῖδες Ps.-Callisth.1.21 (cod. Leid.).

ἀμολγ-άδες βόες, *milch-kine*, S.*Ichn*.5. **–άζει**· μεσημβρίζει, Hsch. **–αῖος**, α, ον, (ἀμέλγω) *made with milk*, μᾶζα ἀ. Hes.*Op*. 590; also expl. as = ἀκμαία (from ἀμολγός, Achaean for ἀκμή), bread *of the best flour*, Ath.3.115a, cf. Eust.1018.21. 2. *full of milk*, μαστός *AP*7.657 (Leon.). **–εύς**, έως, ὁ, *milk-pail*, Theoc.8.87, *AP*9.224 (Crin.). **–ή**, ἡ, *milking*, Hdn.Gr.1.310: but **ἀμόλγη**, ἡ, = ἀμόργη, *Gloss*. **–ιον**, τό, *milk-pail*, Theoc.25.106; also ἀμολγαῖον, Sch.Luc.*Hes*.4.

ἀμολγός, ὁ, Hom. always in the phrase νυκτὸς ἀμολγῷ, usu. of *dead* of night, Il.11.173, 15.324, cf. *h.Merc*.7; also of evening twilight, Il.22.317 (when Venus is seen), and morning twilight, ib.28 (when Sirius rises in autumn); ἱερᾶς νυκτὸς ἀμολγόν A.*Fr*.69; ἀμολγός alone, Orph.*H*.34.12, f.l. in E.*Fr*.781.6:—as Adj., νύξ ib.104. (Derived by Eust.1018.21 from ἀμολγός, Achaean for ἀκμή, but more prob. = *milking-time*.)

ἀμόλυντος, ον, (μολύνω) *undefiled*, Lxx *Wi*.7.22, X.Eph.2.9, Muson.*Fr*.18Bp.105 H., Arr.*Epict*.4.11.8; παρθένος *IG*14.264 (Agrigentum). II. Act., *not leaving any stain*, κινεῖν μέχρι ἀμολύντου Crito ap.Gal.12.487, cf. Antyll.ap.Orib.9.24.4, Olymp.*in Mete*.307.1.

ἀμόμηλις· ἄπιος, ἀχράς, Hsch.

ἀμόμφητος, f.l. in A.*Ch*.510. **ἄμομφος**, ον, (μομφή) *blameless*, A.*Eu*.475; πρὸς ὑμῶν ib.678. II. Act., *having nothing to complain of*, cj. Robortellus for ἄμορφος, ib.413.

ἀμονάδιστος, ον, *not reduced to a unit*, Dam.*Pr*.117.

ἀμόρα, ἡ, *sweet cake*, Philet.ap.Ath.14.646d.

ἀμορβ-αῖος, ον, epith. of χαράδραι, Nic.*Th*.28,489, expl. by Sch. as *rustic*, *pastoral*, or *dark*. **–άς**, άδος, ἡ, fem. of ἀμορβός: ἀμορβάδες Νύμφαι in A.R.3.881 (acc. to Sch.) *rural* or *attendant* Nymphs. **–εύς**, έως, ὁ, = ἀμορβός, Opp.*C*.3.295. **–εύω**, *follow*, *attend*, c. dat., Nic.*Fr*.90:—Med., *let follow*, *make follow*, Id.*Th*. 349:—**ἀμορβέω**, Antim.23. **–ίτης**, ὁ, Sicel for ἀμόρα, Ath.14. 646f; cf. ἀμοργίτης. **–ός**, ὁ, *follower*, *attendant*, Call.*Dian*.45: esp. *herdsman*, *shepherd*, Id.*Hec*.6, Nic.*Th*.49, Opp.*C*.1.132. II. as Adj., *dark*, Sch.Nic.*Th*.28; and ἀμορβῷ is v.l. for ἀμολγῷ, Hom.

ἀμόργεια· χρώματος εἶδος, ἀπὸ νήσου Ἀμοργοῦντος, Suid.

ἀμοργεύς, έως, ὁ, *one who presses olives*, Poll.1.222.

ἀμόργη, ἡ, (ἀμέργω) *watery part which runs out when olives are pressed*, Hp.*Aph*.7.45, Thphr.*CP*6.8.3, Dsc.1.102. 2. kind of *dye* (as expl. of ἀμόργινος, q.v.), Sch.Ar.*Lys*.150. II. = ἀμοργίς, Sch.Aeschin.1.97.

ἀμόργης, ου, ὁ, = foreg. I. 1, Arist.*Col*.$796^{a}27$.

ἀμοργίδιον, τό, Dim. of ἀμοργίς, dub. l. in Paus.Gr.*Fr*.47 (leg. ἀμόργινα).

ἀμόργινος, ον, *made of* ἀμοργίς, χιτώνια Ar.*Lys*.150, Pl.*Ep*.363a; χιτών Antiph.153, *IG*2.754.10; κάλυμμα Clearch.25; τὰ ἀ. (sc. ἱμάτια) Eup.241, Aeschin.1.97:—also expl. as pr. n., *made in Amorgos*, Poll.7.74; or *purple*, St.Byz. s. v. Ἀμοργός, *EM*129.15, cf. 86.16, Sch.Ar.*Lys*.150.

Ἀμόργιον, τό, = Ἀμοργός, Charax 44.

ἀμοργίς, ίδος, ἡ, *stalks of mallow* (*Malva silvestris*), used like hemp or flax, ἄλοπος ἀ. Ar.*Lys*.735: acc. ἄμοργιν, v.l. ἀμοργίδα, ib.737. (Perh. from the pr. n. Ἀμοργός as place of growth.) II. proparox. **ἄμοργις**, εως, ἡ, = ἀμόργη, Hdn.Gr.1.87.

ἀμοργίτας (i.e. ἀμορϝ–, cf ἀμορβίτης)· πλακοῦντας, Hsch. **ἄμοργμα**· σύλλεγμα, ἄρτυμα, Id.

ἀμοργός (A), ὁ, (ἀμέργω) *one who squeezes* or *drains*, ἀμοργοί, πόλεως ὄλεθροι Cratin.214. 2. ἀνέμων λαμπτῆρας ἀμοργούς lanterns *which protect* [the light] *from* winds, Emp.84. II. proparox. **ἄμοργος** (v.l. ἄμεργος), = ἀμόργη, Ph.*Bel*.86.34, al.

ἀμοργός (B), ὁ, = ἀμοργίς, Cratin.96, cf. Paus.Gr.*Fr*.47, Harp.

Ἀμοργός, ὁ, *the island of Amorgos*, Heraclid.*Pol*.47, etc.:—Adj. **Ἀμόργιος**, *IG*1.244, 2.17, etc.:—also **Ἀμοργῖνος**, Suid. s. v. Σιμωνίδης Κρίνεω; **Ἀμοργίτης**, Nic.Dam.p.37 D.

Ἀμοργοῦς, οῦντος, ὁ, = foreg., Suid. s. v. ἀμόργεια, q. v.

ἀμορία, ἡ, v. ἀμμορία.

ἀμορίτης, ὁ, ἄρτος, = ἀμόρα, Lxx 1*Ch*.16.3.

ἀμόρξαι, = ὀμόρξαι, Hsch.

ἄμορος, ον, = ἄμοιρος, c. gen., τέκνων E.*Med*.1395; ὠδίνων *AP*7. 465 (Heraclit.). II. abs., *unlucky*, *wretched*, cj. Pors. for ἄμοιρος in S.*OT*248.

ἀμόρρωτον· ἀθάνατον, Hsch.

ἀμορφ-ία, ἡ, *formlessness*, Thphr.*Metaph*.33; ὕλης Herm.ap.Stob. 1.11.2, cf. Plot.6.7.20. II. *unshapeliness*, *unsightliness*, E.*Or*. 391, Arist.*Ph*.$190^{b}15$. **–ος**, ον, *misshapen*, *unsightly*, γυνή Hdt. 1.196; γῆρας Thgn.1021; στολήν γ' ἄμορφον ἀμφὶ σῶμ' ἔχεις E.*Hel*. 554: metaph., μῦθος Pl.*Lg*.752a: Sup. ἀμορφέστατος (as if from ἀμορφής) Hdt. l.c.: regul. Comp. –ότερος X.*Smp*.8.17: Sup. –ότατος Plu.*Mar*.2, etc. Adv. –φως *uglily*, Luc.*Am*.41. II. *without form*, *shapeless*, Pl.*Ti*.51a: c. gen., ἄ. ἐκείνων ἁπασῶν τῶν ἰδεῶν *without partaking of* their *form*, ib.50d; ἡ ὕλη τὸ ἄ. ἔχει πρὶν λαβεῖν τὴν μορφήν Arist.*Ph*.$191^{a}10$. III. metaph., *degrading*, Pl.*Lg*. 855c. **–όω**, *disfigure*, πρόσωπον δάκρυσι Sch.Il.2.269. **–ύνω**, = foreg., Antim.72. **–ωτος**, ον, *not formed*, *unwrought*, S.*Fr*.249; *without form*, θεός Procl. *in R*.1.40 K.; ἀ. καὶ ἀσχημάτιστος ὕλα Ti. Locr.94a, cf. Plot.6.7.3; *unfigured*, of stars in no constellation, Ptol. *Alm*.7.5. Adv. ἀμορφώτως Procl. *in Prm*.p.780 S.

ἁμός (A) or **ἀμός** [ᾱ], ή, όν, Aeol. **ἄμμος** Alc.105A, *Milet*.3 No. 152.35, = ἡμέτερος (cf. ὑμός for ὑμέτερος, σφός for σφέτερος, A.D.*Pron*. 111.18), freq. used for ἐμός, Il.8.178, Od.11.166, etc.; esp. in Dor., Pi.*P*.3.41, 4.27, Theoc.5.108; Lacon., Ar.*Lys*.1181; Cretan, *GDI* 4952*D*23, etc.; Sicilian, *IG*14.952 (Agrigentum); also Trag., A.*Th*. 417, *Ch*.428, S.*El*.279, *Ph*.1314, etc. (Written ἀμός when = ἐμός by Demetr. ad Il.6.414; but the distn. is not observed.)

ἁμός (B), [ᾰ], old word equiv. to τις, only in Adv. forms ἁμοῦ, ἁμῇ, ἁμοῖ, ἁμῶς, ἁμόθεν, ἁμόθι, and in compds. as οὐδαμός, Hdn.Gr.1. 169. (sm̥–, cf. Goth. *sums* (*some one*), *suman* (*sometime*, *once*).)

ἆμος, Dor. for ἦμος, *as*, *when*, Theoc.4.61, etc.

ἀμόσχευτος, ον, (μόσχος A) *without branches*, Nonn.*D*.22.21.

ἄμοτον, Adv. *insatiably*, *incessantly*, in Hom. always with Verbs expressing passion, desire, etc., esp. ἄ. μεμαώς full of *insatiate* longing, Il.4.440, al.; ἄ. κλαίω τεθνηότα I weep *continually*, 19.300; ἄ. κεχολωμένος *implacably* angered, 23.567; μάχης ἄ. μενεαίνων Hes.*Sc*. 361; ἡμίονοι ἄ. τανύοντο they struggled *restlessly* forwards, Od.6.83: later, *vehemently*, *violently*, λὶς ἄ. κεραΐζει Theoc.25.202; but στῆ δ' ἄ. stood *unwaveringly*, A.R.2.78:—later regul. Adv. –τως Sch.Il.4. 410. II. later, Adj. **ἄμοτος**, ον, *furious*, *savage*, κακόν prob. in Simon.37.16; θήρ Theoc.25.242; πῦρ Mosch.4.104.—Poet. word.

ἁμοῦ, Adv. of ἁμός (B), *somewhere*, ἁμοῦ γέ που *somewhere or other* (Bekk. for ἄλλου γέ που), Lys.24.20; ἄλλοθι μηδὲ ἁμοῦ no-*where* else *at all*, *IG*2.11.

ἀμουργός, όν, v.l. for ἀμοργός (A) I. 2.

ἀμουσ-ία, ἡ, *want of education*, *taste* or *refinement*, *rudeness*, E.*Fr*. 1020, etc., cf. Chor.*Zach.Dial*.2; joined with ἀπειροκαλία, Pl.*R*. 403c. II. *want of harmony*, E.*HF*676. **–ολογία**, ἡ, *inelegance of language*, Ath.4.164f (pl.). **–ος**, ον, *without song*, of fishes, Emp. 74; but usu. *without the Muses*, i. e. *without taste* or *refinement*, *rude*, E.*Ion*526, Ar.*V*.1074; ἄ. καὶ ἀφιλόσοφος Pl.*Sph*.259e; ἄ. ἡδονή, ἁμαρτήματα, *gross* pleasure, faults, Pl.*Phdr*.240b, *Lg*.863c; ἄ. ἐστι, c. inf., it is *incongruous*, Ar.*Th*.159; τῶν Λειβηθρίων ἀμουσότερος, prov. for lowest degree of mental cultivation, Zen.1.79: Sup., γλῶττα –οτάτη Agath.2.28. Adv. –ως Pl.*Hp.Ma*.292c. II. of persons, *unmusical*, Id.*Sph*.253b, al. 2. of sounds, *unmusical*, *discordant*, ἄμουσ' ὑλακτεῖν E.*Alc*.760; ἀμουσόταται ᾠδαί *Ph*.807, etc. Adv. –ως Jul.*Or*.8.247d. **–ωτος**, ον, = ἄμουσος, S.*Fr*.819.

ἄμουχα· καθαρεύουσα (Lacon.), Hsch.; cf. ἀμυσχρός.

ἀμοχθ-εί or **–ί** [ῑ], Adv. *without toil*, A.*Pr*.210, E.*Ba*.194. **–ητος**, ον, = sq., Opp.*C*.1.456. Adv. –τως Babr.9.2. **–ος**, ον, *free from toil and trouble*, of persons, S.*Fr*.410; ἄ. βίος *Tr*.147. Adv. ἀμόχθως Man.2.173, al. 2. *shrinking from toil*, καρδία Pi.*N*.10.30, E.*Fr*. 240. 3. *not tired*, X.*Mem*.2.1.33.

ἀμόω, in aor. part. ἀμώσας, *hang* (Tarent.), Hsch. **ἀμόωλον**, *clean vessel*, Id. **ἀμόωμφος**· ἄπιστος, Id.

ἀμπ–, poet., esp. Ep., Lyr., abbrev. for ἀναπ–, under which will be found words beginning with ἀμπ–.

ἀμπαδίην· ἀμφαδίην, Hsch. **ἀμπάζονται**· ἀναπαύονται, Id. **ἄμπαιδες**, v. ἀμφίπαις.

ἀμπαίνεθαι, v. ἀναφαίνομαι.

ἀμπαιστήρ, ῆρος, ὁ, *door-knocker*, *IG*4.1484.79 (Epid.).

ἀμπαλίνορρος, ον, strengthd. for παλίνορρος, Philetaer.11 (cj. Meineke).

ἄμπαλος, poet. for ἀνάπαλος, *fresh casting of lots*, ἄμπαλον θέμεν Pi.*O*.7.61, cf. Eust.64.43, 1434.28; κατ' ἄνπαλον μισθούντω let *by repeated auction*, *SIG*546.15 (Aetol., iii B.C.).

ἀμπανάμενος, v. ἀναφαίνομαι.

ἄμπανσις, **ἀμπαντός**, **ἀμπαντύς**, v. ἀμφ–.

ἀμπάξαι· παῦσαι (Lacon.), Hsch.; cf. ἀμπάζονται.

ἄμπαυμα, **ἀμπαύω**, etc., v. ἀναπ–.

ἀμπεδίον, **ἀμπεδιήρεις**, **ἀμπέλαγος**, should be written divisim ἀμ πεδίον, i. e. ἀνὰ πεδίον, etc.

ἄμπειρα, = ἀνάπειρα (q. v.). **ἄμπειρος**· ἔμπειρος, Hsch.

ἀμπείρω, poet. for ἀναπείρω.

ἀμπελ-άνθη, ἡ, = οἰνάνθη, Luc.*VH*2.5. **–εία**, ἡ, *vineyard*, *IPE* 1^{2}.418 (Cherson.). **–ειος**, ον, *of vine* or *vineyard*, Suid. **–εών**, ῶνος, ὁ, poet. for ἀμπελών, Theoc.25.157. **–ικός**, ή, όν, *of the vine*, v. l. in Hp.*Acut*.(*Sp*.)5, cf. M.Ant.8.46; χωρίον *IG*7.2808 (Hyettus); ἀμπελικά, τά, *tax on vineyards*, *PPetr*.3 p.243, cf. Vett.Val.76.10; also –κή, ἡ, *PPetr*.3 p.289. Adv. –κῶς Arr.*Epict*.2.20.18. **–ινος**, ον, also η, ον, = foreg., καρπός Hdt.1.212; οἶνος ἀ. *grape*-wine, opp. οἶνος κρίθινος, etc., Id.2.37,60; φύλλα Arist.*PA*$668^{a}23$; ἀ. βακτηρία *vine*-stick, Plb.29.27.5. II. metaph., γραῦς ἀμπελίνη *anus vinosa*, *AP*7.384 (Marc.Arg.). **–ιον**, τό, Dim. of ἄμπελος, Ar.*Ach*. 512, *Pax*596, Hp.*Nat.Mul*.109. **–ιος**, ον, = ἀμπέλειος, μέθυσμα Ph. 1.680; ποτόν Ach.Tat.2.2. **–ίς**, ίδος, ἡ, Dim. of ἄμπελος, *young vine*, *vine-plant*, Ar.*Ach*.995. II. = ἀμπελίων, Id.*Av*.304, cf. Poll.6.

52. III. kind of *sea-plant*, Dionys.*Av*.2.7. **-ιτικός**, ή, όν, *planted with vines*, γῆ *PTeb*.5.17 (ii B.C.). **-ῖτις**, ιδος, ἡ, *of* or *for vines*, ἀ. γῆ *vine-land*, *OGI*90.15 (Rosetta), cf. *Mélanges Holleaux* 105. II. ἀ. γῆ, a bituminous earth (cf. Plin.*HN*35.194) *used to cure* φθειρίασις *in vines*, Posidon.64; as a cosmetic, Dsc.5.160. **-ίων**, ωνος, ὁ, kind of *singing bird*, Dionys.*Av*.3.2.

ἀμπελο-γενής, ές, *of vine kind*, Arist.*Ph*.199ᵇ12. **-δεσμος**, ὁ, Sicilian plant used *for tying up vines*, *esparto*, *Lygeum Spartum*, Plin.*HN*17.209. **-εις**, εσσα, εν, but fem. εις Il.2.561:—*rich in vines*, *vine-clad*, of countries, Il. l.c., 3.184, 9.152, Thgn.784, Pi.*Pae*. 2.25, etc. 2. *of the vine*, ἀ. βάκτρον *vine*-stick, Nonn.*D*.14.102; ἀ. καυλία *vine*-shoots, Nic.*Al*.142. **-εργός**, ὁ, = ἀμπελουργός, *AP* 6.56 (Maced.). **-καρπον**, τό, = ἀπαρίνη, Dsc.3.90. **-κλημα**· *vitis*, and **-κλημία**· *vitis vineae*, *Gloss*. **-μιξία**, ἡ, *intercourse with vines*, Luc.*VH*1.9. **-ποιία**, ἡ, = ἀμπελουργία, Eust.1619. 59. **-πρασον**, τό, *wild leek*, *Allium Ampeloprasum*, Dsc.2.150, Did.ap.Ath.9.371f.

ἄμπελος, ἡ, any climbing plant with tendrils, esp. *grape-vine*, *Vitis vinifera* (ἄ. οἰνοφόρος Dsc.4.181; ἄ. τῆς Ἴδης is a variety, *V. v. apyrena*, *grape-currant*, Thphr.*HP*3.17.4), Hom. (not in Il. exc. in Adj. ἀμπελόεις), etc.; πυροὶ καὶ κριθαὶ καὶ ἄμπελοι Od.9.110, cf. 133, Alc.44, Hdt. 4.195, etc.; ἄ. καὶ ἐλάαν καὶ τἆλλα ἀκρόδρυα Thphr.*HP*4.4.11; ἄ. τὴν περὶ τὸ ἱερὸν κόπτοντες, in collective sense (cf. ἵππος, ἡ), Th.4.90; of wine, ἀμπέλου δρόσος Pi.*O*.7.2; ἀμπέλου παῖς Id.*N*.9.52. 2. ἄ. ἀγρία *wild vine*, *Vitis silvestris*, Dsc.4.181, 5.2, Plin.*HN*23.19:—also = ἄ. λευκή, Thphr.9.14.1, 9.20.3, Gal.14.186. 3. ἄ. λευκή *bryony*, *Bryonia cretica*, Dsc.4.182, Gal.11.826 (but λευκὴ ἄ. white *grape*, Thphr.*CP*1.20.5). 4. ἄ. μέλαινα *black bryony*, *Tamus communis*, Dsc.4.183, Gal.11.827. 5. ἄ. ποντία *wrack*, *Fucus volubilis*, Thphr.*HP*4.6.9. II. *vineyard*, Ael.*NA*11.32. III. *engine for protecting besiegers*, *mantlet*, Apollod.*Poliorc*.141.7. IV. measure of length, = 20 παλαισταί, Hero *Def*.131. V. = αἰγιαλός (Cyren.), Hsch.

ἀμπελο-στᾰτέω, *plant vines*, *GDI*3632 (Cos), Poll.7.141. **-τέμνω** (sic), *prune vines*, *PLond*.1.131.375 (i A.D.). **-τόμον** δρέπανον *pruning-hook for vines*, Hsch. s.v. βίσβη. **-τρόφος**, ον, *nurturing vines*, B.6.5.

ἀμπελουργ-εῖον, τό, *vineyard*, Aeschin.2.156 (v.l. ἀμπελῶνι), Suid. s.v. ἀμπέλειος. **-έω**, fut. -ήσω Philostr.*Im*.2.17; *work in* or *cultivate vineyard*, esp. *dress* or *strip vines*, Ar.*Fr*.43 D., Thphr.*CP*3.7.5, Plu.*Phil*.4, Luc.*VH*1.39:—Pass., ἄμπελος ἀμπελουργουμένη Thphr. *CP*3.14.1. 2. metaph., *strip*, *plunder*, πόλιν D.ap.Aeschin.3. 166. **-ημα**, τό, *vine-dresser's work*, Poll.7.140 (pl.). **-ία**, ἡ, *vine-dressing*, Thphr.*CP*3.14.2, Luc.*Salt*.40: in pl., *vineyards*, Lib. *Or*.11.234, Poll.1.228. **-ικός**, Dor. -ωργικός, ή, όν, *of* or *for culture of vines*, [γᾶ] *Tab.Heracl*.2.43; ἡ -κή (sc. τέχνη), *vine-dressing*, Pl.*R*.333d, Ph.1.329. Adv. -κῶς Poll.7.141. **-ός**, ὁ, *vine-dresser*, Ar.*Pax* 190, Hp.*Epid*.4.25, *IG*2.1055, Thphr.*CP*2.4.8, *PPetr*.3 p.59; title of plays by Amphis and Alexis; cf. ἀμπελοεργός.

ἀμπελο-φάγος [ᾰ], ον, *eating* or *gnawing vines*, ἶπες Str.13.1. 64. **-φόρος**, ον, *bearing vines*, Thphr.*CP*2.4.4, *PTeb*.82, Poll. 1.228. **-φύλαξ**· *custos vineae*, *Gloss*. **-φυλλον**, τό, *vine-leaf*, Hsch. s.v. Κλαρία; = *pampinus*, *Gloss*. **-φῦτος**, ον, *planted with vines*, *growing vines*, D.S.1.36, Str.5.3.1, Ph.2.371. **-φύτωρ**, ορος, ὁ, *vine-planter*, of Bacchus, *AP*6.44 (Leon.). [ῡ metri gr., as in πτεροφύτωρ.]

ἀμπελ-ώδης, ες, *rich in vines*, Poll.1.228, Hsch. s.v. οἰνάδες. **-ών**, ῶνος, ὁ, *vineyard*, Aeschin.2.156 (v.l.), Thphr.*HP*9.10.3, Lxx *Ge*.9. 20, al., *PHib*.151 (iii B.C.), *PTeb*.5.99 (ii B.C.), D.S.4.6, Plu.*Mar*.21, etc.; cf. ἀμπελεών:—Dim. **-ωνίδιον**, τό, *PSI*4.375.7 (iii B.C.).

ἀμπερέως· διαμπάξ, Hsch. **ἀμπέσαι**· ἀμφιέσαι (Lacon.), Id.

ἀμπέτιξ, Adv., (cf. ἀμπί) *round*, dub. l. in *CIG*2554 (Cret.).

ἀμπεχές· ἔνδυμα, Hsch.

ἀμπέχογκος, = γνάφαλλον, Ps.-Dsc.3.117.

ἀμπεχόνη, ἡ, (ἀμπέχω) *fine shawl* worn by women and effeminate men, Pherecr.108.28. 2. *clothing*, X.*Mem*.1.2.5, etc.; in pl., *modes of dress*, Pl.*R*.425b.:—Dim. **-όνιον**, *AB*388, Hsch.

ἀμπεχόνον, τό, = ἀμπεχόνη, Ar.*Fr*.320.7, *IG*2.754, Theoc.15.21.

ἀμπ-έχω (dissimil. fr. ἀμφέχω), Semon.12 (dub.), A.*Pers*.848, S. (v. infr.), later **ἀμφέχω** *AP*7.693 (Apollonid.), *IG*12(3).220 (Thera), Aret.*CA*1.4, etc.; Med., ἀμφέχετο A.R.1.324; also **ἀμπ-ίσχω** E. *Hipp*.192, *Supp*.165: Ep. impf. ἄμπεχον Od.6.225 (late ἄμφεχον Q.S. 3.6, 5.106): fut. ἀμφέξω E.*Cyc*.344: aor. 2 ἤμπεσχον Ar.*Lys*.1156, etc.:—Med., ἀμπέχομαι Ar. (v. infr. II. 2); ἀμπίσχομαι E.*Hel*.422, 3 pl. ἀμπισχνοῦνται Ar.*Av*.1090: impf. ἠμπειχόμην Pl.*Phd*.87b, Ep. ἀμφεχόμην A.R.1.324: fut. ἀμφέξομαι Pherecr.7 D., Philetaer.19: aor. 2 ἠμπεσχόμην E.*Med*.1159, Ar.*Th*.165, 2 sg. subj. ἀμπίσχῃ E.*IA* 1439, part. ἀμπισχόμενος Ar.*V*.1150.—The aor. forms, ἀμπισχεῖν, ἀμπισχών, are sts. falsely written (as if pres.) ἀμπίσχειν, ἀμπίσχων: I. *surround*, *cover*, *enclose*, ἅλμη οἱ νῶτα ἄμπεχεν Od.6.225; κυνῆ πρόσωπα Θεσσαλὶς νιν ἀμπέχει S.*OC*314, cf. A. l.c.: metaph., ἀ. τινὰ σμικρότητι *invest* one with.., Pl.*Prt*.320e: abs., σκότος ἀμπίσχων *surrounding* darkness, E.*Hipp*.192; κρυπτὸν ἀμπισχὼν δόρυ, of the wooden horse, Id.*Tr*.12; τὰ ἀμπέχοντα ὑμένια Aret.*SA*2. 2. 2. *embrace*, γόνυ σὸν ἀμπίσχειν χερί E.*Supp*.165. II. *put round*, esp. *put* clothes and the like *on* another, c. dupl. acc., κρίβανόν μ' ἀμπίσχετε Ar.*V*.1153, cf. *Ra*.1063, *Lys*.1156: with prep., τοίχοισιν δ' ἔπι ἤμπισχεν.. ὑφάσματα *put them* all over.., E.*Ion*1159: metaph., ἡ βασιλικὴ τέχνη δούλους καὶ ἐλευθέρους ἀμπίσχουσα Pl.*Plt*. 311c. 2. Med., *put round oneself*, *put on*, πέπλους E.*Med*.1159; *wear*, τὸ τῆς γυναικὸς ἀμπέχει χιτώνιον Ar.*Ec*.374; λευκὸν ἀμπέχει; do you *wear* a white cloak? Id.*Ach*.1023; χλαίνας οὐκ ἀμπισχνοῦνται Id.*Av*.1090; καλῶς ἠμπίσχετο *was* well *dressed*, Id.*Th*.165; ἐπ' ἀριστερὰ ἀ. Id.*Av*.1567; ἀμπεχόμενοι *with their cloaks on*, opp. γυμνοί (cf. γυμνός I. 5), Pl.*Grg*.523c, Arist.*Pr*.867ᵃ19; ἄνω τοῦ γόνατος ἀ. *wear a tunic* not reaching to the knee, Philetaer. l.c.; περιττῶς ἀ. *to be* gorgeously *dressed*, Plu.*Demetr*.41: c. dat., *clothe* or *cover oneself with* (v. ἔκβολος), E.*Hel*.422.

ἀμπήδησε, poet. for ἀνεπήδησε.

ἀμπί, said to be Aeol. for ἀμφί, Hdn.Gr.2.376, but prob. coined to expl. forms such as ἀμπέχω, which are due to dissimilation.

ἀμπίθυρον (cod. -ουρον)· πυλῶνα (Tarent.), Hsch. **ἀμπιστᾶσθαι**· ἐξετάζειν, and **ἀμπιστάτηρ**· ἐξεταστής, Id. **ἀμπιτίαρ**· παραταττομένη, Id.

ἀμπλᾰκ-εῖν, inf. of aor. ἤμπλακον (ἤμβλακον Archil.73, Ibyc.24), part. ἀμπλ- and ἀπλ-ακών (v. infr.): pf. Pass. ἠμπλάκημαι A.*Supp*. 916:—pres. only later **ἀμπλακίσκω**, Dor. **ἀμβλακίσκω** Theag.ap. Stob.3.1.117: Dor. impf. ἀμβλάκισκον Phint.ap.eund.4.23.61 (ἀμβλακεύω is v.l. for βλακεύω in Hp.*Art*.17; cf. βλάξ): I. c. gen., *miss*, *fail* or *come short of*, ἀνορέας οὐκ ἀμπλακών Pi.*O*.8.67, cf. S.*Ant*. 554, 1234. 2. *lose*, *be bereft of*, εἰ τοῦδ' ἤμπλακον (sc. παιδός) ib. 910; νόστου Simon.119; ἀρίστης ἀπλακὼν ἀλόχου E.*Alc*.242; λέκτρων ἀπλακών Id.*IA*124. II. abs., *do amiss*, *sin*, *err*, παρ θεοῖς Ibyc. 24, cf. Archil.73, E.*Hipp*.892, *Andr*.948, etc.: c. neut. pron., ὡς τάδ' ἤμπλακον when *I committed* these *sins*, A.*Ag*.1212:—Pass., τί δ' ἠμπλάκηται τῶνδέ μοι; Id.*Supp*.916.—Not in Hom. **-ημα**, τό, *error*, *fault*, A.*Pr*.112, 388, S.*Ant*.51, etc.—Poet. and late Prose, Plu. 2.226e, Thd.*Da*.6.4:—metri gr., **ἀπλάκημα** A.*Eu*.934. **-ητος**, v. ἀναμπλάκητος. **-ία**, and **ἀμβλ-** (v. infr.), ἡ, = ἀμπλάκημα, Thgn.204, Emp.115, Hp.*Ep*.22; ἀμπλακίαισι φρενῶν Pi.*P*.3.13; τίνος ἀμπλακίας ποινὰς ὀλέκει; A.*Pr*.564; ἀμπλακίαισι τῶν πάροιθεν E. *Hipp*.835, cf. A.R.4.1082, Rhian.1.20. **-ιον**, τό, = ἀμπλακία, Pi.*P*.11.26. **-ίσκω**, v. ἀμπλακεῖν. **-ιῶτις**, ἡ, = ἱερὰ νόσος, Poet. *de herb*.174.

ἀμπν-είω, Ep. for ἀναπνέω. **-ευμα**, **-οά**, poet. for ἀνάπνευμα, ἀναπνοή. **-υε**, v. ἀναπνέω.

ἄμπνῡτο, Ep. aor. Med., Pass. **ἀμπνύνθη** (better ἀμπνύθη), *recover consciousness* after a swoon, Il.5.697, 22.475, al. (ἀνα-, πνῡ-, cf. πέπνυμαι. Not connected with ἀνα-πνέω, q. v.)

ἀμποίχοιτις· ἐν Συρακούσαις ἀρχή, Hsch.

ἄμποτε, i. e. ἄν ποτε, with opt., *o that!* Sch. rec. A.*Pr*.971.

ἄμποχος, ὁ, = ἀνάδοχος, *guarantor*, *Not.Scav*.1912.452 (Sicily, i B.C.).

ἀμπρακόν· μακρόθεν, Hsch.

ἀμπρ-ευτής, οῦ, ὁ, *hauling*, ὄνος S.*Fr*.820. **-εύω**, *draw along*, *drag*, E.ap.Phot.p.95 R.; αἰχμάλωτον ἤμπρευσαν Lyc.1298; ἄνδρα.. ἀμπρεύοντες Call.*Fr*.234: metaph., λυπρὸν βίον ἀμπρεύσει *will drag on* a wretched life, Lyc.975, cf. 635.

ἀμπρόν (on the accent v. *Et.Gen*., Hsch.), τό, *rope for drawing loads*, Ἐφ.Ἀρχ.1895.59 (v B.C.), *IG*2.678*B* (iv B.C.), cf. Sch.Ar.*Lys*. 289.

ἀμπτᾶσα, **ἀμπταίην**, v. ἀναπέτομαι.

ἀμπῠκ-άζω, *bind front hair*, κισσῷ καὶ στεφάνοισιν ἀμπυκασθεὶς *AP* 13.6 (Phalaec.). **-τήρ**, ῆρος, ὁ, *horse's bridle*, A.*Th*.461. **-τήριον**, τό, = foreg., S.*OC*1069. **-ωμα**, τό, = sq., Id.*Fr*.1002 (pl.).

ἄμπυξ, ῠκος, ὁ (ἡ, S., E., v. infr.):—*woman's diadem*, *frontlet*, Il.22.469, A.*Supp*.431 (lyr., with play on I. 2), E.*Hec*.465, Theoc. 1.33. 2. *horse's headband* (Thess. acc. to Sch.Pi.*O*.5.15), Q.S. 4.511. II. *rim of wheel*, S.*Ph*.680 (lyr.).

ἀμπώλημα (Dor. for ἀναπ-), τό, *indemnification*, *Tab.Heracl*.1. 110, 155.

ἀμπωτίζω, *ebb and flow*, of the sea, Ph.1.298:—Med., Eust.688.52.

ἄμπωτις, ἡ, gen. εως, Ion. ιος, for ἀνάπωτις (ἀναπίνομαι), v. infr.:—*being sucked back*, i.e. of sea, *ebb*, opp., πλημμυρίς or ῥαχία (Ion. ῥηχίη), Hdt.2.11, 7.198, 8.129, Arist.*Mete*.366ᵃ19, *Placit*.3.17, Agatharch. 32, etc.: in pl., *ebb and flow*, *tides*, Arist.*Mu*.396ᵃ26, *Peripl.M.Rubr*. 45, App.*Hisp*.1, Hdn.3.14.6.—The full form **ἀνάπωτις** only Pi.*O*. 9.52, Scymn.110, and later Prose, Plb.10.14.2 (s. v.l.), Arr.*Ind*.22.8: gen. -πώτιδος, Agatharch.101. 2. *retiring of a stream*, Call.*Del*. 130. 3. metaph., τῆς ἀδολεσχίας ὥσπερ ἄμπωτιν λαβούσης Plu. 2.502d. II. *return of humours* inward from surface of body, ἄ. τῶν χυμῶν Hp.*Hum*.1, cf. Erot.*Fr*.8; of blood in the lungs, Gal. *UP*6.10.

ἀμύαλος, ον, for ἀμύελος, *without marrow*, *Tab.Defix.Aud*.162.19, cf. 168.31.

ἀμυγδᾰλ-έα, contr. -ῆ, ἡ, *almond-tree*, *Prunus Amygdalus*, Eup. 70, Thphr.*HP*1.6.3, Dsc.1.123. **-έλαιον**, τό, = ἔλαιον ἀμυγδάλινον, [Gal.]14.519. **-εος**, α, ον, v.l. for ἀμυγδαλόεις in Nic.*Th*.891 (ap. Ath.14.649d). **-η**, ἡ, *almond*, Phryn.Com.68, Hp.*Vict*.2.55, Thphr.*HP*1.11.3, Dsc.1.123, Ath.2.52c. II. *kernel of peach-stone*, *Gp*.10.14.1. **-ινος**, η, ον, *of almonds*, χρῖμα X.*An*.4.4.13; ἔλαιον Thphr.*Od*.14. **-ιον**, τό, Dim. of ἀμυγδάλη, Hp.*Morb*.2.64. **-ιος**, α, ον, *almond-shaped*, ὠτάρια *BGU*781 iii 16 (i A.D.). **-ίς**, ίδος, ἡ, = ἀμυγδάλη, Philox.3.20, Plu.2.624d. **-ίτης** [ῑ], ου, ὁ, = τιθύμαλλος χαρακίας, Dsc.4.164, Plin.*HN*26.70.

ἀμυγδαλο-ειδής, ές, *like the almond* or *almond-tree*, Dsc.4. 164. **-εις**, εσσα, εν, *like an almond*, Nic.*Th*.891. **-κατάκτης**, ου, ὁ, *almond-cracker*, Ath.2.53b.

ἀμύγδαλ-ον, τό, = ἀμυγδάλη, Hp.*Morb.*3.15, Hermipp.63, Arist. *HA*614b15, Dsc.1.123, etc.; = ἀμυγδαλῆ, Lxx *Ec.*12.5. **-ος**, ἡ, = ἀμυγδαλῆ, Luc.*Apol.*5, Hsch. s.v. καρύα. **-ώδης**, ες, *like an almond*, σχήματι Thphr.*HP*4.2.5.

ἄμυγ-μα, ατος, τό, (ἀμύσσω) *scratching, tearing*, πολιᾶς ἄ. χαίτας S.*Aj.*634; ὀνύχων ἀμύγματα E.*Andr.*827. **-μός**, ὁ, = foreg., cj. in A.*Ch.*24.

ἀμυγνόν, v. ἀμυσχρός.

ἄμυδις [ᾰ], Aeol. = ἅμα, Sch.D.T.p.281 H.: I. of Time, *together, at the same time*, Od.12.415, Hes.*Sc.*345, etc. II. more freq. of Place, *all together*, ἄ. κικλήσκετο Il.10.300; ἄ. στήσασα (v.l. καλέσασα) θεούς 20.114, cf. 13.336; ὀστέα.. πάντ' ἄ. 12.385; ἄ. φλόγ' ἔβαλλον threw burning embers *together*, 23.217; freq. in late Ep., A.R.1.961, Arat.581, etc.

ἀμυδρ-ήεις, εσσα, εν, = sq., Nic.*Th.*274. **-ός**, ά, όν, *dim, faint, obscure*: 1. of impressions on the eye, ἀ. χοιράς a rock *dimly seen through water*, Archil.129; ἀ. γράμματα *scarce legible* letters, Th.6.54; ἀ. φέγγος, χρῶμα, Arist.*Mete.*343b13, 372a2; ἀ. τὰ εἴδη τῶν ἰχθύων, σκιὰς μᾶλλον ἢ ἰχθῦς εἰκάσεις (in a painting) Paus.10.28.1. Adv. ἀμυδρῶς, βλέπειν, ὁρᾶν, Arist.*HA*537b11, 556b19; ἀ. μιμεῖσθαί τι represent its form *obscurely*, ib.502b9; ἀ. ἔχειν to be *ill-defined*, *PA* 668a3. 2. generally, *faint, weak*, σφυγμὸς ἀ. τὸν τόνον Aret.*CA*2.3, cf. *SD*1.12; τυπαί Nic.*Th.*358 (Comp.). 3. of impressions on the mind, *vague*, ἀ. εἶδος Pl.*Ti.*49a; ἀ. πρὸς ἀλήθειαν *faint* in comparison with truth, Id.*R.*597a; δι' ἀμυδρῶν ὀργάνων by *imperfect* organs, Id. *Phdr.*250b, cf. *Tht.*195a; μαντεῖα ἀμυδρότερα τοῦ τι σαφὲς σημαίνειν *too obscure*.., Id.*Ti.*72b; ἀ. ἐλπίς Plu.*Alc.*38; ἀ. λόγος [Longin.] *Rh.*p.195 H.; -ότερα σχήματα Aps.p.327 H.; συναίσθησις Dam.*Pr.*81 (Sup.), etc. Adv. -ῶς καὶ οὐθὲν σαφῶς Arist.*Metaph.*985a13, cf. 988a 23; *faintly*, of one near death, Max.Tyr.16.2: Comp. ἀμυδρότερον Pl. *Sph.*250e, Plu.2.1025d. **-ότης**, ητος, ἡ, *dimness*, αἰσθήσεων Ph.2. 432; *faintness*, of the pulse, Gal.9.15; *indistinctness*, opp. τρανότης, Plot.1.4.3. **-όω**, *make indistinct*, Procl.*Inst.*143:—Pass., Ph.1.273, Olymp. *in Mete.*211.11; *become indistinct* or *feeble*, ib.150.4. **-ωσις**, εως, ἡ, *making indistinct* or *feeble*, Anon. *in Cat.*26.9: metaph., Dam. *Pr.*423.

ἀμύελος, ον, *without marrow*, Arist.*PA*655a35, Gal.*UP*1.15.

ἀμυ-ησία, ἡ, *a being uninitiated*, *AB*406, Hsch. s.v. ἀνοργίας. **-ητος**, ον, *uninitiated, profane*, And.1.12, Lys.6.51; ἀ. καὶ ἀτέλεστος Pl.*Phd.*69c: c. gen., ἀ. Ἀφροδίτης *not admitted into mysteries* of Aphrodite, Aristaenet.1.14; ὠδίνων, of Artemis, Orph.*H.*36.4. 2. μυήσεις ἀ. *no true* initiations, Ph.1.156. II. *not closed, open*, Philostr.*Gym.*29 codd.; with play on both meanings, *leaky*, Pl.*Grg.* 493a,b.

ἀμύθητος [ῡ], ον, *unspeakable*, esp. *unspeakably great, untold*, χρήματα D.4.34; κακὰ καὶ πράγματ' ἀ. παρέχων 21.17; ἀ. πλῆθος μυῶν Arist.*HA*580b16; ἀμύθητον ὅσον διαφέρει Id.*Pol.*1263a40, cf. Phld. *Mort.*29; ἀμύθητα περὶ ἕκαστα παρατιθεὶς Id.*Herc.*1005.7.

ἄμῡθος, ον, *without mythic tales*, ποίησις Plu.2.16c.

ἀμυκάλαι· αἱ ἀκίδες τῶν βελῶν, παρὰ τὸ ἀμύσσειν, Hsch. **ἀμύκαρις**· πλῆθος, ἄθροισμα, πλούσιον, πολύ, Id.

ἀμύκητος [ῡ], ον, of places, *where no herds low*, *AP*9.150 (Antip.).

Ἀμύκλαι, ῶν, αἱ, *Amyclae* in Laconia, famous for worship of Apollo, Il., etc.:—**Ἀμυκλ-αῖος**, or **-αεύς**, έως, ὁ, *Amyclean*, X.*HG* 4.5.11, Arist.*Fr.*532:——**-αῖον**, τό, *temple of Amyclean Apollo*, ἐν Ἀ. Foed.ap.Th.5.18 and 23; ἐν τῷ Ἀ. Str.6.3.2; of Artemis, Call.*Aet.* 1.1.24. Adv. **-ᾱθεν** *from Amyclae*, Pi.*N.*11.34. **Ἀμύκλαι**, αἱ, sort of *shoes*, named after *Amyclae*, Theoc.10.35:—also **-ᾱ̆δες**, αἱ, Ar.*Fr.*44 D., Phryn.Com.5 D., cf. Poll.7.88, Hsch. **Ἀμυκλαΐζω**, *speak in the Amyclean* (i.e. *Laconian*) *dialect*, Theoc.12.13.

ἀμυκλίς· γλυκύς, ἡδύς, Hsch. **ἀμύκταν**· γλυκύν, οἱ δὲ ἄμικτον, Id.

ἀμυκτέον, *one must scarify*, Menem.ap.Orib.7.22.6, Archig.ap. Aët.6.27.

ἀμύκτηρ, ηρος, ὁ, ἡ, *without nose*, Str.15.1.57.

ἀμυκτικός, ή, όν, *fit for tearing, lacerating*, Plu.2.642c. Adv. -κῶς Sch.Nic.*Th.*131. II. Medic., of remedies, *irritant*, Sor.2.12, al., Dsc.1.174 (Sup.).

ἀμυλᾶτον, τό, = ἄμυλος II, Sch.Ar.*Pax* 1195.

ἀμυλιδωτόν, τό, kind of *tunic*, Hermipp.2 D.

ἀμύλιον, τό, Dim. of ἄμυλος II, *cake*, Plu.2.466d, Aq.*Ex.*16.31 (cod. A); of ἄμυλος III, *starch*, Hp.*Mul.*2.197, Arist.*Pr.*879a10, Dieuch. ap.Orib.4.7.24.

ἄμῠλος, ον, *not ground at the mill*: hence, *of the finest meal*, ἄρτος Poll.6.72; cf. foreg. II. as Subst., ἄμυλος, ὁ, *cake of fine meal*, Ar.*Ach.*1092, *Pax* 1195, cf. Stratt.2 D., Theoc.9.21, Telecl.32:—also ἄμυλον, τό, Ath.14.647f. III. ἄμυλον, τό, *starch*, Dsc.2.101, Plin.*HN*18.76, *SIG*1171.11 (Lebena), *POxy.*1088 i 5, etc.

ἄμυμος, ον, = sq., Cyr., prob. in Hsch.

ἀμύμων [ῡ], ον, gen. ονος: dat. pl. ἀμύμοσιν *Epigr.Gr.*451 (Trachonitis), dub. l. in *IG*14.1424: (cf. μῦμαρ· αἶσχος, ψόγος, Hsch.):—*blameless, noble, excellent*, οἶκος ὅδ' ἀφνειὸς καὶ ἀ. Od.1.232; ἅμα κρατερὸς καὶ ἀ. ib. 3.111; in Hom. an honorary epithet or title even of Aegisthus, ib.1.29:—never of gods, for Aesculapius is ἀ. as *a physician*, Il.4.194; of a mortal nymph, 14.144. II. of things, ὃς δ' ἂν ἀ. αὐτὸς ἔῃ καὶ ἀμύμονα εἰδῇ Od.19.332; θεῶν ὑπ' ἀμύμονι πομπῇ Il.6.171; μῆτις 10.19; ὀρχηθμός 13.637; νῆσος Od.12.261; ἕρκος 22.442.—Freq. in Hom.; twice in Hes. (*Th.*264,654); once in Pi.*O.*10(11).27; not in B. or Trag.; found in Comic parodies, as Hermipp.82.

ἄμῡνα, ης, ἡ, *warding off an attack, self-defence*, Theopomp.Com. 3 D., Ps.-Phoc.32, Ph.2.31, App.*Pun.*73, etc.: c. gen. obj., ἐχθρῶν Lxx *Wi.*5.17, Ph.1.322. II. *vengeance, requital*, Ps.-Phoc.77, Phld.*Ir.*p.66 W., Nic.Dam.p.104 D., Plot.4.4.17, etc.

ἀμῡν-άθω, pres. assumed by Gramm., cf. Hdn.Gr.1.440, 2.782, as lengthd. form of ἀμύνω: but forms so accented in codd. are best taken to belong to aor. ἠμύναθον and written ἀμυναθεῖν (so Hsch.), -θοῦ, cf. ἀλκαθεῖν:—*defend, assist*, c. dat. pers., εἰ σοῖς φίλοις ἀμυναθεῖν χρῄζεις E.*Andr.*1079, cf. *IA*910; ἀμυνάθετέ μοι Ar.*Nu.*1323: abs., ἄξιαι δ' ἀμυναθεῖν [αἱ ξυμφοραί] S.*OC*1015:—Med., *ward off from oneself, repel*, τόνδ' ἀμυναθοῦ ψόγον A.*Eu.*438; *take vengeance on*, μὴ .. ἀμυνάθοιτό σε E.*Andr.*721. **-ανδρος**, *warding off enemies*, S.*Fr.* 1003. Adv. -ρως A.*Fr.*451 D. **-ητί**, Adv. *in self-defence*, A.D. *Adv.*161.8 (dub.).

Ἀμυνίας [ῡ], ου, ὁ, (ἀμύνω) masc. pr. n. II. Appellat., ὁ θυμὸς εὐθὺς ἦν ἀ. *on its guard*, Ar.*Eq.*570.

ἀμύν-τειρα, ἡ, fem. of ἀμυντήρ, = *cultrix*, *Gloss.* **-τέον**, verb. Adj. of ἀμύνω, *one must assist*, c. dat. pers., X.*Cyr.*8.6.6: also pl., ἀμυντέ' ἐστὶ τοῖς κοσμουμένοις S.*Ant.*677. II. *one must repel*, Ar. *Lys.*661. **-τήρ**, ῆρος, ὁ, lit. *defender*: ἀμυντῆρες, οἱ, *brow-tines* of stag's antlers, Arist.*HA*611b5. **-τήριος**, ον, *defensive*, ὅπλα (i.e. *weapons* in general) Pl.*Lg.*944d, cf. D.S.3.54, D.H.5.46, Str.7.3.17, 17.1.54; τέχναι Pl.*Lg.*920e: c. gen., φάρμακον ἀ. γήρως *antidote for* .., Ael.*NA*6.51; πόαι τῶν δηγμάτων ἀ. 12.32. II. Subst. **-τήριον**, τό, *means of protection*, Pl.*Plt.*279c sq.; *defence, bulwark*, Plb.18. 41a.2; *weapon*, Plu.2.714f; ἀ. τοῦ κακοῦ *antidote for*.., Ael.*NA*3.41; ἀ. ἐξ ἀπόρων *way of escape* from.., ib.3.22. **-της**, ὁ, *defender*, Phot. p.96 R., cf. Hdn.Gr.1.78. **-τικός**, ή, όν, *prompt to repel affront* or *attack*, Arist.*EN*1126a7; of animals, opp. φυλακτικά, *HA*488b8; τὸ ἀ. ὄργανον *PA*683a21; αἱ ἀ. ὁρμαί Plu.2.457c. Adv. -κῶς Procl. *in Prm.*p.555 S., Simp. *in Epict.*p.41 D. 2. *fit for keeping off*: ἡ -τικὴ χειμώνων Pl.*Plt.*280e. **-τρόν**, τό, *reward for defence*, A.*Fr.* 451 E. **-τωρ**, ορος, ὁ, poet. word, *defender, helper*, Il.13.384 (as v.l.), Od.2.326, etc. 2. *repeller*, δυσφροσυνάων Simon.86. 3. *avenger*, πατρός E.*Or.*1588.

ἀμύνω [ῡ], Ep. impf. ἄμῡνον Il.15.731: fut. ἀμῠνῶ, Ion. -ῠνέω Hdt. 9.60, 3 pl. -εῦσι ib.6: aor. 1 ἤμῡνα, Ep. ἄμυνα [ᾰμ] Il.17.615: aor. 2, v. ἀμυνάθω:—**Med.**, Ep. impf. ἀμυνόμην ib.13.514: fut. ἀμυνοῦμαι: aor. 1 ἠμυνάμην: aor. 2, v. ἀμυνάθω:—**Pass.** rare (v. infr. c):—*keep off, ward off*, Hom., mostly in Il.—Construction: 1. c. acc. of the person or thing *to be kept off*, c. dat. pers. *for* or *from whom* danger averted, Δαναοῖσιν λοιγὸν ἄμυνον *ward off* ruin *from* the Danai, Il. 1.456, cf. 341, Od.8.525:—dat. freq. omitted, ὃς λοιγὸν ἀμύνει Il.5. 603; ἄ. τὸν βάρβαρον Pl.*Lg.*692e, cf. *AB*79. b. c. dat. only, *defend, aid, succour*, ἀ. ὥρεσσι, σοῖσιν ἔτησι, Il.5.486, 6.262, cf. Od.11.500, Hdt.8.87, 9.6, etc.; τοιαῦτ' ἀμύνεθ' Ἡρακλεῖ such *aid ye give* to H., E.*HF*219; ἀ. τῇ πόλει, τῷ δήμῳ, Ar.*Eq.*577,790; τῷ νόμῳ E.*Or.*523, Th.3.67:—with inf. added, τοῖς μὲν οὐκ ἠμύνατε σωθῆναι so that they might be saved, Th.6.80. 2. c. acc. et gen., Τρῶας ἄμυνε νεῶν *he kept* the Trojans *off from* the ships, Il.15.731, cf. 4.11, 12.402. b. c. gen. only, ἀ. νηῶν *defend* the ships, ib.13.109. 3. abs., *succour*, χεῖρες ἀμύνειν hands *to aid*, ib.814; ἀμύνειν εἰσὶ καὶ ἄλλοι ib.312; ὦ ξυνδικασταί.. ἀμύνατε *help!* Ar.*V.*197; τὰ ἀμυνεῦντα *means of defence*, Hdt.3.155: c. dat. modi, σθένει ἀ. *defend* with might, Il.13.678. 4. with Preps., once in Hom. with περί, ἀμυνέμεναι περὶ Πατρόκλοιο (cf. B.1.3) ib.17.182; in Prose, ἀ. ὑπὲρ τῆς Ἑλλάδος Pl.*Lg.*692d; ἀ. πρὸ πάντων Plb.6.6.8. II. less freq. like B. II, *requite, repay*, ἔργ' ἀμύνουσιν κακά S.*Ph.*602; ἀμύνειν.. τοῖσδε τοῖς λόγοις τάδε Id.*OC* 1128.

B. Med., *keep* or *ward off from oneself, guard* or *defend oneself against*, freq. with collat. notion of *requital, revenge*: 1. c. acc. rei, ἀμύνετο νηλεὲς ἦμαρ Il.13.514; ἀμύνεσθαι μόρον A.*Ag.*1381; τὸ δυστυχὲς γὰρ ηὑγένει' ἀμύνεται E.*Heracl.*303, cf. S.*Fr.*1004. b. c. acc. pers., ἀ. τὴν Δαρείου στρατιὴν Hdt.3.158; ἐκεῖνον ἠμύναντο S.*Fr.* 589. 2. that from which danger is warded off in gen., as in Act. I. 2, ἀμυνόμενοι σφῶν αὐτῶν Il.12.155; νηῶν ἠμύνοντο ib.179. 3. with Preps., ἀμύνεσθαι περὶ πάτρης ib.243; περὶ τῶν οἰκείων Th.2.39; ὑπέρ τινος X.*Cyn.*9.9. 4. abs., *defend oneself, act in self-defence*, ἀμύνεσθαι φίλον ἔστω Il.16.556; ἢν συλλαμβανόμενος ἀμύνηται Hdt.1.80, cf. 4. 174, al.; ἀλλ' ἀμύνου Ar.*Eq.*244; τοῦ ἄρξαντος καὶ οὐ τοῦ ἀμυνομένου Antipho 4.4.8; οὐδ' ἀμυνόμενος ἀλλ' ὑπάρχων Isoc.16.44, cf. Pl.*Grg.* 456e; κακῶς πάσχοντα ἀ. ἀντιδρῶντα κακῶς Pl.*Cri.*49d; ἂν ᾖ χαρίεις, ἀ. εὖ δρῶν Arist.*EN*1162b10. II. after Hom., ἀ. τινά *avenge oneself on* an enemy: hence, *requite, repay*, Ar.*Nu.*1428, etc.: freq. c. dat. instr., ἔργοις πεπονθὼς ῥήμασίν σ' ἀμύνομαι S.*OC*873; ἀ. τινὰ σιδήρῳ Antipho 4.2.2; τοῖς ὁμοίοις, ἀρετῇ, Th.1.42, 4.63; ὠμότητα ὠμότητι D.S.14.53; ἀ. τινὰς ὑπέρ τινος to *punish for* a thing, Th.5.69; good sense, Simon.229; ἀ. ὁμοίως εὖ παθόντα, ὥσπερ κακῶς Socr.ap. Arist.*Rh.*1398a25: abs., *retaliate*, c. dat. instr., ταῖς ναυσίν Th.1.142; ἀ. ὧν ἔπαθον 1.96.

C. very rarely Pass., ἀμύνονται ἆται *are warded off*, Pi.*P.*11.54; ἀμυνέσθω *let him be driven away*, Pl.*Lg.*845c.

ἀμύξ, Adv., (ἀμύσσω) *scratching, tearing*, ἀ. ἐμφῦσα Nic.*Th.* 131. 2. = μόλις, Euph.146.

ἄμυξ· ἀμυχή, Hsch. (dub.).

ἀμύξανος· ἀνόσιος, Hsch.

ἄμυξις, εως, ἡ, (ἀμύσσω) *tearing, rending, mangling*, Orph.*A.*24, Ach.Tat.8.4; *scarification*, Antyll.ap.Orib.7.16.1; *irritation*, Cass. *Pr.*62.

ἄμυος, ον, *not showing muscle*, σκέλος Hp.*Art.*52, cf. Orib.*Syn.* 5.44.20.

ἀμύριστος [ῠ], ον, *not steeped in unguents*, στέμματα *Epigr.Gr.* 418 (Cyrene). 2. metaph., *rude, rough*, ἀμύριστα φθεγγομένη Heraclit.92.

ἀμυροιραῖνος· ὁ μὴ μυσαττόμενος τὸ ῥαίνεσθαι, Hsch.

ἄμυρον, τό, = ἀτρακτυλίς, Ps.-Dsc.3.93.

ἄμυρος, ον, (ἀ- intens., μύρω) *watery*, τόποι S.*Fr.*512, but perh. (ἀ- priv., μύρον) *not perfumed*, of byres.

ἀμυρτόν· ἱμάτιον (Cret.), Hsch. **ἄμυς**· ὁμοῦ σὺν αὐτῷ (Lacon.), Id.

ἀμύς, ύδος, ἡ, = χελώνη λιμναία, Archig.ap.Gal.12.575.

ἀμύσακτος, ον, (μυσάττω) *without pollution*, *AB*321.

ἀμύσκαρον, v. ἀμυσχρός.

ἄμυσσος· κῆτος (Lacon.), Hsch.

ἀμύσσω, Att. -ττω, Phld.*Lib.*p.57 O.: Ep. impf. ἄμυσσον Il.19. 284: fut. -ξω Il.1.243, Aeschin.*Ep.*12.10: aor. ἤμυξα Nonn.*D.*40. 161, poet. ἄμ- B.16.19, *AP*7.218 (Antip.):—Med., pres., Hp.*Mul.* 1.78: aor. part. ἀμυξάμενος (κατ-) *AP*7.491 (Mnasalc.):—Pass., fut. ἀμυχθήσομαι Aq.2*Ki.*6.19: aor. part. ἀμυχθέν *AP*11.382 (Agath.), Ath.10.433d:—*scratch, tear, lacerate*, χερσὶ δ' ἄμυσσεν στήθεα Il.19. 284; *tear in pieces, mangle*, Hdt.3.76,108; ἀ. τοῖς ὄνυξιν, of the eagle, Arist.*HA*619ᵃ23:—esp. of any slight surface-wound, from whatever cause, *prick* as a thorn, Longus 1.14; *sting* as a fly, Luc.*Musc.Enc.*6: abs., *scratch*, ἀμφοτέραισιν ἀ. Theoc.22.96; *sting*, Hp.*Mul.*1.78. II. metaph., σὺ δ' ἔνδοθι θυμὸν ἀμύξεις χωόμενος *thou wilt tear* thy heart with rage, Il.1.243, cf. Call.*Aet.*3.1.10; καρδίαν ἄμυξεν ἄλγος B.16. 19, cf. 17.11, A.*Pers.*161; φρὴν ἀμύσσεται φόβῳ ib.116; ὑπόμνημα ὃ τὴν γνώμην ἀμύξει Aeschin. l.c., cf. Phld. l.c., Jul.*Or.*2.96a. (For ἀμύχ-yω, cf. ἀμυχή.)

ἀμυστηρίαστος, ον, *not initiated*, Sch.Theoc.3.51, *PLeid.W.*9.38.

ἀμυστ-ί [ῐ], Adv., (μύω) *without closing the mouth*, i.e. *at one draught*, ἀμυστὶ πιεῖν prob. in Hp.*Int.*12, cf. Pherecr.202, *Anacreont.* 8, Luc.*Lex.*8. **-ία**· μέτρον τι, Hsch. **-ίζω**, *drink at one draught*, ἠμύστισα E.*Cyc.*565: pres., Plu.2.650c. **-ις**, ιος and ιδος (Alc. *Supp.*4.20), ἡ, *long draught*, ἄμυστιν προπιεῖν, πίνειν Anacr.63; ἑλκύσαι E.*Cyc.*417; χανδὸν ἄμυστιν οἰνοποτεῖν Call.*Aet.*1.1.11: metaph., ἄμυστιν ὥσπερ κύλικα πίνει τὸν βίον Epich.34. 2. *deep drinking, tippling*, E.*Rh.*438, cf. Sch. II. *large cup*, used by Thracians, ἄμυστιν ἐκλάπτειν Ar.*Ach.*1229, Amips.22, cf. Ath.11.783d.

ἀμύσχεσθαι· τὸ ξέειν τὰς σάρκας τοῖς ὄνυξιν, Hsch. **ἀμυσχῆναι**· καθᾶραι, ἁγνίσαι, Id.

ἀμυσχρός, ά, όν, (μύσος) *undefiled*, Parth.*Fr.*2, prob. l. in S.*Fr.* 1005, cf. Hsch., *EM*87.26 (ἀμυχρόν Phot.p.97 R.; ἀμυχνόν, ἀμυγνόν, ἀμύσκαρον are also cited by Suid.).

ἀμῠχ-ή, ἡ, (ἀμύσσω) *scratch, skin-wound*, Hp.*Epid.*7.32; ἀμυχὰς καταμύξαντες Phryn.Com.3; *of marks of strangling*, D.47.59. 2. Medic., *scarification*, Antyll.ap.Orib.7.18.3, Gal.10.964. II. = ἄμυξις, in sign of sorrow, ἀμυχὰς κοπτομένων ἀφεῖλεν Plu.*Sol.* 21. III. metaph., ἀ. καὶ ἑλκώσεις ἐν ταῖς φιλίαις Iamb.*VP*33. 231. **-ηδόν**, Adv., = ἀμύξ: hence, *slightly*, *EM*88.5. **-ιαῖος**, α, ον, *scratched slightly*: metaph., *superficial*, Pl.*Ax.*366a. **-μός**, ὁ, = ἄμυξις; ἀ. ξιφέων sword-*wound*, Theoc.24.126. **-νός, -ρός**, v. sub ἀμυσχρός. **-ούσης**· στυφούσης ἐπὶ πλέον, Hsch. **-ώδης**, ες, *chapped*, ἐξανθίσματα Hp.*Coac.*435.

ἀμύω (cf. ἠμύω), *sink down, fall*, [φύλλα] ἀμύοντα χαμᾶζε Hes.*Fr.* 96.86. **ἀμύωτος**, ον, dub. sens. in *GDI*4979 (Gortyn).

ἀμφ-, poet. for ἀναφ- (cf. ἀμπ-), but more commonly for ἀμφί before vowels.

ἀμφάγαμαι, *stand round and admire*: aor. -αγάσαντο Q.S.7.722.

ἀμφᾰγᾰπάζω, used by Hom. only in impf. ἀμφαγάπαζον, pres. part. Med. -όμενος; by later Ep. only in pres., impf., cf. *IG*12(9). 289.14 (Eretria, ii/i B.C., prob. l.):—*embrace with love, greet warmly*, Od.14.381, Canthar.2 D. (2 sg. impf. -ηγάπαζες), A.R.3.258, etc.; so Med., Il.16.192, *h.Cer.*290.

ἀμφᾰγᾰπάω, Ep. = foreg., aor. ἀμφαγάπησε *h.Cer.*439; ἑὸν κακὸν ἀμφαγαπῶντες (i.e. Pandora) Hes.*Op.*58; ἀμφαγαπᾷ Orac.ap.D.S.8 *Fr.*21.

ἀμφαγείρομαι, Med., *gather round*, Hom. only in aor. 2, θεαὶ δέ μιν ἀμφαγέροντο Il.18.37, cf. A.R.4.1527: in later Ep. pres. ἀμφαγέρομαι Theoc.17.94, Opp.*H.*3.231, 4.114.

***ἀμφαγνοέω**, pres. assumed by Gramm. for deriv. of ἠμφηγνόουν, but v. ἀμφιγνοέω.

ἀμφάγνυμαι, *to be broken around*, πέλαγος ἕρκεσιν ἀ. prob. l. in J. *BJ*4.10.5.

ἀμφ-άδην, Adv., = ἀμφαδόν, Archil.66. **-άδιος**, α, ον, (poet. for ἀναφάδιος which does not occur, v. sq.):—*public*, γάμος Od.6. 288. II. acc. fem. ἀμφαδίην as Adv., = ἀμφαδόν, *publicly, openly*, Il.13.356, Thgn.90, etc. **-ᾰδόν**, Adv., poet. for ἀναφαδόν = ἀναφανδόν (ἀμφανδόν), *publicly, openly, without disguise*, opp. λάθρῃ, βαλέειν Il.7.243; opp. κρυφηδόν, Od.14.330; opp δόλῳ, κτείνειν 1.296; ἀ. πάντ' ἀγορεύειν Il.9.370; ὡς ἀ. πέπραγα πανταχῇ καλῶς Ion Trag.ap. Phot.p.98 R.—Prop. neut. of Adj. **ἀμφαδός**, ή, όν, which occurs in Od.19.391 μὴ ἀμφαδὰ ἔργα γένοιτο *discovered, known*, cf. A.R.3.615.

ἀμφαεικής· κύκλῳ σειομένης, Hsch.

ἀμφαής, shortened fr. ἀμφιφαής, Hsch.

ἀμφαίνω, poet. for ἀναφαίνω.

ἀμφᾱΐσσομαι, Pass., *rush on from all sides*, ἀμφὶ δέ τ' ἀΐσσονται [κύνες] Il.11.417; *float around*, ἀμφὶ δὲ χαῖται ὤμοις ἀΐσσοντο 6.510.

ἀμφαιωρέω, *cause to float around*, prob. for ἀμφαιρέω, Aret.*CA*1.1.

ἀμφάκανθος, ον, (ἄκανθα) *surrounded with prickles*, ἀ. δέμας, of the hedgehog, Ion Trag.38.

ἀμφάκης [ᾱ], ες, Dor. for ἀμφήκης. **ἀμφακλῆς**· ἀξίνη, Hsch.

ἀμφᾰλᾰλάζω, *shout around*, Nonn.*D.*40.98.

ἀμφᾰλάλημαι, *wander round about*, Opp.*C.*3.423.

ἀμφαλλάξ, Adv. strengthd. for ἀλλάξ, *alternately, reciprocally*, Ath. Mech.22.1, Ps.-Hes.ap.Ath.3.116c, *AP*12.238 (Strat.).

ἀμφαλλάσσω, *change entirely*, Opp.*C.*3.13.

ἀμφανδόν, Adv., poet. for ἀναφανδόν, prob. in Pi.*P.*9.41.

ἀμφανέειν, poet. for ἀναφανεῖν, inf. fut. of ἀναφαίνω, *h.Merc.*16.

ἄμ-φανσις, εως, ἡ, Cret. for ἀνάφανσις, *adoption*, *Leg.Gort.*10. 33. **-φαντός**, *adopted*, ib.50, al. **-φαντύς**, ύος, ἡ, = ἄμφανσις, ib.11.21.

ἀμφάνω, dub. sens., *GDI*5024.58 (Cret.), Hsch.

ἀμφαξονέω, (ἄξων) *go unsteadily, totter*: metaph. from wheels loose on axles, Paus.Gr.*Fr.*50.

ἀμφᾰρᾰβέω, Ep., *rattle* or *ring around*, τεύχεα ἀμφαράβησε Il.21. 408:—**ἀμφᾰρᾰβίζω**, in Ep. impf. ἀμφαράβιζεν Hes.*Sc.*64.

ἀμφαρής· πωρουμένη, κατολιγωρουμένη, Hsch.: also glossed by γυμνός (i.e. ἀφαρής) and ἐπιφανής (i.e. ἀμφιφαής), Id.

ἀμφᾰρίστερος, ον, *with two left hands*, i.e. *utterly awkward* or *clumsy* (cf. ἀμφιδέξιος), Ar.*Fr.*512: hence, *luckless*, Hsch., Eust. 1228.44.

ἀ(μ)φαρμένη· δίκελλα, Hsch.

ἀμφᾰσίη, ἡ, Ep. for ἀφασία, *speechlessness* caused by fear, amazement, or rage, δὴν δέ μιν ἀμφασίη ἐπέων λάβε Il.17.695, Od.4.704, cf. A.R.3.284, Bion *Fr.*13.1.

ἄμφασμα, τό, *cake* soaked in wine and honey (Syrac.), Hsch.

ἀμφαυγεῖ· ἀντιλάμπει, Hsch.

ἄμφαυξις, εως, ἡ, (αὔξειν) *callus* or *overgrowth* on the scar of a removed branch (cf. ἀμφιφύα), Thphr.*HP*3.7.1.

ἀμφαϋτέω, *ring around*, κόρυθες δ' ἀμφ' αὖον ἀΰτευν Il.12.160.

ἀμφαφάω, *touch* or *feel all round*, κοῖλον λόχον ἀμφαφόωσα Od.4. 277; καί κ' ἀλαὸς . . διακρίνειε τὸ σῆμα ἀμφαφόων *by feeling* it, 8.196; *handle*, τόξον ἐΰξοον ἀμφαφόωντας 19.586; 2 sg. ἀμφαφάεις Orph.*L.* 528; Ep. impf. ἀμφαφάασκε Mosch.2.95:—also Med. like Act., τὸν μὲν . . χείρεσιν ἀμφαφόωντο Od.15.461, cf. 19.475; τόξον οἶδα . . ἀμφαφάασθαι (Ep. inf.) 8.215. 2. of persons, μαλακώτερος ἀμφαφάασθαι easier *to deal with*, Il.22.373.—Ep. Verb used by Aret. in forms -όωσι *SD*2.4, *CA*1.1; -όωντα ib.2.4; cf. ἀμφαφᾷς· ψηλαφᾷς, Hsch.

ἀμφεικάς, άδος, ἡ (sc. ἡμέρα), *day next after the twentieth, twenty-first*, *Test.Epict.*3.1, cf. *GDI*3720 (Cos), Hsch. s. v. ἀμφ' εἰκάς.

ἀμφεκτέον· περιβλητέον, Hsch. **ἀμφεκτήρ**· χιτὼν διπλοῦς, Id. **ἀμφελαΐς**· μᾶζα ἐλαίου πλήρης, Id.

ἀμφελελίζω, *shake all round*, γαῖαν Orph.*Fr.*285.6; οὐρανόν Nonn. *D.*13.361; *brandish*, 42.318:—Pass., *swing* or *wave to and fro*, Q.S. 11.465. **ἀμφελικτός**, ον, poet. for ἀμφιελ-, *coiled round*, E.*HF* 398. **ἀμφελίσσω**, poet. and Ion. for ἀμφιελ-, *wrap, fold about*, ἀμφελίξαντες χέρας Id.*Andr.*425; *enwrap*, Aret.*CA*2.4:—Med., τέκνοισιν γνάθους ἀμφελίξασθαι *close their* jaws *upon* the children, Pi.*N.* 1.43.

ἀμφέλκω, *draw around*: Med., ἀμφέλκεσθαί τι *draw* a thing *round one*, i.e. *be surrounded by* it, D.P.268.

ἀμφελόνη· *amictus*, *Gloss.*

ἀμφελυτρ-όω, *wrap round*, Lyc.75. **-ωσις**, εως, ἡ, *wrapper, coating*, Id.845.

ἀμφεμμένος, poet. pf. part. of ἀμφιέννυμι. **ἀμφενέπω**, strengthd. for ἐνέπω, v.l. in Nic.*Th.*627.

ἀμφέπω, v. ἀμφιέπω.

ἀμφερείδω, *fix around*, ζυγόν τινι Lyc.504.

ἀμφερέφω, *cover up*, *AP*11.37 (Antip.).

ἀμφερκής, ές, *fenced round*, πίθος Achae.36.

ἀμφερυθαίνω, *redden, make red all over*, Q.S.1.60.

ἀμφέρχομαι, *surround*, Hom. only aor. 2, c. acc., με κουράων ἀμφήλυθε θῆλυς ἀϋτή Od.6.122; με κνίσης ἀμφήλυθεν ἡδὺς ἀϋτμή 12. 369. II. intr., *pass, elapse*, of time, αἱ φωνίοι πεντεκαίδεκ' ἀμέραυς ἀμφεληλεύθεν (pf. inf.) ὁ ἄρχων τᾶς δίκας *GDI*4999 (Gortyn).

ἀμφέρω, v. ἀναφέρω.

ἀμφεωρία· περισσευομένη, Hsch.

ἀμφεώτας· ὁ Κρητικὸς χιτών, Hsch.

ἀμφηγερέθομαι, Ep. = ἀμφαγείρομαι, ἀμφὶ δ' . . ἠγερέθοντο Od.17. 34.

ἀμφήκης, ες, (ἀκή A) *two-edged*, φάσγανον, ξίφος, Il.10.256, Od.16. 80, B.10.87, etc.; κέντρον, δόρυ, A.*Pr.*692 (lyr.), *Ag.*1149; ἔγχος, γένυς, S.*Aj.*286, *El.*485; of lightning, *forked*, πυρὸς ἀ. βόστρυχος A. *Pr.*1044; κεραυνός Cleanth.1.10. II. metaph., ἀ. γλῶττα tongue *that will cut both ways*, i.e. maintain either right or wrong, Ar.*Nu.* 1160 (parod.); of an oracle, *ambiguous*, ἀ. καὶ διπρόσωπος Luc.*J.Tr.* 43.

ἀμφημερῖνὸς πυρετός, *quotidian fever*, opp. τριταῖος and τεταρταῖος, Hp.*Epid.*1.6, Pl.*Ti.*86a: neut. as Adv., -νὸν πυρεταίνειν Aret. *SD*1.2:—also **-ήμερος** (sc. πυρετός), S.*Fr.*507.

ἀμφην, Aeol. for αὐχήν, q.v. **ἀμφήν**· αὐλήν, Hsch.

ἀμφηρεφής, ές, (ἐρέφω) *covered on both sides, close-covered*, epith. of Apollo's quiver, Il.1.45: in late Prose, ἄντρον Agath.1.10, cf. 3.5; στάδιον ἀ. ὕλαις Zos.2.50.

ἀμφήρης, ες, (ἀραρίσκω) *fitted* or *joined on both sides*; ξύλα ἀ. wood of the funeral pyre *regularly piled all round*, E.*HF*243; ἀ. σκηναί dwellings *well secured*, Id.*Ion* 1128. II. (ἐρέσσω) *with oars on both sides*, Hsch.; ἀ. δόρυ *sculling*-boat, E.*Cyc.*15.

ἀμφηρικός, ή, όν, = ἀμφήρης II: ἀκάτιον ἀ. *sculling*-boat, Th.4.67.

ἀμφήριστος, ον, (ἐρίζω) *contested on both sides, disputed, doubtful*, ἀμφήριστον ἔθηκεν, i.e. made it a dead-heat, Il.23.382; γένος ἀ. Call. *Jov.*5; νεῖκος A.R.3.627; ἐλπίδες Plb.5.85.6; ἐς ἀμφήριστον ἐλθεῖν τινι App.*Pun.*51; *evenly matched*, πόλεις Str.8.4.8, cf. Q.S.5.310, Luc.*Eun.*4, etc.; of stars, *of doubtful position*, Serap. in *Cat.Cod. Astr.*1.100.

ἄμφης· ἀμφίας, Hsch.

ἀμφί, Prep. with gen., dat., acc.: (cf. Skt. *abhitas* 'on both sides', Lat. *ambi-*):—radic. sense, *on both sides*; chiefly Poet. and Ion. Prose, replaced by περί in later Gk.

A. c. GEN. (Poet., Hdt., X.): I. causal, *about, for the sake of*, ἀ. πίδακος μάχεσθαι fight *for the possession of* a spring, Il.16.825; ἀ. γυναικός Pi.*P.*9.105, A.*Ag.*62; ἀ. λέκτρων E.*Andr.*123: like πρός, in entreaties, πρὸς Ζηνός .. Φοίβου τ' ἀ. *for* Phoebus' *sake*, A.R.2. 216. 2. *about, concerning*, once in Hom., ἀμφ' Ἄρεος φιλότητος ἀείδειν sing *of* love, Od.8.267; ἀμφὶ τιμῆς *h.Merc.*172 (cf. c. 4); once in Hdt., ἀμφὶ κρίσιος (as v.l. for κρίσι) μνηστήρων τοσαῦτα ἐγένετο 6.131; more freq. in poets, ἀ. δαιμόνων Pi.*O.*1.35, cf. A.*Th.*1017, E.*Supp.*642, etc.; prob. l. in S.*Ph.*554. II. of Place, *about, around*, post-Hom., ἀ. ταύτης τῆς πόλιος Hdt.8.104; τὸν ἀ. Λίμνας τρόχον E.*Hipp.*1133.

B. c. DAT. (Poet., Ion. and later Prose): I. of Place, *on both sides of*, ἀμφ' ὀχέεσσι Il.5.723; ἀ. κεφαλῇ, ὤμοισιν, στήθεσσι, ποσσί, *about* the head, etc., ib.24.163, 3.328, Od.16.174, Il.13.36; ἁ. δέρᾳ Sapph.*Supp.*23.16; ἀμφί οἱ *around* him, Il.12.396; μοι ἀμφ' αὐτῷ *around* me, 9.470; likewise ἀμφὶ περὶ στήθεσσι Od.11.609:—*all round*, κρέα ἀμφ' ὀβελοῖσι μεμύκει *round*, i.e. *upon*, spits, ib.12.395; πεπαρμένη ἀμφ' ὀνύχεσσι Hes.*Op.*250. 2. more generally, *at, by*, ἀ. πύλῃσι μάχεσθαι *at* the gates, Il.12.175; ἀμφὶ [κόρυθι] διατρυφέν smashed *on* the helmet, 3.362; ἀ. πυρί *on* the fire, 18.344; ἀμφ' ἐμοί *clinging to* me, Od.11.423; esp. of falling *over* one, Il.4.493; of a guardian, *over*, φύλακα ἀ. σοι λείψω S.*Aj.*562; ἀ. γούνασι πίπτειν E.*Alc.*947. II. of Time, ἁλίῳ ἀ. ἑνὶ *in compass of* one day, Pi. *O.*13.37. III. generally, of connexion or association, without distinct notion of place, ἀ. νεκροῖσιν *as concerning* the dead, Il.7. 408; freq. in Pi., ὅσσα δ' ἀμφ' ἀέθλοις *as far as concerns* games, *N.*2. 17; ἐπ' ἔργοισιν ἀ. τε βουλαῖς *in* deeds and counsels, Id.*P.*5.119; *in virtue of*, ἀμφὶ σοφίᾳ 1.12; ἐμᾷ ἀ. μαχανᾷ 8.34; ἀμφ' ἀρετᾷ 1.80, cf. *O.*8.42; σέο ἀμφὶ τρόπῳ *N.*1.29; ἀ. ἰατορίᾳ *in respect of* healing, B.1. 39. IV. causal, *about, for the sake of*, ἀμφ' Ἑλένῃ μάχεσθαι Il.3. 70; ἀ. γυναικὶ ἄλγεα πάσχειν ib.157, cf. Luc.*DDeor.*20.14; ἀ. τοῖσδε καλχαίνων τέκνοις E.*Heracl.*40, cf. *Rh.*457 (lyr.); ἀ. δώλῳ μωλεῖν *Leg.Gort.*1.17; *concerning*, Od.1.48; εἰπὼν ἀμφ' Ὀδυσῆϊ 14.364; ἀρνεύμενον ἀ. βόεσσι *h.Merc.*390; ἀ. Τειρεσίαο βουλαῖς Pi.*I.*7(6).8; ἕξετ' ἀμφ' ἐμοὶ τροφήν S.*OC*1614, cf. *El.*1144; ἔρις ἀ. μουσικῇ Hdt. 6.129; ἀ. σοι A.*Ag.*890; ἀ. τῷ θανάτῳ αὐτῆς λόγος λέγεται *about* her death it is reported, Hdt.3.32, cf. S.*Aj.*303; ἀ. βοῶν ἀγέλαις δόμον αὔξειν B.9.44. 2. of impulses, ἀ. τάρβει, ἀ. φόβῳ *for* very fear, A.*Ch.*547, E.*Or.*825; ἀ. θυμῷ S.*Fr.*565; ἀμφ' ὀδύνῃ A.R.2.96. V. like ἐπί, *added to*, πόνος ἀ. πόνῳ Simon.39.

C. c. ACC., most freq. in Prose (twice only in Th.): I. of Place, *about, around*, mostly with a sense of motion, ἀ. μιν φᾶρος βάλον Il.24.588, cf. Od.10.365; ἀ. βωμίαν ἔπτηξε παστάδα E.*HF* 984. 2. generally, *by, on*, ἀμφ' ἅλα *by* the sea, Il.1.409; ἀ. ῥέεθρα *somewhere by* the banks, 2.461; ἀ. περὶ κρήνην *somewhere about* the fountain, 2.305; ἀ. ἄστυ *all about in* the city, 11.706; Τάρταρον ἀ. μέγαν *somewhere* in Tartarus, *h.Ap.*336, cf. A.*Pr.*1029; ἀ. Εὔβοιαν B.9.34; ἀ. Θρῄκην E.*Andr.*215; ἀ. ψάμαθον *somewhere on* the sand, S.*Aj.*1064; ἀ. βωμόν *at* the altar, E.*IT*705; περὶ πίδακας ἀ. Theoc. 7.142; of motion, *to the neighbourhood of*, ἤλθες ἀ. Δωδώνην A.*Pr.* 830. 3. of persons grouped *about* one, οἱ ἀ. Πρίαμον Priam *and his train*, Il.3.146, cf. 2.417,445; οἱ ἀ. Ξέρξεα his *army*, Hdt.8. 25; but οἱ ἀ. Κορινθίους, οἱ ἀ. Μεγαρέας καὶ Φλειασίους the Corinthians, Megarians, etc., and those *next* them, Id.9.69: hence Att., οἱ ἀ. Πρωταγόραν the *school of* Protagoras or even Protagoras himself, Pl. *Tht.*170c; οἱ ἀ. Εὐθύφρονα Euthyphro's *friends*, *Cra.*399e, cf. Th.8. 65; of a single person, perh. Pl.*Hp.Ma.*281c; so in later Prose, as Luc.*VH*2.18. 4. τὰ ἀ. τι that which *concerns* a thing, τὰ ἀ. τὸ ἄριστον Th.7.40; τὰ ἀ. τὴν δίαιταν domestic arrangements, X.*Cyr.*8. 2.6. 5. causal, *about, for the sake of*, κλαίειν ἀ. τινα weep *about* or *for* one, Il.18.339; μνήσασθαι ἀ. τινα make mention *of* one, *h.Hom.* 7.1, cf. Terp.2, Ar.*Nu.*595; κελαδέοντι φᾶμαι ἀ. Κινύραν Pi.*P.*2.15, cf. *I.*7(6).9, A.*Th.*843; ἀ. νιν γοώμενος S.*Tr.*937. 6. ἀ. τι ἔχειν to be occupied *about* a thing, ἀ. λιτάν' ἔχομεν A.*Th.*101; ἀ. δεῖπνον εἶχεν X.*Cyr.*5.5.44, cf. 5.2.26; εἶναι ἀμφί τι 7.1.1; ἀ. τὰν δαῖσιν *Leg. Gort.*5.46. II. of Time, *throughout, for*, τὸν λοιπὸν ἀ. βίοτον, τὸν ὅλον ἀ. χρόνον, Pi.*O.*1.97, 2.30; *about, at the time of, during*, ἀ. Πλειάδων δύσιν A.*Ag.*826; ἀ. τὸν χειμῶνα X.*Cyr.*8.6.22, etc. 2. of Number, ἀ. τὰς δώδεκα μυριάδας *about* 120,000, ib.1.2.15.

D. POSITION. In poets ἀμφί sts. follows its case, οἱ δέ μιν ἀμφί Od.23.46, cf. 10.218, B.17.53; φρένας ἀ. Hes.*Th.*554, Mimn.1.7; but never suffers anastrophe, Hdn.Gr.1.480.

E. WITHOUT CASE, as Adv., *about, around, on both* or *all sides*, freq. in Ep., ῥῆξεν δέ οἱ ἀ. χιτῶνα Il.13.439; ἀ. δὲ λειμών *around* is meadow, Od.6.292; so ἀ. περί Il.21.10, etc.

F. IN COMPOS.: I. *on both sides*, ἀμφίστομος, ἀμφίαλος. 2. *on all sides*, ἀμφιβάλλω I. 3, ἀμφιλαμβάνω, ἀμφιλαφής. II. causal, *for the sake of*, ἀμφιμάχομαι, ἀμφιτρομέω.

ἀμφιάζω, Plu.*CG*2 (v.l.): fut. -άσω Alciphr.3.42: aor. ἠμφίασα *AP*7.368 (Eryc.), *OGI*200.24 (Axum), Polyaen.1.27.2 (v.l.), (μετ-) Philostr.*Her.Prooem.*2: pf. ἠμφίακα (συν-) Clearch.25:—**Med.**, fut. -άσομαι (μετ-) Luc.*Herm.*86 codd.: aor. ἠμφιασάμην Apollod. 2.1.2, etc.: pf. ἠμφίασμαι in med. sense (μετ-) D.S.16.11 (v.l.):—ἀμφιέζω is a common v.l.: (perh. from ἀμφί, as ἀντιάζω from ἀντί):—later word for ἀμφιέννυμι, *clothe*, τινά Plu. l.c.; ἱματίοις τινά Alciphr. l.c.: metaph., of the grave, ὀστέα ἠμφίασεν *AP* l.c.; σοφίαν ἀσαφείᾳ Them.*Or.*13.235a:—Med., *put on*, ἀμφιάσασθαί τι Lxx *Jb.*40.5, Apollod. l.c.

ἀμφιαλής, ές, (ἅλς B) *sea-girt*, Δῆλος Maiist.6.

ἀμφίᾰλος, ον, = foreg., freq. of Ithaca in Od., as 1.386,395; of Lemnos, S.*Ph.*146; with ref. to Corinth, *of two seas*, ἀ. Ποτειδᾶνος τεθμοί, of Isthmian games, Pi.*O.*13.40. 2. *living amid seas*, ζῷον Plu.2.667e. 3. ἡ ἀ. (sc. ὁδός) dub. l. in X.*HG*4.2.13.

ἀμφιάνακτες, ων, οἱ, nickname of *dithyrambic poets*, because their odes often began thus—ἀμφί μοι αὖθις ἄνακτα or ἀμφί μοι αὖτε, ἄναξ, Sch.Ar.*Nu.*595. **ἀμφιανακτίζω**, *sing dithyrambic hymns*, Cratin. 67, Ar.*Fr.*59, cf. foreg.

Ἀμφιάραος, ου (also Ἀμφιάρης Pi.*N.*9.24, -ηος *O.*6.13), Att. **Ἀμφιάρεως** (choriamb. in S.*OC*1313), ω, *Amphiaraus*, Argive hero and seer, A., etc.; prob. also called Ἄμφις A.*Fr.*410:—hence **Ἀμφιαράϊον**, τό, *sanctuary of A.*, esp. at Oropus, and **Ἀμφιαράϊα**, τά, *festival of A.* held there, *IG*7.48, al., cf. Did.ap.Sch.Pi.*O.*7.153, Str. 9.1.22, etc. **Ἀμφιάρειον**, τό, cj. in Pi.*I.*7(6).33; cf. Ἀμφιεραϊστής.

ἀμφίας, ὁ, a bad Sicilian wine, Nicostr.Com.18, Sosicr.Com.7; cf. ἄμφης.

ἀμφίασ-ις, εως, ὁ, (ἀμφιάζω) *garment*, Lxx *Jb.*22.6, al. **-μα**, ατος, τό, *garment*, Ctes.*Fr.*29.10, Luc.*Cyn.*17. **-μός**, ὁ, = ἀμφίασις, D.H.8.62 (pl.).

ἀμφῐάχυῖα, irreg. part., perh. for ἀμφι-ϝαχυῖα (cf. ἰάχω = ϝιϝάχω), *flying about and shrieking*, of a bird, Il.2.316; later ἀμφ-ιάχω as pres., μέγα ἀμφῐάχων Orph.*A.*819: impf. ἀμφίαχε λαός Q.S.4.147; trans., βοὴ ἀμφίαχεν ἄστυ 13.460.

ἀμφιβαίνω, fut. -βήσομαι, etc.:—*go about* or *around*, ἠέλιος μέσον οὐρανὸν ἀμφιβεβήκει sun *in his course had reached* mid-heaven, Il.8. 68. 2. *bestride*, ἀμφ' ἑνὶ δούρατι βαῖνε *he bestrode* a beam, Od.5. 371; ἵππον ἀ. Call.*Del.*113; ἀ. θηλείαις, of a cock, Babr.5.8: esp., 3. *bestride* a fallen friend, *so as to protect* him, ἀμφὶ κασιγνήτῳ βεβαώς Il. 14.477: hence, b. of tutelary deities, *guard, protect*, Χρύσην ἀμφιβέβηκας ib.1.37; δαίμονες ἀμφιβάντες πόλιν A.*Th.*175:—so, of a wild beast, *guard* its young, Opp.*C.*3.218; or its prey, X.*Cyn.*10. 13. II. *surround, encompass*, c. acc., νεφέλη σκόπελον ἀμφιβέβηκε Od.12.74; σὲ πόνος φρένας ἀμφιβέβηκεν Il.6.355, cf. Od.8.541; ταραγμὸν ἀμφιβάντ' εἶχον μάχης E.*Ph.*1406; ὦ μοῖρα .. οἷά με .. ἀμφιβᾶσ' ἔχεις Id.*Andr.*1082: c. dat., Τρώων νέφος ἀμφιβέβηκε νηυσίν Il.16.66; ἀ. ἀμφί τι, of a slit bandage which *embraces* a tender part without pressing on it, Hp.*Art.*33. 2. metaph., τόδε μοι θράσος ἀμφιβαίνει E.*Supp.*609; ἀμφιβᾶσα φλὸξ οἴνου, metaph. from flame *spreading round* a vessel on the fire, *Alc.*758.

Ἀμφίβαιος, ὁ, epith. of Poseidon at Cyrene, = ἀμφίγαιος, γαιήοχος, Tz.ad Lyc.749.

ἀμφιβάλλω, fut. -βαλῶ, etc.:—**Med.**, Ep. fut. ἀμφιβαλεῦμαι Od. 22.103:—*throw* or *put round*, used by Hom. mostly in tmesi: I. of clothes, etc., *put them on* a person, c. dupl. acc. pers. et rei, ἀμφὶ δέ με χλαῖναν .. βάλεν ἠδὲ χιτῶνα Od.10.365, cf. 451; ἀμφὶ δέ μιν ῥάκος .. βάλεν 13.434: c. dat. pers., ἀμφὶ δέ μοι ῥάκος .. βάλον v.l. in 14. 342; ἀμφὶ δ' Ἀθήνη ὤμοις .. βάλ' αἰγίδα Il.18.204; στολὴν .. ἀμφέβαλλε σῷ κάρᾳ E.*HF*465; γέρας κόμαις Pi.*P.*5.32:—Med., *put round oneself*, δὸς δὲ ῥάκος ἀμφιβαλέσθαι Od.6.178, cf. 22.103, etc.; ἄγραν .. ἀ. πλοκάμοις E.*Ba.*104. b. metaph. and half metaph., τῷ δ' ἐγὼ ἀμφιβαλὼν θάλαμον δέμον I built chamber *over* him, Od.23.192; ζυγὸν Ἑλλάδι ἀ. A.*Pers.*50, cf. 72; ἀνδράσι κρατὴρ ὕπνον ἀμφιβάλλῃ E.*Ba.* 385; ἐξ ὅτου λευκὴν ἐκ μελαίνης ἀμφιβάλλομαι τρίχα since *I have put on* white hair, S.*Ant.*1093; ἀ. νέφος θανάτου Simon.99. c. Act. in med. sense, κρατερὸν μένος ἀμφιβαλόντες [ἑαυτοῖς] 'girding themselves with strength', Il.17.742; δουλοσύναν ἀμφιβαλοῦσα κάρᾳ [ἐμαυτῆς] E.*Andr.*110: reversely, Med. for Act., ἀμφιβάλλεσθαι Ἀΐδαν ἐπί τινι 1191:—Pass., ὕμνος ἀμφιβάλλεται σοφῶν μητίεσσι song *is cast (like a net) over* the minds of poets, Pi.*O.*1.8. 2. *throw* the arms *round*, so as to embrace, c. dat. pers., ἀμφ' Ὀδυσῆϊ .. χεῖρε βαλόντε Od.21.223; ἀμφὶ δὲ χεῖρας δειρῇ βάλλ' Ὀδυσῆϊ 23.208; ἀμφὶ δὲ παιδὶ .. βάλε πήχεε 24.347; but ἀμφὶ δὲ χεῖρας βάλλομεν, of *seizing* or *taking prisoner*, 4.454; also ἀμφὶ δὲ χεῖρα .. βάλεν ἔγχεϊ *grasped* it, 21.433; ἀμφὶ δὲ .. βάλε γούνασι χεῖρας, as a suppliant, 7. 142. 3. c. acc. pers., *encompass, embrace*, ἀμφιβαλόντε ἀλλήλους Il. 23.97; ἀ. τινὰ χερσί E.*Ba.*1363; ἀ. μαστὸν ὠλέναισι *Ph.*306; ἀ. μέλη *Supp.*70. 4. *encompass, beset*, δυσμενὴς ὅρι' ἀμφιβάλλει B.17.6; πόλιν φόνῳ E.*Andr.*799, cf. *Trag.Adesp.*127.6 (lyr.); ἀ. φῦλον ὀρνίθων *surround* them *with nets*, S.*Ant.*344; *strike* or *hit on all sides*, τινὰ βέλεσι E.*HF*422. b. abs., *fish* (cf. ἀμφίβληστρον), *Ev.Marc.*1.16, cf. *PFlor.*2.119.3 (ii A.D.). c. metaph., ἀμφὶ κτύπος οὔατα βάλλει Il.10.535 (unless ἀ. be Adv.). II. *force, move round*, τὸ ἄρθρον v.l. for ἀμφισφάλλω (q.v.), Hp.*Art.*2. III. *doubt*, περί τινος Plb. 39.5.2: also folld. by inf., Hld.5.17; by ὡς .. Ael.*NA*9.33; by ὅτι .. Hermog.*Id.*2.10; περί τινος Id.*Meth.*23. IV. intr., ἀ. εἰς τόπον *go* into *another* place, E.*Cyc.*60. 2. *to be doubtful* or *in dispute*,

Arist.*EE*1243ᵃ12,25; ἀμφιβάλλειν εἴωθε τὰ φίλτρα *are uncertain* in their action, Alciphr.1.37:—Pass., *to be in dispute*, Simp.*in Ph.*21.11. V. Med., *change*, μορφήν Opp.*C.*3.16.

ἀμφιβαρής, gloss on ἀμφικέλεμνον, Hsch., Phot.

ἀμφίβᾰσις, εως, ἡ, *defence of* fallen comrade, δεῖσε δ' ὅ γ' ἀμφίβασιν.. Τρώων Il.5.623.

ἀμφιβάσκω, = ἀμφιβαίνω, Sapph.*Supp.*10.7. **ἀμφιβατεῖν**· ἀμφισβητεῖν, Hsch.

ἀμφίβιος, ον, *living a double life*, esp. *amphibious*, νομή, of frogs, Batr.59; ἀ. στόμα Pl.*Epigr.*2, cf. *Ax.*368b; θήρ Man.4.23; of plants, Thphr.*HP*1.4.3; ἀμφίβιον, τό, = ἀλόη, Ps.-Dsc.3.22:—said by Thphr. (*Fr.*171.12) to have been first used by Democr. 2. metaph., of the soul, *denizen of two worlds*, Plot.4.8.4; of man, Hierocl. *in CA*23 p.468 M.; ὁ κατὰ τὴν ζωὴν κόσμος ἐστὶν οἷον ἀμφίβιον Dam.*Pr.*81, cf. 85; φύσις ἀ. ib.399, cf. 400; of the moon, ἄστρον ἀ. πρὸς νύκτα καὶ ἡμέραν Max.Tyr.40.4; of Tiresias (who lived both as man and as woman), Luc.*Astr.*11.

ἀμφίβλημα, ατος, τό, *something thrown round, enclosure*, E.*Hel.* 70. II. *garment, cloak*, πέπλους τε τοὺς πρὶν λαμπρά τ' ἀμφιβλήματα ib.423; πάνοπλα ἀ. *coats* of panoply, Id.*Ph.*779; *coverlet*, Aret.*SD*2.6.

ἀμφιβληστρ-ευτική (sc. τέχνη), ἡ, *net-fishery*, Poll.7.139. **-εύω**, *catch with a net*, Aq.*Is.*51.20 (Pass.). **-ικός**, ή, όν, *serving for a net*, Pl.*Sph.*235b. **-οειδής**, ές, *net-like*, χιτών prob. *the retina*, Gal. *UP*8.6, 10.2, cf. Ruf.*Onom.*153, Poll.2.71. **-ον**, τό, *anything thrown round*: 1. *casting-net*, Hes.*Sc.*215, Hdt.1.141, 2.95; ἀμφιβλήστρῳ περιβάλλεσθαι Men.27, cf. Stratt.7, Epil.1, Ph.*Bel.*95, *Ev.Matt.*4.18. b. metaph., of *the garment thrown like a net over* Agamemnon, A.*Ag.*1382, *Ch.*492; of the shirt of Nessus, Ἐρινύων ὑφαντὸν ἀ. S.*Tr.*1052; ἀμφίβληστρα σώματος ῥάκη rags *thrown around* body, E.*Hel.*1079. 2. *fetter, bond*, A.*Pr.*81. 3. of *encircling* walls, ἀμφίβληστρα τοίχων E.*IT*96.

ἀμφίβλητος, ον, *put* or *thrown round*, ῥάκη E.*Fr.*697.

ἀμφιβο-άομαι, Pass., *to be celebrated*, *PCair.*67120ᵛ39 (vi A.D.). **-ητος**, ον, *sounding round, resounding*, Call.*Del.*303; κτύπος Nonn. *D.*45.44. 2. *noised abroad, far-famed*, *AP*9.241 (Antip.), cf. Nonn.*D.*26.141.

ἀμφιβολ-εύς, έως, ὁ, (ἀμφιβάλλω) *fisherman*, Lxx *Is.*19.8. **-έω**, *to be in doubt*, Greg.Cor. in Rh.7.1339 W. **-ή**, ἡ, *cast* as of a net, λίνοιο ἀ. *fishing-net*, Opp.*H.*4.149. **-ητικός**, ή, όν, *ambiguous*, φωνή Olymp. *in Cat.*86.39. **-ία**, Ion. **-ίη**, ἡ, *state of being attacked on both sides*, ἀμφιβολίῃ ἔχεσθαι Hdt.5.74. II. *ambiguity*, Arist.*Po.*1461ᵃ25, *SE*165ᵇ26, cf. Epicur.*Nat.*28.5, D.H. *Rh.*8.16, Ael.*Tact.*40(51).1, A.D.*Synt.*311.10, etc.; *double entente*, Cic.*Fam.*7.32.2, cf. Philostr.*VS*2.25.1; ἀ. ἀναιρεῖν remove *doubt*, Plu.2.1050a; *uncertainty of mind*, App.*Pun.*42. **-ος**, ον, *put round, encompassing*, σπάργανα E.*Ion*1490; ὄρη Opp.*C.*3.133: Subst. **-βολον**, τό, κλωστοῦ **-βόλοις** λίνοιο E.*Tr.*537, cf. *AP*6.296 (Leon.). II. *struck* or *attacked on both* or *all sides*, A.*Th.*298; ἀ. εἶναι to be *between two fires*, Th.4.32,36; ἀ. γεγονέναι ὑπὸ τῶν πολεμίων Plu.*Cam.*34, cf. Ph.*Bel.*86.13. 2. Act., *hitting at both ends, double-pointed*, κάμακες *AP*6.131 (Leon.). III. *doubtful, ambiguous*, Pl.*Cra.*437a, X.*Mem.*1.2.35, etc.; τἀγαθὰ ἐς ἀμφίβολον ἀσφαλῶς ἔθεντο prudently accounted their good fortune as *doubtful*, Th. 4.18; ἐς ἀ. θέσθαι call *in question*, Plu.2.756c; τὰ ἅπαξ κεκριμένα ἀ. ποιῆσαι *OGI*664 (Egypt, i A.D.); ἀ. νόμος Arist.*Rh.*1375ᵇ11; τὸ ἀ. *Top.*160ᵃ29; ἀμφίβολα λέγειν *Rh.*1407ᵃ37; δηλώσεις ἀ. Epicur. *Ep.*1p.27U.; συλλογισμοί, λέξεις, Chrysipp.*Stoic.*2.67,107; διάλεκτοι, prob. *contradictory*, ib.56,58; οἰνάριον ἀ. *doubtful* whether it is wine or vinegar, Polioch.2.8; ἐν ἀμφιβόλῳ εἶναι to be *doubtful*, Luc.*DMort.* 1.1; κατὰ δύο ἀμφίβολα Olymp. *in Mete.*22.27. Adv., οὐκ ἀμφιβόλως A.*Th.*863; ἀ. ἔχειν D.H.*Rh.*10.5; δέξασθαι Arr.*Tact.*31.1. IV. of persons, *in doubt, wavering, uncertain*, Luc.*DDeor.*20.11, D.C.37.36, etc.; also ἀ. βίος, of a turncoat, Luc.*Pseudol.*16; ἄνθρωπος, of a eunuch, Lib.*Eth.*26.3.

ἀμφιβόσκομαι, Dep., *eat all about*, Luc.*Trag.*303.

ἀμφίβουλος, ον, *double-minded*: c. inf., *half-minded* to do, A.*Eu.* 733 (cj. Turneb.).

ἀμφιβράγχια, τά, *parts about the tonsils*, Hp.*Int.*53.

ἀμφίβρᾰχυς, εια, υ, *short at both ends*: ὁ ἀ., the metrical foot ⏑ – ⏑, e.g. ἄμεινον, D.H.*Comp.*17, Heph.3.2.

ἀμφίβροτος, η, ον, also ος, ον, *covering the whole man*, Hom. always ἀμφιβρότη ἀσπίς Il.2.389; ἀ. χθών, of body as *surrounding* soul, Emp.148; ἀ. κώδεια (ἡ γὰρ κεφαλὴ συνέχει πᾶν τὸ σῶμα Sch.) Nic. *Al.*216.

ἀμφίβροχος, ον, *thoroughly soaked*, *AP*7.27 (Antip.).

ἀμφιβώμιος, ον, *at the altar*, E.*Tr.*562.

ἀμφίβωτος, ον, contr. from ἀμφιβόητος, Ion Trag.35.

ἀμφιγάνυμαι, = ἀμφιγηθέω, Q.S.1.62.

ἀμφίγειος, ον, *with land on both sides*, θάλασσα Phot., Suid. s.v. πορθμός.

ἀμφιγενής, ές, *of doubtful gender*, Eust.668.48.

ἀμφίγευς, υ, gen. υος, *two-edged*, of an axe, Hsch.

ἀμφιγηθέω, *rejoice throughout*, *h.Ap.*273.

ἀμφίγλωσσος, ον, *ambiguous*, Eust.489.19, al.

ἀμφιγνοέω: impf. ἠμφεγνόουν Pl.*Sph.*236c, X.*An.*2.5.33: aor. ἠμφεγνόησα Pl.*Plt.*291b, *Sph.*228e (ἀμφαγνοέω v.l. in X.*An.* l.c., and Procop.*Goth.*2.16):—*to be doubtful* or *mistaken about* a thing, τι Pl. *Sph.*228e; περί τινος Isoc.2.28; ἐπί τινος πότερον.. Pl.*Grg.*466c; ὑπέρ τινος Procop. l.c.; ἠμφεγνόουν ὅ τι ἐποίουν *they knew not* what they were about, X.*An.* l.c.; οὐκ ἀμφιγνοῶ σε γεγονότα συστρατιώτην *I am* not *mistaken in thinking*.., Plu.*Pomp.*79:—Pass., ἀμφιγνοηθεὶς *unrecognized*, X.*HG*6.5.26; but ἀμφιγνοούμενόν ἐστι *is in dispute*, Arr.*Tact.*6.2, cf. Plot.4.4.12.

ἀμφίγνοια, ἡ, *doubt*, Sch.S.*Aj.*23. **ἀμφιγνωμονέω**, *to be of doubtful mind*, Doroth.ap.*EM*87.48, Sch.Pl.*Grg.*466c.

ἀμφιγόητος, ον, *bewailed all round*, Κωκυτοῦ ὕδωρ *AP*7.700 (Diod.).

ἀμφίγονος, ον, *stepchild*, Hsch., *EM*87.50.

Ἀμφιγυήεις, ὁ, epith. of Hephaestus, *with both feet crooked, lame*, Il.1.607, etc.

ἀμφιγυιόω, *mutilate*, or *impale*, Hsch., cf. *EM*89.17.

ἀμφίγυος, ον, in Hom. always epith. of ἔγχος, either (γυῖον) *with a limb at each end, double-pointed*, or (γύης) *bending both ways, elastic*, Il.13.147, Od.24.527; ἀ. δούρασιν A.R.3.135; prob. (from γυῖον) *stout rivals*, S.*Tr.*504 (lyr.).

ἀμφιδαής, *two-edged knife*, Suid.

ἀμφιδαίω, *kindle around*:—only intr. in pf. and plpf., *burn, blaze around*, ἀϋτή τε πτόλεμός τε ἄστυ τόδ' ἀμφιδέδηε Il.6.329; ἀμφὶ μάχη τ' ἐνοπή τε δεδήει τεῖχος 12.35; of dust, κόνις σφ' ἀμφιδεδήει Hes.*Sc.* 62.

ἀμφιδάκνω, *bite all round*: hence, *grip close*, *APl.*4.118 (Paul.Sil.).

ἀμφιδάκρῡτος, ον, *all-tearful*, πόθος E.*Ph.*330.

ἀμφιδαρκανές· ὁμαλόν, Hsch.

ἀμφιδάσυς, εια, υ, *shaggy* or *fringed all round*, epith. of the Aegis, which was hung with θύσανοι, Il.15.309; also of the head of Marsyas, Simon.177.

ἀμφίδαφος, prob. = ἀμφιτάπης, *POxy.*298.9 (i A.D.).

ἀμφιδέα, ας, ἡ, *anything that binds* or *is bound around, bracelet* or *anklet*, mostly pl., Hdt.2.69, Ar.*Fr.*320.11, *IG*2.652*A*18, cf. 660.11, Aristaenet.1.19, Lib.*Or.*31.12. 2. *iron rings*, by which folding-doors were secured in hinges, Lys.*Fr.*37, *IG*2.834*b* ii 99: sg. **-δῆ** *IG* 11(2).147.7 (Delos, iv B.C.). 3. τὰ ἀμφίδεα, *rim* of the *os uteri*, Hp.*Mul.*1.57, cf. Gal.19.78:—sg. **-δήιον** Ruf.*Onom.*195, **-διον** Erot.

ἀμφιδεής, ές, *afraid on all sides*, Hsch., Phot., Suid.

ἀμφιδεΐδιον, τό, Dim. of ἀμφιδέα, *door-ring*, prob. in *BCH*10.463 (Delos, iv B.C.).

ἀμφιδείκελος, *visible from all sides*, Suid.

ἀμφιδεκάτη, ἡ, Arc. for the *21st of the month*, Hsch. (dub.):—also **ἀμφιδεκατία**, ἡ, *IG*5(1).363 (Sparta); cf. ἀμφεικάς.

ἀμφιδέμω, *build round about*, in aor. 1 Med. ἀμφεδείμαντο J.*BJ* 5.5.1.

ἀμφιδέξιος, ον, *ambidextrous* (cf. ἀμφαρίστερος), Hp.*Aph.*7.43 (wrongly expl. by Glaucias ap.Erot., S.E.*M.*7.50), Arist.*EN*1134ᵇ 34; = περιδέξιος, Hippon.83. Adv. **-ίως**, παίζειν Polem.Hist. 45. 2. *ready to take with either hand*, i.e. *taking either of two things, indifferent*, *Trag.Adesp.*355 (= *Com.Adesp.*360); so ἀμφιδεξίως ἔχει it is *indifferent*, A.*Fr.*266. 3. *two-edged*, σίδηρος E.*Hipp.* 780. b. metaph., *double-meaning, ambiguous*, χρηστήριον Hdt. 5.92.ε', cf. Luc.*JTr.*43. 4. *on either hand, with both hands*, ἀ. ἀκμαῖς with *both* hands *at once*, S.*OT*1243; ἐρείσατ'.. πλευρὸν ἀμφιδέξιον ἐμφύντε τῷ φύσαντι *OC*1112. 5. ἀμφιδέξια, τά, *bracelets*, Hsch.: sg. ἀμφίδεξιν (sic) *IG*3.238*a*.

ἀμφιδεξιότης, ητος, ἡ, *ambidextrousness, dexterity*, Eust.957.30.

ἀμφιδέραιον, τό, *necklace*, Lib.*Decl.*46.17, Hsch.: pl. **ἀμφιδέρρεα**, *AB*388.

ἀμφιδέρκομαι, Dep., *look upon, behold*, *AP*15.22 (Simm.).

ἀμφιδὲσφάγανον (sic)· σκολοπένδρα, Hsch.

ἀμφι-δέτης, ου, ὁ, (δέω A) *yoke* for oxen, Artem.2.24. 2. *necklace*, Procop.Gaz.*Ecphr.*164.21 (pl.). **-δετος**, ον, *bound* or *set all round*, *AP*6.103 (Phil.). **-δέω**, *bind round*, A.R.2.64:—Med. in Hsch.

ἀμφίδηλος, ον, gloss on ἀμφιδείκελος, Suid.

ἀμφιδήμα, ἡ, *foot-wear*, *GDI*4992,5000 (Gortyn).

ἀμφιδηριάομαι, Dep., *fight about*, γυναικὸς εἵνεκα Semon.7.118: c. dat., Lyc.1437.

ἀμφιδήρῑτος, ον, *disputed, doubtful*, νίκη Th.4.134, Plb.4.33.8; μάχη Id.35.2.14.

ἀμφιδήτιοι, prob. = ἀμφιδέαι, Democr.130.

ἀμφιδιαίνω, *moisten all round*, ἱδρῶτι κόμην *AP*9.653 (Agath.).

ἀμφιδῖν-έομαι, Pass., *to be put round in a circle*, Hom. in pf. only, ᾧ πέρι χεῦμα φαεινοῦ κασσιτέροιο ἀμφιδεδίνηται *round* whose edge a stream of tin *is rolled*, Il.23.562; κολεὸν ἀμφιδεδίνηται [ἄορ] scabbard *is fitted close round it*, Od.8.405; of persons, *to be dizzy*, σκοτώδεις ἀμφιδινευόμενοι Aret.*SD*2.3. **-δινεύω**, *whirl around*, πυρήια A.R. 1.1184 (tm.).

ἀμφιδιόρθωσις, εως, ἡ, *guarding oneself both before and after* saying something which may seem too bold, Alex.*Fig.*1.5.

ἀμφιδοκεύω, *lie in wait for*, τινά Bion *Fr.*9.6; *guard*, Orph.*A.* 925.

ἀμφίδομος, ον, *built around*, Opp.*H.*2.351.

ἀμφιδονέω, *whirl round, agitate violently*, Ζέφυρος δένδρεα ἀμφιδονεῖ *AP*9.668 (Marian.), cf. 5.121 (Diod.).

ἀμφι-δοξέω, *to be doubtful*, τὸ ἀμφιδοξεῖν *room for doubt*, Arist.*Rh.* 1356ᵃ8; ἀ. περί τινος Plb.32.16.5. II. c. acc., *doubt about*, Arist. *SE*176ᵇ15:—Pass., *to be doubtful*, τἀληθὲς ἀμφιδοξεῖται ib.176ᵇ20; ἀποφάσεις Plb.36.9.2; ἐλπίδες D.S.19.96, cf. Plu.*Thes.*23. **-δοξος**, ον, of persons, *with doubtful mind*, Ps.-E.*Fr.*1132.52; πρὸς τὸ θεῖον Plu.2.434d; περί τινος ib.11d. 2. of a witness, *of doubtful* *credibility*, Arist.*Rh.Al.*$1431^{b}23$. II. of things, *ambiguous, doubtful*, ἐν ἀμφιδόξῳ Thphr.*CP*1.22.2; ἀ. νίκη, ἐλπίδες, Plb.11.1.8, 15.1.12; of oracles, Luc.*JConf.*14 (v.l.); *causing doubt*, πτοῖαι Onos. 6.5. Adv. -δόξως Gal.1.273, al. 2. in Prosody, *of doubtful quantity*, Lat. *anceps*, Sch.Heph.1.4.

ἀμφίδορος, ον, *quite flayed*, *AP*6.165 (Phalaec.).

ἀμφίδουλος, ον, *slave both by father and mother*, Eub.2 D., Eust. 1445.5.

ἀμφίδοχμος, ον, (δοχμή) *as large as can be grasped*, λίθος ἀ. X.*Eq.* 4.4, cf. Poll.1.200, Hsch.

ἀμφιδρανές, (δρᾶνος) *embroidered on both sides*, ἱμάτιον Hsch., Phot.p.100 R.

ἀμφι-δρόμια, ων, τά, Att. festival at the naming of a child, so called because the parents' friends *carried it round the hearth*, Ar.*Lys.*757, Ephipp.3, Lys.*Fr.*22: on fifth day after birth, Sch.Pl.*Tht.*160e; tenth, acc. to Sch.Ar.*Lys.*l.c.:—hence -**δρομέω**, *AB*207. -**δρομος**, ον, *running both ways*, οἱ κατὰ τὸν πορθμὸν τόποι ἀ. ὄντες *subject to a constant ebb and flow*, Plb.34.2.5; πορθμός with harbour *on both sides*, Pl.Com.24 D. 2. *encompassing, enclosing*, S.*Aj.*352; ἄρκυς ἱστάναι ἀ. X.*Cyn.*6.5 (dub.). II. pr. n. Ἀμφίδρομος, divinity connected with ἀμφιδρόμια, A.*Fr.*222.

ἀμφι-δρύπτομαι, *be torn all round*, Q.S.4.396. -**δρυπτος**, ον, = ἀμφιδρυφής, *AP*6.84 (Paul. Sil.), 9.323 (Antip. ⟨Sid.⟩).

ἀμφίδρυς· *femella*, i.e. *oak-wood handle*, *Gloss.*

ἀμφιδρυτί· δένδρον ἀκῆς, Hsch.

ἀμφι-δρυφής, ές, (δρύπτω) *torn on both sides*, ἄλοχος ἀ. a wife who *has torn both cheeks*, in grief, Il.2.700, Orac.ap.Hdt.6.77. -**δρῠφος**, ον, = foreg., παρειαί Il.11.393.

ἀμφίδῠμος, ον, *two-fold, double*, λιμένες ἀ. Od.4.847; ἀκταί A.R. 1.940; πλάστιγγες Opp.*H.*2.179; ἰσθμός Str.6.1.5; *of double nature*, Opp.*C.*3.483; *with two barbs*, ἄκοντες 1.92. (The termin. -δυμος recurs in δίδυμος, τρίδυμος.)

ἀμφίδῠσις, ἡ, *double cup*, like δέπας ἀμφικύπελλον, Anaxandr.74.

ἀμφιδύω, *put on*, τινί τι Sch.Ar.*Th.*1053:—Med., *put on oneself*, ἀμφιδύσεται χροΐ [πέπλον] S.*Tr.*605.

ἀμφιέζω, freq. as v.l. for ἀμφιάζω, cf. *An.Ox.*2.338.

ἀμφιεκτ⟨ήρ⟩· χιτὼν διπλοῦς, Hsch.

ἀμφίεκτον, τό, measure between ἡμίεκτον and ἀμφορεύς, dub. in Them.*Or.*8.113d.

ἀμφιελικτός, όν, *revolving*, of stars, Arat.378; *winding*, περίπλοος D.P.466. **ἀμφιέλισσα**, ἡ, (ἑλίσσω) Ep. Adj., only fem., in Hom. always of ships, Il.2.165, al., either *curved at both ends* (or *on both sides*), or *wheeling either way, handy*; in late Ep., *twisting, doubling*, ἱμάσθλη ἀ. Nonn.*D.*48.328; μίτρη Jo.Gaz.1.319; *wavering, doubtful*, ἀοιδή Tryph.667.

ἀμφιελίσσω, *wind round*, Arat.996, Orph.*Fr.*115.

ἀμφιελόν· ἄφθονον, Hsch.

ἀμφιέννυμι Pl.*Prt.*321a; -ύω Plu.*Per.*9: fut. ἀμφιέσω Od.5.167, Att. ἀμφιῶ (ἀπ-) Men.339, (προσ-) Ar.*Eq.*891: aor. ἠμφίεσα Od.18. 361 (opt. -έσαιμι), X.*Cyr.*1.3.17:—Med., ib.8.2.21: fut. -έσομαι ib. 4.3.20, Pl.*R.*457a: aor. ἠμφιεσάμην App.*BC*2.122, Ep. ἀμφιέσαντο Od.23.142:—Pass., aor. part. ἀμφιεσθείς Hdn.1.10.5: pf. ἠμφίεσμαι Ar.*V.*1172, etc.; poet. part. ἀμφιεμμένος *Epigr.Gr.*1035.25:—*put round* or *on*, ἀμφὶ δὲ καλὰ λέπαδν' ἔσαν Il.19.393: but mostly c. dupl. acc. pers. et rei, ἐμὲ χλαῖνάν τε χιτῶνά τε εἵματα.. ἀμφιέσασα Od.15.369; in tmesi, ἀμφὶ δέ με χλαῖνάν τε χιτῶνά τε εἵματα ἕσσεν 10. 542; ἀμφὶ δέ μιν μέγα δέρμα.. ἕσσ' ἐλάφοιο 13.436, cf. Ar.*Pl.*936, Pl. *Smp.*219b, X.*Cyr.*1.3.17, etc.:—Pass., ἠμφιεσμένος τι *clothed in*.., *wearing*, Ar.*V.*1172, *Th.*92, *Ec.*879, etc.; τροφαλὶς σκῖρον ἠμφιεσμένη *with* a rind *on*, Eup.277. 2. rarely c. dat. rei, ἀ. τινά τινι *clothe* one *in* or *with*, θριξὶ καὶ δέρμασι Pl.*Prt.*321a: metaph., πονηρὰ χρηστοῖς ἀ. λόγοις *cloak*.., D.H.6.16. II. Med., *put on oneself, dress oneself in*, ἀμφιέσαντο χιτῶνας Od.23.142; ἀμφὶ δ' ἄρα.. ἑανὸν ἕσαθ' Il.14. 178; ἀμφὶ δ' ἄρα.. νεφέλην ὤμοισι ἕσαντο *they put* cloud *round* their shoulders, 20.150; γυίοις ἀμφιέσαντο κόνιν A.*Eleg.*3; λευκὴν ἀμφιέσασθε κόμην *AP*12.93; ἀρετὴν ἀντὶ ἱματίων ἀ. Pl.*R.*457a: abs., οὐ γὰρ παρέχεις ἀμφιέσασθαι τῷ πατρί Ar.*Fr.*17 D.

ἀμφιέπω, poet. also **ἀμφέπω** (the only form in Trag.): impf. or aor. ἀμφίεπον and ἄμφεπον, both in Hom. (v. infr.): poet. Verb only in the tenses cited, and once or twice in Med.: (ἕπω):—*go about, be all round*, γάστρην τρίποδος πῦρ ἄμφεπε Il.18.348, Od.8.437; πρύμνην πῦρ ἄμφεπε Il.16.124; ἕερσ' ἀμφέπει the dew (of milk and honey, metaph. of song) *crowns* [the bowl], Pi.*N.*3.78. 2. *beset, press hard*, Il.11.483; so perh. in Od.3.118 (v. infr. II. 2). II. *to be busy about, look after*, ἀμφίεπον τάφον Ἕκτορος Il.24.804, cf. 5.667; ἀμφὶ βοὸς ἕπετον κρέα *dressed* the meat, 11.776; βοῦς, ὄϊν ἀ., Od.8.61, Il.24.622:—*do honour* or *reverence to*, Δάματρα Pi.*O.*6.95; *tend* or *heal* sick, *P.*3.51; ἀ. σκῆπτρον *sway* the sceptre, *O.*1.12, cf. S.*El.*651; esp. *guard, protect*, Pi.*P.*5.68, prob. in E.*Med.*480, etc.; Βακχεῦ.. ὃς ἀμφέπεις Ἰταλίαν S.*Ant.*1118; μαντεῖον E.*IT*1248; simply, *frequent*, χῶρον Simon.58:—ἀ. κῆδος *cherish* an alliance, E.*Ph.*340; ἀ. μόχθον *go through* toil and trouble, Pi.*P.*4.268; σύμπειρον ἀγωνίᾳ θυμὸν ἀ. *foster* spirit in contests, *N.*7.10; ἀ. ὄλβον *enjoy* happiness, *I.*4(3).59; ἀ. παννυχίδας Critias 1.8. 2. abs., in part., *with good heed, carefully*, ἵππους ἀμφιέποντες ζεύγνυσαν Il.19.392; στίχας ἵστατον ἀμφιέποντες ib.2.525; κακὰ ῥάπτομεν ἀμφιέποντες Od.3.118; ὁ ἀμφέπων δαίμων the fortune *that attends one*, Pi.*P.*3.108. 3. Med., *crowd about*, ἀμφὶ δ' ἄρ' αὐτὸν Τρῶες ἕπονθ' Il.11.473 codd.; *accompany round about*, τινί Q.S.1.47.

Ἀμφιεραϊστής, οῦ, ὁ, *worshipper of Amphiaraus*, $IG2^2$.1322 (iii/ii B.C.). **Ἀμφιεράια**, τά, *festival of A.*, *IG*3.1171.

ἀμφίεργος, ον, *worked* or *prepared in two ways*, ἡμιβρεχῆ καὶ ἡμίελον ἣν καλοῦσί τινες ἀ. Thphr.*CP*3.23.1.

ἀμφιέρχομαι, v. ἀμφέρχομαι.

ἀμφί-εσις, εως, ἡ, *clothing*, Sch.Od.9.51, Simp.*in Cat.*401.21. -**εσμα**, ατος, τό, *garment*: pl., *wraps, clothes*, Hp.*Mul.*2.133, Pl.*Grg.* 523d, *R.*381a; in anatomy, of membranes, Gal.2.554, al. -**εσμός**, ὁ, *clothing*, D.H.8.62 (v.l. -ασμός). -**εστρίς**, ίδος, ἡ, *cloak, wrap*, Poll.6.10, 7.61.

ἀμφι-ετεί, Adv., (ἔτος) *year by year*, prob. in *SIG*963.7 (Amorgos, iv B.C.), cf. Suid., Eust.1385.1. -**ετες**, Adv. = foreg., Moer. 45. -**ετέω**, *offer yearly sacrifices*, *EM*90.26. -**ετηρίς**, ίδος, ἡ, *yearly festival*, *SIG*1109.69 (Athens, ii A.D.), Suid. -**έτηρος**, ον, *celebrated in yearly festivals*, epith. of Dionysus, Orph.*H.*52. 10. -**ετής**, ές, = foreg., Call.*Del.*278, Orph.*Fr.*232. -**ετίδαι**, οἱ, Com. name for stupid persons, Men.13 D. -**ετίζομαι**, Pass., *return yearly*, of festivals, Hsch., *EM*90.27:—also -**ετηρίζομαι**, Cratin.2 D.

ἀμφιζάνω, *sit on*, c. dat., χιτῶνι ἀμφίζανε τέφρη ashes *settled upon* the tunic, Il.18.25.

ἀμφίζευκτος, ον, *joined from both sides*, A.*Pers.*130.

ἀμφιζέω, *boil* or *bubble around*, Q.S.6.104.

ἀμφίζωστος, ον, *girt around*, Nonn.*D.*32.159.

ἀμφιήκης, ες, (ἀκή A) = ἀμφήκης, Hsch.

ἀμφιθάλᾰμος, ου, prob. f.l. for ἀντι-, *corresponding chamber*, Vitr. 6.7.2.

ἀμφιθάλασσος, Att. -**ττος**, ον, *with sea on both sides, sea-girt*, of Rhodes, Pi.*O.*7.33; of Attica, X.*Vect.*1.7, cf. Str.9.1.3.

ἀμφι-θᾰλεύς, έος, ὁ, = παῖς ἀμφιθαλής, hence, in religious ceremonies, *acolyte*, τῶν μεγάλων Ἀντωνίων *BCH*10.415 (Thyatira):—hence -**θαλεύω**, τὰ μεγάλα Ἀσκληπιεῖα ib.11.98 (ibid.). -**θᾰλής**, ές, (θαλεῖν) lit. *blooming on both sides*, of children *who have both parents alive*, Il.22.496, Pl.*Lg.*927d, Call.*Iamb.*3.1.3, *SIG*589.19 (Magn. Mae.), etc. 2. *flourishing on all sides*, χωρίον Poll.1.239: metaph., *all-abounding*, of gods, A.*Ch.*394; Ἔρως Ar.*Av.*1737 (cf. Sch.); of a man, πόσις ἀ. *IG*14.1863: metaph., ἀμφιθαλὴς κακοῖς *abounding in*.., A.*Ag.*1144. II. of things, *complete*, ἀλήθεια Pl.*Ax.* 370d. -**θάλλω**, pf. (with pres. sense) ἀμφιτέθηλα, *to be in full bloom*, *AP*9.231 (Antip.), 12.96.

ἀμφιθάλπω, *warm on both sides, cherish*, Luc.*Trag.*28.

ἀμφιθέατρος, ον, *having seats for spectators all round*, of the Roman *circus*, ἀ. ἱππόδρομος D.H.4.44:—also στοά Id.3.68; στάδιον *IGRom.*4.861 (Laodicea ad Lycum): esp. neut. as Subst., -**θέατρον**, τό, *amphitheatre*, *IGRom.*1.1024.27 (Berenice, i B.C.), Str.14.1.43, J.*AJ*15.8.1, Arr.*Epict.*1.25.27, Procop.*Goth.*3.23, etc.

ἀμφίθετος, ον, in Il.23.270,616 ἀ. φιάλη, acc. to Aristarch., a cup *that will stand on both ends*; acc. to others, *with handles on both sides, that may be taken up by both sides*, cf. Ath.11.501a sq., Eust.1299. 55, Hsch.

ἀμφιθέω, generally pres., *run round about*, ἀμφιθέουσι μητέρας Od. 10.413: c. dat., νόος δέ οἱ αἴσιμος ἀμφιθέει right mind *surrounds* him, Mosch.2.107: impf. ἀμφιθέεσκεν Q.S.5.371.

ἀμφι-θηγής, ές, *sharpened on both sides, two-edged*, ξίφος S.*Ant.* 1309 (lyr.). -**θηκτος**, ον, = foreg., *AP*6.94 (Phil.).

ἀμφί-θλᾰσις, εως, ἡ, *pressure all round*, Aret.*CA*1.6. -**θλασμα**, Ion. -**φλασμα**, ατος, τό, *bruise* of the flesh *round* a spot, Hp.*Art.* 50. -**θλάω**, Ion. -**φλάω**, *crush, contuse round*: in Pass., σὰρξ περὶ ὀστέον Id.*Fract.*11, *Art.*50; of fruit, μήλων σάρκες ἀμφιθλασθεῖσαι Aret.*CD*2.6.

ἀμφιθνήσκω, of flesh, *mortify round* a wound, v.l. in Hp.*Fract.* 33; later, *die around*, τισί Q.S.6.449.

ἀμφιθοάζω, *rush around*, οὐρανόν Man.4.84.

ἀμφίθρεπτος, ον, *clotted round* a wound, αἷμα S.*Tr.*572.

ἀμφιθρύπτομαι, *to be broken up*, dub. l. Aret.*SD*2.4.

ἀμφιθρῴσκω, in aor. part. ἀμφιθορόντες, *leap around*, Eumel.9 (= A.R.3.1373).

ἀμφίθῠρος, ον, *with a door on both sides, with double entrance*, οἶκος S.*Ph.*159; οἰκία Lys.12.15; Boeot. **ἀμφιθίουρος**, ὁ, as Subst., *IG*7.2876 (Coronea). II. Subst. ἀμφίθυρον, τό, *hall*, Theoc.14.42.

ἀμφιθύσανος, ον, *fringed all about*, πρόσλημμα *GDI*5702 (Samos).

ἀμφιίζομαι, *sit upon*, δίφρον Hp.*Mul.*2.114.

ἀμφιΐστημι, v. ἀμφίστημι.

ἀμφικαθίζομαι (v.l. -έζ-), *take a sitz-bath*, Hp.*Mul.*1.13. II. causal, *cause to be seated upon a* πυελός, ib.2.134.

ἀμφικάθημαι, Pass., *sit all round*, Orac.ap.Eus.*PE*4.23.

ἀμφικαίνυμαι, in plpf. Pass. ἀμφεκέκαστο, *to be adorned with*, τεύχεσι Q.S.10.179, cf. 188.

ἀμφικᾰλύπτω, fut. -ψω A.R.2.583: aor. -ψα, v. infr. I. c. acc., *enwrap, enfold*, of garments, Il.2.262; of a coffin, ἀ. ὀστέα 23.91; ἐπὴν πόλις ἀμφικαλύψῃ δουράτεον μέγαν ἵππον *received within* it, Od.8.511, cf. 4.618; ἔρως φρένας ἀμφεκάλυψε *love enfolded* my senses, Il.3.442; θάνατος δέ μιν ἀμφεκάλυψε 5.68, cf. 12.116; θανάτου δὲ μέλαν νέφος ἀμφεκάλυψε 16.350; ἀμφὶ δὲ ὄσσε κελαινὴ νὺξ ἐκάλυψε 11.356; [ὕπνος] βλέφαρ' ἀμφικαλύψας Od.5.493; of a wave, *overwhelm*, A.R.l.c.:—in Pass., ἀμφικεκαλύφθαι ἀμφιέσμασι Hp.*Mul.*2.133. II. ἀ. τί τινι *put round* any one *as a veil, cover*, or *shelter*, ἀ. σάκος τινί Il.8.331; νέφος τινί 14.343; νύκτα μάχῃ ἀ. *throw the mantle* of night over the battle, 5.506; ὄρος πόλει ἀ. *overshadow* a city with a mountain, Od.

8.569. III. after Hom., ἀ. τινά τινι *surround* one *with*, φύλλοις κνήμας Batr.161, cf. Opp.*H*.1.746:—Pass., ἀμφεκαλύφθη κρᾶτα λέοντος χάσματι *he had* his head *covered with* lion's jaws, E.*HF*361. 2. *guard*, μαχαίριον δακτύλῳ Hp.*Mul*.1.70.

ἀμφικάρηνος, ον, *two-headed*, Nic.*Th*.373; in *Al*.417 v.l. for ἀμφίκρηνα, q.v. **ἀμφικᾰρής**, ές, = foreg., Id.*Th*.812.

ἀμφίκαρπος, ον, *fruiting both above and below ground*, *amphicarpic*, Thphr.*HP*1.6.12.

ἀμφίκαρτος, ον, *shorn all round*, Herod.8.24.

ἀμφίκαυστις or **-καυτις**, εως, ἡ: (καίω):—*ripe barley*, Ael.Dion.*Fr*.184, Hsch.s.v. καῦστις. II. Com., *pudenda*, Cratin.381. III. epith. of Demeter, Hsch. l.c.

ἀμφικεάζω, *cleave asunder*, in Ep. aor. part. -κεάσσας Od.14.12.

ἀμφίκειμαι, Pass., *lie round* or *upon*, τινι Pi.*Fr*.92; ἐπ' ἀλλήλοισιν ἀμφικείμενοι *locked in* each other's *arms*, S.*OC*1620; ἐπ' ὀλέθρῳ.. ἀμφικεῖσθαι μόρον slaughter *is heaped on* slaughter, *Ant*.1292 (lyr.).

ἀμφικείρω, aor. 2 Pass. -εκάρην, *shear all round*, *AP*9.56 (Phil.).

ἀμφι-κελεμνίς, *hanging evenly on both shoulders*, Hsch., Theognost.*Can*.163.16. **-κέλεμνον**· ἀμφιβαρές, or, *chair carried by two men*, Hsch.; *satyric dance*, *EM*91.1.

ἀμφίκερως, ων, gen. ω, *two-horned*, Man.1.306, 4.274.

ἀμφίκεστον· περιτμητὸν ἢ περιγραφόμενον, Hsch. (Fort. -ξεστον.)

ἀμφικεύθω, *cover all round*, Hsch.

ἀμφικέφᾰλος, ον, *two-headed*, Eub.107.10 (in poet. form ἀμφικέφαλλος); of the ἀμφίσβαινα, Gal.14.243; σκέλους τὸ ἀ., i.e. the thigh-bone, Arist.*HA*494^{a}5. II. of a couch, *having two places for the head*, i.e. *two ends*, κλίνη *IG*1.277*d* (-κνέφαλλος wrongly cited by Poll.10.36).

ἀμφικίων [κῐ], ον, gen. ονος, *with pillars all round*, S.*Ant*.285.

ἀμφίκλαστος, ον, *broken* (cf. ἀμφιρρώξ), *AP*6.223.

ἀμφίκλαυτος, ον, *mourned around*, Opp.*H*.4.257.

ἀμφικλάω, *break all in pieces*, Q.S.8.345; τρόμος ἀ. γυῖα 12.399.

ἀμφικλῐνής, ές, *unsteady*, *uncertain*, χαρά Ph.2.548. Adv. -νῶς, ἔχειν *to be in doubt*, 2.171.

ἀμφι-κλύζω, *wash* or *flood around*, Orph.*A*.271. **-κλυστος**, ον, *washed on both sides by waves*, ἀκτή, of a promontory, S.*Tr*.752, cf. 780; ἠιών Str.11.4.2; χῶμα App.*BC*5.72.

ἀμφικνέφαλλος, ον, *with cushions at both ends*, v. ἀμφικέφαλος II.

ἀμφικνεφής, ές, *wrapped in darkness*, βυθός *Orac.Chald*.242.

ἀμφίκοιλος, ον, *hollowed on both sides*, Suid. II. *doubly concave*, of a curvilinear angle, Procl.*in Euc.Def*.8 p.127 F., al.

ἀμφίκοιτος· ὁ τάπης, *coverlet*, Suid.

ἀμφίκολλος, ον, *glued on both sides*:—κλίνη ἀ. couch *with two ends fixed on*, Pl.Com.34.

ἀμφικομέω, *tend on all sides* or *carefully*, *AP*7.141 (Antiphil.).

ἀμφίκομος, ον, *with hair all round*, *AP*9.516 (Crin.). 2. *thick-leafed*, θάμνῳ ὑπ' ἀμφικόμῳ Il.17.677, cf. Archestr.*Fr*.9.

ἀμφίκοπος, ον, (κόπτω) *two-edged*, Eust.1531.34.

ἀμφίκορος, ὁ, *middle of three brothers*, Hsch., Suid.

ἀμφίκουρος, ον, *lopped of its branches*, κορμός S.*Fr*.821. 2. *shorn on both sides*, Hsch., Phot.p.102 R. II. *seized by men on either side*, Suid.

ἀμφίκρᾱνος, ον, = ἀμφικάρηνος, E.*HF*1274; ῥάβδος, of Hermes' wand, S.*Fr*.701. II. *surrounding the head*, in Ion. form -κρηνος, *AP*6.90 (Phil.), prob. l. in Nic.*Al*.417.

ἀμφικρατέω, *occupy*, Antioch.Astr. in *Cat.Cod.Astr*.1.112.

ἀμφικρέμαμαι, Pass., *hang round*, φρένας ἀμφικρέμανται ἐλπίδες Pi.*I*.2.43, cf. *O*.7.24. **ἀμφικρεμής**, ές, *overhanging*, σκόπελος *AP*9.90 (Alph.). 2. *hanging round shoulder*, φαρέτρη *APl*.4.212 (Alph.); χλαμύς *App.Anth*.3.166 (Procl.). **ἀμφίκρημνος**, ον, *with cliffs all round*, ἄγκος E.*Ba*.1051. II. metaph., ἀπάτη ἀ. deceit *which is always on the edge of the precipice*, Ps.-Luc.*Philopatr*.16.

ἀμφίκρηνος, ον, Ion. for ἀμφίκρανος, q.v.

ἀμφίκροτος, ον, *struck with both hands*, ψαλμοί *IG*3.82.

ἀμφικρύπτω, *cover* or *hide on every side*, τοῖον νέφος ἀμφί σε κρύπτει E.*Hec*.907.

ἀμφι-κτίονες or **-κτύονες**, ων, οἱ, (v. κτίζω) *they that dwell round* or *near*, *next neighbours*, Hdt.8.104, Pi.*P*.4.66, 10.8, *N*.6.39; cf. sq. (Accented -κτιών or -κτυών by Hdn.Gr.2.724, 1.22, and some codd.)

Ἀμφικτύον-ες, ων, οἱ, *Amphictyons*, deputies of states associated in an ἀμφικτυονία, e.g. at Onchestos, Str.9.2.33; Calauria, 8.6.14; Delos, Ath.6.234e; esp. at Delphi, D.5.14, al., Aeschin.2.115, etc.; Ἀμφικτίονες *IG*2.545.16, al., and this form seems to preserve the etym., v. foreg.: sg. in Lib.*Decl*.17.10, al. **-εύω**, *to be a member of the Amphictyonic Council*, *IG*7.106 (Megara), *SIG*158 (Delos):—Pass., *to be subject to the Amphictyony*, *Gött.Gel.Anz*.1913.175. **-ία** or **-εία**, ἡ, *Amphictyonic League*, D.5.19, 11.4, cf. Did.*in D*.4.6; τὸ δίκαιον τῆς Ἀ. *IG*4.589 (Argos); of the League of Calauria, Str.8.6.14:—τῆς τῶν Λοκρῶν Ἀ. τὸ τρίτον μέρος a third share in *the representation* of Locri *in the Amphictyony*, *Klio*16.163. **-ικός**, ή, όν, *belonging to the Amphictyons* or *their League*, Ἀ. δίκαι trials *in their court*, D.18.322; ἱερά offerings *made at their meeting*, Lex ap. eund. 23.37; πόλεμος D.18.143; τὰ χρήματα τὰ Ἀ. *IG*2.545.6; Ἀ. ἔγκλημα *IG*12(5).526.4 (Ceos, iii B.C.). **-ίς**, ίδος, ἡ, fem. of foreg.; Ἀ. (sc. πόλις), ἡ, *city* or *state in the Amphictyonic League*, Aeschin.2.116. II. name of Demeter at Anthela, Hdt.7.200.

ἀμφι-κύβωται πρόχοι· ἢ ἀπὸ ⟨τῆς⟩ τοῦ ὅλου περιφερείας ἢ ἀπὸ τῆς τῶν ὤτων, Hsch.:—also **-κ[τ]υπος**, ον, *EM*543.7: **-κυφος**, ον, κεραμίδες *BCH*28.159 (Delos, ii B.C.).

ἀμφικῠκάω, *mix up*, Nic.*Th*.602.

ἀμφικυκλόομαι, Pass., *encircle*, *surround*, ἀμφὶ δὲ κυκλοῦντο νῆσον A.*Pers*.458.—Act. in Agath.3.6.

ἀμφικῠλίνδω, aor. -εκύλισα, *roll about*, *round*, or *on*, φασγάνῳ ἀμφικυλίσαις Pi.*N*.8.23.

ἀμφικύμων, ον, gen. ονος, = ἀμφίκλυστος, B.15.16.

ἀμφικῠνέω, *deosculari*, Q.S.7.328, in aor. ἀμφικύσαι.

ἀμφικύπελλος, ον, in Hom. always δέπας ἀ. *double cup*, such as forms a κύπελλον both at top and bottom, Il.1.584, al.: ἀμφικύπελλα are compared with the cell of a honeycomb, as possessing ἀμφίστομοι θυρίδες, Arist.*HA*624^{a}9; but acc. to Aristarch., *two-handled*, cf. Ath.11.783b (post 11.466c).

ἀμφι-κυρτέω, *to be gibbous*, σελήνης -ούσης Olymp.*in Mete*.226.6. **-κυρτόομαι**, Pass., *to be gibbous*, of the moon, Man.6.575 (tm.). **-κυρτος**, ον, *convex on each side*, like the moon in her second or third quarter, *gibbous*, Arist.*Cael*.291^{b}20, Thphr.*Sign*.56, Plu.2.381d. 2. *doubly convex*, of a curvilinear angle, opp. ἀμφίκοιλος, Procl.*in Euc.Def*.8 p.127 F., al.; γραμμαί Gal.2.673; λεπίδες Ph.*Bel*.70.23.

ἀμφιλαγχάνω, *exchange*, τόπους Ptol.*Tetr*.179.

ἀμφίλᾰλος, ον, *talking in two languages*, *in broken Greek*, Ar.*Ra*.979.

ἀμφιλαμβάνω, *grip*, *clasp*, Hp.*Art*.37, Aret.*SD*2.13.

ἀμφιλασθείς· περιελασθείς, Hsch.

ἀμφι-λάφεια or **-ία**, ἡ, *wealth*, *abundance*, Cic.*QF*2.14.3, *Gp*.2.8.1, Hsch., *AB*389. **-λᾰφής**, ές, (prob. from √λαφ-, cf. εἴ-ληφ-α; so) *taking in on all sides*, *wide-spreading*, of large trees, Hdt.4.172; πλάτανος.. ἀ. τε καὶ ὑψηλή Pl.*Phdr*.230b. 2. *thickly grown*, *thick*, ἄλσος δένδρεσιν Call.*Cer*.27, cf. Ael.*NA*7.6; also of hair, Philostr.Jun.*Im*.8, etc.; ἀ. φολίδεσσι δράκων Nonn.*D*.5.153. 3. generally, *abundant*, *enormous*, δύναμις Pi.*O*.9.82; βρονταί, χιών, Hdt.4.28, 50; δόσις ἀ. a *bounteous* gift, A.*Ag*.1015; γόος ἀ. *loud* wail, *Ch*.331; πήματα Id.*Fr*.149A; κατάλυσις Jul.*Ep*.36. Adv. -φῶς *copiously*, Plu.*Eum*.6; ἀ. ἔχειν, c. gen., Alciphr.3.60. 4. *bulky*, *huge*, ἐλέφαντες Hdt.3.114; ἵππος A.R.4.1366; νῆσος ib.983; παστάς Theoc.24.46; χορός Call.*Dian*.3, etc. b. (as if Passive, *held on all sides*), *palpable*, Dam.*Pr*.13, 111. 5. rarely of persons, ἀ. τέχνῃ *great* in art, Call.*Ap*.42; ἀ. τὴν διάνοιαν Dam.ap.Suid.—Not in Hom. or in Early Prose.

ἀμφιλαχαίνω, *dig*, *hoe round*, φυτὸν ἀμφελάχαινεν Od.24.242.

ἀμφιλάων· περικυκλούντων, Hsch.

ἀμφιλέγω, Dor. **ἀμφιλλ-**, *dispute about*, τι X.*An*.1.5.11; χώρας ἃς ἀμφέλλεγον *IG*4.926 (Epid.):—Pass., τὰ ἀμφιλλεγόμενα *GDI*5149 (Cret.). 2. foll. by μή.., *dispute*, *question* that a thing is, X.*Ap*.12: abs., *dispute*, αἴ κ' ἀμφιλλέγωντι τοὶ ταγοί *GDI*2561 *A* 42.

ἀμφιλειπής, ές, *incomplete at both ends*, of the *metrum Choerileum*, [⏑] – ⏑ – – | – ⏑ ⏑ – ⏑ ⏑ – ‖ ⏑ – ⏑ – [–] Sch.Metr.Pi.*N*.11, Mar.Vict.2559.

ἀμφιλείπω, *forsake utterly*, Q.S.12.106.

ἀμφίλεκτος, ον, *spoken both ways*: hence, *doubtful*, ἀ. ὢν κράτει *questioned* in his title to rule, A.*Ag*.1585; *involving dispute*, ἔρις E.*Ph*.500. Adv. -τως A.*Th*.800. 2. *double*, πήματα Id.*Ag*.881.

ἀμφίλῐνος, ον, *bound with flaxen thongs*, κρούπαλα S.*Fr*.44 (apptly. λῑν-, but the line is corrupt).

ἀμφιλίτην· τὸν λιτανευτήν, Hsch.

ἀμφιλιχή· περιμάχητον, Hsch.

ἀμφιλιχμάζω, *lick all round*, Opp.*H*.4.115, 321 (tm.).

ἀμφι-λογέομαι, Dep., *dispute*, *doubt*, περί τινος Plu.*Lys*.22.—Act. in J.*AJ*18.1.4, Hsch. **-λογία**, Ep. **ἀμφιλλ-**, ἡ, *dispute*, *doubt*, Hes.*Th*.229; ἀ. ἔχειν, διαλύειν, Plu.*Comp.Arist.Cat*.4, *Ages*.28, cf. App.*Hann*.46. **-λογος**, ον, *disputed*, *disputable*, ἀγαθά X.*Mem*.4.2.34; τὰ ἀ. *disputed points*, Th.4.118, 5.79; ὀφείλημα Arist.*EN* 1162^{b}28; εἴ τι ἀμφίλογον πρὸς ἀλλήλους γίγνοιτο, δίκῃ διακριθῆναι X.*HG*5.2.10. 2. *uncertain*, *wavering*, neut. pl. ἀμφίλογα as Adv., E.*IT*655 (lyr.). Regul. Adv. -ως A.*Pers*.904. II. Act., *disputatious*, *jarring*, νείκη S.*Ant*.111; ὀργαί E.*Med*.637 (lyr.).

ἀμφίλοξος, ον, *slanting both ways*, ἀμφίλοξα μαντεύεσθαι *utter ambiguous oracles*, Ps.-Luc.*Philopatr*.5, cf. 16.

ἀμφίλοφος, ον, *encompassing the neck*, ζυγόν S.*Ant*.351 (dub.).

ἀμφιλύκη νύξ, ἡ, = λυκόφως, *half-light*, *morning twilight*, Il.7.433; without νύξ, A.R.2.671, Opp.*C*.1.135, *AP*5.280 (Paul. Sil.), Lyd.*Ost*.65. (No masc. is found.)

ἀμφίμακρος, ον, *long at both ends*:—ὁ ἀ. metrical foot *amphimacer*, – ⏑ – (as Οἰδίπους), also called *creticus*, Heph.3.2, Quint.*Inst*.9.4.81, etc.

ἀμφίμαλλος, ον, *woolly on both sides*, Pherecr.1 D., Ael.*VH*3.40, Poll.7.57.

ἀμφιμάντορα· δύσμορον, κακοθάνατον, Hsch.

***ἀμφιμάομαι**, only in aor.; imper. ἀμφιμάσασθε, *wipe all round*, τραπέζας Od.20.152; ind. ἀμφεμάσαντο Q.S.9.428.

ἀμφιμάρπτω, only in pf. -μέμαρπα (-μέμαρφα Q.S.3.614), *grasp all round*, *handle*, A.R.3.147, Opp.*H*.5.636.

ἀμφίμαστα, τά, *cakes of flour and honey* (Lacon.), Hsch.; cf. ἀμφίπαστον.

ἀμφιμάσχᾰλος, ον, *with two arm-holes*, ἀ. χιτών Ar.*Eq*.882, cf. Pl.Com.229, Luc.*Lex*.10.

ἀμφιμάτορες, Dor. for ἀμφιμήτορες.

ἀμφι-μάχητος, ον, *fought for*, *AP*7.705 (Antip.). **-μάχομαι** [ᾰ], Ep. Verb, only pres. and impf., *fight round*: 1. c. acc., *assail*, *besiege*, Ἴλιον ἀμφεμάχοντο Il.6.461; Τρώων πόλιν 9.412; στρατόν

16.73. 2. c. gen., *fight for*, as for a prize, of defenders and assailants, τείχεος ἀμφεμάχοντο 15.391; νέκυος δὲ δὴ ἀ. 18.20; χώρας *SIG*527.151 (Dreros, iii B.C.).

ἀμφιμέλας, -μέλαινα, -μέλαν, *black all round*: Hom. always epith. of φρένες (best written divisim, as by Alex. critics), *darkened on either side*, of strong emotions, as anger, Il.1.103, 17.83, Od.4.661; courage, Il.17.499,573: prob. metaph. from an angry sea. 2. generally, ἀ. κόνις *coal-black* dust, *AP*7.738 (Theodorid.).

ἀμφιμέλει, *to be a care to*, σοι ἀμφιμέμηλε θράσος Q.S.5.190.

ἀμφιμερίζομαι, Pass., *to be completely parted*, *AP*9.662 (Agath.).

ἀμφιμήκης ἀριθμός *containing length of both kinds*, i.e. sum of *odd and even*, Iamb.*in Nic*.p.12.21 P.

ἀμφίμηλον, τό, *probe with two ends*, Antyll.ap.Orib.7.14.5.

ἀμφι-μήτορες, οἱ, αἱ, (μήτηρ) *brothers* or *sisters by different mothers* but the same father, A.*Fr*.76, E.*Andr*.466 (lyr.): sg. in Hsch.; cf. ἀμφιπάτορες. **-μήτριος**, ον, (μήτρα) *round the womb, concerning it*, σημεῖον Hp.*Epid*.7.19 acc. to Gal.19.78 (dub.). 2. ἀμφιμήτρια, τά, *ship's bilge*, = ἐγκοίλια, Artem.4.30, Poll.1.87. II. (μήτηρ) *by different mother*, Lyc.19.

ἀμφι-μῑγής, ές, *well mixed*, Hsch. **-μίγνυμι**, *mix up well*, aor. 2 Pass. ἀμφιμιγεῖσα Orph.*Fr*.238.12.

ἀμφίμῐτος, ον, *with double woof* (cf. *dimity*), Poll.7.57, 10.38.

ἀμφιμῡκάομαι, properly of cattle, *low all around*: metaph., δάπεδον δ' ἅπαν ἀμφιμέμυκε floor *echoed* to song [of Circe], Od.10.227.

ἀμφι-μωλέω, *sue at law concerning*, ἐλευθέρῳ *Leg.Gort*.1.2, cf.9.19:—hence **-μωλος**, ον, *subject of legal process*, 10.27.

ἀμφινάω, *flow round about*, ὕδατος ἀμφιναέντος Emp.84.

ἀμφι-νεικής, ές, *contested on all sides, eagerly wooed*, of Helen, A.*Ag*.686; of Deïanira, S.*Tr*.104 (lyr.). **-νείκητος**, ον, = foreg., ὄμμα νύμφας ib.527 (lyr.).

ἀμφινέμομαι, Med., *dwell round*, c. acc. loci, Ὑάμπολιν ἀμφενέμοντο Il.2.521; Ὄλυμπον ἀ., of gods, 18.186; Ἰθάκην Od.19.132; of constellations, δύ' Ἰχθύες ἀμφινέμονται Ἵππον Arat.282: abs., D.P. 127, al.: metaph., σὲ ὄλβος ἀ. *encompasses* thee, Pi.*P*.5.14.

ἀμφινεύω, *nod this way and that*, *AP*9.709 (Phil.).

ἀμφι-νοέω, *think both ways, be in doubt*, ἀμφινοῶ τόδε, πῶς εἰδὼς ἀντιλογήσω S.*Ant*.376. **-νοος**, ον, *looking at both sides*, Δημόκριτος Timo 46.

ἀμφινωμάω, *surround*, A.*Fr*.304.8. 2. *distribute, turn over* or *peer round*, ἀμφὶ ἓ νωμήσας *h.Cer*.373.

ἀμφι-νωτίζοντα· προσπελάζοντα, προσφερόμενον, Hsch. **-νωτις**, ἡ, kind of χιτών, *EM*93.16. **-νωτοι** χιτῶνες, = foreg., Hsch. (prob.).

ἀμφι-ξέω, *smooth all round*, κορμὸν.. ἀμφέξεσα χαλκῷ Od.23.196. **-ξοος**, ον, contr. **-ξους**, *polishing all round*, σκέπαρνον *AP* 6.205 (Leon.).

ἀμφίον, ου, τό, = ἀμφίεσμα, S.*Fr*.420 (anap.), D.H.4.76, Sch.Arat. 1073 (pl.): ἀμφία καὶ οἰκήσεις *IG*3.60. (From ἀμφί, as ἀντίος from ἀντί; ἄμφιον acc. to Sch.D.T.p.196 H.)

ἀμφιορκία, ἡ, *oath taken by each party* in a lawsuit, Hsch.; also by heliasts, Poll.8.122, *AB*184.

ἀμφιπᾰγής, ές, (πήγνυμι) *set all round*, τινί *with*.., Nonn.*D*.5.362.

ἀμφιπαίω, *spike, transfix*, περὶ σκόλοπας τοὺς ὀπτίλλους *IG*4.951. 92 (Epid.).

ἀμφίπαλτος, ον, *tossed about, re-echoing*, αὐδή *AP*15.27.10 (Besant.).

ἀμφιπᾰλύνω, *sprinkle all over*, A.R.3.1247.

ἀμφιπαρίσταμαι, *stand about and beside*, Epic.ap.Afric.*Cest.Oxy*. 412.42.

ἀμφίπαστον· ἀλφίτοις ἀναδεδευμένοις ἐλαίῳ, Hsch.; cf. ἀμφίμαστα.

ἀμφιπᾰτάσσω, *strike on* or *from all sides*, *AP*9.643.

ἀμφιπάτορες [ᾰ], οἱ, αἱ, *brothers* or *sisters by different fathers* but the same mother, Suid.; cf. ἀμφιμήτορες.

ἀμφιπεδάω, *fetter all round*, Opp.*H*.2.34.

ἀμφίπεδος, ον, *surrounded by a plain*, Pi.*P*.9.55.

ἀμφιπέλεκκον, τό, *double axe*, wrongly read in Il.13.612, cf. Hsch.

ἀμφιπέλομαι, *hover, float around*, of music, ἥτις ἀκουόντεσσι νεωτάτη ἀμφιπέληται Od.1.352; *encompass*, *Sammelb*.5829.16.

ἀμφιπένομαι, Ep. only pres. and impf., = πένομαι ἀμφί τινα, *to be busied about, take charge of*, c. acc. pers., οἱ μεν πατέρ' ἀμφεπένοντο Od.15.467; of people *tending* a wounded man, Il.4.220, 16.28, Od. 19.455: c. acc. rei, δῶρα Il.19.278; τάφον, στόλον, δόρπον, A.R. 2.925, 1199, 4.883; ταῦρον Id.3.271. b. τὸν οὐ κύνες ἀμφεπένοντο dogs *made* not *a meal of* him, Il.23.184, cf. 21.203; λέων.. ὅν τ' ἐν ὄρεσσιν ἀνέρες ἀμφιπένονται *hem in*, A.R.2.27.

ἀμφιπερι-ίσταμαι, Pass., *stand around*, Q.S.3.201. **-κτίονες**, ων, οἱ, *dwellers all around*, Callin.1.2, Thgn.1058, Q.S.6.224.

ἀμφιπέριξ, Adv. *all around*, ὁ ἀ. χῶρος Hp.*Mul*.2.175.

ἀμφιπερι-πλάσσω, aor. -έπλασα, *spread all round*, of a drug, Hp. *Steril*.22. **-πλέγδην**, Adv. *twined round*, *AP*5.275 (Agath.), prob. in Jo.Gaz.1.6; ἀ. πεπεδημένος Nonn.*D*.36.360. **-πλέκομαι**, *to be folded about*, Orph.*L*.80. **-πτώσσω**, *tremble all about*, Q.S.12. 472. **-σκαίρω**, *skip all about*, Opp.*H*.1.190. **-στείνομαι**, Pass., (στεινός, στενός) *to be pressed, crowded on all sides*, Call.*Del*. 179. **-στέφομαι**, Pass., *to be put round as a crown*, ἀλλ' οὔ οἱ χάρις ἀμφιπεριστέφεται ἐπέεσσι grace *crowns* not his words, Od.8. 175. **-στρωφάω**, Frequent. of -στρέφω, *keep turning about all ways*, Ἕκτωρ δ' ἀμφιπεριστρώφα καλλίτριχας ἵππους Il.8.348:—Pass., Q.S.13.11. **-σφίγγω**, *bind all round*, Nonn.*D*.48.338. **-τρομέω**, *tremble all over*, Opp.*H*.4.193. **-τρύζω**, *chirp, twitter round about*, *AP*5.236 (Agath.). **-φθῐνύθω** [ῠ], *decay, die all around*, *h.Ven*. 271. **-φρίσσω**, *bristle all round, all over*, Opp.*H*.4.54.

ἀμφιπετάννυμι, *spread round*, aor. part. ἀμφιπετάσσας Orph.*L*.643.

ἀμφιπέτομαι, *fly around*, c. acc., Opp.*H*.2.448.

ἀμφιπήγνῡμαι, Pass., *to be fixed around*, aor. 2 ἀμφιπαγῆναι Opp. *H*.1.297; *to be pierced by*, ὀδύνῃσι 241.

ἀμφιπήρους· τυφλούς, ἢ μηδὲν λέγοντας, Hsch.

ἀμφιπιάζω, Dor. for -πιέζω, *squeeze all round, hug closely*, [τὰν χίμαρον] χαλαῖς ἀμφεπίαξε λύκος Theoc.*Ep*.6.4.

ἀμφιπίπτω, poet. -πίτνω, *fall upon and embrace, embrace eagerly*, c. acc., φίλον πόσιν ἀμφιπεσοῦσα Od.8.523, cf. Parth.15.2; ἀμφιπίτνουσα τὸ σὸν γόνυ E.*Supp*.278: c. dat., οὔτ' ἀμφιπίπτων στόμασιν *embracing* so as to kiss, S.*Tr*.938; *fall over*, προβάτοις Parth.8.4: metaph., *take to one's heart*, ἔθνος Λοκρῶν ἀμφέπεσον Pi.*O*.10(11).98.

ἀμφιπλάσσω, *spread around*, [ἔμπλαστρον] μήλῃ Hp.*Steril*.221.

ἀμφι-πλεκής, ές, = sq., Orph.*A*.607. **-πλεκτος**, ον, *intertwined*, S.*Tr*.520 (lyr.). **-πλέκω**, aor. 2 part. Pass. -πλακεῖσα Orph. *A*.881:—*twine round*, κείσθω δόρυ μοι μίτον ἀμφιπλέκειν ἀράχναις E.*Fr*.369 (lyr.); αὔραν ἀμφιπλέκειν καλάμοις, of musician, Telest.2.4; *embrace*, Opp.*H*.4.158; so in Pass., Orph.l.c.

ἀμφί-πλευρος, ον, *with traverses on both sides*, θυρίδες Ph.*Bel*.81. 30. **-πλέω**, impf. ἀμφέπλεον, = περιπλέω, Hsch. **-πλη**· ἐμπλεκόμια, Id. **-πληκτος**, Dor. **-πλακτος**, ον, *beaten on both sides*, ἰσθμοί, Id. II. Act., *dashing on both sides*, ῥόθια S.*Ph*.688 (lyr.). **-πλήξ**, ῆγος, ὁ, ἡ, *striking with both sides*, φάσγανον Id.*Tr*. 930: metaph., of a father's and mother's curse, ἀρά *OT*417.

ἀμφι-πλίξ, Adv. *astride*: hence, *gripping with coils*, of serpents, S.*Fr*.596. **-πλίσσω**, *straddle*, Poll.2.172.

ἀμφίπλους, ουν, *which may be sailed round*, γῆ, of islands, Poll. 9.18.

ἀμφιπλύνω, *wash all over*, Hp.*Mul*.2.133, 144.

ἀμφίποκος, ον, = ἀμφίμαλλος, Hsch.

ἀμφιπολ-εῖον, τό, *chamber of the* ἀμφίπολος 1.3, *IG*4.39 (Aegina, v B.C.). **-εύω**, Ep. Verb (used by Hdt.) mostly in pres.: aor., Ἐφ. Ἀρχ.1910.397 (Ambracia):—*serve as an attendant, tend, care for* (not in Il.), βίον, ὄρχατον, ἵππους, Od.18.254, 24.244, *h.Merc*.568; of temple-slaves, *serve, have the care of*, ἀμφιπολεύουσαν ἱρὸν Διὸς Hdt.2.56; of the departed soul, Ὀσίριδος θῶκον *Epigr.Gr*.414 (Alexandria); ψυχὴ σκῆπτρον Ῥαδαμάνθυος ἀ. *IG*14.1389 i 47. 2. abs., [τὰς κούρας] ἔδοσαν.. Ἐρινύσιν ἀμφιπολεύειν Od.20.78, cf. Hes.*Op*.803; *hold the* yearly *office of* ἀμφίπολος, *IG*12(9).906 (Chalcis). 3. c. dat., *minister to*, as priest, Q.S.13.270; Ἀρτέμιτι Ἐφ.Ἀρχ. l.c.; Διί *IG* 14.574 (Centuripa); θεῷ Αὐγούστῳ ib.601 (Malta). 4. *traverse, go about*, ἥλιος μέγαν οὐρανὸν ἀ. Emp.41; δόμον Man.6.273, cf. 3.36, al. **-έω**, later form of ἀμφιπολεύω, mostly in pres. (aor. 1, Pi.*N*. 8.6):—*attend constantly*, ἤδη με γηραιὸν μέρος ἁλικίας ἀ. Id.*P*.4. 158. 2. *attend on, watch, guard*, Ἱμέραν Id.*O*.12.2, cf. Theoc.1. 124; λέκτρον Pi.*N*.8.6; *busy oneself with*, μυρία φρενί B.*Fr*.7.3. 3. *tend, treat gently*, τρώμαν ἕλκεος Pi.*P*.4.271. II. c. dat., *roam with, accompany*, θεαῖς S.*OC*680 (lyr.). **-πολῆσι**· περιπορείαις, *EM*91.7. **-ία** or **-εία**, ἡ, *office of* ἀμφίπολος, D.S.16.70.

ἀμφίπολις, poet. **ἀμφίπτολις**, ὁ, ἡ, *encompassing city*, ἀνάγκη ἀμφίπτολις A.*Ch*.75 (lyr.). II. Subst. ἀ., ἡ, *city encompassed by a river*, as pr. n., Th.4.102, etc.

ἀμφίπολος, ον, (πέλω, πολέω) *busied about, busy*, epith. of Κύπρις, S.*Tr*.860:—in Hom. and Hdt. only as fem. Subst., *handmaid, waiting-woman*, Od.1.331, 6.199, etc.; λάβετ' ἀμφίπολοι γραίας ἀμενοῦς E.*Supp*.1115:—with other Substs., ἀ. ταμίη, γραῦς, Il.24.302, Od.1.191. b. later, *handmaid of gods, priestess*, θεᾶς E.*IT*1114; Διὸς *IG*14.2111. 2. masc., *attendant, follower*, Pi.*O*.6.32. 3. masc., *priest, sacrist*, E.*Fr*.982; ὁ τῶν θεῶν ἀ. Phld.*D*.1.13, cf. Plu. *Comp.Demetr.Ant*.3, *IG*9(1).683 (Corcyra). 4. ἀ. Διὸς Ὀλυμπίου, title of magistrate at Syracuse, D.S.16.70. II. in pass. sense, *frequented*, τύμβος Pi.*O*.1.93.

ἀμφιπονέομαι, (πονέω) *attend to, provide for*, τάδε δ' ἀμφιπονησόμεθ' Il.23.159; κείνου κεφαλὴν.. Ἥφαιστος.. ἀμφεπονήθη, of funeral fire, Archil.120. II. Pass., τὰ ἀμφιπονεόμενα *neighbouring parts affected*, Hp.*Mul*.2.135.

ἀμφιπορφύρεος, α, ον, *edged with purple*, πέπλων prob. in E.*Or*. 1457 (lyr.) (-πόρφυρος Sch. ad loc.).

ἀμφιποτάομαι, *fly round and round*, of a bird, ἀμφεποτᾶτο Il. 2.315, cf. Sapph.*Supp*.14.4, Q.S.5.12.

ἄμφιπποι, ων, οἱ, *cavalry who went into action with a spare horse*, Ael.*Tact*.2.4, Arr.*Tact*.2.3, prob. l. in D.S.19.29. **ἀμφιπποτοξόται**, οἱ, *ἄμφιπποι armed with bows*, prob. l. in D.S.19.29 (codd. ἀφ-, ἐφ-), Plu.2.197d.

ἀμφιπρόστῡλος, ον, *having a portico on either front*, Vitr.3.2.1.

ἀμφιπρόσωπος, ον, *double-faced*, Emp.61; epith. of Janus, = Lat. *bifrons*, Plu.*Num*.19; epith. of Hecate, Orac.Chald.ap.Procl.*in Ti*. 2.246 D. 2. *on two fronts*, μάχη Onos.10.2.

ἀμφί-πρυμνος, ον, *with two sterns*, i.e. *with rudder behind and before*, ναῦς S.*Fr*.131, cf. *Milet*.7 p.60, D.C.74.11, Agath.3.21: metaph., *two-edged*, λόγῳ E.ap.Phot.p.103 R. **-πρῳρος**, ον, *with two prows*, Gal.14.243.

ἀμφιπτολεμοπηδησίστρᾰτος, ον, Com. name in Eup.393.

ἀμφίπτολις, poet. for ἀμφίπολις.

ἀμφι-πτύσσομαι, Med., *embrace*, Opp.*H*.4.289 (tm.). **-πτῠχή**, ἡ, *folding round, embrace*, σώματος δὸς ἀμφιπτυχάς E.*Ion* 519.

ἀμφίπῠλος, ον, *with two entrances*, μέλαθρα E.*Med.*135 (lyr.).

ἀμφίπῡρος, ον, (πῦρ) *with fire at each end*, of the double-pointed thunderbolt, E.*Ion* 212; βροντά Id.*Hipp.*559; δειράδες Παρνασοῦ.. ἵνα Βάκχιος ἀμφιπύρους ἀνέχων πεύκας..πηδᾷ *with twin fires*, of two peaks of Parnassus, Id.*Ion* 716; of Artemis as *bearing a torch in either hand*, S.*Tr.*214 (lyr.). II. *with fire all round*, τρίποδες Id.*Aj.*1405.

ἀμφιρίοστον· ἐξ ἀμφοτέρων ἐρετός, Hsch.

ἀμφιριφές (cod. -ρεφ-), *hurled from either side*, Hsch. **ἀμφιρόν**· ἀμφορέα, Id.

ἀμφιρρεπής, ές, (ῥέπω) *inclining both ways*, Eustr.*in EN* 119.29, Sch.E.*Or.*633; τὸ ἀ. *ambiguity*, Eust.1394.57, cf. Sch.E.*Or.*866. Adv. -πῶς, ἔχειν Eust.200.11.

ἀμφιρρήγνῡμι, *rend all in pieces*, aor. 2 Pass. ἀμφιραγείς Q.S.1.39.

ἀμφιρρηδής, = περιρρηδής, *Lex.Rhet.*ap.Eust.1920.33.

ἀμφίρροπος, ον, *doubtful*, νίκη Polyaen.2.1.23; ἔννοιαι Agath. 4.2. II. *precipitous on both sides*, κρημνοί Malch.p.415 D.

ἀμφιρρώξ, ῶγος, ὁ, ἡ, *jagged*, πέτραι A.R.1.995. 2. *broken*, κλωβοί *AP*6.109.

ἀμφίρῠτος, η, ον, also ος, ον S.*Aj.*134, (ῥέω) *flowed around*, *sea-girt*, Od. always fem. ἀμφιρύτῃ of islands, as 1.50; ἐν Κέῳ ἀμφιρύτᾳ Pi.*I.*1.8; τῆς ἀμφιρύτου Σαλαμῖνος S. l. c.:—**ἀμφίρρυτος**, ον, Hes.*Th.* 983, Orac.ap.Hdt.4.163,164.

ἀμφιρῶτις· περιβόητος, Hsch.

ἀμφίς, Ep. word, once in Pi. (v.infr.), Trag. only E.*Hyps.* (v. infr.), prop. = ἀμφί, but mostly as Adv.: 1. *on both sides*, ἀ. ἀρωγοί helpers *on either hand, to either party*, Il.18.502, cf. 519; ἁμαρτῇ δούρασιν ἀ. βάλεν threw with spears *from both hands* at once, 21.162; σεῖον ζυγὸν ἀ. ἔχοντες having it *on both sides*, Od.3.486. 2. generally, *round about*, ἀ. ἐόντες Il.24.488; ἀ. ἰδών having looked *about*, Hes.*Op.*701 (cf. infr. B. 1); δεσμοὶ..ἀ. ἔχοιεν may bonds *encompass*, Od.8.340; σιδηρέῳ ἄξονι ἀ. *at each end*, Il.5.723; and so (rather than *between*) 3.115, 7.342; μολπὴ ἀ. ἔχει δώματα *fills* the house, Xenoph. 1.12. II. *apart, asunder*, γαῖαν καὶ οὐρανὸν ἀ. ἔχειν Od.1.54; ἀ. ἐέργειν to keep *apart*, Il.13.706; ἀ. ἀγῆναι snap *in twain*, 11.559; τόξων ἀϊκὰς ἀ. μένον 15.709; ἀ. φράζεσθαι think *separately*, each for himself, i.e. *to be divided*, 2.13; ἀ. φρονέοντε 13.345; ἀ. ἕκαστα εἴρεσθαι to ask each *by itself*, i.e. one after another, Od.19.46 codd.; ἀ. ἔμμεναι to be *absent*, Orac.ap.Hdt.1.85.

B. less freq as Prep., like ἀμφί: I. c. gen. (which it may either precede or follow), *around*, ἅρματος ἀ. ἰδεῖν look *all round* his chariot, Il.2.384. b. *concerning*, ἀ. ἀληθείης Parm.8.51; ἀέθλοις..ἐσθᾶτος ἀ. Pi.*P.*4.253. 2. *apart from, far from*, ἀ. ἐκείνων εἶναι Od.14. 352; Διὸς ἀ. ἧσθην Il.8.444; ἀ. φυλόπιδος Od.16.267; ἀ. ὁδοῦ *aside from, out of* road, Il.23.393; πάτρας ἀ. *far from* her fatherland, E.*Hyps.Fr.*3 iii 30. II. c. acc., *about, around*, always after its case, Κρόνον ἀ. Il.14.274; Ποσιδήϊον ἀ. Od.6.266, cf. 9.399.

ἀμφισαλεύομαι, Pass., *toss about*, *AP*5.54 (Diosc.).

ἀμφίσβαινα, ης, ἡ, (βαίνω) kind of *serpent, supposed to go either forwards or backwards*, A.*Ag.*1233, Ar.*Fr.*18 D.; ἀ. ἀμφίκρηνος, δίστομος, Nic.*Th.*372, Nonn.*D.*5.146. II. ἀ. φλέβες veins connecting the breast and generative organs, Pall.*in Hp.*2.103 D.

ἀμφισ-βᾰσίη, ἡ, Ion. for ἀμφισβήτησις, ἐς -βασίας ἀπικνέεσθαί τινι come to *controversy* with one, Hdt.4.14; ἐγένετο λόγων ἀ. Id.8.81, cf. *Inscr.Prien.*37.129. **-βᾰτέω**, Ion. for ἀμφισβητέω, q. v. **-βᾰτος**, ον, = ἀμφισβήτητος, Hellanic.193 J. **-βητέω**, impf. ἠμφεσβήτουν: fut. -ήσω: aor. ἠμφεσβήτησα:—Pass., fut. of med. form -ήσομαι Pl. *Tht.*171b: aor. ἠμφεσβητήθην Id.*Plt.*276b, al., Is.8.44:—Ion. **ἀμφισβᾰτέω** twice in Hdt. (v. infr.), *SIG*279.18 (Zelea): impf. ἀμφεσβάτει *Inscr.Prien.*37.99; also Aeol. pf. part. Pass. ἀμφισβατημένος *IG*12(2).6.25 (Mytilene): (v. βαίνω):—lit. *go asunder, stand apart*: hence, *disagree with*, ὁ ἕτερος τῶν λόγων τῷ πρότερον λεχθέντι -βατέων Hdt.9.74. b. abs., *disagree, dispute, wrangle*, Id.4. 14, etc.: περί τινος And.1.27, Isoc.4.19, Pl.*Prt.*337a; ὑπέρ τινος Antipho 3.4.3; πρός τινα 3.1.1; οἱ ἀμφισβητοῦντες *the parties*, in a lawsuit, Arist.*Rh.*1354a31. 2. c. dat. pers., *dispute* or *argue with* a person, Pl.*Phdr.*263a, al.; τινὶ περί τινος Id.*Plt.*268a. 3. c. gen. rei, *dispute for* or *about* a thing, τοῦ σίτου τοῦ ἡμετέρου D.32.9; *lay claim to*, τῆς ἡγεμονίας Isoc.4.20; τῶν οὐδὲν ὑμῖν προσηκόντων Epist. Phil.ap.D.12.23; τῆς ἀρχῆς D.39.19; τῆς πολιτείας Arist.*Pol.*1280a6, cf. 1283a11; τρία τὰ ἀμφισβητοῦντα τῆς ἰσότητος three things *which claim* equal shares in.., 1294a19; τῆς μεσότητος ἀ. τὰ ἄκρα *EN*1125b 18:—also ἀ. πρός τι *make a claim* with reference to a standard, *Pol.* 1283a24. b. Att. law-term, *lay claim to* property of deceased or guardianship of heiress, χρημάτων Isoc.19.3; κλήρου D.3.5, 44.38; κληρονομίας Is.3.1: abs., 3.61, 6.3; τινὶ περὶ τῶν πατρῴων 3.61; πρὸς διαθήκην in defiance of a will, Isoc.19.1. 4. c. acc. rei, *dispute* point, *be at issue upon* it, ἐν τουτὶ ἀμφισβητοῦμεν Pl.*Grg.*472d; οὐκ ἀληθῆ ἀ. *Mx.*242d; cf. ἀμφισβητητέον. 5. c. acc. et inf., *argue, maintain that*.., ἀ. εἶναί τι Id.*Grg.*452c, cf. D.27.62, etc.; but ἀ. ὅτι ἐστί τι *dispute* the fact that.., Pl.*Smp.*215b: with neg., *argue* or *maintain* that it is not, τὸ μὴ οὐχὶ ἡδέα εἶναι τὰ ἡδέα λόγος οὐδεὶς ἀ. *Phlb.*13a; ἠμφεσβήτει μὴ ἀληθῆ λέγειν ἐμέ D.19.19; ἀ. ὡς οὐκ ἀληθῆ λέγει τις Pl.*R.*476d, al.; οὐδεὶς ἀ. περὶ τούτων, ὡς οὐ.. Arist.*Pol.*1287b 17; σὺ δὲ ἀμφισβητῶν ἀνὴρ εἶναι Aeschin.2.148. II. Pass., *to be the subject of dispute, to be in question*, ἀμφισβητεῖταί τι Pl.*R.*581e, etc.: impers., ἀμφισβητεῖται περί τι *Sph.*225b; περί τινος *R.*457e; ἠμφεσβητήθη μηδεμίαν εἶναι τέχνην *Plt.*276b; ὁ πολίτης ἀ. *is a debatable term*, Arist.*Pol.*1275a2; τὰ ἀμφισβητούμενα, = ἀμφισβητήματα, Th. 6.10, 7.18, Isoc.4.19, Pl.*Lg.*641e, etc. **-βήτημα**, ατος, τό, *point in dispute, question*, Id.*Tht.*158b, Arist.*Pol.*1275b37, etc. 2. *point maintained in argument*, Pl.*Phlb.*11b. **-βητηματικός**, ή, όν, = sq.; τὰ -κά Aps.p.236 H. **-βητήσιμος**, ον, *disputable*, Antipho 3.1.1, etc.; χώρα ἀ. *debatable* ground, X.*HG*3.5.3, D.7.43, *Hell.Oxy.* 13.3, Theopomp.ap.Phot.p.104 R.; τὰ ἀ. *disputed property*, Pl.*Lg.* 954c; ἀ. ἀγαθά Arist.*Rh.*1362b29; *doubtful*, Pl.*Smp.*175e; ἀ. ἐστι πότερον.. Arist.*Metaph.*996b27; οὐκέτ' ἐν -ησίμῳ τὰ πράγματα ἦν D. 18.139. **-βήτησις**, εως, ἡ, *dispute, controversy*, ἀ. γίγνεται, ἔστι περί τινος, Pl.*Phlb.*15a, *R.*533d; ἀ. Δελφῶν πρὸς Ἀμφισσεῖς ὑπὲρ τῶν ὅρων *CIG*1711 (Delph., i A.D.); ἀμφισβήτησιν ὑπολείπειν leave *room for dispute*, Antipho 5.16; ἀμφισβήτησιν ἔχει it admits of *question*, Arist.*EN*1100a18, etc.; ἀ. ἔσται, τίνας ἄρχειν δεῖ *Pol.*1283b3; ἀμφισβητήσεις [εἰσίν], c. acc. et inf., *Rh.*1417a8; ἐξ ὧν ἡ πόλις συνέστηκεν, ἐν τούτοις ποιεῖσθαι τὴν ἀ. make a *claim*, *Pol.*1283a15, etc. 2. as Att. law-term, *claim* to an inheritance, ἀ. ποιεῖσθαι Lys.17.5, cf. Is. 6.4, D.48.26. **-βητητέον**, verb. Adj. *one must argue against*, τοῖς εἰρημένοις Arist.*EN*1113b17; cf. ἀμφισβητέω I. 4. **-βητητικός**, ή, όν, *fond of disputing, disputatious, contentious*, οἱ περὶ λόγους ἀ. Pl.*Plt.* 306a:—ἡ -κή (sc. τέχνη) *art of disputing*, *Sph.*226a; τὸ -κόν *argumentation*, ib.225b. **-βήτητος**, ον, *disputed, debatable*, γῆ Th. 6.6. **-βητος**, ον, = foreg., Antag.1.1.

ἀμφίσγονοι, = ἑτερόγονοι, Hsch.; = ἑτερομήτορες, *EM*87.57.

ἀμφισκέπαρνος, ον, *dressed on both sides*, λίθοι *Milet.*7 p.56; ἱερόν *Rev.Phil.*43.200 (Didyma).

ἀμφίσκιος, ον, (σκιά) *throwing shadow both ways*, sometimes north, sometimes south, of those who live within the tropics, Posidon.70, Cleom.1.7, Ach.Tat.*Intr.Arat.*31. II. *shady all round*, πέτρη Opp. *H.*1.789.

ἀμφίσκω· ἀμπίσχω, Hsch.

ἀμφίσκωμοι, *living around in villages*, Hsch.

ἀμφι-σμίλη, ἡ, and **-σμιλον**, τό, prob. ff.ll. for -μηλον (q. v.), Gal. 2.574, 581.

ἀμφισπάω, *draw about*, Sch.E.*Or.*1457.

ἀμφίσπορα, τά, *boundary lands of which the sowing is disputed* (in Latin form), *CIL*3.586 (Lamia, ii A.D.).

ἀμφιστέλλομαι, Med., *fold round oneself, deck oneself in*, ξυστίδα ἀμφιστειλαμένη Theoc.2.74.

ἀμφιστένω, *roar around*, of the sea, Q.S.9.440; *echo*, of mountains, Id.5.646, 14.82.

ἀμφιστερή· καταρχὴ τῶν θυσιῶν (Lacon.), Hsch.

ἀμφίστερνος, ον, *double-breasted*, Emp.61.

ἀμφι-στεφᾰνόομαι, Pass., ἀμφὶ δ' ὅμιλος..ἐστεφάνωτο the assembly *stood all round*, *h.Ven.*120. **-στεφής**, ές, *placed round like a crown*, Il.11.40 (v.l.). II. *brim-full*, κρατήρ Hsch., Suid. s.v. ἐπιστεφής.

ἀμφίστημι, *place round*: in this sense only poet. in Pass. ἀμφίσταμαι, with intr. aor. ἀμφέστην, Ep. 3 pl. ἀμφέσταν, and 3 pl. pf. ἀμφεστᾶσι, *stand around*, abs., φίλοι δ' ἀμφέσταν ἑταῖροι Il.18.233; κλαίων δ' ἀμφίσταθ' ὅμιλος 24.712: c. acc., ἀμφὶ δέ σ' ἔστησαν Od. 24.58; πεδίον ἀμφεστᾶσι πᾶν S.*OC*1312, cf. *Aj.*724: c. dat., ἀμφίσταμαι τραπέζαις *El.*192. II. Med., *investigate*, *Tab.Heracl.*1.125; cf. ἀμπιστατήρ.

ἀμφίστομος, ον, *with double mouth*, of the ichneumon, Eub.107. 15; ὄρυγμα ἀ. *tunnel*, Hdt.3.60; σπήλαιον Apollod.2.5.1; λαβὰς ἀ. handles *on both sides of bowl* (ἑκατέρωθεν τοῦ στόματος Sch.), S.*OC* 473; ἀ. θυρίδες, of honeycombs, Arist.*HA*624a8; of fistulae, Meges ap.Orib.44.24.11. 2. *two-edged*, ξίφη D.S.5.33; ἕκτορες anchors *with two flukes*, Luc.*Lex.*15. 3. of a body of soldiers, *facing both ways*, δύναμις, τάξις, Plb.2.28.6, 29.4, cf. Ascl.*Tact.*3.5, Onos.21.2; φάλαγξ Ael.*Tact.*37.1, Arr.*Tact.*29.1. Adv. -μως *with* λοχαγοί *in front and rear*, Ascl.*Tact.*11.3, Ael.*Tact.*37.2, Arr.*Tact.*29.2. 4. *pointed at both ends*, ἄκοντες Tim.*Pers.*176.

ἀμφιστρᾰτάομαι, Dep., *beleaguer, besiege*, Ep. impf. ἀμφεστρατόωντο πόλιν Il.11.713.

ἀμφι-στρεφής, ές, *turning all ways*, of a dragon's three heads, Il. 11.40 (v.l. ἀμφιστεφέες):—also **-στραφής**, Diotog.ap.Stob.4.7.62.

ἀμφιστρόγγῠλος, ον, *quite round*, Luc.*Hipp.*6.

ἀμφι-στροφή, ἡ, *wheeling round*, Hsch. **-στροφος**, ον, *turning to and fro, quick-turning*, βᾶρις ἀ. A.*Supp.*882 (Sch. expl. by ἀμφιέλισσα). 2. **Ἀμφίστροφον**, τό, at Delos, possibly a *domed building*, *IG*11(2).142.38 (iv B.C.), al.

ἀμφίσφαιρα, τά, (cf. σφαιρωτήρ) *buttoned boots*, Herod.7.59, Hsch.

ἀμφι-σφάλλω, *treat* a dislocated joint *by circumduction*, Hp.*Art.* 2:—Pass., Id.*Mochl.*5. **-σφαλσις**, εως, ἡ, *circumduction*, *Art.*71.

ἀμφίσφῡρα, τά, kind of *shoes*, Poll.7.94 (prob. f.l. for ἀμφίσφαιρα).

ἀμφίσωπος, ον, = περίωπος, A.*Fr.*41.

ἀμφιτᾰλαντεύω, *cause to weigh evenly on both sides*, Nonn.*D.*1.183, cf. 6.110.

ἀμφιτάμνω, Ion. for ἀμφιτέμνω.

ἀμφιτανύω, = ἀμφιτείνω, *h.Merc.*49 (tm.).

ἀμφιτάπης [ᾰ], ητος, ὁ, *rug* or *carpet with pile on both sides*, Alex. 93, Diph.51; but also ἀμφιτάπητες ψιλαί *CIG*3071 (Teos):—also **ἀμφίταπις**, ιδος, ἡ, Ael.Dion.*Fr.*304, Lyconap.D.L.5.72; and **ἀμφίταπος**, ὁ, *PEdgar*29.4 (iii B.C.), Lxx *Pr.*7.16, Callix.2.

ἀμφιτᾰράσσομαι, Pass., *to be troubled all round*, ἁλὸς ἀμφιταρασσομένας ὀρυμαγδός Simon.51.

ἀμφιτείνομαι, Pass., *to be spread round* or *over*, ἀμφιταθείς Opp. *H.*1.163.

ἀμφιτειχής, ές, *encompassing the walls*, λεώς A.*Th*.291.

ἀμφιτέμνω, Ion. **-τάμνω**, *cut off on all sides, intercept and surround*, in tmesi, τάμνοντ' ἀμφὶ βοῶν ἀγέλας Il.18.528; *clear away*, κόνιν, χοῦν, *AP*7.281 (Heraclid. Sinop.), *IG*4.823.49 (Troezen); *pare all round*, ὀνύχων ἀκίδα *AP*5.227 (Paul. Sil.).

ἀμφίτερμος, ον, *bounded on all sides, hedged about*, Hsch. Adv. -μως S.*Fr*.123.

ἀμφιτεύχω, *make* or *work round about*, plpf. Pass., Τηθὺς δ' ἀμφιτέτυκτο, of sea round shield of Achilles, Q.S.5.14.

ἀμφιτίθημι [τῐ], 3 sg. ἀμφιτιθεῖ Xenoph.1.2, imper. ἀμφιτίθει Thgn.847: aor. ind. ἀμφέθηκα, other moods supplied by aor. 2: (v. τίθημι):—*put round*, Hom. mostly in tmesi, ἀμφὶ δέ οἱ κυνέην κεφαλῆφιν ἔθηκεν Il.10.261, cf. Od.13.431; τοῖς ἀδίκοις ἀμφιτίθησι πέδας Sol.4.34; κἄνπερ κόσμον ἀμφιθῇ χροΐ E.*Med*.787, cf. *El*.512; ἀμφιθεῖναι σῇ δέρῃ θέλω χέρας *Or*.1042; also στέφανον ἀμφὶ κάρα.. ἀμφιθεῖναι Id.*IA*1531:—c. acc. rei only, ζεύγλην δύσλοφον ἀμφιτίθει Thgn. l.c.; cf. Theoc.15.40; δεσμὸν ἀμφέθηκεν πέδης Semon.7.116 (Lyc.1344, τραχήλῳ ζεῦγλαν ἀμφιθεὶς πέδαις, is corrupt):—Med., *put round oneself, put on*, ὁ δ' ἀμφέθετο ξίφος Od.21.431; ἀμφέθετο στεφάνους κρατὸς ἐπὶ σφετέρου Epigr.ap.Ath.1.19b:—Pass., *to be put on*, κυνέη ἀμφιτεθεῖσα Il.10.271. 2. rarely c. dat. rei, *cover* with a thing, ἀμφιθεὶς κάρα πέπλοις E.*Hec*.432.

ἀμφιτιμάομαι, *to be disputed*, of an assessment or estimate, *BCH* 37.184 (Clazomenae, iii B.C.).

ἀμφιτῑνάσσω, *shake around*, δικλίδας ἀμφετίναξε.. προσώποις *swung round* the door in my face, *AP*5.255 (Paul. Sil.).

ἀμφιτιττῠβίζω, *twitter* or *chirp around*, Ar.*Av*.235.

ἀμφίτομος, ον, *cutting on both sides, two-edged*, βέλεμνον A.*Ag*. 1496; λόγχαι, ξίφη, E.*Hipp*.1375, *El*.164; βουπλήξ Q.S.11.190.

ἀμφί-τορνος, ον, *well-rounded*, ἀσπίς E.*Tr*.1156. **-τόρνωτος**, η, ον, = foreg., Lyc.704.

ἀμφίτοροι· ἄλφιτα ἐλαίῳ δεδευμένα (Lacon.), Hsch.

ἀμφιτράχηλος [ᾰ], ον, *round the neck*, Sch.S.*Ant*.351.

ἀμφιτρέμω, *tremble round* one, ἀμφὶ δ' ἄρ' ἀμβρόσιος ἑανὸς τρέμε Il. 21.507.

ἀμφιτρέχω, *run round, surround*, αὐλὴν ἕρκος ἀμφιδέδρομεν Archil. 40; σέλας δ' ἀμφέδραμεν Pi.*P*.3.39; θείη δ' ἀμφιδέδρομεν χάρις Semon. 7.89.

ἀμφι-τρής, ῆτος, ὁ, ἡ, (τετραίνω) = sq.; ἀμφιτρής (sc. πέτρα) rock *pierced through*, cave *with double entrance*, E.*Cyc*.707: also neut., ἀμφιτρῆς αὔλιον S.*Ph*.19. **-τρητος**, ον, *pierced through*, *AP*6.233 (Maec.).

Ἀμφιτρίτη [τρῑ], ἡ, *Amphitrite*, Poseidon's wife, Hom., etc. 2. poet., *sea*, *Hymn.Is*.145, D.P.53, Opp.*H*.1.423: pl., D.P.99. 3. Pythag., = 6, *Theol.Ar*.38 (as if from ἀμφίς, τριάς).

ἀμφίτριψ, ιβος, ὁ, (τρίβω) *rubbed all round*: metaph., like περίτριμμα, *practised knave*, Archil.124, cf. Hsch.

ἀμφιτρομέω, *tremble for*, τοῦ δ' ἀ. καὶ δείδια Od.4.820.

ἀμφιτροχόω, *run round, encompass*, ἀμφιτροχώσας Apollod.1.9. 12, prob. from a poet.

ἀμφιτρυχῆ· κατερρωγότα, Hsch., Phot., Suid.

ἀμφιτύπος, ον, (τύπτω) *pointed at both ends*, βουπλήξ Q.S.1.159.

ἀμφι-φαείνω, *beam around*, αἴγλη δέ μιν ἀ. *h.Ap*.202. **-φαής**, ές, (φάος) *everywhere visible*, Arist.*Mu*.395[b]14; Ἑκάτη *visible from all sides*, Dam.*Pr*.122, cf. *Orac.Chald*.62.

ἀμφίφαλος κυνέη helmet *with double* φάλος, Il.5.743, 11.41, Q.S. 3.334.

ἀμφιφᾰνής, ές, (φαίνομαι) *visible all round, seen by all, known to all*, E.*Andr*.834 (lyr.), *IG*3.1324, *Orac.Chald*.300. 2. of stars, *seen twice in a night*, when they set after and rise before the sun, Gem.14.11, Arr.ap.Stob.1.28.2.

ἀμφιφέρομαι, Pass., *to be borne round, revolve*, in impf., Q.S.5.10.

ἀμφί-φλασμα, -φλάω, v. -θλασμα, -θλάω.

ἀμφιφοβέομαι, Pass., *fear, tremble*, or *quake all round*, ἕταροι δέ μιν ἀμφεφόβηθεν Il.16.290 (al. ἀμφὶ φόβ-), cf. Q.S.2.546, 11.117.

ἀμφιφορεύς, gen. έως, Ep. ῆος, ὁ: (φέρω, φορέω):—*large jar* or *pitcher with two handles*, of gold, Il.23.92, Od.24.74; of stone, 13.105; for wine, 2.290, etc.; for oil, Simon.155.4: used as *cinerary urn*, Il. l.c. II. = μετρητής, Theopomp.Hist.374. (The later form was ἀμφορεύς, q.v.)

ἀμφιφορίτης [ῑ], ὁ, v. ἀμφορίτης.

ἀμφιφράζομαι, Med., *consider on all sides, consider well*, ἀμφὶ μάλα φράζεσθε, φίλοι Il.18.254.

ἀμφιφύα, ἡ, (φύω) = ἄμφαυξις, Thphr.*HP*3.7.1.

ἀμφιφῶν, ῶντος, ὁ, properly part. of *ἀμφιφάω, cake offered to Munychian Artemis *by double light*, i.e. either *surrounded by lighted tapers*, or *offered when sun and moon were both visible*, Pherecr.156, Philem.67, cf. Poll.6.75, *EM*94.55.

ἀμφίχαιτος, ον, *with foliage all round*, D.S.2.53.

ἀμφιχᾰνής, ές, *gaping wide*, Abyden.1.

ἀμφιχᾰράσσω, *scratch, incise around*, γράμματα σκήπτρῳ *PMag. Par*.1.2845; *lance all round*, ῥίζην (sc. ὀδόντος) Marcell.Sid.89; of stars, *mark the course of*, κύκλον Man.2.66.

ἀμφιχάσκω, impf., v. infr.: aor. ἀμφέχᾰνον:—*gape round, gape for*, c. acc., ἐμὲ μὲν Κὴρ ἀμφέχανε Il.23.79; μαστὸν ἀμφέχασκ' ἐμόν, of an infant, A.*Ch*.545; ἀμφιχανὼν λόγχαις ἑπτάπυλον στόμα, of the Argive army round Thebes, S.*Ant*.118; ἀγκίστρου.. πλάνον ἀμφιχανοῦσα, of a fish, *AP*7.702 (Apollonid.): rarely c. dat., Opp.*H*.3.178.

ἀμφιχέω, *pour around, pour* or *spread over*, ἀμφὶ δ' ἄρ' ἑρμῖσιν χέε δέσματα Od.8.278. II. mostly Pass., *to be poured* or *shed around*, πάρος κόνιν ἀμφιχυθῆναι Il.23.764: c. acc., θείη δέ μιν ἀμφέχυτ' ὀμφή ib.2.41; τὴν ἄχος ἀμφεχύθη Od.4.716; ἀμφιχυθὲν γῆρας Mimn.5; ἀμφὶ δὲ σποδὸν κάρᾳ κεχύμεθα *we have* ashes *poured over* our head, E. *Supp*.826. 2. of persons, *embrace*, ἀμφιχυθεὶς πατέρα Od.16.214, cf. 22.498.

ἀμφιχορεύω, *dance around*, abs., Critias19 (anap.), *AP*9.83 (Phil.): c. dat., Opp.*C*.1.27.

ἀμφιχρίομαι, Med., *anoint oneself all over*, ἀμφὶ δ' ἐλαίῳ χρίσομαι Od.6.219.

ἀμφίχρῡσος, ον, *gilded all over*, φάσγανον E.*Hec*.543.

ἀμφίχῠτος, ον, *poured around*; *thrown up around*, τεῖχος ἀ., i.e. an *earthen* wall, Il.20.145, cf. Hellanic.26 J.

ἀμφίχωλος, ον, *lame in both feet*, *AP*6.203.

ἀμφοδ-άρχης, ου, ὁ, (ἄμφοδον II) *officer commanding troops levied in a ward*, Ph.*Bel*.93.8: also a civil official, *OGI*483.82 (Pergam.), Wilcken *Chrest*.61 (i A.D.). **-αρχία**, ἡ, *quarter under the direction of an* ἀ., *CPR*8.7 (iii A.D.).

ἀμφοδέω, *miss, fail to meet*, *Rev.Égypt*.1.208, Hsch. s.v. ἀβροτάξομεν; cf. ἀντ-, δι-, παρ-αμφοδέω.

ἀμφοδικός, ή, όν, *of, belonging to streets*, κέλευθοι Man.4.252.

ἀμφόδιον, τό, Dim. of sq., Luc.*Rh.Pr*.24, *EM*557.46 (as v.l.).

ἄμφοδον, τό, *street*, Ar.*Fr*.327, *OGI*483.80 (Pergam.), *Ev.Marc*.11. 4, Cleom.2.1; = *compitum*, *Gloss*. II. *block of houses surrounded by streets*, Hyp.*Fr*.137, *PMag.Par*.1.349: prov., οὐ θύρα ἀλλ' ἀμφόδῳ διέψευσται Plb.39.3.2: hence, *ward, quarter of a town*, Lxx *Je*.17. 27, *SIG*961.1 (Smyrna), Ph.*Bel*.92.42, *BGU*496 (ii A.D.), etc.:—also **ἄμφοδος**, ἡ, Gal.*UP*16.1, Sm.*Am*.5.16, Procop.*Aed*.2.3.

ἀμφόδων, = ἀμφώδων, Hp.*Art*.8.

ἄμφ-οισμα, ατος, τό, (ἀμφι-φέρω) *revolving figure*, Papp.682.8, 11:—hence **-οιστικός**, ή, όν, *described by revolution*, 682.8, 15.

ἀμφόνη· ἀκρατής, ἁμαρτωλός, μὴ δυναμένη νηστεῦσαι, Hsch.

ἀμφορεᾱ-φορέω, *carry water-pitchers*, Ar.*Fr*.299. **-φόρος**, ου, ὁ, *water-carrier*, Eup.187, Men.431, *IG*2.768.

ἀμφορ-είδιον (not -ίδιον), τό, Dim. of ἀμφορεύς, Ar.*Pax* 202, al. **-είῳ**· φορτίῳ, Hsch. (ἀμφορεῖ· τῷ φορείῳ, Ruhnken). **-εύς**, έως, ὁ: acc. ἀμφορέα Ar.*Fr*.299: dual ἀμφορῆ Telecl.2 D.: pl. ἀμφορῆς Ar.*Nu*.1203:—*jar* with narrow neck (στενόστομον τὸ τεῦχος Id.*Fr*. 108), Hdt.4.163, Ar.*Nu*.1203, etc.; used for various purposes, esp. for keeping wine in, *Pl*.807, *Fr*.299; or milk, E.*Cyc*.327; for pickles, X. *An*.5.4.28. 2. ornament in shape of vase, ὅρμος -έων *IG*11(2).161*B* 38 (Delos, iii B.C.), cf. *SIG*[2]588.199 (ib., ii B.C.). II. liquid measure, = μετρητής (Philyll.7, Moer.45, etc.), 1½ Roman *amphorae* or nearly 9 gallons, Hdt.1.51, *IG*3.38, D.43.8, etc. (Shortened form of ἀμφιφορεύς, q.v., from *having two handles*.) **-ίζω**, dub. sens. in Eust.1924. 13. **-ικός**, ή, όν, *like an amphora*, κάδοι Sch.Ar.*Av*.1032. **-ίξ**, Adv. *like an amphora* (?), Eust.1924.13. **-ιον**, τό, Dim. of ἀμφορεύς, *Gloss*. **-ίσκος**, ὁ, Dim. of ἀμφορεύς, D.22.76; ἀ. Πανιώνιος *IG*2. 818. **-ίτης** [ῑ] ἀγών, ὁ, race *run by bearers of amphorae*, and *of which an amphora was prize*, Call.*Fr*.80 (ap.Sch.Pi.*O*.7.156); ἀμφιφορίτης *EM*95.3. II. *kept in* ἀμφορεῖς, [ἔλαιον] *PSI*5.535.31 (iii B.C.).

ἀμφοτερ-άκις, Adv. *in both ways*, Arist.*Mech*.855[b]32, *Pr*.902[b] 31. **-η**, Adv. *in both ways*, Hdt.7.10.β'; *by both branches*, of a river, 1.75: Argive -εῖ *Mnemos*.47.160 (v B.C.). **-ήκης**, ες, *two-edged*, Epic.Anon.in *PHib*.8. **-ίζω**, *to be in both ways*, ἀ. τῇ χρείᾳ, of figs, *to be good to eat either* fresh or dried, Jul.*Ep*.180.

ἀμφοτερό-βλεπτος, ον, *looking on both sides, circumspect*, Timo 59. **-γλωσσος**, ον, *speaking both ways, double-tongued*, of Zeno the inventor of dialectic, Id.45, cf. Eust.1440.35. **-γνώμων**, ονος, *of two opinions*, βουλή Sch.E.*Hec*.219. **-δέξιος**, ον, = ἀμφιδέξιος, Lxx *Jd*.3. 15, Aristaenet.1.8, Gal.18(1).147. **-δύναμος**, ον, *with power for good or ill*, of Zeus, Eust.1363.29. **-πλοος**, ον, contr. **-πλους**, ουν, *navigable on both sides*, γῆ Poll.9.18. 2. τὸ ἀ. (sc. ἀργύριον or δάνειον) *money lent on bottomry*, when the lender bore the risk *of the outward and homeward voyage*, ἐδάνεισα Φορμίωνι κ' μνᾶς ἀμφοτερόπλουν εἰς τὸν Πόντον D.34.6, etc.; ἀ. κέρδος Ael.*Ep*.18; opp. ἑτερόπλουν, q.v.

ἀμφότερος (Locr. **ἀμφόταρος** *IG*9(1).334.39), α, ον, (ἄμφω) rare in sg., *either*, i.e. *both of two* (opp. ἑκάτερος *each one* of two), ἀμφοτέρας κοινὸν αἶας common to *either* land, A.*Pers*.131; ποίημα ἢ πάθος ἢ ἀμφότερον or *partaking of both*, Pl.*Sph*.248d; τὸ ἀμφότερον ἑκατέρῳ οὐχ ἕπεται Id.*Hp.Ma*.302e. 2. Hom. has sg. only neut. ἀμφότερον as Adv., foll. by τε.. καί; ἀ. βασιλεύς τ' ἀγαθὸς κρατερός τ' αἰχμητής *both together*, prince as well as warrior, ib.3.179; ἀ. γενεῇ τε καὶ οὕνεκα.. Il.4.60; foll. by τε.. δέ.., Pi.*P*.4.79: also neut. pl., ἀμφότερα μένειν πέμπειν τε A.*Eu*.480; φιλοχρήματος καὶ φιλότιμος, ἤτοι τὰ ἕτερα τούτων ἢ ἀ. Pl.*Phd*.68c; ἀ. ἄριστος καὶ στρατηγὸς καὶ ῥαψῳδός *Ion* 541b; by τε.. καί.., Pi.*O*. 1.104. 3. dual in Hom., as ἀ. Αἴαντε Il.12.265, al., less freq. in later writers, X.*An*.1.1.1, Pl.*Prm*.143c, Isoc.4.134, etc.; but pl. is much more freq., and is found with a dual Noun, χεῖρε πετάσσας ἀμφοτέρας Il.21.115.—Phrases: κατ' ἀμφότερα *on both sides*, Hdt.7. 10.β', Pl.*Prm*.159a; ἐπ' ἀμφότερα *towards both sides, both ways*, Hdt. 3.87, al., Th.1.83, al.; ἀμφότερα, abs., *on both sides*, ib.13, al.; ἀπ' ἀμφοτέρων from or *on both sides*, Ξέρξεω ἀπ' ἀ. ἀδελφεός Hdt.7.97; παρ' ἀμφοτέρων D.S.16.7, al.; μετ' ἀμφοτέροισι *one with another* (s.v.l.), Theoc.12.12; ἀμφοτέροις βλέπειν (sc. ὄμμασι) Call.*Epigr*.32. 6; ἀμφοτέραις, Ep. -ῃσι (sc. χερσί) Od.10.264; ἐπ' ἀμφοτέροις βεβακώς (sc. ποσί) Theoc.14.66. II. later, of more than two, *all together*, *Act.Ap*.19.16, *PLond*.2.336.13 (ii A.D.).

ἀμφοτερότης, ητος, ἡ, *duality*, etym. of Ἀμφιτρίτη, Sch.Opp.*H.* 1.385.

ἀμφοτερόχωλος, ον, = ἀμφίχωλος, Apollon.*Lex.* s.v. ἀμφιγυήεις.

ἀμφοτέρ-ωθεν (also -θε Orph.*Fr.*168.14, Androm.ap.Gal.14.39), Adv. *from* or *on both sides*, Il.5.726, Hdt.2.29, Pi.*P.*1.6; of combatants, Th.5.16: c. gen., ἀ. τῆς κεφαλῆς Hp.*VC*1; τῆς ὁδοῦ X.*HG*5.2.6. **2.** *from both ends*, Od.10.167. **-ωθι**, Adv. *in both ways*, X.*Mem.*3.4.12. **-ως**, Adv. *in both ways*, Pl.*Prm.*159a, *Grg.*469a, etc. **-ωσε**, Adv. *to both sides*, γεγωνέμεν ἀ. Il.8.223, 11.6.

ἀμφουδίς, Adv., only Od.17.237 ἀμφουδὶς ἀείρας lifting *by the middle.* (Prob. Adv. from ἀμφί; cf. ἄλλυδις.)

ἀμφούριον, τό, (οὖρος = ὅρος) *acknowledgement paid to neighbours on sale of a plot of land*, PHal.1.253 (iii B.C.).

ἀμφύσκη· τῇ χειρὶ κυρτωθείσῃ, ἔνιοι δὲ τὸ λεῖκνον, Hsch.

ἄμφω, τώ, τά, τώ, also οἱ, αἱ, τά; gen. ἀμφοῖν S.*Ph.*25, etc., dat. ἀμφοῖν *Aj.*1264, etc.:—*both*, of individuals, Il.1.363; of armies or nations, 2.124:—Hom. uses only nom. and acc.: from Hom. downwards freq. with pl. Noun or Verb, Il.2.767, 7.255, etc.; ἐξ ἀμφοῖν, = ἐξ ἀλλήλοιν, S.*OC*1425: sts. indecl., *h.Cer.*15, Arist.*Top.*118ᵃ28, Theoc.17.26, A.R.1.165. (For the root cf. ἀμφί.)

ἀμφώβολος, ὁ, (ὀβολός) *javelin* or *spit with double point*, E.*Andr.* 1133. **2.** as Adj., in neut. pl., *roasted on the spit*, of victims sacrificed in divination, S.*Fr.*1006 (expl. as διὰ σπλάγχνων μαντεῖαι by Eust.1405.30, Hsch.).

ἀμφώδων, οντος, ὁ, ἡ, (ὀδούς) *with incisor-teeth in both jaws*, opp. ruminants, Arist.*HA*501ᵃ11, cf. *PA*675ᵃ5, *HA*495ᵇ31, al. **II.** Subst., *ass*, Lyc.1401. (Freq. written ἀμφόδων; cf. ἀμφόδους.)

ἀμφώης, ες, (οὖς) = ἄμφωτος, Theoc.1.28.

ἀμφωλένιον, τό, (ὠλένη) *bracelet*, Aristaenet.1.25.

ἄμφωμος, ον, *round* or *on the shoulders*, Hsch. **ἀμφωμοσία**, ἡ, = ἀμφιορκία, Id. **ἀμφώνυξ**, v. ἀμφώτιξ. **ἄμφωξις**, v. ἄμφωτις. **ἀμφώτας**· χιτών τις, *EM*93.15: **ἄμφωτος**, Hsch. **ἀμφώτιξ** ἢ **ἀμφώνυξ**· γαστρίμαργος, ἀκρατής, Id.

ἄμφωτις, ιδος, or **ἀμφωτίς**, ίδος, ἡ, (οὖς) *two-handled pail*, Philet. ap.Ath.11.783d: written **ἄμφωξις** in Hsch., *EM*94.7. **II.** *covering for the ears*, A.*Fr.*102; worn by boxers, Plu.2.38b, 706c, cf. Paus.Gr.*Fr.*52.

ἄμφωτος, ον, (οὖς) *two-eared, two-handled*, Od.22.10: neut. as Subst., *jar*, Hierocl.*Facet.*35.

ἄμωκος, ον, *without mockery, serious*, Iamb.*VP*23.105.

ἀμωλεί, *without dispute*, *GDI*4992 (Gortyn).

ἀμώμητος, ον, *blameless*, Il.12.109, Archil.6.2, Pi.*P.*2.73, etc.; *faultless*, ποιημάτιον, λόγοι, D.S.33.5,7; of victims, *unblemished*, Aristeas 93, cf. Ph.*Fr.*69 H.; ἄσπιλοι καὶ ἀ. 2*Ep.Pet.*3.14, cf. Eus. Mynd.*Fr.*21; in epitaphs, *CIG*4642 (Palestine), *IG*14.1937 (Ravenna). Adv. -τως Hdt.3.82.

ἀμωμίς, ίδος, ἡ, plant used for adulterating *amomum*, Dsc.1.15, cf. Plin.*HN*12.49, *Edict.Diocl.Troez.*21.

ἀμωμίτης [ῑ], ου, ὁ, *like amomum*, kind of λίβανος, Dsc.1.68.

ἄμωμον, τό, Indian spice-plant, prob. *Nepaul cardamom, Amomum subulatum*, Arist.*Fr.*110, Thphr.*HP*9.7.2, Dsc.1.15.

ἄμωμος, ον, *blameless*, Semon.4; νόμος Hdt.2.177; *without blemish*, εἶδος ἄ. Hes.*Th.*259; κάλλει A.*Pers.*185; in epitaphs, *CIG*1974 (Thessalonica), al. **2.** *unblemished*, of victims, etc., Lxx *Ex.*29.1, al., 1*Ep.Pet.*1.19, Ph.1.171, al. **3.** *unimpaired, perfect*, ὑγίεια *IG*5(1).1119 (Geronthrae, iv B.C.).

ἀμωμότης, ητος, ἡ, *blamelessness*, Sm.*Ps.*25.1.

Ἀμών, ῶνος, ὁ, sc. μήν, month at Amphissa, *GDI*1684, 1922.

ἀμώνα, Aeol. for ἀνεμώνη, Hsch.

ἀμωρέα, ἡ, kind of *radish*, Thphr.*HP*7.4.2. **ἀμωρεύουσιν**· ἰχθυοφοροῦσιν, *EM*117.26. **ἄμωρος**, kind of *cake*, Hsch.

ἀμῶς or **ἀμῶς**, Adv. from obsol. ἀμός = τίς, only in form ἀμωσγέπως *in some way or other*, Ar.*Th.*429, Lys.13.7, Pl.*Prt.*323c, Epicur. *Fr.*607, etc. (Cf. ἀμός B.)

ἀμώσας· κρεμάσας (Tarent.), Hsch. **ἄμωτον**, τό, = καστάνειον, Ageloch.ap.Ath.2.54d; prob. cj. for μότα, Dsc.1.106.

ἄν (A), [ᾰ], Ep., Lyr., Ion., Arc., Att.; also **κε(ν)** Ep., Aeol., Thess., **κᾱ** Dor., Boeot., El.; the two combined in Ep. (infr. D. II. 2) and Arc., εἰκ ἄν *IG*5(2).6.2,15 (iv B.C.):—modal Particle used with Verbs to indicate that the action is limited by circumstances or defined by conditions. In Hom. κε is four times as common as ἄν, in Lyr. about equally common. No clear distinction can be traced, but κε as an enclitic is somewhat less emphatic; ἄν is preferred by Hom. in negative clauses, κε(ν) with the relative.

A. In Simple Sentences, and in the Apodosis of Compound Sentences; here ἄν belongs to the Verb, and denotes that the assertion made by the Verb is dependent on a condition, expressed or implied: thus ἦλθεν *he came*, ἦλθεν ἄν *he would have come* (under conditions, which may or may not be defined), and so *he might have come*; ἔλθοι *may he come*, ἔλθοι ἄν *he would come* (under certain conditions), and so *he might come.*

I. WITH INDICATIVE: **1.** with historical tenses, generally impf. and aor., less freq. plpf., never pf., v. infr., **a.** most freq. in apodosis of conditional sentences, with protasis implying nonfulfilment of a past or present condition, and apod. expressing what *would be* or *would have been* the case if the condition *were* or *had been* fulfilled. The impf. with ἄν refers to continued action, in Hom. always in past time, exc. perh. καί κε θάμ' ἐνθάδ' ἐόντες ἐμισγόμεθ' Od.4.178; later also in pres. time, first in Thgn.905; πολὺ ἂν θαυμαστότερον ἦν, εἰ ἐτιμῶντο it *would be* far more strange if they were honoured, Pl.*R.*489a; οὐκ ἂν νήσων ἐκράτει, εἰ μή τι καὶ ναυτικὸν εἶχεν he *would* not *have* been master of islands if he had not had also some naval power, Th.1.9. The aor. strictly refers only to past time, Pi.*N.*11.24, etc.; εἰ τότε ταύτην ἔσχε τὴν γνώμην, οὐδὲν ἂν ὧν νυνὶ πεποίηκεν ἔπραξεν if he had then come to this opinion, he *would have* accomplished nothing of what he has now done, D.4.5, al., but is used idiomatically with Verbs of saying, answering, etc., as we say *I should have* said, εἰ μὴ πατὴρ ἦσθ', εἶπον ἄν σ' οὐκ εὖ φρονεῖν S.*Ant.*755, cf. Pl.*Smp.*199d, *Euthphr.*12d, etc.: the plpf. refers to completed actions, as ὃ εἰ ἀπεκρίνω, ἱκανῶς ἂν ἤδη παρὰ σοῦ τὴν ὁσιότητα ἐμεμαθήκη I *should have* already learnt.., ib.14c; εἰ ὁ ἀνὴρ ἀπέθανεν, δικαίως ἂν ἐτεθνήκει Antipho 4.2.3. **b.** the protasis is freq. understood: ὑπό κεν ταλασίφρονά περ δέος εἷλεν fear *would have* seized even the stout-hearted (had he heard the sound), Il.4.421; τὸ γὰρ ἔρυμα τῷ στρατοπέδῳ οὐκ ἂν ἐτειχίσαντο they *would* not *have* built the wall (if they had not won a battle), Th.1.11; πολλοῦ γὰρ ἂν ἦν ἄξια for (if that were so) they *would be* worth much, Pl.*R.*374d; οὐ γὰρ ἦν ὅ τι ἂν ἐποιεῖτε for there was nothing which you *could have* done, i.e. *would have* done (if you had tried), D.18.43. **c.** with no definite protasis understood, to express what *would have been likely to happen*, or *might have happened* in past time: ἢ γάρ μιν ζωόν γε κιχήσεαι, ἤ κεν Ὀρέστης κτεῖνεν ὑποφθάμενος for either you will find him alive, or else Orestes *may* already *have* killed him before you, Od.4.546; ὃ θεασάμενος πᾶς ἄν τις ἀνὴρ ἠράσθη δάϊος εἶναι every man who saw this (the 'Seven against Thebes') *would have* longed to be a warrior, Ar. *Ra.*1022; esp. with τάχα, q.v., ἀλλ' ἦλθε μὲν δὴ τοῦτο τοὔνειδος τάχ' ἂν ὀργῇ βιασθὲν μᾶλλον ἢ γνώμῃ φρενῶν, i.e. it *might* perhaps *have* come, S.*OT*523; τάχα ἂν δὲ καὶ ἄλλως πως ἐσπλεύσαντες (sc. διέβησαν) and they *might* also perhaps *have* crossed by sea (to Sicily) in some other way, Th.6.2, cf. Pl.*Phdr.*265b. **d.** ἄν is freq. omitted in apodosi with Verbs expressing obligation, propriety, or possibility, as ἔδει, ἐχρῆν, εἰκὸς ἦν, etc., and sts. for rhetorical effect, εἰ μὴ.. ἤσμεν, φόβον παρέσχεν it *had* caused (for it *would have* caused) fear, E.*Hec.*1113. This use becomes more common in later Gk. **2.** with fut. ind.: **a.** frequently in Ep., usu. with κεν, rarely ἄν, Il.9.167, 22.66, indicating a limitation or condition, ὁ δέ κεν κεχολώσεται ὃν κεν ἵκωμαι and he *will likely be* angry to *whomsoever* I shall come, ib.1.139; καί κέ τις ὧδ' ἐρέει and in that case men will say, 4.176; ἐγὼ δέ κέ τοι καταλέξω Od.3.80; so in Lyr., μαθὼν δέ τις ἂν ἐρεῖ Pi.*N.*7.68, cf. *I.*6(5).59. **b.** rarely in codd. of Att. Prose writers, σαφὲς ἂν καταστήσετε Th.1.140; οὐχ ἥκει, οὐδ' ἂν ἥξει δεῦρο Pl.*R.*615d, cf. *Ap.*29c, X.*An.*2.5.13; dub. in Hp.*Mul.*2.174: in later Prose, Philostr.*VA*2.21, S.E.*M.*9.225: also in Poetry, E.*El.*484, Ar.*Av.*1313; οὐκ ἂν προδώσω Herod.6.36 (corr. -δοίην):—for ἄν with fut. inf. and part. v. infr.

II. WITH SUBJUNCTIVE, only in Ep., the meaning being the same as with the fut. ind. (I. 2a), freq. with 1st pers., as εἰ δέ κε μὴ δώῃσιν, ἐγὼ δέ κεν αὐτὸς ἕλωμαι in that case *I will* take her myself, Il.1.324; πείθευ, ἐγὼ δέ κέ τοι εἰδέω χάριν obey and *if so* I will be grateful, 14.235 (the subj. is always introduced by δέ in this usage); also with other persons, giving emphasis to the future, οὐκ ἄν τοι χραίσμῃ κίθαρις 3.54, al.

III. WITH OPTATIVE (never fut., rarely pf. πῶς ἂν λελήθοι [με]; X.*Smp.*3.6): **a.** in apodosis of conditional sentences, after protasis in opt. with εἰ or some other conditional or relative word, expressing a fut. condition: ἀλλ' εἴ μοί τι πίθοιο, τό κεν πολὺ κέρδιον εἴη Il.7.28; οὐ πολλὴ ἂν ἀλογία εἴη, εἰ φοβοῖτο τὸν θάνατον; Pl.*Phd.*68b:—in Hom. pres. and aor. opt. with κε or ἄν are sts. used like impf. and aor. ind. with ἄν in Attic, with either regular ind. or another opt. in the protasis: καί νύ κεν ἔνθ' ἀπόλοιτο.. εἰ μὴ.. νόησε κτλ., i.e. he *would have* perished, had she not perceived, etc., Il.5.311, cf. 5.388, 17.70; εἰ νῦν ἐπὶ ἄλλῳ ἀεθλεύοιμεν, ἦ τ' ἂν ἐγὼ.. κλισίηνδε φεροίμην if we were now contending in another's honour, I *should* now carry.., ib.23.274: so rarely in Trag., οὐδ' ἂν σὺ φαίης, εἴ σε μὴ κνίζοι λέχος (for εἰ μὴ ἔκνιζε) E.*Med.*568. **b.** with protasis in pres. or fut., the opt. with ἄν in apodosi takes a simply future sense: φρούριον δ' εἰ ποιήσονται, τῆς μὲν γῆς βλάπτοιεν ἄν τι μέρος they *might perhaps* damage, Th.1.142, cf. 2.60, Pl.*Ap.*25b, *R.*333e; ἢν οὖν μάθῃς.. οὐκ ἂν ἀποδοίην Ar.*Nu.*116, cf. D.1.26, al. **c.** with protasis understood: φεύγωμεν· ἔτι γάρ κεν ἀλύξαιμεν κακὸν ἦμαρ Od.10.269; οὔτε ἐσθίουσι πλείω ἢ δύνανται φέρειν· διαρραγεῖεν γὰρ ἄν for (if they should do so) they *would* burst, X.*Cyr.*8.2.21; τὸν δ' οὔ κε δύ' ἀνέρε.. ἀπ' οὔδεος ὀχλίσσειαν two men *could* not heave the stone from the ground, i.e. *would* not, if they should try, Il.12.447; οὐδ' ἂν δικαίως ἐς κακὸν πέσοιμί τι S.*Ant.*240, cf. D.2.8: in Hom. sts. with ref. to past time, Τυδεΐδην οὐκ ἂν γνοίης ποτέροισι μετείη Il.5.85. **d.** with no definite protasis implied, in potential sense: ἡδέως δ' ἂν ἐροίμην Λεπτίνην but I *would* gladly ask Leptines, D.20.129; βουλοίμην ἄν I *should* like, Lat. *velim* (but ἐβουλόμην ἄν I *should* wish, if it were of any avail, *vellem*); ποῖ οὖν τραποίμεθ' ἄν; which way then *can* we turn? Pl.*Euthd.*290a; οὐκ ἂν μεθείμην τοῦ θρόνου I *will* not give up the throne, Ar.*Ra.*830; idiomatically, referring to the past, αὗται δὲ οὐκ ἂν πολλαὶ εἶεν but these *would* not (on investigation) prove to be many, Th.1.9; εἴησαν δ' ἂν οὗτοι Κρῆτες these *would* be (i.e. *would have* been) Cretans, Hdt.1.2: used in order to soften assertions by giving them a less positive form, as οὐκ ἂν οὖν πάνυ γέ τι σπουδαῖον εἴη ἡ δικαιοσύνη, i.e. it *would* not *prove to be*, etc. (for, it *is* not, etc.), Pl.*R.*

333e. e. in questions, expressing a wish: τίς ἂν θεῶν..δοίη; S.*OC* 1100, cf. A.*Ag.*1448; πῶς ἂν θάνοιμι; S.*Aj.*389: hence (with no question) as a mild command, exhortation, or entreaty, τλαίης κεν Μενελάῳ ἐπιπροέμεν ταχὺν ἰόν Il.4.94; σὺ μὲν κομίζοις ἂν σεαυτὸν ᾗ θέλεις you *may* take yourself off (milder than κόμιζε σεαυτόν), S.*Ant.*444; χωροῖς ἂν εἴσω you *may* go in, *El.*1491; κλύοις ἂν ἤδη, Φοῖβε hear me now, Phoebus, ib.637; φράζοις ἄν, λέγοις ἄν, Pl.*Phlb.*23c, 48b. f. in a protasis which is also an apodosis: εἴπερ ἄλλῳ τῳ ἀνθρώπων πειθοίμην ἄν, καὶ σοὶ πείθομαι if I *would* trust any (other) man (if he gave me his word), I trust you, Id.*Prt.*329b; εἰ μὴ ποιήσαιτ' ἂν τοῦτο if you *would* not do this (if you could), D.4.18, cf. X.*Mem.*1.5.3, Plot.6.4.16. g. rarely omitted with opt. in apodosis: ῥεῖα θεός γ' ἐθέλων καὶ τηλόθεν ἄνδρα σαώσαι Od.3.231, cf. 14.123, Il.5.303; also in Trag., θᾶσσον ἤ λέγοι τις E.*Hipp.*1186; τεὰν δύνασιν τίς..κατάσχοι; S.*Ant.*605. h. ἄν c. fut. opt. is prob. always corrupt (cf. I. 2 b), as τὸν αὐτὸν ἂν ἐπαινέσοι (ἐπαινέσαι Bekk.) Pl.*Lg.*719e; εἰδὼς ὅτι οὐδέν' ἂν καταλήψοιτο (οὐδένα Bekk.) Lys.1.22.

IV. WITH INF. and PART. (sts. ADJ. equivalent to part., τῶν δυνατῶν ἂν κρῖναι Pl.*R.*577b) representing ind. or opt.: 1. pres. inf. or part.: a. representing impf. ind., οἴεσθε τὸν πατέρα..οὐκ ἂν φυλάττειν; do you think he *would* not *have* kept them safe? (οὐκ ἂν ἐφύλαττεν), D.49.35; ἀδυνάτων ἂν ὄντων [ὑμῶν] ἐπιβοηθεῖν when you *would have* been unable, Th.1.73, cf. 4.40. b. representing pres. opt., πόλλ' ἂν ἔχων (representing ἔχοιμ' ἄν) ἕτερ' εἰπεῖν παραλείπω D. 18.258, cf. X.*An.*2.3.18: with Art., τὸ ἐθέλειν ἂν ἰέναι ἄκλητος ἐπὶ δεῖπνον Pl.*Smp.*174b. 2. aor. inf. or part.: a. representing aor. ind., οὐκ ἂν ἡγεῖσθ' αὐτὸν κἂν ἐπιδραμεῖν; do you not think he *would* even *have* run thither? (καὶ ἐπέδραμεν ἄν), D.27.56; ἴσμεν ὑμᾶς ἀναγκασθέντας ἂν we know you *would have* been compelled, Th.1.76, cf. 3.89; ῥᾳδίως ἂν ἀφεθείς when he *might* easily *have* been acquitted, X.*Mem.*4.4.4. b. representing aor. opt., οὐδ' ἂν κρατῆσαι αὐτοὺς τῆς γῆς ἡγοῦμαι I think they *would* not even be masters of the land (οὐδ' ἂν κρατήσειαν), Th.6.37, cf. 2.20; ὁρῶν ῥᾳδίως ἂν αὐτὸ ληφθὲν (ληφθείη ἄν) Id.7.42; οὔτε ὄντα οὔτε ἂν γενόμενα, i.e. things which are not and never *could* happen (ἃ οὔτε ἂν γένοιτο), Id.6.38. 3. pf. inf. or part. representing: a. plpf. ind., πάντα ταῦθ' ὑπὸ τῶν βαρβάρων ἂν ἑαλωκέναι (φήσειεν ἄν) he *would* say that all these *would have* been destroyed by the barbarians (ἑαλώκη ἄν), D.19.312. b. pf. opt., οὐκ ἂν ἡγοῦμαι αὐτοὺς δίκην ἀξίαν δεδωκέναι, εἰ..καταψηφίσαισθε I do not believe they *would* (then) have suffered (δεδωκότες ἂν εἶεν) punishment enough, etc., Lys.27.9. 4. fut. inf. or part., never in Ep., and prob. always corrupt in Att., νομίζων μέγιστον ἂν σφᾶς ὠφελήσειν (leg. -ῆσαι) Th.5.82, cf. 6.66, 8.25,71; part. is still more exceptional, ὡς ἐμοῦ οὐκ ἂν ποιήσοντος ἄλλα Pl.*Ap.*30c (codd.), cf. D.19.342 (v.l.); both are found in later Gk., νομίσαντες ἂν οἰκήσειν οὕτως ἄριστα Plb.8.30.8, cf. Plu.*Marc.*15, Arr.*An.*2.2.3; with part., Epicur. *Nat.*14.1, Luc.*Asin.*26, Lib.*Or.*62.21, dub. l. in Arr.*An.*6.6.5.

B. IN DEPENDENT CLAUSES. I. In the protasis of conditional sentences with εἰ, regularly with the subjunctive. In Attic εἰ ἄν is contracted into ἐάν, ἤν, or ἄν (ᾱ) (q.v.): Hom. has generally εἴ κε (or αἴ κε), sts. ἤν, once εἰ δ' ἄν Il.3.288, twice εἴπερ ἄν 5.224, 232. The protasis expresses either future condition (with apod. of fut. time) or general condition (with apod. of repeated action): εἰ δέ κεν ὣς ἔρξῃς καί τοι πείθωνται Ἀχαιοί, γνώσῃ ἔπειθ' ὅς.. if thus thou shalt do.., ib.2.364; ἢν ἐγγὺς ἔλθῃ θάνατος, οὐδεὶς βούλεται θνῄσκειν if death (ever) come near.., E.*Alc.*671. 2. in relative or temporal clauses with a conditional force; here ἄν coalesces with ὅτε, ὁπότε, ἐπεί, ἐπειδή, cf. ὅταν, ὁπόταν, ἐπήν or ἐπάν (Ion. ἐπεάν), ἐπειδάν: Hom. has ὅτε κε (sts. ὅτ' ἄν), ὁππότε κε (sts. ὁπότ' ἂν or ὁππότ' ἄν), ἐπεί κε (ἐπεὶ ἂν Il.6.412), ἐπήν, εὖτ' ἄν; v. also εἰσόκε (εἰς ὅ κε):—τάων ἥν κ' ἐθέλωμι φίλην ποιήσομ' ἄκοιτιν whomsoever of these I *may* wish.., Il.9.397; ὅταν δὴ μὴ σθένω, πεπαύσομαι when I shall have no strength.., S.*Ant.*91; ἐχθρὸς γάρ μοι κεῖνος.. ὅς χ' ἕτερον μὲν κεύθῃ ἐνὶ φρεσίν, ἄλλο δὲ εἴπῃ whoever conceals one thing in his mind and speaks another, Il.9.312, cf. D.4.6, Th.1.21.—Hom. uses subj. in both the above constructions (1 and 2) without ἄν; also Trag. and Com., S.*Aj.*496, Ar.*Eq.*805; μέχρι and πρίν occasionally take subj. without ἄν in prose, e.g. Th.1.137, 4.16 (μέχρι οὗ), Pl.*Phd.*62c, Aeschin.3.60. 3. in final clauses introduced by relative Advbs., as ὡς, ὅπως (of Manner), ἵνα (of Place), ὄφρα, ἕως, etc. (of Time), freq. in Ep., σαώτερος ὥς κε νέηαι Il.1.32; ὄφρα κεν εὕδῃ Od.3.359; ὅπως ἂν εἰδῇ..φράσω A.*Pr.*824; ὅπως ἂν φαίνηται κάλλιστος Pl.*Smp.*198e; μηχανητέον ὅπως ἂν διαφύγῃ *Grg.* 481a (where ὅπως with fut. ind. is the regular constr.); also after ὡς in Hdt., Trag., X.*An.*2.5.16, al., once in Th.6.91 (but fut. ind. is regular in Att.); ἵνα final does not take ἄν or κε exc. ἵνα εἰδότες ἤ κε θάνωμεν ἤ κεν..φύγοιμεν Od.12.156 (ἵνα = *where* in S.*OC*405). Μή, = *lest*, takes ἄν only with opt. in apodosis, as S.*Tr.*631, Th.2.93.

II. in Ep. sts. with OPTATIVE as with subj. (always κε(ν), exc. εἴ περ ἂν αὐταὶ Μοῦσαι ἀείδοιεν Il.2.597), εἴ κεν Ἄρης ἔλχοιτο Od.8. 353; ὥς κε..δοίη ᾧ κ' ἐθέλοι that he *might* give her to whomsoever he *might* please, ib.2.54: so in Hdt. in final clauses, 1.75,99:—in Od.23.135 ὥς κέν τις φαίη, κέν belongs to Verb in apod., as in ὡς δ' ἂν ἥδιστα ταῦτα φαίνοιτο X.*Cyr.*7.5.81. 2. rarely in *oratio obliqua*, where a relat. or temp. word retains an ἄν which it would have with subj. in direct form, S.*Tr.*687, X.*Mem.*1.2.6, Isoc.17.15; ἐπειδὰν δοκιμασθείην D.30.6:—similarly after a preceding opt., οὐκ ἀποκρίναιο ἕως ἂν..σκέψαιο Pl.*Phd.*101d.

III. rarely with εἰ and INDICATIVE in protasis, only in Ep.: 1. with fut. ind. as with subj.: αἴ κεν Ἰλίου πεφιδήσεται Il.15.213:—so with relat., οἵ κέ με τιμήσουσι 1.175. 2. with εἰ and a past tense of ind., once in Hom., εἰ δέ κ' ἔτι προτέρῳ γένετο δρόμος Il.23.526; so Ζεὺς γάρ κ' ἔθηκε νῆσον εἴ κ' ἐβούλετο Orac.ap.Hdt.1.174, cf. Ar.*Lys.* 1099 (cod. R), A.R.1.197.

IV. in later Greek, ἄν with relative words is used with INDICATIVE in all tenses, as ὅπου ἂν εἰσεπορεύετο *Ev.Marc.*6.56; ὅσ' ἂν πάσχετε *PFay.*136 (iv A.D.); ἔνθ' ἂν πέφυκεν ἡ ὁλότης εἶναι Phlp. *in Ph.*436.19; cf. ἐάν, ὅταν.

C. with impf. and more rarely aor. ind. in ITERATIVE construction, to express elliptically *a condition fulfilled whenever an opportunity offered*; freq. in Hdt. (not in Pl. or A.), κλαίεσκε ἂν καὶ ὀδυρέσκετο she *would* (i.e. *used to*) weep and lament, 3.119; εἶτα πῦρ ἂν οὐ παρῆν S.*Ph.*295; εἴ τινες ἴδοιεν.., ἀνεθάρσησαν ἄν whenever they saw it, on each occasion, Th.7.71; διηρώτων ἂν αὐτοὺς τί λέγοιεν Pl.*Ap.*22b: inf. representing impf. of this constr., ἀκούω Λακεδαιμονίους τότε ἐμβαλόντας ἂν..ἀναχωρεῖν, i.e. I hear they *used to* retire (ἀνεχώρουν ἄν), D.9.48.

D. GENERAL REMARKS: I. POSITION OF ἄν. 1. in A, when ἄν does not coalesce with the relat. word (as in ἐάν, ὅταν), it follows directly or is separated only by other particles, as μέν, δέ, τε, γάρ, καί, νυ, περ, etc.; as εἰ μέν κεν..εἰ δέ κε Il.3.281-4; rarely by τις, as ὅποι τις ἄν, οἶμαι, προσθῇ D.2.14:—in Hom. and Hes. two such Particles may precede κε, as εἴ περ γάρ κεν Od.8.355, cf. Il.2.123; εἰ γάρ τίς κε, ὃς μὲν γάρ κε, Hes.*Op.*280,357; rarely in Prose, ὅποι μὲν γὰρ ἂν D.4.45; ὁπότερος οὖν ἂν Ar.*Ra.*1420: also ὁπόσῳ πλέον ἂν Pl.*Lg.*647e, cf. 850a; ὅπου τὸ πάλαι λεγόμενον ἂν γίγνηται 739c. 2. in apodosis, ἄν may stand either next to its Verb (before or after it), or after some other emphatic word, esp. an interrog., a negative (e.g. οὐδ' ἂν εἷς, οὐκ ἂν ἔτι, etc.), or an important Adjective or Adverb; also after a participle which represents the protasis, λέγοντος ἄν τινος πιστεῦσαι οἴεσθε; do you think they *would have* believed it if any one had told them? (εἴ τις ἔλεγεν, ἐπίστευσαν ἄν), D.6.20. 3. ἄν is freq. separated from its inf. by such Verbs as οἴομαι, δοκέω, φημί, οἶδα, etc., οὐκ ἂν οἴει..; freq. in Pl., *Grg.*486d, al.; καὶ νῦν ἡδέως ἄν μοι δοκῶ κοινωνῆσαι I think that I *should*, X.*Cyr.*8.7.25; οὕτω γὰρ ἄν μοι δοκεῖ ἥ τε πόλις ἄριστα διοικεῖσθαι Aeschin.3.2; ἃ μήτε προῄδει μηδεὶς μήτ' ἂν ᾤηθη τήμερον ῥηθῆναι (where ἄν belongs to ῥηθῆναι) D. 18.225:—in the phrase οὐκ οἶδ' ἂν εἰ, or οὐκ ἂν οἶδ' εἰ, ἄν belongs not to οἶδα, but to the Verb which follows, οὐκ οἶδ' ἂν εἰ πείσαιμι, for οὐκ οἶδα εἰ πείσαιμι ἄν, E.*Med.*941, cf. *Alc.*48; οὐκ ἂν οἶδ' εἰ δυναίμην Pl. *Ti.*26b; οὐκ οἶδ' ἂν εἰ ἐκτησάμην X.*Cyr.*5.4.12. 4. ἄν never begins a sentence, or even a clause after a comma, but may stand first after a parenthetic clause, ἀλλ', ὦ μέλ', ἄν μοι σιτίων διπλῶν ἔδει Ar.*Pax* 137. II. REPETITION OF ἄν:—in apodosis ἄν may be used twice or even three times with the same Verb, either to make the condition felt throughout a long sentence, or to emphasize certain words, ὥστ' ἄν, εἰ σθένος λάβοιμι, δηλώσαιμ' ἂν S.*El.*333, cf. *Ant.*69, A.*Ag.* 340, Th.1.76 (fin.), 2.41, Pl.*Ap.*31a, Lys.20.15; ἀφανεῖς ἂν ὄντες οὐκ ἂν ὑμνήθημεν ἂν E.*Tr.*1244, cf. S.*Fr.*739; attached to a parenthetical phrase, ἔδρασ' ἄν, εὖ τοῦτ' ἴσθ' ἄν, εἰ.. Id.*OT*1438. 2. ἄν is coupled with κε(ν) a few times in Hom., as Il.11.187,202, Od.5.361, al.; cf. ἤν περ γάρ κ' ἐθέλωσιν v.l. ib.18.318. III. ELLIPSIS OF VERB:—sts. the Verb to which ἄν belongs must be supplied, in Hom. only εἰμί, as τά τ' ἔλδεται ὅς κ' ἐπιδευής (sc. ᾖ) Il.5. 481; ἀλλ' οὐκ ἂν πρὸ τοῦ (sc. ἔρρεγκον) Ar.*Nu.*5; τί δ' ἂν δοκεῖ σοι Πρίαμος (sc. πρᾶξαι), εἰ τάδ' ἤνυσεν; A.*Ag.*935:—so in phrases like πῶς γὰρ ἄν; and πῶς οὐκ ἄν (sc. εἴη); also in ὥσπερ ἂν εἰ (or ὡσπερανεί), as φοβούμενος ὥσπερ ἂν εἰ παῖς (i.e. ὥσπερ ἂν ἐφοβήθη εἰ παῖς ἦν) Pl.*Grg.*479a; so τοσοῦτον ἐφρόνησαν, ὅσον περ ἂν (sc. ἐφρόνησαν) εἰ.. Isoc.10.48:—so also when κἂν εἰ (= καὶ ἂν εἰ) has either no Verb in the apod. or one to which ἄν cannot belong, Pl.*R.*477a, *Men.*72c; cf. κἄν:—so the Verb of a protasis containing ἄν may be understood, ὅποι τις ἂν προσθῇ, κἂν μικρὰν δύναμιν (i.e. καὶ ἐὰν προσθῇ) D.2.14; ὡς ἐμοῦ οὖν ἰόντος ὅπῃ ἂν καὶ ὑμεῖς (sc. ἴητε) X.*An.*1.3.6. IV. ELLIPSIS OF ἄν:—when an apodosis consists of several co-ordinate clauses, ἄν is generally used only in the first and understood in the others: πείθοι' ἂν εἰ πείθοι'· ἀπειθοίης δ' ἴσως A.*Ag.*1049: even when the construction is continued in a new sentence, Pl.*R.*352e, cf. 439b codd.: but ἄν is repeated for the sake of clearness or emphasis, ib. 398a, cf. D.19.156 (where an opt. is implied with the third ὡς): rarely expressed with the second of two co-ordinate Verbs and understood with the first, τοῦτον ἂν..θαρσοίην ἐγὼ καλῶς μὲν ἄρχειν, εὖ δ' ἂν ἄρχεσθαι θέλειν (i.e. καλῶς μὲν ἂν ἄρχοι, εὖ δ' ἂν θέλοι ἄρχεσθαι) S.*Ant.*669.

ἄν (B), [ᾱ], Att., = ἐάν, ἤν, Th.4.46 codd., al.; freq. in Pl., ἂν σωφρονῇ *Phd.*61b; ἂν θεὸς θέλῃ ib.80d, cf. D.4.50; ἄν τ'..ἄν τε Arist. *Ath.*48.4: not common in earlier Att. Inscrr., *IG*1.2a5, 2.179b49, al.: but freq. later, *SIG*1044.27 (iv/iii B.C.), *PPetr.*2 p.47 (iii B.C.), *PPar.*32.19 (ii B.C.), *PTeb.*110.8 (i B.C.), *Ev.Jo.*20.23, etc.

ἄν, by crasis for ἃ ἄν, S.*OT*281, 580, etc.

ἂν or **ἄν**, Ep. form of ἀνά, q.v.

ἄν, shortened from ἄνα, v. sub ἀνά G.

ἀν-, negat. Prefix, of which ἀ- privativum (q.v.) is a shortened form.

ἀνά [ᾰνᾰ], Aeol., Thess., Arc., Cypr. ὀν, Prep. governing gen., dat., and acc. By apocope ἀνά becomes ἄν before dentals, as ἂν τὸν ὀδελόν; ἄγ before gutturals, as ἂγ γύαλα; ἂμ before labials, as ἂμ βωμοῖσι, ἂμ πέτραις, etc.; ἀμπεπλεγμένας *IG*5(2).514.10 (Arc.).

A. WITH GEN., three times in Od., in phrase ἀνὰ νηὸς βαίνειν *go on board* ship, 2.416, 9.177, 15.284; ἂν τοῦ τοίχου, τᾶς ὁδοῦ, τοῦ ῥοειδίου, *IG*14.352 i 40, ii 15,83 (Halaesa).

B. WITH DAT., *on, upon*, without any notion of motion, Ep., Lyr., and Trag. (only lyr.), ἀνὰ σκήπτρῳ *upon* the sceptre, Il.1.15, Pi.*P.* 1.6; ἀμ βωμοῖσι Il.8.441; ἀνὰ σκολόπεσσι 18.177; ἀνὰ Γαργάρῳ ἄκρῳ 15.152; ἀνὰ ὤμῳ *upon* the shoulder, Od.11.128; ἀν' ἵπποις, i.e. *in* a chariot, Pi.*O.*1.41; ἀμ πέτραις A.*Supp.*351 (lyr.); ἀνά τε νανσὶν καὶ σὺν ὅπλοις E.*IA*754; ἀγ Κόσσῳ *GDI*1365 (Epirus).

C. WITH ACCUS., the comm. usage, implying *motion upwards*: I. of Place, *up, from bottom to top, up along*, κίον' ἀν' ὑψηλὴν ἐρύσαι Od.22.176; ἀνὰ μέλαθρον *up to*, ib.239; [φλὲψ] ἀνὰ νῶτα θέουσα διαμπερὲς αὐχέν' ἱκάνει Il.13.547; ἀνὰ τὸν ποταμὸν Hdt.2.96; ἂν ῥόον *up*-stream, *GDI*5016.11 (Gortyn); κρῆς ἂν τὸν ὀδελὸν ἐμπεπαρμένον Ar.*Ach.*796 (Megarian); simply, *along*, ἂν τὼς ὅρως *Tab.Heracl.*2.32. 2. *up and down, throughout*, ἀνὰ δῶμα Il.1.570; ἀνὰ στρατόν, ἄστυ, ὅμιλον, ib.384, Od.8.173, etc.; ἀγ γύαλα A.*Supp.*550 (lyr.); ἀνὰ πᾶσαν τὴν Μηδικήν, ἀνὰ τὴν Ἑλλάδα, Hdt.1.96, 2.135, etc.; ὀν τὸ μέσσον Alc.18.3; ἀνὰ τὸ σκοτεινόν *in* the darkness, Th.3.22. 3. metaph., ἀνὰ θυμὸν φρονέειν, ἀνὰ στόμα ἔχειν, to have *continually in* the mind, *in* the mouth, Il.2.36,250; ἀν' Αἰγυπτίους ἄνδρας *among* them, Od.14.286; ἀνὰ πρώτους εἶναι to be *among* the first, Hdt.9.86. II. of Time, *throughout*, ἀνὰ νύκτα *all* night *through*, Il.14.80; ἀνὰ τὰς προτέρας ἡμέρας Hdt.7.223; ἀνὰ τὸν πόλεμον 8.123; ἀνὰ χρόνον *in course of* time, 1.173, 2.151, 5.27; ἀνὰ μέσσαν ἀκτῖνα (i.e. *in* the south) S.*OC*1247. 2. *distributively*, ἀνὰ πᾶσαν ἡμέραν day *by* day, Hdt.2.37,130, etc.; ἀνὰ πᾶν ἔτος 1.136, etc.; ἀνὰ πάντα ἔτεα 8.65: also ἀνὰ πρεσβύτατα *in order of* age, *Test.Epict.*4.28. III. distributively with Numerals, κρέα εἴκοσιν ἀν' ἡμιωβολιαῖα 20 pieces of meat *at* half an obol *each*, Ar.*Ra.*554; τῶν ἀν' ὀκτὼ τὠβολοῦ that sell 8 *for* the obol, Timocl.18; ἀνὰ πέντε παρασάγγας τῆς ἡμέρας [they marched] *at the rate of* 5 parasangs a day, X.*An.*4.6.4; ἔστησαν ἀνὰ ἑκατὸν μάλιστα ὥσπερ χοροί they stood *in bodies of* about 100 men *each*, ib.5.4.12; κλισίας ἀνὰ πεντήκοντα companies *at the rate of* 50 *in each*, *Ev.Luc.*9.14; ἔλαβον ἀνὰ δηνάριον a denarius *apiece*, *Ev.Matt.*20.10; in doctor's prescriptions, ἀνὰ ὀβολὼ β' Sor.1.63, etc.: also ἀνὰ δύο ἥμισυ ζῳδίων *amounting to* 2½ signs, Autol.1.10; *multiplied by*, *PPetr.*3p.198. IV. Phrases: ἀνὰ κράτος *up to* the full strength, i.e. *vigorously*, ἀνὰ κράτος φεύγειν, ἀπομάχεσθαι, X.*Cyr.*4.2.30, 5.3.12; ἀνὰ τὸν αὐτὸν λόγον and ἀνὰ λόγον *proportionately*, Pl.*Phd.* 110d; esp. in math. sense, Id.*Ti.*37a, Arist.*APo.*85^{a}38, etc.; ἀνὰ μέσον *in* the midst, Antiph.13, Men.531.19; ἀνὰ μέρος *by turns*, Arist.*Pol.*1287^{a}17.

D. WITH NOM. of Numerals, etc., distributively, *Apoc.*21.21, v.l. in Sor.1.11, 12, cf. Orib.*Fr.*50,54.

E. WITHOUT CASE as Adv., *thereupon*, Hom. and other Poets:—and with the notion of *spreading all over* a space, *throughout, all over*, μέλανες δ' ἀνὰ βότρυες ἦσαν *all over* there were clusters, Il.18.562, cf. Od.24.343:—but ἀνά often looks like an Adv. in Hom., where really it is only parted from its Verb by tmesis, ἀνὰ δ' ἔσχετο; ἀνὰ δ' ὦρτο (for ἀνῶρτο δέ); ἀνὰ τεύχε' ἀείρας (for τεύχεα ἀναείρας), etc.

F. IN COMPOS. 1. as in C.1, *up to, upwards, up*, opp. κατά, as ἀνα-βαίνω, -βλέπω, ἀν-αιρέω, -ίστημι: poet. sts. doubled, ἀν' ὀρσοθύρην ἀναβαίνειν Od.22.132. 2. hence flows the sense of *increase* or *strengthening*, as in ἀνακρίνω; though it cannot always be translated, as in Homer's ἀνείρομαι:—in this case opp. ὑπό. 3. from the notion *throughout* (E), comes that of *repetition* and *improvement*, as in ἀνα-βλαστάνω, -βιόω, -γεννάω. 4. the notion of *back, backwards*, in ἀναχωρέω, ἀνανεύω, etc., seems to come from such phrases as ἀνὰ ῥόον *up*, i.e. *against*, the stream.

G. ἄνα, written with anastr. as Adv., *up! arise!* ἀλλ' ἄνα Il.6.331, Od.18.13:—in this sense the ult. is never elided; cf. ἀλλ' ἄνα, εἰ μέμονάς γε Il.9.247; ἀλλ' ἄνα ἐξ ἑδράνων S.*Aj.*194. 2. apocop. ἄν after ὤρνυντο, ὦρτο, *and up stood..arose*, Il.3.268, 23.837, etc. 3. when used as Prep. ἀνά never suffers anastrophe.

ἄνα (A), [ᾰνᾰ], voc. of ἄναξ, *king*, only in the phrases ὦ ἄνα, contr. ὦνα, and Ζεῦ ἄνα, and always as address to gods: fem., = ὦ ἄνασσα, Pi.*P.*12.3: ult. elided only in *h.Ap.*526 codd.—Ep., Lyr., and occasionally Trag., as S.*OC*1485 (lyr.).

ἄνα (B), ἡ, = ἄνυσις, Alcm.23.83, Call.*Jov.*90; cf. ἄνη.

ἀνάατος, = ἄνατος, *IG*5(2).357.177 (Stymphalus, iii B.C.); ἀνάατορ ἤστω *Michel*1334 (Elis, iv B.C.).

ἀνα-βάδην [βᾰ], Adv., (ἀναβαίνω) lit. *going up*, but usu. *with one's feet up, lying down*, Ar.*Pl.*1123, D.Chr.62.6, Plu.2.336c, cf. Ath.12.528f, Poll.3.90; so prob. in Ar.*Ach.*399,410, but expl. by a Sch. as *upstairs*. **-βάδισις**, εως, ἡ, *retrogression*, Antyll.ap.Orib.6.22.9. **-βᾰδόν**, Adv. *by mounting*, ἀ. τὴν ὀχείαν ποιεῖσθαι Arist.*HA* 579^{a}19.

ἀναβαθ-μίς, ίδος, ἡ, *step, stair*, Lxx *Ex.*20.26. **-μός**, ὁ, *flight of steps, stair*, Hdt.2.125, Arist.*Oec.*1347^{a}5, D.C.65.21; δι' ἀναβαθμῶν *by degrees*, Ph.2.557. **-ρα**, ἡ, = sq., αἱ ἀ. αἱ στοϊκαί *CIG*4436b (Soli). II. *flight of steps*, Str.7.2.3. III. *going up, ascent*, ᾠδὴ τῶν ἀ. Lxx *Ps.*118(119) tit., al. **-ρον**, τό, *raised seat* or *chair*, *CIG*2924 (Tralles).

ἀναβαίνω, impf. ἀνέβαινον: fut. -βήσομαι: (for aor. 1 v. infr. B): aor. 2 ἀνέβην, imper. ἀνάβηθι, -βῶ, -βῆναι, -βάς: pf. -βέβηκα:—Med., aor. 1 -εβησάμην, Ep. 3 sg. -εβήσετο, v. infr. B:—Pass., v. infr. II.2:—*go up, mount*, c. acc. loci, οὐρανόν, ὑπερῷα ἀ. *go up to* heaven, *to* the upper rooms, Il.1.497, Od.18.302; φάτις ἀνθρώπους ἀναβαίνει *goes up among*, ib.6.29; more freq. with Prep., ἀ. εἰς ἐλάτην, ἐς δίφρον, Il.14.287, 16.657; rarely with ἀνά repeated, ἀν' ὀρσοθύρην ἀ. Od.22.132; after Hom., most. freq. with ἐπί, ἀ. ἐπὶ τὰ ὑψηλότατα τῶν ὀρέων Hdt.1.131: c. dat., νεκροῖς ἀ. *to trample on* the dead, Il.10.493: metaph., ἐπειδὴ ἐνταῦθα ἀναβεβήκαμεν τοῦ λόγου Pl.*R.*445c. II. Special usages: 1. *mount* a ship, *go on board*, in Hom. mostly abs.; ἐς Τροίην ἀ. *embark* for Troy, Od.1.210; ἀπὸ Κρήτης ἀ. 14.252; ἐπὶ τὰς ναῦς Th.4.44, etc.: metaph., ἀναβάσομαι στόλον I *will mount* a prow, Pi.*P.*2.62. 2. *mount* on horseback (cf. ἀναβάτης), ἀ. ἐφ' ἵππον X.*Cyr.*4.1.7, cf. 7.1.3: abs., ἀναβεβηκώς *mounted*; ἀναβάντες (abs.) ἐφ' ἵππων ἐλάσαι 3.3.27; ἀ. ἐπὶ τροχόν *mount* on the wheel of torture, Antipho 5.40. b. c. acc., ἀ. ἵππον *mount* a horse, Theopomp.Hist.2:—Pass., [ἵππος] ὁ μήπω ἀναβαινόμενος that *has* not yet *been mounted*, X.*Eq.*1.1; ἀναβαθείς *when mounted*, ib.3.4; ἐν ἵππῳ ἀναβεβαμένῳ Id.*Eq.Mag.* 3.4, cf. 1.4. 3. of land-journeys, *go up* from the coast into Central Asia, Hdt.5.100, X.*An.*1.1.2; ἀ. παρὰ βασιλέα Pl.*Alc.*1.123b. b. *go up* to a temple, *PPar.*47.19, *Ev.Luc.*18.10; to a town, *Ev.Matt.*20.18, al., cf. *PLond.*3.1170^b.46 (iii A.D.), etc.; in curses, ἀ. παρὰ Δάματρα πεπρημένος *GDI*3536.19 (Cnidus), cf. *SIG* 1180.9 (ibid.). c. *ascend* to heaven, *Ascens.Is.*2.16. 4. of rivers in flood, *rise*, Hdt.2.13; ἀ. ἐς τὰς ἀρούρας *overflow* the fields, Id.1.193. 5. of plants, *shoot up*, ἐπὶ δένδρα X.*Oec.*19.18; *climb* on sticks, Thphr.*HP*8.3.2; generally, *shoot, spring up*, *Ev.Matt.*13.7; of hair, X.*Smp.*4.23. 6. in Att., ἀ. ἐπὶ τὸ βῆμα, or ἀ. alone, *mount the tribune, rise to speak*, D.18.66, 21.205, *Prooem.*56; ἀ. εἰς τὸ πλῆθος, εἰς or ἐπὶ τὸ δικαστήριον *come before* the people, *before* the court, Pl.*Ap.*31c, 40b, *Grg.*486b; ἀ. ἐπὶ τὸν ὀκρίβαντα *mount* the stage, Id.*Smp.*194b: abs., ἀνάβαινε Ar.*Eq.*149; ἀνάβηθι Id.*V.*963; of witnesses in court, Lys.1.29. 7. of the male, *mount, cover*, ἀ. τὰς θηλέας Hdt.1.192, cf. Ar.*Fr.*329; ἀ. ἐπί Ph.1.651, cf. Moer.3:—Pass., *Milet.*3.31(a).6 (vi B.C.). 8. of age, δύο ἀναβεβηκὼς ἔτη τῆς ἡλικίας τῆς ἐμῆς two years *older..*, Ach.Tat.1.7. 9. *ascend to higher knowledge*, ἡ ἀναβεβηκυῖα ἐπιστήμη Simp. *in Ph.*15.34, cf. 9.30; τὰ ἀναβεβηκότα *generalities*, Sor.2.5. 10. c. acc., *surpass*, κάλλει τὴν πᾶσαν διακόσμησιν Lyd.*Ost.*22. III. of things and events, *come to an end, turn out*, Hdt.7.10.θ'; ἀπό τινος ἀ. *result from*, X.*Ath.* 2.17. b. ἀ. ἐπὶ καρδίαν *enter* into one's heart, of thoughts, Lxx 4*Ki.*12.4, *Je.*3.16, 1*Ep.Cor.*2.9, cf. *Ev.Luc.*24.38. 2. *come to, pass over to*, ἐς Λεωνίδην ἀνέβαινεν ἡ βασιληΐη Hdt.7.205, cf. 1.109. IV. *return to the beginning*, of discourse, Democr.144^a; *go back*, ἀναβήσεται ἐπὶ τὰς κτίσεις τῶν προγόνων Hermog.*Inv.*2.2.

B. aor. ἀνέβησα in causal sense, *make to go up*, esp. *put on shipboard*, Il.1.143, Pi.*P.*4.191; so in aor. Med., νὼ ἀναβησάμενοι *having taken* us *on board* with them, Od.15.475: rare in Prose, ἄνδρας ἐπὶ καμήλους ἀνέβησε *he mounted* men on camels, Hdt.1.80.

ἀναβακχεύω, *rouse to Bacchic frenzy, madden*, E.*HF*1086, cf. *Or.* 337. II. intr., *break forth in Bacchic frenzy*, Id.*Ba.*864, Plu.*Crass.* 33, Lib.*Or.*40.23.

ἀναβαλλαγόρας· φάρμακόν τι καὶ λίθος ἐν Σάμῳ, Hsch. **ἀναβαλλίδες**· ταινίαι ἡ σφαῖραι, *EM*95.43, cf. Hdn.Gr.1.91.

ἀναβάλλω, *throw up*, χοῦν ἐξ ὀρύγματος Th.4.90, cf. X.*Cyr.*7.5.10, *Ostr.*1399 (i A.D.); τάφρος ἀναβεβλημένη *foss and dyke*, X.*An.*5.2.5. 2. ἀ. τινὰ ἐπὶ τὸν ἵππον *put on* horseback, *mount* him, Id.*An.* 4.4.4, *Eq.*6.12; of the horse, ἀ. τὸν ἀναβάτην *unseat* his rider, ib.8.7. 3. ἀ. τὰ ὄμματα *cast up* one's eyes, so as to show the whites, Arist.*Pr.*876^{a}31; τὰ λευκά Alex.222.9, Ctes.*Fr.*30. 4. *cause to spring up*, κρήνην Str.8.6.2. 5. *lay* bricks, *SIG*^{2}587.59, cf. Hyp.*Fr.*103. 6. *lift, remove* a tumour, Antyll.(?)ap.Orib.45.17.6. 7. Pass., *to be lifted up*, in prayer, εὔχονται σπλάγχνοισι κακῶς ἀναβαλλομένοισι AristeasEpic.1. II. *put back, put off*, μηκέτι νῦν ἀνάβαλλε..ἄεθλον Od.19.584 (the only place in which Hom. uses the Act.); ἀ. τινά *put off* [with excuses], D.8.52; ἀ. τὰ πράγματα 4.14; *distract* one's attention, Philostr.*Im.*2.24:—Pass., ἀνεβλήθη ἡ ἐκκλησία it *was adjourned*, Th.5.45; ὥστε..εἰς τοὺς παῖδας ἀναβληθήσεσθαι τὰς τιμωρίας *will be put off* to the time of the sons, Isoc.11.25; ὑμεναίους οὐκ ἀναβαλλομένους Call.*Aet.*3.1.43; cf. infr. B. II. 2. pf. part. Pass. ἀναβεβλημένος *slow, measured*, αὔλημα D.Chr.1.1, cf. Hld.2.8: so in Adv. -μένως *slowly*, D.H.*Dem.*54. b. of style, *diffuse*, τὸ ὕπτιον καὶ ἀ. Hermog.*Id.*2.11; λέξις ἀ., opp. συνεστραμμένη, Aristid.*Rh.*2p.540S. III. like B. III, *put on*, ἀ. τὸ Κρητικόν (a short cloak) Eup.311 (s.v.l.). IV. *run* a risk (prob. metaph. from dice), ἐγώ σφε θάψω κἀνὰ κίνδυνον βαλῶ A.*Th.*1033.

B. more freq. in Med., *strike up, begin to play* or *sing* (cf. ἀναβολή II), ἀνεβάλλετο καλὸν ἀείδειν Od.1.155, 8.266, Theoc.6.20: abs., ἀναβάλεο Pi.*N.*7.77; ἀναβαλοῦ Ar.*Pax*1269: c. acc., εὐχὴν ἀ. τῷ Ἔρωτι Philostr.*Im.*1.29. II. *put off, delay* a thing *in which oneself is concerned* (v. supr. II), μηδ' ἔτι δηρὸν ἀμβαλλώμεθα ἔργον Il.2.436, cf. Hes.*Op.*410, Pi.*O.*1.80, *N.*9.29, Hdt.3.85; τὸ μέν τι νυνὶ μὴ λάβῃς, τὸ δ' ἀναβαλοῦ Ar.*Nu.*1139; εἰσαῦθις ἀναβεβλήμεθα *Ec.*983; εἰς τὴν ὑστεραίαν ἀναβαλέσθαι [τὴν δίαιταν] *to adjourn* till the morrow, D.21.84, cf. Pl.*Mx.*234b; ἀ. τινας *Act.Ap.*24.22: abs., *defer payment*, Isoc.3.33: c. fut. inf., ἀ. κυρώσειν ἐς τέταρτον μῆνα Hdt.6.86.β'; ἀ. ἐς τρίτην ἡμέρην ἀποκρινέεσθαι 5.49; ἀ. ποιήσειν τὰ δέοντα D.3.9: c. aor. inf., ἀ. ὑποκρίνασθαι Hdt.9.8; οὐκέτι ἀνεβάλλοντο μὴ τὸ πᾶν οὐ μηχανήσασθαι 6.88. 2. *throw off oneself* on another, *refer* a thing to him, τὶ ἐπί τινα Luc.*Pisc.*15. III. *throw one's cloak up* or *back, throw it over the shoulder*, so as to let it hang in folds, ἀναβάλλεσθαι χλαῖναν Ar.*V.* 1132: so also ἀναβάλλεσθαι alone, Id.*Ec.*97; ἀ. ἐπιδέξια Pl.*Tht.*175e, cf. Ar.*Av.*1568; εἴσω τὴν χεῖρα ἔχοντα ἀναβεβλημένον *with one's cloak thrown up* or *back*, D.19.251; ἀναβεβλ. ἄνω τοῦ γόνατος Thphr. *Char.*4.4; cf. ἀναβολή I.2. IV. = supr. A.IV, ἀναβάλλεσθαι μάχας *risk* battles, Hdt.5.49. V. *to be wroth*, Lxx *Ps.*77(78).21.

ἀναβαπτίζω, *sink*, ναῦς cj. in Plu.*Marc.*15.

ἀναβάπτω, *stain, dye*, τὰς κεφαλάς Thphr.*HP*3.13.6.

ἀναβάσιον, τό, = ἵππουρις, Dsc.4.46 (v.l. ἀνάβασις, and so Ps.-Dsc. l.c.).

ἀνάβἄσις, poet. **ἄμβασις**, εως, ἡ, (ἀναβαίνω) *going up, mounting*, esp. on horseback, X.*Eq.*3.11; *way of mounting*, ib.7.4. b. concrete, πᾶσα ἄμβασις, = πάντες ἀναβάται, all *the horsemen*, S.*OC* 1070. c. *ascension*, εἰς τὸν ἕβδομον οὐρανόν *Ascens.Is.*10.21. d. *ascent* of soul to God, Hierocl. *in CA* 26 p.481 M. 2. *expedition up from* the coast, esp. into Central Asia, as that of the younger Cyrus related by X. 3. *rising* of a river, Heph.Astr.1.23; esp. *inundation* of the Nile, D.S.1.34, *Placit.*4.1, *POxy.*483; δικαία ἀ. normal *rise*, *OGI*666(i A.D.): pl., Str.16.1.24, Plu.2.368b. 4. Medic., *increasing period* of a disease, before the crisis (ἀκμή), Gal.9.556, al. 5. *leaves* of tree, Lxx *Ez.*47.12. II. *way up, ascent* of a tower, mountain, etc., Hdt.1.181, 7.223, Men.*Sam.*20, etc.; ἡ ἀ. τῶν Ἐπιπολῶν Th.7.42; ἀναβῆναι ἐκείνην τὴν ἀ. to make that *ascent*, Pl.*R.* 519d, cf. 515e. 2. *stairs*, Lxx 1*Ch.*26.16, al. III. metaph., *progress*, Artem.4.28; of numbers, *progression*, Id.2.70. IV. = ἵππουρις; cf. ἀναβάσιον. **ἀναβασμός**, ὁ, = ἀναβαθμός, Ar.*Fr.*46 D. (pl.), *Michel*1512 (Piraeus, iv B.C.), cf. Paus.10.5.2: metaph., *progress*, in learning, Plot.6.7.36 (pl.), cf. Them.*Or.*13.177c. (Written ἀναβαζμός *SIG*^{2}587.308.)

ἀναβασσἄρέω, = ἀναβακχεύω II, ἀνὰ δηὖτε βασσαρήσω Anacr.63.

ἀναβαστ-άζω, *raise* or *lift up, carry*, J.*AJ*19.3.1, Luc.*Anach.* 24. **-αξις**, ἡ, gloss on ἀνακωχή, Gal.19.79.

ἀναβἄτ-έον, *one must ascend*, metaph., ἐπὶ τὰ καλὰ ἐπιτηδεύματα Them.*Or.*13.177b; ἐπὶ τὸ θεῖον Porph.*Marc.*27. **-ήριον** (sc. ἱερόν), τό, *sacrifice for fair voyage*, Plu.2.984b. II. *step-ladder*, *Gp.*9.17.8 (pl.). **-ης**, poet. **ἀμβάτης**, ου, ὁ, *one who mounts, one mounted*, of Pentheus in the tree, E.*Ba.*1107; esp. *horseman, rider*, X.*HG*5.3.1, Pl.*Criti.*119b, etc. II. *stallion*, Hsch. III. *firebrand*(?), Sch.Ar.*Ach.*321. **-ικός**, ή, όν, *skilled in mounting, ready at mounting*, ἀναβατικώτεροι ἐπὶ τοὺς ἵππους X.*Mem.*3.3.5. 2. Pass., *fit to be ridden*, κτήνη J.*AJ*15.6.3; ὄνοι Hsch. s.v. ἀστράβη. 3. of the sign Capricornus, *affording an ascent* for souls, Porph.*Antr.* 22. II. of fever, *gradually increasing in heat* (cf. ἀνάβασις I.4), Gal.7.337. III. of irrigation-works, for *raising* water (?), ὕδρευμα *PFlor.*50.15, al. **-ός**, Ep. **ἀμβατός**, όν, *to be mounted* or *scaled, easy to be scaled*, Il.6.434, Od.11.316, Pi.*P.*10.27.

ἀναβεβλημένως, v. ἀναβάλλω A.II.2.

ἀναβέβρῠχε, pf. with no pres. in use, ἀναβέβρυχεν ὕδωρ the water *gushed* or *bubbled up*, Il.17.54 (Zenod. ἀναβέβροχεν).

ἀναβήσσω, *to cough up, expectorate*, Hp.*Prog.*15.

ἀναβῐβ-άζω, fut. -βιβάσω Ph.*Bel.*97.43 (s.v.l.): aor. -εβίβασα:— Med., fut. -βιβάσομαι, Att. -βιβῶμαι Amips.30, Aeschin.2.146: aor. -εβιβασάμην: (v. βιβάζω):—causal of ἀναβαίνω, *make to go up, cause to mount*, ἐπὶ τὴν πυρήν, ἐπὶ πύργον, Hdt.1.86, 3.75, X.*Cyr.*6.1.53; ἐπὶ τὸν τροχόν, of torture, And.1.43; κατὰ τὸ ἀκρότατον X.*HG*4.5.3: metaph., *uplift*, ἐπὶ μετεωροτέραν ἐπίνοιαν Corn.*ND*28. II. Special usages: 1. ἀ. τινὰ ἐφ' ἵππον *mount* one on horseback, Hdt.1.63, 4.72, X.*Eq.*6.12; ἐπ' ἅρμα Hdt.4.180; ἐπὶ τὰ ὀχήματα X.*Cyr.*4.2.28. 2. ἀ. ναῦν *draw* a ship *up* on land, Id.*HG*1.1.2. 3. Med., ἀναβιβάζεσθαί τινας ἐπὶ τὰς ναῦς *have* them *put on board* ship, *embark* for sea, Th.7.33: abs., ἀναβιβασάμενοι ib.35, cf. X.*HG*3.4.10. 4. at Athens, *bring up* to the bar of a court of justice as a witness, Is.9.30:—so in Med., Lys. 12.24, Pl.*Ap.*18d; *bring forward* a fellow-prosecutor, Hyp.*Eux.* 13; but usu. of a culprit, *bring up* his wife and children to raise compassion, And.1.148, Pl.*Ap.*34c, Lys.18.24, 20.34, Hyp.*Eux.*41, Aeschin.3.7, cf. 2.146: so Act., Hyp.*Phil.*9. 5. ἀ. ἐπὶ τὴν σκηνήν *bring upon* the stage, Plb.23.10.16, 29.19.2. 6. ἀ. τὰς τιμάς *raise* the prices, D.S.5.10, cf. *POxy.*513.27. 7. *promote, advance*, στρατιώτην Ph.*Bel.*97.43: c. acc. cogn., ἀ. χώραν *advance* a step, 94. 25:—Pass., ἀναβιβάζεσθαι εἰς τιμήν *ascend* to honour, Plu.*Cat.Ma.* 16. 8. Gramm., ἀ. τὸν τόνον *throw back* the accent, A.D.*Pron.* 49.15, al.; of postpositions, Id.*Synt.*308.10. 9. ἀ. τοὺς φθόγγους *lower, moderate* them, Plu.*TG*2. 10. Astron., ὁ ἀναβιβάζων σύνδεσμος *ascending* node, Ptol.*Alm.*4.9, etc.; without σύνδεσμος, Procl.*Hyp.*5.105. **-ασμός**, ὁ, *the throwing back the accent*, A.D. *Conj.*233.30. 2. Arith., *sum total*, Hero *Geom.*4.13. 3. Medic., *aggravation*, of headache, Steph.*in Hp.*1.223 D. **-αστέον**, *one must cause to mount*, τοὺς ἱππέας X.*Eq.Mag.*1.2; ἐπὶ τοὺς ἵππους ἀ. ὡς νεωτάτους Pl.*R.*467e.

ἀναβῐβρώσκω, aor. -έβρωσα, *gnaw through*, Nic.*Th.*134: aor. Pass. ἀναβρωθῆναι *to be corroded*, ὑφ' ἁλός Philostr.*Im.*2.17; *to be eroded*, of ulcers, Gal.8.392.

ἀναβιοτή, ἡ, *coming to life again*, Sch.E.*Or.*1691.

ἀναβῐ-όω, ἀναβιοῖ Arist.*Mir.*832^{b}6 (but ἀναβιώσκομαι (q.v.) is the common pres.): aor. 2 ἀνεβίων (v. infr.), ἀνεβίουν Luc.*Hist.Conscr.* 40; later aor. 1 ἀνεβίωσα Arist.*HA*587^{a}24, Thphr.*HP*4.14.12: also aor. Med. ἀναβιώσασθαι Lib.*Or.*12.50: pf. ἀναβεβίωκα E.ap. Phot.p.107 R., Luc.*Nec.*1:—*come to life again*, ἀναβιοίην νῦν πάλιν Ar.*Ra.*177; ἐπειδὴ ἀνεβίω And.1.125; ἀναβιοὺς ἔλεγεν Pl.*R.*614b:— also Med., ἀναβιοῦσθαι Plu.2.377b. **-ωσις**, εως, ἡ, *return to life*, Lxx 2*Ma.*7.9, Plu.*Luc.*18, App.*Gall.*1.3, etc. **-ώσκομαι**, as Pass., = ἀναβιόω (q.v.), Pl.*Phd.*71e, al., Aristid.*Or.*20(21).19, Hierocl. *in CA*26 p.479 M.: pf. inf. -βεβιῶσθαι Sannyr.3 D.: aor. part. -βιωθεῖσα Philostr.*VA*4.45. II. causal of ἀναβιόω, *bring back to life*, ἀποκτεινύντων καὶ ἀναβιωσκομένων Pl.*Cri.*48c: aor. inf. ἀναβιώσασθαι *Phd.*89b: fut. ἀναβιώσῃ τὴν μυῖαν Ael.*NA*2.29: later in Act., ἀναβιώσκω Them.*Or.*8.115c, Sch.E.*Alc.*1; Act. ἀναβιώσκω (= ἀναβιόω) only interpol. in Polyaen.6.38.2.

ἀναβλαστ-άνω, fut. -βλαστήσω v.l. in Hdt.3.62: aor. -έβλαστον Id. (v. infr.), -εβλάστησα Eun. (v. infr.):—*shoot up*, of plants, Pl. *Lg.*835d, Plu.2.366b; of monstrous births, ib.991a; *shoot afresh*, Thphr.*HP*4.14.13:—of a city, [αἱ Συρήκουσαι] ἀνά τ' ἔδραμον καὶ ἀνέβλαστον Hdt.7.156; of misfortunes, *spring up*, ἔδει.. κακὰ ἀναβλαστεῖν Id.5.92.δ', cf. 3.62; ἡ ἀναβλαστάνουσα καθ' ἡμέραν τιμή Plu.2. 769a. II. trans., *put forth*, τῆς ψυχῆς ἔρνη διττὰ ἀναβλαστούσης Ph. 1.304, cf. 1.118; ἔρις πολέμους -ησε Eun.*Hist.*p.235 D. **-έω**, = foreg., Emp.146.3. **-ησις**, εως, ἡ, *up-shooting*, Thphr.*HP*8.1.6; κεράτων J.*AJ*10.11.7; τῶν γηγενῶν Agath.3.5 (pl.).

ἀνάβλεμμα, ατος, τό, *looking up*, of dogs, X.*Cyn.*4.4, Poll.2.56.

ἀναβλέπω, fut. -βλέψω Hdt.2.111, -βλέψομαι E.*HF*563: aor. -έβλεψα Hdt.l.c., etc.:—*look up*, Ar.*Nu.*346; πρὸς τὸ φῶς Pl.*R.*515c; εἰς τὸν οὐρανόν *Ax.*370b: esp. as a mark of confidence, ἀ. ὀρθοῖς ὄμμασιν X.*HG*7.1.30; ἀ. πρός τινα ἐκ τοῦ ἴσου *look* him *in the face*, *Cyr.*1.4.12. 2. c. acc., *look up at*, φῶς ἀναβλέψεσθε E. l.c.: c. dat., ἀελίου ἀ. λαμπάσι *Ion*1467; τοῖς κερτομοῦσι γοργὸν ὡς ἀναβλέπει *Supp.*322 codd. 3. c. acc. cogn., ἀ. φλόγα *cast up* a glance of fire, Id.*Ion*1263. II. *recover one's sight*, Hdt.2.111, Pl.*Phdr.* 243b, *Ev.Jo.*9.11; πάλιν ἀ. Ar.*Pl.*95, 117. 2. *open one's eyes*, Pl. *R.*621b, X.*Cyr.*8.3.29. III. metaph., *revive*, ᾧ δῶμ' ἀνέβλεφ' E. *Ba.*1308.

ἀνάβλεψις, εως, ἡ, *looking up, seeing*, Arist.*Ph.*247^{b}8. II. *recovery of sight*, Lxx *Is.*61.1, cf. *Ev.Luc.*4.18.

ἀναβλ-ήδην, = ἀμβλήδην (q.v.), *afresh*, Arat.1070, Max.287. **-ησις**, εως, ἡ, *putting off, delay*, κακοῦ Il.2.380; λύσιος 24.655; θανάτοιο Call.*Ap.*45: abs., *AP*12.184 (Strat.). **-ητικῶς**, gloss on ἀμβολάδην, ἀμβλήδην, Eust.1241.36, 1282.1.

ἀνα-βλύες· πηγαί, Hsch. **-βλύζω**, poet. **ἀμβλ-**, *AP*9.374, Orph.*A.*1130: fut. -βλυήσω prob. in Ezech.*Exag.*137: aor. ἀνέβλυσα Arist.*Mu.*400^{a}32, Q.S.10.108 (tm.); inf. ἀναβλῦσαι (leg. -βλύσαι) Plu.*Sull.*6:—*spout up*, ἔλαιον Arist.*Mir.*841^{a}17; ἄκρητον *AP*7.31 (Diosc.) codd.; ἐέρσην Nonn.*D.*9.58, al. 2. intr., *gush forth*, Arist.*Mu.* l.c., *IG*14.889 (Sinuessa), Heliod.ap.Orib.46.11.9, etc.; Νεῖλος ἀναβλύζων Theoc.17.80.

ἀνάβλῠσις, εως, ἡ, *gushing up*, πηγῶν Arist.*Mu.*396^{a}22, cf. Aët. 16.21. **ἀναβλύσσω**, = ἀναβλύζω, Aq., Sm.*Pr.*18.4.

ἀναβλυστάνω, = ἀναβλύζω, Str.*Chr.*16.22, Procop.*Aed.*2.3, al.:— also **ἀναβλυσθαίνω**, Sch.Pl.*Ti.*22e: **ἀμβλυσθονῆσαι** or **-τονῆσαι**, Eup.105, cf. Eust.1095.8, *EM*200.52.

ἀναβλύω, Ep. impf. ἀναβλύεσκε A.R.3.223, = ἀναβλύζω, *boil over*, Hp.*Mul.*1.78; *gush out*, Plb.34.9.7, Str.3.5.7, Nonn.*D.*48.878 [κρήνη] ἀναβλύεσκε γάλακτι A.R. l.c.: c. acc. cogn., *spout out*, ἀνέβλυον ἰκμάδα, ὕδωρ, Nonn.*D.*9.31, 6.255:—*spurt* foam *from the mouth*, Hp.*Morb.Sacr.*7.

ἀναβό-ᾱμα, poet. **ἀμβ-**, τό, = ἀναβόησις, A.*Ch.*34. **-άω**, fut. -ήσομαι E.*IA*465, Dor. -άσομαι Ar.*Pl.*639: aor. ἀνεβόησα Th.1.53, Ion. ἀνέβωσα Hdt.1.10, al., part. ἀμβώσας 1.8, 3.38:—*cry, shout aloud*, esp. in sign of grief or astonishment, ἀμβώσας μέγα Hdt. ll.cc., cf. Antipho 5.69, E.*Ba.*1079; οἰκτρὸν ἀνεβόασεν *Hel.*184; of the *war-cry*, X.*Cyr.*7.1.38; ἀ. "παρεῖναι τοὺς πρώτους" *call out* 'let the front rank pass', *HG*4.2.22. 2. c. acc., τάδ' ἀναβοάσας E.*Ba.* 525; ἄχη ἀ. *bewail, lament*, A.*Pers.*572; Πανὸς ἀναβοᾷ γάμους E. *Hel.*190. 3. c. acc. pers., *call on*, συμμάχους ib.1592; Ἀσκληπιόν Ar.*Pl.*639. 4. *cry up, extol*, Alex.98.12. **-ησις**, εως, ἡ, *shouting, calling*, D.H.9.10; *invocation*, Sch.S.*OT*80; ἄσημος ἀ. Paul. Aeg.3.13.

ἀναβοθρεύω, *dig up, force up*, *AB*389, Suid., Hsch.

ἀναβολ-άδην, Adv. *bubbling up*, ἀ. ζέοντα ὕδατα Polem.Hist.83 (cf. ἀμβ-). **-άδιον**, τό, Dim. of ἀναβολή I.2, *mantle*, Aq.*Is.*61.3, *POxy.*109, Isid.*Etym.*19.25.7:—also **-αιον**, τό, Sm.*Is.*3.22, *Edict. Diocl.*26.78, 93. **-άς**, άδος, ἡ, v. sub ἀμβολάς. **-εύς**, έως, ὁ, *groom who helps one to mount*, App.*Pun.*106, Plu.*CG*7. 2. *stirrup*, Eust.1406.5, Suid. II. *lever, instrument for lifting*, Heliod.ap. Orib.46.11.26, cf. Paul.Aeg.6.88. **-ή**, poet. **ἀμβολή**, ἡ: (ἀναβάλλω): I. of things: 1. *that which is thrown up, mound of earth, bank*, X.*An.*5.2.5, D.S.17.95; ἀ. χωμάτων *casting up* of dykes, *Arch.Pap.*6.132 (Denderah); διωρύγων *PAmh.*2.91.11 (pl.). 2. *that which is thrown back over the shoulder, mantle*, Pl.*Prt.*342c, *PPetr.*3 p.48 (iii B.C.), Lxx *Ne.*5.13, al.; of the *toga*, Nic.Dam. p.119 D.: also, *fashion of wearing a cloak*, Luc.*Somn.*6. II. of actions, 1. *striking up, prelude* on the lyre preliminary to singing, ὁπόταν προοιμίων ἀμβολὰς τεύχῃς ἐλελιζομένη, addressed to the lyre, Pi.*P.*1.4; esp. of dithyramb, Eup.5 D.: hence, *rambling dithyrambic ode*, Ar.*Av.*1385, cf. *Pax*830, Arist.*Rh.*1409^{b}25; cf. ἀναβάλλω B.I. 2. *putting off, delaying*, οὐκέτι ἐς ἀναβολὰς ἐποιεῦντο τὴν ἀποχώρησιν Hdt.8.21; ὅ τι μέλλετε.. μὴ ἐς ἀ. πράσσετε Th.7.15; οὐκ ἐς ἀμβολάς without *delay*, E.*Heracl.*270; ἐς μηδεμίαν ἀ. *PAmh.* 2.34^d.5; ἐν ταῖς ἀ. τῶν κακῶν ἔνεστ' ἄκη E.*HF*93; ἐπὶ ἀναβολῇ πρᾶσιν, ὠνὴν ποιεῖσθαι sell, buy on *credit*, Pl.*Lg.*915e; ἀναβολήν τινος ποιεῖσθαι Th.2.42; ποιεῖν Pl.*Smp.*201d; εἰς τὸ γῆρας ἀναβολὰς ποιεῖν Men. 235.8; δακρύοις.. ἐμποιεῖν ἀ. τῷ πάθει Id.599; ἀναβολὰν λαβόντες ἔτη τρία *IG*9(2).205.22 (Thess.). b. *deferred payment*, εὐχρηστήσας σῖτον ἐπ' ἀναβολῇ Ἀρχ.Ἐφ.1912.60 (Gonni). 3. ἀ. δίκης ἐπὶ τὸν βασιλέα *reference, appeal*, Str.13.1.55. 4. *lifting*, hence, *removal*, of tumours, Antyll.ap.Orib.45.2.6. III. intr., *going up, ascent, way up*, ἀ. τῶν Ἄλπεων Plb.3.39.9, etc.; τὴν ἀ. ποιεῖσθαι 50.3. 2. *bubbling up*, πομφολύγων Arist.*Pr.*936ᵇ1, Thphr.*Ign.*16; of the Nile, *sources*, ἀμβολαί *CIG*4924 (Philae). -ικός, ή, όν, *filled by a machine*, λάκκος *PLond.*1695.7 (vi A.D.). II. *delayed, deferred*, of payments, *OGI*669.21 (i A.D.): -κόν, τό, *deferment of payments*, *PAmh.*2.131; but λίνον ἀ., perh. = linen *for cloaks*, *PThead.Inv.*15. Adv. -κῶς, = ἀναβλητικῶς (q.v.), Eust.1241.38. -ιμος, ον, *to be delayed*, δίκαι Hsch. -ιον, τό, dub. in *PFay.Ostr.*49.

ἀναβορβορύζω, *grumble loudly*, Ar.*Ec.*433.

ἀναβουλεύομαι, Dep., *change one's opinion*, Eust.1385.59.

ἀναβρ-άζω, intr., *boil* or *foam up*, v.l. for -βράσσω, Procop.*Goth.*3.35: also trans., Aët.1.226. -ἄσις, εως, ἡ, *boiling up, bubbling up*, e.g. of water, v.l. in Str.3.1.9. -ασμός, ὁ, prop. *boiling up*; hence ἀ. γῆς kind of *earthquake*, Suid. s.v. ἐκτιναγμός: metaph., '*réchauffé*', *rehash*, Olymp. *in Mete.*230.11. -άσσω, Att. -άττω, aor. subj. ἀναβράσῃ Dsc.5.14, *boil well, seethe*, ἀναβράττω κίχλας Ar.*Pax* 1197; κρέα ἀνέβραττεν ὀρνίθεια *Ra.*510: abs., ἀναβράττετ', ἐξοπτᾶτε *Ach.*1005, cf. Dsc.l.c.: metaph., ζωὴν.. ζέουσάν τε καὶ ἀναβράττουσαν Dam.*Pr.*86. 2. *throw up*, τὰ ἐν τοῖς λίκνοις ἀναβραττόμενα Arist.*Mete.*368ᵇ29; esp. of the sea, ἅλμη ἀναβρασθεῖσα spray *dashed up*, A.R.2.566, cf. Lxx *Wi.*10.19. II. intr., *jump*, of chariot, ib.*Na.*3.2. -αστος, ον, *boiled*, κρέα Ar.*Ra.*553, Aristomen.8; κίχλαι Pherecr.130.10, cf. 108.23; ὕδωρ Dsc.3.83.

*ἀναβράχω, v. sub ἀνέβραχε.

ἀναβρέχομαι, Pass., *become wet again*, v.l. Arist.*Pr.*927ᵇ6.

ἀναβρομέω, *boil up*, of soup, Ath.3.126d. 2. *roar aloud*, Nonn.*D.*45.330.

ἀναβροντάω, *thunder aloud*, of Odysseus speaking, Tryph.118.

ἀναβρόξειε, ἀναβροχέν, v. βρόχω.

ἀναβροχ-ισμός, ὁ, *extraction of eye-lashes by a loop*, an operation for trichiasis, Paul.Aeg.6.13, cf. Gal.15.918:—-ίζω, 14.784.

ἀναβρυάζω, *neigh aloud*, of horses, ἀνεβρύαξαν Ar.*Eq.*602.

ἀναβρῡχάομαι, Dep., *roar aloud*, Pl.*Phd.*117d; ἀ. ἐλεεινὸν καὶ θρηνῶδες Philostr.*VA*5.42.

*ἀναβρύχω, v. ἀναβέβρυχε, Eust.1095.6.

ἀναβρύω, = ἀναβλύω, Ael.*VH*3.43, f.l. in Ph.1.477: c. acc., ἄνθεα Nonn.*D.*7.346.

ἀνάβρ-ωσις, εως, ἡ, *corrosion* or *erosion*, Sor.2.40, Gal.1.154,239, Antyll.(?)ap.Orib.44.32.11. -ώσκων· κατεσθίων, Hsch. -ωτικός, ή, όν, *corrosive*, Alex.Aphr.*Pr.*1.92.

ἀναβῶνες· βαθμοῦ εἶδος, Hsch. (cod. -ῶδες); cf. ἄμβων.

ἀναγαγγανεύουσιν· ἀναβοῶσιν, Hsch.

ἀνάγαιον· ἀνὰ τὴν γῆν, Hsch. II. **ἀνάγαιον**, τό, = ἀνώγεων, v.l. in *Ev.Marc.*14.15, *Ev.Luc.*22.12.

ἀναγαλλίς, ίδος, ἡ (also ὁ, Hsch.), *pimpernel, Anagallis arvensis*, and *A. caerulea*, Dsc.2.178, Longus 3.12, etc. II. ἀ. ἔνυδρος, = σίον, Ps.-Dsc.2.127.

ἀναγαργαρ-ίζω, *gargle*, χλιαροῖσιν Hp.*Morb.*2.26,27, *Aff.*4:—so also in Med., *Mul.*2.185, *IG*4.955.30 (Epid.), Archig.ap.Gal.12.976 (Pass.). (-γαργαλ- is v.l. in codd. of Hp.) -ισμα, ατος, τό, *gargle*, Dsc.1.128, Archig.ap.Orib.8.1.39. -ισμός, ὁ, *gargling*, Hp.*Int.*38. -ιστέον, *one must gargle*, Philum.ap.Aët.8.48. -ιστον, τό, *gargle*, Hp.*Morb.*2.26.

ἀναγγείωτος, ον, *without blood-vessels*, μέρη Orib.45.17.5.

ἀναγγελία, ἡ, *proclamation*, *SIG*598.11, *OGI*332.44 (Elaea).

ἀναγγέλλω, (v. ἀγγέλλω) *carry back tidings of, report*, τι A.*Pr.*661; πάντ' ἀναγγεῖλαι φίλοις E.*IT*761; τῷ Βρασίδᾳ τὴν ξυνθήκην Th.4.122, etc.; τι τῷ δήμῳ Arist.*EN*1113ᵃ9; ἐν ἁλίᾳ, of valuers, *Tab.Heracl.*1.118; τι πρός τινα Plb.1.67.11: c. part., *tell of* person doing, X.*Ages.*5.6:—Pass., ὡς ἀνηγγέλθη τεθνεώς Plu.*Per.*18. II. *proclaim*, τοὺς στεφάνους *OGI*6 (Scepsis), *SIG*412.13 (Delph.):—Pass., of rewards, ἀνηγγέλθαι αὐτῷ ἀργύριον Aen.Tact.10.15.

ἀνάγγελμα, τό, *proclamation*, *IPE*1².352.49 (Cherson.).

ἀνάγγελος, ον, *from which no messenger returns*, μάχη *AP*7.244 (Gaet.). II. = μυρσίνη ἀγρία, Ps.-Dsc.4.144.

ἀναγγ-ελτικός, ή, όν, *capable of expressing*, δυνάμεις τινὸς ἀ. Anon. *in Prm.*(*Rh.Mus.*47.613). -ελτος, ον, *unannounced, secret*, Hld. ap.Hsch. s.v. ἀνάπαυστα.

ἀνάγειον, τό, = ἀνάγαιον, Petersen-Luschan *Reise in Lykien* p.36 (Myra).

ἀναγείρω, *reassemble*, v.l. Q.S.2.577.

ἀναγελάω, *laugh loud*, X.*Cyr.*5.1.9, Plu.*Arat.*6, Philostr.*VA*5.7; ἐπί τινι *at* one, X.*Cyr.*6.1.34.

ἀναγενν-άω, *beget anew, regenerate*, 1 *Ep.Pet.*1.3, cf. 23:—Pass., prob. in *Corp.Herm.*13.1. 2. metaph., *arouse afresh*, ἀ. πάλιν κακά Phld.*Ir.*p.18 W. -ησις, εως, ἡ, *regeneration*, κόσμου Ph.2.489. -ητικός, ή, όν, *able to produce*, εἰδώλων Iamb.*Myst.*3.28 (dub. l.).

ἀναγεπόπτης, ὁ, perh. *uplifting to full vision*, *PMag.Lond.*121.355.

ἀναγέτρια, ἡ, = μαῖα (Tarent.), Hsch.; cf. ἀγέτρια.

ἀναγεύω, *give* one *a taste*, πρώτους ἠξίωσ' ἀναγεῦσ' ὑμᾶς Ar.*Nu.*523.

ἀναγηρύομαι, Dep., *cry aloud*, Ael.*NA*5.34.

ἀνᾰγής, ές, (ἄγος) = ἐναγής, *wretch*, Herod.2.70, Hsch. (who also glosses it by καθαρός).

ἀναγιγνώσκω, later **ἀναγῑνώσκω**: I. Ep. only in aor. 2 ἀνέγνων, 1. *know well, know certainly*, οὐ γάρ πώ τις ἑὸν γόνον αὐτὸς ἀνέγνω Od.1.216, cf. 21.205, Il.13.734. b. *perceive*, Theoc.24.23. 2. *know again, recognize*, Od.4.250; once in Hdt., *acknowledge, own*, ἀναγνῶναι τοὺς συγγενέας Hdt.2.91, cf. Pi.*I.*2.23: aor. Pass. once in E., εἰ μὲν γὰρ ἔξῃ πόσις, ἀνεγνώσθημεν ἂν *Hel.*290. II. after Hom., fut. ἀναγνώσομαι dub. in *GDI*5075: aor. 2 ἀνέγνων, Cret. 3 pl. subj. -γνῶντι *GDI*5040.43: pf. ἀνέγνωκα:—Pass., fut. -γνωσθήσομαι Lys.17.9: aor. ἀνεγνώσθην Pl.*Prm.*127d: pf. ἀνέγνωσμαι Isoc.15.67, etc.:—of written characters, *know* them *again*, and so, *read*, first in Pi.*O.*10(11).1, cf. Ar.*Eq.*118,1065, Th.3.49, And.1.47, etc. (never in Trag.); ἀναγνώσεται (sc. ὁ γραμματεύς) D.20.27, etc.; λαβὼν ἀνάγνωθι τὸ ψήφισμα Id.18.118; λέγε.. καὶ ἀνάγνωθι Id.19.70; τὴν διαμαρτυρίαν ἀναγνώτω Id.44.45; ἀ. πρὸς ἐμαυτόν Ar.*Ra.*52: abs., οἱ ἀναγιγνώσκοντες *students*, Plu.*Alex.*1, Marin.*Procl.*15; ἀ. παρά τινι Ἀριστοτέλους τὰ περὶ ψυχῆς *attend lectures on* A., ib.12:—Pass., τὰ βιβλία τὰ ἀνεγνωσμένα books *read aloud*, hence, *published*, opp. τὰ ἀνέκδοτα, Lycon ap.D.L.5.73. III. Ion. usage, causal, mostly in aor. ἀνέγνωσα, *induce* one to do a thing, τούτους.. ἀναγνώσας ἕπεσθαι Hdt.5.106, cf. 1.87, 4.158, 6.83, al.; inf. is omitted, ὡς ἀνέγνωσε when *he had persuaded* him, Id.1.68: once in pres., ἀναγιγνώσκεις στρατεύεσθαι βασιλέα Id.7.10; *persuade, convince*, ὅτι.. Hp.*Art.*1:—aor. Pass., ἀνεγνώσθην *to be persuaded* to do a thing, c. inf., Hdt.7.7 and 236: without inf., ὑπὸ τῆς γυναικὸς ἀναγνωσθεὶς 4.154; χρήμασι ἀ. 6.50: plpf. Pass., ὡς οὗτοι.. οἱ ἀνεγνωσμένοι ἦσαν 8.110: rare in Att., ὑπὸ τῶν κυρίων ἀναγιγνωσκόμενον Antipho 2.2.7.

ἀναγκ-άζω, fut. -άσω E.*Andr.*337, Th.5.35 (later 2 pl. -ᾶτε *Arch.Pap.*6.286): pf. ἠνάγκακα Pl.*Hipparch.*232b: plpf. -ειν D.33.28: (ἀνάγκη):—*force, compel*, mostly c. acc. pers. et inf., ἀ. τινὰ κτείνειν, πόλισμα, συνθήκας ποιεῖσθαι, etc., Hdt.1.11, 98, 6.42; δρᾶν, λέγειν, etc., S.*El.*256, *OC*979, etc.: so in Pass., ἠναγκάζοντο ἀμύνεσθαι Hdt.5.101: without inf., κἀμ' ἀναγκάζεις τάδε (sc. δρᾶν) S.*Ph.*1368, cf. *OT*280; ἀναγκάζεσθαί τι *to be forced* [to do] a thing, Pl.*Phdr.*242a, 254b, cf. X.*Mem.*4.5.4; ἀ. τινὰ ἐς τὸ πολεμεῖν Th.1.23; ἐς τὸ ἔργον Id.2.75. 2. c. acc. pers. only, *constrain* a person, τὸ συνδρῶν σ' ἀναγκάσει χρέος E.*Andr.*337; esp. by argument, opp. ῥητορικῶς ἐλέγχειν, Pl.*Grg.*472b; δεινοῖς ἠναγκάσθην *I was constrained, tortured*, S.*El.*221, cf. X.*Hier.*9.2; ἠναγκασμένος, ἀναγκασθεὶς *under compulsion*, Th.6.22, 8.99; ὑπὸ δεσμῶν ἀναγκασθεὶς And.1.2; φανεροὶ ἦσαν ἀναγκασθησόμενοι D.18.19. 3. c. acc. rei only, *carry through by force*, πόλις ἀναγκάζει τάδε E.*IT*595, cf. X.*Mem.*4.5.5, Arist.*Rh.*1392ᵃ27; ἠναγκασμένα λάχανα *forced* vegetables, Philostr. *VA*1.21. 4. c. acc. rei et inf., *contend that* a thing *is necessarily* so and so, μὴ ἀνάγκαζε ὃ μὴ καλόν ἐστιν αἰσχρὸν εἶναι Pl.*Smp.*202b, cf. *Cra.*432c, *Tht.*196b: foll. by Conj., οἱ λόγοι ἀναγκάσειαν ἂν ὅτι ἀθάνατον ψυχή *R.*611b. 5. abs., *apply compulsion*, Arist.*Pol.*1304ᵇ9 (ἀναγκάζω is a gloss in Pl.*Tht.*153c.). 6. in surgery, *use force* to reduce dislocations, etc., Hp.*Art.*3,5, al. -αίη, ἡ, Ep. and Ion. for ἀνάγκη, Il.6.85, Tyrt.6, Sol.36.8, Hdt.1.11, etc. -αίνισμα· ἀνακίνημα, Hsch. -αῖον, τό, *place of constraint, prison*, X.*HG*5.4.8 and 14, cf. Harp., who adds Καλλισθένης δὲ ἀνώγεων εἶπεν, ὃ δεῖ μᾶλλον λέγεσθαι: but correct reading is prob. ἀνάκαιον (preserved in Suid. and *AB*98, as used by Boeotians), or Ἀνάκειον, q.v., as in D.45.80, cf. *EM*98.32. II. = αἰδοῖον, Artem.1.45, Eust.1968.39, *Cat.Cod.Astr.*8(4).133 (pl.). III. *privy*, *Gloss.* IV. = sq., Plaut.*Rud.*363. -αιοπότης, ου, ὁ, kind of *cup*, *SIG*²588.209 (Delos). -αῖος, α, ον, in Att. also ος, ον Th.1.2, Pl.*R.*554a, etc.: *of, with*, or *by force*: I. Act., *constraining, applying force*, μῦθος ἀ. a word *of force*, Od.17.399; χρειὼ ἀ. *urgent* necessity, Il.8.57; ἦμαρ ἀ. day *of constraint*, i.e. life *of slavery*, 16.836; ἀ. τύχη a doom *imposed by fate*, or *fateful* chance, S.*Aj.*485, cf. 803 (but, *fatal* chance, Id.*El.*48); πᾶν γὰρ ἀ. χρῆμ' ἀνιηρὸν ἔφυ Thgn.472, cf. 297, E.*Or.*230; τῆς ἀρχῆς τῷ ἀ. παροξυνομένους by the *compulsory nature* of our rule, Th.5.99; δεσμὸς ἀ. Theoc.24.33; ἐξ ἀναγκαίου under *stress of circumstances*, Th.7.60. 2. *forcible, cogent*, πειθὼ Pl.*Sph.*265d; ἀποδείξεις *Ti.*40e; διαλλακτὰς πολὺ τῶν ἐμῶν λόγων ἀναγκαιοτέρους Th.4.60; τὰ -ότερα τῶν ἀντιγράφων the *more authoritative* copies, Sch.S.*OC*390. II. Pass., *constrained, forced*, twice in Od., πολεμισταὶ ἀ. soldiers *perforce*, Od.24.499; so δμῶες ἀ. ib.210 (where however Eust. expl. it χρειώδεις *trusty, serviceable*, v. infr. 6). 2. *necessary* (physically or morally), οὐκ ἀ. *unnecessary* (on its diff. senses in philosophy v. Arist.*Metaph.*1015ᵃ20ff.), ἀ. [ἐστί] *it is necessary to*.., S.*Ph.*1317, etc.; γίνεταί μοι ἀναγκαιότατον, c. inf., Hdt.3.65; ἀ. κακόν *a necessary* evil, Men.651, cf. Hybreas ap.Str.14.2.24: also c. inf., ἔνιαι τῶν ἀποκρίσεων ἀναγκαῖαι διὰ μακρῶν τοὺς λόγους ποιεῖσθαι Pl.*Grg.*449b; ὁδὸν ἀναγκαιοτάτην εἶναι τρέπεσθαι *Sph.*242b; [μαθήματα] ἀναγκαῖα προμεμαθηκέναι *necessary* for us to have learnt them before, *Lg.*643c. 3. τὰ ἀ. *necessaries of life*, Antipho 4.1.2, Pl.*Lg.*848a; τὰ ἀ. τοῦ βίου Isoc.4.40; ἀ. τροφή Th.1.2. b. τὰ ἀ. *things necessary to be done*, X.*Mem.*1.1.6; τὰ ἐκ θεοῦ ἀ. the *appointed order of things*, *HG* 1.7.33; θεῶν ἀναγκαῖον τόδε E.*Hec.*584 codd.: τὸ ἀ., = ἀνάγκη, Arist.*Ph.*200ᵃ31. 4. *indispensable*, i.e. *a bare minimum*, freq. in Sup., τὸ ἀναγκαιότατον ὕψος *the least* height *that was absolutely necessary*, Th.1.90; ἡ ἀναγκαιοτάτη πόλις *the least that could be called* a city, Pl.*R.*369d; ἐκ τεττάρων ἀναγκαιοτάτων συγκεῖσθαι πόλιν Arist.*Pol.*1291ᵃ12; αὐτὰ τἀναγκαιότατ' εἰπεῖν give *a bare outline* of the facts, D.18.126, cf. 168; ἡ ἀ. συγγένεια *the most distant degree* of kinship *recognized by law*, 44.26: less freq. in Posit., οὐδὲ τἀναγκαῖα ἐξικέσθαι Th.1.70: hence, *scanty, makeshift*, παρασκευή 6.37. 5. of persons, *connected by necessary* or *natural ties*, i.e. *related by blood*, Antipho 1.4, Pl.*R.*574b; ἀ. δόμοις E.*Alc.*533; οἱ ἀ. *kinsfolk*, X.*An.*2.4.1; ἀ. φίλοι E.*Andr.*671; συγγενεῖς καὶ ἀ. ἄνθρωποι D.19.290; τοὺς συγγενεῖς αὐτοῦ καὶ ἀ. φίλους *Act.Ap.*10.24, cf. *PFlor.*2.142.2 (iii A.D.). **6.** Astrol., *efficacious*, Vett.Val.63.1 (Comp.): ἀ. γραμμή line *of fate*, *Cat.Cod.Astr.*7.238. **7.** *costly*, ὄξος *POxy.*1870 (v A.D.); ἐσθής Suid. s.v. βεστιάριον. **III.** Adv. -ως *of necessity, perforce*, ἀ. ἔχει it *must* be so, Hdt.1.89, A.*Ch.*239, S.*Tr.*723, Pl. *Phd.*91e, etc.; ἀ. ἔχει μοι ποιέειν ταῦτα Hdt.8.140.α', al.; ἀ. φέρειν, opp. ἀνδρείως, Th.2.64; *as best might be*, Pl.*Ti.*69d. **2.** γελοίως καὶ ἀ. λέγειν *in a narrow sense* (cf. II.4, but prob. with play on III.1), Id.*R.*527a; πτωχῶς μέν, ἀλλ' ἀ. Babr.55.2:—Sup. ἀναγκαιότατα, λέγεις Pl.*Phlb.*40c. **3.** *strictly*, κελεύειν *OGI*669.41 (i A.D.). **IV.** οἱ ἀ. τόποι *privy* parts, Vett.Val.113.9. **V.** ἀναγκαῖον, τό, v. sub v. **-αιότης**, ητος, ἡ, *blood-relationship*, Lys.32.5 (pl.), Plb.18.51.10, D.H.2.10. **II.** later, *necessity*, S.E.*P.*2.205. **-αιώδης**, ες, = ἀναγκαῖος II.4, in Comp., τὰ -έστερα τῶν λόγων Sch.E.*Ph.*494. **-ασμα**, ατος, τό, *compulsion*, J.*AJ*19.2.5. **-αστέος**, α, ον, *to be compelled*, ἀ. ἄρχειν Pl.*R.*539e. **II.** ἀναγκαστέον *one must compel*, ib.378d, X.*Hier.*8.9, etc. **-αστήρ**, ῆρος, ὁ, *one that constrains*, ἀ. ἄτρακτοι the *constraining* spindles of Fate, *IG*12(7).447 (Amorgos). **-αστήριος**, α, ον, = sq., ἀ. δικαιοσύνης D.H.2.75. **-αστικός**, ή, όν, *compulsory, coercive*, opp. συμβουλευτικός, of law, Pl.*Lg.*930b; ὁ νόμος ἀ. ἔχει δύναμιν Arist.*EN*1180^{a}21. **2.** *cogent*, σημείωσις Phld.*Sign.*4, al.; λόγοι Id.*Rh.*1.247 S., al. Adv. -κῶς Ascl.*in Metaph.*371.8, S.E.*P.*1.193. **3.** Astrol., *having the fixity of law*, Vett.Val.19.34, al. **-αστός**, ή, όν, *forced, constrained*, Hdt.6.58; ἀ. στρατεύοντες Th.7.58, cf. 8.24; ἀ. τροφή Aristid.*Or.*47(23).59. Adv. -τῶς Pl.*Ax.*366a; opp. ἑκουσίως, 1*Ep.Pet.*5.2.

ἀνάγκη, Ion. and Ep. **ἀναγκαίη**, ἡ, *force, constraint, necessity*, κρατερὴ δ' ἐπικείσετ' ἀ. Il.6.458; ἀναγκαίη γὰρ ἐπείγει ib.85; ἀναγκαίη πολεμίζειν 4.300; τίς τοι ἀνάγκη πτώσσειν; 5.633; οἷσιν ἀ. (sc. φυλάσσειν) 10.418, al.: but in Hom. usu. in dat. as Adv., ἀνάγκῃ *perforce, of necessity*, ἀείδειν Od.1.154; φεύγειν Il.11.150: in act. sense, *forcibly, by force*, ἴσχειν, ἄγειν, Od.4.557, 22.353; μνήσασθαι 7.217: strengthd. by καί, 10.434; ὑπ' ἀνάγκης 19.156; opp. ἑκόντες, Pl.*Phdr.*231a; ὑπ' ἀναγκαίης Hdt.7.172, al.; ἐξ ἀνάγκης S.*Ph.*73, Th.3.40, etc.; δι' ἀνάγκης Pl.*Ti.*47e; σὺν ἀνάγκᾳ Pi.*P.*1.51; πρὸς ἀνάγκαν A.*Pers.*569 codd. (lyr.), cf. Epict.*Ench.*29.2; κατ' ἀνάγκην X.*Cyr.*4.3.7: ἀνάγκη ἐστί, c. inf., *it must be that..., is necessary that..*, cf. Il. supr. cit.; πᾶσα ἀ. ἐστὶ ὗσαι Hdt.2.22; τρέφειν τοὺς τοκέας τοῖσι μὲν παισὶν οὐδεμία ἀ., τῇσι δὲ θυγατράσι πᾶσα ἀ. ib.35: c. dat. pers., ἀ. μοι σχεθεῖν A.*Pr.*16, cf. *Pers.*293:—in Trag. freq. in answers and arguments, πολλή γ' ἀνάγκη, πολλὴ 'στ' ἀνάγκη, or πολλή μ' ἀνάγκη, with which an inf. may always be supplied, E.*Med.*1013, *Hec.*396, S.*Tr.*295; so πᾶσ' ἀνάγκη *El.*1497, cf. Pl.*R.*441d; ἀνάγκη μεγάλη [ἐστί] ib.485e, Is.3.6, D.28.9; ἐν ἀνάγκῃ ἐστί Lys.6.8: later ἀνάγκην ἔχω, c. inf., *Ev.Luc.*14.18. **2.** *necessity* in the philosophical sense, Arist.*APo.*94^{b}37, *Metaph.*1026^{b}28, *Ph.*199^{b}34; *logical necessity*, *Metaph.*1064^{b}33: in pl., *laws of nature*, τίσιν ἀνάγκαις ἕκαστα γίγνεται τῶν οὐρανίων X.*Mem.*1.1.11, cf. Hp.*Aër.*21. **b.** *natural need*, γαστρὸς ἀνάγκαις A.*Ag.*726, cf. Ar.*Nu.*1075, X.*Cyn.*7.1; ὑπ' ἀ. τῆς ἐμφύτου Pl.*R.*458d; ἐρωτικαῖς ἀ. ib., etc. **c.** ἡ ἀ. τοῦ τόπου the *lie* of the ground as a *necessary condition*, *PLille*4.14. **d.** ἀνάγκη δαιμόνων, αἱ ἐκ θεῶν ἀνάγκαι, *fate, destiny*, E.*Ph.*1000, 1763: freq. personified in Poets, Parm.8.30, Emp.116, A.*Pr.*105, S.*Fr.*256; Ἀνάγκᾳ δ' οὐδὲ θεοὶ μάχονται Simon.5.21. **3.** *compulsion* exerted by a superior, ἀ. προστιθέναι, ἐπιτιθέναι, X.*Hier.*9.4, *Lac.*10.7. **b.** *violence, punishment*, esp. of torture, mostly pl., ἐς ἀνάγκας ἄγεσθαι Hdt.1.116, cf. Antipho 6.25, Herod.5.5; προσάγειν τινὶ τὰς ἀνάγκας Th.1.99; τὰ πρὸς ἀνάγκας ὄργανα instruments of *torture*, Plb.15.28.2: later in sg., ἡ ἀ. τῶν βασάνων Plu.2.305e; πρὸς ἀνάγκην *under torture*, Id.*Publ.*17: metaph., Hp.*de Arte*13; δολοποιὸς ἀ., i.e. the stratagem of Nessus, S.*Tr.*832; βρόχων πλεκταῖς ἀνάγκαις Xenarch.1.9. **c.** *duress*, '*force majeure*', ὅρκους οὓς ποιέονται ἐν ἀνάγκῃ ὄντες Democr.239; *stress* of circumstances, ἀκούσιοι ἀ. Th.3.82. **d.** *treatment by mechanical force*, τῶν ἀναγκῶν τινὰ προσφέρειν Hp.*Fract.*15, cf. *Art.*73. **4.** *bodily pain, anguish*, κατ' ἀνάγκην ἕρπειν *painfully*, S.*Ph.*206 (lyr.); ὑπ' ἀνάγκης βοᾶν ib.215; ὠδίνων ἀνάγκαι E.*Ba.*89 (lyr.): generally, *distress*, ἐν ἀνάγκαις γλυκὺ γίνεται καὶ τὸ σκληρόν Simon.226; freq. in Lxx, *Jb.*15.24, al.; ἡ ἐνεστῶσα ἀ. 1*Ep.Cor.*7.26: esp. in pl., *IG*12(7).386.23 (Amorgos, iii B.C.), D.S.4.43, 2*Ep.Cor.*6.4, etc. **II.** *tie of blood, kindred*, Lys.32.5. **III.** = ἡ δικαστικὴ κλεψύδρα, Hsch.

ἀναγκό-δακρυς, υ, *shedding forced tears*, A.*Fr.*172A. **-θέτησις**, εως, ἡ, *compulsion*, coined by Oenom.ap.Eus.*PE*6.7 as a parody on νομοθέτησις. **-μόναρχος**· ὁ τύραννος, Hsch. **-πέδη**, ἡ, *fetter*, *PMag. Par.*1.2131. **-σῖτος**, ον, *eating perforce*, i.e. *getting what one can*, epith. of parasites, Crates Com.44, Nicostr.Com.32. **-τροφέω**, (τρέφω) *eat perforce*: hence, *eat by regimen, not after one's own appetite*, like athletes, Epict.*Ench.*29.2. **-φᾰγέω**, = ἀναγκοτροφέω, Arr. *Epict.*3.15.3, Philostr.*VS*2.17: metaph., *stomach*, ἀ. τὰ πράγματα Theopomp.Hist.282, Philostr.*Gym.*44. **-φᾰγία**, ἡ, *strict diet*, of athletes, Arist.*Pol.*1339^{a}6, Them.*Or.*15.185d. **-φορέω**, *bear on compulsion*, apptly. f.l. for -φαγ-, ἀ. τὰ δεινά D.H.10.16.

ἀνάγκῠλος, ον, *without thong* (ἀγκύλη), of a javelin, D.S.3.8.

ἀναγλῠκαίνω, *sweeten*:—Pass., *become sweet*, Thphr.*CP*3.22.3.

ἀνάγλ-υπτος, ον, = ἀνάγλυφος, γρῦπες *SIG*996.10 (Smyrna), cf. Plin.*HN*33.139, Mart.4.39.8. **-υφή**, ἡ, *work in low relief*, Aristeas 58, Str.17.1.28. **2.** *scooped out cavity*, καλάμου Herophil. ap.Gal.2.731. **-ῠφος**, ον, *wrought in low relief*, ἀνδριάντες Ps.-Callisth.3.28; ἱστορίαι *AP*3 tit.: ἀνάγλυφα, τά, Lxx 3*Ki.*6.18. **-ύφω**, aor. -έγλυψα, *carve in relief*, Keil-Premerstein *Dritter Bericht* No.37 (Lydia, i A.D.), J.*AJ*12.2.9, Gal.*UP*16.11: plpf. Pass. ἀναγέγλυπτο J.*AJ*12.2.10.

ἀναγνάμπτω, *bend back*, αἰχμὴ ἀνεγνάμφθη the spear-point *was bent back*, Il.3.348, 7.259, etc. **2.** *undo, loose*, δεσμὸν μὲν ἀνέγναμψαν θεοὶ αὐτοί Od.14.348.

ἀναγν-εία, ἡ, (ἀγνεύω) *abominable wickedness*, Lxx 2*Ma.*4.13. **-ιστος**, ον, *unpurified, unexpiated*, Orph.*A.*1231. **-ος**, ον, *unclean, unholy, defiled*, A.*Ag.*220, *Ch.*994, S.*OT*823; ἄ. καὶ μιαρός Antipho 2.1.10; ἀ. ἀγνεία Ph.1.156. Adv. -νως Id.1.2, Poll.1.32.

ἀνάγνωμα, v. ἀνάγνωσμα.

ἀναγνωρ-ίζω, *recognize*, Pl.*Plt.*258a, *Prm.*127a, al.:—Med., Apollod.3.5.5: Pass., Lxx *Ge.*45.1. **2.** in a tragedy, *recognize* or *come to the knowledge* of a person or thing, so as to produce a *dénouement*, Arist.*Po.*1452^{a}36, al. **b.** *reveal oneself, make oneself known*, ib.1452^{b}5, al. **c.** causal, *cause to recognize, reveal oneself to*, D.S.4.59. **3.** *recognize* a rule in a new instance, Arist.*APr.*67^{a}24. **-ισις**, εως, ἡ, *recognition*, Pl.*Tht.*193c. **2.** in Tragedy, *recognition*, as leading to the *dénouement* (cf. foreg. 2), Arist.*Po.*1452^{a}29, 1454^{b}19. **-ισμα**, ατος, τό, = foreg., Hp.*Flat.*14:—pl. -ίσματα, τά, *tokens of recognition*, Lat. *crepundia*, Charis.p.55 K. **-ισμός**, ὁ, = ἀναγνώρισις, Arist.*Po.*1452^{a}16, Men.*Epit.*581, Hld.7.7. **-ιστικός**, ή, όν, *contributing to recognition*, Sch.Luc.*Laps.*5.

ἀναγν-ωσείω, Desiderat. of ἀναγιγνώσκω, *wish to read*, *Gloss.* **-ωσις**, εως, ἡ, *recognition*, Hdt.1.116. **2.** *reading*, Pl.*Euthd.*279e, Arist.*Po.*1462^{a}17 (prob. l.), *Rh.*1414^{a}18, etc.: pl., Aristeas 283. **b.** *reading aloud*, Hp.*Vict.*2.61, Sor.1.49, *Act.Ap.*13.15, *SIG*959.8 (Chios), D.T.642.11: in pl., *public readings*, Pl.*Lg.*810e; -ώσεις τῷ θεῷ ποιούμενος *BCH*31.351 (Delos). **II.** Gramm., in textual criticism, *reading*, ἡ Ἀρισταρχειος ἀ. A.D.*Synt.*164.2. **III.** = πραγματεία, Olymp.*in Mete.*3.34. **IV.** *persuasion*, Suid. (misunderstanding Hdt.1.116). **-ωσμα**, ατος, τό, *reading*, in concrete, of a book, etc., *read*, D.H.1.8, Luc.*VH*1.2, Plu.2.328d, Orib.*Fr.*67 (pl.). **II.** = ἀνάγνωσις II, A.D.*Synt.*122.8, al. **-ωστέον**, *one must read*, Ph.1.200, D.T.642.12, Gal.18(2).235, Sch.E.*Andr.*1044. **-ωστήριον**, τό, *lectern, reading-desk*, Hsch. **-ώστης**, ου, ὁ, *reader, slave trained to read*, Cic.*Att.*1.12, Phld.*Rh.*1.199 S., Corn.Nep.*Att.*13, Plu.*Crass.*2. **II.** *secretary*, τῆς πόλεως *Inscr. Prien.*111.194; γερουσίας *Inscr.Cos*238. **-ωστικός**, ή, όν, *capable of reading, a good reader*, Arr.*Epict.*2.18.2; *fond of reading*, Plu.2.514a. **2.** *suitable for reading*, Arist.*Rh.*1413^{b}12, cf. *PGrenf.*1.14.12. **-ωστος**, f.l. for ἄγνωστος in Call.*Fr.*422 as cited by Eust.743.7, comparing ἀνάεδνος.

ἀνᾰγόρ-ευσις, εως, ἡ, *public proclamation*, Decr.ap.D.18.118; freq. in Inscrr., as *GDI*3502.4 (Cnidus): = Lat. *renuntiatio*, Plu.*Marc.*4, etc. **-ευτος**, ον, *not to be spoken* or *told*, Sch.S.*Tr.*1093. **-εύω**, Aeschin.3.3: impf. ἀνηγόρευον ib.122: fut. -εύσω Plu.*Galb.*21: aor. -ηγόρευσα Docum.ap.D.18.54, *IG*7.4148, Plb.18.29.4:—**Pass.**, aor. -ηγορεύθην X.*Cyn.*1.14, Plu.2.176e: pf. -ηγόρευμαι Id.*Mar.*45:—fut., aor., and pf. in classic authors are mostly supplied by ἀνερῶ, ἀνεῖπον, ἀνείρηκα, also aor. Pass. ἀνερρήθην Aeschin.3.45:—*proclaim publicly*, ib.122, etc.; ἀ. κήρυγμα *make public* proclamation, Plb. l. c.; ἀ. τινὰ αὐτοκράτορα Plu.*Galb.*2:—Pass., *to be proclaimed*, ἀναγορευέσθω νικηφόρος Pl.*Lg.*730d, cf. D.18.319, Aeschin.3.45: = Lat. *renuntiari*, ὕπατος ἀνηγορευμένος Plu.*Mar.*45, cf. 2.470d. **2.** *designate*, ἀ. τινὰς τῶν δήμων *call after* their demes, Arist.*Ath.*21.4:—Pass., φιλοπάτωρ -ευθῆναι X. l. c.

ἀναγραμματ-ίζω, *write the letters of a name in direct and then in reverse order*, *PMag.Leid.W.*3.21 (Pass.), al. **II.** *transpose the letters* of one word so as to form another, Eust.46.2, 488.12 (Pass.); e.g. Ἥρα ἀήρ, ἀρετὴ ἐρατή, Ἀρσινόη ἴον Ἥρας, Πτολεμαῖος ἀπὸ μέλιτος. **-ισμός**, ὁ, *transposition of this kind*, Artem.4.23, Sch.Lyc. p.5 S., Eust.45 fin.

ἀναγραπτ-έον, *one must inscribe*, εὐεργέτην ἀ. τινά Luc.*DMort.*30.2; generally, *one must count among*, Ph.1.299. **-ος**, ον, *recorded*, εὐεργεσία Th.1.129, Procop.Gaz.*Ep.*16; *registered*, εἴς τινας Procop.*Vand.*2.9. **2.** *rendered famous, immortalized*, Him.*Or.*15.5. **II.** *marked with*, c. dat., βασιλείῳ συμβόλῳ, γράμμασιν ἱεροῖς, Hld.4.8, 8.11; *painted*, in a picture, Chor. in *Philol.*54.111.

ἀναγρᾰφ-εύς, έως, ὁ, *recorder*, esp. as title of commissioners appointed to codify laws, *IG*1.61, cf. Lys.30.2, 25. **II.** *registrar of decrees*, *IG*2.192c, cf. 191. **III.** *plan, pattern, design*, *IG*2.1054b 33, Ph.*Bel.*52.42. **-εύω**, *hold office of* ἀναγραφεύς, *IG*14.757 (Naples). **-ή**, ἡ, *inscribing, registering*, of properties, contracts, etc., Pl.*Lg.*850a; συναλλαγμάτων Arist.*Pol.*1322^{b}34; of names of public benefactors, etc., X.*Vect.*3.11; στήλης *IG*2.14c, cf. 227, etc. **2.** ἀ. τῶν νόμων *codification*, Lys.30.25. **3.** Medic., *prescription, formula*, Hp.*Decent.*10; *formula* for a magic ink, *PMag. Leid.V.*12.16. **4.** *record, description*, Plb.3.33.17, Plu.*Per.*2, etc. **5.** *treatise*, Hero *Bel.*73.5: *composition*, τῶν διαλόγων Phld. *Acad.Ind.*p.4 M. **II.** *register*, esp. in pl., *public records*, *GDI*1743.10 (Delph.), Plb.12.11.4, etc.: also ἀ. ἀρχόντων, φιλοσόφων, D.L.1.22, 42; σταθμῶν Str.15.1.11; *copy of decree*, *SIG*622 A8 (Delph., ii B.C.). **2.** *the Sacred Scriptures*, Ph.1.694. **-ιον**, τό, *list, index*, *PAmh.*2.62. **-ω**, contr. **ἀγγράφω** *IG*7.8, *Tab.Heracl.*1.126: (v. γράφω):—*engrave and set up publicly*, of treaties, laws, and public acts, τὰς ξυνθήκας ἐν στήλῃ λιθίνῃ Th.5.47; τὸν Δράκοντος νόμον IG1.61, cf. And.1.82; ἀ. τι ἐς στήλην, εἰς λεύκωμα, etc., Lycurg.117, Lex ap.D.24.23; ἀναγραψάτωσαν τὸ ψήφισμα IG7.303.44; ἀγγραψάτω ib.7.8; register, τὰ συμβόλαια καὶ τὰς κρίσεις πρὸς ἀρχήν τινα Arist. Pol.1321b34 (Pass.):—Med., ἀναγρψάσθαι συνθήκας have them registered, App.Mith.70. 2. of a person, register or record his name, στηλίτην ἀ. τινά Isoc.16.9:—Pass., to be inscribed or ntered in a public register, ἀναγραφῆναι πατρόθεν Hdt.6.14, cf. 8.90; ἀναγράφεσθαι εὐεργέτης to be registered as a benefactor, as was the custom of the Persians, 8.85, cf. Th.1.129: hence generally, μέγιστος εὐεργέτης παρ' ἐμοὶ ἀναγεγράψῃ Pl.Grg.506c, cf. Lys.20.19, X.Vect.3.11: also, to be registered as a state-debtor, Lys.9.7:—generally, Ἄρθμιον ... ἐχθρὸν αὐτῶν ἀνέγραψαν D.9.43; ἐν τοῖς φίλοις -γεγράφθαι D.C.38.44; Εὐβούλου κούρα ἀνεγραφόμαν became his adopted daughter, Epigr.Gr.205 (Halicarn.):—Med., τὴν εὐεργεσίαν ἀνεγραψάμην εἰς ἐμαυτὸν Corp.Herm.1.30. 3. c. acc. rei, ἀ. στήλην set up a pillar with an inscription on it, Lys.30.21. b. Pass., to be registered, of a deed, PRyl.65.4 (i B.C.). II. of an author, write out, place on record, ὅσα ἄμφω ξυνέγραψαν, ταῦτα ἐγὼ ἀναγράφω Arr.An.Praef.1; describe, X.Ep.1.6, Arr.Tact.1.2, Philostr.VA5.37, Eun.VSp.476B. (Pass.); compose, Epicur.Nat.28.5; of the mind, depict, imagine, Philostr.VA6.19, 7.14. 2. record, πράξεις Plb.1.1.1, cf. D.L.1.40, Longin.13.3, etc.; commemorate, τινά Porph.VP2. 3. describe lines and figures mathematically, ἀ. ἀπό.. upon a base, Pl.Men.83b (Med.), cf. Euc.1.47, etc.; ἀ. τὰς τῆς γῆς περιόδους Arist.Mete.350a17; also of lines used as bases, αἱ ἴσα αὐτοῖς τετράγωνα -ουσαι Euc.10Def.4:—Pass., τὸ τετράγωνον τὸ ἀναγραφησόμενον ἀπό.. that can be described upon.., Id.2.14. 4. reduce to a formula or prescription, δυνάμιες ἀναγεγραμμέναι Hp.Decent.9. III. entitle, Λούκουλλος ἀναγέγραπται τὸ βιβλίον Plu.Luc.42. IV. fill up outlines, opp. περιγράφω, Arist. EN1098a22, cf. Philostr.Im.2.17, Alex.Aphr.in Top.444.6.

ἀναγρετόν· ἀνυπόστροφον, Hsch.

ἀναγρία, ἡ, (ἄγρα) time when hunting was forbidden, close season, X.Cyn.5.34.

ἄναγρον ἢ ἄνιγρον· ἐναγές, Hsch.

ἀναγρύζω, strengthd. for γρύζω, to mutter, grunt, ἢν ἀναγρύζῃ Ar. Nu.945: c. neg., σὲ δὲ χρὴ σιγᾶν μηδ' ἀ. Crates Com.1D., cf. X.Oec.2.11.

ἀναγυμν-όω, strip naked, unveil, metaph. in Pass., Dam.Pr.404. **-ωσις**, εως, ἡ, stripping, Simp.in Ph.226.27.

ἀνάγυρος, ὁ, Anagyris foetida, stinking bean-trefoil, Ar.Lys.68:—also **ἀνάγυρις**, ιος (-εως Gal.16.143), ἡ, Dsc.3.150: prov., μὴ κινεῖν τὸν ἀ. 'let sleeping dogs lie', Lib.Ep.78; ὁ ἀ. κεκινῆσθαι δοκεῖ 'the fat is in the fire', Ar. l. c., cf. Sch. ad loc.—From it the Att. deme **Ἀναγυρ-οῦς** took its name, Adv. **-ουντόθεν** from Anagyrus, Ar.Lys.67 (also **-οῦντάδε** to A., **-οῦντι** at A., St.Byz.); Adj. **-άσιος**, ὁ, man of this deme, Ar.Fr.6D., Pl.Thg.127e, etc. [ῡ, Ar.Fr.6D.]

ἀναγχ-ιππέω, to be forced to serve as knight, Eup.394:—Subst. **-ιπποι**, οἱ, Phot.p.109R.

ἀναγχίστευτος, ον, without heirs, CR11.137 (Phryg.).

ἀνάγχω, hang up, choke, strangle, Nic.Th.475.

ἀνάγω, fut. ἀνάξω Hdt.7.10.θ', etc.: aor. 2 ἀνήγαγον, etc.: (v. ἄγω):—opp. κατάγω, I. lead up from a lower place to a higher, ἐς Ὄλυμπον Thgn.1347, E.Ba.289; πρὸς τὸ ὄρος X.An.3.4.28; ἱερὸν ἀ. ξόανον, of the Trojan horse, E.Tr.525; ὁ πέπλος ἀνάγεται εἰς τὴν ἀκρόπολιν Pl.Euthphr.6c. 2. lead up to the high sea, carry by sea, λαὸν ἀνήγαγεν ἐνθάδ' ἀείρας Il.9.338; γυναῖκ' εὐειδέ' ἀνῆγες ἐξ Ἀπίης γαίης 3.48, cf. 6.292; στρατὸν ἐπὶ τὴν Ἑλλάδα Hdt.7.10.θ': but freq. = simple ἄγω, conduct, carry to a place, Il.8.203, Od.3.272; ἀ. ναῦν put a ship to sea, Hdt.6.12, 7.100, etc.; ἀνάγειν abs. in the same sense, Id.3.41, 8.76, cf. D.23.169:—but this is more common in Med., v. infr. B. I. 3. take up from the coast into the interior, Od.14.272; esp. from Asia Minor into Central Asia, ἀ. παρὰ or ὡς βασιλέα Hdt.6.119, X.HG1.4.6, An.2.6.1, etc.; from Piraeus to Athens, Id. HG2.4.8. 4. bring up, esp. from the dead, ἀ. εἰς φάος Hes.Th.626; εἰς φῶς Pl.R.521c, S.Fr.557 (Pass.); τῶν φθιμένων ἀ. A.Ag.1023, cf. E.Alc.985; κλίνει κἀνάγει πάλιν lays low and brings up again, S.Aj.131; ἐκ λεχέων ἀ. φάμαν παλαιάν waken up, revive, renew, Pi.I.4(3).22. 5. ἀ. χορόν conduct the choir, Hes.Sc.280, E.Tr.326, Th.3.104; ἀ. θυσίαν, ὀρτὴν celebrate.., Hdt.2.48,60, al., cf. Act.Ap.7.41; sacrifice, ταύρους OGI764.47 (ii B.C.). 6. lift up, raise, κάρα S.Ph.866; τὸ ὄμμα ἀ. ἄνω Pl.R.533d; ἀ. τὰς ὀφρῦς, = ἀνασπᾶν, Plu.2.975c; ἂν πυκτεύοντες ἀνάγωσιν ἑαυτοὺς Id.2.541b. 7. ἀ. παιᾶνα lift up a paean, S.Tr.210; ἄναγε πολύδακρυν ἀδονάν, of a song of lamentation, E.El.126; κωκυτὸν Ph.1350. 8. ἀ. εἰς τιμὴν raise to honour, Plu.Num.16; τίμιον ἀ. τινά E.HF1333; elevate, οἱ εἰς φιλοσοφίαν ἀνάγοντες [ἀστρονομίαν] Pl.R.529a. 9. in various senses, φάρμακα ἀνάγοντα expectorants, Hp.Morb.3.15; ἀ. ὀδόντας cut teeth, Id.Aph.3.25; ἀ. πλῆθος αἵματος bring up blood, Plu.Cleom.30; ἀ. μηρυκισμόν chew the cud, Lxx Le.11.3, al.; τὸν Νεῖλον ἀναγέτω bring the Nile up [over its banks], Luc.DDeor.3; ἀ. φάλαγγα deploy, Plu.Crass.23: Geom., draw a line, Arist.Metaph.1051a25; ἀ. τεταγμένως erect as an ordinate, Apollon.Perg.Con.2.49; in building, carry a line of works to a point, Plu.Nic.18: ἀ. ὕδωρ distil, Syn.Alch.p.66B. 10. μύρια τάλαντ' εἰς τὴν ἀκρόπολιν ἀνήγαγον, i.e. paid them into the treasury there, D.3.24. 11. bring up a prisoner for examination, X.HG3.3.11, OGI483.185 (Pergam.), Plb.40.4.2, Act.Ap.12.4. 12. train, rear, θετὸν υἱόν AP9.254 (Phil.):—Pass., εἰς μέτρα ἥβης ἀνηγόμην IG12(7).449 (Amorgos); of plants, ἀ. ἀμπελῶνας S.(?)Fr.1010. II. bring back, ἀνήγαγον αὖθις Ἄργος ἐς ἱππόβοτον Il.15.29, cf. Od.24.401, Pi.P.5.3, etc. 2. τὸν λόγον ἐπ' ἀρχὴν ἀ. carry back, refer to its principles, Pl.Lg.626d; εἰς ἄλλας ἀρχὰς Arist. EN1113b20; εἰς αὐτὸν τὴν ἀρχὴν 1113a6, cf. GA778b1, al.; εἰς γνωριμώτερον Metaph.1040b20; generally, refer, πάντα τοῖς λογισμοῖς εἰς ἀσφάλειαν Plu.Brut.12; εἰς κοινὸν ὄνομα A.D.Synt.266.13; freq. in Pass., ἀνάγομαι εἴς τι Procl.Inst.21; ὑπό τι Olymp.in Mete.326.33; ἀπό, ἔκ τινος to be derived from, A.D.Adv.121.25, Synt.23.26; ἀ. ἀπό, ἐξ.. derive one's subsistence from.., Vett.Val.10.15, 73.11. 3. ἀ. τι εἰς τὸν δῆμον, Arist.Pol.1292a25; of persons, ἀ. τινὰ ἐπὶ τὴν συγγραφήν refer him to the contract, D.56.31. 4. reduce syllogism to another figure, Arist.APr.29b1; reduce an argument to syllogism, ib.46b40, al. 5. in Law, return a slave sold with an undisclosed defect, εἰς πρατῆρα Pl.Lg.915c, cf. Hyp.Ath.15. 6. refer a claimant, πράτορι ἢ εἰς πόλιν ἔνδικον Milet.3 No.140.42: abs., ὁ ἔχων ἀναγέτω Foed.Delph.Pell.2A15; ἀ. ὅθεν εἴληφας D.45.81. 7. rebuild, Plu.Publ.15, Cam.32. 8. restore to its original shape, Parth.Ep.Dedic.; τάφρον PHal.1.5. 9. reckon, calculate, ἀ. τὰς ἡμέρας πρὸς τὸ μαντεῖον Plu.Cim.18; χρόνον ἐκ τῶν Ὀλυμπιονικῶν Num.1. 10. intr. (sc. ἑαυτόν), withdraw, X.Cyr.7.1.45, etc.; ἐπὶ πόδα ἀ. retreat facing enemy, 3.3.69; ἀ. ἐπὶ σκέλος Ar.Av.383: metaph., ἄναγε εἰς τοὐπίσω, perh. nautical, put back again, Pl.R.528a.

B. Med. and Pass., put out to sea, set sail (v. supr. I. 2), Il.1.478, Hdt.3.137, etc.: fut. ἀνάξεσθαι Th.6.30, etc.; ἀναχθέντες Hdt.3.138, 4.152, cf. A.Ag.626. 2. metaph., put to sea, i.e. make ready, prepare oneself, ὡς ἐρωτήσων Pl.Chrm.155d, cf. Erx.392d. 3. in thought, ascend to higher unity, Dam.Pr.117.

ἀναγ-ωγεύς, έως, ὁ, one that brings up from below, ψυχῶν ἀ. Procl. H.1.34. II. strap for holding a shield, Eust.995.26: in pl., straps which keep up the sandal round the foot, Ael.VH9.11, Ath.12.543f. **-ωγή**, ἡ, leading up, esp. taking a ship into the high sea, putting to sea, ἀ. γίγνεται Th.6.30, X.HG1.6.28. b. bringing upstream, of a ship, OGI56.51 (Egypt, iii B.C.). 2. bringing up from the stomach or lungs, πτυάλου ἀ. expectoration, Hp.Acut.54, cf. 58; σιτίων ἀπέπτων ἀ. vomiting, Epid.1.5; φάρμακα τῆς ἀ. expectorants, Morb.3.15; αἵματος Erasistr.ap.Gal.Libr.Propr.1, Plb.2.70.6. 3. bringing up, rearing, φυτῶν Thphr.CP3.7.4. 4. lifting up of the soul to God, Iamb.Myst.3.7; ἡ πρὸς τὸ πρῶτον ἀ. Porph.Sent.30, cf. Eun. VSp.482B. 5. evocation, Σεμέλης Plu.2.293d. 6. sublimation, αἰθαλῶν Zos.Alch.p.141B.; distillation, ὕδατος ibid. II. referring to a principle, Arist.Metaph.1005a1; of phenomena to a cause, 1027b14: generally, ἀ. πρός τι ποιεῖσθαι Epicur.Sent.23; ἐπὶ τὸ κοινωνικὸν τέλος M.Ant.12.20. 2. resolution of definitions into syllogisms, Arist.APo.90a37. 3. reference to a principle, Id. Metaph.1027b14. 4. return of a defective slave to vendor (cf. ἀνάγω A.II.5), ἀ. ἔστω Pl.Lg.916a; ἀναγωγὴν ποιεῖσθαι ib.b; ἀναγωγῆς τυχεῖν ib.a, cf. Hyp.Ath.15. 5. reference of a claimant to a third party, Foed.Delph.Pell.2A17. 6. delivery, payment, γενημάτων PTeb.24.56 (ii B.C.); φόρων Philostr.VS2.12.2 codd. 7. ἀναγωγαί, αἱ, = sq., Ath.9.395a. **-ώγια** (sc. ἱερά), τά, offerings made on embarkation, a feast of Aphrodite at Eryx, Ael.VH1.15. **-ωγία**, ἡ, (ἀ- priv., ἀγωγή) want of discipline, dissoluteness, corruption, Plb.7.10.5, D.Chr.51.7, Eun.Hist.p.244D. 2. lack of breeding, vulgarity, Plu.2.1065c, Demetr.Eloc.171; unpleasantness, E.Ep.5.2. **-ώγιος**, ον, raising the mind to heavenly things, mystical, κέντρα, πῦρ, Procl.H.2.5, 4.2. II. ἀναγώγιον, τό, reward for restoration of a fugitive slave, σώματος Milet.3 No.150.97. **-ωγός**, όν, bringing up, eliciting, πτυάλου Hp.Acut.58. 2. raising or conveying up, ἡ διὰ τοῦ πυρὸς προσαγωγὴ τῶν θυσιῶν ἀ. ἐπὶ τὸ οὐράνιον πῦρ Iamb.Myst.5.11. b. uplifting the soul, elevating, θεός Jul.Or.5.173c, cf. Iamb.Myst.2.6, Syrian.in Metaph.14.36, Procl.Inst.158; σωτηρία Dam.Isid.232; ἀ. τοῦ τρίτου εἰς τὸ πρῶτον Id.Pr.75.

ἀν-άγωγος, ον, ill-bred, Timo 51 (Sup.), Plu.2.147f; καύχησις Phld.Vit.p.27J.; ἀ. καὶ ἀπαίδευτος τρόπος D.S.34/5.2.35; tasteless, σκώμματα Longin.34.2; ῥητορική D.H.Orat.Vett.1; unlearned, Plb.12.25.6; dissolute, περὶ τὰς ἡδονὰς Plu.2.140b; of horses and dogs, ill-broken, unmanageable, X.Mem.3.3.4, 4.1.3, prob. l. in Arist.Ath.49.1. Adv. -γως Macho ap.Ath.13.580e, Lxx 2Ma.12.14 (Comp.); inerudite et ἀ. Tiro ap.Gell.6.3.12.

ἀναγων-ίατος, ον, free from anxiety, PTeb.58.51 (ii B.C.). **-ιστος**, ον, without contest or conflict, ἀ. ἀπιέναι Th.4.92 (v.l.); never having contended for a prize, X.Cyr.1.5.10; ἀ. περὶ τῆς ἀρετῆς failing in the race of virtue, Pl.Lg.845c.

ἀναδαιμονίζειν· τὸ ἐκ δευτέρου κληροῦσθαι, Hsch.

ἀναδαίομαι, v. ἀναδατέομαι.

ἀναδαίω, poet. ἀνδαίω, light up, φλογὸς μέγαν πώγωνα A.Ag.305:—Pass., metaph., ἀνεδαίετο κερτομίη A.R.4.1726.

ἀναδάκνω, stimulate, of salt applied to roots, Thphr.CP3.17.4; ἀ. τὴν κατάποσιν Xenocr.25: generally, irritate, Ruf.ap.Orib.8.39.3, Hippiatr.33; ἀ. σφοδρῶς Dsc.5.136.

ἀναδαρδαίνω, aor. ἀνεδάρδανα, = ἀναμολύνω, Hsch.

ἀναδάρσασθαι, aor. inf. of ἀναδατέομαι.

ἀναδάσ-ιμος, ον, to be distributed afresh, Sch.Ven.Il.1.300. **-μός**, ὁ, redistribution, partition of land, among colonists, Hdt.4.159,163; as a revolutionary measure, freq. coupled with χρεῶν ἀποκοπαί, Pl.R.566a, D.17.15, Jusj.ap.eund.24.149, SIG526.22 (Itanos). **-τος**, ον, divided anew, redistributed, ἀ. γῆν ποιεῖν Pl.Lg.843b; ἀ. ποιεῖν τὴν χώραν Arist.Pol.1307a2; τὰς οὐσίας ἀ. ποιεῖν 1305a5, cf. 1309a15. II. later, ἀ. ποιεῖν τι undo, rescind, OGI669.20 (Egypt, i A.D.),

Luc.*Abd.*11. III. Adv. -τως· ἀνωμάλως ἔχων τις τοῦ σώματος, Hsch.

ἀναδατέομαι, *divide anew, redistribute*, ὁ δῆμος τὴν γῆν ἐπενόει ἀναδάσασθαι Th.5.4 :—Pass., ἀναδαίομαι *to be distributed*, Orac.ap. Hdt.4.159 : aor. -δασθείς Plu.*Agis* 8.

ἀνά-δειγμα, ατος, τό, *image for show*, Hsch. 2. *mouthpiece worn by public criers* to serve the purpose of a speaking-trumpet, Epigr.ap.Poll.4.92, Hsch. -**δείκνῦμι**, also -ύω Plu.2.417e: Ion. aor. -έδεξα Hdt. (v. infr.): pf. -δέδειχα Plb.21.21.3 : (v. δείκνυμι) :—*lift up and show, exhibit, display*, πύλας ἀναδεικνύναι *display by opening* gates, i.e. *throw wide* the gates, S.*El.*1458 ; μυστοδόκος δόμος ἀναδείκνυται Ar.*Nu.*304 ; ἀναδέξαι ἀσπίδα *hold* up shield *as signal*, Hdt.6.115,121sq.; ἀνέδεξε σημήιον τοῖς ἄλλοις ἀνάγεσθαι *made* signal for them to put to sea, Id.7.128 ; [Μίλητος] Θαλῆν ἀ., on a statue, Epigr.ap.D.L.1.34. II. *notify*, esp. *proclaim* any one as elected to office, αὐτὸν ἀναδεδειχὼς βασιλέα Plb.4.48.3 ; ἀ. τινὰ μέγιστον *make* him the greatest man, 22.4.3 ; ἀνέδειξεν ἑτέρους ἑβδομήκοντα *Ev.Luc.*10.1 :—Pass., ἀναδεδεῖχθαι τὸ ἱερὸν ἄσυλον *SIG*630.23 (Delph., ii B.C.). 2. *dedicate*, τῷ Διὶ ταῦρον *SIG*589.6 (Magn. Mae., ii B.C.) ; τὴν Πιερίδα ταῖς θεαῖς Str.9.2.25 ; θέατρον Plu. *Pomp.*52 ; ἱερά *AP*9.340. 3. ἀ. πόλεμον *declare* war, *SIG*742.12 (Ephesus, i B.C.). -**δειξις**, εως, ἡ, *showing forth*: esp. *public proclamation* or *appointment* to an office, ἡ τῶν ὑπάτων ἀ. Plu.*Mar.*8 ; τῶν συναρχόντων ἡ ἀναγόρευσις καὶ ἀ. *CG*12 : abs., ἡ ἀ. *the election*, *Cat.Mi.*44, 46. 2. ἡ ἀ. τοῦ διαδήματος *ceremony* of coronation, Plb.15.25.11 (pl.) ; *dedication* of temple, Str.8.6.23. 3. *declaration*, χρόνων Lxx *Si.*43.6. II. (from Pass.) *manifestation*, of Osiris, D.S.1.85, but rather from Act. in ἡ ἀ. αὐτοῦ πρὸς τὸν Ἰσραήλ *Ev.Luc.*1.80.

ἀναδεῖπνια, τά, *second supper*, or *second course at supper*, ascribed to Lycians by Eust.1141.14.

ἀναδέκ-ομαι, Ion. for ἀναδέχομαι. -**τέον**, *one must take back*, Hyp.*Ath.*15. -**τικός**, ή, όν, *fitted for receiving*, S.E.*M.*7.355.

ἀνάδελφος, ον, *without brother* or *sister*, E.*Or.*310, Ph.2.291, Vett. Val.15.6, etc.

ἀνάδεμα, poet. ἄνδεμα, ατος, τό, = ἀνάδημα, *IG*5(1).1390.22 (Andania, i B.C.), *AP*7.423 (Antip.).

ἀναδέμω, *block by building up*, πύλας Aen.Tact.23.4. II. Med., *build up again*, J.*BJ*2.20.6 ; simply, *build up*, Ph.1.317,324.

ἀναδενδρ-αδικός, ή, όν, *for* ἀναδενδράδες, ἀμπελὼν *PSI*6.697 (ii A.D.), prob. in *BGU*1279 (iii B.C.). -**άς**, άδος, ἡ, *vine that grows up trees*, Pherecr.109, D.53.15, Thphr.*CP*1.10.4, 3.10.8, Chrysipp. *Stoic.*3.180, Aesop.33. 2. = σκιάς, Hsch. -**ίτης** [ῑ] οἶνος, ὁ, wine *from the* ἀναδενδράς, Plb.34.11.1 :—fem. -ῖτις ἄμπελος *Gp.*5.51.1. -**ομαλάχη**, ἡ, *hollyhock*, *Alcea rosea*, Gal.10.960, Orib.14.38.13, cf. 15.1.4.

ἀναδέξαι, v. ἀναδείκνυμι.

ἀναδέρκομαι, Dep., *look up*, aor. 2 Act. ἀνέδρακεν ὀφθαλμοῖσιν, of one who recovers from fainting, Il.14.436, cf. A.R.3.1010.

ἀναδέρω, poet. ἀνδ–, *strip a scab off*, ψῆκτρᾳ *Hippiatr.*68 ; *expose, lay bare*, in dissection, Gal.2.719 ; *strip off*, τὸν φλοιόν *Gp.*10.18.10 ; ἀνδέροντι πόδας *strip skin off* the feet, Pi.*Fr.*203 :—Pass., ἀναδαρέντα μέρεα Aret.*CD*2.13 ; ἀναδέρεται ἡ ἕλκωσις Antyll.ap.Aët.9.40. 2. metaph., *lay bare, expose*, ἀνά ⟨τε⟩ δέρετον τά τε παλαιὰ καὶ τὰ καινά Ar.*Ra.*1106 (al. -δέρεσθον), cf. Luc.*Pseudol.*20 :—Med., ἠρώτα δ' ὑπὲρ αὐτῶν οὐδέν, ὡς μὴ ἀναδέροιτο Philostr.*VS*1.25.3.

ἀνάδεσ-ις, εως, ἡ, *binding on*, στεφάνων Plu.*Sert.*22. 2. *binding up*, or *decking*, κόμης Luc.*JTr.*33. -**μεύω**, *tie up, suspend*, ἔκ τινος D.S.18.42, cf. Mnesith.Cyz.ap.Orib.*Inc.*15.16 :—also -**μέω**, κλήματα πρὸς χάρακας *Gp.*4.7.3, cf. Sch.A.*Pers.*191 : metaph., of religious scruples or *taboos*, Lyd.*Ost.*16. -**μη**, ἡ, *band for women's hair, snood*, πλεκτὴ ἀ. Il.22.469, cf. *AP*5.275 (Agath.), E.*Med.*978 Porson. -**μος**, ὁ, = foreg., *APl.*4.134 (Mel.) ; *bandage* for female breast, Heliod.ap.Orib.48.50 tit.

ἀνάδετος, ον, *binding up* hair, μίτραι E.*Hec.*923. 2. in pass. sense, πῶλον Χαρίτων μίτραις ἀνάδετον Him.*Ecl.*13.36.

ἀναδεύω, *soak, steep*, Thphr.*HP*9.13.3 : metaph., ἤθεσι ἀ. τοὺς νόμους *imbue* them with moral principle, Plu.*Comp.Lyc.Num.*4, cf. Max.Tyr.10.6 : fut. ἀναδεύσομαι in pass. sense, Gal.10.867 2. *mix into a paste*, οἴνῳ καὶ μέλιτι Phylarch.26, cf. Plu.2.997a.

ἀναδέχομαι, fut. -δέξομαι : aor. ἀνεδεξάμην, Ep. aor. ἀνεδέγμην (v. infr.): pf. Pass. ἀναδέδεγμαι :—*take up, catch, receive*, σάκος δ' ἀνεδέξατο πολλά (sc. δόρατα) Il.5.619 ; ἀ. πληγὰς εἰς τὸ σῶμα Plu. *Tim.*4 ; βέλη τῷ σώματι *Marc.*10. 2. *receive, entertain* as a guest, *Act.Ap.*28.7. II. *take upon oneself, submit to*, ἀνεδέγμεθ' ὀϊζύν Od.17.563, cf. Archil.60 ; ἁμαρτήματα D.19.36 ; πόλεμον Plb.1.88.12 ; ἀπέχθειαν Plu.*Eum.*6 ; ἀ. τι ἐφ' ἑαυτόν D.22.64, cf. Din.1.3 : abs., *acknowledge* one's evidence, of an absent witness, D.46.7. 2. *accept, receive*, ἀγγελίαν Pi.*P.*2.41 (al. -δεῖξατ') ; λουτρὰ . . μητρὸς ἀνεδέξω πάρα E.*IT*818 ; χορηγίας, ἡγεμονίαν, Plu.*Arist.*1,23 ; τὸν κλῆρον *Cic.*43 ; τῶν σωμάτων τὰ μανὰ ἀ. θερμότητα *Cat.Mi.*61 (dub.) ; *accept* a statement, Them.*in Ph.*77.8. 3. *admit of*, κλίσιν, ἀριθμόν A.D. *Pron.*29.9, al. ; σχέσιν πρός τι Procl.*Inst.*122. 4. *undertake* to say or do, c. fut. inf., Hdt.5.91, X.*Cyr.*6.1.17, etc. : c. aor. inf., Plu. *Arist.*14. b. *undertake*, c. acc., S.*Ichn.*157 ; ὅσα ὑπισχνεῖτο καὶ ἀνεδέχετο D.35.7 ; *take upon oneself*, αἰτίαν Pl.*Hp.Mi.*365d ; πρεσβείας, κινδύνους, *OGI*339.20 (Sestos, ii B.C.), 441.9 (Stratonicea, i B.C.). 5. *give security to one*, τινί Th.8.81 ; τινί τι Plb.11.25.9 ; *go bail for*, τινά Thphr.*Char.*12.4 ; τινὰ τῶν χρημάτων Plb.5.16.8 ; ἀ. τοὺς δανειστὰς *undertake to satisfy* them, Plu.*Caes.*11 ; ἀ. τὴν πίστιν ὑπέρ τινος Id.*Phoc.*14 : abs., *Leg.Gort.*9.24,41. 6. *take back*, D.59.58. 7. *experience, suffer*, πάθος, ταραχάς, Phld.*Ir.*p.82 W., *D.*1.13 ; σῆψιν Aët.13.3. III. *wait for*, Plb.1.52.8.

ἀναδέω, poet. ἀνδέω, Att. contr. part. ἀναδῶν (infr. I. 2) : fut. -δήσω : aor. ἀνέδησα (v. infr.) : pf. ἀναδέδεκα Nic.Dam.p.113 D. :—Med. and Pass., Att. contr. ἀναδοῦνται, ἀναδούμενος (infr. I. 2, III) :—Pass., pf. -δέδεμαι :—*bind, tie up, wreath*, δάφνᾳ κόμας ἀναδήσαντες Pi.*P.*10.40 ; στέφανοι ἀνέδησαν ἔθειραν *I.*5(4).9 :—Med., ἀναδέεσθαι τὰς κεφαλὰς μίτρῃσι *bind their* heads . ., Hdt.1.195 ; ἀνδησάμενος κόμαν *having wreathed one's* hair, Pi.*N.*11.28, cf. *I.*1.28 :—so in Pass., μίτρᾳ ἀναδεδεμένος τὴν κόμην Luc.*DDeor.*18.1 ; κρωβύλον ἀναδεῖσθαι τῶν τριχῶν *bind one's* hair into a knot, Th.1.6 ; στέμμ' ἀναδησάμενος *having bound his brows* with the fillet, *Epigr.Gr.*873.4 (Cyrene) ; τίς τοσάσδε . . ἀνεδήσατο νίκας ; who *has won* so many *crowns of* victory ? Simon.10 : metaph., τὴν ἀρχήν App.*BC*1.84 ; κλέος, κράτος, Procop.*Vand.*2.27, *Pers.*1.14 ; ἆθλον Chor.*Zach.*6.9. 2. c. acc. pers., *crown*, τινὰ στεφάνοις Pi.*P.*2.6 ; λήροις (Com. for στεφάνοις) ἀναδῶν τοὺς νικῶντας Ar.*Pl.*589 ; ἀ. τινὰ εὐαγγέλια *crown* him for good tidings, 764 ; τὸν ἡνίοχον Th.5.50 :—metaph. in Pass., τροφῇ τε καὶ τοῖς ἄλλοις πᾶσιν, ὅσων βίος δεῖται, ἀναδοῦνται *are well furnished with* . ., Pl.*R.*465d. II. ἀναδῆσαι τὴν πατριὴν ἐς ἑκκαιδέκατον θεόν *trace* one's family to a god in the sixteenth generation, Hdt.2.143. III. Med., *fasten by a rope to oneself*, ὤνευον ἀναδούμενοι τοὺς σταυρούς Th.7.25 ; esp. of a ship, ἀναδούμενος ἕλκειν *take in tow*, 1.50, 2.90, etc. : metaph., ἀναδεῖσθαί τινας *attach* them *to oneself*, Aristid. *Or.*46(3).25, Ael.*VH*4.9, Luc.*Im.*1 ; ἀπὸ τῶν ὤτων τινὰ ἀναδησάμενος Id.*Scyth.*11 ; ἀναδεῖσθαί τι ἔκ τινος *make dependent* upon . ., Plu.2.222e ; ἐκ τοῦ φιλοκάλου μάλιστα τῆς ψυχῆς ἀναδούμενος τὴν πίστιν 343a :—Pass., ἀναδεδέσθαι ἔκ τινος, εἰς τὴν ὀροφήν, Id.*Dio* 26, *Eum.*11.

ἀνάδηγμα, ατος, τό, *bite*, κωνώπων Hp.*Epid.*2.3.1.

ἀνάδηλος, ον, *evident*, Phld.*Rh.*2.246 S.

ἀνάδημα, poet. ἄνδημα, ατος τό, = ἀνάδεσμη, Pi.*Fr.*179, E.*Hipp.*83, *El.*882, *IG*2.758*B* ; ἀ. χρυσοῦν Pl.Com.178 ; βασιλέων ἀ. Aristid. *Or.*19(41).4.

ἀνάδηξις, εως, ἡ, lit. *biting*: hence in Thphr.*CP*3.17.5 of *the stimulating effect* of certain manures.

ἀνάδησις, εως, ἡ, = ἀνάδεσις, Paul.Aeg.3.59.

ἀνα-δῐδακτέον, *one must teach otherwise* or *better*, Ph.1.162. -**δῐδάσκω**, *teach otherwise* or *better*, ἀ. ὡς . . Hdt.4.95 ; τινά τι Luc.*Pseudol.*13 ; simply, *instruct, inform*, Th.1.32, al., Ar.*Pl.*563, etc. :—Pass., *to be better instructed*, ὅτι . . Pl.*Hp.Ma.*301e ; *learn better things, change one's mind*, Hdt.8.63 (dub.) ; *learn anew* or *from the beginning*, J.*AJ* 2.9.1. II. ἀ. δρᾶμα *produce* play *a second time*, *Vit.Aesch.*, Arg. 1 Ar.*Ra.*, Philostr.*VA*6.11. 2. *explain*, ἐν οὐκ ἀναδιδάσκει σε τῶν λογίων Ar.*Eq.*1045.

ἀναδιδράσκω, *run away again*, Plb.29.19.1 (dub.).

ἀναδίδωμι, poet. ἀνδ– : fut. -δώσω, etc. :—*give up, hold up and give*, φιάλαν Pi.*I.*6(5).39, X.*Smp.*2.8. 2. *deliver*, ἐπιστολάς Plb.29.10.7, D.S.11.45, cf. *IG*14.830 ; ψήφισμα *OGI*437.78 (Pergam., i B.C.). II. *give forth, send up*, esp. of the earth, *yield*, καρπόν Plu.*Cam.*15, cf. Hp.*Aër.*12, E.*Fr.*484.4 ; ὡραῖα Th.3.58. 2. *send up*, Φερσεφόνα . . ἀνδιδοῖ ψυχὰς πάλιν Pi.*Fr.*133.3. 3. of a river, ἀ. θρόμβους ἀσφάλτου Hdt.1.179 ; of a volcano, ἀ. πῦρ καὶ καπνόν Th.3.88, etc. ; ἀ. εὐωδίαν Plu.2.645f, cf. Thphr.*Sud.*10. 4. intr., of springs, fire, etc., *burst, issue forth*, Hdt.7.26, Arist.*Mete.*351^{a}15 (also Pass., τὰ ἐν ἄντροις ἀναδιδόμενα ὕδατα Porph.*Antr.*6). 5. *send up to* higher authority, *present* by name, *PFay.*26.13 (ii A.D.), etc. b. Math., in Pass., *to be given*, of elements in calculation, Vett.Val.21.1. III. *deal round, distribute, impart*, διαβούλιον τοῖς φίλοις Plb.5.58.2 ; of one person, τὴν πρᾶξίν τινι 8.17.2 ; τοῖς λόχοις τὰς ψήφους D.H.10.57, cf. Plu.*TG*11, etc. ; ἀ. φήμην *spread* it, Id.*Aem.*25 :—Pass., ἀνεδίδοντο χρυσοῖ στέφανοι Posidon.17. 2. Medic., *distribute* food, juices, etc., throughout the body, Philotim. ap.Orib.2.69.9, al. : esp. in Pass., Dieuch.ib.4.7.1, Phld.*D.*3.14 ; πέττεσθαί τε καὶ ἀναδίδοσθαι Gal.15.457, cf. 6.650, Porph.*Abst.*1.47. IV. Med., *sell*, Arist.*Fr.*558 (prob. f.l. for ἀποδόσθαι). V. in Gramm., ἀ. τὸν τόνον *throw back* accent, *EM*739.22, Sch.Ven.Il.5.182. VI. intr., *go backwards, retrograde* (cf. ἐπιδίδωμι), Arist. *Rh.*1390^{b}28.

ἀναδῐκ-άζω, *decide again, hear on appeal*, τὰ γνωσθέντα Ph.1.299 : abs., *reverse a decision*, *AP*5.221 (Agath.). II. Med., *renew an action after a previous judgement had been cancelled*, Is.*Fr.*145. -**εῖν**, defect. aor., *throw back*, Ep. 3 sg. ἄνδικε *AB*394. -**έω**, *appeal for rehearing of a case*, *PLille*29.4. -**ία**, ἡ, *renewal of an action*, Lys. *Fr.*298 S. -**ος** (Arc. ὄνδικος *IG*5(2).343*B*2), ον, *tried over again*, δίκαι ἀ. γίγνονται And.1.88, Pl.*Lg.*937d, cf. D.40.39, etc. ; ψῆφον ἀ. καθιστάναι render *subject to appeal*, Id.24.191.

ἀναδῑν-εύω, *whirl about*, Opp.*H.*3.296. -**έω**, intr., of the eyes, *roll*, Hp.*Mul.*1.36 :—also **ἀναδινίω**· περιπατῶ, and **ἄνδινος**· περίπατος, Hsch.

ἀναδιπλασι-άζω, *reduplicate*, Choerob. *in Theod.*p.75 H. : Rhet., *repeat*, Anon.*Fig.*p.160 S. -**ασμός**, ὁ, *reduplication*, *EM*45.45, 55.26.

ἀναδιπλ-όω, *double, fold*, Sor.1.84 :—Pass., *to be made double*, φάλαγξ βραχυτέρα ἐγίγνετο ἀναδιπλουμένη *being made twice as* deep, X.*Cyr.*7.5.5. 2. Gramm., of a word or syllable, *reduplicate*, Phryn.*PS*p.32 B. :—Pass., Trypho *Fr.*21, cf. *EM*98.38. 3. Rhet., *repeat*, Phoeb.*Fig.*2.4. -**ωσις**, εως, ἡ, *convolution*, τοῦ ἐντέρου Arist. *HA*508^{b}13, *PA*675^{b}2. 2. *repetition, duplication*, Ph.2.56, Phlp. *in*

Mete.103.37; esp. in Rhet. (cf. ἐπαναδίπλωσις), Demetr.Eloc.66, al., Alex.Fig.2.2, etc. 3. Medic., double infection, in malarial fevers, etc., Gal.7.369, al., cf. Alex.Trall.Febr.2. 4. Gramm., reduplication, Trypho Fr.12.

ἀναδῐφάω, grope after, Cratin.2.

ἀναδιχότομος φάσις last quarter of the moon, Cat.Cod.Astr.8(4).205.

ἀναδοιδῡκίζω, stir up, EM96.7, Hsch.

ἀνάδομα, ατος, τό, product of digestion, cj. in Plu.2.384a (pl.).

ἀνα-δομέω, rebuild, Agath.2.17:—Med., 5.9:—Pass., 2.15. **-δομή**, ἡ, rebuilding, Suid., Zonar.

ἀναδονέω, stir up, agitate, Ph.1.659; ἀνὰ βάρβιτον δονήσω Anacreont.58.1.

ἀναδορά, ἡ, excoriation, Aret.SD2.3,9, Orib.Fr.3.

ἀνά-δοσις, εως, ἡ, (ἀναδίδωμι intr.) sprouting, of plants, Thphr.CP 2.1.4; bursting, issuing forth, of fire, wind, water, Arist.Mu.395^{a}9, D.S.2.12, J.BJ7.6.3; exhalation, Plu.2.31e. 2. sending up, presentation of names, ἀναδόσεις λειτουργῶν POxy.82.2 (iii A.D.). II. (trans.) distribution, Posidon.17; τῶν ὄντων J.Ap.2.39. 2. of food, distribution, assimilation, Plb.3.57.8, Phld.D.3.13 (sg. and pl.), Plu.2.654a, Gal.Nat.Fac.1.2, Jul.Ep.180; πέψις καὶ ἀ. Muson.Fr.18 B p.103H., Porph.Abst.1.45: metaph., digestion of knowledge, Plu. Per.2. III. Gramm., ἀ. τόνου throwing back of the accent, EM 549.30. **-δοτικός**, ή, όν, causing to spring up, σπερμάτων Corn. ND28. 2. Medic., digestive, Gal.6.416. **-δοτος**, ον, given up or to be given up, Th.3.52.

ἀναδουλόω, reduce to slavery again, App.BC4.29.

ἀναδοχ-εύς, = ἀνάδοχος II, Hsch. **-ή**, ἡ, series, succession, πόνων S.Tr.825 (lyr.). 2. reception, τινῶν A.D.Synt.144.10. II. surety, Plb.5.27.4: Cret. ἀνδοκά Leg.Gort.9.34: so prob. ἀνδοκεία IG14.422 (pl.), 423 (Tauromenium). **-ος**, ον, taking upon oneself, giving security for, πρὸς τὴν ἀδελφὴν ἀ. τῶν χρημάτων Men.516. II. as Subst., security, surety, D.H.6.84, Plu.Dio18; τῆς φιλίας Κύπρις ἀ. PGrenf.1.1; περί, ὑπέρ τινος, Phalar.Ep.22,38.

ἀναδρᾰμ-εῖν, aor. 2 inf. of ἀνατρέχω. **-ητέον**, one must run back: metaph., have recourse, ἐπὶ τὴν τῶν ὅλων θεωρίαν Procl.in Ti. 1.103D.

ἀναδράω, aor. inf. -δρᾶσαι, = ἀναπράξαι, Hsch.

ἀναδρέπω, break off, pluck, Nonn.D.9.120:—Med., cull, ῥητορικοὺς λόγους ἀναδρέψασθαι Them.Or.27.332d.

ἀναδρομ-ή, ἡ, running up: hence, sprouting, impulse, Thphr.CP4.5.1; shooting up, of plant, Hermog.Prog.7; bud, burgeon, E.Fr.766, 855: metaph., ascent, of the soul, Procl.Inst.209; εἰς θεόν, εἰς τὸν ὄντως ἑαυτόν, Porph.Marc.7, Abst.1.29. b. climbing up, of a tree, Agatharch.51. 2. Rhet., returning to a point, Corn.Rh.p.376 H. 3. place of refuge, Poet.ap.Plb.Fr.102. 4. running back, retreat, J.BJ5.2.2. b. reflux, γυναικείων Hp.Liqu.6. 5. sudden throb of pain, Id.Coac.308, 310; = πνῖξις, Steph.in Hp.1.316D. **-ος**, ον, running up, of a fish entering a river from the sea, Alex.Trall.1.15.

ἀναδρύγματα· θύματα, Hsch. **ἀναδρύψει**· ἀναξ[ηρ]ανεῖ, Id.

ἀναδύνω, come to the top of the water, Batr.90, Arist.Fr.335; of rivers which have disappeared into the earth, emerge, Id.Mete.356^{a}25.

ἀναδύομαι, Ep. 3 sg. ἀνδύεται [ῠ] Il.13.225: fut. -δύσομαι [ῡ]: aor. ἀνεδῡσάμην, Ep. 3 sg. -ατο or -ετο: aor. intr. ἀνέδυν, subj. ἀναδύῃ or opt. ἀναδύη [ῡ] Od.9.377: pf. ἀναδέδῡκα: (v. δύω):—come up, rise, esp. from the sea, c. gen., ἀνέδυ πολιῆς ἁλὸς ἠΰτ' ὀμίχλη Il.1.359; ἀνεδύσατο λίμνης Od.5.337: c. acc., ἀνεδύσετο κῦμα θαλάσσης Il.1.496: abs., εἴπερ ἀναδύσει πάλιν Ar.Ra.1460; Ἀφροδίτη ἀναδυομένη, a famous picture by Apelles, Str.14.2.19, Plin.HN35.91, cf. AP12.207 (Strat.). II. shrink back, withdraw, Od.9.377; ἀναδῦναι ἂψ λαῶν ἐς ὅμιλον Il.7.217; hesitate, shirk, ἕτοιμός εἰμ' ἔγωγε, κοὐκ ἀναδύομαι, δάκνειν Ar.Ra.860, cf. Lys.16.15, X.Smp.5.2, D.8.50, 19.210, Men.Epit.205; of rivers, fail, Plu.Thes.15. 2. rarely c. acc., draw back from, shun, ἀνδύεται πόλεμον Il.13.225, cf. D.H.5.52; ἀναδύεσθαι τὰ ὡμολογημένα back out of one's admissions, Pl.Tht. 145c.

ἀνάδῠσις, εως, ἡ, drawing back, retreat, Pl.Euthd.302e, Jul.Or. 5.175b: c. gen., shirking, τῆς στρατείας Plu.Cim.18. 2. emergence from underground, J.BJ7.2.2; of land from water, Lxx Wi. 19.7; of bird from lake, Sch.Od.5.337.

ἀναδυσμός, ὁ, = foreg. 2, Sch.Od.5.337.

ἀναδωδωναῖος, title of Zeus, wrong expl. of Il.16.233, Cleanth. ap.Plu.2.31e.

ἀνάεδνος, ἡ, without bride-price, Il.9.146, 13.366; also of the husband, bringing no gifts, Nonn.D.4.43, 48.633. (Prob. misspelt for ἀν-ϝεδνος.)

ἀναείρω, lift up, of a wrestler, ἤ μ' ἀνάειρ', ἢ ἐγὼ σέ Il.23.724; ἀνάειρε δύω χρυσοῖο τάλαντα took them, carried them off, ib.614,778; ἀθανάτοισι φίλας ἀνὰ χεῖρας ἀείραι 7.130:—Med., lift up in one's arms, carry off, A.R.4.94:—Pass., arise, ἀνηέρθησαν ἄελλαι A.R.1. 1078; of a ship, leave the stocks, Orph.A.268.

ἀνάελπτος, ον, = ἄελπτος, unlooked for, ἀνάελπτα παθόντες Hes. Th.660. (Prob. misspelt for ἀν-ϝελπτος.)

ἀναέξω, enlarge, increase, Q.S.1.460; make grow, ἄνθος Coluth. 247:—Pass., grow, Nonn.D.38.184, al.; grow into, be changed into, λαῖφος ἀνηέξητο καλύπτρη ib.44.243.

ἀναερτ-άζω, = sq., Nonn.D.9.55, al. **-άω**, hang up, dedicate, AP6.195 (Arch.), Antip.Sid.Oxy.662.53.

ἀναζάω, inf. -ζῆν, return to life, be alive again, Ev.Luc.15.24 and 32, Sotion p.183W.: in Ep. form -ζώω Nic.Fr.70.5.

ἀνα-ζεμα, ατος, τό, boiling or bubbling up, Sch.Ar.Av.1243. **-ζεσις**, εως, ἡ, boiling up, of fire, Arist.Mir.833^{a}22, Sch.Il.Oxy.221 xiv 18. **-ζεσμός**, ὁ, irritation, τῶν οὐλῶν Aët.9.43.

ἀνα-ζεύγνῡμι and **-ζευγνύω**, yoke or harness again, ἀναζευγνύναι τὸν στρατόν move off the army, Hdt.9.41; ἀ. τὸ στρατόπεδον break up the camp, ib.58; ἀ. πρὸς τὸν Ἰσθμὸν τὰς νῆας withdraw.., Id.8.60. α'. 2. abs., break up, shift one's quarters, mostly in part., ἀναζεύξας ἤλαυνε Th.8.108, cf. X.An.3.4.37, Ph.Bel.103.15; ἀ. ἐκ τῆς Ἀραβίας Plu.Pomp.42; ἀ. διὰ Συρίας march through.., Id.Ant.84; ἐπὶ τὰς πράξεις Chron.Lind.D.43. 3. repel, [ὕβριν] Inscr.Cos350. **-ζευξις**, εως, ἡ, breaking up one's quarters, marching forth, Plu.Ages.22; return home, Id.Cor.31.

ἀναζέω, fut. -ζέσω, boil up, bubble up, ἐκ γῆς S.Tr.702; λέγεται ἀναζέσαι πῦρ Arist.Mir.833^{a}19; of a lake, ib.837^{b}9; of bile in the mouth, Aret.SD1.15. 2. ἀ. εὐλὰς ἀγεννῶν βασιλέων boil, swarm with worms, metaph., of Alexander's empire, Plu.2.337a; εὐλαὶ ἀναζέουσιν Id.Art.16. b. of sores or boils, break out, Lxx Ex. 9.9. 3. metaph., of passion, boil over, Arist.Pr.947^{b}32, Plu.2. 728b; ἀναζείουσα βαρὺν χόλον boil with rage, A.R.4.391; ἀνέζεσεν αἷμα Pherecr.18D.; ἀνέζει ἡ καρδία Them.Or.13.172d. II. causal, make to boil, Hp.Acut.21; ἀναζείουσιν ἀϋτμήν AP9.626 (Marian.).

ἀνάζησις, εως, ἡ, living again, Theol.Ar.40.

ἀναζητ-έω, investigate, τὰς αἰτίας Pl.Lg.693a; τὰ ὑπὸ γῆς Ap.18b:—Pass., Hdt.1.137, Ar.Lys.26, Th.2.8. II. search out, discover, τὰ παραλελειμμένα ὑπὸ τῶν προτέρων ἀρχείων OGI267 (Pergam., iii B.C.); search for, μαστροπούς Ph.1.40. **-ησις**, εως, ἡ, investigation, Pl. Criti.110a: search for, τινός Memn.41; inspection, ὑδάτων, in pl., Just.Nov.26.4 Intr. **-ητέον**, one must search for, σημεῖον S.E.M. 8.248.

ἀναζῠγή, ἡ, = ἀνάζευξις, Plb.3.44.13, Lxx Ex.40.38, etc.

ἀναζῠγόω, push back the bolt (ζύγωθρον), unbolt, τὴν θύραν ἀναζυγώσας Ar.Fr.654; open, unfasten a casket, Hsch.

ἀναζῡμ-όω, raise as by leaven, loosen, χιὼν ἀ. καὶ μανοῖ τὴν γῆν Thphr.CP3.23.4, cf. Gal.11.435:—Pass., ferment, D.S.1.7. **-ωσις**, εως, ἡ, fermentation, γῆς ὑπὸ χιόνος Thphr.Ign.18.

ἀνάζω, Tarent. for ἀνάσσω, Heraclid.ap.Eust.1654.27.

ἀναζωγρᾰφ-έω, paint completely, delineate, Str.8.3.30; picture to oneself, Ph.2.59, Arr.Epict.2.18.16, S.E.M.7.222:—Pass., to be painted on, ἀσπίδες αἷς οὐδὲν ἀνεζωγράφητο μίμημα Ph.2.591; to be represented, Diog.Oen.7. **-ημα**, ατος, τό, memory-image, Peripatetic word, Alex.Aphr.de An.60.6, al. **-ησις**, εως, ἡ, Chrysipp. Stoic.2.9, Posidon.ap.Gal.5.474.

ἀναζωγρ-έω, recall to life, of those in imminent danger of death, Nonn.D.13.119, al.: metaph. of poetical works, rescue from oblivion, AP7.594 (Jul.). 2. restore to life, Ὑάκινθον ἀνεζώγρησεν Ἀπόλλων Nonn.D.19.102. **-ησις**, εως, ἡ, restoration to life, Agath.1.13.

ἀναζώννῡμι or **-ύω**, fut. -ζώσω, gird up again, recall to service, metaph., τινὰ ἐπὶ τοὺς λόγους Them.Or.18.224a; τὸ ἕκτον βιβλίον πρὸς τὴν ἀΐδιαν κίνησιν Simp.in Ph.1118.6:—Med., ἀ. τὰς ὀσφύας gird up one's loins, 1Ep.Pet.1.13; ἀ. πέπλους Nonn.D.19.73; ἀνεζωσμένοι, Lat. alte praecincti, Polycr.ap.Ath.4.139d:—Pass., to be held in check, of passions, Ph.1.117. 2. Med., c. acc., πόλεμον embark on, Eust. Epiph.p.361D.

ἀναζωόω, recall to life, οἱ τοῦ θεοῦ λόγοι ἀ. τὴν ψυχήν Ph.1.643, cf. Sch.E.Med.9, Aq.Ho.6.2, Sm.Ps.29(30).4, al.

ἀναζωπῡρ-έω, rekindle, light up again, in tmesi, ἀν' αὖ σὺ ζωπυρεῖς νείκη νέα E.El.1121; θερμῷ τὸ θερμὸν ἀ. Arist.Spir.484^{a}7; τὴν ὅλην φύσιν Jul.Or.4.151c; τὸ χάρισμα τοῦ θεοῦ 2Ep.Ti.1.6:—Pass., to be rekindled, Pl.R.527d, X.HG5.4.46 (metaph.); to be excited, Iamb. VP25.112. II. intr. in Act., Plu.Pomp.41, etc. **-ησις**, εως, ἡ, restoration of strength, J.AJ12.8.1; regeneration by heat, of metals, Syn.Alch.p.54B. **-όω**, = -έω, Olymp.in Mete.282.4. **-ωσις**, εως, ἡ, = -ησις, Zos.Alch.p.211B.

ἀναζώστρα, ἡ, (ζώννυμι) kind of bandage, Gal.18(1).774.

ἀνα-ζώω, v. ἀναζάω. **-ζώωσις**, εως, ἡ, recalling to life, Eustr. in EN71.25, Sch.E.Or.288.

ἀναθάλλω, aor. ἀνέθηλα Ael.VH5.4, NA2.25: aor. 2 ἀνέθαλον Ep. Phil.4.10:—shoot up again, sprout afresh, Ael. ll. cc.:—fut. Pass. in act. sense, ἀναθαλήσεται στάχυς AP7.281 (Heracl.): metaph., ἡ σὰρξ ἀ. Lxx Ps.27.7. II. trans., make to flourish, revive, Lxx Si.11.22, 50.10, Ep.Phil. l. c.

ἀνα-θάλπω, warm again, cherish, Anacreont.31.21, J.AJ17.6.5, Plu.2.600b. **-θαλψις**, εως, ἡ, heat, τῆς γῆς Olymp.in Phd.p.201N.

ἀναθαρσ-έω, Att. -θαρρέω, regain courage, Ar.Eq.806, Th.6.63, 7.71; τινί at a thing, Id.6.31; πρὸς ἄλλην αὖθις πεῖραν Plu.Alex. 31. **-ησις**, Att. -θάρρησις, εως, ἡ, recovery of courage, Onos.14. 1, Eust.1267.22.

ἀναθαρσύνω, Att. -θαρρύνω, fill with fresh courage, X.Cyr.5.4. 23. 2. intr., = foreg., Plu.Luc.14.

ἀναθαυμάζω, strengthd. for θαυμάζω, v.l. in D.C.43.13.

ἀναθεάομαι, contemplate again, Plu.2.586a, Them.Or.23.290c.

ἀνάθεμα, poet. ἄνθεμα, ατος, τό, (ἀνατίθημι) properly, like ἀνάθημα, anything dedicated, Theoc.Ep.13.2, AP6.162 (Mel.), CIG2693d (Mylasa), al., Phld.Mus.p.85K. 2. anything devoted to evil, an accursed thing, Lxx Le.27.28, De.7.26, 13.17, al.; of persons, Ep.Rom.9.3, 1Ep.Cor.12.3, etc. II. curse, Tab.Defix.Aud.41 B (Megara, i/ii A.D.), cf. sq.

ἀναθεματιαῖος, gloss on ἀνθεμόεις, Sch.Ven.Il.23.885.

ἀναθεμᾰ-τίζω, *devote to evil*, LxxNu.21.2, Jo.6.20, al., Tab.Defix. Aud.41 A, Cod.Just.1.1.5.3; ἀναθέματι ἀ. LxxDe.13.15; but ἀναθέματι ἀ. ἑαυτούς *bind* themselves *by a curse*, c. inf., Act.Ap.23.14:—Pass., *to be devoted to evil*, LxxNu.18.14. **II.** intr., *curse and swear*, Ev.Marc.14.71. **–τικός**, ή, όν, = ἀναθηματικός, πίνακες Roussel Cultes Égyptiens 222 (Delos, ii B.C.), D.S.31.8. **–τισμός**, ὁ, *a cursing*, Just.Nov.42.1.1: pl., Cod.Just.1.3.38, Just.Nov.146.1.2.

ἀναθεραπεύω, *rear with care*, τοὺς βλαστούς Thphr.HP4.13.3.

ἀναθερίζω, *reap again*, τὴν κριθοφόρον γῆν Ph.2.390; *glean*, Hsch. s.v. ἀνεκαλαμήσατο.

ἀναθερμ-αίνω, *warm up, heat again*, AP11.55:—Pass., *become warm again*, Hp.Epid.1.2, cf. 26.β′, Arist.HA569^{b}11: πυρετὸς –όμενος Hp.Prog.17. **–ανσις**, εως, ἡ, *warming again*, Antyll.ap.Orib.6.10.19.

ἀνάθεσις, εως, ἡ, *setting up in public, dedicating* of gifts in temples, ἀ. σκευῆς, τρίποδος, Lys.21.2 and 4, cf. Ph.1.592 (pl.); εἰς ἀνάθεσιν τοῖς θεοῖς as *an offering*, OGI214.14 (Branchidae). **II.** *putting off, adjournment*, Poll.9.137; τοῦ γάμου Ant.Lib.34.1. **III.** *laying on, imposition*, ἄχθεος Aret.SA2.2.

ἀναθετέον, (ἀνατίθημι) *one must put off*, Pl.Lg.935e; ἀ. τὴν ἄμυναν εἰς τὸν χρόνον Plu.2.817c. **II.** *one must ascribe*, τί τινι Pl.Mx.240e.

ἀναθέω, *run up*, ἐπὶ δένδρα Ael.NA5.54, etc.: c. acc., τὰ ἀνάντη ib.13.14. **2.** of plants, *shoot up*, ib.2.36; τὸ ὁμιχλῶδες..ἀναθέον εἰς ὕψος Gal.18(2).178. **II.** *run up, rise*, Pl.Ti.60c.

ἀναθεωρ-έω, *examine carefully*, Thphr.HP8.6.2, D.S.12.15 (Pass.); *consider a second time*, Thphr.HP1.5.1. **–ησις**, εως, ἡ, *close examination*, D.S.13.35, Plu.2.19e; κατὰ τὴν ἀ. on *further reflection*, Longin.23.2. **II.** *attention attracted* by an event, *magnam ἀ. res habet* Cic.Att.14.5.1, cf. ib.9.19.1, 14.6.2.

ἀναθήκη· ἀνάθεσις, Hsch.

ἀναθηλάζω, *suck up* water, of a tree, Ph.Byz.Mir.1.5; τὸ πύον Aët.15.18.

ἀναθηλέω, *sprout afresh*, οὐδ' ἀναθηλήσει Il.1.236.

ἀνάθημα, ατος, τό, (ἀνατίθημι) *that which is set up*: hence, like ἄγαλμα, *votive offering set up* in a temple, Hdt.1.14, 92, S.Ant.286, etc.; ἀ. ἐκ λειτουργιῶν Lys.26.4. **2.** used by Hom. only in first sense of ἄγαλμα, *delight, ornament*, μολπή τ' ὀρχηστύς τε· τὰ γάρ τ' ἀναθήματα δαιτός Od.1.152, cf. 21.430, IG14.1390; τοῖς τεκοῦσιν ἀνάθημα βιότου, of children, E.Fr.518, cf. Pl.Hp.Mi.364b; to help deserving poverty is βασιλικοῦ πλούτου ἀ. καὶ κατασκεύασμα λαμπρότατον D.H.19.14. **3.** of a slave in a temple, ἀ. πόλεως *devoted to* this service by the city, E.Ion 310.—Cf. ἀνάθεμα.

ἀναθηματικός, ή, όν, *consisting of votive offerings*, τιμαί Plb.27.18.2.

ἀνά-θλασις, εως, ἡ, = ἔκθλιψις, Erot. **–θλάω**, *crush in pieces*, in aor. ἀνέθλασσα v.l. in Q.S.8.94.

ἀνα-θλίβω [ῑ], *force up*, ἐκ τῶν φαρύγγων τοὺς ἀκόλους J.BJ5.10.3; μαστὸς ἀ. χεύματα Ναϊάδος AP9.668 (Marian.); [ὕδατα] εἰς κρήνην Str.3.5.7:—Pass., 16.2.13, AP7.23 (Antip.Sid.), Aret.SA1.8. **2.** simply, *press*, βυβλίδιον AP12.208; of *reducing* a rupture, Archig.ap. Aët.9.28. **–θλιψις**, εως, ἡ, *reduction* of rupture, Orib.Fr.85.

ἄναθλος, ον, *unathletic*, Luc.Cal.12.

ἀναθολ-όω, *make turbid*, ᾠά Arist.GA753^{a}30:—Pass., ἀναθολοῦται τὸ ὕδωρ HA592^{a}8, cf. Procop.Aed.1.5; of urine, Gal.6.252. **2.** metaph., ἀ. τινὰ ἐπί τινα *trouble* his mind *with suspicion* against.., Philostr.VS2.1.11:—Pass., *to be troubled*, ὑπὸ τῆς ἀνίας ἀνεθολοῦθ' ἡ καρδία Pherecr.116. **–ωσις**, εως, ἡ, *making turbid*, ἀ. ὀπῶν *thick mixture* of the juices of herbs, Pl.Lg.824; *a stirring up*, χολῆς Stoic. 3.56.

ἀναθορεῖν, aor. 2 inf. of ἀναθρῴσκω.

ἀναθόρνῠμαι, = ἀναθρῴσκω, Ael.NA1.30, 12.18:—act. form **ἀναθορνύω** in D.C.63.28.

ἀναθορῠβέω, *cry out loudly*, commonly in applause, ἀ. ὡς εὖ λέγοι Pl.Prt.334c, cf. X.An.5.1.3; ὡς εὖ εἰπόντος τινὸς ἀ. ib.6.1.30, cf. Pl. Smp.198a: abs., Euthd.276b.

ἀνά-θρεμμα, ατος, τό, *nursling*, λεαίνας Theoc.23.19. **–θρεπτέον**, *one must feed up*, ὄρνεα Gp.14.19.1; *one must restore nutrition*, Philum.ap.Orib.45.29.12. **–θρεπτικός**, ή, όν, *of* or *for feeding up*, Gal.Thras.30. **–θρεπτος**, ον, *foster-child*, of a slave, Lat. *verna*, App.BC4.43. **–θρεψις**, εως, ἡ, *renewal, restoration* in physiological sense, αἱ ἀ. σφαλεραί Hp.Aph.1.3.

ἀναθρέω, *look up at, view narrowly*, E.Hec.808; ἀ. ὃ ὄπωπεν Pl. Cra.399c:—Pass., τὰ ἔργα ἐκ τῶν λόγων ἀναθρούμενα *compared with*.., Th.4.87.

ἀναθρηνέω, *lift up one's voice in wailing*, D.C.74.13, Sch.E.Or. 1335.

ἀνάθρησις, εως, ἡ, *close observation*, Timo 61.

ἀνάθριξ· *licinus, reburrus*, Gloss.

ἀναθρύπτομαι, *indulge in affectation*, pf. inf. Pass. ἀνατεθρύφθαι Poll.6.185.

ἀναθρῴσκω, poet. and Ion. **ἀνθρ–**: aor. 2 –θορεῖν X.Lac.2.3: aor. 1 subj. ἀναθρῴξωσι Opp.H.3.293:—*spring up*, ὕψι δ' ἀναθρῴσκων πέτεται Il.13.140; of blood, Emp.100.8; of men, ὃς δ' ἀμβώσας μέγα ἀναθρῴσκει Hdt.7.18, cf. AP9.774 (Glauc.); ἀναθρῴσκει ἐπὶ τὸν ἵππον Hdt.3.64.

ἀναθυάω, *to be again at heat*, of swine, Arist.HA546^{a}28, 573^{b}8; prov., γραῦς ἀναθυᾷ Diogenian.4.10, cf. Phot.p.118 R., and prob. in Pherecr.35.

ἀναθυμί-αμα, ατος, τό, *result of exhalation*, Chrysipp.Stoic.2.196, cj. in Zeno ib.1.35. **–ασις**, εως, ἡ, *rising in vapour, exhalation*, Arist. Mete.365^{b}22, cf. Thphr.Fr.33, Petron.47, Plu.2.365e, Hdn.3.14.8: pl., Corn.ND7, Porph.Abst.1.47; of sacrifices, Jul.Caes.333d. **2.** of the soul, Heraclit.12. **3.** of bodily processes, ἡ ἐκ τῶν χυμῶν ἀ. Gal. UP11.14, cf. 6.17. **–άω**, *vaporize*, Thphr.Ign.38:—Pass., *steam up, rise in fume* or *vapour*, ἀναθυμιωμένης διὰ τῶν φλεβῶν τῆς τροφῆς Arist.PA652^{b}36, cf. 653^{a}4; of fire, Id.Mete.341^{a}7; of the earth, *send forth vapour*, ib.360^{b}32; οἶνος ἀναθυμιαθεὶς Plu.2.432e; of smoke, Luc.VH1.23: metaph., μῖσος ἀναθυμιᾶται Plb.15.25.24; of the soul, ψυχαὶ ἀπὸ τῶν ὑγρῶν –ῶνται Heraclit.12. **II.** Med., *draw up vapour*, οἱ ἡρακλειτίζοντές φασιν ἐκ τῆς θαλάττης τὸν ἥλιον ἀ. Arist. Pr.934^{b}36.

ἀναθυράζω, only aor. ἀνεθύραξεν· ἀνεθυμώθη, Hsch.

ἀναθυρόω, *dress* vertical joints of masonry so that only their edges are in contact, IG7.3073.121, 142 (Lebad.).

ἀναθύω (A), *dart up, burst forth*, ὕδωρ Call.Cer.30.

ἀναθύω (B), *sacrifice again*, in Pass., D.C.37.46. **2.** *dedicate*, IG5(2).554, 555 (Melpea). **3.** ἀναθύοντες· ἀναιροῦντες, παραβαίνοντες, Hsch.

ἀναθωΰξας· ἀναβοήσας, Hsch.

ἀναίδεια, Ep. and Ion. **ἀναιδείη**; Att. also **ἀναιδείᾱ** Ar.Fr.226, poet. **ἀναιδία** Hdn.Gr.2.453:—*shamelessness*, ἀναιδείην ἐπιειμένε Il. 1.149; ἀναιδείης ἐπιβῆναι Od.22.424; ἡ γαστὴρ φρένας παρήγαγεν εἰς ἀναιδείην Archil.78; ἀναιδείῃ διαχρεώμενοι Hdt.7.210, cf. 6.129; ἀναιδείας πλέα S.El.607; μετ' ἀναιδείας, = ἀναιδῶς, Pl.Phdr.254d; εἰς τοῦθ' ἧκεν ἀναιδείας D.18.22. **II.** in the Areopagus, λίθος ἀναιδείας was the stone of *unforgivingness*, on which stood an accuser who demanded the full penalty of the law against one accused of homicide (v. αἰδέομαι II.3), Paus.1.28.5; cf. ὕβρις.

ἀναίδεστον· ἄμοιρον, ἄτιμον, Hsch.

ἀναιδεύομαι, *behave impudently*, Ar.Eq.397 codd., Phld.Rh.1.251 S.

ἀναιδήμων, ον, *shameless*: in Adv. –μόνως Gal.17(1).895.

ἀναίδην, faulty form for ἀνέδην (q.v.), Procop.Arc.22.

ἀναιδής, ές, (αἰδώς) *shameless*, of Agamemnon, ὦ μέγ' ἀναιδές Il. 1.158; of Penelope's suitors, Od.1.254, al.; ὦ θρέμμ' ἀναιδές S.El. 622. **2.** c. gen., Κυδοιμὸν ἀναιδέα δηϊοτῆτος *ruthless* in havoc, Il.5. 593. **II.** of things, as, in Od.11.598, the stone of Sisyphus is called λᾶας ἀναιδής *the reckless, ruthless* stone, cf. Il.4.521, 13.139; πότμος ἀ. Pi.O.10(11).105; ἐλπὶς ἀ. *greedy*, Id.N.11.45; ἃ πέπονθ' ἀναιδῆ the *shame* that I have suffered, S.OC516; λόγοι τῶν ἀναιδῶν ἀναιδέστεροι Ar.Eq.385: τὸ ἀναιδές = ἀναίδεια, βλέφαρα πρὸς τἀνειδὲς ἀγαγών E.IA379; ἔνθα τἀνειδὲς κρατεῖ Diph.111b; εἰς ἀναιδὲς..δός μοι σεαυτόν S.Ph.83; ἐπὶ τὸ ἀναιδέστερον τραπέσθαι Hdt.7.39. **III.** Adv. –δῶς S.OT354, E.Alc.694, Ar.Th.525, etc.: Sup. –έστατα Heraclit.15.

ἀναίδητος, ον, = foreg., A.R.3.92, 4.360.

ἀναιδίζομαι, v.l. for ἀναιδεύομαι, Ar.Eq.397 ap.AB.

ἀναιδομάχας, ὁ, *ruthless in fight*, κάπρος B.5.105.

ἀναιή· τροφός, τιθήνη, Hsch. (leg. ἀμμίη).

ἀναιθύσσω, *stir up, rouse*, S.Fr.542 (dub.); φλόγα E.Tr.344.

ἀναίθω, *light up, set on fire*, E.Cyc.331; τὸν Ἅλιον αὐτόν Mosch.1. 23:—Pass., *to be inflamed*, Opp.C.2.188: metaph. of anger, Max. Tyr.24.9. **II.** *blaze up*, ἀνῆθον..λαμπτῆρες A.Ch.536 (Sch.).

ἀναίκλεια· ἄδειπνα, Hsch.

ἀναίλιπος (cod. –λειπως)· ἀνυπόδητος, Hsch.; cf. νήλιπος.

ἀναιμακτί, Adv. of sq., *without bloodshed*, Them.Or.7.90a, Hsch.

ἀναίμακτος, ον, *bloodless, unstained with blood*, ἀ. φυγαί A.Supp. 196; χρώς E.Ph.264; βωμός Pyth.ap.D.L.8.22; ἀ. κεν ἰαύοις Nic. Th.90; ἀρχή, νίκη, Them.Or.5.66d, 2.37c, cf. Antyll.ap.Orib.44.23. 32.

ἀναίμᾰτος, ον, = ἄναιμος, A.Eu.302, Aenigm.ap.Ath.2.63b.

ἀναιμία, ἡ, *want of blood*, Arist.PA652^{b}26.

ἀναιμόδιτον, τό, = ἀνδράχνη, Hsch.

ἀναιμορράγητος, ον, *without haemorrhage*, Antyll.ap.Orib.45.24. 15, Leonid.ap.Aët.15.5.

ἄναιμος, ον, (αἷμα) opp. ἔναιμος, *bloodless*, of parts of the body, Pl.Ti.70c, Prt.321b, Arist.HA495^{a}4: Comp., 520^{b}33, al. **II.** of animals, Id.PA678^{a}33, al. **2.** generally, of colour, νᾶπυ ἀναιμότερον κεχρωσμένον Aët.1.298. **3.** metaph., χλωρὰ καὶ ἄ. τὰ πράγματα Gorg.Fr.16. **III.** *shedding no blood*, πολλοὺς δὲ βροντῆς πνεῦμ' ἄ. ὤλεσεν E.Fr.982; ἀ. νίκη D.C.68.19.

ἀναιμόσαρκος, ον, *with bloodless flesh*, of the cicada, Anacreont. 43.17.

ἀναιμότης, ητος, ἡ, = ἀναιμία, Arist.PA676^{a}31.

ἀναιμόχρους, ουν, *of bloodless complexion*, Gal.14.326.

ἀναίμων, ον, = ἄναιμος, *bloodless*, epith. of the gods, Il.5.342; of cuttlefish, Ion Trag.36; of wine, Plu.2.692e.

ἀναιμωτί, Adv. *without shedding blood*, οὐ γὰρ ἀναιμωτί γ' ἐμαχοντο Il.17.363, cf. Od.18.149, Ph.1.323, al., Gal.2.604, Them.Or.16.213a.

ἀναίνομαι, impf. ἠναινόμην, Ep. ἀναινόμην, late also ἀνηνόμην Agath.1.13: aor. ἀνηνάμην Alciphr.3.37, subj. ἀνήνηται, inf. ἀνήνασθαι: **1.** c. acc., *refuse* or *reject with contempt, spurn*, σὲ δ' ἀναίνεται ἠδὲ σὰ δῶρα Il.9.679; ὃς δέ κ' ἀνήνηται [σφέας] ib.510; τῶν ἄλλων οὔτινα ἀναίνομαι *on* no one of the rest *do I turn my back*, Od. 8.212; and without a notion of contempt, πρὶν μὲν ἀναίνετο ἔργον ἀεικὲς *refused, declined to do* it, ib.3.265; χαλεπόν κεν ἀνήνασθαι δόσιν εἴη 'twould be hard *to refuse* a gift, ib.4.651; ὡς μηδὲν ἀναίνοιντο ἔργον X.Cyr.2.1.31. **2.** *renounce, disown*, φάος..οὐκ ἠναίνετο A.Ag.300;

οὐδ' οἷόν τ' ἀνήνασθαι πόσιν E.*Med.*237; of sexual favours, φιλότητα καὶ εὐνήν Hom.*Epigr.*12.2; ἀναίνεται δὲ λέκτρα E.*Hipp.*14, cf. *El.* 311, Pl.Com.181, Men.446; ἡμᾶς..ἀναίνοιτ' ἂν ἡ τοῦ διαλέγεσθαι δύναμις Pl.*Phlb.*57e; εἰ..ἀναίνει Φορμίωνα κηδεστήν D.36.31. II. c. inf., *refuse, decline* to do, ἠναίνετο λοιγὸν ἀμῦναι Il.18.450; ἕζεσθαι μὲν ἀνήνατο 23.204; and with pleon. neg., ἀναίνετο μηδὲν ἑλέσθαι he *declined* to take anything, 18.500; οὐκ ἀναίνομαι θανεῖν A.*Ag.*1652, cf. *Supp.*801; εἰ..ἀναίνεται εἰ ἐγὼ ἔσομαι ὑὸς Μενεκλέους *repudiates the prospect of* my being.., Is.2.27. III. abs., *refuse*, αἴδεσθεν μὲν ἀνήνασθαι Il.7.93; *deny*, οὐδ' αὐτὸς ἀ. 9.116; ἐπειδὴ πάμπαν ἀναίνεαι Od.14.149; ἀναινόμενος ταῦτα D.61.48. IV. c. part., *disown* doing or having done, νικώμενος λόγοισιν οὐκ ἀναίνομαι *I am* not *ashamed*, A.*Ag.*583; ἀναίνομαι τὸ γῆρας ὑμῶν εἰσορῶν *I am ashamed* to look on your old age, E.*Ba.*251; θανοῦσα δ' οὐκ ἀναίνομαι *IA* 1503, cf. *HF* 1124.—Chiefly poet., once in Pl.

ἀναίρ-εμα, ατος, τό, = ἑλώριον, Sch.A.R.2.264. **-εσις**, εως, ἡ, *taking up* or *away*, esp. of dead bodies for burial, ὀστέων E.*Or.*404; νεκρῶν Th.3.109,113; οἳ ἂν μὴ εὑρεθῶσιν ἐς ἀναίρεσιν 2.34, cf. Antipho 5.68, Lys.2.7; ἀναίρεσιν δοῦναι E.*Supp.*18; in a sea-fight, νεκρῶν ἢ ναυαγίων ἀ. Th.7.72; τῶν ναυαγῶν X.*HG*1.7.5. 2. *taking up*, ἀ. καὶ θέσις ὅπλων Pl.*Lg.*814a, cf. Antipho 3.3.6. 3. *undertaking*, ἔργων Pl.*Lg.*847b. II. *destruction*, X.*HG*6.3.5; τειχῶν καὶ πόλεων D.19.141; φθορὰ ἡ κατ' ἀναίρεσιν *Stoic.*3.266. 2. *slaying, putting to death*, Lxx *Nu.*11.15, J.*AJ*5.2.11, Plu.2.1051d; *banishment*, Hp.*Decent.*2. 3. *repeal*, δογμάτων Plu.*Cic.*34; *quashing* of indictment, Hermog.*Stat.*3. 4. *direct confutation* of arguments, opp. διαίρεσις (confutation by drawing a distinction), Arist.*SE*183a10; *destruction* (by argument), τινός Phld.*Sign.*12. 5. Astrol., = ἀκτινοβολία, Thrasyll.ap.Porph.*in Ptol.*189. **-ετέον**, *one must take up* or *take away*, Dsc.5.99; *one must put to death, kill*, Ph.2.313, Porph.*Abst.*3.26. **-ετήριος**, α, ον, = ἀναιρετικός, Tz. ad Hes.*Op.* 142. **-έτης**, ου, ὁ, *destroyer, murderer*, Sch.Ar.*Pl.*1147. II. Astrol., *Anareta*, a planet *cutting short* human life, Balbill. in *Cat. Cod.Astr.*8(4).236. **-ετικός**, ή, όν, *destructive*, Arist.*Rh.*1386a6; ἀ. τινος Ph.*Fr.*103 H.; ἀ. ἀλλήλων mutually *destructive*, Plu.2.427e, Iamb.*Myst.*5.11; of plants, *poisonous*, Gal.14.57, Dsc.1.129; φάρμακα Men.Prot.p.47 D. Adv. -κῶς *negatively* D.L.9.75. 2. Astrol., *having the nature of* ἀναιρέτης II, Ptol.*Tetr.*127. **-έτις**, -έτιδος, ἡ, fem. of ἀναιρέτης II, *Cat.Cod.Astr.*8(4).235.

ἀν-αίρετος, ον, (αἱρέομαι) *incapable of choosing*, Timo 72. II. Pass., opp. αἱρετός, Simp.*in Epict.*p.14 D., al.

ἀναιρέω, pf. ἀνῄρηκα (ἀνειρ- dub. in *Com.Adesp.*18.6 D.): (v. αἱρέω): —*take up*, ἀνελόντες ἀπὸ χθονὸς *having raised* the victim from the ground, so as to cut its throat (cf. αὐερύω), Od.3.453. 2. *take up and carry off, bear away*, esp. prizes, ἄεθλα Il.23.736, cf. 551; στεφανηφόρους ἀγῶνας ἀναραιρηκότα Hdt.5.102; Ὀλύμπια ἀναραιρηκὼς 6.36, cf. B.1.1. 3. simply, *take up*, παῖδα Pi.*P.*9.61; τὰ ὀστᾶ Th.1. 126. 4. *take up* bodies for burial, ἀνελόντες καὶ κατακλαύσαντες Ar. *V.*386, cf. X.*An.*6.4.9; more common in Med., v. infr. B.1.3. II. *make away with, destroy*, of men, *kill*, Hdt.4.66; πολλοὺς ἀναιρῶν A.*Ch.*990; σὲ μὲν ἡμετέρα ψῆφος ἀ. E.*Andr.*517; θανάτοις ἀ. Pl.*Lg.* 870d; ἐκ πολιτείας τοιαῦτα θηρία ἀ. Din.3.19, etc. 2. of things, *abrogate, annul*, ὅρους ἀνεῖλον πολλαχῇ πεπηγότας Sol.36.4; νόμον Aeschin.3.39; διαθήκας Is.1.14; στήλας And.1.103; ἀταξίαν D.3.35, etc.; ἐκ μέσου ἀ. βλασφημίας Id.10.36; τηλικαύτην ἀνελόντας μαρτυρίαν Id.28.5; *abolish*, τὰς τῶν παρανόμων γραφάς Arist.*Ath.*29.4:— Pass., ἀνῄρηνται ὀλιγαρχίαι X.*Cyr.*1.1.1. 3. *destroy* an argument, *confute* it, Arist.; esp. *confute directly*, opp. διαιρέω (v. ἀναίρεσις II. 4), Arist.*SE*176b36, al.; ἀ. ἑαυτὸν *confute* oneself, Olymp.*in Mete.*25. 14. 4. in argument, *do away with*, τὰς ὑποθέσεις Pl.*R.*533c; *deny*, opp. τιθέναι, S.E.*P.*1.192, al. III. *appoint, ordain*, of oracle's answer to inquiry, ὁ θεὸς αὐτοῖς ἀ. παραδοῦναι Th.1.25; οὓς ἂν ὁ θεὸς ἀνέλῃ Pl.*Lg.*865d, cf. 642d; ἀνεῖλεν θεοῖς οἷς ἔδει θύειν X.*An.*3.1.6: also c. acc. et inf., ἣν τὸ χρηστήριον ἀνέλῃ μιν βασιλέα εἶναι Hdt.1. 13, etc.: abs., *answer, give a response*, ἀνεῖλε τὸ χρηστήριον ibid.; ἀ. τι περί τινος *give an oracle* about a thing, Pl.*Lg.*914a; μαντείας ἀ. D. *Ep.*1.16:—Pass., Id.21.51.

B. Med., *take up for oneself, take up, pick up*, οὐλοχύτας ἀνέλοντο Il.1.449; ἀσπίδα, ἔγχος, 11.32, 13.296; κυνέην Hdt.1.84; δίκτυα Arist. *HA*602b9; *achieve, win*, ἀ. τὴν Ὀλυμπιάδα, τὴν νίκην, Hdt.6.70,103, D.H.5.47; generally, ἀ. ἐπιφροσύνας *take* thought, Od.19.22; εὐδαιμονίαν Pi.*N.*7.56, cf. Thgn.281; in bad sense, ὄνειδος σπαργάνων ἀ. S.*OT* 1035; εἴ σ' ἀνελοίμην if *I should take* thee *into my service*, Od.18. 357; σῖτα ἀ. *get* forage, Hdt.4.128; ποινὴν τῆς Αἰσώπου ψυχῆς ἀ. *exact* vengeance for.., Id.2.134. 2. *take up and carry off, snatch*, κούρας ἀνέλοντο θύελλαι Od.20.66; ἀναιρούμενος οἴκαδε φέρειν Pl.*Lg.* 914b; ἀνείλατο (for the form cf. Hsch.) δαίμων *Epigr.Gr.*404.1. 3. *take up for burial* (cf. A.1.4), Hdt.4.14, Th.4.97, etc.; πατέρων ἀρίστων σώμαθ' ὧν ἀνειλόμην E.*Supp.*1167; τὰ ὀστέα Hdt.2.41; of the ashes of the dead, πυρὸς ἀ. ἄθλιον βάρος S.*El.*1140; of one still living, E.*Hel.* 1616, X.*HG*6.4.13; τοὺς ναυαγοὺς ib.1.7.4, cf. 11; τοὺς δέκα στρατηγοὺς τοὺς οὐκ ἀνελομένους τοὺς ἐκ τῆς ναυμαχίας Pl.*Ap.*32b:—Pass., ἀναιρεθέντων τῶν νεκρῶν..ὑγιὴς ἀνῃρέθη Id.*R.*614b, al. 4. *take up in one's arms*, Il.16.8: hence, *take up* new-born children, *own* them, Plu.*Ant.*36, cf. Ar.*Nu.*531; *take up* an exposed child, Men. *Sam.*159, cf. *BGU*1110, etc. 5. *conceive in the womb*, c. acc., Hdt. 2.108, 6.69. 6. *take up* money at interest, D.50.17. 7. *take up* a lease, *Michel* 1359 (Chios), cf. *BCH*37.204. 8. *withdraw* money from a bank, etc., αὐτὸς ἀνελέσθω *IG*5(2).159. II. *take upon oneself, undertake*, πόνους Hdt.6.108; πόλεμόν τινι war *against* one, Id.5.36; πολέμους ἀναιρούμεσθα E.*Supp.*492, cf. D.1.7; ἀ. ἔχθραν Pl.*Phdr.*233c, D.6.20; ἀ. δημόσιον ἔργον *undertake, contract for the execution of* a work, Pl.*Lg.*921d, cf. a, b, D.53.21. 2. *accept as one's own, adopt*, γνώμην Hdt.7.16.α'; τὰ οὐνόματα τὰ ἀπὸ τῶν βαρβάρων ἥκοντα 2.52; ἀ. φιλοψυχίην *entertain* a love for life, 6.29. III. *rescind, cancel*, συγγραφήν, συνθήκας, etc., D.34.31, 48.46, *IG*7.3171 (Orchom. Boeot., iii B.C.).

ἄναιρον· ὄνειρον (Cret.), Hsch.; cf. ὄναρ.

ἀναίρω, *raise, lift up*, Aen.Tact.23.4:—Med., Ἕως γὰρ λευκὸν ὄμμ' ἀναίρεται E.*El.*102:—Pass., ἀναρθείς, of Ganymede, *AP*12.67.

ἀναισθής, ές, = ἀναίσθητος, Max.Tyr.17.5, 37.5.

ἀναισθ-ησία, ἡ, *lack of sensation*, Pl.*Ti.*74e, Epicur.*Fr.*495; μετ' ἀναισθησίας *without the aid of sense-perception*, Pl.*Ti.*52b; *unconsciousness*, *Ax.*365d; *insensibility* to pleasure or pain, Arist.*EN*1109a4, 1119a7; *insensibility* under surgical treatment, Dsc.5.140. 2. *mental obtuseness*, D.22.64. 3. *stupor*, Aret.*SA*1.5. **-ησιολογία**, ἡ, *insensibility-theory*, Phld.*D.*1.24. **-ητεύομαι**, = sq., condemned by Phryn.329. **-ητέω**, *lack perception*, D.18.221; ἀ. ταλαιπωρίας *to be without sense of* weariness, J.*AJ*11.5.8; συμφορῶν ἀ. *BJ*4.3.10: abs., Epicur.*Ep.*1p.21 U., Sor.2.49, prob. in Porph.*Abst.*1.39. **-ητος**, ον, *without sense* or *feeling*, Thrasymach. 1, Pl.*Ti.*75e; ἀ. τινὸς *without sense of* a thing, Id.*Lg.*843a; ἀ. καὶ νεκρός Men.705; ἀ. ψαύσιος καὶ τρώσιος Aret.*SD*2.12; ἀ. ἡ ἁφή *the sense* of touch *is lost*, ib.1.7. Adv. ἀναισθήτως, πάντων ἔχειν Hp. *Epid.*3.17.ιε'; ἀ. ἔχειν to be *insensible* or *indifferent*, Isoc.12.112, cf. Th.1.82; ἀ. διακεῖσθαι Arist.*EE*1231a1. 2. *without perception* or *common sense, wanting tact, stupid*, Th.6.86; οἱ ἀ. Θηβαῖοι *those blockheads*.., D.18.43, cf. Phld.*Rh.*1.215 S.: τὸ ἀναίσθητον, = ἀναισθησία, Th.1.69. Adv. -ως Phld.*Rh.*1.227 S. II. Pass., *unfelt*, θάνατος Th.2.43. 2. *not perceptible by sense*, ἀόρατον καὶ ἄλλως ἀ. Pl.*Ti.*52a, cf. Phld.*Piet.*20, etc.; ἐν ἀ. χρόνῳ in an *unappreciable* time, Arist.*Ph.*222b15, cf. *Po.*1450b39.

ἀν-αίσιμος, ον, *unseemly*, δῆρις Emp.27a.

ἀναισιμ-όω, impf. ἀναισίμουν (v. infr.): aor. subj. ἀναισιμώσωσι (v. infr.): pf. ἀνησίμωκα v.l. in X.*Cyr.*2.2.15:—Pass., aor. ἀναισιμώθην: pf. ἀναισίμωμαι:—*use up, use, spend, consume*, τὸν χοῦν.. ἀναισίμου *he used up* the earth, Hdt.1.185; ἵνα μὴ τὸν σῖτον ἀναισιμώσωσι 3.150:—Pass., οἶνος ἀναισιμοῦται 2.60; εὐζώνῳ ἀνδρὶ πέντε ἡμέραι ἀναισιμοῦνται 1.72, cf. 2.11, 5.53: often ἀ. ἔς τι *to be used* for a purpose, or *spent* upon a thing, τεσσεράκοντα καὶ ἑκατὸν τάλαντα ἐς τὴν ἵππον ἀναισιμοῦτο 3.90; ὅσα ἐς συρμαίην ἀναισιμώθη 2.125; ταλάντων χιλιάδες ἀναρίθμητοι ἀναισίμωνται (sc. ἐς τὴν πυραμίδα) ib.134; also κοῦ ταῦτα ἀναισιμοῦται; where (i.e. how) *are* these *disposed of?* 3.6; δεῖ ἔτι φράσαι ἵνα ἡ γῆ ἀναισιμώθη 1.179. (ἀνα-, αἴσιμος, q.v.; Ion. (and v.l. in X.*Cyr.*2.2.15); κατ- in Com., otherwise not found in Att., who use ἀναλίσκω, δαπανάω.) **-ωμα**, ατος, τό, = Att. δαπάνη, *that which is used up*, τὰ ἀναισιμώματα τῇ στρατιῇ the war-*expenses*, Hdt.5.31.

ἀν-αίσιος, ον, *ill-omened, unfortunate*, Lyd.*Mag.*3.45.

ἀναΐσσω [ᾰνᾱ], Att. contr. **ἀᾴσσω**, used also by Pi.:—*start up*, μὴ πρὶν ἀναΐξειαν Ἀρήϊοι υἷες Ἀχαιῶν Il.4.114; ὅτε δὴ..ἀναΐξειεν Ὀδυσσεύς whenever *he rose to speak*, 3.216; of a spring, *gush forth*, 22.148: so in later Poets, μυελὸς στέρνων ἐντὸς ἀνᾴσσων *springing fresh* within the breast, A.*Ag.*77 cj. Herm., cf. *Pers.*96 cj. Brunck; ὀρθοὶ ἀνῇξαν πάντες E.*Hel.*1600; βωμὸς ἀνᾴσσων an altar *rising up*, Pi.*O.*13.107.—Rare in Prose, ἀναΐσσει νόσημα Hp.*Prog.*19; ἀνᾴξας, of a hare, X.*Cyn.*6.17. 2. c. acc., ἀναΐξας.. ἅρμα καὶ ἵππους *having leapt upon* it, Il.24.440. 3. Act., *cause to start up*, ἀνῄϊξεν δὲ φέβεσθαι Opp.*C.*1.107.

ἀναισχής, ές, = ἀναίσχυντος, *AB*207.

ἀναισχυντ-έω, *to be* ἀναίσχυντος, *to be shameless, behave impudently*, Ar.*Lys.*460, Th.1.37, And.2.4; πρός τινα X.*Smp.*8.33: also c. part., ἀναισχυντεῖ ποιῶν *he is impudent enough* to do, Ar.*Th.*708; ἀ. διαλεγόμενος Pl.*Cri.*53c: c. acc. cogn., ποῖα..ἀναισχυντοῦσιν Arist. *Rh.*1383b12. 2. trans., *treat shamelessly*, and Pass., *to be so treated*, ὁ ἀναισχυντῶν πρὸς τὸν ἀναισχυντούμενον ib.1412a6. **-ημα**, ατος, τό, *impudent act* or *speech*, Hyp.*Fr.*226, Gal.*UP*10.9. **-ία**, ἡ, *shamelessness, impudence*, Ar.*Th.*702, D.20.166, etc.; ὑπ' ἀναισχυντίας Pl.*Smp.*192a.

ἀναισχυντο-γράφος, ὁ, *obscene writer*, Timae.141. **-ποιός**, όν, *doing shameless deeds*, Procop.*Arc.*9.

ἀναίσχυντος, ον, *shameless, impudent*, Alc.*Supp.*21.5, E.*IA*327, etc., Ar.*Pax*182, And.4.17, Pl.*Lg.*671c (Comp.), *Ap.*17b (Sup.), etc.:—τὸ ἀναίσχυντον, = ἀναισχυντία, E.*IA*1144. Adv. -τως Pl.*Ap.* 31b: Sup. ἀναισχυντότατα ἀνθρώπων D.27.18. II. of things, *shameful, abominable*, βορά E.*Cyc.*416; θῆκαι Th.2.52.

ἀναίτητος, ον, *unasked*, Pi.*Fr.*169.7 (fem. -τήτη); *unclaimed*, γῆ *Sammelb.*4298.3.

ἀναιτίατος, ον, *unblamed*, Ion Trag.ap.Phot.p.113 R.

ἀναιτιολόγητος, ον, *for which no cause can be assigned*, Dsc.*Ther. Praef.*, Alex.Aphr.*Pr.*1.52, Ptol.*Tetr.*111.

ἀναίτιος, ον, also α, ον Hdt.9.110, A.*Ch.*873:—in the best authors, only of persons, *not being the fault* or *cause of* a thing, *guiltless*, ἀναίτιον αἰτιάασθαι Il.13.775, cf. Od.20.135, etc.; αἰτία ἑλομένου, θεὸς ἀ. Pl.*R.*617e; ἀναίτιος ἀθανάτοις *guiltless* before the gods, Hes.*Op.*827, cf. E.*Med.*730; ἀ. παρά τινι X.*Cyr.*1.6.10; ἀ. αἷμα ἐκχέαι *SIG*1181. 6. 2. c. gen. rei, *guiltless of* a thing, Hdt.1.129, 7.233, etc.; φόνου, κακῶν, A.*Ag.*1505, *Ch.*873; κακίας Pl.*Ti.*42d; ἀφροσύνης X.*Cyr.*1.

5.10: οὐκ ἀναίτιόν ἐστι, c. inf., *it is blamable* to do, ib.5.5.22. **II.** *not being the cause*, τὸ ἀ. τιθέναι ὡς αἴτιον Arist.*APr*.65^{b}16, cf. *Rh.* 1401^{b}30; *having no cause, unjustifiable*, κολάσεις Phld.*Ir*.p.52 W. Adv. -ως *not in the form of a cause*, ἀ. τὴν αἰτίαν ἔχειν Plot.6.7.2; *without assigning any reason*, ὀλοσχερῶς καὶ ἀ. λεκτέον Simp.*in Cael.*665.11. **III.** *uncaused*, Plot.3.1.1, Phlp.*inPh*.277.1: Sup., Sch.E.*Hipp*.672. Adv. -ως *without a cause*, Gal.10.36, S.E.*P*.3.67, Simp.*inPh*.641.10; ἀ. γίγνεσθαι Alex.Aphr.*inMetaph*.309.15.

ἄναιτος, v. ἄνατος.

ἀναιχμάλωτος, ον, *not made captive*, Hsch. s.v. ἀπόρθητοι.

ἀναιωρέω, *lift up*, ἑαυτὸν..ἐς ἠέρα..ἀνῃώρησε Coluth.155: plpf. Pass. ἀνῃώρητο Nonn.*D*.16.342.

ἀνάκα, dub. in *IG*5(2).p.xxv.72 (Arc. = ἡνίκα).

ἀνακαγχάζω, *burst out laughing*, Hp.*Ep*.17; μέγα πάνυ ἀνακαγχάσας Pl.*Euthd*.300d; ἀνεκάγχασε μάλα σαρδάνιον *R*.337a.

ἀνακαθ-αίρω, *clear out, clear completely*, τοὺς πόρους the ducts, Anaxipp.1.16; *cleanse* ulcer, Paul.Aeg.4.41; τάφρους D.H.8.13; *clear* streets, *OGI*483.79 (Pergam.); τράφως καὶ ῥόως..ἀγκοθαρίοντι (= ἀνακαθαροῦσι) *Tab.Heracl*.1.132; *prune*, Thphr.*HP*1.3.3; *clear* ground for foundations, *SIG*^{2}587.46 (Eleusis, iv B.C.), *BCH*29.468 (Delos, iii B.C.), *IG*12(2).11.3 (Mytilene):—Med., ἀνακαθηράμενον τὸ χωρίον *Ath.Mitt*.31.134 (Athens, iv B.C.), *IG*2.1054.8 (iv B.C.):—Pass., ib.7.3073.64 (Lebad.); of a mine, *to be cleared out*, Arist.*Mir.* 834^{a}27; οἰκόπεδα D.H.14.2; of the air, *become quite clear*, Plu.*Flam.* 8. **II.** Med., *clear* or *sweep away*, τὸ βάρβαρον ἀνακαθαίρεσθαι ἐκ τῆς θαλάσσης Pl.*Mx*.241d (so Act. in D.H.1.12); τὰ πρὸ ποδῶν Plb. 10.30.8; τὴν παραλίαν ἀ. Plu.*Alex*.17. **2.** *extract*, μεταλλεῖα Pl.*Lg.* 678d. **3.** ἀνακαθαίρεσθαι λόγον *clear up* or *enucleate* a subject, μέθης πέρι, σμικροῦ πράγματος, παμμήκη λόγον -όμενος ib.642a. **4.** Medic., *cleanse thoroughly*, Hp.*Aph*.5.8: metaph., *purify*, τῆς κακίας γῆν καὶ θάλατταν Jul.*ad Them*.254a. **-αρμα**, ατος, τό, (in pl.) *rubbish, lumber*, dub. in Hsch. s.v. ὀξυθύμια. **-αρσις**, εως, ἡ, *clearing away*, of rubbish, Plb.5.100.6; λίθων Ph.*Bel*.100.41; *cleaning*, of sewers, D.H.3.67; of streets, etc., *OGI*483.51 (Pergam.); of ground for foundations, *SIG*^{2}587.19. **2.** Medic., *cleansing*, Gal.8.327. **3.** *end of an eclipse*, opp. ἔμπτωσις, Heph.Astr.1.21. **II.** *clearing up an obscure passage, explanation*, Suid. **-αρτικός**, ή, όν, *promoting vomiting*, Dsc.1.71. **II.** *for cleansing*, Meges ap.Orib.44. 24.7, cf. Paul.Aeg.4.41.

ἀνακάθημαι, *sit upright*, Luc.*Ocyp*.112.

ἀνακᾰθίζω, *set up*: whence Med., *sit up*, εἰς τὴν κλίνην Pl.*Phd.* 60b. **II.** intr., *sit up*, Hp.*Prog*.3, Aen.Tact.27.8; δὶς ἑπτὰ [μησὶν] -ει [τὰ βρέφη] *Theol.Ar*.48; of a hare listening, X.*Cyn*.5.7.

ἀνακαθίννῠμαι, = ἀνακάθημαι, Aret.*SA*1.10.

ἀνακαιν-ίζω, *renew*, τὸν πόλεμον Plu.*Marc*.6, cf. App.*Mith*.37; οἶκον Hsch.Mil.4.33; *revive* legend, Str.2.1.9: metaph., ἀ. εἰς μετάνοιαν *Ep.Hebr*.6.6:—Pass., τῆς ἔχθρας ἀνακεκαινισμένης Isoc.7.8; ὑποθέσεις Just.*Nov*.111.1. **-ισις**, εως, ἡ, *a making new, renewal*, Suid.

ἀνακαινουργέω, = ἀνακαινίζω, prob. l. in *AP*14.60.

ἀνακαιν-όω, in Pass., *to be renewed*, 2*Ep.Cor*.4.16, *Col*.3.10:—in Med., *renew*, Heliod.*in EN*221.13. **-ωσις**, εως, ἡ, = ἀνακαίνισις, *Ep.Rom*.12.2, *Tit*.3.5.

ἀνάκαιον, τό, v. ἀναγκαῖον.

ἀνακαίω, Att. -κάω, aor. ἀνέκαυσα E.*Cyc*.383:—*kindle, light up*, ἡ οἱ πῦρ ἀνέκαιε Od.7.13, Hdt.4.145, etc.:—Med., *light oneself* a fire, Id.1.202, 8.19: metaph., *kindle*, ὀρεξιν Plu.2.1089a; μάχην Porph. *Chr*.23. **2.** Pass., *fire up* with anger, Hdt.5.19; στάσις ἀ. D.H. 9.27.

ἀνακαλαμάομαι, = ἀναθερίζω, in aor. 1 -ησάμην, Hsch.

ἀνακαλέω, poet. ἀγκ-, *call up* or *back*, esp. of magical invocations:—in Med., *call up the dead*, A.*Pers*.621, E.*Hel*.966; χαλκοῦ πατάγοις τὸ φῶς [τῆς σελήνης] Plu.*Aem*.17. **II.** *call again and again*; and so: **1.** *invoke again and again, appeal to*, θεούς Hdt.9.90, E. *Ph*.608, al.; τὰς ἐπωνυμίας τοῦ θεοῦ ἀνακαλῶν Pl.*R*.394a; τοὺς προγόνους D.25.97, etc.:—so in Med., τὸν αὐτῆς δαίμον' ἀνακαλουμένη S.*Tr.* 910; *invoke again*, κεκλημένους μὲν ἀνακαλοῦμεθ' αὖ θεοὺς E.*Supp.* 626: c. inf., ἀνακαλοῦμαι ξυμμάχους ἐλθεῖν [ἀράς] S.*OC*1376, cf. E. *Tr*.469. **2.** *summon, cite*, Hdt.3.127, And.1.45; *cite* before a court, Lys.15.5:—Med., *call to oneself, send for, summon*, Hdt.2.121.α', Arist.*Ath*.8.2; εἰς τοὺς μυρίους ἀ. X.*HG*7.4.33. **3.** *call* by a name, Δαναούς Th.1.3; ὀνομαστὶ ἀ. 7.70; ἐξ ὀνόματος ἀ. D.H.8.65; with the Art., ἀνακαλοῦντες τὸν προδότην X.*An*.6.6.7, cf. *Cyr*.3.3.4; ἀνακαλοῦντες ταῦτα τὰ ὀνόματα ἑαυτούς Pl.*R*.471d:—Pass., Ἀργεῖος ἀνακαλούμενος *proclaimed* an Argive, S.*El*.693; so prob. τῷ Λημνίῳ τῷδ' ἀνακαλουμένῳ πυρί yon fire *famed as* Lemnian, Id.*Ph*.800. **4.** *call on, call to*, esp. for encouragement, ἀλλήλους X.*Cyr*.7.1.35, etc.:—Med., *rally*, ὥσπερ πεφευγότας Pl.*Phd*.89a; εἴ τις κύνας ἐν θήρᾳ -οῖτο X.*Cyr*.1.6.19; simply, *call to*, Th.7.73: c. acc. cogn., τίνα στοναχὰν...ἀγκαλέσωμαι; E.*Ph*.1499; ἀνακαλεῖς με τίνα βοάν; with what cry *dost thou call upon* me? Id.*HF*910. **III.** *call back, recall*, mostly in Med., αἷμα τίς ἂν πάλιν ἀγκαλέσαιτ' ἐπαείδων A.*Ag.* 1021, etc.; *recall* a general from his command, Th.1.131; *call back* from battle, ἀνακαλεῖσθαι τῇ σάλπιγγι *sound a retreat*, X.*An*.4.4.22; *call* dogs *to heel*, Pl.*R*.440d (Pass.). **2.** *restore to health*, Dsc.2. 34. **3.** in Med., *recall, recollect oneself*, Hp.*Epid*.1.26.α', cf. Gal. 17(1).259; so ἀ. τὸν νόον ἐξ ἀγνοίας Ti.Locr.104c; ἀνάνηφε καὶ ἀνακαλοῦ σεαυτόν M.Ant.6.31: hence, *recall, make good*, τὰ ἁμαρτήματα Lys.6.49; ἐν ὀλίγῳ πάντα D.C.73.10.

ἀνακαλλύνω, *sweep up*, Phryn.Com.2 D.

ἀνακαλπάζω, *trot, gallop* (?), A.*Fr*.145 A, S.*Fr*.1007, Ar.*Fr*.48 D., Pl.Com.25 D.; prob. in Ar.*Th*.1174.

ἀνακᾰλυπτήρια, τά, *festival of unveiling*, when the bride first took off her maiden veil, and received presents from the bridegroom, Poll.3.36, cf. Timae.149, Hsch.s.v.sq. **II.** *the presents themselves*, subject of a speech attributed to Lysias, Theon *Prog*.2: in sg., Plu. *Tim*.8. **III.** *revelations*, Ph.1.358.

ἀνακάλυπτρα, τά, = ἀνακαλυπτήρια II, D.S.5.2.

ἀνακᾰλύπτω, Dor. ἀγκ-, *uncover*, *IG*4.952.62 (Epid.); *reveal*, τι πρός τινα Plb.4.85.6; τινά, i.e. his character, Philoch.20; ἀ. λόγους *use open* speech, E.*IA*1146; ἀ. κάρα *unveil oneself*, *Or*.294: so in Med., *unveil oneself*, X.*HG*5.4.6. **II.** *remove a covering*, βλεφάρων μὴ ἀνακαλυφθέντων Arist.*Sens*.444^{b}25, cf. 2*Ep.Cor*.3.14.

ἀνακαμπ-ή, ἡ, *bend* at the end of a rod, Bito50.10; of a tube, Hero *Spir*.1.8, 2.33. **-τέον**, *one must return*, Sor.1.98, Philum.ap.Orib. 45.29.19. **-τικός**, ή, όν, *returning*, διαυλωνισμός Eust.1107.63. **-τω**, *bend convexly*, Arist.*Mete*.385^{b}33 (Pass.); *bend back*, τῷ δ' οὐ πάλιν θυμὸς ἀνεκάμπτετ' B.16.82. **II.** *make to return*, Antiph.12. **2.** mostly intr., *bend back, return*, ταύτῃ λῆγον ἀ. ἐς τὰ εἴρηται τὸ ὄρος Hdt.2.8; ἡ περιφορὰ ἐπ' ἀρχὴν ἀ. Arist.*de An*.407^{a}30, cf. Pl.*Phd*.72b; πάλιν ἀ. Arist.*GC*337^{a}6, Men.*Sam*.341, etc. **b.** *walk up and down*, Str.3.4.16, Plu.2.796d, D.L.2.139. **c.** in Logic, of the terms of a proposition, *to be converted*, Arist.*APo*.72^{b}36, *de An*.407^{a}28. **d.** ἀνακάμπτων, name of a *throw of the dice*, Eub.57.

ἀνακάμψερως, ωτος, ὁ, *a herb* the touch of which was said *to bring back love*, *Sedum Anacampseros*, Plu.2.939d, cf. Plin.*HN*24. 167. (Hsch. writes it paroxyt.)

ἀνακαμψίπνοος ἄνεμος *a returning wind*, a kind of *whirlwind*, Arist.*Mu*.394^{b}36.

ἀνάκαμψις, εως, ἡ, *a bending back*, Hp.*Oss*.15, Arist.*Mete*.386^{a}5.

ἀνάκανδα· ἐν ὑπερῴῳ (Lacon.), Hsch.

ἀνάκανθος, ον, *without a spine*, of certain fish, Hdt.4.53; κοχλίας Aenigm.ap.Ath.2.63b. **2.** of plants, *without thorns*, Thphr.*HP* 3.12.9.

ἀνακάπτω, *gulp down*, Hdt.2.93, Ar.*Av*.579, Arist.*HA*541^{a}13, al.

ἀνάκαρ, Adv., (κάρα) *up to* or *towards the head, upwards*, Hp.ap. Gal.19.79. **ἀνακάς**, Adv. = ἄνωθεν, Hsch.

ἀνάκαυσις, εως, ἡ, *setting on fire, kindling*, λύχνων J.*Ap*.2.39, cf. Plu.2.248d (dub.), Anon.*Incred*.8.

ἀνακαχλ-άζω, *boil up, burst forth*, Opp.*C*.1.275. **-ασις**, εως, ἡ, *a bursting forth*, Sch.A.*Pr*.367.

ἀνάκαψις, εως, ἡ, *gulping down*, Arist.*GA*756^{b}4.

ἀνακέαται, Ion. for ἀνάκεινται.

Ἀνάκεια, ων, τά, *festival of the Dioscuri*, Lys.*Fr*.75.3, Poll.1.37; v. Ἄνακες.

ἀνάκειμαι, poet. ἄγκ-, serving as Pass. to ἀνατίθημι, *to be laid up* as a votive offering in the temple, *to be dedicated*, κρητῆρές οἱ..ἓξ χρύσεοι ἀνακέαται Hdt.1.14; ἀ. ἐν ἱρῷ Id.2.135; πρὸς τοῖς ἱεροῖς Lys.10.28: metaph., αἶνος Ὀλυμπιονίκαις ἄγκειται Pi.*O*.11(10).8, cf. 13.36; λόγος τῷ θεῷ ἀ. Pl.*Smp*.197e; ἐν οὐρανῷ παράδειγμα ἀ. *R*.592b. **b.** *to be set up* as a statue in public, Σόλων ἀνάκειται παράδειγμα D.19.251, cf. *IG*14.1389 i 8; χρύσεοί κ' ἀνεκείμεθα Theoc.10.33, cf. Lycurg. 51. **2.** *to be ascribed* or *offered*, αἱ πράξεις ἀ. τινι Plu.*Lyc*.1; ἡ ἡγεμονία ἀ. τινι Id.*Arist*.15; ἐς τοὺς ἀστέρας τοὺς ἑπτὰ..τὰς ἡμέρας ἀνακεῖσθαι D.C.37.18, cf. Polem.*Cyn*.15. **II.** πᾶν or πάντα ἀνάκειται ἔς τινα everything *is referred to* a person, *depends on* his will, Hdt.1.97, 3.31: so c. dat. pers., πάντων ἀνακειμένων τοῖς Ἀθηναίοις ἐς τὰς ναῦς since *they had* their whole fortunes *depending* on their ships, Th.7.71; ἐπὶ σοὶ τάδε πάντ' ἀνάκειται Ar.*Av*.638; ἅπαντα..ἐπὶ τῇ τύχῃ μᾶλλον ἀ. ἢ τῇ προνοίᾳ Antipho 5.6; of persons, σοὶ ἀνακείμεσθα E.*Ba*.934; εἰς θάνατον ἦν ἀνακείμενα τοῖς ἀλογήσασι the death penalty *was reserved* for..., J.*AJ*17.6.5; λιμὸς εἰς ὑστάτην ἀνακείμενος ἀναισχυντίαν 18.1.1. **2.** *to be put aside*, ταῦτα ἀνακείσθω Them.*in Ph*.29.20. **III.** *lie at table, recline*, S.*Fr*.756, Philippid.30, Arist. *Cat*.6^{b}12, *Fr*.607, Diph.40 Mein. (om. Kock), Plb.13.6.8, *Ev.Matt.* 9.10, al.; cf. Phryn.191.

Ἀνάκειον, τό, (Ἄνακες) *temple of the* Ἄνακες or *Dioscuri*, And.1. 45, Th.8.93, D.45.80 (cf. *AB*212), *IG*4.1028.4 (Epid., ii B.C.); ἐν τῷ ϝανακείῳ ib.9(1).129 (Elatea, v B.C.); cf. ἀναγκαῖον.

ἀνακείρω, *shear* or *cut off, rip up*, Str.16.4.15, [Gal.]14.790, Aët. 13.4.

ἀνακεκᾰλυμμένως, Adv. pf. Pass., *openly*, Hsch.

ἀνακέκλομαι, poet. for ἀνακαλέω, *call out*, *h.Hom*.19.5.

ἀνακέλᾰδος, ὁ, *loud shout* or *din*, dub.l. in E.*Or*.185, where Sch. uses the Verb **ἀνακελαδέω**.

ἀνακέομαι, *repair*, τοῖχον *IG*11.203 *A* 56 (Delos, iii B.C.); cf. ἐνακέομαι; *make good*, Ael.*NA*5.19; τάχ' ἄν τι καὶ ἐξαμάρτοις, ὃ μὴ δυνηθήσῃ -ασθαι D.C.52.37.

ἀνακεραμόω, *re-tile*, *IG*11.287 *A* 72,112 (Delos, iii B.C.).

ἀνακεράννῡμι and -ύω, *mix up* or *again*, ἀνὰ κρητῆρα κέρασσεν Od. 3.390; οἶνον ἀνεκεράννυ γλυκύτατον Ar.*Ra*.511: metaph., τὴν πόλιν αὐτὴν πρὸς αὑτὴν ἀ. ταῖς οἰκειότησιν Plu.*Cat.Mi*.25; κοινωνίαις πολέμων -ασθέντες D.H.1.60:—Pass., πολλῷ τῷ θνητῷ ἀνακεραννυμένη Pl.*Criti*.121a: aor. -κεράσθην Id.*Ti*.87a, part. -κρᾱθείς Plu.*Rom*.29.

Ἄνᾰκες, ων, οἱ, *the Dioscuri, Pollux and Castor*, σωτῆροιν Ἀνάκοιν τε Διοσκούροιν *IG*3.195, cf. 1.34.8, 2.699.30, etc., Plu.*Thes*.33, Cic. *ND*3.21: old pl. of ἄναξ; cf. Ἀνάκειον, -εια.

ἀν-άκεστος, ον, = ἀνήκεστος, Hp.ap.Erot. (ἀνηκ- in *Acut*.39).

ἀνακεφαλαι-όομαι, *sum up the argument*, of an orator, D.H.*Lys.* 9; ἀ. πρὸς ἀνάμνησιν Arist.*Fr.*133:—Pass., *to be summed up*, ἐν τῷ λόγῳ τούτῳ *Ep.Rom.*13.9. **-ωσις**, εως, ἡ, *a summary*, D.H. 1.90. **-ωτικός**, ή, όν, *fit for summing up*: τὸ ἀ., = foreg., Id. *Lys.*19. Adv. -κῶς *summarily*, Eust.1579.8, etc.

ἀνακηδής, -ές, = ἀκηδής, Democr.174,254.

ἀνακηκίω, *spout up, gush forth*, ἀνεκήκιεν αἷμα Il.7.262; ἀνακηκίει ἱδρώς 13.705; πέτρης *from..*, A.R.3.227. 2. rare in Prose, *bubble up, throb violently*, Pl.*Phdr.*251b. II. causal, *make to spout out*, freq. in later Ep., A.R.4.600, Nonn.*D.*12.359, Tryph.322. [ῐ Ep., cf. κηκίω.]

ἀνακήρ-υκτος, ον, = ἀκήρυκτος, dub. in Poll.8.139. **-υξις**, εως, ἡ, *proclamation*, Poll.8.139, Just.*Nov.*6.1.9. **-ύσσω**, Att. **-ττω**, *proclaim by voice of herald, publish abroad*, φόνον τὸν Λαΐειον S.*OT*450:—Pass., μὴ ἀνακηρυχθῇ ἡ βδελυρία εἰς πόλιν Aeschin.1.160. 2. c. acc. pers., *proclaim* as conqueror, τοὺς νικῶντας Ar.*Pl.* 585:—Pass., ἀνακηρυχθῆναι Hdt.6.103, cf. Th.5.50; of slaves, ἀνεκαρύχθησαν ἐπ' ἐλευθερίᾳ *GDI*3600 (Calymna). 3. *extol, sing praises of*, τινά Jul.*Or.*1.46a. II. *put up to auction*, Hdt.1.196. III. *offer by voice of herald*, ἀ. σῶστρά τινος X.*Mem.*2.10.2.

ἀνακής, ές, = ἀνήκεστος, Eup.21. II. Subst., an Indian bird, Hsch. **ἀνακῆσαι**· ἡσυχάσαι, Id.

ἀνακίδνᾰμαι, *spread upwards*, Ἄραψ ἀτμὸς ἐς Ὄλυμπον ἀνακίδναται *Pae.Delph.*11.

ἀνακίδωτος, ον, (ἀκίς) *pointless*, Hdn.Gr.1.222.

ἀνακινδῡνεύω, *run a further risk*, D.C.41.25, 42.1 (Pass.); generally, *run risks*, c. inf., Hdt.8.100: c. dat., ἀ. ναυμαχίῃσι ib.68.α': c. part., ἀ. συμβάλλοντα Id.9.26.

ἀνακῑν-έω (once -άω, imper. ἀνακείνα *PHolm.*20.19), *sway* or *swing to and fro*, Hdt.4.94, cf. Hp.*VC*21. II. *stir up, awaken*, νόσον ἀ. S.*Tr.*1259; of cocks or quails, *stir* them *up* (to fight), Pl.*Lg.* 789c; ἀ. πόλεμον Plu.*Luc.*5; ὑπολείμματα στάσεων *Pomp.*16:—Pass., δόξαι ἀνακεκίνηνται Pl.*Men.*85c, cf. Pherecyd.102 J. III. *uproot*, τὰς κρηπῖδας Agath.2.1: metaph., τὰ καθεστῶτα Id.4.27. **-ημα**, ατος, τό, *swinging of the arms* as an exercise, Hp.*Vict.*2.64. **-ησις**, εως, ἡ, *swinging to and fro* of the arms as preparatory exercise of pugilists: metaph., *preparation, prelude*, Pl.*Lg.*722d. II. *stirring up, excitement*, φρενῶν S.*OT*727; ἀλογίας Porph.*Abst.*1.41.

Ἀνάκιον, τό, = Ἀνάκειον, *IG*2.660:—**Ἀνάκια**, τά, *festival of Dioscuri*, ib.570.

ἀνακίρνᾰμαι, *mix*, ἀνακίρναται ποτόν S.*Fr.*255.8: metaph., φιλίας ..ἀνακίρνασθαι *mix the bowl of* friendship, E.*Hipp.*254. II. as Pass., ἀὴρ ἡλίου ἀκτῖσιν ἀνακιρνάμενος *tempered by..*, Pl.*Ax.*371d; *mingle with*, Iamb. *in Nic.*p.73 P.:—Act., ἀνακίρνησιν Ph.1.284, part. -κιρνάς 1.153:—Pass., ἀνακιρνᾶται Id.*Fr.*74 H. (s. v. l.), cf. Alex. Trall.1.13.

ϝανακισία, name of a tribe at Mantinea, *IG*5(2).271.19.

ἀνακκάζω, Locr. for ἀναγκ-, *Jahresh.*14.168 (Tolophon, iii B.C.).

ἀνακλάζω, aor. 2 ἀνέκλᾰγον E.*IA*1062, Call.*Hec.*1.1.10: aor. 1 ἀνέκλαγξα Ael.*NA*12.33:—*cry aloud, scream out*, E. l.c.; of a dog, *bark, bay*, X.*Cyr.*1.4.15; of geese, *cackle*, Ael. l. c.

ἀνακλαίω, Att. -κλάω, fut. -κλαύσομαι Telecl.1 D.:—*weep aloud, burst into tears*, ἀνακλαύσας μέγα Hdt.3.14, cf. 66, D.C.*Fr.*18.10. 2. c. acc., *weep for*, κακὰ μέζω ἢ ὥστε ἀνακλαίειν Hdt.3.14: so in Med., ὑμῖν τάδ'.. ἀνακλαίομαι S.*Ph.*939; τὰς παρούσας ἀτυχίας ἀνακλαύσασθαι πρὸς ὑμᾶς Antipho 2.4.1.

ἀνάκλᾰ-σις, εως, ἡ, (ἀνακλάω) *a bending back, flexure*, Hp.*Fract.*2; of swords, D.S.5.30; *curve*, of the lines of a ship, Callix.1. II. *reflection* of light or *reverberation* of sound, Arist.*APo.*98^{a}29, *Sens.* 437^{b}10, al., *Stoic.*2.199; so of the wind, Arist.*Pr.*945^{a}7; of water, ἀ. ποιεῖσθαι have its course *turned*, Plb.4.43.9; ἀ. τῆς σαρκὸς ποιεῖσθαι make it *elastic*, Arist.*Pr.*966^{b}17. **-σμός**, ὁ, = foreg. 1, Heliod. ap.Orib.46.12.1. II. in metre, *overlapping*, cf. ἀνακλάω II. 2, Sch. Heph.12. **-στος**, ον, *bent back, reflected*: metaph., of participles derived from Nouns or Adjectives, Plu.2.1011d.

ἀνα-κλαυθμός or **-κλαυσμός** (so codd. l. citand.), ὁ, = sq., D.H. 6.46. **-κλαυσις**, εως, ἡ, (κλαίω) *lamentation*, Id.9.33 (pl.).

ἀνακλάω, *bend back*, ξύλα Hp.*Fract.*13; ἀνακλάσας δέρην E.*Or.* 1471 (lyr.); ταὼς ἀ. οὐράν D.Chr.12.2; ἀ. τὴν γλῶσσαν πρὸς τὸν οὐρανόν Aret.*CA*1.7; to a wrestler, ἀνάκλα *POxy.*466.29 (ii A.D.):—Pass., πίοιμι τὸν τράχηλον ἀνακεκλασμένη *with* my neck *bent back*, Theopomp.Com.54, cf. D.Chr.5.25 (Act.); but in Medic., τὴν κεφαλὴν ἀνακεκλασμένην μεσσηγὺ τῶν ὠμοπλατέων κέεσθαι Aret.*SA*1.6; ἀνακεκλασμένοι *with eyelids slightly open*, Hp.*Coac.*64. 2. *break short off*, or more prob., *fend off*, μηχανὰς βρόχους περιβάλλοντες ἀ. Th. 2.76; prob. in D.C.66.4. 3. metaph., ἀ. ἐπ' ἄλλα τὴν διάνοιαν Plu. 2.359a. II. of light, *reflect*, ib.696a, al.:—Pass., Arist.*Mete.*340^{a} 28, al.; τοσοῦτον ἀνακλασθῆναι τῶν ἀδυνάτων εἶναί φασιν *that* [the rays] *should be* so much *reflected*, ib.343^{b}7; of sound, *to be reverberated*, Thphr.*Sens.*53; of a ball, *rebound*, Arist.*Ph.*255^{b}27. 2. ἀνακλώμενος, in metre, of the *overlapping* of Ionic feet, μέτρον ἀνακλώμενον Heph.12, cf. Sch. ad loc.

ἀνάκλεις, ειδος, ἡ, *picklock*, Poll.7.107.

ἀνακλέπτω, *steal*, prob. l. in *h.Merc.*515, cf. *GDI*1586 (Dodona), Theoc.5.9:—Pass., *steal away, retire*, Hsch.

ἀνάκλημα, ατος, τό, = ἀνάκλασις, τοῦ ῥυθμοῦ Jul.*Ep.*186.

ἀνακλήρωσις, εως, ἡ, *re-allotment*, Sch.Pi.*O.*7.110.

ἀνάκλη-σις, εως, ἡ, (ἀνακαλέω) *calling on, invocation*, θεῶν Th.7. 71; *salutation, address*, Plu.2.35a. 2. *calling aloud*, οἱ βάτραχοι ..ἀνακλήσεσι χρῶνται ib.982e; ζητεῖν τινα μετ' ἀνακλήσεως Nymphis 9. II. *recalling*, ἀ. θέρμης ποιέεσθαι Aret.*CD*2.7, cf. *SD*2.12: metaph., ἀπὸ τῶν αἰσθητῶν ἐπὶ τὰ νοητά Porph.*Marc.*10. 2. *restoration, revival*, Aret.*SA*1.6, cf. *SD*1.7. 3. *retreat*, ἀ. σάλπιγγι σημαίνειν Plu.*Fab.*12, cf. *Alex.*33, Onos.10.2. **-τέον**, *one must revive, restore*, Aët.16.36, Orib.*Fr.*56. **-τήρια**, τά, *a festival on a king's proclamation*, Plb.18.55.3, 28.12.8. **-τικός**, ή, όν, *fit for exhorting*, πρὸς ὁμόνοιαν Plu.*Lyc.*4. II. *fit for recalling*; τὸ ἀνακλητικὸν σημαίνειν, σαλπίγξαι sound *a retreat*, D.H.8.65, *AP* 11.136 (Lucill.): metaph., ἐκδίδωσι τὸ ἀ. τῷ Ἄττιδι Jul.*Or.*5.169c. Adv. -κῶς Sch.E.*Ph.*818. **-τος**, ον, *called back to service*, Lat. *evocatus*, D.C.45.12; οἱ ἀ. Id.55.24, 78.5.

ἀνάκλιθρον, τό, gloss on *fulcrum*; of the back of Cassiepeia's chair, Ptol.*Alm.*7.5.

ἀνάκλῐμα, ατος, τό, *slope, ascent*, τῆς γῆς Apollod.*Poliorc.*173.11.

ἀνακλῑνοπάλη, ἡ, Mart.14.201 (f. l. for ἐπι-).

ἀνακλιν-τήρ, ῆρος, ὁ, *neighbour at dinner*, πρῶτος ἦν ἀ. Δαρείου Ps.-Callisth.2.13. **-τήριον**, τό, *head-rest* of a couch, Erot. s. v. ἀνακλισμοῦ:—also **-τρον**, τό, Poll.6.9; condemned by Phryn.130.

ἀνα-κλίνω, poet. ἀγκλ-, (v. κλίνω) *lean* one thing *upon* another, [τόξον] ποτὶ γαίῃ ἀγκλίνας *having laid* it on the ground, Il.4.113; Ἔρως ἀνακλίνας τοῦ τόξου τὸν πῆχυν Philostr.*Im.*2.1; ἀ. ἑαυτοὺς ἐπὶ τὸ ἐναντίον, of sailors struggling against the wind, Arist.*Mech.* 851^{b}13; *cause to recline* at table, Plb.31.4.5, *Ev.Luc.*12.37:—mostly in Pass., *lie, sink*, or *lean back, recline*, ἀνακλινθεὶς πέσεν ὕπτιος Od. 9.371; of persons asleep, 18.189; of rowers, 13.78; of the elephant, Arist.*HA*498^{a}11; to be *strung*, of strings of lyre, Philostr.*Im.*1. 10. 2. Pass., of ground, *lie sloping upwards*, *Gp.*2.3.1. II. *push* or *put back*, and so, *open*, θύρην ἀγκλίνας Od.22.156; so of the door of Olympus, ἠμὲν ἀνακλῖναι πυκινὸν νέφος ἠδ' ἐπιθεῖναι Il.5.751, cf. Call.*Ap.*6; τὴν θύρην τὴν καταπηκτὴν ἀ., i.e. the trap-door, Hdt. 5.16. III. *throw* the head *back*, and so, *lift up*, τὴν τῆς ψυχῆς αὐγήν Pl.*R.*540a. IV. *overthrow*, of earthquake, compared to battering-ram, Paus.7.24.10. **-κλῐσις**, εως, ἡ, *lying* or *leaning back, position in bed*, Hp.*Coac.*487, Arist.*Cat.*6^{b}11. 2. *bending back*, in tetanus, Aret.*SA*1.6. II. *back to lean against*, θρόνοι.. ἀνακλίσεις ἔχοντες.. *IG*2.676, cf. 2.701 ii (iii) 45, cf. Ath.5.192f; βάθρον ἀνάκλισιν ἔχον *IG* 4.39 (Aegina); *bench, seat*, *JHS*12.232, cf. *IG*1.277*d*. **-κλισμός**, ὁ, *back of a chair* or *couch*, Hp.*Art.*7, Erot. s. v. ἕδος. **-κλῐτος**, ον, *for reclining*, δίφρος Hp.*Superf.*8, Aret.*CA*1.4; θρόνος, = ἀνακλιντήριον, Plu.*Rom.*26; τὰ ἀνάκλιτα Ps.-Callisth.3.22.

ἀνακλονέω, *toss up and down*, Opp.*H.*3.478.

ἀνακλύζω, fut. -ύσω, *wash up against*, A.R.2.551. 2. abs., *boil as with waves*, Plu.2.590f:—causal, *stir up*, χερσὶ θαλάσσιον ὕδωρ Sch.Nic.*Al.*165. 3. Med., *rinse* the mouth, Dsc.*Eup.*1.66.

ἀνακλώθω, of the Fates, *undo the thread* of one's life, *change* one's *destiny*, Luc.*Hist.Conscr.*38; Μοιρῶν νῆμ' ἀνέκλωσαν [αἱ Μοῦσαι] *IG* 14.1188.

ἀνακμ-άζω, *break out afresh with renewed vigour*, of στάσις, J.*BJ* 5.1.1. **-αστικός**, ή, όν, = ἀνηβητήριος, Sch.E.*Andr.*552.

ἀνακναδάλλω, *excite by scratching*, of quails, Poll.7.136, 9.108, Hsch.

ἀνακνάπτω, *make* old clothes *fresh by fulling*: metaph., ἀ. τὰς ἀλλοτρίας ἐπινοίας *vamp* them *up as new*, Lysipp.4.

ἀνακνάω, *scratch*, Paul.Aeg.4.25 (in Med.), cf. Phryn.*PS*p.12 B.

ἀνακνίδεσι· τῇ ὀσφύι, Hsch.

ἀνακνισόω, *perfume thoroughly, fill with vapour*, Tryph.349.

ἀνακογχίζω, dub. in Hp.*Mochl.*2.

ἀνακογχῠλ-ιάζω, (κόγχη) *break open* the capsule covering the seal of a will, διαθήκην Ar.*V.*589 (with *double entente*), cf. Aristid.*Or.* 51(27).9. 2. = ἀναγαργαρίζω (sc. ὕδατι), Pl.*Smp.*185d (but ἀνακογχυλίσαι, Hsch.). **-ιασμός**, ὁ, *gargling*, Ath.5.187a, Antyll. ap.Orib.5.28.3; and **-ιαστόν** (sc. φάρμακον), τό, *gargle*, Pl.Com. 196. **-ίζω**, = -ιάζω, Eup.275, Ruf.ap.Aët.2.92, Poll.6.25, Gal.11. 769. **-ισμα**, ατος, τό, *gargle*, Orib.*Eup.*4.69. **-ισμός**, ὁ, = -ιασμός, Aret.*CA*1.7, Orib.*Fr.*74.

ἀνακοιλιασμός, ὁ, in pl., *purgative*, Cael.Aur.*TP*2.14.

ἀνακοινέω, = sq., only in Med. imper. ἀνακοινέο (for -έεο) Thgn.73.

ἀνακοιν-όω, *communicate, impart*, τινί τι, v.l. in Pl.*Cra.*383a. 2. ἀ. τινί *communicate with, take counsel with*, Ar.*Lys.*1177; ἀ. τοῖς μάντεσι Pl.*Lg.*913b; ἀ. τισὶν ὑπέρ τινος Arist.*Mir.*843^{b}20. II. Med., with plpf. Pass. ἀνεκεκοίνωντο X.*An.*5.6.36:—properly, *communicate* what is *one's own* to another, so of a river, ἀνακοινοῦται τῷ Ἴστρῳ τὸ ὕδωρ Hdt.4.48; ἀ. τὸ ὕδωρ πρὸς τὴν πηγήν Paus.5.7.3, cf. 8.28.3. 2. much like Act., *impart*, τῷ θεῷ περί τινος X.*An.* 3.1.5, cf. 5.6.36, etc.; ἀνακοινοῦσθαί τινι *consult* one, Pl.*Prt.*314b; τοῖς συμμάχοις X.*HG*6.3.8; πρὸς τοὺς οἰκέτας ἀνακοινοῦσθαι περὶ τῶν μεγίστων Thphr.*Char.*4.2: abs., βουλομένους ἀνακοινοῦσθαί τε καὶ ἐς λόγον ἐλθεῖν Ar.*Nu.*470, cf. Pl.*Prt.*349a. **-ωσις**, εως, ἡ, *communication*, Sch.Ar.*Pl.*39. **-ωτέος**, α, ον, Sch.E.*Hipp.*295.

ἀνακοιρᾰνέω, *rule* or *command* in a place, Posidipp.ap.Ath.7. 318d.

ἀνακοιτάζομαι, *deflower* a maiden, Sch.Opp.*H.*1.390.

ἀνακολλ-άω, *glue on* or *to, glue together*, τρίχας Dsc.2.133:—Pass., χιτὼν ἐφ' ἑαυτὸν ἀνακεκολλημένος Lyd.*Mag.*2.13. **-ημα**, ατος, τό, *adhesive plaster*, Dsc.2.135, Aët.7.70. **-ησις**, εως, ἡ, *sticking up* or *out* of in-growing eyelashes *with an adhesive*, Gal.6.627, Dsc. 1.71. **-ητικός**, ή, όν, *of* or *for glueing*, Id.2.133; of a plaster, Heras ap.Gal.13.782.

ἀνακολούθητος, ον, prob. f.l. for -ουθος, D.H.*Th.*49.

ἀνακολουθ-ία, ἡ, Rhet., *inconsequence*, esp. employed with humorous effect, Demetr.*Eloc.*153; generally, Demetr.Lac.*Herc.*1012.63, Corn.*Rh.*p.368 H., Diogenian.Epicur.3.26. **-ος**, ον, *inconsequent*, Epicur.*Ep.*2 p.41 U.; μετάβασις ἀ. Aët.6.22; *inconsistent*, τοῖς ἑαυτοῦ λόγοις Muson.*Fr.*10 p.56 H.; v.l. in Arr.*Epict.*1.7.18. 2. Gramm., *anomalous*, of inflexions, A.D.*Pron.*66.1, al.; also of changed constructions, ἀ. σχῆμα, σχηματισμοί, D.H.*Th.*41,42. Adv. -θως Id.*Rh.*8.13, Sch.Il.2.469, *EM*722.2.

ἀνακολπ-άζω, (κόλπος) *tuck up one's gown, gird oneself up*, Ar.*Th.* 1174; but cf. ἀνακαλπάζω. **-όω**, = foreg., *EM*410.20:—Pass., *form a bay*, Anon.*Geog.Comp.*40.

ἀνακολυμβάω, *come up after diving*: trans., *bring up from the bottom*, Thphr.*HP*4.6.5:—Pass., Hsch.

ἀνακομάω, *get hair again*, Luc.*DMeretr.*12.5.

ἀνακομβόομαι, *gird oneself up* for action, *Gp.*10.83.1.

ἀνακομ-ιδή, Dor. **ἀγκομιδά** *IG*4.742.17, ἡ:—*a carrying away again, recovery*, ἡ τῶν πλοίων ἀ. Decr.ap.D.18.75. 2. *recovery*, ἐκ τῶν νούσων Hp.*VM*21. 3. *return*, Arist.*HA*597ᵇ9, *SIG*615.14 (Delph., ii B.C.), Onos.11.3. 4. *bringing up*, τῶν ἐπιτηδείων Str.3.3.1. **-ίζω**, poet. **ἀγκομ-**, *carry up*, X.*HG*2.3.20:—Pass., Din.1.68; esp. *to be carried up-stream*, or *up the country*, Hdt.2.115. II. *bring back, recover*, οἰκέτην v.l. in X.*Mem.* 2.10.1:—Med. (with pf. Pass., Id.*An.*4.7.1 and 17), *bring* or *take back* or *away with one*, Hdt.5.85, Th.6.7:—Pass., *to be brought back*, Hdt.3.129, etc.; and of persons, *return, come* or *go back*, Id.2.107, Th.2.31; *get safe away, escape*, Plb.1.38.5: so in Med., ἑαυτὸν ἀνακομίζεσθαι ἐκ τῆς Φιλίππου συνηθείας *withdraw from*.., Plu.*Arat.* 51. 2. τὸ Μηδείας ἔπος ἀγκομίσαι *bring back safe*, i.e. *redeem, fulfil*, Pi.*P.*4.9 (prob.):—Med., ἀ. τύχαν δαιμόνων *bring* it *back upon oneself*, E.*Hipp.*831 (lyr.). III. *restore to health, strengthen*, Hp.*Fract.*7, cf. Gal.1.405 (Pass.): metaph., πεπονηκυῖαν ἐξ ἀρχῆς ἀνακεκομίσθαι τὴν οἰκουμένην Aristid.*Or.*26(14).98. **-ιστέον**, *one must restore to health*, Paul.Aeg.3.39. 2. of Pass., *one must return*, Ach.Tat.5.11.

ἀνάκομμα, ατος, τό, (ἀνακόπτω) *check*, φλεγμονῶν, ὀδυνῶν Aët.12.20.

ἀνακονεῖν, v. ἀνακωνῆν.

ἀνᾰκοντίζω, intr., *dart* or *shoot up*, αἷμα δ' ἀνηκόντιζε Il.5.113; so of water, Hdt.4.181. 2. causal, θαλασσίους αὔρας Callistr.*Stat.*14.

ἀνα-κοπή, ἡ, *resistance, check* due to collision, Epicur.*Ep.*1 p.7 U. (pl.), Phld.*D.*1.14 (pl.), Plu.2.76f, cf. 1128c. II. *recoil* of the waves, Id.*Pyrrh.*15, cf. J.*BJ*1.21.6; in a tidal river, Str.3.5.9. III. *back-water*, Plu.*Alex.*44. IV. *clashing* of vowels in hiatus, etc., D.H.*Comp.*22, cf. *Dem.*38. **-κοπτέον**, *one must remove, eliminate*, Paul.Aeg.6.90. **-κόπτω**, *drive back, push back*, θυρέων δ' ἀνέκοπτεν ὀχῆας Od.21.47. 2. *beat back* an assailant, Th.4.12, cf. Plu.*Caes.* 38. 3. ἀ. ναῦν *check* a ship's course, v.l. in Thphr.*Char.*25.2. 4. *return* food, διὰ ῥινῶν, εἰς τὰς ῥῖνας, Herod.Med. in *Rh.Mus.*58.86,90 and 96, cf. Aret.*SA*1.6. II. *knock out*, τὰς ὄψεις ἀνακοπείς Philostr. *Her.Prooem.*2. 2. *cut from below*, Hld.9.18. 3. *beat up* eggs, Sor.1.222, *PMag.Lond.*121.180. III. *check, stop*, ἦχον D.H.*Comp.* 22; προσδοκίαν Phld.*Piet.*25; ἀοιδήν Coluth.125:—Pass., *to be stopped, restrained*, τῆς ὁρμῆς Luc.*Alex.*57, cf. *PFlor.*36.3; *stop short* in a speech, Luc.*Nigr.*35. IV. Medic., *take effect*, ἀνακόπτει γὰρ οὕτως ἡ ὠφέλεια Herod.Med. in *Rh.Mus.*58.92 (fort. διακ., cf. *SIG*1170.16).

ἀνακορέω, *sweep again* or *out*, Pherecr.5 D.

ἀνακός, ὁ, = ἄναξ, Hdn.Gr.1.150, 2.647, cf. Ael.Dion.*Fr.*56.

ἀνακοσμέω, *adorn anew, restore*, *IGRom.*4.468.14 (Pergam.), v.l. in Aristid.*Or.*26(14).98.

ἀνάκουστος, ον, *not hearing, deaf*, cj. in Ph.2.417.

ἀνακουφ-ίζω, *lift* or *raise up*, S.*Fr.*23; ἀ. δέμας E.*Or.*218; ἑαυτὸν εἰς ἀνάβασιν, of a horseman mounting, X.*Eq.*7.2; of the ship of state, ἀ. κάρα βυθῶν S.*OT*23; ὁ ἀὴρ ἀ. τὸν ἀσκόν Arist.*Pr.*939ᵃ35:—Pass., *feel lightened* or *lifted up*, ἀνεκουφίσθην δέμας E.*Hipp.*1392; *to be relieved in mind*, X.*HG*5.2.28. **-ισις**, εως, ἡ, *relief*, κακῶν S.*OT* 218. **-ισμα**, ατος, τό, *a relief*, Hp.*Vict.*2.64.

ἀνάκοψις, εως, ἡ, *interval*, τῶν παροξυσμῶν Herod.Med. in *Rh.Mus.* 58.91.

ἀνα-κραγγαίνω· ἀνακράζω, Hsch.:—also **-κραγγάνω**, Phot.p.114 R.

ἀνακρᾰδεύω, *brandish*, Hsch.

ἀνακράζω, fut. -κράξομαι or fut. pf. -κεκράξομαι LXX *Jl.*3(4).16: aor. ἀνέκρᾰγον; late ἀνέκραξα ib.*Jd.*7.20, *BGU*1201.11, *Ev.Marc.*1. 23, al.:—*cry out, lift up the voice, shout*, ἐπεὶ.. ἀνέκραγον Od.14.467; εἴ τι πέραν ἀερθεὶς ἀνέκραγον if I *raised my voice* too high, Pi.*N.*7.76; ἐξ ἑνὸς στόματος ἅπαντες ἀνέκραγον Ar.*Eq.*670, cf. *V.*1311, etc.; οὐκ ἀνέκραγεν, of a dying man, Antipho 5.44; πρῶτος ἐπὶ τοῦ βήματος ἀνέκραγεν Arist.*Ath.*28.3: foll. by a relat., ἀνέκραγον ὡς εὖ λέγοι Ar. *Ec.*431, cf. X.*An.*5.1.14; τηλικαῦτ' ἀνεκράγετε, ὡς.. D.21.215: c. inf., ἀνακραγόντων βάλλειν.. Plu.*Phoc.*34. 2. rarely of animals, ἂν γλαὺξ ἀνακράγῃ Men.534.11.

ἀνάκρᾱσις, εως, ἡ, *mixing with others*, Plu.*Alex.*47, etc.

ἀνακρατέω, *hold up, support*, Sor.1.114.

ἀνακραυγ-άζω, *cry aloud*, Arr.*Epict.*2.19.15. **-ασμα**, ατος, τό, *loud outcry*, Epicur.*Fr.*414 (pl.).

ἀνακρέκομαι, *begin to play*, ἐς σὲ ἅπας ὄρνις ἀνακρέκεται each bird *tunes its voice* for thee, *AP*9.562 (Crin.).

ἀνακρεμ-άννῡμι, poet. **ἀγκρ-**:—Pass., -κρέμᾰμαι:—*hang up on* a thing, πασσάλῳ ἀγκρεμάσασα Od.1.440; τὰς πέδας ἀνεκρέμασαν ἐς τὴν ἀκρόπολιν, as a votive offering, Hdt.5.77; τὰ ὅπλα πρὸς τὸ Ἀθήναιον ib.95; ἀ. τινά *crucify*, Id.9.120; βροχὸν ἑαυτῷ περιθεὶς ἀνεκρέμασε D.S.2.6; *suspend* a wounded limb in a sling, Hp.*Art.*22:—Pass., ἀνακρεμαμένου τοῦ νέκυος *being hung up*, Hdt.2.121.γ'; τούτου.. τοῦ ἀνακρεμασθέντος Id.9.122, cf. 7.194. II. *make dependent*, ἀ. ἐξ ἀλλήλων τὴν δύναμιν Pl.*Ion*536a; ἀνακρεμάσας [ὑμᾶς] ἀπὸ τῶν ἐλπίδων Aeschin.3.100; ἀ. τὴν πίστιν εἴς τινα Plb.8.19.3. **-ασμός**, ὁ, *hanging up*, *AB*447. **-αστήρ**, ῆρος, ὁ, = κρεμαστήρ, Sor.ap. Orib.54.31.20.

Ἀνακρεόντειος, α, ον, *of Anacreon*, μέτρον Heph.15.22, cf. Sch. Heph.p.118 C.

ἀνακρήμνημι, = ἀνακρεμάννυμι, *shore up*, J.*BJ*5.11.4; *undermine*, ὑπονόμοις τὸ τεῖχος App.*Mith.*75:—also **ἀνακρημνάω**, prob. in J.*BJ*2. 17.8, *AJ*7.10.2.

ἀνακρῑβής, ές, *inaccurate*, Eust.878.37, al.

ἀνακρίνω, *examine closely, interrogate*, esp. judicially, Παυσανίαν Th.1.95, cf. Antipho 2.1.9, Pl.*Smp.*201e; ἀ. τινὰ πόθεν ζῇ Diph.32.3; *sound* a person, LXX 1*Ki.*20.12. 2. *inquire into*, ἀ. τοὺς ἐργασαμένους Antipho 2.3.2; τὴν [αἰτίαν] Phld.*Po.*994 *Fr.*21, cf. *Lib.* p.21 O.:—Med., ἀ. ποινὰ τίς ἔσται what remedy there shall be, Pi.*P.* 4.63. II. *examine* magistrates so as to prove their qualification, D.57.66 and 70. 2. of the magistrates, *examine* persons concerned in a suit, so as to prepare the matter for trial, And.1.101, Is.5.32; ὁ ἄρχων ἀνέκρινε πᾶσιν ὑμῖν καὶ ἀνακρίνας εἰσήγαγεν εἰς τὸ δικαστήριον D.48.31, cf. Arist.*Ath.*56.6:—Pass., ἀνεκρίθησαν αἱ ἀμφισβητήσεις D.48.23:—Med., οὐκ ἀνεκρίνατο ταύτην [τὴν γραφήν] *he did* not *have* it *examined*, of the prosecutor, Id.21.103, cf. 53. 17. 3. generally, *examine*, μάρτυρας *SIG*953.46 (Calymna); τινά 1*Cor.*9.3:—Med., *Michel*409.9 (Cos). 4. *select*, Ps.-Callisth.3. 26. III. in Med., abs., ἀνακρίνεσθαι πρὸς ἑωυτούς *dispute, wrangle* one with another, Hdt.9.56.

ἀνάκρισις, poet. **ἄγκρ-**, εως, ἡ, (ἀνακρίνω II. 1) *examination* of the qualifications of magistrates, Poll.8.85. II. (ἀνακρίνω II. 2) *previous examination* of parties concerned in a suit, *preparation* of the matter for trial, X.*Smp.*5.2, etc., cf. *PSI*4.392 (iii B.C.), *OGI*374 (pl.), *Act.Ap.*25.26; of the magistrate, ἀνάκρισιν διδόναι, παραδιδόναι, Pl.*Chrm.*176c, *Lg.*855e; of the parties, εἰς ἀνάκρισιν ἥκειν Is.6.13, etc.; μηδ' εἰς ἄγκρισιν ἐλθεῖν, i.e. should not even *begin proceedings* (where however the Sch. explains ἐς ἄγκρισιν by ἐς μάχην, cf. ἀνακρίνω III), A.*Eu.*364; οὐδ' ἀ. μοι δώσεις you will not allow me *the first forms of law*, Pl.*Chrm.* l.c. III. generally, *inquiry, examination*, Id.*Phdr.*277e. IV. *preliminary examination* of a slave before sale, *POxy.*1463.12, etc. V. *examination, testing* of magical ingredients, etc., *PMag.Par.*1.1992, 2007. VI. *quarrel, dispute*, Hdt.8.69; *disputation*, Phld.*Acad.Ind.*p.72 M.

ἀνακριτήρ, Dor. **ἀνκριτήρ**, ῆρος, ὁ, *examining magistrate*, *GDI* 3055.1 (Chalcedon) (pl.).

ἀνακρίτως, Adv. *with a second* κρίσις, *relapse*, Pall. *in Hp.*2.181 D.

ἀνακροτᾰλίζω, = ἀνακροτέω, Hippoloch.ap.Ath.4.129c.

ἀνακροτέω, *lift up and strike together*, τὼ χεῖρ' ἀνεκρότησ' ὑφ' ἡδονῆς Ar.*Pl.*739; ἀνακροτήσας τὰς χεῖρας Aeschin.2.226; ταῖς χερσὶν ὑφ' ἡδονῆς Plu.*Mar.*44: abs., οἱ δ' ἀνεκρότησαν *applauded vehemently*, Ar.*Eq.*651, *V.*1314, cf. J.*AJ*12.4.9, Alciphr.1.39: aor. part. ἀνακορτήσασα cj. in Hexam.ap.Diogenian.3.67.

ἀνάκρου-μα, ατος, τό, = -κρουσις II, Corn.*Rh.*p.353 H. **-σία**· παιδιᾶς εἶδος ἐπὶ σφαίρας, Hsch. **-σις**, εως, ἡ, *pushing back*, esp. *pushing* a ship *back, backing water*, Th.7.36; ἡ πάλιν ἀ. ib.62; of a horse, with the bit, Plu.2.549c: metaph., *reaction* against depression, -σεις τοῦ φρονήματος ib.78a; *return*, τῆς παλινδρομίας Iamb. *in Nic.*p.76 P. II. in Music, *first beginning of a tune*, Str.9.3. 10. **-στέον**, *one must check*, X.*Eq.*10.12. II. ἀ. τὸν λόγον *put back* for a fresh start, Dam.*Pr.*85. **-στικός**, ή, όν, *capable of reacting*, πληγή Plu.2.936f. **-ω**, poet. **ἀγκρ-**, *push back* a gatepin, βάλανον Aen.Tact.18.6; *stop short, check*, ἵππον χαλινῷ X.*Eq.* 11.3; *back* horses, τὸ ζεῦγος Plu.*Alc.*2:—Pass., Them. *in Ph.*130. 25. 2. ἀπὸ χερσοῦ νῆα.. ἀνακρούεσκον *thrust* her *off* from shore, A.R.4.1650; *throw up*, δίσκον Philostr.*Her.*2.5. II. in Med., ἀνακρούεσθαι πρύμνην *put* one's ship *astern*, by backing water, Ar.*V.* 399, cf. D.S.11.18; or ἀνακρούεσθαι alone, Th.7.38,40; [ἐπὶ] πρύμνην ἀ. Hdt.8.84; but νῆας ἀ., simply *row back*, Tryph.523: metaph., τὸν λόγον πάλιν ἀ. *put back* and make a fresh start, Pl.*Phlb.*13d; παῦε.. μικρὸν ἀνακρουόμενος Luc.*Nigr.*8; ὥσπερ ἁρμονίαν ἐκλελυμένην ἀ. αὖθις ἐπὶ σώφρονα νόμον καὶ βίον Plu.*Cleom.*16. 2. in Music, *strike up*, Theoc.4.31: hence, *begin* a speech, Plb.4.22.11. III. ἀνακρούειν χεροῖν, = ἀνακροτεῖν, Autocr.1.

ἀνακρύπτω, only in aor. 2 ἀνέκρῠφε Nonn.*D.*6.87.

ἀνακρωτηρίαστος, ον, *unmutilated*, Eust.31.41, Sch.Th.3.34.

ἀνακτάομαι, fut. -ήσομαι: pf. ἀνέκτημαι S.*Fr.*358:—*regain for oneself, recover*, τυραννίδα, ἀρχὴν ἀ. ὀπίσω, Hdt.1.61, 3.73; Ἄργος ἐς ἑωυτοὺς ἀ. ὀπίσω 6.83; δῶμα πατρὸς A.*Ch.*237; ἀ. ταῖς πόλεσι τὴν ἐλευθερίαν D.S.16.14; *repair, retrieve*, ἐλαττώσεις Plb.10.33.4. 2. *refresh, revive*, σώματα, ψυχάς, Id.3.60.7, 87.3; τοὺς κεκμηκότας ὑπὸ τραυμάτων D.H.2.42; γλήχων.. λειποθυμοῦντας -κτᾶται Dsc.3.31; ἀ. ἑαυτόν J.*AJ*9.6.4, Arr.*Epict.*3.25.4, etc. 3. *reinstate*, τοὺς ἐπταικότας D.C.44.47; *restore*, ναούς Id.53.2; θυσίας *IG*2.628. II. c. acc. pers., *win* a person *over, gain* his *favour* or *friendship*, τὸν θεόν Hdt.1.50, X.*Cyr.*1.3.9, Men.*Pk.*123, etc.; παμπόλλους φίλους X.*Cyr.*2.2.10. (Act. dub., v. sub ἀνακτίζω.)

ἀνακτένισμα, ατος, τό, *carding, screening, sifting*, *Gloss.*

ἀνακτέον, (ἀνάγω) *one must bring up*, φλέγμα διὰ τοῦ στόματος

Hp.*Dent.*25. II. *one must refer*, εἰς τὴν ὕλην τὰς αἰτίας Arist.*GA* 778^{b}1. III. *one must reduce, bring back*, εἰς τὴν παλαιὰν ἀταξίαν Plu.*Nob.*3.

ἀνά-κτησις, εως, ἡ, *regaining*, ἀγαθῶν Hierocl.*in CA* 24 p.474 M., Herm.ap.Stob.1.41.44, Dam.*Pr.*75; ἀρουρῶν *PTeb.*378.12; *a recovery* of strength, etc., Thphr.*Fr.*166, Porph.*Marc.*4, f.l. in Hp.*VM* 4. **-κτητέος**, α, ον, *able to be recovered*, Philostr.*VA* 2.7. 2. ἀνακτητέον *one must recover, recruit*, Antyll.ap.Orib.7.12.5. **-κτητικός**, ή, όν, *recuperative*: ἀνακτητικόν· γλήχων, Hsch. (cf. ἀνακτάομαι I. 2).

ἀνα-κτίζω, *rebuild*, Str.9.2.5, D.Chr.2.79: fut. ἀνακτίσσω, prob. l. for ἀνακτήσουσι in *App.Anth.*6.75:—Pass., *CIG*8646 (vi A.D.), al. **-κτίσις**, εως, ἡ, *rebuilding*, J.*AJ* 15.11.6. **-κτιστής**, οῦ, ὁ, *refounder*, Sch.Theoc.5.72.

ἀνακτίτης, ου, ὁ, a precious stone, Orph.*L.*194.

ἀνακτόρεος, α, ον, = ἀνακτόριος, *of the emperor*, ἐχθρός *APl.*5.350.

ἀνακτορία, ἡ, (ἀνάκτωρ) *lordship, rule*, A.R.1.839; *management* of horses, *h.Ap.*234.

ἀνακτόριος, α, ον, *belonging to a lord* or *king, royal*, ὕες Od.15.397. II. ἀνακτόριον, τό, = ἀνάκτορον, Hsch., Suid., v.l. in Hdt. 9.65. 2. = ξιφίον, Ps.-Dsc.4.20. III. -ιος, ὁ, = ἀρτεμισία, Id.3.113.

ἀνάκτορον, τό, *king's dwelling, palace*, in pl., *AP*9.657 (Marian.): mostly of the dwelling of gods, *temple, shrine*, Δήμητρος ἀ. ib.147 (Antag.); Θέτιδος εἰς ἀ. E.*Andr.*43: pl., ib.117, al., S.*Fr.*757; τὸ ἐν Ἐλευσῖνι ἀ. Hdt.9.65, cf. Hegesand.8, Posidon.41, Chor.p.86.24 B.

ἀνακτός, ή, όν, *drawn from a spring*, ὕδωρ *Stad.*26, cf. 75.

Ἀνακτοτελέσται, ῶν, οἱ, (τελέω) *presidents of the mysteries of the Corybantes* (cf. Paus.10.38.7), prob. in Hsch. (-τελευταί cod.).

ἀνάκτωρ, ορος, ὁ, = ἄναξ, of gods, A.*Ch.*357, E.*IT* 1414: pl., Cerc. 4.36, cf. Ptol.*Tetr.*122.

ἀνακυΐσκω, *impregnate again*, Arist.*HA* 573^{b}18.

ἀνακυκάω, *stir up and mix, mix up*, Θασίαν (sc. ἅλμην), φάρμακα, Ar.*Ach.*671, *Pl.*302, cf. Thphr.*CP*6.1.5: metaph., τὸν λογισμόν Ph. 1.690.

ἀνακυκλεύω, *reverse*, App.*BC*4.103.

ἀνακυκλ-έω, *turn round again*, ἀνακύκλει δέμας E.*Or.*231; *revolve in one's mind*, πρὸς ἐμαυτόν Luc.*Nigr.*6; *repeat*, τοὺς αὐτοὺς λόγους Plu.*Dem.*29, cf. Phld.*Mus.*p.40 K., Herm.*in Phdr.*p.191 A.:—Pass., *to be renewed*, πόλεμος ἐφ' ἑαυτὸν -ούμενος Procop.*Arc.*11. II. intr. in Act., *come round in a circle*, Arist.*GC* 338^{a}4; αἱ αὐταὶ δόξαι ἀ. ἐν τοῖς ἀνθρώποις Id.*Mete.*339^{b}29:—so in Pass., ἀ. πρὸς αὐτήν Pl.*Ti.* 37a; αἱ τύχαι πολλάκις ἀ. περὶ τοὺς αὐτούς Arist.*EN* 1100^{b}3. **-ησις**, εως, ἡ, *a coming round again, circuit, revolution*, Pl.*Plt.*269e, cf. Plu. *Sol.*4. 2. in Metric, *recurrence* of form, strophic arrangement, Heph.17.4, *Poëm.*3.2. **-ητέον**, *one must employ a cycle of treatment*, Orib.ap.Aët.11.11. **-ικός**, ή, όν, *easy to turn round*, of a verse that will read either backwards or forwards, ἀναστρέφον ἢ ἀνακυκλικόν *AP*6.323 tit. **-ισμός**, ὁ, *circuit, revolution*, ἐνιαυτοῦ μεγάλου D.S.12.36. **-όω**, = ἀνακυκλέω, v.l. in *AP*9.342 (Parmen.), in Pass.—The Act. perh. in Jul.*Ep.*180 p.394c (ἀνακυκλούσης). **-ωμα**, ατος, τό, *cycle, revolution*, μηνιαῖον ἀ., of the moon, Secund.*Sent.* 6. **-ωσις**, εως, ἡ, = ἀνακύκλησις, Ptol.*Tetr.*87; *wheeling about*, ἱππικοῦ τάγματος Hdn.4.2.9; ἀ. τῶν πολιτειῶν *cycle* of constitutions, Plb.6.9.10.

ἀνακυλίνδω, '*reflect*', t.t. in dissection, Gal.2.730.

ἀνακυλίω [ῑ], *roll up*, λίθους Luc.*Luct.*8, cf. D.H.*Comp.*20; *overturn*, ἁμάξας Plu.2.304f: metaph., χιλιοταλάντους ἀνακυλίων οὐσίας Alex.116.7; *roll away* or *back*, ἀνακεκύλισται ὁ λίθος *Ev.Marc.*16.4.

ἀνακυμβαλιάζω, (κύμβαλον), only in Il.16.379 δίφροι ἀνακυμβαλίαζον the chariots *fell rattling over.*

ἀνακυντεῖν· ῥέγχειν, Hsch.

ἀνακυπόω, *overturn, turn upside down*, Lyc.137, Nic.*Th.*705.

ἀνακύπτω, fut. -κύψομαι Ar.*Av.*146, Pl.*Euthd.*302a; -ψω Luc. *DMar.*3.1: aor. ἀνέκυψα Hdt.5.91, etc.: pf. ἀνακέκῡφα E.*Cyc.*212, X. *Eq.*7.10:—*lift up the head*, Thphr.*Char.*11.3; ἀνακεκυφὼς *with the head high*, of a horse, X. l.c.; κἀγκύψας (for καὶ ἀνακύψας) ἔχε and keep *your head up*, Ar.*Th.*236; ἐν ὀροφῇ ποικίλματα θεώμενος ἀνακύπτων *throwing his head back*, Pl.*R.*529b; ἀνακύψατε καὶ ἐπάρατε τὰς κεφαλάς *Ev.Luc.*21.28; esp. in drinking, Arist.*HA* 613^{a}13, cf. E. l.c.; ἐπικύπτειν καὶ ἀ. Gal.6.146. II. *come up out of the water, pop up*, Ar.*Ra.*1068; ἐκ τῆς θαλάσσης εἰς τὸν ἐνθάδε τόπον Pl.*Phd.* 109d; ἀ. μέχρι τοῦ αὐχένος, opp. καταδῦναι, Id.*Tht.*171d, cf. *Phdr.* 249c. b. metaph., *emerge, crop up*, ὅτι ἐξ αὐτῶν καλόν τι ἀνακύψοιτο Id.*Euthd.*302a; αἱ -κύπτουσαι χρεῖαι Ascl.*Tact.*11.7, cf. Ath.1.25e, *Cod.Just.*1.2.17. c. of persons, *rise out of difficulties, breathe again*, Hdt.5.91, X.*Oec.*11.5; τὰ τῶν Καρχηδονίων ἀνέκυψε Plb.1.55. 1, cf. D.Chr.13.35; ἀπὸ τῶν μυχῶν τοῦ σώματος Porph.*Marc.*6.

ἀνακυρίωσις, εως, ἡ, *authoritative demeanour*, Hp.*Decent.*12.

ἀνακυρτᾶσαι· ἀνασκιρτῆσαι, ἀναπηδῆσαι, Hsch.

ἀνάκυρτος, ον, *curved upwards* or *backwards*, *Gloss.*

ἀνακωδωνίζω, *try by the sound, ring*, Ar.*Fr.*303.

ἀνακωκύω [ῡ], *wail aloud*, κἀνακωκύσας λιγὺ A.*Pers.*468, cf. S.*Ant.* 1227; κἀνακωκύει..ὀξὺν φθόγγον *utters a loud* shrill wailing cry, ib. 423.

ἀνάκωλος, ον, *docked, curtailed*, ἀ. χιτωνίσκος a '*cutty* sark', *short* frock, Plu.2.261f, *SIG*1179.8 (Cnidus); of a camel, *short-legged*, D.S. 2.54.

ἀνάκωμα, ατος, τό, f.l. for ἀνακώναμα (?), [Philol.]ap.Stob.1.20.2.

ἀνακωμῳδέω, *to bring on the stage, satirize*, dub. in Plu.2.10c.

ἀνακωνῆν· ἀναστρέφειν, Hsch. (ἀνακονεῖν cod.); cf. κωνᾶν.

ἀνακῶς, Adv. *carefully*, ἀνακῶς ἔχειν τινός look *well* to a thing, give *good heed* to it, Hdt.1.24, 8.109, Th.8.102, Plu.*Thes.*33; ἀ. θεραπεύειν Hp.*Carn.*19; τὰς (τῆς Pierson) θύρας ἀ. ἔχων Pl.Com.202.—Dor. acc. to Erot. s. v., but found in Ion. and Early Att. (Connected with ἄναξ by Plu. l.c., cf. *AB*391, Phot.p.113 R.)

ἀνακωχέω· ἀναχωρέω, Hsch. II. v. ἀνοκωχεύω.

ἀνακωχή, ἀνακωχεύω, v. ἀνοκωχή:—also **ἀνακωχάζω**, *bring to a stop*, ναῦν Dam.*Isid.*272.

ἀναλάζομαι, *take again*, μορφήν Mosch.2.163.

ἀναλάκατα· οὐ πρὸς ἠλακάτην ἐργαζόμενος, Hsch.

ἀναλακεῖν, *cry aloud*, Sch.A.*Ch.*33.

ἀναλακτίζω, *kick upwards*, Antyll.ap.Orib.6.31.2.

ἀν-ᾰλᾰλάζω, *raise a war-cry*, ἀνηλάλαζον [οἱ στρατιῶται] X.*An.*4. 3.19; στρατὸς δ' ἀνηλάλαξε E.*Ph.*1395: generally, *cry aloud*, Id. *Supp.*719.

ἀναλαμβάνω, fut. -λήψομαι: Ion. pf.inf. Pass. -λελάμφθαι or -λελάφθαι Hp.*Off.*11, part. -λελαμμένος Id.*Art.*11:—*take up, take into one's hands*, τὸ παιδίον Hdt.1.111; τὰ τόξα, τὰ ὅπλα, etc., 3.78, 9.46; *take on board ship*, 1.166, Th.7.25, etc.; *take up into heaven*, in Pass., Lxx 4*Ki.*2.9, *Act.Ap.*1.11: and generally, *take with one*, esp. of troops, supplies, etc., Hdt.9.51, Th.5.64, 8.27, etc.; part. ἀναλαβών often = *with*, ἄνδρας ἀναλαβὼν ἡγήσομαι X.*An.*7.3.36, cf. Th.5.7. b. *suspend* in a sling, Hp.*Art.*22. c. metaph., *take up*, for the purpose of examining, Pl.*Ap.*22b, *Men.*87e, al. 2. *receive*, φιλοφρόνως ἀ. Id. *Ep.*329d, etc.; of women, ἀ. τὴν γονήν *conceive*, Plu.2.495e. 3. *take upon oneself, assume*, τὴν προξενίαν Th.6.89; τὴν ἀρχήν *Inscr. Prien.*123; κόσμον, of a king, *OGI*383.135; ἐσθῆτα Plu.*Arist.*21; πρόσωπον, σχῆμα, Luc.*Nigr.*11, *Somn.*13. 4. in Med., *undertake, engage in*, ἀναλαβέσθαι κίνδυνον Hdt.3.69:—also Act., ἀντὶ τῆς φιλίας τὸν πόλεμον ἀναλαβεῖν Philipp.ap.D.18.78. 5. *take up, adopt*, Arist.*Fr.*76:—Pass., Aeschin.1.52, cf. Epicur.*Fr.*172. 6. of money, *confiscate*, in Pass., *OGI*338.24 (Pergam.), *PSI*1.104.10 (late ii A.D.); κλῆρος ἀνειλημμένος εἰς τὸ βασιλικόν *PTeb.*61^{b}74 (ii B.C.), etc., Plu.2.484a, D.L.7.181. 7. *learn by rote*, Arr.*Epict.* 2.16.5, Plu.*Ages.*20, Alex.Aphr.*in Top.*494.31. 8. *include*, τῷ νόμῳ *OGI*629 (Palmyra). 9. Medic., *make up* ingredients, κηρῷ καὶ νάρδῳ Aret.*CA*1.1, cf. 2.3 (Pass.); so in Magic, ἀ. οἴνῳ καὶ μέλιτι, ὄξει, *PMag.Par.*1.1316, 2690. 10. *raise, erect* a wall, *IG*2.1054.9. 11. abs., *lift up* one's voice, Lxx *Nu.*14.1. II. *get back, regain, recover*, τὴν ἀρχήν Hdt.3.73, X.*HG*3.5.10; ἀ. ἐπιστήμην Pl.*Men.*85d; οὐδ' ἀφέντι λίθον δυνατὸν ἀναλαβεῖν Arist.*EN*1114^{a}18. 2. *retrieve, make good*, τὴν αἰτίην Hdt.7.231; ἁμαρτίαν S.*Ph.*1249, E.*Ion* 426; τὴν ἀρχαίαν ἀρετήν X.*Mem.*3.5.14; ταῦτα ἀ. καὶ μεταγιγνώσκειν D. 21.109. 3. *restore, repair*, τὴν προτέρην κακότητα Hdt.8.109: abs., Id.5.121; ἀ. τὴν πόλιν ἐκ τῆς πρόσθεν ἀθυμίας X.*HG*6.5.21; ἀ. ἑαυτόν *recover* oneself, *regain strength*, Th.6.26, Pl.Com.10 D., Men.*Sam.* 243; *collect* oneself, Isoc.5.22: abs., Pl.*R.*467b, D.18.163, Hp.*Mul.* 2.118. 4. *take up again, resume*, in narrative or argument, τὸν λόγον Hdt.5.62, Pl.*R.*544b, al.; πολλάκις ἀ. Id.*Phd.*95e; ἀναλαβεῖν διεξιόντα *repeat* in detail, Id.*Euthd.*275c; at Rome, ἀ. θυσίας, = *instaurare sacra*, Plu.*Cor.*25; ἀ. τῇ μνήμῃ *recollect*, Pl.*Plt.*294d; without τῇ μνήμῃ, Plu.*Lyc.*21; but ἀ. μνήμην *recover* a memory, Arist. *Mem.*451^{a}22; πρὸς ἑαυτὸν ἀ. *run over* in one's mind, Pl.*Ti.*26a. 5. *receive back* into a family, Luc.*Abd.*9, al. III. *pull up short*, of a horse, X.*Eq.*3.5; *check*, οἷόνπερ ἵππον τὸν λόγον ἀ. Pl.*Lg.*701c; τὴν ὁρμὴν τῆς νεώς Plb.16.3.4; ἀ. τὰς κύνας *call* them *back*, X.*Cyn.*7. 10. IV. *win over*, Ar.*Eq.*682, Din.1.28, Plu.*Brut.*24, al.; ἀ. τὸν ἀκροατήν Arist.*Rh.*1354^{b}32. V. ἀγορὰν στοαῖς ἀνειλημμένην διτταῖς, perh. on a terrace *supported* by two colonnades, Dicaearch. 59.23; cf. ἀνάλημμα II.

ἀναλάμπω, *flame up, take fire*, X.*Cyr.*5.1.16; *shine out*, of the sun, Thphr.*CP*4.13.6: metaph., ἀκτῖνες ἀρετῆς ἀ. Ph.1.335; *flame up*, of envy, Jul.*ad Ath.*274d. II. metaph., *break out*, as war, Plu.*Sull.*6, cf. 7. 2. of a person, *come to oneself again, revive*, Id.*Brut.*15, cf. 2.694f; *blaze up* with enthusiasm, Philostr.*VA*5. 30. III. trans., *cause to shine*, φῶς Plu.*Alex.*30; λιθοκαλλέα μορφήν, of a sculptor, *App.Anth.*2.534 (Halic.). 2. *illuminate*, τὸ ζοφερόν Heraclit.*Ep.*6.3.

ἀνάλαμψις, εως, ἡ, *shining forth*, τοῦ νοητοῦ φωτός Ph.1.7; ἀ. εὐμενεῖς ἔχειν Plu.2.419f.

ἀναλγής, ές, = ἀνάλγητος, πρὸς τὸ αἰσχρόν Plu.2.528d: of a mortified state of body, Hp.*Art.*69; *painless*, θάνατος Plu.*Sol.*27.

ἀναλγησία, ἡ, *want of feeling, insensibility*, Democr.193, D.18.35, Arist.*EN*1100^{b}32, Ph.2.318.

ἀνάλγητος, ον, *without pain*, and so: I. of persons, *insensible to pain* or *danger*, Meliss.ap.Arist.*Xen.*974^{a}19, cf. *EN*1115^{b}26. 2. *unfeeling, hard-hearted, ruthless*, S.*Aj.*946 (lyr.); -ότερος εἶναι to feel *less resentment*, Th.3.40: c. gen., ἀ. γενέσθαι τινός to be *insensible to*, Plu.*Aem.*35. Adv. -τως *unfeelingly*, S.*Aj.*1333; *callously*, ἀ. ἀκούειν Plu.2.46c. II. of things, *not painful*, ἀνάλγητα (sc. πράγματα) *a lot free from pain*, S.*Tr.*126. 2. *cruel*, πάθος E.*Hipp.*1386 (lyr.).

ἀναλδής, ές, (ἀλδαίνω) *not thriving, feeble*, καρποί Hp.*Aër.*15; *barren*, Ar.*V.*1045 (anap.); ἄρουραι ἀναλδέα φυλλιόωσαι *without fruiting*, Arat.333.

ἀναλδήσκω, *grow up*, A.R.3.1363; *spring up afresh*, Opp.*C.*2.397.

ἀναλεαίνω, *bruise, crush, pound fine*, v.l. in Dsc.5.74.

ἀναλέγω, Ep. impf. ἄλλεγον (v. infr.): fut. -λέξω Ar.*Av.*591: Ep. aor. inf. ἀλλέξαι:—**Med.**, v. infr.:—*pick up, gather up*, ὀστέα ἀλλέξαι

Il.21.321; ὀστέα..ἄλλεγον ἐς φιάλην 23.253; ἀνά τ' ἔντεα καλὰ λέγοντες 11.755; ἐκ βίβλων ἀ. *collect* materials from books, *IG*3.716:—Med., *pick up for oneself*, τοὺς στατῆρας Hdt.3.130; [σκώληκας] ἀ. τῇ γλώττῃ, of the woodpecker, Arist.*HA*614^{b}1; ἀ. πνεῦμα *collect one's* breath, *AP*12.132 (Mel.); *select* or *take up* a theme for discussion, Ps.-Alex. Aphr.*in SE*17.15. II. in Med., *reckon up*, τὸν χρόνον Plu.*Lyc.*1:—Pass. (with fut. ἀναλέξομαι Them.*in Ph.*132.7), ὅ σοι τιμὴν οἴσει εἰς τὸν ἔπειτα χρόνον ἀναλεγόμενον *being recounted*, X.*An.*2.1.17. III. in Med., *read through*, τὸ περὶ ψυχῆς γράμμ' ἀναλεξάμενος Call.*Epigr.* 25; συχνὰς ἀναλεξάμενος γραφάς D.H.1.89; ἐκ γραμμάτων ἀ. τι Plu. 2.582a:—Pass., Σαπφοῦς -ομένης ib.711d. 2. Med., *recover*, ἀπὸ τῆς καταπλήξεως dub. in D.S.32.6.

ἀναλεῖ· σχολάζει (Tarent.), Hsch.

ἀναλει-όω, *grind, rub down again*, Pelag.Alch.p.255 B. **-ωσις**, εως, ἡ, Id.p.254 B.

ἀν-άλειπτος, ον, *unanointed*, Antyll.ap.Aët.3.9:—also **-άλειφος**, ον, Them.*Or.*20.235d, Archig.ap.Aët.3.194.

ἀναλείφω, *smear on, apply* a drug, Orib.*Fr.*117.

ἀναλείχω, *lick up*, τὸ αἷμα Hdt.1.74.

ἀν-αλειψία, ἡ, *neglect of anointing*, Sm.*Ps.*108.24, prob. l. for **ἀναλειφίῃ** in Hp.*Vict.*2.57. II. *lack of oil*, *CPR*57.16 (iii A.D.).

ἀνα-λεκτέον, *one must collect*, Agath.*Praef.*p.139 D., Eust.1039.47. **-λέκτης**, ου, ὁ, Lat. *-lecta, slave who picked up broken meats*, Mart.7.20. **-λεκτος**, ον, *select, choice*, γυναῖκες ἀ. τὸ κάλλος Socr. *Ep.*9. **-lectris**, -idos, dub. in Ov.*AA*3.273 (v. ἀναλημπτρίς).

ἀν-αλήθης, ες, *untrue, false*, Plb.12.26^{d}6, Plu.*Comp.Alc.Cor.*2. Adv. -θως M.Ant.2.16. II. of styles, *affected*, D.H.*Dem.*4 (Comp.), Longin.3.4.

ἀνά-λημμα, ατος, τό, *that which is used for repairing* or *supporting*; *sling* for a wounded limb, Hp.*Off.*23. II. any high *erection* or *embankment*, esp. of *substructures* or *retaining-walls*, *SIG*²587.20, *SIG*290 (Delph.), 813 *A* 5 (Delph.), *IG*11.163 *A* 38 (Delos), cf. 165.33, D.S.17.71: pl., Id.20.36, D.H.3.69, *IG*4.203.21; τὸ ἀ. τῆς πόλεως Δαυίδ Lxx 2*Ch.*32.5; ἀ. ὑψηλὸν περιβόλου ἱεροῦ ib.*Si.*50.2. III. *sun-dial*, *CIG*2681, Vitr.9.7.7. IV. = μέρος τι τοῦ ἥπατος, Hsch. **-ληπτέον**, *one must take up* a question, Pl.*Phlb.*33c; *recall*, εἰς μνήμην Id.*Lg.*864b; ἀ. ἑαυτούς they *must recover* themselves, Plu.2.136a, cf. Sor.2.59:—Adj. -τέος Plu.2.1116e. **-ληπτήρ**, ῆρος, ὁ, *bucket*, J.*AJ*8.3.7; *ladle* or *bowl*, Lxx 2*Ch.*4.16. **-ληπτικός**, ή, όν, *restorative*, κύκλος, of medical treatment, Sor.2.88, cf. Gal.1.301. Adv. -κῶς Id.14.672. **-ληπτρίς**, ίδος, ἡ, *suspensory bandage*, Gal.18(1).323; *analemptris*, = στρόφιον, prob.l. in Ov.*AA*3.273. **-λῆσαι**· ἀνατρέψαι, Hsch. (fort. -λῦσαι). **-ληψις**, later **-λημψις**, hyperdor. **-λαψις** Ti.Locr.100c, εως, ἡ:—*taking up*, e.g. *suspension* in a sling, *fixing* a bandage, Hp.*Art.*22, *Off.*9; *looping* or *tying up* of vines, *POxy.*1692.20 (ii A.D.), cf. 1631.13 (iii A.D.). 2. *receiving back* into a family, Luc.*Abd.*5. 3. *acquirement* of knowledge, etc., Phld.*Rh.*1.31 S., al., Ti.Locr. l.c., S.E.*P.*1.73, D.S.1.1; ἱερῶν Plu.2.351e. 4. *assumption* of an office, dub. in *Inscr. Prien.*123; διαδήματος *OGI*383.102. 5. Pass., *being taken up* or *away*, *Psalm.Solom.*4.20; *ascension*, *Ev.Luc.*9.51. 6. *reception, entertainment*, *SIG*888.36 (Thrace). 7. *assimilation*, τροφῆς Menon *Iatr.*25.48. II. *recovery*, μνήμης Arist.*Mem.*451^{a}20; *means of regaining*, Plu.*Publ.*9. 2. *making good, making amends*, Th. 5.65; *refreshing* of soldiers after hard work, Plb.3.87.1, cf. Luc. *Par.*40; ἀνάληψιν ποιεῖν Demetr.Com.Nov.1.10:—*recovery* from illness, Hp.*Aph.*4.27, Pl.*Ti.*83e. 3. *repair*, Str.13.1.38, *PSI*1.83.11 (iii A.D.). 4. *repetition*, [Longin.]*Rh.*p.200 H.

ἀναλθ-ής, ές, *not to be healed*, ἑλκύδριον Hp.*Art.*63, cf. Arctin.*Iliup.* 5, Aret.*SD*1.7, Q.S.3.84. 2. *not healing, powerless to heal*, φάρμακα Bion *Fr.*13.4. 3. *deadly, inflicting incurable wounds*, Opp. *C.*2.424. **-ητος**, ον, = foreg., *incurable*, Nonn.*D.*35.296.

ἀν-αλίγκιος, ον, *unlike*, Hsch.

ἀναλικμάω, *winnow out*, of grain, v.l. in Pl.*Ti.*52e.

ἀνάλιος, ον, Dor. for ἀνήλιος.

ἀνάλιπος [ᾰλ], ον, Dor. for ἀνήλιπος, *barefoot*, f.l. in Theoc.4.56.

ἀνᾱλίσκω E.*IT*337, Ar.*Th.*1131, Th.7.48:—also **ἀνᾱλόω** Hp.*VM* 10, A.*Th.*813, E.*Med.*325, Ar.*Pl.*248, Arar.10, Th.2.24, al., Democr. 280, X.*Hier.*11.1: impf. ἀνήλισκον Pl.*R.*552b, X.*Cyr.*1.2.16, ἀνάλισκον App.*BC*3.58, ἀνάλουν Ar.*Fr.*220.2, Th.8.45: fut. ἀνᾱλώσω E. *Cyc.*308, Pl.*R.*568d: aor. ἀνήλωσα S.*Aj.*1049, Lys.19.18, etc., ἀνάλωσα [ᾰ] E.*El.*681 (s.v.l.) and later: pf. ἀνήλωκα Lys.26.3, etc., and ἀνάλωκα [ᾰ] Th.2.64 codd. and later:—**Pass.**, fut. ἀνᾱλωθήσομαι E. *Hipp.*506, D.22.19, wrongly ἀνηλωθήσομαι *PRev.Laws*51.17 (iii B.C.), ἀνᾱλώσομαι Gal.15.129: aor. ἀνηλώθην and ἀνᾱλώθην: pf. ἀνήλωμαι and ἀνάλωμαι:—in Attic Inscrr. both forms are found in cent. v, ἀναλίσκω only from cent. iv onwards. The augmented forms are sts. wrongly used, ἀνηλοῦντι *POxy.*1143 (i A.D.), ἀνηλώσῃ *PStrassb.*92.17 (iii B.C.); cf. ἀνήλωμα: ἀνάλωσα is found at Amorgos, *IG*12(7).22.16, and at Delos, ib.11(2).161 *A* 114:—*use up, spend*, Ar.*Pl.*381: abs., ib.248; τὰ ἀναλωθέντα ἀποδοῦναι Th.1.117; ἀ. εἴς τι *spend upon* a thing, Id.7.83, Ar.*Fr.*220, Pl.*Phd.*78a, *R.*561a, al.; πρός τι D.3.19; ὑπὲρ φιλοτιμίας Id.18.66: c. dat., Ἰσοκράτει ἀργύριον ἀ. *spend* money in paying him, Id.35.40:—Pass., τἀνηλωμένα *the monies expended* Id.18.113; τοῦτο γὰρ μόνον οὐκ ἔστι τἀνάλωμ' ἀναλωθὲν λαβεῖν E.*Supp.* 776. 2. metaph., ἀνήλωσας λόγον *hast wasted* words, S.*Aj.*1049, cf. E.*Med.*325; χρόνον καὶ πόνον ἐπί τινι Pl.*R.*369e; σώματα καὶ πόνους πολέμῳ Th.2.64; τὴν τῶν προγόνων δόξαν Pl.*Mx.*247b; ἀ. ὕπνον *waste time in* sleep, Pi.*P.*9.27; λόγῳ ἀ. τὸν χρόνον τῆς ἡμέρας *diem eximere dicendo*, Plu.*Aem.*30. 3. *consume*, σιτία Hp.*VM*10; κρέα Paus.10.4.10; of animals, in Pass., *to be eaten*, Pl.*Prt.*321b:—Pass., *to be expended*, εἰς τὴν πιμελήν in forming fat, Arist.*GA*727^{b}1, al. II. of persons, *kill, destroy*, τοὺς ἀναλωθέντας A.*Ag.*570, cf. S.*OT*1174, *Fr.*892, E.*El.*681, Th.8.65:—Med., *kill oneself*, Id.3.81:—Pass., *to be consumed, perish*, Pl.*Plt.*272d; *to be disposed of, got rid of*, ib.289c. (ἀνά, ἁλίσκομαι.)

ἀνάλιστος, ον, *unsalted*: *silly*, Timo 35.

ἀναλιχμάομαι, = ἀναλείχω, Philostr.*VA*5.42: aor. ἀνελιχμήσαντο J.*AJ*8.15.6.

ἀναλκάταλλα· ἄνοσον κάτω, Hsch.

ἀνάλκ-εια, ἡ, *want of strength, feebleness, cowardice*, ἀναλκείῃσι δαμέντες Il.6.74, 17.320:—also in sg., ὤ μοι ἀναλκείης Thgn.891. **-ής**, ές, = sq., Hp.*Aër.*16, Arist.*Phgn.*809^{a}39 (Comp.). **-ιμος**, ον, = sq., *POxy.*79. **-ις**, ιδος, ὁ, ἡ: acc. -ιδα Il.8.153, etc., but -ιν Od.3.375, A.*Ag.*1224: (ἀλκή):—*without strength, impotent, feeble*, of unwarlike men, ἀπτόλεμος καὶ ἄ. Il.2.201, cf. 9.35; κακὸν καὶ ἀνάλκιδα 8.153, 14.126; of the suitors, Od.4.334; of Aegisthus, 3.310, cf. A.*Ag.*1224; of Aphrodite, Il.5.331; also ἄ. θυμός 16.656; φύζα 15.62; ὁ πάντ' ἄ. S.*El.*301, cf. Hdt.2.102.

ἀνάλλακτος, ον, *unchangeable*, Orph.*Fr.*248.8.

ἀναλληγόρητος, ον, *without allegory*, Eust.83.23, 549.29.

ἀναλλοίωτος, ον, *unchangeable*, Arist.*Metaph.*1073^{a}11, *Cael.*270^{a}14; ἀ. τὴν φωνήν D.L.4.17; κάλλος Ph.1.649; of undigested food, Gal.6.575; ἀ. ὕλη *Stoic.*2.114; *not permitting change*, Thphr.*CP*6.10.1.

ἀνάλλομαι, *leap, spring up*, Ar.*Ach.*669; ἐπὶ ὄχθους X.*Eq.Mag.*8.3.

ἄναλλος, ον, *topsy-turvy*, Eust.1000.31.

ἄναλμ-ος, ον, *not salted*, X.*Oec.*20.12. **-υρος**, ον, = foreg., Diosc.Gloss.ap.Gal.19.79.

ἀναλογάδην, Adv., (ἀνάλογος) *proportionately*, Hsch.

ἀναλογεῖον, τό, gloss on ἀναγνωστήριον, Hsch.; *manuale lectorium*, *Gloss.*, cf. Poll.10.60, Hdn.Gr.2.457.

ἀναλογ-έω, *to be analogous*, σπλάγχνον οὐκ ἔχει ἀναλογοῦν Arist. *Fr.*334: c. dat., Phld.*Sign.*37, Ph.1.278, etc.; ὁ τεχνίτης ὁ -ῶν τῷ Φειδίᾳ Gal.*Nat.Fac.*2.3: c. acc., ἀ. τὴν ἐπιμέλειαν *to be capable of performing* a service, *PAmh.*64.13; ἀ. τοῖς τᾶς ἀξίας βάσμοις *to keep up* to the degrees of his rank, *IG*12(2).243.17 (Mytilene), cf. *CIG*3486 (Thyatira), J.*AJ*4.8.4, Ath.3.80c, etc. 2. Math., *to be proportionate*, Cleom.1.7. **-ή**, ἡ, *account, bill*, *Sammelb.*4425.3.1 (ii A.D.). **-ητέον**, *one must sum up*, dub. in Arist.*Rh.Al.*1443^{b}15 (fort. leg. ἀναλογιστέον). **-ητικός**, ή, όν, *proportional*, dub. in D.L.1.17. II. of the *analogical* school of grammarians, A.D. *Conj.*241.14. **-ία**, ἡ, (λόγος) *mathematical proportion*, Pl.*Ti.* 31c, 32c; ἡ ἀ. ἰσότης ἐστὶ λόγων Arist.*EN*1131^{a}31; of progressions, ἀ. γεωμετρική ib.^{b}13; ἀριθμητική ib.1106^{a}36, cf. Ael.*Tact.*10.3; ἁρμονική Thrasyll.ap.Theon.Sm.p.85 H., Nicom.*Ar.*2.22; κατὰ τὴν ἀ. *comparing the ratios*, Arist.*Pol.*1282^{b}40; τὸ κατ' ἀ. ἴσον ib.1301^{a}27; ὑπὲρ τὴν ἀ. τινός *out of proportion*, Olymp.*in Mete.*89.22. 2. *proportion* generally, Arist.*Pol.*1296^{b}25, cf. Epicur.*Nat.*11.7,10. II. *analogy*, Arist.*HA*486^{b}19, Epicur.*Fr.*212, etc. 2. esp. *grammatical analogy*, Gell.2.25, A.D.*Synt.*36.23, etc. III. *relation*, ἀ. ἔχειν stand *in relation with*, πρός τι Phld.*Lib.*p.38 O., cf. p.51 O. IV. *correspondence, resemblance*, ὁμοιότης ἢ ἀ. [τινί] Id.*Sign.*37, cf. *Fr.*3; κατ' -ίαν, opp. διαφοράν, Id.*D.*1.22. **-ίζομαι**, *reckon up, sum up*, τὰ ὡμολογημένα Pl.*Prt.*332d, cf. *R.*330e: abs., ἐκ τῶν προειρημένων ἀ. ib.524d; τὰ δεινὰ X.*Mem.*2.1.4, cf. *Ep.Heb.*12.3; τὰ γεγονότα καὶ τὰ παρόντα πρὸς τὰ μέλλοντα ἀ. *calculate* the past and the present *in comparison with* the future, Pl.*Tht.*186a; ἀ. τι πρός τι Arist.*Pol.* 1320^{b}20; ἐκ τούτων ἀ. *make calculations* from.., Id.*Cael.*293^{a}33; *infer*, Epicur.*Nat.*14.4, Phld.*D.*1.13, Diog.Oen.*Fr.*38. 2. *calculate, consider*, Th.5.7, Lys.14.47. 3. foll. by a Conjunction, ἀ. ὡς.. *calculate* or *reflect* that, Th.8.83, X.*HG*2.4.23, etc.; *take into account*, Phld.*Herc.*1251.5. 4. *recapitulate*, Hyp.*Phil.*4. **-ικός**, ή, όν, *based on mathematical ratios*, Plu.2.1144f, cf. Iamb.*in Nic.*p.100 P. ἡ -κὴ τέχνη the art *of applying analogy*, S.E.*M.*1.199; οἱ -κοί *the analogical school of grammarians*, Suid. s.v. Ἀρείδης, Eust.802.38. **-ισμα**, ατος, τό, *a result of reasoning*, τὰ περὶ τούτων ἀ. Pl.*Tht.*186c. **-ισμός**, ὁ, *reconsideration*, Th.3.36; *reckoning, calculation*, 8.84; *course* or *line of reasoning*, X.*HG*5.1.19; ἐν τῷ πρὸς αὐτὸν ἀ. Men.447; opp. ἐπιλογισμός, *Stoic.*2.89. 2. κατὰ τὸν ἀ. according to *proportionate reckoning*, Docum.ap.D.18.106; δι' ἀναλογισμοῦ S.E.*P.*1.147. **-ιστέον**, v. ἀναλογητέον. **-ιστικός**, ή, όν, *judging by analogy, analogical*, S.E.*M.*11.250; ἡ -κὴ τέχνη ib. 1.214. 2. of knowledge, etc., *reflective*, Phld.*Herc.*1003. Adv. -κῶς ibid. II. *teaching analogy*, γραμματικοί S.E.*M.*2.59; αἵρεσις -κή, of the Rational or Dogmatic school of physicians, opp. ἐπιλογιστική (the Empirics), Gal.1.65; *analogisticus sermo* Id.*Subf.Emp.*8 p.52 Bonnet. Adv. -κῶς S.E.*M.*3.40, Gal.18(2).346.

ἀνάλογος, ον, *according to a due* λόγος, *proportionate, conformable*, Pl.*Ti.*69b, cf. Ti.Locr.103d; but ἐὰν τέσσαρα ἀνάλογα ᾖ *in arithmetical progression*, Ascl.*Tact.*3.1: neut. ἀνάλογον freq. in Arist. in adverbial sense, *in proportion*, *EN*1158^{a}35, etc.; freq. as Adj., τὸ ἀνάλογον λέγω, ὅταν.. *Po.*1457^{b}16; παρὰ τὸ ἀ. *EN*1131^{b}11, al., etc.; but ἐκ τοῦ ἀνάλογον *Rh.*1399^{a}33, 1405^{a}11, al.; μεταφοραὶ αἱ ἀνάλογον (sc. οὖσαι) ib.1408^{a}8; τὰ τούτοις ἀνάλογον *HA*487^{a}5, etc.; ἀ. οἰκοδόμοι (as a predicate) *EN*1103^{b}9, cf. *Rh.*1364^{b}11, al.:—so that it is plain that ἀνάλογον is merely equiv. to ἀνὰ λόγον, as it is written in Pl.*Ti.*37a; cf. λόγος:—the regul. Adv. ἀναλόγως Hp.*Ep.*27, Lxx

*Wi.*13.5, S.E.*P.*1.88, Alex.Aphr. *in Metaph.*156.5. II. *well-proportioned, suitable*, σχῆμα Philostr.*Im.*1.10 (Sup.). III. *equivalent to, resembling*, λυπηρὸν ἢ ἀ. λυπηρῷ Phld.*Ir.*p.76 W., cf. *Sign.* 2,37.

ἀναλογούντως, Adv. pres. part., = ἀναλόγως, c. dat., *CIG*2766 (Aphrodisias); *fittingly*, *BGU*248.21 (i A.D.).

ἀναλογχόω, *embroider with points*, Lyd.*Mag.*2.4 (Pass.).

ἀναλοκίζω, *rend, lacerate*, S.*Fr.*376 (Pass.).

ἄνᾰλος, ον, (ἅλς A) *without salt, not salted*, Arist.*Pr.*927ᵃ35, Gal. 10.401. 2. of salt itself, salt *which is no salt*, *Ev.Marc.*9.50.

ἀνᾱλόω, v. ἀναλίσκω.

ἄναλτος (A), ον, *not to be filled, insatiate*, βόσκειν ἣν γαστέρ' ἄναλτον Od.17.228, 18.364, cf. Cratin.382. (ἀ- priv., *ἀλ-τός, cf. Lat. *alo*, etc.)

ἄναλτος (B), ον, (ἅλς A) *not salted*, Hp.*Morb.*2.54, Timocl.14.7, Din.*Fr.*89.7, Dsc.*Eup.*2.51.

ἀναλύζω, lit. *hiccough*: hence, *sob aloud*, Luc.*Somn.*4 (ἀνολύζων codd.), Q.S.14.281 (vulg. ἀνωλύζεσκε). 2. ἀναλύζων· ἀνανύττων (sic), Hsch.; ἀναλύζουσα· στενάζουσα, λυγκαίνουσα, Suid.

ἀνάλῠ-σις, εως, ἡ, (ἀναλύω) *loosing, releasing*, κακῶν *from* evils, S.*El.*142 (lyr.); ὅρκων Timae.23. 2. *dissolving*, Arist.*Mu.*394ᵇ17, Plu.2.915c (pl.); σώματος, of death, Secund.*Sent.*19. 3. *resolution* of a problem *by the analysis of its conditions*, opp. σύνθεσις, Arist.*EN*1112ᵇ23; esp. in Math., Phld.*Acad.Ind.*17, Papp.634.11, Procl.*in Euc.*p.43 F. 4. in the Logic of Arist., *reduction* of the imperfect figures into the perfect one, *APr.*51ᵃ18, al., Chrysipp.*Stoic.*2.7. 5. *solution* of a problem, etc., Plu.*Rom.*12. II. (from Pass.) *retrogression*, Id.2.76d; *retirement, departure*, J.*AJ*19.4.1; *death* (cf. ἀναλύω III), 2*Ep.Ti.*4.6. **-τέον**, *one must dissolve*, *PHolm.*24.23. **-τήρ**, ῆρος, ὁ, *deliverer*, A.*Ch.*160 (lyr.). **-της**, ου, ὁ, *deliverer*, esp. from a magic spell, Magn.4. **-τικός**, ή, όν, *analytical*, ἐπιστήμη Arist.*Rh.*1359ᵇ10; θεωρία, of mathematical analysis, Papp.410.28; συλλογισμός Arr.*Epict.*2.3.4; τὰ ἀναλυτικά *principles of analysis*, ἀπαιδευσίᾳ τῶν ἀ. Arist.*Metaph.*1005ᵇ4; title of A.'s treatises on this subject; so -κή, ἡ, Ammon. *in APr.*7.34. Adv. -κῶς Arist.*APo.*84ᵃ8. 2. *dissolvent*, τῆς διακρίσεως Dam.*Pr.*161. **-τος**, ον, *dissoluble*, Plot.4.7.2.

ἀν-αλύω (A), *cause to wander, unsettle*, βασιλέα Philostr.*VA*5.35.

ἀνα-λύω (B), Ep. ἀλλύω (ἀνλύω *Hymn.Is.*145): (v. λύω for the tenses and prosody: Hom. has ἀλλύουσα, ἀλλύεσκε with ῡ):—*unloose, undo*, of Penelope's web, νύκτας δ' ἀλλύεσκεν Od.2.105; ἀλλύουσαν..ἀγλαὸν ἱστόν ib.109, etc.; ἀνά τε πρυμνήσια λῦσαι ib. 9.178, etc. 2. *unloose, set free*, ἐμὲ δ' ἐκ δεσμῶν ἀνέλυσαν ib. 12.200 (never in Il.), cf. Ant.Lib.22.4; ὀφθαλμόν, φωνάν Pi.*N.*10.90; τινὰ καταδίκης Ael.*VH*5.18. 3. Medic., *relax*, in Pass., Arist. *GA*728ᵃ15, Men.213, Dsc.5.3. II. *undo* in various senses: 1. *unloose*, ζώνην Call.*Del.*237; in Med., *unwind* a cocoon, Arist. *HA*551ᵇ14. 2. Astrol., *nullify*, of planetary influence, Ptol.*Tetr.*133 (Pass.). 3. *dissolve* matter *into its elements*, ἐς αὐτὰ ταῦτα Ti.Locr.102d:—Pass., of snow, *melt*, Plu.2.898a. b. *resolve into its elements*, οὐ καλὸν ἁρμονίην ἀναλυέμεν ἀνθρώποιο Ps.-Phoc.102:—*investigate analytically*, διάγραμμα Arist.*EN*1112ᵇ20, Plu.2.792d, etc.:—Pass., Archim.*Sph.Cyl.*1.4; ὁ -όμενος τόπος the treasury *of analysis*, Papp.634.2; ἀναλύοντες καὶ ἀναλυόμενοι Dam.*Pr.*2; ἀ. τοὺς μύθους ἐς λόγους πιθανούς Jul.*Or.*2.74d. 4. in the Logic of Arist., *reduce* a syllogism, *APr.*47ᵃ4, al.; cf. ἀνάλυσις I. 4. 5. *reduce*, σχοινία εἰς ὀργυιάς Hero *Geom.*5.8. 6. Gramm., *resolve*, κτητικὰ εἰς γενικάς A.D.*Synt.*292.17. 7. *do away, cancel*, μόρσιμ' ἀ. Ζεὺς οὐ τολμᾷ Pi.*Pae.*6.94, cf. D.21.218, Plu.*Sol.*25, etc.: mostly in Med., *cancel faults*, πάντα ταῦτα X.*HG*7.5.18; ἁμαρτίας D.14.34; ἀλλύοιτό κα τὸ χρέος *discharge* the debt, prob. in *GDI*1151 (Olymp.). 8. *suspend*, τὰ περὶ κυνηγέσιον X.*Cyn.*5.34. 9. *solve the problem* of a thing, τὸν Ἰνδὸν ἀ. *trace* its *source*, Plu.2.133c. 10. *release from a spell*, Luc.*Vit.Auct.*25, cf. Hsch.:—Pass., Men.*Her.Fr.*6. 11. *relieve*, Ptol.*Tetr.*133 (Pass.). III. intr., *loose from moorings, weigh anchor*, and so, *depart, go away*, Plb.3.69.14, Babr.42.8, etc.: metaph., of death, ἐς θεοὺς ἀνέλυσα *Epigr.Gr.* 340.7 (Macestus): abs., *die*, *Ep.Phil.*1.23, *IG*14.1794; ἀ. ἐκ τοῦ ζῆν Diog.Oen.2. 2. *return*, *Ev.Luc.*12.36; ἐξ ᾅδου Lxx *Wi.*2.1.

ἀναλφάβητος, ον, *not knowing one's a b c*, Nicoch.2 D.

ἀνάλφιτος, ον, *without barley-meal*, Philyll.1 D.

ἀνάλ-ωμα [ᾰλ], ατος, τό, ἀνήλωμα freq. in Pap. and Inscrr. as *IG*2².1228.12, 12(5).1061.17 (iii B.C.), Wilcken *Chrest.*30 ii (ca. 200 B.C.):—*expense, cost*, A.*Supp.*476; opp. λῆμμα, Lys.32.20, Pl.*Lg.*920c: in pl., *expenses*, Th.7.28, D.21.106, etc.; οὐσίαν, ἧς αἱ πρόσοδοι λύουσι τἀναλώματα Diph.32.5; ἐκ τῶν ἰδίων ἀναλωμάτων καθοπλίζειν at their own private *costs*, Decr.ap.D.18.116, cf. *IG*7.3073, etc.: metaph., σκαιόν γε τἀνάλωμα τῆς γλώσσης τόδε E.*Supp.*547. 2. *exhalation*, Plu.2.384a codd. **-ωμάτιον**, τό, Dim. of foreg., *slight loss*, Ph.*Bel.*67.28. 2. *trifling expenditure*, *PFlor.*131.3 (iii A.D.). **-ωσις**, εως, ἡ, *outlay, expenditure*, Thgn.903, Th.6.31, Pl.*Cri.*48c, etc. II. *wasting, consumption*, ἐγκεφάλου Hp.*Epid.*6.3.1. **-ωτέος**, α, ον, *to be spent*, Pl.*Lg.*847e. **-ωτής**, οῦ, ὁ, *spender, waster*, Id.*R.*552b, c. **-ωτικός**, ή, όν, *expensive, spendthrift*, ἡδοναί, ἐπιθυμίαι, ib.558d, 559c; *consuming*, c. gen., Ph.2.151, Iamb.*Myst.*2.5.

ἀν-άλωτος [ᾰλ], ον, (ἀ- priv., ἁλίσκομαι) *not to be taken, impregnable*, of strong places or forts, Hdt.1.84, 8.51; οὐδὲν ἀ. ἀρετῇ Chor. in *Rev.Phil.*1.70: *not taken, holding out*, Th.4.70. 2. metaph., *unassailable, convincing*, αἰσθήσεις Pl.*Tht.*179c; of persons, ἀ. ὑπὸ χρημάτων *incorruptible*, X.*Ages.*8.8: c. gen., τῶν Ἀφροδίτης παθῶν Men.Rh.p.416 S. 3. of things, *unattainable*, [D.]61.37.

ἀναλωφάω, *to be relieved again, have a respite from suffering*, Aret. *CA*2.11.

ἀναμαιμάω, *rage through*, ὡς δ' ἀναμαιμάει βαθέ' ἄγκεα θεσπιδαὲς πῦρ Il.20.490.

ἀναμᾰλάσσω, *soften thoroughly*, Hp.*Mul.*2.205, Gal.12.419.

ἀναμανθάνω, *inquire closely*, Hdt.9.101; *learn afresh*, Hsch.; simply, *learn*, D.S.34.17, Ph.1.406.

ἀναμαντεύομαι, *take the auspices a second time*, D.C.37.25. 2. *unmake a prophecy*, Phryn.*PS*p.45 B.

ἀναμάξευτος, ον, *impassable for wagons*, Hdt.2.108.

ἀνάμαξις, εως, ἡ, *impression*, τοῦ εἴδους Alex.Aphr. *de An.*137.25.

ἀναμαρμαίρω, *move quickly*, of a smith's bellows, A.R.3.1300.

ἀναμαρτ-ής, ές, *unerring*, Hsch. s.v. νημερτής. **-ησία**, ἡ, *faultlessness, innocence*, App.*Pun.*52. **-ητος**, ον, *making no mistake, unerring*, X.*Cyr.*8.7.22, Pl.*R.*339b. 2. in moral sense, *blameless*, Hp.*Fract.*16 (Comp.), cf. Antipho 3.2.10, Men.*Epit.*487, Phld. *Sto.Herc.*339.17; *sinless*, *Ev.Jo.*8.7, cf. Aristeas 252, Muson.*Fr.*2 p.6 H.; ἀ. πολιτεία a *faultless* form of government, Arist.*Pol.* 1275ᵇ2; ἀ. πρός τινα *having done no wrong to* a person, Hdt.1.117; τινί 5.39; ἀ. τινός *guiltless of* a thing, 1.155: τὸ -ητότατον, = ἀναμαρτησία, X.*Ages.*6.7, cf. Pl.*R.*477e; πρὸς τὸ ἀ. *to preserve from error*, Arist.*EN*1155ᵃ13. Adv. -τως *without fail, unerringly*, X.*Mem.*2.8.5; *without making a mistake*, Ps.-Alex.Aphr. *in SE*15.33; *inoffensively*, [D.]61.21. II. of things, *not done by fault, done unavoidably*, συμφορά Antipho 3.2.11. 2. *unfailing*, Dion.Byz.17.

ἀναμᾱρυκ-άομαι, v. ἀναμηρ-:—also -ίζω, Jul.*Gal.*314d.

ἀναμᾰσάομαι, *chew over again, ruminate*, Ar.*V.*783.

ἀνα-μάσσω, Att. -ττω, fut. -ξω (v. infr.): (v. μάσσω):—*rub* or *wipe off*, ἔργον, ὃ σῇ κεφαλῇ ἀναμάξεις a deed (as if a stain), which thou *wilt wipe off* with or on thine own head (since it was believed that the pollution of murder was avoided by wiping the weapon on the victim's head), Od.19.92; τὰ μὲν ἐμῇ κεφαλῇ ἀναμάξας φέρω Hdt.1.155:—Med., ἀσέβειαν δημοσίᾳ -ξασθαι Paus.10.33.2; ἀναματτομένη τῷ προσώπῳ τοῦ αἵματος *having* [some of] the blood *wiped on her* face, Plu.*Ant.*77; τὸ ἑτέρου κακόν Ph.2.379; ψυχὴ ἀ. πάθος J.*AJ* 16.8.5; τοσαύτας ἀναμεμαγμένος κηλῖδας Porph.*Chr.*88. II. Med., *knead one's bread*, Ar.*Nu.*676 codd., cf. *AB*391. 2. *receive an impression*, Ti.Locr.94a; of the eyes, ἀ. τοὺς τύπους τῶν δρωμένων Arr.*Epict.*2.23.3; ἡ ψυχὴ ἀναμάττεσθαι δύναται τοὺς τῶν αἰσθητῶν τύπους Plot.4.3.26; ἀ. τὸ εἶδος Alex.Aphr. *de An.*137.1. 3. *obtain an impression of*, τὴν ψυχήν τινος διὰ τῶν λόγων Eun.*Hist.* p.266 D. 4. *refurbish*, τὴν μνήμην Max.Tyr.8.2.

ἀναμαστεύω· ἀναζητῶ, Hsch.; *make a search* (for fugitives), Men.Prot.p.131 D.

ἀναμασχᾰλιστήρ, ῆρος, ὁ, (μασχάλη) *shoulder-strap*, an article of female dress, Philippid.1.

ἀναμάχομαι, *renew the fight, retrieve a defeat*, Hdt.5.121, 8.109, Th.7.61, Jul.*Or.*1.24c. II. metaph., ἀ. τὸν λόγον *fight* the argument *over again*, Pl.*Hp.Ma.*286d, cf. *Phd.*89c. 2. *make good* a loss, ἀ. τὰ ἁμαρτανόμενα Thphr.*CP*3.2.5, cf. Plu.*Arat.*28; περιπέτειαν Plb.1.55.5; ἡ φύσις τὴν φθορὰν ἀ. nature *makes good* the waste, Arist. *GA*755ᵃ31; ἀ. ταῖς ἀνελευθέροις συστολαῖς Phld.*Oec.*p.71 J.; *recover*, Id.*Mort.*37; τὴν νίκην Memn.58; *counteract*, Aret.*CD*2.6.

ἀνάμβᾰτος, ον, of a horse, *that one cannot mount, unbroken*, X. *Cyr.*4.5.46.

ἀναμείγνῡμι, later -μίγνυμι and -ύω, poet. ἀμμείγνυμι B.*Fr.* 16: poet. aor. part. ἀμμείξας Il.24.529; cf. ἀναμίσγω:—*mix up, mix together*, ἀνὰ δὲ κρῖ λευκὸν ἔμειξαν Od.4.41; πάντα τὰ κρέα Hdt.4.26; κᾀμοὶ..μἀναμείγνυσθαι (i.e. μὴ ἀναμ-) τύχας τὰς σάς E. *Supp.*591; θεὰς ἀνθρώποις *h.Ven.*52. II. often in Pass., *to be mixed* with, Διονυσίοισι δώροις B. l.c.; πάντες ἀναμεμειγμένοι S.*El.* 715; τοῖσ. πολλὰ ἔθνεα ἀναμεμίχαται Hdt.1.146; Κάδμου παισὶν ἀναμεμειγμέναι E.*Ba.*37; πάντες ἀλλήλοις Arist.*Pol.*1319ᵇ25; ἐν μέσοις τοῖς Ἕλλησιν X.*An.*4.8.8, cf. Pl.*Phlb.*48a. 2. *join company*, ὡς δὲ ἀνεμείχθημεν D.54.8; *have social intercourse*, Plu.*Num.*20.

ἀναμέλγω, *drain sap from*, ἀνὰ φυλλάδ' ἀμέλξαι Nic.*Al.*428.

ἀναμελετάω, *con over*, παράγγελμα πρὸς ἑαυτόν S.E.*M.*11.122.

ἀν-άμελκτος, ον, *unmilked*, Sch.Theoc.1.6; cf. ἀνήμελκτος.

ἀναμέλπω, *raise a strain*, c. acc. cogn., ἀοιδάν Theoc.17.113; ἁρμονίαν Ph.1.312; οἰκτρὸν μέλος Ps.-Callisth.1.46:—Med., *raise a strain*, *Pae.Delph.*13:—Pass., Phld.*Mus.*p.85 K., Plu.*Daed.*6. II. trans., *praise in song*, *Anacreont.*36.2.

ἀναμεμιγμένως, *promiscuously*, Hsch. s.v. ἀναμίξ, Sch.S.*Tr.*519.

ἀναμενετέον, *one must await*, τινά Ach.Tat.5.11.

ἀναμένω, poet. ἀμμένω, Aeol. ὀμμένω Alc.41:—*wait for, await*, ἀνέμεινα..Ἠῶ δῖαν Od.19.342; νύκτα, τὸν ἥλιον, Hdt.7.42,54; τέλος δίκης A.*Eu.*243; freq. in E., and Att. Prose:—οὐδὲ..ἐπιθυμίαν ἀναμένεις *dost* not *wait for* desire to arise, X.*Mem.*2.1.30, cf. *Smp.* 4.41; ἀ. τινά Hdt.9.57; *face* an enemy *in battle*, Pi.*P.*6.31: c. acc. et inf., οὐκ ἀ. τοὺς Ἕλληνας μάχης ἄρξαι Hdt.8.15: ἀ. φῦναι τὰς τρίχας Id.5.35; ἀ. ἡμέραν γενέσθαι Th.4.135, cf. 120: foll. by relat. clauses, ἀ. ἕως ἄν.. Pl.*Ly.*209a; ἀ. αὐτοὺς ἔστ' ἐμφάγοιέν τι X.*Cyr.*8.1.44; ποῖ χρῆν ἀναμεῖναι; i.e. ἐς τίνα χρόνον; Ar.*Lys.*526: abs., *wait, stay*, Ἑρμῆς..οὐκέτ' ἀμμένει S.*El.*1397, cf. 1389, *Tr.*528, Ar.*Ra.*175: c. part., πεινῶν ἀ. Id.*V.*777. 2. *put off, delay*, X.*Cyr.*1.6.10: c. inf., D.19. 224.

ἀναμερ-ίζω, *distribute, distinguish*, πρόσωπα A.D.*Synt.*114.3, al. **-ισις**, εως, ἡ, *distribution*, Lyd.*Mens.*4.67. **-ισμός**, ὁ, *redistribution*, Sch.rec.Pi.*O.*7.110.

ἀνάμεσος, ον, *in the midst, in the heart of a country*, πόλεις ἀνάμεσοι Hdt.2.108; simply, *in the midst, between*, *PLond.*2.267.189; χρόνος ἀ. ἡμέρας καὶ νυκτός Eudox.*Ars*16; τὴν ἀνάμεσον ἀλλήλων χώραν Ph.Byz.*Mir.*1.2.

ἀνάμεστ-ος, ον (fem. -τη Eup.16 codd.), *filled full*, τινός *of* a thing, Ar.*Nu.*984, Eup. l.c., Philum.ap.Aët.5.125, Phld.*Piet.*74, Man.4.82, Eun.*VS* p.454 B.; ἔχθρας πρὸς τὸν δῆμον ἀνάμεστος D.25.32; βίος ἀ. ἰλύος Epict.*Gnom.*1. **-όω**, *fill up, fill full*, Ar.*Ra.*1084 (Pass.).

ἀναμεταξύ, Adv. *between, intermediate*, Arist.*Ph.*243ᵃ15: of Time, *in the meanwhile*, Nic.Dam.p.63 D., Dexipp.p.196 D.: Prep. c. gen., Aq., Sm.3*Ki.*20.3.

ἀναμετρ-έω, *measure back again, re-measure the road, retrace one's steps*, ὄφρ'.. ἀναμετρήσαιμι Χάρυβδιν Od.12.428; ἀ. σαυτὸν ἀπιών *measure yourself off!* Ar.*Av.*1020; πόνοισι πόνους ἀ., i.e. undergo a succession of labours, *IG*3.1374. 2. *enumerate*, Hp.*Ep.*27:—in Med., *recapitulate*, E.*Or.*14. II. *measure over again*, τὸ ὕδωρ Hp.*Aër.*8. 2. *measure carefully*, ἀ. ὅσῳ ἐλάσσων ὁ χῶρος γέγονε Hdt.2.109; ἀ. τὸ ὅλον Arist.*Ph.*221ᵃ3; τινί τι one thing by another, Pl.*R.*531a:—also in Med., ἀ. γῆν Ar.*Nu.*203; ἀνεμετρησάμην φρένας τὰς σάς *took the measure of*.., E.*Ion* 1271; γνώμης πονηροῖς κανόσιν ἀναμετρούμενος τὸ σῶφρον Id.*El.*52:—Pass., ἀ. τινί *to be measured by*, Pl.*Ti.*39d. 3. *measure out*, θοὐμόφυλον ἀ. δάκρυ E.*IT*346. **-ησις**, εως, ἡ, *measurement*, τῆς γῆς Str.1.1.20, cf. *POxy.*918 xi 14 (ii A.D.); τῶν θείων περιόδων Iamb.*Myst.*9.4. 2. *estimate*, τῆς εὐδαιμονίας πρὸς ἀργύριον ἀ. ποιεῖσθαι Plu.*Sol.*27, cf. Hierocl.*in CA*19p.461 M. **-ητέον**, *one must measure*, Iamb.*Protr.*5. **-ητής**, οῦ, ὁ, *official in charge of land-survey*, Wilcken *Chrest.*229.3 (iv A.D.). **-ικῶς**, Adv. *by measurement*, f.l. in Gem.17.5.

ἀναμηλόω, *examine with a probe*, *h.Merc.*41 (Ruhnken), Hsch.

ἀναμηρυκ-άομαι or **ἀναμᾱρ-**, *chew the cud*, Ath.9.390f, Luc.*Gall.* 8. **-ησις**, εως, ἡ, *rumination*, Aristeas 154.

ἀναμηρύομαι, *wind up, draw back*, as a thread, Plu.2.978d.

ἀνά-μῐγα, poet. ἄμμῐγα, Adv. = ἀναμίξ, *promiscuously, confusedly*, A.*Th.*239, S.*Tr.*839 (lyr.), *IG*5(1).726; τινί *with*.., A.R.1.573, *AP* 7.12; also τινός ib.22. **-μιγδα**, = ἀναμίξ, S.*Tr.*519 (lyr.). **-μίγδην**, Nic.*Th.*912. **-μῐγή**, ἡ, *mixture*, Sch.A.*Th.*330. **-μικτέον**, *one must mix*, Orib.*Syn.*1.33.2.

ἀν-αμίλλητος, ον, *undisputed*, Hsch. (ἀναμήλλικτον cod.), Suid.

ἀναμιμέομαι, *imitate*, Plu.2.303a.

ἀναμιμνήσκω, fut. ἀναμνήσω, poet. ἀμμνήσω: Aeol. aor. Act. ὀμναῖσαι Sapph.*Supp.*23.10: aor. inf. Pass. ὀμνάσθην Theoc.29.26:—*remind* one *of* a thing, c. dupl. acc., ταῦτά μ' ἀνέμνησας Od.3.211, cf. Hdt.6.140, S.*OT*1133, Th.6.6: but also c. gen. rei, μή μ' ἀναμνήσῃς κακῶν E.*Alc.*1045, cf. Pl.*Mx.*246a: c. acc. pers. only, Sapph. l.c. 2. c. acc. pers. et inf., *remind* one to do, Pi.*P.*4.54. 3. c. acc. rei only, *recall to memory, make mention of*, Antipho 2.4.11, D.18.213. 4. foll. by Conj., ἀ. ὅτι.. Th.2.89, etc.; ὡς εἶχε τὰ πράγματ' ἀναμνῆσαι D.18.17. 5. ἀναμιμνήσκων, ὁ, *remembrancer*, Lxx 2*Ki.*20.24, al. II. Pass., *remember, recall to mind*, τινός Hdt.2.151, Th.2.54, etc.; less freq. τι, Ar.*Ra.*661, Pl.*Phd.*72e, X.*An.*7.1.26; περί τι Pl.*R.*329a: foll. by a relat., ἀναμνησθέντας οἷα ἐπάσχετε Hdt.5.109: abs., Id.3.51, Ar.*Ec.*552. 2. ἀ. νοσήματος have a *relapse*, Gal.17(2).423.

ἀναμίμνω, poet. for ἀναμένω, c. acc., Il.11.171: abs., 16.363.

ἀναμινυρίζω, *sing languishingly*, Protagorid.2.

ἀνα-μίξ, Adv. *promiscuously, pell-mell*, Hdt.1.103, Hellanic.71(a)J., Th.3.107: c. dat., γυναῖκες ἀ. ἀνδράσιν Str.3.3.7, cf. 4.6.3, Jul.*Gal.* 100c. **-μιξις**, εως, ἡ, *mingling, admixture*, Thphr.*CP*4.15.4, Plu.*Num.*17, Gal.2.850. **-μίσγω**, poet. and Ion. for ἀναμείγνυμι, ἀνέμισγε δὲ σίτῳ φάρμακα Od.10.235; αἷμα δακρύοισι Tim.*Fr.*7:—Med., *have intercourse with*, τινί Hdt.1.199:—Pass., γέλως ἀνεμίσγετο λύπῃ Call.*Aet.Fr.*7.3 P.

ἀναμισθαρνέω, *serve again for pay*, *Com.Adesp.*11.

ἀναμισθ-όομαι, Dor. **ἀμμ-**, Pass., *to be let anew*, *Tab.Heracl.*1. 111. **-ωσις**, εως, ἡ, *renewal of lease, re-letting*, ἱερῶν *LW*483 (Caria), *BGU*1122.32 (13 B.C.).

ἄναμμα, ατος, τό, (ἀνάπτω) *ignited mass*, πυρὸς ἄ. Epicur.*Ep.*1 p.28 U. (cj.); ἄ. νοερὸν ἐκ θαλάττης, of the sun, Heraclit.ap.*Placit.*2. 20.16, cf. Zeno *Stoic.*1.35, Cleanth.ib.112.

ἀνάμματος, ον, (ἅμμα) *without knots*, X.*Cyn.*2.4, Hsch.

ἀναμνημονεύω, *remember*, Anon.*in Rh.*116.30.

ἀνάμνη-σις, εως, ἡ, (ἀναμιμνήσκω) *calling to mind, reminiscence*, Pl.*Phd.*72e, 92d, *Phlb.*34c (pl.), Arist.*Mem.*451ᵃ21; ἀ. τινος λαβεῖν *recall* it *to memory*, *IG*2.628.20; ἀναμνήσεις θυσιῶν *reminders to the gods* of sacrifices offered, Lys.2.39. 2. *memorial sacrifice*, Lxx *Nu.*10.10, cf. *Ev.Luc.*22.19. 3. παλίνδρομος ἀ., of the moon, Secund.*Sent.*6. **-στέον**, *one must remember*, Gal.10.214, Eust.357. 16. **-στικός**, ή, όν, *able to recall to mind readily*, opp. μνημονικός (*of retentive memory*), Arist.*Mem.*449ᵇ7, 453ᵃ5. II. *indicative of the past*, σημεῖα Gal.1.313. **-στός**, όν, *that which one can recollect*, Pl.*Men.*87b.

ἀναμολεῖν, ἀνέμολον, aor. 2 with no pres. in use (cf. βλώσκω), *go through*, ἀνὰ δὲ κέλαδος ἔμολε πόλιν E.*Hec.*928.

ἀναμολύνω, strengthd. for μολύνω, Pherecr.173, cf. Plu.2.580f.

ἀναμονή, ἡ, *patient abiding, endurance*, Sm.*Ps.*38(39).8; *waiting, delay*, Iamb.*VP*31.197, Ps.-Callisth.1.5, Sch.E.*Or.*1101.

ἀναμορμύρω, *roar loudly, boil up*, πᾶσ' ἀναμορμύρεσκε, of Charybdis, Od.12.238, cf. Jul.*Or.*2.60d.

ἀναμορφ-όω, *transform*, εἴς τι Philostr.Jun.*Im.*4. **-ωσις**, εως, ἡ, *forming anew*, Suid. s.v. καινουργισμός. **-ωτής**, οῦ, ὁ, Hsch. s.v. εἰδοποιός.

ἀναμοχλεύω, *raise by a lever*, ἀ. πύλας *force open* the gates, E.*Med.* 1317; τὴν Ὄσσαν Luc.*Cont.*4: metaph. of dislocated limbs, Gal.18 (1).403.

ἀναμπέχονος, ον, *without upper garment*, of a woman, Euph.53, Pythaen.6.

ἀναμπλάκητος, ον, *unerring, unfailing*, Κῆρες ἀνᾰπλάκητοι S.*OT* 472 (lyr.). 2. of a man, *without crime* or *error*, A.*Ag.*345, S.*Tr.* 120.

ἄναμπυξ, ῠκος, ὁ, ἡ, *without head-band* or *fillet*, Call.*Cer.*124.

ἀναμυλλᾶναι· ἀνανεῦσαι, ἀρνήσασθαι, Hsch.

ἀναμυρησάμενος (-μοιρ- Cyr.Dresd.)· χρηματισάμενος, Hsch.

ἀναμυχθίζομαι, *moan loudly*, A.*Pr.*743.

ἀναμύω, *open* the eyes, opp. συμμύω, *AB*391, Hsch.

ἀναμφήριστος, ον, = ἀναμφίβολος, Hsch.

ἀναμφίβολος, ον, *unambiguous*, σύντομα καὶ ἀ. Ascl.*Tact.*12.11; ἀ. νίκη v.l. in D.H.3.57; φύσις Gal.17(1).370(358). Adv. -λως M. Ant.1.8, Luc.*Anach.*24.

ἀναμφιδόξως, Adv. *incontrovertibly*, Plu.2.441f.

ἀναμφίλεκτος, ον, = sq., τιμή D.H.9.44; πίστις Longin.7.4. Adv. -τως *PPar.*15.3.56 (ii B.C.), S.E.*M.*7.5, Luc.*Rh.Pr.*15.

ἀναμφίλογος, ον, *undisputed, undoubted*, X.*Mem.*4.2.34, *Smp.*3. 4 (Sup.); νίκη D.H.3.57. Adv. -γως *without dispute, willingly*, X.*Cyr.*8.1.44; *unquestionably, indisputably*, Id.*Ages.*2.12, D.H.3.41, Luc.*Herm.*36.

ἀναμφισβήτητος, ον (Comp. written ἀναμφισβητότερον Dam.*Pr.* 136; cf. ἀναφίσβητ' *IG*12(9).1273 iii 7), *undisputed, indisputable*, ἀρχή Diog.Apoll.1; τεκμήρια Th.1.132; ἀριστεῖα Lys.2.43; ἀ. ἡ κρίσις Arist.*Pol.*1283ᵇ5; ἀ. καὶ φανερὰ ἡ ὑπεροχή ib.1332ᵇ20; ἀ. χώρα a place *about which there is no dispute*, i.e. *well-known*, X.*Cyr.*8.5.6. II. Act., of persons, *without dispute* or *controversy*, ἀ. διετελέσαμεν Is.8. 44. Adv. -τως Antipho 5.16, Pl.*Euthd.*305d, al.

ἀναμφόδαρχος, ον, *not registered under an* ἀμφόδαρχος (q.v.), *POxy.*257.22.

ἀναμωκάομαι, *mock*, Sch.Ar.*Ra.*1323.

ἀνανάγκαστος, ον, *unconstrained*, Arr.*Epict.*1.6.40, al. Adv. -τως Id.3.24.39.

ἄνανδες· ἄνωθεν (Cypr.), Cyr.Dresd.; but **ἀνανδές**· οὐκ εὐάρεστον, ἢ ἀληθές, Hsch.

ἀνανδρ-ία (in codd. sts. wrongly -εία, and in later Ion. -ηΐη), ἡ, *want of manhood*, Hp.*Aër.*16, E.*Med.*466, Pl.*Phdr.*254c, etc.; of eunuchs, Luc.*Syr.D.*26. 2. *unmanliness, cowardice*, A.*Pers.*755, E.*Or.*1031, Th.1.83, And.1.56, etc.; ἀνανδρίᾳ χερῶν E.*Supp.*314. II. *unmarried womanhood*, Plu.2.302f. **-ιεῖς**, οἱ, *impotent persons*, dub. l. in Hp.*Aër.*22; cf. ἀναριεῖς. **-όομαι**, *become impotent*, Hp.*Aër.*22. **-ος**, ον, (ἀνήρ): I. = ἄνευ ἀνδρός, *husbandless*, of virgins and widows, A.*Supp.*287, *Pers.*289 (lyr.), S.*OT*1506, etc., and in Prose, as Hp.*Mul.*1.4, Pl.*Lg.*930c. 2. = ἄνευ ἀνδρῶν, *without men*, χρήματα ἄνανδρα A.*Pers.*166; πόλις S.*OC*939; ἄνανδρον τάξιν ἠρήμου (a prolepsis, = ὥστε εἶναι ἄνανδρον) A.*Pers.*298. II. *wanting in manhood, cowardly*, Hdt.4.142, Pl.*Grg.*522e, al.; τὸ ἄ., = ἀνανδρία, Th.3.82. 2. of things, *unworthy of a man*, δίαιτα Pl.*Phdr.*239d. 3. Adv. -δρως, opp. ἀνδρικῶς, Antipho 2.1.8, Pl.*Tht.*177b. **-ωτος**, *widowed*, εὐναί S.*Tr.*110 (lyr.).

ἀνανεάζω, *become young* or *new again*, Ar.*Ra.*592, Lxx 4*Ma.*7.14, Sm.*Jb.*29.20, Phryn.*PS* p.59 B., Suid. s.v. ἀνηβᾶν; ἐκ τῶν νόσων Corn.*ND*33.

ἀνανέμω, poet. ἀννέμω, *distribute*: hence, *count up*, in Med., ἀνανεμέεται (Ion. fut.) τὰς μητέρας Hdt.1.173. 2. *read, con over*, Epich.224, Theoc.18.48.

ἀνανέομαι, *mount up*, οὐδ' ὅπῃ [ἠέλιος] ἀννεῖται Od.10.192.

ἀνανε-όομαι, fut. -ώσομαι Plb.22.7.1, al.: aor. ἀνενεωσάμην Th.5. 43,46, poet. inf. ἀννεώσασθαι, v. infr.:—*renew*, τὸν ὅρκον Th.5.18; τὴν προξενίαν ib.43; τὰς σπονδάς ib.80; φιλίαν Id.7.33, D.23.121; ὁμόνοιάν τινι Philipp.ap.D.18.167; συμμαχίαν Plb. l.c., al. II. κἀννεώσασθαι λόγους *revive* them, prob. for καὶ νεώσασθαι, S.*Tr.*396, cf. E.*Hel.*722, Plb.5.36.7.—Act. freq. in Lxx, *Jb.*33.24, al., *IG*14.1078ᵃ, *Delph.*3(1) No.60, cf. *SIG*478.503 (iii B.C.), Dam.*Pr.*391:—Pass., *Ep.Eph.*4.23.

ἀνανέσαι· καταστῆσαι (Cret.), Hsch.

ἀνάνετος, ον, *not relaxed*, διάθεσις *Stoic.*2.129, cf. 3.141; *not capable of diminution*, Porph.*Intr.*20.4.

ἀνά-νευσις, εως, ἡ, (νέομαι) *return, revival*, Lxx *Ps.*72(73).4, cf. Andronic.Rhod.p.571 M., Hsch. II. *upward inclination*, Dam. *Pr.*56. III. *upward motion*, Ath.Mech.26.2. **-νευστικῶς**, Adv. *showing a disposition to refuse*, Arr.*Epict.*1.14.7. **-νεύω**, fut. -νεύσομαι Pl.*R.*350e, -νεύσω Luc.*Sat.*1: aor. ἀνένευσα, etc.:—*throw the head back* in token of denial, *make signs of refusal*, opp. κατανεύω, ἐπινεύω, ὡς ἔφατ' εὐχομένη, ἀνένευε δὲ Παλλὰς Ἀθήνη Il.6.311; ἀνένευε καρήατι 22.205; ὀφρύσι Od.9.468, cf. Hdt.5.51, Ar.*Lys.*126, Pl.*R.* l.c., etc. 2. c. acc. rei, *deny, refuse*, ἕτερον μὲν ἔδωκε πατήρ, ἕτερον δ' ἀνένευσε Il.16.250: c. fut. inf., σόον δ' ἀνένευσε μάχης ἐξ ἀπονέεσθαι 16.252:—Pass., ἀνανενευμένη *rejected*, Ph.1.146. 3. later, c. gen. rei, *look up from*, Alciphr.3.53; *go back from*, ἀπὸ τοῦ ψεύδους Arr.*Epict.*2.26.3. II. generally, *throw the head up*: hence ἀνανενευκώς *upright*, [τὰς σαρίσας] ἀ. φέρουσι Plb.18.13.3, cf. 1.23.5. 2. Astron., *tilt back*, of the pole, opp. κατανεύω, Eudox.*Ars*6.

ἀνανέω, *come to the surface*, Ael.*NA*5.22.

ἀνανέ-ωσις, εως, ἡ, *renewal*, ξυμμαχίας Th.6.82; ἀγώνων *CIG*2932 (Tralles); ὑποθήκης *POxy*.274.20 (i A.D.); of a term of office, *PTeb*. 5.186 (ii B.C.) (pl.). II. *revival* of a suspended ceremony or office, *OGI*764.25 (Pergam., ii B.C.), *POxy*.1252ᵛ16 (iii A.D.). 2. *recalling to memory*, D.S.5.67. **-ωτής**, οῦ, ὁ, *restorer*, *CIG*2804 (Aphrodisias), *Ephes*.2 No.46. **-ωτικός**, ή, όν, *renewing, reviving*, τινός J.*AJ*11.4.7.

ἀνανῆσαι· σφάξαι, Hsch. (fort. ἀμῆσαι).

ἀνανήφω, *become sober again, come to one's senses*, Arist.*Mir*.847ᵇ9; ἐκ μέθης D.H.4.35, cf. Lync.ap.Ath.3.109e; ἐκ τοῦ οἴνου Nic.Dam. p.7 D.; *return to sobriety of mind*, 2 *Ep.Ti*.2.26; *recover from a swoon*, Charito 3.1, D.Chr.4.77. 2. trans., *make sober again*, Luc.*BisAcc*.17.

ἀνανήχομαι, = ἀνανέω, *swim*, Arist.*Resp*.475ᵇ1 (s.v.l.); *rise to the surface*, Plu.2.985b: metaph., *revive, recover*, Ael.*NA*8.4; ὥσπερ ἐκ κλύδωνος Ph.1.260; ἐκ νόσου λοιμώδους Paus.7.17.1. 2. *swim upstream*, Opp.*H*.1.120:—Act. form ἀνανήξας· διαπλεύσας, Hsch.; cf. ἀνήξεις· κολυμβήσεις (fort. ἀννήξεις· ἀνακ.), Id.

ἀνανθέω, *blossom again, continue blossoming*, Thphr.*CP*3.24.3, Lib.*Or*.18.90, *IGRom*.4.1540.25 (Erythrae).

ἀνανθής, ές, *flowerless*, Pl.*Smp*.196a, Thphr.*HP*1.14.3, *CP*3.19. 1, Plu.2.684c; οὐδεὶς χρόνος ἀ. Thphr. *HP*6.8.4.

ἀνάνθρωπος, ον, *inhuman, savage*, *POxy*.1681.6 (iii A.D.).

ἀνάνιος, ον, *without pain*: Act., *not giving pain*, Hsch., *EM*.97. 43. Adv. -ως ib.44. Cf. ἀνήνιος.

ἀνανίσσομαι, = ἀνανέομαι, Opp.*H*.5.410.

ἀνανοέω, *call to mind*, v.l. in X.Eph.1.11.

ἀνανομή, ἡ, *redistribution*, Eur.*Fr*.748.

ἀνανοσέω, *relapse*, ἐς στάσιν J.*BJ*5.6.1.

ἀνανοστέω, *return to the path*, S.*Ichn*.160.

ἄναντα, Adv. *up-hill*, opp. κάταντα (q.v.), Il.23.116.

ἀναντᾰγώνιστος, ον, *without a struggle*, Th.4.92; ἀ. εὔνοια *unchallenged*, i.e. *unalloyed* goodwill, Id.2.45; ἀ. γέρας ἔλαχεν *without having to strive for it*, Ph.1.646. Adv. -τως Plu.2.1128b. II. *irresistible*, Ph.1.454, al., Plu.*Phoc*.14; ἐρώτημα Polem.*Call*.50. III. *without a rival, incomparable*, Ph.2.6, al.

ἀναντάλλακτος, ον, *not to be exchanged*, *Gloss*.

ἀνανταπό-δοσις, εως, ἡ, *suppressed apodosis* in a conditional sentence, Anon.*Fig*.p.157 S. **-δοτος**, ον, *without apodosis*: τὸ ἀ. *hypothetical proposition wanting the consequent clause*, Sch.Ar.*Pl*.469.

ἀνάντης, ες, (ἀνά, ἄντην) *up-hill, steep*, opp. κατάντης, χωρίον Hdt. 2.29; πεδία Hp.*Aër*.19; ὁδός, ἀνάβασις, Pl.*R*.364d, 515e; πρὸς ἀνάντες ἐλαύνειν, opp. κατὰ πρανοῦς, X.*Eq*.3.7, cf. Pl.*Phdr*.247b; πρὸς τὸ ἀ. τῶν πολιτειῶν *in the ascending scale* of our constitutions, Id.*R*.568c; πρὸς ὑψηλὰ καὶ ἀνάντη Id.*Lg*.732c.

ἀναντί-βλεπτος, ον, *what one dares not face*, Plu.2.67b: metaph., *irrefragable*, διαίρεσις Procl.*in Alc*.p.201 C. **-θετος**, ον, *not to be contradicted*, Olymp.*in Phlb*.p.247 S.; αἵρεσις Simp.*in Epict*.p.7 D., al. II. *without contrary* or *opposite*, Dam.*Pr*.26, Anon.*in Cat*.23. 21. **-λεκτος**, ον, *undisputed*, *PHib*.95.13; *incontestable*, Cic.*QF* 2.8.1, Luc.*Eun*.13; *not to be opposed*, δεήσεις J.*AJ*19.1.4. Adv. -τως Aen.Tact.31.9, Str.13.3.6, Luc.*Cal*.6. **-ληπτος**, ον, *insensible to*, ἀλγηδόνων Dsc.*Eup*.1.12. **-ρρητος**, ον, *not to be opposed*, Plb.6. 7.7, 28.13.4; *undeniable*, *Act.Ap*.19.36; λόγοι S.E.*M*.8.160. Adv. -τως *without opposition, by consent*, Plb.22.8.11; *incontrovertibly*, *OGI*335.138 (Pergam.), Aët.15.15; *without gainsaying*, *Act.Ap*.10. 29. **-τῠπος**, ον, *giving no resistance*, S.E.*M*.9.411. **-φωνησία**, ἡ, *not answering*, Cic.*Att*.15.13.2. **-φώνητος**, ον, *unanswered*, ib.6.1.23, *PRyl*.78.30 (ii A.D.).

ἀναντλέω, *draw up* or *out*, ποταμοὺς ἀ. κοχλίαις Str.3.2.9: metaph., *exhaust, go patiently through*, πόνους D.H.8.51; συμφοράς D.Chr.12. 51.

ἄναντος, ον, *not winnowed* or *bruised*, dub. in S.*Fr*.294.

ἄναξ [ᾰ], ἄνακτος (cf. Ἄνακες), ὁ, rarely fem. ὦ ἄνα for ἄνασσα, Pi.*P*.12.4, cf. A.*Fr*.342: (ϝάναξ *IG*4.236 (Corinth), etc., cf. ϝάνακες 4.564 (Argos)):—*lord, master*, 1. of the gods, esp. Apollo, ἄγουσι δὲ δῶρα Ἄνακτι Il.1.390, al.; ὁ Πύθιος ἄναξ A.*Ag*.509; ἄναξ Ἄπολλον ib.513, *Eu*.85, etc.; ὦναξ Ἄπ. S.*OT*80; ὦναξ without Ἀπόλλον, Hdt.1.159, 4.150, al.; of Zeus, Hom. only in voc., Ζεῦ ἄνα Il.3. 351, 16.233; Ζεὺς ἄναξ A.*Pers*.762; ἄναξ ἀνάκτων.. Ζεῦ Id.*Supp*.524; μὰ τὸν Δία τὸν Ἄνακτα D.35.40; Poseidon, A.*Th*.130; ὦ δέσποτ' ἄναξ, of Ἀήρ, Ar.*Nu*.264; of Apollo Ἀγυιεύς, Id.*V*.875; ὦναξ δέσποτα, of Πλοῦτος, Id.*Pl*.748; esp. of the Dioscuri, cf. Ἄνακες, Ἄνακοι; of all the gods, πάντων ἀνάκτων.. κοινοβωμίαν A.*Supp*.222, cf. Pi.*O*. 10(11).49.—The irreg. voc. ἄνα (q.v.) is never addressed save to gods; ὦναξ is freq. in Trag. and Com. II. of the Homeric heroes, esp. of Agamemnon, as general-in-chief ἄναξ ἀνδρῶν Ἀ. Il.1.442, al. (so Euphetes 15.532, while Ortilochos is called πολέεσσ' ἄνδρεσσιν ἄνακτα 5.546):—also as a title of rank, e.g. of Teiresias, Od.11.144, 151, S.*OT*284; of the *sons* or *brothers of kings* (υἱεῖς τοῦ βασιλέως καὶ οἱ ἀδελφοὶ καλοῦνται ἄνακτες Arist.*Fr*.526, cf. Isoc.9. 72, Clearch.25, and so of Creon, S.*OT*85, cf. 911), and esp. of kings, as Xerxes, A.*Pers*.5, Darius, ib.787, cf. *Ag*.42, E.*Ph*.17, *Or*.349, etc.; βασιλῆι ἄνακτι *lord* king, Od.20.194; of the emperors, θεοὶ ἄνακτες *IG*14.2012 *A* 2, 4.1475 (Epid.). III. *master of the house*, οἴκοιο ἄναξ Od.1.397; ἀμφὶ ἄνακτα κύνες 10.216; as denoting the relation of *master* to slave, freq. in Od.; ἄναξ, θεοὺς γὰρ δεσπότας καλεῖν χρεών E.*Hipp*.88; of the Cyclops, as *owner* of flocks, Od.9. 440. IV. metaph., κώπης, ναῶν ἄνακτες *lords* of the oar, of ships, A.*Pers*.378, 383; πύλης ἄ. θυρωρέ, of a porter, S.*Fr*.775; ἄ. ὅπλων E.*IA*1260; ψευδῶν Id.*Andr*.447; ὑπήνης Pl.Com.122; κέντρων, of planets holding cardinal points, Man.1.66.—Poet. word.

Ἀναξαγόρειος, α, ον, *of Anaxagoras*, διάκοσμος Satyr.*Vit.Eur.Fr*. 37; τὸ Ἀ. *the saying of A.*, Plu.2.679a; οἱ Ἀ. Pl.*Cra*.409b.

ἀνα-ξαίνω, *tear open*, ἀ. λύπην Babr.12.24, Antyll.ap.Orib.44.23.4, Them.*Or*.7.98c; τὰ -οντα φάρμακα Phld.*Ir*.p.60 W. (dub.):—Pass., of evils, *break out afresh*, Plb.27.7.6; εἰς κάκωσιν ἀ. Plu.2.610d, cf. *Dem*. 17: but ἀναξανθεῖσαι τοὺς στομάχους, of those whose appetite is *stimulated afresh*, Alciphr.*Fr*.6.18. **-ξασμός**, ὁ, *laceration*, Archig. ap.Gal.12.406.

ἀναξέω, *hew smooth, polish*, *IG*7.3073.123 (Lebad.); part. contr. ἀναξῶν ib.2².463.72:—Pass., λίθου ἀνεξεσμένου J.*AJ*13.6.6.

ἀναξηρ-αίνω, fut. -ᾰνῶ: aor. ἀνεξήρᾱνα, Ion. -ηνα, Ep. subj. ἀγξηράνῃ:—*dry up*, ὡς δ' ὅτ' ὀπωρινὸς Βορέης.. ἀλωὴν αἶψ' ἀγξηράνῃ Il.21. 347; τὰ ὑποζύγια ἀρδόμενα ἀνεξήρηνε [τὴν λίμνην] Hdt.7.109:—Pass., Hp.*Aër*.8, Phylarch.50, Ph.2.511, etc. 2. metaph., *consume, exhaust*, οἶκον ἀ. ὀδόντες Call.*Cer*.114. II. *dry again*, after bathing, in Pass., Hp.*Acut*.65. **-ανσις**, εως, ἡ, *drying up*, Thphr.*HP*3.1. 2. **-αντικός**, ή, όν, *fit for drying*, Dsc.1.7, Crito ap.Gal.12.488, Plu.2. 624d. **-ᾰσία**, ἡ, = ἀναξήρανσις, Thphr.*Fr*.171.12. **-ασμός**, ὁ, *drying up*, Sor.2.10, Leonid.ap.Aët.16.44, Herod.Med.in *Rh.Mus*.58.90.

ἀναξία (A), ἡ, (ἀνάσσω) *command, behest*, Pi.*N*.8.10 (pl.). 2. = βασιλεία, A.*Fr*.283.

ἀναξία (B), ἡ, *lack of value*: *inferiority*, Pl.*Prt*.356a (s.v.l.).

ἀναξί-αλος, ὁ, *lord of the sea*, epith. of Poseidon, B.19.8. **-βρένται**, α, ὁ, *lord of the thunder*, epith. of Zeus, Id.16.66; cf. ἀργιβρένται, βρένται. **-δώρα**, ἡ, = ἡ ἀνάγουσα δῶρα, of Demeter, S.*Fr*.1010; cf. ἀνησιδώρα. **-μολπος**, ἡ, *queen of song*, epith. of Urania, B.6.10.

ἀναξιό-λογος, ον, *inconsiderable*, D.S.31.9. **-πάθεια**, ἡ, *unworthy treatment*, or rather, *just indignation thereat*, J.*AJ*15.2.7, Hp.*Ep*.17. **-πᾰθέω**, *to be indignant at unworthy treatment*, Str. 8.4.7 (v.l.), D.H.4.11, J.*AJ*15.3.2. **-πιστος**, ον, *unworthy of credit*, Eudem.ap.Simp.*in Ph*.115.35, Alex.Aphr.*in Metaph*.317.15.

ἀνάξιος (A), ον, also α, ον freq. in Att.: I. of persons, *unworthy, not deemed* or *held worthy*; ἀνάξιον σοῦ *too good for* thee, S.*Ph*.1009: also c. inf., ἀ. γὰρ πᾶσίν ἐστε δυστυχεῖν *undeserving* in the eyes of all to suffer, S.*OC*1446; νικᾶν Pl.*Prt*.356a. 2. abs., *worthless, despicable*, Hdt.7.9, S.*Ph*.439, etc.; ἀπερεῖ τις ἔποικος ἀναξία Id.*El*. 189 (lyr.). Adv. -ίως Id.*Aj*.1392, etc. 3. *undeserving of evil*, Id.*Ant*.694, E.*Heracl*.526, Th.3.59. II. of things, *undeserved*, ἀνάξια σφέων αὐτῶν πεπονθότες Hdt.1.73, cf. 114, Lys.21.25, Pl.*Cri*. 53e: also abs., ἀνάξια παθεῖν E.*IA*852, al., Pl.*Tht*.184a. Adv. -ίως, ἐφθάρησαν ἀ. ἑωυτῶν Hdt.7.10.ε'. 2. *unworthy*, πολλὰ καὶ ἀ. ἐμοῦ Pl.*Ap*.38e. 3. *worthless*, τὸ ἀ. ἀκερδές Id.*Hipparch*.231e.

ἀνάξιος (B), ον, (ἄναξ) *kingly, royal*, Sch.Il.23.630.

ἄναξις, εως, ἡ, *bringing up, raising up*, *Psalm.Solom*.18.6.

ἀναξιφόρμιγξ, ιγγος, ὁ, ἡ, *ruling the lyre*, ἀναξιφόρμιγγες ὕμνοι Pi. *O*.2.1.

ἀναξῡνόω, (ξυνός) v.l. for ἀνακοινόομαι in X.*HG*1.1.30 (ap.Suid.).

ἀναξῠράω, *shave again*, τὸν τόπον Cleopatra ap.Gal.12.404.

ἀναξυρίδες, ίδων, αἱ, *trousers* worn by eastern nations, Hdt.5. 49, 7.61, X.*An*.1.5.8; by the Scythians, Hdt.1.71, cf. Hp.*Aër*.22; by the Sacae, Hdt.3.87, etc.: sg., Luc.*Hist.Conscr*.19, Philostr.*VA* 1.25. II. sg. **ἀναξυρίς**, ἡ, = ὀξαλίς, Dsc.2.114, Sch.Nic.*Th*. 838. (Derived from ἀνασύρεσθαι by Eust.22.8, but really Persian. Wrongly expl. as a head-covering by Poll.7.58.)

ἀνάξυστον, = γναφάλλιον, Ps.-Dsc.3.117.

ἀναξύω [ῡ], *scrape up* or *off*, τὰ ἐν τῇ γῇ ὄντα [σημεῖα] ἀναξῦσαι Antipho 5.45:—Pass., ἀναξυομένης τῆς γῆς *being scraped up* by fishermen dredging, Arist.*HA*569ᵇ7, cf. 603ᵃ23; ἀναξυσθέντες *having the surface scraped off*, Plu.*Publ*.15; *to be scraped down*, Orib.*Fr*.99.

ἀναοίγω, poet. for ἀνοίγω, Il.24.455.

ἀναπαιδεύω, *educate afresh*, S.*Fr*.487, Ar.*Eq*.1099.

ἀνα-παιστικός, ή, όν, *anapaestic*, D.H.*Comp*.25, Heph.8, Demetr. *Eloc*.189, etc. **-παιστος**, ον, (cf. sq.) *hammered, forged*, κλεὶς *IG*2.678*B*64, al., 11.161*A*94 (Delos, iii B.C.). II. *struck back, rebounding*:—as Subst., *anapaest* (i.e. a dactyl *reversed*), D.H.*Comp*. 25, Heph.8, etc.; ἀ. ἀπὸ μείζους *dactyl*, Aristid.Quint.1.15. 2. *anapaestic verse*, Arist.*Po*.1452ᵇ23, D.H.1.25, etc.: in pl., of the Comic *parabasis*, Ar.*Eq*.504, *Pax*735, al.; ἀνάπαιστοι σύμπτυκτοι Pherecr.79, cf. Sch.metr.Pi.*O*.4.1; ἀνάπαιστόν τι something *in anapaestic metre*, Aeschin.1.158: ἀνάπαιστα, τά, *anapaestic verses*, Alciphr.3.43; esp. of *ribald* or *satirical songs*, D.C.66.8, Plu.*Per*. 33. **-παιστρίς**, ίδος, ἡ, *smiter*, i.e. *smith's hammer*, Hsch.

ἀναπαίτητος, ον, *not reclaimable*, χρήματα Ἀρχ.Δελτ.6.100 (Methymna, ii B.C.).

ἀναπαίω, *drive back*, in Pass., Eust.587.18: metaph., ῥυθμοὶ ἔμμετροί τε καὶ ἀναπαίοντες, = ἀνάπαιστοι, Philostr.*VS*2.20.3.

ἀναπᾰλαίω, *retrieve by contest*, τὰ σφάλματα J.*BJ*4.1.6. II. ἀ. τὰς ὑποσχέσεις *retract*, Sch.Od.8.567.

ἀναπαλεύω, *overthrow, cancel*, μέρισιν *PLond*.2.394.12 (late).

ἀναπάλη [πᾰ], ἡ, name of a *dance*, Ath.14.631b. II. ἀναπάλαι χειρῶν, a form of exercise, Ruf.*Ren.Ves*.2.33.

ἀνάπᾰλιν, Adv. *back again*, ἰέναι Pl.*Plt*.269d, cf. *Phdr*.264a, al.; ἐπὶ τὸ πέρας ἢ ἀ. Arist.*EN*1095ᵇ1; ἀ. στραφῆναι Id.*Cael*.285ᵃ8, etc. II. *over again*, = ἔμπαλιν, Pl.*Tht.*192d. III. *contrariwise, on the opposite side*, Hp.*Coac.*321; ἀ. πορεύεσθαι proceed *in reverse*, i.e. *wrong order*, Pl.*Ti.*82c; ἀ. τιθέναι Arist.*APr.*37^{b}11, etc.; ἀ. ἐστιν ἡμῖν ἢ τοῖς ἄλλοις *in the opposite way to..*, Thphr.*HP*8.3.5; τοῖς πολλοῖς .. καὶ τοῖς ἀ. (i.e. τοῖς ὀλίγοις) Telesp.15.9 H. IV. in proportion, *inversely*; ὁ ἀ. λόγος the *inverse* ratio Euc.5*Def.*13.; ἀ. ἔχειν Arist.*Cael.*273^{b}32. 2. *conversely*, *An.Ox.*4.325.

ἀναπαλινδρομέω, *to be brought back again to the same spot*, of a bandage, Hp.*Fract.*4.

ἀναπάλλακτος, ον, *irremovable*, αἰσχύνη Jul. *ad Them.*265d.

ἀναπαλλοτρίωτος, ον, *inalienable*, ἀγροί *TAM*261 *b*15 (Lycia).

ἀναπάλλω, poet. **ἀμπάλλω**, Ep. aor. part. ἀμπεπαλών:—*swing to and fro*, ἀμπεπαλὼν προΐει δολιχόσκιον ἔγχος Il.3.355, etc.; ἀμπάλλειν κῶλα, i.e. *dance*, Ar.*Ra.*1358; ἀνέπηλεν ἐπὶ θήρᾳ ... μαινάδας *urged* them *on*, E.*Ba.*1190; κλήρους εἰς ἄγγος ἐμβαλοῦσαι ἀνέπηλαν Ant.Lib.10.3:—Med., αἱ.. αἰθέρα ἀμπάλλεσθε *agitate* it *as you fly*, E.*Or.*322:—Pass., *dart, spring* or *bound up*, ὡς δ' ὅθ' ὑπὸ φρικὸς .. ἀναπάλλεται ἰχθύς .. ὣς πληγεὶς ἀνέπαλτο Il.23.692, cf. Eun.*Hist.*p.239D., Agath.3.16,4.18:—Il. l.c. proves that the sync. aor. ἀνέπαλτο (also found in Il.8.85, 20.424, cf. ἀνὰ δ' ἔπαλτ' ὀρθῷ ποδί Pi.*O.*13.72, and metaph., νεῖκος ἀνέπαλτο B.10.65) must be referred to this Verb (cf. ἔκπαλτο, ἐνέπαλτο, κατέπαλτο); but part. ἀνεπάλμενος is formed from ἀνεφάλλομαι in A.R.2.825; those who, like Heyne, refer it to ἀνεφάλλομαι, write it ἀνεπᾶλτο (cf. ἐπᾶλτο):—aor. Med. ἀνεπήλατο Mosch.2.109: aor. part. Pass. ἀναπαλείς Str.8.6.21. II. ἀναπάλλων (sc. σεισμός), ὁ, an earthquake *with an upward movement*, Arist.*Mu.*396^{a}8.

ἀνάπᾰλος, v. ἄμπαλος: κατ' ἄμπαλον μισθοῦν by *auction*, *IG*9(2).205.15 (Thess.). II. a word coined to expl. ἀναπάλη, Ath.14.631d.

ἀνάπαλσις, εως, ἡ, *a flinging up*, Arist.*Mu.*396^{a}9.

ἀναπάντητος, ον, *where one meets no one*, Cic.*Att.*9.1.3.

ἀνα-παντοῦσιν· ἀνακύπτουσιν, Hsch. **-παπλον**· ἀνοίμωξον, Id.

ἀναπαρθένευσις, εως, ἡ, *restoration of virginity*, Sch.A.*Ch.*71.

ἀναπᾰριάζω, *break treaties like the Parians*, prov. in Ephor.107.

ἀναπάρτιστος, ον, *incomplete*, of verbal expression, *Stoic.*2.58.

ἀνάπας, ασα, αν, = ἅπας, *AP*7.343 (Reiske ἅμα πάσῃς).

ἀναπάσσω, *scatter* or *shed upon*, χάριν τινί Pi.*O.*10(11).94.

ἀναπατάσσω, *strike*, κεφαλὴν ἀνεπάταξε Men.*Epit.*468. 2. ἀνεπάταξεν· ἐξ ὕπνου ἀνέβλεψε, Hsch. II. *strike up*, ἀναπατάξασθαι· ἀνακρούσασθαι ᾆσμα, Id.

ἀναπᾰτέω, *go up, go back*, *AB*397; of horses, *jib, shy*, *Hippiatr.*26.

ἀνά-παυλα, ης, ἡ, *repose, rest*, ὕπνον κἀνάπαυλαν ἤγαγεν S.*Ph.*638; κατ' ἀναπαύλας διῃρημένοι divided into *reliefs*, of workmen, Th.2.75. 2. c. gen. rei, *rest from* a thing, κακῶν S.*El.*873, cf. *Ph.*878; πόνων Th.2.38; τῆς σπουδῆς Pl.*Phlb.*30e. II. *resting-place*, E.*Hipp.*1137, Pl.*Lg.*722c; *inn*, Ar.*Ra.*113; ἀνάπαυλαι κατὰ τὴν ὁδόν Pl.*Lg.*625b; εἰς ἀναπαύλας ἐκ κακῶν (where there is a play upon the first sense) Ar.*Ra.*185, cf. 195. **-παύλησις**, εως, ἡ, = foreg., κακοῦ Orac.ap.Phleg.*Mir.*2:—also **-παυλις** (sic), Hsch.

ἀνά-παυμα, poet. **ἄμπ-**, ατος, τό, *repose, rest*, μερμηράων Hes.*Th.*55; κακῶν ἄμπαυμα μεριμνέων Thgn.343; μόχθων *Lyr.Oxy.*9 iii 4; πλάτας E.*Hyps.Fr.*3 iii 14. 2. *resting-place*, *APl.*4.228 (Anyte); of a tomb, *CIG*4623 (Syria), cf. *Epigr.Gr.*453.3. II. *fallow land*, *PTeb.*115.3 (ii B.C.), *PFay.*112.4 (i A.D.). 2. *the state of such land*, ἐν ἀναπαύματι or ἀναπαύμασι *PTeb.*61^{a}385 (ii B.C.), *PLond.*3.1223.8 (ii A.D.), *BGU*1092.16 (iv A.D.). **-παυματικός**, ή, όν, *of* or *for fallow land*, Wilcken *Chrest.*377.11, al., *BGU*860.11 (iii A.D.). **-παύσιμος**, ον, *of* or *for rest*, Eust.1260.53, al. **-παυσις**, poet. **ἄμπ-**, εως, ἡ, *repose, rest*, Mimn.12.2, Pi.*N.*7.52, Hp.*VM* 11, X.*Lac.*12.6: esp. *relaxation, recreation*, Pl.*Ti.*59c, X.*Cyr.*7.5.47. 2. c. gen. rei, *rest from* a thing, κακῶν Th.4.20; πολέμου X.*Hier.*2.11; κακῶν Epicur.*Ep.*3 p.61 U.; λειτουργίας *PFlor.*57.56. 3. Rhet., *cadence* of a period, Hermog.*Id.*1.1, al. **-παυστήριος** or **-παυτήριος**, Ion. **ἀμπ-**, ον, *of* or *for resting*, θῶκοι Hdt.1.181. II. Subst. ἀναπαυτήριον, τό, *time of rest*, οἱ θεοὶ τὴν νύκτα διδόασιν, κάλλιστον ἀ. X.*Mem.*4.3.3. 2. *place of rest*, Luc.*Am.*18. 3. *sound of trumpet for a halt*, opp. τὸ ἀνακλητικόν, Poll.4.86. III. ἀναπαυστηρία, ἡ, *prop* for head of torsion-engine, Ph.*Bel.*76.17, cf. Hero *Bel.*89.6. **-παυστόν**· τὸ μηκώνιον, Hsch. **-παυτικός**, ή, όν, *giving rest*, Ptol.*Tetr.*20. **-παύω**, poet. and Ion. **ἀμπ-**, fut. Med. ἀναπαύσομαι: aor. ἀνεπαυσάμην Att. and Hellenistic (but ἀνεπαύθημεν Lxx *La.*5.5): later, aor. Pass. ἀναπάη *IG*14.158: fut. Pass. ἀναπαήσομαι v.l. *Apoc.*14.13, al.: pres. Med. ἀναπάεται *IG*14.1717, cf. *PTeb.*264:—*make to cease, stop* or *hinder from* a thing, χειμῶνος .. ὅς ῥά τε ἔργων ἀνθρώπους ἀνέπαυσεν Il.17.550; ἀ. τινὰ τοῦ πλάνου *give* him *rest* from wandering, S.*OC*1113; τοὺς λειτουργοῦντας ἀ. (sc. τῶν ἀναλωμάτων) *to relieve* them from.., D.42.25, cf. 42. 2. c. acc. only, *put an end to*, βοήν S.*Tr.*1262; more freq. *rest, make to halt*, ἀ. στράτευμα X.*Cyr.*7.1.4; κατὰ μέρος τοὺς ναύτας ἀ. Id.*HG*6.2.29; κάματον ἵππων ἀ. A.*Fr.*192 (lyr.); σῶμα E.*Hipp.*1353; εἴδωλον ἀ. ἐπὶ ἅμαξαν *lay* it *in a reposing posture*, Ael.*VH*12.64, cf. *NA*7.29: abs., ἀνάπαυσον *give me rest*, Luc.*Tyr.*21. 3. *bring to a close*, τὸν λόγον Hermog.*Id.*1.8. 4. rarely intr. in sense of Med., *take rest*, ἀναπαύοντες ἐν τῷ μέρει Th.4.11; ἡσυχίαν εἶχε καὶ ἀνέπαυεν X.*HG*5.1.21. 5. of land, *cause to lie fallow*, *PSI*400.10 (iii B.C.), *PTeb.*105.3 (ii B.C.). II. in Med. and Pass., *take rest*, ἀναπαύου κακῶν *take rest from..*, Cratin.297; ἀπὸ ναυμαχίας ἀ. *rest* after a sea-fight, Th.7.73; ἐκ μακρᾶς ὁδοῦ Pl.*Criti.*106a; ἀπ' ἄγρας κεκμακὼς ἀμπαύσεται [Πάν] Theoc.1.17; esp. of troops, *halt, rest*, X.*Cyr.*2.4.3, etc.; ἀναπεπ. τῶν εἰσφορῶν *to be relieved from..*, Isoc.8.20. 2. abs., *take one's rest, sleep*, Hdt.1.12, 2.95, al., E.*Hipp.*211, v.l. in Ar.*Pl.*695, cf. Lys. 13.12, etc. b. of land, *lie fallow*, Pi.*N.*6.11. c. of the dead, ἀμπ. σὺν φιλίῃ ξυνῶς ἀλόχῳ *Epigr.Gr.*520.5 (Thessalonica); ὧδε ἀναπάεται *IG*14.1717, cf. Call.*Epigr.*15.1; ἀ. τοῦ βίου Heraclit.*All.*68, Hdn.3.15.2; ἀ. alone, *die*, Id.1.4.7, cf. Plu.2.110f; ἀ. τὸν βίον *POxy.*1121.12 (iii A.D.). d. *regain strength*, dub. l. in X.*Cyr.*6.1.11. 3. *rest* or *settle* upon an object, τὸ τοῦ Θεοῦ πνεῦμα ἐφ' ὑμᾶς ἀναπαύεται 1*Ep.Petr.*4.14, cf. Lxx *Is.*11.2; of shadows, Iamb.*Comm.Math.*8.

ἀναπαφλάζω, *boil* or *bubble up*, Hsch.

ἀναπείθω (Arc. **ἀμπ-** *SIG*306.59), *persuade, convince*, X.*Mem.*1.2.52, al.:—Pass., Th.1.84. 2. *persuade, move* to do a thing, c. acc. pers. et inf., Hdt.1.124,156, etc.; foll. by Conj., ἀ. ὡς χρή .. Id.1.123; ἀ. λόγῳ ὅκως .. 1.37: c. dupl. acc., ἀ. τινά τι *persuade* one *of* a thing, Ar.*Nu.*77, cf. *AP*9.438 (Phil.). 3. *seduce, mislead*, τινά Hdt.3.148, 5.66, etc.; ἀ. χρήμασι, δώροις, *bribe*, Ar.*Pax*622, X.*Cyr.*1.5.3; χρυσίον διδοὺς ἀναπείσεις ὅπως .. Ar.*Eq.*473, cf. *PMagd.*14.3, *Act.Ap.*18.13:—Pass., ἀναπεπεισμένος *bribed*, Ar.*V.*101.

ἀναπεινάω, *to be hungry again*, Lync.ap.Ath.3.109e.

ἀνά-πειρα, ἡ, *trial, proof*, πλοίων Plb.25.4.8, cf. Callix.1. II. in pl., *exercises*, -ρας ποιῶν τοῖς πληρώμασι Plb.1.59.12. III. ἀνάπειρα· ῥυθμὸς αὐλητικός, Hsch. **-πειράομαι**, *try* or *attempt again*: generally, *make a trial, essay*, τοῖς σκάφεσι Plb.25.4.9; ἀναπειρᾶσθαι ναῦν *make trial of* a new ship, *prove* her, D.51.5; also of the ship herself, πάντες ἑωρᾶθ' ὑμεῖς ἀναπειρωμένην τὴν ναῦν ibid.; esp. as a naval term, *manœuvre, exercise*, Hdt.6.12, Th.7.7,12,51.

ἀναπείρω, poet. **ἀμπ-**, *pierce through, fix on a spit*, σπλάγχνα δ' ἄρ' ἀμπείραντες Il.2.426; ἵν' ἀναπείρω τὰς κίχλας Ar.*Ach.*1007; ὅταν ἐπὶ τὸν ὀβελίσκον ἀναπαρῇ Arist.*Mir.*835^{a}18. II. *impale*, ἐπὶ ξύλου ἀ. Hdt.4.103:—Pass., ἀποθανεῖν ἀναπαρείς Id.4.94; μὴ .. τὸν πόδ' ἀναπαρῶ Macho ap.Ath.8.349c. III. *pierce upwards*, opp. καταπείρω, Antyll.ap.Orib.7.10.1.

ἀναπειστήριος, α, ον, *persuasive*, χαύνωσις Ar.*Nu.*875.

ἀναπελάσας· ἀναρρωσθείς, Hsch. (cf. ὀλιγ-ηπελίη).

ἀναπελεκάω, *dress* stone, *IG*7.4255.19 (Oropus).

ἀναπεμπάζομαι, *count again, count over*, Pl.*Ly.*222e; *think over, ponder over*, Id.*Lg.*724b, Plu.2.605a, Ath.6.263b, al.; ἀ. ὅκωσπερ ὄναρ τὴν νοῦσον Aret.*CA*2.3, etc.:—Act. later in same sense, Lyc.9, 1470, *AP*11.382.12 (Agath.), Hld.3.5, etc.

ἀναπέμπω, poet. **ἀμπ-**, *send up*, κάτωθεν A.*Ch.*382 (lyr.), cf. Ar.*Th.*585; Ἀφαίστοιο κρουνοὺς ἀ. *sends forth ..*, Pi.*P.*1.26; χθὼν ἠρινὰ φύλλ' ἀ. ib.9.46; παντοῖα φύματα Pl.*Ti.*85c:—Med., *send up from oneself*, X.*An.*1.1.5. 2. *send up* to higher ground, εἰς τὰς ἄκρας Id.*Cyr.*7.5.34; esp. from the coast inland, into Central Asia, ἀ. ὡς βασιλέα Th.2.67, cf. Isoc.8.98; to the metropolis, εἰς τὴν Ῥώμην Plb.1.7.12, etc. 3. *remit, refer* to higher authority, *PHib.*1.57 (iii B.C.), *PTeb.*7.7 (ii B.C.); ψήφισμα πρὸς βασιλέα *OGI*329.51; τινὰ πρός τινα *Ev.Luc.*23.7; τινά τινι *Ep.Philem.*12; of a higher authority *referring* to delegates, *BGU*613.4 (ii A.D.), cf. 19120, *PLond.*2.196.11 (ii A.D.); *refer* to a book, Gal.18(2).663, etc. 4. *trace up* one's pedigree, γένος εἴς τινα D.S.4.83. 5. *transmit*, in Pass., τῶν κατ' ὄψιν ἀναπεμπομένων Epicur.*Nat.*11.7; αἰσθήσεων ἀναπεμπομένων Plot.4.4.42. II. *send back*, Pi.*I.*7(6).10: metaph., *send back* in discussion to something previously said, Alex.Aphr. *in Top.*445.15. 2. *refer*, τὰ εἰς τὸ θεῖον -όμενα *OGI*194, cf. D.S.4.43; *ascribe*, τι ἐπί τι Dam.*Pr.*37; τί τινι *Corp.Herm.*18.12. 3. *throw back* the accent, of enclitics, Hdn.Gr.2.828.

ἀναπεπταμένος, η, ον, pf. part. Pass. of ἀναπετάννυμι, q. v. Adv. -νως *explicitly*, Plot.5.1.8.

ἀναπεπτωκότως, Adv. pf. part. of ἀναπίπτω, *despondingly*, Poll.3.123.

ἀναπέσσω, Att. -ττω, *digest again*, f.l. in Arist.*HA*565^{b}23.

ἀναπετάννῡμι or -ύω X.*An.*7.1.17 (cf. ἀναπίτνημι), poet. **ἀμπ-**; **ἀναπετάω** Luc.*Cal.*21: fut. -πετάσω, Att. -πετῶ Men.*Fr.*3 D.:—*spread out, unfold*, ἀνά θ' ἱστία λευκὰ πέτασσαν Il.1.480, etc.; ἀ. βόστρυχον E.*Hipp.*202; τὰν ἐπ' ὄσσοις ὀμπέτασον χάριν *unfold, display*, Sapph.29; φάος ἀμπετάσας *having shed* light *abroad*, E.*IA*34; ἀναπετάσαι τὰς πύλας *throw wide* the gates, Hdt.3.146, cf. X.*An.* l.c.:—Pass., ἀναπεπταμέναι σανίδες, θύραι, Il.12.122, Pi.*N.*9.2; βλέφαρα ἀναπετάννυται X.*Mem.*1.4.6; ἀλώπηξ ἀναπιτναμένη a fox *sprawling on its back* to await the eagle's swoop, Pi.*I.*4(3).47: in pf. Pass., *to be open, lie open*, οἰκία πρὸς μεσημβρίαν -πέπταται *lies open* to the south, X.*Oec.*9.4; αὐλῶν ἀναπέπταται πρὸς τὴν θάλατταν Plu.*Fab.*6; freq. in pf. part., *open*, ἐν πελάγεϊ ἀ. ναυμαχήσεις Hdt.8.60.α'; ἀ. ὄμματα X.*Mem.*2.1.22; ἀ. πρὸς τὸ φῶς τὴν εἴσοδον ἔχουσα, of the cave, Pl.*R.*514a; δίαιτα ἀ. *in the open air*, Plu.*Per.*34: metaph., ἀ. παρρησία *open, barefaced* impudence, Pl.*Phdr.*240e; ὄμμα ἀ. *impudent, brazen*, Zeno *Stoic.*1.58; ἀ. τῇ ψυχῇ δέξασθαί τι Luc.*Nigr.*4.

ἀνα-πέτεια, ἡ, *expansion, dilatation*, πόρων Gal.6.848, cf. Alex.Aphr.*Pr.*1.90. **-πετής**, ές, (πετάννυμι) *expanded, wide open*, ἀδένες Hp.*Gland.*9; ὀφθαλμοί Aret.*SA*1.6. II. (πέτομαι), A.*Supp.*782 (in form ἀμπ-).

ἀναπέτομαι, poet. **ἀμπέταμαι** *IG*14.1934*f*, late **ἀναπετάομαι** v.l. in *Gp.*2.5.12: fut. -πτήσομαι: aor. ἀνεπτόμην or ἀνεπτάμην, in Trag. also ἀνέπτην, 3 pl. ἀνέπτησαν Ant.Lib.14.4:—*fly up, fly away*, ἢν .. ἀναπτῆσθε ἐς τὸν οὐρανόν Hdt.4.132, cf. 5.55; οἰχήσονται ἀναπτόμενοι Antipho *Fr.*58; αἰθερία δ' ἀνέπτα E.*Med.*440; ἀν' ὑγρὸν ἀμπταίην αἰθέρα Id.*Ion*796 ; ἀναπέτομαι δὴ πρὸς Ὄλυμπον Anacr.24 = Ar.*Av.* 1372, cf. 35, *Lys.*774 ; εἰ..πτηνὸς γενόμενος ἀνάπτοιτο Pl.*Phd.*109e ; εἰς τὸν οὐρανὸν ἀναπτήσῃ Id.*Lg.*905a, cf. Aeschin.3.209 ; *hurry off*, Luc.*Alex.*30 : metaph., ἀμπτάμενα φροῦδα πάντα κεῖται E.*Andr.* 1219. 2. metaph., *to be on the wing*, περιχαρὴς δ' ἀνεπτάμαν S. *Aj.*693 ; ἀνέπταν φόβῳ Id.*Ant.*1307.—Cf. ἀνίπταμαι.

ἀνάπευσις, εως, ἡ, (ἀναπυνθάνομαι) *inquiry*, Charito 3.4.

ἀναπεφλασμένως, Adv. pf. part. Pass. of ἀναφλάω, q.v.

ἀναπηγάζει· ἀναδίδωσιν, Hsch.

ἀναπήγνυμι, *transfix, fix on a spit*, λαγῷ' ἀναπηγνύασι Ar.*Ec.* 843. 2. *impale, crucify*, τινὰ ἐπὶ τοῦ ξύλου Alex.222 ; τὸ σῶμα διὰ τριῶν σταυρῶν Plu.*Art.*17. 3. intr. pf. ἀναπέπηγα *project sharply*, of headlands, Philostr.*VA*3.23.

ἀναπηδ-άω, poet. ἀμπ–, fut. –ήσομαι Luc.*Asin.*53 :—*leap up, start up*, esp. in haste or fear, ἐκ λόχου ἀμπήδησε Il.11.379 ; ἐκ τοῦ θρόνου Hdt.3.155 ; ἀναπηδῶσιν πάντες ἐπ' ἔργον *jump up* from bed, Ar.*Av.* 490, cf. X.*Cyr.*1.4.2 ; ἀ. πρὸς τὸν πάππον *jump up on* his *knees*, ib.1. 3.9 ; *start up* to speak, ἀ. ἐν δήμῳ Cratin.356, cf. Ar.*Ec.*428 ; ἐπὶ τὸ βῆμα Aeschin.3.173, cf. 1.71. 2. of water, *spring*, Arist.*HA* 596^{b}18. 3. Medic., *swell up*, Hp.*Gland.*2. **–ημα,** ατος, τό, *outburst*, αἵματος Eust.680.23. **–ησις,** εως, ἡ, *leaping up*, ἐκ τῆς κλίνης Hp.*Morb.Sacr.*1. 2. ἀ. τῆς καρδίας *palpitation* of the heart, opp. σφύξις, Arist.*Resp.*480^{a}13.

ἀναπηλέω, aor. part. –ήσας dub. sens. in *h.Merc.*41.

ἀναπηνίζομαι, *unwind, reel off*, of the thread of a silk-worm's cocoon, Arist.*HA*551^{b}14 ; τὸ τῆς πέρκης κύημα ἀ. οἱ ἁλιεῖς ib.568^a 24.

ἀναπηρ-ία, ἡ, *lameness, mutilation*, Cratin.168, Arist.*Rh.*1386^a 11 ; of the crocodile's tongue, *stunted development*, Id.*PA*660^b 26. **–όβιος,** ον, *with maimed life*, Phryn.Com.4 D. **–όομαι,** Pass., *to be maimed*, Pl.*Plt.*310e, Arist.*Pr.*960^{b}37 :—Act., prob. l. in Plu.2. 373d. **–ος,** ον, *maimed, mutilated*, Hermipp.35, Lys.24.13, Pl.*Cri.* 53a, etc. ; ψυχὴ ἀ. πρὸς ἀλήθειαν Id.*R.*535d ; ἀνάπηρα θύειν Id.*Alc.*2. 149a, cf. Arist.*PA*773^{a}13, al. Adv. –ρως Zonar. (Sts. spelt ἀνάπειρος in codd., Lxx *To.*14.2, *Ev.Luc.*14.13,21, cf. Phryn.*PS*p.13 B.)

ἀναπηρτισμένως, *incompletely*, Chrysipp.*Stoic.*2.107.

ἀναπιδάω, = διαπιδάω, prob. in Alex.Aphr. *in Mete.*56.7.

ἀναπιδύω, *spring up, ooze out*, Thphr.*CP*6.4.1. 2. of ground, *send forth water*, Plu.*Aem.*14.

ἀνα-πιέζω, aor. Pass. ἀνεπιέχθην, *press back*, Hp.*Art.*41. II. *force upwards*, Hero *Spir.*1.10. III. *apply, press upon*, Androm. ap.Gal.12.945, cf. Asclep.ib.986. **–πίεσις,** εως, ἡ, *pressure*, Glaucias ap.Erot. s.v. ἀνοκώχησις. **–πίεσμα,** ατος, τό, a kind of *trap-door* on the stage, Poll.4.127,132. **–πιεσμός,** ὁ, = foreg., πρὸς τόπον Hero *Spir.*1.28. 2. *reduction* of hernia, Heliod.(?) ap.Orib. 50.42.6.

ἀναπίμπλημι, 3 sg. –πιμπλᾷ Arist.*Pr.*967^{b}4 :—*fill up*, πίθον Epigr. ap.Luc.*Dips.*6 : but mostly, 2. metaph., *accomplish* what is destined, as always in Hom., πότμον ἀναπλήσαντες *having filled up the full measure* of their fate, Il.11.263 ; αἴ κε θάνῃς καὶ μοῖραν ἀναπλήσῃς βιότοιο 4.170 ; ἀναπλῆσαι οἶτον, κακά, ἄλγεα, κήδεα, ib.8.465, 15.132, Od.5.302, 13.307 (v.l.), cf. Hdt.5.4, 6.12, 9.87, etc. II. c. gen. rei, *fill full of* a thing, καὶ ξυντυχών σ' Ὑπέρβολος δικῶν ἀναπλήσει Ar. *Ach.*847, cf. *Nu.*1023, Pl.*Phlb.*42a, D.20.28. 2. freq. with a notion of *defiling, infecting*, ὡς πλείστους ἀναπλῆσαι αἰτιῶν Pl.*Ap.*32c :—so in Pass., *to be infected with disease*, Th.2.51 ; ἀ. τῆς τούτου [τοῦ σώματος] φύσεως Pl.*Phd.*67a, cf. Iamb.*Myst.*5.15.

ἀναπίμπρημι, *blow, swell up*, in Pass., Nic.*Th.*179 : aor. ἀνεπρήσθην Hp.*Nat.Mul.*41.

ἀναπίνω [ῑ], *drink up, suck in like a sponge*, Hp.*VM*22 ; *absorb again*, of suppurations which do not come to a head, Id.*Art.*40 ; of extravasated blood, ib.50, cf. Gal.7.694.

ἀναπιπράσκω, *sell again*, Poll.7.12 :—Pass. in aor. 1 part. ἀναπραθείσης *IPE*1^2.32 *A* 53.

ἀναπίπτω, poet. ἀμπ–, *fall back*, A.*Ag.*1599, E.*Cyc.*410 ; *lay oneself back*, like rowers, Cratin.345, X.*Oec.*8.8 ; ἀ. ὑπτία Pl.*Phdr.*254b, cf. e ; of riders, ὑπτίους ἀναπεπτωκότας ἐλαύνειν X.*Eq.Mag.*3.14. 2. metaph., *fall back, give ground*, Th.1.70 ; *flag, lose heart*, D.19.224 ; ταῖς σπουδαῖς (vulg. σπονδ–) ἀναπεπτωκέναι D.H.5.53. b. pf. part. ἀναπεπτωκὼς *lifeless*, of style, σχῆμα ἀ. Aristid.*Rh.*2 p.518 S., al. 3. of a plan, *to be given up*, ἀνεπεπτώκει τὰ τῆς ἐξόδου D.21.163. 4. ἀ. ἀπ' οἴκων *to be banished* from one's house, Poet.ap.Athenag.*pro Christo* 22. 5. *recline* at meals, like ἀνάκειμαι, Alex.293, *Com. Adesp.*638, *PPar.*51.4, *Ev.Marc.*6.40, Luc.*Asin.*23. b. *take to one's bed* in sickness, *PMag.Leid.V.*11.1. 6. *recoil*, of the arms of torsion-engines, Hero *Bel.*100.2.

ἀναπισσόω, *cover over again with pitch*, *Gp.*6.8.3.

ἀναπίτνημι, poet. for ἀναπετάννυμι, inf. –πιτνάμεν Pi.*O.*6.27.

ἀναπιτ-ύζω, *cause to spirt out*, Hero *Aut.*13.1. **–υσμός,** ὁ, *spirting out*, ib.4.3 ; cf. ἀναπυτίζω.

ἀναπλάκητος, ον, = ἀναμπλάκητος, q.v.

ἀνά-πλασις, εως, ἡ, *remodelling, new formation*, σαρκῶν Hp.*Off.* 24 ; *adjustment*, ib.15 ; simply, *modelling, shaping*, Hp.*Hebd.*ap.Ph. 1.29. **–πλασμα,** ατος, τό, *shape, form, model*, τὰ ἀ. τῶν σωμάτων D.S.2.56. II. *representation, imagination*, Str.11.14.12 ; ἀ. τῆς διανοίας S.E.*M.*8.354. 2. *correlative term*, Ascl. *in Metaph.*331. 30. **–πλασμός,** ὁ, = ἀνάπλασις, ἀ. ἐκ ματαίων ἐλπίδων *building of castles in the air*, Plu.2.113d. II. = ἀνάπλασμα II ; ἀ. διανοίας Metrod.*Herc.*831.4, S.E.*M.*7.223, Mich. *in PN*9.21. **–πλάσσω,** Att. –ττω, *form anew, remodel, restore* a broken nose, Hp.*Mochl.*2 ; *rebuild*, οἰκίδια *PHal.*1.183 (iii B.C.) : metaph., ἀ. ταύτας [τὰς ἑταίρας] Alex.98.5 :—Med., ἀναπλάσασθαι οἰκίην *rebuild one's* house, Hdt.8. 109. 2. simply, *model, mould, fashion*, τῆς Αἰδοῦς..τἄγαλμ' ἀ. Ar.*Nu.*995, cf. *AP*7.410 (Diosc.), al. ; τὰ μέλη τοῦ παιδός Pl.*Alc.*1. 121d : metaph., τοῖς ψηφίσμασιν ἀ. ['Αλέξανδρον] Demad.11 ; *make up*, τροχίσκους Dsc.1.8, al. 3. metaph., ἀ. διπλάσια τῆς ἀληθείας κακὰ *invent, imagine* them, Philem.160, cf. Plb.3.94.2, D.H.1.53 ; πολλοὺς θεούς Ph.2.262 ; αἰτίας Procop.*Arc.*15 ; ἐπιστολήν ib.12, Philostr.*VA*7.35 : abs., *imagine vainly*, Metrod.*Herc.*831.14, cf. 17, Phld.*D.*1.17 :—also in Med., *AP*9.710 (Diosc.). 4. *compose*, λόγους D.H.*Dem.*46. II. *plaster up*, ὑπὸ τοῖς ὄνυξι κηρὸν ἀναπεπλασμένος Ar.*V.*108. **–πλαστέον,** *one must make up into shapes*, Dsc.5.88. **–πλαστικός,** ή, όν, *imaginative*, Porph.*Sent.*38, Procl. *in Ti.*1.320 D. **–πλαστος,** ον, *that may be moulded, plastic*, Gal. 18(1).670.

ἀναπλατύνομαι [ῠ], *to be spread wide*, Plu.*Daed.*4.

ἀναπλείω, Ep. for ἀναπλέω III, Nic.*Th.*308.

ἀναπλέκω, *enwreath, entwine*, ὅρμοισι χέρας Pi.*O.*2.74 ; ἀ. τὰς τρίχας Poll.2.35 :—Pass., *IG*5(1).1390.22 (Andania, i B.C., in form ἀμπλ–), ib.5(2).514.10 (Lycosura) :—Med., *braid one's hair*, Luc. *Nav.*3. 2. metaph., ἀ. ῥυθμόν *AP*11.64 (Agath.). 3. ἀναπεπλεγμένοι *closely engaged*, Plu.*Brut.*17.

ἀνάπλεος, α, ον, Att. masc. and neut. **ἀνάπλεως,** ων, but fem. ἀναπλέα Pl.*Phd.*83d :—pl., nom. masc. and fem. ἀνάπλεῳ Pl.*Tht.*196e, Eub.98.8, neut. ἀνάπλεα Arist.*de An.*423^{a}27 : acc. masc. ἀνάπλεως Pl.*R.*516e :—*quite full of* a thing, πτερῶν λέγουσι ἀνάπλεον εἶναι τὸν ἠέρα Hdt.4.31 ; ἀ. ψιμυθίου Ar.*Ec.*1072, cf. Eub. l.c. ; σκότους ἀ. οἱ ὀφθαλμοί Pl.*R.*516e, etc. II. *infected*, τοῦ σώματος ἀναπλέα [ἡ ψυχή] *with* the body, Id.*Phd.*83d ; αὐτὸ τὸ καλὸν μὴ ἀ. σαρκῶν Id. *Smp.*211e ; ἀ. ἐσμεν τοῦ μὴ καθαρῶς διαλέγεσθαι Id.*Tht.*196e.

ἀνάπλευσις, εως, ἡ, *separation, splitting off*, ὀστέου Hp.*Coac.* 234. II. *mounting, rising*, of food in vomiting, Archig.ap.Orib. 8.1.20.

ἀναπλέω, Ion. –πλώω, Ep. –πλείω (q.v.), *sail upwards, go upstream*, στεινωπὸν ἀνεπλέομεν we *sailed up* the strait, Od.12.234, cf. Hdt.2.97, 4.89 ; *sail up* the Hellespont, X.*HG*4.8.36 :—Pass., ἀναπλεῖται ἐκ θαλάττης ὁ Πάδος Plb.2.16.10. 2. *put out to sea*, ἐς Τροίην νήεσσιν ἀναπλεύσεσθαι Il.11.22, cf. And.1.76, Decr.ap.D.18. 184 ; ἀ. ἐπὶ τρόπαιον *IG*2.471.28. 3. *float up, rise to the surface*, ναυάγιον ἀ. Arist.*Pr.*932^{a}1. 4. *overflow*, Ael.*NA*10.19. II. *sail back*, Hdt.1.78 ; of fish, *swim back*, Id.2.93. 2. metaph. of food, *return from the stomach*, for rumination, Ael.*NA*2.54. III. *become loose, split off*, of bone-splinters, Hp.*Fract.*24 ; ὀδόντες ἀναπλέουσι the teeth *fall out*, Id.*Epid.*4.19, cf. ἀναπλείω ; of chalk-stones, *come away*, Orib.*Syn.*9.58.2.

ἀνάπλεως, v. ἀνάπλεος.

ἀναπλήθω, poet. for ἀναπίμπλημι, Q.S.11.312. 2. intr., *to be full*, Id.13.22.

ἀναπλημμῡρέω, *overflow*, Philostr.*Im.*1.31.

ἀναπλημμύρω, *make overflow*, ἀνεπλήμμῡρε θάλασσαν Q.S.14.635.

ἀναπληρ-όω, *fill up* a void, Pl.*Ti.*81b, cf. 78d ; τὸ κεχηνὸς τῆς ἑρμηνείας, τοῦ ῥυθμοῦ, A.D.*Synt.*266.22, Luc.*Tim.*1 :—Pass., *to be filled up*, Arist.*Cael.*306^{b}4. 2. *make up, supply*, εἴ τι ἐξέλιπον ἀ. Pl.*Smp.*188e ; τὴν ἔνδειαν Arist.*Pol.*1318^{b}22 ; τοὺς..ἀμόρφους ἀναπληροῖ ἡ τοῦ λέγειν πιθανότης *compensates* them, Id.*Fr.*101 :—Med., δώματ' ἀ. *fill their* houses, E.*Hel.*907. 3. *fill up* the numbers of a body, τὴν βουλήν Plu.*Publ.*11, cf. X.*Vect.*4.24 ; ἀ. τὴν συνηγορίαν *fill* the place of advocate (left vacant by another), Plu.*Crass.*3, cf. 1*Ep. Cor.*14.16. 4. *pay in full*, τὰς ὠνάς, of tax-farmers, *PPar.*62.5.3 (ii B.C.) :—in Med., *get paid, receive*, ἕως ἀνεπληρώσατο τὴν προῖκα D. 27.13. 5. *use expletive particles*, Demetr.*Eloc.*58. 6. *fulfil*, ἀναπληροῦται ἡ προφητεία *Ev.Matt.*13.14 ; of a task, *perform*, *PPetr.* 3 p.104. II. Pass., *to be restored to its former size* or *state*, ἀνεπληρώθη ὁ ἥλιος, after an eclipse, Th.2.28 ; ἀναπληρουμένης τῆς φύσεως *being in process of restoration*, Arist.*EN*1153^{a}2, cf. *HA*548^b 18. **–ωμα,** ατος, τό, *filling*, Id.*Mir.*833^{b}4 ; ἐρημίας Phalar.*Ep.*98 ; λόγων Ph.2.166. **–ωσις,** εως, ἡ, *filling up, means of filling up*, τῆς ἐνδείας Arist.*EN*1118^{b}18 ; τοῦ λείποντος A.D.*Synt.*250.18 ; τῶν κενουμένων τάξεων Ph.2.382. 2. *satisfying*, τῆς ἐπιθυμίας Arist. *Pol.*1267^{b}4 ; *satisfaction* of the wants and appetites, Id.*EN*1173^b 8. 3. *restoration*, τῆς κατὰ τὴν φύσιν αὐταρκείας Id.*Pol.*1257^{a}30, cf. Plu.*Demetr.*45. 4. *fulfilment*, τοῦ ῥήματος τοῦ Κυρίου Lxx 1*Es.*1.54. II. (from Pass.) *becoming full, overflowing*, of the Nile, Thales ap.Ath.*Epit.* ad fin. lib. ii (vol. i p.278 Schw.). **–ωτέον,** *one must fill up, supply*, Plu.*Cim.*2, *Gp.*9.11.3.

ἀναπληρωτικός, ή, όν, *filling up*, Asp. *in EN*24.3 ; δύναμις Dsc.5. 75 ; φάρμακα Gal.14.763.

ἀναπληστικός, ή, όν, (ἀναπίμπλημι) *fit for filling up*, and so, *that which takes the shape of the vessel which it fills, fluid*, Arist.*PA*649^{b}16, cf. *GC*329^{b}34, *Pr.*939^{a}31.

ἀναπλίσσω πόδεσσι *trot*, prob. in Arat.1108.

ἀναπλοκή, ἡ, (ἀναπλέκω) *a braiding*, χαίτης Philostr.*VA*6.10. II. in Music, *progression* of notes ascending in the scale, opp. καταπλοκή, Ptol.*Harm.*2.12.

ἀνάπλοος, contr. –πλους, ὁ, (ἀναπλέω) *sailing up-stream*, Hdt.2.4 and 8 ; ὁ ἀ. ἐκ τῆς θαλάττης, of a *canal* from the sea to an inland harbour, Pl.*Criti.*115d, cf. 117e. 2. *putting out* to sea, Plb.1.53.13, etc. II. *sailing back, return*, Thphr.*HP*4.7.3, cf. Str.1.3.15.

ἀν-απλόω, *unfold, open*, ταρσὸν ἀναπλώσας Mosch.2.60; τὰς θύρας Babr.74.3:—Pass., of pods or flowers, Dsc.2.159, 4.113. 2. *cause to expand*, τῷ -οῦν τὰ σώματα τὴν θερμότητα Anon.*in Cat.*49.26. II. *explain, unravel*, Anon.*in Tht.*23.6, *Corp.Herm.*1.16, Procl.*in Euc.*p.4F.; ἀπορίαν Simp.*in Ph.*441.11. III. *simplify*, μέχρι τοῦ ἑνός Dam.*Pr.*5:—so in Pass., of compounds, *to be resolved into simple elements*, Ph.1.433 (s.v.l.): pf. part. Pass. ἀνηπλωμένος *open, shallow*, λοπάδας *PHolm.*11.17. Adv. -ως, q.v.

ἀνάπλῠσις, εως, ἡ, *washing* or *rinsing out*, Arist.*Insomn.*460a17.

ἀνάπλωσις, εως, ἡ, *unfolding*; *explanation*, Erot.*Praef.*p.9N., Alex.Aphr.*in Metaph.*467.8. II. *unfolding, evolution*, ἡ τῶν λόγων ἐξέλιξις καὶ ἀ. Plot.5.7.3; opp. συνείλησις, Iamb.*Comm. Math.*12. III. *simplification*, Dam.*Pr.*26,70.

ἀναπλώω, Ion. for ἀναπλέω.

ἀνά-πνευμα, poet. ἄμπν-, ατος, τό, *resting-place*, Pi.*N.*1.1. **-πνευσις**, εως, ἡ, *recovery of breath*: *respite from*, ὀλίγη δέ τ' ἀνάπνευσις πολέμοιο Il.11.801, 16.43. II. *breathing in*, ὕδατος, of fishes, Pl.*Ti.*92b; *inhalation*, opp. ἔκπνευσις, Arist.*HA*492b8. **-πνευστικός**, ή, όν, *of* or *for respiration*, ὁ ἀ. τόπος the *respiratory* region, Id.*Sens.*445a27, Thphr.*Sud.*38; τὰ μὴ ἀ. [ζῷα] Arist.*Spir.*482a8; ἀ. δύναμις the power *of breathing*, M.Ant.6.15; τὰ -κά *respiratory organs*, Alex.Aphr.*Pr.*1.119. **-πνευστος**, ον, poet. for ἄπνευστος, *without drawing breath, breathless*, Hes.*Th.*797 codd. II. ἀναπνευστός, όν, Pass., *capable of being breathed*, ὁ ἀήρ Arist.*Top.*135a33. **-πνεύω**, = sq., Hsch.

ἀναπνέω, Ep. impf. ἀμπνείεσκον A.R.3.231: Ep. aor. imper. ἄμπνυε (v. infr.):—*take breath*, στῆθι καὶ ἄμπνυε Il.22.222: more commonly c. gen., *enjoy a respite, recover from*, ἀνέπνευσαν κακότητος 11.382; ὥς κε.. ἀναπνεύσωσι πόνοιο 15.235; τῆς νόσου S.*Aj.*274; ἀ. ἐκ τῆς ναυηγίης Hdt.8.12; ἐκ καμάτων *IG*14.14 (Syrac.); ἀνέπνευσα ἐκ σέθεν by thy help I *recovered*, S.*OT*1221: c. part., ἀ. τειρόμενοι Il.16.42; ἐς τεῖχος ἀλέντες 21.534: abs., *revive*, X.*An.*4.1.22, D.18.195. 2. πυρεῖα ἀ. *revive, burn up again*, Thphr.*HP*5.9.6. II. *draw breath*, ἀ. πάντα καὶ ἐκπνεῖ Emp.100, cf. Pl.*Phd.*112b, etc.; ἀ. πυκνά Hp.*Mul.*2.203; *gather breath* before a race, Pi.*N.*8.19: metaph., ἀ. οὐχ ἅπαντες ἐπὶ ἴσα ib.7.5. 2. c. acc., *draw breath from, inhale*, τὴν οἰκείαν ἀρχήν Dam.*Pr.*8:—Pass., τὸν ἀναπνεόμενον ἀέρα Corn.*ND*32. III. *breathe forth, send forth*, c. acc. cogn., ἀμπνεῦσαι καπνόν Pi.*O.*8.36; πυρὸς σέλας ἀμπνείεσκον A.R.3.231; ἀ. ὑάκινθον *breathe* hyacinth, Pherecr.131.2: abs., *exhale an odour*, Thphr.*Od.*69: impers., ἡδὺ ἀναπνεῖ τῶν φυτῶν Philostr.*Her.Prooem.*2: metaph., ἀ. χρησμούς Id.*VS*1.18.3. 2. of vapour, ἀϋτμὴ ἀ. μυχοῖο A.R.2.737. IV. causal, ἀ. τὸν ἵππον *breathe* the horse, Hld.8.14.

ἀναπνοείτης, ου, ὁ, *one who restores breath* to an athlete after a contest, *BMus.Inscr.*1109 (ii A.D.) (dub. sens.).

ἀνα-πνοή, poet. ἀμπν-, ἡ, *recovery of breath*, μόχθων ἀμπνοά *rest from* toils, Pi.*O.*8.7, cf. E.*IT*92, etc.; ἀμπνοὰν ἔστᾱσαν they recovered *breath*, took *fresh courage*, Pi.*P.*4.199; ἀ. διδόναι, παρέχειν, E.*Andr.*1137, Pl.*Ti.*70d; λαμβάνειν Id.*Phdr.*251e; ἀναπνοὴν ἔχει.. εἰπεῖν has *breath enough* to say, Men.536.6. II. *respiration, breathing*, Pi.*P.*3.57, Ar.*Nu.*627, Pl.*Ti.*33c, etc.; including εἰσπνοή and ἐκπνοή, Arist.*Resp.*471a7; ἀμπνοὰς ἔχειν, = ἀναπνεῖν, *breathe, live*, S.*Aj.*416; τὴν ἀ. ἀπολαβεῖν τινος *strangle*, Plu.*Rom.*27; ὑπὸ τὴν ἀ. *in a breath*, Plb.10.47.9. 2. = εἰσπνοή, *inspiration*, opp. ἐκπνοή, Pl.*Ti.*78e, 79e, cf. Arist.*Resp.*480b10. III. *exhalation*, Thphr.*HP*6.2.4. IV. *breathing organ*, of the nose and mouth, D.S.2.12, Luc.*Nigr.*32. 2. *air-hole, vent*, Pl.*Ti.*85a, 91b, Plu.*Aem.*14.—Only sg. in Pi.; only pl. in Trag. **-πνοια**, ἡ, = foreg. II. 1, Ti.Locr.101d, Arist.*Pr.*962a26. **-πνοϊκός**, ή, όν, *affecting respiration*, νόσος Ptol.*Tetr.*87.

ἀναπό-βλητος, ον, *not capable of being lost*, ἀγαθά S.E.*P.*3.238, cf. Cleanth.*Stoic.*1.129, Alex.Aphr.*Quaest.*121.16. **-γρᾰφος**, ον, *not registered* in the custom-house books, *contraband*, Poll.9.31; ἀ. μέταλλα *unregistered* mines, Hyp.*Eux.*34; *not registered* in the census, *PLond.*2.260.29 (i A.D.); πρόβατα ἀ. *BGU*338 ii 6 (ii A.D.). **-δεικτος**, ον, *not proved, undemonstrated*, Lycurg.129, Arist.*EN*1143b12. Adv. -τως *without proof*, Plu.*CG*10. II. of first principles, *indemonstrable*, Pl.*Def.*415b, Arist.*APr.*53b2, 57b33, al.; ἀ. συλλογισμοί, of syllogisms, Chrysipp.*Stoic.*2.79, al. Adv. -τως S.E.*P.*1.173, Gal.17(2).160. 2. *incapable of proof*, Plu.*Cor.*20. III. Act., *furnishing no proof*, *PPar.*15.3.62, cf. *Stoic.*2.90. **-δεκτος**, ον, *not to be received*, Sch.E.*Ph.*527. **-δέχομαι**, *take responsibility for*, θυσίαν *Inscr.Magn.*61.56 (dub.). **-δήμητος**, ον, *untravelled*, Ph.2.11.

ἀναποδ-ίζω, (πούς) *make to step back, call back and question, cross-examine*, ἐπειρωτῶν τε καὶ ἀ. τὸν κήρυκα Hdt.5.92.ζ'; πολλάκις ἀνεπόδιζον τὸν γραμματέα Aeschin.3.192, cf. Luc.*Abd.*17:—Pass., Antipho Soph.18. 2. οὐδαμῇ ἄλλῃ ἀνεπόδισε ἑωυτόν in no other passage *did* he *correct* himself, *retract* what he before said, Hdt.2.116. 3. *deduct for retrograde motion*, Vett.Val.25.26. II. intr., *step back, return*, ἐπὶ τὴν μονάδα Pythag.ap.Stob.1.10.12 (corr. Heeren), Lxx *Si.*46.4, Luc.*Nec.*7; εἰς τοὐπίσω Hdn.5.6.7; ἀ. πρὸς.. *revert*, Chor. in *Rh.Mus.*49.492; κύκλον ἀ. *recur* in a cycle, Hippod. ap.Stob.4.34.71; of the *retrograde* motion of the planets, Theo Sm. p.147H., Procl.*Hyp.*5.72, etc.: metaph. of festivals which *fall late* in the calendar, Gem.8.19. **-ισμός**, ὁ, *going back*, εἰς μονάδα, opp. προποδισμὸς ἀπὸ μονάδος, Moderat.ap.Stob.1 *Coroll.*8; of the *retrograde* motion of planets, Vett.Val.226.1, Nicom.*Ar.*1.5; in pl., opp. προποδισμοί, Alex.Aphr.*in Metaph.*440.7; generally, *reversal* of planet's motion, Theo Sm.p.148H. II. *calling back, recall*, Lxx *Wi.*2.5. **-ιστής**, οῦ, ὁ, *one who drives back*, Eust.717.16. **-ιστικός**, ή, όν, *in retardation*, Vett.Val.182.31; -κοὶ ἀστέρες *Cat.Cod. Astr.*1.133.23.

ἀν-απόδοτος, ον, *not given back, not returned*, ἀ. δόσις ἢ δωρεά Arist.*Top.*125a18; ἀργύριον ἀ. δόντα *not to be repaid*, *CIG*(add.)4278k (Xanthus), cf. 4300 o (Limyra), *PTeb.*105.20 (ii B.C.), *PRyl.*171.16 (i A.D.); σῖτον *Inscr.Prien.*108.58. II. τὸ ἀ., = ἀνανταπόδοτον, Sch.Ar.*Av.*7, cf. Simp.*in Ph.*45.11.

ἀνα-ποδόω, = ἀναποδίζω II, ἀ. ἐπὶ τὴν μονάδα Plu.2.876f. II. ἀναποδόομαι *grow fresh feet*, of scorpions, Lyd.*Mag.*1.42.

ἀναπό-δραστος, ον, *unavoidable, not to be escaped*, Arist.*Mu.*401b13, Plu.2.166e, Alex.Aphr.*Fat.*166.3; τὸ ἀ. Plot.4.3.13. 2. Act., *unable to run away*, *AB*392, Alb.*Intr.*6. **-θετος**, ον, *not stored up*, Hsch.

ἀνα-ποιέω, *make up, prepare* a medicine, Hp.*Nat.Mul.*36; *mix up, stir up*, *PHolm.*25.22, al.; μετ' ἐλαίου Bilabel 'Οψαρτ.p.11. II. *make fresh, vamp up*, τὰ ἱμάτια Sch.Ar.*Pl.*1063. **-ποίητος**, ον, *made up, wrought up*, ἔκ τινος Ammon.*Diff.*123.

ἀναποικίλλω, *variegate*, Sch.Pi.*O.*11(10).113 Böckh.

ἀν-άποινος, ον, *without ransom*, only once in neut. (as Adv., acc. to Aristarch.) ἀνάποινον Il.1.99.

ἀναποκλύζω, *wash out again*, θαλάσσῃ *PHolm.*20.6.

ἀναπόκρῐτος, ον, *unanswered*, ἀ. ἀποστέλλειν πρέσβεις Plb.4.34.1, cf. Zeno *Stoic.*1.64; ἀ. ἀπελθεῖν Plb.22.10.13. Adv. ἀναποκρίτως, εἰπών Antipho 3.3.2. 2. Act., *not answering*, οἰμωγή Plb.8.23.6.

ἀναπολάζω, *roll about*, of an engine on shipboard, Ath.Mech.32.7.

ἀναπο-λαυστία, ἡ, *non-enjoyment*, Phld.*D.*1.16. **-λαυστος**, ον, *not to be enjoyed*, Plu.2.829d, 1104f. 2. Act., *not enjoying*, Phld.*Mort.*13; ἡδονῶν Heph.Astr.1.1, Hsch.

ἀναπολεμ-έω, *renew the war*, Str.17.3.15, *Mon.Anc.Gr.*15.8. **-ησις**, εως, ἡ, Str.11.8.3.

ἀναπολεύω, *move upwards in an orbit*, opp. καταπολεύω, *PMag. Par.*1.702.

ἀναπολ-έω, poet. ἀμπ-, properly, *turn up* the ground *again* (τρὶς ἀροτριᾶν τὴν γῆν, Hsch. s.v. ὡραπολεῖν): hence, *go over again, repeat*, ταὐτὰ τρὶς τετράκι τ' ἀμπολεῖν Pi.*N.*7.104; δὶς ταὐτὰ βούλει καὶ τρὶς ἀναπολεῖν μ' ἔπη; S.*Ph.*1238; ὅταν [ψυχὴ] αὖθις ταύτην ἀναπολήσῃ [μνήμην] Pl.*Phlb.*34b, cf. Vett.Val.242.20:—aor. 1 Pass., J.*AJ*13.5.8. **-ησις**, εως, ἡ, *repetition*, A.D.*Synt.*29.10, al., Plot.2.9.12; *reconsideration, recalling to mind*, Id.4.6.3, Hierocl.*in CA*19 p.461M. **-ητέον**, *one must recall to mind*, M.Ant.4.32. **-ίζω**, = ἀναπολέω, of a field, Pi.*P.*6.3.

ἀναπο-λόγητος, ον, *inexcusable*, Plb.12.21.10, *Ep.Rom.*1.20, 2.1; *undefended*, τινὰ ἐάσειν D.Chr.2.39, cf. Eun.*VS*p.489B.; *without making a defence*, D.H.7.46. **-λῠτος**, ον, *not able to get loose, sessile*, Arist.*HA*599a15. Adv. -τως Gal.12.8. **-μικτος**, ον, f.l. for ἀνεπι-, Thphr.*CP*6.8.4.

ἀνα-πομπή, ἡ, (ἀναπέμπω) *sending up*, e.g. to the metropolis, Plb.30.9.10. 2. ἀ. θησαυρῶν *digging up* of treasures, Luc.*Alex.*5. II. *restoration*, ἐπὶ τοὺς πεπρακότας Ph.2.290. 2. *reference, reduction*, ἐπὶ γένος S.E.*M.*10.274; *reference* to a book, Jul.Laod. in *Cat.Cod.Astr.*8(4).246. 3. *delegation* of jurisdiction, *PTeb.*489 (ii A.D.), *BGU*1911 (ii A.D.). **-πόμπιμος**, ον, *sent back*, Luc.*Luct.*10, D.C.62.2; of slaves, τοῖς κυρίοις -ους ποιεῖν D.S.14.96. 2. of trials, *referred* to a higher court, Luc.*Eun.*12, D.C.52.33, etc. **-πομπός**, ὁ, *one that sends up* or *back*, epith. of Hades, as *sending up* the shade of Darius, A.*Pers.*650. II. *distributor* of bread to soldiers, *POxy.*1115.2 (iii A.D.).

ἀναπόνιπτος, ον, *unwashen*, Ar.*Eq.*357, Phryn.Com.3D. II. = *not to be washed out*, Suid.

ἀναπορεύομαι, *proceed up-stream*, D.C.75.9.

ἀναπό-ρριφος, ον, (ἀπορρίπτω) *not liable to be rejected, free from blemish*, *PLond.*2.282.13 (i A.D.), etc. **-σβεστος**, ον, *inextinguishable*, Hecat.Abd.14.

ἀνάποσις, εως, ἡ, *swallowing up*, of rivers, Olymp.*in Mete.*218.12, al.

ἀναπό-σπαστος, ον, *inseparable*, τοῦ ἑνός Dam.*Pr.*113. Adv. -τως Simp.*in Epict.*p.6D. **-στᾰτος**, ον, *unable to escape from*, θανάτου *Epigr.Gr.*526 (Beroe): abs., *without means of escape*, *POxy.*1469.5 (iii A.D.). 2. δεσπότης ἀ. *from whom there is no escape*, Plu.2.166e (codd.). 3. *inseparable*, Porph.*Sent.*40. **-στολος**, ον, *without permit*, ἐξὸν ἐκπλεῖν ἀ. *PGnom.*165 (ii A.D.). **-στρεπτος**, ον, *not to be turned away*, Sm.*Jb.*9.13. **-τέλεστος**, ον, *unfinished*, Eust.922.19. **-τευκτος**, ον, *unerring in its aim*, ὄρεξις Arr.*Epict.*2.8.29; of persons, 1.4.11, al. Adv., Comp. -ότερον 4.6.26.

ἀναποτικός, ή, όν, *absorbent*, Ptol.*Tetr.*18.

ἀναποτισμός, ὁ, *watering*, dub. in *PLond.*3.1177.187 (ii A.D.).

ἀναπό-τμητος, ον, *not to be cut off* or *severed*, Arr.*Epict.*1.1.24. **-τριπτος**, ον, gloss on ἀλίαστος, Sch.Il.*Oxy.*1086.74 (fort. -τρεπτος).

ἀναπούλωτος, ον, *not scarred over*, Gal.19.446.

ἀναποφέρω, *bring back again*, in aor. 1 Med. ἀναπηνεγκάμην *PCair. Preis.*32.12 (ii A.D.).

ἀνάπραξις, εως, ἡ, *exaction* of a debt or penalty, δανείων D.H.6.1; τοῦ ἀργυρίου *IG*9(1).694.10 (Corcyra).

ἀνάπρᾱσις, εως, ἡ, *retail dealing*, Poll.7.12.

ἀναπράσσω, Att. -πράττω, contr. ἀμπρ-, *exact, levy* money or debts, Th.8.107, Lys.16.6; ἀ. τό τε κεφάλαιον καὶ τὸν τόκον *IG*9(1).

694.58 (Corcyra); *demand back*, of loans already repaid, *OGI*669.20 (so in Med., of interest already paid, Plu.2.295d); ἀ. ὑπόσχεσιν *exact the fulfilment of* a promise, Th.2.95, cf. Ar.*Av.*1621; *distrain upon*, τὰ ἐμφανέα *SIG*554.16 (Thermon):—Med., *exact for oneself*, δίκας D.H.6.19.

ἀναπρεσβεύω, *send up ambassadors*, J.*AJ*18.2.4.

ἀναπρήθω, *let burst forth*, δάκρυ' ἀναπρήσας Il.9.433, Od.2.81.

ἀνάπρῑσις, εως, ἡ, *sawing off*, Hp.*Ep.*22.

ἀνάπταιστος, ον, = ἄπταιστος, Suid.

ἀναπτέον, *one must attach*, τὸν λόγον ἀπὸ τῶν φανερωτέρων Str.1.3.10.

ἀναπτεροποιέω, *represent as winged*, τὸν Ἔρωτα Men.Rh.p.337 S.

ἀναπτεροφορέομαι, *fly upwards*, Ph.*Fr.*59 H.

ἀναπτερ-όω, prop. *raise its feathers*, of a bird: hence metaph., *raise, set up*, ὀρθίους ἐθείρας ἀνεπτέρωκα E.*Hel.*633. 2. metaph., *set on the wing, put on the tiptoe* of expectation, *excite*, ἀναπτερώσας αὐτὴν οἴχεαι Hdt.2.115, cf. Pl.*Phdr.*255c; μῶν τι.. ἄγγελμ' ἀνεπτέρωκε Δαναϊδῶν πόλιν; E.*Or.*876; φόβος μ' ἀναπτεροῖ Id.*Supp.*89, cf. S.*Fr.*355; ἀ. τινὰ χρηστοῖς λόγοις Ar.*Av.*1449, cf. Men.*Epit.*510:—Pass., *to be in a state of eager expectation*, ἀνεπτερώθης A.*Ch.*228; ἀ. τὴν ψυχήν Cratin.384; ἀνεπτέρωμαι κλύων Ar.*Av.*434; ἀνεπτερωμένων τῶν Λακεδαιμονίων X.*HG*3.4.2; ἀνεπτερωμένος θεᾶσθαι Id.*Smp.*9.5; ἀναπτερωθεὶς ὑπό τινων ὡς.. *being irritated* by the remark of some, that.., Id.*HG*3.1.14. II. *furnish with new wings*, Ar.*Lys.*669:—Pass., *get new wings*, Pl.*Phdr.*249d. **–ωσις**, εως, ἡ, *clamour*, λόγοι ἀναπτερώσεως *clamorous* words, Lxx *Si.*31.1, cf. *Pr.*7.11. **–ωτός**, όν, *excitable, fickle*, χρῆμα ἡ νίκη Men.Prot.p.10 D.

ἀναπτερῠγίζω, *raise the wings and fly away*, Ael.*NA*4.30: metaph., Phld.*Vit.*p.21 J.

ἀναπτερύσσομαι, *to be furnished with wings*, Sch.Ar.*Eq.*1341.

ἀνα-πτησίκερως, ὁ, = ἰκτῖνος, Phot.p.119 R. **–πτησις**, εως, ἡ, *upward flight*, Hierocl. *in CA* 26 p.478 M.

ἀναπτοέω, poet. **–πτοιέω**, *scare exceedingly*, Mosch.2.23, Opp.*C.*1.107, etc.:—Pass., *to be scared*, Plu.*Pel.*16; *to be in great excitement*, Id.2.261a, etc.

ἄναπτος, ον, (ἀ– priv., ἅπτομαι) *not to be touched, impalpable*, Arist.*de An.*424^{a}12. II. ἀναπτός, όν, (ἀνάπτω) *fastened on*, φᾶρος Eust.1774.15.

ἀνά-πτυκτος, ον, *that may be opened*, Arist.*PA*683^{b}15. **–πτυξις**, εως, ἡ, *opening, gaping*, τοῦ στόματος ib.662^{a}29. 2. *explanation*, Id.*Rh.Al.*1435^{b}18, cf. Plu.2.382d, Ath.1.1a.

ἀνάπτῠσις, εως, ἡ, *expectoration*, Gal.15.480, Herod.Med. in *Rh. Mus.*58.93; αἵματος Alex.Trall.5.5; of fistulae, *opening out*, Antyll. ap.Orib.44.23.6.

ἀνα-πτύσσω, pf. inf. Pass. ἀνεπτύχθαι E.*El.*357: aor. Pass. ἀνεπτύχθην Hp.*Judic.*3, but –επτύγην *Int.*48:—*unfold* the rolls on which books were written, *open for reading*, ἀ. τὸ βιβλίον Hdt.1.125, cf. 48; δέλτων ἀναπτύσσοιμι γῆρυν E.*Fr.*370: also ἀ. πύλας, κύτος, *undo, open*, E.*IT*1286, *Ion* 39; χλαμύδα Plu.*Demetr.*42; even χεῖλος Opp.*H.*3.247; ἀναπτύξας χέρας with arms *outspread*, E.*Hipp.*1190; σεισμοὶ –ξαντες τὴν ἁρμονίαν τῶν ὀρῶν Philostr.*Im.*2.17:—Med., *fold up*, Arist.*PA*664^{b}27, al. b. *cut open*, of freshly killed animals, Pherecyd.97 J., Philum.*Ven.*17.3, *PMag.Leid.V.*10.1, etc. c. *ruminate, chew*, Opp.*H.*1.137. 2. *unfold, disclose*, πᾶν ἀ. πάθος A.*Pers.*254, 294; πάντ' ἀναπτύσσει χρόνος S.*Fr.*301; ἀ. πρὸς φῶς Id.*El.*639, cf. E.*HF*1256; φρένα πρός τινα Id.*Tr.*662: in later Prose, Porph.*Antr.*4. II. as military term, τὴν φάλαγγα ἀ. *fold back* the phalanx, i.e. *deepen* it by countermarching from front to rear, X.*Cyr.*7.5.3; conversely, τὸ κέρας ἀ. *open out* the wing, i.e. *extend* the line by countermarching from rear to front, X.*An.*1.10.9, cf. Plu.*Pel.*23, Arr.*Tact.*9.5. **–πτυχή**, ἡ, = ἀνάπτυξις, ἰὼ.. αἰθέρος ἀμπτυχαί oh *wide expanse* of heaven! E.*Ion* 1445; νυκτός τε πηγὰς οὐρανοῦ τ' ἀναπτυχάς S.*Fr.*956; ἡλίου ἀναπτυχαί the sun's *unclouded orb*, E.*Hipp.*601; ἀ. ἐλεύθεροι (sc. ὀμμάτων) *El.*868. **–πτῠχος**, ον, = ἀνάπτυκτος, Arist.*HA*528^{a}14.

ἀναπτύω, *spit up* or *out*, αἷμα Hp.*Aph.*5.13; σίαλον Plb.12.13.11: abs., *sputter*, ξηρὰ δ' ἀναπτύει [ῠ] Nic.*Al.*211; μυδῶσα κηκὶς.. ἔτυφε κἀνέπτῡε S.*Ant.*1009:—Pass., Gal.16.210.

ἀνάπτω, *make fast on* or *to*, Hom. (only Od.), ἐκ δ' αὐτοῦ [ἱστοῦ] πείρατ' ἀνῆπτον Od.12.179, cf. 51, 162; πρυμνήσι' ἀνάψαι 9.137: c. dat., γαίῃ A.R.2.177; ἀ. τι πρός τι E.*HF*1012:—Med., ἐκ τοῦδ' ἀναψώμεσθα πρυμνήτην κάλων to him will we *moor* our bark, i.e. he shall be our protector, Id.*Med.*770, etc.; θεοῖσι κῆδος ἀνάψασθαι *form a close connexion* with.., Id.*Tr.*845; χάριτας ἔς τινα ἀ. *confer* favours on.., Id.*Ph.*569; also, *fasten to oneself*, ἐπιστολὴν ἐκ τῶν δακτύλων ἀ. Din.1.36; *take in tow*, ναῦν D.S.13.19, Plu.*Cam.*8; τὸ κράτος Ph.1.474:—Pass., *to be fastened* or *fasten oneself on to, cling to*, c. gen., πέπλων E.*HF*629: c. dat., κίοσιν ib.1038 (prob., lyr.); *have* a thing *fastened* on one, περιβόλαι' ἀνήμμεθα ib.549. 2. *hang up* in a temple, *offer up*, like ἀνατίθημι, πολλὰ δ' ἀγάλματ' ἀνῆψεν Od.3.274, cf. Arist.*Fr.*572, Lyc.853, Philostr.*VA*1.11, Tryph.256. 3. metaph., *fasten upon, attach to*, μῶμον ἀνάψαι Od.2.86; αἷμα ἀ. τινί a charge of bloodshed, dub. in E.*Andr.*1196, cf. Ps.-Phoc.70, etc.; κήδε' ἀνῆπταί τινι A.R.2.245; *ascribe, refer to*, τοὺς λόγους εἰς ἀριθμοὺς ἀ. Arist.*Metaph.*1078^{b}22; ἀρχήν, αἰτίαν ἀ. εἰς τὸν Πύθιον Plu.*Lyc.*6, etc.; χάριν ἀ. τινί *ascribe* a favour to him, Id.*Ant.*46; τὴν χάριν εἰς Καίσαρα πάντων ἀνῆπτεν Id.*Brut.*6; τοῖς ἐκ τοῦ θεοῦ τὴν εὐδαιμονίαν ἀνάψασι Porph.*Abst.*2.3:—Med., *attach oneself*, πρὸς πολλούς Phld.*Herc.*1457.8. II. *light up, kindle*, λύχνα Hdt.2.133; πῦρ E.*Or.*1137; φῶς Pl.*Ti.*39b; πυρὶ ἀ. δόμους E.*Or.*1594: metaph., νέφος οἰμωγῆς ὡς τάχ' ἀνάψει Id.*Med.*107:—Pass., *to be kindled*, Zeno *Stoic.*1.31, etc. 2. *inflame with anger*, Lib.*Or.*68.35:—Pass., ib.33.15, Ps.-Callisth.3.22; *excite* emotionally, Phld.*Po.*1425.20. 3. intr., *to be lighted* up, Arist.*Mir.*841^{a}32.

ἀνάπτωσις, εως, ἡ, *falling back*: metaph., *slackness*, Eust.1406.8; of machines, *recoil*, Ph.*Bel.*68.45, Hero *Bel.*82.13; of style, *lifelessness*, Eust. ad D.P.69. 2. *reclining at meals*, Aristeas 187, 203; generally, *lying down*, in pl., Onos.10.11.

ἀνάπτωτος, ον, *flat*, of style, v.l. in Eust. ad D.P.69.

ἀναπυνθάνομαι, *inquire closely into*, τὰς πάτρας αὐτῶν ἀνεπύθετο Hdt.6.128; ἀνεπυνθάνετο τὸν ποιήσαντα Id.8.90; ἀναπυθώμεθα τούσδε τίνες ποτὲ καὶ πόθεν ἔμολον Ar.*Av.*403. 2. abs., ἀναπυνθανόμενος εὑρίσκω discover *by inquiry*, Hdt.5.57; also, *learn by inquiry*, ἀ. ταῦτα πρηττόμενα X.*An.*5.7.1 codd.; ἀ. περί τινος Pl.*Hp.Mi.*363b; ἀ. τί τινος *ask of* a person, Ar.*Pax* 693.

ἀναπυρέττω, *suffer from recurrence of fever*, Gal.16.649.

ἀναπυρίζω, in aor. part. ἀμπυρίξας, *kindle*, of fire, *Lyr.Alex.Adesp.*31.

ἀναπῡρόω, *set on fire*, Arist.*Mu.*395^{a}22 (Pass.): intr., metaph., *break out afresh*, πάθη.. πάλιν ἀναπυρώσαντα Gal.16.742.

ἀναπυρσεύω, *make glaring*, τὴν βαφὴν τὴν πορφύρας Poll.1.49.

ἀνάπυστος, ον, *well-known, notorious*, Od.11.274, Hdt.6.64, 66, etc.

ἀναπῡτ-ίζω, *spit up, spout up*, Hero *Spir.*1.28. **–ισμός**, ὁ, Id.*Aut.*4.3 (but see ἀνα-πιτύζω, –υσμός).

ἀναπωλέω, *put up for sale again*, *PPetr.*3 p.109 (Pass.); *sell again*, Poll.7.12:—Pass., prob. in *CIG*2266.11 (Delos).

ἀναπωμάζω, (πῶμα) *lift up the cover*, Hero *Spir.*1 *Praef.*, Crito ap. Gal.12.732.

ἀνάπωσις, εως, ἡ, *a drinking up*, Erot. s.v. ἄμπωτις (οἷον ἀ. τις οὖσα) s.v.l. Cf. ἀνάποσις.

ἀνάπωτις, v. ἄμπωτις:—Adj. **ἀναπωτικός**, ή, όν, Eust.1719.44.

ἄναρ· ὄναρ (Cret.), Phot.p.119 R., Hsch.

ἀναρ–: when ἀνά is compd. with words beginning with ρ, the ρ is usually doubled, as in ἀναρραΐζω, etc., though in Poets and Ion. Greek it is sometimes single, as in sq.

ἀναραγαθῆσαι· ἀναψοφῆσαι, ἀναπηδῆσαι, Hsch.

ἀνάρακτος· δημόσιος, Hsch.

ἀναράομαι, *recall a curse*, Callisth.ap.Suid., Poll.5.130.

ἀνάρβηλα· τὰ μὴ ἐξεσμένα, ἄρβηλοι γὰρ τὰ δέρματα, Hsch.

ἀνάρβῠλος, ον, *without shoes, unshod*, E.*Fr.*530.7.

ἀναργῠρ-ία, ἡ, *want of cash*, Stratt.8 D.; ἡ τῆς ἀ. παραγραφή *non numeratae pecuniae*, *Cod.Just.*4.21.16; ἡ τῆς προικὸς ἀ. Just.*Nov.*100 *Pr.*: pl., ibid. **–ος**, ον, *without silver*: *without money*, Lys.*Fr.*35, Pl.*Lg.*679b. II. *not bought with silver*: *incorruptible*, Poll.6.191.

ἀναρθρ-ία, ἡ, *want of vigour*, Arist.*Pr.*894^{b}21. **–ος**, ον, *not differentiated* or *articulated*, Pl.*Ti.*75a, Arist.*HA*583^{b}10, al. 2. *without strength, nerveless*, S.*Tr.*1103, E.*Or.*228. 3. *without visible joints*, like fat men, Hp.*Aër.*19. II. of sound, *inarticulate*, ψόφοι Thphr.*Sens.*41; ᾠδαί D.S.3.17; ἀλαλαγμός Plu.*Mar.*19, cf. *Caes.*63; φθογγή Id.2.613e, etc.; φθέγματα *Epigr.Gr.*1003 (Memnon). Adv. **–ρως** *confusedly*, Plu.2.611b. III. *avoiding the use of the article*, ἁρμονία D.H.*Comp.*22.

ἀνᾰριθμ-έομαι, Med., *reckon up, enumerate*, D.19.18. II. *reconsider*, Pl.*Ax.*372a:—Act., D.C.36.25. **–ησις**, εως, ἡ, *numbering*, Gal.17(1).314, Simp. *in Ph.*714.28. **–ητος**, ον, *not to be counted, countless*, Pi.*O.*7.25, Hdt.1.126, 7.190, 211, al.; of time, *immeasurable*, S.*Aj.*646. 2. *unregarded*, E.*Ion* 837, *Hel.*1679. **–ιος**, ον, = ἀνάρσιος, and ἀναρίθμιον· ἐχθρόν (opp. ἐναρίθμια· φίλα, συνήθη), Hsch. **–ος** [ᾰρ], poet. **ἀνήριθμος**, ον, *without number, countless*, Sapph.*Supp.*20.10, Pi.*I.*5(4).50; κυμάτων ἀ. γέλασμα A.*Pr.*90; πλῆθος ἀνάριθμοι Id.*Pers.*40: c. gen., ἀ. ὧδε θρήνων *without count* or *measure* in lamentations, S.*El.*232; μηνῶν ἀ. (Herm. for μήλων) *without count* of months, Id.*Aj.*604 (lyr.); ὧν πόλις ἀνάριθμος ὄλλυται *by* [the loss of] *countless hosts* of them.., Id.*OT*179; χρόνον.. ἡμερῶν ἀνήριθμον Id.*Tr.*247. II. *without number*, i.e. *having no assigned number*, Plot.6.6.11. 2. *not numerable*, Dam.*Pr.*117. [ἀνᾰρῐθμος Sapph. l.c., A.*Pers.*40 (lyr.); ἀνᾱρῑθμος in E.*Ba.*1335 (iamb.). S. has ἀνᾰρῐθμος in lyr., *OT*167, 179, *El.*232. S. also uses ἀνήρῐθμος in lyr., *Aj.*604: Theoc. has ἀνᾱριθμος 15.45, but ἀνᾰριθμος 16.90.]

ἀνᾱριστ-έω, *take no breakfast*, v.l. in Hp.*Acut.*28. **–ητος**, ον, *not having breakfasted*, Eup.68, Ar.*Fr.*454, Gal.15.562. **–ία**, ἡ, *want of breakfast*, Hp.*Vict.*3.75 (pl.); prob. for **ἀναρίστησις**, ib.4.90. **–ος**, ον, = ἀναρίστητος, Id.*VM*11, Plb.3.72.3; *dinnerless*, X.*An.*1.10.19. Theoc.15.147.

ἀνᾱρίτης [ῑ], ου, ὁ, = νηρείτης, Ibyc.22, Epich.42, cf. 114, Herod.11 (ἀνηρ–). (ῑ not ει acc. to Hdn.Gr.2.475.)

ἄναρκτος, ον, (ἄρχω) *not governed* or *subject*, Th.5.99; *not submitting to be governed*, βίος A.*Eu.*526 (where Wieseler metri gr. ἀνάρχετος, on analogy of ἀπεύχετος), S.*Fr.*30.

ἀνάρμενος, ον, *unequipped*, *AP*11.29 (Autom.).

ἀναρμόδιος, ον, *unfit*, Zos.1.29, Men.Prot.p.110 D., David *in Porph.*132.23. Adv. –ίως *AB*363.

ἄναρμος, ον, *without joints*, of atoms, Gal.1.416, cf. Heraclid.Pont. ap.eund.19.244; ὄγκοι S.E.*M.*10.318. 2. *loose*, of the groin, prob. l. in Philostr.*Gym.*48.

ἀναρμοστ-έω, *not to fit* or *suit*, τινί Pl.*R.*462a; πρὸς ἄλληλα Id.*Sph.*253a; of musical instruments, *to be out of tune*, Id.*Grg.*

482b (cj.). —ία, ἡ, *discord*, of musical sounds, Id.*Phd.*93c, e, al.: metaph., Dam.*Pr.*341. —ος, ον, *not fitting*, of dress, X.*Mem.*3.10.13; of sound, *out of tune*, Pl.*Ti.*80a; opp. εὐάρμοστος, *Tht.*178d: metaph. of the soul, *Phd.*93c, cf. *Smp.*206c; ἀ. τινί 206d; *incongruous*, μεταβολὴ ἀ. τοῖς θεοῖς Iamb.*Myst.*3.27. Adv. —τως Pl.*R.*590b. II. of persons, *impracticable*, Hdt.3.80, Ar.*Nu.*908. 2. *unfitted, unprepared*, πρός τι Th.7.67.

ἀναροδανισθῆναι· ἀναβληθῆναι, Hsch.

ἀναροιβδέω, v. sub ἀναρρ—.

ἀναρός· ἄγγελος (Tarent.), Hsch. (leg. ἄγγαρος).

ἀναροτρίαστος, ον, *unploughed*, γῆ *EM*175.36.

ἀναρπ-άγδην, Adv. *snatching up violently*, A.R.4.579,1232. **—αγή,** ἡ, *recapture*, E.*Hel.*50 (pl.). **—άζω,** fut. —άσω (v. infr. III) and —άξω, more freq. in Med. form —άσομαι (v. infr. III): aor. —ήρπασα and —αξα, in Hom. as suits the metre: aor. 2 Pass. ἀνηρπάγην D.S.4.75, Plu.*Pyrrh.*7:—*snatch up*, ἀνὰ δ' ἥρπασε Παλλὰς Ἀθήνη (sc. τὸ ἔγχος) Il.22.276, cf. Pi.*P.*4.34; ἀ. τὰ ὅπλα X.*An.*7.1.15; of the sun *causing* the earth's moisture *to evaporate*, Hp.*Aër.*8, cf. Plu.2.658b, Aristid.*Or.*36(48).60. II. *snatch away, carry off*, ὅτε μιν.. ἀνήρπασε Φοῖβος Il.9.564, cf. 16.437, Od.4.515, 5.419; of slave-dealers, ἀλλά μ' ἀνήρπαξαν Τάφιοι *kidnapped* me, 15.427, cf. X.*An.*1.3.14, Aristid.1.161 J., etc.; ἀνήρπασέν ποτε.. Κέφαλον ἐς θεοὺς Ἕως E.*Hipp.*454; ἀ. τοῖς ὄνυξιν, of an eagle, Ar.*V.*17, cf. Epicr.2.10:—Pass., φροῦδος ἀναρπασθείς S.*El.*848 (lyr.), etc.; ὑπὸ τῆς εἱμαρμένης *IG*12(7).51 (Amorgos): in Prose, *to be carried off to prison*, δεῖ με ἀνηρπάσθαι D.21.120,124, cf. 10.18. 2. in good sense, *rescue*, Plu.*Pyrrh.*16:—Pass., ib.7. III. *take by storm, ravage*, σὺ.. ἀναρπάσεις δόμους; E.*Ion* 1303; of persons, ἀναρπασόμενος τοὺς Φωκέας *take* them *by storm* or *at once*, Hdt.8.28, cf. 9.59:—Pass., ἀνήρπασται πόλις E.*Ph.*1079, *Hel.*751, D.9.47; ἐκ μέσης τῆς Ἑλλάδος Aeschin.3.133. IV. *carry off, steal*, πολλοὺς καὶ πολλὰ χρήματα ἔχομεν ἀνηρπακότες X.*An.*1.3.14; τρία τάλαντα ἀνηρπάκασι D.27.29; of regraters, *buy up unfairly*, ἀ. σῖτον Lys.22.15. **—άξανδρος,** f.l. for ἁρπάξανδρος, q.v. **—αστέον,** *one must wipe off*, τοὺς ἱδρῶτας Herod.Med. in *Rh.Mus.*58.92. **—αστός,** όν, also ή, όν E.*Hec.*207 (lyr.):—*snatched up, carried off*, ἀ. γίγνεσθαι to be *carried off*, l.c., Pl.*Phdr.*229c. 2. *carried up the country*, i.e. into Central Asia, ἀ. γίγνεσθαι πρὸς βασιλέα v.l. in X.*Mem.*4.2.33. II. of things, ἀ. ποιεῖν τὸν βίον to give up his substance *as plunder*, Plb.9.26.7, cf. Hdn.7.3.3.

ἀναρραγής, ές, = ἄρρηκτος, Sch.A.*Pr.*6 (s. v.l.).

ἀναρρᾳΐζω, *recover from a bad illness*, Poll.3.108, Hsch.

ἀναρραίνω, *send gushing forth*, πέτρα κρουνὸν ἀ. Arist.*Mir.*841^{a}22.

ἀνα-ρράπτω, *lift up by sewing*, βλέφαρα Gal.*Thras.*23. **—ρράσσω,** *shake up* ingredients, *Hippiatr.*128. **—ρρᾰφή,** ἡ, *lifting by sewing up*, of the eyelid, Leonid.ap.Aët.7.71. **—ρραφικός,** ή, όν, *used in* ἀναρραφή, σμιλίον ibid.

ἀναρραψῳδέω, *begin singing*, προοίμιον Luc.*JTr.*14.

ἀναρρέζω, only aor. 1 ἀνέρεξα· ἔπραξα, Hsch.

ἀναρρέπω, *fly up*, of scales, *Theol.Ar.*29.

ἀναρρέω, *flow, stream back*, Pl.*Ti.*78d; of blood, *IG*12(7).115 (Amorgos); of smoke, Philostr.*Im.*2.27.

ἀναρρήγνῡμι (—ύω App.*BC*4.115), *break up*, μή οἱ ὕπερθε γαῖαν ἀναρρήξειε Ποσειδάων Il.20.63; ἀ. αὔλακας Hdt.2.14; ἀ. τάφον *dig* a grave, E.*Tr.*1153. 2. *break through, break open*, τεῖχος ἀναρρῆξαι Il.7.461; οἴκων μυχούς E.*Hec.*1040; ὑπόνομον Plb.5.71.9; ἐργαστήρια Plu.*Pel.*12:—Pass., νῆες ἀναρραγεῖσαι τὰς παρεξειρεσίας Th.7.34. 3. *tear open* a carcase, of lions, Il.18.582; of hounds, X.*Cyn.*7.9; of Ajax, δίχα ἀνερρήγνυ *was cleaving* them *asunder*, S.*Aj.*236. II. *make to break forth*, λόγον Pi.*Fr.*180; ἔπη Ar.*Eq.*626; νεῖκος Theoc.22.172; πόλιν *make* it *break out, excite greatly*, Plu.*Flam.*10, *Mar.*35:—Pass., with pf. ἀνέρρωγα, *burst forth, break*, of sores, Hp.*Fract.*11; of floods, Arist.*Mete.*368^{a}26; of volcanoes, Id.*Mir.*846^{a}9: metaph., of words, ἀνέρρωγεν τὸ φώνημα Pherecr.10 D.; of persons, ἀναρρήγνυσθαι πρὸς ὀργήν, εἰς ἅπαν τόλμης, Plu.*Brut.*18, *Cic.*19. III. intr., *break* or *burst forth*, δέδοιχ' ὅπως μὴ.. ἀναρρήξει κακά S.*OT*1075: esp. in pf. part. ἀνερρωγώς, of the mouth of carnivorous animals, *with a wide gape*, στόμα ἔχειν ἀνερρωγός Arist.*HA*502^{a}6, *PA*696^{b}34; of the animals themselves, τὰ καρχαρόδοντα πάντα ἀνερρωγότα ib.662^{a}27, cf. 30.—Pres. **ἀναρρήττω,** D.S.17.58.

ἀναρρηθῆναι, aor. inf. Pass. of ἀνειπεῖν, q.v.

ἀνάρρημα, ατος, τό, *proclamation*, Phryn.*PS*p.39 B.

ἀνάρρηξις, εως, ἡ, (ἀναρρήγνυμι) *breaking up*, νεῶν Plu.*Ant.*66 (pl.): αἱμάτων ἀ. *haemorrhage* from lungs, Hp.*Prorrh.*2.7.

ἀνάρρησις, εως, ἡ, *public proclamation*, ἡ ἀ. τοῦ στεφάνου Aeschin.3.32, D.18.58.

ἀναρριζόω, *root, implant in*, θαλάσσῃ dub. in Nonn.*D.*18.36.

ἀνάρρῑνον, τό, = κάρδαμον, *nose-smart*, Arist.*Pr.*925^{a}30, Speus.ap.Ath.9.369b, prob. in Nic.*Fr.*84. II. = ἀντίρρινον, Dsc.4.130 (prob.), Gal.11.834. III. *sternutative*, Hp.ap.Gal.19.79.

ἀναρρῑπίζω, *rekindle*, τὸ θερμόν Arist.*Fr.*233, cf. D.H.1.59: metaph., στάσιν Id.7.15, cf. Ph.2.377; ἐπιθυμίαν Alciphr.1.35; *fan*, Antiph.202.16:—Pass., ἀνὴρ ἀναρριπίζεται Pherecr.4 D.; πόλεμος ἀ. Jul.*Or.*1.13b. 2. *scatter to the winds*, νίκης ἐλπίδα Nonn.*D.*25.307.

ἀναρρίπτω (also —ριπτέω Od.13.78, Hdt.7.50, Th.4.95, etc.), *throw up*, ἀ. ἅλα πηδῷ, i.e. row with might and main, Od.7.328; without πηδῷ, οἱ δ' ἅλα πάντες ἀνέρριψαν 10.130; of a boar *tossing* a dog, X.*Cyn.*10.9; ἀ. τὴν κόνιν, of the bison, Arist.*HA*630^{b}5; ἀ. ὑπὲρ τὴν κεφαλήν Plu.*Aem.*20. II. ἀ. κίνδυνον, metaph. from dicing, *stand the hazard of* a thing, *run* a risk, Hdt.7.50, Th.4.85,95; τὸν περὶ ὀστράκου κίνδυνον Plu.*Nic.*11; τὸν ὑπὲρ τῆς ἡγεμονίας καὶ τοῦ σώματος κίνδυνον Id.*Dem.*20; διὰ μιᾶς μάχης τὸν περὶ τῆς πατρίδος κύβον ἀ. Id.*Brut.*40: with κίνδυνον omitted, ἐς ἅπαν τὸ ὑπάρχον ἀναρρίπτειν *throw for* one's all, *stake* one's all, Th.5.103; ἀ. μάχην *risk* a battle, Plu.*Caes.*40, etc.; also πρὸς ἕνα κίνδυνον τὸ πᾶν ἀ. Id.*Arat.*5:—Pass., ἀνερρίφθω κύβος *jacta sit alea*, Men.65, cf. Ar.*Fr.*673, Plu.*Caes.* 32. III. *set in motion, stir up*, στάσιν D.H.10.17 codd. (prob. —ερρίπιζον).

ἀναρρῑχ-άομαι, impf. ἀνερριχώμην Ar.*Pax*70, Aristaenet.1.20: fut. —ήσομαι Poll.5.82: aor. ἀνερριχησάμην D.C.43.21:—in Suid. and *EM* the augm. tenses are written ἀνηρρ—, cf. ἀρριχάομαι:—*clamber up with the hands and feet, scramble up*, ἀ. ὥσπερ οἱ πίθηκοι ἐπ' ἄκρα τὰ δένδρα Hellanic.197 J.; ἀ. εἰς οὐρανόν Ar.l.c.; also in late Prose, Philostr.*Im.*2.28, Ael.*NA*7.24, 10.29, Aristaenet.1.3, Lib.*Or.*18.238, etc.: rarely c. acc., τοὺς ἀναβασμοὺς τοῖς γόνασιν ἀ. D.C.l.c.; τὸν τοῖχον Aristaenet.1.20 (s. v.l., ⟨πρὸς⟩ add. Pierson):—ridiculed as obsolete by Luc.*Lex.*8. **—ησις,** εως, ἡ, *clambering, swarming up*, ἐπὶ τοὺς οἴκους Arist.*Fr.*84.

ἀνάρριψις, εως, ἡ, *throwing up*, πετρῶν, of a volcano, Plu.2.398e, v.l. ib.951c.

ἀναρροή, ἡ, = ἀνάρροια, κυμάτων Nicoch.6 D. (ἀναρρόη acc. to Hdn.Gr.1.305.)

ἀναρροθιάζω, *dash up*, of the sea, dub. cj. in Eup.324.

ἀνάρροια, ἡ, *back-flow, reflux*, Arist.*Mir.*843^{a}27, Plu.2.929e (of the moon's reflected light); θαλάσσης Thphr.*Metaph.*29.

ἀναρροιβδ-έω, poet. **ἀναροιβδέω,** *swallow back, suck down again*, Χάρυβδις ἀναρροιβδεῖ μέλαν ὕδωρ Od.12.104; τρὶς δ' ἀναροιβδεῖ ib.105, cf. 236:—Pass., Gal.*Sect.Intr.*9; but in S.*Fr.*440, *throw up*, as expl. by Phot.p.120 R., cf. Paul.Aeg.3.10. (The spelling ἀναρρυβδ— has Ms. authority in Hom. and is supported by the assonance with Χάρυβδις, Od. ll. cc.; cf. καταρυβδήσας Hsch.) **—ησις,** εως, ἡ, *a sucking down*, Str.1.2.36.

ἀναρροιζέω, *rush up, rush back*, Plu.2.979e. II. *hurtle in air*, of arrows, Nonn.*D.*29.289. III. trans., *discharge*, οἱ καταπέλται τὰς λόγχας ἀ. J.*BJ*3.7.9.

ἀναρροπ-ία, ἡ, *motion upwards*, Hp.*Hum.*1, cf. *Epid.*2.1.6; *elevation*, Gal.10.318. **—ος,** ον, *tilted up*, like one side of a balance, σχήματα Hp.*Mochl.*35; κατάκλισις Gal.18(2).60, cf. Antyll.ap.Orib.6.1.2; of the motion of humours, *with an upward tendency*, Id.ap. eund.5.28.3. Adv. —πως Pall.*in Hp.Fract.*12.282 C. II. *retrograde*, ἀνάρροπον τιθέναι τὴν τῶν Ἀβάρων κατάβασιν Men.Prot.p.68 D.

ἀνάρρους, ου, ὁ, *upward flow*, opp. κατάρρους, τοῦ αἵματος Hp.*Ulc.*24.

ἀναρροφ-έω, = ἀναρροιβδέω, Cratin.7 D., Arist.*Mete.*356^{b}13, *Placit.*3.5.2, Luc.*VH*1.30; *gulp down*, D.C.71.10. **—ημα,** ατος, τό, *noise of gulping*, Hsch. s. v. ἀναροιβδεῖ (pl.). **—ησις,** εως, ἡ, *sucking up* through a tube, Sch.Opp.*H.*4.462.

ἀναρροχθέω, *retire with a roar*, of waves, Orph.*A.*706.

ἀναρρυβδέω, v. ἀναρροιβδέω.

ἀναρρυθμίζω, *reduce to order*, Philostr.*VA*2.22.

ἀνά-ρρυμα, ατος, τό, *victim*, Sch.Pl.*Ti.*21b:—also **ἀνάρυμα,** *AB* 417. **—ρρῦσις,** εως, ἡ, *rescuing*, Phot.*Bibl.*p.2 B. (prob.); αἰχμαλώτων Just.*Nov.*7.8, cf. 115.3.13: pl., ibid. 2. name of *second day of festival* Ἀπατούρια, Ar.*Pax*890, ubi v. Sch., cf. *AB*417.

ἀναρρύττειν· διδάσκειν, ἀναδιδάσκειν, Hsch.

ἀναρρύω, (ῥύω, ἐρύω) draw the victim's head *back* so as to cut the throat, like Homer's αὐερύω: hence, *sacrifice*, Epich.139, Pi.*O.*13.81, Eup.395. 2. Med., aor. ἀνερρυσάμην, *draw back, rescue*, ψυχὴν ἀ. παθέων *from*.., Hp.*Ep.*23; ἀ. πόλεις Iamb.*VP*7.33; ἀ. ἧτταν *repair* a defeat, D.H.5.46 codd.:—Pass., ἀνερρύσθησαν Just.*Nov.*115.3.13.

ἀναρρώννῡμι, aor. ἀνέρρωσα, *strengthen afresh*, Plu.2.694d, etc.:—Pass., *regain strength*, ἀναρρωσθέντες Th.7.46, Plu.2.75c, etc. 2. intr. in Act., τὴν γονὴν ἀναρρώννυσι Pherecyd.33 J.; νοσήσας ἀνέρρωσε Plu.*Pomp.*57, cf. 2.182b.

ἀναρρώομαι, *rush back*, ἀναρρώσασθαι ὀπίσσω Orph.*A.*1257.

ἀνάρρωσις, εως, ἡ, *recovery*, τῶν κεκμηκότων Simp. *in Ph.*5.1, cf. Philum.ap.Aët.5.123, Hsch. s. v. ἀναστατηρίαι.

ἀνάρσιος, ον, also α, ον S.*Tr.*641 (lyr.): (ἄρσιος):—*incongruous*: hence, I. of persons, *hostile, implacable*, δυσμενέες καὶ ἀνάρσιοι Il.24.365, Od.14.85; ὅσ' ἀνάρσιοι ἄνδρες ἐδηλήσαντ' ἐπὶ χέρσου ib.10.459, 11.401, etc.; ἦσθ' ἀνάρσιος (vulg. ἦλθες), of Apollo, A.*Ag.*511; ἀνάρσιοι *enemies*, S.*Tr.*853 (lyr.); ἀ. καναχά, opp. θεία μοῦσα, ib. 641 (lyr.), cf. Theoc.17.101. II. of events, *untoward, strange*, ἀ. πρήγματα πεπονθέναι Hdt.1.114, cf. 9.37; οὐδὲν ἀ. πρῆγμα συνηνείχθη 3.10, 5.89,90; δεινόν τε καὶ ἀ. ἐποιέετο [τὸ πρῆγμα] 9.110.—Ep., Ion., and (rarely) Trag.

ἀναρτ-άω, *hang to* or *upon*, ὀνάρταις (Aeol. pres. part.) χέρρας ὐμ ἐμμάτων Alc.*Supp.*4.21; λαιμὸν ἀ. μελάθρῳ A.R.3.789; *hang up*, ἑαυτόν Plu.2.841a; τὸ ζῆν ib.314b:—but mostly, 2. metaph., *attach to, make dependent upon*, δήμῳ.. μήτε πᾶν ἀναρτήσῃς κράτος E.*Fr.*626.1; ἀ. ἑαυτὸν εἰς δῆμον D.*Ep.*3.23; ἐς θεοὺς ἀ. τι *leave* it *depending upon* them, E.*Ph.*705; Rhet., ἀ. τι τῇ ὑποστάσει Aristid.*Rh.*1 p.480 S. 3. *keep in suspense*, Alciphr.1.22; *uplift*, ταῖς ὑποσχέσεσι Lib.*Decl.*33.26. 4. *suspend*, i.e. *withhold*, c. dat., τὸ σιτηρέσιόν τινι Just.*Nov.*88.2.1. II. Pass., *to be hung up*, παραδείγματα ἀνηρτημένους as examples, Pl.*Grg.*525c. 2. *depend upon*, ἔκ τινος Id.*Ion*533e: metaph., ἐλπίσιν ἐξ ἐλπίδων ἀναρτωμένους *clinging to* one hope after another, D.19.18; ἀνηρτῆσθαι εἰς.. *to be referred* or *refer-*

able to.., τὰ ἁμαρτήματα..εἰς θεὸν ἀνηρτημένα τιμωρόν Pl.*Lg.*729e; τὰ ἄλλα πάντα εἰς τὴν ψυχὴν ἀ. Id.*Men.*88e; ὅτῳ ἀνδρὶ εἰς ἑαυτὸν ἀνήρτηται πάντα Id.*Mx.*247e; ἀνηρτημένοι ταῖς ὄψεσιν πρός τινα *hanging on* one with their eyes, Plu.*Oth.*3; ταῖς ἐπιθυμίαις εἴς τι Id.2.989d; ἀνηρτημένοι ταῖς ψυχαῖς *in suspense*, D.S.33.5. III. Med., also with pf. Pass., = Act., D.H.11.46: hence, *attach to oneself, make dependent upon one*, τινά X.*Cyr.*1.4.1; *subdue*, ib.1.1.5. **-έομαι**, Ion. Verb, used only in pf. Pass. (cf. ἀρτέομαι), *to be ready, prepared* to do, c. inf., ἀναρτημένου σεῦ χρηστὰ ἔργα ποιέειν Hdt.1.90; ἀναρτημένος ἔρδειν τινὰ κακῶς 6.88; ἀνάρτημαι ἐπ' αὐτοὺς στρατεύεσθαι 7.8.γ'. **-ησις**, εως, ἡ, *suspension*, Thphr.*Lass.*10, Sor.2.85; *crucifixion*, Suid.: metaph., ἡ κατὰ τὴν ὑπόστασιν ἀ. Aristid.*Rh.*1 p.480 S.; ἡ εἰς νοῦν ἀ. Procl.*Inst.*202. 2. metaph., *suspension*, = *withholding*, χορηγίας ἄρτων Just.*Nov.*88 tit.

ἀνάρτιος, ον, *uneven, odd*, Pl.*Phd.*104e, al. 2. *at odds with one, hostile*, Plu.2.1030a.

ἀνάρτῡτος, ον, *unseasoned*, of food, Phld.*Mus.*p.53 K., Diogenian. 2.12, Sm.*Jb.*6.6; ἀ. βίος cj. Coraës in Ath.12.511d.

ἀναρυγή, corrupt for ἀνορυγή (q. v.), *PRyl.*95.8.

ἀνάρῠσις, εως, ἡ, *drawing of water*, Plu.2.951c(pl.).

ἀναρυστῆρα· ἐν ᾧ ὁ οἶνος ἀνιμᾶται, Hsch.

ἀνᾰρύτω [ῠ], aor. 1 ἀνήρυσα Hsch., *draw as from a well*, Plu.2.949f: metaph., ἀ. θριάμβους Cratin.36.

ἀναρχᾱ̆ΐζω, *bring back to old ways*, πόλιν *AP*7.707 (Diosc.).

ἀνάρχετος, v. ἄναρκτος.

ἀναρχ-ία, ἡ, *lack of a leader*, ἀναρχίης ἐούσης since there was *no commander*, Hdt.9.23; οὐκ ἐρεῖτ' ἀ. A.*Supp.*906. II. *lawlessness, anarchy*, δημόθρους ἀναρχία Id.*Ag.*883, cf. Th.6.72; ἀ. καὶ ἀνομία Pl. *R.*575a; opp. ἐλευθερία, 560e; ἀ. καὶ ἀταξία Arist.*Pol.*1302^{b}29; ἀ. δούλων καὶ γυναικῶν their *independence*, ib.1319^{b}28. III. at Athens, *a year during which there was no archon*, X.*HG*2.3.1, Arist.*Ath.* 13.1. IV. *not holding office*, Arr.*Epict.*3.20.17. **-ος**, ον, *without head* or *chief*, Il.2.703; ναυτικὸν στράτευμ' ἄ. E.*IA*914, cf. *Hec.* 607; ἄ. ζῷα, opp. τὰ ὑφ' ἡγεμόνα ὄντα, Arist.*HA*488^{a}11: τὸ ἄ., = ἀναρχία, A.*Eu.*696. 2. ἔτος ἄ. a year *without any regular magistrates*, *GDI*5635 (Teos). II. Act., *holding no office* or *magistracy*, prob. l. Arr.*Epict.*4.6.3. b. *not qualified to hold office*, Max.Tyr. 21.5 (Sup., s. v. l.). III. *without beginning*, Parm.8.27, Ocell. 1.2, S.E.*M.*7.312; κύκλος ἄ. καὶ ἀτελεύτητος Procl.*Inst.*146; ἄ. δίκη *PLips.*33 ii 5 (iv A. D.). b. *without first principles*, S.E.*M.*1.180.

ἀνασαβρῶσαι· εἰς ὀροφὴν ἐμπλῆξαι, Hsch.

ἀνασᾰλεύω, *shake up, stir up*, Luc.*Astr.*29; τὴν ὀσφὺν Alciphr.1.39.

ἀνασάξιμον, τό, *a mine that is reopened and worked*, after having been closed, *IG*2.780,1078*b*.

ἀνάσαρξ, κος, Adj., in sense of ἀνὰ σάρκα, τοὺς ἀνάσαρκας ὕδρωπας Gal.14.275.

ἀνασάττω, *load up, pile up*, pf. part. Pass. ἀνασεσαγμένος Plb.12. 25^h.2; cf. ἀνασάσσει· *luxatur*, *Gloss.Philox.*

ἀνασβέννῡμι, *quench, damp*, ὁρμάς Plu.2.917d.

ἀνασειράζω, *draw back with a hawser*, A.R.1.391: metaph., *hold in check*, φλόγα v.l. in Ar.*Fr.*561; τὴν ὄρεξιν *AP*9.687. 2. *draw off the right road*, E.*Hipp.*237; *draw away*, c. gen., τινὰ χάρμης Nonn. *D.*39.355.

ἀνασεισίφαλλος, ον, *phallum agitans*, Hippon.111.

ἀνά-σεισις, εως, ἡ, *shaking up and down*, esp. for the purpose of threatening, ὅπλων Dexipp.p.182 D.; χειρός Lib.*Or.*18.189. **-σεισμα**, ατος, τό, = foreg., D.H.14.9. **-σεισμός**, ὁ, *threatening gestures*, Id.6.62. **-σειστικός**, ή, όν, *exciting*, τοῦ ὄχλου Eust.211. 7. **-σείω**, poet. ἀνασσείω, Ep. impf. ἀνασσείασκε *h.Ap.*403:—*shake back*, ἀνασείοντά τε κόμας E.*Ba.*240; *swing to and fro, brandish*, αἰγίδα Hes.*Sc.*344; ἀ. τὰς χεῖρας *wave* the hands, Th.4.38; ἀ. φοινικίδας Lys.6.51. 2. *brandish at* one, *threaten with*, εἰσαγγελίαν D.25.47; βοήν Ar.*Ach.*347 (παρὰ προσδοκίαν). 3. *shake out*, ὑδρίαν *IG*2.104*a*36 (iv B. C.); πάντα κάλων *shake out* every reef, Ph. 1.327, al.; ἀ. τὰ ἱστία Philostr.*VA*6.12, cf. *VS*2.32; πάσας τὰς ἡνίας Poll.1.214; τὴν χλαμύδα Philostr.*Im.*1.6. II. *stir up*, τὰ πλήθη Phld.*Rh.*2.290 S., cf. D.H.8.81, D.S.13.91, *Ev.Marc.*15.11, *Ev.Luc.* 23.5:—Pass., *to be incited, encouraged*, c. inf., *PTeb.*28.20 (ii B. C.).

ἀνασεύομαι, Pass., only aor., αἷμα..ἀνέσσυτο the blood *sprang forth, spouted up*, Il.11.458.

ἀνασηκόω, *make up what is wanting by adding weight, compensate for*, τὴν μεταβολήν Hp.*Acut.*29, cf. Ar.*Fr.*743; αἱ γενέσεις ἀ. τὰς φθοράς Arist.ap.Stob.1.34.2 (where in *Mu.*397^{b}3 codd. give ἐπαναστέλλουσι).

ἀνάσηψις, εως, ἡ, *wasting disease*, *Mon.Ant.*24.167.

ἀνασθμαίνω, *breathe with difficulty*, Q.S.4.244, cf. Opp.*H.*5.212 (where it may be trans.).

ἀνασιλλιάομαι, *wear the hair bristling up*, Hsch.

ἀνασιλλοκομάω, = foreg., dub. l. Plu.*Crass.*24.

ἀνάσιλλος (cf. Hdn.Gr.2.446) or **-σῖλος**, ον, *with hair brushed up* on the forehead as the Parthians wore it, τῷ ἀνασίλλῳ κομᾶν Plu. *Crass.*24; restored by Sylburg in Arist.*Phgn.*809^{b}24, 812^{b}35, cf. *PGrenf.*1.10.11 (iii B. C.).

ἀνασῑμαίνομαι, = ἀνασιμόω, Poll.2.73.

ἀνά-σῑμος, ον, *snub-nosed*, Ar.*Ec.*940. 2. generally, *turned up at end*, ὀδόντες ἀ., of the elephant's tusks, Arist.*HA*501^{b}33; ἀ. πλοῖα Id.*Pr.*932^{a}18; of a horse's neck, *curved up*, Simon *Eq.*6. **-σῑμόω**, *turn up the nose, sniff*, esp. of male animals following the females, Hsch.

ἀνασινδης· ἀναπήδησις, Hsch.

ἀνασίτησις, εως, ἡ, *loading with wheat*, πλοίων *PTeb.*486 (ii A. D.).

ἀνασκαίρω, Ep. impf. -εσκαίρεσκε, *hop* or *skip up*, Q.S.8.321.

ἀνασκᾰλεύω, *scrape up*, Hsch., Zen.1.27:—Med., *clean out* the ears, Pl.Com.148. II. metaph., *ransack*, τὴν ὅλην οἰκουμένην *PMag.Par.*1.186.

ἀνασκάλλω, *dig up*, in Pass., f. l. for foreg., Pl.Com.148.

ἀνα-σκάπτω, *dig up*, πλοῦτον Str.9.3.8; τύπον Plu.*Thes.*36; ὅλην πόλιν *Pomp.*62:—Pass., Arist.*Mir.*835^{b}22, Plu.2.924c. 2. *extirpate*, of plants, Thphr.*HP*3.18.5 (prob. l.); *raze to the ground*, of buildings, Plb.16.1.6, *IG*12(2).526*a*4 (Eresus). 3. metaph. of ulcers with 'undermined edges', βεβρωμένα καὶ ἀνεσκαμμένα Archig. ap.Aët.16.106(96). **-σκᾰφή**, ἡ, *digging up*, Str.9.3.8.

ἀνασκεδάννῡμι or **-ύω**, *dissipate*, χροιήν Hp.*Liqu.*1; *scatter abroad*, Plu.*Pyrrh.*22:—Pass., v. l. in Polyaen.1.40.2.

ἀνα-σκεπτέον, *one must consider*, Thphr.*CP*6.13.2. **-σκέπτομαι**, = ἀνασκοπέω, Plu.2.438d, Gal.8.352.

ἀνασκευ-άζω, *pack up the baggage* (τὰ σκεύη), and so, *carry away, remove*, τὴν ἀγορὰν εἴσω X.*An.*6.2.8, etc.; ἀ. τοὺς Ἀθηναίους ἐκ θαλάττης *divert* them from naval enterprise, Philostr.*VS*1.17.3, cf.1.25.7:—in Med., *break up camp, march away*, Th.1.18; κατεσκευάζετο καὶ πάλιν ἀ. X.*Cyr.*8.5.2, etc. 2. *dismantle* a place, Th.4.116:—in Med., *dismantle one's* house or city, Id.1.18. 3. *waste, ravage*, X.*Cyr.*6.2.25 (Pass.); ἀ. τὰς συνθήκας *break* them, Plb.9.31.6:—in Med., τάφον Plu.2.578f. 4. Pass., *to be bankrupt*, τῆς τραπέζης ἀνασκευασθείσης D.33.9, cf. 49.68; οἱ ἀνεσκευασμένοι τῶν τραπεζιτῶν *broken* bankers, ibid.: metaph., ἀνεσκευάσμεθα E.*El.*602. 5. of logicians, *demolish* opponent's arguments, definitions, etc., opp. κατασκευάζειν, Arist.*APr.*43^{a}2, cf. *Rh.*1401^{b}4, Str.1.2.18, Polystr. p.24 W. 6. *reverse* a decision or judgement, Vett.Val.283.23 (Pass.): metaph., ἀ. ψυχάς *disturb*, opp. οἰκοδομέω, *Act.Ap.*15.24, cf. 9.31. 7. Medic., *remove*, νόσον Sor.2.8. II. *build again, remodel*, Str.16.1.5:—also in Med., *build*, οἴκους J.*BJ*6.5.2. **-ασμός**, ὁ, *upsetting, reversal*, πραγμάτων Vett.Val.228.27 (pl.). **-αστέον**, *one must demolish*, Theon *Prog.*5, Aphth.*Prog.*5. **-αστικός**, ή, όν, *destructive*, in Logic, ἀ. τόποι Arist.*Top.*152^{b}37. Adv. -κῶς *destructively, by way of refutation*, Id.*APr.*52^{a}38. 2. c. gen., *destructive of*, ἀλλήλων S.E.*M.*8.196. II. *restorative, curative*, Sor.2.50, Dsc. 1.33. Adv. -κῶς Herod.Med.ap.Orib.5.30.17. **-ή**, ἡ, opp. κατασκευή, *pulling down*: *suppression* of desires, Arr.*Epict.*4.1.175. 2. *refutation* of arguments, S.E.*M.*6.4, cf. Quint.*Inst.*2.4.18, Hermog. *Prog.*5; ὁ κατ' -ὴν τρόπος *negative* mood, proof by *denial* or *argument from non-existence*, Phld.*Sign.*31, al.; *removal, cure*, πυρετῶν Dsc. 3.137; ἰσχιάδος Archig.ap.Aët.12.1. 3. *subversion*, πραγμάτων Vett.Val.2.7, al. (pl.).

ἀνασκηθής, ές, *not free from blemish*, *IG*5(2).3.6 (Tegea, iv B. C.).

ἀνασκ-ησία, ἡ, *want of practice* or *exercise*, Eus.Mynd.39, Muson. *Fr.*4 p.15 H., Poll.1.159. **-ητος**, ον, *unpractised, unexercised*, X. *Cyr.*8.8.24, Plb.1.61.4, Onos.10.3, Plu.*Cam.*18, etc. Adv. -τως Id. 2.112e.

ἀνασκίδνημι, = ἀνασκεδάννυμι, Ph.1.262, al.

ἀνασκινδᾰλεύω or **-υλεύω**, = Att. ἀνασχινδυλεύω, Hsch., *EM*100. 51, Phryn.*PS*p.48 B.

ἀνασκιρτάω, *leap, skip* with joy, D.S.19.55; but of wounded horses, ὑπ' ὀδύνης Plu.*Crass.*25; ἀνεσκιρτηκότες τὴν ὄψιν, of athletes, Philostr.*Gym.*39: pf. part. Pass. ἀνεσκιρτημένος Eup.22.

ἀνασκολοπ-ίζω:—**Pass.**, with fut. Med. -σκολοπιοῦμαι (in pass. sense) Hdt.3.132, 4.43, but Pass. -σκολοπισθήσομαι Luc.*Prom.*7: aor. -εσκολοπίσθην ib.2,10: pf. -εσκολόπισμαι Id.*Peregr.*13:—*fix on a pole* or *stake, impale*, Hdt.1.128, 3.159, al.; in 9.78 it is used convertibly with ἀνασταυρόω, as in Ph.1.237,687, Luc.*Peregr.*11. **-ῐσις**, εως, ἡ, *impaling*, Sch.A.*Pr.*7, Eust.1136.54.

ἀνασκολύπτω· ἀποσκολύπτω, Hsch.

ἀνα-σκοπέω, c. fut. -σκέψομαι, aor. ἀνεσκεψάμην: (cf. ἀνασκέπτομαι):—*look at narrowly, examine well*, πάντ' ἀνασκόπει καλῶς Ar.*Th.*666, cf. Th.1.132, etc.:—also in Med., ἀνασκοπουμένοις Ar. *Ec.*827. II. *look back at, reckon up*, X.*Vect.*5.11 (nisi leg. ἐπανα-). **-σκοπή**, ἡ, *consideration*, Timo 61.

ἀνασκυζάω, *to be at heat again*, *Com.Adesp.*930.

ἀνασμύχω, *consume as by fire*, of disease, Aret.*SD*1.1.

ἀνασοβέω, *scare and make to start up*: generally, *rouse*, ἄγραν Pl. *Ly.*206a; τοὺς ἀκροωμένους Plu.2.44d; τινὰ πρὸς ὀργήν Chor.p.206 B.:—Pass., ἀνασεσοβημένος τὴν κόμην *with ruffled* hair, Luc.*Tim.*54; κόμη ἀνασεσοβημένη Id.*JTr.*30.

ἀνασπάζουσιν· ἀνασπαράσσουσιν, Hsch.

ἀνασπᾰράσσω, *tear up*, ῥίζας E.*Ba.*1104.

ἀνασπάς· (φυ)τὸν ἀνεσπασμένον, Hsch. (ἀνασπάσιον· ἀ. cod.; cf. παρασπάς).

ἀνά-σπασις, εως, ἡ, *drawing back*, Hp.*Art.*48; *tearing up*, τῆς γῆς Thphr.*CP*5.4.7; ἀ. θυρῶν *breaking open*, *Cat.Cod.Astr.*1.97. **-σπασμα**, ατος, τό, *uprooted plant*, σελίνου Eust.679.34. **-σπαστήριος**, ον, *fitted for drawing up*: τὸ ἀ., a machine *for raising* a portcullis, App.*BC*4.78. **-σπαστός**, όν, *drawn up*, Ar.*V.*382: but mostly, *dragged up the country*, of tribes compelled to emigrate into Central Asia, ἀνασπάστους ποιῆσαι τοὺς Παίονας ἐς τὴν Ἀσίην Hdt.5. 12; τούτους ἐξ Αἰγύπτου ἀ. ἐποίησαν παρὰ βασιλέα Id.4.204, cf. 6.9, 32; τοὺς ἀ. κατοικίζειν Id.3.93; εὐθὺς ἀ. *removing* hastily, Plb.2.53. 5. 2. of a door or gate, *drawn back, opened* from inside, S. *Ant.*1186. II. as Subst., οἱ ἀ. (sc. ἱμάντες) *latchets*, Ath.12.

543f. **—σπάω**, poet. **ἀνσπ-**, *draw, pull up*, σπυρίδα Hdt.5.16, cf. 4.154; βύβλον ἐκ τῶν ἑλέων Id.2.92:—Pass., *BGU*1041.8 (iii A.D.). b. *draw* a ship *up* on land, Pi.*P*.4.27, Hdt.7.188, Th.4.9. 2. *draw, suck up greedily*, ὅταν αἷμ' ἀνασπάσῃ κόνις A.*Eu*.647; ἀ. ὑγρόν Hp.*VM*22; ἀ. ποτόν, τροφήν, Arist.*HA*495^{a}26, *PA*661^{a}19; ὕδωρ ἀ. *draw* water, Th.4.97. 3. *draw back*, τὴν χεῖρα Ar.*Pl*.691:—so in Med., ἐκ χροὸς ἔγχος ἀνεσπάσατ' Il.13.574. 4. *tear up, pull down*, τὰ ἀγάλματα ἐκ τῶν βάθρων Hdt.5.86; τὴν σκηνήν Id.7.119; τὸ σταύρωμα Th.6.100; τύμβους E.*Med*.1381, cf. *Ba*.949; δένδρα Arist.*HA*497^{b}29, al.; τὰς σανίδας τῆς γεφύρας Plb.2.5.5; πυλίδας Id.5.39.4, etc. 5. metaph., ἀνασπᾶν λόγους, in S.*Aj*.302, *draw forth* words, *utter wild, incoherent* words; ἀνασπῶντ' αὐτοπρέμνοις τοῖς λόγοισιν Ar.*Ra*.903:—the phrase may be expl. from Pl.*Tht*.180a (ὥσπερ ἐκ φαρέτρας ῥηματίσκια.. ἀνασπῶντες) and Men.429 (πόθεν.. τούτους ἀνεσπάκασιν οὗτοι τοὺς λόγους;); so ἀ. γνωμίδιον Ar.*Fr*.49 D. 6. τὰς ὀφρῦς ἀνασπᾶν *pucker* the eyebrows, and so put on a grave important air, τὰς ὀφρῦς ἀνεσπακὼς ὥσπερ τι δεινὸν ἀγγελῶν Id.*Ach*.1069, cf. Alex.16, D.19.314; ἔβλεψε νᾶπυ καὶ τὰ μέτωπ' ἀνέσπασεν Ar.*Eq*.631; μέχρι νεφέων τὴν ὀφρὺν ἀ. Philem.174, cf. X.*Smp*.3.10; οἱ τὰς ὀφρῦς ἀνεσπασμένοι πρὸς τὸν κρόταφον Arist.*Phgn*.812^{b}27. II. *retract*, ὁ στόμαχος αὐτὸς ἑαυτὸν ἀ. Hp.*Superf*.22, *Steril*.217. III. *carry away from home*, Luc.*Tox*.28 codd.

ἄνασπις, ιδος, ὁ, ἡ, *without a shield*, Nonn.D.30.18, 36.262.

ἀνασπογγίζω, *sponge clean, sponge well*, τὸ ἕλκος Hp.*Ulc*.4; *soak up* drugs, ἀνασπογγίσας εἰρίῳ..πρόσθες Id.*Nat.Mul*.32, cf. 74.

ἄνασσα (Ϝάνασσα *Inscr.Cypr*.101 H., al.), ἡ, fem. of ἄναξ, *queen, lady*, addressed to goddesses, Od.3.380, 6.175; esp. in Att. to Athena, A.*Eu*.228,235,443, etc. 2. to a mortal, Od.6.149, etc.—Common in Poetry from Pi. downwds.; rare in Prose, as Isoc.9.72, Arist.*Fr*.526: c. dat., ἐνέροισιν A.R.3.862. 3. generally, like ἄναξ IV, ἄνασσα πράγους καὶ βουλεύματος *authoress* of this deed, E.*Fr*.704; ὀργίων Ar.*Ra*.387. II. as Adj., *royal*, ἀ. βουλή, of the Roman Senate, *IG*14.1389 i 34.

ἀνασσείασκε, v. ἀνασείω.

ἀνάσσυτος, ον, (ἀνασεύω) *rushing upwards*, of air, Hp.*Mul*.2.124, cf. Hsch.

ἀνάσσω [ᾰ], impf. ἤνασσον Od.11.276, Dor. ἄνασσον [ᾱ] Pi.*O*.6.34, Ep. ἄνασσον [ᾰ] Il.1.252, Aeol. 3 sg. ἐάνασσε Alc.64: fut. ἀνάξω Il.20.180: Ep. aor. ἄναξα Hes.*Th*.837:—rare in Med. and Pass., v. infr.: (Ϝανάσσω, cf. ἄναξ):—poet. Verb, mostly pres., *to be lord, master*, of gods and human rulers: in Hom. mostly c. dat., νήσοισι καὶ Ἄργεϊ *to be lord, hold sway in*.., Il.2.108; κτήμασι, κτεάτεσσι, Od.1.117, 4.93: also c. gen., Ἀργείων, πεδίοιο ἀ. *to be lord of*.., Il.10.33, Od.4.602, cf. Pi. l.c., E.*Andr*.22, etc.: with dat. pers. added, ἐλπόμενον Τρώεσσι ἀνάξειν..τιμῆς τῆς Πριάμου *to be master of* Priam's sovereignty among the Trojans, Il.20.180; γῆς ἀνάσσει βαρβάροισι βάρβαρος E.*IT*31; πάντων μὲν κρατέειν ἐθέλει, πάντεσσι δ' ἀνάσσειν, πᾶσι δὲ σημαίνειν Il.1.288: with Prep., μετ' ἀθανάτοισι ib.4.61, cf. 23.471; ἐν Βουδείῳ 16.572; ἐν Φαίηξι Od.7.62; παρὰ τὸν Ἀχέροντα S.*El*.184; ὑπὸ γαίας ib.841: with neut. Adj., Ζεῦ πάντ' ἀνάσσων Id.*OT*904: in Hom. freq. with ἶφι, Τενέδοιό τε ἶφι ἀνάσσεις Il.1.38, al.: abs., τῶν ἀνασσόντων *the kings*, S.*Ph*.6:—Med. once in Hom., τρὶς ἀνάξασθαι γένε' ἀνδρῶν *to have been king* for three generations, Od.3.245:—Pass., *to be ruled*, ἀνάσσονται δ' ἐμοὶ αὐτῷ 4.177. II. in Trag. sts. metaph. of things, κώπης ἀνάσσων E.*Fr*.705; ὄχων ἀνάσσουσ' *Hel*.1040; στρατηγίας *IT*17; πηδήματος ἀνάσσων *lord of* the leap, dub. in A.*Pers*.96; ἃ τῶν νυκτιπόλων ἐφόδων ἀνάσσεις, of Persephone, E.*Ion* 1049 (lyr.):—Pass., παρ' ὅτῳ σκῆπτρον ἀνάσσεται *is held as lord*, S.*Ph*.140 (lyr.).

ἀν-ᾴσσω, Att. for ἀναΐσσω.

ἀνασταδόν, Adv., (ἀνίστημι) *standing up*, Il.9.671, 23.469.

ἀνασταλάω, *make trickle forth*, Opp.*C*.4.324.

ἀνάσταλ-σις, εως, ἡ, *reduction of diet*, prob. for ἀνάστασις in Herod.Med.ap.Aët.5.129 (pl.). **—τικός**, ή, όν, *fitted for checking*, λύπης Ael.*VH*7.3; θεραπεία Gal.12.664.

ἀνασταλύζω, *sob*, Anacr.43.4. (Etym. dub.; cf. ἀσταλύζω.)

ἀνάσταμα, ατος, τό, dub. sens. in *PPetr*.3 p.291.

ἀναστάς, f.l. for παστάς in A.R.1.789.

ἀνά-στᾰσις, εως, Ion. ιος, ἡ, I. Act., (ἀνίστημι) *making to stand* or *rise up, raising up* the dead, ἀνδρὸς δ' ἐπειδὰν αἷμ' ἀνασπάσῃ κόνις.. οὔτις ἔστ' ἀ. A.*Eum*.648; ἔλαβον..ἐξ ἀναστάσεως τοὺς νεκροὺς αὐτῶν *Ep.Heb*.11.35. 2. *making to rise and leave their place, removal*, as of suppliants, ἀ. ἐκ τοῦ ἱεροῦ Th.1.133; ἀ. τῆς Ἰωνίας *removal* of the Greeks from Ionia [for safety], Hdt.9.106: mostly in bad sense, *desolation*, ἅλωσιν Ἰλίου τ' ἀνάστασιν A.*Ag*.589; πόλεων ἀ. Id.*Pers*.107, cf. E.*Tr*.364; τῆς πατρίδος D.1.5; *disturbance*, Hp.*Decent*.3 (pl.). 3. *setting up, erection*, τειχῶν D.20.72; τροπαίου Plu.2.873a; εἰκόνος *GDI*3505.20 (Cnidus), cf. *IPE*1^{2}.34.8 (Olbia), Arr.*An*.4.11.2; οἰκοδομημάτων Luc.*Phal*.1.3 (pl.). II. (ἀνίσταμαι) *standing* or *rising up*, πόδες ἀναστάσεως χάριν Arist.*Spir*.485^{a}18, cf. Id.*Fr*.156. 2. *rising and moving off, removal*, στρατεύματος Th.7.75, cf. 2.14. 3. *rising up*, ἐξ ὕπνου S.*Ph*.276. b. esp. for the stool, dub. in Hp.*Epid*.6.7.1: hence, *motions*, Id.*Coac*.605, Dieuch.ap.Orib.4.6.2. c. *rising again* after a fall, *Ev.Luc*.2.34. d. *rising from the dead*, Τυνδάρεω Luc.*Salt*.45; εἰς ἀνάστασιν [fort. βλέποντες] *IGRom*.4.743 (Eumeneia, iii A.D.): freq. in N.T., *Ev.Matt*.22.23, al.; ἀ. νεκρῶν *Act.Ap*.23.6; ἀ. ζωῆς, κρίσεως *Ev.Jo*.5.29; ἀπὸ σώματος ἀ. Plot.3.6.6. **—στᾰτέω**, *carry off*, or perh. *seduce*, *POxy*.1836 (vi A.D.). **—στᾰτήρ**, ῆρος, ὁ, *destroyer*, A.*Th*.1020, *Ch*.303. **—στᾰτήρια**, τά, *sacrifice on one's recovery*, Hsch. (cod. -ιαι). **—στάτης**, ου, ὁ, = ἀναστατήρ, A.*Ag*.1227. **—στᾰτος**, ον, (ἀνίσταμαι) *made to rise up and depart, driven from one's house and home*, ἀ. ποιεῖν τινας, ἀ. γίγνεσθαι, Hdt.1.76,177, 7.118, Isoc.4.108, S.*OC*429, *Tr*.39. 2. of cities, *ruined, laid waste*, Hdt.1.155,178, And.1.108, etc.; ἀ. δορὶ χώρα S.*Tr*.240; δόμους τιθέναι ἀ. Id.*Ant*.673; ἀ. ποιεῖν τὰ χωρία Th.8.24; οἴκους ἀ. γεγενημένους Isoc.6.66, cf. Alex.1 D., Men.*Inc*.2.30 Körte. 3. of arguments, *upset*, Pl.*Sph*.252a. 4. c. gen., *driven from, deprived of* a thing, Χαρίτων Plu.2.613b. 5. *unstable*, Olymp.*in Mete*.141.28. II. Subst. ἀνάστᾰτος, ὁ, a kind of *light bread* at Athens, prob. in Ath.3.114a, Paus.Gr.*Fr*.94.

ἀναστᾰτ-όω, *unsettle, upset*, [τὴν γῆν] Lxx *Da*.7.23; τὴν οἰκουμένην *Act.Ap*.17.6, cf. 21.38, *PMag.Par*.1.2244; of the mind, *Ep.Gal*.5.12; ἀναστατοῖ με he *upsets* me, *POxy*.119.10 (ii/iii A.D.); *destroy*, Asp.*in EN*61.28; *drive out*, *BGU*1079.20 (i A.D.):—Pass., ἀναστατωθῆναι Harp. s. v. ἀνεσκευάσατο: ἀναστατοῦ ἐς τὰ ὄρη Aq.*Ps*.10(11).1. **—ωσις**, εως, ἡ, *unsettling*, Heph.Astr.2.32, Eust.81.41. 2. *destruction*, Poll.3.91.

ἀνασταυρ-ίζω, *impale*, Ctes.*Fr*.29.59 (Pass.). **—όω**, = foreg., Hdt.3.125, 6.30, al.; identical with ἀνασκολοπίζω, 9.78:—Pass., Th.1.110, Pl.*Grg*.473c. II. in Rom. times, *affix to a cross, crucify*, Plb.1.11.5, al., Plu.*Fab*.6, al. 2. *crucify afresh*, *Ep.Hebr*.6.6. **—ωσις**, εως, ἡ, *crucifixion*, X.Eph.4.2.

ἀναστᾰχύω, (στάχυς) *shoot up with ears*, A.R.4.271, Procl.*H*.5.10: metaph., κατὰ ὦλκας ἀ. Γίγαντες A.R.3.1054; trans., *cause to spring up*, φυταλίην δρακόντων Nonn.*D*.25.199.

ἀναστείβω, *tread under foot*, *AP*7.544.

ἀν-άστειος, ον, *lacking in wit*, Aristod.ap.Ath.13.585b.

ἀνάστειρος, ον, (στεῖρα) *with a high prow*, ναῦς Plb.16.3.8.

ἀναστείχω, *go up*, ἐπὶ γαῖαν Opp.*H*.1.422; *ascend*, κολώνην ib.4.65.

ἀναστέλλω, *send up, raise*, νέφεα Arat.417:—Med., *gird* or *tuck up* one's clothes, νεβρίδας ἀνεστείλαντο E.*Ba*.696; ἀναστέλλεσθ' ἄνω τὰ χιτώνια Ar.*Ec*.268: abs., ἀναστειλαμένη Artem.4.44:—Pass., ἀνεσταλμένῳ τῷ χιτῶνι with one's frock *girt up*, Plu.2.178c. II. *draw back*, e.g. the flesh in a surgical operation, Hp.*VC*14; *push back* or *up*, τὰς ῥίζας [τῶν ὀρχέων] Arist.*HA*632^{a}17:—Pass., *to be turned up*, of the foot, Hp.*Mochl*.24. 2. *open*, στόμια μεμυκότα Ph.1.278, al. 3. *repulse, check* an assault, E.*IT*1378, Th.6.70, X.*An*.5.4.23: generally, οἱ ἄνεμοι ἀ. τὰ νέφη Arist.*Pr*.943^{a}35, cf. Epicur.*Ep*.2 p.51 U.; φόβος ἀ. τινά Ael.*NA*5.54: Medic., *check* a discharge, etc., Leonid.ap.Aët.16.40, cf. Sor.2.9:—Med., *suppress one's inclinations, dissemble*, Plb.9.22.9:—Pass., Th.3.98, Phld.*Ir*.p.82 W.: c. gen., ἀ. τοῦ.. *to be restrained from*.., Ael.*NA*8.10; ἀνεστάλησαν τὴν ὁρμὴν *VH*6.14. 4. *remove, make away with*, γῆν D.S.17.82; τὰ ἐμποδών Ph.1.407. 5. *lay aside*, Dam.*Pr*.400. III. in Med., *renounce, refuse*, ἀναστέλλεσθαι τροφήν Ael.*NA*11.14.

ἀνα-στενάζω, = ἀναστένω, Hdt.1.86, 6.80, *Ev.Marc*.8.12: c. acc. cogn., τοιά μοι ἀ. ἐχθοδοπά such bitter words *didst* thou *groan forth*, S.*Aj*.930. II. c. acc. pers., *groan for, lament*, A.*Ch*.335, E.*HF*118 (lyr.). **—στενᾰχίζω**, *groan oft and loudly, wail aloud*, Il.10.9. **—στενάχω**, c. acc. pers., *groan aloud over, bemoan, bewail aloud*, ib.23.211:—so in Med., 18.315,355. **—στένω**, *groan aloud*, A.*Ag*.546,1286, S.*Tr*.939. II. *bemoan*, c. acc., Archil.9.8, E.*IT*551.

ἀναστέριστος, ον, *not marked by stars*, of positions in the heavens, Hipparch.1.7.21, 1.8.1.

ἀνάστερος, ον, poet. for ἄναστρος, Arat.349, Man.4.528.

ἀναστέφω, *crown, wreath*, τὸν σὸν κρᾶτα E.*Fr*.243; ἀ. στεφάνοισι ib.362.48; στόρνῃσιν Call.*Hec*.1.1.15:—Pass., ἀνέστεμμαι κάρα φύλλοις I *have* my head *wreathed* with leaves, E.*Hipp*.806; but also δάφνας κλῶνας ἀναστέφεται *Epigr.Gr*.786.

ἀναστηλ-όω, *set up* as or *on a monument*, Lyc.883, Plu.2.1033e. **—ωσις**, εως, ἡ, *setting up of a monument*, Ptol.Heph.ap.Phot.*Bibl*.p.147 B.

ἀνάστημα, ατος, τό, (ἀνίσταμαι) *height*, Thphr.*HP*9.9.5; of animals, D.S.5.17 (pl.); τὸ τῆς ἡλικίας ἀ. J.*AJ*2.9.6; ἀ. βασιλικόν royal *majesty*, D.S.19.92; ἀ. τραγικόν D.Chr.18.7 (prob. l.); ἡ ψυχὴ γαῦρόν τι ἀ. λαμβάνουσα Longin.7.2 (prob.). 2. *protuberance, prominence*, Simp.*in Cael*.480.15. 3. *high ground*, in pl., Str.2.3.2, D.S.2.14, etc. 4. *erection, building*, Epict.*Gnom*.62 (pl.): metaph., *structure*, φιλοσοφίας Phld.*Herc*.1457.10. 5. *eruption*, φλυκταινῶν Lyd.*Ost*.35:—also **ἀνάστεμα**, Lxx *Ju*.9.10, al.

ἀναστηρίζω, aor. 1 -ξα, *set up firmly*, *AP*7.321.

ἀναστησείω, Desiderat. of ἀνίσταμαι, Agath.3.4.

ἀναστίδωνος· ἀνατεταμένος, Hsch.

ἀναστοιχει-όω, *resolve* matter *into its elements*, Chrysipp.*Stoic*.2.188, cf. Ph.1.501,477 (Pass.), Gal.1.508. **—ωσις**, εως, ἡ, *dissolution*, Alex.Aphr.*Pr*.1.79, Lyd.*Mens*.4.26, cf. 40; of the body, Gal.7.251. **—ωτικός**, ή, όν, *dissolvent*, Steph.*in Hp*.1.132 D.

ἀναστολή, ἡ, *putting back*, τῆς κόμης Plu.*Pomp*.2. 2. *opening up* of a fistula, Heliod.ap.Orib.44.23.60.

ἀναστομ-όω, *furnish with a mouth, open up*; τάφρον *clear out* a trench, X.*Cyr*.7.5.15; τὰς Νείλου διώρυγας Plb.5.62.4, cf. S.E.*M*.5.59; ταῦτα τῶν ἡδυσμάτων ἀ. τᾳσθητήρια Diph.18.6; ἀ. μήτραν Dsc.1.19:—Med., φάρυγος ἀναστόμου τὸ χεῖλος *open* your gullet *wide*, E.*Cyc*.357:—Pass., τραυλὴ μέν ἐστιν, ἀλλ' ἀνεστομωμένη *with mouth wide-opened, loud-talking*, Call.Com.19; also, *to be opened, dilated*, ἀ. οἱ πόροι Arist.*HA*581^{b}19, *GA*751^{a}2; ἰχῶρες ἀναστομωθείσης τῆς σαρκὸς ἐξέρρεον Memn.2. 2. of one sea *opening* into another, κατὰ στενοπόρους αὐχένας ἀνεστομωμένος Arist.*Mu.*393^{a}22; ὁ Ἀράβιος κόλπος ἀνεστόμωται εἰς τὸν..Ὠκεανόν D.S.3.38, cf. Ph.2.475, Hld.1.29. **-ωσις**, εως, ἡ, *outlet, opening*, Plu.2.590f, Gal.11.750; *inosculation*, Id.*UP*6.17. 2. *patency*, Cels.4.5, Gal.7.31. 3. *opening up* or *keeping open*, ἕλκους Ruf.*Fr.*118, cf. Procl.*in Alc.*p.119 C. (pl.); αἱμορροΐδων Dsc.1.58; τὰ εἰς ἀ. βρώματα *appetizing* foods (cf. ἀναστομόω 1), Ath.4.132f; ἀ. καὶ δῆξις, of manures, Thphr.*CP*3.17.6. **-ωτέον**, *one must open*, of piles, Gal.17(2).287. **-ωτήριος**, ον, *proper for opening*, τῆς ὑστέρης Hp.*Nat.Mul.*109. **-ωτικός**, ή, όν, = foreg., Dsc.1.4, Antyll.ap.Orib.10.25.2. **-ωτός**, όν, of an abscess, prob. f.l. for ἀστόμωτος, Gal.18(2).795.

ἀνα-στονᾰχέω, = ἀναστένω, Orph.*A.*1287:—also **-στοναχίζω**, Q.S.2.634 (s.v.l.).

ἀναστοφάγος, ον, *not eating the* ναστός (q.v.), Orac.ap.Paus.8.42.6.

ἀναστράπτω, *lighten*, Ph.2.204.

ἀναστρᾰτεύω, *enlist again*, App.*BC*3.66:—Med., *serve again*, of soldiers, D.C.41.35.

ἀναστρᾰτοπεδ-εία, ἡ, *decamping*, Plb.6.40.1. **-εύω**, *move camp*, Id.1.24.4, D.H.5.34, etc.:—Med., J.*AJ*14.15.14, D.C.49.11.

ἀνά-στρεμμα, ατος, τό, f.l. for ἀνάβλεμμα in X.*Cyn.*4.4. **-στρεπτέον**, *one must invert*, τι Isoc.5.132. 2. *one must write with anastrophe*, Hdn.Gr.1.481, etc.

ἀναστρέφω, poet. **ἀνστρέφω**, pf. ἀνέστροφα v.l. in Theognet.1.8, 3 pl. ἀνέστροφαν Cerc.*Fr.*17.30:—*turn upside down*, μήπως.. δίφρους ἀνστρέψειαν *might upset* them, Il.23.436; ὁ θεὸς πάντ' ἀ. πάλιν E.*Supp.*331; ἀ. γένος Ar.*Av.*1240; τὴν ζοήν Cerc. l. c.; ἀ. καρδίαν *upset* the stomach, i. e. cause sickness, Th.2.49; *reverse*, A.*Pers.*333, Ar.*Pl.*779:—Pass., fut. ἀναστραφήσεσθαι τὰ τῆς Ἑλλάδος πράγματα Isoc.5.64: pf. ἀνεστράφθαι τῆς πολιτείας Id.6.66 codd.; ὅρος ἀνεστραμμένον ἐν τῇ ζητήσει *turned up* by digging, Hdt.6.47, cf. X.*Oec.*16.12. 2. *invert* order of words or statements, Demetr.*Eloc.*11, al., Hermog.*Id.*1.11:—also in Pass., with ref. to ἐπαναστροφή (q.v.), ib.12. 3. = ἀρνεῖσθαι, S.*Fr.*1012. II. *turn back*, *Com.Adesp.*22.73 D.; *bring back*, τινὰ ἐξ Ἅιδου S.*Ph.*449, cf. E.*Hipp.*1228; ἀ. δίκην τινί Id.*Ba.*793; ὄμμ' ἀ. κύκλῳ *to roll* it *about*, Id.*Hel.*1557. 2. intr., *turn back, retire*, Hdt.1.80, etc.; esp. in part., ἀναστρέψας ἀπήλαυνεν X.*An.*1.4.5, etc.; but also, *rally*, of troops, Th.4.43, X.*HG*6.2.21, cf. B. III. 1:—ἀναστρέφον, τό, v. ἀνακυκλικός. III. in Gramm., *write with anastrophe*, as πέρι for περί, Hdn.Gr.2.52,66:—Pass., 1.481, al. 2. Math., ἀναστρέψαντι *convertendo*, Euc.5.19*Cor.*; so in Logic, οἱ ἀντιστρέφοντες οὐχ οἱ ἀναστρέφοντες ἀλλήλοις λόγοι συναληθεύονται Gal.11.465.

B. Pass., v. supr. A. I. II. *dwell in* a place, ἀλλά τιν' ἄλλην γαῖαν ἀναστρέφομαι *go to* a place *and dwell there*, Od.13.326, cf. Call.*Lav.Pall.*76, *Aet.*1.1.6 (so ἀναστρέφειν πόδα ἐν γῇ E.*Hipp.*1176); ἀναστρέφεσθαι ἐν Ἄργει Id.*Tr.*993; ἐν φανερῷ, ἐν μέσῳ, *go about* in public, X.*HG*6.4.16, Pl.*R.*558a; ἀ. ταύτῃ Th.8.94; ἐν εὐφροσύναις X.*Ag.*9.4; ἐν τοῖς ἤθεσι Pl.*Lg.*865e; ἀ. ἐν ξυμμαχίᾳ *continue in* an alliance, X.*HG*7.3.2; ἀ. ἐν γεωργίᾳ *to be engaged in*.., Id.*Oec.*5.13; ἐπὶ κυνηγεσίαις Plb.32.15.9; ἀ. ἔν τινι *dwell upon*, in writing, Apollon.Cit.2: generally, *conduct oneself, behave*, ὡς δεσπότης X.*An.*2.5.14; οὑτωσί Arist.*EN*1103^{b}20; θρασέως, ἀχαρίστως καὶ ἀσεβῶς εἴς τινα, Plb.1.9.7, 23.17.10; ἐν ταῖς ἀρχαῖς ὁσίως *IG*12(7).233 (Amorgos); ὡς τὰ παιδία Epict.*Ench.*29.3; πῶς δεῖ ἐν οἴκῳ θεοῦ ἀ. 1*Ep.Ti.*3.15. 2. *revolve*, like the sun in the heavens, X.*Mem.*4.3.8. III. of soldiers, *face about, rally*, Id.*An.*1.10.12, *HG*6.2.20, etc. 2. *to be reversed* or *inverted*, ἐμοὶ τοῦτ' ἀνέστραπται Id.*Hier.*4.5, cf. *Cyr.*8.8.13, Arist.*Mech.*854^{a}10. 3. *return*, Pl.*Plt.*271a; *retreat*, Arist.*HA*621^{b}34.

ἀναστρολόγητος, ον, *ignorant of astronomy*, Str.2.1.19.

ἄναστρος, ον, *carrying no planet*, σφαῖρα Thphr.*Fr.*31,32, cf. Eratosth.*Cat.*22; without σφαῖρα, Jul.*Or.*4.148a; *starless*, νύξ ib. 153c.

ἀναστροφάδην, Adv. *reversely*, Hsch.

ἀνα-στροφή, ἡ, *turning upside down, upsetting, overthrow*, E.*Fr.*301 (pl.); μοῖραν εἰς ἀ. δίδωσι, = ἀναστρέφει, Id.*Andr.*1007; *disorder, confusion*, Posidipp.26.22. 2. *turning back, return*, S.*Ant.*226; πολλὰς ἀ. ποιούμενος, of a hunter, making many *casts backward*, X.*Cyn.*6.25; *wheeling round*, of a horse, Id.*Eq.Mag.*3.14; of soldiers in battle, whether to flee or rally, Id.*Cyr.*5.4.8; μηκέτι δοῦναι αὐτοῖς ἀ. *time to rally*, Id.*HG*4.3.6, cf. *Ages.*2.3; esp. of the *reversal* of a wheeling movement, Ascl.*Tact.*10.6, Ael.*Tact.*25.7, Arr.*Tact.*21.4; of a ship, Th.2.89; ἐξ ἀ. *turning back*, Plb.4.54.4; κατ' ἀναστροφήν *conversely*, S.E.*M.*7.430. 3. in Gramm., *throwing back of the accent*, as in Prepositions after their case, A.D.*Synt.*308.15, etc. 4. Rhet., = ἐπαναστροφή, *repetition* of words which close one sentence at the beginning of another, Hermog.*Id.*1.12, etc. b. *inversion* of the natural order, A.D.*Synt.*71.18, Phoeb.*Fig.*1.4, etc.; τῆς τάξεως Theon *Prog.*4. 5. Math., *conversion* of a ratio, ἀ. λόγου Euc.5 *Def.*16; κατ' ἀναστροφήν Papp.1002.25. II. *dwelling in* a place, Plu.2.216a. 2. *abode, haunt*, δαιμόνων ἀναστροφή A.*Eu.*23. 3. *mode of life, behaviour*, Plb.4.82.1, D.L.9.64; -φὴν ποιεῖσθαι *IG*2.477*b*12, cf. *SIG*491.5, Lxx *To.*4.14, *Ep.Gal.*1.13, *Ep.Eph.*4.22, al.; ἀ. πολιτική *PGiss.*40ii 29 (iii A. D.); ἐξημερωμένης -φῆς civilized *life*, Phld.*Sto.Herc.*339.19. 4. *delay, respite, time for doing* a thing, Plb.1.66.3, al., D.S.10.5. 5. *occupation, concern*, περί τι τὰν ἀ. ἔχειν Archyt.1, cf. Phld.*Po.*5.1425.6. 6. *return, way back*, Arist.*HA*631^{a}26, cf. *Pr.*940^{b}23. 7. *recourse*, ἀ. λαμβάνειν πρός τι Plu.2.112c. **-στροφία**, Ep. **-ίη**, ἡ, = foreg., Man.4.312. **-στρόφιος**, ον, *converse*, of mathematical proportions, Papp.210.15, al. **-στρόφισμα**, ατος, τό, *hinge*, καλυπτῆρας ἐξ ἀ. *hinged* lids *IG*7.3498 (Oropus). **-στροφος**, ον, = ἀναστρόφιος, Papp.828.17 (s.v.l.). **-στρόφως**, Adv. *conversely, vice versa*, *Stoic.*2.71, Iamb.*VP*26.118.

ἀναστρώννυμι, *spread with coverings*, Lyd.*Mag.*1.18 (Pass.).

ἀναστρωπή, ἡ, word coined by Pl.*Cra.*409c, to explain ἀστραπή (ὅτι τὰ ὦπα ἀναστρέφει).

ἀναστρωφάω, Frequentat. of ἀναστρέφω, τόξον ἐνώμα πάντῃ ἀναστρωφῶν *turning* it *constantly*, Od.21.394:—Med., *wander about*, S.*Fr.*945; ἀ. ἐν ἀφθόνοισι *live* in the midst of plenty, E.*Fr.*1063.5. II. intr. in Act., *retire, desist from*, ὀχῆς Arat.1069.

ἀναστῠφελίζω, = στυφελίζω, Nonn.*D.*1.181, Hsch.

ἀναστύφω [ῡ], = στύω, aor. inf. ἀναστῦψαι S.*Fr.*421.

ἀνασύν-ταξις, εως, ἡ, *reassessment of war-tax levied on property*, Poll.6.179, Suid. **-τάσσω**, *reassess war-tax*, Hyp.*Fr.*151.

ἀνασυρίζω, *hiss shrilly*, Orph.*A.*995 (tm.).

ἀνασυρτόλις, εως, ἡ, *lewd woman*, Hippon.110.

ἀνασύρω [ῡ], *pull up*, δοκόν Procop.*Goth.*4.11; another's clothes, D.L.2.116; *expose to view*, τὴν ἀκρασίαν Clearch.14:—Med., *pull up one's clothes, expose one's person*, Hdt.2.60, Thphr.*Char.*11.2, D.S.1.85, etc.; ἀνασυράμεναι τοὺς χιτωνίσκους Plu.2.248b: pf. part. Pass. as Adj., ἀνασεσυρμένος *obscene*, Anacr.ap.Phot.p.123 R.; *lacking in decency*, Thphr.*Char.*6.2. 2. in Pass. also, of Alexander's hair, *to be curly*, Ael.*VH*12.14. II. Med., *plunder, ravage*, Plu.2.330d, cf. Hsch.

ἀνασφᾰδάζω, *struggle violently*, Hsch.

ἀνα-σφάλλω, fut. -σφαλῶ J.*AJ*17.6.5 (v.l. -σφῆλαι), intr., *rise from a fall* or *illness, recover*, συμπτώματος ἀνασφῆλαι Pl.*Ax.*364c; ἐκ τῆς νόσου Nic.Dam.p.98 D., cf. Babr.75.9; νόσου καὶ πόνων Id.78.3, cf. D.Chr.34.5; ἐκ κακῶν Luc.*Abd.*32: abs., J. l. c. **-σφαλσις**, εως, ἡ, *recovery*, Vett.Val.285.20.

ἀνασφηνόω, *tighten with wedges*, Apollod.*Poliorc.*159.6.

ἀνασφίγγω, *bind tight up*, ἵππον χαλινῷ Nonn.*D.*42.51: aor. 1 part. -σφίξας *IG*12(2).11 (Mytilene).

ἀνασφοδάξαι· ἀναπηδῆσαι, ἐξελάσαι, Hsch. (-ῆξαι cod.).

ἀνάσφορον, τό, = πτερίς, Ps.-Dsc.4.184.

ἀνα-σχεθέειν, **-θεῖν**, inf. of the poet. aor. 2 of ἀνέχω. **-σχεσις**, εως, ἡ, (ἀνέχομαι) *holding up, lifting up*, προβοσκίδος, of an elephant, Plu.2.972b. 2. *holding in suspense*, τῶν δεινῶν Id.*Num.*13. 3. ἀ. ἡλίου *rising* of the sun, Arist.*Mu.*393^{b}2 (pl.). **-σχετός**, Ep. **ἀνσχετός**, όν, *enduring, patient*, Plu.2.31a. **-σχετικός**, ή, όν, *enduring, patient*, Plu.2.31a.

-σχετός, Ep. **ἀνσχετός**, όν, *endurable*, Thgn.119: mostly with negat., οὐ γὰρ ἔτ' ἀνσχετὰ ἔργα τετεύχαται Od.2.63; πεσεῖν..πτῶμα' οὐκ ἀ. A.*Pr.*919; θρέμματ' οὐκ ἀ. Id.*Th.*182; so with a question expecting a negative answer, S.*Ph.*987: οὐκ ἀ. [ἐστι], c. acc. et inf., Hdt.1.207, cf. 3.81, 8.142; ζῆν γὰρ κακῶς κλύουσαν οὐκ ἀ. S.*Tr.*721, cf. *OC*1652; οὐκ ἀ. ποιεῖσθαί τι Hdt.7.163: abs., οὐκέτι ἀ. ἐποιοῦντο Th.1.118.

ἀνα-σχίζω, *rip up*, τοῦ λαγοῦ τὴν γαστέρα Hdt.1.123, cf. 124, 3.35; τὰς κυούσας Arist.*EN*1148^{b}20; δέρμα ὀνύχεσσι Theoc.25.277, cf. *IG*4.952.32 (Epid.); *plough up*, νῶτον γᾶς Pi.*P.*4.228 (tm.):—Pass., τρίβος -όμενος track *opened up*, Plu.2.161f. **-σχινδῦλεύω**, = ἀνασκολοπίζω, Pl.*R.*362a; cf. ἀνασκινδυλεύω. **-σχῐσις**, εως, ἡ, *ripping open*, Gal.14.675.

ἀνασῴζω, fut. -ώσω: pf. ἀνασέσωικεν *IG*12(5).1061.9 (Ceos, iii B. C.): aor. ἀνέσωισε ib.1004.5 (Ios, iv/iii B. C.), cf. *OGI*56.11:—*recover what is lost, rescue*, ἀπὸ φόνου ἔρρυτο κἀνέσωσέ μ' S.*OT*1351 (lyr.); ἀ. φίλον ἀλλοιωθέντα Arist.*EN*1165^{b}22:—more freq. in Med., ἀνασῴζεσθαί τινα φόνου *rescue* from death, S.*El.*1133; ἀνασωσάμενός μοι δὸς.. Σάμον Hdt.3.140:—but Hdt. commonly uses the Med. in the proper sense, ἀ. τὴν ἀρχὴν *recover* it *for oneself*, 1.82,106, etc.; in 3.65 he joins Act. and Med., μὴ ἀνασωσαμένοισι δὲ τὴν ἀρχὴν μηδ' ἐπιχειρήσασι ἀνασῴζειν:—Pass., *to be restored, recover*, Pl.*Phlb.*32e; *return safe*, εἰς Κατάνην Lys.20.24; ἀνασωθῆναι ἐς τὰς πατρίδας, of exiles, X.*HG*4.8.28; ἐκ φυγῆς Plb.18.27.2, al. 2. *preserve in mind, remember*, Hdt.6.65.

ἀνασωρεύω, *heap up*, in Pass., Plb.8.33.5.

ἀνά-σωσμα, ατος, τό, *preservation*, Tz. ad Lyc.1297. **-σωσμός**, ὁ, = foreg., Aq.*Ge.*45.1.

ἀνασωφρονίζω, *reduce to sobriety*, in Pass., Hsch. s. v. ἀμπνυτο.

ἀνασώχω, = σώχω, Sch.Nic.*Th.*695.

ἀνατάκται, οἱ, *assessors*, title of financial board at Miletus, *OGI*213 (ca. 300 B. C.), *SIG*577.19, etc.

ἀνατᾰνύω, poet. ἀντ-, = ἀνατείνω, Call.*Jov.*30, *IG*14.1015, *APl.*4.101:—Med., ἀνὰ χεῖρα τανύσσατο A.R.1.344.

ἀνάταξις, εως, ἡ, *financial estimate, assessment*, *SIG*577.21.

ἀνατᾰράσσω, Att. **-ττω**, *stir up* the mud, Arist.*HA*620^{b}16:—Pass., οὖρα ἀνατεταραγμένα *thick* urine, Hp.*Aph.*4.70, cf. *Epid.*1.26.δ'. II. *rouse to frenzy*, S.*Tr.*218; *confound*, Pl.*Phd.*88c:—Pass., ἀνατεταραγμένος πορεύεσθαι march *in disorder*, X.*An.*1.7.20.

ἀνάτᾰσις, εως, ἡ, (ἀνατείνω) *extension*, εἰς ὕψος Plb.5.44.3, etc. b. abs., *height*, J.*BJ*6.9.1; ἀ. ὀρῶν Phlp.*in Mete.*37.10. 2. *stretching out*, Hp.*Art.*11; ἀκοντίων Onos.17: metaph., *threats* of violence, Plb.4.4.7, *Fr.*108 (pl.); μετὰ ἀ. καὶ ἀπειλῆς Epict.*Fr.*25, cf. D.S.38.8. 3. *intensity, inflexibility*, τοῦ φρονήματος Plu.*Mar.*6; *intensity* of passion, Phld.*Lib.*p.29 O.: abs., *courage, steadfastness*, prob. in D.Chr.34.40. 4. *endurance of hunger, fasting*, Sor.1.49, Plu.2.62a. 5. ἀ. τῆς βοῆς *straining*, Sch.E.*Or.*149; κατ' ἀνάτασιν of the *acute accent*, D.T.620.1. 6. metaph., *straining, effort*, Phld.*Rh.*

1.31 S., al.; ἡ πρὸς τὸ ἓν διαγνώσεως ἀ. Dam.*Pr.*27, cf. Procl.*Inst.*21, al.: c. gen., τιμῆς Procop.Gaz.*Pan.*496.4.

ἀνατάσσω, Att. **-ττω**, aor. 2 Pass. ἀνετάγην, *countermand* expenditure, D.C.78.18 (Pass.):—Med., *go regularly through again, rehearse*, Plu.2.968c; *set in order*, διήγησιν *Ev.Luc.*1.1.

ἀνατᾰτικός, ή, όν, *threatening*, Plb.5.43.5, D.S.5.31. Adv. -κῶς Plb.4.4.7.

ἀνατείνω, poet. ἀντ-, *lift up*, χεῖρας ἀ., in swearing, Pi.*O.*7.65; also in prayer, Id.*I.*6(5).41; εὐξόμεθ'.. ἀνατείνοντες τὼ χεῖρ' Ar.*Av.* 623; as token of assent in voting, X.*An.*5.6.33, etc. 2. *stretch forth*, so as to threaten, τὴν μάχαιραν ἀνατεταμένος X.*Cyr.*4.1.3:— Med. (with aor. 1 Pass.), οὐδὲ Πολυδεύκεος βία χεῖρας ἀντείναιτ' ἂν ἐναντίον αὐτῷ Simon.8; οὐδὲν ἂν ὑμῖν εἶχε ἀνατείνασθαι φοβερόν *hold out* any alarming *threat*, D.19.153: abs., *threaten*, Plb.5.55.1: c. dat., 4.82.8: c. fut. inf., 4.18.10. 3. *hold up, offer* as a prize, Pi.*N.*8.25 (Pass.). 4. *present* a document to a magistrate, *BGU*613.3 (ii A. D.). 5. *lift up, exalt*, κῦδός τινος Pi.*N.*8.34; ἀνατείνασθαι ἀρχήν *strain* or *augment* its *force*, Plu.*Cleom.*10. 6. *lift up*, κάρα Pi.*N.*1. 43; ἑαυτόν Ael.*NA*3.21; ἀ. τὰς ὀφρῦς *pucker*, Luc.*Tim.*54. 7. of sound, *strain* to a high pitch, Arist.*Pr.*920ᵇ20 (Pass.). 8. metaph., *excite*, τινά Plu.2.60c:—Pass., Phld.*Lib.*p.44 O.; of the soul, etc., εἰς ἀμέθεκτον αἰτίαν Procl.*Inst.*100, cf. 23. II. *spread out, expand*, e.g. a line of battle, τὰ κέρατα X.*Cyr.*7.1.6, cf. ib.23; ἀετὸς ἐπὶ δόρατος ἀνατεταμένος *spread* eagle, ib.4; ἀ. ἱστία πρὸς ζυγόν Pi.*N.*5.51:— Pass., *to be distended upwards*, Ti.Locr.102a; *extend*, εἰς ὕψος Plb.9. 21.10. III. *hold out, persevere*, esp. in abstinence from food, Sor. 1.56, Arr.*Epict.*2.17.9. IV. intr., *reach up, stretch up*, πέδιλα ἐς γόνυ ἀνατείνοντα Hdt.7.67. 2. *extend, stretch out*, ὄρος... ἀ. ἐς τὴν Οἴτην Hdt.7.176, cf. 8.107, Arist.*HA*524ᵇ19, Epicur.*Nat.*11.5, *Inscr. Prien.*37.160, 42.69: metaph. in Pass., πρὸς ἄφρονας ταῦτ' ἀ. these things only *reach* or *affect* foolish people, Phld.*Herc.*1251.12.

ἀνατειχ-ίζω, *rebuild*, τείχη X.*HG*4.4.18:—in Med., *build up*, τὸ ταπεινότατον J.*BJ*5.5.1. **-ισμός**, ὁ, *rebuilding of walls*, X.*HG*4.8.9.

ἀνατέλλω, poet. ἀντ-, aor. ἀνέτειλα: pf. part. ἀνατεταλκός Plb. 9.15.10:—*make to rise up*, τοῖσιν δ' (sc. ἵπποις) ἀμβροσίην ἀνέτειλε νέμεσθαι Il.5.777; Αἴγυπτος .. Δήμητρος ἀντέλλει στάχυν A.*Fr.*300, cf. Lxx *Ge.*3.18; ὕδωρ ἀ. *make* water *gush forth*, Pi.*I.*6(5).75; τὸν ἥλιον *Ev.Matt.*5.45:—so in Pass., φλὸξ ἀνατελλομένα a flame *mounting up*, Pi.*I.*4(3).83. 2. *bring forth, give birth to*, ἄντειλας Διόνυσον ib.7(6).5; ἰούλους A.R.2.44: of events, μυρί' ἀπ' αἰσχρῶν ἀνατέλλοντα S.*Ph.*1139. II. intr., *rise, appear above the horizon*, of any heavenly body, as sun and moon, Hdt.2.142, S.*OC*1246, Ar.*Nu.* 754; πρὸς ἠῶ τε καὶ ἥλιον ἀνατέλλοντα Hdt.1.204, 4.40; also of constellations, A.R.3.959; ἠὼς ἀντ. Id.2.1007; dist. from ἐπιτέλλω (q.v.), Ptol.*Alm.*8.4; cf. ἀνατολή. b. = ἐπιτέλλω, of the Pleiades, Theoc. 13.25. 2. of a river, *take its rise*, ἐκ ταύτης [τῆς λίμνης] Hdt.4. 52, cf. Ael.*NA*14.16, etc. b. of persons, *originate*, ἐξ Ἰούδα ἀνατέταλκεν ὁ κύριος *Ep.Heb.*7.14. 3. *grow*, of hair, ταρφὺς ἀντέλλουσα θρίξ A.*Th.*535; of teeth, Arist.*HA*501ᵇ29; *spring up*, of plants, Thphr.*HP*3.1.6, al.; cf. ἀνατολή II. 4. of mountains, *rise*, A.R. 1.501; but, *appear on the horizon*, ib.601. 5. *rise up*, ἀνέτειλε σωτήρ prob. in *Epigr.Gr.*978 (Philae).

ἀνατέμνω, *cut up, cut open*, νεκρόν Hdt.2.87, cf. Luc.*Prom.* 21. 2. *dissect*, Hp.*Ep.*17, Arist.*Spir.*478ᵃ21. 3. *open up, clear*, ὁδούς, αὔλακας, Ph.1.16, 20; ὁδὸν καινήν *OGI*701 (Egypt). II. *cut off*, κλήματα Aeschin.3.166; γειτνηπόδισμα *IG*2².463.63.

ἀνατεταμένον, τό, = ἑλξίνη, Ps.-Dsc.4.39.

ἀνατεταμένως, Adv. pf. part. Pass. of ἀνατείνω, *stretched* or *strained to the utmost*, Sch.Ar.*Ra.*1282.

ἀνα-τήκω, *melt*: metaph., *relax*, τὸ σῶμα ἡδοναῖς Plu.2.136b:— Pass., of snow, *thaw*, Plb.2.16.9. **-τηξις**, εως, ἡ, *melting, thawing*, Id.9.43.5.

ἀνᾱτί [ῑ], Adv. of ἄνατος, *without harm, with impunity*, A.*Eu.*59, S.*Ant.*485, E.*Med.*1357, Pl.*Lg.*871e, prob. in Th.8.67, cf. Is.*Fr.*2, D.S.20.58, etc. (Spelling ἀνατεί attested by Hdn.*Epim.*256.)

ἀνατίθημι, pf. ἀνατέθηκα *SIG*1018.9 (Pergam.), etc.:—*lay upon*, once in Hom., ἐλεγχείην ἀναθήσει μοι Il.22.100; ἀ. ἄχθος *lay on* as a burden, Ar.*Eq.*1056 (hex.), cf. X.*An.*3.1.30; κινδύνους ἰδιώταις ἀ. Hyp.*Eux.*9: in good sense, ἀ. κῦδός τινι Pi.*O.*5.8. b. Med., *put on board ship*, *IG*5(1).1421 (Cyparissia). 2. in Prose, *refer, attribute*, a thing to a person, μεγάλα οἱ χρήματα ἀ. Hdt.2.135; οὐ γὰρ ἂν οἱ πυραμίδα ἀνέθεσαν ποιήσασθαι would not *have attributed* to her the erection of the pyramid, ib.134; Φοίβῳ τήνδ' ἀναθήσω πρᾶξιν E.*El.* 1296; εἰ μή, ὅταν.. εὖ πράξητε, ἐμοὶ ἀναθήσετε *will give* me *the credit of* it, Th.2.64; οὐ τῷ συμβούλῳ τὴν τοῦ κατορθοῦν.. ἀνέθηκε δύναμιν D.18.290; ἀ. τινὶ τὴν αἰτίαν τινός Isoc.1.37, Aeschin.2.10; also, *compare*, τινὰ εἴς τι Eun.*Hist.*p.261 D. b. ἀ. τινὶ ἅπαντα πράγματα *lay* them *upon* him, *entrust* them to him, Ar.*Nu.*1453, Th.8.82. II. *set up as a votive gift, dedicate*, τινί τι Hes.*Op.*658, Pi.*O.*3.30, Hdt.2. 159, 7.54, Ar.*Pl.*1089, etc.; Ῥήνειαν ἀνέθηκε τῷ Ἀπόλλωνι Th.1.13; ἀνάθημα ἀνατιθέναι Hdt.1.53, 2.182; ἀ. τι ἐς Δελφοὺς Id.1.92, 2.135, 182, Pl.*Phdr.*235d, etc.; less freq. ἐν Δελφοῖς Theopomp.Com.1 D., Plu.*Sol.*25; *dedicate* a book, Id.*Sull.*6; ἀ. τινά *set up a statue of*.., *SIG*420 (Delos, iii B. C.); incorrectly of burial, *OGI*602 (Jaffa):— Pass., ἀνατεθῆναι Ar.*Eq.*849; cf. ἀνάκειμαι. 2. *set up, erect*, [στήλην] παρὰ βωμόν, νεών, Plb.5.93.10, Plu.*Publ.*14: metaph., *dedicate*, μακραγορίαν λύρᾳ Pi.*P.*8.29; ἀ. τὰς ἀκοὰς τοῖς ἀκροάμασι *give* them *up* to, Plb.23.5.9. 3. *set up and leave* in a place, ἀ. τινὰ ἐπὶ κρημνόν Ar.*Pl.*69; ἀ. ζῶντα (on a cross) Plb.1.86.6. III. *put back*, τί γὰρ παρ' ἦμαρ ἡμέρα τέρπειν ἔχει, προσθεῖσα κἀναθεῖσα τοῦ γε κατθανεῖν; *pushing* us *forward* or *moving* us *back* on the verge of death, S.*Aj.* 476; cf. B. II. 2.

B. Med., *put upon for oneself*, ἀναθέσθαι τὰ σκεύη ἐπὶ τὰ ὑποζύγια X.*An.*2.2.4; *pack* on one's cart, Lys.7.19; τοῖς ὤμοις ἀ. τινά *put on one's* shoulders, Plu.2.983b; freq. like Act., ἀ. τινὰ ἐφ' ἵππον Id.*Art.* 11, etc. 2. *impart, communicate* something *one's own*, τινί τι *Act.Ap.*25.14, *Ep.Gal.*2.2, Plu.2.772d. 3. *remit, refer*, ἀ. περί τινος εἰς σύγκλητον *refer* the consideration of it to the Senate, Plb.21. 46.11, cf. App.*Samn.*4. II. *place differently, change about*, e.g. the men on a draught-board, ἀνὰ πάντα τίθεσθαι v.l. in Orac.ap.Hdt. 8.77. 2. *take back a move* at πεττοί, Pl.*Hipparch.*229e: hence metaph., *retract one's opinion*, X.*Mem.*1.2.44, cf. 2.4.4; freq. in Pl., ἀνατίθεσθαι ὅ τι δοκεῖ Pl.*Grg.*462a, cf. *Prt.*354e, *Chrm.*164d; οὐκ ἀνατίθεμαι μὴ οὐ.. *retract and say* this is not so, Id.*Phd.*87a; οὐκ ἀ. μὴ οὐ καλῶς λέγεσθαι Id.*Men.*89d; ἀνατιθέμενος τὸ διημαρτημένον Luc. *Pseudol.*29.

ἀνατίκτω, *bring forth again*, Ael.*NA*1.17, Hsch.

ἀνατῑμάω, *raise in price*, Hdt.9.33; ἀ. ἑαυτόν D.C.38.5:—Med., Poll.3.125.

ἀνα-τῐναγμός, ὁ, *shaking violently*, Lxx *Na.*2.10(11). **-τῐνάσσω**, fut. -ξω, *shake up and down, brandish*, θύρσον E.*Ba.*80 (lyr., tm.): also of the wind *shaking about* a sail, Id.*Or.*341 (tm.), cf. Gal.14. 638.

ἀνατιταίνω, *brandish*, τόξα Musae.17 (tm.), cf. Opp.*H.*2.90.

ἀνατιτήσαντες· πληρώσαντες, Hsch.

ἀνα-τιτραίνω, = sq., of trepanning, Aët.15.15. **-τιτράω**, *bore through, bore*, Dsc.1.66 (Pass.), Trypho *Fr.*112 V. (Pass.); part. ἀνατιτράς, -άντος, Gal.*UP*16.11, etc., Orib.46.11.10.

ἀνά-τλημα, ατος, τό, *sufferance*, Suid. **-τλῆναι**, inf. of ἀνέτλην, aor. with no pres.: fut. ἀνατλήσομαι: also aor. 1 ἀνέτλησα Orac. ap.Lact.*Inst.*4:—*bear up against, endure*, κήδε' ἀνέτλης Od.14.47; ὀϊζὺς ἣν ἀνέτλημεν 3.104; φάρμακ' ἀνέτλη, i.e. *resisted* the strength of the magic drink, 10.327; πολύθρηνον αἰῶνα.. ἀνατλᾶσα A.*Ag.*716; πατέρα.. οὐκ ἀνέτλατε S.*OC*239, etc.; πόλλ' ἀνατλάς Ar.*Pax*1035; τὴν εἱμαρμένην Pl.*Tht.*169c; τὰ προσήκοντα πάθη Id.*Grg.*525a: c. part., ἀνέτλην μογέουσα *IG*14.1960.

ἄνατλος· ἀκρατής, Hsch.

ἀνα-τμήγω, = ἀνατέμνω, aor. 2 part. Pass. ἀνατμηγείς Marcell.Sid. 85. **-τμητικός**, ή, όν, *fit for cutting up*, Sm.*Ps.*54(55).22.

ἀν-ατμίζομαι, Pass., *evaporate*, Democr.ap.Ath.*Epit.*lib. ii 89 (vol. i p. 281 Schw.).

ἀνατοιχάσαι· περὶ τοῖχον περιπατῆσαι, Hsch.

ἀνατοιχέω, (τοῖχος) *roll from side to side*, esp. of sailors in a storm: metaph., Arr.*Epict.*3.12.7; διατοιχέω is preferred by Phryn.139, Poll.1.114.

ἀνατοκισμός, ὁ, *compound interest*, Cic.*Att.*5.21.11, *CIL*10.3334. 30 (Puteoli, iii A. D.).

ἀνατολάς, Adv. *eastwards*, Lxx *Nu.*10.5 (dub.).

ἀνατολή, poet. ἀντ-, (ἀνατέλλω) *rising* above the horizon, of any heavenly body, e.g. the sun, freq. in pl., ἀντολαὶ ἠελίοιο Od.12. 4, E.*Ph.*504:—also in sg., ἀπ' ἀνατολᾶς ἀλίου ἄχρι δύσεως *IG*4.606; δύσεώς τε καὶ ἀνατολῆς ἡλίου καὶ τῶν ἄλλων ἄστρων Pl.*Plt.*269a, cf. *Lg.*807e; dist. from ἐπιτολή (q.v.), Gem.13.3. 2. = ἐπιτολή, A. *Pr.*457, *Ag.*7; περὶ Ὠρίωνος ἀνατολήν Arist.*Mete.*361ᵇ23; ἀπὸ Πλειάδος ἀ. Id.*HA*599ᵇ11. 3. *the quarter of sunrise, east*, opp. δύσις, freq. in pl., ἀπὸ ἡλίου ἀνατολέων Hdt.4.8; ἡλίου πρὸς ἀντολάς A.*Pr.*707; without ἡλίου, πρὸς ἀνατολάς Thphr.*HP*9.15.2, *Mon.Anc.Gr.*14.12; πρὸς τὰς ἀ. Plb.2.14.4; ἀπὸ ἀνατολῶν Lxx *Nu.*23.7, *Ev.Matt.*2.1, etc. b. the *ascendant*, i.e. the point where the eastern horizon cuts the zodiac, Ptol.*Tetr.*20. c. phase of new moon when 15° distant from sun, *Cat.Cod.Astr.*8(4).204, Paul.Al.*G.*3. 4. in pl., *sources* of a river, Plb.2.17.4. II. *growing*, of the teeth, Arist. *HA*501ᵇ28; of the white at the root of the nails, Poll.2.146: pl., ἀγρὸς ἀνατολὰς καὶ βλάστας ἔχει Ph.1.68, cf. Lxx *Je.*23.5, al.

ἀνατολικός, ή, όν, *eastern*, ἡμισφαίριον Str.2.3.2; στοά J.*AJ*20.9. 7, al.; θάλασσα Epicur.*Fr.*346b: Comp., Str.2.1.27, Marin.*Procl.* 36: Sup., Marcian.*Peripl.*1.6, al. 2. ἀνατολικοί, οἱ, = *Orientales*, title of a *numerus*, *PFlor.*278 v i (iii A. D.). 3. ἀ. χρόνος time occupied *in rising*, Gem.7.18, Ptol.*Alm.*2.11; ἀ. φάσεις Ptol.*Tetr.* 99; but ἀ. σελήνη *waxing moon*, Xenocr.ap.Orib.2.58.77, Ptol.*Tetr.* 116. II. Subst. ἀνατολικόν, τό, = κλύμενον, of a flower *opening at sunrise*, Ps.-Dsc.4.13.

ἀνατόλιος, poet. ἀντ-, η, ον, = foreg., ἄρουρα Nonn.*D.*25.98.

ἀνατολμάω, *regain one's courage*, Plu.*Luc.*31, *Ant.*50; f.l. in E. *Alc.*277.

ἀνα-τομή, ἡ, *dissection*, αἱ ἀ., title of a treatise freq. cited by Arist., as *HA*509ᵇ22, al., cf. Thphr.*HP*1.1.4; ἡ τἀνθρωπίνου σκήνους ἀ. Longin.32.5, cf. Chrysipp.*Stoic.*2.246 (pl.). II. in a logical sense, ἀ. καὶ διαιρέσεις Arist.*APo.*98ᵃ2. **-τομικός**, ή, όν, *relating to anatomy*, ἀ. ἐγχείρησις, title of work by Galen; *skilled in anatomy*, ἄνδρες Gal.4.555. Adv. -κῶς Id.18(2).927.

ἀνάτονος, ον, (ἀνατείνω) *stretching upwards*, Vitr.10.10.6.

ἄνᾱτος, ον, (ἄτη) *unharmed*, B.*Fr.*19 (cj.); Λοξίου κότῳ A.*Ag.* 1211; κακῶν ἄνατος *harmed by no* ills, S.*OC*786, where the Laur. Ms. ἄναιτος. II. Act., *not harming, harmless*, A.*Supp.*356, 359, 410. 2. *immune from punishment*, Ἀρχ.Ἐφ.1920.76 (Crete, vi/v B. C.). Adv. -τως *with impunity*, *IG*9(1).333 (Locr.). (Contr. fr. ἀνάατος, q. v.)

ἀνα-τρεπτέον, *one must overthrow, refute*, Luc.*Herm.*49, Gal.4.620. 2. *one must go back, return*, Orib.*Fr.*142. **-τρεπτικός**, ή, όν, *turning upside down, upsetting*, ἐπιτήδευμα..πόλεως ὥσπερ νεὼς ἀ. Pl.*R.*389d; στομάχου Dsc.2.70; of the pulse (dub. sens.), Gal. 8.928, cf. 644; οἱ ἀ. διάλογοι Plato's *refutative* dialogues, as 'Euthydemus' and 'Gorgias', Thrasyll.ap.D.L.3.59, cf. Hermog.*Meth.* 10. **-τρέπω**, poet. **ἀντρ-**, Aeol. aor. ὀνέτροπε Alc.*Supp.*25.7: pf. -τέτροφα S.*Tr.*1009, And.1.131, later -τέτρᾰφα Din.1.30 codd., v.l. in D.18.296, Aeschin.1.190, 3.158: aor. 2 Med. ἀνετράπετο in pass. sense, Il.6.64, 14.447 (only here in Hom.), Pl.*Cra.*395d, Theoc. 8.90: aor. 2 Pass., Alex.76.3, etc.:—*overturn, upset*, Act., Archil.56. 3, Alc. l. c.; τράπεζαν D.19.198, cf. Sch. ad eund.24.136; in Hom. ἀνετράπετο, = ὕπτιος ἔπεσεν, Il.6.64; ἀνατετραμμένος Ar.*Ra.*543; freq. of ships, Pl.*Lg.*906e, Arist.*Rh.*1398^{b}7, etc.; ἂν ἀναρραπῇ γὰρ πλοῖον Alex. l. c.; τὴν σωφροσύνην, τὸν βίον ἅπαντα And.1.131, cf. Plu. *Pomp.*46. b. Medic., *upset*, στόμαχον Gal.12.911: so abs., *create nausea*, Aristaenet.1.12. 2. *overthrow, ruin*, πρόρριζον ἀνατρέψαι τινά Hdt.1.32, cf. 8.62; μή..δαίμων..ἀντρέψῃ ποδὶ ὄλβον A.*Pers.* 163; λακπάτητον ἀ. χαράν S.*Ant.*1275; πλοῦτον And.1.131; πόλιν Ar.*V.*671; πολιτείαν, οἰκίαν, Pl.*Lg.*709a, *R.*471b; τὰ τῶν Ἑλλήνων D.18.143:—Pass., ἤρυξε πόλιν μἀνατραπῆναι A.*Th.*1082; ὁ βίος ἀνατετραμμένος ἂν εἴη Pl.*Grg.*481c, etc. 3. *upset* in argument, *refute*, Ar.*Nu.*901; ἀ. πρόβλημα Alex.Aphr.*in Top.*514.28. II. Pass., *to be upset, disheartened*, ἀνετράπετο φρένα λύπᾳ Theoc.8.90; ταῖς ψυχαῖς ἀ. Plb.21.25.8. 2. c. acc., *to be checked in, diverted from*, ὁρμήν J.*BJ*2.15.6; τὴν φιλαργυρίαν 2.14.6. 3. *to be turned back*, εἰς χώραν Herm.ap.Stob.1.49.68. 4. *to be made null and void*, Just. *Nov.*2.2 *Intr.* III. *stir up, arouse*, ἀνατέτροφας ὅ τι καὶ μύσῃ S.*Tr.* 1009:—Pass., of the sea in a storm, Arist.*HA*600^{a}4, etc. IV. intr. in Act., *slip, trip up*, Plu.2.631c; of a ship, *capsize*, D.Chr.34.32.

ἀνατρέφω, *bring up, cherish, educate*, A.*Eu.*523, *Ev.Luc.*4.16, al.; ἀ. τὸ φρόνημα *raise* the spirit, X.*Cyr.*5.2.34:—Med., ἀναθρέψασθαι υἱόν *have* him *educated*, Hdn.1.2.1; ἀ. λειμὼν κάλλεα Nic.*Fr.*74.58:—Pass., *grow up*, ἀνατραφῆναι ἐν.. Plu.*Cam.*34, etc.; τῇ Ἑλλάδι φωνῇ Ael.*NA*11.25; ἀνέτραφες in *AP*5.156 (Mel.) = ἀνετράφης. 2. *feed up*, opp. ἰσχναίνω, Hp.*Art.*33, 50: metaph., ἀ. μονῳδίαις Ar.*Ra.* 944:—Pass., ἀνατρέφεσθαι ἐκ νόσου *convalesce*, Hp.*VM*14; of fish after milting, Arist.*HA*608^{a}2.

ἀνατρέχω, fut. -δραμοῦμαι Luc.*Ind.*4, poet. 3 sg. -δράμεται *AP*9. 575 (Phil.): aor. -έδραμον (v. infr.): aor. subj. Med. ἀναδράμηται Hp.*Ep.*19 (*Hermes* 53.69):—*run back*, ὁ μὲν αὖθις ἀνέδραμε Il.16.813, cf. 11.354; ἀνά τ' ἔδραμ' ὀπίσσω 5.599; *return*, of the sea, Plu.2.915a; εἰς τὰς ἐξ ἀρχῆς τάξεις Plb.2.67.6; εἰς τὴν ἑαυτοῦ φύσιν Plu.*Pel.*31; εἰς τὴν προϋπάρχουσαν φιλίαν D.S.20.59; of property, *revert*, ἐπί τινα Just.*Nov.*7.4; in writing, *recur* to a point, ἐπί τι Plb.5.40.4: abs., ἀ. τοῖς χρόνοις 1.12.6, al. 2. c. acc., *retrace, traverse*, κῦδος ἀνέδραμον ὕμνῳ Pi.*O.*8.54, cf. Semon.10; *undo*, ἁμαρτίαν Men.15 D.; ἀ. τὴν τῆς φύσεως ἐλάττωσιν *make amends for*, Plu.2.2c, cf. Luc.*Ind.* 4. 3. *revert*, ἐπὶ τοὺς λόγους, τὴν ὕλην, Plot.5.8.1; *return* to source, of light, 4.5.7; *run back* to (logically), ἐπὶ τὴν κοινοτάτην αἰτίαν Phld. *D.*1.16, cf. Plot.6.1.30. 4. *have recourse to*, ἐπί.. Luc.*Abd.*11, al., Eun.*Hist.*p.251 D. II. *jump up and run, start up*, of men, ἀναδραμὼν ἔθεε Hdt.3.36; ἐκ τῆς κοίτης, ἐκ τοῦ θρόνου, Id.7.15, 212; πρὸς τὰ μετέωρα Th.3.89, cf. X.*HG*4.4.4. 2. of things, ἐγκέφαλος δὲ.. ἀνέδραμεν ἐξ ὠτειλῆς the brains *spurted up* from the wound, Il.17.297; σμώδιγγες..ἀνέδραμον weals *started up* under the blow, 23.717; *slip up*, Gal.18(1).829; *run* or *spread over*, τὸ πάθος ἀ. ἐπὶ τὴν χεῖρα Plu. 2.978c; ἔρευθος ἀ. Call.*Lav.Pall.*27. 3. *run up, shoot up*, of plants, ὁ δ' ἀνέδραμεν ἔρνεϊ ἶσος Il.18.56, cf. Hdt.8.55: hence, of cities and peoples, *shoot up, rise quickly*, ἀνά τ' ἔδραμον καὶ εὐθενήθησαν Hdt.1. 66, cf. 7.156; ἀ. εἰς ἀξίωμα Plu.*Publ.*21; ἀ. τοῖς βίοις, ταῖς ἐλπίσι, D.S.5.12, 18.20; ἀ. ἡ πολυτέλεια *increased*, Plu.*Mar.*34. 4. λίσσῃ δ' ἀναδέδρομε πέτρη the rock *ran sheer up*, Od.5.412. 5. metaph., *soar aloft*, of digression to a nobler theme, ἀνέδραμε πρὸς τὴν ἐν οὐρανῷ λύραν Anon. *in SE*40.23.

ἀνάτρεψις, εως, ἡ, *turning upside down*, Arist.*Mete.*368^{a}32. 2. *refutation*, Phld.*Sign.*11.

ἀνά-τρησις, εως, ἡ, (ἀνατιτράω) *perforation*, Ph.*Bel.*57.16; *trepanning*, Plu.*Cat.Ma.*9, Leonid.ap.Aët.15.12. 2. *hole bored*, Plu.2. 968b. **-τρητος**, ον, *bored through*, ἐμβάδες Suid.

ἀνατριαινόω, (τρίαινα) *shake as with a trident*, Amphis 14.8.

ἀνατριακοσιολόγιστος, ον, *reckoned at* 300 *a head*, *Michel* 731.20 (Ilium).

ἀνα-τρῑβή, ἡ, *education*, τὰ τῆς ἀ., opp. τὰ τοῦ βίου, Ps.-Ptol.*Centil.* 224. **-τρίβω** [ῑ], *rub, chafe*, τὸν ὦμον Hp.*Art.*9:—Med., Id.*Vict.* 3.83; *massage oneself*, Aristid.*Or.*47(23).18, cf. 50, al.:—Pass., sens. obsc., Ar.*Ach.*1149. 2. *rub clean*, κύνας X.*Cyn.*6.26. 3. Med., ἐλαίῳ ὕδωρ συμμείξας ἀ. *rub oneself down*, Arist.*Pr.*881^{a}5. 4. Pass., *to be worn away*, Hdt.3.113.

ἀνατρίζω, *chirp aloud*, of cranes, Q.S.13.107 (al. -τρύζω).

ἀνάτριμμα, ατος, τό, = -τριψις, Aët.8.63.

ἀνατριπλόω, *repeat a third time*, Syr.*in Metaph.*61.8 (Pass.).

ἀνα-τριπτέον, *one must chafe*, Archig.ap.Orib.44.26.9. **-τριπτος**, ον, *rubbed up*: ἀ. ἱμάτια cloths *with rough, raised pile*, like plush or velvet, Dsc.3.33.

ἀνα-τριχόομαι, Pass., *have one's hair grow again*, Suid. **-τρῐχος**, ον, (θρίξ) *with hair bristling backwards*, Porph.ap.Eus.*PE*3. 13. **-τριχοφυέω**, *grow fresh hair*, Cleopatra ap.Gal.12.405.

ἀνάτριψις, εως, ἡ, *chafing, friction*, Hp.*Art.*9, Gal.6.92.

ἀνατροπ-εύς, έως, ὁ, *overturner, destroyer*, τοῦ οἴκου Antipho 2.2.2; τῆς νεότητος Plu.2.5b; *subverter*, τῶν ἐν ἀνθρώποις νομιζομένων D.Chr. 37.32. **-ή**, ἡ, *capsizing*, [τοῦ πλοίου] Arist.*Metaph.*1013^{b}14. 2. *overthrow, ruin*, ἀνατροπαὶ δωμάτων, οἴκων, A.*Eu.*355, Pl.*Prt.*325c; ἀ. βίων Clearch.10. 3. *pouring out*, of drink, Lxx *Ha.*2.15. 4. *upsetting*, στομάχου Sor.1.27, Asclep.Jun.ap.Gal.13.140; ἀ. ναυτιώδεις Plu.2.442f. 5. *refutation*, Str.2.1.22, Hermog.*Prog.*5. 6. *annulment*, Just.*Nov.*2.2 *Intr.*; *undoing*, ἐπ' -ῇ τῆς νοήσεως τοῦ θεοῦ Phld.*D.*3.7. 7. *raising* of body, Cass.Fel.82. **-ιάζω**, *turn back*, *AB*312. **-ος**, ον, dub. l. in *App.Anth.*4.104.15.

ἀνατροφ-εύς, έως, ὁ, *nurturer*, Ps.-Callisth.1.13. **-ή**, ἡ, *education*, Aphth.*Prog.*8; *rearing, nurture*, D.H.*Rh.*5.3, Plu.2.608c, Arr.*Cyn.* 29, Artem.1.16, etc. II. *feeding, diet*, ἡ ἐκ ζῴων ἀ. Porph.*Abst.*3. 17. III. of plants and trees, *cultivation*, *Gp.*4.12.11, 9.14.5.

ἀνατροχ-άζω, = ἀνατρέχω, κοχλιοειδῶς Ph.Byz.*Mir.*1.4. **-ασμός**, ὁ, *running backwards*, Antyll.ap.Orib.6.22.8.

ἀνατρῠγάω, *glean grapes off again*, τοὺς ἀμπελῶνας Ph.2.390.

ἀνατρύζω, v. ἀνατρίζω.

ἀναττικός, όν, *alien to the Attic dialect*, Phryn.ap.St.Byz. s.v. Ἀθῆναι.

ἀνατῠλίσσω, Att. -ττω, *unroll*, βιβλία Luc.*Ind.*16: metaph., ἀ. τοὺς λόγους πρὸς ἑαυτόν Id.*Nigr.*7.

ἀνατυπ-όω, *describe, represent*, Philostr.*VA*1.19, cf. *Her.*2.19 (Pass.):—Med., *form an image of* a thing, *imagine*, Plu.2.329b, 331d; *represent* in writing, εἰς ἐπιστολάς Philostr.*VA*1.32. II. *remodel, transform*, τὴν ἀνθρωπίνην περὶ τοῦ δαιμονίου δόξαν D.Chr. 12.26, cf. Antim.81. **-τομαι**, Med., strengthd. for τύπτω, τὴν κεφαλήν J.*AJ*17.7.1. **-ωμα**, ατος, τό, *mental image*, *Stoic.*1. 214. **-ωσις**, εως, ἡ, = τύπωσις, Hsch. **-ωτικός**, ή, όν, *representing*, Simp.*in Epict.* p.20 D.

ἀνατυρβάζω, *stir up, confound*, Ar.*Eq.*310.

ἀναύγητος, ον, *rayless, sunless*, Ἅιδης A.*Pr.*1028.

ἀναυδάω, *uplift the voice*, *PMag.Par.*1.2532.

ἀναυδ-ής, ές, *speechless*, Epicr.11.20. II. = sq., Hsch. **-ητος**, Dor. **-ᾱτος**, ον, *not to be spoken, unutterable*: hence, *horrible*, ἀναυδάτῳ μένει A.*Th.*897 (lyr.); ἄφατον ἀναύδητον λόγον E.*Ion* 783. 2. *unspoken, impossible*, οὐδὲν ἀναύδατον φατίσαιμ' ἄν S.*Aj.*715 (lyr.). II. *speechless*, Id.*Tr.*968 (cj.). **-ία**, ἡ, *speechlessness*, Hp.*Coac.*353, *Mul.*2.126; *lethargy*, Antigen.ap.Cael.Aur.*AP*2.10. **-ος**, ον, *speechless*, Od.5.456, 10.378, Hes.*Th.*797, etc.; *silent*, ἄ. ἄγγελος, of dust, A.*Th.*82 (lyr.), etc.:—properly, *unable to articulate*, whereas ἄφωνος is *voiceless*, Hp.*Epid.*3.17.γ', but of fishes, A.*Pers.*577; *without speaking*, S.*OC*1274, 1404, Plu.*Pomp.*74, etc. Adv. **-δως** Hp. *Prorrh.*1.90, J.*AJ*16.11.4. 2. *preventing speech, silencing*, χαλινῶν ἄ. μένος A.*Ag.*238 (lyr.). II. *unspeakable, horrible*, ἔργον S. *Aj.*947.

ἀναυλεί, Adv., (ναῦλον) *without passage-money*, Suid.

ἄναυλος (A), ον, *without the flute*, κῶμος -ότατος a procession *unaccompanied by flutes*, i.e. *joyless*, E.*Ph.*791; ἔρωτες Plu.2.406a: neut. pl. as Adv., ἄναυλα ὀρχεῖσθαι Babr.9.9; θύειν Plu.2.277f. 2. *unmusical*, μέλη βοῶν ἄναυλα (as Bgk. for ἄναυδα) S.*Fr.*699. II. *unskilled in flute-playing*, Luc.*Halc.*7.

ἄναυλος (B), ον, (αὐλίον) *weary of its stall*, χοῖρος dub. in Herod. 8.7.

ἀναυλόχητος, ον, *not brought to haven*, Lyc.745.

ἀναυμάχ-ητος, ον, *without sea-fight*, ὄλεθρος ἀ. loss *of a fleet without striking a blow*, Lys.ap.D.H.*Lys.*14. **-ίου**, sc. γραφή, *indictment* of a trierarch *for keeping his ship out of action*, ἀ. ὀφλεῖν And. 1.74.

ἀναυξ-άνω, *increase*, in Pass., *PBaden* 39 iii 16 (ii A. D.). **-ής**, ές, *not increasing*, Thphr.*CP*4.6.3. II. intr., *not waxing* or *growing*, Hp.*Art.*53, *Mochl.*24, al., Arist.*HA*569^{a}30, *Cael.*270^{a}13. **-ησία**, ἡ, Gramm., *omission of the augment*, Greg.Cor.180. **-ητος**, ον, = ἀναυξής, Arist.*Cael.*270^{a}25, Sor.1.47 (Comp.), Aq.*Je.*22.30; μορφαὶ ἀ. πυρός dub. l. in Theodect.17. 2. *without augment*, Eust.19.29. Adv. **-τως** Greg.Cor.180. **-ία**, Ion. **-ίη**, ἡ, *defect in growth*, Hp.*Art.*52 (v. l. ἀναυξήσιος); written **-εια** in Ath.Med.ap.Orib.*Inc.* 21.1. **-ος**, ον, = ἀναυξής I, Plu.2.981f.

ἄναυος, ον, etym. of Att. ἄνεως, A.D.*Adv.*145.4, cf. Eust.387.44.

ἄναυρος, ον, *without air, windless, still*, Hsch.

Ἄναυρος, ὁ, river in Thessaly, Hes.*Sc.*477, etc. II. as Appellat., ἄναυρος, ὁ, *mountain-torrent*, Mosch.2.31, Nic.*Al.*235, Lyc.1424, *IG* 14.1089, etc. (Orig. pr. n., cf. Ἀχελῷος of any river.)

ἄναυς, gen. ἄνᾱος, ὁ, ἡ, only A.*Pers.*680 in nom. pl., νᾶες ἄναες ships *that are ships no more*.

ἄ-ναυτα· ἠπειρωτικά, Hsch. II. ἄν-αυτα· παραχρῆμα (Tarent.), Id. (cf. πάραυτα).

ἀναϋτέω [ῠ], *shout aloud*, Opp.*C.*4.301: c. acc., κρυπτὸν ἀνηΰτησεν ἔπος Nonn.*D.*10.288, cf. Coluth.85.

ἀναυτούργητος, ον, *not to be cultivated* by the lessor *in person*, *PTeb.*378.29 (iii A. D.).

ἀναύχην, ενος, ὁ, ἡ, *without neck* or *throat*, Emp.57.

ἀναύω (αὔω B), = ἀναϋτέω, aor. ἀνήυσα, Dor. ἀνάυσα Theoc.4.37, A.R.4.75.

ἀναφαία· ἡ θερμοπότις παρὰ Κρησίν, Ath.11.783f.

ἀναφαίνω, poet. **ἀμφ-**: fut. -φᾰνῶ, but -φανῶ E.*Ba.*528 codd. (-φαίνω Herm.): aor. ἀνέφηνα, Hellenistic -έφᾱνα: pf. -πέφηνα late, Ps.-Luc.*Philopatr.*3:—*cause to give light, make to blaze up*, ξύλα, δαΐδας Od.18.310. 2. *bring to light, produce*, ὄφιας Hdt.4.

105. b. *show forth, make known, display,* θεοπροπίας, ἀρετήν, ἐπεσβολίας, Il.1.87, 20.411, Od.4.159; πραπίδων καρπόν Pi.*Fr.*211; κἀνέφηνεν οὐ δεδειγμένα S.*Fr.*432.7; ἀ. θυσίας E.*IT*466; ὀργάν Id.*Ba.* 538; ἄστρα X.*Mem.*4.3.4; ἡμέρᾳ καὶ ἡλίῳ.. χάριν οἶδα ὅτι μοι Κλεινίαν ἀ. Id.*Smp.*4.12; rarely of sound, βοὰν ἀμφ. *send forth a loud* cry, A. *Supp.*829; ἀ. μελέων νόμους Ar.*Av.*745:—in Med., νίκαν ἀνεφάνατο Pi.*I.*4(3).71. 3. *proclaim, declare,* βασιλέα ἀ. τινά Id.*P.*4.62; νικάσαις ἀνέφανε Κυράναν ib.9.73, cf. *N.*9.12: c. part., τοὺς πολίτας ἀγαθοὺς ὄντας ἀ. Pl.*Criti.*108c: c. inf., ἀναφαίνω σε τόδε.. ὀνομάζειν I *proclaim that* they call thee by this name, E.*Ba.*528:—Med., in Dor. form ἀμφ–, *adopt* as one's son, *Leg.Gort.*10.34, al. b. of things, *appoint, institute,* ὃς τελετὰς ἀνέφηνε καὶ ὄργια *IG*3.713, cf. *Marm.Par.*28; νῆσον ἀ. τινὶ οἰκεῖν Philostr.*Her.*19.16. 4. ἀναφάναντες τὴν Κύπρον *having sighted..*, *Act.Ap.*21.3. II. Pass., fut. ἀναφᾰνήσομαι Ar.*Eq.*950, Pl.*Prm.*132a, al.; but also –φανοῦμαι Id.*Plt.*289c: pf. ἀναπέφασμαι, but –πέφηνα Hdt. (v. infr.), etc.: aor. ἀνεφάνην Ar.*V.*124:—*to be shown forth, appear plainly,* ἀναφαίνεται ἀστήρ Il.11.62; ἀ. αἰπὺς ὄλεθρος ib.174; τῇ δεκάτῃ.. ἀνεφαίνετο πατρὶς ἄρουρα Od.10.29; τὸ Δέλτα ἐστὶ νεωστὶ ἀναπεφηνός Hdt.2.15, cf. S.*OC*1222 (lyr.), etc.; ἀ. ὁ βλάπτων A.*Ch.*328. b. *reappear,* Hdt.4.195; of rivers which flow underground, Id.6.76, 7.30; simply, *spring up,* ib.198. 2. ἀναφανῆναι μούναρχος *to be declared* king, Id.3.82; στρατηγὸς ἀ. Pl.*Ion* 541e; κλέπτης τις ὁ δίκαιος ..ἀναπέφανται *proved to be..*, Id.*R.*334a, cf. *Smp.*185a; ἀ. λογογράφος ἐκ τριηράρχου from a sea-captain *to come out* a romancer, Aeschin. 3.173:—also c. part., ἀναπέφανται ὢν ἀγαθός Pl.*R.*350c; ἀναφαίνεσθαι ἔχων, σεσωσμένοι, *to be seen* or *found to* have, *to be plainly* in safety, etc., Id.*Sph.*233c, X.*Cyr.*3.2.15, etc. III. the Act. intr. in later Greek, ἀνέφαινεν ἕσπερος Musae.111 (v.l.), cf. Hld.5.22:—ἀναφῆναι is prob. f.l. for ἀναφανῆναι in Hdt.1.165.

ἀναφαίρετος, ον, *not to be taken away,* Men.*Mon.*2, D.H.8.74, D. Chr.31.22; χάρις *POxy.*273.15 (i A.D.); ὠφέλεια Just.*Nov.*68*Pr.*; *inseparable,* opp. *accidental, Stoic.*2.214 (? Diog.Bab.); *not diminished by subtraction, Theol.Ar.*30. Adv. –ως *PFlor.*47a4 (iii A.D.), Just. *Nov.*2.3*Intr.*

ἀναφάλακρος, ον, *forehead-bald, PPetr.*3p.9, Procl.*Par.Ptol.*203, *BGU*998, al.

ἀναφαλαντ-ιαῖος, = foreg., dub. in Antioch.Astr. in *Cat.Cod.Astr.* 7.112.8. **–ίας**, ου, ὁ, = foreg., Luc.*Tim.*47, al., *Cat.Cod.Astr.*8(2). 58.27, etc.:—also **–ανθίας**, Phryn.*PS*p.124B. (cod.). **–ίασις**, εως, ἡ, *forehead-baldness,* Arist.*HA*518ᵃ28. **–ος**, ον, *forehead-bald,* Lxx *Le.*13.41, freq. in Pap., *PPar.*5.1.5 (ii B.C.), etc.:—**–ανθος**, *PPetr.*1p.54 (iii B.C.), etc. **–ωμα**, ατος, τό, *forehead-baldness,* Lxx *Le.*13.42.

ἀναφαν-δά, Adv. *visibly, openly, before the eyes of all,* opp. κρύβδην, Od.3.221, 11.455: as neut. Adj., A.R.4.84. **–δόν**, Adv. = foreg., Il.16.178, Hdt.2.35,46, Pl.*Prt.*348e, etc.: poet. **ἀμφανδόν** Pi.*P.*9.41. **–σις**, εως, ἡ, *appearance,* Anon.in Ptol.*Tetr.*5. II. v. ἄμφανσις.

ἀναφέγγει, gloss on ἀναμαιμάει, Hsch.

ἀναφέρω, poet. **ἀμφ–**, fut. ἀνοίσω: aor. ἀνήνεγκα, Ion. ἀνήνεικα, also inf. ἀνοῖσαι Hdt.1.157: I. *bring, carry up,* [Κέρβερον] ἐξ Ἀΐδαο Od.11.625; ἐκ τῆς ἰλύος ψῆγμα ἀ. χρυσοῦ Hdt.4.195, cf. 3.102 (as v.l. for –φορέω); ἀ. τινὰ εἰς Ὄλυμπον, εἰς θεούς, X.*Smp.*8.30 (Pass.), Plu. *Rom.*28, etc.; in histor. writers, *carry up the country,* esp. into Central Asia, Hdt.6.30; *raise up,* εἰς τὸ ἄνω Hp.*Art.*37; ἀ. πόδα *lift* it, E.*Ph.*1410:—Med., *carry up* to a place of safety, *take with one,* Hdt.3.148; *remove one's goods,* 8.32,36, etc. b. esp. *carry up to the Acropolis, put by,* of treasure, And.3.7, X.*Vect.*5.12, Aeschin.2.174, etc. 2. *bring up, pour forth,* of tears, ἑτοιμότερα γέλωτος ἀ. λίβη A.*Ch.*447; αἵματος πλῆθος ἀ. *spit up,* Plu.*Cleom.*15; ἀ. φωνάς, στεναγμούς, Id.2.433c, *Alex.*52:—Med., ἀνενείκασθαι, abs., *fetch up a deep-drawn breath, heave a deep sigh,* μνησάμενος δ' ἁδινῶς ἀνενείκατο Il.19.314; ἀνενεικάμενόν τε καὶ ἀναστενάξαντα Hdt.1.86 (where others, *having recovered himself, come to himself,* v. infr. II. 7): in Alex. Poets, *utter,* ἀνενείκατο μῦθον, φωνήν, A.R.3.463,635. 3. *uphold, take upon one,* ἄχθος A.*Ch.*841; κινδύνους Th.3.38; διαβολάς, πόλεμον, etc., Plb.1.36.3, 4.45.9, etc.; πολλῶν ἀ. ἁμαρτίας Lxx *Is.* 53.12, *Ep.Heb.*9.28. 4. *offer* in sacrifice, ib.7.27, 13.15, etc.: abs., *make expiation* or *compensation, GDI*3537, al. (Cnidus). 5. *raise up, yield,* ἀρχαῖαι ἀρεταὶ ἀμφέροντ' ἀνδρῶν σθένος Pi.*N.*11. 38. 6. intr., *lead up,* of a road, ἁμαξιτὸς εἰς τὸν Πειραιᾶ ἀ. X.*HG* 2.4.10, cf. Plb.8.29.1, *Inscr.Prien.*37.161. II. *bring* or *carry back,* εἰς τοὔπισθεν ἀ. πόδα E.*Ph.*1410: freq. in Prose, ἀ. τὰς κώπας *recover* the oars (after pulling them through the water), Th.2.84; ἡ εἰρεσία ἀναφέρεται Plu.*Demetr.*53, *Ant.*26. 2. *bring back* tidings, *report,* παρά τινα Hdt.1.47; ἔς τινα Id.1.91, Th.5.28, etc.; τὰ ἐκ τῆς ἐκκλησίας ἀνενεγκόντες Decr.ap.D.18.75:—Pass., Hdt.1.141, al. 3. *bring back from exile,* Th.5.16. 4. *carry back, trace* one's family to an ancestor, τὸ Ἡρακλέους γένος εἰς Περσέα ἀναφέρεται Pl.*Alc.*1. 120e; without γένος, ἀ. εἰς Ἡρακλέα Id.*Tht.*175a. 5. *refer* a matter to another, βουλεύματα ἐς τὸ κοινόν Hdt.3.80; ἐς ἀφανὲς τὸν μῦθον ἀ. Id.2.23; ἁμαρτίαν εἴς τινα ἀ. *ascribe* E.*Or.*76, *Ba.*29, etc.; τῆς κηλῖδος εἰς ὑμᾶς –ομένης Antipho 3.3.11; τὴν αἰτίαν εἴς τινα Lys.22.8; rarely ἀ. τί τινι E.*Or.*432, Lys.12.81; τι ἐπί τινα D.18.224, Aeschin. 3.215; τι ἐπί τι Pl.*Phd.*76d; τι πρός τι Arist.*EN*1101ᵇ19 (Pass.), al.; ποῖ δίκην ἀνοίσομεν; to whom *shall* we *refer* the judgement? E. *Ion* 253; τὴν ἀπόδοσιν εἴς τινα D.34.46:—Pass., *to be attributed* (of authorship), εἰς Μητρόδωρον Phld.*Herc.*1005.8; *to be traced to, derived from,* ἐπί τι ib.1251.11. 6. Pass., *refer to,* of a statement, πρός τι Ps.-Alex.Aphr.*in SE*127.8. b. without acc., ἀ. εἴς τινα *refer* or *appeal* to another, *make reference* to him, Hdt.3.71, Pl.*Ap.*20e; ἔς τινα περί τινος Hdt.1.157, 7.149; ἀ. πρός τι *refer* to something as to a standard, Hp.*VM*9; ἐκεῖσε ἀ. Pl.*R.*484c, cf. *Phdr.*237d. c. *report,* μέτρα καὶ γειτνίας καὶ ἀξίας *PTeb.*14.11 (ii B.C.), etc.:—Pass., ib.10.3 (ii B.C.): abs., *make a report,* τινί *PRyl.*233.8 (ii A.D.), *PFay.* 129.8 (iii A.D.). 7. *bring back, restore,* πόλιν ἐκ πονήρων πραγμάτων Th.8.97; ἀ. ἑαυτόν Ael.*NA*13.12:—Pass., *come to oneself, recover,* μόγις δὴ τότε ἀνενειχθεὶς εἶπε (v. supr. I. 2) Hdt.1.116; ἄφωνος ἐγένετο, ἔπειτα πάλιν ἀνηνέχθη Theopomp.Com.66:—so, b. intr. in Act., *come to oneself, recover,* τῷ πόματι ἀνέφερον (sc. ἑαυτούς) Hdt.3.22, cf. Hp.*Aph.*2.43, D.16.31; ἐκ τραύματος D.H.4.67; ἐξ ὕπνων Plu. *Cam.*23; ἀνέφερέ τις ἐλπὶς ἀμυδρά *revived,* Id.*Alc.*38; ἐκ τοσούτων κυμάτων ἀνενεγκών Eun.*Hist.*p.227D. 8. *bring into account,* εἰς τὸ κοινόν D.41.8, cf. 11, Philonid.1D.; πρὸς ἣν [ἀρχὴν] αἱ πρόσοδοι ἀναφέρονται Arist.*Pol.*1321ᵇ32. 9. *pay over,* εἰς τὸ βασιλικόν *PHib.*50.2, cf. 42.5. 10. *call to mind, consider,* Pl.*Lg.*829e: also c. gen., App.*Pun.*93,112. 11. *repeat,* Pl.*Ti.*26a. 12. *recall a likeness,* ἀ. πρὸς ἀνδριάντα τὴν ὁμοιότητα τῆς ἰδέας Plu.*Brut.*1, cf. 2.53d.

ἀνα-φεύγω, *flee up,* X.*An.*6.4.24, Plu.*Crass.*29, al.: c. acc., *fly to,* Philostr.*VA*1.24. 2. *escape,* X.*HG*6.5.40, cf. 2.3.50: metaph., *retreat,* εἰς τὴν ἀνείδεον φύσιν Plot.6.7.28. 3. of a rumour, *to be lost* in tracing, Plu.*Aem.*25. **–φευκτικός**, ή, όν, *given to flight,* Str.15.1.29. **–φευξις**, εως, ἡ, *fleeing away,* D.C.75.6.

ἀναφήριτον· ἄμαχον, Hsch.

ἀναφής, ές, (ἁφή) *impalpable,* Pl.*Phdr.*247c, Epicur.*Ep.*1 p.6 U., Plu.2.721c, etc.; ἀρεταί Ph.1.689. Adv. –φῶς Iamb.*Myst.*3.31, 5.4, Procl.*in Cra.*p.37 P., Dam.*Pr.*339. II. of wine, *tasteless, insipid,* Plu.2.650b (al. ἀβαφής).

ἀνα-φθέγγομαι, *call out aloud,* Ph.1.74, al., Plu.*Thes.*24, *Caes.*46, etc.: c. acc., Plb.18.5.6; λόγιον Ph.2.177. **–φθεγμα**, ατος, τό, *utterance,* Phld.*D.*3.14 (pl.), Ph.1.661. **–φθεγξις**, εως, ἡ, *mode of utterance,* λύπη καὶ φόβος ἰδίας ἀναφθέγξεις ἔχουσιν ib.618, cf. Diog. Oen.10.

ἀναφθείρομαι, Pass., κατὰ τί δεῦρ' ἀνεφθάρης; *by what ill luck came* you hither? Ar.*Av.*916, cf. Cratin.13D.; cf. φθείρω. II. *to be frustrated, PTeb.*24.32.

ἀναφλᾶ· λάχανον φέρει ἄνθος, ὡς ἡ μαλάχη καὶ τὸ ἄνηθον, Hsch.

ἀνα-φλασμός, ὁ, *masturbation,* Eup.61. **–φλάω**, *masturbari,* Luc.*Peregr.*17: pf. part. Pass. –πεφλασμένος Ar.*Lys.*1099

ἀναφλεγμαίνω, *inflame,* Plu.*Ant.*82, cf. Gal.18(1).73.

ἀνα-φλέγω, *light up, rekindle,* E.*Tr.*320 (lyr.). II. *inflame,* ἐπιθυμίαν Ph.2.48; ἔρωτα Plu.*Alc.*17:—Pass., *to be inflamed with anger,* Pl.*Ep.*349a; ἐξ ὑποψίας Conon 23.1; *to be inflamed,* Ἔρωτος τραῦμα *AP*12.80 (Mel.); *to be excited,* ὑπ' ὀργῆς Plu.2.798f; ὑπὸ λιμοῦ Ael.*NA*15.2; ἀ. τὴν ψυχήν Plu.*Dio*4; δίψος ἀναφλέγεται Id.*Ant.*47, etc.; διανοίας ὑπὸ φιλοτιμίας ἀναφλεγομένης Jul.*Or.*2.83c. **–φλεξις**, εως, ἡ, *lighting up,* Plu.*Lys.*12.

ἀναφλογίζω, = ἀναφλέγω, Call.*Epigr.inc.*2, *AP*12.127 (Mel.).

ἀναφλύω, *bubble, boil up,* ἀνὰ δ' ἔφλυε καλὰ ῥέεθρα Il.21.361: also in Prose, *PHolm.*25.26.

ἀναφοβέω, *frighten away,* Ar.*V.*670.

ἀναφοιβάσας· ἀνακαθάρας, Hsch.

ἀναφοινίσσω, in Pass., *blush, redden,* Lib.*Ep.*225.

ἀναφοιτάω, *go back,* Nic.*Th.*138.

ἀναφορ-ά, ἡ, (ἀναφέρομαι) *coming up, rising,* ἀ. ποιεῖσθαι *rise,* Arist.*HA*622ᵇ7; of vapours or exhalations, *Placit.*3.7.4, *Theol.Ar.* 31, cf. Orib.9.16.3, etc. 2. Astron., *ascent* of a sign measured in degrees of the equator, Ptol.*Tetr.*134. b. Astrol., = ἐπαναφορά, τόπος next to a κέντρον, Vett.Val.19.18. c. *ascendant, Cat.Cod.Astr.*8(3).100; opp. ἀπόκλιμα, Serapion in *Cat.Cod.Astr.* 1.99, S.E.*M.*5.20, etc. d. *rising* of a sign, Ach.Tat.*Intr.Arat.* 39. II. (ἀναφέρω) *carrying back, reference* of a thing *to a standard,* διὰ τὸ γίνεσθαι ἐπαίνους δι' ἀναφορᾶς Arist.*EN*1101ᵇ20; in Law, *recourse,* ἐκείνοις εἶναι εἰς τοὺς ἔχοντας ἀναφοράν D.24.13: abs., Thphr. *Char.*8.5 (pl.), *IG*5(1).1390.111 (Andania, i B.C.); ἡ ἀ. ἡ ἀνοίσω πρός τι Arist.*Cat.*5ᵇ20, al.; ἀ. ἔχειν πρός or ἐπί τι to be *referable* to.., Epicur. *Fr.*409, Plb.4.28.3, Plu.2.290e, al.; ἀ. τινος γίγνεται πρός or ἐπί τι, Plb.1.3.4, Plu.2.1071a; ἐπ' ἀναφορᾷ τῇ πρὸς τὸν δῆμον *BCH*46.312 (Teos); ἀ. ἔχειν ἐπί τι, of writings, *refer to,* Alex.Aphr.*in Mete.*4.1; τούτων εἰς Κυναίγειρον ποιήσασθαι τὴν ἀναφοράν *assign to, give credit for ..*, Polem.*Call.*23. 2. *way of retreat,* ὑπέλιπε ἑαυτῷ ἀναφοράν D.18. 219; νῦν δὲ αὐτοῖς μὲν κατέλιπον τὴν εἰς τὸ ἀφανὲς ἀναφοράν Aeschin. 2.104, cf. Plb.15.8.13, etc. 3. *means of repairing* a fault, defeat, etc., ἀλλ' ἔστιν ἡμῖν ἀ. τῆς ξυμφορᾶς E.*Or.*414; ἀ. ἁμαρτήματος ἔχειν *way to atone for..*, Plu.*Phoc.*2; ἀ. ἔχειν *means of recovery,* Id.*Fab.* 14. 4. *offering,* Lxx *Ps.*50(51).21; ἡ ἀ. τοῦ πνεύματος τοῦ λεκτικοῦ *PMag.Par.*2.281. 5. *report, PLond.*1.17.34 (ii B.C.), etc. 6. *petition, PRyl.*119.28 (i A.D.). 7. *payment on account, instalment, OGI*225 (Milet.), *PEleph.*14.26 (iii B.C.), *PRev.Laws*16.10 (iii B.C.), etc. 8. Rhet., *repetition* of a word, Longin.20.1, Demetr.*Eloc.* 141. 9. *office of ἀναφορεύς,* Lxx *Nu.*4.6,10. 10. Medic., = ἀνάδοσις, opp. πέψις, Aret.*SD*2.7. III. *ceiling* of a wine-press, *Gp.*6.1.3. **–εύς**, ὁ, *bearer, bearing-pole,* Lxx *Ex.*25.12(13) sq., al. II. = τελαμών, Eust.243.31. **–έω**, = ἀναφέρω I, but used in a frequentat. sense, Hdt.3.102,111, Th.4.115. **–ητικός**, ή, όν, = sq. II, of consumption with empyema, Cael.Aur.*TP*2.18. **–ικός**, ή, όν, *standing in relation*: in Gramm., *relative.* Adv. –κῶς *relatively,* A.D.*Pron.*5.20, al., D.T.636.12; *with a reference,* Stob.2.6.6, Gal.

18(1).504. II. Medic., *bringing up blood, phlegm*, Dsc.2.171, cf. *Eup.*2.39, Androm.ap.Gal.13.31. III. ἀναφορικόν, τό, treatise by Hypsicles *on the ascension* of stars; ἀ. πραγματεῖαι Ptol.*Alm.* 8.6. -ιον, τό, Dim. of ἀναφορά, *petition, proposal*, etc., *BGU* 1123.3, *POxy.*294.13, etc.

ἀναφορμίζομαι, *play a prelude*, Apollon.*Lex.* s. v. ἀνεβάλλετο.

ἀνάφορον, τό, = ἀναφορεύς 1, Ar.*Ra.*8, *Ec.*833, *Fr.*559, cf. Phryn. *PS*p.15 B.

ἀναφορύσσω, Ion. for ἀναφυράω, Hp.*Mul.*1.53, 2.205, al.

ἀναφράζω, *relate, describe*, Eun.*Hist.*p.223 D.; Med., *to be aware of*, οὐλὴν ἀμφράσσαιτο Od.19.391.

ἀναφράσσω or **-φράγνῡμι**, *barricade again, block up*, τὰς παρόδους dub. l. in Str.4.3.5, cf. J.*AJ*15.7.10:—Pass., Lxx *Ne.*4.7; λιμένες ἀνεφράγνυντο Them.*Or.*7.91d. II. *remove barriers*, Hsch.

ἀναφρίζω, *cover with foam*, Phryn.*PS*p.46 B.

ἀναφρίσσω, *bristle up*, ἀκάνθαις *with..*, Opp.*H.*4.599; of hair, Poll.2.25.

ἀναφροδῑ-σία, ἡ, *want of power to inspire love, lack of charm*, Philostr.*VA*8.7, Jul.*Mis.*367b. II. *insensibility to love*, Gell. 19.9.9. -τος, ον, *without* Ἀφροδίτη, *not enjoying her favours*, Plu. 2.751e, etc.; ἀ. εἰς τὰ ἐρωτικά *unlucky* in.., Luc.*DDeor.*15.2; *loveless*, μίξεις D.Chr.7.133. 2. *insensible to love*, Plu.2.57d, Jul.*Mis.* 347c. 3. *without charms*, Plu.*Ant.*4, Gell.1.5.3, etc.

ἀνα-φρονέω, *come back to one's senses*, X.*An.*4.8.21, D.C.60.14; ἀναφρονέων· ἀναλογιζόμενος, Hsch. **-φροντίζω**, *think over*, c. inf., ἀ. γάμον σχεθέμεν *meditate how* to get, Pi.*O.*1.69.

ἄναφρος, ον, *without froth*, διαχωρήματα Hp.*Hum.*4; αἷμα Aret. *SA*2.2.

ἀναφρύγω [ῠ], aor. 2 inf. Pass. -φρυγῆναι, *dry up*, Lyd.*Ost.*14.

ἀναφῠγή, ἡ, (ἀναφεύγω) *escape, release from*, ἀναφυγὰς κακῶν A.*Ch.* 943. II. *place of retreat*, Plu.*Aem.*16. III. *withdrawal, retraction*, μήτρας Sor.2.26.

ἀναφύησις, εως, ἡ, *springing up, growth*, Sor.1.87.

ἀναφῠλάσσω, *guard*, prob. in *Epic.Alex.Adesp.*9.2.19.

ἀνάφυξις, εως, ἡ, = ἀναφυγή, ἀ. κακῶν Pl.*Lg.*713e.

ἀνα-φῡράω, *mix up well*, Hp.*Mul.*2.157, Thphr.*Od.*25; τέφραν μετ' οἴνου ἀ. *IG*14.966.8. **-φύρω** [ῡ], *mix up, confound*, τινάς τισι Them.*Or.*21.260c:—Pass., ἀναμὶξ ἦν πάντα ὁμοίως ἀναπεφυρμένα Hdt.1.103, cf. Epicur.*Fr.*250, Metrod.1. 2. *defile*, μάστιξι καὶ αἵματι ἀναπεφυρμένος Hdt.3.157, cf. E.*Ba.*742.

ἀναφῡσ-άω, *blow away*, κέλυφος Hp.*Mul.*1.78; *blow up* or *forth, eject*, ἀποσπάσματα ἀ., of volcanoes, Pl.*Phd.*113b:—Pass., *to be blown upwards*, Arist.*Mete.*367^{a}16. 2. abs., of the elephant going through water, μυκτῆρι ἀ. *blows upward*, Id.*HA*497^{b}30; of whales, Id.*PA*669^{a}7; of Tritons, Philostr.*Im.*1.25. 3. *spray, sprinkle*, οἴνῳ καὶ ἐλαίῳ *Hippiatr.*10. II. metaph. in Pass., *to be puffed up, arrogant*, X.*Cyr.*7.2.23, *HG*7.1.24. III. *blow the flute*, Ath.8.351e; κύκνοι -ῶντες ἡδὺ Philostr.*Im.*1.11. **-ημα**, ατος, τό, *upward blast, eruption* of wind or fire, as in volcanoes, Arist.*Mete.* 367^{a}15, *Mu.*395^{a}8, cf. Plb.34.11.17, Ps.-Luc.*Philopatr.*3. II. Medic., *powder for inflation*, *Hippiatr.*98. **-ησις**, εως, ἡ, *upward blast*, of volcanoes, Arist.*Mu.*395^{b}21, Plb.34.11.17. II. *prelude* in flute-playing, Hsch. s. v. γρόνθων, Eust.1406.50. III. *blowing* a powder *into* the nostrils, *Hippiatr.*98. **-ητός**, ή, όν, *blown up, into*, or *upon*, Eust.1139.58. **-ιάω**, *fetch a deep-drawn breath. blow*, of a dolphin, Hes.*Sc.*211; ἀ. ἆσθμα A.R.2.431.

ἀνάφῠσις, εως, ἡ, *growing again*, κεράτων Ael.*NA*12.18.

ἀναφύσσω, *draw water*: aor. ἀνήφῠσα Nonn.*D.*43.31.

ἀναφῠτεύω, *plant* or *sow again*, Arist.*Mir.*838^{b}29.

ἀναφύω, aor. Pass. ἀνεφύην Lxx 1*Ki.*5.6, part. -φυείς Chor. in *Rev. Phil.*1.75:—*produce again*, ὅμοια κέρατα Arist.*HA*611^{b}1; πτιλὰ νεαρά Ael.*NA*12.4; generally, *let grow*, πώγωνα Theoc.10.40; *foster*, ὄφιν A.R.2.1209; πλῆθος συκοφαντῶν, ἐπιθυμίας, Plu.*Arist.*26, *Arat.*49, etc. 2. abs., *produce* vegetation, Arist.*Fr.*252. II. Pass., with aor. 2 -έφυν and pf. -πέφυκα, *grow up*, Pherecyd.22(a)J., Hdt. 4.58, Pl.*Plt.*272a, etc.; ἦν γὰρ ἀποθάνῃ εἷς τις πονηρός, δύ' ἀνέφυσαν ῥήτορες Pl.Com.186; ἀναφύονταί τινι διαβολαί, δίκαι, Plu.*Thes.*17, *Per.*37. 2. *grow again*, of the hair, Hdt.5.35. 3. metaph., *recover, make a fresh start*, Aeschin.2.177. III. intr. in pres. -φύει, Phlp.*in de An.*195.12.

ἀναφων-έω, *call aloud, shout*, Plb.3.33.4, Lxx 1*Ch.*15.28, al., *Ev. Luc.*1.42; *exercise the voice*, Aret.*CD*1.3: esp. *practise the voice* by declaiming, Plu.2.130c; τὰ πρός τι ἀναπεφωνημένα *declamations* upon.., ib.30e. 2. *proclaim*, βασιλέα Id.*Demetr.*18: c. dat., *decree*, τοῦ ἀναπεφωνημένου Νουμηνίῳ στεφάνου *PFay.*14.2. 3. ἀ. τὴν ἐλευθερίαν *claim* liberty, Artem.1.58, cf. Plu.*Cic.*27. 4. of poetic *utterance*, Arist.*Mu.*400^{a}18, Plu.*Cor.*32; of any *utterance*, c. acc., Epicur.*Ep.*1p.24 U., cf. p.27 U. 5. *invoke*, in Pass., Dam. *Pr.*125 (quater). **-ή**, ἡ, *crying aloud*, Anon.*in Rh.*190.22. **-ημα**, ατος, τό, *acclamation, salutation*, Plu.*Pomp.*13, etc. 2. *exclamation*, Id.*Mar.*19. 3. *interjection*, Heph.*Poëm.*5.3. **-ησις**, εως, ἡ, *vocal exercise*, Sor.1.49, Plu.2.1071c, Aret.*CD*2.7,13. II. *ejaculation*, Plu.*Brut.*24; *utterance*, τὰς πρώτας τῶν ὀνομάτων ἀ. Demetr.Lac.*Herc.*1012.70; τὴν τῆς τέχνης ἀ. *appellation*, Phld.*Rh.*1. 75 S. III. αἱ ἀ., title of work by Epicurus, Id.*Ir.*p.89 W. **-ητής**, οῦ, ὁ, = *nomenclator*, Lyd.*Mag.*3.8. **-ητικῶς**, Adv. *as an exclamation*, Eust.1044.53.

ἀναχάζω, *make to recoil, force back*, found only in poet. aor. 1, οὐδ' ἀνέχασσαν prob. in Pi.*N.*10.69. II. mostly as Pass., **ἀναχάζομαι**, Ep. aor. ἀνεχασσάμην:—*draw back*, freq. in Il. of warriors, ἀλλ' ἀναχασσάμενος λίθον εἵλετο 7.264, cf. 15.728, 16.819, 17.47, etc.; ἀναχασσάμενος νῆχον πάλιν *giving way to* the wave, Od.7.280: c. gen., ἀ. ἠπείροιο *draw back from..*, A.R.4.1241; ἐπὶ πόδα ἀναχάζεσθαι *retire* slowly, of soldiers, X.*Cyr.*7.1.34:—Act. in sense of Pass., Id. *An.*4.1.16.

ἀναχαίνω, v. ἀναχάσκω.

ἀναχαιτ-ίζω, (χαίτη) of a horse, *throw the mane back, rear up*, ἀ. φόβῳ E.*Rh.*786; κόμην ἀ. Hld.2.36: metaph. of men, *become restive*, S.*Fr.*179, Plu.*Demetr.*34; θάλαττα ἀναχαιτίζουσα a *turbulent* sea, Philostr.*Im.*2.17. 2. c. acc., *throw* a rider, φυλάσσων μὴ ἀναχαιτίσειέ νιν, of a branch, E.*Ba.*1072: metaph., *overthrow, upset*, ἔσφηλε κἀνεχαίτισεν Id.*Hipp.*1232, cf. Tim.*Pers.*18; ἀνεχαίτισε καὶ διέλυσε D.2.9; ἀνακεχαίτικεν [ἡμᾶς], of wine, Anaxandr.3; βίος -ισμένος Epicur.*Sent.Vat.*57. 3. c. gen., ἀ. τῶν πραγμάτων *shake off the yoke of, retire from* business, Plu.*Ant.*21; ἀ. ἐκ... 2.611f (cj.). b. *lose, be disappointed of*, ἑνὸς δὲ.. οὐκ ἀνεχαιτίσθην τῆς φιλίας one [sage] did not *disappoint* me, Harp.Astr. in *Cat.Cod.Astr.* 8(3).136.9 (s.v.l.). II. *hold back by the hair*: hence generally, *check*, τοῦ δρόμου τὸ ῥόθιον Luc.*Lex.*15, cf. Procop.*Goth.*4.18; *restrain*, ἐπιδρομάς Id.*Aed.*2.11; πόλεμον Memn.51; ἀ. [τὸ θυμικὸν] τῆς ἀλόγου ὁρμῆς Alex.Aphr.*in Top.*372.17. **-ισις**, εως, ἡ, *restraint*, Jo.Sic. in Rh.6.235 W.; τῆς τάσεως τῆς φωνῆς Anon.*in Rh.* 197.20. **-ισμα**, ατος, τό, = foreg., dub. l. in Plu.2.611f:—also **-ισμός**, ὁ, = foreg., Lyd.*Mag.*2.15, 3.52.

ἀναχᾰλ-ασμός, ὁ, *relaxation*, πνεύματος *Placit.*5.24.4, cf. *Stoic.*2. 215. **-αστικός**, ή, όν, *relaxing*, ὑστέρας Dsc.1.128. **-άω**, poet. ἀγχ-, *relax*, in Pass., *Placit.*5.26.1, Plb.6.23.11, cf. Gal.19.537, Aspasia ap.Aët.16.22. 2. *ease*, [νῆα] ἀγχαλάσας A.R.2.585.

ἀναχαλινόω, gloss on ἀναχαιτίζω, Hsch., Suid.

ἀναχαλκεύω, *forge anew*, τὰς πύλας Ps.-Callisth.3.29.

ἀναχάρ-ᾰγή, ἡ, *scraping up*, Apollod.*Poliorc.*47.27. **-αξις**, εως, ἡ, = foreg., τῆς λεπίδος Plu.2.979c. **-άσσω**, Att. -ττω, *scrape up*, ib.913e; ἀὴρ ἀναχαράσσει ἰόν air *causes the roughness of* rust, ib.396a, cf. 454c.

ἀναχάσκω, only pres. and impf., Ar.*Av.*502, *Fr.*68, Luc.*VH*2.1; poet. ἄγχασκε Pherecr.196:—other tenses from pres. *ἀναχαίνω, fut. -χᾰνοῦμαι Hp.*Superf.*29: aor. 2 ἀνέχᾰνον: pf. ἀνακέχηνα:—*open the mouth, gape wide*, ἀναχανὼν μέγα Ar.*Eq.*641; στόμα ἀνακεχηνός Hp.*Nat.Mul.*45.

ἀναχαυνόω· ἀναλύω, Suid. 2. Pass., *to be puffed up*, Arist.*VV* 1251^{b}18.

ἀναχειοῖ· οἰκειοῦται, Hsch.

ἀναχειρίζομαι, *delay, hinder*, D.C.38.13.

ἀναχελύσσομαι, *cough up*, Hp.ap.Sch.Nic.*Al.*81; expl. as = ἀναπνεῖ, Erot.

ἀναχέω, *pour forth*, ποταμούς Ph.1.50; *cause to overflow*, θάλασσαν Opp.*H.*2.33:—Pass., *to be poured out*, Anacr.42; of floods, Max. Tyr. 8.7; *to be spread over a wide space*, Arist.*Pr.*944^{a}27, *Mu.*393^{a}20, Arr.*An.*6.18.5: metaph., of a rumour, Plu.*Aem.*24. 2. metaph., *relax*, ἡ χάρις ἀναχεῖ τὴν ψυχήν Ph.1.104; ἡ γνῶσις ἀναχεῖται εἰς ἀγνωσίαν *is dissipated, dissolved*, Dam.*Pr.*29. 3. Med., aor. ἀναχέασθαι *anoint oneself*, Gal.*Thras.*46. II. = ἀναχώννυμι, Orph.*A.*568 (tm.), cf. 724.

ἀναχλαινόω, *clothe with a mantle*, Nonn.*D.*11.232.

ἀναχλιαίνω, *warm up*, Hp.*Nat.Mul.* 56, Arist.*Pr.*889^{a}8:—Pass., ib.930^{b}18.

ἀναχλίζω, *warm up*: metaph., *refurbish*, cj. in Phlp.*in de An.* 455.29 (codd. ἂν χλίζεσθαι).

ἀναχνοαίνομαι, (χνοῦς) *get the first down*, Ar.*Ach.*791.

ἀναχοή, ἡ, (ἀναχέω) *eruption*, Αἴτνης Longin.35.4; ἀναχοαί· πόροι, Hsch.

ἀναχορεύω, *begin a choral dance*, Ar.*Th.*994: and c. acc. cogn., ἀ. θίασον, ὄργια, E.*Ph.*1756, *Ba.*482, al. 2. *celebrate in the chorus*, Βάκχιον ib.1153. 3. οὐκ ἄν με.. ἀνεχόρευ' Ἐρινύσι *would* not *have scared* me away by a band of Furies, Id.*Or.*582. II. intr., *dance for joy*, ἀνεχόρευσεν αἰθὴρ Id.*Ion*1079.

ἀναχόω, = ἀναχώννυμι, Luc.*Lex.*2 (in dat. pl. of part. ἀναχοῦσι).

ἀναχράομαι, *use up*, and so, *make away with, destroy*, v.l. in Th.3. 81, cf. D.C.51.8; οἱ ἑαυτοὺς -χρώμενοι 58.16. 2. *use*, *IG*5(1).1390. 60 (Andania, i B.C.).

ἀναχρέμ-πτομαι, *cough up*, D.L.2.75:—Act. in Suid., Zonar. **-ψις**, εως, ἡ, *coughing up*, Hp.*Prorrh.*1.6, Aret.*SA*2.2, etc.

ἀναχρίω, *anoint*, Dsc.*Eup.*1.35.

ἀναχρον-ίζομαι, Pass., *to be an anachronism*, Sch.E.*Hipp.*231, *Ph.*854, Eust.1404.29:—Act. c. part., *to be late in doing*, ἀ. πέμποντες ἐπιστόλια *PTeb.*413.14 (ii/iii A.D.). **-ισμός**, ὁ, *anachronism*, Sch. A.*Pr.*846. 2. *exchange of the quantity* of two syllables, Eust. 1704.8.

ἀνα-χρῡσόω, *regild*, *Ostr.*156, al. **-χρώννῡμι**, *colour anew, discolour*, Plu.2.930f:—Pass., v.l. in Thphr.*Sud.*12: metaph., *to be defiled with*, πολλαῖς γυναιξίν Eust.122.26. **-χρωσις**, εως, ἡ, *discolouring*; *taint, infection*, Plu.2.53c.

ἀνάχυλις, εως, ἡ, = σύμφυτον, Ps.-Dsc.4.9 (dub., cf. ἀνάχυσις III).

ἀνάχῠμα, ατος, τό, *expanse*, ἀ. αἰθέριον Nicom.*Harm.*3. II. = ἀνάχυσις II, Str.*Chr.*7.45.

ἀναχύρωτος [ῠ], ον, *without chaff* or *husks*, Ar.*Fr.*56.

ἀνάχῠσις, εως, ἡ, (ἀναχέω) *expansion, effusion*, χολῆς Aret.*SD*1.15; ἰκτεριώδης Sor.1.48, cf. Ruf.*Fr.*79.9; πύου Erasistr.ap.Gal.8.318;

τῶν εἰδῶν εἰς τὸ ὄν Simp.*in Ph.*503.32: metaph., ἀ. ψυχῆς *exhilaration*, Ph.2.187. b. *exhalation*, τοῦ ὠκεανοῦ (causing fogs) Prisc. p.341 D. 2. ἡ τῆς ἀσωτίας ἀ. *excess* of profligacy, 1*Ep.Pet.*4.4; τοῦ ἀλόγου πάθους Ph.1.695; of enthusiasm, Metrod.*Herc.*831.13. II. *expanse* of water, e.g. *estuary*, Str.3.1.9: pl., ἀ. θαλάττης *inundations*, Max.Tyr.38.3; ἀνάχυσιν λαμβανούσης τῆς θαλάσσης Ocell.3.4. III. an expectorant, = σύμφυτον, Ps.-Dsc.4.9.

ἀνά-χωμα, ατος, τό, *dike, dam*, Aristeas 301, Harp. s.v. ἄνδηρα; cf. ἀνάχωσμα. **-χωματίζω**, *throw up a mound*, Eust.652.30. **-χωμᾰτισμός**, ὁ, *the throwing up a mound*, Sch.A.*Pers.*646, *BGU*199, etc.

ἀναχών-ευσις, εως, ἡ, *melting down*, εἰκόνων *Ephes.*2 No.23. **-εύω**, *smelt over again*, Str.9.1.23, cf. *PHolm.*2.8, *PLeid.X.*6.

ἀνα-χώννῡμι, *heap up into a mound*, κόνιν *AP*7.537 (Phan.):—in Pass., v.l. Th.2.102 (for ἂν κεχῶσθαι); ἀ. ὁδόν *raise* a road *by throwing down rubbish*, D.55.28, cf. *PPetr.*2 p.43 (Pass., iii B.C.), 3 p.111; τάφους Luc.*Tox.*43. **-χωσις**, εως, ἡ, *raising of an embankment*, *PSI*5.488.13 (iii B.C.).

ἀναχωρ-έω, Locr., Cret. **ἀνχ-**, *go back*, πόλινδε ἂψ ἀναχωρήσουσιν Il.10.210, cf. Od.17.461. b. *walk backwards*, of oxen feeding, Hdt.4.183. 2. in Il., mostly, *retire, withdraw* from battle, ἀλλά σ' ἔγωγ' ἀναχωρήσαντα κελεύω ἐς πληθὺν ἰέναι Il.17.30; τόφρ' ἀναχωρείτω 11.189, cf. 4.305, 20.335, etc.: in Prose, μάχης οὔσης εἰς τοὔπίσω ἀ. Lys.14.6; φυγῇ ἀ. Pl.*Smp.*221a; generally, *retire, withdraw*, μεγάροιο μυχόνδε Od.22.270; ὀπίσω ἀ. Hdt.5.94, etc.; ἐς τοὔπισθεν Ar.*Pl.*1208; ἀνεκεχωρήκεσαν *they had retired* or *returned*, Th.8.15, cf. *IG*9(1).334 (Locr.): with Preps. denoting motion to or from, ἐς τὴν ἀκρόπολιν Hdt.3.143; ἐπ' οἴκου Th.1.30; ὑπὸ Βοιωτῶν ἐς Ἀθήνας *were forced* by them *to retire to*.., Hdt.5.61; ἀπό Pl.*Smp.* l.c. II. *come back* or *revert to the rightful heir*, ἡ βασιληίη ἀνεχώρησε ἐς τὸν παῖδα Hdt.7.4; ἡ ποινὴ ἀ. εἰς ἡμᾶς Antipho 2.1.3, cf. *Leg.Gort.*11.10. III. metaph., *withdraw, retire*, ἐξ αἰσθήσεων Pl.*Phd.*83a; ἀ. ἐκ τῶν πραγμάτων *retire from* public life, *from* the world, Plb.29.25.5, cf. Cic.*Att.*9.4.2, *Ev.Matt.*2.14, al.: abs., *withdraw, retire*, Pl.*Smp.*175a, cf. Ar.*Nu.*524; ἀνακεχωρηκυῖα χώρα *inland* spot, Thphr.*HP*9.7.4; ἀ. ἀπὸ θαλάσσης Plb.2.11.16; ἀνακεχωρηκὸς ῥῆμα, ὄνομα *obsolete*, D.H.*Rh.*10.7; *recondite*, ἱστορία Phld.*Rh.*1.157 S. IV. = συγχωρέω, πάντες ἀνεχώρησαν συμπεραίνεσθαι τὸ μίασμα Procop.*Arc.*10. 2. *strike, refuse to work*, *PTeb.*26.18, 41.4, al.; ἀνακεχωρηκότα σώματα ib.5.6. **-ημα**, ατος, τό, *withdrawal, reflux*, θαλάσσης Arist.*Mu.*396ᵃ18. **-ησις**, εως, Ion. ιος, ἡ, *retiring, retreat*, Hdt.9.22, Th.1.12, al.; ἀ. ποιεῖσθαι, of a river, D.S.1.10; of waves, ἐπιδρομαὶ καὶ -σεις Arist.*Mu.*400ᵃ27; τοῦ ποταμοῦ *PPetr.*2 p.45 (iii B.C.). II. *place* or *means of retreat*, Th.1.90, D.19.41. III. *return*, Pl.*Phlb.*32b. IV. *absence*, τὰ ὄντα ἐν -ήσει *BGU*447.6 (ii A.D.), cf. *PTeb.*353.6 (ii A.D.); *retirement*, μετὰ φίλων -ιν εὔσχολον Phld.*Oec.*p.64 J. **-ητέον**, *one must withdraw*, Pl.*Cri.*51b. **-ητής**, οῦ, ὁ, *one who has retired from the world, anchoret*, Just.*Nov.*5.3 (pl.), *Rev.Épigr.*1.159 (Egypt, vi A.D.). **-ητικός**, ή, όν, *disposed to retire*; τὸ ἀ. Arr.*Epict.*2.1.10. **-ίζω**, *make to go back* or *retire*, X.*Cyr.*7.1.41, *An.*5.2.10; ἀγχωρίξαντες (Dor.) τὸν ὅρον *having drawn it back*, *Tab.Heracl.*1.56, 59.

ἀνάχωσμα, ατος, τό, *silted mound*, Sch.Ar.*Eq.*527.

ἀναψᾰθάλλω, *touch up, work up*, Phryn.*PS* p.12 B., cf. Hsch.

ἀναψᾰλάσσω, *tear up, open*, Lyc.343.

ἀνα-ψάω, *wipe up*, σταγόνας ἐρίῳ Ctes.*Fr.*57.28; δάκρυον Dsc.4.64. 2. *clean out*, φρέαρ *PLond.*1.131ʳ631:—Pass., aor. ἀνεψήσθην *BGU*530.17 (i A.D.). **-ψησις**, εως, ἡ, *cleaning out*, φρέατος *PLond.*3.1177.329 (ii A.D.). **-ψησμός**, ὁ, = foreg., λάκκου ib.1.131ʳ621 (i A.D.).

ἀναψηλᾰφ-άω, *retry*, in Law, Just.*Nov.*82.11.1:—Pass., ib.113.1 *Intr.* **-ησις**, εως, ἡ, *close search*, τροφῆς Eust.254.31; *re-examination, retrial*, *Cod.Just.*7.62.35, cf. 12.37.19, Just.*Nov.*82.12, al.

ἀναψηφίζω, *put to the vote again*, Th.6.14; *propose to repeal*, *SIG*194 (Amphipolis), cf. D.C.39.39:—Med., *vote anew*, Pherecr.47. II. *reckon backwards*, εἰς τοὔπίσω Porph.*Plot.*2.

ἄναψις, εως, ἡ, (ἀνάπτω) *lighting up, kindling*, D.H.2.66; of stars, ἄ. καὶ σβέσις Epicur.*Ep.*2 p.39 U.

ἀναψοφέω, *make a noise*, Hsch. s.v. ἀναρραθαγῆσαι.

ἀνα-ψυκτήρ, ῆρος, ὁ, *refresher*, πόνων *from* labours, E.*Fr.*146. **-ψυξις**, εως, ἡ, *cooling*, Posidon.72; *exposure*, ἕλκεος Hp.*Fract.*25. 2. *drying up*, Str.10.2.19. 3. *relief, respite*, Lxx *Ex.*8.15; κακῶν Jul. *ad Them.*258c; καιροὶ -εως *Act.Ap.*3.20. **-ψῡχή**, ἡ, *coolness*, Pl.*Lg.*919a. 2. *relief, respite*, Id.*Smp.*176a, *PLond.*1.42.19 (ii B.C.); κακῶν *from* misery, E.*Supp.*615; πόνων Id.*Ion*1604. 3. *ventilation*, Pl.*Ti.*84d, Arist.*Fr.*219. **-ψύχω** [ῡ], Ep. impf. -εσκον Orph.*L.*562:—*cool, refresh*, ἀήτας Ὠκεανὸς ἀνίησιν ἀναψύχειν ἀνθρώπους Od.4.568; ἀνέψυχον φίλον ἦτορ *were reviving* their spirit, Il.13.84; ἕλκος ἀναψύχοντα 5.795; ἀ. φίλα γούνατα Hes.*Op.*608; ἀ. βάσιν *cool* the feet *in water*, E.*IA*421:—Pass., *to be revived, refreshed*, ἀνέψυχθεν φίλον ἦτορ Il.10.575; of the body, Pl.*Ti.*78e, cf. 70d; ὥστ' ἀνεψύχης [ῠ] Amips.13. 2. ναῦς ἀ. *let* the ships *rest and get dry*, Hdt.7.59, X.*HG*1.5.10; ἀ. τὸν ἱδρῶτα *let* it *dry off*, Plu.*Sull.*29; ἀ. τὰς αὐλαίας *dry* them, Id.*Them.*30:—Pass., *to be dried up*, Str.10.2.19. 3. metaph., c. gen., ἀ. πόνων τινά *give* him *relief from* toil, E.*Hel.*1094; πολέων..μεριμνέων Call.*Hec.*1.1.7; ἀ. κακότητος ψυχάς Orph.*Fr.*230: abs., 2*Ep.Ti.*1.16. 4. Medic., *expose* to air, κατὰ τὸ ἕλκος ἐῶσιν ἀνεψῦχθαι Hp.*Fract.*25; cf. ἀναψύχειν· γυμνοῦν, Erot. II. the Act. is also used intr., *become cool, recover, revive*, Diph.81, *AP*12.132 (Mel.), Opp.*H.*5.623; εὗρεν..δρόμων ἀναψύχουσαν [τὴν ἔλαφον] Babr.95.57; *take relaxation*, *POxy.*1296.7 (iii A.D.).

ἄνδα· αὕτη (Cypr.), Hsch.

ἀνδαβάτης, ου, ὁ, *gladiator*, Lyd.*Mag.*1.46.

ἄνδαιτος, ον, = ἀναδαστός, *SIG*141.11 (Issa).

ἀνδαίω, poet. for ἀναδαίω.

ἁνδάνω [δᾰ], impf. ἥνδανον, Ep. ἑήνδανον, in Ion. Prose ἑάνδανον Hdt.9.5 and 19 (in 7.172, 8.29, codd. give ἥνδανον): fut. ἁδήσω Id.5.39: pf. ἅδηκα Hippon.100, Locr. ϝεϝάδηκα (v. infr. II); ἔαδα A.R.1.867; part. ἑαδώς Il.9.173: aor. ἕαδον Hdt.4.201, 6.106, cf. *SIG*57.40; Ep. εὔαδον (i.e. ἔϝαδον) Il.14.340, Od.16.28; ἅδον [ᾰ] Il.13.748; 3 sg. subj. ἅδῃ Hdt.1.133, opt. ἅδοι Od.20.327, inf. ἁδεῖν Il.3.173, S.*Ant.*89: later, aor. 1 ἧσα Plot.2.3.7:—*please, delight, gratify*, mostly Ion. and poet., used like ἥδομαι, except as to construction: mostly c. dat. pers., Od.2.114, Pi.*P.*1.29, Hdt.5.39: also c. dupl. dat., Ἀγαμέμνονι ἥνδανε θυμῷ Il.1.24, cf. Od.16.28; εἴ σφωϊν κραδίῃ ἅδοι 20.327; Πηνελοπείῃ ἥνδανε μύθοισι *pleased* her *with* words, 16.398:—in ἁδόντα δ' εἴη με τοῖς ἀγαθοῖς ὁμιλεῖν the dat. belongs both to the part. and to the inf., Pi.*P.*2.96: abs., τοῖσι δὲ πᾶσιν ἑαδότα μῦθον ἔειπε Il.9.173, Od.18.422: c. acc., v. dub. in Thgn.26, E.*Or.*1607, both prob. corrupt readings. II. in Hdt. ἁνδάνει expresses *the opinion* of a body of people, οὔ σφι ἥνδανε ταῦτα 7.172, cf. 9.5; τοῖσι τὰ ἀμείνω ἑάνδανε 9.19: c. inf., τοῖσι μὲν ἕαδε βοηθέειν Ἀθηναίοισι 6.106, cf. 4.145, 153, 201; so ἐπεί νύ τοι εὔαδεν οὕτως (sc. ποιεῖν) Il.17.647, cf. Od.2.114:—τὰ ϝεϝαδηκότα *quae placuerunt*, *IG*9(1).334 (Locr.). III. Med., ἣν ἁνδάνηται Hp.*Mul.*2.150; cf. τιμὴ δαίμοσιν ἁνδάνεται *AP*10.7 (Arch.). (Cf. Skt. *svádati*, Lat. *suādeo, suāvis*, O.E. *swēte*, etc.)

ἄνδας· βορέας (Tyrrhen.), Hsch.

ἀνδειράδες, αἱ, = ἄνδηρα, *AB*394, cf. Hsch.

ἄνδεμα, ἀνδεσμός, ἀνδέχομαι, ἀνδέω, ἄνδημα, poet. for ἀναδ-.

ἀνδεργμα· ὁ ἐπὶ τῆς τραγικῆς σκηνῆς παραγόμενος παράκοτος, Hsch.

ἀνδηρευτής, οῦ, ὁ, *workman employed on dikes*, *PRyl.*157.15 (ii A.D.), *PFlor.*369.9 (ii A.D.).

ἄνδηρον, τό, *raised bank* by the side of a river or ditch, *dike*, Mosch.4.102: mostly in pl., ἄνδηρα, τά, Hyp.*Fr.*113, Lyc.629; Πακτωλοῦ χρυσέοισιν ἐπ' ἀνδήροισι Call.*Fr.*45 P., cf. *Fr.anon.*110; τετμῆσθαι καθάπερ ἀνδήροις καὶ ὀχετοῖς Plu.2.650c, cf. Luc.*Lex.*2. 2. *border, edge*, of the sea, dub. in B.1.54 (p.439 J.); ἄ. θαλάσσης Opp.*H.*4.319. 3. *border* for plants or flowers, Thphr.*CP*3.15.4, Theoc.5.93, *AP*12.197 (Strat.), Nic.*Th.*576. 4. = στῆθος χειρός, Poll.2.144.

ἀνδίκα· ὁ βόλος (ἀνδικλόβολος cod.), δίκη ἡ ἐξ ὑπαρχῆς δικαζομένη παρὰ Ταραντίνοις (i.e. ἀνδίκα = ἀναδίκη), Hsch.

ἄνδικε· ἀνάρριψον, Hsch.; cf. ἔδικον.

ἀνδίκτης, ου, ὁ, for ἀναδίκτης (ἀναδικεῖν), *catch of a mousetrap*, Call.*Fr.*233.

ἄνδινος· περίπατος, Hsch. (ἀνδινός· περὶ παντός cod.).

ἄνδῐχα, Adv., (ἀνά, δίχα) *asunder, in twain*, ἡ δ' [κεφαλὴ] ἄνδιχα πᾶσα κεάσθη Il.16.412; ἄνδιχα πάντα δάσασθαι 18.511; opp. ἀμμίγδην, Nic.*Th.*912; *far away*, A.R.4.31. 2. as Prep., c. gen., *apart from*, A.R.1.908, 2.927; ἀλλήλων *AP*5.4 (Stat. Flacc.):—hence **ἀνδιχάζω**, *to be divided in opinion*, of judges, *IG*9(1).333 (Locr.).

ἀνδοκάδην· ἐκ διαδοχῆς, Hsch.

ἀνδοκ-εία, ἡ, = ἀναδοχή II, ἐν ἀνδοκείᾳ Ζωτικοῦ *guaranteed by* Zoticus, *IG*14.423 ii 19: pl., ib.422 iii (Tauromenium). **-εύς**· ἀνάδοχος, Hsch. **-ιάρχης**, ου, ὁ, *officer in charge of* ἀνδοκεῖαι, *IG*14.2417.1.

ἀνδραγαθ-έω, pf. ἠνδραγάθηκα D.S.11.25: aor. -ησα Plb.6.39.2: (ἀνήρ, ἀγαθός):—later form of ἀνδραγαθίζομαι, *behave in a manly, upright manner*, Id.1.45.3, al., *SIG*785.14 (Chios), *BGU*1207.11 (i B.C.), Onos.34.2:—Pass., ἠνδραγαθημένα, opp. ἡμαρτημένα, Plu.*Fab.*20. **-ημα**, ατος, τό, *brave, manly deed*, Str.1.2.8, Plu.*Sert.*10, *IG*14.951, Jul.*Caes.*329c, etc. **-ησις**, εως, ἡ, = sq., Lxx 1 *Ma.*5.56. **-ία**, Ion. -ίη, ἡ, *bravery, manly virtue*, Hdt.1.99, 136, al., Th.2.42; *the character of an upright man*, Ar.*Pl.*191, Phryn.Com.1; ἀνδραγαθίας ἕνεκα στεφανοῦσθαι Hyp.*Lyc.*6. **-ίζομαι**, aor. ἀνδραγαθίσασθαι App.*BC*5.101:—*act uprightly*, εἴ τις ἀπραγμοσύνῃ -ίζεται if any one thinks to sit at home and *play the honest man*, Th.2.63; ἐκ τοῦ ἀκινδύνου ἀ. Id.3.40, cf. Arist.*VV*1250ᵇ4. **-ικός**, ή, όν, *befitting a good man*, Hp.*Art.*78 (Comp.).

ἀνδρ-άγρια, τά, *spoils of a slain enemy*, Il.14.509. **-αγχος**, ὁ, *throttler of men*: *executioner*, Eust.1833.54, 1858.57: ἄνδραχοι· δήμιος Hsch. **-άδελφος**, ὁ, *husband's brother, brother-in-law*, Suid.:—fem. **-αδέλφη**, ἡ, *husband's sister*, Eust.392.2. **-ᾰκάς** (A), Adv. *man by man*, Od.13.14, Cratin.19, cf. Plu.2.151e; ἀ. καθήμενος *apart*, A.*Ag.*1595, cf. Hsch. (-κάς perh. cognate with Skt. *-śás* in *dviśás* 'two by two', etc.) **-ᾰκάς** (B), άδος, ἡ, *a man's portion*, Nic.*Th.*643. **-αλογία**, ἡ, v. ἀνδρολογία.

ἀνδραπόδ-εσσι, v. ἀνδράποδον. **-ηγοί**· οἱ σὺν ἀνδραπόδοις ἀποδημοῦντες, Hsch. **-ίζω**, pres. Act. first in Alciphr.3.40: Att. fut. -ιῶ X.*HG*2.2.20: aor. ἠνδραπόδισα Hdt., Th.:—Med., fut. ἀνδραποδιεῦμαι in pass. sense, Hdt.6.17:—Pass., fut. ἀνδραποδισθήσομαι X.*HG*2.2.14: aor. ἠνδραποδίσθην Lys.2.57: pf. ἠνδραπόδισμαι Isoc.17.14, part. ἀνδραποδισμένος Hdt.6.119: (ἀνδράποδον):—Prose Verb, *enslave*, esp. of conquerors, *sell the free men* of a conquered place *into slavery*, Hdt.1.151, Th.1.98; παῖδας καὶ γυναῖκας Id.3.36; πόλιν 6.62:—Pass., *to be sold into slavery*, Hdt.6.106, 119, 8.29, X.*HG*1.6.14, etc.; πόλις ὑπὸ τῶν βαρβάρων ἠνδραποδίσθη Lys. l.c.:—Med. also in act. sense, Hdt.1.76, al., Th.4.48, And.3.22, etc. II. less freq. of individuals, *kidnap*, Pl.*Grg.*508e, X.*Mem.*4.2.14, *Smp.*4.36. III. metaph., -ίζοντες ἀπὸ τοῦ φρονεῖν τοὺς νέους Alciphr.3.40. **-ιον**, τό, Dim. of ἀνδράποδον, Hyp.*Fr.*227, Diph.80, *POxy.*1102.15 (ii A.D.). —ισις, εως, ἡ, = sq., X.*Ap.*25. —ισμός, ὁ, *selling into slavery, enslaving,* Th.2.68, Isoc.4.100, etc.; πατρίδος D.1.5. II. of individuals, *kidnapping,* whether of free men or other people's slaves, ὑπόδικος —ισμοῦ liable to action *for kidnapping,* Pl.*Lg.*879a, 955a. —ιστήριος, α, ον, *fitted for enslaving,* Tz. ad Lyc.784. —ιστής, οῦ, ὁ, *slave-dealer* or *kidnapper,* Ar.*Eq.*1030, *Pl.*521, Lys.10.10, etc., cf. Poll.3.78; coupled with ἱερόσυλοι, τοιχωρύχοι, etc., Pl.*R.*344b: metaph., ἀ. ἑαυτοῦ *one who sells* his own *independence,* X.*Mem.*1.2.6. —ιστικός, ή, όν, = —ιστήριος: ἡ —κή (sc. τέχνη) *man-stealing, kidnapping,* Pl.*Sph.*222c. Adv., Sup. —ιστικώτατα Eup.396.

ἀνδρᾰποδο-κάπηλος, ὁ, *slave-dealer,* Is.*Fr.*53 S., Luc.*Ind.*24, Gal. *UP*1.9. —**κλέπτης**, ου, ὁ, *slave-stealer,* Men.23 D. —**κλόπος**, ὁ, = foreg., S.*Fr.*1011.

ἀνδράποδον [δρᾰ], τό, *one taken in war and sold as a slave,* whether originally slave or free, *captive,* Hdt.3.125, 129, 5.31, etc.: orig. dist. from δοῦλος, ὅσοι δὲ ἦσαν ξεῖνοί τε καὶ δοῦλοι.. ἐν ἀνδραπόδων λόγῳ ποιεύμενος εἶχε Id.3.125; τὰ ἀ. πάντα, καὶ δοῦλα καὶ ἐλεύθερα Th.8.28; τὰ ἀ. τὰ δοῦλα πάντα ἀπέδοτο X.*HG*1.6.15. II. *low fellow,* 'creature', Pl.*Grg.*483b, *Thg.*130b, X.*Mem.*4.2.39, D.Chr.31.109; of a female slave, Pherecr.16 D. III. as a playful mode of address, Arr.*Epict.*1.4.14, al.—Hom., Il.7.475, has Ep. dat. pl. ἀνδραπόδεσσι (as if from ἀνδράπους), where Aristarch. proposed to read ἀνδραπόδοισι; but it is almost certain that the word was post-Homeric, and the line was rejected on that account by Zenod. and Ar. Byz. (Orig. pl.; formed on the analogy of τετράποδα, cf. τετραπόδων πάντων καὶ ἀνδραπόδων *Foed.Delph.Pell.*1 *B*7. Sg. in X.*Ath.*1.18, etc.)

ἀνδραποδ-ώδης, ες, *slavish, servile, abject,* opp. ἐλευθέριος, Arist. *EN*1128^{a}21; ἀρετή Pl.*Phd.*69b; ἄγροικος καὶ ἀνελεύθερος.. ἀ. τε Id. *Lg.*880a, cf. X.*Mem.*4.2.22; θηριώδης καὶ ἀ. Pl.*R.*430b, cf. Arist. *EN*1118^{a}25; τεχνιτεῖαι Epicur.*Ep.*2 p.40 U.; ἀ. θρίξ *short coarse* hair *like that of slaves,* hence metaph., ἔτι τὴν ἀ. τρίχα ἔχοντες ἐν τῇ ψυχῇ Pl.*Alc.*1.120b. Adv. —δῶς Id.*Smp.*215e. —**ωδία**, ἡ, *servility,* Arist.*Pol.*1336^{b}12, Plu.2.7b. —**ώνης**, ου, ὁ, *slave-dealer,* Ar.*Fr.*312. —**ωνία**, Ion. —ίη, ἡ, *tax on sale of slaves, SIG*4.8 (Cyzicus).

ἀνδράριον, τό, Dim. of ἀνήρ, *manikin, pitiful fellow,* Ar.*Ach.*517.

ἀνδράφαξυς, v. ἀτράφαξυς. **ἀνδραφάσσειν**· κατ' ἄνδρα ἐφάπτεσθαι, Hsch.

ἀνδραφόνος, ὁ, = ἀνδροφόνος, Lex Sol.ap.Phot.p.126 R.

ἀνδραφυστεῖν· φεύγειν, ἢ ἐπὶ φόνῳ διώκειν, Hsch.

ἀνδραχθής, ές, *loading a man, as much as a man can carry,* χερμάδια Od.10.121; βώλακες A.R.3.1334; γόγγροι Eudox.ap.Ath.7.288c.

ἀνδράχλη, ἡ, said to be Att. form for ἀνδράχνη (I), Hellad.ap.Phot. *Bibl.*p.533 B., S.*Fr.*823, but in this passage, as in Thphr.*HP*1.5.2, 1.9.3, = *Arbutus Andrachne.* II. *warming-pan* or *brazier,* Eust. 1571.25, Poet.ap.Suid. **ἄνδραχλος**, ἡ, = ἀνδράχνη, *EM*102.36, v.l. in Thphr.*HP*4.15.2. **ἀνδράχνη**, ἡ, *purslane, Portulaca oleracea,* Id.*CP*1.10.4, al., Dsc.2.124, Luc.*Trag.*151, prob.l. in Pl. Com.44; ἀ. κηπαία Dsc.4.168. 2. ἀ. ἀγρία, = πεπλίς, Dsc.4.168; but = *Sedum stellatum, stonecrop,* ib.90; also = τηλέφιον, Ps.-Dsc.2.186, Gal.19.146. 3. ἀ. θαλασσία, = πεπλίς, Ps.-Dsc.4.168. **ἄνδραχνος**, ἡ, = ἀνδράχλη, Paus.9.22.2 and 28.1.

ἀνδρεάστρια, v. ἀνδρεράστρια.

ἀνδρεία, ἡ, Ion. —ηίη (Hdt.7.99), generally written **ἀνδρία** in the Mss., in agreement with the opinion of A.D.*Adv.*136.8, refuted by Orus ap.*EM*461.53:—ἀνδρεία is required by the metre in Ar.*Nu.*510, and *may* always stand in the few poet. passages where it occurs (Simon.58, A.*Th.*52, S.*El.*983, E.*Tr.*674): ἀνδρία is required in E. *HF*475 μέγα φρονῶν ἐπ' ἀνδρίᾳ (s.v.l., εὐανδρίᾳ Elmsley): ἀνδρεία is also confirmed by the Ion. form ἀνδρηίη:—*manliness, manly spirit,* opp. δειλία, ll.cc., cf. Arist.*Rh.*1366^{b}11, *EN*1115^{a}6; also of women, S.*El.*983, Arist.*Pol.*1260^{a}22; ἀνδρεία ἡ περὶ τὰς ναυτιλίας Str.3.1.8:—in pl., *brave deeds,* Pl.*Lg.*922a; ironically, αἱ διὰ τῶν λόγων ἀνδρεῖαι D.*Prooem.*45. II. in bad sense, *hardihood, insolence,* D. Chr.12.13. III. = ἡ τῶν ἀνδρῶν ἡλικία, Antipho Soph.67^a. IV. *membrum virile,* Artem.1.45. V. *skill,* Lxx *Ec.*4.4.

ἀνδρ-είκελον, τό, *image of a man,* App.*BC*2.147, *APl.*4.221 (Theaet.). II. *flesh-coloured pigment,* Pl.*R.*501b, *Cra.*424e, X.*Oec.*10.5, Arist.*GA*725^{a}26, Thphr.*Lap.*51. —**είκελος**, ον, *like a man,* εἴδωλα D.H.1.38; διατύπωσις Plu.*Alex.*72.

ἀνδρειόθυμος, gloss on ψυχικός, Suid.

ἀνδρεῖος, α, ον, Ion. —**ήιος**, η, ον (codd. of Hdt. have the common form in the Comp. and Sup. ἀνδρειότερος, —ότατος, 1.79, 123), Delph. **ἀνδρέος** *GDI*1724, al.:—*of* or *for a man,* στέγη dub. in A.*Fr.*124; θαἰμάτια Ar.*Ec.*75; opp. γυναικεῖος, Id.*Th.*154, Archipp.6 D., Pl.*R.*451c, X. *Mem.*2.7.5; πέπλοι Theoc.28.10 (where ἀνδρέϊοι); αὐλός (v. αὐλός) Hdt.1.17; ἀ. ἀγορά the *men's* market, *CIG*3657 (Cyzicus); ἀνδρεῖος (sc. σύλλογος) *Test.Epict.*1.22, 2.29; ἀνδρεῖα ἠμπίσχετο *vestem virilem,* D.L.3.46; ἀ. ἱμάτιον, = *toga virilis,* Plu.*Brut.*14. II. *manly, masculine, courageous,* ῥώμη Hdt.7.153, etc.; even of women, Arist.*Pol.*1277^{b}22, *Po.*1454^{a}23; and in bad sense, *stubborn,* ἀναίσχυντος καὶ ἀ. τὰ τοιαῦτα Luc.*Ind.*3: neut., τὸ ἀνδρεῖον, = ἀνδρεία, Th.2.39; καὶ τοῦτ' ἐμοὶ τἀνδρεῖον ἡ προμηθία E.*Supp.*510; ἔβησαν εἰς τἀνδρεῖον Id.*Andr.*683. Adv. —ως Ar.*Pax*498, al.: Sup. —ότατα Pl.*Plt.*262a. 2. of animals, Arist.*HA*488^{b}17, cf. Pl.*La.*196d,e. 3. of things, *strong, vigorous,* λαφυγμός Eup.148; θήρατρον Ael.*VH*1.1. III. **ἀνδρεῖα**, τά, the public meals of the Cretans, also the older name for the Spartan φειδίτια or φιλίτια (q.v.), Alcm.22, Arist. *Pol.*1272^{a}3, Plu.*Lyc.*12, Str.10.4.18 (v.l. ἄνδρια):—also **ἀνδρήιον**, τό, Cretan for *the public hall, GDI*4992 a ii 9, cf. 5040.38, al. IV. ἀνδρεῖον, τό, = σίνηπι ἄγριον, Ps.-Dsc.2.154.

ἀνδρειότης, ητος, ἡ, = ἀνδρεία, X.*An.*6.5.14, Ti.Locr.103d.

ἀνδρει-όω, *fill with courage,* τὰ σπλάγχνα Lxx 4*Ma.*15.23:—Pass., *become a man,* Procl.*Par.Ptol.*89. —**φόντης**, ου, ὁ, *man-slaying,* epith. of Ἐνυάλιος, Il.2.651, etc.; but the metre requires ἀδρι-φόντης, cf. ἀνδρότης. —**ωμα**, ατος, τό, *manly effort,* Metrod.*Herc.*831.12. —**ών**, ῶνος, ὁ, poet. for ἀνδρεών, ἀνδρών, *AP*9.322 (Leon.).

ἀνδρεράστια, v.l. for sq. in Poll.3.70, cf. Phryn.*PS*p.34 B.

ἀνδρεράστρια, ἡ, *woman that is fond of men,* Ar.*Th.*392 (ἀνδρεάστρια cod. R).

ἀνδρεύομαι, = ἀνδρίζομαι, *EM*599.17.

ἀνδρεφόνος, Dor. for ἀνδροφόνος, Hdn.Gr.2.418.

ἀνδρεών, = ἀνδρών, Hdt.1.34, al., *IG*14.291 (Segesta).

ἀνδρηλᾰτ-έω, *banish from house and home,* ἐκ γῆς τῆσδε A.*Ag.*1419, cf. *Eu.*221; ἐκ πόλεώς τε καὶ δόμων *Ag.*1586, cf. S.*OT*100, Pl.*R.*565e, etc.:—Pass., D.C.47.19. —**ης** [ᾰ], ου, ὁ, *he that drives one from his home,* dub. l. in A.*Th.*637, cf. Hsch.

ἀνδρία, v. ἀνδρεία. II. **ἄνδρια**, τά, v. ἀνδρεῖος III.

ἀνδριαντ-άριον, τό, Dim. of ἀνδριάς, *POxy.*1459.58 (iii A.D.), Sch. Luc.*Lex.*3. —**ίδιον**, τό, = foreg., *SIG*^{2}588.167, al. (Delos). —**ιον**, τό, = foreg., *IG*11.161 *B*119 (Delos, iii B.C.), *GDI*5063 (Itanos). —**ίσκος**, ὁ, = foreg., *statuette, IG*2^2.47.5, 20 (iv B.C.), 11.161 *B*17, 60 (Delos, iii B.C.), *GDI*5702 (Samos); *puppet,* Plu.*Thes.*20.

ἀνδριαντο-γλύφος, ὁ, *carver of statues,* Tz. ad Lyc.615. —**ειδής**, ές, *like a statue,* Aethlius 1. —**εργάτης**, ου, ὁ, = ἀνδριαντοποιός, Tz. *H.*10.268. —**θήκη**, ἡ, *niche for a statue, CIG*2749.1 (Aphrodisias). —**πλάστης**, ου, ὁ, *modeller of statues, Cat.Cod.Astr.*8(4).213 (Rhetor.), Eust.206.37. —**πλαστική** (sc. τέχνη), ἡ, *art of modelling,* S.E.*M.*11.188. —**ποιέω**, *make statues,* X.*Mem.*3.1.2. —**ποιΐα**, ἡ, *the sculptor's art, statuary,* Pl.*Grg.*450c, X.*Mem.*1.4.3. —**ποιϊκή** (sc. τέχνη), ἡ, = foreg., Arist.*Ph.*195^{a}6, *Metaph.*1013^{b}6 (v.l. —ποιητική), which is found in Id.*PA*640^{a}30, Ocell.2.3). —**ποιός**, ὁ, *sculptor,* Pi.*N.*5.1, Pl.*R.*540c, etc.; *statuary* in bronze (cf. ἀνδριάς), opp. λιθουργός, Arist.*EN*1041^{a}11.

ἀνδριαντ-ουργία, ἡ, *sculpture,* Tz.*H.*8.348. —**ουργός**, ὁ, (ἔργον) = ἀνδριαντοποιός, Gal.19.162.

ἀνδριάς, ὁ, gen. άντος (Att. ᾶντος, acc. to Hdn.Gr.1.51): (ἀνήρ):—*image of a man, statue,* Pi.*P.*5.40, Hdt.1.183, 2.91, Ar.*Pax*1183, Th.1.134, etc.; ἀνδριάντας καὶ ἄλλα ζῷα λίθινά τε καὶ ξύλινα Pl.*R.*515a; ἀνδριάντας γράφειν paint *statues,* ib.420c; esp. of portrait-statues, ἀ. εἰκονικός Plu.*Lys.*1; ἀ. ὁλοσώματος *IG*12(7).240 (Amorgos); ἀ. ἔφιππος *SIG*730.26 (Olbia); of female figures, Ath.10.425f, etc.; of men, opp. ἀγάλματα of the gods, Gorg.*Hel.*18, Plb.21.29.9; rarely of gods, *GDI*5421 (Delos): prov., λάλος, οὐκ ἀ. Luc.*Vit.Auct.*3; ἀπαθὴς ὡς ἀ. Arr.*Epict.*3.2.4; ἀνδριάντος γυμνότερος D.Chr.34.3: ironically, τὸν καλὸν ἀ., a mother's term of endearment, D.18.129; μακρὸν ἀ. παίζειν, a kind of game, Thphr.*Char.*27.12.

ἀνδρίζω, *make a man of, make manly,* τοὺς γεωργοῦντας X.*Oec.*5.4. II. mostly in Pass. or Med., *come to manhood,* Ar.*Fr.*744, Hyp.*Fr.*228, Luc.*Anach.*15. 2. *play the man,* X.*An.*4.3.34, Pl. *Tht.*151d, Arist.*EN*1115^{b}4, Lxx *Jo.*1.6, al., 1*Ep.Cor.*16.13; *dress like a man,* Philostr.*Im.*1.2. 3. sens. obsc., D.C.79.5; of a eunuch, ἀ. ἐπὶ γυναῖκα Philostr.*VA*1.37, cf. *Ep.*54, Ach.Tat.4.1.

ἀνδρικός, ή, όν, *masculine, manly,* Pl.*R.*474e, etc.; [δίαιτα] σώφρων καὶ ἀ. Id.*Ep.*359a; νοσήματα Hp.*Mul.*1.62; ἀ. ἱδρώς the sweat *of manly toil,* Ar.*Ach.*693; σφηκὸς ἀνδρικώτερον Id.*V.*1090, cf. 1077; ἐσθής D.C.45.2; τὸ τῆς χρόας ἀ. Arist.*Fr.*542: Comp., Anaxandr.1 D. c. inf., πίνειν καὶ φαγεῖν μὲν ἀνδρικοί *like men* to eat and drink, Eub.12. Adv. —κῶς *like a man,* Ar.*Eq.*599, *V.*153, al.: Comp. —ώτερον Id.*Pax*515: Sup. —ώτατα Id.*Eq.*81; opp. ἀνάνδρως, Pl.*Tht.*177b. 2. of things, *large,* Eub.56. II. *composed of men,* χορός X.*HG*6.4.16, Lys.21.1.

Ἀνδρίνεια, τά, festival at Phigalea (prob. from the founder's name), *IG*5(2).422 (ii/i B.C.).

ἀνδρίον, τό, Dim. of ἀνήρ, *manikin,* Ar.*Pax*51; *pitiful fellow,* E. ap.Phot.p.127 R., Theoc.5.40, cf. Eup.316.

ἀνδρίς, ίδος, ἡ, fem. of ἀνήρ, *woman,* Sm.*Ge.*2.23.

ἄνδρ-ισμα, ατος, τό, *genuine, straightforward dealing,* in pl. (opp. εἰρωνεύματα), Max.Tyr.38.4. —**ισμός**, ὁ, = ἀνδρεία, Poll.3.120. —**ιστέον**, *one must play the man,* Pl.*Phd.*90e. —**ιστί** [ῐ], Adv. *like a man, like men,* Ar.*Ec.*149, cf. Crates Com.3 D., Theoc.18.23; *with a male voice,* εἰπεῖν τι D.Chr.33.38.

ἀνδρο-βάμων [βᾰ], ονος, ὁ, *foot-path* or *sidewalk, IGRom.*1.980. —**βᾰρής**, ές, = ἀνδραχθής, Eust.1651.9. —**βασμός**, ὁ, *foot-path,* ὁδὸς ἀ. *GDI*5690 (Erythrae), cf. Hsch. —**βᾰτέω**, = Lat. *paedico, AP*5.207 (Mel.). —**βάτης**, ου, ὁ, = *paedicator,* Hsch. s.v. παιδοπίπας. —**βῐος**, ον, *living like a man,* Anon.ap.Suid. s.v. θρύπτεται. —**βόρος**, ον, *man-devouring, AP*7.206 (Damoch.), Q.S.6.247. —**βουλος**, ον, *of manly counsel, man-minded,* like ἀνδρόφρων, A.*Ag.*11, cf. Phryn.*PS*p.31 B.: opp. γυναικόβουλος. —**βρώς**, ῶτος, ὁ, ἡ, *man-eating, cannibal,* γνάθος E.*Cyc.*93; χαρμοναί Id.*HF*384; ἡδοναί *Fr.*537. —**γαμος**, ὁ, = κίναιδος, *Cat.Cod.Astr.*2.175. —**γένεια**, ἡ, (γένος), κατ' ἀνδρογενείην *of descent by the man's side,* Hp.*Ep.*27; πρεσβύτατος κατ' ἀ. *SIG*1044.20 (Halic.), cf. 1106.25 (Cos). —**γίγας**, αντος, ὁ, *giant-man,* Call.*Cer.*35. —**γόνος**, ον, *begetting men,* ἡμέρα ἀ.

a day *favourable for begetting* (or *for the birth of*) *male children*, Hes. *Op.*783,788. **-γύνης** [ῠ], ου, ὁ, = ἀνδρόγυνος, prob. in Sch.T.Il.13. 291. II. Adj., *common to men and women*, λουτρὰ ἀ. baths *used by both at once*, *AP*9.783. **-γῠνία**, ἡ, Pythag., = πεντάς, i.e. odd and even (3 + 2), *Theol.Ar.*32. **-γῠνος**, ὁ, *man-woman, hermaphrodite*, Pl.*Smp.*189e. 2. *womanish man, effeminate person*, Hp.*Vict.*1.28, Hdt.4.67, Aeschin.2.127, Plu.2.219f, cf. Lxx *Pr.*18.8; ἀνδρογύνων ἄθυρμα Eup.3 D. 3. = *pathicus, cinaedus*, *AP*6.254 (Myrin.), cf. Lib.*Decl.*12.42. b. of women, *Sapphic*, ἀ. ἔρωτες Luc. *Am.*28, cf. Artem.2.12. **-δάϊκτος** [δᾰ], ον, *man-slaying, murderous*, A.*Ch.*860, cf. *Fr.*132. **-δάμας** [δᾰ], αντος, ὁ, ἡ, *man-taming*, φόβος, ῥιπὰ οἴνου, Pi.*N.*3.39, *Fr.*166; *man-slaying*, of Eriphyle, Id. *N.*9.16 (ubi al. ἀνδροδάμαν τ' pro -δάμαντ'). II. *arsenical pyrites*, Ps.-Democr.Alch.p.45 B. **-δμής**· ὕπανδρος γυνή, Hsch. **-δομος**, ὁ, = ἀνδρών, Eust.1573.29, Hsch. **-ελής**, ές, (ἑλεῖν) *subduing men*, ἀνίη *Epigr.Gr.*1034.32 (Callipolis). **-θέα**, ἡ, *man-goddess*, i.e. Athena, *AP*15.22 (Simm.).

ἀνδρόθεν, Adv. *from a man*, ἀ. ἐκκέχυθ' ἵππος, of a Centaur, *APl.* 4.115.

ἀνδρό-θηλυς, υδος, ὁ, ἡ, = ἀνδρόγυνος 1, Philostr.*VS*1.8. **-θνής**, ῆτος, ὁ, ἡ, *murderous*, φθοραί A.*Ag.*814. **-κάπηλος**, ὁ, *slave-dealer*, Gal.6.530, Orib.14.48.1. **-κάπραινα**, ἡ, *lewd woman, wanton*, Pherecr.17 D.

ἀνδροκ-άς, = ἀνδρακάς (B), Hsch.: **-άδες**· πόα τις, Id.

ἀνδρό-κλας, α, ὁ, *weakening men*, of the climacterical year, i.e. the 63rd, Firm.4.20.3:—also **-κλάστης**, ου, ὁ, prob. in Critodem.ap. Vett.Val.237.7. **-κμής**, ῆτος, ὁ, ἡ, *man-wearying*, λοιγός, μόχθοι, A.*Supp.*678, *Eu.*248; *man-slaying*, πέλεκυς Id.*Ch.*889; ἀνδροκμῆτας προσφέρων ἀγωνίας E.*Supp.*525. **-κμητος**, ον, *wrought by men's hands*, τύμβος Il.11.371. **-κόβᾱλος**, ὁ, *rogue*, Hsch., Suid. **-κογχυλευτής**, οῦ, ὁ, v. ἀνδροπορφυρεύς. **-κοιτέω**, *sleep with a man*, *BGU* 1058.30 (i B.C.), Aët.1.142. **-κόνος**, ον, = ἀνδροκτόνος (q.v.), *AB* 394, Hsch. **-κόρινθος**, ὁ, *a Man-Corinth*, in allusion to the lewdness of the men of Heraclea and the women of Corinth, Stratonic.ap.Ath. 8.351c. **-κτᾰσία**, ἡ, (κτείνω) *slaughter of men* in battle, mostly in pl., παύσασθαι..Ἄρην ἀνδροκτασιάων Il.5.909; μάχας τ' ἀνδροκτασίας τε 7.237, etc.: personified, Hes.*Th.*228: in sg., ἀνδροκτασίης ὕπο λυγρῆς by reason of sad *homicide*, Il.23.86, cf. Hes.*Oxy.*1359.1.17, A.*Th.*693 (lyr.). **-κτάστης**, ὁ, prob. f. l. for -κλάστης, Vett. Val.237.7. **-κτονεῖον**, τό, *slaughter-house of men*, Phryn.*PS* p.49 B. **-κτονέω**, *slay men, commit homicide*, A.*Eu.*602. **-κτόνος**, ον, (κτείνω) *man-slaying, murdering*, Hdt.4.110, S.*Fr.*187, E. *Cyc.*22. **-λαλος**, ον, *gossiping about men*, Thphr.*Char.*28.3 (dub. l.).

ἀνδρ-ολέτειρα, ἡ, *murderess*, A.*Ag.*1465: as Adj., Id.*Th.*314 (lyr.).

ἀνδρο-λήμη, ἡ, (λῆμα) = ἀνδρόβουλος, Hsch. **-ληπτέω**, *seize men*, Ἀρχ.Ἐφ.1918.132. **-ληψία**, ἡ, *seizure of foreigners* in reprisal for the murder of a citizen abroad, Lex ap.D.23.82, 51.13, *Ath.Mitt.*32.245 (Pergam.). **-λήψιον**, τό, *right of seizure*, D. 23.83, cf. 6.217; generally, *seizure, arrest*, App.*BC*4.6, Philostr. *Ep.*50. **-λογεῖον**, τό, v. ἀνδρολογία. **-λογέω**, *enlist soldiers*, Alciphr.1.11:—Pass., Luc.*Tox.*58. **-λογία**, ἡ: κατ' ἀνδρολογίαν, κατ' ἀνδραλογίαν, κατ' ἀνδρολογεῖον, ff.ll. in Lxx 2*Ma.*12.43 for κατ' ἄνδρα λογείαν. **-μανέω**, *lust after men*, Eustr. *in EN*274.6. **-μανής**, ές, *mad after men, lustful*, Plu.*Comp.Lyc.Num.*3, *AB*394. **-μάχος** [ᾰ], ον, *fighting with men*, χεῖρες *AP*7.241 (Antip. Sid.): fem. ἀνδρομάχη, ἄλοχος ib.11.378 (Pall.).

Ἀνδρομέδα, ας, ἡ, *Andromeda*, Pherecyd.12 J., etc. II. *the constellation Andromeda*, Eudox.ap.Hipparch.1.2.13, Arat.189, etc.

ἀνδρόμεος, α, ον, (ἀνήρ) *human*, κρέα, αἷμα, χρὼς ἀ., Od.9.297, 22. 19, Il.20.100; ψωμοὶ ἀ. gobbets *of man's flesh*, Od.9.374; ὅμιλος ἀ. throng *of men*, Il.11.538; ἀ. κεφαλή Emp.134; αὐδή, ἐνοπή, A.R.1. 258, 4.581. II. ἀνδρόμεον· ἱμάτιον (Cret.), Hsch. (-μεο- cognate with Skt. *-māya-* in *hiran-māya-* 'golden', etc.)

ἀνδρο-μήκης, ες, *of a man's height*, σταύρωμα X.*HG*3.2.3; φοῖνιξ Thphr.*HP*2.6.7; ὕψος, βάθος, Plb.8.5.6, 10.46.3; θυρεοί Onos.20.1; πυρός Sosith.2.18. **-μηκιαῖος**, ον, = foreg., *POxy.*896 (iv A.D.).

ἀνδρομητὸν (i.e. ἀνα-δρ., cf. ἀνέδραμον) ἐγχειρίδιον a dagger *with a blade slipping back into the haft*, used for stage-murders, Hsch.

ἀνδρόμορφος, ον, *of man's form* or *figure*, Apollod.1.6.3, cf. Eust. 1571.45.

ἄνδρομος, ον, = ἀνδρώδης, Hdn.Gr.1.171.

ἀνδρο-νομέομαι, *to be imperious*, dub. in M.Ant.10.19 codd. **-παις**, αιδος, ὁ, *man-boy*, i.e. *boy with a man's mind*, of Parthenopaeus, A. *Th.*533; of Troilus, S.*Fr.*619, cf. Ar.*Fr.*53 D. **-πλήθεια**, ἡ, *multitude of men*, ἀ. στρατοῦ A.*Pers.*235. **-ποιός**, όν, *making manly*, Plu.2.334f. **-πορνος**, ὁ, *cinaedus*, Theopomp.Hist.17. **-πορφυρεύς**· ἀνδροκογχυλευτής, ἀναλέγων τὰς κόγχλους, Hsch. **-πρόσωπος**, ον, = sq., Hsch. **-πρῳρος**, ον, (πρῷρα) *with man's face*, Emp. 61. **-σάθων**, ὁ, (σάθη) obscene epith. of Priapus, Phot.p.127 R., Eust.1968.43, *AB*394 (prob. l. for -σάνθων), Suid.:—also **-σάθης**, ὁ, *AB* l.c., Hsch.

ἀνδρόσαιμον, τό, (αἷμα) a kind of *St. John's wort, Hypericum perfoliatum*, Dsc.3.156, Gal.11.829. 2. = ὑπερικόν, Dsc.3.154. 3. = ἄσκυρον, ib.155.

ἀνδρόσακες, ους, τό, *sea-navel, Acetabularia mediterranea*, Dsc.3. 133.

ἀνδρό-σῖνις, ιος, ὁ, ἡ, *hurtful to men*, *APl.*4.266. **-στροφος**, ον, *after the manner of men*, ἔργα Man.4.358.

ἀνδροσύνη, ἡ, = ἀνδρεία, Orac.ap.D.S.7.12.

ἀνδρο-σφᾰγεῖον, τό, *slaughter-house of men*, A.*Ag.*1092 (Dobree, for ἀνδρὸς σφαγεῖον). **-σφιγξ**, ιγγος, ὁ, *sphinx with the bust of a man*, not (as usually) of a woman, Hdt.2.175. **-σώτειρα**, ἡ, *saviour of men*, title of Isis, *POxy.*1380.55 (Pap. ἀνδρασ-).

ἀνδροτής, ῆτος, ἡ, *manhood*, Il.16.857, 24.6 (with first syll. shortened; v.l. ἁδροτῆτα). II. = ἀνδρεία, Phintys ap.Stob.4. 23.61.

ἀνδρο-τομέω, *castrate*, τὸν πατέρα S.E.*M.*1.289. **-τῠχής**, ές, *getting a man* or *husband*, ἀ. βίοτος *wedded* life, A.*Eu.*959 (lyr.). **-φᾰγέω**, *eat men*, v.l. for ἀνθρωποφ-, Hdt.4.106. **-φάγος**, ον, *eating men*, Κύκλωψ Od.10.200; οἱ Ἀ., a people north of the Scythians, Hdt.4.18,106, cf. Palaeph.7. **-φθόρος**, ον, *man-destroying, murderous*, μοῖρα Pi.*Fr.*177; ἔχιδνα S.*Ph.*266. II. proparox., ἀνδρόφθορον αἷμα the blood *of a slain man*, Id.*Ant.*1022. **-φονεύς**, έως, ὁ, = ἀνδροφόνος, Man.2.302. **-φονέω**, *slay men*, ἡβηδὸν ἀ. Str.4.6.8: c. acc., Hp.*Ep.*17:—Pass., Ph.2.314. **-φονία**, ἡ, *slaying of men*, Arist.*EN*1107a12, Epicur.*Fr.*237 (pl.), D.H.4.24 (pl.), Plu.*Rom.* 22. **-φόνος**, ον, *man-slaying*, Homeric epith. of Hector, Il.24. 724, etc.; of Achilles, χεῖρες ἀ. 18.317; *homicide*, Pl.*Phd.*114a; generally, *murderous*, ἀ. τὴν φύσιν Theopomp.Hist.217:—rarely exc. of *slaughter in battle*, but in Od.1.261 φάρμακον ἀ. a *murderous* drug:—epith. of αἷμα, Orph.*H.*65.4. 2. of women, *murdering their husbands*, Pi.*P.*4.252. II. as law-term, *one convicted of manslaughter, homicide*, Lys.10.7, D.23.29, cf. ib.216:—hence as a term of abuse, τοὺς ἀ. ἰχθυοπώλας Ath.6.228c, cf. Amphis 30. III. ἀ. Κῶνος, a landmark at Athens, *IG*3.61 *A* ii 15. **-φόντης**, ου, ὁ, = ἀνδρειφόντης, A.*Th.*572. **-φρων**, ονος, ὁ, ἡ, *man-minded*, like ἀνδρόβουλος, γυνή S.*Fr.*943. **-φυής**, ές, *of human shape*, Emp.61, Nonn.*D.*36.94. **-φυκτίς**, ίδος, ἡ, a kind of *mollusc*, Epich.42.

ἀνδρ-όω, *change into a man*, Lyc.176,943. II. *rear up into manhood*, *AP*7.419 (Mel.), Plu.2.490a:—Pass., *become a man, reach manhood*, Hdt.1.123, 2.32, Hp.*Art.*58, E.*HF*42, Ant.Lib.13.3, etc.: metaph., διθύραμβοι ἠνδρωμένοι Macho ap.Ath.8.341c: also in Med., = συγγενέσθαι, Hsch. III. in Pass., also of a woman, *virum experta sum*, ἠνδρώθησαν D.C.*Fr.*87.3; ἠνδρωμέναι Id.67.3. **-ύνω**, = foreg., Ps.-Callisth.1.13 (Pass.). **-ώδης**, ες, *manly*, -έστεροι ἄνδρες Emp.67, cf. Isoc.5.76 (Comp.); ἀ. τὴν φύσιν Arist.*EN*1171b6; -έστεροι τὰ ἤθη Id.*Rh.*1391a22; ἀ. ῥυθμοί, σχήματα, D.H.*Dem.*43, al.; λόγοι Plu.2.110d; δίαιτα Hierocl. *in CA*17 p.458 M.: Sup., J.*BJ*7. 8.6. Adv. -δῶς, διακεῖσθαι Isoc.12.31: Sup. -δέστατα X.*Mem.*4.8. 1. **-ών**, ῶνος, ὁ, *men's apartment* in a house, *banqueting-hall*, Hdt. (v. infr.), etc.; εὐτράπεζοι, εὔξενοι, A.*Ag.*244, *Ch.*712, cf. E.*HF*954, X.*Smp.*1.4, etc.; Ion. -εών (q.v.); Ep. -ειών (q.v.). **-ώνιον**, τό, Dim. of foreg., *IG*11(2).287 *A* 147,154 (Delos, iii B.C.). **-ωνῖτις**, ιδος, ἡ, = ἀνδρών, opp. γυναικωνῖτις, Lys.1.9, X.*Oec.*9.6, *IG*11(2).158 *A*18 (Delos, iii B.C.): as Adj., ἀ. ἑστία Ph.1.312, al. II. among the Romans, *passage between two courts of a house*, Vitr.6.7.5. **-ωνῠμικόν** (sc. ὄνομα), τό, *name transferred* from an animal *to a man*, e.g. Σκύμνος, Πῶλος, Sch.Il.18.319. **-ωνύμιον** [ῠ], τό, *proper name*, Theognost.*Can.*9, Sch.Ar.*V.*1239. **-ῷος**, α, ον, late form of ἀνδρεῖος, Muson.*Fr.*3 p.17 H., Gal.2.888, Sch.Ar.*Ra.*47, Aspasia ap. Aët.16.18; distinguished by Sch.Lib.*Or.*64.54 ἀνδρεῖα ἐσθήματα ἤτοι ἀνδράσι πρέποντα· ἀνδρῷα δὲ οἰκήματα τὰ ἐμπεριέχοντα ἄνδρας.

ἀ-νέαστος, ον, of land, *unploughed*, Str.11.4.3.

ἀνέβρᾰχε, (v. *βράχω), 3 sg. aor. 2, with no pres., τὰ δ' ἀνέβραχε but it [the armour] *clashed* or *rang loudly*, Il.19.13; τὰ δ' ἀνέβραχεν [the door] *creaked* or *grated loudly*, Od.21.48; of water, *gushed roaring forth*, A.R.1.1147.

ἀνεγγάρευτος, ον, = ἀναγγ., *free from obligation to serve as ἄγγαρος*. *Sammelb.*4226 (ii A.D.).

ἀνέγγραφος, ον, *of which no written evidence exists*, ἀδικήματα *IG* 5(2).357.162 (Stymphalus, iii B.C.), cf. Sch.Pl.*Ap.*19b, Suid.

ἀνέγγυος, ον, *not vouched for, not accredited*, ὧρη ἀ., of uncertain weather, Anacr.113; of an illegitimate child, νόθος καὶ ἀ. Pl.*R.*461b; γάμοι *unhallowed*, E.ap.Phot.p.128 R.; of a woman, *unbetrothed, unwedded*, Plu.*Caes.*14, *Comp.Rom.Thes.*6, D.C.59.12, etc.; ἀ. ποιεῖν τὰς μίξεις D.H.2.24.

ἀνεγ-είρω, *wake up, rouse*, ἐξ ὕπνου Il.10.138; ἐκ λεχέων Od.4.730; τὴν ἀηδόνα Ar.*Av.*208:—Pass., E.*HF*1055; ἀνηγέρθη X.*An.*3.1.12, *AP*11.257 (Lucill.): poet. aor. Med. ἀνεγρόμην A.R.1.522; ἀνεγρετο Maiist.31. II. metaph., *wake up, raise*, κῶμον Pi.*I.*8(7).2; μολπήν Ar.*Ra.*370:—Pass., ἀνεγειρομένα φάμα Pi.*I.*4(3).23. 2. metaph. also, *rouse, encourage*, ἀνέγειρα δ' ἑταίρους μειλιχίοις ἐπέεσσι Od.10. 172; *stir, rouse the spirit of*, θυμοειδῆ ἵππον X.*Eq.*9.6:—Med., *take heart*, Ph.2.120. III. of buildings, *raise*, δόμον *AP*9.693a, cf. Lib.*Or.*11.56; ἀπὸ θεμελίων *OGI*422 (Judaea). **-έρμων**, ον, gen. ονος, *wakeful*, κύνες *AP*9.558 (Eryc.). **-ερσις**, εως, ἡ, *raising up*, Plu.2.156b. 2. *waking up*, ib.378f. **-ερτος**, ον, *not broken by waking*, ἀ. ὕπνος Arist.*GA*779a3, *EE*1216a3.

ἀνεγκάλυπτος, ον, *uncovered*, Hsch.

ἀνεγκαρτέρητος, ον, *not to be endured*, κακὸν διὰ τὴν πολυχρονιότητα Phld.*Herc.*1251.4: v. ἀνεκκ-.

ἀνεγκέφαλος, ον, *without brain*, Gal.5.314.

ἀνεγκλη-σία, ἡ, γραφὴ ἀνεγκλησίας deed *of indemnity*, *PLips.*29.13 (iii A.D.), etc. **-τί** [ῐ], Adv. of sq., Pl.Com.231: -τεί Isoc.15. 28. **-τος**, ον, *without reproach, blameless*, X.*HG*6.1.13, D.*Ep.*2. 14; διαφυλάττειν τοὺς πολίτας ἀ. Arist.*Rh.*1360a16; ἀ. ἑαυτὸν παρέχειν *IG*2².1271, cf. *CIG*2270.7 (Delos). Adv. -τως D.17.2, *SIG*436.

6 (Delph., iii B.C.), *PLand.*33.14 (ii A.D.). **II.** *giving no ground for dispute*, ἀ. τὰς οὐσίας πρὸς ἀλλήλους κατασκευάζεσθαι Pl.*Lg.*737a. Adv. -τως, ἔχειν Arist.*Pol.*1321b22. **III.** Act. in Adv. -τως *uncomplainingly*, Plu.2.102e.

ἀνέγκλῐτος, ον, *unchanging*, Plu.2.393a, cf. *Per.*15. **II.** Gramm., *not enclitic*, A.D.*Synt.*136.7, al. **III.** Math., *not inclined*, i.e. at right angles, Ptol.*Alm.*1.16.

ἀνεγκόπτως, Adv. *without hesitation*, of speech, Aët.8.38.

ἀνεγκωμίαστος, ον, *not praised*, Isoc.9.73, J.*AJ*4.6.13.

ἄνεγμα· αἴνιγμα (Tarent.), Hsch.

ἀνέγρομαι, late poet. form for ἀνεγείρομαι, formed from the aor. ἀνηγρόμην, Opp.*H.*2.204, Q.S.5.610.

ἀνεγχώρητος, ον, *impossible*, Sch.Hermog. in Rh.7.135 W.

ἀνεδάφιστος [δᾰ], ον, *not levelled*, γῆ Arist.*Pr.*934b22.

ἀνέδην, Adv., (ἀνίημι) *let loose, freely, without restraint*, Pl.*Prt.* 342c, S.*Ph.*1153 (lyr.); ἀ. φεύγειν flee *pell-mell*, A.*Supp.*14; τῆς πομπείας τῆς ἀ. γεγενημένης D.18.11; ἀ. βακχεύειν *AP*6.172; ἀ. καὶ ὡς ἔτυχε Ael.*NA*3.9. **2.** *licentiously, violently*, Plb.15.20.3. **II.** *without more ado, simply, absolutely*, Pl.*Grg.*494e; *straightforwardly*, ἀ. ἐρωτᾶν Ps.-Alex.Aphr.*in SE*101.22.

ἀνέδραστος, ον, *without firm foundation*, βάσις, of a rhetorical period, D.H.*Comp.*22; δρόμος *IG*7.2543 (Thebes); of a bandage, *liable to slip*, Gal.18(2).379; *unsteady*, ib.819, cf. Plu.2.654a, Procl. *in Prm.*p.794 S., *in Ti.*3.122 D. Adv. -τως, gloss on ἀνέδην, Sch. Philum.ap.Orib.45.29.14.

ἀνέεδνος, ον, v. ἀνάεδνος.

***ἀνέζω**, pres. not found, *set upon*, ἐς δίφρον ἀνέσαντες Il.13.657; εἰς εὐνὴν ἀνέσαιμι 14.209, cf. 1.310 (tm.); *restore to one's place*, οὐκ οἶδ' ἤ κέν μ' ἀνέσει θεός Od.18.265:—Pass., *sit upright*, ἀνὰ δ' ἕζετο σιγῇ A.R.1.1170, 4.1332.

ἀνεθέλητος, ον, *unwished for, unwelcome*, ἐπὶ συμφορὴν ἐνέπεσε ἀνεθέλητον Hdt.7.88; ἀ. γίνεταί τι ib.133.

ἀνεθ-ίζομαι, *become used to* a thing, D.L.2.96. **-ιστέον**, *one must accustom*, Dam.*Pr.*3.

ἀνέθιστος, ον, *unaccustomed*, πόνοι Hp.*Vict.*2.66; ἱερά D.H.2.73.

ἀνείδεος, ον, (εἶδος) *formless*, ὕλη *Placit.*1.2.3, cf. Ph.1.417, al., Plot.1.8.3, al., Ael.*NA*2.56; ὕλη *without specific difference*, Dam.*Pr.* 425; of persons, μικρά τις καὶ ἀνείδεος Aen.Gaz.*Thphr.*p.62 B.

ἀνειδωλόπληκτος, ον, *not afflicted by ghosts*, *PMag.Par.*1.1063.

ἀνειδωλοποι-έω, *represent in imagery*, of poets, Plu.2.1113a; *form a mental image of, imagine*, τὰ μὴ ὄντα ὡς ὄντα Ph.2.59, cf. S.E.*P.* 3.155:—Med., *Placit.*5.2.3:—Pass., τὰ ἀνειδωλοποιούμενα μέτρα patterns *conceived in the mind*, Longin.14.1. **-ησις**, εως, ἡ, S.E. *P.*3.189.

ἀνεικάζομαι, Med., *represent satirically*, Cratin.63 (dub.).

ἀνεικαιότης, ητος, ἡ, *levelheadedness, discretion*, Chrysipp.*Stoic.* 2.40, Arr.*Epict.*3.2.2, D.L.7.46.

ἀνείκαστος, ον, *unattainable by conjecture, immense*, βοή Lxx 3*Ma.* 1.28; πλῆθος Ps.-Callisth.3.20; *incomparable*, στρατιώτης Polem. *Call.*50; f.l. for ἀνήκεστος, D.8.46. **II.** *incapable of artistic representation*, D.Chr.12.59.

ἀνεικής, ές, *uncontested*, v.l. for ἀεικής, Il.12.435.

ἀνεικία, ἡ, Pythag., = πεντάς, as reconciling the feud of odd and even (3 + 2), *Theol.Ar.*27, al.; cf. ἀνικία. **2.** also = ἐννεάς, ib.57.

ἀνεικόνιστος, ον, *not registered with personal description*, *BGU* 258.9 (ii A.D.).

ἄνεικος, ον, *without demur*, φόρον ἄ. τελεῖν *CIG*2693e11 (Cyzicus).

ἀνειλείθυια, ἡ, *without the aid of Eileithyia*, ἀ. ὠδίνων λοχιᾶν *never having invoked her aid* in childbirth, E.*Ion*453, cf. Eust.1861.44.

ἀνειλ-έω, *roll up* or *crowd together*, πολεμίους Philostr.*VA*2.11:—Pass., *crowd* or *throng together*, ἀνειληθέντες εἴς τι χωρίον Th.7.81; αἱ μέλιτται.. αὑτοῦ ἀνειλοῦνται Arist.*HA*627b12; of wind *pent in the bowels*, v.l. in Hp.*Prog.*11; πνεῦμα -ούμενον Epicur.*Ep.*2 p.46 U.; of sound, Arist.*Aud.*804a20; ἀνειλεῖται ἡ γλῶσσα *is kept within bounds*, Plu.2.503c. **II.** *unroll*, ib.109d. **-ημα**, ατος, τό, *rolling up*: in pl., *flatulent colic*, Hp.*VM*22. **II.** *scroll*, Aristeas 177 (pl.). **-ησις**, εως, ἡ, = foreg., Hp.*Epid.*3.8. **2.** *penning up, confinement*, πνεύματος Epicur.*Ep.*2 p.44 U. **3.** *twisting of the body*, in gymnastic exercises, Aret.*CD*1.2, 2.13.

ἀνειλιγμένως, Adv. pf. part. Pass. of ἀνελίσσω, *explicitly*, opp. συνεσπειραμένως, Herm.*in Phdr.*p.137 A., cf. Phlp.*in Ph.*20.5; [ψυχὴ μετέχει θεοῦ] ἀ. Anon.*Incred.*21.

ἀνείλιξις, εως, ἡ, *reversal of motion*, Pl.*Plt.*270d, 286b.

ἀνειλίσσω, v. ἀνελίσσω.

ἀνείλλω or **ἀνείλω**, = ἀνειλέω:—in Pass., *shrink up* or *back*, Pl. *Smp.*206d.

ἀνειλυσπᾶσθαι· ἀναρ⟨ρ⟩ιχᾶσθαι, Hsch.

ἀνείλυστος, ον, *accompanied with gripes*, στρόφοι Aret.*SD*2.3.

ἀνειμάρθαι, pf. inf. Pass., = οὐχ εἱμάρθαι *not to be decreed by fate*, dub. in *Placit.*1.27.4 (ἀνειμαρτά Diels).

ἀνείμασθος· ἄφθορος, ἄπληστος, Hsch.

ἀνειμένως, Adv. pf. part. Pass. of ἀνίημι, *at ease, carelessly*, ἀργῶς καὶ ἀ. X.*Mem.*2.4.7; ἀ. διαιτᾶσθαι *without restraint, freely*, Th.2.39; πίνειν X.*Cyr.*4.5.8; ζῆν Arist.*EN*1114a5; ἀ. ποιεῖσθαι τοὺς λόγους *frankly*, Isoc.8.41; κατηγορίαν τινὸς ποιήσασθαι ἀ. *openly*, Aristid.2. 116 J.; *in a milder form*, Dsc.2.153, 5.159. **2.** *without accent*, opp. περισπωμένως, ὀξυτόνως, Anon.*in SE*8.23.

ἄνειμι, in Att. serving as fut. to ἀνέρχομαι, and ἀνῄειν, Ep. ἀνήϊον, as impf.:—*go up*, ἅμ' ἠελίῳ ἀνιόντι at sun-*rise*, Il.18.136, cf. Hdt.3. 85; ἀνήϊον ἐς περιωπήν *I went up a hill*, Od.10.146, cf. Pl.*R.*614d; γῆ δ' ἄνεισ' εἰς αἰθέρα E.*Fr.*687; ἱδρὼς ἀνῄει χρωτί *came up* upon the skin, S.*Tr.*767: metaph., *reach, attain to*, εἰς προβλήματα Pl.*R.*531c: Medic., ἐπὶ τὰς ϛ' *raised the dose* to six cotylae, Ruf.ap.Aët.5.84. **2.** *sail up*, i.e. *out to sea*, ἐκ Τροίης ἀνιόντα θοῇ σὺν νηΐ Od.10.332; πόντον ἀνήϊον A.R.4.238. **3.** *go up inland* (v. supr. 1), esp. *go up* into Central Asia, ἡ ἀγγελίη ἀνῄιε παρὰ τὸν βασιλέα Hdt.5.108; ἐκ Πειραιῶς Pl.*R.*439e, etc.; εἰς ἄστυ Φαληρόθεν Id.*Smp.*172a. **4.** *come forth*, Ael.*NA*11.33. **5.** *to be promoted*, εἰς Ἄρειον πάγον Hyp.*Fr.* 138, Lex ap.D.24.22. **6.** ἀνιόντα καὶ κατιόντα πρόσωπα *ascendants* and descendants, Just.*Nov.*117.7, 118*Pr.* **II.** *approach*, esp. as a suppliant, ἄνεισι πάϊς ἐς πατρὸς ἑταίρους Il.22.492, 499. **III.** *go back, return*, freq. in Od., ἐξ Αἰθιόπων ἀνιών 5.282; ἀ. ἐπὶ τὸν πρότερον λόγον Hdt.1.140, cf. 7.239; θαλάσσης ἐς τέκνα Pl.Com.173. 11; without Prep., πάλιν δὲ τῶνδ' ἄνειμί σοι γένος *genus repetam*, E. *Heracl.*209.

ἀνείμων, ον, gen. ονος, (εἷμα) *without clothing, unclad*, Od.3.348.

ἀνεινῶς· οἰκτρῶς, Hsch.

ἀνεῖπον, aor. with no pres. in use, ἀναγορεύω being used instead; imper. ἀνειπάτω *IG*2².1186.19, but -έτω ib.1247.13:—*announce, proclaim*, esp. by herald, ἀ. τινά *proclaim* conqueror, Pi.*P.*1.32, 10. 9; στέφανον *IG*12(5).129.33 (Paros), cf. Docum.ap.D.18.55; τῷ ἀπειθοῦντι πάντα τὰ χαλεπὰ ἀνεῖπεν X.*Cyr.*4.2.35; τὸν νόμον ἄνειπε Herod.2.42: c. acc. et inf., *make proclamation that*.., τοὺς γεωργοὺς ἀπιέναι Ar.*Pax* 550; κήρυγμα τόδε ἀνειπών.. τὸν μὲν βουλόμενον.. μένειν κτλ. Th.4.105; also εἴ τις εἴη.. ἐκφαίνεσθαι X.*Cyr.*4.5.56: abs., *proclaim, give notice*, in law-courts, theatres, etc., ἀνεῖπεν ὁ κῆρυξ, εἴ τις βούλεται.. ξυμμαχεῖν, τίθεσθαι τὰ ὅπλα Th.2.2, cf. Pl.*R.* 580b, etc.; ὁ δ' ἀνεῖπεν, εἴσαγ', ὦ Θέογνι, τὸν χορόν Ar.*Ach.*11; ἐν τῷ βουλευτηρίῳ ἀ. Docum.ap.D. l.c. supr.: simply, *say aloud*, τῷ δὲ ἀνεῖπεν ἔνδοθεν, "εἰς κόρακας" Luc.*Alex.*46.—Pass., aor. ἀνερρήθην, ἀναρρηθεὶς ἡγεμών X.*HG*1.4.20, etc.; ἀναρρηθέντος ἐν τῷ θεάτρῳ τοῦ στεφάνου D.18.83, cf. ib.149; τὸν ἐν τῇ ἐκκλησίᾳ στέφανον ἀναρρηθέντα Aeschin.3.47: fut. ἀναρρηθήσεται ib.147: pf. imper. ἀνειρήσθω *let the proclamation be taken as made*, Pl.*R.*580c. **II.** *call upon, invoke*, θεούς Plu.*Comp.Rom.Thes.*6.

ἀνείργω, *keep back, restrain*, used by Hom. always in Ep. impf., Τρώων ἀνέεργε φάλαγγας Il.3.77; μάχην ἀνέεργον ὀπίσσω 17.752; so ἀ. τὸν θυμόν Pl.*Lg.*731d; τοὺς στρατιώτας X.*HG*7.1.31; ταῖς τιμωρίαις τοὺς ἁμαρτάνοντας D.H.*Is.*8; τινὰς ἀπὸ πράξεως Porph.*Abst.*1.7: c. acc. et inf., ἀ. μὴ διασκίδνασθαι τὴν ἀγέλην Luc.*DDeor.*20.5:—f.l. in X.*Cyr.*5.4.45 (leg. ἀνειργμένοις). **II.** *force back*, D.H.3.32.

ἀνειρεσίαν· οὐσίαν πολλήν, Hsch. **ἀνείρετον**· ἀπαραίτητον, Id.

ἄνειρξις, εως, ἡ, *restraint*, Plu.2.584e.

ἀνείρομαι, used by Hom. only in pres., whereas Att. prefer ἀνερωτάω: but Trag. (in lyr.) use aor. ἀνηρόμην S.*Aj.*314, inf. ἀνερέσθαι Id.*OT*1304; Pl.*Men.*85c has fut. ἀνερήσομαι, and Hsch. gives ἀνηρήμεθα· ἠρωτήθημεν: **1.** c. acc. pers., *inquire of, question*, ὅτε κεν δή σ' αὐτὸς ἀνείρηται ἐπέεσσι Od.4.420; so μή μ' ἀνέρῃ τίς εἰμι S.*OC*210, cf. *Aj.*314, Pl.*Ap.*20a, etc. **2.** c. acc. rei, *ask about*, τήνδε τε γαῖαν ἀνείρεαι Od.13.238: in Prose also περί τινος Pl.*Men.*74c. **3.** c. dupl. acc., ὅ μ' ἀνείρεαι what thou *inquirest of* me, Il.3.177; ἀνήρετ'.. Χαιρεφῶντα Σωκράτης ψύλλαν ὁπόσους ἅλλοιτο.. πόδας Ar. *Nu.*145, cf. Pl.*Smp.*173b, etc.

ἀνειρύω, poet. and Ion. for ἀνερύω.

ἀνείρω, (v. εἴρω) *fasten on* or *to, string*, ἀνείρας [τὰ ὦτα] περὶ τὸν χαλινόν Hdt.3.118; ἀ. τὰ κρέα *fasten upon* a spit, Pl.Com.201; ἐνώτια ἀργυρᾶ ἀνειρμένα *IG*11(2).161 *B*61 (Delos); ἀ. στεφάνους *twine* or *wreathe* them, Ar.*Ach.*1006; τρίχας βελόνῃ D.C.51.14.

ἀνεῖσαι· ἐρευνῆσαι, ζητῆσαι, Hsch.

ἀνείσακτος, ον, *not initiated*, = ἀμύητος, Iamb.*VP*17.75; applied by Stoics to their opponents, *Stoic.*2.250.

ἀνεισοδίαστος, ον, ἔσται δὲ ἄπρατον καὶ ἀ. dub.l. in *IGRom.*4. 1475 (Smyrna; prob. ἀνεξ- *inalienable*).

ἀνείσοδος, ον, *without entrance* or *access*, Plu.*Dio* 7, *Pyrrh.*29.

ἀνείσπρακτος, ον, *free from pecuniary liability*, *BGU*1133.13 (i B.C.), *POxy.*270, 286.

ἀνεισφορ-ία, ἡ, *exemption from taxation*, *SIG*612 *B*3 (Delph., ii B.C.), *Jahresh.*14 *Beibl.*126 (Tralles), Plu.*Eum.*4, *IPE*2.36.2, *BGU* 1074.4 (quoting Hadrian's decree), etc. **-ος**, ον, *exempt from taxation*, τῶν εἰς τὰ στρατιωτικὰ ἀναλισκομένων D.H.5.22, cf. Plu. *Cam.*2, *IG*14.951, J.*AJ*13.6.7.

ἀνέκαθεν, before a cons. -θε (Hdt.6.128 codd.), Adv. of Place (cf. ἀνεκάς), *from above*, A.*Ch.*427, *Eu.*369 (lyr.); τἀνέκαθεν ῥεῖ ἐκ.. Hdt. 4.57; cf. ἄγκαθεν. **II.** of Time, *from the first*, ἐόντες ἀ. Πύλιοι being Pylians *by origin*, Id.5.65, cf. 7.221; more often with the Art., γεγονότες τὸ ἀ. ἀπὸ Αἰγύπτου 2.43, cf. 6.128; γένος ἐόντες τὰ ἀ. Γεφυραῖοι 5.55, cf. 1.170, 6.35; τὰ ἀ. λαμπροί of *ancestral* renown, 6.125; πόλις ἀ. συγγενὴς *OGI*566 (Lycia). **2.** ἀ. κατηγορεῖν narrate *from the beginning*, Plb.2.35.10, 5.16.6.

ἀνέκαιρεν· ἀνεβάλλετο, ἀνήρχετο, ἀνεφέρετο, Hsch.

ἀνεκάς, Adv. *upwards*, ὅταν.. μοῖρα πέμπῃ ἀ. ὄλβον Pi.*O.*2.22; ἀσπίδα φέρειν.. ἀ. ἐς τὸν οὐρανόν Ar.*V.*18, cf. *Fr.*188; [τρέπειν] τὸν αὐχέν' ἐκ γῆς ἀ. Crates Com.10; ἀ. δ' ἐπῆρω τὸ σκέλος Eup.50, cf. Pherecr.169 (Valck.); εἰς τὸ ἀ. Hp.*Mul.*1.1. (Plu.*Thes.*33 wrongly derives the name of the Ἄνακες from this word, τὸ γὰρ ἄνω τοὺς Ἀττικοὺς **ἀνέκας** (sic) ὀνομάζειν καὶ **ἀνέκαθεν** τὸ ἄνωθεν, cf. *Num.*13: but -κάς perh. as in ἄνδρα-κάς (A) (q.v.), ἑ-κάς: ἀνεκάς does not contain ἑκάς; ἀνεκάς· ψιλῶς, Phot.p.129.13 R., i.e. not ἀνhεκάς.)

ἀνεκβάλλω, *draw out*, σκόλοπας καὶ ἀκίδας, of a plaster, Gal.14.242.

ἀνέκ-βᾰτος, ον, *without outlet*, χαράδρα Th.3.98; Ἄϊδος εὐνή Opp.*H.*4.392. 2. *not 'coming off'*, ὄνειρος, opp. ἀποβαίνειν, *Cat.Cod. Astr.*5(3).89.31. **-βίαστος**, ον, *not to be overpowered*, Chrysipp. *Stoic.*2.64, v.l. in Gell.1.2.7. **-δαρτος**, ον, *not skinned*, and Adv. **ἀνεκδαρτί**, both in Suid. **-δήμητος**, ον, *unpropitious for a journey*, ἡμέρα Plu.2.269e. **-διήγητος**, ον, *indescribable, ineffable*, 2*Ep. Cor.*9.15, Hsch., v.l. in Aristeas 99. **-δίκητος**, ον, *unavenged*, J.*AJ*20.3.1; *unpunished*, *PGoodsp.*15.5; βλασφημίαι Just.*Nov.*77.1.1, cf.137 *Pr.* **-δοτος**, Arc. **ἀνέσδοτος** *SIG*306.5 (Tegea, iv B.C.), ον, *not given in marriage, unaffianced*, of a girl, Lys.13.45, D.45.74, Is.6.14; ἀ. ἔνδον καταγηράσκειν Hyp.*Lyc.*13. II. *unpublished*, D.S.1.4, Cic.*Att.*14.17.6; of a *secret* remedy, ἀ. δύναμις Philum.*Ven.*10.9. **-δρομος**, ον, *inevitable*, θῶμιγξ *AP*9.343 (Arch.). **-δυτος**, ον, *not to be escaped from*, to interpr. νήδυμος, Eust.1580.13. **-θέρμαντος**, ον, *not warmed* or *to be warmed*, Gal.7.189, Orib.ap.Phot.*Bibl.*p.175 B. Adv. -τως Antyll.ap.Orib. 9.25.27. **-θῦτος**, ον, *not to be removed by sacrifice*, μιάσματα Corn.*ND*9 (codd. ἀνέκπλυτα). **-καρτέρητος**, ον, *unendurable*, κακόν Phld.*D.*1.12. (Less usual spelling of ἀνεγκ-, cf. ἀνέκκλητος 2.) **-κλησίαστος**, ον, *not used for assemblies of the people*, θέατρον Posidon.41. **-κλητος**, ον, *unchallenged*, of a περιοδονίκης (q.v.), *IG*14.1102, 1104. 2. = ἀνέγκλητος. Adv. -τως *GDI*1723, 1729 (Delph.). **-κλῖτος**, ον, *not to be evaded*, Hsch. s.v. ἀλίαστος, Sch.Il.2.797. Adv. -τως *unavoidably*, ibid. **-κόπως**, Adv. *without excision* (but prob. ἀνεκκόπτως), Heliod.ap.Orib.50.9.5. **-κρῖτος**, ον, *not emptied*, γαστήρ Poet. *de herb.*137. **-λάλητος**, ον, *unutterable, ineffable*, 1 *Ep.Pet.*1.8, Eun.*VS* p.486 B., Ar. Byz.*Epit.*26.10, Jul.*Or.*5.158d. 2. *not capable of expression* or *calculation*, δύναμις Dsc.*Eup.Praef.*; ἰδιότης Heliod.ap.Sch.Orib.45.2. **-λειπτος**, ον, *incessant, uninterrupted*, Hyp.*Epit.*20 (dub.), D.S.4.84, *PLond.*3.1166.7 (i A.D.); *infinite*, of divisions of space, S.E.*M.*10.141; *unfailing*, Lxx *Wi.*7.14, *Ev.Luc.*12.33, D.S.1.36, Procl.*Inst.*84. Adv. -τως D.S.18.50, Hero ap.Procl. *Hyp.*4.75. 2. ἀ. μᾶζα, in Alchemy, of the asem alloy, *PHolm.*2.17, *PLeid.X.*7 and 39. **-λεκτος**, ον, *not carefully chosen*, ὀνόματα D.H.*Comp.*3. **-ληπτ[..]·** ἐξαίρεσιν ποιεῖσθαι (Rhod.), Hsch. **-λῐπής**, ές, = ἀνέκλειπτος, Lxx *Wi.*7.14, 8.18. **-λόγιστος**, neut. pl. as Adv., -ιστα *without reckoning*, *BGU*183.24 (i A.D.): regul. Adv. -τως, πίνειν Pherecr.143.1. **-λῦτος**, ον, *indissoluble*, Just.*Nov.*39 *Pr.* **-νιπτος**, ον, *indelible*, Poll.1.44. **-πίμπλημι**, *fill up* or *again*, f.l. in X.*An.*3.4.22. **-πληκτος**, ον, *undaunted, intrepid*, Pl.*Tht.*165b, Hyp.*Fr.*117; ὑπὸ κακῶν Pl.*R.*619a:—τὸ -ότατον X. *Ages.*6.7. Adv. -τως Plu.2.260c, Hierocl. *in CA*10 p.434 M. II. Act., *making no impression*, λέξις Plu.2.7a. **-πληξία**, ἡ, *imperturbability*, Pl.*Def.*412c. **-πλήρωτος**, ον, *incapable of fulfilment*, τἀγαθὸν ⟨οὐκ⟩ -τον Phld.*D.*1.12. **-πλῦτος**, ον, *indelible*, Pl.*Ti.*26c, Poll.1.44. **-ποίητος**, ον, *not alienated*, of property, πράγματα Just.*Nov.*22.20.2, cf. 22.39. **-πραξία**, ἡ, *non-effect*, Sch. A.*Th.*843. **-πύητος**, ον, *not suppurating*, Hp.*Aph.*5.20, Ruf.ap. Orib.7.26.21; δακρυώδης καὶ ἀ. exuding serum *instead of pus*, Hp. *Fract.*25. **-πύρωτος**, *not set on fire*, Olymp. *in Mete.*12.25. **-πυστος**, ον, *not found out by inquiry*, J.*AJ*17.11.2.

ἀνεκτέος, α, ον, *to be borne*, ἀνεκτέα (sc. ἐστι τάδε) S.*OC*883; ἀνεκτέα τάδε (restored for ἀνεκτά) Ar.*Lys.*477: **ἀνεκτέον**, Clearch.4.

ἀνεκτικός, ή, όν, (ἀνέχομαι) *enduring, patient*, τῶν ἰδιωτῶν M.Ant. 1.9; τινός Arr.*Epict.*2.22.36. Adv. -κῶς Hierocl. *in CA*12 p.447 M.

ἀνέκτιτος, ον, *unpaid*, χρέος D.Chr.12.43.

ἀνέκτομος, ον, *not castrated, entire*, prob. in Philotim.ap.Orib.2. 69.3.

ἀνεκτός, όν, later ή, όν *IGRom.*4.293 ii 4 (Pergam.), D.L.2.36: Aeol. **ὄνεκτος** Alc.*Supp.*27.9:—*bearable, sufferable, tolerable*, mostly with a neg. (like ἀνασχετός), λοίγια ἔργα.. οὐδ' ἔτ' ἀνεκτά Il.1.573; χρειὼ.. οὐκέτ' ἀνεκτός 10.118, Thgn.1195, etc.: so mostly in Att., οὐκ ἀνεκτόν A.*Ag.*1364; οὐκ ἀνεκτά S.*Ant.*282, etc.; or with a question, ἦ ταῦτα δῆτ' ἀνεκτά; Id.*OT*429; ταυτὶ δῆτ' ἀνέκτ' ἀκούειν; Ar. *Th.*563:—οὐκ ἀνεκτόν [ἐστι] foll. by inf., with or without μὴ οὐ, Pl. *Tht.*154c, 181b; τὸ μὲν οὐκ ἀ. ἐμοὶ.. γίγνεσθαι Id.*Lg.*861d. 2. without a neg., τὸ μὲν καὶ ἀνεκτὸν ἔχει κακόν *that can be endured*, Od.20.83; ἀ. χοὖτος ἦν ὅμως ἐμοί Pherecr.145.13; ἀνεκτὰ παθεῖν Th.7.77; μέχρι τοῦδε ἀνεκτοὶ οἱ ἔπαινοι ἐς ὅσον.. Id.2.35; παντὶ τρόπῳ ὅστις καὶ ὁπωσοῦν ἀνεκτός in any *tolerable* manner whatsoever, Id.8.90; ἀ. τι λέγειν Isoc.8.65; συμβίωσιν -όν Phld.*Ir.*p.78 W.; ἀνεκτότερα *more tolerable*, Cic.*Att.*12.45.2; ἀνεκτότερον ἔσται τινὶ *Ev.Matt.*10.15, 11.22, etc.: Sup., Phld.*Rh.*2.226 S. b. of persons, μόγις ἀνεκτοί Lys.22.20, cf. D.*Ep.*3.13. II. Adv. -τῶς, in Hom. always οὐκέτ' ἀνεκτῶς, Od.9.350, etc.; οὐκ ἀνεκτῶς ἔχει it is not *to be borne*, X.*HG*7.3.1: without neg., Phld.*D.*3 *Fr.*2, *Oec.*p.31 J.

ἀνεκτότης, ητος, ἡ, *endurableness*, *Gloss.*

ἀνέκ-τριπτος, ον, *indelible*, Poll.1.44. **-φαντος** (v.l. -φατος), ον, *not to be revealed* or *uttered*, i.e. *mystical, obscure*, Procl. *in Prm.* p.549 S., *in Ti.*3.169 D. Adv. -τως Id. *in Prm.*p.589 S., cf. Eust.382.9. **-φευκτος**, ον, *not to be escaped, inevitable*, D.S.20.54, Plu.2.166e, Corn.*ND*13, Phld.*Ir.*p.79 W. **-φοίτητος**, ον, *not proceeding* or *emanating*: hence, *inseparable from...*, τὰ μέρη τῶν ὅλων Procl. *in Ti.*1.6 D., *in Prm.*p.634 S.; τοῦ ὅλου Dam.*Pr.*289; τοῦ ἑνός ib.59; ἀπὸ [τῆς οὐσίας] ib.66; ἑαυτῆς Eustr. *in EN*40.8. **-φορος**, ον, *not to be brought to light*, Iamb.*VP*32.226, Poll.5.147. 2. Medic., ἀνέκφορα πάντα γίγνεται there is a general *stoppage* (of intestinal obstruction), Archig.ap.Aët.9.28. **-φραστος**, ον, *inexpressible, unutterable*, Procl. *in Prm.*p.549 S. 2. *not visiting*, τῶν ἐκεῖ Syrian. *in Metaph.*109.25. **-φώνητος**, ον: in Gramm., ἀνεκφώνητα *unpronounced letters*, as ι subscriptum, *EM*203.7. **-χύμωτος**, ον, *not drained of juices*, Gal.13.194.

ἀνέλαιος, ον, *without oil*, Thphr.*CP*2.3.8; *without olives*, Str.17.1.35.

ἀνέλατος, ον, = ἀνήλατος, Olymp. *in Mete.*326.38.

ἀνελάττωτος, ον, *undiminished*, Procl. *in Alc.*p.16 C. Adv. -τως Id.*Inst.*27.

ἀνέλεγ-κτος, ον, *not cross-questioned, safe from being questioned*, Th.5.85; ἡ γλῶττα ἀ. ἡμῖν ἔσται, ἡ δὲ φρὴν οὐκ ἀ. Pl.*Tht.*154d, cf. *Phlb.*41b. 2. *not refuted*, ἐὰν τινὰ ἀ. Id.*Grg.*467a; ἵνα μοι καὶ ἀ. ἡ μαντεία γένοιτο *irrefutable*, Id.*Ap.*22a, cf. *Ti.*29b. Adv. -τως, λεγόμενον *without refutation* or *reply*, Plu.*CG*10. 3. of persons also, *without trial*, ἀ. διαφυγεῖν Th.6.53. **-ξία**, ἡ, *irrefutableness*, *Stoic.*2.39. **-χω**, *convince, convict utterly*, E.*Ion*1470.

ἀνελεήμων, ον, gen. ονος, *merciless, without mercy*, Arist.*Rh. Al.*1442ᵃ13, *Ep.Rom.*1.31, *Cat.Cod.Astr.*2.173:—also **ἀνηλεήμων**, Nicoch.20; and in *AB*400 **ἀνελήμων**. Adv. ἀνελεημόνως, ἀπολέσθαι Antipho 1.25, Lxx *Jb.*6.21.

ἀνελεής, ές, = sq. Adv. -ῶς *mercilessly*, *PLips.*39.12 (iv A.D.).

ἀνελέητος, ον, *without pity*, Arist.*Phgn.*808ᵇ1; εἰς ἀδελφόν Lib. *Decl.*47.32.

ἀνελελίζω, *shake and rouse*, Opp.*C.*4.302.

ἀνέλεος, ον, *unmerciful*, *Ep.Jac.*2.13.

ἀνελευθερ-ία, ἡ, *illiberality of mind, servility*, joined with κολακεία, Pl.*Smp.*183b, *R.*590b, etc. 2. esp. in money matters, *stinginess*, X.*Cyr.*8.4.32, Arist.*EN*1107ᵇ10, 1121ᵇ13, etc. **-ιος**, ον, = ἀνελεύθερος, Asp. *in EN*101.14. **-ιότης**, ητος, ἡ, = ἀνελευθερία, Arist. *MM*1192ᵃ8. **-ος**, ον, *not free*, σῶμα, of a slave, Pherecr.8 D.; *slavish*, of a shameful death, A.*Ag.*1494 (lyr.); ἀτιμίαι Arist.*Pol.*1336ᵇ12. 2. of actions, *servile, mean*, ἀ. εἶναι νομίζω κακηγορίας δικάζεσθαι Lys.10.2, cf. Pl.*Tht.*182c; ἀ. ἐργασίαι Arist.*EN*1121ᵇ33; παιδιαί *Pol.*1336ᵃ29. 3. esp. in money matters, *niggardly*, Ar.*Pl.*591, Arist.*EN*1107ᵇ13, 1122ᵃ5, etc. 4. *rude, unpolished*, διάλεκτος Ar.*Fr.*685. 5. of animals, *mean, treacherous*, ζῷα ἀ. καὶ ἐπίβουλα, οἷον οἱ ὄφεις Arist.*HA*488ᵇ16. II. Adv. -ρως *meanly*, προσαιτεῖν X.*Ap.*9; ζῆν Alex.265.7.

ἀνέλ-ιγμα, ατος, τό, *anything rolled up*, ἀ. χαίτης *a ringlet*, *AP*6.210 (Philet.), cf. 7.485 (Diosc.). **-ικτος**, ον, *without turns* or *twists*, Aret.*CD*1.4, Gal.*UP*5.3. **-ιξις**, εως, ἡ, *unfolding*: hence, *evolution* in dancing, Plu.*Thes.*21. 2. *unfolding* in growth, Simp. *in Ph.*632.31. 3. logical *unfolding, exposition*, αἱ -ξεις τῶν λόγων Procl. *in Prm.*p.542 S., cf. Syrian. *in Metaph.*97.4, Prisc.Lyd.34.23; ἡ μαθηματικὴ ἐπιστήμη γνῶσίς ἐστι.. διεξόδοις τισὶ χρωμένη καὶ ἀνελίξεσιν Iamb.*Comm.Math.*1. **-ίσσω**, Att. **ἀνελίττω**, Ep. and Ion. **ἀνειλίσσω**: (v. ἑλίσσω):—*unroll*, ἀγαθίδα Pherecyd.148 J.: but mostly, *unroll* a book, Arist.*Pr.*914ᵃ26 (Pass.); *read, interpret* it, X. *Mem.*1.6.14; λόγον Pl.*Phlb.*15e. 2. *unravel, 'explicate'*, τὸ συνεσπειραμένον τῆς νοερᾶς ἐπιβολῆς Procl. *in Euc.*p.4 F., cf. Prisc.Lyd.34.23; ἀνειλιγμένος ὁρισμός *explicit* definition, Simp. *in Ph.*276.28. 3. *cause to move backward*, πόδα E.*Or.*171. II. *roll back*, i.e. *counteract*, ἀνελίττουσαι σφαῖραι Arist.*Metaph.*1074ᵃ2, cf. Simp. *in Cael.*32.17, al., Procl.*Hyp.*4.98, Theo Sm.p.180 H.: metaph., ὅπως ἂν στρέφῃ καὶ ἀνελίττῃ τὸν βίον ὁ θεός Plu.*Num.* 14:—Med., *reverse the direction of motion*, Arist.*GA*741ᵇ21:—Pass., *to be counteracted*, Id.*Metaph.*1074ᵃ7; μίαν δ' ἀνελίσσετ' ἀμοιβήν Opp.*H.*1.420; γλῶσσ' ἀνελισσομένη *moving glibly*, Ar.*Ra.*827. III. intr., πνεύματ' ἀνειλίσσοντα Nic.*Al.*596.

ἀνελκής, ές, *free from ulceration*, Hp.*Off.*18.

ἀνελκόομαι, Pass., *suppurate afresh*, Hp.*Mul.*2.122, *Morb.*1.21, Cass.*Pr.*9.

ἄνελκτος, ον, *inextensible*, Arist.*Mete.*385ᵃ16, 386ᵇ14.

ἀνελκτός, όν, *up-drawn*, ἀ. ὀφρύσι, prob. of Pericles, Cratin.355.

ἀνέλκυστος, ον, *incapable of being pulled*, ὑπὸ φαντασίας Chrysipp. *Stoic.*2.40.

ἀνέλκω, *draw up*, τάλαντα.. ἀνέλκει *holds* them *up* (in weighing), Il.12.434; ἀνελκύσαι νῆας *haul* them *up high and dry*, Hdt.7.59, Th.6.44; νῆες ἀνελκυσμέναι Hdt.9.98; δοκοὺς ἀ. Th.2.76; *haul up* a sail, Epicr.10. 2. *drag up, drag out*, ἀνελκύσαι εἰς τὸ φῶς Ar.*Pax*307; κἆτ' ἀνελκύσας ἐρωτᾷ *having dragged* him *into open court*, Id.*Ach.*687; τὰ παιδάρι' εὐθὺς ἀνέλκει *drags* them *into the witness-box*, Id.*V.*568:—Med., ἀνέλκεσθαι τρίχας *tear one's own* hair, Il.22.77:—Pass., κύνα χερσὶν ἀνελκόμενον D.P.790. II. *draw back*, ὁ δὲ τόξου πῆχυν ἄνελκεν (in act to shoot) Il.11.375, cf. Od.21.128:—Med., ἔγχος ἀνελκόμενον *drawing back his* spear [out of the corpse], ib.22.97; τόξον ἀνέλκεται τοξευτής Arat.305:—Pass., pf. part. ἀνειλκυσμένος Procl.*Hyp.*7.39.

ἀνέλκωσις, εως, ἡ, (ἀνελκόομαι) *suppuration*, Cass.*Pr.*9.

ἀνέλκωτος, ον, *without ulcers*, Dsc.2.32, Aret.*SD*1.12; καρκινώματα, = κρυπτά, Leonid.ap.Aët.16.42, cf. 15.14, Aret.*SD*2.11.

ἀνέλλειπτος, ον, *unfailing*, πρὸς τὰς ὑπηρεσίας *Inscr.Prien.*113.90 (i B.C.). Adv. -ως *ceaselessly*, *IG*14.2498 (Nemausus).

ἀνέλλην, ηνος, ὁ, ἡ, *un-Greek, outlandish*, ὅμιλον ἀνέλληνα στόλον A.*Supp.*234 (ἀνελληνόστολον Bothe).

ἀνελλήνιστος, ον, *not Grecian*, S.E.*M.*1.181, Phryn.300, *EM*777.53.

ἀνελλῐπής, ές, *unfailing, unceasing*, ἀ. παρασχεῖν τὴν ἀγοράν *SIG* 799.17 (Cyzicus), cf. Ael.*VH*1.33; of rivers, Poll.3.103. Adv. -πῶς Plu.2.495c, S.E.*M*.8.439, *CIG*(add.)2775*b*(Aphrodisias). II. *not lacking*, τινός *OGI*194: abs., *lacking nothing*, Plot.5.8.7. Adv. = ἀπερίττως, σημαίνειν mean *exactly*, Alex.Aphr.*in Top*.43.3.—Also spelt **ἀνελλειπής** Eutoc.*in Archim*.3.114.16 H., Ammon.*in APr*.32.22.

ἀνελλίπους, *lame*, Hsch.

ἄνελπις, ιδος, ὁ, ἡ, *without hope*, σωτηρίας E.*IT*487.

ἀνελπιστ-έω, *despair*, Suid. **-ία**, ἡ, *hopelessness*, Ascl.*Tact*. 5.2, Sch.Th.2.51; *non-expectation*, Onos.10.20. **-ος**, ον, *unhoped for*, Heraclit.18; φυγή A.*Supp*.330; θαῦμα S.*Tr*.673; ἔργον Th.6.33; τύχη E.*Hel*.412; τὸ ἀ. τοῦ βεβαίου *the hopelessness* of attaining any certainty, Th.3.83; τὰ ἀ. Arist.*Rh*.1383ᵃ8; οὐκ ἀ. μοι γέγονεν τὸ γεγονός Pl.*Ap*.36a. Adv. -τως *unexpectedly*, γέγονεν ἀ. μέγας Decr.ap.D.18.182, cf. Plu.*Pel*.4. II. Act., 1. of persons, *having no hope, hopeless*, Hp.*Aph*.7.47, *Prog*.19; ἀ. δὲ θανόντες Theoc. 4.42: c. inf., ἀ. σωθήσεσθαι Th.8.1; ἀ. ἐπιγενέσθαι ἄν τινα σφίσι πολέμιον *not expecting that*.., Id.3.30; ἀ. τοῦ ἑλεῖν X.*Cyn*.7.9; ἀ. ἔς τινα Th.6.17; ἀ. καταστῆσαί τινι ὡς.. Id.3.46. Adv. -τως, ἔχει he is *in despair*, Pl.*Phlb*.36b. 2. of things or conditions, *leaving no hope, desperate*, βίοτος S.*El*.186 (lyr.), Th.5.102; πρὸς τὸ ἀ. τραπόμενοι Id. 2.51; ἀ. οὐδέν [ἐστι], c. acc. et inf., it is nowise *unreasonable to expect that*.., And.4.24: Comp., τὰ ἐκ τῆς γῆς ἀνελπιστότερα ὄντα Th.7.4. Adv. -τως, νουσέειν Aret.*CA*2.5.

ἀνέλυτρος, ον, *unsharded*, of bees, wasps, etc., opp. κολεόπτερα (beetles), Arist.*HA*490ᵃ15, 532ᵃ24, al.

ἀνεμαφέτης, ου, ὁ, *wind-releaser*, *PMag.Par*.1.1363.

ἀνέμβᾰτος, ον, *inaccessible*, Eratosth.*Fr*.16.14, D.H.1.3; ἀ. δρυμῶνα Babr.45.11; of a river, σκαφέεσσιν ἀ. *AP*9.641 (Agath.): metaph., ἡ οὐσία τῶν πραγμάτων ἀ. Ocell.1.15; βελέεσσιν ἀ. *AP*5.233.3 (Paul. Sil.). 2. *not to be trodden*, of a spot struck by a thunderbolt, Plu. *Pyrrh*.29. 3. Act., *not going to* or *visiting*, *AP*9.287 (Apollonid.).

ἀνεμέσητος, ον, (νέμεσις) *not incurring the wrath of God*, Pl.*Cra*. 401a: εἰ -ητον εἰπεῖν Id.*Smp*.195a; also, *not liable to blame*, ἀ. [ἐστι] ..τινί, c. inf., Id.*Tht*.175e, Aeschin.3.66, Epicur.*Fr*.161, etc. Adv. -τως Pl.*Lg*.684e.

ἀν-έμετος or **-ήμετος**, ον, *without vomiting*, Hp.*Prorrh*.1.85, *Epid*. 2.3.1. Adv. -τως *Coac*.546.

ἀνεμέω, *vomit up*, Hp.*Prorrh*.1.31, Arist.*HA*594ᵃ29, al.: metaph., Chrysipp.*Stoic*.2.243.

ἀνέμητος, ον, *not distributed*, οὐσία Aeschin.1.102, D.44.10; *undivided*, Max.Tyr.35.7. 2. Act., *having no share*, Plu.*Cat.Mi*.26.

ἀνεμ-ία, ἡ, (ἄνεμος) = ἐμπνευμάτωσις, *flatulence*, Hp.*Epid*.2.5.5. **-ιαῖος**, ον, *windy*, ᾠὸν ἀνεμιαῖον a *wind*-egg, Arar.6, *Com.Adesp*.5 D., Ath.2.57e; ἄγονα καὶ ἀ. ἔκγονα ψυχῆς Them.*Or*.32.356a. 2. metaph., *empty, vain*, γόνιμον ἢ ἀ. Pl.*Tht*.151e; ἀ. τε καὶ ψεῦδος ib. 161a; ἀ. ἐλπίς Alciphr.1.21. **-ίζομαι**, Pass., *to be driven with the wind*, *Ep.Jac*.1.6, Sch.Od.12.336: Act. in Hsch. s.v. ἀναψῦξαι. **-ιος**, ον, f.l. for ἀνεμιαῖος in Ph.1.96, cf. Hsch.

ἀνεμό-δαρτος, ον, *stripped by the wind*, Eust.1095.12. **-δρομος**, ον, *running with the wind, swift as the wind*, Luc.*VH*1.13. **-εις** [ᾰ], v. ἠνεμόεις. **-επάκτης**, ου, ὁ, *wind-bringer*, *PMag.Par*.1. 1360. **-ζάλη** [ζᾰ], ἡ, *strong surging sea*, Sch.Od.5.1 (pl.), Id.E. *Ph*.1154. **-κοῖται**, οἱ, *wind-lullers*, sorcerers at Corinth, Eust. 1645.42, Hsch. **-μᾰχία**, ἡ, *meeting of contrary winds*, Lyd.*Mens*. 4.13. **-ομαι**, Pass., *to be filled with wind*, Pl.*Ti*.83d; ἠνεμωμένος τὴν τρίχα with hair *floating in the wind*, Callistr.*Stat*.14; ἠνεμωμένη πτεροῖς Lyc.1119: of the sea, *to be raised by the wind*, *AP*13.12 (Hegesipp.). II. *to be inflated, swollen*, Hp.*Nat.Mul*.64: metaph., ἠνεμῶσθαι περί τι *to be eager* for.., Ael.*NA*11.7. **-ποιός**, *wind-creating*, *PMag.Lond*.121.776. **-πους**, ουν, gen. οδος, *with feet swift as the wind*, *EM*20.6.

ἄνεμος [ᾰ], ὁ, *wind*, πέτετο πνοιῇς ἀνέμοιο Il.12.207; ἀνέμων ἀτάλαντοι ἀέλλῃ 13.795; ὦρσεν.. ἀνέμοιο θύελλαν 12.253; ἀνέμοιο.. δεινὸς ἀήτης 15.626, cf. 14.254; ἀνέμων ἀμέγαρτον ἀϋτμήν Od.11.407, etc.; ἀνέμων πνεύματα Hdt.7.16.α', E.*HF*102; ῥιπαί S.*Ant*.137,930 (both lyr.); ἀήματα A.*Eu*.905; αὖραι E.*Med*.838; πνοιαί Ar.*Av*.1396; ἀνέμων φθόγγος Simon.37.10; ἀνέμου κατιόντος μεγάλου *a gale* having come on, Th.2.25; ἀνέμου ἐξαίφνης ἀσελγοῦς γενομένου Eup.320; ἄνεμος κατὰ βορέαν ἑστηκὼς *the wind* being set in the north, Th.6.104; ἀνέμοις φέρεσθαι παραδιδόναι τι cast a thing *to the winds*, E.*Tr*.419, cf. A.R.1.1334; κατ' ἄνεμον στῆναι stand *to leeward*, Arist.*HA*541ᵃ26, cf. Plu.2.972a; κατ' ἄνεμον καὶ ῥοῦν νήχεσθαι ib.979c: metaph., ἄνεμος.. ἄνθρωπος 'unstable as the wind', Eup.376; φέρειν τιν' ἄρας (sic l.) ἄ. *a very windy* to carry off, Antiph.195.5 (Lobeck); ἀνέμους θηρᾶν ἐν δικτύοις try to catch *the wind*, and ἀνέμῳ διαλέγεσθαι talk *to the wind*, Zen.1.38; ἀνέμους γεωργεῖν 'plough the sands', ib.100. 2. *cardinal point, quarter*, ἐκ τῶν τεσσάρων ἀ. Lxx *Za*.2.6, *Annales du Service* 19.40 (Theadelphia, 93 B.C.), *Ev.Matt*.24.31, al., Vett.Val. 140.6, *PFlor*.50.104: sg., ib.20.19 (ii A.D.); τὸ κατ' ἄνεμον *aspect*, *POxy*.100.10 (ii A.D.). II. *wind* in the body, Hp.*Mul*.2.179, al. (From ἀνε- 'blow, breathe', cf. Skt. *áni-ti* 'breathes', Goth. *uzanan* 'expire', etc.)

ἀνεμο-σκεπής, ές, *sheltering one from the wind*, χλαῖναι Il.16. 224. **-στροφος**, ον, *whirling with wind*, θύελλα prob. for -τρόπῳ in *Anacreont*.36.14. **-συρις**, ιδος, ἡ, a kind of *fan*: hence, *fan-shaped whirlwind*, Olymp. *in Mete*.200.19. **-σφάρᾰγος** [φᾰ], ον, *echoing to the wind*, κόλποι Pi.*P*.9.5. **-τρᾰφής**, ές, = sq., Eust.1095.12. **-τρεφής**, ές, *fed by the wind*, κῦμα ἀ. Il.15.625; ἔγχος ἀ. a spear from a tree *reared by the wind*, i.e. *made tough and strong by battling with the wind*, 11.256 (v.l. ἀνεμοτρεπές or -στρεφές *turned*, i.e. *shaken by the wind*), cf. Philostr.*Im*.2.3.

ἀνεμούριον, τό, (οὖρος) *windmill*, Hero *Spir*.1.43.

ἀνεμο-φθορία, ἡ, *blasting, blight*, Lxx *De*.28.22, *IG*12(9).955.7, 1179.25 (Euboea). **-φθορος**, ον, *blasted by the wind*, Lxx *Ho*.8. 7, Ph.2.431. **-φοιτος**, ον, v. sub ἠνεμ-. **-φόρητος**, ον, *carried by the wind*, of rumours, Cic.*Att*.13.37.4; of delicate vessels, Luc.*Lex*.7; dub. sens. in *Sammelb*.4324.8(-φόρετος),14.

ἀνέμ-πληκτος, ον, *intrepid*, Sch.E.*Or*.1479. Adv. -τως Plu.*Galb*. 23 (nisi legendum ἀνεκπλήκτως). **-πληστος**, ον, *of which one cannot have one's fill*, θέαμα v.l. in Them.*Or*.2.40b. **-πόδιστος**, ον, *unhindered*, ἐνέργεια Arist.*EN*1153ᵃ15; βίος *Pol*.1295ᵃ37. Adv. -τως D.S.1.36, *PFlor*.370.17 (ii A.D.), Jul.*Or*.6.193d. 2. *not obscured, clear*, Procl.*Hyp*.4.92. Adv. -τως ib.88. II. Act., *offering no impediment*, πρός τι Arist.*PA*663ᵇ11. **-πόλητος**, ον, *unsold*, Sch.S.*Ant*.1036. **-πτωτος**, ον, *not falling into*, εἰς λύπας Pl. *Def*.412c: abs., D.L.7.117. **-υμάχθη**· ὑπείδετο, Hsch. **-φάνιστος**, ον, *without formal notification*, δωρεαί, opp. ἐμφανεῖς, Just.*Nov*.162. 1. **-φαντος**, ον, *not expressive* or *indicative*, ὕβρεως κτλ. Plu.2. 45c; πλήθους Procl. *in Prm*.p.639 S. **-φᾰτος**, ον, v.l. for foreg., Procl. *in Prm*. l.c., cf. eund. *in Ti*.3.1 and 12 D.; *without a tinge of*, Elias *in Cat*.20.26: abs., *lacking in expression*, πλοκή, of melody without rhythm, Aristid.Quint.1.13; λέξις Aristid.*Rh*.2 p.434 S. Adv. -τως Hermog.*Id*.2.10,11, Aristid.*Rh*.2 pp.434,450 S.

ἀνεμ-ώδης, ες, *windy*, Σκῦρος S.*Fr*.553; χώρα Hp.*Aër*.24, cf. Nic. *Th*.96; ἀκρωτήριον Plu.2.967b; ἔτος ἀ. Arist.*Mete*.360ᵇ5; κύματα ἀ. *bringing wind*, Id.*Pr*.932ᵇ29; σημεῖον ἀ. a sign *of wind*, Thphr.*Sign*. 18. 2. metaph., *vain, idle*, Hsch. s.v. κραπαταλίας. **-ώκης**, ες, *swift as the wind*, νεφέλα E.*Ph*.163 (lyr.); δῖναι Ar.*Av*.697; κόρα *Lyr.Adesp*.106. **-ώλιος**, ον, *windy*, Hom., but only metaph., ἀνεμώλια βάζειν talk *words of wind*, Il.4.355, Od.11.464; οἱ δ' αὖτ' ἀνεμώλιοι are *like the winds*, i.e. *empty boasters*, Il.20.123; τί νυ τόξον ἔχεις ἀνεμώλιον αὔτως; why bear thy bow *in vain?* 21.474; δίκη ἀ., of a trial, Maiist.38; ἔπεσεν.. ἀνεμώλιον αὔτως Theoc.25.239; εἶπε δ' ὕδωρ πίνειν, ἀνεμώλιος *the empty fool!* *AP*11.61 (Maced.); ἀ. ἀσπίδα θεῖναι make it *powerless*, i.e. *harmless*, Orph.*L*.512.—Ep. and Ion. word, used by Luc.*Astr*.2. (From ἄνεμος, with Aeol. ending -ώνιος, by dissimilation -ώλιος, Eust.1214.27; cf. μετα-μώνιος.)

ἀνεμ-ώνη, ἡ, *poppy anemone, Anemone coronaria*, Cratin.98, Pherecr.108.25, Theoc.5.92, Thphr.*HP*7.10.2; ἀ. ἥμερος Dsc.2. 176. 2. ἀ. ἀγρία *scarlet wind-flower, Anemone fulgens*, ibid.; also called ἀ. φοινικῆ Crateuas *Fr*.4; ἀ. λειμωνία Thphr.*HP*6.8.1. 3. ἀ. ὀρεία, *mountain wind-flower, Anemone blanda*, ibid.; αἷμα ῥόδον τίκτει, τὰ δὲ δάκρυα τὰν ἀ. Bion 1.66. II. metaph., ἀνεμῶναι λόγων *flowers* of speech (with suggestion of *emptiness*), Luc.*Lex*. 23. **-ωνίς**, ίδος, ἡ, = ἀνεμώνη ἥμερος, Nic.*Fr*.74.64, Nonn.*D*.42. 323.

ἀνεμώτας, α, ὁ, *ass sacrificed to the winds* at Tarentum, Hsch.

Ἀνεμῶτις, ιδος, ἡ, *she that stills the wind*, Ἀθηνᾶ Paus.4.35.8.

ἀνεν-δεής, ές, *in want of naught*, Plu.2.1068c, *AP*10.115; sup., Plot.6.9.6, Dam.*Pr*.13; πάντων ἀ. βίος Hdn.8.7.5; τὸ ἀνενδεὲς τῆς τροφῆς *IG*5(2).268.17 (Mantinea, Aug.). Adv. -εῶς *faultlessly, unexceptionably*, D.H.*Rh*.1.5, D.Chr.12.34; ἀ. ἐκτελέσας *CIG*3989 (Laodicea Combusta), cf. 4085 (Pessinus), *SIG*888.21 (Maced.), *PLond*. 3.974 i 4 (iv A.D.). 2. *completely*, Iamb.*Comm.Math*.10. 3. *with no need of*, βοηθείας Jul.*Mis*.341c. **-δεκτος**, ον, *inadmissible, impossible*, *Ev.Luc*.17.1, Artem.2.70. **-δετος**, ον, *not bound up with*, νοῦς ἀ. σώματι Ph.1.71. **-δοίαστος**, ον, *unhesitating*, Ph.1. 440, 2.36; *indubitable*, Id.1.302, al., Luc.*Herm*.67; *unambiguous*, Anon. *in SE*61.15: Gramm., *unquestionably correct*, ἀ. καὶ ὑγιές A.D. *Synt*.21.1. Adv. -τως 218.19; *without doubt*, Ph.2.319; *unhesitatingly, unequivocally*, 1.351, *POxy*.138.25 (610 A.D.). **-δοτος**, ον, *unyielding, rigid*, τόνος κλίνης Antyll.ap.Orib.9.14.5; *not giving way*, Ph.1.154, al.: metaph., προθυμία Hierocl.p.57.3 A., Orib.*Fr*.55; πάθος Herod.Med.in *Rh.Mus*.58.89. Adv. -τως, διαθλεῖν Ph.2.66, cf. Eustr. *in EN*297.23. **-δῠτος**, ον, *not put on*, Hsch. s.v. ἄφαροι.

ἀνένεικα, Ion. aor. Act. of ἀναφέρω.

ἀνενεκτέον, (ἀναφέρω) *one must refer*, Plot.4.4.38, Dam.*Pr*.277.

ἀνενεργ-ής, ές, *inefficacious*, Thphr.*HP*9.17.1, Dsc.2.111. **-ησία**, ἡ, *want of exercise*, Sor.1.106; *inactivity*, Alex.Aphr. *de An*.74.27; as criticism of Sceptics by Stoics, *Stoic*.2.36. **-ητος**, ον, *inefficacious, inactive*, Ruf.*Anat*.30, S.E.*M*.7.30, cf. Alex.Aphr. *de An*.39.8, Hierocl. *in CA*21 p.466 M.; οὐσία Plot.6.8.21. 2. *not possessing an* ἐνέργεια, of the Good, Plot. 5.6.6. 3. *not actualized* or *realized*, Procl. *in R*.2.160 K., *in Prm*.p.600 S., *in Ti*.3.32 D. **-ος**, ον, = ἀνενεργής, Serapion in *Cat.Cod.Astr*.8(4).228 (Comp.).

ἀνενετεῖ· ἀρνεῖται, ἀπὸ τοῦ ἄνω νεύειν, ἢ ἀπαρνεῖται, Hsch.

ἀνενεχύραστος, ον, *not liable to distraint*, *CPR*1.15 (i A.D.), etc.

ἀνενήνοθεν· ἀνῆγεν ἢ ἀνέβη, Hsch.; cf. ἐνήνοθε.

ἀνεν-θουσίαστος, ον, *unimpassioned*, ἡδοναί Plu.2.751b; βίος ἀ. εἰς τιμήν ib.1098d. Adv. -τως ib.346b. **-θύμητος**, ον, *failing to consider*, τοῦ θνητοῦ Phld.*Mort*.38. **-νόητος**, ον, *without conception of*, τινός Plb.2.35.6, Phld.*Herc*.862.9, D.S.1.8, Plot.6.7.29, Procl. *in Prm*.p.484 S.; foll. by indirect qn., Alex.Aphr. *de An*. 175.14. Adv. -τως *without the use of concepts*, Eustr. *in EN*40.7; *without discursive thought*, i.e. by intuition, Porph.*Sent*.10. II. *inconceivable*, Cleom.2.1; ἐννοεῖν τὰ -τα Dam.*Pr*.7. **-όχλητος**, ον, *undisturbed*, Hdn.5.7.2, Hld.5.19; of a sepulchre, *CIG*2845.9

(Aphrodisias), *BGU*935.3 (iii/iv A.D.). Adv. -τως Ruf. and Aspasia ap.Aët.16.50, Sch.E.*Or.*630, Simp.*in Ph.*1176.24. **-τᾰτος**, ον, *without tension* or *force*, Theopomp.Com.71; *without over-exertion*, Antyll.ap.Orib.6.21.5. **-τᾰφιάστως**, Adv. *without burial*, Eust.1278.60. **-τευκτος**, ον, *unsociable*, ἤθη Plu.2.10a. 2. *inaccessible to persuasion* or *influence*, δικαιοσύνη ib.355a, etc. **-τονον**· ἱμάτιον (Lacon.), Hsch. **-τρέπτως**, *without doubt*, An.Ox.2.341. **-τρεχής**, ές, *ill-adapted, inappropriate*, Hierocl.p.50.22A. **-τροπος**, ον, *not heeding* or *respecting* a thing, Hsch.; δαίμων *Eranos* 13.87 (inc. loc.).

ἀνεξ-άκουστος [ᾰκ], ον, *unheard of*, Sch.S.*Aj.*318. **-άλειπτος** [ᾰλ], ον, *indelible*, Isoc.5.71, Plu.2.1b, *PHolm.*22.43, cf. 1.12. Adv. -τως Hsch. **-άλλακτος**, ον, *unchangeable*, Procl. *in Ti.*1.238 D., Id. *in Prm.*p.599 S. **-αλλοτρίωτος**, ον, *unalienated*, *BGU*1151.43 (i B.C.), *PLond.*2.360.9, etc., cf. *Ath.Mitt.*3.58 (Lydia). **-ᾰπᾰτησία**, ἡ, *freedom from deception* or *mistake*, Arr.*Epict.*3.2.2. **-ᾰπάτητος**, ον, *infallible, not to be deceived*, Arist.*Top.*132a32; πρός τι in a thing, Id.*Pol.*1338a42, cf. Hierocl. *in CA* 23p.470 M., al. Adv. -τως Ph.1.483, Poll.8.11. **-ἀρίθμητος**, ον, *not to be counted* or *told*, Id.3.88, 4.162. **-έλεγκτος**, ον, *incapable of disproof* or *criticism*, Th.1.21; τὸν λόγον ἀ. ποιεῖν Arist.*SE*176b24; ἀ. μᾶλλον ἢ πιθανήν *difficult to disprove* rather than credible, D.S.1.40, etc.; ἀ. ἔχει τὸ ἀνδρεῖον leaves their courage *without any real test* or *proof*, Th.4.126; *unrefuted*, Gal.15.547. Adv. -τως X.*Oec.*10.8, prob. in S.E.*M.*7.191. 2. of persons, *not to be convicted*, Antipho 2.1.10: of conduct, etc., *blameless, unexceptionable*, X.*Cyn.*13.7, D.25.39, Plu.*Pel.*4. **-έλευστος**, ον, = ἀνεξίτητος, Hsch. **-έλικτος**, ον, *whose development cannot be fully exhausted*, ταῖς ἡμετέραις ἐπιβολαῖς Dam.*Pr.*177. Adv. -τως dub. l. S.E.*M.*7.191. **-εράω**, = ἀναπτύω, Sch.Opp.*H.*1.137. **-έργαστος**, ον, *not worked out, unfinished*, Luc.*Fug.*21, Gal.*Nat.Fac.*2.3. **-ερεύνητος** (Hellenistic ἀνεξεραύν–), ον, *not to be searched out*, Heraclit.18, *Ep.Rom.*11.33, D.C.69.14. **-έταστος**, ον, *not searched out, not inquired into* or *examined*, D.4.36, 21.218, Aeschin.3.22. II. *without inquiry* or *investigation*, ὁ ἀ. βίος οὐ βιωτὸς ἀνθρώπῳ Pl.*Ap.*38a. Adv. -τως Ph.1.550, Plu.2.94d, etc. **-εύρετος**, ον, *not to be found out*, ἀριθμός Th.3.87, cf. Hellanic.194 J., Arist.*Mu.*392a17, Plu.2.964a. **-ήγητος**, ον, *not to be told*, μυστήρια Hsch. s.v. σεμνά. 2. *unexplained*, Gal.*UP*2.7, Simp. *in Ph.*241.21, Sch.Pi.*N.*9.95. 3. *unspeakable, ineffable*, πέλαγος κάλλους Them.*Or.*13.177d.

ἀνεξία, ἡ, *endurance, resignation*, Sicilian word, Cic.*Att.*5.11.5.

ἀνεξῐκᾰκ-έω, *to be long-suffering*, Charito 8.4. **-ία**, ἡ, *forbearance*, Plu.2.90e, Luc.*Par.*53, Hld.10.12; ἀ. πόνων *patient endurance under*.., Hdn.3.8.8, cf. Eun.*Hist.*p.258 D. **-ος**, ον, *enduring pain* or *evil*, Herod.Med.ap.Orib.5.30.7, Luc.*Jud.Voc.*9, Vett.Val.38.21, Gal.5.38, Them.*Or.*15.190a (Sup.), Aret.*SA*2.6 (Comp.); *forbearing, long-suffering*, 2*Ep.Ti.*2.24. Adv. -κως Luc.*Asin.*2.

ἀνεξίκμαστος, ον, *not dried up*, Arist.*Pr.*928a29, cf. Gal.8.367.

ἀνεξῐκώμη, ἡ, expl. by Hsch. as ἧς οὐκ ἂν ἀνάσχοιτο ὅλη κώμη, Cratin.383, but rather ἡ ὅλην κώμην ἀνέχουσα.

ἀνεξ-ίλαστος [ῐ], ον, *implacable*, Ptol.*Tetr.*162, Harp. s.v. ἀνίδρυτος. **-ινάσκετο**· ἐξαινάσκετο, ἀνεξηραίνετο, Hsch. **-ιόομαι**, (ἰός) *to be reduced to a metallic state*, Zos.Alch.p.153 B. **-ίτηλος** [ῐ], ον, *indelible*, βαφή Poll.1.44. **-ίτητος** [ῐ], ον, *with no outlet: inevitable*, Hsch. **-ιχνίαστος**, ον, *unsearchable, inscrutable*, Lxx *Jb.*5.9, *Ep.Rom.*11.33, *Ep.Eph.*3.8. **-όδευτος**, ον, *with no issue* or *outlet*, ἀ. ἐς φάος τρίβοι *IGRom.*4.743 (Eumeneia). **-οδίαστος**, ον, *not to be alienated*, *CIG*2050 (Philippopolis), cf. *BCH*27.318, prob. in *IGRom.*4.1475 (Smyrna). **-οδος**, ον, *with no outlet, not to be got out of, impassable*, Ἀχέρων Theoc.12.19; δυσχωρίαι D.H.3.59; λαβύρινθος *AP*12.93 (Rhian.). 2. ἡμέρα ἀ. *unfit for an expedition*, Plu.2.269e. II. of persons, conditions, etc., *not coming into public, unsocial*, ib.242e, 426b, etc.; βίος 1098d; διάνοια 610a; λόγοι ἀ. *without practical result*, 1034b. **-οιστος**, ον, *not to be expressed, ineffable*, ib.728d, Gorg.(?) ap.S.E.*M.*7.82, Jul.*Or.*5.158d. **-ούσιος**, ον, *without power*, *Gloss.*

ἀνεορτ-άζω, *instaurare ludos*, D.C.*Fr.*51 (Pass.). **-αστος**, ον, *without holidays* or *festive joy*, βίος Democr.230, cf. Plu.2.1102b. **-ος**, ον, *without festival*, Alciphr.3.49; ἑορταὶ ἀ. festivals *unkept*, D.H.8.25, but, *impious* festivals, Ph.2.320: c. gen., ἀ. ἱερῶν *without share in festal* rites, E.*El.*310.

ἀνεοστᾰσίη, ἡ, = ἐνεοστασίη, Hsch.

ἀνεπ-άγγελτος, ον, *not announced*, πόλεμος ἀ. a war *begun without formal declaration*, Plb.4.16.4. 2. *uninvited*, ἀ. φοιτᾶν ἐπὶ δεῖπνον Cratin.44. **-αίσθητος**, ον, *unperceived, imperceptible*, Ti.Locr. 100b, Plu.2.1062b, Luc.*Sat.*33. Adv. -τως Simp. *in Cat.*309.3. 2. Act., *not perceiving*, τινός Plb.28.1.6, Longin.4.1, *OGI*194 (Egypt). Adv. -τως Ph.*Fr.*70 H., *Hippiatr.*38, Syrian. *in Metaph.*100.38, Simp. *in Ph.*1198.39. **-άϊστος**, ον, *inaudible*, Agathocl.2. **-αίσχυντος**, ον, *having no cause for shame*, 2*Ep.Ti.*2.15; μηδὲ -τον ἡγοῦ J.*AJ* 18.7.1. **-αιτίᾱτος**, ον, *unimpeached*, ib.4.8.38. **-ακτος**, ον, *not brought in* or *home*, Ph.1.139. **-άλλακτος**, ον, *not alternating*, ἀ. ζῷα animals in which the upper and lower teeth *do not lock into one another*, but meet flat, opp. καρχαρόδοντα, Arist.*HA* 501a17.

ἀνέπαλτο, ἀνεπάλμενος, v. sub ἀναπάλλω.

ἀνεπ-άνακτος, ον, *not to be brought back*, ἀ. ἐκβάλλεσθαι Ph.1.139, cf. 2.338 (dub.). **-ανόρθωτος**, ον, *irreparable*, ἀτύχημα J.*AJ*16.11.3; *incorrigible*, Iamb.*VP*22.102; *uncorrected*, Plu.2.49b, Arr.*Epict.* 3.1.11. II. *not to be amended, perfect*, Ph.2.614. **-αύξητος**, ον, Gramm., *unaugmented*, *An.Ox.*4.180.

ἀνέπᾰφος, ον, *untouched, unharmed*, ἀ. παρέχειν τι D.35.24, cf. Syngr.ib.11; ἀ. σώματα *not liable to seizure*, Men.*Perinth.*8; ἐλευθέρα ἔστω καὶ ἀ. *GDI*1532, cf. Thphr.*Fr.*97.2, *IG*2.584c, *BGU*193.19 (ii A.D.); ὑποθήκη *PHamb.*28.8 (ii B.C.); *unencumbered*, οἰκία *PThead.*1.12 (iv A.D.): c. gen., *unharmed by*, ὕβρεως M.Ant.3.4. Adv. -φως Suid.

ἀνεπαφρο-δῑσία, ἡ, = ἀναφροδισία, *BGU*1197.14 (1 B.C.). **-δῑτος**, ον, = ἀναφρόδιτος, X.*Smp.*8.15, *Com.Adesp.*123, Alciphr.3.60.

ἀνεπαχθής, ές, *not burdensome, without offence*, Plu.*Cat.Mi.*8, *Pomp.*1; σκώμματα Luc.*Ep.Sat.*34. II. Adv. -θῶς, προσομιλεῖν Th.2.37; λέγειν Luc.*Sol.*5. 2. *not taking offence*, ἀνεπαχθῶς φέρειν Plu.2.102e. 3. *without discomfort*, Jul.*Or.*6.191d.

ἀνεπείγομαι, dub. l. in Man.5.97.

ἀνεπ-είσακτος, ον, *not adventitious, native, instinctive*, Sch.Opp. *H.*1.705. **-έκτᾰτος**, ον, *not lengthened*, A.D.*Synt.*110.14, al.; of declensions, *parisyllabic*, D.T.632.10. **-έλευστος**, ον, *not coming back*, Sch.S.*El.*182. **-εξέργαστος**, ον, *not wrought out, imperfect*, Simp. *in de An.*4.13, Eust.499.2. **-εξήγητος**, ον, *unexplained*, ἀ. καταλιπεῖν Gal.15.14 (al. ἀνεπιζήτητος). **-έρειστος**, ον, *not supported*, Iamb.*Comm.Math.*8. **-ερώτητος**, ον, *not asked for* or *arranged for*, τὸ μὴ προσήκειν ἀ. τρέχειν τόκον Just.*Nov.*136.4. **-ηρέαστος**, ον, *free from injury* or *insult, unmolested*, D.S.31.8, Memn.2.3, J.*AJ*14.10.6, *PFlor.*91.17 (ii A.D.), cf. *BGU*1022.24: Medic., *uninjured*, Archig.ap.Orib.8.1.6, Id.ap.Aët.8.73. Adv. -τως J.*AJ* 16.2.5.

ἀνεπής, ές, *without a word, speechless*, Hsch.

ἀνεπι-βάρητος, ον, *unburdened*, πόλις *IGRom.*4.219 (Ilium), cf. *IG* 7.2711, *SIG*799.16 (Cyzicus), *Ath.Mitt.*33.382 (Pergam.). **-βᾰσία**, ἡ, (ἀ- priv.) *prohibition of traffic* or *intercourse*, *IG*4.752.6 (Troezen), Heraclit.*Ep.*9.8. **-βᾰτος**, ον, *not to be climbed*, γυμνῷ ποδί Str. 12.3.11; *inaccessible*, Plu.2.228b. **-βλητος**, ον, *inattentive, heedless*, prob. l. Phld.*D.*1.14, *Mus.*p.80 K. **-βούλευτος**, ον, *without plots*, and so, 1. Act., *not plotting*, τὸ ἀ. πρὸς ἀλλήλους *the absence of intrigue*, Th.3.37; *not insidious*, λόγος Aristid.*Rh.*2 p.445 S. 2. Pass., *not plotted against, not liable to attack*, ἀ. φθόνῳ *Com.Adesp.*1212, cf. Plb.7.8.4, Agatharch.42, Ael.*NA*9.59, etc. Adv. -τως Ph.2.645, Suid. s.v. Ξάνθος. **-βουλος**, ον, *not exposed to treachery*, *PSI*1.96.3 (v A.D.). Adv. -λως *without treachery*, Eust.905.57. **-γνώμων**, ον, gen. ονος, *ignorant, unconscious*, τινός Porph.*Abst.*1.45. **-γνωστος**, ον, *not distinctly known*, Herm.ap. Stob.1.41.44; τὸ ἀ. τῆς συμβολῆς J.*AJ*12.2.11:—Act., *not knowing distinctly*, τινός Simp. *in de An.*299.37. Adv. -τως *not noticeably*, Plb.18.18.16. **-γρᾰφος**, Dor. -γροφος *Tab.Heracl.*1.84, ον, *without title* or *inscription*, χιτωνίσκιον ἀ. (for the names of those who offered vestments were embroidered upon them) *IG*2.754.28, al., ib. 7.303.102 (Oropus), etc.; μέσσοροι *Tab.Heracl.* l. c. 2. *unregistered*: hence, *free of charge*, of a harvest, γένημα ἀ. *PGnom.*234 (ii A.D.), cf. Plb.8.31.6, D.S.1.64, etc.: metaph., *without distinguishing marks*, Luc.*Nec.*15; *unmarked*, *Cat.*25. **-δάνειστος** [δᾰ], ον, *on which no money has been borrowed, not mortgaged*, *IG*12(7).515 (Amorgos), *BGU*193.19 (ii A.D.), Sch.Luc.*JTr.*48. **-δεής**, ές, = ἀνενδεής, v. l. in Pl.*Lg.*947e, cf. Chrysipp.*Stoic.*3.16; ἀ. τινος Ph.1.334, al., Luc.*DMort.*26.2. **-δείκνῡμι**, *make clear, show*, Gal. 1.172.

ἀνεπί-δεικτος, ον, *not able to be shown*, Herophil.ap.S.E.*M.*11.50. 2. *not exhibited*, *IG*7.3073.172 (Lebad.). 3. *unsupported by proof*, αἰτία Gorg.*Pal.*4. **-δεκτος**, ον, *not accepting* or *admitting*, νόμων Phld.*Rh.*1.383 S.; κακοῦ S.E.*M.*9.33, cf. D.L.3.77, Alex. Aphr. *in Metaph.*393.13, Id. *in Top.*210.16. **-δετος**, ον, *not bandaged*, Hp.*Fract.*20; *not requiring a bandage*, of plasters, Dsc.5.85, Democr.ap.Gal.13.915. **-δηκτος**, ον, f.l. for -δετος, Dsc.5.85. **-δηλος**, ον, *not manifest* or *observable*, Ptol.*Harm.*1.4. **-δῐκος**, ον, *without the process of* ἐπιδικασία, by which claims to inheritance or guardianship were enforced, ἀ. ἔχειν τὰ πατρῷα Is.3.59; παραλαμβάνειν ἀ. τὴν ἀγχιστείαν Id.8.34 (cj.); ἀ. ἔχειν κλῆρον D.46.22, cf. Poll.3.33. **-δόκητος**, ον, *unexpected*, Simon.62. **-δοτος**, ον, *not growing* or *sprouting*, Thphr.*HP*7.4.8, *CP*4.6.3. **-είκεια**, ἡ, *unfairness, unkindness*, D.29.3. **-εικής**, ές, *unreasonable, unfair*, Th.3.66, Ar.*Fr.*50 D., Phld.*Ir.*p.57 W., Alex.Aphr. *in Top.*208.9: neut. as Adv., *without consideration*, *PGiss.*39.3 (ca. 200 B.C.): regul. Adv. -κῶς Arr.*An.*7.29.1, Poll.8.13. **-ζητησία**, ἡ, *absence of inquiry*, Andronic.Rhod.p.572 M. **-ζήτητος**, ον, *leaving nothing to be desired*, *IPE*1².39.8 (Olbia). 2. v.l. for ἀνεπεξήγητος, *uninvestigated*, Gal.15.14. **-θετος**, ον, *admitting no addition*, Dicaearch. 59.7. **-θεώρητος**, ον, Astrol., *not overlooked* or *controlled*, Gal.19.548. **-θόλωτος**, ον, *untroubled, unpolluted*, S.E.*M.*1.303, Procl. *in Alc.*p.251 C. **-θύμητος** [ῡ], ον, *without desire*, opp. ἐπιθυμητικός, Stob.2.6.14, Chaerem.Hist.4. **-καλύπτως**, Adv. *openly*, v. l. in D.S.2.21. **-καυτος**, ον, *free from sunburn*, πρόσωπα Dsc.2.50. **-κέλευστος**, ον, *not under orders*, φύσις, metaph. of untilled land, Ph.2.207. Adv. -τως 1.115. **-κηρύκευτος** [ρῡ], ον, = ἀκήρυκτος, Hsch.; πολέμιοι Procop.*Aed.*4.1. **-κινδύνως** [ῡ], Adv. *without danger*, ib.5.3. **-κλήρωτος**, ον, *not assigned by lot*, *IG*2.789a28, al. **-κλητος**, ον, *free from blame, unimpeachable*, X.*Cyr.*2.1.22; πίστις J.*AJ*18.9.4: Comp. -ότερος X.*Ages.*1.5. Adv. -τως D.C.39.22. II. *without preferring any charge*. Adv. -τως Th.1.92. **-κλῖτος**, ον, *unwavering*, Simp. *in Cat.*201.31. **-κλυστος**, ον, *not liable to inundation*, τεῖχος J.*AJ*2.10.2. **-κόητα**· ἀσύνετα, Hsch. (-νόητα cod.). **-κοινώνητος**, ον, *not social* or *gregarious*, Eust.73.38. **-κόρριστος**, ον, *not insulted*, *EM*103.35, cf. Hsch. **-κούρητος**, ον, *without succour*, Philem.213.2, Onos.3.2. **-κράτητος** [ρᾰ], ον, *without dominant planet*, γένεσις Vett.Val.151.5. **-κρῐσία**, ἡ, *inability to form a judgement*, S.E.*M*.11.182. **-κρῐτος**, ον, *not decided, indeterminate*, πράγματα Aristocl.ap.Eus.*PE*14.18, cf. S.E.*P*.1.98, etc. Adv. -τως Id.*M*.11.230. 2. *indistinct, indeterminate*, φαντασία Plot.3.6.4. 3. Medic., *untested, untried*, ἡ διαφωνία ἢ ἀ., t.t. of the Empirics, Gal.1.78. 4. *not officially examined*, *POxy*.257.23 (ii A.D.), etc.; of a question, etc., *unexamined*, Simp.*in Ph*.1148.29. **-κρυπτος**, ον, *unconcealed*, M.Ant.1.14. **-κώλῡτος**, ον, *unhindered*, J.*AJ*18.6.4, Onos.35.2. Adv. -τως *without let or hindrance*, *IPE*2.52 (Panticapaeum); *without restraint*, D.S.17.116, Decr.ap.J.*AJ*19.5.3, Alciphr.3.8. **-λειπτος**, ον, *unfailing*, Alex.Aphr.*in Mete*.89.13, Them.*in Ph*.81.27. **-ληπτος**, ον, *not open to attack*, τοῖς ἐχθροῖς Th.5.17; *not censured, blameless*, βίος v.l. in E.*Or*.922, X.*Cyr*.1.2.15; *perfect*, τέχνη Ph.1.15; ἀνεπιληπτότερον *less open to criticism*, Pl.*Phlb*.43c; ἐξουσία ἀ. *not subject to control*, D.H.2.14; *unassailable, not subject to cancellation*, συγγραφαί *PTaur*.1.7.15. Adv. -τως X.*An*.7.6.37, Ph.2.2, al. **-ληστος**, ον, *not to be forgotten*, Aristaenet.2.13, Hsch. s.v. ἀλαστοῖς. Adv. -τως Sch.Od.14.174. **-λόγιστος**, ον, *unable to consider*, c. gen., τῶν ἐναργειῶν Diogenian.Epicur.3.25; *inconsiderate, thoughtless*, Epicur.*Sent.Vat*.63, Sor.1.48; τῶν παθῶν Phld.*Ir*.p.24 W., Mitteis *Chr*.361 (iv A.D.). Adv. -τως Pl.*Ax*.365d, 369e:—Subst. **-ιστία**, ἡ, Sch.Od.15.225:—Verb **-ιστέω**, Phld.*Ir*.p.19 W. (Pass.). **-λυτος**, ον, *unbandaged*, Crito ap.Gal.13.708. II. *unsolved*, Olymp.*in Cat*.111.15. **-μέλητος**, ον, *uncared for*, Sch.A.R.1.1175, *Gp*.12.29.1. **-μικτος**, ον, *unmixed with*, τῷ ἔξω Arist.*Spir*.483^{b}1; *pure from*, ῥυπαρίας Dsc.5.126, cf. *Eup.Praef*., Eustr.*in EN*294.12: abs., σπέρματα J.*AJ*4.8.20, cf. Max.Tyr.40.6. II. *avoiding contact*, Epicur.*Sent*.39; *not mixing* with others, *unsocial*, βίος ἀ. ὁμιλίαις Plu.2.438c; δίαιτα ἀ. Id.*Rom*.3; τὸ ἀ., = ἀνεπιμιξία, Str.8.1.2: of a country, *unfrequented, unvisited*, ξενικαῖς δυνάμεσι D.S.5.21, cf. Plu.2.604b; ψυχὴ ἀ. πάθεσι ib.989c; ποιῆσαί τι ἀ. ἑαυτῷ to make it *alien from* oneself, D.S.5.17, cf. Phld.*Rh*.1.121 S. **-μιξία**, ἡ, *want of intercourse* or *traffic*, Plb.16.29.12, App.*Mith*.93. **-μονος**, ον, *not enduring long*, Plu.2.7b, Vett.Val.40.22. **-μώμητος**, ον, = ἀμώμητος, Sch.Od.13.42:—also **-μωμος**, ον, Phot. **-νοησία**, ἡ, *inconceivability*, S.E.*M*.3.57. **-νόητος**, ον, *unintelligible*, σημεῖα τοῖς ἄλλοις ἀ. D.S.19.94; *inconceivable, unthinkable*, S.E.*P*.2.104, Dam.*Pr*.22. Adv. -τως *inconceivably*, Procl.*in Prm*.p.864 S., Id.*in Ti*.1.3 D. 2. Act., *having no experience of*, τινός D.S.2.59. 3. = *sine adinventione*, Just.*Nov*.59.7. **-ξεστος**, ον, *not polished, not finished*, δόμος Hes.*Op*.746, Them.*Or*.26.388b. **-πλαστος**, ον, *not plastered over*: metaph., *unaffected*, D.L.2.117. **-πλεκτος**, ον, *without connexion with others, isolated*, Str.2.5.8, al. **-πληκτος**, ον, *not liable to be reproved*, Eup.397; βίος E.*Or*.922, Men.*Epit*.489. Adv. -τως Hsch., f.l. in Ph.2.454. 2. in bad sense, *not reproved, licentious*, τροφῇ ἀ. τραφῆναι Pl.*Lg*.695b, cf. Eus.Mynd.62. II. Act., *not reproving* or *blaming*, τὸ ἀ. *abstinence from blame* or *criticism*, M.Ant.1.10. **-πληξία**, ἡ, *impunity, licentiousness*, Pl.*Lg*.695b. **-πρόσθητος**, ον, *not occultable*, Procl.*Hyp*.5.12, cf. Eustr.*in APo*.192.33: metaph., τῷ ἀσωμάτῳ τὸ ἔνογκον -θητον the material *forms no obstacle to* the incorporeal, Porph.*Sent*.27. Adv. -τως Eust.1138.59. **-ρρεκτος**, ον, (ῥέζω) *not dedicated*, χυτρόποδες Hes.*Op*.748. **-ρρήτως**, Adv. *without demur* or *subterfuge*, *PAmh*.2.147.11 (iv/v A.D.). **-σήμαντος**, ον, *undistinguished*, κατὰ τὴν ἐσθῆτα Plb.5.81.3; *unrecorded, unnoticed*, ἀ. τινα or τι παραλιπεῖν Id.11.2.1, D.S.11.59, cf. Phld.*Sign*.34. Adv. -τως *without notice*, Aps.p.259 H. II. *without an attack of* ἐπισημασία (q.v.), Gal.14.277. III. Act., *not conferring distinction*, σοφοῖς ἀνδράσι Darius ap.D.L.9.14. **-σκεπτεί**, Adv. of sq., Diog.Oen.24. **-σκεπτος**, ον, *inattentive, inconsiderate*, πρᾶγμα Ph.5.143 C.; ἀλογία Porph.*Abst*.1.43; ὁρμή Procop.*Goth*.4.32. Adv. -τως Hdt.2.45; ἀ. ἔχειν τινός to give *no consideration to* ..., Arist.*GA*778^{b}10. II. Pass., *not examined, unregarded*, X.*Mem*.2.4.3; *unobserved*, Anon.*in SE*12.27. **-σκευος**, ον, *without equipment*, *IG*2.789^{b}27, al. **-σκεψία**, ἡ, *disregard*, Arist.*APo*.79^{a}6. **-σκίαστος**, ον, *not in the shade*, Alex.Aphr.*in Mete*.19.15. **-σκόπητος**, ον, *unregarded*, Eustr.*in APo*.202.19. **-σκοπος**, ον, gloss on ἀνεπιστάτητος, Hsch. **-σκότητος**, ον, *not obscured* or *overclouded*, Gal.*UP*10.2, Ptol.*Tetr*.100, Heph.Astr.1.25; and so prob. Procl.*Par.Ptol*.144 (-ιστος codd.). **-σταθμεία**, ἡ, *exemption from billeting*, *IGRom*.4.295, *Sammelb*.4224.15. **-στάθμευτος**, ον, *exempt from billeting*, Plb.15.24.2:—also **-σταθμος**, ον, *OGI*262.13 (Baetocaece), *PTeb*.5.168 (ii B.C.). **-στᾰσία**, ἡ, *inattention, thoughtlessness*, Pl.*Ax*.365d; *distraction, insensateness* (of passion), Phld.*Ir*.p.33 W.; *want of reflection*, Simp.*in Cael*.163.35, al. **-στάτητος**, ον, *without inspector, without tutelary genius*, Max.Tyr.14.8, cf. Hsch. **-στᾰτος**, ον, (ἐφίστημι) *inattentive*, Plb.5.34.4, Phld.*Ir*.p.44 W.; τινός *to* a thing, Porph.*Abst*.1.9. Adv. -τως Plb.1.4.4, Longin.33.4, Herod.Med.ap.Orib.10.5.11; *without a check*, Plb.10.47.9, etc. 2. Pass., *not attended to, unregarded*, Ptol.*Alm*.10.6, cf. Simp.*in Cael*.163.35. Adv. -τως Porph.*in Cat*.65.22. 3. *without guidance*, ὀχεῖαι Ph.2.309. 4. *ill-considered*, Alex.Aphr.*in Mete*.9.2, Simp.*in Cael*.157.11. Adv. -τως ib.89.12. **-στημονέω**, *to be ignorant*, *EM*23.24. **-στημονικός**, ἡ, όν, *non-scientific*, πρᾶξις Arist.*EE*1220^{b}25. **-στημοσύνη**, ἡ, *want of knowledge, ignorance, unskilfulness*, Th.5.7; of bees, Arist.*HA*626^{b}4; τινός Pl.*R*.560b: *want of science*, opp. ἐπιστήμη, ib.350a, al., Plot.6.1.10: pl., X.*Oec*.20.21; of κακία, Chrysipp.*Stoic*.3.60. **-στήμων**, Dor. -άμων Archyt.3, ον, gen. ονος, *ignorant, unskilful*, Hdt.9.62, Th.7.67, etc.; νῆες ἀνεπιστήμονες ships *with unskilful crews*, opp. ἔμπειροι, Id.2.89: so μηδὲν ἀ. ἐᾶν leave no part *untrained*, Pl.*Lg*.795c; ἀ. τινός or περί τινος *unskilled in* a thing, Hp.*VM*1, Pl.*Prt*.350b, *Tht*.202c: c. inf., *not knowing how* to do a thing, X.*Mem*.2.3.7: foll. by relat., ἀ. ὅτι.. *not knowing* that.., Th.5.111; ἀ. ὅπῃ τράπωνται Id.3.112. Adv. -μόνως Pl.*Lg*.636e, X.*Cyn*.3.11, etc. II. *without knowledge, unintelligent*, Pl.*R*.350b, etc.; ἡ δ' ἑτέρη [γνώμη] ἀνεπιστημονεστέρη μέν ἐστι τῆς ἑτέρης *less intelligent*, Hdt.2.21. **-στητος**, ον, *not the object of knowledge*, Eustr.*in APo*.45.9. **-στρεπτέω**, *to be indifferent, pay no heed*, D.L.6.91, Arr.*Epict*.2.5.9, Vett.Val.43.27, Artem.3.42, *POxy*.486.10 (ii A.D.). **-στρεπτος**, ον, prop. *without turning round*: hence metaph., *indifferent, heedless*, πάντων Phld.*Herc*.1251.17, cf. Artem.2.37. Adv. -τως Arr.*Epict*.2.9.4, *PMag.Par*.1.45: also -τεί or -τί Ph.1.90 (-τί), Plu.2.46e, 418b, *PMag.Lond*.121.439. **-στρεφής**, ές, = foreg., ἀ. τινος *careless of*, *Placit*.1.7.7; *inexorable*, τὸ ἀ. τῆς δίκης Corn.*ND*21. **-στρεψία**, ἡ, *want of regard, heedlessness*, Arr.*Epict*.2.1.14. **-στρόφητος**, ον, = sq., *PTeb*.27.168 (ii B.C.). **-στροφος**, ον, = ἀνεπίστρεπτος, αὐχήν Ar.Byz.*Epit*.100.10; ἀ. πρός τι Simp.*in de An*.79.5; τινός Eustr.*in EN*110.2; ἀ. τι ἔχειν *to be inattentive to*, Sophon.*in de An*.20.34. Adv. -φως dub. in Hdn.7.10.4; ἀ. κρέμασθαι, of a bat, Trypho *Trop*.1.4. 2. *not capable of inversion*, Procl.*Inst*.44. **-σφᾰλής**, ές, = ἀσφαλής, Them.*Or*.15.190a, Ps.-Alex.Aphr.*in SE*40.18, 41.3. **-σχετος**, ον, *not to be stopped*, ὁρμή J.*Vit*.51; φορή Aret.*SD*2.5; δακρύων ἀ. πηγαί Aristaenet.2.5; of persons, Ph.2.268. Adv. -τως Id.1.296, Plu.*Ages*.27. **-τακτος**, ον, *subject to no control*, τῆς ἀ. πᾶσιν ἐς τὴν δίαιταν ἐξουσίας Th.7.69, cf. Plu.2.987b. Adv. -τως *without orders* or *command*, J.*AJ*19.2.2, D.L.5.20. **-τᾰτος**, ον, *not to be extended farther*, S.E.*M*.10.272. 2. *not capable of* τὸ μᾶλλον, opp. ἀνάνετος, διαφορά Porph.*Intr*.20.4; ἕξεις *in Cat*.138.5. Adv. -τως *without augmentation* or *intensification*, Procl.*Inst*.52; *without stress*, opp. μετ' ἐπιτάσεως, Ammon.*in Interp*.11.26 (misplaced). **-τάττω**, *enjoin*, Eustr.*in EN*370.24. **-τετελεσμένος**, η, ον, *not properly executed* (incorrect form), *Sammelb*.4512.79. **-τευκτος**, *not hitting the mark, vain*, Sch.E.*Ph*.1387: c. gen., ἀ. ἀγαθῶν βίος Vett.Val.173.14, cf. Ptol.*Tetr*.157. Adv. -τως Heph.Astr.3.20. **-τευξία**, ἡ, *failure to attain*, Id.2.30. **-τέχνητος**, ον, *without design*. Adv. -τως *Placit*.4.11.3. **-τήδειος**, ον (α, ον *Gp*.5.26.3), Ion. -εος, η, ον:—*unserviceable, unfit*, of persons and things, X.*HG*1.6.4, etc.; πρός τι Pl.*Sph*.219a; in a positively bad sense, *mischievous, prejudicial*, Hdt.1.175, Th.3.71; γνῶναί τι ἀ. περί τινος And.2.28; of bad omens, X.*HG*1.4.12; of food, Hp.*Acut*.17 (Comp.), *VM*20: c. inf., *unfitted to*.., Lys.31.2. Adv. -ως, πράττειν fare *ill*, opp. εὖ πράττειν, ib.5; ἀ. ἔχειν Plu.2.819a: Comp. -ότερον Pl.*Lg*.813b. 2. *unkind, unfriendly*, X.*HG*7.4.6; ἄλλους τινὰς ἀ. ἀνήλωσαν, i.e. political *opponents*, Th.8.65; στῆλαι ἀ. *IG*2^2.43 *A*34. **-τηδειότης**, ητος, ἡ, *unfitness, inconvenience, inaptitude*, Ph.1.191, 521, M.Ant.5.5, Procl.*Inst*.143. **-τήδευτος**, ον, *made without care* or *design, artless*, D.H.*Comp*.22, cf. 25, Onos.10.3, Luc.*Hist.Conscr*.44. Adv. -τως Phld.*Rh*.1.156 S., D.H.*Lys*.8, Luc.*Pisc*.12. II. *unpractised, untried*, οὐδὲν ἀμίμητον οὐδ' ἀ. Plu.*Alc*.23. Adv. -τως, γλώττης οὐκ ἀ. εἶχεν Philostr.*VA*7.27. **-τίμητος** [τῑ], ον, *not to be censured*, Arist.*EN*1154^{b}4, etc.; τινός *for* a thing, D.61.54; *uncriticized*, Isoc.12.245. 2. *unpunished*, Plb.35.2.8, Onos.*Praef*.6, Ph.1.219. II. *not estimated* or *rated*, *IG*2^2.1241.14, cf. 2.1059.7. **-τμητος**, ον, *subject to no deduction* or *restriction*, μισθώσεις, ἀπολογία, Hsch. **-τρέπτως**, Adv. *without permission*, Lxx 3*Ma*.1.20. **-τρόπευτος**, ον, *without guardian*, Ph.1.219: metaph., ib.696, cf. Gal.*Nat.Fac*.2.3:—also **-τροπος**, ον, Phryn.*PS* p.12 B. **-φανής**, ές, *undistinguished, obscure*, J.*AJ*17.10.7: Comp., Ptol.*Tetr*.168. **-φαντος**, ον, *without ostentation*, Ph.2.76, Vett.Val.16.21; *insignificant*, ἀποτελέσεις Paul.Al.F.1. Adv. -τως M.Ant.1.9. **-φᾰτος**, ον, *unexpected*, Ph.2.533 (v.l. for -φαντος), Hsch. Adv. -τως Ph.2.521, Suid. **-φθόνητος**, ον, *unenvied*, *EM*81.25. **-φθονος**, ον, *without reproach*, ἔγχος S.*Tr*.1033 (lyr.); ἀ. ἐστι πᾶσιν it is *no reproach to* any one, Th.6.83, cf. Pl.*R*.612b, Epicur.*Fr*.161; οὕτω γάρ μοι.. ἀνεπιφθονώτατον εἰπεῖν *least invidious*, D.18.321; *ungrudging*, ἔπαινος Onos.*Praef*.10. Adv. [τὴν ἀρχὴν] ἀνεπιφθόνως κατεστήσατο *so as not to create odium*, Th.6.54, cf. Plu.*Cam*.1; ἀ. εἰπεῖν Isoc.15.8. **-φραστος**, ον, *unthought of*, δύαι Semon.1.21. **-χάδην**· οὐκέτι χωροῦν, Hsch. **-χαρής**, ές, *lacking in refinement*, Vett.Val.75.23. **-χείρητος**, ον, *unassailable*, Plu.*Caes*.25; = ἀνεπιβούλευτος, Hsch. 2. *unattempted*, Plu.2.1075d.

ἀνεπ-όπτευτος, ον, *not admitted among the* ἐπόπται, Hyp.*Fr*.174, cf. Poll.8.124. **-οπτος**, ον, *not to be discerned* or *distinguished*, Id.5.150. **-οργίζομαι**, *to be roused by anger*, Phld.*Lib*.p.41 O. **-όψιος**, ον, *not in sight*, Suid.

ἀνέραμαι, aor. ἀνηράσθην, *love again, love anew*, c. gen., And.1.127, and perh. X.*Mem*.3.5.7 (cj.).

ἀνεραστ-ία, ἡ, *ignorance of love*, Them.*Or*.13.163d. **-ος**, ον, *loveless*, ἔρωτες D.Chr.7.133, cf. Plu.2.406a, etc.; ἀ. κοινωνία, ὁμιλία, ib.752c, 756e; τὸ ἀ. ἑτέρων *want of love for*..., ib.634b; βίος *AP*12.18 (Alph.). 2. *not loved*, Luc.*DMort*.6.3. 3. *unlovely*, Chor.

in *Rh.Mus.*49.498. II. Act., *not loving*, Hld.3.9, Aristaenet.1.10; *unloving, cruel, harsh*, Call.*Epigr.*34.4 (Sup.), Luc.*DDeor.*14.1; ἀνέραστα ποιεῖν Plu.2.61a.

ἀνεργ-άζομαι, *knead, work up*, Orib.9.39.2. **–ασία**, ἡ, *unemployment, idleness*, in pl., Artem.1.67, 2.28 (v.l. ἀνεργίας). **–αστος**, ον, *not thoroughly wrought, imperfect*, Arist.*Metaph.*1048^{b}4; λίθος ἀ. *unwrought*, D.S.14.18; γῆ ἀ. *untilled*, dub. l. in Luc.*Prom.*11; σῖτος ἀ. *raw*, J.*BJ*5.10.2:—of a subject, *not thoroughly handled* or *treated*, Plb.10.43.1. **–εια**, ἡ, *cessation from work, holiday*, J.*BJ*4.9.12 (dub.). **–ία**, ἡ, = ἀεργία, v.l. for ἀνεργασία, Artem.2.28. **–ος**, ον, *not done*, ἔργα ἄ., Lat. *facta infecta*, E.*Hel.*363. 2. = ἀνέργαστος, δέρμα *Edict.Diocl.*8.13, al. 3. *inactive*, opp. ἐνεργός, v.l. in J.*AJ* 16.2.4.

ἀνέργω, v. ἀνείργω.

ἀνερεθίζω, *provoke, stir up, excite*, J.*AJ*19.7.1, Plu.*Thes.*6:—Pass., *to be in a state of excitement*, Th.2.21, X.*An.*6.6.9, Plu.*Pyrrh.*11; εἴς τι Dam.*Pr.*150.

ἀνερείδω, *prop up, rest* a thing *on*, τὸ πρόσωπον τῇ χειρί dub. in Aristaenet.1.22.

ἀνέρεικτος or **–ικτος**, ον, *not bruised, unground*, Hp.*Aff.*52.

***ἀνερείπομαι**, Ep. Dep., used by Hom. only in 3 pl. aor., *snatch up and carry off*, ἀνηρείψαντο, of the gods, Il.20.234, cf. Pi.*Pae.*6.136, A.R.2.503; of the Harpies, Od.1.241, etc.; of storms, 4.727; so παῖδα..'Αφροδίτη ὦρτ' ἀνερειψαμένη Hes.*Th.*990; τὴν 'Αργὼ οὐρανὸς ἀνηρείψατο Them.*Or.*27.333a:—later, *take upon oneself*, πόνον Orph.*A.*290. (The true spelling is prob. ἀνηρεψ–, which has Ms. authority in Hes. l.c. and A.R.1.214; cf. ἀ[νᾱ]ρέψατο Pi.*Pae.* l.c., and ἀνερεψάμενοι, Hsch.: v. ἅρπυια.)

ἀνερέπτομαι, Pass., στόμαχος ἀνερεπτόμενος the stomach *drawn up spasmodically* so as to cause vomiting, dub. l. in Nic.*Al.*256, cf. *AB*401.

ἀνερεύγω, *throw up, disgorge*, ἀνήρῠγεν ἀτμόν (aor. 2) Nonn.*D.*1.239; ἰωὴν ib.485:—Pass., *discharge itself*, of a river, Arist.*Mu.*392^{b}16, A.R.2.744.

ἀνερευθής, ές, of cancerous ulcers, *pallid*, Archig.ap.Aët.16.106 (bis), but prob. f.l. for ἐν–.

ἀνερευν-άω, *search out, examine, investigate*, λόγους Pl.*Phd.*63a; ἔγγραφα *POxy.*1468.18 (iii A.D.):—in Med., Pl.*Lg.*816c, J.*AJ*19.1.15:—Pass., *BJ*2.8.6. **–ησις**, εως, ἡ, *a searching out*, Tz. ad Lyc. 11. **–ητος**, ον, *not investigated*, Pl.*Hp.Ma.*298c; ἀ. παραλιπεῖν τι Arist.*EN*1181^{b}12. 2. *that cannot be searched* or *found out*, v.l. in Pl.*Cra.*421d; ἀνερεύνητα δυσθυμεῖσθαι harass oneself about *inscrutable things*, f.l. in E.*Ion* 255.

ἀνερίθευτος [ῑ], ον, *unbribed, uncorrupted*, *GDI*3585 (Calymna), *Michel*473 (Mylasa); *not honeycombed by intrigues*, ἡγεμονία Ph.2.555, cf. 538.

ἀνερίναστος [ῑ], ον, *not ripened by caprification*, of figs, Thphr.*HP*2.8.3, *CP*2.9.12, Suid.; cf. ἀνηρίναστος.

ἀνερίνεος, ον, = foreg., Hermipp.59 (s. v.l.).

ἀνερκής, ές, *unprotected*, Q.S.3.494.

ἀνερμάτιστος, ον, *without ballast*, ὥσπερ τὰ ἀ. πλοῖα Pl.*Tht.*144a; *unstable*, Olymp.*in Mete.*147.4, cf. Gal.*UP*2.14. 2. metaph., ἀ. τράπεζα an *empty* table, Plu.2.704b; *unstable*, εἶδος Dam.*Pr.*413; also of persons, *without ballast*, Ph.2.451, Plu.2.501d, Plot.1.8.8; ἀ. ἐαθέντα τὰ μεγάλα Longin.2.2.

ἀνερμήνευτος, ον, *with none to interpret*, E.*Hyps.Fr.*1 iv 18. II. *inexplicable, indescribable*, τῷ πέλας S.E.*M.*7.65; ὀδύνη Aristaenet. 2.5.

ἀνερπύζω, = sq., Opp.*H.*4.289, Dionys.*Av.*1.31.

ἀνέρπω, *creep upwards*, E.*Ph.*1178: aor. ἀνείρπῠσα Ar.*Pax*585, Luc.*Nec.*22, etc.; of ivy, E.*Fr.*88; *spring up*, of water, Call.*Ap.*110; ἀ. πρὸς τὸ μετεωρότερον Arist.*PA*688^{a}10; ἐς τὰς ῥῖνας Hp.*Vict.*3.76.

ἀνέρρω, *go quite away, take oneself off*, Eup.221 (in aor. ἀνήρρησα).

ἀνερυγγάνω· ἀνερεύγω, Suid.

ἀνερυθρίαστος, ον, *unblushing*, Ph.2.664.

ἀνερυθριάω, *begin to blush, blush up*, Pl.*Chrm.*158c, X.*Smp.*3.12.

ἀνερύω, Ion. and Dor. **ἀνειρύω** [ῠ], *draw up*, ἀνὰ θ' ἱστία λευκ' ἐρύσαντες Od.9.77, 12.402; ἀνειρύσαι νῆας, = ἀνελκύσαι, Hdt.9.96, cf. A.R.2.586; ἀ. πέπλως Theoc.14.35:—Med., ἐκ νούσου ἀνειρύσω *AP*6.300 (Leon.).

ἀνέρχομαι, (cf. ἄνειμι): aor. –ήλυθον or –ῆλθον:—*go up*, ἀνελθὼν ἐς σκοπιήν Od.10.97; εἰς τὴν ἀκρόπολιν X.*HG*2.4.39; ἐπὶ τὴν σκηνήν Arr.*Epict.*3.22.26; ἐπὶ βῆμα Hdn.1.5.2: abs., *mount the tribune*, Plu.*Aem.*31; *go up from* the coast inland, Od.19.190; *come up from* the nether world, ἀ. ἐξ 'Αΐδεω Thgn.703; κἀξ 'Αιδου θανὼν πρὸς φῶς ἀ. S.*Ph.*625; ἐξ 'Αιδου εἰς θεούς Pl.*R.*521c. 2. of trees, *grow up, shoot up*, Od.6.163,167; of the sun, *rise*, A.*Ag.*658; ἀ. ὠκεανοῖο A.R.3.1230; of water, *rise*, Arist.*Mete.*358^{b}32, Heph.Astr.1.23: metaph., ὄλβος ἀ. E.*Or.*810. 3. *go up to* a first principle, in argument, ἐπ' ἀρχὴν ἀνελθόντες σκοπεῖν Pl.*R.*511d. II. *go* or *come back, return*, ἂψ or αὖθις ἀ. Il.4.392, Od.1.317. 2. *come back to* a point, *recur to it and say*, ἀνελθέ μοι πάλιν τί.. E.*Ph.*1207, cf. *Ion* 933; πάλιν ἐπ' ἀρχὴν ἀ. v.l. in Pl.*Ti.*69a. 3. νόμος..εἰς σ' ἀνελθὼν εἰ διαφθαρήσεται *being brought home to* you, E.*Hec.*802. [In Il.4.392, A.R.1.821, ἀνερχομένῳ is corrupt.] III. trans., *traverse*, νειόν Call.*Aet.Fr.*7.4 P.

ἀνερῶ, Att. fut. of ἀναγορεύω; v. ἀνεῖπον.

ἀνερωτ-άω, *question*, c. acc. pers., καί μιν ἀνηρώτων Od.4.251, cf. Pl.*R.*454c; ἐμαυτὸν ὑπέρ τινος Id.*Ap.*22d; τινὰ περί τινος Hdt.9.89:—Pass., Pl.*Grg.*455d. 2. c. acc. rei, *inquire into*, τὰς δόξας Id.*Men.*84d, al. 3. c. dupl. acc., *question* a person *about* a thing, E.*IT*664, Ar.*Pl.*499, Pl.*Tht.*143d. **–ητέον**, *one must interrogate*, Id.*Phlb.*63c. **–ίζω**, = ἀνερωτάω, Telecl.52.

ἀνεσθίω, *eat away*, of ulcers, etc., in Pass., Hp.*Epid.*4.1, Aret.*SD*1.13. **ἀνεσθίων**· μηκέτι ἐσθιομένων, Hsch.

ἀνεσία, ἡ, = ἄνεσις, Cratin.20.

ἀνέσιμος, ον, (ἀνίημι) *given up to idleness*, ἀ. ἡμέρα *a holiday*, Sch.Th.7.73; *loose*, Sch.Lyc.18.

ἄνεσις, gen. εως, Ion. ιος, ἡ: (ἀνίημι):—*loosening, relaxing*, τῶν χορδῶν of the strings, opp. ἐπίτασις, Pl.*R.*349e; coupled with χάλασις, ib.590b; τῆς αἰσθήσεως..δεσμὸν τὸν ὕπνον εἶναί φαμεν, τὴν δὲ.. ἄνεσιν ἐγρήγορσιν Arist.*Somn.Vig.*454^{b}27; ἀέρος Thphr.*CP*2.1.6; πάγων ἄ., i.e. a *thaw*, Plu.*Sert.*17; of the *ebb*-tide, Str.7.2.1. 2. metaph., *remission, abatement*, κακῶν Hdt.5.28; opp. θλῖψις, 2*Ep.Cor.*8.13, al.; λύπης, μοχθηρίας, etc., Plu.2.102b, etc.; τὴν ἡδονὴν ἄνεσιν λαμβάνειν Phld.*D.*3*Fr.*1; ἄ. φόρων, τελῶν, *remission* of tribute, taxes, Plu.*Sert.*6, *IG*7.2227 (Thisbe), etc.; κολάσεως Plot.4.3.24; of fevers, opp. παροξυσμός, Gal.7.427. 3. *relaxation, recreation*, opp. σπουδή, Pl.*Lg.*724a, Arist.*Rh.*1371^{b}34, cf. Cleanth.*Stoic.*1.122; ἄ. καὶ σχολή Plb.1.66.10; ψυχῆς Mnesith.Ath.ap.Ath.11.484a. 4. *solution*, Dsc.5.96. 5. = τὸ τελευταῖον τῆς παρακμῆς Archig.ap.Gal.7.424. II. *indulgence, licence*, ἡδονῶν Pl.*R.*561a; ἡ τῶν γυναικῶν παρ' ὑμῖν ἄ. Id.*Lg.*637c, cf. Arist.*Pol.*1270^{a}1; δούλων ib.1313^{b}35; *relaxation of custody*, *Act.Ap.*24.23. III. of musical pitch, Aristid.Quint.1.5; of an unaccented syll., Phld.*Po.*2.18.

ἀνέσπερον· ἀσκότεινον, Hsch.

ἀνέσσῠτο, 3 sg. Ep. aor. Pass. of ἀνασεύω, Il.11.458.

ἀνεσταλμένως, Adv. pf. part. Pass. of ἀναστέλλω, *tucked up*, gloss on ἐπιστολάδην, Sch.Hes.*Sc.*287.

ἀνέστιος, ον, *without hearth and home, homeless*, Il.9.63; ἄπαις τε κἀγύναιξ κἀνέστιος S.*Fr.*4, cf. Ar.*Eq.*1266; ἄοικος καὶ ἀ. Luc.*Sacr.*11, cf. Eus.Mynd.59: metaph., ψυχή Max.Tyr.14.8; *savage*, ἄγρη Opp.*H.*2.417.

ἀνεστραμμένως, Adv. pf. part. Pass. of ἀναστρέφω, *inversely*, *EM* 584.20; *perversely*, *PTeb.*25.16 (ii B.C.).

ἀνέσχεθε, ἀνεσχέθομεν, v. sub ἀνέχω.

ἀνετάζω, *inquire of*, ἀλλήλους τὴν αἰτίαν Lxx *Su.*14 (Thd.), *Jd.*6.29 (cod. A). II. *examine* documents, *POxy.*34 i 13; *examine by torture*, τινά *Act.Ap.*22.24, cf. 29.

ἀνέταιρος, ον, *without friends* or *fellows*, Plu.2.807a.

ἀνετέον, (ἀνίημι) *one must relax*, Pl.*Sph.*254b: c. gen., τῆς ἀκριβεστέρας οἰκονομίας Phld.*Oec.*p.73 J.; *one must loosen*, Gal.17(1).434; *one must let slip*, Pl.*Smp.*217c, *Plt.*291c. 2. *one must permit*, Sor.1.108. 3. *one must dilute*, Orib.*Fr.*54.

ἀνετεροίωτος, ον, *unchangeable*, Arist.*Mu.*392^{a}32; *unaltered*, Phld.*Po.*994.3, S.E.*M.*8.455; *undifferentiated*, Dam.*Pr.*68, Procl.*in Prm.* p.926 S.

ἀνετικός, ή, όν, *relaxing*, Antyll.ap.Orib.6.21.30, cf. Crito ap.Gal.13.1041. Adv. –κῶς Stob.2.6.6.

ἀνέτοιμος, ον, *unready, not ready*, Plb.12.20.6, D.S.12.41, J.*Vit.*22; εἴς τι *APl.*4.242 (Eryc.). Adv. –ως, ἔχειν πρός τι App.*Mith.*12. 2. *out of reach, unattainable*, ἀνέτοιμα διώκειν Hes.*Fr.*219.

ἄνετος, ον, (ἀνίημι) *relaxed, slack*, ἡνίαι γαστρός Philostr.*VA*6.11; of the hair, Luc.*Alex.*13; τὸ ἄ. τῆς κόμης Philostr.*VA*1.32:—of bodily parts, *relaxed*, Arist.*GA*738^{a}2. Adv. ἀνετῶς (sic Hsch.) S.*Fr.*641, Ps.-Alex.Aphr.*in SE*121.32, dub. in Call.*Aet.*3.1.39. 2. *set free from labour*, esp. of men and animals dedicated to a god, Hyp.*Fr.*72; θηρία Philostr.*Im.*1.28, cf. App.*BC*1.110; of land, *consecrated and lying untilled*, Ael.*NA*11.2, Poll.1.10. 3. metaph., τὴν τῶν μειρακίων ὁρμὴν ἄνετον εἴασαν νέμεσθαι f.l. for ἀφ– in Plu.2.12a; *uncontrolled, licentious*, ἐξουσία Hdn.2.4.4; *intemperate*, ἁμάρτημ' ἄνετον Phld.*Lib.*p.6 O.

ἀνετῠμολόγητος, ον, *of unknown derivation*, S.E.*M.*1.245.

ἀνέτῠμος, ον, = foreg., S.E.*M.*1.245. Adv. –μως ib.244.

ἄνευ, Megarian and Hellenistic **ἄνις** (q. v.); ἄνευν *IG*4.1484.58 (Epid.); ἄνευς *GDI*1157 (Olymp.):—Prep. (never used in compos.) c. gen. (c. acc. only *GDI* l. c.), *without*, opp. σύν, ἄνευ ἔθεν οὐδὲ σὺν αὐτῷ Il.17.407; ἄ. κέντροιο *without* the goad, 23.387; μόνος ἄ. τινός Ar.*Lys.*143, Pl.*Smp.*217a; in pregnant sense, ἄ. θεῶν, mostly with neg., οὔτι ἄ. θεοῦ ἥδε γε βουλή Od.2.372; οὔ τοι ἄ. θεοῦ ἔπτατο.. ὄρνις 15.531; οὐκ ἄ. θεῶν τινος A.*Pers.*164; μηδὲ θύεσθαι μέν τιν' ἰδίᾳ ἄ. τοῦ ἄρχοντος Aen.Tact.10.4; also without neg., ἄ. ἐμέθεν *without* my knowledge and will, Il.15.213; ἄ. πολιτᾶν *without* their consent, A.*Ch.*431; ἄ. τοῦ κραίνοντος S.*OC*926; ἄ. τοῦ ὑγιεινοῦ *without reference to* health, Pl.*Grg.*518d, cf. 519a; οὐκ ἐνδέχεται ζῆν ἄ. κακοῦ τινος Diph.32.12, etc. II. *away from, far from*, ἄ. δηΐων Il.13.556; ἄ. ὄψου ποιεῖν τινας ἑστιωμένους Pl.*R.*372c, cf. *Hp.Ma.*290e. III. in Prose, *except, besides*, πάντα ἄ. χρυσοῦ Id.*Criti.*112c; ἄ. τοῦ καλὴν δόξαν ἐνεγκεῖν *praeterquam quod attulerit*.., D.18.89; καὶ ἄ. τοῦ λαμβάνειν even *without* it, X.*Cyr.*5.4.28.—In early writers it rarely follows its case, ὑφηγητοῦ δ' ἄ. S.*OC*502; ὧν ἄ. X.*Cyr.*6.1.14; freq. in later Prose, as always in Arist., *Metaph.*1071^{a}2, al., cf. Plu.2.47c, etc. (Cf. Goth. *inu*, OHG. *āno* 'without'; perh. akin to neg. pref. ἀ–.)

ἀνευάζω, fut. –άξω Nonn.*D.*1.20:—*utter cries of* εὖα, D.P.579, *AP*9.139 (Claud.). II. c. acc. pers., *honour with such cries*, Lyc.207, Arr.*An.*5.2.7.

ἀνευ-δοκησία, ἡ, *discredit*, Phld.*Ir.*p.80 W. **–δόκητος**, ον, *discredited*, ib.p.53 W. **-ένδοτος**, ον, f. l. for εὐένδοτος, Ph.2.269. **-ήκοος**, ον, *disobedient*, *PGen.*50.12.

ἄνευθε, before a vowel **-θεν** : (ἄνευ) :—Ep. and Lyr. word : 1. Prep. c. gen., like ἄνευ, *without*, οἷος ἄνευθ' ἄλλων Il.22.39 ; μούνῳ ἄνευθ' ἄλλων Od.16.239; ἄ. πόνου 7.192 ; ἄ. θεοῦ, = ἄνευ θεοῦ, Il.5.185, cf. Pi.*O.*9.103(v.l.). 2. *away from*, ἄνευθεν ἄγων πατρός τε φίλων τε Il.21.78.—Hom. always puts it before its case, though sts. parted from it, as ἄ. δέ σε μέγα νῶϊν ib.22.88 ; later it freq. follows, as πατρὸς ἄνευθεν A.R.4.746. II. Adv. *far away, distant*, αἱ δέ τ' ἄνευθε [νῆσοι] Od.9.26 ; τοὶ δ' ἄλλοι ἄνευθεν καίοντ' Il.23.241 ; ἐγγύθι μοι θάνατος κακὸς οὐδ' ἔτ' ἄνευθεν 22.300 ; οὐδέ . . ἄνευθ' ἔσαν ἀλλὰ μάλ' ἐγγύς 23.378 ; ἄ. λείπειν leave *far away*, Pi.*P.*1.10 :—often with part., ἄ. ἐών Il.2.27, cf. 4.277.

ἀνεύθετος, ον, *inconvenient*, λιμὴν ἀ. πρὸς παραχειμασίαν *Act.Ap.*27.12.

ἀνεύθῡνος, ον, *not accountable, irresponsible*, opp. ὑπεύθυνος, τῇ [μουναρχίῃ] ἔξεστι ἀνευθύνῳ ποιέειν τὰ βούλεται Hdt.3.80, cf. Arist. *Pol.*1271^{a}5 ; ὑπεύθυνον τὴν παραίνεσιν ἔχοντας πρὸς ἀνεύθυνον τὴν ὑμετέραν ἀκρόασιν Th.3.43 ; *free from liability* or *censure*, *POxy.*906.8 (ii/iii A. D.), Lib.*Or.*59.100 ; *not open to objection*, of a statement, Alex.Aphr.*in Top.*425.5. 2. *guiltless, innocent*, Luc.*Abd.*22 : c. gen., ἀ. ἁμαρτήματος Id.*Nigr.*9 ; *irreproachable*, ἀ. τὸ ἰσχίον, of athletes, Philostr.*Gym.*48. Adv. -νως Poll.3.139, Just.*Nov.*8.12 *Intr.*—In Att., ἀνυπεύθυνος was more common.

ἀνεύθυντος, ον, *which cannot be straightened*, Arist.*Mete.*386^{a}8.

ἀνευθύνω, *straighten*, in Pass., Gal.18(1).776.

ἄνευκτος, ον, *not wishing, not praying*, εὐχομένοις καὶ ἀνεύκτοις *AP* 10.108.

ἀνευλᾰβής, ές, *irreverent, impious*, Aq.*Is.*57.11.

ἀνευνοησία, ἡ, *malevolence*, Vett.Val.37.19.

ἀνευόδωτος, ον, *that does not prosper*, Aq., Sm.*Je.*22.30.

ἀνευπρεπής, ές, *unseemly* :—in Adv. -πῶς Hsch. s. v. σχέδιον.

ἀνεύρ-εσις, εως, ἡ, *discovery*, E.*Ion* 569, v.l. in D.H.11.27, cf. Ph.1.285, Plu.*Thes.*12, etc. **-ετέον,** *one must find out*, Pl.*Plt.* 294d. **-ετής,** οῦ, ὁ, *inspector*, τῶν χωρίων τῶν δημοσίων *SIG*279.3 (Zeleia).

ἀνεύρετος, ον, *undiscovered*, Pl.*Lg.*874a, D.S.5.20, Plu.2.700d, *POxy.*472.14 (ii A. D.), etc.

ἀνεύρ-ημα, ατος, τό, *invention, discovery*, Paus.5.9.2. **-ίσκω,** fut. -ευρήσω : aor. -εῦρον, later -ευράμην A.R.4.1133 :—Pass., aor. -ευρέθην :—*find out, discover*, Hdt.1.67, 2.54, etc. ; ἀγαθὰ ἀ. λογιζόμενος Id.7.8.γ' ; ἀ. φόνον A.*Ag.*1094 ; σὸν χρέος ἀνευρίσκειν πότερον . . E.*IT*883 ; ἀ. τὴν αἰτίαν Pl.*Phd.*100b ; τὴν τοῦ θεοῦ φύσιν *Phdr.* 252e, etc. :—Med., *win, gain*, ἱερὸν χῶρον ἀνευρομένην *Epigr.Gr.* 259 :—Pass., *to be found out* or *discovered*, ὡς ὕστερον ἀνευρέθη Th. 1.128 : c. part., ἀνεύρηται ὁμοῖα παρεχομένη Hdt.4.44. II. *think out, invent*, μόνος ἀνευρηκὼς τέχνην Antiph.113, cf. Timocl.37, Pl. *Phdr.*273c ; ἀ. πρόφασίν τινα Philem.88.10, etc.

ἄνευρος, ον, *without sinews*, Hp.*Mochl.*41. 2. *nerveless, slack*, S.*Ichn.*143, Theopomp.Com.71, Arist.*HA*538^{b}7 (Comp.), al. ; νεῦρα ἄνευρα Phld.*Ir.*p.69 W.

ἀνεύρ-υνσις, εως, ἡ, *dilatation*, Gal.1.402 ; ἀρτηρίας Antyll.ap. Orib.45.24.2. **-ύνω** [ῡ], *dilate*, Hp.*Superf.*29, *Placit.*5.16.2 ; ἡ ῥὶς τοὺς μυκτῆρας ἀνευρύνετο Philostr.*Her.*19.9 ; -υσμένον στόμα ἀγγείου Aët.8.69 ; esp. of arterial aneurism, Antyll.ap.Orib.45.24.1 ; ἀ. πάλιν ὁ Ὠκεανὸς *broadens out*, Arist.*Mu.*393^{b}6 : metaph., νοῦς ἀ. τὰς δυνάμεις Ph.1.249, cf. Dam.*Pr.*74 (Pass.). **-υσμα,** ατος, τό, *aneurism*, Ruf. ap.Aët.14.51, Antyll.ap.Orib.45.24.1, Gal.7.725, 10.335. **-υσματώδης,** ες, *like an aneurism*, Aët.15.10, Paul.Aeg.6.38. **-υσμός,** ὁ, *dilatation*, ἀρτηρίας Antyll.ap.Orib.45.24.2 ; μήτρας Dsc.1.13.

ἀνευφημέω, *shout* εὐφήμει or εὐφημεῖτε : hence, as this was mainly done on sorrowful occasions, *cry aloud, shriek*, ἅπας δ' ἀνηυφήμησεν (so Brunck for ἀνευφώνησεν) οἰμωγῇ λεώς S.*Tr.*783, cf. E.*Or.*1335, Pl.*Phd.*60a. 2. *proclaim*, c. acc. et inf., Alex.Aphr. *in Metaph.* 767.30, cf. Simp.*in Ph.*1360.20 : c. dupl. acc., Dam.*Pr.*58. II. later, *receive* or *honour with auspicious cries*, τινὰ ὡς εὐεργέτην J.*BJ* 4.2.5, cf. 2.21.4, Hdn.6.4.1.

ἀνευφρ-αίνομαι, f.l. for ἐν-, Ph.2.476. **-ανσία,** ἡ, *joylessness*, *Cat.Cod.Astr.*2.161. **-αντος,** ον, *joyless*, ἀπόλαυσις Secund.*Sent.* 9, cf. *Annales du Service* 22.9 (Egypt, i A. D.), Ptol.*Tetr.*158, Suid.

ἀνευφρόσυνος, ον, *joyless*, θήρη Sch.Opp.*H.*4.533.

ἀνεύχομαι, *unsay a prayer*, Pl.*Alc.*2.142d, 148b.

ἀνεφάλλομαι, *leap up at*, used only in part. ἀνεπάλμενος, v. ἀναπάλλω.

ἀνέφαπτος, ον, *not to be claimed as a slave* (cf. ἀνέπαφος), *GDI* 1684 sqq. (Delph.).

ἀνέφεδρος, ον, *without drawing a bye*, ἀ. νικᾶν *SIG*1070.6 (Olymp.), *IG*5(1).680, al. (Sparta).

ἀνεφέλκομαι, Med., *draw up for oneself*, ἐξ ἁλὸς ἰχθύν Man.5.279.

ἀνέφελος, ον, *unclouded, cloudless*, αἴθρη Od.6.45 ; ἀήρ Arist.*Mu.* 394^{a}23 ; νύξ Plu.*Arat.*21, etc. : metaph., *not to be veiled* or *hidden*, κακόν S.*El.*1246 (lyr.). (ἀνν. is v.l. in Arat.415, etc. ; Eust.945.4 has also the form **ἀνεφής,** ές.)

ἄνεφθος, ον, *unboiled*, Antyll.ap.Orib.9.24.3, Gal.6.354 : Comp., Paul.Aeg.1.74, *Gp.*10.67.1. 2. ἄ. πλίνθος *unbaked*, Agath.2.16.

ἀνέφικτος, ον, *out of reach, unattainable*, Ph.1.228, al., Phld.*Rh.* 1.27 S., Plu.2.54d, Luc.*Herm.*67, Jul.*Or.*2.82d.

ἀνεφόδευτος, ον, *undetected, unexamined*, Phld.*Lib.*p.39 O.

ἀνέφοδος, ον, *not liable to invasion*, Lyd.*Mag.*3.32.

ἀνεφριτικὰ συμπτώματα *not-nephritic*, Gal.17(1).136.

ἀνεχέγγυος, ον, *unwarranted*, διὰ τὸ τὴν γνώμην ἀνεχέγγυον γεγενῆσθαι because they had *no sure confidence* in themselves, Th.4.55.

ἀνέχραζεν· ἀνέχριμπτεν, ἀνήρει δ' ἀνεκούφιζεν, Hsch.

ἀνέχω, impf. ἀνεῖχον : also **ἀνίσχω,** impf. ἀνῖσχον : fut. ἀνέξω Archil. 82, Luc.*Hist.Conscr.*4 (s. v. l.), also ἀνασχήσω Hdt.5.106, 7.14, E.*IA* 732 : aor. ἀνέσχον Il.17.310, etc. ; poet. ἀνέσχεθον ib.10.461, E. *Med.*1027, Ep. inf. ἀνσχεθέειν Od.5.320 : pf. ἀνέσχηκα S.E.*M.*7.190, Phalar.*Ep.*105 :—**Med. ἀνέχομαι** : impf. ἠνειχόμην (with double augm.) A.*Ag.*905, S.*Ph.*411, Th.1.77, etc. : fut. ἀνέξομαι Il.5.895 ; S.*El.*1028, D.18.160, etc. ; also ἀνασχήσομαι A.*Th.*252, Ar.*Ach.*299, Ep. inf. ἀνσχήσεσθαι Il.5.104 : aor. ἀνεσχόμην 18.430, A.*Ch.*747 codd., E.*Hipp.*687 (where ἠνέσχου is contra metr.) ; more freq. with double augm. ἠνεσχόμην Hdt.5.48, A.*Ag.*1274 ; and Att., as Ar.*Nu.* 1363, Th.3.28, Lys.3.3, etc. ; sync. ἠνσχόμην S.*Ant.*467 ; 2 sg. imper. ἄνσχεο (v. infr. c. II) :—**Pass.,** D.H.3.55, Lxx 4 *Ma.*1.35.

A. trans., *hold up, lift up*, χεῖρας ἀνέσχον held up their hands *in fight* (v. infr. C. I), Od.18.89 (later of pugilists, *hold up* the hands *in token of defeat*, Theoc.22.129) :—freq. *lift up* the hands *in prayer*, θεοῖσι δὲ χεῖρας ἀνέσχον Il.3.318, cf. 1.450, Archil.82, etc. ; so ἄνακτι εὐχὰς ἀ. *offer* prayers, perhaps *with uplifted hands*, S.*El.*636 ; ἄνεχε χέρας, ἄνεχε λόγον E.*El.*592 ; also ἀ. τὴν χεῖρα *offer* the hand (to shake), Theopomp.Com.82 (dub.). 2. *lift up* as an offering, τά γ' Ἀθηναίῃ ληΐτιδι . . ὑψόσ' ἀνέσχεθε χειρί Il.10.461 ; as a testimony, σκῆπτρον ἀ. πᾶσι θεοῖσι 7.412 ; μαζὸν ἀ., of Hecuba entreating her son Hector, 22.80 ; κενεὰς . . ἀνέσχε γλήνας A.R.2.254 ; ἄκουε δ' ἀν' οὖς ἔχων A.*Fr.*126. 3. ἀ. φλόγα *hold up* a torch, esp. at weddings, E.*IA*732 : hence the phrase ἄνεχε, πάρεχε (sc. τὸ φῶς) *hold up*, pass on the light in procession, Id.*Tr.*308, *Cyc.*203, cf. Ar.*V.*1326 ; also ἀ. φάος σωτήριον E.*Med.*482 ; τὸ σημεῖον τοῦ πυρός Th.4.111. 4. *lift up, exalt*, τὰ κείνων Pi.*P.*2.89. 5. *hold up, prop, sustain*, οὐρανὸν καὶ γῆν, of Atlas, Paus.5.11.5 ; κίων ἀ. τὴν στέγην Oenom.ap.Eus.*PE* 5.34 :—Pass., γέφυρα σκάφαις ἀνεχομένη D.H.3.55 :—but more freq., b. metaph., *uphold, maintain*, εὐδικίας Od.19.111 ; πολέμους Th.1.141 ; ὄργια ἀ. *keep up* the revels, Ar.*Th.*948 ; Βάκχης ἀνέχων λέκτρ' Ἀγαμέμνων *remaining constant to*, E.*Hec.*121 (v. infr. B. 3) ; οἰνῶπ' ἀνέχουσα κισσόν *keeping constant to, haunting* the ivy, S. *OC*674 (s. v. l.) ; βαρὺν ἀνὰ θυμὸν ἔχοισα *keeping up* his anger, Theoc. 1.96. 6. *put forth*, δάφνα ἀ. πτόρθους E.*Hec.*459 (lyr.). II. *hold back, check*, ἄνεχ' ἵππους Il.23.426 ; ἀ. τὰ ὅπλα διὰ τῶν ἀνακλητικῶν D.H.9.21 ; ἀ. Σικελίαν μὴ ὑπ' αὐτοὺς εἶναι *keep* it from being . . , Th.6.86 ; ἑαυτὸν ἀπό τινος Plu.2.514a :—Pass., ἀνέχεται τὰ πάθη ὑπὸ τοῦ λογισμοῦ Lxx 4 *Ma.*1.35.

B. intr., *rise up, emerge*, ἀνσχεθέειν . . ὑπὸ κύματος ὁρμῆς Od.5. 320 ; of a diver, Hdt.8.8 ; σκόπελοι ἐν τῷ Νείλῳ ὀξέες ἀ. Id.2.29 ; ἀ. ἐς ἀέρα A.R.3.1383. b. esp. in form ἀνίσχω, of the sun, πρὸς ἥλιον ἀνίσχοντα Hdt.3.98, etc. ; so λαμπὰς ἀνίσχει A.*Ag.*93 (lyr.) ; ἅμ' ἡλίῳ ἀνίσχοντι X.*Cyn.*6.13, cf. Eub.119.9. c. of events, *arise, happen*, Hdt.5.106, 7.14. d. *appear, show oneself*, ἄελπτον ὄμμα . . φήμης ἀνασχόν S.*Tr.*204 ; *turn out, prove to be*, μελοποιὸς ἢ τραγῳδὸς ἄριστος Eun.*Hist.*p.209 D. e. *stand up*, κίονες περὶ τοίχοις A.R. 3.217. 2. *come forth*, αἰχμὴ παρὰ . . ὦμον ἀνέσχεν Il.17.310, cf. Plu. *Caes.*44 ; of a headland, *jut out* into the sea, Hdt.7.123, Th.1.46, etc. ; ἀ. πρὸς τὸ Σικελικὸν πέλαγος Id.4.53, cf. D.23.166 ; ἐς τὸν πόντον [τὴν ἄκρην] ἀνέχοντα *jutting out* with its headland into the sea, Hdt. 4.99 (dub. l.) ; reversely, κοιλάδες ἐς μεσόγαιαν ἐκ θαλάσσης ἀ. Str. 3.2.4. 3. *hold on, keep doing*, c. part., ἀ. διασκοπῶν Th.7.48 ; σε . . στέρξας ἀνέχει *is constant* in his love for thee, S.*Aj.*212 (lyr., cf. supr. A. I. 5 b) : c. dat., τελεταῖς *practise regularly*, Eun.*Hist.*p.249 D. : abs., *wait*, ταύτῃ ἀνέχειν Th.8.94, cf. 2.18. 4. *hold up, cease*, Ζεὺς οὐθ' ὕων πάντεσσ' ἁνδάνει οὔτ' ἀνέχων Thgn.26, cf. X.*HG*1.6.28 ; dub. l. in Hp.*Epid.*5.20. 5. c. gen., *cease from*, οὐδὲ . . καμάτων ἀνέχουσι γυναῖκες S.*OT*174 ; τοῦ πολέμου App.*Pun.*75 ; τοῦ φονεύειν Plu.*Alex.* 33.—Hom. uses no tense intr. exc. aor.

C. Med., *hold up what is one's own*, ὁ δ' ἀνέσχετο μείλινον ἔγχος Il.5.655 ; δούρατ' ἀνασχόμενοι 11.594, etc. : hence ἀνασχόμενος is often used abs. (sc. ἔγχος, ξίφος, etc.), πλῆξεν ἀ. 3.362 ; κόψε δ' ἀ. Od.14.425 ; πὺξ μάλ' ἀνασχομένω πεπληγέμεν Il.23.660 ; also ἄντα δ' ἀνασχομένω χερσί ib.686. II. *hold oneself up, bear up*, οὐδέ σ' ὀΐω δηρὸν ἔτ' ἀνσχήσεσθαι ib.5.285, cf. Od.11.375 : aor. imper. ἀνάσχεο, = τέτλαθι, *be of good courage*, Il.1.586 ; ἄνσχεο *be patient*, 23.587 ; ἀνὰ δ' ἔχευ is prob. l. for ἀνὰ δ' εὖ in Archil.6.2 : in pres. part., ἀνεχόμενοι φέρουσι τὸν χειμῶνα they bear *with patience*, Hdt.4.28 ; Stoic motto ἀνέχου καὶ ἀπέχου Gell.17.19. 2. c. acc., τοσσάδ' ἐνὶ φρεσὶν ᾗσιν ἀνέσχετο κήδεα Il.18.430 ; ἦ δὴ πολλὰ κάκ' ἄνσχεο σὸν κατὰ θυμόν 24.518 ; τὴν δουλοσύνην οὐκ ἀ. Hdt.1.169 ; τὰ πρὶν κακὰ ἠνειχόμεσθα A.*Ag.*905, etc. ; χαλκὸν ἀνασχέσθαι Il.4.511, etc. : c. acc. pers., οὐ γὰρ ξείνους . . ἀνέχονται they *do not suffer* or *bear with* strangers, Od.7.32, cf. 17.13 ; τῶν ἵππων οὔτι ἀνεχομένων τὰς καμήλους Hdt.7. 87 ; τούτους ἀνάσχου δεσπότας E.*Alc.*304, cf. Eup.6 D. : c. acc. rei et gen. pers., οὐδεὶς ἂν αὐτοῦ ἀγελαστὶ ἠνέσχετο ταῦτα τὰ ἔπη Ath.5. 188c, cf. Ar.*Lys.*507. 3. c. gen., dub. in Hom., δουλοσύνης ἀνέχεσθαι v.l. in Od.22.423 ; so ἅπαντος ἀνδρὸς ἀ. Pl.*Prt.*323a, cf. D.19. 16 ; *to be content with*, τοῦ ἐν σώματι κάλλους Plot.5.9.2. 4. the dependent clause is mostly (always in Hom.) in part., οὐ μάν σε . . ἀνέξομαι ἄλγε' ἔχοντα I *will* not *suffer* thee to have . . , Il.5.895 ; οὐ γὰρ ἀεργὸν [ὄντα] ἀνέξομαι I *will* not *suffer* one [to be] . . , Od.19.27 ; εἰ τὸν . . θανόντ' ἄθαπτον ἠνσχόμην νέκυν S.*Ant.*467 ; οὐκ ἀνέξεται τίκτοντας ἄλλους E.*Andr.*712 ; καὶ γάρ κ' . . ἀνεχοίμην ἥμενος for I *would* *be content* to sit.., Od.4.595; σοῦ κλύων ἀνέξεται A.*Pers.*838, cf. S.*El.*1028, *Ph.*411; ἀνάσχεσθε σιγῶσαι Id.*Fr.*679; also οὐ σῖγ' ἀνέξει; Id.*Aj.*75: freq. in Prose, Hdt.1.80,206, 5.19, al., Th.2.74, etc.; ἄποτος ἀ. Arist.*HA*596ᵃ2; also ἀ. τοῦ ἄλλα λέγοντος Pl.*R.*564d; ἀ. τῶν οἰκείων ἀμελουμένων Id.*Ap.*31b; οὐδ' ἂν ἠνέσχεσθε εἴ τις.. D.21.170:—also in Act., ἀνέσχηκα Phalar.*Ep.*105. 5. rarely c. inf., *suffer*, οὐκ ἀνέξομαι τὸ μὴ οὐ.. A.*Eu.*914; κοκκύζειν τὸν ἀλεκτρυόν' οὐκ ἀνέχονται Cratin.311; ἀνακεκλίσθαι οὐκ ἀ. Aret.*SA*1.9; ἀ. πάντα ὑπομένειν Alciphr.3.34; σὺν ἄλλοις βιοῦν οὐκ ἀ. Ael.*NA*6.30. b. *dare to* do, ἀνέσχοντο τὸν ἐπιόντα δέξασθαι Hdt.7.139. c. οὐκ ἀ., c. inf., *refuse* to do.., *POxy.*903.36, al. III. rarely, *hold on by one another, hang together*, ἀνά τ' ἀλλήλῃσιν ἔχονται Od.24.8.

ἀνεψαινυγμένως· ἐσπουδασμένως, Hsch.

ἀνέψ-ἄνος, ον, (ἕψω) *bad for cooking*, ὕδατα Hp.*Aër.*7. **-ητος**, ον, *unboiled*, Dsc.1.102, Alex.Aphr.*in Mete.*190.34, Tim.*Lex.* s. v. κερασβόλον:—later form ἀνέψετος *PMag.Par.*1.53. II. *undigested*, δόρπος Sch.Nic.*Al.*66.

ἀνεψι-ά, ἡ, fem. of ἀνεψιός, X.*Mem.*2.7.2, Isoc.19.8, etc. **-ἄδῆ**, ἡ, *first cousin's daughter*, Ar.*Fr.*745. **-άδης**, ου, ὁ, = sq., *Sammelb.*176, Iamb.*Protr.*21.κζ', Poll.3.28. **-ἄδοῦς**, οῦ, ὁ, *first cousin's son*, Pherecr.203, Hermipp.86, D.44.26, Is.11.12; also, of *second cousins*, acc. to Poll.3.28, but this rests on a misinterpretation of D. 45.54. **-ός**, ὁ, *first cousin*, or generally, *cousin*, Il.9.464, Hdt.5.30, 7.82, A.*Pr.*856, *Com.Adesp.*58 D., etc., v. esp. And.1.47; ἀ. πρὸς πατρός Is.11.2; ἐκ πατρός Theoc.22.170: comically, ἐγχέλεων ἀ. Stratt.39. [ἀνεψιοῦ κταμένοιο Il.15.554, = ἀνεψιὸ͜ο κτ., cf. Q.S.3.295.] (Cf. Skt. *napāt* 'grandson', Lat. *nepos*, etc.) **-ότης**, ητος, ἡ, *relationship of cousins*, esp. in phrase ἐντὸς ἀνεψιότητος Pl.*Lg.*871b, Lex ap.D.43.57.

ἀνέψω, *boil again*, Arg.E.*Med.* (in aor. part. ἀνεψήσασα); ἔλαιον ἀνεψήτασθαι f.l. for ἀναψ. in Carm.Pop.ap.Sch.Ar.*Eq.*725.

ἀνέω [ᾰ], = πτίσσω, Ar.*Fr.*694 (v.l. αἰνεῖθ'), Ath.10.455e, Paus. Gr.*Fr.*21, prob. in Poll.7.24 (ἀλεῖν codd.). Cf. αἴνω, ἀφᾱνέω.

ἄνεω, Adv. *without a sound, in silence*, δὴν δ' ἄ. ἦσαν Il.9.30,695; τίπτ' ἄ. ἐγένεσθε; 2.323; οἱ δ' ἄ. ἐγένοντο 3.84, Od.7.144, 10.71; ἅπαντες ἧσθ' ἄ. 2.240.—In all the places cited it is joined with a pl. Verb, and is commonly written ἄνεῳ (as if nom. pl. from ἄνεως).

ἀνέῳγα, ἀνέῳγον, v. ἀνοίγνυμι.

ἀνεῳγότως, Adv. pf. part. of ἀνεῳγώς (from ἀνοίγω), *openly*, Gloss.

ἀνέωνται, v. ἀνίημι sub init.

ἄνη, ἡ, (ἄνω) *fulfilment*, A.*Th.*713, Call.*Jov.*90.

ἀνηβ-άσκω, = sq., D.H.*Rh.*2.6 (censured by Thom.Mag.p.171 R.), *POxy.*1381.197. **-άω**, *grow young again*, Hes.*Op.*132 (prob.), A.*Supp.*606 (Tyrwh. ἀνηβῆσαί με for ἂν ἡβήσαιμι), E.*Ion* 1465, Pl.*Lg.*666b; δὶς ἀ. Thgn.1009; πάλιν X.*Cyr.*4.6.7; μόνος ὁ νοῦς παλαιούμενος ἀνηβᾷ Plu.2.5e. II. *grow up, attain to* ἥβη, Call.*Jov.*56. **-ητήριος**, α, ον, *making young again*, ἀ. ῥώμη the *returning* strength *of youth*, E.*Andr.*552. **-ος**, ον, *not yet come to man's estate*, opp. ἔφηβος, παῖς Heraclit.117, cf. *Leg.Gort.*11.19, Lys.14.25, Theoc.8.3; οἱ ἄ. *pueri*, *CIG*2034 (Byzantium), cf. *SIG*1028.32 (Cos); ἄνηβοι καὶ ἄγονοι ἐκ γενετῆς *impotent*, Arist.*HA*581ᵇ22; of a girl, Pl.*Lg.*833c. **-ότης**, ητος, ἡ, *childhood, minority*, Just.*Nov.*159 *Pr.*

ἀνηγεμόνευτος, ον, *without leader, unguided*, ψυχή Ph.1.337, cf. 696, Luc.*Icar.*9; φυρμός M.Ant.12.14.

ἀνηγέομαι, Dor. ἀνᾱγ-, *relate, rehearse*, Pi.*N.*10.19, cf. *I.*6(5).56, Hdt.5.4. 2. intr., ἀ. πρόσφορος ἐν Μοισᾶν δίφρῳ *advance* worthily in the Muses' car, Pi.*O.*9.80.

ἀνήδομαι, *renounce one's enjoyment of* a thing, *no longer enjoy* it, ἃ τόθ' ἥσθην, ταῦτα νῦν ἀ. Hermipp.77.

ἀνήδονος, ον, *disagreeable*, J.*AJ*17.3.1, Them.*Or.*26.319d. II. *without pleasure*, Plot.4.8.8.

ἀνήδυντος, ον, *not sweetened* or *seasoned*, Hp.*Int.*21, al., Arist.*Pr.*925ᵇ18, etc. 2. metaph., Id.*Pol.*1340ᵇ16; ἀ. βραχυλογία Plu.*Phoc.*5; ὕμνος Them.*Or.*18.218b; so, *unpleasant*, Hegesand.26; γυνή, φωνή, Plu.2.142b, 405d; ἦθος ἀ. πρὸς χάριν ib.799d.

ἀνήδυστος, ον, v.l. for foreg., Plu.*Phoc.*5.

ἀνήη, v. ἀνίημι. **ἀνηθείη·** ὁμιλία, Hsch.

ἀνηθέλαιον, τό, *oil of dill*, Gal.19.666, Orib.*Fr.*1.

ἀνηθίκευτος, ον, *without characteristic*, Sch.Lyc.14.

ἀνήθ-ινος, η, ον, *made of dill*, στέφανος (in form ἀνήτ-) Theoc.7.63; οἶνος Dsc.5.65; μύρον Id.1.51, cf. Aret.*CA*1.2; cf. ἀνήτινος, ἀννήθιον. **-ίτης** [ῑ] οἶνος wine *flavoured with dill-seed*, *Gp.*8.3. **-οειδής**, ές, *like dill*, Dsc.4.164.

ἄνηθον or **ἄννηθον**, τό, Aeol. ἄνητον Alc.36, Sapph.78,128, also Anacr.ap.Poll.6.107. **ἄννητον** Thphr.*HP*9.7.3:—*dill, Anethum graveolens*, Ar.*Nu.*982, *Th.*486, Thphr.*HP*1.11.2, Alex.127.5, Theoc.15.119, *Ev.Matt.*23.23, Dsc.3.58, *SIG*1170.26 (ii A. D.), Bilabel Ὀψαρτ. p.10. (ἀνν- in Ar. ll.cc. Not to be confused with ἄννησον, q.v.)

ἀνηθοποίητος, ον, *not giving exact delineation of character*, D.H.*Lys.*8, Longin.34.3. 2. *unprincipled*, Cic.*Att.*10.10.5.

ἀνήιον, v. ἄνειμι (εἶμι).

ἀνήκεστος, ον, (ἀκέομαι) *incurable, desperate, fatal*, ἄλγος, χόλος, Il.5.394, 15.217; ἀ. πάθος ἔρδειν τινά Hdt.1.137; ἀ. λώβην λωβᾶσθαί τινα Id.3.154; λυμαίνεσθαί τινα λύμῃσι ἀ. Id.6.12, cf. A.*Ch.*516, etc.; κακόν, κακά, συμφοραί, Hes.*Th.*612, Archil.9.5, Th.5.111; μίασμα.. ἀ. τρέφειν keep it *till it is past cure*, S.*OT*98; ἁμαρτάδες Hp.*Acut.*39; ἔργον Antipho 5.91; πονηρία X.*Mem.*3.5.18; ἀνήκεστα ποιεῖν τινα *ruin utterly*, Id.*An.*2.5.5; ἀνήκεστα πάσχειν to be *utterly ruined*, Th.3.39; ἀ. τι παθεῖν D.54.5; ἀ. τι βουλεῦσαι περί τινος Th.1.132; ἁπάντων τῶν ἀνηκέστων αἴτιον D.21.70, etc. 2. of persons, ἀ. πλεονέκτας X.*Oec.*14.8; χρήσασθαί τινι τῶν ἐχθρῶν ὡς ἀνηκέστῳ Plu.*Per.*39; ἀ. εἴς τι J.*AJ*18.6.10: Comp. -έστερος f.l. in Antipho 5.91: Sup., Ph.2.316. II. Act., *damaging beyond remedy, pernicious*, πῦρ S.*El.*888; χαρά Id.*Aj.*52. III. Adv. ἀνηκέστως, διατιθέναι treat *cruelly*, Hdt.3.155, cf. 8.28; ἀ. ἔχειν Aret.*SD*1.5, App.*BC*2.123.

ἀνηκής, ές, (ἄκος) = foreg., S.*Fr.*49.

ἀνηκίδωτος, ον, (ἀκῐδωτός) *without point*, A.*Fr.*279; opp. ἠκιδωμένος, βέλη *IG*2.807*b*138.

ἀνηκο-έω, *to be deaf*, Hdn.*Epim.*188. **-ΐα**, ἡ, *not hearing*, Plu.2.38b, Hierocl.*in CA*25 p.477 M. 2. *ignorance*, Plu.2.676f. 3. *disobedience*, Steph.*in Rh.*288.36. **-ος**, ον, *without hearing*, Arist.*Pr.*903ᵇ38; of the dead, Mosch.3.103; πέτραι Lyc.1451. 2. c. gen., *not hearing* a thing, *never having heard* or *learnt* it, Pl.*Phdr.*261b, X.*Mem.*2.1.31: hence, *ignorant of* it, παιδείας Aeschin.1.141; *with no ear for*, τῶν Διονυσίου ῥυθμῶν Philostr.*VS*1.22.3; *not attending the lectures of*.., c. gen., ib.2.2. Adv. ἀνηκόως, ἔχειν ἀστρολογίας Plu.2.145c; ἔς τι Paus.10.17.13. b. c. acc. rei, ἀνήκοος εἶναι ἔνια γεγενημένα (where ἀ. εἶναι = ἀγνοεῖν) Pl.*Alc.*2.141d. c. abs., σκαιὸς καὶ ἀ. *ignorant, untaught*, D.19.312, cf. Sallust.5. 3. *not willing to hear, not listening*, Call.*Del.*116; τὸ ἀ. *disobedience*, D.H.6.35. II. *unheard*, Philostr.*Her.*12.3; *without result*, ἀ. τέθυται Alciphr.3.35.

ἀνηκουστ-έω, *to be unwilling to hear, disobey*, c. gen., οὐδ' ἄρα πατρὸς ἀνηκούστησε Il.15.236; τῶν πατρὸς λόγων A.*Pr.*40; τῶν νόμων Th.1.84: c. dat., ἀ. τοῖσι στρατηγοῖσι Hdt.6.14: also abs., 1.115, Aen.Tact.10.3. **-ία**, Ion. **-ίη**, ἡ, *want of hearing, deafness*, Hp.*Morb.*3.4. 2. *disobedience*, Pl.*Lg.*671b. **-ος**, ον, *not to be heard, inaudible*, Arist.*de An.*421ᵇ5. 2. *unheard of*, ἤκουσ' ἀνήκουστα.. ὥστε φρῖξαι S.*El.*1407, cf. E.*Hipp.*363 (lyr.). 3. of prayers, *not to be granted*, Antipho 1.22. II. Act., *not willing to hear*: τὸ ἀ. *disobedience*, X.*Cyn.*3.8.

ἀνήκω, *to have come up to* a point, *reach up to*, of persons and things, ἐς μέτρον τινὸς ἀ. Hdt.2.127; αἱμασιὴν ὕψος ἀνήκουσαν ἀνδρὶ ἐς τὸν ὀμφαλόν Id.7.60; ἐς τὰ μέγιστα ἀ. ἀρετῆς πέρι 5.49; χρήμασι ἀ. ἐς τὰ πρῶτα 7.134; φρενῶν ἐς τὰ ἐμεωυτοῦ πρῶτα οὔκω ἀ. *have* not yet *reached* the highest point I aim at, ib.13; οὐκ ἐς τοσοῦτο εὐηθίης ἀ. ib.16.γ', cf. 9.γ'; πρόσω ἀρετῆς ἀ. ib.237; ἀ. εἰς τὸ ὀξύ *to rise to* a point, Ael.*NA*1.55; τοῦτο μὲν ἐς οὐδὲν ἀ. *amounts to* nothing, Hdt.2.104; μεῖζον ἀ. ἢ κατ' ἐμὰν ῥώμαν the matter *has gone* too *far*.., S.*Tr.*1018; αἱ πολλαὶ [ζημίαι].. ἐς τὸν θάνατον ἀ. *have gone as far as*.., Th.3.45. 2. ἀ. ἐς σὲ ἔχειν it *has come to* you to have, *has become* yours to have, Hdt.6.109. 3. ἀ. εἴς τι *refer to* or *be connected with*.., D.60.6, Arist.*EN*1167ᵇ4 (v.l.); τὰ εἰς ἀργυρίου λόγον ἀ. ἀδικήματα which *involve* a money consideration, Din.1.60; so ὁ φόνος ἀνήκει εἴς τινα Antipho 3.3.7; ἀ. πρός τι Plb.2.15.4, Callix.2, etc. II. *belong, appertain*, Lxx 1 *Ma.*10.42, al.; τὰ εἰς τιμὴν καὶ δόξαν ἀνήκοντα *OGI* 763.36 (Pergam.); τὰ ἐκείνοις -οντα ib.532 (Paphlag.); τὰ ἀ. τῇ πόλει *Inscr.Magn.*53.65 (iii B. C.); τὰ ἀ. τοῖς ἱεροῖς *PTeb.*6.42 (ii B. C.). 2. abs., *to be fit* or *proper*, *Ep.Eph.*5.4, *Ep.Col.*3.18; τὸ ἀνῆκον, = τὸ προσῆκον, *Ep.Philem.*8. III. *come back*, εἰς τοὺς πρώτους πάλιν ἀ. λόγους Pl.*Tht.*196b.

ἀνηλάκᾰτος, ον, *unable to spin*, γυνή Matro *Parod.Fr.*5.

ἀνήλᾰτος, ον, *not malleable*, Arist.*Mete.*385ᵃ16: metaph., *stubborn*, Anacr.140. 2. *not struck with a hammer*, Lxx *Jb.*41.15.

ἀνηλεγής, ές, *unconcerned, reckless*, πόλεμος Q.S.2.75: neut. in Hsch. Adv. -έως Q.S.2.414.

ἀνηλε-ήμων, v. sub ἀνελεήμων. **-ής**, ές, = ἀνελεής, *without pity, unmerciful*, Men.*Epit.*478, Call.*Del.*106, Parth.14.2, App.*Mith.*38; poet. acc. ἀνηλέα (as if from ἀνηλής) *Epigr.Gr.*418 (Cyrene); gen. ἀνηλέος Man.1.263; ἀνηλής is dub. in Alcm.81, cf. *An.Ox.*1.60. Adv. -εῶς Hp.*Aff.*40, And.4.39. **-ητος**, ον, *unpitied*, Lycurg.148 (ἀνελ- codd.). II. *unmerciful*, Aeschin.2.163, Eub.1 D. Adv. -τως Pl.*Lg.*697d, Ar.*Fr.*51 D.

ἀνήλειπτος, ον, *unanointed*, should be read for ἀνείληπτος in Antyll.ap.Orib.10.13.19:—also **ἀνήλειφος** (so codd.) or **ἀνήλῐφος**, ον, D.C.56.30, Philagr.ap.Orib.5.19.10, Hp.*Ep.*17.

ἀνηλειψία, ἡ, *being unanointed, uncleanliness*, Hp.*Vict.*2.57, Plb.3.87.2.

ἀνηλής, v. ἀνηλεής.

ἀνηλιάζω, *place in the sun*, f.l. in Protagorid.4.

ἀνήλῐκος, ον, *not yet arrived at man's estate*, Ps.-Callisth.1.38, Suid. s.v. ἄνηβος.

ἀνηλιοδείκτης, ου, ὁ, dub. sens. in *PMag.Par.*1.1374.

ἀνήλιος, Dor. -άλιος, ον, *without sun, unsunned, sunless*, of the nether world, A.*Th.*859 (lyr.); μυχοί, δνόφοι, Id.*Pr.*453, *Ch.*51 (lyr.); φυλλάς S.*OC*676 (lyr.); λιβὰς E.*Andr.*534 (lyr.).

ἀνηλιποκαιβλεπέλαιος (fort. -κάλιπ-), ον, *barefoot and unanointed* (?), Epigr.ap.Hegesand.1.

ἀνήλῐπος, Dor. ἀνάλ-, ον, *barefoot*, v.l. for νήλιπος, Theoc.4.56.

ἀνηλῐφής, ές, = ἀνήλειπτος, Suid.: **ἀνήλῐφος**, ον, v. ἀνήλειπτος.

ἀνήλῠσις, εως, ἡ, *going up*: *return*, Hsch.

ἀνήλ-ωμα, ατος, τό, = ἀνάλωμα, *PTeb.*212 (ii B. C.), *PHal.*15.7 (iii B. C.), *BGU*1117.15 (i B. C.), *IG*2.595, etc. **-ωτικός**, ή, όν, = ἀναλ-, *PLond.*2.265.10 (i A. D.); ἀ. μέτρον *PPetr.*3 p.317.

ἀνήλωτος, ον, *not nailed*, Suid. s. v. ἀγόμφωτος.

ἀνήμελκτος, ον, *unmilked*, Od.9.439.

ἀνήμερ-ος, ον, *not tame, wild, savage*, of persons, πολιήτας Anacr.1.7; ἀνήμεροι γάρ, οὐδὲ πρόσπλατοι ξένοις A.*Pr.*716, cf. Carneisc.

*Herc.*1027.16, 2 *Ep.Ti.*3.3, Arr.*Epict.*1.3.7; of a country, A.*Eu.*14; ἐκβολή E.*Hec.*1078; βίος Plu.2.86d; διάθεσις Phld.*Ir.*p.57 W., cf. p.85: Sup., Clearch.37. Adv. -ρως, ἀ. τισὶ χρήσασθαι D.S.13.23. **-ότης**, ητος, ἡ, *wildness, savageness*, Phld.*Oec.*p.68 J., *Gloss.*

ἀνημερ-όω, *to clear of wild beasts*, ἀ. κνωδάλων ὁδόν S.*Fr.*905. **-ωτος**, ον, *untilled*, γῆ ib.825, Cratin.26 D.

ἀνήμετος, ον, v. ἀνέμετος.

ἀνήμυκτος, ον, (ἀμύσσω) *not torn* or *lacerated*, Hsch.

ἀνήνασθαι, ἀνήνατο, v. ἀναίνομαι.

ἀνηνεμ-έω, f.l. for νην-, Str.7.3.18. **-ία**, ἡ, = νηνεμία, *AP*9.544 (Adaeus); noted as an archaic form by Luc.*Pseudol.*29. **-ος**, ον, *without wind*, ἀνήνεμος χειμώνων *without the blast* of storms, S. *OC*677 (lyr.); *gentle*, τυφών Olymp.*in Mete.*201.22.

ἀνήνιος (A), ον, *unbridled*, *EM*107.20.

ἀνήνιος (B), ον, = ἀνάνιος (q.v.), *without pain*, Hp.ap.Gal.19.81.

ἀνήνοθε, Ep. pf. used like an aor.: αἷμ' ἔτι θερμὸν ἀνήνοθεν ἐξ ὠτειλῆς blood *gushed forth from* the wound, Il.11.266; κνίση μὲν ἀνήνοθεν the savour *mounted up*, Od.17.270 (ἐνήνοθε Aristarch.).

ἀνήνυστος, ον, (ἀνύω) *of none effect, ineffectual*, ἀνηνύστῳ ἐπὶ ἔργῳ Od.16.111, cf. A.R.4.1307; κάματοι Opp.*C.*4.196. 2. *impossible of fulfilment*, Emp.12.

ἀνήνυτος, ον, = ἀνήνυστος, ἀ. πόνος, εὐχαί, Pl.*Lg.*735b, 936c; ἀ. ἔργον πράττειν, of Penelope's web, Id.*Phd.*84a, cf. E.*Hel.*1285. Adv., ταῦτ' ἀνηνύτως ἔχει S.*Fr.*557.4. 2. *endless, never-ending*, οἶτος Id.*El.*167, cf. Plb.9.24.4; κακόν Pl.*Grg.*507e; κακοπαθία Phld. *Herc.*1251.17; βυθός, etc., Ph.1.85, etc.: neut. pl. as Adv., ἀνήνυτα μοχθοῦσιν Epicur.*Fr.*470.

ἀνήνωρ, ορος, ὁ, *unmanly*, Od.10.301; ἀνὴρ ἀνήνωρ a man *of no manhood*, Hes.*Op.*751. II. *childless*, Hsch.

ἀνήξεις· κολυμβήσεις, Hsch.; cf. ἀναvήχομαι.

ἀνηπελίη· ἀσθένεια, Hsch.; cf. εὐηπελίη.

ἀνηπλωμένως, Adv. pf. part. Pass. of ἀναπλόω, *at length, in detail*, opp. συνῃρημένως, τὸν λόγον παραδίδωσι Simp.*in Ph.*1215.20; ἀ. καὶ ἀφηγηματικῶς Aps.p.243 H.

ἀνήπυστος, ον, (ἠπύω) *unheard of*, dub. in Zonar.

ἀνηπύω, *sound*, αὐλοῦ ἦχον ἀνηπύοντος Mosch.2.98. 2. c. acc., *sing aloud*, ὑμέναιον A.R.4.1197.

ἀνήρ, ὁ, ἀνδρός, ἀνδρί, ἄνδρα, voc. ἄνερ: pl. ἄνδρες, -δρῶν, -δράσι [ᾰ], -δρας: Aeol. dat. pl. ἄνδρεσι Alc.*Supp.*14.8: late nom. sg. ἄνδρας *Cat.Cod.Astr.*7.109.7: in Att. the Art. often forms a crasis with the Noun, ἁνήρ for ὁ ἀνήρ, τἀνδρός, τἀνδρί for τοῦ ἀνδρός, etc., ἅνδρες for οἱ ἄνδρες; the Ion. crasis is ὡνήρ, ὧνδρες, Hdt.4.161,134: Ep. also ἀνέρα, ἀνέρος, ἀνέρι, dual ἀνέρε, pl. ἀνέρες, ἀνέρας, ἄνδρεσσι. [Ep. Poets mostly use ᾱ in arsi, ᾰ in thesi; but in trisyll. forms with stem ἀνέρ- always ᾱ; so also Trag. in lyr., S.*Tr.*1011, *OT*869. But in Trag. senarians ᾰ always.] (ἀ- in nom. by analogy; cf. Skt. *nar-* from I.-E. *ner-*, *nr-* from *nr̥-*, Gk. ἀνδρ- from *n̥r-*):—*man*, opp. *woman* (ἄνθρωπος being *man* as opp. to *beast*), Il.17.435, Od.21.323; τῶν ἀνδρῶν ἄπαις without *male* children, Pl.*Lg.*877e; in Hom. mostly of princes, leaders, etc., but also of *free* men; ἀ. δήμου *one of* the people, Il.2.198, cf. Od.17.352; with a qualifying word to indicate rank, ἀ. βουληφόρος Il.2.61; ἀ. βασιλεύς Od.24.253; ἡγήτορες ἄ. Il.11.687. II. *man*, opp. *god*, πατὴρ ἀνδρῶν τε θεῶν τε ib.1.544, al.; Διὸς ἄγγελοι ἠδὲ καὶ ἀνδρῶν ib.334, cf. 403, Hdt.5.63, etc.: most common in pl., yet sts. in sg., e.g. Il.18.432:—freq. with a Noun added, βροτοί, θνητοὶ ἄ., Od.5.197, 10.306; ἄ. ἡμίθεοι Il.12.23; ἄ. ἥρωες ib.5.746:—also of *men*, opp. *monsters*, Od.21.303:—of *men* in societies and cities, οὔτε παρ' ἀνδράσιν οὔτ' ἐν ναυσὶ κοίλαις Pi.*O.*6.10; and so prob., ἄλλοτε μέν τ' ἐπὶ Κύνθου ἐβήσαο.., ἄλλοτε δ' ἂν νήσους τε καὶ ἀνέρας.. *h.Ap.*142. III. *man*, opp. *youth*, unless the context determines the meaning, as in οὔ πως ἔστι νεωτέρῳ ἀνδρὶ μάχεσθαι ἄνδρα γέροντα Od.18.53; but ἀ. alone always means *a man in the prime of life*, esp. *warrior*, ἀ. ἕλεν ἄνδρα Il.15.328; so ἀ. ἀντ' ἀνδρὸς ἐλύθησαν Th.2.103; the several ages are given as παῖς, μειράκιον, ἀ., πρεσβύτης X.*Smp.*4.17; εἰς ἄνδρας ἐγγράφεσθαι, συντελεῖν, D.19.230, Isoc.12.212; εἰς ἄνδρας ἀναβῆναι *BMus.Inscr.*898; in Inscrr. relating to contests, opp. παῖδες, *IG*2².1138.10, etc. IV. *man* emphatically, *man indeed*, ἀνέρες ἔστε, φίλοι Il.5.529; freq. in Hdt., πολλοὶ μὲν ἄνθρωποι, ὀλίγοι δὲ ἄνδρες 7.210; πρόσθεν οὐκ ἀ. ὅδ' ἦν; S.*Aj.*77; ἄνδρα γίγνεσθαί σε χρή E.*El.*693; ἀ. γεγένησαι δι' ἐμέ Ar.*Eq.*1255; ὁ μαθὼν ἀ. ἔσει Id.*Nu.*823; ἄνδρας ἡγοῦνται μόνους τοὺς πλεῖστα δυναμένους καταφαγεῖν Id.*Ach.*77; εἰ ἄνδρες εἶεν οἱ στρατηγοί Th.4.27; οὐκέτι ἀ. ἀλλὰ σκευοφόρος X.*Cyr.*4.2.25; τὸν Λυκομήδην .. μόνον ἄνδρα ἡγοῦντο Id.*HG*7.1.24; οὐκ ἐν ἀνδράσι not *like a man*, E.*Alc.*723, cf. 732; ἀνδρὸς τὰ προσπίπτοντα γενναίως φέρειν 'tis *the part of a man..*, Men.771, etc. V. *husband*, Il.19.291, Od.24.196, Hdt.1.146, etc.; εἰς ἀνδρὸς ὥραν ἡκούσης τῆς κόρης Pl. *Criti.*113d; so ἐξοικιεῖν εἰς ἀνδρὸς [οἶκον] θυγατέρα Luc.*Lex.*11:—also of *a paramour*, opp. πόσις, S.*Tr.*551, cf. E.*Hipp.*491, Theoc.15.131; ἀ. ἁπασῶν τῶν γυναικῶν ἐστι νῦν Pherecr.155; αἰγῶν ἄνερ Theoc.8.49. VI. Special usages: 1. joined with titles, professions, etc., ἰητρὸς ἀ. Il.11.514; ἀ. μάντις, ἀ. στρατηγός, Hdt.6.83,92 (dub.); ἀ. νομεύς S.*OT*1118; ἄνδρες λοχῖται, λῃσταί, ἀσπιστῆρες, ib.751,842, *Aj.*565; esp. in disparagement, κλῶπες ἄ. E.*Rh.*645; ἀ. δημότης S. *Ant.*690; with names of nations, as Φοίνικες ἄ. Hdt.4.42; ἀ. Θρῇξ E. *Hec.*19, al.; esp. in addresses, ἄ. ἔφοροι Hdt.9.9; ἄ. πολῖται S.*OT* 513; ἄ. δικασταί D.21.1, etc.; ὦ ἄνδρες *gentlemen* of the jury, Antipho 1.1, Lys.1.1, etc.; ὦ ἄ. Ἀθηναῖοι Id.6.8, etc.: hence in Comedy, ἄ. ἰχθύες Archipp.29; ἄ. θεοί Luc.*JTr.*15; ὦ ἄ. κύνες Ath.4.160b. 2. ὁ ἀνήρ, by crasis Att. ἁνήρ, Ion. ὡνήρ, is freq. used emphatically for αὐτός, ἐκεῖνος Ar.*V.*269, prob. in Pl.*Sph.*216b, etc.: sts. so in oblique cases without the Art., S.*Tr.*55, 109, 293, etc.; but not in Prose. 3. ἀ. ὅδε, ὅδ' ἀ., in Trag., = ἐγώ, S.*Aj.*78, E.*Alc.*690, etc. 4. πᾶς ἀ. every *man*, every *one*, freq. in Pl.*Lg.*736c, al., cf. E.*Or.*1523. 5. *a man, any man*, εἴτ' ἄνδρα τῶν αὐτοῦ τι χρὴ προϊέναι; Ar.*Nu.*1214; οὐ πρέπει νοῦν ἔχοντι ἀνδρί Pl.*Phd.*114d, etc.; οὐ παντὸς ἀνδρὸς.. ἐσθ' ὁ πλοῦς 'tis not *every one* that can go, Nicol.Com.1.26. 6. ὦ δαιμόνι' ἀνδρῶν Eup.316; and often with a Sup., ὦ φίλτατ' ἀνδρῶν Phryn.Com.80, etc. 7. κατ' ἄνδρα *viritim*, Isoc.12.180, *POxy.*1047 iii 11, *BGU*145.5, etc.; so τοὺς κατ' ἄνδρα *individuals*, opp. κοινῇ τὴν πόλιν, D.Chr.32.6. 8. In LXX, ἀνήρ = ἕκαστος, δότε μοι ἀνὴρ ἐνώτιον *Jd.*8.24; ἀ. τῷ ἀδελφῷ αὐτοῦ προσκολληθήσεται '*each to his fellow*', of leviathan's scales, *Jb.*41.8; also ἀ. εἷς 4*Ki.*6.2; with negs., ἀ. μὴ ἐπισκεπήτω ib.10.19; ἀνὴρ ἀνήρ *any one*, *Le.*15.2. 9. ἄνδρας γράφειν· τὸ ἐν διδασκάλου τὰ παιδία ὀνόματα γράφειν, Hsch. VII. *male animal*, Arist.*HA*637ᵇ15.

ἀνηρέμητος, ον, *restless*, Corn.*ND*26, S.E.*M.*3.5. Adv. -τως 10.223.

ἀνηρεοί, οἱ, *rings through which cables were passed*, Hsch.

ἀνήρεστον· οὐκ ἀρεστόν, Hsch.(prob.).

ἀνηρεφής, ές, *not covered*, A.R.2.1171.

ἀνηρήμεθα, v. ἀνείρομαι.

ἀνήρης, ες, = ἀνδρώδης, dub. in A.*Fr.*218.

ἀνηρίθευτος, ον, = ἀνερίθευτος (q.v.), *GDI*5653*B* (Chios, v B.C.).

ἀνήριθμος, v. ἀνάριθμος. **ἀνηρίναστος**, ον, = ἀνερίναστος, Hsch. **ἀνήριστα**· ἀνέριστα, ἄπλαστα, Id.

ἀνηρός, ά, όν, = ἀνιαρός, ὀρθόπνοια Ph.Tars.ap.Gal.13.267; but ἀνηρόν· ἄβλαπτον, *EM*108.22.

ἀνήροτος, ον, *unploughed*, γύαι A.*Pr.*708; *without tillage*, ἀνήροτα πάντα φύονται Od.9.109: neut. pl. as Adv., λειμῶνες ἀνήροτα πορφύρουσι Opp.*C.*1.462: metaph., γυνὴ ἀ. Luc.*Lex.*19.

ἀνηρτημένως, Adv. pf. part. Pass. of ἀναρτάω, *disconnectedly, incoherently*, Herm.*in Phdr.*p.177 A.

ἀνησιδώρα, ἡ, *sending up gifts*, epith. of Earth, *Ath.Mitt.*37.288 (ii A.D.), cf. Sch.Ar.*Av.*971; of Demeter, S.*Fr.*826, Alciphr.1.3, Paus.1.31.4, Plu.2.745a; ἑστία ἀ., of Rome, ib.317a.

ἀνήσσητος, Dor. **ἀνήσσᾱτος**, ον, *unconquered*, Theoc.6.46.

ἄνησσον, τό, v. ἄννησον.

ἄνηστις, ὁ, ἡ, = νῆστις, A.*Fr.*258 A, Cratin.45.

ἄνηστος, ον, (νέω) *unspun*, σίππιον *POxy.*1288.34.

ἀνήσυχος· *inquietus*, *Gloss.*

ἀνήτινος, η, ον, Dor. for ἀνήθ-: **ἄνητον** or **ἄννητον**, v. ἄνηθον.

ἀνήφαιστος, ον, ἀ. πῦρ fire *that is no fire*, i.e. discord, E.*Or.*621.

ἀνηχέω, *raise a shout*, Sch.E.*Or.*1335.

ἀνθαιρ-έομαι, *choose* one person or thing *instead of* another, τὸ δ' εὐσεβὲς τῆς δυσσεβείας ἀνθελοῦ E.*Cyc.*311; ἄλλους ἀ. ἀντὶ τούτων *CIG* 2715.11 (Stratonicea); στρατηγοὺς ἔπαυσαν.. καὶ ἄλλους ἀνθείλοντο Th.6.103, cf. X.*HG*6.2.13, Pl.*Lg.*765d; τὰν εὔδοξον ἀ. φήμαν *prefer, choose rather*, E.*Hipp.*773 (lyr.). II. *dispute, lay claim to*, οὐδεὶς στέφανον ἀνθαιρήσεται Id.*Hec.*660. **-εσις**, εως, ἡ, *choice of* one *to succeed* another, *CIG*2715.12. **-ετιστής**, οῦ, ὁ, of planets, *belonging to the opposite 'condition'*, Jul.Laod. in *Cat.Cod.Astr.*5(1).183.21, cf. 192.36.

ἀνθάλιον, τό, = μαλιναθάλλη, Plin.*HN*21.88,175.

ἀνθᾰλίσκομαι, *to be captured in turn*, i.e. after one has captured others, οὔ τἂν ἑλόντες αὖθις ἀνθαλοῖεν ἄν A.*Ag.*340; *to be convicted in turn*, ἀντικατηγορήθη καὶ ἀνθεάλω D.C.36.40.

ἀνθᾰμαρτάνω [ᾰν], *err in retaliation*, Agath.4.4.

ἀνθᾰμιλλ-άομαι (ἀντ- Hsch.), *vie one with another, be rivals*, Pl. *Lg.*731a; *race*, of triremes, X.*HG*6.2.28:—Act., part. ἀνθαμιλλεῦντες Hp.*Ep.*17. **-ος**, ον, *vying with, rivalling*, E.*Ion*606.

ἀνθάπτομαι, Ion. ἀντ-, *lay hold of in return*, οἱ Πέρσαι.. ἅπτοντο αὐτοῦ·.. οἱ δὲ ἀντάπτοντο Hdt.3.137, cf. E.*Hec.*275: but mostly, II. simply, *lay hold of, grapple with, engage in*, c. gen., ἀ. τοῦ πολέμου Hdt.7.138; ἀ. τῶν πραγμάτων Th.8.97; ἀ. τῆς λογιστικῆς Pl.*R.*525c: generally, *reach, attain*, τερμόνων E.*Med.*1182 (dub.). 2. *lay hold of, seize, attack*, esp. of pain, grief, etc., πλευμόνων S.*Tr.*778, cf. Ar. *Ra.*474; φρενῶν, καρδίας, E.*Med.*55,1360; περὶ τῆς μισθοφορᾶς.. μαλακωτέρως ἀνθήπτετο (sc. Τισσαφέρνους) *attacked* him, Th.8.50 (unless abs., 'was less firm in his *counter-grip*').

ἀνθάριον, τό, *pimple, eruption*, = ἐρύθημα, Hsch.

ἀνθαρμόζω, *fit* one thing *to* another, χειρὶ χεῖρα Sch.Pi.*P.*4.65.

ἀνθάρπαγμα, ατος, τό, *a thing seized by way of reprisal* or *pledge*, Eust.877.37.

Ἄνθεια, ἡ, epith. of Hera at Argos, Paus.2.22.1, *EM*108.47; at Miletus, in dat., Ἥρῃ Ἀνθέῃ *Milet.*3 No.31(a).5 (vi B.C.); of the Ὧραι, Hsch.; also of Aphrodite at Cnossus, Id.

ἀνθεινός, ή, όν, = ἀνθινός, D.S.4.4, Ael.*NA*2.11.

ἄνθειον, τό, *flower, blossom*, dub. in Ar.*Ach.*869 (Boeot.).

ἀνθεκτέον, *one must cleave to*, τούτου ἀ. τοῖς ἐπιμεληταῖς Pl.*R.*424b; ἀ. τῆς μέσης ἕξεως Arist.*EN*1126ᵇ9: so in pl., ἀνθεκτέα ἐστὶ τῆς θαλάσσης Th.1.93.

ἀνθεκτικός, ή, όν, *clinging to, attached to*, τινός Arr.*Epict.*4.11.3.

ἀνθελετός, ή, όν, *preferred*, Poet.*de herb.*194.

ἀνθελιγμός, ὁ, *counter-winding*, *Placit.*3.15.5 (pl.) (ἀντ- codd.).

ἀνθέλιξ, ικος, ἡ, *the interior curvature of the ear*, the exterior being ἕλιξ, Ruf.*Onom.*44.

ἀνθέλκω, aor. inf. -ελκύσαι Herm.*in Phdr.*p.170 A.:—*draw* or *pull against*, Th.4.14; ἀ. ἀλλήλαις *pull against* one another, Pl.*Lg.*644e;

ἀ. τὴν ψυχὴν *draw* it *in a contrary direction*, Id.*R.*439b; φιλανθρώπως τινὰς ἀ. D.S.30.8: metaph., of *resistance* of facts *to* suggested inference, εἰς τοὐναντίον μηδενὸς –κοντος Phld.*Sign.*17, cf. 18; ἀ. τινὰ πρὸς αὐτὰς ἑκάστῃ Luc.*Demon.*63:—Pass., Pl.*Ax.*372, D.H.3.30.

ἄνθεμα, ατος, τό, v. ἀνάθεμα. II. name of *dance*, in Ath.14.629e, unless this be neut. pl. of ἄνθεμον.

ἀνθεμίζομαι, in A.*Supp.*73 γοεδνὰ ἀνθεμίζεσθαι, i.e. (says the Sch.) τὸ ἄνθος τῶν γόων ἀποδρέπεσθαι; cf. ἀπανθίζω.

ἀνθέμ-ιον, τό, = ἄνθος, f.l. for ἄνθεμον in Thphr.*HP*1.13.3, al., cf. *AP*4.1.36 (Mel.), *PMag.Leid.V.*13.9. 2. *honeysuckle pattern* on Ionic columns, *IG*1.322; so ἀ. ἐστιγμένοι tattooed with a similar pattern, of the Mossynoeci, X.*An.*5.4.32: pl., *artificial flowers*, *IG*11.161*B*50 (Delos, iii B.C.). 3. of gold, *the purest quality*, Lxx *Ec.*12.6. **–ίς**, ίδος, ἡ, = ἄνθος, J.*AJ*12.2.10, *AP*6.267 (Diotim.). 2. *camomile*, Nic.*Fr.*74.37; ἀ. λευκὴ *Matricaria Chamomilla*, *wild c.*, ἀ. μελίνη *Anthemis tinctoria*, *dyer's c.*, ibid.; ἀ. πορφυρᾶ *A. rosea*, ibid., Dsc.3.137. b. = ἀνθυλλίς, Ps.-Dsc.3.136; = ἀργεμώνη, Id.2.177; = ἀμάρακον, Id.3.138:—also **ἀνθεμίσιον**, τό, Alex.Trall.9.1. **–οειδής**, ές, = ἀνθεμώδης, Orph.*H.*43.4. **–όεις**, εσσα, εν, also εις as fem., Il.2.695, Hes.*Fr.*16:—*flowery*, of places, ἐν λειμῶνι Σκαμανδρίῳ ἀνθεμόεντι Il.2.467, cf. 695, B.12.88; ἐπ' ἀνθεμόεντι Ἕβρῳ on the *flowery* banks of Hebrus, 15.5. II. of works in metal, *adorned with flowers*, λέβητ' ἄπυρον.. ἀ. Il.23.885; ἐν ἀ. λέβητι Od.3.440; κρητῆρα πανάργυρον ἀ. 24.275; *embroidered*, κύπασσις *AP*6.272 (Pers.). (ἀνθεμεῦντας ps.-Ion. form in Anacr.62.)

ἄνθεμον, τό, = ἄνθος, Sapph.85, Semon.7.66, Pi.*N.*7.79, Cratin.98, Ar.*Ach.*992, *Tab.Heracl.*1.96; ἄνθεμα χρυσοῦ golden *flowers*, Pi.*O.*2.72; ἄνθεμ' ὀρειχάλκου *h.Hom.*6.9; ἄνθεμα κοτταβείων *IG*11.164*B*25 (Delos, iii B.C.). 2. name of a *plant*, ἄ. ἀφύλλανθες *Matricaria Chamomilla* var. *eradiata*, and ἄ. φυλλῶδες *Anthemis chia*, Thphr.*HP*7.8.3. 3. v. ἄνθεμα II. 4. pl., name of *cake*, Poll.6.76, Hsch.

ἀνθεμό-ρρυτος, ον, *flowing from flowers*, ἀ. γάνος μελίσσης, i.e. honey, E.*IT*634. **–στρωτος**, ον, *strewn with flowers*, Id.ap.Phot.p.138 R.

ἀνθεμουργός, όν, *working in flowers*, ἡ ἀ., i.e. *the bee*, A.*Pers.*612.

Ἀνθεμουσία· τάγμα τι παρὰ Μακεδόσιν ἐξ Ἀνθεμοῦντος πόλεως Μακεδονίας, Hsch.

ἀνθεμοφόρον, τό, = βούνιον, Ps.-Dsc.4.123.

ἀνθεμ-ώδης, ες, *flowery, blooming*, μελίλωτος Sapph.*Supp.*25.14; Νεῖλος B.18.39; ἔαρ A.*Pr.*455; Τμῶλος E.*Ba.*462; λειμών Ar.*Ra.*450. **–ωτός**, ή, όν, *adorned with flowers* or *with flower-patterns*, καλυπτήρ *IG*2.807*b*107.

ἄνθεξις, εως, ἡ, *clinging to*, ἀλλήλων Pl.*Ep.*323b (pl.).

ἄνθεο, Ep. aor. 2 imper. Med. of ἀνατίθημι.

ἀνθερεών, ῶνος, ὁ, *chin*, δεξιτερῇ δ' ἄρ' ὑπ' ἀνθερεῶνος ἑλοῦσα, in token of supplication, Il.1.501; παρὰ νείατον ἀνθερεῶνα, i.e. just under the *chin*, 5.293, cf. Hp.*Oss.*18, Nic.*Th.*444. 2. later, *neck, throat*, Euph.92.1 (pl.): sg., *AP*9.129 (Nestor), Q.S.1.110: sg. in both senses, Ruf.*Onom.*47,48. 3. *mouth*, Nonn.*D.*3.247, 25.476.

ἀνθέρ-ῐκος, ὁ, *flowering stem of asphodel*, Thphr.*HP*7.13.2, cf. Hp.*Coac.*491, Hellanic.67 J., Longus 1.10; and so prob. ἐξ ἀνθερίκων in Hdt.4.190, which others refer to ἀνθέριξ. 2. *flower-head of asphodel*, Dsc.2.169. 3. *the plant* itself, *asphodel*, Cratin.325, Eup.14.5. II. = ἀνθέριξ I, Sch.Arat.1060. **–ῐκώδης**, ες, *like asphodel*, καυλός Thphr.*HP*9.10.1. **–ιξ**, ῐκος, ὁ, = ἀθήρ, *beard* of an ear of corn, *the ear* itself, Il.20.227, Hes.*Fr.*117, *AP*12.121 (Rhian.). II. = ἀνθέρικος I. 1 (q.v.), *stalk of asphodel*, v.l. in Theoc.1.52. **–ίσκος**, ὁ, = ἀνθέρικος, dub. in *AB*403.

ἄνθεσαν, Ep. 3 pl. aor. 2 Act. of ἀνατίθημι.

ἀνθεσι-ουργός, όν, *creating flowers*, Orph.*Fr.*197. **–πότᾰτος**, ον, *fluttering round flowers*, μέλεα Antiph.209. **–χρως**, ωτος, ὁ, ἡ, *variegated*, πέρκη Matro *Conv.*51.

Ἀνθεσ-τήρια, τά, *Feast of Flowers*, i.e. three days' festival of Dionysus at Athens, in the month Anthesterion, Apollod.*Fr.*28; also in Ionic cities, *SIG*38.32 (Teos), *CIG*3655 (Cyzicus). (Deriv. from ἀνα-θέσσασθαι is dub.; from ἀνθεῖν acc. to Ister 28.) **–τηριάδας·** τὰς ἐχούσας ὥραν γάμου (Rhod.), Hsch. **–τηριών**, ῶνος, ὁ, the month *Anthesterion*, eighth of the Attic year, answering to the end of February and the beginning of March, in which the Anthesteria were celebrated, Th.2.15, etc.; also in Ionic cities, as Tenos, *IG*12(5).872.48.

ἀνθεστιάω, *entertain in return* or *mutually*, Plu.*Ant.*27, cf. 32 (Pass.), Luc.*Am.*9.

Ἀνθεσ-φόρια, τά, a festival in honour of Persephone, who was carried off while *gathering flowers*, Poll.1.37. **–φόρος**, ον, *bearing flowers, flowery*, μῖλαξ E.*Ba.*703; λείμακες ἀνθεσφόροι Id.*IA*1544. II. ἀνθεσφόροι, αἱ, *women celebrating the Anthesphoria*, Poll.4.78.

ἄνθεται· ἐλεύθεροι (Tarent.), Hsch.

ἄνθετο, Ep. 3 sg. aor. 2 Med. of ἀνατίθημι.

ἀνθέω, *blossom, bloom*, of the youthful beard, πρὶν.. ὑπὸ κροτάφοισιν ἰούλους ἀνθῆσαι Od.11.320 (the only place in Hom.), cf. Orph.*L.*255; of persons, τυτθὸν δ' ἀνθήσαντας ὑπὸ κροτάφοισιν ἴουλον *with* the young down *just showing*, *IG*5(1).1355 (Geraneia), cf. *APl.*5.381. 2. of flowers and plants, first in Hes.*Op.*582, Alc.39; στάχυς S.*Fr.*395; *flourish*, ἀ. κυπάρισσοι Theoc.27.46: c. dat., ἄνθεσιν *h.Ap.*139; ῥόδοις Pi.*I.*4(3).18: metaph., ἀνθοῦν πέλαγος Αἰγαῖον νεκροῖς A.*Ag.*659; ἀφρὸς ἤνσει (Lacon.) dub.l. in Ar.*Lys.*1257. II. metaph., 1. *bloom, be brilliant, shine* with colour, etc., ἤνθει φοινικίσι..ἡ στρατιά X.*Cyr.*6.4.1; of linen garments, Plu.2.352d. 2. *to be in bloom, blooming*, Ἥβας καρπὸν ἀνθήσαντα Pi.*P.*9.110; ἀνθοῦσαν ἀκμὴν ἔχων Isoc.5.10; ἐν ὥρᾳ ἀνθεῖν *to be in the bloom* of youth, Pl.*R.*475a; τὰ σὰ λήγει ὥρας, σὺ δ' ἄρχῃ ἀνθεῖν Id.*Alc.*1.131e, cf. ib.c. 3. *flourish* in wealth and prosperity, λαοί Hes.*Op.*227; ἀνθεύσης Ἐρετρίης Hdt.6.127, cf. Th.1.19, etc.; ὄλβος σμικρὸν ἀνθήσας χρόνον E.*El.*944; ἀνθοῦσα ἐφ' ὥρᾳ πολιτεία Plu.*Per.*16; ἀνθούσης τῆς νέας Ἀκαδημίας Id.*Luc.*42; τὸ ἀνθοῦν τῆς δυνάμεως the *flower* of the force, Id.*Cor.*39: c. dat., ἀ. τῆς Ἀσίας ἀνδράσι *flourish, abound* in men, Hdt.4.1. b. of persons, *flourish, be popular*, οὕτως ἤνθησεν ἐκεῖνος Ar.*Eq.*530, cf. *Nu.*897, 962; πραπίδεσσι, δόξῃ ἀ., Pi.*O.*11(10).10, Plu.*Dem.*5; Ἕκτορος ἤνθει δόρυ E.*Hec.*1210; σφόδρα γε ἤνθησεν ἐπὶ ταῖς ἐλπίσιν D.2.10; ἀ. πρὸς δόξαν, πρὸς χάριν, Plu.*Sert.*18, *Phoc.*3. 4. *to be at the height* or *pitch*, ἀνθεῖ πάθος τινί A.*Ch.*1009 (lyr.); of a disease, ἤνθηκεν S.*Tr.*1089, cf. Hp.*Epid.*1.25; ὕβρις ἐν νέοις ἀνθεῖ S.*Fr.*786; σκωμμάτων ἀνθούντων when they *were in full swing*, Plu.*Ant.*32. 5. c. gen., *swarm with*, φθειρῶν ἤνθησεν Paus.9.33.6.

ἀνθεών, ῶνος, ὁ, *flower-bed* or *garden*, *OGI*365 (Amasia):—also **ἀνθών**, *Gloss.*

ἄνθη, ἡ, *full bloom* of a flower or plant, ἀκμὴν ἔχει τῆς ἄνθης Pl.*Phdr.*230b, cf. Porph.ap.Eus.*PE*3.10: a special Att. form, Moer.4, Thom.Mag.p.10 R. 2. *blossom* or *bloom*, Nic.*Th.*625, Ael.*NA*12.4.

ἀνθηδών, όνος, ἡ, *the flowery one*, i.e. *the bee*, Damocr.ap.Gal.14.91, Ael.*NA*15.1, *EM*108.43. II. *eastern thorn*, *Crataegus orientalis*, Thphr.*HP*3.12.5:—hence **ἀνθηδονοειδής**, ές, as epith. of *Crataegus monogyna*, *hawthorn*, ibid.

ἀνθήεις, εσσα, εν, *bright-coloured*, βασιλίσκος Marcell.Sid.26; σάλπη Id.30; κίστος Ruf.ap.Gal.12.425.

ἀνθηλᾶς, ὁ, prob. *flower-merchant*, *PLond.*2.387.21 (vi/vii A.D.).

ἀνθήλη, ἡ, *the silky flower-tufts* of the reed, Thphr.*HP*4.10.4, Dsc.1.85, cj. for ἀνθίνη in Phan.Hist.25:—ἀνθήλη· πώγων, Hsch. (cf. ἀνθήλη πυρός Id.).

ἀνθήλιον, τό, f.l. for ἀνθύλλιον, Dsc.3.156, 4.121; = κανθήλιον, Charax 21:—ἀνθήλια· περιδέρματα, Hsch. (–ηλά· περίδερμα cod.).

ἀνθήλιος, ον, = ἀντήλιος, q.v.

ἄνθημα (A), ατος, τό, = ἐξάνθημα, Hsch. II. = ἄνθος, κρίνου Sch.Nic.*Al.*406.

ἄνθημα (B), ατος, τό, poet. for ἀνάθημα, *offering*, *IG*12(5).911.21 (Tenos).

ἀνθήμερον, Adv. *to-day*, prob. in S.*Fr.*168; cf. ἀντί A. II, ἀνταλλές.

ἀνθήμων, ον, gen. ονος, = ἀνθηρός, κυτίνοιο.. καρπόν Nic.*Al.*610.

ἀνθηρο-γρᾰφέω, *write in a florid style*, Eust.991.8:—Pass., *to be embellished*, Cic.*Att.*2.6.1. **–ποικίλος**, ον, *brocaded with flowers, flowered*, Ph.1.666.

ἀνθηρός, ά, όν, *flowery, blooming*, ἔαρ Chaerem.9; λειμών, δάπεδον, Ar.*Av.*1093, *Ra.*352; χώρα Str.17.3.12 (Comp.); πρόσοψις, διάθεσις, D.S.5.3, 19; τὰ ἀ. *flowery meads*, Plu.2.770b; but also, *flowering plants*, ib.765d. II. metaph., *fresh, young*, χλόη E.*Cyc.*541; of music, etc., *fresh, new*, X.*Cyr.*1.6.38; of persons, Plu.*Pomp.*69; ἱλαρὸς καὶ ἀ. 2.50b; cf. ἄνθος II. 1 fin. 2. τᾶς μανίας ἀνθηρὸν μένος rage *bursting* (as it were) *into flower*, i.e. *exuberant*, S.*Ant.*960. 3. *bright-coloured, brilliant*, τοῦ χαλκοῦ τὸ ἀ. Plu.2.395b; of colours, τὸ ἀ. τῶν χρωμάτων Luc.*Nigr.*13, cf. Plu.2.79d, etc. 4. *brilliant, splendid*, δειπνάριον Diph.64; ἐδωδή Ph.1.679 (Comp.) (s.v.l.); βίος Max.Tyr.21.1; θεωρία Iamb. *in Nic.*p.35 P.; of personal appearance, dress, etc., ἀνθηρὸς εἱμάτων στολῇ E.*IA*73. Adv. –ῶς Sch.Opp.*H.*1.459. 5. of style, *flowery, florid*, ἀ. *genus dicendi* Quint.*Inst.*12.10.58, cf. Plu.2.648b; of music, ἀ. καὶ μαλακὴ ἁρμονία (metaph. of policy), Id.*Per.*15; ἂν ἀ. ᾖ τὸ πρᾶγμα, ἔστω καὶ ἡ λέξις τοιαύτη Hermog.*Prog.*10. Adv. "ἀνθηρῶς", an exclamation of applause, Plu.2.46a: Comp. ἀνθηρότερον, λέγειν Isoc.13.18. III. ἀνθηρός, ὁ, = ἄλιμον, Ps.-Dsc.1.91. 2. ἀνθηρά, ἡ, name of a *lip-salve*, Plin.*HN*24.69, Gal.13.839; also of a *plaster*, Cels.6.11, Sor.ap.Gal.12.957.

ἀνθηρότης, ητος, ἡ, *brilliancy*, Sch.Pi.*O.*9.72.

ἄνθησις, εως, ἡ, *flowering*, Thphr.*CP*4.10.1, Plu.2.647f.

ἀνθησσάομαι, *give way* or *yield in turn*, τινί Th.4.19, D.C.49.44.

ἀνθησῠχάζω, *to be quiet in turn*, App.*BC*2.93.

ἀνθητικός, ή, όν, = ἀνθικός, τὰ ἀ. *flowering plants*, Thphr.*HP*1.14.3.

ἀνθηφόρος, ἡ, = ἀνθοφόρος II; ἀ. καὶ ἀρχιέρεια *CIG*2821, 2822 (Aphrodisias); but ἀρχιέρεια ἀ. *Rev.Ét.Gr.*19p.137.

ἀνθίας, ου, ὁ, a kind of *sea-fish*, *Labrus* or *Serranus anthias* (Adams), Anan.5.1, Epich.58, Diph.64; = αὐλωπίας, Arist.*HA*570[b]19.

ἀνθιερόω, *consecrate in return*, Epicur.*Fr.*141.

ἀνθ-ίζω, *strew* or *deck with flowers*, E.*Ion*890; κεφαλὴν ῥόδοις Philostr.*Im.*1.15 (but σκευὴ ἠνθισμένη *adorned, embroidered with flowers*, ibid.): metaph., ἀ. τὴν λέξιν D.H.*Isoc.*13:—Med., *gather, cull flowers*, App.*BC*4.105. 2. *colour, dye, stain*, [πορφύρα] ἀ. τὴν χεῖρα Arist.*HA*547[a]18:—Pass., ἠνθισμένοι φαρμάκοισι Hdt.1.98; οὐ γάρ σε μή.. γνῶσ'.. ὧδ' ἠνθισμένον thus *disguised* or with *silvered* hair, S.*El.*43; κρέα πυρὸς ἀκμαῖς ἠνθισμένα meat *browned* at the fire, Epicr.6; οἶνος ἠνθισμένος wine *flavoured with flowers*, Gal.19.81. 3. ἀνθίζουσα, ἡ, a *plaster*, Id.13.856. **–ικός**, ή, όν, *flowering*, τὰ ἀ., opp. τὰ φρυγανικά, Thphr.*HP*6.6.2. **–ιμος**, η, ον, = sq., μελίσσης ἄ. εἶδαρ Orph.*L.*735. **–ινος**, η, ον, *of* or *like flowers, blooming, fresh*, like ἀνθηρός: in Od.9.84 the esculent lotus is called ἄνθινον εἶδαρ, where prob. *vegetable* as opp. to *animal* food is all that is meant; ἀ. κυκεών a drink *flavoured with flowers*, Hp.*Int.*12; ἄ. ἔλαιον oil *of lilies*, Id.

*Mul.*1.35; ἄ. μέλι Arist.*Mir.*831^{b}18; ἄ. οἶνος Gal.19.81; τριμμάτιον Sotad.Com.1.17; στέφανος *SIG*1017.12 (Sinope); εὐωδία Plu.2.645e. II. *flowered*, *bright-coloured*, of women's dress, ἐσθῆτες, στολή, Str.3.3.7, Plu.2.304d; τὰ ἄνθινα (sc. ἱμάτια) *gay-coloured dresses* worn by the ἑταῖραι at Athens, Phylarch.45; forbidden at religious festivals, *IG*11.1300 (Delos), ib.5(2).514.6 (Lycosura, ii B.C.); also of dresses worn at the Anthesteria by the Satyrs: hence τὴν φιλοσοφίαν ἄνθινα ἐνέδυσεν he clothed philosophy *in motley*, of Bion, who delivered his precepts in sarcastic verses, like those used in the satyric drama, Eratosth.ap.D.L.4.52, cf. Thphr.ap.Demetr. Lac.*Herc.*1055.15, Str.1.2.2. (On the accent v. Hdn.Gr.1.182.)

ἄνθιον, τό, in Orphic phraseology, *spring*, Orph.*Fr.*33.

ἀνθιππ-άρχης, ου, ὁ, *deputy-master of the horse*, Lyd.*Mag.*1.38. **-ασία**, ἡ, *sham fight of horse*, X.*Eq.Mag.*1.20, *IG*2.1291, cf. 1305*b*. **-εύω**, *ride against*, ἀλλήλοις, of cavalry, X.*Eq.*8.12.

ἀνθισμός, ὁ, *lustre*, of dyes, *PHolm.*18.25.

ἀνθ-ιστάω, later form of ἀνθίστημι, dub. in Hermog.*Stat.*2:—also **-ιστάνω**, *PPetr.*2p.120. **-ίστημι**, *set against*, Th.4.115; esp. in battle, πελταστικὴν τῇ τοῦ παγκρατίου μάχῃ Pl.*Lg.*834a; ἀ. τροπαῖον *set up* a trophy *in opposition*, Th.1.54,105; *weigh against*, Ar.*Ra.*1389; ἀ. τινὸς τὴν ὀλκήν *outweigh* him, Lxx *Si.*8.2. 2. *match with*, *compare*, ἀντιστῆσαι καὶ παραβαλεῖν Plu.*Thes.*1. II. Hom. uses only Pass., with intr. aor. 2 ἀντέστην: aor. 1 Pass. ἀντεστάθην Hdt.5.72: pf. ἀνθέστηκα *Ep.Rom.*9.19; Att. contr. part. ἀνθεστώς Th.6.70: fut. ἀντιστήσομαι Hdt.8.75, S.*OC*645:—*stand against*, esp. in battle, *withstand*, Ἥρῃ δ' ἀντέστη.. Ἄρτεμις Il.20.70, cf. 72, Hdt.6.117, al.; τοὺς ἀνθισταμένους τοῖς ὑμετέροις βουλήμασι D.18.49; πρὸς τὴν ἀνάγκην οὐδ' Ἄρης ἀ. S.*Fr.*256, cf. Th.1.93, X.*Smp.*5.1: rarely c. gen., δέος.. σοὶ φρενῶν ἀνθίσταται A.*Pers.*703 (ἀνθάπτεται Wakef.), cf. Q.S.1.520. 2. of things, *turn out unfavourably* to one, ἀντιστάντος αὐτῷ τοῦ πράγματος Th.5.4, cf. 38; ἂν τὰ παρ' ὑμῶν τῶν ἀκουόντων ἀντιστῇ D.19.340. 3. abs., *make a stand*, ἀλλ' ἔτ' ἄρ' ἀνθίσταντο Il.16.305; *resist*, *fight on*, Hdt.5.72, etc.; ὑπέρ τινος S.*Aj.*1231, *Ant.*518.

ἀνθο-βαφής, ές, *bright-coloured*, στρωμνή Antyll.ap.Orib.9.14.7, cf. Ph.2.274; ἐσθής S.E.*P.*1.148; πέδιλα Luc.*Am.*41; γῆ *IG*7.1802. **-βαφία**, ἡ, *dyeing in bright colours*, Plu.*Fr.*16p.113B. **-βάφος** [ᾰ], ὁ, *dyer in bright colours*, Id.2.830e, Man.2.326. **-βολέω**, *bestrew with flowers*, χαίτην *AP*5.146 (Mel.); as a mark of honour, ὥσπερ ἀθλητὴν ἀ. Plu.*Caes.*30:—Pass., Id.*Pomp.*57. II. *put forth flowers*, *Gp.*10.2.10. **-βόλησις**, εως, ἡ, *putting forth of flowers*, ib.59.3. **-βολος**, ον, *garlanded with flowers*, θρίξ *AP*9.270 (Marc. Arg.), but codd. have ἀνθοβόλον, i.e. *shedding flowers*. **-βοσκός**, όν, *nourishing*, *growing flowers*, or perh. *feeding on flowers*, S.*Fr.*31. **-γρᾰφέω**, *paint in bright colours*, Ph.1.33. **-δίαιτος**, ον, *living on flowers*, μέλισσα *AP*5.162 (Mel.). **-δόκος**, ον, *holding flowers*, τάλαρος Mosch.2.34. **-κάρηνος**, ον, *crowned with flowers*, Opp.*C.*4.235. **-κομέω**, *produce flowers*, of the earth, βοτάνας ἀ. *AP*7.321. **-κόμος**, ον, *decked with flowers*, *flowery*, λειμῶνες ib.10.6 (Satyr.). 2. *parti-coloured*, οἰωνοί Opp.*C.*2.190. **-κρᾰτέω**, *govern flowers*, Luc.*Pseudol.*24. **-κροκος**, ον, (κρέκω) *worked with flowers*, πῆναι E.*Hec.*471 (lyr.).

ἀνθ-ολκή, ἡ, *pulling in the contrary direction*, *retraction*, Aret.*CA* 1.4; *revulsion* in venesection, Antyll.ap.Orib.7.11.1; *means of drawing back*, D.C.35.5; *counterpoise*, τοῦ βλάπτοντος ἀ. Plu.2.20c; *resistance*, *countercheck*, ἀνθολκαὶ καὶ διατριβαί Id.*Luc.*11. **-ολκός**, όν, = ἀντίρροπος, ἀ. καὶ κωλυσιεργά Iamb.*Protr.*21.κβ'.

ἀνθο-λογέω, *gather flowers*, Plu.2.917f: c. acc., Hp.*Ep.*16, Porph. *Abst.*2.6:—Med., of bees, *gather honey from flowers*, Arist.*HA*628^{b}32:—Pass., *Gp.*11.26.2. **-λογία**, ἡ, *flower-gathering*, Luc.*Pisc.*6. **-λογικά**, τά, *books on floristics*, Plin.*HN*21.13. **-λόγιον**, τό, *collection of extracts*, ἐπιγραμμάτων Suid. s.v. Διογενειανός, cf. eund. s.vv. Ὡρίων, Ὦρος. **-λόγος**, ον, *flower-gathering*, *AP*12.249 (Strat.): c. gen., *culling the flower of*, κάλλευς ib.95 (Mel.).

ἀνθομῑλέω, *associate*, *deal with one another*, Hp.*Ep.*17 (but f.l. for ἀνθαμιλλεῦντες).

ἀνθομοιόω, *compare*, τὸν νόμον τῇ φύσει Philostr.*Dial.*2:—Pass., *to be compared in turn*, πρὸς ἄλληλα Iamb.*in Nic.*p.12P.

ἀνθόμοιος, ον, *like*, ὕδωρ μέλιτος Ps.-Callisth.2.42.

ἀνθομολογ-έομαι, *make a mutual agreement* or *covenant*, πρός τινα D.33.8 (s.v.l.), Plb.5.105.2; ὑπέρ τινος 15.19.9; τινί *PTeb.*21.6 (ii B.C.); περί τινος ib.410.14 (16 A.D.). II. *confess freely and openly*, τὰς ἀρετάς τινος D.S.1.70; ἁμαρτίας J.*AJ*8.10.3; τὸν τοῦ βασιλέως θάνατον Plb.15.25.4: abs., 30.8.7. 2. *admit*, *signify*, πρός τινα μηδὲν ἑωρακέναι 29.17.1; ὡς.. Plu.*Brut.*16. 3. *assent*, *agree*, τοῖς εἰρημένοις Plb.28.4.4. 4. *return thanks* to God, Lxx *Ps.*78(79).13, *Ev.Luc.*2.38; χάριν ἀ. *return* thanks, Plu.*Aem.*11:—Act., -λογέω *admit a claim*, is late, *PGrenf.*2.71 ii 14 (iii A.D.). **-ησις**, εως, ἡ, *mutual agreement*, Plb.31.24.12, 36.4.4. 2. *confession*, *admission*, *testimony*, S.E.*M.*7.184, 8.453. **-ία**, ἡ, = foreg., *Gloss.*

ἀνθο-νομέω, *feed on flowers*, A.*Supp.*44. **-νόμος**, ον, *browsing on flowers*, ib.539.

ἀνθοπλ-ίζω, *arm against*, ἱππεῦσι δ' ἱππῆς ἦσαν ἀνθωπλισμένοι E.*Supp.*666; ἀνθώπλισται πρὸς τὰ πολέμια πλοῖα X.*Oec.*8.12:—Med., *arm oneself*, Id.*HG*6.5.7. **-ῐσις**, εως, ἡ, *counter-arming*, *hostile armament*, Sch.Th.1.141. **-ίτης** [ῑ], ου, ὁ, *one armed in like manner*, Lyc.64.

ἀνθο-πλοκία, ἡ, *plaiting of flowers*, Jul.Laod. in *Cat.Cod.Astr.*5(1).189.9. **-πλόκος**, ὁ, *one who plaits flowers*, Rhetor.ib.8(4).209.9. **-πωλεῖν**· οἰνοπωλεῖν, φαρμακοπωλεῖν, Hsch. **-πώλης**, ου, ὁ, *flower-seller*, Rhetor. in *Cat.Cod.Astr.*8(4).211.

ἀνθορ-ίζω, *make a counter-definition*, in Med., Sch.D.21.28, *PLond.*2.355.4 (i A.D.); *define* terms *by* their *mutual relations*, Elias *in Cat.*138.9. **-ισμός**, ὁ, *counter-definition*, Hermog.*Stat.*4, *Inv.*3.14, cf. Sch.D.21.28; *alternative definition*, Elias *in Cat.*205.25.

ἀνθορμέω, *lie at anchor opposite*, τινί Th.7.19; ἀ. ἀλλήλοις, of two hostile squadrons before fighting, 2.86; ἀ. πρός τινα 7.34.

ἄνθορος, Dor. ἄντ-, ὁ, *corresponding boundary-stone*, *Tab.Heracl.*1.60.

ἄνθος (A), ους, τό: gen. pl. ἀνθέων, freq. used for ἀνθῶν, S.*El.*896, Hermipp.5,6, Eub.105, Aristag.3; but ἀνθῶν Pherecr.46, Pl.*Criti.*115a, X.*Cyn.*5.5:—*blossom*, *flower*, πέτονται ἐπ' ἄνθεσιν εἰαρινοῖσιν Il.2.89; ὑακινθίνῳ ἄνθει ὁμοίας Od.6.231; βρύει ἄνθεϊ λευκῷ Il.17.56; τέρεν' ἄνθεα ποίης Od.9.449; ἐπ' ἄνθεσιν ἵζειν Ar.*Eq.*403; δένδρα καὶ ἄνθη καὶ καρπούς Pl.*Phd.*110d; ἡ κατ' ἄνθη δίαιτα Id.*Smp.*196a; ἄνθεα τεθρίππων *the chaplets of flowers* which graced them, Pi.*O.*2.50, cf. 7.80; [Δάφνιν] φέρβον μαλακοῖς ἄνθεσσι μέλισσαι, i.e. with honey, Theoc.7.81. 2. generally, *anything thrown out upon the surface*, *eruption*, προσώπου Hp.*Coac.*416; cf. ἐξανθέω: *froth* or *scum*, ἄ. οἴνου Gal.11.628, *Gp.*6.3.9, 7.15.6; ἄνθη χαλκοῦ, = χάλκανθος, Nic.*Th.*257; ἄ. χαλκοῦ, v. χαλκός; ἄ. χρυσοῦ, = ἀδάμας, Poll.7.99. 3. in pl., *embroidered flowers* on garments, Hermipp.5,6, Pl.*R.*557c, Cypr. *Fr.*4. II. metaph., *bloom*, *flower* of life, ἥβης ἄ. Il.13.484, Pi.*P.*4.158, A.*Supp.*663; ἥβης ἄνθεσι Sol.25; κουρήιον ἄ. *h.Cer.*108; ὥρας ἄ. X.*Smp.*8.14; παῖς καλὸν ἄ. ἔχων Thgn.994; χροιᾶς ἀμείψεις ἄ. *the bloom* of complexion, A.*Pr.*23; τὸ τοῦ σώματος ἄ. its *youthful bloom*, Pl.*Smp.*183e; ὅταν [τὰ πρόσωπα] τὸ ἄ. προλίπῃ Id.*R.*601b; also, *the flower* of an army and the like, ἄ. Ἄργους A.*Ag.*197; ἄ. Περσίδος αἴας Id.*Pers.*59, cf. 252, 925, E.*HF*876 (lyr.); ὅ τι ἦν αὐτῶν ἄ. ἀπολώλει Th.4.133; ἄνθεα ὕμνων νεωτέρων *the choice flowers* of new songs, Pi.*O.*9.48; τὸ σὸν.. ἄ., παντέχνου πυρὸς σέλας thy *pride* or *honour*, A.*Pr.*7; τὰ ἄνθη *flowers* or *choice passages*, *elegant extracts*, *APl.*4.274, Cic.*Att.*16.11.1. 2. like ἀκμή, *the bloom*, i.e. *height* of anything, bad as well as good, δηξίθυμον ἔρωτος ἄ. A.*Ag.*743; ἀκήλητον μανίας ἄ. S.*Tr.*999; ἀ. τοῦ νοῦ Procl. *in Alc.*p.248C., Dam.*Pr.*70; τῆς οὐσίας Procl. *in Ti.*1.412D.; τῆς ψυχῆς ib.472D. III. *brightness*, *brilliancy*, as of gold, Thgn.452; χαλκήϊον ἄ. Orph.*Fr.*174; of dyes, *lustre*, *PHolm.*17.37; freq. of purple, in sg., Pl. *R.*429d, Arist.*HA*547^{a}7, J.*AJ*3.6.1; ἁλὸς ἄνθεα *AP*6.206 (Antip. Sid.); of *bright colours* generally, περιβόλαια παντὸς ἄνθους D.H.7.72; ἄ. θαλάσσιον seaweed *dye*, Ps.-Democr.Alch.p.42B. IV. ἄ. πεδινόν, = ἀνθεμίς, Ps.-Dsc.3.136.

ἄνθος (B), ὁ, a kind of *bird*, perh. *the yellow wagtail*, Arist.*HA* 592^{b}25, 609^{b}14, Ael.*NA*5.48.

ἀνθοσμ-ίας, ου, ὁ, *redolent of flowers*, almost always of wine, οἶνος ἀ. *with a fine bouquet*, Hp.*Steril.*235, Ar.*Pl.*807, *Ra.*1150, Pherecr.108.30; also ἀ. (sc. οἶνος) X.*HG*6.2.6, Luc.*Sat.*22:—in Id.*Lex.*2 ἀ. λειμῶνες, as a pedantic phrase:—also **-ιος**, ον, Sch.Ar.*Ra.*1150.

ἀνθοσύνη, ἡ, *bloom*, *luxuriant growth*, τεκέων *AP*5.275 (Agath.); ὑλαίη ib.11.365 (Id.).

ἀνθο-τρόφος, ον, = ἀνθοβοσκός, γαῖα Aristonous 1.21. **-φορέω**, *gather honey from flowers*, of bees, Arist.*HA*625^{b}19. II. *produce flowers*, *AP*10.16 (Theaet.). III. *to be an* ἀνθοφόρος II, *IG*12(8).553 (Thasos) (-ίσασα lapis). **-φόρος**, ον, *bearing flowers*, *flowery*, ἄλσος Ar.*Ra.*445, *AP*12.256 (Mel.); opp. κάρπιμος, Thphr.*CP*1.5.5. II. ἀνθοφόρος, ἡ, *flower-bearer*, title of a priestess of Demeter and Kore, *IG*12(8).526 (Thasos), cf. 609 (ibid.) **-φυής**, ές, *parti-coloured*, πτέρυξ, of a parrot, *AP*9.562 (Crin.). II. *producing flowers*, βῶλος *IG*12(9).954.13 (Chalcis).

ἀνθρᾰκ-άριος· *carbonarius*, *Gloss.* **-εία**, ἡ, *making of charcoal*, Thphr.*HP*3.8.7. **-εύς**, έως, ὁ, *charcoal-maker*, Aesop.59, Cic.*Att.*15.5.1 (cj.), Them.*Or.*21.245a, App.*BC*4.40:—also **-ευτής**, οῦ, ὁ, And.*Fr.*4, Ael.*NA*1.8. **-ευτός**, ή, όν, *which can be carbonized*, Arist.*Mete.*387^{b}19. **-εύω**, *make charcoal*, Thphr.*HP*9.3.1, cf. Poll.7.146; τὰ ἀνθρακευόμενα *charcoal*, Antig.*Mir.*136. 2. *burn to a cinder*, ἀ. τινὰ πυρί Ar.*Lys.*340. **-ηρός**, ά, όν, *belonging to charcoal*, Alex.208, *SIG*975.40 (Delos, iii B.C.). **-ιά**, ᾶς, Ep. **-ιή**, ῆς, ἡ, *burning charcoal*, *hot embers*, ἀνθρακιὴν στορέσαι Il.9.213; ὑποθεῖναι Hp.*Nat.Mul.*61; ἀνθρακιᾶς ἄπο a broil hot from *the embers*, E.*Cyc.*358, cf. *AP*6.105 (Apollonid.); ἐπ' ἀνθρακιᾶς ὀπτῆσαι Cratin.143; σου τῆς ἀνθρακιᾶς ἀπολαύει warms himself at your *fire*, Ar.*Eq.*780: metaph. of lovers, τιθέναι τινὰ ὑπὸ ἀνθρακιῇ or ἀνθρακιὴν *AP*12.17, 166 (Asclep.); Κύπριδος ἀ. ib.5.210 (Posidipp.). 2. *black sooty ashes*, ib.11.66 (Antiphil.). **-ίας**, ου, ὁ, *burnt to a cinder*, Luc.*Icar.*13, cf. *DMort.*20.4, al. **-ίδες**, αἱ, *small fish for frying*, Philyll.13.3. **-ίζω**, *make charcoal of*, *roast* or *toast*, Ar.*Pax*1136; *carbonize*, *PHolm.*6.4. **-ινος**, η, ον, *of the nature of*, or *made of*, *a carbuncle*, Lxx *Es.*1.7. 2. ἀνθρακίνου βαφή *blue* dye (*woad*), *PHolm.*18.35. **-ιον**, τό, Dim. of ἄνθραξ, a stone of which mirrors were made, Thphr.*Lap.*33. II. Dim. of ἄνθραξ II.1, *IG*11.161*B*82 (Delos, iii B.C.); of ἄνθραξ II.2, Cass.Fel.22. III. *brazier*, Alex.134. **-ίτης** [ῑ], ου, ὁ, name of a *gem*, Plin.*HN*36.148. II. fem. **-ῖτις**, ιδος, a kind of *coal*, ib.37.99. **-οβότανον**, *betony*, *Gloss.* **-οειδής**, ές, *like*, or *of the colour of*, *coal*, Ph.1.383. **-οθήκη**, ἡ, *coal-cellar*, *Gloss.* **-οκαύστης**, ου, ὁ, = ἀνθρακεύς, Sch.Ar.*Ach.*326. **-όομαι**, Pass., *to be burnt to cinders* or *ashes*, κεραυνῷ Ζηνὸς ἠνθρακωμένος A.*Pr.*374, cf. E.*Cyc.*614, Thphr.*Lap.*12. II. *form a malignant ulcer* (cf. ἀνθράκωσις), Aët.7.2. **-οπώλης**, ου, ὁ, *coal-merchant*, Philyll.

14. **-ώδης**, ες, = ἀνθρακοειδής, Hp.*Mul.*11, Arist.*Sens.*437^{b}17, Diog.Oen.8. **-ωμα**, ατος, τό, *heap of charcoal, coal-fire*, Dsc.*Eup.*1.45. **-ών**, ῶνος, ὁ, *coal-store*, Hdn.Gr.1.30, 2.860. **-ωσις**, εως, ἡ, *malignant ulcer*, commonly in the eye, Paul.Aeg.3.22. 2. *carbuncle*, Gal.14.777. II. *carbonization, charring*, Dsc.*Eup.*1.49.

ἄνθραξ, ἄκος, ὁ, *charcoal*, Sotad.Com.1.12: mostly in pl. ἄνθρακες Ar.*Ach.*34,332, *Nu.*97; ἄ. Παρνήθιοι Id.*Ach.*348; ὀπτωμέναις κόγχαισιν ἐπὶ τῶν ἀ. Id.*Fr.*68; ἄνθρακας ἡμμένους Th.4.100, etc.; their vapour produced stupor, Arist.*Sens.*444^{b}31: prov., ἄνθρακας κατεσθίειν, of a glutton, Euphro 10.14, cf. Ion Trag.29. 2. *coal*, οἷς καὶ οἱ χαλκεῖς χρῶνται Thphr.*Lap.*16, *PHolm.*2.33; ἐπὶ ἀνθράκων μαλακῶν on a slow *fire*, Xenocr.16. II. a precious stone of dark-red colour, including the *carbuncle, ruby*, and *garnet* (Adams), Arist.*Mete.*387^{b}18, Lxx *Ex.*28.18, Phylarch.41, etc. 2. hence, *carbuncle, malignant pustule* (acc. to some, *small-pox*), Hp.*Epid.*3.7, Gal.7.719, al. III. = ἰσάτις, *woad*, *PHolm.*18.34, al.

ἀνθρεῖ· κρύπτει, Hsch.

ἀνθρηδών, όνος, ἡ, *hornet*, D.S.17.75, Hsch.

ἀνθρηκόν, τό, = ἀνθρίσκος (?), Phot.p.140 R.

ἀνθρήν-η, ἡ, *hornet, wasp*, Ar.*Nu.*947; in Arist. the name seems to be given to several diff. species, *HA*628^{b}32, al. **-ιον**, τό, *wasp's nest*, Ar.*V.*1080,1107; Μουσῶν ἀνθρήνιον, of Sophocles, Philostr.Jun.*Im.*13 (= *Com.Adesp.*22). **-ιώδης**, ες, *honeycombed*, ἀ. καὶ πολύπορος Plu.2.916e. **-οειδής**, ές, *like an* ἀνθρήνη, Thphr. *HP*7.13.3.

ἄνθρυσκον, τό, *chervil, Scandix australis*, Sapph.*Supp.*25.13, Cratin.98.6, Pherecr.109 (ἔνθ–), Thphr.*HP*7.7.1 (ἔνθ–):—in Hsch. **ἀνθρίσκιον**, τό; in Poll.6.106 **ἀνθρίσκος**, ὁ.

ἀνθρωπ-άρεσκος [ᾰρ], ὁ, *man-pleaser*, Lxx *Ps.*52(53).6, *Ep.Eph.*6.6, *Ep.Col.*3.22. **-άριον**, τό, Dim. of ἄνθρωπος, *manikin*, Eup.26 D., Ar.*Pl.*416, Demad.51 (of Demosthenes), Arr.*Epict.*1.3.5. **-έη**, contr. **-ῆ** (sc. δορά), ἡ, *man's skin*, like ἀλωπεκῆ, λεοντῆ, etc., Hdt.5.25 codd., Poll.2.5. **-ειος**, α, ον, Ion. **-ήϊος**, η, ον, (ος, ον Luc.*Asin.*46):—*human*, opp. θεῖος, Heraclit.78; τὰ -ήϊα Democr. 37; ἀνθρωπηΐη φωνή Hdt.2.55; ἡ ἀ. φύσις Id.3.65, al.; ἀ. σῶμα Canthar.3 D.; ἀ. τι παθεῖν *IG*5(1).1208.52 (Gythium); ἀ. πήματα *such as man is subject to*, A.*Pers.*706; ἀ. ψόγος reproach *of men*, Id.*Ag.*937; τέχνη ἀ. Th.2.47; ἀνθρωπήϊα πρήγματα *human* affairs, Hdt.1.32, cf. Pl.*Prm.*134e; τὰ ἀ. A.*Fr.*159, Pl.*Phd.*89e; ἅπαντα τἀ. S.*Aj.*132, Antiph.240b, etc.; τὸ ἀ. *mankind, human nature*, πέφυκε τὸ ἀ. ἄρχειν τοῦ εἴκοντος Th.4.61, cf. 5.105. 2. *human, suited to man, within man's powers*, ἡ ἀ. εὐδαιμονίη Hdt.1.5; ἀδύνατον καὶ οὐκ ἀ. not *for man to attempt*, Pl.*Prt.*344c; ὅσα γε τἀ. *in all human probability*, Id.*Cri.*47a; κατὰ τὸ ἀ. (v.l. -πινον) Th.1.22. 3. *human*, opp. *mythical*, ἡ ἀ. λεγομένη γενεή Hdt.3.122. 4. ἀνθρωπείους ἡμέρας· τὰς ἀποφράδας (Rhod.), Hsch. II. Adv. -ως *by human means, in all human probability*, Th.5.103; ἀ. φράζειν to speak *as befits a man*, Ar.*Ra.*1058.—Said to be the correct Attic form by Moer.26. **-εύομαι**, *act as a human being*, as opp. both to gods and beasts, Arist.*EN*1178^{b}7; ψυχὴ ἀνθρωπευομένη a *human* soul, Herm.ap.Stob.1.41.68. **-ήϊος**, η, ον, v. ἀνθρώπειος. **-ίζω**, *act like a man, play the man*, Archyt.ap.D.L.3.22; opp. κυνάω, Luc. *Demon.*21:—so in Med., Ar.*Fr.*37. II. Pass., *become man*, Alex.Aphr.*in Top.*137.27, Simp.*in Ph.*1138.28:—so in Act., *AP*1.105. **-ικός**, ή, όν, *human*, ἔργα Philol.11, cf. Pl.*Sph.*268d; ἡ ἀ. ἀρετή *EN*1102^{b}12, cf. 1178^{a}21, al.: ἀνθρωπικόν [ἐστι], c. inf., *it is like a man, suited to man's nature*, ib.1163^{b}24, al.: Comp. -ώτεροι, οἱ, the *commoner specimens of humanity*, Plot.2.9.9; ἀ. μῦθος a play *dealing with human characters*, Ar.*Fr.*3 D.; παρασκευή Phryn.*PS*p.135 B. Adv. -κῶς Luc.*Zeux.*4, Plu.2.999b, Porph.*Abst.*3.4. **-ινος**, η, ον, also ος, ον Pl.*Lg.*737b:—*of, from*, or *belonging to man, human*, ἀ. βίος Philol.11, cf. Hdt.7.46; ἅπαν τὸ ἀ. all *mankind*, Id.1.86; τὸ ἀ. γένος (v.l. φῦλον) Antipho 4.1.2, Pl.*Phd.*82b; ἀ. κίνδυνοι, opp. θεῖοι, And.1.139; ἀ. δίκη Lys.6.20; ἀ. τεκμήρια, opp. omens, Antipho 5.81; τἀνθρώπινα *human affairs*, Pl.*Tht.*170b, Arist.*EN*1102^{b}3 (v.l. -ικά); ἀνθρώπινόν τι παθεῖν die, *IG*5(2).266.20 (Mantinea, i B.C.), cf. *PPetr.*1 p.33 (iii B.C.), *PRyl.*153.39 (ii A.D.); so ἐάν τι τῶν ἀ. περί τινα γένηται Epicur.*Fr.*217. 2. *human, suited to man*, ἀνθρωπίνη δόξα *fallible, human* understanding, Pl.*Sph.*229a; οὐκ ἀ. ἀμαθία *superhuman, monstrous* folly, Id.*Lg.*737b, etc.; ἀ. καὶ μετρία σκῆψις D. 21.41; οὐ χρὴ ἀνθρώπινα φρονεῖν ἄνθρωπον ὄντα Arist.*EN*1177^{b}32; ἀ. νοῦς Men.482; ἀ. τὸ γεγενημένον X.*Cyr.*5.4.19. 3. ἀνθρώπινα, τά, *secular revenues*, *SIG*527.133; *secular rites*, opp. θεῖα, *Leg.Gort.*10.43. II. Adv. ἀνθρωπίνως, ἁμαρτάνειν commit *human*, i.e. *venial*, errors, Th.3.40; ἀνθρωπινώτερον *more within the range of human faculty*, Pl.*Cra.*392b, D.18.252; ἀνθρωπίνως ἐκλογίζεσθαι, i.e. *with fellow-feeling*, And.2.6; *humanely, gently*, D.23.70; ἀ. χρὴ τὰς τύχας φέρειν *with moderation*, Men.816; εὐτυχίαν D.S.1.60.—Of the three forms, ἀνθρώπειος is used exclusively in Trag. and generally in Th. (but cf. 1.22); ἀνθρώπινος prevails in Comedy and in Prose from Pl. downwds. (though he uses ἀνθρώπειος no less frequently); ἀνθρωπικός is freq. in Arist. **-ιον**, τό, = sq., E.*Cyc.*185, Anaxandr. 34; *paltry fellow*, ὦ πόνηρ' ἀνθρώπια Ar.*Pax* 263, cf. X.*Mem.*2.3.16, *Cyr.*5.1.14, D.18.242. **-ίσκος**, ὁ, Dim. of ἄνθρωπος, *manikin*, E.*Cyc.*316, Pl.*R.*495c; with a shade of contempt, Id.*Phdr.*243a, cf. Luc.*Pisc.*17; ἰδιώτας ἀ. κωμῳδῶν Ar.*Pax* 751. **-ισμός**, ὁ, *humanity*, Aristipp.ap.D.L.2.70. **-ιστί** [τῖ], *in the language of men*, S.*Fr.*827, cf. Sch.Od.6.125, Ps.-Callisth.3.17.

ἀνθρωπο-βορέω, *practise cannibalism*, Chrysipp.*Stoic.*3.186. **-βορία**, ἡ, *cannibalism*, Zeno *Stoic.*1.59 (pl.). **-βόρος**, ον, *man-eating*, Ph.2.423. **-γλωσσος**, Att. **-ττος**, ον, *speaking man's language*, of the parrot, Arist.*HA*597^{b}27. **-γνάφεῖον**, τό, *a place for fulling men*, comic name for a bath, ap.Clem.Al.*Paed.*3.9. **-γονέω**, *beget, produce men*, Ph.2.494. **-γονία**, ἡ, *begetting of men*, title of play by Antiphanes, *POxy.*427; *origin of man*, J.*Ap.*1.8. **-γράφος** [ᾰ], ὁ, *painter of men*, Plin.*HN*35.113. **-δαίμων**, ονος, ὁ, ἡ, *man-god*, i.e. *deified man*, E.*Rh.*971; *semi-devil*, Procop. *Arc.*12. **-δηκτος**, ον, *bitten by a man*, Dsc.1.125, Antig.ap. Philum.*Ven.*5.1. **-ειδής**, ές, *like a man, in human shape*, τύπος Hdt.2.86; θεὸν ἀ. οὐδένα γενέσθαι ib.142; θηρίον Phryn.*PS* p.6 B.; θεοί Arist.*Metaph.*997^{b}10, Phld.*Piet.*15, al.; πίθηκοι Arist. *HA*502^{a}24; of zodiacal signs, Ptol.*Tetr.*145. Adv. -δῶς D.L.10.139. **-είκελος**, ον, *like a man*, Hsch.*Prooem.* **-θεν**· *humanitus*, *Gloss.* **-θηρία**, ἡ, *hunting of men*, Pl.*Sph.*223b. **-θῡμος**, ον, *bold as a man*, opp. θυμολέων, Plu.2.988d. **-θῠσία**, ἡ, *human sacrifice*, ib.857a, al.: in pl., ib.417c, Str.4.4.5, Pallas ap.Porph.*Abst.* 2.56. **-θῠτέω**, *offer human sacrifices*, Ph.2.28, Porph.*Abst.*2.27. **-κομικός**, ή, όν, *belonging to the care* or *government of men*: ἡ -κή (sc. τέχνη) *politics*, Them.*Or.*15.186d:—also **-κόμος**, ον, Anon. in Rh.3.607 W. **-κτονέω**, v.l. for ἀνθρωποσφαγέω, E.*Hec.*260; *offer human sacrifice*, Phylarch.63:—Subst. **-κτονία**, ἡ, Porph.*Abst.* 2.55, Hld.10.7. **-κτόνος**, ον, *murdering men, homicide*, E.*IT*389, 1*Ep.Jo.*3.15, *Ev.Jo.*8.44. II. proparox., ἀνθρωποκτόνος βορά feeding *on slaughtered men*, E.*Cyc.*127. **-λάτρης**, ου, ὁ, *man-worshipper*, Νεστόριος ὁ ἀ. *Cod.Just.*1.1.5.

ἀνθρωπ-όλεθρος, ον, *plague of men, murderous*, Suid.

ἀνθρωπό-λιχνος, ον, *greedy of human flesh*, μυῖα Herm.ap.Stob. 1.41.68. **-λογέω**, *describe* or *represent in the form of man*, Ph.1.282:—Pass., ib.181. **-λόγος**, ον, *speaking of man*, i.e. *fond of personal conversation*, Arist.*EN*1125^{a}5. **-μάγειρος** [ᾰγ], ὁ, *one who cooks human flesh*, Luc.*Asin.*6. **-μῖμος**, ον, *imitating men*, Ps.-Plu.*Fluv.*14.3. **-μορφος**, ον, *of human form*, θεός Epicur.*Fr.* 353, cf. Str.17.1.28, Ph.1.15, Corn.*ND*27, Procop.*Arc.*18; ζῴδια Ptol.*Tetr.*79,181. **-νομικός**, ή, όν, *feeding men*: ἡ -κή (sc. τέχνη) Pl.*Plt.*266e. **-νοος**, ον, contr. **-νους**, ουν, *with human understanding, intelligent*, πίθηκοι Ael.*NA*16.10: Sup. -νούστατος Str.15.1.29.

ἀνθρωποόμαι, *to have the concept* or *idea of a man*, Plu.2.1120d.

ἀνθρωπο-πάθεια [ᾰθ], ἡ, *humanity*, Alciphr.2.1. **-παθέω**, *to have human feelings*, ἄνθρωπος ὢν ἀ. Ph.1.134. **-παθής**, ές, *with human feelings*, ib.182, al. Adv. -θῶς, λέγεσθαι, of the gods, Hermog. *Id.*2.10. **-πλάστης**, ου, ὁ, *fashioner of men*, Ph.1.652. **-ποιέω**, *make, form man* or *men*, Simp.*in Cat.*333.6. **-ποιΐα**, ἡ, *making of man* or *men*, Luc.*Prom.*5,17. **-ποιός**, όν, *making men*, of a portrait-sculptor, opp. θεοποιός, Id.*Philops.*18,20; γυνὴ -ποιὸν ὑπούργημα Secund.*Sent.*8; ἀ. χώρα Simp.*in Epict.*p.64 D. **-πολις**, εως, ἡ, *city of men*, title of Menippean satire by Varro. **-ρραίστης**, ου, ὁ, (ῥαίω) *man-destroyer*, *Drawcansir*, a comedy of Strattis. II. title of Dionysus at Tenedos, Ael.*NA*12.34.

ἄνθρωπος, ὁ, Att. crasis ἅνθρωπος, Ion. ὥνθρωπος, for ὁ ἄνθρ–:—*man*, both as a generic term and of individuals, Hom. etc., opp. *gods*, ἀθανάτων τε θεῶν χαμαὶ ἐρχομένων τ' ἀνθρώπων Il.5.442, etc.; πρὸς ἠοίων ἢ ἑσπερίων ἀνθρώπων *the men* of the east or of the west, Od.8.29; even of the dead in the Isles of the Blest, ib.4.565; κόμπος οὐ κατ' ἄνθρωπον A.*Th.*425, cf. S.*Aj.*761. 2. Pl. uses it both with and without the Art. to denote *man* generically, ὁ ἄ. θείας μετέσχε μοίρας *Prt.*322a; οὕτω.. εὐδαιμονέστατος γίγνεται ἄ. *R.*619b, al.; ὁ ἄ. *the ideal man, humanity*, ἀπώλεσας τὸν ἄ., οὐκ ἐπλήρωσας τὴν ἐπαγγελίαν Arr.*Epict.*2.9.3. 3. in pl., *mankind*, ἀνθρώπων.. ἀνδρῶν ἠδὲ γυναικῶν Il.9.134; ἐν τῷ μακρῷ.. ἀνθρώπων χρόνῳ S.*Ph.*306; ἐξ ἀνθρώπων γίγνεσθαι depart *this life*, Paus.4.26.5, cf. Philostr.*VA*8.31. b. joined with a Sup. to increase its force, δεινότατον τῶν ἐν ἀνθρώποις ἁπάντων D.53.2; ὁ ἄριστος ἐν ἀνθρώποις ὄρτυξ the best quail in *the world*, Pl.*Ly.*211e; freq. without a Prep., μάλιστα, ἥκιστα ἀνθρώπων, most or least *of all*, Hdt.1.60, Pl.*Lg.*629a, *Prt.*361e; ἄριστά γ' ἀ., ὀρθότατα ἀ., Id.*Tht.*148b, 195b, etc. c. τὰ ἐξ ἀνθρώπων πράγματα 'all the trouble in the world', ib.170e; γραφὰς τὰς ἐξ ἀνθρώπων ἐγράφετο Lys.13.73; αἱ ἐξ ἀνθρώπων πληγαί Aeschin.1.59; πάντα τὰ ἐξ ἀνθρώπων κακὰ ἔλεγε D.C.57.23. 4. joined with another Subst., like ἀνήρ, ἄ. ὁδίτης Il.16.263; πολῖτας ἀ. D.22.54; with names of nations, πόλις Μερόπων ἀνθρώπων *h.Ap.*42; in Att. freq. in a contemptuous sense, ἄ. ὑπογραμματεύς, ἄ. γόης, ἄ. συκοφάντης, Lys.30.28, Aeschin.2.153,183; ἄ. ἀλαζών X.*Mem.*1.7.2; ἄ. ὑφάντης Pl.*Phd.*87b; Μενίππου, Καρός τινος ἀνθρώπου D.21.175; ἄ. βασιλεύς *Ev.Matt.*22.2. 5. ἅνθρωπος or ὁ ἄνθρωπος alone, *the man, the fellow*, Pl.*Prt.*314e, *Phd.*117e; ὡς ἀστεῖος ὁ ἄ., with slight irony, ib.116d, al.; with a sense of pity, D.21.91. 6. in the voc. freq. in a contemptuous sense, as when addressed to slaves, etc., ἄνθρωπε or ὤνθρωπε *sirrah! you sir!* Hdt.3.63, 8.125, and freq. in Pl., but in Trag. only S.*Aj.*791,1154; simply, *brother*, *POxy.*215.1, Diog.Oen. 2. 7. *slave*, ἂν ἄ. ᾖ Philem.22; ἄ. ἐμός Gal.14.649; ὁ ἄ. τῆς ἁμαρτίας or ἀνομίας 2*Ep.Thess.*2.3; ἄ. τοῦ Θεοῦ 1*Ep.Tim.*6.11; but τιθέναι τινὰ ἐν ἀνθρώποις make *a man of*, of a freed slave, Herod.5.15. 8. ἄ. ἄ. *any one*, Hebraism in Lxx *Le.*17.3 (cf. ἀνήρ VI.8); ἄ. like Germ. *man* 'one', 1*Ep.Cor.*4.1, al. 9. Medic., name of a *plaster*, ἡ διὰ σάνδυκος ἄ. καλουμένη Aët.15.43. II. as fem., *woman*, Pi.*P.*4.98, Hdt.1.60, Isoc.18.52, Arist.*EN*1148^{b}20; contemptuously, of female slaves, Antipho 1.17, Is.6.20, etc.; with a sense of pity, D.19.197.—Prop. opp. θηρίον, cf. ἀνήρ; but opp. γυνή, Aeschin.3.137; ἀπὸ ἀνθρώπου ἕως γυναικός Lxx 1Es.9.40, etc.

ἀνθρωποσφᾰγέω, *slay men*, E.*Hec.*260.

ἀνθρωπότης, ητος, ἡ, *abstract humanity*, Ph.1.206, S.E.*M.*7.273, Vett.Val.346.29, Plot.6.1.10, Dam.*Pr.*58.

ἀνθρωπο-τρόφος, ον, *nourishing men*, Hsch. **-φᾰγέω**, *eat human flesh*, Hdt.4.106, Porph.*Abst.*2.57; of carnivora, Arist.*HA* 594ᵃ29. **-φᾰγία**, ἡ, *cannibalism*, Arist.*Pol.*1338ᵇ20, Phld.*Sto. Herc.*339.14, Porph.*Abst.*2.57: in pl., Plu.*Luc.*11. **-φᾰγικῶς**, Adv. *like cannibals*, Eust.634.59. **-φάγος** [ᾰ], ον, *man-eating*, Antiph.68.12, Arist.*HA*501ᵇ1, Heraclit.*Incred.*31:—esp. of *cannibal* tribes, Str.4.5.4, etc. **-φθόρος**, ον, *destroying men*, gloss on βροτολοιγός, Sch.Il.5.31. **-φυής**, ές, *of man's nature*, οὐκ ἀνθρωποφυέας ἐνόμισαν τοὺς θεούς Hdt.1.131; Κένταυροι D.S.4.69. **-χειρον**, τό, *herb of mercury* (= πενταδάκτυλον, ἑρμοδάκτυλον, Ps.-Dsc.), *Cat. Cod.Astr.*8(3).162:—also **-χειρ**, ὁ, ib.7.234.

ἀνθρωπώ, ἡ, Lacon. for ἄνθρωπος II, Hsch.

Ἀνθρωφηρακλῆς, -έος, ὁ, title of play by Pherecrates, Phot. p.145R.

ἀνθυβρ-ίζω, *abuse one another, abuse in turn*, E.*Ph.*620 (Pass.), Plu. *Per.*26, Luc.*DMeretr.*33, etc. **-ισις**, εως, ἡ, *counter-abuse*, Mich. *in EN*54.9.

ἀνθυλακτέω, *bark* or *bay in answer*, Ael.*HA*4.19.

ἀνθύλλιον, τό, Dim. of ἄνθος, M.Ant.4.20, Dsc.2.183. II. = sq. 1, Plin.*HN*26.84, cf. 21.175. III. = μυοσωτίς, Ps.-Dsc.4.86.

ἀνθυλλίς, ίδος, ἡ, a plant, *Cressa cretica*, Dsc.3.136. 2. *herb ivie, Ajuga Iva*, ibid., Plin.*HN*26.84.

ἄνθυλλον, τό, = foreg. 1, Ps.-Dsc.3.136, Plin.*HN*21.175.

ἀνθυπ-άγω [ᾰγ], *bring to trial* or *indict in turn*, Th.3.70. 2. *rejoin, reply*, A.D.*Pron.*53.21, al.:—Pass., τὸ -αγόμενον, -αχθησόμενον, Id.*Synt.*118.1, 121.22. b. *substitute*, ib.12.9, etc. 3. *lead under in turn*, αἰχμαλώτους ὑπὸ τὸ ζυγόν D.C.*Fr.*36.22; but in Med., *bring over*, τινὰς ἐς εὔνοιαν ib.35.10. 4. *withdraw in turn*, ἀνθυπῆγε Μαρδόνιος Aristid.1.146J. **-ᾰγωγή**, ἡ, *reply*, A.D.*Synt.*19.12, al. **-ᾰκούω**, *listen to in turn*, τινός Nicol.*Prog.*6.10 in Rh.1. 314W. II. *correspond, answer to*, Iamb.*in Nic.*p.21P. **-αλλᾰγή**, ἡ, Rhet., *substitution of one case for another*, Demetr.*Eloc.*60, A.D.*Synt.*204.27, al. **-αλλάσσω**, Att. -ττω, *substitute*, esp. in Rhet., *substitute one case for another*, Demetr.*Eloc.*59, cf. A.D.*Synt.* 232.2; of *interchange* of moods, in Pass., ib.211.19:—Med., *receive in exchange*, θνητὸν ἀθανάτου βίον Ph.2.440. **-αντάω**, *meet, reply to objections*, πρός τινα Longin.18.1. **-άρχω**, *to be set over against*, of ἀντίστοιχα, Stoic.ap.Plu.2.960b.

ἀνθῠπᾰτ-εία, ἡ, *proconsulate*, *CIG* (add.)3841*f* (Aezani), *BCH* 11.110 (Epist. Hadriani), Hdn.7.5.2, Just.*Nov.*8.1: pl., ib.26.5 *Intr.* **-εύω**, *to be proconsul*, Plu.*Comp.Dem.Cic.*3, *Act.Ap.*18. 12, Hdn.7.5.2. **-ιανός**, = *proconsularis*, Just.*Nov.*30.1. **-ικός**, ή, όν, *proconsular*, ἐξουσία D.C.58.7. 2. ἀ. δεκαδαρχία the body of military tribunes *which took the place of the consulate*, Plu.2. 277f. **-ος**, ὁ, *proconsul*, Lat. *pro consule*, Plb.28.5.6, *Act.Ap.*13. 7, etc., freq. in Inscrr. as *SIG*684.3, and Pap. as *Sammelb.*3924.32 (I A.D.); στρατηγὸς ἀ. *SIG*704*K*, etc. II. as Adj., *proconsular*, ἐξουσία D.H.9.16; ἀρχή Id.11.62.

ἀνθυπ-είκω, *yield in turn* or *mutually*, τινί Plu.*Cor.*18, D.C.45. 8. **-ειξις**, εως, ἡ, *a mutual yielding*, Plu.*Sol.*4.

ἀνθυπερβάλλω, *surpass in turn*, J.*AJ*16.7.2.

ἀνθυπερηφανέω, *to be haughty in return*, August.ap.Suet.*vit. Horat.*

ἀνθυπέρχομαι, *insinuate oneself into, creep upon in turn*, τινά Anon. *Prog.* in Rh.1.601W. II. Gramm., *take the place of*, A.D.*Synt.* 95.9, 112.6.

ἀνθυπηρετέω, *serve in turn*, τινί Arist.*EN*1133ᵃ4, 1170ᵇ25.

ἀνθυπισχνέομαι, *promise in return*, Sch.Ar.*Eq.*694.

ἀνθυπο-βάλλω, *bring objections in turn, retort*, Aeschin.3.209. II. *substitute fraudulently*, Ph.2.630. **-δεικτος**, ον, *brought forward as an instance in opposition*, Phld.*D.*1.16. **-κρίνομαι** [ῑ], Ion. ἀντυπ-, *answer in return*, Hdt.6.86.γ'. II. *put on* or *pretend in turn*, ὀργήν Luc.*Dom.*30. **-λείπω**, *leave on the other side*, f.l. in Ph.2.505 (Pass.). **-λογέω**, *compensate*, *Gloss.* **-λογίζομαι**, *charge against, deduct*, *PPetr.*3p.149. **-λογισμός**, ὁ, *compensation*, *Gloss.*

ἀνθυπ-όμνῡμι, *make a counter-affidavit*, in Med., D.48.25, 58. 43. **-οπτεύω**, *suspect mutually*, ἀλλήλους D.C.45.8: abs., Aen. Tact.24.11 (cj.):—Pass., ἀνθυποπτεύεται.. πλέον ἕξειν *he is met by the suspicion* that.., Th.3.43. **-ορύσσω**, *make countermines*, Aen. Tact.37.5, Polyaen.6.17. **-όρυξις**, εως, ἡ, *countermining*, Ph. *Bel.*100.22 (pl.).

ἀνθυπό-στᾰσις, εως, ἡ, *convertibility of substance*, Dam.*Pr.* 158. **-στρέφω**, *recur*, of an illness, Poll.3.107; *return*, Olymp. *in Mete.*148.1, Pall.*in Hp.Fract.*12.276C.; *turn round upon*, Ps.-Callisth.2.29; *turn back*, ib.31, al. **-στροφή**, ἡ, *return*, of a clyster, Sever.*Clyst.*25. **-στροφέω**, = ἀνθυποστρέφω, Steph.*in Hp.*2.279D. **-τείνομαι**, *maintain by way of rejoinder*, Ulp. ad D.23.88. **-τίθημι**, *interpose to counteract*, πρός.. Aristeas 239. **-τῑμάομαι**, *reply to the* ὑποτίμησις (q.v.), Poll.8.150. **-τίμησις** [τῑ], εως, ἡ, *reply to* ὑποτίμησις, Rh.5.7W.

ἀνθυπουργ-έω, Ion. ἀντυποργέω, *return a kindness*, ἀ. τινὶ τοῦτο τὸ ἂν δεηθῇ Hdt.3.133; χάριν S.*Fr.*339; αἰσχρά τινι E.*Hipp.*999; τι καθ' αὑτὸν Corn.*ND*15. **-ία**, ἡ, *service done in return*, Anon.*in Rh.*109.1. **-ησις**, εως, ἡ, *returning of a kindness*, Hsch.

ἀνθυπο-φαίνω, *reveal in turn*, *CIG*4958 (Egypt). **-φέρω**, *reply, rejoin*, opp. πυνθάνομαι, D.H.*Dem.*54, cf. Hermog.*Inv.*4.14, S.E.*M.* 7.440. II. *use* a word or phrase *in reply* to a question, in Pass., A.D.*Pron.*24.17, *Synt.*73.6. III. *cause to retrogress*, Plu.2.76d:—Pass., ib.939a. **-φορά**, ἡ, *reply*, opp. πεῦσις, D.H.*Dem.*54; esp. *reply to a supposed objection*, Quint.*Inst.*9.3.87, Hermog.*Inv.*3.4, Ulp. ad D.3.10. II. *reply*, A.D.*Synt.*72.26. **-χωρέω**, *give place in turn*, τινί Dam.*Pr.*303, Steph.*in Hp.*2.279D. **-χώρησις**, εως, ἡ, *retiring in turn*, εἰς τὸ ἐκτός Plu.2.903d.

ἀνθυφαίρ-εσις, εως, ἡ, = ἀνταναίρεσις I, Alex.Aphr.*in Top.*545. 16. **-έω**, *take away again* or *in turn*, Iamb.*in Nic.*p.28P., Porph. *in Ptol.*194:—Pass., Lxx *Le.*27.18, *PLond.ined.*2361ᵛ (III B.C.), D.C. 48.33, Procl.*Hyp.*4.12. 2. ἀ. μισθοῦ *deduct* on account of wages, *IG*4.1508*A*8 (Epid.).

ἀνθυφίστᾰμαι, Pass., with aor. 2 ἀνθυπέστην, *undertake for* another, ἀνθυποστῆναι (sc. χορηγός) *undertake to serve* as choragus *in rivalry with* another, D.21.68:—later in Act., *imply reciprocally*, Dam.*Pr.*72.

ἀνθώδης, ες, *flowerlike*, Thphr.*HP*1.13.1. II. *full of flowers*, τόπος Sch.Nic.*Th.*438.

ἀνθωρο-σκοπέω, *to be in a diametric aspect with the horoscope*, Ptol. *Tetr.*200, Vett.Val.135.3. **-σκόπος**, name of the *seventh* τόπος *in an* ἀποτελεσματογραφία, Paul.Al.*M.*2.

ἀνία, Ion. **ἀνίη**, Aeol. **ὀνία**, ἡ, *grief, sorrow, distress, trouble*, Hes. *Th.*611, Sapph.1.3 (pl.), Thgn.76, etc.; ὑπὸ τῆς ἀνίας ἀνεθολοῦθ' ἡ καρδία Pherecr.116; εἰς ἀνίαν ἔρχεταί τινι is like to be *a mischief* to him, S.*Aj.*1138, cf. Pl.*Grg.*477d, *Prt.*355a, al.: in pl., ὀνίαισι Sapph. l.c.; ἀντ' ἀνιῶν ἀνίαι Thgn.344; ἐμοὶ λιπὼν ἀνίας S.*Aj.*973, cf. 1005, *Ph.*1115, Pl.*Prt.*353e. 2. concrete, δαιτὸς ἀνίη *the killjoy* of our feast, Od.17.446; ἄπρηκτος ἀνίη inevitable *bane*, of Scylla, 12.223; ἀνίη καὶ πολὺς ὕπνος *an annoyance*, 15.394. [In Hom. and S. always ῑ, also E.*IT*1031 (s.v.l.). Other Poets made the ι long or short as the verse required, though the Homeric quantity prevailed in Ep.]

ἀνιάζω, only pres. and impf. (exc. aor. ἠνίασα *AP*11.254 (Lucill.)): Ion. impf. ἀνιάζεσκον A.R.3.1138:—Ep. Verb, *grieve, distress*, like ἀνιάω, c. acc. pers., ὅς κεν τοῦτον ἀνιάζῃ Od.19.323; ἀλλ' ὅτε δὴ ῥ' ἀνίαζον.. Ἀχαιούς Il.23.721 (v.l. Ἀχαιοί). II. intr., *to be grieved* or *distressed*, θυμῷ ἀνιάζων *grieving* at heart, Od.22.87; ἀλλ' ὅτε δὴ ῥ' ἀνίαζε *was grieving, growing weary*, 4.460, cf. A.R.4.1347; κτεάτεσσιν ὑπερφιάλως ἀνιάζει he *grieves for* his goods, Il.18.300; ἐπὶ παιδί Arat.196. [ῑ metri gr. in Hom. and other Ep.]

ἀνιακκάς, apptly. the name of a *tune*, Eub.46.

ἀνιάομαι, *cure again, repair*, τὸ παρεὸν τρῶμα ἀνιεῦνται (which in sense at least is an Ion. fut.) dub. in Hdt.7.236 (leg. ἀκεῦνται).

ἀνιαρίζω, Dor. for ἀνιερίζω, *dedicate*, *IG*14.644 (Bruttii).

ἀνιᾱρός, ά, όν, Ion. and Ep. **ἀνιηρός**, ή, όν:—*grievous, troublesome, annoying*, of persons, πτωχὸν ἀνιηρόν Od.17.220; ἐχθροῖς ἀνιαροί Ar. *Pl.*561, cf. Lys.25.20 (Sup.):—of animals, σχέτλια καὶ ἀ. Hdt.3.108. Adv. ἀνιαρῶς, λέγειν S.*Ant.*316. 2. mostly of things, *painful, grievous*, πτωχεύειν πάντων ἔστ' ἀνιηρότατον Tyrt.10.4, cf. Thgn.124; πόλλ' ἀνιηρὰ παθών Id.276; πᾶν γὰρ ἀναγκαῖον χρῆμ' ἀ. ἔφυ Id.472 (= Even.8); opp. ἡδύ, E.*Med.*1095 (lyr.), cf. Pl.*Prt.*355e; τοῖς γεγενημένοις ἀνιαροῖς D.18.291; Comp. ἀνιαρότερος Lys.10.28; irreg. Comp. ἀνιηρέστερος Od.2.190: Sup. -ότατος Pl.*Grg.*477d. II. Pass., *grieved, distressed*, X.*Cyr.*1.4.14. Adv. -ρῶς *wretchedly*, ζῆν Id.*Mem.* 1.6.4; ἔχειν Sor.1.53. [ῑ Hom. and S., ῐ Eleg., E., Com.]

ἀνίᾱτος [ῐ], Ion. **-ίητος**, ον, *incurable*, Hp.*Aph.*7.87; ἕλκος, τραῦμα, Pl.*Lg.*877a, 878c: also in moral sense, πράγματα ib.660c; ἀ. καὶ ἀνήκεστα κακά Aeschin.3.156; ἀνελευθερία ἀ. ἐστιν Arist.*EN*1121ᵇ 13. 2. of persons, *incurable, incorrigible*, Pl.*R.*410a, *Grg.*526b; ἀ. κατὰ τὴν μοχθηρίαν Arist.*EN*1165ᵇ18, al. Adv. ἀνιάτως, ἔχειν to be *incurable*, Pl.*Phd.*113e, D.18.324; οἱ ἀ. κακοί Arist.*EN*1137ᵃ 29. II. Act., ἀ. μετάνοια *unavailing* repentance, Antipho 2.4.12.

ἀνιάτρευτος, ον, = foreg., Suid. s.v. βρύω.

ἀνιᾱτρεύω, *heal again*, Tz.*H.*6.665.

ἀνιᾱτρολόγητος, ον, *uninstructed in medical science*, Vitr.1.1.13.

ἀνίᾱτρος, Ion. **-ίητρος**, ὁ, *no-physician*, Hp.*Praec.*7, Arist.*Ph.* 191ᵇ6, Plot.6.7.37, Alex.Aphr.*in Top.*33.2: Adj., *unworthy of a physician*, ἀ. τι ἔχειν Antyll.ap.Orib.10.23.24.

ἀνίαχος, f.l. for αὔταχος (q.v.) in Hom. and Q.S.

ἀνῐάχω [ᾰχ], *cry aloud*, A.R.2.270, 3.253, Nonn.*D.*15.417. 2. c. acc., *proclaim loudly*, *APl.*4.296 (Antip.); ἔπος Nonn.*D.*44.190.

ἀνιάω [ᾰν], S.*Aj.*266, etc.: 3 sg. impf. ἠνία ib.273, Pl.*Grg.*502a: fut. ἀνιάσω [ᾱσ] X.*An.*3.3.19, Ep. ἀνιήσω Hom.: aor. ἠνίασα And.1. 50, etc.; Dor. ἀνίασα Theoc.2.23: pf. ἠνίακα Hld.7.22:—Pass., ἀνιῶμαι Od.15.335, etc., Ion. 3 pl. opt. ἀνιῴατο Hdt.4.130: 3 pl. impf. ἠνιῶντο X.*Cyr.*6.3.10: fut. ἀνιάσομαι Ar.*Fr.*488.11, X.*Mem.*1.1.8 (ἀνιαθήσομαι only in Gal.*Anim.Pass.*9); Ep. 2 sg. ἀνιήσεαι Thgn.991: aor. ἠνιάθην X.*HG*6.4.20; Ion. -ήθην Il.2.291: pf. ἠνίημαι Mosch. 4.3: the aor. Med. ἀνιάσασθαι is v.l. for ἀνιᾶσθαι in Gal.*UP*6.16: (ἀνία). [ῑ always in Hom. and S.; ῐ in Thgn. and late Poets; ῐ in Ar. l.c., etc.]:—commoner form of the Ep. ἀνιάζω, *grieve, distress*, c. acc. pers., ἀνιήσει.. υἷας Ἀχαιῶν Od.2.115, cf. 20.178; μηδὲ φίλους ἀνία Thgn.1032; φίλους ἀνιῶν S.*Aj.*266: c. acc. rei, ἀνιᾷ μου τὰ ὦτα Pl.*Grg.*485b: c. dupl. acc., ὁ δρῶν σ' ἀνιᾷ τὰς φρένας S.*Ant.*319: c. acc. pers. et neut. Adj., τί ταῦτ' ἀνιᾷς με; ib.550; παῦρ' ἀνιάσας, πόλλ' εὐφράνας (sc. ὑμᾶς) Ar.*Pax*764; ἠνίασά σε οὐδὲν πώποτε And. 1.50:—Pass., *to be grieved, distressed*, c. dat. pers. vel rei, ἀνιᾶται παρεόντι he *is vexed* by one's presence, Od.15.335; ἀ. ὀρυμαγδῷ 1.133;

σύν σοι..παθόντι κακῶς ἀνιώμεθα Thgn.655; πάσχων ἀνιήσεαι Id.991; ἀ. ὑπομιμνήσκων Lys.13.43; δαπανῶντα ἀνιᾶσθαι X.*Cyr.*8.3.44; περί τινος Ar.*Lys.*593: c. neut. Adj., τοῦτ' ἀνιῶμαι πάλαι I *have* long *been vexed at* this, S.*Ph.*906; πολλὰ μὲν αὐτοὺς ἀνιωμένους, πολλὰ δὲ ἀνιῶντας τοὺς οἰκέτας X.*Oec.*3.2: abs., οὐδ' ἂν..ἀνιῷτο Thgn.1205: esp. in aor. part. Pass. ἀνιηθείς *disheartened*, Od.3.117, Il.2.291.

ἀνιγροδέτης· βυρσοδέψης, Hsch. **ἄνιγρον**, v. ἄναγρον.

ἀνιγρός, ά, όν, = ἀνιαρός I, Nic.*Th.*8, Call.*Iamb.*1.164 (prob.), Opp.*H.*3.188; νοῦσος Call.*Aet.*3.1.14; cf. ἀνιγρόν· ἀκάθαρτον, φαῦλον, κακόν, δυσῶδες, ἀσεβές, Hsch.; ἀ. ἀντίπαλοι *AP*7.561 (Jul. Aegypt.); δαίμων *IG*14.2123.

ἀνιδεῖν, aor. inf., *look up*, dub. in A.*Ch.*808.

ἀνῑδ-ῑτί, Adv., (ἰδίω) *without sweat* or *toil*, Pl.*Lg.*718e. **-ίω**, *perspire so that the sweat stands on the surface* Id.*Ti.*74c (prob.).

ἄνιδρος, ον, v. ἀνίδρως.

ἀνῑδρόω, *get into a sweat*, Hp.*Coac.*24.

ἀνίδρ-ῡτος (v. ἀΐδρυτος), ον, Ph.2.451, Dam.*Pr.*413. **-ύω**, *set up*, e.g. a statue, D.C.37.34.

ἀνίδρ-ως [ῐ], ων, *without perspiration*, Ruf.*Ren.Ves.*6.2, Aret.*SD* 1.16, 2.7; and so, with v.l. ἄνιδρος, in Hp.*Acut.*(*Sp.*)17. **-ωσις**, εως, ἡ, *sweating*, Id.*Epid.*7.105. **-ωτί**, Adv. *without sweat*, Id.*Prorrh.* 1.61, X.*Cyr.*2.1.29: metaph., *without toil* or *trouble*, Il.15.228; *lazily, slowly*, X.*Cyr.*2.2.30, *Oec.*21.3. **-ωτος**, ον, *without having sweated* or *exercised oneself*, ἀ. γενόμενοι εἰσίοιεν Id.*Cyr.*2.1.29· *not accompanied by perspirations*, ἴκτερος Hp.*Judic.*9.

ἀνῐέρ-ειος, ον, = ᾧ ἱερεῖα μὴ θύεται, *AB*405, Suid. **-εύω**, = ἀνιερόω, τέμενος Men.Eph.1. **-ος**, ον, *unholy, unhallowed*, A.*Ag.* 220,769, *Supp.*757; ἀνίερος ἀθύτων πελάνων *unhallowed because of* the unoffered sacrifices, E.*Hipp.*146 (all lyr. passages); of a child *born out of wedlock*, Pl.*R.*461b. II. *receiving no victims*, Ἄρης E.*Fr.*992 (lyr.). **-όω**, *dedicate, devote*, Arist.*Oec.*1346^{b}5; τινί τι Plu.*Cor.*3:—Pass., *PTeb.*60.10 (ii B.C.), *BGU*1202.5 (i B.C.), etc.: used of persons invoking the wrath of the gods upon themselves or others in case of breach of faith, *SIG*1179 (Cnidus). **-ωσις**, εως, ἡ, *consecration*, ἱεροῦ D.H.5.35, cf. *SIG*563.9,16 (Teos), *IG*9(1).278 (Locr., ii B.C.); *dedication* of a manumitted slave, Boeot. ἀνιάρωσις *IG*7.3315 (Chaeronea). **-ωτέον**, *one must consecrate*, Ph. 1.184. **-ωστί**, Adv. of ἀνίερος, Heraclit.14.

ἀνίημι, ης (ἀνιεῖς, as if from ἀνιέω, dub. in Il.5.880), ησι: impf. ἀνίην, Hom. and Att. 2 and 3 sg. εις, ει, Ion. 3 sg. ἀνίη *SIG*1 (Abu Simbel, vi B.C.), Iterat. ἀνίεσκε Hes.*Th.*157; also ἠνίει Hp.*Epid.*7.46; 1 sg. ἀνίειν Luc.*Cat.*4: fut. ἀνήσω: pf. ἀνεῖκα: aor. 1 ἀνῆκα; Ion. ἀνέηκα:—the Homeric forms ἀνέσει Od.18.265, aor. opt. ἀνέσαιμι 14.209, part. ἀνέσαντες 13.657 should be referred to ἀνέζω, but ἄνεσαν Il.21.537 is from ἀνίημι: aor. 2, 3 pl. ἀνεῖσαν Th.5.32, imper. ἄνες A.*Ch.*489, S.*Ant.*1101, E.*Hel.*442, subj. ἀνῇς A.*Eu.*183, Ep. 3 sg. subj. ἀνήῃ Il.2.34, opt. ἀνείη, inf. ἀνεῖναι, part. ἀνείς:—Pass., ἀνίεμαι: pf. ἀνεῖμαι Hdt.2.65, A.*Th.*413, 3 pl. pf. ἀνέωνται Hdt.2.165 (v.l. ἀνέονται), inf. ἀνἑῶσθαι (sic) *Tab.Heracl.*1.153: aor. part. ἀνεθείς Pl.*R.*410e: fut. ἀνεθήσομαι Th.8.63. [ἀνῐ- Ep., ἀνῑ- Att.: but even Hom. has ἀνΐει, ἀνῑέμενος, and we find ἀνΐησιν in Pl.Com.153 (anap.).]:—*send up* or *forth*, Ζεφύροιο..ἀήτας Ὠκεανὸς ἀνίησιν Od.4.568; of Charybdis, τρὶς μὲν γάρ τ' ἀνίησιν.. τρὶς δ' ἀναροιβδεῖ 12.105; ἀφρὸν ἀ. *spew up, vomit*, A.*Eu.*183; σταγόνας [αἵματος] ἀ. S.*OT*1277; of the earth, καρπὸν ἀ. *make* corn or fruit *spring up*, *h.Cer.*333; κνώδαλα A.*Supp.*266; also of the gods, ἀ. ἄροτον γῆς S.*OT*270, etc.; so of females, *produce*, ib.1405:—in Pass., σπαρτῶν ἀπ' ἀνδρῶν ῥίζωμ' ἀνεῖται A.*Th.*413: then in various relations, συὸς χρῆμα ἀ. S.*Fr.*401; κρήνην E.*Ba.*766; of a forest, πῦρ καὶ φλόγα Th.2.77; πνεῦμ' ἀνεὶς ἐκ πνευμόνων E.*Or.*277:—*send up* from the grave or nether world, A.*Pers.*650, Ar.*Ra.*1462, Phryn.Com.1 D., Pl.*Cra.*403e, etc.:—Pass., ἐκ γῆς κάτωθεν ἀνίεται ὁ πλοῦτος ibid.; of fruit, Thphr.*CP*5.1.5. 2. *let come up, give access to*, τινά X.*HG*2.4.11; εἰς τὸ πεδίον ib.7.2.12. II. *let go*, from Hom. downwds. a very common sense, ἐμὲ δὲ γλυκὺς ὕπνος ἀνῆκεν, i.e. *left* me, Il.2.71, etc., cf. Pl.*Prt.*310d:—Pass., ἀνίεσθαι *wake up*, D.S.17.56; *set free*, ἐκ στέγης ἀ. S.*Ant.* 1101; *let go unpunished*, ἄνδρα τὴν ὀλιγαρχίαν λυμαινόμενον X.*HG*2.3.51, cf. Lys.13.93; ἄνετέ μ' ἄνετε *leave* me *alone, forbear*, S.*El.* 229 (lyr.); of a state of mind, ἐμὲ δ' οὐδ' ὧς θυμὸν ἀνίει..ὀδύνη Il.15.24; ὅταν μ' ἀνῇ νόσος μανίας E.*Or.*227; ὥς μιν ὁ οἶνος ἀνῆκε Hdt.1.213, etc.; ἀ. ἵππον *to let* him *go* (by slackening the rein), S.*El.*721; ἵππους εἰς τάχος ἀ. X.*Eq.Mag.*3.2; τῷ δήμῳ τὰς ἡνίας ἀ. Plu.*Per.* 11. b. *loosen, unfasten*, δεσμόν Od.8.359 (v.l. δεσμῶν); δεσμά τ' ἀνεῖσαι Call.*Hec.*1.2.13: hence, *open*, πύλας ἄνεσαν Il.21.537; ἀ. θύρετρα E.*Ba.*448; ἀ. σήμαντρα *break* the seal, Id.*IA*325:—Pass., πύλαι ἀνειμέναι D.H.10.14. 2. ἀ. τινί *let loose at* one, *slip at*, ἀ. τὰς κύνας X.*Cyn.*7.7: hence ἄφρονα τοῦτον ἀνέντες Il.5.761, cf. 880: c. acc. et inf., Διομήδεα μαργαίνειν ἀνέηκεν ib.882: generally, *set on* or *urge* to do a thing, c. inf., Μοῦσ' ἄρ' ἀοιδὸν ἀνῆκεν ἀειδέμεναι Od.8.73, cf. 17.425, Il.2.276, 5.422: freq. c. acc. pers. only, *let loose, excite*, as οὐδέ κε Τηλέμαχον..ὧδ' ἀνιείης Od.2.185; μέγας δέ σε θυμὸς ἀνῆκεν Il.7.25; τοῖσιν μὲν Θρασυμήδεα δῖον ἀνῆκεν *urged* Thrasymedes *to* their *aid*, 17.705:—so in Pass., ἅπας κίνδυνος ἀνεῖται σοφίας Ar.*Nu.*955. 3. ἀ. τινὰ πρός τι *to let go for* any purpose, τὸν λεὼν.. ἀνεῖναι πρὸς ἔργα τε καὶ θυσίας Hdt.2.129; ἐς παιγνίην ἑωυτὸν ἀ. ib.173; τὰ μικρὰ εἰς τύχην ἀνείς E.*Fr.*974 (v.l. ἀφείς); τὰ σώματα ἐπὶ ῥᾳδιουργίαν X.*Cyr.*7.5.75; ἐὰν δ' ἀνῇς, ὕβριστον χρῆμα κακόλαστον [γυνή] if you *leave* her *free*, Pl.Com.98. 4. *let, allow*, c. acc. et inf., ἀνεῖναι αὐτοὺς ὅ τι βούλονται ποιεῖν Pl.*La.*179a; ἀ. τρίχας αὔξεσθαι Hdt.2.36, cf. 4.175: with inf. omitted, ἀνεῖσα πένθει κόμαν E.*Ph.*323; ἀ. στολίδος κροκόεσσαν τρυφάν ib.1491; κόμας Plu.*Lys.*1: c. dat. pers. et inf., ἀνεὶς αὐτῷ θηρᾶν *having given* him *leave* to hunt, X.*Cyr.*4.6.3. 5. Med., *loosen, undo*, c. acc., κόλπον ἀνιεμένη *baring her* breast, Il.22.80; αἶγας ἀνιέμενοι *stripping* or *flaying* goats, Od.2.300; so ἀνεῖτο λαγόνας E.*El.*826; so in Act., ἀνιέναι· δέρειν, Hsch. 6. *let go free, leave untilled*, of ground dedicated to a god, τέμενος ἀνῆκεν ἅπαν Th.4.116; ἀργὸν παντάπασι τὸ χωρίον ἀνιέντες τῷ θεῷ Plu.*Publ.*8; generally, τὴν χώραν ἀ. μηλόβοτον Isoc.14.31; ἀρούρας ἀσπόρους ἀ. Thphr.*HP*8.11.9; στέλεχος ἀνειμένον *allowed to run wild*, Lxx *Ge.*49.21:—but this sense mostly in Pass., *devote oneself, give oneself up*, ἐς τὸ ἐλεύθερον Hdt.7.103; esp. of animals dedicated to a god, which *are let range at large* (cf. ἄνετος), ἀνεῖται τὰ θηρία Id.2.65; of a person *devoted to* the gods, νῦν δ' οὗτος ἀνεῖται στυγερῷ δαίμονι S.*Aj.*1214; of places, etc., θεοῖσιν ἀ. δένδρεα Call.*Cer.*47; ἄλσος ἀνειμένον a *consecrated* grove, cj. in Pl.*Lg.*761c; of land, ἀ. εἰς νομάς *PTeb.*60.8,72.36 (ii B.C.): hence metaph., ἀνειμένος εἴς τι *devoted to* a thing, *wholly engaged in* it, e.g. ἐς τὸν πόλεμον Hdt.2.167; ἀνέωνται ἐς τὸ μάχιμον they *are given up* to military service, ib.165; ἐς τὸ κέρδος λῆμ' ἀνειμένον *given up* to.., E.*Heracl.* 3: hence pf. part. Pass. ἀνειμένος as Adj., *going free, left to one's own will and pleasure, at large*, S.*Ant.*579, *El.*516; ἀ. τι χρῆμα πρεσβυτῶν γένος καὶ δυσφύλακτον E.*Andr.*727; πέπλοι ἀνειμένοι *let hang loose*, ib.598; τὸ εἰς ἀδικίαν καὶ πλεονεξίαν -μένον *unrestrained propensity to..*, Plu.*Num.*16; σώματα πρὸς πᾶσαν ἐπιθυμίαν ἀνειμένα Id.*Lyc.*10. 7. *slacken, relax*, opp. ἐπιτείνω or ἐντείνω, of a bow or stringed instrument, *unstring*, as Hdt.3.22, cf. Pl.*R.*442a, *Ly.*209b, X.*Mem.*3.10.7, etc.; esp. of musical scales, ἁρμονίαι ἀνειμέναι, opp. σύντονοι, Arist.*Pol.*1342^{b}22, al.; ἀνειμένα Ἰαστὶ μοῦσα Pratin.Lyr.5: metaph., ὀργῆς ὀλίγον τὸν κόλλοπ' ἀ. Ar.*V.*574, cf. Pherecr.145.4, Pl.*R.*410e; πολιτεῖαι ἀνειμέναι καὶ μαλακαί Arist.*Pol.*1290^{a}28; τοῖς γηράσκουσι ἀνίεται ἡ συντονία *GA*787^{b}13; ἀνειμένη τάσις the *grave* accent, Sch.D.T.p.130 H.; οἱ πάγοι τὰς φλόγας ἀ. *temper*, Arist.*Mu.*397^{b}2: hence, b. *remit, neglect, give up*, στέρνων ἀραγμούς S.*OC*1608; φυλακὰς ἀνῆκα E.*Supp.*1042; φυλακήν, ἄσκησιν, etc., Th.4.27, X.*Cyr.*7.5.70, etc.; ἀ. θάνατόν τινι *to remit* sentence of death to one, let one live, E.*Andr.*531; ἔχθρας, κολάσεις τισί Plu.2.536a; ἀ. τὰ χρέα, τὰς καταδίκας, Id.*Sol.*15, D.C.64.8, cf. 72.2; ἄνες λόγον speak *more mildly*, E.*Hel.*442; so ἀ. τινὸς ἔχθραν Th.3.10; ἀ. ἀρχήν, πόλεμον, etc., Id.1.76, 7.18, etc.:—Pass., *to be treated remissly*, ἀνεθήσεται τὰ πράγματα Id.8.63; ὁ νόμος ἀνεῖται *has become effete, powerless*, E.*Or.*941: freq. in pf. part. ἀνειμένος as an Adj., ἐν τῷ ἀνειμένῳ τῆς γνώμης when their minds are *not strung up for action*, Th.5.9; ἀνειμένῃ τῇ διαίτῃ *relaxed, unconstrained*, of the Athenians, Id.1.6; δίαιτα λίαν ἀ., of the Ephors, Arist.*Pol.*1270^{b}32; ἀ. ἡδοναί *dissolute*, Pl.*R.*573a; ἄνανδρος καὶ λίαν ἀ. ib.549d; ἀ. χείλεα *parched*, Theoc.22.63; of climate, ἀ. καὶ μαλακός Thphr.*CP*5.4.4; ὀσμὴ μαλακὴ καὶ ἀ. 5.7.1: Comp. ἀνειμενώτερος Iamb.*VP*15.67:—but, 8. the sense of *relaxation* occurs also as an intr. usage of the Act., *slacken, abate*, of the wind, ἐπειδὰν πνεῦμ' ἀνῇ S.*Ph.*639, cf. Hdt.2.113, 4.152; ἕως ἀνῇ τὸ πῆμα S.*Ph.*764, cf. Hdt.1.94; ἐμφῦσα οὐκ ἀνίει, of a viper, having fastened on him she *does* not *let go*, Id.3.109: esp. in phrase οὐδὲν ἀνιέναι not *to give way* at all, X.*HG*2.3.46, cf. *Cyr.*1.4.22; τὰς τιμὰς ἀνεικέναι ἤκουον that prices *had fallen*, D.56.25, cf. Arist.*Rh.*1390^{a}15; σιδήρια ἀ. ἐν τοῖς μαλακοῖς *lose* their *edge*, Thphr.*HP*5.5.1. b. c. part., *give up* or *cease* doing, ὕων οὐκ ἀνίει [ὁ θεός] Hdt.4.28, cf. 125, 2.121.β', E.*IT*318, etc. c. c. gen., *cease from* a thing, μωρίας Id.*Med.*457; τῆς ὀργῆς Ar.*Ra.*700, D.21.186; φιλονικίας Th.5.32; ἀνῆκε τοῦ ἐξελθεῖν *forbore to* come forth, Lxx 1*Ki.*23.13. 9. *dilute, dissolve*, διά τινος or τινί, Gal.13.520, al., *Gp.*4.7.3, cf. Arr.*An.*7.20.5 (Phryn.19 says that διΐημι is more correct in this sense); διυγραινομένων καὶ ἀνιεμένων Thphr.*Vent.*58.

ἀνίηρ· βοτάνη τις, Hsch.

ἀνιηρός, ή, όν, Ion. for ἀνιαρός.

ἁνίκα [ῐ], Dor. for ἡνίκα.

ἀνίκᾰνος [ῐ], ον, *insufficient, incapable*, Babr.92 *Subscr.*, Hld.2.30. 2. *dissatisfied with everything*, Arr.*Epict.*4.1.106.

ἀνῑκεί or **ἀνῑκί**, Adv. *without victory*, D.C.61.21.

ἀνῐκέτευτος, ον, *without prayer, not entreating*, E.*IA*1003.

ἀνίκητος [ῑ], Dor. **-ᾱτος**, ον, *unconquered, unconquerable*, Hes.*Th.*489, Tyrt.11.1, Thgn.491, Pi.*P.*4.91, S.*Ant.*781, *Ph.*78, E.*Andr.* 997, etc. Adv. -τως Phld.*Ir.*p.67 W., Hsch. s.v. ἀτρώτως.—Poet., but used by Gorg.*Fr.*11, Pl.*R.*375b, X.*Cyn.*1.17, and in later Prose, Lxx 2*Ma.*11.13, Plu.*Alex.*14, etc.; λεύκη ἀ., name of a *plaster*, Crito ap.Gal.12.487. II. ἀνίκητον, τό, = ἄνηθον, Plin.*HN*20.186, Ps.-Dsc.3.58. 2. = σμῖλαξ τραχεῖα, Id.4.142.

ἀνῑκία, ἡ, *non-victory*, Pythag. term, f.l. for ἀδικία, Arist.*Metaph.* 990^{a}24, cf. Alex.Aphr. ad loc.

ἀνικμ-άζω, *draw up*, Sch.Nic.*Al.*524:—Pass., *evaporate*, Dsc.4.64:—hence **-αστέον**, Philum.*Ven.*16.6.

ἀνίκμαντος, ον, *unmoistened*, Lyc.988.

ἀνικμάω, *winnow, sift out*, in Pass., Pl.*Ti.*53a (ἀνικλ- Hsch.); cf. ἱκμάω, ἀπικμάω.

ἄνικμος, ον, *without moisture*, Arist.*Pr.*906^{b}19, Plu.2.951b; *sapless*, Thphr.*CP*6.20.2.

ἀνίκω, *attain to*, εἰς δόξαν *SIG*560.16.

ἀνίλαστος [ῐ], ον, *unappeased, merciless*, Plu.2.170c.

ἀνίλεως [ῐ], ων, Att. for ἀνίλαος (not in use), *unmerciful*, *Ep.Jac.* 2.13 (s.v.l.), Hdn.*Epim.*257.

ἀνίλλω, = ἀνείλλω, Phryn.*PS* p.31 B., Olymp. *in Phlb.* p.240 S. :—Pass., *shrink back*, of the soul, Plot.1.6.2, cf. Porph.*Plot.*14.

ἀνίλλωμα, ατος, τό, = ἀνάβλεμμα, Poll.2.54.

ἀνιλυσπάομαι, Dep., *wind one's way* or *struggle upwards*, Hsch.; wrongly written ἀνειλ-.

ἀνῐμ-άω, used by early writers only in pres. and impf. (aor. ἀνίμησα Hierocl.p.63.19 A., Plu.*Phoc.*18), *draw up, raise* water by means of leather straps (ἱμάντες), ἀπὸ τροχιλιᾶς Thphr.*HP* 4.3.5, cf. Hierocl. l. c.; generally, *draw out* or *up*, ἀλλήλους δόρασι ἀνίμων X.*An.*4.2.8, cf. *Eq.*7.2; κάδον Sor.1.93 :—Pass., aor. ἀνῑμήθην App.*Mith.*32, D.L.1.116, Antig.*Mir.*157 : pf. ἀνίμημαι Luc.*Pisc.*50 :—freq. used by later writers in Med., ἀνιμῶμαι Id.*Alex.*14; τῇ προβολῇ φόρτον, of an elephant, Aret.*SD* 2.13; of the sun causing evaporation, *Stoic.*1.35, 2.197, *Gp.*1.13.1 : fut. -ήσομαι Longus 1.12 : aor. -ησάμην Plu.2.773d, Luc.*VH* 2.42, etc. II. seemingly intr. (sc. ἑαυτόν), *get up*, X.*Eq.*7.1. **-ησις**, εως, ἡ, *drawing up*, of water, Simp. *in Ph.*571.6, Suid.

ἄνῑος, ον, = ἀνιαρός, A.*Pers.*256,1055,1061; ἄνιος· ἀνατεπείς (sic), Hsch.

ἀνιοχίων, Dor. (Lacon.) for ἡνιοχέων, *IG* 5(1).213.

ἀνιππεύω, *ride on high*, -οντος ἡλίου E.*Ion* 41.

ἀνιππία, ἡ, *tax paid in lieu of service in cavalry*, *PSI* 4.388.36 (ii B.C.), *PPetr.*2 p.129 (iii B.C.), *PTeb.*99.56 (ii B.C.).

ἄνιππος, ον, *without horse, not serving on horseback*, ἱππόται καὶ ἄνιπποι Hdt.1.215, S.*OC* 899; *without a horse to ride on*, Ar.*Nu.*125, Plb.10.40.10; *unable to ride*, Plu.2.100a. 2. of countries, *unsuited for horses*, ἄ. καὶ ἀναμάξευτος Hdt.2.108, cf. Aen.Tact.8.4, D.H.2.13.

ἀνίπταμαι, = ἀναπέτομαι, Max.Tyr.22.6.

ἀνιπτόπους, ὁ, ἡ, gen. ποδος, *with unwashen feet*, epith. of the Σελλοί, Dodonaean priests of Zeus, Il.16.235, cf. *BCH* 7.276 (Lydia); applied to parasites by Eub.139; to the Great Bear, as *metuens aequore tingi*, by Nonn.*D.*40.285.

ἄνιπτος, ον, *unwashen*, χερσὶ δ' ἀνίπτοισιν (v. l. -ησιν) Διὶ λείβειν.. ἅζομαι Il.6.266, cf. Hes.*Op.*725, *Ev.Matt.*15.20 : prov., ἀ. ποσί, i.e. *unprepared*, Luc.*Pseudol.*4. 2. *not to be washed out*, αἷμα A.*Ag.*1459.

ἄνις, = ἄνευ, Megarian in Ar.*Ach.*798,834, cf. *IG* 14.432 (Tauromenium); also in late Poets, Lyc.350, Nic.*Al.*419, *Epigr.Gr.*418.3.

ἀνῐσ-άζω, *equalize*, Hp.*Vict.*3.85, Arist.*IA* 708ᵇ14, *Cael.*293ᵃ2 :—Pass., ib.297ᵇ12. **-άκις** [ᾰκ], Adv. *an unequal number of times*, Theo Sm.p.26 H., al., Nicom.*Ar.*2.17. **-άριθμος** [ᾰρ], ον, *unequal*, ἐτῶν ὅρον X.*Ep.*3.

ἀνισάριον σπέρμα *aniseed*, Damocr.ap.Gal.14.97,124.

ἀνισασμός, ὁ, *equalization*, Eust.42.6.

ἀνῑσᾶτον, τό, *decoction of aniseed*, Alex.Trall.8.2 : also ἀννησᾶτον Orib.5.33.10 (interpol.).

ἀνῐσεπίπεδος, ον, *having unequal plane faces*, of certain solid numbers, e.g. βωμίσκος (q. v.), Iamb. *in Nic.*p.93 P.

ἀνῐσήλικος, ον, *unequal in age*, Procl. *in Prm.*pp.945,949 S.

ἀνῑσίτης, ου, ὁ, *flavoured with aniseed*, οἶνος *Gp.*8.4 tit.

ἀνῐσο-βᾰρής, ές, *unequal in weight*, Simp. *in Cael.*225.34, Alex.Aphr. *in Top.*166.24,173.18. **-γώνιος**, ον, *having unequal angles*, Iamb. *in Nic.*p.93 P. **-διάστᾰτος**, ον, *having their three dimensions unequal*, ibid. **-δρομος**, ον, *of unequal course*, περίοδοι τῶν ἑπτὰ ἀστέρων Ph.1.143. **-δύνᾰμος** [ῠ], ον, *of unequal strength*, Sch.Heph. p.103 C. **-ειδής**, ές, *of uneven form*, Porph.*VP* 50. **-κρᾰτέω**, *to be unequal in strength*, S.E.*M.*10.28. **-λαμπής**, ές, *shining unequally*, κύκλος *PMag.Par.*1.1132. **-μετρος**, ον, *not commensurate with*, τινί Aret.*SD* 2.2. **-μήκης**, ες, *of unequal length*, Gal.13.545.

ἄνῑσον, τό, v. ἄννησον.

ἀνῐσο-πᾰχέω, *to be of unequal thickness*, Hero *Stereom.*2.59.4. **-πᾰχής**, ές, *of unequal thickness*, Gal.13.545. **-πλᾰτής**, ές, *of unequal breadth*, Euc.*Opt.*6. **-πλευρος**, ον, *scalene*, τρίγωνον Ti.Locr.98a, Theo Sm.p.113 H. **-πληθής**, ές, *unequal in number*, ἀ. γωνίας ἔχειν, of polygons, Papp.308.6. **-ρροπος**, ον, *unequally balanced, unfair*, Plu.*Nob.*6, Phlp. *in Ph.*677.25.

ἄνῐσος, ον (η, ον Aesar.ap.Stob.1.49.27), *unequal, uneven*, Hp.*Fract.*37, Pl.*Ti.*36d, etc.; τὸ ἄ. *inequality*, Arist.*EN* 1129ᵇ1, etc.; ἄ. πολιτεία, of an oligarchy, Aeschin.1.30 : so of persons, οἱ ἄ. Arist.*Pol.*1280ᵃ13; ἄ. κατά τι ib.23; but also, *not content with equality* or *justice, unjust*, Id.*EN* 1129ᵃ33, 1129ᵇ10; *unfair*, χεῖρες *AP* 9.263 (Antiphil.). Adv. *unequally*, Hp.*Art.*61; *unfairly*, ἀ. σχεῖν πρός τινας D.24.168; ἀ. νενεμῆσθαι τὰς ἀρχάς Arist.*Pol.*1282ᵇ24.

ἀνῐσο-σθενής, ές, *of unequal strength*, Gal.5.415. **-σκελής**, ές, *with uneven legs*, Sch.D.P.175; *with tails of unequal length*, of a bandage, Heliod.ap.Orib.48.63 tit. **-στροφος**, ον, *revolving unevenly*, Tz.*H.*10.563. **-τᾰχής**, ές, *unequally rapid*, παλμοί Ph.2.637; φορά Theo Sm.p.189 H. Adv. -ῶς Alex.Aphr. *in Mete.*39.17, Them. *in Ph.*133.11, Procl.*Hyp.*2.14.

ἀνῐσότης, ητος, ἡ, *inequality*, Pl.*Phd.*74c, al., Arist.*Pol.*1302ᵃ26, etc.: pl., Procl.*Hyp.*5.3.

ἀνῐσο-τοιχέω, *to be out of trim, lean over to one side*, metaph. from a ship, Simp. *in Epict.*p.108 D. **-τονος**, *unequally stretched*, βρόχος Heliod.ap.Orib.44.14.2; *not in unison*, Ptol.*Harm.*2.2. **-υψής**, ές, *of unequal height*, Apollod.*Poliorc.*142.5, Hero *Dioptr.*12. **-φυές**· ἀνόμοιον, Hsch. **-χρονος**, ον, *of unequal duration*, Herodic.ap. Orib.8.4.6; in Metric, *composed of unequal times*, Aristid.Quint.1.24.

ἀνῐσόω, *equalize, balance*, Pl.*Plt.*289e; ὁ σίδηρος τοὺς ἀσθενεῖς ἀ. τοῖς ἰσχυροῖς *puts* them *on a par with*.., X.*Cyr.*7.5.65; of *giving* late-comers *an equal share of* wine, *AB* 80, Hsch. (cf. ἀνίσωμα) :—Pass., *to be equal in* a thing, πλήθεϊ ἀνισωθῆναι Hdt.7.103 :—Med., *make oneself equal, contend with*, ζυγαίναις Opp.*H.*5.37. II. *make smooth, level*, στενωπούς J.*BJ* 5.5.1 :—Pass., ibid. B. (ἄνισος) *make unequal*, Phlp. *in Ph.*364.16 (Pass.), Dam.*Pr.*401 (Pass.), Elias *in Cat.*200.22.

ἀνίστημι, A. causal in pres. ἀνίστημι (later **ἀνιστάω** S.E.*M.*9.61) : impf. ἀνίστην : fut. ἀναστήσω, poet. ἀνστήσω : aor. 1 ἀνέστησα, Ep. ἄνστησα, Aeol. 3 pl. ὄστασαν Hsch. : pf. ἀνέστακα Lxx 1 *Ki.*15.12, Arr.*Epict.*1.4.30 : also in aor. 1 Med. ἀνεστησάμην (v. infr. I. 5, III. 6). I. *make to stand up, raise up*, γέροντα δὲ χειρὸς ἀνίστη he *raised* the old man *up* by his hand, Il.24.515, cf. Od.14.319; τί μ' αὖ.. ἐξ ἕδρας ἀνίστατε; S.*Aj.*788; ἀ. τινὰ ἐκ τῆς κλίνης Pl.*Prt.*317e; ὀρθὸν ἀ. τινά X.*Mem.*1.4.11; ἀπὸ τοῦ καθαρμοῦ τινα D.18.259. 2. *raise from sleep, wake up*, Il.10.32, etc.; εἰς ἐκκλησίαν ἀ. τινά Ar.*Ec.*740; ἀ. τινὰ ὠμόϋπνον Eup.305 : metaph., ἀ. νόσον S.*Tr.*979. 3. *raise from the dead*, οὐδέ μιν ἀνστήσεις Il.24.551, cf. A.*Ag.*1361, S.*El.*139; from misery or misfortune, Id.*Ph.*666, Aeschin.1.67. 4. *produce* a witness, etc. (cf. III. 6), προφήτην ὑμῖν ἀ. ὁ Θεός *Act.Ap.*3.22, al. 5. after Hom., also of things, *set up, build*, στήλας v.l. in Hdt.2.102; πύργους X.*Cyr.*7.5.12, etc.; τρόπαια Διί E.*Ph.*572; ἀνδριάντα ἐς Δελφοὺς Philipp.ap.D.12.21; so ἀ. τινὰ χρυσοῦν, χαλκοῦν (in pure Attic ἱστάναι), *set up* a golden, brazen *statue* of him, Plu.2.170e, *Brut.*1 (Pass., v. infr. B) :—so in aor. 1 Med., ἀναστήσασθαι πόλιν *build oneself* a city, Hdt.1.165; ἀνεστήσαντο δὲ βωμούς *they set them up* altars, Call.*Dian.*199. b. *build up again, restore*, τείχη D.20.68 : metaph., θεῶν τιμάς E.*HF* 852. 6. *put up for sale*, Hdt.1.196. II. *rouse to action, stir up*, ἀλλ' ἴθι νῦν Αἴαντα.. ἄνστησον Il.10.176, cf. 179, 15.64, etc. : c. dat. pers., *raise up against* another, τούτῳ δὲ πρόμον ἄλλον ἀναστήσουσιν ib.7.116 (v. infr. B. I. 5) : *rouse to arms, raise* troops, Th.2.68,96; ἀ. πόλεμον ἐπί τινα Plu.*Cor.*21; ἀναστήσας ἦγε στρατόν he *called up* his troops and marched them, Th.4.93, cf. 112, etc. III. *make* people *rise, break up* an assembly *by force*, Il.1.191; but ἐκκλησίαν ἀναστῆσαι *adjourn* it, X.*HG* 2.4.42. 2. *make* people *emigrate, transplant* (cf. infr. B. II. 2), ἔνθεν ἀναστήσας ἄγε Od.6.7; ἀνίστασαν τοὺς δήμους Hdt.9.73; Αἰγινήτας ἐξ Αἰγίνης Th.2.27; even γαῖαν ἀναστήσειν A.R.1.1349; οἴκους Plu.*Publ.*21; also ἀ. τινὰ ἐκ τῆς ἐργασίας D.18.129. 3. *make* suppliants *rise and leave sanctuary*, Hdt.5.71, Th.1.137, S.*OC* 276, etc. : also ἀ. στρατόπεδον ἐκ χώρας *make* an army *decamp*, Plb.29.27.10; τὰ πράγματα ἀνίστησί τινα Plu.*Alc.*31. 4. ἀ. ἐπὶ τὸ βῆμα *make to ascend* the tribune, Id.2.784c, cf. *Cam.*32. 5. of sportsmen, *put up* game, X.*An.*1.5.3, cf. *Cyr.*2.4.20 (Pass.), *Cyn.*6.23, D.Chr.2.2. 6. μάρτυρα ἀναστήσασθαί τινα *call* him *as one's* witness, Pl.*Lg.*937a.

B. intr. in pres. and impf. ἀνίσταμαι, -μην, in fut. ἀναστήσομαι, in aor. 2 ἀνέστην (but ἀναστῶ, for ἀναστήσω, Crates Com.4 D.), imper. ἄστηθι (for ἄν-στηθι) Herod.8.1, part. ἀστάς *IG* 4.951.112 (Epid.) : pf. ἀνέστηκα, Att. plpf. ἀνεστήκη; also pf. ἀνεστέασι Hdt.3.62 : aor. Pass. ἀνεστάθην, Aeol. part. ὀσταθείς Hsch. :—*stand up, rise*, esp. to speak, τοῖσι δ' ἀνέστη Il.1.68,101, etc.; ἐν μέσσοισι 19.77 : in Att. c. fut. part., ἀ. λέξων, κατηγορήσων, etc. : so c. inf., ἀνέστη μαντεύεσθαι Od.20.380 : in part., ἀναστὰς εἶπε E.*Or.*885; παραινέσεις ἐποιοῦντο ἐν σφίσιν αὐτοῖς ἀνιστάμενοι Th.8.76; also, *rise from one's seat* as a mark of respect, θεοὶ δ' ἅμα πάντες ἀνέσταν Il.1.533; ἀπὸ βωμοῦ (cf. A. III. 3) Aeschin.1.84. 2. *rise from bed* or *sleep*, ἐξ εὐνῆς ἀνστᾶσα Il.14.336, cf. A.*Eu.*124; εὐνῆθεν Od.20.124; ὄρθρου ἀ. Hes.*Op.*577; ὀψὲ Ar.*V.*217; οὐδ' ἀνιστάμην ἐκ κλίνης, of a sick person, And.1.64 : abs., *rise from sleep*, Hdt.1.31. 3. *rise from the dead*, Il.21.56, cf. 15.287, Hdt.3.62, A.*Ag.*569; παρὰ τῶν πλειόνων Ar.*Ec.*1073. 4. *rise from* an illness, *recover*, ἐκ τῆς νούσου Hdt.1.22, cf. Pl.*La.*195c : abs., Th.2.49. 5. *rise* as a champion, Il.23.709; θανάτων χώρᾳ πύργος ἀνέστα [Oedipus] S.*OT* 1201 : hence c. dat., *stand up* [to fight against..], Ἀγκαῖον.., ὅς μοι ἀνέστη Il.23.635; μή τίς τοι.. ἄλλος ἀναστῇ Od.18.334; Τυφῶνα θοῦρον πᾶσιν ὃς ἀνέστη θεοῖς A.*Pr.*354 codd.; v. supr. A. II. 6. *rise up, rear itself*, πύργοι E.*Ph.*824 (lyr.), cf. Plb.16.1.5; of statues, etc., *to be set up*, Plu.2.91a, 198f : metaph., μή τι ἐξ αὐτῶν ἀναστῇ κακόν Pi.*P.*4.155; πόλεμος D.H.3.23; θορύβου ἀναστάντος App.*BC* 1.56. 7. *to be set up*, βασιλεύς as king, Hdt.3.66 codd. 8. of a river, *rise*, ἐξ ὀρέων Plu.*Pomp.*34. 9. pf. part., γῇ γηλόφοισιν ἀνεστηκυῖα Arr.*Ind.*4.7 : metaph., *lofty*, ἀ. τὴν ψυχὴν γενόμενος Eun.*Hist.*p.233 D. II. *rise to go, set out, go away*, εἰς Ἄργος E.*Heracl.*59, cf. Th.1.87, 7.49,50; ἀνίστατο εἰς οἴκημά τι ὡς λουσόμενος Pl.*Phd.*116a. 2. *to be compelled to migrate* (supr. A. III. 2), ἐξ Ἄρνης ἀναστάντες ὑπὸ Θεσσαλῶν Th.1.12, cf. 8 : of a country, *to be depopulated*, χώρα ἀνεστηκυῖα Hdt.5.29; πόλις.. πᾶσ' ἀνέστηκεν δορί E.*Hec.*494; ἡσυχάσασα ἡ Ἑλλὰς καὶ οὐκέτι ἀνισταμένη no longer *subject to migration*, Th.1.12; τὴν ἀσφάλειαν.. περιειδέτ' ἀνασταθεῖσαν D.19.84. 3. of a law-court, *rise*, Id.21.221. 4. *cease*, οὐκ ἀνέστη ἕως ἐνίκησε σκορπίσαι *Psalm.Solom.*4.13.

ἀνιστορ-έω, *make inquiry into, ask about*, ἄρνησις οὐκ ἔνεστιν ὧν ἀνιστορεῖς S.*OT* 578 : c. acc. pers. et rei, *ask* a person *about* a thing, πεύσει γὰρ οὐδὲν ὧν (= ἐκείνων ἃ) ἀνιστορεῖς ἐμέ A.*Pr.*963, cf. S.*OC* 991, *Ph.*253; σε.. ἀνιστορῶ E.*Supp.*110; ἀ. τινὰ περί τινος Id.*Hipp.*92; *investigate*, τι Thphr.*CP* 1.5.5. **-ησία**, ἡ, *ignorance of history*, Cic.*Att.*6.1.17. **-ητος**, ον, *ignorant of history, uninformed*, περί τινος Plb.12.3.2; τινός Phld.*Rh.*1.188S., Arr.*Epict.*1.6.23, cf. D. Chr.12.59. Adv. -τως, ἔχειν τινός Plu.*Demetr.*1. II. *uninvestigated*, Ph.*Bel.*78.36; *unrecorded*, Phld.*Mus.*p.28K., Plu.2.731c; χώρα, ἰδέαι ὀρνέων, Agatharch.58,84.

ἀνίστωρ, ορος, ὁ, ἡ, late form for ἀΐστωρ, Tz.*H.*3.272.

ἀνίσχαλος· ἄτοκος, ἀνήμελκτος, ἀθήλαστος, *EM*110.32, cf. Hsch. s.v. σχαλίσαι (-αδον *EM*739.43, Suid.).

ἀνισχάνω, like ἀνέχω, poet. for ἀνέχω, Orph.*A.*445.

ἀνίσχιος, ον, *without prominent haunches*, Arist.*HA*499^{b}1.

ἀνίσχ-ῡρος, ον, *not strong, without strength*, Str.2.1.36, v.l. in D.H.4.54, Sch.Theoc.14.15: Comp., ῥῖγος -ότερον Hp.*Flat.*8; *invalid*, of a document, ἄκυρος καὶ ἀ. *PSI*183.9 (v A.D.), Just.*Nov.*72.5. **-ῡρότης**, ητος, ἡ, *want of strength, Gloss.* **-υς**, υ, gen. υος, *without strength*, Lxx *Is.*40.30.

ἀνίσχω, v. sub ἀνέχω.

ἀνίσωμα, ατος, τό, = ἐπίστιος, ἡ, prob. in Ath.10.447a; cf. ἀνισόω.

ἀνίσωσις [ῐ], εως, ἡ, *equalization*, Th.8.87, Pl.*Lg.*740e. II. (ἀ- priv.) *inequality*, Mich.*in EN*15.22.

ἀνῐσωτέον, *one must make equal*, Aristid.1.423J.

ἀνῐτέον, verb. Adj. of ἄνειμι, *one must return*, ὅθεν ἐξέβημεν D.H.*Lys.*13.

ἀνῑΰζω, *squeal*, of swine, Q.S.11.177.

ἄνιχθυς, υ, gen. υος, *without fish*, λίμνη Str.16.1.21.

ἀνίχν-ευσις, εως, ἡ, *tracing out, investigation*, Eust.1437.16. **-ευτος**, ον, *not tracked*, Luc.*Am.*35; βυθοί Ps.-Callisth.2.38. **-εύω**, (ἀνά, ἰχνεύω) *track*, as a hound, Il.22.192, cf. Arist.*HA*624^{a}28 (of bees), *AP*5.301 (Agath.), Porph.*Sent.*43, Jul.*Or.*6.183b: generally, *trace out, search out*, Plu.*Caes.*69; χέρσον ἀ. Lyc.824:—also **ἀνιχνεῖν**, *Epigr.Gr.*270.

ἀνίψᾰλος, ον, (ἵπτομαι) *unhurt*, Stes.76 (v.l. ἀνίψανον).

ἀνίωτος [ῐ], ον, (ἰόω) *not liable to rust*, Arist.*Mir.*833^{b}31, *PLeid.X.*36B.

ἀννεῖται, Ep. for ἀνανεῖται, from ἀνανέομαι.

ἀννέφελος, Ep. for ἀνέφελος.

ἀννήθιον, τό, = neut. of ἀνήθινος, *POxy.*1923.13 (v/vi A.D.).

ἀννησοειδής, ές, *like* ἄννησον: neut., = κώνειον, Hsch., Sch.Nic.*Al.*186.

ἄννησον or **ἄνησσον** (*PSI*4.422.28 (iii B.C.), Dsc.3.56), τό, *anise, Pimpinella Anisum*, Hdt.4.71, Hp.*Acut.*23, Thphr.*HP*1.11.2, 1.12.1 (prob.), Alex.127.7, Nic.*Th.*650, Phaenias ap.Ath.9.371d, *POxy.*1088.67 (i A.D.), Bilabel Ὀψαρτ.p.10.—ἄννισον, ἄνισον, and ἄνησον are variants in codd.

Ἀννιβαϊκός, ή, όν, *of* or *for Hannibal*, Plb.2.71.9, D.S.2.5.

Ἀννιβίζω, *side with Hannibal*, Plu.*Marc.*10.

ἀννίς· μητρὸς ἢ πατρὸς μήτηρ, Hsch.

ἄννισον, τό, v. ἄννησον.

ἀννωδέως· τρυφερῶς, σοβαρῶς, Hsch. **ἄννωμα**· θρυπτόμενα, (Tarent.), Id.

ἀννων-αρχέω, *to be curator annonae*, *IGRom.*3.1412. **-εακὸν** φρόντισμα, = *cura annonae*, Lyd.*Mag.*3.38. **-έπαρχος**, ὁ, *praefectus annonae*, *PFlor.*75.20 (iv A.D.). **-εύομαι**, Pass., *to have as an allowance* (*annona*), ἀ. καθ' ἑκάστην ἡμέραν ἄρτους μβ' *OGI*200.20 (Axum). **-η**, ἡ, = Lat. *annona*, *CIG*4447 (Syria), *OGI*200.16 (Axum), *POxy.*1192.4 (iii A.D.), al. **-ιακός**, ή, όν, *belonging to the annona*, εἴδη *PFlor.*377.15 (vi A.D.). **-ικός**, ή, όν, *concerning the annona*, *PLips.*6 ii 11.

ἀνόδευτος, ον, *impassable*, Aq.*Je.*18.15; πεζῇ φήσαντος ἀνόδευτα εἶναι στρατοπέδοις Str.16.4.23, cf. App.*BC*4.106. II. *trackless*, χεῦμα Hedyl.ap.Str.14.6.3; ἐρημίαι Lyd.*Mag.*1.50.

ἀνοδηγέω, *guide back*, dub. l. in Babr.95.55.

ἀνοδία, ἡ, *a road that is no road*, ὁδὸν ἢ κυριώτερον εἰπεῖν ἀνοδίαν Ph.2.156, al.; ἐρήμην ἀνοδίαν ἑαυτοῖς συντεμεῖν Porph.*Chr.*1; mostly in dat. ἀνοδίᾳ, ἀνοδίαις, *through places with no roads*, Plb.5.13.6, 4.57.8, D.S.19.5, Plu.2.508d, cf. *Mar.*37. II. *ascent*, ἀνοδίαι καὶ στάσεις τοῦ ἡλίου Vett.Val.343.18.

ἄνοδμος, ον, *without smell, having no smell*, Hp.*Acut.*63 (vv. ll. ἄνοσμος, ἄοσμος), Arist.*Pr.*873^{a}2.

ἀνόδοντος, ον, = ἀνόδων, Pherecr.74,82.

ἄνοδος (A), ον, *having no way* or *road, impassable*, ὁδοὶ ἄ. E.*IT* 889 (lyr.); opp. εὔοδος, X.*An.*4.8.10.

ἄνοδος (B), ἡ, *way up*, e.g. to the Acropolis at Athens, Hdt.8.53; τὴν ἄ. οἰκοδομήσασα *CIG*1948 (incert. loc.): metaph., ἡ εἰς τὸν νοητὸν τόπον τῆς ψυχῆς ἄ. Pl.*R.*517b, cf. Phld.*D.*1.6. b. *journey inland*, esp. into Central Asia, like ἀνάβασις, τριῶν μηνῶν ἄ. Hdt.5.50; ἄ. παρὰ βασιλέα ib.51, cf. X.*An.*2.1.1. 2. *rising*, τοῦ ὑγροῦ Arist.*Mete.*355^{a}6; *rising* of a star, κατηλυσίη τ' ἄνοδός τε Arat.536; *slope of a hill*, Plb.5.24.4. II. the first (or second) day of the Thesmophoria, Alciphr.3.39, cf. Sch.Ar.*Th.*86, Hsch. III. *ascent* of the soul to its original source, Hierocl. *in CA*24p.471M. IV. Math., *increasing progression, Theol.Ar.*58.

ἀνόδων, οντος, ὁ, ἡ, *toothless*, Arist.*PA*674^{b}20, *Fr.*294.

ἀνοδύρομαι [ῡ], *break into wailing*, E.*Hyps.Fr.*1 iv 7, X.*Cyr.*5.1.6, Plu.2.123c.

ἀνόδυρτος, ον, *not mourning*, *Trag.Adesp.*303.

ἀνόζεστα· τὰ μὴ ἐζεσμένα, Hsch. (fort. ἀπόζεστα).

ἄνοζος, ον, *with no*, or *very few, branches*, Thphr.*HP*1.8.1, etc.: Comp. -ότερος ib.3.13.3:—also **ἄοζος**, ον, ib.1.5.4, al.

ἀνό-ημα, ατος, τό, *a foolish act*, f.l. for ἀνόμημα, *Stoic.*3.136. **-ήμων**, ον, gen. ονος, *without understanding*, Od.2.270, 17.273, Democr.197, al. **-ησία**, ἡ, *want of understanding*, Suid. s.v. ἀβέλτερος. 2. opp. νόησις, *un-knowing*, i.e. mystical vision, θεωρεῖται ἀνοησίᾳ κρείττονι νοήσεως Porph.*Sent.*25. 3. *mindlessness*, ib.44. **-ηταίνω**, *to be devoid of intelligence*, Pl.*Phlb.*12d, Henioch.5, Plot.5.5.1; opp. νοεῖν, 2.9.1:—also **-ητεύω**, Sch.Ar.*Nu.*1480. **-ητία**, ἡ, Att. for ἀνοησία, Ar.*Fr.*746, cf. Moer.28. **-ητος**, ον, *not thought on, unheard of*, ἄφραστ' ἠδ' ἀνόητα *h.Merc.*80. 2. *not within the province of thought*, νοήματα ὄντα ἀνόητα εἶναι Pl.*Prm.*132c; *not the object of thought, unthinkable*, Plot.5.3.6 and 10. Adv. -τως *without discursive thought*, of vision, βλέψαι ἀ. Id.6.7.16. II. Act., *not understanding, unintelligent, senseless, silly*, Hdt.1.87, 8.24; ὦ ἀνόητοι oh *fools!* Ar.*Lys.*572; ὠνόητε Id.*V.*252; opp. προνοητικός, X.*Mem.*1.3.9: Comp. -ότερος Luc.*Peregr.*33; τὸ ἀ., opp. τὸ νοῦν ἔχον, Pl.*Ti.*30b; τῷ θνητῷ καὶ ἀ. Id.*Phd.*80b; τὸ ἀ. [τῆς ψυχῆς] Id.*R.*605b, etc.:—of animals, τὸ τῶν προβάτων ἦθος εὔηθες καὶ ἀ. Arist.*HA* 610^{b}23, cf. 622^{a}3. b. c. gen., *not understanding*, θεοῦ Max.Tyr.41.5; τῆς φωνῆς Luc.*Asin.*44, cf. Ecphant.ap.Stob.4.7.64. 2. of acts, thoughts, etc., ἀ. γνῶμαι S.*Aj.*162 (lyr.); δόξαι Pl.*Phlb.*12d; εὐχειρίη Hp.*Art.*35; ἀ. καὶ κενόν Ar.*Ra.*530; οἴνου..καὶ τῶν ἄλλων ἀνοήτων and all other *follies*, Id.*Nu.*417. b. *without mind*, ἀνόητα καὶ ἄνευ ζωῆς Plot.5.5.1. III. Adv. -τως Ar.*Lys.*518, Pl.*R.*336e, etc.; ἀ. διακεῖσθαι Lys.10.4: Sup. -ότατα D.C.44.35:—also -ητεί, *AB*1327, *An.Ox.*2.313.

ἀνόθευτος, ον, *pure, genuine*, χρυσίον Ps.-Plu.*Fluv.*7.4: metaph., μαρτυρία D.S.1.72; βίος Ph.2.267; φίλος Gal.14.7. II. *free from adultery*, γάμος Arist.*Mir.*846^{a}30, Ps.-Plu.*Fluv.*5.2.

ἀνόθηρον· νωθρόν, Hsch.

ἄνοθος, ον, = ἀνόθευτος, *pure, genuine, unadulterated*, εὔνοια Ph.1.454; κάλλος 2.156. Adv. -θως ib.216, al., Hsch.

ἄνοια, Ep. ἀνοίη Thgn.453, ἡ:—*the character of an* ἄνοος, *want of understanding, folly*, ἀνοίῃ *in folly*, Hdt.6.69; ὑπ' ἀνοίας A.*Pr.*1079, Philem.143; νεότητι καὶ ἀνοίᾳ Pl.*Lg.*716a; ἄ. λόγου S.*Ant.*603; τὴν ἄ. εὖ φέρειν E.*Hipp.*398; πολλῇ ἀνοίᾳ χρῆσθαι to be *a* great *fool*, Antipho 3.3.2; πολλὴ ἄ. [ἐστι] πολεμῆσαι Th.2.61; ἄνοιαν ὀφλισκάνειν to be thought *a fool*, D.1.26; δύο ἀνοίας γένη, τὸ μὲν μανίαν, τὸ δ' ἀμαθίαν Pl.*Ti.*86b; but opp. μανία, Id.*R.*382c, e, etc.: pl., *follies*, Isoc.8.7. [In Trag. sts. paroxyt. ἀνοίᾱ (cf. ἀγνοίᾱ), cf. A.*Th.*402, S.*Fr.*583.5, E.*Andr.*519.]

ἀνοιγ-εύς, έως, ὁ, *opener*, Dam.*Pr.*125 ter. **-μα**, ατος, τό, *opening, door*, Lxx 3*Ki.*14.6 (cod. Alex.); *valve*, Zos.Alch.p.225B., etc. II. ἄ. σφαίρας, used of the *diameter* of a sphere, *IGRom.*4.503.12 (Pergam.). **-νῡμι** Lys.12.10; **ἀνοίγω** Pi.*P.*5.88, Hdt.3.37,117, and Att. as *IG*1.32 (συν-), al.: later **ἀνοιγνύω** Demetr.*Eloc.*122, Paus.8.41.4: impf. ἀνέῳγον Il.16.221, al., Hdt.1.187, etc.; also ἀνῷγον Il.14.168; rarely ἤνοιγον X.*HG*1.1.2 and 6.21; Ion. and Ep. ἀναοίγεσκον Il.24.455; late ἀνεῴγνυον App.*BC*4.81, etc.: fut. ἀνοίξω Ar.*Pax*179: aor. ἀνέῳξα Id.*V.*768, Th.2.2, Hp.*Vict.*2.56, part. ἀνεῴξας *CIG*(add.)4300*d* (Antiphellus); also ἤνοιξα X.*HG*1.5.13 and in late Prose; Ion. ἄνοιξα Hdt.1.68 (best codd. ἀνῷξα), 4.143, 9.118; poet. ἀνῷξα Theoc.14.15, κἀνῷξε Phld.*Acad.Ind.*p.103M.: pf. ἀνέῳχα D.42.30, Men.229; ἀνέῳγα Aristaenet.2.22 (v. infr.): plpf. ἀνεῴγει Pherecr.86 (Pors.):—**Pass., ἀνοίγνῡμαι** E.*Ion*923, Ar.*Eq.*1326: late fut. ἀνοιχθήσομαι Lxx *Is.*60.11, Epict.*Ench.*33.13 (v.l.); ἀνοιγήσομαι Lxx *Ne.*7.3, *PMag.Par.*1.358; ἀνεῴξομαι X.*HG*5.1.14: pf. ἀνέῳγμαι E.*Hipp.*56, Th.2.4, etc.; ἀνῷγμαι Theoc.14.47; later ἤνοιγμαι (δι-) best reading in Hp.*Epid.*7.80, cf. J.*Ap.*2.9; plpf. ἀνέῳκτο X.*HG*5.1.14 (pf. 2 ἀνέῳγα is used in pass. sense in Hp.*Morb.*4.39, *Cord.*7, and later Prose, as Plu.2.693d, *Ev.Jo.*1.51, 2*Ep.Cor.*6.11, Luc.*Nav.*4 (though he condemns it *Soloec.*8); but in Att., only Din.*Fr.*81): aor. ἀνεῴχθην E.*Ion*1563, subj. ἀνοιχθῇ D.44.37, opt. ἀνοιχθείην Pl.*Phd.*59d, part. ἀνοιχθείς Th.4.130, Pl.*Smp.*216d; later ἠνοίχθην Paus.2.35.7, Lxx *Ps.*105(106).17; and aor. 2 ἠνοίγην *Ev.Marc.*7.35, Luc.*Am.*14, etc.—In late Gr., very irreg. forms occur, ἠνέῳξα Lxx *Ge.*8.6; ἠνέῳχα *PMag.Par.*1.2261; ἠνέῳγμαι *Apoc.*10.8, Hld.9.9; ἠνεῴχθην Lxx *Ge.*7.11; also aor. 1 inf. ἀνῶξαι Q.S.12.331; ἀνῴχθην Nonn.*D.*7.317:—*open*, of doors, etc., ἀναοίγεσκον μεγάλην κληῗδα *they tried to put back* the bolt *so as to open* [the door], Il.24.455, cf. 14.168; πύλας ἀνοῖξαι A.*Ag.*604; θύραν Ar.*V.*768; also without θύραν, ἐπειδὴ αὐτῷ ἀνέῳξέ τις Pl.*Prt.*310b, cf. 314d; χηλοῦ δ' ἀπὸ πῶμ' ἀνέῳγε *took off* the cover *and opened* it, Il.16.221; φωριαμῶν ἐπιθήματα κάλ' ἀνέῳγεν 24.228; so ἀ. σορόν, θήκας, Hdt.1.68,187; κιβωτὸν Lys.12.10; ἀ. σήμαντρα, σημεῖα, διαθήκην, *open* seals, etc., X.*Lac.*6.4, D.42.30, Plu.*Caes.*68; and metaph., καθαρὰν ἀνοίξαντι κλῇδα φρενῶν E.*Med.*660; ἀ. βίβλινον (sc. οἶνον) *tap* it, Theoc.14.15; γῆρυν ἀνοίξας, for στόμα, Tryph.477; ἀ. φιλήματα kiss *with open mouths*, Ach.Tat.2.37. b. *throw open* for use, γυμνάσιον *OGI*529.11; κἀνῷξε σχολὰς *opened* school, Phld.*Acad.Ind.*p.103M.; εἰ ἀνοίξω ἐργαστήριον; shall I *open* a shop? Astramps.*Orac.*43p.5H. 2. metaph., *lay open, unfold, disclose*, ὄνομα A.*Supp.*322; ἔργ' ἀναιδῆ S.*OC*515, cf. E.*IA* 326; λανθάνουσαν ἀτυχίαν Men.674. 3. as nautical term, abs., *get into the open sea, get clear of land*, X.*HG*1.1.2, 5.13, 6.21; but ἁλὸς κέλευθον ἀ. Pi.*P.*5.88 is *to open* or *first show* the way over the sea. II. Pass., *to be open, stand open, lie open*, ὄπισθε τῆς ἀνοιγομένης θύρης Hdt.1.9; ἀνεῳγμένην καταλαμβάνειν τὴν θύραν Pl.*Smp.*174e; ἀνεῳγμένας πύλας Ἅιδου E.*Hipp.*56; δικαστήρια ἀνοίγεται Pl.*R.*405a; παρέξει ταμπόρι' ἀνεῳγμένα Ar.*Av.*1523; ἀνέῳκται τὸ δεσμωτήριον D.24.208; λέων τὰ ἐντὸς ἀνοιχθεὶς *cut open*, Arist.*HA*497^{b}17; κόλποι δι' ἀλλήλων ἀνοιγόμενοι *opening* one into another, Plu.*Crass.*4: metaph., θησαυρὸς ὡς ἀνοίγνυται κακῶν E.*Ion*923.

ἀνοιδ-αίνω, *blow up, inflate*, Poll.4.179: aor. inf. ἀνοιδῆναι Q.S. 14.470. II. intr., = ἀνοιδέω, Nic.*Fr*.68.7. **-ανσις**, εως, ἡ, = ἀνοίδησις, *dilatation*, opp. συστολή, Plot.4.5.7 (pl.). **-έω**, Ep. **-είω** Nic.*Th*.855: fut. -ήσω: aor. ἀνῴδησα E.*Hipp*.1210, Pl.*Ti*.84e: pf. ἀνῴδηκα Hp.*Acut*.10:—*swell up*, Hp. l. c.; of a wave, E. l. c., cf. Alciphr.1.10; of wind in the body, Pl. l. c.; of figs ripening, Nic. l. c.; τὰ στέρνα ἀνῴδει Aeschin.*Ep*.1.2; τὸ κάλυμμα ἀνῳδηκός *swollen out, inflated*, Arist.*HA*625^{a}2, cf. *GA*728^{b}28. 2. metaph., θυμὸς ἀνοιδέει Hdt.7.39; ὀργαῖς..-ούσαις Phld.*Ir*.p.63 W.; of anger, ἀνοιδήσας ὁ βασιλεύς Philostr.*VA*7.33 (so in Med., θυμὸν ἀνοιδήσαντο they *swelled* with rage, Q.S.9.345); ἀνοιδούσης τῆς νόσου Philostr.*VA*4.4. **-ησις**, εως, ἡ, *swelling, intumescence*, τῶν μαστῶν Arist.*HA*574^{b}16, al.; θαλάσσης Id.*Mu*.399^{a}27 (pl.). **-ίσκω**, *make to swell*, σῖτον Thphr. *CP*4.13.7:—Pass., = ἀνοιδέω, Hp.*Acut*.10.

ἀνοίκ-ειος, ον, *not of the family*, S.E.*P*.1.67: Comp. -ότερος *less closely related*, Phlp.*in Ph*.256.14. II. *unfitting, unseasonable*, Cic.*Att*.16.11.4, D.S.3.56, Plu.2.102a: c. gen., *foreign to, incongruous with*, Epicur.*Ep*.3 p.60 U., Plb.6.10.1, 24.5.13, D.S.12.21: c. dat., *dissimilar to*, Plb.5.96.8; *alien from*, κενοδοξίᾳ Porph.*Antr*.4 (Sup.): abs., Phld.*Po*.1676.9, Id.*D*.3.8 (Comp.). Adv. -ως, ῥηθῆναι Simp.*in Ph*.350.27. III. Astrol., *not in its domicile*, Vett.Val. 50.2. Adv. -ως Id.44.5. **-ειότης**, ητος, ἡ, *ineptitude*, Eustr.*in EN*364.18. 2. *incongruity*, Iamb.*Myst*.1.4. **-είωτος**, ον, *not to be adapted, alien*, ἀλλήλοις M.Ant.12.30. **-ῆ**· παρὰ τὸ εἰκὸς εἰρημένον, *EM*110.55, cf. Hsch. s. v. ἀνοκηδεολόγον. **-ητος**, ον, = ἀοίκητος, Hdt.4.31. **-ίζω**, *remove up the country*, ἀ. τὴν Σπάρτην, i. e. *break it up* as a city, Arist.*Rh.Al*.1423^{a}7; ἀ. τινὰς ἐς τὴν Περσίδα Paus.1.25.5, cf. Str.13.3.3; ἀ. [τέττιγας] φθόνου ἐς δένδρα *remove* them *out of* envy's *way*, dub. in Philostr.*VA*7.11 (leg. ἀπ-):—Pass. and Med., *shift one's dwelling up the country, migrate inland* or *to higher ground*, αὐτοὶ δ' ἀνῳκίσανθ' ὅπως ἀνωτάτω Ar.*Pax* 207, cf. *Av*. 1351, Str.9.2.17, App.*Pun*.84; and of cities, *to be built inland* or *away from the coast*, Th.1.7:—generally, *migrate*, ἀνοικίσασθαι εἰς Ὄλυνθον Id.1.58, cf. 8.31. II. *resettle, colonize afresh*, Paus.2.1.2, Memn. 60 (Med.); *rebuild*, Aps.pp.239, 245 H.:—Pass., *to be repeopled*, Plu. *Luc*.29. **-ισις**, εως, ἡ, *shifting* people *upward and inland*, App. *Pun*.84. **-ισμός**, ὁ, = foreg., Str.9.2.17, prob. in Ph.2.526. II. *rebuilding, restoration*, πόλεων Hdn.3.6.9.

ἀνοικο-δεσποτήτος, ον, Astrol., *without a dominant planet*, Vett. Val.134.17, 151.5. **-δομέω**, *build up*, τὰ χείλεα τοῦ ποταμοῦ.. ἀνοικοδόμησε πλίνθοισι Hdt.1.186. 2. *wall up*, λαύρας καιναῖς πλίνθοισιν ἀ. Ar.*Pax* 100; θύραν Lycurg.128; πύλας dub. l. in D.S.11. 21 (in this sense ἀποικ- is a freq. v. l.). II. *build again, rebuild*, πόλιν καὶ τείχη Th.1.89, cf. Jusj.ap.Lycurg.81, X.*HG*4.4.19, etc.; ἀ. χώραν *occupy again with buildings*, D.S.15.66:—Pass., metaph., *to be exalted*, Lxx *Ma*.3.15. **-δομή**, ἡ, *rebuilding, restoration*, *PLond*.2.216.18 (i A. D.), *PAmh*.93.19 (ii A. D.); Dor. **-μά** *IG*12(1).9 (Rhodes). **-δόμησις**, εως, ἡ, = foreg., Arist.*Ath*.23.4. **-δομία**, ἡ, *building up*, *IG*4.823.6 (Troezen), Sch.Th.8.90. **-νόμητος**, ον, *not set in order, unarranged*, Macho ap.Ath.8.341b, Longin.33. 5. II. Act., *managing badly*, Plu.2.517e, v. l. in Gell.12.12.4.

ἄνοικος, ον, *houseless, homeless*, ἄ. ποιέειν τινά Hdt.3.145; cf. ἄοικος.

ἀνοικτεί or **-τί**, Adv. = ἀνοίκτως, Hdn.*Epim*.257.

ἀνοικτέον, *one must open*, E.*Ion* 1387.

ἀνοικτές· ἀταλαιπώρητον, Hsch.

ἀνοίκ-της, ου, ὁ, *one who opens*, A.D.*Synt*.324.6. **-τικός**, ή, όν, *fit for opening*, Lyd.*Mens*.4.64: -κόν *means of opening* the mouth, Orib.*Fr*.48.

ἀνοικτίρμων, ον, gen. ονος, *pitiless, merciless*, S.*Fr*.659.8, *AP*7. 303 (Antip. Sid.).

ἀνοίκτιστος, ον, *unmourned*, σῶμα [Arist.]*Pepl*.28. II. Act., *pitiless*, Περσεφόνης θάλαμοι *IG*2.3765 (*Supp*.p.283). Adv. -τως Antipho 1.25.

ἀνοικτός, ή, όν, *capable of being opened*, Babr.59.11, Luc.*VH*1.24.

ἄνοικτος, ον, *pitiless, ruthless*, E.*Tr*.787, Ar.*Th*.1022. Adv. -τως *without pity, without being pitied*, S.*OT*180, E.*Tr*.756: also ἀνοίκτρως Ant.Lib.39 (s. v. l.).

ἀνοιμ-ώζω, *wail aloud*, A.*Pers*.465, Th.3.113, Telecl.1 D. **-ωκτί** [ῐ], Adv. *without need to wail, with impunity*, S.*Aj*.1227; *without wailing*, Philostr.Jun.*Im*.10. **-ωκτος**, ον, *unmourned, unlamented*, A.*Ch*.433, 511.

ἄνοινος, ον, = ἄοινος, Hdn.*Epim*.216.

ἄνοιξις, εως, ἡ, *opening*, πυλῶν Th.4.67, 68; πόρων Thphr.*Od*. 13; χειλῶν Plu.2.738c, cf. *PMag.Lond*.46.274 (iv A. D.): pl., Porph. *Antr*.27; ἄ. τοῦ στόματος, Hebraism for παρρησία, Lxx *Ez*.29.21, 2 *Ep.Cor*.6.11, *Ep.Eph*.6.19, etc.

ἄνοισ-ις, εως, ἡ, (ἀναφέρω, ἀνοίσω) *bringing back*, Suid. **-τέος**, α, ον, *to be referred*, E.*Fr*.970. II. ἀνοιστέον *one must carry back* or *report*, S.*Ant*.272, E.*HF*1221:—*one must refer*, τι πρός τι Plu. *Phoc*.5; ἐπί τι Thphr.*CP*4.11.8. **-τός**, ή, όν, *brought back*, ἀ. ἔς τινα *referred* to some one *for decision*, Hdt.6.66 (v. l. ἀνώϊστου).

ἀνοιστρέω, *goad to madness*, E.*Ba*.979; ἔρωτι καρδίην ἀνοιστρηθείς Herod.1.57.

ἀνοίσω, v. ἀναφέρω. **ἄνοιτο**, v. ἄνω.

ἀνόκαιον· ὑπερῷον, γράφεται καὶ ἀνώγεων, Hsch.

ἀνοκηδεολόγον, v. ἀνοικῆ.

ἀνόκνως, Adv. = ἀόκνως, *POxy*.743.39 (i B. C.), *PFay*.130.14 (iii A. D.).

ἀνοκωχεύω, Ion. **ἀνακ-**, *hold back, stay, hinder*, ἀ. τὰς νέας *keep* them *riding at anchor*, Hdt.6.116 (cf. Hsch. s. v. ἀνακ-), etc.: metaph., of a chariot, *hold* it *in, keep* it *back*, S.*El*.732; also ἀ. πόλεμον D.H.9. 16. 2. ἀ. τὸν τόνον τῶν ὅπλων *keep up* the tension of the ropes, *keep* them *taut*, Hdt.7.36. 3. *keep afloat*, Arist.*Cael*.313^{a}23. II. also intr. (sc. ἑαυτόν), *keep still*, Hdt.9.13; *hold back*, of ships, D.S. 11.18.—The form **ἀνακωχέω** *support, relieve strain upon*, is found in Hp.*Art*.9, 38, *Mochl*.2.

ἀνοκωχή, ἡ, redupl. form = ἀνοχή (cf. ὄκωχα pf. of ἔχω), *stay, cessation*, κακῶν Th.4.117; ἀ. νομῆς *a stay* in the spreading of the ulcer, Aret.*SD*2.9, cf. 1.8. 2. esp. *cessation of arms, truce*, δι' ἀνοκωχῆς γίγνεσθαί τινι to be at *truce* with one, Th.1.40; ἀ. ἐστί τινι πρός τινα one party has *a truce* with another, Id.5.32. II. *hindrance*, τριβὴ καὶ ἀ. τῶν Ἑλλήνων Id.8.87. (Archaic word used by Th. acc. to D.H.*Amm*.2.3. Mss. generally have the corrupt form ἀνακωχή, which gave rise to a deriv. παρὰ τὸ ἄνω τὰς ἀκωκὰς ἔχειν *EM*96.52: but Hsch. gives the correct form. Ammon.*Diff*.19 attempts to distinguish the forms.)

ἀνοκώχησις, εως, ἡ, glossed by σύμπτωσις, Bacch.ap.Erot. s. v. (ἀνακ- codd.).

ἀνολβ-έω, *to be* ἄνολβος, Epic.*Oxy*.1794.13. **-ία**, Ion. **-ίη**, ἡ, *the state of an* ἄνολβος, *misery*, Hes.*Op*.319 [ῐ]. **-ιος**, ον, = sq., v. l. in Hdt.1.32. **-ος**, ον, poet. Adj. *unblest, wretched, luckless*, ἦμαρ Orac.ap.Hdt.1.85; γαῖα, ὄμμα, E.*Hel*.247, *IA*354; ὤμοι ἐμῶν ἄνολβα βουλευμάτων, for ἐμὰ.. βουλεύματα, S.*Ant*.1265: of persons, Thgn.288 (Comp.), A.*Eu*.551, S.*Aj*.1156, etc. 2. *without means, poor*, Arat.1073.

ἀνόλεθρος, ον, *not ruined, having escaped ruin*, Il.13.761.

ἀνολισθάνω, aor. -ώλισθον, *slip* or *glide back, return*, ἔς τινα Call. *Fr*.96.

ἀνολκή, ἡ, *hauling up*, λίθων Th.4.112; ἀ. καὶ καθολκή Aen.Tact. 10.12.

ἀνολολύζω, *cry aloud, shout aloud*, ἀνωλόλυξα χαρᾶς ὕπο A.*Ag*. 587, cf. Simon.148.2, S.*Tr*.205, E.*Med*.1173, etc. 2. c. acc., *bewail loudly*, S.*El*.750: but c. acc. cogn., βοὴν ἀ. E.*Tr*.1000. II. causal, *excite by Bacchic cries*, πρώτας δὲ Θήβας.. ἀνωλόλυξα Id.*Ba*.24.

ἀνολοφύρομαι [ῡ], *bewail aloud*, Th.8.81, X.*Cyr*.7.3.14, J.*AJ*2. 6.4: c. part., ἀ. ποθῶν.. Pl.*Prt*.327d.

ἀνολόφυρτον· ἀδάκρυτον, Hsch. (ἀνωλόφυκτον cod.).

Ἀνολυμπιάς, άδος, ἡ, *an Olympiad omitted in the list*, Paus.6.22.3.

ἄνομαι, v. ἄνω.

ἀνομαλ-ίζω, *restore to equality, equalize*, Pass., pf. inf. ἀνωμαλίσθαι Arist.*Rh*.1412^{a}16: fut., cj. in *Pol*.1265^{a}40; cf. sq. **-ωσις**, εως, ἡ, *restoration of equality, equalization*, ib.1274^{b}9.

ἀνομβρ-έω, *gush out with water*, πηγή Ph.2.91: metaph., ὥσπερ ἀπὸ γῆς τῆς αἰσθήσεως -ησάντων παθῶν 1.575: c. acc., *pour forth*, ὕδωρ 2.115: metaph., Lxx *Si*.18.29, al., Ph.1.477. **-ήεις**, εσσα, εν, *rainy*, Nic.*Al*.288. **-ία**, ἡ, *want of rain*, Arist.*HA*606^{b}20, D.S.1.29, J.*AJ*8.13.2, Ph.2.383: metaph., [τὴν παίδευσιν] οὔτε ὄμβρος οὔτε ἀ. ἀφαιρεῖται Antipho Soph.60. **-ος**, ον, *without rain*, of countries, Hdt.2.22, 4.185. 2. ἄ. ῥοαί streams *not fed by showers*, E.*Ba*.406.

ἀνομέω, *to be* ἄνομος, *act lawlessly*, περὶ τὸ ἱρόν Hdt.1.144. 2. Pass., *to be unlawfully used*, *POxy*.1465.9 (i B. C.).

ἀνομήλῐκος, ον, *of unlike age*, Procl.*in Prm*.p.949 S.

ἀνόμ-ημα, ατος, τό, *transgression of the law*, Lys.ap.Phot.p.143 R., Lxx *Le*.20.14, al., *Stoic*.3.136, D.S.17.5. **-ία**, Ion. **-ίη**, ἡ, *lawlessness, lawless conduct*, opp. δικαιοσύνη, Hdt.1.96, 97; ἀ. νόμων κρατεῖ E.*IA*1095 (lyr.); ἀ. ἀμύνειν Antipho 4.1.7; ἀ. ὀφλισκάνειν E. *Ion* 443; ἀντὶ αὐτονομίας.. εἰς ἀνομίας ἐμπίπτειν Isoc.6.64, cf. Plu.2. 755b; ζῆν ἐν πάσῃ ἀναρχίᾳ καὶ ἀ. Pl.*R*.575a. 2. *the negation of law*, opp. νόμος, D.24.152.

ἀνομίλητος [ῐ], ον, *having no communion with others, unsociable*, Pl.*Lg*.951a, Plu.2.50b, etc. 2. c. gen., ἀ. παιδείας *uneducated*, Pl. *Ep*.332c: abs., Luc.*Merc.Cond*.14: c. dat., ἀ. τοῖς ἔργοις τῆς τέχνης Gal.15.159, 18(1).287.

ἀνόμιμος, ον, v. l. for ἄνομος, Pl.*Min*.314d.

ἀνόμιστος, ον, *not customary*, Orac.ap.Phleg.*Mir*.10.

ἀνόμιχλος, ον, *without mist*, ἀήρ Arist.*Mu*.394^{a}23.

ἀνόμμᾰτος, ον, *eyeless, sightless*, S.*Ph*.856 (lyr.), Orph.*Fr*.82.

ἀνομο-γένεια, ἡ, *difference in kind*, Epicur.*Fr*.36. **-γενής**, ές, *of different kind*, ibid. (prob.), Chrysipp.*Stoic*.2.81, Arr.*Epict*.1.20.2, Alex.Aphr.*in Top*.116.10, al., S.E.*M*.8.229.

ἀνομο-ειδής, ές, *differing in species*, Plot.4.3.2, Iamb.*Myst*.1.19, Dam.*Pr*.34; v. l. for ἀνόμοιο-, Arist.*EN*1163^{b}32. Adv. -ειδῶς Dam. *Pr*.37.

ἀνομόζηλος, ον, *having a different bent*, S.E.*M*.7.56.

ἀνομοθέτητος, ον, *unregulated by law*, Pl.*Lg*.781a, 785a, Arist. *Pol*.1269^{b}19; ἄγραφον καὶ ἀ. φύσεως δίκαιον D.H.7.41.

ἀνομοιο-βᾰρής, ές, *of unevenly distributed weight*, Arist.*Cael*.273^b 23. **-γενής**, ές, *of different kind*, Ph.2.307. Adv. -νῶς *in a different gender*, Sch.rec.S.*Ant*.74. **-γώνιος**, ον, *with dissimilar angles*, Papp.216.20. **-ειδής**, ές, *of unlike kind, heterogeneous*, φιλίαι Arist.*EN*1163^{b}32, cf. Dam.*Pr*.440:—hence Subst. **-είδεια**, ἡ, A.D.*Pron*.101.22. **-κατάληκτος**, ον, *with different terminations*, Id.*Synt*.167.25. **-μερής**, ές, *consisting of unlike parts, not homogeneous*, esp. of organs, opp. tissues, Arist.*HA*486^{a}7, *Mete*.388^{a}18, *GA*722^{b}31, Thphr.*Fr*.22, Gal.6.844, al. 2. in Metric, [συστήματα] κατὰ περικοπὴν ἀνομοιομερῆ Heph.*Poëm*.4. **-ποιός**, όν, *causing* *unlikeness*, Dam.*Pr*.342. **-πτωτος**, ον, *with unlike inflexions*, Eust.1228.62. Adv. -τως Id.631.27.

ἀνόμοιος, ον, Pl.*Phlb*.13e, etc., also α, ον Isoc.12.225, etc.:—*unlike, dissimilar*, Pi.*N*.8.28; ἀ. τινι *unlike* it, Pl.*Grg*.513b, al.; ἐξ ἀνομοίων ἡ πόλις is composed of *dissimilar elements*, Arist.*Pol*.1277^{a}5. Adv. -ως Th.1.84, Pl.*R*.388c, al.; ἀ. ἔχειν X.*An*.7.7.49. 2. of number, = ἑτερομήκης, *Theol.Ar*.9,58.

ἀνομοιό-στροφος, ον, *consisting of unequal strophes*, Heph.*Poëm*.5.3. **-σχήμων**, ον, gen. ονος, *of unlike form*, Gal.18(1).774, Procl.*Inst*.210, Phlp.*in Ph*.677.2.

ἀνομοιότης, ητος, ἡ, *unlikeness, dissimilarity*, Pl.*Prm*.159e, *Plt*.273d, Thphr.*CP*1.2.2, Hierocl.*in CA* 26 p.481 M.: in pl., Pl.*Plt*.294, Arist.*Po*.1448^{a}10.

ἀνομοιό-τροπος, ον, *differing in modality* (including quantity and quality), πρότασις Eustr.*in APo*.52.17. **-φυλος**, ον, *of different kind*, Sm.*Le*.19.19. **-χρονος**, ον, in Metric, *of dissimilar quantity*, Eust.13.7. **-χρους**, ουν, *of different colour*, Alex.Aphr.*de An*.146.8.

ἀνομοι-όω, (ἀνόμοιος) *make unlike* or *dissimilar*, Pl.*R*.546b, *Prm*.148b:—Pass. (c. fut. Med., Porph.*Abst*.1.37), *to be* or *become so*, Pl.*Tht*.166b, al. II. (ἀνά, ὁμοιόω) *make even again*, *PHal*.1.100 (iii B.C.). **-ώδης**, ες, *unlike*, Procl.*Inst*.203. **-ωσις**, εως, ἡ, *a making unlike, dissimilarity*, Pl.*Tht*.166c.

ἀνομολογ-έομαι, *agree upon* a thing, *come to an understanding*, περί τινος Pl.*R*.442e; πρὸς ἀλλήλους ib.348b; πρός τι with a view to.., Id.*Tht*.164c; τινί *with* a person, Plu.2.1070d (Act. in codd.): abs., *admit*, Muson.*Fr*.17 p.92 H., *Sammelb*.4638.14. 2. *recapitulate, sum up* one's conclusions, τὰ εἰρημένα Pl.*Smp*.200e. 3. *pay money by note of hand* or *order*, Lys.ap.Phot.p.143 R., *IG*1.188.34:—hence Subst. **ἀνομολόγημα**, ατος, τό, *promissory note*, ib.17. II. Act., in later Prose, ἀ. τινί Plu.2.1070d codd.; D.18.86 uses the pf. in pass. sense, ἀνωμολόγημαι..τὰ ἄριστα πράττειν I *am allowed by all* to have done what is best, cf. ib.266, 60.4, and late Prose, Ph.1.161, al.: aor. part. Pass. -ηθείς 2.520. **-ητέον**, *one must admit*, τοῦτο περὶ αὐτῶν Pl.*R*.452e, cf. *Lg*.737c. **-ητος**, ον, *agreed on again, under a renewed bill for both the principal debt and the unpaid interest*, *AB*211. II. (ἀ- priv.) *inconsistent*, τὸ ἀ. Ptol.*Tetr*.47. **-ία**, ἡ, *verbal agreement*, Hsch. II. (ἀνομόλογος) *disagreement*, Str.2.3.3, Plu.*Comp.Nic.Crass*.1. 2. *failure to lead a consistent life*, title of treatise by Chrysipp., *Stoic*.3.94, cf. Posidon. ib.112; generally, *inconsistency*, Hierocl.p.56 A. **-ος**, ον, *not agreeing, incongruous*, S.E.*M*.8.331, cf. Harp. s.v. ἀσυνθετώτατον, Apollon.Cit.3: c. dat., Alex.Aphr.*in Top*.548.17. Adv. -γως Porph.*Abst*.2.40. **-ούμενος**, η, ον, *not agreeing, inconsistent*, ἵνα μὴ ἀ. ᾖ ὁ λόγος Pl.*Grg*.495a; ἀ. τοῖς προειρημένοις Arist.*APr*.48^{a}21, cf. Chrysipp.*Stoic*.3.125. 2. *not admitted, not granted*, τὰ ἀνομολογούμενα συνάγειν Arist.*Rh*.1396^{b}28, cf. 1400^{a}15:—Adj., compd. of ἀ- priv. and ὁμολογούμενος; for a Verb ἀνομολογέομαι, *disagree with*, does not occur. Adv. -νως Gal.5.470.

ἄνομος, ον, *lawless, impious*, τράπεζα Hdt.1.162; of persons, S.*OC*142, al.; στρατός *Tr*.1096; Ἐχίονος γόνος E.*Ba*.995; of things, θυσία A.*Ag*.151; πάθη E.*Or*.1455; μοναρχία Pl.*Plt*.302e: τὰ ἄνομα *lawless acts*, Hdt.1.8: Comp. -ώτερος Pl.*Hp.Ma*.285a. Adv. -μως E.*Med*.1000, Antipho 4.1.2, Th.4.92. 2. c. gen., ἀ. θεοῦ, i.e. *without (the Mosaic) Law* and therefore without God, 1 *Ep.Cor*.9.21. Adv. ἀνόμως, = χωρὶς νόμου, *Ep.Rom*.2.12. 3. *illegal*, κατοχή *POxy*.237 vii 11 (ii A.D.). II. (νόμος II) *unmusical*, νόμος ἄ. A.*Ag*.1142 (lyr.).

ἀνομό-σημος, ον, *contradictory*, *PHib*.31.4.15. **-ούσιος**, ον, *differing in οὐσία*, Ps.-Alex.Aphr.*in SE*12.17. **-τἄγής**, ές, *of a different order*, Dam.*Pr*.119; *not co-ordinated*, of lines of vision, prob. l. in Gal.*UP*10.12; cf. ὁμοταγής. **-ὕλος** [ῠ], ον, *differing in substance*, Phlp.*in de An*.526.18.

ἀνονδόκως· ἄνωθεν, Hsch. (fort. ἀνοκόνδως, cf. ἀνάκανδα).

ἀνονείδιστος, ον, *irreproachable*, Nic.Dam.p.119 D.

ἀνόνητος, Dor. -ᾱτος, ον, *unprofitable*, περισσὰ κἀνόνητα σώματα S.*Aj*.758; ὦ πολλὰ λέξας..κἀνόνητ' ἔπη v.l. ib.1272; ἀ. γάμος E.*Or*.1501 (lyr.), cf. *Hel*.886; ἀ. γίγνεσθαι D.9.40, cf. Plu.2.248a; τινί Arist.*EN*1095^{a}9, cf. *Pol*.1334^{b}40; ἄργυρον εἰς ἀνόνατα ῥέοντα Cerc.4.4:—neut. pl. ἀνόνητα is freq. in E. as Adv., *in vain*, as *Hec*.766, *Alc*.412 (lyr.), al.; ἀνόνητα πονεῖν Pl.*R*.486c: regul. Adv. -τως Pall.*in Hp*.2.147 D., Sch.E.*Or*.1501: Comp., ibid. II. Act., c. gen., τῶν ἀγαθῶν ἀ. τινα ποιῆσαι *deprive of all benefit from*..., D.18.141, cf. 19.315, Plu.2.800d, Nic.Dam.p.13 D.

ἀνονόμαστος, ον, faulty form for ἀνωνόμαστος, Gal.7.425, Hdn.*Epim*.203, Suid.

ἀνόξυντος, ον, *not to be written with the acute accent*, Eust.930.57.

ἄνοος, ον, contr. **ἄνους**, ουν, *without understanding, silly*, κραδίη Il.21.441; ψυχή Pl.*Ti*.44a, etc.; of persons, S.*Ant*.99; ἄνους τε καὶ γέρων ἅμα ib.281; πλοῦτος ἄ. wealth *without wit*, *AP*9.43 (Parmen.): Comp. ἀνούστερος A.*Pr*.987: Sup. ἀνούστατος Pherecr.19 D. Adv., Comp. ἀνουστέρως S.*Fr*.589.1.

ἀνοπαῖα, only in Od.1.320 ὄρνις δ' ὣς ἀνοπαῖα διέπτατο, where it is variously written and explained: 1. acc. to Hdn.Gr.2.133, it is an Adv. (compd. of ἀνά, *ὄπτομαι), she flew away *unseen, unnoticed*; or, acc. to Eust., = ἄνω, ἀνωφερές, *up into the air*, cf. καρπαλίμως ἀνόπαιον Emp.51, and Ἀνόπαια, the name of the pass above Thermopylae (Hdt.7.216). 2. acc. to Aristarch., ἀνόπαια or πανόπαια, a kind of *eagle*, cf. Hebr. *'ānaphā* 'heron'. 3. acc. to Gramm. in *An.Ox*.1.83, ἀν' ὀπαῖα (= ἀνὰ ὀπήν) *up by the hole in the roof, up the smoke-vent*.

ἀνόπιν, Adv. *backwards*, Hsch.; *farther back*, in a book, etc., Eust.1031.46.

ἄνοπλος, ον, *without the* ὅπλον or *large shield*, of the Persians, who bore only γέρρα, Hdt.9.62: generally, *unarmed*, Pl.*Euthd*.299b, Onos.42.17; τὸ ἄ., opp. τὸ ὁπλιτικόν, of citizens *not entrusted with arms*, Arist.*Pol*.1289^{b}32:—of ships, *unarmed*, Plb.2.12.3. (On the form v. ἄοπλος.)

ἄνοπτος, ον, *unseen*, Suid.

ἄνορ· νοῦς, Scythian word, Hsch., cf. Hdn.*Epim*.240.

ἀνόρᾱτος, ον, v.l. for ἀόρ- in Pl.*Ti*.51a, Polycharm.1.

ἀνοργάζω, lit. *knead up*: in Pass., ἀνωργασμένον σῶμα *relaxed*, Hp.*Int*.21. II. *toss, dandle*, παιδία Hsch. (nisi ad ἀνορταλίζειν spectat).

ἀνόργᾰνος, ον, *without instruments*, Plu.*Per*.16; βίος Porph.*Abst*.1.6; κίνησις ἀ. movement *without limbs for the purpose*, of serpents, Plu.2.381b.

ἀνόργητος, ον, Hellenistic for ἄνοργος, Moer.12, cf. Sch.Pi.*P*.10.33.

ἀνοργία, ἡ, = ἀμυησία, Hsch., Suid.

ἀνοργίαστος, ον, *not celebrated with orgies*, ἱερά Ar.*Lys*.898; τελεταί, i.e. *no true* mysteries, Ph.1.156. 2. of a god or person *in whose honour no orgies are held*, Pl.*Epin*.985d. II. *uninitiated*, Ph.2.268; ἀμύητος καὶ ἀ. τῶν ἱερῶν Them.*Or*.13.166c.

ἄνοργος, ον, *not wrathful*, Cratin.385.

ἀνορέα, ἡ, more common in Ion. form ἠνορέη (q. v.), Pi.*O*.8.67, al., Theoc.29.19.

ἀνορ-έγω, *hand up*, of the elephant's use of his trunk, Arist.*HA*497^{b}28. **-εκτέω**, *have no appetite*, Antyll.ap.Orib.5.29.8, Sor.2.43. **-εκτος**, ον, *without appetite for*, ἀπολαύσεως Arist.*VV*1250^{b}9; ἡδονῆς Andronic.Rhod.p.576 M.; περὶ τὰς ἀπολαύσεις Arist.*VV*1250^{a}8: abs., Sor.1.24, Plu.2.460a, etc. Adv. ἀνορέκτως, ἔχειν Gal.10.576. II. Pass., *not desired*, of food, Plu.2.664a. **-εξία**, ἡ, *want of desire* or *appetite*, Ti.Locr.102e, Aret.*CA*2.3.

ἀνόρεος [ᾰ], α, ον, (ἀνήρ) = ἀνδρεῖος, πόλεμος S.*Fr*.436.

ἀνορθιάζω, *call out, shout aloud*, And.1.29. II. *prick up*, τὰ ὦτα Ph.2.188, al.:—Pass., ἐγήγερται καὶ ἀνωρθίασται 1.381.

ἄνορθος, ον, (ἀ- priv.) perh. *sloping*, ἄ. εἰς τὸ εἴσω *IG*2^2.463.60; prob. corrupt in Herophil.ap.Gal.2.571.

ἀνορθ-όω, aor. ἀνώρθωσα E.*Alc*.1138, Isoc.5.64, etc.: plpf. with double augm. ἠνωρθώκει v.l. in Lib.*Ep*.1039: the double augm. is common in the compd. ἐπανορθόω:—*set up again, restore, rebuild*, τὸν νηόν Hdt.1.19; τὸ τεῖχος 7.208; τὸ στρατόπεδον Th.6.88, etc.; τὸ σῶμά τινος E.*Ba*.364:—Med., ἀνορθοῦσθαι τὰ πίπτοντα τῶν οἰκοδομημάτων *have* them *rebuilt*, Arist.*Pol*.1322^{b}20. 2. *restore to health* or *well-being*, πόλιν S.*OT*46; τινά Pl.*Lg*.919d. 3. *set straight again, set right, correct*, τινά E.*Supp*.1228; τὰ ἀλλότρια κακά Pl.*R*.346e. **-ωσις**, εως, ἡ, *restoration*, τειχῶν *PRyl*.157.13 (ii A.D.); = ἐπανόρθωσις, Ph.*Fr*.54 H.; f.l. in Plb.15.20.5, Corn.*ND*16.

ἀνορίνω, Aeol. impf. ὀννώριν⟨ν⟩ε, *stir up, arouse*, (sc. παφλάσμους) Alc.*Supp*.25.8.

ἄνορκος, ον, *bound by no oath*, Poll.1.39.

ἀνορμ-άομαι, Pass., *start up, try eagerly to do* a thing, c. acc. cogn., στόλον Opp.*H*.3.105.—Hsch. has the Act. in neut. signf., and so Ruf.ap.Orib.45.30.40, *mount*, of a disease. **-ητικῶς**, Adv. *with an upward rush*, Sch.Opp.*H*.5.210. **-ητος**, ον, *impetuous*, Erot. s.v. ἀνάσσυτος.

ἀνορμίζω, *take* [ships] *from* their *moorings*, ἐς τὸ πέλαγος τὰς ναῦς D.C.48.48:—Med., *put to sea*, Id.42.7:—Pass., *anchor above*, ὑπὲρ τόπον Id.71.2.

ἄνορμος, ον, *without harbour*, πέτραι Anon.ap.Suid. s.v. λισσάδας πέτρας: metaph., ὑμέναιον ὃν δόμοις ἄνορμον εἰσέπλευσας S.*OT*423.

ἀνορνῦμι, fut. -όρσω, *rouse, stir up*, ἀνὰ μὲν φόρμιγγ', ἀνὰ δ' αὐλὸν ὄρσομεν Pi.*N*.9.8; τινά A.R.4.1352:—Pass., ἂν δ' ἄρα Τυδεΐδης ὦρτο (Ep. aor.) *up he started*, Il.23.812, cf. Od.8.3; ἀνὰ δ' ὤρνυτ' Ἰήσων A.R.1.349.

ἀνορούω, poet. Verb, used by Hom. only in aor. 1 (X.*Eq*.3.7, 8.5 has pres. inf. and part.):—*start up, leap up*, abs., Il.9.193, Od.3.149, Sapph.*Supp*.20a.11, etc.; ἐκ δὲ θρόνων ἀνόρουσαν Od.22.23; ἐξ ὕπνοιο μάλα κραιπνῶς ἀ. Il.10.162, etc.; ἐς δίφρον δ' ἀ. 11.273; so Ἠέλιος δ' ἀνόρουσε..οὐρανὸν ἐς.. Helios *went swiftly up* the sky, Od.3.1; τοῖσι δὲ Νέστωρ ἡδυεπὴς ἀ. Il.1.248; ἀνορούσαις (Aeol. part.) Pi.*O*.7.37.

ἀνόροφος, ον, *roofless*, πέτρα E.*Ba*.38.

ἀνορροπύγιος [ῠ], ον, *without rump*, καρκίνος Arist.*HA*525^{b}31; πτῆσις ἀ. *without help from the tail* or *rump*, of insects, ib.532^{a}24.

ἀνορτᾰλίζω, *clap the wings and crow*, like a cock, Ar.*Eq*.1344.

ἀνόρυκτος, ον, *not obtained by digging*, ἅλες Orib.*Eup*.4.24.

ἀνορύσσω, Att. -ττω, pf. Pass. ἀνορώρυγμαι Men.468:—*dig up* what has been buried, τὰ ὀστέα Hdt.2.41, Lycurg.113; ὑδρίας Ar.*Av*.602; τινά Id.*Pax*372, Plu.*Ages*.20; χρυσόν Luc.*Cont*.11. 2. ἀ. τάφον *dig up, break open, destroy* it, Hdt.1.68, Isoc.16.26.

ἀνορχέομαι, *leap up and dance*, E.*Supp*.719; of the soul, Ph.1.379.

ἄνορχος, ον, *without testicles*, i.e. *castrated*, Hp.*Vict*.2.49. II. *without stones*, φοίνικες Arist.*Fr*.267.

ἀνοσάμικτον· ὀλιγόρρυτον ὕδωρ, Hsch.

ἀνοσήλευτος, ον, *untended*, S.*Fr*.264.

ἀνόσητος, ον, *without sickness*, S.*Fr*.1014, *PIand*.13.11 (iv A.D.).

ἀνοσία, ἡ, (ἀ- priv., νόσος) *freedom from sickness*, Poll.3.107. II. (ἀ- priv., ὅσιος) ἀνοσίjα ϝοι γένοιτυ *may he be accursed*, Inscr.Cypr. 135.29 H. (perh. neut. pl. ἀνόσιjα); cf. sq.

ἀνόσιος, ον, more rarely α, ον E.Tr.1316 (lyr.), Aeschin.2.157 (dub.), and later:—*unholy, profane*, opp. ἄδικος, as ὅσιος to δίκαιος (v. ὅσιος I.1), of persons, A.Th.611, S.OT353, etc.; ἀ. ὁ θεομισής Pl. Euthphr.7a; ἄδικος καὶ ἀ. Id.Grg.505b. 2. of things, ἔργον, μόρος, στόμα, etc., Hdt.2.114, 3.65, S.OC981, etc.; αὐδῶν ἀνόσι' οὐδὲ ῥητά μοι Id.OT1289; ἀνόσια πάσχειν Antipho 2.4.7; ἀσεβὲς μηδὲν μηδὲ ἀ. X.Cyr.8.7.22; οὐ μόνον ἄνομον ἀλλὰ καὶ ἀ. Id.Lac.8.5; ἀ. νέκυς a corpse *with all the rites unpaid*, S.Ant.1071; ἀ. τι γεγένηται ἐμοῦ παρόντος the holy rites have been *profaned*, Antipho 5.84. II. Adv. -ίως *in unholy wise*, S.Ph.257; κάτω γῆς ἀ. οἰκῶν *without funeral rites*, or *through an unholy deed*, E.El.677.

ἀνοσιότης, ητος, ἡ, *unholiness, wickedness*, v.l. in Pl.Euthphr.5d; ἀ. καὶ δεινότης τῶν πεπραγμένων Isoc.12.121.

ἀνοσιουργ-έω, *act impiously, wickedly*, Pl.Lg.905b, Ph.2.128, D.C.56.5, 77.12. **-ημα**, ατος, τό, *impious act*, Ph.2.313, Porph. Chr.58. **-ία**, ἡ, *impiety, wickedness*, Pl.Ep.335b, Plu.Arat.54, D.C.71.30. **-ός**, όν, *acting impiously*, Pl.Ep.352c, Arist.EN1166^{b}5, Ph.2.313.

ἄνοσμος, ον, = ἄνοδμος, *without smell*, v.l. in Hp.Acut.63, cf. Arist. HA634^{b}19, etc.; ἴχνη ἄνοσμα footsteps *that leave no scent*, Poll.5.12:—but ἄοσμος (q.v.) was preferred.

ἄνοσος, Ion. and Ep. **ἄνουσος**, ον, *without sickness, healthy, sound*, of persons, ἀσκηθέες καὶ ἄ. Od.14.255; ἄ. καὶ ἀγήραοι Pi.Fr.143, cf. Pl.Ti.33a; ἄπηρος, ἄ. Hdt.1.32; λῷστον δὲ τὸ ζῆν ἄ. S.Fr.356. Adv. ἀνόσως, διάγειν Hp.Epid.1.1; ζῆν Ph.1.267; ἄ. ᾦχετ' ἐς ἡμιθέους IG 5(2).472.13 (Megalopolis, ii/iii A.D.). 2. c. gen., ἄ. κακῶν *untouched by* ill, E.IA982; ἄ. πρὸς τὰ ἄλλα ἀρρωστήματα, τῶν ἄλλων ἀρρωστημάτων, Arist.HA604^{a}12,22. 3. of a season, *free from sickness*, ἔτος ἄ. ἐς τὰς ἄλλας ἀσθενείας Th.2.49; ἕξις, λόγος ἄ., Plu.Cic.8,2.7b. II. of things, *not causing disease, harmless*, E.Ion1201.

ἀνόστεος, ον, *boneless*, of the polypus, Hes.Op.524 (Lacon. acc. to Clitarch.ap.Procl. ad loc.) cf. Hp.Epid.2.2.19; ἀ. ἡ καρδία Arist.PA 666^{b}17; τὰ περὶ τὴν κοιλίαν ib.655^{a}2; φυὴ μελέων Opp.H.1.639.

ἀνόστ-ητος, ον, *unreturning*, Orph.A.1269. II. *whence none return*, χῶρος ἐνέρων AP7.467 (Antip. Sid.), cf. Opp.H.3.586, etc. **-ιμος**, ον, *not returning*, κεῖνον ἀ. ἔθηκεν *cut off* his *return*, Od.4.182. 2. *not to be retraced*, κέλευθος E.HF431 (lyr.). II. (νόστος II) *giving a low yield*, of corn, Thphr.CP3.21.1 (Sup.); *not nutritious*, Sor.1.91. **-ος**, ον, *unreturning, without return*, πάντας ὄλεσαν καὶ ἔθηκαν ἀνόστους Od.24.528; πάντες ἐγένοντο ἄ. Arist.Fr. 145: Sup., ἡβάσεις ἥβαν ἀνοστοτάταν *never, never to return*, AP7. 482. II. = foreg. II, Thphr.CP4.13.2 (Comp.).

ἀνόστρᾰκος, ον, *with no shell*, ᾠά Sch.Nic.Al.295.

ἀνόσφιστος, ον, *not stolen*, Eust.1768.54.

ἀνόσφρ-αντος, ον, *that cannot be smelt*, Arist.deAn.421^{b}6:—also **-ητος**, ον, Alex.Aphr. de An.52.15.

ἀνοσχήν· ἄνανδρος, Hsch.

ἀνότιστος, ον, *free from moisture, dry*, τόποι Dsc.1 Praef.9; κονιορτός Archig.ap.Orib.8.2.6.

ἄνοτος, ον, *without the south wind*, Hsch. s.v. βορεασμοί.

ἀνοτοτύζω, *break out into wailing*, A.Ag.1074, E.Hel.371 (lyr.).

ἀνοτότυκτον· ἀθρήνητον, Hsch. (ἀνότευκτον cod.).

ἄνου· ἄνω (Ion.), Hsch.

ἀνούᾰτος, ον, *without ear*: *without handle*, Theoc.Ep.4.3.

Ἀνουβ-ιακός, ή, όν, *of Anubis*, epith. of a kind of thread, PMag. Par.1.1083. **-ιάς**, άδος, ἡ, a plant, perh. = στάχυς, ib.901. **-ιδεῖον**, τό, *sanctuary of A.*, Roussel Cultes Égyptiens 224 (Delos, ii B.C.):—also **-ιεῖον**, τό, ib.229,231 (ii B.C.).

ἀνουθέτητος, ον, *unwarned, unadmonished*, Isoc.2.4, D.Ep.3.11. 2. *that will not be warned*, Men.Mon.49, Plu.2.283f.

ἀνούλεγοι· ἀμώλεθροι, Hsch.

ἄνουλος, ον, in Comp. -ότερον *less wavy*, cj. in Thphr.HP3.11.3.

ἄνουροι· ἄβρεκτοι, ὑψηλοί, Hsch.

ἄνους, ουν, contr. for ἄνοος.

ἀνουσίαστος, ον, = ἀνούσιος, opp. οὐσιώδης, Corp.Herm.2.5. II. *without the use of an* οὐσία (q.v.), PMag.Par.1.2441.

ἀνούσιος, ον, *without substance*, οὐδὲ ἄρα ἡ ἑτερότης ἀ. Dam.Pr. 192; ἀ. καὶ νεκροί Procl. in Alc.p.271 C., cf. Olymp. in Alc.p.92 C.; δύναμις, of God, opp. οὐσιώδης, Procl.Inst.121. Adv. -ίως Syrian. in Metaph.114.29. II. in Alchemy, *not affecting substance, superficial in action*, σώματα Zos.Alch.p.160 B., al.

ἀνουσιότης, ητος, ἡ, *unsubstantiality*, Simp. in de An.247.9.

ἀνουσίωσις, εως, ἡ, *conferring of non-existence*, Simp. in Ph.433.18.

ἄνουσος, ον, Ion. for ἄνοσος.

ἀνούτ-ᾰτος, ον, *unwounded* by stroke of sword, ἄβλητος καὶ ἀ. Il.4.540, cf. A.R.2.75. II. *invulnerable*, Nonn.D.16.157, al. III. *where no wounds are inflicted*, ἀγῶνες ib.37.774. **-ητί** [ῐ], Adv. *without inflicting a wound*, οὐδ' ἄρα οἵ τις ἀνουτητί γε παρέστη Il.22.371. II. *without receiving a wound*, Q.S.3.445. **-ητος**, ον, = ἀνούτατος, Nic.Th.719. II. *invulnerable*, Nonn.D.16.382, etc.

ἀνοῦχι, prob. some kind of *brushwood*, PPetr.3 p.101.

ἀνοφθαλμίᾰτος, ον, *free from ophthalmia*, Dsc.Eup.1.29.

ἀνόφθαλμος, ον, *without eyes*, Tz.H.3.219.

ἀνοφρυάζομαι, *arch one's eyebrows*: metaph., *to be supercilious*, Com.Adesp.842.

ἀνοχεύς, έως, ὁ, *suspensory membrane*, in pl., Aret.SA2.6,11.

ἀνόχευτος, ον, *non-copulating*, Arist.HA546^{b}16, al.

ἀνοχέω, *raise up*, Olymp. in Mete.24.13.

ἀνοχή, ἡ, *holding back, stopping*, esp. of hostilities: hence mostly in pl., *armistice, truce*, X.Mem.4.4.17; ἀνοχὰς ποιεῖσθαι Decr.ap.D. 18.164; διδόναι D.H.8.68; σπείσασθαι Plu.Pel.29; αἱ Καλλισθένους ἀ. Aeschin.2.31; αἱ ἑξαετεῖς ἀ. D.H.3.59; cf. ἀνοκωχή. 2. *time, opportunity*, οὐκ ἔδωκεν αὐτοῖς ἀνοχὴν ἐμβατεῦσαι Lxx 1 Ma.12.25; ἡμερῶν ἀ. *delay* of some days, POxy.1068.15 (iii A.D.). 3. pl., ἀνοχαί, = Lat. *feriae*, D.C.39.30. 4. ἀνοχαὶ δικῶν, = Lat. *iustitium*, Id.55.26. II. (ἀνέχομαι) *long-suffering, forbearance*, Ep.Rom.2.4, 3.26. 2. ἀνοχὴν ἀναπαύλης διδόναι *permission* to rest, Hdn.3.6.10. 3. *relief from* disease, Philum.ap.Orib.Syn.8.3.4. III. = ἀνατολή, Poll.4.157, Hsch.

ἀνοχ[ικ]ός· ἀνατολικός, Hsch. II. Adv. -κῶς *connectedly*, Simp. in de An.285.19.

ἀνοχλ-έω, = ἀνοχλίζω, S.E.M.10.83. **-ησία**, ἡ, = ἀοχλησία, Luc.Am.27, D.L.2.87, Gal.6.18. **-ητικός**, ή, όν, *heaving upwards*. Adv. -κῶς S.E.M.10.83. **-ίζω**, *heave up*, A.R.1.1167, Opp.H.5.128, Hsch. 2. *heave out of the way*, A.R.3.1298. **-ος**, ον, *not in the way, not an impediment*, Arist.PA663^{b}20 (Sup.).

ἀνοχμάζω, *hoist, lift up*, AP9.204 (Agath.).

ἄνοχον, τό, *evacuation of the bowels*, Thphr.HP3.18.13. **ἄνοχος**, ον, of weather, *tolerable*, Cat.Cod.Astr.7.184.35.

ἀνοχῠρόομαι, *fortify*, dub. in Polyaen.4.11.2.

ἀνόχῠρος, ον, v. sub ἀνώχυρος.

ἀνοψία, ἡ, *want of fish* (ὄψον) *to eat with bread*, ἔφερον δεινῶς τὴν ἀ. Antiph.190.8; ἀνοψίαν ὑποφέρειν Plu.2.237f. II. Ion. **ἀνοψίη**, ἡ, = τὸ μὴ βλέπειν, Hsch. (ἀνοψοφίην cod.).

ἄνοψος, ον, (ὄψον) *without relish*, Plu.2.123b.

ἄν-περ, = ἐάνπερ, ἤνπερ, v. ἐάν. **-ποτε**, = εἴθε, Sch.E.Or.1580.

ἀνρεία, ἡ, coined by Pl.Cra.413e as etym. of ἀνδρεία.

ἀνσατήρ· βουβών (Lacon.), Hsch. **ἄνσατον**· ἄψασθαι, συνάψαι (Cret.), Id. **ἀνσερίσασθαι**· τὸ μόνον πρὸς τὸ πῦρ στῆναι (Lacon.), Id.

ἀνσπάω, poet. for ἀνασπάω.

ἄνστα, ἀνστάς, ἀνστήμεναι, ἀνστήσεις, ἀνστήσων, ἀνστήτην, poet. forms, v. ἀνίστημι. **ἀνσχεθέειν, ἄνσχεο**, poet. forms, v. ἀνέχω. **ἀνσχετός**, v. ἀνασχετός.

ἄντα, Ep. Adv. *over against, face to face*, in Hom. mostly in the phrases, ἄ. μάχεσθαι fight *man to man*, Il.19.163; ἄ. ἰδεῖν look *before one*, ib.13.184, cf. E.Alc.877 (lyr.); θεοῖς ἄ. ἐῴκει he was like the gods *to look at*, Il.24.630; εἴδεται ἄ. πελιδνή Nic.Th.238; ἄ. τιτύσκεσθαι aim *straight at them*, Od.22.266, cf. Pi.N.6.27; ἄ. πρός τινος Epigr. Gr.223.4 (Milet.). II. as Prep. with gen., like ἀντί, *over against*, Ἤλιδος ἄ. Il.2.626; ἄ. παρειάων σχομένη κρήδεμνα.. *before* her cheeks, Od.1.334; ἄντ' ὀφθαλμοῖϊν 4.115; also of persons, ἄ. σέθεν *before* thee, *to* thy *face*, ib.160, cf. 22.232; so in Il.21.331, with a notion of comparison, *confronted with* thee; ἕρπει ἄ. τῶ σιδάρω τὸ καλῶς κιθαρίσδεν *rivals* it, Alcm.35. 2. in hostile sense, *against*, Διὸς ἄ. πολεμίζειν Il.8.428; Διὸς ἄ... ἔγχος ἀεῖραι ib.424; εἴ κέ μεν ἄ. στήῃς 17.29; Αἴαντος στήμεναι ἄ. ib.166.

ἄνται· ἄνεμοι, and **ἀντάς**· πνοάς, Hsch. (leg. ἀῆται, ἀήτας).

ἀντᾰγανακτέω, *to be indignant in turn*, Oenom.ap.Eus.PE6.7.

ἀντᾰγᾰπάω, *love in turn* or *return*, in Pass., Ph.2.8, Them.Or.4.55d.

ἀντᾰγείρω, *rival as a collector, beggar*, Celsus ap.Orig.Cels.6.42.

ἀνταγλᾱΐζομαι, *shine brightly*, Ps.-Callisth.2.26.

ἀντᾰγοράζω, *buy with money received in payment* for something else, πωλεῖν τι καὶ ἀ. σῖτον X.An.1.5.5; τὰ ἀνταγορασθέντα D.35.24.

ἀντᾰγορεύω, *speak against, reply*, ἀντᾱγόρευσεν Pi.P.4.156. II. *gainsay, contradict*, τοῖς ἄρχουσιν Ar.Ra.1072.

ἀντᾰγωνία, ἡ, *adversity*, dub. in IG14.1977 (pl.).

ἀντᾰγων-ίζομαι, I. *struggle against, prove a match for*, τινί, esp. in war, Hdt.5.109, Th.6.72, X.Cyr.1.6.8, etc.; ἀ. ταῖς παρασκευαῖς τινός D.43.81; πρὸς τοὺς βαρβάρους Inscr.Prien.17.15, cf. Ep.Hebr.12.4. 2. generally, *struggle, vie with*, τινί Th.3.38; περί τινος And.4.2; οἱ ἀνταγωνιζόμενοί τι *the parties in a lawsuit*, X. Cyr.8.2.27; [οἱ ἐλευθέριοι] οὐκ ἀ. περὶ τῶν χρημάτων Arist.Rh. 1366^{b}8. 3. *act a part in rivalry with*, τινί Plu.Dem.29. II. as Pass., *to be set against*, τινί X.Oec.10.12. **-ιστέω**, *oppose, be a rival*, Arist.Rh.1416^{b}14. **-ιστής**, οῦ, ὁ, *opponent, competitor, rival*, Dialex.2.7, X.Cyr.1.6.8, 3.3.36, Alex.272; τινί τινος X.Hier. 4.6, etc.; ἀ. ἔρωτος *a rival* in love, E.Tr.1006, cf. Pl.R.554e, al.; χαλεποὶ ἀ. τοῖς βαρβάροις Isoc.4.75; ἀ. τῆς παιδείας *opponents* of their system of education, Arist.Pol.1338^{b}37; ἀ. ἔχειν τινὰ ταῖς ἐπιβολαῖς Plb.2.45.5. **-ιστος**, ον, in Poll.3.141, is interpreted, *contending as an adversary*:—but ἀνταγωνίστως (Id.1.157) is f.l. for ἀναντ- in Lib.Decl.15.21.

ἀντᾰδῐκ-έω, *injure in return, retaliate upon*, ἀλλήλους Pl.Tht.173a, cf. Cri.49b,c, Max.Tyr.18.5. **-ητέον**, *one must retaliate*, ibid.

ἀντᾴδω, *sing in answer*, esp. of the partridge, *answer* when another calls, ἀ. ὡς μαχούμενος Arist.HA614^{a}11, cf. Mir.845^{b}25, Ael.NA4.16; ἀ. Μούσαις Luc.Pisc.6; τοῖς φθεγγομένοις Plu.2.794c; *cry out at one*, ἐγὼ δ', ἢν τοῦτο δρᾷς, ἀντᾴσομαι Ar.Ec.887:—Pass., στροφῇ ἀντᾳσθῆναι Poll.4.112.

ἀνταείρω, = ἀνταίρω, only in Med., ἀνταείρεσθαι χεῖράς τινι *raise one's* hands *against* one, *make war upon* him, Hdt.3.144, 7.101; or without τινί, 6.44, 7.212; also πόλεμον βασιλέϊ ἀ. 8.140.α΄.

ἀντάεις, Dor. for ἀντήεις.

ἄνταθλος, ον, *contending against, rivalling*, τινός *AP*12.68 (Mel.).

ἀνταιδέομαι, Med., *respect in return*, αἰδουμένας ἀ. X.*Cyr*.8.1.28.

ἀνταῖος, α, ον, (ἄντα) *set over against, right opposite*, ἀνταία πληγή a wound *in front, right in the breast*, S.*El*.195, E.*Andr*.844; ἀνταίαν ἔπαισεν (sc. πληγήν) S.*Ant*.1308. 2. *opposed to, hostile, hateful*, κνώδαλον ἀ. βροτοῖσιν A.*Ch*.588 (lyr.); πομπά E.*IA*1323 (lyr.), cf. S.*Fr*.72,334; θεός ib.335; τἀνταῖα θεῶν their *hostile purposes*, A.*Pers*.604. II. *besought with prayers*, epith. of Hecate, etc., A.R.1.1141, cf. Orph.*H*.41.1; ἀνταία· . . ἱκέσιος, A.(*Fr*.223)ap.Hsch.; ἀνταῖος Ζεύς Sch.Il.22.113.

ἀνταίρω, Ion. **ἀνταείρω** (q.v.), *raise against*, χεῖράς τινι *AP*7.139 (so in Med., Th.3.32, 1.53); πόλεμόν τινι Plb.15.7.8; πρὸς Ἔρωτα μάχην *AP*12.147 (Mel.); *raise in reply*, λαμπτῆρας Aen.Tact.26.13:—Med., ὅπλα ἀνταιρόμενοι Th.1.53, cf. 3.32. II. intr., *rise up* or *rebel against, withstand*, ἀντᾶραί τινι Pl.*Euthd*.272a, D.2.24; πρός τι or τινα, Id.6.5, Plu.*Pyrrh*.15, D.H.6.48:—so in Med., τινί Luc.*Herm*.33, *JTr*.34. 2. of a cliff, *rise opposite to* or *in the same parallel with*, τοῖς κατὰ Μερόην τόποις Str.2.1.2, cf. 20; πρὸς τὴν Λιβύην Plu.*Aem*.6.

ἀνταισχύνομαι [ῡ], *to be ashamed in turn*, Ach.Tat.8.4.

ἀνταιτέω, *demand in return*, Th.4.19, Lib.*Or*.54.75; σμικρὰ τῆς ἀμνηστίας τὴν βουλήν App.*BC*3.35. II. *contest with*, τινὶ τὴν ὑπατείαν D.C.40.53.

ἀνταιτιάομαι, *make a countercharge*, D.C.*Fr*.99.

ἀνταιωρέομαι, *rise over against*, Plot.6.5.11.

ἀντᾰκαῖος, ὁ, a sort of *sturgeon*, Hdt.4.53, Lync.1.9, Ael.*NA*14.23. 2. Adj., τάριχος ἀν καῖον Antiph.186.

ἀντακάς· σήμερον, and **ἀντακές**· σημεῖον(sic), Hsch.; cf. ἀνταλλές.

ἀντᾰκολουθ-έω, *to be reciprocally implied*, of the virtues, Chrysipp. *Stoic*.3.72, cf. S.E.*P*.1.68 (abs.); ἀ. ἀλλήλαις αἱ εὐφυεῖαι Anon.*in Tht*.11.16; οὐδὲ ἀ. ἀλλήλαις [ἀκμὴ καὶ λαμπρότης] Hermog.*Id*.1.10, cf. Them.*inPh*.150.29. **-ησις**, εως, ἡ, *reciprocal implication*, of the virtues, *Stoic*.3.76, Procl.*inAlc*.p.319C. **-ία**, ἡ, = foreg., *Stoic*.2.121; *correspondence*, Iamb.*inNic*.p.39P. **-ος**, ον, *reciprocally implied*, τὸ ἀ. ἀλλήλαις Eustr.*inEN*311.15: abs., *corresponding*, ἕξις dub. in Phld.*Rh*.1.27S. (cf. *Supp*.15).

ἀντᾰκοντίζω, *hurl against in return*, λίθον D.C.59.28.

ἀντᾰκούω, fut. -ούσομαι S.*Aj*.1141, *hear in turn*, ἀντὶ τῶν εἰρημένων ἴσ' ἀντάκουσον Id.*OT*544; ἅ γ' εἶπας ἀντήκουσας E.*Heracl*.1014 (cj.); κἀμοῦ νῦν ἀντάκουσον Id.*Supp*.569; ἀντακούσει τοῦτον ὡς τεθάψεται S.*Aj*.1141: abs., *listen in return*, ἀ. ἐν μέρει A.*Eu*.198, cf. Crates Com.5D.: also in Prose, X.*An*.2.5.16, Lib.*Decl*.5.89.

ἀντακροάομαι, *hear in turn*, Ar.*Lys*.527.

ἀντακρωτήριον, τό, *opposite headland*, Str.6.1.1.

ἀντᾰλαζονεύομαι, *boast in reply*, Eust.590.11.

ἀντᾰλᾰλάζω, *return a shout*, of friendly armies, Plu.*Pyrrh*.32, *Flam*.4; of an echo, A.*Pers*.390.

ἀνταλλᾰγ-ή, ἡ, *exchanging, exchange, barter*, *Gloss*., Simp.*inPh*.1350.32. **-μα**, ατος, τό, *that which is given* or *taken in exchange*, φίλου *for* a friend, E.*Or*.1157, cf. Lxx *Jb*.28.15, al.; τῆς ψυχῆς *Ev.Matt*.16.26, cf. Ph.*Fr*.110H. **-ος**, ον, *exchanged for another*, Men.16,254,513.

ἀνταλλα-κτέον, *one must give in exchange*, τινός *for* a thing, D.19.223. **-κτης**, ου, ὁ, *one who requites*, τῶν κακῶν Phld.*Mort*.17 (pl.). **-κτος**, ον, *taken as equivalent*, πρός τι Porph.*Abst*.1.51. **-σσω**, Att. **-ττω**, *exchange* one thing *with* another, δάκρυα δ' ἀνταλλάσσετε τοῖς τῆσδε μέλεσι E.*Tr*.351; τὴν ἀξίωσιν τῶν ὀνομάτων ἐς τὰ ἔργα ἀ. they *changed* the signification of the names in relation to things, Th.3.82; τὴν ψυχὴν τοῦ χρυσίου Poll.3.113. II. more freq. in Med., *take in exchange*, ἄνδρα A.*Ch*.133; ἀνταλλάσσεσθαί τί τινος *take* one thing *in exchange for* another, E.*Hel*.1088, etc.; τι ἀντί τινος D.16.5; ἀνταλλάσσεσθαι τῇ διανοίᾳ *interchange* in thought, Pl.*Tht*.189c; θάνατον ἀνταλλάξεται *shall receive* death *in exchange*, i. e. as a punishment, E.*Ph*.1633:—so in Pass., ἀντηλλαγμένου τοῦ ἑκατέρων τρόπου *having made an interchange* of each other's custom, i. e. having each adopted the way of the other, Th.4.14. 2. *give in exchange*, μηδεμιᾶς χάριτος μηδ' ὠφελίας τὴν εἰς τοὺς Ἕλληνας εὔνοιαν D.6.10.

ἀνταλλές· ταύτης τῆς ἡμέρας, Hsch.; cf. ἀντακάς, ἀντακές.

ἄνταλλος, ον, *exchanged*, Sch.D.T.p.343H.

ἀντᾰμείβομαι, *exchange* one thing *with* another, ὅταν δελφῖσι θῆρες ἀνταμείψωνται νομόν Archil.74.7. II. c. acc. pers., *repay, requite, punish*, ἀνταμείβεσθαί τινα κακοῖς Id.65; κακαῖσι ποιναῖς A.*Pr*.225; παθὼν κακῶς κακοῖσιν ἀντημείβετο Id.*Th*.1054; ἀνταμειψόμεσθά σ' ὥσπερ εἰκὸς ἀντὶ τῶνδε Ar.*Th*.723. III. *answer again*, τοῖσδε Hdt.9.79; πρὸς τοὺς φίλους οἷ' ἀνταμείβει ῥήματ' S.*OC*814; τινὰ οὐδέν ib.1273; also ὑμᾶς . . τοῖσδ' ἀνταμείβομαι λόγοις E.*Andr*.154.

ἀντάμειψις [ᾰμ], εως, ἡ, *exchanging, requital*, v.l. in Lxx *Ps*.118(119).112, Hsch.

ἀνταμελέω, in fut. Pass. ἀνταμεληθήσομαι, *neglect in turn*, Ph.2.275.

ἀνταμιλλᾶσθαι· ἀντερίζειν, Hsch.

ἀντᾰμοιβαῖος, sc. πούς, the foot ◡ ◡ – – ◡, Diom.1.481K.

ἀντᾰμοιβή, ἡ, *interchange*, πυρὸς ἀ. τὰ πάντα καὶ πῦρ ἁπάντων Heraclit.90. 2. *repayment, requital*, εὐεργεσίας Charito 5.2.

ἀντᾰμοιβός, όν, v. ἀντημοιβός.

ἀντᾰμύνομαι [ῡ], Med., *defend oneself against another, resist*, Th.4.19. II. *requite*, ἐχθρὸν κακοῖς S.*Ant*.643; οἱ ἀνταμυνόμενοι Th.3.84.

ἀνταμφοδέω, (ἄμφοδον) *miss* a person *in the street* going to meet him, *BGU*1030.5 (iii A. D.).

ἀνταναβῐβάζω, *make go up in turn*, X.*HG*3.2.15.

ἀνταναβοάω, *cry out in answer* or *opposition*, App.*BC*2.131.

ἀνταναγιγνώσκω, *read and compare*, Cratin.386; νόμους D.20 Arg. ii 8, cf. *PPetr*.3p.50 (III B.C.).

ἀντανάγω [ᾰγ], *lead up against*, esp. ἀ. νέας *put* ships *to sea against*, Hdt.6.14, cf. Th.7.37: also ἀ. ναυσὶν ἓξ καὶ ὀγδοήκοντα ib.52: more freq. abs. in same sense, whether in Act., as Id.8.38, X.*HG*2.1.23, or in Med., as Th.4.13, X.*HG*1.1.5:—Pass., ναυσὶν ἀνταναχθεὶς D.S.13.71:—generally, *attack*, ἀντανήγετο πρὸς τὸ μειράκιον Pl.*Erx*.398e. 2. *raise in opposition*, [ὅρος] τῇ Οἴτῃ Philostr.*VA*4.23. 3. *bring up instead*, *AP*9.285 (Phil.).

ἀνταναίρ-εσις, εως, ἡ, *corresponding diminution*, Arist.*Top*.158^{b}33. II. *alternate removal*, Eust.1397.44. III. *cancellation*, Simp.*inPh*.1237.23. **-ετέος**, α, ον, *to be struck off*, *PTeb*.61(6).220 (II B.C.). **-ετικός**, ή, όν, *cancelling opposite sides of an account*, *striking a balance*: metaph., εὐλογιστία ἐστὶν ἐπιστήμη -κή *Stoic*.3.64. **-έω**, *strike out of an account*, D.18.231:—Pass., *to be cancelled correspondingly*, Arist.*Metaph*.1040^{a}22, Demad.59; *to be struck off*, *PTeb*.60.111, al. (II B.C.). 2. *kill in return*, Ph.2.321 (Pass.). 3. *set off against, deduct*, *Sammelb*.4369(a).10, al. (III B.C.), *PRyl*.154.33 (I A.D., Pass.); prob. l. for ἀνταναίρειν (= ἀνθυφελεῖν), Ar.*Fr*.12D. 4. Med., *resume*, ἀποβεβληκὼς τὴν ἁλουργίδα οὐκέτι ἀντανείλετο Agath.4.29.

ἀντανά-κλᾰσις, εως, ἡ, *reflection of light*, *Placit*.4.14.3, cf. Vett.Val.1.14, Ath.Med.ap.Orib.9.12.1 (pl.); also, of sound, *echo*, Plu.2.502d. 2. *bending back*, ἀγκίστρου Sch.Opp.*H*.1.216. II. *use of a word in an altered sense*, Lat. *contraria significatio*, Quint.*Inst*.9.3.68, Sch.A.R.1.746. **-κλασμός**, ὁ, *reflexive sense*, of words, A.D.*Pron*.43.12. **-κλαστος**, ον, *reciprocal*, προσηγορία Priscian.*Inst*.11.1. **-κλάω**, *reflect*, φῶς v.l. in Plu.2.696a:—Pass., ἀντανακλᾶται ἀκτὶς S.E.*M*.5.82; ὀφθαλμοὶ ἀλλήλοις ἀντανακλώμενοι *reflected* one in another, Ach.Tat.1.9. 2. of sound, in Pass., *to be reflected* or *echoed*, Lxx *Wi*.17.19, *Placit*.4.20.2. 3. *bend back*, τὸν ἀγκῶνα Heliod.ap.Orib.49.13.8. 4. Gramm., in Pass., *to be reflexive*, of pronouns, A.D.*Synt*.175.12, cf.*Pron*.28.3, al. 5. *cause to revert*, in writing, εἴς τι πάλιν ἀ. τὸ πέρας *CPHerm*.18.11. **-κοπή**, ἡ, *recoil*, κυμάτων Arist.*Mu*.396^{a}19. **-κόπτω**, *throw back again*, Phryn.*PS* p.61B. **-κράζω**, *cry out in turn* or *reply*, App.*Mith*.26. **-λαμβάνω**, *take over instead*, Ptol.*Phas*.p.11H.

ἀντανᾱλίσκω, *destroy in return*, E.*Or*.1165.

ἀντανά-λῠσις, εως, ἡ, *counteraction, incongruity of position*, Vett.Val.186.28, Antioch.Astr. in *Cat.Cod.Astr*.8(3).107. **-λύω**, Astrol., *counteract*, Vett.Val.289.17 (Pass.). **-μένω**, *wait instead of* taking active measures, c. inf., Th.3.12. **-παύομαι**, Med., *rest correspondingly*, Polyaen.1.14. **-πίμπλημι**, *fill in return*, v.l. in X.*HG*2.4.12. **-πλέκω**, *plait in rivalry with*, ἄνθεα τοῖς Μελεαγρείοις στεφάνοις *AP*4.2 (Phil.). **-πληρόω**, *fill up*, τὴν θέσιν τοῦ ὀνόματος A.D.*Synt*.14.1; τὰ ὑστερήματα τῶν θλίψεων τοῦ Χριστοῦ *Ep.Col*.1.24; ἀ. πρὸς τὸν εὐπορώτατον ἀεὶ τοὺς ἀπορωτάτους *put in* the poorest *so as to balance* the richest, D.14.17. **-πλήρωσις**, εως, ἡ, *filling up again*, Epicur.*Ep*.1p.11U.

ἀντανα-σηκόω, *compensate*, *IG*14.956*A*19. **-τρέχω**, *return*, of the foreskin, Paul.Aeg.6.60. **-φέρω**, *bring back in turn*, ἀ. τὴν πίστιν Plu.2.2cc. II. abs., *make compensation*, τῇ λοιπῇ δόξῃ πρὸς τὴν δυσφημίαν Them.*Or*.7.99c. **-χωρέω**, *give ground in turn*, Aristid.*Or*.23(42).47.

ἄντανδρος, ον, *instead of a man, as a substitute*, ἀντί τινος Luc.*DMort*.16.2, etc.

ἀντάνειμι, (εἶμι *ibo*) *rise so as to balance*, τινί Th.2.75.

ἀντανεμία, ἡ, *contrary wind*, Simp.*indeAn*.60.32.

ἀνταν-έχω, *hold up in turn* or *in reply*, πυρσούς Polyaen.6.19.2, cf. 1.40.3, Men.Prot.p.72D. **-ισόω**, *make equal, adjust, compensate*, Lib.*Or*.59.161 (dub.):—Pass., Them.*inPh*.137.21. **-ίστημι**, *set up against* or *in rivalry*, λόγον Plu.2.40e; τρόπαιον D.C.42.48; τί τινι Plu.2.348d. II. Pass., with aor. 2 Act., *rise up against*, τινὶ ἐς χεῖρας S.*Tr*.441, cf. Plu.*Sull*.7; *rise one against another*, Id.2.723b. **-ίσωμα** [ῐ], ατος, τό, *an equivalent*, J.*AJ*18.9.7. **-ίσωσις** [ῐσ], εως, ἡ, *balancing, equalizing*, Boethus ap.Porph.ap.Eus.*PE*11.28, David *Proll*.214.11, Simp.*inCael*.458.2.

ἀντᾰνοίγω, *open against*, ἀ. ὄμματα κεραυνοῖς *face* them, Longin.34.4.

ἀντανταν· ἐπίβουλον, ἀντίδικον, Hsch.

ἀντᾰνύω, v. ἀνατανύω.

ἄνταξ· ἐν μέρει, Hsch. (cf. ὑπαντάξ).

ἀντάξιος, α, ον, also ος, ον Theoc.17.114:—*worth just as much as*, c. gen., ψυχῆς ἀ. *worth* life *itself*, Il.9.401; πολλῶν ἀ. ἄλλων 11.514; ἕκαστος δέκα ἀνδρῶν ἀ. *worth as much as* ten, Hdt.7.103, cf. 2.148, Pl.*Lg*.730d, X.*Mem*.2.10.3, etc.; *worthy of*, τέχνας Theoc. l. c. 2. abs., *worth as much, worth no less*, Il.1.136.

ἀνταξιόω, *demand as an equivalent* or *in turn*, Th.6.16: c. dupl. acc., ἀνταξιῶσαι δωρεὰν αὐτόν Macho ap.Ath.13.579a.

ἀνταπαιτέω, *demand in return*, Th.3.58, 5.17, Plu.*Sol*.3:—Pass., *to be called on for* a thing *in turn*, λόγον Id.*Cat.Mi*.53.

ἀνταπᾰμείβομαι, Med., *obey in turn*, ῥήτραις Tyrt.4.6.

ἀνταπᾰτάω, *deceive in turn*, τινά J.*AJ*5.8.11.

ἀνταπειλέω, *threaten in turn*, τινί Ph.2.469, cf. Them.*Or*.7.95b.

ἀνταπερύκω [ῡ], *keep off in turn*, *AP*15.14 (Theoph.).

ἀνταπέχω, *receive in return*, χάριτάς τινος *Anatolian Studies* p.343.

ἀνταπο-δείκνῡμι or -ύω, *prove in return* or *answer*, X.*Smp.*2.22; τὸ ἀντικείμενον Arist.*Rh.*1403^{a}27. 2. *appoint instead*, D.C.49.43. **-δίδωμι**, *give back, repay, tender in repayment* or *requital*, Batr.186; ἀ. τὸ ὅμοιον, τὸ ἴσον, Hdt.1.18, Th.1.43; χάριν Pherecr. 2 D.; τὴν ἴσην Arist.*Rh.*1379^{b}7; ἀ. τροφεῖα Lys.6.49; ἀρετήν Th. 4.19; ὕβριν Plu.2.825c; τὰ αὐτὰ ἀ. *react* in the same way, Pl.*Ti.* 79e; of counter-arguments, Id.*Prm.*128d: abs., *pay back*, Th.3.40, Arist.*Rh.*1367^{a}21. 2. *take vengeance*, Lxx *De.*32.35, al., *Ep. Rom.*12.19. II. *assign as a balance*, ἐναντίαν γένεσιν Pl.*Phd.* 71e. 2. *make convertible*, τὴν μεταφορὰν τὴν ἐκ τοῦ ἀνάλογον Arist. *Rh.*1407^{a}15:—Pass., Demetr.*Eloc.*79. b. Gramm., *make to correspond*, of correlatives (e.g. τοιοῦτος, οἷος), in Pass., A.D.*Conj.*254.19, *Synt.*54.5, al.; so of μέν..δέ, Arist.*Rh.*1407^{a}23, Demetr.*Eloc.*53, cf. Hermog.*Id.*1.4, al. 3. intr., *answer to, correspond with*, εἰ μὴ ἀνταποδιδοίη τὰ ἕτερα τοῖς ἑτέροις Pl.*Phd.*72a, cf. b; οὐκ ἀνταποδίδωσι τὸ ὅμοιον *there is* no similar *correspondent*, Arist.*Mete.*347^{b}32, cf. *IA* 707^{b}16, Ps.-Alex.Aphr.*inSE*192.14. 4. *give back words, exchange* 'tu quoque's', Pl.*Phdr.*236c. III. *deliver in turn*, τὸ σύνθημα X.*Cyr.*3.3.58 (Pass.); *explain in turn*, Pl.*Ti.*87c. IV. *give back* a sound, of an echo, Plu.*Sull.*19; of troops, κραυγὴν ἀ. Id.*Tim.* 27. **-δομα**, ατος, τό, *repayment, requital*, whether of good or evil, Lxx *Si.*12.2, 14.6, al., *Ev.Luc.*14.12, *Ep.Rom.*11.9. **-δοσις**, εως, ἡ, *giving back in turn*, opp. ἀποδοχή, Th.4.81; *rendering, requiting, repayment*, Arist.*EN*1133^{a}3, 1163^{a}11, al.; χάριτος Men.*Mon.*330, D.S.20.100; τῶν εὐεργεσιῶν Phld.*Piet.*14; *retribution*, Lxx *Is.*61.2, 63.4, al.; *reprisals*, γίγνεται ἀ. ἔκ τινος Plb.5.30.6; *reward*, Lxx *Ps.*18 (19).11, *Ep.Col.*3.24. II. *turning back, opposite direction* or *course*, of a current, ἀ. ποιεῖσθαι Plb.4.43.5, etc., cf. Plu.2.136b. 2. *responsive sound*, Arist.*Aud.*803^{a}31. III. *alternation*, e.g. of action and reaction, περιόδων πρὸς ἀλλήλας Hp.*Aph.*1.12; *reaction*, prob. in Epicur.*Ep.*2 p.48 U., cf. Thphr.*Vent.*10. 2. Rhet., *parallelism* or *opposition of clauses* in a periodic sentence, Demetr.*Eloc.*23, cf. 250; in a simile, *correspondence with* the object of comparison, Quint. *Inst.*8.3.77. b. Gramm., *correlativity* of words such as τοιοῦτος, οἷος, A.D.*Synt.*54.1. c. *answering clause*, Hermog.*Id.*1.11, 2.1; v.l. in A.D.*Synt.*20.6. 3. *capping verses*, as a subject of competition, *Michel* 913 (Teos). **-δοτέον**, *one must repay*, τὴν ἀξίαν ὧν ἔπαθεν Arist.*EN*1163^{a}2; τιμήν 1163^{b}14; χάριν 1164^{b}26; τὰς εὐεργεσίας ib.31. II. ἀ. ἕξιν τινί *one must make* it *correspond to*.., Pl.*Phlb.*40d. **-δοτικός**, ή, όν, = ἀμοιβαῖος, Sch.Opp.*H.*2. 255. II. Gramm., *belonging to* or *marking* ἀνταπόδοσις, Plb. Rh.p.107 S.; of pronouns, *correlative*, A.D.*Adj.*158.24, *Conj.*237.9, al. Adv. -κῶς Sch.A.R.1.5. **-δύομαι** [ῠ], *strip, prepare for a contest with*, τινί Philostr.*Im.*2.19. **-θνῄσκω**, *die* or *am killed in requital*, ἀνταποθανεῖν τὸν ἀποκτείναντα Antipho 5.10; τοῦ ἐμψύχου δόγματος ὃ ἀνεῖλε Ph.1.94.

ἀντάποινα, f.l. for ἀντίποινα, S.*Ph.*316, E.*HF*755; also in *POxy.* 1381.234.

ἀνταπο-κατάστᾰσις, εως, ἡ, *renewal by substitution*, *Corp.Herm.*11. 2. 2. of planets, *the opposite position to* ἀποκατάστασις, Doroth.ap. *Cat.Cod.Astr.*2.196.19. **-καταστᾰτικός**, ή, όν, Astrol., *opposite to the position of* ἀποκατάστασις, σελήνη Max.*Epit.*p.80 L. **-κρίνομαι** [ῑ], Med., *answer again*, Lxx *Jb.*16.8, *Ev.Luc.*14.6; *argue against*, τινί *Ep.Rom.*9.20. II. *correspond to*, Nicom.*Ar.*1.8.10, 11. **-κρίσις**, εως, ἡ, *correspondence* (cf. foreg. II), ib.8, Iamb. *in Nic.*p.36 P. **-κτείνω**, *kill in return*, Hdt.7.136, A.*Ch.*121, E. *Hec.*262, Ar.*Ach.*326, X.*HG*2.4.27, etc. **-λαμβάνω**, *receive* or *accept in return*, ἑστίασιν Pl.*Ti.*27b; χάριν D.20.46.

ἀνταπόλλῡμι, *destroy in return*, E.*Ion* 1328, Pl.*Cri.*51a. II. Pass. and Med., with pf. 2 Act., *perish in turn*, αὐτὸς ἀνταπωλόμην E. *Hel.*106, cf. *IT*715; ὑπὲρ ἀνδρὸς ἑκάστου δέκα ἀνταπόλλυσθαι Hdt.3.14.

ἀνταπο-λογέομαι, *speak for the defence* or *in reply*, Is.5.17, D.C. 50.2. **-παίζω**, *lose what one has won at play*, ἀστραγάλους Menecr. 1 D. **-παλσις**, εως, ἡ, *rebounding, revulsion*, Cass.*Pr.*26. **-πέρδω**, Lat. *oppedere*, πρὸς τὰς βροντάς Ar.*Nu.*293.

ἀνταπορέω, *raise questions in turn*, S.E.*M.*1.231.

ἀνταπο-στέλλω, *send in exchange*, ὁμήρους Plb.21.43.22; *send backwards and forwards*, πρέσβεις D.C.50.2, cf. Aen.Tact.31.9 (Pass.); *refer* one *back again*, ἐπί τι S.E.*M.*8.86; of an echo, τὰς ἀνακλάσεις ἀ. Plu.2.248c. **-στρέφω**, *turn back again*, Tz.*H.*5.903. **-στροφή**, ἡ, *turning away from one another*, of places which face opposite ways, Str.6.1.5. **-ταφρεύω**, *cut off in turn by trenches*, App.*BC* 2.61. **-τειχίζω**, *wall off, fortify on the other side*, D.C.43.7. **-τίνω** [ῑ], *requite, repay*, *AP*9.223 (Bianor), Orph.*Fr.*32d, e. **-τος**· συνδεδεμένος, Hsch. **-φαίνω**, *show on the other hand*, Th.3.38, 67. **-φέρω**, *catch in turn*, of a ball, Poll.9.107.

ἀντάποχον, τό, *counter-receipt*, *POxy.*1542.1 (iv A.D.), *BGU*974. 10 (iv A.D.).

ἀντάπτομαι, Ion. for ἀνθάπτομαι.

ἀνταπ-ωθέω, *repel in turn*, Arist.*Pr.*936^{b}35:—Pass., Id.*Somn.Vig.* 457^{b}23. **-ωσις**, εως, ἡ, *mutual repulsion*, *Placit.*2.23.2.

ἄνταρ· ἀετός (Etruscan), Hsch. 2. = δίασμα, Euph.147.

ἀντάρης, ου, ὁ, *the star α Scorpii*, Heph.Astr.1.3, Ptol.*Calend.* p.214 W., Id.*Alm.*8.1.

ἀντᾰριθμ-έω, *count against one another*, Paus.10.20.1. **-ητέον**, ἑκάστῳ σταγόνι τοὺς ἴσους [ὀδόντας] Poll.2.93.

ἀνταρκέω, *hold out against*, τοῖς παροῦσιν Th.7.15; πρός τι Plu. *Cleom.*30. II. abs., *hold out, persist*, Ar.*Eq.*540, Isoc.6.79, 19. 26: c. part., τρέφουσα.. ἀντήρκεσεν D.C.68.25.

ἀνταρκτικός, ή, όν, *antarctic*, πόλος Arist.*Mu.*392^{a}4; κύκλος Gem. 5.16; without κύκλος, ib.39; ζώνη *Placit.*3.14.1.

ἀντ-αρσία, ἡ, *insurrection*, Lyd.*Ost.*33, *Cat.Cod.Astr.*7.171. **-αρσις**, εως, ἡ, = foreg., Sm.4 *Ki.*11.14. **-αρτης**· τύραννος, ἐπιβαίνων βασιλεῖ, Hsch.

ἄνταρχος, ὁ, *pro-magistrate*, Gloss.

ἀντάρχων, οντος, ὁ, *vice-president*, τοῦ ἀγῶνος *IG*2^{2}.1077, cf. ib.12 (2).35e (Mytil.); *pro-magistrate*, *SIG*785.17 (Chios), *POxy.*907.21 (iii A.D.); ἀ. τῶν στρατηγῶν *AJA*18.329 (Sardes, i B.C.).

ἀντασπάζομαι, *welcome, greet in turn*, X.*Cyr.*1.3.3; *return greeting*, Hierocl.*Facet.*7; *receive kindly*, X.*Cyr.*5.5.42, Pl.Com.12 D., Plu.*Tim.*38.

ἀνταστράπτω, *lighten against*, ἀστραπαῖς D.C.59.28.

ἀντάτας, α, ὁ, (ἄτη) *surety*, *GDI*5015.23 (Gortyn).

ἀντατῑμάζω, *requite with dishonour*, prob. cj. in S.*Aj.*1339.

ἀνταυγ-άζω, = ἀνταυγέω, πρὸς ἥλιον Hld.1.2, cf. 9.14. II. trans., *expose to the light, illuminate*, ἡλίῳ βίον ἀ. Ph.2.260. **-ασία**, ἡ, *reflection of light*, Gloss.:—also **-εια** or **-ία**, ἡ, *Placit.*2.20.12, X. *Cyn.*5.18, Plu.2.921b, Ps.-Hp.*Hebd.*1.52; ἡλίου Onos.29.2; τῆς χιόνος *from* the snow, D.S.17.82; *shining in one's face*, ἡλίου Ascl.*Tact.*12.10. **-έω**, *reflect light*, Hp.*Carn.*17, Arist.*Pr.*932^{a} 27, Chaerem.14; πρὸς Ὄλυμπον Emp.44; φάσγανον ἀνταυγεῖ φόνον *flashes back* murder, E.*Or.*1519; *gleam, glitter*, Eub.56. **-ής**, ές, *reflecting light, sparkling*, κάλλος Sannyr.1 D.; κόραι Ar.*Th.*902; χιών D.S.17.82: pr. n. Ἀνταύγης, of the sun, Orph.*Fr.*237.

ἀνταυδάω, *address face to face*, τινά S.*El.*1478.

ἀνταυλέω, *play on the flute against*, τινί Agath.4.23.

ἀνταΰω, *sound in turn, answer*, οἱ ἀντάΰσε [ῠ] βροντᾶς φθέγμα Pi. *P.*4.197, cf. Opp.*C.*2.78.

ἀνταφαιρ-έω, *take away in return*, in Med., Antipho 4.1.7:—Act., intr., *diminish in turn*, Aristid.*Or.*23(42).50, cf. 2.309 J. II. *subtract from the opposite side*, and **-εσις**, εως, ἡ, *subtraction from the opposite side*, Nicom.*Ar.*1.13.

ἀνταφεστιάω, *feast in return*, Pl.*Ti.*17b.

ἀνταφίημι [φῐ], *let go in turn*, δάκρυ ἀ. *let* the tear *fall in turn*, E. *IA*478. II. *send back*, σφαῖραν Poll.9.107.

ἀντάω, Ep. impf. ἤντεον Il.7.423: I. c. dat. pers., *come opposite to, meet face to face, meet with*, ᾗ οἱ ἔπειτ' ἤντησ' ib.6.399; ἤντεον ἀλλήλοισιν 7.423; so also in Trag., ἀνέμοις ἀ. A.*Supp.*36; πατρί S.*Tr.*902, etc. II. = ἀντιάω, c. gen., 1. c. gen. pers., *meet* in battle, εἴ κεν πάντων ἀντήσομεν Od.16.254, cf. Il.16.423: also without any hostile sense, σπέρμα μὲν ἄντασ' Ἐρεχθειδᾶν by lineage *she reached, went up to* the Erechtheidae, S.*Ant.*982. 2. c. gen. rei, *meet with, take part in, partake in* or *of*, μάχης, δαίτης, Il.7.158, Od.3.44; κατάλεξον ὅπως ἤντησας ὀπωπῆς how thou *hast gained* sight of him, ib.17.44, cf. 3.97; so ἀ. ξεινίων Hdt.2.119; ἀλώσιος Pi. *O.*10(11).42; ἀ. τινὸς ὑπό τινος *meet with* such and such treatment from another, Hdt.1.114; σφῷν.. θεοῖς ἀρῶμαι μή ποτ' ἀντῆσαι κακῶν S.*OC*1445. III. c. acc., ἤν νιν πομπαῖς ἀντήσῃς E.*IA*150 (s.v.l.).—The simple Verb never in Com. or Att. Prose; but cf. ἀπαντάω.

ἀντεγγράφω [ᾰφ], *insert* one name *instead of* another, Arist.*Ath.* 36.2, D.25.73 (Pass.).

ἀντεγείρω, *raise* or *build instead*, D.C.69.12; *build in opposition*, τί τινι App.*Pun.*114.

ἀντεγκᾰλέω, *make a counter-claim*, D.40.14. 2. *bring a counter-charge*, τινί Isoc.17.12, D.H.8.64, Plu.*Ant.*55, etc.; ἀλλήλοις δώρων Hermog.*Stat.*3.

ἀντέγκειμαι, Pass., *to be urgent on the other side*, Eun.*VS* p.470 B. II. *to be inserted in place of* another letter (as θ for ε), Eust.1863.56.

ἀντέγκλημα, ατος, τό, *counter-claim* or *-charge*, Hermog.*Stat.*2, cf. 11: pl., Corn.*Rh.*p.387 H.

ἀντεγκληματικός, ή, όν, *of* or *for a counter-accusation*, ἀντίθεσις Hermog.*Stat.*6, 12; τὸ -κόν Antipho 4.2 Arg.; τὰ -κά Aps.p.235 H. Adv. -κῶς Sch.A.R.1.834.

ἀντεγχειρίζω, *entrust to* another *instead*, τινὶ δίκας D.C.60.24.

ἀντεγχέω, *pour in instead*, Gal.18(1).282.

ἀντεικ-άζω, fut. -άσομαι Pl.*Men.*80c: aor. -ήκασα Ar.*V.*1311, subj. -εικάσω Pl. l. c.:—*compare in return*, τινά τινι Ar. l. c.: c. acc., Pl. l. c.:—hence **-ασία**, ἡ, Sch.Ven.Il.8.560.

ἀντειλέω, *unwind in opposite direction*, Orib.49.22.18 (Pass.).

ἀντεῖν· ὁ ἐναντίος τῇ ἀγωγῇ, Hsch.

ἀντείνω, poet. for ἀνατείνω.

ἀντεῖπον, aor. 2 without any pres. (cf. ἀντερῶ, ἀντιλέγω, ἀνταγορεύω), *speak against* or *in answer, gainsay*, c. dat., S.*OC*999, etc.; ἀ. τινὶ δεομένῳ Th.1.136: abs., οὐδὲν ἀντειπεῖν ἔχω A.*Pr.*51; ἀ. πρός τινα or τι, Th.3.61, X.*HG*3.3.3; *oppose*, Pl.*Thg.*131a; ἀ. ὑπέρ τινος *speak* in one's defence, Ar.*Th.*545: c. acc. cogn., ἀ. ἔπος *utter* a word *of contradiction*, E.*IA*1391; δύο λόγω περὶ τῶν αὐτῶν ἀντειπεῖν *speak on both sides of* a question, Isoc.10.1; τούτῳ ἂν δίκαιον λόγον ἀντείποιμι Pl.*Ap.*28b. 2. κακῶς ἀ. τινά *malign* him *in turn*, S. *Ant.*1053.

ἀντείρομαι, Ion. aor. -ειρόμην, Att. -ηρόμην:—*ask in turn*, Hdt.1. 129, 3.23, X.*Cyr.*2.2.22: in part., Plu.2.739b.

ἀντεισ-άγω [ᾰγ], *introduce, import instead*, D.9.39 (Pass.), Pl.*Ax.* 369e, Men.402.16, etc. II. *bring in to office*, etc., *in turn*, ἀλλήλους εἰς ἐπαρχίας κτλ. Plu.*Caes.*14. III. *restore*, Gal.6.75, al. **-άγωγή**, ἡ, *compensatory antithesis* (as οἰκτρόν.. σεμνὸν δέ), Alex.*Fig.*1.25, Zonae.*Fig.*20. **-ακτέον**, v.l. for ἀντεισενεκτέον, q.v. 2. *one must restore*, Gal.1.393. -βάλλω, intr., *make an inroad in reprisal*, D.C.48.21. -δύνω [ῠ], *enter instead*, εἰς τοὺς πόρους Eust.1111.45. -ειμι, (εἶμι *ibo*) *enter in turn* or *in return*, Simp. *in Ph.*573.4. -ενεκτέον, *one must introduce instead*, Hermog. *Stat.*3. -έρχομαι, *enter in turn* or *instead*, Aristid.*Or.*37(2).27, Hero *Spir.*2.36, Them. *in Ph.*113.26. -κρίνομαι [ῑ], *to be introduced in place of*, Hero *Spir.*1.3. -οδιάζω, *bring in, introduce in turn*, Sch.D.T.p.72 H. -φέρω, *contribute in return*, τὰς εἰσφοράς Ar. *Lys.*654: metaph., οὐδὲ τυχόντα ἔρανον ἀλλήλαις Gal.*UP*8.7. II. νόμον ἀ. *substitute a new* law *for* an old one, D.20.97; καινὰ δαιμόνια D.C.52.36. III. *introduce as a counter-measure*, Onos.42. 12. -φορά, ἡ, *contribution in return*, *Milet.*3 No.147.22 (iii B.C.).

ἀντεκ-βάλλομαι, *to be produced in an opposite direction*, *Theol. Ar.*26; ἀλλήλοις *to be correspondingly projected*, Anon. *in EN*224. 24. -δικος, ὁ, *deputy-defensor*, *POxy.*1987 (vi A.D.), cf. *PLond.*5. 1709.80 (vi A.D.). -θέω, *rush out on the other side from*, Arr.*An.* 1.21.3. -θλίβω [ῑ], *squeeze out in turn*, Hp.*Loc.Hom.*9. -καίω, *kindle in turn*, metaph. of passion, J.*AJ*15.7.3 (Pass.). -κλέπτω, *steal away in return*, Ar.*Ach.*527. -κομίζω, *carry out* or *away in return*, in fut. ἀντεκκομιεῖ, Hsch. -κόπτω, *knock out in return*, ὀφθαλμόν D.24.140; εἴ τις τὸν ὀφθαλμὸν ἐξέκοψέ τινος, ἀντεκκοπῆναι Arist.*MM*1194ᵃ38, cf. D.S.12.17. -κρίνω [ῑ], *excrete in turn*, Gal. 4.517 (Pass.). -πέμπω, *send out in turn*, X.*HG*4.8.25; *expel, discharge in turn*, of respiration, Gal.5.710. -πλέω, *sail out against*, τινί Th.4.13: abs., Plu.*Lys.*10. -πλήσσω, *frighten in return*, Ael. *NA*12.15, Aristid.1.130 J. -πνέω, *breathe out in turn*, Gal.*Nat. Fac.*3.13, al. -ῥέω, *flow out in turn*, ib.1.13, *UP*6.11. -τᾰσις· ἀνταπόδοσις, Hsch. -τάσσω (sc. στρατόν), *draw up troops in opposition*, App.*BC*4.108. -τείνω, *stretch out in rivalry*, ἀ. αὑτόν τινι *match* oneself *with* another, Ar.*Ra.*1042; τῇ ἐκείνου δεινότητι τὸν ἐκείνου πλοῦτον Philostr.*VS*1.21.4. -τίθημι, *set forth* or *state instead*, Plu.*Arat.*1; *publish a counter-edict*, Id.*CG*12. II. *contrast with*, S.E.*M.*1.251. -τίνω [ῑ], *repay*, Ph.2.78, al. -τῖσις, εως, ἡ, *retribution*, Id.1.159; *requital*, Sch.Pi.*P.*1.112. -τιστος, ον, (ἐκτίνω) *punished in turn*, Sch.Il.24.213. -τρέφω, *to maintain in return*:— in Pass., ἀντεκτρέφεσθαι ὑπὸ τῶν ἐκγόνων Arist.*HA*615ᵇ25. 2. *train as a rival*, βότρυν βότρυϊ Lync.ap.Ath.14.654a. -τρέχω, *sally out against*, X.*HG*4.3.17, *Ages.*2.10. -φέρω, *bring out against, oppose*, τί τινι Plu.2.72e. -φύομαι, *grow out, issue opposite*, Gal. 5.537.

ἀντελαττόομαι, *to be worsted in turn*, D.C.44.27.

ἀντελαύνω, intr., *sail against*, τριήρει with a trireme, Plu.*Nic.*24.

ἀντελιγμός, ὁ, Ion. for ἀνθελ- (q.v.).

ἀντελ-λογέω, *deduct*, *POxy.*1578.11 (iii A.D.). -λογισμός, ὁ, *compensation*, *Gloss.* -λογος, ὁ, = foreg.: metaph., ἐν ἀντελλόγῳ σταθμᾶσθαι Eust.997.54.

ἀντελπίζω, *hope instead* or *in turn*, ἄλλα Th.1.70; ἕτερον πλοῦτον Lib.*Decl.*26.28.

ἀντεμ-βαίνω, *fit into each other*, of hinge-joints (γίγγλυμοι), Gal. 2.737:—also -βᾰσις, εως, ἡ, ibid. -βάλλω, *put in instead*, τῇ γῇ παγκαρπίαν Thphr.*HP*9.8.7; *substitute*, Dsc.2.49. 2. intr., *make an inroad in turn*, X.*HG*3.5.4, Plb.5.96.3; *attack in turn*, Plu.*Phil.* 18. -βᾰσις, v. sub ἀντεμβαίνω. -βῐβάζω, *put on board instead*, Th.7.13, cf. D.4.37. -βοάω, *shout at* a person *in answer*, *AB*85, Eust.855.21. -βοή, ἡ, *answering cry*, Anon. in Rh.3. 580 W. -βολή, ἡ, *pipe made of pieces fitted into each other*, *BGU*1117.16 (13 B.C.), cf. 1116.12. 2. = ἀντέμβασις, Hsch. s.v. ἐπαλλάξαντες, Suid. s.v. γίγγλυμοι. 3. *substitute*, κίκεως *PHolm.* 10.11. -βριάζειν· ἀντεξετάζειν, Hsch. -βροχή, ἡ, *remedy for external application*, Orib.*Fr.*90. -μάσασθαι, *requite an injury*, dub. word in E.*Fr.*611 (= Eup.458). -παίζω, *mock at in return*, τινί Sch.Ar.*Pax* 1112. -πείρω, in Pass., *resist and become fixed*, of barbs, Paul.Aeg.6.88. -πήγνῠμαι, aor. 2 -ενεπάγην, Pass., *to be plunged in in revenge*, τισί Ar.*Ach.*230. -πίπλημι, *fill in turn*, ἀντενέπλησαν τὴν ὁδόν X.*HG*2.4.12; *fill in return, by way of compensation*, τί τινος Id.*An.*4.5.28:—Pass., *to be filled with in exchange*, τινός Pl.*Lg.*705b. -πίπρημι, *set on fire in return*, ἀντενεπίμπρᾰσαν τὰ ἱρά Hdt.5.102. -πίπτω, *fall into the place of*, Phlp. *in Ph.*547.19; *attack in return*, Agath.5.19. -πλέκομαι, Pass., *to be entwined together*, ἀλλήλαις Dsc.4.75, cf. Poll.1.184; of *crossed* or *reversed* bandaging, Sor.*Fasc.*12.513 C.:—*return* one's *embraces* or *salutation*, J.*AJ*16.2.5. -πλοκή, ἡ, *mutual entwining*, αἱ ἐν ταῖς ἀτόμοις ἀ. M.Ant.7.50; *crossing* of veins, Gal. *in Pl. Ti.*7; *complication, confusion*, M.Ant.6.10. -φαίνω, *oppose by a counter-statement*, ἀ. ταῖς ἀποφάσεσιν Plb.18.28.12. -φᾰνίζω, = foreg., Hsch. -φᾰσις, εως, ἡ, *difference of appearance*, Str.2.4.8; also pl., ibid.; *opposition, antithesis*, S.E.*M.*1.57; *distinction*, Hdn.Gr.1.941, A.D.*Adv.*159. 19. -φράττω, *obstruct*, Simp. *in Cael.*441.7. -φύομαι, *to be inserted opposite*, Gal.4.384.

ἀντεν-αντίωσις, εως, ἡ, Rhet., *positive statement made in a negative form*, as οὐκ ἐλάχιστα for μέγιστα, Alex.*Fig.*2.23, Zonae.*Fig.* 22. -δείκνῠμαι, *give contrary indications*, of symptoms, Gal.10. 626. -δειξις, εως, ἡ, *counter-indication*, Steph. *in Hp.*2.282 D. -δίδωμι, *give way in turn*, of sawyers, ὁ μὲν ἕλκει, ὁ δ' ἀντενέδωκε Ar. *V.*694 (Dobree, for ἀντανέδωκε). -δύομαι [ῠ], *put on instead*, Plu. 2.139c. -έδρα, ἡ, *counter-ambuscade*, Plb.1.57.3. -εδρεύω, *lay a counter-ambuscade*, Hp.*Ep.*17, D.C.41.51. -εργέω, *to be efficacious against*, θανασίμοις Dsc.1.115. -έχῠρον, τό, *counter-pledge*, Sch.A.R.1.1355:—hence -εχῠράζομαι, *take a counter-pledge*, Hsch. s.v. ῥυσιάζει. -θεσις, εως, ἡ, *insertion instead*, Eust. 1679.12. -ίστημι, *insert instead*, prob. rest. in *IGRom.*4.293 i 37 (Pergam., ii B.C., Pass.). -οικίζω, *introduce as inhabitants instead*:—Pass., αἱ ψυχαὶ ἀγνοῖς πάλιν ἀ. σώμασιν J.*BJ*3.8.5. -τίθημι, *insert in turn* or *instead*, Nicom.*Ar.*2.27.

ἀντεξ-άγω [ᾰγ], *export in return*, X.*Vect.*3.2. 2. *evict in return*, *BGU*1273.34 (iii B.C.; written ἀντιεξ-). II. *lead out against*, τὰ στρατόπεδα Plb.2.18.6, cf. D.H.8.65, Plu.*Publ.*9; v.l. for προσήγαγε, D.S.13.66:—abs., *march out against*, τινί Plb.3.66.11. -αίρω, *raise to an equal height*, λόγοις ἔργα Philostr.*VS*1.19.1. -αιτέω, *demand in return*, Plu.*Alex.*11. -ανίστᾰμαι, Pass., with aor. 2 Act., *rise up against*, πρός τι Hld.7.19. -ᾰπᾰτάω, *deceive in return*, D.C.58.18. -αρμα, ατος, τό, (ἀντεξαίρω) *southerly elevation* (i.e. *latitude*), *corresponding to* a northerly one, *Theol.Ar.*25. -ειμι, (εἶμι *ibo*) *go out against*, X.*HG*4.5.10, Plb.1.24.10. -ελαύνω, *charge against, attack*, Plu.*Phil.*18, al., D.C.47.43. -έρχομαι, = ἀντέξειμι, X.*HG*7.2.12, *Cyr.*6.3.13. -ετάζω, *try* one *by the standard of another*, Aeschin.1.8,37, Arr.*Epict.*2.18.21; τι πρός τι Plu. *Caes.*3, cf. Gal.18(1).229; τινὰ ἀλλήλοις Them. *in Ph.*52.20; *compare*, λόγους Luc.*Herm.*30, cf. Aps.p.247 H., etc.:—Pass., *to be measured* or *compared*, παρά or πρός τι, Plu.*Tim.*36, 2.65b; τινί Ph. 2.45, al., D.Chr.31.126:—Med., *measure one's strength against* another, τινί Luc.*DMort.*12.2: esp. *dispute with* him *at law*, like ἀντιδικέω, ib.29.1: metaph., ἀ. τῇ νόσῳ Id.*Abd.*16. -ετᾰσις, εως, ἡ, *comparison*, A.D.*Synt.*161.10, Aps.p.248 H., al. 2. *term of comparison*, of an integer compared with the sum of the preceding integers, *Theol.Ar.*10. -εταστέον, *one must compare*, Max.Tyr.30. 6. -εταστικός, ή, όν, *comparative*, Aphth.*Prog.*10. Adv. -κῶς Men. Rh.p.403 S. -ήγησις, εως, ἡ, *counter-explanation*, αἱ πρὸς Ἰόβαν ἀ., title of work by Didymus, Ath.14.634c. -ηγητής, οῦ, ὁ, *deputy*-ἐξηγητής *BGU*362 xv 10 (iii A.D.), *PMeyer*6.9 (ii A.D.), *PRyl.*397.1 (iii A.D.). -ιππεύω, *ride out against*, Plu.*Pomp.*7. -ῑσάζω, *make equal, compare*, Sch.Od.11.308. -ίστᾰμαι, Pass., with aor. 2 Act., *yield to an attack, retire from the contest*, Plu.2.946d. -οδος, ἡ, a *military movement*, τὰς δι' ἀλλήλων ἀ. καὶ εἰσόδους Onos.10. 2. -ορμάω, *sail* or *march out against*, D.C.48.47, 63.24. -όρμησις, εως, ἡ, *sailing against*, v.l. in Th.2.91; *countercharge*, Plu.*Pomp.* 69. -ωσις, εως, ἡ, *counter-thrust*, Epicur.*Ep.*2 p.40 U.

ἀντεπ-άγω [ᾰγ], *lead against*: abs. (sc. στρατόν or the like), *advance against, advance to meet an enemy*, Th.4.124, Plb.12.18.11, etc. II. *inflict in return*, ποινήν τινι Aristaenet.2.9. III. *introduce as a counter-measure*, ἀλεξήματα Onos.30. -ακτέον, *one must march against*, πρός τινα Id.21.6. -ᾴδω, *use charms against*, Plot. 4.4.43. -αινέω, *praise in return*, X.*Cyr.*8.3.49. II. Pass., ἀ. τινι *to be extolled in comparison with*, Luc.*Pr.Im.*19. -ανάγομαι [ᾰγ], *put to sea against*, πρός τινα Th.4.25. -αρχος, ὁ, *subpraefectus*, *Gloss.* -αφίημι [φῐ], *let go, let slip against*, τινί Luc.*Zeux.*9. -ειμι, (εἶμι *ibo*) *rush upon, meet an advancing enemy*, Th.4.33,96, etc.; τινί Id.7.6, cf. Lib.*Decl.*37.15, Onos.8.2; πρός τι Id.21.8. -εισάγομαι [ᾰγ], *to be carried in* or *enter instead*, Ti.Locr.102a; f.l. for sq., *Placit.* 4.22.1. -είσειμι, (εἶμι *ibo*) *enter in turn*, εἰς τὰ ἀραιώματα ibid. -είσοδος, ἡ, *entrance in return*, ἀ. παρέχειν ibid. -εισφέρομαι, *come in instead*, ib.2. -έκτᾰσις, εως, ἡ, *stretching in the opposite direction*, Hsch. s.v. τόξου πῆχυν. -εκτείνω, *stretch in the contrary direction*, Gal.18(1).213. -ελαύνω, *rush to meet, attack one*, App.*Pun.*26. -εξάγω [ᾰγ], intr., *sail* or *march out against*, Th.8. 104, Luc.*Bacch.*3: c. acc., στρατιάν, δύναμιν, J.*AJ*6.9.1, 8.14.4:—also in Med., D.C.50.31. -έξειμι, (εἶμι *ibo*) *march out to meet* an enemy, πρός τινα Th.7.37: abs., X.*Cyr.*3.3.30, etc. -εξελαύνω, = foreg., Th. 4.72. -εξέρχομαι, = ἀντεπέξειμι, ib.131, Aristid.1.149 J. -έξοδος, ἡ, *sally in turn*, D.C.47.37. -ερείδομαι· *obnitor*, *Gloss.* -έρχομαι, *march against in return*, Aristid.1.150 J., cf. D.C.36.51. -ερωτάω· *restipulor*, *Gloss.* II. *ask a question in turn*, *PLond.*1.118(1).70 (vi A.D.). -ερώτησις, εως, ἡ, *restipulatio*, *Gloss.* -ηχέω, *clamour against* one, Luc.*Cat.*19.

ἀντεπι-βουλεύω, *form counter-designs*, Th.1.33, 3.12, etc. -γράφω [ᾰ], *write* something *instead*, καλὰ ἐπιγράμματα ἀνελὼν ἀσεβῆ ἀ. D.22. 72:—Med., -εσθαι ἐπὶ τὸ νίκημα *put their own* names *instead of the other party to* the victory, i.e. *claim it*, Plb.18.34.2. -δείκνῡμι, *exhibit in turn*, Pl.*Tht.*162b: c. part., *contrast*, ἀ. ἑαυτὸν ποιοῦντά τι X.*Ages.* 1.12:—Med., *exhibit oneself in competition*, Plu.2.674b: also c. acc. rei, ἀ. τι καλόν τινι *display* a fine *sight in rivalry with*, Id.*Ant.*23; also τι πρός τι Id.*Alex.*21. -θεσις, εως, ἡ, *mutual attack, contention*, Ph. 1.7, al. -θύω, *offer sacrifice as substitute*, *BCH*15.207. -θῡμέω, *desire* a thing *in rivalry with*, τινός And.4.28:—Pass., ἐπιθυμῶν ξυνεῖναι καὶ ἀντεπιθυμεῖσθαι τῆς ξυνουσίας and *have one's* company *desired in turn*, X.*Mem.*2.6.28. -κᾰλέω, *accuse in return*, ἀ. ὅτι.. App. *BC*5.59. -κειμαι, *to be placed upon*, Gal.12.604. -κηρύσσω, *put a price on* one's *head in return*, χρήματά τινι Poll.4.93. -κουρέω, *help in return*, τινί X.*HG*4.6.3. -κράτεια [ρᾰ], ἡ, *alternate mastery*, νείκους καὶ φιλίας *Placit.*2.4.8. -κρᾰτέω, *get the upper hand in turn*, Str.16.1.19, D.C.44.27. -λαμβάνομαι, *lay hold on the other side*, Luc.*Symp.*43. -μελέομαι or -μέλομαι, *attend* or *give heed in turn*, v.l. X.*Cyr.*5.1.18; τινός *to* one, Id.*An.*3.1.16. -μέλλω, v.l. for ἀντιμέλλω (q.v.). -μετρέω, *measure to in return*, Poll.5. 142. -νοέω, *devise in turn*, Ael.*NA*6.23, J.*AJ*10.8.1: c. inf., App.*BC*4.109. -πλέω, *sail against in turn*, Th.1.54 and prob. in 1.50, Poll.1.124. -ρρέω, *admit a counter-fluxion*, Hp.*Loc.Hom.* 29. -ρρημα, ατος, τό, *counter*-ἐπίρρημα, Heph.*Poëm.*8.2, Poll.4.112;

v. ἐπίρρημα. **–σκώπτω**, *mock in return*, τινά Plb.18.7.5. **–σπάω**, gloss on ἀνθέλκω, Hsch.:—Med., Ph.1.247; *absorb* nutriment, Gal.17 (2).312. **–σταλμα**, ατος, τό, *return furnished in reply*, *CPR*20i 20 (iii A.D.). **–σταλτικός**, ή, όν, *of* or *for replying to a letter*: –κή (sc. τέχνη), ἡ, *art of writing replies*, *Epist.Charact.*19. **–στάτης** [ᾰ], ου, ὁ, *vice-president*, τοῦ Μουσείου *Recueil de Travaux* 37.94 (Denderah). **–στέλλω**, *write an answer*, *CPR*20ii5 (iii A.D.): c. inf., J.*AJ*15.6.2, al.; οὐδέν Luc.*Sat.*19:—Pass., τὰ ἀντεπεσταλμένα Paus. 4.22.6, etc. **–στρᾰτεύω**, *take the field against*, X.*HG*4.8.33. **–στρέφω**, *turn against*, *retort*, Plu.2.810e; *turn round and back*, of a needle, Gal.10.418. **–στροφή**, ἡ, *turning back upon*, χειρὸς ἐπὶ τὸν ὦμον *Placit.*4.14.3; κατ' ἀ. Ruf.ap.Orib.49.35.4. **–τάσσω**, *order in turn*, τινὶ ποιεῖν τι Th.1.135; τινί τι Pl.*Ti.*20b. **–τείνω**, *excite by contrast*, τὴν φαντασίαν Plu.2.933c. **–τειχίζω**, *raise a counter-work*: metaph., Λυκείῳ τὴν Ἰταλίαν ἀ. Him.*Or.*7.13: so as Dep. with pf. Pass., *establish a fort in the enemy's country*, Th.1.142. **–τίθημι**, *put on in exchange*, D.C.58.7 (Pass.). 2. ἀ. ἐπιστολὴν πρός τινα *give* a letter *in answer*, Th.1.129, Is.*Fr.*49, cf. J.*AJ*17.5.1. II. Med., *make a counter-attack*, *throw oneself upon*, D.S.36.4, Ph.1.661; simply, *attack*, 2.111:—Act. in same sense, ἀλλήλοισιν *make* mutual *plots*, Hp.*Ep.*17. **–τρέχω**· ἀντεφοδεύω, Suid.; *turn and attack*, of animals at bay, Ph.2.354. **–τροπος**, *sub-procurator*, *Ephes.*2 No.28, cf. *CIL*3.14195⁴, al.; ἀπὸ τῶν ἀ.· *a ramulariis*, *Gloss.* **–φέρω**, *lay*, *inflict in turn upon*, κακὰ πόλεσι Ph.1.407; ἀντεποισόμεθα· ἀντεπενέγκω.., Hsch. (–επονησ– cod.). 2. Pass., *rush upon in turn*, Ti.Locr.102a. **–χειρέω**, *make a counter-attack*, Str.5.2.2, cf. Max. Tyr.18.9; τινί Plu.*Them.*31. II. *make attempts to prove the contrary*, Arist.*Top.*160b10; τὰ ἀντεπιχειρούμενα *controversial efforts to prove* or *disprove*, S.E.*M.*9.191. **–χείρησις**, εως, ἡ, *a counter-attack*, D.H.9.14.

ἀντεπόπτευσις, v.l. ἀντεμπότευσις, εως, ἡ, Lat. *compensatio*, *reputatio*, *Gloss.*

ἀντέρᾰμαι, aor. –ηράσθην, *to be a rival in love*, τινί τινος Luc.*Musc. Enc.*10.

ἀντερᾰνίζω, *contribute one's share in turn*:—Pass., *to be repaid*, ὑμμασιν ἀλλοτρίοις *AP*9.12 (Leon.).

ἀντεραστής, οῦ, ὁ, *rival in love*, τινός Ar.*Eq.*733; generally, *rival*, Pl.*R.*521b, Arist.*Rh.*1388a14:—fem. **ἀντεράστρια**, *Gloss.*

ἀντεράω, *love in return*, τῶν ἀντερώντων ἱμέρῳ πεπληγμένος A.*Ag.* 544; ἐρῶν ἀντερᾶται X.*Smp.*8.3, cf. Bion *Fr.*8.1; ἀντερᾶν τινός Luc. *DMar.*1.5; ἀντερᾶσθαι ὑπό τινος Plu.*Dio* 16. II. *rival in love*, τινί Id.2.972d; ἀ. τινί τινος *rival* one *in love for..*, E.*Rh.*184: abs., τὸ ἀντερᾶν *jealous love*, Plu.*Lyc.*18.

ἀντεργάζομαι, *retaliate*, τὰ αὐτά τινας ἀ. D.C.*Fr.*36.21.

ἀντεργολᾰβέω, *compete with*, τι *in* a thing, Posidipp.3.1.

ἀντερεθίζω, *provoke in turn*, τινὰ πρὸς μάχην Eust.848.17.

ἀντερεί-δω, *set firmly against*, χειρὶ χεῖρ' ἀντερείσαις *clasping* hand in hand, Pi.*P.*4.37; but ἄκναμπτον Ἥρα μένος ἀν[τ]ερείδων Id.*Pae.*6. 87; ἀντέρειδε τοῖς Ἐρεχθείδαις δόρυ E.*Supp.*702; ἀ. ξύλα [τῷ πύργῳ] *set* wooden stays or props *against* it, X.*HG*5.2.5; ἀ. βάσιν *plant* it *firm*, S.*Ph.*1403; λίθοι οἱ –οντες τὰς περιφερεῖς στέγας *springers* of a vault, Demetr.*Eloc.*13. II. intr., *stand firm*, *resist pressure*, *offer resistance*, opp. ὑπείκω, X.*Cyr.*8.8.16, cf. *Cyn.*10.16, Pl.*Ti.*45c, Arist. *MA*698b18, Epicur.*Fr.*76bis; *exert counter-pressure*, θέναρι ἀ. Hp. *Fract.*14; τὸ ὠθούμενον ἀ. ὅθεν ὠθεῖται *offers resistance* in the direction from which the pressure comes, Arist.*Mech.*858a26; πρός or περί τι, Plu.2.924d, 923e. 2. metaph., *exert mutual pressure*, of contending politicians, Phld.*Rh.*2.51 S. (dub.); simply, *argue against*, Sor.2.57. **–σις**, εως, ἡ, *thrusting against*, *resistance*, Hp.*Art.* 50; esp. *the fulcrum* or *resistance* used in reducing a dislocation, ib. 2; of joints, Arist.*IA*705a14; λάμπειν ἀντερείσει τοῦ αἰθέρος *by* its *resistance*, Plu.*Lys.*12; *forward pressure*, Ael.*Tact.*18.8; *repulsion*, Plu.2.396a, cf. Ph.1.153, Plot.4.3.26 (pl.). II. Rhet., *buttressing*, *mutual support*, of clauses in a period, Demetr.*Eloc.*12. **–σμα**, ατος, τό, *prop*, Hsch. s.v. στῆλαι. **–στικός**, ή, όν, *of* or *for resistance*, ἕξις Metop.ap.Stob.3.1.115, Hierocl.p.23A.; κίνησις Simp. *in Ph.*1046.12.

ἀντερέσσω, Att. –ττω, *row against*, πρὸς αὐτὸν τὸν ἄνεμον D.C.48. 48.

ἀντερίζω, *strive against*, *contend*, ταύροις Philostr.*Her.*12b, cf. Hsch.

ἀντερύομαι [ῡ], *make equal in weight with*, *value equally with*, c. gen., χρυσοῦ τε καὶ ἀργύρου ἀντερύσασθαι Thgn.77:—Act., –ερύω *pull in the opposite direction*, Ep. impf. –ερύεσκε Nonn.*D.*46.214.

ἀντερῶ, fut. without any pres. in use: pf. ἀντείρηκα S.*Ant.*47 (cf. ἀντεῖπον):—*speak against*, *gainsay*, S. l. c.; τεθνάναι δ' οὐκέτ' ἀ. θεοῖς A.*Ag.*539; τι πρός τινα Ar.*Nu.*1079; πρός τι *Ach.*701; τινί Pl.*R.* 580a:—Pass., οὐδὲν ἀντειρήσεται no *denial shall be given*, S.*Tr.*1184; τὰ –ημένα Gal.5.477.

ἀντέρως, ωτος, ὁ, *return-love*, *love-for-love*, Pl.*Phdr.*255d, Ach.Tat. 1.9, Them.*Or.*24.305a. II. *Anteros*, personified as *a god who avenged slighted love*, Paus.1.30.1, etc.:—but also (as it seems) *a god who struggled against* Ἔρως, Id.6.23.5. III. name of a *gem*, Plin. *HN*37.123 (pl.).

ἀντερωτάω, *question in turn*, ἐρωτώμενος ἀντερωτᾷς; Pl.*Euthd.* 295b, cf. Aeschin.3.226, Aen.Tact.24.16, Plu.*Cor.*18.

ἀντέσο· ἀντί(α)σον, ἄντικρυς ἐλθέ, Hsch.

ἀντεστραμμένως, Adv. pf. part. Pass. of ἀντιστρέφω (q.v.).

ἀντεταγών, part. (cf. τεταγών), *holding aloft*, prob. in A.R.2.119.

ἀντεταιῶς· ἀναγεγραμμένως, Hsch. (Perh. ἀντ' ἔτεος ἀναγεγραμμένως (Dor. acc. pl.), = *enrolled in the same year.*)

ἀντετοῦς· τοῦ αὐτοῦ ἔτους (Lacon.), Hsch.

ἀντευ-δοκιμέω, *rival in distinction*, Lyd.*Mens.*1.28 (Pass.). **–εργετέω**, *return a kindness*, X.*Mem.*2.6.4; ἀ. τοὺς εὖ ποιήσαντας Arist. *Rh.Al.*1422a32. **–εργέτημα**, ατος, τό, *kindness returned*, Hsch. s.v. ἀνθυπούργησον. **–εργέτης**, ου, ὁ, *one who returns kindnesses*, Asp.*in EN*113.14, Sch.A.R.2.321. **–εργετικός**, ή, όν, *disposed to return kindnesses*, Arist.*EN*1124b11. **–κρᾱτος** ζώνη *south temperate* zone, Cleom.1.2, *Stoic.*2.195. **–νοέω**, *wish well in return*, τινί X.*Cyr.*8.3.49 (divisim). **–πάσχω** and **–ποιέω** are by recent edd. written divisim ἀντ' εὖ π. (v. Pl.*Grg.*520e, X.*An.*5.5.21, D.20. 124), on the ground that εὖ never enters into direct composition with Verbs, v. εὖ fin.; but ἀντευποιεῖν is read in Arist.*EN*1179a28, *Rh.* 1374a24. **–ποιΐα**, ἡ, *requital of benefits*, Mich.*in EN*465.27. **–φρασμα**, ατος, τό, *the opposite of joy*, Agatho 30. **–χαριστητέον**, *one must give thanks in turn*, Porph.*Abst.*2.37.

ἀντεφ-εστιάω, *entertain in return*, Ph.2.139, Philostr.*VS*2.5.3, Ael.*NA*9.45, 15.7; as f.l. for ἀνταφ–, Pl.*Ti.*17b. **–ευρίσκω**, *find out against*, J.*AJ*10.8.1. **–ήδομαι**, aor. inf. –ησθῆναι, *exult over in turn*, Ph.2.313. **–ίστημι**, *appoint against* one, στρατηγούς τισι Aristid.1.173 J. **–οδεύω**, *go forth to meet*, Suid. **–οδιάζομαι**, Pass., *to be furnished instead of provisions*: metaph. in J.*AJ* 15.9.1. **–οράω**, *check*, *verify*, *SIG*1023.89 (Cos). **–ορμάω**, *rush against*, *attack*, Hld.8.16: abs., Ph.2.122. **–ορμέω**, *anchor over against* the enemy, Plu.*Alc.*36. **–όρμησις**, εως, ἡ, *rushing against*, *attack*, Ph.2.31, Hld. l. c.

ἀντέχω or **ἀντίσχω**, fut. ἀνθέξω; part. ἀντισχήσων (in sense II) Lib. *Ep.*33.2: aor. ἀντέσχον:—*hold against*, c. acc. et gen., χεῖρ' ἀ. κρατός *hold* one's hand *against* one's head so as to shade the eyes, S.*OC* 1651: c. dat., ὄμμασι δ' ἀντίσχοις (–έχοις codd.) τάνδ' αἴγλαν *may'st* thou *keep* this sunlight *upon* his eyes, Id.*Ph.*830 (lyr.); τοὺς χαλινοὺς τῶν ἵππων Hdn.5.6.7. II. c. dat., *hold out against*, *withstand*, Ἁρπάγῳ Hdt.1.175, cf. 8.68.β'; τοῖς δικαίοις S.*Fr.*78; τῇ ταλαιπωρίᾳ Th.2.49; πρός τινα Id.6.22; πρὸς τοὺς καμάτους Hdn.3.6.10, etc.: c. acc., *endure*, ἀντέχομεν καμάτους *AP*9.299 (Phil.); but in Th.8.63 ἀ. τὰ τοῦ πολέμου rather belongs to the next signf., *hold out* as regards the war; so πολλὰ ἀ. ib.86. 2. *hold out*, *endure*, c. part., ἡ Ἄζωτος ..ἐπὶ πλεῖστον χρόνον πολιορκουμένη ἀντέσχε Hdt.2.157, cf. 5.115, Th.2.70; μηκέτι ἀντέχωσι τῷ πόνῳ διϊστάμενοι Pl.*Ti.*81d; πολλάκις γιγνομένην ψυχὴν ἀντέχειν *last* through several states of existence, Id.*Phd.*88a. 3. abs., *hold out*, *stand one's ground*, Hdt.8.16, A. *Pers.*413, etc.; πῶς δύσμορος ἀντέχει; S.*Ph.*176 (lyr.); νόσημα ἀντίσχει τὸν αἰῶνα πάντα Hp.*Fract.*11; ἔστ' ἂν αἰὼν ἀντέχῃ E.*Alc.*337; βραχὺν χρόνον D.2.10; ἀ. ἐπὶ πολύ, ἐπὶ πλέον, Th.1.7,65; ἀ. ἐλπίσιν in hope, D.S.2.26; ἀ. περί τινος X.*HG*2.2.16: peculiarly, ἀ. μὴ ὑπακοῦσαι I *hold out against..*, *refuse..*, Plu.2.708a. b. of the rivers drunk by the Persian army, *hold out*, *suffice*, Hdt.7.196, cf. A.*Pers.* 413 (in full ἀ. ῥέεθρον Hdt.7.58; ἀ. ὕδωρ παρέχων ib.108); so ἀντέχει ὁ σῖτος Th.1.65. 4. *extend*, *reach*, ἐς ὅσον ἡ ἐπιστήμη ἀ. Id. 6.69; *prevail*, διὰ τὴν λῃστείαν ἐπὶ πολὺ ἀντίσχουσαν 1.7. III. Med., *hold before one against* something, c. acc. et gen., ἀντίσχεσθε τραπέζας ἰῶν *hold out* the tables *against* the arrows, Od.22.74. 2. c. gen. only, *hold on by*, *cling to*, ἐκείνου τῆς χειρός Hdt.2.121.ε'; πέπλων E.*Tr.*750, cf. *Ion* 1404; τῶν θυρῶν Ar.*Lys.*161: metaph., ἀ. τῶν ὄχθων *cling to* the banks, *keep close to* them, Hdt.9.56; ἀ. Ἡρακλέος *cleave to* Hercules, i.e. *worship* him *above all*, Pi.*N.*1.33; ἀ. τῆς ἀρετῆς, Lat. *adhaerere virtuti*, Hdt.1.134; ἀ. τοῦ πολέμου Id.7.53; τοῦ κέρδους S.*Fr.*354; τῆς θαλάσσης Th.1.13; σωτηρίας Lys.33.6; τῆς ἀληθείας Pl.*Phlb.*58e, cf. *R.*600d, al.; τῶν παραδεδομένων μύθων Arist.*Po.*1451b24; τῆς ἐλευθερίας Decr.ap.D.18.185; τῶν δικαίων *POxy.*1203.30 (i A.D.). b. c. gen. pers., *care for*, *support*, 1*Ep. Thess.*5.14. 3. abs., αὐτὸς ἀντέχου S.*Ph.*893, cf. Ar.*Ach.*1121. 4. c. dupl. gen. pers. et rei, ἀνθέξεταί σου τῶν πατρῴων χρημάτων *will lay claim to* the property *from* you, *dispute* it *with* you, Ar.*Av.* 1658. 5. *resist*, Pl.*R.*574b; φονεῦσαι τοὺς ἀντεχομένους D.S.4. 49. 6. *adhere*, Arist.*HA*583a18: Medic., of constipation, γαστὴρ ἀντίσχετο Hp.*Epid.*4.20; γαστρὸς ἀντεχομένης ib.17.

ἄντη, ἡ, (ἄντομαι II) *prayer*—a word preserved by Hsch. (ἄντησι (cod. ἀντήσει)· λιτανείαις, ἀντήσεσι), and restored by Herm. for λιταῖς (metri gr.) in S.*El.*139 (dub.).

ἀντῆ· δῶρον ἱκέσιον, Hsch.

ἀντήδην, Adv. *in supplication*, Hsch. (–δης cod.).

ἀντήεις, Dor. –άεις, εσσα, εν, (ἄντα) *hostile*, Pi.*P.*9.93.

ἀντήλιος, ον, (ἀντί, ἥλιος) *opposite the sun*, i.e. *looking east*, S.*Aj.* 805, E.*Ion* 1550; δαίμονες ἀντήλιοι statues of gods *which stood in the sun* before the house-door, A.*Ag.*519, cf. E.*Fr.*538. 2. of the moon, *reflecting the sun's rays*, *AB*403 (ἀνθ–), cf. Suid.: hence metaph., *imitation*, *reflection*, Theopomp.Hist.367 (ἀνθ–). II. ἀντήλια, τά, = παρήλια, *parhelia*, Suid., cf. Men.511. 2. *screens* or *parasols*, Eust.1281.3; also, *blinkers* on horses' bridles, Poll.10.54 (ἀνθ–), Eust.1562.39.—The Ion. form ἀντήλιος is always used in Trag.; ἀνθήλιος first in Theopomp. l. c., cf. Ph.1.656, *Placit.*3.6.

ἀντημοιβός, όν, Ep. for ἀνταμοιβός, *corresponding*, Call.*Del.*52.

ἄντην, Ep. Adv., (ἀντί) *against*, *over against*, οὔ μιν ἔγωγε φεύξομαι.. ἀλλὰ μάλ' ἄ. στήσομαι I will *confront* him, Il.18.307, cf. 11. 590; δμοιωθήμεναι ἄ. match himself *openly against* me, 1.187, Od.3. 120; so πειρηθήμεναι ἄ. 8.213; more rarely with Verbs of motion, μηδ' ἔα ἄ. ἔρχεσθαι *straightforwards*, opp. πάλιν τρέπε, Il.8.399; also ἀ. βαλλομένων *in front*, 12.152; οὐδέ τις ἔτλη ἀ. εἰσιδέειν look him *in the face*, 19.15, cf. 24.223; ἀ. λοέσσομαι will bathe *before all, openly*, Od.6.221, cf. 8.158; ἀγαπαζέμεν ἀ. greet *in the face of all*, Il.24.464; νείκεσέ τ' ἀ. 10.158; ὅς μ' εἴρεαι ἀ. 15.247:—θεῷ ἐναλίγκιος ἀ. like a god *in presence*, Od.2.5, 4.310; χελιδόνι εἰκέλη ἀ. 22.240; cf. ἄντα. II. as Prep. c. gen., only in late Ep., as Nic.*Th.*474, Opp.*C.*3.210.

ἀντήνωρ, ορος, ὁ, ἡ, (ἀνήρ) *instead of a man*, σποδὸς ἀ. dust *for men*, A.*Ag.*442.—In Il. as pr. n.

ἀντηρετέω, *row against* or *on the opposite side to* another, *EM*112. 40.

ἀντηρέτης, ου, ὁ, (ἐρέτης) properly, *one who rows against* another, cf. *AB*411: generally, *opponent, adversary*, A.*Th.*284, 595; ἀ. δορός τινι ib.997 (lyr.).

ἀντήρης, Dor. -άρης, ες, poet. Adj. *set over against, opposite*, λαβεῖν τινὰ ἀντήρη meet *face to face* in battle, E.*Ph.*754, cf. 1367; ἀντήρεις στέρνων πληγάς blows *on the breast*, S.*El.*89: c. gen., Φοινίκας ἀ. χώρα *over against, facing* it, E.*Tr.*221 (lyr.): c. dat., ἀ. τινί *opposite to* a thing, Id.*IA*224; ἀ. ὄψεσι, of the bat, *hostile to*, S.*Fr.*747 (lyr.).

ἀντηρίδιον, τό, Dim. of ἀντηρίς, *stanchion* supporting the base of a torsion-engine, Hero*Bel.*89.4. 2. *support, base*, *Milet.*7 p.60 (ii B.C.), Haussoullier *Cinquantenaire de l'École Pratique des Hautes Études* p.89 (ii B.C.).

ἀντήριος· στήμων, καὶ κανὼν ὁ προσκείμενος τῇ θύρᾳ, Hsch.

ἀντηρίς, ίδος, ἡ, *prop, stay, support*, E.*Fr.*1111: pl., Plb.8.4.6; *stanchion* or *strut* in torsion-engines, Ph.*Bel.*76.16, Hero*Bel.*101.9; ἀρκύων X.*Cyn.*10.7; in Th.7.36 ἀντηρίδες are *stay-beams* fixed inside a ship's bow, and projecting beyond it, so as to support and strengthen the ἐπωτίδες. II. = θυρίς, *window*, Suid.:—and in E.*Rh.*785 it must mean *nostrils*, if it be the right reading. [ῑδος E. ll.cc.: hence ἀντήρειδες in Apollod.*Poliorc.*178.4, Hero*Bel.*101.9, is wrong; so -είδιον ib.89.4 is f.l. for -ίδιον as Inscrr. show.] (-ηρῐδ- = -ερῐδ-, weak form of stem of ἐρείδω (cf. ἔρις).)

ἄντησις, εως, ἡ, *entreaty, prayer*, Hsch.

ἄντηστις, εως, ἡ, *confronting*, κατ' ἄντηστιν θεμένη Od.20.387.

ἀντηχ-έω, Dor. -αχέω Theoc.*Ep.*4.11 (Scal.):—*sing in answer*, παιᾶνα θεῷ E.*Alc.*423; ἀντάχησ' ἂν ὕμνον ἀρσένων γέννᾳ would *have sung* a song *in answer to*.., Id.*Med.*426. II. abs., *sound responsively*, of a musical string, Arist.*Pr.*919ᵇ16; of bronze vessels, Aen.Tact. 37.7, Plb.22.11.12; *resound*, Hp.*Morb.*4.56, cf. *Carn.*18, Luc.*VH*1. 38; *echo*, φωναῖς ἀ. Plu.2.414c. III. *shout in opposition*, Id.*Mar.* 19, cf. J.*BJ*2.19.8, Them.*Or.*21.255d. 2. *contradict*, Plu.2.925e, cf. 1000c. -ημα, ατος, τό, *echo*, Sch.Philostr.*Her.*19.12. -ησις, εως, ἡ, *a re-echoing*, Plu.2.589d. -ος, ον, *sounding in response*, ἁρμονία Ph.1.312, 2.485.

ἀντί, Prep. governing gen.:—orig. sense, *over against*. (Cf. Skt. *ánti* 'opposite', 'facing', Lat. *ante*, etc.)

A. Usage: I. of Place, *opposite, over against*, formerly quoted from several places of Hom., as Il.21.481 ἀντὶ ἐμεῖο (where now ἀντί' ἐμεῖο, i.e. ἀντία); Τρώων ἀνθ' ἑκατόν (i.e. ἄντα) 8.233; so ἀντ' Αἴαντος (i.e. ἄντα) 15.415, cf. Od.4.115, Hes.*Op.*727; but ἀντί is so used in X.*An.*4.7.6, *IG*2.835*c*–*l*68; αἱ ὀπαὶ αἱ γιγνόμεναι ἀ. τόρμων mortises *facing* tenons, Hero*Bel.*97.5; ἀντὶ μαιτύρων *in the presence of* witnesses, *Leg.Gort.*1.40; ἀντὶ τῆς ὄψεως ἡμῶν Eudox.*Ars*18. II. of Time, ἀντὶ νυκτός *the same* night, *SIG*1025.43 (Cos); ἀντὶ ϝέτεος *GDI*2561 *A* 45 (Delph.); ἀντ' ἐνιαυτοῦ *IG*5(2).266.8 (Mantinea, i B.C.); ἀνθ' ἡμέρας· δι' ὅλης τῆς ἡμέρας, Hsch.; cf. ἀντετοῦς. III. *instead, in the place of*, Ἕκτορος ἀντὶ πεφάσθαι Il.24.254; ἀντὶ γάμοιο τάφον Od.20.307; so later πολέμιος ἀντὶ φίλου καταστῆναι Hdt.1.87; ἀντὶ ἡμέρης νὺξ ἐγένετο Id.7.37; ἀντὶ φωτῶν σποδὸς A.*Ag.*434; τὸν πόλεμον ἀντ' εἰρήνης μεταλαμβάνειν Th.1.120, cf. 4.20, 7.75; βασιλεύειν ἀντί τινος X.*An.*1.1.4; also ἀντὶ ἄρχεσθαι ὑπ' ἄλλων ἄρχειν ἁπάντων Hdt.1.210, cf. 6.32, 7.170 (where the usual constr. would be ἀντὶ τοῦ ἄρχεσθαι, cf. Th.7.28, X.*Cyr.*6.2.19, etc.); ὀργίλοι ἀντὶ θυμοειδοῦς γεγένηνται Pl.*R.*411c: sts. used elliptically, ἦ 'τολμήσατ' ἀντ' ἐμοῦ δοῦναί τινι; i.e. ἀντὶ τοῦ ἐμοὶ δοῦναι, S.*Ph.*369, cf. *OC*448, Ar.*Av.*58. 2. in Hom. often to denote equivalence, ἀντί νυ πολλῶν λαῶν ἐστιν ἀνήρ he is *as good as* many men, Il.9.116; ἀντὶ κασιγνήτου ξεῖνος..τέτυκται a guest is *as much as* a brother, Od.8. 546; ἀντί τοί εἰμ' ἱκέταο I am *as* a suppliant, Il.21.75, cf. 8.163; so later τοῦτό σφι ἀντὶ λουτροῦ ἐστί serves *as* a bath, Hdt.4.75; ὑπάρχειν ἀντὶ τῶν ἔνδον to be *as hostages for*.., Th.2.5; δουλεύειν ἀντὶ ἀργυρωνήτων *just like* bought slaves, D.17.3; ἀντὶ [πλεύμονος] βράγχια Arist. *PA*669ᵃ4. 3. to denote exchange, *at the price of, in return for*, σοὶ δὲ θεοὶ τῶνδ' ἀντὶ χάριν..δοῖεν Il.23.650; νῆσον ἀντὶ χρημάτων παρέλαβον *for* money paid, Hdt.3.59; ἀντ' ἀργυρίου ἀλλάξασθαι Pl.*R.* 371d; ἀμείβειν τι ἀντί τινος Pi.*P.*4.17, cf. E.*Or.*646, 651; ἀντὶ ποίας εὐεργεσίας; Lys.6.40, etc.; τί δ' ἐστὶν ἀνθ' οὗ..; S.*Ant.*237; ὄνειδος ἀνθ' ὅτου Id.*OC*967; δοίην ἀντ' ἀνιῶν ἀνίας grief *for* grief, Thgn.344; ἀντ' ἀγαθῶν ἀγαθοῖσι βρύοις A.*Supp.*966:—hence ἀνθ' ὧν *wherefore*, A.*Pr.*31, S.*OT*264, Th.6.83, *Ev.Luc.*12.3; ἀντὶ τούτου *therefore*, *Ep.Eph.*5.31; but ἀνθ' ὧν also for ἀντὶ τούτων ὅτι.., *because*, S.*Ant.* 1068, Ar.*Pl.*434: ἀντὶ τοῦ; *wherefore? why?* S.*OT*1021; also ἀνθ' ὧν ὅτι ἦτε.. *instead of being as you were*.., Lxx *De.*28.62. 4. *for the sake of*, Pl.*Mx.*237a, Arist.*EN*1110ᵃ21; with Verbs of entreaty, like πρός c. gen., ἀντὶ παίδων ἱκετεύομέν σε S.*OC*1326. 5. to mark comparison, ἓν ἀνθ' ἑνός one *set against* the other, *compared with* it, Pl.*R.*331b, *Lg.*705b; χάριν ἀντὶ χάριτος, i.e. ever-increasing grace, *Ev.Jo.*1.16; *in preference to*, ἀφνεὸν βούλεται ἀντ' ἀγαθοῦ Thgn.188; ἀντὶ αὐλοῦ καὶ ἀντὶ κιθάρας ὁ ἦχος ἀκούεται Demetr.*Eloc.* 71; αἱρεῖσθαί τι ἀντί τινος Isoc.9.3, D.1.1, cf. X.*Lac.*9.1: even after Comparatives, πλέον ἀντὶ σοῦ S.*Tr.*577; μείζον' ὅστις ἀντὶ τῆς αὑτοῦ πάτρας φίλον νομίζει Id.*Ant.*182; so (esp. after a neg.) ἄλλος ἀντ' ἐμοῦ A.*Pr.*467, S.*Aj.*444, Ar.*Nu.*653; δόξαν ἀντὶ τοῦ ζῆν ἠγαπηκώς Plu.*Alex.*42.

B. Position: ἀντί rarely follows its case, as in Il.23.650, A. *Ag.*1277, *IG*5(1).1119 (Geronthrae, iv B.C.), *AP*7.715 (Leon.); but the Gramm. hold that it never suffers anastrophe.

C. in Compos. it signifies, 1. *over against, opposite*, as ἀντιβαίνω, ἀντίπορος. 2. *against, in opposition to*, as ἀντιλέγω, ἀντίβιος. 3. *one against another, mutually*, as ἀντιδεξιόομαι. 4. *in return*, as ἀντιβοηθέω. 5. *instead of*, as ἀντιβασιλεύς, ἀνθύπατος. 6. *equal to, like*, as ἀντίθεος, ἀντίπαις, ἀντίδουλος. 7. *corresponding, counter*, as ἀντίφορτος, ἀντίτυπος.

ἀντία, v. sub ἀντίος.

ἀντιάζω, impf. ἀντίαζον Hdt.1.166 (but ὑπ-ηντίαζον 4.121), ἠντίαζον (ὑπ-) X.*An.*6.5.27, etc.: fut. ἀντιάσω [ᾰ]; Dor. -άξω (v. infr.): aor. ἠντίασα Hdt.4.80, 9.6; but these two tenses belong also to ἀντιάω: (ἀντί):—*meet face to face*: I. c. acc. pers., *encounter*, whether as friend or foe, τὸν ἐπιόντα Id.4.118, cf. 2.141, 4.80, etc.; ἀ. [τινὰ] ἐς τόπον Hdt.1.166, cf. 9.6; πατέρ' ἀντιάσασα πρὸς..πόρθευμα A. *Ag.*1557: abs., κόρος..βαρὺς ἀντιάσαι Pi.*N.*10.20; μολπὰ πρὸς κάλαμον ἀντιάξει song *shall answer to* the pipe, Id.*O.*10(11).84. 2. *approach as suppliants*, ἀ. τινὰ δώροισι Hdt.1.105: hence simply, *entreat, supplicate*, Ἄρεα ἀντιάζω S.*OT*192; καί σ' ἀντιάζω πρὸς..Διός Id.*Aj.*492, cf. E.*Andr.*572, etc.; freq. with acc. omitted, ἀλλ' ἀντιάζω S.*El.*1009, cf. *Ph.*809, E.*Alc.*400; βᾶθι καὶ ἀντίασον γονάτων *entreat* [her] by her knees, Id.*Supp.*272. II. = ἀντιάω II, ἀντάω, c. dat. pers. et acc. rei, ὅταν θεοὶ..Γιγάντεσσιν μάχαν ἀντιάζωσιν *in* fight, Pi. *N.*1.68.—This Verb is never used in correct Att. Prose.

ἀντιάνειρα, ἡ, (ἀντί, ἀνήρ), fem. form of a masc. in -άνωρ or -ήνωρ: in Il. always as epith. of the Amazons, *a match for men*, 3.189, 6.186, etc.; so of Athena, Coluth.170. II. in Pi.*O.*12.16 στάσις ἀντιάνειρα faction *wherein man is set against man*.

ἀντιάς, άδος, ἡ, *tonsil*, mostly in pl., Hp.*Morb.*2.11 and 30: esp. when inflamed, Cels.7.12, Gal.7.263; cf. παρίσθμια.

ἀντιαττικιστής, οῦ, ὁ, *Anti-Atticist*, title of grammatical work, *AB*77.

ἀντιαχάτης [ᾰτ], ου, ὁ, a stone *like an agate*, dub. in Orph.*L.*637 (Abel).

ἀντ-ιᾰχέω, *cry* or *call against*, Theoc.*Ep.*4.11 codd. (ἀνταχεῦσι Scal.), A.R.2.828. -ιάχω [ᾰ], = foreg., Orph.*A.*828; ἀμοιβήδην ἀντίαχεν A.R.4.76.

ἀντιάω, Hom. uses pres. only in the Ep. forms ἀντιόω, inf. ἀντιάαν, 3 pl. imper. ἀντιοώντων, part. ἀντιόων, όωσα, όωντες; but ἀντιόω, which is pres. in Il.1.31, 23.643, serves as fut. in 13.752: fut. ἀντιάσω [ᾰ] Od.22.28, Thgn. (v. infr.): aor. ἠντίασα Hom. (these two tenses in form belong to ἀντιάζω; but such instances as belong in sense to ἀντιάω are given here):—Med., once in Hom. (v. infr.), A.R. 1.470, 2.24: (ἀντί, ἀντίος):—Ep. Verb: I. *go for the purpose of meeting* or *receiving*: 1. c. gen. rei, *go in quest of*, when an aim or purpose is implied, πολέμοιο μενοίνα ἀντιάαν Il.13.215; ὄφρα πόνοιο..ἀντιάσητον 12.356; οὐκέτ' ἀέθλων ἄλλων ἀντιάσεις Od.22.28, al.: metaph. of an arrow, *hit*, ἀλλά κεν ἢ στέρνων ἢ νηδύος ἀντιάσειε Il.13.290:—often of the gods, *come* (as it were) *to meet* an offering, and so, in past tenses, *to have received, accepted* it, ἀντιόων ταύρων τε καὶ ἀρνειῶν ἑκατόμβης Od.1.25; ἀρνῶν κνίσης αἰγῶν τε τελείων..ἀντιάσας Il.1.67; generally, *partake of, enjoy*, αἲ γὰρ.. ὀνήσιος ἀντιάσειεν Od.21.402; so ἔργων ἀντιάσεις χαλεπῶν Thgn.1308; οὔτε του τάφου ἀντιάσας οὔτε γόων S.*El.*869: abs., ἀντιάσαις *having obtained* [his wishes], Pi.*I.* 6(5).15:—once in Med., ἀντιάασθε, θεοί, γάμου Il.24.62. 2. more rarely c. gen. pers., *match* or *measure oneself with*, ἡμεῖς δ' εἰμὲν τοῖοι οἳ ἂν σέθεν ἀντιάσαιμεν ib.7.231; δήων ἀντιάσειν Thgn.552. b. rarely, *come to aid*, οὗ παιδὸς τεθνηότος ἀντιόωσα Od.24.56. II. c. dat. pers., *meet with, encounter*, as by chance, μηδ' ἀντιάσειας ἐκείνῳ ib.18.147; δυστήνων δέ τε παῖδες ἐμῷ μένει ἀντιόωσιν Il.6. 127. 2. c. gen., *encounter*, ψύχεος Emp.65. III. abs. in aor. part., ἀλλά τιν' ὕμμ' ὀΐω δόμεναι θεὸν ἀντιάσαντα *having haply met* you, Il.10.551, cf. Od.6.193, 13.312, 17.442. IV. c. acc. rei, only in ἐμὸν λέχος ἀντιόωσα, euphem. for *sharing* it, only in Il.1.31. V. *approach as a suppliant, supplicate*, like ἀντιάζω I.2, only in later Ep., c. gen. pers., A.R.1.703: also c. acc. pers., Id.3.694: c. acc. rei, ib. 717. VI. ἀντιόωσα σελήνη dub. in Orph.*Fr.*168.16.

ἀντιβάδην [ᾰ], Adv. *going against, opposite*, ἀ. ὠθεῖν Plu.2.381a.

ἀντιβαδίζω, *go against, the contrary way*, Phot. s.v. ῥαβάττειν.

ἀντιβαιβάζω· *obvagio*, Gloss.

ἀντιβαίνω, fut. -βήσομαι, *go against, withstand, resist*, c. dat., Hdt. 5.40, A.*Pr.*236, Decr.ap.D.18.186, etc.; πλευραῖσιν ἀντιβᾶσα *having set her foot against*.., E.*Ba.*1126: abs., ἀντιβὰς ἐλᾶν row *with foot planted against* the stretcher, Ar.*Ra.*202. 2. abs., Hdt.3.72, 8.3, E.*IA*1016, etc.; βιασθεὶς πολλὰ κἀντιβάς *reluctant*, S.*El.*575; εἰ..μὴ περὶ σοῦ μάχομαι μόνος ἀντιβεβηκώς Ar.*Eq.*767 (ἀμφι- Dawes); ἀ. πρὸς τἀριστερὰ μόνον Pl.*Lg.*634a.

ἀντι-βάκχειος (sc. πούς), ὁ, the foot – – ᴗ, Diom.1.513 K., al.: —also -**βακχος**, ὁ, Ter.Maur.1411.

ἀντιβάλανος· ἡ κικκίς, Hsch.

ἀντιβάλλω, *throw against* or *in turn*, Th.7.25 (the acc. pers. being understood); βέλος Plb.6.22.4: c. dat., ἀ. ἀκοντίοις Plu.*Nic.*25; ἀ.

τῷ κωρύκῳ *practise by striking against* the sack, in the gymnasium, Luc.*Lex.*5; *put back* a protruding bone, Pall.*in Hp.Fract.*12. 285 C. II. *put one against the other, compare, collate*, of Mss., Str.13.1.54, 17.1.5, *POxy.*1479 (i B.C., Pass.); *match, compare with*, λέοντι τίς αἰετὸν ἀντιβάλοιτο; Opp.*C.*1.68; λόγους ἀ. πρὸς ἀλλήλους *exchange* words in conversation, *Ev.Luc.*24.17; πρὸς ἑαυτὸν ἀ. τὸ γεγονός *weigh* with oneself, Lxx 2*Ma.*11.13. III. in Med., *change*, μορφήν dub. l. Opp.*C.*3.16.

ἀντιβάλμους· ἀντιστρόφους, Hsch.

ἀντιβαρνικί, τό, *cassia*, Hsch.

ἀντιβᾰσῐλεύς, έως, ὁ, = Lat. *interrex*, D.H.9.69.

ἀντιβᾰσῐλεύω, *reign as a rival king*, τισί J.*BJ*4.7.1.

ἀντίβᾰσις, εως, ἡ, *resistance*, Ph.*Bel.*73.14, Plu.*Caes.*38, etc.; πρός τι Id.2.584f; ἡ κατ' ἀντίβασιν ἀφή S.E.*M.*10.2; opp. ἐπέρεισις, Sor.2.10, cf. Antyll.ap.Orib.9.23.11. 2. *ground of opposition* (?), διαφόρου τετευχότα -σεως Phld.*Sign.*27. II. in the ballista, *counter-prop*, Vitr.10.11.9.

ἀντιβαστάζω, *support, prop*, Eust.1933.37.

ἀντιβάτης [ᾰ], ου, ὁ, *bolt of a door*, Sch.Ar.*V.*202.

ἀντιβᾰτικός, ή, όν, *contrary, opposite*, φορά Plu.*Phoc.*2. II. of contact, *firm, thorough*, -κωτέρα ἡ κατὰ τὴν κίνησιν τοῦ οὐρανίου σώματος ἀφή Simp.*in Cael.*440.19, cf. 9; *resistent*, Hierocl. p.23 A., Alex.Aphr.*Quaest.*62.4, Olymp.*in Mete.*18.30; of the pulse, Gal.8.949, cf. 644. Adv. -κῶς ib.668: Comp., κλίνης -κώτερον ἐστρωμένης Sor.2.61.

ἀντιβῐάζομαι, *use force against*, *AP*12.183 (Strat.): abs., Ph.1.295, al.:—Pass., ῥώμῃ -βιασθέντες κραταιοτέρᾳ 2.423.

ἀντιβιβλίον, τό, *counter-account*, *PFlor.*388.48 (i A.D.); *counter-summons*, Just.*Nov.*53.3.2 (ἀντιβίβλῳ codd.).

ἀντιβῐβρώσκω, fut. Pass. -βρωθήσομαι, *eat in turn*, Ath.7.343c.

ἀντιβίην [βῐ], Adv., (βία) *against, face to face*, ἐριζέμεναι βασιλῆϊ ἀντιβίην Il.1.278; Ἕκτορι πειρηθῆναι ἀ. 21.226, cf. 5.220, Orph.*L.*26.

ἀντίβῐος, α, ον, also ος, ον: (βία):—*opposing force to force*: as Adj. in Hom. only in the phrase ἀντιβίοις ἐπέεσσι with *wrangling* words, Il.1.304, Od.18.415, etc.; ἀ. ὅμιλος *hostile*, Tryph.624. b. Subst., *enemy*, Jul.*Caes.*319b (anap.), Nonn.*D.*2.508, al., Opp.*H.*5.114. 2. as Adv., ἀντίβιον, = ἀντιβίην, ἀ. μαχέσασθαι Il.3.20; Μενελάῳ ἀντίβιον.. πολεμίζειν ib.435; εἰ μὲν ἀντίβιον.. πειρηθείης 11.386.

ἀντιβλάπτω, *harm in return*, Arist.*EN*1138ᵃ8, Ph.2.371.

ἀντιβλασφημέω, *retaliate with abuse*, Sch.Aristid.p.673 D.

ἀντι-βλεπτέον, *one must look in the face*, μοι πρός τι Luc.*Dem. Enc.*17. **-βλέπω**, fut. -βλέψομαι D.25.98:—*look straight at, look in the face*, c. dat. pers., τῷ ἐμῷ πατρὶ οὐδ' ἀντιβλέπειν δύναμαι X.*HG*5.4.27; τοῖς φίλοις *Com.Adesp.*22.41 D.; εἰς or πρὸς τὸν ἥλιον, X.*Mem.*4.7.7, Thphr.*Sens.*18: metaph., πρὸς δωρεὰς βασιλέων Plu.*Comp.Dem. Cic.*3: c. acc., ἀντιβλέπειν ἐκεῖνον οὐ δυνήσομαι Men.586: abs., part., ἀντιβλέπουσαι.. αἱ αἶγες *facing one another*, Arist.*HA*611ᵃ5. **-βλεψις**, εως, ἡ, *looking in the face, look*, X.*Hier.*1.35, Plu.2.681b.

ἀντίβλημα, ατος, τό, *stone inserted in vacant space* in masonry, *POxy.*498.16 (ii A.D.).

ἀντιβοάω, *return a cry*, of an echo, Bion 1.38; *call aloud in answer*, J.*BJ*3.5.4: c. acc., ἰήϊον ἀντεβόησαν prob. in Euph.80; ἴακχον θρήνοις Him.*Ecl.*2.4.

ἀντιβοηθέω, *help in turn*, τινί Th.6.18, 7.58, Pl.*R.*559e, X.*HG*7.4.2.

ἀντίβοιος, ον, (βοῦς) *worth an ox* or *in place of an ox*, of offerings, S.*Fr.*405.

ἀντιβολεύς· *dictator*, *Gloss.*

ἀντιβολέω, impf. ἠντιβόλουν Ar.*Eq.*667 codd., Lys.1.25: fut. ἀντιβολήσω Od. (v. infr.), Lys.14.16: aor. in Hom., ἀντεβόλησα; with double augm., ἠντεβόλησα Ar.*Fr.*38:—*meet*, esp. in battle, c. dat. pers., Il.16.847, al.: abs., 11.365, al. 2. rarely c. dat. rei, *to be present at*, φόνῳ ἀνδρῶν ἀντεβόλησας Od.11.416; τάφῳ ἀνδρῶν ἀ. 24.87; cf. ἀβολέω. 3. c. gen. rei, *partake of, have one's share of*, μάχης καυστείρης ἀντιβολῆσαι Il.4.342; οὐ γάρ τευ ἐπητύος ἀντιβολήσεις Od.21.306; οὐ δέ κεν τάφου ἀντιβολήσαις 4.547; γάμου ἀ. Hes. *Op.*784, cf. Pi.*O.*13.30; even πυκινοῦ νόου ἀ. Timo 59.1. 4. rarely of the thing, *fall to one's lot*, c. gen. pers., στυγερὸς γάμος ἀντιβολήσει.. ἐμέθεν Od.18.272. 5. c. acc. pers., *meet as a suppliant, entreat, supplicate*, freq. in Com., Ar.*Nu.*110, *Pl.*444: c. acc. et inf., Id.*Eq.*667, *Ach.*147, D.21.188: abs., περὶ τῶν ἀντιβολούντων those who *supplicate*, Ar.*V.*559; freq. in parenthesis, εἶτ', ἀντιβολῶ, Id.*Eq.*109, cf. *Pl.*103 (freq. also ἀντιβολῶ σε Pl.Com.43.5, 173.3; also in Lys. 1.25, 29, X.*Ath.*1.18):—Pass., *to be supplicated*, ἀντιβοληθείς Ar.*V.*560. II. causal, *cause to meet*, τινά τινι *IG*14.2431 (Fréjus).

ἀντιβολ-ή, ἡ, *confronting, comparing, collation*, ἀντιγράφων Str. 17.1.5; *opposition*, ἐξ ἀντιβολῆς παραβάλλειν Hsch. s.v. παραβλήδην. II. *discussion*, A.D.*Conj.*213.20. III. *substitute*, *PHolm.*10.14. **-ήρ**· στρωτὴρ μικρός (Lacon.), Hsch. **-ησις**, εως, ἡ, = sq., Pl.*Ap.*37a, *Smp.*183a. **-ία**, ἡ, *an entreaty, prayer*, Eup.317, Th.7.75. **-ον**, τό, = ἀντίγραφον, Sch.Il.18.490, Sch.Od.12.556.

ἀντιβομβέω, *return a humming sound*, Ach.Tat.3.2, cf. Eust.1885.19.

ἀντιβόρειον, τό, name of a *sundial*, Vitr.9.8.1.

ἀντιβουλεύομαι, Med., *give contrary advice*, Polyaen.1.30.4.

ἀντιβρᾰδύνω [ῡ], *delay in turn*, Sch.Th.3.10.

ἀντιβρίθω [ρῑ], *press down in the opposite scale*, Ph.2.170.

ἀντιβροντάω, *rival in thundering*, τινί Luc.*Tim.*2; βρονταῖς ἀ. D.C.59.28.

ἀντιγᾰμέω, *marry in turn*, Eust.1796.53.

ἀντιγέγωνα, pf. in pres. sense, *return a cry*, *AP*9.177.

ἀντιγενεηλογέω, Ion. form, *give a different pedigree*, Hdt.2.143.

ἀντιγένεσις, εως, ἡ, Astrol., *recasting of nativity in a later year*, Vett.Val.213.20, al.

ἀντιγεννάω, *generate in rivalry*, Lync.ap.Ath.7.285f; or *in return*, τοὺς γονεῖς Ph.1.89.

ἀντιγεοῦχος, ὁ, *land-agent*, *BGU*303.4 (vi A.D.), *POxy.*943.8 (vi A.D.).

ἀντιγεραίρω, *honour in turn*, App.*BC*2.140.

ἀντιγηροτροφέω, *support in old age in turn*, Lesb.Rh.2.10.

ἀντιγλαυκισμός, ὁ, *substitute for blue dye*, *PLeid.X.*100.

ἀντιγνωμονέω, *to be of a different opinion*, τινί D.C.46.44; ἀ. μὴ οὐκ εἶναί τι *think* that a thing is *otherwise*, X.*Cyr.*4.3.8.

ἀντι-γόνιον· βοτάνη, καὶ ἄνθος, Hsch. **-γόνιος**· βόλος τις οὕτως ἐκαλεῖτο, Id. **-γονον**· ἀκακία, Id.

Ἀντίγονος, ὁ, name of several Macedonian kings:—hence **Ἀντιγόνειος**, α, ον, *of Antigonus*, Polyaen.4.9.1; **Ἀντιγόνεια**, τά, name of a *festival in his honour*, Plb.28.19.3, *IG*11.154*A*42 (Delos, iii B.C.): also **Ἀντιγονικός**, ή, όν, Plu.*Arat.*54:—fem. **Ἀντιγονίς**, ίδος, a kind of *cup named from him*, Polem.Hist.57, Plu.*Aem.*33:—**Ἀντιγονίζω**, *to be on Antigonus' side, of his party*, Polyaen.4.6.13, D.T.638.16.

ἀντίγραμμα, ατος, τό, *duplicate letter*, Luc.*Herm.*40; = ἀντίγραφον, Gal.17.59.

ἀντιγρᾰφ-εία, ἡ, *office of* ἀντιγραφεύς, *PPetr.*3 p.162, *PTeb.*5.85 (ii B.C., pl.), cf. *Inscr.Prien.*108.222 (ii B.C.; -ία lapis). **-εῖον**, τό, *office whence* ἀντίγραφα *were issued*, *Jahresh.*7 *Beibl.*44 (Ephesus), cf. ib.18 *Beibl.*286. **-εύς**, έως, ὁ, *checking-* or *copying-clerk*, a public officer, Aeschin.3.25, cf. *IG*2.408, al., cf. 575 (of a deme), *SIG*364.22 (Ephesus), etc., Plb.6.56.13, *PRev.Laws* 12.1; ἀ. τῶν εἰσενεγκόντων *one who keeps a check upon* their *accounts*, D.22.70. **-ή**, ἡ, *a reply in writing*, such as Caesar's *Anticato* in reply to Cicero's *Cato*, Plu.*Caes.*3, cf. *Sol.*1, Id.2.1059b, Herm.*in Phdr.*p.189 A. II. as law-term, *answer put in by the defendant, plea*, D.45.46 (where a specimen is found); sts. of *the plaintiff's plea, indictment*, Pl.*Ap.*27c, Hyp.*Eux.*31:—sts. ἀντιγραφή was used indifferently of both parties, cf. Harp.:—in Ar.*Nu.*471, generally, *counter-pleas*, cf. Poll. 8.58. III. *transcribing*, D.H.4.62. 2. = ἀντίγραφον, Plu.2.577e. IV. *rescript, imperial decree*, *OGI*262.27. **-ικός**, ή, όν, τὸ ἀ. κεφάλαιον *concerning the indictment*, Sch.Aristid.p.441 D. **-ος**, ον, *copied, in duplicate*, στῆλαι, διαθῆκαι, etc., D.20.36, 45.10, etc. II. as Subst., ἀντίγραφον, τό, *transcript, copy*, Decr.ap.And.1.79, Lys. 32.7, D.25.47, Arist.*Pol.*1309ᵃ11; esp. of *copies* of a book, Ἀττικιανὰ ἀντίγραφα *copies* of an edition issued by Atticus, Harp. s.v. Ἀργᾶς, al.; *certified copy* of official document, *CPR*1.4 (i A.D.); εἰκόνος ἀ. *copy* of a picture, Luc.*Zeux.*3 (but -φος Jac.). **-ω**, *write against* or *in answer, write back*, v.l. in Th.1.129 (Pass.), Phld.*Ir.*p.86 W., Plu.*Luc.*21, D.Chr.2.18, *PFlor.*278 ii 30 (iii A.D.), etc.; ἀ. τῇ γραφῇ *vie in description* with painting, Longus *Prooem.* II. Med., with pf. Pass. (Aeschin.1.154, D.45.45), as law-term, *put in as an* ἀντιγραφή, *plead against*, τι περί τινος Is.11.17, cf. D.48.31; also ἀ. τινί, c. inf., *plead against* another *that* such is the case, Lys.23.5, D.44.39:—also, *bring a counter-accusation*, Poll.8.58, cf. Aeschin.1.119, 154; later in Act., *plead in answer to* a charge, -γράψαι ὡς οὐκ ἔπραξεν D.S.1.75. 2. *keep a counter-reckoning* of money paid or received (cf. ἀντιγραφεύς), Arist.*Ath.*54.3; simply, *check* accounts, *PTeb.*89.13 (ii B.C.). 3. *issue a rescript*, *SIG*888.8. III. Pass., aor. ἀντιγραφῆναι *to be copied*, εἰς στήλας *Milet.*3.148.93. **-γραψις**, εως, ἡ, *putting in of an* ἀντιγραφή, v.l. in Lys.23.10.

ἀντιγυμνᾰσιαρχέω, *to be deputy-gymnasiarch*, *AJA*19.324 (Locr.).

ἀντιγώνιος, ον, *marking opposite angles*, of stars in a quadrilateral, Hipparch.3.4.3, Ptol.*Alm.*7.1.

ἀντιδάκνω, fut. -δήξομαι Muson.*Fr.*10 p.55 H.: the aor. ἀντέδακα dub. in Luc.*Ocyp.*27:—*bite in turn*, Hdt.4.168, Ael.*NA*4.19, Muson. l.c.

ἀντιδάκτῠλος, ὁ, *thumb*, Aq.*Ex.*29.20. II. in Metric, *dactyl reversed, anapaest*, Diom.1.478 K., Choerob.*in Heph.*p.215 C.

ἀντιδᾰνειστέον, *one must lend in return*, τῷ δανείσαντι Arist.*EN* 1165ᵃ8.

ἀντιδᾰπᾰνάω or **-αομαι**, *spend in turn upon*, τοὺς δαπανωμένους Lib.*Ep.*843 (dub. l.).

ἀντίδειξις, εως, ἡ, *refutation*, *Corp.Herm.*16.1.

ἀντίδειπνος, ον, *taking anothers place at dinner*, Luc.*Gall.*9.

ἀντιδεξιόομαι, *give the right hand in turn, return one's salute*, τινά X.*Cyr.*4.2.19, D.Chr.38.47, Luc.*Laps.*13.

ἀντιδέομαι, *entreat in return*, Pl.*La.*186d.

ἀντιδέρκομαι, = ἀντιβλέπω, c. acc., E.*HF*163.

ἀντιδέχομαι, *receive in return*, A.*Ch.*916; ἀμοιβὰς κακάς *Cat.Cod. Astr.*2.211; ἔδωκα κἀντεδεξάμην E.*IA*1222.

ἀντιδέω, *fetter in turn*, Diog.Oen.39.

ἀντιδημᾰγωγέω, *practise counter-demagogy*, πρὸς τὴν Κίμωνος εὐπορίαν Arist.*Ath.*27.3, cf. Plu.*CG*8.

ἀντιδημηγορέω, *harangue in opposition to*, τινί Eust.1029.1.

ἀντιδημιουργέομαι, Med., *manufacture in competition*, πρός τι Lync.ap.Ath.11.469b.

ἀντιδια-βαίνω, *cross over in turn*, X.*Ages.*1.8, dub.l. J.*AJ*13.1.3. **-βάλλω**, *to attack in return*, τὸν διαβάλλοντα Arist.*Rh.*1416ᵃ26. **-γράφω** [ᾰφ], *pay in money instead of kind*, *PPetr.*2 p.102

(iii B.C., Pass.) :—Med., *Inscr.Magn.*103.68 (ii B.C.) :—hence **-γρᾰφή**, ἡ, *Ostr.*1509, al. (ii B.C.). **-ζεύγνῡμαι**, *pair off with*, in dichotomy, S.E.*M.*11.15 ; *to be subjoined in turn*, A.D.*Synt.*126.10.

ἀντιδιαίρ-εσις, εως, ἡ, in Logic, *division by dichotomy*, Plot.4.4.28, 6.3.10, D.L.7.61, Iamb.*Myst.*1.15. **II.** in Surgery, *counter-incision*, Paul.Aeg.4.48. **-έω**, *distinguish logically*, βαρβάρους πρὸς Ἕλληνας Str.14.2.28, cf. Demetr.Lac.*Herc.*1012.68, Phld.*Oec.*p.35 J.; τὸ σύνθετον τῷ ἁπλῷ Plot.6.3.10, cf. Iamb.*Comm.Math.*4 :—Pass., *to be opposed as the members of a natural classification*, Arist.*Cat.*14^{b}34, *Top.*143^{a}36, cf. Iamb.*Myst.*9.7. **II.** Med., τροφὴν τοῖς νεύροις, perh. *distribute*, Theo Gymn.ap.Gal.6.208.

ἀντιδιάκειμαι, *to be different*, of mixed stuffs, Aq.*De.*22.11.

ἀντιδιάκονος [ᾱ], ον, *serving in return*, τοῖς ἄλλοις Str.16.4.26.

ἀντιδιακοσμέω, *arrange* or *array in opposition*, of troops, App.*BC*2.75.

ἀντιδιαλέγομαι, *reply to, answer in discussion*, in Pass., περὶ τῶν ἀντιδιαλεγομένων τοῖς διαλεκτικοῖς, title of work by Chrysipp., D.L.7.202.

ἀντιδιαλλάσσομαι, Med., *exchange* prisoners, τινά τινος D.H.19.13. **II.** of historians, *differ* in an account, πρός τι Id.1.84.

ἀντιδια-λογίζομαι, *set off in compensation*, *Gloss.* **-νυκτερεύω**, *bivouac opposite to*, τινί App.*BC*4.130. **-πλέκω**, *retort*, ἀντιδιαπλέκει ὡς.. Aeschin.3.28, cf. *AB*406. **-σταλτικός**, ή, όν, *distinctive*, A.D.*Pron.*24.12, *Synt.*97.17. Adv. -κῶς Id.*Pron.*40.4. **-στᾰτέω**, *be at variance*, ἀλλήλοις Ammon.*Diff.*45. **-στέλλω**, *distinguish, discriminate*, Str.10.2.17 ; ἁπλᾶ καὶ σύνθετα Plot.6.1.29 ; τι ἀπό τινος Longin.*Proll.Heph.*p.83 C.:—Med., *controvert*, Sor.2.54. **II.** *contrast, oppose*, τί τινι S.E.*P.*1.9 ; τινὰς πρός τινας D.H.*Th.*32 ; τι πρός τι Alex.Aphr. *in Metaph.*400.17 :—Pass., A.D.*Synt.*14.24. **-στολή**, ἡ, *opposition, distinction*, Id.*Pron.*23.24, *Synt.*15.17, al., Alex.Aphr. *in Metaph.*11.12, etc. **II.** Medic., *counter-dilatation*, ἀρτηριῶν πρὸς καρδίαν Gal.8.760. **-ταξις**, εως, ἡ, *comparison of arguments* for and against a thesis, Iamb.*Comm.Math.*35. **-τάσσομαι**, Med., *oppose*, τινὶ πρὸς τὰ ὅλα Arr.*Epict.*3.24.24 ; τινὶ περί τινος S.E.*M.*7.159 : abs., ib.8.126. **-τίθημι**, *retaliate upon* a person, D.S.34.12 ; κακῶς παθόντα ἀ. Eust.546.28 :—Med., *offer resistance*, πρὸς τὴν πειθώ Longin.17.1 ; τοὺς ἀντιδιατιθεμένους *opponents*, 2 *Ep.Ti.*2.25.

ἀντιδῐδάσκᾰλοι, οἱ, *poets who are rivals in dramatic* or *lyric contests*, Sch.Pi.*N.*4.60.

ἀντιδῐδάσκω, *inform, instruct in turn* or *on the other side*, App.*BC*5.19, *AP*6.236 (Phil.). **II.** of dramatists, etc., *contend for the prize*, Ar.*V.*1410, cf. Satyr.*Vit.Eur.Fr.*38.19, D.Chr.37.40.

ἀντιδίδωμι, *give in return, repay*, τινί τι Hdt.1.70, 3.135, A.*Ch.*94, etc.; πόνον, οὐ χάριν, ἀντιδώσειν ἔχειν S.*OC*232, cf. A.*Ch.*498, *Eu.*264 ; νέκυν νεκρῶν ἀμοιβὸν ἀ. S.*Ant.*1067 ; ἀ. χάριν E.*HF*1337, cf. Th.1.41, 3.63 ; τιμωρίαν Id.2.53 ; λαμβάνων ἀντεδίδου X.*Cyr.*8.6.23 :—Pass., ἔλεος πρός τινα δίκαιος ἀντιδίδοσθαι Th.3.40. **2.** *give for* or *instead of*, τί τινος E.*Alc.*340, *IT*28 ; τι ἀντί τινος Ar.*Pax*1251. **II.** at Athens, ἀ. [τὴν οὐσίαν] *offer to change fortunes with* one (cf. ἀντίδοσις II), Lys.24.9, D.20.130 ; ἀ. τριηραρχίαν Id.21.78 ; *accept such an offer*, Id.28.17. **III.** *give as an antidote*, Democr.ap.Gal.14.90.

ἀντιδιέξειμι, (εἶμι *ibo*) *go through, recount in turn*, ὀνόματα Aeschin.1.155.

ἀντιδιεξέρχομαι, *go through in opposition*, ἀ. λόγῳ Pl.*Tht.*167d.

ἀντιδιεσταλμένως, Adv. pf. part. Pass. of ἀντιδιαστέλλω, *as distinguished from, opposed to*, Iamb.*in Nic.*p.12 P.

ἀντιδιηγέομαι, *introduce a counter-narration*, Corn.*Rh.*p.364 H. **b.** *relate in turn*, X.Eph.5.9.

ἀντιδιήγησις, εως, ἡ, *counter-narration*, Fortunat.*Rh.*2.19.

ἀντιδιΐστημι, = ἀντιδιαστέλλω, Dam.*Pr.*67, Hsch., Suid. s. v. ἀντιδιαστέλλεται.

ἀντιδῐκ-άζομαι, *implead one another*, Lys.*Fr.*300 S. **-ᾰσία**, ἡ, *litigation*, Aq.*Pr.*20.3. **-έω**, impf. ἠντιδίκουν Lys.6.12, but ἠντεδίκουν (acc. to the best Ms.) D.39.37, 40.18 : aor. ἠντεδίκησα Id.47.28 :—*to be an* ἀντίδικος, *dispute, go to law*, περί τινος X.*Mem.*4.4.8 ; οἱ ἀντιδικοῦντες ἑκάτεροι *the parties to a suit*, Pl.*Lg.*948d : abs., of the defendant, ἀντιδικῶν Ar.*Nu.*776 ; ἀ. πρός τι or πρός τινα *to urge one's suit against*.., D.28.17, 41.10, Is.11.9 ; *join issue*, ἠντιδίκει ἢ μήν.., c. acc. et inf., Lys. l. c. ; *oppose, rebut*, διαβολαῖς D.41.13 ; ἀλλήλοις prob. in Thugen.1 D. **II.** Pass., *to be an object of dispute*, Phot.p.147 R. **-ησις**, εως, ἡ, = sq., *Gloss.* **-ία**, ἡ, *litigation, contention*, πρός τινα ὑπέρ τινος Plu.2.483b ; ὁ ἐξ -ίας *the opponent in a process*, Mitteis *Chr.*88.14 (ii A.D.) ; Astrol., opp. συναφεῖαι, συνάψεις, Ptol.*Tetr.*191. **-ος**, ον, *opponent* or *adversary in a suit*, Aeschin.2.165, cf. Pl.*Phdr.*273c : fem., ἡ ἀ. *POxy.*37 i8 (i A.D.) : properly, *the defendant*, Antipho 1.2 ; but also, *the plaintiff*, Lys.7.13 ; ἀ. πρός τινα Antipho 1.5 :—generally, *opponent, adversary*, A.*Ag.*41 ; ἀληθινῶν ἀ. [Heraclit.]133, cf. 1 *Ep.Pet.*5.8, Phld.*Ir.*p.65 W.

ἀντιδικτάτωρ, ορος, ὁ, = Lat. *pro dictatore*, Lyd.*Mag.*1.38.

ἀντιδιορίζω, *define in turn, give a counter-definition*, Gal.18(2).837.

ἀντιδιορύσσω, Att. -ττω, *countermine*, Str.12.8.11.

ἀντιδίσκωσις, εως, ἡ, *doubling of the sun's disk*, Lyd.*Ost.*9^{c}.

ἀντιδοκέω, *think oneself equal to*, κύμασιν Lxx 2 *Ma.*9.8.

ἀντιδόκιον, τό, Archit., *course supporting beams*, ἀ. λίθινον *Milet.*3 p.172 (iii B.C.).

ἀντιδομή, ἡ, (δέμω) *opposed* or *substituted building*, Aen.Tact.23.5.

ἀντι-δοξάζω, *to be of a contrary opinion*, Pl.*Tht.*170d, Epicur.*Nat.*14.8, Phld.*Sign.*19, cf. 31, D.L.9.18. **-δοξέω**, = foreg., τινί or πρός τινα, Plb.2.56.1, 16.14.4 ; τινὶ περί τινος D.S.2.29 : abs., Boeth. *Stoic.*3.267. **-δοξος**, ον, *of a different opinion* or *sect*, Luc.*Herm.*17, Aristaenet.1.10 ; μάχη φορᾶς ἀ. Luc.*Par.*29.

ἀντίδορος, ον, (δορά) *instead of skin*, κάρυον χλωρῆς ἀντίδορον λεπίδος with a green husk *as integument*, *AP*6.22 (Zon.).

ἀντί-δοσις, εως, ἡ, (ἀντιδίδωμι) *giving in return, exchange*, Arist.*EN*1133^{a}6, Call.*Fr.*221 ; φορτίων D.S.2.54 ; αἰχμαλώτων 12.63 ; καρπῶν D.Chr.38.22 ; κακῶν App.*BC*1.3 ; ἡ εἰς τὴν σιωπὴν ἀ. Ael.*NA*5.9 :—*repayment, requital*, ὕβρεως Orac.ap.Luc.*Alex.*50 ; ἀντίδοσίν τινος *in return for*.., *IG*3.172. **II.** at Athens, *a form by which a citizen charged with a* λειτουργία or εἰσφορά *might call upon any other citizen*, whom he thought richer than himself, *either to exchange properties, or to submit to the charge himself*, Lys.3.20, etc., cf. Cratin.14 D. ; καλεῖσθαί τινα εἰς ἀ. τριηραρχίας ἢ χορηγίας X.*Oec.*7.3 ; καταστὰς (sc. χορηγὸς) ἐξ ἀντιδόσεως D.21.156 ; ποιεῖσθαι ἀ. τινι Id.4.36 ; ἀ. ἐπ' ἐμὲ παρεσκεύασαν 28.17 ; cf. Isoc.15, D.42. **-δοτος**, ον, (ἀντιδίδωμι) *given in lieu of*, πυρός *AP*9.165 (Pall.). **II.** *given as a remedy for*, κακῶν φάρμακον ἀ. ib.10.118. **2.** as Subst., ἀντίδοτος (sc. δόσις), ἡ, *an antidote, remedy*, *AP*12.13 (Strat.), Gal.14.1, etc. : in other places the gender is uncertain, Plu.2.42d, 54e, etc. :—hence Dim. **ἀντιδότιον**, τό, Archig.ap.Philum.*Ven.*14.7.

ἀντιδουλεύω, *serve in turn*, τοῖς τεκοῦσι γὰρ δύστηνος ὅστις μὴ ἀντιδουλεύει τέκνων E.*Supp.*362.

ἀντίδουλος, ον, *instead of a slave*, neut. pl. as Adv., ταύρων γονὰς δοὺς ἀντίδουλα A.*Fr.*194. **II.** of persons, *being as a slave, treated as a slave*, Id.*Ch.*135.

ἀντίδουπος, ον, *re-echoing*, ᾄδειν A.*Pers.*121 (lyr.) ; βοᾶν ἀντίδουπά τινι ib.1040, parodied by Pl.Com.27 D.

ἀντιδράσσομαι, Att. -ττομαι, *lay hold of*, καρδίας Them.*Or.*32.357b.

ἀντί-δρᾱσις, εως, ἡ, *retaliation*, Anon. *in Rh.*91.30. **-δράω**, fut. -δράσω [ᾱ], *act against, retaliate*, παθὼν μὲν ἀντέδρων S.*OC*271, cf. 953, E.*Andr.*438, Antipho 4.2.2, etc. ; πρὸς τὰς πράξεις ἀ. S.*OC*959 :—Pass., Iamb.*Myst.*3.29. **II.** c. acc. pers., *repay, requite*, ἀ. τινὰ κακῶς S.*OC*1191, cf. Pl.*Cri.*49d ; γενναῖα γὰρ παθόντες ὑμᾶς ἀντιδρᾶν ὀφείλομεν E.*Supp.*1179.

ἀντιδρομέω, *run in a contrary direction*, Luc.*Astr.*12.

ἀντιδύνᾰμος [ῠ], ον, = ἀντίβιος, Sch.Opp.*H.*5.267.

ἀντιδύνω [ῡ], *set opposite to*, *Intr.Arat.*p.328 Maass.

ἀντιδυσχεραίνω, *to be angry in turn*, τοῖς δυσχεραίνουσιν M.Ant.6.26.

ἀντι-δωρεά, ἡ, *a return-gift, recompense*, Arist.*EN*1123^{a}3. **-δωρέομαι**, *present in return*, ἀ. τινά τινι one *with* a thing, Hdt.2.30 ; τινί τι a thing *to* one, θεοὶ δέ σοι ἐσθλῶν ἀμοιβὰς ἀντιδωρησαίατο E.*Hel.*159, cf. Pl.*Euthphr.*14e ; *offer instead*, τούτου ἐφιέμενος ἀ. ἄλλο Arist.*EN*1159^{b}14. **-δωρον**, τό, *return-gift*, Men.Prot.p.20 D., Just.*Nov.*120.11, v.l. for ἀντίδουλα in A.*Fr.*194.

ἀντιζεύγνῡμι, *annex*, e. g. a word in the corresponding clause of a sentence, D.H.*Amm.*2.11.

ἀντι-ζηλία, ἡ, *rivalry*, Vett.Val.39.27, Heph.Astr.2.28. **-ζηλος**, ὁ, ἡ, *rival, adversary*, Lxx *Le.*18.18, *Si.*26.6 : as Adj., *controversial, in rivalry*, παράδοσις Vett.Val.198.11 : Astrol., ὁ διάμετρος ἀ. Porph. in Ptol.*Tetr.*186. **-ζηλόω**, in Pass., *to be emulous of, rival*, Vett.Val.47.15.

ἀντιζητέω, *seek one who is seeking us*, X.*Oec.*8.23.

ἀντίζομαι, Ion. for ἀνθίζομαι.

ἀντιζῠγ-ής, ές, = διάμετρος, Petos.ap.Vett.Val.128.25. **-ία**, ἡ, *equivalence*, *Theol.Ar.*57. **II.** *diametrical opposition*, Vett.Val.123.26. **-ος**, ον, *put in the opposite scale* : hence, *balancing, correspondent*, Arist.*PA*666^{a}27, Plu.2.723c ; ζῴδια Anon.*II Intr. Arat.*p.128 Maass. **II.** ἀντίζυγα, τά, *vertical cross-pieces*, in building, *IG*2^{2}.463. **-όω**, *insert cross-pieces*, ibid. **II.** *counterbalance*, πρός τι Eust.60.29.

ἀντιζωγρέω, *save alive in turn*, Babr.107.16.

ἀντιθάλπω, *warm mutually*, ἀλλήλους J.*BJ*4.4.6.

ἀντιθᾰνᾰτάω, *devise death in turn*, Eust.1029.40.

ἀντιθάπτω, *bury opposite* :—Pass., aor. ἀντετάφην *IG*14.1721.

ἀντίθεμα, ατος, τό, = ἀντίθημα, *IG*4.823.69, Haussoullier *Milet* p.163.

ἀντίθεος, η, ον, *equal to the gods, godlike* (cf. S.E.*M.*7.6) : Homeric epith. of heroes, Il.5.663, etc. ; of nations, ib.12.408, Od.6.241 ; of women, only ib.11.117 ; applied even to Polyphemus and the suitors, ib.1.70, 14.18 ; ἥρωες ἀ. B.10.79. **II.** *contrary to God*, Ph.1.566, al. **2.** Subst. ἀντίθεος, ὁ, *hostile deity*, Hld.4.7, Iamb.*Myst.*3.31, *PMag.Lond.*121.635 (unless Adj., *disguised as a god*).

ἀντιθερᾰπεύω, *take care of in turn*, γονέας X.*Cyr.*8.3.49. **2.** *court in return*, in Pass., J.*AJ*17.2.4, Max.Tyr.20.6.

ἀντιθερμαίνω, *warm in turn*, Alex.Aphr.*Pr.*1.115, Gal.1.656.

ἀντιθέσιον, τό, = ξάνθιον, Dsc.4.136.

ἀντί-θεσις, εως, ἡ, *opposition*, Pl.*Sph.*257e, 258b ; ἀντίθεσιν ἔχειν πρός τι *correspond to*.., Arist.*HA*503^{a}25 ; *resistance*, *AP*12.200 (Strat.). **2.** in Logic, *opposition* of propositions, in pl., Arist.*Int.*19^{b}20, *Top.*113^{b}15, *Metaph.*1054^{a}23. **b.** *substitution of the contradictory*, as 'not-man' for 'man', ἡ σὺν -θέσει ἀντιστροφή, *conversion by negation*, e. g. 'man is an animal ∴ what is not an animal cannot be a man', Anon. *in SE*15.23, al. **3.** Rhet., *antithesis*, Isoc.12.2, Arist.*Rh.*1410^{a}22 ; in forensic oratory, *counter-proposition*, Hermog.*Id.*1.4, al. **4.** Gramm., *change* or *transposition* of a letter, Hdn.Gr.2.945, Diom.1.442 K. **-θετέον**, *one must oppose*, πρός τι ὅτι.. Arist.*Pol.*1286^{b}2. **-θετικός**, ή, όν, *setting in opposition, contrasting*, ἀ. δύναμις φαινομένων τε καὶ νοουμένων S.E.*P.*1.8 ;

antithetical, Eust.1325.19; ἀντιθετικά, τά, D.21 Arg.ii 9; ἀ. στάσις Hermog.*Stat.*4, al. II. *contrasted, correspondent*, of poems in which a number of κῶλα are repeated in reversed order, Heph. *Poëm.*4.6. **-θετος**, ον, *opposed, antithetic*, ἀ. εἰπὼν οὐδέν Timocl. 127; φύσιν ἔχειν ἀ. πρός τι Plu.2.672c; ἀρεταῖς κακίαι ἀ. S.E.*M.*9.156, cf. Plot.2.5.2, Phld.*Ir.*p.87 W.: c. gen., *inconsistent with*, *PTeb.*24.63. Adv. -τως, συζυγεῖν Plu.2.1022e, cf. Demetr.*Eloc.*24; ἀ. ἔχειν, of bones in arm, Heliod.ap.Orib.44.23.27; ἀ. ἀντικεῖσθαι, of ὑγίεια and νόσος, opp. ἀντιφατικῶς, Alex.Aphr. *in Top.*580.1. 2. = διάμετρος, Vett.Val.340.23. 3. ἀ. ψῆφος *blackball*, *GDI*4 p.1204 (Itanos). 4. ἀντίθετον, τό, *antithesis*, Ar.*Fr.*326, Arist.*Rh.Al.*1435ᵇ26, Aeschin. 2.4.

ἀντιθέω, fut. -θεύσομαι Hdt.5.22:—*run against* another, *compete in a race*, l.c. II. *run contrary ways*, *AP*9.822.

ἀντιθήγω, *whet against* another, ὀδόντας ἐπί τινα Luc.*Par.*51.

ἀντίθημα, ατος, τό, *revetment* of wall, *IG*1.321, cf. 11.203*A*45 (Delos).

ἀντιθλίβω [λῐ], *press against, counteract*, ἀλλήλους Archyt.ap. Stob.2.13.120:—Pass., ἀντιθλίβεται τὸ θλῖβον crushing *produces counter-crushing*, Arist.*GA*768ᵇ20.

ἀντιθνῄσκω, *die in turn* or *for* another, *EM*114.14.

ἀντιθρηνέω, *wail in return*, τινί *An.Ox.*3.180.

ἀντίθροος, ον, *echoing, resounding*, Coluth.118, *APl.*4.153 (Satyr.).

ἀντιθρῴσκω, *leap to meet*, Emp.105.1.

ἀντιθῡμόομαι, *show anger in turn*, Ael.*NA*17.13 codd. (ἀντιφιλοτιμ– Hercher).

ἀντίθῠρος, ον, (θύρα) *opposite the door*, κατ' ἀντίθυρον κλισίης *opposite the door* of the house, Od.16.159, as the Sch.; or it may be a neut. Subst. ἀντίθυρον *the part facing the door, vestibule*, as it is in βᾶτε κατ' ἀντιθύρων S.*El.*1433, ubi v. Herm.: in Luc.*Symp.*8, *the side of a room facing the door*, cf. *Alex.*16, *Dom.*26.

ἀντιθύω, *sacrifice in turn*, Philox.10 (Pass.).

ἀντικαθαιρέω, *pull down* or *destroy in turn*, D.C.46.34.

ἀντικαθεύδω, *sleep again* or *instead*, *AP*11.366 (Maced.).

ἀντικάθημαι, Ion. **ἀντικάτ–**, properly pf. of ἀντικαθίζομαι, but used as pres.:—*to be set over against*, τινί Archyt.ap.Stob.4.1.138. 2. mostly of armies or fleets, *lie over against*, so as to watch each other, ἡμέραι σφι ἀντικατημένοισι ἐγεγόνεσαν ὀκτώ Hdt.9.39, cf. 41, Th.5.6, X.*Eq.Mag.*8.12, etc.: metaph., λόγος ἀ. τινι S.E.*M.*1.145.

ἀντικαθίζομαι, Ion. **ἀντικατ–**, fut. -εδοῦμαι: aor. -εζόμην:—Med., *sit* or *lie over against*, of armies or fleets watching one another, Hdt. 4.3, 5.1, Th.1.30, 4.124. II. Act., *place* or *settle instead of* another, Lxx 4*Ki.*17.26.

ἀντικαθίστημι, Ion. **ἀντικατ–**, fut. -καταστήσω:—*replace, substitute*, ἄλλα Hdt.9.93; μὴ ἐλάσσω ἀντικαταστῆσαι πάλιν *replace* an equal quantity of gold, Th.2.13; ἄλλους ἀ. *set up* others *in their stead*, Arist.*Mir.*838ᵃ3. 2. *set against, oppose*, τινὰ πρός τινα Th. 4.93; *establish as a counterpart*, τινά τινι Pl.*R.*591a. 3. *set up* or *bring back again*, ἀ. ἐπὶ τὸ θαρρεῖν Th.2.65; *rally*, τοὺς θορυβηθέντας D.H.6.11. II. Pass., with aor. 2 and pf. Act.; also aor. 1 κατεστάθην X.*An.*3.1.38:—*to be put in another's place, reign in his stead*, Hdt.2.37, X.l.c. 2. *to be pitted against* another, *opposed*, abs., Th.1.71, 3.47, etc.; τινί X.*Eq.Mag.*7.5. b. in lawsuits, *to be confronted with*, τινί, πρός τινα, *POxy.*97.9 (ii A.D.), *BGU*168.11 (ii A.D.).

ἀντίκαινον· ἰσόκαινον, Hsch.

ἀντικαίω, Att. **-κάω**, *set on fire in turn*, Pl.*Ti.*65e.

ἀντικᾰκουργέω, *damage in return*, τινά Pl.*Cri.*49c, 54c.

ἀντικᾰκόω, = foreg., J.*BJ*3.7.30.

ἀντικᾰλέω, *invite in turn*, X.*Smp.*1.15 (in fut. Pass. -κληθήσομαι), cf. *Ev.Luc.*14.12.

ἀντικαλλωπίζομαι, *adorn oneself in rivalry with*, πρὸς τὴν πολυτέλειαν εὐτελείᾳ Plu.2.406d.

ἀντικάνθαρον, = ἡμεροκαλλές, Ps.-Dsc.3.122. II. perh. *cost of carriage*, Just.*Edict.*13.15.

ἀντικάρδιον, τό, in Poll.2.165, *pit of the stomach*: but Ruf.*Onom.* 68 makes it *the depression in the throat above the clavicle*, = σφαγή, λαυκανίη, cf. Hsch. (ἀντικαραῶν cod.).

ἀντικαρτερέω, *hold out against*, πρός τι D.C.39.41.

ἀντικαταβάλλω, in Med., *repay, render*, τὴν προσήκουσαν χάριν Lib.*Decl.*43.3.

ἀντικατάγω [ᾰγ], *bring in instead*:—Pass., ἀντικαταχθῆμέν τινι *come into the place of* another, Ti.Locr.101d.

ἀντικατα-δύνω [ῡ], *set over against*, of stars setting at sunrise, Hipparch.2.2.11, al., Theo Sm.p.137 H. **-δύομαι**, *stoop down in turn* or *in opposition*, Ach.Tat.6.18. **-δῠσις**, εως, ἡ, *setting in the opposite quarter*, in pl., Hipparch.2.1.14, 2.2.1. **-θνῄσκω**, aor. 2 -έθανον, *die* or *be slain in turn*, τοὺς κτανόντας ἀντικατθανεῖν A.*Ch.* 144. **-κλείω**, in Pass., *to be enclosed in turn*, Ruf.*Oss.*38. **-λαμβάνω**, *take possession of in turn*, Ti.Locr.102d. II. = ἀντιλαγχάνω, δίκην Pl.Com.9 D. III. *occupy in opposition*, λόφον D.C.36.47, cf. 42.31. **-λέγω**, *enroll instead*, soldiers or senators, Id.40.65, 54.14. **-λείπω**, *leave in one's stead*, Pl.*R.*540b, Pyth.*Sim.*36.

ἀντικατ-αλλᾰγή, ἡ, *exchange*, τινὸς πρός τι Plu.2.49d, cf. *PFlor.* 47.15 (iii A.D.); *requital*, Sch.Opp.*H.*2.687. **-άλλαγμα**, ατος, τό, *satisfaction*, J.*AJ*15.9.2, Onos.34.4 (pl.). **-αλλακτέον**, *one must exchange*, τινά τινων Arr.*Epict.*4.3 tit. **-άλλαξις**, εως, ἡ, *profits of commerce*, D.L.7.99, *BGU*1210.177 (ii A.D., pl.). **-αλλάσσομαι**, Att. **-ττομαι**, Med., *exchange* one thing *for* another: 1. *give* one thing *for* another, τὴν ἰδίαν ψυχὴν ἀντὶ τῆς κοινῆς σωτηρίας Lycurg.88; τὸ ζῆν ὑπὲρ ἄλλου οὐδενός Isoc.5.135. 2. *receive* one thing *in exchange for* another, τι ἀντί τινος Id.6.109, Aeschin.3.92, D.Chr.40. 30. 3. *set off* or *balance* one thing *against* another, εὐεργεσίας κρίσεως Din.1.14; ἀ. τι πρὸς τὴν περὶ τὰ θεῖα φιλοσοφίαν *afford* some *compensation for*.., Arist.*PA*645ᵃ3; ἀ. ἀδικοῦντα, εἰ βλαβερόν, ἀλλὰ καλὸν *submit in justification a balance* in case of injury.., Id.*Rh.*1416ᵃ 11. 4. *interchange*, Id.*EN*1157ᵃ12. II. Pass., ἀντικαταλλαγῆναι (sc. τῇ τύχῃ) *to be reconciled*, Plb.15.20.5: abs., *come to an agreement*, περὶ οὗ ἀντικατηλλάγη *PFlor.*47.13. III. Act., *come to an agreement*, ὁμολογῶμεν ἀντικατηλλαχέναι πρὸς ἀλλήλους ib.3 (iii A.D.).

ἀντικατα-μετρέω, *assign* land *in compensation* or *exchange*, *PTeb.* 61ᵇ111, 72.39 (ii B.C., Pass.). **-μύω** [ῡ], *shut one's eyes in turn*, Poll.9.113. **-πλήσσω**, *frighten in turn*, App.*BC*3.91, Onos.29. 2. **-ρρέω**, *flow down, drip in turn*, Olymp. *in Mete.*80.36, al., Steph. *in Hp.*1.130 D., al.; *run back again*, Gal.8.285. **-σκευάζω**, *establish instead*, D.H.1.5. 2. 'paint in the opposite colours', πολλὰ τῶν ἀδίκων J.*AJ*16.7.1. 3. *prepare in opposition*, D.C.49.37, 77. 15. **-στᾰσις**, εως, ἡ, *being confronted with one another*, Plb.4. 47.4; *opposition*, J.*AJ*16.2.5; λόγοι ἐξ ἀντικαταστάσεως γενόμενοι Decr.ib.14.10.21, cf. *SIG*785.7 (Chios). **-στρᾰτοπεδεύω**, *to encamp opposite*, D.H.8.84. **-σχεσις**, εως, ἡ, *holding in by force*, τοῦ πνεύματος Arist.*Pr.*961ᵇ22. **-τᾰσις**, εως, ἡ, *counter-extension*, Hp.*Art.*72. II. *confronting*, πρός τινα *BGU*1138.3 (i B.C.), *POxy.*260.10 (i A.D.). **-τείνω**, *make counter-extension*, Hp.*Fract.* 14, *Art.*3. II. metaph., ἂν ἀντικατατείναντες λέγωμεν αὐτῷ λόγον παρὰ λόγον if we speak *setting* speech *directly* in contrast with speech *against* him, Pl.*R.*348a, cf. Plu.2.669e. **-τρέχω**, aor. -έδρᾰμον, *overrun in turn*, D.C.60.9. **-φέρομαι**, *to be carried down again*, Gal.17(2).57. **-φρονέω**, *despise in turn*, τινός D.C.54.33. **-φῠτεύω**, *plant instead*, ἕτερα ἀντὶ τῶν ἐκλειπόντων [δένδρων] *BGU*1120. 33 (i B.C.). **-χωρισμός**, ὁ, *replacement*, Antyll.ap.Orib.6.10.14.

ἀντικατ-έχω, *hold fast on the other side*, Hp.*Art.*74. 2. Astrol., *occupy incongruous position*, τοὺς οἴκους ἢ τὰ ὑψώματα *Cat.Cod.Astr.* 8(3).115. **-ηγορέω**, *accuse in turn, recriminate upon*, τινός Gorg. *Pal.*27, Lys.6.42, Aeschin.1.178:—in Pass., D.C.36.40. II. Pass., in Logic, *to be convertible*, ἀ. τοῦ πράγματος Arist.*Top.*102ᵃ 19, al.; *reciprocate*, of cause and effect, Id.*APo.*73ᵃ16, cf. 78ᵃ 28. **-ηγορητικός**, ή, όν, *contradictory*, sermo (i.e. λόγος) Gal. *Subf.Emp.*12 p.65 Bonnet. **-ηγορία**, ἡ, *countercharge*, Quint. *Inst.*3.10.4. **-ημαι, ἀντικατίζομαι, ἀντικατίστημι**, Ion. for ἀντικάθ–. **-ολισθαίνω**, *slip down correspondingly*, Paul.Aeg.6.65.

ἀντικάτων, ωνος, ὁ, *Anticato*, name of a book written by Caesar in reply to the *Cato* of Cicero, Plu.*Caes.*54, App.*BC*2.99.

ἀντίκειμαι, 3 pl. ἀντικέαται Archyt.ap.Stob.2.2.4, used as Pass. of ἀντιτίθημι:—*to be set over against, correspond with*, τιμὰ ἀγαθοῖσιν ἀ. *is held out to* them *as a fitting reward*, Pi.*I.*7(6).26:—ἀντικείμενος, ὁ, name of a *bandage*, Sor.*Fasc.*12.515 C. II. *to be opposite to*, of places, τινός Hp.*Aër.*4; τινί Str.2.5.15; of things, *to be opposite* or *opposed*, πρὸς ἄλληλα Pl.*Sph.*258b; ἀ. κατὰ διάμετρον in a circle, Arist.*Cael.*277ᵃ23, al. Adv. -μένως, συνέστηκεν *PA*654ᵃ11. 2. *to be opposed*, in various ways, *Cat.*11ᵇ17, *Metaph.*1055ᵃ38, al.; in Logic, αἱ -κείμεναι προτάσεις *APr.*63ᵇ24, al. Adv. ἀντικειμένως *Metaph.*1054ᵇ15, etc.; propositions are *opposed* either contradictorily (ἀντιφατικῶς) or contrarily (ἐναντίως), *Int.*17ᵇ16; ἀντικείμενα defined as ὧν τὸ ἕτερον τοῦ ἑτέρου ἀποφάσει πλεονάζει *Stoic.*2.70, cf. 82, al. 3. Rhet., ἀντικειμένη [λέξις] *antithetical*, Arist.*Rh.*1409ᵇ 35; ἀντικειμένως εἰπεῖν ib.1401ᵃ5, cf. 1410ᵇ29; ἀντικείμενα κῶλα Demetr.*Eloc.*22. III. *resist, be adverse*, ἀντικείσομαι τοῖς ἀντικειμένοις σοι Lxx *Ex.*23.22, cf. *Is.*66.6, al., *Ev.Luc.*13.17, al.; *to be hurtful*, τοῖς σώμασι Procop.Gaz.*Ep.*27.

ἀντικέλευθος, ον, *pursuing an opposite path*, φάος Man.4.74; simply, *opposite*, τοῖχος Nonn.*D.*8.191: c. gen., Καρκίνος ἀ. Αἰγοκερῆος 2.658. II. *opposing, hostile*, αἰχμή 2.459, cf. 23.35, al.

ἀντικελεύω, *bid, command in turn*, Th.1.128:—Pass., *to be bidden* to do a thing *in turn*, ib.139.

ἀντίκεντρον, τό, *that which acts as a goad*, A.*Eu.*136, 466.

ἀντικέφᾰλον, τό, *back of the head*, Lyd.*Mens.*4.54, *Hippiatr.* 115. II. as Adj., κροκοδείλους -κεφάλους αὐτοῖς *back to back*, *PMag.Par.*1.2954.

ἀντικηδεύω, *mind, tend instead of* another, τινός E.*Ion* 734:—also **ἀντικήδομαι**, Poll.5.142.

ἀντικῆρυξ, υκος, ὁ, *deputy-herald*, *IG*3.1295.

ἀντικηρύσσω, *proclaim in answer to*, οὐδὲν ἀντεκήρυξεν λόγοις E. *Supp.*673; *in opposition to*, τινί Lib.*Decl.*39.45.

ἀντικῑν-έω, *move in opposition*, Arist.*Mem.*453ᵃ26, cf. Ph.2.22:—Med. or Pass., ἀνάγκη τὸ κινοῦν ἀντικινεῖσθαι must *suffer a countermovement*, Arist.*Ph.*257ᵇ23, cf. *GA*768ᵇ19, *Cael.*272ᵇ4. II. in Pass. also, *make counter-movements*, πρὸς πᾶν Plb.2.66.3; σφοδρότερον -ηθῆναι *retaliate* more ruthlessly, Chor.p.226 B. **-ησις**, εως, ἡ, *contrary motion*, *Corp.Herm.*2.6, Simp. *in Ph.*677.20, Id. *in Cael.*366. 8, 395.29. **-ητος**, ον, *moved in return*, Phlp. *in Ph.*355.15.

ἀντικῐχάνω [χᾰ], *encounter*, only aor. Med. ἀντικ[ι]χομένην *BGU* 1024 vii 29 (iv/v A.D.).

ἀντικλάζω, *sound by striking against*, κραυγὴ.. πέτραισιν ἀντέκλαγξ' *is echoed* by them, E.*Andr.*1145. 2. c. acc. cogn., ἀ. ἀλλήλαις μέλος *sing against* one another, Id.*Ba.*1057.

ἀντικλαίω, Att. **-κλάω**, *weep in return*, Hdt.3.14 (v.l. ἀνέκλαιον), Eust.37.14.

ἀντικλάω, *bend back*, Sch.Opp.*H.*1.152.

ἀντικλείομαι, *to be enclosed,* εἰς τὴν κοιλότητα Ruf.*Oss.*32.

ἀντίκλεις, ειδος, ἡ, *false key,* Poll.10.22, Palch. in *Cat.Cod.Astr.* 1.97.13:—also **-κλειθρον,** τό, *Gloss.*

ἀντίκλησις, εως, ἡ, *calling upon, summoning in return,* Jul.*Ep.*192.

ἀντικλίνω [ῑ], *turn* or *bend again,* Musae.107.

ἀντίκλῐσις, εως, ἡ, *alternative inflexion,* Sch.Opp.*H.*1.59.

ἀντικνημιάζω, *strike on the shin,* S.E.*M.*1.217 (s.v.l.).

ἀντικνήμιον, τό, *part of the leg in front of the* κνήμη (τῆς κνήμης τὸ πρόσθεν Arist.*HA* 494ᵃ6; but τὸ ὄπισθεν Sch.Ar.*Pl.*784), *shin,* Hippon.49, Hp.*Fract.*18, Ar.*Ach.*219, *Eq.*907.

ἀντίκοιλον, τό, *hollow of the instep,* dub. l. in Polem.*Phgn.*85.

ἀντικολάζω, *punish in return,* Luc.*Tyr.*12 (Pass.).

ἀντικολᾰκεύω, *flatter in turn,* Plu.*Alc.*24.

ἀντικομίζω, *bring back as an answer,* λόγον Plu.*Lys.*26:—Med., *receive in exchange,* J.*BJ*2.8.4, App.*BC*4.70.

ἀντικομπάζω, *boast in opposition,* τινί Plu.*Ant.*62.

ἀντικοντόω, *support with a pole* or *stick,* ξύλῳ ἀ. τῷ σώματι Hp. *Mochl.*20 (ἀντικονταίνουσι prob. l. for -κοταίνουσι Erot., -κοτέουσι or -κοντέουσι codd.).—But -όω is confirmed by **ἀντικόντωσις,** εως, ἡ, *the support of a stick* to a lame man, Id.*Art.*52,58.

ἀντι-κοπή, ἡ, *beating back, hindrance, check,* Epicur.*Ep.*1 p.10 U.; *resistance,* Id.*Nat.Herc.*908.4; προσκρούσει καὶ ἀ. Plu.2.77a; *clashing,* of streams meeting, Str.5.2.5. **-κοπτικός,** ή, όν, *resisting, repellent,* S.E.*M.*10.137. **-κόπτω,** *cut down mutually,* ἀλλήλους D.C.43.37 (nisi leg. ἀνακ-). **II.** *beat back, resist,* **1.** in a physical sense, c. acc., ὁκόταν νέφεα.. ἀντικόψῃ πνεῦμα ἐναντίον Hp.*Aër.* 8: abs., ὅταν πνεῦμα ἀντικόπτῃ νότιον Arist.*HA*599ᵃ1, cf. *PA*642ᵇ1; *check growth,* ὅταν ἀντικόψῃ ὁ χειμών Thphr.*CP*1.12.6, cf. Epicur. *Ep.*1 p.11 U., al.:—in Pass., *meet with resistance,* Id.*Nat.Herc.*908.2; ἀ. ἀλλήλοις, of winds, Thphr.*Vent.*53. **2.** of persons, ὁ δὲ Θηραμένης ἀντέκοπτε λέγων.. X.*HG*2.3.15, cf. Aristid.*Or.*43(1).10: c. dat., Phld.*Vit.*pp.9,25 J. **3.** of things, ἤν τι ἀντικόψῃ *if there be* any *hindrance,* X.*HG*2.3.31; ἡ πυκνότης ἀ. πρὸς τοῦτο *militates against* this, Demetr.Lac.*Herc.*1055.18.

ἀντικορύσσομαι, Med., *take arms against,* ἀνέμοις *AP*7.668 (Leon.), Ath.15.701b.

ἀντικοσμ-έω, *arrange in turn,* Plu.2.813d. **2.** *adorn in turn,* ib.828a:—Pass., Aristid.*Or.*25(43).33:—Subst. **-ησις,** εως, ἡ, Suid. **-ήτης,** ου, ὁ, *deputy-*κοσμητής (signf. I. 2), *IG*3.1120, al.:—hence **-ητεύω,** *discharge this office,* ib.1126.

ἀντικοτ-έω· *obstrigillo, obtrecto, officio, Gloss.*:—also **-ησις·** *offensio,* ib.

ἀντίκοψις, εως, ἡ, *opposition,* ἀνέμων Thphr.*Vent.*55.

ἀντικράζω, pf. ἀντικέκραγα, *to shout in return,* πολλὰ βλάσφημά τισι J.*BJ*6.2.3.

ἀντικρᾰτέω, *hold, have instead of something else, AP*11.298.

ἀντικρίνω [ῑν], *judge in turn,* τινά Aristid.*Or.*34(50).40; *compare, match,* τί τινι Ael.*NA*5.56, al.:—Pass., πρός τι 2.43, al.:—Med., *contend against,* Lxx *Jb.*9.32, 11.3.

ἀντίκριος, ὁ, *counter-ram,* Aen.Tact.22.7.

ἀντίκρῐσις, εως, ἡ, = ἀπόκρισις, Anaxil.41, Poll.4.113.

ἀντί-κρουσις, εως, ἡ, *abrupt close,* in a rhetorical period, Arist. *Rh.*1409ᵇ22; *hindrance, check,* Plu.2.721b; dub. sens. in Aeschin. 1.168, perh. *repartee.* **-κρουσμός·** *offensio, Gloss.* **-κρουστία,** ἡ, dub. sens. in Phld.*Po.*1677.23. **-κρούω,** *strike* or *clash against, come into collision,* **1.** in a physical sense, ὀλίγα.. τὰ ἀντικρούοντα αὐτοῖς Arist.*Cael.*313ᵇ2: abs., Id.*PA*642ᵃ36, al., cf. Pl. *Lg.*857c; ἀσπὶς ἀσπίδι Lib.*Decl.*37.8. **2.** in a general sense, αὐτοῖς.. τοῦτο ἀντεκεκρούκει *had been a hindrance to* them, *had counteracted* them, Th.6.46; ἀ. τοῖς λογισμοῖς J.*AJ*2.4.3; ἀ. ταῖς συμβουλίαις Plu.*Ages.*7; ἀ. πρός τι Id.*Cat.Ma.*24: abs., *prove a hindrance, offer resistance,* ἀντέκρουσέ τι καὶ γέγον' οἷον οὐκ ἔδει D.18.198; ἐὰν ἀντικρούσῃ τις Arist.*Rh.*1379ᵃ12; ἀντέκρουον αἱ γυναῖκες *Pol.*1270ᵃ7.

ἀντικρύ, Adv. = ἄντην, *over against, right opposite,* θεοῖς ἀντικρὺ μάχεσθαι Il.5.130: c. gen., Ἕκτορος ἀντικρύ ib.8.301. **II.** = ἄντικρυς, *straight on, right on,* ἀντικρὺ δόρυ χάλκεον ἐξεπέρησεν Od.10.162; ἀντικρὺ μεμαώς Il.13.137: mostly followed by a Prep., ἀντικρὺ δ' ἀν' ὀδόντας 5.74; ἀντικρὺ δι' ὤμου 4.481, cf. Od.22.16; ἀντικρὺ κατὰ μέσσον *right* in the middle, Il.16.285; once in X., ἀντικρὺ διάττων *Cyr.*7.1.30; cf. καταντικρύ. **2.** *outright, utterly, quite,* ἀντικρὺ δ' ἀπόφημι Il.7.362; ἀντικρὺ δ' ἀπάραξε 16.116; ἀντικρὺ μακάρεσσιν ἔϊκτο A.R.4.1612, etc. (Cf. ἄντικρυς sub fin.) [ῡ generally, but ῠ Il.5.130, 819; ῐ by nature (cf. καταντῐκρύ Ar.*Ec.*87), ῑ by position in Ep.]

ἄντῐκρῠς, Adv. *straight on, right on,* ἄντικρυς ἰὼν παρεκαθέζετο ἐκ δεξιᾶς he came *straight up* and.., Pl.*Euthd.*273b, cf. Ar.*Lys.*1068, Th.2.4; also εἰς τὸ ἄ. πορεύεσθαι Pl.*Smp.*223b. **2.** *outright, openly, without disguise,* ὅπως ἄ. τάδ' αἰνέσω A.*Ch.*192; ὁ χρησμὸς ἄ. λέγει Ar. *Eq.*128; εὔχονταί γε πλουτεῖν ἄ. Id.*Pl.*134; ἄ. ἔφη χρῆναι πλεῖν Th. 6.49; ἃ ἠδικοῦντο οὐ δηλοῦντες ἄντικρυς Id.5.30; οὐδὲν ἢ ἄ. δουλείαν *downright* slavery, Id.1.122; ἡ ἄ. ἐλευθερία Id.8.64; οὐκ ἄ. not *at all,* οὐ διοίσοντ' ἄ. τῶν Ἡρακλειδῶν Ar.*Pl.*384. **3.** sts. of Time, *straightway,* συλλαβόντες ἄγουσιν ἄ. ὡς ἀποκτενοῦντες Lys.13.78, cf. Men.*Pk.*38, Pl.*Ax.*367a. **II.** later, = ἀντικρύ, *opposite,* ἄ. εἶναι to *oppose,* Arist.*EE*1243ᵃ37; ἄ. ἐπιέναι *against,* D.H.3.24; καταστῆναι Plu.*Sol.*27; κατακλιθῆναί τινος Lxx 3*Ma.*5.16; ἐν τῇ ἄ. πυλίδι *CIG* (add.)4224*e* (Cragus): c. gen., ἄ. Χίου *Act.Ap.*20.15, cf. *PTeb.*395.4 (ii A.D.), etc.—Gramm. distinguish ἀντικρύ, = ἐξ ἐναντίας, and ἄντικρυς, = φανερῶς, διαρρήδην, cf. *AB*408, but ἀντικρύ (q.v.) has both senses in Hom. (-κρυ(ς) prob. akin to κέρας, κάρα.)

ἀντικρύσιον, dub. sens., Theognost.*Can.*125.2 (from ἄντικρυς).

ἀντίκτησις, εως, ἡ, *acquisition of* one thing *for* another, ἀδελφοῦ ἀ. οὐκ ἔστιν Plu.2.481e.

ἀντικτόνος, ον, (κτείνω) *in requital for murder,* ἀντικτόνοις ποιναῖσι.. πατρός A.*Eu.*464.

ἀντικτῠπέω, aor. ἀντέκτυπον, *ring in response, AP*14.10.3; *clash against,* τινί *APl.*4.221 (Theaet.): abs., Procop.*Goth.*2.23.

ἀντικῠδαίνω, *praise in turn,* Them.*Or.*4.57d.

ἀντικῠμαίνομαι, Pass., *boil with conflicting waves, dash hither and thither,* Plu.2.897c; of wind in a cul-de-sac, *surge back,* Orib.9. 20.3.

ἀντικῠματόω, *surge against,* Procop.*Aed.*4.8.

ἀντικύπριος, sc. πούς, the foot – ⏑ – – ⏑, Diom.1.482 K.

ἀντικύπτω, *occur, crop up,* τὰς ἀντικυπτούσας χρείας Ascl.*Tact.*12. 10 (fort. ἀνα-).

ἀντικυρία, ἡ, *hellebore,* Suid.:—also **ἀντικύρικον·** ὁ ἐλλέβορος, Hsch. (From the place-name Ἀντικύρα.)

ἀντικύρω [ῠ], aor. ἀντέκυρσα, *hit upon, encounter, meet,* τινί Pi. *O.*12.12, S.*OC*99, etc.: abs., Id.*Ph.*545.

ἀντικύων· ἀλώπηξ, Hsch.

ἀντικωλύω, *hinder by resisting,* Hp.*Loc.Hom.*10:—hence **-ῡτέον,** Gal.18(2).390.

ἀντικωμάζω, *celebrate by a festival in turn,* Sch.Pi.*P.*9.156.

ἀντικωμῳδέω, *ridicule in turn,* Plu.*Flam.*9, Max.Tyr.9.3.

ἀντικωπηλάτης, ου, ὁ, = ἀντηρέτης, Sch.A.*Th.*283.

ἀντιλᾰβ-εύς, έως, ὁ, = πόρπαξ, Hsch. **-ή,** ἡ, *thing to hold by, handle,* ὅπως ἂν.. μὴ ἔχοι ἀντιλαβὴν ἡ χείρ Th.7.65; of a shield, οὔτε πόρπακας οὔτ' ἀντιλαβὰς ἔχει Str.3.3.6. **2.** *grip,* of a dog, Ael.*NA*8. 1. **3.** metaph., πολλὰς.. ἔχει ὑποψίας καὶ ἀντιλαβάς gives many *handles against* one, *points of attack,* Pl.*Phd.*84c; so ἀ. διδόναι D.H. *Rh.*8.15; παρέχεσθαι Luc.*Tim.*29. **4.** Gramm., in dramatic dialogue, *division of a line between two speakers,* Hsch. **5.** *apprehension,* Dam.*Pr.*6.

ἀντιλαγχάνω, pf. -είληχα D.40.3:—as law-term, *move for a rehearing of a suit,* when the case had gone by default, ἀ. δίαιταν Id. 21.86; ἀ. τὴν μὴ οὖσαν (sc. δίαιταν) ib.90, cf. Poll.8.61, Hsch.; τὴν ἔρημον (sc. δίκην) ἀ. D.32.27. **II.** *enter an exceptive plea,* οἱ νόμοι διδόασι τὰς παραγραφὰς ἀντιλαγχάνειν Id.37.33. **III.** *bring counter-action,* Procop.*Arc.*17.

ἀντιλάζομαι or **-ῠμαι,** poet. and Dor. Prose for ἀντιλαμβάνομαι, *take hold of, hold by,* c. gen., E.*IA*1227; πραγμάτων Theag.ap.Stob. 3.1.67, cf. Archyt.ib.117; *take a share of, partake in,* πόνων E.*Or.* 452, etc. **2.** c. acc., *to receive in turn, to be repaid,* ἀντιλάζυται.. τοιάδ' ἂν τοκεῦσι δῷ Id.*Supp.*363. (-λάζυμαι l.c., *Or.*753, *IA*1109; -λάζομαι ib.1227, *Or.*452 (-λάζου); both forms in codd. *Med.*1216.)

ἀντιλακτίζω, *kick against,* τινί Ar.*Pax*613; τῷ νῷ Phld.*Rh.Supp.* p.52 S. **2.** *kick back in return,* ὄνον Plu.2.10c.

ἀντιλᾰκωνίζω, *answer in Laconian fashion,* Eust.1642.51.

ἀντι-λᾰλέω, *speak against* one, dub. in Men.*Epit.*529, Sm.*Ps.*138 (139).20. **-λᾰλος,** dub. in *Epic.Alex.Adesp.*9ix 15.

ἀντιλαμβάνω, *receive instead of,* χρυσοῦ δώματα πλήρη τᾶς ἥβας ἀ. E.*HF*646 (lyr.); mostly without a gen., οὔτε κακοὺς εὖ δρῶν εὖ πάλιν ἀντιλάβοις *receive in turn,* Thgn.108; κἂν.. ᾖ σώφρων.. σώφρον' ἀντιλήψεται E.*Andr.*741; ἡδονὴν δόντας.. κακίαν.. ἀ. Th.3.58; ἔρανον Arist.*Pol.*1330ᵇ40; ἀ. ἄλλην [χώραν] *seize in return, get instead,* Th.1.143; ἀ. ἄλλους τινάς X.*Cyr.*5.3.12, cf. 8.7.16; χάριτα *AP*6. 191 (Longus). **II.** mostly in Med., with pf. Pass. -είλημμαι Lys.28.15, Pl.*Prm.*130e: c. gen., *lay hold of,* σαπροῦ πείσματος ἀντελάβου Thgn.1362; ἄκρου τοῦ στύρακος ἀ. Pl.*La.*184a, cf. *Prt.* 317d, al.; τῇ ἀριστερᾷ ἀ. τοῦ τρίβωνος ib.335d; φιλίου χωρίου ἀ. *gain* or *reach* it, Th.7.77, cf. Ar.*Th.*242: abs., -όμενος Th.3.22. **b.** metaph. c. gen., *lay hold of,* τῆς σωτηρίας, τῆς ἐλευθερίας, τοῦ ἀσφαλοῦς, Id.2.61,62, 3.22; *lay claim to,* τοῦ θρόνου Ar.*Ra.*777,787; τοῦ πατρικοῦ μέρους *BGU*648.10 (ii A.D.). **2.** *help, take part with, assist,* οὐκ ἀντιλήψεσθ'; E.*Tr.*464; of persons, ἀ. Ἑλλήνων *to take* their *part,* D.S.11.13; ἀ. τῶν ἀσθενούντων *Act.Ap.*20.35, etc.: abs., Th.7.70:—also in Pass., ἀντειλημμένη *having received help, BGU*1105.21 (Aug.), al. **3.** *take part* or *share in* a thing, *take in hand,* τῶν πραγμάτων X.*Cyr.*2.3.6, D.1.20, etc.; τοῦ πολέμου Isoc.6.101; τῆς θαλάττης Plb.1.39.14; τῆς Ἀφροδίτης Alex.219.15; τῆς παιδείας Pl.*R.*534d; ἀ. τοῦ λόγου *seize on the* conversation (to the interruption of the rest), ib.336b: abs., ἀρχόμενοι πάντες ὀξύτερον ἀ. Th.2.8, cf. 8. 106. **4.** *take hold of for the purpose of finding fault, reprehend, attack,* ἡμῶν Pl.*Sph.*239d, cf. *R.*497d, etc.; τοῦδε ἀντιλαβώμεθα *let* us *attack* the question, Id.*Tht.*169d; ἀ. ὡς ἀδύνατον.. *to object* that.., Id.*Sph.*251b: abs., Id.*Grg.*506a. **5.** *take fast hold of,* i.e. *captivate,* ὁ λόγος ἀντιλαμβάνεταί μου Id.*Phd.*88d, cf. *Prm.*130e, Luc.*Nigr.*19. **6.** of plants, *take hold,* Thphr.*HP*4.1.5; of scions, *unite, CP*1.6.4. **7.** *grasp with the mind, perceive, apprehend,* Pl.*Ax.* 370a; noted as an obsol. word for συνίημι by Luc.*Sol.*7:—so of the senses, ἀ. κατὰ τὴν ἀκοήν, ὀσφρήσει, S.E.*P.*1.50,64, cf. Phot.p.148 R., Alex.Aphr.*in Top.*103.1, al. **III.** in Med. also, *hold back,* ἵππου τῷ χαλινῷ X.*Eq.*10.15, cf. Arist.*MM*1188ᵇ6; *interrupt, Aud.*802ᵇ 26. **IV.** Act. in sense of Med., Alex.Aphr.*Pr.*1.38.

ἀντι-λάμπω, inf. -λάμπην Sapph.*Supp.*3.6:—*light up in turn,* οἱ δ' ἀντέλαμψαν (sc. οἱ φύλακες) A.*Ag.*294. **II.** intr., *reflect light, shine,* X.*Cyn.*5.18; πρὸς τὴν σελήνην Plu.*Arat.*21; of the rainbow, Anaxag. 19. **2.** *shine opposite to* or *in the face of,* ὁ ἥλιος ἀ. τινί Plu.*Mar.* 26, etc., cf. Arr.*Tact.*27.4: metaph., *dazzle,* τῷ ἀκροάτῃ λέξις ἀ. Plu.

2.41c. III. *vie in brilliance with*, τινί Philostr.*Ep.*32. **-λαμψις,** εως, ἡ, *reflection of light*, Plu.2.930d, 931b.

ἀντιλαοί· τῶν ἄρτων κλάσματα, Hsch.

ἀντιλέγω, Hdt., Com., and Att. Prose (cf. ἀνταγορεύω): fut. ἀντιλέξω E.*Hipp.*993, Ar.*Ra.*998, Lys.8.10 (but the common fut. is ἀντερῶ): aor. ἀντέλεξα S.*OT*409, Ar.*Nu.*1040 (but the aor. commonly used is ἀντεῖπον): pf. ἀντείρηκα: fut. Pass. ἀντειρήσομαι:—*speak against, gainsay, contradict*, τινί Th.5.30, Pl.*Smp.*216b, X.*Mem.*4.6.13, etc.; περί τινος Th.8.53, X.*Mem.*4.4.8; ὑπὲρ τῶν δικαίων ib.3.5.12; πρός τι 1.2.17; πρὸς πάντα τὰ δίκαια Ar.*Nu.*888:—often folld. by a dependent clause, ἀ. ὡς.. *declare in opposition* or *answer* that.., χρησμοῖσι οὐκ ἔχω ἀντιλέγειν ὡς οὐκ εἰσὶ ἀληθέες Hdt.8.77, cf. Ar.*Eq.*980, Th.8.24, X.*An.*2.3.25, etc.; οὐ τοῦτό γ' ἀντιλέγουσιν, ὡς οὐ.. Arist.*Pol.*1287^b23; also ἀ. ὑπέρ τινος ὡς.. Th.8.45: so c. inf., ἀ. ποιήσειν ταῦτα, ἤν.. *to reply* that they will.., if.., Id.1.28; ἀ. μὴ κτεῖναι Μυτιληναίους Id.3.41; ἀ. τὸ μὴ οὐ ἀξιοῦσθαί τινα X.*Cyr.*2.2.20. 2. c. acc. rei, ἴσ' ἀντιλέξαι S.*OT*409; ἀ. τὸν ἐναντίον λόγον Lys.8.11; μῦθον ἀ. τινί *tell* one tale *in reply to* another, Ar.*Lys.*806; ἀντιλέγομεν πρᾶγμά τι Men.*Epit.*8:—Pass., *to be disputed, questioned*, X.*HG*6.5.37; of a place, ὑπό τινος ἀντιλεγόμενον *counter-claimed*, ib.3.2.30; ἀντιλέγεσθαι μικρὸν πρός τινα περί τινος D.27.15; τὰ ἀντιλεγόμενα *points in dispute*, Aeschin.2.44; πρὸς τὰ ἀντειρημένα κτλ., title of work by Chrysippus, *Stoic.*2.8; τόπος ἀντιλλεγόμενος (sic) *IG*5(2).443.15 (Megalopolis, ii B.C.): abs., -λέγεται περί τινος Str.8.6.6; of the genuineness of literary works, *to be disputed*, Plu.2.839c. 3. abs., *speak in opposition*, Hdt.9.42, E.*Hipp.*993, Ar.*Ra.*1076, etc.; ὁ ἀντιλέγων *the opponent*, Pl.*Prt.*335a; οἱ ἀντιλέγοντες Th.8.53; λαὸς ἀπειθῶν καὶ -λέγων Lxx*Is.*65.2.

ἀντιλειτουργέω, *render service in return*, *PPar.*63.183 (ii B.C.).

ἀντι-λεκτέον, *one must gainsay*, οὐδὲν ἀ. E.*Heracl.*975, cf. Hp.*Ep.*27:—Adj. **-τέος,** α, ον, Luc.*Anach.*17. **-λεκτος,** ον, *questionable, to be disputed*, ὅρος οὐκ ἀ. Th.4.92. **-λεξις,** εως, ἡ, *answer*, Hp.*Decent.*12. 2. *dialogue*, ἀντιλέξεις τῶν ὑποκριτῶν, opp. μονῳδίαι, Philostr.*VA*6.11. 3. *contradiction*, J.*AJ*18.1.3.

ἀντιλεσχαίνω, *chatter against*, Perict.ap.Stob.4.25.50.

ἀντιλέων, οντος, ὁ, *lion-like*, formed like ἀντίθεος, Ar.*Eq.*1044; where, however, it is in fact a pr. n.

ἀντιλημματίζω, *set off in accounts, deduct*, *POxy.*1577.11 (iii A.D.), cf. 1578.17 (iii A.D., Pass.).

ἀντιλήμ-πτωρ, -ψις, v. ἀντιλή-πτωρ, -ψις.

ἀντίληξις, εως, ἡ, *motion for a new trial*, D.39.38; cf. ἀντιλαγχάνω.

ἀντι-ληπτέον, *one must take part in* a matter: abs., Ar.*Pax* 485; τῶν πραγμάτων αὐτοῖς ἀ. D.1.2, cf. 14. II. *one must hold back*, ἀ. τοῦ ἵππου τῷ χαλινῷ X.*Eq.*8.8. III. Adj. **-ληπτέος,** α, ον, ὁ λόγος Plu.*Nob.*3. **-ληπτικός,** ή, όν, Dor. **-λαπτ-,** *able to apprehend*, λόγων Ti.Locr.100c; χρωμάτων Phld.*Herc.*19.18; δύναμις ἀ. πληγῆς ἀέρος Plu.2.98b; ἀ. δύναμις, of the soul, Aristo *Stoic.*1.86, cf. *Stoic.*2.230; *assisting* a scion *to unite*, γλισχρότης Thphr.*CP*1.6.4; of the hand, *prehensile*, Gal.*UP*2.6. Adv. -κῶς, ἔχειν to be *aware, apprehend*, Hierocl.p.19A. 2. *taking hold of*, i. e. *impressing itself upon* the senses, φωνή Thphr.*Fr.*89.3, cf. Cass.*Pr.*35 (Comp.); τὸ ἀ. Iamb.*Comm.Math.*8. II. *able to check*, Pl.*Def.*416a. 2. abs., *self-controlled*, Ptol.*Tetr.*188. **-ληπτός,** ή, όν, *which can be apprehended*, τῇ ἁφῇ Alex.Aphr.*in Mete.*201.4; τῇ ὄψει Phlp.*in Ph.*417.16; τὰ -ληπτὰ *objects of sense-perception*, Plot.4.5.8. **-λήπτωρ,** later **-λήμπτωρ,** ορος, ὁ, *helper, protector*, Lxx 2*Ki.*22.3, *BGU*1139.17 (i B.C.), Eustr.*in APo.*93.19; θεοὶ ἀ. *UPZ*14.18 (ii B.C.). **-ληψις,** later **-λημψις,** εως, ἡ, *receiving in turn* or *exchange*, Th.1.120; *counter-claim*, X.*HG*3.5.5. II. (from Med.) *laying hold of in turn, reciprocation*, Democr.ap.Arist.*Fr.*208; of cultivated plants, *giving a return*, Thphr.*CP*3.6.6; of a vine *laying hold* by its tendrils, ib.2.18.2. b. *taking in hand*, τοῦ λ(ε)ιτουργήματος *POxy.*900.13 (iv A.D.). 2. = ἀντιλαβή, *hold, support*, X.*Eq.*5.7; of a bandage, Hp.*Off.*9; ἀντίληψιν βοηθείας ἔχειν D.S.1.30; ἀ. διδόναι τινί give one *a handle*, Plu.2.966e; ἀ. παρέχειν Luc.*Anach.*2. 3. *defence, succour*, *UPZ*42.38 (ii B.C.), *PAmh.*35.58 (ii B.C.), *BGU*1187.27 (i B.C.), Lxx*Ps.*21(22).20, al., 1*Ep.Cor.*12.28, Iamb.*Myst.*7.3. 4. *claim to* a thing, X.*HG*3.5.5. 5. *objection*, Pl.*Phd.*87a, *Sph.*241b, *Hp.Ma.*287a, Plu.*Alex.*18, Iamb.*Myst.*1.1, al.: in forensic oratory, *plea of justification*, Hermog.*Stat.*2, al., Syrian.*in Hermog.*2 p.79R.; *discussion*, θεολογικὴ ἀ. Iamb.*Myst.*1.8. 6. *grasping with the mind, apprehension*, Epicur.*Fr.*250, *Stoic.*2.206, Diog.Oen.4; φυσικὴν -ψιν ποιεῖσθαί τινος D.S.3.15; οὐκ ἐπιστρέφει τὴν ἀ. does not attract the *attention*, [Longin.]*Rh.*p.190H.; of sensuous *perception*, *Stoic.*2.230, Ti.Locr.100b, Anon.*in Tht.*59.48, Phld.*Herc.*1003, Alex.Aphr.*in Top.*91.5; ποιοτήτων Plu.2.625b, cf. Metrod.1. 7. of disease, *seizure, attack*, τῶν ἀκρωτηρίων Th.2.49.

ἀντιλῐτᾰνεύω, *entreat in return*, Plu.2.1117c.

ἀντι-λόβιον, τό, *upper edge of the ear*, opp. προλόβιον, Gal.14.701, Poll.2.86. **-λοβίς,** ίδος, ἡ, = foreg., Ruf.*Onom.*44.

ἀντιλογ-έω, = ἀντιλέγω, *deny*, S.*Ant.*377 (lyr.). 2. = ἀντιλέγω 3, Ar.*Nu.*321, al.:—in Med., Democr.85, Antipho Soph.98. **-ητικός,** ή, όν, = ἀντιλογικός, Gal.7.281, Hsch. **-ία,** ἡ, *contradiction, controversy*, ἀ. χρησμῶν πέρι λέγειν Hdt.8.77; ἡμέας.. ἐς ἀ. παρέξομεν will offer ourselves to *argue the point*, Id.9.87; ἐδόκεον ἀντιλογίης κυρήσειν expected to be allowed *to argue it*, ib.88; εἰς -ίαν κατέστησαν Lys.*Fr.*75.1; -ίας ἅπτεσθαι Pl.*R.*454b; ἐς -ίαν τινὶ γενέσθαι Th.1.73; ἀ. καὶ λοιδορία D.40.32; ἀντιλογίαν ἔχει it is open to *contradiction*, Arist.*Rh.*1418^b25, cf. 1414^b3: in pl., *opposing arguments*, Ar.*Ra.*775; δι' ἀντιλογιῶν καταλλαγῆναι Th.4.59; ἀ. πρός τινα X.*HG*6.3.20; ἐς -ίαν ἐλθεῖν Th.1.31; ἀντιλογίαν ἐν αὑτῷ ἔχειν to have *grounds for defence* in itself, Id.2.87; ἄνευ -ίας without *dispute*, *BGU*1133.15 (Aug.), etc. 2. later, *quarrel, dispute*, *PPetr.*2 p.56 (iii B.C.), *PGrenf.*1.38.8 (ii/i B.C.), *Ep.Hebr.*12.3, etc. 3. *right, claim*, τοῦ αὐτοῦ λάκκου *POxy.*1892 (vi A.D.). **-ίζομαι,** *count up* or *calculate on the other hand*, Antipho 2.2.8; ἀ. ὅτι.. X.*HG*6.5.24. (Act. dub. in Phld.*D.*1.21 (ἀντιλογικῶν Diels).) **-ικός,** ή, όν, *given to contradiction, disputatious*, Ar.*Nu.*1173, Isoc.15.48, Ph.1.412, Sor.1.14, Pl.*Tht.*197a, al.: ἡ -κή (sc. τέχνη) *the art of disputation*, Id.*R.*454a, *Phdr.*261d; τὸ -κόν Id.*Sph.*225b: οἱ -κοί *persons skilled in this art*, Id.*Ly.*216a, *Phd.*101e; of arguments, οἱ περὶ τοὺς ἀντιλογικοὺς λόγους διατρίψαντες ib.90c: [λόγοι] -κοί, οἱ, title of work by Protagoras, D.L.3.37. Adv. -κῶς *in the manner of such disputants*, Pl.*Tht.*164c. **-ισμός,** ὁ, *countercharge*, Philostr.*VS*2.1.4. **-ος,** ον, *contradictory, reverse*, τύχαι E.*Hel.*1142 (lyr.); φιλονεικίαι love *of contradiction*, Simp.*in Ph.*1135.28, cf. Epicur.*Nat.*28*Fr.*8.

ἀντιλοιδορέω, *rail at* or *abuse in turn*, *PPetr.*3 p.48 (iii B.C.), Plu.2.88f (Pass.), 1*Ep.Pet.*2.23:—Med., c. acc. rei, Luc.*Symp.*40.

ἀντίλοξος, η, ον (or ος, ον), name of a *bandage*, Sor.*Fasc.*12.512, cf. 516C.

ἀντιλοχέω, *lay counter-ambush*, Ph.1.664 (s.v.l.).

ἀντιλῡπ-έω, *vex in return*, Plu.*Demetr.*22, Luc.*DMeretr.*3.3, 12.5. **-ησις,** εως, ἡ, *vexing in return*, Arist.*de An.*403^a30, Plu.2.442b.

ἀντίλῠρος, ον, *responsive to the lyre* or *like that of the lyre* (Sch.), καναχά, of the flute, S.*Tr.*643.

ἀντίλυτρ-ον, τό, *ransom*, 1*Ep.Ti.*2.6. 2. *antidote, remedy*, Orph.*L.*593. **-ωτέον,** *one must ransom in return*, Arist.*EN*1164^b35.

ἀντιλωβάω, *maltreat in return*, Eust.757.59 (Pass.).

ἀντιμαίνομαι, pf. part. ἀντιμεμηνώς, *to be filled with passion for a lover in return*, Luc.*DMeretr.*12.2. 2. *rage against*, βρονταῖς Διός *APl.*1.30 (Gem.).

ἀντιμανθάνω, *learn in turn* or *instead*, Ar.*V.*1453.

ἀντιμαντεύομαι, *divine, predict, in reply*, Them.*Or.*13.163a.

ἀντιμαρτ-ῠρέω, *appear as witness against*, Ar.*Fr.*437; *contradict*, τινί Plu.2.418a; opp. συμφωνεῖν, Polystr.p.10W.; esp. in Epicurus' Logic, *disprove* by fact or experience, *Ep.*1 p.10U., al.; so ἀ. πρὸς τὴν αἴσθησιν Plu.2.447c: abs., Id.*Alc.*21, cf. Gal.4.735: c. acc., ἀ. τὰ εἰρημένα Plot.6.4.4:—Pass., *to be disproved, invalidated*, Epicur.*Ep.*1 p.11U., al. **-ύρησις** [ῠ], εως, ἡ, *counter-evidence*, Id.*Fr.*247: in pl., Id.*Nat.*28*Fr.*7, Plu.2.1121e. **-ύρομαι** [ῡ], *protest on the other hand*, Luc.*Symp.*47.

ἀντιμᾰχ-έω, *resist by force of arms*, D.S.23.7. 2. as law-term, *resist, demur*, *AB*184. **-ησις,** εως, ἡ, *conflict, struggle*, ἐπ' ἀλλήλοις D.H.8.58. **-ητύς,** ύος, ἡ, = foreg., Eratosth.31 (v.l. -ηστύς). **-ομαι,** *fight against* one, Th.4.68: abs., D.S.22.10. **-ος,** ον, *capable of meeting in war*, τινί App.*Hisp.*9.

ἀντιμεγᾰλοφρονέω, *vie in pride* or *boasting with*, τινί Eust.676.5.

ἀντιμεθέλκω, *drag different ways, distract*, τὰ -οντα πράγματα Ph.1.231, cf. *APl.*4.136 (Antiphil.), 139 (Jul. Aegypt.), in Pass.; τῇ καὶ τῇ *AP*10.74 (Paul. Sil.).

ἀντιμέθεξις, εως, ἡ, *reciprocal participation*, Simp.*in Ph.*101.18.

ἀντιμεθίστημι, *move from one side to the other, revolutionize*, ψηφίσματα καὶ νόμον Ar.*Th.*362. II. Pass., with aor. 2 and pf. Act., *exchange places*, ἀ. ἀλλήλοις τό τε ὕδωρ καὶ ὁ ἀήρ Arist.*Ph.*209^b25, cf. 211^b27, *Mete.*366^b20; ἀλλήλαις Jul.*Or.*8.241a. 2. *make counter-moves*, Luc.*Dem.Enc.*37.

ἀντιμειρᾰκιεύομαι, *behave petulantly in return*, πρός τινα Plu.*Sull.*6.

ἀντιμελίζω, *compete in music with*, τινί *AP*5.221 (Agath.).

ἀντιμέλλω, *wait and watch against* one, ἀντιμελλῆσαι Th.3.12 (Sch. for ἀντεπι-).

ἀντιμέμφομαι, *blame in turn, retort upon* one, ἀ. ὅτι.. Hdt.2.133.

ἀντιμερίζομαι, *impart in turn*, χάριν *AP*6.209 (Antip. Thess.). 2. *distinguish*, Hsch.

ἀντιμερίτης, ου, ὁ, *rival claimant*, τινῶν Jul.*Gal.*148c.

ἀντιμεσουρᾰν-έω, *to be in the opposite meridian*, as the sun at midnight, Plu.2.284e, Ptol.*Tetr.*33, Vett.Val.116.5, al., Man.4.613. **-ημα,** ατος, τό, *opposite meridian*, S.E.*M.*5.12, Ptol.*Tetr.*201; name of the *fourth* τόπος in a '*nativity*', Paul.Al.*L.*3. **-ησις,** εως, ἡ, *occupation of the opposite meridian*, Heph.Astr.1.2.

ἀντιμετα-βαίνω, *pass over in turn*, ἐπί τι Alex.Trall.5.6. **-βάλλω,** *meet one change with another*, Hp.*Acut.*26. **-βάσις,** εως, ἡ, *rowing up-stream*, πρὸς τὸ ῥεῦμα τοῦ ποταμοῦ Plu.2.319c. **-βᾰτικός,** ή, όν, *resilient*, Sor.2.31. **-βολή,** ἡ, *transposition*, as a figure of speech, as in 'non ut edam vivo sed ut vivam edo', Quint.*Inst.*9.3.85, cf. Alex.*Fig.*2.22, Phoeb.*Fig.*2.4.

ἀντιμετ-άγω [ᾰγ], *countermarch*, λόχον Onos.33.6; *press in contrary direction*, Heliod.ap.Orib.49.8.20. **-αγωγή,** ἡ, *counter-extension*, τοῦ σώματος ib.9.3.

ἀντιμετά-δοσις, εως, ἡ, *mutual contribution*, Dam.*Pr.*17. **-θεσις,** εως, ἡ, *interchange*, προσώπων Longin.26.1; of meanings, Alex.*Fig.*2.22. **-κλίνω** [ῑ], *turn aside* or *the opposite way*, Ph.1.678. **-λαμβάνω,** *assume in turn* or *in exchange*, πρόσωπον Plu.2.785c; τὸν τόπον τινός Ascl.*Tact.*10.15; ὥσπερ ἐκ κληρονομίας τὸ μῖσος J.*AJ*16.3.1. 2. *receive back in return*, Phld.*Oec.*p.65J., cf. *Piet.*113. 3. *take* arguments *in reverse order*, Dam.*Pr.*350. II. Gramm., *use* a form *in place of* another, A.D.*Adv.*130.14:—Pass., 154.22, al.; also, *to be changed*, εἰς.. 130.11. **-ληπτέον,** *one must use instead, substitute*, λέξεις ἀντὶ λέξεων Phld.*Rh.*1.159S. **-ληψις,** εως, ἡ, *partaking* *of the opposite*, Plu.2.438d (fort. ἀντίληψις); ἀ. τῶν βίων *experience of divers kinds* of life, ib.466c. 2. *double reflex movement*, Heliod.ap. Orib.8.28.28, 29. 3. Gramm., *interchange of forms*, A.D.*Adv.* 155.1.

ἀντιμεταλλακτέον, *one must substitute*, Thphr.*Metaph.*16 codd.

ἀντιμεταλλεύω, *countermine*, Ph.*Bel.*99.13, Plb.1.42.12; τοῖς πολεμίοις 16.31.8.

ἀντιμετα-ρρέω, *flow off in turn* or *back*, *Placit.*4.22.2, but ἀντιμετερᾷ (cj. Bernardakis) is prob. **-σπάω**, *draw off in a different direction*, εἰς φροντίδας J.*AJ*13.5.3. **-στᾰσις**, εως, ἡ, *counter-change, reciprocal replacement*, Arist.*Ph.*208^{b}2; *reverse movement*, εἰς τὸ ἀντίπαλον D.H.3.19, Simp.*in Ph.*1352.14. **-ταξις**, εως, ἡ, *interchange of gender*, D.H.*Amm.*2.10. **-τάσσω**, *change the order of battle so as to meet the enemy*, in Med., D.H.3.25. **-τίθεμαι**, *to be changed, replaced*, J.*AJ*16.7.6, cf. Numen.ap.Eus.*PE*14.5. **-χωρέω**, *go away to the other side*, ταῖς ἐλπίσι *make room for new* hope, J.*AJ* 15.2.2. **-χώρησις**, εως, ἡ, *interchange*, of letters, etc., Eust.1618.36.

ἀντιμετειλέομαι, *to be unrolled in reverse direction*, of cables, Orib. 49.22.14.

ἀντιμέτ-ειμι, (εἶμι *ibo*) *compete with* others: οἱ ἀντιμετιόντες *rival competitors*, Plu.*Comp.Arist.Cat.*2. **-εράω**, v. ἀντιμεταρρέω.

ἀντιμετέχω, *participate reciprocally*, Dam.*Pr.*14, 33, 65.

ἀντιμετρ-έω, *measure out in turn, give* one thing *as compensation for* another, τί τινι Luc.*Am.*19:—Pass., ἀντιμετρηθήσεται ὑμῖν *it shall be measured in turn*, *Ev.Matt.*7.2, *Ev.Luc.*6.38. II. Astrol., *correspond in ascension*, *Cat.Cod.Astr.*8(4).187. **-ησις**, εως, ἡ, *reciprocal measurement*, Simp.*in Ph.*733.29.

ἀντιμέτωπος, ον, *front to front, face to face*, X.*HG*4.3.19, *Ages.*2.12, Hld.9.16.

ἀντίμηνα· κατὰ μῆνα, Hsch.

ἀντιμηνίω, *rage, be wrathful against*, Ael.*Fr.*205.

ἀντιμηνύω, *testify in return*, *BMus.Inscr.*4.481*.388 (Ephesus, ii A.D.).

ἀντιμηχᾰν-άομαι, *contrive against* or *in opposition*, ἄλλα ἀ. Hdt.8.52, cf. E.*Ba.*291; σβεστήρια κωλύματα Th.7.53: abs., Arist.*HA*613^{b}27; πρός τι X.*HG*5.3.16. **-ημα**, ατος, τό, *counter-engine* or *device*, μηχανήμασιν ἀ. εὐτρεπίζειν Polyaen.4.2.20, cf. Ath.Mech.9.1.

ἀντιμῑμ-έομαι, abs., *follow an example*, App.*BC*5.41, 94. **-ησις**, εως, ἡ, *close imitation of* a person *in* a thing, c. dupl. gen., Th.7.67. **-ος**, ον, *closely imitating*, ἠχή, of an echo, Callistr.*Stat.*9; τινός Alcid.ap.Arist.*Rh.*1406^{a}29; of man as a microcosm, ἀ. τῆς οὐρανίου τάξεως Ruf.*Anat.*1; ἀ. οὐρανοῦ ποταμός Hld.9.9, cf. Ph.2.164, Sthenidas ap.Stob.4.7.63: c. dat., ὀφθαλμὸν ἀ. ἡλίου τροχῷ Ar.*Th.*17. II. = μανδραγόρας, Dsc.4.75; = ὠκιμοειδές, Ps.-Dsc.4.28.

ἀντιμῑσέω, *hate in return*, Ar.*Lys.*818.

ἀντιμισθ-ία, ἡ, *requital, recompense*, *Ep.Rom.*1.27, *2Ep.Cor.*6.13. **-ιον**, τό, *reward*, Ps.-Callisth.3.26. **-ος**, ον, *as a reward, in compensation*, μνήμην ἀντίμισθον ηὗρετ' ἐν λιταῖς A.*Supp.*270. **-ωτός**, όν, *hired as a substitute*, Hsch.

ἀντιμίσιον, τό, (*mensa*) *table in a court of justice*, Suid.

ἀντιμνηστεύω, *rival in love*, D.S.8.19.

ἀντιμοιρ-εί, Adv. *in proportionate shares*, D.36.8. **-έω**, *receive a proportionate share*, Poll.4.176. **-ία**, ἡ, *compensation*, v.l. for ἀντιμοιρεί, D.36.8. **-ος**, ον, prob. for ἰσοτίμοιρος, A.*Ch.*319.

ἀντιμολεῖν, (v. βλώσκω) *go to meet*, Apollon.*Lex.* s. v. ἀντιβολῆσαι.

ἀντίμολπος, ον, *sounding instead of*, ἀ. ὀλολυγῆς κωκυτός a shriek *of far other note than* the cry of joy, E.*Med.*1176; ὕπνου τόδ' ἀντίμολπον..ἄκος *song*, sleep's *substitute*, A.*Ag.*17.

ἀντίμορος, ον, *corresponding*, of stones in a building, *IG*1.322.

ἀντίμορφος, ον, *formed after, corresponding to* a thing, Luc.*Am.*44. Adv. -φως, τινί Plu.*Crass.*32.

ἀντιμῡκάομαι, *low in answer*, τινί D.H.1.39. 2. *roar against*, ἀλλήλοις, of sea and lake, Procop.*Aed.*4.8.

ἀντιμυκτηρίζω, *answer mockery*, gladio Cic.*Fam.*15.19.4.

ἀντιμῶλος, ὁ, Cret., = ἀντίδικος, *Leg.Gort.*6.25.

ἀντιναυπηγέω, *build ships against*, Th.7.36, 62 (Pass., as v.l.).

ἀντινέμομαι, *bestow in return*, τὰν αὐτὰν χάριν *Epigr.Gr.*205.

ἀντινεοποιός, ὁ, *deputy-νεοποιός*, *Rev.Ét.Gr.*19.251 (Aphrodisias).

ἀντινήχομαι, *swim against*, πρὸς κῦμα Plu.2.979b.

ἀντινῑκάω, *conquer in turn*, A.*Ch.*499, cf. D.C.48.21.

Ἀντινόεια, τά, festival *in honour of Antinous* at Athens and Eleusis, *IG*3.1129, 1147 (ii A.D.).

ἀντινομ-έω, *disobey*, θεοῖς Philostr.*VA*6.20 (fort. ἀντινομ⟨οθετ⟩εῖν). **-ία**, ἡ, *conflict of laws*, Quint.*Inst.*7.1.15, Hermog.*Stat.*2, D.22 Arg.ii 12; ἐν ἀντινομίᾳ γίγνεσθαι to be *in a strait between two laws*, Plu.*Caes.*13; *ambiguity in the law*, Id.2.742a. **-ίζομαι**, Pass., νόμοι ἀντινομιζόμενοί τινος, prob. laws *enacted against* one, Archyt.ap. Stob.4.1.132. **-ικός**, ή, όν, *relating to ambiguity in the laws*, Plu. 2.741d. Adv. -κῶς *by citing a contrary law*, D.22 Arg.ii 24.

ἀντινομοθετέω, *make laws in rivalry with*, τινί Plu.2.1044c, etc.

ἀντίνοος, ον, *opposite in character, resisting*, τινί Hp.*Epid.*6.5.4.

ἀντινουθετέω, *warn in return*, Plu.2.72e.

ἀντίνωτος, ον, in pl., *back to back*, D.S.2.54, Ael.*Tact.*37.1, Arr.*Tact.*29.1.

ἀντιξενίζω, *entertain in return*, ξενισθεὶς μὴ -ίσαι Phld.*Vit.*p.30 J., cf. Eust.1961.37.

ἀντιξηραίνω, prob. f.l. for ἀνα-, Gal.18(2).804.

ἀντι-ξοέω, *set oneself against, oppose*, Pi.*O.*13.34. **-ξοος**, ον, contr. **-ξους**, ουν:—Ion. word, *opposed to, adverse*, ἐλπόμενοι οὐδέν σφι φανήσεσθαι ἀντίξοον Hdt.7.218, cf. 6.50; τὸ..τοῖσι Σκύθῃσι ἀ. 4.129; στρατὸν..ἀ. Πέρσῃσι 6.7:—abs., ἐν μυρίῃσι γνώμῃσι μίαν οὐκ ἔχω ἀντίξοον 8.119; δοῦρα ἀ. γόμφοις A.R.2.79; τὸ ἀντίξοον *opposition*, Hdt.1.174; τὸ ἀ. συμφέρον Heraclit.8; of diseases and remedies, Aret.*SA*2.4, *CA*2.1. Adv. ἀντιξόως *in hostile spirit*, Philostr.*VA* 7.36. II. τὸ ἀ. the *opposite side* of the compass, *Placit.*2.12.1. (Prob. from ξέω 'hew'.)

ἀντιξύω [ῡ], *scrape in turn*, ἀ. τὸν ξύοντα 'claw me, claw thee', Sophr.149, Aristid.2.84 J.

ἀντίον, as Adv., = ἄντην, v. ἀντίος. **ἀντίον**, τό, a part of the loom, Ar.*Th.*822, cf. Poll.7.36, 10.125. 2. generally, *loom*, ἀντίον ὑφαινόντων Lxx *2Ki.*21.19, al.

ἀντιόομαι, fut. -ώσομαι Hdt.7.9.γ', 102, al.: aor. Pass. ἠντιώθην, Ion. ἀντ- Id.4.126, 7.9.α', al.:—*resist, oppose*, τινί Id.1.76, A.*Supp.*389, etc.; τινὶ ἐς μάχην Hdt.7.102: abs., οἱ ἀντιούμενοι, = οἱ ἐναντίοι, Id.1.207, 4.1. 2. in Id.9.7.β' (dub.), c. acc., τὸν Πέρσην ἀντιώσεσθαι ἐς τὴν Βοιωτίην that ye *would meet* him in Boeotia. (ἐναντ- is used in pure Att., ἀ. in Aen.Tact.36.7. The Homeric forms ἀντιόω, ἀντιόωσι, etc., belong to ἀντιάω.)

ἀντίος, ία, ίον, (ἀντί) *set against*, and so, I. in local sense, *face to face, opposite*, ἀντίοι ἔσταν ἅπαντες Il.1.535; ἀντίος ἦλθε θεῶν went *to meet them*, 6.54; ἡ δ' οὐκ ἀθρῆσαι δύνατ' ἀντίη *though she faced him*, Od.19.478; esp. in battle, Il.11.216, etc.: ἐχώρεον..οἱ Πέρσαι ἀντίοι Hdt.9.62; ἐκ τοῦ ἀντίου προσφέρεσθαι X.*Cyr.*1.4.8; ἀντίος ἐλαύνειν ibid.; ἐκ τῆς ἀντίης προσπλέειν Hdt.8.6; κατ' ἀντίον Hp.*VC*11:—freq. c. gen., which often precedes, Ἀγαμέμνονος ἀντίος ἐλθών Il.11.231, cf. 5.301, 7.98; but also follows, ἀ. ἦλθεν ἄνακτος Od.16.14, cf. Il.17.31, etc.: less freq. in Hom. c. dat., ὅς ῥά οἱ ἀ. ἦλθε 15.584, cf. 7.20; but mostly so after Hom., ἀντίαι ἵζοντο τοῖσι Πέρσῃσι Hdt.5.18, cf. Pi.*N.*10.79, E.*Supp.*667, X.*An.*1.8.17, etc.; ἀ. ἐς.. *h.Merc.*345; = διάμετρος, Man.3.339. b. *direct*, opp. πλάγιος, Antyll.ap.Orib.44.23.9, cf. Heliod.ib.28. 2. *opposite, contrary*, τὸν ἀ. τοῖσδε λόγον A.*Ag.*499; τούτοις ἀντία opinions *opposed to* these, E.*Supp.*466; ἀδεῖα μὲν ἀντία δ' οἴσω with pleasure [I speak], though I shall offer *reproof*, S.*Tr.*122; οἱ ἀντίοι, = οἱ ἐναντίοι, Pi.*P.*1.45 (so later, *PTeb.*43.21 (ii B.C.)); εἰς τὸ ἀντίον X.*Eq.*12.12; also λόγοι ἀντίοι ἢ οὓς ἤκουον words *the very reverse* of those I have heard, Id.*An.*6.6.34. II. as Adv. in neut. ἀντία and ἀντίον, *against, over against*, abs., ἀντίον ἵζεν Od.14.79, cf. 17.334, etc.: more freq. like a Prep. c. gen., ἀντί' ἐμεῖο στήσεσθαι Il.21.481; ἀντία δεσποίνης φάσθαι *before* her, Od.15.377; so ἀντία σευ *in* thy *presence*, Hdt.7.209, cf. 1.133; ἀντίον τοῦ μεγάρου *facing* it, Id.5.77; τὰς καμήλους ἔταξε ἀντία τῆς ἵππου Id.1.80, cf. 3.160, al.; τἀνδρὸς ἀντίον μολεῖν S.*Tr.*785: so, 2. *against*, ὅς τις σέθεν ἀντίον εἴπῃ Il.1.230; ἀντίον αὐτῶν φωνὴν ἱέναι Hdt.2.2; ἐρίζειν ἀντία τοῖς ἀγαθοῖς Pi.*P.*4.285: c. dat., ἰέναι ἀντία τοῖσι Πέρσῃσι ἐς μάχην Hdt.7.236; ὕδωρ καπνῷ φέρειν ἀντίον Pi.*N.*1.25. 3. in the phrase τὸν δ' ἀντίον ηὔδα *answered*, Od.15.48, etc. (more freq. in Od. than Il.). 4. ἀντία εἶναι *to be present, help*, of a god, *Milet.*7 p.64 (ii/iii A.D.).—The word is almost confined to Poets and Ion. Prose; in Att. Prose ἐναντίος is preferred, though X. uses ἀντίος.

ἀντιο-στατέω, = ἀνθίσταμαι, *to be contrary*, of a wind, S.*Ph.*640. **-τόμον**, τό, *tonsillotome*, Gal.14.785, *Hermes* 38.281. **-φρων**· ἐναντίον φρονῶν, Hsch. **-χεῖ**· ἐναντιοῦται, Id.

Ἀντιόχειος, α, ον, *of Antiochus*, τέτραχμον *IG*11.203 *B* 40, 46 (iii B.C.).

ἀντιοχεύομαι, Pass., *contrario more futuo*, *AP*11.284 (Pall.).

ἀντιόω, ἀντιόωσα, etc., v. sub ἀντιάω.

ἀντιπᾰγές· ἐναντίως συνεστηκός, *EM*114.10.

ἀντιπαγκρᾰτιάζω, *contend in the* παγκράτιον, Sch.Philostr.*Im.*2.6.

ἀντιπάθ-εια [ᾰθ], ἡ, *suffering instead*, λυπεῖ τὸν στερόμενον τῶν ἀγαθῶν ἡ ἀ. κακῶν Pl.*Ax.*370a. II. *opposition, contrast*, τῆς γῆς πρὸς τὴν αἰθέρα Plu.2.952d. III. *counteraction, antipathy*, S.E.*P.*1.43, Archig.ap.Philum.*Ven.*14.4, Sor.2.42. IV. in Metric, of *opposed* rhythms, ἡ κατ' ἀντιπάθειαν μεῖξις Heph.14, cf. Aristid.Quint.1.28. V. *contrary affection*, Str.3.5.7; περὶ συμπαθειῶν καὶ ἀντιπαθειῶν, title of work by Bolus, Suid. s. v. Βῶλος, etc. **-έω**, *have an aversion*, Alex.Aphr.*Pr.Prooem.* 2. *to be opposed, reversed* in metric, as iambus or trochee, Sch.Heph.p.115 C. II. *to be affected*, ὑπὸ τῶν ἔξωθεν A.D.*Synt.*291.14. 2. *to be affected in a contrary manner*, τινί Plb.34.9.5, cf. Str.3.5.7. **-ής**, ές, *in return for suffering*, A.*Eu.*782; *felt mutually*, ἡδονή Luc.*Am.*27. 2. *of opposite feelings* or *properties*, δύναμις Plu.2.664c; φύσιν ἔχειν ἀ. πρός τι ib.940a. Adv. -θῶς *Gp.*5.11.4, Alex.Trall.8.2. 3. in Metric, of *opposed* rhythms, Sch.Heph.p.122 C., al. II. Subst. ἀντιπαθές, τό, *remedy for suffering*, Plu.*Ant.*45, cf. ἀντίτομον· φάρμακον ἀντιπαθές, Hsch.; λίθος ἀντιπαθὴς καλούμενος Ps.-Plu.*Fluv.*21.5:—name of a *black kind of coral*, Dsc.5.122. **-ητικός**, ή, όν, *opposed to passivity*, Sch.Opp.*H.*1.653. **-ιον**, τό, = ἀντιπαθής II, Hsch. s. v. μῶλυ.

ἀντιπαιανίζω, v. ἀντιπαιωνίζω.

ἀντιπαιδεύω, *teach as a rival master*, τινί Suid. s. v. Γενέθλιος.

ἀντιπαιδονόμος, ὁ, *deputy-παιδονόμος*, *IG*12(2).259 (Mytil.).

ἀντιπαίζω, *play one with another*, X.*Cyn.*5.4, Pl.*Erx.*395b.

ἀντίπαις, αιδος, ὁ, ἡ, *like a child*, γραῦς A.*Eu.*38; *little more than a child*, θυγατρὸς ἀντίπαιδος E.*Andr.*326; ἡλικία Luc.*Am.*2. II. *instead of a boy*, i. e. *no longer a boy*, S.*Fr.*564 (s.v.l.). 2. Subst., *a mere boy*, Plb.15.33.12, 27.15.4, D.H.4.3, Plu.*Aem.*22, Luc.*Somn.*16, Ant.Lib.13.5.

ἀντιπαίω, *strike against, resist,* τὸ ἀντιπαῖον Hp.*VM*22, cf. Arist. *Pr.*902^{b}13: metaph., πρός τι Plb.18.46.15; τινί Iamb.*in Nic.*p.22 P.:—Pass., ib.p.24 P.

ἀντιπαιωνίζω or **-ᾱνίζω,** *sing the battle song against,* ἀλλήλοις Max. Tyr.32.2, cf. Aen.Tact.27.4 (-παιαν-).

ἀντιπᾰλαιστής, οῦ, ὁ, *antagonist in wrestling,* Ael.*VH*4.15.

ἀντιπᾰλαίω, *wrestle against, POxy.*1099, Sch.Ar.*Ach.*570, Eustr. *in EN*117.34.

ἀντιπάλλομαι, *rebound,* Cass.*Pr.*26, Eust.948.12.

ἀντίπᾰλος, ον, (πάλη) properly, *wrestling against*: hence, *antagonist, rival,* κράτος ἀ. A.*Pr.*528 (lyr.); ἀ. θεοῖς E.*Ba.*544 (lyr.): c. gen., μένος γήραος ἀντίπαλον Pi.*O.*8.71; γοητείας φάρμακον ἀ. *AP*10.50 (Pall.):—Subst. ἀντίπαλος, ὁ, *antagonist, rival, adversary,* Pi.*N.*11. 26, S.*Ant.*126 (lyr.): mostly in pl., Hdt.7.236, Ar.*Ra.*365, 1027, Pl. *Alc.*1.119e, al.; cf. φθόνος πρὸς τὸ ἀ. Th.2.45, etc.; ὁ δ' ἦλθεν ἐπὶ τἀντίπαλον E.*Ba.*278 (dub.). **2.** of things, *nearly matched, nearly balanced,* ἀπὸ ἀ. παρασκευῆς Th.1.91; ἀ. τριήρης *equally large,* Id.4. 120; ἀ. τινι Id.1.11, Pl.*Mx.*240a; γνῶμαι μάλιστα ἀ. πρὸς ἀλλήλας Th.3.49; ἀ. δέος fear *caused by the balance of the power of the parties, mutual* fear, ib.11; ἀ. ποιναί *adequate* punishment, E.*IT*446; ἤθεα ἀ. [τῇ πόλει] habits *corresponding to . .,* Th.2.61; ὑμεναίων γόος ἀ. E. *Alc.*922; ἀντίπαλόν τι τῆς ναυμαχίας a point *where* the action *was evenly balanced,* Th.7.71, cf. 38, Lys.2.38; ἀντίπαλα καταστῆσαι bring to *a state of balance,* Th.4.117; εἰς ἀ. καταστῆναι to be in *such state,* Id.7.13. Adv. -λως Id.8.87: also neut. pl., ναυμαχήσαντες ἀντίπαλα Id.7.34. **II.** τὸν ἀμὸν ἀ. *him who fights for* me, my *champion,* A.*Th.*417 (lyr.).

ἀντιπαρα-βαίνω, *transgress, PLips.*298 (iii A.D.). **-βάλλω,** *place side by side* so as *to compare* or *contrast,* τι πρός τι Pl.*Ap.*41b; λόγον παρὰ λόγον *Hp.Mi.*369c, cf. Isoc.5.142; τί τινι Arist.*Fr.*91; βίον τινὸς καί τινος Plu.*TG*1:—Pass., c. dat., *measure oneself against, rival,* App.*BC*2.15. **II.** *contribute instead,* X.*Lac.*5. 3. **-βλητέον,** *one must compare,* prob. for -τόν in *An.Ox.*3. 216. **-βολή,** ἡ, *reply by comparison* or *contrast,* Arist.*Rh.*1414^{b}10, 1419^{b}34, Plu.2.40f, Longin.*Fr.*11, Ruf.ap.Orib.49.30.9.

ἀντιπαρ-αγγελία, ἡ, *competition for a public office,* Plu.*Arat.* 35. **-αγγέλλω,** *give orders, command in turn,* X.*HG*4.2.19, D.C. 65.1. **II.** *compete for a public office,* Plu.*Caes.*7; δημαρχίαν Id. *Mar.*29; τινί *with* one, Id.*Cat.Mi.*49.

ἀντιπαρα-γρᾰφή, ἡ, *counter-*παραγραφή, *perscriptio, replicatio, Gloss.* **-γράφω** [ᾰφ], *add* or *insert on the other side,* Ptol.*Geog.* 8.1.3:—Med., as law-term, *reply to a* παραγραφή, *remancipo, Gloss.*

ἀντιπαρ-άγω [ᾱγ], *shift in order to meet attacks,* τοὺς σάκκους J.*BJ* 3.7.20:—Pass., *to be shifted in the other direction,* Paul.Aeg.6.3. **2.** Pass., *to be produced correspondingly,* Plot.2.4.11. **3.** *adduce, allege on the other side,* Plu.2.719c: abs., *argue on the other side,* Phld. *Rh.*2.267 S., cf. *Vit.*p.4 J. **II.** more freq. intr., *lead an army against, advance to meet the enemy,* X.*Cyr.*1.6.43. **2.** *march parallel with, skirt,* ταῖς ὑπωρείαις Plb.1.77.2, cf. 3.53.4. **-ᾰγωγή,** ἡ, *flank march,* Id.9.3.10 (pl.), 11.18.2, Plu.*Pyrrh.*21. **2.** metaph., *machinations, UPZ*20.44 (ii B.C.). **II.** in pl., *hostility,* πρός τινα Plb.10.37.2, al.

ἀντιπαρα-δέχομαι, *admit instead* or *in place of,* A.D.*Synt.*108. 13. **2.** *receive in turn, BGU*977.15 (ii A.D.); dub. sens. in Ph.2. 508. **-δίδωμι,** *deliver up in turn,* τὴν ἀρχήν τινι J.*AJ*15.3.1, cf. *PFlor.*384.74 (v A.D.). **-δοσις,** εως, ἡ, *mutual accommodation,* of heavenly bodies, Vett.Val.162.31. **-θεσις,** εως, ἡ, *comparison, contrast,* J.*Ap.*2.33, A.D.*Synt.*49.21, al., Herm.*in Phdr.*p.183 A. **-θέω,** *outflank,* X.*An.*4.8.17. **II.** *run parallel to* a thing, Plot.6.5.11.

ἀντιπαρ-αινέω, *advise contrariwise,* c. inf., D.C.65.11. **-αιτέομαι,** *deprecate in answer,* A.D.*Synt.*296.18.

ἀντιπαρα-κᾰλέω, *summon in turn* or *contrariwise,* ἐπὶ ἀληθεστέραν γε σωτηρίαν Th.6.86, cf. X.*Cyr.*2.2.24, Pl.*Grg.*526e; ὑπέρ τινος *change one's attitude and petition,* J.*BJ*1.25.5. **-κειμαι,** *lie just opposite,* τινί Plb.3.37.7. **2.** Gramm., *correspond with, to be correlative to,* τινί A.D.*Adv.*155.1, al.; *to be opposed, Synt.*118.23. **-κελεύομαι,** *exhort in turn* or *contrariwise,* τοῖς πρεσβυτέροις μὴ καταισχυνθῆναι Th.6.13, cf. X.*Cyr.*3.3.42 and 59. **-κλησις,** εως, ἡ, *mutual exhortation,* Plb.11.12.2.

ἀντιπα[ράκρ]ῐσις, εως, ἡ, *comparison,* Diog.Oen.38 (dub. rest.).

ἀντιπαραλαμβάνω, *compare by contrasting,* Gal.14.221. **II.** Astrol., *take* a function *in exchange,* Vett.Val.174.7.

ἀντιπαραλλάσσω, *pass from side to side,* χεῖρας περὶ τὸ στέρνον Sor. 1.103.

ἀντιπαράλληλος, sc. πούς, = διτρόχαιος, Sch.Heph.p.219 C.

ἀντιπαρα-λῡπέω, *annoy in turn,* Th.4.80. **-πέμπομαι,** ἀ. τῇ μνήμῃ *to be cheered on one's way* [to death] by the remembrance, Plu. 2.1099d. **-πήγνῡμι,** *set up as a standard of comparison* or *reference,* A.D.*Synt.*37.22 (Pass.). **-πλέω,** *sail along on the other side,* Th.2.83. **-πορεύομαι,** *march on the flank,* ταῖς χώραις Plb. 5.7.11. **-σκευάζομαι,** Med., *prepare oneself in turn, arm on both sides,* Th.1.80, D.10.29, etc.; ἀ. ἀλλήλοις ὡς ἐς μάχην Th.7.3. **II.** later, in Act., *instigate in return,* τινὰ ἐναντιωθῆναί σφισι D.C.38. 14. **-σκευή,** ἡ, *hostile preparation,* Th.1.141. **-στᾰσις,** εως, ἡ, as a figure of speech, *counter-objection, rejoinder, retort,* Hermog. *Stat.*3, al., Aps.p.270 H., Olymp.*in Cat.*78.26, Alex.Aphr.*in Metaph.* 518.28; *indirect reply,* Procl.*in Alc.*p.303 C.:—Adj. **-στᾰτικός,** ή, όν, Hermog.*Inv.*3.6. Adv. -κῶς ibid., Eust.704.36. **-στρᾰτοπεδεύω,** *encamp opposite,* D.H.8.25. **-ταξις,** εως, ἡ, *hostile demonstration,* ἀντιπαρατάξεις κατὰ τὴν ἀγοράν Id.6.22; ἀ. τῆς γνώμης *stubborn determination to resist,* J.*AJ*18.8.5. **-τάσσομαι,** Att. **-ττομαι,** Med. and Pass., *stand in array against,* ἀλλήλοις Th.6.98, cf. X.*HG*1.3.5; ἀντιπαρατεταγμένους πρὸς τὴν τούτων ἀσέλγειαν Aeschin.3.257: metaph., *hold one's ground against,* Epicur.*Fr.*138: abs., *stand in hostile array,* Th.1.63; ἀπὸ τοῦ ἀντιπαραταχθέντος in *hostile array,* Id.5.9; in a Com. metaph., ἡ δημιουργὸς ἀντιπαρατεταγμένη κρεάδι' ὀπτᾷ Men.518.12; λίαν -τεταγμένοι, of a *hostile* audience, Corn.*Rh.*p.360 H.: c. acc., ἀντιπαρετάξαντο φάλαγγα X.*An.*4.8. 9. **II.** Act., = Med., is dub. l. in Plb.9.26.4. **-τείνω,** *stretch side by side* so as *to compare* or *contrast,* ἄλλον [λόγον] πρὸς αὐτὸν ἀ. Pl.*Phdr.*257c. **2.** intr., *extend beside,* Anon.*Geog.Comp.*7; and Pass. in same sense, ib.21. **-τίθημι,** *contrast and compare,* τὰς ἄλλας νύκτας ταύτῃ ἀ. Pl.*Ap.*40d, cf. Men.325.15, Phld.*Po.*2.28, *Hom.*p.12 O., Jul.*Gal.*99d. **-χωρέω,** *yield, give up in turn,* τινὰ ἀλλήλοις Phlp.*in Ph.*553.20; *give place in turn,* ἀλλήλοις Gal.19.474: Astrol., *yield to adverse influence,* Vett.Val.125.10; *return a pledge, BGU*1158.6 (i B.C.). **-χώρησις,** εως, ἡ, *making way for each other,* Simp.*in Cael.*459.16; *mutual concession,* Eust.445.11: Astrol., *yielding to adverse influence,* Vett.Val.274.19.

ἀντιπάρ-ειμι, (εἶμι *ibo*) *march on opposite sides of* a river or entrenchments, X.*An.*4.3.17, *HG*5.4.38. **-εισᾰγωγή,** ἡ, *introduction of a second* soul, Plot.2.9.5 (as v.l.). **-έκτᾰσις,** εως, ἡ, *interpenetration* of two or more bodies in κρᾶσις, Chrysipp.*Stoic.*2.153. **-εκτείνομαι,** *to be reciprocally interpenetrated,* τὰ ἀλλήλοις δι' ὅλων -όμενα Id.ib.154:—also Act., [αἱ ψυχαὶ] δι' ὅλων τῶν σωμάτων -ουσιν Id.ib. 153. **2.** Act., *extend in line with,* τῷ τείχει τὸ ἱππικόν J.*BJ*3.7. 24. **3.** Pass., *extend in the contrary direction,* Iamb.*in Nic.* p.13 P. **-εξάγω** [ᾰγ], *lead on against* the enemy, τὴν δύναμιν, τὸν ἵππον, Plu.*Luc.*27, *Pyrrh.*16: metaph., *cite* an authority *in contradiction of* another, Gal.8.715; *incite to rivalry,* Them.*Or.*22.275d. **2.** *bring into action as an enemy,* τὸν θεόν J.*AJ*18.8.1. **3.** (sc. στρατόν) *march against,* Philipp.ap.D.18.39: metaph., *adduce arguments against,* [τοῖς ποιηταῖς] D.Chr.7.98, cf. Ael.*VH*4.9, S.E.*M.*7.166. **b.** *march parallel with,* τινί Plu.*Aem.*30, cf. Arr.*An.*5.17.1: c. acc., τὴν δύναμιν Plu.*Luc.*27. **II.** *compare,* ἑαυτὸν πρός τινα Id.2. 470b. **-εξᾰγωγή,** ἡ, *a means of attack in controversy,* πρός τινα S.E.*M.*7.150. **-έξειμι,** (εἶμι *ibo*) *proceed in a parallel direction,* J.*AJ*2.9.4, Plu.2.195c. **II.** *make hostile demonstrations,* Id.*Cic.* 43. **-εξέρχομαι,** = foreg., D.C.47.46. **-εξετάζω,** *compare,* τοὺς βίους τῶν πόλεων ἀλλήλοις D.H.3.11; βύβλον βύβλῳ Id.*Th.* 16. **-έρχομαι,** *pass by on the opposite side, Ev.Luc.*10.31: c. acc. loci, *AP*12.8 (Strat.). **II.** *come up and help,* as *against* an enemy, Lxx *Wi.*16.10. **III.** *enter in place of,* Diog.Oen.29. **IV.** *penetrate,* Chrysipp.*Stoic.*2.248. **-έχω,** *furnish* or *supply in turn,* Th. 6.21:—also in Med., X.*Hier.*7.12; *supply mutual need,* τοὐλλιπὲς ἀλλήλοις *AP*9.12 (Leon.). **2.** *cause in return,* τοὺς ἀντιπαρέξοντας πράγματα D.21.123. **-ηγορέω,** *persuade, comfort in turn,* Plu.2. 118a. **-ήκω,** = ἀντιπαρεκτείνομαι, Chrysipp.*Stoic.*2.153, 230; *stretch parallel to,* c. dat., Arist.*Mu.*393^{a}31, Str.2.5.28; *outflank,* τῷ στρατεύματι Paus.8.10.6. **-ιππεύω,** *bring their cavalry against,* Arr. *An.*5.16.3. **-ίστημι,** Rhet., *retort,* τινί τι Aps.p.270 H., Ps.-Alex. Aphr.*in SE*102.15 (-ιστῶντος):—Pass., νόμος -ίσταται νόμῳ Aps. p.271 H.; *correspond,* Ptol.*Geog.*8.1.14. **-οδεύω,** *meet on a march,* ἀλλήλοις App.*Pun.*107. **-ονομάζομαι,** *to be opposite in expression,* Iamb.*in Nic.*p.29 P.

ἀντιπαρρησιάζομαι, *speak freely in turn,* Plu.2.72e.

ἀντιπαρ-ῳδέω, *write a parody against,* Str.9.1.10:—Subst. **-ῴδησις,** εως, ἡ, Steph.*in Rh.*319.19. **-ωνῠμέομαι,** Pass., *to be opposite in name* or *expression,* Nicom.*Ar.*1.8:—Act. in same sense, Iamb.*in Nic.* p.18 P., al.:—Subst. **-ωνῠμία,** ἡ, ib.p.13 P., al.; and Adj. **-ώνῠμος,** ον, Nicom.*Ar.*2.3.

ἀντιπάσχω, *suffer in turn,* κακὰ ἀ. *suffer* evil *for* evil, Antipho 4.2.3; δεσμούς X.*Hier.*7.12; τί ἂν δράσειαν αὐτούς, ὅ τι οὐκ ἂν μεῖζον ἀντιπάθοιεν; Th.6.35; δρῶν ἀντιπάσχω χρηστά I *receive* good *for* good done, S.*Ph.*584; καλὸν τὸ εὖ ποιεῖν μὴ ἵνα ἀντιπάθῃ Arist.*EN*1163^{a}1; ἀ. ἀντί τινος Th.3.61: abs., *suffer for* one's acts, X.*An.*2.5.17. **b.** *to be affected in a contrary manner,* ἡ ψυχὴ τοῖς σώμασιν ὡς ἀσώματος ἀντιπέπονθε Sallust.8; opp. συντρέχειν, Alex.Aphr.*in Top.*437.16. **2.** τὸ ἀντιπεπονθός *requital,* Arist.*EN*1132^{b}21 (Pythag.); of persons, εὔνοιαν ἐν ἀντιπεπονθόσι φιλίαν εἶναι ib.1155^{b}33. **3.** *to be in the same proportion,* πρός τι Id.*Mech.*850^{b}2. **4.** *to be reciprocally proportional,* Euc.6.14, al.; -πεπονθότα σχήματα figures *having* the sides about the equal angles *reciprocally proportional,* Id.6 *Def.*2, cf. Hero *Deff.* 118. Adv. -πεπονθότως *reciprocally,* Archim.*Aequil.*1.6, 7, al., cf. Iamb.*in Nic.*p.11 P. **II.** *counteract,* δυσουρίαις, θανασίμοις φαρμάκοις, Dsc.3.62, 64. **III.** *to be of opposite nature to,* τινί Thphr.*Lap.* 14. **IV.** Gramm., ἀντιπεπονθώς *reflexive,* κατηγορήματα *Stoic.*2. 59. **V.** *to be adversely affected,* Agathin.ap.Orib.10.7.11, Archig. ap.eund.8.2.15.

ἀντιπᾰτᾰγέω, *rattle so as to drown* another sound, ψόφῳ Th.3.22; τοῖς ὅπλοις Dam.*Isid.*63.

ἀντιπᾰτάσσω· *repercutio, Gloss.*

ἀντιπᾰτέω, *trample upon in turn,* Sch.Ar.*Pl.*973.

ἀντιπατρίς, ίδος, ἡ, name of a kind of *silver vessel, IG*11.110, al. (Delos, iii B.C.). (Prob. from pr. n. Ἀντίπατρος.)

ἀντιπειστικός, ή, όν, *availing to persuade to the contrary, An.Bachm.* 2.291.

ἀντιπελαργ-έω, *cherish in turn*, Iamb.*VP*5.24, Zen.1.94; *cherish in place of* another, of a sister acting as parent, Aristaenet.1.25:—Subst. **-ωσις**, εως, ἡ, *Com.Adesp.*939.

ἀντι-πέμπω, *send back an answer*, Hdt.2.114; πέμψασιν ἀντέπεμψεν S.*OT*306:—Pass., Hdt.6.4. 2. *send back* sound, *echo*, Arr.*An.*6.3.3. 3. *send in requital* or *repayment*, οἰκούρια S.*Tr.*542; τινὶ θηρίον Philem.47. II. *send against*, στρατιάν τινι Th.6.99. III. *send in the place of* another, στρατηγοὺς ἐπὶ τὰς ναῦς Id.8.54. **-πεμψις**, εως, ἡ, *sending back* of sound, *echo*, Arr.*An.*6.3.3.

ἀντιπενθής, ές, *causing grief in turn*, A.*Eu.*782.

ἀντιπεπόνθησις, εως, ἡ, *reciprocal proportion*, Nicom.*Ar.*1.7, Iamb.*Comm.Math.*7.

ἀντιπέρā, Adv. for ἀντιπέρāν, Plb.1.17.4 (dub.): c. gen., ἀ. τῆς Γαλιλαίας *Ev.Luc.*8.26: proparox. in Hsch.

ἀντιπεραίνομαι, *accomplish in turn*, τὸ δρᾶν καὶ τὸ παθεῖν, sens. obsc., *AP*12.238 (Strat.).

ἀντιπέρ-αιος, α, ον, *lying over against*, ἀντιπέραι' ἐνέμοντο *the lands lying over against*, Il.2.635:—in late Ep. also fem. ἀντιπέραιά A.R.2.351, D.P.962, Nonn.*D.*24.148:—also **ἀντιπεραῖτις**, ιδος, ἡ, Tz.*H.*1.896. **-αλαχεῖν**· ἀντιτρέφειν, Hsch. **-āν**, Ion. **-ην**, Adv. = ἀντιπέρāς, v.l. in X.*HG*6.2.9, cf. A.R.2.177, al.; also κατ' ἀντιπέραν, c. gen., Plb.9.41.11. II. Adj., Ἀσίδα τ' ἀντιπέρην τε Asia and *the opposite coast*, Mosch.2.9. **-āς**, Adv. *over against, on the other side*, c. gen., Th.2.66, etc.; εἰς τὸ ἀ. X.*Cyn.*9.3: abs., ἡ ἀ. Θρᾴκη Th.1.100, cf. 4.92. **-ηθεν** (-θε Man.6.579), Adv. *from the opposite side*, A.R.1.613, *AP*9.551 (Antiphil.): c. gen., A.R.2.1030.

ἀντιπερι-άγω [ᾰγ], *bring round*, τὸν δὲ [σκορπίον] τὸ κέντρον ἐπαίροντα ἀντιπεριάγειν Arist.*Mir.*844^{b}27; of the *corvus* employed on the Roman ships, Plb.1.22.8; τὸν αὐχένα τοῦ ἵππου Ph.1.311. **-άγωγή**, ἡ, *contrary revolution*, Ptol.*Alm.*5.2, Procl.*Hyp.*4.34. 2. in midwifery, *rotatory movement* used in extracting the afterbirth, Sor.1.73. **-βάλλω**, *put round in the other direction*, e.g. a bandage, Hp.*Fract.*11. 2. *embrace in return*, Ach.Tat.5.8:—Pass., *to be clothed about*, θανάτῳ Lxx *Si.*23.12. **-ειλέομαι**, *to be rolled in the contrary direction*, Orib.49.22.24. **-ειμι**, (εἶμι *ibo*) *come round as in a cycle*, Aret.*SA*2.2. **-έλκω**, *draw round to the other side*, S.E.*M.*7.189. **-ηχέω**, *echo around*, Plu.2.502d. **-ίστημι**, *oppose by surrounding, compress*, Arist.*Mete.*382^{b}10, 347^{b}6:—Pass., with intr. tenses in Act., *to be compressed*, ib.348^{b}6, al. 2. Pass., *to be replaced by another substance*, ib.382^{a}14; ἀ. ἀλλήλοις *change places with*, Id.*Resp.*472^{b}16, cf. Gal.17(2).292. 3. Pass., *to be opposed*, in general sense, Iamb.*in Nic.*p.19 P.; of the shadow of the earth, Theo Sm. p.121 H. II. *bring all round*, φόβους ἀ. τινί Plb.4.50.1; εὐδαιμονίαν τισί Lib.*Decl.*43.6. **-λαμβάνω**, *embrace in turn*, X.*Smp.*9.4. **-πλέω**, *sail round on the other side*, Str.1.1.8. **-ποιέομαι**, *express reciprocal action*, of certain verbs, A.D.*Synt.*429.3. **-ποιητικός**, ή, όν, *expressive of a claim*, *An.Bachm.*2.291. **-σπασμα**, ατος, τό, as military term, *diversion*, ἀ. ποιεῖν τινί Plb.3.106.6. **-σπασμός**, ὁ, = foreg., D.S.14.49. **-σπαστός**, ή, όν, *drawn through*, of cautery, Paul.Aeg.6.42. **-σπάω**, *draw off, divert*, D.S.3.37; esp. as military term, Plb.2.24.8, etc.:—Pass., Arist.*PA*670^{b}10. 2. *divert, distract*, ἑαυτὸν ἄβακι Iamb.*VP*5.24. **-στᾰσις**, εως, ἡ, *surrounding so as to compress*, Arist.*Somn.Vig.*457^{b}2, 458^{a}27, *Pr.*867^{b}32, 962^{a}2. 2. *reciprocal replacement, interchange*, Id.*Ph.*215^{a}15, 267^{a}16 (v. Simp. ad loc.), *Mete.*348^{b}2, Thphr.*Ign.*18, *Sud.*23. 3. *alternation*, Nicom.*Ar.*1.8 and 13. **-στροφή**, ἡ, *turning round to the other side*, *Placit.*4.14.2. **-σχίζομαι**, *to be broken up and return*, of sputum, Steph.*in Hp.*1.174 D. **-φορά**, *contrary revolution*, Procl.*in Ti.*1.76 D., al., Simp.*in Cael.*473.19: pl., Procl.*in Prm.*p.571 S. **-χωρέω**, *move round in turn* or *in opposition*, Plu.*Ages.*39. **-ψύχω** [ῡ], *cool* or *chill in turn*, Plu.2.691f. **-ωθέω**, *push* or *press back any surrounding body*, ib.1005f:—hence Subst. **-ωσις**, εως, ἡ, ibid.

ἀντιπέσσομαι, Att. **-ττομαι**, Pass., of food, *to be quite digested*, Arist.*Pr.*884^{a}2.

ἀντίπετρος, ον, *like stone, rocky*, S.*OC*192 codd. (lyr.). II. in Theoc.*Syrinx* 2 (acc. to Sch.), *exchanged for a stone*, of Zeus in his infancy.

ἀντιπήγνῡμι, in pf. -πέπηγα, *to be fixed opposite*, ἀλλήλοις, of crocodile's teeth, Tim.Gaz. in *An.Ox.*4.264.

ἀντίπηξ, ηγος, ἡ, (πήγνυμι) *wheeled cradle* or *perambulator* for infants, κοίλης ἐν ἀντίπηγος εὐτρόχῳ κύκλῳ E.*Ion*19; κύτος ἑλικτὸν ἀντίπηγος ib.40. (Mytil., = κιβωτός, acc. to Eust.1056.46.)

ἀντιπηρ-όομαι, Pass., *to be blinded in return*, Ph.2.332. **-ωσις**· *talio*, Gloss.

ἀντιπίνω [πῑ], *drink to, pledge in turn*, Sch.Opp.*H.*3.226.

ἀντιπίπτω, *collide*, Arist.*Pr.*915^{b}18; *fall upon*, ταῖς σπείραις Plb.3.19.5. 2. *resist*, ἀντιπῖπτον *resisting body*, Arist.*Pr.*961^{b}3; ἀ. τινί *Act.Ap.*7.51; μηδὲν ἀντιπεσόντα without *demur*, *UPZ*36.21 (ii B.C.); τῆς φράσεως οὐκ -ούσης A.D.*Adv.*123.5; εἰ μηδὲν -πίπτει *POxy.*1473.20 (iii A.D.), cf. Aët.16.73; ἀντιπῖπτον an *objection*, Phlp.*in Mete.*58.3; ἡ τοῦ ἀντιπίπτοντος λύσις Aps.p.238 H. 3. of circumstances, *to be adverse*, τινί Plb.16.2.1, etc.: abs., τῆς τύχης -ούσης ib.28.2; of contrary winds, 4.44.9; *tell against, conflict with* (fact or theory), Phld.*Sign.*8, al. II. *to fall in a contrary direction*, αἱ σκιαί Str.2.1.19.

ἀντιπιστεύω, *trust in return*, Charito 2.11.

ἀντιπῐφάσκω· ἀνταποδίδωμι, Hsch.

ἀντιπλᾰγιάζομαι, *to be placed athwart*, of bars in lattice-work, Lyd.*Mag.*3.37.

ἀντιπλάδη, ἡ, *substance* or *process for protecting walls from damp*, *Ath.Mitt.*26.110.

ἀντίπλαστος, ον, lit. *similarly formed*; generally, *like*, νόμος S.*Fr.*284.

ἀντιπλέκω, *intertwine*, in Pass., Gal.18(2).748; of crossed or reversed bandaging, Sor.*Fasc.*12.513 C.

ἀντιπλεονεκτέω, *have equal precedence* or *privilege*, ἐν τῷ οὐρανῷ τό τε μέσον αὐτοῦ καὶ τὸ πέριξ Simp.*in Cael.*515.5; *have respective advantages over each other*, Id.*in Cat.*335.1, Elias *in Cat.*98.1:—hence **-ησις**, εως, ἡ, Simp.*in Cat.*341.2.

ἀντίπλευρος, ον, *with its side opposite, parallel*, κῆπος Εὐβοίας S.*Fr.*24.4; ἀ. παριππεύειν Hld.10.29.

ἀντιπλέω, *sail against* an enemy, v.l. in Th.1.50 and 54; ἀ. ἀνέμοισιν Ps.-Phoc.113.

ἀντιπληκτίζω, *struggle with*, πρός τινα Tz. ad Lyc.930.

ἀντιπλήξ, ῆγος, ὁ, ἡ, *beaten by the waves*, ἀκταί S.*Ant.*592 (lyr.).

ἀντιπληρόω, *fill in turn* or *against*, τὰς ναῦς *man* them *against* the enemy, Th.7.69, etc.:—Med., ἀ. φιλοτησίαν πρός τινα *fill one's* cup in his honour, *pledge* him, Aristid.2.115 J. II. *fill up by new members*, ἀ. τάξεις ἐκ πολιτῶν X.*Cyr.*2.2.26; *replenish after exhaustion*, Thphr.*CP*1.13.3.

ἀντιπλήσσω, *strike in turn*, in Pass., Arist.*EN*1132^{b}29, *MM*1194^{a}33.

ἀντίπλοια, ἡ, *sailing close to the wind*: metaph. of a mixed constitution, dub. l. in Plb.6.10.7 (fort. -πνοια).

ἀντί-πνευσις, εως, ἡ, *opposite current of air*, Orib.9.20.3. **-πνέω**, of winds, *blow against*, πρός τι Arist.*Pr.*940^{b}34; ἀλλήλοις Thphr.*Vent.*53: impers., ἀντιπνεῖ, διὰ τὸ ἀντιπνεῖν Arist.*Mete.*370^{b}22. 2. *to be adverse* or *contrary*, Ph.1.593, Plu.*Cic.*32, Luc.*Nav.*7: metaph. of fortune, Plb.25.3.9, Clitomachus ap.Stob.4.41.29: c. dat., Luc.*Tox.*7. 3. trans., πνεῦμα ταῖς ναυσί Plu.2.309b. **-πνοή**, ἡ, = sq., Sch.A.R.4.820. **-πνοια**, ἡ, *conflicting wind*, τῷ βορέᾳ Thphr.*Vent.*28. 2. *contrary wind*, Ph.1.352, Hdn.5.4.11. **-πνοος**, ον, contr. **-πνους**, ουν, *caused by adverse winds*, ἀντιπνόους . . ἀπλοίας A.*Ag.*147 (lyr.); στάσις ἀ. Id.*Pr.*1087 (lyr.). Adv. -νόως Tz. ad Lyc.739.

ἀντίποδες, οἱ, v. ἀντίπους.

ἀντιποθέω, *long for in turn*, X.*Mem.*2.6.28 (Pass.).

ἀντιποι-έω, *do in return*, ταῦτα Pl.*Cri.*50e; ἀντ' εὖ ποιεῖν Id.*Grg.*520e; οἱ μὴ ἀντιποιοῦντες εὖ Arist.*Rh.*1397^{b}7; κακῶς μὲν πάσχοντας, ἀντιποιεῖν δὲ οὐ δυναμένους X.*An.*3.3.12, cf. ib.7; ἀ. κακῶς τὸν ἄρξαντα Muson.*Fr.*10p.56 H.; ἀ. τὸ αὐτό Arist.*EN*1138^{a}22:—Pass., *to have done to one in turn*, Lxx *Le.*24.19. II. Med. (aor. Pass. in Luc.*DMort.*29.2), c. gen., *exert oneself about* a thing, *seek after* it, ἀ. τῶν σπουδαίων Isoc.1.2; *lay claim to*, τῆς πόλεως Th.4.122; ἀρετῆς Isoc.6.7; τῆς τέχνης, τῶν νικητηρίων, Pl.*Men.*90d, *Phlb.*23a; τοῦ πρωτεύειν D.10.52; τῆς θαλάττης Antiph.190.11; τῶν ἐν τῇ Ἑλλάδι πραγμάτων D.Chr.11.62; οἱ Δωριεῖς ἀντιποιοῦνται τῆς τραγῳδίας Arist.*Po.*1448^{a}30: also c. inf., ἀ. ἐπίστασθαί τι *lay claim to* knowing.., Pl.*Men.*91c, cf. *Hp.Mi.*363a: c. acc., τὴν κληρονομίαν *Michel* 546.16 (Cappad., i B.C.). 2. *contend with* one *for* a thing, ἀ. τινὶ τῆς ἀρχῆς X.*An.*2.1.11, 2.3.23; more rarely τινὶ περί τινος ib.5.2.11; τινὸς πρός τινα Arr.*Epict.*1.29.9. 3. abs., *set up opposition*, Pl.*Prt.*336c, Arist.*Pol.*1314^{a}12; *maintain resistance*, Plb.2.9.5, 21.25.6. **-ησις**, εως, ἡ, *laying claim to*, τινός D.H.11.30, cf. S.E.*M.*6.27, *PLond.*2.251.25 (iv A.D.).

ἀντίποινα, τά, *requital, retribution*, ἀντίποιν' ὡς τίνης ματροφόνου δύας prob. in A.*Eu.*268; ἀντίποινά τινος πράσσειν, λαμβάνειν, to exact *retribution for*.., Id.*Pers.*476, S.*El.*592; ἀντίποιν' ἐμοῦ παθεῖν suffer *retribution for* me, Id.*Ph.*316, cf. Nech. in *Cat.Cod.Astr.*7.145.—In codd. sts. written ἀντάποινα, q. v. Later in sg., as Lib.*Decl.*43.69.

ἀντίποινος, ον, *for recompense*, Lyc.271. 2. *in substitution*, Id.1201.

ἀντιπολεμέω, *wage war against*, Th.3.39: c. dat., Pl.*Criti.*112e, X.*Cyr.*7.2.24: c. acc., Lxx *Is.*41.12:—Pass., *to be warred against*, D.C.38.40.

ἀντιπολέμιος, ον, *warring against*, οἱ ἀντιπολέμιοι *enemies*, Th.3.90 codd. (but -πόλεμοι Poll.1.150); in Hdt.4.134, 140, codd. vary between ἀντιπόλεμοι and -μιοι; but in 7.236, 8.68.β' ἀντιπόλεμοι occurs without v.l., and is the only form cited by Hsch., cf. Onos.10.9, al.

ἀντιπολίζω, *build up as an opposing city*, ἑαυτόν J.*BJ*5.2.4.

ἀντιπολιορκέω, *besiege in turn*, τόπον Th.7.28; τινά Plu.*Marc.*7:—Pass., J.*BJ*3.7.19.

ἀντίπολις, εως, ἡ, *rival city*, τινί Str.3.5.3, v.l. in D.S.11.81.

ἀντιπολῑτ-εία, ἡ, *political opposition*, τινὶ πρός τινα Plb.20.5.5, cf. Plu.*Caes.*11. II. in pl., *opposite parties*, Plb.11.25.5. **-εύομαι**, *to be a political opponent*, Arist.*Pol.*1274^{a}14; οἱ -όμενοι *the opposite party*, Din.1.97: in sg., *political opponent*, Cic.*Att.*7.8.5: metaph., ὁ φθόνος ταῖς πράξεσιν ἀ. Aristonym.ap.Stob.3.38.36; ἀ. τινι Plu.*Them.*19, *Per.*8.

ἀντιπονέομαι, *exert oneself in opposition*, App.*BC*5.33.

ἀντίπονον, τό, *return for labour, wages*, Iamb.*VP*5.22.

ἀντιπορεία, ἡ, *marching against*, Ascl.*Tact.*10.2, Ael.*Tact.*25.1.

ἀντιπορεῖν, aor. with no pres. in use, *give instead*, *APl.*5.341.

ἀντιπορεύομαι, *march to meet* another, X.*HG*7.3.5.

ἀντιπορθέω, *ravage in return*, E.*Tr.*359, Lyc.1398.

ἀντίπορθμος, ον, *over the straits*, ἠπείροιν δυοῖν πεδία plains *on opposite sides of the straits*, E.*Ion* 1585; Πελοπίας χθονὸς ἐν ἀντιπόρθμοις *in the parts opposite* Peloponnesus, Id.*Fr.*515, cf. Arist.*Mu.*392ᵇ23, Lyc.1071 : c. dat., Str.8.6.21.

ἀντιπορνόβοσκος, ὁ, title of a comedy by Dioxippus, Ath.3.100e.

ἀντίπορος, ον, = ἀντίπορθμος, *on the opposite coast,* ἐς ἀ. γείτονα χώραν, i.e. Europe, as separated by a strait from Asia, A.*Pers.*66, cf. *Supp.*544, E.*Med.*210; Ἄρτεμιν Χαλκίδος ἀντίπορον, i.e. her temple at Aulis *over against* Chalcis in Euboea, Id.*IA*1494 (all lyr. passages): —in X.*An.*4.2.18 τὸν ἀ. λόφον τῷ μαστῷ, simply, *over against, opposite to.*

ἀντίπορπος, ἡ, *seton* for keeping incision open, *Hippiatr.*24,26.

ἀντίπους, ὁ, ἡ, πουν, τό, gen. οδος, *with the feet opposite,* στὰς ἀ., of one *at the Antipodes,* Pl.*Ti.*63a; so ἀ. ἔσται πορευόμενος ἕκαστος αὐτὸς αὑτῷ Arist.*Cael.*308ᵇ20, cf. Eratosth.16.19; οἱ ἀ. *the Antipodes,* Str. 1.1.13, Cleom.1.2, Cic.*Acad.Pr.*2.39.123, Plu.2.869c.

ἀντι-πρακτικός, ή, όν, *counteracting,* M.Ant.2.1: Comp. -ώτερος Xenocr.ap.Orib.2.58.72. **-πραξις,** εως, ἡ, *counteraction, resistance,* Plb.6.17.8, D.H.11.53, Plu.*Publ.*11, Demetr.Lac.*Herc.*1012.71.

ἀντίπρᾱσις, εως, ἡ, *contract of sale executed by the purchaser, PLond. ined.*2227 (iv A.D.).

ἀντιπράσσω, Att. -ττω, Ion. **-πρήσσω,** *act against, seek to counteract,* τινί X.*Ath.*2.17, Alex.264 (Med.); πρός τι Arist.*Pol.*1320ᵃ6, etc. 2. abs., *act in opposition,* D.32.14; ὁ ἀντιπρήσσων, = ἀντιστασιώτης, Hdt.1.92; ἀ. τι *oppose* in any way, X.*HG*2.3.14; ἐάν τε ἀντιπράττῃ τις ἐάν τε μὴ συμπράττῃ Arist.*Rh.*1379ᵃ13; *conflict with, tell against* a theory, Demetr.Lac.*Herc.*1055.20:—Med., X. *Hier.*2.17.

ἀντιπρεσβεύ-ομαι, Med., *send counter-ambassadors,* Th.6.75, Luc. *Peregr.*16: c. dat., Paus.7.9.5:—Act. in Aristid.1.372 J., App.*Mith.* 87. **-τής,** οῦ, ὁ, = Lat. *pro legato, Gloss.*

ἀντιπρίασθαι [ῐ], aor., *buy in return, SIG*²861 (Delph.).

ἀντιπρο-αίρεσις, εως, ἡ, *mutual preference,* πρὸς ἀλλήλους Arist.*EE* 1236ᵇ3. **-βάλλομαι,** *propose instead of* another, τὸν ἕτερον Pl.*Lg.* 755d:—Act., Gal.19.64. **-βολή,** ἡ, *proposing instead of* another, Pl.*Lg.*755e, 756a (cj.). **-εῖδον,** aor. 2, *recognize before meeting,* ἀλλήλους Ph.2.544. **-ειμι,** (εἶμι *ibo*) *come forward against* or *to meet,* τινί Th.6.66: abs., App.*Pun.*107. **-ηγέομαι,** *precede instead of following, EM*462.35, Hdn.Gr.2.394. **-θυμέομαι,** *to be hostilely disposed,* Aen.Tact.11.1.

ἀντίπροικα, Adv. *for next to nothing, cheaply,* X.*Ages.*1.18, Poll. 7.10.

ἀντιπροικῷον, τό, *compensation, PFlor.*294.74 (vi A.D.).

ἀντιπρο-ΐσχομαι, *hold out before one, present,* as weapons, ἡ λύπη ἀ. τὰ ἄμαχα κέντρα τῆς φύσεως Them.*Or.*32.357b:—Hsch. has the Act. ἀντιπροΐσχειν· ἀντιδοῦναι. **-κᾰλέομαι,** Med., *retort a legal challenge* (πρόκλησις), D.37.43; *challenge in turn,* c. acc. et inf., D.H. 15.8. **-καταληπτέον,** *one must reply to an anticipation,* Arist.*Rh.Al.* 1433ᵇ1. **-κλησις,** εως, ἡ, *retorting of a* πρόκλησις, Hsch. **-πίνω** [ῑ], *drink in turn,* αἷμα ἀλλήλοις J.*BJ*5.10.4. II. *present in return* (cf. προπίνω I. 2), ἀοιδάς Dionys.Eleg.1; τὰ ὅμοια Ath.4.128a.

ἀντιπροσ-ᾰγορεύω, *return salute,* Plu.*Crass.*3 (in aor. -ευσα):— but in earlier Prose, aor. 2 ἀντιπροσεῖπον Thphr.*Char.*15.3:—Pass., ἀντιπροσερρήθην X.*Mem.*3.13.1. **-άγω** [ᾰγ], *adduce on the other side,* τι πρός τινα Phld.*Rh.*1.377 S. **-αμάομαι,** Med., *heap in turn,* ἀ. τὴν γῆν *scrape up new* soil *upon,* X.*Oec.*17.13. **-βάλλομαι,** Pass., *to be impinged upon in return,* Hierocl.p.23 A. **-ειμι,** (εἶμι *ibo*) *march against,* X.*Cyr.*3.3.24. **-εἶπον,** v. ἀντιπροσαγορεύω. **-ελαύνω,** intr., *charge against,* of cavalry, D.C.46.37. **-έρχομαι,** *come to meet,* τινί Id.60.6. **-κᾰλέομαι,** Med., *summon in turn,* D.47. 45. **-κρίνω** [ῑ], *join instead,* Alex.Aphr.*de An.*134.32:—Pass., *to be added to in exchange,* c. dat., Id. *in Sens.*57.2. **-κῠνέω,** *fall down and worship in turn,* Plu.2.1117c. **-οψις,** εως, ἡ, *appearing instead,* glossed by ὁμηρεία, Suid., Zonar. **-φέρω,** *bring near in turn,* λύχνον τινί X.*Smp.*5.9. **-φθέγγομαι,** *accost in return,* Ph. 1.36. **-ωπος,** ον, *with the face towards, facing,* τοῖς πολεμίοις X. *Cyr.*7.1.25, cf. Aen.Tact.22.11; *face to face,* ἀντιπρόσωποι μαχόμενοι X.*HG*6.5.26; φιλήματα *AP*12.251 (Strat.); of images, *reflected,* Phlp.*Sens.*52,53; of winds, *blowing in a contrary direction, Placit.* 4.1.1. Adv. -πως Arist.*Mir.*835ᵇ11, Steph. *in Hp.*1.95 D., al. II. Subst. -ωπον, τό, *prow,* Artem.2.23, 4.24.

ἀντιπρό-τᾰσις, εως, ἡ, *counter-proposition,* Hermog.*Inv.*3.4, Steph. *in Int.*24.1. **-τείνω,** *hold out in turn,* τὴν δεξιάν X.*HG*4.1.31; ἱκετηρίας D.H.8.19 codd. 2. *propose in turn,* D.C.48.11 (Med.). 3. *adduce on the other side,* Gal.10.112. **-τίθημι,** *publish, post up in opposition,* γράμματα D.C.65.1. **-φέρω,** in Med., *adduce in reply,* Demetr.Lac.*Herc.*1012.49.

ἀντίπρῳρος, ον, *with the prow towards,* ἀ. τοῖσι βαρβάροισι γενόμενοι Hdt.8.11; τοὺς ἔσπλους ταῖς ναυσὶν ἀντιπρῴροις κλῄειν Th.4.8; [ἐμβολαῖς] μὴ ἀντιπρῴροις χρῆσθαι not to charge *prow to prow,* Id.7.36; τὸ ἀ. ξυγκροῦσαι ibid.; ἀ. ἐμβάλλεσθαι ib.34; τῶν πολεμίων ἀ. ἐφορμούντων Id.8.75; of ships, *ready for action,* ib.53; ἀ. καταστῆσαι τὰς τριήρεις X.*HG*6.2.28; τὸ στράτευμα ἀ. ὥσπερ τριήρη προσῆγε ib.7.5. 23. 2. *face to face,* τάδ' ἀντίπρῳρα..βλέπειν πάρεστ' S.*Tr.*223 (lyr.); κατ' ἀντίπρῳρα ναυστάθμων *in front of* them, E.*Rh.*136 (lyr.); ὀργῆς ἀντιπρῴρου κυλινδουμένης Plu. *de Ira Fr.*27 B.

ἀντιπταίω, *obstruct, stand in the way,* πρός τι Onos.17.

ἀντί-πτωμα, ατος, τό, *stumble against,* Lxx *Si.*34(31).29; *accident,* Ptol. *Tetr.*116, Paul.Al.*N.*3b. **-πτωσις,** εως, ἡ, *opposition, resistance,* Hp.*Decent.*3 (pl.). II. Gramm., *interchange of cases,* Priscian. *Inst.*17.155, Sch.Ar.*V.*135. **-πτωτικός,** ή, όν, *of* or *belonging to* ἀντίπτωσις II, Anon.*Fig.*p.151 S. Adv. -κῶς *with such interchange,* Eust.29.39.

ἀντίπῡγος, ον, *rump to rump,* Arist.*HA*540ᵃ14, 542ᵃ16. 2. c. gen., *turned away from,* λιμὴν ἀ. λιμένος Scyl.46, cf. 108.

ἀντιπυκτεύω, *wrestle against,* τῷ ἔρωτι Sch.S.*Tr.*441.

ἀντίπῠλος, ον, *with the gates opposite,* ἀλλήλῃσι Hdt.2.148.

ἀντίπυργος, ον, *like a tower* or *fort,* E.*Ba.*1097. II. Subst. ἀ., ὁ, *repository, cupboard,* ἀ. ξύλινοι Lib.*Or.*11.254.

ἀντιπυργόω, *build a tower over against,* c. acc. cogn., πόλιν τήνδ' ἀντεπύργωσαν *reared up* this *rival* city, i.e. the Areopagus as a rival to the Acropolis, A.*Eu.*688.

ἀντιπυρσεύω, (πυρσός) *return signals,* Plb.8.28.3, 10.46.1.

ἀντιρρέπω, *counterpoise, balance,* A.*Ag.*574; τινί Hp.*Art.*4: metaph., *vacillate,* ὥσπερ ἐπὶ πλάστιγγος Ph.2.170, etc.

ἀντιρρέω, *flow* or (of wind) *blow contrariwise,* Poll.1.111.

ἀντιρρήγνῡμι, *break opposite ways,* Plu.2.1005b.

ἀντί-ρρησις, εως, ἡ, *gainsaying, altercation,* ἀ. γίγνεταί τινι πρός τινα περί τινος Plb.2.7.7; *controversy,* Gal.*Phil.Hist.*24 D.; *refutation of,* D.S.1.38, J.*Ap.*2.1, Hermog.*Id.*1.8, Gal.1.131; *counter-statement, POxy.*68.11 (ii A.D.); *reply,* Phld.*Rh.*1.384 S., al., *Sign.*7, cf. 11. **-ρρητέον,** *one must speak against,* Pl.*Plt.*297b. **-ρρητικός,** ή, όν, *controversial,* λόγος S.E.*P.*1.21. Adv. -κῶς, ἔχειν πρός τινας Steph. *in Hp.*1.72 D.

ἀντιρρητορεύω, *speak against, dispute with,* τινί Max.Tyr.9.3.

ἀντίρρῑνον, τό, *calf's snout, Antirrhinum Orontium,* Thphr.*HP* 9.19.2 (codd. -ριζον, cf. Hsch.), Dsc.4.130.

ἀντίρροια, ἡ, *back-current,* Thphr.*Vent.*53.

ἀντιρροπ-ή, ἡ, *counterpoise,* Hp.*Art.*38,39 (v.l. -ίη, as in Gal.18 (1).481). **-ία,** ἡ, in pl., τύχης ἀ. *vicissitudes* of fortune, Agath. *Praef.*p.134 D.

ἀντίρροπος, ον, like ἰσόρροπος, *counterpoising, compensating for,* τινός D.1.10; ἄγειν..λύπης ἀ. ἄχθος to balance the *counterpoising* weight of sorrow, S.*El.*120 (lyr.); Θεανοῖ..ἀ. *balancing* her, *weighing as much as..,* Antiph.26.24; κτῆμα πόνοις ἀ. Max.Tyr.6.6; ῥώμη πρὸς κίνδυνον ἀ. Pl.*Def.*412a. Adv. ἀντιρρόπως, πράττειν τινί *so as to balance* his power, X.*HG*5.1.36: also neut. pl. as Adv., ψυχὰς δ' ἀντίρροπα θέντες *as a counterpoise, IG*1.442. 2. like ἀντίζυγος, *equivalent to,* c. dat., X.*Oec.*3.15.

ἀντίρρους, ουν, *flowing directly opposite to,* Νείλῳ Str.11.2.2.

ἀντίρρωται· ἀποπέμπεται, Hsch.

ἀντίς, (ἀντί) *opposite,* c. gen., *POxy.*941.4 (vi A.D.).

ἀντῐσάζω, *to be equal with, compensate,* c. gen., Sch.E.*Alc.*859.

ἀντισέβομαι, *revere in turn,* Epicur.*Fr.*141.

ἀντισεμνύνομαι [ῡ], Med., *meet pride with pride,* Arist.*Pol.*1314ᵃ 7. II. Act., *extol in return,* Eust.1563.40.

ἀντισήκ-ος, ον, *compensating, equivalent,* χάρις Eust.1075.8. **-όω,** *counterbalance, compensate for,* c. dat. rei, ὡς τοῖσδε (sc. κακοῖς) δὶς ἀντισηκῶσαι A.*Pers.*437: c. gen., ἀντισηκώσας δέ σε φθείρει θεῶν τις τῆς πάροιθ' εὐπραξίας some god ruins thee, *making compensation for, balancing,* thy former happiness, E.*Hec.*57, cf. D.S.31.12: c. acc., τιμαῖς ἀντισηκώσω χάριν I *will compensate* the favour by honours, Luc.*Trag.*243; *support by way of compensation,* τινά Hp.*Acut.*29, cf. *Art.*6:—Pass., ἡ ὠφέλεια πολλαῖς ὀδύναις -οῦται Simp. *in Epict.* p.27 D. **-ωμα,** ατος, τό, *equipoise, compensation, PSI*238.10 (vi/vii A.D.), Eust.546.24. **-ωσις,** εως, Ion. ιος, ἡ, = foreg., ἀ. γίνεται Hdt.4.50; *equivalence,* Plot.1.4.14.

ἀντισημαίνω, *give a countersign,* J.*AJ*19.1.10. II. *give hostile signs,* τοῖς βαρβάροις ἀντεσήμαινε τὰ ἐκ τοῦ θεοῦ Paus.10.23.1.

ἀντισήπω, *make to putrefy in turn,* Gal.11.608.

Ἀντισθέν-ειοι, οἱ, *followers of Antisthenes,* Arist.*Metaph.*1043ᵇ24; ὁ Ἀ. Ἡρακλῆς, referring to a book *by A.,* Plu.2.536b. **-ισμός,** ὁ, *a way of life according to the teaching of Antisthenes,* Jul.*Or.*6.187c.

ἀντίσιγμα, ατος, τό, *sigma reversed,* as a critical mark, D.L.3.66, Sch.Od.5.247. 2. *symbol for ps,* Priscian.*Inst.*1.42.

ἀντισιωπάω, *to be silent in turn,* Ar.*Lys.*528.

ἀντισκαιωρέω, *lay snares for,* τινά Tz.*H.*3.256.

ἀντισκευάζομαι, Med., *furnish for oneself in opposition,* τὸν οἶκον X.*Ages.*8.6:—Pass., Ph.*Bel.*92.11.

ἀντίσκηνος, ον, *opposite the stage-buildings,* prob. sc. στοά, *Ephes.* 2.41 (iii A.D.).

ἀντίσκιος, ον, *throwing a shadow the opposite way,* Ach.Tat.*Intr. Arat.*31, Vett.Val.142.28, Jul.*Or.*4.147c; ζόφον..ἀ. Ἠοῦς Nonn.*D.* 7.311.

ἀντισκόροδον, τό, = σκόροδον τὸ Κύπριον, Plin.*HN*19.112.

ἀντισκοτ-έω, *obstruct,* τῷ δικαίῳ S.E.*M.*2.78. **-ησις,** εως, ἡ, *obstruction, Gloss.*

ἀντισκώπτω, *mock in return,* Plu.*Tim.*15, *Ant.*24:—Pass., *take a gibe in return for one's own,* ἡδέως D.C.66.11.

ἀντῐσόομαι, Pass., *oppose on equal terms,* Th.3.11.

ἀντισοφ-ίζομαι, *use counter-devices,* πρός τι Arist.*Pol.*1297ᵃ36: abs., Ph.1.364. **-ιστεύω,** = foreg., τῷ θείῳ λόγῳ Id.1.449, cf. Numen.ap.Eus.*PE*14.8. **-ιστής,** οῦ, ὁ, *one who seeks to refute,* c. gen., μαγγανείας Luc.*Alex.*43, cf. *Cal.*16.

ἀντί-σπασις, εως, ἡ, *revulsion,* esp. of bodily humours, Hp.*Hum.*1, *Vict.*2.56, Gal.10.315, etc. **-σπασμα,** ατος, τό, in war, *distraction, diversion,* Plb.2.18.3, D.S.20.86, J.*AJ*19.1.10; ἀ. τῆς φυγῆς Ph.1. 549. II. *cause of dissension,* J.*AJ*17.2.4. **-σπασμός,** ὁ, *convulsion,* Ar.*Lys.*967. II. *counter-movement* (ebb and flow), of the sea, *Placit.*3.17.7. **-σπαστέον,** *one must draw off by another out-*

let, Hp.Vict.4.90, Gal.16.153. **-σπαστικός**, ή, όν, able to draw back, retractile, Arist.HA638^{a}31. II. revulsive, βοηθήματα Gal. 17(1).907. Adv. -κῶς Id.11.305. III. in Metric, antispastic, Heph.10,al. **-σπαστος**, ον, drawn in the contrary direction, νεφέλαι πνεύμασιν ἀ. Orph.H.21.5. 2. spasmodic, convulsive, ὀστέων ἀδαγμὸς ἀ. S.Tr.770. II. ἀντίσπαστος (sc. πούς), ὁ, in Prosody, antispast, a foot made up of an iambus and trochee, ⏑ – – ⏑, Heph. 3, Aristid.Quint.1.22. 2. = ἀντίφθογγος, ἀντίσπαστα μέλη Phryn. Trag.11; ἀντίσπαστα ἐφυμνεῖ πηκτίδος συγχορδίᾳ S.Fr.412 (unless 'doubly twanged', of an instrument with two registers). III. ἀντίσπαστον· φιλήματος ὄνομα, Hsch. IV. Subst. -σπαστος, ὁ, tackle, pulley-rope, Ath.Mech.9.13, al. **-σπάω**, draw the contrary way, hold back, ἀ. ὁρμώμενον A.Pr.339; τοὺς μὲν τείνειν τοὺς δ' ἀ. Ar. Pax493, cf. Luc.Cat.4; opp. σπάω, Arist.HA542^{a}15, al.:—Pass., suffer a check, Id.Rh.1409^{b}21; to be drawn in a contrary direction, Epicur.Ep.2p.53U., Ph.2.171: metaph., περίοδοι -σπώμεναι dragging, Phld.Rh.2.95S. 2. draw to itself, X.Cyn.5.1; εἰς αὑτό Arist. Pr.929^{a}39:—Med., draw over to one's own side, Plb.22.10.14. II. intr., = ἀντέχομαι, seize, c. gen., A.R.2.598.

ἀντισπεύδω, oppose eagerly, contend against, πρός τινα Antipho 1.7; τοῖς ἐπιθυμήμασί τινος D.C.59.13.

ἀντισπόδιον, τό, (σποδός) substitute for [mineral] ashes, vegetable ashes, Orib.15.1.27(36), Gal.12.234:—also **ἀντίσποδον**, Dsc.1.109, 5.75.

ἀντισπουδάζω, = ἀντισπεύδω, τινί D.C.40.55.

ἀντισπουδία, ἡ, opposite exertion, Oenom.ap.Eus.PE5.24.

ἀντιστᾰδιαῖος, α, ον, a furlong long, i.e. enormous, Sch.Od.12.90.

ἀντισταθμ-άω, = ἀντισηκόω, Sm.Jb.28.19:—in Med., Eust.1875.8. **-ησις**, εως, ἡ, = ἀντισήκωσις, Id.1625.27, Sch.Od.4.612. **-ίζω**, = ἀντισηκόω, Incert.Jb.28.19. **-ος**, ον, (σταθμός) counterpoising, balancing, τινί Pl.Sph.229c; χρυσὸν ἀ. τῆς κεφαλῆς οὐκ ἐδέξαντο D.S. 5.29: metaph., in compensation for, ὡς πατὴρ ἀ. τοῦ θηρὸς ἐκθύσειε τὴν αὑτοῦ κόρην S.El.571.

ἀντιστᾰσ-ιάζω, form a party against, τινί X.An.4.1.27; οἱ ἀντιστασιάζοντες, = οἱ ἀντιστασιῶται, Id.Cyr.7.4.3; ἀ. πρὸς πάντα to offer opposition to.., D.C.37.54. **-ιαστής**, οῦ, ὁ, = ἀντιστασιώτης, J. BJ1.7.5, D.C.73.4, Fr.84.1. **-ιμος**, ον, sloping, Anon.Alch. p.26B. **-ιος**, ον, of equal weight: metaph., λόγοι Max.Tyr.4.1; τὸ ἀ. Id.39.1. **-ις**, εως, ἡ, counter-faction, στάσις καὶ ἀ. καὶ μάχη Pl.R.560a. II. opposition, αἰώνιος Ph.1.577; ἐπὶ τῇ ἀρχῇ J.AJ 17.11.2; τύχης Plu.Aem.36; ἐξ ἀ. ἀγωνίζεσθαι in pitched battle, Hdn. 5.4.4; ἴσην ἀ. ἔχειν weigh equally, Arist.Mu.397^{a}1. III. counter-plea, set-off, e.g. benefit conferred balanced against injury done, Hermog.Stat.2, cf. 6 (pl.), Arg.Lycurg. **-ιώτης**, ου, ὁ, one of the opposite faction or party, Hdt.1.92, 4.164, X.An.1.1.10, Aen.Tact. 11.7, etc.

ἀντιστᾰτέον, one must check, ταῖς κενώσεσι Philum.ap.Aët.9.6.

ἀντιστᾰτ-έω, = ἀνθίσταμαι, resist, oppose, esp. as a political partisan, Hdt.3.52; τινί Pl.Grg.513c, J.AJ18.9.2, cf. Ph.1.205, al.; πρός τι Plu.2.802b; trans., τῷ φόβῳ τὸ κλέος Lib.Vit.1.7. **-ης** [ᾰ], ου, ὁ, opponent, adversary, A.Th.518, Plu.2.1084b. II. vertical beam in plinth of torsion-engine, HeroBel.91.11. **-ικός**, ή, όν, of or for a counter-plea (cf. ἀντίστασις III), Hermog.Stat.5,10.

ἀντίστερνον, τό, the part of the spine opposite the breast, Sor.2.63 (pl.), Ruf.Anat.25.

ἀντιστήκω, = ἀνθίσταμαι, Hsch. s.v. ἀντεξάγω.

ἀντιστήρ-ιγμα, ατος, τό, a prop or support, Hp.Art.9,16: metaph., support, stay, Lxx Ps.17(18).18. **-ιγμός**, ὁ, blocking the way, resistance, ἀνακοπαὶ καὶ -μοί D.H.Dem.38; -μοὶ γραμμάτων Id.Comp. 16. **-ίζω**, press against, Hp.Art.47; offer resistance, Democr.9, Arist.Pr.940^{a}11.

ἀντιστίλβω, shine by reflection, Zen.3.8.

ἀντιστοιχ-είωσις, εως, ἡ, change of a letter, e.g. φιτρῶν for φυτρῶν, Sch.Il.12.29. **-έω**, stand opposite in rows or pairs, χοροὶ ἀντιστοιχοῦντες ἀλλήλοις X.An.5.4.12; ἀ. τινί stand vis-a-vis to a partner in a dance, Id.Smp.2.20. II. of letters, correspond, ἀ. τὰ δασέα τοῖς ψιλοῖς EM443.17. **-ία**, ἡ, standing opposite in pairs, τῶν ποδῶν Arist.Pr.894^{a}19; πραγμάτων Plu.2.474a. II. of letters, correspondence, of the relation of tenuis, media, and aspirate to each other, Ascl.Myrl.ap.Ath.11.501b. **-ος**, ον, ranged opposite in rows or pairs, Arist.IA708^{b}8, al. 2. standing over against, σκιὰ ἀντίστοιχος ὥς E.Andr.745; ἀντίστοιχα λέγων.. τούτοισι corresponding with, D.H.Rh.9.7. II. of letters, corresponding, as tenuis, media, and aspirate, A.D.Synt.55.14, cf. Fr.7b, D.T.631.27; also of vowels, Hdn.Epim.2; κατ' ἀντίστοιχον Lyd.Mag.1.7.

ἀντίστομος, ον, drawn up face to face, διφαλαγγία Ascl.Tact.11.3, cf. Ael.Tact.37.3, Arr.Tact.29.2, Hsch.

ἀντιστορέννῡμι, aor. 1 inf. ἀντιστρῶσαι, lay paving instead, SIG^2 587.48 (Eleusis).

ἀντιστοχαστικός, ή, όν, conjecturing in turn, Sch.D.8.17.

ἀντιστρᾰτεύομαι, take the field, make war against, τινί X.Cyr.8.8. 26:—later in Act., D.S.22.15, J.AJ2.10.1(abs.): metaph., Ἔρωτες ἀ. τοῖς ὑπερηφανοῦσι Aristaenet.2.1.

ἀντιστρᾰτηγ-έω, act against as general or (generally) make war against, τινί D.H.11.37; τοῖς ἐπιχειρήμασί τινων J.Vit.55, cf. Max. Tyr.41.3. **-ησις**, εως, ἡ, hostile manœuvre, Onos.32.9.

ἀντιστράτηγος [ρᾰ], ὁ, enemy's general, Th.7.86, D.H.6.5, Plu. Sert.12. II. at Rome, acting commander or governor, either pro consule, Plb.28.3.1, or pro praetore, D.C.41.43. 2. propraetor, i.e. governor of a province with rank of pro praetore, IG12(5).722 (Andros, ii B.C.). 3. lieutenant of a commander, Lat. legatus pro praetore, OGIii p.551 (Bargylia, ii B.C.), Plb.3.106.2, 15.4.4, Plu. Comp.Lys.Sull.4, etc.; in full, πρεσβευτὴς καὶ ἀ. J.AJ14.12.13; ἀντιταμίας καὶ ἀ. proquaestor pro praetore, OGI448 (i B.C.); πρεσβευτὴς Σεβαστοῦ ἀ., = Lat. legatus Augusti pro praetore, IGRom.3.186 (Ancyra, ii A.D.), etc.

ἀντιστρᾰτιώτης, ου, ὁ, soldier of the enemy, Gal.19.180, Chor. in Lib.4.522 Reiske.

ἀντιστρᾰτοπεδ-εία, ἡ, = sq., Plb.3.101.8. **-ευσις**, εως, ἡ, an encamping opposite, the position of two armies in sight of one another, D.C.78.26. **-εύω**, encamp over against, τινί Isoc.6.80, Plb.1.74. 13, Onos.10.19, etc. II. more freq. in Med., τινί Hdt.1.76: abs., Th.1.30: so pf. Pass., Id.4.124, X.HG7.4.13.

ἀντιστρεπτ-έος, α, ον, in Logic, to be converted, Arist.APr.51^a 23. II. one must reverse, τὴν δόξαν Plot.5.5.11. **-ος**, ον, that can be turned about: τὰ ἀ. machines that move on a pivot or swivel, D.S.20.91.

ἀντιστρέφω, pf. -έστροφα, turn to the opposite side:—Pass., to be turned in the opposite direction, μόχλος ἀντεστραμμένος reversed lever, Ph.Bel.59.25; turn and look at, Aristaenet.1.4: also c. acc., οὐδ' ἀ. ὃ λέγουσιν cast a glance at, Phld.Rh.1.245S. Adv. ἀντεστραμμένως Arist.IA712^{a}4. 2. intr., wheel about, face about, X. Ages.1.16. II. retort an argument, τοὺς λόγους Arist.Top.163^{a}30, cf. APr.59^{b}1; αἰτίας Procop.Pers.1.16. III. correspond, ἀλλήλοις Anon. in Tht.19.47. IV. in Logic, to be convertible, Arist. Cat.14^{b}11, al.; τὰ γένη κατὰ τῶν εἰδῶν κατηγορεῖται, τὰ δὲ εἴδη κατὰ τῶν γενῶν οὐκ ἀντιστρέφει are not conversely predicable of genera, ib. 2^{b}21: impers., ἀντιστρέφει the relation is reciprocal, Id.GC337^{b}23, cf. de An.423^{a}21, Pr.883^{b}8; περὶ ἀντιστρεφόντων λόγων καὶ συνημμένων complementary propositions, title of work by Chrysipp.; so of metaphors, Anon.Fig.p.228S. 2. most freq. in the doctrine of syllogism, of reduction by conversion of one of the premisses, Arist. APr.50^{b}25; either of the terms, τὸ Β τῷ Α ἀντιστρέφει the term B is convertible with A, ib.67^{b}30, al.; τὸ Γ πρὸς τὸ Α ἀ. ib.38; ἀ. τὸ καθόλου τῷ κατὰ μέρος ib.31^{a}27, al.; or of the propositions, ib.25^{a}8, al.; ἀ. καθόλου to be simply convertible, ib.28; ἀ. ἐπὶ μέρους, ἐν μέρει, κατὰ μέρος, ib.39^{a}15, 25^{a}8,10. 3. in Pass., of propositions, to be converted or changed into their opposites, Id.APr.45^{b}6, APo.80^{b}25, al. 4. to be interdependent, have a reciprocal nexus, τὰ μὲν οὖν ἀ.. καὶ ποιητικὰ ἀλλήλων καὶ παθητικὰ ὑπ' ἀλλήλων Id.GC328^{a}19: hence of cyclical argument, ἐν μόνοις τοῖς ἀ. κύκλῳ καὶ δι' ἀλλήλων (sc. αἱ ἀποδείξεις) Id. APr.58^{a}13, cf. APo.95^{b}40, GC337^{b}23. 5. generally, to be suited conversely for one or another purpose, ὁ τόπος ἀντιστρέφει πρὸς τὸ ἀνασκευάζειν καὶ κατασκευάζειν Id.Top.109^{b}25; ἀ. πρὸς ἄμφω ib.112^a 27, al. V. pf. part. Pass., conversely opposed, of concavities, facing one another, ἀντεστραμμένα πρὸς ἄλληλα Id.HA498^{a}8; but, back to back, Plb.6.32.6. 2. in Logic, converted, συλλογισμὸς -μμένος Arist.APr.44^{a}31; πρότασις ib.58^{a}1; ἀ. τῇ πάχνῃ ὁ εὐρὼς its converse, Id.GA784^{b}16; ἡ ἀ. πρόσθεσις Id.Ph.207^{a}23. 3. Adv. ἀντεστραμμένως inversely, ib.206^{b}5; conversely, PA684^{b}35, IA712^{a}4, al.: in Logic, opposedly, Id.Int.22^{a}34. VI. of lyrics, possess strophe and antistrophe, Aristid.Quint.1.29, Sch.Ar.Ach.1037, Sch.Heph. p.167C. VII. of grammatical construction, to be inverted, A.D. Synt.180.16, al.

ἀντιστροφ-ή, ἡ, a turning about: I. in choruses and dances, strophic correspondence, D.H.Comp.25; in later writers, = ἀντίστροφος, ἡ (q.v.), Sch.Ar.Nu.595, al. II. Rhet., repetition of closing words in successive members, Phld.Rh.1.195S., Hermog.Id.1.12, cf. 2.1, Eust.945.60; ἀ. τὸ ἐναντίον τῆς ἐπαναφορᾶς Alex.Fig.2.4. 2. inversion, of construction, e.g. ἠχῶν ἔπεσα for πεσὼν ἤχησα Phoeb. Fig.1.5. 3. Gramm., inversion of letters (e.g. ἀκήν, ἧκα), EM 424.8. III. inversion, κατὰ τὴν ἀ. τῆς ἀναλογίας in inverse ratio, Arist.Ph.266^{b}18:—in Logic, conversion of terms of a proposition, Id.APr.25^{a}40; ἀ. δέχεσθαι to be convertible, ib.50^{b}32. b. Math., τῶν θεωρημάτων ἡ ἀ. Procl. in Euc.p.251F., cf. Apollon.Perg.Con.2. 49; ἀ. προηγουμένη complete conversion, Procl. in Euc.p.253F.; ἀ. ἀξιωμάτων Stoic.2.64; generally, κατ' -φήν conversely, Metrod.Herc. 831.14. 2. retortion of an argument, Arist.APr.61^{a}22. 3. change of a proposition into its opposite, ib.38^{a}3, 39^{a}28. **-ος**, ον, turned so as to face one another: hence, correlative, co-ordinate, counterpart, Pl.Tht.158c, etc.; τινί to a thing, Id.Grg.464b, R.605a; ἡ ῥητορική ἐστιν ἀ. τῇ διαλεκτικῇ Arist.Rh.1354^{a}1, Pol.1293^{a}33, etc.; ἰατρικῇ ἀ. δικαιοσύνη Aristid.2.37J.; also τινός the correlative or counterpart of.., Pl.R.530d, Grg.465d, Isoc.5.61, etc.; ἀ... ὥσπερ Arist.Pol.1292^{b}7. Adv. -φως in a manner corresponding, τινί Pl.R. 539d; ἡ γλῶττα ὥσπερ -φως ἔχουσα τῷ μυκτῆρι being the counterpart of.., Arist.PA661^{a}27; συμβαίνει δ' ἀντιστρόφως the result follows by a reversible proof, Id.Ph.265^{b}8. 2. in Logic, converse, λόγος Phld.Rh.1.179S. Adv. -φως Id.Sign.6: also in Math., converse, θεώρημα Papp.970.20; τὰ ἀ. the converse proposition, Apollon.Perg.Con. 4.55. Adv. -φως conversely, ib.1.38, Max.Tyr.34.4. 3. contrary, opposed, τινός D.Chr.4.87; πρός τι Luc.Merc.Cond.31. Adv. -φως in the opposite way, Phld.Lib.p.31O., Ps.-Luc.Philopatr.18. II. that can be retorted, D.H.Rh.9.5 (as v.l., cf. ἀγχι-). III. ἐξ ἀντιστρόφου by an inverted construction (cf. ἀντιστροφή II. 2), Hdn.Fig. p.102S. IV. in lyrics, antistrophic, Arist.Pr.918^{b}27, etc.: esp. Subst. ἀντίστροφος (sc. ᾠδή), ἡ, antistrophe, Id.Rh.1409^{a}26, D.H. Comp.19, etc.; also of members in a rhet. period, ἐν στροφῇ καὶ ἀντιστρόφῳ Hermog.*Id.*1.11. V. f.l. for ἀμφίστροφος, *wheeling both ways*, A.*Supp.*882 codd. VI. *retorting* a charge, Procop.*Arc.* 17. VII. ἀντίστροφος, ἡ, = ἀπόστροφος Sch.Ar.*Pl.*3. 2. ἀντίστροφοι, name for the *two upper ribs*, Poll.2.182. VIII. Adv. -φως *crosswise*, τὰς χεῖρας ἀλλήλαις ἐπιβάλλειν Gal.*UP*5.14; *inversely*, Herod.Med.ap.Orib.10.5.4, cf. Diogenian.3.30.

ἀντισύγκλητος, ἡ, *counter-senate*, name given by Marius to his body-guard, Plu.*Mar.*35, *Sull.*8.

ἀντισυγκρίνω [ρῑ], *compare* one *with* another, Nicom.*Ar.*1.13:— Pass., ib.20, Charito6.1.

ἀντισυζῠγία, ἡ, = συζυγία, of signs rising and setting at the same point of the horizon, Gem.2.1.

ἀντισυλλογίζομαι, *answer by syllogism*, Arist.*Rh.*1402ᵃ31, al.

ἀντισυμβολ-έω, *give a counter-receipt*, *PFay.*73.1 (ii/iii A.D.), al. **-ον**, τό, *counter-receipt*, ib.73, al., *PGrenf.*2.23, *PLond.*1.15.3.

ἀντισυμβουλεύω, *give contrary advice*, Stob.2.6.2.

ἀντισυμμᾰχέομαι, Pass., *to be helped in return*, ὑπό τινος Longin. 17.1.

ἀντισυμποσιάζω, *write a Symposium in rivalry of* Plato, Luc. *Lex.*1.

ἀντισυν-ᾰλείφω, *anoint in return*, τὸν συναλείψαντα Phld.*Vit.* p.30J. **-αντάω**, *meet face to face*, *AP*12.227. **-άπτω**, *meet in opposite directions*, dub. in Gal.18(2).727.

ἀντισῡριγγιακός, ή, όν, *protecting against fistula*, κολλύριον Aët. 15.13.

ἀντισφαιρίζω, *play at ball against*, οἱ ἀντισφαιριοῦντες *parties about to play in a match*, X.*Lac.*9.5.

ἀντισφάττω, *slaughter in turn*, D.C.45.47 (in aor. 2 Pass.).

ἀντισφήν, ῆνος, ὁ, *counter-wedge* which drives out another, Ph.*Bel.* 67.32.

ἀντισφίγγω, ἔνθεν καὶ ἔνθεν ἀ. *form an obstacle by tension*, Hp.*Art.*3.

ἀντισφράγισμα, ατος, τό, *sealed copy*, *SIG*785.12 (Chios).

ἀντισχηματ-ίζω, *meet one figure by another*, D.H.*Rh.*9.14. **-ισμός**, ὁ, *the use of such figures in turn*, ibid.

ἀντισχῡρίζομαι, Med., *to be stiff in maintaining a contrary opinion*, Th.3.44; πρός τι Plu.2.535e.

ἀντίσχῡρος, ον, *strong to resist*, Hsch.

ἀντισχύω, fut. -ύσω [ῡ], *repel by force*, Lxx *Wi.*7.30, D.C.48.11.

ἀντίσχω, = ἀντέχω (q.v.), Hp.*Fract.*11, S.*Ph.*830 (lyr.), Th.1.7 [codd. often confuse -ίσχων, -ισχών].

ἀντισῴζω, *preserve in turn*, Anon.ap.Suid. s.v. δυσκλεές, Aristid. 1.418J.

ἀντίσωσις [ῐσ], εως, ἡ, *equalization*, Iamb.*Protr.*21.ιθ'.

ἀντί-ταγμα, ατος, τό, *opposing force*, D.S.11.67, Plu.*Cleom.*23; of a person, 'a political force', *Nic.*2, *Luc.*38. **-τακτέον**, (ἀντιτάσσω) *one must array against*, τι πρός τι Id.2.127f. 2. (from Pass.) *one must make resistance*, πρός τινα Arist.*Top.*134ᵃ4. **-τακτικός**, ή, όν, *fit for resistance*, πρός τι Plu.2.759e. **-τακτος**, ον, *contrary, opposed*, τῶν πραγμάτων ἐχόντων τι -ον Hierocl.p.60A.

ἀντιτᾰλαντεύω, = ἀντισηκόω, *APl.*4.221 (Theaet.); *put into the opposite scale*, Lib.*Decl.*43 *Intr.*2.

ἀντιτάλαντον· ἀντίσταθμον, ἴσον, Hsch.

ἀντιτᾰμίας, ου, ὁ, = Lat. *pro quaestore*, *SIG*745 (Rhodes, i B.C.), J. *AJ*14.12.13, D.C.41.43, etc., prob. in *IG*14.356 (Halaesa); cf. ἀντιστράτηγος.

ἀντίταξις, εως, ἡ, *a setting in array against*, ἡ σφετέρα ἀ. τῶν τριήρων their ships *ranged for battle*, Th.7.17; ἀ. ποιεῖσθαι πρός τινα, = ἀντιτάσσεσθαι, Id.5.8, cf. Phld.*Piet.*12; *contest*, of bulls fighting, Hierocl. p.11A. 2. generally, *opposition*, D.H.10.57, Plu.2.663b, Andronic. Rhod.p.572M.

ἀντιτᾰράττω, *stir up in opposition*, Max.Tyr.14.7.

ἀντίτᾰσις, εως, ἡ, (ἀντιτείνω) *stretching the contrary way*, e.g. in the setting of a dislocated limb, Hp.*Art.*75. 2. *opposition, resistance*, πᾶσαν ἀ. ἀντιτείνειν Pl.*Lg.*781c.

ἀντιτάσσω, Att. -ττω, *set opposite to, range in battle against*, τὸ ἄριστον ἀ. Πέρσῃσι Hdt.5.110; τίν' ἀντιτάξεις τῷδε; A.*Th.*395, cf. 408, etc.; ἀ. τὸν νόμον πρὸς τὴν ἀναίδειαν *set* the law *in opposition to* their impudence, Aeschin.3.16, cf. Isoc.9.61, etc.:—so in Med., πρὸς τὸ ἐμπειρότερον αὐτῶν τὸ τολμηρότερον ἀντιτάξασθε Th.2.87; τῶν Ἑλλήνων τινὰ ἀρετὴν τῇ Ξέρξου δυνάμει ἀντιτάξασθαι Id.3.56. II. Med., *set oneself against, meet face to face*, ἀντιτάξομαι κτενῶν σε E.*Ph.*622, cf. Th.4.55, etc.; περὶ τῶν πρωτείων ἡμῖν ἀντιτάξασθαι D.3.27:—Pass., *to be drawn out in array against*, τινί Hdt.4.134, X.*HG*3.1.6; πρὸς τὸ διπλήσιον Hdt.7.103; πόλιν -ομένην πρὸς πόλιν X.*Cyr.*3.1.18, etc.; κατά τινας Id.*HG*4.2.18; τὸ ἀντιτετάχθαι ἀλλήλοις τῇ γνώμῃ Th.3.83: abs., dub. in E.*Supp.*1144. 2. generally, *oppose, resist*, Plb.31. 25.8, *Act.Ap.*18.6, *Ep.Rom.*13.2, etc. 3. *set against, compare*, Lxx *Pr.*3.15 (Pass.).

ἀντιταφρεύω, *dig a trench in opposition*, Ph.*Bel.*93.26.

ἀντιτείνω, fut. -τενῶ Pl.*R.*604a (v.l.):—*stretch, strain back*, εἰς τοὔπισθεν τὰ σπαρτία Arist.*Pr.*888ᵃ20; τὰς ἡνίας Plu.2.13d. 2. *stretch out* or *offer in return*, νήπι' ἀντὶ νηπίων E.*Med.*891. II. intr., *act* or *strive against, resist*, ἐπιβουλίᾳ Pi.*N.*4.37; τινί Hdt.7.161, Pl.*R.*547b, etc.; παντὶ λόγῳ Id.*Phd.*91c; πρός τι *Phdr.*256a, Arist. *EN*1126ᵇ15 (πρός = *with respect to*): abs., Hdt.7.219, S.*Ant.*714, etc.; οὐκ ἀντέτεινον, ἀλλ' εἶκον Hdt.8.3; ὑπείκει καὶ οὐκ ἀ. Pl.*Lg.*727d; δύο ἄνδρες ἀντιτείνοντες *pulling one against the other*, Hp.*Fract.*15. 2. of countries and places, *lie over against*, τινι Plu.*Them.*8.

ἀντιτειχ-ίζω, *erect counter-fortifications*, πρὸς τὰς μηχανάς J.*AJ*14. 16.2; trans., *fortify instead*, τὸ καταρριφθὲν τοῖς σώμασι Id.*BJ*5.8.2: metaph., τῷ τέλει τῆς ἡδονῆς Ph.1.426 (Pass.). **-ισμα**, ατος, τό, *counter-fortification*, Th.2.77, Ath.13.602d (pl.).

ἀντιτέμνω, *cut against*, i.e. *as a remedy* or *antidote*, φάρμακα.. ἀντιτεμὼν βροτοῖσι E.*Alc.*972 (lyr.).

ἀντιτέρπω, *delight in return*, Plu.2.334a (Pass.).

ἀντιτεταγμένως, Adv. pf. part. Pass. of ἀντιτάσσω, *in the opposite sense*, τῷ ποιεῖν Plot.5.3.15.

ἀντίτευχος, (gend. uncertain), name of a *throw at dice*, Eub.57.3.

ἀντιτεύχω, *make in opposition*, ἀντιτέτυκτο Antim.35 codd.

ἀντιτεχν-άζω, *use art in turn*, D.H.*Rh.*9.5:—also in Med., πρός τι J.*AJ*1.19.8. **-άομαι**, *contrive in opposition, counter-plan*, τάδε Hdt.5.70; τινί Max.Tyr.32.9: abs., Plu.*Sert.*18; πρός τι J.*AJ*14. 16.2. **-έω**, *to be a rival in art*, Sch.Ar.*V.*1402. **-ησις**, εως, ἡ, *counter-manœuvring, emulation*, Th.7.70, D.H.14.10. **-ίτης**, ου, ὁ, *professional rival*, Gal.5.655. **-ος**, ον, *rival in an art* or *craft*, Ar.*Ra.* 816, Pl.*R.*493a, etc.; οὐκ ἐκείνῳ οὐδὲ τοῖς ποιήμασιν αὐτοῦ Id.*Phd.* 60d, cf. *Lg.*817b; ἀ. καὶ ὁμότεχνος τοῖς ποιηταῖς D.Chr.12.46: c. gen., τῆς μαγγανείας αὐτοῦ Luc.*Alex.*43.

ἀντιτηρέω, *maintain in turn*, Arr.*Epict.*2.20.14.

ἀντιτίθημι (pres. part. -τιθοῦντας Ps.-Callisth.1.29), *set against* or *so as to oppose*, θαλασσαίαισι δίναις ἀντιθέντα μένος στάλας Simon.57 (dub.). b. *set against so as to balance, contrast*, or *compare*, τῶυτὸ ἀντιθήσω ἐκείνῳ Hdt.1.207, cf. 8.66; δύο γὰρ ἀντίθες δυοῖν E.*Or.*551: also c. gen., ἀ. τὴν Ἀθηναίων ἐκ πολλοῦ ἐμπειρίαν τῆς σφετέρας ἐξ ὀλίγου μελέτης Th.2.85, cf. 3.56: with a Prep., ἀ. τι πρός τι D.21.175:— Pass., *to be contrasted*, τινί or πρός τι, Pl.*Sph.*257d, 258e. 2. ἀ. τινί τινα *match* one *against* the other *in battle*, ἴσους ἴσοισι.. ἀντιθεὶς E.*Ph.* 750, cf. Ar.*Eq.*353:—Pass., *to be matched* one *against* another, of counteracting tendencies, Hdt.4.50; of opposing motives, Id.8. 83. 3. *retort, rejoin*, ἀντίθες παρρησίᾳ ὅπως.. E.*El.*1049; ἀντιθεῖσ' ἀμείψομαι Id.*Tr.*917; ἀ. ὅτι.. Th.6.18. 4. intr., *oppose, resist*, πρὸς τὸν Δία Arr.*Epict.*3.24.24, etc. II. *place* or *deposit in return*, ἀντιθέντας ἐν ναοῖς ἢ χαλκὸν ἢ.. E.*Hipp.*620, cf. X.*Mem.*3.14.1; ἀ. τί τινος *give* one thing *for* another, τὴν ἐνθάδ' Αὖλιν ἀντιθεῖσα τῆς ἐκεῖ E. *IT*358.

ἀντιτῑμ-άω, *honour in return*, τινά X.*HG*3.1.13; τινὰ πᾶσι τοῖς καλοῖς Id.*Cyr.*5.2.11, etc.:—fut. Med. in pass. sense, Id.*Oec.*9.11. II. Med. as law-term, *make a counter-estimate of damages*, c. gen. pretii, Pl.*Ap.*36b, D.24.138. **-ημα**, ατος, τό, glossed by **-ησις**, εως, ἡ, Hsch.

ἀντίτῑμος, ον, *of equal worth*, Ἀθηνᾶ 20 p.163 (Chios), and **ἀντίτῑμα**· τὰ ἄποινα, τὰ ἀντέκτιτα, Hsch.

ἀντιτῑμωρ-έομαι, *avenge oneself on*, τινά E.*IT*357, Th.3.82, Plb.1. 81.9: abs., *revenge oneself, take vengeance*, Ar.*Pax*134, 626:—a fut. Pass. occurs in Sch.Lyc.1337. **-ημα**, ατος, τό, and **-ία**, ἡ, *vengeance, revenge*, ib.1297. **-ησις**, εως, ἡ, = foreg., Gal.6.138, al. **-ητέον**, dub. in Gal.*UP*2.8 codd. (misquoting Hp.*Acut.*37. β'). **-ητος**, η, ον, gloss on ἄντιτος, Eust.1346.3, Hsch.

ἀντιτίνω, fut. -τείσω, *suffer punishment for* a thing, τι Thgn.741: abs., S.*Aj.*1086: generally, *repay*, χάριτάς τινι Eust.142.15. II. Med., *exact* or *inflict in turn*, ἐμῆς ἀγωγῆς ἀντιτείσασθαι φόνον *exact* death *as a punishment for*.., A.*Ag.*1263; πόσιν δίκην (codd. δίκῃ) τῶνδ' ἀντιτείσασθαι κακῶν *exact* a penalty from him *for* these evil deeds, E.*Med.*261, cf. Lyc.1367. [On the quantity v. τίνω.]

ἀντίτιτος, v. ἄντιτος.

ἀντιτιτρώσκω, *wound in turn*, Sch.E.*Hipp.*507: plpf. Pass. ἀντετέτρωτο Hld.7.27.

ἀντίτοιχος, ον, *striking full on the bulwarks*, ἀκτίς Tim.*Pers.*12.

ἀντιτολμ-άω, *dare to stand against* another, abs., Th.2.89; πρὸς τολμηρούς Id.7.21. **-ος**, ον, *boldly attacking*, A.*Eu.*553 (lyr.).

ἀντίτομος, ον, (ἀντιτέμνω) *cut as a remedy for* an evil:—Subst. ἀντίτομον, τό, *remedy, antidote*, *h.Cer.*229, Hsch.; ἀντίτομα ὀδυνᾶν *antidotes for* pains, Pi.*P.*4.221. II. *having opposite curvatures for cutting*, Paul.Aeg.6.30.

ἀντιτονέομαι or **-όομαι**, Pass., *to have a different accent from*, τινί Eust.1025.4.

ἀντίτονος, ον, (ἀντιτείνω) *strained against, resisting*, Pl.*Ti.*62c; of a bow, *APl.*4.211.4 (Stat. Flacc.). 2. Subst. ἀντίτονα, τά, *guy-ropes* securing torsion-engines, Plu.*Marc.*15, Ph.*Bel.*99.47.

ἀντιτοξεύω, *shoot arrows in return*, X.*An.*3.3.15, Philostr.*Im.*1.6.

ἀντιτορ-έω, (cf. τετορεῖν) *bore right through*, c. gen., δόρυ χροὸς ἀντετόρησεν Il.5.337: c. acc., πυκινὸν δόμον ἀντιτορήσας *having broken* it *open*, ib.10.267, cf. *h.Merc.*178. **-ησις**, εως, ἡ, *piercing*, Eust. 672.30.

ἄντῑτος (by haplology for ἀντίτιτος, which occurs in Hsch.), ον, = παλίντιτος, *requited, revenged*, ἄ. ἔργα the work *of revenge*, Od.17. 51, 60; ἄ. ἔργα παιδός *revenge for* her son, Il.24.213, cf. Call.*Iamb.* 1.160.

ἀντίτρᾱγος, ὁ, (cf. τράγος) *the eminence of the external ear*, Aret. *CD*1.2, Poll.2.85, Ruf.ap.Orib.25.1.7.

ἀντιτρᾱχύνομαι [ῡ], Pass., *to be exasperated in turn*, πρός τινα Eust.467.9.

ἀντιτρέφω, *sustain, maintain in turn*, X.*Cyr.*8.3.38.

ἀντιτρίβω [ρῑ], *rub in return*, Plot.6.1.20 (Pass.).

ἀντιτρῡπάω, gloss on ἀντετόρησεν, Sch.Opp.*H*3.556.

ἀντιτυγχάνω, aor. -έτῠχον, *meet with in return*, τινός Simon.128, Thgn.1334; ἀ. ἐπικουρίας ἀπό τινος Th.6.87; ἀ. μάχας *fall into* quarrel, Pi.*N.*7.42; κρείττονος Prov.ap.Plb.15.16.6; ἀ. χοιράδος *hit* *upon* a rock, Opp.*H.*4.480; πλείστων ἀ. ἀέθλων *IG*4.682 (Hermione). **II.** ὁ ἀντιτυγχάνων *any chance person*, *GDI*1918, al. (Delph.). **2.** ἁ βωλὰ ἀντιτυχόνσα the council *for the time being*, *IG*4.554 (Argos); οἱ ἔφοροι.. ἀεὶ οἱ ἀντιτυγχάνοντες ib.5(1).1146 (Gythium, i B.C.), cf. 7.3080 (Lebad.), 5(2).266 (Mantinea, i B.C.), *Delph.*3(1).294 v 5.

ἀντιτυμπᾰνίζω, *beat drums in rivalry with*, βρονταῖς prob. cj. in Anon.Vat.42.

ἀντιτῠπ-έω, *strike against*, esp. of a hard body, τινί Arist.*Mete.* 370b18; *resist*, τὰ ἁπτὰ ἀ. τὴν ἁφήν Phld.*Sign.*18; πεδίου μὴ ἀντιτυποῦντος τῇ ὁπλῇ Luc.*Dom.*10; προσάλληλα Ach.Tat.2.38: abs., Hp.*Mul.*2.177; τὸ εἶκον καὶ μὴ ἀντιτυποῦν Pl.*Cra.*420d:—also in Med., Hp.*Mul.*1.61. **–ής**, ές, *resisting, repellent*, Hdn.6.7.7; συγκρίσεις Epicur.*Nat.*2.9; of αἴσθησις, *Stoic.*2.115. **2.** metaph., *hard*, Alex.Aphr.*de An.*125.9; ἀ. καὶ στερρὸν ὁ πόνος Ph.2.162. **II.** of sounds, *clashing, dissonant*, D.H.*Comp.*22, al. **–ησις**, εως, ἡ, *collision*, Olymp.*in Mete.*204.19. **–ία**, ἡ, *resistance of a hard body*, Phld.*Sign.*34, *Mus.*p.30 K., S.E.*P.*3.39, Aret.*SD*1.14, *Corp.Herm.* 2.6, Plot.2.6.2, Plu.2.599d (pl.); *repercussion*, Cass.*Pr.*26. **2.** of light, *reflection*, Plot.4.4.29. **3.** *surface* of a solid, *Theol.Ar.*18, Iamb.*Comm.Math.*8. **–ος**, ον, rarely η, ον, v. infr. II. 1a: (τύπτω): —*repelled* by a hard body, τύπος ἀ. *blow and counter-blow*, of the hammer and anvil, Orac.ap.Hdt.1.67, cf. 68; of sound, *echoed, echoing*, στόνος S.*Ph.*694 (lyr.), 1460 (lyr.), cf. *APl.*4.154 (Luc. or Arch.); κατὰ τὸ ἀ. by *repercussion*, of an echo, Luc.*Dom.*3; of light, *reflected*, ἀκτῖνες Tryph.519, cf. *AP*9.822. **2.** *corresponding*, as the stamp to the die, ἅγια ἀ. τῶν ἀληθινῶν *figuring* or *representing* the true, *Ep.Hebr.*9.24, cf. 1*Ep.Pet.*3.21; ἀ. τοῖς δακρύοις χάριτα *IG*14.1320; *resembling*, c. dat., Nonn.*D.*26.327; μίμημα ib.8.23: hence, *feigned, counterfeit*, 1.423, al. **b.** *corresponding*, φιλότης *mutual* affection, 13.552. **c.** Subst. ἀντίτυπος, ὁ, or ἀντίτυπον, τό, *image*, Ἄμμωνος κεραοῦ χάλκεον ἀ. *Epigr.Gr.*835 (Berytus); ἀντίτυπον, τό, = ἀντίγραφον, *reproduction, copy*, *POxy.*1470.6 (iv A.D.): metaph., *antitype*, Plot.2.9.6. **II.** Act., *repelling*, as a hard body does: hence, **1.** *firm, resistent*, χωρίον Hp.*Art.*43; *rigid, inelastic*, *AP*9.739 (Jul. Aegypt.); –ώτερα ὄντα, of a horse's fetlocks, X.*Eq.*1.4; ἀντιτύπᾳ δ' ἐπὶ γᾷ πέσε S.*Ant.*134; οἱ ἐν ἀντιτύποις περίπατοι walking *on hard ground*, Arist.*Pr.*885a36; ἀντιτυπώτατον εἶδος, expl. of σκληρόν, *most resistent*, Pl.*Ti.*62c. **b.** metaph., *stubborn, obstinate*, ἄνθρωποι Id.*Tht.*156a; μάχη ἀ. X.*Ages.*6.2; *harsh-sounding*, ἁρμονίαι D.H.*Comp.*22, cf. 16; ἀ. ἀκοῦσαι Ael.*NA*12.15; of colour, *glaring*, Plu.*Dem.*22. **2.** *opposed to*, ἦθος δόλιον πίστιος ἀντίτυπον *the reverse of*.., Thgn.1244; ἀ. Διός *the adversary of* Zeus, A.*Th.*521 (lyr.); *adverse*, of events, X.*HG*6.3.11: simply, ἀ. τινι *opposite, over against*, Plb.6.31.8. **–όω**, *express as by a figure*, χρώμασι.. χάριν *AP*1.36 (Agath.).

ἀντιτύπτω, fut. –τήσω Ph.*Bel.*85.10, *beat in turn*, Ar.*Nu.*1424, Antipho 4.4.3; τυπτόμενον ἀντιτύπτειν Pl.*Cri.*51a.

ἀντιτύπωσις [ῠ], εως, ἡ, *an image impressed, impression*, Orib.45.3.3.

ἀντιτῠραννέω, *set up a counter-tyranny*, Lyd.*Mag.*2.1.

ἀντιτυφλόω, *blind in return*, Mich. *in EN*31.27.

ἀντιτωθάζω, *ridicule in turn*, Conon 49.3.

ἀντιφαίνω, *reflect light*, Thphr.*Sens.*26:—Pass., ἀντιφαίνομαι, aor. ἀντεφάνην, *appear face to face*, Hes.*Cat.Oxy.*1359 i 5.

ἀντιφάνεια [φᾰ], ἡ, *reflection*, Damian.*Opt.*12.

ἀντιφάρα, ἡ, (φάρω, Dor. for φέρω) *dispute*, *EM*114.19, Hsch.; so ἀντιφαρές· ἐναντίον, Id.

ἀντιφάρμᾰκον, τό, *antidote*, Arist.*Mir.*837a18, Ceb.26, Ath.3.84f, Ruf.*Fr.*58.1, Apollon.ap.Philum.*Ven.*33.6, Dsc.1.125:—Adj. –κός, ή, ἀ. ῥίζα D.S.17.90.

ἀντί-φᾰσις, εως, ἡ, (ἀντίφημι) in Logic, *contradiction* of propositions, Arist.*Int.*17a33, *APo.*72a12, *Metaph.*1011b23, 1055b1, al.; ἐξ ἀντιφάσεως *per contra*, Porph.*Chr.*58; ἐξ ἀντιφάσεως συλλογισμός, e.g. 'either there is day or there is not day', Chrysipp.*Stoic.*2.87; ἡ κατ' ἀντίφασιν ἐρώτησις, e.g. 'Does A possess B or not?', Ps.-Alex. Aphr. *in SE*81.35, cf. 103.16. **II.** *contradictory proposition*, Arist. *Int.*22a39, *APr.*34b29, al. **–φάσκω**, *contradict*, ἑαυτῷ Olymp. *in Mete.*181.11; *to be in contradiction*, Simp. *in Ph.*1155.28; τὰ ἀντιφάσκοντα *contradictories*, Id. *in Cat.*44.21, cf. 19.21; ὁ ἀντιφάσκων *the opponent* in argument, Phld.*Po.*2.54. **–φᾰτικός**, ή, όν, in Logic, *contradictory*, only in Adv. –κῶς Arist.*Int.*17b17, 22a34.

ἀντιφερίζω, *set oneself against, measure oneself with*, οὔ τις σοί γε.. δύνατ' ἀντιφερίζειν Il.21.357; κακὸν ἐσλῷ Hes.*Th.*609; ὅτι μοι μένος ἀντιφερίζεις Il.21.488; σὺ Θεμιστοκλεῖ ἀντιφερίζεις; Ar.*Eq.*813, cf. 818; ἀ. πὰρ σοφόν Pi.*P.*9.50.

ἀντίφερνος, ον, (φερνή) *instead of a dower*, ἀ. φθορά A.*Ag.*406 (lyr.). **II.** ἀντίφερνα, τά, = *donatio propter nuptias*, *Cod.Just.*5.3.20.

ἀντιφέρω, *set against*, Pl.*Erx.*395b; ἀ. πόλεμον ἐπί τινι *AP*7.438 (Damag.): used by Hom. only in Med. or Pass., *set oneself against, fight against* another, ἀντεφέροντο μάχῃ Il.5.701; ἀργαλέος γὰρ Ὀλύμπιος ἀντιφέρεσθαι hard *to oppose*, 1.589, cf. Od.16.238: c. acc. cogn., μένος ἀ. τινί *match oneself with* another in strength, Il.21.482; τίς Ὁμηρείοις ἀντιφέροιτο λόγοις; *AP*9.625 (Maced.). **II.** Pass., *to be borne in a contrary direction to*, τῷ οὐρανῷ Arist.*Cael.*291b2, cf. *Ph.*215a30; τῷ παντὶ τὴν φοράν Theo Sm.p.134 H.

ἀντιφεύγω, *flee* or *go into exile in turn*, ἀντί τινος E.*El.*1091.

ἀντίφημι, *say 'no', contradict*, abs., Pl.*Grg.*501c, Arist.*APr.*65b1; ἀ. τινί *contradict* a thing, Id.*Insomn.*462a7; πρός τι ib.460b19.

ἀντι-φθέγγομαι, *return a sound, echo, repeat*, E.*Hipp.*1216; τὸ ἀκουσθέν Arist.*GA*781a26. **II.** *speak against, contradict*, J.*AJ* 18.7.2, Luc.*Salt.*23, *Pisc.*31, S.E.*M.*7.332, al. **III.** *answer*, Pi. *O.*6.61. **IV.** *raise a shout in reply*, D.S.17.33. **–φθεγμα**, ατος, τό, *echo*, Sch.rec.S.*El.*109. **–φθογγος**, ον, *of answering sound, concordant*, c. gen., Pi.*Fr.*125; *imitative*, *AP*7.191 (Arch.).

ἀντιφῐλ-έω, *love in return*, Pl.*Ly.*212d, Theoc.12.16, 28.6, Arist. *EN*1157b30:—Pass., Pl.*Ly.*212c, X.*Mem.*2.6.28, Arist.*EN*1159a30, al. **II.** *kiss in return*, *AP*5.284 (Agath.). **–ησις**, εως, ἡ, *return of affection*, Arist.*EN*1155b28. **–ία**, ἡ, *mutual affection*, Id. *EE*1236b2.

ἀντιφῐλο-δοξέω, *vie in ambition*, πρός τινα Plb.1.40.11. **–νεικέω**, *strive jealously against*, πρὸς πάντα Id.3.103.7; τῇ συγκλήτῳ 32.3.16: abs., J.*AJ*2.9.1. **–σοφέω**, *hold contrary tenets*, τῇ στοᾷ Luc. *Bis Acc.*21; τῷ τυράννῳ Lxx 4 *Ma.*8.15. **–τῑμέομαι**, Pass., *to be moved by jealousy against*, πρὸς τὴν βουλήν D.H.6.96, cf. Plu.*Per.*14; τῇ ἀρετῇ Max.Tyr.14.7: plpf. ἀντεπεφιλοτίμητο D.C.59.19; in good sense, *show public spirit in return*, D.Chr.32.95. **2.** Medic., *set up a vicious circle with*, ταῖς νόσοις Sever.*Clyst.*4. **–φρονέομαι**, *receive kindly in turn*, J.*AJ*14.11.5; also, *rival*, Plu.*Sert.*20.

ἀντιφλέγω, *light up again* or *to meet* one, αὐτῷ ὅλον ὀφθαλμὸν ἀντέφλεξε Μήνα Pi.*O.*3.20.

ἀντιφλῠᾱρέω, *talk nonsense against*, τοῖς φλυαροῦσιν ἀ. Gal.8.696, 9.923.

ἀντιφοβέω, *frighten in turn*, Ael.*NA*12.15.

ἀντιφολκός· μέρος τῆς πολεμικῆς νεώς, Hsch.

ἀντιφον-εύω, *murder in return*, Sch.E.*Or.*415. **–ος**, ον, *in revenge for blood*, ποινὰς ἀντιφόνους ἄτας A.*Eu.*982; δώσουσ' ἀντιφόνους δίκας S.*El.*248; ἀντίφονον κορέσαι στόμα Id.*Ph.*1156. **II.** θάνατοι ἀ. deaths *by mutual slaughter*, A.*Th.*893.—Trag. word, but only in lyric passages.

ἀντιφορά, ἡ, *contrary motion*, Simp. *in Cael.*156.20.

ἀντιφορικῶς, as Adv., = ἀντιφραστικῶς, Sch.Th.3.15.

ἀντιφορτ-ίζω, *take in a return-cargo*, Str.5.3.5, *Peripl.M.Rubr.* 32; but the Med. is more usual in same sense, D.35.25 and 37: so metaph., Hp.*Ep.*17; τίμημα ἀ. τοῦ ἔργου Procop.*Arc.*20. **II.** in Med. also, *import in exchange for* exports, X.*Vect.*3.2; *take as return-freight*, ἀργύριον Arist.*Mir.*844a18. **2.** Pass., χρήματα .. ἀντιφορτισθέντα goods *received in exchange for the cargo*, Syngr.ap.D.35.11, cf. ib.24. **–ος**, ὁ, *return-freight*, Arg. 1 Ar.*Ach.* **II.** Subst. ἀντίφορτον, τό, *load which balances* another, *BGU*248.27 (i A.D.).

ἀντίφραγμα, ατος, τό, *counter-fence, bulwark*, πρός τι Plu.2.558d.

ἀντιφράζω, *translate*, Gal.11.793. **II.** *express by antithesis* or *negation*, Trypho *Trop.*2.15 (Pass.).

ἀντίφραξις, εως, ἡ, (ἀντιφράσσω) *barricading*, γῆς ἀ. *the interposition* of the earth, so as to cause a lunar eclipse, Arist.*APo.*90a16, cf. *Mete.* 367b21; so ἥλιον ἐκλείπειν σελήνης ἀντιφράξει Id.*Fr.*210, cf. Plu.2.169a. **II.** Pythag. name for *seventeenth day of the month*, ib.367f.

ἀντίφρᾰσις, εως, ἡ, (ἀντιφράζω) Rhet. and Gramm., *antiphrasis*, i.e. the use of words of good sense in place of those of a contrary sense, Εὐμενίδες for Ἐρινύες, πόντος εὔξεινος for ἄξεινος, Ath.3.90b; or οὐδ' ἄρα.. γήθησεν for ἐλυπήθη, Trypho *Trop.*2.15; κατ' ἀντίφρασιν Corn.*ND*4, Erot. s. v. ἀσήμοις, Herm. *in Phdr.*p.176 A., Porph.*Chr.* 87. **II.** *expression by means of negation*, Anon.*Fig.*p.212 S.

ἀντιφράσσω, Att. –ττω, *barricade, block*, τὴν ὁδόν τισι Plu.2.548d:—Pass., *to be screened*, ἀντιπεφραγμένος λαμπτήρ *lantern*, Philist. 15; τόπος ὑπὸ τῆς γῆς -φραττόμενος Plu.*Nic.*23. **II.** c. dat., *stand in the way of*, τῷ ἀέρι Arist.*Juv.*470a13, cf. *Pr.*929a38; esp. of a body intercepting the sun's light, ὅσοις ἀντιφράττει ἡ γῆ ὥστε μὴ ὁρᾶσθαι ὑπὸ τοῦ ἡλίου... Id.*Mete.*345a29: c. acc., ἕκαστον ἀντιφράττειν αὐτήν (sc. τὴν σελήνην) Id.*Cael.*293b25: abs., X.*Smp.*5.6, Thphr.*Ign.*49; ἡ γῆ ἀ. Arist.*APo.*87b40; ἡ θάλαττα ἀ. Id.*Mete.*368b10; κωλύει τὸ ἀλλότριον καὶ ἀ. Id. *de An.*429a20. **2.** Pass., *to be placed as an obstacle*, τινὸς ἀντιφραχθέντος περὶ τὴν ἀναπνοήν Pl.*Ti.*66e.

ἀντιφραστικῶς, Adv. *by way of* ἀντίφρασις, Eust.399.38.

ἀντιφρίσσω, *bristle up in self-defence*, Arist.*HA*630a2.

ἀντίφρουρος· τὴν ἴσην ἔχων φρουράν, Hsch.

ἀντιφῠλ-ακή, ἡ, *a watching against* one another, πρὸς ἀλλήλους Th.2.84: pl., D.C.77.2, Luc.*Hist.Conscr.*28. **–άσσω**, Att. –ττω, *watch in turn*, Pl.*Lg.*705e:—Med., *to be on one's guard in turn*, X. *An.*2.5.3, cf. Plu.*Demetr.*36.

ἀντιφῡσάω, *blow against*, Antyll.ap.Orib.9.23.11.

ἀντιφῠτεύω, *implant in turn*: metaph., ἔρις ἔριν ἀ. Ps.-Phoc.78.

ἀντιφύω, in pf. part. ἀντιπεφυκότων, *to be of contrary nature*, Hsch.

ἀντιφων-έω, *sound in answer, reply, rejoin*, abs., A.*Eu.*303, S.*Ant.* 271, etc.; esp. *answer in a loud voice*, Plu.*Mar.*19, etc. **2.** c. acc. cogn., ἀ. ἔπος *utter* a word *in reply*, S.*Aj.*773; πόλλ' ἀ. Id.*El.*1501; ἀ. Ἔρωτας, of a lute, *sound* love strains *in reply*, Anacreont.23.9. **3.** c. acc. pers., *reply to, answer*, μή μ' ἀντιφώνει μηδέν S.*Ph.*1065. **4.** *answer by letter*, τινί Plb.8.16.11, *POxy.*805 (i B.C.), al.: abs., Plb.8.17.8:—Pass., *to be received in answer*, ἐκ Ῥώμης Id.15.18.6, cf. J.*AJ* 14.10.26; but –πεφωνημένα ἐκ τῶν δημοσίων δέλτων ἀντίγραφα copies *taken from*.., *OGI*453.26 (M. Antonius). **5.** *controvert, disagree with*, τινί S.E.*M.*7.327; *to be discordant with*, –φωνοῦντος τοῦ νῦν βίου τῷ βιβλίῳ Luc.*Apol.*4. **II.** legal t. t., = *constituere*, Anon. *de Actionibus* in *Zeitschr.d.Savigny-Stiftung* 1893 p.92. **–ησις**, εως, ἡ, *answer by letter*, *POxy.*294.12 (i A.D.), *BGU*1204.4 (i B.C.). **–ητής**, οῦ, ὁ, *one who answers for, is responsible for* another, *POxy.*136.39 (vi A.D.). **–ος**, ον, (φωνή) *sounding in answer, concordant*, as in the octave, ὀξύτητα βαρύτητι σύμφωνον καὶ ἀ. Pl.*Lg.*812d: abs., ἁρμονίαι Ph.2.485. 2. *responsive to*, c. gen., στεναγμάτων E.*Supp.*800 (lyr.). II. *discordant, contradictory*, Plu.2.361a, *Corp.Herm.*16.1: c. gen., τῶν γενησομένων Plu.2.412b. III. as Subst., ἀντίφωνον, τό, *concord in the octave*, τὸ ἀ. σύμφωνόν ἐστι διὰ πασῶν Arist.*Pr.*918b30, 921a8.

ἀντιφωτ-ίζομαι, *to be directly exposed to light*, -ομένου ὄμματος Dam.*Pr.*29. -ισμός, ὁ, *reflection of light*, Plu.2.625e; πρὸς τὴν σελήνην Id.*Nic.*21.

ἀντιχαίνω· *rehisco*, *Gloss.*

ἀντιχαίρω, *rejoice in turn* or *answer*, Νίκα ἀντιχαρεῖσα Θήβᾳ S.*Ant.*149.

ἀντιχᾰλεπαίνω, *to be embittered against*, D.H.17.5, Plu.2.468b.

ἀντιχάλημα (leg. -χέλυσμα)· μέρος τι τῆς μακρᾶς νεώς, Hsch.

ἀντιχαλκεύω, *forge against*, in Med., πρὸς τὰς μαχαίρας κράνη ὁλοσίδηρα Polyaen.8.7.2.

ἀντι-χᾰρίζομαι, *show kindness in return*, τινί Hdt.7.114, X.*Cyr.*4.1.20, Ph.2.26, etc. -χᾰρις, ιτος, ἡ, *acknowledgement of a favour*, Heliod. *in EN*95.18, Lib.*Decl.*43.29.

ἀντιχασμάομαι, *yawn in answer to*, τοῖς χασμωμένοις Arist.*Pr.*886a24, 887a4.

ἀντίχειρ (sc. δάκτυλος, which is supplied in Heliod.ap.Orib.48.54.1, S.E.*M.*1.137, *Gp.*4.12.13), ὁ, *thumb*, as being *opposite to* the fingers, Sor.1.103, Dsc.5.79, Plu.2.761c, etc. II. *responsive to the touch*, βόμβοι κυμβάλων Diog.Trag.1.4 (Casaubon). III. Subst. (sc. σωλήν), *inverse tube* of alembic, Zos.Alch.p.225B.

ἀντίχειρον, τό, *thumb-breadth*, Hero *Geom.*4.11; also ὁ ἀντίχειρος δάκτυλος *thumb*, Antyll.ap.Orib.7.9.8.

ἀντιχειροτον-έω, *vote against*, abs., Th.6.13,24, Ar.*Ec.*423; ἀ. ὡς.. D.59.5; τινί Max.Tyr.17.5. -ία, ἡ, *contrary vote*, Poll.2.150.

ἀντίχθων (sc. γῆ), ονος, ἡ, *opposite* or *counter-earth*, in the Pythag. system, Arist.*Cael.*293a24, *Metaph.*986a12, *Placit.*2.7.7. 2. *southern hemisphere*, Cic.*Tusc.*1.28.68; ἀ. ζώνη Jul.*Or.*5.173c: in pl., *people of the southern hemisphere*, Ach.Tat.*Intr.Arat.*30, Plin.*HN*6.81.

ἀντίχορδος, ον, *concordant*, Hsch.: but, II. metaph., *in reply* or *opposition to*, τοῖς πεφιλοσοφημένοις Plu.2.663f.

ἀντιχορεύω, *dance in harmony*, Nonn.*D.*22.44.

ἀντιχορηγ-έω, *to be a rival choragus*, And.4.42; ἀ. τινί *rival* him *in the choragia*, D.21.62. II. *furnish in return*, J.*BJ*2.20.8 (Pass.). -ος, ὁ, *rival choragus*, And.4.20, D.21.59.

ἀντιχόρια, τά, *odes sung alternately by two semichori*, Poll.4.107.

ἀντιχόρτοις· συνόροις, Hsch.

ἀντι-χράω, (χράω B) *to be sufficient*, only in aor. 1, ὁ ποταμὸς οὐκ ἀντέχρησε τῇ στρατιῇ πινόμενος Hdt.7.127, cf. 187. -χρημᾰτίζομαι, *transact business instead of* another, *PFlor.*382.59 (iii A.D.). -χρησις, εως, ἡ, *substitution of usufruct for interest*, *Dig.*20.1.11.1.

ἀντίχριστος, ὁ, *Antichrist*, 1*Ep.Jo.*2.18,22, etc.

ἀντιχρον-ία, ἡ, *use of one tense for another*, Sch.E.*Or.*82. -ισμός, ὁ, = foreg., ib.48, Hdn.in *An.Ox.*3.274.

ἀντιχρώζω, *colour, tinge in turn*, [Lib.] *Descr.*30.13.

ἀντιχώννῡμι, *raise an embankment against*, πόλει Amynt.ap.Ath.12.529e.

ἀντιχωρέω, *move in opposite direction*, dub. l. in Porph.*Sent.*11.

ἀντι-ψάλλω, *play a stringed instrument in accompaniment* of song, ἀ. ἐλέγοις φόρμιγγα Ar.*Av.*218. -ψαλμος, ον, *responsive, harmonious*, ᾠδάς E.*IT*179 (lyr.).

ἀντιψαύω, = ἀνθάπτομαι, Sch.E.*Hec.*275.

ἀντιψέγω, *blame in turn*, Sch.A.*Eu.*416.

ἀντιψηλᾰφάω· *obtrecto*, *Gloss.*

ἀντιψηφ-ίζομαι, *vote against*, πρός τι Plu.*Lys.*27; τὸ ἀληθὲς τῷ λόγῳ ἀ. Lib.*Or.*64.37. -ος, ον, *voting against*, τῷ θεῷ Pl.*Alc.*2.150b.

ἀντίψῡχος, ον, *given for life*, Luc.*Lex.*10. 2. ἀ. ἀποθανεῖν *giving one's own life for another's*, D.C.59.8. 3. name for οἱ Μέμνονος ὄρνιθες, Hsch.

ἀντιψύχω [ῡ], *cool, chill in turn*, Alex.Aphr.*Pr.*1.113.

ἀντιψωμίζω, *feed with dainty morsels in rivalry*, Arg.1 Ar.*Eq.*

ἀντλ-έω, (ἄντλος) *bale out bilge-water, bale the ship*, Thgn.673, Alc.19. 2. generally, *draw water*, ἀντλέει καὶ ἐγχέει Hdt.6.119, *Ev.Jo.*2.8, etc.; οἷον ἐκ κρήνης ἐπ' ὀχετοὺς ἀ. *draw* as from a well, *and pour into*.., Pl.*Ti.*79a; διὰ χώνης τοῖσι βουλομένοις πιεῖν Pherecr.108.31: prov. of labour in vain, ἠθμῷ ἀντλεῖν *draw water* in a sieve, Arist.*Oec.*1344b25; εἰς τετρημένον πίθον ἀ. X.*Oec.*7.40; but ἐκ πίθω ἀ., of one who has abundance in store, Theoc.10.13; ἕτοιμον ἀ. Herod.4.14. II. metaph., *drain dry*, i.e., 1. *use the utmost, make the most of*, τὰν ἔμπρακτον ἄντλει μαχανάν Pi.*P.*3.62: but more commonly, 2. of toil, suffering, etc., *drain to the dregs*, τὴν παροῦσαν ἀντλήσω τύχην A.*Pr.*377; τλημόνως ἤντλουν κακά Id.*Ch.*748; λυπρὸν ἀντλήσει βίον E.*Hipp.*898; δέκα ἀντλήσας ἔτη v.l. Id.*Tr.*433. 3. *squander*, πατρῴαν κτῆσιν ἀντλεῖν S.*El.*1291. III. Pass., ἀντλούμενος ὄλβῳ *flooded with*, Man.4.92. -ημα, ατος, τό, *bucket for drawing water*, Plu.2.974e, Sch.Ar.*Ra.*1332, *Ev.Jo.*4.11. -ησις, εως, ἡ, *drawing up* or *emptying*, Ruf.ap.Orib.5.3.1, *POxy.*971 (i/ii A.D.), Ael.*VH*1.24. -ησμός, ὁ, = foreg., *PFlor.*16.21 (iii A.D.). -ητήρ, ῆρος, ὁ, *one who draws water*, Poll.10.31; ληνῶν Man.4.257. 2. = κάδος ναυτικός, Hsch. II. *ladle*, Ath.10.424a. -ητήριος, α, ον, *of* or *for drawing up*: τὸ ἀ. (sc. ἀγγεῖον) *bucket*, D.C.50.34. -ητής, οῦ, ὁ, = ἀντλητήρ I, *PLond.*1.131r311 (i A.D.), al., Ptol.*Tetr.*179. -ητικός, ή, όν, *for irrigation*, ἄξων *POxy.*137.20 (vi A.D.); *suitable for irrigation*, κτήματα *PFlor.*148.3 (iii A.D.). -ητός, όν, *irrigated*, *PAmh.*2.96.3, *PFlor.*369.6 (ii A.D.). -ήτρια, ἡ, *she who draws up*, priestess at the Thesmophoria, Sch.Luc.*DDeor.*2.1. -ία, ἡ, = ἄντλος, i.e., 1. *hold of a ship*, S.*Ph.*482; τὴν ἀντλίαν φυλάξω Ar.*Eq.*434; δεῖπνον.. ἐξ ἀντλίας ἥκοντα, i.e. the coarse food used by seamen, Dionys.Com.2.41. 2. *bilge-water, filth*, Ar.*Pax*17. 3. *reservoir*, *BGU*1120.26 (i B.C.), *PRyl.*92.5 (ii/iii A.D.). 4. = καδίσκος, Hsch.

ἀντλιαντλητήρ, ῆρος, ὁ, *bucket*, Men.30.

ἀντλίον, τό, = foreg., Ar.*Fr.*470, Epil.5.

ἄντλος, ὁ, in Poll.1.92 also ἄντλον, τό:—in Hom., *hold of a ship*, Od.12.411, 15.479. 2. *bilge-water*, πόλις.. ἄντλον οὐκ ἐδέξατο let in no *water*, metaph. for 'let no enemy come in', A.*Th.*796; ἄντλον εἴργειν ναός pump out *water* from a ship, E.*Tr.*691; εἰς ἄντλον ἐμβαίνειν πόδα, metaph. for getting into a difficulty, Id.*Heracl.*168. 3. a *flood* of water, Pi.*O.*9.53; ἀλίμενον ὥς τις εἰς ἄντλον πεσών E.*Hec.*1025 (lyr.); ἐν ἄντλῳ τιθέναι *scuttle, sink*, metaph., ὕβριν Pi.*P.*8.12. II. *bucket*, Man.6.424. III. *heap of corn*, threshed but not yet cleansed, Nic.*Th.*114,546, Q.S.1.352, *AP*6.258 (Adaeus).

ἀντοδῠνάω, *hurt in return*, Sch.Theoc.3.13.

ἀντοδύρομαι [ῠ], *lament in return*, App.*BC*1.10.

ἀντοικέω, *to be ἄντοικος* (q.v.):—Pass., ἡ ἀντοικουμένη, Ptol.*Geog.*1.8.1, cf. Ach.Tat.*Intr.Arat.*30, Olymp. *in Grg.*p.541 J.

ἀντοικοδομ-έω, *build* or *fortify against*, Plb.1.42.12, D.S.16.49; τινά App.*BC*2.61:—Med., Arr.*An.*1.21.4: metaph., ἀ. τινι διατριβήν Ael.*VH*4.9. -ητέον, *one must build against*, Ph.*Bel.*92.22. -ή, ἡ, = sq., *IG*12(1).420 (Thera). -ία, ἡ, *building against*, ib.11.165.15 (Delos, iii B.C.), Plb.1.48.1.

ἄντοικος, ον, *living on the same side of the equator, but under the opposite meridian*, Gem.16.1, Cleom.1.2.

ἀντοικτίζω, *pity in return*, Th.3.40.

ἀντοικτίρω, = foreg., τινά E.*Ion* 312.

ἀντοίομαι, aor. ἀντῳήθην, *to be of contrary opinion*, Pl.*Tht.*178c.

ἀντολ-ή, ἡ, poet. for ἀνατολή, q.v. -ίη, ἡ, collat. poet. form of ἀνατολή, Androm.ap.Gal.14.37, *APl.*4.61 (Crin., pl.), *Epigr.Gr.*441 (Trachonitis), al.; personified, *PMag.Berol.*2.9.3. 2. as Adj., *eastern*, ἐν ἀντολίῃ.. ἀρούρῃ Nonn.*D.*25.98. -ίηθε, Adv. for ἀνατολίηθε, *from the east*, Opp.*C.*2.123; -θεν ib.1.43, Man.2.11, 3.49. -ίηνδε, *towards the east*, D.P.260.

ἀντολοφύρομαι [ῠ], *bewail in turn*, J.*BJ*4.5.1.

ἄντομαι, only pres. and impf.: (ἀντί, ἄντα):—poet. Verb (Hom. only in Il.), = ἀντάω, *meet*, Il.2.595, al.; esp. in battle, c. dat., ἀλλήλοισιν ἄντεσθ' ἐν πολέμῳ 15.698, cf. 16.788; ἀργύρῳ ἀντομένη.. ἐτράπετ' αἰχμή 11.237; so χαλεπῇ ἤντ. θευμορίῃ Call.*Ep.*32: abs., διπλόος ἤντετο θώρηξ the breastplate *opposed* or *stopped* (the dart), Il.4.133. 2. *meet with favour, greet*, Pi.*P.*2.71. II. c. acc. pers., = ἀντιάζω I.2, *approach with prayers, entreat*, πρός σε.. ἄντομαι Διός E.*Alc.*1098; πρός σε γενειάδος.. ἄντομαι Id.*Supp.*279 (lyr.); πρός σ' ὅ τι σοι φίλον ἐκ σέθεν ἄντομαι S.*OC*250; ἄ. Ἑρμῆν Ar.*Th.*977; ἄ. ὑπέρ τινος *beg* in another's behalf, S.*OC*243 (lyr.): abs., ἔλθετον, ἀντόμεθ' Ar.*Th.*1155 (lyr.).

ἀντόμνῡμι, *swear in turn, swear on the other part*, in a treaty, c. fut. inf., X.*HG*3.4.6, *Ages.*1.10. II. as Att. law-term, *make an affidavit*, both of the accuser and the defendant (cf. ἀντωμοσία), Antipho 1.18, Is.9.1, D.43.3, etc.:—in Med., Is.5.16.

ἄντομος, ὁ, dialectic form of ἀνάτομος, *stake* or *pale*, cf. ἄντομοι· σκόλοπες (Sicel), Hsch.: hence collectively, *paling, boundary-fence*, *Tab.Herad.*1.15, al.; also, *road adjoining such a fence*, ib.2.13, al.

ἀντομῶσαι· παρακαλέσαι, Hsch. **ἀντοναί**· αἱ τῶν χειρῶν φοραί, Id.

ἀντονειδίζω, *upbraid in return*, τινί Eust.1042.46.

ἀντονίνημι [νῐ], fut. -ονήσω, *serve mutually*, dub. in Lib.*Or.*5.53 codd.

ἀντονομ-άζω, *name instead, call by a new name*, c. dupl. acc., Th.6.4. 2. ὁ -άζων ὅρος plea *of avoidance and confession*, Arg.Lycurg., cf. Hermog.*Stat.*4. 3. *nominate instead*, Pass., *POxy.*1405.17 (iii A.D.). II. *use ἀντονομασίαι* or *rhetorical figures*, Ar.*Th.*55. 2. *use the pronoun*, Eust.103.23; ἀ. τινά A.D.*Synt.*192.21:—Pass., ib.98.11. III. Arith., in Pass., *to be of a contrary denomination*, Nicom.*Ar.*1.23. -ασία, ἡ, *use of an epithet, patronymic*, or *appellative for a proper name*, and vice versa, Tryph.*Trop.*2.17, Ps.-Plu.*Vita Hom.*24; ἀ. καὶ μετάληψις Demetr.Lac.*Herc.*1014.19,20. 2. *nomination of his successor by retiring official*, *POxy.*1642.15 (iii A.D.). II. Gramm., = ἀντωνυμία, *pronoun*, or *the use of it*, D.H.*Comp.*2, A.D.*Pron.*4.18. III. Arith., *contrary denomination*, Nicom.*Ar.*1.23. -αστικός, ή, όν, *pronominal*, cj. for ἀντωνυμικός (q.v.), D.H.*Amm.*2.12.

ἀντόπτρα, ἡ, name of a *surgical instrument*, *Hermes* 38.281.

ἀντοργίζομαι, *to be angry in turn*, M.Ant.6.26, Gal.19.211.

ἀντορέγω, *stretch out, present in turn*, Them.*Or.*11.153a.

ἀντορθιάζω, *rise up in opposition*, Hierocl.p.17A.

ἄντορος, ὁ, dialectic form of ἄνθ-ορος, *opposite boundary, counter-fence*, *Tab.Herad.*1.60, al.

ἀντορύσσω, *dig a countermine*, Hdt.4.200, Aen.Tact.37.7: metaph., ἀ. ὀφθαλμούς Paus.3.14.10.

ἀντορχέομαι, *imitate one's dancing*, Arist.*HA*597b24, cf. Metrod.Sceps.13.

ἄντος· εὖρος, οἱ δὲ Εὐριπίδης, Hsch.

ἀντοφείλω, *owe a good turn, to be indebted*, Th.2.40.

ἀντοφθαλμ-έω, *look in the face, meet face to face*, ἀ. κατὰ πρόσωπον

Plb.18.46.12: hence, *defy, withstand*, τινί and πρός τινα, Id.1.17.3, 2.24.1, etc., cf. Lxx *Wi.*12.14; ἀ. τῷ ἀνέμῳ, of a ship, *Act.Ap.*27.15; πάθεσι Longin.34.4. **–ησις**, εως, ἡ, *looking straight in the face*: hence, *straightforward dealing*, ἀ. πεποίηται πρὸς τοὺς πολίτας *IG*5(1).1114.17. **–ος**, ον, *looking in the face*, Hsch. s. v. ἀντωπόν.

ἀντόφρυς, name of a *plant*, Hsch.

ἀντοχέομαι, *drive* or *ride against*, f.l. in Mosch.2.119.

ἀντοχεύς· πόρπαξ ἀσπίδος, Hsch.

ἀντοχή, ἡ, *adhesion*, Orib.45.2.6, Gal.19.440. II. *attachment*, c. gen., ἑαυτῶν, of rings, Alex.Aphr.*Pr.*2.67: metaph., Procl. *in Ti.* 1.75 D.

ἀντοχῠρόω, *fortify in turn*, τὸ καταρριφθέν J.*BJ*3.7.23.

ἀντραῖος, α, ον, *haunting caves* or *grots*, E.*Fr.*13.

ἀντρέπω, poet. for ἀνατρέπω.

ἀ(ν)τρέσας· ἀναφοβηθείς, Hsch.

ἀντρηΐς, ΐδος, ἡ, *cave-dwelling*, Antip.Sid.*Oxy.*662.50.

ἀντριάς, άδος, ἡ, = fem. of ἀντραῖος, Νύμφαι ἀ. *grot*-Nymphs, *AP*6.224 (Theodorid.), cf. Phryn.*PS*p.27 B.

ἀντρίτης, ου, ὁ, = ἀντραῖος, coined by St.Byz. s. v. Ἄντρον.

ἀντρο-δίαιτος [ῐ], ον, *living in caves*, Orph.*H.*32.3; of Pan, ib.11.5. **–ειδής**, ές, *like caves*, Epicur.*Ep.*2 p.48 U., *Placit.*3.15.11.

ἄντροθε, *from a cave*, Pi.*P.*4.102.

ἄντρον, τό, poet. word, *cave*, Hom. only in Od., as 9.216, al., cf. Hes.*Th.*483, Pi.*P.*1.17, etc.; of a lion, A.*Eu.*193; of a serpent, E.*Ph.*232. II. *inner chamber, closet*, Lxx 3*Ki.*16.18.

ἀντρο-φυής, ές, *born in caves*, ἀνθίαι Opp.*H.*3.212. **–χᾰρής**, ές, *cave-haunting*, epith. of nymphs and Pan, Orph.*H.*11.12, 51.5.

ἀντρώδης, ες, *full of caves*, πέτρα X.*An.*4.3.11; τόπος Arist.*Pr.*932^{a}2; ὑπώρειαι Ph.*Fr.*36 H.; τὰ ἀ. Corn.*ND*28. 2. *like a cave*, οἰκίαι Philostr.*VS*2.23.3.

ἀντύα· τὸ ὑποπόδιον, Hsch.

ἀντῠγωτός, όν, *wearing a frontlet*, Hsch.

ἀντυκάρτερα· ἀντίσχυρα (Lacon.), Hsch.

ἄντυξ, ῠγος, ἡ, *edge* or *rim of anything round* or *curved*; and so, I. in Hom. (only in Il.): 1. *rim* of round shield, Il.6.118, al., E.*Rh.*373 (lyr.). 2. *rail* round front of chariot, ἐξ ἄντυγος ἡνία τείνας 5.262,322; δοιαὶ δὲ περίδρομοι ἄντυγές εἰσι 5.728; καὶ ἄντυγες αἱ περὶ δίφρον 11.535: in pl. also S.*Aj.*1030, Pl.*Tht.*207a: in sg., μάρπτει δὲ.. ἡνίας ἀπ' ἄντυγος E.*Hipp.*1188. II. post-Hom.: 1. pl., *the chariot* itself, S.*El.*746, E.*Ph.*1193: sg., κατ' ἄντυγα Νυκτὸς ὀπαδοί Theoc.2.166, cf. Jul.*Or.*3.122b. 2. *bridge of the lyre*, E.*Hipp.*1135 (lyr.). 3. *orbit* of a planet, *h.Hom.*8.8, Procl.*H.*2.17; *vault* of heaven, ἄ. οὐρανίη *AP*9.806, cf. 11.292 (Pall.); ἄ. αἰθερίη *IGRom.*4.607; *orb, circle* of the world, Nonn.*D.*38.108; ἄ. ἡμίτομος ..σελάνας the *disk* of the half-moon, Mosch.2.88. 4. in Nonnus, of the *curve* of the body, ἄ. μαζοῦ, μηρῶν, *D.*1.348, 15.228, so perh. in Herod.8.29. 5. *outermost tier*, in a theatre, ἡ ἐσχάτη ἄ. τοῦ θεάτρου Eun.*VS*p.489 B.—Poet. word, used by Pl. l.c., Luc.*DDeor.*25.2, in signf. I. 2, cf. also II. 5.

ἀντυποκρίνομαι, ἀντυπουργέω, Ion. for ἀνθυπ–.

ἄντυπος· ἴσος, ὅμοιος, ἡ ἐναντίος, Hsch.

ἀντ-ῳδή, ἡ, in Comic Parabasis, *lyric passage responding to* ᾠδή, ἀ. καὶ ἀντιστροφή Sch.Ar.*V.*1091, *Nu.*298. **–ῳδός**, όν, *singing in answer, responsive*, ἠχὼ λόγων ἀντῳδός Ar.*Th.*1059; ἀ. Πανὶ κρέκων κέλαδον *AP*7.196 (Mel.); μέλος ἀ. ἠχεῖν, of birds, Ael.*NA*4.16.

ἀντωθ-έω, *push in the contrary direction*, Hp.*Fract.*39, cf. Ph.2.354:—Pass., τὸ ὠθοῦν ἀντωθεῖται Arist.*GA*768^{b}19, cf. *Mech.*851^{a}3:—Med., *push one against another*, Theopomp.Hist.283. **–ησις**, εως, ἡ, *counter-thrust*, Gal.18(1).324, Phlp. *in Ph.*646.19; prob. cj. for ἀντίθεσις in Paul.Aeg.6.117.

ἄντωμος, ον, *shoulder to shoulder*: ἄντωμοι, οἱ, = ἄντοικοι (q.v.), Cleom.1.2.

ἀντωμοσία, ἡ, (ἀντόμνυμι) *oath* or *affidavit* made by the prosecutor, Pl.*Ap.*19b, Lys.23.13; also, by the defendant, Is.3.6, cf. Harp. s. v., Poll.8.55.

ἀντωνέομαι, *buy instead*, X.*Oec.*20.26, Men.438.3: metaph., κλέος ἀείμνηστον ἀ. Jul.*Or.*1.42b. 2. *bid against*, ἐπεὶ οὐδεὶς ἀντεωνεῖτο And.1.134; ἀ. ἀλλήλοις Lys.22.9; ὁ ἀντωνούμενος *rival bidder*, D.18.239.

ἀντωνῠμ-έω, *have an opposite denomination*, Theol.Ar.41. **–ία**, ἡ, *pronoun*, D.H.*Comp.*6, Plu.2.1009c, etc.; περὶ ἀντωνυμίας, title of work by A.D. II. *interchange of names*, Dam.*Pr.*73. **–ικός**, ή, όν, *pronominal*, D.H.*Amm.*2.12. Adv. **–κῶς** *like a pronoun*, A.D.*Synt.*156.7, al.

ἀντ-ωπέω, = ἀντοφθαλμέω, Hld.1.21, Heph.Astr.1.24; πρὸς τὸ ἕν Dam.*Pr.*118. **–ώπιος**, ον, = ἀντωπός, A.R.4.729, Man.4.336, Nonn.*D.*5.485, al.: c. gen., 5.78: c. dat., 33.184. **–ῶπις**, ιδος, = fem. of sq., ib.6.76. **–ωπός**, όν, (ὤψ) *with the eyes front, facing*, ἀντωπὰ βλέφαρα E.*IA*564; ἀντωπὸς βλέψαι *AP*12.196 (Strat.); τῆς ὄψεως ἀντωπά *front parts* of the face, Luc.*Im.*6; *opposite*, *AP*10.14 (Agath.); *full in the face*, βέλος *APl.*4.134 (Mel.); of an eagle, ἁλίῳ Ecphant.ap.Stob.4.7.64. 2. *like*, Opp.*H.*5.7.

ἀντωρύομαι [ῡ], *roar against* or *at*, Sch.Luc.*Par.*51.

ἄντωσις, εως, ἡ, *pushing against* or *back*, Arist.*Resp.*480^{a}14.

ἀντωφέλ-εια, ἡ, *benefit in return*, Mich. *in EN*469.18. **–έω**, *assist* or *benefit in turn*, τινά X.*Mem.*2.10.3:—Pass., *derive profit in turn*, ib.2.8.3, *Cyr.*1.6.11.

ἀνυβριστί, Adv. of sq. II, Anacr.63.

ἀνύβριστος, ον, *not insulted*, *PRyl.*117.26 (iii A.D.); τελευτή Plu.*Pel.*9, cf. *Luc.*18. Adv. **–τως** Ps.-Phoc.157. II. Act., *not insulting, decorous*, παιδιαί Plu.*Sert.*26; σκῶμμα Id.2.46c; τὸ ἀ. τοῦ βίου 92d: Sup., D.Chr.3.98. Adv. **–τως** Democr.73.

ἀνῠγίαστος, ον, = ἀναλθής, *incurable*, Hsch. s. v. ἀναλθές.

ἀνῠγιής, ές, *unhealthy*, *Gloss.*

ἀνυγρ-αίνω, *moisten*, Hp.*Int.*51, Thphr.*CP*2.6.1. 2. metaph., *melt, soften*, τὰ ἤθη Plu.2.156d:—Pass., ib.566a. **–ασμός**, ὁ, *moistening*, Archig.ap.Orib.8.2.6.

ἀνύδᾰτος [ῠ], ον, *without water*, Man.1.144.

ἀνυδρ-εύομαι, *draw up from a well*, τὸν κάδον Pherecr.76. **–ευτος**, ον, *unwatered*, Thphr.*HP*7.4.6. **–ία**, ἡ, *want of water, drought*, Hp.*Aër.*12, Th.3.88, *PPetr.*2 p.22; *lack of irrigation*, *PLond. ined.*2179 (iii A.D.). **–ις**, ἡ, fem. of sq., κώμη *PThead.*20.5 (iv A.D.). **–ος**, ον, (ὕδωρ) *waterless*, of arid countries, Hes.*Fr.*24, Hdt.4.185; γῆ Hp.*Aër.*1; δάπεδα Trag.ap.Phot.p.151 R.; esp. *without spring-water*, Hdt.2.7 codd., cf. 149, 3.5; ἡ ἄνυδρος (sc. γῆ) Id.3.4 and 9, Arist.*Fr.*103, Lxx *Is.*44.3; of seasons, Hp.*Aph.*3.14; θέρος Id.*Aër.*10; in E.*Tr.*1085 (lyr.), of a corpse, *deprived of funeral lustrations; unwatered*, σμύρνα Id.*Ion*89 (anap.). II. ἄνυδρον, τό, = στρύχνον μανικόν, Dsc.4.73.

ἀνύλακτος [ῠ], ον, *without barking*, Suid. s. v. μαιουμᾶς.

ἄνῡλος, ον, (ὕλη) *treeless*, τόποι Thphr.*CP*1.5.2 (v.l. ἄϋλος). 2. *immaterial*, Ascl. *in Metaph.*26.4.

ἀνῠμέναιος, ον, *without the nuptial song, unwedded*, S.*Ant.*876, 917, E.*Hec.*416, Men.548, etc.; μοῖρα ἀ. S.*OC*1221 (lyr.): neut. pl. as Adv., Id.*El.*962, E.*Ph.*347 (lyr.). Adv. **–ως** Sch.ad loc.

ἀνυμεναιόω, *celebrate with nuptial ode*, γάμους S.*Fr.*725.

ἀνυμνέω, *proclaim by an oracle*, δίκαν E.*El.*1190 (lyr.). II. *celebrate in song*, γάμον D.H.*Rh.*2.1, cf. Jul.*Or.*5.172d, Chor.p.127 B., Procop. Gaz.*Ep.*52, Ps.-Luc.*Philopatr.*4 (Pass.): **–είω** Orac. in *App.Anth.*6.261.18, Nonn.*D.*24.328. III. *declaim*, Eun.*VS*p.468 B. IV. c. dupl. acc., *proclaim as*, ὅπερ ὂν –οῦμεν Dam.*Pr.*48, cf. 58:—Pass., ib.34.

ἀνύμφευτος, ον, *unwedded*, S.*El.*165 (lyr.); ματρὸς ἔχοντες ἀ. γονάν born *of an ill marriage*, Id.*Ant.*980, v. Sch.: transf. of things, κάρηνον (of Zeus), Nonn.*D.*46.48, cf. 20.155, al.

ἀνυμφής, ές, acc. sg. ἀνυμφέα cj. for ἄνυμφο[ν], *Milet.*6.46 (*Mnemos.*50.255).

ἄνυμφος, ον, *not bridal*, ἄ. τροφή S.*El.*1183 (lyr.); νύμφη ἄ. a bride *that is no bride, unhappy* bride, E.*Hec.*612, cf. *Hipp.*547 (lyr.), Men.548. II. *without bride* or *mistress*, μέλαθρα E.*Hel.*1125 (lyr.), cf. *Sammelb.*4301.

ἀνύξιον· ἄβρωτον, Euclid.ap.Hsch.

ἀνῠόδρομος, ον, *swiftly-running, fleet*, Sapph.71.

ἀνυπαίτιος, ον, *blameless*, Ph.1.4, al., Hld.9.11; ἡ κατ' ὀρθὸν λόγον ἀ. διοίκησις Boeth.*Stoic.*3.266. Adv. **–ίως** Ph.1.206.

ἀνυπάκουστος, ον, *not suited for hearing*, i. e. *for declamation*, λέξις Phld.*Rh.*1.198 S.

ἀν-ύπαρκτος, ον, *non-existent, unreal*, Epicur.*Fr.*27, Zeno *Stoic.*1.19, Phld.*Mus.*p.65 K., Ph.2.307, Plu.2.1124a, *PGiss.*7.8 (ii A.D.), etc. **–υπαρξία**, ἡ, *non-existence, nonentity*, Phld.*Mort.*28, Antip.*Stoic.*3.252, S.E.*P.*1.21, Plot.5.5.2. 2. *absence of predication*, ἡ ἀπόφασις said to be ἀναίρεσις (τῆς φάσεως) καὶ ἀ. Alex.Aphr. *in Top.*409.19.

ἀνυπείκαστον, sine expl., Hsch.

ἀνύπ-εικτος, ον, *unyielding, hard*, Suid. **-εξαιρέτως**, Adv. *without exception*, M.Ant.8.41.

ἀνυπέρ-αρτος, ον, *not ostentatious*, ἐν δαπάναις καὶ παρασκευαῖς ἀ. Andronic.Rhod.p.576 M. **–βᾰτος**, ον, *impassable*, κρημνοί D.Chr.64.21. 2. *not to be overcome, unsurpassable*, S.E.*M.*9.153; ἀηδία Phld.*Vit.*p.12 J. 3. Act., *not transgressing the bounds*, διάθεσις ἀ. τῶν κατ' ὀρθὸν λόγον D.L.7.93. Adv. **–τως** *without omission*, of numerical progression, Nicom.*Ar.*2.23; *unfailingly*, Gal.19.544. **–βλητος**, ον, *not to be surpassed* or *outdone*, φιλία X.*Cyr.*8.7.15; ἀρετή Isoc.4.71; φιλοτιμία D.2.18; εὔνοια Lycurg.101; ἄνθρωπος ἀ. εἰς πονηρίαν Antiph.168.5; τάχη Epicur.*Ep.*1 p.10 U. Adv. **–τως** Arist.*Rh.*1370^{b}31, Pyth.*Sim.*144. 2. *persistent, obstinate*, of disease, Gal.13.61. **–εκτος**, ον, *unsurpassable*, ἀκρότης Phld.*D.*3.5.

ἀνυπερθε-σία, ἡ, *immediateness, haste*, Aq.*Ps.*7.7 (pl.). **–τέω**, *do immediately, to be hasty*, ib.77(78).21. **–τος**, ον, *immediate*, Ph.2.58, al., Dsc.*Ther.Praef.* Adv. **–τως** *forthwith, without delay*, *BGU*1167.51 (i B.C.), Lxx 3*Ma.*5.20, *IG*3.77, Ph.1.599, etc. II. *unsurpassed by*, c. dat., Democr.275; *incomparable*, [Philol.]21.

ἀνυπέροχος, ον, *without superiority on either side*, Eust.832.3.

ἀνυπ-εύθῡνος, ον, *not liable to a* εὔθυνα, *not accountable*, of persons, esp. magistrates or statesmen, Ar.*V.*587, Pl.*Lg.*761e; ἀ. ἄρχειν ib.875b, cf. Arist.*Pol.*1295^{a}20; = Lat. *dictator*, Plu.*Fab.*3. Adv. **–νως** Andronic.Rhod.p.574 M., D.S.1.70. 2. of things, *beyond human control* or *criticism*, τὰ τῆς τέχνης ἀ. Hp.*Praec.*7; ἀνάγκη Epicur.*Ep.*3 p.65 U.; ἐξουσία ἀ. *unchartered* freedom, Phld.*Herc.*1251.3. II. *that will not bear investigation*, ἔργα Ph.2.266. **–ήκοος**, ον, *not obeying*, τοῦ λόγου Pl.*Ti.*91b, cf. 73a. **–ηλῐφής**, ές, *EM*61.6, or **–ήλῐφος**, ον, Phryn.*PS*p.34 B., *not anointed with pitch*.

ἀνυπήνηος [ῡ], ον, *beardless*, Eust.1353.47, Hsch.

ἀνυπηρε-σία, ἡ, *unserviceableness*, Simp. *in Epict.*p.49 D. **–τητος**, hyperdor. **–τᾰτος**, ον, *without attendance*, Euryph.ap.Stob.4.39.27.

ἀνυπογρᾰφος, ον, *without subscription, unsigned*, *PFlor.*16.38 (iii A.D.).

ἀνυπο-δεσία, –δετέω, –δετος, = ἀνυποδησία, –δητέω, –δητος, found in codd. and Inscrr., as -*δετος* *IG*5(1).1390.15 (Andania, i B.C.), but condemned by Phryn.409, Id.*PS*p.27 B., etc. **-δήματος,** *ον*, = *ἀνυπόδητος*, *AB*82. **-δησία,** *ἡ*, *a going barefoot*, Pl.*Lg*.633c, X.*Lac*.2.3. **-δητέω,** *go barefoot*, Arist.*Fr*.74, Luc.*Cyn*.1. **-δητος,** *ον*, *unshod*, *barefoot*, as the philosophers and Spartans, Epich.108, Lys.32.16, Pl.*Phdr*.229a, *Smp*.173b, Ar.*Nu*.103, etc.; ἀ. ὄρθρου περιπατεῖν Aristopho 10.8. **2.** *having the feet unprotected*, Pl.*Prt*. 321c.

ἀνυπό-δῐκος, *ον*, *not liable to action*, Plu.*Cat.Mi*.11; ἀ. πάσας δίκας καὶ ζαμίας *GDI*1685,al. (Delph.), cf. 5170 (Cret.). **-ζωστος,** *ον*, of ships, *without ὑπόζωμα* (q.v.), *IG*2.789*b*79,83. **-θετος,** *ον*, *not hypothetical*, *unconditioned*, *absolute*, ἀρχή Pl.*R*.510b, cf. Phld. *D*.1.19; τὸ ἀ. Pl.*R*.511b, al. Adv. -*τως* *not hypothetically*, Plu.2. 399b. **II.** *without foundation*, ib.358f.

ἀνύπ-οιστος, *ον*, *insupportable*, Timae.60, D.H.7.15, J.*AJ*19.2.2, Eus.Mynd.54; *irresistible*, φάλαγξ Ascl.*Tact*.5.1. Adv. -*τως* Poll.3. 130. **II.** Act., *impatient*, Ptol.*Tetr*.159. **-οιστότης·** *intolerabilitas*, *Gloss.*

ἀνυπό-κρῐτος, *ον*, *without dissimulation*, Lxx *Wi*.5.18, *Ep.Rom*. 12.9, *Ep.Jac*.3.17. Adv. -*τως* M.Ant.8.5. **II.** *undramatic*, Demetr.*Eloc*.194. **III.** in punctuation, of a stop in a simple sentence, opp. *ἐνυπόκριτος* (q.v.), Sch.D.T.p.24H. **-ληπτος,** *ον*, perh. f.l. for *ἀνυπόδητος*, Anon.*in Rh*.82.38. **-λογος,** *ον*, *subject to no claim* or *charge*, *POxy*.71 i 6 (iv A.D.): c. gen., ἀ. παντὸς κινδύνου *BGU*1119.7 (i B.C.). **II.** *without deduction*, φόρος *CIG*2693*e* (Mylasa). **-μενετέος,** *α*, *ον*, *not to be sustained*, Stob.2.6.6:—also **-μενετός,** *ή*, *όν*, ibid. **-μένητος,** *ον*, = *ἀνυπομόνητος*, Phld.*Mus*. p.91 K. **-μνηστος,** *ον*, dub. sens. in Id.*Piet*.98. **-μόνητος,** *ον*, *unbearable*, κακόν Chrysipp.*Stoic*.3.131; ἀ. θεάσασθαι Arist.*Mir*. 843^{a}15, cf. D.S.3.29, D.H.6.51, Crates *Ep*.29, etc. Adv. -*τως* Hsch. s.v. *ἀστέκτως*. **II.** Act., *not enduring*, Procl.*Par.Ptol*.224. **-νόητος,** *ον*, *unsuspected*, *πρός τι* *in* a thing, D.61.11; ἄνθρωποι Plb.13. 6.8. **2.** *unexpected*, ἐλπίς Id.2.57.6. Adv. -*τως* Id.1.84.9. **II.** Act., *unsuspecting*, τοῦ μέλλοντος Id.4.10.7, cf. Phld.*Mort*.13, cf. 39. Adv. -*τως* *unsuspiciously*, Plb.5.39.2. **-παστος,** *ον*, of a stone, *with nothing spread below it*, *IG*7.3073.164 (Lebad.).

ἀνύποπτος, *ον*, *without suspicion*, i.e., **1.** Pass., *unsuspected*, Th.3.43 (Comp.), X.*Cyr*.5.3.11; λεηλασίαι *unexpected*, Arr.*Tact*.17. 5. Adv. -*τως* *unsuspectedly*, Aen.Tact.10.20, al., Men.666. **2.** *free from risk*, κίνησις Sor.1.55; θάνατος Phld.*Sto.Herc*.339.4. **3.** Act., *unsuspecting*, πράξεως Plb.8.27.2, Plu.*Brut*.8. Adv. -*τως* Th. 1.146; ἀ. ἔχειν Arist.*Top*.156^{b}18; *unhesitatingly*, Plu.2.614b.

ἀνυπό-πτωτος, *ον*, (ὑποπίπτω) *not coming under the cognizance of*, τῇ αἰσθήσει S.E.*M*.7.345, etc. **2.** = *ἀμετάπτωτος*, Herill.*Stoic*.1. 191. **-στάλτως,** Adv. = *ἀνυποστόλως*, ἐλευθεριάζοντες interpol. in Ammon.*in Cat*.2.8. **-στασία,** *ἡ*, gloss on *ἀτλησία*, Hsch. **-στασις,** *εως*, *ἡ*, *unsubstantiality*, Sch.E.*Hec*.702 (leg. -*στασίαν*). **-στᾰτος,** *ον*, *not to be withstood*, *irresistible*, δύναμις Pl.*Lg*.686b; ἀνάγκη X.*Lac*.10.7; φρόνημα, πόλις, Id.*Cyr*.5.2.33, *Mem*.4.4.15; τολμήματα D.54.38; ἀ. τισὶν ἀνταγωνισταί D.Chr.8.17. Adv. -*τως* Aristobul.ap. Eus.*PE*8.10. **II.** *without sure foundation*, ἡ τῆς ὑποθέσεως ἀρχὴ ἀ. Plb.1.5.3, cf. 12.25^f.4; ἀ. εἶναι τὰς τῶν ὅλων ἀρχάς D.L.9.99, cf. Ath. 3.98c. **2.** *without sediment*, οὖρα Aret.*SD*1.13, cf. *CD*1.13, Hp. *Epid*.2.2.23. **3.** *unsubstantial*, *Stoic*.2.117, Syrian.*in Metaph*.25. 3; of accidental or secondary qualities, Syn.Alch.p.62 B.; *non-existent*, Ps.-Archyt.ap.Simp.*in Ph*.785.17; μαντικαί D.L.7.149; τὸ ἀ... τῆς μαντικῆς Diogenian.Epicur.4.79; κειμήλιον Secund.*Sent*. 11. **4.** *without significance*, φωνή Them.*in Ph*.124.27. **-στολος,** *ον*, *using no concealment*, *frank*, *fearless*, ῥήτωρ Poll.4.21; τὸ ἀ. τῆς ὀργῆς J.*AJ*16.3.1. Adv. -*λως* D.Chr.13.16, Phld.*Rh*.1.109 S., Alciphr.3.39, etc. **-στρεπτος,** *ον*, *unreturning*, Suid. s.v. *ἄνοστος*. Adv. -*τί* *without turning back*, Pythag.ap.Phlp.*in de An*.116. 32. **-στροφος,** *ον*, *from which none return*, Orph.*H*.56; ὁδός Lyd.*Mag*.3.14. **2.** of diseases, *without relapse*, Hp.*Epid*.6.3. 4. **-τακτέω,** *to be unruly*, *insubordinate*, Sch.Od.19.179. **-τακτος,** *ον*, of persons or things, *not made subject*, τινί *Ep.Hebr*.2.8, cf. J.*AJ*11.6.6, Arr.*Epict*.4.1.161; ἀ. ὁ βασιλεύς Artem.2.30; *unrestrained*, *free*, Ph.1.473, cf. Arr.*Epict*.2.10.1. **2.** *not to be classified under heads*, *confused*, Plb.3.36.4; *irregular*, ποιήματα, of dithyrambs, Demetr.Lac.*Herc*.1014.12, Zen.2.15. **II.** of persons, *independent*, Ptol.*Tetr*.61; in bad sense, *unruly*, 1*Ep.Ti*.1.9, *Ep.Tit*.1.6 and 10, *PMag.Par*.1.1367. Adv. -*τως* *impatiently*, Hsch. s.v. *ἀστέκτως*. **III.** of Verbs, *having no first aorist*, *AB*1087. **-ταξία,** *ἡ*, *indiscipline*, Phld.*Lib*.p.63 O. **-τίμητος** [ῑ], *ον*, *that cannot be adequately punished*, ἀσέβεια J.*AJ*16.11.8, cf. 15.7.10. Adv. -*τως* *without fear of punishment*, 16.9.1. **-τλητος,** *ον*, *not to be borne*, Sch.E.*Ph*.93.

ἀνύπουλος, *ον*, *without disguise*, Ph.2.435; γνώμη *without arrière-pensée*, Chor.*Milt*.50.

ἀνύπους, *ὁ*, *ἡ*, only in Hsch. ἀνύποδας· ταχύποδας, ἀπὸ τοῦ τοῖς ποσὶν ἀνύειν, prob. due to a misreading of S.*Aj*.837 Ἐρινῦς τανύποδας.

ἀνυπο-φόρητος, *ον*, *insufferable*, *EM*115.18. **-χώρητος,** gloss on *ἀνύπεικτος*, Hsch.

ἀνύπτιος, *ον*, *not passive*, of reciprocal Verbs, D.L.7.64.

ἄνυρις· ἄδικος, ἀσεβής, and **ἄνυρος·** ἄδικος, Hsch.

ἀνῠ-σιεργός, *όν*, *finishing work*, *industrious*, Theoc.28.14 [ᾱ metri gr.], cf. Phld.*Hom*.p.30 O. **-σιμος,** *ον*, (ἀνύω) = *ἀνυστικός*, *efficacious*, *effectual*, *πρός τι* Pl.*Lg*.716d: Comp., εἴς τι οὐδὲν -*ώτερον* X. *Cyr*.1.6.22, cf. Aret.*CA*1.10, Jul.*Or*.5.178a: Sup. -*ώτατος* Pl. l.c., Luc.*Cal*.16; λόγος D.Chr.39.8. Adv. -*μως* Pl.*Tht*.144b, Ps.-Alex. Aphr.*in SE*164.33: Sup. -*ώτατα* Pl.*R*.518d. **2.** Pass., *capable of accomplishment*, J.*BJ*5.5.1, cf. Porph.*VP*27, Serapion in *Cat.Cod. Astr*.1.100. **-σις,** *εως*, *ἡ*, (ἀνύω) *accomplishment*, ἄ. δ' οὐκ ἔσσεται αὐτῶν Il.2.347; οὐκ ἄνυσίν τινα δήομεν we find no *end*, *accomplish* nothing, Od.4.544; χρήμασιν ὧν ἄ. γίνεται οὐδεμία Thgn.462; οὐδ' ἄνυσις there is no *respite*, Theoc.25.93.—Poet. and late Prose, as Plu.2.77b. **-σμα,** *ατος*, *τό*, *accomplishment*, *end*, Sch.Od.5. 299. **-στέον** or **-στέα,** *one must accomplish*, Suid. **-στικός,** *ή*, *όν*, *effective*, *practical*, Arist.*Phgn*.813^{a}4; τὸ ἀ. D.H.*Vett.Cens*.5.2: Comp. -*ώτερος* Plb.8.5.3, cf. Archig.ap.Gal.8.154: Sup., [Longin.] *Rh*.p.182 H. **-στός,** *όν*, *to be accomplished*, *practicable*, οὔκ ἐστ' ἀνυστὸν τόνδε σοι κατακτανεῖν E.*Heracl*.961, cf. D.Chr.12.34; τί γὰρ μερόπεσσιν ἀ.; Opp.*H*.2.4: neut., ὡς ἀνυστόν [ἐστι], like ὡς δυνατόν, ὡς ἀ. κάλλιστα Diog.Apoll.3; ὡς ἀ. ἀνθρωπίνῃ γνώμῃ Hp. *Nat.Puer*.29; σιγῇ ὡς ἀ. as silently *as possible*, X.*An*.1.8.11; ᾗ ἀ. μετριωτάτῳ Id.*Lac*.1.3; τὰ ἀνθρώπῳ ἀ. Arist.*Fr*.44. **2.** of persons, *able*, *ready*, πρὸς λόγους Hp.*Decent*.3. **-τής,** *οῦ*, *ὁ*, = Lat. *exactor*, Just.*Nov*.163(2) (pl.). **-τικός,** *ή*, *όν*, = *ἀνυστικός*, *effective*, X.*Eq.Mag*.2.6 (Comp.), *Oec*.20.22 (Sup.), Plb.8.3.3 (Comp.); λόγοι S.E.*M*.9.182 (Sup.); of persons, J.*BJ*5.9.1 (Comp.), 1.17.8 (Sup.). **2.** *rapid*, ἀνυτικωτέραν ποιεῖν τὴν κίνησιν Arist.*PA*682^{b}1. Adv. -*κῶς* [Longin.] *Rh*.p.190 H. **-τω** or **ἀνύτω,** Att. form of *ἀνύω*.

ἀνῠφ-αίνω, *weave anew*, ἀ. τὸ ἀνατριβόμενον *renew* that which wears out, Pl.*Phd*.87d, cf. Olymp.*Vit.Pl*.p.3 W., *in Alc*.p.198 C. **-άντης,** *ου*, *ὁ*, *one who weaves anew*, Suid.:—fem. **-άντρια,** Eust.1764.60.

ἀνυφαίρετος, *ον*, f.l. for *ἀναφ-*, D.H.*Dem*.34.

ἀνύφαντος, *ον*, *not woven*, Ael.Dion.*Fr*.80.

ἀνυψόω, *raise up*, *exalt*, Lxx *Ps*.112(113).7, al., *PGen*.51.27 (iii A.D.):—Med., *AP*7.748 (Antip. Sid.):—Pass., ὁ λόγος -*οῦται* πρὸς θεῖον δικαστήν Lyd.*Mag*.2.16.

ἀνύω (ἄνῠ), Il.4.56, Ar.*Ra*.606, Att. **ἀνύτω** or **ἁνύτω** Th.2.75, Pl.*R*.486c, al.: impf. ἤνυον Hdt.9.66, E.*Hec*.1167: fut. ἀνύσω [ῠ], S.*Aj*.607, Ar.*Ra*.649, Ep. ἐξ-ανύω Il.11.365: aor. ἤνῠσα Od.24. 71, A.*Pers*.726, etc.; poet. ἤνυσσα (Dor. ἀν-) Pi.*P*.12.11, A.R.4. 413, Ep. ἄνυσσα [ᾰ] Hes.*Th*.954, Maiist.57 (ὑπ-): pf. ἤνῠκα Pl.*Plt*. 264b:—**Pass.**, pf. ἤνυσμαι Plb.8.29.1, etc., δι-ήνυσμαι X.*Cyr*.1.4.28: aor. ἠνύσθην Plb.32.3.17, D.Chr.3.127: fut. ἀνυσθήσομαι J.*AJ*1.19.1, Ael.*VH*1.21:—**Med.**, ἀνύομαι Pi.*P*.2.49, Bion *Fr*.4.6: impf. ἠνυτόμην A.*Ag*.1159: fut. ἀνύσομαι (v. infr.): aor. ἠνυσάμην A.*Pr*.700, S.*Tr*. 995 (lyr.), inf. ἀνύσασθαι X.*An*.7.7.24 (Valck.)—Non-thematic forms are found in poets: impf. Act. ἄνῠμες, Dor. for ἤνυμεν, Theoc.7.10: pres. Pass. ἄνυται Opp.*H*.3.427, Nic.*Al*.599: impf. Pass. ἤνῠτο Od.5. 243 (nisi leg. ἤνετο); Dor. ἄνῠτο Theoc.2.92. [ῠ in all parts: hence ἀνῦσαι in Tryph.126, ἀνῡσάμενοι in *AP*10.12 should be written with σσ: ἀνῦων is corrupt in Nonn.*D*.21.16]:—*effect*, *accomplish*, ἤνυτο δ' ἔργον Od.5.243 (v. supr.), cf. A.*Pers*.726, etc.; πρὸς θανάτῳ θάνατον ἀνύσασα S.*Tr*.886; ἀρωγάν Id.*Ph*.1145 (lyr.); τοὔπος ὡς ἄρ' ὀρθὸν ἤνυσας Id. *Ant*.1178, cf. *OC*454: abs., οὐδὲν ἤνυε he *did* no *good*, Hdt.9.66; εἴ τι ἔμελλεν ἀνύτειν whatever was likely *to forward the work*, Th.2.75; σμικρὸν ἀνύτειν Pl.*Sph*.230a, al.; ἧσσον ἁνύτειν Th.2.76; οὐδὲν ἤνυε τούτοις D.21.104; ἀ. εἴς τι *to conduce* towards.., Pl.*Ax*.369d: c. acc. et inf., Ἀπόλλων.. ἐκεῖνον ἤνυσε φονέα γενέσθαι *brought it to pass* that.., S.*OT*720:—Med., *accomplish for one's own advantage*, ἀνύσσεσθαι τάδε ἔργα (if not in pass. sense, *will be accomplished*) Od.16.373, cf. Hp.*Ep*.27; θεός.. τέκμαρ ἀνύεται Pi.*P*.2.49, cf. Ar.*Pl*.196, dub. in Pl.*Phd*.69d. **2.** *make an end of*, *destroy*, φλόξ σε ἤνυσεν Od.24.71; *kill*, Pi.*P*.12.11. **3.** c. dupl. acc., *make*, *cause to be*, ἠνύσατ' ἐκτοπίαν φλόγα S.*OT*166 (lyr.), Nic.*Al*.400. **4.** *make*, εἰκόνα *AP* 12.56 (Mel.). **5.** *finish a journey*, ὅσσον τε πανημερίη γλαφυρὴ νηῦς ἤνυσεν (sc. ὁδοῦ) as much as a ship *gets over* in a day, Od.4.357; so πολλὴν κέλευθον ἤνυσεν A.*Pers*.748; πορείαν Onos.6.1: c. acc. loci, ὄφρα τάχιστα νηῦς ἀνύσειε θαλάσσης.. ὕδωρ Od.15.294, cf. Thgn.511, S.*Ant*.231. **6.** in Trag. freq. abs. (sc. ὁδόν or κέλευθον), *make one's way*, *win*, πρὸς πόλιν Id.*Tr*.657 (lyr.); ἐπὶ ἀκτάν E.*Hipp*.743; also θάλαμον ἀνύτειν (i.e. εἰς θάλαμον) *reach* the bridal chamber, S.*Ant*. 805 (lyr.); ἀ. Ἅιδαν Id.*Aj*.607 (lyr.), E.*Supp*.1142 (lyr.): metaph., ζυγὰ ἤνυσε δούλια Τροία (s.v.l.) Id.*Tr*.599 (Τροίᾳ Sch.): rarely with inf. instead of acc., στρατὸς ἤνυσε περᾶν *succeeded in* crossing, A.*Pers*. 721: with Adj., *come to be*, εὐδαίμων ἀνύσει καὶ μέγας S.*Ph*.720 (lyr.). **7.** in Pass. of Time, *come to an end*, χρόνος ἄνυτο Theoc. 2.92, cf. Eus.Mynd.63. **8.** in Pass. of persons, *grow up*, ἠνυτόμαν τροφαῖς (lyr.) A.*Ag*.1159. **9.** *get*, *obtain*, γαστρὶ φορβάν S.*Ph*.711 (lyr.), cf. Theoc.5.144; τίνος χρείας ἀνύσαι; i.e. τίνος χρείας προσπίτνετε, ὥστε ἀνύσαι αὐτήν; S.*OC*1755:—Med., χρείαν ἠνύσασθε ye *obtained* it, A.*Pr*.700, cf. *Ch*.858, S.*Tr*.995 (lyr.); τοῦτο ἐκ Μοιρέων ἠνύσατο *AP*7.506 (Leon.). **II.** c. part., οὐκ ἀνύω φθονέουσα *I gain* nothing by grudging, Il.4.56. **2.** in Com., *do quickly*, *make haste*, οὐ μέλλειν.., ἀλλ' ἀνύειν Ar.*Pl*.607, cf. *Ra*.606; οὐκ ἀνύσεις τι; *make haste!* ib.649; ἀλλ' ἄνυσον, οὐ μέλλειν ἐχρῆν *Fr*.102: c. part., ἄνυε πράττων *make haste* about it, *Pl*.413; ἄνυσον ὑποδησάμενος *make haste* and get your shoes on, *V*.1168, cf. *Av*.241; ἄνυσόν ποτ' ἐξελθών Pherecr.40: more freq. in part. ἀνύσας, or ἀνύσας τι with a Verb, ἄνοιγ', ἄνοιγ' ἀνύσας *make haste* and open the door, Ar.*Nu*.181; ἀνάβαιν' ἀνύσας *V*.398; σὺ δ' ἔγχεον πιεῖν ἀνύσας τι *Eq*.119, cf. *V*.202,847, 1158, *Pl*.648,974; βοηθησάτω τις ἀνύσας *Ach*.571; νῦν οὖν ἀνύσαντε φροντίσωμεν *Eq*.71; ἀκολουθήσεις ἐμοὶ ἀνύσας τι *Nu*.506, cf. 1253; ἀπόδωμεν ἀνύσαντε *Pax*872. (The distinction of meaning ἀνύτω *accomplish*, *make way*, ἀνύω *hasten*, is doubtful, cf. *AB*411.—Att.

ἀνύω acc. to Hdn.Gr.1.541, Phryn.PSp.23B., cf. καθανύσαι X.HG 7.1.15 (Hsch.); but κατανύειν (q.v.) occurs in Trag., cf. ταῦτ' ἀνύσηται Ar.Pl.196.) (I.-E. sen-, pres. stem snneu-, cf. Skt. sanoti 'wins'.)

ἄνω (A), imper. ἀνέτω S.Ichn.70, inf. ἄνειν Pl.Cra.415a, part. ἄνων, impf. ἦνον, etc. (v. infr.): aor. ἤνεσα IG7.3226 (Orchom. Boeot.), Hymn.Is.35, prob. in AP7.701.1 (Diod.) (ἤνεσ' codd.):—= ἀνύω, ἀνύτω, *accomplish, finish*, ἦνον ὁδόν Od.3.496; οὔτ' ἄν τι θύων οὔτ' ἐπισπένδων ἄνοις A.Fr.161 (Dobree, cf. AB406); ἀλλ' οὐδὲν ἦνεν E.Andr. 1132; ἢ τὸ δέον..ἤνομεν; S.Ichn.98; ταῦτα πρὸς ἀνδρὸς ἔστ' ἄνοντος εἰς σωτηρίαν (cf. ἀνύω I.6) Ar.V.369; ἀρυσσάμενοι ποτὸν ἤνομεν AP 11.64 (Agath.). II. Pass., *come to an end, be finished*, mostly of a period of time, μάλα γὰρ νὺξ ἄνεται night *is quickly drawing to a close*, Il.10.251; ἔτος ἀνόμενον the *waning* year, Hdt.7.20; ἦμαρ ἀνόμενον A.R.2.494; ἀνομένου τοῦ μηνός SIG577.30 (Milet., iii/ii B.C.); also ὅππως..ἔργον ἄνοιτο Il.18.473; ἤνετο τὸ ἔργον Hdt.1.189, 8.71; ἀνομένων βημάτων A.Ch.799; ὁππόταν θήρης..ἔργον ἄνηται Opp.H.5. 442: impers., λιταῖς ἄνεται, = λιταὶ ἀνύονται, Pi.O.8.8. [ᾱ Hom., exc. Il.18.473: afterwds. common, cf. A. l.c., Opp.H. l.c. Orig. ἄνϝω, cf. ἀνύω.]

ἄνω (B), Aeol. ὄνω, Adv., (ἀνά): I. with Verbs implying Motion, *upwards*, ἄ. ὤθεσκε ποτὶ λόφον Od.11.596; ἄ. ἀπὸ θαλάσσης ἀναπλεῖν *up* stream, Hdt.2.155; ἄ. ποταμῶν χωροῦσι παγαί E.Med.410 (lyr.), hence "ἄ. ποταμῶν", proverbial, D.19.287, etc.; κόνις δ' ἄ. φορεῖτο S. El.714; κονιορτὸς ἄ. ἐχώρει Th.4.34; ἡ ἄ. ὁδός the *upward* road, Pl. R.621c; ἄ. ἰόντι going *up the country* (i.e. *inland*, v. infr. II.1f), Hdt.2.8; ἄ. κάτω, v. infr. II.2; πέμπειν ἄ., i.e. from the nether world, A.Pers.645 (lyr.), cf. Ch.147; σύριγγες ἄ. φυσῶσι μέλαν μένος S. Aj.1412 (lyr.). II. with Verbs implying Rest, *aloft, on high*, ib.240, etc.; τὸ ἄ. Pl.Phdr.248a, etc. b. *on earth*, opp. *the world below*, νέρθε κἀπὶ γῆς ἄ. S.OT416; ἡνίκ' ἦσθ' ἄ. Id.El.1167; ἄ. βλέπειν Id. Ph.1348; ἄ. ἐπὶ [τῆς] γῆς Pl.Phd.109c; οἱ ἄ. the *living*, opp. οἱ κάτω the *dead*, S.Ant.1068, cf. Ph.1348, etc.; τὰ ἄ. πράγματα the world *above*, Luc.Cont.1. c. *in heaven*, opp. *earth*, οἱ ἄ. θεοί the gods *above*, S.Ant.1072; κῆρυξ τῶν ἄ. τε καὶ κάτω A.Ch.124: esp. in NT, ἐκ τῶν ἄ. εἰμί Ev.Jo.8.23; ἡ ἄ. Ἰερουσαλήμ Ep.Gal.4.26; ἡ ἄ. κλῆσις Ep.Phil.3.14. d. generally, of relative position, ὁ δῆμος ἄ. καθῆτο *in the upper quarter* of the city, i.e. the Pnyx, D.18.169; ἡ ἄ. βουλή, i.e. the Areopagus, Plu.Sol.19; βαλλόμενοι ὑπὸ τῶν ἄ. by those *above on the roofs*, Th.4.48; τὰ ἄ. X.An.4.3.25; τὰ ἄ. τῆς οἰκίας, opp. θεμέλια, Id.Eq.1.2; οἱ ἄ. τόποι OGI111.17. e. geographically, *on the upper side*, i.e. *on the north*, ἄ. πρὸς βορέην Hdt.1.72; οὔτε τὰ χωρία οὔτε τὰ κάτω [οὔτε τὰ πρὸς τὴν ἠῶ οὔτε τὰ πρὸς τὴν ἑσπέρην] Id.1.142; ὁ ἄ. τόπος Pl.R.435e. f. *inward from the coast*, ἡ ἄ. Ἀσίη Hdt.1.95; τὰ ἄ. τῆς Ἀσίης ib.177; ἡ ἄ. ὁδός the *upper* or *inland* road, Id.7.128, X.An.3.1.8; ἡ ἄ. πόλις, opp. *the Piraeus*, Th.2.48; in full, οἱ ἀπὸ θαλάσσης ἄ. ib.83; ἡ ἄ. Μακεδονία Plu.Pyrrh.11; ὁ ἄ. βασιλεύς the king *of the upper country*, i.e. of Persia, X.An.7.1.28. g. in the race-course, τὰ ἄ. *turning-post*, Pl.R.613b; cf. κάτω. h. in the body, τὰ ἄ. the *upper* parts, opp. τὸ κάτω, Arist.GA741^{b}28, al.; ἡ ἄ. κοιλία Id.Mete.360^{b}23. i. of Time, *formerly, of old*, εἰς τὸ ἄ. reckoning *upwards* or *backwards*, of generations, Pl.Tht.175b; οἱ ἄ. men *of olden time*, Id.Criti.110b; οἱ ἄ. τοῦ γένους Id.Lg.878a; αἱ ἄ. μητρός the mother's *lineal ancestors*, Id.R.461c, cf. infr. C; ἐν τοῖς ἄ. χρόνοις D.18.310. k. *above*, in referring to a passage, Pl.Grg. 508e; ἐν τοῖς ἄ. λόγοις R.603d, cf. Arist.Rh.1412^{b}33, etc. l. of tones in the voice, οἱ ἄ. τόνοι Plu.Cic.3. m. metaph., ἄ. βαίνειν walk *proudly*, Philostr.VA1.13; ἄ. φρονεῖν Hld.7.23. n. *higher, more general*, of κατηγορίαι, Arist.APo.82^{a}23. 2. ἄ. καὶ κάτω *up and down, to and fro*, εἶρπ' ἄ. τε καὶ κάτω E.HF953; ἄ. καὶ κ. φεύγειν Ar.Ach.21; ἄ. τε καὶ κ. κυκᾶν Id.Eq.866; περιπατεῖν ἄ. κ. Id.Lys. 709. b. *upside-down, topsy-turvy*, τὰ μὲν ἄ. κ. θήσω, τὰ δὲ κ. ἄ. Hdt.3.3; πάντ' ἄ. τε καὶ κ. στρέφων τίθησιν A.Eu.650; τρέπουσα τύρβ' ἄ. κ. Id.Fr.311, cf. Ar.Av.3; ἄ. κ. συγχεῖν E.Ba.349; ἄ. καὶ κ. ποιεῖν τὰ πράγματα D.9.36; τοὺς νόμους στρέφειν 21.19; πόλλ' ἄ., τὰ δ' αὖ κ. κυλίνδοντ' ἐλπίδες Pi.O.12.6; πολλάκις ἐμαυτὸν ἄ. κ. μετέβαλλον *backwards and forwards*, Pl.Phd.96a, cf. Prt.356d. 3. ἄ. ἔχειν τὸ πνεῦμα *pant* or *gasp*, Men.23, cf. Sosicr.1.

B. as Prep. with gen., *above*, ἡ ἄ. Ἅλυος Ἀσίη Hdt.1.130, cf. 103, Call.Jov.24; αἱ ἄ. μητρός (v. supr. II.1i); ἄ. τοῦ γόνατος *above* the knee, Thphr.Char.4.4; ἀπὸ ἄ. τῆς χθονὸς ταύτης Lxx 3Ki.14. 15. 2. with partitive gen., αἰθέρος ἄ. ἐλεῖν dub. in S.Ph.1092, cf. E.Or.1542; γῆς ἥκοντ' ἄ. Id.HF616; μικρὸν προαγαγὼν ἄ. τῶν πραγμάτων Aeschin.2.34.

C. Comp. ἀνωτέρω, abs., *higher*, ἀ. θακῶν..Ζεύς A.Pr.314; ἀ. οὐδὲν τῶν πρηγμάτων προκοπτομένων not getting on any *farther*, Hdt. 1.190; ἀδελφῷ ἢ πατρὶ ἢ ἔτι ἀ. Pl.Lg.880b; οὐ προήϊσαν ἀ. τὸ πρὸς ἑσπέρης Hdt.8.130. 2. c. gen., ἀ. Σάμου ib.132; ἀ. γίγνεσθαί τινων X.An.4.2.25; ἀ. τῶν μαστῶν *above* them, ib.1.4.17; later ἀνώτερον Plb.1.7.2, etc.; cf. ἀνώτερος. II. Sup. ἀνωτάτω, ἐς τοὺς ἀ. (sc. στάντας) Hdt.7.23; ἡ ἀ. κώμη X.An.7.4.11; ἀνῳκίσανθ' ὅπως ἀ. Ar.Pax 207; ἡ ἀ. ἄσκησις the *highest*, Arr.Epict.3.24.84, cf. Ph.1.33, al.; τὰ ἀ. τῶν γενῶν Arist.Metaph.998^{b}18, cf. Zeno Stoic.1.51, S.E.P. 1.138; τὰ ἀ. τρία Ph.1.321; ἡ ἀ. διαίρεσις Ps.-Alex.Aphr.in SE20.27.

ἄνωγα, old Ep. pf. with pres. sense: ἄνωγα, -ας, -ε, without augm., Il. and Trag., Hdt.3.81; 1 pl. ἄνωγμεν h.Ap.528: imper. ἄνωγε E.Or.119, more freq. ἄνωχθι Il.23.158, A.Ch.772, E.Alc.1044; 3 sg. ἀνωγέτω Od.2.195, ἀνώχθω Il.11.189; 2 pl. ἀνώγετε Od.23.132, ἄνωχθε 22.437, E.Rh.987; subj. ἀνώγῃ Il.7.74, Hdt.7.104, ἀνώγωμεν Herod.3.31; inf. ἀνωγέμεν Il.13.56; part. ἀνώγουσα Herod.7.101: plpf. with impf. sense, 3 sg. ἠνώγει Il.6.170, S.OC1598; without augm. ἀνώγει Od.2.385; Ion. ἠνώγεα ib.9.44, 17.55:—but ἀνώγει in Il.6. 439, 19.102, Od.5.139, 357, Hes.Th.549, Hdt.7.104 is pres. in sense, and must be referred to pres. ἀνώγω (unless corrected to ἄνωγεν); also 2 dual ἀνώγετον Il.4.287, and (later) 2 sg. ἀνώγεις Q.S.13.238:—from this pres. are formed impf. ἤνωγον Il.9.578, Od.14.237, or ἄνωγον Il.5.805, Od.3.35, etc.; ἤνωγες Maiist.17; ἤνωγε h.Cer.297, Hes.Op.68; 3 pl. ἄνωγον Inscr.Cypr.135 H.: fut. ἀνώξω Od.16.404: aor. ἤνωξα Hes.Sc.479; subj. ἀνώξομεν, Ep. for -ωμεν, Il.15.295; inf. ἀνῶξαι Od.10.531. Il.7.394, the impf. ἠνώγεον implies pres. ἀνωγέω:—Pass., ἄνωκται· κελεύεται, Hsch.:—poet. and Ion. Verb, also in Cypr., Inscr.Cypr. l.c., *command, order*, esp. of kings and masters, Il.5.899, etc.; also of equals and inferiors, *advise, urge*, 16.8, Od.2.195, etc.: constr. c. acc. pers. et inf., σιωπᾶν λαὸν ἀνώγει *bade* the people keep silence, Il.2.280, cf. 4.287, etc.; πατὴρ ἄνωγέ σ'.. αὐδᾶν A.Pr.947, cf. 1037, etc.; πράσσειν ἄνωγας οὖν με..τάδε; S.Tr. 1247; σιγᾶν ἄνωγα (sc. σε) Id.El.1458: in Hom. also c. dat. pers., Od.10.531, 20.139 sq., cf. A.R.1.693: c. acc. pers. only, θυμὸς ἄνωγέ με my spirit *bids, prompts* me, freq. in Hom.: abs., ἐποτρύνει καὶ ἀνώγει Il.15.43; κέλομαι καὶ ἄνωγα Od.3.317.

ἀνώγαιον or **ἀνώγεον**, τό, (ἄνω, γαῖα) *anything raised from the ground: the upper floor of a house*, used as a granary, X.An.5.4.29 (s.v.l.), Antiph.312; as a dining-room, Ev.Marc.14.15, Ev.Luc.22. 12. 2. *prison*, Suid. (ἀνώγεον in GDI1581 (Dodona); ἀνάγαιον and ἀνόκαιον are also found in codd., cf. AB405, Suid.)

ἀνωγή, ἡ, (ἄνωγα) *command, exhortation*, A.R.1.1134; θεῖαν δι' ἀνωγάν Philol.71.6 (Argos).

ἄνωδα, Arc., = ἄνωθε, dub. in IG5(2).262.17 (Mantinea, v B.C.).

ἀνωδίνω [ῑ], *to be in labour, bring forth*, Nonn.D.41.167.

ἀνωδόρκας· βρίγκος ἢ ἰχθύς (Theb.), Hsch.

ἄνῳδος, ον, *songless*, Arist.HA488^{a}34.

ἀνωδῠν-ία, ἡ, *freedom from pain*, Protag.9, Plot.1.4.6: in pl., *pain-free periods*, Philagr.ap.Aët.12.20. **-ος**, ον, (ὀδύνη) *free from pain*, οἰδήματα Hp.Prog.7, cf. D.Chr.32.57; τὸ ἓν ἀ. καὶ ἀνάλγητον Arist.Xen.974^{a}19; of persons, S.Ph.883; -ώτερος γίγνεσθαι *suffer less pain*, Hp.Prorrh.2.7; τὸ ἀνώδυνον, = ἀνωδυνία, Plu.2.102d. Adv. ἀνωδύνως, τίκτεσθαι Hp.Coac.527, cf. Plu.Cic.2; ἴᾶσθαι D.Chr.41.9: Sup. -ώτατα Hp.Acut.4. 2. *causing no pain, harmless*, τὸ μὴ φρονεῖν γὰρ κάρτ' ἀ. κακόν S.Aj.554b; ἁμάρτημα ἢ αἶσχος ἀ., definition of τὸ γελοῖον, Arist.Po.1449^{a}35. Adv. -ως, ἰάσασθαι τὴν πατρίδα Plu. Cleom.10. II. Act., *allaying pain*, Hp.Aph.5.22, Dsc.4.68 (Comp. and Sup.); φάρμακον ἀ. *anodyne*, Plu.2.614c:—the epitaph of a physician in IG14.1879 combines both signfs., πολλούς τε σώσας φαρμάκοις ἀνωδύνοις, ἀνώδυνον τὸ σῶμα νῦν ἔχει θανών.

ἄνωθεν and **ἄνωθε** (Ar.Ec.698), Dor. **ἄνωθα** Tab.Heracl.1.17: (ἄνω):—Adv. of Place, *from above, from on high*, θεοὺς ἄ. γῆς ἐποπτεύειν ἄχη A.Ag.1579; ὕδατος ἄ. γενομένου Th.4.75; βάλλειν ἄ. Id.7. 84; *from the interior* of a country, Id.1.59, X.An.7.7.2; esp. from inner Asia, Plu.Dem.14; from the north, Hdt.4.105. 2. like ἄνω, *above, on high*, opp. κάτωθεν or κάτω, A.Ag.871 (dub.): of the gods, Id.Supp.597 (lyr.), Pl.Lg.717b; of men on earth, οἱ ἄ. the *living*, A.Ch.834 (lyr.), E.Hel.1014; those *on deck* (in a ship), Th.7.63; of birds *of the air*, S.El.1058 (lyr.); ἡ ἄ. Φρυγία *upper* Phrygia, D.23. 155. b. rarely c. gen., ἄ. τοῦ στρατοπέδου Hdt.1.75; τοῦ καρποῦ Hp.Art.80; τῆς νεώς Plu.Them.12. II. in narrative or inquiry, *from the beginning, from farther back*, ἄ. ἄρχεσθαι, ἐπιχειρεῖν, Pl.Phlb. 44d, Lg.781d; ἄ. ἐξετάζειν τὸ γένος D.44.69, cf. Men.Epit.23; in quotations, *above, earlier*, Sch.E.Ph.249, etc.: οἱ ἔμπροσθεν καὶ ἄ. γονεῖς *ancestors*, Pl.Ti.18d; Κορίνθιαι εἰμὲς ἄ. *by descent*, Theoc.15.91, cf. 22. 164, Call.Aet.3.1.32; πονηρὸς ἄ. a *born* rogue, D.45.80; ἐκ προγόνων ἄ. τετιμημένος IG2^2.1072; ἄ. ἀναμάρτητον *from early life*, Phld. Sto.Herc.339.17.16; ἐν τοῖς ἄ. χρόνοις D.9.41. 2. τὰ ἄ. *higher, more universal principles*, Pl.Phd.101d, cf. Arist.APo.97^{a}33. 3. *over again, anew, afresh*, φιλίαν ἄ. ποιεῖται J.AJ1.18.3, Artem.1.14, cf. Ev.Jo.3.3; πάλιν ἄ. Ep.Gal.4.9, cf. Harp. s.v. ἀνάδικοι κρίσεις; κτίστης ἄνωθε γενόμενος IG7.2712.58.

ἀνωθέω, *push up* or *forth*, ἀνώσαντες πλέον (sc. ναῦν) they *pushed off from shore* and sailed, Od.15.553; ἀ. τὴν πόλιν εἰς τοὺς πολεμίους Th.8.93:—Pass., *to be thrust upwards*, Arist.Pr.931^{b}35. 2. *push back*, Hp.Art.80; ὅστις σῖτον..ἐσαχθέντα ἀνωθεοίη SIG37 A 10 (Teos): —Med., *repel, repulse*, οὗτοι ἦσαν οἱ βασιλέα..ἀνωσάμενοι Hdt.7.139, cf. 8.109. 3. *support*, of buoyant water, Olymp. in Mete.81.23, al. 4. metaph., *hand over*, τὰ πράγματα πρὸς τὸν δῆμον D.C.52. 17; *refer*, τὰς ἐλαττώσεις εἰς τοὺς στρατηγήσαντας Id.Fr.43.18. 5. intr., *push one's way up*, εἰς τὸ πρόσαντες J.BJ3.7.5.

ἄνωθον· ὀξύν, Hsch. (fort. ἄνωθρον).

ἀνωΐσ-τί [ῐ], Adv. of sq., *unlooked for*, Od.4.92. **-τος** (A), ον, (οἴομαι) *unlooked for, unexpected*, ἀ. κακόν Il.21.39; ἀνωΐστων πολέων περ Hom.Epigr.5; βέλεα Mosch.2.75; κλάδοι Epic.Anon.Oxy. 214.1. Adv. -τως A.R.1.680. **-τος** (B), ον, prob. f.l. for ἀνοιστός, *referred*, ἀνωΐστου γενομένου ἐς τὴν Πυθίην the matter having been *referred to*.., Hdt.6.66. 2. *lifted up, raised*, Aret.SA2.11.

ἀνώλεθρος, ον, (ὄλεθρος) *indestructible*, Parm.8.3; ἀθάνατος καὶ ἀ. Anaximand.15, Pl.Phd.88b, 95b, Arist.Mu.396^{a}31, Ocell.1.2; of roots, Thphr.HP3.12.2. II. Act., *not deadly, harmless*, ὄφεις Paus.10.17.12; of symptoms, *not fatal*, Aret.SD1.5.

ἀνωλέως· ἰσχυρός, Hsch.

ἀνωλόφυκτος, ον, (ὀλοφύζω) *unbewailed*, Hsch.

ἀνωμᾰλ-έω, *suffer ups and downs of fortune*, Nech.ap.Vett.Val. 279.28, cf. 65.6, Heph.Astr.2.28. **-ής**, *ές*, = ἀνώμαλος, Epicur. *Ep.*2 p.53 U., Arist.*Pr.*918a11; ἡ φωνὴ μεταβάλλει ἐπὶ τὸ.. ἀνωμαλέστερον Id.*HA*581a18. Adv. -λῶς Id.*Ph.*265b12. **-ία**, ἡ, *unevenness, irregularity*, Pl.*R.*547a, Arist.*HA*495b2; of shape, Str.16.1.21; ἀ. τῶν στοιχείων, as cause of disease, Diocl.*Fr.*30: pl., Epicur.*Ep.*2 p.53 U. 2. Astron., *irregular motion, anomaly*, ἀ. τῆς κινήσεως Gem.1.20, cf. Ptol.*Alm.*3.3, etc.; ἀ. ἐκλειπτικαί, of the moon's orbit, Plu.*Aem.*17. II. of conditions, *irregularity*, ἀ. καὶ ταραχή Isoc.2.6; ἀ. τῆς κτήσεως Arist.*Pol.*1270a15; τύχης D.S.20.30, cf. 18.59: pl., Vett.Val.38.17. III. of persons, *inconsistency*, Aeschin.2.7 and 54, Plb.6.44.2, Plu.*Alc.*16; of style, *unevenness*, Id.2.45b. IV. Gramm., *deviation from rule, irregularity*, title of work by Chrysipp., *Stoic.*2.6, cf. Gell.2.25, etc.; *variety, diversity*, Arist.*GA*788a24, A.D.*Adv.*205.18. V. *indisposition*, '*malaise*', Hld.7.19, Gal.7.435. **-ίζω**, *to be subject to vicissitude*, Vett.Val.57.4, 85.28. **-οκράς**, *unevenly mixed*, Hsch. **-ος**, *ον*, (ἀ- priv., ὁμαλός) *uneven, irregular*, χώρα Pl.*Lg.*625d; φύσις Id.*Ti.*58a; τὸ ἀ. τῆς ναυμαχίας Th.7.71 (cj.), cf. Arist.*Pr.*885a15: and in Sup., Hp.*Aër.*13; of movements, Arist.*Ph.*228b16, al.; of periods of time, Id.*GA*772b7; of the voice, ib.788a1. Adv. -λως, κινεῖσθαι Id.*Ph.*238a22, cf. Pl.*Ti.*52e. II. of conditions, fortune, and the like, φεῦ τῶν βροτείων ὡς ἀ. τύχαι E.*Fr.*684; πόλις, πολιτεία, Pl.*Lg.*773b, *Mx.*238e; θέα Plot.6.7.34. Adv. -λως Hp.*Prog.*3, Isoc.7.29; ἀ. διατεθῆναι τὸ σῶμα fall into *precarious* health, Prisc.p.333 D. III. of persons, *inconsistent, capricious*, ὁμαλῶς ἀ. Arist.*Po.*1454a26; ὄχλος, δαιμόνιον, App.*BC*3.42, *Pun.*59; πίθηκος Phryn.Com.20; τύχη *AP*10.96. Adv. -λως Isoc.9.44. IV. Gramm., of words *which deviate from a general rule, anomalous*, Diom.1.327 K.; but τὸ ἀ. τῆς συντάξεως *diversity* of construction, A.D.*Synt.*291.17. Adv. -λως Sch.Th.*Oxy.*853 v 18. **-ότης**, *ητος*, ἡ, = ἀνωμαλία, Pl.*Ti.*57e, 58c, *Placit.*2.30.2. **-ωσις**, v. ἀνομάλωσις.

ἀνωμολογ-ημένως, Adv. *admittedly*, Lib.*Decl.*50.39 (s.v.l.). **-ητος**, *ον*, *inconsistent*, Ptol.*Tetr.*47.

ἄνωμος, *ον*, *without shoulder*, Πελοπίδαι Suid.

ἀνωμο-τί, Adv. of sq., *without oath*, καὶ ὀμνύντας καὶ ἀ. Hdt.2.118. **-τος**, *ον*, (ὄμνυμι) *unsworn, not bound by oath*, ἡ γλῶσσ' ὀμώμοχ', ἡ δὲ φρὴν ἀ. E.*Hipp.*612; ἀ. μάρτυρες Antipho 5.12, cf. D.21.86; θεῶν ἀνώμοτος E.*Med.*737. Adv. -τως Aristid.*Or.*28(49).94. II. *not sworn to*, εἰρήνη D.19.204.

ἀνωνίς, *ίδος*, ἡ, = ὄνωνις, Dsc.3.18, v.l. in Poet.ap.Plu.2.44e, cf. 485a.

ἀνωνόμαστος, *ον*, *nameless, ineffable*, E.*Hec.*714 (lyr.); ἀ. ὀσμή Ar.*Av.*1715.

ἀνωνῠμ-εί and **-ί**, Adv. *without name*, v.l. in Sch.D.T.p.18 H., *EM*764.22. **-ία**, ἡ, *namelessness*, Arat.146. **-ος**, *ον*, (from ὄνυμα, Aeol. for ὄνομα) *without name*, οὐ μὲν γάρ τις πάμπαν ἀ. ἐστ' ἀνθρώπων Od.8.552; ἡ Εὐρώπη.. ἦν ἀ. Hdt.4.45; θεαί, i.e. the Furies, E.*IT*944; Ὅρκου παῖς ἐστὶν ἀ. Orac.ap.Hdt.6.86, cf. Pl.*Ti.*60a, Arist.*EN*1107b2, prob. in *Po.*1447b9, cf. Tz.*Diff.Poet.*11. 2. *anonymous*, μήνυσις Lys.13.22, cf. D.C.66.11. 3. *not to be named, unspeakable*, Aristid.*Or.*50(26).8. 4. *difficult to name*, in Comp., Arist.*EE*1221a40, Alex.Aphr.*in Mete.*197.23. 5. Adv. -μως *without mentioning a name*, Men.Rh.p.391 S. II. *nameless, inglorious*, γῆρας Pi.*O.*1.82; γῆ πατρὶς οὐκ ἀ. E.*Hel.*16, cf. *Hipp.*1; ὄνομα ἀ. Ar.*Lys.*854; of persons, S.*Tr.*377, Pl.*Lg.*721c; ἀ. καὶ ἄδοξοι D.8.66, cf. Herod.6.14. Adv. -μως Poll.5.160.

ἄνωξις, *εως*, ἡ, = ἀνωγή, Hsch.

ἀνώξω, v. ἄνωγα.

ἀνώπιον, τό, (ὀπή) *the part above the door*, Poll.2.53 (pl.).

ἀνώπιστος, *ον*, *unseen, unnoticed*, Hsch.

ἀνωρέας· οὐκ ἀπολλυμένους, Hsch.

ἀνωρ-ία, Ion. -ίη, ἡ, *untimeliness*, ἀ. τοῦ ἔτεος πολεμέειν *the bad season* of the year for war, opp. ὥρα ἔτους, Hdt.8.113. **-ος**, *ον*, v.l. for ἄωρος, ἀ. ἀποθανών Id.2.79, cf. *Leg.Gort.*7.29.

ἀνώροφος, *ον*, (ὄροφος) *unroofed, uncovered*, Lyc.350, D.C.37.17.

ἀνωρύομαι [ῡ], *howl aloud, utter with a howl*, πένθος *AP*7.468 (Mel.), Hld.10.16.

ἀνῷσαι, v. ἀναφέρω.

ἀνωστικῶς, Adv. *by pushing upwards*, S.E.*P.*3.69.

ἀνωστόν· ἔγκλητον, Hsch.

ἀνώτατος, *η*, *ον*, Sup. Adj. formed from ἄνω (B), *topmost*, τὰ ἀνώτατα Hdt.2.125; θεῶν τῶν ἀνωτάτων νοητικός Euryph.ap.Stob.4.39.27 (ἀνωτάτω Mein.); ἡ ἀ. χάρις D.Chr.31.32. Adv. **ἀνωτάτω**, v. ἄνω (B).

ἀνωτερικός, *ή*, *όν*, *upper* in point of place, *inland* (v. ἄνω (B) A. II. 1 f), *Act.Ap.*19.1. 2. of a medicine, *given by the mouth*, τροχίσκος Archig.ap.Aët.9.42, cf. Cass.Fel.48. II. τὸ -κόν *medicine which takes effect upwards, emetic*, Hp.*Superf.*29, Gal.10.969.

ἀνώτερος, *α*, *ον*, Comp. Adj. from ἄνω (B), *upper, higher*, Arist.*HA* 496b35, D.H.*Rh.*1.1, Luc.*Asin.*9; ἐπιβουλῆς ἀ. γέγονεν got *the better of*, Nic.Dam.p.25 D.; neut. as Adv., Arist.*HA*503b18; *above*, Lxx *Le.*11.21; *earlier* in a book, *Ep.Hebr.*10.8, cf. Plb.3.1.1; *to a higher place*, *Ev.Luc.*14.10. Adv. **ἀνωτέρω**, v. ἄνω.

ἀνωτέρωθεν, Adv. *from above, from a higher place*, Hp.*Oss.*5.

ἀνωτικός, *ή*, *όν*, = ἀνωτερικός I, *CIG*6849 (Ilium), cf. *Eranos* 13.89.

ἀνωφάλακρος [φᾰ], *ον*, *bald on top*, Ptol.*Tetr.*143.

ἀνωφέλ-εια, ἡ, *uselessness*, D.L.9.78, Aq.*Je.*4.14; *inconvenience*, *PHaw.*56.20 (i A.D.). **-ής**, *ές*, *unprofitable, useless*, ἁβροσύναι Xenoph.3.1; γόοι A.*Pr.*33; σκιά S.*El.*1159; πάντα ἀ. ἦν Th.2.47; ἀ. αὐτῷ τε καὶ τοῖς ἄλλοις Pl.*R.*496d, al. 2. *hurtful, prejudicial*, Th.6.33; τινί Pl.*Prt.*334a, X.*HG*1.7.27: Comp. -έστερος E.*Fr.*48, X.*Cyn.*13.11, Pl.*Hp.Ma.*284e. Adv. -λῶς Arist.*EN*1095a5, *PLond.*3.908.28 (ii A.D.). **-ητος**, *ον*, *unprofitable, useless*, τινί *to* one, A.*Ch.*752: abs., S.*Ant.*645, *El.*1144; γῆ X.*Cyr.*1.6.11. II. *helpless*, ἄνθρωπος Eup.377; ἀ. καὶ θεοῖς ἐχθρός Stratt.9 D. **-ιμος**, *ον*, = foreg., Phld.*Rh.*2.69 S.

ἀνωφέρ-εια, ἡ, *motion upwards*, opp. κατωφ., Alex.Aphr.*Pr.*1.92. **-ής**, *ές*, *borne upwards, ascending*, opp. κατωφερής, of air and fire, Chrysipp.*Stoic.*2.143, cf. 290, Aristid.Quint.3.19; ὀσμαί Arist.*Pr.*908a25, cf. Herm.*in Phdr.*p.178 A.; τὸ ἀ. Plu.2.649c. 2. of wine, *heady, intoxicating*, Ath.1.32c. II. Act., *bearing upwards*, Arist.*Ph.*217a3.

ἀνώφλῐον, τό, (φλιά) *lintel* of a door, Suid.

ἀνώ-φοιτος, *ον*, *mounting upwards*, of air and fire, Zeno *Stoic.*1.27, cf. Ph.2.513, etc. **-φορέω**, *bear up, raise*, freq. in Eust., esp. in Pass. as 40.36, al.:—Act., 695.54. **-φορος**, *ον*, = ἀνωφερής, S.E.*M.*10.9, Alex.Aphr.*Pr.*1.96, Herm.*in Phdr.*p.132 A.

ἄνωχθι, ἀνώχθω, ἄνωχθε, v. ἄνωγα.

ἄνωχμον· κελευστικόν, Hsch.

ἀνώχῠρος, *ον*, = ἀνόχυρος, *not fortified*, X.*Ages.*6.6, *SIG*569.7 (Halasarna, iii B.C.). II. *open, clear*, χώρα, f.l. for ἄνυδρος, Hp.*Aër.*24.

ἄξαλλα, ἡ, a herb found on the Euphrates and used as a remedy for fever, Chryserm.ap.Ps.-Plu.*Fluv.*20.3 (translated by θερμόν).

ἄξεινος, *ον*, Ion. for ἄξενος, q.v. **ἀξ-έμεν, -έμεναι**, v. sub ἄγω.

ἀξενάγητος, *ον*, *without a guide*, ψυχή Diog.*Ep.*39.2.

ἀξενᾰγώγητος, *ον*, *not received* or *guided as a guest*, Eust.*Prooem.*1.10.

ἀξεν-ία, ἡ, *inhospitality*, Eratosth.ap.Str.17.1.19, D.S.1.67. **-ος**, Ion. and poet. **ἄξεινος**, *ον*, *inhospitable*, of persons, opp. πολύξεινος, Hes.*Op.*715; ἀνὴρ ξένοισιν ἄ. E.*Fr.*736; ἄ. καὶ ἄγριον Pl.*Sph.*217e; of places, ὅρμος S.*Ph.*217 (lyr.); γῆ, στέγη, E.*IT*94, *Cyc.*91: Comp. and Sup. -ώτερος, -ώτατος, Id.*Alc.*556, *Med.*1264. II. Ἄξεινος (sc. πόντος) *the Axine*, afterwds. called *the Euxine*, Pi.*P.*4.203, E.*Andr.*793 (lyr.); in full, πόρος, πόντος Ἄ., Id.*IT*253, 341.

ἄξεστος, *ον*, *unwrought*, πέτρος S.*OC*19, cf. *Fr.*322, *AP*7.657 (Leon.): metaph. of a poet, *rough, uncouth*, Sch.Ar.*Ra.*86.

ἀξία, Ion. -ίη, ἡ, (ἄξιος) *worth, value*, τῶν φορτίων Hdt.4.196; τοῦ τιμήματος τῆς ἀξίας E.*Hipp.*623; ἡ ἀ. τοῦ δούλου Pl.*Lg.*936d; then, simply, *money-value, price, amount*, κατ' ἀξίην ἑκάστου ἀδικήματος ἐδικαίευ Hdt.1.100; ὑποτελέειν ἀξίην βασιλέϊ Id.4.201; τῆς ἀ. τιμᾶσθαι estimate the penalty *at the real amount*, Pl.*Ap.*36b, cf. e; τὴν ἀξίαν τῆς βλάβης ἀπογράφεσθαι Id.*Lg.*845e; προσάπτειν ἑκάστῳ τῶν ἁμαρτημάτων τὴν ἀ. τοῦ πάθους ib.876d; μὴ κατ' ἀξίαν τῆς οὐσίας X.*Cyr.*8.4.32; σκοποῦμαι.. εἰ ἄρα ὥσπερ τῶν οἰκετῶν, οὕτω καὶ τῶν φίλων εἰσὶν ἀξίαι Id.*Mem.*2.5.2; κατὰ τὴν τῆς ὀλιγωρίας ἀ. according to *the amount* of his neglect, Decr.ap.D.18.74; ἡ κατ' ἀ. ἰσότης *proportionate* equality, Arist.*Pol.*1302a8; τὸ κατ' ἀ. ἴσον ib.1301b30; παρὰ τὴν ἀ. Id.*EN*1122b29, al. 2. of persons, *reputation, dignity*, Th.6.68, D.13.18, cf. 18.63; ἡ τῆς ἀρχῆς ἀ. Pl.*Lg.*945b; ἡ τῆς ἀ. τιμή ib.744b; οἱ ἐπ' ἀξίας persons *of dignity, official* personages, Luc.*Nigr.*24; ἐξεπορεύετο μετὰ μεγάλης ἀ. with great *dignity, pomp*, Plb.38.8.6; κατὰ δουλικὴν ἀξίαν κοσμεῖσθαι D.S.5.40. 3. generally, a man's *due, merit, deserts*, τὴν μὲν ἀ. οὐ λάμψεαι, ἐλάσσω δὲ τῆς ἀξίης Hdt.7.39; εἰ τῆς ἀ. ἐτύγχανες Ar.*Av.*1223; κατ' ἀξίαν according to *desert* or *merit, duly*, E.*Hec.*374, Pl.*R.*496a, cf. *Phd.*113e, al.; ὑπὲρ τὴν ἀ. beyond *desert, undeservedly*, E.*HF*146, D.2.3; παρὰ τὴν ἀ., οὐ κατ' ἀ., Th.7.77, cf. D.1.23. b. *penalty*, τὴν ἀ. ἀποτίνειν, ὑπέχειν, Luc.*DMort.*30.1, *Pisc.*8. 4. *moral value*, *Stoic.*3.30: pl., Cleanth.ib.1.129. II. *estimate of* a thing's *worth, opinion*, κατὰ τὴν ἰδίαν ἀ. D.S.14.10, cf. 107; esp. *estimate* of the moral value of actions, αἱ τῶν ἐκτὸς ἀξίαι Arr.*Epict.*1.2.7, cf. 1.25.17.

ἀξι-άγαστος [ᾰγ], *ον*, *worth admiring, admirable*, X.*Lac.*10.2, Ael.*Fr.*116, Jul.*Or.*6.190d. **-άκουστος** [ᾰκ], *ον*, *worth hearing*, X.*Smp.*4.44. **-ακρόᾱτος**, *ον*, *worth listening to*, Id.*Lac.*4.2 (in Sup. -ότατος). **-απόλαυστος**, *ον*, *delectable*, *Stoic.*3.180. **-αφήγητος**, Ion. **-απήγητος**, *ον*, *worth telling*, Hdt.1.16, 177 (Sup.), J.*AJ*15.11.5 (Sup.), Arr.*An.*1 *Praef.*1 (Comp.).

ἀξιάω, = ἀξιόω, *Hoffmann Inscr.*2 No.160.33 (Lampsacus), No.130.5 (Tenedos).

ἀξι-ελέητος, *ον*, *pitiable*, Diog.*Ep.*27. **-επαίνετος**, *ον*, = v.l. for sq., in X.*HG*4.4.6. **-έπαινος**, *ον*, *praiseworthy*, Id.*Cyr.*3.3.6, D.61.15; χρῆμα, of a dead ox, Ael.*NA*2.57, etc.: Sup. -ότατος X.*HG*4.4.6. Adv. -νως Apollon.*Vit.Aeschin.*11. **-επιθύμητος** [ῡ], *ον*, *worthy of desire*, Hsch. s.v. ἀξιέραστον. **-έραστος**, *ον*, *worthy of love*, X.*Cyr.*5.2.9, Chrysipp.*Stoic.*3.181, Plu.*Comp.Thes.Rom.*1, Luc.*DMar.*1.2, Aristaenet.1.27; οἰκονομία *PMag.Par.*1.2010: Comp., X.*Smp.*8.14. **-ήκοος**, *ον*, (ἀκοή) = ἀξιάκουστος, Diog.*Ep.*35 and 36. **-θεος, -θέωρος**, v. ἀξιόθεος.

ἀξῑν-άριον, τό, Dim. of sq., J.*BJ*2.8.7. **-η**, ἡ, *axe-head*, ἀξίνην εὔχαλκον ἐλαΐνῳ ἀμφὶ πελέκκῳ Il.13.612. 2. *battle-axe* (expl. as δίστομος πέλεκυς by Hsch.), ib.15.711, cf. Hdt.7.64. 3. *axe* for hewing wood, X.*An.*1.5.12, *Ev.Matt.*3.10, *Ev.Luc.*3.9. (Cf. Goth. *aqizi*, OE. *æx*, Lat. *ascia* (fr. *acsia).) **-ίδιον**, τό, Dim. of foreg., J.*BJ*2.8.9.

ἀξῑνο-κράτημα [ρᾰ], *ατος*, τό, *helve of an axe*, Zonar. s.v. στελεός. **-πληκτος**, *ον*, *struck by an axe*, *An.Par.*3.114, Sch.Il.1.1.

ἀξινῶρυξ· *acisculus, ligo*, Gloss.

ἀξιο-βίωτος, *ον*, *worth living for*, οὐκ ἀξιοβίωτόν ἐστιν X.*HG*4.

4.6. **-δάκρῦτος**, ον, *worthy of tears*, Sch.E.*Med.*1221. **-δοτος**, ον, *deserving, honourable*, *IGRom.*4.1398 (Smyrna). **-εργός**, όν, *fit for, capable of work*, X.*Oec.*7.34. **-ζηλος**, ον, *enviable*, Ael. *VH*12.64, Them.*Or.*13.175b (Sup.). Adv. -λως Suid. **-ζήλωτος**, ον, = foreg., Phld.*Piet.*66 (Sup.); νίκη Plu.*Flam.*20. 2. *worthy of emulation*, Dsc.*Praef.*4. **-ζήτητος**, ον, *worth inquiry*, Oenom.ap.Eus.*PE*6.7. **-θάνᾰτος** [θᾰ], ον, *worthy of death*, Sch.A. *Th.*582. **-θαύμαστος**, ον, *wonder-worthy*, X.*Mem.*1.4.4 (Comp.), Callix.1, Aristeas 282. **-θέᾱτος**, Ion. -ητος, ον, *well worth seeing*, Hdt.1.14,184, al., X.*Smp.*1.10, Corn.*ND*17: Comp. -ότερος Plu. *Demetr.*43: Sup. -ότατος Hdt.2.176, X.*Lac.*4.2. **-θεος** (A), ον, (θεός) *worthy of God*, Oenom.ap.Eus.*PE*5.34. **-θεος** (B), ον, (θέα) *worth seeing*, Alciphr.3.55:—in poet. forms **ἀξίθεος** *Epigr.Gr.*981; **ἀξιθέωρος**, ον, ibid. (Philae). **-θρηνος**, ον, *worthy of lamentation*, E.*Alc.*904 (lyr.). **-θρῐάμβευτος**, ον, *worth being led in triumph*, Suet.*Calig.*47. **-καταφρόνητος**, ον, *deserving contempt*, Iamb.*VP* 31.206. **-κοινώνητος**, ον, *worthy of our society*, Pl.*R.*371e; *worthy to share in*, τοῦ συλλόγου *Lg.*961a. **-κτητος**, ον, *worth getting*, X.*Cyr.*5.2.10, Paus.1.9.5, Philostr.*Ep.*9; ἐς φιλίαν Aristid.Quint. 3.18. **-ληπτος**, ον, *worth acceptance, precious*, Hsch. **-λογος**, ον, *worthy of mention, remarkable*, ὁ ἐν Ἐφέσῳ νηός Hdt.2.148, etc.; πόλεμος -ώτατος Th.1.1; τοῦτο -ώτερον X.*Cyr.*8.2.13; ἁλίθοι Suid. Adv. -γως X.*Mem.*1.5.5, Aristeas 72, Phld.*Rh.*1.2 S., al., Plu.2. 128e. 2. of persons, *of note, important*, τοὺς μάλιστα ἐν τέλει καὶ ἀξιολογωτάτους Th.2.10, etc. 3. ἀ. μιμήματα imitations of *worthy* objects, Pl.*Lg.*669e. **-μᾰθής**, ές, = sq., X.*Ep.*7 (Comp.). **-μάθητος** [ᾰ], ον, *worth being learnt*, Iamb.*VP*3.14. **-μᾰκάριστος** [κᾰ], ον, *worthy to be deemed happy*, X.*Ap.*34 (Sup.). **-μανεῖς**· δυνατώτεροι, Hsch. **-μᾰχος**, ον, *a match for* another *in battle* or *war*, τινί Hdt.7.157, Th.8.38; πρός τινα Plu.*Cat.Ma.*12, etc.: abs., Hdt. 3.19, 8.63, Th.8.80, Aen.Tact.2.5. 2. c. inf., *sufficient in strength* or *number*, νέες ἀξιόμαχοι τῇσι Αἰγινητέων συμβαλεῖν Hdt.6.89; νεῶν ..ἀξιομάχων δέκεσθαι τὸν ἐπιόντα Id.7.138, cf. 101; ἀξιόμαχόν τι δρᾶν D.C.43.4. Adv. -χως, τινὶ συνεστάναι Plu.*Sull.*19. **-μίμητος** [ῑ], ον, *worthy of imitation*, Ecphant.ap.Stob.4.7.65. **-μῑσής**, ές, *worthy of hate, hateful*, D.C.78.21. **-μίσητος** [ῑ], ον, = foreg., Plu.2. 10a, 537d, D.C.38.44:—also **ἀξιόμῑσος**, ον, A.*Eu.*366 (lyr.). **-μνημόνευτος**, ον, *worthy of mention*, Pl.*Prt.*343a, *Smp.*178a, X.*HG*4.8. 1, etc. **-μνηστος**, ον, = foreg., *Gloss.* **-μορφος**, ον, *shapely, beautiful*, Man.4.513. **-νῑκος**, ον, *worthy of victory, worthy of being preferred*, X.*Cyr.*1.5.10: c. inf., -ότερος ἔχειν τοῦτο τὸ κράτος *more worthy* to hold this supremacy, Hdt.7.187, cf. 9.26: Sup., Luc. *Anach.*36. **-πενθής**, ές, *lamentable*, E.*Hipp.*1465. **-πιστεύομαι**, *to be worthy of belief*, Phld.*Po.*1676.11. **-πιστία**, ἡ, *trustworthiness*, Hipparch.1.1.7, Phld.*Rh.*1.45 S., D.S.1.23, Longin. 16.2, etc. 2. *plausibility*, J.*BJ*1.32.2; *credibility*, Alex.*Fig.*1. 17. **-πιστος**, ον, *trustworthy*, Pl.*Alc.*1.123b; ἀ. ἂν εἰκότως φαίνοιτο D.1.3; Κτησίας οὐκ ὢν ἀ. Arist.*HA*606ᵃ8, al.; ἀ. εἴς τι X.*Mem.* 1.5.2; ναύλοχα ἀ. πρὸς τοσαύτην ναυτιλίαν *sufficient for*.., Plu.*Caes.* 58: Comp., Phld.*Mus.*p.77 K. 2. of evidence, *trustworthy*, Arist. *GA*741ᵃ37. Adv. -τως, ἀ. συνῶπται 741ᵃ34. 3. in bad sense, *plausible*, in Adv. -τως Timae.70, Gal.17(2).139. **-πιστοσύνη**, ἡ, = -πιστία, Man.4.505. **-ποινος**, ον, *exacting due punishment*, of Athena at Sparta, Paus.3.15.6. **-πρεπής**, ές, *proper, becoming*, σῶμα X.*Smp.*8.40 (Sup.), cf. Phld.*Rh.*2.30 S. **-προστάτευτος** [ᾰ], ον, *worthy of command*, Poll.1.178.

ἀξιόρᾱτος, ον, *worth seeing*, Luc.*Hist.Conscr.*32, Ph.1.441.

ἄξιος, ία, ιον (ος, ον Nonn.*D.*8.314), for *ἄγ-τιος, *counterbalancing*, cf. ἄγω VI: hence prop. *weighing as much, of like value, worth as much as*, c. gen., βοὸς ἄ. Il.23.885; νῦν δ' οὐδ' ἑνὸς ἄξιοί εἰμεν Ἕκτορος we are not—all together—*worth* one Hector, 8.234, cf. Hdt. 1.32, 7.21; πάντων Ζεὺς ἄξιον ἦμαρ ἔδωκεν Il.15.719; so πολλοῦ ἄ. *worth* much, X.*An.*4.1.28, Pl.*Smp.*185b, etc.; πλείονος ἄ. Id.*Phdr.* 235b, etc.; πλείστου ἄ. Th.2.65, Pl.*Grg.*464d, etc.; παντός, τοῦ παντὸς ἄ., E.*Fr.*275, Pl.*Sph.*216c; παντὸς ἄ., c. inf., Ar.*Av.*797; λόγου ἄ., = ἀξιόλογος, Hdt.1.133, Th.1.73, etc.; σπουδῆς, μνήμης ἄ., Plu.2. 35a, 172e:—opp. to these are οὐδενὸς ἄ. Thgn.456; ἢ παντὸς ἢ τὸ παράπαν οὐδενός Pl.*Phlb.*64d; ὀλίγου Id.*Grg.*497b, etc.; σμικροῦ Id. *R.*504d, etc.; βραχέος Id.*Lg.*692c; μείονος, ἐλάττονος ἄ., X.*Vect.*4.50, *Cyr.*2.2.14; πολλαπλασίου τιμήματος ἄ. κτήσεις Arist.*Pol.*1306ᵇ12; also εἰς ὀγδοήκοντα μνᾶς ἄ. *worth* up to a sum of.., D.27.10. 2. c. dat. pers., σοὶ δ' ἄξιόν ἐστιν ἀμοιβῆς 'tis *worth* a return to thee, i.e. will bring thee a return, Od.1.318; πολέος δέ οἱ ἄξιος ἔσται Il.23.562; βασιλεῖ ἂν πολλοῦ ἄξιοι γένοιντο X.*An.*2.1.14. 3. abs., *worthy, goodly*, ἄξια δῶρα Il.9.261; ἄ. ὦνος a *goodly* price, Od.15.429; ὅθεν κέ τοι ἄξιον ἄλφοι it would bring thee *a good price*, 20.383; φέροντες ὅ τι ἕκαστος ἄξιον εἶχε X.*Cyr.*3.3.2. b. in Att. in an exactly opposite sense, 'good value for the money', i.e. *cheap*, Ar.*Eq.*672,895: Comp., ib.645; ὡς ἀξιώτατον πρίασθαι Lys.22.18; ὡς ἄ. γεγόνασιν οἱ πυροὶ ἐν τῇ ἀγορᾷ Thphr.*Char.*3.3, cf. X.*Vect.*4.6. 4. *deserved, meet, due*, δίκη S.*El.*298, X.*Oec.*12.19; χάρις Id.*HG*1.6.11; ἄξια δράσας ἄξια πάσχων *fit* suffering for *fit* deeds, A.*Ag.*1527, cf. E.*Ion*735. 5. of persons, οἱ ἑωυτοῦ ἄξιοι those of one's own *rank*, his *peers*, Hdt.1.107. 6. *sufficient for*, c. gen., ἄ. τοῦ πολέμου τὰ χρήματα D.14.27. 7. αἰδοῦς ἀξίαν..τὴν προθυμίαν μᾶλλον ἢ θράσους more *like* modesty than rashness, Arist.*Cael.*291ᵇ 25. II. after Hom., in moral relation, *worthy, estimable*, of persons and things, Hdt.7.224, etc.; οὐδὲν ἀξία nothing *worth*, A.*Ch.* 445; ἀξίαν κἀπ' ἀξίων Id.*Eu.*435; ἀξίων γεννητόρων ἤθη φυλάσσεις E. *Ion*735. 2. *worthy of, deserving*, mostly c. gen. rei, ἄξιον φυγῆς, ἄξια στεναγμάτων, γέλωτος, Id.*Med.*1124, *Or.*1326, *Heracl.*507; ἐγκωμίων τί ἀξιώτερον ἤ..; X.*Ag.*10.3: c. gen. pers., ποιεῖν ἄξια οὔτε ὑμῶν οὔτε πατέρων Th.2.71; ἄξιον τοῦ πατρός Isoc.9.80; ἄξια τοῦ Μαραθῶνος διανοεῖσθαι Plu.*Cim.*5. b. c. gen. rei et dat. pers., ἡμῖν δ' Ἀχιλλεὺς ἄξιος τιμῆς *is worthy of* honour *at* our *hands*, E.*Hec.*309; πολλῶν ἀγαθῶν ἄ. ὑμῖν Ar.*Ach.*633; ἄ. πλείστου Λακεδαιμονίοις Th. 4.81; θανάτου τῇ πόλει X.*Mem.*1.1.1, cf. 1.2.62; εἰμὶ δ' οὐ τούτων ὑμῖν ἄ. D.21.217; χάριτος ἄ. τῇ πόλει Antipho 6.10; later τιμῆς ἄ. παρὰ πάντων Luc.*Tox.*3. 3. c. inf., Προθοήνορος ἀντὶ πεφάσθαι ἄ. *worthy* to be killed instead of him, Il.14.472, cf. Th.1.76; τίεσθαι δ' ἀξιώτατος A.*Ag.*531; ἄ. θρήνων τυχεῖν S.*Aj.*924; ἄξιοι δουλεύειν *only fit* to be slaves, Arist.*Pol.*1254ᵇ36; also ἄ. σέβειν E.*Heracl.*315 (Elmsl.). b. ἄξιός εἰμι, like δίκαιός εἰμι, I *deserve* to.., ἄξιός εἰμι πληγὰς λαβεῖν Ar.*Ec.*324; ἄξιός εἰμι ἀπολαῦσαι X.*Cyr.*5.4.19: abs., the inf. being supplied, *authorized* to act, And.1.132; ἄ. γάρ, emphatically, Pl.*Tht.*143e. c. later ἄ. ἵνα *Ev.Jo.*1.27. 4. ἄξιόν [ἐστι] 'tis *meet, fit, due*, ἄξιον εἶναι τρεῖς ἑνὸς ἀντὶ πεφάσθαι Il.13.446; ἄ. μνήμην ἔχειν Hdt.1.14: later c. fut. inf., ἄ. διαπορήσειν Did.*in D.*9. 15. b. c. dat. pers. et inf., τῇ πόλει γὰρ ἄξιον ξυλλαβεῖν τὸν ἄνδρα 'tis *meet* for the city, is *worth* her *while*.., Ar.*Ach.*205; τί σοι ζῆν ἄξιον; Id.*Nu.*1074, cf. *Av.*548; ἄξιόν γε πᾶσιν ἐπολολύξαι Id.*Eq.*616; freq. in X. as ὡς οὐκ ἄξιον εἴη βασιλεῖ ἀφεῖναι κτλ. that it was not *meet* for him.., *An.*2.3.25. c. the inf. is sts. omitted, ἄξιον γὰρ Ἑλλάδι 'tis *meet* in the eyes of Hellas [so to do], Ar.*Ach.*8; and sts. the dat., ἄξιόν ἐστι *operae pretium est*, it is *worth while*, ἐνθυμηθῆναι D.1.21; γαμεῖν οὐκ ἄξιον E.*Alc.*628. III. Adv. ἀξίως, c. gen., ἐμάχοντο ἀξίως λόγου Hdt.6.112; οὔτε ἑωυτοῦ ἀ. Id.3.125; οὐκ ἀ. ἀπηγήσιος ibid.; τῆς ἀδικίας Th.3.39; ἀ. τοῦ θεοῦ, τῆς θεᾶς, *OGI*331.9 (Pergam.), *Inscr.Magn.*33.30, cf. 1*Ep.Thess.*2.12: abs., S.*OT*133, etc.; κολάσετε ἀξίως *as* they *deserve*, Th.3.40.

ἀξιο-σέβαστος, ον, *worthy of reverence, worshipful*, Eust. ad D.P. p.72.22. **-σκεπτος**, ον, *worth considering*, X.*HG*6.1.13. **-σπούδαστος**, ον, *worthy of zealous endeavours*, X.*Lac.*10.3 (Comp.), Plu. 2.5d. **-στράτηγος** [ρᾰ], ον, *worthy of being general* or *worthy of a great commander*, X.*An.*3.1.24 (Comp.), D.C.36.24 codd. (Sup.):—**-στρᾰτηγικός** is found as v.l. in Arr.*An.*4.11.9 and D.C.41.55, and **-στρᾰτήγητος** Id.45.42. **-σῦλος**, ον, *liable to seizure*, *GDI*1151.6 (Elis). **-τέκμαρτος**, ον, *worthy of being brought in evidence, credible*, ἀξιοτεκμαρτότερον τοῦ λόγου τὸ ἔργον deeds are *stronger proof* than words, X.*Mem.*4.4.10. **-τίμησις** [τῐ], εως, ἡ, *valuing, appraisement*, Sch.Aristid.p.281 F. **-τίμητος** [ῑ], ον, *highly prized, valuable*, Ph.1.461:—also **-τῑμος**, ον, Nic.Dam.p.94 D., X.*Ep.*2.3 (Comp.), App.*BC*3.19 (Sup.). **-φᾰνής**, ές, (φανῆναι) *reputable*, *PLond.*2.483.72 (vii A. D.). **-φίλητος** [φῐ], ον, *worth loving*, X.*Oec.* 10.3, *Stoic.*3.180. **-χρεία**, ἡ, *sufficiency, guarantee*, in pl., *CPH* 97.13 (iii A. D.). **-χρείων**, ονος, = sq., ἐνέχυρα *SIG*672.30 (Delph.).

ἀξιόχρεως, εων, gen. εω, Ion. **ἀξιόχρεος**, ον, Hdt. (though the other form occurs as v.l. 1.156, al.) and Hp.*Art.*11; both forms in *Foed. Delph.Pell.*1 *A* 15, cf. 1 *B* 9: Boeot. acc. pl. ἀξιοχρειέας, implying nom. ἀξιοχρη(ϝ)ής, prob. rest. in *IG*7.1739.9: neut. pl. ἀξιόχρεα Hdt. 5.65: dat. sg. written ἀξιοχρείῳ *IG*2².1183.28: Comp. and Sup. ἀξιοχρεώτερος, -ώτατος, Plb.4.3.3 (s.v.l.), 10.27.1: (χρέος):—*worthy of a thing*: hence, I. abs., like ἀξιόλογος, *noteworthy, considerable*, πόλις Th.1.10; of a person, ὑπὸ ἀξιοχρέου καὶ ἀποθανεῖν ἡμίσεα συμφορή Hdt.5.111. 2. *serviceable, sufficient*, ἀξιόχρεον πρόφασιν προτείνειν Id.1.156; ἐπ' οὐδεμιῇ αἰτίῃ ἀξιόχρεῳ Id.3.35; also of persons, ἀ. ἐγγυηταί *trustworthy, substantial*, Ar.*Ec.*1065, Pl.*Ap.*38c, cf. *Foed. Delph.Pell.* ll.cc.; εἰς ἀ. τὸν λέγοντα ἀνοίσω Pl.*Ap.*20e; στρατόπεδα ἀ. πρὸς μάχην Plb.1.19.1; τόλμα ἀ. πρὸς ἡγεμονίαν Plu.*Caes.*56. II. c. inf., *able, sufficient to* do.., Hdt.4.126, Th.5.13; ἀξιόχρεω..ἡμῖν ἀντιτάξασθαι D.3.27; ἢ οὐκ ἀξιόχρεως ὁ θεὸς..τὸ μίασμα λῦσαι; E.*Or.* 598. Adv. -χρέως Hsch. III. c. gen. rei, *worthy, deserving of*, ἀξιόχρεα ἀπηγήσιος, = ἀξιαπήγητα, Hdt.5.65; ἀ. τηλικούτου πράγματος *worthy of credit* in.., D.8.49, cf. 19.131.—Rare in poets, as E. l.c.

ἀξιόω, pf. ἠξίωκα Isoc.18.24:—Med., v. infr. III. 2:—Pass., fut. ἀξιωθήσομαι Id.9.6, but also ἀξιώσεται S.*Ant.*637: aor. ἠξιώθην: pf. ἠξίωμαι: (ἄξιος):—*think, deem worthy*, I. c. acc. et gen., whether in good sense, *think worthy of a reward*, ἡμᾶς ἀξιοῖ λόγου E.*Med.*962; ἑαυτὸν τῶν καλλίστων X.*An.*3.2.7; or in bad, *of a punishment*, γοργύρης Hdt.3.145; ἀ. τινὰ ἀτιμίας Philipp.ap.D.18.166; κακοῦ Pl.*Ap.* 38a:—Pass., ἀξιεύμενος θυγατρὸς τῆς σῆς Hdt.9.111; λέχη..τυράννων ἠξιωμένα *deemed worthy of* kings, E.*Hec.*366; ἀξιοῦσθαι κακῶν Antipho 3.2.10; τοῦ αὐτοῦ ὀνόματος Pl.*Phd.*103e, al. 2. c. acc. only, *esteem, honour*, S.*Aj.*1114, E.*Heracl.*918; ἀ. τινὰ προσφθέγμασιν *honour* one with words, A.*Ag.*903; of things, *value*, οὐκ ἐξ ἴσου πάσας ἀξιοῦμεν ὑπολήψεις Phld.*Herc.*1251.12:—Pass., καλοῖς ὑμεναίοις ἀξιοῦσθαι E.*Or.*1210: abs., τύμβον ἀξιούμενον δρᾶσθαι Id.*Hec.*319, cf. Th. 5.16. 3. *value at* a certain price, ὁπόσης ἂν τιμῆς ἀξιώσῃ τὸ πωλούμενον Pl.*Lg.*917d. II. c. acc. pers. et inf., *think* one *worthy* to do or be, σέ τοι ἠξίωσε ναίειν E.*Alc.*572; οὐκ ἀξιῶ 'γὼ 'μαυτὸν ἰσχύειν μέγα Ar.*Eq.*182; τί σαυτὸν ἀποτίνειν ἀξιοῖς; Pherecr.93:—Pass., Pi. *N.*10.39, A.*Pr.*242; διδάσκαλος ἀξιοῦσθαι *to be esteemed as* a teacher, Pl.*Tht.*161d. 2. *think fit, expect, require that*.., ἀ. τινὰ ἰέναι Hdt. 2.162; ἀ. τινὰ ἀληθῆ λέγειν Antipho 2.3.4; οὐκ ἀ. [ὑμᾶς] τὰ μὴ δεινὰ ἐν ὀρρωδίᾳ ἔχειν we *expect* that you do not.., Th.2.89, cf. 3.44; ἀ. σωτηρίαν ἐμοὶ γενέσθαι And.1.143; ἀ. καὶ παρακαλεῖν τινα c. inf., Decr.ap.D.18.165; ἀ. ἵνα.. *Inscr.Prien.*53.58, al.; simply, *ask, request*, *PEleph.*19.18, Apollon.Perg.1 *Praef.* (Pass.); esp. *pray*, τὸν θεὸν ὅπως.. Aristeas 245, cf. Lxx *Je.*7.16, *SIG*1181.1; τὰ -ούμενα *prayers*, Aristeas 18; also, *ask, inquire* of an oracle, Ps.-Callisth. 1.3. III. c. inf. only, ἀ. κομίζεσθαι, τυγχάνειν *think one has a right to* receive, *expect* to receive, Th.1.43, 7.15; προῖκα θεωρεῖν ἀ. Thphr. *Char.*6.4; ἄλλο τι ἀξιοῖς ἢ ἀποθανεῖν; Lys.22.5: with a neg., οὐκ ἀξιῶ ὑποπτεύεσθαι I *think* I do not *deserve* to be suspected, *have a right* not to be.., Th.4.86:—Pass., ὥστε ἀξιοῦσθαι λητουργεῖν so as *to be required* to.., D.27.64; υἱῷ προθύμως τἀξιούμενον ποιῶν *one's duty*, Men. 663. 2. *think fit, expect, consent, resolve*, etc., and so in various senses, ἀξιῶ θανεῖν I *consent* to die, S.*OT*944, etc.; *dare*, ἀξιῶσαι μάχην συνάψαι A.*Pers.*335; *deign* to do, εἴ τις ἀξιοῖ μαθεῖν Id.*Ag.*1661, cf. S.*OT*1413; ἀξιῶ χρήματα λαμβάνειν I *do not hesitate* to receive, Pl.*Hp.Mi.*364d, etc.; οἶμαι πάντας.. φέρειν ἀξιοῦν ἔρανον I think that all *should be glad* to bring, D.21.101:—freq. with neg., οὐδ' ἀξιῶ μνησθῆναι I do not *think* them *worth* mentioning, Hdt.2.20; οὐκ ἠξίωσαν οὐδὲ προσβλέψαι A.*Pr.*217; οὐκ ἀξιώσαντες.. τοῦτο παθεῖν Th.1.102 (but ἀξιοῦντε μὴ ἀντιδοῦναι δίκην 3.66); πείθεσθαι οὐκ ἀξιοῦντες *refusing*, X.*Oec.*21.4:—also in Med. (not in Att. Prose), ἀξιοῦσθαι μέλειν *deign* to care for, A.*Ag.*370; φονεὺς γὰρ εἶναι ἠξιώσατο *thought fit* to be, Id. *Eu.*425; οὐκ ἀξιεύμεναι ἀναμίσγεσθαι τῇσι ἄλλῃσι not *condescending* to.., Hdt.1.199; οὐκ ἀξιεύμενος ἐς τὸν.. θρόνον ἵζεσθαι not *deeming oneself worthy* to.., Id.7.16. 3. *think, deem*, ἀξιοῦντες ἀδικέεσθαι Id.6.87, cf. S.*OC*579, E.*HF*1343; ἑκάτεροι νικᾶν ἠξίουν *claimed* the victory, Th.1.55. IV. *make a claim*, Id.4.58; πάντες καθ' ὑπεροχὴν -οῦσιν Arist.*Pol.*1288^{a}23; ἀξίωσιν ἀ. Plb.38.7.7; ἀξιοῦν τινά τι *make a claim on* a person, X.*Mem.*3.11.12. 2. ἐγὼ μὲν οὑτωσὶ περὶ τῆς τύχης ἀξιῶ *hold* this *opinion*.., D.18.255; ἐγὼ μὲν οὐκ ἀξιῶ I *think* not, Id.20.12: in philosophic language, *lay down, maintain* (cf. ἀξίωμα II. 2), Arist.*APr.*37^{a}10, cf. 41^{b}10, Polystr.p.24 W.; ἐν τῷ τοιῷδε ἀξιοῦντι in such a *state of opinion*, v.l. in Th.3.43.

ἄξῐφος, ον, *without sword*, Lyc.50, A.D.*Synt.*187.10. Adv. **ἀξιφεί** Hdn.*Epim.*257.

ἀξιώλεθρος, ον, *pernicious*, ἐνθύμημα Procop.*Aed.*6.5, cf. *Goth.*4.30.

ἀξί-ωμα, ατος, τό, *that of which one is thought worthy, an honour*, γάμων.. ἀξίωμ' ἐδέξατο E.*Ion*62; οἱ τὰς πόλεις ἔχουσι κἀξιώματα ib.605; κοινῆς τραπέζης ἀ. ἔχειν Id.*Or.*9; τὸ τῆς πόλεως ἀ. the *dignity* of the city's representative, D.18.149. 2. *honour, reputation*, E.*Supp.* 424, Th.2.65, etc.; ὧν ἐν ἀξιώματι ὑπὸ τῶν ἀστῶν Id.6.15; τὸ τῶν ἐλευθέρων γυναικῶν ἀ. D.59.113: c. gen. objecti, ἀ. ἔχειν ἀρετῆς *claim* on ground of merit, Arist.*Pol.*1281^{b}25. 3. *rank, position*, ἀξιώματος ἀφάνεια Th.2.37; γένει καὶ τοῖς ἄλλοις ἀξιώμασιν Isoc.19.7. 4. of things, *worth, quality*, οὐ τῷ πλήθει ἀλλὰ τῷ ἀ. Th.5.8. 5. concrete, *things of dignity*, Philostr.*VS*2.5.4. II. *that which is thought fit, decision, decree*, δαιμόνων S.*OC*1452, cf. 1459; τὰ τῶν προγόνων ἀ. D.18.210; ἀ. κενὰ καὶ νομοθεσίαι Epicur.*Ep.*2 p.36 U. 2. in Science, *that which is assumed as the basis of demonstration, self-evident principle*, Arist.*Metaph.*997^{a}7, 1005^{b}33, *APo.*72^{a}17, Polystr. p.16 W.:—Math., *axiom*, Arist.*Metaph.*1005^{a}20, etc.; philosophical *doctrine*, τὸ Ζήνωνος ἀ. ib.1001^{b}7, cf. *Xen.*979^{b}22; logical *proposition*, Chrysipp.*Stoic.*2.53,63, etc. 3. *request, petition*, ἱκετικὸν ἀ. *BGU*1053 ii 7 (i B.C.), cf. Plu.2.633c. **-ωμᾰτικός**, ή, όν, *dignified, honourable*, προστασία Plb.10.18.8, etc.; *high in rank*, Plu. 2.617d: Comp., Dam.*Pr.*54. 2. in Literary Criticism, *dignified*, D.H.*Dem.*18, al.; ῥυθμός *Comp.*13: Comp., *Isoc.*3. Adv. -κῶς, κατεσκευάσθη *Dem.*43; λέγειν Hermog.*Id.*2.6. 3. *concerned with dignities*, Ptol.*Tetr.*163. II. *supplicatory*, Plb.20.9.9. III. *employing logical propositions*, ἐκφορά *Stoic.*2.61: Sup., D.L.4. 33. Adv. -κῶς *self-evidently*, Steph. *in Hp.*1.59 D. **-ωμάτιον**, τό, Dim., *petty dignity*, Arr.*Epict.*2.2.10. **-ωσις**, gen. εως, Ion. ιος, ἡ, *thinking worthy*, τῆς ἀξιώσιος εἵνεκα τῆς ἐξ ἐμεῦ γῆμαι for your *deeming* it *fit* to marry from my family, Hdt.6.130. 2. *being thought worthy*, one's *reputation, character*, διὰ τὴν προϋπάρχουσαν ἀ. Th.1.138, cf. 6.54; τὴν ἀ. μὴ ἀφανίζειν Id.2.61; *excellence*, τῶν ποιημάτων D.H.*Comp.*4. 3. *dignity, rank*, Id.6.71, al., App.*BC*1.79; λοχαγοῦ τάξις καὶ ἀ. Arr.*Tact.*12.4. 4. *dignity* of style, D.H.*Comp.* 18. II. *demand, claim*, on grounds of merit (opp. χρεία, on grounds of necessity), Th.1.37; ἀ. χάριτος ib.41, cf. Plb.1.67.10, *PRyl.*120.17 (ii A.D.), etc.; generally, *request*, ἐχθροῦ δεηθέντος μὴ ἀποστραφῇς τὴν ἀ. Epicur.*Fr.*215. b. *petition*, ἀ. ἔγγραφος Plu. *Demetr.*42; = *libellus*, D.C.60.30. III. *opinion, principle, maxim*, τὴν ἀ. ταύτην εἰλήφεσαν.. Th.2.88, cf. Aeschin.3.220. IV. ἀ. τῶν ὀνομάτων ἐς τὰ ἔργα *the established meaning* of words, Th.3. 82. **-ωτέον**, *one must think worthy*, τινά Arist.*EN*1159^{b}18, Jul. *Ep.*89b; *insist on*, c. inf., Phld.*D.*3.2.

ἀ-ξόᾰνος, ον, *without carved images*, Luc.*Syr.D.*3.

ἀξονήλᾰτος, ον, *whirling on the axle*, σύριγγες A.*Supp.*181.

ἀξόν-ιον, τό, Dim., *small bolt* or *pin*, Hero *Spir.*1.30, Poll.10.31; of *bolts* used in twisting the strands of torsion-engines, Hero *Bel.*82. 7:—also **-ίσκος**, ὁ, Id.*Spir.*2.32, Ph.*Bel.*76.24. **-ιος**, α, ον, (ἄξων) *belonging to the axle*, *AP*9.117 (Stat. Flacc.).

ἄξοος, ον, *unwrought, not carved*, σανίς Call.*Fr.*105.

ἄξος, ὁ, Cret., = ἀγμός, St.Byz. s.v. Ὄαξος. B. Maced. word for ὕλη, Hsch.

ἀξουγγία, ἡ, *tallow, grease*, Crateuas *Fr.*3, al., Gal.12.419:—also **ἀξούγγιον**, τό, Aët.12.1, Gal.13.57, *Hippiatr.*105; cf. ὀξούγγιον.

ἀξουγγιασμός, ὁ, *treatment with* ἀξούγγιον, *Hippiatr.*129.

ἀξυγκρότητος, ον, for ἀσυγ-, *not welded together by the hammer*: metaph. of rowers, *not trained to pull together*, Th.8.95; of style, *not compact, rambling*, D.H.*Dem.*19.

ἀξῠλ-ία, Ion. -ίη, ἡ, *want of wood*, Hes.*Fr.*206, Str.15.2. 10. **-ιστος**, ον, = sq. 1, Hsch. **-ος**, ον, *with no timber cut from it*, ἄξυλος ὕλη an *unthinned*, i.e. *thick*, wood, Il.11.155 (ἀφ' ἧς οὐδεὶς ἐξυλίσατο Sch.Ven. ad loc.), wrongly expl. (as if ἀ- intens.) *thick with trees*, Corn.*ND*13. II. *without wood*, Hdt.4.61,185, *AP*9.89 (Phil.); also, *without a load of wood*, Luc.*Asin.*32. III. *free from woody matter*, of galbanum, Dsc.3.83, Democr.ap.Gal.13.916.

ἀξυμ-, ἀξυν-, v. sub ἀσυμ-, ἀσυν-.

ἄξῡνος, ον, = ἀκοινώνητος, Hsch., Suid.

ἀξῠρής, ές, and **ἄξῠρος**, ον, *not cutting, blunt*, Hsch.

ἀξύστατος, ον, v. sub ἀσύστατος.

ἄξυστος, ον, *not scraped*, Antyll.ap.Orib.4.11.13.

ἄξων, ονος, ὁ, *axle*, Il.16.378; σιδήρεος 5.723; φήγινος ib.838, cf. Hes.*Op.*424, A.*Th.*153 (lyr.), etc. 2. *axis*, of a cone, Arist.*Mete.* 375^{b}22; of a conic section, Apollon.Perg.1 *Def.*7; of a cylinder, Archim.*Con.Sph.Def.*1.260. 3. *axis of the celestial sphere*, Arist.*Mu.* 391^{b}26, Arat.22, D.H.2.5; ἄ. νοητός Eust.1389.59. 4. metaph., *course, path* of action, Lxx *Pr.*2.9, 2.18. II. οἱ ἄξονες *the wooden tablets of the laws* in Athens, *made to turn upon an axis*, Plu.*Sol.*25: sg. in *IG*1.61, D.23.31. 2. in pl., *door-jambs*, Parm.1.19. III. in pl., *part of a bridle-bit*, X.*Eq.*10.9 and 10. IV. *the second cervical vertebra*, Poll.2.132. (Cf. Skt. *ákṣas*, Lat. *axis*, OHG. *ahsa*, Lith. *ašis* 'axle'.)

ἀογκέω, *diminish in bulk*: hence, *weaken* an arch or vault, *BCH* 23.178 (Pisidia).

ἄογκος, ον, *not bulky, attenuated*, σῶμα ὡς ἀογκότατον Hp.*Nat.Hom.* 9. 2. *immaterial*, Syrian. *in Metaph.*143.22; *without mass* or *bulk*, Plot.6.1.26, 6.4.5, Porph.*Sent.*27: Comp., Dam.*Pr.*372.

ἄοδμος, ον, v. ἄνοδμος.

ἀοζ-έω, *serve, wait on*, A.*Fr.*54. **-ία**, Ion. -ίη, ἡ, *attendance* on a god, *service*, *Epigr.Gr.*425 (Phryg.). **-ος**, ὁ, = θεράπων, *servant, attendant*, esp. belonging to a temple, A.*Ag.*231 (lyr.), cf. Call.*Del.*249, *IG*9(1).976 (Corc.). (*sm̥-sod-yos*, root *sed-* 'go', Slav. *chodŭ*, cf. ὁδός.)

ἄοζος, ον, = ἄνοζος, q.v.

ἄοῖα, τά, trees cut down and dedicated to Aphrodite, Nassandros (sic) ap.Hsch. **ἄοιγον**· ὀλέθριον, Hsch. (leg. λοιγόν).

ἀοιδάω, = ἀοιδιάω, dub. in Simon.174, cf. Hdn.Gr.1.439.

ἀοιδ-ή [ᾰ], Att. contr. ᾠδή (q.v.), ἡ, (ἀείδω):—*song*, whether: 1. *art of song*, αὐτὰρ ἀοιδὴν θεσπεσίην ἀφέλοντο Il.2.599; ὡς ἄρα τοι.. θεὸς ὤπασε θέσπιν ἀ. Od.8.498. 2. *act of singing, song*, οἱ δ' εἰς ἱμερόεσσαν ἀ. τρεψάμενοι 18.304; ὑπ' ὀρχηθμῷ καὶ ἀοιδῇ Hes.*Sc.*282. 3. *thing sung, song*, στονόεσσαν ἀ. οἱ μὲν ἄρ' ἐθρήνεον Il.24.721, cf. Od. 1.351, Hdt.2.79, Alc.*Supp.*4.24, Pi.*N.*11.18 (pl.), etc.; whether of joy or sorrow, cf. A.*Eu.*954 (lyr.) with S.*Ant.*883; λύρας ἀ. E.*Med.* 425 (lyr.). 4. *theme of song, person sung of*, ἵνα ᾖσι καὶ ἐσσομένοισιν ἀ. Od.8.580, cf. Thgn.252, Theoc.12.11; στυγερὴ δέ τ' ἀ. ἔσσετ' ἐπ' ἀνθρώπους [Κλυταιμήστρα] Od.24.200. 5. = ἐπῳδή, *spell, incantation*, ὀχῆες ὠκείαις.. ἀναθρῴσκοντες ἀοιδαῖς A.R.4.42, cf. 59. Cf. ᾠδή. [Dissyll. in Hes.*Th.*48 (unless λήγουσί τ' ἀοιδῆς be read) and in Pi. l.c. (unless μελίζεν be read).] **-ιάω**, poet. for ἀείδω, Od.5.61, 10.227, Hermesian.7.13. **-ικός**, ή, όν, *musical*, prob. coined by Sch.Heph.p.130 C. **-ιμος**, ον, *sung of, famous in song* or *story*, Hdt.2.79,135, Pi.*P.*8.59, etc.; προφάταν Id.*Pae.*6.6; from Pi. (*Fr.*76) downwds. a favourite epith. of Athens; ἀ. πόμα a *glorious* draught, Id.*N.*3.79, etc.; ἀ. εὐνομίῃσιν *famous* for his justice, *IG*7.94 (Nisaea), cf. Luc.*Tim.*38, App.*BC*2.82, etc.: Sup., Plu.*Ant.*34:—only once in Hom., and in bad sense, *notorious, infamous*, ὡς.. ἀνθρώποισι πελώμεθ' ἀοίδιμοι Il.6.358. II. *won by song*, ἄγρα, of the Sphinx's victims, E.*El.*471 (lyr.).

ἀοιδο-θέτης [ᾰ], ου, ὁ, *lyric poet*, *AP*7.50 (Archim.). **-κῆρυξ**, Dor. -κᾱρυξ, ὁ, *herald who announces singers*, *IG*5(1).1314.15 (Thalamae, ii A.D.). **-μάχος** [ᾰ], ον, *fighting with verses*, λογολέσχαι *AP*11.140 (Lucill.). **-πόλος**, ὁ, *one busied with song, poet*, like μουσοπόλος, *AP*7.594,595 (Jul. Aegypt.), cf. *APl.*4.75 (Antip.). 2. *ode-devoted*, of lyric poetry, Aus.*Ep.*14.

ἀοιδός [ᾰ], ὁ, (ἀείδω) *singer, minstrel, bard*, Il.24.720, Od.3.270, 8.,Hes.*Th.*95, *Op.*26, Sapph.92, etc.; ἀ. ἀνήρ Od.3.267; θεῖος ἀ. 4.17, 8.87, al.; τοῦ ἀρίστου ἀνθρώπων ἀ. Hdt.1.24; πολλὰ ψεύδονται ἀ. Arist.*Metaph.*983^{a}4: c. gen., γόων, χρησμῶν ἀοιδός, E.*HF*110, *Heracl.* 403; πρᾶτος ἀ., of the cock, Theoc.18.56. 2. fem., *songstress*, πολύϊδρις ἀ. Id.15.97; of the nightingale, Hes.*Op.*208; of the Sphinx, S.*OT*36, E.*Ph.*1507 (lyr.); ἀοιδὸς Μοῦσα Id.*Rh.*386 (lyr.). 3. *enchanter*, S.*Tr.*1000. II. as Adj., *tuneful, musical*, ἀοιδοτάταν ὄρνιθα E.*Hel.*1109 (lyr.), cf. Theoc.12.7, Call.*Del.*252, *IG*12(2). 443. 2. Pass., = ἀοίδιμος, *famous*, πολλὸν ἀοιδοτέρη Arcesil.ap. D.L.4.30. III. = εὐνοῦχος, Hsch.; cf. δοῖδος.

ἀοιδοτόκος [ᾰ], ον, *inspiring song*, *AP*9.364 (Nestor).

ἀοίκ-ητος, ον, *uninhabited*, ἀ. καὶ ἔρημος ἡ Λιβύη Hdt.2.34, cf. 5.10, Pl.*Lg.*778b; *uninhabitable*, Arist.*Mete.*362^{b}9. II. *houseless*, ποιεῖν τινα ἀοίκητον *banish* one *from home*, D.45.70, cf. Luc.*Gall.*17. **-ος**, ον, *houseless, homeless*, Hes.*Op.*602, E.*Hipp.*1029, Pl.*Smp.*203d, etc.; ἐπὶ ξένης χώρας ἄοικος S.*Tr.*300; of animals, Arist.*HA*488^a 21: Comp., D.Chr.6.62. II. ἄ. εἰσοίκησις a *homeless*, i.e. *miserable*, home, S.*Ph.*534, cf. Nonn.*D.*17.42.

ἄοιμος, ον, = ἄρρητος, acc. to Hsch.; but also ἄοιμος· ἄπορος ἢ ἀληθὴς ἢ ἀπρόστυχος, Id.

ἀοιν-έω, *abstain from wine*, Hp.*Morb.*3.7. **-ία**, ἡ, *abstinence from wine*, Str.15.1.45. **-ος**, ον, *without wine*, ἄοινοι χοαί, offered to the Erinyes, A.*Eu.*107 (whence they are themselves called ἄοινοι, S. *OC*100); ἀοίνοις ἐμμανεῖς θυμώμασιν frenzied with the *wine* of wrath, A.*Eu.*860; ἄ. συμπόσιον Thphr.ap.Plu.2.679a; νηφαντικὴ καὶ ἄ. κρήνη Pl.*Phlb.*61c. 2. of men, *having no wine, sober*, X.*Cyr.*6.2.27; also of a place, *having none*, ib.26. 3. *without use of wine*, ἀοινοτέρα τροφή Arist.*Pol.*1336^{a}8; ἄοινος μέθη Plu.2.716a.

ἀοκν-ία, ἡ, *not shrinking from*, c. gen., πόνων Hp.*Epid.*6.4.18; censured by Poll.3.120. **–ος**, ον, *without hesitation, resolute*, ἀνήρ Hes.*Op.*495; φύλακα τροφῆς ἄοκνον S.*Aj.*563; ἄ. πρὸς μελλητάς Th.1.70; ἕψομαί γ' ἀ. Cleanth.*Stoic.*1.118; πρὸς τὰς ἀναγκαίας χρήσεις Epicur.*Ep.*3 p.64 U.; πρὸς τοὺς πόνους Plu.*Pel.*3; ἄ. βλάβη *pressing, present* mischief, S.*Tr.*841. Adv. **–νως** *without hesitation*, Hp. *Art.*38, Pl.*Lg.*649b, Orib.*Syn.Praef.*: Sup. –ότατα X.*Cyr.*1.4.2.

ἀολλεῖ· συνάγει, Hsch.

ἀολλήδην, Adv. of sq., *in a body, together*, Epic. in *Arch.Pap.*7.7, Opp.*H.*1.788; of two only, Mosch.2.49, cf. sq.

ἀολλής, ές, (v. εἴλω) *all together, in throngs* or *crowds*, freq. in Hom., esp. of warlike hordes, always in pl., Ἀργεῖοι δ' ὑπέμειναν ἀολλέες Il.5.498; βάλλον δ' εἰν ἐλεοῖσιν ἀολλέα they put [the joints] *all together* on the dressers, Od.14.432; τύραννον μέγ' ἐπαίνεντες ἀόλλεες Alc.37A, cf. Sapph.*Supp.*20b.2; χωρῶμεν δὴ πάντες ἀολλεῖς S.*Ph.*1469 (lyr.); of two only, *together*, Id.*Tr.*514 (lyr.); cf. foreg.

ἀόλλησις, εως, ἡ, etym. of ἀλλᾶς, *EM*68.31.

ἀολλίζω, *gather together*, ἀόλλισσαν κατὰ ἄστυ γεραιάς Il.6.287; ἀολλίσσασα γεραιάς ib.270; ἀ. τὸν ὄχλον Pherecyd.11 J.:—Pass., *come together, assemble*, πάντες ἀολλίσθησαν Ἀχαιοί Il.19.54; πρίν περ ὅμιλον ἀολλισθήμεναι 15.588; νῆσοι ἀολλίζονται Call.*Del.*18. 2. later of things, *gather together, heap up*, ὄλβον *AP*9.649 (Maced.); Βάκχον ib.772 (Phoc.).

ἀολλόπους, ἀόξοος, ff.ll. for ἀελλόπους, ἄξοος, Hsch.

ἀόμμᾰτος, ον, = ἀνόμματος, Tz.*H.*1.538.

ἄοπλος, ον, *without heavy armour on* (cf. ὁπλίτης), Th.4.9, etc.: generally, *unarmed*, Pl.*Prt.*321c; τὰ τυφλὰ τοῦ σώματος καὶ ἄοπλα καὶ ἄχειρα, i.e. the back, X.*Cyr.*3.3.45; ἅρμα ἄ. a chariot *without scythes*, ib.6.4.16. Cf. ἄνοπλος.

ἄοπος, ον, (ὄψ) *speechless*, Hsch. II. = sq., Id.

ἄοπτος, ον, *unseen*, Antipho Soph.4.

ἄορ or **ἆορ**, ἄορος, τό (on the accent see Hdn.Gr.1.391): (ἀείρω):—properly, *hanger* or *sword hung in a belt* (cf. ἀορτήρ), Od.11.24; synon. with ξίφος, 10.294, cf. 321.—The masc. acc. pl., οὐκ ἄορας οὐδὲ λέβητας 17.222 (cf. Hsch.), is prob. f.l. for ἀοράγ'; Eust.1818.5 and the Scholl. ad loc. expl. ἄορας as = ὄαρας, *women* given as prizes (cf. ἀόρων· γυναικῶν, Hsch.), or = τρίποδας. 2. later, *any weapon*, ἄορ τριγλώχιν *the trident*, Call.*Del.*31; of *the horn* of the rhinoceros, Opp. *C.*2.553. [Hom. has ᾰ in dissyll. forms, as also Hes.*Sc.*457, Call. *Hec.*1.1.1; in the trisyll. forms, ᾰ Od.17.222, al., ᾱ Il.10.484, al. In Hes.*Sc.*221, and later Poets, ᾱ even in ἄορ, which must then be written ἆορ. Hes.*Th.*283 has ἄορ as monosyll., unless we read with Tricl. γένθ', ὁ δ' ἄορ χρύσειον...]

ἀορᾱ-σία, ἡ, *inability to see, blindness*, Plb.12.25^g.4, Lxx *Ge.*19.11, al., *IG*12(9).955.8, 1179.26 (Euboea); *failure to observe*, στάσεων *Inscr.Magn.*114.4. **–τος**, ον, *unseen, invisible*, Pl.*Phd.*85e, etc.; ἀόρατος ὄψιν Alex.240.5; τραῦμ' ἀ., ἔρως *APl.*4.198 (Maec.); ἀ. τὸ μέλλον Isoc.1.29; τὸ ἀόρατον *the unseen world, the unseen*, ἐξ οὐρανοῦ καὶ τοῦ ἀ. Pl.*Sph.*246a, cf. *Tht.*155e, al.: τὰν ἀ. ἀτραπιτὸν βιότου *obscure*, *Epigr.Gr.*223 (Milet.); ἀ. κατὰ δόξαν Ath.12.511d; τὸν ἀ. ὡς ὁρῶν *Ep.Hebr.*11.27. Adv. **–τως** Ph.1.157, *Placit.*2.24.5. II. Act., *not having seen, without experience of*, παντὸς κακοῦ, δεινοῦ, Plb. 2.21.2, 3.108.6: abs., Luc.*Halc.*3.

ἀόρβιτος, ον, (*orbis*) *without tyres*, τροχοί *Edict.Diocl.*15.31a.

ἀοργ-ησία, ἡ, *a defect in the passion of anger*, 'lack of gall', Arist. *EN*1108^{a}8, cf. 1126^{a}3:—in good sense, Plu., who wrote a treatise περὶ ἀοργησίας, cf. Nic.Dam.p.150 D., Andronic.Rhod.p.575 M., Gal. 5.30. **–ητος**, ον, *not irascible*, Arist.*EN*1108^{a}8:—in good sense, Phld.*Ir.*p.71 W., Plu.2.10c, Luc.*Herm.*12, Aret.*CD*1.4, etc. Adv. **–τως** Phld. *Lib.*p.7 O., Arr.*Epict.*3.18.6, Hierocl. *in CA*12 p.447 M. **–ιστος**, ον, = foreg., Sor.1.88.

ἀοριστ-αίνω, = sq., Procl.*Inst.*124, Phlp. *in GA*191.34, Sch. Hermog.*Stat.* in Rh.4.82 W., Dam.*Pr.*436; *to be undecided, uncertain* (of a fact), Ps.-Alex.Aphr. *in SE*57.24. 2. *make ἀόριστος*, Iamb. *in Nic.*p.78 P. **–εύω**, = sq., Arc.142.4. **–έω**, *to be indeterminate*, Arist.*Pr.*941^{b}26. 2. *to be without definite ideas, uncertain*, Phld.*Mus.*p.48 K., cf. S.E.*P.*1.28, Porph.*Sent.*33, Asp. *in EN*74.27. 3. *to be immoderate*, opp. ἔχεσθαι ὅρου καὶ μέτρου, Epicur. *Fr.*465. **–ία**, ἡ, *indefiniteness, indeterminateness*, τῆς ὥρας Arist. *Pr.*941^{b}32, cf. *Mete.*361^{b}34, Thphr.*Vent.*52, Gal.4.406. 2. *illimitability*, Epicur.*Sent.Vat.*63. 3. *indecision*, τῆς ψυχῆς Plot.2.4. 10. 4. *lack of limit*, κατὰ τὰς ἐπιθυμίας Carneisc.*Herc.*1027.14, cf. Phld.*Herc.*1251.3. 5. pl., *irregularities*, τὰς κατὰ τῶν φασμάτων τῶν τοῦ ἡλίου ἀοριστίας Epicur.*Nat.*11.6. **–ος**, ον, *without boundaries, debatable*, γῆ Th.1.139. 2. *limitless*, ὀρέξεις, φόβοι, ἐπιθυμίαι, Epicur.*Fr.*202, 203. II. *indeterminate*, Pl.*Lg.*643d, Arist.*Metaph.* 1087^{a}17, al.; οὐδὲν ἀνεξέταστον οὐδ' ἀ. D.4.36; ἄτακτα, ἀδιόρθωτα, ἀόρισθ' ἅπαντα ibid.; ἀ. ἀξιώματα *indefinite* propositions, Chrysipp. *Stoic.*2.5, al.; ἀ. καὶ κρίσεως προσδεόμενον, opp. ὡρισμένον, Epicur. *Nat.*p.31 G.; ἀ. [ἄρχων] one who holds office *without limit of time*, Arist.*Pol.*1275^{a}26; *uncertain*, ζωῆς τελευτή *AP*9.499: Comp. πρόληψις Phld.*Rh.*2.189 S., cf. Plot.3.9.2. Adv. **–τως** Pl.*Lg.*916e, Arist. *Cat.*8^{b}9, al. 2. ἀ. ὄνομα or ῥῆμα an *indefinite* term, as οὐκ-ἄνθρωπος Id.*Int.*16^{a}32, 16^{b}14; of pronouns, A.D.*Pron.*7.1, al. 3. ὁ ἀ. (sc. χρόνος) *the aorist tense*, D.T.638.24, A.D.*Synt.*276.5, al. **–όω**, in Pass., *to be indefinite*, ib.70.4, al. **–ύς**· ὁμιλία, Zonar.; cf. ἀόρκτους (leg. ὀαριστύς). **–ώδης**, *indefinite*, φαντασία Hierocl. p.39 A., cf. A.D.*Pron.*5.14, *Synt.*27.4, al.; ἀ. χρόνος Eust.1755.58. Adv., A.D.*Synt.*70.1.

ἀόρκτους· ὁμιλίας, Hsch.; cf. ἀοριστύς.

ἀόρμητος, ον, *without impulse*, Ph.1.278.

ἄορνος, ον, (ὄρνις) *without birds*, λίμνη S.*Fr.*748; ἄ. ὕψη heights *no birds can reach*, Plu.2.327c; ἄ. λίμνη lake *Avernus*, Arist.*Mir.*839^{a}13; called ὁ Ἄορνος by Str.5.4.5; ἡ ἄ. πέτρα, a hill-fort on the Indus, D.S. 17.85, Plu.2.181c.

ἄορον· μοχλόν, πυλῶνα, θυρωρόν (Cypr.), Hsch. **ἄορος**· ἄυπνος (Methymn.), Id.

ἀορτ-εύς [ᾰ]· ἀορτήρ, Hsch. **–έω**, lengthd. form of ἀείρω, found only in aor. 1 part. Pass. ἀορτηθείς *hung up, suspended*, *AP*7.696 (Arch.). **–ή**, ἡ, (ἀείρω) in pl., = βρόγχια, Hp.*Loc.Hom.*14 (where Littré reads ἀορτρέων, –τρησι), *Coac.*394, cf. Ruf.*Onom.*159. 2. the *arteries* springing from the heart, i.e. aorta and pulmonary artery, Hp.*Cord.*10; esp. in sg., the *aorta*, Arist.*HA*496^{a}7, 513^{b}4, etc.: in pl., *arteries*, Poll.2.205. II. *knapsack that hung from* the shoulders, Men.331, Diph.40, Posidipp.10, cf. Poll.7.79, 10. 139. III. *point of suspension* of a balance, *Theol.Ar.*29. **–ήρ**, ῆρος, ὁ, (ἀείρω) *strap to hang* anything *to, sword-belt*, Od.11.609: in pl., κουλεὸν.. χρυσέοισιν ἀορτήρεσσιν ἀρηρός Il.11.31 (also expl. as οἱ κρίκοι τῆς θήκης, Hsch.). 2. in Od.13.438 *knapsack-strap*, στρόφος ἀορτήρ, v. στρόφος. **–ης**, ὁ, = ἀορτή II (Maced.), Hsch. 2. = ἀορτήρ I, Id. **–ρα**, τά, *lobes of the lungs*, Hp.*Morb.*2.54.

ἀόρχης, ες, *without ὄρχεις, gelded*, D.C.75.14.

ἆος· πνεῦμα ἢ ἄημα (cod. ἴαμα), Hsch.

ἀοσμ-ία, ἡ, *want of perfume*, opp. εὐοσμία, Thphr.*CP*6.16.3. **–ος**, ον, *having no smell*, v.l. in Hp.*Acut.*63, Arist.*Sens.*443^{a}10: Comp., ib.19; opp. εὔοσμος, Thphr.*CP*6.16.5; cf. ἄνοδμος, ἄνοσμος.

ἀοσσ-έω, aor. inf. ἀοσσῆσαι, *help*, τινί Mosch.4.110; cf. ἀοζέω. (*sm-soqᵘ-i̯o-*, cf. Lat. *socius*, ἕπομαι.) **–ητήρ**, ῆρος, ὁ, *assistant, helper, aider*, Il.15.254, 22.333, Od.4.165, A.R.1.471, etc.

ἄοστον· ἄριστον, Hsch. (i.e. λῷστον). **ἀούματα**, τά, *chaff* (Cypr.), Id. (fort. λούματα, = λύματα).

ἄουτος, ον, (οὐτάω) *unwounded, unhurt*, Il.18.536, Hes.*Sc.* 157. II. = ἀνήκοος, Hsch.

ἀοχλ-ησία, ἡ, *freedom from disturbance*, τοῦ σώματος Epicur.*Ep.*3 p.62 U.; ψυχῆς S.E.*P.*1.10, cf. Posidon.*Stoic.*3.5. **–ητος**, ον, *undisturbed, calm*, διαγωγή D.H.1.8: an Epicurean term, Epicur. *Sent.Vat.*79, cf. Luc.*Par.*11; τὸ τῆς σαρκὸς ἀ. Alciphr.3.55. Adv., Comp. –ότερον Gal.13.597: Sup. –ότατα Id.15.707. **–ος**, ον, *not troublesome*, Hp.*Art.*78 (Sup.). Adv. –ως Id.*Fract.*31.

ἄοψ, οπος, ὁ, ἡ, *without eyes*, Hsch.

ἀπαβοιδῶρ (Lacon., = ἀπαοιδῶς), *out of tune*, Hsch.

ἀπαγγ-ελεύς, έως, ὁ, = ἀπαγγελτήρ, Man.2.263. **–ελία**, ἡ, *report*, e.g. of an ambassador, D.19.5, al., Arist.*Rh.Al.*1438^{b}10; ἀ. ποιεῖσθαι Lycurg.14; in Psychology, *reports* of the senses, Plot.4. 6.3. 2. *narrative, recital, description*, ὧν.. βραχεῖα ἡ ἀ. ἀρκεῖ Th. 3.67; lyric poetry is said to be δι' ἀπαγγελίας αὐτοῦ τοῦ ποιητοῦ Pl. *R.*394c, cf. Phld.*Po.*5.1425.2; dramatic poetry is expressed by action καὶ οὐ δι' ἀπαγγελίας Arist.*Po.*1449^{b}26, cf. ib.11, D.H.*Comp.* 20. II. *diction*, Id.*Dem.*25, Plu.*Dem.*2.

ἀπαγγ-έλλω, fut. –αγγελῶ, Ion. –έω Simon.5.18: aor. 1 –ήγγειλα: pf. –ήγγελκα Plu.*Fab.*16:—Pass., pf. –ήγγελμαι Pl.*Chrm.*153c: aor. –ηγγέλθην Hdt.2.121.ε', E.*Hec.*672, later –ηγγέλην Plu.*Galb.*25: 1. of a messenger, *bring tidings, report*, τινί τι Il.9.626, etc., Pi.*P.*6.18, Hdt.3.25, etc.; τι πρός τινα A.*Ch.*266, X.*An.*6.3.22, etc.; ἀ. εἰς τὴν Ἑλλάδα, εἰς τὸ στρατόπεδον, ib.2.4.4, 6.4.25; τὰ παρά τινος ib.2. 3.4; ταῦτα περί σου οἴκαδε Pl.*Men.*71c, cf. Hp.*de Arte*11, Th.4.122; ἀ. ἡδονάς, φόνον, E.*IT*642, *Andr.*1241: folld. by relat. clause, ἐκέλευε τὸν ἄγγελον ἀπαγγέλλειν ὅτι.. Hdt.1.127, cf. X.*An.*2.3.5; ἀ. ὡς.. Lys.9.6: abs., πάλιν ἀ. *bring back tidings, report in answer*, Od.9.95: —Pass., ἐξ ὧν.. ἀπηγγέλλετό μοι as *he was reported* to me, D.21.25: c. part., ἀπηγγέλθη.. ὁ νέκυς ἐκκεκλεμμένος *was reported* to have been stolen away, Hdt.2.121.ε'. 2. of a speaker or writer, *report, relate*, ὄψις ἀπαγγέλλει Id.1.210, cf. Arist.*Rh.*1417^{b}9, *Po.*1448^{a}21, D.H. *Comp.*20; ὧν ὁ παθὼν ἔνια.. οὐδ' ἂν ἀπαγγεῖλαι δύναιθ' ἑτέρῳ D.21. 72; *describe*, Hp.*Prorrh.*2.3 (Pass.), cf. Plu.*Fab.*16; [Ῥωμαίους] ἡττημένους ὑπὸ τοῦ συγγραφέως ἀπηγγέλθαι Plb.1.15.11. 3. *recite, declaim*, Chor. in *Rev.Phil.*1.220. II. *explain, interpret*, a dream or riddle, Lxx *Ge.*41.8, *Jd.*14.12. **–ελσις**, εως, ἡ, = ἀπαγγελία, *AB*438. **–ελτήρ**, ῆρος, ὁ, *one who reports, messenger*, Phryn. Trag.(?) ap.Phot.p.154 R.: metaph. of a cork, ἀ. κύρτου *AP*6.5 (Phil.). **–ελτικός**, ή, όν, *reporting*, αἴσθησις Plot.4.4.17; *narrative*, Sch.Ar.*Ach.*9. II. Rhet., *of* or *for expression*: τὸ ἀ. *power of expressing*, Arr.*Epict.*2.23.2. Adv. –κῶς S.E.*P.*1.197.

ἀπαγγή· φανερὸν ποιῶ, Hsch.

ἄπᾰγε, (imper. of ἀπάγω) *away! begone!* Lat. *apage!* ἄ. ἐς μακαρίαν Ar.*Eq.*1151; κἄπαγ' ἀπὸ τῆς ὀσφύος *hands off!* Id.*Pax*1053: abs., Luc.*Prom.Es*7, *Am.*38, etc.: rarely c. part., ἄπαγε τὰ πάρος εὐτυχήματ' αὐδῶν E.*Ph.*1733: pl., D.C.38.46.

ἀπαγελάζω· *abgrego*, *Gloss.*

ἀπάγελος [ᾰγ], ον, *not yet received into the ἀγέλη*, of boys under 17, Cret. word, Palch. in *Cat.Cod.Astr.*5(1).188.31 (prob. l.), Hsch.

ἀπᾰγής, ές, (πήγνυμι) *not firm* or *stiff*, πῖλοι ἀπαγέες Hdt.7.61;

of water, ἀ. καὶ ἀσύστατον Plu.2.949b, cf. Gal.8.677; ὀστοῦν ἔτι ἄ. Antyll.ap.Orib.46.27.5; of flesh, *flabby*, D.L.7.1, Poll.1.191.

ἀπᾰγῑνέω, Ion. for ἀπάγω, esp. *pay* tribute, ἀ. φόρον Hdt.3.89,94.

ἀπαγκῠλόω, *make crooked*, χεῖρα v.l. in Ath.15.667c; σπάρτον *make a loop in* a rope, Hero *Aut*.27.4.

ἀπαγκωνίζομαι, *bare the elbows*, aor. -ισάμενος Archipp.1 D.; ἀπηγκωνισμένη πάντα *elbowing* all *aside*, utterly *unabashed*, Philostr. *VA*6.11; γλῶττα ἀπηγκωνισμένη καὶ γυμνή Id.*VS*2.1.11. II. Act. in Eust.1221.58, *bind* one's *hands behind* him.

ἀπαγλαΐζω, *deprive of ornament*, τινά τινος *AP*5.219 (Agath.), cf. Poll.1.217:—Pass., Tim.*Pers*.20. II. *honour to the full*, *IG*.12(5).292 (Paros).

ἀπάγλαυται· διόλου κατάνυται, Hsch.

ἄπαγμα, ατος, τό, *fracture at a joint*, Gal.ap.Orib.46.6.1, Gal.10.424.

ἀπαγνίζω, Ion. for ἀφαγνίζω, q.v.

ἀπάγνῡμαι, *to be fractured at a joint*, Gal.ap.Orib.46.6.3.

ἀπαγοράζω· *redimo*, *Gloss*.

ἀπαγόρευ-μα, ατος, τό, *prohibition*, *interdict*, Plu.2.1037d; προστάγματα καὶ ἀ. Arr.*Epict*.3.24.98. **-σις**, εως, ἡ, *prohibition*, ἐπίρρημα -εύσεως D.T.642.5, cf. A.D.*Synt*.246.4, al. II. *failure of strength*, *exhaustion*, Luc.*Anach*.37, Plu.*Ant*.45. **-τέον**, *one must give up*, Luc.*Herm*.47; *one must issue a prohibition*, περί τινος D.Chr.7.133 (dub.). **-τικός**, ή, όν, *prohibitory*, Plu.2.1037f; τινός Corn.*ND* 16; of particles, A.D.*Conj*.229.16. Adv. -κῶς Aristeas 131; gloss on ἀπηλεγέως, Sch.Il.1.309. **-ω**, mostly in pres. and impf. only (ἀπερῶ being used as fut. by correct writers, ἀπεῖπον as aor., ἀπείρηκα as pf., and ἀπορρηθήσομαι, ἀπερρήθην, ἀπείρημαι as Pass. fut., aor., and pf.): aor. ἀπηγόρευσα Pl.*Tht*.200d (v.l.), D.40.44, 55.4, freq. in later writers: pf. ἀπηγόρευκα Arist.*Phgn*.808^{a}11, Plu.2.1096f, etc.; Arist. (v. infr.) has pf. Pass. ἀπηγορευμένος:—*forbid*, μὴ ποιεῖν τι Hdt.1.183, 3.51, Ar.*Ach*.169, etc.; ἀ. τινὶ μὴ ποιεῖν Hdt.4.125, Pl.*Prt*.334c, al.; ἀ. μηδένα βάλλειν X.*Cyr*.1.4.14; τινὶ ποιεῖν τι D.S.20.18; ἔμοιγε ἀπηγόρευες ὅπως μὴ.. ἀποκρινοίμην Pl.*R*.339a; τοῦ νόμου ἀπαγορεύοντος ἐάν τις.. Lys.9.6; ἀ. τι Id.10.6; περὶ ὧν ὁ νόμος ἀ. μὴ κινῶσιν Arist.*Pol*.1298^{a}38; τὰ ἀπηγορευμένα things *forbidden*, ib.1336^{b}9, cf. S.E.*P*.1.152. 2. *dissuade*, πολλὰ ἀπαγορεύων οὐδὲν ἤνυε Hdt.9.66, cf. 3.124; ἀ. τινί τι Plu.*Arat*.35. II. intr., *bid farewell to*, c. dat., ἀ. τῷ πολέμῳ *give up*, *renounce* war, Pl.*Mx*.245b: c. acc., τὴν ἀγκιστρείαν Aristaenet.1.17; *lose*, στρώματα εἰς τὴν βαφὴν Eun.*VS*p.487 B.: c. part., *give up doing*, οὔτε λέγων οὔτε ἀκούων ἀ. X.*Cyn*.1.16: also, *grow weary of*, ἀ. θεώμενος Id.*Eq*.11.9: abs., *give up*, *flag*, *fail*, Pl.*R*.368c, 568d, *Tht*.200d (answering to ἀπεροῦμεν above); ἀ. γήρᾳ *by* old age, X.*Eq.Mag*.1.2; ἀ. ὑπὸ πόνων *to be exhausted* by.., Id.*An*.5.8.3; ταχὺ ἀ. οἱ ἵπποι Arist.*IA*712^{a}32; ἀ. πρὸς στρατείαν Plu.*Cor*.13; πρὸς κρύος Luc.*Anach*.24, cf. Eun.*Hist*. p.272 D.: also of things, τὰ ἀπαγορεύοντα *worn out and useless*, X.*Cyr*.6.2.33. III. *make an announcement*, *proclamation from*, ἀπὸ τῶ λάω ὦ ἀπαγορεύοντι *Leg.Gort*.10.36, 11.13.

ἀπαγορία, Dor. for ἀπηγορία, dub. in Pi.*Fr*.122.6.

ἀπαγρεύω, *carry off*, *take away*, Hsch.

ἀπαγρι-όομαι, *become wild* or *savage*, μή μ' ἐκπλαγῆτ'.. ἀπηγριωμένον S.*Ph*.226, cf. Pl.*Plt*.274b; ὑπὸ τῶν στατήρων ἦν ἀπηγριωμένη had been *made saucy* by riches, Epicr.3.16. II. of plants, *revert to wild state*, Thphr.*HP*2.2.9, 3.2.2. **-ωσις**, εως, ἡ, *reversion to wild state*, Id.*CP*4.5.6.

ἄπαγρος, ον, (ἄγρα) *unlucky in the chase*, Hsch.

ἀπαγχον-άω, = sq. in Pass., D.C.72.7:—also -έω, in Pass., Steph. *in Hp*.2.334 D. **-ίζω**, *hang by a noose*, *strangle*, Ant.Lib.13.7; αὐτόν *AP*11.111 (Nicarch.):—Pass., Hp.*Virg*.1; γυναῖκας ἀπ' ἐλαίας ἀπηγχονισμένας D.L.6.52. II. *release from a noose*, Luc.*Lex*.11.

ἀπάγχω, *strangle*, *throttle*, ὁ μὲν λάε νεβρὸν ἀπάγχων Od.19.230; γαλῆν ἀ. Ar.*Pax*795, cf. Plu.*Mar*.27, Luc.*Lex*.11; ὃ μάλιστά μ' ἀπάγχει *chokes* me *with anger*, Ar.*V*.686:—Med., aor. ἀπηγξάμην, and Pass., *hang oneself*, *to be hanged*, Archil.67, Hdt.2.131, Hp.*Aph*.2.43, A.*Supp*.465, And.1.125, Philem.130, etc.; ἐκ δένδρων Th.3.81; ὥστε μ' ἀπάγχεσθ' *am ready to choke*, Ar.*Nu*.988; ἀπάγξασθαι ῥηγνύμενος Arr.*Epict*.2.20.31.

ἀπάγω [ᾰγ], *lead away*, *carry off*, ἀπάγουσι βόας καὶ ἴφια μῆλα Od.18.278; ἀ. τινὰ ἐκτόπιον S.*OT*1340 (lyr.), cf. 1521, etc.; προσάγειν.., ἀπάγειν, bring near.., *hold far off*, Arist.*GC*336^{a}18; ἀ. ἀχλὺν ἀπ' ὀφθαλμῶν *remove* it, Thphr.*HP*7.6.2; τὸ ἱμάτιον ἀπὸ τοῦ τραχήλου Plu.*Ant*.12; οὐκ ἀπάξετε ταῦτα; *stop* this *fooling!* Jul.*Or*.7.225a:—Med., *take away for* or *with oneself*, παρθένον Hdt.1.196, cf. 4.80, Ar.*Nu*.1105, etc.; or *that which is one's own*, X.*Cyr*.3.1.37, etc.:—Pass., ἐς ὀξὺ ἀπηγμένας *brought to a point*, *tapering off*, Hdt.7.64, cf. 2.28, Arist.*PA*658^{b}30. 2. *lead away*, *draw off* troops, τῆς στρατιῆς τὸ πολλόν Hdt.1.164, cf. Th.1.28, al.; ἄπαγε τὸν ἵππον Ar.*Nu*.32. b. elliptically, *retire*, *withdraw*, Hdt.5.126, X.*HG*1.1.34, al.; 'go off', Apollod.*Epit*.3.3. 3. *abduct*, Aeschin.1.80, Luc.*Tim*.16:—Pass., πρὸς ὕβριν -εσθαι Id.*Anach*.13. II. *bring back*, *bring home*, Il.18.326; ἀπήγαγεν οἴκαδε Od.16.370, cf. S.*Ph*.941, X.*An*.1.3.14; ἀ. ὀπίσω Hdt.9.117. III. *return*, *render what one owes*, *pay*, τὸν φόρον Ar.*V*.707, cf. X.*Cyr*.2.4.12, Th.5.53; *render* service, honour, etc., κώμους πρὸς τάφον E.*Tr*.1184; θεωρίαν εἰς Δῆλον Pl.*Phd*.58b. IV. *arrest and carry off*, ἀπάγετε αὐτὸν παρ' ἐμέ Hdt.2.114, cf. 6.81; δεῖν κἀπάγειν ἐφίετο E.*Ba*.439:—Pass., ἀπαχθέντας παρ' ἑωυτόν Hdt.6.119. 2. law-term, *bring before a magistrate and accuse* (cf. ἀπαγωγή III), Antipho 5.85; ἀσεβείας *for* impiety, D.22.27; ἀ. ὡς θεσμοθέτας Id.23.31; ἀ. τοῖς ἕνδεκα Id.24.113; τὴν ἐπὶ θανάτῳ -εσθαι Sch.Arist.*Rh*.1397^{a}30 ap.D.H.*Amm*.1.12. 3. *carry off to prison*, Pl.*Grg*.486a, Ar.*Ach*.57; εἰς τὸ δεσμωτήριον And.4.181, D.23.80, 35.47 (Pass.): abs., ὡς γόης ἀπαχθῆναι Pl.*Men*.80b; ἀπαχθεὶς Lys.25.15. V. *lead away*, *divert* from the subject, esp. by sophistry, ἀπὸ τοῦ ὄντος ἐπὶ τοὐναντίον Pl.*Phdr*.262b; ἀ. τινὰ ἀπὸ τῆς ὑποθέσεως D.19.242; ἀ. τὸ ὀργιζόμενον τῆς γνώμης *divert*.., Th.2.59; ἀπὸ δεινῶν ἀ. τὴν γνώμην ib.65. b. in Logic, *reduce*, εἰς ἀδύνατον Arist.*APr*.29^{b}9:—impers. in Pass., ἀπῆκται ἄρα εἰς.. Papp.798.11. c. in later Greek, *reduce*, *drive* an opposing disputant, ἐπὶ ψεῦδος S.E.*P*.2.233; εἰς ἀντίφασιν, εἰς ἄτοπον, Phlp.*in APr*.21.31, 58.14:—Pass., εἰς ἀδύνατον ἀπαχθῆναι Arr.*Epict*.1.7.25, cf. Phlp. *in APr*.129.2. 2. *receive*, ἀπ' ὄψεως.. τὰ δοξάζοντα ἀ. Pl.*Phlb*.39b. 3. *separate*, ἀπάγεται καὶ χωρίζεται Id.*Phd*.97b. VI. simply, *carry*, ἐν ἀριστερᾷ τόξον Id.*Lg*.795a.

ἀπαγωγή, ἡ, *leading away*, of troops, X.*An*.7.6.5; *dragging away*, *rape*, γυναικῶν Luc.*Phal*.1.3 (pl.). b. *leading into captivity*, Lxx *Is*.10.4, al. c. *separation*, *withdrawal*, σώματος (from the soul), Plot.4.4.19. II. *payment*, κατεστρέψατο ἐς φόρου ἀ. subjected them to *payment* of tribute, Hdt.1.6.27, 2.182. III. as Att. law-term, 1. *a summary process by which a person* caught in the act (ἐπ' αὐτοφώρῳ) *might be arrested* by any citizen and brought before the magistrates, Antipho 5.9, And.1.88, Lys.13.85f, D.24.113; ἀπαγωγῆς ἄξια Hyp.*Eux*.16. 2. *written complaint* handed in to the magistrates, ἀπάγειν τὴν ἀ. lay such *accusation*, Lys.13.86; παραδέχεσθαι ἀ., of the Eleven, *admit it*, ibid. IV. in Logic, *shifting* of the basis of argument: hence of argument based on a probable or agreed assumption, Arist.*APr*.69^{a}20, cf. Anon.*in SE*65.35; *reduction*, ἡ εἰς τὸ ἀδύνατον ἀ. *reductio per impossibile*, *APr*.29^{b}6; ἡ ἀ. μετάβασίς ἐστιν ἀπ' ἄλλου προβλήματος ἢ θεωρήματος ἐπ' ἄλλο, οὗ γνωσθέντος ἢ ποριοθέντος καὶ τὸ προκείμενον ἔσται καταφανές Procl. *in Euc*.p.212 F.; τῶν ἀπορουμένων διαγραμμάτων τὴν ἀ. ποιήσασθαι ib. p.213 F. b. *reduction* of a disputant (cf. ἀπάγω v.1c), ἡ ἐπὶ τὸ ἄδηλον ἀ. S.E.*P*.2.234.

ἀπᾰγωγός, όν, *leading away*, *diverting*, λύπης Gorg.*Hel*.10, cf. Iamb.*Myst*.2.5.

ἀπᾰγώνιος, v. ἐπαγώνιος.

ἀπᾰδεῖν, Ion. -έειν, v. sub ἁφανδάνω.

ἀπᾰδῐκέω, *withhold wrongfully*, μισθὸν ἀ. τινός Lxx *De*.24.14. II. *wrong*, *PLond*.2.354.7 (i B.C., Pass.).

ἀπᾰδόντως, Adv. *unbefittingly*, Plot.3.5.5.

ἀπᾴδω, fut. -ᾴσομαι Pl.*Ti*.26d:—*sing out of tune*, ὅλῃ ἁρμονίᾳ Id.*Lg*.802e; ἐπὶ τὸ ὀξὺ Arist.*Pr*.919^{b}23: abs., Pl.*Hp.Mi*.374c, D.Chr.13.20, etc. II. metaph., *dissent*, ἀπ' ἀλλήλων Pl.*Lg*.662b; πρὸς τὴν καθεστῶσαν πολιτείαν Plu.*Lyc*.27: c. gen., ἐθῶν Luc.*Anach*.6; *to be at variance with*, τῆς ἀληθείας Ph.1.235; *fall short of*, τῆς διὰ τῶν νεύρων ἰσχύος Hero *Bel*.112.16. 2. *wander away*, πολὺ ἀπῇσας ἀπὸ τοῦ ἐρωτήματος Pl.*Hp.Ma*.292c. 3. in part., *unbefitting*, ἀπᾴδοντα τῷ θεῷ ἐγκώμια Jul.*Or*.4.132b; τῷ πράγματι Lib.*Or*.10.34; ξένον καὶ ἀπᾷδον τὸ ῥῆμα Porph.*Chr*.69.

ἀπαείρω, aor. -ήειρα, poet. form of ἀπαίρω, *depart*, E.*Fr*.773.68:—in Med., ἀπαειρόμενον πόλιος Il.21.563. II. trans., *remove*, ὀθόνην ἀπὸ γυίων Orac.ap.Porph.ap.Eus.*PE*5.9.

ἀπαέξομαι, poet. for ἀπαυξάνομαι, *grow out of*, Semon.7.85; plpf. ἀπηέξηντο Q.S.14.198 (dub.).

ἀπᾰθᾰνᾰτ-ίζω, *aim at immortality*, Pl.*Chrm*.156d, v.l. in Arist.*EN*1177^{b}33. II. trans., *deify*, D.S.2.20, Vett.Val.150.17; ἑαυτόν Inscr.ap.Str.15.1.73; ἀ. τὴν ψυχήν *represent it as immortal*, Ascl. *in Metaph*.90.26; *make perpetual*, θεὸς ἀ. τὰ γένη Ph.1.9; διὰ τοῦ πυρὸς ἀ. τοῖς θεοῖς τὰς τιμάς Porph.*Abst*.2.5:—Pass., *become immortal*, *earn immortality*, ψυχαὶ ἀπαθανατιζόμεναι, opp. φθαρτὰ σώματα, Ph.1.427; *become a god*, D.C.45.7. **-ισις**, εως, ἡ, *immortalization*, *deification*, dub. l. in Id.60.35. **-ισμός**, ὁ, = foreg., Corn.*ND*31, *PMag.Par*.1.741, al.

ἀπάθ-εια [πᾰ], ἡ, *impassibility*, of things, opp. πάθος, Arist.*Ph*.217^{b}26, *Metaph*.1046^{a}13: pl., opp. πάθη, Epicur.*Ep*.1 p.25 U., S.E.*M*.10.224. II. of persons, *insensibility*, *apathy*, Arist.*EN*1104^{b}24, *de An*.429^{a}29; ἀ. τῶν κακῶν *insensibility to*.., Thphr.*HP*9.15.1; ἀ. περί τι Arist.*APo*.97^{b}23, *Rh*.1383^{b}16. 2. as Stoic term, *freedom from emotion*, Dionys.*Stoic*.3.35, cf. Arr.*Epict*.4.6.34, al., Plu.2.82f; spelt ἀπαθία in Antip.*Stoic*.3.109, Phld.*Sto.Herc*.339.7. III. *absence of injury*, σῴζεσθαι δι' ἀπάθειαν ἀνακαμπτόμενα for the sake of *immunity*, Arist.*PA*682^{b}21. **-έω**, *to be free from* πάθος, Phld.*Lib*. p.40 O.

Ἀπᾰθηναῖοι, ων, οἱ, *degenerate Athenians*, Theopomp.Hist.308; censured by Poll.3.58.

ἀπαθής, ές, *not suffering* or *having suffered*, c. gen., ἀ. ἔργων αἰσχρῶν Thgn.1177; κακῶν Hdt.1.32, 2.119, X.*An*.7.7.33, etc.; ἀεικείης Hdt.3.160; τῶν σεισμῶν τῶν τοῦ σώματος Pl.*Phlb*.33e; νόσων D.60.33, etc.; but also, *without experience of*, πόνων Hdt.6.12; καλῶν μεγάλων Id.1.207: abs., A.*Pers*.862 (lyr.), Th.1.26; πρός τινος Pi.*P*.4.297; χάριν ἴσθι ἐὼν ἀ. be grateful for going *unpunished*, Hdt.9.79: generally, *unaffected*, τὸ οἰκεῖον ὑπὸ τοῦ οἰκείου ἐστὶν ἀ. Arist.*Pr*.872^{a}11, cf. Thphr.*Ign*.42; πρός τι Plu.*Alc*.13, etc.: c. dat. modi, Luc.*Nav*.44. b. Medic., of organs, *unaffected*, *sound*, μόρια Aret.*SD*1.7, cf. Gal.5.122; τὰ ἀπαθῆ τῶν ᾠῶν *good* eggs, Alex.Aphr.*Pr*.2.76. II. *without passion* or *feeling*, *insensible*, *free from emotion*, Arist.*Top*.125^{b}23, cf. *Rh*.1378^{a}5, 1383^{a}28, *Stoic*.3.109, al., Pers.*Stoic*.1.99; of the Cynics, Polystr.p.20 W.; *unmoved by*.., τινός Phld.*Acad.Ind*.p.51 M. Adv. -θῶς, ἔχειν Plu.*Sol*.20: Comp. -έστερον Plot.

3.6.9: Sup. -έστατα Longin.41.1. 2. of things, *not liable to change, impassive*, Arist.*Metaph.*1019^{a}31, al.; ἀ. αἱ ἰδέαι Id.*Top.*148^{a}20, cf. *Metaph.*991^{b}26; Ἀναξαγόρας τὸν νοῦν ἀ. φάσκων Id.*Ph.*256^{b}25; ὁ δὲ νοῦς ἴσως θειότερόν τι καὶ ἀπαθές ἐστιν Id.*de An.*408^{b}29, cf. 430^{a}18; οὐσία ἀσώματος καὶ ἀ. Plu.2.765a; ἀ. ὑπὸ τῶν πολλῶν *unaffected* by the many, Dam.*Pr.*60. 3. Medic., *unaffected by disease, healthy*, περιταμὼν ἄχρι τῶν ἀπαθῶν Gal.5.122, cf. Antyll.ap.Orib.44.23.13. III. *exciting no feeling*, Arist.*Po.*1453^{b}39; τὰ ἀπαθῆ *unemotional topics*, Id.*Fr.*134. IV. Gramm., *not modified*, of uncontracted verbs, Theodos.*Can.*p.36 H.; of patronymics, Eust.13.17; in Metric, *free from metrical licences*, Ps.-Plu.*Metr.*p.472 B. V. ἀπαθῆ, τὰ μὴ ὡς ἀληθῶς γεγονότα πάθη Antipho Soph.5.

ἀπαθία, v. ἀπάθεια.

ἀπαί, = ἀπό, Emp.134, D.P.51. **ἀπαιάζει**, corrupt in Hsch.

ἀπαιγειρόομαι, *to be changed into a poplar*, Str.5.1.9.

ἀπαιδᾰγώγητος, ον, *without teacher* or *guide*, Arist.*EN*1121^{b}11; *uneducated, untaught*, τινός *in* a thing, Id.*Pol.*1338^{b}33 (v.l. ἀπαιδάγωγος): -ητον, τό, *lack of education*, Sor.1.33.

ἀπαιδ-ευσία, Ion. -ιη, ἡ, *want of education*, Democr.212, Pl.*R.*514a, al.; μετὰ ἀπαιδευσίας Th.3.42; δι' ἀπαιδευσίαν Arist.*Rh.*1356^{a}29; δι' ἀ. τῶν ἀναλυτικῶν Id.*Metaph.*1005^{b}3, cf. 1006^{a}6; ἀ. πλούτου ἐστὶ τὸ νεόπλουτον εἶναι Id.*Rh.*1391^{a}17. 2. *stupidity*, Pl.*Grg.*527e, al., Aeschin.1.144; ἀπαιδευσίᾳ ὀργῆς *from bigotry* of passion, Th.3.84. -ευτέω, *to be* ἀπαίδευτος, A.D.*Conj.*235.19, Iamb.*in Nic.*p.9 P.; *to be foolishly said*, Id.*Comm.Math.*7. -ευτος, ον, *uneducated*, παιδεύσωμεν τὸν ἀ. E.*Cyc.*493, cf. Pl.*Tht.*175d; πιθανώτεροι οἱ ἀ. τῶν πεπαιδευμένων ἐν τοῖς ὄχλοις Arist.*Rh.*1395^{b}27, cf. E.*Hipp.*989: c. gen. rei, *uninstructed in..*, X.*Cyr.*3.3.55. 2. *boorish, rude*, Pl.*Grg.*510b, etc.; ῥῆμα ἀ. Id.*Phdr.*269b; ἀ. βίος Alex.284; πνεῦμα Philem.213.11; ἀ. μαρτυρία *clumsy* evidence, Aeschin.1.70; ζητήσεις 2*Ep.Ti.*2.23: Comp., Nicoch.3. II. Adv. -τως Pl.*R.*559d; ἀ. ἔχειν E.*Ion* 247, Alex.267.4, cf. Philostr.*VA*6.36; φληναφᾶσθαι Phld.*Rh.*1.227 S.

ἀπαιδία, ἡ, (ἄπαις) *childlessness*, Hdt.6.139, S.*OT*1024, Antipho 3.1.2, etc. II. = ἀπαιδευσία, *POxy.*33 ii 13 (ii A.D.) (s.v.l.).

ἀπαιδοιόω, = ἀποσκολύπτω (Aeol.), Poll.2.176 (Pass.); ἀπαιδοίωται· ἀπηναισχύντηκε, τέτμηται, Hsch.

ἀπαιδοτρίβητος [ρῐ], ον, *not taught by a* παιδοτρίβης, *AB*419.

ἀπαιθᾰλόω, *burn to cinders* or *ashes*, f.l. in Thphr.*CP*4.12.8.

ἀπαίθομαι, *take fire*, Q.S.1.693.

ἀπαιθριάζω, *expose to the air, air*, Hp.*Morb.*3.17:—Pass., Herod. Med.ap.Orib.5.30.33. 2. ἀ. τὰς νεφέλας *clear away* the clouds, Ar.*Av.*1502. 3. intr., *clear up, grow fine*, of weather, Lib.*Or.*11.215: metaph., M.Ant.2.4.

ἀπαιθύσσομαι, *flare, stream*, of a torch, D.S.2.53.—Act. in *EM* 233.34, intr., of the eyes.

ἀπαίνομαι, v.l. for ἀναίνομαι, Il.7.185.

ἀπαίνῠμαι, = ἀποαίνυμαι (q.v.), Mosch.2.66.

ἀπαιοθήκη, ἡ, dub. sens., *PGrenf.*2.111.39 (inventory of church property).

ἀπαιολάω, *perplex, confound*, E.*Ion* 549; ἀ. τινὰ τῆς ἀληθείας Babr.95.99:—also **ἀπαιολέω**, Sch.Ar.*Nu.*1150.

ἀπαιόλ-η, ἡ, (αἰόλος) *loss by fraud*, τέθνηκεν.. χρημάτων ἀπαιόλῃ A.*Fr.*186. II. *fraud*, cj. Herm. in E.*Hel.*1056; personified in Ar.*Nu.*1150. -ημα, ατος, τό, = foreg., A.*Ch.*1002, S.*Fr.*1018, Ar.*Nu.*729:—also -ησις, εως, ἡ, Hsch.

ἀπαιρεθέω, Ion. aor. 1 subj. Pass., and **ἀπαραιρημένος**, Ion. pf. part. Pass., from ἀφαιρέω.

ἀπαίρω (cf. ἀπαείρω), fut. ἀπᾰρῶ: aor. 1 ἀπῆρα E.*IT*967: pf. ἀπῆρκα Th.8.100, Aeschin.2.82: Ion. impf. ἀπαιρέεσκον, v.l. ἀπαίρεσκον, Hdt.1.186:—*lift off*, and so, *carry off, take away*, τὰ ξύλα ibid.; *remove*, τί τινος E.*Or.*1608; τινὰ Σπάρτης Id.*Hel.*1671; in *IT*967, perh. *get rid of*, νικῶν ἀπῆρα φόνια πειρατήρια:—Pass., ἀπαίρεται τράπεζα Achae.17.5; ἀπό τινος *Ev.Matt.*9.15. II. *lead* or *carry away*, τὰς νέας ἀπὸ Σαλαμῖνος Hdt.8.57; μελάθρων ἀ. πόδα E.*El.*774; ἀ. τινὰ ἐκ χθονὸς Id.*Hel.*1520. 2. elliptically (sc. ναῦς, στρατόν, etc.), *sail away, march away, depart*, ἀπαίρειν ἀπὸ Σαλαμῖνος Hdt.8.60, freq. in Th., X., etc.: c. gen., ἀπαίρειν χθονός *depart from* the land, E.*Cyc.*131; Σπάρτης ἀπῆρας νηῒ Κρησίαν χθόνα Id.*Tr.*944: c. acc. cogn., ἀ. πρεσβείαν *to set out on* an embassy, D.19.163.

ἄπαις, αιδος, ὁ, ἡ, *childless*, Hdt.6.38, S.*Fr.*4; τὰς ἄπαιδας οὐσίας, perh. *childless* estate, dub.l. in Id.*Tr.*911:—often c. gen., ἄ. ἔρσενος γόνου *without* male heirs, Hdt.1.109 (so ἄ. alone, 5.48,67); ἀ. ἔρσενος καὶ θήλεος γόνου Id.3.66; τέκνων ἄπαιδα E.*Supp.*810; ἄ. ἀρρένων παίδων And.1.117, X.*Cyr.*4.6.2; ἀρρένων τε καὶ θηλειῶν Pl.*Lg.*925c. II. Νυκτὸς παῖδες ἄπαιδες children of Night, *yet children none*, dub. l. in A.*Eu.*1034.

ἀπαίσιος, ον, *ill-omened*, ἡμέρα App.*BC*1.78; φωνή Plu.2.266d; ἄχθος ὑαίνης Opp.*H.*1.372; ἡμέρα Luc.*Pseudol.*12; ὄνομα Procl. *in Cra.*p.39 P. Adv. ἀπαξίως, αἰσίως καὶ ἀ. ἐπιγενησόμενα Gal.1.292.

ἀπαΐσσω, Att. -ᾴσσω, *spring from* a height, κρημνοῦ ἀπαΐξας Il.21.234. II. *dart away*, ὁπόταν μὲν ἀπαΐξῃ τέρεν αἷμα Emp.100.6, cf. ib.23; τοῦ δ' ἐγὼ κλύων ἀπῆξα S.*Tr.*190, cf. Ar.*Ra.*468; ἀπῆξε πέμφιξ S.*Fr.*337; φρένες.. γνώμης ἀπῆξαν Id.*Aj.*448. [ἀπᾱ- Hom., cf. ἀΐσσω.]

ἀπαισχύνομαι [ῡ], *shrink back* or *refuse through shame*, Pl.*Grg.*494c, Phld.*Lib.*p.34 O.

ἀπαισχυντέω, = foreg., Hld.8.5 (but better ἀπαναισχ-).

ἀπαιτ-έω, *demand back, demand to have returned*, esp. of things forcibly taken or rightfully belonging to one, Hdt.1.2; εἰ μὲν βούλεσθε, αἰτῶ, εἰ δὲ μὴ βούλεσθε, ἀπαιτῶ And.2.22; τὸ μισθάριον γὰρ ἂν ἀπαιτῇς Diph.43.34; τὸ τέλος ὁ χρόνος ἀπαιτεῖ *BCH*7.278 (Tralles); τὴν ψυχὴν *Ev.Luc.*12.20; ἀ. τινά τι *demand* something *of* one, Hdt.8.122, E.*Hel.*963, Ar.*Av.*554, D.1.22; εὐθύνας ἀ. τινά Id.18.245; also ἀ. ὅπλα τοῦ πατρός S.*Ph.*362; χάριν ἀ. τινά Pl.*Phdr.*241a, etc.; τι παρά τινος Arist.*de An.*408^{a}18; also ἀ. δίκην ἐξ ἀδίκων A.*Ch.*398; λόγον ἀ. τινὰ περί τινος Pl.*R.*599b; ἀ. ὑπέρ τινος ib.612d; ἀ. ὑποσχέσεις Arist.*EN*1164^{a}17: c. inf., ἀ. τινὰ ποιεῖν τι E.*Supp.*385. b. *call down on oneself*, ποινάς Jul.*Or.*2.59a (and so Med., ib.58a). c. of things, *require*, νοῦσοι -έουσι σικύην Aret.*CA*1.10; περίοδος ἀ. μῆνα τρισκαιδέκατον Plu.*Agis* 16: abs., ὅταν αἱ χρεῖαι -ῶσιν Ael.*Tact.*15.1. 2. *inquire*, ἀπαιτήσομεν αὐτὸν τίνες εἰσίν Str.12.3.24. II. Pass., of things, *to be demanded in payment*, Hdt.5.35. 2. of persons, *have demanded of one*, ἀπαιτεῖσθαι εὐεργεσίαν X.*Ap.*17; τὸ τῆς ψυχῆς χρέος Lxx *Wi.*15.8; ἀποδώσειν ὅταν ἀπαιτῆται *BGU*1058.33 (i B.C.); *yield to a request*, οὐκ ἀπαιτούμεσθα, answering to ἀπαιτῶ σκῆπτρα, E.*Ph.*602. -ημα, ατος, τό, *demand*, *BGU*1113.15 (i B.C.); *requirement*, Arr.*Epict.*4.6.35, M.Ant.5.15. II. *that which is demanded*, [ἄνθρωπος] γῆς ἀ. Secund.*Sent.*7. -ήσιμον, τό, *list of lands subject to dues*, *PTeb.*72.218 (ii B.C.), *BGU*457.4 (ii A.D.), *PFay.*40.3 (ii A.D.). 2. *demand* for services, *POxy.*136.17 (vi A.D.). -ησις, εως, ἡ, *demanding back*, Hdt.5.85; Ἑλένης ἀ., name of a play by S.; ἀ. ποιεῖσθαι make a *formal demand*, D.33.26, cf. *POxy.*272.13 (i A.D.); *claim, right to demand* a thing, τινὸς ἔχειν ἀ. ἀπὸ τῆς πόλεως *IG*9(1).61 (Daulis). -ητέον, *one must demand* or *require*, Arist.*EN*1098^{a}33, Jul.*Or.*2.86a. 2. -τέος, α, ον, *to be demanded, required*, Arist.*EN*1104^{a}3. -ητής, οῦ, ὁ, *tax-gatherer*, *PAmh.*2.72, *POxy.*514.1 (ii A.D.), etc. -ητικός, ή, όν, *requiring*: -κόν, τό, *state of need*, Gal.1.205. -ίζω, = ἀπαιτέω, *demand back*, of things forcibly taken away, χρήματα Od.2.78, cf. Call.*Fr.*178; simply, *demand*, τινά τι Nonn.*D.*42.382, cf. Opp.*H.*5.443.

ἀπαίων, ωνος, ὁ, ἡ, *without the paean, cheerless*, ἀκτὰς ἀπαίωνας.. Ἀχέροντος S.*Fr.*523.

ἀπαιώνιστος, ον, = foreg., E.*Fr.*77.

ἀπαιωρ-έομαι, *hang down from, hover about*, Hes.*Sc.*234; ἀ. ἔνθεν καὶ ἔνθεν *hang without support* at either end, as a fractured limb supported only by the bandage at the fracture, Hp.*Fract.*7, cf. *Art.*63, J.*AJ*15.11.3, Antyll.ap.Orib.44.23.6, Meges ap.eund.44.24.13; τῆς ὕλης ἡ κόμη μετέωρος ἀπῃώρηται Procop.Gaz.*Ecphr.*p.158 B. 2. *to be uplifted*, Luc.*Astr.*19. II. later in Act. ἀπαιωρέω, *let hang down*, πλοκάμους Alciphr.3.55; *lift up* a garment, J.*AJ*11.6.9. -ημα, ατος, τό, *holder* for splints in surgical apparatus, Hp.*Fract.*30.

ἀπακμάζω, *go out of bloom, fade away*, v.l. in Pl.*Ax.*367b (ap. Stob.).

ἀπακμή, ἡ, *decline*, of genius, Longin.9.14.

ἀπᾰκονάω, *sharpen*, τὴν γλῶτταν καθάπερ μάχαιραν Porph.*Chr.*31:—Pass., *to be sharpened to a point*, ἄκραι εἰς λεπτὸν ἀπηκονημέναι J.*AJ*6.6.2.

ἀπᾰκοντίζω, *shoot away like a javelin, shoot off*, τὰς ἀποφυάδας Arist.*HA*501^{a}32 (= Ctes.*Fr.*64); *spirt out* blood, Antyll.ap.Orib.7.10.2; *dart forth*, μαρμαρυγήν Nonn.*D.*40.414.

ἀπάκρας μάχη *single* combat (Lacon.), Hsch.

ἀπακρῑβόομαι, *to be highly wrought* or *finished*, πρὸς κάλλος Pl.*Lg.*810b; λόγος ἀπηκριβωμένος Id.*Ti.*29c, Isoc.4.11, cf. Pl.*Phlb.*59d; παιδεία Isoc.15.190; τὰ μάλιστ' ἀπηκρ. the most *perfect creatures*, Arist.*PA*666^{a}28; of persons, ἀπηκριβωμένος ἐπί τινι *accurately versed* in a thing, Isoc.12.28; cf. ἀπηκριβωμένως. II. Med., *finish off, make perfect*, of sculpture, *APl.*4.172 (Alex.Aet.), cf. 5.342; ἀ. ταῖς γραμμαῖς Luc.*Im.*16 (Pass.).

ἀπακταίνω, *to be unequal to violent exercise*, Hsch.

ἀπακ-τέον, *one must lead away*, τινά τινος Plu.2.9f. -τός, όν, *that may be dragged to prison*, Arr.*Epict.*3.24.105 (Schweigh. for ἀπότακτος, q.v.).

ἀπάλαιστος [πᾰ], ον, *not to be thrown in wrestling, unconquerable*, Pi.*N.*4.94.

ἀπάλαιστρος [πᾰ], ον, *not trained in the palaestra, unskilled in wrestling*, *AP*12.222 (Strat.); opp. οἱ μετέχοντες τοῦ γυμνασίου, *CIG* 3086 (Teos). 2. generally, *awkward, clumsy*, Cic.*Or.*68.229, Quint.*Inst.*9.4.56, Phld.*Rh.*1.8 S. (Sup.). II. *not customary in the palaestra, contrary to its rules*, *AP*5.213 (Mel.).

ἀπᾰλαίωτος, ον, *not growing old* or *decaying*, Hsch. s.v. ἀγήραος.

ἀπάλαλκε [πᾰ], 3 sg. aor. 2, opt. ἀπαλάλκοι: (with no pres., v. ἄλαλκε and cf. ἀπαλέξω):—*ward off, keep off* something *from* one, τί τινος Il.22.348, cf. Od.4.766; νόσους Pi.*O.*8.85: later inf. ἀπαλαλκέμεν Theoc.28.20: 2 sg. ἀπάλαλκες Q.S.5.215.

ἀπάλαμνος [πᾰ], ον, poet. for ἀπάλαμος (cf. παλαμναῖος from παλάμη, νώνυμνος from νώνυμος), properly, *without hands*, i.e. *helpless*, ἀνὴρ ἀ. Il.5.597, cf. Simon.53; also οὐκ ἀ. λόγος Alc.49. Adv. -νως *AB*418. II. in Lyr. and Eleg., *reckless, lawless*, ἀ. φρένες Pi.*O.*2.57; of acts, ἔρδειν ἔργ' ἀ. Sol.28.12; ἀπάλαμνα μυθεῖσθαι Thgn.481; ἀνελέσθαι Id.281; ἀ. τι παθεῖν E.*Cyc.*598.

ἀπάλᾰμος [πᾰ], ον, = foreg., *helpless*, Hes.*Op.*20; βίος ἀ., of Tantalus, Pi.*O.*1.59. [ᾰπ metri gr., Hes. l. c.]

ἀπᾰλάομαι, *go astray, wander*, ἀ. ἄλλῃ Hes.*Sc.*409.

ἀπαλασίξαι (i.e. ἀπαληθίσαι)· ὀμόσαι (Lacon.), Hsch.

ἀπᾰλαστέω, (ἄλαστος) *complain of grievous usage*, Hsch. (ἀτταλ- cod.).

ἀπαλαύξινα· εἰς αὐτὸν καταστρέφοντα, Hsch.

ἀπαλγ-έω, *put away sorrow for*, τὰ ἴδια Th.2.61; ἀ. τὸ πένθος Plu. *Cleom.*22; τὸ πάθος Procop.*Arc.*16. II. generally, *to be despondent*, ἀ. ταῖς ἐλπίσιν Plb.9.40.4; πρὸς ἐλπίδα D.C.48.37: abs., Plb.1.35.5, *Ep.Eph.*4.19. **-ησις**, εως, ἡ, *ceasing to feel pain*, Hld.6.5.

ἀπαλεῖν· ἀμελεῖν, and **ἀπαλέντες**· ἀμελοῦντες, Hsch.

ἀπ-ᾰλειπτέον, *one must expunge*, M.Ant.11.19. **-ᾰλείφω**, pf. ἀπαλήλιφα D.52.29:—*wipe off, expunge*, esp. from a record or register, Id.45.44; ἀ. ἀπὸ ὀφλήματος καθ' ὅτι ἂν ἐκτίνῃ Id.58.50; ἀ. τι τῶν δεδογμένων *cancel* it, Aeschin.2.160; ἀ. ἀπὸ τῶν παρακαταθηκῶν *embezzle* part of the deposits, D.52.27:—Med., *erase*, Themist.*Ep.* 8:—Pass., *to be erased*, *POxy.*34 i 14 (i A.D.). 2. metaph., μυρίας ἐπιστολὰς ἓν δάκρυον ἀπαλείφει μητρός Plu.*Alex.*39.

ἀπᾰλέξ-αι, -ασθαι, v. ἀπαλέξω. **-ησις**, εως, ἡ, *defence*, τινός *against* a thing, Phot., Suid. **-ητικός**, ή, όν, *helping, defending*, *EM*56.10. **-ίκᾰκος**, ον, = ἀλεξίκακος, f.l. in Orph.*H.*67.5, dub. in *IG*12(7).253 (Amorgos); ἥλιος Porph.ap.Eus.*PE*3.11. **-ω**, *ward off from*, c. acc. rei et gen. pers., καὶ δέ κεν ἄλλον σεῦ ἀπαλεξήσαιμι Il. 24.371: c. dat. pers., Ζεὺς.. μοι ἀπαλέξαι γάμον *may* he *avert* it *from* me, A.*Supp.*1053. 2. c. acc. pers. et gen. rei, οὐδ' ὥς τιν' ἔμελλεν ἀπαλεξήσειν κακότητος Od.17.364. II. Med., *defend oneself*, πρὸς ταῦτ' ἀπαλέξασθαι S.*Aj.*166 (lyr.), cf. *Fr.*303, Nic.*Th.*829.

ἀπᾰλεύομαι, *keep aloof from*, v.l. Nic.*Th.*395 (Sch.).

ἀπᾰληθεύω, *speak the whole truth*, πρός τινα X.*Oec.*3.12: c. acc., χρόνος ὁ πάντα ἐκκαλύπτων καὶ ἀπαληθεύων Ael.*Fr.*62.

ἀπαλθαίνομαι, fut. -ήσομαι, *heal thoroughly*, ἕλκε' ἀπαλθήσεσθον (-ονται Aristarch.) Il.8.419: impf., Q.S.4.404.

ἁπᾰλία, ἡ, (ἁπαλός) *softness*, τοῦ ἀέρος *Gp.*1.8.2.

ἁπᾰλίας, ου, ὁ, *a sucking pig*, D.L.8.20 (prob.); cf. **ἁπάλιον**· θῦμα δελφάκιον, Hsch.

ἀπαλλ-ᾰγή, ἡ, (ἀπαλλάσσω) *deliverance, release, relief from* a thing, πόνων, πημάτων, ξυμφορᾶς, A.*Ag.*1, 20, *Pr.*754, S.*Ant.*1338, etc.: in pl., A.*Pr.*318, E.*Heracl.*811; ἀ. πραγμάτων Antipho 6.35; ἀ. τοῦ πολέμου *putting an end to* the war, Th.7.2; οὐκ ἦν τοῦ πολέμου πέρας οὐδ' ἀ. D.18.145; of contracts, *release, discharge*, ἀ. συμβολαίων Id. 33.3; generally, *relief from*, τινός Arist.*HA*582ᵇ12. 2. abs., *divorce*, in pl., E.*Med.*236, 1375: sg., *PRyl.*154.29 (i A.D.), etc. II. *removal*, Pl.*Lg.*736a. III. (from Pass.) *going away, means of getting away* or *escape*, Hdt.1.12, 7.207, al.; τέλος τῆς ἀ. the final *departure*, Id.2.139; ἡ ἀ. ἐγένετο ἀλλήλων *separation* of combatants, Th.1.51; ἐκ τῆς Αἰγύπτου τὴν ἀ. ποιήσασθαι D.S.15.43. 2. τοῦ βίου *departure* from life, Hp.*Epid.*7.89, X.*Cyr.*5.1.13; ψυχῆς ἀπὸ σώματος Pl.*Phd.*64c: hence ἀ. alone, *death*, Thphr.*HP*9.8.3, etc. 3. *avoidance*, τῆς μίξεως Sor.1.31. **-ακτέον**, *one must release from*, τινά τινος Plu.*Cor.*32. 2. *one must remove, make away with*, τι ἐκποδών D.H.6.51. II. (from Pass.) *one must withdraw from, get rid of*, τινός Lys.6.8, Pl.*Phd.*66e. **-ακτής**, οῦ, ὁ, *liberator from*, κακοῦ Max.Tyr.13.5. **-ακτιάω**, = ἀπαλλαξείω, M.Ant.10. 36. **-ακτικός**, ή, όν, *fit for ridding, removing*, στρόφων Dsc.3.72; νοσήματος Phld.*Rh.*1.345 S. 2. *fit for curing illness*, Arist.*Pr.* 959ᵇ26. 3. Adv. -κῶς, ἔχειν, = ἀπαλλαξείειν, *wish to depart*, D.H. *Rh.*11.8. **-αξείω**, Desiderat. of ἀπαλλάσσομαι, *wish to be delivered from* or *get rid of*, τινός Th.1.95, 3.84, Procop.*Arc.*4. **-αξίκακος**, = Ἀλεξίκακος, epith. of Heracles, Roussel *Cultes Égyptiens* 200 (Delos). **-αξις**, εως, ἡ, = ἀπαλλαγή III, Hdt.9.13, Porph.*Marc.*9; ἀ. χροιῆς *loss of* colour, Hp.*Hum.*5, cf. Epicur.*Nat.*139 G.

ἀπαλλᾶσθαι· ἀπαντλεῖν, Hsch. (fort. ἐπαμᾶσθαι· ἐπαντλεῖν).

ἀπαλλάσσω, Att. -ττω, fut. -ξω Isoc.5.52: pf. ἀπήλλαχα X.*Mem.* 3.13.6: aor. ἀπήλλαξα Hdt.1.16, Ar.*V.*1537, etc.:—**Pass.**, pf. ἀπήλλαγμαι Id.*Pax* 1128, Isoc.5.49, Ion. ἀπάλλαγμαι Hdt.2.144, 167: aor. ἀπηλλάχθην, Ion. ἀπαλλ- Id.2.152, etc.; in Att. ἀπηλλάγην [ᾰ] as always in Prose; also in Trag. (for the most part metri gr., cf. however S.*Ant.*422, *El.*783 (v.l.), E.*Ph.*592 (v.l.), *Andr.*592): fut. ἀπαλλαχθήσομαι Id.*Hipp.*356, Ar.*Av.*940; in Prose, ἀπαλλαγήσομαι Th. 4.28, etc.:—**Med.**, fut. (in pass. sense) ἀπαλλάξομαι Hdt.7.122, E. *Hel.*437, Th.8.83, etc.: aor. ἀπηλλάξαντο E.*Heracl.*317, cf. Plu.*Cat. Mi.*64.

A. Act., *set free, deliver from* a thing, παιδίον δυσμορφίης Hdt. 6.61; τινὰ πόνων, κακῶν, A.*Eu.*83, *Pr.*773; τινὰ ἐκ γόων S.*El.*292; ἐκ φόβου καὶ κακῶν And.1.59: c. acc. only, *release*, S.*Ant.*596, etc.; κόπος μ' ἀ. Id.*Ph.*880. 2. *put away from, remove from*, τί τινος, as ἀ. γῆς πρόσωπον, φρενῶν ἔρωτα, E.*Med.*27, *Hipp.*774 (lyr.); σφαγῆς χεῖρα *IT*994; χρυσὸν χερὸς *Hec.*1222; ἀ. τινά τινος *take away* or *remove from* one, Ar.*Ec.*1046; τινὰ ἀπὸ τῆς πολιορκίας D.C.43.32. 3. c. acc. only, *put away, remove*, τι E.*Hec.*1068, Pl.*Prt.*354d, etc.; μύθοις ἔργ' ἀ. κακά *do away* ill by words, E.*Fr.*282.26; *get rid of* creditors, And. 1.122; τοὺς χρήστας Is.5.28; *get rid of* an opponent, by fair means or foul, D.24.37; ἀ. τοὺς κατηγόρους Lys.29.1; τοὺς Πελοποννησίους ἐκ τῆς χώρας Th.8.48; *dismiss, send away*, τινά Id.1.90; *remove* or *displace* from an office, ib.129; ἀ. τοὺς ὑπηρέτας καὶ θεραπευτῆρας Plu. *Lyc.*11; also, *make away with, destroy*, Thphr.*HP*9.15.2; ἑαυτόν Plu.*Cat.Mi.*70; *bring to an end*, λόγον E.*Med.*790. 4. in Law, *give a release, discharge*, D.36.25, cf. 37.1; τοὺς δανείσαντας ἀ. 34.22, cf. *PTeb.*315.16 (ii A.D.); *discharge* a debt, D.C.59.1, etc.:—so in Pass., Id.51.17. II. intr., *get off free, escape*, esp. with an Adv. added, ῥηιδίως, χαλεπῶς ἀ., Hp.*VM*10, 20, cf. X.*Cyr.*4.1.5; ὁ στόλος οὕτως ἀ. *came off, ended*, Hdt.5.63, cf. A.*Ag.*1288, E.*Med.*786; οὐκ ὡς ἤθελε ἀπήλλαξεν Hdt.1.16; κάκιον ἀ. Pl.*R.*491d, cf. Men.*Epit.*199; καταγελάστως ἀ. Aeschin.2.38; ἀλυσιτελῶς ἀ. Thphr.*Char.*8.11; ἀλύπως ἀ. *get along* well, *PPetr.*3 p.58: with part. or Adj., χαίρων ἀ. Hdt.3.69; ἀθῷοι ἀ. Pl.*Sph.*254d, etc.: c. gen., *depart from*, βίου E.*Hel.*302 (dub. l.); τοῦ ζῆν Pl.*Ax.*367c; so πῶς ἀπήλλαχεν ἐκ τῆς ὁδοῦ; X.*Mem.*3.13.6; ἄριστ' ἀπαλλάττεις ἐπὶ τούτου τοῦ κύβου *in respect of*.., Diph.73.

B. Pass. and Med., *to be set free* or *released from* a thing, *get rid of* it, ἀπαλλαχθέντας δουλοσύνης Hdt.1.170; τυράννων Id.5.78; τῶν παρεόντων κακῶν Id.2.120; πημονῆς A.*Pr.*471; φόβου S.*El.*783; πραγμάτων τε καὶ μαχῶν Ar.*Pax* 293; στρατιᾶς Id.*Ach.*251; Κλέωνος Th.4.28; τῆς κακουχίας ἐπὶ τὴν αὐτοῦ σκηνήν Plb.5.15.6. 2. *get off, escape*, mostly with some Adj. or Adv. added (as in Act. II), ῥηιδίως ἀ. Hp.*VM*3; ἀγῶνος ἀ. καλῶς E.*Heracl.*346; ἀζήμιος ἀπαλλαγῆναι, ἀπαλλάττεσθαι, Ar.*Pl.*271, Pl.*Lg.*721d. 3. abs., *to be acquitted*, D.22.39. 4. of a point under discussion, *to be dismissed as settled*, τοῦτο ἀπήλλακται μὴ.. τὸ φίλον φίλον εἶναι Pl.*Ly.*220b, cf. *Phlb.* 67a. II. *remove, depart from*, ἐκ τῆς χώρης, ἐξ Αἰγύπτου, Hdt.1. 61, 2.139, al.; μαντικῶν μυχῶν A.*Eu.*180; γῆς ἀπαλλάσσεσθαι πόδα E.*Med.*729; δόξης, δέους Th.2.42; ἀ. παρά τινος Aeschin.1.78; *depart, go away*, ἐς τὴν ἑωυτοῦ Hdt.1.82, al.; ἐπὶ τῆς ἑωυτοῦ Id.9.11, cf. 5.64; πρὸς χώραν Pl.*Lg.*938a: abs., Hdt.2.93, al., Aen.Tact.10.19, 15.9. 2. ἀπαλλάσσεσθαι τοῦ βίου *depart from* life, E.*Hel.*102, *Hipp.*356; βίου ἀπαλλαγὴν ἀ. Pl.*R.*496e; freq. without τοῦ βίου, *depart, die*, E.*Heracl.*1000, Pl.*Phd.*81c, etc. 3. ἀ. λέχους *to be divorced*, E.*Andr.*592; ἀ. γυναῖκά τε ἀπ' ἀνδρὸς καὶ τὸν ἄνδρα ἀπὸ γυναικός Pl.*Lg.*868d. 4. ἀ. τῶν διδασκάλων *leave* school, Id.*Grg.*514c, cf. X.*Mem.*1.2.24. 5. ἀ. ἐκ παίδων *become a man*, Aeschin.1. 40. 6. *to be removed from, free from* the imputation of, ἀπηλλαγμένος εὐηθίης *many removes from* folly, Hdt.1.60; ξυμφορῶν Th.1. 122; αἰσχύνης Id.3.63: c. inf., κρῖναι ἱκανῶς οὐκ ἀπήλλακτο *was* not *far from* judging adequately, Id.1.138. b. πολλὸν ἀπηλλαγμένος τινός *far inferior* to him, Hdt.2.144. 7. *depart from, leave off from*, τῶν μακρῶν λόγων S.*El.*1335; σκωμμάτων Ar.*Pl.*316; ἀ. λημμάτων *give up the pursuit of*.., D.3.33; οὐκ ἀπήλλακται γραφικῆς *is* not *averse from*.., Luc.*Salt.*35. b. abs., *have done, cease*, of things, S.*Ant.*422; ὅταν ἡ μέθη ἀπαλλαγῇ Arist.*MM*1202ᵃ3. c. *throw up one's case, give up a prosecution*, D.21.151, 198. d. c. part., εἰπὼν ἀπαλλάγηθι speak and *be done with it*, Pl.*Grg.*491c, cf. *Tht.*183c; ταῦτα μαντευσάμενος ἀπαλλάττομαι Id.*Ap.*39d; ἀπαλλάχθητι πυρώσας E. *Cyc.*600: also in part., with a Verb, οὐκοῦν ἀπαλλαχθεὶς ἄπει; *make haste* and begone, S.*Ant.*244. 8. *to depart from enmity*, i.e. *to be reconciled, settle a dispute*, πρὸς ἀλλήλους Pl.*Lg.*915c: abs., ib. 768c. 9. *recover from an ailment*, Aret.*SD*1.14.

ἀπαλλητός, όν, *marvellous*, Hsch.

ἀπαλλοιόω, *differentiate*, Phld.*Sto.Herc.*339.9.

ἀπαλλότρι-ος, α, ον, *given over to strangers*, πολιτεῖαι D.S.11. 76. **-όω**, pf. ἀπηλλοτρίωκα Aeschin.2.194:—*estrange, alienate*, ἀφ' ὑμῶν τὸν ἐπὶ Θρᾴκης τόπον l.c.; λόγον -οῦντα κακίας Aristo *Stoic.*1.80; τινά τινος J.*AJ*4.1.1:—Pass., *to be alienated*, τινός *from* one, Plb.1.79.6, cf. Alex.Aphr.*in Top.*389.12; πρός τινα towards one, Isoc.*Ep.*7.13, D.S.18.48; ἀπηλλοτριωμένην πρὸς φυτείαν ἀμπέλου χώραν *ill-suited for*.., Id.3.73. 2. of property, *alienate*, Arist. *Rh.*1361ᵃ22, *IPE*1².32 *B*68 (Olbia, iii B.C.):—Pass., *PLond.*3.1157ᵛ iii 3 (iii A.D.). 3. of things, *separate, distinguish*, Hp.*Art.*58 (Pass.). b. *alter*, Pl.*Ti.*65d (Pass.). c. *remove*, in Surgery, Archig.ap.Orib.46.26.13 (Pass.):—Act., Gal.14.789. **-ωσις**, εως, ἡ, *alienation*, λέγω ἀπαλλοτρίωσιν δόσιν καὶ πρᾶσιν Arist.*Rh.*1361ᵃ 22, cf. *CIG*3281 (Smyrna). 2. *estrangement*, γονέων Vett.Val.2. 37 (pl.); φιλτάτων Gal.19.181.

ἁπαλοανθής, v. ἁπαλοβραχέα.

ἀπᾰλοάω, poet. -οιάω, *thresh out*, σῖτος ἀπηλοημένος D.42.6. 2. metaph., *bruise, crush*, Il.4.522; generally, *destroy*, Nonn.*D.*9.320.

ἁπᾰλο-βραχέα· ἁπαλοανθῆ, Hsch. **-θριξ**, τρῐχος, ὁ, ἡ, *soft-haired*, E.*Ba.*1186 (lyr.).

ἀπαλοῖξαι· ὀμόσαι (Lacon.), Hsch. (cf. ἀπαλασίξαι).

ἀπᾰλοιφή, ἡ, (ἀπαλείφω) *effacing, expunging*, *Gloss.* II. prob. l. for ἀπαλειφή (sic), *paste, amalgam*, Zos.Alch.p.222 B. [Perh. ἀπαλῐφή; cf. καταλιφή.]

ἁπᾰλο-κουρίς, ίδος, ἡ, = ἁπαλὴ κουρίς, or καρίς, cj. in Epich.44. 3. **-κροκῶδες**, τό, name of an *eye-salve*, Sichel *Pierres sigillaires* p.59.

ἄπαλον· ἀνοχὴ ἀπὸ τοῦ παλαίειν, Hsch.

ἀπαλ-όνυχος, ον, dub. l. in Ph.2.397.

ἁπᾰλό-παις, αιδος, ὁ, *delicate child*, Hsch. s. v. δρυψόπαιδα. **-πάρηος** [ᾰρ], ον, *with soft cheeks*, Eust.691.52. **-πλόκᾰμος**, ον, *with soft tentacles*, of cuttlefish, Philox.2.14. **-πους**, οδος, ὁ, ἡ, *tender-footed*, *Hippiatr.*116.

ἁπᾰλός, ή, όν, *soft to the touch, tender*: in Hom. mostly of the human body, ἁπαλὴν ὑπὸ δειρήν Il.3.371; παρειάων ἁπαλάων 18.123; ἁπαλοῖο δι' αὐχένος ἤλυθεν ἀκωκή 17.49; ἁ. πόδες 19.92; ἁ. τέ σφ' ἦτορ ἀπηύρα, i.e. the life of *young* animals, 11.115; ἴεσαν αὐδὴν ἐξ ἁπαλῶν στομάτων Hes.*Sc.*279; δέρα Sapph.*Supp.*23.16; of persons, *delicate*, παῖδες Alc.*Supp.*14.5; εὐμορφοτέρα.. τᾶς ἀπάλας Γυρίννως Sapph.76; of flowers, ἄνθρυσκα Ead.*Supp.*25.13; rare in Trag., and only in lyr., παρειά A.*Supp.*70; βρέφος ἁ. E.*IA*1285; βλέφαρον τέγγουσ' ἁ. *El.* 1339; more freq. in Com., σισύμβριον Cratin.239; κρέα Ar.*Lys.* 1063; δάκτυλοι Alex.48; θερμολουσίαις ἁπαλοί *Com.Adesp.*56; so in Prose, ἁ. ψυχή Pl.*Phdr.*245a; of *raw* fruit, Hdt.2.92, cf. X.*Oec.*19. 18; of *tender* meat, Id.*An.*1.5.2; *soft-boiled*, of eggs, Cael.Aur. *AP*2.18; of a *gentle* fire, Philem.79.8, D.S.3.25. II. metaph., *soft, gentle*, ἁπαλὸν γελάσαι laugh *gently*, Od.14.465; ἁ. δίαιτα *soft*, *delicate*, Pl.*Phdr*.239c; τῷ αὐτῷ..χρησώμεθα τεκμηρίῳ περὶ Ἔρωτα ὅτι ἁπαλός Id.*Smp*.195e (also in Sup.); ἁ. εἴσπλους λιμένος, opp. τραχύς, Cratin.357. Adv. ἁπαλῶς, ὀπτᾶν to roast *moderately*, Sotad. Com.1.16: Comp. ἁπαλωτέρως, ἅπτεσθαι Hp.*Art*.37. 2. in bad sense, *soft, weak*, ὡς ἁ. καὶ λευκὸς [οἶνος] Cratin.183; λευκός, ἐξυρημένος, γυναικόφωνος, ἁ. Ar.*Th*.192. [ᾰπᾰλος; for καλάμῳ..ὑπᾰπάλῳ, in Theoc.28.4, is corrupt.]

ἁπᾰλό-σαρκος, *with soft* or *tender flesh*, Hp.*Liqu*.6, *Mul*.1.1; Diph.Siph.ap.Ath.8.355e. **-στομος**, ον, *delicate to the mouth*, Hsch. s.v. γλύξις. **-σύγκρῐτος**, ον, *of delicate texture*, σώματα Orib.44.14.4. **-σώματος**, ον, *of tender body*, Ar.*Fr*.54 D. **-της**, ητος, ἡ, *softness, tenderness*, Hp.*VM*22, Pl.*Smp*.195d, X.*Mem*.2.1.22; δι' ἁπαλότητα Arist.*Pol*.1336a10. **-τρεφής**, ές, *well-fed, plump*, σίαλος Il.21.363; λειμῶνες *rich* pastures, *IG*14.1389 ii 11. **-φόρος**, ον, *wearing soft raiment*, *EM*4.16. **-φρων**, ον, gen. ονος, *soft-hearted*, *AP*7.403 (Marc. Arg.). **-χροος**, ον, contr. **-χρους**, χρουν; with heterocl. gen. ἁπαλόχροος, dat. -χροΐ, acc. -χροα:—*soft-skinned*, *h.Ven*.14, Hes.*Op*.519, Thgn.1341, E.*Hel*.373 (lyr.):—also **-χρως**, χρωτος, ὁ, ἡ, Phryn.*PS*p.30 B.

ἁπᾰλ-υντής, οῦ, ὁ, *worker of hides, currier*, Zonar. **-ύνω** [ῡ], *soften*, ἵππου τὸ στόμα, τὰς τρίχας, X.*Eq*.4.5, 5.5; *make plump*, opp. ἰσχναίνω, Hp.*Art*.50. 2. *make tender* or *delicate*, τοὺς πόδας ὑποδήμασι X.*Lac*.2.1:—Pass., *to be softened*, metaph., Lxx 4*Ki*.22.19, *Ps*.54(55).21.

ἁπᾰλύσκομαι, = ἀπαλεύομαι: ἀπαλύξασθαι v.l. for ἀπαλέξασθαι, Nic.*Th*.829.

ἁπᾰλυσμός, ὁ, *making plump*, Hp.*Art*.50.

ἀπαλφῐτίζω, *mix* wine *with barley-meal* or *groats*, in the Persian fashion, f.l. in Ath.10.432d.

ἀπᾰμαλδύνω [ῡ], *bring to naught, plunge into obscurity*, *AP*9.24 (Leon.); *quench*, μαρμαρυγήν Nonn.*D*.33.24; *turn pale*, ἔρευθος Q.S.8.209.

ἀπᾰμαυρόω, *remove darkness*, ὅσσων..ἀπημαύρωσας ὁμίχλην Orph.*H*.6.6. II. *make obscure*, *Hymn.Is*.21. 2. Pass., *fall into obscurity, become antiquated*, μάθημα ἀπημαυρωμένον Ael.*Tact.Praef*.2. b. Pass., *lose its power*, of a drug, Agatharch.97. III. Pass., *to be deprived of sight*, ἀ. τοῦ βλέπειν Lxx *Is*.44.18.

ἀπᾰμάω (A), fut. -ήσω, *cut off*, ἀπ' οὔατα νηλέϊ χαλκῷ ῥῖνάς τ' ἀμήσαντες Od.21.300, cf. Hes.*Th*.181; ἀπάμησον [τὸν πόδα] S.*Ph*.749:—in Med., Thphr.*Lap*.21; ἀπὸ στάχυν ἀμήσασθαι Q.S.13.242:—Pass., Nonn.*D*.4.413. [ᾰπᾱ- in Ep.; but in S. ᾰπᾰ-.]

ἀπᾰμάω (B), *sweep away*, γῆν *Gp*.2.6.44.

ἀπαμβλίσκω, *make abortive*, καρποὺς *produce abortive* fruit, Plu.*Arat*.32. II. intr., *miscarry*, aor. ἀπήμβλωσε, Id.*Pomp*.53.

ἀπαμβλύνω [ῡ], fut. -ῠνῶ (v. infr.), *blunt* or *dull the edge of*, τὰ ξίφη D.C.40.24 (Pass.). 2. mostly metaph., ἐλπίδα Pi.*P*.1.82 (tm.); of a person, τεθηγμένον τοί μ' οὐκ ἀπαμβλυνεῖς λόγῳ A.*Th*.715; τὰ λευκὰ τῶν τριχῶν ἀπαμβλύνει τὸν νοῦν Herod.1.67; φάος ὅσσων Opp.*H*.4.525; *tone down, take the edge off* a phrase, Plot.3.6.12:—more freq. in Pass., *to be blunted, lose its edge* or *force*, ὥρη μὲν ἀπήμβλυνται, θυμὸς δὲ μενοινᾷ Hom.*Epigr*.12, cf. S.*Eleg*.6; γηράσκοντι συγγηράσκουσι αἱ φρένες καὶ ἐς τὰ πρήγματα πάντα ἀπαμβλύνονται Hdt.3.134; ἀπαμβλυνθήσεται γνώμην A.*Pr*.866; ἡμῖν -ύνεται ἡ δικαιοσύνη *is indistinctly seen*, Pl.*R*.442d. II. = foreg., J.*BJ*4.8.3 (s.v.l.).

ἀπαμβρᾰκόομαι, *to be patient, endure* (cf. ἀμβρακόομαι), Pl.Com.5 D.

ἀπαμβροτεῖν, v. ἀφαμαρτάνω.

ἀπᾰμείβομαι, fut. -ψομαι: aor. ἀπημείφθην X.*An*.2.5.15: plpf. ἀπάμειπτο *AP*14.2, Nonn.*D*.8.165:—*reply, answer*, freq. in Hom., but always with a second more definite Verb, as ἀπαμειβόμενος προσέφη Il.1.84, al.; ἀπαμείβετο φώνησέν τε 20.199, al.; ὧδε ἀ. X. l.c.; τινά Theoc.8.8.

ἀπᾰμείρω, *deprive one of share in* a thing, τινά τι A.R.3.186:—Med., τί τινος Nonn.*D*.29.158:—Pass., *to be bereft*, τίνος *of* a thing, prob. l. in Hes.*Th*.801, cf. *Op*.578; v.l. for ἀποαίνυται, Od.17.322.

ἀπᾰμέλγω, *suck out* milk from the breast, Sor.1.105.

ἀπᾰμελέομαι, Pass., *to be neglected utterly*, ἀπημελημένος Hdt.3.129, 132, S.*Ph*.652.

ἀπᾰμέργομαι, Med., only pres. and impf., *take* or *carry off for oneself*, Nic.*Th*.861, *Al*.306.

ἀπᾰμέρδω, = ἀπαμείρω, Q.S.4.422, Man.3.26, Agamestor ap. Sch. Lyc.179.

ἀπᾰμεύς, έως, ὁ, *harvester*, *PStrassb*.35.14 (iv/v A.D.).

ἀπᾰμήτωρ, ορος, *shearing off*, μηδέων ἀ. ἄνδρες Man.4.220.

ἀπαμμένος, Ion. pf. part. Pass. of ἀφάπτω.

ἀπᾰμοιβή, ἡ, *alternation*: ἐξ -ῶν masonry laid in courses *of headers and stretchers*, *IG*2.1054c60.

ἀπαμπαίομαι, Cret. for ἀπαναπ., *beat off*, of dogs, *GDI*4998 ii 17 (Gortyn).

ἀπαμπίσχω, *take off*, ἐσθῆτα Ph.2.43:—Med., *doff*, 1.653: and metaph., ψυχὴ ἀ. τὸ ἀδικεῖν ib.569. II. metaph., *lay bare, reveal*, 2.74, al.

ἀπαμπλᾰκεῖν, inf. of aor. ἀπήμπλακον (no pres. in use), = ἀφαμαρτεῖν, *fail utterly*, S.*Tr*.1139.

ἀπαμυνταί· βοηθοί, Hsch. (-τοί cod.).

ἀπᾰμύνω [ῡ], *keep off, ward off*, with collat. notion of defence, τί τινι something *for* (i.e. *from*) another, Αἰτωλοῖσιν ἀπήμυνεν κακὸν ἦμαρ Il.9.597; ἡμῖν ἀπὸ λοιγὸν ἀμύνειν 1.67; later τί τινος Luc.*Cyn*.13: c. acc. only, ἀ. τῶν ἐπιόντων κακῶν τὰ ἡμίσεα Hdt.7.120; ἀ. τὸν βάρβαρον *repulse* him, 9.90; τὰς μυίας Ar.*V*.597; τοὺς ἔξωθεν Pl.*R*.415e. 2. *requite, take vengeance on*, τινά *AP*5.6 (Asclep.). II. Med., *keep off from oneself, drive back, repel*, ἄνδρ' ἀπαμύνασθαι Od.16.72; so ἀ. μίαν [ναῦν] καὶ ὀλίγῳ πλεῦνας Hdt.5.86; τὴν πενίην καὶ τὴν δεσποσύνην Id.7.102, cf. 3.110. 2. abs., *defend, protect oneself*, ὁ δ' οὐκ ἀπαμύνετο χερσίν Od.11.579; πόλις ᾗ ἀπαμυναίμεσθα by which we *may protect ourselves*, Il.15.738; μεγέθει Arist.*Long*.467a3.

ἀπαμφι-άζω, *take off* a garment, *doff* it, Plu.2.406d, Ph.2.393: metaph., γαῖαν *AP*7.49 (Bianor); ἀπαμφιάσαντες τὴν ψυχήν Them.*Or*.21.249d:—Med., ἀπαμφιάσασθαι τὰ περίαπτα Ph.1.288: metaph., *lay bare, reveal*, τὰ κεκρυμμένα Id.2.310:—Pass., γυμνὴ καὶ ἀπημφιασμένη ἀλήθεια Id.1.362. 2. *strip off*, βῶλον *AP*7.76 (Diosc.):—hence Subst. **-ασις**, εως, ἡ, *putting off*, dub. in J.*AJ*19.2.5. **-ασμός**, ὁ, = foreg., metaph., τοῦ τρόπου Corn.*ND*30.

ἀπαμφιέννυμι [ῠ], *strip off garments*, στέρν' ἀπημφιεσμέναι having them *stripped bare*, Xenarch.4.5. 2. *strip off*, τοίχους Plu.2.516f, cf. Ph.1.117.

ἀπαμφίζω, Att. fut. -ιῶ, = ἀπαμφιάζω, *strip from* one, τί τινος Men.339:—also **ἀπαμφίσκω**, Ph.2.319.

ἀπαναγιγνώσκω, *read amiss*, A.D.*Synt*.126.15.

ἀπᾰναγκάζω, *force away*, τι ἀπό τινος Hp.*Art*.2; opp. προσαναγκάζω, ib.14; simply, = ἀναγκάζω, ib.58, cf. Str.2.1.31, *PFay*.122.18 (100 A.D.):—freq. as f.l. for ἐπαν-, as Plb.4.46.6, 5.24.1, Them.*Or*.33.367a.

ἀπανάγνωσμα, ατος, τό, *fault in reading, faulty reading*, A.D.*Synt*.146.24, al.

ἀπαναιδεύομαι, Dep., = ἀναισχυντέω, mentioned by Thom.Mag. p.21 R. as an Att. word.

ἀπᾰναίνομαι, *disown, reject*, οἱ δ' οὐ γιγνώσκοντες ἀπηνήναντο Il.7.185; ἀπανήνασθαι θεοῦ εὐνήν Od.10.297; εὐθὺς δ' ἀπανάνατο νύμφαν Pi.*N*.5.60; part. ἀπανηνάμενος A.*Eu*.972 (lyr.); of a woman, τὸν ἄνδρα ἀπαναίνεται Hp.*Mul*.2.179; pres. also in Plu.2.132c.

ἀπαναισιμόω, *use up, consume*, [ὑγρασίη] -οῦται Hp.*Gland*.9.

ἀπαναισχυντέω, *behave with effrontery*, c. acc. cogn., ἀ. τοῦτο Pl.*Ap*.31b; c. inf., Alex.Aphr.*in Top*.524.5: abs., D.29.20, cf. 54.33; *put away shame*, Hld.8.5.

ἀπᾰνᾱλ-ίσκω, fut. -ανᾱλώσω, Alciphr.3.47: pf. ἀπανάλωκα Th.7.11: aor. 1 Pass. -ηλώθην ib.30: plpf. ἀπανηλώμην D.S.12.40: pf. -ηλωμένος J.*AJ*12.9.5:—*use quite up, utterly consume*, ll.cc.:—part. Pass. ἀπαναλούμενος in Ti.Locr.101d. II. *spend from* a given sum, *IG*1.32.26. **-ωσις**, εως, ἡ, *consumption*, D.S.1.41, Sor.1.42, Antyll.ap.Orib.6.10.18.

ἀπανᾶν· καλεῖν, Hsch.; cf. ἀπανεῖ.

ἀπαναπαύομαι, *take one's rest*, Sch.Opp.*H*.3.236.

ἀπανάστᾰσις, εως, ἡ, *migration*, Str.4.1.13, J.*BJ*1.15.3; *departure*, D.H.9.6, Philostr.*Ep*.11.

ἀπαναστομόω, = ἀναστομόω, for which it is v.l. in D.H.3.40.

ἀπανατέλλω, poet. ἀπαντ-, *make to rise, raise up from*, v.l. in Opp.*C*.2.97, 563.

ἀπαναχωρ-έω, *pass away*, Olymp.*in Grg*.p.367 J.; v.l. for ἐπ-, J.*BJ*2.21.5:—Subst. **-ησις**, εως, ἡ, v.l. for ἐπ-, D.S.25.6.

ἀπανδόκευτος, ον, *without an inn to rest at*, ὁδός Democr.230.

ἀπανδρίζομαι, *stand manfully*, πρός τι Callistr.*Stat*.4.

ἀπανδρόομαι, *become a man, come to maturity*, E.*Ion* 53, Luc.*Am*.26; ἀπηνδρώθησαν αἱ μῆτραι *viro maturae factae sunt*, Aret.*SD*1.6.

ἀπανεῖ· καλεῖ, and aor. imper. ἀπάνεσον· κάλεσον (Lacon.), Hsch.; cf. ἀπανᾶν.

ἀπᾰνεμία, ἡ, *shelter from wind*, Sch.Opp.*H*.1.602.

ἀπᾰνεμόομαι, *to be blown down*, Hsch. (leg. ἀπηνεμώθη for -ήθη).

ἀπάνευθε [ᾰν], and before vowels -θεν, strengthd. for ἄνευθε, Adv. *afar off, far away*, ἀ. κιών Il.1.35; φεῦγον ἔπειτ' ἀ. 9.478, etc. II. as Prep. with gen., *far from, aloof from*, τῶν ἄλλων ἀ. θεῶν ib.14.189, cf. 20.41; ἀ. τοκήων Od.9.36; ἀ. θεῶν *without* their *knowledge*, Il.1.549. 2. *out from, issuing from*, τοῦ δ' ἀ. σέλας γένετ' 19.374.

ἀπανθ-έω, *finish blooming*, Thphr.*HP*1.13.3, al.; *fade*, Hp.*Genit*.9: mostly metaph., Ar.*Ec*.1121; ἀνανθεῖ..καὶ ἀπηνθηκότι καὶ σώματι καὶ ψυχῇ Pl.*Smp*.196a; so in Arist.*Rh*.1410b15, old age is compared to straw, ἄμφω γὰρ ἀπηνθηκότα, cf. Luc.*DMort*.18.2, al.; of athletes, ἀ. ὑπὸ τῶν πόνων Philostr.*Gym*.48. II. of wine, *lose its sweetness*, i.e. *ripen*, Alex.45. III. *break out*, of skin-eruptions, Sor.1.121, Orib.*Inc*.24.2. **-ησις**, εως, ἡ, *time of blossoming*, ταχεῖαν εἶναι τὴν ἀ. Thphr.*HP*7.7.4.

ἀπανθ-ίζω, *pluck off flowers*: metaph., ματαίαν γλῶσσαν ἀπανθίσαι *cull the flowers of* idle talk, A.*Ag*.1662; Ἄρης φιλεῖ..τὰ λῷστα πάντ' ἀπανθίζειν (Kidd for πάντα τἀνθρώπων) *cut off* all the best, Id.*Fr*.100; ἀπανθίζειν ἐπεχείρει τοὺς Φρύγας Ἀχιλλεύς Polion ap.Phryn.*PS*p.162 B.:—Med., *gather honey from flowers*, Luc.*Pisc*.6; *pick out flowers*, *Asin*.54: metaph., *cull the best of* a thing, Plu.2.30d, Luc.*Merc.Cond*.39, Philostr.*VS*2.1.14. 2. Pass., *to be withered*, Phryn.*PS*p.9 B. **-ισμα**, ατος, τό, *inflorescence*, τὸ ἀκρότατον τῆς ψυχῆς καὶ τὸ ἀ. Olymp.*in Alc*.p.226 C.; *flower plucked* or *culled*, Eust.782.21; τὸ τερπνὸν τῆς πορφύρας ἀ., rhetorical description of the emperor Constant. Porphyrog., *Gp.Prooem*.11. **-ισμός**, ὁ, *plucking of flowers*, Sch.Il.5.629.

ἀπανθρᾰκ-ίζω, *broil on the coals, roast*, βοῦν ἀπηνθράκιζ' ὅλον Ar.*Ra*.506, cf. *Av*.1546, Ph.1.665, Philostr.*VA*5.25. **-ίς**, ίδος, ἡ, *cake baked on coals*, Diocl.*Fr*.116 (v.l. ἐπ-), cf. Hsch. **-ισμα**, ατος, τό, *broil*, Hsch. s.v. χναύματα. **-όω**, *burn to a cinder*, ἀπηνθράκωσεν Luc.*DMort*.20.4:—Pass., Id.*DMar*.11.1, *Peregr*.1.

ἀπανθρωπ-έομαι, *shun like a misanthrope*, rejected by Poll.2.5, but used by Hp.*Ep.*12 ἀπανθρωπέονται ξύμφυλον ὄψιν, cf. Tz.*H.*7.880, 885 (ubi -οῦνται). **-ία** (-εία Poll.8.14), ἡ, *dislike of men*, Luc. *Tim.*44. 2. *unfitness for social intercourse*, J.*BJ*2.17.3. II. *unsociability, moroseness*, Hp.*Coac.*472 (pl.); *inhumanity*, *POxy.*298.52 (i A.D.), J.*AJ*17.11.2. **-ίζομαι**, *become a man*, opp. a *beast*, Herm.ap.Stob.1.49.69. **-ος**, ον, *far from man*: hence, I. *desert, desolate*, τῷδ' ἀπανθρώπῳ πάγῳ, of Caucasus, A.*Pr.*20; ἀ. ἡ γῆ Luc.*Prom.*11. 2. ἀπάνθρωπον, τό, *violence, drastic nature*, of remedies, Philum.*Ven.*2.5. II. of men and their deeds, *inhuman, savage*, S.*Fr.*1020; ἀπάνθρωπα διαπεπραγμένοι D.H.6.81; ἀ. ἐπιστολαί *PFlor.*367.4 (iii A.D.); *unsocial, misanthropic*, τρόπος Pl.*Ep.*309b (Comp.), cf. J.*AJ*8.4.3, Gal.5.54 (Comp.). Adv. -πως J.*AJ*6.13.6, Luc.*Tim.*35, Philostr.*VA*1.21. 2. χρόα οὐκ ἀ. not *unpleasing*, Plu.2.54e, *Cat.Mi.*5. III. ἀπάνθρωπον, τό, = σταφὶς ἀγρία, Ps.-Dsc.4.152.

ἀπανιζόμενοι· ξηραινόμενοι, Hsch.

ἀπανίστημι, *make rise up and depart, send away*, τὴν στρατιὴν Hdt. 3.156, 6.133; *cause to depart*, τοὺς Ἀθηναίους Th.2.70. II. Pass., with aor. 2 and pf. Act., and fut. Med., *arise and go away, depart again*, Hdt.9.87; ἀπὸ τῆς πόλιος ib.86; ἐκ τῆς Μακεδονίας Th.1.61; Ποτειδαίας ib.139; esp. *leave one's country, emigrate*, ib.2.

ἀπάνουρ-γευτος, ον, *guileless*, *EM*163.6. Adv. -τως Sch.D.22.20. **-γος**, ον, = foreg., Plu.2.966b. Adv. -γως S.E.*M.*2.77.

ἄπαντᾰχ-ῆ, Adv., (ἅπας) *everywhere*, E.*Fr.*218, Jul.*Or.*4.134b. **-όθεν**, *from all sides*, D.S.20.57, Jul.*Or.*1.35b, al.: c. gen., γῆς Luc. *DMort.*9.2. **-όθι**, = ἀπανταχοῦ, Luc.*Prom.*12, Them.*Or.*25.310b. **-οῖ**, *to every quarter*, Is.9.14 (Reiske for -χῇ). **-οῦ**, *everywhere*, E.*IT*517, Alex.152, Men.*Epit.*16; ἀ. γῆς D.C.69.13.

ἀπαντάω, impf. ἀπήντων Th.4.127, Dor. 3 sg. ἀπάντη Bion *Fr.*9.7: fut. ἀπαντήσω Arist.*Rh.Al.*1432b35, Plb.4.26.5, etc.; but better -ήσομαι Th.4.77, 7.2 and 80, X.*HG*1.6.3, Lys.2.32, etc.: aor. ἀπήντησα E.*Ph.*1392, Th.2.20: pf. ἀπήντηκα Ar.*Lys.*420, D.18.15:—the Med., used in act. sense by Polyaen.1.21.1 (impf.), al., is censured by Luc.*Lex.*25; so also pf. ἀπήντημαι Plb.2.37.6, D.H.6.88, etc. I. mostly of persons, *move from* a place *to meet* a person, and generally, *meet, encounter*, τινί Hdt.8.9, E.*Supp.*772, etc.; ἐξ ἐναντίας ἀ. Pl.*Lg.*893e; ἀ. ταῖς ὁμοίαις φύσεσι *encounter, fall in with* them, D.60.20: abs., ὁ ἀεὶ ἀπαντῶν *any one that meets you, any chance person*, Pl. *R.*563c; οἱ ἀπαντῶντες D.36.45, Alex.78, cf. 87. b. freq. with a Prep., ἀ. τινὶ εἰς τόπον *come* or *go* to a place *to meet* him, *meet* him at a place, Hdt.2.75; ἐς τὠυτὸ 6.84; ἐπὶ Τριποδίσκον Th.4.70; τὸν μὲν ἐς τὰς Σίφας ἀ., τὸν δ' ἐπὶ τὸ Δήλιον ib.89: without dat. pers., *present oneself* at a place, Id.7.1; εἰς Κύζικον X.*HG*1.3.13; ἀ. ἐνθάδε Ar.*Lys.*13; δεῦρο πάλιν ἀ. Pl.*Tht.*210d, etc. c. c. dat. loci, *light upon, come to*, τόπῳ Lxx *Ge.*28.11. 2. freq. in hostile sense, *meet* in battle, ἀ. δορί (dat. pers. being omitted) E.*Ph.*1392; ὅπλοις *HF*542; τοῖς βαρβάροις Μαραθῶνάδε And.1.107; ἀ. Ἀθηναίοις ἐς Τάραντα Th.6.34, cf. 2.20, 3.95; ἀ. πρός τινα Isoc.4.86,90; generally, *resist, oppose* in any way, νομοθέτῃ ἀ. λέγων.. Pl.*Lg.*684d; διὰ λόγων νουθετικῶν ἀ. prob. ib.740e; ἀ. τραχέως πρὸς τὰς τῶν πλησιαζόντων ὀργάς Isoc.1.31; ἀ. τοῖς εἰρημένοις *rejoin, reply*, Id.11.30; τοῖς θορύβοις Arist.*Rh.Al.* l.c.; πρὸς ἕκαστον D.21.24. b. abs., *present oneself* in arms, *attend the muster*, E.*Ba.*782. c. *face, meet*, αἰκίαις καὶ θανάτοις Hecat.Abd.ap.J.*Ap.*1.22. 3. freq. as a law-term, *meet in open court*, τῷ καλεσαμένῳ Pl.*Lg.*937a, cf. D.39.3, etc.: without dat. pers., ἀ. πρὸς τὴν δίκην *present oneself* at the trial, Pl.*Lg.*936e; πρὸς ἣν [δίκην] οὐκ ἀπήντα *did not appear to defend* his cause, D.21.90; ἀ. πρὸς τὸν διαιτητήν, etc., *come before* him, Id.40.11, etc.; εἰς ἡμέραν τὴν συγκειμένην ἀ. εἰς τὸ Ἡφαιστεῖον 33.18; ἐπὶ τὰ ἱερά 42.7; ἐπὶ τὴν δίαιταν Test.ap.eund.21.93; ἀ. ἐπὶ τοῖς ἀλλοτρίοις ἀγῶσι *to be present* at other people's suits, *meddle with* them, D.21.205: abs., *appear in court*, 40.16, etc. 4. ἀ. εἰς.. *enter into* a thing, *attempt* it, εἰς τὸν ἀγῶνα Pl.*Lg.*830a; ἀ. εἰς τὴν τίμησιν *come to* the question of rating, Aeschin.3.198; ἀ. εἰς τὰς χρείας Arist.*EN*1158a8; ἀ. πρὸς τὰς μαθήσεις Pl.*Tht.*144b; πρὸς τὴν ἐρώτησιν, τὸ πρόβλημα, Arist. *Metaph.*1036a14, *Ph.*213b3; ἀ. πρὸς τὴν τροφήν *go to seek* it, Id. *deAn.* 421b12; ἀ. ἐπί.. *have recourse to*.., D.21.151, 24.193, etc.; ἐπὶ ταύτας τὰς οἰκίας ἀ. οἱ τραγῳδοποιοί Arist.*Po.*1454a12. II. of things, *come upon* one, *meet* or *happen to* one, ἀ. δάκρυά μοι E.*Ion*940, cf. Bion l.c.; τοῖς πρὸς ὑμᾶς ζῶσι τοσαύτην κωφότητα.. παρ' ὑμῶν ἀπαντᾶν D.19.226; ἐπὶ τῷ κεφαλαίῳ τῶν πραγμάτων ἀ. [ἡ ῥαθυμία] 'comes home to roost', 10.7; ἀ. αὐτῷ κραυγὴ παρὰ τῶν δικαστῶν Aeschin.1.163; μή τίς σοι ἐναντίος λόγος ἀ. Pl.*Phd.*101a, cf. D.H.4.33, etc. 2. abs., *happen, occur, turn out*, Ar.*Lys.*420, Pl.*Ep.*358e, Arist.*Pol.*1302a6, *Top.*160a23, al.; τούτων ἀπαντώντων Hdt.8.142:—Pass., Plb.2.7.4, Phld.*Herc.*1251.9.

ἀπαντή, ἡ, = ἀπάντησις, Lxx *Jd.*4.22, al.

ἀπάντη, Adv., (ἅπας) *everywhere*, κύκλῳ ἀ. *all* round about, Od. 8.278; κῆρυξ δὲ φέρων ἀν' ὅμιλον ἀ. δεῖξε (sc. τὸν κλῆρον) Il.7.183, cf. 186; ἀ. πλανώμενος Pl.*Lg.*752a.

ἀπάντ-ημα, ατος, τό, (ἀπαντάω) *meeting*, E.*Or.*514. II. *chance*, Lxx *Ec.*9.11. **-ησις**, εως, ἡ, = foreg., S.*Fr.*828, Epicur.*Ep.*1 p.10 U., Plb.5.26.8, D.S.18.59; εἰς -σίν τινι ἐξελθεῖν Lxx *Jd.*11.31, *Ev.Matt.*25.6; *escort*, Plb.5.43.3, etc. II. *meeting* in argument, *reply*, πρός τι Arist.*SE*176a23, *Metaph.*1009a20, cf. Phld.*Sign.*19,28; ἀ. ποιεῖσθαι to *reply*, Plb.5.63.7; προσφιλὴς κατ' ἀ. in *conversation*, Id. 10.5.6, cf. Phld.*Vit.*p.13 J., Id.*Herc.*1457.4, Plu.2.803f (pl.). III. *steadfastness in face of opposition*, Hp.*Decent.*5. **-ητέον**, *one must present oneself, appear*, ἀ. μοι εἰς τὴν στοάν Pl.*Tht.*210d; *one must rejoin, reply*, πρὸς τοὺς λόγους Arist.*SE*182b5; τοῖς θορύβοις *Rh.Al.*1432b33; *one must counteract*, Antyll.(?)ap.Orib.8.6 tit. **-ητήριον**, τό, *hostelry, inn*, *PSI*3.175.5 (v A.D.), *PLand.*17 (vi/vii A.D.), *Gloss.* **-ητής**· *deversorianus*, ib. **-ητικός**, ή, όν, *combative*, Asp. in *EN*82.27. Adv. -κῶς *obviam*, *Gloss.* **-ιάζω**, *meet*, ἀλλάλοις Archyt.1; v.l. for ὑπ- in Procop.*Goth.*3.6. **-ίζορα**· ἐναντία, Hsch.

ἀπαντικρύ, Adv. (in Att. Inscr. ἀπαντροκύ *IG*2.834b i 25, cf. 2(5) p.204), strengthd. for ἀντικρύ, *right opposite*, τῆς Ἀττικῆς D.8.36, cf. Hp.*Cord.*2, Thphr.*Char.*21.7, Luc.*Am.*5; ὁ ἀ. λόφος X.*HG*6.4.4. 2. *in the first instance*, opp. ἀνὰ χρόνον, Hp.*Art.*41.

ἀπαντινά· ἀνέντροπα, ἐκτετημένα (sic), Hsch.

ἀπαντίον, Adv., strengthd. for ἀντίον, like ἀπεναντίον, *right opposite*, ἐς τὴν ἀ. ἀκτήν Hdt.7.34, cf. Scyl.111.

ἀπαντλ-έω, *draw off from*, ἀ. χθονὸς ὕβρισμα θνητῶν E.*Or.*1641; *lighten*, τί σοι οἷοί τε θνητοὶ τῶνδ' ἀπαντλῆσαι πόνων; A.*Pr.*84; ἀ. τὸ ὑγρόν Arist.*Pr.*870b16; opp. ἐπιχέω, Pl.*R.*407d. II. c. acc. only, *lighten, lessen*, βάρος ψυχῆς E.*Alc.*354; τῶν ἐγκαλουμένων ἀπηντληκώς τι *having shed* some of his faults, Phld.*Lib.*p.35 O.:—in Pass., Ph. 1.266, Plu.*Alex.*57. **-ησις**, εως, ἡ, *drawing off*, of moisture, Arist. *Pr.*869b38; of blood, with menses, Sor.1.29. **-ητέον**, *one must draw off*, as water, *Gp.*6.18.

ἀπάντομαι, *entreat* one *not* to do a thing, E.*Rh.*901 (lyr., tm.). II. poet., = ἀπαντάω, Phryn.254.

ἀπάντοτε, Adv. *always*, A.D.*Synt.*263.2, al.

ἀπαντροκύ, v. ἀπαντικρύ.

ἀπᾰνύω [ῡ], *finish entirely*, νῆες ἀπήνυσαν οἴκαδε (sc. ὁδόν) the ships *performed the voyage* home, Od.7.326:—Pass., Q.S.5.1.

ἀπάνωθεν, *from above, from the top*, τοῦ τείχους Lxx *2Ki.*11.20, al.

ἅπαξ [ᾰπ], Adv. *once, once only, once for all*, first in Od., ὅτε τ' ἄλλοι ἅ. θνήσκουσ' ἄνθρωποι 12.22; ἅ... ἀπὸ θυμὸν ὀλέσσαι ib.350; ἀπαλλάχθηθ' ἅ. E.*Cyc.*600; οὐχ ἅ. μόνον more than *once*, A.*Pr.*211; ἅ... κοὐχὶ δίς S.*OC*1208; πολλάκις καὶ οὐχὶ ἅ. Hdt.7.46; πολλάκις τε κοὐχ ἅ. S.*OT*1275; μὴ ἅ. ἀλλὰ πολλάκις Antipho 1.3, cf. Pl.*Lg.*711a; μὴ δίς, ἀλλ' ἅ. μόνον Arist.*Pol.*1299a10; of the self-creation of Νοῦς, τὴν ποίησιν αὐτοῦ.. ἅ. εἶναι Plot.6.8.21; ἅ. ἔτι *yet* this *once*, A.*Ag.*1322; τὸ ἅ. τοῦτο *at* this *moment*, Lxx *2Ki.*17.7; ἅ. δυοῖν ποδοῖν, i.e. *two* square feet (1 × 2), opp. δυοῖν δίς (2 × 2), *four*, Pl.*Men.*82c. 2. c. gen., ἅ. τοῦ ἐνιαυτοῦ, ἔτεος ἑκάστου ἅ., Hdt.2.59, 4.105; also ἐν τῷ ἐνιαυτῷ ἅ. Id.2.132. 3. *once on a time, formerly*, ἅ. καὶ ἅ. Lxx *Jd.*20.30. II. without any notion of number, after conditional and temporal Particles, if *once*, when *once*, εἴπερ ἐσπείσω γ' ἅ. if *once* you have made a treaty, Ar.*Ach.*307, cf. 923; ἢν ἅ. ἀλῷ Id.*V.*898, cf. *Av.*342; ἂν ἅ. τις ἀποθάνῃ Amphis 8; ἐπειδήπερ γ' ἅ. ἐμοὶ σεαυτὸν παραδέδωκας Ar.*V.*1129; ἐπεὶ ἅ. ἐταράχθησαν Th.7.44; ὡς ἅ. ἤρξατο X.*HG*5.4.58; ἐπεὶ ἅ. αὐτοῖς φίλος ἐγένετο Id.*An.*1.9.10, cf. 3.2.25, Isoc.12.242; ὡς ἅ. ἐγκλήματα ἐταράχθη D.18.151: so with part., ἐπὶ γᾶν ἅ. πεσὸν.. αἷμα A.*Ag.*1019 (lyr.); ἅ. θανόντος οὔτις ἔστ' ἀνάστασις Id.*Eu.*648; ἅ. ἐλθόντες Pl.*Prm.*165e, cf. *Ep.Hebr.*6.4, etc. (ἁ- = sm̥ (cf. εἷς); -παξ akin to πήγνυμι.)

ἁπαξ-άπᾱς [ξᾰ], ασα, αν, *all together, the whole*, περιτρέχων τὴν γῆν ἁπαξάπασαν Hermipp.4.3; ἡμέρα ἁ. Stratt.36.2; ἁπαξάπαν Xenarch. 7.16: ἁπαξαπάσης τιμῆς Phld.*Mort.*23: mostly in pl., *all at once, all together*, Ar.*Pl.*111,206, etc. **-απλῶς**, Adv., strengthd. for ἁπλῶς, *in general*, Hierocl.p.51 A., *PLips.*27.29 (ii A.D.), S.E.*M.*7.428, Luc. *Peregr.*3, etc.

ἀπαξί-α, ἡ, (ἄξιος) opp. ἀξία, *disvalue*, Zeno *Stoic.*1.48, cf. Antip. ib.3.251, Arr.*Epict.*1.2.10, S.E.*M.*11.62. **-ος**, ον, = ἀνάξιος, *unworthy of*, τινός Pl.*Lg.*645c. II. οὐκ ἀ. [ἐστι], c. inf., Id.*Ep.*324b. Adv. -ίως Iamb.*Myst.*5.6. **-όω**, *disclaim as unworthy, disown*, τι or τινά, Th.1.5, Plb.1.67.13, Plot.5.8.3; ἀ. τινὸς μή, c. inf., Paus. 10.14.6. 2. ἀ. ἑαυτὸν τῶν καλλίστων Arist.*Mu.*391a6; but τί τινος *deem* a thing *unworthy* of one, Luc.*Dom.*2:—Med., λέσχας ἃς ἀπηξιώσατο *deemed* them *unworthy of*.., *banished* them *from*..., A.*Eu.*367.

ἄπαξις, εως, ἡ, = ἀπαγωγή, *arrest*, *POxy.*33 iii 15 (ii A.D.).

ἀπαξίωσις, εως, ἡ, *rejection, contempt*, Plb.*Fr.*10, D.H.1.9; τῆς ἀρχῆς 5.71.

ἀπαξοί· μοναχοί, Hsch.; perh. to be read in Hdt.2.79, 7.96.

ἀπάορος, ον, Dor. for ἀπήορος, q.v.

ἀπᾰπαῖ, = ἀππαπαῖ, Ar.*V.*309.

ἀπάπη, ἡ, *dandelion, Taraxacum officinale*, Thphr.*HP*7.7.1, 7.8.3 and 11.3 (ex cod. Urb. pro vulg. ἀπάτη vel ἀφάκη), cf. Plin.*HN*21.99.

ἀπαππᾰπαῖ, = ἀππαπαῖ, S.*Ph.*746.

ἄπαππος, ον, *with no grandfather*: metaph., φάος οὐκ ἄπαππον Ἰδαίου πυρός light not *unfathered* by the Idaean flame, A.*Ag.*311.

ἀπάπτω, Ion. for ἀφάπτω.

ἀπαρά-βᾰτος, ον, *unalterable*, εἱρμὸς αἰτιῶν *Stoic.*2.266; ἐπιπλοκή, of causation, Chrysipp.ib.293; τάξις Plu.2.410f; ἡ τῆς κινήσεως ἰδέα Ocell.1.15; *infallible*, προρρήσεις Iamb.*VP*28.135, cf. Philum.*Ven.* 4.14; also of persons, *Cat.Cod.Astr.*8(4).215. Adv. -τως Chrysipp.*Stoic.*2.279. 2. *inviolable*, κύρια καὶ ἀ. *PRyl.*65.18 (i B.C.), cf. *PGrenf.*1.60.7 (vi A.D.). 3. *permanent, perpetual*, ἱερωσύνη *Ep.Hebr.*7.24. 3. Act., *not transgressing*, J.*AJ*18.8.2; ἀ. τῶν καθηκόντων Hierocl. in *CA*10 p.435 M. Adv. -τως Arr.*Epict.*2.15.1. **-βλαστος**, ον, *not branching laterally*, Thphr.*HP*1.2.5, *CP*1.1.3; *not budding laterally*, Id.*HP*3.17.2. **-βλητος**, ον, *incomparable*, *PLond.*2.232.5 (iv A.D.), f.l. for -βατος in Ph.2.509. **-βολος**, ον, *without deposit made*, κρίσιν ἀπάρβολον *IG*9(1).694.115; δίκα *GDI*5017 (Gortyn, prob.). II. Adv. -λως *without danger*, Sch.Il.13.141.

ἀπαράγγελτος, ον, *without formal declaration*, πόλεμος Ἀρχ.Ἐφ. 1920.84 (Itanos, ii B.C.). Adv. -τως *without signal of battle*, Plb.16. 3.1, *Fr.*11.

ἀπαρα-γνώστως, Adv. *without reading*, Suid. s.v. Πουλχερία. **-γράφος**, ον, *incapable of definition*, ποσότης Plb.16.12.10.

ἀπαράγωγος [ᾰγ], ον, *not to be turned aside*, Hierocl.*in CA* 13 p.450 M. Adv. -γως ib.8 p.431 M.

ἀπαρα-δειγμάτιστος, ον, *not liable to censure*, Ptol.*Tetr.*170. **-δεικτος**, ον, *not returned, unregistered*, ἐδάφη *BGU* 915.6 (ii A.D.). **-δεκτος**, ον, *inadmissible*, Phld.*Sign.*17 (-δεικτον Pap.), A.D.*Synt.*59.18, al.; *unacceptable*, Olymp.Hist.p.465 D. II. Act., *not receiving* or *admitting*, c. gen., μαθημάτων Memn.2.2; [τῶν ἀγαθῶν] Phld.*D.*3 *Fr.*42 (dub. rest.); τέχνης Ph.1.311; διαβολῆς *Stoic.*3. 153; esp. in Gramm., τῶν ἄρθρων A.D.*Synt.*16.18, al. **-δίσκευτος**, ον, *not defeated in discus-throwing*, *Ephes.*2 No.72 (iii A.D.). **-θετος**, ον, *not padded out with quotations*, D.L.7.181: hence in Gramm., ἀπαράθετα *words* or *phrases without quoted authority*, prob. for ἀπαρένθ-, *Et.Gud.* s.v. ἀεί. **-θραυστος**, ον, *unshaken, not to be shaken*, Olymp.*in Phlb.*p.274 S., Eustr.*in EN*297.26.

ἀπαραιρημένος, Ion. pf. part. Pass. of ἀφαιρέω.

ἀπαραίτητος, ον, I. of gods or persons, *not to be moved by prayer, inexorable*, δαίμων Lys.2.78; θεοί, θεαί, Pl.*Lg.*907b, *IG*12(2). 484 (Lesb.); Δίκη D.25.11; ἀνάγκη Epicur.*Ep.*3p.65 U.; δικασταί Lycurg.2; ἀ. εἶναι περί τι Plu.*Pyrrh.*16:—τὸ ἀ. τινος πρὸς τοὺς πονηρούς Id.*Publ.*3. Adv. -τως *implacably, inexorably*, Th.3.84; ἀ. ἔχειν πρός τινα Plb.21.31.15. II. of punishments, etc., *not to be averted by prayers, inevitable, unmerciful*, τιμωρίαι Din.1.23; κολάσιες Ti. Locr.104d; νόμος J.*Ap.*2.30; ὀργή, κατηγορία, Plb.1.82.9, 12.12.6; = ἀνήκεστος, βουλεύεσθαί τι ἀ. Id.4.24.6; ἁμαρτία *unpardonable*, Id. 33.10.5. Adv. -τως *obstinately*, Sor.1.107. 2. *not to be evaded*, ἱκέτευμα Plu.2.950f; χρεία *POxy.*900.12 (iv A.D.), cf. *PFlor.*6.11 (iii A.D.); *indispensable*, ἀριθμός Philostr.*VA*3.30; *irresistible*, προθυμία Orib.*Fr.*57. Adv. -τήτως *without evasion*, *PMag.Leid.W.*17.2.

ἀπαρα-κάλυπτος [κᾰ], ον, *undisguised*, γυμνὴ καὶ ἀ. κατηγορία Hld. 10.29. Adv. -τως Pl.*R.*538c, *Euthd.*294d: Comp. -ότερον D.C.67. 3. 2. *open-hearted*, ἀ. τὰς ψυχάς Ptol.*Tetr.*155. **-κλητος**, ον, *unsummoned, volunteering*, Th.2.98; εὔνοια *Inscr.Prien.*108.43 (ii B.C.); καὶ παρακαλούμενος καὶ ἀ. Plu.2.403b, cf. *CIG*2271.27 (Delos). II. *not to be consoled*, Sch.A.*Pr.*185.

ἀπαρᾰκολούθητος, ον, *not to be reached* or *attained*, Tz.ad Lyc. 5. II. Adv. -τως *inconsequently*, M.Ant.2.16, Plot.4.3.28.

ἀπαρᾰκόντιστος, ον, *not defeated in javelin-throwing*, *Ephes.*2 No. 72 (iii A.D.).

ἀπάρακτος, ον, (παράγω) gloss on ἀνώπιστος, Hsch.

ἀπαρά-λειπτος, ον, *unintermittent*, Simp.*in Ph.*213.34. Adv. -τως Syrian.*in Metaph.*132.23, Procl.*in Prm.*p.833 S. 2. *complete*, Alex.Trall.5.1. **-λεκτος**, ον, *with disordered hair*, Pherecr. 195. **-λήκτως**, Adv. *unceasingly*, *CIG*2271.7 (Delos).

ἀπαράλλακτος, ον, *precisely similar, indistinguishable*, *Stoic.*2.26, al., cf. Phld.*Sign.*15, al., D.H.2.71, D.S.1.91, Plu.*Alex.*57, Plot.5. 7.3; ἀ. ἁρμονία πρὸς τὸ ἀρχέτυπον Jul.*Or.*2.93a: c. gen., *indistinguishable from*, Phld.*Po.*994.26: c. dat., *exactly like*, D.S.2.50. Adv. -τως *unchangeably*, Lxx *Es.*3.13, *BMus.Inscr.*481*.402 (Ephesus), Theo Sm.p.172 H.; *in precisely similar terms*, Ath.1.26a, etc.; *indistinguishably*, *Stoic.*2.190, al., Plot.2.1.2.

ἀπαραλλαξία, ἡ, *indistinguishability*, *Stoic.*2.34 (pl.), cf. Phld. *Sign.*6,37; ὁμοιότης κατ' -ίαν S.E.*M.*7.108. II. *unshakable determination*, *Stoic.*3.73.

ἀπαρα-λόγιστος, ον, *not to be deceived*, τῶν καθηκόντων τήρησις Hierocl.*in CA*10p.437 M.; *not liable to error*, Nicom.*Harm.*6. Adv. -τως *undoubtedly*, Ruf.ap.Orib.45.30.55. II. Act., *not deceiving*, Hsch. s.v. ἀπαράσημον. **-λογος**, ον, *not without reason* or *method*, Iamb.*VP*30.182. **-λῡτος**, *irrevocable*, λόγος *PGrenf.*1.60.31 (vi A.D.). **-μῑγής**, ές, *unmixed*, Sch.Od.2.341.

ἀπαρᾰμίλλητος, ον, *unrivalled*, J.*AJ*8.7.3.

ἀπαρά-μονος, ον, *not abiding, transient*, Secund.*Sent.*14, Vett.Val. 39.30, al. **-μύθητος** [ῡ], ον, *not to be persuaded* or *entreated, inexorable*, Pl.*Epin.*980d, Plu.2.629a. 2. *incorrigible*, in Adv. -τως Pl.*Lg.*731d. II. of conditions, *comfortless*, Plu.2.332d; *not admitting consolation*, πάθος Jul.*Or.*8.245c; κακόν Hld.1.14. 2. of persons, *inconsolable*, Id.2.33. Adv. -τως Jul.*Or.*8.252a. **-μῦθος**, ον, = foreg., *inexorable*, κέαρ A.*Pr.*185 (lyr.); *restive*, ὄμμα πωλικόν E.*IA*.620. [In A. ᾰπ- metri gr.]

ἀπαράντινα· ἀπαράλλακτα, Hsch.

ἀπᾰράομαι, *propitiate*, τοῖς θεοῖς Mim. in *POxy.*413ᵛii 133.

ἀπαρά-πειστος, ον, *not to be seduced*, D.H.8.61. **-πόδιστος**, ον, *free from embarrassment* or *interference*, Arr.*Epict.*1.1.10, al., *BGU* 1124.44 (i B.C.); ὁρμή Hld.3.13; *clear*, διάνοια Hices.ap.Ath.15. 689c. Adv. -τως Arr.*Epict.*2.13.21, S.E.*M.*1.178, *PLond.*3.1168.12 (i A.D.), Gal.4.725.

ἀπαραποιήτως· ἀπλάστως, Hsch.

ἀπαρα-σήμαντος, ον, *unnoticed*, ἀ. τι ἀφιέναι, ἐᾶσαι, Lxx 2*Ma.*15.36, *Mon.Ant.*23.61 (Seleucia), cf. *Michel* 546.21 (Anisa, i B.C.). **-σημείωτος**, ον, = foreg., Dsc.*Prooem.*1. **-σημος**, ον, *not counterfeit*, Hsch. II. κατηγορία φόνου ἀ. with *no* defendant *named*, Antipho 2.1 tit. **-σκευᾰσία**, ἡ, *want of preparation*, Hp.*Acut.*65. **-σκεύαστος**, ον, = sq., X.*An.*1.5.9 (Comp.), 2*Ep.Cor.*9.4, J.*AJ*4.8.41. Adv. -τως Arist.*Rh.Al.*1430ᵃ3. **-σκευος**, ον, *without preparation, unprepared*, Antipho 5.18 (Sup.), Th.2.87; ἀπαράσκευόν τινα λαβεῖν X. *Cyr.*7.5.25; ἀ. ληφθῆναι D.40.30; ἀ. πρὸς τὸ μέλλον Plb.1.49.4: c. gen., *unprovided with*, τῶν ἐπιτηδείων J.*BJ*3.7.32; also of things, ἀπόστασις Th.3.13: Sup., X.*An.*1.1.6. Adv. ἀπαρασκευῶς, ἔχειν, διακεῖσθαι, Plb.1.45.7, 14.10.7. **-στᾰτος**, ον, *not having appeared in person*, *PLond.*2.260.128 (i A.D.).

ἀπᾰράσσω, Att. -ττω, *strike off*, ἀντικρὺ δ' ἀπάραξε [τὴν αἰχμήν] Il.16.116; ἀπήραξεν δὲ χαμᾶζε.. κάρη 14.497; ἀ. τοῦ ἵππου τοὺς πόδας Hdt.5.112; κρᾶτα S.*Tr.*1015 (lyr.). 2. *knock* or *sweep off*, τοὺς ἐπιβάτας ἀπὸ τῆς νεὸς Hdt.8.90; τοὺς ἀπὸ τοῦ πολεμίου καταστρώματος ὁπλίτας ἀ. Th.7.63:—Pass., aor. part. ἀπαραχθείς D.H.8. 85. 3. *crush*, ἀπὸ δ' ὀστέον ἄχρις ἄραξε Il.16.324:—Pass., -άσσεται τὴν κεφαλήν J.*BJ*3.7.23.

ἀπαρα-σχημάτιστος, ον, *not parallel in formation*, *EM*13.33: c. dat., ἀ. οὐδετέρῳ *having no corresponding* neuter, Eust.94. 30. **-τᾰτος**, ον, *unextended*, Simp.*in Ph.*640.21. Adv. -τως *without extension*: of Time, *in a moment*, τὴν ἀφὴν ἀθρόως καὶ ἀ. γίνεσθαι Id.*in Cael.*313.22. **-τήρητος**, *not observed*, *IG*2².1035.11 (i B.C.). Adv. -τως *without precautions*, Plb.3.52.7, 14.1.12, J.*BJ*4.3. 3, Ph.*Fr.*105 H. **-τιλτος**, ον, *with hairs not pulled out*, Ar.*Lys.* 279, Luc.*Salt.*5. **-τρεπτος**, *not turned*, of clothes, Phryn.*PS* p.52 B. II. of laws, *not to be perverted*, Plu.2.745d; of persons, Poll.8.10. Adv. -τως M.Ant.1.16.1.

ἀπάραυξος, ον, *not subject to increase*, dub. in Gal.8.913.

ἀπαρά-φθορος, ον, *free from damage*, ἔργον *IG*12(3).326 (Thera). **-φύλακτος** [ῠ], ον, *not to be guarded against*, Sch.Il.11.297. II. (from Med.) *careless, heedless*, Sch.E.*Hipp.*657. **-χάρακτος** [χᾰ], ον, *not counterfeit*, Damocr.ap.Gal.14.135, Hsch. s.v. ἀπαράσημον. **-χῠτος**, ον, *without anything poured in, unmixed*, οἶνος Gal.13.721, cf. 10.832; ὕδωρ Hld.5.16: generally, *pure*, Plu.2. 968c. **-χώρητος**, ον, *not giving ground, staunch*, Plb.1.61.3. Adv. -τως, διακεῖσθαι περί τινος Id.5.106.5. 2. *refusing to retire, unyielding*, τὸ ἀ. τῆς ἐξουσίας D.H.10.19; φιλαρχία ἀ. 10.54, cf. Plu. 2.10a. II. Pass., *not permitted*, Sch.Opp.*H.*5.416.

ἀπάρβολος, v. ἀπαράβολος.

ἀπαργία, ἡ, *hawk's-beard, Crepis Columnae*, Thphr.*HP*7.8.3.

ἄπαργμα, ατος, τό, = ἀπαρχή (q.v.), in pl., Ar.*Pax*1056, Lyc. 106. II. = μασχαλίσματα, *EM*118.22.

ἀπαργῠρ-ίζω, *appraise at cash value*, ὄψα Them.*Or.*23.292d:—Med., *buy off*, πολέμους Lyd.*Mag.*3.45. **-ισμός**, ὁ, *selling for ready money*, *Gloss.* II. = Lat. *adaeratio*, *PFlor.*377.4 (vi A.D.), Just.*Nov.*43.1 *Intr.*, 130.4. **-όω**, = ἀπαργυρίζω, Artem.1.50.

ἀπαρ-έγκλῑτος, ον, *direct*, Gal.*UP*15.8; *inflexible*, νόμοι φυσικοὶ ἀ. Nicom.*Ar.*1.23; πρόνοια Hero *Deff.*136.57. 2. *straight*, εὐθεῖα (sc. γραμμή) Phlp.*in Mete.*21.10, cf. Ammon.*in Porph.*9.1. Adv. -τως Gal.18(2).726; *not diverging from the perpendicular*, Eustr.*in EN*74. 9. II. *unimpaired*, ὑγίεια Iamb.*VP*3.13. **-εγχείρητος**, ον, *not to be tampered with, inviolable*, Ti.Locr.95a, Arr.*Epict.*4.1.161, J.*AJ*15.8.1. Adv. -τως *inimitably, perfectly*, D.S.4.78. **-έγχῠτος**, ον, = ἀπαράχυτος, Ath.1.27a. **-εμπόδιστος**, ον, = ἀπαραπόδιστος (for which it occurs as a v.l.), Sor.1.3; ἡ τοῦ κόσμου διοίκησις Chrysipp.*Stoic.*297, cf. S.E.*M.*1.147. Adv. -τως Aët.16.61, Hdn.*Fig.* p.96 S., Alex.Aphr.*in Top.*46.3. **-έμφᾰτος**, ον, (παρεμφαίνω) *not determinative* or *indicative*, c. gen., A.D.*Synt.*239.8, cf. Herm.*in Phdr.* p.124 A., Ps.-Alex.Aphr.*in SE*36.17. Adv. -τως Hsch. II. ἡ ἀπαρέμφατος (sc. ἔγκλισις) the *infinitive mood* (cf. παρεμφατικός), D.H.*Comp.*5, A.D.*Synt.*226.20, Ps.-Alex.Aphr.*in SE*34.28; τὸ ἀ. S.E.*P.*1.204. Adv. -τως *in the infinitive mood*, ἀναγνῶναι take *as an infinitive*, A.D.*Synt.*76.16. **-ενθύμητος** [ῡ], ον, *not considering, carelessly*, M.Ant.10.8. Adv. -τως Id.6.53. **-ενόχλητος**, ον, *undisturbed*, συμβίωσις Phld.*Ir.*p.78 W.; ὑπό τινων *BGU*1140.24 (i B.C.), cf. *IGRom.*4.2927 (Pergam.), *PTeb.*41.24, Plu.2.118b.

ἀπαρές· ὑγιές, Hsch.; cf. ἀπηρής.

ἀπᾰρέσκω, *to be disagreeable to*, τινί Th.1.38, Plu.2.6b. 2. c. acc. pers., *displease*, Pl.*Tht.*202d, Jul.*Mis.*365d. 3. abs., τὰ ἀπαρέσαντα J.*AJ*8.14.1. II. Med., οὐ.. γάρ τι νεμεσσητὸν βασιλῆα ἄνδρ' ἀπαρέσσασθαι it is no disgrace for a king *to approve* a man (or, *to appease* a man of royal birth), Il.19.183, cf. Sch. and Eust. ad loc. III. ἀπαρέσκεσθαί τινι *to be displeased with*, Hdn.5.2.5, cf. 5.6.1, 6.1.10, Lyd.*Mag.*2.7.

ἀπᾰρεστός, όν, *unpleasing*, Stob.2.7.11ᵏ.

ἀπαρηγόρητος, ον, *unconsoled*, Plu.*Dem.*22; *admitting of no consolation*, συμφορά J.*AJ*7.6.1. II. *not to be controlled*, Men.798, Plu.*Mar.*2, *Ant.*6; *inexorable*, Hp.*Decent.*4. Adv. -τως *inflexibly*, Ph.2.196.

ἀπαρήγορος, ον, *unconsoling*, θρῆνος *Epigr.Gr.*344.2 (Mysia).

ἀπαρθένευτος, ον, *unmaidenly, unfitting a maiden*, E.*Ph.*1739 (lyr.), neut. pl. as Adv., cf. Id.*IA*993. II. *deflowered*, Sch.Theoc. 2.41. III. *virginal* (as if from παρθενεύω, = κορεύω), S.*Fr.*304, *Carm.Pop.*8.

ἀπάρθενος, ον, *no more a maid*, Theoc.2.41; νύμφην ἄνυμφον παρθένον τ' ἀπάρθενον 'virgin wife and widowed maid', E.*Hec.*612.

ἀπαρθρ-όομαι, Pass., *to be jointed*, ἀπό τινος Hp.*Art.*30. **-ωσις**, εως, ἡ, *articulation*, Gal.18(1).433.

ἀπᾰριθμ-έω, *count over, take an inventory of*, X.*Oec.*9.10; *reckon up*, Id.*Cyr.*5.2.35; μύθους ἀ. *recount*, Arist.*Po.*1453ᵃ18:—Pass., Ps.-Alex. Aphr.*in SE*64.11, al. II. *reckon* or *pay back, repay*, X.*Cyr.*3.1.42, D.H.4.10, etc. III. Med., *secure payment of* a sum owing, *IG*1. 32, cf. ib.2².1122; but, 2. = Act. in Men.*Epit.*164, cf. Alex.Aphr. *in Top.*422.3; ἀ. προγόνους δυνάστας Jul.*Or.*2.83b; *enumerate*, σοφῶν ὀνόματα Id.*Gal.*176b. **–ησις,** εως, ἡ, *counting over*, ὀνομάτων Th. 5.20, cf. Alex.Aphr. *in Top.*425.8, Procl. *in Prm.*p.908 S., *in Ti.*1. 15 D., al.:—Adj. **–ητικός,** ή, όν, Sch.Hermog.*Id.* in Rh.7.1027 W.

ἀπαρίνη [ῐ], ἡ, *cleavers*, *Galium Aparine*, Thphr.*HP*7.14.2, Plu.2. 709e, Dsc.3.90, Gal.11.834. 2. = ἄρκιον, Ps.-Dsc.4.106. 3. = ξάνθιον, Dsc.4.136.

ἀπαρῑνής, ές, *of the* ἀπαρίνη, χυλός Nic.*Th.*953.

ἀπ-άριστα, neut. as Adv., (ἄριστον) *after luncheon*, *Tab.Defix.Aud.* 187.63. **–αριστάω,** *finish luncheon*, *Gloss.*

ἀπαρκέω, *suffice*, *be sufficient*, Sol.5 (ap.Arist.*Ath.*12.1), A.*Pers.* 474, S.*OC*1769 (lyr.), E.*Fr.*892; πρός τι S.E.*P.*1.185: abs., οὐκ ἀπήρκει *it was* not *enough*, Ar.*Fr.*457, cf. D.H.11.1. II. *to be contented*, *acquiesce*, ὥστ' ἀπαρκεῖν A.*Ag.*379 (lyr.):—Pass., Cerc.18 ii 13, Lyc. 1302.

ἀπαρκής, ές, *sufficient*, Hsch.

ἀπαρκίας, v. ἀπαρκτίας.

ἀπαρκούντως, Adv., (ἀπαρκέω) *sufficiently*, Poll.9.154 (perh. f.l. for ἐπ–).

ἀπαρκτεῖν· ἀποτυχεῖν, Hsch.

ἀπαρκτέον, (ἀπάρχομαι) *one must offer as first-fruits*, *sacrifice*, Ph. 1.533, Them.*Or.*11.142a, Porph.*Abst.*2.61.

ἀπαρκτίας, ου, ὁ, (ἄρκτος) *north wind*, Arist.*Mete.*363^{b}14, al., Thphr.*Sign.*2.35. The form **ἀπαρκίας,** mentioned by Eust.1156. 17, 1535.16, but censured by Phryn.*PS* p.31 B., occurs (= *Septentrio*) in *IG*14.1308, *Gloss.*

ἀπάρκτιος, α, ον, *northerly*, πνοαί Lyc.27.

ἀπαρν-έομαι, fut. –ήσομαι Pl.*Grg.*461c: aor. ἀπηρνησάμην Call.*Cer.* 75, 107, A.R.3.1133 (v.l.), *Ev.Matt.*16.24, al., but in Trag. and Att., –ηρνήθην S.*Tr.*480, E.*Hipp.*1266, Th.6.56, etc.:—*deny utterly*, Hdt. 6.69; κλέψαντες ἀπαρνεῖσθαι Antipho 2.3.4; μὴ.. ἀπαρνηθεὶς γένῃ Pl. *Sph.*217c; ἀπαρνηθῆναί τι *to refuse*, *reject* it, Th. l.c., etc.; ἀ. μή c. inf., τὸν.. ἀπαρνηθέντα μὴ χρᾶναι E. l.c.; οὐκ ἀπαρνοῦμαι τὸ μή (sc. δρᾶσαι) S.*Ant.*443, *Aj.*96; τίνα οἴει ἀπαρνήσεσθαι μὴ οὐ..; Pl. *Grg.*461c; οἷός ἐστι μὴ ἂν ἀ. χαρίσασθαι Id.*Phdr.*256a. 2. in Logic, opp. κατηγορεῖν, *deny*, Arist.*APr.*41^{a}9:—Pass., ib.63^{b}37. 3. ἀ. ἑαυτόν *deny* oneself, *Ev.Matt.*16.24, al. II. Pass., fut. ἀπαρνηθήσεται it *shall be denied* or *refused*, S.*Ph.*527, cf. *Ev.Luc.*12.9, dub. in Lxx *Is.*31.7: aor. ὥνθρωπος ἐν μὲν οἶδεν, ἐν δ' ἀπηρνήθη *was refused*, Herod.4.74. **–ησις,** εως, ἡ, *denial*, *renunciation*, Ph.2.438. **–ητής,** οῦ, ὁ, *one who denies*, *Gloss.* **–ητικός,** ή, όν, *denying*, Eust.29.44.

ἄπαρνος, ον, (ἀρνέομαι) *denying utterly*, ἄ. ἐστι μὴ νοσέειν Hdt.3. 99, cf. Antipho 1.9 and 10: c. gen., ἄ. οὐδενὸς καθίστατο she *denied* nothing, S.*Ant.*435. II. Pass., *denied*, ᾇ.. οὐδὲν ἄπαρνον τελέθει to whom nothing is *denied*, A.*Supp.*1039 (lyr.).

ἀπαρ-όδευτος, ον, *inaccessible*, κρημνοί D.S.17.67. **–όξυντος,** ον, *without paroxysms*, Alex.Trall.8.2. **–όρμητος,** ον, *not excitable*, Theag.ap.Stob.3.1.116. **–ουσιάστως,** Adv., (παρουσία) *without bodily presence*, Olymp. *in Alc.*p.13 C. **–οχος,** ον, *niggardly*, Vett. Val.85.24; *impraestans*, *Gloss.*

ἀπαρόω, aor. ἀπήροσα, *plough up*, Suid. (expl. by ἀπηροτρίασα).

ἀπαρρενόω, *produce male plants*, opp. ἀποθηλύνομαι, Thphr.*HP*7. 4.3 (Pass.).

ἀπαρρησίαστος, ον, *deprived of freedom of speech*, Thphr.*Fr.*103; πολιτεία Plb.22.12.2; *having no right of speech*, Cic.*Att.*9.2.2; *not frank*, Phld.*Herc.*1457.12, Id.*Rh.*2.158 S. II. *not speaking freely*, J.*BJ*4.5.4, Plu.2.51c, al., Luc.*Cal.*9. Adv. –τως, εὐλαβεῖσθαι Ph.1. 477. b. *not acting freely*, of reptiles, Herm.ap.Stob.1.49.69. III. Pass., *not freely spoken of*, Ph.2.428.

ἄπαρσις, εως, ἡ, (ἀπαίρω) *setting out*, *departure*, D.H.3.58, Lxx *Nu.*33.2, J.*AJ*17.9.3.

ἀπαρτάω, *hang up*: ἀ. δέρην *strangle*, E.*Andr.*412; *swing freely*, of a stone in a sling, Arist.*Mech.*852^{b}1:—Pass., *hang loose*, X.*Eq.*10. 9, Arist.*Aud.*802^{a}38; ἀπό τινος πρός τι Id.*GA*740^{a}29; ἔκ τινος Luc. *Pisc.*48; τινός Babr.17.2. 2. metaph., *make dependent upon*, ἀ. ἐλπίδας ἐξ ἑαυτοῦ Luc.*Tim.*36:—Med., *make dependent on oneself*, νόμοις τὸ πλῆθος Plu.*CG*8. II. *detach*, *separate*, τὸν λόγον τῆς γραφῆς D.18.59, cf. Arist.*Rh.*1407^{a}24:—Pass., ὥστε τὴν χώραν πολὺ τῆς πόλεως ἀπηρτῆσθαι Id.*Pol.*1319^{a}34; ὁ πλεύμων.. πολὺ ἀπηρτημένος τῆς καρδίας Id.*HA*508^{a}33; οἱ πόροι.. ἀπήρτηνται ἀλλήλων, opp. συμπίπτουσι, ib.495^{a}18:—but that from which one is separated is often omitted, and the Pass. used absolutely, ἀπηρτημένοι καὶ ταῖς παρασκευαῖς καὶ ταῖς γνώμαις *detached*, D.4.12; συνεχεῖς καὶ οὐκ ἀπηρτημένοι not *detached*, Arist.*HA*509^{b}13, cf. 506^{b}19, al.; of Time, τοῖς καιροῖς οὐ μακρὰν ἀπηρτῆσθαι Plb.12.17.1, cf. Plu.*TG*3; λόγος ἀπηρτημένος *discrepant*, Str.7.3.2; λίαν ἀπηρτ. far *different*, Ph.1.300, cf. Phld.*Rh.*1.288 S. III. intr. in Act., *remove oneself*, *go away*, ἐς ἀλλοτρίαν ἀπαρτᾶν Th.6.21, cf. D.C.40.15; *to be away*, *distant*, ἀπό τινος Id.51.4; πρὶν ἀπαρτηθῆναι 44.38 is perh. f.l. for ἀπαντ–.

ἀπαρτής, ές, *raised up*, ῥίς Hp.*Art.*38 (v.l. ἀπαρτητήν).

ἀπάρτησις, εως, ἡ, *hanging from*, *appendage*, τῶν πτερυγίων Arist.*GA*720^{b}12. 2. *attachment*, Hp.*Art.*8 (with v.l. ἀπάρτισις): metaph., *dependence*, Plot.5.1.2. II. *detachment*, *separation*, Ph. 1.209.

ἀπαρτί [ῐ], Adv. *completely*, and, of numbers, *exactly*, *just*, ἡμέραι ἀ. ἐνενήκοντα Hdt.5.53, cf. 2.158; φρόνιμος ὢν ἀ. ταύτης τῆς τέχνης Telecl.37; ἀ. ἐναρμόζειν πρός τι Hp.*Art.*73: of Time, ἀ. ἐν καιροῖσι.. Id.*Acut.*41. II. *just the contrary*, τί.. ἀποτίνειν τῷδ' ἀξιοῖς;—ἀ. δή που προσλαβεῖν παρὰ τοῦδ' ἐγὼ μᾶλλον *on the contrary*, I expect to receive.., Pherecr.93, cf. 71, Ar.*Pl.*388. III. ἀπάρτι, properly ἀπ' ἄρτι, of Time, *from now*, *henceforth*, *Ev.Matt.*23.39, etc. 2. *just now*, *even now*, *Ev.Jo.*13.19, etc. (This is not an Att. use, hence Pl.Com.143 must be incorrectly interpr. by *AB*79.)

ἀπαρτία, Ion. –ίη, ἡ, = ἀποσκευή, *household utensils*, *movables*, *chattels*, Hippon.26, Thphr.ap.Poll.10.19, Lxx *Ex.*40.36. 2. *spoil*, including captives, ib.*Nu.*31.17, 18. II. *public auction*, *PStrassb.* 59.3 (i B.C.), *PGnom.*241 (–εία, ii A.D.), Poll. l.c. III. ἀπαρτίαν· μετάβασιν, ἀποσκευήν, τέλος, ἀπαρτισμόν, Hsch.

ἀπαρτιζόντως, Adv. *adequately*, *precisely*, λόγος κατ' ἀνάλυσιν ἀ. ἐκφερόμενος Antip.*Stoic.*3.247, cf. Apollod.ib.3.260; Alex.Aphr. *in Top.*42.27; of division, *without remainder*, Theo Sm.p.76 H.

ἀπαρτίζω, fut. ἀπαρτιῶ Mitteis *Chr.*88 iii 13 (ii A.D.):—*make even*, σπουδῇ.. οὐκ ἀπαρτίζει πόδα *does* not *allow* his feet *to move evenly*, *regularly*, A.*Th.*374 (Herm. οὐ καταργίζει); *produce an even result*, Arist.*GA*780^{b}10; ἀ. ὥστε σφαιροειδῆ εἶναι *make* it *perfectly* spherical, Id.*Mete.*340^{b}35; *fasten off* the ends of a phylactery, *PMag.Par.*1. 2703. II. generally, *get ready*, *complete*, Plb.31.12.10; *finish*, λόγον Iamb. *in Nic.*p.35 P.; *dispose of*, δίκας Mitteis *Chr.* l.c., cf. Charito 6.1; *educate* an apprentice *thoroughly*, *POxy.*724.11 (ii A.D.):—Pass., *to be brought to perfection*, Arist.*Fr.*282; *to be completed*, *be exactly made up*, ἀπηρτισμένης ⟨τῆς⟩ πρώτης περιόδου Hp.*Morb.*4.48; ἀπαρτίζεται εἰς ἑπτὰ κεφαλάς, of the golden candlestick, J.*AJ*3.6.7: metaph., *end*, *result in*, εἴς τι ib.16.8.2; of multiplication, *make*, Paul.Al.*E.*1; ἀπηρτισμένος *complete*, *perfect*, D.H.*Dem.*50; στίχος verse *coinciding with a sentence*, Hdn.*Vers.*86; πρὸς τὸ τέλος Phld. *Mus.*p.31 K., cf. *Piet.*66. 2. intr., *to be complete*, τῆς ὀκταμήνου ἀπαρτιζούσης Hp.*Epid.*2.3.17; ἀ. ὁ τόπος καὶ τὸ σῶμα *fit exactly*, Arist. *Ph.*205^{a}32; ἀ. πρός τι *square with*, *suit exactly*, Id.*Pol.*1313^{a}7; ἡ ἀπαρτίζουσα ὥρα the *fitting* season, Id.*HA*542^{a}31; τῶν ὀργάνων οὐθὲν ἀπαρτιζόντων Epicur.*Nat.*11.6; οἱ –οντες *corresponding precisely to definition*, *Stoic.*2.128. Adv. ἀπαρτισμένως (sic) Simp. *in Ph.*949.17; cf. ἀπηρτισμένως.

ἀπαρτικός· πρὸς ἄπαρσιν καὶ ἀποδημίαν ἕτοιμος, Hsch.

ἀπαρτι-λογέω· ἄρτια βάζω, Eust.1594.1. **–λογία,** Ion. –ίη, ἡ, *an even number* or *sum*, Hdt.7.29, Lys.*Fr.*28 S., Antipho Soph. 99.

ἀπάρτιον προγράφειν, (ἀπαρτία) put up *goods to public sale*, Plu.*Cic.* 27, 2.205c.

ἀπάρτ-ισις, εως, ἡ, *arrangement*, νεύρων Hp.*Art.*8 (with v.l. ἀπάρτησις, q.v.). **–ισμα,** ατος, τό, = sq., Sm.3*Ki.*7.9(46). **–ισμός,** ὁ, *completion*, *Ev.Luc.*14.28; ἔργων *PGiss.*67.9 (ii A.D.); λογοθεσίας Mitteis *Chr.*88 iv 25 (ii A.D.); κατ' ἀπαρτισμόν *precisely*, Chrysipp. *Stoic.*2.164; οὐ κατ' ἀπαρτισμὸν ἀλλ' ἐν πλάτει *not narrowly but broadly*, D.H.*Comp.*24. 2. *rounding off*, βαλάνου Antyll.ap.Orib. 50.3.1.

ἀπαρτίως, Adv., (ἄρτιος) = ἀπαρτί, Gal.17(2).437; f.l. in Hp. *Hum.*6 (to which Gal. refers).

ἀπαρτύειν· ἀποκηρύσσειν (Tarent.), Hsch.; ἀπαρτῦναι· τάξαι, Id.

ἀπαρυστέον, (ἀπαρύω) *one must draw off*: metaph., ἀ. τῶν ἀπειλῶν Ar.*Eq.*921.

ἀπάρυστρον, τό, = ἀρυστήρ, *IG*11(2).110.27 (Delos, iii B.C.).

ἀπαρύω or –ύτω [ῠ], fut. –ύσω, *draw off*, τὸ ἐπιστάμενον ἀπαρύσαντες *having skimmed off* the cream, Hdt.4.2, cf. D.S.5.37. 2. metaph., *draw off*, *take off the force of* a thing, χαλκῷ ἀπὸ ψυχὴν ἀρύσας Epic.ap.Arist.*Po.*1457^{b}14; *exhaust*, *come to the end of*, Plu.2.463c, etc.:—Med., c. gen., ὁ τῆς μνήμης τῶν ἀγαθῶν ἀπαρυτόμενος *skimming the cream of* memory, ib.610e:—Pass., aor. part., ἀπαρυθεὶς τὴν ἄνω ... ἄνοιαν ἐπιπολάζουσαν *having* it *skimmed off* the surface, Alex.45.

ἀπαρχαΐζω, *compare to something ancient*, τινί τι Ath.1.20c. II *assign antiquity to*, αἵρεσιν Gal.14.683; τὸ παγκράτιον Sch.Pi.*N.*3.27.

ἀπαρχαιόομαι, Pass., *to be* or *become ancient*, ἀπηρχαιωμένα *old-fashioned songs*, Antiph.85; ἀ. λέξις, φράσις, D.H.*Th.*24, Aristid.*Rh.* 2p.508 J.

ἀπαρχή, ἡ, mostly in pl. ἀπαρχαί (cf. ἄπαργμα): 1. *beginning of a sacrifice*, *primal offering* (of hairs cut from the forehead), ἀπαρχαὶ κόμης E.*Or.*96, cf. *Ph.*1525 (lyr.); later, a *banquet* held on this occasion, Plu.2.40b. 2. *firstlings* for sacrifice or offering, *first-fruits*, ἁπάντων ἀπαρχαί Hdt.4.71; ἀπαρχὰς ἄγειν θεοῖσι S.*Tr.*183; ἀπαρχὰς θύειν E.*Fr.*516; ἀ. σκυλευμάτων *Ph.*857; ἐπιφέρειν ἀ. τῶν ὡραίων Th. 3.58; τῶν ὄντων Is.5.42, cf. Epicur.*Fr.*130, etc.:—so also in sg., λείας ἀ. S.*Tr.*761; ἀ. τῶν πατρώων χρημάτων Hdt.1.92, etc.; ἀνθρώπων ἀ. εἰς Δελφοὺς ἀποστέλλειν Arist.*Fr.*485; ἀ. ἀπό τινος ἀνατιθέναι Hdt. 4.88; inscribed on votive offerings, [ἀνέθηκεν].. τόδ' ἀ. *IG*1.382, etc.; freq. in Lxx, as *Ex.*25.2, al., cf. *Ep.Rom.*11.16, and metaph., ἀ. τῶν κεκοιμημένων 1*Ep.Cor.*15.20; τῶν κτισμάτων *Ep.Jac.*1.18. 3. metaph., ἀπαρχαὶ τῶν ἐμῶν προσφθεγμάτων E.*Ion*402; ἀπαρχὴν τῆς σοφίας ἀνέθεσαν Pl.*Prt.*343b, etc.; ἀ. ἀπὸ φιλοσοφίας Plu.2.172c. 4. *tax on inheritances*, *PTaur.*1.7.10; *tax* paid by Jews, *Stud.Pal.*4.72 (i A.D.). 5. *entrance fee*, *PTeb.*316.10 (i A.D.), al. 6. *board of officials* (cf. sq.), *IG*12(8).273 (Thasos). 7. *birth-certificate* of a free person, *PTeb.*316.10 (i A.D.), *PGnom.*131 (ii A.D.): perh. metaph. in *Ep.Rom.*8.23.

ἀπάρχης, ου, ὁ, title of *official* (or perh. *ex-magistrate*) in Lesbos, *IG*12(2).68.5, 69 b 6 (Mytil.).

ἀπάρχομαι, *make a beginning*, esp. in sacrifice; τρίχας ἀπάρχεσθαι *begin the sacrifice with* the hair, i.e. by cutting off the hair from the forehead and throwing it into the fire, κάπρου ἀπὸ τρίχας ἀρξάμενος Il.19.254; ἀλλ' ὅ γ' ἀπαρχόμενος τρίχας ἐν πυρὶ βάλλεν Od. 14.422: abs., 3.446. II. later c. gen., *cut off part* of a thing, *offer* *it*, τοῦ ὠτὸς τοῦ κτήνεος Hdt.4.188; ἀ. κόμης E.*El*.91; τῶν κρεῶν καὶ σπλάγχνων *offer part of* them, Hdt.4.61: hence, 2. *offer the first-lings* or *first-fruits*, πάντων of all sacrifices, Id.3.24: abs., *begin a sacrifice*, Ar.*Ach*.244, *Pax* 1056, etc.; ἀ. τοῖς θεοῖς X.*Hier*.4.2; ἀπηργμένοι, of eunuchs, *having had their first-fruits offered*, Anaxandr.39.11. 3. metaph., *take as the first-fruits, take as the choice* or *best*, δικαστήν Pl.*Lg*.767c: abs., *offer first-fruits*, Theoc.17.109. III. generally, *offer, dedicate*, χρυσᾶς (sc. δραχμάς) *IG*2.652*B*19, cf. Plu. *Sull*.27, *AP*7.406 (Theodorid.). IV. later, = ἄρχομαι, *begin*, c. gen., πημάτων Lyc.1409: c. inf., v.l. in Luc.*Nigr*.3; *practise, prelude on*, ὀργάνων Him.*Or*.17.2.

ἄπαρχος, ὁ, f.l. for ἔπαρχος, A.*Pers*.327.

ἀπάρχω, fut. -ξω (v. infr.), *lead the way*, εἰς νᾶσον B.11.6 (s.v.l.): esp. in dancing, ὁ ἀπάρχων τῶν ὀρχηστῶν dub. l. in D.H.7.73; ὔμμι δ' ἀπάρξει *shall lead* you *in the dance*, *AP*9.189. II. prob. *reign far away* from home, of Teucer, Pi.*N*.4.46.

ἀπᾰρφδήτως, Adv. *without alteration*, Eust.1090.12.

ἅπᾱς, ἅπᾱσα (also ἅπανσα *SIG*56.25 (Argos, v B.C.)), **ἅπαν** (ἁ- = *sm*-, cf. εἷς), strengthd. for πᾶς, *quite all, the whole*, and in pl. *all together*, freq. from Hom. downwds.; ἅπασι *in all things*, Hdt.1.1; τοῖσι ἅπασι 91; ἐν ἅπασι Hp.*Coac*.156; ἐφ' ἅπασι Ph.2.365. 2. with Adj., ἀργύρεος δὲ ἔστιν ἅ. *all* silver, i.e. of *massive* silver, Od.4.616, 15.116; ἅ. δὲ τραχὺς ὅστις ἂν νέον κρατῇ A.*Pr*.35; μικκός γα μᾶκος.. ἀλλ' ἅπαν κακόν Ar.*Ach*.909, cf. Theoc.15.19,148; ἡ ἐναντία ἅπασα ὁδός the *exactly* contrary way, Pl.*Prt*.317b. 3. with abstract Subst., *all possible, absolute*, ἅπασ' ἀνάγκη Ar.*Th*.171; σπουδῇ D.H.6.23; ἀτοπία Plb.39.1.7; εἰς ἅπαν ἀφικέσθαι ἀνοίας Paus.7.15.8. 4. sts. c. Art., Hdt.3.64, al., A.*Pr*.483, Th.2.13. II. after Hom. in sg., *every one*, neut. *everything*, Pl.*Phd*.108b; οὐ πρὸς [τοῦ] ἅπαντος ἀνδρός not in the power of *every* man, Hdt.7.153; οὐκ ἐξ ἅπαντος δεῖ τὸ κερδαίνειν φιλεῖν S.*Ant*.312; ἐξ ἅπαντος εὖ λέγει *in any cause whatever*, Id.*OC*807; σῖγα νῦν ἅπας ἔχε σῖγαν Cratin.144; ἅπαν γένοιτ' ἂν ἤδη *nihil non*.., Ar.*Th*.528: with Subst., ἅπαντι λόγῳ in *every* matter, Cratin.231; τὸ ἅπαν, as Adv., *altogether*, Pl.*Phdr*.241b; καθ' ἅπαν as *a whole*, Ti.Locr.96d; ἐς ἅπαν Th.5.103; εἰς ἅπαν *at all*, Lib.*Or*.18.266; πρὸς ἅπαν Ph.2.493; ἐξ ἅπαντος Luc.*Merc.Cond*.41. [ᾰπᾱν Od.24.185, etc., Pi.*P*.2.49; but ᾰπᾰν Men.129, Metrod.57, Theoc.2.56, and Att. acc. to Hdn.Gr.2.12; ᾰπᾰν in anap., Ar.*Pl*.493: the use of ἅπας for πᾶς is chiefly for the sake of euphony after consonants.]

ἀπασβολόομαι, *turn to soot, become sooty*, Dsc.5.76.

ἀπασιτόν· τὸ δεσμωτήριον, Hsch. (fort. ἀπλίκιτον).

ἀπασκᾰρίζω, fut. -ιῶ Men.839:—*struggle, be convulsed*, like a dying fish, ἀ. ὥσπερεὶ πέρκην χαμαί Ar.*Fr*.495; ἀπασκαριῶ γέλωτι Men. l.c.; ἀπησκάρισεν *gave up the ghost*, prob. for ἀπεσκ-, *AP*11.114 (Nicarch.).

ἀπασπάζομαι, *take leave of*, ἀλλήλους *Act.Ap*.21.6, v.l. in Lxx *To*.10.13; ᾠδῇ καὶ μέλει χορόν Him.*Ecl*.11.1.

ἀπασπαίρω, *gasp away*, θνήσκει δ' ἀπασπαίρουσα E.*Ion*1207.

ἀπασσεῖον (sic)· παμποίκιλον, οἱ δὲ λινοῦν χιτῶνα, οἱ δὲ μαλλωτόν, Hsch.

ἀπαστακώς· ἁμαρτών, Hsch.

ἀπαστ-ί, Adv. of ἄπαστος, *fasting*, Hsch. **-ία**, ἡ, *abstaining from food, fast*, ἀ. ἄγειν Ar.*Nu*.621. **-ος**, ον, (πατέομαι) *not having eaten, abstaining from food, fasting*, Il.19.346, Arist.*HA*563ᵃ23, Call.*Cer*.6, Euph.57, v.l. in *h.Merc*.168. 2. c. gen., ἄπαστος ἐδητύος ἠδὲ ποτῆτος *without having tasted* meat or drink, Od.4.788, cf. 6.250, *h.Cer*.200: ἐδητύος ἔργον ἄπαστον a meal *which feeds not*, Opp.*H*.2.250. II. Pass., *not eaten*, Ael.*NA*11.16.

ἀπαστρά-πτω, *flash forth*, Arat.430, Opp.*C*.1.220; αὐγὴ ἀ. λίθων J.*AJ*3.8.9: c. acc. cogn., φέγγος Ph.1.150, al.; αἴγλην Opp.*C*.3.479; φάος Procl.*Hymn*.7.31, cf. Luc.*Gall*.7, Iamb.*Myst*.2.3. **-ψις**, εως, ἡ, *lightning*, Tz.*H*.9.106.

ἀπαστύς, ύος, ἡ, = ἀπαστία, *EM*118.50.

ἀπασφᾰλίζω, *make secure, fasten* or *shut up*, Ps.-Porph. in Bentley *Epistola ad Millium* p.303 (where ἀποσφαλίσει for ἀπασφαλίσῃ), Sch.E.*Or*.1108.

ἀπασχολ-έω, *leave* one *no leisure, keep* him *employed*, Luc.*Philops*.14, Hld.2.21:—Pass., *to be wholly occupied* or *engrossed*, so as to attend to nothing else, περί τινα Luc.*Charid*.19, cf. Olymp. *in Mete*.108.22; τινί ib.107.13; ἀ. ἐπὶ τῆς ἀλλοδαπῆς *to be absent* on foreign service, *POxy*.71 ii 8 (iv A.D.). II. τῆς συνεχείας τῶν φυτῶν ἀπασχολούσης ἐς ἑαυτὴν τὰ βέλη *rendering* them *of none effect*, Hdn.7.2.5. III. ἀ. τινὰ τῶν ἡδίστων *detain* him *from*.., Hld.10.23. **-ητέον**, *one must be engrossed*, βιωτικαῖς πράξεσι Aët.9.23. **-ία**, ἡ, *detention by business*, Str.6.4.2 (pl.).

ἀπᾰτᾰγί, Adv., (πάταγος) *noiselessly*, Suid.

ἀπᾰτάω [ᾰπ], late Ion. -έω Luc.*Syr.D*.27 (Pass.): impf. ἠπάτων E.*El*.938, Ion. ἐξ-απάτασκον Orac. in Ar.*Pax*1070: fut. -ήσω: aor. ἠπάτησα, Ion. ἀπ- Il.9.344, S.*Tr*.500 (lyr.): pf. ἠπάτηκα Id.*Ph*.929:—Pass., fut. ἀπατηθήσομαι Arist.*APr*.67ᵃ38, cf. (ἐξ-) Pl.*Cra*.436b, Aeschin.2.123; also in Med. form ἀπατήσομαι Pl.*Phdr*.262a, (ἐξ-) X.*An*.7.3.3: aor. ἠπατήθην Pl.*Cri*.52e: pf. ἠπάτημαι Th.5.46, etc.: (ἀπάτη):—*cheat, deceive*, Il.19.97, Od.17.139, etc.; *cheat* one's *hopes*, Hes.*Op*.462; οἷ' ἠπάτηκας S.*Ph*.929; κλέμματα.. ἃ τὸν πολέμιον ἀπατήσας Th.5.9: abs., *to be deceptive* or *fallacious*, Arist.*Rh*.1376ᵇ28:—Pass., *to be self-deceived, mistaken*, Pi.*Fr*.182, S.*OT*594, Pl.*Phdr*.262a, etc.; ἔγνωκα.. φωτὸς ἠπατημένη S.*Aj*.807; τί γὰρ οὐκ.. ἔρχεται ἀγγελίας ἀπατώμενον; comes not *belied by* the result? Id.*El*.170; ἀ. περί τι Arist.*Rh*.1368ᵇ22; περί τινος Id.*Sens*.442ᵇ8; ἀ. ταύτην τὴν ἀπάτην Id.*APo*.74ᵃ6; also ἀπατᾶσθαι ὡς.. *to be deceived into thinking* that.., Pl.*Prt*.323a.—The compd. ἐξαπατάω is more common, esp. in Hdt. and Att. Prose; the simple Verb is used in Lxx *Ge*.3.13, al., but not by Plb., and is rare in later Greek, Plu.2.15d.

ἀπάτειρα [πᾰ], fem. of ἀπάτωρ, epith. of Isis, *POxy*.1380.19.

ἀπάτερθε [πᾰ], before a vowel -θεν, Adv. *apart, aloof*, ἀ. δὲ θωρήσσοντο Il.2.587, cf. Thgn.1059, Pi.*O*.7.74. II. as Prep. c. gen., *far away from*, ἀπάτερθεν ὁμίλου Il.5.445, cf. Thgn.1153; γόων ἀ. *IG*14.2123.

ἀπᾰτ-εύω, = ἀπατάω, Xenoph.11. **-εών**, ῶνος, ὁ, *cheat, rogue*, Hp.*Art*.42, Democr.63, Pl.*R*.451a, X.*Cyr*.1.6.27, Epicur.*Fr*.236, etc.:—as Adj., ἀ. λόγος Max.Tyr.2.1. **-η**, ἡ, *trick, fraud, deceit*, νῦν δὲ κακὴν ἀπάτην βουλεύσατο Il.2.114, cf. 4.168: in pl., *wiles*, οὐκ ἄρ' ἔμελλες.. λήξειν ἀπατάων, says Athena to Ulysses, Od.13.294, cf. Il.15.31; σκολιαὶ ἀπάται Pi.*Fr*.213. 2. *guile, treachery*, ἄταν ἀπάτᾳ μεταγνούς A.*Supp*.111, cf. S.*OC*230; ἀπάτης δικαίας οὐκ ἀποστατεῖ θεός A.*Fr*.301, cf. *Pers*.93; ἀ. ἐρώτων S.*Ant*.617; διαβολὴ καὶ ἀ. Antipho6.7, etc.; ἀ. εὐπρεπής, opp. βία ἐμφανής, Th.4.86; ἢ βίᾳ ἢ ἀπάτῃ 2.39; ἀ. λεχέων *a being cheated out of* the marriage, S.*Ant*.630; ἄνευ δόλου καὶ ἀπάτης 'without fraud or *covin*', Hdt.1.69; μετὰ σκότους καὶ ἀ. Pl.*Lg*.864c. 3. Ἀπάτη, personified, Hes.*Th*.224, Luc.*Merc.Cond*.42. II. *beguiling* of time, *pastime* (not Att., Moer.65), Plb.4.20.5; ψυχῆς Dicaearch.1.1; ψυχαγωγίαι καὶ ἀπάται τῆς πόλεως D.Chr.32.5. III. as name of a plant, f.l. for ἀπάπη (q.v.). **-ήλιος**, ον, poet. Adj. *guileful, wily*, ἀπατήλια εἰδώς skilled in *wiles*, Od.14.288; ἀ. βάζειν ib.127; of a person, Nonn.*D*.46.10, al. **-ηλογεῖν**, gloss on γελγιθεύειν, Hsch. **-ηλός**, ή, όν (ος, ον Pl.*Criti*.107d), = ἀπατήλιος, Il.1.526; κόσμος Parm.8.52; λόγου στόλος Emp.17.26; δέσποινα X.*Oec*.1.20; κακοῦργος καὶ ἀπατηλή Pl.*Grg*.465b; ἀ. λόγος Id.*Lg*.892d; τὸ ἀ. ἐν λόγοις Id.*Cra*.407e; σκιαγραφία ἀ. *producing illusion*, Id.*Criti*.107d; στρατηγός App.*BC*1.112 (Sup.); also, *deceptive*, opp. γνήσιος, Eus. Mynd.63. Adv. -λῶς Iamb.*Myst*.3.26, Poll.9.135. **-ημα**, ατος, τό, *deceit, stratagem*, Aen.Tact.23.6; *beguilement*, δόξης Gorg.*Hel*.10 (pl.); πόθων *AP*7.195 (Mel.). **-ήμων**, ον, gen. ονος, = ἀπατήλιος, Orac.ap.Zos.1.52. **-ήνωρ**, ορος, ὁ, ἡ, (ἀνήρ) *beguiling men*, τέχνη Tryph.137. II. epith. of Dionysus, Call.*Fr*.36P. **-ησις**, εως, ἡ, *beguiling*, Lxx *Ju*.10.4, Phld.*Ir*.p.9W. (pl.), Id.*D*.1.16. **-ητής**, οῦ, ὁ, *deceiver*, *Gloss*. **-ητικός**, ή, όν, *fallacious*, of sophistry, Pl.*Sph*.240d, 264d, Arist.*APo*.80ᵇ15, al.: Comp. -κώτερος *more effective in deceiving*, X.*Eq.Mag*.5.5. Adv. -κῶς Poll.4.24.

ἀπάτητος [πᾰ], ον, *untrodden*, *AP*6.51. II. *not trodden down*: hence metaph., *unusual*, Democr.131.

ἀπᾰτῑμ-άζω, = sq., ἀπητιμασμένη A.*Eu*.95. **-άω**, *dishonour greatly*, ἀπητίμησε Il.13.113.

ἀπατμ-ίζω, *evaporate*, ἀπατμίζει τὸ ὑγρόν Arist.*Mete*.359ᵃ31, cf. *Somn.Vig*.457ᵇ31, *PA*653ᵃ36. **-ισις**, εως, ἡ, *evaporation*, Mich. *in EN*55.6.

ἄπᾰτος, ον, (ἄτη) *immune from punishment*, *Leg.Gort*.2.1, al.

ἀπατουργόν· κωλυτικόν, Hsch.

Ἀπᾰτουρεών, ῶνος, ὁ, name of a *month*, answering to Att. Pyanepsion, *CIG*3661 (Cyzicus), *IPE*1².47 (Olbia):—written -ιών *IG*11.203*A*32,53 (Delos, iii B.C.), ib.12(5).824.33 (Tenos), *SIG*169.1 (Iasus): Ἀπατοριών *IG*12(7).412 (Amorgos, iii B.C.).

Ἀπᾰτούρια, τά, *the Apaturia*, a festival celebrated by the members of φρατρίαι at Athens and most Ionic cities, Hdt.1.147, And.1.126, X.*HG*1.7.8, D.39.4, Thphr.*Char*.35, etc.

Ἀπᾰτουρία, ἡ, title of Aphrodite at Troezen, Paus.2.33.1:—also **Ἀπατούρη** *IPE*2.28 (Panticapaeum); **Ἀπατουριάς** ib.352 (Phanagoria):—also **Ἀπάτουρον** (leg. -ούριον) τὸ τῆς Ἀφροδίτης ἱερόν, at Phanagoria, Str.11.2.10. (ἀ- copul., πατήρ, cf. ὁμοπάτορες.)

ἀπατρία (Ep. -ίη), ἡ, *exile*, *CIG*3632 (Ilium).

ἄπᾰτρις, ιδος, ὁ, ἡ, *without country*, Tz.*H*.7.436.

ἀπάτυλλα [πᾰ], ἡ, Dim. of ἀπάτη, dub. in Cerc.*Oxy*.1082*Fr*.39.

ἀπάτωρ [πᾰ], ορος, ὁ, ἡ, (πατήρ) *without father*, of deities, αὐτοπάτωρ, ἀ. Orph.*H*.10.10; ἀ... ἀμήτωρ Nonn.*D*.41.53, cf. *Ep.Hebr*.7.3; *fatherless, orphan*, ἀοίκους ἀπάτοράς τε S.*Tr*.300; ἀμήτωρ ἀ. τε E.*Ion*109 (lyr.); ἀ. πότμος Id.*IT*864 (lyr.), cf. Vett.Val.103.35: neut. pl., ἀπάτορα τέκεα E.*HF*114 (lyr.); *disowned by the father*, Pl.*Lg*.929a: also c. gen., ἀ. ἐμοῦ *not having* me *for a father*, S.*OC*1383. 2. *of unknown father*, like σκότιος, Plu.2.288e, *PGrenf*.2.56.3 (ii A.D.).

ἀπάτωρος, ον, = foreg., [Hes.] ap.Sch.Il.*Oxy*.1087.50.

ἀπαυαίνω, aor. part. ἀπαυάνας Orph.*Fr*.31.20:—*make to wither away*, Thphr.*CP*3.10.7; *parch* with thirst, Orph. l.c.:—Pass., *to be withered*, Q.S.1.66, al.; cf. ἀφ-.

ἀπαυγ-άζω, *flash forth*, ἀπὸ τῶν ὀφθαλμῶν σέλας Hld.3.4; χροιάν, χρῶμα, Id.4.8, Philostr.*VA*3.8. II. Med., *see from far*, Call.*Del*.125,181. **-ασμα**, ατος, τό, *radiance, effulgence*, of light *beaming from* a luminous body, φωτὸς ἀϊδίου Lxx *Wi*.7.26; δόξης *Ep.Hebr*.1.3, cf. Ph.1.337, al., Hld.5.27, Dam.ap.Simp. *in Ph*.775.15. **-ασμός**, ὁ, *efflux of light, radiance, effulgence*, Plu.2.83d, 934d.

ἀπαυγής, ές, *bright*, Hsch.

ἀπαυδ-άω, *forbid*, abs., ἐγὼ δ' ἀπαυδῶ γ' S.*Ph*.1293; freq. folld. by μή c. inf., τὸν ἄνδρ' ἀπηύδα.. στέγης μὴ ἔξω παρήκειν Id.*Aj*.741; τὸν ἄνδρ' ἀπαυδῶ τῆσδε γῆς.. μὴ εἰσδέχεσθαί τινα Id.*OT*236, cf. E.*Rh*.934, *Supp*.468, Ar.*Eq*.1072: with implied neg., ἀ. ἐξίστασθαι μύσταισι χοροῖς Id.*Ra*.369. II. *decline, refuse*, οὔκουν ἀπαυδᾶν δυνατόν ἐστι μοι πόνους E.*Supp.*342; *renounce*, νεῖκος ἀ. Theoc.22.129; *say no*, *APl.*4.299. III. *to be wanting towards*, *fail*, φίλοισι E.*Andr.*87: hence abs., *fail*, of wood, Thphr.*HP*5.6.1; ἀ. πρὸς τὸ περίπατον Antyll.ap.Orib.6.21.11; *become speechless*, of hysterical patients, Hp.*Mul.*1.74, cf. Ps.-Luc.*Philopatr.*18; ἀ. τὰ μαντεῖα the oracles *are dumb*, Plu.2.431b; *faint*, *fail*, Thphr.*Char.*8.14; ἀ. ὑπὸ λιμοῦ Luc. *Luct.*24; κόπῳ Babr.7.8; πόνοις *AP*5.167; *die* (of patients), Herod. Med. in *Rh.Mus.*58.80. **–ησις**, εως, ἡ, *exhaustion*, Agathin.ap. Orib.10.7.10.

ἀπαυθᾰδιάζοντες· μεγαλοφρονοῦντες, *AB*419, Hsch., Suid.:—Med., -ιάζομαι, = sq., Phlp. *in Mete.*7.35; *reject boldly*, Hld.7.19.

ἀπαυθᾰδίζομαι, *speak* or *act boldly*, Pl.*Ap.*37a; freq. in late Prose, in bad sense, Ph.2.441; μέχρι παντὸς J.*BJ*3.7.11, cf. Plu.2.766c, Them.*Or.*10.131d, 135a, 23.29cc.

ἀπαυθημερίζω, *do on the same day*; esp. *go* or *return the same day*, εἰς τὸ στρατόπεδον X.*An.*5.2.1; ἐκ Πίσης εἰς Αἴγιναν Ael.*VH*9.2.

ἀπαυλεῖσθαι· τὸ μὴ προαυλεῖν κατὰ τρόπον, Hsch.

ἀπαύλια, ων, τά, (αὐλή) *sleeping alone*, esp. the night before the wedding, when the bridegroom slept alone in the father-in-law's house, Poll.3.39; cf. ἐπαύλια:—*EM*119.14 is confused.

ἀπαυλ-ίζομαι, aor. -ηυλίσθην, *sleep* or *live away from*, τῆς πόλεως D.H.8.87; ἀπὸ τῆς νύμφης Poll.3.39. **–ισμός**, ὁ, seems to be used of *a moon-stroke* or *fit caused by sleeping in the moonlight*, Poet. *de herb.*173. **–ιστήριος**, α, ον, *belonging to the* ἀπαύλια, ἀ. χλανίς a garment *presented on this day*, Poll.3.40.

ἄπαυλος, ον, *lying alone*, Hsch.

ἀπαυλόσῠνος, ον, *away from the* αὐλή, *AP*6.221 (Leon.).

ἀπαυξάνομαι, pf. part. ἀπηυξημένος *in 'irrational' proportion to the* χρόνοι πρῶτοι, Gal.8.913.

ἀπαύξησις, εως, ἡ, *decrease*: hence, *disesteem*, πίπτειν εἰς ἀ. Longin.7.3.

ἀπαυράω, v. ἀπούρας.

ἀπαυρίσκομαι, *derive nourishment*, ἀπὸ τῆς ἰκμάδος Hp.*Nat.Puer.* 26.

ἀπαυστί, Adv. of sq., *unceasing*, *incessant*, D.C.37.46.

ἀπαυστίας· παραχύτας, Hsch.

ἄπαυστος, ον, *unceasing*, *never-ending*, Parm.8.27; αἰών A.*Supp.* 574 (lyr.); βίος Pl.*Ti.*36e; ἄτα S.*Aj.*1187 (lyr.); ἁ. καὶ ἀθάνατος φορά Pl.*Cra.*417c, etc. Adv. -τως Arist.*Mu.*391ᵇ18, Corn.*ND*34. 2. *not to be stopped* or *assuaged*, *insatiable*, δίψα Th.2.49; γνάθοι Antiph. 237.4; ἐπιθυμίη χρημάτων Eus.Mynd.1. II. c. gen., *never ceasing from*, γόων E.*Supp.*82 (lyr.).—Cf. ἄπαυτος.

ἀπαυτίκα, Adv. strengthd. for αὐτίκα, *on the spot*, dub. l. in D.C. 40.15.

ἀπαυτομᾰτίζω, *do* a thing *of oneself*, Plu.2.717b; *produce spontaneously*, Ph.1.36:—Pass., Id.2.182:—Act., intr., *occur spontaneously*, Id.1.571; -ίζουσα φορά ib.387; of the menses, Orib.7.20.1.

ἀπαυτομολέω, *go of one's own accord*, *desert*, Th.7.75; πρός τινα D.H.*Orat.Vett.*2; τινός D.C.36.17.

ἄπαυτος, ον, *unceasing*, Thphr.*Metaph.*5; cf. ἄπαυστος.

ἀπαυχενίζω, *cut off by the neck*, D.S.34.2.22. II. ταῦρον ἀ. *tame* a bull *by forcing back his neck*, Philostr.*Her.*12ᵇ, cf. Philostr. Jun.*Im.*2. III. *shake off* the yoke *from the neck*, *get free by struggling*, Phld.*Lib.*p.34 O., Ph.1.305.

ἀπαφίνιον, τό, *stone kneading-trough* (Lacon.), Hsch.

ἀπᾰφίσκω, *cheat*, *beguile*, mostly in compos. with παρά and ἐξ:—of the simple word Hom. has only ἀπαφίσκει Od.11.217: aor. opt. ἀπάφοιτο in act. sense, 23.216:—later, ἀπάφῃ *APl.*4.108 (Jul.); ἀπαφών Opp.*H.*3.444; ἤπαφες, ἤπαφε, Q.S.3.49, Nonn.*D.*5.512: aor. 1 ἀπάφησε ib.8.129, Q.S.13.280, 2 sg. ἀπάφησας 3.502.

ἀπαφός· ἔποψ, Hsch.

ἀπαφούλιστορ· σταφυλῖνος (Lacon.), Hsch.

ἀπαφρίζω, *skim*, esp. of honey, *Gp.*8.29 and 32, Orib.5.33.4:—Pass., Gal.6.283, *Gp.*8.27.2, Philagr.ap.Orib.5.21.1.

ἀπάχεια [πᾰ], ἡ, *thinness*, Eust.641.33.

ἀπᾰχής, ές, *without thickness* or *solidity*, Eust.641.35.

ἀπαχλυόομαι, *have blurred vision*, Aret.*SD*2.3.

ἀπαχλύω, *free from darkness*, Q.S.1.79.

ἄπᾰχος, ον, paraphrase of νεαρός, f. l. in Procl.*Par.Ptol.*43.

ἀπᾰχῠρίζω, (ἄχυρον) *winnow*, Sch.Nic.*Th.*114.

ἀπεγγυᾰλίζω, *give up*, *deliver again*, Hsch.

ἀπεγνωσμένως, Adv. pf. part. Pass. of ἀπογιγνώσκω, *desperately*, Plu.*Nic.*21.

ἀπεδᾰνός, όν, = ἠπεδανός, Hsch. s. h. v.

ἀπέδεσθαι, **ἀπεδήδοκα**, v. ἀπεσθίω.

ἀπεδίζω, (ἄπεδος) *level*, ἠπέδιζον τὴν ἀκρόπολιν Clitod.22.

ἀπέδῐλος, ον, *unshod*, A.*Pr.*135, Nonn.*D.*5.407, al.:—also **-δίλωτος**, ον, Call.*Cer.*124.

ἀπεδοποιέω, v. ἀπειδοποιέω.

ἄπεδος, ον, (ἀ- copul., πέδον) *level*, *flat*, χώρη Hdt.1.110, cf. 9.25, 102, Th.7.78, X.*Cyn.*6.9:—Subst. ἄπεδον, τό, *flat surface*, Hdt.4.62.

ἄπεζος, ον, (πέζα) *footless*, Lyc.629.

ἀπεθίζω, *disaccustom*, τιμωρίαις ἀ. τινά Aeschin.1.58: c. inf., ἀ. μὴ ποιεῖν *accustom* or *teach not* to do something, ib.152; τινός τινα Philostr.*VS*1.25; τινὸς τὸ σῶμα Epicur.*Fr.*458, cf. Gal.16.141: pf. part. ἀπειθικώς Plu.*Alex.*40:—Pass., ἀπειθισμένος J.*BJ*5.13.4.

ἀπεθιστέον, *one must disuse*, *unteach*, *Gp.*14.7.5.

ἀπεῖδον, inf. ἀπῐδεῖν, aor. 2 with no pres. in use, ἀφοράω being used instead:—*look away from other things at*, and so simply, *look at*, πρός or ἔς τι Th.7.71, Luc.*DMar.*9.2, al.; πόρρωθεν ἀπιδεῖν Timocl. 21. II. *look away from*, and so, *despise*, Plu.2.107of (dub. l.). (In later Greek ἀφ-, ἀφίδω *Ep.Phil.*2.23.)

ἀπειδοποιέω, *construct according to a pattern*, *Inscr.Milet.* (Haussoullier p.163), in form ἀπειδοποιήθη; but more prob. from **ἀπεδοποιέω**, *make flat*, *smooth*, κατεξέσθη τὸ ὑπέρθυρον καὶ ἀ.

ἀπειθ-αρχία, ἡ, *disobedience to command*, Antipho Soph.72, D.C. *Fr.*57.17. **–εια**, ἡ, *disobedience*, X.*Mem.*3.5.5, D.H.9.41, Arr. *Epict.*3.24.24; υἱοὶ τῆς ἀπειθείας *Ep.Eph.*5.7; later **ἀπειθία**, ἡ, *BGU* 747 ii 14 (ii A.D.), etc., *Gloss.* **–έω**, Att. form of ἀπῐθέω (though even Trag. preferred ἀπιστέω, q.v. II), *to be disobedient*, *refuse compliance*, A.*Ag.*1049; opp. πείθομαι, Pl.*Phdr.*271b: freq. c. dat., *disobey*, οὐκ ἀπειθήσας θεῷ E.*Or.*31; ἀ. ἅμα νόμῳ καὶ τῷ θεῷ Pl.*Lg.*741d, etc.; τὰ μεγάλα ἀ. τινί *in* great matters, Id.*R.*538b; ἀ. ταῖς ἐνεχυρασίαις *not to abide by* them, Id.*Lg.*949d: later c. gen., ψαφίσματος *GDI*3705.111 (Cos); ἐντολῶν Lxx *Jo.*5.6. 2. of animals, X.*Cyr.* 7.5.62; of ships, τοῖς οἴαξιν ἀ. D.S.13.46. 3. of a woman, *refuse compliance*, Aristaenet.2.20.

ἀπείθη, **ἀπείθησαν**, Ion. aor. 1 Pass. of ἀφίημι.

ἀπειθήνιος, ον, *disobedient*, *BGU*747 i 6 (ii A.D.).

ἀπειθής, ές, *disobedient*, S.*Fr.*45; ἀ. τοῖς νόμοις Pl.*Lg.*936b; of ships, τοῖς κυβερνήταις ἀπειθεστέρας τὰς ναῦς παρεῖχον *less obedient to* them, Th.2.84, cf. D.C.50.29 (Comp.), Orph.*A.*247; στράτευμα X.*Eq.* 3.6; of horses, Id.*Eq.Mag.*1.3; ἀπειθέα τεύχειν work *disobedience*, Call.*Dian.*66. Adv. ἀπειθῶς, ἔχειν πρός τινα Pl.*R.*391b. b. *unbelieving*, Nonn.*D.*8.306. 2. of things, *inflexible*, *rigid*, κέντρον Ael. *NA*1.55; σιδήρου καὶ ἀδάμαντος ἀπειθέστεροι Ph.2.87; ὀδόντες ἀ. *unyielding*, Opp.*C.*2.511; χῶρος ἀ. *impracticable*, of Hades, Hermesian. 7.3; δίκη ἀ. Νεμέσεως *IG*4.444. II. Act., *not persuasive*, *incredible*, μῦθος Thgn.1235; *uninviting*, πρὸς τὴν γεῦσιν Hices.ap.Ath.3.87b, c; τὴν γεῦσιν Id.323a; of places, *difficult of access*, Ael.*Fr.*120.

ἀπεικ-άζω, fut. -άσομαι X.*Mem.*3.11.1, -άσω Plu.2.1135a:—Pass., aor. ἀπεικάσθην E.*El.*979, Pl.*Cra.*419d: fut. -ασθήσομαι Them.*Or.*2. 33a: pf. ἀπείκασμαι Pl.*Cra.*420d (on the augment v. εἰκάζω):—*form from a model*, *represent*, *express*, *copy*, of painters, ἀ. τὰ καλὰ τῶν ζῴων Isoc.1.11; τὸ σὸν χρῶμα καὶ σχῆμα Pl.*Cra.*432b, cf. *Criti.*107d, e; διὰ χρωμάτων ἀ. X.*Mem.*3.10.1; χρώμασι καὶ σχήμασιν Arist.*Po.*1447ᵃ 19: metaph., ἀ. ἑαυτόν τινι *conform* oneself *to*.., Pl.*R.*396d:—Pass., *become like*, *resemble*, τινί ib.563a, *Cra.*419c; ἀπεικασθεὶς θεῷ *in* a god's *likeness*, E.*El.*979. 2. *express by a comparison*, ἔχοιμ' ἂν αὐτὸ μὴ κακῶς ἀπεικάσαι S.*Fr.*149.2, cf. Pl.*Tht.*169b; οἷος γὰρ Ἀχιλλεὺς ἐγένετο ἀπεικάσειεν ἄν τις Βρασίδαν Id.*Smp.*221c; τὸ θάλλειν τὴν αὔξην μοι δοκεῖ ἀπεικάζειν τὴν τῶν νέων the word θάλλειν seems *to express* the growth.., Id.*Cra.*414a; ἀ. διὰ τοῦ ῥῶ *to express* by the sound of ῥ, ib. 426e:—Pass., *to be copied* or *expressed by likeness* τοῖς ὑπὸ τῶν κάτω ἀπεικασθεῖσι Id.*R.*511a; τὰ ἄλλα ἀπείργαστο εἰς ὁμοιότητα ᾧπερ (sc. τούτου ᾧ) ἀπεικάζετο Id.*Ti.*39e; ἀ. πρός τι *to be copied* in reference to.., i.e. from.., ib.29c. 3. *liken*, *compare with*, τινί τι E.*Supp.* 146, Pl.*Phd.*76e, *Grg.*493b, *Smp.*221d, al.; οὐ τοιοῦτόν ἐστιν ᾧ σὺ ἀπεικάζεις not such [as that] to which you *compare* it, Id.*Phd.*92b:—Pass., *to be likened* or *compared*, ἄρχουσιν Id.*Lg.*905e, al.; [τὸ ἀναγκαῖον] ἀπείκασται τῇ πορείᾳ Id.*Cra.*420d; [τὸ ψεῦδος] ἀπείκασται τοῖς καθεύδουσι ib.421b. II. ὡς ἀπεικάσαι, = ὡς ἐπεικάσαι, *as one may guess*, *to conjecture*, S.*OC*16, *Tr.*141, E.*Or.*1298. III. *imagine*, ἀ. χειρώσεσθαι (-ασθαι codd.) τὴν Σπάρτην D.S.15.65. **–ᾰσία**, ἡ, *representation*, μίμησις καὶ ἀ. Pl.*Lg.*668b, *Criti.*107b, Hierocl *in CA*27 p.484 M. **–ασμα**, ατος, τό, *copy*, *representation*, Pl.*Cra.*402d, 420c. **–ασμός**, ὁ, *representation*, Porph.*Abst.*4.7. **–αστέον**, *one must represent as like*, τινά τινι Pl.*Phdr.*27ce; ἀπειλητικὰ τὰ ὄμματα ἀ. X.*Mem.*3.10.8; *one must compare*, τί τινι Plot.5.6.4, cf. Men. Rh.p.349 S.

ἀπεικον-ίζω, (εἰκών) *represent in a statue*, *AP*12.56 (Mel.); *express*, ψυχῇ κάλλος ib.127 (Mel.); generally, *represent*, Porph.*Sent.*44:—Pass., *to be modelled*, Ph.1.106, al.; *to be described*, 1.561. 2. Med., *reflect*, *symbolize*, τὴν [τῶν ἀπορρήτων] δύναμιν Procl. *in Alc.* p.25 C., cf. *Inst.*209, Aristaenet.2.5. **–ισμα**, ατος, τό, = ἀπείκασμα, Socr.*Ep.*20, Ph.1.4, al., *BMus.Inscr.*481*.24 (Ephesus, ii A.D.), Phlp. *in Ph.*316.24.

ἀπεικότως, **ἀπεικώς**, v. ἀπέοικα.

ἀπειλέω (A), Elean ἀποϝηλέω, *keep away*, ἀπὸ τῶ βωμῶ *GDI*1159, cf. 1150; ἀπὸ μαντείας 1154:—Pass., ἐς ἀπορίην ἀπειληθείς or ἀπειλημένος *brought* into great straits, Hdt.1.24, 2.141; ἐς ἀναγκαίην ἀπειλημένος Id.8.109; ἀπειληθέντες ἐς στεινὸν *forced* into narrow compass, Id.9.34. II. *unroll*, *roll off*, Hero *Aut.*5.5.

ἀπειλέω (B), 3 dual impf. Act. ἀπειλήτην, Ep. for ἠπειλείτην, Od. 11.313: later Ep. pres. **ἀπειλείω** Musae.122, Nonn.*D.*20.204:—*hold out* either in the way of *promise* or *threat*, and therefore: I. sts. in good sense, *promise*, οὐδ' ἠπείλησεν ἄνακτι..ῥέξειν κλειτὴν ἑκατόμβην Il.23.863, cf. 872; also, *boast* or *brag*, ὥς ποτ' ἀπειλήσει 8.150; ἦ μὲν ἀπείλησας βητάρμονας εἶναι ἀρίστους Od.8.383, cf. Jul.*Or.*2. 57a. II. commonly in bad sense, *threaten*, in Hom. either abs., as Il.2.665, Od.21.368: or (more freq.) c. dat. pers., ib.20.272, etc.: c. acc. cogn., αἶψα δ' ἀναστὰς ἠπείλησεν μῦθον *spake a threatening* speech, Il.1.388; ἀπειλὰς ἀ., v. ἀπειλή; δείν' ἀπειλήσων ἔπη E. *Supp.*542: freq. with neut. Pron. or Adj., ἀ. τόγε θυμῷ Il.15.212; ταῦτα, πολλὰ ἀ., Hdt.7.18, 1.111, Th.8.33, etc.; πύργοις ἀ. δεινά A. *Th.*426; τοῦτ' ἀπειλήσας ἔχεις S.*OC*817. 2. with acc. of the thing threatened, θάνατον ἀ. ὃς ἂν.. Hdt.4.81; ξίφος Plu.*Pomp.*47; ζημίας ἀ. κατά τινος Id.*Cam.*39; ἠπείλησαν τοὺς ἄρχοντας *threatened* *them with* the prefects, Lib.*Or.*47.7. 3. dependent clauses were added in fut. inf., γέρας..ἀφαιρήσεσθαι ἀπειλεῖς Il.1.161, cf. 15.179, Od.11.313; σφέας..ἀπείλεε ἐκτρίψειν Hdt.6.37; ἀ. δράσειν τι E.*Med.* 287; ἀ. ἀποκτενεῖν Lys.3.28: rarely in pres. inf., ἠπ...ἑλκέμεν Il. 9.682: after Hom. in aor. inf., X.*Mem.*3.5.4, *HG*5.4.7, Theoc.24. 16. 4. ἀ. ὅτι.., ὡς.., Ar.*Pl.*88, X.*An.*5.5.22, etc.; ἀ. τινί, εἰ μή .. Id.*Cyr.*4.5.12. III. Pass., ἀπειλοῦμαι, of persons, *to be terrified by threats*, Id.*Smp.*4.31. 2. of things, τὰ ἀπειληθέντα, = ἀπειλαί, Pl.*Lg.*823c. IV. later in Med., with aor. 1 -ησάμην App.*BC*3.29, Polyaen.7.35.2: c. inf., *forbid with threats*, ἀπειλησώμεθα αὐτοῖς μηκέτι λαλεῖν *Act.Ap.*4.17.

ἀπειλ-ή, ἡ, mostly in pl., *boastful promises, boasts*, ποῦ τοι ἀπειλαὶ ἃς..ὑπίσχεο οἰνοποτάζων; Il.20.83; μέχρι τῶν ἀπειλῶν γενναῖος Lib. *Or.*59.118, cf. Eust.704.28. II. commonly in pl., *threats*, ποῦ τοι ἀπειλαὶ οἴχονται τὰς Τρωσὶν ἀπείλεον υἷες Ἀχαιῶν; Il.13.219; οὐδὲ.. λήθετ' ἀπειλάων τὰς ἀντιθέῳ Ὀδυσῆι πρῶτον ἐπηπείλησεν Od.13.126, cf. Il.16.200, Hdt.6.32; εὐθύνειν ἀπειλαῖς καὶ πληγαῖς Pl.*Prt.*325d, cf. A.*Pr.*175(lyr.): in sg., S.*Ant.*753, Th.4.126; ἀπειλῆς ἕνεκα τοῖς ἐν τῷ Ταρτάρῳ Arist.*APo.*94ᵇ33. 2. of threatening conditions, ἀ. πνιγμοῦ Alex.Aphr.*Pr.*2.60; τὰ ἐν ἀπειλῇ ἀποστήματα Heras ap.Gal.13. 815; of storms, J.*BJ*1.21.5, Ael.*NA*7.7. **-ημα**, ατος, τό, = ἀπειλή, S.*OC*660(pl.). **-ησις**, εως, ἡ, *threat*, Phld.*Herc.*1251.8. **-ητήρ**, ῆρος, ὁ, *threatener, boaster*, Il.7.96, Call.*Del.*69, *AP*6.95 (Antiph.): as Adj., Nonn.*D.*4.378, al.:—fem. **-ήτειρα**, ib.2.257. **-ητήριος**, α, ον, *of* or *for threatening*, λόγοι Hdt.8.112. **-ητής**, οῦ, ὁ, = ἀπειλητήρ, D.S.5.31, J.*BJ*1.10.4. **-ητικός**, ή, όν, = ἀπειλητήριος, ῥήσεις Pl.*Phdr.*268c; νόμιμα Id.*Lg.*823c; ὄμματα X.*Mem.*3.10.8. Adv. -κῶς Phryn.*PS*p.61 B.

ἀπείλλω, v. ἀπίλλω.

ἄπειμι (A), (εἰμί *sum*), impf. ἀπῆν (later ἀπήμην *POxy.*1204.23 (iii A.D.)), 2 sg. ἀπῆσθα S.*Ph.*379; Ep. ἀπέην Il.20.7, 3 pl. ἄπεσαν ib.10. 357: fut. ἀπέσομαι Ar.*Nu.*887; Ep. ἀπέσσομαι Od.8.150, 3 sg. ἀπεσσεῖται ib.19.302:—*to be away* or *far from*, c. gen., ὁππότε πάτρης ἧς ἀπέησιν ἀνήρ ib.169, cf. 20.155, al.; ἐὰν δ' ἀπῇ τούτων σὺ χαίρειν S. *Ant.*1169; ἀ. ἀπὸ τῶν ἰδίων Th.1.141: c. dat., φίλοισιν E.*Med.*179 (lyr.), cf. *Tr.*393, Hdt.4.1, Th.2.61, etc.: but mostly, 2. abs., *to be away* or *absent*, and of things, *to be wanting*, οἵ τ' ὄντες οἵ τ' ἀπόντες, i.e. all that are, every one, S.*Ant.*1109; τὰς οὔσας τέ μου καὶ τὰς ἀπούσας ἐλπίδας Id.*El.*306; of the dead, v.l. in E.*Hec.*312; τοῦ θεοῦ ἀπεόντος the god *not being counted*, Hdt.6.53:—in 3 pl. impf., ἀπῆσαν and ἀπῇσαν are freq. confused in codd., as in Th.4.42.

ἄπειμι (B), (εἶμι *ibo*), serving as fut. of ἀπέρχομαι: inf. ἀπιέναι, in *AP*11.404 (Lucill.) ἀπίναι:—*go away, depart*, Od.17.593, al.; οὐκ ἄπει; = ἄπιθι, *begone*, S.*OT*431; ἀπιὼν οἴχεσθαι D.18.65, Isoc.17.43; οἱ πρέσβεις περὶ τῶν σπονδῶν ἀπῇσαν Th.4.39; of soldiers, ἀπίασι οὐδενὶ κόσμῳ *will retreat*, Hdt.8.60.γ'; ἀ. πρὸς βασιλέα *desert* to him, X.*An.* 1.9.29; ἀ. πάλιν *return*, ib.1.4.7, cf. 15; ἄπιτε ἐπὶ τὰ ὑμέτερα αὐτῶν *return* to your homes, Hdt.6.97; ἄπιμεν οἴκαδε Ar.*V.*255; ἀπῇσαν ἐπ' οἴκου Th.5.36; εἰς τὴν πατρίδα Arr.*Epict.*2.23.36; of the Nile, *recede*, Hdt.2.108; ἀ. ἐπί τι *go* in quest of.., X.*Cyr.*7.5.80; μηνὸς ἀπιόντος, for the common φθίνοντος, Decr.ap.D.18.37, *CIG*3658 (Cyzicus); *die*, Luc.*Tim.*15, Philostr.*Im.*2.9. 2. c. acc. cogn., πολλὴν καὶ τραχεῖαν ἀπιέναι (sc. ὁδόν) Pl.*Phdr.*272c. 3. *to be discharged*, Hp.*Mul.*8, al.

ἀπεῖπον, inf. ἀπειπεῖν, Ep. ἀπόειπεῖν, ἀπόειπέμεν, and part. ἀποειπών, i.e. ἀποϝειπών, Il.19.35, etc.: less freq. aor. 1 ἀπεῖπα Hdt.3.153, S.*Ant.*405: fut. in use is ἀπερῶ, pf. ἀπείρηκα, mostly in signf. IV. 3:—**Med.**, aor. 1 ἀπειπάμην Hdt.1.59, 5.56, Arist.*EN*1163ᵇ19, but never in correct Att.:—**Pass.**, fut. ἀπορρηθήσομαι Lys.22.14: aor. ἀπερρήθην Pl.*Lg.*929a, D.33.21:—pres. and impf. are supplied by ἀπαυδάω, ἀπόφημι, and in Att. Prose by ἀπαγορεύω:—*speak out, tell out, declare*, μῦθον Il.9.309, cf. 431; ἀγγελίην 7.416; ἀληθείην 23.361; ἐφημοσύνην Od.16.340; μνηστήρεσσιν ἀπειπέμεν (prob. μνηστῆρσ' ἀποειπέμεν) *to give* them *full notice*, ib.1.91; ἀπηλεγέως ἀποειπεῖν Il. 9.309, cf. Od.1.373; ῥῆσιν ἀπερέοντα *to deliver* a *verbal* message, Hdt. 1.152: in aor. Med., ἀπείπασθαι θανάτῳ ζημιοῦν τοὺς πλευσομένους Arist.*Mir.*837ᵃ2. II. *deny, refuse*, ὑπόσχεο καὶ κατάνευσον, ἢ ἀπόειπ' Il.1.515, cf. 9.510, 675; σύμφαθι ἢ ἄπειπε Pl.*R.*523a: c. acc., βοήθειαν Plu.*Tim.*2. III. *forbid* (cf. ἀπαγορεύω I), freq. in Prose, ἀ. τινι μὴ ποιεῖν *forbid* one *to do, tell* him *not to* do, Hdt.1.155, S.*OC*1760, Ar. *Av.*556; also without μή, Plb.2.52.8: with inf. omitted, ἀπειπὼν εἴργει μελάθρων A.*Ag.*1333, cf. S.*Ant.*405; ἀ. τινί τι *forbid* him *the use of* it, Arist.*Pol.*1264ᵃ21:—Pass., ἀπειρῆσθαι γάρ οἱ..μηδενὶ ἐπιδεικνύναι Hdt.6.61; τὸ ἀπειρημένον a *forbidden* thing, Id.3.52, Antipho 3.2.7; ἀπείρηται δὲ τοῦτο τῷ νόμῳ Xenarch.7.7; ἀπειρημένον, abs., *contrary to orders*, Arist.*Rh.*1373ᵇ10. IV. *renounce, disown, give up*, c. acc. rei, ἀ. μῆνιν Il.19.35; and not seldom in Prose, as εἴτε.. ἀπερέουσι..τὴν συμμαχίην Hdt.7.205; ἀπειπεῖν..κηρύκων ὕπο..πατρῴαν ἑστίαν *renounce* it by public proclamation, E.*Alc.*737; τὸν υἱὸν ὑπὸ κήρυκος ἀ. Pl.*Lg.*928d; πόνους E.*HF*1354; προξενίαν Th.5.43, 6.89; ὁμιλίαν Lys.8.6; ταῦτα μὲν οὖν ἀπείποι τις ἂν D.21.113; ἀ. τὴν στρατηγίαν *to resign* it, X.*An.*7.1.41; τὴν ἀρχήν Arist.*Pol.*1272ᵇ5; ἐλπίδας Plb.14.9.6; ἀ. γυναῖκα *divorce* her, Plu.*Luc.*38:—in Pass., αἱ σπονδαὶ οὐκ ἀπείρηντο *had* not *been renounced*, remained in force, Th.5.48; τὰς σπονδὰς μέλλειν ἀπορρηθήσεσθαι Lys.22.14:—in Med., ἀπείπασθαι παῖδα Hdt.1.59; συμμαχίην 4.120, 125; φιλίαν Plb.33.10. 5; ἀ. ὄψιν *averruncare*, Hdt.5.56; ἀ. υἱόν, πατέρα, Arist.*EN*1163ᵇ 19; ἀποϝειπάθθω (Cret. for ἀπειπάσθω) *let him renounce* the inheritance, *Leg.Gort.*11.11; ἀ. γνώμας *withdraw, retract* them, Plu.*Caes.* 8. 2. *refuse*, c. inf., Nonn.*D.*4.30. 3. intr., *fail, tire, sink from exhaustion*, ἐπεὶ δ' ἀπεῖπε S.*Tr.*789, cf. Ar.*Pax* 306, Pl.*Phdr.*228b, etc.; ἀπειρηκὸς σῶμα Antipho 5.93; γῆ ἀπειρηκυῖα Thphr.*CP*3.20.3; οὐ γάρ που ἀπεροῦμέν γέ πω *shall* not *give in* yet, Pl.*Tht.*200d; ἕως ἂν ἀπείπωσιν D.54.25, cf. 27; οἱ διὰ τὸν χρόνον ἀπειρηκότες Arist.*Pol.* 1329ᵃ33; οὐδ' ἀπεῖπεν..φάτις *was* not *unfulfilled*, A.*Th.*840. b. c. dat. pers., *fail* or *be wanting to* one, οὐκ ἀ. φίλοις E.*Med.*459. c. c. dat. rei, *fail* or *fall short in* a thing, ἀπειρηκότων δὲ χρήμασι *now that they are bankrupt*, D.3.8; ἀ. σώμασι Isoc.4.92, Lycurg.40; but, d. ἀ. κακοῖς, ἄλγει, *give way to, sink under* them, E.*Or.*91, *Hec.*942; ἀ. ὑπὸ πλήθους κακῶν X.*HG*6.3.15. e. ἀ. πρὸς τὸν φόνον *to be tired* of butchery, Plu.*Cam.*18; ἀ. ἐν τοῖς δράμασι Antiph.191. 14. f. c. pres. part., ἀ. ταλαιπωρούμεναι Ar.*Lys.*778; φέροντες ἀπεροῦσιν they *will be tired of* paying, Th.1.121; ἀ. λέγων *give over* speaking, Pl.*Lg.*769e; ἀπειρήκη τὰ ὄντα σκοπῶν I *had failed to*.., Id.*Phd.*99d, etc.

ἀπειρ-ἄγᾰθέω, *act without right knowledge*, Paul.Aeg.6.50. **-ᾰγᾰθία**, ἡ, *ignorance of goodness, folly*, Hierocl.p.54 A. **-άγᾰθος**, ον, *unacquainted with goodness, foolish*, Lxx *Es.*8.13. Adv. -θως D.S.15.40.

Ἀπειραῖος, α, ον, *Apeiraean*, and **Ἀπείρηθεν**, Adv. *from Apeire*, both in Od.7.8,9 γρηῢς Ἀπειραίη.., τήν ποτ' Ἀπείρηθεν νέες ἤγαγον. *Apeire* seems to be *Limitless-land* (from ἄπειρος B), an imaginary place; Hsch. expl. by ἠπειρωτική.

ἀπειράκις, Adv., (ἄπειρος B) *times without number*, Arist.*Ph.*193ᵃ 28, *Xen.*975ᵃ26, Plu.2.426e; πολλάκις, μᾶλλον δ' ἀ. Arist.*Pol.*1329ᵇ 27; οὐχ ἅπαξ οὐδὲ δὶς ἀλλ' ἀ. Id.*Cael.*270ᵇ19, cf. Phld.*D.*3 *Fr.*35; ἀπειράκις ἄπειρος Ph.1.499, Dam.*Pr.*21.

ἀπείρανδρος, ον, *that has not known man*, Hsch. s.v. μνηστή.

ἀπείραστος, ον, *incapable of being tempted*, κακῶν *Ep.Jac.*1. 13. II. *without experience*, τῶν ἀβουλήτων Alciphr.3.37. III. *not experienced*, Gal.13.459; *untried*, τέχνη Phld.*Rh.*1.45 S.

ἀπείρᾱτος, ον, Dor. and Att. for ἀπείρητος.

ἀπείρᾱτος, ον, (-π-τος, cf. πειραίνω) *impenetrable*, Pi.*O.*6.54. II. = ἄπειρος (B), v.l. in Hp.*Flat.*3, dub. in Dam.*Pr.*107.

ἀπειρᾰχῶς, Adv. *in an infinite number of ways*, Plu.2.732f, Procl. *in Prm.*p.581 S.

ἀπείργᾰθον, Ep. ἀποέργαθον (also ἀπεργ– Hsch.), poet. aor. 2 of ἀπείργω:—*keep away*, Πηλείωνα δόλῳ ἀποέργαθε λαοῦ Il.21.599; ῥάκεα μεγάλης ἀποέργαθε οὐλῆς he *pushed back* the rags *from* the scar, Od. 21.221; ἣν μή μ' ὁ κραίνων τῆσδε γῆς ἀπειργάθῃ S.*OC*862.

ἀπείργω, Ion. and Ep. **ἀπέργω**, in Hom. also ἀποέργω (i.e. ἀποϝέργω), also ἀπεέργει Hsch.: fut. ἀπείρξω: aor. ἀπείργαθον (q.v.); aor. also ἀπεῖρξα S.*Aj.*1280, Th.4.37, etc.:—**Pass.**, pf. inf. ἀπεῖρχθαι Phld.*Mus.*p.19 K.:—*keep away, debar from*, c. gen., ὁ δὲ Τρῶας.. αἰθούσης ἀπέεργεν Il.24.238; σφέας θυσιέων ἀπέρξαι Hdt.2. 124; ἀ. πόλεως ζυγόν A.*Th.*471; ἐγώ σφ' ἀπείργω..χαρᾶς S.*Aj.*51 (dub. sens.); οὐκ ἔστιν ὅτε ἀπειργομέν τινα..μαθήματος ἢ θεάματος Th.2.39, cf. 3.45; νόμων ἡμᾶς ἀπείργεις; do you *exclude* us *from* their benefit? Ar.*V.*467; δείπνου ἀ. τινά Cratin.57; ἀ. τινὰ ἀπό τινος Hdt.9.68:—Med. like Act., ἱκέτην ἀπείργεται A.*Ch.*569; but also, *keep one's hands off, keep away from*, ξένου Pl.*Lg.*879d. 2. *keep from* doing, *prevent* (ἀπείργω τὸν βουλόμενον ἐνεργεῖν τι, ἀνείργω τὸν ἀρξάμενον *AB*1331), c. acc. et inf., αὐγὰς ἀπείρξω σὴν πρόσοψιν εἰσιδεῖν S.*Aj.*70, cf. E.*Rh.*432, Antiph.126; μὴ ποιεῖν E.*Hel.*1559; ἀ. τι μὴ γίγνεσθαι Pl.*Lg.*837d:—Pass., *to be debarred from* doing, ἅπτεσθαί τινος Id.*Prm.*148e. 3. c. acc., *keep back, keep off, ward off*, μικρὸς δὲ λίθος μέγα κῦμ' ἀποέργει Od.3.296; ἀπὸ πάμπαν εἴργοντες (sc. τοὺς πολεμίους) Pi.*O.*13.59; τίς ταῦτ' ἀπεῖρξεν; S.*Aj.*1280; νόσους ἀ. E.*Ion*1013: abs., ἀλλ' ἀπείργοι θεός God *forfend!* S.*Aj.*949; ὅπου μὴ..καῦμα ἀπείργει Pl.*Ti.*22e, etc. b. νόμος οὐδεὶς ἀπεῖργε *checked* them, Th.2.53, cf. Democr.259; τὴν βίαιον τροφὴν ἀ. *prohibit* it, Arist.*Pol.*1338ᵇ41:—Pass., φυγῇ ἀπειργόμενος X.*HG*1.4.15. c. τὸ ἀπεργμένον the old bed of the Nile laid dry by *barring* or *damming off* the river, Hdt.2.99; ὁ ἀγκὼν..ὡς ἀπεργμένος ῥέῃ *dammed off*, ibid. II. *part, divide, separate*, ὅθι κληῖς ἀποέργει αὐχένα τε στῆθός τε Il.8.325:—and so, *bound, skirt*, of seas and rivers, etc., ὁ Ἅλυς ἔνθεν μὲν Καππαδόκας ἀπέργει, ἐξ εὐωνύμου δὲ Παφλαγόνας Hdt.1.72; πρὸς βορῆν ἄνεμον ὁ Κεραμεικὸς κόλπος ἀπέργει ib.174, cf. 204, 2.99, 4.55. 2. of travellers, ἐπορεύετο ἐν ἀριστερῇ μὲν ἀπέργων Ῥοίτειον πόλιν κτλ. *keeping* Rhoeteium on the left.., Id.7.43; ἐκ δεξιῆς χειρὸς τὸ Πάγγαιον ὄρος ἀ. ib.112, cf. 109, 8.35. III. *shut up, confine*, αἱ ἐσχατιαὶ τὴν ἄλλην χώρην ἐντὸς ἀ. Id.3.116; ἀπεργμένον ἐν τῇ ἀκροπόλει Id.1.154, cf. 5.64; ἐν τῷ ἱρῷ Id.6.79.

ἀπειρέσιος, α, ον, *boundless, immense*, γαῖα, ὀϊζύς, Il.20.58, Od.11. 621; δῆρις Batr.4; *countless*, ἄνθρωποι πολλοί, ἀπειρέσιοι Od.19.174, cf. Hes.*Fr.*134.4, Theoc.25.100; ὄρνιθες Simon.40; ἀ. εἶδος *untold* beauty, Hes.*Fr.*33; once in Trag., ἀ. πόνοι S.*Aj.*928 (lyr.): neut. as Adv., Q.S.2.179, 3.386. (Like ἀπερείσιος, by metrical lengthening for *ἀπερέσιος; root *per–* in πεῖραρ, ἄπειρος B.)

Ἀπείρηθεν, v. Ἀπειραῖος. **ἀπείρηκα**, v. ἀπεῖπον.

ἀπείρητος, Dor. and Att. **ἀπείρᾱτος**, ον, also η, ον *h.Ven.*133; *without trial*, and so: I. Act., *without making trial of, without making an attempt upon*, c. gen., ἀπείρητος..σταθμοῖο, of a lion, Il. 12.304: abs., *making no attempt* or *venture*, Pi.*I.*4(3).30. 2. *without trial* or *experience of, unknowing of*, φιλότητος *h.Ven.* l.c., cf. J.*BJ*3.4.1, Plu.2.681c, etc.; στρατὸν μὴ ἀπείρατον καλῶν Pi.*O.*11 (10).18; ἀλλοδαπῶν οὐκ ἀ. δόμοι not *unvisited by*.., Id.*N.*1.23; ἀ. πολεμίας σάλπιγγος *that never heard* an enemy's bugle, Demad.12: abs., *inexperienced*, opp. εὖ εἰδώς, Od.2.170, cf. Pi.*O*.8.61. Adv. ἀπειράτως, ἔχειν τινός Paus.10.7.1. II. Pass., *untried, unattempted*, οὐ μὰν ἔτι δηρὸν ἀ. πόνος ἔσται..ἦτ' ἀλκῆς ἦτε φόβοιο Il.17.41 (where however Nicanor took it in signf. 1.2); ἔστω μηδὲν ἀ. Hdt.7.9.γ'; οὐδὲν ἦν ἀπείρατον τούτοις κατ' ἐμοῦ D.18.249, cf. J.*BJ*7.8.1, Luc. *Tox*.3.

ἀπειρία (A), ἡ, (ἄπειρος A) opp. ἐμπειρία, *want of skill, inexperience, ignorance*, Hp.*Lex*4, Th.1.80; ἐμπειρία τε τῆς ἀπειρίας κρατεῖ E.*Fr.* 619; ἡ μὲν ἐμπειρία τέχνην ἐποίησεν ἡ δ' ἀπειρία τύχην Polus ap. Arist.*Metaph*.981a5; ὑπὸ ἀπειρίας Pl.*Tht*.167b; δι' ἀπειρίαν Id.*Grg.* 518d. 2. c. gen. rei, τοῦ θανεῖν E.*Fr*.816.10; ἀ. μέθης *want of skill to carry it discreetly*, Antipho 4.3.2; ἀ. ἔργου And.3.2; μουσικῆς ἀπειρίᾳ Philetaer.18; δι' ἀπειρίαν τοῦ ἐρωτᾶν καὶ ἀποκρίνεσθαι Pl.*R.* 487b; ἀπειρείῃσι νόοιο (sic) *Epigr.Gr*.1078.5 (Adana).

ἀπειρία (B), ἡ, (ἄπειρος B) *infinity, infinitude*, τὴν τῶν ὁμοιομερῶν ἀ. Anaxag.ap.Arist.*Metaph*.988a28; opp. πέρας, Pl.*Phlb*.16c; ἡ ἀ. καὶ ὁ αἰών Metrod.37, cf. Phld.*D*.3.11; ἀ. χρόνου Pl.*Lg*.676a; ἀ. τῶν κόσμων Epicur.*Ep*.1p.9U.; τῶν ἀτόμων Dam.*Pr*.98; τῶν ἀριθμῶν Ph. 1.10. 2. *eternity*, Arist.*Cael*.279a26.

ἀπείρῐτος, ον, = ἀπειρέσιος, Od.10.195, Hes.*Th*.109; *boundless, immense*, νῆσος D.P.4; γαῖα Orph.*Fr*.91, al.: neut. pl. as Adv., ἀπείριτα δηριόωντες Timo 12.

ἀπειρκτικός, ή, όν, *keeping out*, Alex.Aphr.*in Sens*.23.18.

ἀπειρο-βίως, Adv. *without experience of life*, Hierocl.p.55 A. **-γᾰμος**, ον, *unwedded*, νύμφα Eub.35; of Athene, Nonn.*D*.47.416, *Cat.Cod.Astr*.7.227. **-γονος**, ον, *infinitely generative*, δύναμις Dam. *Pr*.98,99. **-γρᾰφος**, ον, f.l. for ἀπερίγραφος, ib.272. **-γωνος**, ον, *with an infinite number of angles*, *Theol.Ar*.1. **-δακρυς**, υ, *ignorant of tears*, A.*Supp*.71. **-διοικήτης**, ου, ὁ, *director of the infinite*, *PMag.Par*.1.1354(pl.). **-δροσος**, ον, *unbedewed, parched*, E. *El*.735 (lyr.). **-δύναμος** [ῠ], ον, *of infinite potentiality*, ἡ τῆς ψυχῆς φύσις Porph.*Sent*.37, cf. Procl.*Inst*.84, Id.*in Prm*.p.642 S., Dam.*Pr.* 117, al., Simp.*in Ph*.608.36:—Subst. **-δῠναμία**, ἡ, *infinite potentiality*, Procl.*in Prm*.p.873 S., Simp.*in Ph*.1329.10. **-ειδής**, ές, *resembling the infinite*, Procl.*Inst*.159, Dam.*Pr*.210, Simp.*in Ph*.528. 13. **-θάλαττος** [θᾰ], ον, *unused to the sea*, Philostr.Jun.*Im.* 12. **-κᾰκος**, ον, *without experience of evil*: τὸ ἀ. *unsuspiciousness*, Th.5.105. II. *unused to evil* or *misery*, E.*Alc*.927. **-κᾰλεύομαι**, *lack taste*, Aeschin.*Ep*.10.1. **-κᾰλία**, ἡ, *ignorance of the beautiful, want of taste*, ἀμουσία καὶ ἀ. Pl.*R*.403c; ὑπ' ἀπειροκαλίας ib.405b; ἀ. περὶ χρήματα *vulgar* extravagance, Arist.*EN*1107b19; of literary style, D.H.*Dem*.23: in pl., *vulgarities*, X.*Cyr*.1.2.3. **-κᾰλος**, ον, *ignorant of the beautiful, tasteless, vulgar*, ἀ. καὶ ἀπαίδευτος Pl.*Lg.* 775b, cf. D.H.*Pomp*.2, etc.; περὶ λόγους ἀ. Plu.2.44d; ἀ. ἡγοῦμαι πάντων μεμνῆσθαι Ael.*Tact*.1.2; τὸ ἀ., = ἀπειροκαλία, X.*Mem*.3.10. 5. Adv. -λως Pl.*Phdr*.244c, etc.; *foolishly, rashly*, Onos.11. 4. **-λεχής**, ές, (λέχος) = ἀπειρόγαμος, Ar.*Th*.119; Φοίβη Orac. ap.Eus.*PE*4.23. **-λογία**, ἡ, (λόγος) *interminable argument*, S.E. *P*.2.151(pl.), prob. l. in Phld.*Rh*.1.7 S. **-μάχας** [μᾰ], α, ὁ, (Dor.) *unused to battle, untried in war*, Pi.*N*.4.30. **-μεγέθης**, ες, *immensely large*, S.E.*P*.3.44; διαστήματα Ph.1.605, cf. Cleom.2.1: metaph., χωρίον ἐπιστήμης Ph.1.627. **-μείζων**, ον, *infinitely greater*, v.l. for ἀπείρῳ μείζων, Cleom.2.1.

ἀπειρόμενος· ἀποφεύγων, Cyr., cf. Hsch.

ἀπειρό-μοθος, ον, *unused to toil*, Κυθερείη Nonn.*D*.24.294. 2. = ἀπειρομάχης, κεμάδες ib.20.260. **-πλᾰσίων**, ον, gen. ονος, *infinitely more, many thousand-fold*, Phlp.*in Mete*.17.15, Eust.89. 8. **-πληθής**, ές, *infinitely great or numerous*, Id.562.37, Sch.Nic. *Th*.310:—Subst. **-πλήθεια** or **-πληθία**, ἡ, Eust.202.43. **-πλους**, ουν, *ignorant of navigation*, Luc.*Dom*.12. **-ποιός**, όν, *producing infinitude*, δυνάμεις Procl.*in Prm*.p.567 S., cf. p.602 S., Dam.*Pr*.91 bis. **-πόλεμος**, ον, *inexperienced in war*, App.*Mith*.51; τὸ ἀ. D.H.8.37. Adv. -μως App.*BC*2.71. **-πονος**, ον, *unused to toil*, Κυθερείη Nonn.*D*.24.276.

ἄπειρος (A), ον, (πεῖρα) *without trial* or *experience of* a thing, *unused to, unacquainted with*, ἄθλων Thgn.1013; καλῶν Pi.*I*.8(7).70; κακότητος Emp.112.3; τυράννων Hdt.5.92.α'; τῆς ναυτικῆς Id.8.1; Περσέων Id.9.58, cf. 46; πόνων, νόσων, A.*Ch*.371, *Fr*.350.2; γνώμης S. *Ant*.1250; δικῶν Antipho 1.1; πολέμων Th.1.141; τοῦ μεγέθους τῆς νήσου Id.6.1; γραμμάτων Pl.*Ap*.26d; ἀνδρῶν ἀγαθῶν Lys.2.27; of a woman, ἄ. ἄλλων ἀνδρῶν *not having known* other men (beside her husband), Hdt.2.111; ἄ. λέχους E.*Med*.672: abs. in same sense, ib. 1091 (lyr.). 2. abs., *inexperienced, ignorant*, Pi.*I*.8(7).48, etc.; γλυκὺ δ' ἀπείροισι πόλεμος Id.*Fr*.110; δίδασκ' ἄπειρον A.*Ch*.118. Adv. ἀπείρως, ἔχειν τῶν νόμων Hdt.2.45; πρός τι X.*Mem*.2.6.29; περί τινος Isoc.5.19: Comp. ἀπειρότερον, παρεσκευασμένοι Th.1.49; -οτέρως Isoc.12.37, Arist.*Resp*.470b9.

ἄπειρος (B), ον, (πεῖραρ, πέρας) *boundless, infinite*, σκότος Pi.*Fr.* 130.8; τὸν ὑψοῦ τόνδ' ἄ. αἰθέρα E.*Fr*.941; ἤπειρον εἰς ἄ. ib.998; of number, *countless*, πλῆθος Hdt.1.204; ἀριθμὸς ἄ. πλήθει Pl.*Prm*.144a; ἄ. τὸ πλῆθος Id.*R*.525a, al.; εἰς ἄ. τὴν ἀδικίαν αὐξάνειν Id.*Lg*.910b; χρόνος ἄ. *OGI*383.113 (i B.C.): Comp. -ότερος Dam.*Pr*.50, Phlp.*in Mete*.17.15; τὸ ἄ. *the Infinite*, as a first principle, Arist.*Ph*.203a3, etc.; esp. in the system of Anaximander, D.L.2.1, etc.; but τὰ ἄπειρα *individuals*, opp. τὰ εἴδη, Arist.*Top*.109b14, cf. *Metaph*.999a27, al.; ἄπειρος, opp. πεπερασμένος, *Ph*.202b31; εἰς ἄ. ἰέναι, προϊέναι, ἥκειν, etc., *APo*.81b33, *Ph*.209a25, *EN*1113a2, etc.; [γῆ] ἐπ' ἄπειρον ἐρριζωμένη Str.1.1.20; also, *indefinite*, ὕλη *Stoic*.2.86. 2. in Trag., freq. of garments, etc., *in which one is entangled past escape*, i.e. *without outlet*, ἀμφίβληστρον A.*Ag*.1382; χιτών S.*Fr*.526; ὕφασμα E.*Or*.25. 3. *endless*, i.e. *circular*, ἀ. δακτύλιος a simple hoop-ring, = ἅλιθος (Poll. 7.179), Arist.*Ph*.207a2; cf. ἀπείρων (B) 1.3. Adv. -ρως, θρυφθῆναι *into an infinite number of* fragments, Id.*Pr*.899b16.

ἀπειροσύνη, ἡ, = ἀπειρία (A), E.*Hipp*.196, *Med*.1094, Cleanth.1.33.

ἀπειρο-τέρμων, ονος, ὁ, *limitless*, of God, *Corp.Herm*.18.12. **-τεχνής**, f.l. for -λεχής in Orac.ap.Eus.*PE*4.23. **-τοκος**, ον, *not having brought forth*, παρθενίη *AP*6.10 (Antip. Sid.). **-χρόνιος**, ον, *of infinite duration*, διαμονή Phld.*D*.3*Fr*.24.

ἀπειρόω, *multiply to infinity*, Dam.*Pr*.25 bis (Pass.).

ἀπειρωδίν, ῖνος, ἡ, *knowing not the pains of child-birth*, Nonn.*D*.16. 152.

ἀπείρων (A), ον, gen. ονος, (πεῖρα) = ἄπειρος (A), *without experience, ignorant*, S.*OT*1088 (lyr.), *Fr*.266.

ἀπείρων (B), ον, gen. ονος, (πεῖραρ, πέρας) Ep. form of ἄπειρος (B), *boundless, endless*, ἐπ' ἀπείρονα γαῖαν Od.1.98, Hes.*Th*.187; Ἑλλήσποντος ἀ. Il.24.545; δῆμος ἀ. a *countless* people, ib.776; ὕπνος ἀ. *seeming endless*, i.e. *profound* sleep, Od.7.286; ἀπείρονα γῆς βάθη Emp.39, cf. 28; τῶν ἀλιθίων ἀ. γενέθλα Simon.5.6; δόξα Pi.*P*.2.64; κύκλος a *vast* concourse, B.8.30. 2. = ἄπειρος (B) 2, *without end* or *escape*, δεσμοὶ ἀπείρονες Od.8.340. 3. In Att., = ἄπειρος (B) 3, *having no end, circular*, δακτύλιος ἀ. Ar.*Fr*.250, cf. *IG*2.709.5, 11(2). 161*B*81 (Delos, iii B.C.); ἐν λόχῳ ἀπείρονι, of persons standing in *a circle*, A.*Fr*.379.

ἀπείς, v. sub ἀφίημι.

ἀπεισουτῆρες· σκόλοπες, Hsch.

ἄπειστος, ον, (πείθω) *not to be persuaded*, πρὸς δωροδοκίαν Hyp. *Dem.Fr*.4.

ἀπέκ, Prep. with gen., *away out of*, v.l. in *h.Ap*.110.

ἀπεκ-βαίνω, *turn out, come to be*, ὥσπερ τι τέρας Eust.1062. 61. **-βάλλω**, *turn out*, Sch.A.*Pr*.84. **-βιόω**, aor. ἀπεξεβίω, *cease living*, Hsch. **-βολή**, ἡ, (ἀπεκβάλλω) *expulsion*, Sch.Dosiad. *Ara.* **-γονος**, ὁ, ἡ, *great-great-grandchild*, Simon.112.3. **-δέχομαι**, *expect anxiously, await eagerly*, σωτῆρα *Ep.Phil*.3.20; θάνατον Alciphr.3.7; τὸ μέλλον Hld.2.35, cf. S.E.*M*.2.73. II. *misunderstand, misinterpret*, Hipparch.1.6.11, al. b. *understand* a word *from* the context, A.D.*Conj*.226.20. **-δίδωμι** *relet* (after cancelling a contract), *CIG*2266 (Delos); simply, *contract for*, στήλην *Michel*468.72 (Iasus); ὅπως στήλη κατασκευασθῇ ib.481.31 (Priene). **-δῐκέω**, = τιμωρέω, Sch.E.*Hec*.749. **-δοσις**, εως, ἡ, *contract*, -σιν ποιῆσαι *Milet*6.36 (-έγδ- lapis), cf. *PPetr*.2p.34; *performance of* work *contracted for*, ἐν τῇ ἀ. τῶν ἔργων *PSI*4.352.5 (iii B.C.). **-δύομαι**, fut. -δύσομαι [ῡ]: aor. 1 -εδῡσάμην:—*strip off oneself*: metaph., *put off*, τὸν παλαιὸν ἄνθρωπον *Ep.Col*.3.9. II. *strip off for oneself, despoil*, τινά ib.2.15. **-δῠσις**, εως, ἡ, *putting off* (like clothes), ib.11.

ἀπεκεῖθεν, Adv. *thence*, Olymp.*in Mete*.119.28 (better divisim).

ἀπεκέλλερεν· ἀπέκλεψεν, Hsch.

ἀπέκιξα, v. κίκω.

ἀπεκ-λανθάνομαι, *forget entirely*, τινος, found only in aor. 2 imper., ἀπεκλελάθεσθε δὲ θάμβευς Od.24.394. **-λέγομαι**, *pick out and reject*, Dsc.1.7, Antip.*Stoic*.3.252, Arr.*Epict*.4.7.40. **-λεκτικός**, ή, όν, *fit for rejection*, ἀπαξία *Stoic*.3.28, cf. Antip.ib.251. **-λογή**, ἡ, *rejection*, opp. ἐκλογή, Diog.Bab.*Stoic*.3.219, cf. S.E.*M*.11.133: pl., Ph.*Fr*.8 H. **-λούομαι**, v.l. for ἐκλ. in Dsc.1.99. **-λύω**, *relax, weaken*, Alex.Aphr.*Pr*.1.120 (dub.). **-ρίπτω**, *throw away*, *PMag.Par*.1.59. **-ρῦσις**, f.l. for ἀπέρασις, q.v. **-τᾰσις**, εως, ἡ, *spreading out*, Lxx *Jb*.36.29, Gal.19.447; f.l. for ἐπέκτασις in Ph. *Bel*.72.28:—also **-τανσις**, Anon.*in Rh*.146.1. **-τείνω**, *draw off*, τῆς θερμασίας ἐν τοῖς ἀγγείοις ἀπεκταθείσης Gal.17(1).114.

ἀπέκτητος, ον, = sq., *AP*5.269 (Paul. Sil.).

ἄπεκτος, ον, lit. *uncombed*: hence, *unshorn*, of sheep less than a year old, μὴ σφάττειν πρόβατον ἄ. ἢ ἄτοκον Androt.41, cf. Philoch.64.

ἀπεκφορέω, gloss on ἀπεξινησάμην, Hsch.

ἀπελᾰσία, ἡ, (ἀπελαύνω) *driving away*, *POxy*.1252r6 (iii A.D.), *PLond*.2.403.12 (iv A.D.).

ἀπέλᾰσις, εως, ἡ, *retirement* of cavalry, Arr.*Tact*.16.10(pl.).

ἀπέλαστος, ον, *unapproachable*, dub. in Simon.29.

ἀπελᾰτέος, α, ον, *to be driven away*, Philostr.*VA*6.16.

ἀπελάτης [λᾰ], ου, ὁ, *driver away, cattle-lifter*, Ptol.*Tetr*.180, Just. *Nov*.22.15.1.

ἀπελαύνω, also ἀπέλα as imper. from pres. ἀπελάω, X.*Cyr*.8.3.32; Dor. impf. ἀπήλαον vulg. in Ar.*Lys*.1001 (but prob. ἀπήλααν, = ἀπήλασαν, should be read): fut. -ελάσω Lxx *Ez*.34.12; Att. -ελῶ (also in Hdt.8.102): pf. -ελήλακα X.*Cyr*.4.2.10:—**Pass.**, aor. -ηλάθην [ᾰ]: pf. part. ἀπεληλαμένος Artem.4 *Prooem.*:—**Med.**, aor. -ηλασάμην *AP*7.303 (Antip. Sid.):—*drive away, expel from* a place, τινὰ δόμων, πόλεως, etc., E.*Alc*.553, etc.; ἀπὸ τόπου X.*Cyr*.3.2.16; ἀ. τινά *drive away, banish* him, S.*OC*93,1356, etc.; *expel* (from a society), X.*An.* 3.1.32; *exclude, keep at a distance*, Ar.*Eq*.58; *remove*, φόβον τινὶ X. *Cyr*.4.2.10; *exclude from* a thing, Id.*HG*3.2.31:—Med., ἀ. τί τινος *ward off, avert from* him, *AP* l.c. 2. ἀ. στρατιήν *lead away* an army, Hdt.4.92: freq. abs. like ἀπάγω, *march, depart*, ἐς τὰς Σάρδις Id.1.77, cf. 5.25, etc.; πυρώσας τὰς Ἀθήνας ἀπελᾷς Id.8.102; also (sc. ἵππον) *ride away*, X.*Smp*.9.7, etc. II. Pass., *to be driven away*, ἐνθεῦτεν Hdt.5.94; ἐντεῦθεν εἰς ἄλλον τόπον X.*Cyr*.1.2.3; γῆς ἐμῆς πρός τινος S.*OC*599; *to be excluded from* a thing, ἀπάσης [τῆς στρατιῆς] *from* the command, Hdt.7.161, cf. X.*Cyr*.1.2.15; τῆς πολιτείας Lys.18.5; τῶν ἀρχῶν Pl.*R*.564d; ἀ. τῆς φροντίδος *to be far* *from*, Hdt.7.205; ἐς πατέρ' ἀπηλάθην τύχης *was barred from* [good] fortune on my father's side, E.*HF*63; ἀ. φιλίας Them.*Or*.7.90c.

ἀπελεγκτής, οῦ, ὁ, *one who refutes*, Oenom.ap.Eus.*PE*6.7.

ἀπελεγμός, ὁ, *refutation, exposure*, *Act.Ap*.19.27.

ἀπελέγχω, strengthd. for ἐλέγχω, *convict, expose, refute*, Antipho 5.19; τινά τινος Ph.1.205; εὐχέρειαν ἑαυτοῦ ib.193; τὴν διάνοιαν, εἰ .. M.Ant.8.36: abs., *procure a conviction*, *CIG*4325*k* (Olympus); *vindicate*, ἀ. τὸν τόκον γνήσιον Jul.*Or*.2.81d:—Pass., *to be convicted*, πείσας *of* having persuaded, Antipho 5.21.

ἀπέλεθρος, ον, *immeasurable*, ἶν' ἀπέλεθρον ἔχοντας Il.5.245, cf. Od. 9.538; ἀπέλεθρον ἀνέδραμε sprang back *immeasurably*, Il.11.354; *countless*, Nonn.*D*.19.330.

ἀπελέκητος, ον, *unhewn, unwrought*, Lxx 3*Ki*.6.1, al.: metaph., φωνή Crantor ap.D.L.4.27.

ἀπελευθερ-ία, Ion. -ίη, ἡ, *enfranchisement of a slave*, Aeschin.3.41, Man.4.600. II. *status of a freedman*, Poll.3.83. **-ιάζω**, *to be free, act freely*, -άζουσα κίνησις Ph.1.419, cf. 277; in bad sense, ὑπ' αὐθαδείας Id.2.31. **-ικός**, ή, όν, *in the condition of a freedman*, ἄνθρωπος Plu.*Sull*.1, *Cic*.7; γυνή *PGnom*.83 (ii A.D.); γένος Str.8.6.23. II. *relating to freedmen*, νόμοι D.ap.Poll.3.83. **-ισμός**, ὁ, *manumission*, *IG*9(1).109 (Elatea). **-ίωσις**, εως, ἡ, = foreg., ib.190 (Phocis). **-ιωτής**, οῦ, ὁ, *freedman*, Str.5.3.7 (v.l. ἀπελευθέρων). **-ος**, ὁ, *restored to freedom*, S.*Ichn*.193; *emancipated slave, freedman*, Pl.*Lg*.930d; ἀ. τινος Lys.7.10; opp. δοῦλος and μέτοικος, X.*Ath*.1.10, Arist.*Pol*.1278ᵃ2; ἀ. ἀφιέναι τινά Aeschin.3.41: metaph., ἀ. Κυρίου 1*Ep.Cor*.7.22:—fem. **ἀπελευθέρα**, Ion. -έρη, ἡ, Hp.*Epid*.5.75, Is.6.19, D.59.18, Men.436. **-όω**, *emancipate* a slave, Pl.*Lg*.915a sq., *POxy*.722.18 (i A.D.):—Pass., Pl.*Lg*.915b; αἱρεῖται ἐπίτροπον ὁ ἀπελευθερούμενος Arist.*Rh*.1408ᵇ25. **-ωσις**, εως, ἡ, *emancipation*, δούλων D.17.15, cf. Plu.*Publ*.7, *PGnom*.60 (ii A.D.), *BGU*96.10 (iii A.D.). **-ωτικός**, ή, όν, *concerning manumission*, νόμοι *SIG*1210 (Calymna); δίκαια *SIG*²868.9 (ibid.).

ἀπέλευσις, εως, ἡ, *dropping out*, of a letter, Eust.191.13.

ἀπέληκα (cf. λακίς)· ἀπέρρωγα (Cypr.), Hsch.

ἀπελίσσω, *unroll, unwind*, ἀγαθίδα Aen.Tact.18.15:—Pass. in Ion. form ἀπειλισσομένης Hero *Aut*.2.7. II. *roll up*, aor. 1 ἀπείλιξαν D.C.46.36.

ἀπέλκω, Ion. for ἀφέλκω.

ἀπελλάζω, Lacon. for ἐκκλησιάζω, Plu.*Lyc*.6.—Hsch. writes ἀπελάζειν, but quotes **ἀπέλλαι**· σηκοί, ἐκκλησίαι; ἐν ταῖς μεγάλαις ἀπέλλαις *IG*5(1).1144.21, 1146.41 (Gythium, i B.C.).

ἀπελλαῖα, τά, *sacrifice at meeting* of a φρατρία, *Michel*995*A*4 (Delph.).

Ἀπελλαῖος, ὁ, sc. μήν, name of a month in various Dorian states, as Delphi, *GDI*1721, al.; Epidaurus, *IG*4.925.1, etc.:—also **Ἀπελλαιών**, ῶνος, ὁ, at Tenos, ib.12(5).872.15.

ἀπελλακάς· ἱερῶν κοινωνούς, Hsch. **ἀπέλλειν**· ἀποκλείειν, Id.

ἀπέλλητος, ὁ, = ἀνταγωνιστής, A.*Fr*.415.

ἀπελλόν· αἴγειρος, Hsch.

Ἀπέλλων, ὁ, Dor. form of Ἀπόλλων, *IG*5(1).145 (Amyclae), *GDI* 5075 (Cret.), etc.; cf. Ἀπείλων *Inscr.Cypr*.140 H.

ἄπελος, τό, *wound not skinned over*, Call.*Fr*.343.

ἀπελπ-ίζω, Att. fut. -ιῶ D.S.19.50: pf. -ήλπικα:—*despair of*, τῆς πόλεως τὴν σωτηρίαν Hyp.*Ath*.35; τὸ μέλλον Epicur.*Ep*.3p.62 U.; πράξεις Plb.1.19.12, etc.:—Pass., *to be given up in despair*, τὰ πράγματα Id.10.6.10; of persons, *to be despaired of*, οἱ ἀπηλπισμένοι Lxx *Is*.29.19, cf. Plb.9.5.2; ὑπὸ τῶν ἰατρῶν D.S.1.25, D.L.8.69, cf. *IG* 14.966 (ἀφηλπ-). 2. ἀ. τινός *despair of*, Plb.1.55.2, al.; οὐκ ἀ. τινός *to be confident of*, Gal.8.365; περὶ τῆς νίκης D.S.2.25. 3. abs., *hope* that a thing will *not* happen, D.L.1.59. II. causal, *drive to despair*, τινά *AP*11.114 (Nicarch.). III. *hope to receive back*, μηδὲν (v.l. μηδένα) ἀπελπίζοντες *Ev.Luc*.6.35 (dub.). **-ισμός**, ὁ, *hopelessness, despair*, Plb.30.32.11. **-ιστέον**, *one must despair*, Posidon. ap.Aët.6.20, Ph.2.422, Orib.14.42.3. **-ιστία**, ἡ, *despair*, Tz.*H*. 11.18 (pl.). **-ιστος**· *desperatus*, *Gloss*.

ἀπεμέσω· ματαίῳ, Hsch.

ἀπεμέω, Ep. aor. -εσσα, *spit up, vomit forth*, Il.14.437, Hp.*Aff*.15, Opp.*H*.1.560, Arist.*Pr*.871ᵃ21, Ael.*NA*9.66, Luc.*Cont*.7, Gal.14. 163:—Pass., ἀπεμούμενα Arist.*Pr*.926ᵇ26.

ἀπεμπολ-άω, *sell*, ἀπημπόλα με λάθρα E.*Ion*1371; ἀ. τι ἀντί τινος *to sell for* a thing, Id.*Cyc*.257; τί τινος X.*Smp*.8.21, cf. Herod.7.65; ἀ. τινὰ εἰς λατρείαν Luc.*Merc.Cond*.23; *sell*, i.e. *betray*, ἡ μὲν Ἄργος βαρβάροις ἀπημπόλα E.*Tr*.973; ἀ. ψυχάς *barter* your lives, Id.*Ph*. 1228; τίς ὢν σὺ τήνδ' ἀπεμπολᾷς χθονός; *dost* thou *smuggle* her *out of* the country? Id.*IT*1360; ἀ. νόμους τοῖς δεομένοις Procop.*Pers*.1. 24:—Pass., ἀπεμπολώμενοι 'bought and sold', Ar.*Ach*.374.—An Ion. form ἀπεμπολέω is found in D.H.7.63, Max.Tyr.33.8, Luc.*Tox*. 28. **-ή**, ἡ, *sale*, Hsch.; also, = sq., Id. **-ησις**, εως, ἡ, *riddance*, ἀκαθαρσίας Hp.*Decent*.5. **-ητής**, οῦ, ὁ, *seller, dealer*, Lyc.341.

ἀπεμ-φαίνω, *to be incongruous, inconsistent*, Plb.6.47.10, A.D. *Synt*.324.23; ἀπεμφαῖνον *incongruous*, *Stoic*.2.51, Str.8.3.17, Jul.*Or*. 7.217c, Dam.*Pr*.229; *to be absurd*, A.D.*Synt*.47.8, S.E.*P*.3.112; -οντες θρῆνοι *discordant*, Marin.*Procl*.33; of verses faulty in metre, Aristid.Quint.1.28; τοῦ ἀπεμφαίνοντος ὀνόματος of a word similar in meaning but *different in form* (?), Demetr.Lac.*Herc*.1012.74:—Pass., *to be distinguished*, A.D.*Pron*.46.1. II. *display*, ἀλαζονείαν.. διὰ τῶν προσώπων Malch.p.397 D. **-φασις**, εως, ἡ, *incongruity, absurdity*, Str.10.2.12; *contradiction*, εἰς -σιν περικλείεσθαι S.E.*M*. 11.162. **-φερής**, ές, *unlike*, Thphr.*HP*8.8.5.

ἀπέναντι, Adv., (ἔναντι) *opposite*, c. gen., Plb.1.86.3, Lxx *Ge*.21. 16, *PGrenf*.1.21.14 (ii B.C.), *IG*2.489*b*17, *Ev.Matt*.27.61; *before, in the presence of*, ἀ. ὑμῶν *Act.Ap*.3.16; *against*, c. gen., Lxx *Si*.37.4, *Act.Ap*.17.7. 2. abs., εἰς τὸν ἀ. βουνόν *Inscr.Prien*.37.168. 3. = κατὰ ἀνατολὰς νότου, Hsch.

ἀπεναντίον, Adv. = foreg., ἡ ἀ. (sc. χώρα) the *opposite* shore, ἐς τὴν ἀ. Hdt.7.55, cf. Str.7.6.2, D.S.19.38: c. dat., Gal.*UP*1.9: c. gen., *from before*, Lxx *Ca*.6.4: Geom., of angles, ἡ ἀ. γωνία the *opposite* angle, Euc.1.16, al.; of sides of a figure, Archim.*Aequil*.2.1, hence, II. Adj. **ἀπεναντίος**, ον, Procop.*Aed*.1.11. Adv. -ίως v.l. in Luc.*Nigr*.36.

ἀπενᾰρίζω, (ἔναρα) *strip of arms*, c. dupl. acc., τοὺς ἐνάριζον ἀπ' ἔντεα Il.12.195, 15.343.

ἀπενάσσατο, 3 sg. aor. 1 Med. of ἀποναίω.

ἀπενδονικώς· φυγών, Hsch.

ἀπένεικα, ἀπενείχθην, v. ἀποφέρω.

ἀπενεόομαι, Pass., (ἐνεός) *become mute*, Thd.*Da*.4.16.

ἀπενέπω, v. ἀπεννέπω.

ἀπενθ-ής, ές, *free from grief*, A.*Pr*.956; νεβρός B.12.87; θυμός *Fr*.7.2, cf. Plu.*Flam*.11, Tryph.599. **-ητος**, ον, = foreg., A.*Ag*. 895, *Eu*.912. 2. Pass., *unlamented*, Lxx 2*Ma*.5.10, *Epigr.Gr*. 436 (Berytus).

ἀπενῐαυτ-έω, = -ίζω, Pl.*Lg*.866c, 868c. **-ησις**, εως, ἡ, *banishment for a term of years*, τριετεῖς ἀ. ib.868e (v.l. -ισις). **-ίζω**, *go into banishment for a term of years*, X.*Mem*.1.3.13, Nic.Dam. p.18 D., Philostr.*VA*1.13; ἐνιαυτοὺς τρεῖς ἀ. Pl.*Lg*.868d. II. *outlive the year* after a thing, D.C.46.49. **-ισμός**, ὁ, = ἀπενιαύτησις, *AB*421, Hsch.

ἀπεννέπω, Trag. word, also **ἀπενέπω** (only lyr. E.*IA*552), *forbid*: abs., A.*Th*.1058, E.*Ph*.1657; ἀ. τι *forbid* it, S.*OC*209; more freq. c. acc. et inf., ἀ. τινὰ ποιεῖν E.*Med*.813, *Heracl*.556; ἀ. τινὰ μὴ ποιεῖν Id.*Ion*1282, *HF*1295; ἀ. τινὰ θαλάμων *order* him *from* the chamber, Id.*IA*552 (lyr.). 2. c. acc. rei, *deprecate*, ἀνδροκμῆτας δ'.. ἀπεννέπω τύχας A.*Eu*.957 (lyr.).

ἀπεντάσσω, *put back in its place*, of the prolapsed uterus, Sor.2.88.

ἀπεντεῦθεν, Adv. *at this point*, Plb.39.1.1. II. *henceforth*, *POxy*.93.16 (iv A.D.), Eustr. *in EN*339.16.

ἀπέξ, v. ἀπέκ.

ἀπεξ-αιρέω, *take out, remove*, τί τινος E.*IT*1278 (tm.). **-αρτάω**, *hang out*, τι ἐκ τόπου Anon.ap.Suid. s. v. κυνζόμενον. **-έβαι**· τὸ ἀποπατεῖν (Cret.), Hsch. **-ηγέομαι**, *narrate*, cj. in X.Eph.5. 9. **-ῑνόω**, *purge*, prob. in Timocl.39; also aor. Med. ἀπεξινησάμην (from -αω) Hsch. **-ῐσάζω**, *equalize*, Steph. *in Int*.16. 33. **-ωθέω**, *drive out, expel*, *AB*1454.

ἀπέοικα, *to be unlike, differ from*, c. gen., Plu.*Per*.8, Arr.*Ind*.6.8, Lib.*Or*.59.157:—in early writers found only in part. **ἀπεοικώς**, Att. **ἀπεικώς**, υῖα, ός, *unreasonable, unnatural*, οὐκ ἀπεικός (v.l. ἀπεοικός) Hp.*VM*4, Antipho 2.2.5; οὐκ ἀπεικός not *unlikely*, Plb.2.62.8, cf. Philostr.*VA*3.34; ἀπεοικὼς πρὸς τὰ καλά *unfitted, indisposed* for noble deeds, Plb.6.26.12: c. dat., *unlike*, Heph.15.4. Adv. ἀπεοικότως *unreasonably*, Th.6.55; but οὐκ ἀπεικότως Th.1.73, 2.8, 8.68, cf. Porph.*Abst*.1.46; D.Chr. has ἀπεοικότως 12.35, ἀπεικότως 31.116.

ἀπέπαντος, ον, (πεπαίνω) *not ripened, unripe*, Thphr.*CP*2.8.4, *AP* 9.561 (Phil.), Dsc.5.34; cf. ἀπεπαν[ό]τος· ὁ μὴ παλαιούμενος, Hsch.

ἀπεπείγομαι, *hasten away*, ἄλλοσε Man.5.239.

ἀπέπειρος, ον, *unripe*, ὀπώρα *AP*9.78 (Leon.).

ἄπεπλος, ον, *unrobed*, i.e. *in her tunic only*, of a girl, ἄπεπλος ὀρούσαισ' ἀπὸ στρωμνᾶς Pi.*N*.1.50; λευκῶν φαρέων ἄπεπλος, i.e. clad in black, E.*Ph*.324 (lyr.).

ἀπεπορίανεν· ἀπεχλωρίασεν, Hsch.

ἀπεπτέω, *suffer from indigestion*, Luc.*Par*.57, Plu.2.136d, Arr. *Epict*.1.26.16, Cass.*Pr*.74. 2. Pass., of food, *to remain undigested*, Gal.6.628, Mich. *in EN*56.21.

ἄπεπτος, ον, (πέσσω) *uncooked*: *undigested*, of food, Hp.*Epid*.1. 26.β', Arist. *de An*.416ᵇ5, al.; of humours, *crude, unconcocted*, Hp. *VM*19; οὖρον Id.*Acut*.42; φύματα Id.*Art*.41, cf. Arist.*Mete*.384ᵃ33: Comp., Id.*GA*750ᵇ25: Sup., ib.745ᵇ20. Adv. -τως Hp.*Epid*.1. 5. 2. metaph., Arist.*Mete*.371ᵃ3, Plu.2.495b. II. *suffering from indigestion*, Ruf.ap.Orib.7.26.99, Aret.*SD*2.3; τὸ στόμα τῆς γαστρὸς Alex.Aphr.*Pr*.1.45. III. χῶραι ἄ. countries *where fruits ripen ill*, Thphr.*CP*6.18.12 (Comp.).

ἄπερ, neut. pl. of ὅσπερ, q. v.

ἀπεραντο-λογέω, *talk without end*, Str.13.1.41. **-λογία**, ἡ, = ἀπειρολογία, Cic.*Att*.12.9, Luc.*DMort*.10.10, Gal.18(1).254. **-λόγος**, ον, *talking without end*, γλῶσσαι Thal.4 Bgk., cf. Ph.1.216: Comp. -ώτερος Gal.18(1).254.

ἀπέραντος, ον, (περαίνω) *boundless, infinite*, of space, πεδίον Pi.*N*. 8.38 (who also has ἀπείραντος ἀλκά *P*.9.35); πόντου κλῇδ' ἀ. E.*Med*. 213 (lyr.); τὸν ἀέρα τόνδ' ὄντ' ἀ. Ar.*Nu*.393; ὁδός Pl.*Tht*.147c; of time, *endless*, τὸ χρῆμα τῶν νυκτῶν ὅσον· ἀπέραντον Ar.*Nu*.3; χρόνος Pl.*Plt*.302a; of number, *countless, infinite*, ἀ. ἀριθμὸς ἀνθρώπων Id. *Criti*.119a; ἀ. κακά Id.*R*.591d, al.; λῦπαι Plu.*Sol*.7; πένθη *Fab*.17; *unlimited*, τιμωρίαι D.23.39; generally, of events, business, etc., ἀπέραντον ἦν there was *no end to it*, Th.4.36; μακρὸν καὶ ἀ. φαίνεται Arist.*EN*1101ᵃ26; ἀπέραντα περαίνειν represent as concluded *what is not concluded*, Luc.*Philops*.9 (with allusion to signf. III); μηδὲν ἀβασάνιστον μηδ' ἀ. Plb.4.75.3. Adv., τὸ ἀπεράντως διεστηκός of *unlimited* dimensions, Arist.*Ph*.204ᵇ21, *Metaph*.1066ᵇ33. II. *allowing no escape, whence none can pass*, Τάρταρος, δίκτυον, A.*Pr*.153, 1087 (both lyr.). III. in Logic, *inconclusive*, λόγος Phld.*Ir.*p.97 W., cf. *Stoic.*2.77. IV. *incomplete, imperfect*, of persons, ἀτελὴς καὶ ἀ. Artem.1.12.

ἀπέρᾰσις, εως, ἡ, (ἀπεράω) *spitting out, vomiting*, Plu.2.134e, Philum.*Ven.*17.6: metaph., Str.8.8.4 (ἀπέκρυσις codd.). II. *carrying off of moisture*, Thphr.*CP*2.9.8: metaph., Iamb.*Myst.*3.9.

ἀπέραστος, ον, *unsurpassed*, Aristeas 156 (v.l. ἀπέραντον).

ἀπερᾰτέον, *one must vomit*, Orib.*Fr.*53.

ἀπέρᾰτος, ον, (περάω) *not to be crossed* or *passed*, ποταμός Plu.2.326e, Luc.*VH*2.30: metaph., Διὸς οὐ παρβατός ἐστιν μεγάλα φρὴν ἀ. A.*Supp.*1049.

ἀπέρᾰτος, ον, (πέρας) *boundless*, Ph.1.554, al.; v.l. for ἀπέραντος in Pl.*Tht.*147c (Anon.*in Tht.*23.48), Sch.Ar.*Nu.*3.

ἀπεράτωτος [ᾰτ], ον, *unbounded*, Plu.2.424d, Dam.*Pr.*178; of fate (with play on πεπρωμένη), Plu.2.1056d.

ἀπεράω, fut. -άσω [ᾱ], *vomit, disgorge*, Archig.ap.Gal.13.174, Philum.*Ven.*17.6, Alciphr.3.7. II. of moisture, generally, *carry off*, Str.1.3.6:—Pass., prob. in Thphr.*CP*1.17.10.

ἀπεργ-άζομαι, pf. -είργασμαι, sts. Act., Pl.*Lg.*704c, *Ti.*30b, al., sts. Pass., *R.*566a, *Phdr.*272a, al.: aor. -ειργάσθην always in pass. sense, Id.*R.*374c, al.:—*finish off, complete, bring to perfection*, τὰ ξύλινα τοῦ τείχους Ar.*Av.*1154; freq. in Pl., ἔργον ἀ. *Grg.*454a, *R.*353c, 603a, al.; εὐδαίμονα πόλιν ἀ. *Lg.*683b; τόν τε πολιτικὸν ἀ. καὶ τὸν φιλόσοφον *Plt.*257a; ἡ τέχνη ἐπιτελεῖ ἃ ἡ φύσις ἀδυνατεῖ ἀπεργάσασθαι Arist.*Ph.*199ᵃ16. 2. of a painter, *fill up with colour, represent in a finished picture*, opp. ὑπογράψαι (*sketch*), ἀ. ἀκριβῶς Pl.*R.*548d. 3. *finish a contract*, X.*Mem.*1.6.5. II. *cause, produce*, Pl.*Ti.*28e, al.; τὸ πλέον καὶ τὸ ἔλαττον Id.*Phlb.*24e; δόξαν ψευδῆ ib.40d; νίκην καὶ σωτηρίαν Id.*Lg.*647b; πανουργίαν ἀντὶ σοφίας ib.747c; ὀσμήν Arist.*Fr.*368, etc.; folld. by inf., *enable*, τὸ ἀπεργαζόμενον ὀρθῶς χρῆσθαι Pl.*Euthd.*281a. III. c. dupl. acc., *make* so and so, ἀγαθὸν ἀ. τινα X.*Smp.*8.35; τοὺς παῖδας ἀ. δειλοτέρους Pl.*R.*381e, cf. *Plt.*287a, al.: pf. in pass. sense, ἀπειργασμένος τύραννος *finished* tyrant, *R.*566a; τέχνη ἀπειργασμένη *Phdr.*272a; ἀνὴρ ἀ. καλὸς κἀγαθός X.*Oec.*11.3. 2. ἀ. τινά τι *do* something *to* one, ὅ τι ἀγαθὸν ἡμᾶς ἀπεργάζεται Pl.*Chrm.*173a, cf. *Riv.*135e; ὅπερ ὕδωρ γῆν ἀ. as water *acts upon* earth, Id.*Ti.*61b. IV. *work off* a debt, Men.*Her.*36. **-ασία**, ἡ, *finishing off, completing*, of painters, πρὸς τὴν ἀ. τὴν τῶν εἰκόνων Pl.*Prt.*312d; *execution, workmanship*, Arist.*Po.*1448ᵇ18. II. *causing, producing*, ἀ. χάριτος καὶ ἡδονῆς Pl.*Grg.*462c; ἔργου, ὑγιείας, *Euthphr.*13d, e; ἐνύλων εἰδῶν Iamb.*Comm.Math.*9. III. *working off* of a debt, *IG*5(1).1390.77. IV. ἡ ἀ. τῶν νόσων *treatment*, Pl.*Alc.*2.140b; τοῦ χώματος *upkeep*, *POxy.*729.8 (ii A.D.). V. *efficacy*, ἡ ἐν ταῖς θυσίαις ἀ. Iamb.*Myst.*5.8, al. **-αστικός**, ή, όν, *fit for finishing, effecting, causing*, c. gen., Pl.*R.*527b, Epicur.*Sent.*26, Phld.*Rh.*1.345 S., S.E.*M.*4.4, etc.: ἡ -κή (sc. τέχνη) *the art of making*, τινός Pl.*Epin.*975c.

ἄπεργος, ον, *idle*, f.l. for ἀργός, Artem.1.42. II. *obsolete*, Phld.*Rh.*1.354 S.

ἀπέργω, v. ἀπείργω.

ἀπέρδω, *bring to an end, finish*, ἱρήϊα Hdt.4.62.

ἀπερεί, Adv. = ὥσπερεί, from ἅπερ, S.*El.*189 (lyr.).

ἀπερείδω, *fix, settle*, τὰς ὄψεις Plu.2.681f; τὴν ὄψιν πρός τι Luc.*Dem.Enc.*17; δι' ἄλλα τὴν γνῶσιν *support*, Iamb.*Protr.*5. 2. intr., = Pass., ἔνθα ἡ ὄψις ἀπερείδῃ Luc.*DDeor.*20.8; but, II. used by earlier writers in Med. with pf. Pass. in med. sense, *support oneself upon, rest upon*, ἀ. ἐν τῷ χαλινῷ, of a horse, *lean upon* the bit, X.*Eq.*10.7; ὀκτὼ τοῖς μέλεσι ἀ. *supporting himself on..*, Pl.*Smp.*190a, cf. *Ti.*44e, Arist.*PA*684ᵃ3; πείσμασιν, of a ship, Archimel.ap.Ath.5.209d, al.; ἀ. εἰς τοῦτο *to be fixed steadily on..*, Pl.*R.*508d; εἰς ἓν κεφάλαιον ἀ. *rest entirely on..*, ib.581a; ἀ. ἐπί τι *rely on*, Plb.28.20.8; πρὸς τὴν γῆν Hp.*Art.*52: abs., Arist.*IA*705ᵃ9. III. Med. in act. sense, ἀ. εἰς τοῦτο [τὸ οὖς] X.*Cyn.*5.32; τὴν χεῖρα πρός τινα Plu.*Sull.*35; τὰς ὄψεις εἴς τι Id.2.521d; ἀ. ἐλπίδας εἴς τινα, ἐπί τινα, *fix one's* hopes *upon* one, Plb.23.5.3, 28.2.3, cf. Plu.*Dio*42; ἀ. ὀργὴν εἴς τινα, χάριν ἐπί τινα, *direct one's* anger, *one's* gratitude, *towards* him, Plb.1.69.7, 23.3.6, cf. Plu.2.775e; ἀ. εἰς Περικλέα τὴν ὑπόνοιαν Id.*Per.*32; of Fortune, τὴν νέμεσιν εἰς τὸν οἶκον Id.2.198d; ἀ. ἄγνοιαν ἐπί τινας *throw the blame of* their ignorance *upon..*, Plb.38.9.5; ἐπὶ τὴν τύχην τοὺς ὀδυρμούς Plu.2.168a. 2. ἀ. λείαν εἰς τόπον *place, deposit in..*, Plb.3.92.9; τὰς δυνάμεις εἰς ἀσφαλὲς ἀπηρεῖσθαι Id.3.66.9; ὠδῖνας Call.*Del.*120.

ἀπερείσιος, ον, = ἀπειρέσιος (q.v.); ἀπερείσι' ἄποινα *countless* ransom, Il.1.13, al.; ἔδνα 16.178; δῶρα A.R.1.419; ἄλγος *AP*7.363.

ἀπέρει-σις, εως, ἡ, *leaning upon, pressure, resistance*, Pl.*Cra.*427a; ἀ. πρὸς τὰς χεῖρας Arist.*IA*705ᵃ18, cf. *Pr.*885ᵇ1. II. *infliction*, τιμωρίας Plu.2.1130d. **-σμα**, ατος, τό, *prop, stay*, Hsch.

ἀπερεύ-γομαι, *belch forth, disgorge*, τι Hp.*Morb.*2.60, Nic.*Al.*380, etc.; ἀ. ἄχνην, of a river, *empty itself*, D.P.693, 981. **-ξις**, εως, ἡ, *belching forth*, Aret.*SA*1.9.

ἀπερημόομαι, *to be left destitute of*, τῆς τοῦ δαίμονος ἐπιμελείας Pl.*Plt.*274b; *to be isolated*, ἀπὸ τῶν ὄντων Id.*Sph.*237d; ἀπηρημωμένος *in isolation*, ἐν ψιλὸν ἀ. Plot.6.6.11.

ἀπέρημος, ον, strengthd. for ἔρημος, Sch.Pi.*N.*4.88.

ἀπερητύω [ῠ], *keep back, hinder*, A.R.1.772.

ἀπερι-άγνιστος, ον, *not purified*, prob.l. for ἀπεριόριστος, Hsch. **-βλεπτος**, ον, *not looked at from all sides*: hence, *limitless*, ἀ. καὶ παμπληθῆ θεωρίας ἔκτασιν Iamb.*VP*29.162, cf. *AB*421; *incomprehensible*, Hsch., Suid. II. Act., *regardless*, Phryn.*PS*p.10 B. **-βλητος**, ον, *without* περιβολή (q.v.), λόγος Hermog.*Id.*1.11. **-γένητος**, ον, *not to be overcome*, D.S.3.30; φύσις Corn.*ND*31. **-γραπτος**, ον, *not cancelled, valid*, διαθήκη *PLond.*1.77.51. **-γρᾰφος**, ον, *not rounded*, περιόδου βάσις D.H.*Comp.*22. 2. *not circumscribed*, Ph.1.5, al., Procl.*Inst.*93, Dam.*Pr.*71; *undetermined*, of time, Chrysipp.*Stoic.*2.67. 3. *unlimited*, ἀριθμῷ *Stoic.*3.79. Adv. -φως Ph.1.47, Corn.*Rh.*p.396 H. **-έργαστος**, ον, *not wrought carefully, simple*, in Adv. -τως Hierocl.*Prov.*p.464 B. **-εργία**, ἡ, *artlessness*, Perict. ap.Stob.4.28.19. **-εργος**, ον, *not over-busy, artless, simple*, Hp.*Decent.*3; ἀγωγή Gal.13.168; of things, Dsc.*Eup.*1.35, Sor.2.11; ἀφελὴς καὶ ἀ. χρῆσις Ath.6.274a: Sup., ib.b; τὸ ἀ. *simplicity*, Plu.2.1144f, Ach.Tat.5.27. Adv. -γως Ceb.21, D.H.*Dem.*9, Sor.1.46, S.E.*P.*1.240, Ael.*VH*12.1.

ἀπερίζομαι, *contend*, Suid.

ἀπερι-ήγητος, ον, *not traced out*, ἀ. καθάπερ τινὶ περιγραφῇ Pl.*Lg.*770b; ἀ. τῷ πλήθει *innumerable*, Simp.*in Ph.*178.29. **-ήχητος**, ον, *not encompassed by sound*, *AB*422. **-θλάστως**, Adv. *without crushing*, Sor.2.60. **-κάθαρτος** [κᾰ], ον, *unpurified, impure*, Lxx *Le.*19.23, Ph.1.346. **-κάλυπτος** [κᾰ], ον, *uncovered, exposed*, in Adv. -τως *undisguisedly*, Hld.8.5. **-κοπος**, ον, *without hindrance* or *interruption*, in Adv. -πως Tz.ad Lyc.1432. **-κτητος**, ον, *not gaining wealth*, Ptol.*Tetr.*182. **-κτύπητος** [ῠ], ον, *not surrounded with noise*, Suid. **-λάλητος** [λᾰ], ον, *not to be out-talked* or *without skill in circumlocution*, Ar.*Ra.*839:—cf. Hsch. ἀπεριλάλητον (ἀπεριάλλητον cod.)· ἀνεξαπάτητον, ἀφελῆ. **-ληπτος**, ον, *uncircumscribed*, ἐξουσία ἀ. *absolute* power, Plu.*Pomp.*25; *indeterminate*, Theol.*Ar.*58; *not to be embraced* or *comprehended*, λόγῳ Ph.2.24; ἐπιστήμη Iamb.*VP*29.159: abs., τῷ ἀ. τῆς δυνάμεως Plot.6.9.6, cf. Procl.*Inst.*150; *incomprehensible*, Iamb.*Myst.*1.7, Dam.*Pr.*7; ἀ. κατὰ τὸν ἀριθμὸν κόσμοι Gal.8.159, cf. A.D.*Synt.*5.14; *indefinite* (opp. *infinite*) οὐχ ἁπλῶς ἄπειροι ἀλλὰ μόνον ἀ. Epicur.*Ep.*1 p.8 U., cf. *Placit.*1.3.8, Corn.*ND*9. **-λῦτος**, ον, *not annulled* or *cancelled, valid*, *BGU*1170.58 (i B.C.), *POxy.*713.39 (i A.D.). **-μάχητος** [μᾰ], ον, *not worth contending for*, δόγμα Ph.1.2. II. *free from need of contention*, βίος Max.Tyr.36.1. **-μέριμνος**, ον, in Adv. -νως *unthinkingly*, Ar.*Nu.*136. **-νόητος**, ον, *incomprehensible*, v.l. in S.E.*P.*2.70, Ph.1.581, Dam.*Pr.*4, *PMag.Par.*1.1138. 2. *inconceivable*, i.e. *indefinitely short*, χρόνος Epicur.*Ep.*1 p.10 U. II. *unintelligent*, Eust.644.43. III. Adv. -τως *inadvisedly*, Plb.4.57.10. 2. *imperceptibly*, S.E.*P.*3.145 codd. **-οδος**, ον, *not periodic*, D.H.*Comp.*23, cf. 26. **-οπτος**, ον, *unregarding, reckless of*, πάντων Th.1.41, J.*AJ*19.1.11: abs., Onos.1.22. Adv. -τως Poll.3.117. **-όριστος**, ον, *unlimited, infinite*, Longin.16.1, 44.6, Ph.1.187; ἐπιστήμαις ἀ. *undefinable*, Iamb.*Comm.Math.*7. Adv. -τως Gal.7.469. 2. of poems in uniform metre, *indefinite in length*, Heph.*Poëm.*6.2. **-ουσίαστος**, ον, *without wealth*, Eust.1768.54. **-πλάνητος** [λᾰ], ον, *without wandering* or *deviating*, Id.1308.46. **-πνευστος**, ον, *sheltered from wind*, Agathin.ap.Orib.10.7.16. **-πτυκτος**, ον, *not wrapped up*, J.*AJ*3.7.5. **-πτωτος**, ον, *not liable to*, τινός or τινί (dub. l.) Dsc.2.47; τινί D.L.7.122, cf. *Stoic.*3.152. II. *not stumbling*, of the Stoic sage, Arr.*Epict.*1.1.31, al. Adv., Comp. -ότερον 4.6.26. **-σάλπιγκτος**, ον, *not surrounded by the sound of trumpets*, Pyrrhus ap.Stob.4.13.60. **-σκεπτος**, ον, *inconsiderate, thoughtless*, Th.4.108, D.C.*Fr.*57.25. Adv. -τως Th.4.10, 6.57, Ph.2.340, al., D.H.6.10: Comp. -ότερον Th.6.65, Chrysipp.*Stoic.*3.125. II. Pass., *uninvestigated*, πολλὰ ἀ. καταλιπεῖν Ph.1.387. **-σκοπος**, ον, = foreg., Suid. s.v. ἀπερίγραπτοι. **-σπαστος**, ον, *not drawn hither and thither, not distracted* or *hindered*, Plb.2.67.7; ὕπνος Philum. ap.Orib.45.29.57; θεωρία Porph.*Abst.*1.36; τὸ ἀ. *freedom from distractions*, Plu.2.521c, Lxx *Si.*41.1; παρέχεσθαί τινα ἀ. *guarantee against annoyance*, *BGU*1057.22 (i B.C.); but ἀ. τῆς σῆς εὐεργεσίας *not able to be roused by* it, Lxx *Wi.*16.11. Adv. -τως Plb.2.20.10, 1 *Ep.Cor.*7.35; καθῆσθαι Arr.*Epict.*1.29.59. 2. *uninterrupted, free from digressions*, D.H.*Th.*9; τὸ ἀ. τῆς ἐξουσίας *the fact of* power *not passing from hand to hand*, Plu.*Arist.*5. Adv. -τως *continually*, ἐπαινεῖ τὸν οἶνον Ath.1.1cc.

ἀπερίσσευτος, ον, = ἀπέριττος, Phint.ap.Stob.4.23.61ᵃ.

ἀπέρισσος, ον, v. ἀπέριττος.

ἀπερισσοτρύφητος [ῠ], ον, *not luxuriously fed*, ὀϊζύς Timo 3.

ἀπερί-στᾰτος, ον, *not stood around*: and so, I. *unguarded*, ῥᾳστῶναι Plb.6.44.8. 2. *solitary*, Ps.-Phoc.26, Arr.*Epict.*4.1.159; *not crowded*, D.L.7.5. 3. Medic., of wounds or ulcers, *free from complications*, Gal.13.498, al. II. *without explanatory circumstances*, Hermog.*Stat.*1. III. *not encompassed by dangers*, βίος Max.Tyr.36.3. **-στικτος**, ον, *not dotted round*, opp. περιεστιγμένος, ἀ. διπλῆ Sch.Il.p.xliii Dind., etc.; εὐθεῖα Gal.19.750. **-τμητος**, ον, *uncircumcised*, Lxx *Ge.*17.14, al., J.*BJ*1.1.2: metaph., καρδία Lxx *Ez.*44.7, cf. *Act.Ap.*7.51, al. II. *not clipped* or *circumscribed*, φύσις Plu.2.495c. **-τρεπτος**, ον, *not to be turned* or *moved, immutable*, Sm.*Ps.*95(96).10, Plu.2.983c. Adv. -τως S.E.*M.*1.53. **-τροπος**, ον, *unheeding*, S.*El.*182 (lyr.).

ἀπέριττος, ον, *without superfluity, plain, simple*, λιτοὶ καὶ ἀ. Zeno *Stoic.*1.57, cf. D.H.*Lys.*15, Plu.2.267f, Philostr.*VS*1.23.2; τὸ ἀ. τῆς τροφῆς Luc.*Nigr.*26; μηροί, γαστήρ, *perfectly modelled*, Philostr.*Jun.Im.*14, 15. Adv. -ττως *plainly*, D.S.12.26; *frugally*, Simp.*in Epict.*p.33 D.

ἀπεριττότης, ητος, ἡ, *simplicity*, λόγου S.E.*M.*2.23.

ἀπερίττωτος, ον, *without* περιττώματα, φύσις, τροφή, Thphr.*CP*6.10.3, 17.9.

ἀπερι-φερής, ές, *not round* or *rounded*, Thphr.*CP*6.1.6. **-φραστος**, ον, *without circumlocution*, Eust.1941.59. Adv. -τως ib.1112.42. **-φρονήτως**, Adv. *without malice prepense*, ἀ. καὶ ἀκαταγνώστως *Sammelb.*4774.5. **-ψυκτος**, ον, *free from chill*, τηρεῖν Gal. 11.475, cf. Sor.2.14.

ἀπερκτικός, = ἀπειρκτικός, prob.l. for παρεκτικός, Alex.Aphr.*in Sens.*97.

ἀπεροπεύς, έως, ὁ, = ἠπεροπευτής, *EM*433.45.

ἀπερριμμένως, Adv. pf. part. Pass. of ἀπορρίπτω, *negligently*, Aristeas 28.

ἀπέρρω, *go away, be gone*, E.*HF*260; ἄπερρε *away! begone!* Ar. *Nu.*783, *Ec.*169; οὐκ ἀπερρήσεις σὺ θᾶττον; Cratin.123.

ἀπερρωγώς, υῖα, ός, (ἀπορρήγνυμι) *broken*, i.e. *unsound, unreliable*, σημεῖον S.E.*M.*8.165.

ἀπερυγγάνω, aor. ἀπήρῠγον, *belch forth, disgorge*, τὴν κραιπάλην Alciphr.3.32, cf. Nic.*Th.*253: metaph., *vent*, D.L.5.77, Ph.1.639. II. abs., *eructate*, Arist.*Pr.*962ᵃ8.

ἀπερυθριάω, *to put away blushes, to be past blushing*, Ar.*Nu.*1216; ἀπερυθριᾷ πᾶς, ἐρυθριᾷ δ' οὐδεὶς ἔτι Men.782, cf. Plu.2.547b, Luc.*Jud. Voc.*8, Lib.*Decl.*15.43; πρὸς πάντας Jul.*Or.*6.196d. Adv. **ἀπηρυθριᾰκότως**, *shamelessly*, Apollod.Com.13.10. 2. *cease to be red* or *flushed*, Luc.*Lex.*4.

ἀπερῠκάνω, = sq., Epic.Anon.*Oxy.*422.6.

ἀπερύκω [ῠ], impf. ἀπήρυκον Plb.16.1.3: aor. ἀπήρυξα X.*An.*5.8.25, Isyll.74 (tm.), Maiist.45 (tm.):—*keep off* or *away*, εἰ γὰρ Ἀθήνη.. βελέων ἀπερύκοι ἐρωήν Il.17.562; σύας τε κύνας τ' ἀ. Od.18.105; ἀπερύκοι.. Φοῖβος κακὰν φάτιν S.*Aj.*186 (lyr.); πολέμιον X. l.c., cf. Plb.16.1.3: c. gen., στρατὸν.. Μήδων ἀπέρυκε τῆσδε πόλεος Thgn. 775: c. acc. et inf., *prevent* one *from*.., οὔτε σε κωμάζειν ἀπερύκομεν οὔτε καλεῦμεν Id.1207:—less freq. in Prose, ἀ. τινί τι *keep off from*, ταῦτα ἡ εὐτυχίη οἱ ἀπερύκει Hdt.1.32, cf. X.*Oec.*5.6; τοὺς λύκους ἀπὸ τῶν προβάτων *Mem.*2.9.2, cf. Arist.*HA*620ᵃ12:—Pass., πατρῴης γῆς ἀπερυκόμενος *debarred from*.., Thgn.1210:—Med., ἀλλήλων ἔριδος (v.l. ἔριδας) δὴν (δῆγμ' Bgk.) ἀπερυκόμενοι *desisting from*.., Id. 494; ἀπερύκου (sc. φωνῆς) *abstain from* speech, S.*OC*169 (lyr.):—later in act. sense, ἀπερύκεο νούσους, to be read in Maced.*Pae.*23. 2. *withhold*, σῖγα νόον βουλήν τ' ἀπερύκων A.R.3.174.

ἀπερῠσῑβόω, (ἐρυσίβη) *destroy by mildew*, Thphr.*CP*5.10.3 (Pass.). 2. *produce mildew*, ib.5.9.13.

ἀπερύω [ῠ], *tear off from*, ῥινὸν ἀπ' ὀστεόφιν ἐρύσαι Od.14.134; πόρτιν μητρὸς ἀπειρύσσαντες Q.S.14.259:—Med., *AP*7.730 (Pers.) (tm.).

ἀπέρχομαι, fut. -ελεύσομαι (Att. fut. ἄπειμι): pf. -ελήλυθα: aor. -ῆλθον:—*go away, depart from*, c. gen., πάτρης Il.24.766; οἴκου Od. 2.136, cf. S.*OC*1165, etc.; λόγου E.*IT*546; ἀ. ἀπὸ τοῦ βουλευτηρίου Th.8.92; ἐκ τῆς χώρας Id.1.89, etc.: metaph., ἀ. ἐκ δακρύων *cease from* tears, E.*Or.*295. 2. with εἰς, implying *departure from* one place *and arrival at* another, ἀ. ἐς τὰς Σάρδις Hdt.1.22; ἀ. εἰς Θουρίους οἰκήσοντες And.4.12; παρά τινα Luc.*Tim.*11; ἀ. ἐπ' οἴκου *depart* homewards, Th.1.92; ἀθῷος οἴκαδε Archipp.40; ἀπῆλθεν ὅθεν.. *went back to* the place whence he came, Men.481.3: metaph., ἀ. εἰς τὴν ἀρχαίαν φύσιν Pl.*Smp.*193c. 3. abs., Hdt.1.199, etc.; ταχεῖ' ἀπέρχεται (sc. ἡ νόσος) S.*Ph.*808; κἀτ' ὀφλὼν ἀ. Ar.*Ach.*689; ἄπελθε τουτονὶ λαβών take him and *be off!* Id.*Av.*948; ἀπελθόντος ἐνιαυτοῦ Pl.*Lg.*954d; νυκτὸς -ομένης Arat.315. 4. c. part., ἀ. νικῶν *come off* conqueror, Aristid.2.2 J., cf. Plu.*Ages.*7, etc. 5. *spread abroad*, ἀπῆλθεν ἡ ἀκοὴ αὐτοῦ εἰς Συρίαν *Ev.Matt.*4.24. II. *depart from life*, ἀ. κάτω E.*Alc.*379, cf. S.*Ant.*818 (lyr.): abs., D.L.3.6, *AP*11.335, cf. Ph.1.513, Plot.4.7.15; εἰς τοὺς θεούς *PPetr.*2 p.45 (iii B.C.).

ἀπερῶ, Ion. ἀπερέω, v. ἀπεῖπον.

ἀπερωεύς, έως, ὁ, *thwarter*, ἐμῶν μενέων ἀπερωεύς Il.8.361.

ἀπερωέω, *retire* or *withdraw from*, τῷ κε τάχα.. πολέμου ἀπερωήσειας Il.16.723.

ἀπερωπός, όν, *inconsiderate, cruel*, A.*Ch.*600; expl. by ἀναιδής, σκληρός, οἷον ἀπερίοπτος καὶ ἀπερίβλεπτος by Phryn.*PS* p.10 B., cf. *EM*120.41, Hsch. Adv. -πῶς· θαυμαστῶς, ἀδοκήτως, Id.

ἀπέρωτος, ον, (ἔρως) *loveless, unloving*, ἔρως ἀπέρωτος, like γάμος ἄγαμος, read by M² in A.*Ch.*600; but v. foreg.

ἄπες, Ion. for ἄφες, v. sub ἀφίημι.

ἄπεσθαι (= ἕπ-)· ἀκολουθῆσαι, Hsch.

ἀπεσθέομαι, Med., (ἐσθής) *undress oneself*, Luc.*Lex.*5 (in pf. part. ἀπησθημένοι).

ἀπεσθίω, fut. ἀπέδομαι Ar.*Av.*26: aor. part. ἀποφαγών Id.*Eq.*497: pf. ἀπεδήδοκα Id.*Ra.*984:—Pass., aor. 1 ἀπηδέσθην Pl.Com.138: pf. ἀπεδήδεμαι Arist.*HA*591ᵃ5:—*eat, gnaw off*, τοὺς δακτύλους Hermipp. 24, cf. Ar.*Av.*26; ἀπεσθίει μου τὴν ἀκοήν Hermipp.52; τίς τὴν κεφαλὴν ἀπεδήδοκεν τῆς μαινίδος; Ar.*Ra.*984; ἀπεσθίει τὴν ῥῖνα τἀνθρώπου D.25.61. II. *leave off eating*, τὰ πετραῖα τῶν ἰχθυδίων Theopomp. Com.62.

ἀπεσκής, ές, (πέσκος) *without a bow-case*, τόξα S.*Fr.*626.

ἀπέσκληκα, v. ἀποσκλῆναι.

ἀπεσκληρυμμένως, Adv., (ἀποσκληρύνω) ἀ. ἔχων, = ἀπεσκληκώς, *AB*422.

ἀπεσσία, = ἄφεσις, Hsch. (dub.).

ἀπεσσούα, *he is gone off*, Lacon. for ἀπεσσύη, ἀπεσσύθη, aor. Pass. of ἀποσεύω, X.*HG*1.1.23 (dub.).

ἀπεσσύμεθα, -συτο, Ep. sync. aor. Pass. of ἀποσεύω.

ἀπεστύς, ύος, ἡ, = sq., Hsch.

ἀπεστώ, οῦς, ἡ, Ion. Noun, (ἄπειμι, cf. εὐεστώ) *absence*, ἐπαισχυνομένους τῇ ἀπεστοῖ τῆς μάχης Hdt.9.85, cf. Call.*Fr.*340.

ἀπεσχᾰρ-όω, *remove a scab*, Zopyr.ap.Orib.14.61.2:—Pass., Eust. 1575.43. **-ωτικός**, ή, όν, *removing scabs*, Paul.Aeg.4.34, 6.66.

ἀπέτηλος, ον, *leafless*, *AP*6.190 (Gaet.).

ἄπετρος, ον, *without stones*, Eust.1736.9.

ἀπευδιασμός, ὁ, (εὐδιάζω) *making calm*, Porph.*VP*29 (pl.).

ἀπευδοκιμῶ· *depudesco*, *Gloss.*

ἀπευήκασιν· ἐξηραμμέναι εἰσίν, Hsch.

ἀπευθᾰνᾰτίζω, *die well* or *happily*, Lxx 2 *Ma.*6.28.

ἀπευθής, ές, (πυνθάνομαι) *not inquired into, unknown*, κείνου δ'.. ὄλεθρον ἀπευθέα θῆκεν Od.3.88, cf. Arat.259, etc.; ἀ. ἀκοῇ Max.Tyr. 17.9. II. Act., *not inquiring, ignorant*, ἦλθον.. ἀπευθής Od.3.184, cf. Cerc.5.3: c. gen., D.P.194, *APl.*4.303.

ἀπευθ-υνσις, εως, ἡ, *adjustment, setting*, Paul.Aeg.6.92. **-υντέον**, *one must set straight, adjust*, Sor.2.60. **-ύνω**, fut. -ῠνῶ S. *Ichn.*169:—*make straight, restore*, πάντα ὀρθὰ ἀ. Pl.*Ti.*71d; χέρας δεσμοῖς ἀ. *bind* his arms *straight*, i.e. *behind* him, S.*Aj.*72: metaph., ἀπευθύνεται τὸ ὑποκλάζον τοῦ πυρετοῦ Paul.Aeg.2.47. b. in military drill, *dress*, λόχον Ascl.*Tact.*12.11, etc. 2. *guide aright, direct*, δεῦρ' ἀ. μολεῖν A.*Ag.*1667; ἀ. βροτῶν τοὺς ἀγνωμοσύναν τιμῶντας *corrects, chastises* them, E.*Ba.*884 (lyr.); ἐκ πρύμνης ἀ. *to steer*, Pl.*Criti.* 109c; πλήκτροις ἀ. τρόπιν S.*Fr.*143, cf. *Ichn.* l.c.; ἀ. πόλιν *govern, rule*, Id.*OT*104; ἀ. τὰ κοινά Aeschin.3.158; κλήρῳ ἀ. [τὴν ἰσότητα] *regulate*, Pl.*Lg.*757b, cf. *Plt.*282e; ἀ. τι πρός τι *to adjust*, Arr.*Epict.*4.12.16, cf. Luc.*Im.*12; ταῖς συλλαβαῖς ἀ. τοὺς χρόνους D.H.*Comp.*11. II. τὸ ἀπευθυσμένον (sc. ἔντερον) *intestinum rectum*, Dsc.1.99, Heliod.ap. Orib.44.23.55, Gal.2.573, etc.

ἄπευκος, ον, *without resin*, Thphr.*HP*3.9.3 (in Comp. -ότερος).

ἀπευκτ-αῖος, α, ον, = ἀπευκτός, Pl.*Ax.*369b (Sup.), Plu.2.289b; τάραχοι *CPHerm.*119ʳiv 16 (iii A.D.), cf. A.D.*Synt.*252.10. Adv. -αίως *to the loss of our hopes*, [τελευτῆσαι] *POxy.*1114.24 (iii A.D.). **-ικός**, ή, όν, *deprecatory*, ὕμνοι Men.Rh.p.342 S. **-ός**, ή, όν, Luc.*Pseudol.*12, Hld.7.25: (ἀπεύχομαι):—*to be deprecated, abominable*, πήματα A.*Ag.*638; ἀ. τὸ δεηθῆναι τούτων Pl.*Lg.*628c; τὰ ἀ. Id.*Ep.*353e.

ἀπεύλογον, τό, *of irregular shape*, dub. in Hero *Stereom.*2.32.

ἀπευλῡτέω· *expedio, explico, exploro*, *Gloss.*

ἀπευνάζω, *lull to sleep*, ἀπευνασθέντος κακοῦ (ἀπ' εὐνασθέντος κ. cod. L) S.*Tr.*1242.

ἄπευστος, ον, = ἀπευθής, Hsch.

ἀπευτακτέω, *deliver* or *pay regularly*, τοὺς φόρους Str.4.6.9:—Pass., Id.7.4.6, *UPZ*42.15 (ii B.C.).

ἀπευτελεῖσθαι· ἀπάρξασθαι, Hsch.

ἄπευτος, ον, = ἄπευστος, Hsch.

ἀπευφημ-έω, *deprecate*, v.l. for ἐπ-, Philostr.*VA*5.19, 7.10. **-ισμός**, ὁ, -οῦ χάριν out of *politeness*, Phld.*Lib.*p.56 O.

ἀπευχᾰριστέω, *show gratitude*, τινί *IG*5(1).1145.35 (Gythium).

ἀπεύχετος, ον, = ἀπευκτός, A.*Ch.*155, 625 (lyr.).

ἀπευχή, ἡ, *deprecation*, Men.Rh.p.343 S. (pl.).

ἀπεύχομαι, *wish* a thing *away, wish* it *may not happen*, c. acc. rei, ἀπεύχου ταῦτα, πρὸς θεῶν E.*Hipp.*891; τί μάλιστ' ἂν ἀπευξαίμεθα; D.20.157; ἀ. τι τοῖς θεοῖς μηδαμῶς γίγνεσθαι *pray* the gods it *may not be*, Pl.*Lg.*687d, cf. D.8.51: without μή, ἀπεύχεσθε ἰδεῖν Id.6.23, cf. 20.106: also τοῦτο.. μὴ γένοιτο.. ἀπεύχομαι Ar.*Th.*714. II. *reject, despise*, μητρὸς αἷμα A.*Eu.*608. III. *avert by prayer*, Philostr.*VA* 6.41.

ἀπεύω, *scorch off*, v. ἀφεύω.

ἀπευωνίζω, *cheapen*, dub. in Luc.*Nigr.*23.

ἀπεφεισμένως, *abundantly*, dub. in Str.15.1.24.

ἀπέφθῑθον, v. ἀποφθίθω.

ἄπεφθος, ον, by dissimilation for ἄφεφθος, (ἀφέψω) *boiled down*, ἄ. χρυσός *refined* gold, Thgn.449, Hdt.1.50; χρυσίον Th.2.13; ὕδωρ ἄ. water *purified by boiling*, Alex.198; μέλι ἄ. *despumated*, Sor.1.118.

ἀπέφρυσεν· ἀπέζεσεν, ἀπέβαλεν, Hsch.

ἀπεχθαίρω, *hate utterly, detest*, τινά Il.3.415, Opp.*H.*5.420, Jul.*Or.* 2.86b, Vett.Val.349.14:—Med., aor. 1 ἀπηχθήραντο Q.S.13.255. II. *make utterly hateful*, ὅς τέ μοι ὕπνον ἀ. καὶ ἐδωδήν Od.4.105.

ἀπεχθάνομαι, Od.2.202, Ar.*Pl.*910, Pl.*Ap.*24a, etc.: impf. ἀπηχθανόμην Cratin.36, X.*An.*7.7.10: fut. ἀπεχθήσομαι Hdt.1.89, E.*Alc.*71, Pl.*Phlb.*28d, etc.; ἀπεχθᾰνοῦμαι Them.*Or.*26.322c: pf. ἀπήχθημαι Th.1.75, 2.63, X.*An.*7.6.34, etc.: aor. ἀπηχθόμην Il.24.27, etc.; subj. ἀπέχθωμαι ib.4.53; inf. ἀπεχθέσθαι (not ἀπέχθεσθαι), v. ἀπέχθομαι; part. ἀπεχθόμενος Pl.*Min.*321a: (ἔχθος):—Pass., *to be hated, incur hatred*, ἀπεχθάνεαι δ' ἔτι μᾶλλον Od.2.202; elswh. in Hom. always in aor., mostly c. dat. pers., *to be* or *become hateful to* one, *incur* his *hate*, ἀπήχθετο πᾶσι θεοῖσι Il.6.140; ἶσον γάρ σφιν πᾶσιν ἀπήχθετο κηρὶ μελαίνῃ 3.454; οὔτε τί μοι πᾶς δῆμος ἀπεχθόμενος χαλεπαίνει nor does the people *roused to hate against* me distress me, Od.16.114; σοὶ ἐμέθεν ἀπήχθετο φροντίσδην Sapph.41, Hdt.1.89, 3.1, Antipho 6.11, Th.1.136, etc.; ἀ. πρός τινα *to be hateful* in his eyes, E.*Med.*290; *to be irritated* against, πρὸς τὴν ἡγεμονίαν Plu.*Galb.*18, cf. J.*AJ*13.9.3: c. dat. rei, *to be hated for* a thing, Pl.*Ap.*24a, cf. Th.2.63 (but also in act. sense, *dislike*, τῇ φιλοσοφίᾳ, τῷ οἴνῳ Philostr.*VA*3.22, *Im.*2.17): c. part., ἀ. ποιῶν And.4.10; θριάμβους ἀναρύτουσ' ἀπηχθάνου Cratin. 36. II. causal, λόγοι ἀπεχθανόμενοι language *that causes hatred*, opp. οἳ πρὸς φιλίαν ἄγουσι, X.*Smp.*4.58.

ἀπέχθεια, ἡ, *hatred*, 1. felt towards another, πρός τινα D.18.36, Arist.*Pol.*1305ᵃ23; διὰ τὴν ἀ. τοῦ πάθους *for* it, ib.1274ᵃ40. 2. felt by others towards one, *enmity, odium*, ὁ πράξας τὴν ἀ. αὐτῶν δίκαιος φέρεσθαι Antipho 3.4.2, cf. Pl.*Ap.*28a, D.3.13, etc.: in pl., *enmities*, Pl.*Ap*.23a, interpol. in D.9.64; θεοῖς δι' ἀπεχθείας ἐλθεῖν to be *hated* by them, A.*Pr*.121 (lyr.); δι' ἀ. γίγνεταί τι it becomes *hateful*, X.*Hier*.9.2; οὔτ' ἐκείνου πρὸς χάριν οὔτ' ἐμοῦ πρὸς ἀπέχθειαν D.5.7; ἀπέχθειαν φέρει τι it brings *odium*, Id.*Prooem*.44; πολλὴν ἔχει ἀ. Arist.*Pol*.1322a2; δείσας τὴν πρὸς ὑμᾶς ἀ. *enmity* with you, Isoc.8.38; μετὰ πολλῆς ἀ. Plb.1.66.9.

ἀπεχθές, Adv. *yesterday*, A.D.*Synt*.235.26:—divisim ἀπ' ἐχθές *AP*11.35 (Phld.).

ἀπεχθ-ήεις, εσσα, εν, Adj. *odious*, *noxious*, Androm.ap.Gal.14.33. **-ημα**, ατος, τό, *object of hate*, E.*Tr*.425. **-ήμων**, ον, gen. ονος, worse form for sq., Poll.8.153. **-ής**, ές, *hateful*, S.*Ant*.50; *hostile*, Theoc.1.101; τὸ ἀ. Onos.37.3: Sup., Ph.1.604. II. *hated*, Isoc.1.12 (dub. l.); δάκρυα *IG*4.622 (Argos). Adv. -θῶς, ἔχειν τινί D.5.18; διακεῖσθαι D.Chr.32.70; πρός τινας D.H.7.31: Sup. -έστατα Poll.5.116. **-ητικός**, ή, όν, *full of hatred*, *envious*, opp. κόλαξ, Arist.*MM*1193a22, *EE*1221a26, 1233b32. **-ομαι**, later form of ἀπεχθάνομαι, Theoc.7.45, Lyc.116, *AP*5.176 (Mel.), Plu. *Marc*.22, etc.; for in E.*Hipp*.1260 ἐπάχθομαι is the better reading; and the inf. ἀπέχθεσθαι freq. found in codd. should be written ἀπεχθέσθαι, cf. ἀπεχθάνομαι. **-ρεύω**, *to be hostile*, Phld.*Rh*.2.162 S. **-ρῶς**· ἐχθρωδῶς, Hsch.

ἀπέχω, fut. ἀφέξω, and (Od.19.572) ἀποσχήσω: aor. ἀπέσχον:—*keep off* or *away from*, αἴ κεν Τυδέος υἱὸν ἀπόσχῃ Ἰλίου ἱρῆς Il.6.96, 277; ἑκὰς νήσων ἀπέχων εὐεργέα νῆα Od.15.33; κληῖδες ἀπ' ὤμων αὐχέν' ἔχουσιν the collar-bone *parts* the neck *from* the shoulders, Il.22.324; Εὐβοίης ἀπέχειν.. αἶγας Orac.ap.Hdt.8.20, cf. 22; ἄπεχε τῆς βοὸς τὸν ταῦρον A.*Ag*.1125 (lyr.), cf. *Pr*.687 (lyr.). 2. c. dat. pers., τοι.. χεῖρας ἀφέξω Od.20.263. 3. with a Prep., ἀ. φρένα περισσῶν παρὰ φωτῶν E.*Ba*.427 (lyr.); ῥῖνα ἀπὸ κάκκης Ar.*Pax*162. 4. c. acc. only, *keep off* or *away*, σκοτεινὸν ἀ. ψόγον Pi.*N*.7.61; ἀ. φάσγανον E.*Or*.1519. 5. οὐδὲν ἀπέχει c. inf., nothing *hinders*, *debars* one *from* doing, Pl.*Cra*.407b, Plu.2.433a. II. Med., κακῶν ἄπο χεῖρας ἔχεσθαι *hold one's* hands *off* or *away from*.., Od.22.316; κυάμων ἄπο χεῖρας ἔχεσθε Emp.141; ἀθανάτων ἀ. χεῖρας A.*Eu*.350 (lyr.), cf. *Supp*. 756, Pl.*Smp*.213d, 214d:—but mostly, 2. ἀπέχεσθαί τινος *hold oneself off* a thing, *abstain* or *desist from* it, πολέμου Il.8.35, al.; βοῶν Od. 12.321; οὐδὲ.. σεῦ ἀφέξομαι *will* not *keep my hands off* thee, ib.19.489; Δεκελέης *abstain from ravaging* D., Hdt.9.73, cf. 1.66, 4.118, al., Th. 1.20, etc.; *keep away from*, πόλεως X.*HG*7.3.10: in pf. Pass., μηδὲ τῶν μικρῶν ἀπεσχημένον D.27.47; ἀγορᾶς ἀπεσχ. Arist.*Pol*.1278a 25. 3. c. inf., ἀπέχεσθαι μὴ στρατεῦσαι *abstain from* marching, Th.5.25; λαμβάνειν ἀπέσχετο Philem.94.3; ἀπέχεσθαι τοῦ ποιεῖν X. *Mem*.4.2.3; οὐκ ἀ. τὸ μὴ οὐ ποιεῖν Id.*Cyr*.1.6.32, Pl.*R*.354b: also c. part., Jul.*Or*.1.43d. 4. abs., *refrain oneself*, D.21.61. III. intr. in Act., *to be away* or *far from*, c. gen. loci, τῶν Ἐπιπολῶν ἓξ ἢ ἑπτὰ σταδίους Th.6.97; ἀ. ἀπὸ Βαβυλῶνος, etc., Hdt.1.179, cf. 3.26, al.; ἀπὸ θαλάττης.. δώδεκα ὁδὸν ἡμερῶν ἀ. Euphro11.3; ἀ. παμπόλλων ἡμερῶν ὁδὸν X.*Cyr*.1.1.3; τὸ μέσον ἴσον τῶν ἐσχάτων ἀ. Pl.*Prm*.145b; πλεῖστον ἀ. κατὰ τόπον Arist.*Mete*.363a31; ἀ. τὴν ἡμίσειαν διάμετρον Id. *Cael*.293b30, etc. b. *project*, *extend*, Id.*GA*781a11; τὰ ἀπέχοντα *prominent parts*, *PA*655a32. c. ἀποσχὼν τεσσαράκοντα μάλιστα σταδίους μὴ φθάσαι ἐλθὼν *failing to arrive in time by*.., Th.5.3. 2. of actions, *to be far from*, ἀπεῖχον τῆς ἐξευρέσιος οὐδὲν ἔλασσον *were just as far from* the discovery, Hdt.1.67; τοσοῦτον ἀπέχω τοῦ ποιεῖν τι ὥστε.. Isoc.6.70; τοσοῦτῳ πλέον ἡμῶν ἀπέχεις τοῦ πιστὰ λέγειν ὅσον.. ib.11. 32; ἀπέχει τοῦ μὴ μετ' ὀργῆς [πράττειν] D.21.41; πλεῖστον ἀ. τινός to *be* as *far* as possible *from* doing, X.*Mem*.1.2.62; but τοσοῦτ' ἀπέχει τῶν χορηγῶν so far *is it from the thoughts of*.., D.21.59. 3. generally, *to be far removed from*, πολιτείας, μοναρχίας, Arist.*Pol*.1289b2, 1293a17; τοῦ μέσου Id.*EN*1109a10. 4. *differ from*, οὐδέν τι ἀπεῖχε γαμετῆς γυναικός Hdn.1.16.4. 5. διαφύσιες.. ἧσιν οὐδὲν ἀπέχει ἀγγεῖα εἶναι nothing *is wanting*, Hp.*de Arte*10. IV. *have* or *receive in full*, τὴν ἀπόκρισιν Aeschin.2.50; τὸ χρέος ἀ. *receive* payment *in full*, Call.*Epigr*.55; χάριτας ib.51; ἀπέχω in receipts, *BGU*612.2 (i A.D.), etc.; ἀ. τὸν μισθόν Plu.*Sol*.22, *Ev.Matt*.6.2, al.; καρπὸν ἀ. τῶν πονηθέντων Plu.*Them*.17; ἀ. τὸ μέτριον Id.2.124e. 2. impers., ἀπέχει *it sufficeth*, *it is enough*, *Ev.Marc*.14.41, cf. *Anacreont*.15.33.

ἀπεψία, ἡ, (ἄπεπτος) *indigestion*, etc.; δι' ἀπεψίαν Arist.*PA*668b8: in pl., Id.*Mete*.381b9, Plu.2.127d, Gal.8.34, S.E.*P*.1.131.

ἀπέψω, Ion. for ἀφέψω.

ἀπέωσε, v. ἀπωθέω. **ἀπεωστόν**· ἀπόθητον, Hsch. **ἀπηγενέες**· ἀποτεταγμένοι, Id.

ἀπηγέομαι, ἀπήγημα, ἀπήγησις, Ion. for ἀφηγ–.

ἀπηγορ-έομαι, Med., *defend oneself*, like ἀπολογέομαι, Arist.*Pr*. 951a23:—Act., *defend*, Simp.*in Cat*.17.2. **-ευμα**· ἀπολόγημα, Hsch. **-ημα**, ατος, τό, *defence*, opp. κατηγόρημα, Pl.*Lg*.765b. **-ία**, Dor. **ἀπαγ-**, ἡ, dub.l. in Pi.*Fr*.122.6 (pl.).

ἀπήδᾰλος, ον, *without rudder*, Arist.*IA*710a8.

ἀπηθ-έω, *strain off*, *filter*, Ar.*Ra*.943, Thphr.*HP*9.8.3. **-ημα**, ατος, τό, *that which is filtered off*, Asclep.ap.Gal.14.142, *Hippiatr*.6, 11. **-ητέον**, *one must strain off*, Dsc.5.88.

ἀπήκει· ἀπέχει, ἢ εἰς ὀξὺ συνάγει, Hsch. **ἀπηκολλύρισεν**· ἐν τῷ παραβεβλῆσθαι ἀπέστρεφε (Lacon.), Id.

ἀπήκοος, ον, (ἀκοή) *disobedient*, opp. ὑπήκοος, Hsch.

ἀπηκρῑβωμένως, Adv., (ἀπακριβόω) *exactly*, Plu.*Agis* 2 (v.l.); *sparingly*, Alex.213.4.

ἄπηκτος, ον, *not capable of being solidified*, Arist.*Mete*.385b1, *GA* 735b30, *HA*520a8. 2. *not solid*, θεμέλια Sor.1.47.

ἀπηλγημένως, Adv., (ἀπαλγέω) gloss on ἀπηλεγέως, Sch.Il.9.309.

ἀπηλεγ-έω, *neglect*, A.R.2.17. **-έως**, Adv. *without caring for anything*, *outright*, *bluntly*, Hom. only in phrase μῦθον ἀπηλεγέως ἀποειπεῖν Il.9.309, Od.1.373; ἀ. πεπύθοιτο A.R.4.1469; νίσσετ' ἀπηλεγέως *straightforwards*, *without looking about*, Id.1.785; *sternly*, 4.687; prob. f.l. for ἀνηλ–, Q.S.1.226:—also **ἀπηλεγές**, Nic.*Th*.495, Opp.*C*.2.510. (From ἀλέγω, like νηλεγής, ἀνηλεγής.)

ἀπηλιαστής, οῦ, ὁ, opp. φιληλιαστής, *one who keeps away from the* Ἡλιαία, i.e. an enemy to law, with a play on ἥλιος (*not fond of basking in the sun*), Ar.*Av*.110.

ἀπηλῐθιόομαι, Pass., *become stupid*, *fatuous*, Dsc.5.17.

ἀπῆλιξ, Ion. for ἀφῆλιξ.

ἀπηλῐ-ώτης (with or without ἄνεμος), ου, ὁ, *east wind*, Hdt.4.22, 7.188, E.*Cyc*.19, Th.3.23; opp. ζέφυρος, Arist.*Mete*.363b13, cf. *Mu*. 394b23, *Vent*.973a13, al.—The Ion. form ἀπηλιώτης is retained in Att., and appears on the Tower of Andronicus Cyrrhestes, *CIG* 518; ἀφηλιώτης on a later table of the winds, *IG*14.1308, and in Latin authors, Catull.26.3, Seneca *QN*5.16.4, Gell.2.22.8. **-ωτικός**, ή, όν, *from the quarter of the* ἀπηλιώτης, Arist.*Mete*.364a21, *POxy*. 985 (i A.D.), Ptol.*Geog*.1.11.1.

ἀπηλλαγμένως, Adv., (ἀπαλλάσσω) c. gen., *apart from*, ὀργῆς dub.l. in J.*AJ*17.5.6.

ἀπηλλάζεις· ἀπηλλαγμένος ἔσῃ, Hsch.

ἀπήμαντος, ον, *unharmed*, *unhurt*, Od.19.282, cf. Hes.*Th*.955; ἀ. βίοτος a life *free from misery*, Pi.*O*.8.87; ἔστω δ' ἀπήμαντον be *misery far away*, A.*Ag*.378 (lyr.). II. Act., *unharming*, σθένος Id.*Supp*. 576 (lyr.); of snakes, Nic.*Th*.492. Adv. -τως Tz. ad Lyc.886.

ἀπήμβροτον, v. ἀφαμαρτάνω.

ἀπημελημένως, Adv., (ἀπαμελέω) *carelessly*, Procop.*Vand*.1.4, al.

ἀπήμιος, ὁ, *averter of ill*, Ζεύς Paus.1.32.2.

ἀπημονία, ἡ, = sq., Call.*Jov*.92.

ἀπημοσύνη, ἡ, *freedom from harm*, *safety*, Thgn.758, *IG*12(5).215 (Paros). 2. *harmlessness*, Opp.*H*.2.647.

ἀπήμων, ον, gen. -ονος, (πῆμα) like ἀπήμαντος, *unharmed*, *unhurt*, ἀδάκρυτος καὶ ἀ. Il.1.415, al.; σὺν νηυσὶν ἀπήμονες ἦλθον Ἀχαιοί Od. 4.487; νόστος ἀ. ib.519, cf. νῆες ἀπήμονες Opp.*H*.5.676; ὄλβος Pi. *Pae*.9.8; μοῖρα A.R.1.422; *without sorrow* or *care*, ἀ. κραδία κᾶδος ἀμφ' ἀλλότριον Pi.*N*.1.54, cf. *P*.10.22: c. gen., ἀ. πάσης οἰζύος A.*Eu*.893.—Rare in Prose, as Hdt.1.42, 4.179, Pl.*Phdr*.248c, Ph.1.393. II. Act., *doing no harm*: hence, *kindly*, *propitious*, οὖρον ἀπήμονά τε λιαρόν τε Od.7.266, cf. 12.167; πόντος Hes.*Op*.670; ὕπνον ἀπήμονά τε λιαρόν τε Il.14.164; μῦθος 13.748; πομποί Od.8.566; *without hostile intent*, A.*Supp*.186; πλοῦς νεῶν ἀ. *free from harm to* them, E.*IA* 1575.

ἀπηναῖος· ἀπήνης, Hsch.

ἀπήνεια, ἡ, (ἀπηνής) *rudeness*, *discourtesy*, Thphr.*Char*.15.1: in pl., A.R.2.1202. 2. *stiffness*, Heliod.ap.Orib.44.23.56, Sor.1. 44.

ἀπήνεμος, ον, (ἄνεμος) *without wind*, D.Chr.6.33, *AB*424; ἀ. λιμήν Poll.1.100.

ἀπήνη [ᾰ], ἡ, *four-wheeled wagon*, drawn by mules, ἡμίονοι ἕλκον τετράκυκλον ἀπήνην Il.24.324, cf. Od.6.57 with 69, 72, 73, 82; much the same as ἅμαξα, cf. Il.24.266 with 324, Od.6.72 with 73: of a *racing-car*, drawn by mules, ἡμιόνοις ξεστᾷ τ' ἀπήνᾳ Pi.*P*.4.94, cf. *O*. 5.3, Arist.*Fr*.568; ἦν γὰρ δὴ ἀπήνη.. ἡμιόνους ἀνθ' ἵππων ἔχουσα Paus. 5.9.2. 2. later, any *car* or *chariot*, A.*Ag*.906, S.*OT*753; ἀ. πωλική ib.803; *war-chariot*, Str.4.5.2; cf. καπάνα. 3. metaph., *any conveyance*, ναΐα ἀ. *ship*, E.*Med*.1123; πλωταῖς ἀπήναις *Lyr. Adesp*.117 (= *Trag.Adesp*.142); τετραβάμονος ὡς ὑπ' ἀπήνας, of the Trojan horse, E.*Tr*.517 (lyr.). 4. metaph., like ζεῦγος, *pair*, e.g. of brothers, ἀ. ὁμόπτερος Id.*Ph*.329 (lyr.). 5. in pl., the *alae nasi*, Poll.2.80.

ἀπηνής, ές, Ep. Adj. *ungentle*, *rough*, *hard*, of persons, Il.1.340; ὅτι τοι νόος ἐστὶν ἀ. 16.35, cf. Od.18.381; θυμὸς ὑπερφίαλος καὶ ἀ. Il. 15.94; μῦθον ἀπηνέα τε κρατερόν τε ib.202, cf. Od.18.381, al.; ὃς μὲν ἀπηνὴς αὐτὸς ἔῃ καὶ ἀπηνέα εἰδῇ *cruel* himself and full of *cruel thoughts*, 19.329.—Rare in Att. (never in Trag.), ὅπως τοῖς ἔξωθεν μηδὲν δείξειαν ἀπηνές Ar.*Nu*.974 (anap.); ἀπηνές τι εἰπεῖν Pl.*Phdr*.257b (but ἀπηχές (q.v.) Hermias ad loc.), cf. *Lg*.950b, Call.*Iamb*.1.257; freq. in later Prose, as Onos.42.23, Phld.*D*.3 *Fr*.69, D.S.9.24, Plu.2.678b, 970c, Luc.*Nec*.18; τὸ ἐς ἀλλήλους ἀ. Procop.*Goth*.4.35: Comp. -έστερος J.*BJ*5.7.4, Adam.2.44: Sup. -έστατος Ael.*NA*3.26; τοῖς φίλοις J.*BJ* 1.24.8. Adv. -νῶς D.Chr.32.53, Plu.2.19b; πρὸς φίλους ἀπηνῶς ζῆν ib.525d: Comp. -έστερον J.*AJ*11.6.9. II. in physical sense, σπλὴν ἀ. *hard*, Aret.*SD*1.14, cf. 2.12; *unpleasant to taste*, *CA*1.5. (Cf. προσ-ηνής, Goth. *ansts* 'favour'.)

ἀπῆνθον, Dor. aor. 2 of ἀπέρχομαι, Theoc.2.84, al.

ἀπηνόφρων, ον, gen. ονος, *harsh-minded*, Sch.A.*Pr*.159.

ἀπηξία, ἡ, (πήγνυμι) *want of solidity*, *liability to flux*, σώματος Ptol. *Tetr*.204; *incapacity for solidification*, Ar.Byz.*Epit*.15.9.

ἀπηόριος, α, ον, = sq., *hanging*, of branches, *AP*9.71.

ἀπήορος, Dor. **ἀπάορος**, ον, (ἀείρω) *hanging on high*, *far distant*, ἀστέρες οὔτε τι πολλὸν ἀ. οὔτε μάλ' ἐγγύς Arat.396: c. gen., ἀπάορος ἐχθρῶν *aloof from* them, Pi.*P*.8.86.

ἀπηρεμέω, *take a thorough rest*, Sor.1.80, Orib.*Fr*.74.

ἀπηρής, ές, = ἄπηρος, *unharmed*, A.R.1.888 (ap.*EM*122.4; ἀπήμοσιν codd.), v.l. A.R.1.556 (on the accent v. Hdn.Gr.1.7).

ἀπήρῑνος, ον, (πηρίν) *without scrotum*, restored (for ἀπύρηνος) by Coraës in Archestr.8.9.

ἄπηρος, ον, *unmaimed*, Hdt.1.32, *AP*7.110 (D.L.), Hsch.

ἀπηρτημένως, Adv., (ἀπαρτάω) *consistently with*, τινί Plu.2.105e. II. ἀ. ἔχειν to be *discontinuous*, M.Ant.4.45.

ἀπηρτισμένως, Adv., (ἀπαρτίζω) *adequately, completely*, D.H.1.90; *precisely*, Procl.*Hyp*.4.80.

ἀπηρυθριακότως, v. ἀπερυθριάω.

ἀπήρωτος, ον, *intact, unimpaired*, Thphr.*CP*3.5.1, Gal.5.234. Adv. -τωί Theognost.*Can*.159.

ἀπήτρια, Dor. for ἠπ-, Hsch.

ἀπηύρων, ας, α, v. sub ἀπούρας.

ἀπήχ-εια, ἡ, *discord, enmity*, Lys.*Fr*.88: **ἀπηχία**, Phryn.*PS* p.25 B. **-έω**, *sound back, re-echo*, Arist.*Pr*.899^{a}24, 918^{a}35. 2. *utter*, φωνάς Arr.*Epict*.2.17.8. II. *to be out of tune*, Phryn.*PS* p.25 B., Suid.; *to be discordant*, Ph.1.693, 2.44. **-ημα**, ατος, τό, *echo*: metaph. of *sayings repeated by rote*, Pl.*Ax*.366c; *faint echo*, τῆς ἐκεῖ ζωῆς Procl.*in Alc*.p.99C., cf. p.135 C. 2. *echo*, 'ring', μεγαλοφροσύνης Longin.9.2. 3. Medic., *fracture from contre-coup*, Sor.*Fract*.8. **-ής**, ές, (ἦχος) *discordant*, v.l. in Pl.*Phdr*.257b (Hermias), cf. Aristid.*Or*.40(5).8, Luc.*Vit.Auct*.10; *out of tune with* one's surroundings, Alciphr.3.70. **-ησις**, εως, ἡ, *echo*: metaph. of *posthumous fame*, M.Ant.4.3. 2. *sounding, resonance*, φωνῆς, πνεύματος, D.T.629.26, Gal.19.380, cf. Phlp.*in Ph*.47.1 (pl.).

ἀπηχθημένως, Adv., (ἀπεχθάνομαι) *hostilely*, Philostr.*VA*7.36.

ἀπήωρος, ον, *high in air*, ἀ. δ' ἔσαν ὄζοι Od.12.435; cf. ἀπήορος.

Ἀπία γῆ, v. sub ἄπιος (B).

Ἀπιακός, ή, όν, *of Apis*, ἄρτοι *PSI*4.425.40 (iii B.C.); cf. Ἀ. ἄρτος· Μεμφιτικός, Hsch.

ἀπιάλλω, fut. -ιαλῶ Hsch., Dor. for ἀποπέμπω, Th.5.77; μεγάλου δ' ἀπὸ χεῖρας ἴαλλε *keep* them *off*, Archestr.*Fr*.29.

ἀπίαλος, Dor. for ἠπ-, Hsch.

ἀπιάπτω, *tear away*, only in tmesi, ὀπόσων ἀπὸ θυμὸν ἴαπτε Q.S.1.9.

ἀπίαστος, ον, *not to be caught*, Hsch. s. v. ἄναπτος.

ἀπιᾶτον, τό, *wine flavoured with celery*, *Gp*.8.30, Alex.Trall.10.

ἀπιδέα, ἡ, *pear-tree*, *Gp*.10.3.6 (ἀππ- codd.).

ἀπίδιον, τό, Dim. of ἄπιον, *pear*, Sch.Od.7.115 codd., Alex.Trall.*Febr*.3.

Ἀπιεῖον, τό, *the temple of Apis*, *OGI*90.33 (Rosetta).

ἀπίεστος [ῐ], ον, (πιέζω) *incompressible*, Arist.*Mete*.385^{a}15, 386^{b}8, Thphr.*Lap*.8.

ἀπίθᾰνος [ῐ], ον, *incredible, unlikely*, Pl.*Lg*.663e, Arist.*Po*.1461^{b}12; φαντασίαι *Stoic*.2.25: Comp. ἔτι -ώτερον εἰ.. Str.1.2.22. 2. of persons, *not to be trusted* or *relied on*, πρός τι in a matter, Aeschin.2.3. b. *unpersuaded, unconvinced*, ἀ. ἂν εἴη Pl.*Prm*.133c. II. *not having confidence* to do a thing, c. inf., Plu.*Nic*.3. III. *not persuasive, unconvincing*, λόγος Pl.*Phdr*.265b, cf. Arist.*Rh*.1406^{b}14, 1408^{b}22; ὁρίζειν τὸν ἀριθμὸν ἀπίθανον Ael.*Tact*.8.1; ἀ. λέγειν, of persons, Plu.2.812e, cf. 819c; ἀ. ζωγράφος Luc.*Ind*.22; ἀ. ἐν τῇ ὑποκρίσει Id.*Pseudol*.16. Adv. -νως *not persuasively, coarsely, rudely*, Isoc.5.26, D.H.*Lys*.17, Epicur.*Ep*.2 p.35 U., etc.

ἀπῐθᾰνότης, ητος, ἡ, *improbability*, αἰτίας Aeschin.2.64, J.*Ap*.1.34.

ἀπῑθέω, (πείθω) Ep. form of ἀπειθέω, c. dat., freq. in Hom. usu. with neg., οὐκ ἀπίθησε μύθῳ he *disobeyed* not the words, Il.1.220, cf. 6.102, al.: abs., ib.16.458: once c. gen., οὐδ' ἀπίθησε θεὰ.. ἀγγελιάων *h.Cer*.448: used in S.*Ph*.1447 (anap.). II. *fail to persuade*, οὐδ' ἀπίθησέ νιν (ϝιν Herm.) Pi.*P*.4.36.

ἀπῑθής, ές, poet. for ἀπειθής I, *AP*5.86 (Rufin.); for ἀπειθής II, *lacking in persuasion*, Timo 26.

ἀπῑθύνω, = ἀπευθύνω, of setting bones, in pf. Pass., Hp.*Fract*.7; of drawing lines, *AP*6.67 (Jul. Aegypt.); ἀ. τῆς ὄψιος τὰ διάστροφα Aret.*CA*1.5.

ἀπικμάω, *winnow*, σῖτον Thphr.*CP*4.16.2.

ἄπικρος, ον, *not bitter*, τῷ ἤθει Arist.*VV*1250^{a}42, cf. Ptol.*Tetr*.158.

ἀπικρόχολος, ον, *free from bitter bile*, Hsch.

ἀπίλητος, ον, (πιλέω) *not to be pressed close*, i.e. either *incompressible* or *elastic*, Arist.*Mete*.385^{a}17, 387^{a}16.

ἀπίλλω, *exclude*, Lys.10.18 (nisi leg. ἀπείλλ-).

ἀπίμελος, ον, (πιμελή) *without fat, not fat*, Diocl.*Fr*.136, Arist.*HA* 519^{b}8, *PA*675^{b}11, al.: Comp. -ώτερος ib.672^{a}23: Sup. -ώτατος *HA* 520^{a}19.

ἀπῑνής, ές, (πίνος) *without dirt, clean*, Ath.14.661d.

ἀπῑνόω, (ἀπινής) *clean*, Hsch. (Pass.).

ἀπῑνύσσω, (πινυτός) *lack understanding*, δοκέεις δέ μοι οὐκ ἀπινύσσειν Od.5.342, 6.258; κῆρ ἀπινύσσων, of one *lying senseless*, Il.15.10; cf. Apollon.*Lex*. s. v. ἀπινυτέω.

ἀπινύτως, Adv. *unwisely*, Hsch. s. v. ἀπινύσσων.

ἄπιξις, εως, ἡ, Ion. for ἄφιξις.

ἀπιοειδής, ές, φύλλα *like those of the pear-tree*, Thphr.*HP*3.10.3, cf. Gal.19.137.

ἄπιον, τό, (ἄπιος A) *pear*, Pl.*Lg*.845b, Theoc.7.120, Thphr.*CP*6.14.4. 2. = ἄπιος (A), *pear-tree*, ib.1.15.2.

ἄπιος (A), [ᾰ], ἡ, *pear-tree*, *Pyrus communis*, Arist.*HA*552^{b}2, Thphr.*HP*1.3.3, *CP*1.15.2, Dsc.1.116, Gal.11.834. 2. = ἄπιον, *pear*, Ar.*Fr*.569.3; ἀπ' Εὐβοίας ἀπίους Hermipp.63.17, Alex.33, Gal.6.603. II. *Euphorbia Apios, tuberous spurge*, Thphr.*HP*9.9.5, Dsc.4.175. III. = ἀστράγαλος, Ps.-Dsc.4.61.

ἄπιος (B), η, ον, *far away, far off, distant*, τηλόθεν ἐξ ἀπίης γαίης Il.1.270, 3.49, Od.16.18, cf. S.*OC*1685. II. Ἄπιος, α, ον, *Apian*, i.e. *Peloponnesian*, said (in this sense) to be derived from Ἆπις, Apis, a mythical king of Argos, A.*Supp*.260, cf. Paus.2.5.7; Ἀπία γῆ, Ἀπία χθών, or Ἀπία alone, *the Peloponnese*, esp. *Argolis*, A.*Ag*.256, S.*OC*1303, Ath.14.650b, etc.; cf. Ἀπίς prob. in A.R.4.1564. [The former word has ᾰ, the latter ᾱ; yet S.*OC*1685 uses signf. I with ᾱ, and later Ep. Poets have signf. II with ᾰ, cf. Rhian.13.] (Commonly derived from ἀπό, as ἀντίος from ἀντί; and Hsch. expl. ἐξ ἀπίης γαίης by ἀλλοτρίας ἢ ξένης ἢ μακρὰν οὔσης, cf. Str.8.6.9.)

ἀπῑπόω, *press* the juice *from* anything, Hdt.2.94.

Ἆπις, ιδος, εως, and Ion. ιος, ὁ, *Apis*, a bull worshipped in Egypt, Hdt.2.153, etc. 2. a mythical king of Argos, v. ἄπιος (B) II. II. **Ἀπίς**, = Ἀπία γῆ, Theoc.25.183, prob. in A.R.4.1564.

ἀπῐσόω, *make equal*, αὐτὸν ἀ. τοῖς κλιντῆρσιν, in reference to Procrustes, Plu.*Thes*.11, cf. Luc.*Pr.Im*.13:—Pass., *to be made equal*, τῇ ἀξίῃ τῶν φορτίων *to* their value, Hdt.4.196, cf. Sch.Il.*Oxy*.1086 i 22 (in form ἀφ-).

ἀπίσσωτος, ον, (πισσόω) *unpitched*, ἄγγη Str.11.10.2, cf. Dsc.1.71 (interpol.).

ἀπιστ-εύω, incorrect form for sq., ἀ. εἰ.. *POxy*.237^{v}5 (ii A.D.). **-έω**, fut. Pass. ἀπιστηθήσομαι D.S.32.10, but ἀπιστήσομαι in pass. sense, Pl.*R*.450c:—*to be* ἄπιστος, and so: I. *disbelieve, distrust*, ἐγὼ τὸ μὲν οὔ ποτ' ἀπίστεον Od.13.339; τύχην ἀ. E.*Alc*.1130; πάντα Ar.*Ec*.775, cf. Th.7.28 (s. v.l.), X.*Ages*.5.6, 8.7:—Pass., τὴν γνῶσιν τοῦ οἰκείου ἀπιστεῖσθαι *was distrusted*, i.e. no one could be sure of knowing, Th.7.44; ἀ. ἐν μαρτυρίαις Antipho 2.2.7; ἐπειδὰν γνῶσιν ἀπιστούμενοι, οὐ φιλοῦσι τοὺς ἀπιστοῦντας X.*Cyr*.7.2.17, cf. *Hier*.4.1; ὑπὸ τῆς πατρίδος Id.*Smp*.4.29, cf. Pl.*Plt*.271b, Isoc.5.49:—but mostly, 2. c. dat. pers., κρατέουσιν Emp.5.1, cf. Th.8.83, Pl.*Prt*.319b, etc.: so c. dat. rei, τῷ χρησμῷ Hdt.1.158; πῶς ἀπιστήσω λόγοις; S.*Ph*.1350, cf. Th.6.86; ἀ. τῇ ἐξ αὐτῶν ξυνέσει Id.3.37; τοῖς ἰάμασιν *IG* 4.951.24 (Epid.); ἡμῖν αὐτοῖς Arist.*EN*1112^{b}10; ἀ. τινί τι *disbelieve* one in a thing, Hdt.3.122; περί τινος Id.4.96; οἷς ἠπίστησαν ἔχειν.. whom they *suspected of* having, Plb.4.18.8. 3. c. inf., οὐδέν σ' ἀπιστῶ καὶ δὶς οἰμῶξαι I nothing *doubt* that.., S.*Aj*.940; ἀ. μὴ γενέσθαι τι *to doubt* that it could be, Th.1.10; ἀπιστοῦντες αὐτὸν μὴ ἥξειν Id.3.2.101, cf. 4.40, Pl.*Plt*.301c, *R*.555a; also ἀ. μὴ οὐκ ἐπιστήμη ᾖ ἡ ἀρετή Id.*Men*.89d; ἀ. πῶς.. *Phd*.73b; ἀ. εἰ.. *APl*.4.52 (Phil.), Ph.2.555; ὅτι.. Pl.*Men*.89d; ὡς *R*.450c:—Pass., τὸ ἐπιτήδευμα ἀπιστεῖται μὴ δυνατὸν εἶναι it *is not believed* to be possible, Id.*Lg*.839c, cf. *Chrm*.168e. 4. abs., *to be incredulous*, Hdt.8.94, cf. *Ev.Marc*.16.16, etc.; νᾶφε καὶ μέμνασ' ἀπιστεῖν Epich.250; ἐπὶ τοῖς λεγομένοις Ph.2.92. II. = ἀπειθέω, *disobey*, τινί Hdt.6.108, freq. in Trag. and Pl., A.*Pr*.640, S.*Ant*.381 (lyr.), *Tr*.1183, 1224, Pl.*Ap*.29c, al.: abs., *to be disobedient*, τοῖς ἀπιστοῦσιν τάδε *in* these things, S.*Ant*.219, cf. 656; ἢν δ' ἀπιστῶσι but if they *refuse to comply*, E.*Supp*.389, cf. Pl.*Lg*.941c. 2. *to be faithless*, εἰ ἡμεῖς ἀπιστοῦμεν, ἐκεῖνος πιστὸς μένει 2*Ep.Tim*.2.13. 3. νεκρὸς τὸν θάνατον ἀπιστούμενος *belying* death, Polem.*Call*.55. III. τὸ σῶμ' οὐκ ἀπιστήσω χθονί, i.e. I *will* not *hesitate to commit* it.., E.*Heracl*.1024; τούτῳ ἠπίστησεν ἀποθανοῦσαν ἑαυτὴν ἐπιτρέψαι Lys.31.21. **-ητέον**, *one must mistrust, disbelieve*, c. dat., Plb.4.41.8; of persons, Str.8.4.10, etc.; ἀ. ἡμῖν περί.. Hp.*Cord*.2. **-ητικός**, ή, όν, *incredulous*, M.Ant.1.6.

ἀπιστία, Ion. -ίη, ἡ, *unbelief, distrust*, πίστεις.. ὁμῶς καὶ ἀπιστίαι ὤλεσαν ἄνδρας beliefs and *disbeliefs*, Hes.*Op*.372; πίστει χρήματ' ὄλεσσα, ἀπιστίῃ δ' ἐσάωσα Thgn.831 [ῑ]; τῶν θείων τὰ πολλὰ ἀπιστίῃ διαφυγγάνει μὴ γινώσκεσθαι Heraclit.86, cf. Pl.*Grg*.493c; τοῖσι παρεοῦσι ἀ. πολλὴ ὑπεκέχυτο Hdt.3.66, cf. 2.152; ὑπὸ ἀπιστίης Id.3.153, al.; ὑπὸ ἀ. μὴ γενέσθαι τι from *disbelief* that.., Id.1.68; ἀ. πρὸς ἑαυτόν *lack of* self-*confidence*, Th.8.66; ἀπιστίᾳ λόγους ἐνδέχεσθαι E.*Ion* 1606; πέφευγε τοὔπος ἐξ ἀπιστίας A.*Ag*.268; ἀπιστίαν ἔχειν περί τινος to be *in doubt*, Pl.*Phd*.107b; σώφρων ἀ. E.*Hel*.1617; πρὸς -ίαν τοῦ κατηγόρου to *discredit* him, Arist.*Rh*.1398^{a}10; ἡ ἀ. ἡ πρὸς ἀλλήλους Id.*Pol*.1297^{a}4; ἀ. ἡ καθ' αὑτοῦ Longin.38.2; πρός τι Pl.*Sph*.258c. 2. of things, τὰ εἰρημένα ἐς ἀ. πολλὴν ἀπῖκται Hdt.1.193; πολλὰς ἀπιστίας ἔχει it admits of many *doubts*, Pl.*R*.450c; ὁ λόγος εἰς ἀ. καταπίπτει Id.*Phd*.88d; καταβαλεῖν τινὰ εἰς ἀ. ib.c; ἀ. παρέχειν ib.86e (interpol.); ἀτοπία καὶ ἀπιστία *incredibility*, Isoc.17.48; ταῦτ' ἀπιστίαν ἔχει D.10.44. II. *want of faith, faithlessness*, θνῄσκει δὲ πίστις βλαστάνει δ' ἀ. S.*OC*611; *treachery*, And.3.2, X.*An*.2.5.21; βλέπειν ἀπιστίαν Eup.309.

ἄπιστος, ον, I. Pass., *not to be trusted*, and so: 1. of persons and their acts, *not trusty, faithless*, ὑπερφίαλοι καὶ ἄ. Il.3.106; θεοῖσίν τ' ἐχθρὲ καὶ ἀνθρώποισιν ἄπιστε Thgn.601; ἄ. ὡς γυναικεῖον γένος E.*IT*1298; ἄ. λῄστορες *Sammelb*.4309.14 (iii B.C.); δολοπλοκίαι Thgn.226; ἄ. ποιεῖν τινά *mistrusted*, Hdt.8.22, cf. 9.98; τὰ ἑαυτοῦ πιστὰ ἀ. ποιεῖν X.*An*.2.4.7; ἄπιστος ἑταιρείας λιμήν S.*Aj*.683; θράσει ἀ. ἐπαιρόμενος by *untrustworthy, groundless* confidence, Th.1.120; *shifty, unreliable*, Pl.*Lg*.775d. 2. of reports and the like, *incredible*, dub. in Archil.74.5, cf. Pi.*O*.1.31, Hdt.3.80; τέρας A.*Pr*.832; ἄ. καὶ πέρα κλύειν Ar.*Av*.418; ἄ. ἐνόμιζον εἰ.. Ph.2.556; τὸ ἐλπίδων ἄ. *undreamed of* even in hope, S.*Ph*.868: Comp. -ότερος, λόγος Aeschin.3.59: Sup., πίστις ἀπιστοτάτη And.1.67, cf. Pl.*Ep*.314b. II. Act., *mistrustful, incredulous, suspicious*, θυμὸς δέ τοι αἰὲν ἄ. Od.14.150; ὦτα.. ἀπιστότερα ὀφθαλμῶν *less credulous*, Hdt.1.8; ἄ. πρὸς Φίλιππον *distrustful* towards him, D.19.27; ἄ. εἶ.. σαυτῷ you do *not believe* what you say yourself, Pl.*Ap*.26e; ἤθη ἄ. Id.*Lg*.705a; τὸ ἄ., = ἀπιστία, Th.8.66; δούλοις πῶς οὐκ ἄπιστον; Gorg.*Pal*.11. b. in *NT*, *unbelieving*, 1*Ep.Cor*.6.6, al. 2. *disobedient, disloyal*, S.*Fr*.627: c. gen., A.*Th*.876; ἔχειν ἄπιστον.. ἀναρχίαν πόλει, i.e. ἀναρχίαν ἔχειν ἀπειθοῦσαν τῇ πόλει, ib.1035, cf. E.*IT*1476. III. Adv. ἀπίστως: 1. Pass., *beyond belief*, ἀ. ἐπὶ τὸ μυθῶδες ἐκνενικηκότα Th.1.21; οὐκ ἀ. not *incredibly*, Arist.*Rh.Al*.1438^{a}22, 1438^{b}2. 2. Act., *distrustfully, suspiciously*, Th.3.83; ἀ. τινὰ διαθεῖναι D.20.22. b. *treacherously*, Ph.1.516.

ἀπιστοσύνη, ἡ, = ἀπιστία, E.*Med.*422 (lyr.).

ἀπιστούντως, Adv. = ἀπίστως 2, Numen.ap.Eus.*PE*14.7.

ἀπιστόφιλος, ον, *loving unbelief*, Orac.ap.Phleg.*Mir.*10.

ἀπισχν-αίνω, *make lean* or *thin*, Philem.98.7, Arist.*HA*574^{b}6. **-αντέον**, *one must make thin*, Id.*Pr.*865^{a}37. **-όω**, in Pass., *shrink*, Hp.*Int.*3, *Morb.Sacr.*8, cf. Sor.1.53.

ἀπισχῡρ-ίζομαι, *oppose firmly, give a flat denial*, πρός τινα Th.1.140, cf. Plu.*Per.*31; πρὸς τὰς ἡδονὰς Id.*Agis*4, al.; *hold out against*, πρὸς δίψος Them.*Or.*11.149c. II. *set oneself to affirm, maintain* a thing, ib.28.342c, Eust.1278.53, etc. III. *cling firmly*, of the λεπάς, Sch.Ar.*Pl.*1096. **-ιστικῶς**, Adv. *positively*, Eust.1861.41.

ἀπίσχω, = ἀπέχω, *keep off, hold off*, Od.11.95; χεῖρας ἔργου J.*BJ* 1.7.3.

ἀπίσωσις [πῐ], εως, ἡ, *equalization*, Nicom.*Ar.*1.23; as a rhetorical figure, coupled with παρίσωσις, Poll.4.27 (pl.).

ἀπῐτέον, (ἄπειμι B) *one must go away*, Hp.*Ep.*13, X.*An.*5.3.1, Amphis 1, Luc.*Herm.*82.

ἀπίτευτος, ον, *unwatered*, *BCH*21.554 (Thesp.); cf. πιτεύω.

ἀπίτης [ῑ], (sc. οἶνος), ου, ὁ, (ἄπιον) *perry*, Dsc.5.24, *Gp.*8.5 (ἀππ-).

ἀπῐτητέον, pl. έα, = ἀπιτέον, Luc.*Lex.*2.

ἀπιχθυόομαι, Pass., *to become a fish*, Herm.ap.Stob.1.49.69.

ἄπιχθυς, υ, *eating no fish*, Ar.*Fr.*564 (= E.*Fr.*366). 2. Subst., *paltry little fish*, Eust.1720.24.

ἀπίων [ῑ], ον, gen. ονος, *not fat*, Diph.Siph.ap.Ath.4.120e, Aret. *CD*1.5.

ἀπλᾰγιάστως, Adv., (πλαγιάζω) *not obliquely*, Eust.1229.41.

ἄπλαγκτος [λᾰ], ον, = ἀπλανής, Nonn.*D.*4.313.

ἁπλαῖ, v. sub ἁπλοῦς.

ἀπλακέω, ἀπλακία, etc., v. sub ἀμπλακέω, etc.

ἀπλάκουντος [λᾰ], ον, *without cakes*, Pl.Com.113.

ἀπλάν-εια [λᾰ], ἡ, *constancy, unchangeableness*, Suid. **-ῆ**· πολλά (Cypr.), Hsch. **-ής**, ές, *not wandering, steady, fixed*, Pl.*Plt.*288a, al.: c. gen., ἀπλανὲς ἀπηργάσατο ἐκείνων [κινήσεων] made it *free from* their *influence*, Id.*Ti.*34a. 2. Astron. of stars, *fixed*, opp. *planets*, ib. 40b, cf. Arist.*Mete.*343^{b}9, *Metaph.*1073^{b}19, Arat.461, *AP*9.25 (Leon.); ἡ ἀ. σφαῖρα *Corp.Herm.*2.6. II. of a line, *straight*, *AP*6.65 (Paul. Sil.). III. *unwavering*, θεωρία Epicur.*Ep.*3 p.62 U. 2. *not erring*, S.E.*M.*7.195, Longin.2.2 (Sup.), etc. Adv. **-νῶς** *without going astray*, Max.Tyr.5.2; *accurately*, Alciphr.3.59. **-ησία**, ἡ, *freedom from error*, S.E.*M.*7.394. **-ητος**, ον, *that cannot go astray* or *err*, Lxx *Jb.*12.20, Babr.50.20, *POxy.*237 vi 30 (ii A. D.).

ἄπλαντα· ῥυπαρά, Hsch. (leg. ἄπλυντα).

ἀπλαστία, ἡ, *sincerity*, Pl.*Def.*412e.

ἄπλαστος, ον, *not capable of being moulded*, Arist.*Mete.*385^{a}15. 2. *not moulded*: hence, *natural, unaffected*, φρόνημα, εὔνοια, προθυμία, ἦθος, etc., Plu.*Aem.*37, *Vit.Philonid.*p.10 C., Them.*Or.*4.56d, etc.; of persons, Lxx *Ge.*25.27, Ceb.20. Adv. **-τως** *naturally, without disguise*, γελᾶν Pl.*Ep.*319b codd.; αὐλεῖν Thphr.*HP*4.11.4; λέγειν D.H. *Rh.*10.11; ἀποκρίνεσθαι Ael.*VH*9.27. 3. *not feigned*: hence, *true*, opp. *mythical*, Plu.2.16c, 62c. 4. *not fully shapen, unformed*, Ph. 2.317. II. v.l. for ἄπλᾱτος (q.v.).

ἀπλᾰτής, ές, *without breadth*, γραμμή Arist.*APr.*49^{b}36; μῆκος ἀ., opp. πλάτος ἔχον, Id.*Top.*143^{b}14: metaph., Gal.7.410; ἀ. ὑγίεια *without latitude*, i.e. variation, Id.6.28. Adv. **-τῶς** Iamb. *in Nic.*p.56 P.

ἄπλᾱτος, Dor. and Trag. for Ep. ἄπλητος (q.v.), ον, (πελάζω) *unapproachable*, always with a notion of *terrible, monstrous*, Hes.*Op.*148, *Th.*151; ἄ. πῦρ Pi.*P.*1.21 (whence it must be restored for ἀπλήστου in A.*Pr.*373); ὀφίων κεφαλαί, Τυφών, Pi.*P.*12.9, *Fr.*93; Ἔχιδνα B.5.62, cf. 12.51; θρέμμα S.*Tr.*1093; αἶσα Id.*Aj.*256 (lyr.); ἄπλατον ἀξύμβλητον ἐξεθρεψάμην Id.*Fr.*387.—In many places ἄπλαστος is a v.l., Id.*Aj.*256, E.*Med.*151 (lyr.); cf. ἄπληστος. 2. = ἄπλετος, κυψέλη *Com.Adesp.*620; ἄπλατοι ὅσοι Phld.*Rh.*1.3 S., al.; γάλα Diog.Oen. 39, cf. Epicur.*Nat.*11.154.14, Phld.*Oec.*p.41 J., Porph.*Abst.*1.55; cf. ἄπλητος.

ἀπλέητον· ἀπροσπέλαστον, Hsch.

ἀπλεκής, ές, = sq., Nonn.*D.*42.87.

ἄπλεκτος, ον, *unplaited*, χαίτη *AP*7.412 (Alc. Mess.), *Epigr.Gr.* 790.8 (Dyme).

ἀπλεόναστος, ον, *without an extra letter*, Eust.947.16.

ἀπλεονέκτητος, ον, *free from avarice*, Chaerem.ap.Porph.*Abst.* 4.6. 2. *without excess*, *Theol.Ar.*34.

ἀπλετομεγέθης, ες, *unapproachably great*, λίθος Sch.A.R.3.41.

ἄπλετος, ον, *boundless, immense*, ἠέρος ὕψος Emp.17.18; αὐγή Id. 135; δόξα Pi.*I.*4(3).11; βάρος S.*Tr.*982; also found in Prose, χρυσὸς ἄ. Hdt.1.14, 50, al.; ἅλες, ὕδωρ, 4.53, 8.12; οἰμωγή 6.58; μάχη Pl.*Sph.* 246c; ἄ. καὶ ἀμήχανον [χρόνου πλῆθος] Id.*Lg.*676b; ἐν χρόνου μήκεσιν ἀπλέτοις ib.683a; χιών X.*An.*4.4.11; πλῆθος Arist.*GA*755^{b}26; ποταμοὶ ἄπλετοι τὸ μέγεθος Id.*Mete.*355^{b}23; ῥαφανίδες ἄ. τὸ πάχος Id.*Pr.* 924^{a}27; θόρυβος Plb.1.50.3, al.; φύσις Plot.5.5.6; δύναμις 4.8.6.

ἄπλευρος, ον, *without sides* or *ribs*, ἄ. στῆθος *narrow* chest, Arist. *Phgn.*810^{a}3, cf. 809^{b}7 (Comp.); of persons, *narrow-chested*, opp. εὔπλευροι, ib.810^{b}13, Teles p.55.3 H., Mnesith.ap.Orib.21.7.6 (Sup.).

ἄπλευστος, ον, *not navigated*: τὸ ἄ. part of the sea *not yet navigated*, X.*Cyr.*6.1.16.

ἀπληγής, ές, of verses, *free from metrical defect*, Diom.p.498 K.

ἁπλήγιος, ον, *clad in a single garment*: generally, = ἁπλοῦς, Eup. 222.

ἁπληγίς, ίδος, ἡ, = ἁπλοΐς (as Subst.), *a single upper garment* or *cloak*, opp. διπληγίς, S.*Fr.*777, Ar.*Fr.*54, Herod.5.18.

ἄπληγος, ον, (πληγή) *not smitten* with disease, etc., *PMag.Par.* 1.1063.

ἀπλήθυντος, ον, *not multiplied, without plurality*, Porph.*Sent.*33, Procl. *in Prm.*p.535 S. Adv. **-τως** Porph.*Sent.* l.c., Procl.*Inst.*62.

ἄπληκτος, ον, *unstricken*, of a horse *needing no whip* or *spur*, Eup. 232, Pl.*Phdr.*253d: metaph., Plu.2.721e; *unwounded, without receiving a blow*, φρουδοι δ' ἄ. E.*Rh.*814; *immune from stings*, Dsc. 2.118; of a plant, *uninjured*, Thphr.*HP*9.14.1. 2. Act., *not striking*, in Adv. **-τως** *without pulsation*, Procl. *in Cra.*p.37 P. II. Act., *not irritating* or *pungent*, Sor.2.59: Comp., *not too stimulating*, Herod.Med.ap.Aët.5.116. Adv. **-τως** Ruf.ap.Orib.8.24.53.

ἀπλημμελῶς, Adv. *without discord*, Dam.*Pr.*434.

ἀπλήμων, ον, = ἄπληστος, Hsch.

ἀπλήξ, ῆγος, ὁ, ἡ, = ἄπληκτος 1, Arr.*Epict.*4.1.124; sens. obsc., Luc.*Am.*54.

ἀπλήρωτος, ον, *insatiable*, Phld.*Mus.*p.78 K., Ph.2.266, al., Luc. *Merc.Cond.*39; Ἅιδης *IG*14.1754; πάντων Plu.2.524b; *unsatisfied*, Gal.17(1).597. 2. *unfilled*, Poll.1.121; τὸ ἀ. *absence of satiety*, Plot.5.8.4.

ἀπλησίαστος, ον, = ἄπλατος, Sch.Pi.*P.*12.15, Sch.S.*Aj.*247.

ἀπληστ-εί, Adv. of ἄπληστος, Hdn.*Epim.*257. **-εύομαι**, *to be insatiable*, τινός in a thing, Hipparch.ap.Stob.4.44.81; ἔν τινι Lxx *Si.*34(31).17. **-ία**, ἡ, *insatiate desire, greediness*, whether of food or money, ὑπὸ τῆς ἀπληστίας Pherecr.156; εἰς τοσαύτην ἀ. ἀφίκοντο Lys.12.19, cf. D.36.44; διὰ τὴν ἀ. Pl.*Grg.*493b; ἀ. τρόπων D.22. 67 (interpol.); γαστρός Ph.1.360. 2. c. gen. rei, *insatiate desire of*, πλούτου, χρυσοῦ, Pl.*R.*562b, *Lg.*831d; λέχους E.*Andr.*218; τῆς εὐχῆς, referring to Midas, Arist.*Pol.*1257^{b}16; τοῦ θεωρεῖν Ph.1. 12. **-οινος**, ον, *insatiate in wine*, ἀρύταιναι Timo 4. **-ος**, ον, *insatiate, greedy*, Thgn.109, S.*El.*1336, Arist.*HA*591^{b}2, etc.; sts. confounded with ἄπλαστος (i.e. ἄπλατος), q.v. 2. c. gen., ἄ. χρημάτων, αἵματος, Hdt.1.187, 212, Pl.*Lg.*773e, etc.; κακῶν A.*Eu.* 976 (lyr.). II. Adv. **-τως**, ἔχειν Pl.*Grg.*493c, al.; ἀ. διακεῖσθαι or ἔχειν πρός τι X.*Cyr.*4.1.14, Isoc.5.135, 8.7: also neut. pl. as Adv., αἰάζεις ἄπληστα *CIG*2240 (Chios).

ἄπλητος, Ep. and Ion. form of ἄπλᾱτος (q.v.), ον, dub. in *h.Cer.* 83; μαίνεται ἄπλητον Semon.7.34; = ἄπλετος, *great*, χεύματα Orph. *A.*1051; αἰθήρ Q.S.8.222; δῶρα Id.9.510.

ἄπλια, name of a *throw at dice*, Poll.7.204.

ἀπλίκιτ-ον, τό, *camp-prison*, *PLond.ined.*2487 (iv A. D.):—hence **-άριοι**, οἱ, *warders*, Lyd.*Mag.*3.8.

ἁπλοδίσημος, ον, (also written ἀπλοτίσ-) dub. sens., ἔργον, apptly. of embroidery or weaving, *PLond.ined.*2132.

ἁπλο-ειδής, ές, *simple* or *single*, *Theol.Ar.*52 (Comp.). **-θριξ**, ὁ, ἡ, gen. τριχος, *with plain hair*, Ptol.*Tetr.*143, Alex.Aphr.*Pr.* 1.2.

ἄπλοια, ἡ, Ion. and poet. ἀπλοΐη, Call.*Dian.*230, prob. in *AP*7.640 (Antip.): (ἄπλοος):—*impossibility of sailing, detention in port*, esp. from stress of weather, A.*Ag.*188; ἀπλοίᾳ χρῆσθαι E.*IA*88, cf. *IT* 15; ἡσύχαζεν ὑπὸ ἀπλοίας Th.4.4, cf. 6.22: pl., ἀποπλέειν .. ὁρμημένον αὐτὸν ἴσχον ἄπλοιαι Hdt.2.119.

ἁπλοΐδιον, τό, Dim. of ἁπλοΐς, *PPetr.*3 p.18 (iii B. C.).

ἁπλοΐζομαι, (ἁπλοῦς) *behave simply, deal frankly*, πρὸς τοὺς φίλους X.*Mem.*4.2.18; *to be simple in habits*, D.C.65.7; *to be reduced to simplicity*, Dam.*Pr.*32.—Act. in same sense, Sch.Od.6.187.

ἁπλοϊκός, ή, όν, *simple, natural, plain*, Phint.ap.Stob.4.23.61^{a}, Luc.*Tim.*56, A.D.*Synt.*200.18, Hermog.*Id.*2.9, Demetr.*Eloc.*244, etc.: Comp. **-ώτερος** Simp. *in Ph.*337.11: Sup. **-ώτατος** Philostr. *VS*2.9.2, Luc.*Alex.*4. Adv. **-κῶς** D.H.*Dem.*45.

ἄπλοιοι· οἱ μὴ δυνάμενοι πλεῖν, Hsch.

ἁπλοΐς, ίδος, ἡ, *simple, single*, ἁπλοΐδες χλαῖναι Il.24.230, Od.24. 276: as Subst., *single garment*, = ἁπληγίς, *AP*5.293 (Agath.).

ἁπλόκᾰμος, ον, *having shorn her hair*, *AP*7.146 (Antip. Sid.).

ἄπλοκος, ον, (πλέκω) = ἄπλεκτος, Opp.*H.*3.469: metaph., *unconnected*, cj. in Longin.19.1.

Ἁπλοκύων, ὁ, nickname of *a Cynic who wore his coat single* instead of double, Plu.*Brut.*34, D.L.6.13.

ἁπλόος, η, ον, contr. **ἁπλοῦς**, ῆ, οῦν, opp. διπλόος *twofold*, and so, I. *single*, ἁπλῆ γὰρ οἶμος εἰς Ἅιδου φέρει A.*Fr.*239, cf. X. *Cyr.*1.3.4 (Comp.); ἁπλῷ τείχει περιτειχίζειν Th.3.18; δὶς τόσ' ἐξ ἁπλῶν κακά S.*Aj.*277; ὅπως ἂν ἡ χάρις ἐξ ἁπλῆς διπλῆ φανῇ Id.*Tr.* 619; ἁπλᾶς δὲ λύπας ἐξὸν οὐκ οἴσω διπλᾶς E.*IT*688. b. ἁπλαῖ (sc. κρηπῖδες), αἱ, *single-soled shoes*, Stratt.24, D.54.34. II. *simple, plain, straightforward*, κελεύθοις ἁπλόαις ζωᾶς Pi.*N.*8.36; ἁ. ὁ μῦθος A.*Ch.*554; ἁ. λόγῳ Id.*Pr.*610, al.; ὡς ἁ. λόγῳ ib.46, Ar.*Ach.*1151; ἁ. λόγος the matter is *simple*, E.*Hel.*979; ἁ. διήγησις *simple* narrative (without dialogue), Pl.*R.*392d; οὐκ ἐς ἁπλοῦν φέρει leads to no *simple issue*, S.*OT*519; ἁπλᾶ γε καὶ σαφῆ λέγω μαθεῖν Alex.240.7; οὐδὲν ἔχω ἁπλούστερον λέγειν X.*Cyr.*3.1.32; of *single-membered* periods, Demetr.*Eloc.*17, etc.; of habits, ἁπλούστατος βίος Plb.9.10. 5; νόμοι λίαν ἁ. καὶ βαρβαρικοί Arist.*Pol.*1268^{b}39; ἁπλοῦν ἦν .. ἀποθανεῖν *a plain course*, Men.14. b. of persons, or their words, thoughts, and acts, *simple, open, frank*, ἁπλᾶ γάρ ἐστι τῆς ἀληθείας ἔπη A.*Fr.*176; ἁ. καὶ γενναῖος Pl.*R.*361b, etc.; ἁ. τρόποι E.*IA*927; opp. δόλος, Ar.*Pl.*1158; πρὸς τοὺς φίλους ὡς ἁπλούστατον εἶναι X. *Mem.*4.2.16. c. *simple-minded*, ὁ κριτὴς ὑπόκειται εἶναι ἁ. Arist. *Rh.*1357^{a}12, cf. *HA*608^{b}4 (Comp.), *Rh.*1367^{a}37; in bad sense, *simple, silly*, Isoc.2.46; λίαν γὰρ ἁπλοῦν τὸ νομίζειν.. Arist.*Mete*.339^{b}34. **III.** *simple*, opp. *compound* or *mixed*, Pl.*R*.547e, etc.; opp. μεμιγμένος, κεκραμένος, Arist.*Metaph*.989^{b}17, *Sens*.447^{a}18; ἁ. χρώματα Id.*Col*.791^{a}1; ἁ. ὀνόματα, opp. διπλᾶ, Id.*Po*.1457^{a}31; also of nouns, *without the article*, A.D.*Synt*.98.17, al.; of the *positive* adjective, Plu.2.412e, etc. **b.** ἁ. βιβλία rolls *containing a single author*, Id.*Ant*.58. **c.** of precious metals, *unalloyed, pure*, *SIG*901.9 (Delph., iv A.D.), *PCair*.67041. **d.** ἁ. ἐπίδεσμος, a kind of *bandage*, Hp.*Off*.7, etc. **2.** *absolute, sheer*, ἀκρασία Arist.*EN*1149^{a}2; συμφορά Lys.24.8, etc. **3.** *simple, unqualified* (cf. ἁπλῶς II. 3), οὐ πάνυ μοι δοκεῖ..οὕτως ἁπλοῦν εἶναι ὥστε.. Pl.*Prt*.331b, cf. *Smp*.206a, *Tht*.188d, al. **4.** *general*, opp. ἀκριβής, Arist.*Metaph*.1025^{b}7 (Comp.), cf. 1030^{a}16. **IV.** Adv. ἁπλῶς, v. sub voc. **V.** Comp. and Sup. ἁπλούστερος, ἁπλούστατος, v. supr.; irreg. Sup. ἁπλότατος *AP*6.185 (Zos.). (Cf. δι-πλόος; ἁ- = *sm̥*; -πλόος perh. identical with πλοῦς 'voyage', cf. Serb. *jedan put* '(one journey, hence) *once*'; transition from 'once' to 'simple' as in Lett. *vienkaŕšs* 'simple' (cf. Lith. *vienkart* 'once').)

ἄπλοος, ον, contr. **ἄπλους**, ουν: **I.** Act., of ships, *unseaworthy*, τριήρεις And.3.5; ναῦς ἄπλους ποιεῖν Th.7.34; νῆες ἄπλοι ἐγένοντο ibid.: of persons, ναύκληρον..ποιήσας ἄπλουν Crito Com.3: Comp., ἀπλοώτεραι νῆες *less fit for sea*, Th.7.60 (codd.; ἀπλούστεραι Suid.). **II.** Pass., of the sea, *not navigable, closed to navigation* (cf. ἄπλοια), ἄπλους ἡ θάλαττα ὑπὸ τῶν..λῃστῶν γέγονεν D.18.241; ἅλμη A.R.4.1271; Πόντος Plb.4.38.7: metaph., αἰθήρ Nonn.*D*.6.358. **III.** *no seafarer*, Ἠχώ ib.319.

ἁπλοπᾰθής, ές, (πάθος) *simply passive*, S.E.*P*.3.108 (**-πάθεια**, ἡ, is f.l. ib.47).

ἁπλός, ή, όν, late form for ἁπλόος, *An.Ox*.2.331.

ἁπλοσύνη, ἡ, = ἁπλότης, Lxx *Jb*.21.23.

ἁπλοσχήμων, ον, *of simple form*, Str.*Chr*.2.28.

ἁπλότης, ητος, ἡ, *singleness*, τῆς φωνῆς Arist.*Aud*.801^{a}19. **II.** *simplicity*, πόλεως X.*HG*6.1.18; κατὰ τὴν μουσικὴν Pl.*R*.404e; τῆς τροφῆς D.S.3.17: of literary style, D.H.*Rh*.9.14: pl., ἁπλότητες λόγων ibid. **2.** of persons, *simplicity, frankness, sincerity*, X.*Cyr*.1.4.3, Lxx *Wi*.1.1, Plb.1.78.8, D.S.5.66, etc.; ἡ εἰς τὸν Χριστὸν ἁ. 2*Ep.Cor*.11.3. **3.** *open-heartedness*: hence, *liberality*, ib.8.2, 9.11, cf. *IG*14.1517.

ἁπλο-τομέω, *cut by a simple incision*, τι Antyll.ap.Orib.44.8.1:—Pass., Aët.8.26:—hence **-τομητέον**, Id.16.123. **-τομία**, ἡ, *simple incision*, Antyll.ap.Orib.44.8.6, Gal.14.781.

Ἄπλουν, ὁ, Thess., = Ἀπόλλων, Pl.*Cra*.405c, *IG*9(2).512.19 (Larissa), etc. **ἁπλοῦς**, v. ἁπλόος.

ἄπλουτος, ον, *without riches*, S.*Fr*.835; ἁβρὸς καὶ οὐκ ἄ. Philostr.*VA*6.36; ἄ. ἀπεργάσασθαι τὸν πλοῦτον Thphr.*Fr*.78.

ἁπλόφυλλον, τό, = ἄλυσσον, Ps.-Dsc.3.91 (prob.l.).

ἁπλόω, (ἁπλοῦς) *make single, unfold, spread out*, οὐρήν Batr.74 (v.l.), cf. 80; σῶμα *AP*11.107 (Lucill.); ἱστία Orph.*A*.360, etc.; σαγήνην Alciphr.3.3; φάλαγγα Paus.4.11.2; δακτύλους Sor.1.73; ἁ. τὸν ἄργυρον *beat* it *thin*, *Anacreont*.4.5; *expose* a wound, Just.*Nov*.111*Pr*.:—Pass., ἀγρευθεὶς εἰς τὸ πλοῖον ἡπλώθη [the fish] *lay stretched out*.., Babr.4.5; ἀσπάραγος χαίρει γῇ ἡπλωμένῃ *open* ground, *Gp*.12.18.1; ἁπλωθέντων ἱστίων Lib.*Or*.11.264:—Med., *AP*10.9, Orph.*A*.278, D.P.235. **2.** metaph., ἅπλωσον σεαυτόν *be simple*, M.Ant.4.26:—Pass., *to be simplified*, Plot.6.7.35; but, *to be expanded*, Id.3.5.9 (fort. ἐξαπλ-). **3.** *make plain*, ὁδόν Lxx *Jb*.22.3.

ἀπλῠσία (A), ἡ, (ἄπλυτος) *filthiness, filth*, *AP*7.377 (Eryc.).

ἀπλῠσία (B), ἡ, a kind of *sponge*, so called because it *cannot be cleaned*, Arist.*HA*549^{a}4, Plin.*HN*9.150, prob.l. in Thphr.*HP*4.6.10.

ἄπλῠτος, ον, (πλύνω) *unwashen, unwashed*, of clothes, ἄλουτος ἀπλύτοις ἐν εἵμασιν Semon.7.5; ῥαφανίδες Eup.312, cf. Pherecr.175; of sponges, Arist.*HA*548^{b}29; of parts of the body, Ar.*V*.1035; ἀ. ποσὶ διεξιέναι τὰ φανερώτατα D.Chr.12.43; ἄ. ἄρτος Gal.6.500. Adv. -τως, λοιδορεῖν with *foul* language, Phld.*Ir*.p.45 W.

ἅπλ-ωμα, ατος, τό, (ἁπλόω) *that which is unfolded, expanse*, Sch.Ar.*Av*.1218. **-ῶς**, Adv. of ἁπλοῦς, *singly, in one way*, μένειν ἁ. ἐν τῇ αὑτοῦ μορφῇ Pl.*R*.381c, etc.; ἁ. λέγεσθαι *in one sense*, opp. πολλαχῶς, Arist.*Top*.158^{b}10; ἁ. λεγόμενα, opp. συμπλεκόμενα, Id.*Metaph*.1014^{a}19, cf. *Ph*.195^{b}15; opp. κατ' ἀλλήλων λέγεσθαι, *without distinction of subject and predicate*, *Metaph*.1041^{b}1; ἐσθλοὶ μὲν γὰρ ἁ. παντοδαπῶς δὲ κακοί Poët.ap.*EN*1106^{b}35, etc. **II.** *simply, plainly*, ἀλλ' ἁ. φράσον A.*Supp*.464; ἁ. τι φράζουσ' Id.*Ch*.121; ἁ. εἰπεῖν Isoc.4.154; λαλεῖν Anaxil.22.23. **b.** *openly, frankly*, Isoc.3.52, X.*HG*4.1.37; *in good faith*, D.18.308, etc.: in bad sense, ἁ. ἔχειν to be *a simpleton*, Isoc.4.16. **c.** *in its natural state, uncooked*, of food, Jul.*Or*.6.192b. **2.** *simply, absolutely*, ἁ. ἀδύνατον Th.3.45; τῶν νεῶν κατέδυ οὐδεμία ἁ. no ship was *absolutely* sunk (though some were disabled), Id.7.34; ἁ. οὐδὲ ἕν..συνίημι Philem.123; ὅσ' ἐστὶν ἀγαθὰ..ἁ. *simply* all the good things there are, Ar.*Ach*.873; ἔδωκ' ἐμαυτὸν ὑμῖν ἁ. D.18.179; ἁ. *absolutely*, opp. κατά τι (*relatively*), Arist.*Top*.115^{b}12; opp. πρός τι, *APr*.41^{a}5; opp. πρὸς ἡμᾶς, *APo*.72^{a}3; opp. τινί, *Top*.116^{a}21; ἁ. βαρύ, κοῦφον, μαλακόν, etc., *Cael*.311^{a}17, 27, *Mete*.386^{b}32, al.; τὸ ἁ. καλόν, τὸ ἁ. ἀγαθόν, etc., *EN*1136^{b}22, 1134^{b}4, al.; opp. ὁτιοῦν (*in some particular*), *Pol*.1301^{a}29; strengthd. ἁ. οὕτως Pl.*Grg*.468c, D.21.99; τὴν ἁ. δίκην *absolute, strict* justice, opp. τοὐπιεικές and χάρις, S.*Fr*.770; ἡ τελεία καὶ ἁ. κακία Arist.*EN*1138^{a}33; τὸ ἁ. the *absolute*, Dam.*Pr*.5: Comp. ἁπλούστερον Is.4.2; -τέρως Str.6.2.4: Sup. ἁπλούστατα Pl.*Lg*.921b. **3.** *in a word*, E.*Rh*.851, X.*Cyr*.1.6.33, *Mem*.1.3.2, etc. **4.** *generally*, opp. σαφέστερον, Arist.*Pol*.1341^{b}39, al.; ὡς ἁ. εἰπεῖν ib.1285^{a}31, *EN*1115^{a}8, al.; ἁ. δηλῶσαι *Hell.Oxy*.11.4; τὸν ἀκριβῶς ἐπιστάμενον λέγειν ἁ. οὐκ ἂν δυνάμενον εἰπεῖν Isoc.4.11, cf. Demetr.*Eloc*.100, 243: in bad sense, *loosely, superficially*, λίαν ἁ. Arist.*Metaph*.987^{a}21, *GA*756^{b}17, al.; οὐχ ἁ. φέρειν not *lightly*, E.*IA*899. **5.** *foolishly*, Plu.2.72b. **-ωσις**, εως, ἡ, *simplification*, Plot.6.9.11. **-ωτέον**, *one must simplify* Dam.*Pr*.256. **-ωτικός**, ή, όν, *simplifying*, c. gen., ib.39.

ἄπλωτος, ον, (πλώω) *not navigated, not navigable*, Arist.*Mir*.839^{b}13; πελάγη Ph.2.108; ἄπλωτα πάντα ἦν *navigation* was *stopped*, App.*Mith*.93.

ἀπνεής, ές, corrupt in *AP*9.420 as epith. of πῦρ (metaph. of love).

ἀπνεύ-μᾰτος, ον, (πνεῦμα) *without wind* or *current of air*, μεσημβρία Arist.*Pr*.911^{b}2, cf. Thphr.*CP*1.8.3. **-μων**, ον, gen. ονος, *without breath* or *life*, νεκρὰ καὶ ἀ. Simp. *in Epict*.p.6 D., Orac.ap.Dam.*Pr*.453, *Tab.Defix.Aud*.22.8 (Curium, iii A.D.). **-στί**, Adv. of ἄπνευστος, *without breathing*, ζῆν Arist.*Pr*.898^{b}24, *Resp*.475^{a}23; ἀ. ἔχειν *hold* one's *breath*, Pl.*Smp*.185d; *without drawing breath*, Hp.*Int*.12; λόγους συνείρειν σαφῶς καὶ ἀ. D.18.308 (-τεί), cf. Thphr.*Char*.2.9; ἀ. ἕλκειν, ἐκπίνειν, Antiph.74.14, Alex.244.3; *without breathing*, i.e. *lifeless*, ἀ. κεῖσθαι Plu.2.642d; φεύγειν ἀ. *breathlessly*, Porph.*Chr*.49. **-στία**, ἡ, *holding of the breath, not breathing*, Arist.*Pr*.881^{b}13, 961^{b}21. **-στιάζω**, *hold the breath*, ib.962^{b}31. **-στος**, ον, *breathless*, ἄ. καὶ ἄναυδος Od.5.456, cf. Theoc.25.271. **2.** *lifeless, dead*, Nonn.*D*.26.115; *without life*, φαρέτρη ib.15.269. **II.** = ἀπνεύματος, τόποι Thphr.*CP*5.12.7 (Sup.). Adv. -τως, = ἀπνευστί (q.v.), Plu.2.844f.

ἄπνιγμος, ον, = οὐ πεπνιγμένος, κνώδων Anon.ap.Hsch.

ἀπνοέω, *suffer from breathlessness*, Orib.*Syn*.9.44.1.

ἄπνοια, ἡ, *freedom from wind*, Hp.*Epid*.3.2. **2.** *windlessness, calm*, Arist.*Pr*.944^{b}12, Plb.34.11.19 (v.l.); *want of wind*, Thphr.*CP*2.7.5; *shelter from wind*, Arist.*GA*785^{a}29. **3.** *absence of respiration*, Gal.7.959.

ἄπνοος, ον, contr. **ἄπνους**, ουν:—*without wind, with but little air*, ἔαρ Hp.*Epid*.3.2, cf. Arist.*Mete*.361^{b}6, Thphr.*CP*2.9.1. **2.** *unventilated*, οἰκία Plu.2.515b; *air-tight*, κώρυκος Herod.8.74. **II.** *breathless*, Theopomp.Com.71. **2.** *lifeless*, *AP*7.229 (Diosc.), *IG*14.1787. **3.** *without breathing* or *respiration*, Heraclid.Pont.*Fr*.72, 75 Voss, Arist.*HA*492^{a}13.

ἀπό, Aeol., Thess., Arc., Cypr. **ἀπύ** Sapph.44, cf. 78, Alc.33, Theoc.28.16, *IG*12(2).6.45 (Mytil.), ἀπυδόμεναι ib.9(2).594 (Larissa), 5(2).6 (Tegea), etc.:—Prep. usually with Gen. but v. infr. B. (Cf. Skt. *ápa*, Lat. *ab*, Umbr. *ap-ehtre* 'ab extra', Goth. *af*, OE. *af*, *æf*, *of*, etc.) Orig. sense, *from*. [ᾰπὸ: where ἀπō is found in Ep. before ϝ or liquids (as ἀπὸ ἕθεν Il.6.62, ἀπὸ νευρῆς 11.664, Hes.*Sc*.409) ἀπαί was sometimes written in later texts, cf. Eust.625.11:—ᾱ metri gr. in Ep. compds., such as ἀπονέεσθαι.]

I. OF PLACE, the earliest, and in Hom. the prevailing sense: **1.** of Motion, *from, away from*, ἐσσεύοντο νεῶν ἄπο καὶ κλισιάων Il.2.208; pleonastic, ἀ. Τροίηθεν ib.24.492; ἀπ' οὐρανόθεν 8.365 (later with Advbs., ἀπὸ ἔμπροσθεν Lxx *Ec*.1.10, etc.); strengthd., ἐκτὸς ἀ. κλισίης Il.10.151; also ἀπ' αἰῶνος νέος ὤλεο, implying *departure from* life, ib.24.725; opp. ἐξ, of relatively superficial motion, λαμβάνομεν οὔτε ἐκ τῆς γῆς οὐδέν, οὔτ' ἀπὸ τῶν οἰκιῶν X.*Mem*.2.7.2; similarly of the cause or ground, ἐξ ὧν προηγώνισθε καὶ ἀφ' ὧν εἰκάζω Th.4.126:—freq. of warriors fighting *from* chariots, etc., οἱ μὲν ἀφ' ἵππων, οἱ δ' ἀ. νηῶν.. μάχοντο Il.15.386; ἀφ' ἵππων μάρνασθαι Od.9.49; so ἡ μάχη ἦν ἀφ' ἵππων Hdt.1.79; λαμπὰς ἔσται ἀφ' ἵππων *on horseback*, Pl.*R*.328a; ἀφ' ἵππου θηρεύειν X.*An*.1.2.7; ἀ. νεῶν πεζομαχεῖν Th.7.62; ἐν ταῖς ναυσὶν αἰρόμενος τοὺς ἱστοὺς ἀ. τούτων ἐσκοπεῖτο X.*HG*6.2.29; ὀμμάτων ἄπο..κατέσταζον γένυν, of tears, E.*Hec*.240: joined with ἐκ, ἐκ Κορίνθου ἀ. τοῦ στρατοπέδου Pl.*Tht*.142a. **2.** of Position, *away from, far from*, μένων ἀ. ἧς ἀλόχοιο Il.2.292 (cf. ἀπ' ἀνδρὸς εἶναι to live *apart from* a man or husband, Plu.*CG*4); κεκρυμμένος ἀπ' ἄλλων Od.23.110; μοῦνος ἀπ' ἄλλων *h.Merc*.193; ἀπ' ὀφθαλμῶν, ἀπ' οὔατος, *far from* sight or hearing, Il.23.53, 18.272, cf. 22.454; ἀ. θαλάσσης ᾠκίσθησαν Th.1.7, cf. 46; αὐλίζεσθαι ἀ. τῶν ὅπλων Id.6.64; ἀπ' οἴκου εἶναι Id.1.99; σπεύδειν ἀ. ῥυτῆρος *far from*, i.e. *without using* the rein, S.*OC*900; in Hom. freq. strengthd., τῆλε ἀ..., νόσφιν ἀ..., Il.23.880, 5.322; in measurement of distances, ὅσον ιε' στάδια ἀ. Φυλῆς X.*HG*2.4.4, etc.; but later the numeral follows ἀ., πηγὰς ἔχων ἀ. μ' σταδίων τῆς θαλάσσης D.S.4.56; ἀ. σταδίων κ' τῆς πόλεως Plu.*Phil*.4; κατεστρατοπέδευσεν ἀ. ν' σταδίων fifty stades *away*, Id.*Oth*.11, cf. D.Chr.17.17. **3.** of the mind, ἀ. θυμοῦ *away from*, i.e. *alien from*, my heart, Il.1.562; ἀ. δόξης 10.324; οὐ..ἀ. σκοποῦ οὐδ' ἀ. δόξης Od.11.344; ἀ. τοῦ ἀνθρωπείου τρόπου Th.1.76; οὐδὲν ἀ. τρόπου not *without* reason, Pl.*R*.470b; οὐκ ἀ. σκοποῦ, καιροῦ, Id.*Tht*.179c, 187e; οὐκ ἀ. γνώμης S.*Tr*.389; οὐκ ἀ. τοῦ πράγματος D.24.6; μάλα πολλὸν ἀπ' ἐλπίδος ἔπλετο A.R.2.863. **4.** in pregnant sense, with Verbs of rest, previous motion being implied (cf. ἐκ), ἀνὰ δ' ἐβόασεν..ἀ. πέτρας σταθεὶς E.*Tr*.523; ἀ. τῆς ἐμῆς κεφαλῆς τὴν [ἐκείνου] κεφαλὴν ἀναδήσω, i.e. taking the chaplet *off* my head, and placing it on his, Pl.*Smp*.212e: with Verbs of hanging, where ἐκ is more common, ἁψαμένη βρόχον ἀ. μελάθρου Od.11.278. **5.** with the Article, where the sense of motion often disappears, οἱ ἀ. τῶν οἰκιῶν φεύγουσιν, i.e. οἱ ἐν ταῖς οἰκίαις φεύγουσιν ἀπ' αὐτῶν, X.*Cyr*.7.5.23; οἱ ἀ. τῶν πύργων..ἐπαρήξουσι ib.6.4.18; αἴρειν τὰ ἀ. τῆς γῆς Pl.*Cra*.410b; αἱ ἵπποι αἱ ἀ. τοῦ ἅρματος v.l. in Hdt.4.8; ὁ Ἀθηναῖος ὁ ἀ. τοῦ στρατεύματος X.*An*.7.2.19; τὸν ἀ. γραμμᾶς κινεῖ λίθον Theoc.6.18. **6.** partitive, λαχὼν ἀ. ληΐδος αἶσαν part *taken* *from* the booty, a share *of* it, Od.5.40; αἱρεσθαι ἀ. τῶν καλπίδων Ar. *Lys*.539; ἀ. ἑκατὸν καὶ εἴκοσι παίδων εἷς μοῦνος Hdt.6.27; ὀλίγοι ἀ. πολλῶν Th.7.87, cf. A.*Pers*.1023. 7. Math., of figures described *upon* a base, κῶνον ἀναγράφειν ἀ. κύκλου Archim.*Sph.Cyl*.1.19, etc.; τὸ ἀ. τῆς AB τετράγωνον the square *on* AB, Euc.1.47, cf. 48; εἴδεα ἀ. .. Archim.*Spir*.10,11. 8. ἀ. ἀνθρώπου ἕως γυναικός man *and* woman, Lxx 1*Es*.9.40; ἀ. ἀρσενικοῦ ἕως θηλυκοῦ ib.*Nu*.5.3. 9. *from being, instead of*, ἀθανάταν ἀ. θνατᾶς.. ἐποίησας Βερενίκαν Theoc.15.106. 10. privative, *free from, without*, ἀ. πάσης ἀκαθαρσίας *PLips*.16.19 (ii A.D.); ἀ. ζημίας *PTeb*.420.4 (iii A.D.). II. OF TIME, *from, after*, Hom. only in Il.8.54 ἀ. δείπνου θωρήσσοντο rising up *from*, i.e. *after*, cf. Hdt.1.133; ἀ. δείπνου εἶναι or γενέσθαι, Id.1.126, 2.78, 5.18, al.; ἀ. τοῦ σιτίου πίνειν Hp.*Salubr*.5; ἀ. τῶν σίτων διαπονεῖσθαι X.*Lac*. 5.8; in narrative, τὸ ἀ. τούτου or τοῦδε, *from* this point *onwards*, Hdt.1.4, 2.99; ἀ. τούτου τοῦ χρόνου Id.1.82, X.*An*.7.5.8; τὸ ἀπ' ἐκείνου Luc.*Tox*.25; ἡμέρῃ δεκάτῃ ἀφ' ἧς.. Hdt.3.14, etc.; δευτέρῃ ἡμέρῃ ἀ. τῆς ἐμπρήσιος Id.8.55, cf. X.*An*.1.7.18, etc.; ἀφ' οὗ χρόνου Id.*Cyr*. 1.2.13; more often ἀπ' or ἀφ' οὗ, Hdt.2.44, Th.1.18, etc.; ἀφ' οὗπερ A.*Pers*.177; ἀφ' ἧς Plu.*Pel*.15; εὐθὺς ἀ. παλαιοῦ, ἀ. τοῦ πάνυ ἀρχαίου, *of* olden time, Th.1.2, 2.15; ἀπ' ἀρχᾶς Pi.*P*.8.25, etc.; ἀ. γενεᾶς X. *Cyr*.1.2.8; ἀφ' ἑσπέρας *from the beginning of* evening, i.e. *at* eventide, Th.7.29; ἀ. πρώτου ὕπνου ib.43; ἀ. μέσων νυκτῶν Ar.*V*.218; ἀπ' ἀγροῦ *fresh from* field-work, *Ev.Marc*.15.21, cf. 7.4; ἀ. νουμηνίας X.*An*.5.6.23; χρονίζειν ἀ. τοῦ καιροῦ tarry *beyond* the time, Lxx 2*Ki*. 20.5; ἀ. τέλους ἐννέα μηνῶν *at* the end of.., ib.24.8; γενόμενος ἀ. τῆς ἀρχῆς Plu.*Caes*.5: hence ἀ. ἀγωνοθετῶν an *ex*-ἀγωνοθέτης, *IG*3. 398; ἀ. λογιστῶν *POxy*.1103.3 (iv A.D.); οἱ ἀ. ὑπατείας, = *consulares*, Hdn.7.1.9, etc.; but ἀ. τινος the *freedman of*.., *IG*5(2).50.59 (Tegea, ii A.D.), cf. ib.5(1).1391 (Andania), 1473. III. OF ORIGIN, CAUSE, etc.: 1. of that *from* which one is born, οὐ γὰρ ἀ. δρυός ἐσσι οὐδ' ἀ. πέτρης not *sprung from* oak or rock, Od.19.163; γίγνονται δ' ἄρα ταί γ' ἔκ τε κρηνέων ἀ. τ' ἀλσέων 10.350, cf. S.*OT*415, *OC*571, etc.: sts. ἀπό denotes remote, and ἐκ immediate, descent, τοὺς μὲν ἀ. θεῶν, τοὺς δ' ἐξ αὐτῶν τῶν θεῶν γεγονότας Isoc.12.81, cf. Hdt.7.150; πέμπτη ἀπ' αὐτοῦ γέννα A.*Pr*.853; τρίτος ἀ. Διός third *in descent from* Zeus, Pl.*R*. 391c; οἱ ἀ. γένους τινός his descendants, Plu.*Them*.32; Περσέως ἀφ' αἵματος E.*Alc*.509: of the place one *springs from*, ἵπποι.. ποταμοῦ ἄπο Σελλήεντος Il.2.839, cf. 849; Ἡρακλεῖδαι οἱ ἀ. Σπάρτης Hdt.8.114, cf. Th.1.89, etc.; τοὺς ἀ. Φρυγίας X.*Cyr*.2.1.5, etc.: hence, b. metaph. of things, Χαρίτων ἄπο κάλλος ἔχουσαι Od.6.18; θεῶν ἄπο μήδεα εἰδώς ib.12; γάλα ἀ. βοός A.*Pers*.611; μῆνις ἀφ' ἡμῶν Id.*Eu*.314; ἡ ἀφ' ὑμῶν τιμωρία Th.1.69; ὁ ἀ. τῶν πολεμίων φόβος fear *inspired by* the enemy, X.*Cyr*.3.3.53. c. of persons, οἱ ἀ. τῆς χώρας, τῆς πόλεως, country *folk*, towns*folk*, Plb.2.6.8, 5.70.8; and so of connexion with the founder or leader of a sect, οἱ ἀ. Πυθαγόρου Luc.*Herm*.14; οἱ ἀ. Πλάτωνος Plu.*Brut*.2; οἱ ἀ. τοῦ περιπάτου, ἀ. τῆς Στοᾶς, etc., Luc.*Conv*. 6; generally οἱ ἀ. φιλοσοφίας καὶ λόγων philosophers and learned men, ibid.; οἱ ἀ. σκηνῆς καὶ θεάτρου stage players, Plu.*Sull*.2; οἱ ἀ. τῆς βουλῆς Id.*Caes*.10, etc.; ὁ ἀφ' ἑστίας παῖς, v. ἑστία; ἀπ' ἐξωμίδος *with only* an ἐξωμίς, S.E.*P*.1.153. 2. of the material *from* or *of* which a thing is made, εἵματα ἀ. ξύλου πεποιημένα Hdt.7.65; ἀπ' ὀμφακος τεύχειν οἶνον A.*Ag*.970, cf. S.*Tr*.704; ὅσσα ἀ. γλυκερῷ μέλιτος Theoc.15.117; ἔνδυμα ἀ. τριχῶν καμήλου *Ev.Matt*.3.4: hence στέφανος ἀ. ταλάντων ἑξήκοντα *of* or *weighing* 60 talents, Decr.ap.D. 18.92, cf. Plb.24.1.7, *IG*2.555.10, al.: hence of value, θύεν αἶγα ἀ. δραχμᾶν εἴκοσι *GDI*3707 (Cos); κρᾶσις ἀ. τε τῆς ἡδονῆς συγκεκραμένη καὶ ἀ. τῆς λύπης Pl.*Phd*.59a; so, by an extension of this use, εἰδεχθής τις ἀ. τοῦ προσώπου ugly *of* countenance, Thphr.*Char*.28.4; θῆλυν ἀ. χροιῆς Theoc.16.49; σεμνὸς ἀ. τοῦ σχήματος Luc.*DMort*.10. 8. 3. of the instrument *from* or *by* which a thing is done, τοὺς.. πέφνεν ἀπ' ἀργυρέοιο βιοῖο by arrow *shot from* silver bow, Il.24.605; τόξου ἄπο κρατεροῦ ὀλέκοντα φάλαγγας 8.279; ἐμῆς ἀπὸ χειρός 10.371, 11.675; so ἀ. χειρὸς ἐργάζεσθαι μεγάλα Luc.*Hist.Conscr*.29; γυμνάζεσθαι ἀ. σκελῶν, χειρῶν, τραχήλου, X.*Lac*.5.9; μάχεσθαι ἀ. ἄκοντος Str.17.3.7; ἡ ἀ. τοῦ ξίφους μάχη D.S.5.29; βάπτειν τὸν δάκτυλον ἀ. τοῦ αἵματος Lxx *Le*.4.7. 4. of the person *from* whom an act comes, i.e. *by* whom it is done, οὐδὲν μέγα ἔργον ἀπ' αὐτοῦ ἐγένετο Hdt.1.14; ζήτησιν ἀ. σφέων γενέσθαι Id.2.54; ἐπράχθη οὐδὲν ἀπ' αὐτῶν ἔργον ἀξιόλογον Th.1.17, cf. 6.61; ἀ. τινος ὄνασθαι Pl.*R*.528a, etc.; so τἀπ' ἐμοῦ, τἀπὸ σοῦ, E.*Tr*.74, S.*OC*1628; τὰ ἀ. τῶν Ἀθηναίων Th.1.127: in later Greek freq. of the direct agent, Plb.1.34.8, Str.5.4.12, D.H.9.12, *Ev.Luc*.9.22, J.*AJ*20.8.10, etc.; in codd. this may sts. be due to confusion with ὑπό, but cf. *PMag.Par*.1.256, *BGU* 1185.26 (Aug.), *SIG*820.8 (Ephesus, i A.D.), etc. 5. of the source *from* which life, power, etc., are sustained, ζῆν ἀπ' ὕλης ἀγρίης Hdt.1. 203; ἀ. κτηνέων καὶ ἰχθύων ib.216; ἀ. πολέμου Id.5.6; ἀπ' ἐλαχίστων χρημάτων X.*Mem*.1.2.14; ἀ. τῆς ἀγορᾶς Id.*An*.6.1.1; τρέφειν τὸ ναυτικὸν ἀ. τῶν νήσων Id.*HG*4.8.9, cf. Th.1.99; ἀ. τῶν κοινῶν πλουτεῖν Ar.*Pl*.569, cf. D.24.124; ἀ. μικρῶν εὔνους.. γεγένησαι Ar.*Eq*. 788, cf. D.18.102; ἀφ' ὥρας ἐργάζεσθαι *quaestum corpore facere*, Plu. *Tim*.14. 6. of the cause, means, or occasion *from, by*, or *because of* which a thing is done, ἀ. τούτου κριοπρόσωπον τὤγαλμα τοῦ Διὸς ποιεῦσι Hdt.2.42; ἀ. τινος ἐπαινεῖσθαι, θαυμάζεσθαι, ὠφελεῖσθαι, Th.2.25, 6.12, X.*Cyr*.1.1.2; ἀ. τῆν ξυμφορῶν διαβάλλεσθαι Th.5.17; τὴν ἐπωνυμίαν ἔχειν ἀ. τινος Id.1.46; ἀ. λῃστείας τὸν βίον ἔχειν X.*An*. 7.7.9; ἀπ' αὐτῶν τῶν ἔργων κρίνειν D.2.27; ἀ. τοῦ πάθους *in consequence of*.., Th.4.30; βλάπτειν τινὰ ἀ. τινος Id.7.29; κατασκευάσαντα τὸ πλοῖον ἀφ' ὧν ὑπελάμβανε σωθήσεσθαι D.18.194; τρόπαιον ἀ. τινος εἱστήκει *on occasion of* his defeat, Id.19.320; τλήμων οὐδ' ἀπ' εὐτόλμου φρενός A.*Ag*.1302, cf. 1643; ἀ. δικαιοσύνης *by reason of* it (v.l. for ὑπό), Hdt.7.164; ἀ. τῶν αὐτῶν λημμάτων *on* the same *scale of* profits, D.3.34, etc.; for ὅσον ἀ. βοῆς ἕνεκα, v. ἕνεκα: hence in half adverbial usages, ἀ. σπουδῆς in earnest, eagerly, Il.7.359; ἀ. τοῦ ἴσου, ἀ. τῆς ἴσης, or ἀπ' ἴσης, equally, Th.1.99, 15, D.14.6, etc.; ἀπ' ὀρθῆς καὶ δικαίας τῆς ψυχῆς Id.18.298; ἀ. ἀντιπάλου παρασκευῆς Th.1.91; ἀ. τοῦ προφανοῦς openly, ib.35; ἀ. τοῦ εὐθέος straightforwardly, Id. 3.43; ἀ. τοῦ αὐτομάτου *of* free-will, Pl.*Prt*.323c; ἀ. γλώσσης *by* word of mouth, Hdt.1.123 (but also, *from* hearsay, A.*Ag*.813); ἀ. στόματος Pl.*Tht*.142d; ἀπ' ὄψεως *at* sight, Lys.16.19; ἀ. χειρὸς λογίζεσθαι *on* your fingers, Ar.*V*.656; πεύθομαι δ' ἀπ' ὀμμάτων νόστον A.*Ag*. 988; ὀμμάτων ἄπο *in* the public gaze, E.*Med*.216; ἀ. τοῦ κυάμου ἄρχοντας καθίστασθαι X.*Mem*.1.2.9; ἡ βουλὴ ἡ ἀ. τοῦ κυάμου Th.8.66, cf. *IG*1.9; τοὺς ἀ. τοῦ κυάμου δισχιλίους ἄνδρας Arist.*Ath*.24.3; τριηράρχους αἱρεῖσθαι ἀ. τῆς οὐσίας Decr.ap.D.18.106; ἀφ' ἑαυτοῦ *from* oneself, *on* one's own *account*, Th.8.6, etc.; ἀφ' ἑαυτοῦ γνώμης Id.4.68; ἀ. συνθήματος, ἀ. παραγγέλματος, *by* agreement, *by* word of command, Hdt.5.74, Th.8.99; ἀ. σάλπιγγος *by sound of* trumpet, X.*Eq.Mag*.3. 12 (s.v.l.); ἐπίτροπος ἀ. τῶν λόγων, = Lat. *procurator a rationibus*, *Ann.Épigr*.1913.143*a* (Ephesus, ii A.D.). 7. of the object spoken of, τὰ ἀ. τῆς νήσου οἰκότα ἐστί the things *told from* or *of* the island.., Hdt.4.195, cf. 54, 7.195; νόμος κείμενος ἀ. τῶν τεχνῶν Ar.*Ra*.762.

B. in Arc., Cypr., ἀπύ takes dat., ἀπὺ τᾷ [ἀμέρᾳ] *IG*5(2).6 (Tegea); ἀπὺ τᾷ ζᾷ *Inscr.Cypr*.135.8 H. (Idalion). 2. in later Greek ἀπό is found c. acc., *PLond*.1.124.30 (iv/v A.D.).

C. in Hom. frequent with Verbs in tmesi, as Il.5.214, etc., and sts. in Prose, as Hdt.8.89.

D. IN COMPOS.: 1. *asunder*, as ἀποκόπτω, ἀπολύω, ἀποτέμνω: and hence, *away, off*, as ἀποβάλλω, ἀποβαίνω; denoting, *removal* of an accusation, as ἀπολογέομαι, ἀποψηφίζομαι. 2. *finishing off, completing*, ἀπεργάζομαι, ἀπανδρόω, ἀπανθρωπίζω, ἀπογλαυκόω. 3. *ceasing from, leaving off*, as ἀπαλγέω, ἀποκηδεύω, ἀπολοφύρομαι, ἀποζέω, ἀπανθίζω, ἀφυβρίζω. 4. *back again*, as ἀποδίδωμι, ἀπολαμβάνω, ἀπόπλους: also, *in full*, or *what is one's own*, as ἀπέχω, ἀπολαμβάνω: freq. it only strengthens the sense of the simple. 5. *by way of abuse*, as in ἀποκαλέω. 6. almost = ἀ- priv.; sts. with Verbs, as ἀπαυδάω, ἀπαγορεύω; more freq. with Adjectives, as ἀποχρήματος, ἀπότιμος, ἀπόσιτος, ἀπόφονος.

E. ἄπο, by anastrophe for ἀπό, when it follows its Noun, as ὀμμάτων ἄπο S.*El*.1231, etc.; never in Prose. 2. ἄπο for ἄπεστι, Semon.1.20, Timocr.9.

ἀποαγνέω· ἀποκαθαίρω, Hsch.

ἀποαίνυμαι, v. ἀπαίνυμαι.

ἀποαιρέομαι, poet. for ἀφαιρέομαι, Il.1.275.

ἀποᾰφύσσω, aor. 1 ἀποήφυσα, *draw off*, Euph.131.

ἀπόβα, v. ἀποβαίνω.

ἀποβᾰδίζω, Att. fut. -ιῶ, *go away*, οἴκαδε Ar.*Fr*.475.

ἀποβάθρα, Ion. **-βάθρη**, ἡ, *ladder for disembarking, gangway*, Hdt.9.98, Th.4.12, Luc.*DMort*.10.1. II. = λάσανον 1, Suid.

ἀπόβαθρα, τά, *sacrifices on disembarkation*, D.C.40.18; perh. to be read in S.*Fr*.415.

ἀποβαίνω, fut. -βήσομαι, with Ep. aor. 1 -εβήσετο Il.2.35: aor. 2 ἀπέβην: pf. ἀποβέβηκα—in these tenses intr. (pres. not in Hom.):—*step off from* a place, νηὸς ἀ. *alight, disembark from* a ship, Od.13.281; ἀπὸ τῶν νεῶν, ἀπὸ τῶν πλοίων, Hdt.5.86, 4.110; ἐκ τῶν νεῶν X.*HG*5.1. 12: abs., *disembark*, Hdt.2.29, Th.1.111, etc.; ἀ. ἐς χώρην Hdt.7.8.β', cf. E.*Fr*.705, Th.4.9, Lys.2.24; ἐς τὴν γῆν Th.1.100; ἐξ ἵππων ἀ. ἐπὶ χθόνα *dismount* from a chariot, Il.3.265, cf. 11.619; ἵππων 17.480; but in D.61.23 τὸ ἀποβαίνειν seems to be the art of *leaping from* horse to horse (cf. ἀποβάτης); τῇ συνωρίδι τοῦ ἀποβάντος *IG*9(2).527.10 (Larissa): generally, ἀβάτων ἀποβάς *having stepped off* ground on which none should step, S.*OC*167. 2. *go away, depart*, Il.1.428, 5.133, etc.; ἀπέβη πρὸς μακρὸν Ὄλυμπον 24.468; πρὸς δώματα, κατὰ δῶμα, Od.4.657, 715; μετ' ἀθανάτους Il.21.298: c. gen., ἀ. πεδίων E. *Hec*.142; ἀπὸ τῆς φάτνης X.*Eq.Mag*.1.16; of death, ἀπὸ δὲ φθίμενοι βεβᾶσι E.*Andr*.1022; of hopes, *vanish, come to nought*, Id.*Ba*.909 (lyr.). II. of events, *issue, result from*, τὰ ἔμελλε ἀποβήσεσθαι ἀπὸ τῆς μάχης Hdt.9.66; τἀναντία ἀπέβη *resulted*, Pl.*Phlb*.39a, cf. *Lg*. 782e; ὅ τι ἀποβήσεται Id.*Prt*.318a, etc.; τὸ ἀποβαῖνον, contr. τὠποβαῖνον, *the issue, event*, Hdt.2.82, etc.; τὰ ἀποβαίνοντα, τὸ ἀποβάν, *the results*, Th.1.83, 2.87; τὰ ἀποβησόμενα *the probable results*, Id.3. 38, cf. S.E.*M*.5.103. 2. freq. with an Adv. or other qualifying phrase, σκοπέειν.. τὴν τελευτὴν κῇ ἀποβήσεται how it will *turn out, issue*, Hdt.1.32; ἀ. τῇ περ εἶπε ib.86; ἀ. κατὰ τὸ ἐόν ib.97; ἀ. παρὰ δόξαν, ἀ. τοιοῦτον, Id.8.4, 7.23; τοιόνδ' ἀπέβη τόδε πρᾶγμα E. *Med*.1419, cf. X.*Cyr*.1.5.13; πολέμου τοιοῦτον ἀπέβη τὸ τέλος Plb.26. 6.15; οὐδὲν αὐτῷ.. ὡς προσεδέχετο ἀπέβαινεν Th.4.104, cf. 3.26; παρὰ γνώμην ἀ. 5.4; opp. κατὰ γνώμαν ἀ. Theoc.15.38; πῶς ἡ φήμη δοκεῖ ὑμῖν ἀποβῆναι; And.1.131. 3. abs., *turn out well, succeed*, ἡ ὑπόσχεσις ἀπέβη Th.4.39, cf. 5.14; of dreams, *turn out true*, Arist.*Div. Somn*.463ᵇ10. 4. of persons, with an Adj., *turn out, prove to be* so and so, ἀ. οὐ κοινοί *prove* partial, Th.3.53; ἀ. χείρους Pl.*Lg*.952b; φρενιτικοὶ ἀ. Hp.*Coac*.405; τύραννος ἐκ βασιλέως ἀ. Plb.7.13.7; also of a wound, ἰάσιμον ἀ. Pl.*Lg*.878c. b. with εἰς.., ἀ. εἰς τὰ πολιτικὰ οἱ τοιοῦτοι *prove fit* for public affairs, Id.*Smp*.192a; ἐς ἀλαθινὸν ἄνδρ' ἀ. Theoc.13.15. c. of conditions, etc., ἀπέβη ἐς μουναρχίην *things ended in* a monarchy, Hdt.3.82; εἰς ἓν τέλεον καὶ νεανικόν Pl.*R*.425c; ἀποβήσεται εἰς μαρτυρίαν *Ev.Luc*.21.13. 5. of space, μέγεθος μὲν ἦν πρὸς τὸν Ἠριδανὸν ἀποβεβηκυῖα *reaching, extending to*

..., Pl.Criti.112a. 6. τῷ ἀποβεβηκότι ποδί with the hind foot, opp. τῷ προβεβηκότι, Arist.IA706ᵃ9.

B. causal, in aor. 1 ἀπέβησα, cause to dismount, disembark, land (in which sense ἀποβιβάζω serves as pres.), ἀ. στρατιήν Hdt.5.63, 6.107; ἐς τὴν Ψυττάλειαν Id.8.95. II. hence, in Pass., τὸ ἀποβαινόμενον σκέλος a leg put out so as not to bear the weight of the body, Hp.Art.52:—Act., Id.Mochl.20.

ἀποβάλλω, fut. -βαλῶ, throw off, ἀπὸ δὲ χλαῖναν βάλε Il.2.183, cf. 21.51; ἀπὸ φροντίδος ἄχθος .. βαλεῖν A.Ag.166: c. gen., throw off from, ἀ. ὀμμάτων ὕπνον E.Ba.692:—Med., throw off from oneself, cast off, δύναμιν βασιλέως And.3.29. 2. throw away, h.Merc.388, Hdt. 3.40, etc.; ἀ. τὴν ἀσπίδα Ar.V.22, And.1.74, Lys.10.9, etc.; τὸν ἄνδρα τὸν πάρος ἀ. reject him, E.Tr.663, cf. Pl.Tht.151c, etc.; ἀ. τὰ κέρατα, τὰς ὁπλάς, cast, shed, Arist.HA500ᵃ10, 604ᵃ15, al.:—Med., Pl.Lg.802b; οὐδεὶς ἀ. ἑκὼν jettisons cargo, Arist.EN1110ᵃ9; ἀ. τὸν φιλέοντα Theoc.11.19; expose a child, Leg.Gort.4.9; despise, reject, Hp.Ep.10:—Pass., ἀποβληθεὶς τῆς τυραννίδος Plu.Comp.Dion.Brut. 3. b. throw away, sell too cheap, X.Oec.20.28. 3. lose, τὴν τυραννίδα Hdt.1.60; τὰ πατρῷια, τὸν στρατόν, τὴν κεφαλήν, Id.3.53, 8.65, al.; βιοτάν S.Fr.593; τὴν οὐσίαν Ar.Ec.811, Pl.Cri.44e, etc.; ἱκανὸν μέρος τῶν ὄντων Antipho 2.1.6, etc.; opp. κτᾶσθαι, Isoc. 6.57, Arist.Pol.1291ᵇ41; ἀ. δόξαν, τέχνην, Id.de An.428ᵇ5, Metaph. 1047ᵃ1, al.; ἀ. τι ὑπό τινος X.Smp.4.32; ἀ. πολλοὺς τῶν στρατιωτῶν Th.4.7; τὸν εὐεργέταν E.HF878:—in Med., ἀγαθὸν πολίτην SIG730.20 (Olbia). b. Gramm., drop a letter, etc., A.D.Pron.36.21, al. 4. degrade, Pl.Lg.630d.

ἀπόβαμμα, ατος, τό, water drawn from a sacred spring, IG4.1607 (Cleonae). II. tincture, infusion, Sch.Nic.Al.51.

ἀποβάπτω, dip, plunge, ἑωυτόν Hdt.2.47; ἐς τὴν κύλικα ἀκινάκεα Id.4.70; εἰς ποταμὸν τὰ γιγνόμενα Arist.Pol.1336ᵃ16; λίθον ἐν οἴνῳ Id.HA607ᵃ25; φαρμάκῳ τοὺς ὀϊστούς Id.Mir.845ᵃ1: metaph., ἀ. τὴν λέξιν εἰς νοῦν Plu.Phoc.5:—Pass., ὅστις ἐν ἅλμῃ.. ἀπεβάφθη Ar.Fr. 416; περιστερὰς ἀποβεβαμμένας εἰς μύρον Alex.62.3. 2. ἀ. ὕδωρ draw water, Lxx 2Ma.1.21.

ἀποβᾰσῐλεύς, έως, ὁ, ex-king, AB1089.

ἀπόβᾰσις, εως, ἡ, (ἀποβαίνω) stepping off, disembarking, ἀπὸ τῶν νεῶν ἐς τὴν Λοκρίδα ἀποβάσεις ποιησάμενοι Th.3.103, cf. 115; ἡ ναυτικὴ ἐπ' ἄλλους ἀ. landing from ships in the face of an enemy, Id.4.10: abs., ποιεῖσθαι ἀ. disembark, land, Id.2.26; ἀ. ἐστι a landing is possible, Id.4.13, cf. 6.75; οὐκ ἔχει ἀπόβασιν does not admit of landing, or has no landing-place, Id.4.8; ἐν ἀποβάσει τῆς γῆς, = ἀποβάντες ἐς τὴν γῆν, Id.1.108. 2. in Plb.8.4.4 ἐξ ἀποβάσεως ἰσοϋψὴς τῷ τείχει, of a ladder, equal in height to the wall, when planted at the proper distance from its foot, cf. Id.9.19.7. II. way of escape, Plu.Sol.14. III. result, issue, τῶν εἰρημένων Aret.SA2.4, Luc.Hes.6 (pl.), Artem.4. 83; of prophecies, Phld.D.1.25; success in a race (prob.), Tab. Defix.Aud.234.59 (Carthage, i A.D.), al. IV. = ἀγὼν ἀποβατικός, IG7.4254 (Oropus, iv B.C.). V. numerical sequence, Theol.Ar. 60.

ἀπόβασκε· ἄπελθέ, Theodos.Gramm.p.64 G.

ἀποβᾰ-τήριος, α, ον, of Zeus, as protector of persons landing, Arr. An.1.11.7; of Artemis, IGRom.4.1539 (Erythrae). II. τὰ ἀ. (sc. ἱερά) offerings made on landing, St.Byz. s. v. Βουθρωτός, Poll.2. 200. III. ἀ. τόπος place of landing, of Mt. Ararat, J.AJ1.3. 5. **-της**, ου, ὁ, one that dismounts; but in usage, one who rode several horses leaping from one to the other, ἀποβάτην ἀγωνίσασθαι Plu.Phoc.20, cf. IG2.966, al., D.H.7.73, AB198,426, EM124.31, Suid. **-τικός**, ή, όν, of or for an ἀποβάτης, ἀγών IG9(2).527,531 (Larissa). Adv. -κῶς EM124.31.

ἀποβδελύττομαι, reject with abhorrence, Eustr. in EN19.4.

ἀποβελίζω, take off the spit, f.l. in Sotad.Com.1.10.

ἀποβημᾰτίζω, degrade from one's rank or station, Plu.Nob.21.

ἀποβήσσω, cough up, Hp.Aph.5.11, Prog.23: fut. -βήξομαι Id. Mul.1.41.

ἀπο-βῐάζομαι, force away, force back, τὸ ὑγρόν Arist.IA714ᵃ19; τὸ κωλῦον Id.Pr.903ᵇ5, cf. GA737ᵇ29, Mete.368ᵇ10, PPetr.3p.39 (iii B.C.):—Pass., to be forced away or back, X.Cyr.4.2.24, Arist.Mete. 364ᵃ29; ἀ. εἰς ἐλάττω τόπον to be forced into.., ib.366ᵇ11. 2. treat with violence, τινά Plb.16.24.5: abs., 33.9.5, cf. SIG629.20 (Delph., ii B.C.), Wilcken Chr.11A 30 (ii B.C.): metaph., κατὰ τὰς λέξεων ὁμιλίας Phld.Oec.p.59 J. II. abs., use force, X.Cyr.3.1.19, Arist. Mete.364ᵇ8, al.; force its way, ib.351ᵃ6:—Act. **-βιάζω**, Sch.Theoc. 6.18. **-βιάομαι**, = foreg., Hp.Morb.1.24.

ἀποβῐβ-άζω, causal of ἀποβαίνω B, make to get off, esp. from a ship, disembark, put on shore, τινά Th.6.97, etc.; τινὰ εἰς τόπον Hdt.8.76, Pl.Grg.511e; ἐς τὴν πολεμίαν ἀποβιβάζων τὸν πόδα Ar.V.1163; ἀ. τινὰ ὅποι αὐτὸς κελεύοι X.HG7.4.3:—Med., ἀποβιβάσασθαί τινας ἀπὸ τῶν νεῶν cause them to be put on shore, Hdt.9.32. **-ασμός**, ὁ, disembarkation, Iamb.VP3.17.

ἀποβιβρώσκω, eat off, in aor. Pass. χεῖρας ἀποβρωθέντα AP7.294 (Tull. Laur.).

ἀποβι-όω, cease to live, λάθε ἀποβιώσας Philostr.VA8.28; ἀπεβίω Hld.4.7, cf. Ant.Diog.10. **-ωσις**, εως, ἡ, ceasing to live, death, Plu.2.389a, CIG4253 (Lycia), al. **-ώσκομαι**, = ἀποβιόω, Herm. in Phdr.p.202 A.

ἀποβλάπτω, ruin utterly, Pi.N.7.60, Pl.Lg.795d:—Pass., ἀποβλαφθῆναι φίλου to be robbed of a friend, S.Aj.941.

ἀποβλαστ-άνω, shoot forth from, spring from, ἀπέβλαστον ματρὸς ὠδῖνος S.OC533, cf. Plu.2.954c, Hierocl. in CA17 p.459 M., Iamb. Myst.3.20. **-ημα**, ατος, τό, shoot, Thphr.CP1.20.1: metaph., τὸ ἑαυτοῦ ἀ. πᾶς φιλεῖ Pl.Smp.208b. **-ησις**, εως, ἡ, shooting forth, growth, νεύρων Hp.Art.45, cf. Gal.UP8.6; of roots, Dsc.2.183.

ἀπό-βλεμμα, ατος, τό, steadfast gaze, Phryn.Com.75. **-βλεπτέον**, one must consider, Gal.11.407. **-βλεπτος**, ον, gazed on by all, admired, E.Hec.355, Procop.Arc.9, al. **-βλέπω**, fut. -βλέψομαι Luc.Somn.12, etc., but -βλέψω Hero Spir.2.34: pf. -βέβλεφα Antip. Stoic.3.254 codd. Stob.:—Med., pres., Luc.VH2.47 (v. l.): aor., Sch.Od.12.247:—Pass., Ar.Ec.726:—look away from all other objects at one, gaze steadfastly, ἐς ἐμέ Hdt.7.135; εἰς σε E.Andr.246, cf. Pl.Chrm.162b, al.; ἐς ἀκτάς E.Hipp.1206; ἐς μίαν τύχην Id.Hel. 267; πρὸς τὸ Ἥραιον Hdt.9.61, cf. Pl.R.431b; πρός τινα Id.Phd.115c, Phdr.234d, al. 2. pay attention to, regard, ἐς τὸ κακόν Ar.Ra. 1171; πρὸς τὰ κοινὰ E.Supp.422; εἰς τὰ πράγματα ἀ. φαύλως ἔχοντα D. 2.29; εἰς τὸ κέρδος μόνον Demetr.Com.Vet.4; εἰς τὴν μισθαποδοσίαν Ep.Hebr.11.26; ἐπί τι Pl.Phlb.61d; κατά τι Luc.DMort.18.1; πρός τι Pl.R.477c, al.; εἰς τὰ πράγματα καὶ πρὸς τοὺς λόγους ἀ. D.3.1: c. acc., Thphr.Vert.8, Plu.Luc.26, etc. 3. of places, etc., look, face in a particular direction, πρὸς ὁδόν D.C.76.11 (of a statue); Ῥήνου προχοάς AP9.283 (Crin.); ἐπὶ τὴν ἀνατολήν J.AJ11.5.5. 4. look upon with love, wonder or admiration, look at as a model, c. acc., οὐ χρὴ.. μέγαν ὄλβον ἀ. S.Fr.593; ἀ. τινά Luc.Vit.Auct.10, cf. D.19. 265; προϊόντα ἴσα θεῷ ἀπέβλεπον Philostr.VA5.24; more freq. with a Prep., εἰς ἔμ' Ἑλλὰς.. ἀ. E.IA1378; ἡ σὴ πατρὶς εἰς σὲ ἀ. X.HG6. 1.8, cf. Th.3.58; εἰς τὴν εὐσέβειαν τῆς θεοῦ SIG867.11 (Ephesus); so ἀ. πρός τινα E.IT928, X.Mem.4.2.30, Thphr.Char.2.2; of a vain person, ἀ. εἰς τὴν ἑαυτῆς σκιάν X.Mem.2.1.22; of entire dependence, πάντα ἀ. εἰς τὸν ἐραστήν Pl.Phdr.239b; εἰς ἀλλοτρίαν τράπεζαν X.An. 7.2.33; look longingly, ἐς τὸν ἀγρόν Ar.Ach.32:—Pass., to be looked up to, Id.Ec.726, Aeschin.Socr.Fr.56 D.; ὡς εὐδαίμων ἀ. Luc.Nigr. 13, cf. Somn.11. 5. ἐς τοιόνδ' ἀποβλέψας μόνον τροπαῖον αὐτοῦ στήσομαι with a single look, E.Andr.762. II. look away, D.Chr.21. 13: c. gen., Philostr.Im.1.1; ἀ. ἀπ' ἀμφοτέρων face both ways, dub. in X.HG2.3.31; ἀπὸ τοῦ συμφέροντος Antip. l.c. III. Med., look at each other, ταυρωπὸν ἀποβλεψάμενοι Ph.1.602. **-βλεψις**, εως, ἡ, of a place, ἀ. ἔχειν πρὸς βορρᾶν look towards..., Gp.2.3.7.

ἀπό-βλημα, ατος, τό, anything cast away, Lxx Wi.13.13, Sch.Ar. Eq.412. **-βλήσιμος**, ον, fit to be cast away, CPHerm.119ʳ vi 5 (iii A.D.). **-βλησις**, εως, ἡ, outpouring; μέθης ἀ., of exclamations uttered in liquor, Eust.1767.59. **-βλητέος**, α, ον, to be thrown away, rejected, Pl.R.387b, Luc.Herm.18. II. ἀποβλητέον one must reject, A.D.Conj.226.10. **-βλητικός**, ή, όν, apt to throw off, καρπῶν Thphr.CP2.9.3. **-βλητος**, ον (η, ον D.L.7.127, Iamb.Myst.1.19), to be thrown away or aside, as worthless, οὔ τοι ἀπόβλητ' ἐστὶ θεῶν ἐρικυδέα δῶρα Il.3.65; οὔ τοι ἀπόβλητον ἔπος ἔσσεται 2.361; γίγαρτον Simon.88, etc., cf. Hp.Ep.10 and late Prose, as Ph.2.294, Luc.Tox. 37, Plu.2.821a, Plot.6.7.31, Procop.Arc.11. 2. capable of being thrown off, Iamb. l. c.; capable of being lost, D.L. l. c.

ἀποβλίττω, cut out the comb from the hive: hence, steal away, carry off, ὁ δ' ἀπέβλισε θοἰμάτιόν μου Ar.Av.498: aor. Med. ἀπεβλίσατο cj. Reisk. in AP7.34 (Antip. Sid.).

ἀπο-βλύζω, spirt out, ἀ. οἴνου spirt out some wine, Il.9.491, cf. Archil.32; ὕδαρὲς ἀ. Aret.SD2.6. II. intr., flow forth, πηγαὶ ἀ. τῶν ὀρῶν Philostr.Im.1.9, cf. Procop.Aed.2.2, al. **-βλυστάνω**, = foreg., πηγαὶ ἀ. ὕδωρ ib.1.11. **-βλύω**, = foreg., Orph.A.1066.

ἀποβλώσκω, go away, A.R.3.1143.

ἀποβολ-εύς, έως, ὁ, one who has lost, ὅπλων Pl. Lg.944b. **-ή**, ῆς, ἡ, throwing away, e.g. ὅπλων ib.943e sq.; jettison, Ph.2.413; in Gramm., dropping of a letter, etc., A.D.Pron.55.7, al.; τόνου Synt. 130.1. 2. loss, opp. κτῆσις, χρημάτων Pl.La.195e, Arist.EN1115ᵃ 21, etc.; ἐπιστήμης Pl.Phd.75d, cf. Euphro 1.27: pl., τὰς τῶν κακῶν ἀ. Arist.Rh.1362ᵃ36, cf. Isoc.3.32. **-ιμαῖος**, ον, apt to throw away, c. gen., τῶν ὅπλων Ar.Pax678. 2. Pass., usually thrown away, worthless, Gloss. **-ον**· ἀποβεβλημένον, Hsch.

ἀποβόομαι, Pass., of Io, become a cow, Eust.278.32.

ἀποβορρότατος, ον, most northerly, POxy.506.26 (ii A.D.).

ἀπο-βοσκέω, = sq., EM120.5. **-βόσκομαι**, feed upon, καρπόν Ar.Av.749,1066.

ἀποβουκολ-έω, lead astray, as cattle, βοῦς ἐς τὴν ἰδίαν ἀγέλην Longus 1.27. 2. lead away shepherds from the sheep, τῶν θρεμμάτων Chor.p.92 B. 3. let stray, lose (as a bad shepherd does his sheep), χαρίεν γὰρ εἰ.. τῇ θυγατρὶ τὸν παῖδα ἀποβουκολήσαιμι.. if I were to lose my daughter her son, X.Cyr.1.4.13:—Pass., stray, lose one's way, Luc.Nav.4. 4. beguile, soothe, Id.Am.16; lead astray, seduce, Id.Bis Acc.13. **-ίζω**, = ἀποβουκολέω 3, Chor. in Rh.Mus. 49.522.

ἀπό-βρασμα, ατος, τό, that which is thrown off, Alex.Trall.Febr. 6; scum, Hsch.; chaff, Id., Suid. **-βρασμός**, ὁ, throwing off of scum, S.E.M.9.103. **-βράσσω**, Att. -ττω, Poll.6.91: mostly in aor. -έβρᾱσα:—throw out froth, like boiling water, and metaph., shake, sift out the bran from the meal, Call.Fr.232:—Pass., spirt out, Hp.Nat.Puer.31; to be cast ashore, Thphr.Fr.30.3; νεκροὶ ἀπεβράσθησαν εἰς τοὺς αἰγιαλούς Ph.2.174. 2. metaph., εἰς τὰ τῆς ἐσχατιᾶς ib.354. II. intr., cease to boil, Alciphr.1.23.

ἀπό-βρεγμα, ατος, τό, infusion, Agatharch.61, Str.16.4.17, Dsc.4. 81, Aret.CA1.1, Plu.2.614b. **-βρεξις**, εως, ἡ, moistening, Aq., Sm.Nu.6.3, Gal.6.652. **-βρέχω**, steep well, soak, Thphr.CP2.5.5, IG4.955.9 (Epid.): metaph., τὴν γλῶσσαν εἰς νοῦν ἀ. Zeno Stoic.1.67, cf. Suid. s. v. Ἀριστοτέλης:—Pass., aor. part. -βρεχθείς Thphr.HP

5.9.5; -βραχεῖς Dsc.1.110: metaph., ὡς τὰ ἄχη τῆς ψυχῆς ἀποβρέχοιτο Philostr.*VA*7.22.

ἀποβρίζω, *go off to sleep, go sound asleep*, Od.9.151: aor. imper. ἀπόβριξον Theoc.*Ep.*19; ὕπνον ἀ. Call.*Epigr.*18; βαιὸν ἀποβρίξαντες Q.S.5.661.

ἀποβρόξαι, aor. of *ἀποβρόχω, *swallow, gulp down part of a thing* (cf. ἀναβρόξειε), prob. l. *AP*7.506 (Leon.); cf. ἀποβρύκω.

ἀποβροχή, ἡ, v.l. for βροχή (q. v.), Dsc.1.43.

ἀποβροχθίζω, *gulp down*, Ar.*Fr.*236.

ἀποβροχ-ίζω, *ligature*, Sor.1.80, Gal.14.784. II. *bind tightly*, λαιμόν *AP*9.410 (Tull. Sab.). III. *strangle*, ἑαυτόν Polyaen. 8.63. **-ισμός**, ὁ, *making a ligature*, Antyll.ap.Orib.45.24. 3. **-ιστέον**, *one must make a ligature*, Archig.ap.Orib.47.13.5.

ἀποβρύκω [ῡ], *bite off, eat greedily of*, τῶν κρεῶν (partit. gen.) Eub. 42: abs., *bite in pieces*, Archipp.35; ἀπέβρυξεν is v. l. (Planud.) for -έβροξεν in *AP*7.506 (Leon.).

ἀπόβρωμα, ατος, τό, *something devoured*, Ps.-Callisth.3.15.

ἀποβύω [ῡ], *stop up*, *AB*426.

ἀποβώμιος, ον, *far from an altar, godless*, Κύκλωψ E.*Cyc.*365. II. in Eust.1720.28, literally, *not offered on an altar*, but on the ground. 2. *not suitable for an offering*, *IG*5(2).403 (Lusi, dub.).

ἀπόγαιος, v. ἀπόγειος.

ἀπογαιόω, *make into land*, Heraclit.*All.*22 (Pass.): Medic., *form a stone*, Gal.19.648,672; cf. ἀπογεόομαι.

ἀπογᾰλακτ-ίζω, *wean from the mother's milk*, Diph.74, Lxx *Ge.*21. 8, Sor.1.116, *POxy.*37 i 22 (i A.D.), *PLips.*31.20 (ii A.D.). **-ισις**, εως, ἡ, *weaning*, Ar.Byz.*Epit.*42.14. **-ισμός**, ὁ, = foreg., Hp. *Dent.*16. **-ιστέον**, *one must wean*, Sor.1.78. **-όομαι**, Pass., *to become milky*, Antyll.ap.Orib.4.11.6. **-ος**, ον, *weaned*, Aët. 4.29.

ἀπογᾰληνίζω, *calm down*, ἑαυτόν prob. in Plu.2.655b.

ἀπογᾰληνιόομαι, Pass., *become calm*, Ps.-Democr.*Symp.Ant.* p.4 G.

ἀπογᾰληνόομαι, *calm down*, of physical disturbances, Sor.1.46.

ἀπόγαλον, τό, = ἀβρότονον, Ps.-Dsc.3.24.

ἀπόγειος, α, ον, (γῆ) *from land, coming off land*, ἄνεμοι, πνεῦμα, Arist.*Mu.*394^{b}14, *Mete.*363^{a}1, cf. Thphr.*CP*2.3.1; ἡ ἀ. (sc. αὔρα) *land-breeze*, Arist.*Pr.*940^{b}24; αἱ ἀπόγεαι ib.945^{a}4; τὰ ἀ. ib.940^{b}18. 2. ἀπόγαιον or ἀπόγειον, τό, *mooring cable*, Plb.33.9.6, Luc.*VH*1.42, Polem.*Call.*26, Lib.*Or.*59.139, 61.21, etc.; in full, ἀπόγεια (-γυια cod.) σχοινία Hsch. s. v. γύαια; cf. ἀπόγυον. II. *far from the earth*, Plu.2.933b, cf. Olymp.*in Mete.*10.14, al.: Comp., Cleom.2.6, Ptol.*Alm.*9.1: Sup., Theo Sm.p.157 H.; τὸ ἀ. (sc. σημεῖον), in Astronomy, a planet's *greatest distance from the earth, apogee*, Ptol. *Alm.*3.3. 2. *from the shore*, Luc.*Lex.*15.

ἀπογεισ-όω, *crown with a cornice*, γείσοις Κορινθίοις *IG*2^2.463.71, cf. *BCH*35.12 (Delos): metaph., *make to jut out like a cornice*, ὀφρύσι ἀ. τὰ ὑπὲρ τῶν ὀμμάτων X.*Mem.*1.4.6:—Pass., *jut out like a cornice*, Arist.*GA*781^{b}13. **-ωμα**, ατος, τό, *projecting cornice*: metaph. of eyebrows, Arist.*PA*658^{b}16.

ἀπογεμε· ἄφελκε (Cypr.), Hsch.

ἀπογεμίζομαι, Pass., of a ship, *discharge her cargo*, D.H.3.44; *to be emptied of contents*, Ps.-Luc.*Philopatr.*24.

ἀπογενεσία, ἡ, = sq., *PMag.Par.*1.721.

ἀπογένεσις, εως, ἡ, *decease*, τὰς τῶν ψυχῶν γενέσεις καὶ ἀ. Porph. *Antr.*31, cf. 24, Plot.3.4.6.

ἀπογενν-άω, *produce*, Hp.*Morb.*1.25 (Pass.); τὸ ὅμοιον Thphr.*CP* 1.16.12; γάλα Sor.1.27; συμπτώματα Gal.7.200; of atoms *generating* bodies, Epicur.*Nat.*22 G., cf. Diog.Oen.20, Aen.Gaz.*Thphr.* p.42 B.; ἀ. δυσμένειαν Demad.15:—Pass., Epicur.*Ep.*2 p.40 U.; τὰ ὑπὸ μεγαλοφροσύνης -ώμενα Longin.15.12, cf. Ph.1.144, Plot.6.1.6, etc. II. *destroy*, ἐγώ εἰμι ὁ γεννῶν καὶ ὁ ἀπογεννῶν *PMag. Lond.*46.155. **-ημα**, ατος, τό, *offspring*, Ti.Locr.97e, Ael.*NA* 15.8. **-ησις**, εως, ἡ, *generation*, Sch.Epicur.*Ep.*3 p.47 U., Jul. *Or.*4.153c, Procl.*Inst.*152.

ἀπογεόομαι, Pass., *to be changed into earth*, Ph.2.508 (cj.).

ἀπογεύ-ω, *give* one *a taste of*, *AP*4.3.39 (Agath.); opp. ἀποπληρόω, Herod.Med.ap.Orib.5.30.21. II. Med., *take a taste of*, σιτίων, Hp.*Epid.*7.2, cf. Pl.*R.*354b, *Tht.*157d, X.*Cyr.*1.3.4, Plb.3.57.8; ἑκάστου μικρὸν ἀ. Eub.42, cf. Antiph.326: metaph., ἐλπίδος Ph.2. 338. **-σις**, εως, ἡ, *tasting*, τῶν παθῶν Olymp.*in Alc.*p.6 C., cf. *PMag.Leid.W.*9.34.

ἀπογεφῡρόω, *bank off, fence with dykes*, τὴν Μέμφιν Hdt.2.99.

ἀπογηράσκω, *grow old*, Thgn.821, Hp.*Aph.*2.20; part. ἀπογηράς dub. l. Alex.278; inf. ἀπογηρᾶν, of senile dementia, Gal.16.696; ἀπεγήρασα Thphr.*HP*7.13.6; of vines, ὅσσαι δέ κα..ἀπογηράσκωντι *fail from old age*, *Tab.Heracl.*1.170.

ἀπογίγνομαι, Ion. and later Att. -γίνομαι, fut. -γενήσομαι:—*to be away from, have no part in*, τῆς μάχης Hdt.9.69; τῶν ἁμαρτημάτων Th.1.39; *to be freed from*, κακῶν ἀπογεγονότες J.*AJ*19.2.2. II. abs., *to be taken away*, opp. προσγίγνομαι, Zeno Eleat.2, Pl.*Ti.*82b, *Lg.*850a; ἀπεγίγνετο οὐδέν..προσεγίγνετο δέ Th.2.98: generally, *to be away, absent*, Antipho 2.3.5, Pl.*Phd.*69b, D.8.35; ἀπό τινος Aeschin.2.126; of diseases, opp. προσπίπτω, Hp.*Morb.Sacr.*1 (dub. l.). 2. esp. of death, ἀ. ἐκ τῶν οἰκίων *depart* from the house, *die* out of it, Hdt.2.85; ἀπογενέσθαι alone, *to be dead*, ib.136, cf. *IG*9(1).334. 37 (Locr.), Ocell.1.14; οἱ ἀπογενόμενοι *the dead*, Th.2.34; ὁ ὕστατον αἰεὶ ἀ. he who *died* last, Hdt.6.58, cf. 5.4; οἱ ἀπογιγνόμενοι *the dying*, Th.2.51, Hdt.3.111. 3. *fall away, be lost*, Th.5.74; opp. ἐκβλαστάνω, Paus.5.12.1. III. *arrive at*, ἀ. δωδεκαταῖος Hp.*Epid.* 4.11. IV. *turn out, become*, τράχηλος σκληρὸς ἀ. ib.12 (dub. l.); νωθροὶ ἀ. Id.*Prorrh.*1.117 (dub. l.). V. ἀ. τὸ ἕκτον μέρος εἰς τρίχας καὶ αἷμα *goes into, is consumed in forming*.., Arist.*HA*595^{b}1.

ἀπογιγνώσκω, Ion. and later Att. -γῑνώσκω, fut. -γνώσομαι:—*depart from a judgement, give up a design* or *intention* of doing, τοῦ μάχεσθαι X.*An.*1.7.19, cf. Plb.1.29.5, etc.; ἀ. τὸ κατὰ γῆν πορεύεσθαι X.*HG*7.5.7; ἀ. διώκειν Plu.*Ant.*34, cf. *Thes.*6; ἀ. μὴ βοηθεῖν *resolve not* to help, D.15.9, cf. *IG*2^2.457.30: c. gen., *give up* a notion, Simp. *in Ph.*610.9. II. c. gen. rei, *despair of*, τῆς ἐλευθερίας Lys.2. 46; οὐδενὸς χρὴ πράγματος ὅλως ἀπογνῶναι Men.131; ὡς ἀνιάτων D.Chr.32.97; ὑπὲρ σφῶν Jul.*Or.*2.61c: abs., *despair*, D.4.42 (where some codd. supply ἑαυτῶν), Babr.43.18: c. fut. inf., αἱρήσειν ἀ. Arr. *An.*3.20.3; ἀκούσεσθαι Luc.*Icar.*10: c. aor. inf., τὴν πόλιν ἀπέγνω ἑλεῖν Arr.*An.*1.5.8, cf. D.Chr.32.9. 2. c. acc., *give up as hopeless* or *desperate*, τὴν σωτηρίαν Arist.*EN*1115^{b}2; τὰς πρεσβείας Plb.5.1.5, al.; τὰς ἐλπίδας Id.2.35.1; ἀ. τι ἀπὸ τῶν παρόντων App.*Hisp.*37; ἀρετῆς ἀκρίβειαν Porph.*Antr.*36; ἀ. αὐτόν Plb.21.26.14:—Pass., *to be given up*, τὰ παρ' ὑμῶν D.19.54; ἐλπίς D.H.5.15; ἐλευθερία Luc. *Tyr.*6; ἀπεγνωσμέναι ἐλπίδες *forlorn* hopes, Plb.30.8.3; ἐπιβουλὴ -μένη Hdn.4.4.3; ἀπεγνωσμένοι ἄνθρωποι *desperate* men, Id.1.16.4 (but ἄνθρωποι ἀπεγνωκότες Plu.*Alex.*16); ὑπὸ τῶν ἰατρῶν ἀ. *to be despaired of*.., Id.*Per.*13. Adv. ἀπεγνωσμένως *in despair*, Id.*Nic.*21. b. *renounce, reject*, τι Hp.*Medic.*4, cf. D.3.33; τινάς Id.6.16, cf. D.C.73. 15; φιλίαν Iamb.*VP*22.102. III. as law-term, *refuse to receive* an accusation, *reject*, γραφήν, ἔνδειξιν, D.22.39, 58.17: hence, 2. ἀ. τινός (sc. δίκην vel γραφήν) *reject* the charge *brought against* a man, i. e. *acquit* him, opp. καταγιγνώσκειν τινός, Id.40.39, cf. Aeschin.2.6, etc.; ἀ. τί τινος Is.5.34: c. inf., ἀ. τινὸς μὴ ἀδικεῖν *acquit* him of wrong, Lys.1.34; also οὐκ ἀπέγνω τῆς δίκης D.34.21.

ἀπογκ-έω, (ὄγκος) *swell up*, Hp.*Aff.*5. **-όω**, *stuff*, χόρτῳ dub. l. in Porph.*Abst.*2.30 (ἐπ- Nauck).

ἀπογλαυκ-όομαι, Pass., *suffer from* γλαύκωμα of the eyes, Aristeas 316, D.S.3.24, Plu.*Tim.*37; τοὺς ὀφθαλμοὺς Vett.Val.69.10; Ἀπεγλαυκωμένος, title of a play of Alexis. 2. *become grey-blue*, of the pupil, Dem.Ophth.ap.Aët.7.53; *to be dyed blue*, *PHolm.*26. 32. **-ωσις**, εως, ἡ, *formation of a* γλαύκωμα, Dsc.1.54, Ptol.*Tetr.* 149 (pl.), Orib.*Syn.*3.151.

ἀπογλάφομαι [λᾰ], *scrape off from oneself, obliterate*, τὸν ἄνδρα.. ἀπεγλαψάμην *Com.Adesp.*574, cf. Paus.Gr.*Fr.*109.

ἀπόγλουτος, ον, *with small rump*, Suid. s. v. λίσποι.

ἀπογλῠκαίνω, *sweeten*, D.S.1.40, cf. Ruf.ap.Orib.8.47b7; ἀπεγλυκασμένος Diph.Siph.ap.Ath.2.55f.

ἀπογλῠφ-ή, ἡ, *place scraped bare*, Asclep.Jun.ap.Gal.12.694. **-ω**, *scrape* or *peel off*, Aret.*CD*1.2, Alciphr.3.60; *scrape thin*, Heliod. ap.Orib.48.33.3; *carve*, of sculpture, *Rev.Phil.*44.251 (Didyma, ii B. C.).

ἀπογλωττίζομαι, Pass., *to be deprived of tongue*, Luc.*Lex.*15.

ἀπόγνοια, ἡ, (ἀπογιγνώσκω) *despair*, τοῦ κρατεῖν Th.3.85.

ἀπογνώμων, ον, = ἀγνώμων III, Hsch., Suid.

ἀπο-γνώσιμος, ον, *desperate*, of errors of conduct, Phld.*Lib.* p.22 O. **-γνωσις**, εως, ἡ, = ἀπόγνοια, τοῦ βίου D.H.1.81, Aret.*SA* 2.2; πραγμάτων Luc.*Somn.*17; ἐλπίδος Ph.2.300: abs., Aristaenet. 1.13. II. *rejection*, φίλου Iamb.*VP*22.102. **-γνωστέον**, *one must give up in despair*, ἐλπίδας Ph.1.455, cf. Aristaenet.1.17. 2. *one must reject the view*, Plot.4.9.2: c. gen., Simp.*in Ph.*610.9. **-γνωστής**, οῦ, ὁ, *desperate man*, Hsch. **-γνωστικῶς**, Adv. *in a desperate way, as in a hopeless case*, Arr.*Epict.*3.1.24.

ἀπο-γομή, ἡ, *discharge* of cargo, *PBaden* 26.73,75. **-γομόω**, *unload* cargo, *Stud.Pal.*8 No.1094.

ἀπογονή, ἡ, *issue, posterity*, *Gloss.*

Ἀπογονικός, ὁ (sc. μήν), name of a month in Cyprus, *Hemerolog. Flor.*

ἀπόγονος, ον, *born* or *descended from*, Γλαύκου οὔτε τι ἀ. ἔστι has no *descendant*, Hdt.6.86.δ′: in pl., *descendants*, Id.1.7, 4.148, al., Th.1. 101; σαὶ..ἀπόγονοι thy *offspring*, S.*OC*534 (lyr.): metaph., ἀ. τοῦ ἐφθαρμένου πνεύματος Hp.*Ep.*19 (*Hermes* 53.65); ἀ. τέταρτος, ἕβδομος Paus.4.15.3: fem. ἀπογόνη *Milet.*3 No.176. II. *viable*, Hp.*Epid.* 2.3.17.

ἀπογραΐζω, *skim off*, ἀφρὸν γάλακτος Sch.Nic.*Al.*91.

ἀπογρᾰφ-εύς, έως, ὁ, *registrar*, Sch.Pl.*Lg.*850c. **-ή**, ἡ, *register, list*, of lands or property, Pl.*Lg.*745d, 850d, etc.; of the πεντηκοστολόγοι, D.34.7; ἀ. τῆς οὐσίας *IG*2.476.14; ἐφήβων *CIG*(add.) 1997c (Maced.); *list* of moneys claimed by the state from private persons, Lys.17.4, D.20.32. 2. *register of persons liable to taxation*, *Ev.Luc.* 2.2, J.*AJ*18.1.1; ἡ κατ' οἰκίαν ἀ. *PLond.*2.260.79 (i A.D.), etc.; of the Roman *census-lists*, Plu.*Cat.Ma.*16 (pl.); *muster-roll* of soldiers, Plb.2.23.9. 3. generally, ἐξ ἀπογραφῆς λέγειν from *a written list*, Sotad.Com.1.35. II. as Att. law-term, *copy of a declaration* made before a magistrate, *deposition* or *information* laid, Lys.9.3, 29.1, Lex ap.D.35.51; ποιεῖσθαι ἀ., = ἀπογράφειν, D.53.1; τινὸς κατά τινος And.1.23, cf. Harp. s. v. 2. any *written declaration* before a magistrate, ἀ. ποιείσθωσαν δηλοῦντες κτλ. *POxy.*237 vii 33 (i A.D.), etc.; esp. *declaration* of property or persons liable to taxation, *BGU*1147. 26 (i B.C.), etc. **-ος**, ον, *copied*:—as Subst., ἀ., ὁ, *a copy*, D.H.*Is.* 11, D.L.6.84; ἀπόγραφον, τό, Cic.*Att.*12.52.3. **-ω**, *write off, copy*, and in Med., *have* a thing *copied, have a copy made of*, τι Pl.*Chrm.* 156a, Plu.2.221b; *commit to writing*, ὀνόματα Pl.*Criti.*113b. II. *enter in a list, register*, ἔθνος ἐν ἕκαστον ἀπέγραφον οἱ γραμματισταὶ Hdt.

7.100:—Pass., *to be registered*, παρὰ τοῖς ἄρχουσι Pl.*Lg*.914c, cf. Men. 272; πρὸς τὸν ἄρχοντα Is.6.44:—freq. Med., *register as one's own property*, ἄρνας δέκα δύο *POxy*.246.10 (i A.D.); *declare* as liable to taxation, *PTaur*.1 vii 11 (ii B.C.), etc. 2. Med. also, *register, note for one's own use*, τὰ ἔτεα Hdt.2.145, 3.136, cf. Heraclid.Pont.ap. Ath.11.554e, etc. 3. Med., *register oneself*, οἱ Ἐλευσῖνάδε ἀπογραψάμενοι Lys.25.9; πρὸς τὸν ταξίαρχον εἰς τὴν τάξιν X.*Cyr*.2.1.18; ἔξεστι πᾶσιν ἀπογραψαμένοις ἐκκλησιάζειν Arist.*Pol*.1297a24; φυλῆς ἧστινος ἂν ἀπογράψηται *IG*2.54*b* 11 (iv B.C.); ἀπεγράψανθο ἐμ πελτοφόρας ib.7.2823 (Boeot.); ἀ. εἰς ἀγῶνας πυγμὴν ἢ παγκράτιον *enter oneself for*.., Plb.39.1.8; but ἀπογραψάμενος πύκτης *AP*11.75 (Lucill.); γέρδιος -όμενος *POxy*.252.4 (i A.D.); ἐπὶ στρατηγίαν ἀ. *enter as candidate for*.., Plu.*Sull*.5; also ἀπογράψομαι ἐμαυτόν *PGrenf*.1.45.6 (ii B.C.); αὐτοὺς ἀ. Plu.*Nic*.14. b. metaph., *subscribe to*, τῇ ἐμῇ αἱρέσει Vett.Val.271.18. III. as Att. law-term, 1. ἀ. τινά *enter* a person's name for the purpose of accusing him, *give in a copy of the charge* against him, And.1.12, etc.; generally, *inform against, denounce*, X.*HG*3.3.11: c. acc. et inf., ἀ. τινὰ μορίαν ἀφανίζειν Lys.7. 29:—Med., *enter one's name as an accuser, indict*, τινά Antipho 6.37: abs., ibid.; of the magistrate who receives the charge, ἀπογράφεσθαι τὴν δίκην Antipho 6.41:—in Pass., of the person accused, ἀ. φόνου δίκην ib.36, Lys.7.2, etc. 2. *hand in a list* or *inventory* of property alleged to belong to the state, but held by a private person, Id. 17.4, al., D.53.1,2; ἀ. οὐσίαν τινὸς ὡς δημοσίαν οὖσαν Hyp.*Eux*.34; generally, *give in a list* or *statement* of property, τοῖς ἄρχουσι τὸ πλῆθος τῆς αὑτῶν οὐσίας Pl.*Lg*.754d; τὰ χωρία καὶ τὰς οἰκίας D.22.54:—Pass., 40.22:—Med., *have such list given in, see it done*, Lys.12.8, al.; ἀπογραφὴν ἀπογράψασθαι D.42.16; τίμημα μικρόν Is.7. 39, cf. 11.34; ἀ. ἀπόλειψιν *have* it *registered*, D.30.17. b. c. acc. pers., ἀπέγραψεν ταῦτα.. ἔχοντα αὑτόν *gave a written acknowledgement* that he was in possession of.., Id.27.14; but ἔχειν ib.47:—in Pass., *to be entered in the list* [of debts], Id.25.71.

ἀπόγυιοι· εὐχαί· σιωπώμεναι, Hsch.

ἀπογυιόω, *enfeeble, unnerve*, μή μ' ἀπογυιώσῃς μένεος Il.6.265, cf. Ath.1.10b; *tire out*, cj. for ἀπογυμνώσῃ, Thphr.*Char*.7.4.

ἀπογυμνάζω, *bring into hard exercise*, ἀ. στόμα *ply* one's tongue *hard*, A.*Th*.441; αὐτούς Arist.*HA*624a25.

ἀπογυμν-όω, *strip bare*, esp. of arms: hence, in Pass., μή σ' ἀπογυμνωθέντα κακὸν καὶ ἀνήνορα θήῃ Od.10.301; ἀπογυμνωθεὶς *with the person exposed*, Hes.*Op*.730; ἀ. τινά *vanquish*, Thphr.*Char*.7.4:—Med., *strip oneself*, X.*Mem*.3.4.1; ἀπογυμνοῦσθαι τὰ ἱμάτια *strip off one's* clothes, Arist.*Pr*.866a21:—Pass., τῆς σχέσεως Them.*in Ph*. 26.8. 2. metaph., *lay open, reveal, explain*, Paus.4.22.4, App.*BC* 1.57; σόφισμα Jul.*Mis*.357c. 3. Pass., *become visible*, of land from the sea, Str.1.1.20. **-ωσις**, εως, ἡ, *stripping bare*, Plu.2.751f; ξιφιδίων App.*BC*1.64.

ἀπογῡναίκωσις, εως, ἡ, *making womanish*, Plu.2.987f.

ἀπόγυον, τό, *mooring cable*, Poll.1.93 (v.l.); cf. ἐπίγυον, ἀπόγειος 2.

ἀπογώνιον, τό, = ὡροσκοπικὴ μοῖρα, Vett.Val.349.22: in pl., *tables* of such degrees for calculating expectation of life, Critodem.ibid., cf. 304.21.

ἀπογωνιόομαι, Pass., *become angular*, Thphr.*CP*2.16.4.

ἀποδαιμονίζει· ἀποκαρτερεῖ ἐν τῷ ἐνθουσιᾶν, Hsch.

ἀποδάκνω, *bite off a piece of*, ἄρτου Aristomen.14:—Pass., μῆλα ἀποδεδηγμένα *with pieces bitten out*, Luc.*Tox*.13: also c. acc., *bite off*, τὴν αὑτῆς γλῶσσαν Polyaen.8.45. 2. abs., *bite, gnaw*, ὀδάξ Cratin.164, cf. X.*Smp*.5.7, *Tab.Defix.Aud*.237.18 (Carthage, i A.D.):—Pass., *have one's tongue bitten*, as by a pungent substance, Arist.*Pr*.958b7.

ἀποδάκρ-ῡσις, εως, ἡ, *flow of tears*, Cass.*Pr*.18. **-ῡτικός**, ή, όν, *calling forth tears*, κολλύρια ibid., cf. Antyll.ap.Orib.8.14.1. **-ύω** [ῡ], *weep much for, lament loudly*, τινά Pl.*Phd*.116d; τι Plu.*Sull*. 12. 2. ἀ. γνώμην *weep away* one's judgement, *be melted to tears contrary to* it, Ar.*V*.983. 3. *to be made to weep* by the use of collyrium, and so *have* the eyes *purged*, Arist.*Pr*.958b6, Luc.*Peregr*.45, Gal.12.751. 4. of trees, *weep, drip* gum, etc., ἀ. ῥητίνην Plu.2. 640d. II. *cease to weep*, ἀπολοφυράμενοι καὶ ἀποδακρύσαντες Aristox. *Fr.Hist*.90, cf. *AB*427.

ἀποδᾰπανάω, *waste*, τὸν καιρόν Herod.Med.ap.Orib.7.8.2.

ἀποδάπτω, = ἀποκόπτω, Hsch.

ἀποδαρθάνω, aor. -έδαρθον, inf. -δραθεῖν Them.*Or*.7.91a (but v. infr.):—*sleep*, μικρόν Plu.*Dio* 26; ἀποδαρθεῖν τὸν ἀηδόνιον ὕπνον Nicoch.4 D. (cf. ἀηδόνιος). II. *wake up*, Ael.*NA*3.13.

ἀπόδαρ-μα, ατος, τό, *hide*, Hdt.4.64 (v.l. -δερμα). **-μός**· *ingluvies*, Gloss.

ἀποδάσ-μιος, ον, *parted off*, Φωκέες ἀ. *parted from* the rest, Hdt. 1.146; ἀ. αἶσα a share *apportioned*, Opp.*H*.5.444. **-μός**, ὁ, (ἀποδατέομαι) *division, part of a whole*, Th.1.12; *separation*, χώρας ἀποδασμῷ ζημιωθῆναι by *loss* of territory, D.H.3.6. **-τος**, ον, *divided off*, Hsch. (-δατοι cod.). **-τύς**, ύος, ἡ, = ἀποδασμός, Id.

ἀποδᾰτέομαι, fut. -δάσομαι [ᾰ], Ep. -δάσσομαι: Ep. aor. -δασσάμην Theoc.17.50, inf. -δάτταθθαι *Leg.Gort*.4.29:—*portion out* to others, *apportion*, ἥμισυ τῷ ἐνάρων ἀποδάσσομαι Il.17.231; Ἀχαιοῖς ἄλλ' ἀποδάσσεσθαι 22.118; σοὶ δ' αὖ.. τῶνδ' ἀποδάσσομαι ὅσσ' ἐπέοικεν 24.595; πάντων ἴσον Pi.*N*.10.86, cf. Call.*Del*.9, etc. II. *part off, separate*, ἀποδασάμενος μόριον ὅσον δὴ τῆς στρατιῆς Hdt.2.103.

ἀποδαυλίζω, f.l. for ἀποκαυλίζω, E.*Supp*.717.

ἀποδαψῐλεύομαι, *to be liberal of* a thing, Gloss.

ἀποδέδεγμαι, pf. of ἀποδέχομαι: also Ion. for ἀποδέδειγμαι, pf. Pass. of ἀποδείκνυμι.

ἀποδεδειγμένως, Adv., (ἀποδείκνυμι) *demonstrably*, Cyr.

ἀποδεδειλιᾱκότως, Adv., (ἀποδειλιάω) *in a cowardly way*, censured by Poll.5.123.

ἀποδεής, ές, (δέω B) *empty*, ἀγγεῖον Arist.*Fr*.224, Plu.2.967a; ναῦς ἀ. *not fully manned*, Id.*Ant*.62: metaph. of persons, Id.2.473e.

ἀποδεῖ, Ion. **ἀποδέει**, v. ἀποδέω.

ἀποδειδίσσομαι, *frighten away*, Il.12.52 (tm.).

ἀποδείκ-νῡμι (and -ύω X.*Smp*.8.20, Plb.7.14.3), Ion. **-δέκνῡμι** *GDI*5653*b*14 (Chios, v B.C.), fut. -δείξω, Ion. -δέξω:—*point away from* other objects *at* one, and so: I. *point out, display, make known*, whether by deed or word, σφι γνώμας Hdt.1.171, al.; τάφους καὶ συγγένειαν Th.1.26; ἦθος τὸ πρόσθε τοκήων A.*Ag*.727; ἀρετήν Hyp.*Epit*.29; τὰ τῆς τέχνης ἐξευρήματα Hp.*Praec*.9; *proclaim*, τὴν ἡμέρην *GDI* l.c.:—Pass., τῶν οὔρων ἀποδεχθέντων *SIG*134.2 (Milet., iv B.C.). 2. *bring forward, produce*, μαρτύρια τούτων Hdt.5.45; πολλοὺς παῖδας Id.1.136, cf. S.*OT*1405, Isoc.19.6, X.*Cyr*. 1.2.5; ἐπόχους 8.1.35; ἀ. τρόπαια And.1.147; χρήματα πλεῖστ' ἀ. ἐν τῷ κοινῷ Ar.*Eq*.774; μορφὴν ἑτέραν E.*Fr*.839.14 (v.l. ἐπέδειξεν): c. part., ὑγιέα τινὰ ἐόντα ἀ. *produce* him safe and sound, Hdt.3.130, cf. 134. 3. *produce, deliver* accounts, τὸν λόγον Id.7.119; ἀ. τετρακόσια τάλαντα τετελεσμένα ib.118. 4. *publish* a law, Lys. 30.11, X.*HG*2.3.11. 5. *appoint, assign*, τέμενος ἀ. τινί Hdt.5.67, 89; βωμόν τινι Id.7.178; ἐν βουλευτήριον Th.2.15; γῆς ὅρους ib.72; τὴν τρίτην ἀ. ἐκκλησίαν *to fix, prescribe* it, D.24.25:—Pass., τοῖσί ἐστι χῶρος ἀποδεδεγμένος Hdt.1.153; τροφὴ αὐτοῖσι τοιαύτη ἀποδέδεκται Id.2.65. b. c. inf., κώμας ὅθεν ἀπέδειξαν οἱ ἡγεμόνες λαμβάνειν τὰ ἐπιτήδεια whence *they appointed* that they should receive.., X.*An*.2.3.14:—Pass., τοῖσι ἀποδεδέχθαι.. ἕλκειν (impers.) *it had been appointed* them to draw, Hdt.2.124. 6. *show by argument, prove, demonstrate*, Ar.*Nu*.1334, Arist.*APo*.75b37, etc.; ἀ. σαφεῖς τὰς ἀποδείξεις And.2.3; ἀ. ὡς.. Ar.*V*.548, Pl.*R*.472d; ὅτι.. Id.*Prt*.323c, etc.; πότερον.. ἤ.. Id.*Alc*.1.114b: c. dupl. acc., *prove* one so and so, οὓς ἀποδείξω λέκτρων προδότας E.*Ion* 879, etc.; τοιούτους τινάς Hp.*Decent*.4: folld. by part., ἀ. λόγῳ.. οὐδὲν μετεόν Hdt.5.94; ἀ. τινὰ λέγοντα οὐδέν *make it evident* that.., 7.17, cf. 2. 133. II. *show forth* a person or thing *as* so and so, hence: 1. *appoint, proclaim, create*, ἀ. τινὰ στρατηγόν X.*An*.1.1.2, al.: c. inf., στρατηγὸν εἶναι Hdt.5.25; ἀ. τούτους τὴν πόλιν νέμειν ib.29; ἑαυτὸν ὅτι ἐστὶ θεός 2*Ep.Thess*.2.4:—Pass., *to be so created*, Hdt.1.124,162; μελεδωνοὶ ἀποδεδέχαται τῆς τροφῆς 2.65; ἀπεδέχθη εἶναι ἵππαρχος 7.154; αὐτοκράτωρ ἀποδέδεικται *POxy*.1021.7 (i A.D.); ὕπατος ἀποδεδειγμένος, = Lat. *consul designatus*, *OGI*379.5 (Tiflis), etc. 2. *make, render*, mostly with an Adj., ἀ. τινὰς μοχθηροτάτους *make* them finished rascals, Ar.*Ra*.1011; ἀ. κρατίστους τοὺς λόχους X.*Cyr*.2. 1.23; γοργότερον ἀ. τὸν ἵππον Id.*Eq*.1.10; ζῷον ἀγριώτερον Pl.*Grg*. 516b: with a Subst., γέλωτα ἀ. τινά Id.*Tht*.166a, cf. *Phd*.72c: c. part., βλέποντ' ἀποδείξω σ' ὀξύτερον τοῦ Λυγκέως Ar.*Pl*.210; ἀ. τινὰς ἀλλοτρίους ὄντας Pl.*Smp*.179c:—Pass., πολέμιοι ἀποδεδειγμένοι *declared* enemies, X.*An*.7.1.26, cf. D.23.200. 3. *represent as*, ἀ. παῖδα πατρὸς ἑωυτῶν ἕκαστον ἐόντα Hdt.2.143, cf. Lys.32.17:—Pass., ἀνδραγαθίη δ' αὕτη ἀποδέδεκται *is represented, considered as*.., Hdt.1.136; οὐδὲ.. οὗτοι ἐν τοῖσι ἄλλοισι θεοῖσι ἀποδεδέχαται *have not been considered, admitted* among.., 2.43:—these two last examples may be pass. usages of ἀποδέχομαι. 4. c. inf., *ordain* a thing or person to be, X.*Oec*.7.30, *Lac*.10.7. 5. *dedicate, consecrate*, θέατρον Plu.*Luc*.29:—Pass., νεὼς ἀποδείκνυται Luc.*Tox*.5.

B. Med., *show forth, exhibit* something of one's own, ἀποδέξασθαι τὴν γνώμην *deliver one's* opinion, Hdt.1.170,207, cf. Th.1.87; also ἀ. μεγάλα ἔργα Hdt.1.59, al.; ἀξιαπηγητότατα ib.16; οὐδὲν λαμπρὸν ἔργον ib.174; ἀ. ἀρετάς *display* high qualities, Pi.*N*.6.49 (cf. supr. A. I. 2); πνεύματα εἰς ἄλληλα στάσιν.. ἀποδεικνύμενα A.*Pr*. 1088; of buildings and the like, μνημόσυνα ἀ. Hdt.2.101; χώματα ἀξιοθέητα 1.184; οὐδεμίαν στρατηΐην ἀ. not *to have* any military service *to show*, 2.111:—Pass., ἔργα μεγάλα καὶ θαυμαστὰ.. ἀποδεχθέντα Id. *Prooem*., cf. 9.27. 2. Med. in act. sense, ἀποδεδειγμένοι ἦσαν ὅτι *had declared* that.., X.*An*.5.2.9.

C. Pass., v. supr. I. 5, II. 1,2,3: aor. ἀπεδείχθην is always Pass., as Hdt.7.154; and so mostly pf. ἀποδέδειγμαι, 1.136, Antipho 2.4.10, X.*An*.7.1.26; but the part. of the latter is sts. Act., v. supr. B. 2. **-τέον**, *one must show, prove*, Pl.*Phdr*.245b. 2. c. dupl. acc., *one must make* one so and so, σκαπανέα αὐτὸν ἀ. Luc.*Vit.Auct*. 7. **-τικός**, ή, όν, *affording proof, demonstrative*, ὁ ἀ. συλλογισμός Arist.*APo*.74b10; ἕξις ἀ. Id.*EN*1139b31; πίστεις ἀ. Id.*Rh*.1358a1, etc.: Comp. -ώτερος Phlp.*in Ph*.9.20: Sup. -ώτατος, λόγος Ph.2.499. Adv. ἀποδεικτικῶς, ἐπίστασθαι Arist.*APo*.75a12; εἰρηκέναι Phld.*Mus*. p.12 K. 2. ἀ. ἱστορία, διήγησις, in which the facts are *regularly set forth and explained*, Plb.2.37.3, 4.40.1, cf. Plu.2.243a. Adv. -κῶς Sch.Iamb. *in Nic*.p.129 P. 3. of persons, *scientific, exact*, Gal.4. 649. 4. ἀ., τά, *sights, attractions*, *SIG*685.70 (Crete, ii B.C.). **-τός**, ή, όν, *demonstrable* or *to be demonstrated*, Arist.*APo*.76b33, al. 2. *demonstrated*, Id.*EN*1140b32.

ἀποδειλ-ίᾱσις, εως, ἡ, *cowardice*, Plb.3.103.2; ἀ. πρός τινα Plu.*Alex*. 13. **-ιᾱτέον**, *one must flinch*, Pl.*R*.374e, Marin.*Procl*.31. **-ιάω**, fut. -άσω [ᾱ], *to be very fearful, play the coward, flinch from danger or toil*, X.*Mem*.3.12.2, Pl.*Grg*.480c, al.; ἀ. ἐν ἰσχυροῖς μαθήμασιν Id.*R*. 535b, cf. 504a; ταῖς ψυχαῖς Plb.1.15.7; πρός τινα or τι Id.11.16.2, cf. Onos.33.6, Luc.*DMort*.10.9, etc. 2. ἀ. τοῦ διαπονεῖσθαι *shrink from*.., X.*Lac*.10.7. 3. ἀ. τὴν μάχην *to be afraid of*, Plb.5.84.5.

ἀπόδειξις, Ion. **-δεξις**, εως, ἡ, (ἀποδείκνυμι) *showing forth, making* *known, exhibiting,* δι' ἀπειροσύνην.. κοὐκ ἀπόδειξιν τῶν ὑπὸ γαίας E.*Hipp.*196. 2. *setting forth, publication,* Ἡροδότου.. ἱστορίης ἀπόδεξις Hdt.*Prooem.*; ἀρχῆς ἀ. *an exposition, sketch* of it, Th.1.97; ἀ. περὶ τὸν πολιτικόν Pl.*Plt.*277a; περί τινος *R.*358b. 3. *proof,* βουλομένοισί σφι γένοιτ' ἂν ἀ. Hdt.8.101; ἀ. ποιεῖσθαι Lys.12.19, etc.; esp. by words, ἀποδείξεις εὑρίσκειν τινός Isoc.10.3; ἀ. λέγειν Pl.*Tht.* 162e; -ξεις φέρειν Plb.12.5.5; χρῆσθαί τινι ἀποδείξει τινός use it *as a proof* of a thing, Plu.2.160a: in pl., *proofs,* or *arguments in proof* of, τινός D.18.300, cf. Pl.*Phd.*73a; λέγειν τι ἐς ἀπόδειξιν τοῦ περιέσεσθαι τῷ πολέμῳ Th.2.13; ἄνευ ἀποδείξεως Pl.*Phd.*92d; μετ' ἀ. Plb.3.1.3, al.; ἀ. λαμβάνειν.. τῶν μανθανόντων *test* them by examination, etc., Plu.2.736d; ἀ. ποιεῖσθαι τῶν ἐφήβων *IG*2.470.40; ἀ. τέχνης *specimen,* Dionys.Com.3.4; ἀ. αὐτοῖς δοῦναί τινος Plu.2.79f, etc.; *citation,* ποιητῶν καὶ ἱστοριαγράφων ἀποδείξεις *SIG*685.93 (Crete, ii B.C.). b. in the Logic of Arist., *demonstration,* i.e. *deductive proof by syllogism, APo.*71^{b}17, al., cf. Epicur.*Ep.*1 p.25 U., *Stoic.*2.89; opp. inductive proof (ἐπαγωγή), Arist.*APo.*81^{a}40:—sts. in a loose sense, ἀ. ῥητορικὴ ἐνθύμημα Id.*Rh.*1355^{a}6. 4. *appointment,* θεωρῶν *SIG*402.29 (Delph., iii B.C.). II. (from Med.) ἀ. ἔργων μεγάλων *display, achievement* of mighty works, Hdt.1.207, cf. 2.101, 148.

ἀποδειπν-έω, *finish supper,* Ath.15.622e, Iamb.*VP*21.98. **-ίδιος,** ον, *of* or *from supper, AP*6.302 (Leon.). **-ος,** ον, = ἄδειπνος, Hsch.

ἀποδειρο-τομέω, *slaughter by cutting off the head,* or *cutting the throat,* of men, Il.18.336, 23.22, Luc.*DMeretr.*13.3; μῆλα ἐς βόθρον Od.11.35; κεφαλὴν ἀ. Hes.*Th.*280. **-τόμησις,** εως, ἡ, *slaughtering,* Eust.1145.63.

ἀποδείρω, Ion. for ἀποδέρω.

ἀποδεισιδαιμονέω, *brood over with superstitious fear,* Sch.Th.7.50.

ἀποδεκάτ-ευσις, έως, ἡ, *tithing, Gloss.* **-εύω,** v.l. for sq., *Ev. Luc.*18.12.

ἀποδεκᾰτίζω, = sq., δεκάτην Lxx *To.*1.7.

ἀποδεκᾰτόω, *tithe, take a tenth of,* τι Lxx 1*Ki.*8.16; πάντα *Ev.Luc.* 18.12; ἀ. τὸν λαόν *take tithe of* them, *Ep.Hebr.*7.5; δεκάτην ἀ. τινός Lxx *De.*14.22. II. *pay tithe of,* τι Lxx *Ge.*28.22, *Ev.Matt.*23.23, etc.

ἀποδέκομαι, Ion., etc., for ἀποδέχομαι.

ἀποδεκ-τέον, (ἀποδέχομαι) *one must receive from others,* τὰ εἰσφερόμενα X.*Oec.*7.36. 2. *one must accept, allow, admit,* c. acc. rei, λόγον Pl.*Lg.*668a: c. gen. et part., ἀ. τινὸς λέγοντος Id.*Tht.*160c, *R.*379c; μὴ ἄλλως ἀ. λεγομένης τέχνης; Id.*Phdr.*272b. 3. Adj. -τέος, α, ον, Vett.Val.329.16, Zos.Alch.p.229 B. **-τήρ,** ῆρος, ὁ, = sq., X.*Cyr.* 8.1.9, Arist.*Mu.*398^{a}25. **-της,** ου, ὁ, *receiver*: in pl., *financial officials,* established by Cleisthenes, *IG*2.38, D.24.162, Arist.*Ath.*48, *Pol.*1321^{b}33, Harp.: also at Thasos, *IG*12(8).608; in Egypt, σίτου *Ostr.*1217; ἀχύρου *POxy.*43^r iii 8 (iii A.D.), cf. Poll.8.114; ἀ. τῶν πολιτικῶν χρημάτων *Jahresh.*21/2 *Beibl.*255 (ii A.D.):—hence -τεύω, *hold office of* ἀποδέκτης, *IG*12(8).391, 610 (Thasos). **-τός,** όν (ἡ, ὁν prob. l. in Phld.*Ir.*p.60 W.), *acceptable, welcome, OGI*441.100, 1*Ep.Ti.*2.3, S.E.*M.*11.83, Plu.2.1061a: Comp. -ότερος Dsc.*Eup.*1 *Praef.* Adv. -τως *An.Ox.*3.139, Sch.E.*Or.*1680.

ἀποδενδρόομαι, Pass., *grow into a tree,* Thphr.*HP*3.17.2, cf. 1.3. 2; *to be turned into a tree,* Luc.*VH*1.8, Heraclit.*All.*36.

ἀποδέξασθαι, aor. 1 of ἀποδέχομαι, but also, II. Ion. for ἀποδείξασθαι, cf. ἀποδείκνυμι.

ἀπόδεξις, εως, ἡ, (ἀποδέχομαι) *acceptance,* τῶν ἀπονεμομένων M.Ant. 10.8; πρὸς τοὺς φίλους *OGI*227.13 (Milet., iii B.C.). II. Ion. for ἀπόδειξις.

ἀποδέρκομαι, = ἀποβλέπω, Trag. (Satyric) in *POxy.*1083.21.

ἀπόδερμα, v. ἀπόδαρμα.

ἀποδερμᾰτ-ίζω, *flay, strip,* Androm.ap.Gal.12.991, Sch.Nic.*Al.* 301, Hsch. **-ισμός,** ὁ, *flaying, Gloss.* **-όομαι,** Pass., of shields, *to have their leather covering destroyed,* ὑπ' ὄμβρου Plb.6.25.7: —late in Act., *flay,* κεφαλὴν ξίφει Zos.Alch.p.108 B.

ἀποδερτρόω, (δέρτρον) *disembowel, eviscerate,* Sch.Od.11.579.

ἀποδέρω, Ion. -δείρω (also in Ar.*V.*1286):—*flay, skin completely,* τὸν βοῦν Hdt.2.40, cf. 42, 4.60; ἀ. τὴν κεφαλήν *scalp,* 4.64:—Pass., πρόβατα ἀποδαρέντα X.*An.*3.5.9; *become excoriated,* Philum.ap.Orib. 45.29.61. 2. *flay by flogging, fetch the skin off one's back,* Ar.*Lys.* 739. 3. sens. obsc., ib.953. 4. Medic., *separate by avulsion,* Gal.2.896. II. *strip off,* ἀ. πᾶσαν ἀνθρωπηΐην (sc. δορήν) Hdt.5.25.

ἀπόδεσις, εως, ἡ, *tying up,* ἡ τοῦ ὀμφαλοῦ ἀ. τοῖς παιδίοις Arist.*HA* 587^{a}12; ἀ. ἐκ τοῦ πασσάλου Nicom.*Harm.*6, cf. Iamb.*VP*26.118.

ἀποδεσμ-εύω, *bind fast,* Lxx *Pr.*26.8, *Hippiatr.*77. **-έω,** = foreg., Pherecyd.119 J., Tim.Gaz.ap.Ar.Byz.*Epit.*143.14, Olymp.*in Mete.*96.7. **-ίς,** ἴδος, ἡ, prob. f.l. for ὑπο-, Gal.14.794. **-ος,** ὁ, *band, breastband, girdle,* Ar.*Fr.*320.13, Luc.*DMeretr.*12.1. II. *bag, case, receptacle,* Plu.*Dem.*30, Paul.Aeg.3.41; σταχτῆς *sachet,* Lxx *Ca.*1.13. 2. *bundle,* ἐπιστολῶν *PRyl.*78.36 (ii A.D.), etc.

ἀποδεχθείς, Ion. for ἀποδειχθείς, Hdt.

ἀποδέχομαι, Ion. -δέκομαι, fut. -δέξομαι: aor. -εδεξάμην: pf. -δέδεγμαι (for possible pass. usages of this tense v. ἀποδείκνυμι A. II. 3): —*accept,* καὶ οὐκ ἀπεδέξατ' ἄποινα Il.1.95, cf. Ar.*Ec.*712, X.*An.*6.1.24, etc.; ἀ. γνώμην παρά τινος *accept* advice from him, Hdt.4.97; ἀπόδεξαί μου ὃ λέγω Pl.*Cra.*430d. 2. *accept as a teacher, follow,* X.*Mem.*4.1. 1, etc.; ἀ. τινὰ σύμβουλον Pl.*Prt.*323c. 3. *admit* to one's presence, τοὺς πρεσβευτάς Plb.21.35.5; ἀ. αὐτὸν καὶ τὰ ῥηθέντα φιλοφρόνως 21. 22.1, cf. 3.66.8. 4. mostly of *admitting into the mind,* a. *receive favourably, approve,* ἀπολογίαν Antipho 3.2.2; κατηγορίας, διαβολάς, Th.3.3, 6.29; τοῖσι μὴ ἀποδεκομένοισι, c. acc. inf., those who do not *accept the story* that.., Hdt.6.43; freq. in Pl., δοῦναί τε καὶ ἀ. λόγον *R.*531e; τὴν ἀπόκρισιν *Prt.*329b; λόγον παρά τινος *Smp.*194d, etc.; τι παρά τινος *Ti.*29e; τί τινος Th.1.44, 7.48, Pl.*Phlb.*54a, etc.: c. gen. pers. mostly with part. added, ἀ. τινὸς λέγοντος *receive* or *accept* a statement *from* him, i.e. *believe* or *agree with* his statements, Id.*Phd.*92a,e; μὴ ἀποδέχεσθε τούτου φενακίζοντος ὑμᾶς D.56.31; ἀ. μαθηματικοῦ πιθανολογοῦντος Arist.*EN*1094^{b}26, cf. *Rh.*1395^{b}8: without part., οὐκ ἀποδέχομαι ἐμαυτοῦ ὡς τὸ ἓν δύο γέγονεν I cannot *satisfy* myself *in thinking* that.., Pl.*Phd.*96e, cf. *Euthphr.*9e, *R.*329e: abs., *to accept a statement, to be satisfied,* D.18.277, Arist.*Pol.*1263^b 16; ἀ. ἐάν.. Pl.*R.*336d, 525d: c. gen. rei, *to be content with,* τῆς προαιρέσεως Lib.*Or.*24.2; τῶν εἰρημένων ib.59.9. b. generally, *approve, acknowledge,* τὴν τῶν ἐφήβων ἀρετὴν *IG*2.481.60, al. c. *take* or *understand* a thing, ὀρθῶς ἀ. τι X.*Mem.*3.10.15, cf. *Cyr.*8.7.10; ἱκανώτατα Pl.*R.*511d; τὰ τοιαῦτα δυσχερῶς πως ἀποδέχομαι Id.*Euthphr.* 6a; ὑπόπτως Th.6.53: c. gen. pers. (the acc. rei being understood), οὕτως αὐτοῦ ἀποδεχώμεθα let us *understand* him thus (referring to what goes before), Pl.*R.*340c; μὴ χαλεπῶς ἀλλὰ πρᾴως ἀποδεχώμεθα ἀλλήλων Id.*Lg.*634c. II. *receive back, recover,* Hdt.4.33; opp. ἀποδιδόναι, Th.5.26. III. *sustain, hold out against,* Plb.3.43.3, 5.51.1.

ἀποδέω (A), *bind fast, tie up* the navel, Pl.*Smp.*190e; generally, *bind,* Lxx *Jo.*9.4, J.*AJ*4.8.21:—Pass., ἐν δερματίῳ ἀποδέδεταί τι Pl. *Erx.*400a, cf. Arist.*HA*587^{a}14, Erasistr.ap.Gal.11.148.

ἀποδέω (B), *to be in want of, lack,* often in accounts of numbers, τριακοσίων ἀποδέοντα μύρια 10,000 *lacking* or *save* 300, Th.2.13, cf. 4.38, etc.; δυεῖν χιλιάδων ἀποδέοντες εἶναι δισμύριοι D.H.7.3; generally, τοσοῦτον ἀποδέω τινός so *far am I from..,* Pl.*Ax.*366b, 372a: c. inf., ὀλίγον ἀποδεῖν εἶναι *want* little *of* being, Plu.2.978f; *fall short of, be inferior to,* τινός Luc.*Merc.Cond.*36, cf. Plu.2.1088c; πλήθει οὐ πολὺ ἀποδέοντες ἀλλήλων not *differing* much in number, D.H.3.52, cf. Plu.*Luc.*28; *come short of, miss,* τῆς ἀληθείας Pl.*Ax.*369d.

ἀποδηλ-όω, *make manifest,* A.*Fr.*304.2, Hp.*Int.*23; *indicate,* πλῆθος Corn.*ND*13; *explain, expound,* ὅτι.. Plb.21.37.8, cf. Plu.*Phil.* 13:—Pass., Str.2.5.16. II. intr., *become manifest,* Arist.*Mir.* 834^{b}33. **-ωσις,** εως, ἡ, *communication by speech,* Diog.Oen.10.

ἀποδημ-έω, Dor. -δᾱμέω, pf. ἀπεδήμηκα dub. in Hermipp.66:—*to be away from home, be abroad* or *on one's travels,* Hdt.1.29, 4.1, 152, Ar.*Nu.*371, etc.; of foreign service, Id.*Lys.*101; opp. ἐπιδημεῖν, X. *Cyr.*7.5.69: metaph., *to be absent,* Pi.*P.*10.37; ὁ νοῦς παρὼν ἀποδημεῖ Ar.*Eq.*1120: sts. c. gen., ἀποδημεῖν οἰκίας Pl.*Lg.*954b; ἀπὸ τῆς ἑωυτῶν Hdt.9.117; ἐκ τῆς πόλεως Pl.*Cri.*53a; οὐκ ἔξεστι ἀποδημεῖν τοῖς Λακεδαιμονίοις Arist.*Fr.*543. 2. *go abroad,* παρά τινα to visit him, Hdt.3.124; ἀ. ἐς Αἴγιναν κατὰ τοὺς Αἰακίδας *go abroad* to Aegina to fetch the Aeacidae, Id.8.84; ἀ. ἐπὶ δεῖπνον εἰς Θετταλίαν Pl.*Cri.*53e; ἐνθένδε εἰς ἄλλον τόπον Id.*Ap.*40e; κατ' ἐμπορίαν Lycurg.21, 57 (v.l. ἐπί); πρὸς τὰ ἱερά X.*HG*4.7.3; ποῖ γῆς ἀπεδήμεις; Ar.*Ra.*48; ἄλλοσε ἀ. Pl.*Lg.*579b; ἐκεῖσε Id.*Phd.*61e. **-ησις,** εως, ἡ, = ἀποδημία, Alciphr.1.29, *CIG*1813*b*8 (Nicopolis, dub.). **-ητής,** οῦ, ὁ, *one who goes abroad, is not tied to his home,* opp. ἐνδημότατος, Th.1.70. **-ητικός,** ή, όν, *fond of wandering* or *travelling,* Dicaearch.1.9, Vett.Val. 98.7; παράστασις ἀ. banishment *to foreign parts,* of ostracism, Arist. *Pol.*1308^{b}19: metaph., *migratory,* i.e. *mortal,* Arr.*Epict.*3.24.4, cf. ib.60, 105. **-ία,** Ion. -ίη, ἡ, *going* or *being abroad,* ἀ. ἐξ οἴκου Hdt. 6.130, cf. Lys.3.10; ἀ. ποιεῖσθαι Pl.*Cri.*52b; ἔξω τῆς χώρας Id.*Lg.* 949e, cf. 950a; ἀ. ἡ εἰς Ὀλυμπίαν And.4.30; περὶ τῆς ἀ. τῆς ἐκεῖ as to my *life in* that *foreign land,* i.e. beyond the grave, Pl.*Phd.*61e, cf. 67c, *Ap.*41a (but in pl. of earthly life, as *exile from* heaven, Porph. *Marc.*5); ἐξ ἀποδημίας τινὸς προσῄει from *a long journey,* X.*Cyr.*3. 1.7. **-ος,** Dor. -δᾱμος, ον, *away from one's country, abroad,* οὐκ ἀ. Ἀπόλλωνος τυχόντος Pi.*P.*4.5, cf. Plu.2.799f, etc.; ἀ. ἐπέρχεσθαι *from abroad, CIG*3344*A* (Smyrna); ἀ. στρατεία Luc.*Am.*6: metaph., τῆς ἐμῆς γνώμης Hp.*Ep.*17:—less Att. than ἔκδημος, Moer.143, cf. Poll.1.177.

ἀπόδησις, f.l. for ἐπίδησις, Sor.ap.Gal.13.43.

ἀποδία, ἡ, (πούς) *absence of feet,* Arist.*PA*642^{b}23, 690^{b}15.

ἀποδιαγράφω [ρᾰ], *order payment to be made, SIG*976.30 (Samos, ii B.C.), *PTheb.Bank* 12.7 (ii B.C.).

ἀποδιαιρέω, *distribute,* v.l. in Lxx *Jo.*1.6; *divide off, distinguish from,* δημιουργοῦ τὸν Ἄττιν Jul.*Or.*5.165b; ἐγχέλυας ἰχθύων Eust. 1221.36:—Pass., *PStrassb.*92.6 (iii B.C.).

ἀποδιαιτάω, *pronounce in* one's *favour in an arbitration,* opp. καταδιαιτάω (q.v.), ὅπως τὴν δίαιταν αὐτῷ ἀποδιαιτήσομεν Test.ap.D.21. 93:—Pass., ib.96: hence ἀ. τινός (sc. τὴν δίκην) *decide for* one, Id. 40.17; τὰ ἀποδιαιτηθέντα μου λύσας ib.43.

ἀποδιά-κειμαι, Pass., *have a distaste,* πρός τι Aët.8.76. **-κλασμός,** ὁ, *mental perturbation,* Gal.19.514. **-κρίνω** [ρῐ], *separate completely,* Dam.*Pr.*36. **-λαμβάνω,** *set apart,* Syrian.*in Metaph.* 64.40; *discuss separately,* Dex.*in Cat.*59.16, Herm.*in Phdr.*p.115 A., etc. **-ληπτός,** ή, όν, *separable,* ἀ. καθ' ἑαυτήν *Stoic.*2.126. **-ληψις,** εως, ἡ, *division into parts,* Iamb.*Myst.*1.9, Procl.*in Prm.*p.674 S.; *abstraction,* Dex.*in Cat.*40.9 (pl.). **-λύω,** *dissipate,* νωθρότητας Antyll.ap.Orib.6.21.36. II. *confute utterly,* λόγον Phld.*Herc.* 19.16. **-νομή,** ἡ, *distribution, assignment,* Ecphant.ap.Stob. 4.7.66. **-πέμπομαι,** *divert,* ἡμᾶς τῆς ματαίας πλάνης Syn.Alch. p.59 B. **-σείω,** gloss on ἀπεστυφέλιξεν, Hsch. **-στᾰσις,** εως, ἡ, *distance,* τῶν ἀστέρων Vett.Val.227.14. **-στέλλω,** *divide, PTaur.* 8.22.48 (ii B.C.), Lxx *Jo.*1.6 (v.l.):—Pass., *to be set apart, forbidden,* ib.2*Ma.*6.5. **-στολή,** ἡ, *division, PRyl.*65.4 (ii B.C.). **-στρέ-**

φω, *divert*, Phld.*Lib*.p.29 O. **-τίθεμαι**, *to be weaned*, *Theol.Ar.* 49. **-τρίβω** [ῐ], *waste time*, Aeschin.2.49; *spend time*, περὶ ὀρχηστάς D.C.54.17 (Pass.); ἐν πόλει Agath.1.19, cf. 3.16, 4.13. II. c. acc. pers., *detain*, D.C.44.19; *defer*, τὰς χειροτονίας App.*BC*2.20: abs., *delay*, ib.13. III. *divert*, τὰς χεῖρας ἀπὸ τῶν σφαγῶν D.C. 77.14.

ἀποδῐδάσκω, *teach not* to do, Hp.*Fract*.1.

ἀποδιδρασκίνδα (sc. παιδιά), Adv. *a game in which all but one ran away*, described by Poll.9.117.

ἀποδῐδράσκω, Ion. -ήσκω, fut. -δράσομαι, Ion. -δρήσομαι: pf. -δέδρᾱκα Men.*Sam*.143, Phld.*Rh*.1.199 S.: aor. ἀπέδραν, Ion. -έδρην, opt. ἀποδραίην Thgn.927, imper. ἀπόδρᾱθι Ph.1.90, inf. ἀποδρᾶναι, Ion. -δρῆναι, part. ἀποδράς—the only form found in Hom.; the other tenses in Hdt., etc., pf. part. ἀποδεδρακότες X.*An*.6.4.8:—*run away*, *escape* or *flee from*, esp. *by stealth*, Hom. (never in Il.), ἐκ νηὸς ἀποδράς Od.16.65; νηὸς ἀ. 17.516; ἀ. ἐκ τῆς Σάμου Hdt.3.148; ἐς Σάμον 4.43; ἐπὶ θάλασσαν 6.2; ἀποδρᾶσα ᾤχετο And.1.125, cf. 4.17, Ar.*Ec*.196, Pl.*Tht*.203d; of runaway slaves, X.*An*.1.4.8 (ἀποδρᾶναι τὸ ἀναχωρήσαντά τινα εὔδηλον εἶναι ὅπου ἐστίν, ἀποφεύγειν δὲ τὸ μὴ δύνασθαι ἐπιληφθῆναι Ammon.p.19 V.); σώματα ἀποδράντα *IG*2².584; of soldiers, *desert*, X.*An*.5.6.34; ἀποδιδράσκοντα μὴ δύνασθαι ἀποδρᾶναι *attempting to escape* not to be able *to escape*, Pl.*Prt*.317a, cf. 310c. 2. c. acc., *flee*, *shun*, Hdt.2.182, Ar.*Pax*234, etc.; ἀπέδρασαν αὐτόν Th.1.128; *evade*, τὸν νόμον Arist.*Pol*.1270ᵇ35; οὐκ ἀπέδρα τὴν στρατείαν D.21.165; ὅτε..τὸ σὸν ὄμμ' ἀπέδραν (poet. for ἀπέδρασαν) S.*Aj*.167.—Rare in Trag. (Cf. Skt. *drāti* 'run'.)

ἀποδῐδύσκω, = ἀποδύω, τινάς Artem.2.69:—Med., Parth.15.3; *cast off*, *slough off*, γῆρας Artem.2.13, 14.

ἀποδίδωμι, fut. -δώσω: aor. 1 ἀπέδωκα: aor. 2 ἀπέδων A.D.*Synt*. 276.9, shortened inf. ἀποδοῦν prob. in Hsch.:—*give up* or *back*, *restore*, *return*, τινί τι Hom., etc.: esp. *render what is due*, *pay*, as debts, penalties, submission, honour, etc., τοκεῦσι θρέπτρα Il.4.478; ἀ. τινὶ λώβην *give* him *back* his insult, i.e. *make atonement for* it, ib.9.387 (tm.); τὴν πλημμέλειαν Lxx*Nu*.5.7; εὖ ἔρδοντι κακὴν ἀ. ἀμοιβήν Thgn.1263; ἀ. τὴν ὁμοίην τινί Hdt.4.119; ἀμοιβάς Democr.92; κακὸν ἀντ' ἀγαθοῦ Id.93; ἀ. τὸ μόρσιμον *pay the debt of* fate, Pi.*N*.7.44; τὸ χρέος Hdt.2.136; τὸν ναῦλον Ar.*Ra*.270; τὴν ζημίαν, τὴν καταδίκην, Th.3.70, 5.50; τὴν φερνήν *PEleph*.1.11 (iv B.C.); εὐχάς X.*Mem*.2.2.10; ἀ. ὀπίσω ἐς Ἡρακλείδας τὴν ἀρχήν Hdt.1.13, etc.; πόλεις ἀ. τοῖς παρακαταθεμένοις Aeschin.3.85; ἀ. χάριτας Lys.31.24; οὐκ ἐς χάριν ἀλλ' ἐς ὀφείλημα τὴν ἀρετὴν ἀ. Th.2.40; ἀ. χάριν τινός Isoc.6.73; [τὴν πόλιν] ἀ. τοῖς ἐπιγιγνομένοις οἵανπερ παρὰ τῶν πατέρων παρελάβομεν X.*HG*7.1.30:—Pass., ἕως κ' ἀπὸ πάντα δοθείη Od.2.78; ἀ. μισθός, χάριτες, Ar.*Eq*.1066, Th.3.63. 2. *assign*, ταῖς γυναιξὶ μουσικὴν καὶ γυμναστικήν Pl.*R*.456b; τὸ δίκαιον καὶ τὸ συμφέρον Arist.*Rh*.1354ᵇ3, cf. 1356ᵃ15; τὸ πρὸς ἀλκὴν ὅπλον ἀ. ἡ φύσις Id.*GA*759ᵇ3, etc. b. *refer* to one, as belonging to his department, εἰς τοὺς κριτὰς τὴν κρίσιν Pl.*Lg*.765b; ἀ. εἰς τὴν βουλὴν περὶ αὐτῶν *refer* their case to the Council, Isoc.18.6, cf. Lys.22.2, etc. 3. *render*, *yield*, of land, ἐπὶ διηκόσια ἀποδοῦναι (sc. καρπόν) *yield fruit* two hundred-fold, Hdt.1.193; τἄλλα δ' ἄν τις καταβάλῃ ἀπέδωκεν ὀρθῶς Men.*Georg*.38; ἢν ἡ χώρη κατὰ λόγον ἐπιδιδοῖ ἐς ὕψος καὶ τὸ ὅμοιον ἀποδιδοῖ ἐς αὔξησιν *renders*, *makes* a like increase in extent, Hdt.2.13:—hence perh. metaph., τὸ ἔργον ἀ. Arist.*EN*1106ᵃ16; ἀ. δάκρυ E.*HF*489. 4. *concede*, *allow*, c. inf., *suffer* or *allow* a person to do, ἀ. τισὶ αὐτονομεῖσθαι Th.1.144, cf. 3.36; εἰ δὲ τοῖς μὲν..ἐπιτάττειν ἀποδώσετε D.2.30; ἀ. κολάζειν Id.23.56; τῷ δικαστηρίῳ ἀποδέδοται τοῦ φόνου τὰς δίκας δικάζειν Lys.1.30; ἀ. τινὶ ζητεῖν Arist.*Pol*.1341ᵇ30, cf. *Po*.1454ᵇ5; also οὔτε ἀπολογίας ἀποδοθείσης And.4.3; ἐπειδὰν αὐτοῖς ὁ λόγος ἀποδοθῇ when right of speech is *allowed* them, Aeschin.3.54. 5. ἀ. τινά with an Adj., *render* or *make* so and so, like ἀποδείκνυμι, ἀ. τὴν τέρψιν βεβαιοτέραν Isoc.1.46; τέλειον ἀ. τὸ τέκνον Arist.*GA*733ᵇ1; δεῖ τὰς ἐνεργείας ποιὰς ἀ. Id.*EN*1103ᵇ22; μετριωτέραν τὴν ὑπερηφανίαν D.H.7.16. b. *exhibit*, *display*, τὴν ὑπάρχουσαν ἀρετήν And.1.109; ἀ. τὴν ἰδίαν μορφήν *render*, *express* it, Arist.*Po*.1454ᵇ10; ἀ. φαντασίαν τινός *present* appearance of, Phld.*Ir*.p.71 W., al. 6. *deliver over*, *give up*, e.g. as a slave, E.*Cyc*.239; ἀ. τὸν μιαρὸν τῷ χρόνῳ φῆναι Antipho4.4.11. 7. ἀ. ἐπιστολήν *deliver* a letter, Th.7.10, cf. E.*IT*745. 8. ἀ. τὸν ἀγῶνα ὀρθῶς καὶ καλῶς *bring* it *to a conclusion*, Lycurg.149. 9. λόγον ἀ. *render* an account, D.27.48:—Pass., μαρτυρίαι ἀ. Test.ap.D.18.137. 10. ἀ. ὅρκον, v. ὅρκος. 11. *give an account* or *definition* of a thing, *explain* it, E.*Or*.150; ἀ. τί ἐστί τι Arist.*Cat*.2ᵇ8, cf. 1ᵃ10, *Metaph*.1040ᵇ30, al.; ἑπομένως τούτοις ἀ. τὴν ψυχήν Id.*deAn*.405ᵃ4, cf. *Ph*.194ᵇ34, al.; also, *use by way of definition*, ὁ μὲν τὴν ὕλην ἀποδίδωσιν, ὁ δὲ τὸ εἶδος Id.*deAn*.403ᵇ1; simply, *define*, τὸν ἄνθρωπον S.E.*M*.7.272; *expound*, Phld.*D*.3.14, cf. Epicur.*Nat*.14.3, 119 G., 143 G.; *render*, *interpret* one word *by* another, ἀ. τὴν κοτύλην ἄλεισον Ath.11.479c; *explain*, *interpret*, τὸ "φωνὴν αἵματος βοᾶν" Ph.1.209:—Pass., βέλτιον ἀποδοθήσεται Epicur.*Ep*.1 p.15 U.; ἀκριβεστέρως ἀποδοθήσεται A.D.*Synt*.45.21; ἀ. τι πρός τι *use with reference to*, Olymp.*in Mete*.281.10, cf. Sch.Ar.*Pl*.538. 12. *attach* or *append*, *make dependent upon*, τί τινι or εἴς τι Hero *Aut*.24.5, 6.2. 13. ἀ. τί τινος *assign* a property *to* a thing, Arist.*Top*.128ᵇ28. II. intr., *return*, *recur*, Id.*GA*722ᵃ8, *HA*585ᵇ32. 2. Rhet. and Gramm., *introduce a clause answering to the* πρότασις, Id.*Rh*.1407ᵃ20; διὰ μακροῦ ἀ. D.H.*Dem*.9, etc.; cf. ἀπόδοσις II.2; οὐκ ἀποδίδωσι τὸ ἐπεί *has* no *apodosis*, Sch.Od.3.103; esp. in similes, *complete the comparison*, Arist.*Rh*.1413ᵃ11. 3. in Tactics, *turn back to face the enemy*, εἰς ὀρθόν Ascl.*Tact*.10.12, etc. 4. Medic. in Pass., *to be evacuated*, σὺν τοῖς περιττώμασιν Dsc.4.82. III. Med., *give away of one's own will*, *sell*, Ar.*Av*.585, Hdt.1.70, etc.; ἀ. τι ἐς τὴν Ἑλλάδα *take* to Greece *and sell* it there, Id.2.56: c. gen. pretii, Ar.*Ach*.830, *Pax*1237; οὐκ ἂν ἀπεδόμην πολλοῦ τὰς ἐλπίδας Pl.*Phd*.98b; ἀ. τῆς ἀξίας, τοῦ εὑρίσκοντος, *sell for* its worth, *for* what it will fetch, Aeschin.1.96; ὅταν τις οἰκέτην πονηρὸν πωλῇ (= offer for sale) καὶ ἀποδῶται τοῦ εὑρόντος X.*Mem*.2.5.5, cf. Thphr. *Char*.15.4; διδοῦσι [τὰς νέας] πενταδράχμους ἀποδόμενοι Hdt.6.89; ἀ. εἰσαγγελίαν *sell*, i.e. *take a bribe to forgo*, the information, D.25.47; οἱ δραχμῆς ἂν ἀποδόμενοι τὴν πόλιν X.*HG*2.3.48; at Athens, esp. *farm out* the public taxes, D.20.60, opp. ὠνέομαι: metaph., οἷον πρὸς ἄργυρον τὴν δόξαν τὰς ψυχάς Jul.*Or*.1.42b:—Act. and Med. are distinguished in Lex ap.And.1.97 πάντα ἀποδόμενος τὰ ἡμίσεα ἀποδώσω τῷ ἀποκτείναντι: but Act. is used in med. sense in Th.6.62 (s.v.l.), cf. *Foed.Delph.Pell*.2 *A* 22, and possibly in E.*Cyc*.239, Ar.*Ra*.1235: Med. for Act. in Antipho *Fr*.54:—Pass., *to be sold*, Hsch.

ἀποδιηθέω, *strain off*, *filter*, *Gp*.9.20.

ἀποδιΐστημι, *separate*, ἀποδιαστῆσαι καὶ διαχωρίσαι Plu.2.968d, cf. Vett.Val.214.17:—Pass., Hsch. II. intr., *to be distant*, [πόλεις] θαλάσσης ἀποδιέστησαν Lib.*Descr*.8.1, cf. Paul.Al.*F*.1.

ἀποδῐκάζω, *acquit*, opp. καταδικάζω, Antipho6.47, Arist.*Pol*.1268ᵇ18; ἀ. δίκην Critias71 D., *PPetr*.3 p.44 (iii B.C.).

ἀποδῐκεῖν, inf. of ἀπέδικον, poet. aor. with no pres., *throw off*, E.*HF*1205; *throw down*, A.*Ag*.1410.

ἀποδῐκέω, (δίκη) *defend oneself on trial*, X.*HG*1.7.21, Antiph.313.

ἀπόδῐκος, ον, = ἀπολελυμένος τοῦ ἐγκλήματος, πόλις *GDI*1432 (Hypata). 2. *rejected*, δίκα *IG*9(1).692.3 (Corcyra, ii B.C.).

ἀποδῐνέω, (δῖνος III) *thresh* corn, Hdt.2.14; 3 pl. subj. -δίνωντι *Tab.Heracl*.1.102.

ἀποδίομαι, poet. for ἀποδιώκω, αἴ κεν Ἄρηα..μάχης ἐξ ἀποδίωμαι (with ᾰ metri gr.) Il.5.763.

ἀποδιοπομπ-έομαι, fut. -ήσομαι (in pass. sense, Themist.*Ep*.4.5; act. form in Eust.1935.12):—*escort out of* the city the δῖον κῴδιον (v. κῴδιον): hence generally, *conjure away*, Pl.*Cra*.396e, Onos.5, Ph.1.239, Lib.*Decl*.15.34; μετ' εὐπρεπείας τοὺς φιλοσόφους ἐκ τῆς πόλεως Plu.*Cat.Ma*.22; τινὰς τοῦδε τοῦ γράμματος Gal.*Thras*.37. 2. generally, *set aside*, *waive*, τὸ προβληθέν Ath.9.401b, cf. Theo Sm. p.200 H. II. καθήρασθαι καὶ ἀ. τὸν οἶκον *free* it *from pollution*, Pl.*Lg*.877e; πόλιν καθαίρειν καὶ ἀ. Lys.6.53. **-ησις**, εως, ἡ, *offering of an expiatory sacrifice*, Pl.*Lg*.854b. **-ητέον**, *one must reject with abhorrence*, Plu.2.73d.

ἀποδιορ-ίζω, *mark off by dividing* or *defining*, Arist.*Pol*.1290ᵇ26; (sc. ἑαυτούς) *Ep.Jud*.19. **-ισμός**, ὁ, *division*, *separation*, v.l. for ἀπομερισμός, Herm.*in Phdr*.p.166 A. **-ιστέον**, *one must mark off*, *separate*, τινὰ τινος Sever.*Clyst*.p.35 D.

ἀποδιπλόομαι, Pass., *to be unfolded*, Eust.1661.60.

ἀποδίς, Adv. *twice*, A.D.*Synt*.339.14, al.

ἀποδισκεύω, *throw like a discus*, in Pass., Eust.1591.31.

ἀποδιφθερόομαι, Pass., *to be covered with hides*, δέρμασι Lyd.*Ost*.45.

ἀποδιψάω, *cease from thirst*, *be relieved of it*, Eust.871.5.

ἀποδιωθέω, *thrust away*, Hices.ap.Ath.3.87d, cf. Hp.*Mul*.2.201, Aspasia ap.Aët.16.72:—Med., Ar.Byz.*Epit*.10.9.

ἀπο-δίωγμα [ῐ], ατος, τό, *pursuit*, a ceremony performed at the Thesmophoria, Hsch. s.v. δίωγμα. **-διωκτέον**, *one must drive away*, κύνας Lib.*Fab*.1.1. 2. -διωκτέος, α, ον, *to be driven away*, Hdn.*Epim*.165. **-δίωκτος** [ῐ], ον, *thrust out*, ib.103. **-διώκω**, fut. -διώξομαι, *chase away*, Th.3.108, 6.102; ἀπὸ τῆς θηλείας Arist.*HA*614ᵃ16; οὐκ ἀποδιώξει σαυτὸν ἐκ τῆς οἰκίας; *take* yourself *off*, Ar.*Nu*.1296; τὸ λυποῦν ἀποδίωκε τοῦ βίου Men.410; intr., *move*, Olymp.*in Mete*.43.2:—Pass., *to be ridden at full speed*, of a horse, Aët.3.7. **-δίωξις** [ῐ], εως, ἡ, *expulsion*, πνεύματος Antyll.ap.Orib.6.36.4, cf. *Gp*.13.1.1.

ἀποδοκεῖ, impers., (δοκέω) mostly c. μή et inf., ἀπέδοξέ σφι μὴ τιμωρέειν *it seemed good* to them *not* to do, they *resolved not*.., Hdt.1.152; ἐπεί σφι ἀ. μὴ ἐπιδιώκειν Id.8.111; without μή, X.*An*.2.3.9: sts. with inf. omitted, ὥς σφι ἀπέδοξε when they *resolved not* (to go on), when they *changed their mind*, Hdt.1.172.

ἀποδοκῐμ-άζω, *reject on scrutiny* or *trial*, *reject* a candidate *from want of qualification*, Hdt.6.130, Lys.13.10, Archipp.14:—Pass., λαχὼν ἀπεδοκιμάσθη ἄρχειν Din.2.10, cf. D.25.30. 2. generally, *reject as unworthy* or *unfit*, πασσόφους ἄνδρας Pl.*Tht*.181b; ἵππον X.*Eq.Mag*.1.13; νόμους Id.*Mem*.4.4.14; ἀργύριον Thphr.*Char*.4.11; τὴν [τοῦ αὐλοῦ] χρῆσιν ἐκ τῶν νέων Arist.*Pol*.1341ᵃ26, cf. 37 (Pass.); [ἡ ὄρνις] ἀ. τὰ αὑτῆς Id.*HA*618ᵃ17; τὴν τοιαύτην διατριβήν Timocl.8.12; τὸ ποιεῖν τι X.*Cyr*.8.1.47: c. inf., Phlp.*in Ph*.584.26. II. *conclude*, *judge*, Dam.*Pr*.117. **-ᾰσία**, ἡ, *rejection after trial*, etc., *Gloss*. **-αστέον**, *one must reject*, Xen.*Eq*.3.8, Onos.1.19. 2. -αστέος, α, ον, *to be rejected*, Arist.*Po*.1462ᵃ8, Luc.*Herm*.18. **-αστής**, οῦ, ὁ, *one who rejects*, *Gloss*. **-αστικός**, ή, όν, *rejecting*, *disapproving*, δύναμις δοκιμαστικὴ ἢ ἀ. Arr.*Epict*.1.1.1. **-άω**, = ἀποδοκιμάζω, *reject*, Hdt.1.199. **-ος**, ον, *worthless*, Dsc.1.64; *rejected*, λίθος *BCH*20.324 (Lebad.); πῶροι ib.6.20 (Delos, ii B.C.).

ἀπόδομα, ατος, τό, *gift*, *offering*, Lxx*Nu*.8.13 sq.

ἄποδον· βραδύ, ἢ ἀπαγόρευσις, Hsch.

ἀποδόντωσις, εως, ἡ, *cleansing of the teeth*, Poll.2.48.

ἀποδορά, ᾶς, ἡ, *peeling of the skin*, Agathin.ap.Orib.10.7.18 (pl.).

ἄποδος, ἡ, Ion. for ἄφοδος. II. = ἄπους, *not having the use of one's feet*, *Tab.Defix.Aud.*159A44 (Rome, ca. 400 A.D.).

ἀπο-δόσιμος, ον, *restored*, ἀ. γίγνεσθαι Sch.Th.3.52. 2. -μον, τό, *receipt*, *PSI*3.237.6 (v/vi A.D.). **-δοσις**, εως, ἡ, (ἀποδίδωμι) *giving back, restitution, return*, τῶν ἵππων Hdt.4.9; τῶν χωρίων Th.5.35, Pl.*R.*332b; dist. from δόσις, Arist.*Pr.*950ᵃ37. 2. *payment*, *IG*1.32*A*5, etc.; ἡ ἀ. τοῦ μισθοῦ Th.8.85; φόρου Luc.*VH*1.36: generally, *giving*, Pl.*Lg.*807d; *rendering*, i.e. *performance*, ἔργου Dam.*Pr.*64. 3. *assignment, attribution*, Plot.5.1.6. II. *rendering by way of definition*, Arist.*Cat.*7ᵃ8, *Top.*108ᵇ9, al.; *definition*, S.E.*P.*3.242, etc. 2. in a sentence, *clause answering to* the πρότασις, διὰ μακροῦ τὰς ἀ. λαμβάνειν D.H.*Th.*52, al.; cf. ἀποδίδωμι II. 2. 3. Gramm., *interpretation, explanation*, A.D.*Synt.*155.25, cf. Heliod.ap. Orib.48.70.5: generally, *account, explanation*, Epicur.*Ep.*2p.41U. (pl.), Simp.*in Ph.*614.13; but ψιλὴ ἀ. bare *statement*, Theodor.ap. Corn.*Rh.*p.363H. III. (from Med.) *sale*, Poll.3.124. **-δόσιμος**, Arc. **ἀπυδόσμιος**, *saleable*, κόπρος *IG*5(2).3 (Tegea, iv B.C.). **-δοσμός**, Arc. **ἀπυ-**, (ἀποδίδωμι) *sale*, ib.343.28 (Orchom. Arc., iv B.C.). **-δοτέον**, *one must give* to another *as* his *due*, Arist.*EN*1163ᵃ8, ᵇ20; *one must refer, assign*, τί τινι Pl.*R.*452a, etc. 2. *one must describe, represent*, οἷος τυγχάνει ὁ θεὸς ὤν..ἀ. ib.379a. 3. *one must explain, interpret*, Sch.Pi.*N.*5.25. 4. *one must allow, permit*, Jul.*Or.*2.73c. II. -δοτέος, α, ον, *to be referred, ascribed, assigned*, Pl.*R.*456b; ἕτερος ἂν εἴη ὁρισμὸς -τέος Arist.*Top.*142ᵃ1. **-δοτήρ**, ῆρος, ὁ, *a giver back, repayer*, Epich.116. **-δοτικός**, ή, όν, *productive of*, τινός Sor.1.28, S.E.*M.*11.253; *assigning*, Iamb.*in Nic.* p.18P. 2. *concerning* ἀπόδοσις II.1, S.E.*P.*1.67. 3. *of* or *for* ἀπόδοσις III, *EM*763.8. Adv. -κῶς Eust.920.55. **-δοτος**, ον, *liable to be repaid*, φερναί *SIG*364.60 (Ephesus).

ἀποδοῦ· ἀπόδυσον, Hsch.

ἀπόδουλος, ὁ, *freedman*, Suid. s. v. Ἀριστοφάνης.

ἀποδοχ-εῖον, τό, *storehouse*, Lxx*Si.*1.17. 2. *cistern*, ib.50.3; also ἀποδόχιον *PHib.*1.85 (iii B.C.), *BCH*1.55 (Tralles). **-εύς**, έως, ὁ, = ἀποδέκτης, *IG*5(2).434 (Megalopolis), Epist.ap.J.*AJ*16.6.2, Them.*Or.*15.192c. 2. *keeper of archives*, ἀ. δημοσίων γραμμάτων *IGRom.*4.1248 (Thyatira), *Jahresh.*21/2 *Beibl.*255 (ii A.D.). **-ή**, Aeol. **ἀπυδοχά**, ἡ, *receiving back, having restored to one*, opp. ἀπόδοσις, Th.4.81. 2. *entertainment, reception*, ξένων J.*AJ*12.2.12 (s.v.l.). 3. *place of reception*, γῆ ἀ. πάντων Secund.*Sent.*15. II. *acceptance, approbation, favour*, ἀποδοχῆς τυγχάνειν παρά τινι Plb.1.5.5, cf. J.*AJ*6.14.4; ἀ. ἀξιοῦσθαι Plb.2.56.1, cf. D.S.12.53; μετ' εὐχαριστίας καὶ ἀποδοχῆς Phld.*D.*3.2; εἶναι ἐν ἀ. τῷ δήμῳ *SIG*807.21 (Magn. Mae., i A.D.); εἶναι ἐν τῇ καλλίστῃ ἀ. *AJA*18.324 (Sardes); ἐν ἀ. ἔχειν τινά *GDI*311 (Cyme); πάσης ἀ. ἄξιος 1*Ep.Ti.*1.15, cf. *SIG*867.21 (Ephesus, ii A.D.), Hp.*Ep.*20. III. *acceptation, meaning* of terms, S.E.*M.*1.232.

ἀποδοχμόω, *bend sideways*, Od.9.372, Orph.*Fr.*149.

ἀπόδραγμα, ατος, τό, *part taken off*, Hsch.

ἀποδρᾰθεῖν, v. ἀποδαρθάνω.

ἀποδρᾱπετεύω, *run away from*, τι Tz.*in An.Ox.*4.80.

ἀποδράς, v. ἀποδιδράσκω.

ἀπόδρᾱσις, Ion. **-δρησις**, εως, ἡ, (ἀποδιδράσκω) *running away, escape*, τὴν ἀ. ποιεῖσθαι Hdt.4.140; βουλεύειν Luc.*DMort.*27.9; οὐκ ἔστιν ἀ. Plu.*CG*1. 2. c. gen., *escape from, avoidance of*, στρατείας D.21.166; *evasion*, τῆς ἐρωτήσεως Plu.2.641c.

ἀποδρασκάζω, = ἀποδιδράσκω, Tz.*H.*1.502.

ἀποδρεπᾰνίζω, *prune, lop with a* δρέπανον, Suid. s. v. δρεφθῆναι.

ἀπο-δρέπτομαι, = sq., σοφίην *AP*10.18 (Marc. Arg.). **-δρέπω**, *pluck off*, ἀπόδρεπε οἴκαδε βότρυς *pluck and take* them home, Hes.*Op.*611; *pluck off* hair, Hp.*Mul.*2.106: metaph., ἀ. καρπὸν ἥβας Pi.*P.*9.110, cf. *O.*1.13; τὸν ἀφροδισίων κῆπον Archipp.2D.:—Med., μαλθακᾶς ὥρας ἀπὸ καρπὸν δρέπεσθαι Pi.*Fr.*122.8, cf. *AP*6.303 (Aristo), Plu.2.79d. **-δρεψις**, εως, ἡ, *plucking off*, *Corp.Herm.*18.11.

ἀπο-δρῆναι, Ion. for -δρᾶναι, v. ἀποδιδράσκω. **-δρησις**, v. ἀπόδρᾱσις.

ἀποδρομή, ἡ, *harbour of refuge*, σκάφαις dub. in *Peripl.M.Rubr.*3.

ἀπόδρομος, ον, (δραμεῖν) *apart from the race*, whether as *too old* or *too young* (as in Crete, *Leg.Gort.*7.35) *to share it*, Eust.727.18, 1592.55 sqq.; or *left behind by others*, Hsch., cf. S.*Fr.*73.

ἀποδρύπτω, aor. 1 ἀπέδρυψα: aor. 2 ἀπέδρῠφον:—*tear off the skin, lacerate*, μή μιν ἀποδρύφοι ἑλκυστάζων Il.23.187; μή σε νέοι διὰ δώματ' ἐρύσσωσ'..ἀποδρύψωσί τε πάντα Od.17.480; σάρκας ὀνύχεσσι Theoc.25.267:—Pass., ἀπὸ χειρῶν ῥινοὶ ἀπέδρυφθεν Od.5.435, cf. 426; ἀποδρυφθῆναι χαλάζῃ *AP*11.365 (Agath.):—Med., *scrape oneself, grow thin*, dub. in Alciphr.3.51.

ἀποδῠνᾰμία, ἡ, *lack of power*, Olymp.*in Grg.*p.251J.

ἀποδύνω [ῡ], = ἀποδύω, *strip off*, ἀπέδυνε βοείην Od.22.364.

ἀπ-οδυρμός, ὁ, *bewailing, lamentation*, *Gloss.* **-οδύρομαι** [ῡ], *lament bitterly*, τι πρὸς τὤγαλμα Hdt.2.141; τύχας A.*Pr.*637; ἐμαυτὴν καὶ γένος τὸ πᾶν S.*El.*1122; τινί *to* a person, Apollod.1.9.8 (dub.): abs., Pl.*R.*606a. 2. *take one's fill of lamentation* (cf. ἀπολοφύρομαι), *IG*1.463.

ἀπόδῠσις, εως, ἡ, (ἀποδύομαι) *stripping, undressing*, J.*AJ*12.5.1, Plu.2.751f, Porph.*Abst.*1.31. II. gloss on Lat. *obitus*, *POxy.*1099ᵛ42.

ἀποδυσ-πετέω, *desist through impatience*, Arist.*Top.*163ᵇ19; περὶ αὐτὴν τὴν ἐπιθυμίαν Plu.2.502e; πρός τι Luc.*Rh.Pr.*3; σχέτλια ἀ. Alciphr.3.74. (πετ-, root of πίπτω.) **-πέτημα**, ατος, τό, = sq., Sch.Luc.*Tim.*3 (pl.). **-πέτησις**, εως, ἡ, *discouragement, despair*, Corn.*ND*35.

ἀπο-δῠτέον, *one must strip*, τινά Luc.*Herm.*38; *one must put off*, χιτῶνας Porph.*Abst.*1.31. II. (from Pass.) ἀ. ταῖς γυναιξίν they *must strip off their clothes*, Pl.*R.*457a. **-δῠτήριον**, τό, *undressing room* in the bath, X.*Ath.*2.10, Pl.*Ly.*206e, etc.; in the palaestra, Id.*Euthd.*272e. **-δύω**, I. in fut. -δύσω, aor. 1 -έδῡσα (for pf. -δέδῠκα v. infr. II. 1), trans. used by Hom. (esp. in Il.) of *stripping* armour *from* the slain, 1. c. acc. rei, *strip off*, τεύχεα δ' Ἕκτωρ δῃώσας ἀπέδυσε Il.18.83, cf. 4.532, etc.; ἀπὸ μὲν φίλα εἵματα δύσω 2.261; ἀ. τί τινος Pl.*Chrm.*154e. 2. c. acc. pers., *strip*, ἀπέδυσε τὰς...γυναῖκας Hdt.5.92.η', cf. Pl.*Epigr.*12.3; ἵνα μὴ ῥιγῶν ἀποδύῃ (sc. τοὺς ὁδοιπόρους) Ar.*Av.*712, cf. *Th.*636, *Ec.*668: c. dupl. acc., τὴν ἐσθῆτά τινα ἀ. Luc.*Nigr.*13:—Pass., *to be stripped of* one's clothes, οὔ τοι τοῦτον ἀποδυθήσομαι (sc. τὸν τρίβωνα) Ar.*V.*1122; ἵνα μή ποτε κἀποδυθῇ μεθύων Id.*Ra.*715, cf. *Pl.*930; θοἰμάτιον ἀποδεδύσθαι Lys.10.10; ἀποδυόμενος *stripped of its shell*, of the nautilus, Arist.*HA*622ᵇ18. II. Med., fut. -δύσομαι: aor. 1 -εδυσάμην Od.5.349 (v.l.), Pl.*R.*612a (v.l.), Lys.*Fr.*232S., etc.; mostly with intr. aor. 2 Act. ἀπέδυν, pf. ἀποδέδῡκα (used trans. by X.*An.*5.8.23 πολλοὺς ἤδη ἀποδέδυκεν):—*strip off oneself, take off*, εἵματα ταῦτ' ἀποδὺς Od.5.343; ἀπόδυθι..θοἰμάτιον Ar.*Th.*214; τῶν ἱματίων ἀποδύσας (aor. 2 part. pl. fem.) *having stripped off* some of them, ib.656; σῶμ' ἀποδυσάμενος *Epigr.Gr.*403 (Galatia): metaph., ἀ. τὴν ὑπόκρισιν J.*AJ*13.7.1. 2. abs., ἀποδυσάμενος *having stripped*, v.l. for ἀπολυσ-, Od.5.349; ἀποδύντες *stripped naked*, Th.1.6, cf. Pl.*Mx.*236d: metaph., ἀποδύεσθαι πρὸς τὸ λέγειν, εἰς ἀγορανομίαν, Plu.*Dem.*6, *Brut.*15; οἱ ἀποδυόμενοι εἰς τὴν παλαίστραν those who *strip for* the palaestra, who *practise* there, Lys.*Fr.*45.1; εἰς τὸ γυμνάσιον *IG*14.256 (Phintias); πρὸς τὸ ἀχανὲς πέλαγος Jul.*Or.*4.142c; ἀποδύντες τοῖς ἀναπαίστοις ἐπίωμεν *let us strip* and attack the anapaests, Ar.*Ach.*627, cf. *Ra.*641.

ἀποδωρέω, *give away*, Ἀρχ.Ἐφ.1918.170.106 (Epid., iv B.C.), Critias6.3D.

ἀποδωσείω, Desiderat., *wish to give back*, Procop.*Goth.*3.34.

ἀποείκω, *withdraw from*, θεῶν ἀπόεικε κελεύθου Il.3.406 (Aristarch.).

ἀπο-ειπεῖν, -ειπών, v. ἀπεῖπον. **-εργάθω**, v. ἀπειργαθον. **-έργω**, v. ἀπείργω.

ἀπόερσε, Ep. aor. almost always in 3 pers. (imper. ἀπόερσον Nic. *Th.*110):—*swept away*, ἔνθα με κῦμ' ἀπόερσε Il.6.348; ὅν ῥά τ' ἔναυλος ἀποέρσῃ 21.283; μή μιν ἀποέρσειε μέγας ποταμός ib.329; cf. ἀπούρας.

ἀποζάω, *live off*, ὅσον ἀποζῆν enough *to live off*, Th.1.2: c. dat., ἀ. ἐλύμοις Procop.*Pers.*1.12, al. 2. *live poorly*, Luc.*Tox.*59, Ael.*NA*16.12, Lib.*Or.*11.253. 3. *live out*, ἰδιώτην βίον J.*AJ*9.10.4.

ἀπό-ζεμα, ατος, τό, (ἀποζέω) *decoction*, *Gp.*13.12.2, Apollon.ap. Philum.*Ven.*33.5. **-ζέννῡμι**, = ἀποζέω, Dsc.1.94 (Pass.), etc. **-ζεσμα**, ατος, τό, = ἀπόζεμα, *PHolm.*15.40, al.

ἀπο-ζευγέω, aor. inf. -ῆσαι, lit. *unyoke*: metaph., *discontinue treatment*, Hp.*Loc.Hom.*12. **-ζεύγνῡμι**, *separate, part*, ἀ. συνεύνων Man.3.85; ἀ. τὸ τείχισμα Malch.p.412D. II. mostly in Pass., -ζεύγνῠμαι, aor. -εζύγην [ῠ] (v.infr.), also -εζεύχθην E.*El.*284, *AP*12.226 (Strat.):—*to be loosed from the yoke*, [βοῦς] εἰς νομὰς ἀπεζεύχθη Babr.37.6; but usually metaph., *to be parted from*, τέκνων γυναικός τ' E.*HF*1375, cf. *Med.*1017; εἰ γάμων ἀπεζύγην if I *were free from*.., Id.*Supp.*791; ὀρφανὸς ἀποζυγεὶς Id.*Ph.*988; ὥσπερ δεῦρ' ἀπεζύγην πόδας as I *unharnessed* my feet, i.e. took rest, A.*Ch.*676. **-ζευκτέον**, *one must part, separate*, τινά τινος Them.*Or.*13.179c. **-ζευξις**, εως, ἡ, *unyoking*, Sch.Od.6.88.

ἀποζέω, *boil till the scum is thrown off*, Hp.*Acut.*(*Sp.*)63, Diph.17.9; simply, *boil*, κρέα *IG*12(7).515.78 (Amorgos). 2. intr., *cease boiling* or *fermenting*: metaph., Alex.45.3.

ἀποζημιόω, v. ἀπίθετο.

ἀποζίννυνται· ἀποσβέννυνται, Hsch. (-ξινν- cod.).

ἀπο-ζῠγή, ἡ, *deed of divorce*, *PGrenf.*2.76.19 (iv A.D.). **-ζῠγος**, ον, of numbers, *odd*, Vett.Val.361.13.

ἀπόζῡμος, ον, *in a state of fermentation*, Hp.*Prorrh.*2.23.

ἀπόζω, *smell of* something, τινός Luc.*DMar.*1.5, Plu.2.13f: abs., Longus4.1. II. impers., ἀπόζει τῆς Ἀραβίης *there comes an odour from* Arabia, Hdt.3.113, cf. Luc.*Cyn.*17.

ἀποζωγρᾰφέω, *portray*, τἀναντία φαντάσματα Pl.*Ti.*71c.

ἀπο-ζώννῡμι and -ύω, aor. -έζωσα, *take the girdle off* one, Chor. p.28B.; esp. when *discharging* him *from service*, Hdn.2.13.8. **-ζωσις**, εως, ἡ, *ungirding*, *Gloss.*

ἀποϝειπάθθω, v. ἀπεῖπον.

ἀποϝηλέω, v. ἀπειλέω.

ἀποθᾰλασσόω, *make into sea*, Eust.ad D.P.511.

ἀποθᾰνετέον, (ἀποθνήσκω) *one must die*, Arist.*EN*1110ᵃ27.

ἀποθαρρέω and -θαρσέω, *take courage, have full confidence*, X.*Oec.*16.6: c. inf., *to have the boldness to*.., Longin.32.8, J.*AJ*15.7.3: c. acc., ἀ. τὸ πρόσω τῆς πορείας Paus.10.19.5: c. dat., *use rashly*, Aët.12.23.

ἀποθαρρύνω, *encourage*, τοὺς φίλους App.*Hann.*12.

ἀποθαυμάζω, Ion. -θωυμάζω or -θωμάζω, *marvel much at* a thing, ἄφαρ δ' ἀπεθαύμασ' ὄνειρον Od.6.49; ἀ. τὰ λεγόμενα, τὸ λεχθέν, Hdt.1.11,30; πολλὰ ἄλλα Id.2.79: abs., *wonder much*, Id.1.68, X.*Oec.*2.17, Luc.*Am.*13, *POxy.*1242 iii 53 (iii A.D.): c. part., ἀ. ὁρέων Hdt.1.88; folld. by εἰ, *wonder* that.., Aeschin.1.94, 119.—Rare in Trag., A.*Ag.*318, S.*OC*1586.

ἀποθεάομαι, *look attentively at*, τι J.*BJ*2.15.1.

ἀποθειάζω, = ἀποθεόω, Them.*Or.*20.239d.

ἀποθει-όω, *clothe in mystical language*, λόγον Philostr.*Im.*16.2; = ἀποθεόω, in Pass., *AP*12.177. **-ωσις**, εως, ἡ, *fumigation*, Onos. 10.28 (pl.).

ἀποθεμελιόω, *destroy utterly*, Suid. s.v. ἀπογαιῶσαι.

ἄποθεν, freq. as f.l. for ἄπωθεν (q.v.) in codd., as Th.2.81, Arist. *Pol.*1280^{b}18, etc., cf. Hsch.

ἀπόθε-ος, ον, *far from the gods, godless*, S.*Fr.*267. **-όω**, *deify*, *PTeb.*5.78 (ii B.C.), Plb.12.23.4, Plu.*Num.*6, etc.:—Pass., Γανυμήδης.. ἀποθεούμενος Nicol.Com.1.35; μετὰ τὸ ἀποθεωθῆναι *CIG*2831.7 (Aphrodisias); cf. -θειόω. 2. in magic, *drown* a sacred animal and thus liberate its divine element, *PMag.Berol.*1.5, *PMag.Lond.* 121.629 (Pass.); ἀ. ἱέρακα ἐν ὕδατι Afric.ap.Sch.Tz.*H.*9.161.

ἀποθερᾰπ-εία, ἡ, *regular worship*, θεῶν Arist.*Pol.*1335^{b}15. II. *restorative treatment* after fatigue, Antyll.ap.Orib.6.21.1, Gal.*Thras.* 47. **-ευσις**, εως, ἡ, = θεράπευσις, Hsch. s.v. ἀκέσεων (pl.). **-ευτέον**, *one must treat by* ἀποθεραπεία, τὸ σῶμα Sor.2.11: abs., *one must conclude the treatment*, σὺν ἀλείμματι Id.1.49. **-ευτικός**, ή, όν, *of, connected with* ἀποθεραπεία, Antyll.ap.Orib.6.21.4, Gal.6.197. Adv. -κῶς ib.262. **-εύω**, *treat with attention and honour*, D.H.3.71, Phld.*Herc.*1457.11, etc. 2. *cure*, τινά Hp.*Praec.*5; τὸ ἀλγοῦν τινι Plu.2.118c; *apply* ἀποθεραπεία *to*, τὰ μέρη Antyll.ap.Orib.7.16.10, Gal.6.201 (Pass.).

ἀποθερίζω, poet. aor. ἀπέθρῐσα (also in late Prose, Porph.*Abst.*2. 10):—*cut off*, ἶνας μεδέων ἀπέθρισεν Archil.138; ἄκρας ὡς ἀπέθρισεν κόμας E.*Or.*128, cf. *Hel.*1188, *AP*6.107 (Phil.), etc.; καυλόν Dsc.3. 70; of persons, μνηστῆρας Nonn.*D.*48.96; regul. form -θέρισα in Ael.*NA*1.5, Apollod.1.9.22; ἀπεθέρισα τοὺς προφήτας σου Lxx *Ho.*6. 6(5):—Med., aor. ἀπεθρισάμην *AP*5.236 (Agath.); ἀποθρίξασθαι, of the *tonsure* of monks, Procop.*Arc.*1, al., perhaps from a mistaken etymology, cf. ἀποθρίξαντες τὴν χαίτην Ael.ap.Ar.Byz.*Epit.*149.13.

ἀποθέρισμα, ατος, τό, v. sub ἀπόθρισμα.

ἀπόθερμος, ον, = ἄθερμος, Aret.*SD*2.1. II. as Subst., = μελιτοῦττα, Sch.Ar.*Pl.*1122; = ἄμυλος, Sch.Theoc.9.21. 2. a kind of *drink*, Hp.*Mul.*1.44, 2.207. 3. a *condiment*, Gal.6.519.

ἀποθέσιμος, ον, *stored away*, χρήματα J.*AJ*16.7.1.

ἀπόθεσις, εως, ἡ, (ἀποτίθημι) *laying up in store*, σκευῶν *SIG*1106. 107 (Cos); εἰς ἀ. γενέσθαι to be *stored up*, Pl.*Lg.*844d; γάλα χρήσιμον εἰς ἀ. Arist.*HA*522^{a}26; ἡ ἀ. τῆς τροφῆς, of bees, 622^{b}26; τὴν ἀ. τῆς θήρας ποιεῖσθαι 623^{a}12; *preserving*, of fish, Philum.ap.Aët.9. 23. 2. *the final movement in setting* a dislocated or fractured limb, Gal.18(2).332, al., Pall.*in Hp.Fract.*12.273C.; f.l. in Hp.*Off.* 19. 3. κατ' ἀπόθεσιν, of *internal* abscesses, Gal.17(1).103. II. *putting aside, making away with, getting rid of*, ῥύπου 1*Ep.Pet.*3. 21, cf. 2.1.14. 2. *exposure* of children, Arist.*Pol.*1335^{b}19; cf. ἀποτίθημι II.7. 3. *resignation* of an office, App.*BC*1.3, cf. *SIG* 900.16 (iv A.D.). 4. ἀ. κώλου, περιόδου, *close* or *cadence* of a phrase, Demetr.*Eloc.*19, cf. Sch.Ar.*Nu.*176; so in metres, = κατάληξις, Heph.4 tit. III. = ἀποδυτήριον, Luc.*Hipp.*5.

ἀπο-θεσπίζω, *utter as an oracle*, ἀ. ἔμμετρα Str.9.3.5, cf. Plu.*Luc.* 2; *prophesy*, D.H.6.43. **-θέσπισις**, εως, ἡ, *oracle given*, Str.17. 1.43.

ἀπόθεστος, ον, *despised*, δὴ τότε κεῖτ' ἀ. Od.17.296, cf. Lyc.540, Call.*Fr.*302, Plu.2.159f. (From θέσσασθαι, cf. πολύθεστος.)

ἀπό-θεται, ων, αἱ, a place in Lacedaemon, into which misshapen children were thrown as soon as born, Plu.*Lyc.*16. **-θετέον**, *one must set aside, lay by*, Dsc.2.76. **-θετικός**, ή, όν, *completing*, τῆς διανοίας Sch.Ar.*Pl.*8. II. of verbs, *deponent*, *An.Bachm.* 2.303,304. **-θετος**, ον, (ἀποτίθημι) *laid by, stored up*, Dsc.5.9, Plu.*Caes.*35, Luc.*Merc.Cond.*5: ἀπόθετα, τά, *stores*, *PRyl.*153.16 (ii A.D.). 2. *hidden, secret, mysterious*, ἔπη Pl.*Phdr.*252b; βίβλοι D.H.11.62, cf. Philostr.*Im.*1.10, 2.16, Plu.*Crass.*16. 3. *reserved for special occasions, special*, φίλος Lys.8.17; δωρεά D.59.93. 4. ἀπόθετος, ὁ (sc. νόμος), name of an aulodic nome, Plu.2.1132d, Poll. 4.79. II. f.l. for ἀπόθεστος, Plu.2.159f. III. ἀπόθετον· *deponens*, *Gloss.*; cf. foreg. II.

ἀποθέω, *run away*, Hdt.8.56, X.*Cyr.*7.5.40.

ἀποθεωρ-έω, = ἀποθεάομαι, Arist.*Mir.*839^{b}3, Plb.27.4.4, D.S.4.38, Polycharm.1; *observe*, Plu.*Lyc.*25; *examine, consider*, πίστεις Phld. *Rh.*2.116 S., cf. *Oec.*p.74 J. **-ησις**, εως, ἡ, *serious contemplation*, Plu.*Pel.*25; *wide view*, τόπος τὴν ἀ. πανταχόθεν εὐφυής D.S.19. 38. **-ητέον**, *one must consider, contemplate*, Plu.2.30a. 2. ἀ. μή.. *one must take care* not.., Herod.Med.ap.Orib.7.8.10.

ἀποθέωσις, εως, ἡ, *deification*, Str.6.3.9, *CIG*2832 (Aphrodisias), Cic.*Att.*1.16.13, Senec.*Apoc.* tit., *PGen.*36.18 (ii A.D.), Hierocl.*in CA*27 p.483 M.

ἀπο-θήκη, ἡ, *any place wherein to lay up* a thing, *magazine, storehouse*, Th.6.97; ἀ. βιβλίων Luc.*Ind.*5; ἀ. σωμάτων *burial-place*, Id.*Cont.*22. 2. *refuge*, Philist.59. II. *anything laid by, store*, ἀποθήκην ποιεῖσθαι ἐς τὸν Πέρσην lay up *store* of favour with him, Hdt. 8.109. **-θήκιον**, τό, *larder*, Cael.Aur.*CP*1.11.93.

ἀποθηλ-άζω, *suck*, Sor.1.118, Paul.Aeg.3.28. **-ασμός**, ὁ, (θηλάζω) *sucking, sucking out*, Erasistr.ap.Dsc.*Ther.Praef.*, Sor.1. 77, Paul.Aeg.3.35.

ἀποθηλύνω, *make effeminate, enervate*, Plu.*Ant.*53; *weaken*, τὰς ὀσμάς Thphr.*Od.*66; ἄκρατον Plu.2.692d:—Pass., Clearch.6. II. *produce female* plants, Thphr.*HP*7.4.3.

ἀποθηρευτής, οῦ, ὁ, *drinking-cup used after hunting*, *IG*11(2).113. 17 (Delos, iii B.C.), al.

ἀποθηρι-όω, *change into a beast*, τινά Eratosth.*Cat.*1:—Pass., Str. 3.2.7; prob. in Herm.ap.Stob.1.49.69. 2. *make quite savage*, τὸν βίον Plu.2.995d; *exasperate*, τινὰ πρός τινα Plb.1.79.8:—Pass., *to become* or *be so*, ib.67.6; τὴν ψυχήν D.S.17.9; of wounds, Plb.1.81. 5. II. Pass., *to be full of savage creatures*, ἀποτεθηρίωται ὁ Νεῖλος Alciphr.2.3. **-ωσις**, εως, ἡ, *changing into a wild beast*, Hsch. s.v. Αἰαίη. II. (from Pass.) *fury* or *rage* against any one, πρός τινα D.S.34/5.20.

ἀποθησαυρ-ίζω, *store, hoard up*, Lxx *Si.*3.4, D.S.5.40, Luc. *Alex.*23; ἑαυτοῖς τι 1*Ep.Ti.*6.19:—Pass., J.*BJ*7.8.4, Vett.Val.16. 21. **-ισμός**, ὁ, *laying by, storing up*, D.S.3.29.

ἀπόθητος, ον, *not desired*, Hsch., dub. in Call.*Fr.*302 (leg. ἀπόθεστος).

ἀποθῑνόομαι, Pass., *to be silted up*, Plb.1.75.8.

ἀπο-θλίβω [ῑ], *squeeze out*, τοὺς ὄρχεις Arist.*HA*632^{a}17; ὑπόστασιν Thphr.*Od.*29; τὸν ἐκ τοῦ βότρυος ἀποθλιβόμενον οἶνον D.S.3.62; τῆς χώρας *from* the place, Luc.*Jud.Voc.*2. 2. *press* or *force back*, τὸ αἷμα Arist.*HA*587^{a}22:—in E.*Cyc.*237 Ruhnken restored ἀπολέψειν. 3. *press tightly*, τὰ κράσπεδα Diph.43.30; ἀ. τινά *press upon, crowd*, *Ev.Luc.*8.45. 4. *crush*, Lxx *Nu.*22.25. II. Gramm., *drop* a letter in the middle of a word, A.D.*Adv.*185.3 (Pass.). III. *oppress much*, Aq.*Ex.*3.9, Sm.*Jd.*10.12:—Pass., πρὸς τὸ τὴν πόλιν ἀποθλιβῆναι Wilcken *Chr.*11 *A* 9 (ii B.C.). **-θλιμμα**, ατος, τό, *expressed juice*, Dsc.1.110. II. *solid residue after expression of juice*, Gal.11.845. **-θλιμμός**, ὁ, *oppression*, Aq.*Ex.* 3.9. **-θλιψις**, εως, ἡ, *pressing*, βοτρύων D.S.3.63. II. *squeezing out of one's place*, Luc.*Jud.Voc.*2.

ἀποθνήσκω, fut. -θᾰνοῦμαι, Ion. -θανέομαι or -εῦμαι Hdt.3.143, 7.134:—strengthd. for θνήσκω, *die*, Hom. (v. infr.), Pi.*O.*1.27, and once in Trag. (E.*Fr.*578.6); in Com. and Prose the usual form of the pres.; σεῦ ἀποτεθνηῶτος Il.22.432; ἀποθνήσκων περὶ φασγάνῳ Od.11. 424; βόες δ' ἀποτέθνασαν ἤδη 12.393; ἐκ τῶν τρωμάτων Hdt.2.63; ὑπὸ λιμοῦ Th.1.126: c. dat., βρόμῳ κεραυνοῦ Pi. l.c.; νόσῳ Th.8.84: c. acc. cogn., θάνατον ἀ. X.*Mem.*4.8.3, etc.; εἰς ἕτερον ζῆν ἀ. Pl.*Ax.* 365d; *to be ready to die*, of laughter, etc., Ar.*Ach.*15; ἀ. τῷ δέει Arist.*MM*1191^{a}35. II. serving as Pass. of ἀποκτείνω, *to be put to death, slain*, ὑπό τινος Hdt.1.137, 7.154; esp. by judicial sentence, ἀποθανεῖν ὑπὸ τῆς πόλεως Lycurg.93, cf. Pl.*Ap.*29d, 32d, al., Arist. *Rh.*1397^{a}30 (v.l.). III. *renounce*, νόμῳ *Ep.Gal.*2.19; ἀπό τινος *Ep.Col.*2.20.

ἀποθορεῖν, aor. 2 inf. Act. of ἀποθρῴσκω.

ἀποθρᾰσύνομαι, *to be very courageous, dare all things*, D.61.20:— later -θαρρύνομαι, Diog.*Ep.*32.3.

ἀπό-θραυσις, εως, ἡ, *breaking, fracture*, Paul.Aeg.6.89,117; κατὰ ἀπόθραυσιν Sor.*Fract.*10. II. *breaking up*, νεφῶν Arist.*Mu.*394^a 33. **-θραυσμα**, ατος, τό, *piece broken off*, Str.10.5.16. **-θραύω**, *break off*, νεὼς κόρυμβα A.*Pers.*410; τοὺς ὑπερέχοντας τῶν σταχύων D.H.4.56: metaph., τῆς ἐλευθερίας τὸ κεφάλαιον Jul.*Mis.*356b; τοῦ ἑνὸς τὸ μερικόν Dam.*Pr.*51:—Pass., *to be broken off*, Arist.*Pr.*967^{b}5, Arr.*Tact.*2.4: metaph., ἀποθραυσθῆναι τῆς εὐκλείας *to be broken off from* one's fair fame, *make shipwreck of* it, Ar.*Nu.*997.

ἀπόθρεκτα· φευκτά, Hsch.

ἀποθρηνέω, *lament much*, Plu.*Fab.*18, *Crass.*27, Babr.12.3.

ἀποθρῑάζω, properly, *strip of fig-leaves*: metaph., *circumcise*, Ar. *Ach.*158; cf. θρῖον.

ἀποθριγκόω, *furnish with coping*, τοῖχον *IG*11(2).144 *A* 84, al. (Delos, iv B.C.). 2. *wall off*, Procop.*Aed.*5.7, al.

ἀποθρίζω, v. ἀποθερίζω.

ἀπόθριξ, τρῐχος, ὁ, ἡ, = ἄθριξ, Call.*Fr.*341; = ἄνηβος, Poll.2.22.

ἀπόθρισμα, ατος, τό, *that which is cut off*, Orph.*A.*1000.

ἀποθρύπτω, *crush, crumble to pieces*, J.*BJ*3.7.23: metaph., *break in spirit, enervate*, τὰς ψυχὰς συγκεκλασμένοι τε καὶ ἀποτεθρυμμένοι Pl. *R.*495e.

ἀποθρῴσκω, aor. ἀπέθορον, *leap off from*, νηός Il.2.702; ἀπὸ τῶν ἵππων, ἀπὸ νεός, Hdt.1.80, 7.182; ἰοὶ ἀπὸ νευρῆφι θορόντες Il.16.773: abs., *spring away*, Opp.*H.*1.206. 2. *leap up from, rise from*, καπνὸν ἀποθρῴσκοντα νοῆσαι ἧς γαίης Od.1.58. 3. *rebound from*, ἔρως ἀντιτύπου κραδίης ἀ. *AP*9.443 (Paul. Sil.). 4. *break off*, of rocks, ἀφ' ὑψηλῆς κορυφῆς Hes.*Sc.*375.

ἀποθυμαίνω, dub. in S.*Ichn.*122.

ἀποθῡμίασις, εως, ἡ, *rising of smoke* or *vapour*, Plu.2.647f (nisi leg. ὑπο-).

ἀποθῡμιάω, *smoke out*, [μῦς] Arist.*HA*580^{b}23.

ἀποθύμιος [ῡ], ον (fem. -ίη in Semon.7.35): (θυμός):—*not according to the mind, unpleasant, hateful*, ἔπος Hes.*Op.*710; ἀποθύμια ἔρδειν τινί to do one *a disfavour*, Il.14.261; οὔ τι ἀποθύμιον ποιῆσαι Hdt.7.168; μή μοι τι τέκνοις ἀ. ἕρπῃ Mosch.4.93.

ἀπόθυμος, ον, f.l. for ἀπρόθυμος, Plu.2.87f.

ἀποθυννίζω, *dismiss as worthy of a tunny*, in Pass., Luc.*JTr.*25, cf. Eust.1720.63.

ἀποθῠρίζω, *put out of doors*, *Gloss.*:—also **-θυρόω**, Hsch. (Pass.).

ἀπο-θύσσειν· ἀποτυγχάνειν, Hsch. **-θύσσει**· ἀποπνεύσει, Id.

ἀποθυστάνιον, τό, *drinking-vessel*, Polem.Hist.20.

ἀπο-θῠτέον, *one must perform a sacrifice*, Them.*Or.*11.142a. **-θύω**, fut. -θύσω *IG*4.951.45 (Epid.):—*offer up* as a votive sacrifice, χιμαίρας X.*An.*3.2.12; ἡγεμόσυνα 4.8.25; εὐχήν Diph.43.10; ἴατρα *IG* l. c.

ἀποθωρᾱκίζομαι, *put off one's coat of mail*, Procop.*Goth.*4.32.

ἀποθωυμάζω or **-θωμάζω**, Ion. for ἀποθαυμάζω.

ἀποιδ-έω, *swell up*, Hp.*Mul.*1.52. **-ησις**, εως, ἡ, *swelling*, ὑφάλου γῆς Str.1.3.10 (pl.). **-ίσκομαι**, = ἀποιδέω, Hp.*Int.*41.

ἀποϊερόω, = ἀφιερόω, *CIG*2827.9 (Aphrodisias).

ἀποίζειν· ἀπομωκᾶσθαι, Hsch.

ἀποιητικός, ή, όν, *unpoetical*, Sch.D.P.289.

ἀποίητος, ον, *not done, undone*, πεπραγμένων ἀποίητον θέμεν ἔργων τέλος Pi.*O*.2.18; ἀ. πάμπολλ' ἐστίν Men.113. 2. *not to be done, impossible*, Plu.*Cor*.38. II. *not artificial, unpolished*, D.H.*Lys*.8; esp. *unpoetical*, ἀ. λόγος, opp. ποιητική, Id.*Comp*.1; τὰ ἀποίητα, opp. τὰ πεποημένα, Phld.*Po*.1081; ἀ. ὑπόθεσις *not used as material for poetry*, ibid.; τὸ ἀ. *simplicity, naïveté*, Aristid.*Or*.31(11). 4. Adv. -τως D.H.*Dem*.39. III. of land, *unsuitable*, εἴς τι *Gp*.10.75.12.

ἀποικει-όω, *absorb completely, assimilate*, Anon.Lond.24.26:—hence -**ωσις**, εως, ἡ, ib.24.35. II. *keep apart*, Hero *Spir.Praef*. p.146 S. (Pass.), s.v.l.

ἀποικ-εσία, ἡ, = ἀποίκησις, esp. of *the Captivity*, Lxx 4*Ki*.24.15, al. -**έω**, *go away from home*, esp. as a colonist, *settle in a foreign country, emigrate*, ἐκ πόλεως Isoc.4.122; ἐς Θουρίους Pl.*Euthd*.271c: so c. acc. loci, Καλλίσταν ἀπῴκησαν νᾶσον Pi.*P*.4.258, cf. Porph.*VP* 2. II. *dwell afar off*, μακρὰν ἀ. Th.3.55; πρόσω ἀ. X.*Oec*.4.6; ἀ. τινὸς πρόσω E.*HF*557, cf. *IA*680; ἐν νήσῳ Arist.*Pol*.1272^{b}1; ἀ. τῶν πεδίων Philostr.*Im*.1.9: c. acc., *live a long way off* a person, Theoc.15.7 (s.v.l.):—Pass., ἡ Κόρινθος ἐξ ἐμοῦ..μακρὰν ἀπῳκεῖτο Corinth *was inhabited* by me *at a distance*, i.e. I *settled far from* Corinth, S.*OT*998. -**ησις**, εως, ἡ, = sq., *emigration*, Hsch., Suid.; dub. in D.H.2.36. -**ία**, Ion. -ίη, ἡ, (ἄποικος) *settlement far from home, colony*, Pi.*O*.1.24, S.*Fr*.373.6, Hdt.1.146, *IG*1.31, etc.; correlative to μητρόπολις, Th.1.34; εἰς ἀ. στέλλειν, ἄγειν, send, lead to form *a settlement*, Hdt.4.147, 5.124; ἀ. κτίσαι A.*Pr*.814; ἀ. ἐκπέμπειν Th.1.12; ἀ. κηρύσσειν ἐς τόπον ib.27; ἀ. ποιεῖσθαι Pl.*Lg*.702c; στέλλειν (of the οἰκιστής) Str.8.6.22; ἀποστέλλειν (of the μητρόπολις) Aeschin.2.176; ἡ κώμη ἀ. οἰκίας is *an offshoot from*.., Arist.*Pol*.1252^{b}17. 2. *migration*, Ph.2.410. II. *charter* granted to a colony, Hyp.*Fr*.73. -**ίζω**, Att. fut. ἀποικιῶ A.*Fr*.304.10:—*send away from home*, ἐς νῆσον Od.12.135; ἐκ τόπων S.*Tr*.955 (lyr.), cf. *OC*1390; ἀ. δόμων τινά E.*El*.1008, cf. *Hipp*.629; of the queen-bee, X.*Oec*.7.34:—Pass., *to be settled in a far land*, ἐν μακάρων νήσοις ἀπῳκίσθαι Pl.*R*.519c; *emigrate*, ἐκ τῆσδε τῆς πόλεως Id.*Euthd*.302c; ἀπὸ πατρὸς ἀποικισθῆναι *dwell apart from*.., Arist.*GA*740^{a}7. 2. metaph., *banish*, τὰς ψευδεῖς δόξας Ph.2.221:—Pass., εἰς τὸ μέσον ἀπῳκίσθη τῶν ἐσχάτων Pl.*Plt*.284e; ἀνάγκης οὐκ ἀ. πολύ *is* not far *removed from*.., Chaerem.18. II. *colonize* a place, *send a colony to* it, c. acc., Hdt.1.94, Th.1.24; δρυμοὺς ἐρήμους καὶ πάγους ἀποικιεῖ A. l. c.

ἀποίκῐλος, ον, *unadorned, simple*, ἀληθείας στολή Ph.1.369, al.; *homogeneous*, σῶμα ὁμοιομερὲς καὶ ἀ. Plot.6.7.13, cf. Iamb.*VP*23.103. Adv. -λως Vett.Val.343.36.

ἀποίκιλτος, ον, *not elaborated, without convolutions*, ἐγκέφαλος Gal.*UP*8.13. 2. = foreg. in Adv. -τως Sch. A.*Pr*.317.

ἀποίκ-ις, ίδος, ἡ, pecul. fem. of ἄποικος, ἀ. πόλις *a colony*, Hdt.7.167, Plu.*Cor*.28; and without πόλις, Str.10.4.17. -**ισις**, εως, ἡ, *leading out a colony*, D.H.3.31 (s.v.l.). -**ισμός**, ὁ, *settlement of a colony*, ἀ. εἰς Ἐλέαν, title of work by Xenoph., D.L.9.20; μετὰ τὸν ἀ. Arist.*Pol*.1304^{b}32. II. = ἀποικεσία, Lxx *Je*.26(46).19, al. -**ιστέον**, *one must send away*, Paul.Aeg.4.1. -**ιστής**, οῦ, ὁ, *leader of a colony*, *IG*1.31.4, Men.Rh.p.356 S.

ἀποικοδομέω, *cut off by building, wall up, barricade*, τὰς θύρας, τὰς ὁδούς, Th.1.134, 7.73; χαράδραν D.55.5:—Pass., Plu.*Caes*.49. 2. *rebuild* (nisi leg. ἀν-), Jul.*Or*.2.66a.

ἀποικονομ-έω, *manage so as to get rid of* a thing, Antyll.ap.Orib.6.6.1:—Med., πᾶν πάθος καὶ νόσημα τῆς ἑαυτοῦ ψυχῆς *get rid of* them *by one's manner of life*, Hierocl.p.51 A., cf. Plot.1.4.6, 5.9.1, Procl. *in Prm*.p.497 S.:—Pass., *to be removed*, Herod.Med.ap.Orib.10.37.17. -**ησις**, εως, ἡ, *getting rid of* a thing, Cass.*Pr*.70. -**ητέον**, *one must get rid of*, φλεγμονήν Orib.*Fr*.42, cf. Herod.Med.in *Rh.Mus*.58.76. -**ητος**, ον, *to be got rid of*, Arr.*Epict*.4.1.44. -**ία**, ἡ, *rejection*, opp. ἐκλογή, Alex.Aphr.*de An*.160.25.

ἄποικος, ον, *away from home, abroad*, ἄ. πέμπειν τινὰ γῆς to send *away from* one's native land, S.*OT*1518. II. mostly as Subst., 1. of persons, *settler, colonist*, Hdt.5.97, Th.1.25, 38, 7.57, etc. 2. of cities, πόλιν Σινωπέων ἄποικον ἐν τῇ Κολχίδι χώρᾳ X.*An*.5.3.2, cf. 6.2.1, Ar.*Lys*.582: hence A. calls iron Χάλυβος Σκυθῶν ἄ. *Th*.729 (lyr.).

ἀποικτίζομαι, *complain loudly of* a thing, πρὸς πατέρα ἀποικτίζετο τῶν..ἤντησε (sc. ταῦτα ὧν ἤντησε) Hdt.1.114.

ἀποίμαντος, ον, *untended*, ἀγέλη, of bees, *AP*6.239 (Apollonid.).

ἀποιμώζω, *bewail loudly*, τι A.*Ag*.329, S.*Ph*.278; τινά A.*Fr*.138, Antipho 5.41; ἀ. τι πρός τινα E.*Med*.31; ἀ. ἑαυτόν τινος D.H.5.8.

ἄποινα, τά, (by haplology for ἀπό-ποινα (ποινή), cf. ἀπετίνυτο ποινήν Il.16.398; τὰ χρήματα ἄποινα ὠνόμαζον οἱ παλαιοί D.23.33): I. Hom. (only in Il.), *ransom* or *price paid*, whether *to recover one's freedom* when taken prisoner, φέρων ἀπερείσι' ἄ. Il.1.13; οὐκ ἀπεδέξατ' ἄ. ib.95, al., cf. Hdt.6.79; or *to save one's life*, Il.6.46, 10.380, al., Thgn.727; or *for the corpse of a slain friend*, ὅς ἄ. φέροι καὶ νεκρὸν ἄγοιτο Il.24.139: freq. with gen. of the person ransomed, ἄ. κούρης, υἷος, *ransom for* them, 1.111, 2.230; νεκροῖο δὲ δέξαι ἄ. 24.137. II. generally, *atonement, compensation, penalty*, ἂψ ἐθέλω ἀρέσαι δόμεναί τ' ἀπερείσι' ἄ. 9.120, cf. Hdt.9.120; ὕβρεως, μιασμάτων ἄ., *for* violence, etc., A.*Pers*.808, *Ag*.1420, cf. 1670, E.*Ba*.516, *Alc*.7; in *IT* 1459 τῆς σῆς σφαγῆς ἄ. prob. *redemption, rescue* from death.—Rare in Prose, ἀποίνοις ἐξιλασθῆναι Pl.*Lg*.862c, cf. Hdt. l. c., Parth.8. 5. 2. in good sense, *recompense, reward*, freq. c. gen., ἄποιν' ἀρετᾶς Pi.*P*.2.14, cf. *O*.7.16, al.: in sg., τοῦτο γὰρ ἀντ' ἀγαθοῖο νόου εἴληχεν ἄποινον *IG*14.1389 i 10.

ἀποινάω, *demand the fine* due from the murderer (cf. ἄποινα II), Lex ap.D.23.28, cf. 33:—Med., *hold to ransom*, E.*Rh*.177, cf. 66 (lyr., dub.).

ἀποινέω, *cease to ferment*, v.l. in Alex.45.4.

ἀποινί, Adv. *unpunished*, Agath.4.19.

ἀποινό-δῐκος, ον, *exacting penalty, atoning*, δίκαι E.*HF*888. -**δορπος**, ον, *ransom-devouring*, Lyc.902.

ἄποινον, τό, v. ἄποινα II. 2.

ἄποινος, ον, = ἄοινος, Eust.727.19.

ἄποιος, ον, (ποιός) *without quality* or *attribute*, στοιχεῖα *Placit*.1.15.8; ὕλη Zeno *Stoic*.1.24, Chrysipp.*Stoic*.2.111; ποιότης Plot.1.8.10; γεῦσις Aret.*SA*2.7; τὸ ἄ. Porph.*Abst*.1.30; ἀ. ὕδωρ *pure* water, Ath.1.33c (Sup.); ἄ. βοτάνη Orib.*Fr*.52. II. (ποιεῖν) *inert*, ἄ. δὲ καὶ ἀδύναμον (v.l. ἀδύνατον) τὸ σῶμα καθ' αὑτό Procl.*Inst*.80, cf. eund. *in Ti*.3.337 D.

ἀποιστέον· *perferendum*, *Gloss*.

ἀποϊστεύω, *kill with arrows*, *AP*7.743 (Antip.).

ἀποίσω, v. ἀποφέρω.

ἀποίχομαι, fut. -οιχήσομαι: impf. -ῳχόμην:—*to be gone away, to be far from, keep aloof from* a thing, c. gen., ἀποίχονται πολέμοιο Il.11.408; ἀποίχεαι ἀνδρός *hast forsaken* him, 19.342. 2. abs., *to be gone, to have departed*, ὅππως δὴ δηρὸν ἀποίχεται how long *he has been gone*, Od.4.109; ἀνδρὸς ἀποιχομένοιο πολὺν χρόνον 21.70, cf. 1.253; περὶ πατρὸς ἀποιχομένοιο ἐρέσθαι his *absent* father, 1.135, cf. E.*Hel*.1306 (lyr.); ἀ. εἰς τάξιν πάλιν Id.*Heracl*.818: imper. ἀποίχεσθε *begone!* Hecat.30 J. 3. *to have perished*, ἀποίχεται χάρις E.*HF*134 (lyr.); of persons, *to be dead and gone*, ἀπολιπὼν μ' ἀποίχεται Ar.*Ra*.83; in full, ἀ. βιότοιο v.l. in *AP*10.59 (Pall.); οἱ ἀποιχόμενοι, = οἱ τελευτήσαντες, Pi.*P*.1.93, cf. 3.3, *SIG*1219.10 (iii B.C.). 4. μηνὸς ἀποιχομένου, = φθίνοντος, Arat.810. 5. ἀποιχομένου μίτου, of a *broken* lyre-string, *AP*6.54 (Paul. Sil.).

ἀποιων-ίζομαι, *shun as an ill-omen*, Lat. *abominari*, *Gloss*. -**ισμός**, ὁ, = *deprecatio*, Charis.p.553 K.

ἀποκαθαίρω, aor. inf. -ῆραι Gal.11.129, but subj. -άρῃ Thphr.*CP* 1.17.10:—*clear, cleanse* or *clean quite*, ἀ. τὴν χεῖρα εἰς τὰ χειρόμακτρα upon the towels, X.*Cyr*.1.3.5; τοῖς προσθίοις ἀ. σκέλεσιν, of flies, Arist.*PA*683^{a}29:—Pass., Id.*Pr*.958^{b}5:—Med., *rid oneself of*, ib.880^{a}32. 2. *refine* metal *by smelting*, Str.9.1.23; ῥητίνη ἀποκεκαθαρμένη *purified*, Dsc.1.25: metaph., ἀποκεκαθάρθαι τὴν φωνήν *to be pure in* dialect, Luc.*Hist.Conscr*.21. II. *cleanse off, clear away*, τὰς τραπέζας Ar.*Pax*1193; ἀ. τὰς βαναύσους τέχνας εἰς οἰκετῶν καὶ μετοίκων χέρας Plu.*Comp.Lyc.Num*.2; *remove by purging* or *clearing*, ἴκτερον Dsc.4.71; ἀ. ἄνω *purge* by emetics, Hp.*Morb*.3.9:—Pass., *to be removed by purging*, Id.*VM*19: generally, *to be got rid of*, Pl.*Ti*.72d, Arist.*HA*568^{b}9; *to be thrown off*, Id.*Mete*.383^{a}34:—Med., ἀποκαθήρασθαί τι *get rid of* a thing, Ti.Locr.104b, Demoph.*Sim*.25; τινός *rid oneself of*.., X.*Cyr*.2.2.27.

ἀποκαθαριεύω, = sq., Sch.Il.1.1.

ἀποκᾰθᾰρ-ίζω, fut. -ιῶ, *cleanse, purify*, Lxx *Jb*.25.4. -**ισμα**, ατος, τό, = κάθαρμα, *EM*483.12. -**μα**, ατος, τό, *that which is cleared off, excretion*, ἀ. ἡ χολή Arist.*PA*677^{a}29, cf. *HA*546^{b}24; *by-product, dross*, 624^{a}15; *dregs*, τῶν ὄντων Jul.*Or*.5.170d; *offscourings, slops*, St.Byz. s.v. Ἀζανία (pl.). -**σις**, εως, ἡ, *purging*: hence, of *dross*, Arist.*Mete*.383^{b}4, cf. Str.4.2.1; of animal *secretions*, Arist.*GA*726^{a}13, cf. *HA*587^{b}1; ἀποκαθάρσεις χολῆς Th.2.49. 2. *cleansing*, πνεύματος *Gp*.12.22.11; *sifting* of grain, *PRev.Laws*39.10 (iii B.C.), *PLond.ined*.2361^{r} (iii B.C.). II. *lustration, expiation*, Plu.*Rom*.21, Iamb.*Comm.Math*.15; νείκους Hierocl. *in CA* 24 p.473 M. -**τέον**, *one must purify*, Aristid.*Or*.46(3).3. -**τικός**, ή, όν, *clearing off, cleansing*, c. gen., Dsc.3.23; ψυχῶν Iamb.*Myst*.2.5.

ἀποκαθέζομαι, *sit down*, *Gloss*.

ἀποκαθεύδω, *sleep away from home*, ἐς τὸ ἱερόν Philostr.*VS*2.4.1; of a woman separated from her husband, *sleep apart*, Eup.399. II. *fall asleep over* a thing, Them.*Or*.1.13d.

ἀποκάθ-ημαι, *sit apart*, ἀτιμώμενοι ἀποκατέαται (Ion. for -κάθηνται) Hdt.4.66; ἐν τῷ τεύχει Arist.*HA*625^{a}26; ἐν τῷ γυμνασίῳ *SIG*739.7 (Delph., i B.C.); ἀποκαθημένη, = αἱμορροοῦσα, Lxx *Le*.20.18, al., cf. Ph.1.578; θεαταὶ ἀ. τῶν κινδύνων J.*BJ*4.6.2. II. *sit idle*, Ael.*VH*6.12. -**ίζω**, *sit apart*, of a judge, ἐν τῷ γυμνασίῳ Plb.31.6.3. II. *sit down*, Plu.2.649c; of the uterus, *slip down*, Sor.2.85. -**ισμα**, ατος, τό, *residuatio*, *Gloss*.

ἀποκαθιστάνω, = sq., *SIG*^{2}588.56 (ii B.C.), Plb.3.98.9, D.S.18.57:—also -**ιστάω**, v.l. in Arist.*Metaph*.1074^{a}3.

ἀποκαθίστημι, fut. -καταστήσω: aor. ἀποκατέστησα, later ἀπεκατέστησα *PTeb*.413.4 (ii/iii A.D.): pf. -καθέστᾰκα Plb.21.11.9, *SIG*798.7 (i A.D.):—*re-establish, restore, reinstate*, X.*Lac*.6.3; τὰν πολιτείαν Decr.Byz.ap.D.18.90; πολίτας Plu.*Alex*.7; συνθήκας εἰς τὸ ἐξ ἀρχῆς D.H.3.23; ἀ. τινί τι *restore, return* it *to* one, Plb.3.98.7, D.S.18.65, etc.; ἀ. εἰς αὑτὰν (sc. φύσιν) Ti.Locr.100c, cf. Arist.*MM*1204^{b}37; εἰς τὸ αὐτό Id.*Metaph*.1074^{a}3; εἰς ἀκέραιον, = *restituere in integrum*, *CIL*1.203; τινὰ ἐς οἶκον Plb.8.27.6, cf. Thphr.*Char*.7.6; ἀ. σαυτὸν εἰς ἐκεῖνον τὸν χρόνον *carry* yourself *back*.., Plu.2.610d; ἐπί .. D.S.5.23; *cure*, δασυσμοὺς φωνῆς Dsc.1.64, etc. 2. *pay* what is due, ἀργύριον Lxx *Ge*.23.16. 3. *hand over, deliver*, τοῖς φυλακίταις τὸ σῶμα *PSI*4.359.9 (iii B.C.). 4. in drill, *restore* a formation, etc., εἰς ὀρθὸν ἀ., = εἰς ὀρθὸν ἀποδοῦναι, Ael.*Tact*.26.3 (cf. ἀποδίδωμι

11.3); ἀποκατάστησον *as you were!* Ascl.*Tact.*12.11, etc. **II.** Pass., with pf. ἀποκαθέστᾰμαι, aor. -εστάθην [ᾰ]: also aor. 2 Act. -κατέστην:—*to be restored*, Arist.*Cat.*9^{b}25, al.; τῷ θεῷ *SIG*459.7 (Beroea, iii B.C.); *return* from captivity, Vett.Val.68.24; μέχρι τοῦ τὰ πράγματ' ἀποκατασταθῆναι till affairs *are settled*, Wilcken *Chr.*10 (ii B.C.); ἀ. εἰς τὴν ἐξ ἀρχῆς κατάστασιν *return, settle down* into.., Plb.25.1.1, cf. 2.41.14, Porph.*Antr.*34; of planets, *complete a revolution*, Cleom. 2.7, al.; of the periodic *return* of the cosmic cycle, *Stoic.*2.190; of stars, *return* to their place in the heavens, Phlp.*in Mete.*112.21; of a revolving figure, *return* to the original situation, Archim.*Con. Praef.*; of sicknesses, *subside*, Hp.*Aph.*6.49; ἀ. εἴς τι *turn out* so and so, Thphr.*HP*4.14.5; of sediment, *settle*, Dsc.5.89; of a spring, *recoil*, Ph.*Bel.*70.46, cf. 71.2. **2.** *to be detached from* the mainland, of an island, Anon.Vat.40.

ἀποκαίνῠμαι, *surpass, vanquish*, τῇ δ' αὖτ'.. ἀπεκαίνυτο πάντας in wrestling again he *vanquished* all, Od.8.127; οἷος δή με.. ἀπεκαίνυτο τόξῳ ib.219, cf. A.R.2.783.

ἀποκαίριος, ον, = ἄκαιρος, *unseasonable*, S.*Ph.*155 (lyr.).

ἀποκαισᾰρόομαι, Pass., *assume the monarch*, M.Ant.6.30.

ἀποκαίω, Att. -κάω, aor. ἀπέκηα Il. (v. infr.), -έκαυσα D.25.95, Philippid.25.4:—*burn off*, of cautery, X.*Mem.*1.2.54, D. l. c.; of intense cold, θέλλαν ἤ κεν ἀπὸ Τρώων κεφαλὰς.. κήαι Il.21.336; ἄνεμος βορρᾶς.. ἀποκαίων πάντα X.*An.*4.5.3; ἀπέκαυσεν ἡ πάχνη τοὺς ἀμπέλους Philippid. l. c., cf. Thphr.*CP*2.3.1, al.:—Pass., ἀπεκαίοντο αἱ ῥῖνες their noses *were frozen off*, X.*An.*7.4.3. **2.** *calcine*, Dsc. 5.125.

ἀποκᾰκ-έω, (κάκη) *sink under a weight of misery*, Lxx *Je.*15.9. **-ησις**, εως, ἡ, *cowardice*, Hsch. s.v. ἀπόκνησις.

ἀποκᾰλᾰμουργέω, *free from reeds*, in Pass., *PLond.*3.1003.7 (vi A.D.).

ἀποκᾰλέω, *recall*, esp. from exile, Hdt.3.53, X.*Cyr.*1.4.25. **2.** *call away* or *aside*, Id.*An.*7.3.35. **II.** *call by a name*, esp. by way of disparagement, *stigmatize as..*, τὸν τοῦ μανέντος.. ξύναιμον ἀποκαλοῦντες S.*Aj.*727; ὀλιγαρχικοὺς καὶ μισοδήμους ἀ. And.4.16; ὡς ἐν ὀνείδει ἀ. μηχανοποιόν Pl.*Grg.*512c; ἀργόν, σοφιστήν ἀ. τινά, X. *Mem.*1.2.57, 1.6.13; οὓς νῦν ὑβρίζει καὶ πτωχοὺς ἀ. D.21.211; ὡς ἐν αἰσχρῷ φιλαύτους ἀ. Arist.*EN*1168^{a}30; παράσιτον ἀ. Timocl.19; χαριεντισμὸν ἀ. *call* it a *sorry* jest, Pl.*Tht.*168d; sts. without any bad sense, τοὺς χαλεπαίνοντας ἀνδρώδεις ἀ. Arist.*EN*1109^{b}18, cf. X.*Eq.* 10.17, Plu.2.776e.

ἀποκαλλωπίζω, *strip of ornament*, esp. of foliage, Poll.1.236.

ἀπο-κάλυμμα [κᾰ], ατος, τό, *a revelation*, Lxx *Jd.*5.2. **-κᾰλυπτέος**, α, ον, *to be revealed*, Them.*Or.*23.294c. **-κᾰλύπτω**, aor. 2 Pass. -καλύφην *CPR*1.239.5 (iii A.D.), etc.:—*uncover*, τὴν κεφαλήν Hdt.1.119; τὰ στήθη Pl.*Prt.*352a:—in Pass., of land *left* cultivable by the Nile (cf. ἀποκάλυφος), ἀρούρας β' ἀποκαλυφείσης.. αἰγιαλοῦ *PIand.*27.12, cf. 27.60 (i/ii A.D.):—Med., ἀποκαλύπτεσθαι τὴν κεφαλήν Plu. *Crass.*6. **2.** *disclose, reveal*, τόδε τῆς διανοίας Pl.*Prt.*352a; τὴν τῆς ῥητορικῆς δύναμιν Id.*Grg.*455d, cf. 460a:—Med., *reveal one's whole mind*, Plu.*Alex.*55, 2.880e:—in Pass., Lxx 1*Ki.*2.27, al.; ἀποκαλύπτεσθαι πρός τι *let one's designs* upon a thing *become known*, D.S.17.62, 18.23:—Pass., *to be made known*, *Ev.Matt.*10.26, etc.; of persons, 2*Ep.Thess.*2.3,6,8, etc.; λόγοι ἀποκεκαλυμμένοι *naked*, i.e. *shameless*, words, Ps.-Plu.*Vit.Hom.*214. **3.** *unmask*, τινά Luc.*Cat.*26, *Vit.Auct.*23. **II.** of the epiglottis, *raise*, Arist. *de An.*422^{a}2 (Pass.). **-κάλῠφος** [κᾰ], ον, *uncovered*, κεφαλή Ph.1.141 (s.v.l.); ἀ. αἰγιαλός land cultivable only *when* the water *receded*, *BGU*640, *CPR* 32.7 (s.v.l.); ὀψ[ί]μως ἀποκάλυφο(ι) (ἄρουραι) ε̄ *CPHerm.*45.6. **-κάλυψις** [κᾰ], εως, ἡ, *uncovering*, of the head, Phld.*Vit.*p.38 J.; *disclosing*, of hidden springs, Plu.*Aem.*14: metaph., ἁμαρτίας Id.2.70f; *revelation*, esp. of divine mysteries, *Ep.Rom.*16.25, etc.; of persons, *manifestation*, 2*Ep.Thess.*1.7, etc.; title of *the Apocalypse*.

ἀποκάμνω, *grow quite weary, fail, flag utterly*, mostly abs., S.*OC* 1776 (lyr.), Pl.*R.*445b, *AP*5.46 (Rufin.); τῷ μήκει τοῦ χρόνου Jul. *Or.*2.91d: c. part., ἀ. ζητῶν, μηχανώμενος, *to be quite weary of* seeking, etc., Pl.*Men.*81d, X.*Mem.*2.6.35. **2.** c. inf., *cease* to do, μοχθεῖν οὐκ ἀ. E.*Ion* 135 (lyr.); μὴ ἀποκάμῃς σαυτὸν σῶσαι *do not hesitate..*, Pl.*Cri.*45b. **3.** c. acc., ἀ. πόνον *flinch from* toil, X.*HG* 7.5.19; ἀ. πρὸς τὰς διαμαρτίας *to be disheartened by..*, Plu.*Arat.*33.

ἀπο-καμπτός, όν, *bent*, Sch.Opp.*H.*1.205. **-κάμπτω**, intr., *turn aside, wheel*, opp. ὀρθοδρομεῖν, X.*Eq.*7.14; ἀ. ἐκ τῆς ὁδοῦ Thphr. *Char.*22.9; ἀ. ἔξω τοῦ τέρματος, of chariots, Arist.*Rh.*1409^{b}23. **2.** ἀποκεκαμμένον ῥάμφος *curved* beak, Horap.2.96.

ἀποκαπν-ίζω, *fumigate*, *PMag.Par.*2.23. **-ισμός**, ὁ, *fumigation* (v.l. for ὑπο-), Dsc.3.112.

ἀποκᾱπύω, (v. καπνός) *breathe away*, aor. 1 in tmesi, ἀπὸ δὲ ψυχὴν ἐκάπυσσεν she *gasped forth* her life, Il.22.467, cf. Q.S.6.523.

ἀποκᾰρᾱδοκ-έω, *expect earnestly*, c. acc., Plb.16.2.8, al., Aq.*Ps.* 36(37).7, J.*BJ*3.7.26. **-ία**, ἡ, *earnest expectation*, *Ep.Rom.*8.19, *Ep.Phil.*1.20.

ἀποκᾰρᾱτομέω, *behead*, Sch.Pi.*O.*10(11).19.

ἀποκαρδιουργέω, *extract the heart of a victim*, Hsch. s.v. ὁσιουργῆσαι.

ἀπόκαρμα, ατος, τό, in pl., *hair-clippings*, Iamb.*Protr.*21.λβ'.

ἀποκαρόω, *stupefy*, prob. in Dsc.4.75.

ἀποκαρπ-ίζω, *gather fruit*:—Pass., *to be stript of fruit*, Poll.1.236. **II.** metaph. in Med., *reap the fruits of, enjoy*, c. acc. rei, *IG* 14.1934f 12. **-όω**, *throw off, send out*, φλέβας Hp.*Oss.*17:—Med., *enjoy the fruits of*, τι *PAmh.*2.142.15 (iv A.D.).

ἀποκαρτέον, (ἀποκείρω) *one must clip off*, Eup.400.

ἀποκαρτερ-έω, *kill oneself by abstinence, starve oneself to death*, Hp. *Acut.*56; Ἀποκαρτερῶν, title of work by Hegesias, Cic.*Tusc.*1.34.84, cf. Plu.*Num.*21, Luc.*Macr.*19; -οῦντα ἀποθνήσκειν Phld.*Mort.*6; ὥστε μᾶλλον ἂν θέλειν ἀποκαρτερεῖν ἢ τοῦτ' ἀκούων καρτερεῖν *Com. Adesp.*336.8; οὐκ ἀπεκαρτέρησε.., ἀλλ' ἐκαρτέρησ' Timocl.18. **-ησις**, εως, ἡ, *suicide by hunger*, Quint.*Inst.*8.5.23. **-ητέον**, *one must abstain from food*, Philum.ap.Aët.9.23.

ἀποκαρφολογέω, = καρφολογέω, v.l. in Hp.*Prog.*4.

ἀποκαρφόομαι, Pass., *to be parched, dried up*, Sever.*Clyst.*p.12 D.

ἀποκαταβαίνω, *dismount*, D.H.9.16.

ἀποκάτ-αγμα, ατος, τό, *fragment broken off*, φιάλης *IG*7.3498.60 (Oropus). **-άγνῡμι**, *break, rend off*, Hsch. s.v. ἀπαράσσεται. **-άγω** [ᾰγ], *bring back*, Vett.Val.319.19.

ἀποκαταλαμβάνω, *intercept*, Autol.2.13 (Pass.).

ἀποκαταλλάσσω, Att. -ττω, *reconcile again*, *Ep.Eph.*2.16; τὰ πάντα εἰς αὐτόν *Ep.Col.*1.20.

ἀποκαταπτῦσαι· τελειῶσαι, Hsch.

ἀποκατα-ρρέω, *flow down from*, ἀπό τινος Hp.*Aph.*7.30. **-ρρίπτω**, *plunge*, σιδηρᾶ εἰς ὕδωρ Gal.14.208.

ἀποκατα-στᾰσία, ἡ, *restitution*, *PTeb.*424.7 (iii A.D.). **-στᾰσις**, εως, ἡ, *restoration, re-establishment*, τοῦ ἐνδεοῦς Arist.*MM*1205^{a}4; εἰς φύσιν ib.1204^{b}36, 1205^{b}11; *return to* a position, Epicur.*Ep.*1 p.8 U.; esp. of military formations, *reversal* of a movement, Ascl.*Tact.*10.6, etc.; generally, πάντων *Act.Ap.*3.21; of the soul, Procl.*Inst.*199 (pl.); τῆς φύσιος ἐς τὸ ἀρχαῖον Aret.*CD*1.5; *recovery from sickness*, Id. *SA*1.10; τῶν ὁμήρων εἰς τὰς πατρίδας Plb.3.99.6; εἰς ἀ. ἐλθεῖν, of the affairs of a city, Id.4.23.1; *return* to original position, Ascl.*Tact.* 10.1; ἀ. ἄστρων *return* of the stars to the same place in the heavens as in the former year, Plu.2.937f, D.S.12.36, etc.; *periodic return* of the cosmic cycle, *Stoic.*2.184,190; of a planet, *return* to a place in the heavens occupied at a former epoch, Antioch.Astr.ap.*Cat.Cod.Astr.* 7.120,121; but, *zodiacal revolution*, Paul.Al.*T.*1; opp. ἀνταπ. (q.v.), Doroth.ap.*Cat.Cod.Astr.*2.196.9; *restoration* of sun and moon after eclipse, Pl.*Ax.*370b. **-στᾰτικός**, ή, όν, *bringing back* to a point, σελήνης Ph.1.24; χρόνος Gem.18.17; μοῖρα Vett.Val.213.27; ἀ. ἀριθμοί *recurrent*, in which the last digit is identical in all powers, Nicom.*Ar.*2.17; πᾶσα περίοδος τῶν ἀϊδίων -κή Procl.*Inst.*199; ἀ. βίος Herm.*in Phdr.*p.152 A.; ἀ. διάλαμψις, of star positions at the nativity of the terrestrial universe, Paul.Al.*T.*1. **II.** *for restitution*, *POxy.*144.9 (vi A.D.). **-σχεσις**, εως, ἡ, *abstentatio*, *Gloss.* **-τίθημι**, *lay aside*, ἀποκάτθετο (sync. aor. Med.) κυνέην A.R.3.1287: c. gen., ib.817. **-φαίνομαι**, Pass., *to be clearly visible*, Aristaenet. 1.3. **-ψύχω** [ῡ], *cool*, Gal.11.555.

ἀποκατεῖδον, inf. -ιδεῖν cited from Hp.*Prog.*7 (where ἐπι- codd.) by Metrod.*Herc.*831.2.

ἀποκατ-έχω, *hold bound*, ἐσχάταις τιμωρίαις *IG*14.872 (Cumae, dub. l.). **-ημαι**, Ion. for ἀποκάθημαι. **-ορθόω**, *recover one's prosperity*, Arist.*EE*1247^{b}10.

ἀπο-κάτω [κᾰ], *from below*, Sch.D.T.p.23 H. **-κάτωθεν** [κᾰ], *from the bottom upwards*, Olymp.*in Mete.*179.17, al., *PMag.Leid.W.* 5.49:—better written divisim.

ἀποκαυλ-ίζω, (καυλός) *break off by the stalk*: hence, *break short off*, E.*Supp.*717, Th.2.76:—Pass., *to be so broken, to be fractured across*, Hp.*Fract.*45, *Art.*33. **-ισις**, εως, ἡ, *breaking off by the stalk*: *snapping*, πηδαλίων Luc.*Merc.Cond.*1. **-ιστέον**, *one must break off*, Antyll.ap.Orib.44.23.20.

ἀπόκαυλος, ον, f.l. in Thphr.*HP*7.2.4.

ἀπό-καυμα, ατος, τό, *firebrand*, Sm.*Ps.*101(102).4. **2.** *blister* caused by a burn, Hierocl.*Facet.*135, Eust.1123.24; *chilblain*, Id. ad D.P.916, Sch.Nic.*Th.*677. **-καυσις**, εως, ἡ, (ἀποκαίω) *burning, scorching*, Str.16.4.20. **-καυσμός**, ὁ, *burning*, πάπων Judeich *Altertümer von Hierapolis* p.142. **-κάω**, v. ἀποκαίω.

ἀπόκειμαι, fut. -κείσομαι, used as Pass. of ἀποτίθημι, *to be laid away from*, προμαθείας ἀπόκεινται ῥοαί the tides of events *lie beyond* our foresight, Pi.*N.*11.46, cf. Arat.110. **II.** abs., *to be laid up in store*, of money, ἀ. ἔνδον ἀργύριον Philetaer.7.6; σῖτος D.42.6; παρά τινι Lys.19.22; τινί for one's use, X.*An.*2.3.15; χάρις.. ξύν' ἀπόκειται (as Reisig for ξυναπόκειται) *is laid up* as a common possession, S.*OC*1752: hence, *to be kept in reserve*, X.*Cyr.*3.1.19, etc.; πολύς σοι [γέλως] ἐστὶν ἀποκείμενος you have great *store* of laughter *in reserve*, ib.2.2.15; ἀ. εἰς.. *to be reserved for* an occasion, Pl.*Lg.*952d; τὸ τῆς συγγνώμης ὠφέλιμον, ἔλεος ἀ. τινί, D.23.42, D.S.13.31; σοφία ἐς ἐκείνας [τὰς τέχνας] ἀποκείσθω *let* the name of wisdom *be reserved for..*, Philostr.*Gym.*1; ἐφ' ὑμῖν ἀπόκειται τὸ πεισθῆναι you *reserve* your acquiescence, D.Chr.38.5: c. inf., ἀτυχήματα ἀπόκειταί τινι ἐνευδοκιμεῖν D.18.198; ὅσα τοῖς κακουργοῖς ἀ. παθεῖν D.H.5.8, cf. Luc. *Syr.D.*51; ἀ. τοῖς ἀνθρώποις ἅπαξ ἀποθανεῖν *Ep.Hebr.*9.27; πᾶσι.. τὸ θανεῖν ἀπόκειται *Epigr.Gr.*416.6 (Alexandria). **2.** *to be buried*, *Not. Scav.*1923.49. **III.** *to be laid aside, neglected*, ἀ. πόρρω Cratin.367, cf. Plu.2.159f, Philostr.*VA*8.21. **2.** ἀποκειμένη καὶ παλαιὰ φύσις *stale*, of perfume, D.S.3.46. **IV.** *to be exposed, lie open, to*, χώρα ἀ. βαρβάροις Procop.*Aed.*4.2, cf. 2.9.

ἀποκείρω, aor. -έκειρα, Ep. -έκερσα (v. infr.):—Pass., pf. -κέκαρμαι E.*Hec.*910:—*clip, cut off*, properly of hair, mostly in Med., ξανθὴν ἀπεκείρατο χαίτην Il.23.141; ἀποκείρασθαι τὰς κεφαλάς *to have their* hair *shorn close*, Hdt.6.21: abs., ἀποκείρασθαι *cut off one's* hair, Ar. *Nu.*836; esp. in token of mourning, Is.4.7:—in Act., X.*Eq.*5.8, Thphr.*Char.*21.3, Luc.*Pisc.*46; *tear out*, ἧπαρ Id.*Prom.*2:—Pass., δὶς ἀποκαρέντα πρόβατα twice *shorn* or *clipped*, D.S.1.36; ἀποκεκαρμένος ἐν χρῷ, ἀ. σκάφιον, of peculiar fashions of *hair-cutting*, Ar.*Th.* 838, Luc.*DMeretr.*5.3: c. acc., ἀπὸ στεφάναν κέκαρσαι πύργων thou *hast been shorn of* thy crown of towers, E.*Hec.*910; but ἀ. τινὰ τῶν γενείων Philostr.*VA*7.34. 2. metaph., *cheat*, τοὺς παχεῖς Luc. *Alex.*6. II. generally, *cut through, sever*, ἀπὸ δ' ἄμφω κέρσε τένοντε Il.10.456; ἀπὸ δὲ φλέβα πᾶσαν ἔκερσεν 13.546. III. metaph., *cut off, slay*, ἀποκείρεται σὺν ἄνθος πόλεως E.*HF*875 (lyr.); ἀπέκειρε τὴν ἀκμὴν τῆς Σπάρτης Demad.12.

ἀποκεκᾰλυμμένως, Adv. *openly*, Isoc.8.62, D.H.*Rh.*8.3, Lib.*Or.* 1.37, al.

ἀποκεκινδῡνευμένως, Adv. *venturously*, Them.*Or.*8.107c.

ἀποκεκρυμμένως, Adv. *by stealth*, Theon *Prog.*8, Procop.*Goth.*4.27.

ἀποκέλλω, *get out of the course* or *track*, *AB*428.

ἀπόκενος, ον, *not quite full*, ἀγγεῖα Dsc.5.36, cf. Gal.17(2).163; *empty*, Hero *Spir.*2.24.

ἀποκενόω, *drain, exhaust*, Hp.*Nat.Puer.*15; ἀ. τοὺς πόδας (where τοὺς π., more Hebraico, = τὴν γαστέρα) Lxx *Jd.*3.24; *evacuate*, τὸ περιττὸν γυμνασίοις Sor.1.27:—Pass., Arist.*Fr.*224.

ἀποκεντ-έω, *pierce through*, Hp.*Ulc.*25, Lxx *Nu.*25.8, al., D.L. 9.26. **-ησις**, εως, ἡ, *piercing*, Lxx *Ho.*9.13.

ἀπόκεντρος, ον, *away from a cardinal point*, Man.3.269.

ἀποκένωσις, εως, ἡ, *evacuation*, αἵματος Orib.7.20.11, cf. Sor.1.36, Gal.1.392.

ἀποκερᾰμόω, *cover with tiles*, τὴν πάροδον τοῦ τείχους *SIG*[2]587.110.

ἀποκερδαίνω, pf. -κεκέρδαγκα D.C.43.18:—*have benefit, enjoyment from* or *of* a thing, c. gen., ποτοῦ E.*Cyc.*432; ἀ. βραχέα *make* some small *gain* of a thing, And.1.134: abs., ἔνεσται ἀποκερδᾶναι Luc. *DMort.*4.1.

ἀποκερμᾰτίζω, *break into small pieces*, Porph.*Sent.*37. 2. metaph., ἀ. τὸν βίον *dissipate* one's whole substance, *AP*7.607 (Pall.).

ἀποκεστίλλαι· ἐκδεῖραι, Hsch. **ἀπόκετον**· ἀποκομίζων, Id.

ἀποκεφᾰλαιόομαι, Pass., *to be summed up*, Eust.1769.4.

ἀποκεφᾰλ-ίζω, *behead*, Arr.*Epict.*1.1.24, Lxx *Ps.*151.7, v. l. in Artem.1.35; of a fish, Dorio ap.Ath.7.287e:—Pass., Phld.*Sign.*13, 29, Arr.*Epict.*1.1.19. **-ισμα**, ατος, τό, *dirt that comes off the head*, Poll.2.48. **-ισμός**, ὁ, *beheading*, Plu.2.358e, Procl.*Par.Ptol.* 280. **-ιστής**, οῦ, ὁ, *headsman*, Str.11.14.14.

ἀποκεχωρισμένως, Adv. *separately*, Apollon.*Lex.* s. v. τμήδην.

ἀποκηδεύω, *cease to mourn for*, τινά Hdt.9.31.

ἀποκηδέω, Dor. -κᾱδέω, = ἀκηδέω, *to be remiss*, Il.23.413; *to be faint*, Sophr.78.

ἀποκηδής, ές, = ἀκηδής, *negligent*: Adv., Comp. -έστερον Hp.ap. Gal.19.84.

ἀποκήλειν· ἀποδιώκειν, Hsch.

ἀπόκηρος, (κήρ) *free from fate* or *death*, prob. l. in Emp.147.

ἀποκηρ-υκτος, ον, *publicly renounced*: 1. of a son, *disinherited, disowned*, Theopomp.Hist.309, Poll.4.93, Luc.*Icar.*14, Hermog.*Stat.* 2. **-ύξιμος**, ον, *to be sold by public auction*, *IG*2.476. **-υξις**, εως, ἡ, *public announcement*, esp. *public renunciation* of a son, *disinheriting*, Plu.*Them.*2, Luc.*Abd.*5, Hermog.*Inv.*4.13. **-ύσσω**, Att. -ττω, *offer* a thing *for public sale, sell by auction*, Hdt.1.194, Pl.Com. 121; ἀ. ὅ τι ἂν ἀλφάνῃ Eup.258:—Pass., *to be sold by auction*, Lys. 17.7, Luc.*Pisc.*23, D.Chr.66.4. II. *renounce publicly*, ἐξέστω τῷ πατρὶ τὸν υἱὸν ἀ. Pl.*Lg.*928e sq., cf. D.39.39, Luc.*Abd.*1:—Pass., *to be disinherited*, ὑπὸ τοῦ πατρός Aeschin.Socr.*Oxy.*1608.39. 2. *declare outlawed, banish*: metaph., φιλοσοφίας Max.Tyr.32.2; τῆς σοφίας Philostr.*VA*4.30. III. *forbid by proclamation*, ἀποκεκήρυκται μὴ στρατεύειν X.*HG*5.2.27, cf. Thphr.*HP*4.4.5. IV. *manumit* by public renunciation of ownership, οἱ ἀποκαρυχθέντες ἐλεύθεροι, ἀπελεύθεροι, *IG*5(2).274,342*a* (Mantinea, i/ii A. D.).

ἀποκῐδᾰρόω, *take the* κίδαρις *off*, τὴν κεφαλήν Lxx *Le.*10.6, 21.10.

ἀποκίδνᾰμαι, *spread abroad from* a place, A.R.4.133, Arat.735, D.P.48.

ἀποκίκω, 3 pl. aor. ἀπέκιξαν, *dash to the ground*, Ar.*Ach.*869 (Boeot.).

ἀποκινδύν-ευσις [ῠ], εως, ἡ, *venturous attempt*, τύχης Th.7.67 codd. **-ευτέον**, *one must make a desperate venture*, τῇ βίᾳ τῶν σωμάτων Polyaen.1 *Praef.*4. **-εύω**, *make a desperate venture, try a forlorn hope*, πρός τινα *against* another, Th.7.81; οὐ τῶν εὐτυχούντων ἦν τὸ ἀ. Arist.*Fr.*159; ἀ. ἔν τινι *to make trial in* his case, *upon* him, X.*Mem.* 4.2.5, Aeschin.2.104; ἀ. πάσαις ταῖς δυνάμεσι D.H.3.52; ἀ. περὶ τῶν ὅλων Plu.*Alex.*17: c. acc. cogn., ἀ. τοῦτο *to make* this *venture*, Lys. 4.17: c. inf., ἀποκινδυνεύετον.. σοφόν τι λέγειν Ar.*Ra.*1108:—Pass., ἡμῖν.. ἀποκεκινδυνεύσεται τὰ χρήματα *will be put to the uttermost hazard*, Th.3.39. II. *shrink from the dangers of* another, *abandon* him *in danger*, τινός Philostr.*VA*7.15.

ἀποκῑνέω, *remove* or *put away from*, ἀποκινήσασκε τραπέζης Il.11. 636; μή μ' ἀποκινήσωσι θυράων Od.22.107; τῆς ὀδύνης Hp.*Morb.*2. 69. II. intr., *move off, abscond*, Aen.Tact.10.5, Polyaen.1.43.2.

ἀπόκῑνος, ὁ, (κινέω) *comic dance*, of an indecent nature, Cratin.120, Ar.*Fr.*275, Poll.4.101, Ath.14.629c: metaph., ἀπόκινον εὑρέ find *some way of dancing off* or *escaping*, Ar.*Eq.*20.

ἀποκιρνάομαι, *become unmixed*, κιρνᾶται πάντα καὶ ἀποκιρνᾶται Zos. Alch.p.110 B.

ἀποκιρσ-όομαι, Pass., *become varicose*, φλέβες ἀ. Archig.ap.Gal. 8.90. **-ωσις**, εως, ἡ, *formation of a varex*, Paul.Aeg.6.64.

ἀποκισσόομαι, Pass., *develop into* κισσός, of ἕλιξ, Thphr.*HP*3.18. 7. II. *to be deprived of the ivy-wreath*, *IG*3.80.

ἀπόκιστος, ον, gloss on ἀπέκτητος and ἄποκος, Hsch.

ἀποκλᾰδεύω, *lop off the branches*, Ph.Bybl.ap.Eus.*PE*1.10.

ἀπο-κλάζω (A), aor. -έκλαγξα, *ring* or *shout forth*, A.*Ag.*156 (lyr.), *AP*7.191 (Arch.).

ἀπ-οκλάζω (B), *bend one's knees*: hence, *rest*, Ar.*Fr.*109 (but cf. ἀποκλάω 2).

ἀποκλαίω, Att. -κλάω [ᾱ], fut. -κλαύσομαι: aor. -έκλαυσα:—*weep aloud*, Hdt.2.121.γ', etc.; ἀ. στόνον S.*Ph.*695 (lyr.). 2. ἀ. τινά or τι *bewail much, mourn deeply for*, Thgn.931, A.*Pr.*637; ἐμαυτόν Pl.*Phd.*117c:—Med., ἀποκλαύσασθαι κακά *bewail one's* woes, S.*OT* 1467; τὴν πενίαν Ar.*V.*564; τερπνὸν τὸ λέξαι κἀποκλαύσασθαι E.*Fr.* 563. II. Med., also, *cease to wail*, Luc.*Syr.D.*6.

ἀπόκλαξον, v. ἀποκλείω.

ἀπόκλᾱρος, ον, Dor. for ἀπόκληρος.

ἀπό-κλᾰσις, εως, ἡ, *breaking*, of a wave, *EM*8.41. **-κλασμα**, ατος, τό, *fracture near a joint*, Hp.*Off.*23. 2. *morsel* of bread, Alex.Trall.7.9.

ἀπόκλαυμα, ατος, τό, *loud wailing*, γραῶν Arr.*Epict.*2.16.39 (pl.).

ἀποκλάω, *break off*, τὸ κέρας Str.10.2.19: aor. 2 part. ἀποκλάς Anacr.17:—Med., *AP*7.506 (Leon.):—Pass., σὺν ἱστίῳ.. ἄρμεν' ἀποκλασθέντα Theoc.22.14. 2. *dress vines*, Ar.*Fr.*109 (unless from ἀπ-οκλάζω (B), q. v.). 3. dub. sens. in Hp.*Off.*14 (s. v. l.).

ἀποκλάω [ᾱ], v. sub ἀποκλαίω.

ἀπό-κλεισις or **-κλησις**, εως, ἡ, (ἀποκλείω) *a shutting up*, ἀ. μου τῶν πυλῶν *a shutting* the gates *against* me, Th.4.85. II. *a shutting out*, ἀποκλήσεις γίγνεσθαι (sc. ἔμελλον) there would be *a complete stoppage to their works*, Id.6.99. **-κλεισμα**, ατος, τό, *guard-house*, Lxx *Je.*36(29).26. **-κλεισμός**, ὁ, *exclusion*, Arr.*Epict.*4.7.20, Artem.3.54; but, *prison*, Aq.*Ps.*141(142).8. **-κλειστος**, ον, *shut off, enclosed*, Lxx 3*Ki.*6.21.

ἀποκλείω, fut. -κλείσω X.*An.*4.3.20: Ion. -ηίω: Att. -ῄω, fut. -κλῄσω Ar.*V.*775: Dor. aor. imper. -κλαξον Theoc.15.43:—*shut off from* or *out of*, τινὰ τῶν πυλέων Hdt.5.104; δωμάτων A.*Pr.*670; ἀ. τινά *shut* her *out*, Theoc.15.43,77; τινὰ τῇ κιγκλίδι Ar.*V.*775; τῇ θύρᾳ Id.*Ec.*420:—Med., ἀ. τινὰ τῆς διαβάσεως Th.6.101:—Pass., ἀ. τῆς διεξόδου [ὕδωρ] Hdt.3.117; τῆς ὀπίσω ὁδοῦ ib.55; τοῦ ἄστεος ib. 58; ἀ. τῶν πυλῶν Ar.*Lys.*423 codd.; τῆς θύρας Timocl.23; ὑπὸ τῆς ἵππου Hdt.9.50. 2. *shut out* or *exclude from*, τούτων Id.1.37, etc.; ἀ. τινὰ τῶν ὑπαρχόντων D.28.17; ἀπὸ τῶν ἀγαθῶν Ar.*V.*601; also ἀποκεκλῄκαμεν.. θεοὺς μηκέτι.. διαπερᾶν πόλιν Id.*Av.*1263:—Pass., ἀ. τοῦ σίτου, τῶν προσηκόντων, *turn away from* food, *have no appetite*, Hp.*Int.*1; τῶν σιτίων Id.*Vict.*3.81, cf. D.54.11; ἀ. τοῦ λόγου τυχεῖν Id.45.19; πρὸς τὰς ὁτουδήποτε ἀποκλείονται μεταδόσεις *refuse*, Phld.*Herc.*1251.17. II. c. acc. only, *shut up, close*, τὰς πύλας, τὰ ἱρά, Hdt.1.150, 2.133; τά.. πρὸς τὴν ἠῶ ἔχοντα τό τε Πήλιον ὄρος καὶ ἡ Ὄσσα ἀποκληΐει, of Thessaly, 7.129; ἀ. τὰς ἐφόδους τῶν ἐπιτηδείων X.*HG*2.4.3:—Pass., *to be closed*, ἀ. αἱ πύλαι Hdt.3.117; ἀ. ἡ Σκυθικὴ ὑπὸ Ἀγαθύρσων, i. e. *is bounded* by them, Id.4.100; of a road, Babr. 8.4. 2. *shut up*, as if in prison, δέμας S.*OT*1388, Ar.*V.*719; τὴν πόλιν ἀ. μοχλοῖς Id.*Lys.*487; ἀ. τινὰ ἔνδον D.59.41:—Pass., ἀποκλῄεσθαι ἐν δωματίῳ Lys.1.17. 3. *shut out*, ἀ. τὴν ὄψιν *intercept*, Hdt.4.7; ἀ. τὴν βλάστην τοῦ πτεροῦ *bar* its growth, Pl.*Phdr.*251d:—Pass., τὸ φῶς ἀποκέκλεισται Arist.*Pr.*904[b]18.

ἀποκλέπτω, fut. -ψω, *to steal away, run away with*, τι *h.Merc.*522:—Pass., aor. 2 ἀπεκλάπην, *to be robbed of*, τι interpol. in Artem.2.59.

ἀποκληΐω, v. -κλείω: later -κλήζω, *IG*3.900.

ἀπο-κληρόνομος, ον, = sq., *disinherited*, Arr.*Epict.*3.8.2, *BGU*326. 7 (ii A. D.), Just.*Nov.*2.3 *Intr.* **-κληρος**, Dor. -κλᾱρος, ον, *without lot* or *share of*, πόνων Pi.*P.*5.54; ἀχέων Emp.147. II. abs., *disinherited*, Arist.*Top.*112[b]19.

ἀποκληρ-όω, *choose by lot from* a number, Hdt.2.32; ἀ. ἕνα ἐκ δεκάδος Id.3.25; ἀπὸ πάντων τῶν λόχων Th.4.8: at Athens, *choose* or *elect by lot*, πρυτάνεις Id.8.70, cf. And.1.82; σιτοφύλακας ἀ. Lys.22. 16:—Pass., *to be so chosen*, D.25.27, *Marm.Par.*16: hence, *choose at random*, prob. in Phld.*Rh.*1.114 S.:—Med., much like Act., Ph.2. 508, Plu.2.826f. 2. *allot, assign by lot*, χώραν τινί Plu.*Caes.*51, cf. Hld.4.2:—Pass., *to be allotted, fall to* one's *share*, τινί Luc.*Merc. Cond.*32, Ph.2.577; *have allotted to one*, τι Ph.1.214. II. *eliminate by lot*, Arist.*Pol.*1298[b]26. **-ωσις**, εως, ἡ, *selection by lot*, δικαστῶν D.C.39.7; *choice by lot* or *chance, unreasoning choice*, Plu.2.1045f: hence, *absurdity, absence of reason*, in the phrase τίς ἡ ἀ. τοῦ..; what is there *unreasonable* in.., A.D.*Synt.*267.17, cf. Alex.Aphr. *de An.*22.25, S.E.*M.*8.351, Dam.*Pr.*34, al.; κατ' ἀποκλήρωσιν *without reason, at random, fortuitously*, Gal.1.135, al. **-ωτέον**, *one must decide by lot*, Arist.*Pol.*1318[b]1. **-ωτικός**, ή, όν, *choosing* or *acting by lot* or *chance, at random*, τὸ -κόν S.E.*P.*3.79; *absurd*, λόγος Phlp. *in Mete.*82.35, cf. Simp. *in Cael.*158.3, 161.21. II. *assigning, allotting*, δυνάμεις τοῦ κατ' ἀξίαν ἀ. Simp. *in Epict.*p.104 D.

ἀπόκλησις, ἀποκλῄω, v. ἀπόκλεισις, ἀποκλείω.

ἀπόκλητος, ον, (ἀποκαλέω) *called* or *chosen out, select*; οἱ Ἀπόκλητοι, in the Aetolian League, *members of the select council*, Plb.20.1.1, etc.

ἀπόκλῐμα, ατος, τό, *a slope*, *EM*374.35, Aristeas 59. II. Astrol., *cadent place*, preceding one of the four κέντρα, *Cat.Cod.Astr.* 1.100; opp. ἐπαναφορά (q. v.), S.E.*M.*5.14, Paul.Al.*P.*2, etc.

ἀποκλῐμάκωσις, εως, ἡ, *ladder*, *JHS*12.232 (Cilicia).

ἀπο-κλῑνής, ές, *on the decline*, Man.6.62. **-κλίνω** [ῑ], fut. -ῐνῶ:—Pass., aor. -εκλίθην, poet. -εκλίνθην Theoc.3.37:—*turn off* or *aside*, ὄνειρον Od.19.556; αὐγήν Sor.1.100; *turn back*, *h.Ven.*168: metaph., τὴν διάνοιαν Simp. *in Ph.*1164.39:—Pass. (cf. III. 1), *slope away*, of countries, τὰ πρὸς τὴν Γελῴαν ἀποκεκλιμένα D.S.13.89; of the day, *decline towards evening*, ἀποκλινομένης τῆς μεσαμβρίης, τῆς ἡμέρης, Hdt.3.104,114,4.181. **II.** Pass., *to be upset*, D.55.24, Plu.*Galb.* 27. **III.** more freq. intr. in Act., **1.** of countries, *slope*, ὡς πρὸς τὰς ἄρκτους Plb.3.47.2. **2.** *turn aside* or *off the road*, X.*An.* 2.2.16, Theoc.7.130: hence, τὸ πρὸς τὴν ἠῶ ἀποκλίνοντι *as one turns* to go eastward, Hdt.4.22. **3.** *slip off*, στέφανον -κλίνοντα τῆς κεφαλῆς Philostr.*Im.*1.14. **4.** with a bad sense, *fall away, decline*, S.*OT*1192 (lyr.); ἐπὶ τὸ ῥαθυμεῖν D.1.13; πρὸς θηριώδη φύσιν Pl.*Plt.* 309e: generally, *tend, incline*, πρὸς τὰς ἡδονάς Arist.*EN*1121^{b}10, cf. Pl.*R.*547e; ἀ. ὡς πρὸς τὴν δημοκρατίαν, πρὸς τὴν ὀλιγαρχίαν, Arist. *Pol.*1293^{b}35, 1307^{a}15; ἀ. εἴς τινα τέχνην Pl.*Lg.*847a; πρὸς τὸ κόσμιον ib.802e; *to be favourably disposed*, πρός τινα D.23.105. **5.** Astrol., of planets, *enter the* ἀπόκλιμα (q.v.), opp. ἐπίκεντρος εἶναι, Plot.2.3.1, cf. 3, Ptol.*Tetr.*115. **-κλῐσις**, εως, ἡ, *slope*, Cleom.1.1, Ph.1. 459. **II.** *turning off, decline*, of fortune, Plu.2.611a; of disease, Gal.7.424, Herod.Med. in *Rh.Mus.*58.98. **III.** *stooping, descent*, Plu.2.970d; of the sun, Id.*Aem.*17; of a ship, *rolling*, Id.*Pomp.*47 (pl.); of a crowd, *swaying to and fro*, Id.*Pyrrh.*33. **IV.** Astrol., *passing away from* a κέντρον, Vett.Val.57.14. **V.** *turning aside*, Corn.*Rh.*p.384 H. **-κλῐτέον**, *one must incline*, πρός τι Arist.*EN* 1165^{a}4. **-κλῐτος**, ον, *declining, waning*, Plu.2.273e.

ἀπο-κλύζω, *wash off*, [πίσσαν] εἰς οἶνον Erasistr.ap.Philum.*Ven.*17. 12: metaph., τὸν λόγον ἀ. τῆς ψυχῆς Plu.*Cic.*32; *wash clean*, σέρεις Diog.*Ep.*32.1; ἔρια *PHolm.*27.2; *rinse* the mouth, *Gp.*14.17.5:— Pass., Thphr.*HP*8.6.5, Arist.*Mu.*397^{a}34. **II.** in Med., D.S.4.51: metaph., ποτίμῳ λόγῳ ἁλμυρὰν ἀκοὴν ἀ. Pl.*Phdr.*243d: hence, *avert by purifications*, ὄνειρον Ar.*Ra.*1340. **-κλῠσις**, εως, ἡ, *washing off*, ἐπικλύσεις καὶ ἀ. flow and *ebb*, Them.*Or.*13.167b.

ἀπό-κλωμα· ἀπολογία ἐπὶ τὸ χεῖρον, Hsch. **-κλωνεῖ**· ἀποστροφεῖ (Tarent.), Id.

ἀποκμητέον, (ἀποκάμνω) *one must grow weary*, Pl.*R.*445b (Bekk. for ἀποκνητέον).

ἀπό-κναισις, εως, ἡ, *affliction, vexation*, Hsch. **-κναίω**, Att. **-κνάω**, inf. -κνᾶν dub. l. Pl.*Phlb.*26b: aor. -έκναισα Id.*R.*406b:— *scrape, rub off*, τι Antiph.245:—Med., Hsch. **II.** ἀ. τινά *wear* one *out, worry to death*, Ar.*Ec.*1087, Pl. ll. cc., f.l. in Thphr.*Char.*7.4; σύ μ' ἀποκναίεις περιπατῶν Men.341; ἀποκναίει γὰρ ἀηδίᾳ δήπου καὶ ἀναισθησίᾳ D.21.153, cf. D.H.*Dem.*20:—Pass., *to be worn out*, Pl.*R.* 406b; εἰσφοραῖς X.*HG*6.2.1.

ἀποκν-έω, *shrink from*, c. acc., τὸν κίνδυνον Th.3.20; τὸν πλοῦν Id.8.12; πρός τι Zos.5.40:—c. inf., *shrink from* doing, Th.4.11, Pl. *Phd.*84c, *Tht.*166b. **2.** abs., *shrink back, hesitate*, Th.3.55, 6.18, Pl.*Lg.*780d, etc. **-ησις**, εως, ἡ, *shrinking from*, στρατειῶν Th. 1.99; ἀ. πρὸς τοὺς πολιτικοὺς ἀγῶνας Plu.2.783b. **-ητέον**, Pl. *R.*349a, 372a, Isoc.8.62; οὐκ ἀ. τὸ φάναι μὴ συνιέναι Arist.*Top.* 160^{a}21.

ἀπο-κνίζω, fut. -ίσω, *nip* or *snip off*, τι Hp.*Steril.*214, Ar.*Ach.*869, Sotad.Com.1.23, Thphr.*HP*6.8.2; κηφῆνος πτερόν Arist.*HA*554^{b}5; ἀπό τινος D.S.2.4; τινός Plu.2.977b; *wring off*, κεφαλὴν Lxx *Le.*1.15; ἀ. τὰ ὄμματα, perh. f.l. for ἀπόκναισον, *Tab.Defix.Aud.*242.59 (Carthage, iii A.D.). **-κνῐσις**, εως, ἡ, *nipping off*, Thphr.*CP*5.9.11 (pl.). **-κνισμα**, ατος, τό, *that which is nipped off, a little bit*, Ar. *Pax*790.

ἀποκογχίζω, *draw out with a* κόγχη I.2, Dsc.1.30.

ἀποκοιμάομαι, Pass. with fut. Med. -ήσομαι:—*sleep away from home*, νύκτα -ηθείς Pl.*Lg.*762c; ἐν Λακεδαίμονι Eup.208. **II.** *get a little sleep*, esp. of troops on duty, Hdt.8.76, Ar.*V.*213, X.*Cyr.*2.4. 22 and 26, Plb.3.79.10; simply, *fall asleep*, Polyaen.8.23.1. **III.** *die an easy death*, Vett.Val.126.28.

ἀποκοιμίζω, *put to sleep*, Alciphr.1.39:—Pass., *go to sleep*: metaph., Socr.*Ep.*1.6.

ἀπο-κοιτέω, *sleep away from* one's post, Decr.ap.D.18.37, cf. *PPetr.*3 p.204 (iii B.C.). **-κοιτος**, ον, *sleeping away from*, τῶν συσσίτων Aeschin.2.127; οὐκ ἀ. παρὰ Ῥέας Luc.*DDeor.*10.2; μήτε ἀ. μηδ' ἀφήμερος ἀπὸ τῆς οἰκίας *BGU*1098.34 (i B.C.): abs., Men.*Inc.* 2.10. **2.** *separate from*, c. gen., ἀρουρῶν *BGU*915.14 (i/ii A.D.).

ἀποκολᾰκεύω· *eblandior*, *Gloss.*

ἀποκόλαστος, ον, *unpunished*, Zos.Alch.p.241 B.

ἀποκολλάω, *unglue, dissolve*, Gal.18(1).481 (Pass.): metaph., σῶμα διαλυόμενον ἤδη καὶ ἀποκολλώμενον, Eun.*Hist.*p.264 D.; *strip off*, τί τινος Eust.854.33.

ἀποκολοκύντωσις, εως, ἡ, (κολοκύνθη) *transformation into a pumpkin*, a travesty of the ἀποθέωσις of the Emperor Claudius, attributed to Seneca, D.C.60.35.

ἀποκολούω, *cut short off*, πόδας dub. in Hp.*Nat.Mul.*8, cf. Call. *Jov.*90 (tm.), *AB*435, Hsch. s.v. ἀποσκόλυπτε.

ἀποκολπόομαι, Pass., *form a bay*, Arist.*Mu.*393^{a}26.

ἀποκολυμβάω, *dive and swim away*, Th.4.25, D.C.49.1.

ἀποκομάω, *lose one's hair*, Luc.*Lex.*5.

ἀποκομ-ιδή, ἡ, *carrying away*, Plb.24.6.3. **II.** (from Pass.) *getting away* or *back, return*, Th.1.137. **-ίζω**, *carry away, escort*, X.*Cyr.*7.3.12; *carry away captive*, ἐς πόλιν Th.7.82:—Pass., *to be carried off*, οἴκαδε And.1.61, cf. D.54.9; *take oneself off, get away*, ἐς τὴν Ἠιόνα Th.5.10; ἐπ' οἴκου Id.4.96. **II.** *carry back*, A.R.4. 1106:—Pass., ὀπίσω ἀ. *return*, Hdt.5.27. **-ιστής**, οῦ, ὁ, *one who leads away*, Sch.E.*Andr.*1268: pl., ib.*Hec.*222. **II.** *messenger, bearer* of a letter, *Cat.Cod.Astr.*2.193. **-ιστικός**· *ablativus*, *Gloss.*

ἀπόκομμα, ατος, τό, *splinter, chip*, πέτρας ἀπόκομμ' ἀτεράμνου (of a man) Theoc.10.7; ἀ. τῶν τοῦ χαλκοῦ πετάλων *PHolm.*1.40; ἀ. ἀραχνίου *shred*, Luc.*VH*1.18; *block* of wood, of an idol, Aq.*Ez.*20.7; of stone, πώρων ἀ. *IG*11.158*A* 32 (Delos, iii B.C., pl.).

ἀποκομπάζω, of lyre strings, *break with a snap*, *AP*6.54 (Paul. Sil.); *declare blatantly*, Simp.*in Ph.*1143.8.

ἀποκονδῠλόομαι, *become condylomatous*, Paul.Aeg.3.75.

ἀποκονίω [ῑ], said to be an Aetol. word for *kick up the dust*, i.e. *run*, dub. in Hygin.*Astr.*3.11.

ἀποκοντόω, (κοντός) *thrust away* or *out*, τὰ ὀπίσω Procop.*Arc.*9.

ἀπο-κοπέομαι, = ἀποκόπτομαι III, Hsch. **-κοπή**, ἡ, (ἀποκόπτω) *cutting off*, κρατός A.*Supp.*841, cf. Hp.*Mochl.*34; *lopping off* a shoot *for grafting*, M.Ant.11.8: Medic., *amputation*, Archig.ap. Orib.47.13.3; *stoppage*, ἐμμήνων Sor.1.26. **2.** πεδίων ἀ., prob. their *abrupt terminations*, Plu.*Phil.*4, cf. *Gp.*12.41.1. **3.** φωνῆς ἀ. *loss* of voice, Dsc.2.120, cf. Gal.13.31. **II.** ἀποκοπαὶ χρεῶν *cancelling* of all debts, And.1.88, Pl.*R.*566a, Jusj.ap.D.24.149, etc. **III.** *abruptness*, esp. of literary style, Demetr.*Eloc.*238; ἀ. ῥυθμοῦ *broken* rhythm, ib.6; ἐξ ἀποκοπῆς *abruptly*, D.H.*Th.*52; also of disease, ἐξ ἀ. λυθῆναι to be *suddenly* cured, Gal.7.441. **IV.** *section, extract*, λόγου Tryph.*Trop.*7. **V.** in Gramm., *apocope, cutting off of* one or more letters, esp. at the end of a word, Arist.*Po.*1458^{b}2 (pl.), cf. A.D.*Synt.*6.11; κατ' ἀποκοπήν Str.8.5.3; also of elliptical expressions, such as νὴ τόν, Ph.2.271. **-κοπος**, ον, *castrated*, Str.13.4. 14, Vett.Val.113.28; τὸ ἀ. *castration*, Ph.2.264. **II.** *abrupt, precipitous*, ὄρη *Peripl.M.Rubr.*32.

ἀποκοπρόομαι, *turn into excrement*, Anon.Lond.25.41.

ἀπο-κοπτέον, *one must hew off*, χεῖρα Ph.1.668, cf. Paul.Aeg.6. 74. **-κοπτικός**, ή, όν, *fit for cutting off*, Procl.*in R.*2.182, 296 K. **-κοπτός**, ή, όν, *severed from others, special*, νίκη Eust. 1468.3. **-κόπτω**, *cut off, hew off*, freq. in Hom., of men's limbs, κάρη ἀπέκοψε Il.11.261; ἀπό τ' αὐχένα κόψας ib.146, al.; in Prose, χεῖρας ἀ. Hdt.6.91, etc.; ἀγκύρας X.*HG*1.6.21; γεφύρας Plu.*Nic.*26; *amputate*, Archig.ap.Orib.47.13.2; νηῶν ἀποκόψειν ἄκρα κόρυμβα Il.9.241; ἀπὸ πείσματ' ἔκοψα νεός Od.10.127; ἀΐξας ἀπέκοψε παρήορον he *cut loose* the trace-horse, Il.16.474:—Pass., ἀποκεκόψονται, of buds, *will be cut off*, Ar.*Nu.*1125, cf. M.Ant.11.8; ἀ. τὴν χεῖρα *have it cut off*, Hdt.6.114; ἀ. τὰ γεννητικά, of eunuchs, Ph.1.89: abs., ἀποκεκομμένος *eunuch*, Lxx *De.*23.1, cf. Luc.*Eun.*8:—Med., *make oneself a eunuch*, *Ep.Gal.*5.12, cf. Arr.*Epict.*2.20.19. **2.** metaph., ἀπ' ἐλπίδα φημὶ κεκόφθαι ναυτιλίης νόστου τε A.R.4.1272, cf. Plb.3.63.8; ἔλεον D.S.13.23; ἀ. τὸ ἀμφίβολον τῆς γνώμης *decide summarily*, Alciphr.1.8; also ἀποκοπῆναι τῆς ἐλπίδος Plu.*Pyrrh.*2; διὰ τὸ μὴ ἀποκόπτειν τὴν πολυχρόνιον ζωήν *exclude from the reckoning, despair of*, Phld.*Herc.*1251.22; *reject, exclude*, Id.*Sign.*7, *D.*3.13:—Med., dub. in Id.*Mort.*23. **3.** esp. of voice or breath, *cut short*, τὸν τοῦ πνεύματος τόνον D.H.*Comp.*14, cf. 22:—Pass., ἀποκέκοπταί τινι ἡ φωνή Plu.*Dem.*25, cf. Dsc.*Eup.*1.85. **4.** of literary periods or phrases, *bring to an abrupt close*, δεῖ τῇ μακρᾷ -κόπτεσθαι Arist.*Rh.* 1409^{a}19, cf. Demetr.*Eloc.*18,238. **5.** Gramm., in Pass., *to be cut short by* ἀποκοπή (q.v.), Eust.487.10, *EM*609.54. **6.** *abstract* an idea or word from its context, τὸ "ἀγαθὸς" ἀποκοπέν Anon.*in SE*57. 31. **II.** ἀ. τινὰ ἀπὸ τόπου *beat off from* a strong place, of soldiers, X.*An.*3.4.39, 4.2.10. **III.** Med., *smite the breast in mourning*: c. acc., *mourn for*, νεκρόν E.*Tr.*628.

ἀποκορέννυμι, *make quite satisfied*, *Gloss.*

ἀποκορέω, *wipe off*, Hsch.

ἀποκορσόομαι, Med., (κόρση) = ἀποκείρομαι, A.*Fr.*248.

ἀποκορῠφ-όω, *bring to a point*, Plb.3.49.6:—Pass., *rise to a head*, εἰς ὀξὺ Hp.*Prog.*7; *run to a point*, φλὸξ ἀ. Thphr.*Ign.*53: metaph., *culminate*, εἰς ἓν -κορυφοῦται ἡ νόησις Dam.*Pr.*213. **2.** metaph., ἀπεκορύφου σφι τάδε *gave* them this *summary answer*, Hdt.5.73; *cause to culminate*, διδασκαλίαν εἰς θεολογίαν Simp.*in Ph.*1359.8, cf. *in Cael.*126.3. **-ωσις**, εως, ἡ, *concentration*, εἰς ἓν Prisc.Lyd.22.3.

ἄποκος, ον, *without nap*, *An.Ox.*2.238; *not shorn*, Suid.

ἀποκοσμέω, *restore order by clearing away, clear away*, ἀπεκόσμεον ἔντεα δαιτὸς Od.7.232; *dismantle*, ἡρῷον *IG*3.1423; *deform*, ἀμπέλους Corn.*ND*30; πόλιν Lib.*Or.*30.23; τὸ βασίλειον τῆς πρώτης εὐδαιμονίας J.*AJ*16.8.5, cf. Longus 4.7:—Pass., *to be disfigured*, D.C.*Fr.* 102.9:—Med., *put off one's ornaments*, Paus.7.26.9:—Pass., *to be stripped of them*, Aristid.*Or.*43(25).39. **II.** *remove from the world, kill*, Lxx *2Ma.*4.38.

ἀποκοττᾰβ-ίζω, *dash out the last drops of wine*, as in playing at the cottabus, X.*HG*2.3.56, cf. Ath.15.665e. **2.** metaph., *vomit*, Herod.Med.ap.Orib.10.8.12. **-ισμός**, ὁ, *dashing out the last drops*, Ath.15.666a, cf. 667c (pl.). **2.** *vomit*, Herod.Med.ap.Orib.5.27.9.

ἀποκουφίζω, *lighten, set free from*, τινὰ κακῶν, παθέων, E.*Or.*1341, *Hec.*104 (lyr.), cf. *AP*9.372; *relieve*, Plu.*Cleom.*18; *lighten* a cargo, Str.5.3.5 (Pass.).

ἀποκόψιμος, *that can be cut off*, *Gloss.*

ἀπόκοψις, εως, ἡ, *cutting off*, ὀστέων Hp.*Art.*68.

ἀπο-κρᾰδίζω, (κράδη) *pluck from the fig-tree*, ἐρινούς Nic.*Al.* 319. **-κράδιος** [ρᾰ], ον, *plucked from the fig-tree*, *AP*6.300 (Leon.).

ἀποκράζω, *cry out under, complain of*, βίαν Simp.*in Epict.*p.132 D.

ἀποκραιπᾰλ-άω, *sleep off a debauch*, Plu.*Ant.*30. **II.** *waste in debauch*, Theognet.2. **-ίζομαι**, = foreg., Suid. **-ισμός**, ὁ, *sleeping off a debauch*, Hsch.

ἀποκρᾱνίζω, *strike off from the head*, κέρας *AP*6.255 (Eryc.). **II.** *cut off the head*, Eust.1850.30.

ἀποκρᾰτέω, *exceed all others*, ὁ Νεῖλος πλήθεϊ [ὕδατος] ἀ. Hdt.4.50, cf. 75. II. trans., *control, remedy*, ἐντεροκήλας Dsc.4.9. 2. *withhold, retain*, τροφήν Plu.2.494d; *keep one's hands from*, ξιφῶν J.*BJ*4.5.4. 3. *retain* in memory, c. gen., μαθημάτων Sor.1.3.

ἀπόκρᾰτος, ον, *without strength, exhausted*, Ph.1.209.

ἀπο-κρεμάζω, = ἀποκρεμάννυμι, Suid. s. v. Ὑπέρβολον. **-κρέμᾰμαι**, Pass., *hang down from, hang on by*, Arist.*HA*553^{b}3; τὰ ἀποκρεμάμενα *appendages*, ib.620^{b}14; impf. ἀπεκρεμάμην Q.S.11.197; aor. ἀπεκρεμάσθην Luc.*DDeor*.21.1; ἀποκρεμάμενος τὴν ῥῖνα *hook-nosed*, Philostr.*Her*.3.3. **-κρεμάννῡμι**, fut. -κρεμάσω, Att. -κρεμῶ:—*let hang down*, αὐχέν' ἀπεκρέμασεν, of a dying bird, Il.23.879; χορδὰν πλῆκτρον ἀπεκρέμασε the plectrum *broke* the string *so that it hung down*, *AP*9.584; ἡ προβολὴ τῶν χειρῶν ἀ. τὸ σῶμα *renders unsteady*, Philostr.*Gym*.34; ἰσχύν *relax*, ib.53:—Pass., *hang down*, Arist.*Pr*.948^{b}4; *break forth from*, πηγὰς -υμένας τῶν ὀρῶν Philostr.*VA*6.26: metaph., *become detached*, γνώμη μὴ -ύσθω οὗ ζητεῖ Id.*VS*2.9.2; οὐσίαι ἀποκεκρεμασμέναι τῶν οἰκείων ἐνάδων Dam.*Pr*.213. II. *hang up, suspend*, τὸν φαρετρεῶνα Hdt.1.216. **-κρέμᾰσις**, εως, ἡ, *hanging down*, Aët.3.7. **-κρέμασμα**, ατος, τό, = foreg., αὐχένος Eust.1334.2. **-κρεμαστός**, ή, όν, *hanging from* a thing, Epigr.ap. Philostr.*Her*.19.17 (tm.). **-κρεμάω**, = ἀποκρεμάννυμι, Arist.*HA*540^{b}26, Luc.*Asin*.30. **-κρεμής**, ές, *hanging down*, Ruf.*Onom*.101, Eust.1587.20.

ἀποκρήμνημι, = ἀποκρεμάννυμι, Sor.1.71, Diog.*Ep*.30.3.

ἀπο-κρημνίζω, *throw from a cliff's edge*, Hld.2.8. **-κρημνος**, ον, *sheer, precipitous*, ὄρος ἄβατον καὶ ἀ. Hdt.7.176, cf. 3.111; χῶρος ἀ. Id.8.53, cf. Th.4.31, etc.: Sup., Diog.*Ep*.37.4: metaph. of an advocate's case, *full of difficulties*, πάντα ἀ. ὁρῶ D.25.76. **-κρημνόω**, *walk over a precipice*, David *Proll*.148.26.

ἀπο-κρῐδόν, Adv., (ἀποκρίνω) *apart from*, c. gen., A.R.2.15: abs., Opp.*H*.1.548, cf. *IG*3.1416*a*:—also **-κριδά**, Hdn.Gr.1.496.

ἀπόκρῐμα, ατος, τό, *judicial sentence, condemnation* (= κατάκριμα, Hsch.), τὸ ἀ. τοῦ θανάτου 2*Ep.Cor*.1.9. 2. (from Med.) *answer*, δοῦναί τισι Plb.12.26^b.1; esp. of the *answers* given by Emperors to *legationes*, ὁ ἐπὶ τῶν Ἑλληνικῶν ἀ. *SIG*804.5 (Cos, i A.D.); ἐπὶ τῶν ἐπιστολῶν καὶ πρεσβειῶν καὶ ἀ. Suid. s.v. Διονύσιος, cf. *IG*12(1).24 (Rhodes, i A.D., pl.), J.*AJ*14.10.6; also of a proconsul of Asia, *OGI*494.18 (Milet., ii A.D.). b. *rescript*, θεοῦ Ἁδριανοῦ *PTeb*.286.1 (ii A.D.).

ἀποκρίνω [ῑ], fut. -κρῐνῶ, *separate, set apart*, prob. in Alc.*Supp*.5.7, Pherecr.23, Ael.*VH*12.8; χωρὶς ἀ. Pl.*Plt*.302c, al.:—Pass., *to be parted* or *separated*, ἀποκρινθέντε *parted from the throng* (of two πρόμαχοι), Il.5.12 (nowhere else in Hom.); πίθηκος ᾔει θηρίων ἀποκριθεὶς Archil.89.3; of the elements in cosmogony, Emp.9.4, Anaxag.2, Democr.167; ἀπεκρίθη..τοῦ βαρβάρου ἔθνεος τὸ Ἑλληνικόν Hdt.1.60; χωρὶς θηρίων ἡ δίαιτα ἀποκέκριται Id.2.36; ἀποκεκρίσθαι εἰς ἓν ὄνομα *to be separated and brought* under one name, Th.1.3; οὐ βεβαίως ἀπεκρίθησαν, of combatants, *separated* without decisive result, Id.4.72. 2. Medic. in Pass., *to be distinctly formed*, Hp.*Prog*.23; of the embryo, Arist.*HA*561^{a}17; τὰ ἐν τῷ σώματι -όμενα bodily *secretions*, Hp.*VM*14; τὰ ἐς τὴν κοιλίην ἀ. Id.*Vict*.4.89; but ἐς τοῦτο πάντα ἀπεκρίθη all illnesses *determined* or *ended* in this *alone*, Th.2.49; also ᾗ τὰ περιττώματα ἀποκρίνεται *are voided*, Arist.*PA*665^{b}24, cf. *GA*773^{b}35. 3. *mark by a distinctive form, distinguish*, πρύμνην Hdt.1.194; νόσημά τι ἀποκεκριμένον *specific*, Pl.*R*.407d, cf. Arist.*Mete*.369^{b}29. II. *choose*, ἕνα ὑμέων ἀ. ἐξαίρετον Hdt.6.130; ἀ. τοῦ πεζοῦ, τοῦ στρατοῦ, *choose from*.., Hdt.3.17,25; δυοῖν ἀποκρίνας κακοῖν *having set apart*, i.e. *decreed*, one of two, S.*OT*640. 2. *exclude*, πλήθει τῶν ψήφων Pl.*Lg*.946a. III. *reject on examination*, κρίνειν καὶ ἀ. ib.751d; ἐγκρίνειν καὶ ἀ. ib.936a; ἀ. τινὰ τῆς νίκης *decide* that one *has lost* the victory, *decide* it *against* one, Arist.*Pol*.1315^{b}18:—Med., Pl.*Lg*.966d. IV. Med., ἀποκρίνομαι, fut. -κρῐνοῦμαι, etc.: Pl. uses pf. and plpf. Pass. in med. sense, *Prt*.358a, *Grg*.463c, etc., but also in pass. sense (v. infr.):—*give answer to, reply to* a question, dub. l. in Hdt.5.49, 8.101 (elsewh. ὑποκρ-), cf. E.*Ba*.1271, *IA*1354; ἀ. τινί Ar.*Nu*.1245, etc.: metaph., ἀ. τοῖς πράγμασιν ὡς ἐπὶ τῶν ἐρωτημάτων Arr.*Epict*.2.16.2; ἀ. πρός τινα, πρὸς τὸ ἐρωτώμενον, *to* a questioner or question, Th.5.42, Pl.*Prt*.338d; ἀ. εἰ.. Ar.*V*.964; ἀ. ὅτι.. Th.1.90: c. acc., ἀποκρίνεσθαι τὸ ἐρωτηθὲν *to answer* the question, Id.3.61, cf. Pl.*Cri*.49a, *Hp.Ma*.287b, Arist.*Metaph*.1007^{a}9: c. acc. cogn., ἀ. οὐδὲ γρῦ Ar.*Pl*.17; οὐδὲν ξυμβατικόν Th.8.71; ἀ. ἀπόκρισιν Pl.*Lg*.658c:—Pass., τοῦτό μοι ἀποκεκρίσθω *let* this *be* my *answer*, Id.*Tht*.187b; καλῶς ἄν σοι ἀπεκέκριτο your *answer would have been* sufficient, Id.*Grg*.453d, cf. *Men*.75c, *Euthd*.299d. 2. *answer charges, defend oneself*, Ar.*Ach*.632; ὁ ἀποκρινόμενος *the defendant*, Antipho 6.18, cf. 2.4.3; ἀπεκρινάμην freq. in legal documents, *PHib*.1.31.24 (iii B.C.), etc. 3. aor. Pass. ἀπεκρίθη, = ἀπεκρίνατο, he *answered*, condemned by Phryn.86, is unknown in earlier Att., exc. in Pherecr.51, Pl.*Alc*.2.149b; but occurs in Macho ap.Ath.8.349d, *UPZ*6.30 (ii B.C.), *SIG*674.61 (Narthacium, ii B.C.), *IG*4.679 (Hermione, ii B.C.), Plb.4.30.7, etc.; once in J., *AJ*9.3.1, twice in Luc., *Sol*.5, *Demon*.26; regular in Lxx (but sts. ἀπεκρινάμην in solemn language, as 3*Ki*.2.1) and prevails in *NT* esp. in the phrase ἀποκριθεὶς εἶπεν *Ev.Matt*.3.15; ἀ. λέγει *Ev.Marc*.8.29, al., cf. X.*An*.2.1.22 codd.: fut. ἀποκριθήσομαι in same sense, Lxx*Is*.14.32, al., *Ev.Matt*.25.45, Hermog.*Inv*.4.6.

ἀπο-κρῐσιάριος, ὁ, *secretary*, *POxy*.144.15 (vi A.D.). **-κρῐσις**, εως, ἡ, *separation*, Anaxag.4; κάθαρσις ἀ. χειρόνων ἀπὸ βελτιόνων Pl.*Def*.415d. 2. Medic., *excretion* or *secretion*, γονῆς Hp.*Genit*.2, σιτίων *Vict*.4.93, cf. Arist.*HA*582^{a}4, *Pr*.878^{a}23, etc.; ἀ. σπερματική, περιττωματική, *PA*681^{b}35; σπέρματος Epicur.*Nat.Herc*.908.3. 3. ἀ. νοσηρή *exhalation, miasma*, Hp.*Nat.Hom*.9. II. (from Med.) *decision, answer*, first in Thgn.1167, cf. Hdt.1.49, 5.50 codd. (ὑπόκρισις edd.), Hp.*Decent*.3, *Steril*.213, E.*Fr*.977; ἀ. πρὸς τὸ ἐρώτημα Th.3.60, cf. X.*Hier*.1.35. 2. *defence*, Antipho 5.65. 3. *rescript*, Procop.*Pers*.2.23; = *responsum*, *Gloss*. 4. *embassy, commission*, Chor. in *Rev.Phil*.1.79. III. a kind of *dance*, Hsch. **-κρῐτέον**, *one must reject*, opp. ἐγκριτέον, Pl.*R*.377c, 413d, cf. Lib.*Or*.25.53. II. *one must answer*, Pl.*Prt*.351d, *Alc*.1.114e, etc. **-κρῐτικός**, ή, όν, *secretory*, δύναμις τῶν περιττωμάτων ἀ. Gal.8.9; ἀ. δύναμις faculty *of ejection*, Olymp. *in Mete*.201.7; *separative*, Simp. *in Ph*.1190.22. II. *proper to answers*, Theon *Prog*.5. **-κρῐτος**, ον, *separated, chosen*, Inscr. in Sauciuc *Andros* 130, Opp.*H*.3.266.

ἀποκροτ-έω, *snap the fingers*, Str.14.5.9. II. *dash against the ground*, χαμαί Babr.119.4. **-ημα**, ατος, τό, *snap of the finger*, Aristobul.6.

ἀπόκροτος, ον, *beaten* or *trodden hard*, γῆ, χωρίον, Th.7.27, X.*Eq*.7.15, cf. Hero *Aut*.2.1: generally, *hard*, χηλαὶ καὶ ὁπλαί Plu.2.98d: Medic., ἀρτηρία Gal.19.405; πῶρος ib.442: metaph., ψυχὴ λιθίνη καὶ ἀ. Ph.2.165, cf. Ptol.*Tetr*.155. Adv. -τως *without fail*, *PGrenf*.2.89.3 (vi A.D.), etc.; cf. Hsch. s. v. διακρότως. II. of style, *sonorous*, Anon. *in Rh*.191.20, 225.11.

ἀποκρουνίζω, *spout, gush out*, Plu.2.699d.

ἀπό-κρουσις, εως, ἡ, (ἀποκρούομαι Pass.) *retiring, waning*, τῆς σελήνης Colum.2.10.10, Alex.Trall.8.2, *PMag.Leid.V*.11.28, Horap.1.4, etc. **-κρουστέον**, *one must repel*, Them.*Or*.22.278a. **-κρουστικός**, ή, όν, *able to drive off, dispel*, Dsc.1.116; δυνάμεις Gal.1.396; *repulsive*, D.L.2.87. 2. *waning*, ἀ. σελήνη Ptol.*Tetr*.149, cf. Paul.Al.*G*.4; δέλτος ἀ. πρὸς σελήνην *PMag.Par*.1.2241.

ἀπόκρουστος, ον, *beaten back*, Nic.*Th*.270.

ἀποκρούω, *beat off, drive away, from* a place or person, X.*HG*5.3.22, *AP*11.351 (Pall.); ὕπνον, νόσον, Porph.*Abst*.1.27,53:—more freq. in Med., *beat off from oneself*, τὰς προσβολάς Hdt.4.200, Th.2.4; αὐτοὺς ἐπιόντας Hdt.8.61, etc.; generally, *repel*, opp. ἐπισπᾶσθαι, S.E.*M*.7.400; *shake off*, Plot.4.7.10, Hierocl. *in CA*19 p.461 M.; τινάς Jul.*Or*.2.67b; ἀλληλοφαγίας τοὺς ἀνθρώπους Porph.*Abst*.1.23; *refute* an opponent, D.H.*Comp*.25; κατηγορίαν Chor. in *Rev.Phil*.1.245:—Pass., *to be beaten off*, of an assault, Th.4.107, etc.; ἀποκρουσθέντες τῆς πείρας Id.8.100, cf. X.*HG*6.4.5; ἀ. τῆς μηχανῆς dub. in Plb.21.28; τῆς Ἰβηρίας Plu.*Sert*.7, etc. II. *knock off*, *IG*3.1417.12:—Pass., κοτυλίσκιον τὸ χεῖλος ἀποκεκρουμένον a cup *with* the lip *knocked off*, Ar.*Ach*.459. III. Pass., also, *to be thrown from horseback*, X.*Eq.Mag*.3.14; *to be stranded*, πρὸς χωρίον λιμνῶδες ἀπεκρούσθη Gal.2.221.

ἀποκρῠβή, ἡ, *concealment*, Lxx*Jb*.24.15, Aq.*Is*.16.4, *Cat.Cod.Astr*.2.161, Eust.974.45.

ἀποκρύβω, = ἀποκρύπτω, v.l. in D.S.3.25.

ἀποκρύπτω, used by Hom. only in aor. 1, Ep. impf. ἀποκρύπτασκε Hes.*Th*.157:—Pass., aor. -εκρύβην [ῠ] Lxx*Jb*.3.23: fut. -κρῠβήσομαι ib.*Ps*.18(19).6, Gal.*UP*10.12:—Med., aor. 2 -εκρυβόμην Apollod.3.2.1:—*hide from, keep hidden from*, c. acc. et gen., αἲ γάρ μιν θανάτοιο.. δυναίμην νόσφιν ἀποκρύψαι Il.18.465: c. dat. pers., ἀπέκρυψεν δέ μοι ἵππους 11.718: c. dupl. acc., *hide* or *keep back from* one, οὔτε σε ἀποκρύψω τὴν ἐμὴν οὐσίαν Hdt.7.28; τι ἀπό τινος Lxx 4*Ki*.4.27:—Med., ἀποκρύπτεσθαί τινά τι Pl.*Lg*.702c, X.*Mem*.2.6.29, etc.; ἀ. τι *keep* it *back*, Pl.*Prt*.348e, cf. 327a: c. acc. pers., X.*Cyr*.8.7.23, *Smp*.1.6. 2. *hide from sight, keep hidden, conceal*, Od.17.286, etc.; ἔθηκε νύκτ' ἀποκρύψας φάος Archil.74.3; τὸν ἥλιον ὑπὸ τοῦ πλήθεος τῶν ὀϊστῶν ἀ. Hdt.7.226; ἀποκρύψει φάος νύξ A.*Pr*.24; χιὼν ἀ. τι X.*An*.4.4.11; ἀ. τὴν σοφίαν Pl.*Ap*.22e; ἀ. τὴν οὐσίαν ἐν ταῖς οἰκίαις Isoc.1.42; εἰς τὸ ἄδηλον -κρύπτων X.*Eq.Mag*.5.7:—Med., Ar.*Eq*.424,483; ἀ. ἑαυτὸν *efface* oneself, Pl.*R*.393c: c. inf., ἀποκρύπτεσθαί τι μὴ καθ' ἡδονὴν ποιεῖν *to conceal* one's doing, Th.2.53; περὶ ὧν ἀποκρυπτόμεθα μηδένα εἰδέναι Lys.7.18; pf. Pass. in med. sense, οὐκ ἀποκέκρυπται τὴν οὐσίαν D.28.3: abs., ἀποκρύψασθαι πρός τινα Isoc.11.2:—Pass., τὸν Ἑλλήσποντον ὑπὸ τῶν νεῶν ἀποκεκρυμμένον Hdt.7.45; τοὺς ἀποκρυπτομένους those who *withdraw from public*, Alex.265. 3. *obscure*, E.*Fr*.153, Arist.*Po*.1460^{b}4, Alcid.*Soph*.30, Lib.*Or*.63.26, Jul.*Or*.1.44c. II. ἀ. γῆν *lose from sight*, of ships running out to sea, opp. ἀνοίγνυμι 1.3, φεύγειν εἰς τὸ πέλαγος.. ἀποκρύψαντα γῆν Pl.*Prt*.338a, cf. Lib.*Or*.59.147; ἐπειδὴ ἀπεκρύψαμεν αὐτούς when we *got out of sight of* them, Luc.*VH*2.38, cf. Th.5.65 (sc. αὐτούς); τὴν θάλατταν (i.e. by marching inland) Aristid.1.473 J.; ἀποκρύπτουσι Πελειάδες (sc. ἑαυτούς) *disappear*, Hes.*Fr*.179; ἄστερες ἄμφι σελάνναν ἀ. εἶδος Sapph.3; but also Pass. of ships, Hero *Aut*.22.5.

ἀποκρυσταλλόομαι, Pass., *become all ice*, Sch.Il.23.281.

ἀποκρῠφή, ἡ, *hiding-place*, Lxx*Jb*.22.14, al.

ἀπόκρῠφος, ον, *hidden, concealed*, E.*HF*1070 (lyr.); ἐν ἀποκρύφῳ in *secret*, Hdt.2.35; ἀ. θησαυροὶ *hidden, stored up*, *Ep.Col*.2.3; *underhand*, μηδὲν ἀ. πεποιῆσθαι *Vit.Philonid*.p.2 C. 2. c. gen., ἀπόκρυφον πατρός *unknown to* him, X.*Smp*.8.11. II. *obscure, recondite, hard to understand*, Id.*Mem*.3.5.14; γράμματα Call.*Fr*.242; ἀ. σύμβολα δέλτων, of hieroglyphics, *Hymn.Is*.10; στήλη *PMag.Par*.1.1115; [βίβλος] *PMag.Leid.W*.25.14; -κρύφων μύσται Vett.Val.7.30; ἀ. αἰτία Procl. *in Ti*.1.53 D., cf. eund. *in Prm*.p.549 S. III. Adv. -φως *secretly*, Aq.*Hb*.3.14, Vett.Val.301.5.

ἀπόκρυψις, εως, ἡ, *disappearance*, ἀ. ποιεῖσθαι Arist.*Cael*.294^{a}2.

ἀποκτάμεν, -κτάμεναι, -κτάμενος, v. ἀποκτείνω.

ἀποκτάομαι, *lose possession of, alienate*, Hsch. **II.** metaph., *clear out of the way, refute*, Gal.1.132.

ἀποκτείνῦμι or **-κτίννῦμι** (the former is the more correct spelling, cf. best codd. in Pl.*Grg.*469a, Plb.2.56.15, etc., Hdn.Gr.2.539), = sq., Crates Com.17, Lys.12.7, Pl. l. c., X.*An.*6.3.5, D.20.158, etc.: —also **-κτιννύω**, X.*HG*4.4.2, 5.2.43, etc.

ἀποκτείνω (later -κτέννω (q.v.): -κταίνω 2*Ep.Cor.*3.6, etc.), fut. -κτενῶ, Ion. -κτενέω Hdt.3.30: aor. 1 ἀπέκτεινα Il.: pf. ἀπέκτονα Isoc.12.66, Pl.*Ap.*38c, X.*Ap.*29, D.22.2; plpf. 3 pl. -εκτόνεσαν Id. 19.148, Ion. 3 sg. -εκτόνεε Hdt.5.67; later ἀπεκτόνηκα Arist.*SE* 182^{b}19, Parth.24.2, Plu.*Tim.*16; also ἀπέκταγκα Men.344, Arist. *Pol.*1324^{b}16,18, Lxx 1*Ki.*24.12, etc.; ἀπέκτᾰκα Plb.11.18.10: aor. 2 -έκτᾰνον Il., poet. 1 pl. ἀπέκταμεν Od.23.121, inf. -κτάμεναι, -κτάμεν, Il.20.165, 5.675:—**Pass.**, late (ἀποθνήσκω being used as the Pass. by correct writers), pres. in Palaeph.7: aor. ἀπεκτάνθην D.C.65.4, Lxx 1*Ma.*2.9: aor. 2 inf. ἀποκτανῆναι Gal.14.284: pf. inf. ἀπεκτάνθαι Plb.7.7.4, Lxx 2*Ma.*4.36:—but aor. Med. in pass. sense ἀπέκτατο Il. 15.437, 17.472; part. ἀποκτάμενος 4.494, etc.; cf. ἀποκτείννυμι:—stronger form of κτείνω, *kill, slay*, Ep., Ion., and the prevailing form in Att. (cf. ἀποθνήσκω): once in A.*Ag.*1250, never in S., freq. in E., *Hec.*1244, al. **2.** of judges, *condemn to death*, Antipho 5.92, Pl.*Ap.*30d sq., etc.; also of the accuser, And.4.37, X.*HG*2.3.21, Th.6.61; *put to death*, Hdt.6.4: generally of the law, Pl.*Prt.* 325b. **3.** metaph., τὸ σεμνὸν ὥς μ' ἀ. τὸ σόν E.*Hipp.*1064; σὺ μή μ' ἀπόκτειν' Id.*Or.*1027.

ἀποκτενείω, Desiderat. of ἀποκτείνω, dub. in Lib.*Narr.*18.

ἀποκτέννω, later form for ἀποκτείνω, Plb.1.69.11, *AP*.11.395 (Nicarch.), Lxx *To.*6.13.

ἀπόκτησις, εως, ἡ, *deed of gift*, *PGrenf.*2.70.26 (iii A.D.). **2.** *loss*, θάνατος ἀ. βίου Secund.*Sent.*19, cf. Paul.Al.*N.*4.

ἀπόκτῐσις, εως, ἡ, *planting of a colony*, Call.*Ap.*74, D.H.1.49.

ἀποκτῠπέω, *sound loudly from*, τῆς γλώττης Philostr.*VS*1.25.7; *make a noise by striking*, μάστιξι Suid. s. v. τύμπανα, cf. *AB*208.

ἀποκῠᾰμεύω, *select by lot*, ταμίας *IG*1.32.13.

ἀποκῠβεύω, *run hazard* or *risk*, περὶ βασιλείας D.S.17.30, Polyaen. 8.14.1.

ἀποκῠβιστάω, *plunge headlong off* a place, εἰς ὕδωρ Clearch.73 (dub.).

ἀποκῠδαίνω, *glorify greatly*, Hierocl.p.59 A., *IG*3.1367.

ἀποκῠ-έω, *bear young, bring forth*, c. acc., Arist.*Fr.*76, interpol. in D.H.1.70, Plu.*Sull.*37: abs., Luc.*DMar.*10.1: metaph., ἡ ἁμαρτία ἀ. θάνατον *Ep.Jac.*1.15, cf. Ph.1.214:—Pass., of the child, Plu. *Lyc.*3, Hdn.1.5.5 (Pass. part. ἀποκυόμενα Ph.2.202,397). **-ησις**, εως, ἡ, *bringing forth, birth*, Plu.2.907c, Dsc.2.120, Ph.2.396, Sor. 1.46, etc. **-ητικός**, ή, όν, *favourable for bringing forth*, ἡμέρα Paul.Al.*R.*1; ὥρα Palch.in *Cat.Cod.Astr.*1.114. **-ΐσκω**, = ἀποκυέω, Ael.*NA*9.3, D.L.8.29: metaph. in Pass., ἀριθμὸς ἀ. Herm.*in Phdr.*p.134 A.

ἀπο-κῠλινδέω, = ἀποκυλίω, J.*BJ*3.7.28 (Pass.). **-κύλισμα** [ῠ], ατος, τό, *rolling-machine*, Longin.40.4. **-κῠλίω**, *roll away*, Lxx *Ge.*29.3, al., D.S.14.116, *Ev.Matt.*28.2, Apollod.3.15.7:—Pass., Luc. *Rh.Pr.*3.

ἀποκῠμᾰτίζω, *make to swell with waves, boil up*, Plu.2.734e: metaph., ἀ. τὰς ψυχάς ib.943d; ἦχον D.H.*Comp.*23.

ἀπόκῡνον, τό, (κύων) *dog's-bane, Marsdenia erecta*, Dsc.4.80, Gal. 11.835. **II.** name of a *poisoned cake for dogs*, Hsch.

ἀποκῠνόω, *turn into a dog*, Eust.1714.42.

ἀποκυπαρῶσαι· ἀποκτεῖναι, Hsch.

ἀποκύπτω, *stoop away from* the wind, Ar.*Lys.*1003, in pf. ἀποκέκῡφα, but Reiske ἐπικεκύφαμες (prob. l.).

ἀποκῡριάζειν· ἀποκακεῖν, ἀποφεύγειν, ἀποσκιρτᾶν, Hsch.; cf. ἀνακυρτᾶσαι.

ἀποκῡρόω, *annul*, Lat. *abrogare*, *Gloss.*

ἀποκυρτόομαι, *rise to a convex shape*, v.l. for ἀποκορυφόομαι, Hp. *Prog.*7.

ἀποκύρωσις [ῡ], εως, ἡ, *ratification by vote*, Sch.E.*Hec.*259.

ἀποκωκύω, *mourn loudly over*, τινά A.*Ag.*1544.

ἀποκώλ-ῡσις, εως, ἡ, *hindering*, X.*Eq.*3.11, J.*AJ*14.11.5. **-ῡτέον**, *one must forbid*, Sor.2.42. **-ύω**, fut. -ύσω [ῡ], *hinder* or *prevent from* a thing, or its use, τινὰ τῆς ὁδοῦ X.*An.*3.3.3; ἀπό τινος Lxx *Ec.*2.10: c. inf., *prevent from* doing, E.*Med.*1411, Pl.*Tht.*150c, al.; ἀ. τοῦ ποιεῖν X.*Hier.*8.1; ἀ. μὴ ἐλθεῖν Id.*An.*6.4.24. **II.** c. acc. only, *keep off, hinder*, Orac.ap.Hdt.1.66, cf. Th.3.28. **III.** abs., *stop the way*, Id.1.72: impers., οὐδὲν ἀποκωλύει *there is* nothing *to prevent* it, Pl.*R.*372e, al. **IV.** *shut up*, τέκνα εἰς οἶκον Lxx 1*Ki.*6.10.

ἀποκωφόομαι, *become deaf*, Lxx *Mi.*7.16, Arr.*Epict.*2.20.37, etc.

ἀπολάβειον [λᾰ], τό, *clamp, holdfast*, Ph.*Bel.*61.15.

ἀπο-λᾱγαίω, *set at liberty*, ἐλεύθερον *GDI*5008, al. (Gortyn). **-λάγαξις**, εως, ἡ, *setting at liberty*, ib.5010.

ἀπολαγνεύω, *spend in debauchery*, in pf. Pass., Hsch. (-λαχν- cod.).

ἀπολαγχάνω, *obtain a portion of* a thing *by lot*, λαγχάνειν ἄπο μοῖραν ἐσθλῶν B.4.20; τῶν κτημάτων τὸ μέρος ἀ. Hdt.4.114, cf. 115; τὴν Ταναγρικὴν μοῖραν Id.5.57; τῆς γῆς Id.4.145; μόριον ὅσον αὐτοῖσι ἐπέβαλλε Id.7.23; ὡς ἀλλὰ ταῦτά γ' ἀπολάχωσ' οἴκων πατρός that they *may obtain*.., E.*HF*331; cf. Antipho *Fr.*63, *Leg.Gort.*5.4, al. **II.** *fail in drawing lots*, ἀ. κριτής Lys.4.3, cf. Plu.*Cat.Mi.*6, 2.102e: generally, *lose one's all, be left destitute*, E.*Ion*609.

ἀπολάζυμαι, poet. for ἀπολαμβάνω, E.*Hel.*911.

ἀπολαΐζομαι, *become stone*, prob. l. in Hsch. s. v. ἀπολελασμένον.

ἀπολάκημα, ατος, τό, *box on the ear*, Hsch.

ἀπολακτ-ίζω, *kick off* or *away, shake off*, ἀνίας Thgn.1337; ὕπνον A.*Eu.*141; βαρεῖαν κωφείαν Phld.*D.*1.24 (dub.); *inimicos* Plaut.*Epid.* 678. **2.** *spurn*, λέχος τὸ Ζηνός A.*Pr.*651; τὰ καλὰ καὶ σωτήρια Plu. *Ant.*36. **II.** abs., *kick out, kick up*, ἀμφοτέροις with both legs, Luc. *Asin.*18. **-ισμα**, ατος, τό, *kick*, Theodos.Gramm.p.6 G. **-ισμός**, ὁ, *a kicking off* or *away*, ἀ. βίου, of a violent death, A.*Supp.*937: Medic., of a form of haemorrhage, *diapedesis*, Steph.*in Hp.*1.124 D.

ἀπολᾰλέω, *blurt out*, πρός τινα ὅτι J.*AJ*6.9.2, cf. Luc.*Nigr.*22, Poll.2.127.

ἀπολαμβάνω, fut. -λήψομαι, in Hdt. -λάμψομαι 3.146, 9.38: Att. pf. ἀπείληφα, Pass. ἀπείλημμαι, Ion. ἀπολέλαμμαι: in Act. aor. 2 ἀπέλαβον, but in Pass. aor. 1 ἀπελήφθην, Ion. ἀπελάμφθην Hdt.:—*take* or *receive from* another, correlat. to ἀποδιδόναι, Pl.*R.*332b; οὐδὲν ἀ. τοῦ βίου χρηστόν (v.l. ἀπολαύ-) Plu.2.258b. **2.** *receive what is one's due*, μισθόν Hdt.8.137; ἀ. τὸν ὀφειλόμενον μισθόν X.*An.*7.7.14; τὴν σὴν ξυνάορον E.*Or.*654; τὰ χρήματα Ar.*Nu.*1274; τὰ παρὰ τοῦ πατρός Antiph.196; ἀ. χρέα *have* them *paid*, And.3.15; ὑπόσχεσιν παρά τινος ἀ. X.*Smp.*3.3; τὰ δίκαια Aeschin.1.196: opp. λαμβάνω, Epist.Phil.ap.D.12.14, cf. D.7.5; ἀ. ὅρκους *accept* them *when tendered*, Id.5.9, 18.27. **3.** *take of, take a part of* a thing, Th.6.87, Pl.*Hp.Mi.*369b; ἀ. μέρος τι Id.*R.*392e, cf. Arist.*Po.*1459^{a}35: abs. in aor. part., ἀπολαβὼν σκόπει consider it *separately*, Pl.*Grg.*495e, cf. *R.*420c. **4.** *take away*, Plb.21.43.8,17; *take off*, τὸ βάρος Arist. *IA*711^{a}24. **5.** *hear, learn*, Pl.*R.*614a. **II.** *regain, recover*, τὴν τυραννίδα, τὴν πόλιν, Hdt.1.61, 2.119, 3.146, al.; τι παρά τινος Th.5. 30; τὴν ἡγεμονίαν Isoc.4.21; τὴν αὐτὴν εὐεργεσίαν 14.57: metaph., ἀ. ἑαυτόν *recover* oneself, Porph.*Sent.*40, al. **2.** *have rendered to one*, λόγον ἀ. *demand* an account, Aeschin.3.27,168. **III.** *take apart* or *aside*, of persons, ἀ. τινὰ μοῦνον Hdt.1.209; αὐτὸν μόνον Ar. *Ra.*78, cf. Lxx 2*Ma.*6.21; of things, μὴ μόνος τὸ χρηστὸν ἀπολαβὼν ἔχε E.*Or.*451:—Med., ἀπολαβόμενος *taking* him *aside*, *Ev.Marc.*7. 33:—Pass., οἱ ἀπειλημμένοι those *set apart, recluses*, *UPZ*60.10 (ii B.C.). **IV.** *cut off, intercept*, λέγων ὡς ἀπολάμψοιτο συχνούς Hdt.9. 38; ἀ. τείχει wall *off*, Th.4.102; ἰσθμούς Id.1.7, cf. 4.113; ἀ. εἴσω *shut up* inside, Id.1.134; of contrary winds, ὅταν τύχωσιν οἱ ἄνεμοι ἀπολαβόντες αὐτούς Pl.*Phd.*58c; κἂν ἄνεμοι τὴν ναῦν ἀπολάβωσιν Philostr.*Her.*14; τὴν ἀναπνοὴν ἀ. τινός *stop* his breath, *choke* him, Plu.*Rom.*27; τὸν ἀντίπαλον ἐς πνῖγμα Philostr.*Im.*1.6; ἀ. τῶν σιτίων *spoil the appetite*, Hp.*Prorrh.*2.22:—freq. in Pass., ὑπ' ἀνέμων ἀπολαμφθέντες *arrested* or *stopped* by contrary winds, Hdt.2.115, 9.114; ὑπὸ ἀπλοίας Th.6.22; νόσῳ καὶ χειμῶνι καὶ πολέμοις ἀποληφθείς D.8.35; ἐν ὀλίγῳ ἀπολαμφθέντες Hdt.8.11; ἀπολαμφθέντες πάντοθεν Id.5.101; ἐν τῇ νήσῳ Id.8.70,76; ἐν τῇ Εὐρώπῃ ib.97,108; ἐν τοῖς ἰδίοις λόγοις ἀ. *to be entangled* in.., Pl.*Euthd.*305d; ἐν τούτῳ τῷ κακῷ Id.*Grg.* 522a; ἐς στενόν Philostr.*VS*1.19.1; of an afflux of blood, *to be checked*, Hp.*Fract.*4; κοιλίη, κύστις ἀπολελαμμένη, Id.*Prorrh.*1.88,115, etc. **V.** Math., *cut off*, ἡμικύκλιον ἀποληφθήσεται Arist.*Mete.*375^b 27, cf. Archim.*Quadr.*15, etc.; *intercept*, Id.*Sph.Cyl.*1.10; -ομένη, ἡ, *abscissa*, Apollon.Perg.*Con.*1.11, al.—A prose word, used by E. ll. cc.

ἀπολαμπρύνω, *make bright* or *famous*, Lib.*Or.*64.87:—Pass., *become so*, ἔργοισι by one's deeds, Hdt.1.41; ἔργοισί τε καὶ γνώμῃσι Id.6.70.

ἀπολάμπω, *shine* or *beam from*, αἰχμῆς ἀπέλαμπ' εὐήκεος (sc. φῶς) Il.22.319, cf. Ar.*Av.*1009; ἀστὴρ ὣς ἀπέλαμπεν Il.6.295, Od.15.108: —Med., χάρις ἀπελάμπετο grace *beamed from* her, Il.14.183, cf. Od. 18.298; χρυσοῦ ἀπολάμπεται *gleams with* gold, Luc.*Syr.D.*30. **2.** *reflect light*, Epicur.*Ep.*2 p.51 U. **II.** c. acc. cogn., αὐγὴν ἀ. Luc. *Dom.*8; ἀστραπῆς κάλλος Callistr.*Stat.*5; θεῖόν τι Philostr.*Im.*1.16.

ἀπόλαμψις, εως, ἡ, Aeol., = ἀπόληψις, *IG*12(2).28 (Mytil.).

ἀπολανθάνομαι, dub. for ἐκλ-, Longus 3.7.

ἀπολάντιον, τό, perh. name of a grass, σπάρτα ἀπολαντίου *PMag. Lond.*1.121.209.

ἀπολάπτω, *lap up* like a dog, *swallow greedily*, Ar.*Nu.*811.

ἀπό-λαυσις, εως, ἡ, *act of enjoying, fruition*, Th.2.38, *OGI*669. 8 (Egypt, i A.D.); ἀ. ἀνεύφραντος Secund.*Sent.*9. **II.** *result of enjoying, pleasure*, αἱ ἀ. αἱ σωματικαί Arist.*Pol.*1314^{b}28, cf. *EN* 1148^{a}5, etc.; ὁ κατ' ἀπόλαυσιν βίος a life of *pleasure*, Id.*Top.*102^b 17. **2.** c. gen., *advantage got from* a thing, σίτων καὶ ποτῶν X.*Mem.*2.1.33, cf. Hp.*VM*11; ἀγαθῶν Isoc.1.27; ἀπόλαυσιν εἰκοῦς (acc. abs.) *as a reward for* your resemblance, E.*Hel.*77, cf. *HF*1370; ἀ. ἑαυτῶν ἔχειν Pl.*Ti.*83a; ἀ. ἀδικημάτων *advantage, fruit* of them, Luc.*Tyr.*5. **-λαυσμα**, ατος, τό, *enjoyment*, Aeschin.*Ep.*5.4 (pl.), J.*AJ*18.6.10, Plu.2.125d, *Aem.*28. **-λαυστέον**, *one must enjoy*, τῶν θεωρημάτων Iamb.*Protr.*2. **-λαυστικός**, ή, όν, *devoted to enjoyment*, βίος Arist.*EN*1095^{b}17; οἱ -κοί Plu.2.1094f; *producing enjoyment*, ἀρεταί Arist.*Rh.*1367^{a}18. Adv. -κῶς, ζῆν Id.*Pol.*1312^b 23. **II.** *choice*, οἶνος Plb.12.2.7; μήκωνες Hices.ap.Ath.3.87e (Comp.); *luxurious*, δίαιτα Gal.18(2).463. **-λαυστός**, όν, *enjoyed, enjoyable*, Epicur.*Ep.*3 p.60 U., Phld.*Ir.*p.84 W., Ph.1.572, Diotog. ap.Stob.4.7.62, Plu.*Comp.Arist.Cat.*4. **-λαύω**, fut. -λαύσομαι Ar. *Av.*177, Pl.*Chrm.*172b, etc.; later -λαύσω D.H.6.4, Plu.*Pyrrh.*13, etc. (in earlier writers corrupt, as Hyp.*Epit.*30): aor. ἀπέλαυσα E.*IT*526, Ar.*Av.*1358, etc.: pf. -λέλαυκα Pl.Com.169, Isoc.19.23: —**Pass.**, pf. -λέλαυται Philostr.*VA*6.19, but ἀπολελαυσμένος Plu.2. 1089c, 1099e (ἐν-): aor. ἀπελαύσθην Ph.1.37.—The double augm.

ἀπήλαυον, ἀπήλαυσα, is found in codd. of Id.1.435, etc., prob. in *LW* 1046.5 (Blaudos). (The simple λαύω is not found, but was = λάϝω, expl. by Aristarch. as ἀπολαυστικῶς ἔχω, cf. Apollon.*Lex.*, Sch.Od. 19.229) :—*have enjoyment of* a thing, *have the benefit of* it, c. gen. rei, τῆς σῆς δικαιοσύνης Hdt.6.86.α΄; τῶν σιτίων Hp.*VM*11, cf. Pl.*R.* 354b; ἰχθύων, λαχάνων, ἐδεσμάτων, etc., *enjoy* them, Amphis 26, Aristopho 10.3, Antiph.8; ποτῶν, ὀσμῶν, X.*Cyr.*7.5.81, *Hier.*1.24, etc.; τῶν ἀγαθῶν Isoc.1.9, Pl.*Grg.*492b; σχολῆς Id.*Lg.*781e; τῆς σιωπῆς ἀ. *take advantage of* it, D.21.203; τῆς ἐξουσίας Aeschin.3. 130. 2. with acc. cogn. added, ἀ. τί τινος *enjoy* an advantage *from* some source, τί γὰρ.. ἂν ἀπολαύσαιμι τοῦ μαθήματος; Ar.*Nu.* 1231, cf. *Th.*1008, *Pl.*236; ἐλάχιστα ἀ. τῶν ὑπαρχόντων Th.1.70; τοῦ βίου τι ἀ. Id.2.53; ζῴων τοσαῦτα ἀγαθὰ ἀ. ὁ ἄνθρωπος X.*Mem.*4.3. 10, cf. Pl.*Euthd.*299a, etc.; τοσοῦτον εὐερίας ἀπολέλαυκε Pl.Com. 169. 3. c. acc. (instead of gen.), ἀ. τὸν βίον Diph.32.6 (ἀποβάλλειν cj. Kock); ἀ. καὶ πάσχειν τι Arist.*Sens.*443^{b}3. 4. abs., οἱ ἀπολαύοντες, opp. οἱ πονοῦντες, Id.*Pol.*1263^{a}13; ἧττον ἀ. *to have* less *enjoyment*, Id.*HA*584^{a}21; ἡδόμενοι καὶ -οντες Plu.2.69e. II. in bad sense (freq. ironically), *have the benefit of*, τῶν Οἰδίπου κακῶν ἀ. E.*Ph.*1205; ἀ. τι τῶν γάμων Id.*IT*526; ἧς ἀπολαύων Ἅιδην.. καταβήσει Id.*Andr.*543 (lyr.); τῶν ἁμαρτημάτων, τῶν ἀσεβῶν ἀ., Hp.*VM* 12, Pl.*Lg.*910b; φλαῦρόν τι ἀ. Isoc.8.81, cf. Pl.*Cri.*54a: with Preps., ἀπὸ τῶν ἀλλοτρίων [παθῶν] ἀ. Id.*R.*606b; ἐκ τῆς μιμήσεως τοῦ εἶναι ἀ. ib.395c; ἀπ' ἄλλου ὀφθαλμίας ἀ. Id.*Phdr.*255d. 2. abs., *have a benefit, come off well*, Ar.*Av.*1358. III. *make sport of*, συνοδοιπόρου Thphr.*Char.*23.3, cf. Lys.6.38.—Chiefly Att.; Trag. only in E. (Cf. Lat. *lu-crum*, Goth. *laun* 'payment', Slav. *loviti* 'capture'; cf. Dor. λᾶία, Att. λεία 'booty'.)

ἀπολεαίνω or **-λειαίνω**, *smooth*, παρειάς D.S.5.28: metaph., *polish*, περιόδους Plu.2.350e, cf. 384a. II. *erase, cancel* an entry, *IG*7.1737.17 (Thesp.).

ἀπολέγω, *pick out from* a number, and so: 1. *pick out, choose*, τὸ ἄριστον Hdt.5.110, cf. 3.14, Ar.*V.*580, Aen.Tact.1.5, 3.2:—freq. in Med., *pick out for oneself*, τριήκοντα μυριάδας τοῦ στρατοῦ *from* the army, Hdt.8.101; ἐκ πάντων Th.4.9:—Pass., ἀπολελεγμένοι *picked men*, Hdt.7.40; ἀπειλεγμένοι X.*Eq.Mag.*8.12. 2. *pick out* for the purpose of rejecting, τριβόλους Ar.*Lys.*576; ἀ. τινὰ ἐκ τῶν δικαστῶν Plu.*Cat.Mi.*48. II. later, *decline, refuse*, ἀ. τὸ χορηγεῖν Plb.2.63.1; ἀ. περί τινος Id.4.9.3:—Med., *decline* something *offered to one*, ἀρχήν Id.*Fr.*16; ἱκεσίαν, δέησιν, Plu.*Sol.*12, *Cat.Mi.*2; *renounce, give up*, τὰ πρωτεῖα, τὴν νίκην, τὸν βίον, Id.*Luc.*42, *Nic.*6, 2. 1060d; τὴν ψυχήν Lxx *Jn.*4.8: abs. (sc. τὸ ζῆν), Ph.1.274; also, *give in, make no resistance*, Plu.*Lyc.*22, *Pomp.*23:—so in Act., *lose heart*, as pres. of ἀπεῖπον, τῇ ταλαιπωρίᾳ Procop.*Vand.*2.19; ταῖς δυνάμεσι Herod.Med.ap.Orib.10.5.9. III. *speak of fully*, Ael.*NA* 8.17 (Pass.), cf. ἀπολέγει· παραγγέλλει, and ἀπολέξω· ἐρῶ, δηλώσω, Hsch.

ἀπολειαίνω, v. ἀπολεαίνω.

ἀπολείβραξαι· ἀπολεῖψαι, ἐκνοτίσαι· ἄλλοι, πορρωτέρω ἀπελθεῖν, Hsch.

ἀπολείβω, *let drip*: hence, *pour a libation*, ἀπολλείψας Hes.*Th.* 793; δένδρον ἀπολεῖβον μέλι *dropping* honey, D.S.17.75; δάκρυα τῶν ὀφθαλμῶν Alciphr.3.21: metaph., ἴχνη ὥραν ἀπολείβει *Com.Adesp.* 39:—Pass., *drop* or *run down from*, τινός Od.7.107; ἔραζε Hes.*Sc.* 174.

ἀπόλειμμα, ατος, τό, *a remnant*, Ar.Byz.*Epit.*22.18, D.S.1.46.

ἀπολεῖνα· ἀποστρέφειν (Lacon.), Hsch.

ἀπολειόω, *erase*, ἐπιγραφήν *CIG*3966 (Apamea Cibotus); Arc.

ἀπυλιῶναι (pres. inf.) dub. in *IG*5(2)p.xxxvi *D*1.20 (Tegea, iv B.C.).

ἀπολειπής, f.l. for ἐπιλειπής, Hp.*Nat.Puer.*20.

ἀπο-λειπτέον, (ἀπολείπομαι) *one must stay behind*, X.*Oec.*7. 38. 2. (from Act.) *one must leave behind*, Hld.2.17; *one must desert, abandon*, οὐκ ἀ. Plu.2.263f; *one must omit, pass over*, Jul.*Or.* 3.106c. **-λείπω**, aor. ἀπέλῐπον (ἀπέλειψα late, Them.*Or.*25.310d, Ps.-Phoc.77):—*leave over* or *behind*, οὐδ' ἀπέλειπεν ἔγκατα Od.9.292, cf. Heraclit.56, etc.; κλέος καὶ φήμην Critias 44 D.; *bequeath*, *Test. Epict.*2.3, cf. Mosch.3.97; ἀ. κληρονόμον *leave as* one's heir, *POxy.* 105.3 (ii A.D.); *bequeath to posterity*, of writings, D.L.8.58, cf. 7. 54. 2. *leave hold of, lose*, ψυχάν Pi.*P.*3.101 (tm.); βίον S.*Ph.* (lyr., tm.); νέαν ἁμέραν ἀπολιπὼν θάνοι E.*Ion*720 (lyr.): conversely, ἐμὲ μὲν ἀπολέλοιπεν ἤδη βίοτος S.*El.*185 (lyr.). 3. *leave behind* in the race, *distance*: generally, *surpass*, X.*Cyr.*8.3.25, Lys.2.4; τινὰ περί τι Isoc.4.50:—more freq. in Med. and Pass., v. infr. 4. *leave undisputed*: hence, *admit*, Chrysipp.*Stoic.*3.173, Phld.*Piet.*17, S.E.*M.*7.55, D.L.7.54; αἰτίαν νόσων ἀ. τὸ αἷμα Meno *Iatr.*11.43; [ὁ Διοκλῆς] τὴν φρόνησιν περὶ τὴν καρδίαν ἀ. Herod.Med. in *Rh.Mus.*49. 540. 5. *leave, allow*, ὑπερβολὴν οὐδὲ ταῖς ἑταίραις Jul.*Or.*7. 210d. II. *desert, abandon*, one's post, etc., οὐδ' ἀπολείπουσιν κοῖλον δόμον, of bees, Il.12.169, cf. Hdt.8.41, al.; ἀ. (sc. τὴν πολιορκίην) Id.7.170; τὴν ξυμμαχίαν, τὴν ξυνωμοσίαν, Th.3.9,64; of persons, καί σ' ἀπολείψω σου λειπόμενος E.*El.*1310; ξεῖνον πατρώϊον ἀ. *leave* him *in the lurch*, Thgn.521; ἀπολιπὼν οἴχεται Hdt.3.48, cf. 5.103, Ar.*Ra.* 83; of a wife, *desert* her husband, And.4.14, D.30.4 (not of the husband, Luc.*Sol.*9); of sailors, *desert*, τὴν ναῦν D.50.14. 2. c. inf., ἀ. τούτους κακῶς γηράσκειν *leave* them to grow old, X.*Oec.* 1.22. 3. *leave undone* or *unsaid*, ὅσα ἀπέλιπε κτείνων τε καὶ διώκων.. σφέα ἀπετέλεσε Hdt.5.92.η΄; ὕβρεως οὐδ' ὁτιοῦν ἀ. D.54. 4, cf. Pl.*R.*420a; *omit*, συχνὰ ἀπολείπω ib.509c. III. *leave open*, *leave a space*, ἀ. μεταίχμιον οὐ μέγα Hdt.6.77; ἀ. ὡς πλέθρον X.*An.* 6.5.11; μικρὸν ἀ. *leaving* a small *interval*, Hero *Aut.*27.1. IV. intr., *cease, fail*, τάων οὔποτε καρπὸς ἀπόλλυται οὐδ' ἀπολείπει Od.7. 117; opp. γίνεται, Diog.Apoll.7; of rivers, *fall, sink*, Hdt.2.14,93; ἀ. τὸ ῥέεθρον Id.2.19; τῆς θαλάττης τὰ μὲν ἀπολειπούσης, τὰ δ' ἐπιούσης Arist.*Mete.*353^{a}22; of swallows, δι' ἔτεος ἐόντες οὐκ ἀπολείπουσι Hdt.2.22; of youth, *begin to decay*, X.*Smp.*8.14; *fail, flag, lose heart*, Id.*Cyr.*4.2.3; of the moon, *wane*, Arist.*APo.*98^{a}33. 2. c. gen., *to be wanting of* or *in* a thing, προθυμίας οὐδὲν ἀ. Th.8.22, cf. Pl.*R.* 533a: freq. of numbers, μηδὲν ἀ. τῶν πέντε κτλ. Id.*Lg.*828b; τῶν εἴκοσιν ὀλίγον ἀ. Arist.*HA*573^{b}16, etc.; ἀπὸ τεσσέρων πηχέων ἀ. τρεῖς δακτύλους *wanting* three fingers *of* four cubits, Hdt.1.60, cf. 7.117; μήτ' ἄρ' ὑπερβάλλων βοὸς ὀπλὴν μήτ' ἀπολείπων Hes.*Op.*489: c. inf., ὀλίγον ἀπέλιπον ἐς Ἀθήνας ἀπικέσθαι *wanted* but little of coming, Hdt.7.9.α΄; βραχὺ ἀ. διακόσιαι γενέσθαι Th.7.70; οὐδὲν δ' ἀπολείπετε οὕτω πολεμεῖν D.4.40; ἡ πόλις μικρὸν ἀπέλιπεν ἔρημος εἶναι Plu.*Tim.* 1. 3. c. part., *leave off* doing, ἀ. λέγων X.*Oec.*6.1: abs., ὅθεν ἀπέλιπες from the point at which.., Pl.*Grg.*497c, cf. *Phd.*78b, Is.5. 12. 4. *depart from*, ἐκ τῶν Συρακουσῶν Th.5.4; ἐκ τοῦ Μηδικοῦ πολέμου Id.3.10, cf. Pl.*Phd.*112c.

B. Med. (aor. ἀπελιπόμην in A.R.1.399 (tm.)), like Act.1.1, *bequeath to posterity*, Hdt.2.134 codd.; cf. ἀπολείψεται· ἐάσεται, Hsch.

C. Pass., *to be left behind, stay behind*, Th.7.75 (v.l. for ὑπο-), X. *Cyr.*1.4.20; μόνος ἀπολελειμμένος Antipho 1.3; *to be unable to follow* an argument, *be at a loss*, Pl.*Tht.*192d. 2. *to be distanced by, inferior to*, ἀ. [ἀπὸ] τῶν ἄλλων θηρίων Diocl.*Fr.*145; *to be inferior*, ἔν τισι Isoc.12.61. II. *to be absent* or *distant from*, c. gen., πολὺ τῆς ἀληθηΐης ἀπολελειμμένοι Hdt.2.106, cf. Pl.*R.*475d; ἥβας E.*HF* 440 (lyr.): c. gen. pers., X.*Mem.*4.2.40, Pl.*Smp.*192d: abs., E.*Or.* 80, Pl.*Phdr.*240c; *to be deprived of*, τοῦ σοῦ.. μὴ ἀπολείπεσθαι τάφου S.*El.*1169; πατρῴας μὴ ἀ. χθονός E.*Med.*35; τῶν πρὶν ἀπολειφθεὶς φρενῶν Id.*Or.*216. 2. *to be wanting in, fall short of*, ὅτι τοῦ σκώπτειν ἀπελείφθη Ar.*Eq.*525; τοῖς ἀπολειφθεῖσι (sc. τῆς παιδείας) D.18. 128, cf. Isoc.12.209; ἀπολειφθεὶς ἡμῶν *without* our *cognizance*, D.19. 36; ἀπολειφθῆναι τῶν πραγμάτων *to be left in ignorance of*.., Id.27.2; καιροῦ ἀ. *miss* the opportunity, Id.34.38, cf. Isoc.3.19; θεάματος, ἑορτῆς ἀ., Luc.*DMar.*15.1, *Sacr.*1; εἰσβολῆς Isoc.14.31. 3. *remain to be done*, Plb.3.39.12: impers., ἀπολείπεται λέγειν, διδάσκειν, D.L.7.85, S.E.*M.*7.1.

ἀπολειτουργέω, *complete required service*, D.L.3.99, M.Ant.10.22.

ἀπολείχω, *lick off*, ἕλκη, v.l. for ἐπι-, A.R.4.478, cf. Epic. in *Arch. Pap.*7.6, Ath.6.250a, Sch.Il.*Oxy.*221 ii 33; *lick clean*, c. gen. partit., φόνου *Ev.Luc.*16.21.

ἀπόλειψις, εως, ἡ, (ἀπολείπω) *abandonment*, ἡ ἀ. τοῦ στρατοπέδου Th.7.75; *defection*, Id.4.126; *desertion* of a husband by his wife (cf. ἀπολείπω II. 1), D.30.15; ἀπόλειψιν ἀπογράφεσθαι (v. ἀπογράφω III. 2) ib.17 (but also, = ἀπόπεμψις, ἀ. γράψασθαι Plu.2.100e); *desertion* by soldiers, seamen, etc., X.*HG*4.1.28, D.50.11. II. intr., *deficiency*, of rivers, *failing*, Arist.*Mete.*351^{a}21 (pl.); of the moon, *waning*, Id. *GA*767^{a}5; of the sun, *departure to southern hemisphere*, Jul.*Or.*4. 137d. 2. *death*, δοιὴ δὲ θνητῶν γένεσις, δοιὴ δ' ἀ. Emp.17.3; ἀ. τοῦ ζῆν Hyp.*Epit.*24; ἐκ τοῦ ὄντος Porph.*Sent.*20. III. in Law, *default*, *Cod.Just.*1.4.18.

ἀπόλεκτος, ον, (ἀπολέγω) *chosen, picked*, Th.6.68, X.*An.*2.3.15, Aen.Tact.26.10. II. ἀπόλεκτον, τό, *choice cut off* the πηλαμύς (q.v.), Xenocr.70.

ἀπολέλασται· ἀπολέλεκται, Hsch.

ἀπολελεγμένως, gloss on ἀπηλεγέως, Hsch.

ἀπολελῠμένως, Adv. *absolutely*, opp. κατὰ σχέσιν, S.E.*M.*8.162, cf. Ptol.*Tetr.*127. II. Gramm., *in the positive degree*, opp. κατὰ σύγκρισιν ('in the comparative'), Phryn.*PS*p.1 B. III. Rhet., *without regular pauses*, ἀ. λέγειν, opp. διακόψαι, Hermog.*Id.*1.9.

ἀπολέμητος, ον, *not warred on*, Plb.3.90.7, Luc.*DDeor.*20.12.

ἀπόλεμμα, ατος, τό, (ἀπολέπω) *skin*, D.C.68.32.

ἀπόλεμος, Ep. **ἀπτόλεμος**, ον, *unwarlike*, ἀ. καὶ ἄναλκις Il.2.201, al., cf. X.*Cyr.*7.4.1, Jul.*Or.*2.87a; ἀ. χειρὶ λείψεις βίον, i.e. by *a woman's* hand, E.*Hec.*1034 (lyr.). 2. *unwarlike, peaceful*, εὐνομία Pi.*P.*5.66; εὐναί E.*Med.*640; ἡσυχία D.H.2.76, etc. Adv. -μως, ἴσχειν Pl.*Plt.*307e. II. *invincible*, A.*Ag.*768, *Ch.*55 (lyr.). III. πόλεμος ἀ. a war *that is no war*, a hopeless struggle, Id.*Pr.*904 (lyr.) (Dind. metri gr. proposes ἀπολέμιστος), E.*HF*1133.

ἀπολεοντόομαι, Pass., (λέων) *become a lion*, Heraclit.*Incred.*12.

ἀπολεπιδόομαι, Pass., *exfoliate*, of bones, Hp.*Fract.*33.

ἀπολεπ-ίζω, = ἀπολέπω, *peel*, *Gp.*10.58. **-ισμα**, ατος, τό, *husk*, Sch.Ar.*Ach.*469.

ἀπολεπτ-ύνω, *fine down*, esp. *of reducing temperature* or *fever*, Plu.2.695e, Alex.Trall.*Febr.*5:—more freq. in Pass., *become quite fine* or *thin*, ἀπολεπτυνθέντος τοῦ πικροῦ *being fined away*, Pl.*Ti.*83b; πλάτος ἀπολελεπτυσμένον Arist.*HA*489^{b}33; of fever, v.l. in Hp. *Epid.*1.25. **-υσμός**, ὁ, *attenuation*, Antyll.ap.Orib.6.10.17.

ἀπολέπω, aor. 2 Pass. ἀπελέπην Hsch.:—*peel, skin*, ἀ. μάστιγι τὸ νῶτον cj. Ruhnk. in E.*Cyc.*237; ὥσπερ ᾠὸν τὸ λέμμα Ar.*Av.*673; θρίδακας ἀπολελεμμένας τὸν καυλόν *with* the stalk *peeled*, Epich. 158. 2. *lop off*, στεῦτο ἀπολεψέμεν οὔατα χαλκῷ Il.21.455 (dub. l.).

ἀπολέσκετο, Ep. iterative of ἀπόλλυμι.

ἀπολευκ-αίνω, *make all white*, Hp.*Prorrh.*2.20; τὸν ἀέρα Plu.*Eum.* 16:—Pass., *to be* or *become so*, Arist.*Fr.*350, Archig.ap.Orib.44.26. 1. **-όω**, = foreg., *Hippiatr.*69.

ἀπό-ληγμα, ατος, τό, *skirt, hem* of a robe, Aq.*Ex.*28.33. **-λήγω**, *leave off, desist from*, c. gen., ἀλλ' οὐδ' ὣς ἀπέληγε μάχης Il.7.263; οὐκ ἀπολήγει ἀλκῆς ib.21.577; νέον δ' ἀπέληγεν ἐδωδῆς ib.24.475; ἀ. ἔρωτος Pl.*R.*490b. **2.** c. part., *leave off* doing, Il.17.565, Od.19.166; [γενεὴ] ἡ μὲν φύει, ἡ δ' ἀπολήγει Il.6.149: abs., *cease, desist*, ib.13.230, 20.99; κλέος..οὐδ' ἀπολήξει Xenoph.6.3; opp. γίνεται, Emp.17.30; of the wind, *fall*, Theoc.22.19. **3.** ἀ. εἰς ἓν *end* in.., Arist.*Mu.*399^{a}13, cf. Str.13.4.1, Plu.2.496a, Luc.*Im.*6; ἐς ὀξὺ *taper* to a point, Arr.*Tact.*16.7: Rhet., of the close of a sentence, ἀ. εἰς συνδέσμους Demetr.*Eloc.*257. **b.** τὸ ἀπολῆγον [τοῦ βουνοῦ] the *extremity* of the hill, *Inscr.Prien.*37.168 (ii B.C.): so Medic., τὰ ἀ. μέρη the *extremities*, Ruf.ap.Orib.49.33.11, al. **II.** trans., = ἀποπαύω, A.R.4.767. [ἀπολλ. Il.15.31, Od.13.151, 19.166, Theoc. l.c., al.] **-ληκέω**, *snap the fingers*, Hellanic.63(b) J., Hsch. (-λεκ- cod.), Suid. s. v. Σαρδαναπάλλους. **-ληξις**, εως, ἡ, *cessation*, ἐνεργείας M.Ant.9.21; καταμηνίων Sor.1.62; esp. *decline* of life, Hp. *Praec.*14. **II.** *close* of a sentence or period, Demetr.*Eloc.*182, al. **III.** *termination* of a fistula, Antyll.ap.Orib.44.22.7.

ἀποληπτ-έον, *one must admit, accept*, κριτήριον τὴν φαντασίαν (nisi leg. -λειπτέον, cf. ἀπολείπω I.4) S.E.*M.*7.388. **-ικός**, ή, όν, *pertaining to the receipt of a debt*, ὁμολογία *Cod.Just.*4.21.16.

ἀποληρέω, *chatter at random*, D.19.182, Longus 1.17; ἔς τινα D.C.53.23; τι Id.72.4. **2.** *outdo in foolish talk*, τινά Plb.34.6.15.

ἀπόληρος· ἡ τοῦ θανάτου γραφή (Tarent.), Hsch.

ἀπόληψις, εως, ἡ, (ἀπολαμβάνω IV) *intercepting, cutting off*, ὁπλιτῶν Th.7.54; *stoppage*, ἐπιμηνίων, οὔρων, Hp.*Prorrh.*1.51, 2.7, etc.; ὑδάτων Thphr.*CP*3.21.1; *imprisonment*, πνεύματος ἐν τῇ γῇ Epicur.*Ep.*2 p.48 U.; ἀ. ποδὸς *constrained position*, Hp.*Art.*62. **b.** *refutation*, Gal.5.261. **2.** *reception*, τῆς φιλίας Phld.*D.*3*Fr.*84, cf. Str.10.2.25. **3.** *clamp, holdfast*, Ph.*Bel.*57.44. **4.** *repayment*, Phalar. *Ep.*27.

ἀπολῐβάζω, *cause to drop off, throw away*, Pherecr.42. **II.** intr., *drop off, vanish*, οὐκ ἀπολιβάζεις εἰς ἀποικίαν τινά; Eup.206, cf. Ar.*Av.*1467.

ἀπολῐγαίνω, *speak with a shrill voice, bluster*, ἦν δ' ἀπολιγαίνῃ Ar. *Ach.*968. **II.** *make shrill music*, Plu.2.713a.

ἀπολῐγωρέω, *esteem little*, πόλεμον Sch.Th.1.140, cf. Steph. *in Gal.* 1.285 D.

ἀπολῐθ-όω, *turn into stone, petrify*, Arist.*Pr.*937^{a}17, cf. Hellanic. 191 J., Pherecyd.77 J.:—Pass., ἀ. ὑπὸ τοῦ ἡλίου Thphr.*HP*4.7.2; *become stone*, Arist.*Pr.*937^{a}14, *Mir.*838^{a}14, Str.5.4.13, Palaeph.31; *become hard*, *PHolm.*4.38. **-ωσις**, εως, ἡ, *petrifaction*, Pherecyd. 12 J., Thphr.*Lap.*50, Sch.Il.2.319: metaph., Arr.*Epict.*1.5.3.

ἀπολιμνόομαι, Pass., *become a lake* or *pool*, Eust.267.47.

ἀπολιμπάνω, Aeol. ἀπυ-, collat. form of ἀπολείπω, ἀέκων σ' ἀ. Sapph.*Supp.*23.5, cf. Luc.*Cat.*7, Gal.*UP*4.11, *POxy.*1426.12 (iv A.D.):—Pass., Plu.*Them.*10.

ἀπόλινον, τό, = θυμελαία, Dsc.4.172 (v.l.).

ἀπολῐν-όω, *tie up with a thread*, of surgeons, Paul.Aeg.6.5. **-ωσις**, εως, ἡ, *operation by ligature*, ibid.

ἀπόλιον· θαῦμα, Hsch. (fort. θῦμα, cf. ἀπάλιον).

ἀπολῐόρκητος, ον, *impregnable*, Str.12.3.31, Plu.2.1057e.

ἀπολιόω, v. ἀπολειόω.

ἀπολῐπαίνω, *oil*, Antig.*Mir.*135.

ἄπολις, ι: gen. ιδος or εως, Ion. ιος: dat. ἀπόλι Hdt.8.61:—*without city, state* or *country*, Id.7.104, 8.61, etc.; *outlaw, banished man*, ἄ. τινα τιθέναι, ποιεῖν, S.*OC*1357, Antipho 2.2.9, Pl.*Lg.*928e, etc.; προβαλέσθαι S.*Ph.*1018; ἀ. ἀντὶ πολιτῶν Lys.20.35; ἄ. τῆς ἀρχαίας (sc. πόλεως) Aristid.*Or.*26(14).75. **2.** *no true citizen*, opp. ὑψίπολις, S.*Ant.*370. **II.** of a country, *without cities*, Plu.*Tim.*1, Philostr.*VA*1.24. **III.** πόλις ἄπολις a city *that is no city*, a ruined city, ἄ. Ἰλίου πόλιν ἔθηκας A.*Eu.*457, cf. E.*Tr.*1292; also, one *that has no constitution, no true* city, Pl.*Lg.*766d.

ἀπολισθ-άνω, later -αίνω Poll.1.116, v.l. in Hp.*Acut.*17, Plu.*Alc.*6, etc.: aor. ἀπώλισθον Ar.*Lys.*678, etc.; later ἀπωλίσθησα *AP*9.158:—*slip off* or *away*, Th.7.65, Arist.*Pr.*961^{a}27, Plot.3.6.14: c. acc. cogn., ἐκ τέγεος πέσημα *AP* l.c. **2.** c. gen., *slip away from*, τινός Ar.*Lys.*678; τῆς μνήμης prob. in Alciphr.3.11; ἀ. τινός, also, *cease to be intimate with* one, τοῦ Σωκράτους Plu. l. c.; ἀ. εἴς τι Luc.*Dem. Enc.*12; ἐπὶ τὴν δόξαν Iamb.*Myst.*9.8. **b.** ἀ. τοῦ ρ *make a slip* in pronouncing ρ, Plu.2.277d. **-ησις**, εως, ἡ, *slipping off*, Plot.6.6.3.

ἀπόλιστος, ον, = ἄπολις, Man.4.282.

ἀπολῐταργίζω, Att. fut. -ιῶ, *hop off, pack off*, οὔκουν ἀνύσας τι.. ἀπολιταργιεῖς; Ar.*Nu.*1253.

ἀπολ-ίτευτος [ῐ], ον, *without political constitution* (πολιτεία), of nations, Arist.*Pol.*1327^{b}26. **II.** *not fitted for public affairs, unstatesmanlike*, Plu.*Mar.*31; ὑπατεία, λόγοι, Id.*Crass.*12, 2.1034b. **2.** *withdrawn from public life, private*, βίος ib.1098d; θάνατος Id.*Lyc.*29. **3.** *not in current use*, λέξις Id.2.7a. **-ίτης** [ῐ], ου, ὁ, v.l. for ἀποπολίτης, q.v. **-ιτικός**, ή, όν, *unstatesmanlike*, Cic.*Att.*8.16.1 (Sup.).

ἀπολίτρωσις, εως, ἡ, = ἀπονίτρωσις, Orib.*Fr.*74.

ἀπολιχμάζω, = sq., Opp.*C.*2.175 (tm.).

ἀπολιχμάομαι, *lick off*, αἷμα Il.21.123:—later in Act., D.H.1.79. **II.** *lick*, τὸ πρόσωπον Longus 1.5.

ἀπολλαπλάσιος, ον, *without multiplicity*, Dam.*Pr.*47.

Ἀπολλόδωρος, ὁ, pr. n., *Apollodorus*, Th.7.20, etc.:—hence Adj. **-δώρειος**, ον, αἵρεσις Str.13.4.3.

ἀπόλλῡμι or -ύω (Th.4.25, Pl.*R.*608e, Arist.*Pol.*1297^{a}12, but f.l. in Men.580; the form is rejected by Phryn.*PS*p.10 B., Moer.12), impf. ἀπώλλυν A.*Pers.*652 (lyr.), S.*El.*1360, ἀπώλλυον And.1.58: fut. ἀπολέσω, Ep. ἀπολέσσω, Att. ἀπολῶ, Ion. ἀπολέω Hdt.1.34, al.: aor. ἀπώλεσα, Ep. ἀπόλεσσα: pf. ἀπολώλεκα:—freq. in tmesi in Ep.; Prep. postponed in Od.9.534:—stronger form of ὄλλυμι, *destroy utterly, kill*, in Hom. mostly of death in battle, ἀπώλεσε λαὸν Ἀχαιῶν Il.5.758, al.; ἐκπάγλως ἀπόλεσσαν ib.1.268; also of things, *demolish, lay waste*, ἀπώλεσεν Ἴλιον ἱρήν ib.5.648, etc.; generally, βίοτον δ' ἀπὸ πάμπαν ὀλέσσει *will waste* my substance, Od.2.49; οἵ μ' ἀπωλλύτην *sought to destroy* me (impf. sense), S.*OT*1454; in pregnant sense, ἐπεί με γᾶς ἐκ πατρίας ἀπώλεσε *drove* me *ruined* from.., E.*Hec.*946; τῆς παρ' ἡμέραν χάριτος τὰ μέγιστα τῆς πόλεως ἀ. for the sake of.., D.8.70. **2.** λόγοις or λέγων ἀ. τινά *talk* or *bore* one *to death*, S.*El.*1360, Ar.*Nu.*892 (lyr.): hence, alone, in fut. ἀπολεῖς με Id.*Ach.*470; οἴμ' ὡς ἀπολεῖς με Pherecr.108.20; ἀπολεῖ μ' οὑτοσί by his questions, Antiph.222.8, etc. **3.** *ruin* a woman, Lys.1.8. **II.** *lose*, πατέρ' ἐσθλὸν ἀπώλεσα Od.2.46, cf. Il.18.82, Democr.272; ἀπώλεσε νόστιμον ἦμαρ Od.1.354; ἀπὸ θυμὸν ὀλέσσαι *lose* one's life, Il.16.861, Od.12.350; θυμὸν οὐκ ἀπώλεσεν *loses* not his spirit, S.*El.*26; ἔλεον ἀπώλεσεν Il.24.44; freq. of things, ἡ τοῦ πλέονος ἐπιθυμίη τὸ παρεὸν ἀπόλλυσι Democr.224; ἵππους ἑβδομήκοντα ἀπολλύασι Th.7.51; ἀπώλεσαν τὴν ἀρχὴν ὑπὸ Περσῶν X.*An.*3.4.11, cf. 7.2.22; μηδὲν ἀπολλὺς τοῦ ὄγκου Pl.*Tht.*155c; ἀ. οὐσίαν, = ἀπόλλυσθαι, Id.*Prm.*163d.

B. Med., ἀπόλλῠμαι: fut. -ολοῦμαι, Ion. -ολέομαι Hdt.7.218: aor. 2 -ωλόμην: pf. -όλωλα, whence the barbarous impf. ἀπόλωλο Ar.*Th.*1212: plpf. in Att. Prose sts. written ἀπωλώλειν in codd., as Th.4.133, 7.27:—*perish, die*, Il.1.117, etc.; *cease to exist*, opp. γίγνεσθαι, Meliss.8, Pl.*Prm.*156b, etc.: sts. c. acc. cogn., ἀπόλωλε κακὸν μόρον Od.1.166; ἀπωλόμεθ' αἰπὺν ὄλεθρον ib.9.303: c. dat. modi, ἀπώλετο λυγρῷ ὀλέθρῳ (v.l. λυγρὸν ὄλεθρον) ib.3.87; ἀ. ὑπό τινος Hdt.5.126; simply, *to be undone*, αὐτῶν.. ἀπωλόμεθ' ἀφραδίῃσιν Od.10.27; ἀπωλώλει τῷ φόβῳ μή.. X.*Cyr.*6.1.2: freq. in Att., esp. in pf., ἀπόλωλας you *are lost*, Ar.*Nu.*1077; ἀπωλόμεθ' ἂν εἰ μὴ ἀπολώλειμεν Plu.2.185f; ἱκανὸν χρόνον ἀπολλύμεθα καὶ κατατετρίμμεθα Ar.*Pax*355; βλέπειν ἀπολωλός Philostr.Jun.*Im.*2:—as an imprecation, κάκιστ' ἀπολοίμην εἰ.. Ar.*Ach.*151, al.; κακὸς κακῶς ἀπόλοιθ' ὅστις.. Eub.116; ἐξώλης ἀπόλοιθ' ὅστις.. Men.154; ἀπολλύμενος, opp. σῳζόμενος, Isoc.6.36, cf. Plu.2.469d: freq. in part. fut., ὦ κάκιστ' ἀπολούμενε O *destined to* a miserable *end!* i.e. O *thou villain, scoundrel, knave!* Ar.*Pl.*713, cf. 456, *Ach.*865, *Pax*2; ὁ κάκιστ' ἀνέμων ἀ. Luc.*DDeor.*14.2. **2.** in *NT*, *perish*, in theol. sense, *Ev.Jo.*3.16, al.; οἱ ἀπολλύμενοι, opp. οἱ σῳζόμενοι, 1*Ep.Cor.*1.18. **II.** *to be lost*, ὕδωρ ἀπολέσκετ' (of the water eluding Tantalus) Od.11.586; οὔποτε καρπὸς ἀπόλλυται never *falls untimely*, ib.7.117; ἀπό τέ σφισιν ὕπνος ὄλωλεν Il.10.186; γέλως ἐξ ἀνθρώπων ἀπόλωλεν X.*Smp.*1.15; ἀπολόμενον ἀργύριον Antipho Soph.54; ἀπώλοντο οἱ ὄνοι Lxx 1*Ki.*9.3.

ἀπόλλω, late form of ἀπόλλυμι, Lxx 4*Ma.*6.14, v.l. in Eust.712.55, etc.

Ἀπόλλων, ὁ, *Apollo*: gen. ωνος (also ω *An.Ox.*3.222): acc. Ἀπόλλω *IG*1.9, al., A.*Supp.*214, S.*OC*1091, *Tr.*209 (lyr.) (mostly in adjurations, νὴ τὸν Ἀπόλλω, etc.), Ἀπόλλωνα Pl.*Lg.*624a, freq. later, Agatharch.7, etc.: voc. Ἄπολλον Alc.1, A.*Th.*159 (lyr.), Cratin.186, etc.; Ἀπόλλων A.*Ch.*559; cf. Ἀπέλλων, Ἄπλουν. **II.** Pythag. name of a number, Porph.*Abst.*2.36.

Ἀπολλ-ώνεια, τά, = Lat. *ludi Apollinares*, D.C.47.18. **-ωνιακός**, ή, όν, = Ἀπολλώνιος I, Ph.2.560, Dam.*Pr.*95, Olymp.*Vit.Pl.* p.1 W. **-ωνιασταί**, οἱ, *worshippers of Apollo*, *IG*12(1).163 (Rhodes). **-ώνιος**, α, ον, *of* or *belonging to Apollo*, Pi.*P.*6.9, etc.:—fem. **-ωνιάς** (sc. πόλις or νᾶσος), άδος, ἡ, i.e. Delos, Id.*I.*1.6: also, = δάφνη, Hsch. **II. -ώνιος**, ὁ, (sc. μήν) name of month at Elis, Methymna, etc., Sch.Pi.*O.*3.35, *IG*12(2).505, etc. **III. -ώνιον**, τό, *temple of Apollo*, Th.2.91, Arist.*Mir.*840^{a}21, *GDI*5726.45 (Halic.):—also **-ώνειον**, D.S.14.16, etc., cf. Eust.1562.54. **IV. -ώνια**, τά, *festival of Apollo*, *IG*11(2).105 (Delos), etc. **-ωνίσκος**, ὁ, Dim. of Ἀπόλλων, Ath.14.636f. **2.** *statuette of Apollo*, Roussel *Cultes Égyptiens* 221 (Delos, ii B.C.). **-ωνιών**, ῶνος, ὁ, (sc. μήν) name of month at Halicarnassus, *BCH*14.106.

Ἀπολλωνό-βλητος, ον, *stricken by Apollo*, = ἡλιόβλητος, Macrob.1.17.11. **-ννησοι**, formed in illustration of ἑκατόννησοι, Str.13.2.5. **-τραφής**, ές, *nourished by Apollo*, Sch.Il.23.291.

ἀπολογ-έομαι, aor. ἀπελογησάμην E.*Ba.*41, Antipho 5.13, but f.l. in Pl.*Sph.*261c, X.*An.*5.6.3; also aor. Pass. ἀπελογήθην Antipho 2.3.1, al., Alex.12 (prob. spurious in X.*HG*1.4.13): pf. ἀπολελόγημαι And.1.33, Isoc.12.218 (in pass. sense, Pl.*R.*607b):—*speak in defence, defend oneself*, opp. κατηγορεῖν, περί τινος *about* a thing, Antipho 5.7, Th.1.72; πρὸς τὴν μαρτυρίαν *in reference* or *answer to* the evidence, Antipho 2.4.3, cf. Th.6.29; πρός τινας *before*.., Eup.357, cf. Plb.22.6.4: later, c. dat., κατηγορίαις Plu.*Them.*23; ἀ. ὑπέρ τινος *speak in* another's *behalf*, Hdt.7.161, E.*Ba.*41, Pl.*R.*488a, etc.; ἀ. ὑπέρ τινος *speak in support of* a fact, Antipho 3.2.1; ὑπὲρ τῆς ἀδικίας Pl.*Grg.*480b; πρὸς Μέλητον *in answer to* him, Id.*Ap.*24b: abs., παρὼν ἀ. Hdt.6.136, Ar.*Th.*188; ὁ ἀπολογούμενος *the defendant*, Id.*V.*778, And.1.6. **2.** c. acc. rei, *defend oneself against*, ἀ. τὰς διαβολάς Th.8.109; τὰς πράξεις *defend* what one has done, Aeschin.1.92. **3.** ἀ. τι ἔς τι *allege in one's defence* against a charge, Th.3.63; ἀ. πρὸς τὰ κατηγορημένα μηδέν Lys.12.38; τί ποτε ἀπολογήσεσθαι μέλλει μοι; Antipho 1.7 codd.; ταῦτα ἀ. ὡς.. Pl.*Phd.*69d; ἔργοις καλλίστοις ἀ. ὡς.. Lys.2.65; ἀ. ὅτι οὐδένα ἀδικῶ X.*Oec.*11.22; ἀ. ἀπολογίαν Luc.

Hes.6. 4. ἀ. δίκην θανάτου *speak against* sentence of death *passing on one*, Th.8.68.—Prose word, used once in Trag., v. supr.—The Prep. ἀπό implies the *removal* of a charge. **-ή**, ἡ, (ἀπολέγω) *selection*, or possibly *challenging of jurors*, ἐξ ἀπολογῆς *OGI*484.54 (Pergam.). **-ημα**, ατος, τό, *plea alleged in defence*, Pl.*Cra.*436c; ὑπὲρ τῆς πόλεως πρὸς Ῥωμαίους Plu.*Cim.*1. **-ητέον**, *one must make one's defence*, Antipho 4.4.1; *one must defend*, Pl.*Ap.*19a: also in pl., -ητέα Philostr.*VA*8.7; ἐκεῖνα -ητέα ἦν ὅτι... D.H.6.44. **-ητικός**, ή, όν, *suitable for defence, apologetic*, Arist.*Rh.Al.*1421ᵇ10. **-ία**, ἡ, *speech in defence*, opp. κατηγορία, Antipho 6.7, Th.3.61, Pl.*Ap.*28a, etc.; ἀ. ποιεῖσθαι to make *a defence*, Is.6.62; ἀ. ποιεῖσθαι τὸν ἑαυτοῦ βίον τῶν τοῦ πατρὸς ἀδικημάτων Lys.14.29; τῶν κατηγορηθέντων τὸ μὴ λαβὸν ἀπολογίαν Hyp.*Eux.*31; ἀ. τοῦ εὐαγγελίου *Ep.Phil.*1.16; expl. by πληροφορία, Hsch. **-ίζομαι**, fut. -ιοῦμαι Phld.*Lib.* p.50O., D.C.*Fr.*109: aor. ἀπελογισάμην Pl.*Sph.*261c (prob.); Dor. -ιξάμην *IG*9(1).694.97 (Corcyra): pf. ἀπολελόγισμαι ib.2.594.19, 329.16, D.H.*Pomp.*1.17 codd.: in pass. sense, X.*Oec.*9.8:—*render an account*, ἀ. κατ' ἐνιαυτόν Id.*HG*6.1.3; ἀ. τὰς προσόδους *render an account of* the receipts, Aeschin.3.25, cf. *IG*7.303.21 (Orop.); τῇ βουλῇ καὶ τῷ δήμῳ ib.2.594.19:—Pass., τὰ ἀπολελογισμένα *the estimates*, X.*Oec.*9.8. 2. ἀ. εἴς τι *refer to* a head or class, Pl.*Phlb.* 25b. II. *reckon on* a thing, *calculate that* it will be.., c. acc. et inf., D.19.20; ἀπολογιεῖται πεῖσαι.. *will count on* persuading, Phld. l.c.; *calculate fully*, ἀ. πότερον.. Pl.*Sph.* l.c. III. *give a brief account of*, τι Arist.*Rh.Al.*1433ᵇ38; περί τινος ib.1444ᵇ31; but, *recount at length*, τι Plb.21.3.2; περί τινος Id.8.24.7; ὡς... Id.4.25.4.—Prose word: Act., *reject*, Suid. **-ισμός**, ὁ, *giving account, statement of reasons*, etc., v.l. in Aeschin.3.247, Plb.10.11.5. 2. *account kept, record*, ἀναλωμάτων Luc.*Dem.Enc.*33; ἀπολογισμὸν ποιήσασθαι *Klio*18.276 (Delph., ii B.C.), cf. Plu.*Per.*23, *POxy.*297.5 (i A.D.): in pl., Plu.2.822e. 3. *narration*, Plb.10.21.8. 4. = ἀπολογία, Zeno *Stoic.*1.55; τοῦ βίου, τῶν πράξεων, Plu.2.726b, *Sull.*34. **-ιστής**, οῦ, ὁ, *accountant, bookkeeper*, *POxy.*34 vi 8 (ii A.D.). **-ος**, ὁ, *story, tale*, Ἀλκίνου ἀπόλογος, of long and tedious stories (from that told by Odysseus to Alcinous in Od.9–12), Pl.*R.*614b, Arist.*Rh.*1417ᵃ13, *Po.*1455ᵃ2. II. *fable, apologue, allegory*, Cic.*Orat.*2.66.264, Quint. *Inst.*6.3.44, Gell.2.29.20. III. *account rendered*, *Test.Epict.*8.36, *IG*14.952 (Agrigent.), Hsch. IV. = λογιστής, *IG*12(8).267 (Thasos), *BCH*45.154 (ibid., iii B.C.), *AJA*19.446 (Halae, iii B.C.).

ἀπολοιδορέω, *abuse violently*, Plb.15.33.4.

ἀπολοίμιον φανόν· τὸν ἐπὶ δόλῳ, Hsch.

ἀπολοιπασία, ἡ, *remainder*, in subtraction, Hero *Geom.*12.32. II. *list of arrears*, *POxy.*1147.1 (vi A.D.), cf. ib.1855.4 (vi A.D.).

ἀπόλοιπος, ον, *remaining over, left behind*, Lxx *Ez.*41.15, al.; ἀπόλοιπα, τά, *unpaid arrears*, = Lat. *residua*, *IG*5(1).1434 (Messene).

ἀπολοίφειν· ἀποτελεῖν, Hsch.

ἀπολοπίζω, = ἀπολέπω, *skin, peel*, prob. l. for -λογίζειν, -λογίζων, Ar.*Fr.*135, Antiph.128, cf. Phryn.*PS* p.44 B.

ἄπολος, ον, = ἀκίνητος, ἀστρεφής, *immovable*, Hsch.

ἀπό-λουμα, ατος, τό, = ἀποκάθαρμα, Sch.Ar.*Eq.*1401, Eust.1560.32. **-λουσις**, εως, ἡ, *ablution*, Pl.*Cra.*405b, Sor.1.83. **-λούτριος**, ον, *washed off*: τὰ ἀπολούτρια (sc. ὕδατα) water *which has been used for washing*, Ael.*NA*17.11:—also **-λουτρον**, τό, Sch.Ar.*Eq.* 1401. **-λούω**, I. c. acc. rei, *wash off*, λούειν ἄπο βρότον Il. 14.7:—Med., ὄφρ'.. ἅλμην ὤμοιιν ἀπολούσομαι that I *may wash* the brine *from off my* shoulders, Od.6.219; of baptism, ἀ. τὰς ἁμαρτίας *Act.Ap.*22.16. 2. c. acc. pers., *wash clean*, Ar.*V.*118 (ἀπέλου for ἀπέλοε, v. λούω), Pl.*Cra.*405b, 406a:—Med., *wash away from oneself*, λούσασθαι ἄπο βρότον αἱματόεντα Il.23.41; τὸ σῶμα ἀπελούετο Longus 1.13: in archaic style, ἀπολούμενος Luc.*Lex.*2, cf. Ath.3.97e, 98a. 3. c. acc. pers. et rei, ὄφρα τάχιστα Πάτροκλον λούσειαν ἄπο βρότον *might wash* the gore *off* him, Il.18.345: c. gen. rei, καί μ' ἀπέλουσε λύθρου *Epigr.Gr.*314.6 (Smyrna). 4. ἀπολουσέμεναι· κολ[λ]οβώσειν (Cypr.), Hsch.; cf. ἀπολέπω.

ἀπολοφ-ύρομαι [ῡ], *bewail loudly*, ἐμαυτόν And.3.16, cf. X.*HG* 1.1.27; συμφοράν Antipho Soph.54: abs., *indulge one's sorrows to the full*, Th.2.46, Pl.*Mx.*249c. **-υρσις**, εως, ἡ, *lamentation*, Sch. S.*Aj.*596.

ἀπολοχμόομαι, *make too much wood*, Thphr.*HP*6.6.6.

ἀπόλυγμα[τος]· ἀπογύμνωσις (Cypr.), Hsch.

ἀπόλῡμα, ατος, τό, *filth*, Harp. s.v. ὀξυθυμία: in pl., *fragments of tissue*, Heliod.ap.Orib.44.10.13, Gal.19.422.

ἀπολῡμ-αίνομαι, Med., (λῦμα) *cleanse oneself by bathing*, esp. *from an* ἄγος, Il.1.313, 314, A.R.4.702, cf. Paus.8.41.2; ἀπολυμήνασθαι καὶ ἀφαγνίσαι τὸ μίασμα Agath.2.7. **-αντήρ**, ῆρος, ὁ, (λύμη) *destroyer*: δαιτῶν ἀ. *one who destroys* one's pleasure at dinner, *kill-joy* (or *a devourer of remnants, lick-plate*), Od.17.220, 377.

ἀπολύουσα, = κώνειον, Ps.-Dsc.4.78.

ἀπολυπραγμ-όνητος, ον, *not meddled with*, prob. in *SIG*399.24 (Delph.). Adv. -τως Hsch. s.v. ἀπεριέργως. **-ων**, ον, gen. ονος, *not meddlesome*, M.Ant.1.5, Ptol.*Tetr.*159.

ἄπολυς, υ, *without plurality*, expl. of ἁπλοῦς, Dam.*Pr.*21, 26.

ἀπο-λῠσίδιον, τό, *order for delivery*, *PFlor.*131.7 (iii A.D.), al.; οἴνου *PFay.*133.14. **-λύσιμος** [ῠ], ον, (ἀπολύω) *deserving acquittal*, Antipho 4.4.9. II. *released from* public service, *PLond.*2.445.7 (i A.D.); ἀπὸ στρατείας *CPR*1.3 (i A.D.). **-λῠσις**, εως, ἡ, *loosing*, e.g. of a bandage or cord, Hp.*Fract.*10, Hero *Aut.*2.9. 2. *release, deliverance*, Pl.*Cra.*405b, Plb.33.1.5: c. gen., κατὰ τὴν ἀ. τοῦ θανάτου as far as *acquittal from* a capital charge went, Hdt.6.136; ἀ. κακῶν θάνατος Plu.*Arat.*54; ἀ. πένθους *end* of mourning, *OGI*56.53 (Canopus). 3. *getting rid of a disease*, Hp.*Coac.*378, etc. 4. *spell for releasing* a divine being, *PMag.Par.*1.1056, al. II. (from Pass.) *separation, parting*, Arist.*GA*718ᵃ14; τῆς ψυχῆς Id.*R.*479ᵃ22: abs., *decease, death*, Thphr.*HP*9.16.8, Lycon ap.D.L.5.71; ἀ. ποιεῖσθαι to take one's *departure*, of an army, Plb.3.69.10. **-λῠτέον**, *one must acquit*, τινά τινος Gorg.*Hel.*6; *one must disengage*, ὀστέον Heliod.ap.Orib.46.12.2. **-λῠτήριον**, τό, = ἐκλ., Sch.E.*Ph.* 969. **-λῠτικός**, ή, όν, *disposed to acquit*. Adv. -κῶς, ἔχειν τινός *to be minded to acquit* one, X.*HG*5.4.25. **-λῠτος**, ον, *loosed, free*, Plu.2.426b; ἀ. ψυχαί souls *at large* before being embodied, Porph. ap.Stob.1.49.40; ἀ. θεοί Dam.*Pr.*351, cf. Procl.*in Cra.*p.74 P. 2. *absolute, unconditional*, Arr.*Epict.*2.5.24, S.E.*M.*8.273, Plot.6.1.18 and 22. Adv. -τως S.E.*M.*8.161, Men.Rh.p.434 S., Lyd.*Mens.*4.7; opp. κατὰ σχέσιν, Procl.*in Prm.*p.733 S. 3. τὸ ἀ. the *positive* degree of comparison, Hdn.*Fig.*p.85 S., Sch.Ar.*Av.*63. 4. ἀ. χάραγμα *independent* coinage of Alexandria, Just.*Edict.*11, *POxy.* 1448 (vi A.D.). 5. Rhet., *unfinished*, μερισμός, e.g. μέν not folld. by δέ, Hermog.*Id.*2.7. b. ἀ. χαρακτήρ *loose, unconstrained* style, Aphth.*Prog.*11. 6. Medic., = ἀπολελυμένος (ἀπολύω c. II. 1), Heliod.ap.Orib.46.14.2, Ruf.*Syn.Puls.*3.4. Adv. -τως ib.5.

ἀπολυτρ-όω, *release on payment of ransom*, Men.*Mis.*21: c. gen. pretii, ὡς ἐχθροὺς ἀ. τῶν μακροτάτων λύτρων Pl.*Lg.*919a, cf. Philipp. ap.D.12.3; *restore for a ransom*, τὰ ἐλεύθερα σώματα καὶ τὴν πόλιν αὐτοῖς Plb.2.6.6, cf. J.*BJ*2.14.1:—Med., Polyaen.5.40. **-ωσις**, εως, ἡ, *ransoming*, αἰχμαλώτων Plu.*Pomp.*24 (pl.), cf. J.*AJ*12.2.3, Ph.2.463. II. *redemption by payment of ransom, deliverance*, *Ev. Luc.*21.28, *Ep.Rom.*3.24, al.; of Nebuchadnezzar's *recovery*, Lxx *Da.*4.30c; in *NT*, *redemption*, *Ep.Rom.*3.24, al. **-ωτικός**, ή, όν, *for ransom*, Suid. s.v. θυσία.

ἀπολύω [v. λύω], fut. -λύσω, etc.: fut. Pass. ἀπολελύσομαι X.*Cyr.* 6.2.37:—*loose from*, ἱμάντα θοῶς ἀπέλυσε κορώνης Od.21.46; ὄφρ' ἀπὸ τοίχους λῦσε κλύδων τρόπιος the sides of the ship *from* the keel, ib.12.420; *undo*, ἀπὸ κρήδεμνον ἔλυσεν ib.3.392; ἐπιδέσματα Hp. *Fract.*25. 2. *set free, release, relieve from*, ἀ. τινὰ τῆς φρουρῆς Hdt. 2.30; τῆς ἐπιμελείας X.*Cyr.*8.3.47; τῶν ἐκεῖ κακῶν Pl.*R.*365a; τὴν ψυχὴν ἀπὸ τῆς τοῦ σώματος κοινωνίας Id.*Phd.*65a, cf. 67a; ἀ. τῆς μετρήσεως *save* them *from the trouble* of measuring, Arist.*Pol.*1257ᵃ40:—Pass., *to be set free*, τῶν δεινῶν, φόβου, Th.1.70, 7.56, etc. b. freq. in legal sense, ἀ. τῆς αἰτίης *acquit of* the charge, Hdt.9.88, X.*An.*6.6.15; opp. καταψηφίζω, Democr.262; τῆς εὐθύνης Ar.*V.*571: c. inf., ἀ. τινὰ μὴ φῶρα εἶναι *acquit of* being a thief, Hdt.2.174; so ἀπολύεται μὴ ἀδικεῖν Th.1.95, cf. 128: abs., *acquit*, Ar.*V.*988, 1000, Lys.20.20, etc. II. in Il. always, = ἀπολυτρόω, *release on receipt of ransom*, οὐδ' ἀπέλυσε θύγατρα καὶ οὐκ ἀπεδέξατ' ἄποινα 1.95; Ἕκτορ' ἔχει.. οὐδ' ἀπέλυσεν 24.115, al.:—Med., *set free by payment of ransom, ransom, redeem*, χαλκοῦ τε χρυσοῦ τ' ἀπολυσόμεθ' *at a price of*.., Il.22.50 (but Act. in Prose, ἀπολύειν πολλῶν χρημάτων X.*HG*4.8.21). 2. *let go, let alone, leave* one, of an illness, Hp.*Coac.*564. III. *discharge, disband* an army, ἀ. οἴκαδε X.*HG*6.5.21; generally, *dismiss, discharge*, ἐμὲ.. ἀπέλυσ' ἄδειπνον Ar.*Ach.*1155, cf. Bion 1.96. 2. *divorce* a wife, *Ev.Matt.*1.19, etc.; τὸν ἄνδρα D.S.12.18. 3. *do away with, remove*, αἰσχύνην D.20.47:—Pass., Antipho 2.1.5. 4. *discharge* or *pay* a debt, Pl.*Cra.*417b; *pay*, ἀ. τὸν χαλκόν *PTeb.*490 (i B.C.); *pay off* a mortgage, *POxy.*509.15. 5. *dismiss* a charge, εἰσαγγελία ὑπὸ τοῦ κατηγόρου ἀπολελυμένη Hyp.*Eux.*38. IV. ἀ. ἀνδράποδα Θρᾳξίν *sell*, Antipho 5.20; ἀ. οἰκίαν τινί *sell* a mortgaged house *outright*, Is.6.33. V. *deliver*, τί τινι *PFlor.*123.2 (iii A.D.):—Pass., ib.228.6 (iii A.D.). VI. *begin to count*, [μοίρας] ἀπό.. Vett.Val.135: abs., Id.19.19, Paul.Al.*Q.*2. VII. intr., *depart* (cf. B. IV, C. 2), Plb.3.69.14, al.

B. Med. with aor. 2 ἀπελύμην (in pass. sense), Opp.*C.*3.128:—*redeem*, v. supr. A. II. II. ἀπολύεσθαι διαβολάς *do away with, refute* calumnies *against one*, Th.8.87, Pl.*Ap.*37b, al.: abs., Arist.*Rh.*1416ᵇ 9. 2. τὴν αἰτίαν, τὰς βλασφημίας, τὰ κατηγορημένα, Th.5.75, D. 15.2, 18.4: c. gen., τῶν εἰς Ἀριστόβουλον -σασθαι J.*AJ*15.3.5. b. *refute*, τοὺς ἐναντίους λόγους Dam.*Pr.*126 ter: abs., ὁ δὲ ἀπολυόμενος ἔφη *in defence*, Hdt.8.59. III. like Act., *acquit*, τοῦ μὴ κακῶς ἔχειν ἀλλ' ὀρθῶς Pl.*Lg.*637c. 2. *release from*, τοὺς Ἕλληνας ἀ. δουλείας Id.*Mx.*245a. IV. like Pass. (c. II), *depart*, S.*Ant.*1314; also, *put off*, πνεῦμα ἀ. *AP*9.276 (Crin.); but πνεῦμα μελῶν ἀπέλυε *IG*14.607e (Carales).

C. Pass., *to be released*, ἐλπίζων τοὺς υἱέας τῆς στρατηίης ἀπολελύσθαι *from* military service, Hdt.4.84, cf. X.*Cyr.*6.2.37; τῆς ἀρχῆς ἀπολυθῆναι βουλόμενοι *to be freed from* their rule, Th.2.8; τῶν δεινῶν μηδέποτε οἴεσθαι ἀπολυθήσεσθαι Id.1.70; τῆς ὑποψίας Antipho 2.4.3; τῆς μιαρίας ib.3.11: abs., *to be acquitted*, Th.6.29; *to be absolved from*, τῶν ἀδικημάτων Pl.*Phd.*113d. II. of combatants, *to be separated, part*, οὐ ῥᾳδίως ἀπελύοντο Th.1.49; generally, *to be separated* or *detached*, ἀλλήλων or ἀπ' ἀλλήλων, Arist.*Metaph.*1031ᵇ3, *Ph.*185ᵃ28; ἀ. τὰ ᾠὰ τῆς ὑστέρας Id.*GA*754ᵇ18, al.; ἀπολελυμένος, abs., *detached*, αἰδοῖον, γλῶττα, ὄρχεις, Id.*HA*500ᵇ2, 533ᵃ27, 535ᵇ2; τὴν γλῶτταν ἀ. *having* its tongue *detached*, Id.*Fr.*319, al.; also, *distinct, differentiated*, Id.*HA*497ᵇ22. 2. *depart*, ἔθανες, ἀπελύθης, S.*Ant.*1268 (lyr.), cf. Plb.6.58.4, al., Lxx *Nu.*20.29, al.; cf. supr. B. IV. III. of a child, *to be brought forth*, Hp.*Superf.*11, cf. 24, Arist.*GA*745ᵇ11; of the mother, *to be delivered*, Hp.*Epid.*2.2.17. IV. *to be annulled*, Arist. *EN*1156ᵃ22. V. ἀπολελυμένος, η, ον, *absolute*, esp. in Gramm., D.T. 636.15, A.D.*Synt.*97.20, al.: also, *general*, of meaning, Olymp.Alch.

p.72 B. VI. of metres, *irregular, without strophic responsion*, Heph.*Poëm*.5.

ἀπολῦώρητος, ον, *not highly esteemed*, Phld.*Oec*.p.67 J.

ἀπολωβάω, *dishonour*, aor. Pass. ἀπελωβήθην S.*Aj*.217 (lyr.).

ἀπολωπίζω, (λῶπος) = λωποδυτέω, S.*Fr*.1021.

ἀπολωτίζω, = ἀπανθίζω, *pluck off flowers*: generally, *pluck off*, κόμας E.*IA* 792; ἀ. νέους *cut off* the young, Id.*Supp*.449.

ἀπολωφ-άω, Ion. -έω, *appease*, Hp.*Ep*.17 (Pass.); δίψαν A.R.4.1418 (tm.). II. intr., *abate*, Procop.*Aed*.1.1, 5.5:—Subst. **-ησις**, εως, ἡ, *lightening, relief*, *An.Ox*.3.188.

ἀπόλωψεν· ἀπώλετο, Hsch.

ἀπομαγ-δᾰλία or **-ιά**, ἡ, (ἀπομάσσω) *the crumb* or *inside of the loaf*, on which the Greeks wiped their hands at dinner, and then threw it to the dogs: hence, *dog's meat*, Ar.*Eq*.415, Alciphr.3.44, Plu.*Lyc*.12. **-δᾰλίς**, ίδος, ἡ, = foreg., Eust.1857.17. **-μα**, ατος, τό, *anything used for wiping* or *cleaning*, Hp.*Medic*.2. 2. *dirt washed off*, S.*Fr*.34. II. *impression of a seal*, Thphr.*CP*6.19.5, *Lap*.67.

ἀπομᾰδ-άω, of the hair, *fall off*, Arist.*Mir*.836^{a}1. **-ίζω**, *make quite bald*, Crito ap.Gal.12.454, Sch.Ar.*Eq*.373.

ἀπομάζιος, (μαζός) *taken from the breast*, Opp.*C*.4.93.

ἀπομάθημα [ᾰθ], ατος, τό, *unlearning*, Hp.*Fract*.25.

ἀπομαίνομαι, aor. 2 ἀπεμάνην [ᾰ], *go mad*, Luc.*DDeor*.12.1.

ἀπομᾰκᾰρίζω· *ebeo*, *Gloss*.

ἀπομακ-τέον, *one must wipe*, τὰ μέλη Aët.9.1. **-της**, ου, ὁ, *one who wipes, rubs*, or *cleans*, *Com.Adesp*.589, *AB*431; esp. in magical rites, Poll.7.188. **-τρια**, ἡ, fem. of ἀπομάκτης, Poll.7.188. **-τρον**, τό, *strickle*, Ar.*Fr*.712.

ἀπομᾰλᾰκίζομαι, *to be weak* or *cowardly, show weakness*, πρός τι in a thing, Arist.*HA*613^{a}1, cf. Plu.*Lyc*.10.

ἀπομαλθᾰκίζομαι, = foreg., Plu.2.1097a, prob. l. (for -όομαι) Id.*Pel*.21.

ἀπομανθάνω, *unlearn*, ταῦτα ἃ πρὸ τοῦ ᾤμην εἰδέναι Pl.*Phd*.96c, cf. *Prt*.342d, X.*Cyr*.4.3.14, Antisth.ap.D.L.6.7: c. inf., Plu.*Lyc*.11.

ἀπομαντ-εία, ἡ, *negative divination*, opp. κατα-, Jul.Laod. in *Cat. Cod.Astr*.5(1).190. **-ευμα**, ατος, τό, *divination*, v.l. in Hp.*Ep*.27. **-εύομαι**, *divine by instinct, presage*, τὸ μέλλον ἥξειν Pl.*R*.516d; τι εἶναι ib.505e; τρίτον ἀ. τι τὸ ὄν Id.*Sph*.250c, cf. Plot.5.5.12, Jul.*Or*.4.149c. **-ευτικός**, ή, όν, *of negative divination*, *PAmh*.2.14.15.

ἀπόμαξις, εως, ἡ, (ἀπομάσσω) *wiping off*, Plu.*Rom*.21. II. *taking an impression*: metaph., *copying, imitation*, Iamb.*Protr*.21.

ἀπομᾰρ-αίνω, *cause to waste away*, αἱ συλλήψεις ἀ. τὰ σώματα Sor.1.30, cf. Chor.p.22 B.; τὴν ἀκμὴν τῶν αἰσθήσεων Callistr.*Stat*.2; ἡδονὰς τὰς τὸ θυμοειδὲς -ούσας Philostr.*VA*7.4; *obliterate* from memory, Chor.*Milt*.19:—Pass., *waste, wither away, die away*, ἡ ῥητορικὴ ἐκείνη ἀ. Pl.*Tht*.177b; αἱ κατὰ τὸ σῶμα ἡδοναὶ ἀ. Id.*R*.328d; of a tranquil death, X.*Ap*.7, cf. Plu.*Num*.21; of comets, ἀπομαρανθέντες κατὰ μικρὸν ἠφανίσθησαν Arist.*Mete*.343^{b}16; of wind, *die down*, ib.367^{b}11; ἡ φύσις ἀ. Ocell.1.12, etc. **-ανσις**, εως, ἡ, *wasting* or *dying away, disappearance*, opp. φάσις, παρηλίων Thphr.*Vent*.36.

ἀπομαρξάμενοι· ἀπομαξάμενοι, Hsch.; cf. ὀμαρξον.

ἀπομαρτῠρ-έω, *testify, bear witness*, ἀ. τισὶν ὅτι εἰσὶν πολῖται *Milet*.3 No.313 (iii B.C.): c. acc. et inf., Plb.30.31.20; τι Plu.2.860c:—Pass., περὶ τούτων ἀπομεμαρτύρηται αὐτῷ ὅτι *IG*2.377.9. **-ομαι** [ῠ], *maintain stoutly*, τι Pl.*Sph*.237a.

ἀπομάσσω, Att. -ττω, *wipe off*, δάκρυα χλαμύδι Plb.15.26.3, cf. Plu.*Rom*.21:—Med., *wipe off oneself*, ὕδατος ἄχνην Call.*Del*.14; τὸν κονιορτὸν τισι *Ev.Luc*.10.11; *wipe*, τι *POxy*.1381.133: abs., *dry oneself*, Jul.*Or*.6.203b. 2. *wipe clean*, esp. in magical ceremonies, ἀπομάττων [αὐτοὺς] τῷ πηλῷ καὶ τοῖς πιτύροις D.18.259, cf. Luc.*Nec*.7, Hsch. s. vv. μαγίδες, μαγμόν:—Med., *wipe for oneself*, Ἀχιλλείων ἀπομάττει *you wipe your hands on* the finest bread, Ar.*Eq*.819; χεῖρας χειρομάκτρῳ ἀ. Ath.9.410b: abs., *wipe one's mouth*, Eratosth.30; of a serpent, ἀ. τὸν ἰὸν *get rid of* its poison, Arist.*Fr*.372. II. *wipe off* or *level* corn in a measure *with a strickle*: hence χοίνικα ἀ. *give scant* measure, Luc.*Nav*.25; κενεὰν ἀπομάξαι (sc. χοίνικα) *level* an empty measure, i.e. labour in vain, Theoc.15.95. III. *take an impression of*, ἔν τισι τῶν μαλακῶν σχήματα ἀ. Pl.*Ti*.50e:—Med., *model*, as a sculptor, Philostr.*VA*6.19, *APl*.4.120 (Arch. or Asclep.): metaph., *take impressions*, ὅθεν ἡμὴ φρὴν ἀπομαξαμένη Ar.*Ra*.1040; τὰς ἰδέας Gal.18(2).655; ἀ. παρ' ἀλλήλων one from another, Arist.*EN*1172^{a}12: generally, *copy, imitate*, D.H.*Vett.Cens*.3.2; ἤθεα ἀ. τεκούσης Nonn.*D*.46.18, cf. 48.229: c. gen., *model oneself upon*, Call.*Epigr*.27.

ἀπομαστῑγόω, *scourge severely*, Hdt.3.29, 8.109.

ἀπομαστίδιον, τό, *suckling*, E.*Hyps.Fr*.64.94.

ἀπομᾰτᾰΐζω, *behave idly* or *unseemly*, euphem. for ἀποπέρδω, Hdt.2.162, Favor.ap.Stob.4.50.25; cf. ἀποματαιάσαι· ἐξευτελίσαι, Hsch.

ἀπομαύρωσις, εως, ἡ, *dullness*, διανοίας Archig.ap.Aët.6.27.

ἀπο-μάχομαι [μᾰ], fut. -μαχοῦμαι, *fight from* the walls of a fort or town, τεῖχος ἱκανὸν ὥστε ἀπομάχεσθαι ἐκ τοῦ ἀναγκαιοτάτου ὕψους Th.1.90; βασίλεια ἱκανὰ ἀ. high or strong enough *to fight from*, X.*Cyr*.3.1.1: abs., *fight desperately*, Id.*An*.6.2.6; πρός τι Plu.*Brut*.5, Hld.5.1; τινί *against* a thing, Plu.*Caes*.17. II. ἀ. τι *fight off* a thing, *decline* it, ἀπεμαχέσαντο τοῦτο Hdt.7.136: abs., ὁ μὲν δὴ ταῦτα λέγων ἀπεμάχετο Id.1.9; ἀ. μὴ λαβεῖν τὴν ἀρχήν D.H.2.60. III. ἀ. τινά *drive off in battle*, X.*HG*6.5.34. IV. *finish a battle, fight it out*, Lys.3.25; *resist*, Arist.*Pr*.870^{b}23. V. metaph., *counteract*, ταῖς ἀποφοραῖς Aët.16.24. **-μᾰχος**, ον, (μάχη) *unfit for service, disabled*, X.*An*.3.4.32, 4.1.13, Arr.*Tact*.12.4, Agath.3.22. II. *absent from the fight*, of Achilles, *AP*9.467 tit., cf. Agath.2.7.

ἀπομεθίημι ψυχήν *give up* the ghost, A.R.1.280 (tm.).

ἀπομειλίσσομαι, Att. -ττομαι, *appease, allay*, θεοῦ μῆνιν D.H.1.38; πεῖναν Ph.2.477; τινά J.*AJ*19.9.2; θεούς Porph.*Marc*.2. II. *expiate*, τὰς τῶν πολλῶν ἁμαρτίας Id.*Abst*.4.5.

ἀπομειουρ-ίζω or **-μυουρίζω**, (μείουρος) *make to taper off to a point*, Nicom.*Ar*.2.13; of a root, Herod.Med.ap.Orib.8.4.3. **-ισμός**, ὁ, *curtailment*, Dam.*Pr*.59 (pl.).

ἀπομειόω, *diminish*, Aët.3.162.

ἀπομείρομαι, *distribute*, αἶσαν Hes.*Op*.578. 2. Pass., *to be parted from*, Id.*Th*.801, Arat.522:—in each place with v.l. ἀπαμείρομαι (q.v.).

ἀπομελ-αίνομαι, *turn black*, of grapes, Thphr.*HP*2.7.5; of cinders, Ruf.*Fr*.70.14. 2. *to be blackened by mortification*, Hp.*Art*.69. **-ανσις**, εως, ἡ, = λεύκωσις, Olymp.Alch.p.91 B.

ἀπόμελι, ιτος, τό, *honey-water*, an inferior kind of *mead*, Dsc.5.9. 2. = ὀξύγλυκυ, τό, Antyll.ap.Orib.5.29.8, Philagr.ib.5.17, Gal.6.274.

ἀπομελίζω, *enervate*, = ἀπογυιόω, Eust.641.23.

ἀπομέμφομαι, *rebuke*, E.*Rh*.900 (lyr.); φανερῶς J.*BJ*1.24.2, Plu.2.229b (s.v.l.); τῇ ἀποτυχίᾳ Oenom.ap.Eus.*PE*5.20 (v.l.).

ἀπομένω, dub. sens. in *PFlor*.378.6 (V A.D.); *remain behind*, Alciphr.3.60, dub. l. in Polyaen.4.6.13.

ἀπομερίζω, *divide off, separate*, Pl.*Plt*.304a; ἑαυτοὺς τῆς ὁμιλίας Hierocl.*in CA*24 p.472 M.:—Pass., *to be distinguished*, ἑτέρων συγγενῶν Pl.*Plt*.280b. 2. *detail* for special service, Plb.8.30.1; πρός or ἐπί τι, Id.3.101.9, 16.21.8:—Pass., πρός τι, Id.10.16.2; ἀπομερισθῆναι ἀριστίνδην *to be selected* by merit, Pl.*Lg*.855d:—also in Act., *take as one's special province*, Bito 56.3. b. *assign a detachment to* a commander, τῆς δυνάμεώς τινι Plb.3.35.5. 3. *impart*, δεκάτην τινί J.*AJ*4.4.4. 4. *send out branches*, [ἡ ἀορτή] ἀ. ἑαυτῆς ἀπάσας τὰς ἀρτηρίας Gal.5.199.

ἀπομεριμνάω, *rest from labour*: hence, *die*, Eust.821.36.

ἀπομερισμός, ὁ, = ἀπονομή, of water from an aqueduct, *Ephes*.2 No.18 (I A.D.), cf. Hsch. s. v. ἀπόδραγμα, al. 2. *fragmentation*, οὐ γὰρ ἀ. τοῦ παράγοντος τὸ παραγόμενον Procl.*Inst*.27. 3. *division*, τῆς ψυχῆς Herm. *in Phdr*.p.166 A. 4. *banishment*, ἐλλογίμων ἀνδρῶν *Cat.Cod.Astr*.8(3).185.25, al. 5. v.l. for ἐπιμερίζω (q.v.), Vett.Val.164.19, al.

ἀπομερμηρίζω, aor. -ιξα *AB*431:—*sleep off care, forget one's cares in sleep*, Ar.*V*.5, D.C.55.14.

ἀπομεστόομαι, Pass., *become filled to the brim*, Pl.*Phdr*.255c, Plot.2.3.18.

ἀπομετρ-έω, fut. Med. -ήσομαι *IG*7.3073.77 (Lebad.):—*measure off* or *out*, θριγκούς l.c.; δακτυλίους μεδίμνοις Luc.*DMort*.12.2:—Med., μεδίμνῳ ἀπομετρήσασθαι τὸ ἀργύριον X.*HG*3.2.27:—Pass., *to be measured off*, Plb.6.27.2, Str.2.1.27. II. *measure out, distribute*, X.*Oec*.10.10; σῖτόν τινι J.*AJ*2.5.7, cf. Ath.Med.ap.Orib.*Inc*.5.6. **-ημα**, ατος, τό, *servant's allowance*, *Gloss*. **-ησις**, εως, ἡ, *measuring out, distribution*, Vett.Val.346.13. **-ον**, τό, in pl., *emoluments* of a priest, *IG*2^2.1357, 1363 (Eleusis), *Leg.Sacr*.2.10 B 10.

ἀπομήκης, ες, prob. f.l. for ἐπι-, Sophon. *in de An*.75.13.

ἀπομηκύνω, *prolong, draw out*, λόγον Pl.*Sph*.217e, cf. *Prt*.336d, Luc.*Herm*.67, etc.: abs., *to be prolix*, Them.*Or*.2.39d, etc.:—Pass., *to be prolonged, extended*, Sor.1.57, Luc.*DMar*.1.2.

ἀπομηνίω, *to be very wroth, persevere in wrath*, κεῖτ' ἀπομηνίσας Ἀγαμέμνονι (where Eust. expl., *having departed from wrath* against him) Il.2.772; ἐμεῦ ἀπομηνίσαντος ib.9.426, 19.62; opp. μεθησέμεναι, Od.16.378; ἀ. εἴς τινα *PBodl.ined*.32478. II. *cease from wrath*, *AB*431, Suid.

ἀπομηρῡκάομαι, aor. -ήσατο, *ruminate*, Porph.*Chr*.32.

ἀπομηρύομαι [ῡ], *draw up from, out of*, βυθῶν Opp.*C*.1.50.

ἀπομῑμ-έομαι, *express by imitation, copy* or *represent faithfully*, ἦθος X.*Mem*.3.10.3; πρᾶξιν Pl.*Lg*.865b; τὴν Κλεοφῶντος πολιτείαν Aeschin.3.150; τὸ ἵεσθαι διὰ τοῦ ῑ ἀ. *endeavour to express* motion by the sound of *i*, Pl.*Cra*.427a sq.: pf. in pass. sense, Moschio ap.Ath.5.207f. **-ημα**, ατος, τό, *imitation, copy*, Hp.*Vict*.1.22, Bato Sinop.4, D.S.16.26. **-ησις**, εως, ἡ, *imitation*, Hp.*Vict*.1.10, Arist.*Rh.Al*.1420^{b}16, Phld.*Lib*.p.45 O., J.*AJ*3.7.7, Plu.*Num*.14.

ἀπομιμνήσκομαι, fut. -μνήσομαι, aor. -εμνησάμην:—*remember, recognize*: hence, *repay*, τῷ οἱ ἀπεμνήσαντο [χάριν] Il.24.428; ἀπεμνήσαντο χάριν εὐεργεσιάων *for* benefits, Hes.*Th*.503; αὐτῷ δὲ.. χάριν ἀπομνήσεσθαι ἀξίαν Th.1.137, cf. E.*Alc*.299.

ἀπομίμνω, *remain away from*, c. gen., παρθενικῆς Nonn.*D*.42.439.

ἀπομῑνύθω, = μινύθω, Orph.*L*.624.

ἀπομίσγομαι, *draw off and mix*, οἶνον Max.Tyr.1.5.

ἀπομῑσέω, = μισέω, Eratosth.*Cat*.9, Them.*Or*.15.189c.

ἀπόμισθ-ος, ον, *away from* (i.e. *without*) *pay, unpaid* or *underpaid*, X.*HG*6.2.16; ἄθλιοι ἀ. ξένοι D.4.46; *defrauded of pay*, Lys.*Fr*.138 S. II. *paid off, discharged*, ἀ. γίγνεται παρὰ Τιμοθέου D.23.154, cf. Aen.Tact.5.2 and 11.4; λευκή με θρὶξ ἀ. ποιεῖ *Com.Adesp*.226. **-όω**, *let out for hire*, γῆν ἐπὶ δέκα ἔτη Th.3.68; χωρίον τινί Lys.7.9; ὥσπερ..ἀπομεμισθωκότες τὰ ὦτα Pl.*R*.475d; *farm out* by contract, *IG*1.26a10, al.; ἀναγραφήν *Milet*.7.69 (Didyma), etc.: c. inf., ἀ. ποιεῖν τι ὡς ἂν δύνωνται ὀλιγίστου *contract for*.., Lex ap.D.43.58.

ἀπομιτρόω, *take away the mitre*, Lxx *Le*.21.10, Ph.1.562.

ἀπομνημόν-ευμα, ατος, τό, *memorial, record*, τινός D.S.1.14, Plu.

*Pomp.*2; ἀ. σύντομον *memorandum*, *PSI*1.85 (iii A.D.): in pl., *memoirs*, as those of Socrates by X., D.H.*Rh.*9.12, Plu.*Cat.Ma.* 9. **-ευσις**, εως, ἡ, *recounting, summarizing*, τῶν λόγων Arist.*Top.* 164ᵃ3, cf. Plu.2.44e. II. *commemoration*, *BSA*17.233 (Pamphyl.). **-εύω**, *relate from memory*, Pl.*Phdr.*228a, etc.:—Pass., *to be recorded*, ἀπομνημονεύεται ὁκόσος ἐγένετο X.*Ages.*1.2. 2. *remember, call to mind*, Pl.*Plt.*268e, *Phd.*103b, *Ly.*211a, D.19.13, Aeschin.3.16, etc.; *keep in mind*, διδαχήν Pl.*Plt.*273b, al. 3. ἐπὶ τούτου τὠυτὸ οὔνομα ἀπεμνημόνευσε τῷ παιδὶ θέσθαι *gave* his son the same name *in memory of* a thing, Hdt.5.65. 4. ἀ. τινί τι *bear* something *in mind against* another, X.*Mem.*1.2.31, Aeschin.1.129, 3.208; οὐδὲ μνησίκακος· οὐ γὰρ μεγαλοψύχου τὸ ἀ. Arist.*EN*1125ᵃ 4. 5. τινί τι *bear in mind favourably*, πατρικὰς εὐεργεσίας D.*Ep.* 3.19; χάριν Luc.*Sacr.*2, *JTr.*40.

ἀπομνησικᾰκέω, *bear a grudge against*, τινί Hdt.3.49; πρός τινα Eus.Mynd.45.

ἀπόμνῡμι or -ύω (Pi.*N.*7.70), fut. -ομοῦμαι: 3 impf. ἀπώμνυ Od. 2.377:—*take an oath away from*, i.e. *swear that one will not do* a thing, ἡ δ' αὐτίκ' ἀπώμνυεν ib.10.345, cf. 12.303, 18.58; μέγαν ὅρκον ἀπόμνυ ib.2.377; ἀπώμοσα καρτερὸν ὅρκον ib.10.381. 2. *deny on oath*, Hdt.2.179, 6.63; ἀ. Ζηνὸς σέβας S.*Ph.*1289; ταῦτ' ἀ. μοι τοὺς θεούς Ar.*Nu.*1232, cf. *Eq.*424; also ἀ. τἀναντία κατὰ τῆς θυγατρός *swear to the contrary by..*, D.29.52: freq. c. μή et inf., ἀ. μὴ ὅρσαι Pi. l.c., cf. E.*Cyc.*266; τοὺς θεοὺς ἀ. ἦ μὴν μὴ εἰδέναι.. Pl.*Lg.*936e, cf. X.*Cyr.*6. 1.3; ἀ. μηδὲ ὀβολόν (sc. ἔχειν) Id.*Smp.*3.8; ἀ. ὡς οὐκ εἴρηκε D.21. 120. 3. c. acc., ἀ. υἱόν *deny, disown* a son *on oath*, And.1.127:—Med., ἀπωμόσατο τὴν ἀρχήν, = Lat. *eieravit, solemnly laid it down*, Plu.*Cic.*19. II. strengthd. for ὄμνυμι, *take a solemn oath*, ἦ μήν .. Th.5.50 codd.

ἀπό-μοιρα, ἡ, *portion*, σιτηρᾶς *OGI*55.15 (iii B.C.); esp. of a *revenue assigned* to the gods, τὰς καθηκούσας ἀ. τοῖς θεοῖς..μένειν ib. 90.15 (Rosetta), cf. *PEleph.*14.3 (iii B.C.), *PRev.Laws*25.15, al., *PLond.*2.195.9 (i A.D.), etc.: generally, λαφύρων J.*AJ*6.14.6; ὀρνίθων Paus.8.22.6. b. θεία ἀ. *particle* of divinity, M.Ant.2.1. 2. *distribution* of parts of a victim, *BCH*29.524 (Delos). **-μοιράζω**, =sq., Sch.A.*Th.*727. **-μοιράομαι**, *give as a share*, J.*AJ*18.8. 7. **-μοίρια**, τά, *portion dedicated to a god*, *AP*6.187 (Alph.). **-μοιρος**, ον, *forming a branch* or *portion* of a nation, etc., Zos.3.6.

ἀπομολῠβόω, *turn into lead*, Lyd.*Mens.*4.107:—also written **-μολυβδόω**, *detach by melting off the lead*, Gloss.

ἀπομονόομαι, Pass., *to be excluded*, τῆς ξυμβάσεως *from* the agreement, Th.3.28; ἐκ συμμείξεως Pl.*Ti.*60d. 2. *to be left alone*, ἐν πολεμίοις Plu.*Phil.*18.

ἀπόμοργ-μα, ατος, τό, *that which is wiped off*, Eust.218.12. **-νῡμι**, fut. -μόρξω, *wipe off* or *away from*, ἀπ' ἰχῶ χειρὸς ὀμόργνυ Il.5.416; αἷμ' ἀπομόργνυ ib.798; πεύκης ἀπὸ δάκρυ' ὀμ. v.l. in Nic.*Al.*547:—Med., *wipe off from oneself*, ἀπομορξαμένω κονίην Il.23.739; ἀπομόρξατο δάκρυ *wiped away his* tears, Od.17.304; ἀφρὸν ἀπὸ στομάτων Mosch. 2.96; abs. in same sense, ἀπομόρξασθαι Ar.*Ach.*706; ἀ. ἱδρῶτα ib. 696:—Pass., τὴν ὀργὴν ἀπομορχθείς *having* my anger *wiped off*, Id.*V.* 560; ἀπωμοργμένος *rubbed bare*, Arist.*Phgn.*810ᵇ3. 2. *wipe clean*, σπόγγῳ δ' ἀμφὶ πρόσωπα.. ἀπομόργνυ Il.18.414:—Med., ἀπομόρξατο χερσὶ παρειάς *wiped her* cheeks, Od.18.200.

ἀπο-μορφόομαι, Pass., *receive their form*, Thphr.*Fr.*171.9. II. late in Act., ἀ. τινὰ εἰς πτηνόν *change* one *into the form of..*, Eust. 1598.64. **-μορφος**, ον, *of strange form, strange*, S.*Fr.*1022. **-μόρφωσις**, εως, ἡ, *form*, Sch.Ptol.76.

ἀπομοσία στήλη record *of an oath*, *OGI*573.22 (Cilicia).

ἀπομοτικός, ή, όν, *of abjuration*, λόγος Simp.*in Cat.*406.9.

ἀπόμουσος, ον, *away from the Muses, untutored, rude*, E.*Med.* 1089. Adv., κάρτ' ἀπομούσως ἦσθα γεγραμμένος wast *unfavourably* painted, A.*Ag.*801.

ἀπομοχλεύω, *move as with a lever*, Hp.*Art.*70, cf. Ph.*Bel.*70.47.

ἀπομυζ-άω, *suck away*, Artem.5.49:—Pass., Them.*Or.*22.282c. **-ουρις**, ιδος, ἡ, obscene name of a courtesan, *Com.Adesp.*1352.

ἀπομῡθέομαι, *dissuade*, μάλα γάρ τοι ἔγωγε πόλλ' ἀπεμυθεόμην Il. 9.109. II. = ἀπολογέομαι, Stratt.72.

Ἀπόμυιος, ὁ, *Averter of flies*, epith. of Zeus and Heracles, Paus. 5.14.1, *EM*131.23.

ἀπομῡκάομαι, *bellow loud*, *AP*9.742 (Phil.).

ἀπο-μυκτέον, (ἀπομύσσομαι) *one must wipe one's nose*, E.*Cyc.* 561. **-μυκτηρίζω**, *turn up the nose at*, Hsch. s.v. ἀποσκαμυνθίζειν:—also **-μυκτίζω**, Luc.*DMeretr.*7.3 (s.v.l.).

ἀπομυλλαίνω, *make mouths at*, *EM*125.25; μὴ ἀπομυλλαίνῃ ἡ γνάθος, of a broken jaw, in which the fractured parts *override* each other, Hp.*Art.*33 (-σμιλ- in Gal. ad loc.).

ἀπομυξία, ἡ, *dirt from the nose*, *AB*432, Hsch.

ἀπόμυξις, εως, ἡ, *blowing one's nose*, Plu.2.1084c.

ἀπομύσσω, Att. -ττω, *wipe* the nose, ῥῖνα *AP*11.268; σεαυτόν Arr.*Epict.*1.6.30:—Med., *blow one's nose*, Ar.*Eq.*910, X.*Cyr.*1.2.16, Thphr.*Char.*19.4, *AP*7.134, etc.; ὑδατώδη ἀ. Arist.*Pr.*897ᵃ31; βραχίονι, ἀγκῶνι ἀ., Plu.2.631d, D.L.4.46. II. metaph., *stop* his *drivel*, Pl.*R.*343a. 2. Pass., *to be wiped clean*, i.e. *cheated*, γέρων ἀπεμέμυκτ' ἄθλιος Men.493 (Act. in Hsch.). III. *snuff* a wick, *Com. Adesp.*847. (Cf. μυκτήρ, μύξα, Lat. *mūcus, emungo.*)

ἀπομύω, fut. -ύσω [ῠ], *shut* the eyes *close*: hence, *die*, Call.*Epigr.* 41.

ἀπομφολύγωτος [ῠ], ον, *making no bubbles*, Dsc.5.99.

ἀπομωκάομαι, v. ἀποίζειν.

ἀπομωλέω, *contend*, of litigants, *Leg.Gort.*6.26.

ἀπομωλύνομαι, *to be absorbed, disappear*, Hp.*Epid.*7.105.

ἀπομωρόω, *stupefy*, Dsc.4.75:—Pass., Asclep.ap.Aët.6.16.

ἀπόναϝε, perh. for ἐπόνησε, *wrought*, *IG*5(1).920 (Sellasia).

ἀπόναιο, ἀποναίατο, v. ἀπονίναμαι.

ἀποναίω, *remove, send away*, used by Hom. only in aor. 1, ὡς ἂν.. περικαλλέα κούρην ἂψ ἀπονάσσωσιν Il.16.86, cf. A.R.4.1492:—Med., *wend one's way back*, Δουλίχιόνδ' ἀπενάσσατο Il.2.629, cf. Od.15. 254. II. aor. Med. in trans. sense, ἀπενάσσατο παῖδα *sent away her* child, E.*IT*1260 (lyr.):—Pass., aor. ἀπονασθῆναι, *to be taken away, depart from* a place, σᾶς πατρίδος ib.175 (lyr.); πατρὸς καὶ πόλεως Id. *Med.*166.

ἀποναρκ-άω, *to be quite torpid*, πρὸς πόνους Plu.2.8f. **-ησις**, εως, ἡ, = ἀπονάρκωσις, Plu.2.652e. **-όομαι**, *become torpid, stupefied*, Hp.*Coac.*478, cf. *Acut.*(*Sp.*)55; ἀπονεναρκωμένος Pl.*R.*503d, Hp.*Ep.* 21. **-ωσις**, εως, ἡ, *insensibility*, Id.*Art.*46, Arist.*Pr.*875ᵇ7.

ἀπονείφω, *snow* or *rain down*, δρόσον Ph.2.112 (dub. l.).

ἀπονεκρ-όω, *destroy*, Dsc.*Eup.*1.204; esp. of cold, *benumb*, Tz.*H.*1.332:—Pass., *to be quite killed, be benumbed*, τοὺς πόδας D.S. 2.12, cf. Luc.*VH*2.1: metaph., τὸ αἰδῆμον ἀπονενέκρωται Arr.*Epict.* 4.5.21; τῆς ψυχῆς -ουμένης ib.1.5.4. **-ωσις**, εως, ἡ, *benumbing*, ibid.

ἀπονέμ-ησις, εως, ἡ, (ἀπονέμω) *distribution*, M.Ant.8.6, Porph. *Sent.*40, Hierocl.*in CA*7 p.430 M. II. *branch*, Gal.4.565, Orib. 22.2.6, cf. 8.62. **-ητέον**, *one must assign*, Arist.*EN*1165ᵃ18. 2. **-ητέος**, α, ον, *to be assigned*, φρόνησις ἐν -τέοις Zeno *Stoic.*1.49, Chrysipp.ib.3.72. **-ητής**, οῦ, ὁ, *distributor*, Gloss. **-ητικός**, ή, όν, *disposed to distribute*: τὸ ἀ. [ἦθος] disposition *to give every one his due*, M.Ant.1.16; ἑκάστῳ τῶν πρὸς ἀξίαν Gal.19.384; *distributive*, Asp.*in EN*158.22. Adv. -κῶς D.L.7.126. (ἀπονεμετ- is a f.l.) **-ω**, fut. -νεμῶ Pl.*Phlb.*65b:—*portion out, impart, assign*, ἡμῖν.. ταῦτ' ἀπένειμε τύχη Simon.100; βωμοὺς καὶ ἀγάλματα θεοῖσι Hdt.2.4; τὸ πρέπον ἑκατέροις Pl.*Lg.*757c; τῷ θεῷ τοῦτο γέρας Id.*Prt.*341e; τοῖς θεοῖς χάριτας *SIG*708.33, cf. 1*Ep.Pet.*3.7; τὸ καλῶς ἀποθανεῖν ἴδιον τοῖς σπουδαίοις ἡ φύσις ἀπένειμεν Isoc.1.43; aor. imper. ἀπόνειμον *render, impart*, Pi.*I.*2.47; τῇ συγγνώμῃ πλέον ἢ τῷ δικαίῳ ἀπονέμειν Din.1. 55:—Med., *assign* or *take to oneself*, τι Pl.*Sph.*267a, *Lg.*739b; ἀπονέμεσθαί τι *feed on*, Ar.*Av.*1289; ἀπονέμεσθαι τῶν πατρῴων *help oneself to a share* of.., Pl.*R.*574a:—Pass., *to be assigned*, τοῖς ἀγαθοῖς Arist. *EN*1123ᵇ35; *to be rendered*, θεῷ Porph.*Marc.*11. II. *part off, divide*, of logical division, ἐπὶ τἀναντία ἀ. τοῖς ὀνόμασι Pl.*Plt.*307b:—in Pass., ib.276d, 280d. III. Pass., *to be taken away, subtracted*, Id.*Lg.*771c, 848a.

ἀπονένεται· ἀποστρέφεται, Hsch.

ἀπονενοημένως, Adv., (ἀπονοέομαι) *desperately*, X.*HG*7.2.8, Luc. *DMort.*19.2, etc.; ἀ. ἔχειν πρὸς τὰ γεύματα to be *obstinately averse* to food, Hp.*Epid.*3.17.β'; ἀ. διακεῖσθαι πρὸς τὸ ζῆν to be *recklessly indifferent* to life, Isoc.6.75.

ἀπονέομαι, *go away, depart*, freq. in Hom., only in pres. (sts. with fut. sense, as Il.2.113) and impf., always at the end of the line, with the first syll. long, metri gr., ἀπονέεσθαι Il. l.c., etc.; ἀπονέωνται Od. 5.27; ἀπονέοντο Il.3.313, al.

ἀπονεοττεύω, *hatch the young*, Arist.*HA*563ᵃ3.

ἀπόνευμα, ατος, τό, *slope*, Suid. s.v. ἀπόκλιμα.

ἀπονευρ-όομαι, Pass., *become tendinous*, Gal.2.252, etc. 2. *become a nerve*, Id.5.191. 3. ἀπονευρούμενος· ὁ τὰ νεῦρα κοπτόμενος, Hsch.; *to be unnerved*, Suid. **-ωσις**, εως, ἡ, *end of the muscle*, where it becomes *tendinous*, Gal.4.368, 13.603.

ἀπόνευσις, εως, ἡ, *bending* or *turning off*, *Stoic.*2.289, Them.*Or.*20. 236b. II. *dissent*, opp. κατάνευσις, Anon.*Fig.*p.179 S.

ἀπονεύω, *bend away from* other objects towards one, *turn off* or *incline towards*, εἰς τοὐπίσω Plb.3.79.7; σκηναὶ ἀπονενευκυῖαι πρὸς ἓν μέρος τῆς πόλεως Id.15.29.2: metaph., πρὸς τὴν γεωμετρίαν Pl.*Tht.* 165a; πρὸς τὸ δικολογεῖν Arist.*Rh.*1355ᵃ20; πρός τινα Plb.21.6.4; ἐπὶ τὴν ἁρπαγήν Id.16.6.7; ἀπὸ τοῦ ἀληθοῦς Arr.*Epict.*4.10.2. II. abs., *hang the head*, of barley, Thphr.*CP*3.22.2. III. Astron., *pass away from* a cardinal point, Vett.Val.95.1.

ἀπονέω (A), *unload*:—Med., *throw off a load from*, στέρνων ἀπονησαμένη (expl. by ἀποσωρεύσασα in *AB*432, Hsch.) E.*Ion*875; ἀπενήσω· ἀπέβαλες *AB*421; ἀπὸ δ' εἵματα..νήσαντο A.R.1.364.

ἀπονέω (B), (ἄπονος) *to be without pain*, Hsch. s.v. ἀωδυνεῖν.

ἀπονήμενος, v. ἀπονίναμαι.

ἀπονήνισι· τιμὴν ἀποδοῦναι, Hsch.

ἀπονηρευσία, ἡ, (πονηρεύομαι) *innocence*, gloss on εὐήθεια, Sch.D. 2.6.

ἀπόνηρος, ον, (πονηρός) *not vicious, harmless*, Ptol.*Tetr.*163. 2. Medic., *not malignant*, πυρετοί Antyll.ap.Orib.5.29.8. II. (πόνηρος) *not taking pains*, c. inf., D.H.*Lys.*15.

ἀπονηστίζομαι, *break one's fast*, Herod.9 tit.

ἀπονητί, Adv. of ἀπόνητος, *without fatigue*, Hdt.3.146, E.*Fr.lyr.*3, Luc.*Rh.Pr.*8, al.

ἀπόνητο, v. ἀπονίναμαι.

ἀπόνητος, ον, *without toil* or *trouble*. Adv., Sup. ἀπονητότατα *with least toil* or *trouble*, Hdt.2.14, 7.234. 2. *without suffering*, S.*El.* 1065 (lyr.).

ἀπονήχομαι, *escape by swimming, swim away*, Plb.16.3.14, Luc. *Pisc.*50: metaph., τοῦ σώματος *escape from..*, Plu.2.476a; πόλεως J.*BJ*2.20.1.

ἀπονία, ἡ, (ἄπονος) *non-exertion, laziness*, X.*Cyr.*2.2.25, Arist.*Rh.*

1370a14 (pl.); *exemption from toil*, of women, Id.*GA*775a37, cf. Plu. *Rom*.6. **II.** *freedom from pain*, Epicur.*Fr*.2, Chrysipp.*Stoic*.3.33, Dsc.*Eup*.1.67, Aret.*SA*2.1, etc.

ἀπονίζω, later **-νιπτω** D.S.4.59, Plu.*Phoc*.18, and once as v.l. in Hom., v. infr.:—*wash off*, ἀπονίψαντες.. βρότον ἐξ ὠτειλῶν Od.24.189, cf. Il.7.425 (tm.):—Med., *wash off from oneself*, ἱδρῶ πολλὸν ἀπονίζοντο θαλάσσῃ ib.10.572. **II.** *wash clean*, esp. of the hands and feet, τὴν ἀπονίζουσα φρασάμην I perceived it (the scar) *as I was washing his feet*, Od.23.75; ὅταν ἡ θυγάτηρ μ' ἀπονίζῃ καὶ τὼ πόδ' ἀλείφῃ Ar.*V*.608, cf. Men.*Georg*.60; ἕ μὲν ἔφη ἀ. τὸν παῖδα Pl.*Smp*. 175a:—Med., χρῶτ' ἀπονίπτεσθαι *wash one's* body, v.l. in Od.18.179, cf. 172; χεῖράς τε πόδας τε ib.22.478: abs., οἷον εἴ τις εἰς πηλὸν ἐμβὰς πηλῷ -νίζοιτο Heraclit.5; *wash one's hands* (esp. after meals, cf. Ar.Byz.ap.Ath.9.408f), Hp.*Mul*.1.89; ἐγὼ μὲν ἀποτρέχων ἀπονίψομαι Ar.*Av*.1163; ἀπονίψασθαι δοτέον *water to wash with*, Alex.250, cf. Antiph.136; so in pf. Pass., ἀπονενίμμεθ' Ar.*V*.1217; ἀπονενιμμένος Id.*Ec*.419; also in late Prose, v. supr.; τῆς κρήνης -νιψάμενος Alciphr.3.1; but ἀπονίψασθαι τὸ πρόσωπον ἀπὸ τᾶς κράνας *IG*4.951.63 (Epid.). **2.** rarely of things, ἀ. τὴν κύλικα Pherecr.41.

ἀπονῑκάω, *overpower*, J.*AJ*15.3.4:—Pass., Arist.*MA*703a27.

ἀπόνιμμα, ατος, τό, (ἀπονίπτω) = ἀπόνιπτρον, Plu.*Sull*.36: esp. *water for purifying the dead* or *the unclean*, Clidem.(or Anticlid.)ap. Ath.9.409f, cf. 410a.

ἀπονίνᾰμαι, Med., fut. ἀπονήσομαι Hom.: Ep. aor. 2 without augm. ἀπονήμην, ἀπόνητο Hom.; 2 sg. opt. ἀπόναιο Il.24.556, 3 pl. ἀποναίατο *h.Cer*.132, S.*El*.211 (lyr.); inf. ἀπόνασθαι A.R.2.196; part. ἀπονήμενος Od.24.30: later aor. 1 ἀπωνάμην Luc.*Am*.52, Procl.*in Alc*.p.89C.:—*have the use* or *enjoyment of* a thing, ἧς ἥβης ἀπόνητο Il. 17.25; τῶνδ' ἀπόναιο *mayest* thou *have joy of* them, ib.24.556; τιμῆς ἀπονήμενος Od. l. c.; μηδέ ποτ' ἀγλαΐας ἀποναίατο S.*El*.211: without gen., ἦγε μὲν οὐδ' ἀπόνητο married her but *had* no *joy* [of it], Od.11. 324; θρέψε μὲν οὐδ' ἀπόνητο ib.17.293, cf. 16.120; πόλιν κτίσας οὐκ ἀπόνητο Hdt.1.168.

ἀπό-νιπτρον, τό, *water used for washing, dirty water*, ἀ. ἐκχεῖν Ar. *Ach*.616. **-νίπτω**, v. ἀπονίζω.

ἀπονίσσομαι, *go away*, Thgn.528, A.R.3.899: aor. -νισσαμένη *AP*9.118.

ἀπονιτρόω, *rub off with* νίτρον (q. v.), Hp.*Ulc*.18.

ἀπόνιψις, εως, ἡ, *washing off* or *away*, Herod.Med.ap.Orib.*Fr*.106, prob. l. for ἄποψις in Callix.2.

ἀπονοέομαι, *have lost all sense*, **1.** of fear, *to be desperate*, ἀπονοηθέντας διαμάχεσθαι X.*HG*6.4.23; ταῖς γνώμαις Plb.16.31.1; ἄνθρωποι ἀπονενοημένοι *desperate* men, Th.7.81, cf. X.*HG*7.5.12. **2.** of shame or duty, ἀπονενοημένος *abandoned fellow*, Thphr.*Char*. 6.1, cf. Isoc.8.93, D.19.69:—later in Act., *make desperate*, J.*AJ*18. 1.6.

ἀπόνοια, ἡ, (νοῦς) *loss of all sense*, **1.** of fear and hope, *desperation*, εἰς ἀ. καταστῆσαί τινα to make one *desperate*, Th.1.82, 7.67, cf. Nicol.Com.1.43, Plb.2.35.2, D.H.6.23. **2.** of right perception, *madness*, D.18.249, 25.32, Phld.*Lib*.p.11O., *PGiss*.8.7.8 (ii A.D.), Alciphr.1.3: in pl., Plb.1.70.5. **3.** *rebellion*, ἀ. καὶ στάσις Antig. ap.Heph.Astr.2.18.

ἀπόνοιμον· ἀπογύμνωσιν, Hsch.

ἀπονομή, ἡ, = ἀπονέμησις, *distribution, assignment*, τινός τινι Ph. 2.345. **2.** *a portion*, Harp.

ἀπονομίζω, *forbid by law*, Mnaseas 32.

ἄπονος, ον, *without toil* or *trouble*, βίος Simon.36; χάρμα Pi.*O*.10 (11).22; οἶκος A.*Pers*.862 (lyr.); τύχη S.*OC*1585; ἄ. ὕπνον εὕδεις *Eranos* 13.87; ἀπονώτατος τῶν θανάτων *easiest*, Pl.*Ti*.81e; ἄ. τινι χάρις *costing* one *no trouble*, And.2.22; ἄ. τὸ εὖ πάσχειν Arist.*EN*1168a24; -ώτερον τὸ ὀξύ, in playing the flute, Thphr.*Fr*.89.6; opp. μετὰ βίας, Arist.*PA*668b19. **b.** *painless*, τοξικόν Str.3.4.18. **2.** of persons, *work-shy, lazy*, μαλακὸς καὶ ἄ. X.*HG*3.4.19; ἄ. πρός τι Pl.*R*.556b; of the heaven, *free from the necessity of labour*, Arist.*Cael*.284a15. **b.** *free from pain*, Dsc.3.96, Aret.*SA*2.1; in Sup., *least painful*, Id.*CA*1. 6. **3.** *relieving pain*, Id.*CD*2.12. **II.** Adv. -νως Hdt.9.2; ἀπόνως ἔχειν feel *easy*, of a sick person, Hp.*Prog*.23 (but with v.l. ἀποβήσσειν ἀ.); ἀπόνως λιπαροί, opp. ἐπιπόνως αὐχμηροί, X.*Mem*.2.1.31. **III.** irreg. Comp. ἀπονέστερος Pi.*O*.2.68; regul. Comp. -ώτερος Hp.*Art*. 79, cf. supr. Adv., Comp. -ώτερον Th.1.11.

ἀπονοσέω, *fall into a morbid state*, Hp.*Septim*.6.

ἀπονοστ-έω, *return, come home*, Hom. in phrase ἂψ ἀπονοστήσειν Il.1.60, al.; ἀ. ἀπὸ τάφου Hes.*Op*.735; ἀ. ὀπίσω Hdt.4.33; ἀ. σῶς Id. 3.124, 4.76; ἀπήμων Id.1.42, al.; ἐς Σπάρτην Id.1.82; rare in Trag. and Prose, ἀπονοστήσας χθονὸς *when he returns from*.., E.*IT*731; ἀ. ἐπ' οἴκου Th.7.87; ἐκ πυρός Iamb.*Protr*.21.ι': abs., X.*An*.3.5. 16. **-ησις**, εως, ἡ, *return*, Arr.*An*.7.4.3, 7.12.1.

ἀπονόσφι, before a vowel **-νόσφιν**, Ep. Adv. *far apart, aloof*, ἀ. κατίσχεαι Il.2.233; ἀ. τραπέσθαι Od.5.350. **II.** c. gen., following its case, *far away from*, ἐμεῦ ἀ. ἐόντα Il.1.541; φίλων ἀ. ὀλέσθαι Od. 5.113; φίλων ἀ. ἑταίρων ib.12.33.

ἀπονοσφίζω, *put asunder, exclude from*, τινὰ δόμων *h.Cer*.158. **2.** *bereave* or *rob of*, ὅπλων τινά S.*Ph*.979:—Pass., *to be robbed of*, ἐδωδῆν *h.Merc*.562. **3.** Med., *embezzle*, τὰ κοινά *OGI*515.49 (Mylasa), prob. in *SIG*37 (Teos, v B.C.). **II.** c. acc. loci, *flee from, shun*, S.*OT*480 (lyr.), cf. *Ichn*.131.

ἀπονυκτερεύω, *pass a night away from*, τοῦ στρατοπέδου Plu.*Fab*. 20: abs., Id.2.195e.

ἀπονύμφης, ου, ὁ, or **-νυμφος**, ον, = μισογύνης, Poll.3.46.

ἀπονυστάζω, *to be sleepy and sluggish*: metaph., Plu.*Cic*.24, cf. Arr.*Epict*.4.9.16.

ἀπονῠχ-ίζω, *pare the nails*, Men.996:—Med., ἀπονυχίσασθαι τὰς χεῖρας Hp.*Mul*.1.70:—Pass., *have them pared*, ἀκριβῶς ἀπωνυχισμένος *with* carefully *pared nails*, Thphr.*Char*.26.4; ὑπὸ σμίλης ἀπωνυχίσθη Babr.98.14, cf. Sor.1.69. **2.** metaph., *scratch out*, τὰ σιτία Ar. *Eq*.709. **II.** = ὀνυχίζω III, *polish by the nail*, τὰ ῥήματα Jul.*Or*.2. 77a. **III.** = ἐξονυχίζω, Paul.Aeg.3.59. **-ισμα**, ατος, τό, *nail-paring*, D.L.8.17, Iamb.*Protr*.21.λβ'. **-ιστικός**, ή, όν, *polishing to the nail*: -κή (sc. -τέχνη), ἡ, Sch.D.T.p.110H.

ἀπονωτίζω, *turn one's back and flee*, S.*Fr*.713; trans. in causal sense, ἀ. τινὰς φυγῇ E.*Ba*.763.

ἀποξαίνω, *scarify, tear*, in Pass., Lxx 4*Ma*.6.6, Asclep.Jun.ap.Gal. 13.1022.

ἀποξανᾶν· κακοπαθεῖν, Hsch.

ἀποξενῑτεύομαι, *dwell away from home*, Sch.E.*Hec*.1208.

ἀπο-ξενολογέω, *hire for mercenary service*, J.*AJ*13.16.2; *finish recruiting*, prob. in *Vit.Philonid*.p.12C. **-ξενος**, ον, *alien to guests, inhospitable*, stronger than ἄξενος, ὅρμος S.*OT*196 (lyr.). **2.** c. gen. loci, *far from* a country, τῆσδε γῆς ἀπόξενος A.*Ag*.1282, *Ch*.1042; τοῦδ' ἀ. πέδου *banished from*.., Id.*Eu*.884. **-ξενόω**, *drive from house and home*: generally, *estrange, banish from*, εἰς βαρβάρους τινὰ τῆς Ἑλλάδος Plu.2.857e, cf. Id.*Alex*.69; *drive into exile*, τινά Id.*Phil*.13:—Pass., *live away from home*, φυγὰς ἀπεξενοῦτο S.*El*.777; γῆς ἀπεξενωμένοι E.*Hec*.1221; of troops on service, ἀ. ἔξω τῆς οἰκείας Arist.*Pol*. 1270a2; ἑτέρωσε ἀ. *migrate* to some other place, Pl.*Lg*.708b: generally, *alienate oneself from, be averse from*, τινός D.S.3.47, cf. Luc. *Dom*.2. **2.** *wean*, Sor.1.117:—Pass., *become disused to*, λουτρῶν Agathin.ap.Orib.10.7.1. **3.** *to be convicted of* ξενία, Is.*Fr*.46. **4.** Med., *disguise oneself*, Lxx 3*Ki*.14.5. **II.** metaph., τοῦ ποιητοῦ ἀ. τὰ ἔπη *estrange* the verses *from* him, i. e. *deny that* they *are* his, Ath. 2.49b; but in Pass., ἀπεξενωμένος *outlandish*, of words, Hdn.Gr.2. 910; μαθήματα Iamb.*VP*1.2. **-ξένωσις**, εως, ἡ, *living abroad*, Plu. *Pomp*.80. **2.** *exile*, Paul.Al.*E*.2 (pl.), al. **-ξενωτέος**, α, ον, *to be rejected*, Aret.*CD*1.2.

ἀπό-ξεσις, εως, ἡ, *smoothing, polishing*, *SIG*244ii39 (Delph., iv B.C.). **-ξεσμα**, ατος, τό, *scraping, shred*, ἐντέρων Orib.8.26.1, cf. Eust.230.4. **-ξέω** (contr. ἀποξοῦσιν *SIG*2587, subj. ἀποξῶμεν Herod.Med.ap.Orib.10.37.17), *cut off*, ἀπὸ δ' ἔξεσε χεῖρα Il.5.81. **II.** *wipe, scrape*, τινὰ σπόγγοις Herod.Med. l. c. **2.** *scrape off*, ἀποξέων τὸν κηρόν Luc.*Somn*.2; *scrape*, τὸ ὀστοῦν Aët.15.11. **3.** metaph., ἀπέξεσας τὴν αἰδῶ τοῦ προσώπου *strip* it *off* like a mask, Alciphr.3.2, cf. Luc.*Vit.Auct*.10 (v.l. -ξυσον). **III.** *scrape to a point*, in pf. part. Pass. -εσμένος Hp.*Nat.Mul*.109. **2.** metaph., *polish, finish off*, Eust.1.16, al.; ἀπεξεσμένος *polished, precise*, Suid.

ἀποξηραίνω, *dry up*, τὸ ἀρχαῖον ῥέεθρον -ξηρῆναι Hdt.2.99:—Pass., *to be dried up*, of rivers, ἀποξηρανθῆναι Id.1.75; ἀπεξηρασμένου τοῦ.. ῥεέθρου ib.186, cf. 7.109. **2.** generally, *dry completely*, τὰς ναῦς *lay* them *up*, Th.7.12:—Pass., ἀπεξηραμμένα κρεάδια Alex.124.11, cf. Thphr.*HP*8.11.3.

ἀποξίννυται, v. ἀποζίννυται.

ἀποξῐφίζομαι, = ἀπορχέομαι, *AB*432: but ἀπεξίφισται· ἀποδεδοκίμασται, Hsch.

ἀποξῠλίζω, *deprive of its woody fibre*, κράμβην Arist.*Pr*.873b4 (v.l. ἀποχυλίζοντες).

ἀποξῠλόομαι, *become hard like wood*, *Gp*.17.2.1, 19.2.5.

ἀποξύνω, *bring to a point, make taper*, ἀποξύνουσιν ἐρετμά Od.6. 269, cf. 9.326, Luc.*DMar*.2.2:—Pass., Thphr.*Ign*.52: pf. part. ἀπωξυμμένος or -υσμένος, Plb.18.18.13, 1.22.7; ὦτα -ξυσμένα Gal.7. 30. **II.** *make sharp and piercing*, τὴν φωνήν Plu.*TG*2. **b.** *intensify*, θερμότητα Id.2.695d. **III.** *make sour*, [τὴν τροφήν] Hp. *Vict*.3.76, cf. Asclep.Jun.ap.Gal.13.164:—Pass., Sor.1.107.

ἀποξῠρ-άω or **-έω**, *shave clean*, c. dupl. acc., τὸν δοῦλον ἀποξυρήσας τὴν κεφαλήν Hdt.5.35; ἀποξυρεῖν ταδί Ar.*Th*.215; ἀπεξύρησε ib.1043; τὴν κόμην ἀπεξύρησε Luc.*Sacr*.15:—Pass., τὰς κεφαλὰς ἀπεξυρημένοι Polyaen.7.35.1. **-ησις**, εως, ἡ, *shaving off*, τριχῶν Orib.46.8.1. **-ίζω**, *scalp*, Sch.E.*Tr*.1026. **-ος**, ον, (ξυρόν) *cut sharp off, abrupt, sheer*, πέτραι Luc.*Rh.Pr*.7, *Prom*.1, cf. *Peripl.M.Rubr*.40. **-ω**, = ἀποξυράω, aor. part. -ξύρας Polyaen.1.24:—Med., -ξυράμενος *get shaved*, ibid., cf. Plu.*Oth*.2:—Pass., opp. κείρεσθαι, D.C.57.10.

ἄποξυς, υ, *tapering*, Hp.*Art*.33, *Off*.9 (with vv. ll. ἀπόξυρα, ἀπόξηρα), Dsc.2.114, Gal.15.330.

ἀπόξῠσις, εως, ἡ, *sharp point*, *Gp*.10.75.11. **II.** *making smooth*, of stone, *IG*4.481 (Nemea).

ἀπόξυσμα, ατος, τό, (ἀποξύω) *that which is shaved* or *scraped off*: *shavings, filings*, Dsc.*Eup*.1.175, Sch.Ar.*Pax*48.

ἀποξυσμός, ὁ, *becoming acid*, Aët.9.10.

ἀποξυστρόομαι, Pass., *become bent* or *blunted*, Plb.2.33.3.

ἀποξύω [ῡ], fut. -ξύσω, = ἀποξέω, *scrape off*, τι Thphr.*HP*9.4.4; τὸν καττίτερον *IG*7.303.15 (Oropus), cf. Dsc.5.79:—Med., φάρμακον D.Chr.32.44: abs., *scrape oneself*, Plin.*HN*34.62. **2.** metaph., *strip off* as it were a skin, γῆρας ἀποξύσας θήσει νέον Il.9.446, cf. Nosti *Fr*.6; κόρυζαν ἀποξύσας (prob. f.l. for ἀπομύξας) Luc.*Nav*.45; τὸ ἐρυθριᾶν ἀ. τοῦ προσώπου v.l. in Id.*Vit.Auct*.10: so in Pass., ἀπέξυσται τὴν αἰδῶ τοῦ προσώπου Alciphr.3.40:—Med., *scrape off*, φάρμακον D.Chr.32.44.

ἀποπᾰγιόομαι, gloss on ἀποκλεΐζομαι, Gal.15.129 (ad Hp.*Nat. Hom*.10).

ἀποπαιδᾰγωγέω, *lead away*, ἀπό τινος Iamb.*Protr*.21.

ἀποπαιδαριόω, dub. sens. in *PSI* 4.418.17 (iii B.C.).

ἀπόπᾰλαι, Adv. *from of old*; condemned by Phryn.32.

ἀποπᾰλαιόω, *abrogate*, dub. in Hsch.

ἀποπάλησις, εως, ἡ, gloss on ἐκπάλησις, read by Erot. in Hp. *Fract.*42, cf. Gal.19.84.

ἀπο-πάλλω, *hurl* or *cast*, βέλη Luc.*Am.*45; *radiate*, αὐγήν J. *BJ* 5.5.6:—Pass., *rebound*, Epicur.*Fr.*293; ἀ. πάλιν Arist.*Pr.*891ᵃ 3, cf. Plu.*Alex.*35, S.E.*M.*10.73, etc. **–παλμός**, ὁ, *rebounding*, Epicur.*Ep.*1 p.8 U. **–παλσις**, εως, ἡ, = foreg., ib.2 p.50 U.; gloss on ἐκπάλησις, Gal.19.84; *shock*, Archig.ap.Orib.8.2.10. **–παλτικός**, ή, όν, *rebounding*. Adv. –κῶς S.E.*M.*10.223.

ἀποπαλώσει· ἀποπαλαιώσει, Hsch.

ἀπόπαξ· ξύμπαν, Hsch.

ἀποπαππόομαι, Pass., *become pappose*, of dandelions, Thphr.*HP* 7.11.4.

ἀποπαπταίνω, *look about one, look round*, as if to flee, Ion. fut. ἀποπαπτανέουσιν Il.14.101.

ἀποπάρδαξ, ακος, ὁ, *qui crepitum ventris emittit*, Hsch. (ἀποπαρδακᾶ cod.).

ἀποπαρθεν-εύομαι, *lay aside virginity*, Hp.*Aër.*17:—also –όω, *deflower*, νεανίδα Lxx *Si.*20.4.

ἀπόπαστος, ον, *fasting*, Opp.*H.*1.299.

ἀποπάσχω, opp. πάσχω, a Stoic term, *reject an impression*, ἀπόπαθε ὅτι ἡμέρα ἐστί Arr.*Epict.*1.28.3.

ἀποπᾰτ-έω, fut. –ήσομαι Ar.*Pl.*1184, but –ήσω Hp.*Morb.*2.66: aor. subj. –πατήσω Ar.*Ec.*354:—*retire to ease oneself*, Cratin.49, Ar. ll. cc., M.Ant.10.19, D.C.78.5, etc. II. *pass with the excrement, void*, τι Ar.*Ec.*351. **–ημα**, ατος, τό, *dung*, ἀλώπεκος Eup.284, cf. Ael. *NA* 3.26. **–ησις**, εως, ἡ, *going to stool*, Gal.15.607. **–ητέον**, *one must ease oneself*, Ar.*Ec.*326. **–ος**, ὁ (ἡ only in Greg.Cor. p.521 S.) *ordure*, Hp.*Prorrh.*2.4, Plu.2.727e, Luc.*Trag.*168. 2. = ἄφοδος, *privy*, Ar.*Ach.*81, Poll.10.44.

ἀπό-παυσις, εως, ἡ, (from Med.) *cessation* of an attack, Aret.*SA* 1.5. **–παύστωρ**, ορος, ὁ, = ἀποπαύων, Orph.*H.*39.3. **–παύω**, *stop* or *hinder from, make to cease from*, τοὺς μὲν... εἴασαν ἐπεὶ πολέμου ἀπέπαυσαν Il.11.323; πένθεος ἀ. τινά Hdt.1.46; ἐρώτων S.*Aj.*1205 (lyr.); λόγου δέ σε μακροῦ 'ποπαύσω E.*Supp.*639: c. inf., *hinder from* doing, ἀ. τινὰ ἀλητεύειν, ὁρμηθῆναι, Od.18.114, 12.126:—Med. and Pass., *leave off, cease from*, c. gen., πολέμου δ' ἀποπαύεο πάμπαν Il.1.422, cf. 8.473; ἀοιδῆς Od.1.340; τοῦ δάκνειν X.*Cyr.*7.5.62; ἐκ καμάτων S.*El.*231 (lyr.): abs., *leave off*, opp. ἄρχεσθαι, Thgn.2; *terminate*, Arat.51. 2. c. acc., *stop, check*, νὺξ ἀπέπαυσε.. Πηλεΐωνα Il. 18.267; Ἀλκμήνης δ' ἀ. τόκον 19.119, al.; so ἀ. κῶμον Thgn.829; μερίμνας E.*Ba.*381 (lyr.); ὠδῖνα Pl.*Tht.*151a, etc. II. intr. in Act., ἀπόπαυσον *stop! cease!* E.*Fr.*118; οὐκ ἀπὸ πυγμαχίης ἀποπαύσετε; *AP* 9.217 (Scaev.).

ἀποπεῖν· ἀπελθεῖν, Hsch.

ἀπό-πειρα, ἡ, *trial, venture*, ἀ. ποιεῖσθαι τῆς μάχης make *trial* of their way of fighting, Hdt.8.9; ναυμαχίας ἀ. λαμβάνειν Th.7.21; δοῦναι ἀ. εὐσεβείας give *proof* of it, Ph.1.650. **–πειράζω**, *make trial of, prove*, ἀ. εἰ.. Arist.*Mir.*831ᵃ29. 2. *make an attempt upon*, Μεγάρων App.*Pun.*117. **–πειράομαι**, fut. –άσομαι [ᾱ]: aor. Pass. ἀπεπειράθην, Ion. –ήθην, v. infr.:—*make trial* or *proof of*.., τῶν μαντηΐων, τῶν δορυφόρων, Hdt.1.46, 3.128; ἀ. ἑκάστου εἰ ναυμαχίην ποιέοιτο Id.8.67, cf. 9.21; ἀ. γνώμης [ἑκάστου] Id.3.119; τῆς γνώμης ἀποπειρῶ Ar.*Nu.*477, cf. And.1.105; ἀ. τινὸς εἰ δύναιτο ἀληθεύειν X. *Cyr.*7.2.17, cf. 2.3.5; ναυμαχίας ἀποπειρᾶσθαι *to venture* it, Th.4.24: abs., ἐπεὰν ἀποπειρηθῇ Hdt.2.73; freq. in Pl., to express the dialectical *trial* of an opponent, *Prt.*311b, 349c, al. II. Act., esp. in Th., τῆς Καρχηδονίων ἀρχῆς καὶ αὐτῶν ἀποπειράσοντες 6.90; ὅπως ναυμαχίας ἀποπειράσωσι 7.17; ἀποπειρᾶσαι τοῦ Πειραιῶς *make an attempt on* the Piraeus, 2.93, cf. 4.121: abs., κατὰ γῆν ἀ. 4.107, cf. 7.36; τῶν τειχῶν App.*BC* 5.36, etc. **–πειρᾱτέον**, *one must make trial of*, τῶν λόγων Isoc.9.11, cf. Gal.10.376.

ἀποπέκω, *shear off* wool:—Pass., ἀποπέπεκται Hsch.:—Med., ἀπὸ χαίταν πέξηται *comb* her hair, Call.*Lav.Pall.*32, cf. *AP* 6.155 (Theodorid.).

ἀποπελεκ-άω, *hew* or *trim with an axe*, Ar.*Av.*1156, Thphr.*HP* 5.5.6:—also –ίζω, *AB* 438. **–ημα**, ατος, τό, *chip*, Hsch. s. v. λατύπη.

ἀποπελιόομαι, (πελιός) *become livid*, Hp.*Acut.*(*Sp.*)9.

ἀποπεμπτικός, ή, όν, *valedictory*, ὕμνοι Men.Rh.p.336 S.

ἀπόπεμπτος, ον, *dismissed*, dub. in *PPetr.*2 p.52 (iii B.C.); cf. Hsch.

ἀποπεμπτόω, *give a fifth part of*, τι Lxx *Ge.*47.26. II. *take a fifth part of*, ib.41.34.

ἀποπέμπω, *send off* or *away, dispatch, dismiss*, Il.21.452, Od.24.312, al.; τῷ κε τάχα στυγερῶς μιν ἐγὼν ἀπέπεμψα νέεσθαι 23.23; ἐπί τι, ἐς τι, for a purpose, Hdt.1.38,47; ἀ. τοὺς πρέσβεις *dismiss* them, Th.5.42, cf. Ar.*Nu.*1244; ἀ. ἀσινέας Hdt.7.146:—Med., *send away from oneself*, τὸν παῖδα ἐξ ὀφθαλμῶν ἀ. Id.1.120; ἀ. τὴν γυναῖκα *put away, divorce* her, Id.6.63 (so in Act., D.59.52, Men.994); ἀ. τὰς ναῦς ὁμολογίᾳ *get rid of*.., Th.3.4; ἀ. ἡδονὴν *get rid of* it, Arist.*EN* 1109ᵇ 11; *send from home*, A.*Pers.*137. II. of things, *send back*, Od. 17.76; ἀ. ἐξοπίσω Hes.*Op.*87. 2. *send off, dispatch*, ἀναθήματα ἐς Δελφοὺς Hdt.1.51; *export*, τἀπόρρητα Ar.*Ra.*362:—so in Med., X. *Vect.*1.7. 3. Med., *get rid of*, τὸ ὕδωρ Hdt.2.25. 4. *emit, discharge*, Pl.*Ti.*33c. 5. Med., *avert* by sacrifice, etc., ἔννυχον ὄψιν E.*Hec.*72 (lyr.), cf. Orph.*H.*39.9; *banish, exorcise* disease, αἶγας ἐς ἀγριάδας τὴν ἀποπεμπόμεθα Call.*Aet.*3.1.13.

ἀπόπεμψις, εως, ἡ, *sending away, dispatching*, τῶν κατασκόπων Hdt 7.148. 2. *dismissal, divorcing*, D.59.59; δίκη ἀποπέμψεως Lys. *Fr.*307 S.

ἀποπενθέω, *mourn for*, τινά Plu.*Cor.*39.

ἀποπεραίνω, *complete, finish*, in fut. ἀποπερᾰνῶ, Hsch.

ἀπο-περαιόω, *terminate*, Ammon. *in Int.*54.29. **–περᾰτίζω**, = foreg., Sch.Ar.*Nu.*1454. **–περᾰτόω**, = foreg., Porph. *in Cat.* 132.33, Sch.Ar.*Th.*1033:—freq. in Pass., –οῦσθαι εἴς τι Hierocl. *in CA* 26 p.478 M., Paul.Aeg.6.77, Steph. *in Hp.*1.188 D., al.; ἔν τινι Phlp. *in Mete.*31.1. **–περάτωσις**, εως, ἡ, *termination* of a fistula, Antyll.ap.Orib.44.22.9, Paul.Aeg.6.77: generally, *completion, end*, Syrian. *in Metaph.*49.29; *final term*, Procl.*Inst.*147 (pl.), Dam.*Pr.* 114, al.

ἀποπεράω, *carry over*, Plu.*Pomp.*62, *Mar.*37, al.

ἀποπέρδομαι, fut. –παρδήσομαι Ar.*Ra.*10: aor. Act. –έπαρδον Id. *Eq.*639, *Pl.*699, etc.:—*break wind*, Ar. ll. cc., etc.: metaph., ἀνὴρ ἀποπέρδεται ἵππον, i. e. *desinit in equum*, of a Centaur, *APl.*4.115.

ἀποπερισπάω, *draw off, divert*, τὴν διάνοιαν Sor.1.117, cf. Sch.Ar. *Nu.*721.

ἀποπερκόομαι, (πέρκος) *colour*, of ripening grapes, S.*Fr.*255.6.

ἀποπέρνημι, *sell*, Aeol. aor. subjunct. ἀποπεράσσει Schwyzer 646. 13 (Cyme, ii B.C.): Ion. aor. inf. ἀποπεράσαι *GDI* 5533*f* 2 (Zelea); 3 pl. ἀπεπέρασαν *SIG* 45.32 (Halic., v B.C.).

ἀποπερονάω, *fix with a buckle* or *pin*, Hp.*Mochl.*5:—Pass., πρὸς τοὺς παραστάτας Ph.*Bel.*66.43.

ἀποπετάννῡμι, *spread out*, τρίβωνα D.L.6.77:—also **ἀποπετάζω**, Aq.*Ex.*5.4, al.

ἀποπέτομαι, fut. –πετήσομαι Ar.*Pax* 1126: aor. ἀπεπτάμην, part. –πτάμενος, inf. –πτάσθαι Hdt.7.13: also ἀπεπτόμην Ar.*Av.*90; aor. 2 ἀπέπτην, 3 pl. ἀπέπταν Emp.2.4; inf. ἀποπτῆναι *AP* 5.211 (Mel.):—*fly off* or *away*, esp. of dreams, ᾤχετ' ἀποπτάμενος Il.2.71; ψυχὴ δ' ἠΰτ' ὄνειρος ἀποπταμένη πεπότηται Od.11.222; ἀπέπτετο Ar.*Av.*90; ἐς τἀπὶ Θρᾴκης ἀποπέτου ib.1369; οἴχεται ἀποπτάμενος Pl.*Smp.*183e; συχνὸν ἀποπτάς Arist.*HA* 619ᵃ32; ψυχῆς ἐκ μελέων ἀποπταθείσης *IG* 9(1).883.6 (Corcyra).

ἀποπεφασμένως, Adv., (ἀποφαίνω) *openly, clearly, plainly*, D.59.67.

ἀποπήγνῡμι, *make to freeze, freeze*, τἀντικνήμια Ar.*Ra.*126:—Pass., of men, *to be frozen*, in fut. –πᾰγήσομαι X.*Mem.*4.3.8. 2. of blood, *congeal*, Hp.*Morb.Sacr.*9:—Pass., X.*An.*5.8.15.

ἀποπηδ-άω, *leap off*, esp. of riders, *dismount*, Plu.*Fab.*16, Jul.*Or.* 2.60a, etc. II. *start off from, turn away from*, ἀπό τινος Hp.*Art.* 47; ἀ. ἀπὸ τῆς φύσιος *from* its natural position, of a joint, ib.61; metaph., ἀπὸ τοῦ λόγου Pl.*Tht.*164c; Σωκράτους X.*Mem.*1.2.16: abs., *leap off*, Pl.*R.*613b; *stalk off*, οἴχεται ἀποπηδήσας πρὸς ἄλλον Id.*Lg.* 720c; ἐς τὰ Περσῶν ἤθη Procop.*Goth.*1.24. 2. *rebound*, Arist. *Aud.*803ᵇ1, Ph.1.610. **–ησις**, εως, ἡ, *leaping off*, Plu.2.769f.

ἀποπηλώσειν· ἀποπηδώσειν, Hsch.

ἀποπηνίζομαι, *become unwound, unrolled*, Thphr.*HP* 8.10.4.

ἀποπήσσω, late form for ἀποπήγνυμι, *benumb*, τὸν νοῦν Herm.ap. Stob.1.49.45.

ἀποπῑδύω, *ooze out, spread*, Hp.*Nat.Puer.*21.

ἀπο-πῐέζω, *squeeze out*, τὸ αἷμα ἐκ.. Arist.*Pr.*889ᵇ28. II. *squeeze tight*, Hp.*Aph.*5.46, al.; *press outwards* or *away from* a spot, Id. *Fract.*30:—Pass., ὅταν [οἱ πόδες] ἀποπιεσθῶσιν ἀπὸ καθέδρας Thphr.*Fr.* 11:—also –πῐάζω, Lxx *Jd.*6.38, Archig.ap.Orib.8.1.21. **–πίεσις** [πῐ], εως, ἡ, *squeezing* or *wringing out*, Thphr.*Ign.*11, cf. Archig.ap. Gal.8.110. **–πίεσμα** [ῐ], ατος, τό, *pressure outwards* or *off*, used of rods slightly bent, Hp.*Fract.*30.

ἀποπιμπλάνω, rare form of sq., Agath.5.21.

ἀποπίμπλημι, later **–πιμπλάω**: poet. also **ἀποπίπλημι, –άω**:—*fill up* a number, τὰς τετρακοσίας μυριάδας Hdt.7.29. II. *satisfy, fulfil*, in Pass., ἀποπλησθῆναι τὸν χρησμόν Id.8.96. 2. *satisfy, appease*, ἀ. αὐτοῦ τὸν θυμόν Id.2.129, cf. Th.7.68; ἀ. τὰς ἐπιθυμίας Pl. *Grg.*492a, al. 3. *satisfy* an inquirer, τινά Id.*Cra.*413b.

ἀποπίμπρημι, only in aor. ἀπέπρησεν· ἀπεδάκρυσεν, ἀπεφύσησεν, ἀπέμαρεν, Hsch.

ἀποπῑνόω, *dirty, soil*, prob. l. for ἀπινοῦται, Hsch.

ἀποπίνω [ῑ], *drink up, drink off*, Hdt.4.70; ὅσον ἂν ἀποπίῃ Critias 33: abs., Philostr.*Ep.*60.

ἀποπιπράσκω, *sell off*, ξύλων τῶν ἀποπραθέντων *BCH* 6.20 (Delos, ii B.C.).

ἀποπίπτω, *fall off from*, ἐκ πέτρης Od.24.7; ἀπὸ τῶν φιαλέων Hdt. 3.130; τοῦ κολεοῦ ἀ. ὁ μύκης ib.64, cf. Hecat.22 J.; ἀ. τῶν ἵππων *slip off*, Plb.11.21.3. 2. abs., *fall off*, στιλπναὶ δ' ἀπέπιπτον ἔερσαι Il. 14.351, cf. Th.4.4, Arist.*HA* 557ᵇ29. II. *miss* or *fail in obtaining*, τῆς ἐλπίδος ἀ. Plb.9.7.1; τἀγαθοῦ Procl.*Inst.*13; *fail to record, let slip*, τῶν ἀναγκαιοτέρων D.S.13.84: abs., *to be disappointed, fail*, Plb.4.36. 5, *UPZ* 70.27 (ii B.C.).

ἀπόπισθεν, *from behind*, better divisim, Sch.E.*Hec.*900.

ἀποπιστεύω, *trust mistakenly*, τοῖς ἐπιπέδοις Plb.3.71.2, cf. 12.26ᵈ. 4, J.*AJ* 15.7.6; τοῖς ἰδίοις λογισμοῖς (opp. τῷ θεῷ πεπιστευκέναι) Ph. 1.132, cf. Gal.8.90. 2. *confide strongly in*, τῇ τῶν ἰδεῶν ὑποθέσει Procl. *in Prm.*p.480 S.

ἀποπλάζω, *lead away from*, ἀοιδῆς A.R.1.1220, cf. Hsch.:—Pass., only aor., *stray away from*, πολλὸν ἀπεπλάγχθης σῆς πατρίδος Od. 15.382; Τροίηθεν 9.259; ἀπὸ θώρηκος.. πολλὸν ἀποπλαγχθεὶς [ὀϊστός] *glancing off* the hauberk, Il.13.592; –πλαγχθέντες ἑταίρων Theoc.22. 35; τῆλε δ' ἀπεπλάγχθη σάκεος δόρυ Il.22.291: abs., *wander*, Od.8.573; *to be separated*, Emp.22.3; τρυφάλεια ἀποπλαγχθεῖσα a helm *struck off*, *falling from the head*, Il.13.578:—also ἀποπλασθεῖσα· ἀποκρουσθεῖσα, Hsch.

ἀποπλᾰν-άω, fut. -ήσω, *lead astray, make to digress*, λόγον Hp. *Art.*34, Luc.*Anach.*21; ἀ. τινὰ ἀπὸ τῆς ὑποθέσεως Aeschin.3.176:—Pass., *wander away from*, τῆς ὑποθέσεως Isoc.7.77: abs., of leaderless wasps, Arist.*HA*554b23; *wander from the truth*, Alex.Aphr. *in Metaph.*139.12, Chrysipp.*Stoic.*3.33. II. *distribute*, in Pass., ἀποπλανᾶται ἐς πάντα αἷμα καὶ πνεῦμα Hp.*Alim.*33. III. metaph., *seduce, beguile*, τοὺς ἐκλεκτούς *Ev.Marc.*13.22. **-ημα**, ατος, τό, *deception*, Hsch., Suid. s.vv. ἀπαιόλημα, αἰόλημα. **-ησις**, εως, ἡ, *digression*, Pl.*Plt.*263c, Licymn.ap.Arist.*Rh.*1414b17. II. *wandering*, Lxx*Si.*31(34).11. **-ίας**, ου, ὁ, *a wanderer, fugitive*, *AP*9.240 (Phil.), 548 (Bianor). **-ος**, ὁ, *fallacy*, Cratin.Jun.7. 2. *impostor*, Hsch.

ἀποπλάσσομαι, Med., fut. -πλάσομαι, aor. -πλασάμην:—*model* or *mould from* a thing: hence, *represent, model, portray*, Plu.*Aem.*28, *AP*5.14 (Rufin.), 7.34 (Antip. Sid.), etc.; ἀ. πρᾶξιν Call.*Fr.*194.

ἀποπλάστωρ, ορος, ὁ, *copier*, Man.4.343.

ἀποπλέκω, *separate*, Pass., συμπλέκονται τὰ πάντα καὶ -ονται Zos. Alch.p.110 B.: esp. in pf. part. -πεπλεγμένος, η, ον, *divorced, separated*, γυνή *PGen.*19.3 (ii A.D.); ἀνήρ *BGU*118ii 11 (ii A.D.).

ἀποπλευστέον, *one must sail away*, Ar.*Fr.*142.

ἀποπλέω, Ep. -πλείω, Ion. -πλώω v.l. in Hdt.4.156,157, cf. Arr. *Ind.*26.9: fut. -πλεύσομαι Hdt.4.147; -πλευσοῦμαι Pl.*Hp.Mi.*371b:—*sail away, sail off*, οἴκαδ' ἀποπλείειν Il.9.418, etc.; ἐπ' Αἰγύπτου Hdt. 1.1, cf. Ar.*Ra.*1480; ὀπίσω ἀ. Hdt.4.156; ἐκ τῆς Σικελίας ὡς ἐς τὰς Ἀθήνας Th.6.61; ἐπ' οἴκου Id.1.55.

ἀπο-πληγία, ἡ, = ἀποπληξία, Gal.16.672. **-πληκτεύομαι**, *to be senseless*, Phld.*Po.*2.40. **-πληκτικός**, ή, όν, *paralysed*, ἀ. τὰ δεξιά, τὰ ἀριστερά, Hp.*Coac.*467, cf. Arist.*Rh.*1411a21; τὰ ἐξαίφνης ἀ. *apoplectic seizures*, Hp.*Coac.*470; τὰ ἀ. νοσήματα Arist.*Pr.*954b 30. **-πληκτος**, ον, (ἀποπλήσσω) *disabled by a stroke*, 1. in mind, *struck dumb, astounded*, Hdt.2.173, cf. S.*Ph.*731; ἀ. ποδί Id. *Fr.*248; *senseless*, οὐχ οὕτως ἄφρων οὐδ' ἀ. D.21.143, cf. Men.*Epit.* 344, Phld.*Ir.*p.82 W., D.Chr.11.100; ἀ. καὶ παντελῶς μαινόμενος D. 34.16; ὃ νυνὶ ποεῖς ἀ. ἐστι Men.*Pk.*246; -τότερος μῦθος D.Chr.11. 54. 2. in body, *paralysed, crippled*, Hdt.1.167, Pl.Com.130; ἀ. τὰς γνάθους *struck dumb*, Ar.*V.*948. 3. Medic., *stricken with paralysis*, Hp.*Aph.*6.57; μέρος *paralysed*, Id.*Flat.*13: so σκέλος Id.ap. Aret.*SD*1.7; ἀπόπληκτοι *cases of apoplexy*, Id.*Aph.*3.16. **-πληκτώδης**, ες, = ἀπόπληκτος, Gal.19.110. **-πληξία**, Ion. -ίη, ἡ, *madness*, Phld.*Rh.*1.145 S., *Vit.*p.7 J.; μάντεων Phleg.*Mir.*2. 2. of body, *apoplexy*, Hp.*Aph.*2.42, Aret.*SD*1.7; ἀ. μέρους *paralysis*, Arist.*Pr.*905a17: in pl., ib.860a33, al. **-πλήξιος**, ον, *apoplectic*, πυρετός Alex.Aphr.*Pr.*2.42 (s. v. l.). **-πληξις**, εως, ἡ, = ἀποπληξία, σώματος Hp.*Aph.*6.56.

ἀποπληρ-όω, = ἀποπίμπλημι, *fill up*, Hp.*Art.*45 (in irreg. form -πληρέουσιν), *VM*22. 2. *satisfy*, τὰς βουλήσεις, τὰς ἐπιθυμίας, Pl. *R.*426c, *Lg.*782e; *satisfy* an inquirer, κἀμὲ τάχ' ἂν ἀποπληρώσαις ὡς .. Id.*Chrm.*169c, cf. *Plt.*286a; τοῦτό μοι ἐν τῇ ψυχῇ ἀποπλήρωσον *make* this *complete* for me, *satisfy* me in this, Id.*Prt.*329c:—Pass., Arist.*Rh.*1369b14. II. *complete*, ἑβδομήκοντα ἔτη *PFlor.*382.10 (iii A.D.). III. *discharge* a function, ib.2.23 (iii A.D.). 2. *pay* a debt, Hsch. s. v. ἐκτετικότας. 3. *fulfil* a promise, Hdn.2.7.1.—Prose word, also in E.*Oen.*4.6 A. (Pass.). **-ωματικός**, ή, όν, = -ωτικός, δύναμις Iamb.*Myst.*3.10. **-ωσις**, εως, ἡ, *filling, satisfying*, Plu.2.48c, Porph.*Abst.*3.18, Jul.*Or.*4.144d. 2. *accomplishment, fulfilment*, ἐνέργεια ἡ τοῦ οἰκείου ἔργου ἀ. Dam.*Pr.*64, cf. Iamb.*Myst.* 5.26, al. **-ωτής**, οῦ, ὁ, *one who completes* or *fulfils*, τῶν αἱρεθέντων Pl.*R.*620e, cf. Jul.*Or.*2.90c, Iamb.*Myst.*5.10, al. **-ωτικός**, ή, όν, *completing, fulfilling*, Jul.*Or.*4.137b; τῶν εὐχῶν Iamb.*Myst.*5.26; *supplying with content*, τὸ νοητὸν -κὸν τοῦ νοῦ Dam.*Pr.*70.

ἀποπλήσσω, Att. -ττω, *cripple by a stroke, disable in body* or *mind*:—Pass., *lose one's senses, become dizzy* or *astounded*, S.*Ant.*1189. 2. Med., *push off from oneself*, Arist.*Pr.*899b24.

ἀποπλίσσομαι, *trot off*, Ar.*Ach.*218.

ἀπόπλοια, ἡ, = ἀπόπλους (A), Lib.*Eth.*4.1.

ἀποπλοκή, ἡ, *chemical separation*, opp. συμπλοκή, Zos.Alch.p.110 B.

ἀποπλοκίαι· ἐμπλοκαί (Lacon.), Hsch.

ἀπόπλοος (A), contr. -πλους, ὁ, *sailing away*, ἐνθεῦτεν Hdt.8.79, Arist.*Po.*1454b2. 2. *voyage home* or *back*, X.*An.*5.6.20; of the Greeks at Troy, Arist.*Po.*1457b7.

ἀπόπλοος (B), ον, contr. -πλους, ουν, *starting on a voyage*, *AP*5. 177 (Mel.). II. *unseaworthy*, Hsch.

ἀπό-πλῠμα, ατος, τό, *water in which anything has been diluted* or *dissolved*, ἀ. κηρίων *mead*, ἀ. τιτάνου *lime-water*, D.S.5.26,28; κρεῶν Sor.1.59. **-πλυνσις**, εως, ἡ, *cleansing*, Sophon.*in deAn.*96. 2. **-πλύνω** [ῡ], fut. -ῠνῶ, *wash well, wash away*, λαΐγγας.. ἀποπλύνεσκε θάλασσα Od.6.95; τὸ περὶ τὴν γλῶτταν Pl.*Ti.*65d; τὰς χεῖρας Ath.9.409c; τινὰ βαφῆς ἀτόπου Philostr.*VA*8.22. 2. *wash away*, Arist.*Sens.*443b7 (Pass.). **-πλῠσις**, εως, ἡ, *washing away*, Alex. Aphr. *inSens.*94.13. **-πλῠτέον**, *one must wash, cleanse*, *Gp.*16. 18.2.

ἀποπλώω, Ion. for -πλέω: **ἀποπνείω**, Ion. for -πνέω.

ἀποπνευματ-ίζω, *breathe out, expire*, in Pass., Hsch. s. v. ἀπεψύχη: also, = ἀποπέρδω, Sch.Ar.*Pax*891. **-ισμός**, ὁ, Hsch. s. v. πετραδεῖλαι. **-ωσις**, εως, ἡ, = foreg., Eust.866.18. **-ος**, ον, *away from the wind, sheltered*, Thphr.*Vent.*30.

ἀποπνέω, Ep. -πνείω (as always in Hom.), fut. -πνεύσομαι, later -πνεύσω *Gp.*2.21.3:—*breathe forth*, of the Chimaera, δεινὸν ἀποπνείουσα πυρὸς μένος Il.6.182; [φῶκαι] πικρὸν ἀποπνείουσαι ἁλὸς.. ὀδμήν Od.4.406; ἀ. ἔπος στόματος Pi.*P.*4.11; θυμὸν ἀποπνείων *giving up* the ghost, Il.4.524; so without θυμόν, Batr.99, Nic.Dam.p.61 D., Phleg.*Mir.*3; ἀ. ψυχήν Simon.52; ἡλικίαν Id.115, Pi.*I.*7(6).34; ἀ. τὴν δυσμένειαν *to blow* it *off*, *get rid of* it, Plu.*Them.*22:—Pass., ἀποπνεῖται ἡ ἀτμίς Arist.*Pr.*937a7. b. causal in Pi.*N.*1.47 χρόνος ἀπέπνευσεν ψυχάς *made* them *give up* the ghost. 2. *breathe hard, take breath*, Arist.*HA*587a5; *exhale, evaporate*, ψυχὰς ὥσπερ ὁμίχλας ἀποπνεούσας τῶν σωμάτων Plu.2.560c. 3. in Com., = ἀποπέρδω, *AB*439. II. *smell of a thing*, c. gen., Luc.*Hist.Conscr.*15; χθιζῆς μέθης Plu.2.13f; but also τοῖον ἀπέπνεε λείψανα so they *smelt*, A.R. 2.193; τοῦ χρωτὸς ἥδιστον ἀ. Plu.*Alex.*4; ἀ. τι τοιοῦτον Id.2. 695e. 2. *exhale* (*and so lose*) *the scent*, Thphr.*HP*9.16.2, cf. Plu. 2.692c; τὸ βρομῶδες ib.791b. III. *blow from* a particular quarter, αὔρη οὐκ ἀ. ἀπὸ θερμῶν χωρέων Hdt.2.27, cf. 19; ἀπὸ τῆς γῆς Arist. *Mete.*366a33, al.; τὸ ἀποπνέον Id.*Pr.*933a39: impers., ἀποπνεῖ ἀπὸ τῆς θαλάττης *there is a breeze from* the sea, ib.933a27, 943b4. IV. Pass., *to be blown out*, of a light, Plu.2.281b.

ἀποπνίγω [ῑ], fut. -πνίξω Pl.Com.198, Antiph.171: aor. inf. ἀποπνεῖξαι *GDI*2171.18 (Delph., i B.C.):—*choke, throttle*, Hdt.2.169, al.; τὰς ἀναπνοάς Hp.*Morb.Sacr.*9; τοὺς πατέρας τ' ἦγχον.. καὶ τοὺς πάππους ἀπέπνιγον Ar.*V.*1039; *suffocate*, Id.*Eq.*893; of plants, *choke*, *Ev.Matt.*13.7, *Ev.Luc.*8.7:—Pass., fut. -πνῐγήσομαι Ar.*Nu.*1504; also -πεπνίξομαι Eun.*VS* p.463 B.: aor. 1 ἀπεπνίχθην Aret.*SA*1.7: aor. 2 ἀπεπνίγην [ῐ] (v. infr.): pf. part. -πεπνιγμένος Hdt.4.72:—*to be choked, suffocated*, τρώγων ἐρεβίνθους ἀπεπνίγη Pherecr.159, cf. Alex. 266; *to be drowned*, Democr.172, D.32.6, Aesop.352. b. generally, *cut off, kill*, λιμῷ τινα Aret.*CA*1.9:—Pass., πόλις ἀ. τῇ τῶν ἀναγκαίων σπάνει Procop.*Arc.*26. 2. metaph., *choke one with vexation*, ἀποπνίξεις με λαλῶν Antiph. l. c.; ἡ γάρ [με] γειτονεῦσ' ἀποπνίγεις Call.*Iamb.*1.300:—Pass., *to be choked with rage*, ἐπί τινι *at* a thing, D.19.199, cf. Alex.16.7; πρός τι Lib.*Or.*63.15.

ἀπο-πνοή, ἡ, *exhalation, evaporation*, Arist.*Pr.*863a7, Thphr.*HP* 9.7.2, al. II. *breeze blowing from* a place, Arist.*Pr.*943b12. III. *death*, D.L.4.21 (prob. for ἀναπνοῆς). **-πνοια**, ἡ, = foreg. I, Hp. *de Arte* 12. 2. = foreg. II, Thphr.*CP*5.12.2.

ἀποποι-έω, *unmake*, *Corp.Herm.*9.6. 2. *deduct*, τὸ ἀποποιηθέν *BGU*475r5 (ii A.D.). II. Med., *put away from oneself, reject*, Lxx*Jb.*14.15, Plu.2.152a; *refuse*, δῶρον Plot.4.3.14; *deny, disclaim*, εἰδέναι τι Max.Tyr.24.4; *do away with, kill*, *Cat.Cod.Astr.*7.135. 29. **-ησις**, εως, ἡ, *disclaimer, disavowal*, Phoeb.*Fig.*2.3.

ἀποπολεμέω, *fight off* or *from*, (sc. τοῦ ὄνου) *from* ass-*back*, Pl. *Phdr.*260b.

ἀπόπολις, poet. -πτολις, ι, gen. ιδος and εως, *far from the city, banished*, ἀ. ἔσει A.*Ag.*1410 (lyr.), cf. S.*OT*1000, *OC*208, E.*Hyps.* *Fr.*44; ἀπόπτολιν ἔχειν τινά S.*Tr.*647 (lyr.).

ἀποπολῑτεύω, *dissolve political community*, *IG*9(2).205.16 (Melitaea):—in Med., ib.9(1).32 (Stiris).

ἀποπομπ-αῖος, α, ον, *carrying away evil*, of the scapegoat, Lxx *Le.*16.8 sq., Ph.1.338, al.; ἀ. θεοί Hsch. II. *to be cast out, abominable*, Ph.1.238. **-έω**· ἀποπέμπομαι, Hsch. **-ή**, ἡ, (ἀποπέμπω) *sending away*, Lxx *Le.*16.10. b. *valediction*, Men.Rh.p.333 S. 2. *divorce*, *PSI*1.36a16 (i A.D.), etc., Poll.8.31. 3. *averting* an ill omen, etc., ἀ. ποιεῖσθαι Isoc.5.117; *getting rid*, πυρετῶν Luc.*Philops.* 9. **-ιμος**, ον, = ἀποπομπαῖος, πάθος Ph.1.75: ἡμέραι, = ἀποφράδες, Hsch.

ἀποπονέω, *finish a work*, τὰ πλεῖστα γὰρ ἀποπεπόνηκας Ar.*Th.*245.

ἀποποντόω, (πόντος) *cast into the sea*, Sch.S.*Aj.*1297.

ἀποπορδή, ἡ, *crepitus ventris*, prob. in Alex.Aphr.*Pr.*1.144.

ἀποπορ-εία, ἡ, *return*, πορεία καὶ ἀ., of machinery at work, Hero *Aut.*12.1. 2. *departure*, D.C.*Fr.*104.4, Agath.2.31, 3.23; *retreat*, Procop.*Pers.*1.23, al. **-εύομαι**, Pass., *depart*, X.*An.*7.6.33, *IG* 9(2).205.18 (Melitaea), etc. II. *go back, return*, ἐκ βαλανείου Plb. 24.7.6; of machinery (cf. foreg.), Hero *Aut.*6.3. **-ευτέα**, *one must go away*, Agath.2.22.

ἀποπορπάω or -ίζω, *fix in the safety-pin and excise*, *Hippiatr.*12.

ἀπόπρᾱμα, ατος, τό, *sub-letting*, *PRev.Laws*18.16 (iii B.C.), *UPZ* 112.3 (ii B.C.).

ἀποπράσσω, *demand the return of*, χρήματα *IG*12(7).42 (Amorgos):—Pass., ib.4.752.9 (Troezen):—Med., *exact to the uttermost*, τὸν μισθόν Them.*Or.*21.260b.

ἀποπρᾱτίζομαι, (πιπράσκω) *sell*, Lxx *To.*1.7.

ἀποπρᾱΰνω, *soften matters down*, Plu.*Sert.*25.

ἀποπρεσβ-εία, ἡ, *an ambassador's report*, Plb.23.9.5, al., cf. *AJA* 18.324f (Sardes, 5 B.C.). **-εύω**, *report as ambassador*, τὰ παρ' ἐκείνων Pl.*Lg.*941a: abs., *make such a report*, Plb.7.2.5.

ἀποπρηνίζω, (πρηνής) *throw headlong*, Nonn.*D.*18.271 (aor. -ιξεν).

ἀποπρίασθαι [ῐ], aor. with no pres., ἀποπρίω (for -πρίασο) τὴν λήκυθον *buy* it *off* or *up*, Ar.*Ra.*1227.

ἀπό-πρῑσις, εως, ἡ, *sawing off*, Paul.Aeg.6.77. **-πρισμα**, ατος, τό, *shavings*, prob. l. Arist.*Mir.*841a16. **-πριστέον**, *one must saw off*, Paul.Aeg.6.77. **-πρίω** [ῑ], *saw off*, Hdt.4.65, *AP*11.14 (Ammian.); ὀστέον Hp.*Fract.*33:—Pass., Isid.Char.20, Plu.2.924b, prob. in Archil.122.

ἀποπρό, Adv. *afar off*, πολλὸν ἀ. φέρων Il.16.669. 2. as Prep. c. gen., *away from*, τυτθὸν ἀ. νεῶν ib.7.334, cf. E.*HF*1081, *Or.*142, etc.

ἀποπρο-άγω [ᾰγ], only in pf. Pass., mostly part., ἀποπροηγμένα *in* *the second rank*, of things neither good nor bad, opp. προηγμένα, Zeno *Stoic.*1.48; the distn. was rejected by Aristo ib.1.83, but cf. *Stoic.*3.29, al.: inf. -ῆχθαι Aristo l.c. **-αιρέω**, *take away from*, σίτου ἀποπροελὼν δόμεναι *having taken some of* the bread to give it away, Od.17.457. **-βάλλω**, *throw far away*, A.R.3.1311.

ἀπόπροθε, before vowels **-θεν**, Adv., prop. *from afar*, ἰύζουσιν ἀ. οὐδ' ἐθέλουσιν ἀντίον ἐλθέμεναι Il.17.66; ἀ. εἰς ἓν ἰόντες A.R.1.39, cf. 1244, etc.; but in Hom., = ἀπόπροθι, *afar off, far away*, αὖθι μένειν παρὰ νηυσὶν ἀ. Il.10.209, cf. 17.501; στῆθ' οὕτω ἀ. Od.6.218; ἀ. εἰν ἁλὶ κεῖται 7.244, cf. 9.188, 17.408, Thgn.595, S.*Ichn.*3. 2. c. gen., *far away from*, ὀφθαλμῶν Archil.25; αἰζηῶν Q.S.1.414.

ἀποπροθέω, *run away from*, *AP*9.679 (better divisim).

ἀπόπροθι, Adv. *far away*, ἀ. δώματα ναίεις Od.4.811, al., cf. Theoc. 13.61, etc.; μάλα πολλοὶ ἀ. πίονες ἀγροί fields *extending far and wide*, Il.23.832, cf. Od.4.757.

ἀποπρο-θορεῖν, aor. 2 inf. of ἀποπροθρῴσκω, *spring far from*, νηός A.R.3.1280, Orph.*A.*545. **-ΐημι**, *send away forward, send on*, [κύνα] ἀποπροέηκε πόλινδε Od.14.26; ἑταίρους Orph.*A.*1216. 2. *send forth, shoot forth*, ἰὸν ἀποπροίει Od.22.82; *let fall*, [ξίφος] ἀποπροέηκε χαμᾶζε ib.327.

ἀποπροικίζω, (προίξ) *give a dowry*, Sch.Od.2.53.

ἀποπρο-λείπω, *leave far behind*, Ἄργος ἀποπρολιπών Hes.*Fr.*144, cf. A.R.1.1285, Hermesian.7.21,44. **-νοσφίζω**, Att. fut. -ἰῶ, *remove afar off, carry far away*, E.*IA*1286 (lyr., better divisim ἀποπρὸ νοσφ-).

ἀπόπροσθεν, Adv. = ἀπόπροθε, Hp.*VC*10. 2. c. gen., νεφῶν καὶ ὑδάτων ἀ. Pl.*Epin.*987a.

ἀποπροσποιέομαι, Med., *reject*, τὸ προβληθέν Ath.9.402a, Eust. 769.14; *dissemble*, ἑκοντὶ ἀποπροσποιησάμενος τὰ λεχθέντα πρὸς αὐτοῦ εἰδέναι Men.Prot.p.44 D., cf. p.125 D.

ἀποπροσωπίζομαι, Med., *clean one's face*, Pherecr.9: also, = ἐσοπτρίζεσθαι, Hsch.

ἀποπρο-τέμνω, *cut off from*, νώτου ἀποπροταμών *after he had cut a slice from* the chine, Od.8.475, cf. Nic.*Th.*572. **-φεύγω**, *flee away from, escape*, δίψαν *AP*12.133 (Mel.).

ἀποπρωΐ, *early*, *Gloss.*

ἀποπτάω, *roast sufficiently*, Sor.1.51, Lyd.[*Mens.*]p.182 W.; of ores, *smelt*, in Pass., Ph.*Bel.*70.4 and 6.

ἀποπτερνίζω, *thrust off with the heel*, Philostr.*Her.*6.

ἀπο-πτερῠγίζομαι, *clap the wings vehemently*, Thphr.*Sign.*18; *spread the wings and fly away*, metaph. of ἔρως, Eust.397.5. **-πτερῠγόομαι**, *lose the* πτέρυγες, of a rudder, Vett.Val.287.36. **-πτερύσσομαι**· ἀποπτερυγίζομαι, Hsch.

ἀποπτεύω, *have a view*, εἰς θάλασσαν J.*AJ*15.9.6.

ἀποπτήσσω, strengthd. for πτήσσω, f.l. for ὑπο-, Hsch. s.v. καταμεμυκέναι, dub. in Opp.*H.*4.370.

ἀπό-πτισμα, ατος, τό, (πτίσσω) *chaff, husks*, dub. l. for ἀπόπρισμα, Arist.*Mir.*841^{a}16. **-πτίσσω**, *strip the husk off*, Dieuch.ap.Orib. 4.6.4 (Pass.).

ἀποπτοέω, poet. **-πτοιέω**, *scare* or *drive away*, Call.*Fr.anon.*93:—Pass., *to be startled, to shy*, of horses, Plb.3.53.10.

ἀπόπτολις, v. ἀπόπολις.

ἄποπτος, ον, (ἀπόψομαι) *seen* or *to be seen from* a place, ὅπως μὴ ἄ. ἔσται ἡ Κορινθία ἀπὸ τοῦ χώματος Arist.*Pol.*1274^{a}40, cf. Arr.*Ind.*4.7; ἐν ἀπόπτῳ ἔχειν *in a conspicuous place*, Id.*An.*2.10.3; ἐν ἀ. εἱστιᾶσθαι J.*AJ*13.14.2, etc. II. *out of sight of, far away from*, τοῦδ' ἄποπτος ἄστεως S.*OT*762; ἄποπτος ἡμῶν Id.*El.*1489: abs., *far away*, ἐξ ἀπόπτου μᾶλλον ἢ 'γγύθεν σκοπεῖν Id.*Ph.*467; ὡς ἐξ ἀ. θεώμενος Pl.*Ax.* 369a; τόπος ἐξ ἀπόπτου καταφανής Plu.*Eum.*15; οὐδ' ἐξ ἀ. Phld.*Rh.*1. 149 S., *Piet.*27, cf. Gal.4.628. 2. *dimly seen*, S.*Aj.*15. 3. *out of sight*, ἐν ἀπόπτῳ τίθενται τὸν χάρακα D.H.2.54; ἐξ ἀπόπτου τῶν Ῥωμαίων παρεμβαλόντες Id.6.14.

ἀπόπτυγμα, ατος, τό, (πτύσσω) *portion of the* χιτών *folded back*, *IG* 2.652 *A* 20.

ἀποπτύρω, *scare*, *Gloss.*

ἀπό-πτυσμα, ατος, τό, *that which is spat out*, *AB*223; v.l. in Arist. *Mir.*841^{a}16. **-πτύσσω**, *fold back*, -πτύξαντες τοῦ χιτωνίσκου Aen. Tact.31.23. **-πτυστήρ**, ῆρος, ὁ, *one that spits out*: ἀ. χαλινῶν a horse *that will not bear* the bit, Opp.*H.*2.11. **-πτυστος**, ον, *spat out*: hence, *abominated, detested*, θεοῖς A.*Eu.*191: abs., S.*OC*1383, E. *Med.*1373, Ar.*Eq.*1285, etc. **-πτύω**, *spit out*, ὄνθον ἀποπτύων Il. 23.781; of the sea, ἀποπτύει ἁλὸς ἄχνην 4.426, cf. Emp.115.10; ἀ. σίαλον ἐκ τοῦ στόματος X.*Mem.*1.2.54: abs., *spit*, A.*Fr.*354, X.*Cyr.* 1.2.16 codd., Thphr.*Char.*19.11:—Pass., Ph.1.29, Gal.15.472; *to be washed ashore*, Alciphr.1.10. 2. *abominate, spurn*, ἀποπτύουσι δέ τ' ἀράς Hes.*Op.*726; ἀποπτύεις λόγους A.*Eu.*303; ἀπέπτυσαν εὐνὰς ἀδελφοῦ Id.*Ag.*1192, cf. *Pr.*1070 (lyr.), Ar.*Pax* 528, E.*Andr.*607; *disown*, A.*Ch.*197:—aor. ἀπέπτυσα freq. used in pres. sense, ἀπέπτυσα μὲν λόγον E.*Hel.*664, cf. *IA*874: freq. abs., ἀπέπτυσα *omen absit*, Id. *Hipp.*614, *Hec.*1276, *IT*1161; ἀ. χαλινόν, of a horse, Philostr.*Im.*1. 12. 3. *ward off*, Epic. in *BKT*5(1).122. [ῠ of pres. long in Ep.; ῠ of fut. and aor. short in Trag.]

ἀπό-πτωμα, ατος, τό, *unlucky chance, misfortune*, Plb.11.2. 6. II. *error*, Vett.Val.238.26. **-πτωσις**, εως, ἡ, *falling off* or *away*, ὀστέων Hp.*Mochl.*35; ἀνθέων Dsc.*Praef.*8. 2. ἀ. τῆς ἀρχῆς *deposition*, Ath.12.530a. 3. *direction in which a force is exerted*, Ph. *Bel.*73.7. 4. *vanishing, disappearance, negation*, τὸ μηδαμῶς ὂν ἀ. ἐστι τοῦ ὄντος Dam.*Pr.*8; *eclipse*, τοῦ εἰδώλου ib.433. II. *declension from*, καθήκοντος Chrysipp.*Stoic.*2.51, M.Ant.10.12, Procl.*Inst.*209 (pl.); τῆς εὐσεβείας Hierocl. *in CA*11 p.442 M.; κατὰ ἀπόπτωσιν, opp. κατὰ κατόρθωσιν, Herm. *in Phdr.*p.166 A.

ἀποπῠδαρίζω, v. πυδαρίζω, Ar.*Eq.*697.

ἀποπῡ-έω, *suppurate*, Hp.*Epid.*2.2.6. **-ημα**, ατος, τό, *suppuration*, ib.4.25. **-ητικός**, ή, όν, *suppurative*, Id.*Coac.*282, *Epid.*2.3. 6. **-ΐσκω**, (πυέω) *to promote suppuration*:—Pass., *suppurate*, Id. *Morb.*2.28.

ἀποπυκνόομαι, Pass., *to be condensed, consolidated*, f.l. in Epicur. *Ep.*2 p.49 U.

ἀποπυνθάνομαι, *inquire* or *ask of*, ἀ. [αὐτοῦ] εἰ.. *asked of* him whether.., Hdt.3.154; παρά τινος J.*AJ*12.4.9.

ἀποπυργίζοντες λόγοι, title of work by Diagoras, Suid. s.v. Διαγόρας.

ἀπο-πῡρίας (sc. ἄρτος), ου, ὁ, a kind of *toasted bread*, Cratin.99, Ath.3.111e. **-πῡριατέον**, *one must foment*, Gal.12.840, Aët. 8.16. **-πῡριάω**, *foment*, Antyll.ap.Orib.7.22.21, Gal.13.245, al. **-πῡρίζω**, *roast on the fire*, Epich.124, cf. Hsch. **-πῡρίς**, ίδος, ἡ, small fish like ἐπανθρακίς, Clearch.16. II. *fry*, τῶν μαινίδων ἀπόπυριν ποιήσας Teles p.41 H. III. *sacrifice of fish*, *SIG*1106.42 (Cos).

ἀποπῡτίζω, stronger form of πυτίζω, Hp.*Epid.*7.25, Ar.*Lys.*205, Arist.*HA*527^{b}22.

ἀπο-πωμάζω, *remove lid*, Zos.Alch.p.221 B., *PHolm.*9.40, al. **-πωμᾰτίζω**, = foreg., Gal.14.268.

ἀπόρανθρον, τό, v. ἀπόρρανθρον.

ἀποράξ· ἀπόρροια, ἀπόσπασμα, ἀπότμημα, Hsch.

ἀπορᾰφᾰνίδωσις, εως, ἡ, v. ῥαφανιδόω, Sch.Ar.*Pl.*168.

ἀποργάζω, *work up* mortar, *IG*2^2.463.84.

ἀποργ-ής, ές, *wrathful*, Antiph.73 (dub.):—Comp. -έστερον Erot. is a variant for ἀστεργέστερον Hp.*Fract.*16. **-ίζομαι**, Pass., *to be angry*, Men.*Sam.*338, Lxx 2*Ma.*5.17.

ἀπορέγχω, *snore to the end*, *AP*11.4 (Parmen.).

ἀπορέγω, *stretch out*, Hp.*Fract.*1.

ἀπορέπω, *slink away*, *AP*9.746 (Polem. Rex).

ἀπόρευτος, ον, *that cannot* or *may not be travelled*, ὁδός Plu.*Cam.* 26, *Mar.*39. 2. *not to be traversed*, πέλαγος Ph.2.112, al. 3. *pathless*, Λιβύη Agatharch.7.

ἀπορέω (A), Ion. for ἀφοράω.

ἀπορ-έω (B), Lacon. 1 pl. ἀπορίομες X.*HG*1.1.23: aor. ἠπόρησα Th.1.63, etc.: pf. ἠπόρηκα Pl.*Sph.*244a, etc.:—**Pass.**, fut. ἀπορηθήσομαι (συν-) S.E.*M.*10.5, but Med. in pass. sense ἀπορήσομαι Arist. *MM*1200^{a}11: aor. ἠπορήθην, pf. ἠπόρημαι, both in act. and pass. sense (v. infr.):—*to be* ἄπορος, i.e. *without means* or *resource*: hence, 1. *to be at a loss, be in doubt, be puzzled*, mostly folld. by relat. clause, ἀ. ὅκως διαβήσεται Hdt.1.75; ὅτῳ τρόπῳ διασωθήσεται Th.3.109; ὅ τι λέξω δ' ἀπορῶ S.*OT*486 (lyr.); ἀ. ὅπῃ, ὁπόθεν, ὅποι, Th.1.107, 8.80, X. *HG*5.4.44; ὅ τι χρὴ ποιεῖν Id.*Cyr.*4.5.38; τίνα χρὴ τρόπον.. D.3.3; ἀ. εἰ.. Pl.*Prt.*326e; πότερα.. X.*Mem.*1.4.6; ἀ. ὁποτέραν τῶν ὁδῶν τράπηται ib.2.1.21; ἀ. μή.. *fear* lest.., Pl.*Alc.*2.142d: with acc. added, ἀ. τὴν ἔλασιν ὅκως διεκπερᾷ *to be at a loss about* his march, how to cross, Hdt.3.4: c. acc. only, ἀ. τὴν ἐξαγωγήν *to be at a loss about* it, Id.4. 179, cf. Ar.*Ec.*664, Pl.*Prt.*348c, al.: also c. inf., *to be at a loss how* to do, Ar.*V.*590, Pl.*Plt.*262e, Lys.9.7:—also ἀ. περί τινος Pl.*Phd.*84c, *Grg.*462b, al.; ἀ. διὰ τὸ πλῆθος τῶν ἁμαρτημάτων ὅθεν ἄρξωμαι And. 4.10; ἐς πολλὰ S.*Tr.*1243: abs., Hdt.6.134; οὐκ ἀπορήσας without *hesitation*, Id.1.159; τὸ δ' ἀπορεῖν ἀνδρὸς κακοῦ E.*HF*106, etc.:—Med. used like Act., Hdt.2.121.γ'; ὡς ἠπόρημαι... τάδε E.*IA*537; ἠπορούμην ὅτι χρησαίμην Lys.3.10, cf. Pl.*Prt.*321c: so in aor. Pass., πολλὰ.. ἀπορηθείς D.27.53. 2. in Dialectic, *start a question, raise a difficulty*, ἀπορία ἣν ἀπορεῖς Pl.*Prt.*324d; ἀ. περί τινος Arist.*Ph.* 194^{a}15, al.; τὰ αὐτὰ περί τινος *Metaph.*1085^{a}35; ἀ. πότερον.. *Pol.* 1283^{b}36; ἀπορήσειε δ' ἄν τις τί.. *EN*1096^{a}34, cf. 1145^{b}21, Plb.1.64. 1, al.:—Pass., τὸ ἀπορούμενον, τὸ ἀπορηθέν, *the difficulty just started, the puzzle before us*, Pl.*Sph.*243b, *Lg.*799c, cf. Hp.*VM*1; τὰ ἠπορημένα Arist.*Pol.*1281^{a}38; ἀπορεῖται *there is a question* or *difficulty*, πότερον.. Id.*EN*1099^{b}9; μή.. ib.1159^{a}6. 3. Pass., of things, *to be left wanting, left unprovided for*, τῶν δεομένων γίγνεσθαι οὐδὲν ἀπορεῖται X.*Lac.*13.7, cf. *Oec.*8.10; *to fail, turn out a failure*, opp. εὐπορεῖσθαι, Hp.*Art.*47. II. c. gen. rei, *to be at a loss for, in want of*, ἀπορεῖς δὲ τοῦ σύ; S.*Ph.*898; ἀλφίτων Ar.*Pax*636; πάντων Id.*Pl.*531; τροφῆς Thuc.8.81; ξυμμάχων X.*Cyr.*4.2.39; τοσαύτης δαπάνης Id. *Mem.*1.3.5; λόγων Pl.*Smp.*193e:—Med., Id.*Lg.*925b. III. ἀ. τινί *to be at a loss* by reason of, by means of something, X.*An.*1.3.8, Isoc.4. 147. IV. *to be in want, be poor*, opp. εὐπορέω, in Med., ὅταν ἀπορῆταί τις Antiph.123, but Act., Timocl.11, E.*Fr.*953.19; opp. πλουτέω, Pl. *Smp.*203e:—Pass., ἄνθρωπος ἠπορημένος *Com.Adesp.*249.—Chiefly Prose and Com.; never in A., thrice in S., twice in E. **-ημα**, ατος, τό, *matter of doubt, question, puzzle*, Pl.*Phlb.*36e, Arist.*Metaph.* 1011^{a}6, etc. 2. esp. in the Dialectic of Arist., *objection raised to an* ἐπιχείρημα (q.v.), Id.*Top.*162^{a}17. 3. *practical difficulty*, Plb. 31.13.8. **-ηματικός**, ή, όν, = ἀπορητικός, S.E.*P.*1.221, v.l. in Gal. *Nat.Fac.*2.9. 2. *expressive of doubt*, of particles, D.T.642.26, A.D. *Conj.*258.15. Adv. -κῶς S.E.*M.*8.1. **-ησία**, ἡ, = ἀπορία, Eub. 141:—also **-ησις**, εως, ἡ, Thphr.*Od.*12. **-ητέον**, *one must raise the question*, τί δήποτε.. Ph.1.336; περί τινος Plu.*Fr.*2.6. **-ητικός**, ή, όν, *inclined to doubt*, Id.*Aem.*14, S.E.*P.*1.221, al.; ἀ. καὶ σκεπτικοί D.L.9.69, cf. Gell.11.5.6. Adv. -κῶς S.E.*M.*7.30, Procl. *in Prm.* p.562 S. 2. *dubitative*, ἐπίρρημα Gal.7.661; ὕμνοι Men.Rh.p.343 S.

ἀπόρθητος, ον, *not sacked, unravaged*, Πριάμοιο.. ἀ. πόλις ἔπλεν

Il.12.11; ἀρχαγοὺς ἀπορθήτων ἀγυιῶν B.8.52, cf. 99; Θάσον ἀ. λείπειν Hdt.6.28; ἀ. χώρα *Hell.Oxy.*16.3; of Attica, E.*Med.*826, cf. A.*Pers.* 348; of Laconia, Din.1.73, cf. Lys.33.7; οὐκ ἐφύσων οἱ Λάκωνες ὡς ἀπόρθητοί ποτε; Antiph.117.

ἀπορθ-όω, *make straight*, τὸ στόμα τῶν μητρέων Hp.*Nat.Mul.* 40. II. *guide aright*, γνώμας S.*Ant.*636; πρός τι according to a standard, Pl.*Lg.*757e. III. *restore to health*, dub. in Men. *Georg.*59. **-ωμα**, ατος, τό, *erection*, *IG*9(1).691.2 (Corcyra, iii B.C.). **-ωσις**, εως, ἡ, *guiding aright*, τῆς γνώσεως Eust.1531.66.

ἀπορία, Ion. -ίη, ἡ, (ἄπορος) *being* ἄπορος: hence, I. of places, *difficulty of passing*, X.*An.*5.6.10. II. of things, *difficulty, straits*, in sg. and pl., ἐς ἀπορίην πολλὴν ἀπιγμένος, ἀπειλημένος, Hdt.1.79, 2.141; ἐν ἀπορίῃ or ἐν ἀπορίῃσι ἔχεσθαι, Id.9.98, 4.131, cf. Antipho 5.66; ἀπορίῃσιν ἐνείχετο Hdt.1.190; ἀπορίην ἐρωτηθέντι παρασχεῖν Hp.*VM*13, cf. Lys.19.1; ἀπορίᾳ τελέθει, c. inf., Pi.*N.*7.105, cf. Pl. *Lg.*788c; εἰς φρέατα καὶ πᾶσαν ἀ. ἐμπίπτων Id.*Tht.*174c: c. gen. rei, ἀ. τοῦ μὴ γινώσκειν Hp.*Morb.Sacr.*1; ἀ. τοῦ μὴ ἡσυχάζειν *impossibility* of keeping quiet, Th.2.49; ἀ. τῆς προσορμίσεως Id.4.10; ἀ. τοῦ ἀνακαθαίρεσθαι Pl.*Lg.*678d. 2. *not providing* a thing, Id.*Men.* 78e. III. of persons, *difficulty of dealing with* or *getting at*, τῶν Σκυθέων Hdt.4.83; τοῦ ἀποκτείναντος Antipho 2.4.2. 2. *being at a loss, embarrassment, perplexity*, ἀ. τοῦ δυστυχεῖν E.*Ion*971, cf. Th. 7.44,75, etc.; ἀ. ἐν τῷ λόγῳ συμβᾶσα Aeschin.2.41; *distress, discomfort*, in illness, Hp.*Epid.*5.42, Aret.*SA*2.5: hence metaph., ὠδίνουσι καὶ ἀπορίας ἐμπίμπλανται Pl.*Tht.*151a. 3. ἀ. τινός *lack of* a person or thing, σοφῶν ἀνδρῶν Ar.*Ra.*806; τροφῆς, χρημάτων, etc., Th.1.11, 7.48; ἀπώλλυντο.. ἀπορίᾳ τοῦ θεραπεύοντος *for want of one* to attend to them, Id.2.51; ἀ. λόγων Pl.*Ap.*38d; ἀ. πλοίων *shortage* of ships, *CPHerm.*6.10: abs., *need, poverty*, Th.1.123; ἀ. καὶ πενία And.1.144; opp. εὐπορία, Arist.*Pol.*1279b27: in pl., D. 19.146. IV. in Dialectic, *question for discussion, difficulty, puzzle*, ἀπορίᾳ σχόμενος Pl.*Prt.*321c; ἀ. ἣν ἀπορεῖς ib.324d; ἡ ἀ. ἰσότης ἐναντίων λογισμῶν Arist.*Top.*145b1, al.; ἔχει ἀπορίαν περί τινος Id. *Pol.*1285b28; αἱ μὲν οὖν ἀ. τοιαῦταί τινες συμβαίνουσιν Id.*EN*1146b6; οὐδεμίαν ποιήσει ἀ. Id.*Metaph.*1085a27; ἀ. λύειν, διαλύειν, Id.*MM* 1201b1, *Metaph.*1062b31; ἀπορίᾳ ἀπορίαν λύειν D.S.1.37.

ἀπορικός, ή, όν, *of* or *for persons without means*, ὀνόματα *BGU*390.8 (iii A.D.), cf. *PTeb.*267 *Intr.* (ii A.D.).

ἀπορνε-όω, *turn into a bird*, Apollod.1.7.4, Sch.Ar.*Av.*251:—Pass., Herm.ap.Stob.1.49.69, Apollod.1.8.3. **-ωσις**, εως, ἡ, *being changed into a bird*, Sch.Ar.*Av.*212.

ἀπορνῑθόομαι, *become a bird*, Str.6.3.9, Heraclit.*Incred.*35, Sch. Ar.*Av.*100.

ἀπόρνῠμαι, *start from* a place, ἀπορνύμενον Λυκίηθεν Il.5.105, cf. Hes.*Th.*9, A.R.1.800.

ἀποροποίητος, ον, *impermeable*, S.E.*M.*8.309.

ἄπορος, ον, first in Hdt. and Pi. (v. infr.), *without passage, having no way in, out,* or *through*: hence, I. of places, *impassable*, πέλαγος, πηλός, Pl.*Ti.*25d, *Criti.*108e; ὁδός, ὄρη, X.*An.*2.4.4, 2.5.18. II. of states or circumstances, *impracticable, difficult*, Hdt. 5.3, etc.; ἄ. ἀλγηδών, πάθη, S.*OC*513 (lyr.), *Ph.*854; τἄπορον ἔτος ib.897; ἄ. χρῆμα E.*Or.*70; ἀγών, κίνδυνος, Lys.7.2 and 39 (Sup.); αἰσχύνη Pl.*Lg.*873c; σωτηρία λεπτὴ καὶ ἄ. ib.699b, cf. *R.*453d; φόβος *Lg.*698b; βίος Men.*Kith.Fr.*1.10; νύξ Longin.9.10:—ἄπορον, τό, and ἄπορα, τά, as Subst., ἐκ τῶν ἀπόρων in the midst of their *difficulties*, Hdt.8.53, cf. Pl.*Lg.*699b; εὔπορος ἐν τοῖς ἀ. Alex.234.6; ἄπορα πόριμος A.*Pr.*904; ἐν ἀπόροις εἶναι to be in *great straits*, X.*An.* 7.6.11; εἰς ἄπορον ἥκειν, πεσεῖν, E.*Hel.*813, Ar.*Nu.*703; ἐν ἀπόρῳ εἴχοντο, ἦσαν, they were *at a loss* how to.., Th.1.25, 3.22; ἐτεῇ οἷον ἕκαστον γιγνώσκειν ἐν ἀπόρῳ ἐστί Democr.8: ἄπορόν [ἐστι] c. inf., Pi.*O.*10(11).40, Th.2.77, Aeschin.Socr.53, etc.; ἄπορα [ἐστι] Pi.*O.*1.52: Comp. -ώτερος, ἡ λῆψις Th.5.110. 2. *hard to discover* or *solve*, ἀνεξερεύνητον καὶ ἄπορον Heraclit.18; ἄ. ἐρωτήσεις, = ἀπορίαι IV, Plu.*Alex.*64, Luc.*DMort.*10.8; ζήτησις Pl.*Plt.*284b; λόγοι D.L. 7.44. 3. *hard to get, scarce*, ἐν δυστυχίῃ [φίλον εὑρεῖν] πάντων -ώτατον Democr.106; θῦμα Pl.*R.*378a; ἄπορα [ὀφλήματα] *bad* debts, D.50.9. III. of persons, *hard to deal with, unmanageable*, E.*Ba.* 800, Pl.*Ap.*18d (Sup.), cf. Th.4.32 (Sup.): c. inf., ἄ. προσμίσγειν, προσφέρεσθαι, *impossible* to have any dealings with, Hdt.4.46, 9.49; βορῆς ἄνεμος ἄ. *against which nothing will avail, which there is no opposing*, Id.6.44; ἄ. τὸ κακὸν καὶ ἀνίκητον Id.3.52. 2. *without means* or *resources, helpless*, ἔρημος, ἄ. S.*OC*1735 (lyr.), cf. Ar.*Nu.*629, etc.; ἄ. ἐπὶ φρόνιμα S.*OT*691 (lyr.); ἐπ' οὐδέν Id.*Ant.*360 (lyr.); ἄ. γνώμῃ Th.2.59. 3. *poor, needy*, Id.1.9, Pl.*R.*552a; opp. εὔπορος, Arist.*Pol.* 1279b9, 1289b30; ἄ. λειτουργεῖν *too poor* to undertake liturgies, Lys. 31.12, cf. *PRyl.*75.5 (ii A.D.), etc.; ἄ. καὶ τῶν ἐλαχίστων κατέστησαν D.Chr.17.18; also of states of life, δίαιτα ταπεινὴ καὶ ἄ. Pl.*Lg.* 762e. IV. Adv. -ρως Simon.46, etc.; τὸ πρᾶγμα ἀ. εἶχε πατρί E. *IA*55; ἀ. ἔχει μοι περί τινος Antipho 1.1; ἀ. ἔχειν, c. inf., D.H.6.14; ἀ. διατεθῆναι Lys.18.23: Comp. -ώτερον Th.1.82; but -ωτέρως διακεῖσθαι Antipho 3.2.1: Sup. -ώτατα Pl.*Ti.*51b, etc.

ἀπορούω, *dart away*, Ἰδαῖος δ' ἀπόρουσε Il.5.20, etc.; esp. *start back*, Od.22.95; ἀλλήλων Orph.*A.*705. 2. *spring up from*, πρέμνων Pi.*Fr.*88.

ἀπορρ-, ρ is regularly doubled in all compds. after ἀπό; but in Poets it sts. remains single.

ἀπορραγεῖς· οἱ καθαρμοί, Hsch.

ἀπορρᾱθῡμ-έω, *leave off in faintheartedness* or *laziness*, τινός X. *Mem.*3.7.9: abs., Pl.*R.*449c, D.8.75. Adv. **-ήτως**, v.l. for ἀπαραμυθήτως, Jul.*Or.*8.252a.

ἀπορραίνω, *spirt out, shed about*, τοῦ θοροῦ, τῶν ᾠῶν (partit. gen.), Hdt.2.93: c. acc., Arist.*HA*567a31:—Pass., Dsc.*Eup.*1.235, al. II. *sprinkle, douche*, Epict.*Ench.*4:—esp. in Med., *sprinkle* by way of lustration, *IG*1.121, al. III. Pass., *to be dissolved*, Olymp.*in Mete.*228.6 (dub.).

ἀπορραΐς, v.l. for αἱμορροΐς in Arist.*HA*530a19: in *Gloss.* expld. by *murex*.

ἀπορραίω, *bereave* one *of* a thing, c. dupl. acc., ὅστις σ' ἀέκοντα βίῃφι κτήματ' ἀπορραίσει' Od.1.404; ἀπορραῖσαι [αὐτὸν] φίλον ἦτορ *bereave* him *of* life, 16.428; θυμὸν ἀπορραῖσαι (sc. ἄνδρας) Emp.128: c. gen. rei, μή τιν' ἀπορραίσειν γεράων Hes.*Th.*393.

ἀπόρρανθρον, τό, = sq., *IG*12(3).248.18 (Anaphe; ἀπόρανθρον lapis), *Inscr.Prien.*158.

ἀπορραντήριον, τό, (ἀπορραίνω) *a vessel for sprinkling with holy water*, E.*Ion*435, *IG*1.143, al.

ἀπορραντίζω, = ἀπορραίνω, Alex.Trall.1.13.

ἀπόρραξις, εως, ἡ, *a game of ball*, Poll.9.103,105, Eust.1601.33.

ἀπορρᾰπίζω, *beat back, drive away*, Apollod.*Poliorc.*141.1; *reject*, Mich.*in EN*56.22, Eust.561.41:—Pass., Arist.*Div.Somn.*464a26. II. τῆς γλώσσης ἄκρας ἀπορραπιζούσης τὸ πνεῦμα *causing* the breath *to vibrate*, in the pronunciation of *r*, D.H.*Comp.*14 (but v. ἀπορριπ-).

ἀπορρᾰπιστέον, *one must reject*, Eust.310.23.

ἀπορράπτω, *sew up again*, τοῦ λαγοῦ τὴν γαστέρα Hdt.1.123: metaph., τὸ στόμα τινός Aeschin.2.21, cf. Ph.1.476; γεράνων ὄμματα Plu.2.997a:—Pass., τὰ ἀπερραμμένα Gal.18(2).671.

ἀπορράσσω, *beat off*, τοὺς Ῥωμαίους ἀπὸ τοῦ λόφου D.H.6.5, cf. D.C.56.14.

ἀπορραψῳδέω, *speak in fragments of epic poetry*, X.*Cyr.*3.3.54.

ἀπορρέζω, fut. -ρέξω, *sacrifice*, χίμαρον v.l. in Theoc.*Ep.*4.15; *offer part of*.., Is.*Fr.*105.

ἀπορρέμβομαι, *wander from*, c. gen., τῆς παρατηρήσεως M.Ant.3.4: abs., *hesitate*, Id.4.22.

ἀπό-ρρευμα, ατος, τό, *that which distils*, as from a tree, Theognost. *Can.*79. **-ρρευματίζω**, v.l. for -φλεγματίζω, Ps.-Diocl.*Epist.ad Antig.*ap.Paul.Aeg.1 fin. **-ρρευσις**, εως, ἡ, *flowing from*, ἔχειν τὰς ἀ. to be *the source of streams*, Plb.10.28.4; ἀέρος οὐ δεχομένου τὰς ἀ. Plu. 2.933c. II. Astrol., = ἀπόρροια 3, Vett.Val.146.32; μανίας καὶ λύττης ἀ. Junc.ap.Stob.4.50.27. (ἀπόρρυσις (q.v.) shd. perh. be read in these passages.) III. *folly*, = ἀφροσύνη, Aq.*De.*22.21, 1*Ki.*25.25.

ἀπορρέω, Ep. -ρείω Nic.*Th.*404, fut. ἀπορρεύσω Serapio in *Cat. Cod.Astr.*1.101,102, but ἀπορρυήσομαι Dsc.5.75: aor. ἀπερρύην, part. ἀπορρυείς A.*Ag.*1294; ἀπέρρευσα Plb.5.15.7, Ath.9.381b:—Pass., ἀπορρέοιτο Gal.6.709:—*flow* or *run off*, ἀπό τινος Hdt.4.23; ἐκ κρήνης Pl.*Criti.*113e, etc.: abs., *stream forth*, of blood, A.*Ag.*1294; τὸ ἀπορρέον *the juice that runs off*, Hdt.2.94, 4.23; φλόγα τῶν σωμάτων -ουσαν Pl.*Ti.*67c; λιγνὺς ἀπὸ τῆς φλογὸς ἀ. *emanating from*, Arist.*Mete.*374a25, cf. *Mu.*394a13: metaph., ὥσπερ ἐκ πηγῆς ἀ. τῆς ἡμερότητος Plu. *Cat.Ma.*5; τὸ ἀπορρέον ἐκ νοῦ λόγος Plot.3.2.2. II. *fall off*, of fruit, Hdt.1.193; feathers, Pl.*Phdr.*246d; leaves, D.22.70; hair, Arist. *HA*518a14; flesh, σάρκες ἀπ' ὀστέων ἀπέρρεον E.*Med.*1201: generally, *run to waste*, Plot.2.1.3; of riders, ἀπορρυέντες εἰς γῆν Plu.*Eum.* 7, cf. *Pyrrh.*30, al. 2. *fall away, decay, perish*, ἀ. δαίμων, ἀ. μνῆστις, S.*El.*999, *Aj.*523; τῶν καλῶν ἡ μνήμη ταχέως ἀπορρεῖ Longin.33.3. 3. of persons, *fall away, drop off from*, ἀλλήλων Pl.*Lg.*776a; ἀπό τινος Plb.5.26.11; τῆς αὐλῆς Plu.*Arat.*51: abs., *slip away, decamp*, Plb.5.15.7. 4. *fall away, decline from*, τῆς δόξης Plu.2.199a. 5. Astrol., *to be 'separated'*, ἀπό.. Serapio ll. cc.

ἀπόρρηγμα, ατος, τό, *fragment*, Plu.*Dio*46, Sch.Il.2.755.

ἀπορρήγνῡμι or -ύω, *break off*, δεσμὸν ἀπορρήξας Il.6.507, cf. Hdt. 3.32; ἧκε δ' ἀπορρήξας κορυφὴν ὄρεος Od.9.481; πνεῦμ' ἀπέρρηξεν βίου *snap the thread* of life, *die*, A.*Pers.*507; ἀ. πνεῦμα, βίον, E.*Or.*864, *IT*974, cf. *Tr.*756; ἀ. ψυχὴν *AP*7.313; τὰ μακρὰ τείχη ἀ. ἀπὸ τῆς τῶν Μεγαρέων πόλεως Th.4.69; ἀ. τῆς εἰρήνης τὴν ξυμμαχίαν, a phrase of D. censured by Aeschin.3.72; ἀ. πάνυ τείνουσαι τὸ καλῴδιον Luc. *DMeretr.*3.3. 2. causal, ἀ. τὸν θυμόν *let* one's rage *burst forth*, D.H.*Rh.*9.5, cf. Luc.*Am.*43; *burst out with* a remark, App.*BC*2.81:—Pass., πόλεμος.. ἀπερρήγνυντο ἐς ἔργον Id.*Syr.*15. 3. ἀ. ἑαυτόν τινος *tear* oneself *away, break away* from, Plu.*Marc.*27; τῶν τοῦ πατρὸς ἐπιτηδευμάτων J.*AJ*10.3.1; *deprive*, τοὺς ἀδελφοὺς τῆς βασιλικῆς ἐλπίδος Id.*BJ*1.23.2. II. Pass., freq. in aor. ἀπερράγην [ᾰ] Hdt.8.19, etc.: pf. ἀπέρρηγμαι Ph.2.510; but 3sg. ἀπορέρηκται Gal.ap.Orib. 46.21.22:—*to be broken off* or *severed from*, ἀπό τινος Hdt.l.c., ib.37: abs., *to be broken off, severed*, Id.2.29, Th.5.10, etc.; *break away from* one's allegiance, *rebel*, J.*BJ*2.14.3. 2. Act., pf. ἀπέρρωγα in pass. sense, Archil.47, etc.; φωνὴ ἀπερρωγυῖα a *broken* voice, Hp. *Acut.*(*Sp.*)10, Arist.*Aud.*804b20; ἀπερρωγὼς *broken in character, dissolute*, Luc.*Pseudol.*17; οἵ γε μὴ τελέως -ότες Muson.*Fr.*12 p.64 H.; *absurd*, S.E.*M.*8.165. III. intr. in aor. 1 Act., ἀπορρήξας ἀπὸ δεσμῶν *AP*9.240 (Phil.); κακὸν ἀπέρρηξε Luc.*Abd.*6.

ἀπορρηθῆναι, aor. 1 inf. Pass. of ἀπερῶ.

ἀπόρρημα, ατος, τό, (ἀπερῶ) *prohibition*, Pl.*Plt.*296a.

ἀπόρρηξις, εως, ἡ, *bursting*, e.g. of an abscess, Aret.*SA*2.1. 2. *breaking away from*, ὁδῶν J.*AJ*19.3.1.

ἀπόρρησις, εως, ἡ, (ἀπερῶ) *forbidding, prohibition*, Pl.*Sph.*258c; *interdiction* of judgement, παρὰ τὴν ἀ. D.33.31; δίκη τῆς ἀ. Is.2.29. II. (ἀπείρηκα) *giving up*, Pl.*R.*357a; ἀ. μαρτυρίας *refusal* to give testimony, Plu.*Mar.*5; *renunciation of a truce*, Plb.14.2.14. III. *disowning* of a son, = ἀποκήρυξις, Suid. IV. *giving in, flagging*, -σιν ποιήσασθαι Aristid.1.374 J.

ἀπορρήσσω, late form of ἀπορρήγνυμι, Paus.10.15.5, Iamb.*Myst.* 3.16.

ἀπο-ρρητέον, (ἀπερῶ) *one must prohibit*, D.Chr.7.133. **-ρρητος**, ον, *forbidden*, ἀπόρρητον πόλει *though it was forbidden to* the citizens, S.*Ant.*44, cf. E.*Ph.*1668; τἀπόρρητα δρᾶν Ar.*Fr.*622; τὰ ἀ. *forbidden exports*, τὰ. ἐξάγειν, ἀποπέμπειν, Id.*Eq.*282, *Ra.*362; ἀπόρρητον μηδὲν ποιούμενοι Pl.*Lg.*932c; πράξεις ἀ. Phld.*Ir.*p.54 W. II. *not to be spoken, secret*, ἀ. ποιεῖσθαι make *a secret of*, Hdt.9.94; esp. of state *secrets*, Ar.*Eq.*648; ἐν -τῳ ποιεῖσθαι X.*An.*7.6.43; τἀπόρρητα ποιοῦνται Lys.12.69; ὁ ἐπὶ τῶν ἀπορρήτων τοῦ βασιλέως Plu.*Luc.*17, cf. *OGI* 371; ὁ τῶν ἀ. γραμματεύς, = *a secretis*, Procop.*Pers.*2.7; ἀπόρρητα ποιεύμενος πρὸς μηδένα λέγειν ὑμέας keep them *secret* so that you tell them not to any one, Hdt.9.45; ἐν ἀπορρήτῳ τὴν ἀλήθειαν λέγειν tell *as a secret*, Pl.*Tht.*152c; ἐν ἀ. εἰδέναι And.2.19; φυλάττειν ἐν ἀπορρήτοις keep *as a secret*, Arist.*Fr.*662; ἐν ἀπορρήτῳ ξυλλαμβάνειν arrest *secretly*, And.1.45; δι' ἀπορρήτων ἐξαγγέλλειν, ἀκούειν, Lycurg.85, Pl.*R.*378a; κύριον καὶ ῥητῶν καὶ ἀπορρήτων D.1.4; τἀπόρρητ' οἶδεν Id. 21.200; ὁ ἐν ἀπορρήτοις λεγόμενος λόγος of *the esoteric doctrines* of the Pythagoreans, Pl.*Phd.*62b; τὰ ἀ. τῆς κατὰ τὰ μυστήρια τελετῆς *SIG* 873.9 (Eleusis, ii A.D.); ἐν ἀπορρήτοις in *cipher*, D.S.15.20: Comp. -ότερος Paus.2.17.4, Philostr.*VA*6.19. 2. of sacred things, *ineffable, secret*, φλόξ E.*IT*1331; μυστήρια Id.*Rh.*943; τἀπόρρητ'.. ἐκφέρειν Ar.*Ec.*442, cf. Pherecr.133; ἐνεργείας Jul.*Or.*4.151b. b. γόης καὶ ἀ. a 'man of mystery', Philostr.*VA*8.7.9. 3. *unfit to be spoken, abominable*, Lys.10.2; ἀ. ἀδικίαι Pl.*Lg.*854e; τίς οὐκ οἶδεν.. τὰς ἀπορρήτους, ὥσπερ ἐν τραγῳδίᾳ, τὰς τούτου γονάς; D.21.149; of *foul abuse*, κακῶς τὰ ἀπόρρητα λέγειν ἀλλήλους Id.18.123, etc.; in Att. Law of words (e.g. ῥίψασπις) whose use was punishable, Isoc.20.3. 4. of words, *not in common use*, ἀ. καὶ ἔξω πάτου Luc.*Hist.Conscr.* 44. 5. τὰ ἀπόρρητα, = τὰ αἰδοῖα, Plu.2.284a, cf. Ar.*Ec.*12, Longin. 43.5. III. Adv. ἀπορρήτως *ineffably, inexpressibly*, Philostr.*VS* 2.18; *covertly*, ἀπορρήτως τὰ γραφόμενα κατεχλεύαζε διὰ τῆς εἰκόνος Eun.*Hist.*p.263 D.

ἀπορρῑγ-έω, 2 pf. ἀπέρρῑγα, *shrink shivering from* a thing: generally, *shrink from doing* it, c. inf., νέεσθαι Od.2.52. **-όω**, *shiver with cold*, Arist.*Pr.*862^{b}37.

ἀπορριζόω, *pull out by the roots*, τρίχας Alciphr.3.66.

ἀπορρῑν-άω, *file off*, κέρατα Str.7.3.18. **-ήματα**, τά, *filings, scraps*, Daphitas ap.eund.14.1.39.

ἀπορριπίζω, *blow away*, τὴν ἀναθυμίασιν Arist.*Pr.*947^{a}20; *blow out* or *back*, v.l. in D.H.*Comp.*14; cf. ἀπορραπίζω.

ἀπο-ρριπτέον, *one must reject, cast aside*, Hld.7.17; ὄκνον Them.*Or.* 22.274c. **-ρριπτος**, ον, *cast aside*, Procop.Gaz.*Ep.*116. **-ρρίπτω**, poet. **ἀπορίπτω** Pi.*P.*6.37, later **ἀπορριπτέω** X.*HG*5.4.42, Plu.*Caes.* 39, *Cat.Ma.*5, Luc.*Tim.*12, Hdn.4.9.2, D.C.74.1, fut. -ρίψω Hes.*Sc.* 215: pf. ἀπέρριφα Plb.1.40.15:—*throw away, put away*, μῆνιν, μηνιθμόν, Il.9.517, 16.282; ἀπὸ κρόκεον ῥίψαις.. εἷμα Pi.*P.*4.232; ἀπορρίψοντι ἐοικώς like one *about to cast* [a net], Hes.*Sc.*215; ἀ. ἀπὸ τοῦ στόματος *spit*, Thphr.*Char.*19.4; *vomit*, τὴν τροφήν Asclep.Jun.ap. Gal.13.162; *cast up*, of a river, τοὺς νεκροὺς τῶν ῥευμάτων Jul.*Or.*2. 60c. II. *cast forth from* one's country, A.*Ch.*914; ἄπωστος γῆς ἀπορριφθήσομαι S.*Aj.*1019; ἀπερριμμένοι *outcasts*, D.18.48, cf. D.H. 9.10; of things, *reject*, *PBaden* 19.12 (ii A.D.); τὰ φαῦλα καὶ ἀπερρ. τῶν ἐδεσμάτων Hdn.4.12.2. 2. *disown, reject*, Pi.*O.*9.38, S.*El.* 1018. 3. *throw aside, set at naught*, ἡ ἡμετέρη εὐδαιμονίη οὕτω τοι ἀπέρριπται ἐς τὸ μηδέν Hdt.1.32; Κύπρις δ' ἄτιμος τῷδ' ἀ. λόγῳ A.*Eu.* 215; ὅταν.. τὰ χρηστὰ ἀπορρίπτηται D.25.75. III. of words, *utter*, esp. in disparagement, ἔς τινα Hdt.1.153, 4.142 (Pass.), 8.92: generally, ἀ. ἔπος *let fall* a word, Id.6.69; χαμαιπετὲς ἔπος ἀ. Pi.*P.* 6.37; λόγον ἀχρεῖον Ant.Lib.11.3; μηδ' ἀπορριφθῇ λόγος A.*Supp.* 484. IV. intr., *throw oneself down, leap off*, *Act.Ap.*27.43, Charito 3.5. **-ρρῑφή**, ἡ, *being cast out*, Sch.E.*Hec.*675. **-ρρίψιμος**, ον, *that should be thrown away*, Artem.5.85. **-ρριψις**, εως, ἡ, *throwing off*, ἱματίων Hp.*Acut.*42 (pl.), cf. Luc.*Symp.*15.

ἀπο-ρροή, ἡ, (ἀπορρέω) *flowing off, stream*, αἵματος ἀπορροαί E.*Hel.* 1587; *outflow*, Sabin.ap.Orib.9.15.6; *surface from which water flows off*, D.S.2.8. 2. *falling* of a river, Aristid.*Or.*36(48).36. 3. *exhalation*, Plu.*Sol.*23. 4. *effluence, emanation*, ἀπορροὴ τοῦ κάλλους Pl.*Phdr.*251b; πάντων ἀπορροαὶ ὅσσ' ἐγένοντο Emp.89, cf. Arist. *Pr.*908^{a}21, Plot.2.3.2; ἔστι χρόα ἀπορροὴ σχημάτων ὄψει ξύμμετρος Pl. *Men.*76d. II. *falling away, loss*, τὰ ἐκεῖ ταχθέντα κατὰ φύσιν μένοντα οὐδεμίαν πάσχει ἀ. Plot.2.1.4. **-ρροια**, ἡ, = foreg. I. 1, X.*HG* 5.2.5. 2. = foreg. I. 4, Arist.*Sens.*438^{a}4, al., Epicur.*Ep.*1 p.9 U., Porph.*Abst.*2.46, etc.; αἴγλης Orph.*L.*173; Medic., *effluvia*, Gal.15. 625 (pl.), etc. 3. Astrol., *separation*, opp. συναφή, Serapio in *Cat. Cod.Astr.*1.100: but, *influence* of planets, Gem.2.14. II. = foreg. II, Plot.2.3.11. (Less correct than ἀπορροή, Phryn.*PS*p.50 B.)

ἀπορροιβδέω, *shriek forth*, οὐκ εὐσήμους ἀ. βοάς, of birds of prey, S.*Ant.*1021; ἰωήν Nonn.*D.*2.257.

ἄπορρον· πάλιν, Hsch. (fort. ἄψορρον).

ἀπόρροος, ον, contr. **-ρρους**, ουν, (ἀπορρέω) *streaming out of*, αἰγῶν ἀ. θρόμβος Antiph.52.8. II. Subst., *outflow*, κρήνης E.*Antiop.* iv B 57 Arn.; *branch* of a river or sea, Νείλου Aristid.*Or.*36(48).74; θαλάσσης ib.87, cf. 44(17).17 (pl.).

ἀπορροφέω, *swallow some of*, τοῦ οἴνου X.*Cyr.*1.3.10 codd.

ἀπο-ρρῡ́σκω, *run off*, of whey in making cheese, Eust.1625. 65. **-ρρῠπαίνω**, *tarnish*, prob. in S.*Ichn.*153 (Pass.). **-ρρῠπόω**, = sq., Hsch. s.v. ἀπινοῦται. **-ρρύπτω**, *cleanse thoroughly*, Asp.*in EN*25.1, Luc.*Gall.*9; τοὺς πόρους Gal.11.745:—Med., *cleanse oneself*, Plu.*Sull.*36, Ael.*NA*9.62: c. acc., ἀ. τὰς ἐκ παθῶν καὶ νοσημάτων κηλῖδας Ph.2.487, cf. Iamb.*Protr.*21.ια'. 2. *wash away*, μελεδωνάς prob. cj. in *AP*9.815. **-ρρῠσις**, εως, ἡ, *sinking down*, τῶν προσκεφαλαίων Herod.Med. in *Rh.Mus.*58.74; cf. ἀπόρρευσις.

ἀπορρυταλίξαι· ἀποσπάσαι, Hsch.

ἀπόρρῠτος, ον, = ἀπόρροος, *running*, κρήνη Hes.*Op.*595; ἀ. ὕδωρ, opp. στάσιμον, Hp.*Aër.*7. II. *subject to efflux*, opp. ἐπίρρυτος, Pl.*Ti.*43a; οὐκ ἀ., of the sea, Arist.*Mete.*353^{b}32; *having an outflow*, πηγή Porph.*Sent.*44. III. ἀ. σταθμά stables *with drains* or *a sloping floor*, X.*Eq.*4.3.

ἀπόρρυψις, εως, ἡ, *cleansing*, Ath.9.409c; in medic. sense, Philagr.ap.Orib.5.21.4, Ruf.ib.8.24.5: metaph., *purification*, τῆς ψυχῆς Iamb.*VP*17.74 (pl.).

ἀπο-ρρωγάς, άδος, v.l. for sq., Lxx 2 *Ma.*14.45. **-ρρώξ**, ῶγος, ὁ, ἡ, (ἀπορρήγνυμι) *broken off, abrupt, sheer, precipitous*, ἀκταί Od.13. 98; πέτρα X.*An.*6.4.3, cf. Arist.*HA*611^{a}21, Call.*Lav.Pall.*41. 2. Subst., *cliff, precipice*, Plb.7.6.3, etc.; ἀκμή *AP*7.693 (Apollonid.); *abyss*, J.*BJ*1.21.3. II. fem. Subst., *piece broken off*, Κώκυτός θ' ὃς δὴ Στυγὸς ὕδατός ἐστιν ἀ. *branch* of the Styx, Od.10.514, cf. Il. 2.755; ἀλλὰ τόδ' ἀμβροσίης καὶ νέκταρός ἐστιν ἀ. is *an efflux, a distillation* of nectar (ἀπόσταγμα Hsch.), Od.9.359; ἀ. Ἐρινύων *limb* of the Furies, Ar.*Lys.*811 (lyr.); ἡ δὲ προφητείη δίης φρενός ἐστιν ἀ. Orac.ap.Luc.*Alex.*40; μελέων ὀλίγη τις ἀ. some small *portion* of melody, *AP*7.571 (Leont.); ἀ. δραχμαίη *portion* of a drachm's weight, Nic.*Th.*518; ἀπορρῶγες σπλάγχνου Aret.*SD*1.10; ἀπορρὼξ τῆς πόλεως, of Samos, Demad.ap.Ath.3.99d; μουνογενής τις ἀ. φύλου ἄνωθεν Χαλδαίων Orph.*Fr.*247.23.

ἀπορύσσω· *refodio*, Gloss.

ἀπορφᾰνίζω, *bereave*, τινὰ παιδός *BCH*46.345:—Pass., *to be orphaned*, A.*Ch.*249; ἀπό τινος ἀ. *to be torn away from*.., 1 *Ep.Th.*2.17.

ἀπόρφῠρος, ον, *without purple attire*, Plu.2.528b; esp. of a garment, *without purple border*, Id.*Ant.*71, *POxy.*1741.21 (iv A.D.).

ἀπορχέομαι, *dance away, lose by dancing*, γάμον Hdt.6.129.

ἆπος, v.l. for αἶπος (q.v.).

ἀποσᾰλεύω, *lie in the roadstead, ride at anchor*, Th.1.137; ἐπ' ἀγκύρας D.50.22, cf. Arist.*HA*523^{b}33, *PA*685^{a}34: metaph., ἀ. ἐν φόβοις J. *BJ*7.3.4; *keep aloof from*, τινός Plu.2.493d. b. ἀποσαλεύσας· ἐπιτηρήσας, Hsch., *EM*125.48. 2. trans., *shake, cause to move*, Gal. 6.141:—Pass. (with fut. -σαλεύσομαι), *to be loosened, shaken away*, Ruf.*Ren.Ves.*12.3; *be shaken from one's opinion*, Arr.*Epict.*3.26.16.

ἀποσαρκόομαι, dub. sens., σὰρξ ἀποσαρκοῦται Arist.*Pr.*865^{b}30 (fort. ἀποστρακοῦται), cf. 966^{a}26.

ἀποσάττω, *unsaddle, unpack*, opp. ἐπισάττω, Lxx *Ge.*24.32. II. *stop up, caulk*, Din.*Fr.*89.10; *stuff with food*, σαυτὸν ἀποσάξεις (Casaub. for -τάξεις) Diph.43.41:—Med., *stuff oneself*, Philem.68.

ἀποσᾰφέω, (σαφής) *make clear, indicate*, οὐδὲν ἀπεσάφει.. ὁπότερα ποιήσοι Pl.*Prt.*348b, cf. *Cra.*384a, Gal.8.678, Luc.*Hist.Conscr.*52; ὑπέρ τινος Jul.*Gal.*138a.

ἀποσᾰφηνίζω, = foreg., Luc.*JTr.*27.

ἀποσβαίω· νεκρῷ, Hsch.

ἀπο-σβέννῡμι (-ύω A.D.*Pron.*36.4, Plu.2.681e), *extinguish, quench*, τὸ φῶς *Trag.Adesp.*9; τοὺς λύχνους Ar.*V.*255; τὸ πῦρ Pl.*Hp. Ma.*290e, etc.; also ἀ. τὸ κακόν Id.*R.*556a; τὸ γένος καὶ ὄνομα X.*Cyr.* 5.4.30; ψυχήν *AP*7.303 (tm.); ἰόν ib.11.321 (Phil.); τὰς ὁράσεις Plu. l.c.; Gramm., *extinguish*, i.e. *lose*, τὸν τόνον, of enclitics, A.D.*Pron.* l.c. II. Pass., pres. in Heraclit.30, Hp.*Aër.*4, X.*Lac.*13.3, etc.:—Med., fut. ἀποσβήσομαι Pl.*Lg.*805c: aor. 2 and pf. Act. intr., ἀπέσβην E.*Med.*1218, X.*Cyr.* l.c., Call.*Fr.*1.10 P., Theoc.4.39, etc.; ἀπέσβηκα X.*Cyr.*8.8.13, Pl.*Plt.*269b, etc.: aor. 1 Pass. ἀπεσβέσθην Ar.*Lys.* 293, Lys.1.14, v.l. in Luc.*Cat.*27: pf. ἀπέσβεσμαι Parm.8.21, Porph. *Abst.*3.7:—*to be extinguished, go out, vanish, die, cease*, ll.cc.; of a woman's milk, Hp.*Aër.* l.c., Arist.*GA*777^{a}14; ἀ. ὁ μαστός Id.*HA* 618^{b}7: metaph., ἔρωτος ἀπέσβη πυρσός *AP*12.182 (Strat.). **-σβεσις**, εως, ἡ, *extinction*, πυρός Arist.*APo.*93^{b}10; ζωῆς Procl.*in R.*2.113 K.

ἀποσειρόω, *strain, filter off*, Philum.*Ven.*23.3, Aët.1.113, *PMag. Leid.V.*6.19, *PHolm.*23.21, etc.

ἀπό-σεισις, εως, ἡ, *shaking off*: *licentious dance*, Poll.4.101. **-σεισμα**, ατος, τό, f.l. for ὑπο-, Gal.13.784. **-σείω**, *shake off*, Men.61, Thphr.*CP*1.20.3:—Pass., ξίφος ἀποσεσεῖσθαι τοῖς αὐχέσιν ἐπαιωρούμενον Hdn.5.2.1:—Med., *shake off from oneself*, πάντ' ἀποσεισάμενος Thgn.348; of a horse, *throw* his rider, Hdt.9.22, X.*Cyr.* 7.1.37; τειχέων θριγκοὺς ἀ. *throw* them *off*, S.*Fr.*506: metaph., ἀποσείεσθαι λύπας, γῆρας, Ar.*Ra.*346, *Lys.*670; νέφος Id.*Nu.*288; ἑταίρους Luc.*DMeretr.*13.2; ὕπνον Id.*Tim.*6:—Pass., ὑπὸ τῶν ἐρωμένων Them.*Or.*24.302c. 2. Med., *shake oneself*, Arist.*HA*560^{b}8.

ἀποσεμνύνω, *extol, glorify*, Pl.*Tht.*168d, D.S.2.47, etc. II. Pass., with fut. Med., *give oneself solemn airs*, Ar.*Ra.*703; ἀποσεμνῠνεῖται πρῶτον ib.833, cf. Procop.*Arc.*17; ὀψὲ ἀπεσεμνύνθη, of Tragedy, *assumed a dignified form*, Arist.*Po.*1449^{a}20; ἀποσεμνυνάμενοι Aristid.26(14).63. 2. c. dat., *pride oneself on*, πατρίδι, κάλλει, etc., Procop.*Aed.*4.1, 1.1, al.

ἀποσεύω, *chase away*, Nic.*Th.*77, *AP*9.642 (Agath.):—Pass., *run away, flee*, Hom. only in syncop. aor. 2 ἀπέσσυτο Il.6.390, etc.; ἀπεσσύμεναι θύγατρες B.10.82: also aor. ἀπεσσύθην [ῠ] Hes.*Th.*183; ἀποσυθὲν αἷμα, *haemorrhage*, v.l. for ἀποχυθέν in Hp.*Acut.*(*Sp.*)29:—Med., = Act., ἀπεσσεύοντο γυναῖκας A.R.1.805.

ἀποσήθω, *sift off, separate by sifting*, Dsc.5.88. 2. metaph., *riddle completely, rob*, Herodic.ap.Ath.13.591c.

ἀποσηκόω, (σηκός) *shut up in a pen*, Hsch.

ἀποσημ-αίνω, *announce by signs* or *signals, give notice*, περί τινος Hdt.5.20: abs., *give a sign* or *signal*, Pl.*Euthd.*276b; νοσήματα ἀ. *show themselves*, Arist.*Pr.*954ᵇ30. 2. c. acc., *indicate by signs* or *symptoms*, οὐδὲν ἀ. Hp.*Epid.*1.9; = δηλῶσαι, S.*Fr.*676; *denote, represent*, J.*AJ*3.7.7, Plu.*Sull.*7, etc.; *indicate*, J.*AJ*1.3.8, al.; *declare*, ib.1.8.1, al.:—Med., *show by signs* or *proofs*, Hdt.9.71; *guess by signs*, Ael.*NA*6.58. II. ἀ. εἴς τινα *allude to* him, Th.4.27, cf. Plu.2.177b; πρός τινα Philostr.*VA*6.10. III. *give adverse signs, be unpropitious*, τινί ib.2.33. IV. in Med., *seal up as confiscated, sequestrate*, Ar.*Fr.*432, X.*HG*2.3.21; of persons, *proscribe*, ib.2.4.13 (also Act., ἀποσημανῶ· ἀποδιώξω, Hsch.). 2. generally, *seal up*, γράμματα Hdn.4.12.6. **-άντωρ**, ορος, ὁ, *a sealer, recorder*, Eust.1590.6. **-ασία**, ἡ, *enunciation*, Phld.*Po.*2.16.

ἀποσημει-όομαι, *note down, make notes*, Phlp.*in Cat.*3.29. **-ωσις**, εως, ἡ, *record, note, abstract*, second title of Hippocrates' προγνωστικόν, Steph.*in Hp.*1.54 D., cf. Herm.*in Phdr.*p.96 A.

ἀποσήπομαι, Pass., aor. ἀπεσάπην [ᾰ] Hp.*Aph.*6.58: fut. -σᾰπήσομαι Id.*Prorrh.*2.1: with pf. Act. ἀποσέσηπα (v. infr.):—*lose by rotting* or *mortification*, ὑπὸ τοῦ ψύχους τοὺς δακτύλους τῶν ποδῶν ἀποσεσηπότες *having lost* the toes by frost-bite, X.*An.*4.5.12, cf. 5.8.15, Luc.*Ind.*6. 2. of water, *throw off impurities* by boiling, joined with ἀφέψεσθαι, Hp.*Aër.*8. II. causal in Act., *cause to putrefy, remove by putrefaction*, Id.*Haem.*2; γάλα Id.*Gland.*17; τινὰ ἐκ τοῦ σώματος Gal.11.820, cf. Aët.1.18.

ἀποσήχειν· ἀποδιώκειν, Hsch.

ἀπόσηψις, εως, ἡ, *rotting away*, Plu.9.1087e (pl.).

ἀποσῑγ-άω, *keep silent about, make no mention of*, c. acc., Demetr.*Eloc.*149, Ps.-Plu.*Vit.Hom.*213. **-ησις**, εως, ἡ, *keeping silence*, Hp.*Decent.*3 (pl.).

ἀποσῑμ-όω, *make flat-nosed*:—Pass., ἀποσεσιμώμεθα τὴν ῥῖνα we *have snub* noses, Luc.*DMort.*24.2. 2. = τὸ ἐπικύψαι καὶ τὴν πυγὴν προτεῖναι γυμνήν Philippid.1. II. ἀ. τὰς ναῦς *cause to swerve*, Th.4.25, cf. Gal.18(2).347. **-ωσις**, εως, ἡ, *turning* a ship *aside*, App.*BC*4.71 (pl.).

ἀποσιόομαι, Ion. for ἀφοσιόομαι.

ἀποσῑτ-έω, *cease to eat, starve*, Luc.*Asin.*33; *lose appetite*, Orib.*Inc.*6.25. **-ία**, ἡ, *aversion to food, want of appetite*, Hp.*Aph.*6.3, Aret.*SD*1.12. 2. *fasting*, Porph.*Abst.*1.27. **-ίζομαι**, *get to eat*, f.l. for ἐπι-, τι Aristaenet.1.3. **-ικός**, ή, όν, *exciting distaste for food*, Hp.*Prorrh.*1.100. **-ος**, ον, = ἄσιτος, *having eaten nothing*, ἡμερῶν τοσούτων ἀ. Hld.8.7, cf. Ael.ap.Ar.Byz.*Epit.*82.14, Luc.*Hist.Conscr.*21. 2. *hungry*, Philonid.1. II. *having an aversion for food, without appetite*, Hp.*Epid.*1.26.ς', Plu.2.635c, Gal.16.654, Jul.*Or.*6.190d.

ἀποσῑωπ-άω, *maintain silence*, Isoc.12.215, Plb.30.19.9, etc.; *cease speaking and be silent*, μεταξὺ λέγων ἀ. Plu.*Alc.*10; as a rhetorical figure (cf. sq.), Demetr.*Eloc.*44, 253. II. trans., *keep secret*, ὄνομα Luc.*Pseudol.*21; *leave unsaid*, Id.*Pisc.*29; *leave unnoticed*, *POxy.*237 vii 24 (ii A.D.). **-ησις**, εως, ἡ, *becoming silent*, Plu.*Alex.*52, Herod.Med. in *Rh.Mus.*58.71. 2. a rhetorical figure, when for emphasis, modesty, etc., the sentence is *abruptly broken off*, Quint.*Inst.*9.2.54, Demetr.*Eloc.*103, 264, Plu.2.1009e, Hermog.*Id.*2.7. 3. *breaking off* of friendship, Ptol.*Tetr.*192 (pl.).

ἀποσκάλλω, *scratch, scrape off*, *AB*428.

ἀποσκαμυνθίζειν· ἀπομυκτηρίζειν, Hsch.

ἀποσκάπτω, fut. Pass. -σκᾰφήσομαι Polyaen.5.10.3:—*cut off* or *intercept by trenches*, X.*An.*2.4.4. II. strengthd. for σκάπτω, Pl.*Lg.*760e.

ἀποσκᾰρίζω, = ἀπασκαρίζω (q. v.), Lxx *Jd.*4.21.

ἀποσκεδάννῡμι or **-ύω**, fut. -σκεδάσω, contr. -σκεδῶ S.*OT*138 (poet. also ἀποκεδ- A.R.3.1360, tm.):—*scatter abroad, disperse*, ἄλλους μὲν ἀπεσκέδασεν βασιλῆας Il.19.309; ψυχὰς μὲν ἀπεσκέδασ' ἄλλυδις ἄλλῃ Od.11.385; σκέδασον δ' ἀπὸ κήδεα θυμοῦ 8.149; ἀ. μύσος S. l. c.; ἀντιπάλων ὕβριν ἀπεσκέδασαν Epigr.ap.D.18.289:—Pass., *to be scattered*, τῶν ἐκ Τροίης ἀποσκεδασθέντων Hdt.7.91; *straggle away from*, ἀπὸ τοῦ στρατοπέδου X.*An.*4.4.9; τῆς φάλαγγος Id.*HG*5.4.42:—Med., *repel and scatter*, τὸν τοιόνδε φλύαρον Pl.*Ax.*365e.

ἀποσκελίσαι· παιδικὴν ὄρχησιν ὀρχήσασθαι, Hsch. (-ῆσαι cod.).

***ἀποσκέλλω**, v. ἀποσκλῆναι.

ἀποσκεπάζω, *uncover*, Sch.A.*Pr.*83, *Gp.*7.15.4 (Pass.).

ἀποσκεπαρνισμός, ὁ, (σκέπαρνον) *chipping off with an adze*: name for a particular kind of *wound in the head*, Gal.ap.Orib.46.21.3, Sor.*Fract.*1, 7.

ἀπο-σκεπτέον, *one must look*, πρός τι Arist.*Pol.*1327ᵇ4. **-σκέπτομαι**, not found in pres. (v. ἀποσκοπέω), fut. ἀποσκέψομαι: aor. ἀπεσκεψάμην:—*examine*, Plu.2.582d, ἔς τι Hp.*Mul.*1.11.

ἀποσκέπω, *give shelter from*, τὸν βορέαν Arr.*Epict.*3.22.65. II. *strip*, τὸ δέρμα Hsch. s. v. ἀπεσκόλυπτεν.

ἀποσκευάζω, *pull off*, τὴν ὀροφήν Lycurg.128; *clear away* tables, Suid.; *strip of furniture*, οἰκίαν Lxx *Le.*14.36. 2. = ζημιόω, Hsch. II. mostly in Med., *pack up and carry off*, ἀ. τι τῶν ἰδίων *SIG*633.68 (Milet., ii B. C.), cf. 588.50 (ib., ii B. C., Pass.), Plb.2.26.6, D.H.9.23: abs., *pack up and depart*, *Act.Ap.*21.15. 2. *get rid of*, τὰ ἐνοχλοῦντα (= ἀποπατέω, cf. Poll.5.91), Hdn.4.13.4; *remove*, τῆς φιλίας τινά Luc.*Cal.*12; *make away with, kill*, Id.*Tyr.*1, Hdn.2.5.1; *get rid of, confute*, τοὺς σοφιστάς Gal.8.19:—Pass., *to be expelled*, τῶν σωμάτων Dsc.*Ther.Praef.* 3. *repel*, αἰτίαν, διαβολάς, J.*BJ*2.16.5, 1.24.4. 4. *reject*, Simp.*in Ph.*888.15. 5. *defer*, διήγησιν Hld.5.1. 6. *transfer*, ἔς τινας τὰς αἰτίας Jul.*Or.*2.66d.

ἀποσκευή, ἡ, *removal, riddance*, i.e. *assassination*, J.*AJ*18.2.4. II. *baggage*, in sg. and pl., Plb.2.3.7, 1.66.7, Plu.2.174a, etc.; *household stuff*, Lxx *Ge.*34.29, *UPZ*110 iii 90 (ii B. C.), etc.; δόμων ἀ. Ezek.*Exag.*209. III. *ordure, filth*, v.l. Str.14.1.37. [Scanned ⏑ – ⏑ – by Ezek. l. c.]

ἀπόσκημμα, ατος, τό, *support, prop*, A.*Fr.*18. II. = ἀπόσκηψις, Ruf.ap.Orib.45.30, Gal.18(2).133, Simp.*in Epict.*p.37 D.

ἀποσκην-έω, *encamp apart*, πόρρω ἀπεσκήνουν τῶν Ἑλλήνων X.*An.*3.4.35. **-ος**, ον, (σκηνή) *encamping apart, living and messing alone*, opp. σύσσιτος, Id.*Cyr.*8.7.14. **-όω**, *keep apart from*, τὰ ὦτα τῶν Μουσῶν Plu.2.334b: also intr. in Act., μακρὰν ἀ. τῶν ἰδίων Id.2.627a, cf. *Eum.*15, *Demetr.*9. 2. *remove one's habitation*, Lxx *Ge.*13.18.

ἀποσκήπτω, *hurl from above*, ἐς οἰκήματα τὰ μέγιστα.. ἀποσκήπτει βέλεα (sc. ὁ θεός) Hdt.7.10.ε': metaph., ἀ. τὴν ὀργὴν εἴς τινα *discharge* one's rage upon one, D.H.6.55, cf. J.*AJ*13.1.5; φθορὰν εἰς τὴν πόλιν ib.6.1.1; ἀ. τιμωρίαν D.S.1.70. II. intr., *fall suddenly*, ὀργαὶ δ' ἔς σ' ἀπέσκηψαν θεᾶς her wrath *fell* upon thee, E.*Hipp.*438; μὴ οὖν εἰς ἀθρόους ἀλλ' εἰς ἕνα ἀποσκήψατε Aeschin.1.182; ἀ. τὸ ὕδωρ εἰς τοὺς ὀφθαλμούς Arist.*Mir.*846ᵃ2; αἱ πληγαὶ τῶν ξιφῶν εἰς τὰς χεῖρας Plu.*Pomp.*19; ἡ δίκη ἀ. ἐς ὀφθαλμοὺς καὶ ἐς χεῖρας Philostr.*VA*1.6; ἀποσκήψαντος τοῦ ἐνυπνίου ἐς φλαῦρον *come to* a sorry *ending*, Hdt.1.120; ποῖ ταῦτα ἀποσκήψει; Cic.*Att.*12.5.1; εἰς μέγα τι κακόν, ἐς ὄλεθρον ἀ., D.H.7.15, Alciphr.1.37. 2. Medic., of humours, *determine*, εἴς τινα τῶν ἀκυροτέρων μορίων Gal.15.783, cf. 17(1).54; ἐς τὸ πᾶν Aret.*SD*1.12.

ἀπόσκηψις, εως, ἡ, *determination* of humours to one part of the body, Hp.*Aph.*6.56, *Prorrh.*2.7; ἀ. νούσου ἐς ἕν τι Aret.*SD*1.9; wrongly expl. as = ἀπόσχασις by Gal.19.84.

ἀποσκῐ-άζω, *cast a shade* or *shadow*, σκιαὶ δι' ἑτέρου.. φωτὸς ἀποσκιαζόμεναι shadows *cast*.., Pl.*R.*532c, cf. D.C.36.49. II. *cloud over, dull the brightness* of metallic surfaces, Zos.Alch.p.223 B. **-ασμα**, ατος, τό, *shadow*, ἀ. τροπῆς *a shadow cast by* turning, *Ep.Jac.*1.16, cf. Porph.*in Ptol.*193, Suid. s. v. ἀνθήλιος. II. *illusion, deceit*, Men.Prot.p.118 D. **-ασμός**, ὁ, *the casting a shadow*, ἀ. γνωμόνων *measures of time by the shadow* on the sun-dial, Plu.*Per.*6 (pl.).

ἀπο-σκίδνημι, *scatter*, Ph.2.100:—elsewh. in Pass., **-σκίδνᾰμαι**, Μυρμιδόνας δ' οὐκ εἴα ἀποσκίδνασθαι Il.23.4; of soldiers, ἀ. ἔς τι *to disperse* for a purpose, Hdt.4.113: abs., Th.6.98; cf. ἀποκίδναμαι.

ἀποσκίμπτω, = ἀποσκήπτω:—Pass., δύο ἄγκυραι ἀγαθαὶ ἐκ ναὸς ἀπεσκίμφθαι it is good *to have* two anchors *fastened to* the ship, Pi.*O.*6.101.

ἀποσκίρρωμα, ατος, τό, *a callous, hard lump*, Sch.Ar.*Ach.*553.

ἀποσκιρτάω, *skip away*, τῆς ἀγελῆς Hellanic.111 J.; in Str.17.1.31 *to have a bout of skipping* or *capering*: metaph., *to be restive* or *rebellious*, Luc.*Merc.Cond.*23, Them.*Or.*7.87b.

ἀποσκλῆναι, aor. 2 inf. of *ἀποσκέλλω (cf. σκέλλω), *to be dried up, wither*, Ar.*V.*160: pf., λιμῷ ἀπεσκληκέναι Luc.*DMort.*27.7: and abs., ἀπέσκλη *died of starvation*, Men.*Her.*30: fut. ἀποσκλήσῃ *AP*11.37 (Antip.).

ἀπόσκληρ-ος, ον, strengthd. for σκληρός, *very hard*, Philum.*Ven.*15.4, 22.1, Simp.*in Ph.*304.27. 2. *harsh* to the taste, of water, Myia *Ep.*4. **-ύνω**, *harden*, Hp.*Coac.*515:—Pass., Arist.*Mir.*836ᵇ5, Thphr.*CP*3.16.2; ἀπεσκληρυμμένοι, gloss on ναρκώδεις, Erot.

ἀπόσκλησις, εως, ἡ, *drying up, withering*, Corn.*ND*33.

ἀποσκνίπτω, aor. subj. ἀποσκνίψῃς, *scatter*, Hsch.

ἀποσκνῐφόω, *obscure, darken*, Emp.42.2.

ἀποσκολοπίζω, *remove stumbling-blocks*, Aq.*Is.*57.14, al.

ἀποσκολύπτω, *skin, strip off*, Archil.124 (sens. obsc.), S.*Fr.*423; also ἀπεσκολυμμένος, = περιτετμημένος, Hsch., Ael.Dion.*Fr.*432.

ἀπο-σκοπεύω, = sq., Lxx *La.*4.17, Ph.1.677 codd., etc.; cf. ἀποσκωπεύω. **-σκοπέω**, (with fut. -σκέψομαι) *look away from* other objects *at* one, and so *look steadily*, πρός τινα or τι, S.*OT*746, Pl.*Plt.*291e, Arist.*Pol.*1284ᵇ5, etc.; εἴς τι S.*OC*1195; πόρρω ποι ἀ. Pl.*R.*432e; *keep watch*, Luc.*DMar.*6.2. 2. c. acc., *look to, regard*, E.*Hec.*939 (lyr.), D.H.6.72, Procop.*Goth.*4.15:—Med., ἀποσκοπεῖσθαι τὸ μέλλον Plu.*Pomp.*79; πρός τι Procl.*in Prm.*p.549 S. 3. ἀποσκοπεῖν εἰ.. E.*Supp.*236. 4. Pass., ἡ πόλις ἐκ περιωπῆς -εῖται *is visible from a distance*, Procop.*Aed.*1.1. **-σκοπιάζω**, = foreg., Q.S.6.114. **-σκόπιος**, ον, *far from the mark*, ἀ. ἀφάμαρτον *App.Anth.*3.59 (Ptol.). **-σκοπος**, ον, *erring from the mark*, οὐκ.. ἀ. οὐδ' ἀδαήμων Emp.62.3. II. *beholding from afar*, Hsch.

ἀποσκορᾰκ-ίζω, (ἐς κόρακας) *wish* one *far enough, curse, damn*, Lxx *Is.*17.13, Plu.2.740a, Alciphr.1.38, Iamb.*VP*25.112. **-ισμός**, ὁ, *casting off utterly*, Lxx *Is.*66.15, Hsch.

ἀποσκορπίζω, = σκορπίζω, Lxx 1 *Ma.*11.55, *Gp.*20.12.1, Aët.15.15.

ἀποσκοτ-ίζω, *darken*, c. gen., τῆς ἐκείνου [θεοῦ] ἐνοράσεως ἑαυτὸν ἀπεσκότισε Porph.*Marc.*13. II. *remove darkness*, σμικρὸν ἀποσκοτίσαι κελεύοντος *stand out of his light*, Plu.2.605e; ἀποσκότησόν μου is f.l. in D.L.6.38. **-όομαι**, *to be darkened, blinded*, ὑπὸ λιγνύος Plb.1.48.6; of the mind, Ath.10.446b; σελήνη ἀποσκοτοῦται Eust.1769.19; ἀποσκοτοῦσθαι τὰς ὄψεις Plu.*Sert.*17, Sch.Pi.*P.*4.89.—The Act. only in Poll.1.118, ἀ. τὰ ὄμματα. II. *to be shaded off*, in painting, Ar.*Fr.*712. **-ωσις**, εως, ἡ, *darkening, loss of sight*, Nech.ap.Vett.Val.279.33.

ἀποσκουτλόω, *deprive of its paving*, ἡρῷον *IG*3.1423 sq.

ἀποσκῠβᾰλ-ίζω, *treat as vile refuse,* Sch.Pi.*P.*3.22; *pollute* a tomb, prob. in *CIG*3927 (Hierapolis):—Pass., *to be cast forth as excrement,* Epict.*Gnom.*19:—hence Subst. **-ισις,** εως, ἡ, Sch.Ar.*Pl.*1184.

ἀποσκυδμαίνω, *to be enraged with,* μὴ..ἀποσκύδμαινε θεοῖσι Il.24.65.

ἀποσκύζω, = foreg., Procop.*Arc.*10, Hsch.

ἀποσκῠθίζω, *scalp* (*as the Scythians did*), Lxx 4*Ma.*10.7. 2. metaph. in Pass., *to be shaved bare,* κρᾶτ' ἀπεσκυθισμένη E.*Tr.*1026; τὴν ἐφ' ὕβρει κουρὰν ἀπεσκυθίσθαι Ath.12.524f.

ἀποσκῡλεύω, *carry off as spoil from,* τί τινος Theoc.24.5.

ἀποσκύλλω, *pull, tear off,* aor. Med. ἀποσκύλαιο λάχνην Nic.*Th.*690.

ἀπόσκωμμα, ατος, τό, *banter, raillery,* Hsch.

ἀποσκωπεύω, *dance the figure* σκώπευμα (q. v.); ὁ -εύων, painting by Antiphilus, Plin.*HN*35.138; confused with ἀποσκοπεύω by Ath. 14.629f.

ἀποσκωπτικῶς, Adv. *in a jeering way,* Sch.Luc.*Lex.*15.

ἀποσκώπτω, *banter, rally,* Θαλῆν ἀστρονομοῦντα..θεραπαινὶς ἀποσκῶψαι λέγεται Pl.*Tht.*174a; ἀ. πρός or εἴς τινα, *jeer* at one, D.C.48.38, Luc.*Herm.*51, etc.; ἐπί τινι D.C.60.33; εἴς τινα ἐπίγραμμα D.L. 5.11.

ἀποσμ-άω, *wipe off,* οὐλάς Dsc.5.91, Diocl.*Fr.*141, Apollon.ap. Gal.12.477; ῥύπον Luc.*Anach.*29. II. *wipe clean,* Id.*Pisc.* 14 (Pass.). **-ηκτέον,** *one must wipe clean,* Sor.1.78, Aët.12.1. **-ηξις,** εως, ἡ, *wiping, cleaning,* Archig.ap.Aët.9.35, Hsch. s.v. ἔκνιψις. **-ήχω,** = ἀποσμάω, Pherecyd.33J., Sor.1.81, Paus. 5.5.11, Luc.*Tim.*54, Them.*Or.*32.359c:—Pass., c. dat., *to be smeared with,* *Gp.*16.18.2.

ἀποσμῑκρύνω, *diminish,* Luc.*Merc.Cond.*21, etc.:—also **ἀποσμῑκρόω,** Tim.*Lex.* s.v. ὑποκορίζεσθαι.

ἀποσμιλαίνω, f.l. for ἀπομυλλαίνω.

ἀποσμίλ-ευμα [ῐ], ατος, τό, *a chip, shaving,* Suid. **-εύω,** *plane off, polish off,* ῥήματα, λέξιν, Jul.*Or.*2.77a, Them.*Or.*21.251b.

ἀποσμύχομαι [ῡ], Pass., *to be consumed as by a slow fire, waste, pine away,* Luc.*DMort.*6.3.

ἀποσοβ-έω, *scare away,* as one does birds, τοὺς ῥήτορας Ar.*Eq.*60, cf. *V.*460: metaph., ἀποσοβῆσαι τὸν γέλων Id.*Ra.*45; ἀ. ἀπὸ τῶν ὀφθαλμῶν τὰ λυποῦντα *to keep off,* X.*Eq.*5.6; ἀ. τινὰ ὁμιλίας Plu.2.11d:—Med., *keep off from oneself,* X.*Eq.*5.7:—Pass., *to be scared,* ἀποσοβηθῆναι ταῖς διανοίαις Plb.30.5.16. II. intr., *to be off in a hurry,* οὐκ ἀποσοβήσεις; i.e. *be off!* Ar.*Av.*1032,1258, cf. Luc.*Nav.* 4; ἀποσοβῶμεν *let's be off,* Men.997. **-ημα,** ατος, τό, *that which averts evil,* Sch.Opp.*H.*1.46, Sch.E.*Med.*1322; = sq., Sch.rec.A.*Th.* 69. **-ησις,** εως, ἡ, *scaring away,* Sch.A.*Pers.*215. **-ητέον,** *one must shun,* v.l. Phryn.295. **-ητήρ,** ῆρος, ὁ, *one that scares away,* Sch.Od.14.531. **-ητήριος,** α, ον, gloss on ἀλεξητήριος, Hsch. **-ητής,** οῦ, ὁ, = -ητήρ, Sch.Ar.*Pl.*359. **-ητικός,** ή, όν, *driving away, averting,* μιασμῶν Iamb.*Protr.*21.ις', cf. Sch.Pi.*O.*9.143.

ἄποσος, ον, *non-quantitative,* Plot.4.7.5, Phlp.*in Ph.*401.4.

ἀποσοφόομαι, *become wise,* Arr.*Epict.*1.18.10.

ἀποσπάδιος [ᾰδ], α, ον, (ἀποσπάω) *torn off* or *away from,* τινός Orph.*H.*18.13; τὸ ἀ. = ἀπόσπασμα, *AP*6.102 (Phil.).

ἀποσπάδων, οντος, ὁ, = σπάδων, Suid.

ἀποσπαίρω, *beat convulsively,* σφυγμῶν -οντων Aët.16.67.

ἀποσπᾰλᾰκόω, (σπάλαξ) *blind*: metaph. in Pass., ὁ τᾶς Δίκας ὀφθαλμὸς ἀπεσπαλάκωται Cerc.4.17.

ἀποσπάρ-αγμα [πᾰ], ατος, τό, = ἀπόσπασμα, *AP*13.21 (Theodorid.). **-άσσω,** *tear off,* E.*Ba.*1127.

ἀποσπαργᾰνόω, *take off the swaddling-clothes,* Sor.1.100:—Pass., Lyd.*Mens.*4.26.

ἀποσπαρθάζω, *quiver,* Hp.*Morb.*2.10.

ἀπο-σπάς, άδος, ἡ, *torn off from,* τινός Nonn.*D.*1.289, al.: metaph., βασσαρίδες ἀποσπάδες ἠθάδος ὕλης ib.34.347, etc. II. as Subst., *slip for propagating,* *Gp.*11.9, etc.; *vine-branch* or *bunch of grapes,* *AP*6.300 (Leon.): metaph., *branch* of a river, Eust.1712.6. **-σπᾰσις,** εως, ἡ, *avulsion, separation,* αὐτόματος ἀ. Aret.*CD*1.4. **-σπασμα,** ατος, τό, *that which is torn off, a piece, rag, shred,* Pl.*Phd.* 113b; *branch, division of a tribe,* Str.9.5.12, cf. Agatharch.57: generally, *a detached portion* or *particle,* ψυχῆς καὶ σώματος ἀ. τὸ σπέρμα Epicur.*Fr.*329, Zeno *Stoic.*1.36, Chrysipp.ib.2.191, Ph.1.119; μύθου Corn.*ND*17. 2. *avulsion, tearing apart* of bones, Hp.*Off.*23, cf. Gal.18(2).887. **-σπασμάτιον,** τό, Dim. of foreg., *fragment,* Cic.*Att.*2.1.3. **-σπασμός,** ὁ, *tearing away, severing,* Plu.2. 77c; νεύρου Gal.18(1).736. II. *being torn away, separation, severance,* ὁ τῆς συνοδίας ἀ. Str.8.3.17; τῶν ἀναγκαιοτάτων D.H.5.55, cf. Phld.*Lib.*p.4O.; -μοὶ τῆς ψυχῆς ἀπὸ τοῦ σώματος Id.*Mort.* 9. **-σπαστέον,** *one must sever,* Ph.*Bel.*92.30. **-σπαστος,** ον, *separated,* ἀπ' ἀλλήλων prob. l. in Theag.ap.Stob.3.1.117. **-σπάω,** fut. -σπάσω [ᾰ], *tear* or *drag away from,* τινός S.*Aj.*1024, Pl.*R.* 491b, etc.; ἀ. τινὰ ἀπὸ γυναικὸς καὶ τέκνων Hdt.3.1, cf. 102; ἀποσπάσας..περόνας ἀπ' αὐτῆς S.*OT*1268; μή μου τὸ τέκνον ἐκ χερῶν ἀποσπάσῃς E.*Hec.*277: rarely ἀ. τινά τι *tear* a thing *from* one, S.*OC* 866; ἀ. τινά *tear* him *away,* Hdt.6.91; ἀ. τι τῆς λείας *detach, abstract* some of it, Plb.2.26.8: metaph., ἀ. τινὰ ἐλπίδος S.*OT*1432; and reversely also ἀ. τῆς φρενὸς αἵ μοι μόναι παρῆσαν ἐλπίδων Id.*El.*809; *detach, withdraw,* πλήρωμα a gang of labourers, *PPetr.*3 p.129 (iii B.C.); τινὰ ἀπό τινος *BGU*1125.9 (i B.C.), cf. infr. 5; μαθητάς *Act.Ap.*20.30; ἀ. πολίτας τῆς θαλάσσης Plu.*Them.*19; ἀπὸ τοῦ φρονεῖν τινά Ar.*Ra.*962:—Med., τὴν μάχην οὕτω μακρὰν τῆς ναυτικῆς βοηθείας Plu.*Pomp.*76:—Pass., *to be dragged away, detached, separated from,* τινός Pi.*P.*9.33, E.*Alc.*287, etc.; ἐξ ἱροῦ Hdt.1.160; ἀπὸ τῶν ἱερῶν Th.3.81; of a bone, *to be torn off,* Hp.*Art.*13; ἀκρώμιον -σπασθέν Id.*Mochl.*6. 2. ἀ. τινὰ κόμης *drag away* by the hair, A.*Supp.*909. 3. ἀ. πύλας, θύρας, *tear off* the gates, doors, Hdt.1.17, 3.159, etc.: metaph., πινακηδὸν ἀποσπῶν [ῥήματα] Ar.*Ra.*824. 4. ἀ. τὸ στρατόπεδον *draw off, divert* the army, X.*HG*1.3.17: abs., ἀποσπάσας *having drawn off,* Id.*An.*7.2.11:—Pass., of troops, *to become separated* or *broken,* Th.7.80, Plb.1.27.9. 5. *withdraw, reclaim,* *POxy.*496.9. 6. ἀπεσπασμένος, ὁ, *eunuch,* Lxx *Le.*22.24. II. intr. (sc. ἑαυτόν), *separate* (i.e. *be separated*) *from,* Ael. *NA*10.48, Luc.*Icar.*11, D.C.56.22; and in X.*An.*1.5.3 the best Mss. give πολὺ γὰρ ἀπέσπα (for ἀπέπτα) φεύγουσα [στρουθός].

ἀποσπείρω, *scatter like seed,* τι ἐς γῆν Luc.*Somn.*15, cf. *Theol.Ar.*6.

ἀποσπένδω, *pour out wine,* as a drink-offering, at sacrifices, εὔχετ' ἀποσπένδων Od.3.394; ὤμοσ' ἀποσπένδων 14.331; ἀ. μέθυ E.*Ion* 1198, cf. Antipho 1.20; τινί Pl.*Phd.*117b:—Pass., *AP*5.54 (Diosc.).

ἀποσπερμ-αίνω, aor. -ηνα, *shed semen,* εἴς τι Apollod.3.14.6, Palaeph.51. **-ᾰτίζω,** = foreg., Arist.*GA*728ᵃ11; δυνάμεις Porph. *Antr.*16. **-άτισις** [ᾰτ], εως, ἡ, *emission of semen,* Sch.Aristid. p.329 F. **-ᾰτισμός,** ὁ, = foreg., Tz. ad Lyc.598.

ἀποσπερμᾰτόομαι, *to be converted into semen,* Steph.*in Hp.*1. 124 D.

ἀποσπεύδω, fut. -σπεύσω, *to be zealous in preventing, dissuade earnestly,* τὴν συμβολήν the engagement, Hdt.6.109: c. acc. et inf., ἀ. Ξέρξεα στρατεύεσθαι Id.7.17: abs., opp. ἐπισπεύδω, ib.18, Th.6.29.

ἀποσπινθηρ-ίζω, *emit sparks,* Arist.*Mete.*341ᵇ30. **-ισμός,** ὁ, *the emission of sparks,* Hsch.

ἀπόσπληνος, ἡ, *rosemary,* Apul.*Herb.*79.

ἀποσπογγ-ίζω, *wipe off as with a sponge,* Antipho 5.45, Antyll.ap. Orib.6.9.1:—Med., Sch.Od.8.88. **-ισμα,** ατος, τό, *dirt wiped off with a sponge,* Rh.3.530 W. **-ισμός,** ὁ, *sponging off,* Antyll.ap. Orib.9.23.2, Sor.1.67. **-ιστέον,** *one must wipe off,* Orib.*Fr.*38.

ἀποσποδέω, *wear quite off,* τοὺς ὄνυχας *walk* one's toes *off,* Ar. *Av.*8:—Pass., = ἀπερρίφθαι, ἀποθανεῖν, Hsch. II. ἀπεσποδηκότων· φλεγομένων ἐν τῇ τέφρᾳ, Id. (-ικώτων cod.).

ἀπόσπονδος, ον, (σπονδή) stronger form for ἄσπονδος (q.v.), Poll. 6.30.

ἀπόσπορος, ον, *born from,* θαλάσσης Musae.249, cf. Nonn.*D.*11. 145.

ἀποσπουδάζω, *dissuade eagerly,* τινά τινος Philostr.*VA*4.2. II. *slight, despise,* τοὺς Ἐπικούρου λόγους ib.1.7; *show lack of interest in,* τινός Id.*VS*1.17.2.

ἀποσσεύω, poet. for ἀποσεύω.

ἀπόσσῡτος, ον, *rushing away,* Opp.*H.*2.560, Nonn.*D.*2.686, al.; *thrown out of* a chariot, ib.28.165; *starting from* a mark, of racers, Opp.*H.*4.102; *departing from,* ὠκεανοῖο Tryph.668.

ἀπόστα, for ἀπόστηθι, aor. 2 imper. of ἀφίστημι.

ἀπόσταγμα, ατος, τό, *that which trickles down,* κυκεῶνος Tz. ad Lyc. 607, *EM*538.16.

ἀποστᾰδά [δᾱ], *standing apart,* Od.6.143.

ἀποστᾰδόν, Adv., (ἀφίσταμαι) *from afar,* Il.15.556. II. ἀπόσταδον· δίκτυον μεμολυβδωμένον καὶ καλάμῳ περιεννημένον, Hsch.

ἀποστάζω, *let fall drop by drop, distil away,* δακρύων ἀποστάζει αἰδῶ A.*Supp.*579 (lyr.); ἀμβροσίαν ἀ. Theoc.15.108: of grains, κρῖμνον κυκεῶνος ἀποστάζοντος ἔραζε Call.*Fr.*205: metaph., φάος Id. *Dian.*118; φωνήν *AP*15.9 (Cyrus). II. intr., *trickle,* Hp.*Coac.*328; μανίας ἀποστάζει μένος fury *distils from* madness, or *trickles away,* i.e. *passes off,* S.*Ant.*959 (lyr.); λόγων ἀ. χρυσός Luc.*Electr.*6; of grain, Herod.6.6: metaph., ῥίνημ' αὐτῆς ἂν οὐκ ἀποστάξαι not a brass farthing would *come off* the price, Id.7.82.

ἀποστάλ-αγμα [τᾰ], ατος, τό, = ἀπόσταγμα, αἰγείρων Scymn.397. **-άζω,** = ἀποστάζω II, Luc.*Am.*45: c. acc., ἀποσταλάξει τὰ ὄρη γλυκασμόν Lxx *Jl.*3(4).18 (= *Am.*9.13). **-άω,** = ἀποστάζω I, Opp.*C.* 3.370, 4.198.

ἀπόσταλ-μα, ατος, τό, gloss on ἄφεμα, *EM*176.4. **-τέον,** *one must send away,* Alex.*Fig.*1.1.

ἀποστάνομαι, = ἀφίσταμαι, *PGen.*53.21 (iv A.D.).

ἀποστάξις, εως, ἡ, *nose-bleeding,* Hp.*Acut.*(*Sp.*)29.

ἀπο-στᾰσία, ἡ, late form for ἀπόστασις, *defection, revolt,* v.l. in D.H.7.1, J.*Vit.*10, Plu.*Galb.*1; esp. in religious sense, *rebellion against God, apostasy,* Lxx *Jo.*22.22, 2*Ep.Th.*2.3. 2. *departure, disappearance,* Olymp.*in Mete.*320.2. 3. *distinguishing,* c. gen., Elias *in Cat.*119.7. 4. *distance,* Archim.*Aren.*1.5. **-στᾰσίου** δίκη action against a freedman *for having forsaken his* προστάτης and chosen another, ἀ. ὀφλεῖν D.25.65, cf. 35.48, Arist.*Ath.*58.3, prob. in *IG*2.776. II. ἀποστασίου βιβλίον writing or bill *of divorce,* Lxx *De.*24.1, *Ev.Matt.*19.7, *Ev.Marc.*10.4: so ἀποστάσιον *Ev.Matt.*5.32. III. ἀποστασίου συγγραφή deed *of cession, conveyance,* *PHib.*1.96.3 (iii B.C.), cf. *PGiss.*36.21 (ii B.C.), etc.; ἀντίγραφον -ίου *BGU*919.23 (ii A.D.); with συγγραφή omitted, esp. in phrase πρᾶσις καὶ ἀποστασίου *PTeb.*561ᵛ (i A.D), etc. **-στᾰσις,** εως, ἡ, (ἀφίστημι) *causing to revolt,* συμμάχων Th.1.122; Ἰώνων ἀπὸ τῆς Λακεδαιμονίων συμμαχίας Arist.*Ath.*23.4. B. (ἀφίσταμαι) *emanation,* εἰδώλων -σεις Epicur.*Fr.*320. 2. *slackness,* of bandages, Gal.18(2).806. 3. *defection, revolt,* ἀπό τινος Hdt.3.128; τὴν Κυπρίων ἀ. πρῆξαι Id.5.113; τὴν Αἰγύπτου ἀ. παρασκευάζεσθαι Id.7.4; ἀ. ἐκ τῆς ξυμμαχίας Th.5.81; ἀ. πρός τινα Id.1.75; διπλῆν ἀ. ἀποστήσεσθαι Id.3.13; ἀ. τῶν Ἀθηναίων, for ἀπὸ τ. Ἀ., Id.8.5; but τὰς

Μεσσηνίων ἀ. Pl.*Lg.*777c. 4. *departure from*, βίου E.*Hipp.*277; *separation* of effect *from* cause, Procl.*Inst.*35; *giving up, cession*, ἀ. τῶν κτημάτων D.19.146; *desisting from, disuse of*, φάσεως S.E.*P.*1.192; τῶν ἀπροαιρέτων Arr.*Epict.*4.4.39. 5. *distance*, ἁ ἀφ' ἡμῶν ἀ. Archyt.1; ἀφεστάναι τῇ αὐτῇ ἀ. ᾗπερ.. Pl.*Phd.*111b; ἀπόστασιν ὅσην ἀφεστηκὼς γίγνεται Id.*R.*587d, cf. 546b; ἐκ μικρᾶς ἀ. Arist.*Aud.*800b7; τῇ ἀπὸ τῆς γῆς ἀ. Id.*HA*503a21; ἐκ τῶν ἀ. according to their *distances*, Id.*Cael.*290b22; of time, κατὰ τὴν πρὸς τὸ νῦν ἀ. Id.*Ph.*223a5; ἐξ ἀποστάσεως at *a certain distance*, Plb.3.114.3; ἐν ἀποστάσει Id.3.113.4, Phld.*Herc.*19.25; κατ' ἀποστάσεις Hanno *Peripl.*13. 6. Rhet., *employment of detached phrases*, Hermog.*Id.*1.10, Aristid.*Rh.*1 p.462 S., Philostr.*VS*1.9.1 (pl.), *Ep.*73. 7. *lapse, declension*, Plot.1.8.7, 5.1.1. II. *place where something is put away, repository, storehouse*, Str.17.1.9, Philippid.14, Heraclid.*Pol.*72. III. Medic., *suppurative inflammation, throwing off* the peccant humours left by fever, etc., Hp.*Epid.*3.4 (pl.), Aret.*SD*1.9, Aristid.*Or.*47(23).68. 2. of diseases, *transition from one to another*, Hp.*Epid.*1.6; στραγγουριώδης ἀ. ib.3.1α'. 3. *lesion* of continuity, Gal.18(2).820. 4. *degree* of heat, cold, etc., Id.11.561, al. **-στᾰτέον**, (ἀφίσταμαι) *one must stand off from*, i.e. *give up, abandon*, πολέμου Th.8.2, etc.; οὐκ.. ἀ. τῇ πόλει τούτων D.18.199: abs., οὐκ ἀ. πρὶν.. Pl.*Plt.*257c. II. later, (ἀφίστημι) *one must keep apart, detain*, ἵππον ἀπὸ τῶν ἔργων *Gp.*16.1.4. **-στᾰτέω**, *stand aloof from*, τινός A.*Ch.*826 (lyr.), *Fr.*161, 301; οὔκουν πάρος γε σῆς ἀπεστάτουν φρενός S.*Ant.*993; μορφῆς δὲ τῆς σῆς οὐκ ἀπεστάτει *was* not *far from*.., Id.*OT*743; *fall off from, fail* one, κοὐκ ἀποστατῶ φίλων Ar.*Av.*312; βουλευτέον ὅπως μηδεὶς τῶν νῦν παρόντων ἀποστατήσει ἡμῶν συμμάχων X.*Cyr.*4.5.24; ἀ. τῶν ὄντων *to be absent from*, Pl.*Prm.*144b, cf. *Tht.*205a. 2. of the soul, etc., *fall away* from the divine, Plot.5.1.5, 5.3.16. II. abs., *stand aloof, be absent*, A.*Ch.*444 (lyr.); ἑκάς, πρόσω ἀ., Id.*Ag.*1104 (lyr.), *Eu.*65; σμικρὸν ἀ. Pl.*Cra.*428d. **-στᾰτήρ**, ῆρος, ὁ, *one who has power to dissolve an assembly*, or *to decide a question*, Lex Lyc.ap.Plu.*Lyc.*6; cf. ἀφίστημι. **-στάτης** [τᾰ], ου, ὁ, *deserter, rebel*, ἀ. τοῦ βασιλέως Plb.5.57.4, cf. Wilcken *Chr.*10 (ii B.C.), Plu.*Cim.*10; *seceder*, *SIG*705.41,50 (Delph., ii B.C.). II. *runaway slave*, Plu.*Rom.*9; ἀ. κύων *runaway* dog, Id.2.821d. III. Lat. *apostata, apostate*, *Cod.Theod.*16.7.7. **-στᾰτικός**, ή, όν, *of* or *for rebels, rebellious*, θράσος Plu.*Rom.*7. Adv. -κῶς, ἔχειν to be *ready for revolt*, Id.*Pel.*15: Comp. -ώτερον, φρονούντων *PLond.*2.354.6 (i B.C.); -κῶς πράττειν τοῦ λόγου Chrysipp.ap.Gal.5.406. II. *disposed to exfoliate*, of bones, Hp.*Fract.*25, Antyll.ap.Orib.6.1.6. III. Rhet., *belonging to* ἀπόστασις B.1.6; -κόν, τό, Hermog.*Id.*1.10; σχήματα ibid., Aps.p.259 H.; λόγος Eust.1389.28. Adv. -κῶς Id.635.58. **-στάτις** [τᾰ], ιδος, ἡ, pecul. fem. of ἀποστάτης, ἀ. πόλις Lxx 1*Es.*2.18, J.*AJ*11.2.1.

ἀποσταυρόω, *fence off with a palisade*, Th.4.69, 6.101, X.*HG*7.4.32, Plb.4.56.8, Plu.*Arat.*40:—Pass., Pherecr.17.

ἀποστᾰφῐδόομαι, Pass., = σταφιδόομαι, Thphr.*CP*2.8.3.

ἀποστᾰχύω, *to be in the ear*, of corn, *Gp.*2.24.3.

ἀποστεγ-άζω, *uncover*, πυκινὸν ῥόον Emp.100.14 (prob. in 42.1); ἀ. τὸν νεών *unroof* it, Str.8.3.30, cf. 4.4.6 (Pass.), *IG*12(3).325.30 (Thera, ii A.D., Pass.); ἀ. τὸ τρῆμα *open* it, Sotad.2. 2. *take off* a covering, τὴν στέγην *Ev.Marc.*2.4. II. = ἀποστέγω I, *cover closely*, Thphr.*CP*5.6.5, Arist.*Pr.*924a37. **-ασμα**, ατος, τό, *protection against*, ψύχους Thphr.*CP*5.13.3. **-ασσις** (Dor. for -στέγασις), εως, ἡ, *plastering*, πλίνθων, τοίχων, *IG*4.823.24,25 (Troezen). **-νόω**, *cover close*, Moschio ap.Ath.5.207b:—Pass., *to be blocked*, of the intestines, Hp.*Acut.*(*Sp.*)51; *to be luted* or *sealed up close*, Hero *Spir.*1.23, 2.10. **-ω**, *shelter* or *protect*, αἱ ὀφρύες ἀ., οἷον ἀπογείσωμα, τῶν ὑγρῶν Arist.*PA*658b16: c. acc. only, *protect*, Id.*Pr.*924b1; ἀ. καὶ τηρεῖ τὴν ζωήν [ὁ φλοιός] Thphr.*CP*1.4.5. II. *keep out* or *off*, τὸ ὕδωρ Arist.*Pr.*924a26, cf. Emp.84.10, Pl.*Lg.*844b; τὸ ψῦχος Arist.*Pr.*939b17; τὴν ἁλμυρίδα Thphr.*CP*3.6.3, al.; θερμότητα καὶ ὑγρότητα ib.4.12.2, cf. 5.12.9, Plu.2.665f: metaph., ὄχλον πύργος ἀποστέγει A.*Th.*234 (lyr.); ἀ. πληγὰς λίθων Plb.6.23.5.

ἀποστείνομαι, gloss on ὀρέχθεον, Sch.Il.23.30.

ἀποστεινόω, poet. for ἀποστενόω.

ἀποστείχω, aor. ἀπέστῐχον, *go away, go home*, οἴκαδ' ἀ. Od.11.132, etc.; imper. ἀπόστιχε Il.1.522: aor. part. ἀποστιχόντων Hdt.9.56; ἐς νύκτ' ἀποστείχοντος ἡλίου A.*Supp.*769, cf. S.*El.*799, etc.

ἀποστέλλω, fut. -στελῶ: aor. ἀπέστειλα (v. infr.):—*send off* or *away from*, μή μ'.. τῆσδ' ἀποστείλητε γῆς S.*El.*71, cf. E.*Med.*281; τῆσδ' ἀ. χθονὸς Id.*Cyc.*468; ἔξω χθονὸς Id.*Ph.*485; ἐκ τῆς πόλεως Pl.*R.*607b; *send away, banish*, τὰ δίκαια S.*Ph.*450; τινά E.*Hec.*731:—Pass., *go away, depart*, S.*OT*115; ἀποστέλλου χθονὸς E.*Supp.*582; δόμων.. τῶν ἐμῶν ἀπεστάλης Id.*Hel.*660; φυγὰς ἀποσταλείς Id.*Ph.*319 (lyr.); πρὸς σὲ δεῦρ' ἀπεστάλην Id.*IT*1409. II. *dispatch*, on some mission or service, S.*Ph.*125, 1297, etc.; freq. of messengers or forces, Hdt.1.46, 123; νέας ἐπὶ χώρην Id.7.235, cf. 8.64; στρατὸν παρά τινα Id.5.32; ναῦς αὐτοῖς ἀ. βοηθοὺς Th.1.45: also ἀ. ἀποικίην Hdt.4.150; οἰκιστάς (as a form of banishment), Arist.*Pol.*1306b31; πρεσβείαν Th.3.28; ἀγγέλους X.*An.*2.1.5, etc.; ἀπαρχὴν εἰς Δελφοὺς Arist.*Fr.*485:—Pass., c. inf., οἱ ἀποσταλέντες στρατεύεσθαι Id.3.26, cf. 5.33; ἀποσταλθέντες *GDI*5186.4 (Cret.). III. *put off, doff*, θαἰμάτια Ar.*Lys.*1084. IV. intr., *retire, withdraw*, of the sea, Th.3.89; of persons, οἴκαδε D.32.5.

ἀποστενοχωρέω, *straiten, cramp*, Ath.Mech.40.1, Gal.19.408.

ἀποστενόω, poet. -στεινόω, *straiten*, Thphr.*Ign.*54 (Pass.), Alex.Aphr.*Pr.*1.75; ὄμματα ἀπεστείνωτο Theoc.22.101; τόπος ἀπεστενωμένος D.S.3.37: metaph. in Pass., *to be contracted*, γνῶσις ἀπεστενωμένη Simp.*in Ph.*18.4; ἐπιχείρησις -μένη *hampered*, Alex.Aphr.*in Top.*56.3; τὸν τοῦ ἑνὸς ἀπεστενωμένον ἰδιασμόν Dam.*Pr.*28 bis.

ἀποστένω, *bewail*, πόθον Aristaenet.2.18.

ἀποστέν-ωσις, εως, ἡ, *straitening, straits*, Sch.Il.23.330. 2. *contraction*, Dam.*Pr.*59 (pl.). **-ωτικός**, ή, όν, *straitening*, i.e. *condensing*, opp. πλατυντικός, Eust.315.11.

ἀποστεπτικός, ή, όν, *of* or *for discrowning*, ᾆσμα, a bridal chant, *EM*131.38.

ἀποστέργω, *get rid of love, love no more*, Theoc.14.50; μητέρα ἀ. Philostr.*VS*2.25.2; *loath, reject*, τι A.*Ag.*499; ἀοιδάν Terpand.5; πόθους τινός Theoc.*Ep.*4.14; πίστιν Doroth. in *Cat.Cod.Astr.*2.175. II. *empty of love, harden*, καρδίαν Lxx *De.*15.7.

ἀποστερεόω, *harden*, Ph.*Bel.*79.4, 81.4:—Pass., *become solid*, Arist.*Mir.*837b13, 844a14: metaph., -όομαι πρός τι *persist stubbornly in*, Phld.*Rh.*2.31 S.

ἀποστέρ-εσις, εως, ἡ, = ἀποστέρησις II, *POxy.*71.10 (iv A.D.). **-έω**:—Pass., fut. -στερηθήσομαι Lys.12.70, v.l. in D.1.22; also -στερήσομαι E.*HF*137 (lyr.), Th.6.91, D.24.210; ἀποστεροῦμαι And.1.149: pf. ἀπεστέρημαι, etc.:—*rob, despoil, defraud* one *of* a thing, c. acc. pers. et gen. rei, χρημάτων ἀ. τινά Hdt.5.92.ε'; τὸν πατέρα τῆς τυραννίδος Ar.*Av.*1605; τῆς ψυχῆς Antipho 4.1.6: c. acc. pers. et rei, μή μ' ἀποστερήσῃς ἡδονάν S.*El.*1276 (lyr.), cf. Antipho 3.3.2, X.*An.*7.6.9, Is.8.43, etc.: abs., *commit fraud*, Ar.*Nu.*487; ἀπεστερηκὼς ὑπ' ἀνάγκης being constrained to *become a defaulter*, Pl.*Phdr.*241b; συνέστιον ὢν ἔκγονον ἢ ἀδελφὸν ἀπεστέρηκε γίγνεσθαι Id.*Lg.*868d:—Pass., *to be robbed* or *deprived of*, c. gen., Ἑλλάδος ἀπεστερημένος Hdt.3.130; σοῦ τ' ἀπεστερημένη καὶ πατρός S.*El.*813; ἡδονῶν Ar.*Nu.*1072; ἁπάντων ἂν ἀπεστερήμην D.21.106: c. acc., ἵππους ἀπεστέρηνται X.*Cyr.*6.1.12, etc.: abs., εἰ δ' ἀπεστερήμεθα if we *have been frustrated*, S.*Aj.*782. 2. ἀ. ἑαυτόν τινος *detach, withdraw* oneself *from* a person or thing, τῶν [ἀγαλμάτων].. ἀπεστέρησ' ἐμαυτόν Id.*OT*1381; οὐκ ἀποστερῶν γε τῶν ἐς τὴν πόλιν ἑαυτὸν οὐδενός Antipho 5.78; ἄλλον ἑαυτὸν ἀ. Th.1.40; ἀ. ἑαυτὸν τοῦ φρονεῖν Crobyl.3; ἐκείνους.. ἀ. μὴ ἂν.. ἀποτειχίσαι *deprive* them *of* the power of walling off, Th.7.6:—reversely, ἀ. τὸν ἔλεον ἑαυτοῦ Plu.*Aem.*26, cf. *Dem.*4. 3. c. acc. pers., *defraud, rob*, Hdt.7.155, Ar.*Pl.*373, 1*Ep.Cor.*6.7, etc.; θεούς Pl.*Lg.*917d. 4. c. acc. rei only, *filch away*, S.*Ph.*931; *withhold*, A.*Pr.*777, S.*OT*323, Ar.*Nu.*1305; *refuse payment* of a debt, D.21.44, etc.; *refuse to give up*, παρακαταθήκην Arist.*Rh.*1383b21; Ζεὺς ἀποστεροίη γάμον *may* he *avert* it, A.*Supp.*1063 (lyr.). 5. τὸ σαφές μ' ἀποστερεῖ certainty *fails* me, E.*Hel.*577. II. in Logic, *draw a negative conclusion*, Arist.*APr.*44b23. (ἀποστερέω is f.l. in Isoc.12.243.) **-ησις**, εως, ἡ, *deprivation*, τῆς ἀκοῆς Th.7.70; ἐπ' ἀποστερήσει τοῦ δούλου for the purpose of *depriving* him *of* the slave, Pl.*Lg.*936d. II. *withholding what is due*, Antipho Soph.107, D.24.111; ἐπ' ἀποστερήσει τῶν ἐμῶν in order to *avoid payment* of my claims, Id.30.5. **-ητέον**, *one must defraud*, τινά τινος Plu.2.931d. **-ητής**, οῦ, ὁ, *one who withholds*, Arist.*EE*1232a15; esp. *one who withholds what is due, a defrauder, cheat*, Pl.*R.*344b, *POxy.*745.7 (i A.D.); ἀποστερητὴν ἀγοράσας ἀγρόν a farm *that costs money* instead of bringing it in, *Com. Adesp.*109. **-ητικός**, ή, όν, *of* or *for withholding* by fraud, γνώμη ἀ. τόκου a device *for cheating* one of his interest, Ar.*Nu.*747, cf. 728. **-ητρίς**, ίδος, ἡ, fem., *for cheating*, γνώμη ib.730. **-ίζω**, = sq., *carry off*, ἀ. τὴν πλεονεξίην τοῦ σώματος Hp.*Gland.*17 (s.v.l.). **-ίσκω**, = ἀποστερέω, S.*OC*376.

ἀποστερνίζω, *expectorate*, Gloss.

ἀποστεφᾰνόω, *rob of the crown, discrown*, Charito 1.5, etc.:—Med., aor. inf. -ώσασθαι *lay aside one's crown*, D.L.2.54, Max.Tyr.5.9:—Pass., Luc.*JTr.*10, Jul.*Caes.*310c.

ἀποστηθίζω, (στῆθος) *repeat by heart*, *EM*277.56, David *Proll.*5.22.

ἀπό-στημα, ατος, τό, *distance, interval*, ἀ. τοῦ ἡλίου πρὸς τὴν γῆν Arist.*Cael.*294a4; τῶν σφαιρῶν Id.*Metaph.*1073b33, cf. Phld.*Sign.*9, etc.; ἐξ ἀ. θεωρεῖσθαι Epicur.*Ep.*2 p.39 U.; ὅπλα τὰ ἐξ ἀ. λεγόμενα Ascl.*Tact.*1.2. 2. *degree* of descent from an ancestor, τοῖς ἀ. πρὸς τοὺς γονεῖς παντοδαπῶς ἔχειν Arist.*EN*1100a26. 3. *abscess*, Hp.*Aph.*7.36, Arist.*Pr.*885b31, Thphr.*Od.*59. **-στημᾰτίας**, ου, ὁ, *one who has an abscess*, Aret.*SD*1.9. **-στημᾰτικός**, ή, όν, *due to an abscess*, Heliod.ap.Orib.44.23.74. II. *at a distance*, οὐδὲν ἀ. παρεμφαίνουσα Chrysipp.*Stoic.*2.245. **-στημάτιον** [ᾰτ], τό, Dim. of ἀπόστημα, Gal.17(1).326, Heliod.ap.Orib.44.14.10. **-στημᾰτώδης**, ες, *of the nature of an abscess*, Hp.*Coac.*141.

ἀποστήρ-ιγμα, ατος, τό, *stay, support*, Hp.*Off.*25, cf. *EM*125.17. 2. *determination* of humours, Hp.*Flat.*9. **-ίζομαι**, Med., *fix firmly*, βάκτρον ἐς γᾶν *APl.*4.265.9. 2. *support oneself firmly, throw one's weight upon*, τοῖς μηροῖς Arist.*Pr.*882b30: πρὸς τὸ ὑποκείμενον Id.*IA*705a8, cf. *MA*699a5. II. Medic., of diseases, *to be confirmed*, Hp.*Prorrh.*2.2. 2. ἀ. ἐς.., of humours, *determine* towards a particular part of the body, Hp.*Hum.*7; of labour pains, Arist.*HA*586b28: also in Act., Hp. l.c., cf. *Prorrh.*2.14. **-ιξις**, εως, ἡ, *fulcrum* or *rest for a lever*, Hp.*Mochl.*42.

ἀποστῐβής, ές, (στίβος) *off the road, solitary*, S.*Fr.*558.

ἀποστίζω, *mark with points* or *lines*, f.l. for ὑπ- in Gal.17(1).560, al.

ἀποστιλβόω, *make to shine*, κύπελλον *AP*7.339.

ἀπο-στίλβω, Ep. impf. ἀπεστίλβεσκε Epic. in *Arch.Pap.*7.7:—*to be bright from* or *with*, ἀποστίλβοντες ἀλείφατος Od.3.408: c. dat., Lyc.253; ἐθείραις *AP*5.25, cf. Luc.*Asin.*47: c. gen., χρυσοῦ Id.*JTr.*8, cf. *Hipp.*6; φῶς ἀπό τινος Plot.2.1.7. 2. abs., φαίνεται τὸ ὕδωρ ἀποστίλβον τῆς νυκτὸς *phosphorescent*, Arist.*Mete.*370a14; *shine brightly*, Thphr.*Sign.*26, Agatharch.95, Luc.*DMar.*14.2, etc.; ἀκτὶς ἀ. εἰς πέλαγος Alciphr.1.1. 3. Act., *shed* light, etc., Μήνη σέλας -ουσα κεραίης Nonn.*D*.5.165; καθαρότητα Iamb.*Myst*.2.8. **-στιλ-ψις**, εως, ἡ, *emission of light*, Sch.A.R.3.1377 (pl.), Hsch. s. v. αἰγίς.

ἀποστλεγγ-ίζω, *scrape with a* στλεγγίς (q. v.), Philostr.*Gym*.18, 51:—Med., *scrape oneself clean*, X.*Oec*.11.18; pf. part. Pass. ἀπεστλεγγισμένοι *scraped clean, fresh from the bath*, Ar.*Eq*.580; -ισάμενοι Arist. *Pr*.867^{b}4; censured as archaic by Luc.*Rh.Pr*.17. **-ισμα**, ατος, τό, *scrapings with the* στλεγγίς, Str.5.2.6.

ἀποστολ-εύς, έως, ὁ, *one who dispatches*, ἀ. τῶν ἐνσωματωμένων ψυχῶν Herm.ap.Stob.1.49.69: but mostly, 2. at Athens, *magistrate who had to fit out* a squadron for service, D.18.107, 47.26, Aeschin.2.177, Philoch.142, *IG*2.809^{b}20. **-ή**, ἡ, (ἀποστέλλω) *sending off* or *away*, E.*IA*688, *Ph*.1043 (lyr., pl.); *dispatching*, νεῶν Th.8.9; *sending forth on their journey*, ξένων ὑποδοχὰς καὶ ἀ. Arist. *EN*1123^{a}3, cf. *IG*2.238.15; δοῦναί τι ἀποστολάς τινι *as a parting gift*, Lxx 3*Ki*.9.16, cf. 1*Ma*.2.18. 2. *shooting, discharge*, βέλους Ph.*Bel*. 68.33. 3. *discharge from service*, οὐκ ἔστιν ἀ. ἐν ἡμέρᾳ πολέμου Lxx *Ec*.8.8. 4. *payment* of tribute, Jul.*Ep*.204. II. (from Pass.) *expedition*, Th.8.8. 2. *apostleship*, 1*Ep.Cor*.9.2, *Ep.Gal*.2.8. **-ικός**, ή, όν, *sung on departure*, μέλη Procl.ap.Phot.p.322 B. **-ιμαῖος**, α, ον, *sent off, missive*, φίλημα Ach.Tat.2.9. II. *connected with dismissal*, φράσις Eust.790.44. **-ιον**, τό, *tax for escort* of caravans, *OGI*674.4 (Coptos, i A.D.). **-ος**, ὁ, *messenger, ambassador, envoy*, ὁ μὲν δὴ ἀ. ἐς τὴν Μίλητον ἦν Hdt.1.21; ἐς Λακεδαίμονα τριήρεϊ ἀ. ἐγίνετο he went off *on a mission* to Laced., Id.5.38. b. *commander of a naval force*, Hsch. 2. *messenger from God*, Lxx 3*Ki*.14.6; esp. of the *Apostles*, *Ev.Matt*.10.2, al. II. = στόλος, *naval squadron* or *expedition*, Lys.19.21; ἀπόστολον ἀφιέναι, ἀποστέλλειν, ποιεῖσθαι, D.3.5, 18.80, 107, *IG*2.809^{b}190. 2. *colony*, D.H.9.59. 3. = ἀποστολή, of envoys, J.*AJ*17.11.1. 4. ἀπόστολον, τό, with or without πλοῖον, *packet*, Pl.*Ep*.346a, Ps.-Hdt.*Vit.Hom*.19. 5. ἀπόστολος, ὁ, *order for dispatch*, of a vessel, *CPHerm*.6.11 (iii A.D., pl.), *PAmh*. 2.138.10 (iv A.D.), cf. *Dig*.49.6.1. 6. *export-licence*, *PGnom*.162 (ii A.D.). 7. gen. dub., *cargo dispatched by order*, *POxy*.522.1, al. (ii A.D.), *PTeb*.486 (ii/iii A.D.).

ἀποστομ-ατίζω, (στόμα) *teach by word of mouth, teach by dictation*, γράμματα ἀ. Pl.*Euthd*.277a: abs., ὅταν ἀ. ὑμῖν ὁ γραμματεύς ib.276c:—Pass., τὸ ἀποστοματιζόμενον *dictated lesson*, ibid., Arist.*SE*165^{b}32. 2. *interrogate, catechize*, as a master his pupil, *Ev.Luc*.11.53, cf. Pl.ap.Poll.1.102 (Pass.). II. *repeat by heart*, Ath.8.359d, Antyll. ap.Orib.6.9.4: generally, *recite, repeat*, Plu.*Thes*.24. **-ίζω**, *deprive of an edge*, πέλεκυς ἀπεστομισμένος Philostr.*Im*.2.17. II. = foreg. II, Hsch. III. = φιμόω, Id. **-όω**, *stop the mouth of*, Cerc.11.7: hence, *block, stop up*, τὰς διώρυχας Plb.*Fr*.117. II. = ἀποστομίζω I, ὅπλα ἀπεστομωμένα τὰς ἀκμάς D.H.6.14, cf. Luc.*Tim*.10. **-ωσις**, εως, ἡ, *laying open, opening*, τῶν πόρων Arist.*Pr*.888^{a}28.

ἀπόστοργος, ον, *devoid of affection*, ἀ. γίγνεσθαι Plu.2.491c. Adv. -γως, ἔχειν τινός Lib.*Decl*.51.13. II. = ἀπεχθής, *unlovable*, Hsch.

ἀποστράβοομαι [ᾰ], Pass., *become squinting*, Sor.1.106.

ἀποστραγγᾰλίζω, *kill by strangling*, D.S.14.12, Str.17.1.11.

ἀποστραγγίζω, *check*, *Theol.Ar*.49 (Pass.).

ἀποστρᾰκ-ίζω, *bake to a hard crust*, of a quick fire, Gal.6.484. II. *banish by ostracism*, Hsch., Suid. **-όομαι**, *become dry like a potsherd*, Hp.*VC*16, Dsc.2.4, *Hippiatr*.25; *to be ossified*, Phlp.*in GA*113.1.

ἀποστράπτω, *flash forth*, φλόγα A.R.3.1018 (tm.).

ἀποστρᾰτεύομαι, *to be discharged from military service*, App.*BC* 5.26.

ἀποστράτηγος [ρᾰ], ὁ, *retired general*, ἀ. ποιεῖν τινά to *remove* him *from the command, supersede* him, D.23.149; also, *general who has completed his term of office*, Plu.*Marc*.22.

ἀποστρᾰτοπεδεύομαι, *remove one's camp from, encamp away from*, τινός X.*An*.3.4.34; ἀ. προσωτέρω *encamp at a* greater *distance*, ib. 7.7.1.

ἀποστρεβλόομαι, Pass., *to be horribly tortured*, Lxx 2*Ma*.9.7.

ἀπο-στρεπτικός, ή, όν, *repellent*, Gal.4.819. **-στρεπτος**, ον, *turned back*, = ἀποστραφείς, Phryn.*PS*p.15 B. 2. *hostile, unacceptable*, Diogenian.Epicur.4.62. **-στρέφω**, Dor. aor. ἀποστράψαι *SIG* 244 ii 16 (Delph.); Ion. aor. ἀποστρέψασκε Il.22.197, etc.: pf. ἀπέστροφα Lxx 1*Ki*.6.21:—Pass. and Med., fut. -στρέψομαι X.*Cyr*.5.5. 36, Plu.2.387c: aor. -εστράφην [ᾰ], S.*OC*1272, etc.; later -εστρεψάμην Lxx *Ho*.8.3, prob. in Ar.*Nu*.776: fut. -στρᾰφήσομαι Lxx *Nu*.25. 4, al.: pf. -έστραμμαι Hdt.1.166, etc.: Ion. 3 pl. plpf. -εστράφατο ibid.; -έστρεμμαι *PSI*4.392.11 (iii B.C.):—*turn back*: hence, either *turn to flight*, ὄφρ᾽..᾽Αχαιοὺς αὖτις ἀποστρέψῃσιν Il.15.62, etc., cf. Hdt. 8.94; or *turn back from flight*, X.*Cyr*.4.3.1; *send home again*, Th.4. 97, 5.75; ῥῆμα *bring back* word, Lxx 4*Ki*.22.9; ἀποστρέψαντε πόδας καὶ χεῖρας *having twisted back* the hands and feet so as to bind them, Od.22.173, 190, cf. S.*OT*1154; τὸν ὦμον Ar.*Eq*.263; ἀποστρέφετε τὰς χεῖρας αὐτῶν, ὦ Σκύθαι Ar.*Lys*.455; ἀ. τὸν αὐχένα Hdt.4.188; *guide back again*, ἀποστρέψαντες ἔβαν νέας Od.3.162; ἴχνι᾽ ἀποστρέψας *having turned* the steps of the oxen *backwards* so as to make it appear that they had gone the other way, *h.Merc*.76; *turn away, avert*, αὐχέν᾽ ἀποστρέψας Thgn.858; ἀπέστρεψ᾽ ἔμπαλιν παρηΐδα E.*Med*. 1148; but τὸ πρόσωπον πρός τινα Plu.*Publ*.6; *bring back, recall*, ἐξ Ἰσθμοῦ X.*An*.2.6.3; φῶτας ἀπέστρεψεν Περσεφόνης θαλάμων [Emp.] 156.4. 2. *turn away* or *aside, divert*, v.l. in Th.4.80, etc.; ὕδατα *cut off* water from a besieged town, Ph.*Bel*.97.4; τὸν Καΰστρον *SIG* 839.14 (Ephesus); τὸν πόλεμον ἐς Μακεδονίαν Arr.*An*.2.1.1; *avert* a danger, an evil, etc., πῆμ᾽ ἀ. νόσου A.*Ag*.850 (Porson); *prevent*, Dsc. 2.136; *rebut*, δίκην Ar.*Nu*.776 (v. supr.); ἀ. τύχην μὴ οὐ γενέσθαι Antipho6.15 codd.; ἀ. εἰς τοὐναντίον τοὺς λόγους Pl.*Sph*.239d; τὰς πράξεις εἰς τοὺς ἀντιδίκους Arist.*Rh.Al*.1442^{b}6. 3. ἀ. τινά τινος *dissuade from*, X.*Eq.Mag*.1.12; τινὰ ἀπὸ τοῦ λήμματος Din.2.23; πότων ἀ. τοὺς στομάχους D.H.*Dem*.15. II. as if intr. (sc. ἑαυτόν, ἵππον, ναῦν, etc.), *turn back*, Th.6.65; ἀ. ὀπίσω Hdt.4.43; ἀ. πάλιν S.*OC* 1403. 2. *turn away* or *aside*, Hdt.8.87; of a river, Id.4.52; τἀναντία ἀ. X.*HG*3.4.12.

B. Pass., *to be turned back*, ἀπεστράφθαι τοὺς ἐμβόλους, of ships, *to have* their beaks *bent back*, Hdt.1.166; ἀποστραφῆναι..τὼ πόδε *to have* one's feet *twisted*, Ar.*Pax*279; τρίχες ἀπεστραμμέναι *close-curled*, Arist.*Phgn*.809^{b}26. II. Med. and Pass., *turn oneself from* or *away*, ἀπεστραμμέναι ἀπ᾽ ἀλλήλων Id.*HA*611^{a}6; ἀπεστραμμένοι *back to back*, Apollod.*Poliorc*.145.2: esp., 1. *turn one's face away from, abandon*, c. acc., Phoc.2, Sallust.3; ἐχθροῦ ἀξίωσιν Epicur. *Fr*.215; μή μ᾽ ἀποστραφῇς S.*OC*1272; μή μ᾽ ἀποστρέφου E.*IT*801, cf. Ar.*Pax*683, X.*Cyr*.5.5.36, *PSI* l. c.; τὸ θεῖον ῥᾳδίως ἀπεστράφης E. *Supp*.159: also c. gen., ἄψορρος οἴκων τῶνδ᾽ ἀποστραφείς S.*OT*431: c. dat., ἀστεφανώτοισι ἀπυστρέφονται Sapph.78: abs., μὴ πρὸς θεῶν ..ἀποστραφῇς S.*OT*326; ἀπεστραμμένοι λόγοι *hostile* words, Hdt.7. 160; τὴν διάνοιαν ἀποστρέφεσθαι *to be alienated*, Phld.*Lib*.p.8 O. 2. *turn oneself about*, X.*Cyr*.1.4.25; ἅρματα ἀπεστραμμένα ὥσπερ εἰς φυγήν ib.6.2.17; ἀποστραφῆναι λυγιζόμενος *escape* by wriggling, Pl.*R*. 405c. 3. ἀποστραφῆναί τινος *fall off from* one, *desert* him, X. *HG*4.8.4. **-στροφή**, ἡ, *turning back*, X.*Eq*.9.6; ἀ. νώτων Max. Tyr.9.8; ἀ. λαμβάνειν make *a bend*, of a stream, Plu.*Luc*.27, cf. Luc.*Hipp*.2. 2. *twisting*, ὀρχεων ἀποστροφαί Trag.(Satyr.)*Oxy*. 1083.10. II. *turning away from, escape, refuge*, c. gen., τύχης, κακῶν, A.*Pr*.769, E.*Fr*.444; ζημίας Id.*Med*.1223. 2. *resort, recourse*, Hdt.8.109, Th.4.76; ἥκει βίου τελευτὴ κοὐκέτ᾽ ἔστ᾽ ἀ. S.*OC* 1473, cf. E.*Med*.603; οὐκ ἔχων ἀ. D.4.8, cf. Hyp.*Dem.Fr*.5; in pl., Antip.*Stoic*.3.255: c. gen. objecti, οὔ σφί ἐστι ὕδατος οὐδεμία ἄλλη ἀ. no other *means for getting* water, Hdt.2.13; so σωτηρίας ἀ. Th.8.75; βίου Luc.*DMeretr*.6.1; ἀ. τοῦ δήμου ποιεῖσθαι secure a *refuge with*.., Philostr.*VS*2.1.4. III. Rhet., *apostrophe*, when *one turns away from all others to one*, and addresses him specially, Phld.*Lib*.p.11 O., Quint.*Inst*.9.2.38, Longin.16.2, Hermog.*Inv*.4.4, *Id*.1.10 (pl.), Phoeb. *Fig*.1.1, Alex.*Fig*.1.20. IV. *aversion*, Plot.1.1.1; opp. ἐπιθυμία, Simp.*in de An*.15.36; γευμάτων Aret.*SD*2.6; σιτίων Gal.11.261; ὀσμῆς *Gp*.12.39.8. V. *diversion, amusement*, Plu.2.133b (pl.). VI. *elision*, A.D.*Pron*.46.1 (ubi leg. ἐ). VII. = προδοσία, Hsch. **-στροφία**, ἡ, *she that turns away*, epith. of Aphrodite, Paus.9.16.3. **-στροφος**, ον, *turned away, averted*, ἀποστρόφους αὐγὰς ἀπείρξω S.*Aj*.69: *turned away from*, c. gen., σελήνης Man.1.57: also c. dat., δισσοῖς σελάεσσιν ἀ. οἶμον ἰοῦσα Id.6.127. Adv. -φως Lyd.*Ost*.15. b. Astrol., *not conjoined*, Vett.Val.53.24, etc. 2. *to be turned from, dreadful*, epith. of the Erinyes, Orph.*H*.70.8. II. as Subst., **-στροφος**, ἡ, *apostrophe*, Sch.D.T.p.135 H., etc.; *mark of elision*, *EM*638.19, etc. 2. *turning away* of chorus from stage in Comic parabasis, Platon.*Diff.Com*.8.

ἀποστρυθάομαι, perh. = *disturb, move*, dub. in *IG*5(1).1155.2 (Gythium).

ἀποστρώννῡμι, *pave*, τὸ καταπεσὸν ἀνοικοδομήσαντι καὶ -ώσαντι *IG*11(2).203 *A* 41 (Delos, iii B.C.). II. *take off the trappings*, Hsch. s. v. ἀπέσαξεν.

ἀποστῠγ-έω, aor. 1 -εστύγησα S.*OC*692 (lyr.), -έστυξα Opp.*H*.4. 370: aor. 2 ἀπέστῠγον Call.*Aet*.1.1.11, *Del*.223, Nic.*Al*.406, Parth. 36.2: pf. with pres. sense, -εστύγηκα Hdt.2.47:—*hate violently, abhor*, Hdt. l. c., S.*OC*186, 692, E.*Ion*488 (lyr. in S. and E.); ἀ. ὕδωρ (in comparison with wine) Melanipp.4; ἄμυστιν Call.*Aet*.l. c.: c. inf., ἀ. γαμβρὸν ἄν οἱ γενέσθαι Ἱπποκλείδεα Hdt.6.129. **-ησις**, εως, ἡ, *abhorrence*, Sch.A.*Ch*.79.

ἀποστῡπάζω, *drive off with blows*, Archil.127. (Cf. στύπος.)

ἀποστῠφελίζω, *drive away by force from*, τινά τινος Il.18.158, *AP* 7.603 (Jul. Aegypt.).

ἀποστύφω [ῡ], *draw up, contract*, of the effect of astringents, δριμέα..ὥστε ἀποστύφειν Arist.*Pr*.863^{a}18, cf. Thphr.*CP*2.8.1; χείλεα ἀ. *screw* them *up*, *AP*7.536 (Alc.):—Pass., pf., οὖρα δ᾽ ἀπέστυπται *are stopped*, Nic.*Th*.433. 2. of preparing tissues for dyes, *mordant*, *PHolm*.9.14. 3. ἀποστύφων· τῇ φωνῇ σκληρός, Hsch.

ἀποσυγχωρέω, *give up, withdraw*, Sch.Ar.*Nu*.107.

ἀποσῡκ-άζω, *gather figs*, Amips.33 (Pass.). 2. *squeeze figs*, to try whether they are ripe: metaph. of informers, with a play on συκοφαντία, Ar.*Eq*.259. **-ίζω**, = foreg. 1, Sch.Nic.*Al*.319.

ἀποσῡλάω, *strip off spoils from* a person: hence, *strip off* or *take away from*, τί τινος Pi.*P*.4.110. II. *rob, defraud* one *of* a thing, ὅς μ᾽..ἀπεσύλησεν πάτρας S.*OC*1330; ὅτε ἐκράτησεν ἡμῶν ἀπεσύλησεν ἃ ἐδύνατο Is.5.30; ἀ. τινά τι E.*Alc*.870 (lyr.), X.*An*.1.4.8:—Pass., ἀποσυλᾶσθαί τι A.*Pr*.172 (lyr.); ἱερὰ -συληθέντα τῶν ἀναθημάτων Jul. *Or*.7.228b. III. *carry off*, τὴν Ἄρτεμιν Luc.*Tox*.2.

ἀποσυμβαίνω, *to be absent*, of an accidental quality, S.E.*M*.7.282; ἀποσυμβεβηκότα *negative symptoms*, e.g. absence of pain, Gal.18(2). 86.

ἀποσυμβιβ-άζω, *make good a deficiency*, *POxy*.136.25 (vi A.D.):—hence -ασμός, ὁ, ib.2035 (vi A.D.).

ἀποσυμβολ...· συναντᾶν, Hsch.

ἀποσυμβουλεύω, *dissuade*, τινὶ ποιεῖν τι Arr.*Epict*.1.23.3, cf. Phalar.*Ep*.58. II. metaph., *divert*, of a stream of blood meeting another, ἀ. τῷ ἐπιρρέοντι Hp.*Loc.Hom*.3.

ἀποσυμμίγνῡμι, *mingle*, Thd.*Da.*11.6.

ἀποσυν-άγω [ᾰγ], *recover* a man *from*, ἀπὸ λέπρας Lxx 4*Ki.*5.3. **-άγωγος** [ᾰγ], ον, *expelled from the synagogue*, *Ev.Jo.*9.22, etc. **-εθίζω**, *wean* one *from*, τὸ βρέφος τοῦ μαστοῦ Sor.1.116:—Pass., ibid. **-εργέω**, *thwart, oppose*, ib.27, al., S.E.*P.*1.212; of planetary influence, Ptol.*Tetr.*3. **-έργησις**, εως, ἡ, *adverse influence*, Id.*Phas.Praef.*8. **-ίστημι**, *appoint a representative*, τινὰ κατελθεῖν εἰς Ἀλεξάνδρειαν *POxy.*1274.9 (iii A.D.):—Pass., *PGen.*44.28 (iii A.D.). 2. *recommend, introduce* one person to another, c. acc. et dat., *PHamb.*27.1, *AB*436. **-τάσσω**, *order to be supplied*, *PSI*4.418 (iii B.C.).

ἀποσῡριγγόω, *make a channel for*, Hp.*Oss.*18:—Pass., Id.*Loc.Hom.*12.

ἀποσῡρίζω, *whistle aloud* for want of thought, or to show indifference, μάκρ' ἀποσυρίζων *h.Merc.*280:—Pass., *sound like whistling*, Luc.*VH*2.5.

ἀπόσυρμα, ατος, τό, *that which is peeled off, abrasion*, Hp.*Liqu.*2, Dsc.1.30. 2. *mark left by a rope dragged along*, *POxy.*69.8 (ii A.D.). II. *rubbish* left in working mines, Arist.*Mir.*833^{a}29.

ἀποσύρω [ῡ], *tear away*, S.*Fr.*416, *EM*127.19; φλυκταίνας Philum.*Ven.*33.3; τὸ -σεσυρμένον *torn flesh*, Gal.13.457, cf. Orib.44.18.2 (Pass.); τὰς ἐπάλξεις Th.7.43; but τοὺς πολεμίους (sc. ἀπὸ τοῦ τείχους) Plb.10.15.1; *lay bare, strip*, μέτωπον ἐς ὀστέον Theoc.22.105; τὴν ἐπιπολῆς γῆν Plb.34.10.10; *skim off*, τὸ πιμελῶδες Sor.2.13.

ἀποσυσσῑτέω, *absent oneself from the public table* (συσσίτια), Pl.*Lg.*762c.

ἀποσυστᾰτικὰ γράμματα letter *of recommendation, power of attorney*, *PSI*3.236.20 (iii/iv A.D.), *PLond.ined.*2222 (iv A.D.); τὸ ἀ. *POxy.*1642.8 (iii A.D.), *PLond.*ibid.

ἀπόσφαγμα, ατος, τό, = ὑπόσφαγμα, Ael.*NA*1.34.

ἀποσφάζω, in Att. Prose **-σφάττω** Lys.13.78, Pl.*Euthphr.*4c, etc.: plpf. -εσφάκειν D.C.78.7:—**Pass.**, aor. -εσφάγην [ᾰ] Hdt.4.84: fut. -σφᾰγήσομαι Ar.*Th.*750:—*cut the throat of* a person, ἀ. τινὰ ἐς ἄγγος so that the blood runs into a pail, Hdt.4.62: generally, *slay*, Ar.*Ach.*327, Th.7.86, Pl. l. c., etc.:—Med., *cut one's throat*, X.*Cyr.*3.1.25:—Pass., ἀποσφαγείην πρότερον ἂν ἢ καθυφείμην Men.*Epit.*184.

ἀποσφαιρ-ίζομαι, Pass., *to be thrown off like a ball*, Arist.*Pr.*936^{b}36. II. later in Act., *jerk away like a ball*, Tz. ad Lyc.17. **-ισις**, εως, ἡ, *throwing off, flinging as a ball*, ibid.

ἀποσφαιρόω, *round off, make into balls*, Ath.2.42f.

ἀποσφᾰκελ-ίζω, *to have one's limbs frost-bitten and mortified*, ἵπποι ἐν κρυμῷ ἑστεῶτες ἀ. Hdt.4.28, cf. Ar.*Fr.*424. II. *fall into convulsions*, Plu.*Lyc.*16. **-ισις**, εως, ἡ, *gangrene*, σαρκῶν Hp.*Art.*69 (pl.).

ἀποσφάλλω, aor. 1 -έσφηλα (v. infr.):—*lead astray, drive in baffled course*, ὅντινα πρῶτον ἀποσφήλωσιν ἄελλαι ἐς πέλαγος Od.3.320; μή ..σφας ἀποσφήλειε πόνοιο lest he *balk* them *of* the fruits of toil, Il.5.567. 2. *cause to err*, Lib.*Or.*59.147. II. mostly in Pass., esp. in aor. 2 ἀπεσφάλην [ᾰ], *to be balked* or *disappointed of*, τῆς ἐλπίδος Hdt.6.5; *to be deprived of*, φρενῶν Sol.33.4, A.*Pr.*472; γνώμης Id.*Pers.*392; οὐσίας ἀρετῆς ἀπεσφαλμένοι *mistaken as to* the nature of.., Pl.*Lg.*950b; *fail in reaching*, Ἰταλίας Plu.*Pyrrh.*15: abs., *make a mistake*, D.26.3; ἀποσφάλλεσθαι εἴς τι *go astray*, Plu.2.392b: rare in literal sense, *miss one's footing*, ἀποσφαλεὶς ἐξ ὕψους ἔπεσε Id.*Per.*13.

ἀποσφαλμάω, *fall headlong*, of a horse, Plb.*Fr.*18.

ἀποσφάξ, άγος, ὁ, ἡ, *broken off, abrupt*, βῆσσα Nic.*Th.*521.

ἀποσφάττω, v. ἀποσφάζω.

ἀποσφενδον-άω, *hurl from* or *as from a sling*, D.S.2.50, Luc.*JTr.*33:—Pass., Lxx 4*Ma.*16.21, Plu.2.1062a. **-ητος**, ον, *driven away by the sling*, ib.293b.

ἀποσφηκόω, *untie, loosen*, Nonn.*D.*21.152, al.

ἀποσφήλωσις, εως, ἡ, *failure*, Suid.

ἀποσφην-όω, *wedge tight in*, ἀποσφηνωθεὶς δένδρῳ τὰς χεῖρας Eust. ad D.P.369; λίθος εἰς φυτὸν -ωθεὶς Aët.16.21; *compress as by a wedge*, Ph.*Bel.*76.25, Hero *Bel.*77.3. 2. sens. obsc., Mim.*Oxy.*413.17. II. *plug* a tooth, Paul.Aeg.6.28. **-ωμα**, ατος, τό, *wedge-shaped block*, *PFay.*331 (ii A.D.). **-ωσις**, εως, ἡ, *impaction* of an infant in childbirth, Paul.Aeg.3.76.

ἀπο-σφίγγω, *squeeze tight, compress, bind up*, τραῦμα cj. Littré in Hp.*Art.*69; σιαγόνας Luc.*Luct.*19; λόγος ἀπεσφιγμένος a *close-packed* style, Id.*Rh.Pr.*9. **-σφιγξις**, εως, ἡ, *squeezing tight*, Hp.*Fract.*11 (pl.), *Art.*69 (pl.):—in form **-σφιξις**, *ligature* above a poisonous bite, Philum.*Ven.*22.4, cf. Leonid.ap.Orib.45.23.78, Antyll.ib.7.9.2.

ἀποσφρᾱγ-ίζω, *seal up*, Plu.*Alex.*2 (Pass.):—Med., E.*Or.*1108, Theopomp.Hist.265. II. *unseal*, D.L.4.59. **-ισμα**, ατος, τό, *impression of a seal*, Plin.*Ep.Traj.*74, Ath.13.585d; also, *the seal itself, signet*, Lxx *Je.*22.24. II. *sealed copy*, *IG*12(7).237.69 (Amorgos, i B.C.). III. *stamped receipt* for goods taken, *PRev.Laws*31.19 (iii B.C.). **-ιστής**· *resignator*, *Gloss.*

ἀποσφρ-αίνω, *make to smell*, γλήχωνι αὐτὸν ἀποσφραίνει he *gives* himself *a whiff of* pennyroyal, *AP*11.165 (Lucill.), cf. Sor.2.85, Orib.8.6.1:—Pass., ἥρμοσεν ἀποσφρανθὲν *when smelt at*, Dsc.1.54. **-αντέον**, *one must cause to smell*, αὐτὰς τοῖς δυσώδεσι Aspasia ap.Aët.16.72.

ἀποσφύδου· καρτερεῖν *AB*436, Suid.

ἀποσφῡρηλᾰτέω, *shape on the anvil*, Lib.*Decl.*51.16.

ἀποσχάζω, stronger form of σχάζω, ἀ. φλέβα *open* a vein, Crates Com.41, Arist.*HA*514^{b}2:—Pass., *to be lanced*, of a γαργαρεών, Hp.*Prog.*23. 2. *scarify*, Antyll.ap.Orib.7.18.2. II. *let go*, σχαστηρίαν Hero *Bel.*79.3:—Med., *let go* a stage machine, Id.*Aut.*20.4.

ἀποσχᾰλίδωμα, ατος, τό, (σχαλίς) *forked piece of wood for propping hunting-nets*, X.*Cyn.*10.7.

ἀπό-σχᾰσις, εως, ἡ, *opening of a vein*, Hp.*Epid.*7.66 (but possibly *scarification*). II. *letting go*, in an engine, Ph.*Bel.*74.51. **-σχαστέον**, *one must scarify*, Paul.Aeg.4.21. **-σχάω**, = ἀποσχάζω I, Hp.*Morb.*2.38, Arist.*HA*512^{a}30.

ἀποσχεδιάζω, = αὐτοσχεδιάζω, *make offhand*, νόμος ἀπεσχεδιασμένος Arist.*EN*1129^{b}25, cf. Ael.*Tact.*21.2. 2. *act offhand* or *at random*, τὰ πολλά Jul.*Ep.*89a, cf. Sch.Ar.*Pax*990, etc. 3. *write offhand*, περί τινος Plb.12.3.7; *extemporize*, Ath.3.125c, Philostr.*VA*5.37:—Pass., τὰ μυθικῶς -εσχεδιασμένα Phld.*Sign.*38.

ἀπό-σχεσις, εως, ἡ, *abstinence*, τινός Plu.2.123c (pl.): abs., ib.125d (pl.); τῶν βρωμάτων Str.16.2.37 (pl.). II. *division*, χρόνου Artem.4.2 (pl.). **-σχετέον**, (ἀπέχομαι) = ἀφεκτέον, *one must abstain*, οἴνου Hp.*Acut.*63. **-σχετική**· *dimissoria*, *Gloss.*

ἀποσχετλιάζω, strengthd. for σχετλιάζω, Phryn.*PS*p.63 B.

ἀπόσχημα, ατος, τό, *figure, copy*, τινός Sch.Stob.p.463 Heeren.

ἀποσχημᾰτίζω, *shape, fashion*, in Pass., ἐργασίαι εἰς ζῷα -εσχηματισμέναι Socr.*Ep.*28, cf. Philostr.*VS*1 *Praef.*

ἀπο-σχίζω, *split, cleave off*, ἀπὸ δ' ἔσχισεν αὐτήν [τὴν πέτρην] Od.4.507; *tear off*, E.*Alc.*172, Opp.*H.*2.623. 2. *sever, detach from*, τινὰ ἀπὸ τοῦ συμμαχικοῦ Hdt.6.9; ἀ. Λυδοὺς *part* them *off, separate* them, Pl.*Plt.*262e; τὴν ἰδίαν ψυχὴν τῆς τῶν λογικῶν M.Ant.4.29:—Pass., ἀποσχισθῆναι ἀπό.., of a river *being parted from* the main stream, Hdt.2.17, 4.56; of a tribe *detached from* its parent stock, Id.1.58, 143; ἀπὸ τῆς μεγάλης φλεβὸς -σχίζεται Arist.*HA*514^{b}10: c. gen., ἀποσχισθέντες τῆς ἄλλης στρατιῆς Hdt.8.35, cf. 7.233, Pl.*Plt.*267b, etc.:—Med., *separate oneself*, Id.*Lg.*728b; τοῦ σοφιστοῦ Lib.*Or.*3.24. 3. metaph., ἀ. τινὰ τοῦ λόγου *cut* him *off from* his speech, *interrupt* him *in* it, Ar.*Nu.*1408. **-σχίς**, ίδος, ἡ, mostly in pl., ἀποσχίδες *branches* of veins, Hp.*Oss.*6, Aret.*CA*2.2; ὀστῶν Gal.18(2).781; of a mountain, *spurs*, Str.11.12.4. II. sg., *branch* of the bile-duct, Gal.2.578. **-σχίσις**, εως, ἡ, *division, branching*, of a vein, Arist.*HA*514^{a}13, Aret.*CA*2.2. **-σχισμα**, ατος, τό, *that which is severed*, M.Ant.4.29.

ἀποσχοινίζω, *separate by a cord*: hence generally, *bar, exclude*, ἀπεσχοινισμένος πᾶσι τοῖς ἐν τῇ πόλει δικαίοις D.25.28: abs., Plu.2.443c; ἀρετῆς Ph.1.205; ἀ. τινά τινος ib.219, cf. Lib.*Decl.*23.45.

ἀποσχολάζω, *rest, recreate* oneself, ἔν τινι Arist.*EN*1176^{b}17. 2. *have leisure for, devote oneself to*, τῷ οἴνῳ Ael.*VH*12.1. 3. *spend one's leisure with* one, *go to* him *for teaching*, Ps.-Hdt.*Vit.Hom.*5, 34.

ἀπόσχολος, ον, *shunning the schools*, f.l. in Timo 50.

ἀποσῴζω, *save* or *preserve from*, νόσου S.*Ph.*1379; ἐκ τῶν ναυαγίων -σωθέντες Luc.*Herm.*86; ἀ. οἴκαδε *bring safe* home, X.*HG*7.2.19, cf. *An.*2.3.18. 2. *keep safe*, Pl.*Phlb.*26c, *Lg.*692c, *IG*2.268; ἀ. πατρὸς γνώμας *keep* them *in mind, remember*, E.*Fr.*362.2. 3. *preserve*, τὴν τάξιν, of the pulse, Gal.14.635. II. Pass., ἀποσωθῆναι ἐς.. *to get safe* to a place, Hdt.5.87, 7.229, X.*HG*1.3.22; ἐπὶ θάλατταν ib.3.1.2: abs., *get off safe*, Hdt.2.107, al. III. intr. in Act., ἀ. γενομένη *come safely* into being, Pl.*Ep.*336b.

ἀποσωμάτωσις [ᾰτ], εως, ἡ, *conversion from corporeal substance*, ὑδάτων Zos.Alch.p.107 B.

ἀποσωρεύω, *heap up, accumulate*, *AB*432, Hsch. s. v. ἀποθησαμένη.

ἀποτᾰγή, ἡ, (ἀποτάσσω) *renunciation* of a claim, *PLond.*3.1007.18 (vi A.D.). II. *disinheriting*, *PMasp.*97 ii 53 (vi A.D.).

ἀποτᾰγηνίζω, v. ἀποτηγανίζω.

ἀπόταγμα, ατος, τό, *prohibition*, Iamb.*VP*28.138 (pl., dub.).

ἀποτάδην [ᾰδ], Adv., (τείνω) *stretched at length*, Luc.*Zeux.*4, Ael.*NA*4.21; ἀ. τρέχειν Poll.6.175. 2. *diffusely, prolixly*, Philostr.*VS*1 *Praef.*, cf. 1.15.4; ξυνέστειλε τοὺς χοροὺς ἀ. ὄντας Id.*VA*6.11; ἀ. φθεγγόμενον [φθέγμα κηρύκων] Poll.4.94; also with κατά, τῶν κατὰ ἀ. λόγων ἀκήκοας Herm. *in Phdr.*p.184 A.

ἀποτάδων· ἐκτεταμένων, Hsch.

ἀπο-τακτέον, *one must exclude*, Ἡρακλέα τῶν χθονίων θεῶν Philostr.*VA*8.7.9. **-τακτήρ**, ῆρος, ὁ, *anchorite, hermit*, *POxy.*1311 (v A.D.). **-τακτικός**, ὁ, = foreg., *PFlor.*71.722 (iv A.D.). **-τακτῖται**, οἱ, name of a heretical sect, *Anatolian Studies* p.86 (iv/v A.D.):—**-τισταί** (= -τῆρες) is f.l. in Jul.*Or.*7.224b. **-τακτος**, ον, *set apart for a special use*, σιτία Hdt.2.69; ἀπότακτον, τό, 'speciality', Philem.76; ἀ. χρεία Heliod.ap.Orib.49.4.7. 2. *settled, appointed*, ἡμέρα Critias 6.27 D.; *fixed*, ἐκφόριον *PTeb.*42.12 (ii B.C.); φόρος *POxy.*280.17 (i A.D.), etc.:—Subst. **-τακτον**, τό, *fixed rent*, ib.1124.9 (i A.D.); *prescribed sum*, *PFay.*39 (ii A.D.), Porph.*Abst.*4.17; ἱερὸν ἀ. imperial *assessment*, *POxy.*1662.14 (iii A.D.). 3. *set apart* for punishment, Herod.3.69; cf. ἄπακτος. II. Adv. **-τως** *in isolation*, Phld.*D.*3 *Fr.*1.

ἀπο-τᾰμία, ἡ, *larder*, Cael.Aur.*CP*3.21 (fort. -ιεία):—Adj. **-τᾰμιακός**, ή, όν, *Cat.Cod.Astr.*8(4).338.

ἀποτᾰμιεύομαι, *lock up, keep*, Ael.*VH*1.12, cf. *PSI*4.428.28 (iii B.C.).

ἀποτάμνω, Dor. and Ion. for ἀποτέμνω.

ἀποτᾰνύω, = ἀποτείνω, τὴν χεῖρα Hp.*Fract.*8.

ἀποτάξιον· ἀπόπομπον, Hsch.

ἀπόταξις, εως, ἡ, (ἀποτάσσω) *separate assessment* for tribute, Antipho *Fr.*55.

ἀποταρτᾰρόομαι, metaph., *suffer hell*, ἐν ταῖς ἀποβολαῖς ταῖς χρημάτων Phld.*Herc.*1251.20.

ἀπότᾰσις, εως, ἡ, *lengthening, prolongation*, ὅσων ἔστιν ἀ. τῆς φωνῆς, i.e. ὅσων ἀποτείνεται ἡ φωνή, Arist.*HA*545ᵃ17, cf. *de An*.420ᵇ8. 2. *stretching out*, τῆς χειρός Sor.1.101 ; τῶν ποδῶν Plu.2.670d ; τετάνου ἴδιον ἡ ἐς εὐθὺ ἀ. Aret.*SA*1.6. 3. *distension*, of the breast, Sor.1.87. 4. *reference*, ἡ ἀ. πρὸς Κλυταιμήστραν Sch.S.*El*.1070, cf. A.D.*Synt*.35.28, al.

ἀποτάσσω, Att. -ττω, *set apart, assign specially*, χώραν τινί Pl.*Tht*.153e ; *detach* soldiers, Plb.6.35.3, etc., cf. *POxy*.475.27 (ii A.D.):—Pass., ἀποτεταγμένη ἀρχή *distinct* office, Arist.*Pol*.1322ᵃ26 ; ἀποτεταγμένοι τῇ κατοικίᾳ χρηματισταί *PFay*.12 (ii B.C.): generally, *to be fixed, appointed*, χῶρος Plu.2.120b ; *ear-mark*, ἀργύριον εἰς δημοθοινίαν -τεταγμένον *IG*12(7).515.91 (Amorgos), cf. *BCH*46.397 (Mylasa). II. *appoint, settle definitely*, Arist.*HA*585ᵇ36. III. *remove, exclude*, τόπον τοῦ κόσμου Philostr.*VA*3.35 ; ἑαυτόν τινων Id.*Im*.2.19. IV. Med., ἀποτάσσομαί τινι *bid adieu to* a person, *part from* them, *Ev.Luc*.9.61, *Act.Ap*.18.21, *Ev.Marc*.6.46, J.*AJ*11.8.6, *BGU*884 ii 14 (ii/iii A.D.), Aesop.64, Lib.*Ded*.45.28 ; *have done with, get rid of* a person, *POxy*.298.31 (i A.D.) ; ἀ. τῷ βίῳ *commit suicide*, *Cat.Cod.Astr*.8(3).136.17 : also c. dat. rei, *renounce, give up*, τοῖς ἑαυτοῦ ὑπάρχουσιν *Ev.Luc*.14.33 ; τροφῇ J.*AJ*11.6.8 ; ταῖς μίξεσι, of the Vestals, Sor.1.32 ; πάθεσι Ph.1.116, cf. Iamb.*VP*3.13, Phryn.15.

ἀποταυρόομαι, Pass., *to be like a bull*, δέργμα λεαίνης ἀποταυροῦται δμωσίν *casts* the *savage* glance of a lioness on them, E.*Med*.188 (lyr.). 2. of Io, *to be changed into a heifer*, Erot. s. v. κερχνώδεα.

ἀπόταυρος, ον, *apart from the bull*, Arist.*HA*595ᵇ19.

ἀπότᾰφος, ον, *not buried in one's ancestral tomb*, Din.*Fr*.16.5. II. *buried separately*, *IG*12(1).656 (Rhodes), Hsch., *EM*131.43.

ἀποτάφρ-ευσις, εως, ἡ, *circumvallation*, D.H.9.9 (pl.). **-εύω**, *fence off with a ditch*, X.*An*.6.5.1, *HG*5.4.38 ; for defence or offence, D.H.2.37, 3.41.

ἀποτέγγω, *dip*, Hp.*Morb*.2.56.

ἀπότεγμα, ατος, τό, (τίκτω) *product*, νοῦ καὶ λόγου Sophon.*in de An*.52.30.

ἀποτείνω, 3 pl. pf. Pass. ἀποτέτανται Luc.*Zeux*.4 :—*stretch out, extend*, μέρος τι αὑτοῦ Arist.*GA*723ᵇ22 ; ἀ. ἐκεῖ τὴν διάνοιαν Id.*Mem*.452ᵇ10 ; τὼ πόδε Luc.*Merc.Cond*.13 :—Pass., δρέπανα ἐκ τῶν ἀξόνων εἰς πλάγιον ἀποτεταμένα X.*An*.1.8.10 ; ἡ ὄψις ἀπὸ μικροῦ ἐνόπτρου πόρρω ἀποτεινομένη Arist.*Mete*.377ᵇ33, etc. 2. *extend, prolong*, of the line of an army, X.*HG*5.2.40 (Pass.) ; μακροτέρους ἀ. μισθούς *extend* rewards much further, Pl.*R*.363d ; esp. of speeches, λόγον Id.*Grg*.466a ; ἀ. μακροὺς λόγους *to make long* speeches, Id.*Prt*.335c, al. ; συχνὸν λόγον Id.*Grg*.465e ; μακρὰν ῥῆσιν ἀ. Id.*R*.605d ; of brazen vessels, μακρὸν ἠχεῖ καὶ ἀ. [τὴν ἠχήν] Id.*Prt*.329a ; φωνὴ σάλπιγγος ὀξὺν ἀ. φθόγγον Plu.*Sull*.7 ; ἱστορίας μέχρι μέσων νυκτῶν ἀ. Id.2.60a :—Pass., προοίμια ἀποτεταμένα ὡς ἐν διηγήσεως τρόπῳ D.H.*Rh*.10.13 ; ἀποτεινομένου τοῦ ποτοῦ Luc.*Merc.Cond*.18. 3. *strain, tighten* :—Pass., παραδείγματα ἀκριβῶς ἀποτεταμένα ταῖς γραμμαῖς severely *drawn*, Luc.*Rh.Pr*.9 :—Med., *exert oneself*, ὑπέρ τινος about a thing, Id.*Am*.17 ; ἀποτείνεσθαι πρός τινα *inveigh* against.., D.L.5.17, Gal.18(1).255. 4. *refer, allude*, πρός τινα Luc.*Nigr*.13 :—Med., Simp.*in Ph*.242.23 :—Pass., impers., ἀποτείνεται ἐπί.. *the reference is* to.., Sch.Il.*Oxy*.221 xi 25. II. intr., *extend*, ἀπό.., εἰς.., Arist.*HA*503ᵇ16, 514ᵃ34 ; μέχρι.. Id.*Mete*.343ᵇ22 ; ἀ. πόρρω *to go* too *far*, Pl.*Grg*.458b : c. part., *continue doing*, ἀ. μαχόμενοι Plu.2.60a.

ἀπό-τεισις, v. ἀπότισις. **-τεισμα**, ατος, τό, *payment*, *IG*2.1058.26, 12(7).62.15 (Amorgos).

ἀποτειχ-ίζω, *wall off*, 1. by way of *fortifying*, ἀ. τὸν Ἰσθμόν Hdt.6.36 :—Pass., Id.9.8. 2. by way of *blockade*, ὁ τοὺς θεοὺς ἀποτειχίσας Ar.*Av*.1576 ; τοὺς ἐν τῇ ἀκροπόλει Th.4.130, cf. 1.64, X.*HG*1.3.4, 2.4.3 :—Pass., Th.6.96 : metaph., *shut out*, ἑαυτῷ τὴν φυγήν Hld.9.20. 3. *keep off by fortification*, τὰς καταδρομάς Plu.*Per*.19. 4. *wall off, separate*, ὄρη ἀποτειχίζοντα τὴν Ἰταλίαν ἀπό τε Ἰλλυρίων καὶ Γαλατῶν Jul.*Or*.2.72b. 5. Med., *build a party-wall*, πρὸς ἀλλήλους Luc.*Am*.28. II. *unblock by razing a wall*, χάσμα Polyaen.1.3.5 ; *dismantle*, τὴν ἀκρόπολιν Arr.*Epict*.4.1.88. **-ισις**, εως, ἡ, *walling off of a town, blockading*, τῆς Ποτειδαίας Th.1.65. II. *razing of fortifications*, Polyaen.2.22.3. **-ισμα**, ατος, τό, *lines of blockade*, Th.6.99, 7.79, X.*HG*1.3.7. **-ισμός**, ὁ, = ἀποτείχισις I, Plu.*Nic*.18, etc. **-ιστέον**, *one must wall off*: metaph., διαβολήν Them.*Or*.22.278a.

ἀποτεκμαίρομαι, *draw signs* or *proofs from* a thing, *conclude*, c. acc. et inf., A.R.4.1538.

ἀποτεκνόομαι, Pass., *to be deprived of children*, Lxx *Ge*.27.45.

ἀπότεκνος, ον, *sterile*, Vett.Val.119.30.

ἀποτέλει-ος, ὁ, (τέλος) title of a *magistrate* of the Achaean League, Plb.16.36.4: in pl., Id.10.23.9 ; ἀ. τῶν πεζῶν *subordinate commander*, *IG*5(2).293 (Mantinea). **-όω** or **-τελεόω**, *bring to maturity*, Aristid.*Or*.43(1).13 :—Pass., *come to maturity*, Arist.*HA*576ᵇ7. **-ωσις**, εως, ἡ, *bringing to perfection*, Plu.*Nob*.7.

ἀποτελ-έσιμος, η, ον, *effective*, Hsch. s. v. θεμινήσασα. **-εσις**, εως, ἡ, *production*, ὑγρασίας Epicur.*Ep*.2 p.50 U., cf. *Theol.Ar*.44. 2. Astrol., *influence*, Paul.Al.*F*.1. **-εσμα**, ατος, τό, *full completion*, μηνός Arist.*Mu*.397ᵃ14 ; τέχνης Plb.4.78.5, Plu.*Lyc*.30. 2. *event, result*, Plb.2.39.11, D.S.1.89, Phld.*Rh*.1.129 S. (pl.), Antyll.ap.Orib.45.26.4, M.Ant.6.42, etc. ; *effect*, opp. αἰτία, *Stoic*.2.118, al., Herm.ap.Stob.1.41.6, Procl.*Inst*.18. 3. *finished product*, Olymp.*in Mete*.143.15 ; *created objects*, in pl., Ph.2.472. II. Astrol., *result of certain positions of the stars on human destiny*, τἀπὸ ἀποτελεσμάτων προρρηθέντα Phld.*D*.1.25, cf. Plu.*Rom*.12, Artem.1.9, *PTeb*.276 (ii/iii A.D.) ; title of works by Helicon and others, Suid. s. v. **-εσμᾰτικός**, ή, όν, *productive of material objects*, τέχνη ἀ., opp. θεωρητική and πρακτική, S.E.*M*.11.197 : generally, *productive*, τινός Sor.1.48, Gal.19.475. II. *astrologically influential*, Ptol.*Tetr*.90 ; *of* or *for astrology*, λόγος Vett.Val.332.1 ; -κή (sc. τέχνη), ἡ, Eust.900.34, Simp.*in Ph*.293.11 ; ἀποτελεσματικά, name of a *work on astrology* by Paul.Al. ; οἱ -κοί *astrologers*, Eust.193.7. **-εσμᾰτογρᾰφία**, ἡ, *nativity plan*, Vett.Val.29.10, Paul.Al.*L*.1, Porph.*in Ptol*.201. **-εσμᾰτολόγος**, ὁ, *writer on astrology*, *Theol.Ar*.53. **-εστέον**, *one must complete*, τὴν ἐκτομήν Dsc.*Ther*.2. **-εστικός**, ή, όν, *causative, productive*, τινός Epicur.*Ep*.1 p.14 U., *Stoic*.2.149, Polystr.p.32 W., Pl.*Def*.412c, Plu.2.652a, etc. ; *final, conclusive*, ἀποχή *PTeb*.397.25 (ii A.D.). 2. prob. f.l. for -ματικός II, Porph.*Plot*.15. II. Gramm., *final*, σύνδεσμος A.D.*Synt*.265.27, al. Adv. -κῶς ib.268.28.

ἀποτελευτ-άω, intr., *end*, ἐς τεταρταίους Hp.*Aër*.10, cf. Alex.Aphr.*Pr*.2.57 ; εἰς ἀνίας, εἰς ἡδονάς, Pl.*Prt*.353e, 354b ; ἀποτελευτῶν *at last*, Id.*Plt*.310e ; εἰς τοὐναντίον καὶ τὸ ἄμεινον Arist.*Metaph*.983ᵃ18 ; ἡ ὀλιγαρχία εἰς δῆμον ἀπετελεύτησεν Id.*Pol*.1305ᵇ11. **-ή**, ἡ, = sq., ἀ. εἴς τι ποιεῖσθαι Antyll.ap.Orib.44.22.1. **-ησις**, εως, ἡ, *ending*, εἴς τι Hp.*Loc.Hom*.3, Thphr.*Ign*.54. II. *result*, δόξα διανοίας ἀ. Pl.*Sph*.264a ; *completion, accomplishment*, Dam.*Pr*.67, 113.

ἀποτελέω, fut. -τελέσω, Att. -τελῶ, *bring to an end, complete* a work, Hdt.5.92.η', X.*HG*3.2.10, Pl.*Plt*.308e, etc. :—Pass., Th.4.69 : pf. part. ἀποτετελεσμένος *perfect*, ἐπίτροπος X.*Oec*.13.3. 2. *produce*, νοσήματα Pl.*Ti*.84c, cf. Epicur.*Ep*.1 p.20 U., M.Ant.10.26, etc. :—Pass., Arist.*Cael*.268ᵇ26. 3. *pay* or *perform what is due*, τὰς εὐχάς σφι ἀ. Hdt.2.65 ; τῷ θεῷ τὰ πάτρια Id.4.180 ; of rent or tribute, τὰ νομιζόμενα X.*Cyr*.3.2.19 ; ἀπαρχὴν τῶν ἐκ τῆς γῆς Pl.*Lg*.806e ; *pay* or *suffer*, παραπλήσια τοῖς Καμβύσου παθήμασιν ib.695e. 4. *accomplish, perform*, τὰ καθήκοντα X.*Cyr*.1.2.5 ; προσταχθέντα Pl.*Lg*.823d ; τὰ προσήκοντα Id.*Criti*.108d ; ἀ. ἄρτον *accomplish the making of* bread, Hp.*VM*3 ; ἐν ὑφ' ἑνὸς ἔργον ἄριστ' ἀποτελεῖται Arist.*Pol*.1273ᵇ10. b. esp. of astral influences, Ptol.*Tetr*.1, D.C.45.1, etc. ; cf. ἀποτέλεσμα. c. Astrol., *make a forecast*, περὶ ζωῆς Ps.-Ptol.*Centil*.215. 5. *render* of a certain kind, τὴν πόλιν ἀ. εὐδαίμονα *make* the state *quite* happy, Pl.*Lg*.718b ; ἀμείνους ἐκ χειρόνων ἀ. Id.*Plt*.297b, cf. *Lg*.823d ; τοιούτους ἄνδρας ὥστε.. Plb.6.52.11 :—in Med., ἄμεμπτον φίλον ἀποτελέσασθαι *make* him without blame *towards himself*, X.*Lac*.2.13 :—Pass., τύραννος ἀντὶ προστάτου ἀποτετελεσμένος Pl.*R*.566d ; ἐνύπνιον τέλεον ἀ. *turns out* .., ib.443b. 6. *fill up, satiate*, τὰς ἐπιθυμίας Id.*Grg*.503d :—Pass., Id.*R*.558e, al. II. Pass., *to be worshipped*, Id.*Smp*.188d.

ἀποτελωνέομαι, *get discharge from the customs*, *PLond.ined*.2092 (iii B.C.).

ἀποτεμᾰχίζω, (τέμαχος) *cut a portion off, sever*, Herm.*in Phdr*.p.92 A. :—Pass., τῆς ἀποτετεμαχισμένης ψυχῆς ib.p.166 A., cf. Syrian.*in Metaph*.40.35.

ἀποτέμνω, Ep., Ion., and Dor. -τάμνω, fut. -τεμῶ : aor. 2 Ion. and Dor. -έταμον, Att. -έτεμον :—**Pass.**, fut. ἀποτμηθήσομαι Lys.6.26 :—*cut off, sever*, παρηορίας ἀπέταμνε Il.8.87 ; ἀπὸ στομάχους ἀρνῶν τάμε 3.292, etc. ; χρῶτ' ἀπὸ πάντα καὶ ἄρθρα τεμῶ χερί S.*Ph*.1207 ; τὴν κεφαλήν Hdt.2.39, cf. *IG*4.952.2 (Epid.) ; τὰ σκέλεα Hdt.2.40 ; τὴν ῥῖνα καὶ τὰ ὦτα Id.3.154, etc. ; *amputate*, X.*Mem*.1.2.54, Hp.*Art*.69 ; *excise*, Id.*Haem*.2, cf. Dsc.*Eup*.1.12 (Pass.) ; *decapitate*, ἀλεκτρυόνα *PMag.Par*.1.38 :—Pass., *to be cut off*, τὰ ἀκρωτήρια ἀποτμηθήσεσθαι Lys.6.26 ; τὴν γλῶτταν ἀποτμηθείς Aeschin.1.168 (s. v. l. ; ἐκτμ. Suid.) ; τὴν κεφαλήν Luc.*Nav*.33 ; τὸν τράχηλον Arr.*Epict*.1.2.27. 2. *cut off, divide, sever*, in a geographical sense, ὁ Ἅλυς.. ἀποτάμνει σχεδὸν πάντα τῆς Ἀσίης Hdt.1.72 ; ὄρεα ὑψηλὰ ἀ. [τὴν χώρην] Id.4.25 : mathematically, ἥμισυ.. ἡ γραμμὴ ἀ. Pl.*Men*.85a, cf. Arist.*Mech*.849ᵃ37 :—Med., Pl.*Phlb*.42b :—Pass., of troops, *to be cut off from* the main body, X.*An*.3.4.29. 3. *cut off, check, put an end to*, τὰς μηχανάς Cratin.289 (s. v. l.). 4. *cut off, separate* in argument, Pl.*Lg*.653c :—Med., Arist.*Metaph*.1003ᵃ24 :—Pass., *to be so cut off* or *abstracted*, Id.*Ph*.202ᵇ8. 5. ἀ. τὰ βαλλάντια *to be* a *cut*-purse, Pl.*R*.348d. 6. *cut open*, ἱερεῖον Plu.*Cim*.18. b. ἀποτεμεῖν· ἀγνίσαι, Hsch. II. Med., *cut off for oneself*, ἀποταμνόμενον κρέα ἔδμεναι Il.22.347 ; ἀ. πλόκαμον Hdt.4.34 ; τὴν χώρην ἀ. τάφρον ὀρυξάμενοι ib.3 ; ἀ. τοῦ ὠτός *cut off a bit of*.., ib.71. 2. *cut off*, with a view of appropriating, πεντήκοντ' ἀγέλης ἀπετάμνετο.. βοῦς *h.Merc*.74 ; τὰς Θυρέας ἐούσας τῆς Ἀργολίδος μοίρης ἀποταμόμενοι ἔσχον Hdt.1.82 ; χώραν, ὀργάδα, Isoc.5.122, D.13.32, etc. (in Pass., of the country *cut off*, Hdt.1.82, etc.) ; ἀ. ὡς μέγιστα τῶν Ἀθηναίων *cut off* as much power as possible *from* them, Th.8.46 : also c. gen., χώρας ἀποτάμνεσθαι *cut off a part of*.., *SIG*56.24 (Argos, v B.C.), cf. Isoc.1.88 ; Φοινίκης ἀ. Ἀραβίας τε *to have a slice* or *portion of*.., Theoc.17.86. 3. *cut off from common use, consecrate*, ὕλας Luc.*Sacr*.10. 4. *subtend*, of the chord of an arc, S.E.*M*.1.304.

ἀπότεξις, εως, ἡ, *bringing to the birth*, Ph.2.466, Hierocl.p.7 A., Sor.1.6, S.E.*M*.5.53, Olymp.*Vit.Pl*.p.1 W.

ἀποτερᾰτεύομαι, Pass., (τέρας) *to be astonished as by a prodigy*, Ps.-Callisth.3.17.

ἀποτερμᾰτ-ίζω, *bound, limit, define*, Anon.*Geog.Comp*.19, cf. 10 (Pass.) ; *bring to an end*, λόγον dub. in Phld.*D*.3.14. II. Med., *look towards*, εἴς τι prob. for ἀποτελμ- in Hp.*Decent*.3. **-ισμός**, ὁ, *limitation*, τῆς ὁράσεως Gem.16.5 **-ωσις**, εως, ἡ, = foreg., *EM*583.17.

ἀποτετερμᾰτισμένως, Adv. *definitely*, Hsch. s. v. ἀμφιτέρμως.

ἀποτετρᾰγωνίζω, *square*, Hero *Stereom*.2.60.3.

ἀποτετραίνω, aor. 1 part. -τρήσας, *perforate*, Hp.*Steril*.222.

ἀπό-τευγμα, ατος, τό, *failure*, Arist.*VV*1251^{b}20, Phld.*Rh.*1.67 S., *Vit.*p.35 J., D.S.1.1, Cic.*Att.*13.27.1, etc. **-τευκτέω**, = ἀποτυγχάνω, Phot. s.v. οὐκ ἀποτευκτήσεις. **-τευκτικός**, ή, όν, *causing failure* or *miscarriage*, τινός Hippod.ap.Stob.4.39.26; *liable to failure*, Phld.*Rh.*1.72 S., Arr.*Epict.*3.6.6, 3.26.14, Ptol.*Tetr.*161. Adv. -κῶς *without success*, Arr.*Epict.*4.10.6. **-τευξις**, εως, ἡ, *miscarriage, failure*, Pl.*Ax.*368d, Phld.*Mus.*p.14 K. (pl.); ἐλπίδος Plu.*Galb.*23; of an electoral *defeat*, Id.*Mar.*5.

ἀποτεφρόω, *reduce to ashes*, Dsc.5.81, Poll.1.167:—Pass., τῶν -τεφρουμένων ὑλῶν Lyd.*Mag.*3.70.

ἀποτηγᾰνίζω, (τήγανον) *eat off the gridiron, eat broiled*, Pherecr. 123, Phryn.Com.57, Machoap.Ath.13.582e; written ἀπεταγήνισα in Sotad.Com.1.1.

ἀποτήκω, *melt away from*, αὐτῆς τῆς φύσεως ἀ. *melt away a part of*.., Pl.*Ti.*65d; τετυλωμένα βλέφαρα ἀ. *reduce* them, Dsc.5.99: metaph., Plu.2.451f:—Pass., ἀπετάκη αὐτοῦ τρία τάλαντα Hdt.1.50, cf. Epicur. *Ep.*2 p.49 U.; ἀπετάκησαν οἱ μασθοί (prob. for ἀπετάθησαν), Luc. *DMort.*28.2.

ἀπο-τῆλε, *afar off*, ἠϊόνων *AP*7.637 (Antip.), cf. *APl.*4.86. **-τηλόθεν**· μακρόθεν, Hsch. **-τηλόθι**, = foreg., A.R.4.728. **-τηλοῦ**, = foreg., Od.9.117, A.R.4.1092, etc.

ἀπότηξις, εως, ἡ, *melting away, discharging*, Hp.*Morb.Sacr.*5; of snow, Str.4.1.12.

ἀποτηρέω, *wait for, watch for*, D.S.14.21 (Dind. ἐπιτ-).

ἀποτίβᾰτος, ον, Dor. and poet. for ἀπρόσβατος, S.*Tr.*1030 (lyr.).

ἀποτίθημι, *put away, stow away*, δέπας δ' ἀπέθηκ' ἐνὶ χηλῷ Il.16. 254, cf. X.*An.*2.3.15; ἀ. εἰς δεσμωτήριον Lycurg.112: metaph., 'pigeon-hole', *class*, Phlp.*in Ph.*361.22. 2. *expose* a child, Pl.*Tht.* 161a. II. Med. (aor. 1 part. ἀποθησαμένη Hsch.), *put away from oneself, lay aside*, τεύχεα κάλ' ἀποθέσθαι ἐπὶ χθονί Il.3.89; τὴν Σκυθικὴν στολὴν ἀ. *put* it *off*, Hdt.4.78; ἀ. κόμας *cut* it *off*, in mourning, E.*Hel.* 367 (lyr., tm.); ἀ. τὸν νόμον *set aside*, i.e. *disregard*, the law, Th.1.77; ἀ. τὰν Ἀφροδίταν *quell* desire, E.*IA* 558 (lyr.); ἀ. ῥᾳθυμίαν D.4.8, 8.46; ὀργὴν Plu.*Cor.*19; ἀρχὴν Id.*Pomp.*23. 2. *put away from oneself, avoid*, ἀποθέσθαι ἐνιπὴν *wipe away* the reproach, Il.5.492, cf. Hes.*Op.* 762; νόστον ἔχθιστον ἀπεθήκατο Pi.*O.*8.68, cf. 10(11).40. 3. *put by for oneself, stow away*, Ar.*Eq.*1219, X.*Cyr.*6.1.15; ἀ. τροφὴν τοῖς νεοττοῖς Arist.*HA*619^{a}20; ἀ. τινὰ εἰς φυλακήν Plb.23.10.8; freq. of drugs, Dsc.4.136, al., cf. *PEleph.*12 (iii B.C.); ἐν φυλακῇ *Ev.Matt.* 14.3. b. *bury*, *IG*14.1974. 4. ἀποτίθεσθαι εἰς αὖθις *put off, defer*, E.*IT*376, Pl.*Grg.*449b, X.*Smp.*2.7, etc.; εἰς τοὺς παῖδας ἀ. τὰς τιμωρίας Lys.*Fr.*53.3. 5. *reserve, keep back*, Pl.*Lg.*887c, Din.1. 30. 6. ἀπεθήκατο κόλπων, of a woman, *laid down the burden of* her womb, i.e. bore a child, Call.*Dian.*25; ἀ. ὠδῖνας Str.10.5.2: but, 7. μηδὲν ἀποτίθεσθαι τῶν γιγνομένων *expose* none of *one's* children, Arist.*Pol.*1335^{b}22. 8. ἀ. χρόνον εἴς τι *employ, bestow* time upon it, Plb.18.9.10. 9. *set* a fracture, Pall.*in Hp.Fract.*12. 276 C.; cf. ἀπόθεσις.

ἀποτίθησιν· ἀποθνήσκει, Hsch.

ἀποτίκτω, *bring to the birth*, Pl.*Tht.*150c, 182b, Arist.*HA*544^{a}3, al.:—Pass., ib.10, Philostr.*VA*1.5, Iamb.*Comm.Math.*4; χθονὸς ἧς ἀπετέχθην *IG*9(1).882.5 (Corcyra).

ἀποτῐλάω, *pass*, of excrement, τι αἱμοειδές *Hippiatr.*75; *defile*, Suid.

ἀπο-τίλλω, fut. -τιλῶ Cratin.123: aor. ἀπέτιλα Ar.*Fr.*686:—*pluck, pull out*, τὰς τρίχας Hdt.3.16; οὐδὲν ἀποτίλας without *pulling off* any of the fur, Id.1.123. II. *pull the hair off, pluck bare*, τὰς κεφαλάς Ar.*Lys.*578, cf. Luc.*Gall.*28; ἀποτιλῶ σε τήμερον Cratin. l.c.:—Pass., ἀποτετιλμένος σκάφιον Ar.*Av.*806, cf. *Ec.*724. 2. of a fish, σαπέρδην ἀποτῖλαι Id.*Fr.*686. **-τιλμα**, ατος, τό, *piece plucked off*, γραιᾶν ἀποτίλματα πηρᾶν *pluckings*, Theoc.15.19. **-τιλμός**, ὁ, *tearing away*, Sor.1.71.

ἀποτίμαστος [ῑ], ον, *dishonoured*, Hsch.

ἀποτῑμ-άω, *fail to honour, slight*, *h.Merc.*35, Call.*Fr.*103, *IG*14. 1389 ii 33. 2. Pass., *to be disfranchised*, Phleg.*Olymp.Fr.*14. II. *value*, τὰ χρήματα, of the owner, J.*AJ*18.1.1:—Med., of the valuer, ibid., cf. 17.13.5; *fix a price by valuation*, δίμνεως ἀποτιμησάμενοι *having fixed their price* at two minae a head, Hdt.5.77; ἀ. πολλοῦ αἰσχροὶ εἶναι *value it* at a high price (i.e. to offer a great deal) *that they may not* be ugly, Hp.*Art.*37:—Pass., *to be valued*, πλειόνων χρημάτων Catalog.ap.D.18.106. 2. *measure*, μέτρον γῆς J.*AJ*5.1. 21. III. as law-term, 1. in Act., *mortgage* a property, D.30. 28, 41.7. 2. Pass., of the property, *to be pledged* or *mortgaged*, Id.30.4; τινὶ εἰς προῖκα *IG*12(7).57 (Amorgos), cf. ib.2.1138. **-ημα**, ατος, τό, *mortgaged property, security*, Lys.*Fr.*84 S., Is.6.36, D.30.7, *IG*2.1059.4. **-ησις**, εως, ἡ, *pledging of a property, mortgaging*, D. 31.11. II. = Lat. *census*, Plu.*Crass.*13, J.*AJ*.18.2.1. 2. *valuation*, Just.*Nov.*2.4. III. *tax*, *AB*437, cf. *OGI*476.2 (Dorylaeum, i A.D.). **-ητής**, οῦ, ὁ, *one who receives in pledge*, *AB*437. II. official *valuer* of property, Lys.*Fr.*84 S., Harp.

ἀπότῑμος, ον, *put away from honour*, stronger than ἄτιμος, Hdt.2. 167 (Comp.), S.*OT*215 (lyr.).

ἀποτίν-αγμα [ῐ], ατος, τό, *tow*, Lxx *Jd.*16.9, Sm.*Is.*1.31. **-άσσω** [ῐ], *shake off*, E.*Ba.*253:—Med., ἀποτινάξασθαι Gal.6.821; ἀποτετίνακται τὸ ῥῆμα τῶν ὄνων *has got rid of* it, Lxx 1*Ki.*10.2.

ἀπο-τίνῡμι [ῐ, cf. sq.], Dor. inf. -τινύμεν *Supp.Epigr.*1.410.9 (Crete, iv B.C.); 3 sg. imper. ἀποτεινύτω *GDI*5100.11 (ib.), *SIG*²680. 8 (Syros):—later **-τίννῡμι**, inf. -τιννύναι, part. -τιννύντες, Them.*Or.* 23.289c, 3.40d, imper. -τιννύτω J.*AJ*4.8.36, *SIG*1109.79 (Athens, ii A.D.):—also **-τιννύω** Lxx *Ge.*31.39, al., Ph.2.596; ἀποτειννυέτω *PAvrom.*1 *A* 26:—for Med. v. sq. II.1.

ἀποτίνω, Arc. ἀπυτείω *IG*5(2).6.43 (Tegea, iv B.C.), fut. -τείσω: aor. -έτεισα; Thess. 3 sg. aor. imper. ἀππεισάτου ib.9(2).1229 (ii B.C.):—*repay*, τιμὴν δ' Ἀργείοις ἀποτινέμεν Il.3.286; εὐεργεσίας ἀποτίνειν Od.22.235. 2. *pay for* a thing, πρὶν.. μνηστῆρας ὑπερβασίην ἀποτεῖσαι ib.13.193; Πατρόκλοιο δ' ἕλωρα.. ἀποτείσῃ *may atone for* making a prey of Patroclus, Il.18.93; σύν τε μεγάλῳ ἀπέτεισαν *made atonement* with a great price, ib.4.161; ἀ. αἷμα A.*Ag.*1338 (lyr.); πληγὰς τῶν ὑπεραύχων S.*Ant.*1352. 3. more freq., *pay in full*, τίσιν οὐκ ἀποτείσει Orac.ap.Hdt.5.56, cf. 3.109; ζημίην Id.2.65; ἀργύριον Ar.*V.*1255; ἐγγύας Antipho 2.2.12, cf. 5.63; χρήματα Lys. 1.29; ἀξίαν Luc.*DMort.*30.1; ἀπότεισον *pay* the wager! Ar.*Pl.*1059; in Law παθεῖν ἢ ἀποτεῖσαι are opposed to denote personal or pecuniary penalties, e.g. Lexap.D.21.47, cf. ib.25; τί ἄξιός εἰμι παθεῖν ἢ ἀ.; Pl.*Ap.*36b, cf. *Plt.*299a, *Lg.*843b, al. 4. c. acc. pers., ἀλάστωρ.. τόνδ' ἀπέτεισεν *made* him *the price*, A.*Ag.*1503 (lyr.). 5. τὸ πεπρωμένον ἀ. *pay the debt of* fate, i.e. *die*, *Epigr.Gr.*509 (Thess.). II. Med., ἀποτίνομαι, poet. ἀποτίνῡμαι (freq. written -τίννυμαι) Il.16. 398, Hes.*Op.*247 (s.v.l.), Thgn.362, Hdt.6.65: fut. -τείσομαι:—*to get paid one, exact* or *require* a penalty *from*, πόλεων δ' ἀπετίνυτο ποινήν Il.16.398, etc.: c. dupl. acc., ἀποτείσασθαι δίκην ἐχθρούς E. *Heracl.*852; δέκα τάλαντ' ἀ. Eup.317 (dub.), etc. 2. c. acc. pers., ἀποτείσασθαί τινα *avenge oneself on* another, *punish* him, Od.5.24, X. *Cyr.*5.4.35, etc. 3. c. acc. rei, *take vengeance for* a thing, *punish* it, εἴ κέ ποτέ σφι βίας ἀποτείσεται Od.3.216, cf. 16.255; τὰ παράνομα ..θεὸς ἀ. Ar.*Th.*684: c. gen. rei, ἀ. τῶν..ἱρῶν κατακαυθέντων Hdt.6. 101, v. supr. I.2: abs., *take vengeance*, Thgn. l.c., Sol.4.16. [ἀποτίνω has ῑ by position before νϝ in Ep., ῐ in Att. For ἀποτίνυμαι, which has ῑ by nature, ἀποτείνυμαι should perh. be read in early texts; cf. foreg.]

ἀποτίπλαστος, ον, Dor. for ἀπροσπέλαστος, Hsch.

ἀπότῐσις (better ἀπότεισις), εως, ἡ, *repayment*, Ath.11.503b.

ἀποτιστέον (better ἀποτειστέον), *one must pay*, ζημίαν X.*Lac.*9.5, cf. *PTeb.*71, Aristid.*Or.*46(3).2.

ἀπότιστος, ον, *unwatered*, *PTeb.*1.71.8–9 n. (ii B.C.).

ἀπότιτθος, ον, *put from the breast, weaned*, Ph.2.83, 332.

ἀπο-τμήγω, Ep. for ἀποτέμνω, *cut off from*, μοῦνον ἀποτμήξας πόλιος Il.22.456; τὸν.. λαοῦ ἀποτμήξαντε 10.364, etc. 2. *cut off, sever*, χεῖρας ἀπὸ ξίφεϊ τμήξας 11.146; μήδεα Hes.*Th.*188; κλιτῦς τότ' ἀποτμήγουσι χαράδραι *plough* the hill-sides, Il.16.390:—Pass., μοῦνοι ἀποτμηγέντες A.R.4.1052: c. gen., τοῦ ἑνός Dam.*Pr.* 34. **-τμημα**, ατος, τό, *anything cut off, piece*, Hp.*Art.*38, *Gp.*1.14. 12. **-τμήξ**, ῆγος, ὁ, ἡ, *cut off, sheer*, like ἀπορρώξ, σκοπιή A.R.2. 581. **-τμηξις**, εως, ἡ, *cutting off*, Anon.Lond.32.51. **-τμησις**, εως, ἡ, *cutting off*, ἀγκυρίων Ph.*Bel.*100.33 (pl.). **-τμητέον**, *one must cut off*, τῆς τῶν πλησίον χώρας *a portion of* it, Pl.*R.*373d; *one must excise*, τὴν μήτραν Sor.2.89.

ἄποτμος, ον, *unhappy, ill-starred*, Il.24.388, Od.20.140; βοά A. *Pers.*280 (lyr.); πότμος ἄ. E.*Hipp.*1144 (lyr.): Comp. -ότερος Mosch. 4.11: Sup. -ότατος Od.1.219.

ἀπότοκος (A), ὁ, *propagation*, νοσήματος Hp.*Art.*49 (pl.).

ἀπότοκος (B), ον, *resulting from*, τινός Aret.*SD*1.16, 2.3.

ἀποτολμ-άω, *make a bold venture upon*, τινί Th.7.67: c. inf., ἀ. ἐπιχειρῆσαι Lys.7.28; λέγειν Aeschin.3.131, cf. Plb.2.45.2, Ph.1. 233, etc.:—pf. part. Pass. in act. sense, δι' ἐλευθερίας λίαν ἀποτετολμημένης *too presumptuous* liberty, Pl.*Lg.*701b, cf. Plu.*Galb.*25: in pass. sense, εἰπεῖν τὰ νῦν ἀποτετ. Pl.*R.*503b: abs., ἀποτολμᾷ καὶ λέγει *Ep.Rom.*10.20: c. acc., ἀναίρεσιν J.*AJ*7.8.3. **-ητέον**, *one must venture*, c. inf., λέγειν Plu.2.11d.

ἀπότολμος, ον, *bold, daring*, Heph.Astr.3.34, Sch.Opp.*H.*1.112.

ἀποτομ-άς, άδος, ἡ, pecul. fem. of ἀπότομος, *abrupt, sheer*, πέτρα D.S.4.78, cf. 2.13. 2. as Subst., *split* or *hewn piece of wood*, J. *AJ*3.1.2; *javelin used in athletic games*, Poll.10.64, Hsch. 3. fiery *dart*, prob. l. in Tim.*Pers.*28. **-εύς**, έως, ὁ, = foreg. 2, Poll. 3.151. **-ή**, ἡ, *cutting off*, τῶν χειρῶν X.*HG*2.1.32: in pl., Ti. Locr.97d. 2. *piece, segment*, ἀπὸ τοῦ ἀπείρου Epicur.*Ep.*2 p.37 U.; γῆς Ph.2.77, cf. ib.124 (pl.), Diog.Oen.24; κόσμου Ocell.3.3; τοιαύτας ἔχειν τὰς ἀ., of the moon in eclipse, Arist.*Cael.*297^{b}25, cf. 294^{a}4, Plot.6.4.7; *end cut off*, Dsc.5.120. b. in Music, *difference between* λεῖμμα *and* τόνος, Gaud.*Harm.*14; τοῖς ἡμιτονίοις τῷ τε ἐλάσσονι καὶ τῷ μείζονι, τουτέστι τοῦ τε λείμματος καὶ τῇ ἀ. ib.16. c. Math., *compound irrational straight line equivalent to binomial surd with negative sign*, Euc.10.83, al. 3. *branching off*, τῶν φλεβίων Arist.*HA*497^{a}17; *place where roads intersect*, Plb.6.29.9. 4. *division* of an argument *into sections*, D.H.*Is.*15. 5. in Tactics, = φαλαγγαρχία (q.v.), Ascl.*Tact.*2.10, etc. **-ία**, ἡ, *severity*, νόμων D.S.12.16, *POxy.*237 vii 40 (i A.D.); ἐπιτιμημάτων Plu.2.13d; ἀναβάσεως *BGU*1208.16 (Aug.); Φαλάριδος Demetr.*Eloc.*292; περὶ τὰ δίκαια D.H.8.61; of tortures, Ph.2.287; καῦσις διὰ τὴν ἀ. Archig.(?) ap.Aët.9.35. II. *cutting off*, Dem.Ophth.ap.Aët.7.81. III. *sheer madness*, Ps.-Callisth.2.12. **-ος**, ον, *cut off*, στροφέων ἀ. μῆκος πήχεων πέντε *IG*11(2).287 *A* 49 (Delos, iii B.C.); esp. *sheer, precipitous*, ἀ. ἐστι ταύτῃ ἡ ἀκρόπολις Hdt.1.84, cf. 4.62; ἀ. ἐκ θαλάττης Pl.*Criti.*118a; τὰ ἀ. *precipices*, Philostr.*VA*3.4; ἀπότομον ὤρουσεν εἰς ἀνάγκαν, metaph. from one who comes suddenly *to the edge of a cliff*, S.*OT*877 (lyr.). Adv. -μως, ἔχειν Philostr.*VA*2.5. 2. metaph., *severe, relentless*, λῆμα E.*Alc.*981 (lyr.); κρίσις Lxx *Wi.*6.6. Adv. -ως ib.5.22, Plb.18.11.2, Plu.*Crass.*3, etc.; *brusquely*, prob. l.

in Cic.*Att.*10.11.5. b. of persons, *severe*, Ph.2.268. c. of gladiatorial combats, a fight *to a finish*, ἐνόζυγον ἀπότομον *IGRom.* 4.1632; ἀπότομα alone, Μουσεῖον καὶ Βιβλ.1876/8 No.153; μονομαχιῶν τρεῖς ἡμέρας ἀποτόμους *Inscr.Magn.*163.10, cf. *IGRom.*3.360.9 (Sagalassus), *CIG*2880 (Branchidae). 3. *concise*, συγκεφαλαίωσις Plb.9.32.6. 4. c. gen., οἱ καθηγητῶν οὕτως ἀπότομοι γενηθέντες *offshoots* of our founders, Phld.*Lib.*p.22 O. 5. ἀπότομοι· οὐκ ἐνεργοί, Hsch.: ἀπότομον· τὸν μὴ ἄξιον προσόψεως, Id. II. *absolute*: Adv. -μως *absolutely*, οὐδὲν τῶν τοιούτων ἐστὶν ἀ. οὔτε κακὸν οὔτ' ἀγαθόν Isoc.6.50, cf. D.61.4; ἀ. ἀληθής Phld.*Mus.*p.98 K.; *precisely, in the strictest sense*, τοῖς ὀνόμασι χρῆσθαι Isoc.9.10.

ἀποτοξεύω, *shoot off arrows*, ἀπὸ δένδρων D.C.37.2: metaph., *shoot off like an arrow*, ῥηματίσκια Pl.*Tht.*180a, cf. Luc.*Rh.Pr.*17:—Pass., Id.*Prom.Es*2. 2. *shoot* a person, τινά τινι Id.*Vit.Auct.*24 (codd., κατατοξ– Cobet). II. *keep off by shooting*, λοιμόν Id.*Alex.*36.

ἀποτορεύω, dub. l. for sq., Ph.1.505 (Pass.), Jul.*Or.*3.112a.

ἀποτορν-εύω, *round off* as by the lathe, εἰς σφαῖραν –τετορνευμένος Ph.1.505: metaph. of *polished* language, σαφῆ καὶ στρογγύλα.. τὰ ὀνόματα ἀποτετόρνευται Pl.*Phdr.*234e (imitated by Plu.2.45a); κέγχρους Jul.*Or.*3.112a; περιόδους ib.2.77a. **–ωσις**, εως, ἡ, *rounding off* as by the lathe, Heliod.ap.Orib.49.7.4.

ἄποτος, ον, *not drinkable*, ὕδωρ Hdt.4.81, Pherecr.70, etc. 2. *not drunk from*, ποτήριον Philostr.*VA*4.20. II. Act., *never drinking*, ὄνοι Hdt.4.192; of grasshoppers, Pl.*Phdr.*259c; of birds of prey, Arist.*HA*594^{a}1. 2. *not drinking, without drink*, ἄσιτος ἀνήρ, ἄ. S.*Aj.*324, cf. X.*Cyr.*7.5.53; ἄ. ἀνέχεσθαι Arist.*HA*596^{a}1; *not given to drinking*, ἐδωδοὶ καὶ ἄ. Hp.*Aër.*1; but, *unable to drink*, Id.*Epid.*2.2.7. 3. in Architecture, ἁρμοὶ ἄ. *not admitting water*, of close-fitting joints, *IG*2^2.244.90.

ἀποτρᾰγεῖν, v. ἀποτρώγω.

ἀποτράγημα [ᾰγ], ατος, τό, *remains of a dessert*, v.l. for ἀποπάτημα, Eup.284.

ἀποτρᾰγοπώγων, = λάδανον, Gal.12.423.

ἀποτρᾰχηλίζω, *strangle*, σχοινίοις Eun.*Hist.*p.272 D.

ἀποτρᾰχύνω, pf. ἀποτετράχυκα D.H.*Comp.*22:—*make rough* or *hard*: metaph., τὴν ἁρμογήν l.c.; but ἀ. τὴν ἀκοήν *grate on* the ear, Id.*Dem.*43:—Pass., *to be* or *become rough* or *hard*, Thphr.*HP*6.4.2.

ἀποτρέκω, = ἀποτρέχω, barbarism in Ar.*Th.*1214.

ἀποτρεπ-τέον, *one must turn away, divert*, Arist.*Rh.Al.*1425^{a}35; τὴν ὄρεξιν ἐπὶ τὰ λιτά Plu.2.125d. 2. –τέος, α, ον, *to be diverted*, ῥεύματα Gal.16.152. **–τικός**, ή, όν, *fit for dissuading from* a thing, τινός Ps.-Luc.*Philopatr.*8; ἀ. εἶδος τῶν λόγων Arist.*Rh.Al.*1421^{b}9. 2. *preventive*, τῶν νομῶν Dsc.1.70. **–τος**, ον, *abominable*, Them.*Or.*13.170c. **–ω**, *turn away from*, εἰ δὲ σύ.. τιν' ἄλλον.. ἀποτρέψεις πολέμοιο Il.12.249, cf. 20.256; ὅθεν.. ἀπέτραπε λαὸν Ἀθήνη 11.758; *deter* or *dissuade from*, τινός τινα Th.3.39; τινὰ τῆς κακουργίας Id.6.38; τῆς γνώμης And.3.21, etc.: c. inf., ἀ. προσωτέρω τὸ μὴ πορεύεσθαι Hdt.1.105; ἀ. βοᾶν A.*Supp.*900 (lyr.); δηλοῦν D.60.26, cf. X.*Mem.*4.7.5,6: c. part., ἀ. τινὰ ὑβρίζοντα A.*Supp.*880:—Pass., ὁ παραβαίνειν τι βουλόμενος τῷ μὴ προὔχων ἂν ἐπελθεῖν –τρέπεται Th. 3.11, cf. Plu.*Fab.*19. 2. c. acc. pers. only, *turn away* or *back*, πάντας ἀπέτραπε καὶ μεμαῶτας Il.15.276: c. dat. modi, οὔ μ' ἐπέεσσιν ἀποτρέψεις μεμαῶτα 20.256, cf. 109; τοὺς ἀλαζόνας ἀ. *deter* them, Pl.*Chrm.*173c; opp. παροξῦναι, D.21.37; opp. συμβουλεύω, Arist.*Rh.*1391^{b}33, etc. 3. c. acc. rei, *turn back again*, ποτὶ χέρσον ἔντεα ναός Pi.*N.*4.69. 4. *turn aside, avert*, ἀπὸ δὲ.. ἔγχεος ὁρμὴν ἔτραπε Hes.*Sc.*455; *pervert*, δίκας κέλευθον ὀρθᾶς B.10.27; τὸ σφάλμα ἀ. *prevent, avert* it, Hdt.1.207; τὸ μέλλον γενέσθαι Id.3.65, cf. 8.29, al.; ἀ. βλάβην, συμφοράν, Pl.*Grg.*509b, *Phdr.*231d; ἀ. τὴν εἰρήνην *prevent* its being made, X.*HG*6.3.12. 5. *turn from* others *against* one, ἐπὶ τῷδε.. οὐκ ἔγχος τις.. ἀποτρέψει; v.l. in S.*Tr.*1013 (lyr.):—Pass., ἀποτετράφθαι πρὸς τὴν ἄλλην Ἰταλίαν Plu.*Fab.*19:—Med., ἀποτραπόμενος πρὸς θυσίαν, i.e. *turning away from other objects to* this one, Id.*Rom.*7; εἰς τὴν μεσογείαν –τραπόμενος Luc.*Tox.*52. II. Med. and (later) Pass., *turn from, desist from*, c. part., ἀπετράπετ' ὄβριμος Ἕκτωρ ὀλλὺς Ἀργείους Il.10.200: c. inf., λέγειν E.*Or.*410, cf. Antipho 5.32, D.*Prooem.*23 (*b*); ἀ. ἐκ κινδύνων Th.2.40; ἀ. τοῦ ἐρωτήματος X.*Oec.*15.13. 2. *turn away, turn a deaf ear*, οὐδ'.. ἀπετράπετ' οὐδ' ἀπίθησεν Il.12.329: abs., Pl. *Smp.*206d. 3. c. acc. rei, *turn away from, shrink from*, δεῖμα πολιτῶν A.*Th.*1065 (anap.); τἀληθές E.*IA*336 (lyr.), cf. Th.3.68, and late Prose, Plu.*Cleom.*9, etc. 4. *turn back, return*, ἐπ' οἴκου Th.5.13; ἐς τὴν πόλιν Id.3.24; ἀποτρεπόμενοι ἵεντο X.*HG*7.2.13. 5. *dissuade, deter*, τινά Plb.7.13.1. 6. *beat off, repulse*, Plu.*Brut.*42.

ἀποτρέφω, *feed, support*, τὴν στρατιὰν ἡ χώρα ἀ. Str.16.2.10; τινά Lyd.*Mag.*1.34, al.; γαμετάς Just.*Nov.*43.1.2:—Pass., *live off* a thing, Poll.6.32, Just.*Nov.*80.5 *Intr.*; συσσιτίων ἀ. Eust.1.14.

ἀποτρέχω, fut. –θρέξομαι Ar.*Nu.*1005, but –θρέξω Pl.Com.232; also –δρᾰμοῦμαι X.*An.*7.6.5: aor. 2 ἀπέδρᾰμον Hdt.4.203:—*run off* or *away*, ll. cc., X.*An.*5.2.6; οἴχεσθαι ἀποτρέχων Pl.*Tht.*171d. II. *run hard*, of one training for a race, Ar. l.c. III. *run home*, οἴκαδε X.*Oec.*11.18; *run off the track*, Pl.*R.*613c. IV. *depart*, Foed.ap.Plb.3.24.11; of manumitted slaves, ἀποτρεχέτω ἐλευθέρα *GDI*2038 (Delph.), etc. V. of workers, *abscond, strike*, *PSI*4.421.8 (iii B.C.).

ἀπότρεψις, εως, ἡ, (from Med.) *aversion*, Hp.*Liqu.*2 (pl.).

ἀποτριάζω, *to be victorious in wrestling* (cf. τριακτήρ), Sch.A.*Ch.* 339 (Pass.); *to be victorious in the* πένταθλον, Poll.3.151: = τρεῖς πληγὰς δοῦναι, *AB*438, Hsch.

ἀπο-τρῑβή, ἡ, *rubbing away, wearing out, depreciation*, τῶν σκευῶν D.50.28; *damage*, ὥστε μηδεμίαν ἀ. τῷ δημοσίῳ συμβῆναι, = ne quid detrimenti res publica caperet, D.C.37.31. **–τρίβω** [ῑ], fut. –ψω, strengthd. for τρίβω, *wear out*, πολλά οἱ.. σφέλα.. πλευραὶ ἀποτρίψουσι his ribs will *wear out* many a footstool (thrown at him), Od.17.232. II. *rub clean*, ἀ. ἵππον *rub down* a horse, X.*Eq.*6.2:—Med., ἀ. τὸ αἰδοῖον Plu.2.1044b. III. *rub off*, ἰόν Theoc.16.17: metaph., πρὶν γῆρας ἀποτρῖψαι νεότητα Id.24.133:—Pass., *to be rubbed off*, Arist. *Col.*793^{a}25:—Med., *get rid of*, ἀδοξίαν D.1.11; ἐγκλήματα Aeschin. 1.179; τὸ πάθος Arist.*EN*1105^{a}2; διαβολάς D.S.17.5; τὸν πόλεμον, τὸν κίνδυνον, Plb.3.8.10, 10.14.1; τοὺς πελάζοντας ἀ. *brush* them *away*, Id.3.102.5; τὴν ἄνθρωπον Plu.*Mar.*40; *quartanam* Cic.*Att.*7.5.5; λιμὸν τῆς γαστρός Plu.2.1044b; *decline, reject*, ἡμέραν *Inscr.Prien.* 27.17; τὴν πεῖραν Plu.*Thes.*26; δεήσεις Id.*Brut.*17; τὰ διδόμενα *OGI* 315.82 (Pessinus, ii B.C.). 2. in Pass., ὥστε μηδὲν ἀπ' αὐτῆς ἀποτριβῆναι, = ne quid detrimenti resp. caperet, D.C.40.49, etc. **–τριμμα**, ατος, τό, *that which is rubbed off*, ἀκόνης Ναξίας *emery powder*, Dsc. 5.149, Critoap.Gal.12.447. **–τριπτος**, ον, *worn out*, *PLond.*2.191.12 (ii A.D.).

ἀποτρίς, Adv. *thrice*, A.D.*Synt.*339.14.

ἀποτρῐτ-όω, *boil down to a third part*, v.l. in Ps.-Dsc.4.137 (Pass.), cf. *Gp.*7.13.5, Alex.Trall.1.15. **–ωσις**, εως, ἡ, *boiling down to a third part*, ἑψέσθω εἰς –σιν Orib.*Fr.*51, cf. Aët.3.77.

ἀπό-τρῐχος, ον, *hairless*, Eust.581.13. **–τριψις**, εως, ἡ, *mashing*, *PSI*4.332.24 (iii B.C.).

ἀποτροπ-άδην [ᾰδ], Adv. *turned away*, Opp.*H.*3.612. **–αιος**, ον, *averting evil*, freq. of Apollo, Ar.*Eq.*1307, *Av.*61, *Pl.*359, Orac.ap.D. 21.53, *CIG*464: generally, θεοὶ ἀ. Hp.*Vict.*4.89, Pl.*Lg.*854b, X.*HG*3.4, Paus.2.11.1. 2. of sacrifices, D.H.5.54, Plu.2.290d, 292a. II. Pass., *that ought to be averted, ill-omened*, φαντασίαι Ph.2.433; δυσφημίαι Plu.2.587f; θέαμα Luc.*Tim.*5; ἄκουσμα Id.*Gall.*2, etc. **–άομαι**, poet. for ἀποτρέπω, Ps.-Phoc.133 codd., Numen.ap.Ath.7.304f. **–ή**, ἡ, *turning away, averting*, A.*Pers.*217; ἄλλοσ' ἀποτροπὰ κακῶν γένοιτο, i.e. ἄλλοσε ἀποτρέποιτο κακά, E.*Hel.*360; λυπῶν ἀπαλλαγάς τε καὶ ἀποτροπάς Pl.*Prt.*354b; τεράτων ἀ., Lat. *procuratio*, Plu.*Fab.*18. 2. *diverting*, of water, Pl.*Lg.*845d. 3. *prevention*, Th.3.45; ἀποτροπῆς ἕνεκα κολάζειν Pl.*Prt.*324b, cf. *R.*382c. 4. *dissuasion*, Id.*Thg.*128d; opp. προτροπή, Arist.*Rh.*1358^{b}9, Chrysipp.*Stoic.*3.3. II. (from Med.) *desertion of one's party*, 'ratting', Th.3.82. **–ία**, Ep. –ίη, ἡ, poet. for foreg. 1, οὐ γάρ τις ἀ. θανάτοιο A.R.4.1504. **–ιάζω**, *utter a deprecatory prayer for*, τινά Aristaenet.1.1:—Med., *avert evil by sacrifice*, Lxx *Ez.*16.21; σημεῖον *POxy.*885.53, cf. Phleg.*Mir.*1, Sch. A.*Pers.*203. **–ίασμα**, ατος, τό, *sacrifice to avert evil*, Hsch. **–ιασμός**, ὁ, *averting by expiatory sacrifice*, *PTeb.*140: in pl., Beros.ap.J.*AJ* 1.3.6, Aesop.112b, D.L.8.32. **–ιαστής**, οῦ, ὁ, *averter*, Sch.A. l.c. **–ιαστικός**, ή, όν, *fit for averting*, Eust. ad D.P.723. **–ιμος**, ον, = ἀποτρόπαιος, Hsch. s. v. ὀξυθυμία. **–ιος**, ον, = foreg., Orph.*A.* 481. **–ος**, ον, (ἀποτρέπω) *turned away, far from men*, ἐγὼ παρ' ὕεσσιν ἀπότροπος Od.14.372; *turned away in flight*, Opp.*H.*4.254. 2. *from which one turns away, horrible*, ἀ. ἄγος A.*Ch.*155 (lyr.); τὸν ἀ. Ἅιδαν S.*Aj.*608 (lyr.); σκότου νέφος Id.*OT*1314; πῦρ Ar.*Ec.*792; γνώμη ἀ. a *stern, hostile* decree, Pi.*P.*8.94; κασιγνήτης ἀπότροπον.. εὐνήν Ps.-Phoc.182. II. Act., *turning away, averting*, κακῶν A. *Ch.*42, E.*Ph.*586; ἀ. δαίμονες A.*Pers.*203. 2. *preventing, saving from*, ἀ. αὐτοῖς ἐγένετο μή.., c. inf., Pl.*Lg.*877a.

ἀποτροφ-ή, ἡ, *nourishment, support*, *PSI*1.76.6 (vi A.D., pl.); f.l. for ἀποστρ– in D.H.7.28, dub. in Ph.1.617 (leg. ἀπ' ο(ὐρανοῦ) τροφήν). **–ιμος**, ον, (prob. for –τρόφιμος) *furnishing sustenance*, ἐπιτήδευμα τοῦ ζῆν ἀ. *means of* subsistence, *PFlor.*295.2 (vi A.D.). **–ος**, ον, *reared away from home*, Hdt.2.63; of birds, Arist.*HA*536^{b}16: c. gen., ἀ. ἀλλήλων *reared apart from*, Plu.2.917c.

ἀποτροχίζω· *deporto*, Gloss.

ἀπότροχος, ὁ, (ἀποτρέχω) *race-course*, Ar.*Fr.*637 (pl.).

ἀποτρῠγ-άω, *pluck grapes* or *fruit*, Philostr.*VA*3.5; ἀ. πέπερι ib. 3.4: metaph., ἀρχὰς ἐθνῶν ἀ. Lxx *Am.*6.1. **–ίζω**, (τρύξ) *rack off, decant*, εἰς ἀγγεῖα *Gp.*8.23.2.

ἀποτρύζω, *emit a sound*, σύριγμα Nonn.*D.*25.47.

ἀποτρυπῶν· λάθρα ἐξιών, Hsch.

ἀποτρύχω [ῡ], = sq., τινὰ πόνοις Ph.2.231:—Pass., ib.288, Plu. *Ant.*24; of land, Ph.2.371. (The form **–χόομαι** is dub. in Plu. *Ant.*38.)

ἀποτρύω [ῡ], *rub away, wear out*, ἐλπίδα S.*Tr.*125 (lyr.); ζῷον πόνοις Ph.2.341; χρόνῳ καὶ δαπάνῃ τινὰ ἀ. Plu.*Aem.*13:—Med., γῆν ἀποτρύεσθαι S.*Ant.*339 (lyr.):—Pass., ἀποτετρυμένος *harassed*, Hierocl.p.53 A., cf. Plu.*CG*6.

ἀπο-τρώγω, aor. 2 ἀπέτρᾰγον Ph.1.224, Gal.6.864, D.L.9.27:—*bite* or *nibble off*, πτόρθους Eup.14; τὸ ἱππομανὲς ἀ. Arist.*HA*605^{a}4; γλῶτταν Ph. l.c., cf. Gal. l.c.: metaph., μισθοὺς ἀ. Ar.*Ra.*367, cf. Men.303; ἀ. τὸ ἀπορηθέν 'gulp down', 'bolt' the difficulty, i.e. pass it by without trying to get at the heart of the matter, Arist.*Metaph.* 1001^{a}2. 2. c. gen., *nibble at*, πόης Babr.46.6: metaph., τᾶς αὔλακος οὐκ ἀποτρώγεις, i.e. you don't *gobble* your swathe, Theoc.10.6. **–τρωκτος**, ον, *bitten off*: metaph., *with the end cut off by apocope*, e.g. ἄλφι for ἄλφιτον, Hsch. and Suid. s.v. ἄλφι. **–τρωμάξαι**· ἀποφράξαι, Hsch. **–τρωξις**, εως, ἡ, *biting off*, μυκτήρων Phld.*Ir.* p.34 W.

ἀποτρωπάω, Frequentat. of ἀποτρέπω, τινὰ ὀπίσσω Il.20.119: abs., εἰ δέ κ' ἀποτρωπῶσι θεοί, παύσασθαι ἄνωγα Od.16.405. B. Med., c. inf., Il.18.585: c. gen., τανυστύος Od.21.112, etc.: c. acc., πεῖραν A.R.3.16.

ἀποτυγχάνω, fut. -τεύξομαι Pl.*Lg.*898e:—Med., aor. ἀποτεύξασθαι· ἀποτυχεῖν, Hsch.: pf. Pass. in med. sense, Phld.*Rh.*1.220 S.:—*fail in hitting* or *gaining*, τινός Hp.*VM*2, Pl.*Lg.*744a, X.*Mem.*4.2.27, etc.; τοῦ ὠφελιμωτάτου Pl.*Tht.*179a; τούτων τριῶν ἑνός γ' ἀ. Alex. 211; μήτ' ἀξίως τυχεῖν τῆς ἀληθείας μήτε πάντως ἀ. Arist.*Metaph.*993^{b}1; *lose*, ὧν εἶχον ἀπέτυχον X.*Cyr.*1.6.45; κακοῦ ἀποτυχεῖν *escape from*, Philem.93.9. 2. Pass., ἀποτυγχάνεται *a failure ensues*, Arist.*Ph.*199^{b}3; of things, *to be missed*, τὸ μὴ ἐπιτευχθὲν ἀ. D.H. *Pomp.*2.14; τὰ προτεθεσπισμένα καὶ ἀποτετευγμένα prophesied and *not come to pass*, Luc.*Alex.*28; ἀποτετευγμένος *rejected, not finding a purchaser*, Dsc.5.79. II. abs., *miss one's object, fail*, X.*HG*7. 5.14; ὅλως ἀ. D.11.12; λέγοντες οὐκ ἀποτευξόμεθα *shall* not *miss the truth* in saying, Pl.*Lg.*898e; ἀ. περί τινος X.*Eq.*1.16; τυγχάνειν καὶ ἀ. κατά τι Arist.*Po.*1450^{a}3; τῷ γάμῳ D.S.12.12; ἐν ταῖς ἐπιβολαῖς Plb.5.98.6:—Med., ἀποτυγχανομένῳ πρὸς τὸν γάμον Ant.Lib.39.3.

ἀποτῡλόω, = ἀναφλάω, Pherecr.204, *AB*423.

ἀποτύμβιος, ον, *away from the tomb*, λώβην ῥεθέων ἀ. ἴσχειν *BCH* 23.281 (Termessus).

ἀποτυμπᾰν-ίζω (later -τυπ- *UPZ*119 (ii B.C.), *POxy.*1798.1.7), *crucify on a plank*, D.8.61, 9.61:—Pass., Lys.13.56, D.19.137, Arist. *Rh.*1383^{a}5, Beros.ap.J.*Ap.*1.20. 2. generally, *destroy*, Plu.2. 1049d. **-ισμός**, ὁ, *crucifixion*, *Cat.Cod.Astr.*7.140.11.

ἀπό-τῠπος, ον, *moulded*, εἰκόνες J.*AJ*20.9.4. 2. Subst. ἀπότυπος, ὁ, *image*, Ἀπόλλωνος ἀ. ἀργυροῦς *IG*11(2).223*B*17 (Delos, iii B.C.); also as neut., Ἀπόλλωνος ἀπότυπον ἀργυροῦν ἐπίχρυσον ib.203 *B*83 (ib.). **-τῠπόω**, *impress*, σφραγῖδα Luc.*Alex.*21; of stars, εἴδωλον *form* a constellation, Phlp.*in Mete.*112.36. 2. *represent*, τὴν ἀσώματον θεόν Lib.*Eth.*11.3, cf. Porph.ap.Eus.*PE*3.7. II. Med., *stamp an impression* as on wax, *form as in an impression*, εἴς τι Pl.*Tht.*191d, cf. *Lg.*681b; πρὸς τὴν τοῦ παραδείγματος φύσιν Id.*Ti.* 39e, cf. Hierocl.*in CA*23 p.468 M., Iamb.*Myst.*1.11. 2. *model one's style on, imitate*, Ἰσοκράτην D.H.*Din.*8.

ἀποτύπτω, *incise, open*, τὰς φλέβας Hp.*Morb.*2.55; *scarify*, τὴν ὄσχην ib.71. 2. Med., *cease to beat oneself, cease mourning*, Hdt. 2.40.

ἀποτύπ-ωμα [ῠ], ατος, τό, *impression*, Pl.*Tht.*194b, Iamb.*Myst.*2. 10 (pl.). **-ωσις**, εως, ἡ, *impression*, ἀ. ποιεῖν ἀπό τινος Longin. 13.4, cf. Thphr.*Sens.*51; v.l. for διατύπωσις, J.*AJ*12.2.8.

ἀποτῡρόω, *make into cheese*, Erot. s.v. ὀρὸν πίσσης (Pass.).

ἀποτυφλ-όω, *make quite blind*, τινά Arist.*Mir.*845^{a}23; τὴν ὅρασιν D.S.3.37: metaph. of anger, Phld.*Ir.*p.68 W.:—Pass., *to be blinded*, Arist.*HA*602^{a}2, 618^{b}7; τῶν ὄψεων Porph.*Abst.*1.17: metaph., χρήμασι πολλοῖς ὑπό τινων J.*AJ*20.6.1. 2. metaph., *cut out the bud* of a tree, Plu.2.529b. 3. *make* a spring *fail*, ib.703b:—Pass., *to be obstructed*, ἀποτυφλωθῆναι τοὺς πόρους Arist.*Pr.*879^{b}7; τὰς πηγάς Str. 1.3.16; τὸν μαστόν Antig.*Mir.*45; τὰ ἀγγεῖα Aët.16.26. **-ωσις**, εως, ἡ, *making blind*, Lxx *Za.*12.4: metaph. of the veins, *blocking*, Herod.Med. in *Rh.Mus.*49.555.

ἀποτύφω [ῡ], *burn*, in pf. part. Pass. ἀποτεθυμμένος, Hsch.

ἀποτῠχ-ής, ές, *missing*, Pl.*Sis.*391c (Comp.). **-ία**, Ion. -ίη, ἡ, *failure*, Democr.243, Din.1.29 (as v.l.), Plb.5.98.5, Phld.*Rh.*1. 73 S., J.*AJ*16.9.1, etc.: c. gen., *failure to obtain*, στεφάνου, ὕδατος, Artem.5.78. **-ίζω**, (τύχος, = τύκος) = ἀποπελεκάω, Paus.Gr.*Fr.* 62:—Pass., Hsch.

ἀπουλ-όω, *cicatrize*, ἕλκη Dsc.5.79: metaph., τὴν ἀβελτερίαν Plu. 2.46f:—Pass., of sores, ἀπουλωθῆναι Arr.*Epict.*2.21.22, cf. Alex. Aphr.*Pr.*1.114; ἀπουλωθήσεται Gal.13.719. **-ωσις**, εως, ἡ, *cicatrization*, v.l. in Dsc.2.4, cf. Crito ap.Gal.12.448, Aret.*CD*2.3, Alex. Aphr.*Pr.*1.111. **-ωτικός**, ή, όν, *causing to scar over, healing*, Dsc. 2.4: c. gen., ἑλκῶν Id.5.84, cf. Gal.4.770. **-ωτος**, ον, *free from scar*, prob. in Plu.2.1091e (for ἀπουλώτιστος: ἀμωλώπιστος Bern.).

ἀπουρᾱγέω, *cover the rear*, τινί Plb.3.49.13, al.

ἀπουρίσαι, = ἀφορίσαι, Eust.1774.36.

ἀπούρας, Homeric aor. part. Act., cf. ἀπούραις Pi.*P.*4.149: aor. ind. ἀπηύρων, ας, α, Hom.; pl. ἀπηύρων Il.1.430: aor. part. Med. ἀπουράμενος Hes.*Sc.*173: fut. ἀπουρήσω Il.22.489 (Sch.Ven.B):—*take away* or *wrest from, rob of*, c. dupl. acc. pers. et rei, ἄμφω θυμὸν ἀπηύρα 6.17; ἁπαλόν τέ σφ' ἦτορ ἀπηύρα 11.115; τοὺς μὲν Τυδεΐδης.. τεύχε' ἀπηύρα ib.334; λάθον δέ ἑ θυμὸν ἀπούρας Od.13.270, etc. 2. c. gen. pers., a doubtful construction in Ἀχιλλῆος γέρας αὐτὸς ἀπηύρων Il.19.89; κούρην..Ἀχιλῆος ἔβης κλισίηθεν ἀπούρας 9.107, cf. Od.18. 273; τήν ῥα βίῃ ἀέκοντος ἀπηύρων Il.1.430 (where β. ἀ. may be taken together, 'in spite of him unwilling', cf. ἥ σε βίῃ ἀέκοντος ἀπηύρα νῆα Od.4.646). 3. c. dat. pers., πολέεσσιν.. θυμὸν ἀπηύρα Il.17. 236; οἱ οὔ τιν' ἀπηύρα Od.3.192. 4. c. acc. only, ἔχει γέρας αὐτὸς ἀπούρας Il.1.356; ἐλεύθερον ἦμαρ ἀ. 6.455, etc.:—Med., ἀπουράμενοι ψυχάς *having taken away each other's* lives, Hes.*Sc.*173. II. after Hom., *receive* good or ill, *enjoy* or *suffer*, first in Hes.*Op.*240 ξύμπασα πόλις κακοῦ ἀνδρὸς ἀπηύρα (v.l. ἐπαυρεῖ); φόνον πρὸς τέκνων ἀπηύρα E.*Andr.*1030 (lyr.). (ἀπο-ϝρᾱ-, augmented ἀπ-η-ϝρᾱ- (cf. ηἑίδη, ἑώρων for ἠϝόρων); perh. cogn. with ἀπό-(ϝ)ερσε.)

ἄπουργοι γωνίαι corners *used to shoot rubbish*, Suid., *AB*434.

ἀπουρ-έω, *pass urine*, Aret.*SD*2.2, Luc.*VH*1.23, etc.: c. acc., *pass in urine*, αἷμα Ruf.*Ren.Ves.*3.10; πηλόν Gal.13.330. **-ημα**, ατος, τό, *urine passed*, Anon.Lond.30.32. **-ησις**, εως, ἡ, *making water*, ib.30.6, Sor.1.66, Ruf.ap.Aët.11.29, Aret.*SD*2.3.

ἀπουρία, ἡ, *issue of free and slave*, Suid., Zonar.

ἀπουρ-ίζω, (οὖρος = ὅρος) only in Il.22.489 ἄλλοι γάρ οἱ ἀπουρίσσουσιν (Ion. for ἀφοριοῦνται, Sch.Ven.A) ἀρούρας others *will mark off the boundaries of* his fields, i.e. *take* them *away from* him; better ἀπουρήσουσι *will take away*; cf. ἀπούρας. II. v.l. for ἐπουρίζω, Ph.1. 668. **-ικτικῶς**· ἀφελομένως, Hsch.

ἄπουρος, ον, (οὖρος = ὅρος) *far from the boundaries*, ἄ. πάτρας v.l. in S.*OT*194 (lyr.).

ἀπουρόω, (οὖρος A) *to be driven by foul winds*, Plb.16.15.4.

ἄπους, ὁ, ἡ, πουν, τό, gen. οδος, *without foot* or *feet*, Pl.*Phdr.*264c, Arist.*HA*487^{a}23, Corn.*ND*16, etc. 2. *without the use of one's feet, lame*, S.*Ph.*632; *bad of foot*, κύνες X.*Cyn.*3.3; κακόποδες οἱ διὰ τοῦτο καλοῦνται ἄποδες Arist.*HA*487^{b}24, cf. *Metaph.*1022^{b}35, *de An.* 422^{a}29. II. as Subst., = κύψελος, *sand-martin, Hirundo riparia*; possibly also, *the swift, Cypselus apus*, Id.*HA*618^{a}31.

ἀπουσία, ἡ, (ἄπειμι) *absence*, A.*Ag.*1259, E.*Hec.*962, Th.1.70, *Ep. Phil.*2.12, etc. II. *waste*, as in smelting ore, Arist.*Mete.*383^{b}3, Agatharch.28; τρῖψις καὶ ἀ. *POxy.*1273.32 (iii A.D.). III. = ἀποσπερματισμός, Plu.2.364d.

ἀπουσιάζω, *waste one's goods*, Suid.; εἴς τινα Artem.1.78: c. gen., *lose substance*, σωμάτων Zos.Alch.p.235 B.:—Pass., *to be expended*, εἰς τροφήν Sor.1.87.

ἀποφᾰγεῖν, aor. 2 inf. of ἀπεσθίω, *eat off, eat up*, Ar.*Eq.*497: later fut. ἀποφάγονται *POxy.*465.74.

ἀποφαιδρύνω, *cleanse off*, Q.S.5.616, 8.487:—Med., *bathe*, λουτροῖς *AP*9.419 (Crin.).

ἀποφαίνω, *show forth, display*, Sol.15.33, etc.; ἀ. τινὶ ἐς ὄψιν Hdt. 4.81; ἀ. τὴν φύσιν αὐτοῦ Ar.*Nu.*352; τινά S.*Fr.*1023, cf. 74 (Pass.); ἀ. παῖδας ἐκ γυναικός, i.e. *have* children by her, Is.6.22; of the woman, *produce*, ἔφεδρον βασιλέα.. ἀ. Hdt.5.41; also of the descendants, ἑπτὰ πάππους πλουσίους ἀ. *produce* seven generations of wealthy ancestors, Pl.*Tht.*174e. II. *make known, declare*, ὡς εἰπὼν ἀπέφηνε Batr.144; γνώμην ἀ. περί τινος Hdt.1.40; δικαίην ζόην ἀ. *give evidence of* a legitimate mode of living, Id.2.177; cf. B. II. 2. *show by reasoning, prove*, c. part., τοὺς μὲν ἀ. πεφευγότας Id.1.82; ἀπέφαινε τῷ λόγῳ μιν σκαιότατον ἐόντα ib.129; πόλλ' ἂν ἀποφήναιμ' ἐκείνους.. ἀδικουμένους Ar.*Ach.*314; ἀποφαίνω ὑμᾶς κυριωτάτους ὄντας Th.2.62; ἀ. ἀγαθῶν.. οὖσαν αἰτίαν ἐμέ Ar.*Pl.*547, cf. Isoc.4.139, Plb.1.15.7; with part. omitted, ἀ. τινὰ ἔνοχον Antipho 4.2.3, cf. And.1.41; ἀ. τινὰ ἐχθρόν Philipp.ap.D.12.8. b. *represent, proclaim*, ἀ. σεαυτὸν ἀρετῆς διδάσκαλον Pl.*Prt.*349a; σοφὸν ἀ. τὸν Ἡσίοδον Id.*Lg.*718e; ἀντὶ φιλοσόφων μισοῦντάς τι ἀ. τινάς Id.*Tht.*168b; ἀ. ἡδονὴν τῶν φαύλων (sc. οὖσαν) Arist.*EN*1172^{a}30, cf. *Rh.Al.*1438^{b}19, etc. 3. c. acc. et inf., *make plain that*.., Pl.*R.*338e, al.; *show*, ἀ. λόγῳ ὡς.. Hdt.5.84; ἀ. ὡς.., ὅτι.., Th.3.63, Pl.*Phd.*95c, etc. 4. *denounce, inform against*, Antipho 6.9, Lys.31.2; πρίν γ' ἂν τοῦτον ἀποφήνω.. οἷος ὢν θρασύνεται Ar.*Ra.*845; ὃν ἡ ἐξ Ἀρείου πάγου βουλὴ ἀποπέφαγκεν χρήματ' ἔχειν Din.1.15:—Pass., ἀποπέφανται μισθαρνῶν ibid. III. *give an account of*, τὴν πρόσοδον, τὴν οὐσίαν, D.27.47, 42.11: esp. *pay in money* (to the treasury) *according to accounts delivered*, of public officers, Id.20. 77, 80: generally, of private persons, ἕνδεκα μνᾶς τοῦ ἐνιαυτοῦ ἀπέφηνεν Id.27.19; ἅπαντα ἐς τὸ κοινὸν ἀ. X.*Oec.*7.13. IV. *render, make* so and so, Ἀθηναίους μικροπολίτας ἀ. Ar.*Eq.*817, cf. X.*Eq.*1.11, 10.5, Luc.*Somn.*8. 2. *declare elected*, τινὰς ἄρχοντας Pl.*Lg.*753d; τοὺς πεντακισχιλίους Th.8.93:—in Med., ἀποφήνασθαί τινα ταμίαν v.l. in Pi.*N.*6.25 (cf. B. III):—Pass., ἀποφαίνεσθαι εὐδοκίμου στρατιᾶς *to be named* (chief) of a glorious army, A.*Pers.*858 codd.

B. Med., *display something of one's own*, Μοῦσαν στυγεράν A.*Eu.* 309; καλὰ ἔργα Pl.*Smp.*209e: abs., *make a display of oneself, show off*, X.*Cyr.*8.8.13. 2. ἀ. μαρτύρια *produce* evidence, Hdt.5.45; ἀ. νόμους *set forth, propound*, Pl.*Lg.*780a. II. ἀποφαίνεσθαι γνώμην *declare one's* opinion, Hdt.1.207, 2.120, al., E.*Supp.*335, Pl.*Grg.*466c, D.4.1; ἀ. δόξαν Pl.*R.*576e; δόξαν περί τινος Id.*Tht.*170d. 2. abs., *give an opinion*, ταύτῃ ἀ. Hdt.7.143; ἀ. περί τινος Pl.*Ly.*214a: c. inf., ἀ. κινεῖσθαι τὰ πάντα Id.*Tht.*168b:—Pass., καθόλου ἀ. ἐπί τινος Arist. *Int.*17^{b}3. 3. *give a decision* or *award*, ὁ κριτὴς ἀ. Pl.*R.*580b; ἀ. περί τινος Id.*Phdr.*274e; ἀ. δίαιταν, of an arbitrator, D.33.19, 20:—Pass., τῆς διαίτης -φαινομένης Id.54.27. III. Med. used like the Act., Pi.*N.* l.c. supr.; ἀ. λογισμόν X.*Mem.*4.2.21: c. inf., *advise*, τὸν ..ὑπακούειν ἀποφηνάμενον D.18.204. IV. *define*, ἀ. τἀγαθὸν οὗ πάντες ἐφίενται Arist.*EN*1094^{a}2.

C. Pass., *disappear, shade off*, θάλασσα κατὰ μικρὸν εἰς πέλαγος ἀποφαινομένη *Peripl.M.Rubr.*26.

ἀποφᾰλακρόομαι, Pass., *become bald*, Phryn.*PS* p.26 B.

ἀπόφαν-σις, εως, ἡ, (ἀποφαίνω) *declaration, statement*, Arist.*APo.* 72^{a}11, *Rh.*1395^{b}6 (as v.l.); δι' ἀποφάνσεων περαίνειν τὸ πᾶν Hermog. *Id.*2.11. II. in Logic, *predication*, κατά τινος or ἀπό τινος, *affirmative* or *negative*, Arist.*Int.*17^{a}25, cf. Chrysipp.*Stoic.*2.59. **-τέον**, *one must pronounce*, Ph.2.461, Aristid.Quint.1.28, Plot.2.1.8. **-τικός**, ή, όν, *categorical*, λόγος ἀ. Arist.*Int.*17^{a}8, cf. *Stoic.*2.61, al.; *declaratory*, ἐπιστήμη πάντων ἀληθῶν -κή ib.2.42. Adv. -κῶς dub. in Aristid. *Rh.*1 p.462 S., cf. Sch.E.*Ph.*624, al.; λέγειν Hermog.*Id.*2.11. **-τος**, ον, *declared, asserted*, λεκτὸν αὐτοτελὲς ἀ. Chrysipp.*Stoic.*2.62; σχῆμα διηγήματος Hermog.*Prog.*2; χρεῖαι ib.3.

ἀποφάργνῡμι, v. ἀποφράγνυμι. **ἀπόφαρσις**· ἡ ἑταίρα, Hsch.

ἀπόφᾰσις (A), εως, ἡ, (ἀπόφημι) *denial, negation*, opp. κατάφασις, Pl.*Sph.*263e; ἀ. ἐστιν ἀπόφανσίς τινος ἀπό τινος *a predication* of one thing *away from* another, i.e. *negation* of it, Arist.*Int.*17^{a}25, cf. *APo.* 72^{a}14; ἀ. τινός *negation, exclusion* of a thing, Pl.*Cra.*426d; δύο ἀ.

μίαν κατάφασιν ἀποτελοῦσι Luc.*Gall.*11. II. *negative particle*, e.g. οὐ, A.D.*Adv.*124.8, al.; *sign of negation*, *Stoic.*2.52 (pl.).

ἀπόφᾰσις (B), εως, ἡ, (ἀποφαίνω) = ἀπόφανσις, *sentence, decision*, of an arbitrator's *award*, διαίτης D.47.45, cf. 33.21; κατά τινος, of an Amphictyonic decree, D.S.16.24; ἀ. ἔγγραφος *OGI*335.72 (Pergam.); of an emperor, *PTeb.*286.11 (ii A.D., pl.). 2. *catalogue, inventory*, ἀ. δοῦναι D.42.1,14. 3. = ἀπόφανσις, *assertion, judgement*, Arist.*Rh.* 1365b27, Epicur.*Ep.*3p.60U., Phld.*Ir.*p.75W., Plb.1.14.8 (pl.), al.; περί τινος Plu.*Comp.Sol.Publ.*1, cf. Str.2.1.19; καταληπτικὴ ἀ. S.E. *P.*2.123. b. *answer*, Plb.22.13.7; πρὸς τὰ κατηγορούμενα Id.24.2.5. 4. *oracle*, Jul.*Ep.*89. 5. = φάσμα, *appearance, image*, sc. τοῦ ἡλίου, Diog.Oen.8.

ἀποφάσκω, = ἀπόφημι, only in pres. inf. and part., and impf.:—*deny*, Plu.2.393c; τί τινος Simp.*in Ph.*218.11:—Pass., Dam.*Pr.*445; in S.*OT*485 οὔτε δοκοῦντ' οὔτ' ἀποφάσκονθ' is interpreted by Sch. οὔτε πιστὰ οὔτε ἄπιστα 'neither commanding assent nor *suffering denial*' (but better referred to ἐμέ understood, 'neither assenting nor *denying*'):—ὁ ἀποφάσκων [λόγος], name of a sophism, Arr.*Epict.*3.9.21; title of work by Chrysippus, *Stoic.*2.8.

ἀποφᾰτικός, ή, όν, (ἀπόφημι) *negative*, opp. καταφατικός, λόγος Arist.*Cat.*12b8, cf. Chrysipp.*Stoic.*2.55,69; ἐπίρρημα A.D.*Synt.*245.24. Adv. -κῶς Arist.*APr.*64a14; also written for ἀποφαντικῶς, A.D. *Pron.*27.16. II. *conclusive*, *PLond.*5.1902v (vi A.D.).

ἀποφαυλίζω, = ἀποφλαυρίζω, Lib.*Decl.*48.68, *EM*789.51.

ἀποφεῖν· ἀπατῆσαι, Hsch. (fort. ἀπαφεῖν, sed cf. ἀποφώλιος).

ἀποφενᾱκίζω, *delude, mock*, Men.Prot.p.90D.

ἀποφέρβομαι, *feed on*, σοφίαν dub.l. in E.*Med.*826 (lyr.).

ἀποφέρω, Hom. only in fut. -οίσω (Dor. -οισῶ Ar.*Ach.*779, Med. -οίσομαι Theoc.1.3, Luc.*Bis Acc.*33) and Ion. aor. ἀπένεικα: Att. aor. -ήνεγκα Th.5.10: aor. 2 -ήνεγκον Ar.*Ach.*582, etc.: pf. -ενήνοχα D.27.20:—*carry off* or *away*, τεύχεα δέ σφ' ἀπένεικαν Od.16.360, etc.; of a wind, Il.14.255, Hdt.4.179: metaph., Plu.2.374e; of a disease, Hdt.3.66, 6.27; generally, ἀ. σῆμα S.*Tr.*614; βρέφος ἐς ἄντρον E.*Ion*16, cf. *Ev.Marc.*15.1, etc.:—Pass., *to be carried from one's course*, ὑπ' ἀνέμων Hdt.2.114, cf. 116; ἀπενεχθέντες ἐς Λιβύην Th.7.50, cf. 6.104. 2. *exhale, evaporate*, Anon.Lond.22.25:—Pass., *to be wafted*, Plu.2.681a. II. *carry* or *bring back*, αὖτις ἀποίσετον ὠκέες ἵπποι Il.5.257; ἂψ Ἕκτορι μῦθον ἀποίσειν 10.337; ἀ. οἴκαδις Ar.*Ach.*779;—so in Pass., of oracles, ταῦτα ἀπενειχθέντα Hdt.1.66,158,160: but in Pass., also of persons, *return*, Id.4.164, Th., etc.; ἀπηνέχθη εἰς.. ἔτι ζῶν *was carried home*, of a sick man, X.*HG*3.3.1; τεθνεὼς ἐκ δεσμωτηρίου ἀ. Lys.12.18. 2. *pay back, return*, Hdt.1.196, etc.: hence, *pay what is due* as tribute, etc., Id.4.35, 5.84, Th.5.31. 3. *bring in, return*, of slaves let out to labour for their master's profit, v.l. Aeschin.1.97, cf. Philostr.*Her.*2. 4. generally, *bring, hand over as required*, τί τινι Hdt.4.64; ὅπλα X.*Cyr.*7.5.34; εἰς τὰ δημόσια ἀ. ἱερὰ τὰ ἴδια Pl.*Lg.*910c. III. *hand in* an accusation, *render* accounts, returns, etc., ἀ. παρανόμων (sc. γραφήν) πρὸς τὸν ἄρχοντα Docum.ap.D.18.54, cf. 52.30; ἀπήνεγκε παρανόμων (sc. γραφήν) Δημοσθένει Decr.ap.D.18.105; λόγον.. ἀπενήνοχεν ἀναλωμάτων D.27.20; λόγον πρὸς τοὺς λογιστάς, λόγον τῇ πόλει, Aeschin.3.22; ἀ. τοὺς ἱππεύσαντας *hand in a list of..*, Lys.16.6; ναύτας D.50.6; ἀ. ἐν τῷ λόγῳ δεδωκώς *having entered in* the account, Id.49.16:—Pass., *to be returned as* so and so, ἀπηνέχθη ἀνώμοτος Id.21.86; διαιτητὴς ἀπενηνεγμένος Id.52.30. 2. *deliver* a letter, Id.34.8. IV. *bring home, receive as wages*, Luc.*Tim.*12 (which others refer to signf. II. 2).

B. Med., *take away with one*, Hdt.1.132, Isoc.6.74, etc.; *carry off* a prize, μετὰ Πᾶνα τὸ δεύτερον ἆθλον ἀποισῇ Theoc. l.c.; κάλλευς πρῶτ' ἀπενεγκαμέναν *APl.*4.166 (Even.); ἀ. δόξαν Hdn.1.5.7; *carry home* delicacies from a banquet, Luc.*Symp.*38 (less freq. in Act., Id. *Nigr.*25). 2. *take for oneself, gain, obtain*, λέχη ἀλλότρια E.*El.* 1089 codd.; *receive to oneself*, μόρον Id.*Ph.*595. 3. *obtain* a decision, *win* a lawsuit, δίκην κενὴν θελόντων ἀ. *Inscr.Prien.*111.150 (i B.C.). II. *bring back for oneself*, ὀπίσω Hdt.7.152; ἀ. σημεῖα τοῦ θυμῷ μάχεσθαι X.*Ages.*6.2; ἀ. βίον μητρί, i.e. *return to* her alive, E. *Ph.*1161; νόστον Id.*IA*298 (lyr.).

C. Intr. in Act., *be off*, ἀπόφερ' ἐς κόρακας Ar.*Pax*1221.

ἀπο-φεύγω, fut. -φεύξομαι Pl.*Ap.*39a; -οῦμαι Ar.*Av.*932: pf. -πέφευγα X.*An.*3.4.9, etc.:—*flee from, escape*, c. acc., Batr.42,47; σοφίην ὁ σοφώτατος οὐκ ἀποφεύγει Thgn.1159; τὴν πεπρωμένην μοῖραν Hdt.1.91; τὴν μάχην Id.5.102; κῆρα S.*Ph.*1166 (lyr.), cf. Pl.*Ap.*39a; νόσον D.28.15; ἀ. ἐκ τῶν πλησίον κωμῶν X.*An.*3.4.9; ἐς Νίσαιαν Th.1.114: rarely c. gen., ἀ. τῆς φθορᾶς *2Ep.Pet.*1.4: c. inf., *avoid*, λέγειν Phlp. *in Ph.*617.14: abs., *get safe away, escape*, Hdt.1.1, 9.102, etc.; *go free*, of manumitted slaves, *IG*2.786, al. II. as law-term, ἀ. πολλὸν τοὺς διώκοντας Hdt.6.82; τινά And.1.123; φεύγων ἂν ἀποφύγοι δίκην Ar.*Nu.*167, cf. 1151; γραφάς Antipho 2.1.16; εὐθύνας Pl.*Lg.*946d: c. dupl. acc. pers. et rei, ἀπέφυγον αὐτοὺς τὰς δίκας ἅς μοι ἐνεκάλουν D.40.19. 2. abs., *get clear off, be acquitted*, opp. ἁλίσκομαι, Hdt.2.174, Pl.*Ap.*35c, D.18.103; κἂν.. εἰσέλθῃ φεύγων οὐκ ἀποφεύγει Ar.*V.*579. 3. of a woman in child-birth, *bring to birth*, ἀ. τὸ παιδίον ἐν τῷ τόκῳ Hp.*Mul.*1.25; also ἀ. τοῦ παιδίου ib.33: intr., ἢν τὰ ὕστερα μὴ δύνηται ἀποφυγεῖν Id.*Nat.Mul.*56. **-φευκτικός**, ή, όν, *useful in escaping*, τὰ ἀ. *means of acquittal*, X.*Ap.*8. **-φευξις** or **-φυξις** (cod. Rav. in Ar.*V.*558,562,645 and *Nu.*874, cf. D.Chr.1.41), εως, ἡ, *escaping, means of getting off*, ἀ. δίκης *acquittal*, Ar.*Nu.* l.c., al., cf. Antipho 5.66.

ἀποφηλικίζω· ἀποπλανάω, *AB*439, Suid.

ἀπόφημι, fut. -φήσω: aor. 1 ἀπέφησα Pl.*Tht.*166a, al.:—*speak out, declare flatly* or *plainly*, ἀντικρὺ δ' ἀπόφημι γυναῖκα μὲν οὐκ ἀποδώσω κτλ. Il.7.362:—Med., ἀγγελίην ἀπόφασθε 9.422.—In this sense only Ep. II. *say no*, S.*OC*317, etc. 2. c. acc., *deny*, οὔτε σὺ φῂς ἃ ἐρωτῶ οὔτε ἀπόφῃς Pl.*Prt.*360d, cf. X.*Cyr.*6.1.32, Arist.*APo.*71a14, al.; opp. κατάφημι, Id.*Int.*17a31, al.; ἀ. τι κατά τινος, opp. καταφάναι, Id.*Metaph.*1007b22; *negative*, τι Id.*Rh.*1412b10, *Po.*1457b31; μὴ γεγονέναι Plu.*Alc.*23.

ἀπόφημος, ον, = δύσφημος, Ael.*NA*6.44.

ἀποφθαλμόομαι, *look askance at*: hence, *covet, envy*, *PLond.*1674.17 (vi A.D.).

ἀποφθαναῖνον· ἀποθνήσκοντα, Hsch.

ἀποφθαράξασθαι, *snort*, Hsch.

ἀπόφθαρμα, ατος, τό, *abortion*, Hp.*Epid.*2.2.13, 5.53.

ἀπο-φθέγγομαι, *speak one's opinion plainly*, Luc.*Zeux.*1; *utter an apophthegm*, Plu.2.405e, Iamb.*VP*11.55; χρησμόν Luc.*Alex.*25, cf. D.S.16.27, Vett.Val.73.24: metaph. of vessels when struck, *ring*, σαπρὸν ἀ. Luc.*Par.*4. II. *chant hymns*, Lxx *1Chr.*25.1. **-φθεγκτήριον**, τό, *an utterance*, Man.4.550. **-φθεγκτος**, ον, = ἄφθεγκτος, E.*IT*951. **-φθεγμα**, ατος, τό, *terse pointed saying, apophthegm*, of Theramenes, X.*HG*2.3.56; of Anaxagoras, Arist.*Metaph.*1009b26; of Pittacus, Id.*Rh.*1389a16; of the Spartans, ib.1394b34: in pl., title of work by Plu. **-φθεγματίας**, ου, ὁ, *dealer in saws and proverbs*, Metrod.45. **-φθεγματικός**, ή, όν, *dealing in apophthegms, sententious*, Plu.*Lyc.*19, *Brut.*2, Demetr.*Eloc.*9; θορύβους ἐνθυμηματικοὺς καὶ -κούς, i.e. bare assertions, Epicur.*Nat.*14.9. Adv. -κῶς Eust.1870.46.

ἀποφθείρω, fut. -φθερῶ, *destroy utterly, ruin*, A.*Ch.*256; δέμας ἀσιτίαις E.*Supp.*1106. 2. *have an abortion, miscarry*, Hp.*Epid.*1.16. II. Pass., with fut. Med., *to be lost, perish*, E.*Tr.*508, v.l. in Th.2.49. 2. *to be gone, make off*, ἀποφθαρεὶς ἐκ τῆς πόλεως Men. *Sam.*282, cf. Alciphr.*Fr.*6.3: freq. in imprecations, οὐ γῆς τῆσδ' ἀποφθαρήσεται; i.e. *let him begone with a plague* to him, E.*HF*1290; οὐκ εἰς κόρακας ἀποφθερεῖ; Ar.*Eq.*892, *Nu.*789; ἀποφθείρου ταχύ Men. *Sam.*158; ἀποφθάρηθι Lib.*Decl.*33.28.

ἀπο-φθῐνύθω [ῠ], poet. Verb, *perish*, ἀποφθινύθουσι δὲ λαοί Il.5.643, Hes.*Op.*243, cf. A.R.1.683. II. causal, *make to perish*, θυμὸν ἀποφθινύθουσι *lose* their life, Il.16.540. 2. *diminish*, τὰ μὲν αὔξεις τὰ δ' ἀ. E.*Fr.*916. **-φθίνω** [ῐ], I. intr. in pres., *perish utterly, die away*, A.*Ag.*857; ἀποφθίνει τὰ χρηστὰ S.*Ph.*457: also in pf. ἀπέφθῐκα Them.*Or.*28.341d: but mostly, II. causal, in fut. -φθίσω, aor. ἀπέφθισα [ῑ Ep., ῐ Trag.]:—*make to perish, waste away, destroy*, ἄνδρας ἀποφθίσειε θάλασσα Hes.*Op.*666; πρὸς γυναικὸς δ' ἀπέφθισεν βίον *had* his life *taken* by a woman's hand, A.*Ag.*1454 (lyr.); ἔμελλέ σ' Ἕκτωρ καὶ θανὼν ἀποφθίσαι S.*Aj.*1027; τὸν βαλόντ' ἀποφθίσαι χρῄζων Id.*Tr.*709; of disease, *cause death, be fatal*, Hp.*Aër.*11. 2. most freq. in Pass., = Act. intr., *perish, die*, esp. in aor. with plpf. form ἀπέφθιτο [ῐ] Od.15.268; imper. ἀποφθίσθω Il.8.429; opt. ἀποφθίμην [ῑ] Od.10.51; Ep. and Lyr. part. ἀποφθίμενος [ῐ] *dead*, Il.3.322, al., Ibyc.27, B.8.79 (not in Trag.): also in Ep. aor. 3 pl. ἀπέφθιθεν Od.5.110,133, 7.251 (v.l. ἀπέφθιθον). 3. Med., aor. 1 -φθίσασθαι [ῑ] Q.S.14.545. **-φθῐσις**, εως, ἡ, *waning* of the moon, Sch. Arat.799.

ἀποφθορά, ἡ, (ἀποφθείρω) = φθορά, σπέρματος A.*Eu.*187; esp. *abortion, miscarriage*, Hp.*Epid.*3.1.ι', ια'.

ἀποφῑμόω, *muzzle completely*, *AB*421.

ἀποφλάσαι· ῥογχάσαι (Cret., Sam.), Hsch.

ἀποφλαυρίζω, *treat slightingly, make no account of, disparage*, τι Pi.*P.*3.12, Hdt.1.86.

ἀποφλεγμαίνω, *cease to burn*, of inflammation, Hp.*Aph.*6.49: metaph. of anger, Plu.2.13d.

ἀποφλεγμᾰτ-ίζω, *purge away phlegm* or *cleanse from it*, Dsc.2.159, Antyll.ap.Orib.8.10.2; *promote the discharge of phlegm* or *mucus*, Gal.11.769, etc. **-ικός**, ή, όν, *promoting such discharge*, ibid. **-ισμός**, ὁ, *purging of phlegm*, Dsc.5.3, Antyll.ap.Orib.8.10 tit., Archig.ap. Gal.12.582. **-ιστέον**, *one must promote the discharge of phlegm*, Id.12.650.

ἀπόφλησις, εως, ἡ, *discharge of a debt*, Anon. *in Rh.*206.3.

ἀποφλογίζω, *burn up*, Hsch. s.v. εὔστρα (Pass.).

ἀποφλογόομαι, Pass., *grow fiery*, ἀ. τὰ ὄμματα Max.Tyr.24.8.

ἀποφλοιόω, (φλοιός) *peel, strip off*, καλύπτρην Nonn.*D.*14.380:—Med., λέοντος δέρμα *AP*6.263 (Leon.):—also **-φλοιάω**, *peel*, κύπερον Aët.1.129.

ἀποφλύζω, *give vent to, sputter out*, ὄφρ' ἀλεγεινὴν ὕβριν ἀποφλύξωσιν A.R.3.583: aor. ἀπέφλυσαν Archil.35 (-φλοσαν codd. Phot.):—Hsch. has **ἀποφλύειν**· ἀπερεύγεσθαι.

ἀπόφλω, *owe*, Tz.*H.*13.613.

ἀποφοβέομαι, *to be scared away*, Sch.Opp.*H.*3.510.

ἀποφοιβάζω, *utter by inspiration*, ποιήματα ὥσπερ ἀ. Str.14.5.15; *foretell*, τὰ μέλλοντα D.S.34.2; τὸν λόγον Id 31.10; ταῦτα περὶ τοῦ μέλλοντος ἀποπεφοίβακεν Plb.29.21.7.

ἀποφοιβάομαι, = foreg., *PMag.Par.*1.738.

ἀποφοιτ-άω, fut. -ήσομαι Thom.Mag.p.7R.:—*cease to attend* a master, ἀ. παρά τινος, of scholars, Pl.*Grg.*489d; ἀ. πρός τινα *go away to a new master*, Din.*Fr.*6.13: abs., *cease to go to school*, Lys.*Fr.*116; also ἀ. τῶν ἐκκλησιῶν Philostr.*VS*1.17.2, cf. *VA*7.25, Hld.3.13. 2. *desert, abscond*, πρός τινα Plu.*Lys.*4, cf. Aristid.*Or.*21(22).15; of ships in battle, Procop.*Goth.*4.23; simply, *depart*, Dionys.*Av.*1.11. **-ησις**· χωρισμός, ἀναχώρησις, Hsch.

ἀπόφονος, ον, φόνος, αἷμα ἀ., *unnatural* murder, E.*Or.*163, 192 (both lyr.).

ἀποφορ-ά, ἡ, (ἀποφέρω) *payment of what is due, tax, tribute*, Hdt. 2.109, Plu.*Thes.*23, etc.: esp. *money* which slaves let out to hire *paid* to their master, ἀποφορὰς πράττειν X.*Ath.*1.11; ἀ. κομίσασθαι And.1.38; φέρειν Aeschin.1.97, Men.431; ἀποδόντες Id.*Epit.*163: generally, *return, profit, rent*, ἀποφορὰν φέρειν Arist.*Pol.*1264^{a}33; ἀποφέρειν Plu.2.239e; ἀ. βαλανείου *BGU*362 ix 2 (iii A.D.); *contribution, war-tax*, ἀ. τελεῖν Plu.*Arist.*24. II. *effluvia*, D.H.10.53, D.S.24.12, Plu.2.647f, Aret.*SA*1.10; ἡ ἀ. τοῦ πυρός Sch.Il.*Oxy.*221 xvii 8. 2. *absorption* of περίττωμα, Anon.Lond.*Fr.*1.6. III. in Logic, = στέρησις, *privation*, Arist.*Metaph.*1046^{b}15, cf. Alex.Aphr. ad loc. IV. *right to carry away* portions of sacrifice, *SIG*1025. 46, al., 1026.4 (Cos, iv/iii B.C.). **-έω**, *carry away*, χοῦν *SIG*^{2}587.45 (dub.). **-ησις**, εως, ἡ, = ἀποφορά II, S.E.*P.*1.126. **-ητος**, ον, *carried away*; τὰ ἀ. *presents which guests received* at table *to take home*, Ath.6.229c, cf. Petron.56, Suet.*Calig.*55, *Vesp.*19. **-ος**, ον, *not to be borne* or *suffered*, μίασμα Phalar.*Ep.*141 (ἀπότροπον Ruhnk.). 2. *past bearing*, δένδρα Hsch.; cf. ἀποφόρος· ἀσθενέστερος, Id.

ἀποφορτ-ίζομαι, Med., *discharge one's cargo*, τὸν γόμον *Act.Ap.*21. 3; *jettison*, abs., Ph.2.413; τῇ θαλάσσῃ τὰ περιττὰ τῶν φορτίων Timae. 61; *unload one's stomach*, Artem.2.26:—Pass., of περιττώματα, Sor. 1.40: generally, *jettison, get rid of*, τι Ph.2.434, etc. **-ισμός**, ὁ, *unloading*: hence of *vomiting*, Archig.ap.Orib.8.23.1.

ἀποφράγνῡμι (better -φάργ-), *fence off, block*, τὰς ὁδοὺς ἀπεφάργνυσαν Th.7.74: metaph., ἀποφάργνυσαι κύκλῳ τὸ πρᾶγμα S.*Ant.*241.

ἀποφράζω, *explain*, Dam.*Pr.*111 (Pass.).

ἀπόφραξις, εως, ἡ, *blocking up*, τῆς ὁδοῦ X.*An.*4.2.25: pl., πόρων Ph.2.432.

ἀποφράς, άδος, ἡ, (φράζω) *not to be mentioned, unlucky*; ἀ. ἡμέραι, opp. καθαραὶ ἡμ., Pl.*Lg.*800d, cf. Lys.*Fr.*53.2, Plu.*Alc.*34, Luc.*Pseudol.* 12; ἀ. πύλαι at Rome, = *portae nefastae*, Plu.2.518b. II. rarely as masc. Adj., *impious, wicked*, ἄνθρωπος Eup.309; βίος Luc.*Pseudol.*32.

ἀποφράση, ἡ, Cretan word for δούλη, Seleuc.ap.Ath.6.267c:—Eust.1090.57 writes -φράτη.

ἀποφράσσω, Att. -ττω, fut. -ξω, = ἀποφράγνυμι, *block up, stop up*, Hp.*Carn.*18, *Mul.*1.1; τὰς διεξόδους Pl.*Ti.*91c; ἀ. καὶ παροικοδομεῖν D.55.17; τὰς φυγάς Onos.32:—Med., ἀποφάρξασθαι αὐτοὺς *bar* their *passage*, Th.8.104.

ἀποφρέω, aor. -έφρησα, = ἐκφρέω, Cratin.78.

ἀπόφρικτος, ον, (φρίσσω) *shivering*, Aret.*SD*1.12.

ἀποφρύγω [ῡ], *dry up*, ὑφ' ἡδονῆς ἀπεφρύγοντο Eun.ap.Suid. s.v. ἀπεφρύγοντο. II. aor. 2 Pass. -φρῠγῆναι *cool down*, Maria ap. Zos.Alch.p.238 B.

ἀποφυάς, άδος, ἡ, = ἀπόφυσις, *appendage*, τῶν ἐντέρων, of the *caeca* of birds and fishes, Arist.*HA*507^{b}33, 509^{a}17. 2. *outgrowth*, Thphr. *HP*7.2.5. 3. *branch* of a blood-vessel, Hp.*Oss.*11, Arist.*PA*667^b 17. 4. *one of the spines* on the tail of the martichoras, Id.*HA*501^{a}31.

ἀποφυγγάνω, = ἀποφεύγω, D.23.74, Them.*Or.*18.220b, al.

ἀποφυγή, ἡ, like ἀπόφευξις, *escape* or *place of refuge*, βραχείας τὰς ἀποφυγὰς παρέχειν Th.8.106; ἀ. κακῶν, λυπῶν, *escape from* ills, griefs, Pl.*Phd.*107d, *Phlb.*44c (pl.). 2. *excuse, plea*, Aristid.2.85 J.; *shift, subterfuge*, *PStrassb.*40.44 (vi A.D.).

ἀποφῠλάττω, *store up*, Hsch. s.v. ἀποταμιεύεται:—Med., *ward off*, Id. s.v. ἀπαλέξασθαι.

ἀποφύλιος [ῠ], ον, *having no tribe*, i.e. *foreign*, A.*Fr.*287, Poll.3.56.

ἀποφυλλίζω, *strip* a plant *of its leaves*, Thphr.*HP*7.12.2, Dsc.1. 49, Sch.Ar.*Pax*1147.

ἀπόφυλλον τραχύ, = ἄλυσσον, Ps.-Dsc.3.91.

ἀπόφυξις, εως, ἡ, v. ἀπόφευξις.

ἀποφῡσ-άω, *blow away*, Ar.*V.*330 (anap.); τὰ νέφη Arist.*Mete.*364^b 8. II. *breathe out*, ἀ. ψυχίδιον Luc.*Nav.*26. 2. *throw off*, κονιορτόν Archig.ap.Orib.8.2.6. III. ἀποφυσήσασα· ἐγκρύψασα, Hsch. **-ησις**, εως, ἡ, *blowing away*, τῆς φλογός Sch.Pi.*P.*4. 412. **-ητέον**, *one must blow off, away*, Dsc.5.99.

ἀπόφῠσις, εως, ἡ, *side-shoot*, Thphr.*HP*6.4.4, Plb.18.18.10 (pl.): metaph., μιᾶς φύσεως ἀποφύσεις Dam.*Pr.*100. II. in Anatomy, *process* of a bone, i.e. the *prominence* to which a tendon is attached, Hp.*Art.*45; ἀ. ὀδοντοειδής *processus dentatus*, Gal.*UP*12.7, etc.; ἀ. στυλοειδεῖς Ruf.*Onom.*142; of the βρογχίαι, ib.159. 2. *branch* of an artery, Gal.8.319; of a nerve, Id.*UP*9.9; of the urethra, ib.15.3 (but ἀ. σκωληκοειδής is f.l. for ἐπίφυσις, ib.8.14; the two words distd. by Id.2.733). III. Archit., member connecting shaft and base of column, Vitr.4.7.3.

ἀποφῠτ-εία, ἡ, *propagation by slips*, Arist.*Long.*467^{a}28, *Juv.*468^b 18, Thphr.*CP*1.4.3. **-εύω**, *strike slips* or *cuttings*, Arist.*GA*761^b 28, al., Thphr.*HP*7.2.1.

ἀποφύω, *produce*, ῥίζας Thphr.*HP*1.6.4; of veins, *send out* branches, ἀ. τὰς φλέβας Gal.15.532; τένοντας Id.18(2).979:—Pass., with aor. 2 and pf. Act., *grow afresh*, ἀπὸ τῶν ῥιζῶν Thphr.*CP*4.8. 5; of branching veins, Gal.15.389; τρίχες ἀ. Archig.ap.Aët.6.55: metaph., Dam.*Pr.*89. II. *part asunder, separate*, Hsch.

ἀποφώζω, *dry*, λίνου σπέρμα ἀποπεφωσμένον Hp.*Mul.*1.63.

ἀποφώλιος, ον, acc. to the Ancients, = ἀνεμώλιος, μάταιος, *empty, vain, idle*, Hom. only in Od., νόον ἀποφώλιός ἐσσι 8.177; οὐκ ἀποφώλια εἰδώς 5.182; οὐκ ἀ. ἦα οὐδὲ φυγοπτόλεμος 14.212; ἐπεὶ οὐκ ἀ. εὐναὶ ἀθανάτων are not *barren*, 11.249; νέκυς ἀ. Opp.*C.*3.447; ἀποφώλια μητιόων Man.6.565; ῥέξουσ' ἀποφώλια Orac.ap.Jul.*Ep.*89; of the Minotaur, ξύμμικτον εἶδος κἀποφώλιον τρέφος a *monstrous*, hybrid birth, E.*Fr.*996; in Nic.*Al.*524 στομίων ἀ. ἆσθμα is expld. by Sch. χαλεπόν, but perh. there is a play on φωλεύοντα (φωλεός, cf. Eust.) which occurs just before. (Perh. from ἀποφεῖν (q.v.), cf. ἁμαρτωλός: ἁμαρτεῖν; Hsch. has ἀποφώλια· ἀποφίλια (i.e. -φύλια).) **-φωλος**, ον, = foreg., Man.4.316.

ἀποφωνέω, Cret. ἀποπωνίω, *depose in evidence*, *Leg.Gort.*1.13, al.

ἀποφώρ, ῶρος, ὁ, *thief*, Hsch.

ἀποχάζομαι, *withdraw from*, βόθρου Od.11.95; γραφίδων *APl.*4. 181 (Jul. Aegypt.): abs., ἀποχασθῇ· ἀποθάνῃ, Hsch.:—Act., only in aor. imper. ἀπόχασον· ἀποχώρησον, Id.

ἀποχαιρετίζω, (χαῖρε) *say farewell, take leave*, Sch.rec.S.*Tr.*532.

ἀποχᾰλάω, *slack away*, ἀποχάλα τὴν φροντίδ' ἐς τὸν ἀέρα λινόδετον ὥσπερ μηλολόνθην τοῦ ποδός Ar.*Nu.*762; ἑαυτὸν ἀ. Plu.2.655b (s.v.l.).

ἀποχᾰλῑνόω, *unbridle*, X.*Eq.*11.7: metaph., ἀ. τὴν αἰδῶ Plu.2.794c.

ἀποχαλκ-εύω, *forge of copper*, X.*Cyn.*10.3. **-ίζω**, *strip of brass*, i.e. *of money*, pun on Χαλκίς in *AP*11.283 (Pall.).

ἀποχᾰρακόω, = ἀποσταυρόω, D.H.5.58, Plu.*Pomp.*35 (Pass.).

ἀποχάρ-αξις [χᾰ], εως, ἡ, *incision*, πολλὰς -ξεις λαμβάνειν Democr. 155; *scarification*, Gal.11.305, al. II. *enclosure*, Haussoullier *Milet* p.187, cf. *Rev.Phil.*44.251, 264. **-άσσω**, Att. -ττω, *erase, obliterate*, στήλην D.Chr.31.86. II. *incise*, *Hippiatr.*52. III. *characterize, mark*, ἀποχαράττει ταῦτα τὸν ἀγαθὸν ποιητήν prob. in Phld.*Po.*5.1425. 10.

ἀποχᾰρ-ίζομαι, *confer upon, present*, τί τινι *IGRom.*4.182 (Lampsacus), Alex.Aphr. *in Metaph.*483.25:—Pass., τάλαντον -ισθέν σοι *POxy.*1208.16 (iii A.D.). **-ισμα**, ατος, τό, *deed of gift*, *PMonac.* 8.29 (vi A.D.).

ἀποχᾰριστέω, *return thanks*, *Delph.*3(1).152 (ii B.C.).

ἀποχειμάζω, *blow over*, ὅταν ἀποχειμάσῃ when the wind *drops*, Arist.*Pr.*943^{b}31.

ἀπο-χειρίζω, *cut off the hand*, only in Pass., ἀπεχειρίσθη τὴν δεξιάν Anon.ap.Suid., cf. Eust.1960.10. **-χειρόβῐος**, ον, = sq., Poll.1.50, Hsch. **-χειροβίοτος** or **-ωτος** [ῐ], ον, *living by the work of one's hands*, Hdt.3.42, X.*Cyr.*8.3.37. **-χειρος**, ον, *unprepared*, Plb.22.14. 8. **-χειροτονέω**, *vote by show of hands away from*; and so, I. *vote a charge away from* one, *acquit* him, τινός D.21.214. II. *reject as unfit*, ἀ. τινὰ ἀπὸ τῆς τῶν ἐφήβων ἐπιμελείας Din.3.15, cf. Arist. *Ath.*49.1; αὐτὸν ἀ. τῆς ἀρχῆς Plu.*Nic.*8: metaph., ἀ. τῆς ἡδονῆς τὸν ἄνδρα you vote his poetry *devoid of* sweetness, Max.Tyr.23.5. 2. *supersede, depose*, τὸν στρατηγόν D.23.168, cf. Arist.*Ath.*61.2:—Pass., D.49.9, Hp.*Ep.*10. 3. *abrogate, annul*, τὰς συνθήκας D.23.172:—Pass., of laws, Id.24.21; of a peace, *to be rejected*, ἐν τῇ ἐκκλησίᾳ Ar.*Pax*668. III. ἀ. μὴ φίλ' εἶναι.. *vote* that a thing is *not*.., D.24.12; μὴ μισθοῦν τοὺς οἴκους Is.6.37; ἀ. τῶν δικαστῶν ὡς οὐδὲν αὐτοῖς προσῆκεν ib.45. **-χειροτονητέον**, *one must reject a claim to*, τοῦ ἀρίστου Max.Tyr.22.5. **-χειροτονία**, ἡ, *deposition* of an official, D.58.28.

ἀποχέτ-ευμα, ατος, τό, *branch*, τῆς θαλάσσης Eust.ad D.P.38. **-ευσις**, εως, ἡ, *drawing off*, περιττωμάτων Ph.1.29. **-εύω**, *draw off* water *by a canal*, Pl.*Lg.*736b:—Pass., ὥσπερ ῥεῦμα ἀπωχετευμένον Id.*R.*485d, cf. Arist.*Pr.*867^{b}13, M.Ant.12.2:—Med., metaph., Πλάτων ἀπὸ τοῦ Ὁμηρικοῦ νάματος εἰς αὑτὸν μυρίας παρατροπὰς -σάμενος Longin.13.3:—so in Act., 'canalize', τὴν Ὁμήρου ποίησιν Jul.*Or.*2. 51a. 2. metaph., ἀ. τὸ βάσκανον Plu.2.485e.

ἀποχέω, imper. ἀπόχει Dsc.1.53: aor. ἀπέχεα, Ep. -έχευα:—*pour out* or *off, spill, shed*, ἀπὸ δ' εἴδατα χεῦεν ἔραζε Od.22.20, 85: poet. pres. Med., παγὰν ἂν ἀποχεύονται Κασταλίας δίναι E.*Ion*148 (lyr.). 2. *pour off*, Hp.*Ulc.*12; τι εἴς τι Dsc.1.53. II. Pass., *to be poured off*, Plb.34.9.10; τοῦ μὲν ἀποχεομένου ὕδατος, τοῦ δὲ ἐπιχεομένου Dsc.2.76; *to be shed, fall off*, ἀποχυθέντα φύλλα Plu.2. 332b. 2. of plants, *come into ear*, Thphr.*HP*8.8.1, etc.; οὐκ εἰς στάχυν ἀλλ' οἷον φόβην ib.4.4.10:—Med., *make to shoot*, ἀ. ποίην Nic. *Th.*569 (s.v.l.); χαίτην ib.658.

ἀποχή, ἡ, (ἀπέχω) *distance*, Phld.*Rh.*1.168 S., Ptol.*Geog.*1.11.2, al. II. *abstinence*, Phld.*Ind.Sto.*67, cf. *Piet.*36, Arr.*Epict.*2.15.5; ἀ. τροφῆς Plu.*Demetr.*38; ἐμψύχων Porph.*Abst.*tit. III. *receipt, quittance*, *PTeb.*11.14 (ii B.C.), *BGU*1116.41 (i B.C.), *AP*11.233 (Lucill.), Ulp.ap.*Dig.*46.4.19, etc.: metaph., ἡ τελευταία ἀ., title of work by Zos.Alch.p.239 B.

ἀποχηρόομαι, Pass., *to be bereft of*, τινός Ar.*Pax*1013 (parod.).

ἀπόχιμος, ον, *of* or *for a receipt*, γράμματα *PCair.Preis.*14.13 (iv A.D.).

ἀποχλωρίας, ου, ὁ, *one whose complexion has become pale*, Hsch.

ἀποχοιρ-ιάζειν· ἀποσοβεῖν, ὡς χοῖρον ἐλαύνειν, Hsch., cf. *AB*439; ἀπεχοιρίασεν· ἀπεσκίρτησεν, Hsch. **-ωσις**, εως, ἡ, *transmutation into swine*, Eust.1656.32.

ἀπόχοον, τό, prob. = ἀπόχυμα, *PFay.*123.12 (i/ii A.D.).

ἀποχορτάζω, *feed to the full*, Sosith.2.13.

ἄποχος, ον, = ἀπόχιμος, γράμματα *PThead.*28.13 (iv A.D.), al. II. ἄποχον· ἀπότεχνον, ἄγροικον, μάταιον, Hsch.

ἀποχραίνω, *colour, tint evenly*, Pl.*Lg.*769a, cf. Tim.*Lex.* s.v. χραίνειν:—Pass., *take a tone*, Pl.*R.*586b; of fruit, *colour*, Arist.*Col.*796^a 24.

ἀπόχρανος· ἀκάλυπτος, ἀπροφάσιστος, Hsch.

ἀποχράω, Dor. -χρέω Archim.*Aren.*3.3, [Epich.]253: inf. -χρῆν D.4.22, Antiph.161, Luc.*Herm.*24 (-χρῆναι v.l. in D.H.3.22, condemned by *AB*81), Ion. -χρᾶν Hdt.3.138, but -χρῆναι Hp.*VC*14; part. -χρῶν, -χρῶσα, v. infr.: impf. ἀπέχρη, Ion. -έχρα Hdt.1.66: fut. -χρήσω: aor. -έχρησα:—*suffice, be sufficient, be enough*: 1. abs., in persons other than 3 sg., 1 sg. only in εἷς ἐγὼν ἀποχρέω [Epich.] l.c.; [θανάτῳ] δύ' ἀποχρήσουσιν μόνῳ Ar.*Pl.*484; ἀποχρήσει (sc. ἡ ὑφαντική) Pl.*Plt.*279b; τηλικαύτην ἀποχρῆν οἶμαι τὴν δύναμιν D.4.22; ἀποχρῶν ἀνὴρ ἔμοιγε πρὸς τὰ νῦν κακά Pherecr.145.6; ἡλικία ἀποχρῶσα Ar.*Fr.*489; σύμβουλος ἀποχρῶν τῇ πόλει Pl.*Alc.*2.145c; of ἀρετή, *Stoic.*3.50: c. inf., ἀποχρῶσι.. ἑκατὸν νέες χειρώσασθαι Hdt.5.31; Κνιδίους μούνους ἀποχρᾶν οἵ τοὺς κατάγοντας γίνεσθαι Id.3.138, cf. 9.48; πεδίον ἀποχρῶν τὴν Ἀσίαν πρὸς τὴν Εὐρώπην ἀντιτάξαι Philostr. *Im.*1.1. 2. mostly in 3 sg., c. dat., a. with a nom., [ποταμὸς] οὐκ ἀπέχρησε τῇ στρατιῇ πινόμενος *was* not *enough to supply* the army with drink, Hdt.7.43,196; often in the phrase ταῦτ' ἀπόχρη μοι Ar. *Av.*1603, cf. Pl.*Phdr.*279a; ἀπόχρη μοι τοσοῦτον ἐὰν.. Isoc.5.28; οὐκ ἀπέχρησε δὲ αὐτῷ τοῦτο D.21.17; οὐδὲ ταῦτ' ἀπέχρησεν αὐτοῖς Isoc. 4.97. b. impers., c. inf., ἀποχρᾷ (-χρη) μοι ἡσυχίην ἄγειν, ποιέειν τι, etc., *'tis sufficient* for me to.., Hdt.1.66, 6.137, 9.79, Hp.*Mochl.*38; [ἔφασαν] ἀποχρήσειν σφι τὴν ἑωυτῶν φυλάσσειν Hdt.8.130: c. dat. part., ἀποχρᾶν σφι κατὰ τὸ ἥμισυ ἡγεομένοισι *it was enough* for them if they shared the command, Id.7.148; μέρος βαιὸν ἐχούσῃ πᾶν ἀπόχρη μοι *'tis* all *sufficient* for me to have a little, A.*Ag.*1574 (nowhere else in Trag.); τοσαῦτ' ἀπόχρη προσθήσειν Str.9.1.20. c. impers., ἀπόχρη τινός *there is enough of* a thing, Hp.*Mul.*1.12, *Vid.Ac.*4; ἀποχρῆν ἐνίοις ὑμῶν ἄν μοι δοκεῖ εἰ.. methinks *it would have satisfied* some of you, D.4.42: abs. in part., οὐκ ἀποχρῆσαν αὐτῷ *since it did* not *suffice* him, Arist.*Xen.*976^{b}21. 3. Pass., *to be contented with* a thing, c. dat., ἀποχρεωμένων τούτοισι τῶν Μυσῶν the Mysians *being satisfied* therewith, Hdt.1.37; τοῖς ὀνόμασι μόνον D.17.31. b. impers., οὐκ ἀπεχρᾶτο μούνων Μήδων ἄρχειν Hdt.1.102; ἀπεχρᾶτό σφι ἡσυχίην ἄγειν Id.8.14. II. *deliver an oracle*, Ael.*Fr.*59.

B. ἀποχράομαι *use to the full, avail oneself of*, ἐπικαιρότατον χωρίον.. ἀποχρῆσθαι Th.1.68; ἀποχρήσασθε τῇ.. ὠφελίᾳ Id.6.17, cf. 7.42; ὅταν.. ἀποχρήσωνται χρῶνται λοιπὸν ὡς προδόταις when they *have made all the use they can of* them, then they deal with them.., Plb.18.15.9. 2. *abuse, misuse*, c. dat., εἰς ταῦτα ἀποχρῆσθαι τῷ πλουτεῖν D.21.124; πλεονεκτικῶς ταῖς ἐξουσίαις ἀ. *OGI*665.16 (Egypt, i A.D.); ἀποχρωμένων μᾶλλον ἢ χρωμένων αὐτῷ Plu.*Comp.Alc.Cor.*2; οἷς μὲν χρῆσθαι, οἷς δ' ἀ. Id.2.178c: c. gen., θυγατρός Id.*Nob.*13. 3. c. acc., *destroy, kill*, Ar.*Fr.*358, Th.3.81, Poll.8.74, etc. 4. ἀ. τὰ χρήματα *make use of*, Arist.*Oec.*1349^{b}17. 5. ἀποχρησαμένοις· ἀποσεισαμένοις, Hsch.

ἀπό-χρεμμα, ατος, τό, *expectoration*, Hp.*Loc.Hom.*16. **-χρέμπτομαι**, *cough up, expectorate*, Id.*Acut.*58, *Loc.Hom.*14. **-χρεμψις**, εως, ἡ, *expectoration*, Id.*Aph.*4.47.

ἀποχρεόντως, v. ἀποχρώντως.

ἀποχρέω, -χρη, v. ἀποχράω.

ἀποχρημᾰτ-ίζω, *carry to an end, close* a discussion, λόγον dub. in Phld.*D.*3.14; cf. ἀποτερματίζω. II. Pass., *to be deposited, registered*, of an official copy, ἐν τοῖς ἀρχείοις *Inscr.Magn.*293.5. **-ος**, ζημία ἀ. forfeiture *of my inheritance*, A.*Ch.*275.

ἀπό-χρησις, εως, ἡ, *getting rid of*, τῶν περιττῶν dub. in Plu.2. 267f. II. *consumption, using up*, *Ep.Col.*2.22. **-χρηστικῶς**, f.l. for -χρώντως, D.L.7.160.

ἀποχριμφθέντα· ἀποχωρισθέντα, Hsch.

ἀποχρίω· *relevio, relino*, *Gloss.*

ἀποχρῡσόω, *turn into gold* or *money*, Pass., Artem.1.50, cf. Poll. 7.102.

ἀποχρωμένως, = ἀποχρώντως, dub. in Phld.*Rh.*2.87 S.

ἀποχρώννῡμι, = ἀποχραίνειν, Poll.7.129.

ἀποχρώντως, Dor. **-χρεόντως** Archim.*Aren.*3.2, Adv. pres. part. of ἀποχράω:—*enough, sufficiently*, Th.1.21, 7.77, Pl.*R.*429a; ἀ. ἔχει τινί Antiph.191.16; ἀ. ἔχειν τιμῆς J.*AJ*15.2.7; μέρος ἀ. ἐξειργασμένον Phld.*Piet.*22.

ἀπόχρωσις, εως, ἡ, (ἀποχρώννυμι) *laying on colour*, ἀ. σκιᾶς Plu.2. 346a.

ἀποχῡλ-ίζω, *extract the juice*, prob. in Arist.*Pr.*873^{b}4, cf. Dsc.1.86:—Pass., Antyll.ap.Orib.4.11.3. **-ισμα**, ατος, τό, *juice*, μαλάχης ἀγρίας *Gp.*15.6.1. **-όω**, = ἀποχυλίζω, Hp.*Mul.*1.93.

ἀπόχῠμα, ατος, τό, (χέω) *that which is poured out*, Ti.Locr.100a, *PFay.*95.25 (ii A.D.). 2. = ζώπισσα, Dsc.1.72. 3. Ὀρειβασίου ἀ., name of a kind of *plaster*, Aët.15.24.

ἀποχύνω, later form of ἀποχέω, Lxx 3*Ki.*22.35.

ἀποχῠρόω, *fortify*:—Pass., ἀποχυρωθέντος τοῦ περιπολίου *SIG*569. 9 (Cos, iii B.C.); ἀπωχυρῶσθαι *form a fence*, of trees, Thphr.*HP* 4.7.7: metaph., ἀπωχυρωμένος πρὸς τὸ λαμβάνειν *incorruptible*, Plu. *Dem.*14.

ἀπό-χῠσις, εως, ἡ, (ἀποχέω) *pouring out* or *forth*, ἀκτίνων ἢ χρωμάτων S.E.*P.*3.51, cf. Gal.*UP*6.2, al.; of corn, *coming into ear*, ἐκβιάζεσθαι τὴν ἀ. Thphr.*HP*8.10.4: generally, *inflorescence*, ἡ καλαμώδης ἀ. φόβη ib.8.3.4. **-χῠτήριον**, τό, *sewer*, Charis.p.553 K. **-χῠτος**, ον, *poured out*, Hsch. s.v. ἀράμενοι.

ἀποχωλεύω, *make quite lame*, X.*HG*7.2.9, *Oec.*11.17.

ἀποχωλόομαι, Pass., *to be made quite lame*, Hp.*Aër.*22, Th.7.27, Paus.10.1.3.

ἀποχώννῡμι, *bank up* a river, etc., X.*HG*2.2.4, 5.2.4; λιμένας ἀπεχώννυσαν Plu.*Phoc.*11.

ἀποχωρ-έω, fut. -ήσομαι Th.3.13, D.25.78:—*go from* or *away from*, δόμων Ar.*Ach.*456; ἐκ τοῦ στρατοπέδου Pl.*R.*394a. 2. abs., *depart*, πάλιν ἀ. E.*IT*265; *withdraw*, ἐπὶ τὰ ἀναγκαῖα v.l. in X.*Cyr.* 1.6.36: esp. after a defeat, *retire, retreat*, Th.2.89, etc.; πρὸς τὴν πόλιν X.*HG*4.4.11; ἐπὶ τῆς Κορίνθου Th.2.94. 3. ἀ. ἐκ τῶν πόλεων.. *withdraw from*.., *give up possession of*, X.*HG*5.2.13. b. metaph., *withdraw* or *dissent from* opinions, δοξῶν Gal.15.356, cf. Arr.*Epict.*4. 1.53. 4. *turn out, succeed*, Phld.*Rh.*1.105 S.; of persons, κατὰ τρόπον ἀ. *to be successful*, ib.2.259 S. 5. *have recourse*, εἰς, ἐπί τι, D.25.78, 37.21. II. *pass off*, esp. of the excretions of the body, Hp.*Judic.*10, X.*Cyr.*1.2.16; τὰ ἀποχωροῦντα *excrements*, Id.*Mem.*1. 4.6; τὸ ἀποχωροῦν *excretion*, Arist.*GA*725^{b}15. III. of places, *to be distant*, μέρη ἀποκεχωρηκότα Plb.15.27.8; ἀ. ὡς πόδα *to be* a foot *apart*, Apollod.*Poliorc.*165.1. **-ήματα**, τά, *excretions*, Meno *Iatr.* 12.41. **-ησις**, εως, ἡ, *retreat*, Th.5.73; ποιεῖσθαι ἀ. Hdt.8.21; *place* or *means of safety*, Th.8.76 (pl.); *line of retreat*, Aen.Tact.16.4. 2. *death*, Eun.*VS* p.469 B. II. *voidance*, opp. πλήρωσις, Pl.*Ti.*65a, 81a; esp. of excretions, Arist.*GA*726^{a}21, al.; = ἀπόπατος 2, Plu.*Lyc.* 20. **-ητέον**, *one must depart*, Hld.7.11. **-ίζω**, *separate from*, τὸ χεῖρον ἀπὸ βελτίονος Pl.*Sph.*226d:—Pass., *to be separated from*, πυρός Id.*Ti.*59d; ἐξ ἰνῶν αἷμα ἀ. ib.84a. 2. *separate, set apart, detach*, Lys.16.16; ἀ. ὡς ἓν εἶδος *separate and put* into one class, Pl. *Plt.*262e; ἀπὸ βασιλικῆς τε καὶ πολιτικῆς πράξεως ib.289d. 3. Pass., *to be vomited*, Herod.Med. in *Rh.Mus.*58.99. **-ισις**, εως, ἡ, *separation*, Antyll.(?)ap.Orib.45.17.3. **-ιστέον**, *one must separate, remove*, *Gp.*16.1.5. **-ιστής**, οῦ, ὁ, *separator*, *Gloss.*

ἀπόχωσις, εως, ἡ, *damming up*, ἀ. ποταμοῦ *bar*, Plu.*Ant.*41.

ἀποψάλακτος, = ἀκρότητος II, Phot. s.v. οὐκ ἀ.

ἀποψᾰλίζω, = ψαλίζω, *cut off with shears*, Dsc.1.99, Heliod.ap. Orib.48.50.1.

ἀπο-ψάλλω, *pluck off*, τρίχας Hsch.; ἀ. πάγην *spring* a trap that is set, Lyc.407; *twang* a string, Id.915; ἡ γλῶττα ἀ. τὴν ἄκραν Ἀτθίδα *rings out* the purest Attic, metaph. from the lyre, Philostr.*VS* 2.1.7. **-ψαλμα**, ατος, τό, *the part of the string which the musician plucks*, Ptol.*Harm.*1.8 (pl.), al., Porph. *in Harm.*295.

ἀποψαύω, prob. f.l. for ἐπι-, Suid. s.v. μουσομανία.

ἀποψάω, fut. -ήσω: impf. 3 sg. ἀπέψη E.*IT*311 (Elmsl.: ἀπέψα codd., cf. Hsch.): aor. ἀπέψησα Dsc.1.68.8, Luc.*Gall.*6. I. c. acc. rei, *wipe off*, ἀφρόν τ' ἀπέψη E. l.c.; δάκρυ *AP*5.65 (Rufin.), cf. Nonn. *D.*8.205:—Med., *wipe* or *rub off from oneself*, τι Ar.*Eq.*572. 2. ἀ. νούσους *cure* diseases, of Apollo, Herod.4.17. II. c. acc. pers., *wipe clean*, Ar.*Lys.*1035:—Med. (v. ψάω) *wipe oneself, wipe one's nose*, μου πρὸς τὴν κεφαλὴν ἀποψῶ *wipe your nose* on my head, Id.*Eq.*910; *podicem detergere*, ἀποψώμεσθα Id.*Pl.*817; ἀπεψησάμην Id.*Ra.*490; ἀ. τὴν χεῖρα εἴς τι X.*Cyr.*1.3.5; prov. τὴν κόνιν ἀποψησάμενος ἀγωνίζεσθαι *renew the struggle*, Eust.1327.29. III. τὰ ἐπιτήδεια σφόδρα ἀποψῶν giving short measure, of a skinflint, Thphr.*Char.*30.11.

ἀποψέ, Adv. *late*, A.D.*Synt.*304.16.

ἀποψεύδομαι, *cheat grossly*: c. acc., *forge*, πρόφασιν J.*BJ*4.3.5:—Pass., *to be quite cheated of*, τῆς ἐλπίδος Plu.*Marc.*29.

ἀπό-ψηκτέον, *one must wipe clean*, ὦτα καὶ ῥῖνας *Gp.*17.20.3. **-ψηκτος**, ον, *wiped clean*: hence metaph., *keen-witted, sharp*, S.*Ichn.*363 (lyr.). **-ψηκτρον**, τό, *cleanser*, name of a remedy for ὑπώπια, Gal. 12.818. **-ψημα**, ατος, τό, *wipings, refuse*, Dsc.5.75, Hsch. s.v. μαριλοκαυτῶν. **-ψηξις**, εως, ἡ, *scraping, scratching*, Orib.*Fr.*79, Paul.Aeg.4.15. **-ψηστρον**, τό, *strickle*, Hsch.

ἀποψηφ-ίζομαι, Att. fut. -ιοῦμαι D.22.45: Dep., c. pf. Pass., D.C. 39.55:—*vote away from*, opp. καταψηφίζομαι, θάνατον ἀ. τινός *vote* death *away from* him, *refuse to condemn* him to death, Lycurg. 149. 2. *refuse to elect*, τινά Plu.*Cor.*15. II. ἀ. τινός (gen. pers.), 1. *vote a charge away from* one, i.e. *acquit*, Antipho 5.96, Lys.12.90, D.18.250; τινός Id.19.212: abs., *vote an acquittal*, Pl.*Ap.* 34d, 39e; ἀ. τινὸς ὡς οὐκ ἀδικεῖ Arist.*Pr.*951^{b}1. 2. *vote the franchise away from* one, *disfranchise*, D.57.11; τοῦ παιδός Id.59.59, cf. Aeschin.1.114; ἀ. μὴ εἶναι ἐλεύθερον Arist.*Ath.*42.1:—Pass., τὸν ἀποψηφισθέντα Ἀντιφῶντα D.18.132; δικαίως ἔστ' ἀπεψηφισμένος Aristopho 11.1; ἀ. τοῦ πολιτεύματος Plu.*Phoc.*28. III. c. acc. rei, *reject*: of judges, ἀ. γραφήν *vote against receiving* the indictment, Aeschin.3.230; ἀ. τὸν νόμον (with play on νόμος 'tune') Pl.*Lg.*800d; ἀ. ἃ Διοπείθης κατεψηφίσατο Is.5.34, cf. D.20.164; ἀποψηφιζόμενον μὲν κύριον δεῖ ποιεῖν τὸ πλῆθος to give them an absolute power *of rejection*, Arist.*Pol.*1298^{b}35. IV. folld. by μή c. inf., *vote against* doing, X.*HG*3.5.8, D.19.174; so ἢν δ' ἀποψηφίσωνται (sc. μὴ ἕπεσθαι) X.*An.*1.4.15; ἀποψηφίσασθαι ἔφη Id.*HG*7.3.2.—Act. only -ψηφίζοντες· *refragantes*, *Gloss.* **-ισις**, εως, ἡ, *acquittal*, Antipho 5.9. 2. *disfranchisement*, D.57.2 and 4 (pl.), cf. *IG*2.841 *b* 102. 3. *final vote*, *SIG*344.120 (Teos). **-ιστέον**, *one must acquit*, D.22.44. **-ος**, ον, *voting in the negative*, ἀ. ἐγένοντο τοῦ ἀποκτεῖναι Phryn.*PS* p.13 B.

ἀποψήχω, *wipe away*, Eun.*VS* p.481 B. II. *scrape* or *rub off*, Dsc.2.76, 5.78 (-ψώχω Wellm.):—Pass., Arist.*HA*630^{b}11.

ἀποψῑλ-όω, *strip off hair, make bald*, Ar.*Th.*538; of a barber, ἀ. τὸ πύκνωμα τῶν τριχῶν Alciphr.3.66:—Pass., Ar.*Lys.*827. 2. *strip bare*, τὸ ὀστέον Hp.*Foet.Exsect.*1; τὸν Κύρου οἶκον ἀ. Hdt.3. 32. II. c. gen., *strip bare of*, φίλων τινά A.*Ch.*695. **-ωσις**, εως, ἡ, *stripping*, ἀμπέλων Thphr.*CP*5.9.11.

ἀπόψιος, α, ον, *far seen, conspicuous*, prob. l. in Dicaearch.1.1.

ἄποψις, εως, ἡ, *outlook, view*, πεδίον πλῆθος ἄπειρον ἐς ἄποψιν boundless in view, Hdt.1.204; παραπλησίους πάντας ἐκ τῆς ἀ. all alike *to look at*, Plb.11.31.8; ἐν ἀπόψει εἶναι, γίγνεσθαι, to be *within view*, Str. 6.1.5, *AP*9.412 (Phld.). 2. *lofty spot* or *tower which commands a view, belvedere*, Str.17.1.16, Plu.*Comp.Cim.Luc.*1. II. *that on which one looks, view, prospect*, Arist.*Mir.*843^{a}17, Plu.2.133b.

ἀποψιώ, pf. Pass. ἀπέψισται, *strip bare*, *EM*818.36.

ἀποψοφ-έω, *break wind*, Hp.*Epid.*6.3.14, Arist.*HA*633^{b}7, *Pr.*895^b

17, Macho ap.Ath.8.349e. II. *sound loudly*, φωνὴ ἐν λιμένι-ψοφοῦσα Thphr.*Sign*.40. **-ησις**, εως, ἡ, *crepitus ventris*, Plu.2.866c.

ἀπό-ψυγμα, ατος, τό, *ordure*, Hsch. **-ψυξις**, εως, ἡ, *cooling, evaporation*, Thphr.*Fr*.171.10. II. *shivering fit, rigor*, Simp.*in Epict*. p.50 D. (pl.). **-ψῦχος**, ον, *frigid*, of literary style, Longin. 42. **-ψύχω** [ῡ] :—Pass., aor. ἀπεψύχθην and ἀπεψύχην [ῠ], v. infr., also ἀπεψύγην [ῠ] Hld.2.3 :—*leave off breathing, faint, swoon*, τὸν δὲ.. εἷλεν ἀποψύχοντα Od.24.348; ἀ. ἀπὸ φόβου *Ev.Luc*.21.26. 2. c. acc., ἀπέψυξεν βίον *breathed out* life, S.*Aj*.1031; πνεῦμα *AP*12.72 (Mel.): abs., *expire, die*, Th.1.134, cf. Lxx 4 *Ma*.15.17, D.C.43.11, al.; λεπτὸν ἀ. faintly *breathing out his life*, Bion 1.9 :—also Pass., ἀποψύχεται Hp. *Morb*.1.19: aor. 2 ἀπεψύχη A.*Fr*.104. II. *cool, chill*, ὄψα Sosip. 54 :—Pass. or Med., *to be cooled*, Hom. only in phrase ἱδρῶ ἀπεψύχοντο χιτώνων στάντε ποτὶ πνοιήν they *got* the sweat *dried off* their tunics, Il.11.621; ἱδρῶ ἀποψυχθείς (by bathing) 21.561 (also in Act., ἱδρῶ ἀποψύχοντε Orph.*A*.1091): generally, *grow cold*, Thphr.*HP*4. 7.3, etc.: metaph., ἀπεψυγμένοι πρὸς τὸ μέλλον *cold and indifferent* as to.., Arist.*Rh*.1383ᵃ4; ἀποψυχόμενοι *shivering with terror*, Arr.*Epict*. 4.1.145, cf. Alciphr.2.2; but, *to be refreshed*, Phryn.*PS* p.27 B. 2. impers., ἀποψύχει *it grows cool*, ἐπειδὰν ἀποψύχῃ Pl.*Phdr*.242a, ap. Phryn.*PS* p.45 B., sed leg. ἀποψυχῇ (aor. 2 Pass.). III. ἀποψύχειν· ἀποπατεῖν, ἀφοδεύειν, Hsch.; cf. ἀπόψυγμα. **-ψωλέω**, (ψωλός) sens. obsc., *praeputium retrahere alicui*, Ar.*Ach*.592; ἀπεψωλημένος *a lewd fellow*, ib.161. **-ψώχω**, v. ἀποψήχω.

ἄππα, = πάππα, ἄττα (Maced., acc. to *EM*167.32), Call.*Dian*.6, *BGU*714.15, al.

ἀππαλλάζειν· ἐκκλησιάζειν (Ion.), Hsch.; cf. ἀπελλάζω.

ἀππαπαῖ, an exclamation of grief or pain, Ar.*V*.235,309.

ἄππας, ὁ, religious official, τοῦ Διονύσου *Inscr.Magn*.117.8 (ii A.D.), cf. *Ath.Mitt*.17.200, Buresch *Aus Lydien* 131. II. = τροφεύς, Hsch.

ἀππασάμενος, = ἀνακτησάμενος (cf. πάομαι), Corinn.*Supp*.2.78. (From ἀμ-πα-.)

ἀππέμψει, rare poet. contr. for ἀποπέμψει, Od.15.83.

ἄππιλος· ἀσπάργαντος, Hsch. **ἄππιρ**· ὕσπληξ (Lacon.), Id.

ἀπρᾱγ-έω, *do nothing, remain quiet*, θεοὺς ἀπρηγεῦντας (-ται Pap.) Call.*Iamb*.1.198, Plb.3.70.4, 4.64.7; *hold no office or employment*, Heph.Astr.2.28. II. *fare ill*, Pittac.ap.Stob.3.1.172. **-ία**, ἡ, *inaction*, Plb.3.103.2; *want of energy*, Plu.*Fab*.1 (so in physical sense, Aret.*SD*2.7); *unemployment*, Vett.Val.189.8.

ἀπραγμ-άτευτος [μᾰ], ον, *impracticable*, πόλις ἀ., i.e. an *impregnable* city, D.S.17.40; χωρίον Plb.4.75.2. II. *deprived of commerce*, Anon.ap.Suid. s. v. διακλεισθέντες. III. *costing no trouble*, Muson. *Fr*.18 B p.105 H., Eun.*VS* p.504 B. IV. *free from trouble*, Phld. *Piet*.66. V. *inexperienced*, *UPZ*39.21 (ii B.C.). VI. *not elaborate, simple*, *Vit.Aesch*. Adv. -τως D.H.*Is*.16; *without taking pains*, Jul.*Or*.6.191c. **-οσύνη**, ἡ, *freedom from politics, love of a quiet life*, Ar.*Nu*.1007, X.*Mem*.3.11.16; of states, Th.1.32; ἡ Νικίου τῶν λόγων ἀ. Id.6.18. 2. = ἀτέλεια λειτουργιῶν, *SIG*876.8 (Smyrna), Poll. 8.156. II. *love of ease, easiness of temper*, Th.2.63, D.21.141. III. *inexperience*, *POxy*.71 ii 16 (iv A.D.). IV. name of a *weed* which grew ἐν Ἀκαδημίᾳ, Ar.Byz.ap.Sch.Ar.*Nu*.1007. **-ων**, ον, gen. ονος, *free from business* (πράγματα), *easy-going, fond of quiet*, esp. of those who *refrain from meddling in politics*, opp. πολυπράγμων, ὅστις δὲ πράσσει πολλά.. μωρὸς παρὸν ζῆν ἡδέως ἀπράγμονα E.*Fr*.193; τῶν ἀ. γε πόρνων κοὐχὶ τῶν σεμνῶν [τις ὤν] Eup.8.4 D.; esp. with political connotation, *not meddling in public affairs*, 'mugwump', ἄν τιν' αὐτῶν γνῷς ἀπράγμον' ὄντα καὶ κεχηνότα Ar.*Eq*.261, cf. Antipho 3.2.1; αὐτουργοί τε καὶ ἀ. Pl.*R*.565a; ἀ. καὶ οὐ φιλόδικος D.40.32; ἀκάκους καὶ ἀ. Id.47.82; οἱ ἀ. οὐκ ἄδικοι Arist.*Rh*.1381ᵃ25; τὸν μηδὲν τῶνδε [τῶν πολιτικῶν] μετέχοντα οὐκ ἀπράγμονα ἀλλ' ἀχρεῖον νομίζομεν Th.2.40; πόλις ἀ. *keeping clear of foreign politics*, Id.6.18; ἡσυχία ἀ. Id.1.70; βίος ἀνδρὸς ἰδιώτου ἀπράγμονος Pl.*R*.620c; τὸ ἀ. Th.2.63; τόπος ἀ. a place *free from law and strife*, Ar.*Av*.44; ἀπόλαυσις ἀ. X. *Mem*.2.1.33. Adv. -μόνως *without trouble* or *care*, E.*Fr*.787; ἀ. ζῆν ἡδύ Apollod.Com.1.1. II. of things, *not troublesome* or *painful*, τελευτὴν.. ἀπραγμονεστάτην τοῖς φίλοις X.*Ap*.7. Adv. -μόνως *without trouble*, Th.4.61, X.*HG*6.4.27; σῴζεσθαι Th.6.87; ὁ λόγος ἀ. εἴρηται *carelessly*, Arist.*Mete*.369ᵇ27: Comp. -έστερον X.*Ages*.4.1. 2. *simple*, ἐσθής Muson.*Ep*.4.

Ἀπρᾱγόπολις, εως, ἡ, *Castle of Indolence, Sans-souci*, as Augustus called his retreat on an island near Capri, Suet.*Aug*.98.

ἄπρᾱγος, ον, = ἀπράγμων, Sm.*Jd*.9.4.

ἀπρακτέω, *do nothing, to be idle*, Arist.*EN*1095ᵇ33; opp. πράττειν, Id.*Pol*.1325ᵃ31. 2. *gain nothing*, παρά τινος X.*Cyr*.1.6.6. 3. *waste one's time*, Lyd.*Mag*.1.22. 4. *lose power*, of a drug, Paul. Aeg.3.4.

ἄπρακτος, Ion. **ἄπρηκτος**, ον, Pi.*I*.8(7).7 codd.: I. Act., *unavailing, unprofitable*, ἄπρηκτον πόλεμον Il.2.121; ἀπρήκτους ἔριδας ib.376; ἄ. ἐλπίς Simon.5.16, cf. Pi. l. c.; ἄ. γίγνεταί τι D.9.40; ἄ. ἡμέραι days *when no business is done, holidays*, Plu.2.270a, cf. *BGU* 255.8 (vi A.D.); *restful*, παῦλα B.9.8; ἄ. ἑορτή *Proll.Hermog*. in Rh. 4.15 W. (s. v. l.); ἀ. χρόνος period *of inaction*, Plb.2.31.10. b. of a farm, *untilled*, Lys.7.6. 2. of persons, *unsuccessful*, ἄπρηκτος νέεσθαι Il.14.221; ἄ. ἀπιέναι, ἀπελθεῖν, ἀποχωρεῖν, Th.4.61,99,1.111; ἄ. γίγνεσθαι *gain nothing*, Id.2.59; ἄ. ἀποπέμπειν τινά Id.1.24: Comp., Socr.*Ep*.6.7. Adv. -τως *unsuccessfully*, Th.6.48; ἄπρακτ' ὀδυρόμενον *in vain*, B.*Fr*.8. 3. *not taking part in the action*, ἄ. κηδευτὴς ὁ χορός Arist.*Pr*.922ᵇ26; *doing nothing, idle*, Ti.Locr.104e, Arr.*Epict*.1.10.7. Adv. ἀεργῶς καὶ ἀ. *PFlor*.295.5 (vi A.D.). 4. *impotent*, μόρια Orib. *Fr*.67, cf. Dsc.3.101. Adv. -τως, βοηθεῖ οὐκ ἀ. Orib.*Fr*.129. II. Pass., *against which nothing can be done, unmanageable, incurable*, ὀδύναι, ἀνίη, Od.2.79, 12.223; μεληδόνες Simon.39; φθόνων -ότατος καὶ ἀπορώτατος ὁ τῆς δεισιδαιμονίας Plu.2.165d. 2. *not to be done, impossible*, πρᾶγμα, ἔργμα, Thgn.1075,1031; ἄπρηκτα *impossibilities*, Id.461. 3. *not done, left undone*, X.*Mem*.2.1.2, D.19.278; ἄ. ποιῆσαί τι *undo* it, Id.*Prooem*.41. 4. c. gen., κοὐδὲ μαντικῆς ἄ. ὑμῖν εἰμί not *unassailed* even by your divining arts, S.*Ant*.1035.

ἀπραξία, ἡ, *non-action*, τὸ μέλλον ἴσον ἀπραξίᾳ λέγω intending to act is the same as *not-acting*, E.*Or*.426; οὐδεμίαν.. πρᾶξιν οὐδ' ἀπραξίαν Pl.*Sph*.262c. 2. *rest from business, leisure*, Men.633: in pl., = Lat. *justitium*, Plu.*Sull*.8. II. *want of success*, κοινὴ ἀ. Aeschin. 1.188. 2. in pl., *futilities*, Phld.*Rh*.1.38 S.

ἀπρᾱσία, ἡ, *want of purchasers, no sale*, Eup.62, D.27.21, 34.8.

ἄπρᾱτος, ον, *unsold, unsaleable*, dub. in Lys.7.6, cf. D.34.9, *BGU* 18.4 (ii A.D.), al.; *unprostituted*, Aeschin.2.23. Adv. ἀπρατί Sch. Il.1.99.

ἀπρέπ-εια, Ep. ἀπρεπίη, ἡ, *unseemliness*, Pl.*R*.465b, etc. 2. *impropriety* in writing, Id.*Phdr*.274b. II. *ugliness*, εἴδεος ἀπρεπίη *APl*.4.319, cf. Dsc.*Alex*.27. **-ής**, ές, *unseemly, unbecoming*, ἀ. τι ἐπιγνῶναι, πάσχειν, Th.3.57,67; ἀ. καὶ ἄσχημον Pl.*Lg*.788b; μέθη.. φύλαξιν -έστατον Id.*R*.398e; τὸ.. τοιαυτὶ ποιεῖν ἀπρεπές Epicr.11. 33; τὸ ἀ., = ἀπρέπεια, Th.5.46, 6.11. Adv. -πῶς, poet. -πέως, *h.Merc*. 272, Pl.*Phdr*.274b, etc.: Comp. -έστερον Hdn.3.13.1. II. of persons, *disreputable, indecent*, ἀνδρίον Theoc.5.40.

ἄπρηκτος, Ion. for ἄπρακτος. **ἄπρητον**· ἀφλόγιστον, Hsch.

ἀπρήϋντος, ον, *implacable*, *AP*7.287 (Antip.), Nonn.*D*.28.1, al.

ἀπρῐάτην [ᾰ] (ἀπριάδην read by Rhian. in Hom.), Adv. of πρίασθαι, *without purchase-money*, ἔνθα με.. ἐκομίσσατο Φείδων ἥρως ἀ. (speaking of a man) Od.14.317; so in late Prose ἥδετο ἀ. εὐωχούμενος Agath.4.22:—also as fem. of Adj. **ἀπρίατος**, μή με ἀπριάτην περάσαντες (sc. Δημήτερα) *h.Cer*.132; δόμεναι.. κούρην ἀπριάτην ἀνάποινον Il.1.99: acc. pl., ἀπριάτας Pi.*Fr*.169.7.

ἄπριγδα, = ἀπρίξ, A.*Pers*.1057,1063 (lyr.).

ἀπριγδόπληκτος, ον, *struck unceasingly*, prob. l. for ἄπριγκτοι πληκτά in A.*Ch*.425 (lyr., Blomfield).

ἀπρίξ, Adv. *fast, tight*, ἀ. ὄνυξι συλλαβών S.*Aj*.310; ἀ. ἔχεσθαι τοῦ κερδαίνειν Id.*Fr*.328, cf. Theoc.15.68, Luc.*Nec*.5, Eun.*VS* p.475 B.; τοῖν χεροῖν λαβέσθαι τινός Pl.*Tht*.155e, cf. Plb.12.11.6; ἔχειν χείρεσσι Theoc.24.55; δράξασθαι *AP*5.247 (Paul. Sil.). II. Subst., a kind of ἄκανθα (Cypr.), *EM*132.53.

ἄπριστος, ον, *not to be sawed*, μοχλός Aen.Tact.20.2. 2. *unsawed*, Q.S.12.137, prob. in *CPHerm*.28.11 (iii A.D.).

ἀπρίωτος [ῐ], ον, in Surgery, *without the use of the trepan*, Hp.*VC*14; *not trephined*, ib.20.

ἀπροαιρ-εσία, ἡ, *inconsistency*, Hp.*Ep*.17; prob. in *Sammelb*. 4317.5 (ii/iii A.D.), for τῆς σῆς σαπροεραισει. **-ετος**, ον, *without set purpose, not deliberate*, of actions, Arist.*EN*1135ᵇ10, Arr.*Epict*.2. 16.1, Plot.1.2.5, etc. Adv. -τως Hp.*Prog*.2, Arist.*EN*1106ᵃ3, Phld. *Ir*.p.93 W., etc. 2. of things, *incapable of choice* or *purpose*, Hermog.*Id*.2.4; *not under the control of will*, Phld.*D*.3 *Fr*.75, M.Ant.6. 41, al.

ἀπρόβᾰτος, ον, *making no progress*, of persons, Phld.*Ir*.p.43 W. II. *not advancing matters, inconclusive*, λόγος Id.*Sign*.6 and 35.

ἀπρόβολος, ον, *unprotected*, Pall. *in Hp.Fract*.12.285 C.

ἀπροβουλ-ευσία, ἡ, *failure to look forward*, Phld.*Herc*.1251. 7. **-ευτος**, ον, *unpremeditated*, Arist.*EN*1135ᵇ11; λόγοι Thphr. *Char*.3.1; *not deliberated upon*, D.H.4.72, J.*BJ*3.5.6. 2. *not submitted to the* βουλή, D.22.5, Hyp.*Fr*.231, Plu.*Sol*.19; of the Roman Senate, App.*BC*1.59. II. Act., *without forethought* or *premeditation*, Arist.*EN*1151ᵃ3, Ceb.8. Adv. -τως Pl.*Lg*.867a,b; ἀ. τοῦ ἀποκτεῖναι *without purpose of*.., ib.866e. **-ία**, ἡ, *want of premeditation*, ib.867b. **-ος**, ον, = ἀπροβούλευτος, only in Adv. -λως *rashly*, A.*Ch*.620 (lyr.).

ἀπρό-γρᾰφος, ον, *not promulgated*, Hyp.*Fr*.231. **-διηγήτως**, Adv., (διηγέομαι) *without preface*, Tz.*Proll.Hes*.10. **-δῐκος**, ον, *without preliminary trial*, [δίκα] *GDI*5017 (Gortyn). **-εδρος**, ον, *without president*, ἐκκλησία Eun.*Hist*.p.209 D. **-θεσμος**, ον, *not fixed to any definite time*, opp. ἐμπρόθεσμος, Sor.1.33. **-θέτως**, Adv., (προτίθημι) *undesignedly*, Plb.9.12.6. **-θῡμία**, ἡ, *want of readiness*, Suid. s. v. ἀρρωστία. **-θῡμος**, ον, *unready, backward*, Hdt.7.220, Th.4.86, X.*An*.6.2.7, etc. Adv. -μως Pl.*Lg*.665e. **-ϊδής** [ῐ], ές, (προϊδεῖν) *unforeseen*, Nic.*Th*.2,18, *AP*7.213 (Arch.), 9.111 (Id.). Adv. -ῶς Archig.ap.Orib.8.2.19. 2. Act., *unforeseeing*, prob. in Nonn.*D*.9.102, 48.757.

ἄπροικος, ον, (προίξ) *without portion* or *dowry*, ἄ. τὴν ἀδελφὴν διδόναι Is.3.29, cf. D.40.20; λαβεῖν Lys.19.15, Diod.Com.3.4, cf. Men.*Mon*. 371.

ἀπρό-ϊτος [ῐ], ον, *not proceeding* or *emanating* (cf. ἀπρόοδος), Dam. *Pr*.34; θερμή Gal.14.729. Adv. -τως Hsch. **-κάλυπτος** [κᾰ], ον, *undisguised*. Adv. -πτως Chio *Ep*.7.3, 13.3. **-κατασκεύαστος**, ον, *not elaborately prepared*, D.H.*Is*.14. **-κοπία**, ἡ, *lack of progress*, Sch.Luc.*Bis Acc*.21. **-κοπος**, ον, *making no progress*, Man.3. 375, Ptol.*Tetr*.156. **-κρίτως** [ῐ], *without discussion, admittedly*, *POxy*.1467.22 (iii A.D.). 2. = Lat. *sine praejudicio*, Just.*Nov*.17. 8. **-ληπτος**, ον, *unanticipated*, *Stoic*.3.149, Onos.8.1. 2. *not prejudged*, τὸ ἀ. τῶν πράξεων Hierocl. *in CA*24 p.459 M. 3. *unprejudiced*, Syrian. *in Metaph*.1.15.

ἀπρομήθ-εια or **-ία**, ἡ, *want of forethought*, Pl.*La.*197b, J.*BJ*3.5.6. **-ευτος**, ον, later form for ἀπρομήθητος. Adv. -τως Suid. s. v. ἀφειδῶς. **-ης**, ες, *not known beforehand*, τὸ ἀ. τῶν γεγονότων J.*AJ* 19.3.1; τὸ ἀ. *failure to take previous account in time*, ib.18.6.5. **-ητος**, ον, *unforeseen*, A.*Supp.*357.

ἀπρονο-ησία, ἡ, *improvidence*, Epicur.*Fr.*368, Alex.Aphr. *de An.* 178.22, Procl. *in Prm.*p.746 S. **-ητέω**, *to be imprudent*, Sch.Il. 4.2. **-ητος**, ον, *unpremeditated*, ἀκρασία Arist.*MM*1203^{a}30; χώρα ἀ. an *unguarded* country, Plb.4.5.5; τόποι ἀ. *unreconnoitred*, Id.3.48.4; *not the work of providence*, κόσμος Ph.2.411, cf. Hierocl. *in CA*11 p.442 M. II. Act., *not considering beforehand*, ἡ ὀργὴ -τον X.*HG* 5.3.7; ἀ. καὶ ἀπαράσκευοι Plb.5.7.2, cf. Orph.*Fr.*233; ἀ. τῶν ἐσομένων J.*Vit.*13; τῶν ἐπὶ γῆς πραγμάτων Luc.*Bis Acc.*2, etc.; of the gods, *not exercising providence*, Epicur.*Fr.*368. Adv. -τως X.*Cyr.*1.4.21, etc.; ἀ. τινὸς ἔχειν Str.2.5.1; opp. προνοίᾳ, S.E.*P.*1.151; οἱ ἀ. θεώμενοι *without previous acquaintance*, Plb.10.14.8.

ἀπρονόμευτος· οὐ πρυτανευθείς· ἀπρονομή (sic) γὰρ ἡ ἐπὶ τῆς χώρας ἁρπαγή, Hsch.

ἀπρόξενος, ον, *without* πρόξενος, A.*Supp.*239.

ἀπροξίς, ίδος, ἡ, *burning bush*, *Dictamnus albus*, Pythag.ap.Plin. *HN*24.158.

ἀπρό-οδος, ον, *not proceeding* or *emanating*, ἡ [τοῦ ἑνὸς] φύσις Dam. *Pr.*34. **-οιμίαστος**, ον, *without preface*, Luc.*Hist.Conscr.*23, Corn. *Rh.*p.358 H. Adv. -τως D.H.*Lys.*17. **-οπτος**, ον, *unforeseen*, A.*Pr.*1074 (lyr.); ἐξ -όπτου Aesop.330. Adv. -τως *PAmh.*2.154.7 (vi A. D.). II. Act., *not foreseeing, unwary*, Poll.1.179; ἀ. τοῦ μέλλοντος Id.3.117. Adv. -τως Sor.1.71, Ael.*NA*1.8. **-ὁρᾱτος**, ον, = foreg. I, D.S.20.96, Corn.*ND*10, Iamb.*Protr.*21. 2. *not previously seen*, Gal.14.279. II. = foreg. II, Ph.2.268, Max.Tyr. 11.6; τοῦ μέλλοντος Ph.2.159. Adv. -τως Onos.22.1, D.L.9.62, Ach. Tat.2.6, Max.Tyr.31.1. **-πετία**, ἡ, *freedom from precipitancy*, Ti. Locr.102e.

ἄπροπον· ἀπρεπές, Hsch.

ἀπρο-πτωσία, ἡ, *freedom from precipitancy, deliberateness*, *Stoic.* 2.39, Chrysipp.ib.40, M.Ant.3.9. **-πτωτος**, ον, *not precipitate*, Chrysipp.*Stoic.*2.40; συγκατάθεσις Arr.*Epict.*2.8.29, cf. M.Ant.4.49. Adv. -τως Chrysipp.*Stoic.*3.50. **-ρρητος**, ον, *not foretold*, Pl.*Lg.* 968e, as Ast for ἀπόρρητος.

ἀπροσ-ᾱγόρευτος, ον, *without appellation*, *Proll.Hermog.* in Rh.4.21 W. **-άρμοστος**, ον, *not befitting*, τινί Eust.1271.58. **-άρτητος**, ον, *detached*, ζῷον ἤδη ἀ. *Theol.Ar.*46. **-αύδητος**, ον, *not accosted*, Plu.2.29b,921f; *unapproachable*, Aristocl.ap.Eus.*PE*11.3. **-βᾰτος**, Dor. **ἀποτίβατος**, ον, *inaccessible*, πέτραι Arist.*HA*563^{a}5, cf. Plu.*Alex.* 58, Luc.*Prom.*1; ἀποτίβ. νοῦσος *unapproachable*, S.*Tr.*1030 (lyr.), cf. Max.Tyr.18.1. **-βλεπτος**, ον, *not to be looked at*, *EM*433.49. **-βλητον**· γενναῖον, Hsch. **-δεής**, ές, *without want of* anything, Lxx 1 *Ma.*12.9, al., Phld.*D.*3.13; φιλοσοφίας Plu.2.122f, cf. 381b, Luc.*Hist.Conscr.*36: abs., *self-sufficient*, Plu.*Comp.Arist.Cat.* 4, Plot.5.9.4. **-δέητος**, ον, = foreg., Plb.21.23.4; διδασκαλίας Phld.*Rh.*1.194 S. **-δεικτος**, *not to be pointed out*, A.*Supp.*794 cod. (lyr., -μεικτος Headlam). **-δεκτος**, ον, *inadmissible*, *BGU* 1113.21 (i B. C.), S.E.*P.*2.229. II. Act., *not giving heed to*, συμβουλίας Phld.*Vit.*p.34 J., dub. in Id.*D.*3 *Fr.*42; *unacceptable*, Plb.36.12.4; θυσία *IG*3.73.14,74.8; εὐχὴ ἀ. ὑπὸ θεοῦ Porph.*Marc.*24. **-διόνῡσος**, ον, *unconnected with the worship of Dionysus*, Plu.2.671f. II. *not to the point, mal à propos*, proverbial like οὐδὲν πρὸς Διόνυσον, Cic.*Att.* 16.13^a.1, Plu.2.612e, Luc.*Bacch.*6. **-διόριστος**, ον, *undefined*, Ulp. ad D.24.68; *unqualified*, Heliod. *in EN*109.19; of propositions, *indefinite in quantification*, Ammon. *in APr.*14.37. Adv. -τως *without distinction*, Gal.16.558; *par excellence*, Olymp. *in Mete.*123.3. **-δόκητος**, ον, *unexpected, unlooked for*, A.*Pr.*680, S.*El.*1017, etc.; εὐπραγία Th.3.39; πρᾶγμ' ἡμῖν ἰδεῖν ἀ. Ar.*Lys.*352; κακοπάθεια Antipho 3.2. 11; τύχη Pl.*Lg.*920d; ἀ. [ὁδὸν] πορευθείς X.*HG*6.4.3; ἐξ ἀπροσδοκήτου Hdt.1.191, 7.204. Adv. -τως Th.4.29, Lys.1.11, etc. II. Act., *not expecting, unaware*, ἐπιθέσθαι τισὶ ἀπροσδοκήτοις Th.2.33, cf. 7.39; ὡ. ἦσαν ὡς ἤδη μαχούμενοι Id.6.69; ἀ. μὴ ἄν ποτέ τινα σφίσιν ἐπιθέσθαι Id.7.29. **-δοκία**, ἡ, *non-expectation*, Pl.*Def.*412c. **-έγγιστος**, ον, gloss on ἀπρόσιτος, Hsch. **-ειλος**, *unsunned*, E.*Fr.* 845. **-εκτέω**, *to be heedless, inattentive*, Eustr. *in APo.*258.6. **-εκτος**, ον, *heedless, careless*, Tz. ad Lyc.314. Adv. -τως *unconcernedly*, Porph.*Sent.*32. **-έλευστος**, ον, *not taken up*, of an inheritance, Just.*Nov.*1.1.3, cf. Suid. **-εξία**, ἡ, *want of attention*, Arr.*Epict.* 4.12.5, Sext.*Sent.*280a, etc. **-ηγορία**, ἡ, *want of intercourse*, Poet.ap.Arist.*EN*1157^{b}13. **-ήγορος**, ον, *not to be accosted, unapproachable*, of a man, S.*OC*1277; of a lion, Id.*Tr.*1093; *without intercourse* or *conversation*, Plu.2.679a. **-ηνής**, ές, *ungentle, harsh*, Sch.Pi.*P.*2.10. **-θετέω**, *suspend judgement*, Timo 80. **-θετος**, ον, *not added to*, *Theol.Ar.*30. **-θικτος**, ον, *untouched, not to be touched*, Hsch. s. v. ἀπροτίμαστος. **-ικτος**, ον, *unattainable*, ἔρωτες Pi.*N.*11. 48. **-ῑτος**, ον, *unapproachable, inaccessible*, ὄρη Plb.3.49.7, cf. Str. 1.3.18; φῶς 1 *Ep.Ti.*6.16; of persons, Cic.*Att.*5.20.6, cf. Plu.2.68e; καταφυγή D.S.19.96: metaph., λόγοις ἀ. παρρησία Plu.*Alc.*4; δύναμις τοῦ λόγου Luc.*Dem.Enc.*32. Adv. -τως Plu.2.45f. **-καίρως**, *unseasonably*, Sch.Ptol.*Tetr.*158.

ἀπρό-σκεπτος, ον, *unforeseen, not thought of*, X.*Lac.*13.7. II. Act., *improvident*, D.51.15. Adv. -τως Antiph.195.

ἀπρόσ-κλητος, ον, *without summons to attend a trial*, *IG*1.27a10, Hyp.*Fr.*2; ἀ. δίκη a prosecution *in support of which no* πρόσκλησις *has been issued*, D.53.15; ἐπιβολή ib.14; γνῶσις Id.21.92; *without notice*, ὑμέναιος Hld.6.8; *unsummoned*, Id.8.1. **-κόλλητος**, ον, *not adhering*, τινί Eust.1940.20.

ἀπροσκοπεῖν· μὴ προορᾶν, Hsch.

ἀπρόσ-κοπος (A), ον, *not stumbling, void of offence*, *Ep.Phil.*1.10; συνείδησις *Act.Ap.*24.16. 2. *free from harm*, ἄτρωτος καὶ ἀ. *IG*5(2). 20.19 (Tegea, i B. C.); [θεοί] σε διαφυλάσσουσιν ἀ. *PGiss.*17.7 (ii A. D.), cf. *PBaden* 39 iii 14 (ii A. D.). Adv. -πως ib.79 iv 8 (ii A. D.). II. *giving no offence*, τινί S.E.*M.*1.195, 1 *Ep.Cor.*10.32.

ἀπρό-σκοπος (B), ον, *unseeing*, A.*Eu.*105. II. *unexplored*, ὁδός Lxx *Si.*35(32).21.

ἀπρόσ-κοπτος, ον, *without offence*, *IG*14.404. Adv. -τως *without stumbling*, τρέχειν Eust.925.28. **-κορής**, ές, *not satiating* or *disgusting*, Men.Rh.p.340 S., Hld.6.1. II. *insatiate*, πρὸς τὰς ἡδονάς *Cat.Cod.Astr.*8(4).178.19. **-κρουστος**, ον, *free from blows*, ἕλκη φυλάττειν ἀ. Hierocl.p.25 A. II. *not taking offence*, πρός τινα Plu. *in Hes.*65. **-ληπτος**, ον, *not taking* or *admitting* a construction, A.D.*Pron.*14.15, *Synt.*63.21. **-λογος**, ον, *not to the point*, Sch.Ar. *V.*1311, al. Adv. -γως Plb.9.36.6. **-μᾰχος**, ον, *irresistible*, S. *Tr.*1098; τινί Luc.*Tox.*48. **-μηχάνητος** [χᾰ], ον, *against whom no device avails*, Sch.Il.16.29. **-μήχᾰνος**, ον, = foreg., Sch.A.R.1. 1053. **-μῑγής**, ές, = sq., Steph.Byz. s. v. Σῆρες, Eust. ad D.P. 752. **-μικτος** (-μεικτος), ον, *holding no communion with*, ξένοισι Hdt.1.65: abs., *solitary, isolated*, Poll.3.64. Adv. -τως Id.5. 139. **-όδευτος**, ον, *not turned to profit*, *JHS*38.188 (Iconium, dub.). **-οδος**, ον, *without approach, inaccessible*, βίος Phryn.Com. 18; ὄρη Procop.*Goth.*4.16. II. *not yielding a return, unproductive*, Phld.*Oec.*p.35 J. **-οιστος**, ον, *hard to associate with* or *deal with*, A.*Pers.*91 (lyr.). Adv. -τως *unsociably*, Isoc.9.49. **-όμῑλος**, ον, *unsociable*, γῆρας S.*OC*1236. **-οπτος**, ον, *not to be looked at, faced*, ἀστραπή Poll.1.117. **-όρᾱτος**, ον, *not to be looked on, frightful*, πόνος Pi.*O.*2.67; epith. of Κύρβας, Orph.*H.*39.2. **-όρμιστος**, ον, *where one cannot land*, D.S.20.74, Sch.S.*Ph.*214. **-πᾰθής**, ές, *without affection* or *passion*, Hierocl. *in CA*11 p.438 M. **-πέλαστος**, ον, *unapproachable*, Str.1.2.9, Plu.*Ant.*70. **-πληστος**, = foreg., Hsch. **-πλοκος**, ον, *not to be interwoven*, Sch.Ar.*Ra.*1340. **-ποίητος**, ον, *unfeigned*, in Adv. -τως D.S.32.24. **-πταιστος**, ον, = ἀπρόσκοπος (A), Hp.*Ep.*17. **-πτωσία**, ἡ, *freedom from error*, Alex. Aphr. *de An.*150.35. **-ρητος**, ον, *unaddressed*, ἀ. τινὰ καταλιπεῖν Jul.*Ep.*182, cf. Poll.5.137,138.

ἀπρο-στᾰσίαστος, ον, *without* προστάτης or *guardian*, Ph.1.170; of the universe, ib.696. **-στασίου γραφή** indictment of a μέτοικος *for not having chosen a* προστάτης or *patron*, D.35.48; ἀ. δίκη Arist.*Ath.* 58.3, Hyp.*Fr.*15. **-στάτευτος** [τᾰ], ον, *without a leader* or *guide*, J.*AJ*20.8.8, Ael.*NA*15.8, f. l. for sq. in Hierocl.p.54 A. **-στάτητος** [τᾰ], ον, = foreg., M.Ant.12.14; οἶκος Hierocl.p.54 A. **-στᾰτος**, ον, = foreg., dub. in D.C.78.20.

ἀπροστίμητος [ῐ], ον, *without penalty*, Ἀρχ.Δελτ.2.269 (Coronea, i B. C.). II. ἀπροστίματον· ἀπροσδόκητον, ἀπρόσβατον, Hsch.

ἀπρόστομος, ον, *without sharp edge*, ξίφος Magn.7.

ἀπρόστυχος, gloss on ἄσιμος, Hsch.

ἀπρόσ-φῐλος, ον, *unfriendly, hostile*, Hld.5.7. **-φορος**, ον, *dangerous*, νῆσους ναύταις ἀπροσφόρους E.*IA*287 (lyr.); *unsuitable*, Herod. Med.ap.Orib.10.18.6; *incongruous*, Tz. ad Hes.*Op.*735. Adv. -ρως Steph. *in Hp.*1.223 D. **-φυής**, ές, *incongruous*, Eust.178.37; *unrelated*, Tz.*H.*8.158. Adv. -ῶς Eust.529.31. **-φῡλος**, ον, (φῦλον) *not belonging to the tribe*, Hld.4.8 (dub. l.). **-φωνητί**, Adv. of sq., *without accosting*, Aesop.35. **-φώνητος**, ον, *not accosted*, Cic.*Att.* 8.8.1. 2. *unnoticed, unremarked*, Plu.2.575b, Sch.A.R.1.645.

ἀπρόσχημος, = *aequiformis*, of verses, Diom.p.498 K.

ἀπρόσ-χωρος, ον, *arrogant*, *Gloss.* **-ψαυστος**, ον, *not to be touched*, Hdn.*Epim.*57.

ἀπροσωπόληπτος, ον, *not respecting persons*, Suid. s. v. ἀδυσώπητος. Adv. -τως *without respect of persons*, 1 *Ep.Pet.*1.17.

ἀπρόσωπος, ον, *without a face*, i. e. *without beauty of face*, opp. εὐπρόσωπος, Pl.*Chrm.*154d, cf. Ael.*NA*14.18; of a country, Chor. p.223 B. II. *without a mask, undisguised*, ἀγνωμοσύνη Aristid. 1.409 J. III. *impersonal*, Phld.*Lib.*p.29 O., *AB*420. Adv. -πως Aphth.*Prog.*4.

ἀπροτί-ελπτος, ον, Ep. for ἀπρόσ-, *unhoped for*, Opp.*C.*3.422 (v. l. ἀπροτίοπτον). **-μαστος**, ον, Ep. for ἀπρόσμαστος, (μαίομαι) *untouched, undefiled*, of Briseis, Il.19.263. II. *unapproachable*, of Homer, Euph.118. **-όπιστος**· ἀπρονόητος, Hsch. **-οπτος**, ον, = ἀπρόσοπτος, *invisible, obscure*, Man.2.19, Opp.*H.*3.159, Q.S.7. 73, *Ath.Mitt.*27.339 (Acarn.).

ἀπρο-φᾰνής, ές, = ἀπρόφατος, *unexpected*, f. l. in Orph.*A.*787. **-φάσιστος** [φᾰ], ον, *offering no excuse, unhesitating, ready*, προθυμία Th.6.83; εὔνοια Lys.*Fr.*114; σύμμαχοι X.*Cyr.*2.4.10; συνεραστής Timocl.8. Adv. -τως *without disguise*, Th.1.49, etc.: *without evasion, honestly*, Id.6.72, *IG*2.243, etc.; *unhesitatingly*, D.C.38.39. II. *admitting no excuse, implacable*, θάνατος E.*Ba.*1002. III. *inexcusable*, κακία Plu.*Cat.Mi.*44, cf. 2.742c. **-φᾰτος**, ον, *unforetold, unexpected*, Arat.424,768, A.R.2.268, Nic.*Al.*598. Adv. -τως A.R. 1.1201, 2.580, Orph.*A.*787. II. *unutterable, terrific*, A.R.1. 645. III. *without parley*, in Adv. -τως Id.2.62, 4.1005. **-φύλακτος** [ῠ], ον, *not guarded against, unforeseen*, Th.4.55. Adv. -τως D.C.38. 41, Ach.Tat.8.1. 2. *unguarded*, Opp.*H.*5.106. II. Act., *using no precautions*, Hld.6.13. **-φώνητος**, ον, *not announced beforehand*, Sch.Od.4.727. **-χωστος**, ον, *not silted up*, λιμένες Men.Rh.p.351 S.

ἀπρῠτάνευτος [τᾰ], ον, *without payment of* πρυτανεῖα (q. v.), δίκαι *Milet.*3 No.147.31.

ἀπταισία, ἡ, *smoothness* of rhythm in music, Pl.*Lg.*669e.

ἄπταιστος, ον, *not stumbling*, ἀπταιστότερον παρέχειν τὸν ἵππον make a horse *less apt to stumble*, X.*Eq.*1.6: metaph., ἄ. ἐν τῷ βίῳ Epict. *Gnom.*52; δώμασιν ἀ. Limen.43, cf. M.Ant.5.9; βίος Luc.*Am.*46; *infallible*, Plot.5.3.17, Alex.Aphr.*in Metaph.*713.12; ἀλήθεια Iamb.*Myst.* 3.31; θεοὶ διδασκάλων -ότατοι Max.Tyr.38.1. Adv. -τως Pl.*Tht.*144b; *inevitably*, Gal.14.230: Comp. -ότερον *with greater precision*, Ptol.*Tetr.* 177:—also -τί, Hdn.*Epim.*256. 2. *intact*, Plu.2.691d. II. *not causing to stumble, giving a good footing*, λεία καὶ ἄ. ὁδός Max.Tyr.5.2.

ἀπτάν· ἀναχωρήσιον, Hsch. II. cf. sq., Id.

ἀπταντίτας, derived from ἀπτάν, = πένης, τιτάν, = παιδεραστής, Hsch. **ἀπταρύσσεται**· πέτεται, Id.; cf. ἀπτερύσσομαι.

ἀπτέον, (ἅπτομαι) *one must cling to* a thing, *bestow pains upon* it, μουσικῆς Pl.*R.*377a, cf. Epicur.*Fr.*461; *one must partake of*, πλακοῦντος Alex.250, cf. Gal.11.371, Porph.*Abst.*2.44.

ἀπτερέως, Adv., (ἀ-, = sm̥-, πτερόν) *quickly, swiftly*, Hes.*Fr.*96.46, Parm.1.17, A.R.4.1765. (Expld. as = αἰφνιδίως by Hdn.Gr.2.230; cf. ἄπτερος III, ἀπτέρωτος II.)

ἄπτερος, ον, *without wings, unwinged*, Hom. only in Od., and always in phrase τῇ δ' ἄπτερος ἔπλετο μῦθος the speech was to her *without wings, remained unuttered*, opp. ἔπεα πτερόεντα, 17.57; ἄ. φάτις *unspoken* rumour, A.*Ag.*278; ἄπτερα πωτήματα *wingless* flight, Id.*Eu.*250; ἄ. δρόμος, of the Trojan horse, v.l. in Tryph.85. 2. ἄπτερα, opp. πτερωτά, *without wings*, of insects, Arist.*HA*523b17; ἄπτερον, τό, Id.*PA*642b33. II. *unfeathered*, of Harpies, A.*Eu.*51; ἄνθρωπος ζῷον ἄ. Pl.*Def.*415a; ὄρνις (i.e. the Chorus) E.*IT*1095 (lyr.); of arrows, Hdt.7.92. 2. of young birds, *unfledged, callow*, ἄ. ὠδὶν τέκνων E.*HF*1039, cf. Pl.*Phdr.*256d. III. (ἀ-, = sm̥-) ἄ. τάχος of great speed, *Trag.Adesp.*429; cf. ἄπτερα· ἰσόπτερα, ταχέα, ἡδέα, Hsch. Adv. -ρως Lyc.627 (δμοπτέρως, ταχέως, Sch.).

ἀπτέρῠγος, ον, *without wings*, Hedyle ap.Ath.7.297b.

ἀπτερύομαι, = πτερύσσομαι, *flap the wings*, Arat.1009.

ἀπτερύσσομαι, = foreg., Archil.49 Diehl (ap.Sch.Arat.1009); cf. ἀπταρύσσεται.

ἀπτέρωτος, ον, *unfeathered*, of arrows or bolts, *IG*2.809e19. II. ἀπτέρωτα· ταχέα, αἰφνίδια, Hsch.; cf. ἀπτερέως, ἄπτερος III.

ἀπτήν, ῆνος, ὁ, ἡ, (πτηνός) *unfledged, callow*, ἀπτῆσι νεοσσοῖσι Il.9.323: metaph. of men, ἀπτῆνα τυτθὸν *Com.Adesp.*1291. II. *unwinged*, βροτοί Ar.*Av.*687; πεζοῖς τε καὶ ἀπτῆσι (sc. ζῴοις) Pl.*Plt.*276a.

ἀπτικός, ή, όν, (ἅπτομαι) *able to come into contact with*, ἀλλήλων Arist.*GC*322b27. 2. abs., τὴν ἀ. αἴσθησιν the sense *of touch*, Id. *de An.*413b9, cf. Alex.Aphr.*Pr.Praef.*; τὸ ἁ. Arist.*de An.*415a3; γλῶττα ἀπτικωτάτη *most sensitive to touch*, Id.*PA*660a21. Adv. -κῶς Olymp.*in Alc.*p.40C. 3. of medicines, *acting on*, c. gen., τοῦ νευρώδους Dsc.2.179.

ἄπτῖλος, ον, *unfledged*, Jul.*Ep.*191.

ἄπτιστος, ον, *not winnowed* or *ground*, Hp.*VM*14.

ἀπτοεπής, ές, *reckless in speech*, Il.8.209 (v.l. ἀπτοεπής: fort. ἀεπτο-επής *uttering unspeakable words* (for ἀϝεπτο-, cf. ϝέπος)).

ἀπτόητος, poet. **ἀπτοίητος**, ον, *undaunted*, Lxx *Je.*26(46).28, Nonn.*D.*22.355, Sch.Il.1.56, etc. Adv. -τως, θνήσκειν Phalar.*Ep.* 103.2.

ἀπτολέμ-ιστος, ον, *unwarlike*, Orac.ap.Ath.12.524b. **-ος**, ον, poet. for ἀπόλεμος, Il.2.201, E.*Med.*640 (lyr.), etc.

ἄπτορος· ἰσόπτερος, Hsch. (leg. ἄπτερος).

ἀπτός, ή, όν, (ἅπτω) *tangible*, ὁρατὰ ἢ ἁ. σώματα Pl.*R.*525d, cf. *Ti.* 32b, al., Arist.*de An.*424a12, Thphr.*Od.*64, etc. II. ἀπτά· φάρμακα, Hsch.

ἄπτρα, ἡ, Dim. **ἄπτριον**, τό, (ἅπτω B) *wick of a lamp*, Sch.D.T. p.195H.

ἄπτυστος, ον, *without expectoration*, πλευρῖτις Hp.*Coac.*375, cf. Gal. 17(1).491.

ἅπτω, fut. ἅψω: aor. ἧψα:—**Pass.**, pf. ἧμμαι, Ion. ἅμμαι Hdt.1. 86: fut. ἅψομαι Od.9.379, ἀφθήσομαι (συν-) Gal.3.311:—**Med.**, v. infr. (cf. ἑάφθη):—*fasten* or *bind to*, used by Hom., once in Act., ἅψας ἀμφοτέρωθεν.. ἔντερον οἰός (of a lyre-string) Od.21.408; once in Med., ἁψαμένη βρόχον.. ἀφ' ὑψηλοῖο μελάθρου *having fastened* the noose to the beam (to hang herself), 11.278; so later ἅψεται ἀμφὶ βρόχον.. δείρᾳ E.*Hipp.*770; ἁψαμένη βρόχον αὐχένι A.R.1.1065:—Act., βρόχους ἅ. κρεμαστούς E.*Or.*1036; but βρόχῳ ἅ. δέρην Id.*Hel.*136, cf. *AP*7.493 (Antip. Thess.). 2. *join*, ἅ. χορόν A.*Eu.*307; πάλην τινὶ ἅ. *fasten* a contest in wrestling *on* one, *engage with* one, Id.*Ch.*868: —Pass., ἅπτεσθαι τὴν Μεγαρέων πόλιν καὶ Κορινθίων τοῖς τείχεσιν Arist.*Pol.*1280b14. II. more freq. in Med., ἅπτομαι, fut. ἅψομαι, aor. ἡψάμην E.*Supp.*317, with pf. Pass. ἧμμαι S.*Tr.*1010 (lyr.), Pl. *Phdr.*260e:—*fasten oneself to, grasp*, c. gen., ἅψασθαι γούνων Il.1.512; χειρῶν 10.377; ἁψαμένη δὲ γενείου Ὀδυσσῆα προσέειπεν Od.19.473; ἅπτεσθαι νηῶν Il.2.152; βρώμης δ' οὐχ ἅπτεαι οὐδὲ ποτῆτος; Od.10.379, cf. 4.60; ὡς δ' ὅτε τίς τε κύων συὸς.. ἅπτηται κατόπισθε.. ἰσχία τε γλουτούς τε Il.8.339; ἅπτεσθαι τοῦ ἐπεόντος ἐπὶ τῶν δενδρέων καρποῦ Hdt.2.32; τῶν τύμβων ἁπτόμενοι Id.4.172; ἅπτεσθαί τινος, Lat. *manus inicere alicui*, Id.3.137; οὔτ' ἔθιγεν οὔθ' ἥψαθ' ἡμῶν E.*Ba.*617; τῶν σφυγμῶν *feel* the pulse, Arr.*Epict.*3.22.73: metaph., *take hold of, cleave to*, Pl.*Lg.*967c. b. abs., τῶν μὲν γὰρ πάντων βέλε' ἅπτεται for the spears of all the Trojans *reach their mark*, Il.17.631; ἀμφοτέρων βέλε' ἥπτετο 8.67. c. ἅ. τῆς γῆς *land*, D.S.4.48. III. metaph., *engage in, undertake*, βουλευμάτων S.*Ant.*179; ἀγῶνος E. *Supp.*317; πολέμου *prosecute* it *vigorously*, Th.5.61; ἧπται τοῦ πράγματος D.21.155; ψυχὴ ἡμμένη φόνων Pl.*Phd.*108b, cf. E.*IT*381; τῶν μεγίστων ἀσεβημάτων Plb.7.13.6; so ἅ. τῆς μουσικῆς καὶ φιλοσοφίας Pl.*R.*411c; ἐπιτηδεύματος ib.497e; γεωμετρίας Id.*Plt.*266a; τῆς θαλάττης Plb.1.24.7; ἅπτεσθαι λόγου E.*Andr.*662, Pl.*Euthd.*283a (but ἅπτεσθαι τοῦ λόγου *attack, impugn* the argument of another, Id.*Phd.* 86d); τούτων ἥψατο *touched on* these points, *handled* them, Th.1.97; ἅ. τῆς ζητήσεως Arist.*GC*320b34; but also, *touch on, treat superficially*, Pl.*Lg.*694c, Arist.*EE*1227a1. b. abs., *begin, set to work*, ταῖς διανοίαις Ar.*Ec.*581. 2. *fasten upon, attack*, Pi.*N.*8.22, A.*Ag.* 1608, etc.; μόνον τῷ δακτύλῳ Ar.*Lys.*365; τῆς οὐραγίας Plb.2.34.12; esp. with words, Hdt.5.92.γ'; of diseases, ἧπταί μου S.*Tr.*1010, cf. Gal.15.702; ἥψατο τῶν ἀνθρώπων Th.2.48; ὅσα ἅπτεται ἀνθρώπων all that *feed on* human flesh, ib.50. b. *lay hands on*, χρημάτων Pl.*Lg.* 913a; τῶν ἀλλοτρίων Id.*R.*360b, etc. 3. *touch, affect*, ἄλγος οὐδὲν ἅπτεται νεκροῦ A.*Fr.*255, cf. S.*OC*955; ἅπτει μου τοῖς λόγοις τῆς ψυχῆς Pl.*Ion* 535a; τῆς ἐμῆς ἥψω φρενὸς E.*Rh.*916; ὥς μου χρησμὸς ἅ. φρενῶν Ar.*Eq.*1237; *make an impression upon*, ἡμῶν *OGI*315.56 (Pessinus, ii B.C.). 4. *grasp with the senses, perceive*, S.*OC*1550, Pl.*Phd.*99e; *apprehend*, τῆς αἰτίας Arist.*Resp.*472a3. 5. *have intercourse with* a woman, Pl.*Lg.*840a, Arist.*Pol.*1335b40, 1*Ep.Cor.* 7.1; εὐνῆς E.*Ph.*946. 6. *come up to, reach, overtake*, X.*HG*5.4.43; *attain*, τῆς ἀληθείας Pl.*Phd.*65b; τοῦ τέλους Id.*Smp.*211b: in Pi., c. dat., ἀγλαΐαις *P.*10.28; στάλαισιν Ἡρακλείαις Id.*I.*4(3).12; but also c. gen., Ἡρακλέος σταλᾶν Id.*O.*3.44. 7. *make use of, avail oneself of*, τῆς τύχης E.*IA*56. 8. Geom., of bodies and surfaces, *to be in contact*, Arist.*Ph.*231a22, cf. *Metaph.*1002a34, al., S.E.*M.*3. 35; of lines or curves, *meet*, Euc.3 *Def.*2; *touch*, Id.4 *Def.*5, Archim. *Sph.Cyl.*1.28; *pass through* a point, Euc.4 *Defs.*2,6; of points, *lie on* a line or curve, ib.*Defs.*1,3; ἅπτεται τὸ σημεῖον θέσει δεδομένης εὐθείας *the locus* of the point *is* a given straight line, Id.ap.Papp.656.6, al.

B. Act., *kindle, set on fire* (i.e. by *contact* of fire), Hdt.8.52, etc. (so in Med., Call.*Dian.*116); ἐρείκης θωμὸν ἅψαντες πυρί A.*Ag.*295: metaph., πυρσὸν ὕμνων Pi.*I.*4(3).43:—Pass., *to be set on fire*, ὁ μοχλὸς ἐλάϊνος ἐν πυρὶ μέλλεν ἅψεσθαι Od.9.379; ὡς ἅφθη τάχιστα τὸ λήιον.. ἅψατο νηοῦ as soon as the corn *caught fire*, it *set fire to* the temple, Hdt.1.19; πυρῆς ἤδη ἁμμένης ib.86; ἧπται πυρί E.*Hel.*107. II. ἅ. πῦρ *kindle* a fire, ib.503:—Pass., ἄνθρακες ἡμμένοι *red-hot* embers, Th.4.100; δᾷδ' ἐνεγκάτω τις ἡμμένην Ar.*Nu.*1490, cf. *Pl.*301. III. *cook*, Alex.124.1.

ἀπτώδιον, τό, *brooch*, *POxy.*1273.8 (iii A.D.).

ἀπτώξ, ῶκος, ὁ, ἡ, *without hares*, Hdn.Gr.1.46.

ἀπτώς, ῶτος, ὁ, ἡ, (πίπτω) *not falling* or *liable to fall*, ἀ. δόλος, of a wrestler's art, Pi.*O.*9.92; λόγος Pl.*R.*534c; ἀ. ἑστάναι M.Ant.7.61; ἀ. ἑαυτὸν διατηρεῖν Plu.*Comp.Arist.Cat.*2.

ἄπτωτος, ον, = ἀπτώς, *never thrown*, of a wrestler, *IG*14.1106, *TAM*2.301. 2. metaph., *faultless*, Longin.33.4, cf. Ph.1.678. II. *without cases*, ῥῆμα στοιχεῖον λόγου ἄ. Apollod.*Stoic.*3.213, cf. D.T. 638.3, A.D.*Synt.*176.5, al. 2. *not involving different cases*, of a geometrical problem, Procl.*in Euc.*p.222F. III. Adv. -τως, ἔχειν to be *secure*, Corn.*ND*9; *infallibly, with certainty*, S.E.*M.*8.187.

ἀπύ, Aeol., Arc., Thess. for ἀπό:—**ἀπυδόσμιος, -δοσμός**, v. ἀπο-.

ἄπῡγος, ον, *without buttocks*, Semon.7.76, Pl.Com.184.3.

ἄπυθεν, Aeol. for ἄποθεν, Hsch.

ἀπύθμενος, ον, *without bottom* or *base*, κύλιξ Thphr.*Fr.*94; φιάλη Parth.ap.Ath.11.501a, cf. Dsc.*Eup.*1.235; γῆ ἀπύθμενον θεώρημα Secund.*Sent.*14:—also **ἀπυθμένιστος**, ον, Eust.870.28: **ἀπύθμην**, ενος, ὁ, ἡ, Theognost.*Can.*86.

ἀπύκαστον· ἀσκέπαστον, Phot.

ἄπυκν-ος, ον, *not dense, not compressed*, Ptol.*Geog.*8.1.4. 2. in Music, of notes, *not included in the* πυκνόν (q. v.), Cleonid.*Harm.*4, etc. **-ωτος**, ον, = foreg. 1, Eust.972.39.

ἄπῠλος, ον, = sq., metaph., Vett.Val.334.13.

ἀπύλωτος [ῠ], ον, *not secured by gates*, X.*HG*5.4.20; στόμα Ar. *Ra.*838 (v.l. ἀθύρωτον).

ἀπυνδάκωτος [δᾰ], ον, = ἀπύθμενος, S.*Fr.*611.

ἄπῡος, ον, *not suppurating*, Suid.

ἄπυργ-ος, ον, *untowered, unfortified*, E.*Fr.*749. **-ωτος**, ον, = foreg., *not girt with towers*, Od.11.264.

ἀπύρεκτος [ῠ], ον, = ἀπύρετος, Arr.*Epict.*4.6.21 (ex corr.), *Gp.*13. 8.9, Gal.10.378, Aët.9.31.

ἀπῠρεξία, ἡ, *absence of fever, time* or *state free from fever*, Gal.17(1). 69, cf. 19.399.

ἀπύρετος [ῠ], ον, *free from fever*, Hp.*Aph.*4.20, Luc.*Philops.*25, *POxy.*1582.9 (ii A.D.); *not inducing fever*, δίαιτα Hp.*Art.*69; βίος Antiph.226.6; *relieving fever*, ἀντίδοτος Archig.ap.Gal.13.173:—perh. to be read for **ἀπύρευτος** f.l. in Thphr.*Char.*3.6.

ἀπῡρηνομήλη, ἡ, *probe without a knob* (πυρήν), Hp.ap.Gal.19.85.

ἀπύρηνος [ῡ], ον, *without stone* or *kernel, pipless*, ῥοά Ar.*Fr.*118, Thphr.*HP*4.13.2; φοῖνιξ Arist.*de An.*422a29, *Fr.*267. II. *with no spine*, ἰχθύς (i.e. ἔγχελυς) Archestr.*Fr.*8 codd.

ἀπυρίτης (sc. ἄρτος), ὁ, a kind of *loaf*, Poll.6.33.

ἄπῡρος, ον, *without fire*, in Hom. only of pots and tripods, *that have not yet been on the fire, brand-new*, ἕπτ' ἀπύρους τρίποδας Il.9.122, cf. 23.267. b. *not capable of standing on the fire*, σκευῶν ἐμπύρων καὶ ἀ. Pl.*Lg.*679a, cf. Ar.*Fr.*532. c. *not wasted by fire*, Max.Tyr. 41.4. 2. ἄ. οἶκος *fireless*, i.e. *cold, cheerless*, Hes.*Op.*525. 3. *unfermented*, οἶνος Alcm.117; *uncooked*, σιτία Plu.2.349a; ἄκολος *AP* 9.563 (Leon.), etc. 4. ἄ. χρυσίον *unsmelted*, opp. ἄπεφθον, Hdt.

3.97, IG2.652B28 (but ἄ. χρυσός, of nuggets, or gold-dust, Arist.Mir. 833^{b}8, D.S.2.50, al.); ἄ. κύανος Thphr.Lap.55; ἄ. τέχναι Aristid.Or. 37(2).13; θεῖον ἄ. native sulphur, Gal.12.903. 5. ἱερὰ ἄ. sacrifices in which no fire was used, i.e. offerings of fruit, grain, and wine, Pi.O. 7.48, cf. A.Ag.70 (lyr.), S.Fr.417; θυσίαν ἄπυρον παγκαρπείας E.Fr. 912.4; ἄ. βωμοί Ph.1.345; ἱερουργία Plu.2.578b. 6. in A.Pr.880 (lyr.) ἄ. ἄρδις an arrow-point but one not forged in fire, i.e. the sting of the gad-fly; ἄ. δᾴς, of love, Luc.DDeor.19.1. II. Medic., without fever, Hp.Epid.1.1, cf. Aret.SD1.9. Adv. ἀπύρως Hp.Prorrh. 1.119. III. = νεκρός, Hsch.

ἀπύρωτος [ῠ], ον, not exposed to fire, brand-new, φιάλη Il.23.270; uncooked, Thphr.Od.10; of the moon in eclipse, not fiery, Placit.2. 29.2; incombustible, Thphr.Lap.19,22.

ἄπυστος, ον, not heard of, ᾤχετ' ἄϊστος ἄ. Od.1.242, cf. Sapph. Supp.25.19, Opp.C.1.236. 2. of words, inaudible, ἄπυστα φωνῶν S.OC489. II. Act., without hearing or learning a thing, οὐδὲ δὴν ἦεν ἄ. Ζεύς Od.5.127: c. gen., μύθων 4.675; κακῶν ἔτι πάμπαν ἀπύστῳ IG14.1389ii16.

ἀπύω, Dor. for ἠπύω.

ἀπφά or **ἄπφα**, a term of endearment used by brothers and sisters, also by lovers, Eust.565.23.

ἀπφάριον [φᾰ], Dim. of ἀπφά, Xenarch.4.15, CIG3277 (Smyrna).

ἀπφίδιον [φῐ], τό, Sch.Luc.Cat.12, and **ἀπφίον**, τό, Eust.565.23, Dim. of ἀπφά; also **ἀπφία** Poll.3.74, cf. Hsch.

ἀπφῦς (for the accent cf. Hdn.Gr.2.936), gen. ύος, ὁ, a term of endearment used by children to their father, papa, Theoc.15.14:— Eust. (v. foreg.) expld. as ὁ ἀφ' οὗ ἔφυ.

ἀπώγων, ωνος, ὁ, ἡ, beardless, Suid.

ἀπῳδ-έω, v.l. for ἀπᾴδω in Plu.2.1043b: metaph., go wrong, τοσοῦτον μόνον.. ἀπῴδησεν ὁ ἄνθρωπος prob. in Phld.Po.994.4. **-ός**, όν, out of tune, E.Cyc.490 (lyr.), Ph.1.375, Luc.Icar.17: metaph., out of harmony with, c. gen., Id.Salt.65: abs., Ph.2.170, Luc.Pisc.34, A.D. Synt.307.14. II. having ceased to crow or sing, ἀλεκτρυών Luc. Lex.6; of a person, Him.Or.22.5.

ἄπωθεν (in late Poets also **ἄπωθε**, Q.S.6.647, AP7.172 (Antip. Sid.)), Adv. from afar or afar, S.Ant.1206, Tr.816, E.Heracl.674, Ar.Av.1184, etc.; οἱ ἄπωθεν strangers, outsiders, Arist.Rh.1371^{a}12, al. 2. c. gen., far from, νεώς E.IT108, cf. Ar.Pl.674, Th.3.111, Babr.1.12; cf. ἄποθεν.

ἀπωθέω, fut. inf. ἀπωσέμεν Il.13.367: aor. ἀπέωσα Od.9.81, ἀπῶσα prob. corrupt in S.Fr.479:—**Med.**, fut. ἀπεώσομαι Lxx 4Ki.21.14: aor. ἀπεωσάμην Hom. (v. infr.), ἀπεωσάμην Th.1.32, etc., ἀπωθησάμην D.C.38.28 codd.: pf. ἀπῶσμαι· ἀπώθησα, Hsch., inf. ἀπεῶσθαι Th.2. 39:—**Pass.**, pf. part. ἀπωσμένος Phld.Ir.p.33 W.:—thrust away, push back, ὤϊξε πύλας καὶ ἀπῶσεν ὀχῆας Il.24.446, cf. 21.537; ἀ. ἐπάλξεις pushed them off the wall, Th.3.23:—Med., thrust away from oneself, χερσὶν ἀπώσασθαι λίθον Od.9.305; ἀπώσατο ἦκα γέροντα pushed him gently away, Il.24.508; αἱ χεῖρες τὸ τόξον -οῦνταί τε καὶ προσέλκονται Pl.R.439b. 2. drive away, ἠέρα μὲν σκέδασεν καὶ ἀπῶσεν ὁμίχλην [Ζεύς] Il.17.649; of the wind, beat from one's course, Βορέης ἀπέωσε Od.9.81 (so in Med., σφέας κεῖθεν ἀπώσατο ἶς ἀνέμοιο 13.276). 3. c. gen., εἴ κέ μιν οὐδοῦ ἀπώσομεν 22.76, cf. 2.130; γῆς ἀπῶσαί [με] πατρίδος S.OT641:—Med., thrust from oneself, drive away, μνηστῆρας ἀπώσεαι ἐκ μεγάροιο Od.1.270:—Pass., to be expelled, Hdt.1.173; ἀπωθοῦμαι δόμων Ar.Ach.450; γῆς S.OT670. 4. thrust aside, spurn, Id. Aj.446, al.:—Pass., τὸν δῆμον πρότερον ἀπωσμένον pushed aside, Hdt. 5.69. 5. repel, drive back, in Med., Τρῶας ἀπώσασθαι Il.8.206; νεῖκος ἀπωσαμένους 12.276; ἀπώσασθαι κακὰ νηῶν 15.503; νηῶν μὲν ἀπωσάμενοι δήϊον πῦρ 16.301; πένθος Archil.9.10; νοῦσον AP6.190 (Gaet.):— also in Prose, Antipho 4.4.6, etc.: c. dupl. acc., τὴν ναυμαχίαν ἀπεωσάμεθα Κορινθίους Th.1.32. 6. in Med., reject, τὸ ἀργύριον Hdt.1.199; τὸν αὐλὸν S.Tr.216 (lyr.); φιλότητα Id.Ph.1122 (lyr.); τὰς σπονδάς Th.5.22; τὰ ἐξ ἀδικίας κέρδη Pl.R.366a; ἀ. πόνους decline them, E.Fr. 789; τὴν δουλοσύνην shake off slavery, Hdt.1.95; ὕπνον shake off sleep, Pl.R.571c: abs., refuse, ποιήσω κοὐκ ἀπώσομαι S.Tr.1249.

ἀπώθ-ησις, εως, ἡ, rejection, repulsion, χυμῶν Steph.in Hp.1.72 D. **-ητής**, οῦ, ὁ, one who repels, Gloss. **-ητος**, ον, thrust or driven away, rejected, Suid. **-ία**, ἡ, refusal, PFay.21.24 (ii A.D.) (fort. ἀπειθίας).

ἀπώλεια, ἡ, destruction, Arist.EN1120^{a}2, etc.: pl., Id.Mete.351^{b} 11. II. loss, Id.Pr.952^{b}26; opp. τήρησις, Plb.6.59.5 Schweigh., cf. BGU1058.35, al. (i B.C.); τῶν χρόνων ἀ. Diog.Oen.1. 2. perdition, Ep.Rom.9.22, 2Ep.Thess.2.3. 3. thing lost, Lxx Le.6.3(5.22).

ἀπωλεσίοικος, ον, ruining one's house, μειράκιον Com.Adesp.848.

ἀπώλευτος, ον, of horses, unbroken, Anon.ap.Suid.

ἀπωλία, ἡ, = ἀπώλεια, Pl.Com.199.

ἀπώμ-αστος, ον, (πῶμα) without a lid, Babr.60.1, Gal.17(2). 161. **-ος**, ον, = foreg., Gp.6.1.4, Zos.Alch.p.113 B.

ἀπωμ-οσία, ἡ, (ἀπόμνυμι) denial upon oath, as law-term, opp. ἐξωμοσία, Poll.8.54, cf. Hsch. **-οτικός**, ή, όν, of or for denial on oath, ἐπίρρημα (i.e. μά) D.T.642.15, Eust.54.23. Adv. -κῶς Id.92. 22, Sch.Il.1.85. **-οτος**, ον, abjured, declared impossible on oath, χρημάτων ἄελπτον οὐδέν ἐστιν οὐδ' ἀ. Archil.74; βροτοῖσιν οὐδέν ἐστ' ἀ. S.Ant.388; πρᾶγμ' ἀ. Eup.217; οὐδὲν ἀ. οὐδὲ ἄπρακτον ποιεῖσθαι D.Chr.4.102. II. of persons, under oath not to do a thing, καίπερ ὢν ἀ. S.Ant.394; κἂν ἀ. τις ᾖ Trag.Adesp.566.

ἀπωνέομαι, buy, purchase, ἀπωνηθήσεται Theopomp.Com.84.

ἀπωρῠγ-ίζω, dig up, PFlor.369.5 (ii A.D.). **-ισμός**, ὁ, layering of ἀπώρυγες II, POxy.1692.14 (ii A.D.), cf. 1631.10 (iii A.D.).

ἀπῶρυξ, υγος, ἡ, (ἀπορύσσω) canal from a place, ἀπώρυγες συχναί Procop.Vand.2.19 (Scalig., for ἀπορρῶγες): metaph. of Samos, ἀ. τῆς πόλεως Demad.Fr.4 S., cf. Phld.Rh.1.181 S. II. layer of a vine, Lxx Ez.17.6, Gp.5.18.1, POxy.1631.10 (iii A.D.).

ἀπωρ-ωσία, ἡ, absence of callus, Paul.Aeg.6.110. **-ωτος**, ον, not forming a callus, of fractured bones, Dsc.1.70.

ἀπωσί-κᾰκος [ῐ], ον, repelling evil, θεοί IG14.957; ἄνεμοι ἀ. BMus. Inscr.370 (Delos). **-κύμᾰτος** [ῡ], ον, repelling waves, AP6.90 (Phil.)

ἄπ-ωσις, εως, ἡ, thrusting or driving away, διὰ τὴν τοῦ ἀνέμου ἄπωσιν αὐτῶν Th.7.34, cf. Aret.SD1.14. 2. repulsion, opp. ἕλξις, Arist.Ph.243^{a}19. **-ωσμός**, ὁ, = foreg., Lxx La.1.7. **-ωστέον**, one must reject, E.HF294. **-ώστης**, ου, ὁ, one that drives away, ἄνεμος Eust.1741.22; cf. ἐξώστης. **-ωστικός**, ή, όν, rejecting, δύναμις Gal.Nat.Fac.3.8. **-ωστός**, ή, όν, thrust or driven away from, τῆς ἑωυτοῦ (sc. γῆς) Hdt.6.5, cf. S.Aj.1019. II. that can be driven away, οὐδὲ ἀπωστοὶ ἔσονται Hdt.1.71.

ἀπωτάτω, Sup. Adv. of ἄπωθεν, farthest from, τῆς Θρᾴκης D.23. 166, cf. Trag.Adesp.130 (lyr.).

ἀπώτερος, α, ον, Comp., (ἀπό) farther off, = μακρότερος, Suid.: neut. as Adv., ἡ ἀπώτερον (sc. γραμμή) Euc.3.15, al.; opp. ἔγγιον, Id. Phaen.p.4 M.

ἀπωτέρω, Comp. Adv. of ἄπωθεν, farther off, S.OT137, Ar.Nu. 771, Pl.Phdr.254c, etc.; γένει ἀ. ὄντες D.43.50: prov., ἀ. ἢ γόνυ κνάμα Theoc.16.18. 2. c. gen., farther from, Cratin.229.

ἀπωτέρως, = foreg., Gloss.

ἄπωτος, ον, deaf, dub. in GDI104 (Cypr.) (= Inscr.Cypr.171 H.); λιταῖς ἄπωτε cj. in Moschio Trag.2.

ἀπωχραίνω, make pale, v.l. for ἀποχραίνω, Arist.Col.796^{a}24.

ἄρ, v. sq.

ἄρα, Ep. **ῥα** (which is enclitic and used after monosyllables, ἦ, ὅς, γάρ, etc., or words ending in a vowel or diphthong, e.g. ἐπεί), before a consonant **ἄρ** (perh. cf. Lith. ir̃ 'and'): expressing consequence, then, or mere succession, there and then, and in many derived uses.

A. Earlier usage: to denote, I. immediate transition, there and then, straightway, ὣς φάτο βῆ δ' ἄρ' Ὄνειρος Il.2.16: after a part., ὣς εἰπὼν κατ' ἄρ' ἕζετο 1.68, al.; πυθόμενος.. εἶπε ἄ. Hdt.4.134, cf. 9.9; ἐρωτώσης τῆς μητρὸς ἀπεκρίνατο ἄρα X.Cyr.1.3.2; with other Particles, δέ, ἤ, ὡς, etc., cf. ὁ δὲ Ἀστυάγης ἄ. εἶπεν ib.4.10: also after Advbs. of Time, τότε δή ῥα, τῆμος ἄρα, etc.; οὕτως ἄρα Pl.Phdr.259b; often in apodosi, as αὐτὰρ ἐπεὶ δὴ θηήσατο.. αὐτίκ' ἄρ' ἤλυθεν Od.5. 77; repeated τὼ μὲν ἄρ'.. κεῖντο ἡ δ' ἄρ'.. ἀγόρευε Il.21.426: in enumerations, e.g. in Homer's catalogue, then, next, οἳ δ' ἄρ' Ἀθήνας εἶχον 2.546; so in genealogies, Σίσυφος.. ὁ δ' ἄ. Γλαῦκον τέκεθ' υἱόν 6.154. 2. to draw attention, mark you! τὸν τρεῖς μὲν ἐπιρρήσσεσκον.. τῶν ἄλλων Ἀχιλεὺς δ' ἄρ' ἐπιρρήσσεσκε καὶ οἶος 24.456; with imper., ἀλλ' ἄγε δὴ κατ' ἄρ' ἕζευ 24.522: to point a moral or general statement, φευγόντων δ' οὔτ' ἂρ κλέος ὄρνυται οὔτε τις ἀλκή 5. 532. II. connexion, such as, 1. that of antecedent and consequent, οἰνοχόει.. ἄσβεστος δ' ἄρ' ἐνῶρτο γέλως 1.599, cf. 24.507; τοὔνεκ' ἄρ' ἄλγε' ἔδωκε 1.96; freq. with οὕνεκα in protasi, 7.140, al.: also in questions, τίς τ' ἂρ τῶν ὄχ' ἄριστος ἔην; who then (say you) was..? 2.761: with demonstr. Pronoun in recapitulation, ἀλλ' υἱὸν Πριάμοιο.. τόν ῥ' Ὀδυσεὺς βάλε he it was, whom.., 4.501: freq. in such phrases as ὣς ἄρα φωνήσας 2.35, al.; ὣς ἄρ' ἔφη 1.584, al.; ἦ ῥα 3. 355, al., thus, then he spoke.—This usage is universal in Greek. 2. explanation of that which precedes, χωόμενον κατὰ θυμὸν ἐϋζώνοιο γυναικὸς τήν ῥα.. ἀπηύρων whom (and for this cause he was angry) they had taken away, 1.429; εἰ μὴ ὑπερφίαλον ἔπος ἔκβαλε.. φῆ ῥ' ἀέκητι θεῶν φυγέειν for he said, Od.4.504: freq. with οὕνεκα; so with relatives, ἐκ δ' ἔθορε κλῆρος ὃν ἄρ' ἤθελον αὐτοί the very one which.., Il.7.182.

B. Later usage, always with inferential force: 1. in drawing conclusions (more subjective than οὖν), ἄριστον ἄ. ἡ εὐδαιμονία Arist.EN1099^{a}24; δῆλον ἄ. Id.Pol.1295^{b}33; in pseudo-syllogistic conclusions, Id.SE174^{b}11, Rh.1401^{a}3, al.: esp. by way of informal inference, as it seems, οὐκ ἄ. σοί γε πατὴρ ἦν Πηλεύς Il.16.33; οὐδ' ἄ. πως ἦν ἐν πάντεσσ' ἔργοισι δαήμονα φῶτα γενέσθαι 23.670; μάτην ἄρ', ὡς ἔοικεν, ἥκομεν S.El.772; οὕτω κοινόν τι ἄ. χαρᾷ καὶ λύπῃ δάκρυά ἐστιν so true is it that.., X.HG7.1.32; πολὺ γὰρ ἀμείνων ἄ. ὁ τοῦ ἀδίκου ἢ ὁ τοῦ δικαίου βίος Pl.R.358c; ἦν ἄ. πυρὸς γ' ἕτερα.. θερμότερα Ar.Eq. 382; ὦ τλῆμον ἀρετή, λόγος ἄρ' ἦσθα Trag.Adesp.374; so in announcing the discovery or correction of an error, as οὐκ ἐννενοήκαμεν ὅτι εἰσὶν ἄ... Pl.R.375d; φαίνεται πρὸ ποδῶν ἡμῖν κυλινδεῖσθαι καὶ οὐχ ἑωρῶμεν ἄρ' αὐτό ib.432d; εἰκότως ἄ. οὐκ ἐγίγνετο· ὡς γὰρ ἐγὼ νῦν πυνθάνομαι.. X.An.2.2.3. 2. in questions, expressing the anxiety of the questioner, τίς ἄ. ῥύσεται; who is there to save? A.Th.92; so in exclamations to heighten the expression of emotion, οἵαν ἄρ' ἥβην.. ἀπώλεσεν what a band of youth was that..! Id.Pers.733; so ὡς ἄρα ib.472, S.Fr.577; τί μ' ἄ. τί μ' ὀλέκεις; Id.Ant.1285; τί οὖν.. ἄ. X.Oec.6.2; πῶς ἄ.; οὕτως ἄ., etc.; ἄ. alone, ἔζης ἄ. S.Fr.686: esp. in ironical comments, Ar.Av.476, 1371, etc. 3. epexegetic, namely, ἐρῶ, ὡς ἄ... Pl.Tht.152d, cf. 156e. 4. for τοι ἄρα, τἄρα, v. sub τοι II.2. 5. εἰ (or ἐάν) μὴ ἄ. unless perhaps, Pl.Ap.38b, D.58.4; separated from εἰ μή, Id.9.20; with irony, εἰ μὴ ἄ. ἡ τῆς ἀρετῆς ἐπιμέλεια διαφθορά ἐστιν X.Mem.1.2.8. 6. in hypothetical clauses, to indicate the improbability of the supposition, ἢν ἄ. ποτὲ κατὰ γῆν βιασθῶσιν Th.1.93, etc.; or simply, perhaps (sts. separated from εἰ), εἴ τις οὖν ὑμῶν ἄ... ὑπελάμβανεν D.21.8: εἴ τις ἰδίᾳ τινὰ δεδιὼς ἄ. ἀπρόθυμός ἐστιν Th.4.86.

C. IN CRASIS, freq. τἄρα, μεντἄρα, οὐτἄρα: also δήξομἄρα for δήξομαι ἄ., Ar.*Ach.*325; οἰμώξετἄρα, κλαύσἄρα, Id.*Th.*248, *Pax* 532: also in Trag., E.*Hyps.Fr.*34.86.

D. ἄρα never stands first in the sentence in Classical Greek (Arist.*Mech.*851ᵃ22 is corrupt), but is found at the beginning of an apodosis in *Ev.Matt.*12.28, *Ep.Rom.*10.17, and first in a sentence, *Ev.Luc.*11.48, Vett.Val.305.20; in conclusion of syllogism, Herm. ap.Stob.3.11.31.

ἆρᾰ, interrog. Particle, implying *anxiety* or *impatience*, = Ep. and Lyr. ἦ ῥα: 1. alone, it simply marks the question, the nature of which is determined by the context: e.g. in D.35.44 a *negative* answer is implied in the question ἆρ' ἂν οἴεσθε..; but an *affirmative* in X.*Cyr.*4.6.4 ἆ. βέβληκα δὶς ἐφεξῆς; cf. ἆρ' εὐτυχεῖς..ἢ δυστυχεῖς; E.*Ph.*424.—To make it plainly neg., we have ἆ. μή..; A.*Th.*208, Pl.*Phd.*64c; and to make it plainly affirmative, ἆρ' οὐ; ἆρ' οὐχί; S. *OC*791, *OT*540; ἆρ' οὐχ οὕτως; Pl.*Phlb.*11d. 2. ἆ. οὖν; is used to draw an affirmative inference, Id.*Grg.*477a, *La.*190b; also when a neg. answer is expected, Id.*Chrm.*159b; with a neg., ἆρ' οὖν οὐ..; Id.*Phdr.*263a, etc. 3. in ἆρά γε, each Particle retains its force, γε serving to make the question more definite, Ar.*Pl.*546, X.*Mem.*1.5.4, etc. 4. less freq. with τίς interrog., τίνος ποτ' ἆρ' ἔπραξε χειρί S.*Aj.*905; τί δ' ἆρ' ἐγὼ σέ; E.*IA*1228; τίς ἆρ' ὁ φεύγων; Ar.*V.*893; with ἦν, E.*Rh.*118. 5. in indirect questions, σκεψώμεθα τοῦτο ἆ... Pl.*Phd.*70e, cf. *R.*526c, al., Arist.*Ph.*204ᵇ3, etc. II. in Poets sts. like ἄρα, Archil.86,89, Pi.*P.*4.78, Ar.*V.*3; τοιοῖσδε χρησμοῖς ἆ. χρὴ πεποιθέναι; A.*Ch.*297, cf. 435; τῷ δὲ ξιφήρης ἆρ' ὑφειστήκει λόχος E.*Andr.*1114: in exclamations, βραδεῖαν ἡμᾶς ἆρ' ὁ τῆνδε τὴν ὁδὸν πέμπων ἔπεμψεν S.*Aj.*738; ὀδυνηρὸς ἆρ' ὁ πλοῦτος E.*Ph.*566, cf. *El.*1229, *Hipp.*1086; ἦ δεινὸν ἆρ' ἦν Id.*Fr.*931; ἔμελλόν σ' ἆ. κινήσειν Ar.*Nu.*1301, cf. *Ach.*347.

B. In Prose, ἆ. almost always stands first in the sentence, but cf. Pl.*Grg.*467e; καὶ ὑπὲρ τούτων ἆ... Jul.*Or.*2.61c: in Poetry greater licence is taken, v. supr. 1.4, 11.

ἀρά, Ion. **ἀρή**, ἡ, *prayer*, Il.15.378,598, 23.199, Hes.*Op.*726, Pi.*I.*6(5).43; ἀρὴν ἐποιήσαντο παῖδα γενέσθαι Ἀρίστωνι offered *prayers* that a child should be born, Hdt.6.63. 2. *vow*, *Inscr.Cypr.*83, 147 H. 3. *curse, imprecation*, ἐξ ἀρέων μητρὸς..ἥ ῥα θεοῖσι πόλλ' ἀχέουσ' ἠρᾶτο Il.9.566; freq. in Trag., mostly in pl., A.*Pr.*910, S.*OT* 295; ἀρὰς ἀρᾶσθαι, προστιθέναι, ἐξανιέναι, E.*Ph.*67, S.*OC*952,154(lyr.), 1375; ἐπεύχεσθαι Pl.*Criti.*119e; θέσθαι ἐπί τινας Plu.*Cam.*13: also in sg., πατρὸς δ' ἀ. κρανθήσεται A.*Pr.*910, cf. *Ag.*457 (lyr.), etc.; ἡ τοῦ νόμου ἀ. Pl.*Lg.*871b; ἀρᾷ..ἔνοχος ἔστω ib.742b, etc.: in pl., *imprecations*, freq. in Inscrr. on those who shall mutilate or remove them, *Inscr.Magn.*105.53(ii B.C.), *IG*3.1417 sqq. II. Ἀρά personified as the goddess of destruction and revenge, ὦ πότνι' Ἀρὰ σεμναί τε θεῶν παῖδες Ἐρινύες S.*El.*111; δεινόπους Ἀρά Id.*OT*418; but in A.*Eu.*417 the Erinyes say that Ἀραί is their own name γῆς ὕπαι; Ἀρά τ' Ἐρινὺς πατρὸς ἡ μεγασθενής Id.*Th.*70; Ἀρᾶς ἱερόν Ar.*Fr.*575. (Hence the Verb ἀράομαι.) [Ep. always ᾰρ, Att. always ᾱρ.] (From ἀρϝά, cf. κατάρϝος.)

Ἀρᾰβ-άρχης, v. Addenda. **-αρχία**, ἡ, *office of* Ἀραβάρχης, *BGU*665 ii 5 (i A.D.).

ἄραβδος, v. ἄρραβδος. **ἀράβδωτος**, v. ἀρράβδωτος.

ἀρᾰβέω [ᾰρ], (ἄραβος) *rattle, ring*, Hom. (mostly in Il.), always of armour, δούπησεν δὲ πεσὼν ἀράβησε δὲ τεύχε' ἐπ' αὐτῷ Il.5.42, al.; of the teeth, *gnash*, Theoc.22.126; ἀραβεῖ δ' ἁ γνάθος Epich.21.2. 2. trans., *gnash, grind*, ὀδόντας Hes.*Sc.*249, A.R.2.281.

Ἀρᾰβ-ία, ἡ, *Arabia*, Hdt.2.8, etc. (also, = κόσμος γυναικός, Hsch.): poet. **Ἀρραβία** Theoc.17.86:—Adj. **Ἀράβιος**, α, ον, *Arabian*, οἱ Ἀ. Hdt.1.198, al.:—also **Ἀρᾰβικός**, ή, όν, χάραγμα *PGen.*29.8 (ii A.D.), Plu.*Ant.*69, Hsch.:—later **Ἄραβες** (v. Ἄραψ):—pecul. fem. **Ἀρᾰβίς**, ίδος, Them.*Or.*34.56: **Ἀράβισσα**, St.Byz. **-ίζω**, *take part with the Arabs*, Suid. **-ιστί**, Adv. *in Arabic*, Eust. ad D.P.954.

ἀραβίδες· αἱ μετὰ κονιορτοῦ πνοαί, Hsch.

ἀραβίς, ίδος, ἡ, = δράβη, Dsc. (post 2.185).

ἄρᾰβος [ᾰρ], ὁ, *gnashing* or *chattering* of teeth, ἄ. δὲ διὰ στόμα γίγνετ' ὀδόντων Il.10.375, cf. Hes.*Sc.*404, Hld.5.3; prob. f.l. for ἄραδος in Plu.2.654b. 2. generally, *rattling, ringing*, σάκεος Call.*Del.* 147. (Prob. onomatop.)

ἀρᾰβοτοξότης, ου, ὁ, *Arab archer*, employed for police duty in Egypt, *PAmh.*2.77.4 (ii A.D.), etc.

ἀραβύλη· ἀρβύλη, Hsch.

ἀραβών, v. ἀρραβών.

ἀράγ-δην [ᾰρ], Adv., (ἀράσσω) *with a rattle*, Luc.*Lex.*5. **-ειν**· σπαράσσειν, Hsch. **-μα**, ατος, τό, = sq., τυμπάνων ἀ. E.*Cyc.*205. II. = κάταγμα, Sor.*Fract.*10. **-μός**, ὁ, *clashing, clattering, rattling*, A.*Th.*249; ἀ. πετρῶν *crashing shower* of stones, E.*Ph.*1143; στέρνων ἀ. *beating* of the breast in grief, S.*OC*1609; ἀ. χεροῖν Lyc.940.—Rare in Prose, Hellanic.167(c) J.

ἀραδ⟨ήσ⟩ει· θορυβήσει, ταράξει, and **ἀράδηται**· κεκόνηται (prob. -κίν-), συγκέχυται, Hsch.; cf. ἄραδος.

ἀρᾱδιούργητος, ον, *not dishonestly done*, *AB*357, Suid. s.v. ἀκαπήλευτον. Adv. -τως, = *sine fraude*, Just.*Edict.*7.7.

ἄρᾰδος [ᾰρ], ὁ, *disturbance*, τοῦ χρωτὸς ἄ. ποιεῖν Hp.*Morb.*4.56; ἄ. ἐμποιεῖν Id.*Acut.*(*Sp.*)47; also of foods, ἄ. ἔχειν Id.*VM*15; ἔχον ἄ. κακόν Id.*Acut.*10; *palpitation* of the heart, ἄ. κακός Nic.*Th.*775: generally, ὁ ἐκ τῆς συνουσίας ἄ. καὶ παλμός prob. in Plu.2.654b. (Prob. onomatop., like ἄραβος.)

ἀράδους· βλαβεράς, λεπτάς, Hsch.

ἀράζω or **ἀρράζω**, *snarl, growl*, of dogs, Ael.*NA*5.51, Poll.5.86, Ph.1.694 codd. (Onomatop., = *make the sound* ἀρα, ἀρρα.)

ἀράη· φιάλην, καὶ ἀράκτην, Hsch.; cf. ἀράκη, ἀρακτήρ.

ἀραιά, ᾶς, ἡ, *belly*, v. ἀραιός.

ἀραιάκις, = ὀλιγάκις, prob. in Hsch. s.vv. ἀδράκις, ἀρβάκις.

ἀραιόδους, οντος, ὁ, ἡ, *with thin-set teeth*, Arist.*HA*501ᵇ23, cf. *Pr.* 963ᵇ20 (dub. l.).

ἀραιό-θριξ, τρῐχος, ὁ, ἡ, *with thin hair*, Hsch. s.v. ψεδνή, cf. Moer. 421. **-πορος**, ον, *thinly porous, flaccid*, Alex.Aphr.*Pr.*1.2.

ἀραῖος [ᾰ], α, ον, also ος, ον S.*Ant.*867 (lyr.): (ἀρά): I. Pass., *prayed to* or *entreated*, Ζεὺς ἀ., = ἱκέσιος, S.*Ph.*1182 (lyr.). 2. *prayed against, accursed*, γονά A.*Ag.*1565 (lyr.); πότμος ἀ. ἐκ πατρός Id.*Th.*898 (lyr.); μ' ἀραῖον ἔλαβες you adjured me *under a curse*, S. *OT*276. II. Act., *cursing, bringing mischief upon*, c. dat., φθόγγος ἀ. οἴκοις A.*Ag.*237 (lyr.); δόμοις ἀ. S.*OT*1291, cf. E.*Med.*608, *IT* 778; ἀ. γονεὺς ἐκγόνοις ὡς οὐδεὶς ἕτερος ἄλλος Pl.*Lg.*931c: abs., A. *Ag.*1398, S.*Tr.*1202.—Almost confined to Trag., exc. Pl. l.c.

ἀραιός [ᾰ], ά, όν, (ἀρ- Hdn.Gr.2.108, v.l. in Il.18.411, al.) *thin, slender*, κνῆμαι, χείρ, γλῶσσαι, Il. l.c., 5.425, 16.161; γαστήρ Nic.*Th.* 133; *narrow*, εἴσοδος Od.10.90; of ships, Hes.*Op.*809; φάλαγγες ἀ., opp. βαθύτεραι, X.*Lac.*11.6, cf. Plu.*Crass.*23; ἀραιᾷ τροφῇ χρῆσθαι *meagre*, of diet, Arist.*Pol.*1335ᵇ13. II. later, of the substance of bodies, *of loose texture*, opp. πυκνός, Anaximen.1, Meliss.7, Anaxag. 12,15, cf. Emp.104 (Sup.), Thphr.*CP*2.4.7, etc.; opp. πίων, Arist. *Pr.*880ᵃ38; freq. in Hp., as *VM*22; δέρμα *Aph.*5.71; ὀστέον *Art.*33; εἴρια *Mul.*1.1; ὁμίχλη..νέφους ἀραιοτέρα Arist.*Mu.*394ᵃ21, cf. *Mete.* 364ᵇ25 (Comp.); σπογγοι D.S.3.14. b. φλύκταιναι ἀ. *empty* blisters, Nic.*Th.*240 (v. Sch. ad loc.), cf. Theoc.12.24. 2. in Tactics, *in open order*, opp. πυκνός, τὸ ἀραιότατον [διάστημα] Ascl.*Tact.*4.1, etc. III. *intermittent*, πνεῦμα Hp.*Epid.*1.26.α', β'; ἆσθμα, βήξ, Aret.*SD*1.11, etc. Adv. -ῶς Hp.*Nat.Puer.*24; of the pulse, Gal.9.444, al. IV. *scanty, few and far between*, τρίχες Arist.*Col.*797ᵇ27; ἀκτῖνες ib.791ᵃ 27; φωναί Id.*Aud.*803ᵇ28; ὀδόντες Poll.2.94, etc. V. ἀραιά (sc. γαστήρ), ἡ, *flank, belly*, Ruf.*Onom.*171. VI. of the voice, *thin*, Theoc.13.59. (Homeric metre proves ϝαραιός.)

ἀραιό-σαρκος [ᾰρ], ον, *with porous, spongy flesh*, Hp.*Nat.Puer.*21, *Mul.*1.1, Hices.ap.Ath.7.288c (Comp.). **-στημος**, ον, *of thin warp, fine*, Hsch. s.v. μανοστήμοις. **-στῡλος**, ον, *with columns widely spaced*, Vitr.3.3.1. **-σύγκρῐτος**, ον, *with loose tissues*, Gal.6.407. **-της**, ητος, ἡ, *looseness of substance, porousness, rarity*, opp. πυκνότης, Hp.*Aph.* 5.63, al., Arist.*Pr.*869ᵇ30: pl., Id.*Ph.*260ᵇ10, Epicur.*Ep.*2 p.49 U., *Placit.*3.12.1; τῶν πόρων Arist.*Aud.*802ᵃ24; opp. πύκνωσις, Plu.*Fr.inc.* 149. **-τρητος**, ον, *with few pores*, opp. πολύτρητος, Gal.*UP*8.6 codd.

ἀραι-όφθαλμος [ᾰρ], ον, *with few eyes* or *buds*, κλῆμα *Gp.*5.8.2.

ἀραιό-φυλλος [ᾰρ], ον, *with scanty leaves*, Zonar. s.v. μανόφυλλον.

ἀραιόω [ᾰρ], *make porous, rarefy*, τὴν ἐπιδερμίδα Hp.*Nat.Puer.*20; τὴν σάρκα Id.*Vict.*3.78; opp. πυκνόω, Arist.*Pr.*884ᵃ27, Aret.*CA*2.1, cf. *SA*2.2, etc. II. Pass., *to be rarefied*, Hp.*Vict.*1.13, Arist.*Mu.* 394ᵃ36; ἀραιουμένων τῶν σωμάτων Ph.*Bel.*71.43.

ἀραίρ-ηκα, -ημένος, -ητο, v. αἱρέω.

ἀραιώδης [ᾰρ], ες, *loose of substance, porous*, Gal.14.680.

ἀραί-ωμα [ᾰρ], ατος, τό, (ἀραιόω) *interstice, crevice, chink*, Str.4.4.1, D.S.1.39, Luc.*VH*1.30, *Placit.*3.3.11, Plu.2.980c, etc.; of the body, Hp.*Morb.*4.45; *pore*, σώματος Hero *Spir.*1 *Praef.*, al., cf. Sor.1.115; *a little bit*, Longin.10.17. **-ωσις**, εως, ἡ, *becoming* or *making porous, rarefaction*, opp. πύκνωσις, dub. in Epicur.*Nat.*14 *Fr.*11 (cf. *Fr.*6), cf. Plu.*Strom.*3, D.L.9.8 (Heraclit.), Corn.*ND*17, etc. 2. Medic., *porosity*, of the lungs, Hp.*Oss.*13, etc. 3. *mordanting*, *PHolm.* 8.3. **-ωτικός**, ή, όν, *of* or *for rarefying*, ὑγρῶν, v.l. in Dsc.1.62.

ἀράκη, ἡ, = φιάλη, Hsch. s.v. ἀράη (leg. ἀράκην), and s.v. ἐξ ἀρκιάων (leg. ἀρακάων): so in Ath.11.502b Αἰολεῖς τὴν φιάλην ἀράκην (ἀρακίν cod.) καλοῦσιν.

ἀρᾰκικός, ή, όν, *of* or *from aracus*, φόρος *PFlor.*27.6 (iv/v A.D.).

ἀράκιον [ᾰκ], τό, = sq., *POxy.*119.12 (ii/iii A.D.), Gal.13.68.

ἀρᾰκίς, ίδος, ἡ, and **ἀρᾰκίσκος**, ὁ, Dims. of ἄρακος, Gal.19.85.

ἄρᾰκος [ᾰρ], ὁ, a leguminous plant, *wild chickling, Lathyrus annuus*, Ar.*Fr.*412c, *BGU*636.12 (i A.D.), Gal.6.524. II. neut., ἄ. τὸ τραχὺ καὶ σκληρόν, a variety which grew as a weed among lentils, Thphr.*HP*8.8.3. III. Tyrrhen. word for ἱέραξ, Hsch.

ἀρᾰκό-σπερμον [ᾰρ], τό, *aracus-seed*, *PRyl.*143.16 (i A.D.). **-σπορος**, ον, *sown with aracus*, *BGU*1292.54 (i B.C.). **-χερσος**, ον, *dry and fit for sowing aracus* (sc. γῆ), *CPHerm.*120ʳ iii 5.

ἀρακτῆρα· ἀμελκτῆρα, Hsch.: **ἀράκτης**, Id. s.v. ἀράη.

ἀρᾰκώδης [ᾰρ], ες, *like* ἄρακος: -ῶδες, τό, *tine-tare, Lathyrus tuberosus*, Thphr.*HP*1.6.12.

ἄραμα· βόρβορος, Hsch. **ἄραμεν**· μένειν, and **ἀράμεναι**· ἡσυχάζειν, Id. (perh. for ἠρεμεῖν). **ἀράμενοι**· τὰ ἀπόχυτα ὕδατα, Id. **ἄραμος**· ἐρῳδιός, Id. **ἀράνη**· μεσάγκυλον, Id. (order requires ἀραύη). **⟨ἄ⟩ρανις**· ἔλαφος, Id. **ἀράντισιν**· ἐρινύσι (Maced.), Id.

ἄραξ, ακος, ὁ, = ἄρακος, *PMeyer* 12.23 (ii A.D.), *PTeb.*423.4 (iii A.D.), etc.

ἀράξα, ἡ, fabulous plant which grows by the Araxes, Ps.-Plu. *Fluv.*23.2.

ἄραξις, εως, ἡ, *dashing, beating*, Cass.*Pr.*25. II. kind of *bread* used in Athamania, Ath.3.114b.

ἀραξίχειρος [ᾰ] [ῐ], ον, (ἀράσσω) *beaten with the hand*, τύμπανα *AP* 6.94 (Phil.).

ἀράομαι, Aeol. inf. ἄρασθαι Sapph.*Supp.*5.22: fut. ἀράσομαι [ᾱ],

Ion. ἀρήσομαι: aor. ἠρησάμην, Aeol. 3 pl. ἀράσαντο Sapph.51: pf. ἤρᾱμαι (only in compds. ἐπήραμαι, κατήραμαι): (ἀρά): [ᾱρ Hom., ἄρ Lyr., Trag.]:—poet. Verb (v. infr.), *pray to* a god, Ἀπόλλωνι Il.1.35; δαίμοσιν 6.115: once c. acc., *invoke*, στυγερὰς ἀρήσετ' Ἐρινῦς Od.2.135. 2. c. acc. et inf., *pray* that.., ἀρᾶται δὲ τάχιστα φανήμεναι Ἠῶ Il.9.240; τὰ ἐναντία.. ἀρέομαι ὑμῖν γενέσθαι Hdt.3.65 codd.; ἠρῶντο (sc. σφέας) ἐπικρατῆσαι *prayed* that they might prevail, 8.94; ἥ σε θεοῖς ἀρᾶται.. μολεῖν S.*Aj.*509, cf. Ar.*Th.*350. b. c. inf. only, πάντες κ' ἀρησαίατ' ἐλαφρότεροι πόδας εἶναι *would pray* to be, Od.1.164. c. folld. by optat., ἀρώμενος εἶος ἵκοιο *praying* till thou should'st come, ib.19.367. 3. *pray for*, ἔσλα τῷ γάμβρῳ Sapph.51; ἀ. τινὶ ἀγαθά Hdt.1.132: c. inf., σφῷν.. θεοῖς ἀρῶμαι μή ποτ' ἀντῆσαι κακῶν S.*OC* 1445; more freq. in bad sense, *imprecate*, τί τινι Id.*OT*251; ἀρὰς ἀ. τινί Id.*OC*952, And.1.31, cf. A.*Th.*633, *Pr.*912; and without an acc., ἀρᾶσθαί τινι *to curse* one, E.*Alc.*714, cf. S.*OT*1291. 4. c. fut. inf., *vow* that.., πατὴρ ἠρήσατο Πηλεὺς.. με.. σοί τε κόμην κερέειν ῥέξειν τε Il.23.144. II. Act. only in Ep. aor. inf., ἀρήμεναι μέλλεις you are like *to have prayed*, Od.22.322. III. the part. ἀρημένος (q.v.) does not belong to this Verb.

ἀραρίζω, = ἀράζω, Ammon. s.v. φωνεῖν. **ἄραριν**· ἀράχνην, Hsch. **ἀραρινοί** (sc. λίθοι), stones used *to fill chinks* in walls, Id. **ἄραρις**· ἔνορκος, Id.

ἀρᾰρίσκω (redupl. form of √αρ, *join, fit together*), only impf. ἀράρισκε Od.14.23, Theoc.25.103: the tenses in use (from *ἄρω) are mostly poet., v. infr.

A. trans.:—Ion. aor. 1 ἦρσα Il.14.167 (ἐπ-), Ep. ἄρσα Od.21.45, imper. ἄρσον 2.289, pl. ἄρσετε A.R.2.1062, part. ἄρσας Il.1.136 (also inf. ἀράραι· ἁρμόσαι, πλέξαι, Hsch.): aor. 2 ἤρᾰρον, Ion. ἄρᾰρον, inf. ἀρᾰρεῖν, part. ἀρᾰρών (but ἄρᾰρον is used intr. in Il.16.214, Od.4.777, Simon.41; while for ἄρηρεν, in trans. sense (Od.5.248), ἄρασσεν is the true reading; ἐς οὐρανὸν ἤραρεν ὄσσε Orph.*A.*984 is by confusion with αἴρω:—**Med.**, fut. ἄρσομαι Lyc.995 acc. to Sch. (possibly fr. αἴρω): aor. 1 ἠρσάμην, part. ἀρσάμενος Hes.*Sc.*320: 3 pl. aor. 2 opt. (in pass. sense) ἀραροίατο A.R.1.369: pf. subj. ἀρήρεται Hes.*Op.*431 (προσ-):—**Pass.**, pf. part. ἀρηρεμένος or -έμενος A.R.3.833, al.; later incorrectly written ἀρηράμενος Q.S.2.265, Opp.*C.*2.384, etc.: aor. 1 ἤρθην, only 3 pl. ἄρθεν, for ἤρθησαν, Il.16.211:—*join together, fasten*, οἱ δ' ἐπεὶ ἀλλήλους ἄραρον βόεσσι when they had *knitted* themselves one to another with their shields, Il.12.105 (in Pass., μᾶλλον δὲ στίχες ἄρθεν 16.211); ἄγγεσιν ἄρσον ἅπαντα *pack up*, Od.2.289. II. *fit together, construct*, ὅτε τοῖχον ἀνὴρ ἀράρῃ πυκινοῖσι λίθοισιν Il.16.212:—Med., ἀρσάμενος παλάμῃσι Hes.*Sc.*320. 2. μνηστῆρσιν θάνατον καὶ Κῆρ' ἀραρόντες *having prepared, contrived*, Od.16.169. III. *fit, equip, furnish* with a thing, νῆ' ἄρσας ἐρέτῃσιν 1.280; καὶ πώμασιν ἄρσον ἅπαντας *fit* all [the jars] with covers, 2.353, cf. A.R.2.1062; καὶ ἤραρε θυμὸν ἐδωδῇ *furnished*, i.e. *satisfied*, his heart with food, Od.5.95:—in Pass., esp. pf. part., *fitted, furnished with*, πύλας ἀρηρεμένας σανίδεσσι A.R.1.787. 2. *please, gratify*, ἐμέ γ' ἁ στονόεσσ' ἄρᾰρεν φρένας S.*El.*147 (lyr.); ἁ Νεμέα ἄρᾱρε Nemea *smiled on* [him], Pi.*N.*5.44. IV. *make fitting* or *pleasing*, ἄρσαντες κατὰ θυμόν (sc. τὸ γέρας), Il.1.136.

B. intr.:—pf. ἄρᾱρα with pres. sense, Ion. and Ep. ἄρηρα, part. ἀρᾱρώς, ἀρηρώς, Hom., Trag., and late Prose (except that X. has προσαραρέναι *HG*4.7.6), Ep. fem. part. ἀρηρυῖα Hes.*Th.*608, and metri gr. ἀρᾰρυῖα Hom., εὖ ἀραρός Opp.*H.*3.367: Ion. and Ep. plpf. ἀρήρειν or ἠρήρειν, with impf. sense, Il.10.265, 12.56, etc.:—**Med.** only aor. 2 part. sync. ἄρμενος, η, ον, also ος, ον Hes.*Op.*786 (cf. however ἀρηρεμένος): on aor. 2 used intr. v. supr. A. I:—*to be joined closely together*, ἀρηρότες *in close order*, Il.13.800; ἄραρον κόρυθές τε καὶ ἀσπίδες 16.214; ἑξείης ποτὶ τοῖχον ἀρηρότες [πίθοι] *piled close* against the wall, Od.2.342: c. dat. instr., κόλλῃσιν ἀρηρότα Emp.96.4; in Tactics, ἀραρός, τό, = ὀμφαλός (q.v.), Ascl.*Tact.*2.6, etc. 2. abs., *to be fixed*, φρεσὶν ᾗσιν ἀρηρώς Il.10.553; θυμὸς ἀρηρὼς Theoc.25.113; ἄρᾱρε φέγγος *shines for ever*, Pi.*N.*3.64; ἄραρεν ἥδε γ' ὠλένῃ τις *is fixed*, A.*Pr.*60: or metaph., θεῶν.. οὐκέτι πίστις ἄραρε E.*Med.*414 (lyr.); ὡς ταῦτ' ἄραρε ib.322; τὸ σόν τ' ἄραρε *is fixed*, ib.745: abs., ἄραρε *it is fixed, my mind is made up*, Id.*Or.*1330, Men.*Epit.*185; τὸ ἀραρὸς ἦθος *steadfastness*, J.*AJ*14.12.3; δόγματα ἀραρότα D.Chr.12.56; also of persons, ἀραρὼς τὴν γνώμην *steadfast*, Plu.*Dio*32; [θεοὶ] ἀραρότες τοῖς κρίμασιν Hierocl.p.48 A.; τοῖς λογισμοῖς ἀ. Id.p.51 A. II. *fit well* or *closely*, ζωστὴρ ἀρηρώς a *close-fitting* belt, Il.4.134; πύλαι εὖ, στιβαρῶς ἀραρυῖαι, 7.339, 12.454; σανίδες πυκινῶς ἀ. 21.535; *fit* or *be fitted to* a thing, ἔγχος παλάμηφιν ἀρήρει *fitted* the hands, Od.17.4; κόρυθα κροτάφοις ἀραρυῖαν, κνημῖδες ἐπισφυρίοις ἀραρυῖαι, Il.13.188, 19.370; κυνέη ἑκατὸν πολίων πρυλέεσσ' ἀραρυῖα *fitting* a hundred champions, i.e. *large enough for* them, 5.744; also with Preps., κυνέη ἐπὶ κροτάφοις ἀραρυῖα Od.18.378, Hes.*Sc.*137; ὄφρ' ἂν.. δούρατ' ἐν ἁρμονίῃσιν ἀρήρῃ Od.5.361; κεραυνὸς ἐν κράτει ἀ. *fit* emblem in victory, Pi.*O.*10(11).83; ἀνθρώποισιν ἀρηρότα μυθίζεσθαι *befitting* men, Orph.*A.*191. III. *to be fitted, furnished with* a thing, [τάφρος] σκολόπεσσιν ὀξέσιν ἠρήρει Il.12.56; πόλις πύργοις ἀραρυῖα 15.737; ζώνη θυσάνοις ἀραρυῖα 14.181: hence, *furnished, endowed with*, χαρίτεσσιν ἀραρώς Pi.*I.*2.19; ἔθνεα θνητῶν παντοίαις ἰδέῃσιν ἀρηρότα Emp.35.17; κάλλει ἀραρὼς E.*El.*948; πολλῇσιν ἐπωνυμίῃσιν ἀρηρὼς D.P.28. IV. *to be fitting, agreeable, pleasing*, (cf. ἀρέσκω) once in Hom., ἐνὶ φρεσὶν ἤραρεν ἡμῖν it *fitted* our temper *well*, Od.4.777; ἄκοιτιν ἀρηρυῖαν πραπίδεσσι Hes.*Th.*608. V. syncop. aor. 2 part. Med. ἄρμενος, η, ον (ος, ον Id.*Op.*786), *fitting, fitted* or *suited to* (cf. ἀρμένως), c. dat., ἱστὸν.. καὶ ἐπίκριον ἄρμενον αὐτῷ *fitted* or *fastened to* the mast, Od.5.254 (cf. ἄρμενα, τά); τροχὸν ἄρμενον ἐν παλάμῃσιν Il.18.600; πέλεκυν.. ἄ. ἐν π. Od.5.234. 2. *fit, meet*, μάλα γάρ νύ οἱ ἄρμενα εἶπεν Hes.*Sc.*116: rarely c. inf., ἡμέρα κούρῃσι γενέσθαι ἄρμενος a day *meet* for girls to be born, Id.*Op.*786. 3. *prepared, ready*, χρήματα δ' εἰν οἴκῳ πάντ' ἄ. ποιήσασθαι ib.407; ἄ. πάντα παρεῖχον Id.*Sc.*84, cf. Thgn.275; ἄ. ἐς τόδε ἔργον A.R.4.1461; ἄ. ἐς πόλεμόν τε καὶ ἐν νήεσσι μάχεσθαι Hermonax 1.3, cf. 8. 4. *agreeable, welcome*, ἄρμενα πράξαις, = εὖ πράξας, Pi.*O.*8.73; ἐν ἀρμένοις θυμὸν αὔξων Id.*N.*3.58; so of men, ἄ. ξείνοισιν Pl.*Epigr.*6. (Cf. Lat. *arma, armus, artus*, Goth. *arms*, etc.)

ἀρᾱρότως [ᾰρ], (ἀραρίσκω) *compactly, closely, strongly*, A.*Supp.*945, E.*Med.*1192, Pl.*Phdr.*240d, D.Chr.3.79, Iamb.*Protr.*12: Comp. ἀραρότερον (-ώτερον Dind.) Them.*Or.*22.27cc.

ἀράσιμος [ρᾱ], ον, (ἀράομαι) *accursed*, Suid.

ἀράσσω, Att. -ττω [ᾰρ], Ion. and poet. impf. ἀράσσεσκον Pi.*P.*4.226: fut. ἀράξω (συν-) Hom., Dor. ἀραξῶ Theoc.2.160: aor. ἤραξα (ἀπ-) Hom., Ep. ἄραξα Hes.*Sc.*461:—Pass., aor. ἠράχθην, Ep. ἀράχθην (συν-) Hom.: fut. Med. in pass. sense, κατ-αράξεσθαι Plu.*Caes.*44:—*smite, dash in pieces*, (Hom. only in compds. ἀπαράσσω, συναράσσω); of any violent impact, with collat. notion of *rattling, clanging*, as of horses, ὁπλαῖς ἀ. χθόνα Pi. l. c.; ἄρασσε (sc. πύλας) *knock at* the door, E.*Hec.*1044; τὴν θύραν Ar.*Ec.*978, cf. Theoc.2.6 (Pass., of the door, *open with a crash*, Luc.*DMeretr.*15.2); *pound* in a mortar, ὅλμῳ ἀ. Nic.*Th.*508; ἀράσσειν στέρνα, κρᾶτα, *beat* the breasts, the head, *in mourning*, A.*Pers.*1054 (lyr.), E.*Tr.*279 (lyr.); ἄρασσε μᾶλλον *strike* harder, A.*Pr.*58; ὄψεις ἀράξας S.*Ant.*52; ἤρασσε βλέφαρα Id.*OT*1276:—in Pass., ὀμμάτων ἀραχθέντων Id.*Ant.*975 (lyr.); also ἀ. πέτροις τινά *strike with* a shower of stones, E.*IT*327:—Pass., πέτροισιν ἠράσσοντο A.*Pers.*460:—ἀ. κιθάρην *strike* the lyre, Orph.*A.*382; ὕμνον, μέλος, etc., Nonn.*D.*1.15, 440, etc. 2. c. dat. modi, ἀράσσειν τινὰ ὀνείδεσι, κακοῖς, *assail with* reproaches or threats, S.*Aj.*725, *Ph.*374, cf. ἐξαράσσω. II. Pass., *to be dashed against*, πρὸς τὰς πέτρας Hdt.6.44; πρὸς τὴν γῆν Luc.*Anach.*11; of things, *dash one against the other*, A.R.2.553, Ael.*NA*16.39.—The simple Verb is poetic, used once by Hdt. and in late Prose, v. supr. (Akin to ῥάσσω, Ion. ῥήσσω (q.v.), cf. προσαρασσόμενον· προσρησσόμενον, Hsch.).

ἀρασύνη· πύελος, Hsch. **ἀρασχάδες**· τὰ περυσινὰ κλήματα, Id.

Ἀράτειον [ᾱτ], τό, *shrine dedicated to Aratus*, Paus.2.9.4, Plu.*Arat.*53: -**ειος**, ὁ, kind of *fig*, Thphr.ap.Ath.3.77a.

ἀρατειχεύειν· καταρᾶσθαι, οἱ δὲ στρατεύεσθαι, Hsch.

ἀρᾱτ-ήριον, τό, v. ἀρητήριον. -**ικός**, ή, όν, *of, for prayer* or *cursing*: ἀρατικόν, τό, *deprecation*, as a form of proposition, *Stoic.*2.60. -**ός**, Ion. **ἀρητός**, ή, όν, (ἀράομαι) *prayed against, accursed*, ἀρητὸν γόον Il.17.37, 24.741; ἀρατὸν ἕλκος S.*Ant.*972 (lyr.). II. *prayed for, desirable*, Sapph.*Supp.*6.3; ἀ. καὶ σωτήριος γνώμη *SIG*656.17 (Abdera): hence Ἄρητος, Ἀρήτη, as pr. nn., *the Prayed-for*, Hom.: later Ἄρᾱτος. [ᾱρ Ep., ᾰρ Att.]

ἄρατρον, τό, Cret., = ἄροτρον, *GDI*4992 a ii 5 (Gortyn).

Ἀράτυος, ὁ (sc. μήν), name of month in Locris, *SIG*²855.

ἀράχιδνα, ἡ, *ground-pease, Lathyrus amphicarpos*, Thphr.*HP*1.1.7, 1.6.12.

ἀραχν-αῖος [ᾰρ], α, ον, *of* or *belonging to a spider*, νήματα *AP*6.206 (Antip. Sid.); *like a spider's web*, μίτος ib.39 (Arch.); ἀραχναίη, = ἀράχνη, ib.9.233 (Eryc.). -**άομαι**, *weave the spider's web*, Eust.285.41. -**η**, ἡ, = ἀράχνης, ἀράχνης ἐν ὑφάσματι A.*Ag.*1492 (lyr.), cf. *AP*11.110 (Nicarch.); αἱ λειμώνιαι ἀ. Arist.*HA*555ᵇ7 (elsewh. ἀράχνης, q.v.). II. *spider's web*, Hp.*Cord.*10, S.*Fr.*286, *AP*11.106 (Lucill.). III. ἀ. λεπταί thin *lines*, Gal.*UP*10.12. IV. = σφονδύλιον, Ps.-Dsc.3.76. V. kind of *sundial*, Vitr.9.8.1. -**ήεις**, εσσα, εν, = ἀραχναῖος, Nic.*Th.*733, *Al.*492. -**ηκες**· ἀράχναι, Hsch. -**ης**, ου, ὁ, *spider*, Hes.*Op.*777, Pi.*Fr.*296, A.*Fr.*121, Call.*Com.*2, Arist.*HA*623ᵃ30, al.; ἀραχνᾶν ἱστοί B.*Fr.*3.7. II. a kind of *pulse*, Hsch. -**ικός**, ή, όν, = ἀραχναῖος, dub. ibid. -**ιον**, τό, *spider's web*, Od.8.280, 16.35, Cratin.190, Pherecr.142, Pl.Com.22, X.*Mem.*3.11.6, Arist.*HA*623ᵃ30. 2. a *disease* in olive-trees, prob. due to the tent-caterpillar, *Clisiocampa neustria*, Thphr.*HP*4.14.10, *CP*5.10.2. II. Dim. of ἀράχνη, *small spider*, Arist.*HA*555ᵃ27, 622ᵇ27. [ᾰρᾰχν Hom., ᾰρᾰχν Com. ll. cc.] -**ιόω**, *spin a cobweb*, Arist.*HA*605ᵇ10:—Pass., *to be covered with cobwebs*, ib.625ᵃ8:—Act. in same sense, Nonn.*D.*38.14. II. *form a venous network over*, ἡ φλὲψ ἠραχνίωκε τοῦ σπληνὸς ἐναίμοισι φλεβίοισι Hp.*Oss.*18. -**ιώδης**, ες, *like a cobweb*, Id.*Dent.*24, Arist.*HA*622ᵇ12. 2. of liquids, *filled with filaments*, οὖρον Hp.*Coac.*571; γάλα Arist.*HA*583ᵃ34; ἀραχνιῶδες οὐρεῖν Dsc.4.65.

ἀραχνοειδής [ᾰρ], ές, *like a cobweb*, of the scum of urine, λιπαρότητες Hp.*Prog.*12; also used of a *feeble* pulse, Gal.19.411; of *capillary* veins, Id.2.808; of nerves, ib.400; ἀπόφυσις -εστάτη ib.366; ἀ. χιτών in Medic., older name for the ἀμφιβληστροειδὴς χ. (q.v.), i.e. the *retina*, Herophil.ap.Cels.7.7.13, Ruf.*Onom.*153; but distinguished from it by Gal.10.47.

ἄραχνος, ὁ, = ἀράχνης, A.*Supp.*887.

ἀραχνοϋφής [ῠ], ές, *spun as by spiders*, i.e. *fine-spun*, ἀμπεχόναι Ph.1.666, cf. 2.479, 637.

ἀραχνώδης, ες, = ἀραχνοειδής, Arist.*HA*554ᵇ28, Ael.*NA*8.16.

ἄραχος, ὁ, *wild vetch, Vicia Sibthorpii*, Gal.6.541.

Ἄραψ, ὁ, pl. Ἄραβες, οἱ, *Arab*, Str.1.2.34, J.*BJ*1.19.4:—as Adj., Ἄραψ ἀτμός, of incense, *Pae.Delph.*11; θώρηξ Nonn.*D.*36.326: dat. pl. Ἀράβεσσι ib.26.23.

ἀράω, *plough*, οὐδὲ τὰς ὁδὼς.. ἀρασόντι *Tab.Heracl.*1.133. (Cf. Lat. *arare.*)

ἀρβάκις· ὀλιγάκις, Hsch.

ἀρβάλη· τήγανον ὀστράκινον (Tarent.), Hsch.

ἄρβηλος, ὁ (Sch.Nic. l. c.), *semicircular knife,* used by cobblers, i.e. leather-workers (ἄρβηλοι γὰρ τὰ δέρματα Hsch. s. v. ἀνάρβηλα), Nic.*Th.*423. **II.** Geom., *figure resembling it in shape,* contained by three semicircles with coincident diameters, Papp.208.12.

ἀρβίννη· κρέας (Sicel), Hsch.; cf. Lat. *arvina.* **ἀρβόν·** διεστός, ἀραιόν, ἐλαφρόν, Id. **ἀρβύκη·** τοῦ ὑποδήματος, Id.

ἀρβύλη [ῠ], ἡ, *strong shoe* coming up to the ankle, *half-boot,* used by country people, hunters, travellers, A.*Ag.*944, *Fr.*259, E.*Or.* 1470 (lyr.); πηλοπατίδες ἀ. Hp.*Art.*62; αὐταῖσιν ἀρβύλαισιν ἁρμόσας πόδα *with shoes* and all, E.*Hipp.*1189 (wrongly expld. by Eust. as = δίφρος, *the stand of the charioteer*), cf. *Ba.*1134; cf. ἄρμυλα.

ἀρβῠλικός, ή, όν, in form of an ἀρβύλη, ὀβελοί *IG*11(2).158*A*6, al. (Delos, iii B.C.).

ἀρβῠλίς, ίδος, ἡ, = ἀρβύλη, Theoc.7.26, *APl.*4.306 (Leon.).

ἀρβῠλόπτερος, ον, *with winged shoes,* Lyc.839.

ἀρβύνδα· λήκυθον (Lacon.), Hsch. (leg. ἀρυβαλλίδα).

ἀργάδες· εἶδος φυτοῦ, καὶ ἀργαὶ γυναῖκες, Hsch.

Ἀργᾰδῆς, οἱ, name of *one of the four Ionic tribes,* in Attica and elsewh., E.*Ion* 1580, cf. Hdt.5.66, *CIG*3664 (Cyzicus), etc.; also of a χιλιαστύς at Ephesus, *SIG*353.10 (sg.).

ἀργάεις, v. ἀργήεις.

ἀργαίνω, *to be white,* E.*Fr.*73, Philod.Scarph.126 (prob.), Opp.*C.* 3.299:—in Pass., Nonn.*D.*34.145 (s. v. l.).

ἀργαλεῖον, τό, later form for ἐργαλεῖον (q. v.).

ἀργᾰλέος, α, ον, *painful, troublous,* ἄνεμοι Il.13.795; Ἔρις 11.3; νοῦσος 13.667; Ἄσκρη, χεῖμα κακῇ, θέρει ἀργαλέῃ (trisyll.), οὐδέποτ' ἐσθλῇ Hes.*Op.*640; νύξ Alc.*Supp.*12.11; *difficult* of attainment, ἀληθείη Emp.114.2; κάθοδος Anacr.43.5:—never in Trag., sts. in Com., ἀ. πρᾶγμα Ar.*Pl.*1; στάσις Id.*Th.*788; ἀργαλέας νύκτας ἄγειν Id.*Lys.* 764: rare in Prose, πρᾶγμα X.*Hier.*6.4: Comp., Ph.1.224: Sup., Id.2.300. **2.** of persons, *troublesome, vexatious,* Thgn.1208 codd. (ἀρπ– Bgk.); βιότοιο κέλευθοι Emp.115.8, cf. Ar.*Nu.*450, Men.403. 5: Sup., Ar.*Eq.*978: rare in Prose, ἀ. τὴν ὄψιν Aeschin.1.61. **II.** ἀργαλέον ἐστί, c. dat. et inf., ἀ. δέ μοί ἐστι διασκοπιᾶσθαι ἕκαστον Il.17. 252, cf. 12.410, Od.13.312, etc.: rarely c. acc. et inf., ἀργαλέον δέ με πάντ' ἀγορεῦσαι Il.12.176; or without case, ἀ. δὲ πληκτίζεσθ' ἀλόχοισι Διός 21.498, cf. Od.7.241, etc.; also, **2.** agreeing with the object, ἀ... θεὸς βροτῷ ἀνδρὶ δαμῆναι God is *hard* to be subdued by mortal man, 4.397; ἀ. γὰρ Ὀλύμπιος ἀντιφέρεσθαι Il.1.589. **III.** Adv. –ως *AP*9.499. (By dissimilation from *ἀλγαλέος, cf. ἄλγος.)

ἀργᾰλεότης, ητος, ἡ, *grievousness,* Ph.1.346, Eust.892.32.

ἀργαπέτης, ου, ὁ, *commandant of a fort, IGRom.*3.1043, 1044 (Palmyra, iii A.D.) (Persian word).

ἀργᾶς, Dor. contr. for ἀργάεις, v. ἀργήεις.

Ἀργεῖος, α, ον, *of* or *from Argos, Argive*: Ἀργεῖοι in Hom., like Ἀχαιοί, for *the Greeks* in general:—ἡ Ἀργεία (sc. γῆ) *Argolis,* Th.2. 27, al.; ἀργεῖαι, αἱ, *women's shoes,* Hsch.; ἀργεῖος (sc. βόλος), ὁ, name of a *throw at dice,* Id.

ἄργειτε, = ἄγρειτε, Antim.82.

Ἀργειφόντ-ης, ου, ὁ, voc. –φόντα *h.Hom.*29.7, Orph.*H.*28.3, Luc. *Tim.*32: (Ἄργος, *φόνος):—*slayer of Argus,* epith. of Hermes, Od. 1.38, al., Hes.*Op.*77, etc.: variously expld. by Gramm., cf. Corn. *ND*16. **II.** acc. to Paus.Gr.*Fr.*65, from ἀργής, *serpent-slayer,* i. e. Apollo, S.*Fr.*1024, cf. Sch.A.*Pr.*569; of Telephus, Parth.*Fr.* 33. **–ιάδας,** gen. αο, *son of Hermes,* Pancrat.*Oxy.*1085.9.

Ἀργείωνας· τοὺς Ἀργείους, Hsch.

ἄργελλα, ἡ, *vapour bath* (Maced.), Suid.

ἀργέλοφοι, οἱ, *the legs and feet of a sheep-skin,* and so generally, *offal,* Ar.*V.*672.

ἄργεμον, τό, *albugo,* a white speck on the eye, S.*Fr.*233, Hp.*Loc. Hom.*13, Thphr.*HP*7.6.2, 9.9.5, Dsc.2.78.2. **II.** = *Lappa canaria, Geum urbanum Avens,* Plin.*HN*24.176:—also **ἄργεμος,** ὁ, = λεύκωμα, Poll.2.65. **2.** *upper part of the finger-nail,* ib.146.

ἀργεμώνη, ἡ, *Papaver Argemone, wind-rose,* Crateuas *Fr.*9, Dsc.2. 177, Orib.14.60.2, Gal.11.835. **2.** ἀ. ἑτέρα, = ἄργεμον II, Ps.-Dsc. 2.178; written *argemonia* by Plin.*HN*25.102.

ἀργεμώνιον, τό, = ἀστὴρ Ἀττικός, Plin.*HN*26.92. **II.** = ἀνεμώνη, Dsc.2.176.

ἀργένναος, ον, = ἀργεννός, *AP*15.35 (Theoph.).

ἀργεννός, ή, όν, Aeol. for ἀργός, *white,* in Hom. almost always of sheep, ἀργεννῇς ὀΐεσσι Il.6.424, etc.; of woollen cloths, ἀργεννῇσι καλυψαμένη ὀθόνῃσι 3.141; later, ἀ. μόσχοι E.*IA*574 (lyr.); κρίνη Chaerem.8, cf. *AP*9.384.11; ὀθόναι ib.5.259 (Paul. Sil.); σέλα ib.9. 46 (Antip. Thess.); γαῖα Opp.*H.*1.795.

ἀργέντινος, *silvery,* δελματικομαφόρτης *POxy.*1273.12 (iii A.D.):—also **ἀργέντιος,** ib.1310.

ἀργεστής, οῦ, ὁ, *clearing, brightening,* epith. of the south wind, Il. 11.306, 21.334. **II.** *the north-west wind,* ἀ. Ζέφυρος Hes.*Th.*379, 870, cf. Acus.15 J.; Ἀργέστης, pr. n., Arist.*Mete.*363^b24, Thphr. *Sign.*35, D.S.1.39, Plu.*Sert.*8, *AP*9.42 (Jul.). **III.** = ἀργής, *white,* ἀργέσταο λίπευς ἰσόμοιρον ἐλαίου Nic.*Th.*592.

ἀργέτι, ἀργέτα, v. ἀργής:—nom. **ἀργέτις,** ἡ, = ἀργήεσσα, Ἠώς Nonn.*D.*16.124; voc. ἀργέτι *AP*5.253 (Paul. Sil.):—also nom. **ἀργέτᾰ** Μήνη Max.587; ἀργέται ἵπποι Orac.ap.Phleg.*Mir.*3.

ἄργετος, ὁ, = ἄρκευθος (Cret.), Hsch.

ἀργεύομαι, = ἀργέω: metaph. of a woman, Gal.17(1).498.

ἀργεφάντης, coined as etym. of ἀργειφόντης, Corn.*ND*16.

ἀργέω, fut. –ήσω: aor. ἤργησα *BGU*698.4 (ii A.D.): pf. ἤργηκα *POxy.*1160.14 (iii/iv A.D.): (ἀργός, ἀεργός):—*to be unemployed, do nothing,* Hp.*Mochl.*23, E.*Ph.*625, X.*Cyr.*1.2.15, Pl.*R.*426a, etc.; *keep Sabbath,* Lxx 2*Ma.*5.25; ἀ. τὴν ἑβδόμην J.*BJ*7.3.3; οἱ ἀργοῦντες *the idle, Trag.Adesp.*527; γῆ ἀργοῦσα *lying fallow,* X.*Cyr.*1.6.11, *PFlor.*262.9 (iii A.D.); ἀργῆσαν ἤμυσε στέγος S.*Fr.*864; φησὶν ἀργῆσαι τὸ ἐργαστήριον *is out of work,* D.27.19; of the senses, *to be at rest,* νυκτὸς τῆς ὄψεως ἀργούσης Arist.*Pr.*903^a21, cf. *Somn.Vig.*455^a30: c. gen. rei, ἀργήσει.. τῆς αὑτοῦ δημιουργίας *will be unoccupied in* his own work, Pl.*R.*371c. **II.** Pass., *to be left undone,* X.*Cyr.*2.3.3; *to be fruitless,* ἡ σκέψις ἂν ἀργοῖτο Id.*Hier.*9.9.

ἀργεώτας, ὁ, title of Apollo in Messenia, Paus.4.34.7.

ἀργήεις, εσσα, εν: Dor. **ἀργάεις,** contr. **ἀργᾶς,** gen. ᾶντος: (v. ἀργός):—*white, shining,* ταῦρον ἀργάντα Pi.*O.*13.69; ἐν ἀργάεντι (v.l. ἀργινόεντι) μαστῷ Id.*P.*4.8; οἰωνὸς.. ἔξοπιν ἀργᾶς, = πύγαργος, prob. in A.*Ag.*115 (lyr.). **2.** = ἀργεστής, ἀργήεσσιν ἀέλλαις Orph. *A.*128, cf. 685.

ἀργής, ῆτος, ὁ, ἡ, Ep. dat. and acc. ἀργέτι, ἀργέτα (v. infr.), gen. ἀργέος Nic.*Al.*305, and v. l. *Th.*856:—*bright, glancing,* mostly of *vivid* lightning, κεραυνός Il.8.133, Od.5.128, al., Ar.*Av.*1747; opp. ψολόεις κεραυνός, Arist.*Mete.*371^a20; Ζεὺς ἀργής, i.e. *fire,* Emp.6.2; ἀργέτι αὐγῇ Id.21.4; φύσις Orph.*H.*10.10. **2.** *shining, white,* of fat, ἀργέτι δημῷ Il.11.818; ἀργέτα δημόν 21.127; of a robe, ἑανῷ ἀργῆτι φαεινῷ 3.419; ἀργῆτι μαλλῷ A.*Eu.*45, cf. S.*Tr.*675; ἀργὴς Κολωνός because of its *chalky* soil, Id.*OC*670 (lyr.): neut., ἀργῆτος ἐλαίου Nic. *Th.*105; ἀργῆτα κέλευθα Opp.*C.*2.140.—Poet. word, cf. Arist. l. c.

ἀργῆς, Dor. **ἀργᾶς** (ἄργας *AB*442), ὁ, a kind of *serpent,* Achae.1, *Trag.Adesp.*199; ὄφις ἀργῆς Hp.*Epid.*5.86: also an obscure nickname of Demosthenes, Aeschin.2.99, Plu.*Dem.*4.

ἀργηστής, οῦ, ὁ, = ἀργής, *glancing, flashing,* πτηνὸς ἀ. ὄφις, of an arrow, A.*Eu.*181. **2.** *white,* ἀφρός Id.*Th.*60; κύκνοι Theoc.25.131.

ἀργία, ἡ, = ἀεργία, *want of employment,* πεσσοὺς κύβους τε, τερπνὸν ἀργίας ἄκος S.*Fr.*479.4; νεύρων καὶ ἄρθρων Hp.*Mochl.*23; τοῦ καλοῦ Hierocl. *in CA*19 p.461 M.; ψυχῆς ἀργίη Democr.212; *idleness, laziness,* E.*HF*592; νόμος περὶ τῆς ἀργίας against those who *would not work,* D.57.32; γραφὴ ἀργίας *AB*310, cf. Plu.*Sol.*17, 31: in pl., Isoc. 7.44. **b.** *quietism,* E.*Med.*296. **2.** in good sense, *rest, leisure,* τῶν οἰκείων ἔργων *from..,* Pl.*Lg.*761a (pl.), Lxx *Wi.*13.13, etc. **3.** in pl., *holidays,* Arr.*Epict.*4.8.33, = *feriae* or *justitium,* App.*BC*1.56, *PPetr.*3; sg., of the Sabbath, Lxx *Is.*1.14. **4.** *lapse of cultivation,* Thphr.*CP*4.5.6.

ἀργῐ-βόειος, ον, *with white kine,* of Euboea, Poet.ap.Ael.*NA*12.36 (ἀργίβοιος Lobeck). **–βρέντας,** ὁ, (βρέμω, βροντή) = sq., Pi.(?)*Oxy.* 1792; cf. ἀναξιβρέντας. **–κέραυνος,** ον, *with bright, vivid lightning,* epith. of Zeus, Il.19.121, al., Orph.*Fr.*21a, 168, Pi.*O.*8.3, Cleanth. *Stoic.*1.122. **–κερως,** ὁ, ἡ, *white-horned,* αἶγες Orac.ap.D.S.7 *Fr.*16.

ἀργικός, ή, όν, = ἀργός (B), θάκοις ἀ. καθήμενοι E.*Fr.*795 codd. Stob.

ἀργῐλῑπής, ές, Archil.160:—and **ἀργίλιψ,** ιπος, Nic.*Th.*213 (of serpents), *white.*

ἄργιλλα or **ἄργῐλα,** ἡ, *underground dwelling,* so called in Magna Graecia, Ephor.45, Eust. ad D.P.1166; cf. ἄργελλα. **II.** = ἄργιλλος, Gal.12.438, 19.90.

ἀργίλληψιν· γῆ μὴ βλαστάνουσά τι, Hsch.

ἄργιλλος or **ἄργῐλος** (so Ἐφ.Ἀρχ.1893.31 (Acarn.)), ἡ, (ἀργός A) *white clay, potter's earth,* Arist.*Pr.*890^a26, Thphr.*CP*3.20.3, Opp.*H.* 4.658.

ἀργιλλοφόρητος γῆ, dub. sens. in *PTeb.*702.

ἀργιλλώδης or **ἀργῑλώδης,** ες, *clayey,* ἀργιλωδεστέρην γῆν Hdt.2. 12, cf. Arist.*Mete.*352^b10, Thphr.*HP*3.18.5, Antyll.ap.Orib.9.11.4; ὄχθαι Euph.11 (= Archyt.Amph.2).

ἀργιλόεις, = ἀργινόεις, Eust. ad D.P.1166.

ἀργῐ-λοφος [ῐ], *white-crested,* κολώνα Pi.*Fr.*200. **–μήτας,** ὁ, (*quick-witted,* acc. to Hsch.) epith. of bull which carried Europa, Phryn. Trag.16. **–νεφής,** ές, *clouded with white,* ὀπός S.*Fr.*534.2 (anap.).

ἀργῐνόεις, εσσα, εν, = ἀργός, *bright-shining, white,* epith. of Lycastus and Camirus, from their lying on *chalky* hills, Il.2.647, 656; νῆσοι Ἀργινοῦσαι X.*HG*1.6.27; of milk, *AP*7.23 (Antip. Sid.); χαλινά A.R.4.1607; μαστός, v.l. for ἀργάεις (q. v.), Pi.*P.*4.8.

ἀργῐ-όδους, όδοντος, ὁ, ἡ, *white-toothed, white-tusked,* λευκοὶ ὀδόντες ἀργιόδοντος ὑός Il.10.264, cf. Od.8.60, etc.; κύνες Il.11.292:—also **–όδων,** A.R.2.820.

ἄργιον, = ἀδίαντον, Ps.-Dsc.4.134. **ἀργιόπους·** ἀετός (Maced.), Hsch. **ἄργιος·** λευκός, ταχύς, Id.

ἀργῐ-πόδης, ου, Dor. **–ας,** ὁ, = sq., χίμαρος *AP*6.299 (Phan.). **–πους,** ὁ, ἡ, –πουν, τό, gen. ποδος, *swift-footed,* ἀργίποδας κύνας Il.24. 211; of rams, S.*Aj.*237 (lyr.) (= λευκόποδας, Sch.); = ἀετός (Maced.), Hsch.

ἀργίς, ίδος, ἡ, = νύξ (διὰ τὴν ἀνάπαυσιν), Orph.*Fr.*33.

ἀργῖτις (sc. ἄμπελος), ιδος, ἡ, vine with *white* grapes, Virg.*G.*2.99, Plin.*HN*14.35, Isid.*Etym.*17.5.23.

ἄργμα, ατος, τό, (ἄρχω) only in pl. ἄργματα, = ἀπάργματα, *firstlings* at a sacrifice or feast, Od.14.446.

ἀργό-βῐος, ον, *sedentary,* Archig.ap.Aët.13.120. **–θάνᾰτος** [θᾰ], ον, *slow of dying,* Sch.Opp.*H.*1.142.

Ἀργόθεν, Adv. *from Argos,* S.*Ant.*106 (lyr.), E.*IT*70, *Heracl.*775 (lyr.).

ἀργόθριξ, τρῐχος, ὁ, ἡ, τό, *white-haired,* Archim.*Bov.*9.

ἀργόλας, α, ὁ, a kind of *serpent,* Suid.; cf. ἀργῆς. **II.** v. Ἄργος.

Ἀργολ-ίζω, *take the part of the Argives*, X.*HG*4.8.34, Ephor. 137. **-ίς** (sc. γῆ), ίδος, ἡ, *Argolis*, Hdt., etc. 2. as Adj., ὁ, ἡ, *of Argolis*, *Argolic*, ἐσθής A.*Supp*.236 :—later **Ἀργολικός**, ή, όν, Plu. *Rom*.21. Adv. -κῶς Eust.722.63.

Ἀργολιστί, Adv. *in Argive fashion*, S.*Fr*.462.

ἀργομέτωπος, ον, *with rough-hewn faces*, λίθοι Ph.*Bel*.82.5.

Ἀργοναύτης, ου, ὁ, *a sailor in the ship Argo*, *an Argonaut*, Arist. *Pol*.1284^{a}23, etc.; Ἀπολλώνιος ὁ τοὺς Ἀργοναύτας ποιήσας Str.14.2.13.

ἀργο-ποιός, όν, *making idle*, Plu.*Num*.22. **-πρακτος**, ον, *slothful*, Paul.Al.*N*.4.

Ἄργος, εος, τό, name of several Greek cities, Ἄ. Ἀχαιϊκόν Il.9.141; Ἄ. Πελασγικόν 2.681, etc.; ἄργος = πεδίον acc. to Str.8.6.9, cf. Dionys. Epic.ap.St.Byz. s.v. Δώτιον, Call.*Fr*.45 :—hence Adjs. Ἀργεῖος, Ἀργολίς, Ἀργολικός, qq. v.: **Ἀργόλας**, ὁ, E.*Rh*.41 (lyr.), Ar.*Fr*.298.

ἀργός (A), ή, όν, *shining*, *glistening*, of a goose, Od.15.161; of a sleek, well-fed ox, Il.23.30; in Hom. mostly in the phrase πόδας ἀργοί, of hounds, *swift-footed*, because all swift motion causes a kind of glancing or flickering light, 18.578, Od.2.11, etc.; κύνες ἀργοί Il. 1.50, 18.283, cf. D.S.4.41, Corn.*ND*16. 2. *white*, Arist.*Top*.149^a 7. II. parox. as pr. n., Ἄργος, ὁ, name of a dog, *Swift-foot*, Od. 17.292: also of the herdsman *Argus* (i. e. *bright-eyed*, A.*Pr*.567 (lyr.), *Supp*.305) who was so called from his eyes being ever open and *bright*. (By dissimilation from *ἀργρός, cf. Skt. *ṛjrá-*, = (1) *shining*, (2) *swift*, Vedic pr. n. *Ṛji-śvan-*, lit. = *possessing* κύνες ἀργοί.)

ἀργός (B), όν, later ή, όν Arist.*EN*1167^{a}11, *Mete*.352^{a}13, Thphr. *Lap*.27, Ath.Mech.12.11, etc.: (contr. from ἀεργός) :—prop. *not working the ground*, Hdt.5.6; *idle*, *lazy*, opp. ἐργάτις, S.*Ph*.97, cf. Ar. *Nu*.53, etc.; γαστέρες ἀ. Epimenid.1; ἀ. ἐπιθυμίαι Pl.*R*.572e; ἀ. τὴν διάνοιαν ib.458a; τὸ πρὸς ἅπαν ξυνετὸν ἐπὶ πᾶν ἀ. Th.3.82; ἂν ἀ. ᾖ if he have *no trade*, Antiph.123.3; πότερον ἀνθρώπου οὐδέν ἐστιν [ἔργον] ἀλλ' ἀργὸν πέφυκεν; Arist.*EN*1097^{b}30: c. gen. rei, *idle at* a thing, *free from* it, τῶν οἴκοθεν *from* domestic toils, E.*IA*1000; πόνων σφοδρῶν Pl.*Lg*.835d; γυναῖκας ἀργοὺς ταλασίας ib.806a; ἀ. αἰσχρῶν *slow to* evil, A.*Th*.411; ἀργότεραι ἐς τὸ δρᾶν τι Th.7.67; ἀ. περί τι Pl.*Lg*. 966d. 2. of things, δόρυ E.*Ph*.1387; of money, *lying idle*, *yielding no return*, opp. ἐνεργός, D.27.7 and 20; of land, *lying fallow*, Isoc.4. 132, X.*Cyr*.3.2.19, Thphr.*HP*9.12.2; opp. πεφυτευμένος, *IG*7.2226*B* (Thisbe, iii A. D.); διατριβὴ ἀ. *in which nothing is done*, *fruitless*, Ar. *Ra*.1498 (lyr.), Isoc.4.44; χρόνον ἀργὸν διάγειν Plu.*Cor*.31. Adv. ἀργῶς, ἐπιμέλεσθαι X.*Mem*.2.4.7; ἔχειν D.6.3: Comp. and Sup. ἀργότερον, -ότατα, X.*Oec*.15.6 and 1. b. ἀ. λόγος, name of a *sophism*, Chrysipp.*Stoic*.2.277, cf. Plu.2.574e. II. Pass., *unwrought*, ἁρμός, κυμάτιον, *IG*1.322*b* 23,59; πυροὶ ἀ. *unprepared for eating*, Hp.*VM*13; ἄργυρος Paus.3.12.3; βύρσαι *undressed* hides, Ath.Mech. l. c.; *unpolished*, Thphr.*Lap*.27. 2. *not done*, *left undone*, κοὐκ ἦν ἔτ' οὐδὲν ἀ. S.*OC*1605; ἓν δ' ἐστὶν ἡμῖν ἀ. E.*Ph*.766; οὐκ ἐν ἀργοῖς not among *things neglected*, S.*OT*287; τὰ μὲν προβέβηκεν ἀμήχανόν ἐστι γενέσθαι ἀργά Thgn.584. 3. *unattempted*, μάχη Pl.*Euthd*.272a. 4. Astrol., τόπος ἀ., name of the 8th of the 12 'houses', Ptol.*Tetr*.128, Paul.Al.*M*.4; πλανήτης Plot.2.3.3; ζῴδιον S.E.*M*.5.15.

ἀργῠρ-άγχη, ἡ, (formed after κυνάγχη) *silver-quinsy*, which Demosthenes was said to have, when he abstained from speaking on the plea of quinsy, but really because he was bribed, Demad.*Fr*.5S., Plu.*Dem*.25. **-ἀμοιβικός**, ή, όν, *of* or *for a money-changer*: ἡ -κή (sc. τέχνη), Poll.7.170; personified, Luc.*BisAcc*.13,24. Adv. -κῶς Id.*Hist.Conscr*.10. **-ἀμοιβός**, ὁ, *money-changer*, *banker*, Pl.*Plt*. 289e, Theoc.12.37, etc.: as Adj., ἀ. τιμή Maiist.32. **-άνθρωπος**, ὁ, '*silver-man*', symbol in alchemy, Zos.Alch.p.112B. **-άσπῐδες**, οἱ, *the silver-shielded*, a corps in the army of Alexander, D.S.17.57, Arr.*An*.7.11.3, Ath.12.539e, etc.; also in the armies of the Diadochi, Plb.5.79.4, etc. **-άφιον** [ᾰ], τό, Dim. of ἄργυρος, Theognost. *Can*.126.34, *AB*1339. **-ειος**, ον, = ἀργύρεος, ἀργύρεια μέταλλα *silver-mines*, Th.2.55, 6.91; τὰ ἀ. ἔργα X.*Vect*.4.5; τὰ ἔργα τὰ ἀ. D.21.167; τὰ ἀ. alone, X.*Mem*.2.5.2, Aeschin.1.101, Pl.*Lg*.742d. **-ένδετος**, ον, *overlaid with silver*, κύλικες *IG*11(2).161*B*79 (Delos, iii B. C.).

ἀργύρεος [ῠ], α, ον, contr. **ἀργῠροῦς**, ᾶ, οῦν: *of silver*, of the bow of Apollo, Il.1.49, cf. Pi.*O*.9.32; κρητήρ Il.23.741, Od.4.615, cf. A.*Fr*. 184; τάλαρον Od.4.125; λάρναξ Il.18.412; ἀσάμινθοι Od.4.128, etc.; γένος Hes.*Op*.144, etc.; ἀ. πλοῦτος Pl.*Lg*.801d. 2. *silver-plated*, κλῖναι Hdt.9.82. II. as Subst., ἀργυροῦς, ὁ, *silver coin*, Lxx*Za*. 11.12, al., *SIG*731.20 (Tomi, i B. C.), Hero*Mens*.60.1, al.

ἀργῠρ-ευτική, ἡ, *silversmith's art*, Eustr. *in EN*296.10. **-εύω**, *dig for silver*, D.S.5.36, Str.3.2.9. **-ηλάτης** [ᾰτ], ου, ὁ, *silversmith*, Hsch. **-ήλᾰτος**, ον, *of wrought silver*, A.*Fr*.185; φιάλαι E.*Ion* 1181; *bearing silver*, πρὼν [Παγγαίου] A.*Fr*.25A. **-ηρός**, ά, όν, = ἀργυρικός, ἔρανος *IG*2.621.14. **-ίδιον** [ρῐ], τό, = ἀργύριον, generally (but not always, cf. Alciphr.3.38) in a contemptuous sense, Ar. *Pl*.147, *Fr*.547, Eup.113; ἀ. καὶ χρυσίδιον τὸν πλοῦτον ἀποκαλοῦντες Isoc.13.4, cf. Socr.*Ep*.36, Olymp.*in Grg*.p.275J. **-ίζομαι**, Med., *get* or *extort money*, πάντοθεν Din.1.40, cf. *OGI*669.52 (Egypt, i A. D.); ἀργυρισάμενοι *for a bribe*, *Sammelb*.4416.19 (ii A. D.); τινά *from* one, J.*AJ*14.14.6. **-ικός**, ή, όν, *of*, *for*, or *in money*: φόρος *cash* rental, *AJA*16.13 (Sardes, iv B. C.); ἀργυρικά, τά, *taxes paid in money*, ἀργυρικῶν πράκτωρ, πρακτορεία, *BGU*15 i 13 (ii A. D.), *PLond*.2.306 (ii A. D.); ζημίαι ἀ. *IG*2^2.1028.81 (i B. C.), cf. D.S.12.21, Plu.*Sol*.23; τέλος Str.11.13.8, cf. *PRyl*.133.16 (i A. D.), etc. Adv. ἀργυρικῶς ἢ σωματικῶς κολασθήσονται *OGI*664.17 (Egypt, i A. D.).

ἀργύριον [ῠ], τό, *small coin*, *piece of money*, Ar.*Fr*.262, X.*Oec*.19. 16, etc.: pl. (v. Poll.9.89), Ar.*Av*.600, Eup.155, X. l. c.: then, 2. collectively, *money*, Ar.*Pl*.156,158, al.; ἀ. ῥητόν a fixed *sum*, Th.2. 70; εἰς ἀ. λογισθέντα calculated in *our money*, X.*Cyr*.3.1.33; ἀ. καθαρόν 'hard *cash*', Theoc.15.36: in Com. with Art., τἀργύριον *the money*, *the cash*, δανείζεσθαι Ar.*Nu*.756; ἀπαιτεῖν ib.1247; κατατιθέναι Antiph.124.14, etc.; so τὰ. καταβάλλειν Th.1.27, etc. II. = ἄργυρος, *silver*, πεντηκοσίας μνέας ἀργυρίου Hdt.3.13; ἀ. ἐπίσημον and ἄσημον Th.2.13; χρυσίον καὶ ἀ. Pl.*Alc*.1.122e; ἀργυρίου ἄνθος *lead oxide*, Hp.*Nat.Mul*.33.

ἀργύριος [ῠ], name of a *plant*, Hsch.; cf. ἄργυρος III. II. Aeol., = ἀργύρεος, πρόσωπον Alcm.23.55.

ἀργῠρ-ίς, ίδος, ἡ, *silver cup* or *vessel*, Pi.*O*.9.90, Pherecr.129, *IG* 1.127.16, *SIG*^{2}588.142 (Delos, ii B. C.), Ath.11.502a. 2. *plate* in general, πίνειν ἐξ ἀργυρίδων χρυσῶν Anaxil.40. II. = δραχμή, Heraclid.Lemb.5. **-ισμός**, ὁ, *getting money*, Str.7.3.7, Ph.1.145, al., D.C.59.15; ἀργυρισμοῦ πρόφασιν *OGI*669.37 (Egypt, i A. D.); ἐπ' ἀργυρισμῷ *Sammelb*.4416.11 (ii A. D.). **-ίτης**, ου, ὁ, fem. **-ῖτις**, ιδος, ἡ, *of* or *belonging to silver*, γῆ *containing silver-ore*, Posidon. 48, cf. Gal.12.184; ψάμμος Dsc.5.94; βῶλος Plb.34.9.10; more freq. ἀργυρῖτις, ἡ, as Subst., *silver-ore*, φλὲψ ἀργυρίτιδος X.*Vect*.1.5, cf. 4.4; κατεργασάμενος τὴν ἀ. Docum.ap.D.37.28; also a form of λιθάργυρος, Dsc.5.87. II. *of* or *for money*, ἀγὼν ἀργυρίτης a contest *in which the prize was money* (cf. στεφανίτης), Plu.2.820d, Lync. ap.Ath.13.584c. 2. *a moneyed man*, *AB*442. 3. fem. -ῖτις, = λινόζωστις ἄρρην, Ps.-Dsc.4.189.

ἀργῠρό-βῐος, ον, (βιός) *with the silver bow*, Eust.41.11. **-γνωμονικός**, ή, όν, *skilled in assaying silver*, Arr.*Epict*.2.3.2. **-γνώμων**, ονος, ὁ, ἡ, *assayer of silver*, Pl.*Virt*.378e, Arist.*Rh*.1375^{b}5, Plu.*Crass*. 2, Max.Tyr.2.2, etc. **-γρᾰφία**, ἡ, *writing in silver letters*, *PLeid*.*X*. 78. **-δάμας** [δᾰ], αντος, ὁ, name of a *precious stone*, Plin.37. 144. **-δίνης** [ῑ], ου, Dor. **-δίνας**, α, ὁ, (δίνη) *silver-eddying*, epith. of rivers, Il.2.753, 21.8,130, Hes.*Th*.340, B.7.48, Call.*Cer*.13, *Epic.Alex. Adesp*.5, Nonn.*D*.19.304; late Prose, Philostr.*VS*2.1.14. **-ειδής**, ές, *like silver*, *silvery*, δῖναι E.*IA*752 (lyr.), *Ion*95 (anap.); ὕδωρ Orph.*A*. 599; ἀργυροειδεῖ (prob. for ἀργυροδινεῖ) χαλκῷ Tryph.98; of the pupils in disease, Hp.*Prorrh*.2.20. **-εις**, εσσα, εν, = ἀργύρεος, Epigr.ap. Zonar.13.13, v.l. in Nic.*Al*.54. **-ηλος**, ον, *silver-studded*, ξίφος Il.2.45; θρόνος Od.7.162, etc. **-θήκη**, ἡ, *money-chest*, Diocl.Com. 1 D., Antiph.157, Thphr.*Char*.10.14, Poll.4.19. **-θρονος**, ον, *silver-throned*, Ἥρα Him.*Or*.1.20 (Sapph.133). **-θώραξ**, ᾱκος, ὁ, *with a silver breastplate*, Iamb.post Polem.p.49 Hinck. **-κοπεῖον**, τό, *silversmith's shop*, *mint*, Antipho*Fr*.36, And.*Fr*.5, Aeschin.Socr.39, Arist.*Pr*.936^{b}26, Plb.26.1.2 :—also **-κόπιον**, *IG*2^2.1013.30, 12(5). 480. **-κοπέω**, *coin money*, Lxx *Je*.6.29. **-κοπία**, ἡ, *minting*, *coinage*, *SIG*253*U* (Delph., iv B. C.). **-κοπιστήρ**, ῆρος, ὁ, *coiner*, metaph., λόγων Cratin.226; *money-changer*, Hsch. **-κόπος**, ὁ, (κόπτω) *coiner*, Phryn.Com.5. II. *silversmith*, Plu.2.830e, *SIG* 1263 (Smyrna), Poll.7.102,103, Lxx*Jd*.17.4, *Act.Ap*.19.24, *PHaw*. 68.3 (i A. D.). **-κορίνθιος**, *of Corinthian silver*, *cratera* *CIL*6.302 (ii A. D.). **-κυκλος**, ον, *silver-wheeled*, Nonn.*D*.18.10. **-λογέω**, *levy money*, X.*HG*1.1.12: c. acc., *levy money upon*, *lay under contribution*, τὰ τῶν ἐχθρῶν χωρία Th.8.3, cf. 2.69; τοὺς Ἕλληνας Aeschin. 3.159, etc.; ἀ. ἐκ πόλεων X.*HG*4.8.30; παρά τινος Them.*Or*.23. 289d. **-λόγητος**, ον, *subject to a levy in money*, Lxx 2*Ma*.11. 3. **-λογία**, ἡ, *levying of money*, X.*HG*1.1.8, etc. **-λόγος**, ον, (λέγω) *levying money*, ναῦς Ar.*Eq*.1071, Th.3.19, etc. **-μῐγής**, ές, *mixed with silver*, γῆ Str.3.2.9 codd. **-παστος**, ον, *silver-broidered*, ὅπλα Polyaen.4.16. **-πεζα**, ἡ, *silver-footed* (or *-sandalled*), epith. of Thetis, Il.1.538, al.; of Aphrodite, Pi.*P*.9.9, cf. Orph.*Fr*. 275; of Artemis, Nonn.*D*.34.47:—hence Adj. **-πεζος**, ον, *AP*5.59 (Rufin.). **-πηχυς**, υ, *silver-armed*, Nonn.*D*.42.419. **-ποιΐα**, ἡ, *production of silver*, in Alchemy, Ps.-Democr.Alch.p.49B. **-ποιός**, ὁ, *worker in silver*, *AP*14.50. **-πους**, ὁ, ἡ, πουν, τό, gen. ποδος, *with silver feet* or *legs*, κλίνη X.*An*.4.4.21; δίφρος *IG*2.646, D.24.129; φορεῖα Plb.30.25.18. **-πράτης** [ᾰ], ου, ὁ, *money-dealer*, *PSI*1.76. 2 (vi A. D.) :—hence **-ᾱτικός**, ή, όν, Just.*Nov*.136. **-πρυμνον** (sc. πλοῖον), τό, *vessel with silver-plated stern-post*, *PSI*6.551.1 (iii B. C.). **-ριζος**, ον, (ῥίζα) *with silver root*, παγαὶ Ταρτησσοῦ ἀ., i. e. *having silver in the soil*, Stesich.5. **-ρρῠτος**, ον, (ῥέω) *beside a silver stream*, ὄχθαι Ἕβρου E.*HF*386 (lyr.).

ἀργῠρορῠχή, ἡ, (prob. for -υκή) in pl., *silver-mines*, *Mon.Ant*.23. 8 (Adalia).

ἄργῠρος, ὁ, (ἀργός A) *white metal*, i. e. *silver*, ἐξ Ἀλύβης ὅθεν ἀργύρου ἐστὶ γενέθλη Il.2.857; so πηγὴ ἀργύρου A.*Pers*.238, etc.; ἄ. κοῖλος *silver plate*, Theopomp.Hist.283a, Arist.*Oec*.1350^{b}23, etc. 2. ἄ. χυτός *quicksilver*, Id. *de An*.406^{b}19, *Mete*.385^{b}4, Thphr.*Lap*.60. II. = ἀργύριον, *silver-money*, generally, *money*, A.*Supp*.935; ἐπ' ἀργύρῳ γε τὴν ψυχὴν προδούς S.*Ant*.322; εἴ τι μὴ ξὺν ἀργύρῳ ἐπράσσετ' by *bribery*, Id.*OT*124; in later Prose, coupled with χρυσός, *Ev.Matt*. 10.9, Alciphr.2.3. III. = λινόζωστος ἄρρην, Ps.-Dsc.4.189.

ἀργῠρο-σκόπος, ὁ, ἡ, = ἀργυρογνώμων, *IG*5(1).1390.48 (Andania, i B. C.), Phryn.*PS*p.30B. **-στερής**, ές, (στερέω) *robbing of silver*, βίος ἀ. *a robber's* life, A.*Ch*.1002. **-τᾰμεία** (for -ταμιεία), ἡ, *office of* ἀργυροταμίας, *CIG*2787, 2817 (Aphrodisias). **-τᾰμίας**, ου, ὁ, *treasurer* of a city, *IG*2^2.1100, *IGRom*.4.774,775 (Apamea), etc.; of a club, *PLond*. 3.1178.74 (ii A. D.). **-τᾰμιευτικός**, ή, όν, *controlled by the treasurer*, χρήματα *IG*9(1).144 (Elatea, ii A. D.). **-τᾰμιεύω**, *hold office of* ἀργυροταμίας, *IGRom*.4.785 (Apamea), *IG*12(9).20.7 (Carystus). **-τέχνης**, ου, ὁ, *silversmith*, *Jahresh*.1 *Beibl*.107. **-τοιχος**, ον, *with silver sides*, δροίτη A.*Ag*.1539 (lyr.). **-τοξος**, ον, *with silver bow*, Homeric epith. of Apollo, Il.2.766, al.; also simply Ἀργυρότοξος *bearer of the silver bow*, ib.1.37. **-τράπεζα** [ρᾰ], ἡ, *bank*, Just.*Edict*.9.2.1. **-τρύφημα** [ῠ], ατος, τό, a sort of *blanc-mange*, Chrysipp.Tyan.ap.Ath. 14.647d, prob. in Gal.6.811. **-φάλᾰρος** [φᾰ], ον, *with silver trappings*, ἱππεῖς Plb.30.25.6. **-φεγγής**, ές, *silver-shining*, δίφρος Nonn. *D*.4.24; λιμός, of a poor dinner served on *silver* plate, *AP*11.313 (Lucill.). **-φλεψ**, φλεβος, ὁ, ἡ, *with veins of silver ore*, Sch.Pl.*Ti*. 25b. **-χάλῑνος** [ᾰ], ον, *with silver-mounted bridle*, ζεῦγος Philostr. *VS*1.25.2. **-χαλκος**, ὁ, *silver-copper alloy*, Maria ap.Zos.Alch. p.169 B. **-χόος**, ὁ, (χέω) *melter of, worker in, silver*, Lxx *Wi*.15. 9. **-χροος**, ον, *silver-coloured*, Tz.*H*.11.483.

ἀργῠρόω, *to cover with silver*, ὀστέον *Dialex*.2.13; βωμόν *IG*3.899.4: —Pass., *to be silvered, silver-plated*, ῥύπος ἠργυρωμένος Men.*Mon*.469; ἀργυρούμενα ἢ ἐνηργυρωμένα σκεύη Timae.Astr. in *Cat.Cod.Astr*.1.97. 4. **II.** metaph. of persons, ἀργυρωθέντες σὺν οἰνηραῖς φιάλαις *rewarded with silver* wine-cups, Pi.*N*.10.43; also ἀοιδαὶ ἀργυρωθεῖσαι πρόσωπα songs *with silvered* brow, i.e. *mercenary*, Id.*I*.2.8.

ἀργῠρ-ώδης, ες, *rich in silver*, τόπος X.*Vect*.4.3. **-ωμα**, ατος, τό, *silver plate*, mostly in pl., Lys.*Fr*.56, Antiph.243.3, Men.475, Plb.5. 2.10, etc.: dat. pl. -ωμάτοις *IG*14.427 ii 15 (Tauromenium). **II.** *imitation silver*, an alloy of tin, copper, and silver, *PHolm*.1. 35. **-ωματικὴ** γῆ *earth for making moulds for silver reliefs*, *BMus. Inscr*.481*,542,549 (Ephesus, ii A.D.). **-ωμάτιον**, τό, Dim. of ἀργύρωμα, Arr.*Epict*.3.26.36. **-ώνητος**, ον, *bought with silver*, θεράποντες Hdt.4.72; ὑφαὶ A.*Ag*.949; ὁ ἀ., i.e. *slave*, Isoc.14.18; ἀ. σέθεν E.*Alc*.676; ἀ. ἄμπελος *PAvrom*.1 *A* 16 (i B.C.), cf. *PLond*.2.198 (ii A.D.). **-ωρῠχεῖον**, τό, *silver-mine*, Sch.Aeschin.1.100. **-ωταί**, οἱ, name of a *board of officials*, *GDI*1267.16 (Sillyon).

ἀργ-ύφεος [ῠ], η, ον, Ep. Adj. *silver-shining, silver-white*, σπέος Il. 18.50; φᾶρος Od.5.230; ἐσθής Hes.*Th*.574; νάματα *AP*9.633 (Damoch.); ᾠεόν Orph.*Fr*.70, cf. *Mus.Belg*.16.71 (Athens, ii A.D.), Epic. in *POxy*. 421.6. **-ῠφος**, ον, = foreg., epith. of sheep, Il.24.621, Od.10.85.

Ἀργώ, όος, contr. οῦς, ἡ, (ἀργός, ή, όν) *Argo*, the ship in which Jason sailed to Colchis, *the Swift*, first in Od.12.70:—Adj. **Ἀργῷος**, α, ον, *of the Argo*, δόρυ, σκάφος, E.*Andr*.793 (lyr.), *Med*.477. 2. the constellation *Argo*, Eudox.ap.Hipparch.1.2.20, Arat.342, etc. 3. tree of whose timber the *Argo* was built, Hsch.

ἀργώδης, ες, *lazy*, Aesop.413.

ἀργωπός, όν, *white*, Nic.*Fr*.74.19.

ἄρδᾰ, ης, ἡ, *dirt*, τὴν ἄρδαν ἀπ' ἐμοῦ σπόγγισον Pherecr.53.

ἀρδάλιον, τό, *water-pot* or *trough*, Hsch.

ἄρδαλος· ὁ μὴ καθαρῶς ζῶν, Erot.; cf. ἀρδάλους· εἰκαίους, Hsch.:— also **ἄρδαλος**· μόλυσμα, Id.

ἀρδᾰλόω, *smear*, Hp.*Nat.Mul*.67, Philem.59; *spread* a plaster, Hp.*Mul*.1.20:—Pass., ἠρδαλωμένος *filthy*, Lxx *Si*.22.1; also ἀρδαλωμένους· ταρασσομένους, Hsch.

ἀρδάνιον, τό, = ἀρδάλιον, Ael.Dion.*Fr*.66, Poll.8.66, *AB*441.

ἀρδ-εία, ἡ, *irrigation*, Str.4.6.7, Plu.2.688a (pl.), *BGU*283.6 (ii A.D.); εἰς ἀρδείαν τῆς γῆς Wilcken *Chr*.461.24 (iii A.D.); of a horse, εἰς ἀρδείαν ἄγειν Ael.*NA*7.12. **-εύσιμος**, η, ον, *irrigated*, Hsch. s.v. κατάρρυτα. **-ευσις**, εως, ἡ, (ἀρδεύω) = foreg., Hp.*Hebd*.1.87, Plb.9.43.5 (pl.), Moschio ap.Ath.5.207d, J.*AJ*3.1.3. **-ευτέον**, *one must water, irrigate*, *Gp*.9.11.3. **-ευτής**, οῦ, ὁ, *waterer*, Man. 4.258. **-ευτός**, ή, όν, *watered*, Sosith.7. **-εύω**, = ἄρδω, *water, irrigate*, A.*Pr*.852, Arist.*HA*601^{b}13, *Pr*.924^{b}15, Thphr.*HP*7.5.2, etc.:—Pass., *Com.Adesp*.29 D., Plb.10.28.3, *PThead*.16.10 (iv A.D.); βόσκομαι καὶ ἀρδεύομαι M.Ant.5.4: metaph., [Θουκυδίδης] ὁ τὸν Δημοσθένην πολλάκις ἀρδεύσας Chor. in *Philol*.54.120:—Pass., Plot.2.9. 3. **-ηθμός**, ὁ, = ἀρδμός, Lyc.622, Nic.*Th*.401.

ἄρδην, Adv. contr. for ἀέρδην, (ἀείρω) *lifted up on high*, of a vase carried on the head, S.*Ant*.430; φέρειν ἄ. E.*Alc*.608; πηδῶντος ἄ. Ἕκτορος τάφρων ὕπερ S.*Aj*.1279. **II.** *utterly, wholly*, εἰς Τάρταρον ἄ. ῥίψειε δέμας A.*Pr*.1051, cf. E.*Hec*.887; πᾶσαν ἄ. πόλιν ἀπολλύναι Pl.*R*.421a; ἄ. διαφθείρεσθαι Id.*Lg*.677c; Φωκέων ἄ. ὄλεθρος D.19.141; πεπτωκὸς ἄ. πολίτευμα Plb.1.35.5; ὄμνυμι πάντας ἄ. τοὺς θεούς *all together*, all *at once*, Ar.*Th*.274, cf. X.*An*.7.1.12; later εἰς ἄ., πόλιν ἐξελεῖν Hld.9.2.

ἀρδικός· φαρέτρα, Hsch.

ἀρδῐοθήρα, ας, ἡ, (ἄρδις) *forceps to extract arrow-heads*, etc., Serv. ad Virg.*Aen*.8.453, 12.404.

ἄρδις, ιος, ἡ, *point of an arrow*, acc. ἄρδιν Hdt.4.81; acc. pl. ἄρδις (Ion.) 1.215; gen. ἀρδίων 4.81:—on A.*Pr*.880 v. ἄπυρος. **II.** *arrow*, Lyc.63.

ἀρδμός, ὁ, *means of watering*, Il.18.521, Od.13.247, Nonn.*D*.26. 185; *watering-place*, A.R.4.1247. **II.** *draught*, νέκταρος prob. in Orph.*Fr*.189.

ἀρδρομηκιαῖος, α, ον, dub. in *POxy*.896.12 (iv A.D.); cf. ἀνδρο–.

ἄρδω, impf. ἦρδον Pl.*Ti*.76a, Ion. 3 sg. ἄρδεσκε Hdt.2.13: aor. ἦρσα Id.5.12, subj. ἄρσῃ Id.2.14, part. ἄρσας Id.2.14, 5.12: used by Att. only in pres. and impf.:—*water*: hence, 1. *give drink to* cattle, ἵππους ἄρσασα βαθυσχοίνοιο Μέλητος *from* or at the Meles, *h.Hom*. 9.3; ἄ. Σιμόεντος Euph.66; ἦρσε τὸν ἵππον Hdt. l. c.; of rivers, *furnish drink for* men, Pi.*O*.5.12:—Pass., *drink*, ἀρδόμενοι οὐρῆες ἀπὸ πηγέων *h.Ap*.263: metaph., ἄ. φωτί *to be drunk with* light, Plot. 2.9.3. 2. *water* land, of rivers, Hdt.2.14, A.*Pers*.487,806, etc.; of men, *irrigate*, μισθωτὸς ἄρδει πεδία Timocl.15.5, cf. Arist.*GC*335^{a} 14; θεὸς ἄ. γῆν Ph.1.50:—Pass., *to be watered*, of countries, Hdt.2. 13; σῖτος χερσὶ ἀρδόμενος *watered* by hand, Id.1.193; ἐκ τοῦ ποταμοῦ ibid., cf. Ibyc.1, Ath.2.43c; καρποὺς ἀρδομέναν . . χθόνα *having its* corn *watered*, Ar.*Nu*.282; Νυμφάων ὅθεν ἄρδεται ἄστυ Ἀθήνης *IG*3.1354. 5. **II.** metaph., *foster, cherish*, ὄλβον ἄ. Pi.*O*.5.23; πάτραν Χαρίτων ἄρδειν δρόσῳ, i.e. cover with glory, Id.*I*.6(5).64; τὸ λογιστικὸν ἄ. καὶ αὔξειν Pl.*R*.550b, cf. 606d, etc.; ἄ. νοῦν οἴνῳ Ar.*Eq*.96; συμποσίοις ἄρδοντες αὐτούς Pl.*Phdr*.276d, cf. X.*Smp*.2.24. **III.** *guzzle*, πολὺν ἄκρατον Ph.1.639. **IV.** *pour forth*, θεὸς ἄ. χάριτας Id.2. 294:—Pass., ib.244. (ᾱ acc. to Hdn.Gr.2.109.)

Ἀρέθουσα [ᾰρ], ἡ, name of several fountains, e.g. in Ithaca, Od. 13.408; at Syracuse, Str.6.2.4: pl., κρῆναι ἀρέθουσαι Choeril.2:— Adj. **Ἀρεθούσιος**, α, ον, ὕδωρ *AP*9.362.18. (A participial form; **ἀρέθω** is cited by Hdn.Gr.1.440 without expl.)

ἀρειά [ᾰρ], Ion. and poet. **ἀρειή**, ἡ, collective noun, *menaces, threats*, λευγαλέοις ἐπέεσσιν . . καὶ ἀρειῇ Il.20.109, but μειλιχίοις ἐπέεσσιν . . καὶ ἀρειῇ 21.339; πολλὰ δὲ μειλιχίοισι . . πολλὰ δ' ἀρειῇ 17.431.

ἀρειάω [ᾰρ], (ἀρειά) = ἀπειλέω, Hippon.65. (Cf. ἄρος· βλάβος ἀκούσιον, Hsch., Skt. *irasyā* 'malevolence'.)

Ἀρειθύσᾱνος [ῠ], ὁ, *tassel of Ares*, word for a brave warrior, A. *Fr*.203. (Cf. Paus.Gr.*Fr*.67.)

Ἀρεῐκός, ή, όν, *belonging to Ares*, Dam.*Pr*.97 bis; κάλλος Them. *Or*.13.165b; δόξα Paul.Al.*M*.1.

Ἀρει-μᾰνής [ᾰρ], ές, (μαίνομαι) *full of warlike frenzy*, Simyl.ap.Plu. *Rom*.17; Ἀριμασποί D.P.31; Οὖννοι *AP*9.210. **II.** Ἀρειμανής· ὁ Ἀΐδης, παρὰ Πέρσαις, Hsch.; cf. sq. II. **-μάνιος** [μᾰ], ον, = foreg., θρασύτης Ph.1.375; δυνάστης Plu.2.321f, cf. 758f; κριός D.L.6.61; φῦλα J.*BJ*2.16.4. **II.** Ἀρειμάνιος, ὁ, as pr. n., = Avest. *angrō mainyuš*, a name given by the Magi to *the Spirit of Evil*, opp. Oromasdes (= Ahuramazda), Arist.*Fr*.6, Plu.2.369e, Dam.*Pr*.125 bis. **-μᾰνιότης**, ητος, ἡ, opp. ἀψυχία, Stob.2.7.25.

ἀρεῖνος, η, ον, (ἀρία) *made of oak*, ξύλον *IG*11(2).161 *A* 70 (Delos, iii B.C.).

Ἀρειο-πᾰγίτης, **-πᾰγος**, v. Ἄρειος πάγος.

Ἄρειος [ᾰ], ον, also α, ον E.*HF*413 (lyr.); Ion. **Ἀρήϊος**, η, ον; Aeol. **Ἀρεύϊος** Alc.*Supp*.1a.10: (Ἄρης) :—*devoted to Ares, warlike, martial*; in Hom., mostly of warriors, Μενέλαος Ἀρήϊος Il.3.339, al.; Ἀρήϊοι υἷες Ἀχαιῶν 11.800, al.; of arms, Ἀρήϊα τεύχεα δύω 6.340, cf. 10.407; the Att. form only in the phrase τεῖχος Ἄρειον 4.407, al.; also in Hdt., ἀρήιοι ἀγῶνες conflicts *in real war*, opp. γυμνικοί, 9.33; ὅπλον ἀ. 4.23; of a man, as Subst., *warrior*, 6.98; Ἀθηνᾶ Ἀρεία *OGI* 229.70 (Smyrna), cf. *IG*12(5).913 (Tenos): Comp. ἀρειότερος (q.v.) Thgn.548 is prob. formed from ἀρείων, as χερειότερος from χερείων. 2. Ἄρειος (also Ἄρεος, Ἄρηος), ὁ (sc. μήν), name of month in Thessaly, *GDI*1449, etc. 3. Ἄρειον πεδίον, = *Campus Martius*, D.H.7.59, Plu.*Pomp*.53 (also name of a plain in Thrace, Plb.13.10. 7); τῶν τελῶν τὸ καλούμενον Ἄρειον, = *legio Martia*, App.*BC*3.45; Ἄρεια, τά, = *ludi Martiales*, D.C.56.46. 4. Ἄρειον, τό, = ξιφίον, Ps.-Dsc.4.20; = ἰσάτις, Id.2.184. **II.** = Ἄριος, Μάγοι καὶ πᾶν τὸ Ἄρειον γένος Dam.*Pr*.125.

Ἄρειος πάγος [πᾰ], ὁ, *the hill of Ares*, at Athens, Ἀρήϊος π. Hdt.8. 52, cf. A.*Eu*.685,690, etc.; ἡ βουλὴ ἡ ἐξ Ἀρείου πάγου *IG*1.38a (prob.), 2.476.59, al., D.18.133, cf. Lys.26.12, Arist.*Ath*.4.4; ἡ ἐν Ἀ. πάγῳ βουλή D.20.157, Aeschin.1.81, Arist.*Pol*.1273^{b}39; βουλὴ Ἀρεία *IG*3. 824; εἰς τὸν Ἄ. πάγον ἀναβῆναι become a member of the court, Isoc. 7.37, 12.154; ἐν Ἀ. πάγῳ δοῦναι δίκην Arist.*Rh*.1398^{b}26; ψευδομαρτύρια τὰ ἐξ Ἀ. πάγου Id.*Ath*.59.6.—The compd. **Ἀρειόπᾰγος** only in a late Att. Inscr., *IG*3.1005; but we find the noun **Ἀρεοπαγίτης** (Ἀρευ- ib.2.839.7) [ῑ], ου, ὁ, *Areopagite*, Aeschin.1.81, *IG*3.746, cf. 635, Arist.*Ath*.3.6, etc.: prov., Ἀρεοπαγίτου σιωπηλότερος 'as silent as the grave', Them.*Or*.21.263a; στεγανώτερος Alciphr.1.13:—Adj. **Ἀρεοπᾰγῖτις**, βουλή Arist.*Ath*.41.2, Alciphr.2.3; **Ἀρεοπᾰγῑτικός**, ή, όν, Isoc.7 tit., Str.6.1.8.

ἀρειότερος [ᾰ], α, ον, prob. = ἀρείων, Thgn.548, etc.: cf. Ἄρειος.

Ἀρεί-τολμος, ον, *warlike, bold*, *AP*9.40 (Zos.). **-φᾰτος**, Ep. **Ἀρηΐφατος**, ον, (cf. φόνος, πέφαται) *slain by Ares*, i.e. *slain in war*, Il.19.31, etc.; ψυχαί [Heraclit.]136, cf. 24; φόνοι Ἀ. E.*Supp*.603 (lyr.). 2. later, = Ἄρειος, *martial*, Ἀ. ἀγών, λῆμα, A.*Eu*.913, *Fr*. 147; κόποι E.*Rh*.124. 3. *slaying in war*, ἀνέρες Orph.*A*.514.

ἀρείων [ᾰ], ον, gen. ονος, used as Comp. of ἀγαθός, cf. ἄριστος: —*better, stouter, braver*, in Hom. of all advantages of body, birth, and fortune, Il.1.260, al., cf. Hes.*Op*.207, Pi.*N*.7.101, A.*Th*.305 (lyr.), *Ag*.81 (lyr.):—rare in Prose, ἃ ὑμῖν ἄρειον μὴ γνῶναι Arist.*Fr*. 44. **II.** ἀρείονες, οἱ, a kind of *snail* or *slug*, Ael.*NA*10.5.

ἄρεκτος, ον, poet. for ἄρρεκτος, *unaccomplished*, Il.19.150, Simon. 69.

ἀρέομαι, Ion. for ἀράομαι (q.v.), v.l. in Hdt. **II.** fut. of ἄρνυμαι (q.v.), prob. l. in Pi.*P*.1.75.[ᾰ].

Ἀρεοπαγίτης, ου, ὁ, v. Ἄρειος πάγος.

Ἄρεος, α, ον, collat. form of Ἄρειος, Ἀρέα (sc. κρήνη) *the spring of Ares*, Pi.*N*.9.41.

ἀρέσαι, ἀρέσασθαι, v. ἀρέσκω. **ἀρεσίπονον**· σύμμετρον, ἀρέσκον, Hsch.

ἄρεσις [ᾰ], εως, ἡ, *good pleasure, favour*, ἀπόδειγμα τῆς πρὸς τὴν πόλιν ἀρέσεως *Inscr.Prien*.108.30 (ii B.C.).

ἀρέσκ-εια [ᾰρ], ἡ, (ἀρεσκεύομαι) *obsequiousness*, Arist.*EE*1221^{a}8, *MM*1192^{b}30, Thphr.*Char*.5, Plb.31.26.5, Phld.*Herc*.1457.5, Polystr. p.16 W.; ἀ. βασιλέως Plb.6.11^{a}.7, cf. J.*AJ*18.8.7. 2. in pl., = δόξαι, ἀρέσκοντα, αἱ ἀ. τῶν πολλῶν, of false *superstitions*, Ph.2.191; τὰ ταῖς κεναῖς σοφιστῶν ἀρεσκήαις (sic) ὑπεναντία Demetr.Lac.*Herc*.1012. 73. 3. in good sense, πρὸς θεὸν καὶ ἀρετήν Ph.1.168; ἡ εἰς τὸ πλῆθος ἀ. *Inscr.Prien*.113.73 (i B.C.), cf. *IPE*2.5, *Ep.Col*.1.10; πρὸς τὴν ἑτέρων ἀ. βιοῦν Hld.10.14. -ευμα, ατος, τό, *act of obsequiousness*, Plu.*Demetr.*11, Epicur.*Fr.*177. -εύομαι, *to be complaisant to*, τινί Clearch.25, Hsch.: abs., *to be obsequious*, Plu.2.4d, M.Ant.5.5. -ευτικός, ή, όν, *obsequious*, Id.1.16, prob. in Phld.*Herc.*1457.11. -όντως, (ἀρέσκω) *agreeably*, ἀ. ἔχειν E.*IT*463 (lyr.), 581; ῥηθῆναι Pl.*R.*504b, X.*Oec.*11.19.

ἄρεσκος [ᾰ], η, ον, *pleasing*, mostly in bad sense, *obsequious, cringing*, Arist.*EN*1108a28, 1126b12, Thphr.*Char.*5.1. II. ἄρεσκος, ὁ, the staff borne by πορνοβοσκοί on the stage, Poll.4.120.

ἀρέσκω [ᾰ], impf. ἤρεσκον Th.5.37, etc.: fut. ἀρέσω D.39.33, Ep. ἀρέσσω (συν-) A.R.3.901: aor. ἤρεσα Hdt.8.19, *Com.Adesp.*19.4 D., etc., Ep. ἄρεσσα A.R.3.301, inf. ἀρέσαι Il., X.: pf. ἀρήρεκα Corn.*ND*24, S.E.*M.*1.238:—**Med.**, fut. ἀρέσομαι A.*Supp.*655 (lyr.), Ep. ἀρέσσομαι Il.4.362: aor. ἠρεσάμην, Ep. ἀρ- Hes.*Sc.*255, Ep. part. ἀρεσσάμενος Il.9.112, Thgn.762: aor. Pass. in med. sense, S.*Ant.*500:—**Pass.**, aor. ἠρέσθην Paus.2.13.8, J.*AJ*12.9.6. I. of pers. only, *make good, make amends*, ἂψ ἐθέλω ἀρέσαι Il.9.120:—Med., ταῦτα δ' ὄπισθεν ἀρεσσόμεθ' εἴ τι κακὸν νῦν εἴρηται 4.362, cf. Od.22.55, Q.S.4.377, 9.510; σπονδὰς θεοῖς ἀρέσασθαι *make full* drink-offerings to the gods, Thgn. l. c. 2. in Hom. also freq. in Med., c. acc. pers. et dat. modi, *appease, conciliate*, αὐτὸν ἀρεσσάσθω ἐπέεσσι καὶ δώρῳ Od.8.396; τὸν ξεῖνον ἀρέσσομαι ὡς σὺ κελεύεις ib.402; ὥς κέν μιν ἀρεσσάμενοι πεπίθωμεν δώροισι Il.9.112, cf. 19.179; καθαροῖσι βωμοῖς θεοὺς ἀρέσονται A.*Supp.*655; καί σε φίλως θυέεσσιν ἀρέσσατο Maiist.11: c. gen. rei, ἀρέσαντο φρένας αἵματος they *sated their* heart with blood, Hes.*Sc.*255. 3. after Hom., c. dat. pers., *please, satisfy*, οὔτε γάρ μοι Πολυκράτης ἤρεσκε δεσπόζων.. Hdt.3.142; δεῖ μ' ἀρέσκειν τοῖς κάτω S.*Ant.*75, cf. 89; ἀεὶ δ' ἀρέσκειν τοῖς κρατοῦσιν *to be obsequious to* them, E.*Fr.*93, cf. X.*Mem.*2.2.11; ἀ. τρόποις τινός *conform to* his ways, D.61.19; τὸ κολακεύειν νῦν ἀρέσκειν ὄνομ' ἔχει Anaxandr.42; πᾶσιν ἀρέσκω 1*Ep.Cor.*10.33; ἑαυτοῖς *Ep.Rom.*15.1:—Med., μάλιστα ἠρέσκοντό ⟨οἱ⟩ οἱ ἀπ' Ἀθηνέων *pleased* him most, Hdt.6.128. II. of things, c. dat. pers., *please*, εἴ τοι ἀρέσκει τὰ ἐγὼ λέγω Hdt.1.89; κάρτα οἱ ἤρεσε ἡ ὑποθήκη Id.8.58, cf. 3.40, 6.22; τῷ τοῦτ' ἤρεσεν; S.*El.*409; σοὶ ταῦτ' ἀρέσκει Id.*Ant.*211, etc.; τοῖς..πρέσβεσιν ἤρεσκεν [the proposal] *pleased* them, Th.5.37, cf. Pl.*Tht.*157d, al.: also in aor. Pass., μηδ' ἀρεσθείη ποτέ (sc. μηδὲν τῶν σῶν λόγων) S.*Ant.*500. III. c. acc. pers., οὐ γάρ μ' ἀρέσκει γλῶσσά σου τεθηγμένη Id.*Aj.*584; οὐδέ σ' ἀρέσκει τὸ παρόν E.*Hipp.*185 (lyr.), cf. *Or.*210; τουτὶ.. μ' οὐκ ἀ. Ar.*Pl.*353, cf. *Ach.*189, *Ra.*103, Th.1.128; πότερός σε ὁ τρόπος ἀ.; Pl.*Cra.*433e, cf. 391c, *R.*557b, *Tht.*172d: hence in Pass., *to be pleased, satisfied*, οὐκ ἠρέσκετο λειπομένου Μαρδονίου ὑπὸ βασιλέος Hdt.9.66; τῇ κρίσι *with* the decision, Id.3.34; διαίτῃ Σκυθικῇ Id.4.78; τοῖς λόγοις Th.1.129, cf. 2.68; τῇ σῇ συνουσίᾳ Pl.*Thg.*127b; later in aor., ἠρέσθη τῇ γνώμῃ J. l. c., al.; ἀρεσθεὶς τῷ πώματι Paus. l. c. IV. ἀρέσκει is used impers. to express *the opinion* or *resolution* of a public body, ταῦτα ἤρεσέ σφι ποιέειν Hdt.8.19; ἦν δ' ἀρέσκῃ ταῦτ' Ἀθηναίοις Ar.*Eq.*1311; ἀρέσκει.. εἶναι Δελφῶν *it is resolved* that.., *SIG*827*D*10; also of *prevailing opinions*, ἀρέσκει περὶ τρίψεως παραγγέλλοντας.. writers on massage *lay down the rule* that.., Gal.6.96; τὰ ἀρέσκοντα the *dogmas* of philosophers, Plu.2.448a, 1006d, etc.:—Med., ἐξεῖναι παρ' ὁποτέρους ἂν ἀρέσκηται ἐλθεῖν Th.1.35. V. part. ἀρέσκων, ουσα, ον, *grateful, acceptable*, ὅσοις τάδ' ἔστ' ἀρέσκονθ' S.*OT*274; μηδὲν ἀρέσκον λέγειν Th.3.34; ἀρέσκοντας ὑμῖν λόγους Isoc.8.5. 2. of persons, *acceptable*, τὸν ἀρέσκοντα αὐτῷ προσλαμβάνειν Pl.*Lg.*951e; τῇ πόλει ἀ. Lys.19.13. (Cognate with ἀραρίσκω.)

ἀρέσμιον, τό, *honorarium, perquisite*, *IG*9(1).32.25 (Stiris).

ἀρεστέον [ᾰ], *one must be pleased*, c. inf., Tz.*H.*8.212.

ἀρεστ-ήρ [ᾰ], ῆρος, ὁ, *a cake*, as a *propitiatory* offering, *IG*2.1651*B* 6, cf. 1662, Ael.Dion.*Fr.*68, Poll.6.76. -ήριος, α, ον, *propitiatory*, θυσίαι D.H.1.67:—hence **ἀρεστηρία** (sc. θυσία), ἡ, *SIG*2587.223, and -ήριον, τό, *IG*2.198c18 (iv B. C.). -ής, οῦ, ὁ, *EM*138.57.

ἀρεστός [ᾰ], ή, όν, *acceptable, pleasing*, Semon.7.46, Hdt.1.119, Men.*Epit.*71, Phld.*Po.*1676.1, etc.; ἔμοιγε οὐκ ἀρεστά Hdt.2.64; τῶν σῶν λόγων ἀ. οὐδέν S.*Ant.*500, cf. *OT*1096 (lyr.); τἀρεστὰ ὑμῖν αὐτοῖς αἱρεῖσθαι Lys.14.15; τὸ αἱρετὸν ἀρεστόν Chrysipp.*Stoic.*3.9; οἶνον παρέχειν ἀρεστόν *a sufficient* quantity, *IG*12(5).647.17 (Ceos); *satisfactory*, *PSI* 3.171.16 (ii B. C.); of persons, *acceptable, approved*, τινί X.*Cyr.*2.3.7, *SIG*577.58 (Milet., iii/ii B. C.), etc. Adv., ἑωυτῷ ἀρεστῶς *quite to* his own *satisfaction*, Hdt.6.129; ἀ. τοῖς ναοποιοῖς *IG*7.3073.52 (Lebad.); ὄχλοις ἀρεστῶς λέγειν Plu.2.6b; ἐσθίειν ἀ. θεοῖς Arr.*Epict.*1.13.1.

ἀρέσχαι· κλήματα, βότρυες, Hsch.

ἀρεταίνω, = ἀρετάω, Hsch., Eust.1599.32.

ἀρέταιχμος, ον, *valiant with the spear*, ἥρως B.16.48.

ἀρετᾱ-λογία [ᾰρ], ἡ, *celebration of divine* ἀρεταί, Lxx*Si.*36.19(16), cf. Sm.*Ps.*29(30).6; as a profession, *recitation of* ἱεροὶ λόγοι, Str.17.1.17 (prob. l.), Man.4.447. -λόγος, ὁ, (ἀρετή, λέγω) *professional expounder of* ἀρεταί (v. ἀρετή), *writer of* ἱεροὶ λόγοι, μιμογράφου καὶ ἀρεταλόγου ἢ ἄλλου συγγραφέως prob. in Phld.*Po.*5.1425.9; ὀνειροκρίτης καὶ ἀ. *SIG*1133, cf. Suet.*Aug.*74, Juv.15.16, Aus.*Ep.*13.

ἀρετάω [ᾰρ], *thrive, prosper*, οὐκ ἀρετᾷ κακὰ ἔργα Od.8.329; λαοὶ ἀρετῶσι 19.114: in late Prose, ἀρετῶσα γῆ Ph.2.372, al.; διάνοια ib.280:—Med., ἐὰν ἀρετήσηται αὐτοῦ τὰ.. *PGiss.*67.15 (ii A. D.). II. *choose the path of valour*, Procop.*Goth.*4.35, cf. *Aed.*1 *Prooem.*

ἀρετή [ᾰ], ἡ, *goodness, excellence*, of any kind, in Hom. esp. of *manly* qualities, ποδῶν ἀρετὴν ἀναφαίνων Il.20.411; ἀμείνων παντοίας ἀρετὰς ἠμὲν πόδας ἠδὲ μάχεσθαι καὶ νόον 15.642; so of the gods, τῶν περ καὶ μείζων ἀ. τιμή τε βίη τε 9.498; also of women, Od.2.206; ἀ. εἵνεκα for *valour*, Hdt.8.92: pl., ἀ. ἀπεδείκνυντο displayed *brave deeds*, Id.1.176, 9.40. b. later, of the gods, chiefly in pl., *glorious deeds, wonders, miracles*, *SIG*1172, Str.17.1.17; ζῶσαι ἀ. *IG*14.966, cf. 1*Ep. Pet.*2.9: also in sg., ὄψιν ἰδοῦσα ἀρετὴν τῆς θεοῦ *IG*2.1426b, cf. Isyll.62, *BSA*21.169,180. 2. generally, *excellence*, ἡ ἀ. τελείωσίς τις Arist.*Metaph.*1021b20, cf. *EN*1106a15, etc.; of persons, ἄνδρα πὺξ ἀρετὰν εὑρόντα Pi.*O.*7.89, cf. *P.*4.187, B.9.13, etc.; τὸ φρονεῖν ἀ. μεγίστη Heraclit.112: in pl., *forms of excellence*, μυρίαι ἀνδρῶν ἀ. B.13.8, cf. Gorg.*Fr.*8, etc.; δικαστοῦ αὕτη ἀ. Pl.*Ap.*18a; esp. *moral virtue*, Democr.179, 263, al., Gorg.*Fr.*6; opp. κακία, X.*Mem.*2.1.21, cf. Pl.*R.*500d, *Lg.*963a, c sq., D.60.17, Arist.*EN*1102a6, *Pol.*1295a37, etc.; *good nature, kindness*, etc., E.*Fr.*163. b. of animals, things, as land, Hdt.4.198, 7.5, Th.1.2; ἡ ἐν ἀρετῇ κειμένη γῆ *productive* land, *PTeb.*5.165 (ii B. C.); ἵππου Hdt.3.88; κυνῶν, ἵππων, Pl.*R.*335b; σκεύους ib.601d; [ἀστακοῦ] Archestr.*Fr.*24; ἀ. βίου Pl.*R.*618c; πολιτείας *Lg.*886b, etc. 3. *prosperity*, Od.13.45. II. ἀ. εἴς τινα *active merit, good service* done him, ἐς τοὺς Ἕλληνας Th.3.58, cf. 2.40; ἀ. περί τινα X.*An.*1.4.8; ἀνταποδοῦναι ἀ. Th.4.19; ἀρετὰς παρασχέσθαι ὑπέρ τινος D.19.312; ἀρετῆς ἕνεκα, freq. in honorary Inscrr., *IG*2².107.14, etc. III. *reward* of excellence, *distinction, fame*, πλούτῳ δ' ἀρετὴ καὶ κῦδος ὀπηδεῖ Hes.*Op.*313, cf. Sapph.80, Pi.*N.*5.53, al.; ἀθάνατος ἀ. S.*Ph.*1420, Pl.*Smp.*208d; ἃ ἆθλα τοῦ πολέμου τοῖς ἀνδράσιν ἐστίν, ἐλευθερία καὶ ἀ. Lycurg.49; of God, δόξα καὶ ἀ. 2*Ep.Pet.*1.3: in pl., *glories*, Thgn.30, Pi.*N.*10.2, al.; πλοῦτος ἀρεταῖς δεδαιδαλμένος Id.*O.*2.53; γενναίων ἀ. πόνων E.*HF*357 (lyr.), cf. Lys.2.26; προγόνων ἀ. Pl.*R.*618b; in Lxx freq. of the *praises* of God, Is.42.8, al. IV. Ἀρετή personified, Prodic.1, Arist.*Fr.*675, Callix.2, *CIG*2786, *SIG* 985.10, etc. V. ἡ ἀ. σου as a title, Your *worship*, *PLips.*13 ii 20, etc. VI. an *engine of war*, Ath.Mech.38.11. VII. a *plaster*, Androm.ap.Gal.13.531.

ἀρετηφόρος [ᾰ], ον, *virtuous*, Phld.*Rh.*1.217 S., *Mort.*35.

ἀρετίδιον [ᾰ], τό, Dim. of ἀρετή, Anon.*in Rh.*174.6.

ἀρετόομαι [ᾰ], Pass., *become excellent, grow in goodness*, Simp.*in Epict.*p.10 D., Id.*in Ph.*1066.5.

ἀρή [ᾱ], ἡ, *bane, ruin*, ἀρὴν ἑτάροισιν ἀμύνειν Il.12.334; ἀρῆς ἀλκτῆρα γενέσθαι 18.100; ἀρὴν καὶ λοιγὸν ἀμῦναι 24.489, cf. Od.2.59; so in A.*Supp.*84 (lyr.), where the gloss of the Sch., βλάβης, confirms the reading ἀρῆς for ἄρης. (Cf. pf. part. ἀρημένος = βεβλαμμένος, and pr. n. Ἄρης (cf. Corn.*ND*20), perh. also ἄρος, ἀρειά, ἐπήρεια; perh. an old ē stem.)

ἄρηαι, Ep. 2 sg. subj. aor. 2 Med. from ἄρνυμαι, Il., Hes.

ἀρηβώ, a kind of *cassia*, *Peripl.M.Rubr.*12, Gal.14.72.

ἀρηγοσύνη [ᾰ], ἡ, *help, aid*, *AP*9.788.8, *Epigr.Gr.*1050 (Ephesus).

ἀρήγω [ᾰ], fut. -ξω *Com.Adesp.*12.5 D., etc.:—*aid, succour*, τινί Il.2.363, al. (never in Od.); in Hom. always, *succour in war*, freq. c. dat. pers. et modi, μάχῃ Τρώεσσιν ἀ. 1.521, 5.507; ὅμοσσον ἦ μέν μοι.. ἔπεσιν καὶ χερσὶν ἀ. 1.77: generally, *help, succour*, λέχει Ἀλκμήνας Pi.*N.*1.49; νεότατι ἀ. θράσος Id.*P.*2.63; θνητοῖς A.*Pr.*269, etc.; in mock Trag. passages of Com., γυναῖκες, οὐκ ἀρήξετ'; Ar.*Th.*696, cf. *Pl.*476: rare in Prose, Hecat.30 J., etc.; ὁ ναυτικὸς τῷ πεζῷ ἀρήξει Hdt.7.236; τοῖς φίλοις ἀ. X.*Cyr.*1.5.13; ἀ. σὺν ὅπλοις τῇ χώρᾳ Id.*Oec.*5.7; *to be good for* a patient or his case, Hp.*Prorrh.*2.30, cf. *Acut.*65. 2. impers., c. inf., *it is good* or *fit*, φέρειν ἀρήγει Pi.*P.*2.94; σιγᾶν ἀρήγει A.*Eu.*571. II. c. acc. rei, *ward off, prevent*, ὄλεθρον v.l. in Batr.279; ἄρηξον.. ἅλωσιν A.*Th.*119 (lyr.); ἀ. τινί τι *ward off from* one, φόνον τέκνοις E.*Med.*1275 (lyr.), cf. *Tr.*777. (Perh. cognate with Lat. *rēx*, Skt. *rājati* 'rule'.)

ἀρηγών [ᾰ], όνος, ὁ, ἡ, *helper*, Il.4.7, 5.511, in fem.; masc. in Batr. 280, etc.; ἀρηγόνος ἡνιόχοιο Opp.*H.*5.108.

Ἀρηΐ-θοος [ᾰ], ον, *swift in war*, αἰζηοί Il.8.298, 15.315, A.R.1.1042; ἄνδρες Simon.104. -κτάμενος [ᾰρ], η, ον, (κτείνω) *slain by Ares*, Il.22.72.

Ἀρήϊος [ᾰ], η, ον, also ος, ον, Ion. for Ἄρειος, Hom., etc.; δαίμων Ἀ. Jul.*Or.*4.154c:—pecul. fem. **Ἀρηϊάς**, άδος, Q.S.1.187.

Ἀρηΐ-φᾰτος [ᾰ], ον, Ep. and Ion. for Ἀρείφατος (q. v.). -φθορος, ον, *slain in war*, πτώματα Corn.*ND*21. -φῐλος, η, ον, *dear to Ares*, epith. of warriors in Hom., Il.2.778, al., cf. Hes.*Th.*317, Pi.*I.*8(7).25, etc.; of the river Thermodon, Tryph.33.

ἀρήμεναι, v. ἀράομαι. **ἀρημένος** [ᾱ], η, ον, pf. part. Pass., expld. by Gramm. by βεβλαμμένος, *distressed, worn out*, once in Il., γήραϊ λυγρῷ κεῖται ἐνὶ μεγάροις ἀ. 18.435; more freq. in Od., ὕπνῳ καὶ καμάτῳ ἀ. 6.2; τίπτε τόσον, Πολύφημ', ἀρημένος ὧδ' ἐβόησας; 9.403; γήρᾳ ὑπὸ λιπαρῷ ἀ. 11.136; δύῃ ἀ. 18.53. [Prob. akin to ἀρή, Ἄρης.]

ἀρήν (nom. only in Inscrr., *IG*1.4, 11.154*A*11 (Delos, iii B. C.), *SIG*1027.9 (Cos), ϝαρήν *GDI*4964.2 (Gortyn)); also ἄρης *PGurob.*22.40, 42 (iii B. C.), and ἄρνον ib.3, al.; acc. ἄρνα, gen. ἀρνός, dat. ἀρνί, dual. ἄρνε: pl. ἄρνες, ἄρνας, ἀρνῶν, dat. ἀρνάσι J.*AJ*3.8.10, Ep. ἄρνεσσι:—*lamb* (under a year old, Max.515, Istros ap.Eust.1672.12); ἀ. πρωτογόνων Il.4.102, etc.; γαλαθηνῶν Crates Com.1. II. *sheep* of either sex, ἄρν' ἕτερον λευκόν, ἑτέρην δὲ μέλαιναν Il.3.103; ἄρνες κεραοί Od.4.85. III. in pl., *stunted ears* of wheat, Thphr.*HP*8.7.5. (Skt. *ūrā* 'sheep', *úraṇas* 'ram', 'lamb', *urabhras* 'ram', Arm. *garn* 'lamb'; cf. -ϝρην in πολύρρην.)

ἀρηνοβοσκός, ὁ, *shepherd*, Paus.Gr.*Fr.*69, dub. in S.*Fr.*655.

ἄρηξις [ᾰ], εως, ἡ, (ἀρήγω) *help, succour*, τινός *from* a person, A.*Pr.*547 (lyr.), S.*OC*829. II. c. gen. rei, *help against* a thing, *means of averting* it, πημάτων S.*El.*876.

ἄρηρα, ἀρήρειν, ἀρηρεμένος, v. ἀραρίσκω.

ἀρηρομένος, η, ον, v. ἀρόω.

Ἄρης, ὁ, Ep. gen. Ἄρεος, Att. Ἄρεως A.*Th.*64, E.*El.*1258; but Ἄρεος (never contr.) is required by the metre in A.*Th.*115 (lyr.), S.*OC*947, *Ant.*125 (lyr.), *El.*1423 (lyr.), E.*Heracl.*275, *El.*950, *Fr.*16; dat. Ἄρεϊ, contr. Ἄρει; acc. Ἄρεα S.*OT*190 (lyr.), Att. Ἄρη (never Ἄρην, which is not found in Attic Inscrr. and is never required by the metre; Ἄρη' is the true reading in Il.5.909, Hes.*Sc.*59, cf. *AP*7.237 (Alph.), D.S. 5.72); voc. Ἄρες, Ep. (metri gr.) Ἀρές:—Ion. and Ep. declens. **Ἄρης**, ηος, ηι, ηα: Aeol. **Ἄρευς**, ευος, ευα, ευι, ευ, Sapph.66, Alc. 28 ff.:—*Ares*: in Trag., *the god of destruction* generally, S.*OT*190, etc.; ἐς Οἰδίπου παῖδε..Ἄρης κατέσκηψ' Ar.*Fr.*558; in Com., Ἄρεως νεοττός chicken *of Ares*, Id.*Av.*835. 2. the planet *Mars*, Arist. *Cael.*292ᵃ5, Cleom.1.11.59, etc.; Ἄρεος ἡμέρα D.C.37.19. II. in Poets, Appellat. for *war, slaughter*, ξυνάγωμεν Ἄρηα Il.2.381; Ἄρη μείζουσιν S.*OC*1046 (lyr.); χρονίῳ σὺν Ἄρει Pi.*P.*11.36; Ἄρης ἐμφύλιος, Ἄ. τιθασός, A.*Eu.*862, 355; θηλυκτόνῳ Ἄρει δαμέντων Id.*Pr.*861; ναύφαρκτος Ἄ. Id.*Pers.*951 (lyr.); λιθόλευστον Ἄρη *death* by stoning, S.*Aj.*254 (lyr.); ἔνθα μάλιστα γίγνετ' Ἄ. ἀλεγεινὸς ὀϊζυροῖσι βροτοῖσι, of a *mortal wound*, Il.13.569. 2. *warlike spirit*, A.*Ag.*78, E.*Ph.* 134; κἂν γυναιξὶν..Ἄ. ἔνεστιν S.*El.*1242; οὔτ' ὄλβος οὔτ' Ἄ. Id.*Ant.* 952; μέγαν ἐκ θυμοῦ κλάζοντας Ἄ. A.*Ag.*48; Ἄρη βλέπειν Ar.*Pl.*328, Timocl.12.7: in Prose, ἔμφυτος Ἄ. Gorg.*Fr.*6. 3. *the sword*, ὀξὺς Ἄ. Il.7.330, cf. *AP*.7.531 (Antip. Thess.), Plu.2.23c. III. epith. of Zeus, as the *avenger* of perjury, in oaths, *IG*5(2).343c (Arc.); of Ἐνυάλιος, ibid., Poll.8.106. (Akin to ἀρή, q.v.) [ᾰ in Hom., but α of voc. may be long, e.g. Ἄρες, Ἄρες βροτολοιγέ Il.5.31, and gen. Ἄρηος 2.767, Call.*Jov.*77 (s.v.l.), Ἄρεος A.R.3.1187, dat. Ἄρηϊ Id.2. 991: in Trag., regularly ᾰ, but A. uses ᾱ even in dialogue, as *Th.*244, 469; and S. in lyr., *Aj.*252, 614, *Ant.*139.]

Ἀρησιών, ῶνος, ὁ (sc. μήν), name of a month at Delos, *IG*11.158*A* 48 (iii B.C.).

ἀρήτ-ειρα [ᾱρ], ἡ, fem of ἀρητήρ, Call.*Cer.*43, Musae.68, A.R.1. 312, etc. **-εύω**, *to be president*, βωλᾶς *IG*12(3).1259 (Cimolus); Dor. ἀϝρ- ib.4.497.4 (Mycenae), *SIG*56.43 (Argos). (Always in 3 sg. impf. ἀϝρήτευε, ἀρήτευε, hence perh. for ἐ-ϝρήτευε, from ϝρητεύω, cf. ϝρήτρα.) **-ήρ** [ᾱ], ῆρος, ὁ, (ἀράομαι) *one that prays*: poet. for ἱερεύς (Arist.*Po.*1457ᵇ35), *priest*, Il.1.11, 5.78, al.; also in metr. Inscrr., *IG*4.1007 (Epid.), 1538 (Apollo Maleatas), etc., cf. Orac.ap. Jul.*Ep.*89. **-ήριον** [ᾱ], τό, *a place for curses*, Plu.*Thes.*35. **-ός**, ή, όν, Ion. for ἀρατός: **Ἀρήτη**, ἡ, as pr.n., Od.7.54, etc.

ἀρητυμένος, f.l. for ἀρυτήμενος, Alc.47.

ἄρθεν, v. ἀραρίσκω.

ἄρθεος· τράγος, Hsch.

ἀρθμέω, intr., *to be united*, ἐν φιλότητι ἀρθμήσαντε Il.7.302:—Pass., ἀρθμηθέντες A.R.1.1344.

ἄρθμιος, α, ον, *united*, οἱ δ' ἡμῖν ἄρθμιοι ἦσαν *in league with* us, Od. 16.427, cf. Hdt.7.101, al.; ἁ. ἥδε φίλος Thgn.1312; ἄρθμια, τά, *peaceful relations, friendship*, τέως μὲν δή σφι ἦν ἄ. ἐς ἀλλήλους, ἐκ τούτου δὲ πόλεμος Hdt.6.83; ἄ. ἔργα Emp.17.23, cf. 22.1. 2. *calm*, βολαὶ ὀφθαλμῶν Hdn.1.7.5.

ἀρθμός, ὁ, (ἀραρίσκω) *a bond, league, friendship*, ἀρθμῷ καὶ φιλότητι *h.Merc.*524, cf. A.*Pr.*193 (lyr.), Call.*Fr.*199.

ἀρθρέμ-βολέω, *insert* part of a machine, in Pass., Ath.Mech.34. 6. **-βόλησις**, εως, ἡ, *setting of a limb*, Apollon.Cit.1.1:—also **-βολία**, ἡ, Orib.49.9.5. **-βολον**, τό, (ἐμβάλλω) *instrument for setting limbs*, Gal.14.781: in pl., *instruments of torture*, Lxx 4*Ma.*8.13.

ἀρθρίδιον, τό, Dim. of ἄρθρον, v.l. for ἀγρίδιον, M.Ant.4.3.

ἀρθρικός, ή, όν, (ἄρθρον I) *of* or *for the joints*, Gal.19.85. II. (ἄρθρον II) *of, belonging to the article*, in Gramm., A.D.*Synt.*6.5, al. Adv. -κῶς ib.33.6.

ἀρθρῑτικός, ή, όν, (ἄρθρον) *of* or *for the joints*, νόμος Hp.*Art.* 18. II. *diseased in the joints, gouty*, Id.*Epid.*6.4.3, Damox.2.32, Cic.*Fam.*9.23: τὰ -κά Hp.*Epid.*7.100; ἀ. ἀλήματα Gal.17(2).125.

ἀρθρῖτις, ιδος, ἡ (acc. -ῖτιν Porph.*Abst.*1.53), as if fem. of ἀρθρίτης, which does not occur:—*of* or *in the joints*, νόσος Hp.*Aff.*30; ἡ ἀ. *gout*, Id.*Aph.*3.16 (pl.), Aret.*SD*2.12, etc.

ἀρθροκηδής, ές, *limb-distressing*, πόνοι Luc.*Trag.*15.

ἄρθρον, τό, (ἀραρίσκω) *joint*, Emp.17.22, etc.; ἄρθρων πόνοι Hp. *Aph.*3.31, al.; ἅπαν κατ' ἄρθρον S.*Tr.*769; κρᾶτα καὶ ἄρθρα the head and *joints of the neck*, Id.*Ph.*1208 (lyr., codd.); esp. *the socket of the ankle-joint*, ὁ ἀστράγαλος ἐξεχώρησε ἐκ τῶν ἄ. Hdt.3.129; in Hp.*Art.* 1, al., *ball* of a joint, opp. *socket* (κοτύλη), cf. Gal.18(2).487 (but *socket* in Hp.*Loc.Hom.*6); μάρψας ποδός νιν ἄρθρον ᾗ λυγίζεται S.*Tr.*779, cf. *Ph.*1202 (lyr.). 2. generally, *of limbs*, etc., esp. in pl., ἄ. ποδοῖν the ankles, Id.*OT*718, cf. 1032; of the legs, βραδύπουν ἤλυσιν ἄρθρων προτιθεῖσα E.*Hec.*67 (lyr.); ἄ. τῶν κύκλων eyes, S.*OT*1270; ἄ. στόματος the mouth, E.*Cyc.*625; θέναρ διηρημένον ἄρθροις *lines*, Arist.*HA*493ᵇ33; τὰ ἄ. alone, *genitals*, Hdt.3.87, 4.2, Arist.*HA*504ᵇ23, al.; τὰ ἐντὸς ἄ. the internal *organs*, Mnesith.ap.Orib.8.38.7: metaph., ἄ. τᾶν φρενῶν Epich.250: in sg., ἄρθρον τῆς φωνῆς vocal *articulation*, Arist.*HA*536ᵃ 3. II. Gramm., *connecting word*, Id.*Po.*1457ᵃ6; esp. of the *article*, Id.*Rh.Al.*1435ᵃ35, Chrysipp.*Stoic.*2.45, D.H.*Th.*37, al.

ἀρθροπέδη, ἡ, *band for the limbs, fetter*, *AP*6.297 (Phan.).

ἀρθρόω, (ἄρθρον) *fasten by a joint*:—Pass., *to be jointed*, κνημὶς περὶ σφυρὸν -οῦται Hermipp.47.3; σώματα ἠρθρωμένα *well-jointed, well-knit*, Hp.*Aër.*20; κνῆμαι ἠρθρωμέναι Arist.*Phgn.*810ᵃ28. II. mostly of words, *utter distinctly*, γλῶσσα ἀρθροῖ τὴν φωνήν *produces articulate* sounds, X.*Mem.*1.4.12 (but ἀρθρῶσαι γλῶσσαν καὶ νόον *nerve* the tongue and mind, v.l. in Thgn.760); of persons, *render articulate*, καί μ' εἰς τοῦτο..ἠρθρωσαν οἱ θεοὶ ὅπως.. Nic.Dam.p.65 D.

ἀρθρ-ώδης, ες, *well-jointed, well-knit*, X.*Cyn.*4.1, Arist.*Phgn.*810ᵇ 26. 2. *articulated*, opp. ἄναρθρος, Id.*PA*667ᵃ9 (Comp.); esp. in sense of sq., Gal.2.735. Adv. -δῶς ibid. **-ωδία**, ἡ, a particular kind of *articulation*, where the surfaces are only slightly concave and convex, ib.736. **-ωσις**, εως, ἡ, *jointing, compact connexion*, prob. in Str.2.1.30, cf. Ph.2.408. 2. *articulation*, of speech, Phld.*D.* 3.14, cf. *Po.*994.6.

ἀρθύσανοι· ἀποσχίσματα καὶ ἀποκλαστήματα, Hsch.

ἀρῐ- [ᾰ], insep. prefix, like ἐρι-, strengthening the notion conveyed by its compd.: cogn. with ἀρείων, ἄριστος, chiefly denoting *goodness, excellence*: mostly in older Ep. and Lyr.

ἀρία, ἡ, Dor. for φελλόδρυς, Thphr.*HP*3.16.3, al. (Prob. for ἀρέα, cf. ἀρεΐνος.)

ἀριβάσκανος, ον, *very envious*, Hsch.

ἀρί-γνως [ᾰ], ωτος, ὁ, ἡ, = sq., in nom. pl. ἀριγνῶτες, Pi.*N.*5. 12. **-γνωτος**, η, ον, Od.6.108, Aeol. α, ον Sapph.*Supp.*25.4, also ος, ον Il.15.490:—*easy to be known*, ἀρίγνωτοι δὲ θεοί περ 13.72, cf. 15.490, Sapph. l.c.; δώματα Od.6.300; ῥεῖά τ' ἀριγνώτη πέλεται ib.108. 2. in bad sense, *infamous*, ὦ ἀρίγνωτε συβῶτα 17.375.

ἄρῑγος or ἄρρ-, ον, *insensible to cold*, Arist.*Pr.*959ᵇ17, Aret.*SD*1.14.

ἀρίγων, ωνος, ὁ, a kind of *spear*, Hdn.Gr.1.24, 2.279.

ἀρῐ-δάκρυος [ᾰρ], ον, = sq., Arist.*Pr.*874ᵇ8. **-δακρῠς**, υ, gen. υος, *very tearful*, γόος A.*Pers.*947 (lyr.); of persons, Arist.*HA*608ᵇ9, *Pr.* 953ᵇ11: prov., ἀριδάκρυες ἀνέρες ἐσθλοί Sch.Ven.Il.1.349; but in bad sense, Ph.2.269. **-δάκρῡτος**, ον, *much wept*, Hsch. **-δείκετος**, ον, *famous, glorious*: in Hom. mostly c. gen., ἀριδείκετος ἀνδρῶν Il. 11.248, al.; also υἱὸν..ἀριδείκετον εἶναι Od.11.540; ἀ. τέκνα Hes.*Th.* 385; ἀριδείκετε δαῖμον Orph.*Fr.*155; of things, σκῆπτρον ib.101. II. *clear, distinct*, Emp.20.1. (Metr. lengthd. for ἀρι-δέκ-ετος, cf. Lat. *decus.*)

ἀρίδες· αἱ μετὰ κονιορτοῦ πνοαί, Hsch.

ἀρί-δηλος [ᾰρῐ], Dor. **-δηλος** (v. infr.), also **-δᾱλος**, ον, in pr. n., *IG*12(1).741 (Rhodes):—*clear, distinct, far seen*, Ὄσσα Simon.130, cf. Arat.94; *bright*, Ἀνταύγης Orph.*Fr.*237; ἀρίδηλον μνᾶμα *IG*7.52 (Megara), cf. Charito 4.1. II. *manifest*, τάδε γὰρ ἀ. Hdt.8.65, Ph. 1.276, al., Porph.*Chr.*35: Comp., Ph.1.331: Sup., ib.690; also f.l. for ἀΐδηλα in Tyrt.11.7. III. *conspicuous, magnificent*, ἀγῶνα τῶν πρόσθεν -ότερον Arr.*An.*7.14.10; *famous*, Eun.*VS* p.456 B. (Comp.). Adv. -λως Them.*Or.*2.26c, Sch.Ar.*Pl.*948: Comp., Ph.1.451: Sup. -ώτατα (sic) Hsch.—Ep., Ion., and later Prose.

ἀρίδιον, τό, Dim. of ἆρις, *Hermes* 38.281.

ἀρί-ζηλος [ᾰ], ον (Dor. -ζηλος *IG*9(1).270), also η, ον, v. infr.:—Ep. for ἀρίδηλος (-ζηλος from δηλος, cf. δῆλος from δεγαλος and δέατο), *conspicuous*, of lightning, ἀρίζηλοι δέ οἱ αὐγαί Il.13.244, cf. Pi.*O.*2.61, S.*Ichn.*72; of sound, ὡς δ' ὅτ' ἀριζήλη φωνή Il.18.219; of persons whom all admire, ὥς τε θεὼ περ ἀμφὶς ἀριζήλω ib.519, *AP*4.1.3 (Mel.), etc.; ῥεῖα δ' ἀρίζηλον μινύθει καὶ ἄδηλον ἀέξει Hes.*Op.*6. Adv. ἀριζήλως, εἰρημένα a *plain* tale, Od.12.453. II. Dor. ἀρίζαλος (ζῆλος), = sq., Call.*Epigr.*52, Hsch. s. v. ἀρι-. **-ζήλωτος**, ον, *much to be envied*, Ar.*Eq.*1329 (anap.): -ζήλητος in Orac.ap.Eus.*PE*9.10.

ἄριζος· τάφος (Cypr.), Hsch.

ἀριήκοος [ᾰ], ον, *much heard of*, Call.*Del.*308. II. Act., *far-hearing, hearing readily*, A.R.4.1707, Dam.*Isid.*279; οὖας Procl.*H.* 2.14.

ἀριῆνας· ἀρισπώλους, Hsch.

ἀριθμ-έω [ᾰ], impf. ἠρίθμεον as trisyll., Od.10.204, 3 sg. ἠρίθμει 13. 218:—Med., aor. ἠριθμησάμην Pl.*Phdr.*270d:—Pass., fut. Med. in pass. sense ἀριθμήσομαι E.*Ba.*1318; fut. ἀριθμηθήσομαι Lxx 3*Ki.*3.8, Gal.10.68: Ep. aor. inf. ἀριθμηθήμεναι (for -ῆναι) Il.2.124:—*number, count, reckon up*, Od.4.411, Pi.*N.*10.46, etc.; αὐτὰρ ἐγὼ δίχα πάντας .. ἑταίρους ἠρίθμεον *counted* them so as to halve them, Od.10.204; ἀριθμήσαντες *after numbering* the army, Hdt.7.60; οὐδεὶς πώποτ'.. ἠρίθμησε *stopped to count* the enemy, Ar.*Eq.*570: poet., ἀριθμήσεις γαῖαν ἀπειρεσίην, = μετρήσεις, *AP*11.349 (Pall.):—Pass., Hdt.6.111, 9.32:—Med., ἠριθμοῦντο *counted each for himself*, πλίνθους Th.3. 20. 2. *count out, pay*, χρυσίον, ἀργύριον, X.*Smp.*4.44, D.49.30, *IG* 5(1).1390.51 (Andania), *Mon.Anc.Gr.*7.22. 3. *reckon, account*, ἐν εὐεργεσίας μέρει D.21.166; ἀ. τινὰ κλυτόπαιδα *AP*9.262 (Phil.); κέρδος τι ἀ. D.Chr.31.158:—Pass., *to be reckoned*, ἐν τοῖσι γενναίοισιν E.*Hel.* 729; ἐν γράμμασι Luc.*Jud.Voc.*2; εἴς τινας Hdn.1.1.1; ἀριθμεῖσθαι τῶν φιλτάτων *as one of..*, E.*Ba.*1318; μακάρων Theoc.13.72. [-ῑθμ- Ar.*V.*333, *Com.Adesp.*21.28 D.] **-ημα**, ατος, τό, *reckoning, number*, τῶν πάλων A.*Eu.*753; ἡμέρα ἀ. αἰώνιον Secund.*Sent.*4. **-ησις**, εως, ἡ, *counting, reckoning up*, Hdt.2.143, Str.9.5.3, *POxy.*1258.7 (i A.D.), Plot.4.4.11; *counting out, payment* of money, *IPE*1².32*B*35 (Olbia). 2. *account*, *BGU*328 i 24 (ii A.D.), etc. II. = ἀριθμητική, ἡ, Hp.*Ep.*22. **-ητέος**, α, ον, *to be reckoned, counted*, Id.*Epid.* 2.3.17. 2. ἀριθμητέον, *one must reckon, count*, Thphr.*Ign.*3, Porph. *Abst.*2.38. **-ητής**, οῦ, ὁ, *calculator*, Pl.*Just.*373b. **-ητικός**, ή, όν, *of* or *for reckoning, skilled therein*, ἄνθρωπος Id.*Grg.*453e. II. *arithmetical*, μέσα Archyt.2; ἀναλογία Arist.*EN*1106ᵃ35; τὸ ἓν ἁπλῶς οὐκ ἦν ἀ. Dam.*Pr.*117; ἡ ἀριθμητική (sc. τέχνη) *arithmetic*, Pl.*R.*525a, al.; as a subject of competition, *Inscr.Magn.*107; ἡ ἀ. ἐπιστήμη Plu. 2.979e. Adv. -κῶς ib.643c, Theo Sm.p.116 H. III. -κόν, τό, *land-tax* in Egypt, τὸ τέλειον ἀ. *Sammelb.*4415.14 (ii A.D.), etc.; ἡμιτέλειον ἀ. *BGU*330.6 (ii A.D.). **-ητός**, ή, όν, *that can be counted*, οὐκ ἀ. Cratin.153, cf. *AP*12.145; ἠριθμημένον ἢ ἀ. Arist.*Ph.*223ᵃ24; opp. μετρητόν, Id.*Metaph.*1020ᵃ9. 2. *easily numbered, few in number*, ἀριθμητοὺς ἀπὸ πολλῶν Theoc.16.87. 3. οὐκ ἀ. *of* no *account*, Id.14.48. **-ιος**, α, ον, = *numerical*, Iamb.*Comm.Math.*9;

by number, ἀρίθμια σῦκα ρ' *POxy.*529.6 (ii A.D.). 2. Astrol., *determining number*, κλῆρος Vett.Val.145.23; τόπος Id.278.30. II. *reckoned, counted*, μέτ' ἀθανάτοισιν ἀ. Rhian.1.16; ἐν καὶ ὄνος κείνοισιν ἀ. prob. in Opp.*H.*1.151; ἀνέρες ἐν Λιβύεσσιν ἀ. D.P.263; cf. μεταρίθμιος, ἐναρίθμιος. III. Subst. ἀρίθμιον, τό, *set, series*, *BGU*544.23 (iii A.D.).

ἀριθμοποιός [ᾰ], όν, *creating number*, Dam.*Pr.*245.

ἀριθμός [ᾰ], (ᾱρ- *IG*1.164), ὁ, *number*, first in Od., λέκτο δ' ἀριθμόν 4.451; ἀριθμῷ παῦρα Semon.3; ἐν ἀριθμῷ Hdt.3.6; ἀριθμὸν ἓξ Id.1.14, cf. 50; ἐς τὸν ἀ. τρισχίλια Id.7.97; πλῆθος ἐς ἀ. the amount in point of *number*, ib.60; τὸν ἀ. δώδεκα Euphro 11.11; δύο τινὲς ἢ τρεῖς ..εἰς τὸν ἀ. Men.165; ἔλαττον μήτε ὄγκῳ μήτε ἀριθμῷ Pl.*Tht.*155a; οὔτ' ἀριθμοῖς οὔτε μεγέθεσιν ἐλάττους Id.*Lg.*861e; σταθμῷ καὶ ἀ. X.*Smp.*4.45; δι' ἀ. καὶ μέτρου Plu.*Per.*16, cf. E.*Tr.*620: prov., λέγειν ποντιᾶν ψάφων ἀριθμόν 'count the pebbles on the shore', Pi.*O.*13.46, cf. 2.98; οὐ γιγνώσκων ψήφων ἀριθμούς, of a blockhead, Ephipp.19; οὔτ' ἀριθμὸν οὔτ' ἔλεγχον..ἔχων Dionys.Com.3.13. 2. *amount, sum*, πολὺς ἀ. χρόνου Aeschin.1.78; ἀ. τῆς ὁδοῦ X.*An.*2.2.6; ἀ. [χρυσίου] a *sum* of money, Id.*Cyr.*8.2.16. 3. ἀριθμῷ, abs., *in certain numbers*, Hdt.6.58; but δένδρα ἀριθμῷ ὑμέτερα *by tale*, Th.2.72; ἀ. διδόναι Dionys.Com.3.6. 4. *item* or *term* in a series, ὁ δεύτερος ἀ. E.*Ion* 1014; τρίτον ὠδίνων ἀ. *Epigr.Gr.*574; ναῦς πολλοὺς ἀ. ἄγνυται ναυαγίων E.*Hel.*410, cf. Arist.*Po.*1461^{b}24; τοὺς ἀ. τοῦ σώματος *points* of the body, Pl.*Lg.*668d; τοὺς ἀ. ἑκάστου τῶν νοσημάτων Hp.*Acut.*3; τὸ καλὸν ἐκ πολλῶν ἀ. ἐπιτελεῖσθαι Plu.2.45c: hence as a mark of *completeness*, πάντας τοὺς ἀ. περιλαβών Isoc.11.16; τοῦ καθήκοντος τοὺς ἀριθμούς the *sum total* of duty, M.Ant.3.1. 5. *number, account*, as a mark of station, worth, rank, μετ' ἀνδρῶν ἵζει ἀριθμῷ takes his place *among* men, Od.11.449; εἰς ἀνδρῶν μὲν οὐ τελοῦσιν ἀ. E.*Fr.*492; εἰς ἀ. τῶν κακῶν πεφύκαμεν Id.*Hec.*1186; ξενίας ἀριθμῷ πρῶτ' ἔχειν ἐμῶν φίλων *in regard of* friendship, ib.794; δειλοὶ γὰρ ἄνδρες οὐκ ἔχουσιν ἐν μάχῃ ἀριθμόν have no *account* made of them, Id.*Fr.*519; οὐδ' εἰς ἀ. ἥκει λόγων she comes not into my *account*, Id.*El.*1054; ἀ. οὐδεὶς οὐδὲ λόγος ἐστί τινος Plu.2.682f, cf. Call.*Epigr.*27.6, Orac.ap. Sch.Theoc.14.48. 6. *mere number, quantity*, opp. *quality*, ταῦτ' οὐκ ἀ. ἐστιν, ὦ πάτερ, λόγων *a mere set* of words, S.*OC*382; of men, οὐκ ἀ. ἄλλως not *a mere lot*, E.*Tr.*476; ἀριθμός, πρόβατ' ἄλλως Ar.*Nu.*1203; sometimes even of a single man, οὐκ ἀριθμὸν ἀλλ' ἐτητύμως ἄνδρ' ὄντα not *a mere unit*, E.*Heracl.*997; also ἀριθμὸν πληροῦν to be *a mere cipher*, Chor.*Milt.*66. II. *numbering, counting*, μάσσων ἀριθμοῦ past *counting*, Pi.*N.*2.23; esp. in phrases, ἀ. ποιεῖσθαι τῶν νεῶν to hold *a muster* of.., Hdt.8.7; ποιεῖν X.*An.*7.1.7, etc.; παρεῖναι εἰς τὸν ἀ. ib.11; εἴ τι δυνατὸν ἐς ἀ. ἐλθεῖν can be stated *in numbers*, Th.2.72. III. *the science of numbers, arithmetic*, ἀριθμόν, ἔξοχον σοφισμάτων A.*Pr.*459; ἀριθμῶν καὶ μέτρων εὑρήματα S.*Fr.*432; ἀ. καὶ λογισμὸν εὑρεῖν Pl.*Phdr.*274c, cf. *R.*522c: prov., εἴπερ γὰρ ἀριθμὸν οἶδα E.*Fr.*360.19. IV. in Philos., *abstract number*, Arist.*Cat.*4^{b}23, *Metaph.*990^{a}19, al.; ἀ. μαθηματικός ib.1090^{b}35; ἀ. οὐσιώδης, opp. τοῦ ποσοῦ, Plot.5.5.4; ἀ. ἑνιαῖος, οὐσιώδης, ἑτεροῖος, Dam.*Pr.*228. V. Gramm., *number*, *Stoic.*3.214, D.T.634.16, A.D.*Synt.*32.2, al.; cf. ἑνικός, δυικός, πληθυντικός. VI. *numeral*, ib.36.6, etc.; ὁ τέσσαρα ἀ. S.E.*M.*7.96; παιδὸς ἀ., = δεκάτη, E.*El.*1132. VII. *unknown quantity* (x), defined as πλῆθος μονάδων ἀορίστων, Dioph.*Def.*2. VIII. Rhet., *rhythm* in Prose, in pl., D.H.*Comp.*23, *Dem.*52, cf. Arist.*Rh.*1408^{b}29; but also ἀριθμοὶ τῶν ἀρχαίων ποιητᾶν *SIG*703.7 (Delph.). IX. *line* of a book, Apollon. Cit.2. X. *sum of numerical values* of letters in a name, *Apoc.*13.17, al.; φιλῶ ἧς ἀριθμὸς φμε' Pompeian Inscr. in *Rend.Linc.*10(1901).257. XI. *unit* of troops, = Lat. *numerus*, *CIG*5187 (vi A.D.), *BGU*673 (vi A.D.), etc.; = *legio*, Jul. *ad Ath.*280d, Zos.5.26, *PLond.*5.1711.69 (vi A.D.). XII. Astrol., mostly in pl., *degrees traversed in a given time*, Ptol.*Tetr.*112, Doroth. in *Cat.Cod.Astr.*6.107.30; τοῖς ἰδίοις ἀ. at her normal *speed*, of the moon, Gal.19.531; also of *degrees* of latitude, Heph.Astr.2.8, 3.1. XIII. Medic., in pl., *precise conditions*, παρόντων τῶν πρὸς τὴν φλεβοτομίαν ἀριθμῶν Herod.Med. in *Rh.Mus.*58.71, cf. Aret.*CA*2.3, prob. in Herod.Med.ap.Aët.9.2; cf. supr. I.4. [ῑ E.*El.*1132, Ar.*Nu.*1203.] (ἀρῐ-θμός from root ἀρι-, cf. ἐπάριτος (q.v.), νήριτος.)

ἀριθμοστόν [ᾰ], τό, *fraction whose denominator is unknown* ($\frac{1}{x}$), Dioph.*Def.*2.

ἀρίκεσι· χαλεπαῖς, Hsch.

ἀρῐκύμων [ᾰ] [ῡ], ον, gen. ονος, (κύω) *prolific*, Hp.*Superf.*23, prob. in *Aër.*5.

ἄριλλα, ἡ, dub. sens. in *IGRom.*4.1349.

ἀριμάζω, = ἀρμόζω, Hsch.

Ἀριμασποί, οἱ, Scythian word, meaning *one-eyed*, derived by Hdt. 4.27 from **ἄριμα** = ἕν, σποῦ = ὀφθαλμός; by Eust.ad D.P.31 from **ἀρί** = ἕν, μασπός = ὀφθαλμός: Ἀ. ἱπποβάμων A.*Pr.*805.

ἀρίμηλον, τό, a kind of *apple*, Antig.Car.ap.Ath.3.82b (sed leg. εἰαριμήλων).

ἄριμος, Tyrrhen., = πίθηκος, Str.13.4.6.

ἀρῖν, v. ἄρριν.

ἀρίξαι· ὑποστηρίξαι, Hsch.

Ἄριοι, οἱ, ancient name of the *Medes*, Hdt.7.62; Μάγοι καὶ πᾶν τὸ Ἄριον (Ἄρειον codd.) γένος Eudem.ap.Dam.*Pr.*125bis; ἔκοψα κομμὸν Ἄριον (Ἄρειον codd.) a *Median* lament, A.*Ch.*423 (lyr.):—hence **Ἀριανή**, ἡ, name of the eastern *Iranian* highlands, Str.15.2.1: **Ἀριανοί**, οἱ, its inhabitants, D.S.2.37, cf. 1.94, Ael.*NA*16.16 (cf. Avest. *Airyana*). II. inhabitants of the Persian satrapy of Ἀρεία (Arr.*An.*3.25.1), Pers. *Haraiva*, Hdt.7.66; written Ἄρειοι, Id.3.93, Arr.l.c.

Ἀριοντία, ἡ, divinity worshipped at Sparta, *IG*5(1).213.40.

ἀρί-πικρος [ᾰρῐ], ον, *very bitter*, Hsch. **-πρέπεια**, ἡ, *glory*, of God, *Corp.Herm.*18.14. **-πρεπής**, ές, (πρέπω) *very distinguished*, ὡς καὶ σοὶ εἶδος μὲν ἀριπρεπές Od.8.176; δότε δὴ καὶ τόνδε γενέσθαι..ἀριπρεπέα Τρώεσσιν Il.6.477; ἵππον ἀ. προὔχοντα 23.453; ἀ. βασιλῆες Od.8.390. 2. of things, *very bright*, ἔχε δ' αἰγίδα..ἀριπρεπέα Il. 15.309; ἄστρα..φαίνετ' ἀ. 8.556; ὅρμοι *Lyr.Alex.Adesp.*9.3; of a mountain, *conspicuous*, Νήριτον ἀ. Od.9.22; ἀ. εἶδος ἔχουσα Orph.*Fr.*114: Comp., Them.*Or.*18.223b. 3. *famous*, σκῆπτρον Orph.*Fr.*102. Adv. -πῶς, Ion. -πέως *IG*7.1684 (Plataea), etc. **-πρεπτος**, ον, = foreg., Ὑγίεια Maced.*Pae.*21.

ἄρῐς, v. ἄρριν.

ἀρίς [ᾰ], ίδος, ἡ, *bow-drill*, Hp.*Art.*12, Call.Com.16, Apollod.*Poliorc.*148.7, *AP*6.103 (Phil.), 205 (Leon.), Heliod.(?)ap.Orib.46.11.7. II. = φράκτης, *shrine*, Procop.*Aed.*2.3. III. = δρακοντία μικρά, Ps.-Dsc.2.167, Gal.19.85, *PMag.Par.*1.2308. 2. = sq., Plin.*HN*24.151.

ἀρίσαρον, τό, *hooded arum*, *Arisarum vulgare*, Dsc.2.168.

ἀρίσημος [ᾰρῐ], ον, (σῆμα) *notable*, ἀρίσημα δὲ ἔργα τέτυκτο *h.Merc.*12; καὶ τύμβος καὶ παῖδες ἐν ἀνθρώποις ἀρίσημοι Tyrt.12.29; ἀνήρ Hp.*Ep.*10; εἰκών *Epigr.Gr.*260 (Cyrene). II. *plain, visible*, τρίβος Theoc.25.158. Adv. -μως Hld.6.14.

ἀρισθάρμᾰτος [ᾰρ], ον, (ἄριστος, ἅρμα) *best in the chariot-race*, ἀ. γέρας the prize *of the best chariot*, Pi.*P.*5.30.

ἀρίσκος· κόφινος, Hsch.; cf. ῥίσκος.

ἀρισκῡδής [ᾰ], ές, (σκύζω) *very wrathful*, Call.*Fr.*108.

ἀρίσπης, f.l. for ἀρτιεπής, Hsch. **ἀρισπώλους**, v. ἀριῆνας.

ἀρίσταθλος [ᾰ], ον, *victorious in the contest*, *APl.*4.94 (Arch.).

ἀρισταίνω· ἀριστεύω, *AB*1340.

Ἀρισταῖος, ὁ, pr. n., Hes.*Th.*977: also epith. of Apollo, Pi.*P.*9.65; of Zeus, Call.*Aet.*3.1.33.

ἀρισταλκής [ᾰρ], ές, *eminent in power*, σθένος B.7.7.

ἀρισταρχαμία· ἀριστία, Hsch.

Ἀριστάρχειος, α, ον, *of Aristarchus* (the critic), Str.2.3.8; αἱ Ἀ. (sc. ἐκδόσεις) Sch.Il.*Oxy.*221 iv 22, xi 15.

ἀριστ-αρχέω [ᾰρ], *rule in the best way*, Arist.*Pol.*1273^{b}5 codd. **-αρχος**, ὁ, *best-ruling*, epith. of Zeus, Simon.231, B.12.58.

ἀριστάφῡλος [ᾰρ], ον, (σταφυλή) *rich in grapes*, *AP*9.580.

ἀριστάω, inf. ἀριστᾶν, Ion. -ῆν Hp.*Vict.*3.68: pf. ἠρίστηκα X.*Cyr.*4.2.39, Antiph.212.25; of this tense the Com. also used 1 pl. ἠρίσταμεν Ar.*Fr.*496, Theopomp.Com.22, inf. ἠριστάναι Hermipp.60:—Pass., pf. ἠρίστημαι, v. infr. [ᾰρ Ar.*Eq.*815, etc.; ᾰρ only late, *AP*11.387 (Pall.)]:—*take the* ἄριστον or *midday meal*, Ar.*Nu.*416, *Eq.*815; ἠρίστων, opp. ἐδείπνουν, X.*Mem.*2.7.12, cf. *An.*4.6.21: c. acc. rei, *breakfast on*, ἴα καὶ ῥόδα Diod.Com.2.37, cf. Pherecr.122.5: pf. Pass. impers., ἠρίστηται δ' ἐξαρκούντως Ar.*Ra.*377. 2. *eat a second meal*, opp. μονοσιτέω, Hp.*VM*10, *Acut.*30.

ἀριστεία [ᾰρ], Ion. -είη, ἡ, *excellence, prowess*, S.*Aj.*443, *AP*7.312 (Quadr.); γέρας ἀριστείας Alciphr.3.36: in pl., Gorg.*Fr.*11a, Pl.*Lg.*942d: Il.5, 11, 17 are called respectively Διομήδους, Ἀγαμέμνονος, Μενελάου ἀριστεία; cf. Cic.*Att.*16.9.

ἀριστεῖα [ᾰρ], Ion. -ήϊα, τά, *the meed of valour*, ἀ. διδόναι τῷ ἀξιωτάτῳ Hdt.8.123, cf. 124; ἀπαίτεε τοὺς Αἰγινήτας τὰ ἀ. demanded of them *the reward* (they had received) *for prowess*, ib.122; τὰ ἀ. τῆς νίκης φέρεσθαι Hp.*Aër.*23, cf. S.*Aj.*464, Pl.*Lg.*919e, Isoc.9.16, etc.; ἀ. τῆς θεοῦ offered to her, *IG*2.652 *A*30, al.; ἀριστεῖον τῷ θεῷ ib.814^a*A* 32, cf. *SIG*276 *A* 9 (Delph.), D.22.72: less freq. in sg. in same sense, Hdt.8.11, Luc.*DDeor.*22.3. 2. in sg., *monument of valour, memorial*, τοῦ πρὸς τοὺς βαρβάρους πολέμου D.19.272, cf. 59.97.

ἀριστεῖος [ᾰ], ον, Adj. *belonging to the bravest, bestowed as the prize of valour*, στέφανοι, τιμαί, D.H.6.94, 9.13; γέρας Plu.*Thes.*26; Ἡρακλεῖ ποιήσειν θυσίαν ἀριστεῖον Id.*Pyrrh.*22.

ἀριστερᾰχόθεν [ᾰρ], *on the left*, *IG*7.3073.129, 151 (Lebad.).

ἀριστερεών, ῶνος, ἡ, a plant, = περιστερεών, Plin.*HN*27.21, Orph.*A.*916, Ael.*NA*1.35.

ἀριστερο-μάχος [ᾰρ] [μᾰ], ον, *fighting left-handed*, Herm.ap.Stob. 1.49.45. **-πηρος**, ον, *paralysed on the left side*, *BGU*367.8 (vi A.D.).

ἀριστερός [ᾰ], ά, όν, *left, on the left*, ἐπ' ἀριστερά towards, i.e. on, *the left*, Il.2.526, al.; ἐπ' ἀριστερὰ χειρός Od.5.277; ἐπ' ἀ. χειρῶν A.R. 2.1266; ἐξ ἀριστερῶν Hp.*Epid.*2.4.1; ἐν τοῖσι ἀριστεροῖσι ibid. 2. ἀριστερά (with or without χείρ), ἡ, *left hand*, ἐξ ἀριστερῆς χειρός on *the left hand*, Hdt.2.30; simply ἀριστερῆς χ. Id.4.34; ἐξ ἀριστερᾶς S.*Ph.*20, Pl.*Ti.*72c, etc.; οὐξ ἀριστερᾶς..ναός S.*El.*7; ἐς ἀριστερὴν χεῖρα ἥιε, ἐν ἀριστερῇ ἔχειν, Hdt.7.42. 3. metaph., *boding ill, ominous*, because to a Greek, looking northward, unlucky signs came from the left, ἀ. ἤλυθεν ὄρνις Od.20.242. 4. *awkward, erring*, φρενόθεν ἐπ' ἀριστερὰ ἔβας turnedst to *the leftward* of thy mind, S.*Aj.*182 (lyr.); ἐπ' ἀριστερὰ εἴληφας τὸ πρᾶγμα in a *sinister* sense, *Com. Adesp.*22.67 D.; τῷ ἀριστερῷ δέχεσθαι [λόγους] Plu.2.378b. (Prop. 'better', cf. ἄριστος; euphemism (cf. εὐώνυμος) to avoid ill-luck.)

ἀριστεροστάτης [ᾰρ] [τᾰ], ου, ὁ, *standing on the left*, esp. in the Trag. chorus, Cratin.215, Aristid.2.161 J.

ἀριστερόφιν, Ep. gen. of ἀριστερός, ἐπ' ἀ. Il.13.309.

ἀριστερόχειρ [ᾰ], χειρος, ὁ, ἡ, *left-handed*, Sor.1.111.

ἀρίστ-ευμα [ᾰ], ατος, τό, = ἀριστεία, *deed of prowess*, Eust.115.14 (pl.), *Gp.Praef.*2 (pl.). **-εύς**, έως, ὁ, dual ἀριστέοιν S.*Aj.*1304: (ἄριστος):—used by Hom. mostly in pl. ἀριστῆες *those who excel in valour*, *chiefs*, Il.2.404, al.; ἄνδρας ἀριστῆας Od.14.218, cf. Hdt.6.81, Alc. *Supp.*1a.8, Pi.*P.*9.107, Ant.Lib.2.2, etc.: sg., A.*Pers.*306; ἀνδρὸς ἀριστέως E.*IA*28 (lyr.); as an honorary title, *CIG*2881 (Milet.), *IG Rom.*4.914 (Cibyra). **-ευτής**, οῦ, ὁ, *improver*, πεδίων ἀ., of a husbandman, Secund.*Sent.*16. **-ευτικός**, ή, όν, *of, belonging to valiant deeds*, Max.Tyr.29.1, Plu.2.319b. **-εύω**, *to be best* or *bravest*, αἰὲν ἀριστεύειν καὶ ὑπείροχον ἔμμεναι ἄλλων Il.6.208; ὃς δέ κ' ἀριστεύησι μάχῃ ἔνι 11.409; ἐν ἀέθλοισιν ἀ. Pi.*N.*11.14; *gain the prize for valour* (v. ἀριστεῖα, τά), *gain the highest distinction*, Hdt.3.55, 9.105, Pl.*R.*468b, Isoc.9.16. 2. c. gen., ἀριστεύεσκε μάχεσθαι Τρώων he *was the best of* the Trojans.., Il.6.460, cf. Hdt.5.112, 7.106, al.; οὕνεκα βουλῇ ἀριστεύεσκεν ἁπάντων Il.11.627, cf. Pi.*N.*10.10. 3. c. inf., ἀριστεύεσκε μάχεσθαι *he was best at* fighting, Il.16.292, 551, etc.; ἀριστεύεσκε μάχεσθαι Τρώων, v. supr. 4. c. acc. rei, ἀ. τι *to be best in* a thing, στάδιον Pi.*O.*10(11).64, cf. 13.43; ἰάλεμον Theoc.15.98. 5. c. acc. cogn., *win as* ἀριστεῖα, τὰ πρῶτα καλλιστεῖ' ἀριστεύσας S.*Aj.*435, cf. 1300; πάντα ἀ. Id.*Tr.*488, Pl.*R.*540a; μεμιγμένην ἀριστείαν ἀ. Plu.*Pel.*34. II. of things, *to be best*, ἀριστεύοισαν εὐκάρπου χθονός *best of all lands* on fruitful earth, Pi.*N.*1.14; τὸ κηδεῦσαι καθ' ἑαυτὸν ἀριστεύει μακρῷ A.*Pr.*890 (lyr.); of an opinion, *prevail*, Hdt.7.144.

ἀριστέφᾰνος [ᾰρ], ον, *highly honoured with crowns*, *IGRom.*4.1273 (Thyatira).

ἀριστήρ, ῆρος, ὁ, title of magistrate at Elatea, *IG*9(1).101.9. (Perh. a mistake for ἀρτιστήρ.)

ἀριστ-ητήριον [ᾰ], τό, (ἀριστάω) *refectory*, τὸ ἱερὸν ἀ. τοῦ θεοῦ *BCH* 15.184. **-ητής**, οῦ, ὁ, *one who breakfasts*, i.e. *takes more than one full meal in the day*, Hp.*Aër.*1. **-ητικός**, ή, όν, *fond of one's breakfast*, Eup.130: Comp., Id.7.13 D. **-ίζω**, *give one breakfast*, ἀπὸ σμικρᾶς δαπάνης ὑμᾶς ἀριστίζων ἀπέπεμψεν Ar.*Eq.*538; τούτους ἀρίστισον εὖ Id.*Av.*659; τὴν πόλιν ἀ. ἐπὶ πενταετίαν *IG*7.2712.62 (Acraephia):—Med., *breakfast*, Hp.*VM*10.

ἀριστίνδας, ὁ, title at Sparta, *IG*5(1).680.6.

ἀριστίνδην [ᾰ], Adv., (ἄριστος) *according to birth* or *merit*, αἱρεῖσθαι *IG*1.61, cf. 9(1).333.12 (Locr. -δαν), Lex ap. D.43.57, Theopomp. Hist.217a; Ἀθηναίων πολλοὺς ἀπολέσαντες ἀ. καὶ τῶν συμμάχων And. 3.30, cf. Isoc.4.146, Pl.*Lg.*855c; κατ' ἐκλογὴν ἀ. κεκριμένοι Plb.6.10.9; opp. πλουτίνδην, Arist.*Pol.*1273^{a}23, cf. *Ath.*3.1, Plu.*Lys.*13.

ἀριστό-βῐος [ᾰ], ον, *living best*, Orac.ap.Hld.2.35. **-βουλος**, η, ον, *best in counsel*, epith. of Artemis at Melite, Plu.*Them.*22, cf. Artem.2.37; at Rhodes, Porph.*Abst.*2.54:—hence **Ἀριστοβουλῐασταί**, οἱ, a confraternity of her worshippers, *IG*12(1).163 (Rhodes). **-γᾰλᾰτίας**, ου, ὁ, title of *chief citizen of the province of Galatia*, *Class.Rev.*22.214. **-γένεθλος**, ον, *producing the best*, χῶρος *AP*9.686. **-γόνος**, ον, *bearing the best children*, μάτηρ Pi.*P.*11.3.

ἀριστόδειπνον [ᾰ], τό, *breakfast-dinner*, Alex.294, Men.998.

ἀριστό-καρπος [ᾰ], ον, *bearing fairest fruit*, Σικελία B.3.1. **-κρᾰτέομαι**, Pass., *to be governed by the best-born, live under an aristocracy*, Ar.*Av.*125, Pl.*R.*338d, Arist.*Pol.*1288^{a}41, etc. **-κράτης** [ρᾰ], ου, ὁ, *aristocrat*, Asp.*in EN*182.8. **-κρᾰτία**, ἡ, *rule of the best-born, aristocracy*, ἀ. σώφρων Th.3.82, cf. Henioch.5.17, Isyll.1, etc.; *rule of the rich*, Pl.*Plt.*301a. II. *ideal constitution, rule of the best*, Arist. *Pol.*1293^{b}1 sqq., *EN*1160^{a}33, Pl.*Mx.*238c, d, Plb.6.4.3. **-κρᾰτικός**, ή, όν, *aristocratical*, Pl.*R.*587d; ἀ. πολιτεία Arist.*Pol.*1288^{a}21, 1265^{b}33 (Comp.); κοινωνία, of man and wife, Id.*EN*1160^{b}32; παῖς Cic.*Att.*2.15.4 (Sup.). Adv. -κῶς Arist.*Pol.*1300^{a}41, 1317^{a}6, Cic.*Att.*2.3.4, Str.10.1.8. **-λόχεια** (-λοχία Thphr.*HP*9.20.4), ἡ, herb *promoting child-birth, birthwort, Aristolochia*, Nic.*Th.*509, 937; ἀ. στρογγύλη, = *A. rotunda*, ἀ. μακρά, = *A. longa*, ἀ. κληματῖτις, = *A. Clematitis*, Dsc.3.4; ἀ. Κρητική, = *A. cretica*, Plin.*HN*25.95:—also **-λόχιον**, τό, Hp.*Nat.Mul.*32 (s.v.l.): **-λόχιος**, ἡ, Crateuas *Fr.*1, 2. **-λοχος**, ον, *well-born*, *App.Anth.*3.162. **-μαντις**, εως, ὁ, *best of prophets*, S.*Ph.*1338. **-μάχος** [μᾰ], ον, (μάχη) *best in fight*, Pi.*P.*10.3. 2. as pr. n., Hdt., etc.:—hence Adj. **-μάχειος**, ον, *AP*13.8 (Theodorid.).

ἄριστον, τό, *morning meal, breakfast*, twice in Hom., ἐντύνοντ' ἄ. ἅμ' ἠοῖ Od.16.2, cf. Il.24.124; ἄριστα, δεῖπνα, δόρπα θ' αἱρεῖσθαι τρίτα A.*Fr.*182, cf. *Ag.*331: later, *breakfast* was called ἀκράτισμα, and ἄριστον was the midday meal, our *luncheon*, cf. Th.4.90, 7.81; ἄ. αἱρεῖσθαι, ποιεῖσθαι, Hdt.3.26, 6.78; ἀπ' ἀρίστου μέχρι δείλης Arist. *HA*619^{a}15. [ᾰ; contr. from ἄ(γ)ερι-στον, cf. Goth. *air*, OHG. *ēr* 'early', Avest. *ayarə* 'day'; also ἄ(γ)ερ- in ἦρι, ἠέριος; -στο- from -*d-to*-, root *ed*- 'eat'.]

ἀριστό-νῑκος [ᾰ], ον, *gaining glorious victory*, κράτος *Trag.Adesp.* 97. **-νομία**, ἡ, (νέμω) = ἀριστοκρατία, Suid., Hsch. **-νοος**, ον, *excellent in wisdom*, *AP*9.213, *IG*5(2).156 (Tegea, iii/iv A.D.). **-πάλας** [πᾰ], ὁ, *best of wrestlers*, Epigr. in *BKT*5(1).77. **-πάτρα**, ἡ, *daughter of a peerless line*, of Artemis, B.10.106.

ἀριστο-ποιέω [ᾰ], *prepare breakfast*, τὰ ἀριστοποιούμενα things *prepared for breakfast*, X.*HG*4.5.1:—mostly in Med., *get one's breakfast*, Th.4.30, 8.95, X.*An.*3.3.1, 4.3.9, Onos.42.10, etc.; ἠριστοποίηντο X. *HG*4.5.8. **-ποιΐα**, ἡ, *preparation of breakfast*, Onos.12.1.

ἀριστο-πολῑτευτής [ᾰ], οῦ, ὁ, (πολιτεύω) *best of citizens*, honorary title, esp. at Sparta, *IG*5(1).335, al.:—also **-πολίτης** [λῑ], ου, ὁ, *best citizen*, αἰώνιος ἀ. ib.468, *IPE*2.29 (Panticapaeum; -πυλίτης lapis):—hence **-πολῑτεία**, ἡ, *privileges of an* ἀ., *IG*5(1).65 (Sparta), *SIG*893 *A* 9 (Messene). **-πόνος**, ον, *working excellently*, χεῖρες Pi.*O.*7.51; μέλισσα Ps.-Phoc.171; ὑμέναιοι *AP*9.466: pl., ἀριστοπονῆες, as if from -πονεύς, Man.4.512. Adv. -νως *App.Anth.*3.182. II. *excellently wrought*, μέλαθρον Nonn.*D.*44.79. **-πόσεια**, ἡ, (πόσις) νύμφη wife *of a noble husband*, Opp.*C.*1.6. **-πρᾱγέω**, (πρᾶγος) = ἀριστεύω, Eust.621.39.

ἄριστος [ᾰ], η, ον, (with Art. Ep. ὥριστος Il.11.288, Att. ἅριστος) *best* in its kind, and so in all sorts of relations, serving as Sup. of ἀγαθός: I. of persons, 1. *best* in birth and rank, *noblest*: hence, like ἀριστεύς, *a chief*, Ἀργείων οἱ ἄριστοι Il.4.260, cf. 6.209; ἄ. ἔην πολὺ δὲ πλείστους ἄγε λαούς 2.580; θεῶν ὕπατος καὶ ἄ. 19.258; πατρὸς πάντων ἀ. παῖδα S.*El.*366; ἀνδρῶν τῶν ἀ. ὁμιλίῃ, opp. δῆμος, Hdt.3.81, cf. Cic.*Att.*9.4.2. 2. *best* in any way, *bravest*, ἀνδρῶν αὖ μέγ' ἄ. ἔην Τελαμώνιος Αἴας Il.2.768, cf. 7.50, etc.; οἰωνοπόλων, σκυτοτόμων ὄχ' ἄ., 6.76, 7.221. b. c. dat. modi, βουλῇ μετὰ πάντας.. ἔπλευ ἄ. 9.54, al.; ἔγχεσιν εἶναι ἀρίστους Od.4.211. c. c. acc. rei, εἶδος ἄριστε Il.3.39; ψυχὴν ἄ. Ar.*Nu.*1048. d. c. inf., ἄριστοι μάχεσθαι X.*Cyr.*5.4.44; ἄ. διαβολὰς ἐνδέκεσθαι *readiest* to give ear to calumnies, Hdt.3.80; ἄ. ἀπατᾶσθαι *best*, i.e. *easiest*, to cheat, Th.3.38. 3. *morally best*, εἴς τινα E.*Alc.*83 (lyr.); οἱ ἄ. ἁπλῶς κατ' ἀρετήν Arist.*Pol.*1293^{b}3. 4. *best, most useful*, πόλει E.*Fr.*194 codd. (leg. ἀρεστός); αὐτῷ Id.*Heracl.*5. II. of animals, things, etc., *best, finest*, ἵπποι Il.2.763; μήλων, ὑῶν, Od.9.432, 14.414; τεύχε' ἄριστα Il.15.616; χῶρος Od.5.442; ποταμῶν ἄ. τά τε ἄλλα καὶ ἀκέσασθαι Hdt.4.90; ἄριστα φέρεσθαι win an *excellent* reward, S.*El.*1097 (lyr.). III. neut. pl. as Adv., ἄριστα *best, most excellently*, ὄχ' ἄ. Il.3.110, Od.13.365, cf. Hdt.1.193, al., etc.; ἄριστά γε, in answers, *well said!* Pl.*Tht.*163c: later also ἀρίστως Iamb.*Myst.*3.14.

ἀριστοσαλπιγκτής [ᾰρ], οῦ, ὁ, *best of trumpeters*, Poll.4.87.

ἀριστότατος, η, ον, late superlative formation from ἄριστος, *Rev. Phil.*46.127 (Miscamus).

Ἀριστοτελίζω, *follow* or *imitate Aristotle*, Str.13.1.54:—Adj. **Ἀριστοτέλειος**, α, ον, *Aristotelian*, Cic.*Att.*13.19.4:—also **Ἀριστοτελικός**, ή, όν, Luc.*Demon.*56. Adv. -κῶς Iamb.*Comm.Math.*27.

ἀριστο-τέχνης [ᾰ], Dor. **-τέχνας**, ου, ὁ, *best of artificers*, of Zeus, Pi.*Fr.*57, cf. Hsch. **-τόκος**, ον, *bearing the best children*, γαστήρ Opp.*C.*3.62:—poet. fem. **ἀριστοτόκεια** [ᾰρ], Theoc.24.73, Tryph. 401, *IG*12(5).292 (Paros). II. Pass., ἀριστότοκος, ον, *born of the best parents*, γέννα E.*Rh.*909, cf. *Epigr.Gr.*896 (Syria).

Ἀριστοφάνειος [φᾰ], α, ον, *of Aristophanes*, μέτρον, the anapaestic tetrameter, D.H.*Rh.*11.10, Heph.8, Theon *Prog.*3.

ἀριστοφόρον [ᾰ], τό, *breakfast-tray*, *PGrenf.*1.14.7, *PEdgar*9.39 (iii B.C.), *PSI*4.428.47.

ἀριστο-φυής [ᾰ], ές, *of best nature*, Ecphant.ap.Stob.4.7.64 (in Sup. -έστατος). **-χαλκος**, ον, *with, producing finest brass*, Sch. Lyc.854. **-χειρ**, χειρος, ὁ, ἡ, *won by the stoutest hand*, ἀγών S.*Aj.*935 (lyr.). **-χειρουργός**, ὁ, *best of surgeons*, *POxy.*437.

ἀριστώδῑν [ᾰ], ῖνος, ὁ, ἡ, *bearing the best children*, Ἀθῆναι *APl.*4.221 (Theaet.).

ἀρι-σφᾰλής [ᾰρ], ές, *very slippery* or *treacherous*, οὐδός Od.17.196. **-τῑμος**, ον, *highly honoured*, *IG*5(1).add.722.

ἀριτριλλίς, = λινόζωστις, dub. l. in Ps.-Dsc.4.190 (ἀργυρῖτις Wellm.).

ἀρι-φρᾰδής [ᾰρ], ές, (φράζομαι) *clear, manifest*, σῆμα Il.23.326; ὀστέα..ἀριφραδέα τέτυκται ib.240: so poet. Adv. -δέως *plainly*, ἀ. ἀγορεύει Theoc.25.176. 2. *clear to the sight, bright*, Id.24.39. II. *very thoughtful, wise*, S.*Ant.*347 (as cited by Eust.135.25). **-φρων**, ον, gen. ονος, (φρήν) *very wise* or *prudent*, Suid.

ἄριχα· ἄρρεν πρόβατον, Hsch. **ἀρῑχάομαι** or **ἀρρῑχ-**, v. ἀναρριχάομαι. **ἀρίχεται**· γλίχεται, ἐπιθυμεῖ, Hsch. **ἀριχῶταν**· ἐκδύειν ζητῶν, Id.

Ἀρκᾰδάρχης, ου, ὁ, *president of Arcadian council*, *IG*5(2).132 (Tegea, iii A.D.).

Ἀρκᾰδίζω, *take the side of the Arcadians*, Polyaen.6.36.

ἄρκαλα, τά, *ear-rings* or *dry wood*, Hsch. **ἀρκαλέον**· ξηρόν, ῥυσσόν, Id. **ἀρκάνη**, ἡ, *bar to which the threads of the warp are fastened*, Id.

ἀρκαρικός, ή, όν, *of an arcarius*, *POxy.*126.14 (vi A.D.).

ἀρκάριος, ὁ, = *arcarius*, *POxy.*126.15 (vi A.D.).

Ἀρκαδία, ἡ, *Arcadia*, Il.2.603, etc.:—hence -ίηνδε A.R.2.1052: -ίηθεν Id.1.161. **Ἀρκᾰδικός**, ή, όν, *Arcadian*, Men.462.8. **Ἀρκάς**, άδος, ὁ, *Arcadian*, pl. Ἀρκάδες ἄνδρες Il.2.611: also as Adj., ὁ, ἡ, Ἀ. κυνῆ prob. in S.*Fr.*262.

ἀρκεθέωρος, = ἀρχιθέωρος, *IG*2.181 *a*, 11(2).219 *B* (Delos, iii B.C.); cf. ἀρχεθέωρος, ἀρκιθέωρος.

ἄρκειος, α, ον, = ἄρκτειος, *of a bear*, στέαρ Dsc.1.125.3, 2.19; δέρματα D.Chr.7.43, cf. *Edict.Diocl.*8.33. 2. πνοὴ ἄρκειος a *northern* blast, A.*Fr.*127 (Lob. for ἄρκιος).

ἀρκεόντως, Att. contr. **ἀρκούντως**, (ἀρκέω) *enough, abundantly*, ἀ. ἔχει A.*Ch.*892, Th.1.22, Hp.*Mul.*2.162; ἀ. λέγεται Arist.*EN*1102^{a}27; τοῦ βίου ἀ. ἔχειν Ps.-Hdt.*Vit.Hom.*7; ἀ. ποδώκης swift *enough*, X.*Eq.*3.12.

ἀρκεσίβουλος, ον, *availing in council*, Cerc.*Oxy.*1082 *Fr.*24 (prob.).

ἀρκεσίγυιος, ον, *limb-strengthening*, οἶνος dub. in Antiph.207.7 (= Philox.17).

ἀρκ-έσιμος, η, ον, *assisting*, θεός *CIG*9899 (Syria, Jewish). **-εσις**, εως, ἡ, (ἀρκέω) *help, aid*, S.*OC*73; οὐδὲ γὰρ -σιν ἔσχεν *IG*12(3).868 (Thera). **-εσμα**, ατος, τό, = foreg., Hsch. **-ετός**, ή, όν, *sufficient*, Chrysipp.Tyan.ap.Ath.3.113b, *Ev.Matt.*6.34, Herm.ap. Stob.1.49.44: c. inf., J.*BJ*3.6.3; of persons, *satisfactory*, ἀ. γενοῦ *BGU*33.5 (ii/iii A.D.); ἀρκετόν [ἐστι] *it is enough*, c. inf., *AP*9.749 (Oenom.). Adv. -τῶς *Theol.Ar.*38.

ἀρκευθιδίτης οἶνος wine *made from* ἀρκευθίδες, Dsc.5.46 Sprengel (om. Wellm.).

ἀρκεύθινος, η, ον, *of juniper*, οἶνος Dsc.5.36. II. in Lxx, *of oleaster*, 3*Ki*.6.31; *of fir*, 2*Ch*.2.8.

ἀρκευθίς, ίδος, ἡ, *juniper-berry*, Hp.*Nat.Mul*.32, Thphr.*Od*.5 (prob. for -θος), Nic.*Th*.585, Plu.2.383e, Dsc.1.75. II. = sq., Ps.-Dsc. 1.75.

ἄρκευθος, ἡ, *juniper, Juniperus macrocarpa*, Hp.*Nat.Mul*.63, Theoc. 5.97, Nic.*Th*.584; ἀ. μεγάλη Dsc.1.75. II. *Phoenician cedar, Juniperus phoenicea*, Thphr.*HP*3.3.1, 3.12.3, *AP*6.253 (Crin.). III. *prickly cedar, Juniperus oxycedrus*, Musae.*Fr*.2 D. IV. ἀ. μικρά *dwarf juniper, Juniperus communis*, Dsc. l. c.

ἀρκέω, impf. 3 sg. ἤρκει Il.13.440, A.*Pers*.278: fut. ἀρκέσω: aor. ἤρκεσα, Dor. ἄρκεσα Pi.*O*.9.3:—**Med.**, aor. ἠρκεσάμην, 2 sg. ἠρκέσω dub. in A.*Eu*.213 (s. v. l.):—**Pass.**, inf. ἀρκέεσθαι Hdt.9.33, ἀρκεῖσθαι Poet.ap.Greg.Cor.p.425 S.: pf. ἤρκεσμαι Sthenid.ap.Stob.4.7.63: aor. ἠρκέσθην Plu.*Pel*.35, Luc.*Salt*.83: fut. ἀρκεσθήσομαι D.H.6.94, D.S.1.8, etc.:—*ward off, keep off*, c. dat. pers. et acc. rei, σάκος τό οἱ ἤρκεσε λυγρὸν ὄλεθρον Il.20.289, cf. 6.16; πατρίδι δουλοσύνην Simon. 101; κῆρας μελάθροις E.*El*.1300 (lyr.); ὅς οἱ ἀπὸ χροὸς ἤρκει ὄλεθρον Il.13.440, cf. 15.534; τοῦτό γ' ἀρκέσαι S.*Aj*.535; ὡς οὐκ ἀρκέσοι τὸ μὴ οὐ.. θανεῖν *would* not *keep off* death, ib.727. 2. c. dat. only, *defend*, πυκινὸς δέ οἱ ἤρκεσε θώρηξ Il.15.529; οὐδ' ἤρκεσε θώρηξ, without dat., 13.371. 3. *assist, succour*, 21.131, Od.16.261, S.*Aj*.824, *El*. 322, E.*Hec*.1164. II. c. acc. cogn., *make good, achieve*, οὐδ' ἔργα μείω χειρὸς ἀρκέσας ἐμῆς S.*Aj*.439. III. mostly in Trag., and always in Prose, *to be strong enough, suffice*, c. inf., first in Pi.*O*.9.3; ἀρκῶ σοι σαφηνίσαι (-σας Linwood) A.*Pr*.621 codd., cf. S.*OT*1209 (lyr.): c. part., ἀρκέσω θνήσκουσ' ἐγώ my death *will suffice*, Id.*Ant*.547; cf. ἀρκοῦμεν ἡμεῖς οἱ προθνῄσκοντές σεθεν E.*Alc*.383; ἔνδον ἀρκείτω μένων *let him be content* to stay within, S.*Aj*.76; ἀρκεῖν γὰρ οἶμαι μίαν ψυχὴν τάδ' ἐκτίνουσαν Id.*OC*498; οὔτε ἰατροὶ ἤρκουν θεραπεύοντες Th.2.47; ellipt., σοφοὺς ὥσπερ σύ, μηδὲν μᾶλλον· ἀρκέσουσι γὰρ [σοφοὶ ὄντες] E.*Heracl*.576; ἀ. εἴς τι X.*Cyr*.8.2.5; πῶς ἡ πόλις ἀρκέσει ἐπὶ τοιαύτην παρασκευήν; Pl.*R*.369d; ταὐτὸν ἀρκεῖ σκῶμμα ἐπὶ πάντας *holds* equally for all, Id.*Tht*.174a; ὅτ' οὐκέτ' ἀρκεῖ [ἡ μάθησις] when it *avails* no more, S.*Tr*.711. 2. c. dat., *suffice for, satisfy*, οὐδέ ταῦτά τοι μοῦνα ἤρκεσε Hdt.2.115, cf. S.*Ant*.308, etc. 3. *to be a match for*, c. dat., ψιλὸς ἀρκέσαιμι σοί γ' ὡπλισμένῳ Id.*Aj*.1123; πρὸς τοὺς πολεμίους Th. 6.84. 4. abs., *to be enough, avail, endure*, ἀρκείτω βίος A.*Ag*.1314; οὐδὲν γὰρ ἤρκει τόξα Id.*Pers*.278; *hold out, last*, ἐπὶ πλεῖστον ἀρκεῖν Th. 1.71, X.*Cyr*.6.2.31; οὐδ' ἔτ' ἀρκῶ I *can hold out* no longer, S.*El*.186 (lyr.); ὥστε ἀρκεῖν πλοῖα *to be sufficient* in number, X.*An*.5.1.13: freq. in part., ἀρκῶν, οῦσα, οῦν, *sufficient, enough*, βίος ἀρκέων ὑπῆν Hdt.1. 31, cf. 7.28; τἀρκοῦντα *a sufficiency*, E.*Supp*.865; ἀρκοῦσα ἀπολογία Antipho 2.4.10; ἀρκοῦντα or τἀρκοῦντα ἔχειν, X.*Mem*.1.2.1, *Smp*.4. 35; τῶν ἀρκούντων περιττὰ κτᾶσθαι Id.*Cyr*.8.2.21. 5. impers., ἀρκεῖ μοι '*tis enough* for me, I *am well content*, c. inf., οὐκ ἀρκέσει ποθ' ὑμῖν.. εἴκειν S.*Aj*.1242, cf. X.*An*.5.8.13: c. acc. et inf., ἐμοὶ μὲν ἀρκεῖ τοῦτον ἐν δόμοις μένειν S.*Aj*.80; ἀρκεῖ ἦν.., ὅτι.., X.*Cyr*.8.1.14, *Mem*. 4.4.9; ἔμ' ἀρκεῖ βουλεύειν '*tis enough* that I.., A.*Th*.248; οὐκ ἀρκοῦν μοί ἐστι, c. acc. et inf., Antipho 2.2.2; ἀρκεῖν δοκεῖ μοι it seems *enough*, seems *good*, S.*El*.1364. IV. in Pass., *to be satisfied with*, c. dat. rei, Poet.ap.Greg.Cor. l. c.; ἔφη οὐκέτι ἀρκέεσθαι τούτοισι Hdt.9.33, cf. Pl.*Ax*.369e, Arist.*EN*1107^{b}15, *AP*6.329 (Leon.), Plot.5.5.3: abs., ib.3.6, etc. 2. later, c. inf., *to be contented to* do, Plb.1.20.1, Ps.-Luc.*Philopatr*.29, etc.

ἄρκη, ἡ, Lat. *arca*, *CIG*3484 (Thyatira).

ἄρκηλα, *egg*, Hsch.; *hedgehog* (Cret.), Id.

ἄρκηλος, ὁ, *young panther*, Callix.2, Ael.*NA*7.47 (or a species of panther, ibid.); cf. ἄρκιλος.

ἀρκής· ταχύς, Hsch.

ἀρκίθεωρος, = ἀρχιθέωρος, *IG*11.287*B*33, al. (Delos, iii B.C.); cf. ἀρκεθέωρος.

ἄρκιλος, ὁ, *bear's cub*, Eust.1535.15; cf. ἄρκηλος, ἀρκτύλος.

ἄρκιον, τό, *burdock, Arctium Lappa*, Dsc.4.106.

ἄρκιος (A), α, ον Arat.741, ος, ον *AP*11.59 (Maced.): (ἀρκέω):—Ep. Adj. *to be relied on, sure, certain*, οὔ οἱ ἔπειτα ἄρκιον ἐσσεῖται φυγέειν he shall have no *hope* to escape, Il.2.393; νῦν ἄρκιον ἢ ἀπολέσθαι ἠὲ σαωθῆναι one of these is *certain*, to perish or be saved, 15.502; μισθὸς δέ οἱ ἄ. ἔσται a *sure* reward, 10.304, cf. Od.18.358, but, a *sufficient* reward in Hes.*Op*.370; βίος ἄ. ib.501, 577. II. *enough, sufficient*, ἄρκιον εὑρεῖν to be sure of having enough, ib.351, A.R.2.799, Theoc. 8.13; ὄφρα... σφίσιν ἄρκιος εἴη that he might be *sufficient* for them, Id. 25.190; δέμας ἄρκιος Opp.*C*.3.185, cf. *H*.3.601; *helpful, useful*, παντὶ γὰρ ἄ. ἐστι Nic.*Th*.508, cf. Opp.*C*.3.173; ἄρκια νούσων *remedies against*..., Nic.*Th*.837: c. inf., *able to*.., Call.*Fr*.51a, cf. *Cer*.35. Adv. -ίως Hsch. III. in comp. sense, ἄρκιον ἦν θνάσκειν *it were better*.., *AP*9.154 (Agath.).

ἄρκιος (B), v. ἄρκειος.

ἀρκόν· σχολήν (Maced.), Hsch.

ἄρκος (A), ὁ and ἡ, = ἄρκτος, *bear*, Lxx 4*Ki*.2.24, *Apoc*.13.2, *AP*11. 231 (Ammian.), *IG*14.1302 (ii A.D.), *Tab.Defix.Aud*.249 (Carthage, i A.D.), Ael.*NA*1.31, Eust.1156.16, Suid. II. = ἄρκτος III, Hp. *Vict*.2.48. III. ἄρκου σταφυλή a plant, *bear-berry, Arctostaphylos Uva-ursi*, Gal.13.83.

ἄρκος (B), εος, τό, (ἀρκέω) *defence*, Alc.67: c. gen., βέλευς Id. 15.4.

ἀρκούντως, contr. for ἀρκεόντως (q. v.).

ἀρκόφθαλμον, = χρυσόγονον, Ps.-Dsc.4.56.

ἄρκτειος, α, ον, *of a bear*, στέαρ Heras ap.Gal.12.399.

ἀρκτέον, I. (ἄρχομαι) *one must begin*, τι πρᾶγμα S.*Aj*.853; πάλιν ἀ. ἀπ' ἀρχῆς *one must make a* fresh *start*, Pl.*Ti*.48b; ἀπὸ τοῦ πρώτου, τῶν πρώτων, τῶν γνωρίμων ἀ., Arist.*Metaph*.1013^{a}3, *GA*737^{b}25, *EN* 1095^{b}2, cf. Str.15.1.1. II. (ἄρχω) *one must govern*, τινί τινος Isoc. 14.10: abs., S.*OT*628, al. (*you must be ruled*, i. e. *obey*).

ἀρκτεύω, *serve as an* ἄρκτος II, Lys.*Fr*.82:—in Med., Sch.Ar. *Lys*.645.

ἀρκτῆ (sc. δορά), ἡ, *bearskin*, Anaxandr.65.

ἀρκτικός (A), ή, όν, (ἄρκτος I. 2) *near the Bear, arctic, northern*, πόλος Arist.*Mu*.392^{a}3; κύκλος Hipparch.1.7.6, etc.: pl., Gem.5.10; -κά, τά, *the northern constellations*, Str.1.1.21: Comp. -ώτερος ib. 12, Gem.14.10: Sup., Str.1.1.6. II. *connected with the Great Bear*, δύναμις *PMag.Par*.1.1275.

ἀρκτικός (B), ή, όν, (ἄρχομαι) *initial, placed at the beginning*, of a sentence, A.D.*Synt*.28.19; ἀ. τεθεὶς σύνδεσμος Demetr.*Eloc*.56; of a word, συλλαβή Heph.1. 2. *originative*, c. gen., πυρετοῦ Gal. 17(2).299.

ἀρκτικός (C), ή, όν, (ἄρχω) *imperious*, Vett.Val.9.16.

ἄρκτιον, τό, *bearwort, Inula candida*, Dsc.4.105, Nic.*Th*.840, Plin. *HN*27.33.

ἄρκτιος, ον, *arctic, northern*, Nonn.*D*.38.329.

ἀρκτόμορφος, ον, *bear-like*, Tz.ad Lyc.481.

ἄρκτος, ἡ, *bear*, esp. *Ursus arctos, brown bear*, Od.11.611, *h.Merc*. 223, *h.Ven*.159, Hdt.4.191, etc.: the instances of the masc. are dub. (Arist.*Col*.798^{a}26 is inconclusive), the fem. being used even when both sexes are included, Id.*HA*539^{b}33. 2. Ἄρκτος, ἡ, the constellation *Ursa Major*, Ἄρκτον θ', ἣν καὶ Ἅμαξαν ἐπίκλησιν καλέουσιν Il.18.487, Od.5.273, cf. Heraclit.120, E.*Ion*1154, etc.; τὰ ὑπὸ τὴν Ἄ. ἀοίκητα Hdt.5.10; Ἄρκτου στροφάδες κέλευθοι S.*Tr*.131 (lyr.); Ἄρκτου στροφάς τε καὶ Κυνὸς ψυχρὰν δύσιν Id.*Fr*.432.11: in pl., *the Greater and Lesser Bears*, Arat.27; Ἄ. μικρά, μεγάλη, Str.2.5.35, 36, cf. Cic.*ND*2.41.105. 3. *the north*, πρὸς ἄρκτον τετραμμένος Hdt. 1.148, cf. E.*El*.733 (lyr.), Aeschin.3.165, etc.; ἀπὸ ἄ. *IG*5(2).444.11 (Megalopolis), al.: pl., Hp.*Aër*.5 and 19, Pl.*Criti*.118b, etc. b. ἡ ἑτέρα ἄ. *the south pole*, Arist.*Mete*.362^{a}32. II. ἄρκτος, ἡ, at Athens *a girl appointed to the service of Artemis Brauronia* or Ἀρχηγέτις, E. *Hyps.Fr*.57, Ar.*Lys*.645. III. a kind of *crab*, prob. *Scyllarus arctus*, Arist.*HA*549^{b}23, cf. Speus.ap.Ath.3.105b, Mnesim.4.45, Archestr.*Fr*.56. IV. ἄρκτου δένδρον, = ἀκτῆ, Ps.-Dsc.4.173. (Cf. Skt. *ṛkṣas*, Lat. *ursus*, etc.)

ἀρκτοτρόφος, ον, *keeping bears*, Procop.*Arc*.9.

Ἀρκτοῦρος, ὁ, (οὖρος *guard*) the star *Arcturus, Bearward* (v. ἄρκτος I. 2), Hes.*Op*.566, 610, Anaxag.20, etc. II. *the time of his heliacal rising*, i. e. *the middle of September*, Hp.*Aër*.10, S.*OT*1137; τὴν ὥραν τὴν τοῦ τρυγᾶν Ἀρκτούρῳ σύνδρομον Pl.*Lg*.844e (cf. Τρυγητής); Ἀρκτούρου ἐπιτολαί Th.2.78, etc.

Ἀρκτο-φύλαξ [ῠ], ακος, ὁ, *the constellation* Βοώτης, Eudox.ap. Hipparch.1.2.5, Arat.92. **-χειρ**, χειρος, ὁ, ἡ, *with bear's paws for hands*, Artem.5.49.

ἀρκτύλος, ὁ, *bear's cub*, Poll.5.15; cf. ἄρκιλος, ἄρκυλλος.

ἀρκτῷος, α, ον, (ἄρκτος) *of a bear*, γενύεσσιν Nonn.*D*.2.44. 2. *arctic, northern*, βορέας D.P.519, etc.; κρυμός Lib.*Or*.59.128; τὰ ἀ. *the arctic regions*, Luc.*Cont*.5.

ἄρκυια, dub. sens., epith. of Hecate, *Tab.Defix.Aud*.38.14 (Alexandria, iii A.D.).

ἄρκυλλος, ὁ, *young of the bear*, Sch.Opp.*H*.2.248; cf. ἄρκιλος.

ἄρκυλον· δίκτυον, Hsch. **ἄρκυμα**· ἀκρίς (Perga), Id. **ἄρκυον**, τό, = ἄρκυς, Id., *EM*144.11.

ἀρκυοστασία, v. ἀρκυστασία.

ἄρκυς (ἀρκ- *Et.Gen*., cf. Paus.Gr.*Fr*.73), υος, ἡ: pl., nom. and acc., ἄρκυες, -υας, Att. acc. ἄρκυς (v. infr.):—*net, hunter's net*, A.*Ag*.1116, *Ch*.1000: more freq. in pl., ἐξ ἀρκύων πέπτωκεν Id.*Eu*.147 (lyr.); ἀρκύων μολεῖν ἔσω E.*Cyc*.196; ἄρκυς ἱστάναι to set *nets*, X.*Cyn*.6.5; διωκόμενον τὸν λαγὼ εἰς τὰς ἄρκυς ib.10; πλεξάμενος ἄρκυς Ar.*Lys*. 790: metaph., ἄρκυες ξίφους *the toils*, i. e. *perils*, of the sword, E.*Med*. 1278. 2. *woman's hair-net*, Hsch.

ἀρκυ-στασία, ἡ, *line of nets*, in pl., X.*Cyn*.6.6. (Also ἀρκυο- Artem. 2.11, 3.59.) **-στάτος**, η, ον, E.*Or*.1421 (lyr.): (ἄρκυς, ἵστημι):—*beset with nets*, ἐς ἀρκυστάταν μηχανὰν ἐμπλέκειν παῖδα into *the hunter's toils*, E. l. c. II. ἀρκύστατα, τά, *surrounding toils, a place beset with nets*, A.*Eu*.112, S.*El*.1476, cf. A.*Ag*.1375 Elmsl. **-ωρέω** [ῠ], *watch the nets*, of a spider, Ael.*VH*1.2. II. metaph., *keep carefully*, καλώδια Eup.313 (ἀρκ- Eust.1535.18). **-ωρός** [ῠ], ὁ, *watcher of nets*, Cratin.79, X.*Cyn*.6.5, Lycurg.*Fr*.79, Poll.5.17, etc.

ἅρμα, ατος, τό, *chariot*, esp. *war-chariot*, Il.5.231, etc.; freq. in pl. for sg., ἑσταότ' ἐν θ' ἵπποισι καὶ ἅρμασι 4.366, etc.; τὰ Λυδῶν ἅρματα Sapph.*Supp*.5.19; ἵππους ὑφ' ἅρμασι ζευγνύναι A.*Pers*.190, E.*Hipp*.111; ἵππους ὑφ' ἅρματα ἄγειν A.*Pr*.465; πῶλον.. ζυγέντ' ἐν ἅρμασιν Id.*Ch*.795 (lyr.); opp. ἁρμάμαξα (q. v.); also, *racing-chariot* drawn by horses, opp. ὄχημα (a mule-car), Pi.*Fr*.106.5; ἅ. τέλειον *IG*2.967.45; ἁρμάτων ὀχήματα E.*Supp*.662, cf. *Ph*.1190; *travelling-chariot*, *Act.Ap*.8.28. 2. *chariot and horses, yoked chariot*, Il.2. 384, etc.; ἅ. τέθριππον Pi.*I*.1.14; ἅ. τετράορον, τέτρωρον, Id.*P*.10.65, E.*Alc*.483: metaph., τρίπωλον ἅ. δαιμόνων of three goddesses, E. *Andr*.277 (lyr.). 3. *team, chariot-horses*, ἅρμασιν ἐνδίδωσι κέντρον Id.*HF*881 (lyr.); ἅρματα.. φυσῶντα καὶ πνέοντα Ar.*Pax*902; ἅρματα τρέφειν keep *chariot-horses for racing*, X.*Hier*.11.5; ἅρματος τροφεύς

Pl.*Lg.*834b. **4.** metaph., ἅ. θαλάσσης *a ship*, Nonn.*D.*4.230,al., Opp.*H.*1.190. **II.** *a mountain district in Attica*, where omens from lightning were watched for: hence prov., ὁπόταν δι' Ἅρματος ἀστράψῃ, i.e. *seldom* or *never*, Str.9.2.11; δι' Ἅρματος alone, Plu.2.679c. **III.** Pythag. name for *unity*, *Theol.Ar.*6.

ἅρμα (A), ατος, τό, (αἴρω) *that which one takes*: *food*, used by Hp., acc. to Hellad.ap.Phot.p.533 B., cj. in Hes.*Th.*639 (pl.). **II.** *burden, load*, Aq.*De.*1.12, al.

ἅρμα (B), ἡ, (ἀραρίσκω) *union, love*, Delphic word, Plu.2.769a, Hsch.

ἁρμακιάς· στοάς, Hsch.

ἁρμαλά, = πήγανον ἄγριον, Dsc.3.46; Syrian for π. κηπαῖον, Ps.-Dsc.3.45:—also **ἁρμαρά,** *PMag.Par.*1.1294,1990. (Cf. Arabic *harmal* 'rue'.)

ἁρμαλιά, ἡ, *sustenance allotted, food*, Hes.*Op.*560,767; ἁ. ἔμμηνος Theoc.16.35; *stores* in a ship, A.R.1.393:—also **ἁρμολία,** ἡ, *PTeb.*112 (ii B.C.), 121.78 (i B.C.).

ἁρμαλόομαι, in aor. ἡρμαλώσατο, = συνέλαβεν, Hsch.

ἁρμάμαξα [μᾰμ], ης, ἡ, *covered carriage*, esp. used by Persians; [Ξέρξης] μεταβαίνεσκε ἐκ τοῦ ἅρματος ἐς ἁρμάμαξαν Hdt.7.41, cf. 83; of ambassadors to Susa, ἐφ' ἁρμαμαξῶν μαλθακῶς κατακείμενοι Ar.*Ach.*70; used by women, X.*Cyr.*3.1.40, 6.4.11.

ἁρμάν· πόλεμος (Phryg.), *EM*145.42.

ἁρμαρίτης, ου, ὁ, *bank-manager*, Just.*Edict.*9.2.1.

ἁρμᾰσίδουπος [ῐ], ον, *sounding in the chariot*, Pi.*Fr.*17.

ἁρμᾰτάρακτα, τά, (for ἁρματο-ταρ-) *spells for upsetting chariots in races*, *PMag.Par.*1.2210.

ἁρμᾰτ-αρχία, ἡ, *squadron of sixteen war-chariots*, Ascl.*Tact.*8, Ael.*Tact.*22.2. **-ειος,** ον, *of* or *belonging to a chariot*, σύριγγες E.*IA*230; δίφρος X.*Cyr.*6.4.9, Ant.Lib.11.3 (ἁρμάτιον codd.); ἁρμάτινον, Apoll.*Lex.* s.v. δίφρον, is prob. corrupt; τροχὸς *Placit.*2.20.1; νόμος ἁ. name of a *melody for the flute*, Plu.2.335a, 1133e; ἁ. μέλος, stage-direction in E.*Or.*[1384]. **-εύω,** *drive a chariot*, ib.994. **-ηγός,** όν, (ἄγω) *driving a chariot*, τροχοί Parth.6.14. **-ηλᾰσία,** ἡ, *chariot-driving*, X.*Cyr.*6.1.27, Luc.*Dem. Enc.*23. **-ηλᾰτέω,** *go in a chariot, drive it*, Hdt.5.9, X.*Smp.*4.6. **-ηλάτης** [λᾰ], Dor. **-τας,** ου, ὁ, *charioteer*, Pi.*P.*5.115, S.*El.*700, X.*Smp.*2.27, etc. **-ηλᾰτικός,** ή, όν: μονομερής, διμερής, τετραμερὴς ἁ., names of *bandages*, Sor.*Fasc.*12.513 C. (tit.). **-ήλᾰτος,** ον, *driven round by a chariot* or *wheel*, of Ixion, E.*HF*1297 Musgr. (-την codd.). **2.** ὁδὸς ἁ. road *for chariots*, Archyt.ap.Iamb.*Protr.*4. **-ίζομαι,** *place in a chariot*: metaph., εἰς λάληθρον κίσσαν, i.e. the Argo, Lyc.1319. **-ιον,** τό, Dim. of ἅρμα, *Gloss.* **II.** name of an *eyesalve*, Gal.12.779, Aët.7.41. **-ίτης** [ῑ], ου, ὁ, *using chariots*, Λυδοί Philostr.*Im.*1.17.

ἁρμᾰτο-δρομέω, *race in a chariot*, Apollod.3.5.5. **-δρομία,** ἡ, *chariot-race*, Str.5.3.8. **-δρόμος,** ον, *running a chariot-race*, Sch.A.R.1.1333. **-εις,** εσσα, εν, = ἁρμάτειος, δίφρος Critias 2.11 D. **-εργός,** όν, (ἔργον) *building chariots*, Sch.Il.24.277. **-θεσία,** ἡ, (τίθημι) *chariot-race*, Eust.226.6. **-κτῠπος** ὄτοβος *rattling* din *of chariots*, A.*Th.*204 (lyr.). **-μᾰχέω,** *fight in* or *from a chariot*, Eust.1088.27. **-πηγέω,** *build chariots*, Poll.7.115. **-πηγός,** όν, (πήγνυμι) *building chariots*: ἁ. ἀνήρ *wheelwright, chariot-maker*, Il.4.485, Theoc.25.247. **-πήξ,** ῆγος, ὁ, ἡ, = foreg., Theognost. in *AB*1340. **-ποιέω,** = ἁρματοπηγέω, Poll.7.113. **-ποιός,** όν, = ἁρματοπηγός, J.*AJ*6.3.5. **-τροφέω,** *keep chariot-horses*, esp. for racing, X.*Ag.*9.6, D.L.4.17, Phld.*Acad.Ind.*p.47 M. **-τροφία,** ἡ, *keeping of chariot-horses*, X.*Hier.*11.5. **-τροχιά,** Ep. **-ιή,** ἡ, *wheel-track of a chariot*, Il.23.505, Ph.1.312, Luc.*Dem.Enc.*23, Ael.*VH*2.27, Q.S.4.516.

ἁρματωλία, ἡ, acc. to the Sch. for ἁρματηλασία, with a play on ἁμαρτωλία, Ar.*Pax*415.

ἁρμ-ελᾰτέω, = ἁρματηλατέω, Ps.-Callisth.1.18. **-ελᾰτήρ,** ῆρος, ὁ, *charioteer*, κόσμοιο, of the Sun, *IG*14.2012.1 (Sulp. Max.). **-ελάτης** [λᾰ], ου, ὁ, = foreg., Orac.ap.Eun.*Hist.*p.229 D. **2.** name of a *bandage*, Gal.12.497 Chart.

ἄρμενα, τά, *tackle* of a ship, *sails*, etc., Hes.*Op.*808, Aen.Tact.11.3, Theoc.22.13, *IPE*I².32 *B* 52 (Olbia). **2.** *accoutrements*, Alc.94. **3.** *implements*, ὁπόσα ἀνθρώποις ἄ. μεμηχάνηται Hp.*Fract.*31, cf. Aen.Tact.18.11, *AP*6.205 (Leon.), etc.: in sg., πρὸς τὸ ἄ. Hp.*Fract.*2; ἄ. ἐργασίης *AP*6.47 (Antip. Sid.), 11.203. **b.** esp. of *surgical apparatus*, Hp.*Off.*2, cf. Bacch.ap.Erot.*Fr.*37. **4.** *food*, Numen.ap.Ath.7.306c. Neut. of ἄρμενος, part. of ἀραρίσκω (q.v.).

Ἀρμεν-ία, ἡ, *Armenia*, ἡ μεγάλη and ἡ μικρά Str.11.12.3 and 4 sq., cf. App.*Mith.*105:—Adj. **Ἀρμένιος,** α, ον, *Armenian*: also **Ἀρμενιακός,** ή, όν, Str.11.14.12: **-κόν,** τό, *apricot, Prunus Armeniaca*, Dsc.1.115, Gal.6.593 (also **Ἀρμενική** (sc. μηλέα) Id.12.76): **-κὸς λίθος** *limestone coloured blue by copper carbonate*, Id.5.105; χρυσόκολλα Ἀ. Dsc.5.89. **-ιάρχης,** ου, ὁ, *president of the* κοινὸν τῆς Ἀρμενίας, *Anatolian Studies* p.116. **-ιστί,** Adv. *in Armenian fashion*, ἐσκευάσθαι Str.11.3.3.

ἀρμενίζω, *sail*, *Gloss.*

Ἀρμένιον, τό, *copper carbonate, azurite*, Dsc.5.90. **II.** ἀρμένια, τά, Dim. of ἄρμενα, *small tools*, Hero *Aut.*24.2, Sch.Opp.*H.*1.222.

ἀρμενοθήκη, ἡ, *store for ship's tackle*, Hsch. s.v. καραδάλη.

ἄρμενον, v. ἄρμενα.

ἀρμενοποιέω, *sail*, Dosith.432.21.

ἄρμενος, v. ἀείρω III.1.

ἀρμενοφόρος, gloss on ἱστιοφόρος, Hsch.

ἁρμή, ἡ, (ἀραρίσκω) *junction*, Chrysipp.*Stoic.*2.154 (prob. for ὁρμήν); *fitting together*, of shields, Q.S.11.361; *suture* of a wound, Hp. ap.Erot.; of the skull-bones, Id.ap.Gal.19.86.

ἁρμογή, ἡ, (ἁρμόζω) *joining, junction*, Luc.*Zeux.*6; *fitting, arrangement*, Plb.6.18.1. **2.** *joint* in masonry, J.*AJ*15.11.3, Hdn.3.3.7. **3.** Lit. Crit., κώλων ἁ. *getting together, junction, arrangement* of clauses, D.H.*Comp.*8, cf. 23; ὀνομάτων ib.26; of letters, ib.22; *adjustment* of parts in an organized whole, ἁ. τοῖς ὅλοις Phld.*Po.*2.17; ἑλληνισμὸς ἀποτελεῖται καὶ ἁ. τις ib.18. **4.** Medic., *joining of two bones without motion*, = σύμφυσις, opp. ἄρθρον, Gal.19.460. **5.** in Music, = ἁρμονία, *method of tuning* a stringed instrument, Ptol.*Harm.*2.6; *modulation*, Eup.11; opp. ἀναρμοστία, Plot.3.6.2. **6.** in Painting, *gradation* of tints in transition, Plin.*HN*35.29.

ἁρμόδιος, α, ον, (ἁρμόζω) *fitting together*, θύραι, metaph. of the lips, Thgn.422. **II.** *fitting*, ἥβη Id.724; δεῖπνον Pi.*N.*1.21; ἀνθρώποις ἁρμόδιόν [ἐστι] c. inf., Democr.187, cf. Aeschin.Socr.52; μέρη τῆς πολιτείας ἁ. τοῖς τηλικούτοις Plu.2.793a; πᾶν σῶμα ἁ. εἶναι ψυχῇ Aen.Gaz.*Thphr.*p.60 B.: Comp. -ώτερος, γάμος Hld.1.21: Sup. -ώτατος, ἔς τι Arr.*Tact.*16.4; also, *agreeable*, Parth.16.2. Adv. -ως Plu.*Arist.*24, *PGiss.*57.6 (vi/vii A.D.).

ἁρμοδιοτῠπής, ές, *of accordant mould* or *cast*, Hsch.

ἁρμοζόντως, *suitably*, χρείᾳ τινῶν D.S.3.15, cf. *SIG*559.10 (iii B.C.), *BGU*1060.31 (i B.C.); τοῖς παροῦσι J.*AJ*6.1.2; τῷ πάθει Gal.18(1).773; Att. **ἁρμοττόντως** Ph.*Bel.*82.4, Iamb.*Comm.Math.*17, Sch.Ar.*Nu.*253.

ἁρμόζω, Att. **ἁρμόττω,** Dor. **ἁρμόσδω** Theoc.1.53 (ἐφ-); part. ἁρμόσσον Hp.*Art.*37: impf. ἥρμοζον, Dor. ἅρμ- Pi.*N.*8.11: fut. ἁρμόσω S.*Ant.*1318 (lyr.), Hp.*Fract.*31, Ar.*Th.*263: aor. ἥρμοσα Il.3.333, etc., Dor. ἅρμοξα Pi.*N.*10.12 (συν-): pf. ἥρμοκα Arist.*Po.*1459ᵇ32:—**Med.,** Ep. imper. ἁρμόζεο Od.5.162, -όζου Philem.187: fut. -όσομαι Gal.10.971: aor. ἡρμοσάμην Hdt.5.32, etc., Dor. ἁρμοξάμην Alcm.71:—**Pass.,** pf. ἥρμοσμαι E.*Ph.*116 (lyr.), Pl.*La.*193d, Ion. ἅρμοσμαι Hdt.2.124; Dor. inf. ἁρμόχθαι Ocell.ap.Stob.1.13.2; Dor. 3 sg. ἅρμοκται Ecphant.ap.Stob.4.7.64: aor. ἡρμόσθην Pl.*Phd.*93a, Dor. ἁρμόχθην D.L.8.85: fut. ἁρμοσθήσομαι S.*OC*908:—*fit together, join*, esp. of *joiner's* work, ἥρμοσεν ἀλλήλοισιν (sc. τὰ δοῦρα) Od.5.247 (also in Med., *put together*, ἁρμόζεο χαλκῷ εὐρεῖαν σχεδίην ib.162; ναυπηγίαν ἁρμόζων E.*Cyc.*460; ἁρμόζειν χαίταν στεφάνοισι Pi.*I.*7(6).39; ἀρβύλαισιν ἁ. πόδα E.*Hipp.*1189; ἁ. πόδα ἐπὶ γαίας *plant* foot on ground, Id.*Or.*233; ἁ. ποδὸς ἴχνια Simon.182; ἐν ἀσυχαίᾳ βάσει βάσιν ἅρμοσαι (aor. imper. Med.) S.*OC*198; στόμ' ἅρμοσον *kiss*, E.*Tr.*763; ἁ. ψαλίοις ἵππους *furnish* them *with* .., Id.*Rh.*27 (lyr.). **b.** generally, *adapt, accommodate*, ἁ. δίκην εἰς ἕκαστον *award* each his just due, Sol.36.17; σφισὶν βίοτον ἁ. *accord* them life, Pi.*N.*7.98; *apply* a remedy, S.*Tr.*687; *make ready*, τοὐπτάνιον Hegesipp.Com.1.19:—Med., *accommodate, suit oneself*, πρὸς τὴν παροῦσαν πάντοθ' ἁρμόζου τύχην Philem. l.c.; πρός τινα Luc.*Merc.Cond.*30; ἁ. σύνεσιν *acquire* it, Hp.*Lex*2. **2.** of marriage, *betroth*, Hdt.9.108; ἁ. κόρᾳ ἄνδρα Pi.*P.*9.117; ἁ. γάμον, γάμους, ib.13, E.*Ph.*411:—Med., *betroth to oneself, take to wife*, τὴν θυγατέρα τινός Hdt.5.32,47 (but Med. = Act., 2*Ep.Cor.*11.2); ἁ. ὡς ἐὰν αἱρῆται γάμῳ *POxy.*906.7 (ii/iii A.D.):—Pass., ἁρμόσθαι θυγατέρα τινὸς γυναῖκα *have her betrothed* or *married to* one, Hdt.3.137; ὡς ἐκείνῳ τῇδέ τ' ἦν ἡρμοσμένα as *troth was plighted* between him and her, S.*Ant.*570. **3.** *bind fast*, ἁ. τινὰ ἐν ἄρκυσι E.*Ba.*231. **4.** *set in order, regulate, govern*, στρατόν Pi.*N.*8.11:—Pass., [νόμοις] οὐκ ἄλλοισιν ἁρμοσθήσεται S.*OC*908; κονδύλοις ἡρμοττόμην I *was ruled* or *drilled* with cuffs, Ar.*Eq.*1236. **b.** in the Spartan Constitution, *act as harmost*, ἐν ταῖς πόλεσιν X.*Lac.*14.2, etc.: c. acc., ἁρμοστὴν ὃς ἥρμοζε τὴν Ἀσίαν Luc.*Tox.*17. **5.** in Music, *tune* instruments, τὸ σύμφωνον Pl.*Phlb.*56a, etc.:—Med., ἁρμόττεσθαι ἁρμονίαν Id.*R.*591d; ἁ. λύραν *tune one's* lyre, ib.349e; Δωριστὶ ἁ. λύραν Ar.*Eq.*989; αὐλόν Luc.*Harm.*1 (but μέλη ἔς τι ἁ. *adapt* them *to* a subject, Simon.184):—Pass., of the lyre, ἡρμόσθαι *to be tuned*, Pl.*Tht.*144e, cf. *Phd.*85e; ἁρμονίαν καλλίστην ἡρμ. Id.*La.*188d; ὁμονοητικὴ καὶ ἡρμοσμένη ψυχή *at harmony with itself*, Id.*R.*554e. **6.** *compose*, ᾆσμα Philostr.*Her.*19.17. **II.** intr., *fit well*, of clothes or armour, ἥρμοσε δ' αὐτῷ [θώρηξ] Il.3.333; Ἕκτορι δ' ἥρμοσε τεύχε' ἐπὶ χροΐ 17.210; ἐσθὰς ἁρμόζοισα γυίοις Pi.*P.*4.80; ἆρ' ἁρμόσει μοι (sc. τὰ ὑποδήματα); Ar.*Th.*263; τοῖς τρόποις ἁ. ὥσπερ περὶ πόδα *fit* like a shoe, Pl.Com.129; θώραξ περὶ τὰ στέρνα ἁρμόζων X.*Cyr.*2.1.16. **b.** Math., *coincide with*, c. dat., Papp.612.14; *correspond*, Hero *Aut.*1.4. **2.** *suit, be adapted for*, τινί S.*OT*902 (lyr.), *El.*1293, And.4.6; τόδ' οὐκ ἐπ' ἄλλον ἁρμόσει *shall* not *be adapted* to another, S.*Ant.*1318; κἂν ἐπὶ τῶν θηρίων ἁρμόσειε λόγος Arist.*Pol.*1281ᵇ19; εἴς τι, πρός τι, Pl.*Plt.*289b, 286d; πρὸς τὰς συνουσίας Isoc.2.34, cf. D.61.24; of medicines, Dsc.1.2, al.; of an argument, *apply*, Arist.*Ph.*209ᵃ9, al.; τὸ τοῦ Ξενοφάνους ἁρμόττει *is applicable*, Id.*Rh.*1377ᵃ19. **3.** impers., ἁρμόζει *it is fitting*, c. acc. et inf., σιγᾶν ἂν ἁρμόζοι σε S.*Tr.*731: c. inf. only, λόγους οὓς ἁρμόσει λέγειν D.18.42; πάντα τὰ τοιαῦτα ἁρμόττει καλεῖν Id.21.166; οὔτε ἁ. μοι οἰκεῖν μετὰ τοιούτων Id.40.57; τὰ τοιαῦτα ῥηθῆναι μάλιστ' ἂν ἁρμόσειεν Isoc.9.72. **4.** part. ἁρμόζων, ουσα, ον, *fitting, suitable*, Pi.*P.*4.129; ἡ ἁρμόζουσα ἀπόφασις the *appropriate* verdict, Archim.*Sph.Cyl.*1 *Praef.*; ἀλλήλοις Pl.*La.*188d, al.: c. gen., Plb.1.44.1; πρός τι X.*Mem.*4.3.5, etc. **5.** *to be in tune*, λύραν ἐπιτείν' ἕως ἂν ἁρμόσῃ Macho 2.9.

ἁρμοῖ, Adv. *just, lately*, A.*Pr.*615, Theoc.4.51, Lyc.106, Call.*Fr.*44; *at once*, Hp.*Mul.*1.36. **2.** *just, a little*, ib.4, *Steril.*213. **3.** *tightly*, Id.*Cord.*12.—Written ἁρμῷ Pi.*Fr.*10, Pherecr.111, Hp.*Cord.* l.c., cf. *EM*144.49. (Old locative of ἁρμός.)

ἁρμοίματα· ἀρτύματα, Hsch.

ἁρμο-κ[όπος], ὁ, *locksmith*, prob. in *BGU*344.14 (ii/iii A. D.). **-λογέω**, *join, pile together*, τάφον *AP*7.554 (Phil.):—Pass., τὰ μέλαθρα τῶν θυρίδων ἡρμολόγηται *PRyl.*233.6 (ii A. D.): metaph., ἡρμολογημένον τῷ πρὸ ἑαυτοῦ *closely connected with*.., S.E.*M.*5.78. **-λόγησις**, εως, ἡ, *joining, Gloss.* **-λόγος**, ον, *joining together*, Id.

ἁρμονία, ἡ, (ἁρμόζω) *means of joining, fastening*, γόμφοις μιν.. καὶ ἁρμονίῃσιν ἄρηρεν Od.5.248; of a ship, ὄφρ' ἂν.. ἐν ἁρμονίῃσιν ἀρήρῃ ib.361. 2. *joint*, as between a ship's planks, τὰς ἁ. ἐν ὧν ἐπάκτωσαν τῇ βύβλῳ caulked the *joints* with papyrus, Hdt.2.96; τῶν ἁρμονιῶν διαχασκουσῶν Ar.*Eq.*533; also in masonry, αἱ τῶν λίθων ἁ. D.S.2.8, cf. Paus.8.8.8, 9.33.7. 3. in Anatomy, *suture*, Hp.*Off.*25, *Oss.*12; *union* of two bones by mere apposition, Gal.2.737; also in pl., *adjustments*, πόρων Epicur.*Fr.*250. 4. *framework*, ῥηγνὺς ἁρμονίαν .. λύρας S.*Fr.*244; βοός Philostr.*Im.*1.16; esp. of the *human frame*, ἁρμονίην ἀναλυέμεν ἀνθρώποιο Ps.-Phoc.102; νεύρων καὶ κώλων ἔκλυτος ἁ. *AP*7.383 (Phil.); τὰς ἁ. διαχαλᾷ τοῦ σώματος Epicr.2.19. b. of the mind, δύστροπος γυναικῶν ἁ. women's perverse *temperament*, E.*Hipp.*162 (lyr.). c. *framework* of the universe, *Corp.Herm.* 1.14. II. *covenant, agreement*, in pl., μάρτυροι .. καὶ ἐπίσκοποι ἁρμονιάων Il.22.255. III. *settled government, order*, τὰν Διὸς ἁ. A.*Pr.*551 (lyr.). IV. in Music, *stringing*, ἁ. τόξου καὶ λύρας Heraclit.51, cf. Pl.*Smp.*187a: hence, *method of stringing, musical scale*, Philol.6, etc., Nicom.*Harm.*9; esp. *octave*, ἐκ πασῶν ὀκτὼ οὐσῶν [φωνῶν] μίαν ἁ. συμφωνεῖν Pl.*R.*617b; ἑπτὰ χορδαὶ ἡ ἁ. Arist. *Metaph.*1093ᵃ14, cf. *Pr.*919ᵇ21; of the planetary spheres, in Pythag. theory, *Cael.*290ᵇ13, *Mu.*399ᵃ12, etc. 2. generally, *music*, αὐτῷ δὲ τῷ ῥυθμῷ μιμοῦνται χωρὶς ἁ. Id.*Po.*1447ᵃ26. 3. *special type of scale, mode*, ἁ. Λυδία Pi.*N.*4.46; Αἰολὶς or -ηΐς Pratin.Lyr.5, Lasus 1, cf. Pl.*R.*398e, al., Arist.*Pol.*1276ᵇ8, 1341ᵇ35, etc. b. esp. *the enharmonic scale*, Aristox.*Harm.*p.1 M., Plu.2.1135a, al. 4. ἁρμονίαν λόγων λαβών *a due arrangement* of words, fit to be set to music, Pl.*Tht.*175e. 5. *intonation* or *pitch* of the voice, Arist.*Rh.* 1403ᵇ31. 6. metaph. of persons and things, *harmony, concord*, Pl.*R.*431e, etc. V. personified, as a mythical figure, *h.Ap.*195, Hes.*Th.*937, etc.; Philos., like φιλότης, *principle of Union*, opp. Νεῖκος, Emp.122.2, cf. 27.3. VI. Pythag. name for *three*, *Theol. Ar.*16. VII. name of a *remedy*, Gal.13.61; of a *plaster*, Paul. Aeg.3.62.

Ἁρμον-ίδης, ου, ὁ, Patron., *son of a carpenter*, Il.5.60. **-ίζω**, *frame*, in Pass., μεμνημένος.. ἐξ οἵης ἡρμόνισαι (prob. for -ισας) καλάμης *AP*7.472.16 (Leon.). **-ικός**, ή, όν, *skilled in music*, Pl.*Phdr.* 268d; ἁ. οὐ μάγειρος *musician*, Damox.2.49 codd. II. *musical*: τὰ -κά *theory of music*, Pl.*Phdr.*268e, Arist.*Metaph.*1077ᵃ5; ἡ ἐν τοῖς μαθήμασιν -κή (sc. ἐπιστήμη) mathematical *theory of music*, ib.997ᵇ21; ἁ. πραγματεία a treatise *thereon*, Plu.2.1142f; ἁρμονικὰ στοιχεῖα, title of work by Aristoxenus; ἁρμονικοί, οἱ, *students of -κή*, οἱ κατὰ τοὺς ἀριθμοὺς ἁ. Arist.*Top.*107ᵃ16; with play on (b), Aristox. *Harm.*p.1 M. b. *of* or *in the enharmonic scale*, νόμος Plu.2. 1133e. c. ἁ. κίνησις, of the pulse, *in harmony with* physical state, Gal.19.376. III. Arith., *harmonic*, μέσα Archyt.2; ἁ. ἀναλογία Ph.1.27, Nicom.*Ar.*2.22, Theo Sm.p.114 H.; μεσότης Arist.*Fr.*47; λόγοι Ph.1.22 (Sup.); λόγοι κατ' ἀριθμὼς ἁ. συγκεκραμένοι Ti.Locr. 96a, cf. Arist.*de An.*406ᵇ29. IV. ἁ. γυμνάσιον training *by rule of thumb*, Philostr.*Gym.*53. V. metaph., *capable of harmonizing*, τακτικοὶ καὶ ἁ. Plu.2.618c; of God, ib.946f. VI. Adv. -κῶς ib.1138e, Iamb.*Comm.Math.*32. **-ιος**, ον, *fitting, harmonious*, Lxx *Wi.*16.20, dub.l. in D.H.*Dem.*22. Adv. -ίως J.*AJ*8.3.2, Ph.1. 179, Iamb.*VP*5.20. (Mostly with v.l. ἁρμοδ-.) **-ιώδης**, ες, = ἁρμόνιος, of friends, Socr.*Ep.*15 (Sup. -ωδέστατος).

ἁρμοποιός, όν, *uniting, joining*, Sch.Lyc.832.

ἁρμός, ὁ, (ἀραρίσκω) *joint*, in masonry, *IG*1.322; in metal-work, Ph.*Bel.*77.39; ὁ προσιὼν, ἀπιὼν ἁ., front and back *faces* of blocks, *IG* 7.3073.106, 112 (Lebad.), cf. 2².463.40: pl., *fastenings* of a door, E. *Med.*1315, *Hipp.*809; ἁ. χώματος λιθοσπαδής a fissure in the tomb made by tearing away the stones *at their joining*, S.*Ant.*1216; *chink in the fitting* of a door, ἁρμῷ τὴν ὄψιν προσβαλεῖν D.H.5.7, cf. Plu. *Alex.*3. 2. *bolt, peg*, ἁ. ἐν ξύλῳ παγείς E.*Fr.*360.12. 3. *shoulder-joint*, *Hippiatr.*34.

ἅρμ-οσις, εως, ἡ, *tuning*, Phryn.*PS*p.24 B. (pl.): metaph. of numbers, *Theol.Ar.*54 (pl.). **-οσμα**, ατος, τό, *joined work*, τρόπις δ' ἐλείφθη ποικίλων ἁρμοσμάτων E.*Hel.*411. **-οστέον**, *one must adapt*, A.D.*Pron.*79.9 codd.; *one must apply*, Ps.-Democr.Alch. p.47 B. **-οστήρ**, ῆρος, ὁ, = sq., X.*HG*4.8.39, *IG*5(1).937.2 (Cythera). II. = κοσμητής 1.2, Pl.Com.126. III. of stones, *laid with the grain*, Hsch. **-οστής**, οῦ, ὁ, *one who arranges* or *governs*, esp. *harmost, governor* sent out by the Lacedaemonians to the περίοικοι and subject cities, Th.8.5, X.*HG*2.4.28, etc.; *governor of a dependent colony*, Id.*An.*5.5.19. 2. title of officials at Thessalonica, *IG*11(4).1053 (iii B. C.). 3. = *triumvir*, App.*BC*4.7; = *praefectus*, Luc.*Tox.*17, 32. 4. *betrothed husband*, Poll.3.35. **-οστικός**, ή, όν, *fitted for joining*, v.l. for ἁρμονικός, *Theol.Ar.*34. **-οστός**, ή, όν, *joined, adapted, well-fitted*, Hero *Spir.*1.16, al.; τινὶ κατὰ τὸ πλάτος Plb.21.28.12; *suitable, fit*, ἁρμοστόν μοι λέγειν τοῦτο Philem. 4.4. Adv. -τῶς Plu.2.438a. **-οστρα**, τά, *sponsalia*, *Gloss.* **-όστωρ**, ορος, ὁ, *commander*, ναυβατῶν A.*Eu.*456.

ἁρμόσυνοι· ἀρχή τις ἐν Λακεδαίμονι ἐπὶ τῆς εὐκοσμίας τῶν γυναικῶν, Hsch.

ἁρμόττω, ἁρμοττόντως, Att. for ἁρμόζω, -ζόντως, qq. v.

ἅρμυλα, τά, *shoes* (Cypr.), Hsch. **ἁρμώατος**· σπασμός (Cypr.), Id. **ἅρμωλα**· ἀρτύματα (Arc.), Id.:—also **ἁρμώμαλα**, Id.

ἄρνα, acc. sg., dual ἄρνε, pl. ἄρνες; v. ἀρήν.

ἀρναβώ, ἡ, *zedoary*, Posidon.Jun.ap.Paul.Aeg.7.3:—also **ἀρναβόν**, τό, Aët.7.135.

ἀρνᾰκίς, ίδος, ἡ, *sheepskin coat*, Ar.*Nu.*730, Pl.*Smp.*220b, Aristonym.6, Theoc.5.50. (Formed as if from *ἄρναξ, Dim. of ἀρνός.)

ἄρναν· τὸν ὅρκον (Clazom.), Hsch. **ἄρναπον**· τὸν ἄρνα, Id.

ἀρνέα, ἡ, = ἀρνακίς, Hdn.*Philet.*p.445 P. II. *lambing*, *POxy.* 297.8 (i A. D.).

ἄρνειος, α, ον, (ἀρήν) *of a lamb* or *sheep*, κρέα Orac.ap.Hdt.1.47, Pherecr.45.3, X.*An.*4.5.31; σπλάγχνα Eub.75.5; ἁ. φόνος slaughtered *sheep*, S.*Aj.*309. 2. Ἀρνεῖος, ὁ (sc. μήν), name of month at Argos, *Schwyzer* 90.3 (-ῆος lapis), Conon 19. 3. ἄρνειον, τό, = ἀρνόγλωσσόν, Ps.-Dsc.2.126. II. **ἀρνεῖον**, τό, *a shop where lamb is sold, butcher's shop*, Didym.ap.*EM*146.39.

ἀρνειός, ὁ, *ram, wether* (= τριετὴς κριός, Hsch.), Il.2.550, al., Ister 53; ἀ. ὄϊς, opp. θῆλυς, Od.10.572, al.; but later, θῆλυς ἀ. A.R. 3.1033. 2. the constellation *Aries*, Max.72. (Orig. ἀρνηϝός, cf. ἀρνηάς and Att. ἀρνεώς. Deriv. of ἄρσην, as ἀρσν-ηϝ-ό-ς, cf. ἀρνευ-τήρ. No initial ϝ-.)

ἀρνεοθοίνης, ου, ὁ, *feasting on rams*, *APl.*4.235 (Apollonid.).

ἀρνέομαι, fut. -ήσομαι A.*Pr.*268, Ar.*Ec.*365; also ἀρνηθήσομαι S.*Ph.*527 (ἀπ-), *Ev.Luc.*12.9: aor. Pass. ἠρνήθην freq. in Att., Th. 6.60, etc.: also aor. Med. ἠρνησάμην Hom. (v. infr.), Hdt.3.1; rare in Trag. and Att., E.*Ion* 1026, Aeschin.2.69, 3.324: pf. ἤρνημαι D. 28.24:—*deny, disown*, τεὸν ἔπος ἀρνήσασθαι Il.14.212, Od.8.358, etc.; ἀ. ἀμφὶ βόεσσιν *h.Merc.*390; ἀ. ἃ εἶπον E.*Hec.*303: abs., Hdt.2.174; ἀρνούμενοι ἔπαινοι *negative* praises, Plu.2.58a. 2. *refuse*, τόξον.. δόμεναί τε καὶ ἀρνήσασθαι Od.21.345, cf. Hes.*Op.*408, Hdt.3.1; ἀ. γάμον Od.1.249; ἀ. χρείαν *decline, renounce* a duty or office, D.18.282; διαθήκην Id.36.34; κληρονομίαν *PFlor.*61.49 (i A. D.); ζωὰν ἀ., of a suicide, *AP*7.473 (Aristodic.); δυνάμει τὸν βίον ἀ. S.E.*M.*11.163; ἀ. ἀνθρώπους *cast aside* humanity, Him.*Or.*2.10. 3. abs., *say No, decline*, ὁ δ' ἠρνεῖτο στεναχίζων Il.19.304; αὐτὰρ ὅ γ' ἠρνεῖτο στερεῶς 23.42, etc. 4. in expressing *denial*, c. inf., either without μή, *deny that*.., A.*Eu.*611, E.*IA*966; or with μή, *say that.. not*.., Ar.*Eq.*572, Antipho 3.3.7, etc.; οὐδ' αὐτὸς ἀρνεῖται μὴ οὐ.. D.C.50.22; also οὐκ ἂν ἀρνοίμην τὸ δρᾶν S.*Ph.*118; ἀ. ὅτι οὐ.., ὡς οὐ.., X.*Ath.*2.17, Lys. 4.1, D.9.54. 5. in expressing *refusal*, c. inf., ἀ. εἶναι χρηστούς Hdt.6.13: poet. also c. part., οὐ γὰρ εὐτυχῶν ἀρνήσομαι E.*Alc.*1158, cf. *Or.*1582.

ἀρνεός, ὁ, = ἀρνειός, *PStrassb.*24.44 (ii A. D.).

ἀρνευ-τήρ, ῆρος, ὁ, *tumbler, acrobat*, Herod.8.42: metaph. of one falling headlong, ὁ δ' ἀρνευτῆρι ἐοικὼς κάππεσε Il.12.385, 16.742, Od. 12.413. 2. *diver*, Arat.656, Hsch. **-τήρια**, τά, *tumbling* or *diving tricks*, Id. (s. v. l.). (Acc. to D.H.ap.*Et.Gen.*, from ἀρήν, *one that plunges and butts like a lamb*; but rather from ἀρνεύω *butt* or *dive headlong like a ram* (*ἀρνεύς, cf. ἀρνειός).) **-τής**, οῦ, ὁ, = ἀρνευτήρ, epith. of the fish ἵππουρος, Numen.ap.Ath.7.322f, Eust. 1083.59. **-ω**, *frisk, tumble*, Lyc.465; *plunge, dive*, Id.1103.

ἀρ(ν)εώνιον· ὅρκον βασίλειον, Hsch.

ἀρνεώς, ὁ, *ram*, *IG*2.844.5: gen. pl. ἀρνέων read by Zenod. in Il. 3.273. (From ἀρνηϝός, cf. ἀρνειός.)

ἀρνηάς, άδος, ἡ, prob. some sort of *sheep*, ἔπεροι καὶ ἀρνηάδες ἐρίων ἀτελέες, ἀρνηάδων ἔταλα ἀτελέα *Schwyzer* 644.15 (Aeol.). (Fem. of ἀρνεώς, q. v.)

ἀρνηΐς, ΐδος, ἡ, = ἀρνίς, Ael.*NA*12.34.

Ἀρνῆος, v. ἄρνειος 1. 2.

ἀρν-ήσιμος, ον, *to be denied*, τούτων δ' οὐδέν ἐστ' ἀ. S.*Ph.*74. **-ησις**, εως, ἡ, *denial*, τούτου δ' οὔτις ἀ. πέλει A.*Eu.*588; τῶνδ' ἀ. οὐκ ἔνεστί μοι S.*El.*527, cf. *OT*578: foll. by τὸ μή c. inf., D.19.163. II. Gramm., *negation*, D.T.642.3, Lesb.Gramm.26; δύο ἀ. μίαν συγκατάθεσιν ποιοῦσι two *negatives* make an affirmative, Sch.S.*OT*1053. **-ητέον**, *one must deny*, Arist.*Top.*160ᵃ25, Hld.1.26. **-ητικός**, ή, όν, *denying, negative*, μόριον ἀξιώματος Chrysipp.*Stoic.*2.66, cf. Alex.Aphr.*in Metaph.*333.26; φαντασίαι Numen.ap.Eus.*PE*14.8; ἐπίρρημα Eust. 211.37. Adv. -κῶς Porph.*in Cat.*136.27, Simp.*in Ph.*812.17, Sch. Ar.*Ra.*1455.

ἀρνίον, τό, Dim. of ἀρήν, *a little lamb*, Lys.32.21, Eub.150.4, *PStrassb.*24.7 (ii A. D.). II. *sheepskin, fleece*, Luc.*Salt.*43.

ἀρνίς, ίδος, ἡ, festival at Argos, in which dogs were slain, Conon 19; cf. ἀρνηΐς.

ἀρνό-γλωσσον, τό, (γλῶσσα) *plantain*, *Plantago major*, Thphr. *HP*7.8.3, 7.10.3, Crateuas *Fr.*6, Luc.*Trag.*150; ἀ. τὸ μεῖζον Dsc.2. 126. 2. *haresfoot plantain*, *P. Lagopus*, ἀ. τὸ μικρόν ibid. **-κόμης**, ου, ὁ, *with lamb's hair*, i.e. *curly hair*, epith. of Apollo, Macr.*Sat.*1. 17.45. **-πολέμιον**, τό, = σταφὶς ἀγρία, Ps.-Dsc.4.152.

ἀρνορ(κ)ίη· ὁ μετὰ τοῦ ἀρνὸς αἰρομένου γινόμενος ὅρκος, Hsch.

ἀρνός, ὁ, late nom., = ἀρήν, Aesop.274.

ἀρνο-τροφία, ἡ, *rearing of lambs*, *Gp.*18.1.2. **-φάγος** [ᾰ], ον, *lamb-devouring*, Man.4.255.

ἄρνυθεν· ἠγωνίζοντο, ἐνήργουν, Hsch.

ἄρνῠμαι, imper. ἄρνυσο Sapph.75, *Trag.Adesp.*4: fut. ἀρέομαι [ᾰ] Pi.*P.*1.75, Att. ἀροῦμαι S.*OC*460, *Aj.*75, Pl.*Lg.*969a: aor. 2 ἀρόμην [ᾰ] Il.11.625, 23.592 (augm. 3 sg. ἤρετο only as v.l. for ἤρατο, cf. ἀείρω); subj. ἄρηαι Hes.*Op.*632, ἄρηται Il.12.435; opt. ἀροίμην 18. 121, S.*El.*34, etc.; inf. ἀρέσθαι Il.16.88, S.*Aj.*246 (lyr.); part. ἀρόμενος A.*Eu.*168 (lyr.):—*win, gain*, esp. of honour or reward, in pres. and impf. often with additional idea of *striving*, ἀρνύμενος πατρός τε μέγα κλέος *maintaining*.., Il.6.446; κλέος ἐσθλὸν ἄροιτο 5.3; κῦδος ἀρέσθαι 9.303, Od.22.253, Pi.*N.*9.46; ἵν' οἴκαδε κέρδος ἄρηαι Hes.*Op.* 632; οὐχ ἱερήϊον οὐδὲ βοείην ἀρνύσθην Il.22.160; ἀέθλια ποσσὶν ἄροντο 9.124; ἀρνύμενος ἥν τε ψυχὴν καὶ νόστον ἑταίρων *trying to win, striving to secure*.., Od.1.5; *exact*, of atonement, τιμὴν ἀρνύμενοι Μενελάῳ Il. 1.159; ὅτῳ τρόπῳ πατρὸς δίκας ἀροίμην τῶν φονευσάντων πάρα S.*El.*34; simply, *receive*, καί κεν τοῦτ' ἐθέλοιμι Διός γε διδόντος ἀρέσθαι Od.1.390; ὧν.. τὴν μάθησιν ἄρνυμαι S.*Tr.*711, etc.; κράτος ἄρνυται Id.*Ph.*838 (lyr.); τὴν δόκησιν ἄ. E.*Andr.*696; ἕλκος ἀρέσθαι Il.14.130; = λαβεῖν in ποδοῖν κλοπὰν ἀ. S.*Aj.*247 (lyr.); ἄγος ἀ. A.*Eu.*168 (lyr.); *win reputation for*.., δειλίαν ἀρῇ S.*Aj.*75 (cf. Hsch.); τόλμαν.. ἀρομένῳ Pi.*N.*7.59: rare in Prose, exc. in the phrase μισθὸν ἄρνυσθαι Pl.*Prt.*349a, *R.*346c, *Lg.*813e, Arist.*Pol.*1287ᵃ36, cf. ἀρ[έσ]θαι μισθόν *IG*12(9).1273–4iii 1 (Eretria); also ἢ δ' ἂν ἄνδρα ἑωυτῇ ἄρηται Hp.*Aër.*17; δίκαν ἀρέσται καὶ δόμεν (= λαβεῖν καὶ δοῦναι) *IG*9(1).334.32 (Locr.); ζωὴν αἰσχρὰν ἄ. *strive to save*, Pl.*Lg.*944c: rarely in bad sense, ἀρνύμενος λώβαν λύμας ἀντίποιν' ἐμᾶς *reaping* destruction as the penalty of.., E.*Hec.*1073 (lyr.). II. *take up, bear, carry* (perh. by confusion with ἄρασθαι), οὐδ' ἂν νηῦς.. ἄχθος ἄροιτο Il.20.247. (Root ϝ: *er*: *or*, cf. τιμά-ορος 'one who *exacts* atonement'.)

ἀρνυτός· εὔπνους, εὔνους, Hsch.

ἀρνῳδός, ὁ, *one who sings for the prize of a lamb*, Eust.6.26, cf. Hsch., *EM*146.55.

ἀρνών· *agnile, Gloss.*

ἄρξ, ὁ, *bear*, ἐγὼ εἰς κάτω μέρη λέων εἰμὶ καὶ εἰς ἄνω μέρη ἄ. εἰμί *OGI* 201.15 (Nubia), cf. *PMag.Lond.*121.782.

ἄρξιφος, Persian word, = *eagle*, Hsch. **ἀροάτους·** ἀβάτους, καὶ ἀνιαρούς, Id.

ἄροκλον, τό, = φιάλη, Nic.*Fr.*129 (dub.l.).

ἄρομα, ατος, τό, f.l. for ἄρωμα (q.v.), Luc.*Lex.*2, Ael.*NA*7.8, cf. *AB*450.

ἄρον, τό, *cuckoo-pint, Arum italicum*, Arist.*HA*600ᵇ11, Thphr.*HP* 1.6.10, Ph.*Bel.*89.44 (pl.), Ps.-Dsc.2.167. II. *Egyptian arum, Colocasia antiquorum*, Plin.*HN*19.96, Gal.6.650. III. = δρακόντιον, Thphr.*HP*7.12.2, Phan.ap.Ath.9.371d. IV. *Arum Dioscoridis*, ἄ. τὸ καλούμενον παρὰ Σύροις λοῦφα Dsc.2.167, cf. Gal.11.839.

ἀροπῆσαι· πατῆσαι (Cret.), Hsch. (fort. τροπῆσαι).

ἄρος [ᾰ], εος, τό, *use, profit, help*, f.l. in A.*Supp.*885, cf. Hsch., Eust.1422.19; cf. ἄρ-νυμαι. 2. = κοιλὰς ἐν αἷς ὕδωρ ἀθροίζεται ὀμβριον, Hsch. 3. = ἀκούσιον βλάβος, Id.; cf. ἀπαρές, ἀπηρής.

ἀρ-όσιμος [ᾰ], ον, (ἀρόω) *arable, fruitful*, γῆ *corn*-land, *POxy.*137.14 (vi A.D.), cf. Max.Tyr.5.4; ὀροπέδια Str.6.2.6; ἡ ἀ. Id.9.5.19, Hld. 9.5, Ph.Byz.*Mir.*1.3. II. metaph., *fit for engendering* children, S.*Ant.*569 (in form ἀρώσιμος). **–οσις**, εως, ἡ, *arable land, corn-land*, Il.9.580, Od.9.134, Thphr.*CP*3.2.2, A.R.1.826. II. *ploughing*, Arat.1055, Arist.*Mu.*399ᵇ17, Ael.*NA*13.1.

ἀροσμός, ὁ, = ἄροσις, *PTeb.*49.10.

ἀρ(ο)σπάκες· δρύες ἐπικεκομμέναι, Hsch.

ἀρ-οτήρ [ᾰ], ῆρος, ὁ, *plougher, husbandman*, Il.18.542, 23.835, Hecat.335 J., E.*El.*104, etc.: in Prose, Σκύθαι ἀροτῆρες, opp. νομάδες, Hdt.4.17, cf. 191, 1.125, 7.50. 2. as Adj., βοῦς ἀροτὴρ steer *for ploughing*, Hes.*Op.*405, Arat.132, Plu.*Pyrrh.*5, *OGI*519.21 (Asia Minor, iii A.D.), etc.; ὁλκός Nonn.*D.*3.192; τένων Orph.*H.*40.8. II. metaph., *begetter, father*, τέκνων E.*Tr.*135 (lyr.); εὐτεκνίης *IG*14. 1615. **–ότης**, ου, ὁ, = foreg., Pi.*I.*1.48, Hdt.4.2, Pherecr.130; βόες ἀ. Hp.*Art.*8, cf. Ael.*VH*5.14; Πιερίδων ἀρόται *workmen* of the Muses, i.e. *poets*, Pi.*N.*6.32; ἀ. κύματος *seaman*, Call.*Fr.*436. **–οτήσιος**, ον, *of* or *for ploughing*, ἀ. ὥρη Arat.1053. **–οτικός**, ή, όν, *capable of ploughing*, βόες Gal.19.245.

ἄρ-οτος [ᾰ], ὁ, *corn-field*, οὔτ' ἄρα ποίμνῃσιν καταΐσχεται οὔτ' ἀρότοισιν Od.9.122: metaph., Ἄρη τὸν ἀρότοις θερίζοντα βροτοὺς ἐν ἄλλοις A. *Supp.*638 (lyr.). 2. *crop*, S.*OT*270: metaph., *seed*, τέκνων ὃν ἔτεκες ἄροτον E.*Med.*1281 (lyr.); ὅσον εὐσεβίᾳ κρατοῦμεν ἄδικον ἄροτον (cj. Barnes for ἄροτρον) ἀνδρῶν Id.*Ion*1095. 3. *tillage, ploughing*, Hes.*Op.*384, 458; ζῆν ἀπ' ἀρότου live by *husbandry*, Hdt.4.46; ἄ. ἱερός ritual *ploughing*, ceremonial at Athens, Plu.2.144a: pl., Ar.*Ra.* 1034. 4. metaph., *procreation of children*, ὁ ἄ. ὁ ἐν γυναικί Pl. *Cra.*406b; παίδων ἐπ' ἀρότῳ γνησίων, in Athen. marriage-contracts, Men.720, cf. *Pk.*436, Luc.*Tim.*17; τέκνων ἀρότοισιν E.*Hyps.Fr.*1 iii 25. II. *season of tillage, seed-time*, Hes.*Op.*450, Thphr.*HP*8.1.2, Arat.267, etc.: hence, *season, year*, τὸν παρελθόντ' ἄ. S.*Tr.*69; δωδέκατος ἄ. ib.825 (lyr.). **–οτός**, ή, όν, *arable*, Theognost.*Can.*95. II. ἀροτόν· τὸν ὁλκὸν τοῦ Ἕκτορος ἢ τὸ ἀντίσταθμον A.*Fr.*270 (ap.Hsch.).

ἀροτρ-αῖος [ᾰρ], α, ον, *of corn-land, rustic*, θαλάμη *AP*7.209 (Antip.). **–ευμα**, ατος, τό, *ploughing*: metaph., *generation*, φύσεως ἀ. καινοῖς Poet.ap.Stob.1.49.46. **–εύς**, έως, ὁ, = sq., Theoc.25.1, 51, Bion *Fr.*9.8, etc. **–ευτήρ**, ῆρος, ὁ, = ἀροτήρ, ἀρούρης *AP*9.299 (Phil.); πόντου ib.242 (Antiphil.). **–εύω**, *plough*, Pherecyd.105 J., Lyc. 1072, Nic.*Th.*6, Babr.21.5. **–ήτης** (or **–ίτης**), ου, ὁ, *belonging to the plough*, βίοτος, χαλκός, *AP*9.23 (Antip.), 6.41 (Agath.). **–ιάζω**, *plough*, in Pass., *PFlor.*383.89 (iii A.D.). **–ίαμα**, ατος, τό, *ploughed land*, Sch.Ar.*Pax*1158. **–ίασις**, εως, ἡ, = sq., Lxx *Ge.*45.6, Ps.-Ptol.*Centil.*214. **–ιασμός**, ὁ, *ploughing, tillage*, Sch.Opp.*H.*2. 19. **–ιαστής**, οῦ, ὁ, *husbandman*, *EM*207.31. **–ιάω**, = ἀρόω, Call. *Dian.*161, Thphr.*HP*8.6.3, Babr.55.2, Corn.*ND*28 (Pass.). **–ιος**, ον, *of husbandry*, epith. of Apollo, Orph.*H.*34.3. **–ιόω**, = **–ιάω**, in Pass., v.l. in Lxx*Is.*7.25, cf. Ps.-Plu.*Fluv.*21.2. **–ίτης**, v. **–ήτης**.

ἀροτρο-δίαυλος [ᾰρ] [ῐ], ὁ, *plougher*, who goes backwards and forwards *as in the* δίαυλος, *AP*10.101 (Bianor). **–ειδής**, ές, *like a plough*, D.S.3.3.

ἄροτρον [ᾰ], τό, (ἀρόω) *plough*, Od.18.374; πηκτὸν ἄ. Il.10.353, cf. Thgn.1201, Pi.*P.*4.224, etc.; ἰλλομένων ἀρότρων S.*Ant.*340; ἀρότρῳ ἀναρρηγνύντες αὔλακας Hdt.2.14: pl., Ar.*Pl.*515, Mosch.*Fr.*4.6. b. ἡ ἀπ' ἀρότρου πληγή, in boxing, *right-handed* blow, Paus.6.10.2, Philostr.*Gym.*20. 2. in pl., metaph. of the *organs of generation*, Nonn.*D.*12.46, al. II. ἄροτρα· γῆ, χώρα, πλέθρα, Hsch.

ἀροτρο-πόνος [ᾰ], ον, *working with the plough*, *AP*9.274 (Phil.). **–πους**, ποδος, ὁ, *ploughshare*, Lxx*Ju.*3.31. **–φορέω**, *draw the plough*, *AP*9.347 (Leon.).

ἀρότται, οἱ, *serfs* at Syracuse, Eust.295.33.

ἄρουρα [ᾰρ] (ἀρωραῖος in Ar.*Ach.*762 is hyperdor., as shown by Aeol. ἄρουρα Sapph.*Supp.*25.11, Cypr. *a ro u ra i* (dat. sg.) *Inscr. Cypr.*135.20 H.), ἡ, (ἀρόω) *tilled* or *arable land*, Il.11.68, etc.; φυταλιῆς καὶ ἀρούρης 6.195; οὖθαρ ἀρούρης 9.141, al.; τέλσον ἀρούρης 18.544: in pl., *corn-lands, fields*, 14.122, 23.599: rare in Prose, Pl.*Ti.*22e, Arist.*Pol.*1284ᵃ30, *Inscr.Cypr.* l.c. 2. generally, *earth, ground*, ὀλίγη δ' ἦν ἀμφὶς ἄ. Il.3.115; σέο δ' ὀστέα πύσει ἄ. 4.174. 3. *land*, generally, = γῆ; πατρὶς ἄ. father-*land*, Od.1.407; ἄ. πατρία, πατρῴα, Pi.*O.*2.14, *I.*1.35. 4. *the earth*, ἐπὶ ζείδωρον ἄ. Il.8.486, Od.7.332; ἄχθος ἀρούρης Il.18.104, al. 5. metaph. of a woman as receiving seed and bearing fruit, Thgn.582, A.*Th.*754 (lyr.), S.*OT*1257, cf. *Tr.* 32; ἄ. θήλεια Pl.*Lg.*839a, cf. *Ti.*91d. II. *measure of land* in Egypt, 100 *cubits square*, Hdt.2.168, cf. 141, *OGI*90.30, *POxy.*45.12, Hecat. Abd.ap.J.*Ap.*1.22, *PRyl.*143.17 (i A.D.), etc. III. = σωρὸς σίτου σὺν ἀχύροις (Cypr.), Hsch.

ἀρουρᾰβάτης [ᾰρ] [βᾰ], ου, ὁ, *traversing the tilled land*, epith. of the Nile, Epic. in *BKT*5(1).119.

ἀρουρ-αῖος [ᾰρ], α, ον, *of* or *from the country, rural, rustic*, μῦς ἀ. *field*-vole, Hdt.2.141; σμίνθος A.*Fr.*227; ὦ παῖ τῆς ἀ. θεοῦ, of Euripides as the reputed son of a *herb*-seller, Ar.*Ra.*840; ἀ. Οἰνόμαος, of Aeschines, who played the part of Oenomaüs 'in the provinces', D. 18.242, cf. *AB*211 sq.; ἀ. λίθοι *rough* stones, *SIG*²587.21; φυτὰ ἀ. *field*-weeds, Thphr.*HP*7.6.1. **–είτης** (or **–ίτης**), ὁ, = foreg., μῦς ἀ. Babr.108.27. **–ηδόν**, τό, *surface measured in* ἄρουραι, *PRyl.* 157.5 (ii A.D.), *PStrassb.*112.10 (ii A.D.), etc. **–ιον**, τό, Dim. of ἄρουρα, *AP*11.365 (Agath.). **–ισμός**, ὁ, *measuring in* ἄρουραι, *PLond.*3.1171ᵛ(a)3 (i A.D.). **–ίτης**, v. **–είτης**.

ἀρουροπόνος [ᾰ], ον, *working in the field*, *AP*6.36, 104 (both Phil.).

ἄρους· τὰ λιβάδια, Hsch. **ἀρόχεται·** γλίχεται, ἐπιθυμεῖ, Id.

ἀρόω [ᾰ], pres. inf. ἀρώμεναι Hes.*Op.*22: fut. ἀρόσω *AP*9.740 (Gem.), –ώσω or –όσσω ib.7.175 (Antiphil.): aor. ἤροσα Hes.*Op.*485, Pi.*N.*10.26, S.*OT*1497, etc. (ἄροσε Call.*Cer.*137), Ep. inf. ἀρόσσαι A.R.3.497:—**Pass.**, pres. ἀροῦται Din.1.24: aor. ἠρόθην A.*Supp.*1007, S.*OT*1485: Ion. pf. part. ἀρηρομένος Il.18.548, Hdt.4.97:—*plough, till*, οὔτε φυτεύουσιν.. οὔτ' ἀρόωσιν Od.9.108: metaph. of poets, Μοίσαισιν ἔδωκ' ἀρόσαι gave them *work to do* (cf. ἀρότης), Pi.*N.*10.26; πόντος.. ἠρόθη δορί A. l.c. II. *sow*, ἀροῦν εἰς Ἀδώνιδος κήπους Pl. *Phdr.*276b:—metaph. in Pass., ἐν Διὸς κήποις ἀροῦσθαι.. ὄλβους S.*Fr.* 320. 2. metaph. of the man, ἀλλοτρίην ἄρουραν ἀροῦν Thgn.582; τὴν τεκοῦσαν ἤροσεν S.*OT*1497; of the mother, *IG*7.581.1 (Tanagra): —Pass., of the child, ἔνθεν αὐτὸς ἠρόθη *was begotten*, S.*OT*1485. (Root ἀρο–, cf. Lat. *arāre*, Goth. *arjan*, Lith. *árti*, etc., 'plough'.)

ἁρπάγ-δην, Adv. *hurriedly, violently*, A.R.1.1017; *greedily*, Opp. *H.*3.219, Aret.*SA*2.12. **–εύς** [πᾰ], έως, ὁ, = ἅρπαξ, Them.*Or.*21. 247a. **–ή**, ἡ, *seizure, robbery, rape*, first in Sol.4.13; ὀφλὼν ἁρπαγῆς δίκην found guilty *of rape*, A.*Ag.*534; αἰτέειν δίκας τῆς ἁ. Hdt.1.2; ἁρπαγῇ χρησαμένους ib.5; ἁρπαγὴν ποιεῖσθαι, ποιεῖν, Th.6.52, X.*Cyr.* 7.2.12; ἐφ' ἁ. τραπέσθαι Th.4.104, X.*Cyr.*4.2.25; τοῦ κρητῆρος ἡ ἁ. Hdt.3.48: pl., of a single act, συνεπρήξαντο τὰς Ἑλένης ἁ. Id.5.94, cf. A.*Th.*351 (lyr.), *Supp.*510; Καδμείων ἁ., of the Sphinx, E.*Ph.*1021 (lyr.). II. *thing seized, booty, prey*, τοῦ φθάσαντος ἁ. A.*Pers.*752; ἁ. κυσί, θηρσί, Id.*Th.*1019, E.*El.*896; ἁρπαγὴν ποιεῖσθαί τι to make *booty* of a thing, Th.8.62. III. *greediness*, X.*Cyr.*5.2.17. IV. ἐν ἁρπαγῇ σελήνης when the moon is *invisible*, *PMag.Par.*1.750. **–η**, ἡ, *hook* for drawing up buckets, etc., Men.829, Poll.6.88; *grappling-iron*, D.C.66.4, 74.11. 2. *rake*, E.*Cyc.*33. **–ιμαῖος**, α, ον, = sq., Orph.*H.*29.14, Phryn.*PS* p.6 B.; σελήνη *scarcely visible*, at close of month, Sch.Arat.735. **–ιμος**, η, ον, *ravished, stolen*, Call.*Cer.*9, *Fr.*1.46 P., *AP*11.290 (Pall.), Doroth.20. **–ιον**, τό, = κλεψύδρα 1, Alex.Aphr.*Pr.*1.95. **–μα**, ατος, τό, *booty, prey*, Lyc. 87, Lxx*Jb.*29.17, al.: in pl., ib.*Ez.*22.25. 2. ἅ. εὐτυχίας *wind-fall*, Plu.2.330d; οὐχ ἁ. οὐδ' ἕρμαιον ποιεῖσθαί τι Hld.7.20. **–μός**, ὁ, *robbery, rape*, Plu.2.12a; ἁ. ὁ γάμος ἔσται Vett.Val.122.1. 2. concrete, *prize to be grasped*, *Ep.Phil.*2.6; cf. ἅρπαγμα 2. **–ος**, ὁ, *hook*, ἅρπαγοι χεροῖν A.*Fr.*258 B:—as Adj., χερσὶν ἁρπάγοις S.*Fr.* 706.

ἁρπάζω, fut. –άξω Il.22.310, Babr.89.2, –άσω X.*Eq.Mag.*4.17, (ἀν–) E.*Ion*1303; in Att. more commonly ἁρπάσομαι Ar.*Pax*1118, *Ec.*866, *Av.*1460, X.*Cyr.*7.2.5, (ἀν–) Hdt.9.59; contr. ἁρπῶμαι, ἁρπᾷ Lxx *Le.*19.13, al.: aor. ἥρπαξα Il.3.444, Pi.*N.*10.67, *IG*4.951.11 (Epid.); Trag. and Att. ἥρπασα E.*Or.*1634, Th.6.101 (also Il.13.528, 17.62, Hdt.2.156): pf. ἥρπακα Ar.*Pl.*372, Pl.*Grg.*481a:—**Med.**, aor. ἡρπασάμην Luc.*Tim.*22, etc. (ὑφ-αρπάσαιο Ar.*Ec.*921):—**Pass.**, pf. ἥρπασμαι X.*An.*1.2.27, E.*Ph.*1079 (ἀν–): 3 plpf. ἥρπαστο Id.*El.*1041; later ἥρπαγμαι Paus.3.18.7, inf. –άχθαι Str.13.1.11: aor. 1 ἡρπάσθην

Hdt.1.1 and 4, etc., -χθην Id.2.90 (v.l.), 8.115, D.S.17.74; later, aor. 2 ἡρπάγην [ᾰ] Lyc.505, etc.: fut. ἁρπᾰγήσομαι 1*Ep.Thess.*4.17, *J.BJ*5.10.3; part. ἁρπάμενος (as if from ἅρπημι) *AP*11.59 (Maced.), Nonn.*D.*1.340, al., (ὑφ–) *AP*9.619 (Agath.):—*snatch away, carry off*, ὅτε σε πρῶτον Λακεδαίμονος ἐξ ἐρατεινῆς ἔπλεον ἁρπάξας Il.3.444; ὡς δ' ὅτε τίς τε λέων.. ἀγέλης βοῦν ἁρπάσῃ ib.17.62; τοὺς δ' αἶψ' ἁρπάξασα φέρεν πόντονδε θύελλα Od.10.48, cf. 5.416; κλέψαι τε χἀρπάσαι βίᾳ S.*Ph.*644; ἁ. τοῦ βασιλέος τὴν θυγατέρα Hdt.1.2; ἁ. [χρυσὸν] ὑπὲκ τῶν γρυπῶν Id.3.116; ἁ. καὶ φέρειν Lys.20.17: abs., *to be a robber*, ὁτιὴ 'πιώρκεις ἡρπακὼς Ar.*Eq.*428, cf. *Pl.*372; ἁρπάζειν βλέπει looks *thievish*, Men.*Epit.*181:—Pass. (or Med.), ἐκ χερῶν ἁρπάζομαι I *have* her *torn* from my arms, E.*Andr.*661. 2. *seize hastily, snatch up*, λᾶαν Il.12.445; δόρυ A.*Th.*624; τὰ ὅπλα X.*An.*6.1.8; ἁ. τινὰ μέσον *seize* him by the waist, Hdt.9.107; λίθος ἥτις τὸν σίδηρον ἁρπάζει, of the magnet, Hp.*Steril.*243: c. gen. of the part seized, ἁ. τινὰ τένοντος ποδός E.*Cyc.*400: c. gen. partit., ἁ. τούτων ἐνέτραγον Timocl.16.7: abs., ἀπογεύονται ἁρπάζοντες *greedily*, Pl.*R.*354b:—Med. in Luc. *Sacr.*3. 3. *seize, overpower, overmaster*, γλῶσσαν ἁ. φόβος A.*Th.* 259; *seize, occupy* a post, X.*An.*4.6.11; ἁρπάσαι πεῖραν *seize* an opportunity of attacking, S.*Aj.*2; ἁ. τὸν καιρόν Plu.*Phil.*15; *snap up*, ὥσπερ εὕρημα Herod.6.30. 4. *seize, adopt* a legend, of an author, Hdt.2.156. 5. *grasp with the senses*, ὀσμαὶ -όμεναι ταῖς ὀσφρήσεσιν Plu.2.647e. 6. *captivate, ravish*, Lxx *Ju.*16.9, Plu. *Ant.*28. 7. *draw up* by means of a vacuum, Simp.*in Ph.*647.28. II. *plunder*, πόλεις, τὰ ἐκ τῶν οἰκιῶν, τὴν Ἑλλάδα, etc., Th.1.5, X.*Cyr.*7.2.5, D.8.55, etc.

ἁρπάκ-τειρα, ἡ, fem. of sq., *AP*7.172 (Antip. Sid.). **-τήρ**, ῆρος, ὁ, *robber*, Il.24.262, Opp.*H.*1.373; Περσεφονείης Nonn.*D.*6.92, Jul. *Or.*2.87a. **-τήριος**, ον, = ἁρπακτικός, Lyc.157. **-τής**, οῦ, ὁ, *robber*, Call.*Epigr.*2.6, *Gloss.* **-τί**, Adv. = ἁρπάγδην, *greedily*, ἁρπακτὶ πίε *CIG*8470b (vase). **-τικός**, ή, όν, *rapacious, thievish*, Luc.*Pisc.* 34, Eun.*Hist.*p.243 D.: c. gen., ἁ. πυρός *readily catching* fire, Dsc.1.73. Adv. -κῶς, gloss on ἁρπαλέως, *EM*148.6, Hsch. **-τός**, ή, όν, *gotten by rapine, stolen*, Hes.*Op.*320. 2. *to be caught*, i.e. *to be got by chance, hazardous*, ib.684. **-τύς**, ύος, ἡ, Ion. for ἁρπαγή, Call.*Ap.*95.

ἅρπαλα· ἁρπακτικά, Hsch.

ἁρπάλᾰγος [πᾰ], ὁ, *hunting implement*, Opp.*C.*1.153.

ἁρπᾰλ-έος, α, ον, Ep. Adj., (ἁρπάζω): *devouring, consuming*, νοῦσος *IPE*2.167.3 (Panticapaeum); *greedy*, παλάμη *AP*9.576 (Nicarch.); ἁ. καὶ οἷον δὴ οὖν ἀεὶ τῶν ὀθνείων ἐφίεσθαι Agath.4.13: elsewh. only in Adv., *greedily, eagerly*, ἦ τοι ὁ πῖνε καὶ ἦσθε.. ἁρπαλέως Od.6.250, cf. 14.110; δέξεται ἁρπαλέως Thgn.1046; ἁ. εὕδειν *gladly, pleasantly*, Mimn.12.8; ἁ. ἐπεχήρατο *vehemently*, A.R.4.56; once in Ar., ἁ. ἁραμένη *Lys.*331 (lyr.). II. *attractive, alluring, charming*, κέρδεα Od.8.164; ἁ. ἔρως, opp. ἀπηνής, Thgn.1353; ἄνθεα ἥβης ἁρπαλέα Mimn.1.4; δόσιν gift *to be eagerly seized*, Pi.*P.*8.65, cf. 10.62. **-ίζω**, *catch up, be eager to receive*, τινὰ κωκυτοῖς A.*Th.*243:—also in Med., Hsch. 2. *exact greedily*, A.*Eu.*983 (lyr.). 3. ἁ. τὰ μετέωρά σου *settle* your outstanding transactions, *PLond.ined.* 1561. **-ιμος**, η, ον, = ἁρπακτός, προσφιλής, Hsch.

ἁρπάμενος, η, ον, v. ἁρπάζω.

ἁρπάναι· μάνδραι βοσκημάτων, Hsch.

ἅρπαξ, ἄγος, ὁ, ἡ, (ἁρπάζω) *robbing, rapacious*, Ar.*Eq.*137, v.l. in *Fr.*628, X.*Mem.*3.1.6; λύκοι Lyc.1309 (v.l. Ἄτρακας): also c. Subst. neut., ἅρπαγι χείλει *AP*9.272 (Bianor): Sup. ἁρπαγίστατος Pl.Com. 57. II. mostly as Subst., 1. ἅρπαξ, ἡ, *rapine*, Hes.*Op.*356. 2. ἅρπαξ, ὁ, *robber, peculator*, τῶν δημοσίων Ar.*Nu.*351; ὁ μὲν κλέπτης ὁ δ' ἅ. Myrtil.4; πάντες εἰσὶν ἅρπαγες (sc. οἱ Ὠρώπιοι) Xeno 1. 3. species of *wolf*, Opp.*C.*3.304. 4. *grappling-iron*, used in sea-fights, App.*BC*5.118, Moschio ap.Ath.5.208d; *flesh-hook*, J.*AJ*8.3.7.

ἁρπάξανδρος, α, ον, *snatching away men*, A.*Th.*776, restored by Herm. (in fem. form ἁρπαξάνδραν) for ἀναρπ–.

ἁρπαξίβιος [ξῐ], ον, *living by rapine*, στρατιῶται Archestr.*Fr.*61.

ἁρπαξομίλης [ῑ], ὁ, = ὁ ἁρπάζων τὰς ἀφροδισίους ὁμιλίας, *Com. Adesp.*949.

ἅρπᾰσ-ις, εως, ἡ, = ἁρπαγμός, Phryn.*PS*p.65 B. **-μα**, ατος, τό, Att. form of ἅρπαγμα, Pl.*Lg.*906d, Men.*Epit.*542; prob. in Aeschin. 3.222, cf. Plu.*Cat.Ma.*13, *IG*12(7).123 (Amorgos). **-μός**, = ἁρπαγμός, Plu.2.644a. **-ος**, ὁ, *a bird of prey*, Ant.Lib.20.6. **-τικός**, ή, όν, *rapacious*, like birds of prey, Arist.*Phgn.*813ᵃ19; κέρδους Phld. *Oec.*p.69 J.

ἁρπάστιον, Dim. of sq. 2, Arr.*Epict.*2.5.19.

ἁρπαστός, ή, όν, *carried away* (as by a storm), *AP*12.167 (Mel.) (but ἁρπασταί, nom. pl. of **ἁρπαστής**, ὁ, *ravisher*, is prob. l.). 2. neut. as Subst., ἁρπαστόν, τό, *handball*, Ath.1.14f, Artem.1.55.

ἀρπεδ-ής, ές, *flat, level*, Nic.*Th.*420. **-ίζω**· ὁμαλίζω, ἐδαφίζω, Hsch. **-όεις**, εσσα, εν, = ἀρπεδής, Antim.Col.2 P. (From ἀρι-πέδον acc. to Did.ap.*EM*148.9, Hdn.Gr.2.247, but the best codd. of Nic. l.c. have ἀρπ–; cf. ἐρπεδίζω.)

ἁρπεδον-άπται, ῶν, οἱ, *rope-fasteners*, applied to Egyptian geometers, [Democr.]299. **-η**, ἡ, *cord*, for binding or snaring game, X.*Cyr.*1.6.28, *AP*9.244 (Apollonid.). 2. *yarn* of which cloth is made, Hdt.3.47, Aristias 2 (ap.Poll.7.31), *AP*6.160 (Antip. Sid.); *silk-worm's thread*, Paus.6.26.8; *bow-string*, *AP*5.193 (Posidipp. or Asclep.). II. ἁρπεδόναι· τῶν ἀμαυρῶν ἄστρων σύγχυσις (i.e. band of stars connecting Pisces), Hsch., cf. Vitr.9.5.3. **-ίζω**, *snare with a* ἁρπεδόνη, Hsch.: also, = λωποδυτέω, Id.

ἁρπεδών, όνος, ἡ, = ἁρπεδόνη, *AP*6.207 (Arch.), J.*AJ*3.7.2, Jul. *Gal.*135c.

ἅρπεζα, ἡ, *hedge*, Nic.*Th.*393, 647 (pl.) (expl. by Sch. as *foot-hill*): —also **ἅρπεζος**, ἡ, *BCH*46.405 (Mylasa).

ἀρπετόν· ἀκόμιστον, Hsch.

ἅρπη, ἡ, unknown *bird of prey*, prob. *shearwater*, [Ἀθήνη] ἅρπῃ ἐϊκυῖα τανυπτέρυγι λιγυφώνῳ Il.19.350; a *sea-bird* acc. to Arist.*HA* 609ᵃ24, cf. Ael.*NA*2.47, Dionys.*Av.*1.4 (describing the *Lämmergeier*). II. *sickle*, = δρέπανον, Hes.*Op.*573, S.*Fr.*424; καλαμητόμος A.R.4.987: hence, the *scimitar* of Perseus, Pherecyd.11 J., cf. E.*Ion* 192 (lyr., pl.). 2. *elephant-goad*, Ael.*NA*13.22. 3. metaph. of a hippopotamus' *tooth*, Nic.*Th.*567. 4. *bill-hook*, J.*AJ*14.15.5. 5. kind of *fish*, Marc.Sid.22. (Cf. Lat. *sarpio, sarpo*, etc.)

ἅρπιξ· εἶδος ἀκάνθης (Cypr.), Hsch.; cf. ἄπριξ.

ἁρπίς, ῖδος (but nom. pl. ἁρπίδες *EM*148.36, nom. sg. ἅρπις Suid.), ἡ, = κρηπίς, Call.*Fr.*66.

ἅρπισαι· αἱμασιαί, ἢ τάφρους, Hsch. **ἀρπίσθος**· φοῖνιξ· καὶ **ἀρπίαθος**, Id.

Ἅρπυιαι, (Ἀρεπ– on a vase from Aegina, *Arch.Zeit.*40.197, cf. *EM* 138.21, and prob. ἀρέπυιαι ἀνηρέψαντο shd. be read in Od. ll. cc.; v. ἀνερείπομαι) αἱ, *the Snatchers*, a name used in Od. to personify *whirlwinds* or *hurricanes* (so τυφῶσι καὶ ἁρπυίαις Ph.1.333); ἅρπυιαι ἀνηρείψαντο Od.1.241, 20.77: acc. pl., Hes.*Th.*267; πτηνά τ' Ἁρπυιῶν γένη Anaxil.22.5, cf. A.R.2.188: rarely in sg., Euph.113: as pr. n., Ἅρπυια Ποδάργη, mother of the horses of Achilles, Il.16.150; also name of one of Actaeon's hounds, A.*Fr.*245; cf. ἁρπυίας· ἁρπακτικοὺς κύνας, Hsch. 2. as Adj., ἁ. σκύλακες *Inscr.Perg.*203. (A quasi-participial form.)

Ἁρπυιόγουνος, ον, *Harpy-legged*, ἀηδόνες, of the Sirens, Lyc.653.

Ἄρπυς, ὁ, = Ἔρως, Parth.*Fr.*9 (Aeol. acc. to Hsch.).

ἀρρ–, in words beginning with ρ, ρ is doubled after a Prefix.

ἀρρᾰβάσσω, = ῥαβάσσω, and **ἀρράβαξ**, ὁ, = ὀρχηστής, Paus.Gr.*Fr.* 74, Hsch.

ἀρράβδωτος, ον, *not ribbed*, Arist.*HA*528ᵃ26, *Fr.*304; of columns, *not fluted*, *IG*1.322.55 (ἀρά–), 65.

ἀρράβη· θύρα, οἷον γέρρον, Hsch.

ἀρρᾰβών, ῶνος, ὁ, *earnest-money, caution-money*, deposited by the purchaser and forfeited if the purchase is not completed, ἁ. δοῦναί τινος Is.8.20, cf. Arist.*Pol.*1259ᵃ12, Stilpo ap.D.L.2.118, *BGU*446.18 (ii A.D.): pl., *deposits* required from public contractors, *IPE*1².32*B* 34 (Olbia). 2. generally, *pledge, earnest*, τὴν τέχνην ἔχοντες ἀ. τοῦ ζῆν Antiph.123.6; τοῦ δυστυχεῖν.. ἀ. ἔχειν Men.697, cf. Lxx *Ge.* 38.17, 18, *Ep.Eph.*1.14. 3. *present, bribe*, Plu.*Galb.*17. (Semitic, prob. Phoenician, word, Hebr. *'ērābōn*: freq. written ἀραβών, *UPZ* 67.14 (ii B.C.), *Ep.Eph.* l.c., etc.) II. ἀρραβών· πρόδομα, καὶ ἄγκιστρον, Hsch.

ἀρρᾰβωνίζεται· ἀρραβῶνι δίδοται, Hsch.

ἀρρᾰγάδωτος, ον, (ῥαγάς) *without chink*, Apollod.*Poliorc.*157.1.

ἀρρᾰγής, ές, (ῥήγνυμι) *unbroken*, ὀστέον Hp.*VC*12; βάσεις, ἁρμοί, *IG*7.3073.103, 117 (Lebad.); τάξις Ael.*Tact.*13.3; φάλαγξ Arr.*Tact.* 12.4; σίδηρος Plu.*Demetr.*21; τὸ ἀ. *unbroken surface*, Arist.*Pr.*899ᵇ 20. 2. *that cannot be rent* or *broken*, ξύλα Thphr.*HP*5.5.6; τείχεα D.P.1006: metaph., πόνος παιδείας Ph.1.471 (Sup.); νοῦς Max.Tyr. 41.2; ὁμολογία *Anatolian Studies* p.39 (Sardes, v A.D.), cf. *PLond.* 1731.34. II. ἀ. ὄμμα an eye *not bursting into tears*, S.*Fr.*736.

ἀρραγίδες· στήμονες, κρόκαι, Hsch.

ἀρράζω, = ἀράζω, Ael.*NA*5.51, D.H.16.2.

ἀρραθάγησεν· ἐψόφησεν, Hsch.

ἄρραιστος, ον, *unhurt*, Sch.Od.13.259.

ἄρραντος, ον, (ῥαίνω) *unwatered, unwet*, Arat.868, Str.11.7.5.

ἄρρᾰτος, ον, = σκληρός, ἀμετάστροφος, Pl.*Cra.*407d; ἅ. καὶ μνήμων Id.*R.*535c; θάρσος prob. l. in Id.*Ax.*365a; ἀνέρος ἀρράτοιο Euph. 24.

ἀρρᾰφής, ές, = sq. 2, κεφαλαί Arat.*Iatr.*ap.Poll.2.38.

ἄρρᾰφος, ον, (ῥάπτω) *without seam*, *Ev.Jo.*19.23, J.*AJ*3.7.4. 2. *without sutures*, Gal.*UP*11.19.

ἀρραχθές· ἀσύνετον, Hsch.

ἄρρεκτος, ον, v. ἄρεκτος.

ἀρρεν–, see also ἀρσεν–.

ἀρρενική, ἡ, and **ἀρρενικόν**, τό, v. ἀρσενικόν.

ἀρρενικός, ή, όν, (ἄρρην) *male*, σωμάτιον *POxy.*3717 (i A.D.); ᾠόν *PMag.Lond.*121.522, cf. Luc.*DDeor.*16.1; opp. θηλυκός, *IG*14.872.5 (Cumae): less Att. form ἀρσενικός Call.*Epigr.*27, *POxy.*38.7 (i A.D.), *AP*5.115 (Marc. Arg.); λίβανον ἀ. *PMag.Par.*1.906; cf. λίβανος. 2. *virile*, M.Ant.11.18 (Comp.); *of masculine gender*, Plu.2.1011c; πτῶσις Ph.1.294; (ἀρσ–) D.T.634.17, etc. Adv. -κῶς, opp. θηλυκῶς, Phld. *Piet.*12, cf. Ath.13.590b, (ἀρσ–) Str.8.3.11.

ἀρρενο-γᾰμέω, = τοὺς ἄρρενας γαμεῖν, Anon.*in EN*428.16. **-γονέω**, *beget* or *bear male children*, Thphr.*HP*9.18.5, Ph.1.262. **-γονία**, ἡ, *begetting* or *bearing of male children*, Arist.*HA*585ᵇ11. **-γόνος**, ον, *begetting* or *bearing male children*, ib.573ᵇ32, 585ᵇ13; αἱ σμικραὶ κοτυληδόνες ἀρσ. Hp.*Steril.*230; of drugs, *promoting the conception of males*, Dsc.3.140. 2. ἀρρενογόνον, τό, = φύλλον III, *dog's mercury, Mercurialis perennis*, Thphr.*HP*9.18.5, Dsc.3.125, Plin.*NH*26.162. **-κοίτης**, ου, ὁ, *sodomite*, *AP*9.686; (ἀρσ–) 1*Ep.Cor.*6.9. **-κυέω**, *bear male children*, Str.4.6.8. **-μᾰνής**, ές, *mad after males*, of men, *Cat.Cod.Astr.*8(2).43, v.l. in Heph.*Astr.*1.1. **-μίκτης**, ου, ὁ, = ἀρρενοκοίτης, (ἀρσ–) Man.4.590. **-μιξία**, ἡ, *sodomy*, S.E.*P.* 1.152, 3.199.

ἀρρενόομαι, *become a man, do the duties of one*, Luc.*Am.*19; of a woman, πλέον τῆς φύσεως ἀ. Ph.2.328; φρόνημα ἠρρενωμένον ib.53;

Astrol., of stars (cf. ἄρρην), *become masculine*, Heph.*Astr.*1.2, Ptol. *Tetr.*20.

ἀρρενόπαις, παιδος, ὁ, ἡ, *of male children*, γόνος (ἀρσ–) *APl.*4.134 (Mel.); γονή (ἀρσ–) *Epigr.Gr.*218. II. ἀ. Κύπρις, = *paedicatio*, *AP* 5.55 (Diosc.).

ἀρρεν-οπίπης [ῐ], ου, ὁ, *one who looks lewdly on males*, Eust.827.30.

ἀρρενο-ποιέω, *make masculine*, Ptol.*Tetr.*69. **–ποιός**, όν, *favouring the generation of males*, Ael.*NA*7.27. **–πρεπής**, ές, *befitting men, manly*, Aristid.Quint.2.13.

ἀρρενότης, ητος, ἡ, *manhood, manliness*, *Stoic.*3.66, Andronic. Rhod.p.575 M., Hierocl.p.63 A.; *masculinity*, opp. θηλύτης, Dam. *Pr.*198.

ἀρρενο-τοκέω, *bear male children*, Arist.*HA*574^{a}1, *GA*765^{a}24, Dsc. *Eup.*2.96. **–τοκία**, ἡ, *bearing of male children*, Aët.16.36. **–τόκιον**, τό, *drug promoting conception of males*, Dsc.*Eup.*2.96. **–τόκος**, ον, *bearing male children*, Arist.*GA*723^{a}27.

ἀρρενουργός, όν, = ἀρρενοποιός, Nicom.ap.Phot.*Bibl.*p.144 B.

ἀρρενο-φανής, ές, *masculine-looking*, Lyd.*Mag.*3.62. **–φθορία**, ἡ, = ἀρρενομιξία, Arg.A.*Th.*, Sch.Luc.*Am.*36. **–φρων**, ον, gen. ονος, (φρήν) *of manly mind*, Suid. s. v. Δεββώρα.

ἀρρέντερος, v. ἄρσην.

ἀρρεν-ώδης, ες, *brave*. Adv. –δῶς Lxx 2*Ma.*10.35. **–ωνῠμέω**, (ὄνομα) *use in masculine gender, change into it*, of a feminine noun, Eust.560.15. **–ωπία**, ἡ, *manly look, manliness*, Pl.*Smp.*192a, Zeno *Stoic.*1.58. **–ωπός**, όν, also ἡ, όν Luc.*Fug.*27: (ὤψ):—*masculine-looking, manly*, Pl.*Lg.*802e; γυναῖκες Arist.*GA*747^{a}1, cf. Sor. 1.35, Ruf.ap.Orib.*Inc.*2.15; εὐμορφία Luc.*Scyth.*11; τὸ ἀ., = ἀρρενωπία, D.S.4.6. 2. of things, *befitting a man, manly*, στολή Ael.*NA* 2.11; τὸ ἀ. τῆς ψυχῆς *manliness*, Chor.*Lyd.*8. Adv. –πῶς *Gloss.*:— irreg. fem. **–ωπάς**, άδος, ἡ, = ἀνδρόγυνος, Cratin.389, cf. Hsch.

ἀρρεπής, ές, of a balance, *inclining to neither side*: hence, *without weight* or *influence*, ἀρρεπὲς πρὸς εὐδαιμονίαν Plu.2.1070a, cf. 1015a; *insignificant*, *Stoic.*3.35; *firm, unwavering*, of ἰσότης, ib.159, Dam. *Pr.*283. Adv. –πῶς Ph.1.409, Hierocl.p.31 A.:—also **–πί**, Hdn.*Epim.* 256.

ἀρρευμάτιστος [μᾰ], ον, *arresting discharge, astringent, styptic*, Gal.13.77. II. *not accompanied by discharge, free from discharge*, Ruf.ap.Orib.8.24.54, Aët.7.38, 12.68.

ἄρρευστος, ον, *without flux* or *change*, Dam.ap.Simp. *in Ph.*644.32, Eustr. *in EN*50.25. II. *not flowing*, Sch.A.*Ch.*185 (v.l. ἄγευστος); *not fusible*, Ps.-Democr.Alch.p.45 B.

ἀρρεψία, ἡ, *equilibrium* of the soul, *absence of bias*, D.L.9.74, S.E. *P.*1.190, etc.

ἀρρήδην, Adv. *negatively*, οὐ κατατιθέμενος τῇ ῥήσει, Hsch., cf. Poll.2.129.

ἄρρηκτος, ον, (ῥήγνυμι) *unbroken, not to be broken*, δεσμὸν... χρύσεον ἄ. Il.15.20, cf. 13.37; τεῖχος χάλκεον ἄ. Od.10.4, cf. Il.14.56; ἵν' ἄ. πόλις εἴη 21.447; ἄ. νεφέλην 20.150; πτολέμοιο πεῖραρ... ἄρρηκτόν τ' ἄλυτόν τ' 13.360; φωνή τ' ἄ. 2.490; ἄ. πέδαι A.*Pr.*6; σάκος Id.*Supp.* 190, S.*Aj.*576; ἄρρηκτος φυάν, i.e. *invulnerable*, Pi.*I.*6(5).47; δέρμα ἄ. ἐπὶ τοῦ νώτου, of the crocodile, Hdt.2.68, cf. Arist.*HA*503^{a}10; ἄ. χάλαζαι Theoc.22.16: metaph., θυμός Id.25.112; of land, *unploughed*, *Tab.Heracl.*1.19. Adv. –τως, ἔχειν Ar.*Lys.*182; *with unbroken courage*, Phld.*Mort.*39.

ἀρρήμων, ον, gen. ονος, *without speech, silent*, Poll.2.128.

ἄρρην, v. ἄρσην.

ἀρρηνεῖν· λοιδορεῖν, Hsch.; cf. sq.

ἀρρηνής, ές, *fierce, savage*, of dogs, Theoc.25.83, Hsch.

ἄρρης, late form for ἄρρην, *PMag.Par.*1.361; cf. ἄρσης.

ἀρρῆσαι· ἀβουλῆσαι, ἀπαγορεῦσαι, Hsch.

ἀρρησία, ἡ, (ἄρρητος) *silence*, Nicopho 23.

ἀρρητο-ποιέω, *practise unmentionable vice*, Artem.1.79. **–ποιός**, όν, *practising such vice*, Anon. *in EN*172.29. II. pedantically, *celebrating mysteries*, Luc.*Lex.*10.

ἀρρητόρευτος, ον, *not taught rhetoric*, Tz.*H.*11.217; *unworthy of an orator*, Sopat.Rh. in Rh.8.58 W.

ἄρρητος, ον, also η, ον E.*Hec.*201:—*unspoken*, ἔπος προέηκεν ὅ πέρ τ' ἄρρητον ἄμεινον Od.14.466; ἄνδρες... ῥητοί τ' ἄ. τε Hes.*Op.*4; ἔστω ἄ. τὰ εἰρημένα Pl.*Smp.*189b, etc., cf. Aeschin.3.217; οὐκ ἐπ' ἀρρήτοις γε τοῖς ἐμοῖς λόγοις not *without* warning *spoken* by me, S.*Ant.*556; ἄ. κατελῆ φυλάξομαι Id.*El.*1012. Adv. –τως, σιγᾶν Arist.*Fr.*44 codd. (ἀρρήκτως Reiske, ἀρράτως Bernays). II. *that cannot be spoken* or *expressed*, ἀδιανόητον καὶ ἄ. καὶ ἄφθεγκτον καὶ ἄλογον Pl.*Sph.*238c: hence, *unspeakable, immense*, App.*BC*3.4; ἐπιθυμία Phld.*Ir.*p.50 W.; εὐχαριστία Id.*Lib.*p.51 O. III. *not to be spoken*: hence, 1. *not to be divulged*, ἱοργίαι, ἱρά, Hdt.5.83, 6.135; σέβας ἀρρήτων ἱερῶν Ar. *Nu.*302; ἄ. σφάγια E.*IT*41; ἄ. ἀβακχεύτοισιν εἰδέναι Id.*Ba.*472; διδακτά τε ἄρρητά τ', i.e. things profane and *sacred*, S.*OT*301; ἄ. κόρη the maid *whom none may name* (i.e. Persephone), E.*Fr.*63, cf. *Hel.* 1307; ἀρρήτων θέσμια, sc. of Demeter and Persephone, *IG*3.713. 6. 2. *unutterable, horrible*, δεῖπνα S.*El.*203 (lyr.); λῶβη E.*Hec.*200 (lyr.); ἄρρητ' ἀρρήτων 'deeds without a name', S.*OT*465 (lyr.). 3. *shameful to be spoken*, ῥητόν τ' ἄ. τ' ἔπος Id.*OC*1001, cf. *Aj.*214 (lyr.), 773; ῥητὰ καὶ ἄ. ὀνομάζων 'dicenda tacenda locutus', D.18.122; πάντας ἡμᾶς ῥητὰ καὶ ἄ. κακὰ ἐξεῖπον Id.21.79. Adv. –τως D.L.7. 187. IV. of numbers, ἄρρητα, τά, *irrationals, surds*, opp. ῥητά, Pl.*Hp.Ma.*303b, cf. *R.*546c.

ἀρρητ-ουργέω, = ἀρρητοποιέω, *An.Ox.*3.188. **–ουργία**, ἡ, *filthy lewdness*, Jul.*Or.*7.210d.

ἀρρητο-φόρια, τά, = ἀρρηφόρια, Sch.Luc.*DMeretr.*2.1. **–φόρος**, v. ἀρρηφόρος.

ἀρρη-φορέω, *serve as* ἀρρηφόρος, Ar.*Lys.*642, Din.*Fr.*6.4, *IG*2. 453^{b}14. II. applied to the service of the Jewish High Priest, Ph.1.377. **–φορία**, ἡ, *procession of* ἀρρηφόροι, Lys.21.5. **–φόρια**, τά, *festival at which this took place*, prob. for foreg. in Sch.Ar.*Lys.* 642, *EM*149.13. **–φόρος**, ἡ, at Athens, *maiden who carried the symbols* of Athena Polias in procession, Paus.1.27.3, Plu.2.839c, etc. (wrongly expl. by Gramm. as shortd. for ἀρρητο–: ἀρρη–, = ἔρση, q.v.; cf. Ἐρσηφόροι).

ἀρρῑγ-ής, ές, = sq. Adv. –γέως Hp.*Acut.*29. **–ητος**, ον, *not shivering, daring*, *AP*6.219 (Antip.). **–ος**, ον, *insensible to cold*, Arist.*Sens.*438^{a}22 (Sup.). II. *without shivering*, Aret.*SD*1.14.

ἄρρῑζος, ον, *without roots*, Arist.*Resp.*478^{b}31, Thphr.*CP*3.5. 4. II. metaph., ῥῆμα ἄ. ἐκ τῆς ὀργῆς *not rooted* in..., Them.*Or.* 8.111b; ἄ. καὶ ἀνέστια ἐᾶν Str.1.2.18.

ἀρρίζω· ἀράζω, *AB*1452.

ἀρρίζωτος [ῑ], ον, *not rooted*, Arist.*HA*548^{a}5, Thphr.*CP*3.7.3.

ἄρρῑνον, τό, = νᾶπυ, Nic.*Fr.*84 (s. v. l.); cf. ἀνάρρινον.

ἀρρίπιστος [ῑ], ον, *not cooled* or *ventilated*, Gal.10.745.

ἄρρῑς, ῑνος, ὁ, ἡ, *without power of scenting*, X.*Cyn.*3.2 (with v.l. ἄρινες). II. *noseless*, Str.2.1.9.

ἀρριχάομαι, v. ἀναρριχάομαι.

ἀρρῑχίς, ίδος, ἡ, = sq., Ath.4.139c.

ἄρρῑχος, ἡ, *wicker basket*, Ar.*Av.*1309, Thphr.*CP*1.7.2: masc. in *AP*7.410 (Diosc.):—also **ἄρσῑχος**, D.S.20.41, *Marm.Par.*55, *IG*12 (7).162.22,42 (Amorgos).

ἄρροια, ἡ, *amenorrhoea*, Hp.*Loc.Hom.*47.

ἄρροιζος, ον, *without whistling*, Eust.1538.31.

ἄρρυ, a cry of boatmen, Theognost.*Can.*161: ἀρῦ, Eust.855.23.

ἀρρυθμ-έω, *to be out of rhythm*, ῥυθμῷ ἀ. Pl.*Lg.*802e. **–ία**, ἡ, *want of rhythm or proportion*, Pl.*R.*401a. **–ιστος**, ον, *not reduced to form, unorganized*, Arist.*Metaph.*1014^{b}27, *Ph.*193^{a}11. II. of stone, *undressed, rough-hewn*, Plot.5.8.1.

ἀρρυθμοπότης, ου, ὁ, *immoderate drinker*, Timo 4.2.

ἄρρυθμος, ον, of sounds, *unrhythmical*, opp. εὔρυθμος, Pl.*R.*400d; λέξις... μήτ' ἔμμετρος μήτ' ἄ. Arist.*Rh.*1408^{b}22. Adv. –μως, βαδίζειν *step out of time*, Alex.263.2; *ungracefully*, Plu.*Ant.*29. II. metaph., *in undue measure*, E.*Hipp.*529 (lyr.); *ill-proportioned*, σώματα X. *Mem.*3.10.11; of persons, ἄ. ἐν τοῖς συγγράμμασιν Phld.*Rh.*2.135 S.

ἀρρύπαντος [ῠ], ον, *unsoiled*, Eust.598.43. Adv. –τως, gloss on καθαρῶς, Tz. ad Hes.*Op.*337.

ἄρρῠπος, ον, *clean*, δίαιτα Hierocl. *in CA*17 p.459 M.

ἄρρυπτος, ον, *unwashen*, Nic.*Al.*469.

ἀρρύπωτος [ῠ], ον, = ἀρρύπαντος, dub. l. in Sch.A.*Pers.*614.

ἀρρῠσίαστος, ον, *not carried off as a hostage*, A.*Supp.*610; *not liable to distraint*, D.H.6.41.

ἀρ(ρ)ύσιος, ον, = ἀρρυσίαστος, *Schwyzer* 366 *A*3 (Tolophon, iii B.C.).

ἀρρύσωτος, ον, = sq., Sor.1.88.

ἀρρῠτίδωτος [ῐ], ον, *unwrinkled*, *AP*5.12 (Phld.), 6.252 (Antiphil.), Dsc.3.102, 4.122, Sor.1.56.

ἀρρωδέω, ἀρρωδίη, Ion. for ὀρρωδέω, ὀρρωδία.

ἀρρώξ, ῶγος, ὁ, ἡ, *without cleft* or *breach, unbroken*, γῆ S.*Ant.*251: also c. Subst. neut., ὅπλοις ἀρρῶξιν, like ἀρρήκτοις, Id.*Fr.*156.

ἀρρωστ-έω, *to be unwell*, Heraclit.58, X.*Mem.*3.11.10, D.19.124: c. acc. cogn., ἀρρωστίην, ἀρρώστημα, Hp.*Coac.*579, Arist.*Rh.*1372^a 28. **–ημα**, ατος, τό, *illness, sickness*, Hp.*Flat.*9, D.2.21, 26.26, Arist.*PA*671^{b}9: pl., of *epidemics*, *SIG*943.6 (Cos, iii B.C.). 2. moral *infirmity*, Plu.*Nic.*28. 3. Stoic, = νόσημα (of σῶμα or ψυχή) μετ' ἀσθενείας συμβαῖνον, *Stoic.*3.103, cf. Chrysipp.ib.121. **–ηματικός**, ή, όν, *sickly*, Vett.Val.68.17. **–ήμων**, ον, gen. ονος, = ἄρρωστος, Eup.63. **–ία**, ἡ, *weakness, sickness*, Hp.*VM*6, etc.: pl., Arist.*EN* 1115^{a}2, *SIG*731.7 (Tomi, i B.C.): esp. *lingering ailment, bad state of health*, Phryn.*PS*p.10 B.; ἀ. τοῦ ἀδικεῖν Pl.*R.*359b. 2. *moral weakness*, D.*Prooem.*53; *loss of morale*, Th.7.47; ἀ. τις διανοίας Arist. *Ph.*253^{a}33: c. gen., ἀ. τοῦ στρατεύειν *lack of eagerness* to serve, Th. 3.15, cf. Phryn.*PS*p.10 B. **–ος**, ον, (ῥώννυμι) *weak, sickly*, Arist. *HA*634^{b}14, Plu.2.465c. Adv. –τως, ἔχειν Aeschin.2.14, cf. D.H.7. 12; διακεῖσθαι Isoc.19.20. 2. in moral sense, *weak, feeble*, τὴν ψυχὴν X.*Ap.*30, cf. *Oec.*4.2 (Comp.). 3. ἀρρωστότερος ἐς τὴν μισθοδοσίαν *remiss* in payment, Th.8.83. [ἄρωστος *AP*11.206 (Lucill.).]

ἄρσαι, ἄρσον, ἄρσαντες, ἀρσάμενος, v. ἀραρίσκω.

ἄρσακες· οἱ βασιλεῖς Περσῶν, Hsch.

ἀρσενάκανθον, = γλήχων, Ps.-Dsc.3.31.

ἀρσενίκιον, τό, Dim. of sq., Eust.913.59.

ἀρσενικόν, τό, *yellow orpiment*, Arist.*Pr.*966^{b}28, Thphr.*Lap.*40 (ἀρρεν–), Dsc.5.104, Str.15.2.14, Lyc.ap.Orib.8.25.15:—also ἀρρενική, ἡ, Gall.12.212. (Cf. Hebr. *zarnīq.*)

ἀρσενικός, v. ἀρρενικός.

ἀρσένιον, τό, Dim. of ἄρσην, *male child*, *PGiss.*77.9 (ii A.D.).

ἀρσένιος, = ἀρσενικός, *IG*5(2).498 (Teuthis, iii A.D.).

ἀρσενο-γενής, ές, *male*, γένος A.*Supp.*818 (lyr.). **–θηλυς**, υ, gen. εος, *hermaphrodite, of both sexes*, Plu.2.368c; Pythag. epith. of unity, *Theol.Ar.*5:—also **ἀρρενόθηλυς**, Orph.*Fr.*56, Porph.ap.Eus. *PE*3.11, Man.5.140; of a vine twining about a wild fig, D.S.8 *Fr.*23. **–θῡμος**, ον, *man-minded*, Procl.*H.*7.3, Nonn.*D.*34. 352. **–κοίτης**, v. ἀρρενοκοίτης. **–μίκτης**, v. ἀρρενομίκτης. **–μορφος**, ον, *of masculine form* or *look*, Orph.*H.*36. 7. **–πληθὴς** ἑσμός *crowding* swarm *of men*, A.*Supp.*29 (anap.).

ἀρσέν-ωμα, ατος, τό, *seed of the male*, Sch.Opp.*H*.1.494. **-ωπή**, = σταφὶς ἀγρία, Ps.-Dsc.4.152.

ἄρσην, ὁ, ἡ, ἄρσεν, τό, gen. ἄρσενος, Ep., Ion., and Trag.: Att. **ἄρρην** *IG*2.678*B*55, Pl.*Smp*.191c, etc.: Aeol., Cret., Epid., and Hdt. **ἔρσην**, q.v.; ἀρσ– prevails in Lxx and *NT*, ἀρρ– is more common in Pap. (exc. Pap. Mag.): nom. **ἄρσης** *IG*5(1).364.10 (Lacon.), *POxy*.465.147 (ii A.D.):—*male*, μήτε τις οὖν θήλεια θεὸς.. μήτε τις ἄρσην Il.8.7; βοῦν.. ἄρσενα 7.315; ἄρσενες ἵπποι 23.377, etc.; ἄρσην σπορά E.*Tr*.503; νηδύς Id.*Ba*.527 (lyr.) (of the birth of Bacchus); γονή Hp.*Genit*.7: ἄρσην, ὁ, or ἄρσεν, τό, *the male*, A.*Ag*.861, *Supp*. 393 (lyr.), Pl.*Lg*.665c, *Smp*.191c, etc.; Ἀπόλλωνι.. θῆλυ καὶ ἄρσεν ..προσέρδειν *IG*12(8).358 (Thasos, v B.C.); οἱ ἄρσενες *the male sex*, Th.2.45; τὸ ἄρσεν A.*Eu*.737. 2. *masculine*, Id.*Supp*.951; φρένες E.*Or*.1204: metaph., *mighty*, κτύπος ἄρσην πόντου S.*Ph*. 1455 (lyr.); Ἀχέροντος ἄρσενας χοάς Id.*Fr*.480.3; ἄρσην βοή Ar.*Th*. 125 (lyr.); ἄ. φθόγγοι Aristid.Quint.2.12; of plants, *robust, coarse*, opp. θῆλυς (*tender, delicate*), Thphr.*HP*3.9.3, cf. 2.2.6, Dsc.3.1, al., S.*Tr*.1196. 3. of gender of nouns, *masculine*, ὀνόματα Ar.*Nu*. 682. 4. of sex in plants, ἀπὸ τοῦ ἄρρενος τοῖς θήλεσι βοήθεια Thphr. *HP*2.8.4:—but also, *coarse, tough*, γογγυλίς ib.7.4.3, cf. 3.9.3: Comp. form **ἀρρέντερος** (cf. θηλύτερος), κὰ τὠρρέντερον γένος in the *male* line, *IG*5(2).262.21 (Mantinea, v B.C.). 5. Adv. ἀρρένως Diog.ap.Stob. 4.44.71. (Occurs without ϝ– on Cret. Inscrr. which preserve ϝ–; cf. Skt. *ṛṣabhás* 'bull', Avest. *aršan–* 'man'.)

ἄρσηνος, = ἄρσην, *PLond*.3.909^{a}5. **ἄρσης**, v. ἄρσην.

Ἀρσινόεια, τά, *festival in honour of Arsinoe*, *PSI*4.364.5 (iii B.C.).

ἄρσιος, ον, (ἀραρίσκω) *fitting, meet, right*, Hsch.

ἀρσίπους [ῐ], ὁ, ἡ, πουν, τό, gen. ποδος, contr. for ἀερσίπους, *raising the foot, active*, *h.Ven*.211, *AP*7.717.

ἄρσις, εως, ἡ, (αἴρω) *raising* or *lifting*, τῶν σκελῶν Arist.*IA*711^{b}25; πᾶσα πορεία ἐξ ἄρσεως καὶ θέσεως συντελεῖται Id.*Pr*.885^{b}6; βοῶν, as an athletic feat, *IG*2.471.78 (pl.); μηχανήματος Plb.8.4.6; *taking up, examination*, δειγμάτων *POxy*.708.5, 18 (ii A.D.); *plucking, pulling up* of a herb, *PMag.Par*.1.2977. b. *distillation*, ὕδατος Ps.-Democr. ap.Zos.Alch.p.152B.; *sublimation*, νεφέλης ibid. 2. (from Pass.) *rising*, κυμάτων Arist.*Mu*.396^{a}26. 3. *that which is lifted, burden*, Lxx 4*Ki*.8.9, al.; *that which is taken*, ἄ. βασιλέως *portion* from the king's table, ib.2*Ki*.19.42, cf. 11.8. 4. *dignity*, Aq.*Ge*.49.3. II. *removal*, τὴν ⟨ἐκ⟩ θαλάττης ἄ. [τῶν κητῶν] D.S.3.41; ἀκανθῶν *POxy*. 909.25 (iii A.D.); τριχῶν Dsc.5.146. 2. *taking away, removal, abolition*, dub. in Arist.*Metaph*.1019^{b}16; τοῦ ὄντος Plu.2.1130a; τοῦ φόβου Metrod.*Herc*.831.16. b. Gramm., *omission*, e.g. of the reduplication, Rh.3.566 W. 3. *negation*, Phld.*Sign*.14, Procl.*in Prm*.p.850 S.; opp. θέσις, S.E.*P*.1.192, cf. Plot.5.5.6; = στέρησις, Id. 2.4.13. 4. *destruction, ruin*, *OGI*315.59 (Pessinus, ii B.C.). III. *raising of the foot* in beating time, opp. θέσις, *downward beat*, Aristox.*Rhyth*.12.17, D.H.*Dem*.48, Aristid.Quint.1.13, Luc.*Harm*.1, etc. IV. ἄρσις· ζύμη, Hsch.

ἄρσιχος, v. ἄρριχος.

ἄρσος, εος, τό, only pl. **ἄρσεα**· λειμῶνες, Hsch.; cf. ἄλσος.

ἄρσω, Aeol. fut. of αἴρω.

ἀρσωμίδες· ὑπόδημα γυναικεῖον, Hsch.

ἀρτάβη, ἡ, Persian measure, *artaba*, = 1 medimnus + 3 choenices, Hdt.1.192; or exactly 1 medimnus, Suid., Hsch. II. Egyptian measure of capacity, varying from 24 to 42 χοίνικες, *OGI*90.30 (Rosetta), *PLond*.2.265 (i A.D.), *POxy*.9^{v}8 (iii/iv A.D.), etc.

ἀρταβί-ειος, α, ον, *of an* ἀρτάβη, σφυρίς *PFlor*.369.14 (ii A.D.). 2. **-εία**, ἡ (later **ἀρταβία**, ἡ, *CPR*1.16 (i A.D.)), *tax of one artaba per* ἄρουρα, *PTeb*.119.11 (ii B.C.), *PLond*.3.1171^{v}ii 15 (i A.D.), *PFay*.99: —also neut. pl. -εια, τά, *PTeb*.5.59 (ii B.C.).

ἀρτάδες· οἱ δίκαιοι, ὑπὸ Μάγων, Hsch. **ἀρταῖοι**· οἱ ἥρωες, παρὰ Πέρσαις, Id.

ἀρτᾰμ-έω, *cut in pieces*, ταῦρον E.*El*.816; ἄνδρας γνάθοις Id.*Alc*. 494. **-ησις**, εως, ἡ, *slaughtering*, βοός *IG*7.2426.15 (Thebes).

Ἄρταμις, Ἀρταμίτιος, -μίτιον, v. Ἀρτεμ–.

ἄρτᾰμος, ὁ, *butcher, cook*, X.*Cyr*.2.2.4, Epicr.6, *IG*14.643; βοός Orac.ap.Phleg.10.39. 2. metaph., *murderer*, S.*Fr*.1025, Lyc.236, 797. (For ἀρτι-ταμος, = ὁ εἰς ἄρτια τέμνων, acc. to Eust.577.45.)

ἀρτάνη [ᾰ], ἡ, (ἀρτάω) *that by which something is hung up, rope, noose, halter*, A.*Ag*.875, 1091 (lyr.), etc.; ἀ. κρεμαστή S.*OT*1266; πλεκταῖσιν ἀ. Id.*Ant*.54.

ἀρτάρια, τά, *felt shoes*, Suid.; cf. ἀρτήρ.

ἀρταχήλας· τὰ χέμνια (leg. χελύνια), τὰ χείλη, Hsch.

ἀρτάω, fut. -ήσω *AP*6.245 (Diod.): aor. 1 ἤρτησα E.*Andr*.811, etc.: pf. ἤρτηκα (προσ–) Arr.*Epict*.1.1.14:—**Pass.**, pf. ἤρτημαι E. *Hipp*.857, Ion. 3 pl. ἀρτέαται Hdt.1.125: aor. ἠρτήθην (προσ–) Man. 4.199: —*fasten to* or *hang* one thing *upon* another, τι ἀπό τινος Th.2. 76; ἀ. δέρην *hang*, E.*Andr*. l. c.; ἱμᾶσιν.. ἀρτήσας δέμας *having bound*, Id.*Hipp*.1222:—Med., βρόχους ἀρτωμένη *fastening* halters *to one's neck*, Id.*Tr*.1012; ἀρτήσαντο Orph.*A*.1096: but, II. more freq. Pass., *to be hung upon, hang upon*, ἠρτῆσθαι ἔκ τινος E.*Hipp*. 857, Pl.*Ion*533e, etc.; ἐν βρόχοις E.*Hipp*.779. 2. ἀρτᾶσθαι ἔκ τινος *depend upon*, Hdt.3.19, 6.109, al.; ἐξ ὧν ὧλλοι ἀρτέαται Πέρσαι on whom the rest of the Persians *depend*, i.e. whom they acknowledge as their chiefs, Id.1.125; so παρρησία ἐξ ἀληθείας ἠρτημένη D. 60.26; ἀπὸ ταὐτοῦ ἠ. Arist.*MM*1209^{a}22; ἐντεῦθεν Id.*Juv*.469^{b}15; τοῦ στόματος Ael.*NA*4.51; τῶν χειρῶν Philostr.*Im*.2.23, etc.; αἰτίου, ἀπ' αἰτίας, Porph.*Sent*.14. (Contr. from ἀερτάω (cf. ἀν-αερτάω), cf. ἀείρω 'attach'.)

ἀρτεμ-έω, *to be safe and sound*, Nonn.*D*.35.387. **-ής**, ές, *safe and sound*, ζωόν τε καὶ ἀρτεμέα Il.5.515; σὺν ἀρτεμέεσσι φίλοισι Od. 13.43, cf. A.R.1.415, Call.*Iamb*.1.227.—Ep. word; etym. of Ἄρτεμις, Pl.*Cra*.406b. **-ία**, ἡ, *soundness, health*, *AP*9.644 (Agath.), Procl. *H*.1.42: pl., *recovery*, Max.184.

ἀρτεμίδιον or **-ιδήιον**, = δίκταμνος, Ps.-Dsc.3.32.

Ἀρτεμῑδόβλητος, ον, *stricken by Artemis*, Macr.*Sat*.1.17.11.

Ἄρτεμις, ἡ, gen. ιδος, also ιτος, dat. ιτι *SIG*671 *A* 6 (Delph., ii B.C.), *GDI*1679 (Zacynthus), etc.: acc. ιν, also ιδα *h.Ven*.16: Dor. **Ἄρταμις**, ιτος (or ιδος as in Boeot. Inscrr. *IG*7.546, al.), *SIG*765 (Rhodes, i B.C.), *IG*2.545.12 (Delph.), etc.; dat. Ἀρτάμι ib.4.577 (Argos): pl., Ἀρτέμιδες πραεῖαι, = Εἰλειθυῖαι, ib.7.3101 (Lebad.):—*Artemis*, Od.11.172, etc. (Deriv. uncertain, but more prob. connected with ἄρταμος than with ἀρτεμής.)

ἀρτεμισία, ἡ, *wormwood*, ἀ. πλατυτέρα, = *Artemisia arborescens*, ἀ. λεπτοτέρα, = *A. campestris*, Dsc.3.113. 2. ἀ. μονόκλωνος, = *A. scoparia*, Ps.-Dsc.3.113. II. = ἀμβροσία, ib.114.

Ἀρτεμισιασταί, οἱ, guild of *worshippers of Artemis* at Athens, *Berl.Sitzb*.1888.324.

Ἀρτεμίσιον, τό, *temple of Artemis, place sacred to her*, Hdt.8.8 sq., Plu.2.264c, etc.: Dor. **Ἀρταμίτιον** Ar.*Lys*.1251, *SIG*56.26 (Argos, v B.C.); **Ἀρτεμίτιον** *IG*14.217.14 (Acrae). 2. Ἀρταμίτια, τά, *festival of Artemis*, *Michel*995 *D* 8 (Delph., v B.C.). II. Dim. of Ἄρτεμις, *small figure of Artemis*, as device on a signet, *SIG*^{2}588.191 (Delos, ii B.C.); *image of A.*, Hyp.*Fr*.74.

Ἀρτεμίσιος, Dor. **Ἀρταμίτιος**, ὁ (sc. μήν), a Spartan and Macedonian month, Th.5.19, Plu.*Alex*.16:—also **Ἀρτεμισιών**, ῶνος, ὁ, at Erythrae, *SIG*410.1 (iii B.C.), etc. [The first ι in Ἀρτεμίσιον, –ίσιος, –ισιών, etc., is long (cf. Ar.*Th*.1200, Diph.124) and written ει in Inscrr. of late ii B.C., *IG*12(9).234.23, *SIG*708.1, etc.]

ἀρτέμ-ων, ονος, ὁ, (ἀρτάω) *foresail* of a ship, *Act.Ap*.27.40, dub. sens. in Lyd.*Mens*.2.12. II. *principal pulley* in a system, Vitr. 10.2.9 (in Latin form, = Gk. ἐπάγων). **-ώνιον**, τό, Dim. of foreg. I, Tz. ad Lyc.359. II. name of an *eye-salve*, Gal.12.780.

ἀρτέομαι, Ion. Verb, Pass., *to be prepared, make ready*, c. inf., οἱ δὲ αὖτις πολεμέειν .. ἀρτέοντο Hdt.5.120; ἀρτέετο ἐς πόλεμον Id.8. 97. II. Med., c. acc., οἳ οὐκ ἔων ναυμαχίην ἀρτέεσθαι Id.7.143. (Cf. ἀν–, παρ-αρτέομαι. Akin to ἀρτίζομαι, not to ἀρτάομαι.)

ἀρτέον, (αἴρω) *one must take away*, Socr.ap.Stob.3.13.63; τράπεζαν *one must clear*, Alex.250.1. 2. *one must deny*, Polystr. p.24W.

Ἀρτεπίβουλος [ῐ], ὁ, *Bread-thief*, name of a mouse in Batr.261.

ἄρτημα, ατος, τό, (ἀρτάω) *hanging ornament, ear-ring*, Hdt.2.69; cf. λίθινος. II. *cord for suspension*, e.g. of the steelyard, Arist. *Mech*.853^{a}34, ^{b}25, *IG*2.834*c*13, al.; ἐπὶ τὸ αὑτοῦ ἄ. νεύειν Str.1.1. 20. 2. *buoy*, Plu.*Cat.Mi*.38. 3. in pl., *ligaments*, Gal.8.125.

ἀρτήρ, ῆρος, ὁ, a kind of *felt shoe*, Pherecr.38. II. *that by which anything is carried*, Lxx *Ne*.4.17(11).

ἀρτηρία, Ion. -ίη, ἡ, *wind-pipe*, ἡ ἀ. μόλις ἀναπνεούσῃ ὑπεσύριζε Hp.*Epid*.7.25, cf.39, Pl.*Ti*.70d, Arist.*HA*493^{a}8, *deAn*.420^{b}29; ἡ τραχεῖα ἀ. (cf. II) Timoth.ap.Menon.*Iatr*.8.29, v.l. in Dsc.2.50, Luc.*Hist. Conscr*.7, S.E.*M*.9.178, etc.: in pl., *bronchial tubes*, ἆσθμα.. περὶ στήθεα καὶ ἀρτηρίας Hp.*Epid*.7.12 (vulg. but prob. l. -ίην, = *trachea*), cf. Pl.*Ti*.78c; πλεύμονος ἀρτηρίαι S.*Tr*.1054. II. *artery*, as distinct from a vein, αἱ φλεβῶν καὶ ἀρτηριῶν κοινωνίαι Hp.*Art*.45, cf. 69; τὰς δὲ φλέβας καὶ τὰς ἀ. συνάπτειν εἰς ἀλλήλας.. τῇ αἰσθήσει φανερὸν εἶναι Arist.*Spir*.484^{a}1; ἀ. λεῖαι (cf. I) Gal.*UP*8.1, al.; ἀ. φλεβώδης *pulmonary vein*, ib.6.10; believed to contain πνεῦμα by Erasistr., ib. 17, and derived fr. ἀήρ, τηρέω by Bacch.ap.Erot. s.v. ἀορτέων. III. = ἀορτή, *aorta*, δύο εἰσὶ κοῖλαι φλέβες ἀπὸ τῆς καρδίης, τῇ μὲν οὔνομα ἀρτηρίη τῇ δὲ κοίλη φλέψ Hp.*Carn*.5. IV. in pl. of the *ureters*, Id.*Oss*.10. (Contr. from ἀερτηρία, from ἀείρω 'attach' (q.v.), cf. ἀορτήρ, etc.)

ἀρτηριακός, ή, όν, *of* or *for the trachea* or *bronchi*, esp. -κή (sc. ἀντίδοτος), ἡ, *medicament for their treatment*, Plin.*HN*20.207, 23.136, Gal.13.1; δυνάμεις Androm.ib.14; φάρμακα Aët.8.54; -κὸν ἴσχαιμον styptic for *arterial* haemorrhage, Id.3.19; ἀ. πάθος, τὰ ἀ., affections *of these organs*, Paul.Aeg.3.28; ἡ -κή a medicine, Aët.8.54 sq.; ἡ ἀ. κοιλία τῆς καρδίας *left ventricle*, *Placit*.4.5.7; ἀ. φωνή, of the human voice, opp. ἡ τῶν ὀργάνων, Nicom.*Harm*.2.

ἀρτηρίασις, εως, ἡ, *bronchitis*, Isid.*Etym*.4.7.14.

ἀρτηριο-τομέω, *cut an artery*, in Pass., *have it cut*, Antyll.ap.Orib. 7.14.2, Gal.8.202. **-τομία**, ἡ, *severing of an artery*, Antyll.ap. Orib.7.14 tit., Gal.11.312.

ἀρτηριώδης, ες, *like an* ἀρτηρία, μέρη Gal.8.737; κοιλία τῆς καρδίας *left ventricle*, ibid.; ἀ. φλέψ *pulmonary artery*, Herophil.ap.Ruf.*Onom*. 203, cf. Gal.*UP*6.10.

ἄρτ-ησις, εως, ἡ, (ἀρτέομαι) *equipment*, Hdt.1.195 (v.l. ἄρτισις, q.v.). II. (ἀρτάομαι) *suspension*, Papp.1044.14. **-ησμός**, ὁ, (ἀρτάω) *hanging, suspension*, *AB*447. **-ητός**, όν, = κρεμαστός, Hsch.

ἄρτι [ῐ], Adv. *just, exactly*, of coincidence of Time, *just now* (not in Hom.): 1. mostly of the present, with pres. tense, Thgn.998, Pi.*P*.4.158, A.*Th*.534; opp. πάλαι, with pf., τέθνηκεν ἄ. S.*Ant*.1283; βεβᾶσιν ἄ. Id.*El*.1386; ἄ. ἥκεις ἢ πάλαι; Pl.*Cri*.43a; more fully ἄ. νυνί Ar.*Lys*.1008; ἄ... νῦν or νῦν.. ἄ., Pl.*Plt*.291a, b; later, = νῦν, Theoc.23.26, *Ep.Gal*.1.9, J.*AJ*1.6.1; ἄ. καὶ πρώην *to-day* and yesterday, i.e. *very lately*, Plu.*Brut*.1, etc.; ἕως ἄ. till *now*, *Ev.Matt*.11.12, *POxy*.936.23 (iii A.D.): with Subst., ὁ ἄ. λόγος Pl.*Tht*.153e; ἡλικίαν.. τὴν ἄ. ἐκ παίδων X.*HG*5.4.25; ἡ ἄ. ὥρα 1*Ep.Cor.*4.11, *PMag. Lond.*1.121.373; ἄ. μὲν.. ἄ. δὲ.. *now.. now..*, *at one time.. at another..*, Luc.*Nigr.*4. 2. of the past, *just now*, with impf., ἄ. βλάστεσκε dub. in S.*Fr.*546, cf. E.*Ba.*677, Pl.*Grg.*454b: with aor., λέξας ἄ. S.*Aj.*1272; καθημάτωσεν ἄ. E.*Ph.*1160; opp. νῦν, ὃ ἄ. ἐρρήθη.. νῦν δὲ.. Pl.*Alc.*1.130d, cf. 127c; ἐν τῷ ἄ., opp. ἐν τῷ νῦν καὶ ἐν τῷ ἔπειτα, Id.*Men.*89c. 3. in Antiph.26.7 (s.v.l.) and later also of the future, *just now, presently*, Luc.*Sol.*1, App.*Mith.*69, Astramps.*Orac.* 94.2; condemned by Phryn.12; also, *just at present*, πλεύσεις, ἄ. δὲ οὔ Astramps.*Orac.*92.7: with imper., Nonn.*D.*20.277, etc. (Perh. cogn. with Skt. *ṛtám* 'ordinance', *ṛtás* 'correct'.)

ἀρτῐ-άζω, (ἄρτιος) *play at odd and even*, Ar.*Pl.*816; ἀστραγάλοις ἀ. Pl.*Ly.*206e, prob. in Arist.*Div.Somn.*463ᵇ20. II. *count*, *AP* 12.145. **-άκις** [ᾰ], Adv. *an even number of times*, opp. περιττάκις, Pl.*Prm.*144a, Plu.2.429d; ἄρτια ἀ. *even times even*, of powers of two, Pl.*Prm.*143e, cf. Ascl.*Tact.*2.7. **-ᾰκός**, ή, όν, *of even numbers*, only in Adv. -κῶς, τὸ ἥμισυ ἀ. ὠνομασμένον the half called *after the even number*, Nicom.*Ar.*1.9.

ἀρτίαλα, τά, Aeol., *ear-rings*, Poll.5.97.

ἀρτιάλωτος, ον, *newly caught*, Xenocr.34.

ἀρτιασμός, ὁ, *game of odd and even*, Arist.*Rh.*1407ᵇ3.

ἀρτι-βλαστής, ές, *newly budding*, Thphr.*CP*2.3.1. **-βλαστος**, ον, *recently sprouted*, Callix.1, Dsc.1*Praef.*9. **-βρεφής**, ές, *of young children*, v. ἀρτιτρεφής. **-βρεχής**, ές, *just steeped*, *AP*5.174 (Mel.). **-γάλακτος** [γᾰ], ον, *just weaned*, τέκνον *Epigr.Gr.*205 (Halic., ii B.C.), cf. *Ath.Mitt.*24.448 (Phryg.). **-γάλαξ** [γᾰ], ὁ, ἡ, gen. ακτος, = foreg., Hdn.Gr.1.352. **-γᾰμος**, ον, *just married*, κούρη *IG*14.1835, cf. Opp. *H.*4.179, Nonn.*D.*48.298, al. **-γένεθλος**, ον, *just born*, Orph.*A.* 386. **-γένειος**, ον, *with the beard just sprouting*, *AP*9.219 (Diod.), Nonn.*D.*18.135; as Subst., ἀ. ἐπίλεκτοι App.*Pun.*8; incorrectly used, = ἀρτιγέννητος, σολοικισμοί Luc.*Sol.*2. **-γενής**, ές, *just born* or *made*, Nic.*Al.*357, Ael.*NA*4.34, Sor.1.87. **-γέννητος**, ον, = foreg., βρέφη 1*Ep.Pet.*2.2, cf. Luc.*Alex.*13, Longus 1.9, al. **-γλῠφής**, ές, *newly carved*, Theoc.*Ep.*4. **-γνωστος**, ον, *newly known*, App.*BC*3.12. **-γονος**, ον, = ἀρτιγενής, μῆλα *AP*6.252 (Antiphil.); κάλυκες Nic.*Fr.*74.34, cf. Nonn.*D.*7.143, Opp.*C.*3.9. **-γρᾰφής**, ές, *just written*, Luc.*Lex.*1. **-δᾰής**, ές, *just taught*, *AP*6.227 (Crin.). **-δᾰΐκτος** [δᾰ], ον, *just slain*, Nonn.*D.*15.393, al. **-δακρυς**, υ, *ready to weep*, E.*Med.*903, Luc.*Lex.*4. **-δίδακτος** [δῐ], ον, *just taught*, τῶν Ἑλληνικῶν App.*BC*3.20.

ἀρτί-διον, τό, Dim. of ἄρτος, *small loaf*, D.L.7.13; *piece of bread*, Sor.1.115; *food*, *POxy.*738.8 (i A.D.). **-δορος**, ον, *just stript off* or *peeled*, cj. Toup in *AP*6.22 (Zon.) for ἀντίδορος (q.v.). **-δρεπής**, ές, *just plucked*, Hld.2.23. **-δροπος**, ον, = foreg., v. ἀρτίτροπος. **-έπεια**, ἡ, Ep. fem. of sq., Hes.*Th.*29. **-επής**, ές, (ἄρτιος, ἔπος) *ready of speech, glib of tongue*, ἀ. καὶ ἐπίκλοπος ἔπλεο μύθων Il.22. 281: in good sense, ἀπεφθέγξατο δ' ἀρτιεπής answered *clearly*, Pi.*O.* 6.61; ἀ. γλῶσσα Id.*I.*5(4).46. **-ζῠγία**, ἡ, *recent union*, ἀνδρῶν ἀ., i.e. *newly married* husbands, A.*Pers.*542.

ἀρτί-ζω, pf. ἤρτικα *PMag.Leid.W.*10.42:—*get ready, prepare*, *AP*10. 25 (Antip.), *PMag.* l.c.:—Med., χορὸν ἀρτίζοντο Theoc.13.43; πρός τι D.S.14.20:—Pass., πρός τι *CIG*3601.9 (Ilium), S.E.*M.*11.208. **-ζωος**, ον, *not likely to live*, Hp.*Superf.*15. **-θᾰλής**, ές, *just budding* or *blooming*, *AP*5.197 (Mel.); ἐλπίδες *Epigr.Gr.*348 (Cius); of persons, Nonn.*D.*3.312, al. **-θᾰνής**, ές, *just dead*, E.*Alc.*600 (lyr.), Men. Prot.p.89 D. **-θέριστος**, ον, *newly reaped*, κριθή *Hippiatr.*1. **-θηρος**, ον, *newly caught*, Democr.ap.Gal.14.93. **-καυστος**, ον, *freshly roasted*, Thphr.*Ign.*65. **-κολλος**, ον, *close-glued, clinging close*, ἀρτίκολλος ὥστε τέκτονος χιτών, = ἀρτίως κολληθεὶς ὡς ὑπὸ τέκτονος, S.*Tr.*768. II. metaph., *fitting well together*, ἀ. συμβαίνει τάδε turn out *exactly right*, A.*Ch.*580; εἰς ἀ. ἀγγέλου λόγον μαθεῖν *in the nick of time*, Id.*Th.*373. **-κόμιστος**, ον, *newly nursed*, Nonn.*D.*9.53, al. **-κροτέω**, = συγκροτέω, *equip*, στόλον Str.15.1.32; λόγους prob. in Pl.*Ax.*369d, cf. Phld.*Rh.*2.75 S.:—Pass., *to be brought to an agreement*, γάμοι Men.904. 2. *keep time*, of rowers, Hsch. **-ληπτος**, ον, *just taken*, App.*Mith.*108. **-λῐθία**, ἡ, *exact superposition of joints*, in masonry, *IG*7.4255.27 (Oropus). **-λογία**, ἡ, *ready speech*, Poll.6.150. **-λόγως**, Adv. *speaking readily*, ibid. **-λόχευτος**, ον, *just born*, *APl.*4.122, Nonn.*D.*14.27, al. **-μαζές·** νέον, Hsch. **-μᾰθής**, ές, *having just learnt*, κακῶν E.*Hec.*687; λογικῆς θεωρίας Gal.11.466: abs., *beginner*, Sor.1.4, cf. Longus 3.20. **-μελής**, ές, *sound of limb*, Pl.*R.*536b, Sor.1.3, D.C.69.20; *perfect in all members*, τέχναι Them.*Or.*26.316c. **-μήτας·** νέους, Hsch.

Ἄρτιμις, barbarism for Ἄρτεμις, Tim.*Pers.*172.

Ἀρτίμπασα, ἡ, Scythian name for Aphrodite Urania, Hdt.4.59 (vv.ll. Ἀργίμπ-, Ἀρίππ-).

ἀρτινεστέραν· ὑγιεστέραν, Hsch.

ἀρτίνοος [ῐ], ον, contr. **-νους**, ουν, *sound of mind*, D.C.69.20.

ἀρτῐο-γενής, ές, *of the even class* (of powers of 2), Nicom.*Ar.*1.8 (v.l. ἀρτιοπληθής). **-γώνιος** (or **-γωνος**), ον, *having an even number of angles*, Archim.*Sph.Cyl.*1.44, al. **-δύνᾰμος** [ῠ], ον, *of even power*, of numbers the halves of which are *even*, Nicom.*Ar.*1. 8. **-λογέω**, *speak distinctly*, Eust.1151.59. **-πᾰγής**, ές, v. -ταγής. **-πέρισσος**, Att. **-ττος**, ον, *even-odd*, of *even* numbers, the halves of which are *odd*, as 6, 10, etc., Philol.5, Ph.1.3, Plu.2.1139f; of unity, Arist.*Fr.*199. **-πλευρος**, ον, *having an even number of sides*, of polygons, Archim.*Sph.Cyl.*1.21, al. **-πληθής**, v. ἀρτιογενής.

ἄρτιος, α, ον (ος, ον Aristid.Quint.1.25): (ἄρτι):—*complete, perfect of its kind, suitable, exactly fitted*, ἄ. ἀλλήλοισι σπόνδυλοι Hp.*Art.*45; ἄρτια βάζειν speak *to the purpose*, Il.14.92, Od.8.240; ὅτι οἱ φρεσὶν ἄρτια ᾔδη thought things *in accordance with* him, was of *the same* mind *with* him, Il.5.326, Od.19.248; ἄρτια μήδεσθαι Pi.*O.*6.94; *meet, right, proper*, Sol.4.40, Thgn.946; ἄ. εἴς τι *well-suited* for.., *IG*14.889.7 (Sinuessa); ἀρτιωτάτην ἔχειν τάξιν *most perfect*, Philostr.*VS*1.21.3. 2. *full-grown*, Thphr.*HP*2.5.5; *sound*, of body and mind, νόος, σώμασιν, Thgn.154, D.S.3.33, cf. 2*Ep.Ti.*3.17. 3. *prepared, ready*, c. inf., ἄρτιοι πείθεσθαι, ποιέειν, Hdt.9.27,48; καταβιῶναι Philostr.*VS*1.9. II. of numbers, *perfect*, i.e. *even*, opp. περιττός (*odd*), Epich.170.7, cf. Pl.*Prt.*356e, al.; ἄ. πόδες *even number of* feet, Arist.*HA*489ᵇ22; ἐν ἀρτίῃσι (sc. ἡμέρῃσι) happening on *the even* days, Hp.*Epid.*1.18; ἄ. χώρα, of the *even* feet in iambic and trochaic verse, Heph.5.1, Aristid.Quint. l.c. 2. *exact, precise*, ἐτῶν ἀριθμὸν ὀγδοήκοντ' ἀρτίων *Epigr.Gr.*222*b* (Milet.). III. Adv. ἀρτίως *just, newly*, = ἄρτι, [Epich.]251, freq. in S. 1. of present time, with pres., *Aj.*678, *OT*78, al.: with pf., *OC*892, al. 2. of the past, with impf., *Tr.*664,674, etc.: with aor., ib.346, *OT*243, etc. 3. with an Adj., ἀ. νεοσφαγής *Aj.*898. 4. *closely fitting*, καθηλῶσαί τί τινι Polyaen.3.11.13. IV. neut. pl. ἄρτια, = ἀρτίως 2, *AP*6.234 (Eryc.).

ἀρτῐοταγής, ές, *occupying the even places* in a series, Iamb.*in Nic.* p.59 P., al.; prob. for -παγής in Nicom.*Harm.*11.3. II. *even in number*, Id.*Ar.*2.24.

ἀρτῐότης, ητος, ἡ, *soundness, entireness*, Arr.*Epict.*1.22.12, Gal. *Thras.*12, Stob.2.7.7ᵃ. 2. of numbers, *evenness*, opp. περιττότης, Arist.*Metaph.*1004ᵇ11.

ἀρτῐ-πᾰγής, ές, *just put together* or *made*, στάλικες Theoc.*Ep.*3; ναῦς *AP*9.32; σκῆνος Them.*Or.*4.6ca. II. *freshly coagulated*, ἁλὶ τυρός *AP*9.412 (Phld.). **-παις**, παιδος, ὁ, *lately a boy*, prob. f.l. for ἀντίπαις, Thom.Mag. s.v. παῖς. **-πλακέες·** οἱ πεινῶντες, Hsch. **-πλουτος**, ον, *newly gotten*, χρήματα E.*Supp.*742. **-πνουν·** ὀρθόπνουν, Hsch. **-πόλεμος**, ον, *new to war*, App.*Syr.*37. **-πους**, ὁ, ἡ, πουν, τό, gen. ποδος: Ep. nom. **ἀρτίπος**: I. (ἄρτιος, πούς) *sound of foot*, ὁ μὲν καλός τε καὶ ἀρτίπος, opp. χωλός, Od.8.310, cf. Hdt.3.130, Them.*Or.*21.255c. 2. generally, *strong* or *swift of foot*, ἡ δ' Ἄτη σθεναρή τε καὶ ἀρτίπος Il.9.505; ἀρτίποδες καὶ ἀρτίχειρες Pl.*Lg.*795d. II. (ἄρτι, πούς) *coming just in time*, S.*Tr.*58.

ἄρτῐσις, εως, ἡ, (ἀρτίζω) *equipment*, v.l. for ἄρτησις, ἡ περὶ τὸ σῶμα ἄ. Hdt.1.195.

ἀρτίσκαπτος, ον, *just dug*, *AP*7.465 (Heraclit.).

ἀρτίσκιον, τό, Dim. of sq. 2, Democr.ap.Gal.14.96.

ἀρτίσκος, ὁ, Dim. of ἄρτος, *little loaf*, Hp.*Steril.*216, Sch.Ar.*Pax* 1196. 2. *pastille*, Dsc.2.172, Gal.12.317.

ἀρτιστῆρες, οἱ, magistrates at Elatea, *IG*9(1).97.22.

ἀρτι-στομέω, *to speak in good idiom, accurately*, Str.14.2.28. **-στομία**, ἡ, *distinctness* or *precision in speech*, Poll.6.150. **-στομος**, ον, *speaking in good idiom*, or *with precision*, Plu.*Cor.*38, Suid. Adv. -μως Poll.6.150. II. *with a good mouth* or *opening*, κόλπος Str.5.4.5; λιμήν Id.17.1.6. III. ἀ. βέλεα *evenly tipped*, i.e. *not sharp* or *jagged* (πανταχόθεν ὁμαλά Gal.19), Hp.*VC*11; so ἀ. ξοΐς *plain* chisel (not toothed), *IG*7.3073.148 (Lebad.). **-στράτευτος** [ρᾰ], ον, *young in military service*, App.*BC*3.49. **-σύλληπτος**, ον, *newly conceived* in the womb, Dsc.*Eup.*2.81. **-τέλεστος**, ον, *just completed*, Nonn. *D.*5.579, al. **-τελής**, ές, *newly initiated*, Pl.*Phdr.*251a. II. *fully formed*, Thphr.*HP*2.5.5; *just finished*, Nonn.*D.*26.46. **-τοκέω**, *produce normal issue*: metaph. of vines, *Gp.*5.41.1. **-τοκος**, ον, *new-born*, *AP*6.154 (Leon. or Gaet.), Luc.*DDeor.*7.1, Them. *Or.*25.311a; *new-laid*, ᾠά Aret.*CA*1.10: metaph., σελήνη Opp.*C.* 4.123. II. parox. ἀρτιτόκος, ον, *having just given birth*, ib.3. 119, *AP*7.729 (Tymn.), 9.2 (Tib. Ill.). **-τομος**, ον, *just cut* or *severed*, A.R.4.1515. II. parox. ἀρτιτόμος, ον, *having just cut* or *hewn*, Suid. **-τόνον·** εὔτονον, εὐάρμοστον, Hsch. **-τρεφής**, ές, *just nursed*, ἀρτιτρεφεῖς βλαχαί wailings *of young children*, A.*Th.* 350 cod. Med. (v.l. ἀρτιβρεφεῖς). **-τροπος**, ον, (ἄρτιος, τρόπος) *of modest manners* (but, *just of age*, acc. to Sch.), A.*Th.*333 cod. Med. (v.l. ἀρτιδρόποις *just plucked, of tender age*). **-φᾰής**, ές, *newly shining*, μήνη Nonn.*D.*5.165. **-φᾰνής**, ές, *just seen, having newly appeared*, ib.12.5, al. **-φᾰτος**, ον, *just killed*, Opp.*H.*4. 256. **-φονος**, ον, *just slain*, Nonn.*D.*44.275 (prob.), Sch.Opp.*H.* 2.617.

ἄρτιφος· ὀρίγανον, Hsch.

ἀρτί-φρων [ῐ], ον, gen. ονος, (ἄρτιος, φρήν) *sound of mind, sensible*, οὔτε μάλ' ἀ. Od.24.261, cf. E.*Med.*294; ἀρτιμελεῖς καὶ ἀρτίφρονας Pl. *R.*536b; ἀ... πλὴν.. *quite in one's senses* except.., E.*IA*877: c. gen., ἐπεὶ δ' ἀ. ἐγένετο.. γάμων when he came *to full consciousness of..*, A.*Th.*778 (lyr.). **-φυής**, ές, *just born*, ἀ. ἔθανον *Epigr.Gr.* 334.11 (Ilium), cf. *Inscr.Cos* 343; *fresh*, κράμβη *AP*6.21, cf. Dsc.3.15; κύκλος ἰούλων Nonn.*D.*3.416. II. of number, *even*, Hp.*Septim.* 9. **-φῠτος**, ον, *just born, fresh*, ἄνθεα *AP*4.2.14 (Phil.); ἔρνεα Nonn.*D.*41.5. **-φωνία**, ἡ, = ἀρτιλογία, Poll.6.150. **-φωνος**, ον, only in Adv. -νως, = ἀρτιλόγως, ibid. **-χᾰνής**, ές, *just opening*, *AP* 6.22 (Zon.). **-χάρακτος** [χᾰ], ον, *newly graven*, γράμμα Epigr. ap.Ath.5.209d. 2. *newly ploughed*, Nonn.*D.*2.65. 3. *freshly wounded*, ib.25.498. 4. metaph. of darkness, *newly cleft* by light, ib. 27.5; of colour on ripening grapes, ib.12.311. **-χείλης·** ὑπερέχων τοῖς χείλεσιν, ὑπόμακρος, Hsch. **-χειρ**, ὁ, ἡ, gen. χειρος, *strong of hand* (cf. ἀρτίπους), Pl.*Lg.*795d. **-χνους**, ουν, gen. ου, = ἀρτιγένειος, *with the first bloom on*, μῆλον *AP*6.22 (Zon.); ἀ. ἴουλος *a young* beard, Philostr.Jun.*Im.*6; ἔρνος ἀρτίχνουν γονέων ἐλπίδα *Epigr.Gr.*

201.6 (Cos). **-χόρευτος**, ον, *recently celebrated in the dance*, Nonn.*D.* 7.46, al. **-χριστος**, ον, *fresh-spread*, φάρμακον S.*Tr.*687. **-χυτος**, ον, *just poured* or *shed*, φόνος Opp.*H.*2.617; αἷμα Nonn.*D.*39.226. II. Act., μαζός ib.13.431. **-ώνυμος**, ον, *of even denomination*, epith. of all *even* numbers, Nicom.*Ar.*1.8:—hence **-ωνῠμέω**, *to be even*, Iamb.*in Nic.*p.22 P.

ἀρτίως, v. sub ἄρτιος III.

ἀρτιωτά· βραχυτάτῳ χρόνῳ συντετελεσμένα, Hsch.

ἀρτο-δότης, ου, ὁ, *giver of bread*, Tz.ad Lyc.435. **-ζήτης**, ου, ὁ, *one who begs for bread*, Sch.Lyc.775. **-θήκη**, ἡ, *pantry*, *PFlor.*15.17 (vi A. D.); *bread-basket*, Sch.Ar.*Pl.*763. **-κάπηλος** [ᾰ], ὁ, *bread-seller*, *Stud.Pal.*10.233c6 (v A. D.). **-κλασμα**, ατος, τό, *morsel of bread*, Tz.*H.*8.49. **-κοπεῖον**, τό, *bake-house*, Dsc.2.36, *BGU*1202.5 (i B. C.), *Gp.*1.6.2; -κόπιον Charis.p.553 K.; -κόπιν (sic) *OGI*177.19. **-κοπία**, ἡ, *baking*, *PThead.*31.35, 36.21 (iv A. D.). **-κοπικός**, ή, όν, *belonging to a baker* or *baking*, Lxx 1 *Ch.*16.3; τὸ ἀ., name of work by Chrysipp.Tyan.in Ath.14.647c. **-κόπισσα**, ἡ, fem. of sq., *POxy.*1146.8,9 (iv A. D.). **-κόπος**, ὁ, ἡ, *baker*, whether fem., Hdt.1.51; or masc., Id.9.82, Pl.*Grg.*518b (v.l. -ποιός), X.*An.*4.4.21 (v.l. -ποιός), *HG*7.1.38, *IG*3.1452, *IGRom.*4.1244. (Dissim. from ἀρτοπόπος, cf. Phryn.198, Hsch., Poll.7.21; cf. πέσσω.) **-κρεας**, τό, *bread and meat*, prob. = Lat. *visceratio*, *IGRom.*4.1348 (Lydia), Pers.6.50, *Gloss.*; *artocrea* *CIL*9.5309. **-λάγανον** [λᾰ], τό, *savoury cake* made with spices, wine, oil, and milk, Cic.*Fam.*9.20.2, Ath.5.113d. **-λάγῡνος** [λᾰ] πήρα bag *with bread and bottle*, *AP*11.38 (Polem. Rex). **-μελι**, μέλιτος, τό, *plaster* or *poultice of bread and honey*, Gal.10.692, Aët.3.177. **-πίναξ** [ῐ], ακος, ὁ, *platter*, *PTeb.*140 (i B. C.). **-ποιέω**, *make into bread, bake*, c. acc., πόαν App.*BC*2.61, cf. *POxy.*1459.9 (ii A. D.): abs., *bake bread*, Longus 3.10:—Med., Str. 3.3.7; σῖτον J.*AJ*4.4.4:—Pass., Dsc.2.189. **-ποιΐα**, ἡ, *baking*, Ar.*Fr.*313, X.*Mem.*2.7.6; -ποιεία *PFlor.*168.3 (iii A. D.), al. **-ποιϊκός**, ή, όν, *of* or *for baking*: -κόν, τό, title of work by Chrysipp.Tyan., Ath.3.113a, cf. Poll.10.112:—later **-ποιητικός**, ή, όν, Sch.E.*Hec.*359. **-ποιός**, ὁ, *bread-maker, baker*, X.*Cyr.*5.5.39, J.*AJ*15.9.2. **-πονος**, ὁ, *one who bakes loaves* for Apollo Maleatas, *IG*4.1549 (Epid.). **-ποπέω**, *to be a baker*, Phryn.Com.27. **-πόπος**, v. ἀρτοκ-. **-πράτης** [ᾱ], ου, ὁ, *dealer in bread*, Hierocl.*Facet.*225, *BGU*317.15 (vi A. D.).

ἀρτ-οπτεῖον, τό, *place* or *vessel for baking*, Poll.10.112. **-όπτης**, ου, ὁ, (ὀπτάω) *baker*, Hsch. s. v. πάσανος. 2. *pan for baking bread*, Plin.*HN*18.107. **-οπτίκιος** ἄρτος bread *baked in a pan*, Chrysipp. Tyan.ap.Ath.3.113a, Plin.*HN*18.105.

ἀρτο-πωλέω, *deal in bread*, Poll.7.21. **-πώλης**, ου, ὁ, *baker*, *AJA*18.33 (Sardes, iii A. D.), Poll.7.21. **-πωλία**, ἡ, *dealing in bread*, ib.24, Phryn.*PS*p.33 B. **-πωλικόν**, τό, *tax on bakeries*, *IG*2.860. **-πώλιον**, τό, *baker's shop*, Ar.*Ra.*112, *Fr.*155: -εῖον, Suid. **-πωλις**, ιδος, ἡ, fem. of -πώλης, Ar.*V.*238, *Ra.*858, *PTeb.*119.50 (ii B. C.). 2. as Adj., τηλία ἀ. *baker's tray*, Poll.9.108.

ἄρτος, ὁ, *cake* or *loaf of wheat-bread*, mostly in pl., Od.18.120, al.; ἄρτος οὖλος a whole *loaf*, 17.343; collectively, *bread*, δούλιον ἄρτον ἔδων Archil.*Supp.*2.6; ἀ. τρισκοπάνιστος Batr.35; opp. μᾶζα (*porridge*), Hp.*Acut.*37.—Freq. in all writers. II. ἄρτος· βόλος τις, καὶ ὁ Ἀθηναίων ξένος, Hsch.

ἀρτο-σῑτέω, *eat wheaten bread*, opp. ἀλφιτοσιτέω, X.*Cyr.*6.2.28. 2. *eat bread*, opp. ὀψοφαγέω, Pl.Com.172, Hp.*Vict.*3.68, v.l. in *Nat.Hom.*9. **-σιτία**, ἡ, *feeding on bread*, Id.*Mul.*1.66 (pl.), *Epid.*5.52. **-στάσιον** [ᾰ], τό, *fee for weighing bread*, *PTeb.*612 (ii/iii A. D.). **-στροφέω**, *turn bread*, as in baking, Ar.*Fr.*748. **-τῡρος**, ὁ, *bread and cheese*, *PMag.Lond.*46.181; perh. an Adj. (sc. καθαρμός).

ἀρτουργός, όν, = ἀρτοποιός, Tz.*H.*5.535.

ἀρτο-φᾰγέω, *eat bread*, Hdt.2.77, Hp.*Aff.*61; esp. *eat wheaten bread*, Id.*Acut.*37. **-φάγος** [φᾰ], ον, *bread-eater*, Hecat.*Fr.*323 (b) J.: name of a mouse in Batr.210. **-φοῖνιξ**, ῑκος, ὁ, *cake of bread and dates*, *PLond.*2.90.37 (iii A. D.). **-φόριον**, τό, *bread-basket*, S.E.*M.*1.234: the form **-φορίς**, ibid., is prob. corrupt. II. ἀρτοφόρια, τά, a festival, *An.Ox.*3.277. **-φόρος**, ον, *holding bread*, κανοῦν Poll.6.32; τὸ ἀρτοφόρον, = foreg. 1, Ath.4.129e. **-χᾰρις**, kind of *cake*, Hsch. s. v. χάρις.

ἀρτυλία· διαθήκη, Hsch. (leg. ἄρτυμα). **ἀρτύλλεν**· λόγχην, ἀγκύλην, Id.

ἄρτ-ῡμα, ατος, τό, *condiment, seasoning*, ἀρτύμασι παντοδαποῖσι Batr.41, cf. Hp.*Aff.*43, Dsc.3.36, etc.; βορᾶς ἀρτύματα S.*Fr.*675, cf. 709; τὰ παλαιὰ καὶ θρυλούμενα ἀρτύματα Anaxipp.1.5: metaph., ἡ ἀνάπαυσις τῶν πόνων ἄ. Plu.2.9c. II. = διαθήκη, δίκη, Hsch. (cf. ἄρτημα). **-ῡμᾶς**, ὁ, = sq., *BGU*9 iv 5 (iii A. D.). **-ῡματᾶς**, τᾶτος, ὁ, *dealer in condiments*, *POxy.*1517.14 (iii A. D.), al. **-ῡματικός**, ή, όν, *spicy, savoury*, Suid. s. v. ἄνηθον. **-ῡμάτιον**, τό, Dim. of ἄρτυμα, prob. in *PFay.*117.8 (ii A. D., pl.). **-ῡματοποιΐα**, ἡ, *making of condiments*, *POxy.*1731.16 (iii A. D.). **-ῡματοπώλης**, ου, ὁ, *dealer in condiments*, *Sammelb.*699 (i A. D.). **-ῡματώδης**, ες, *spicy*, Sor.1.115, Dsc.3.34.

ἀρτύνας [ῡ], α, ὁ, a *magistrate* at Argos and Epidaurus, Th.5.47:—also **ἄρτῡνος**, ὁ, Plu.2.291d, Hsch., cf. Hdn.Gr.1.56.

ἀρτύνω [ῡ], fut. -ῠνῶ, Ion. -ῠνέω Od.1.277: aor. Act. ἤρτῡνα, Med. -υνάμην, Pass. -ύνθην:— = ἀρτύω, chiefly used in Ep. (in later Prose, γηράσκουσα ἡ ἐπιστήμη σοφίαν ἀρτύνει Philostr.*VS*1.25.11), ψευδέα τ' ἀρτύνοντες Od.11.366; λόχον ἀρτύναντες 14.469; μνηστῆρσιν θάνατον κακὸν ἀρτύναντε 24.153; ὑσμίνην ἤρτυνον Il.15.303; ἀρτύνθη δὲ μάχη 11.216; ἀρτυνέουσιν ἔεδνα Od.1.277; πυργηδὸν σφέας αὐτοὺς ἀρτύναντες *putting* themselves *in order, dressing* their ranks, Il.12.43, cf. 86, 13.152:—Med., πυκινὴν ἠρτύνετο βουλὴν *prepared his* counsel, 2.55; ἠρτύναντο ἐρετμὰ τροποῖς ἐν δερματίνοισι *fitted* them with.., Od.4.782, 8.53.

ἀρτύς· σύνταξις, Hsch.; cf. ἀρτύν· φιλίαν καὶ σύμβασιν ἢ κρίσιν, Id. (cf. ἀραρίσκω, ἀρθμός).

ἀρτῡσία, ἡ, *art of seasoning*, cj. Mein.in Alex.36.9.

ἀρτῡσί-λᾱος or **-λεως**, ὁ, *a public servant* at Delos, Ath.4.173a (pl.):—also **ἀρτῡσιτρᾰγοι** (s. v.l.), ibid.

ἄρτ-ῡσις, εως, ἡ, (ἀρτύω) *dressing, seasoning*, Ph.*Bel.*86.32, D.S.2.59, Plu.2.99c, Gal.6.478; *mixing of metals in smelting*, Plu.2.395c. **-ῡτήρ**, ῆρος, ὁ, *director*, official of a college at Thera, *Test. Epict.*4.37, al. **-ῡτικός**, ή, όν, *fit for dressing, seasoning*, Sch.Ar.*Eq.*894: -κόν, τό, *spice*, *Sammelb.*5224.50.

ἀρτῡτοπώλης, ου, ὁ, dub. l. for ἀτυρτοπώλης in *Sammelb.*1805.

ἀρτῡτός, ή, όν, *seasoned, flavoured*, Str.15.1.59; ἅλες Dsc.2.147.

ἀρτύω Od.4.771, impf. ἤρτῠον Hom. (v. infr.), the only tenses in Hom.: fut. ἀρτύσω [ῡ] S.*Fr.*1122: aor. ἤρτῡσα Hdt.1.12, Cratin. 303: pf. ἤρτῡκα (κατ-) A.*Eu.*473:—Pass., pf. ἤρτῡμαι Pherecr., Eup., Hp., v. infr.: aor. ἠρτύθην [ῡ] Ruf.ap.Orib.4.2.4: in Att. this Verb is chiefly used in compds. with κατά and ἐξ: (cf. ἀραρίσκω):—like ἀρτύνω, *arrange, prepare, make ready*, of things requiring skill or cunning, e. g. of a smith, τὰ δ' ἤρτυε Il.18.379; σοὶ δὲ..δόλον ἤρτυε Od.11.439; τῷδ' ἤρτυεν..ὄλεθρον 16.448, cf. 20.242; γάμον... ἀρτύει 4.771; ἤρτυσαν τὴν ἐπιβουλὴν Hdt.1.12; φόνον τινί Plb.15.25.2. II. in culinary sense, *dress savoury* meat, *season*, S.*Fr.*1122, Cratin.303; ἀ. τὰ ὄψα Arist.*EN*1118ᵃ29:—Pass., κίχλαι..εἰς ἀνάβραστ' ἠρτυμέναι Pherecr.108.23; ὄψῳ πονηρῷ πολυτελῶς ἠρτυμένῳ Eup.335; τὰ πρὸς ἡδονὴν ἠρτυμένα Hp.*VM*14; ἠρτυμένος οἶνος Thphr.*Od.*51. III. *administer* property, *Leg.Gort.*12.32, *IG*5(2).3.27 (Tegea, iv B. C.), Epich.192. IV. *bequeath*, *Tab.Heracl.*1.106.

ἀρῦ, v. ἄρρυ. **ἄρυα**, τά, *walnuts*, Hsch.

ἀρῠβαλλίς, ίδος, ἡ, = sq., Hsch., *EM*150.54 (prob. l.).

ἀρύβαλλος [ῠ], ὁ, *bag* or *purse*, made so as to draw close, Stesich.11, Antiph.50. II. *globular oil-flask*, Ar.*Eq.*1094, Ath.11.783f.

ἀρυβάσσαλον· κοτύλη, Hsch.

ἀρύπᾰρος [ῠ], ον, *not sordid*, γάμος *Cat.Cod.Astr.*1.149.8.

ἀρῠσαῖα, τά, *remains of ladles*, *SIG*²588.97 (Delos, ii B. C.).

ἀρῠσάνη [ᾰρ] [σᾰ], ἡ, v.l. for ἀρύταινα, Timo 4.

ἀρῠσᾶς, ᾶ, ὁ, = ἀρυστήρ, *IG*11(2).110, al. (Delos, iii B. C.).

ἀρύσιμος [ᾰρῠ], ον, *that may be drawn*, gloss on ἀφυσγετός, Sch. Nic.*Al.*584.

ἀρύσιος, v. ἀρρ-.

ἀρυσμεῖ (Ion. for ἀρρυθμεῖ)· ἀσχημονεῖ, ἀκοσμεῖ, Hsch.

ἀρυσμίη, ἡ, Ion. = ἀρρυθμία, Hsch.: **ἄρυσμος** (= ἄρρυθμος)· εὐσχήμων (leg. ἀσχήμων), *EM*151.1.

ἄρυσος, ὁ, *wicker-basket*, Hdn.Gr.1.213. II. = ἄρρυσος, *not wrinkled, smooth*, Aët.3.126.

ἀρύσσομαι [ᾰρ], Med., *draw for oneself*, Hdt.6.119; cf. ἀρύω.

ἀρυστήρ [ᾰ], ῆρος, ὁ, = ἀρυτήρ, Alc.*Supp.*4.9, Semon.25, Hp.*Genit.* 9, *Inscr.Cos*42ᵇ, *IG*11.154 *A* 66, 161 *C* 63 (Delos, iii B. C.): dat. pl. ἀρυστήρεσσι Call.*Aet.*1.1.17: name of a *liquid measure*, Hdt.2.168.

ἀρυστικός [ᾰ], ή, όν, *for drawing liquids*, ἀγγεῖον Ael.*NA*17.37.

ἄρυστις [ᾰ], ἡ, = ἀρυτήρ, acc. pl. ἀρύστεις S.*Fr.*764:—also = ἄμυστις, *bumper*, Hsch.

ἀρύστῐχος [ᾰ], ὁ, Dim. of ἀρυτήρ, Ar.*V.*855, Phryn.Com.40, *IG*4.39 (Aegina).

ἀρυστρίς [ᾰ], ίδος, ἡ, = ἀρύταινα, *AP*6.306 (Aristo).

ἀρύταινα [ᾰρῠ], ης, ἡ, fem. of ἀρυτήρ, Ar.*Eq.*1092, Antiph.25.3, Thphr.*Char.*9.8, *PMagd.*33.3 (iii B. C.).

ἀρῠταινοειδής [ᾰ], ές, *shaped like an* ἀρύταινα, χόνδρος ἀ. *arytenoid* cartilage of the larynx, Gal.*UP*7.11, cf. 18(2).951.

ἀρῠτήρ [ᾰ], ῆρος, ὁ, (ἀρύω) *ladle* or *cup*, Dsc.2.74. 2. perh. *irrigation*, ἐμίσθωσεν..εἰς τὸν ἀρυτῆρα τοῦ ἐνεστῶτος ἔτους τὰς ἀρού[ρας... *PLond.ined.*2210 (i B. C.).

ἀρῠτήσιμος [ᾰ], ον, *that can be drawn*: *drinkable*, *AP*9.575 (Phil.).

ἀρῠτός, ὁ, *dragging*, cj. in A.*Fr.*270.

ἀρυφῆνα· ῥυτίδα, Hsch.

ἀρύω (A) [ᾰ], Simon.45, Att. **ἀρύτω** [ῠ] Pl.*Phdr.*253a; Aeol. part. ἀρυτήμενοι Alc.47: impf. ἤρῠον Hes.*Sc.*301; ἄρυον Hsch.: aor. ἤρῠσα Pherecr.138, X.*Cyr.*1.3.9:—Med., ἀρύτομαι Ar.*Nu.*272; ἀρύομαι Aeschin.Socr.11, *AP*9.37 (Tull. Flacc.), etc.: fut. ἀρύσομαι [ῠ] *AP*9.230 (Honest.), Luc.*DMar.*6.1: aor. ἠρῠσάμην Plu.2.516c; opt. ἀρῠσαίμην E.*Hipp.*209 (lyr.); inf. ἀρύσασθαι X.*Cyr.*1.2.8; part. ἀρῠσάμενος Hdt. 8.137, Ep. ἀρυσσάμενος Hes.*Op.*550:—Pass., aor. ἠρύθην, ἀπ-αρῠθείς Alex.45.6; also ἀρυσθείς Hp.*Nat.Puer.*25, Plu.2.690b:—*draw* water, wine, etc., τοὶ δ' ἤρυον others *drew off* the must, Hes.*Sc.*301; ἀρυόντεσσιν..ὕδωρ Simon.45; ἐκ πιθῶνος ἤρυσαν ἄκρατον Pherecr.l.c.; ἀρύσαντες ἀπ' αὐτῆς [τῆς φιάλης] τῷ κυάθῳ X.*Cyr.*1.3.9; μέλισσαι νέκταρ ἀρύουσιν *Lyr.Alex.Adesp.*7.18: metaph., κἂν ἐκ Διὸς ἀρύτωσιν if they *draw inspiration* from Zeus, Pl.*Phdr.*253a. II. Med., *draw water for oneself*, ἀρυσσάμενος ποταμῶν ἄπο *having drawn water* from .., Hes.*Op.*550; σφῷν ἀρύσασθαι Pherecr.130.5; ἀρύσασθαι ἀπὸ τοῦ ποταμοῦ X.*Cyr.*1.2.8; ἐκ τοῦ κρατῆρος Pl.*Criti.*120a: c. acc., ἀρύσασθαι ὑδάτων πῶμα E.*Hipp.*209; ἀ. ἐκ τῶν ποταμῶν μέλι καὶ γάλα Pl. *Ion* 534a: c. gen. partit., ὑδάτων ἀ. πρόχοισι Ar.*Nu.*272; ἐς τὸν κόλπον τρὶς ἀρυσάμενος τοῦ ἡλίου *having* (as it were) *drawn* the rays of the sun into *his* bosom, Hdt.8.137: generally, *draw in*, τροφῆς καὶ πνεύματος Diog.Bab.ap.Gal.5.281; μαντικῆς Plu.2.411f; πλοῦτον Id.*Caes.*

29; καιροῦ καὶ τύχης Eun.*Hist.*p.256 D. **2.** of stars *rising from* the sea, οἵ τ' ὠκεανοῦ ἀρύονται ἀστέρες Arat.746.

ἀρύω (B), only in Lexx., ἀρύει· ἀντὶ τοῦ λέγει, βοᾷ, Hsch.; ἀρύουσαι· λέγουσαι, κελεύουσαι, Id. (Syrac., acc. to *EM*134.12):—Med., ἀρύσασθαι· ἐπικαλέσασθαι, Hsch.

ἄρφα· ἀρραβών (i.e. *arrha*), Hsch. **ἀρφύς·** ἱμάς (Maced.), Id. **ἀρφύταινον·** δίσκος (Lyd.), Id. **ἄρχα·** ἀρραβών, Id.; cf. ἄρφα.

ἀρχάγγελος, ον, *archangel*, Lxx *Da.*10.13, al., *Ep.Jud.*9, *PMag. Lond.*121.257 (iii A.D.), Nicom.ap.*Theol.Ar.*43, Dam.*Pr.*96, Procop. *Pers.*2.11, al.:—Adj. **-γελικός,** ή, όν, θεοί Dam.*Pr.*130, cf. Procl. *in Cra.*p.37 P.

ἀρχᾱγέτας, ἀρχᾱγός, Dor., etc., = Att. ἀρχηγέτης, ἀρχηγός.

ἀρχᾱΐζω, *to be old-fashioned, copy the ancients* in manners, language, etc., D.H.*Rh.*10.7, Plu.2.558a.

ἀρχᾱϊκός (ἀρχαϊκός interpol. in Phryn.28), ή, όν, *old-fashioned*, in manners, etc., ἀρχαϊκὰ φρονεῖν Ar.*Nu.*821; ἐν τοῖς δ' ἐκείνων ἔθεσιν ἴσθ' ἀρχαϊκός Antiph.44; of literary style, D.H.*Comp.*22: Sup., Plu. 2.238c; τὰ Ἀρχαϊκά, title of work by Epicurus, *Juvenilia*, Phld.*Sto. Herc.*339.17. Adv. -κῶς Arist.*Metaph.*1089^{a}2; ἀ. ἔχειν τοῖς σχήμασι *Chron.Lind.*B.90; *stupidly*, Aristid.1.482 J.

ἀρχαιο-γονία, ἡ, *origin* of a race, Eust.1156.54, etc. **-γονος,** ον, *of ancient race, of old descent*, S.*Ant.*981. **II.** (perh. parox. ἀρχαιογόνος) *original, primal*, αἰτία Arist.*Mu.*399^{a}26 (nisi leg. ἀρχέγονον). **-γράφος** [ρᾰ], ον, *writing of antiquities*, *Gloss.* **-ειδής,** ές, *old-fashioned, archaic*, Demetr.*Eloc.*245. **-λογέω,** *discuss antiquities* or *things out of date*, Th.7.69; ἀ. τὰ Ἰουδαίων J.*BJProoem.* 6:—Pass., ἱστορία ἀρχαιολογουμένη a history *treated in an antiquarian manner*, D.H.1.74. **II.** *use an old-fashioned style*, Luc.*Lex.* 15. **-λογία,** ἡ, *antiquarian lore, ancient legends* or *history*, Pl. *Hp.Ma.*285d, D.S.2.46, D.H.1.4, Str.11.14.12; title of works by Cleanthes, Josephus, and Hieronymus Aegyptius, cf. J.*AJ*1.3. 6. **-λογικός,** ή, όν, *skilled in antiquarian lore*, Str.10.2.9 (Comp.).

ἀρχαιο-μελῐ-σῑδωνο-φρῡνῐχ-ήρᾰτος, ον, prob. in Ar.*V.*220 μέλη ἀ. *dear honey-sweet old* songs *from Phrynichus' Phoenissae* (ἀρχαῖα μελι- codd.).

ἀρχαῖον, τό, v. sub ἀρχαῖος.

ἀρχαιό-νομος, ον, *old-fashioned*, ἤθη Anon.ap.Suid. s.v. αἵρεσις. **-πῐνής,** ές, *with the patina of antiquity*, D.H.*Dem.*38. **-πλουτος,** ον, *rich from olden time, of hereditary wealth*, A.*Ag.*1043, S.*El.*1393 (lyr.), Lys.19.49, Arist.*Rh.*1387^{a}24. **-πρεπής,** ές, *time-honoured, venerable*, A.*Pr.*409, Pl.*Sph.*229e; παράκλησις Iamb.*Protr.*17: Comp., Dam.*Pr.*131. Adv. -πῶς ib.337. **2.** of literary style, *old-fashioned*, σχήματα D.H.*Comp.*23; ὀνόματα Id.*Pomp.*2; ἑρμηνεία Simp.*inPh.* 233.10 (Comp.). Adv. -πῶς ib.111.15.

ἀρχαῖος, α, ον, (ἀρχή I) *from the beginning* or *origin*: **I.** mostly of things, *ancient*, σκότος S.*OC*106; ἐσθής Hdt.5.88; δόμοις ἐπασσάλευσαν ἀρχαῖον γάνος A.*Ag.*579 codd.; Ζηνὸς ἀρχαίοις νόμοις S.*OC*1382; χερὸς σῆς πίστιν ἀρχαίαν faith *firm for ever*, ib.1632 codd. **2.** *old-fashioned, antiquated*, A.*Pr.*317 (lyr.), Ar.*Nu.*984, D.22.14; of literary style, Demetr.*Eloc.*244. **b.** *simple, silly*, Ar.*Nu.*915, al., Pherecr. 205; -ότερος εἶ τοῦ δέοντος Pl.*Euthd.*295c, etc. **3.** *ancient, former*, τὸ ἀ. ῥέεθρον Hdt.1.75; τοῦ ἀ. λόγου Id.7.160; οὐ γὰρ δὴ τό γ' ἀ. δέμας S.*OC*110; οἱ ἀ., opp. οἱ ὕστερον, Th.2.16; ἀ. φύσις A.*Ch.*281, Hp. *Art.*53, Pl.*Smp.*193c, etc.; φύσις καὶ κατάστασις ἀ. Democr.278; coupled with παλαιός, παλαιὸν δῶρον ἀρχαίου θηρός S.*Tr.*555, cf. Lys. 6.51, D. l.c. **4.** *old, worn out*, ὑποδήματα X.*An.*4.5.14; πινάκια *BGU*781 II (i A.D.). **II.** of persons, Θέμιν.. ἀρχαίαν ἄλοχον Διός Pi.*Fr.*6.5; ἀ. θεαί, of the Erinyes, A.*Eu.*728; Πέλοψ S.*Aj.*1292; οἱ ἀ. *the Ancients*, name given by Arist. to the pre-Socratics, *Metaph.* 1069^{a}25, *GC*314^{a}6; in Lit. Crit., *ancient, classical* writers, Demetr. *Eloc.*15,67; in Plot., the philosophers down to Aristotle, 5.1.9; in *NT, the Fathers, Ev.Matt.*5.21, al. **2.** *ancient, old*, βαλὴν ἀ., of Darius, A.*Pers.*657 (lyr.); λάτρις E.*Hec.*609; ἑταῖρος X.*Mem.*2.8.1; οἱ ἀ. κύριοι the *original* owners, *BGU*992 ii 6 (ii B.C.); τὰς ἀ. πόλεις (banished from) their *original* cities, Polystr.p.22 W.; ἀ. μαθητής an *original* disciple, *Act.Ap.*21.16; ἀ. μύστης *Inscr.Magn.*215 *b*; παιδαγωγὸς ἀ., i.e. *of old, formerly*, E.*El.*287, cf. 853. **III.** neut. as Adv., τὸ ἀρχαῖον, Ion. contr. τὠρχαῖον, *anciently*, Hdt.1.56, 173, al., Att. τἀρχαῖον A.*Supp.*326; ἀπὸ τοῦ ἀ. Hdt.4.117; ἐξ ἀρχαίων D.S.1.14. **2.** regul. Adv. ἀρχαίως *in olden style*, καινὰ ἀ. λέγειν Pl.*Phdr.*267b, cf. Isoc.4.8, D.9.48; ἀ. καὶ σεμνῶς Aeschin.1.183. **IV.** irreg. Comp. ἀρχαιέστερος Pi.*Fr.*45 (on ἀρχέστατος v. h. v.); usual Comp. -ότερος Ar.*Av.*469: Sup. -ότατος Hdt.1.105, etc. **V.** as Subst., τὸ ἀρχαῖον, of money, *prime cost*, πλέον τοῦ ἀ. X.*Vect.*3.2; *principal*, mostly in pl., Ar.*Nu.*1156, etc.; τἀρχαῖα ἀποδιδόναι D.34.26, etc.; τῶν ἀρχαίων ἀπέστησαν lost their *capital*, Id.1.15: opp. ἔργον, Id.27. 10; opp. πρόσοδοι, Is.6.38. **2.** ἀρχαίη, ἡ, = ἀρχή, Eust.475.1, etc.

ἀρχαιότης, ητος, ἡ, *antiquity, old-fashionedness*, Pl.*Lg.*657b, D.H. *Pomp.*2; *simplicity*, Alciphr.3.64; *pristine state*, ἀποκαταστῆσαι εἰς τὴν ἀ. τῆς αὐτονομίας *SIG*814.42 (Nero); *ancient history*, J.*Ap.*1.1, al.; *antiquity, ancient times*, D.Chr.31.94.

ἀρχαιο-τροπία, ἡ, *old fashioned ways*, Plu.*Phoc.*3. **-τροπος,** ον, *old-fashioned*, ἐπιτηδεύματα Th.1.71, cf. Ph.2.458, Iamb.*Protr.*21; of a person, D.C.59.29. Adv. -πως Dam.*Pr.*5. **-φᾰνής,** ές, *seeming ancient*, Lyd.*Mag.*1.18.

ἀρχαιόομαι, *become ancient*, ἐξ ἀρχαιωθέντος καὶ ἀμνημονεύτου χρόνου *POxy.*1915.5, al. (vi A.D.).

ἀρχαιρ-εσία, Ion. -ίη, ἡ, (αἵρεσις) *election of magistrates*, ἀ. συνίζει *an election* is held, Hdt.6.58: mostly in pl., Pl.*Lg.*752c, X.*Mem.* 3.4.1, Is.7.28, Arist.*Pol.*1281^{b}33, etc. **II.** later neut. **-έσια,** τά, Plb.4.67.1, D.H.10.17, *OGI*458.82; = Lat. *comitia*, Plb.3.106.1, etc. **-εσιάζω,** *hold an assembly for the election of magistrates*, Is. *Fr.*47, Plu.*Cam.*9, etc.; *elect* a magistrate *in the assembly*, ib.42, D.H.2.14; simply, *vote*, Plu.*Crass.*14: c. acc. inf., ib.11. **2.** *canvass for a magistracy*, Plb.26.1.5. **-εσιακός,** ή, όν, *for* ἀρχαιρεσίαι, ἐκκλησία *IGRom.*3.474 (Lycia), al. **-εσιάρχης,** ου, ὁ, *leader of a political party*, Hdn.*Epim.*167. **-ετικός,** ή, όν, = ἀρχαιρεσιακός, ἐκκλησία *SIG*730.29 (Olbia), *IGRom.*4.293 *a* ii 69 (Pergam., ii B.C.), *AJA*18.326 (Sardes, 4 B.C.).

ἀρχαϊσμός, ὁ, *old-world charm* of style, D.H.*Comp.*22. **2.** *use of obsolete expressions*, ἀ. οὗτος ῥημάτων Men.11 D., cf. Sch.E.*Hipp.* 23. **3.** *ancient custom*, περὶ ἀρχαϊσμοῦ, title of work by Manetho, Porph.*Abst.*2.55.

ἀρχε-, insep. Prefix (from ἄρχω), = ἀρχι-, with which it is sometimes interchanged, cf. ἀρχιθέωρος, etc.

ἀρχέβακχος, ὁ, *leader of* Βάκχοι, title of Dionysus, *WienerDenkschr.*44(16).104 (Seleucia ad Calycadnum).

Ἀρχεβούλειον μέτρον metre used by Archebulus, ⏑⏑–⏑⏑–⏑⏑–⏑⏑–⏑––, Heph.8.9.

ἀρχέγονος, ον, *original, primal*, τὸ ἀ. ὑγρόν Corn.*ND*17, cf. Nonn. *D.*24.48, al.; οὐσία Gal.5.418: Comp. -ώτερος Ph.2.472: Sup., Id. 1.237. **II.** (perh. parox. ἀρχεγόνος) *first author* or *origin*, ἡ φύσις πάσης τέχνης ἀρχέγονόν ἐστ' Damox.2.8, cf. D.S.1.88; τῶν ὅλων Procl.*Inst.*152; Ὠκεανὸς ἀ. πάντων Corn.*ND*8.

ἀρχ-εδέατρος, ὁ, *chief seneschal* at the Ptolemaic court, *OGI*169.4 (Alexandria), 181.4 (Paphos).

ἀρχε-δίκας [ῐ], α, ὁ, *first, legitimate possessor*, Pi.*P.*4.110. **-ζώστις,** ἡ, = ἄμπελος λευκή, Ps.-Dsc.4.182, Plin.*HN*23.21. **-θέωρος,** = ἀρχι-, *IG*11(2).205 *A*^{a}9, al. (Delos, iii B.C.); cf. ἀρκεθέωρος.

ἀρχείνη, ἡ, title of *priestess*, *SIG*890.20 (Syros, iii A.D.).

ἀρχεῖον, Ion. **ἀρχήϊον,** τό, neut. of an Adj. ἀρχεῖος, α, ον: (ἀρχή II):—*town-hall, residence*, or *office of chief magistrates*, Hdt.4.62 (dub.), Lys.9.9, X.*Cyr.*1.2.3, Isoc.5.48, Arist.*Mu.*400^{b}16; τὰ ἀ. καὶ βουλευτήρια D.10.53, cf. *IG*2.475.21, al., *OGI*268.18 (Nacrasa, iii B.C.), *PGrenf.*2.30, al. (ii B.C.). **2.** τὰ ἀ. *public records, archives*, prob. in *SIG*684.7 (Dyme, ii B.C.), cf. D.H.2.26, *PTeb.*397.19 (ii A.D.). **II.** *college* or *board of magistrates, magistracy*, Arist.*Pol.*1298^{b}28, 1304^{a} 19: but in pl., *special boards*, ib.1299^{a}36, 1331^{a}25, Plu.*Ages.*33; ὀμόσαι τὰ ἀ. *IG*2.332.45, cf. *OGI*218.149 (Ilium), etc.; ὅσοι ἀρχείων μετέχουσιν καὶ δικαστηρίων *SIG*286.20 (Milet., iv B.C.). **III.** in the Roman camp, = *principia, head-quarters*, Plu.*Galb.*12.

ἀρχειοφύλαξ [ῠ], ακος, ὁ, *keeper of archives*, = Lat. *censualis*, Lyd. *Mag.*2.30 (ἀρχαιο- codd.).

ἀρχεῖτις, ἡ, acc. -τιν, title of *priestess* at Thasos, *IG*12(8).526.

ἀρχειώτης, ου, ὁ, Lat. *archeota, a municipal recorder*, *Dig.*50.4.18. 10:—hence **ἀρχειωτικὰ** δικαστήρια courts *of record*, Lyd.*Mag.*2.15 (ἀρχαιοτ- codd.).

ἀρχέ-κᾰκος, ον, *beginning mischief*, Il.5.63, Plu.2.861a, Hld.1.9, Ph.1.359, al., Porph.*Chr.*49.22. **-λᾱος,** ον, *leading the people, chief*, A.*Pers.*297 (in Ion. form ἀρχελείων for -λῃῶν); contr. **ἀρχέλᾱς** Ar.*Eq.*164.

ἀρχελληνοδίκης [ῐ], ου, ὁ, *chief* Ἑλληνοδίκης, *CPHerm.*121.4 (iii A.D.).

ἀρχέμπορος, ὁ, *president of a guild of merchants*, *OGI*646.8 (Palmyra, iii A.D.).

ἀρχενόμενα· ξύλα, Hsch. (perh. ἀρχενομέας *principal ribs*, cf. νομεύς).

ἀρχεντᾰφιαστής, οῦ, ὁ, *president of guild of embalmers*, *UPZ*108. 10,22 (i B.C.).

ἀρχέ-πλουτος, ον, = ἀρχαιόπλουτος, S.*El.*72. **-πολις,** ι, *ruling a city*, Pi.*P.*9.54. **-πρόβουλος,** ὁ, *chairman of* πρόβουλοι, *IG*12 (9).11 (Carystus), *IG*3.1306.

ἀρχεράν-ίζω, *to be president of an* ἔρανος (q.v.), *IG*12(5).672.3 (Syros). **-ιστέω,** = foreg., ib.83, 12(1).155 (Rhodes). **-ιστής,** οῦ, ὁ, *president of an* ἔρανος, ib.2.630.4 (**ἀρχιερᾰνιστής** ib.2^{2}.1369, Hdn.Gr.1.82). **-ος,** = foreg., *IG*12(7).58.9 (Amorgos).

ἀρχεσίμολπος [ῐ], ον, *beginning the strain*, Μοῦσα Stesich.77.

ἀρχέσπερος, ον, v. ἀκρέσπερος.

ἀρχέστατος, irreg. Sup. of ἀρχαῖος, *most ancient*, A.*Fr.*187.

ἀρχέτας, ὁ, Dor. for ἀρχέτης, *leader, prince*, E.*El.*1149: as Adj., ἀ. θρόνος *princely* throne, Id.*Heracl.*753.

ἀρχέ-τῠπικῶς, Adv. *as a model*, Eust.931.22. **-τῠπος,** ον, *first-moulded as a pattern* or *model, archetypal*, σφραγίς, παράδειγμα, Ph.1. 5, al.: Comp. -ώτερος Plot.6.8.14; *exemplary, ideal*, μαῖα Sor.1. 4. **2.** Astrol., ἀ. κλῆρος, = κλῆρος τύχης, Serapio in *Cat.Cod.Astr.* 8(4).226, Vett.Val.67.3. **II.** ἀρχέτυπον, τό, *archetype, pattern, model*, opp. ἀπόγραφον, D.H.*Is.*11, cf. *APl.*4.204 ([Simon.]), Cic. *Att.*16.3.1; Philos., Plot.5.1.4, Procl. *in R.*2.296 K.; *figure on a seal*, Luc.*Alex.*21; ἀ. Διδοῦς *a portrait* of Dido *as she really was*, *APl.*4.151; δαίδαλον ἀ. *IG*14.1188; of the nominative case, *Stoic.* 2.48.

ἀρχεύω, (ἄρχω) *command*, c. dat., ἀρχεύειν Τρώεσσι Il.5.200, cf. 2. 345: c. gen., ὁμάδοιο A.R.1.347: μετὰ παισίν Poet. in *POxy.*1015. 13. **2.** *to be chief magistrate* or *official*, ἠρχευκὼς τῆς πόλεως *OGI* 166.3 (Paphos), cf. *SIG*1023.87 (Cos).

ἀρχ-εφηβεύω, *to be head of the* ἔφηβοι, *IG*4.589 (Argos). **-έφηβος,** ὁ, *head of the* ἔφηβοι, ib.5(2).52 (Tegea, ii A.D.). **-εφοδεία,**

ἡ, *function of an* ἀρχέφοδος, *POxy.*1063.5 (ii/iii A.D.). **-έφοδος,** ὁ, *chief of police*, *PTeb.*90 *Intr.* (i B.C.), *PRyl.*127.20 (i A.D.), *PTeb.* 331.15 (ii A.D.).

ἀρχέχορος, ον, *leading the chorus* or *dance*, πούς E.*Tr.*151; of a person, *IG*14.1618.

ἀρχή, ἡ, (v. ἄρχω) *beginning, origin*, νείκεος ἀ. Il.22.116; πήματος Od.8.81; φόνου 21.4, etc.; opp. τέλος, Hdt.7.51, etc.; opp. τελευτή, Thgn.607, cf. Pl.*Lg.*715e, Hp.*Morb.*1.1; ἀ. γενέσθαι κακῶν Hdt.5.97; ἀ. ποιήσασθαί τινος Th.1.128, And.2.37, Isoc.12.120, etc.; ἀ. λαβεῖν τινός Aeschin.1.11; τὰς ἀρχὰς εἰληφέναι Plb.4.28.3; ἀρχὴν ὑποθέσθαι lay *a foundation*, D.3.2, etc.; βαλέσθαι Pl.*Ep.*326e (and Pass., ἀρχαὶ βέβληνται Pi.*N.*1.8); ἀρχὴν ἄρχεσθαί τινος Pl.*Ti.*36e; *source* of action, [ὁ ἄνθρωπος] ἔχει ἀρχὴν ἐλευθέραν Plot.3.3.4. b. with Preps. in adverbial usages, ἐξ ἀρχῆς from *the beginning*, from *the first*, from *of old*, Od.1.188, Xenoph.10, etc.; οὐξ ἀ. φίλος S.*OT*385; ἡ ἐξ ἀ. ἔχθρα D.54.3; τὸ ἐξ ἀ. X.*Cyn.*12.6; but πλουτεῖν ἐξ ἀ. πάλιν *anew, afresh*, Ar.*Pl.*221; λόγον πάλιν ὥσπερ ἐξ ἀ. κινεῖν Pl.*R.*450a; ὁ ἐξ ἀ. λόγος the *original* argument, Id.*Tht.*177c, etc.; τὰ ἐξ ἀ. the *principal sum*, Arist.*Pol.*1280^{a}30:—also ἀπ' ἀ. Hes.*Th.*425, Hdt.2.104, Pi.*P.*8.25, A.*Supp.*344, Pl.*Tht.*206d; κατ' ἀρχάς in *the beginning*, at *first*, Hdt.3.153, 7.5; αὐτίκα κατ' ἀ. Id.8.94; τὸ κατ' ἀ. Pl.*Lg.*798a, al. c. acc. ἀρχήν, abs., *to begin with, at first*, Hdt.1.9, 2.28, 8.132; τὴν ἀρχὴν And.3.20: pl., τὰς ἀρχάς Plb.16.22.8: freq. followed by a neg., not *at all*, ἀρχὴν μηδὲ λαβών Hdt.3.39, cf. 1.193, al.; ἀ. δὲ θηρᾶν οὐ πρέπει τἀμήχανα S.*Ant.*92; ἀ. κλύειν ἂν οὐκ.. ἐβουλόμην Id.*Ph.*1239, cf. *El.*439, Philol.3, Antipho 5.73, Pl.*Grg.*478c; sts. c. Art., τοῦτο οὐκ ἐνδέκομαι τὴν ἀ. Hdt.4.25; τὴν ἀ. γὰρ ἐξῆν αὐτῷ μὴ γράφειν D.23.93. 2. *first principle, element*, first so used by Anaximander, acc. to Simp. *in Ph.*150.23, cf. Arist.*Metaph.*983^{b}11, etc.; Ἡράκλειτος τὴν ἀ. εἶναί φησι ψυχήν Id. *de An.*405^{a}25; of ὕλη and θεός, opp. στοιχεῖα, *Placit.*1.3.25; *practical principle* of conduct, τῶν πράξεων τὰς ἀρχὰς καὶ τὰς ὑποθέσεις D.2.10; *principles* of knowledge, Arist.*Metaph.*995^{b}8, al. 3. *end, corner*, of a bandage, rope, sheet, etc., Hdt.4.60, Hp.*Off.*9, E.*Hipp.*762, Aen.Tact.18.14, *Act.Ap.*10.11; of a compound pulley, Hero *Bel.*84.14. 4. Math., *origin* of a curve, τῆς ἕλικος Archim.*Spir.*11 *Def.*2, etc.; ξυνὸν ἀ. καὶ πέρας ἐπὶ κύκλου περιφερείας Heraclit. 103. 5. *branch* of a river, Lxx*Ge.*2.10 (pl.). 6. *sum, total*, ib.*Nu.*1.2. 7. *vital organs* of the body, Gal.1.318, al. II. *first place* or *power, sovereignty* (not in Hom.), Διὸς ἀρχά Pi.*O.*2.64, cf. Hdt.1.6, etc.; γενέσθαι ἐπ' ἀρχῆς Arist.*Pol.*1284^{b}2: metaph., μεγάλην μεντἂν ἀ. εἴης εὑρηκώς, of a stroke of fortune, D.21.196: pl., ἀρχαὶ πολισσονόμοι A.*Ch.*864 (lyr.); τὰς ἐμὰς ἀρχὰς σέβων S.*Ant.*744, etc.: c. gen. rei, τῆσδ' ἔχων ἀρχὴν χθονός S.*OT*737; ἀ. τῶν νεῶν, τῆς θαλάσσης, *power over* them, Th.3.90, X.*Ath.*2.7, etc.: prov., ἀ. ἄνδρα δείξει Bias ap.Arist.*EN*1130^{a}1, cf. D.*Prooem.*48; *method of government*, οὐδὲ τὴν ἄλλην ἀ. ἐπαχθής Th.6.54. 2. *empire, realm*, Κύρου, Περδίκκου ἀ., Hdt.1.91, Th.4.128, etc. 3. *magistracy, office*, ἀρχὴν ἄρχειν, παραλαμβάνειν, Hdt.3.80, 4.147; καταστήσας τὰς ἀ. καὶ ἄρχοντας ἐπιστήσας Id.3.89; εἰς ἀ. καθίστασθαι Th.8.70; εἰς τὴν ἀ. εἰσιέναι D.59.72, etc.; ἀ. λαχεῖν to obtain *an office*, Id.57.25; Ἑλληνοταμίαι τότε πρῶτον κατέστη ἀ. Th.1.96; ἐνιαύσιος ἀ. Id.6.54; ἀ. χειροτονητή, κληρωτή, Lex ap.Aeschin.1.21; with sg. Noun, Κυθηροδίκης ἀ. ἐκ τῆς Σπάρτης διέβαινεν αὐτόσε Th.4.53; *term of office*, ἀρχῆς λοιποὶ αὐτῷ δύο μῆνες Antipho 6.42; ἀρχαὶ καὶ λειτουργίαι *POxy.*119.16 (iii A.D.). 4. in pl., αἱ ἀρχαί *the authorities, the magistrates*, Th.5.47, cf. Decr.ap.And.1.83; ἐν ταῖς ἀ. εἶναι Th.6.54; ἡ ἀρχή collectively, 'the board', D.47.22, cf. *IG*1.229, etc.; παραδιδόναι τινὰ τῇ ἀ. Antipho 5.48; but ἡ ἀ., of a single *magistrate*, *PHal.*1.226 (iii B.C.); κατ' ἀρχῆς γὰρ φιλαίτιος λεώς against *authority*, A.*Supp.*485; πομποὺς ἀρχάς Id.*Ag.*124 (anap.). 5. *command*, i.e. *body of troops*, Lxx 1*Ki.*13.17, al. 6. pl., *heavenly powers*, *Ep.Rom.*8.38, al., cf. Dam.*Pr.*96; *powers of evil*, *Ep.Eph.*6.12, al. III. = εἶδος μελίσσης ἀκέντρου, Hsch.

ἀρχηγενής, ές, *originating, causing*, κλαυμάτων A.*Ag.*1628.

ἀρχηγ-έσια, τά, *festival of Apollo Archegetes*, *Inscr.Cos*105.16. **-ετεύω,** *to be chief leader*, τῶν κάτω Hdt.2.123. **-ετέω,** *make a beginning*, ἀπὸ τῶνδε S.*El.*83. **-έτης,** ου, ὁ, fem. **ἀρχηγέτις,** ιδος (dat. ἀρχηγέτι Ar.*Lys.*644); Dor. **ἀρχᾱγέτας:** (ἡγέομαι):—*first leader, author*, esp. *founder* of a city or family, Hdt.9.86, Pi.*O.*7.78, *IG*9(1).61.49 (Daulis); title of Apollo at Cyrene, Pi.*P.*5.60; at Naxos in Sicily, Th.6.3; of Heracles at Sparta, X.*HG*6.3.6; Asclepius in Phocis, Paus.10.32.12; Helios at Rhodes, Aristid.*Or.*24(44).50; freq. of ἥρωες, *IG*2.1191, *SIG*1024.40 (Myconos), etc.; so at Athens of ἥρωες ἐπώνυμοι, Ar.*Fr.*126, Orac.ap.D.43.66; ὁ δήμου ἀ. the *tutelary hero* of the deme, Pl.*Ly.*205d; at Sparta of the kings, ῥήτρα ap.Plu.*Lyc.*6; so at Thera, *IG*12(3).762; fem. ἀρχηγέτις, of Athena, *IG*3.65, al., cf. *BMus.Inscr.*481*.20 (Ephesus, ii A.D.); τἀρχηγέτι, = τῇ ἀρχηγέτιδι, Ar.*Lys.*644. 2. generally, *leader, chief*, A.*Supp.*184, 251, S.*OT*751, etc.; later, *governor*, Chor. in *Rev.Phil.*1.67: metaph., ἀ. φιλοσοφίας Jul.*Or.*6.188b; of a philosophical school, τῆς ἀγωγῆς Phld.*Sto.Herc.*339.12. 3. *first cause, author*, τύχης E.*El.*891; γένους Id.*Or.*555.

ἀρχηγικός, ή, όν, *original, primary, principal*, αἴτιον Ph.2.168 (Sup.), cf. Max.Tyr.17.8 (Sup.), Syrian. *in Metaph.*65.17, Procl. *in Alc.*p.250C., Jul.*Or.*5.175b (Comp.); -κά, τά, Procl.*Inst.*70.

ἀρχηγός, Dor. **ἀρχᾱγός,** όν, *beginning, originating*, λόγος ἀρχηγὸς κακῶν E.*Hipp.*881; *primary, leading, chief*, Τροίας ἀ. τιμάς Id.*Tr.*196 (lyr.); δύο φλέβες ἀ. Arist.*PA*666^{b}25. II. as Subst., *founder*, of a tutelary hero, S.*OC*60; as fem., *ancestral heroine*, B.8.51; τοῦ γένους Isoc.3.28, cf. D.S.5.56; τῆς πόλεως θεὸς ἀ. τίς ἐστιν Pl.*Ti.*21e; *founder of a family*, Arist.*EN*1162^{a}4. 2. *prince, chief*, Δία ἀ. θεῶν B.5.179, cf. A.*Ag.*259; *chief captain, leader*, Ἑλλάνων Simon.138; Βεβρύκων Theoc.22.110; ἀ. ἱερέων *CIG*6798 (Dijon), cf. 2882 (Milet.). 3. *first cause, originator*, κοπίδων Heraclit.81; πράγματος X.*HG*3.3.4, cf. Din.3.7, Isoc.12.101; συγχύσεως *SIG*684.8 (Dyme, ii B.C.); φόνου *POxy.*1241 iii 35; σωτηρίας *Ep.Hebr.*2.10; Θαλῆς ὁ τῆς τοιαύτης ἀ. φιλοσοφίας Arist.*Metaph.*983^{b}20; τῆς τέχνης Sosip.1.14; τὸ ἀ. *the originating power*, Pl.*Cra.*401d, cf. *Sph.*243d; *primary, fundamental*, ἀρχηγὸν ἡ φωνή Phld.*Po.*2.19.

ἀρχῆθεν, Dor. **-ᾶθεν,** Adv. *from the beginning, from of old*, Pi.*O.*9.55, *I.*4(3).7, Hdt.1.131, 2.138, Hp.*Epid.*6.7.5; rare in Trag., A.*Fr.*416, S.*Fr.*126; condemned by Phryn.75; freq. in later Prose, as Plb.1.50.5, al., Plu.2.238e, etc.; *immediately*, Id.*Cat.Mi.*28. 2. with neg., κρέσσον.. ἀρχῆθεν μὴ ἐλθεῖν not *at all*, Hdt.5.18; cf. ἀρχή I. 1 c.

ἀρχηΐα, ἁ, Cret., = ἀρχεία, *term of office*, *GDI*5007 (Gortyn), al. (unless name of a tribe). **ἀρχήϊον,** τό, v. sub ἀρχεῖον. **ἀρχηΐς,** ίδος, ἡ, title of *priestess*, *IG*5(1).586 (Amyclae).

ἀρχήν, Adv., v. ἀρχή I. 1 c.

ἀρχῐ-, insep. Prefix, like ἀρχε-, from the same Root as ἄρχω, ἀρχός.

ἀρχ-ῐαριστάς, ὁ, = ἀρχιερεύς, *IG*12(1).705 (Camirus), cf. *Michel* 1187 (Peraea). **-ιᾱτρεία,** ἡ, *office of* ἀρχιατρός, *archiatriae dignitas* *Cod.Theod.*13.3. **-ιᾱτρός** (on the accent v. Hdn.Gr.1.229), Ion. **-ιητρός,** ὁ, *court* or *official physician*, *OGI*256.5 (Delos, ii/i B.C.), etc.; of the Roman Emperors, Gal.14.2, al.; of communities, *arch. populares* *Cod.Theod.*13.3, *Cod.Just.*10.52.10, al.: generally, *responsible practitioner*, Aret.*CA*2.5; cf. ἀρχίατρος.

ἀρχί-βακχος, ὁ, *chief of college of* ἰόβακχοι, *IG*2^2.1368.12, al. **-βασσάρα** [σᾰ], ἡ, *leader of Bacchanals*, *CIG*2052 (Apollonia in Thrace). **-βδέλλιον,** τό, = ἄγχουσα, Ps.-Dsc.4.23 Wellm.; spelt archebion in Plin.*HN*22.51. **-βούκολος,** ὁ, *chief herdsman*, Sch.Il.1.39. II. *president of college of* βουκόλοι, *SIG*1115.3 (Pergam., i A.D.): hence **-βουκολέω,** *Inscr.Perg.*487.5. **-βουλευτής,** οῦ, ὁ, *president of council*, *Sammelb.*1106. **-βουλος,** ον, *chief in council*, Suid. **-γαλλος,** ὁ, *head of college of* γάλλοι *in mystery-cult*, *Jahresh.*14 *Beibl.*136 (Cyme, i A.D.), *JHS*19.280 (Lycaonia), etc. **-γένεθλος,** ον, = ἀρχέγονος, Orph.*H.*14.8; Ζεύς Id.*Fr.*168.5. **-γέρων,** οντος, ὁ, *chief of a* γερουσία, *Sammelb.*2100 (i B.C.), *Cod.Just.*1.4.5. **-γεωργός,** ὁ, *chief cultivator*, *POxy.*477.4 (ii A.D.), *Ostr.Strassb.*727.6 (ii A.D.). **-γραμμᾰτεύς,** έως, ὁ, *chief clerk* or *secretary*, Plb.5.54.12, Plu.*Eum.*1, etc. **-δαίμων,** ονος, ὁ, *arch-demon*, *PMag.Par.*1.1349 (pl.). **-δαφνηφορέω,** Thess. **-δαυχναφορέω,** *to be chief* δαφνηφόρος, *IG*9(2).1234 (Phalanna). **-δενδροφόρος,** ὁ, *chief of* δενδροφόροι, *IGRom.*1.614 (Tomi). **-δεσμοφύλαξ** [ῠ], ακος, ὁ, *chief gaoler*, Lxx*Ge.*39.21, Ph.1.290 (pl.):—also **-δεσμώτης,** ου, ὁ, Lxx*Ge.*40.4. **-διάκονος** [ᾱ], ὁ, *chief deacon*, Just.*Nov.*123.3. **-δῐκαστεία,** ἡ, *function of* ἀρχιδικαστής, *PLond.*3.1222.4 (ii A.D.). **-δῐκαστής,** οῦ, ὁ, *chief judge*, D.S.1.48, Plu.2.355a; at Alexandria, *BGU*1155.6 (i B.C.), *OGI*136, 682, etc. **-διοικητής,** οῦ, ὁ, *chief administrator*, *Michel*546.13 (Anisa, i B.C.).

ἀρχίδιον, τό, Dim. of ἀρχή II. 3, *petty office*, Ar.*Av.*1111; ὑπηρετεῖν τοῖς ἀ. serve *the petty magistrates*, D.18.261. II. Dim. of ἀρχή I, ἐξ ἀρχιδίου dub. in Philol.21 (ἐξ ἀρχᾶς ἀιδίω Rose).

ἀρχιεπίσκοπος, ὁ, *archbishop*, Just.*Nov.*3.2.1.

ἀρχιεράνιστής, v. ἀρχερανιστής.

ἀρχῐερ-άομαι, Med., *to be high-priest* or *priestess*, Lxx 4*Ma.*4.18, J.*AJ*17.19.1, *OGI*544.14 (Ancyra), *IG*14.1878, *BSA*16.120 (Pisidia, iii A.D.), etc.: pf. part. ἠρχιεραμένος *IGRom.*3.1475 (Iconium). **-ᾱτεία,** ἡ, = Lat. *pontificatus maximus*, *Mon.Anc.Gr.*5.22. **-ᾱτεύω** (Ion. **-ητεύω** *Inscr.Magn.*221.2 (ii B.C.)), *to be high-priest*, Lxx 1*Ma.*14.47, *PTeb.*407 (ii A.D.), *OGI*485.4 (Magn. Mae.), *IG*14.1045, etc. **-ᾱτικός,** ή, όν, *of the* ἀρχιερεύς, ἐκ γένους ἀ. *Act.Ap.*4.6, cf. J.*AJ*15.3.1, *OGI*470.21, *Jahresh.*15.51, etc.; θρόνοι Just.*Nov.*42.1.1. **-εια,** ἡ, *chief-priestess*, *SIG*846 (Delph.), 882 (Olympia), etc.: misspelt **ἀρχιερεῖα** *IG*5(2).313 (Mantinea, ii A.D.): = Lat. *virgo Vestalis maxima*, D.C.79.9. **-εύς,** έως, ὁ: Ion. **ἀρχιέρεως,** εω, Hdt.2.37, also in Pl.*Lg.*947a: acc. pl. ἀρχιρέας v.l. in Hdt.2.142:—*arch-priest, chief-priest*, ll. cc., freq. in Inscrr., νήσου *OGI*93.3 (Cyprus), etc.: esp. in Roman provinces, of the Imperial cult, ἀ. Ἀσίας ib. 458.31, etc., cf. *PRyl.*149.2 (i A.D.), etc.:—at Rome, = *pontifex*, Plu.*Num.*9, etc.; ἀ. μέγιστος, = *pontifex maximus*, *SIG*832, etc. (but ἀρχιερεύς alone, *IG*7.2711, etc.):—at Jerusalem, *high-priest*, Lxx*Le.*4.3, *Ev.Matt.*26.3, etc. (Spelt **ἀρχι-ιερεύς** *IGRom.*4.882 (Themisonium)). **-εύω,** = ἀρχιερατεύω, Gal.13.600.

ἀρχιερμηνεύς, έως, ὁ, *chief dragoman*, *Izv.Arch.Comm.*40.113 (Panticapaeum, ii/iii A.D.).

ἀρχῐερο-θῠτέω, *to be president of* ἱεροθύται (q.v.), *IG*12(1).836 (Lindus):—Subst. **-θύτης** [ῠ], ου, ὁ, *president of* ἱεροθύται, ib.788, al.

ἀρχῐερωσύνη, ἡ, *high-priesthood*, Ἀπόλλωνος *OGI*244.21 (Daphne, ii B.C.), cf. *BGU*362^{v}11 (iii A.D.), etc.; = *pontificatus maximus*, Plu.*Pomp.*67; of the Jewish *high-priesthood*, Lxx 1*Ma.*7.21, J.*AJ*15.3.1, al.

ἀρχι-εταῖρος, ὁ, *chief friend* or *companion*, Lxx 2*Ki.*16.16 (due to mistranslation of pr.n. *'Arkî*). **-ευνοῦχος,** ὁ, *chief of the eunuchs*, ib.*Da.*1.3, Hld.8.3. **-ζάκορος,** ὁ, ἡ, *chief keeper of a temple*, *CIG* 4470 (Laodicea). **-ζάπφης** or **-ος,** ὁ, title of *religious official* at

Delos, Roussel *Délos Colonie Athénienne* 416. **-θάλασσος** [θᾰ], ον, *ruling the sea*, Ποσειδῶν *AP* 6.38 (Phil.). **-θεωρέω**, *to be* ἀρχιθέωρος, D.21.115, *IG* 12(5).946 (Tenos). **-θεώρησις**, εως, ἡ, = sq., Is.*Fr.* 148. **-θεωρία**, ἡ, *the office of* ἀρχιθέωρος, Lys.21.5, *Inscr.Prien.* 174.27 (ii B.C.). **-θέωρος**, ὁ, *chief of a* θεωρία or *sacred embassy*, And.1.132, Arist.*EN* 1122^{a}25, *SIG*[2]588.15, al. (Delos, ii B.C.):—also **ἀρχεθέωρος, ἀρκιθέωρος, ἀρκεθέωρος** (q.v.); Dor. **ἀρχιθέᾱρος** *SIG* 558.24 (Ithaca). **-θῐᾰσίτης** [ῑ], ὁ, *leader of a* θίασος, *IG* 11(4).1228.4 (Delos, ii B.C.):—hence **-θῐᾰσῑτεύω**, *OGI* 591.5 (Delos), etc.; and **-θῐᾰσεύω**, *BCH* 31.446. **-θρονος**, ὁ, *occupying the chief seat, presiding*, Choerob. in *An.Ox.* 2.182. **-θύρα** [ῠ], ἡ, *principal door* of a temple, *BCH* 27.271 (Argos). **-θῠρωρός**, ὁ, *chief door-keeper*, *Sammelb.* 327. **-ίᾱτρος**, ὁ, = ἀρχίατρος, *IG* 5(2).385 (Cleitor, i/ii A.D.), *POxy.* 126.23 (vi A.D.). **-κᾰμῑνευτής**, οῦ, ὁ, *chief smelter*, *Ath.Mitt.* 19.243 (Laureion). **-κέραυνος**, ον, *ruling the thunder*, Cleanth.1.31, v.l. for ἀργι- in Orph.*Fr.* 21a. **-κερδέμπορος**, ὁ, *president of guild of merchants*, *IG* 12(8).581 (Thasos). **-κήπουρος**, ὁ, *head-gardener*, *PHamb.* 117 (iii B.C.), *BGU* 1479 (ii B.C. (?)). **-κλοπος**, ὁ, *master-thief*, Suid. **-κλωψ**, ωπος, ὁ, *robber-chief*, Plu.*Arat.* 6. **-κοιτωνίτης**, ου, ὁ, *chief chamberlain*, *IPE* 2.428 (Tanais).

ἀρχικός, ή, όν, (ἀρχή) *of* or *for rule, royal*, πυθμήν A.*Ch.* 260; γένος Th.2.80; *official*, δικαστήριον Chor. in *Rev.Phil.* 1.219: neut. pl. ἀρχικά as Subst., perh. *presents demanded by officials on entering office*, *PTeb.* 3.57 *A* 22. 2. of persons, *fit for rule, command*, or *office*, Pl.*Prt.* 352b, al., Isoc.2.24; *having served as magistrates*, *CIG* 2774 (Aphrodisias): c. gen., ἀνθρώπων X.*Mem.* 1.1.16; νεώς Pl.*R.* 488d; φύσει ἀρχικὸν πατὴρ υἱῶν Arist.*EN* 1161^{a}18; ἔστιν -κώτατα τῶν γενῶν Σκύθαι καὶ Θρᾷκες καὶ Πέρσαι Isoc.4.67. Adv. -κῶς, ἔχοντες Lib.*Or.* 11.148; ἱερατικῶς καὶ ἀ. φυλαττόμενα Just.*Nov.* 58. 3. *dominant, sovereign*, ἡ ἀρχικωτάτη ἐπιστήμη the *sovereign* science, i.e. σοφία, Arist.*Metaph.* 982^{b}4; τὴν ἀ. χώραν ἔχειν Id.*PA* 665^{b}18; ἀ. ἀρετή, opp. ὑπηρετική, Id.*Pol.* 1260^{a}23:—Math., *principal*, ἀ. συμπτώματα, of the properties of a curve, Apollon.Perg.*Con.* 1 *Praef.*; ἀ. διάμετροι *principal* diameters, ib.1.51. II. *belonging to* ἀρχαί II. 6, Dam.*Pr.* 130, 344. III. *primal, original*, γένεσις Phld.*D.* 3.14; -κώτατον αἴτιον S.E.*M.* 9.5. Adv. -κῶς ib.1.46. 2. ἀ. σχῆμα ποιήσεως in which the poet *commences with* an invocation of the Muses, Zeus, etc., Anon.*Fig.* p.149 S.

ἀρχι-κῠβερνήτης, ου, ὁ, *chief pilot*, Str.15.1.28, Plu.*Alex.* 66, *PGrenf.* 2.80.8 (v A.D.). **-κῠνηγός**, ὁ, *chief-huntsman*, a Ptolemaic court official, *OGI* 99.2 (Ptol. V), 143.3 (Cyprus, Ptol. VIII), *Ostr.* 1530, J.*AJ* 16.10.3. **-ληστής**, οῦ, ὁ, *robber-chief*, Id.*BJ* 1.10.5, Ps.-Callisth.1.36, *PMasp.* 2 iii 22 (vi A.D.).

ἀρχιλλάν· ἀρχιποίμενα (Cret.), Hsch.

Ἀρχιλόχειος, α, ον, *of* or *used by Archilochus*, μέτρον Heph. 15.2.

ἀρχι-μάγειρος [ᾰ], ον, *chief cook*, Lxx *Ge.* 39.1, al., cf. Ph.2.63; title of a great officer in Oriental courts, Lxx *Da.* 2.14, cf. J.*AJ* 10.10.3, Plu.2.11b:—also **-μᾰγειρεύς**, έως, ὁ, *dignitary* in Mithraic cult, *BCH* 37.97 (Thessalonica). **-μᾰγος**, ὁ, *chief of the magi*, *Epigr.Gr.* 903 *b* 7 (Hypaepa), Rhetor. in *Cat.Cod.Astr.* 8(4).147. **-μανδρίτης**, ου, ὁ, *chief of a* μάνδρα, *abbot*, Just.*Nov.* 5.7. **-μάχιμος** [ᾰ], ὁ, *officer of native Egyptian troops*, *PTeb.* 112.86 (ii B.C.), 121.128 (i B.C.). **-μηχᾰνικός**, ὁ, *chief engineer*, *Sammelb.* 1113 (ii A.D.). **-μῖμος**, ὁ, *chief comedian*, Plu.*Sull.* 36. **-μύστης**, ου, ὁ, *chief of the mystae*, *CIG* 2052 (Apollonia in Thrace), *Arch.Anz.* 30.175 (Kara-Ornan), *BCH* 11.483 (Lydia), Jul.Laod. in *Cat.Cod.Astr.* 4.105.33:—hence **-μυστέω**, *Eph.Epigr.* 3.236 (Perinthus). **-νᾱκορέω**, *to be chief of* νακόροι (= νεωκόροι), *BCH* 37.94 (Thessalonica). **-ναυφύλαξ** [ῠ], ακος, ὁ, *chief of naval guard*, *Annuario* 2.136 (Rhodes, i B.C.). **-νεᾱνίσκος**, ὁ, *chief of* νεανίσκοι, *CIL* 6.2180. **-νεώκορος**, ὁ, *chief of* νεωκόροι, *Milet.* 7.65 (i A.D.), *BCH* 37.97 (ii/iii A.D.). **-νεωποιός**, ὁ, *chief of* νεωποιοί, *CIG* 2811 (νεοπ- ib. 2781, 2795). **-νυκτοφύλαξ** [ῠ], ὁ, *chief of night-guard*, *Sammelb.* 4636.33 (iii A.D.). **-οινοχοεία**, ἡ, *office of chief cup-bearer*, Lxx *Ge.* 40.13. **-οινοχόος**, ὁ, *chief cup-bearer*, ib.1 sq., Plu.*Alex.* 74. **-ονηλάτης** [ᾰ], ου, ὁ, *chief donkey-driver*, *CPHerm.* 127^{r} *Fr.* 2 vii 19:—also **ἀρχονηλάτης**, *PLond.* 1.131^{r}321 (i A.D.). **-παραφύλαξ** [ῠ], ακος, ὁ, *chief of* παραφύλακες (q.v.), *OGI* 476.8. **-παρθένος**, ον, *chief among virgins*, *EM* 702.6. **-παστοφόρος**, ὁ, *head of college of* παστοφόροι (q.v.), *Ostr.* 1174, *POxy.* 241.10 (i A.D.). **-πατριώτης**, ου, ὁ, *head of a family*, Lxx *Jo.* 21.1. **-πεδῐοφύλαξ** [ῠ], ακος, ὁ, *chief of field-guards*, *Sammelb.* 4525. **-πειράτης**, ου, ὁ, Lat. *archipirata* Cic.*Off.* 2.11.40, al.:—*pirate-chief*, D.S.20.97, Plu.*Pomp.* 45, Petron.101. **-πλᾰνος**, ὁ, *nomad chieftain*, Luc.*Tox.* 39. **-ποίμην**, ενος, ὁ, *chief shepherd*, 1 *Ep.Pet.* 5.4, Sm.4 *Ki.* 3.4, *PLips.* 97 xi 4 (iv A.D.). **-πολῐάρχέω**, Thess. **ἀρχι-ττολιάρχεω**, *to be president of board of magistrates*, *IG* 9(2).1233 (Phalanna). **-πρεσβευτής**, οῦ, ὁ, *chief ambassador*, D.S.14.25, Str.17.1.11, *SIG* 810.20 (Rhodes, i A.D.). **-πρόβουλος**, ὁ, *president of* πρόβουλοι, *CIG* 4364 (Termessus). **-προστᾰτέω**, *hold office of chief* προστάτης συναγωγῆς, *Sammelb.* 626 (Ptolem.). **-προστάτης** [ᾰ], ου, ὁ, *chief official of a synagogue*, *Arch.Pap.* 2.430. **-προυρέω**, v. -φρουρέω. **-προφήτης**, ου, ὁ, *chief prophet*, Ph.1.594; *chief of* προφῆται (q.v.), *PGen.* 7.5 (i A.D.), Ps.-Callisth.3.34:—hence **-προφητεία**, ἡ, *PGen.* 36.5 (ii A.D.). **-πρύτᾰνις** [ῠ], εως, ὁ, *chief president*, *OGI* 494.3 (Milet.), *PTeb.* 397.8 (ii A.D.), *Inscr.Prien.* 246.20 (iii A.D.), etc.:—hence **-πρῠτᾰνεύω**, *BCH* 11.70 (Isaura). **-ραβδοῦχος**, ὁ, *chief lictor*, *Gloss.*:—fem. **-ραβδούχισσα**, *leader of wand-bearers*, in cult of Cybele, *IG Rom.* 1.614 (Tomi).

ἀρχιρεύς, v. ἀρχιερεύς.

ἀρχίς, ίδος, ἡ, fem. of ἄρχων, *IG* 12(5).909, al. (Tenos).

ἀρχι-σῑτοποιός, ὁ, *chief baker*, Lxx *Ge.* 40.1 sq., Ph.1.661. **-σκηπτοῦχος**, ὁ, *chief staff-bearer*, *CIG* 2987.21 (Ephesus). **-στάτωρ** [ᾰ], ορος, ὁ, *chief usher*, *POxy.* 294.17 (i A.D.). **-στολιστής**, οῦ, ὁ, *keeper of the sacred vestments*, *OGI* 111.18 (ii B.C.), *Sammelb.* 4011. **-στράτηγος** [ᾰ], ὁ, *commander-in-chief*, Lxx *Jo.* 5.15, al., J.*AJ* 6.11.9, etc. **-συνάγωγος** [ᾰ], ὁ, *ruler of a synagogue*, *Ev.Marc.* 5.22, al., *IG* 14.2304, Ramsay *Cities and Bishoprics* No. 559:—hence **-συνᾰγωγέω**, *BCH* 8.463 (Thessalonica, ii A.D.). II. *master of a guild* or *company*, *IGRom.* 1.782 (Thrace), etc. **-σωμᾰτοφύλαξ** [ῠ], ακος, ὁ, *chief of the body-guard*, Lxx *Es.* 2.21, *OGI* 99.1 (ii B.C.), *PTeb.* 79.52 (ii B.C.), J.*AJ* 12.2.5. **-ταβλάριος**, ὁ, (*tabularium*) *keeper of records*, ἀ. Αἰγύπτου *OGI* 707.6 (Tyre, ii A.D.).

ἀρχιτεκτον-εύμα, ατος, τό, *construction*, Bito 61.2. **-εύω**, = sq., Id.45 (Pass.). **-έω**, *to be architect, chief constructor*, or *commissioner of works*, Plu.*Per.* 13, Sosip.1.16, *OGI* 656, etc.: c. acc., *design, construct*, τριακοντήρη ib.39 (iii B.C.); βιβλιοθήκην Afric.*Cest.* *Oxy.* 412.67:—Pass., τὴν οἰκίαν.. εὖ ἠρχιτεκτονῆσθαι Thphr.*Char.* 2.12. 2. generally, *contrive*, Ar.*Pax* 305, *Fr.* 195; *supervise, direct*, -τεκτονοῦντος τοῦ Πλάτωνος Phld.*Acad.Ind.* p.15 M. **-ημα**, ατος, τό, *stroke of art, artifice*, Luc.*Asin.* 25. **-ία**, ἡ, *architecture, construction*, Lxx *Ex.* 35.32, Bito 49.2, Gal.5.68. **-ικός**, ή, όν, *of* or *for an* ἀρχιτέκτων or his business and art, Pl.*Plt.* 261c; of persons, *fit to be a master-builder, skilled in his art*, Arist.*Pol.* 1282^{a}3. II. ἡ -κή (sc. τέχνη or ἐπιστήμη) *architecture*, Sosip.1.36. 2. *master-art* or *science*, which prescribes to all beneath it, as an ἀρχιτέκτων to his workmen, Arist.*EN* 1094^{a}14, *Metaph.* 1013^{a}14, al.; *professional knowledge*, Id.*Po.* 1456^{b}11.

ἀρχι-τεκτοσύνη, ἡ, *conduct of office of* ἀρχιτέκτων, *BCH* 10.500 (Pisidia). **-τέκτων**, ονος, ὁ, *chief-artificer, master-builder, director of works*, τοῦ ὀρύγματος, τῆς γεφύρας, Hdt.3.60, 4.87; opp. χειροτέχνης, Arist.*Metaph.* 981^{a}30; opp. ἐργατικός, Pl.*Plt.* 259e; *commissioner of works*, *IG* 2.403, al., ib.9(1).694.145 (Corcyra), *SIG* 284.12 (Chios, from Erythrae), etc.; ἀ. τοῦ ναοῦ ib.494.3 (Delph.); ἀ. ἐπὶ τὰ ἱερά *IG* 2.404. b. pl., *board of naval constructors*, Arist.*Ath.* 46.1. 2. generally, *author, contriver*, E.*Cyc.* 477; ἀ. κύριος τῆς ἡδονῆς Alex. 149.2; ἀ. τῆς ἐπιβουλῆς D.56.11; τοῦ τέλους Arist.*EN* 1152^{b}2; τοὺς ταῖς διανοίαις ἀ. τινός *those that direct activities* by thought, Id.*Pol.* 1325^{b}23. II. at Athens, *manager of the state theatre and of the Dionysia*, D.18.28, *IG* 2.335. **-τελώνης**, ου, ὁ, *chief toll-collector, chief-publican*, *Ev.Luc.* 19.2. **-τρίκλῑνος**, ὁ, *president of a banquet* (*triclinium*), *Ev.Jo.* 2.9. 2. *head-waiter*, Hld.7.27. **-υπασπιστής**, οῦ, ὁ, *chief of the men-at-arms*, Plu.*Eum.* 1. **-υπηρέτης**, ου, ὁ, *chief minister*, *IG* 14.914 (iii A.D.), *BGU* 21 iii 9 (iv A.D.):—also **ἀρχυπηρέτης**, *Sammelb.* 599.61, *Ostr.* 1538. **-φερεκίτης** [κῑ], ου, ὁ, *head of Jewish school*, Just.*Nov.* 146.1.2. (Aram. *pirkā* 'lesson'.) **-φῐλος**, ὁ, *principal friend*, dub. l. in J.*AJ* 7.9.6 (prob. ἀρχαῖον φίλον). **-φρουρέω**, *command a* φρουρά, *IG* 9(2).1059 (Thess.): also in form **-προυρέω**, ib.1058. **-φρουρος**, ὁ, *commandant of a* φρουρά, Ἀρχ.Ἐφ. 1911.124 (Gonnos). **-φῠλᾰκέω**, *hold office of* ἀρχιφύλαξ (q.v.), *OGI* 565.12 (Oenoanda); ἠρχιφυλακηκότα Λυκίων τοῦ κοινοῦ *TAM* 2.143 (Lydae). **-φῠλᾰκία**, ἡ, *office of* ἀρχιφύλαξ, *OGI* 566.17 (Oenoanda):—written **-φῠλᾰκεία**, *IGRom.* 3.593 (Sidyma). **-φῠλᾰκίτης**, ὁ, *commandant of* φυλακῖται (q.v.), *PRev.Laws* 37.5 (iii B.C.), *PHib.* 1.73, *PTeb.* 5.142 (ii B.C.):—hence **-φῠλᾰκιτεία**, ἡ, *office of* ἀ., ib.27.22 (ii B.C.), and **-φῠλᾰκιτεύω**, *hold such office*, *PAlex.* 9.4 (iii B.C.(?)). **-φύλαξ** [ῠ], ακος, ὁ, *commandant of guards*, in Egypt, *PGiss.* 9.13 (ii A.D.). II. title of an *official of the Lycian league*, *TAM* 2.199 (Sidyma). **-φύλαρχος** [ῠ], ὁ, *chief of the* φύλαρχοι, Zos. 3.22. **-φῦλος**, ὁ, *chief of a tribe*, Lxx *De.* 29.10(9). **-φωρ**, ωρος, ὁ, = ἀρχίκλωψ, D.S.1.80. **-χορος**, ὁ, *leader of chorus*, *IG* 12(2).484.20 (Mytil.).

ἄρχματα· ἀπάρχματα θεοῖς, Hsch.

ἀρχο-γλυπτάδης, ου, ὁ, *son of a place-hunter*, *Com.Adesp.* 84. **-ειδής**, ές, *of the nature of a principle*, Arist.*Metaph.* 999^{a}2, *APo.* 86^{b}38, Plu.2.1085c, *Theol.Ar.* 8, al.: Comp., Alex.Aphr.*Febr.* 21, Simp. *in Ph.* 7.21: Sup., Alex.Aphr.*Febr.* 7, Dam.*Pr.* 52 ter. Adv. -δῶς Procl.*Inst.* 65, Syrian. *in Metaph.* 3.23.

ἀρχοινόχοος, contr. -χους, ὁ, *chief butler*, *IG* 9(1).486 (Thyrrheum), *PTeb.* 72.447 (ii B.C.).

ἀρχολαβῶν· ἡ ἐργολαβῶν, Hsch.

ἀρχονηλάτης, v. ἀρχιονηλ-.

ἀρχολῖπᾰρος [ῐ], ον, *grasping at office*, *Com.Adesp.* 84.

ἀρχοντ-εύω, *hold office of* ἄρχων, *IPE* 1[2].130.17 (Olbia, ii/iii A.D.). **-ιάω**, *wish to be ruler*, Sch.Ar.*V.* 342, Lyd.*Mag.* 1.28. **-ικός**, ή, όν, *of an archon*, πέλεκυς *AP* 9.763 tit. (Jul. Aegypt.); ὑπηρεσία *PGrenf.* 2.82.15 (400 A.D.): generally, *of a ruler*, *Corp.Herm.* 1.25. 2. *ex-archon*, *IG* 14.756^{a} (Naples), cf. 1789. **-ίς**, ίδος, ἡ, fem. of ἄρχων, *Cat.Cod.Astr.* 2.177.8.

ἀρχός, ὁ, *leader, chief*, εἷς δέ τις ἀρχὸς ἀνὴρ Il.1.144: c. gen., νηῶν 2.493; οἰωνῶν Pi.*P.* 1.7; *ruler*, Τειχιούσσης *SIG* 3 *d* (Milet., vi B.C.); πόλεως (opp. ἔτης), prob. in E.*Fr.* 1014. 2. = ἄρχων, *IG* 7.3301, al. 3. ἀ. ἑῴας, = *dux Orientis*, ib.14.1073 (iv A.D.). 4. of a god, *SIG* 56.26 (Argos, v B.C.). II. *the rectum*, Hp.*Aph.* 5.58, Arist. *HA* 507^{a}33, *Theol.Ar.* 51. 2. *the anus*, Hp.*Haem.* 2, *Epid.* 5.20.

ἀρχο-στάσια [ᾰ], τά, = ἀρχαιρέσια, *IG* 5(2).437 (Megalop., ii B.C.), Ἀρχ.Ἐφ. 1917.2, 10 (Perrhaebia). **-στάσιος** [ᾰ], ὁ (sc. μήν), month *in which elections were held* at Erineos, *GDI* 2030. **-στάται** [ᾰ], οἱ, *electoral college for the appointment of magistrates* in Lycia, *IGRom.* 3.473.44.

ἀρχυπηρέτης, v. ἀρχιυπηρέτης.

Ἀρχύτειος [ῡ], α, ον, *belonging to Archytas*, Iamb.*Comm.Math.* 7 (-ιος cod.).

ἄρχω, Ep. inf. ἀρχέμεναι Il.20.154: impf. ἦρχον ib.2.378, etc.; Dor. ἆρχον Pi.*O.*10(11).51: fut. ἄρξω Od.4.667, A.*Pr.*940, Th.1. 144: aor. ἦρξα, Ep. ἄρξα Od.14.230, etc.: pf. ἦρχα *CIG*3487.14 (Thyatira), Decr.ap.Plu.2.851f:—**Med.**, Od.8.90, etc.; non-thematic part. ἄρχμενος Call.*Aet.*3.1.56, al.: impf., Il.9.93, Hdt.5.28: fut. ἄρξομαι (in med. sense, v. infr.) Il.9.97, E.*IA*442, X.*Cyr.*8.8.2; Dor. ἀρξεῦμαι Theoc.7.95: aor. ἠρξάμην Od.23.310, etc.:—**Pass.**, pf. ἦργμαι only in med. sense, v. infr. I. 2: aor. ἤρχθην, ἀρχθῆναι Th.6. 18, Arist.*Pol.*1277^{b}13, v. infr. II. 4:—*to be first*, I. in Time, *begin, make a beginning*, Act. and Med. (in Hom. the Act. is more freq., in Att. Prose the Med., esp. where personal action is emphasized), πολέμου ἄρχειν *to be the aggressor*, Th.1.53; π. ἄρχεσθαι *to begin one's* operations, X.*HG*6.3.6; ἄρχειν τοῦ λόγου *to open* a conversation, Id.*An.*1.6.6; ἄρχεσθαι τοῦ λόγου *to begin one's* speech, ib.3.2.7. Constr.: 1. mostly c. gen., *make a beginning of*, ἄρχειν πολέμοιο Il.4.335; μύθων Od.3.68; τῶν ἀδικημάτων πρῶτον τοῦτο ἄρξαι Hdt. 1.2; ἦρξεν ἐμβολῆς A.*Pers.*409; τοῦ κακοῦ ib.353; ἄρχειν χειρῶν ἀδίκων, ἄρχειν τῆς πληγῆς, *strike the first* blow, Antipho 4.2.1 and 2:—in Med. in religious sense, = ἀπάρχεσθαι, ἀρχόμενος μελέων *beginning with* the limbs, Od.14.428, cf. E.*Ion*651; but Act., σπονδαῖσιν ἄρξαι Pi.*I.*6(5).37. 2. c. gen., *begin from* or *with...*, ἐν σοὶ μὲν λήξω σέο δ' ἄρξομαι Il.9.97; ἄρχεσθαι Διός Pi.*N.*5.25; πόθεν ἄρξωμαι; A.*Ch.* 855; πόθεν ποτὲ ἦρκται Hp.*VM*5; ἄρχεσθαι, ἦρχθαι ἔκ τινος, Od.23. 199, Hp.*Off.*11; ἀπό τινος freq. in Prose, ἀρξάμενοι αὐτίκα ἀπὸ παιδίων *even* from boyhood, Hdt.3.12; but more commonly ἐκ παίδων, ἐκ παιδός, etc., Pl.*R.*408d, *Thg.*128d:—ἀπό in non-temporal relations, ἀρξάμενος ἀπὸ σοῦ, i.e. *including* yourself, Pl.*Grg.*471c, cf. D.18.297; ἀπὸ τῶν πατέρων X.*Mem.*3.5.15; μέχρι τῶν δώδεκα ἀπὸ μιᾶς ἀρξάμενος Pl.*Lg.*771c; ἀφ' ἱερῶν ἠργμένη ἀρχή ib.771a; ἀφ' Ἑστίας ἀρχόμενος Ar.*V.*846. 3. c. gen. rei et dat. pers., ἄρχε θεοῖς δαιτός *begin* a banquet to the gods, Il.15.95; τοῖς ἄρα μύθων ἦρχε 2.433, etc.; τῇσι δὲ.. ἄρχετο μολπῆς Od.6.101; ἦρξε τῇ πόλει ἀνομίας τὸ νόσημα Th.2. 53, cf. 12; τὴν ἡμέραν ἄρχειν ἐλευθερίας τῇ Ἑλλάδι X.*HG*2.2.23; ἡμῖν οὐ σμικρῶν κακῶν ἦρξεν τὸ δῶρον S.*Tr.*871. 4. c. acc., ἄρχειν ὁδόν τινι, *show* him the way, Od.8.107 (but also ἄρχειν ὁδοῖο *lead* the way, 5.237): abs. (sc. ὁδόν), ἄρχε δ' Ἀθήνη 3.12; σὺ μὲν ἄρχε Il.9.69; ἦ ῥα καὶ ἄρχε λέχοσδε κιών 3.447; ἦρχε δ' ἄρα σφιν Ἄρης 5.592, cf. infr. II. 2: with other accusatives, ἄρχειν ὕμνον Pi.*N.*3.10; ἅπερ ἦρξεν A.*Ag.*1529 (lyr.); λυπηρόν τι S.*El.*552; ὕβριν Id.*Fr.*368. 5. of actions, σέο δ' ἕξεται ὅττι κεν ἄρχῃ Il.9.102: freq. c. inf., τοῖσιν δ' ἦρχ' ἀγορεύειν among them, Il.1.571, etc.; ἦρχε νέεσθαι, ἦρχ' ἴμεν, 2.84, 13.329; ἄρχετε νῦν νέκυας φορέειν Od.22.437, etc.; ὑφαίνειν ἤρχετο μῆτιν Il.7.324; ἤρξαντο οἰκοδομεῖν Th.1.107; ἡ νόσος ἤρξατο γενέσθαι Id.2.47: c. part., of continued action or condition, ἦρχον χαλεπαίνων Il.2.378; ἢν ἄρξῃ ἀδικέων Hdt.4.119; ἡ ψυχὴ ἄρχεται ἀπολείπουσα X.*Cyr.*8.7.26; πόθεν ἂν ὀρθῶς ἀρξαίμεθα ἐπαινοῦντες; Pl.*Mx.*237a, cf. *Tht.*187a (but ἄ. ἐπαινεῖν Id.*Phdr.*241e); ἄρξομαι διδάσκων X.*Cyr.*8.8.2 (but ἦρξω μανθάνειν Id.*Mem.*3.5.22). 6. abs., ἄρχε *take the lead!* Il.9.69: generally, *begin*, ἄρχειν [τὴν ἐκεχειρίαν] τήνδε τὴν ἡμέραν Indut.ap.Th.4.118, cf. Lex ap.D.24.42; τὸ ἄρχον, opp. τὸ ἑπόμενον, Dam.*Pr.*234: part. ἀρχόμενος *at first*, X.*Eq.*9.3, *Cyn.*3.8, Isoc.2.54; *at the beginning*, ἀρχομένου δὲ πίθου καὶ λήγοντος Hes.*Op.*368, cf. *Fr.*192.4; ἀρχομένοισιν ἢ καταπαυομένοισι Ar.*Eq.* 1246; ἄρχεται ὁ πόλεμος ἐνθένδε Th.2.1; ἅμα ἦρι ἀρχομένῳ ibid.; θέρους εὐθὺς ἀρχομένου ib.47. 7. Gramm., of a word, ἄ. ἀπὸ φωνήεντος D.T.633.27; ἡ ἄρχουσα (sc. συλλαβή) A.D.*Synt.*130. 13. II. in point of Place or Station, *rule, govern, command*, 1. mostly c. gen., *rule, be leader of...*, Βοιωτῶν Il.2.494, cf. Hdt.5.1, etc. 2. less freq. c. dat., ἀνδράσιν ἦρξα Od.14.230, cf. 471, Il.2. 805, Pi.*P.*3.4, A.*Pr.*940, E.*Andr.*666, *IA*337, *IG*7.2830 (Hyettus), etc.; also ἐν δ' ἄρα τοῖσιν ἦρχ' *held command* among them, Il.13. 690, cf. Pl.*Phdr.*238a: c. inf. added, ἄρχε Μυρμιδόνεσσι μάχεσθαι *led* them *on* to fight, Il.16.65. 3. abs., *rule*, ὅσον τό τ' ἄρχειν καὶ τὸ δουλεύειν δίχα A.*Pr.*927, cf. *Pers.*774; esp. *hold a magistracy*, ὁκοῖόν τε εἴη ἄρχειν μετὰ τὸ βασιλεύειν Hdt.6.67; at Athens, etc., *to be archon*, D.21.178; ἀρχάς, ἀρχὴν ἄρχειν, Hdt.3.80, Th.6.54; ἄρχειν τὴν ἐπώνυμον (with or without ἀρχήν) *IG*3.659,693, *SIG*872.7. 4. Pass., with fut. ἄρξομαι Hdt.7.159, Pi.*O.*8.45, A.*Pers.*589, Lys.28.7; but ἀρχθήσομαι Arist.*Pol.*1259^{b}40, D.C.65.10:—*to be ruled, governed*, etc., ὑπό τινος Hdt.1.127; ἔκ τινος S.*El.*264, *Ant.*63; ὑπό τινι Hdt.1.91, 103; σφόδρα ὑπό τινος Lys.12.92; ἄρχε πρῶτον μαθὼν ἄρχεσθαι Sol. ap.D.L.1.60, cf. Pl.*Prt.*326d; δύνασθαι καὶ ἄρχεσθαι καὶ ἄρχειν Arist. *Pol.*1277^{b}14; οἱ ἀρχόμενοι *subjects*, X.*An.*2.6.19, etc.

ἄρχων, οντος, ὁ, (part. of ἄρχω) *ruler, commander*, νεός Hdt.5.33: abs., A.*Th.*674, S.*Aj.*668, etc.; *chief, king*, Ἀσίας A.*Pers.*73; ἄ. τοῦ κόσμου τούτου, of Satan, *Ev.Jo.*16.11, al. II. as official title, *chief magistrate*, esp. at Athens, Th.1.126, etc.; οἱ ἐννέα ἄρχοντες *IG*2. 163; οἱ ἄ., at Sparta, *the authorities*, Hdt.6.106: sg., ὁ ἄρχων the *eponymous magistrate of the year*, *IG*1.52, al., Arist.*Ath.*3.3, etc.; so in Boeotia, at Delphi, Delos, and elsewhere, *IG*7.2407, *SIG*295. 18, *IG*2.814, etc.; = Lat. *consul*, Plb.1.39.1. 2. *governor* of a dependency or province, e.g. in the Athenian Empire, *IG*1.62^{b}19, etc.; of a Roman *governor*, *OGI*441.59; = *praefectus*, Plb.6.26.5. 3. generally, *magistrate, official*, Aeschin.3.29, etc.; opp. ἰδιώτης, *SIG* 672.16 (Delph.); *ruler* of a synagogue, *Ev.Matt.*9.18; *president* of a club, *PLond.*3.1178.6 (ii A.D.).

ἀρχ-ωνέω, *to be an* ἀρχώνης, *PRev.Laws* 14.3, al., *BCH*1.410 (Callipolis). **-ώνης**, ου, ὁ, *chief contractor* or *farmer of revenue*, And.1.133 (ἄρχων εἷς codd.), *PRev.Laws* 10.10, al., *CIG* (add.) 3912; ἀ. λιμένων, = *promagister portorii*, *Ephes.*2 No.29; ἀ. τεσσαρακοστῆς λιμένων Ἀσίας *promagister quadragesimae...*, *OGI*525.5 (Halic.).

ἀρχωνίδας, = δρῦς, Pl.Com.233.

ἀρωγή [ᾰ], ἡ, (ἀρήγω) *aid, succour*, Ζηνὸς ἀρωγῇ Il.4.408; ἐς μέσον... δικάσσατε μηδ' ἐπ' ἀρωγῇ judge impartially and not in any one's *favour*, ib.23.574; πέμπειν ἀ. A.*Ch.*477 (lyr.); οὐδ' ἔχων ἀ. S.*Ph.*856 (lyr.); in parody of A., Ar.*Ra.*1267 sq.; ἀ. νόσου, πόνων, *help against...*, Pl. *Lg.*919c, *Mx.*238a. II. of persons, *an aid, succour*, διπλᾶς ἀρωγὰς μολεῖν, of Apollo and Artemis, S.*OC*1094 (lyr.); στρατιῶτιν ἀ., of the Greek host, A.*Ag.*47, cf. 73 (lyr.).—Poet. word, rare in Prose.

ἀρωγοναύτης [ᾰ], ου, ὁ, *helper of sailors*, *AP*9.290 (Phil.).

ἀρωγός [ᾰ], όν, (ἀρήγω) *aiding, succouring, propitious*, τινί Pi.*O.*2. 49, A.*Eu.*289: abs., Id.*Pr.*997, S.*OT*206 (lyr.):—rare in Prose, *beneficial*, medically, Hp.*Aër.*10; ἔλαιον.. ταῖς θριξὶ ἀ. Pl.*Prt.*334b. 2. c. gen., *serviceable, useful towards* a thing, ἀρωγὰ τῆς δίκης ὁρκώματα A.*Eu.*486; γένος ναΐας ἀρωγὸν τέχνας *serviceable* in sea-craft, S.*Aj.* 357; δίψους ἀ. *against* thirst, Antiph.150; πόνων Luc.*Trag.*54: with Preps., ἐπὶ ψευδέσσι Il.4.235; πρός τι Th.7.62: and c. dat., ῥίζας ἐχίεσσιν ἀ. *serviceable against*, Nic.*Th.*636. II. as Subst., *helper*, esp. in battle, ὅσοι Δαναοῖσιν ἀρωγοί Il.8.205, etc.; also, *defender* before a tribunal, *advocate*, ib.18.502; ἀρωγοὺς ξυνδίκους θ' ἥξω λαβών A.*Supp.*726.

ἀρῳδιός, v.l. for ἐρῳδιός, Lxx*Le.*11.19, al.

ἄρωμα (A) [ᾰρ], ατος, τό, *aromatic herb* or *spice*, Hp.*Aph.*5.28, X. *An.*1.5.1, prob. in *Supp.Epigr.*1.414 (Crete, v/iv B.C., pl.), Arist.*Pr.* 907^{a}13, *IG*5(2).514.17 (Lycosura, ii B.C., pl.), Plu.*Phoc.*20.

ἄρωμα (B) [ᾰρ], ατος, τό, (ἀρόω) *arable land, corn-land*, S.*Fr.*75 (pl.), Ar.*Pax*1158, Eup.304.

ἀρωμᾰτ-ίζω [ᾰρ], *spice*, στέαρ Dsc.1.66:—Pass., Id.2.76.10; ἠρωματισμένον ἔλαιον *Inscr.Prien.*112.62 (i B.C.). 2. intr., *have a spicy flavour or scent*, D.S.2.49, Str.16.2.41, Plu.2.623e. **-ικός**, ή, όν, *aromatic*, δυνάμεις Dsc.2.171, Plu.2.383f; -κόν, τό, ib.791b; -κή (sc. ὠνή), ἡ, *contract for supply of spices*, *Röm.Mitt.*13.121. **-ιστέον**, *one must spice, perfume*, Dsc.2.76.8. **-ίτης**, ου, ὁ, fem. **-ῖτις**, ιδος, ἡ, = ἀρωματικός, οἶνος Id.5.54; σχοῖνος Str.16.2.16.

ἀρωμᾰτο-πώλης [ᾰρ], ου, ὁ, *dealer in spices*, Ptol.*Tetr.*179, Artem. 2.22. **-φόρος**, ον, *spice-bearing*, [γῆ] Str.1.2.32; Ἀραβία Dsc.1. 13, cf. Plu.*Alex.*25, Luc.*Macr.*17. 2. Subst. -φόρος, ὁ, *servant in charge of spices*, J.*AJ*17.8.3.

ἀρωμᾰτώδης [ᾰρ], ες, *likespice, spicy*, Dsc.1.13, Gal.1.399, Ath.1.33e.

ἀρώμεναι, v. ἀρόω.

ἀρωνία, ἡ, = ἄρον, corrupt in Phan.ap.Ath.9.371d. 2. = **μέσπιλον**, Dsc.1.118.

ἀρωραῖος, hyperdor. for ἀρουραῖος, Ar.*Ach.*762.

ἀρώσιμος [ᾰ], ον, poet. for ἀρόσιμος (q.v.), S.*Ant.*569.

ἄρωσις, εως, ἡ, = ἄροσις, *POxy.*280.16 (i A.D.).

ἄρωστος [ᾰ], ον, poet. for ἄρρωστος, *AP*11.206 (Lucill.).

ἆς, Aeol., and **ἄς**, Dor., = ἕως, Sapph.25, Pi.*O.*10(11).51, Ar.*Lys.* 173, Theoc.14.70; esp. in sense *as long as*, *Leg.Gort.*4.27, al., *Tab. Heracl.*1.100.

ἀσαγεύω, dub. in B.8.13.

ἀσάζειν· λυπεῖσθαι, Hsch.

ἆσαι, contr. for ἀάσαι, v. ἀάω. **ἆσαι, ἄσαιμι**, v. ἄω. **ᾆσαι, ᾄσας**, v. ᾄδω. **ἀσαίνων**· ὑβρίζων, λυπῶν, Hsch.

ἄσακτος, ον, (σάττω) *not trodden down*, γῆ X.*Oec.*19.11.

ἀσᾰλάμινιος [μῐ], ον, *not having been at Salamis*, Ar.*Ra.*204.

ἀσάλγαν· ὕβριν, ἀμέλειαν, Hsch. **ἀσαλγάνας**· φοβερός, Id.; cf. ἀσελγής.

ἀσάλεια [σᾰ], ἡ, (ἀσαλής) *carelessness*, Sophr.113.

ἀσάλειν [σᾰ]· ἀφροντισθῆναι, σάλα γὰρ ἡ φροντίς, Hsch.

ἀσάλευτος [σᾰ], ον, *unmoved, unshaken*, ἀ. ἡ γῆ Arist.*Mu.*392^{b}34; of Delos, *AP*9.100 (Alph.); ἔσται ἀσάλευτον πρὸ ὀφθαλμῶν Lxx*Ex.* 13.16, al.; πρῷρα *Act.Ap.*27.41; of the sea, prob. in Plu.2.982f: metaph. of the mind, E.*Ba.*391 (lyr.); ἀ. ἡσυχία Pl.*Ax.*370d; πίστις Polystr.p.10 W.; βασιλεία *Ep.Hebr.*12.28; στάλα ἀ. *Hymn.Is.*4; νίκη *IG*9(1).270 (Atalante); ἀ. μένειν, of ordinances, *PLips.*34.35 (iv A.D.), cf. *Sammelb.*4324.12. Adv. -τως Plb.9.9.8: neut. pl. as Adv., χείλεσι ἀσάλευτα μεμυκόσι *AP*12.183 (Strat.).

ἀσαλής, ές, *unthinking, careless*, μανία A.*Fr.*319; cf. ἀσάλειν.

ἄσᾰλος, ον, = ἀσάλευτος, Plu.2.981c.

ἀσάλπικτος, ον, *without sound of trumpet*, ὥρα ἀ. the hour *when no trumpet sounds*, i.e. midnight, S.*Fr.*389.

ἀσάμβᾰλος, = ἀσάνδαλος, Nonn.*D.*32.256, 44.14.

ἀσάμινθος [ᾰσᾰ], ἡ, *bathing-tub*, ἐς ῥ' ἀσάμινθον ἕσασα having made sit in it, Od.10.361; ἐκ ῥ' ἀ. βῆ 3.468; ἐς ῥ' ἀσαμίνθους βάντες ἐυξέστας Il.10.576, al.; ἀργυρέας ἀ. Od.4.128: rare in Att., ἐξ ἀ. κύλικος λείβων from a cup *as large as a bath*, Cratin.234; later, Artem.1.56, *PStrassb.*29.37 (iii A.D.).

ἄσᾱμος, Dor. for ἄσημος.

Ἀσάνα, Ἀσᾶναι, Ἀσᾱναῖος, Lacon. for Ἀθην-, Ar.*Lys.*1300,980, al.

ἀσάνδᾰλος, ον, *unsandalled, unshod*, Pherecyd.105 J., Bion 1.21.

ἄσαντος, ον, (σαίνω) *not to be soothed, ungentle*, θυμός A.*Ch.*422 (lyr.). II. = οὐ σαίνων, Hsch.

ἀσᾰπής, ές, (σήπομαι) *not decayed*, Hp.*Epid.*5.27, Arist.*Pr.*909^{b}4, Thphr.*HP*3.12.3. Adv. -έως, = ἀπέπτως (acc. to Gal. ad loc.), Hp. *Acut.*16.

ἄσαρ, = ἄσαρον (q.v.), Aët.1.131, Suid.

ἀσᾰρίτης [ᾰσ] οἶνος wine *made from hazelwort* (ἄσαρον), Dsc.5. 58, *Gp.*8.6 tit.

ἀσαρκ-έω, causal, *make lean*, Hp.*Vict.*1.35. **-ία**, ἡ, *want of flesh, leanness*, Arist.*HA*493^{b}23, Aret.*SD*1.8,16, Luc.*Anach.*25. **-ος**, ον, *without flesh, lean*, opp. σαρκώδης, Hp.*VM*8, X.*Cyn.*4.1, Arist. *Pr.*867^{b}34 (Sup.), Opp.*C.*1.474 (Sup.); φύλλον Thphr.*HP*3.11.1 (Comp.); *bare of flesh*, Hp.*Fract.*18; ὀστᾶ *Com.Adesp.*1205; τέττιξ *AP*9.264 (Apollon. or Phil.): Comp., ib.5.101 (Marc. Arg.). 2. *not consisting in flesh*, δίαιτα Epicur.*Fr.*464; τροφή Porph.*Abst.*1. 1. II. (ἀ- copul.) *fleshy*, Lyc.154. **-ώδης**, ες, *lean, meagre-looking*, Aret.*SD*1.8.

ἄσᾰρον [ᾰσ], τό, a plant, *hazelwort, Asarum europaeum*, Crateuas *Fr.*7, Dsc.1.10, Gal.11.840, Androm.ap.Gal.14.52. 2. = βάκχαρις, Ps.-Dsc.3.44.

ἄσᾱρος, Aeol. for ἀσηρός, Sapph.77 (Comp.). **ἄσᾰρος**, ον, = sq., Hsch.

ἀσάρωτος [σᾰ], ον, *unswept*, οἶκος a room *paved in mosaic to look as if strewn with crumbs*, Plin.*HN*36.184.

ἄσασθαι, ἄσεσθε, v. ἄω. **ἄσατο**, contr. for ἀάσατο, v. ἀάω, *hurt*. **ἀσαυτόν**, v. αὑσαυτόν.

ἀσάφ-εια [σᾰ], ἡ, *want of clearness, uncertainty, obscurity*, opp. σαφήνεια, Pl.*R.*478c, cf. Plu.*Sol.*19, Arr.*Tact.*1.3; personified, Emp.122. 4:—later **ἀσᾰφία**, ἡ, Plb.1.67.11; Ion. **ἀσαφίη** Hp.*Praec.*14. **-ήνιστος**, ον, *not explained, declared*, Sch.E.*Med.*722 (dub.). **-ής**, ές, *indistinct* (to the senses), *dim, faint*, σημεῖα Th.3.22; σκιαγραφία Pl.*Criti.*107d; *indistinct* (to the mind), *uncertain, obscure*, πάντ' .. αἰνικτὰ κἀσαφῆ λέγεις S.*OT*439; νὺξ διὰ τὸ σκοτεινὴ εἶναι ἀσαφεστέρα ἐστίν by night one sees *less distinctly*, X.*Mem.*4.3.4; ἀ. πέλαγος *AP* 12.156; *inarticulate*, γλῶσσα Hp.*Epid.*1.26.ιγ'; of sounds, Arist. *Aud.*801^{b}21; φθέγματα *Epigr.Gr.*1003.6. 2. of persons, *obscure*, διδάσκαλος Pl.*R.*392d. II. Adv. -φῶς *obscurely*, Id.*Cra.*427d; πολεμοῦνται ἀσαφῶς ποτέρων ἀρξάντων *without knowing* which began, Th.4.20.

ἀσάω [ᾰσ], Thgn.593; elsewh. Pass. **ἀσάομαι**, imper. ἀσῶ, part. ἀσώμενος: aor. ἠσήθην: (ἄση):—orig. *glut oneself, take a surfeit*, and so perh. in Sapph.*Supp.*2.7; but usu., *feel loathing* or *nausea*, caused by surfeit, ἀσᾶται Hp.*Morb.Sacr.*25, *Int.*35; of pregnant women, Arist.*HA*584^{a}22: metaph., *to be disgusted* or *vexed at* a thing, c. dat., μηδὲν ἄγαν χαλεποῖσιν ἀσῶ φρένα Thgn.657, cf. 593; ὅταν δέ τι θυμὸν ἀσηθῇς Id.989; ἄσαιο Sapph. l. c.; ἐδίζητο ἐπ' ᾧ ἂν μάλιστα τὴν ψυχὴν ἀσηθείη Hdt.3.41; ἀσώμενος ἐν φρεσί Theoc.25.240; Aeol. ἀσάμενοι [σᾰ] *disgusted*, Alc.35.—Never in good Att.; in later Prose, πολλὰ ἀσώμενοι καὶ ἀδημονοῦντες Ph.*Fr.*74 H.

ἄσβεσθε· διέφθειρε (Cret.), Hsch.

ἀσβεστήριοι, οἱ, (ἄσβεστος II) *plasterers*, Hsch. s. v. κονιαταί.

ἀσβέστινον (sc. λίνον), τό, a *non-combustible* material, dub. l. in Plin.*HN*19.20.

ἄσβεστος, ον, also η, ον Il.16.123:—*unquenchable, inextinguishable*, φλόξ Il. l. c.; *not quenched*, πῦρ ἄ. D.H.3.67, Plu.*Num.*9; κλέος Od.4.584; γέλως Il.1.599; βοή 11.50; ἐργμάτων ἀκτὶς καλῶν ἄ. αἰεί Pi.*I.*4(3).42; ἄ. πόρος ὠκεανοῦ ocean's *ceaseless* flow, A.*Pr.*532 (lyr.); πῦρ, of hell, *Ev.Marc.*9.43. II. as Subst., ἄσβεστος (sc. τίτανος), ἡ, *unslaked lime*, Dsc.5.115, Plu.*Sert.*17, *Eum.*16; ἄ. κονία Lyc.ap. Orib.8.25.16. 2. a mineral or gem, Plin.*HN*37.146. **ἀσβεστώδης**· *tofus, Gloss.*

ἀσβέστωσις, εως, ἡ, *plastering*, Hsch. s. v. κονίασις.

ἀσβηνοί· ὄρνιθες, Hsch.

ἀσβολαίνεται· *fuscatur, Gloss.*

ἀσβολάω, = foreg., Aesop.59.

ἀσβόλη, ἡ, = ἄσβολος, Semon.7.61, Dsc.5.161, Gal.8.378.

ἀσβολθέν· μέγα, ὑψηλόν, μέλαν, Hsch.

ἀσβολοποιός, όν, *turning into soot*, Eust.1949.36.

ἄσβολος, ἡ (ὁ, Hippon.105), more Att. form for ἀσβόλη, *soot*, Ar. *Th.*245, Alex.98.16, Thphr.*Ign.*39, Luc.*Tim.*2.

ἀσβολόω, *cover with soot*, in pf. part. Pass. ἠσβολωμένος Macho ap. Ath.13.581e, cf. Plu.*Cim.*1, Arr.*Epict.*3.16.3.

ἀσβολώδης, ες, *sooty*, Dsc.1.68.6.

Ἀσγελάτας, epith. of Apollo, *IG*12(3).248.8,27 (Anaphe); cf. Αἰγλάτας:—hence **Ἀσγελαῖα**, τά, festival of Apollo, ib.249.22.

ἄσδος, = στήλη λιθίνη, Arc.45.5.

ἆσε, contr. for ἄασε, v. ἀάω.

ἀσέβ-εια, ἡ, *ungodliness, impiety*, opp. ἀδικία, διὰ τὴν ἐκείνων περὶ μὲν θεοὺς ἀ. περὶ δὲ ἀνθρώπους ἀδικίαν X.*Cyr.*8.8.7; ἀ. εἰς τοὺς θεούς Antipho 5.88, cf. Pl.*R.*615c, etc.; also ἀ. ἀπὸ τοῦ θεοῦ Lxx 2*Ki.*22. 22; ἀ. ἀσκεῖν E.*Ba.*476; δίκη ἀσεβείας πρὸς τὸν βασιλέα Lys.6.11; ἀσεβείας γράφεσθαί τινα Pl.*Euthphr.*5c: at Rome, *disloyalty to the Emperor* (as θεός), D.C.57.9; of Christianity, Id.68.1: in pl., ἀσέβειαι ἀνθρώποις ἐμπίπτουσι νέοις Pl.*Lg.*890a. **-έω**, *to be impious, act profanely, commit sacrilege*, Hdt.1.159; opp. ἀδικέω, Ar.*Th.*367; ἀ. ἐς τὸν νηόν Hdt.8.129, cf. E.*Ba.*490, Antipho 5.93; περὶ τὰ ἱρά, τοὺς θεούς, Hdt.2.139, Antipho 4.1.2, cf. X.*Ap.*22, etc.; πρὸς τὰ θεῖα Id. *Cyn.*13.16: c. acc. cogn., ἀ. ἀσέβημα Pl.*Lg.*910e; ἀγγελίας καὶ ἐπιτάξεις παρὰ νόμον ἀ. ib.941a; περὶ οὗ τὴν ἑορτὴν ἀσεβῶν ἑάλωκε D.21. 227. 2. c. acc. pers., *sin against*, ἢ θεὸν ἢ ξένον τιν' ἀσεβῶν A.*Eu.* 271 (lyr.); ἀ. θεούς D.S.1.77, Plu.2.291c; τὸ ἱαρὸν *IG*7.2418 (Thebes, iv B.C.); τὸν Καίσαρα *POxy.*1612.23 (iii A.D.):—Pass., ἀσεβοῦνται οἱ θεοί Lys.2.7; ἠσεβῆσθαι πρός τινος D.C.57.9; of households, *to be affected with the consequences of sin*, ὅταν τις ἀσεβηθῇ τῶν οἴκων Pl. *Lg.*877e. 3. Pass. also of the act, ἐμοὶ ἠσέβηται οὐδὲν περί τινος And.1.10; τὰ ἠσεβημένα Lys.6.6. **-ημα**, ατος, τό, *impious* or *profane act, sacrilege*, opp. ἀδίκημα, Antipho 2.1.3, Th.6.27, D.21. 104; τὰ περὶ τοὺς θεοὺς ἀσεβήματα Id.16.130. **-ής**, ές, (σέβω) *ungodly, unholy, profane, sacrilegious*, opp. εὐσεβής, Pi.*Fr.*132.1, A. *Supp.*9 (anap.); τὸν ἀσεβῆ, of Oedipus, S.*OT*1382,1441; σκοπῶν τί ἀ. X.*Mem.*1.1.16: c. gen., θεῶν ἀσεβής *against* them, Paus.4.8.1; ἀσεβέστεροι περὶ θεούς X.*Cyr.*8.8.27; πρὸς ἀλλοτρίους J.*BJ*5.10.5. Adv. -βῶς, Sup. -έστατα D.C.79.9.

ἄσειρος, ον, *without trace*, ἵππος Eust.1734.2.

ἀσείρωτος, ον, *not drawn by a trace* (but by the yoke, cf. σειραφόρος), ὄχημα E.*Ion* 1150.

ἄσειστος, ον, *unshaken*, γῆ Max.Tyr.41.4: metaph., εὐδαιμονία Id. 4.5, cf. D.L.8.26. Adv. -τως *unshakably*, Epicur.*Ep.*2 p.36 U., Arr. *Epict.*2.17.33.

ἄσεκτος, ον, Dor. for ἄψεκτος, Rhinth.15.

ἀσελγ-αίνω, impf. ἠσέλγαινον D.21.31: fut. ἀσελγανῶ Id.24.143: aor. inf. ἀσελγᾶναι D.C.52.31:—Pass., pf. ἠσέλγημαι (v. infr.): plpf. ἠσέλγητο J.*AJ*17.5.6:—*to be* ἀσελγής, *behave licentiously*, And.4.7, Pl.*Smp.*190c; εἴς τινα D.54.5:—Pass., of acts, τὰ εἰς ἐμὲ ἠσελγημένα *outrageous acts*, Id.21.19. **-εια**, ἡ, *licentiousness, wanton violence*, Pl.*R.*424e, Is.3.13, etc.; οἳ προελήλυθ' ἀσελγείας ἄνθρωπος D.4.9: joined with ὕβρις, Id.21.1; *insolence*, opp. κολακεία, Phld.*Lib.*p.42 O.; τῶν δημαγωγῶν Arist.*Pol.*1304^{b}22: Astrol., epith. of certain ζῴδια, Vett.Val.335.34. II. *licentiousness*, περὶ τὰς σωματικὰς ἐπιθυμίας Plb.36.15.4, etc. **-έω**, late form of ἀσελγαίνω, Sch.Ar.*Pl.* 1093. **-ημα**, ατος, τό, *licentious act*, prob. in Plb.38.2.2, cf. Plu. *in Hes.*64, Suid. s. v. ἀστυάνασσα; *vulgar abuse*, in pl., *POxy.*903. 21 (iv A.D.). **-ής**, ές, *licentious, wanton, brutal*, And.4.40 (Sup.), D.2.19 (Comp.); εἰς ἔμ' ἀ. καὶ βίαιος Id.21.128, cf. Is.8.43; σκῶμμα Eup.244: generally, *outrageous*, ἄνεμος Id.320. Adv. -γῶς, πίονες *extravagantly* fat, Ar.*Pl.*560; ἀ. ζῆν D.36.45; ἀ. διακείμενος Lys.24. 15; ἀ. τινὶ χρῆσθαι D.9.35. II. *lascivious, lewd*, Jul.*Caes.*315c.

ἀσελγό-κερως, ὁ, ἡ, *with outrageous horn*, κριός Pl.Com.210. **-μᾰνέω**, *to be madly dissolute*, Ps.-Luc.*Philopatr.*7. **-ποιός**, όν, *producing licentious persons*, δεκανοί Antioch.Astr. in *Cat.Cod.Astr.*8 (3).109.13.

ἀσέληνος, ον, *moonless*, νύξ Th.3.22, cf. Plb.7.16.3, App.*BC*5.114.

ἀσέλῑνος, ον, *without crown of celery*, νίκη D.C.68.19.

ἀσεμνολόγητος, ον, *not solemnly extolled*, Eust.342.39.

ἄσεμνος, ον, *undignified, ignoble*, Arist.*Mu.*398^{b}4, Ph.2.406, Hdn. 2.7.1; esp. in Lit. Crit., D.H.*Comp.*7, al., Demetr.*Eloc.*189, Longin. 43.1; *indecent*, Eust.1950.63. Adv. -νως A.D.*Conj.*232.9, al.; βίον ἀ. διῆγεν *BGU*1024 vii 22 (iv/v A.D.).

ἀσεπτέω, = ἀσεβέω, εἰς θεοὺς μηδὲν ἀσεπτεῖν S.*Ant.*1350 (lyr.).

ἄσεπτος, ον, *unholy*, τὰ ἄσεπτα S.*OT*890 (lyr.); Πρωτέως ἀσέπτου παιδός E.*Hel.*542, cf. *Pae.Delph.*22.

ἄση [ᾰ], Aeol. **ἄσα**, ἡ, *surfeit, loathing, nausea*, Hp.*Aph.*5.61 (pl.), *Acut.*(*Sp.*)14; ἄση περὶ τὴν καρδίαν *Epid.*7.10; ἄ. πλησμονή Sch.Il. *Oxy.*221 xi 18. 2. *distress, vexation*, Hdt.1.136, Andronic.Rhod. p.570 M.; ἔπαυσε καρδίαν ἄσης E.*Med.*245: pl., μή μ' ἄσαισι μήτ' ὀνίαισι δάμνα θῦμον Sapph.1.3, cf. Alc.*Supp.*14.11; λύπας καὶ ἄσας παρέχειν Pl.*Ti.*71c, cf. *Stoic.*3.100. 3. *longing, desire*, κῆρ ἄσᾳ βόρηται Sapph.*Supp.*25.17. II. = ἄσις, Luc.*Cyn.*1, Poll.1.49, Opp. *H.*3.433. (Cf. ἄω *satiate*.)

ἀσηκορίς· ἀδικία, Hsch. **ἀσήκορος**· ἀκηδιαστής, Id.

ἀσημ-άνθρωπος, ὁ, 'electron-man', Zos.Alch.p.207 B.; cf. ἀργυράνθρωπος. **-αντος**, ον, *without leader* or *shepherd*, μήλοισιν ἀσημάντοισιν ἐπελθών Il.10.485, cf. Tryph.616; δόμος Opp.*H.*3. 361. II. *unsealed, unmarked*, Hdt.2.38, Pl.*Lg.*954a, Hyp.*Fr.*4; = ἀφύλακτος, Hsch. 2. *giving no sign*: hence, *unseen, unknown*, Nonn.*D.*3.95, 5.232; *unintelligible*, ἔπεα ib.10.31. III. ἀσήμαντοι τούτου ὃ .. σῶμα ὀνομάζομεν *not entombed* in this, which we call body, Pl.*Phdr.*250c, with play on signf. II. 1, cf. Dam.*Pr.*161. IV. *uncoined*, χρυσὸς καὶ ἄργυρος App.*Hisp.*23, *Pun.*66. V. Act., opp. σημαντικός, *without significance*, λέξις Diog.Bab.*Stoic.*3.213; φωνή Plu.2.1026a. Adv. -τως Paul.Aeg.3.15. **-αντρος**, ον, *without seal*, *PMasp.*151.10 (vi A.D.).

ἀσημείωτος, ον, *unnoticed*, πηγὴν παρελθεῖν Ph.1.121; ἀσαμήωτον αὐτοῦ τὰν παρουσίαν ἀφέμεν *GDI*3059.22 (Byzantium, i A.D.). II. *without signposts*, of a road, Demetr.*Eloc.*202. III. *not capable of being inferred by signs*, ἀσημείωτα πάντα ποιοῦσι τἀφανῆ Phld.*Sign.* 30.

ἀσημοκλέπτης, ου, ὁ, *thief of plate*, *AP*11.360.

ἄσημος, Dor. **ἄσᾱμος**, ον, *without mark* or *token*, ἄ. χρυσός *uncoined* gold, bullion, or plate, Hdt.9.41; ἄ. χρυσίον, ἀργύριον, Th.2. 13, 6.8, Alex.69; freq. in Inscrr., opp. ἐπίσημον, *IG*1.170.6, 2.652 *B* 22, etc., cf. Luc.*Cont.*10; also of cattle, *not branded*, *IG*7.3171; of persons, *without distinguishing marks* (e.g. οὐλαί), *PGrenf.*1.27.7, al.; ἄ. ὅπλα arms *without device*, E.*Ph.*1112: generally, *shapeless, formless*, Opp.*C.*3.160. 2. later τὸ ἄσημον (sc. ἀργύριον) *plate, silver*, Lxx *Jb.*42.11, *AP*11.371 (Pall.); μέταλλα ἀσήμου *silver*-mines, Ptol.*Geog.*7.2.17: also, = *electron*, alloy of gold and silver, or an imitation thereof, Ps.-Democr.Alch.p.49 B., etc.:—masc. **ἄσημος**, ὁ, *PLeid.X.*6, al. II. of sacrifices, oracles, and the like, *unintelligible*, χρηστήρια Hdt.5.92.β'; χρησμοί A.*Pr.*662; ἄ. ὀργίων μαντεύματα S.*Ant.*1013. **III.** *leaving no mark, indistinct,* a. to the hearing, πτερῶν γὰρ ῥοῖβδος οὐκ ἄ. ἦν ib.1004; of sounds and voices, *inarticulate, unintelligible,* ἄσημα φράζειν Hdt.1.86; ἄ. κνυζήματα Id.2.2; ἄσημα βοῆς, = ἄσημος βοή, S.*Ant.*1209. b. *without significance, meaningless,* [τοῦ διπλοῦ ὀνόματος] τὸ μὲν ἐκ σημαίνοντος καὶ ἀσήμου Arist.*Po.*1457ᵃ33, *Rh.*1405ᵃ35; ἄσημα τρίζειν, of a mouse, Babr.108.23; μόριον *Stoic.*2.46; λέξις Simp.*in Ph.*1164.4. c. to the eye, ἄσημον ἔχειν μυελόν Arist.*PA*652ᵃ1: generally, πρὸς τὴν αἴσθησιν -ότερα Id.*Aud.*802ᵃ14. d. generally, *unperceived, unnoticed,* A.*Ag.*1596, S.*Ant.*252; ἀσήμων ὑπὲρ ἑρμάτων *hidden, sunken* rocks, Anacr.38. **IV.** of persons, cities, etc., *of no mark, obscure, insignificant,* οὐκ ἄ. E.*HF*849, cf. *Ion* 8; νὺξ οὐκ ἄ. a night *to be remembered* (being a feast), Antipho 2.4.8; τὸ τῆς πατρίδος ἢ τοῦ γένους ἄσημον Phld.*Sto.Herc.*339.16. **V.** Adv. -μως *without leaving traces,* Hp.*Epid.*1.1, *Morb.Sacr.*11; ἀ. πορεύεσθαι X.*Cyn.*3.4; ἀ. καὶ κενῶς φθέγγεσθαι *inarticulately,* Theopomp.Hist.250. **2.** *ignobly,* οὐκ ἀ. D.S.5.52, Hdn.1.10.4.

ἀσημότης· *ignobilitas, Gloss.*

ἀσήμων, ον, gen. ονος, = ἄσημος III, S.*OC*1668.

ἀσημωνία, ἡ, *farming of trade in silver bullion,* *BGU*1242 (iii/ii B.C.).

ἄσηπτος, ον, *not liable to decay* or *corruption,* Hp.*Fist.*4, X.*Cyn.*9.13 (Sup.), Arist.*HA*521ᵃ1, etc.; ξύλα ἄ., of *Acacia tortilis,* Lxx *Ex.*25.5, cf. Thphr.*HP*4.2.8: Sup., κέδρος Ph.2.147. **2.** *undigested,* σιτία Hp.*Aff.*24.

ἀσηρής, ές, = sq., *causing discomfort,* Gal.18(2).850.

ἀσηρός [ᾰ], όν, (ἄση) *causing discomfort,* Hp.*Fract.*22,33, Plu.2.713a. Adv. -ρῶς Poll.3.99. **2.** *feeling disgust, disdainful,* Sapph.77 (Comp.): Medic., *feeling discomfort,* Ruf.ap.Orib.45.30.22.

ἄσηρος, ον, (σῆρες) *without worms,* Suid.

ἄσηστος, ον, (σήθω) *unsifted,* Diph.Siph.ap.Ath.3.115d, Sor.1.50.

ἀσθέν-εια, ἡ, *want of strength, weakness,* Th.1.3, etc.: in pl., ἰσχύες καὶ ἀ. Pl.*R.*618d; esp. *feebleness, sickliness,* Hdt.4.135; ἀ. τοῦ γήρως Antipho 4.3.2, Pl.*R.*330e; σωμάτων Th.4.36, etc. **2.** *disease, sickness,* Id.2.49 (pl.), *OGI*244.11 (Daphne, ii B.C.), etc.; δι' ἀσθένειαν *Ep.Gal.*4.13. **3.** ἀ. βίου *poverty,* Hdt.2.47, 8.51. **4.** in moral sense, *feebleness, weakness,* τῆς ἀνθρωπίνης φύσεως Pl.*Lg.*854a, cf. Arist.*EN*1150ᵇ19; τοῦ ἀκροατοῦ Arist.*Rh.*1419ᵃ18.—Rare in poetry, as E.*HF*269. **-έω,** *to be weak, feeble, sickly,* ἀ. μέλη *to be weak* in limb, E.*Or.*228; τοὺς ὀφθαλμοὺς ἀ. Pl.*Ly.*209e; ἀ. ἀσθένειαν Id.*Chrm.*155b: abs., E.*Hipp.*274, Th.7.47, *Ev.Matt.*10.8, etc.; ἠσθένησε he *fell sick,* D.1.13; ἀσθενέων *sick man,* Hp.*VM*12 (Phot. says that μαλακίζεσθαι is used of women); ἠσθενηκότα Plb.31.13.7. **2.** *to be needy,* Ar.*Pax*636; ἠσθενηκότες, of those *unable to pay* taxes, *PTeb.*188 (i B.C.). **3.** c. inf., *to be too weak* to do a thing, *not to be able..,* J.*BJ*2.15.5; εἰς τὸ θεωρεῖν Plot.3.8.4. **4.** *decline,* ἠσθένησεν ἡ ἡμέρα εἰς τὴν ἑσπέραν Lxx *Jd.*19.9. **-ημα,** ατος, τό, *weakness, ailment,* Arist.*GA*726ᵃ15, *Gp.*1.12.27 (pl.); *weakness* of conscience, *Ep.Rom.*15.1 (pl.). **-ής,** ές, *without strength, weak,* **1.** in body, *feeble, sickly,* τοὺς ἀσθενέας τῆς στρατιῆς Hdt.4.135, cf. Hp.*VM*12; ἀσθενεῖ χρωτὶ βαίνων Pi.*P.*1.55, etc.; ὁ παντάπασιν ἀ. τῷ σώματι D.21.165; ἀ. περὶ τὸν ὀφθαλμόν Luc.*Nigr.*4; τοὺς ἀσθενεστάτους ἐς τὰς ταλαιπωρίας *least able to bear* hardship, Hdt.4.134; ἀσθενέστερος πόνον ἐνεγκεῖν *too weak* to.., D.23.54. Adv. ἀσθενῶς, ἴσχειν Pl.*Lg.*659e, cf. *OGI*751.8 (Amblada, ii B.C.). **2.** in mind, and the like, τὸ ἀ. τῆς γνώμης *the weakness,* Th.2.61. **3.** in power, *weak, feeble,* ἀ. δύναμις Hdt.7.9.α', cf. 1.58; τέχνη δ' ἀνάγκης -εστέρα μακρῷ A.*Pr.*514; πόλιν ἑνὸς -εστέραν S.*OC*1033; εἰς ὠφέλειαν ἀ. D.*Ep.*2.15. **4.** in property, *weak, poor,* οἱ χρήμασιν ἀσθενέστεροι Hdt.2.88: abs., ὅ τ' ἀ. ὁ πλούσιός τε E.*Supp.*433; οἱ ἀσθενέστεροι *the weaker sort,* i.e. *the poor,* X.*Cyr.*8.1.30, cf. Lys.1.2. **5.** *insignificant,* οὐκ ἀσθενέστατος σοφιστὴς Ἑλλήνων Hdt.4.95; *paltry,* ἀ. σόφισμα A.*Pr.*1011; of streams, *petty, small,* Hdt.2.25; of fluids, *of small specific gravity,* Id.3.23; ἐς ἀσθενὲς ἔρχεται comes to *nothing,* Id.1.120. Adv. -νῶς *feebly, without energy,* Pl.*R.*528b; *on slight evidence,* ἀπαγγέλλεσθαι Onos.*Praef.*: Comp. ἀσθενεστέρως, ἐπιθυμεῖν Pl.*Phdr.*255e; -έστερον Id.*Chrm.*172b; -έστερα Th.1.141. **-ικός,** ή, όν, *weakly,* παιδίον Arist.*HA*587ᵃ20, Timo 26.1, Luc.*Tox.*19. Adv. -κῶς, αἰσθάνεσθαι Arist.*Insomn.*462ᵃ20.

ἀσθενο-ποιέω, *make weak,* App.*Mac.*9.6. **-ποιός,** όν, *causing weakness,* Archig.ap.Aët.12.1, Sch.A.R.2.205, Sch.Nic.*Th.*158. **-ρρῖζος,** ον, *with weak roots,* Thphr.*CP*4.14.4.

ἀσθεν-όφθαλμον ζῴδιον, of the Ram, Rhetor. in *Cat.Cod.Astr.*7.194.2, cf. 1.166.19.

ἀσθενό-ψῡχος, ον, *weak-minded,* Lxx 4*Ma.*15.5.

ἀσθεν-όω, *weaken,* X.*Cyr.*1.5.3. **-ωσις,** εως, ἡ, *weakness, faintness,* Hp.*Judic.*20.

ἆσθμα, ατος, τό, *short-drawn breath, panting,* ἆσθμα καὶ ἱδρώς Il.15.241; ἀργαλέῳ ἄσθματι ib.10; ὑπ' ἄσθματος κενοί A.*Pers.*484; ἄσθματι στρευγόμενος Tim.*Pers.*93; ὑπὸ ἄσθματος ἀδυνατεῖν Pl.*R.*568d, cf. 556d; as symptom of anger, Phld.*Ir.*p.27 W.; *death-rattle,* Pi.*N.*10.74. **II.** Medic., *asthma,* Hp.*Aph.*3.22 (pl.), etc. **III.** *breath, breathing,* Mosch.3.53, Luc.*DDeor.*11.2, Philum.*Ven.*36.3; *blast,* ἀρκτῴοις ἄσθμασι *AP*9.677 (Agath.); ἀ. φλογός Coluth.179; κεραυνοῦ Nonn.*D.*1.2. (On the accent v. Hdn.Gr.1.522.)

ἀσθμ-άζω· ἀσθμαίνω, *AB*451. **-αίνω,** *breathe hard*: used by Hom. in pres. part., *panting,* as after running, τὼ δ' ἀσθμαίνοντε κιχήτην Il.10.376; *gasping for breath,* of one dying, ὅ γ' ἀσθμαίνων.. ἔκπεσε δίφρου 5.585, cf. 10.496, Pi.*N.*3.48: pres. ind., Hp.*Morb.*3.7, Arist.*Pr.*905ᵇ33: impf., Luc.*DMeretr.*5.4; οὐδὲν ἀσθμαίνων without *an effort,* A.*Eu.*651; ἀ. τι *pant for* a thing, Hld.4.3: c. acc. cogn., ἀ. πυρὸς δριμεῖαν ὁμοκλήν Opp.*H.*4.14. **-άομαι,** = foreg., prob. in *PMag.Leid.W.*12.28. **-ατίας,** ου, ὁ, = sq., Adam.2.41. **-ατικός,** ή, όν, *suffering from dyspnoea* or *asthma,* Herod.Med.ap.Orib.10.8.9, Antyll.ib.6.8.4, Dsc.1.25, Gal.13.106; *panting,* Man.4.274. **-ατώδης,** ες, = foreg., Hp.*Epid.*2.2.19, 4.21. **-ησις,** εως, ἡ, = ἆσθμα, *Gloss.*

Ἀσία [ᾰ], Ion. -ίη, ἡ, *Asia,* Pi.*O.*7.18, Hdt.1.4, 4.45, A.*Pr.*412; γῆ Ἀσία S.*OC*694, etc.:—Adj. **Ἀσιᾱνός,** ή, όν, *Asian, Asiatic,* Th.1.6, etc.; Ἀ. ῥήτορες Theon *Prog.*2; Ἀ. ζῆλος Str.14.1.41, Plu.*Ant.*2. Adv. -νῶς, ἐστιᾶν τινά D.C.46.30:—fem. **Ἀσιάς,** άδος, and **Ἀσίς,** ίδος [the latter with ᾰ], freq. in A. and E., never in S., Ἀσιάς being required by the metre in E.*Or.*1397 (lyr.), *Ba.*1168 (lyr.), *Cyc.*443, Ἀσίς in A.*Pers.*270 (lyr.), *Supp.*547 (lyr.), cf. Euph.34: Ἀσιάς (sc. γῆ), = Ἀσία, E.*Tr.*748, *Ion* 1356; also (sc. κιθάρα), *the Asian harp,* Ar.*Th.*120, cf. E.*Cyc.*443, Plu.2.1133c:—also **Ἀσιάτης,** -ᾱτις, Ion. **-ήτης, -ῆτις,** A.*Pers.*61 (lyr.), E.*Andr.*1, etc.: **Ἀσιᾱτικός,** ή, όν, Str.15.2.8: **Ἀσίηθεν,** Adv. *from Asia, CIG*6336. (Fem. of ἄσιος (q.v.).)

Ἀσιᾱγενής, ές, *of Asiatic descent,* D.S.17.77; = *Asiaticus,* cognomen of Scipio, Id.35.33: Ion. **Ἀσιηγενής,** Opp.*C.*1.235.

ἀσίαρος· ἐπισκάζων, ἢ ἀσίδαρος, Hsch.

Ἀσι-άρχης, ου, ὁ, *an Asiarch,* priest of the Imperial cult in the province of Asia, Str.14.1.42, *Act.Ap.*19.31, *IG*12(3).531, 14.2405, etc.; Ἀ. ναῶν τῶν ἐν Ἐφέσῳ *OGI*525.8 (Halic.):—hence **-αρχέω,** *BMus.Inscr.*481*.240 (Ephesus, ii A.D.), etc. **-αρχία,** ἡ, *office of* Ἀσιάρχης, *Dig.*27.1.6.14. **-αρχος,** ὁ, = Ἀσιάρχης, *CIG*2990ᵃ (Ephesus).

Ἀσιᾱτογενής, ές, *of Asian birth,* A.*Pers.*12, Critias 6.6 D.

ἀσῑγ-ησία, ἡ, *inability to keep silence,* Plu.2.502c. **-ητος,** ον, *never silent,* Call.*Del.*286, Nonn.*D.*42.405, al.

ἄσιγμος, ον, *without sigma,* ᾠδαί D.H.*Comp.*14; ἄ. ᾠδή, name of a poem of Lasus *without a sigma in it,* Ath.10.455c:—hence **ἀσιγμοποιέω,** *compose such a poem,* ibid.

ἀσίδα, ἡ, = Hebr. *hᵃsidhah, stork,* Lxx *Jb.*39.13, *Je.*8.7: cf. ἄσιδον· ἐρωδιόν, Hsch.

ἀσίδηρος [ῐ], ον, *not of iron,* μοχλοί E.*Ba.*1104; *not made by iron,* αὖλαξ *AP*9.299 (Phil.). **II.** *without sword,* χείρ E.*Ba.*736; μάχη *sham* fight, Onos.10.4; βίος Max.Tyr.36.1.

Ἀσιῆτις, Ion. for Ἀσιᾶτις.

ἄσικχος, ον, *not nice as to food,* Plu.*Lyc.*16. **II.** *not easily causing satiety* or *disgust,* of food, Id.2.132b (Sup.).

ἄσιλλα, ἡ, *yoke,* like that of a milk-man, to carry baskets, pails, etc., Simon.163; ἄ. ἐπωμίους ἀνελόμενοι Alciphr.1.1 (prob.).

ἀσιλλο-φορέω, *carry a yoke,* Democr.132, prob. in *EM*160.34. **-φόρος,** ον, *carrying a yoke, PLond.*1.44.33 (ii B.C.).

ἄσιλος, ον, v. ἀνάσιλος.

ἀσῑνής, ές, *unhurt, unharmed,* τὰς εἰ μέν κ' ἀσινέας ἐάᾳς Od.11.110; ἀσινέα τινὰ ἀποπέμπειν Hdt.2.181; ἀ. ἀπικέσθαι, ἀναχωρέειν, Id.8.19, 116; ἀ. δαίμων *secure, happy* fortune, A.*Ag.*1341; βίοτος Id.*Ch.*1018; ἀσινῆ αἰῶνα διοιχνεῖ Id.*Eu.*315. **2.** less freq. of things, *undamaged,* οἴκημα Hdt.2.121.γ'; ἐὰν τὰ ἐπιθέματα..ἀσινῆ *IG*3.1418, 1419; ὑγιῆς καὶ ἀ. *POxy.*278.18 (i A.D.); of ships, App.*BC*5.98: metaph., κανόνες ἀληθείας Ph.1.215. **II.** Act., *doing no harm,* Sapph.80, Hdt.1.105, Hp.*Fract.*28, *Schwyzer* 197.46 (Crete, iii B.C.); ἀσινέστεραι πηρώσιες Hp.*Art.*61; *harmless,* of wild asses, X.*Cyr.*1.4.7; *innocent,* ἡδοναί Pl.*Lg.*670d; ἀσινέσταται τῶν ἡδονῶν Id.*Hp.Ma.*303e. **2.** *protecting from harm,* πόλεως ἀσινεῖ σωτῆρι A.*Th.*826. **3.** Adv. -νῶς, Ion. -νέως Hp.*Epid.*1.1, Arist.*HA*617ᵃ3: Sup. -έστατα X.*An.*3.3.3.

ἀσῑνότης, ητος, ἡ, *innocence,* Eun.*VS*p.480 B.

ἀσιογεῖαι, αἱ, *mud-walls,* Sch.Il.21.231.

ἄσιος, α, ον, epith. of λειμών, Il.2.461, prob. *Asian,* but also expld. as ἰλυώδης, Eust. adloc., or *meadow of Asias* (reading Ἀσίῳ), Str.14.1.45, St.Byz.131.7.

ἀσίρακος, ὁ, *locust* without wings, = τρωξαλλίς, Dsc.2.52 codd.: **ἀσείρακος,** Gal.12.366.

ἄσις [ᾰ], εως, ἡ, *slime, mud,* Il.21.321, Nic.*Th.*176; ἐκ θαλάσσης Charito 2.2; cf. ἄσις· κόνις, ἢ εἶδος ὀρνέου, Hsch.

ᾆσις, εως, ἡ, *singing, song,* Ptol.ap.Eust.1312.41.

Ἀσίς [ᾰ], ίδος, ἡ, v. Ἀσία.

ἀσῑτ-έω, *abstain from food, fast,* E.*Hipp.*277, Pl.*Smp.*220a; ἀ. ἡμέρας δύο Arist.*HA*594ᵇ20. **2.** *have no appetite,* Hp.*Aph.*2.32. **-ία,** Ion. -ίη, ἡ, *want of food,* Hdt.3.52, E.*Supp.*1105 (both pl.). **II.** *abstinence from food,* Hp.*Acut.*34, Arist.*EN*1180ᵇ9. **2.** *want of appetite,* Hp.*Aph.*7.6. **-ος,** ον, *without food, fasting,* Od.4.788, S.*Aj.*324, E.*Med.*24, Th.7.40, Phryn.Com.3 D., etc.; ἰχθύς Pl.Com.29. Adv. -ως *Mantiss.Prov.*1.47: **ἀσιτί** Lxx *Jb.*24.6. **II.** *of forbidden food,* εὐωχία ἄ. Ph.2.398 (dub. l.).

ἀσιχήρ· δοτικός, Hsch.; cf. ἤσιχερ.

ἀσιώπητος, ον, *not to be left unspoken,* τὸ ἀληθὲς ἀ. Eun.*Hist.* p.261 D.

ἀσκαίρω, = σκαίρω (with ἀ- euph.), Q.S.5.495 (dub.).

ἀσκάλᾱβος [κᾰ], ὁ, = sq., *GDI*3123 (Corinthian vase), Nic.*Th.*484, Ant.Lib.24.3.

ἀσκᾰλᾱβώτης, ου, ὁ, *spotted lizard, gecko, Platydactylus mauretanicus,* Ar.*Nu.*170, Arist.*HA*538ᵃ27, 607ᵃ27; cf. σκαλαβώτης, καλαβώτης.

ἀσκάλαφος, ὁ, an unknown bird, perh. a kind of *owl,* Arist.*HA*509ᵃ21.

ἀσκάλευτος [ᾰ], ον, *unhoed*, Sch.Theoc.10.14. **ἀσκαλεῶς**· ἄγαν σκληρῶς, ἐπιμόνως, Hsch. (i.e. ἀσκελέως).

ἀσκᾰληρής, ές, *equilateral*, Democr.132 (prob. ἀσκαληνές, cf. σκαληνός).

ἀσκάληρον, τό, v.l. (ap.Ath.) for σκαλίας (q.v.), Thphr.*HP*6.4.11:—also **ἀσκαλία**, Plin.*HN*21.97.

ἀσκᾰλίζω, *hoe*, Phryn.*PS*p.42 B.

ἀσκάλιστος [ᾰ], ον, = ἀσκάλευτος, Sch.Theoc.10.14.

ἄσκᾰλος, ον, = ἀσκάλευτος, Theoc.10.14:—also **ἄσκαλτος**, ον, Hsch.

ἀσκᾰλώνιον κρόμυον *Syrian* onion, *Allium Cepa*, Diocl.*Fr.*120, Thphr.*HP*7.4.7, Pl.*HN*19.101. (Hence Eng. *shallot*, which however is applied to κρόμυον σχιστόν; v. κρόμυον.)

ἀσκαλώπας, ὁ, prob. *woodcock*, *Scolopax ruricola*, Arist.*HA*617^{b}23.

ἀσκᾰμωνία, ἡ, = σκαμωνία, *Gp.*12.19.18, *Hippiatr.*31, Suid.

ἀσκανδάλιστος [δᾰ], gloss on ἀπρόσκοπος and ἀπρόσπταιστος, Hsch.

ἀσκανδής· ἄγγελος, Hsch.; cf. Mandaic *ashganda* 'messenger'.

ἀσκάνη· ἀγανάκτησις, Id.

ἀσκάντης, ου, ὁ, *pallet*, Ar.*Nu.*633, Luc.*Lex.*6. II. *bier*, *AP* 7.634 (Antiphil.).

ἀσκαρδᾰμυκτ-έω, *look without winking*, Sch.Ar.*Eq.*292. **-ης**, ου, ὁ, *one who does not blink*, Hp.*Epid.*2.6.1 (pl.). **-ί**, Adv. of sq., *without winking, with unchanged look*, X.*Cyr.*1.4.28, Luc.*Tim.*14, Gal.7.91, Poll.2.67, v.l. in Ar.*Eq.*292. **-ος**, ον, *not blinking* or *winking*, Ar.*Eq.*292, Adam.1.21. Adv. -τως Eust.756.59, v.l. in Ar. l. c.

ἀσκᾰρής, ές, *not hopping* or *skipping*, Hsch.:—also **ἄσκαρθμος**, ον, Id.

ἀσκᾰρῐδώδης, ες, *full of ascarides*, Hp.*Coac.*160.

ἀσκᾰρίζω, fut. -ιῶ, Att. form of σκαρίζω (with ἀ- euph.), Hp.*Nat. Puer.*30, Cratin.26.

ἀσκαρίς, ίδος, ἡ, *worm in the intestines*, Hp.*Aph.*3.26, Arist.*HA* 551^{a}10. II. *larva of the* ἐμπίς, ib.551^{b}27.

ἀσκάριστος, ον, *without struggling*, Sch.S.*Aj.*833.

ἄσκαρος, ὁ, a kind of *castanet*, Poll.4.60, Hsch.; also a kind of *shoe*, Id.

ἀσκαροφόρον· φορτηγόν, Hsch.

ἄσκαστος, v. ἄσχαστος.

ἀσκαύλης, ου, ὁ, (ἀσκός) *bagpiper*, Mart.10.3, *Gloss.*

ἄσκᾰφος, ον, *not dug about*, ἄμπελοι Str.11.4.3.

ἀσκέδαστος, ον, *not scattered*, τὸ ἓν ἀ. Eustr. *in EN*51.13; *that cannot be dissipated*, Procl.*Inst.*48.

ἀσκεθής, ές, v.l. for ἀσκηθής (q.v.), Od.14.255.

ἀσκεία, ἡ, (ἀσκέω) = ἄσκησις, Hsch.

ἀσκελής, ές, (ἀ- euph., σκέλλω) *dried up, withered, worn out*, ἀσκελέες καὶ ἄθυμοι Od.10.463. 2. neut. ἀσκελές as Adv., *toughly, stubbornly*, ἀ. αἰεί ib.1.68, 4.543; ἀ. αὔτως Nic.*Th.*278:—also **ἀσκελέως** αἰεί Il.19.68. II. (ἀ- priv., σκέλος) *without legs*, Pl.*Ti.*34a, Arist.*GA*717^{b}17. 2. (ἀ- copul., σκέλος) = ἰσοσκελής, *even*, of a balance, Nic.*Th.*42.

ἀσκελόν· ἄγαν τὰ αὐτά, Hsch.

ἀσκελοποιός, όν, (ἀ- priv., σκέλλω, ποιέω) *not allowing to pine*, etym. of Ἀσκληπιός, Tz. ad Lyc.1054.

ἀσκέπαρνος, ον, *without the axe, unhewn*, βάθρον S.*OC*101.

ἀσκέπαστος, ον, *uncovered*, Dsc.5.114, Antyll.ap.Orib.6.23.10, *Gp.* 7.19.3, *PLond.*5.1722 (vi A.D.).

ἀσκεπής, ές, = foreg., *Lyr.Alex.Adesp.*7.17, *AP*5.259 (Paul. Sil.), Nonn.*D.*46.279, al.; γυμνὸς καὶ ἀ. Max.Tyr.2.4. 2. *not covering*, ἀ. νεφέων γυμνούμενος ἀήρ Nonn.*D.*22.214:—also **ἄσκεπος**, ον, *defenceless*, Amynt.*Epigr.* in *POxy.*662.37; *bare-headed*, Ps.-Luc.*Philopatr.* 21.

ἄσκεπτος, ον, *inconsiderate, unreflecting*, οὐκ ἄσκεπτα λέγειν Ephipp. 14.5, cf. Pl.*R.*438a, Plu.2.45d: mostly in Adv. -τως *inadvisedly*, Th.6.21, Pl.*Chrm.*158e, etc.; ἀ. ἔχειν Id.*Cra.*440d; ἀ. ἔχειν τινός Id. *Grg.*501c: Comp. -ότερον Arist.*Pol.*1274^{a}30, Plu.*Demetr.*1. II. *unconsidered, unobserved*, Ar.*Ec.*258, X.*Mem.*4.2.19; μὴ τὸ μέγιστον ἐπιστήμης πέρι τί ποτ' ἐστὶν ἄσκεπτον γένηται Pl.*Tht.*184a. 2. *unseen, hidden*, γάμοι Opp.*H.*1.773. 3. *too small to be observed, negligible*, ἐν ἀσκέπτῳ χρόνῳ Arist.*APo.*89^{b}10.

ἀσκέρα, ας, ἡ, *winter shoe with fur lining*, Hippon.19, Lyc.855, 1322, Herod.2.32:—Dim. **ἀσκερίσκος**, ὁ, metapl. pl. ἀσκερίσκα Hippon.18.

ἀσκεύαστος, ον, *not made by art, natural*, κάλλος Philostr.*Im.*2.9.

ἀσκευής, ές, *without the implements of his art*, Hdt.3.131. II. *without furniture*, Muson.*Fr.*14p.71 H.

ἄσκευος, ον, *unfurnished, unprepared*, οὐ ψιλὸν οὐδ' ἄ. S.*OC*1029; [τριήρης] *IG*2.804.268, al.: c. gen., ἄ. ἀσπίδων τε καὶ στρατοῦ *unfurnished with..*, S.*El.*36. II. ἄσκευοι, οἱ, *light-armed troops*, Paus.8.50.2.

ἀσκευώρητος, ον, *not searched thoroughly*, Str.8.6.23.

ἀσκεψία, ἡ, *want of consideration, heedlessness*, Plb.2.63.5.

ἀσκέω, *work* raw materials, εἴρια, κέρα, Il.3.388, 4.110; *work curiously, form by art*, [κρητῆρα] Σιδόνες πολυδαίδαλοι εὖ ἤσκησαν ib. 23.743; ἑρμῖν' ἀσκήσας Od.23.198; πτύξασα καὶ ἀσκήσασα χιτῶνα having folded and *smoothed* it, ib.1.439; ἅρμα.. χρυσῷ καὶ ἀργύρῳ εὖ ἤσκηται Il.10.438; χορὸν ἤσκησεν ib.18.592; γόμφοις ἀ. Emp.87: added in aor. part. to Verbs, [θρόνον] τεύξει ἀσκήσας *elaborately*, Il.14. 240; [χρυσὸν] βοὸς κέρασιν περίχευεν ἀσκήσας Od.3.437; [ἑανὸν] ἔξυσ' ἀσκήσασα Il.14.179. 2. of personal adornment, *dress out, trick out*, ἀ. τινὰ κόσμῳ Hdt.3.1; ἐς κάλλος ἀσκεῖ *decks herself*, E.*El.*1073; δέμας Id.*Tr.*1023:—freq. in Pass., σκιεροῖς ἠσκημένα γυίοις *furnished with..*, Emp.61.4; πέπλοισι Περσικοῖς ἠσκημένη A.*Pers.*182; οὐ χλιδαῖς ἠσκημένον S.*El.*452; of buildings, παστὰς ἠσκημένη στύλοισι Hdt.2.169; Παρίῳ λίθῳ ἠσκημένα Id.3.57: abs., οἴκημα ἠσκημένον Id. 2.130; σῶμα λόγοις ἠσκ. *tricked out* with words only, not real, S.*El.* 1217:—Med., σῶμ' ὅπλοις ἠσκήσατο *adorned his own* person, E.*Hel.* 1379, cf. *Alc.*161. 3. in Pi., *honour* a divinity, *do him reverence*, δαίμον' ἀσκήσω θεραπεύων *P.*3.109; ἀσκεῖται Θέμις *O.*8.22. II. *practise, exercise, train*, esp. in Prose and Com., properly of athletic exercise, 1. c. acc. of person or thing, ἀ. τὸν υἱὸν τὸν ἐπιχώριον τρόπον Ar.*Pl.*47; ἀ. τὰ σώματα εἰς ἰσχὺν X.*Cyr.*2.1.20, cf. *Mem.*1.2.19; ἐχθρὸν ἐφ' ἡμᾶς αὐτοὺς τηλικοῦτον ἠσκήκαμεν D.3.28:—Pass., σώματα εὖ ἠσκημένα X.*Cyr.*1.6.41; εἰς ἀγῶνα ἄμεινον ἡμῶν ἤσκηνται D.9.52; ἀσκεῖσθαι λέγειν Luc.*Dem.*4; τὴν Κυνικὴν ἄσκησιν Id.*Tox.*27; λόγοις D.C.45.2; ἐν παιδείᾳ Id.60.2; πρός τι D.S.2.54. 2. c. acc. of the thing practised, ἀ. τέχνην, πεντάεθλον, Hdt.3.125, 9.33; λόγους Democr.53^a, 110; μανθάνειν καὶ ἀ. τι Pl.*Grg.*509e; ἀ. παγκράτιον, στάδιον, etc., Id.*Lg.*795b, *Thg.*128e; ἠσκηκέναι μηδεμίαν ἄσκησιν κυριωτέραν τῆς πολεμικῆς Arist.*Pol.*1271^{b}5: metaph., ἀ. τὴν ἀληθείην, δικαιοσύνην, Hdt.7.209, 1.96; δίκαια S.*OC*913; ἀρετήν E.*Fr.*853, Pl. *R.*407a; κακότητα A.*Pr.*1066 (lyr.), cf. S.*Tr.*384; ἀσέβειαν E.*Ba.*476; τὰ δίκαια Crates Theb.12; λαλιάν Ar.*Nu.*931 (anap.): c. dupl. acc., ἀ. αὐτόν τε καὶ τοὺς σὺν αὐτῷ τὰ πολεμικά X.*Cyr.*8.6.10. 3. c. inf., ἄσκει τοιαύτη μένειν *practise, endeavour* to remain such, S.*El.*1024; λέγειν ἠσκηκότες Id.*Fr.*963; εὐσεβεῖν ἠσκηκότα E.*Fr.*1067; ἀ. γαστρὸς κρείττους εἶναι, τοὺς φίλους ἀγαθὰ ποιεῖν, X.*Cyr.*4.2.45, 5.5.12, cf. *Mem.*2.1.6; ἤσκει ἐξομιλεῖν παντοδαποῖς he *made a practice of* associating.., Id.*Ag.*11.4. 4. abs., *practise, go into training*, Pl.*R.*389c, X.*Cyr.*2.1.29; οἱ ἀσκέοντες *those who practise gymnastics*, Hp.*Acut.* 9; περὶ τὰς βαναύσους τέχνας Plb.9.20.9.

ἄσκη, ἡ, = ἄσκησις, Pl.Com.234.

ἀσκηθής, ές, *unhurt, unscathed*, in Hom. of persons, ἂψ εἰς ἡμέας ἔλθοι ἀ. Il.10.212; ἀ. ἱκόμην ἐς πατρίδα γαῖαν Od.9.79, cf. Epich.99. 10, Call.*Aet.*3.1.69; ἀσκηθέες (trisyll.) καὶ ἄνουσοι Od.14.255 (v.l. ἀσκεθέες); *sound, healthy*, *IG*4.952.109 (Epid.); ἀ. τινὰ πέμπειν Sol. 19.4; *unblemished*, *IG*5(2).3.5 (Tegea, iv B.C.); = ἀπαθής, θεός Timo 60, etc.; later of things, ἀ. νόστος *safe* return, A.R.2.690; ἀ. μέλι *pure, virgin* honey, Antim.16.2. (Perh. from ἀ- priv., and the root of *scathe*, Germ. *schaden* 'hurt'.)

ἄσκημα, ατος, τό, *exercise, practice*, Hp.*Off.*7, X.*Cyr.*7.5.79; τὰ εἰς τὸν πόλεμον ἀ. Id.*Oec.*11.19, cf. *PLond.*3.1164*i*21 (iii A.D.); in warfare, *branch of the service, arm* (e.g. elephants or chariots), Arr. *Tact.*19.6.

ἄσκηνος, ον, *without tents, not under canvas*, Plu.*Sert.*12, App.*BC* 5.117.

ἀσκηπτος, ον, *that cannot be feigned*, μανία Ph.2.522.

ἀσκηρά· εἶδός τι τῶν καστανίων, Hsch.

ἄσκ-ησις, εως, ἡ, (ἀσκέω) *exercise, practice, training*, ἐξ ἀσκήσιος ἀγαθοὶ γίνονται Democr.242, cf. Protag.3, Pl.*Prt.*323d, al.; γυμνασίων καὶ ἀσκησίων ἐπιμελόμενοι Hp.*VM*4, cf. Th.2.39; πολεμικὴ X. *Cyr.*8.1.34; ἱππικὴ *IG*2.478^{b}18: in pl., *exercises*, ἔθεσι καὶ ἀσκήσεσι Pl. *R.*518e, cf. *Plt.*294d. II. c. gen., ἄ. τινος *practice of* or *in* a thing, Th.5.67; ἀρετῆς X.*Mem.*1.2.20; δειλίας ἀλλ' οὐκ ἀνδρείας Pl.*Lg.* 791b. III. generally, *mode of life, profession*, Luc.*Vit.Auct.*7; of a philosophical sect, ἡ Κυνικὴ ἄ. Id.*Tox.*27. 2. of religious sects, *asceticism*, Str.15.1.61, 17.1.29, Ph.1.643, J.*BJ*2.8.10. IV. *adornment*, τῶν τριχῶν Aeschin.Socr.18. **-ητέος**, α, ον, *to be practised*, X.*Cyr.*5.3.43, Jul.*Ep.*89. II. ἀσκητέον *one must practise*, σοφίαν, σωφροσύνην, Pl.*Grg.*487c, 507d; ποῖα πρὸς ποίους ἀ. Arist.*Pol.*1325^a 13. **-ητήρ**, ῆρος, ὁ, = sq., Poet.ap.Gal.*Protr.*13 (leg. ἀσκήτορες). **-ητής**, οῦ, ὁ, *one who practises any art* or *trade*, ἀ. τῶν καλῶν κἀγαθῶν ἔργων, opp. ἰδιώτης, X.*Cyr.*1.5.11; λόγων D.H.*Is.*2; σοφίης *IG*3.1322; esp. = ἀθλητής, Ar.*Pl.*585, Pl.*R.*403e sq., Isoc.2. 11; Διόνυσος ἀ., title of comedy by Aristomenes. II. *hermit* or *monk*, Ph.1.643. **-ητικός**, ή, όν, *laborious*, βίος Pl.*Lg.*806a; ἀ. νόσημα *such as is incident to an athlete*, Ar.*Lys.*1085; of persons, Ph.1. 552. Adv. -κῶς Poll.3.145. II. *ascetic*, μελέται Ph.1.646. **-ητός**, ή, όν, *curiously wrought*, νῆμα Od.4.134; λέχος 23.189; χρίματα Xenoph.3.6; εἵματα Theoc.24.140; *adorned, decked*, πέπλῳ *with..*, Id. 1.33, cf. *AP*6.219.3 (Antip.). Adv. -τῶς prob.l. in Simon.157. 2. *to be got* or *reached by practice*, οὐ διδακτὸν ἀλλ' ἀ., of virtue, Pl.*Men.* 70a, cf. X.*Mem.*1.2.23; μαθητὸν ἢ ἐθιστὸν ἢ καὶ ἄλλως πως ἀ. Arist.*EN* 1099^{b}10. II. of persons, *exercised, practised in* a thing, Ἀθηναίης παλάμῃσιν Simon. l. c. (codd. D.L.); ἀνὴρ ἀ. καὶ σοφός Plu.*Lyc.* 30. **-ήτρια**, ἡ, fem. of ἀσκητής II, ἀ. γυναῖκες *Cat.Cod.Astr.*7.225. 29, cf. *Anatolian Studies* p.81. **-ήτωρ**, v. ἀσκητήρ.

ἀσκίαστος [ῐ], ον, *unshaded*, Onos.10.5, Eust.1550.63. II. *not clouded by rust*, etc., Maria ap.Zos.Alch.p.152 B., cf. ib.182 B.

ἀσκῐαστ-όω, *clear from rust*, Zos.Alch.p.183 B.:—hence **-ωσις**, εως, ἡ, ib.217 B.

ἀσκίδιον, τό, = sq., Ar.*Ec.*307, Posidon.30.

ἀσκίον, τό, Dim. of ἀσκός, Hp.*Liqu.*6, *Aff.*21, Plu.*Art.*12: prov. of *empty threats*, οὐκ ἀσκίῳ μορμολύττεσθαι Crates Com.8.

ἄσκῐος, α, ον, *unshaded*, ὄρεα Pi.*N.*6.45 (v.l. δασκίοις): αὐγή, ἀκτῖνες, Ph.1.485, 579. II. *shadowless*, Theopomp.Hist.313, Cleom.1.10, Str.17.1.48, Hld.9.22. III. = ἀσκίαστος II, Zos.Alch.p.183 B. IV. (ἀ- intens.) *dull*, of colour, Thphr.*Sens.*78. 2. ἄσκιος ὕλη· ἡ δασεῖα ὕλη, Hsch.

ἀσκίπων [ῐ], ον, gen. ονος, *not leaning on a staff*, *AP*9.298 (Antiphil.), 7.732 (Theodorid.); but ἀσκείπωνι γονῇ γῆρας ἐρειδόμενοι a child *too young to serve as a staff*, *BMus.Inscr.* 2.390.

ἀσκίτης [ῑ], ου, ὁ, (ἀσκός) kind of *dropsy*, *ascites*, Epicur.*Fr.*190, Aret.*SD*1.16, Gal.17(2).670. II. *patient suffering from the disease*, Herod.Med.ap.Orib.10.8.9.

ἀσκληπιάς, άδος, ἡ, *swallow-wort*, *Vincetoxicum officinale*, Dsc.3.92, Gal.11.840. 2. = ἐλλέβορος λευκός, Ps.-Dsc.4.148 Wellm. 3. = δάφνη, Hsch.

ἀσκληπιασμός, ὁ, *bleeding from haemorrhoids*, Sever.*Clyst.*p.35 D.

Ἀσκληπιός, Dor. -ᾱπιός, ὁ, *Asclepios*, Il.2.731, *h.Hom.*16, etc.:—hence **Ἀσκληπιάδης**, ου, ὁ, *son of Asclepios*, Il.4.204, al.: in pl., as a name for *physicians*, Thgn.432, Pl.*R.*405d: also **Ἀσκληπίδης**, ου, ὁ, in pl., S.*Ph.*1333:—**Ἀσκληπιασταί**, Dor. Ἀσκλᾱπ-, οἱ, *guild of worshippers of A.*, *IG*2.617*b*, 12(1).162 (Rhodes), etc.:—**Ἀσκληπιεῖον**, τό, *temple of Asclepios*, Plb.1.18.2, Str.17.3.14; -ίεια, τά, *festival of A.*, Pl.*Ion* 530a, *IG*2.741 *A*[a] 14, etc. (also **Ἀσκληπίδεια** ib.5(1).659 (Sparta)):—**Ἀσκληπιακός**, ή, όν, Aristid.*Or.*47(23).58, Dam.*Pr.*95:—**Ἀσκληπιάδειος** [στίχος], ὁ, metre *employed by* Ἀσκληπιάδης, *POxy.*220 xiv 9, Heph.10.3: also Ἀ., ὁ, *physician of the school of Asclepiades*, Gal.11.794. (Ἀσκληπιοῦ is for -ιόο in Il.2.731. D. is said to have made it proparox. Ἀσκλήπιος, deriving it from ἤπιος, Plu.2.845b.)

ἀσκο-δέτης, ου, ὁ, *string for wineskins*, Nic.*Th.*928. **-δορέω**, *flay a person and make a bag of his skin*, Ps.-Callisth.3.8. **-θύλακος** [ῠ], ὁ, *leathern bag*, Ar.*Fr.*174, Archipp.4, Diocl.Com.3.

ἀσκόλαχα· ἀσκαλαβώτης, Hsch. **ἀσκόομαι**, only aor. 1 ἀσκώσατο (sic)· ἠχθέσθη, Id.

ἀσκόπευτος, ον, *free from intrusions*, πενία ἀ. οὐσία Secund.*Sent.*10.

ἀσκοπήρα, ἡ, *scrip*, *wallet*, Ar.*Fr.*577, Diph.55.2, prob. in Suet.*Ner.*45.

ἄσκοπος (A), ον, (σκοπέω) *inconsiderate*, *heedless*, Il.24.157, Timo 5, etc.; ὄμμα Parm.1.35; ἄσκοποί τινος *unregardful of..*, A.*Ag.*462 (lyr.). Adv. -πως *heedlessly*, Babr.95.39. II. Pass., *not to be seen*, *invisible*, πλάκες ἄ., of the nether world, S.*OC*1682 (lyr.), cf. E.*Hyps.Fr.*57.21 (lyr.). 2. *not to be understood*, *unintelligible*, ἔπος A.*Ch.*816 (lyr.), cf. S.*Ph.*1111 (lyr.); πρᾶγος Id.*Aj.*21; ἄ. χρόνος *unknown* time, Id.*Tr.*246; *unimaginable*, ἄ. ἁ λώβα Id.*El.*864 (lyr.); *bewildering*, *strange*, ἤργασαι δέ μ' ἄσκοπα ib.1315. 3. = ἄσκεπτος, *unconsidered*, Gal.7.432.

ἄσκοπος (B), ον, (σκοπός) *aimless*, βέλος D.H.8.86; κίνησις Phlp.*in Ph.*846.25; ἄσκοπα τοξεύειν Luc.*Tox.*62. Adv. -πως, εἰκῇ καὶ ἀ. χρήσασθαι τοῖς πράγμασιν Plb.4.14.6; πλανώμενος ἀ. Plu.*Dio*49; ἀ. λόγους ῥίπτειν Longus 4.31, cf. Ath.Mech.3.9, Cleom.2.4, Phlp.*in Ph.*902.19; οὐκ ἀ. εἰκάζειν J.*AJ*2.2.3, cf. Gal.18(1).768, Alex.Aphr.*Pr.Anecd.*1.

ἀσκοπῡτίνη [ῐ], ἡ, *leathern canteen*, Antiph.150, Men.266, Lxx *Ju.*10.5.

ἀσκορδίνητος [ῐ], ον, *not stretching one's limbs*, *Com.Adesp.*952.

ἀσκός, ὁ, *skin*, *hide*, *PFay.*121.9 (i/ii A.D.); but usually, *skin made into a bag*, esp. *wineskin*, οἶνον .. ἀσκῷ ἐν αἰγείῳ Il.3.247, Od.6.78; ἀσκὸν .. μέλανος οἴνοιο 5.265, 9.196; ἀσκὸς βοός, of the *bag* in which Aeolus bottled up the winds, Od.10.19, cf. 45, 47; ἀσκοὺς καμήλων *skins of* camel's *hide*, Hdt.3.9; ἀ. Μαρσύεω *bag made from the skin* of Marsyas, Id.7.26; ἀ. ἀφύσητος Hp.*Art.*47; εἴ μοι ἡ δορὰ μὴ εἰς ἀσκὸν τελευτήσει ὥσπερ ἡ Μαρσύου Pl.*Euthd.*285c; ἀσκοῖς καὶ θυλάκοις X.*An.*6.4.23, cf. Th.4.26; ἀσκοὶ πεφυσαμένοι, of mankind, Epich.246; ἄνθρωποι κενεῆς οἰήσιος ἔμπλεοι ἀ. Timo 11; ἀσκός, of the human *skin*, Ph.2.462. 2. *paunch*, *belly*, Archil.72; in oracular language, E.*Med.*679, Plu.*Thes.*3. 3. *bellows*, Plb.21.28.15, Ath.10.456d. 4. *bagpipes*, Gal.4.459. 5. prov., *wineskin*, of a toper, Antiph.19: prov., ἀεί ποτ' εὖ μὲν ἀ. εὖ δὲ θύλακος ἄνθρωπός ἐστι Alex.85; "ἀσκός, πέλεκυς" in a child's game, Thphr.*Char.*5.5; ἀσκὸν δείρειν *flay alive*, hence, *abuse*, *maltreat*, Ar.*Nu.*442:—Pass., ἀσκὸς δεδάρθαι Sol.33.7.

ἀσκότονοι· κυνορραῖσται, κρότωνες, Hsch. **ἀσκουρῶτις**· ἄ(ρ)κτος ἡ (cod. ἢ) μικρά Id.

ἀσκο-φορέω, *bear wineskins* at the feast of Bacchus, *AB*214:—Adj. **-φόρος**, ον, ibid.

ἄσκρα· δρῦς ἄκαρπος, Hsch.

ἀσκύλευτος [ῡ], ον, *not pillaged* or *stripped*, D.H.11.27, Hld.1.1.

ἄσκυλτος, ον, *not pulled about*, Heliod.ap.Orib.50.47.5, Philum. ap.Aët.9.23; *undisturbed*, S.E.*P.*1.71, *POxy.*532.14 (ii A.D.); ἱερὸν ἄ. *IG*12(9).15 (Carystus). Adv. -τως *without being mangled* or *hurt*, Eust.1252.55. II. Act., *without causing laceration*, Herod.Med. ap.Orib.10.7.1: Comp. -ότερον Sor.1.3.

ἀσκυροειδές, τό, = sq., Ps.-Dsc.3.155.

ἄσκυρον, τό (also **ἄσκυρος**, ὁ, Hsch.), *St. John's wort*, *Hypericum perforatum*, Dsc.3.155, Gal.11.829. II. = ἄλισμα, Ps.-Dsc.3.152.

ἄσκῡφος, ον, *without cup*, Hippoloch.ap.Ath.4.129f.

ἀσκωληκόβρωτος, ον, *not worm-eaten*, *PGrad.*7.11 (iii B.C.).

Ἀσκώλια, τά, second day of the rural Dionysia, Sch.Ar.*Pl.*1129.

ἀσκωλι-άζω, *hop on greased wineskins at the* Ἀσκώλια, Ar.*Pl.*1129 (cf. Sch.). II. *hop on one leg*, ἀσκωλιάζειν ῥᾷον ἐπὶ τοῖς ἀριστεροῖς Arist.*IA*705[b]33, cf. Ael.*NA*3.13, Plu.2.621f, Gal.11.106; also, *jump up and down with legs held together*, Sch.Orib.3 p.689 D. (Signf. II may be original and the connexion with ἀσκός due to popular etymology.) **-ασμός**, ὁ, *leaping on greased wineskins*, Poll.9.21.

ἀσκωλίζω, = -ιάζω II, Pl.*Smp.*190d, Phryn.*PS* p.42 B.

ἄσκωμα, ατος, τό, (ἀσκός) *leather padding* or *lining* of the hole which served for the rowlock, Ar.*Ach.*97, *Ra.*364. 2. any *swelling*, such as on the female *breast*, Ruf.*Onom.*92, cf. Poll.2.163. 3. *leathern bellows*, Apollod.*Poliorc.*153.3:—Dim. **-άτιον**, τό, Hero *Spir.*1.39.

ἄσμα, ατος, τό, = δίασμα, *AB*452; cf. ἄττω.

ᾆσμα, ατος, τό, (ᾄδω) *song*, esp. *lyric ode*, *hymn*, Pl.*Prt.*343c sq., Alex.19, Luc.*Salt.*16; ᾆ. μετὰ χοροῦ *SIG*648*B*7 (Delph., ii B.C.).

ἀσμάρᾰγος [μᾰ], ον, *noiseless*, Opp.*H.*3.428.

ᾀσμάτιον, τό, Dim. of ᾆσμα, Pl.Com.235.

ᾀσμᾰτο-κάμπτης, ου, ὁ, *twister of song*, of Trag. and Dithyrambic poets, Ar.*Nu.*333:—hence **-καμπέω**, Tz. in *An.Ox.*3.339.

ᾀσμᾰτο-λογέω, *repeat songs*, Artem.1.76. **-ποιός**, ὁ, *composer of songs*, Ath.5.181e.

ἀσμεναίτατα, -έστατα, v. sub ἄσμενος.

ἀσμεν-έω, (ἄσμενος) = ἀσμενίζω, only in Din.1.34 ἀσμενεῖν μεταβολὴν *wish for* a change. **-ής**, ές, dub. l. in Arist.*Phgn.*807[b]35. **-ίζω**, *take* or *receive gladly*, τι Plb.6.8.3; ἀγλαΐαν Plot.5.8.12; ἐπιστήμην, λόγους, Them.*Or.*33.364d, 8.107b; τὸν Ἰουδαϊσμόν Porph.*Chr.*27: intr., *to be satisfied with* a thing, τινί Plb.3.97.5; τῇ ἡδονῇ Muson.*Fr.*6 p.27 H., cf. Agathin.ap.Orib.10.7.10, Ph.2.37, etc.; ἀ. εἰ.. Plb.4.11.5: c. part., ἀ. ἐσθίοντες Plu.2.101d; ὡς χρησόμενοι App.*BC*3.40:—Med. as Dep., Aesop.45. **-ισμός**, ὁ, *gratification*, Ph.1.450; a form of ἡδονή, *Stoic.*3.97. **-ιστέον**, *one must take* a thing *gladly*, Hp.*Dent.*25, Gal.8.816, 10.648. **-ιστός**, ή, όν, *acceptable*, *welcome*, S.E.*M.*11.85, Plot.6.7.30, Them.*Or.*16.205c; τινί J.*AJ*19.6.4.

ἄσμενος, η, ον, *well-pleased*, *glad*, always with a Verb, φύγεν ἄ. ἐκ θανάτοιο he was *glad to* have escaped death, Il.20.350, cf. Od.9.63, Pi.*O.*13.74: freq. in Trag. and Att., ἄσμενος δὲ τἂν .. κάμψειεν γόνυ A.*Pr.*398; ἐκ θαλάσσης ἀσμένους πεφευγότας E.*Hel.*398; ἄ. αἱρεθεὶς Th.6.12; ἐκάθευδον ἄ. ἥκων ἐξ ἀγροῦ Lys.1.13; ἀσμένας εἰς τὸν λειμῶνα ἀπιούσας Pl.*R.*614e: freq. in dat., ἐμοὶ δέ κεν ἀσμένῳ εἴη *glad* would it make me! Il.14.108; ἀσμένῳ δέ σοι .. νὺξ ἀποκρύψει φάος *glad* wilt thou be when night shuts out the light, A.*Pr.*23; ὡς σφι ἀσμένοισι ἡμέρα ἐπέλαμψε Hdt.8.14; ἀσμένῃ δέ μοι .. ἦλθε S.*Tr.*18; ὡς ἀσμένοισιν ἦλθες Ar.*Pax* 582, cf. Pl.*Cra.*418c, etc. Adv. ἀσμένως *gladly*, *readily*, A.*Pr.*728, D.18.36, Alex.142, Timocl.14 (this Adv., which is common in later Greek, *Act.Ap.*21.17, etc., has sts. been substituted for the Adj., as in Th.4.21 (v.l.)): Sup. ἀσμεναίτατα (v.l. -έστατα) Pl.*R.*329c; -έστατα ib.616a (though the Adj. makes -ώτερος, -ώτατος, Hp.*Art.*8, cf. Phryn.*PS* p.18 B.). (Not to be connected with ἁνδάνω, since there is no ancient authority for rough breathing ἁσμ-.)

ἄσμηκτος, ον, *not cleansed with soap*, Pherecr.195.

ᾀσμός, ὁ, = ᾆσμα, Pl.Com.235.

ἀσμόσσει· ἀγνοεῖ, ἀναπνεῖ, Hsch.: **ἀσμωλεῖν**· ἀγνοεῖν, *EM*155.33: **ἀσμωλή**· ἀναπνοὴ ὀλίγη, ibid.

ἀσολοίκ-ιστος, ον, = sq., Eust.591.9. Adv. -τως Id.316.32. **-ος**, ον, *not barbarous*, S.*Fr.*629. 2. *correct*, *without solecism*, Zeno *Stoic.*1.23. Adv. -κως *AB*452. II. metaph., *uncorrupted*, *unspoiled*, κρέας Eub.7.8; ἀ. παιδιὰ *not coarse*, *refined*, Plu.*Cleom.*13; of persons, *unexceptionable*, Phld.*Acad.Ind.*p.52 M. Adv. -κως Id.*Vit.*p.7 J.

ἀσοῦρ or **ἀσούρ**, = κρατήρ (Phoenician word), Hsch., *EM*155.34.

ἀσοφία, ἡ, *folly*, *stupidity*, Plu.*Pyrrh.*29, Luc.*Astr.*2; rejected by Poll.4.13.

ἀσόφιστος, ον, *not deluded by fallacies*, Arr.*Epict.*1.7.26; ἀ. λόγων παρασκευαῖς J.*Ap.*2.41.

ἄσοφος, ον, *unwise*, *foolish*, Thgn.370, Pi.*O.*3.45, *Ep.Eph.*5.15, Plu.2.330a: Comp., Them.*Or.*15.185a. Adv. -φως D.S.2.29, Lib.*Decl.*2.27.

ἄσπα· ἵππιος, ἡ ἐγγία, Hsch. (Perh. Persian *asp* = ἵππος.) **ἀσπάζει**· συμπεριπατεῖ, Id.

ἀσπάζομαι, Ep. aor. ἀσπάσσατο *Epigr.Gr.*990.9:—*welcome kindly*, *greet*, τινά Hom., etc.: freq. c. dat. modi, δεξιῇ ἠσπάζοντο ἔπεσσί τε μειλιχίοισι Il.10.542; χερσίν Od.3.35, al.; ἀδυπνόῳ φωνᾷ Pi.*I.*2.25; μεγάλως ἠσπάζοντο αὐτὸν *received* him *with* great *joy*, Hdt.1.122, cf. 3.1; παρὰ τὴν πόσιν φιλοφρόνως ἀ. Id.2.121.δ'; εὖ νιν ἀσπάσασθε A.*Ag.*524: freq. with no modal word, S.*OT*596, etc.; esp. as the common form on meeting, Στρεψιάδην ἀσπάζομαι Ar.*Nu.*1145, cf. *Pl.*1042 (v. Sch.), Pl.*Euthd.*273c; αὐτὸν ἠσπάζοντο καὶ ἐδεξιοῦνθ' Ar.*Pl.*752; πόρρωθεν ἀ. *salute* from a distance, Pl.*Chrm.*153b; πρόσωθεν αὐτὴν ἁγνὸς ὢν ἀ. I *salute* her at a respectful distance, i.e. keep away from her, E.*Hipp.*102, cf. Pl.*R.*499a; ἀ. ταῖς κώπαις, of the *saluting* of ships, Plu.*Ant.*76; ἀ. τινὰ βασιλέα *to hail* or *salute as* king, D.H.4.39: metaph., ἀ. συμφοράν *to bid* the event *welcome*, E.*Ion* 587. b. *take leave of*, Id.*Tr.*1276; τὰ ὕστατα ἀ. *take a* last *farewell*, Lys.13.39. c. as a formula in closing letters, *Ep.Rom.*16.22,23, *BGU* 1079.33 (i A.D.), etc. 2. from the modes of salutation in use, *kiss*, *embrace*, Ar.*V.*607; ἀ. τοῖς στόμασι Plu.*Rom.*1; of dogs, *fawn*, X.*Mem.*2.3.9, Pl.*R.*376a; *cling fondly to*, ἴσον σ' ὡς τεκοῦσ' ἀσπάζομαι E.*Ion* 1363, cf. X.*Cyr.*1.3.2; ἐγὼ ὑμᾶς ἀ. καὶ φιλῶ Pl.*Ap.*29d: metaph., φιλεῖν καὶ ἀ. τὸ ἄδικον Id.*Lg.*689a. 3. of things, *follow eagerly*, *cleave to*, ἀ. τὸ ὅμοιον, οἶνον, Id.*Smp.*192a, *R.*475a, cf. S.E.*M.*11.44; of dogs, ἀ. τὰ ἴχνη X.*Cyn.*3.7. 4. ἀ. ὅτι .. *to be glad* that.., Ar.*Pl.*324. 5. c. inf., *to be ready to..*, εὐωχεῖσθαι Philostr.*VA*2.7, cf. 31, *VS*2.25.4. (Act. ἀσπάζω in letters (cf. I.c), *POxy.*1158.18 (iii A.D.), al., cf. ἀσπάζομαι· ἀσπάζω, Hsch.

ἀσπάθητος [ᾰ], ον, (σπᾰθάω) *not struck close with the* σπάθη: hence, either *loosely woven* or *not woven* (i.e. of skin), χλαῖνα S.*Fr.*877: generally, *not in close order*, φάλαγξ D.H.16.3.

ἀσπαίρω, impf. ἤσπαιρον, Ion. and Ep. ἀσπαίρεσκον Q.S.11.104: (ἀ- euph., σπαίρω):—*pant, gasp, struggle*, in Hom. always of the dying (so κραδίη ἀσπαίρουσα must be taken, Il.13.443), περὶ δουρὶ ἤσπαιρ' ὡς ὅτε βοῦς κτλ. ib.571; ζωὸν ἔτ' ἀσπαίροντα 12.203, cf. Od. 19.229, A.*Pers.*977 (lyr.), E.*IA*1587; νεκροὶ -οντες Antipho 2.4.5; ἀ. ἄνω κάτω E.*El.*843; of an infant, Hdt.1.111; of fish taken out of the water, Id.9.120, Babr.6.5:—but in Hdt.8.5 Ἀδείμαντος ἤσπαιρε μοῦνος was the only one who still *made a struggle, resisted*; ἐβόων τε καὶ ἤσπαιρον D.H.7.25.—Poet. and Ion. word.

ἀσπᾰκάζομαι, = ἀσπάζομαι, *Com.Adesp.*953:—**ἀσπᾰκῶς**· φιλοφρόνως, Hsch.

ἀσπάλᾰθος [πᾰ], ὁ, Ar.*Fr.*749, but more commonly ἡ, as Pherecr. 109 (s. v. l.), Thphr.*Od.*33:—name of a *spinous shrub*, yielding a fragrant oil, = ἐρυσίσκηπτρον, *camel's thorn, Alhagi maurorum*, Thphr.9.7.3, *Od.*33, Dsc.1.20. 2. *thorny trefoil, Calycotome villosa*, Thgn.1193 (pl.), Arist.*Pr.*906[b]11, Theoc.4.57 (pl.), 24.89. 3. *Genista acanthoclada*, used as an instrument of torture, ἐπ' ἀσπαλάθων τινὰ κνάμπτειν Pl.*R.*616a.

ἀσπάλαξ [πᾰ], ακος, ὁ, elsewh. σπάλαξ (q. v.), *blind-rat, Spalax typhlus*, Arist.*HA*533[a]3, Antig.*Mir.*10, *Stoic.*2.51, Ael.*NA*17.10; ἀσπαλάκων αὐτόχθονα φῦλα Opp.*C.*2.612: prov., τυφλότερος ἀσπάλακος Diogenian.8.25.

ἀσπᾰλία, ἡ, *angling*, Hsch., Suid.; perh. f.l. for -ιεία.

ἀσπᾰλι-εύομαι, *angle*, Suid.:—Act., fut. -εύσω, metaph. of a lover, Aristaen.1.17; ἀσπαλίσαι· ἁλιεῦσαι, σαγηνεῦσαι, *AB*183, may be f.l. for ἀσπαλιεῦσαι. **-εύς**, έως, ὁ, = sq., Nic.*Th.*704, Opp.*H.*3. 29, al. **-ευτής**, οῦ, ὁ, *angler*, Pl.*Sph.*218e, Aen.Gaz.*Thphr.* p.16 B. **-ευτικός**, ή, όν, *of* or *for an angler*: -κή (sc. τέχνη), ἡ, *angling*, Pl.*Sph.*219d, 221a, Gal.*Thras.*30.

ἄσπαλον· σκῦτος, Hsch. **ἄσπαλος**, ὁ, = ἰχθύς (Athaman.), Id. **ἀσπάνιον**· πάσσαλον, Id.

ἀσπᾰνιστία, ἡ, *superfluity*, Telesp.44 H.

ἀσπᾰραγία, ἀσπάραγος, ἀσπαραγωνία, v. sub ἀσφ-.

ἀσπάρακτος [πᾰ], ον, *not causing laceration*, τάσις Heliod.(?)ap. Orib.49.4.46.

ἀσπαρίζω, for σπαρίζω, = ἀσπαίρω, Arist.*PA*696[a]20, *Resp.*471[b]13.

ἄσπαρτος, ον, of land, *unsown, untilled*, Od.9.123; but ἡ ἄ. the *sea*, Lib.*Eth.*24.4. 2. of plants, *not sown, growing wild*, Od.9. 109, Numen.ap.Ath.9.371b.

ἀσπ-άσιος [πᾰ], α, ον, also ος, ον Od.23.233, Luc.*Nec.*1:—*welcome, gladly welcomed*, ἀσπασίη τρίλλιστος ἐπήλυθε νύξ Il.8.488, cf. 10.35; ὡς δ' ὅτ' ἂν ἀσπάσιος βίοτος παίδεσσι φανήῃ πατρός Od.5.394, etc. Adv. -ίως, ἀ. δ' ἄρα τῷ κατέδυ φάος ἠελίοιο 13.33. II. *well-pleased, glad*, ἀσπάσιοι δ' ἐπέβαν γαίης 23.238; ἀσπάσιον δ' ἄρα τόν γε θεοὶ κακότητος ἔλυσαν they released him *to his joy*, 5.397. Adv. -ίως *gladly*, Hom. with a Verb, to be *glad to . .*, as φημί μιν ἀσπασίως γόνυ κάμψειν Il.7. 118, cf. 18.232, Od.4.523, etc.—Ep., exc. in Adv. -ίως *with glad welcome*, A.*Ag.*1555 (lyr.); *gladly*, Hdt.7.152, Jul.*Or.*2.71a. **-ασμα**, ατος, τό, = sq., esp. in pl., *embraces*, E.*Hec.*829, Ph.2.77, Artem.1.10, etc. II. *thing embraced, dear one*, Plu.2.608e. **-ασμός**, ὁ, *greeting, embrace*, Thgn.860 (pl.); οἱ ἔσχατοι, οἱ τελευταῖοι ἀ., D.H.4.4, Ph.2.45: generally, *salutation*, *Ev.Matt.*23.7, *Ev.Marc.*12.38, *POxy.* 471.67 (ii A.D.), Gal.10.76, Prisc.p.316 D. 2. *affection*, opp. μῖσος, Pl.*Lg.*919e. **-αστέον**, *one must welcome*, Id.*Phlb.*32d, Iamb.*Protr.* 5. **-αστικός**, ή, όν, *friendly*, ἔντευξις Plb.28.3.10; *used in salutation*, δάκτυλος Gal.14.451. Adv. -κῶς, ἐδέξατο τὴν ἀπόκρισιν Phld.*Acad. Ind.*p.41 M. **-αστός**, ή, όν, = ἀσπάσιος, *welcome*, Hom. (only in Od.), Ὀδυσῆ' ἀσπαστὸν ἔδυ φάος ἠελίοιο 13.35, cf. 5.398, 23.239; κάρτα ἀ. [τὸ πρᾶγμα] ἐποιήσαντο Hdt.5.98; τοῖσι ἡ τυραννὶς πρὸ ἐλευθερίης ἦν ἀσπαστότερον 1.62, cf. E.*Rh.*348 (lyr.), Them.*Or.*15.184d (Comp.). Adv. -τῶς Hdt.4.201, Lyc.1090; τὸ τῆς ζωῆς ἀ. Epicur.*Ep.*3 p.61 U.; neut. ἀσπαστόν as Adv., Hes.*Sc.*42. 2. *to be welcomed*, Pl.*Phlb.* 32d. II. ἄσπαστον, τό, an instrument of uncertain use, *BGU*544. 25 (ii/iii A.D.). **-αστύς**, ύος, ἡ, Ion. for ἀσπασμός, Call.*Fr.*427.

ἄσπεδος, ὁ, dub. in Epich.42; perh. ἀσπέτους as Adj. shd. be read.

ἄσπειστος, ον, (σπένδω) *to be appeased by no libations, implacable*, D.25.52; κότος Nic.*Th.*367; πόλεμοι ἄσπειστοι, = ἄσπονδοι, Plu.2. 537b, cf. S.E.*P.*3.175.

ἀσπερμί or -εί, *without the right to a loan of seed*, *PTeb.*61.307, 67.97, *PAmh.*2.90.6, etc.

ἄσπερμος, ον, *without seed*, i. e. *posterity*, Il.20.303, Luc.*Am.*35: metaph., καρπὸς λόγου Max.Tyr.31.5:—in literal sense, opp. πολύσπερμος, Arist.*GA*725[b]29; of plants, Thphr.*HP*7.4.4.

ἀσπερχές, *hotly, unceasingly*, Hom., who uses only the neut. form as Adv., esp. in phrase ἀσπερχὲς μενεαίνεις Il.4.32; ἀ. κεχολῶσθαι 16.61, al. (ἀ- intens., σπέρχομαι.)

ἄσπετος, ον, Ep. Adj. *unspeakable, unutterable*; mostly in sense of *unspeakably great*, ἄ. αἰθήρ, ῥόος Ὠκεανοῖο, ὕλη, ὕδωρ, Il.8.558, 18.403, 23.127, Od.5.101; ἀλκή Il.16.157; less freq. of number, *countless*, ἄσπετα πολλά Od.4.75; κρέα ἄσπετα 9.162; τρεῖτ' ἄσπετον ye tremble *unspeakably*, Il.17.332, cf. Q.S.11.127; φωνὴ ῥεῖ ἄσπετος flows on *unceasingly*, *h.Ven.*237; ἄσπετος αἰών *endless* time, Emp.16.—Chiefly Epic, but found in Lyric, ἄσπετοι μέριμναι B.18.34, and rarely in Trag., θαῦμα S.*Tr.*961 (lyr.); χάλαζα E.*Tr.*78; δρυὸς ἄ. ἔρνος *Cyc.* 615 (lyr.); later Prose, λείας ἄ. πλῆθος f.l. for ἄπλετον, Plb.3.92.8. (ἀ- priv. + root seq[u], cf. ἔννεπε, ἔσπετε (*ἐν-σπετε), Lat. *insece.*) A lengthd. form **ἀάσπετος** is used by Q.S.3.673, 7.193, al.

ἀσπῐδαποβλής, ῆτος, ὁ, *one that throws away his shield, runaway*, Ar.*V.*592.

ἀσπῐδεῖον, τό, part of *shield*, *IG*2.720*B* i 16 (iv B.C.), cf. *Rev.Épigr.* 1.239 (Naples, ii A.D.): pl., defined as αἱ πτυχαὶ τῶν ἀσπίδων, Hsch. II. part of the *prow of a ship*, Id. III. = ἀσπίδιον (?), *POxy.*473.8 (ii A.D.), *BGU*362 x 6 (iii A.D.).

ἀσπῐδής, v. σπιδής.

ἀσπῐδη-στρόφος, ον, *shield-wielding*, λεώς A.*Ag.*825. **-φόρος**, ον, *shield-bearing*, of warriors, Id.*Th.*19; κῶμος ἀ. E.*Supp.*390: Subst., Id.*Ba.*781.

ἀσπίδιον [πῐ], τό, Dim. of ἀσπίς, *small shield*, Hermipp.16, *IG*2. 61.34, Men.765, etc. 2. = ἀτρακτυλίς, Ps.-Dsc.3.93. 3. = ἄλυσσον, ib.91.

ἀσπῐδ-ίσκος, ὁ, Dim. of ἀσπίς, *boss*, Sch.Il.5.743; *wide end of a clyster-pipe*, Cael.Aur.*TP*4.3:—also -ίσκη, ἡ, *boss, disk*, *Jahresh.* 16 *Beibl.*51 (Athens, iii B.C.), *SIG*[2]588.31 (Delos, ii B.C.), *Ausonia* 10. 171 (Perga), Lxx *Ex.*36.26(39.18); *small shield*, Ascl.*Tact.*1.2, Hero *Dioptr.*5, etc.; name of a *constellation*, Ptol.*Alm.*8.1: **-ίσκιον**, τό, *IG*2.733 *A* ii 7, Dsc.3.91, Gal.14.724; and **-ισκάριον**, τό, Lyd.*Mag.* 1.11.

ἀσπῐδιώτης, ου, ὁ, *shield-bearing, a warrior*, ἀνέρες ἀσπιδιῶται Il.2. 554, 16.167, Theoc.14.67, Plb.10.29.6, *AP*9.116: in pl., = Lat. *scutati*, Lyd.*Mag.*1.9:—so **ἀσπῐδίτης** [δῑ], ου, ὁ, S.*Fr.*426.

ἀσπῐδό-δηκτος, ον, *bitten by an adder* or *asp*, Dsc.2.34, Vett.Val. 127.20, Gal.14.300. **-δουπος**, ον, *clattering with shields*, Pi.*I.*1. 23. **-ειδής**, ές, *shaped like a shield*, Agatharch.105. II. *adorned with serpents*, βασιλεῖαι *OGI*90.44 (Rosetta). **-εις**, εσσα, εν, = foreg., Poet.ap.S.E.*M.*1.316, cf. Opp.*H.*1.397; but perh. *shield-covered*, and so of the *testudo, formed by shields*, Id.*C.*1.214. **-θήρας**, ου, ὁ, *snake-hunter*, *Gloss.* **-θρέμμων**, ον, gen. ονος, = ἀσπιδοφέρμων, Sch.E.*Ph.*796.

ἀσπῐδο-πήγιον, τό, *shield-manufactory*, D.36.4, Poll.7.155, Lib. *Or.*33.17. **-πηγός**, ὁ, *shield-maker*, Poll.1.149, Them.*Or.*15. 197c. **-ποιία**, ἡ, *the making of the shield*, Gramm. name for Il.18, Hermog.*Prog.*2, Eust.1154.41. **-ποιός**, ὁ, *shield-maker*, Poll.7. 155. **-τροφος**, ον, *feeding on adders* or *asps*, Gal.11.143.

ἀσπῐδοῦχος, ὁ, (ἔχω) *shield-bearer*, S.*Fr.*427, E.*Supp.*1144.

ἀσπῐδο-φέρμων, ον, gen. ονος, (φέρβω) *living by the shield*, i. e. *by war*, ἀ. θίασος E.*Ph.*796 (lyr.). **-φορέω**, *bear a shield*, Sch.Ar.*Nu.* 984. **-φορικός**, ή, όν, = sq.: -κή (sc. τέχνη), ἡ, Eustr.*in EN*11. 27. **-φόρος**, ον, *bearing a shield*, Thd.2 *Ki.*11.4.

ἀσπίζω, *shield, protect*, τόπον *IGRom.*4.1349 (Lydia): pf. part. ἠσπικότες Hsch., Suid.

ἄσπῐλ-ος, ον, lit. *stainless*: hence, *faultless, without blemish*, λίθοι *IG*2.1054*c*4, cf. *AP*6.252 (Antiphil.), 1*Ep.Ti.*6.14, 1*Ep.Pet.*1.19, etc.; ἄ. ἀπὸ παντὸς κινδύνου *PMag.Leid.V.*8.11: Comp. and Sup. vv.ll. for sq. in Dsc.2.167. II. ἄσπιλος· χειμάρρους (Maced.), Hsch. **-ωτος**, ον, = foreg. 1, Sext.*Sent.*449, Suid.; *without spots*, Dsc.2.167.

ἀσπί⟨ν⟩θιον, τό, prob. a vulgar form of ἀψίνθιον, Hsch.:—also **ἀπίνθιον**, *EM*183.25.

ἀσπίς, ίδος, ἡ, *shield*, εὔκυκλος Il.14.428, al.; κυκλοτερής Hdt.1.194; ἀσπίδος κύκλος A.*Th.*489; ὀμφαλόεσσα Il.4.448, al.; opp. Thracian πέλτη and Persian γέρρον, X.*An.*2.1.6, *Mem.*3.9.2; ἀσπίδα ῥῖψαι, ἀποβαλεῖν, Anacr.28, Ar.*V.*19, cf. Hdt.5.95: to estimate a victory, ἀσπίδας ἔλαβον ὡς διακοσίας X.*HG*1.2.3: metaph., οὗτος γὰρ ἡμῖν ἀ. οὐ μικρὰ θράσους A.*Ag.*1437; τὴν ἀ. ἀποβέβληκεν τοῦ βίου Nicostr. Com.29, cf. Lib.*Or.*62.47. 2. collective, *body of men-at-arms*, ὀκτακισχιλίη ἀ. Hdt.5.30, cf. E.*Ph.*78, X.*An.*1.7.10. 3. military phrases, ἐπ' ἀσπίδας πέντε καὶ εἴκοσι τάξασθαι to be drawn up twenty-five *deep* or *in file*, Th.4.93; στρατιὰν τεταγμένην οὐκ ἐπ' ὀλίγων ἀσπίδων Id.7.79; ἵστασθαι ἐπὶ τρεῖς ἀσπίδας Ar.*Fr.*66; ἐπὶ μιᾶς ἀσπίδος in single line, Isoc.6.99; ἐπ' ἀσπίδα, παρ' ἀσπίδα (opp. ἐπὶ δόρυ), *on the left, towards* or *to the left*, because the *shield* was on the left arm, X.*Cyr.*7.5.6, *An.*4.3.26; παρ' ἀσπίδος A.*Th.*624; ἐξ ἀσπίδος Plb.11.23.5; but παρ' ἀσπίδα, literally, beside the *shield*, Il. 16.400; παρ' ἀ. στῆναι stand in *battle*, E.*Med.*250, *Ph.*1001; παρ' ἀ. βεβηκέναι ib.1073; ἐκπονεῖν Id.*Or.*653, cf. *Hel.*734; ἐς ἀσπίδ' ἥξειν Id.*Ph.*1326; ἀσπίδας συγκλείειν (cf. συγκλείω); ἀσπίδα τίθεσθαι *serve in the ranks*, Pl.*Lg.*756a; but θέσθαι τὰς ἀ. pile *shields*, X.*HG*2.4. 12; ἐπειδὰν ἀ. ψοφῇ when the *shields* ring, i. e. when two bodies of men meet in a charge, Id.*An.*4.3.29; ἀσπίδα ἀναδέξαι, ἆραι, as a signal, Hdt.6.115, X.*HG*2.1.27. 4. of a round, flat bowl, Aristopho 14. 5. *boss* on a door, *IG*4.1484.79 (Epid.). II. *asp, Egyptian cobra, Coluber haie*, Hdt.4.191, Men.702, Nic.*Th.*158, Ph.2.570, Ael.*NA*10.31; a play on signff. I and II, Ar.*V.*23. 2. *ornament* in this form, *OGI*90.43 (Rosetta).

ἀσπ-ιστήρ, ῆρος, ὁ, = sq., S.*Aj.*565, E.*Heracl.*277. **-ιστής**, οῦ, ὁ, *one armed with a shield, warrior*, Hom. (in Il.) always in gen. pl. ἀσπιστάων, Il.4.90, al.:—as Adj., ἀσπισταὶ μόχθοι τευχέων, i. e. the *shield* of Achilles, E.*El.*444 (dub. l.). **-ιστικός**, ή, όν, *composed of warriors*, φάλαγξ D.H.20.3. **-ίστωρ**, ορος, ὁ, = ἀσπιστής, κλόνοι ἀσπίστορες turmoil *of shielded warriors*, A.*Ag.*404 (lyr.).

ἀσπλαγχν-έω, *to be unmerciful*, Aq., Th.*Jb.*41.2. **-ος**, ον, *without bowels*, or rather, *without heart*: metaph., *dastard*, S.*Aj.*472; *unsympathetic, merciless*, Chrysipp.*Stoic.*2.249. Adv. -νως Hsch. s. v. ἀνηλεῶς. II. *not eating* σπλάγχνα, Pl.Com.113.

ἀσπλῆνις· βοτάνης εἶδος, Hsch.

ἄσπληνον, τό (and -ος, ὁ, Dsc.3.134), (ἀ- euph., σπλήν) *miltwaste, Asplenium Ceterach*, supposed to be a cure for the *spleen*, Dsc. l. c., Zopyr.ap.Orib.14.50.1. 2. = ἄκορον, Dsc.1.2.

ἄσπληνος, ον, *spleenless*, Aët.15.14. 2. ἄσπληνος, ὁ, = κισσός, Ps.-Dsc.2.179.

ἀσπόλην· ἀρίστην, Hsch.

ἀσπονδ-εί (also –ί, *SIG*110 (Rhodes, v B.C.), 187 (Cnidus, iv B.C.), Adv. of ἄσπονδος :—*without truce, implacably*, πολεμεῖν Ph.2.195; φονᾶν ib.423. II. of peace, *without formal treaty*, ἀσυλεὶ καὶ ἀ. *SIG*168.9 (Erythrae, iv B.C.), *IPE*2.1 (Panticapaeum, iv B.C.), etc. **–ία**, ἡ, *being without truce* or *treaty*, *IG*2².28, Poll.8.139. II. *implacability*, Lib.*Vit.*1.22 (–εία codd.). **–ος**, ον, *without* σπονδή or *drink-offering*: hence, I. of a god, *to whom no drink-offering is poured*, ἄ. θεός, i.e. death, E.*Alc.*424. II. *without a regular truce* (ratified by σπονδαί), ἀνοκωχή Th.5.32; of persons, *without making a truce*, ἄ. ἀπιέναι Id.3.111, cf. 113; ἀσπόνδους τοὺς νεκροὺς ἀνελέσθαι take up their dead *without leave asked*, Id.2.22; τὸ εὐπρεπὲς ἄσπονδον the specious plea *of neutrality*, Id.1.37. 2. *admitting of no truce, implacable*, ἄσπονδόν τ' Ἄρη (ἀράν codd.) A.*Ag.*1235 (Pors.); πόλεμος D.18.262, Plb.1.65.6, etc.; ἔχθρα Plu.*Per.*30; ἀσπόνδοισι νόμοισιν ἔχθραν συμβάλλειν E.*El.*905 (lyr.); of persons, *implacable*, 2*Ep.Ti.*3.3. Adv. –δως, ἔχειν Ph.*Fr.*24H.

ἀσπορ-έω, *to be unsown*, of land, *PTeb.*61ᵇ34 (ii B.C.), etc.; ἀσπορίσαι, written for –ῆσαι, Wilcken *Chr.*11 *A* 8. **–ία**, ἡ, *barrenness*, Man.4.585. **–ος**, ον, = ἄσπαρτος, χώρα D.19.123, *IG*2.379.9, Plu. *Alex.*66, *PRyl.*133.22 (i A.D.), etc. II. of plants, *unsown, growing without cultivation*, Luc.*Rh.Pr.*8, Nic.*Fr.*74.58. III. *begotten without impregnation*, of Hephaestus, Nonn.*D.*9.229; but, *producing without impregnation*, ἰλύς ib.40.433. IV. *barren*, Luc.*Am.* 28, Nonn.*D.*2.221, al.; *not having issue*, ib.40.119. 2. Act., *preventing production*, αὐχμός ib.39.139.

ἀσπούδ-αστος, ον, *not zealously pursued* or *courted*, γυνή E.*Fr.* 501; ἀσπούδαστα, τά, *matters of no interest*, Hp.*Ep.*17. 2. *not to be sought for, mischievous*, σπεύδειν ἀσπούδαστα E.*Ba.*913, *IT* 202. II. Act., *not in earnest*, τὸ ἀ. *want of earnestness*, περί τι D.H. 5.72. Adv. –τως *carelessly*, Ael.*NA*10.30, *PFlor.*187.3 (iii A.D.). **–ί** [ῐ] or –εί, Adv. *without effort* or *trouble*, Il.8.512, 15.476; *without a struggle, ignobly*, μὴ μὰν ἀσπουδί γε.. ἀπολοίμην 22.304, cf. Arr.*An.* 6.9.5; *carelessly*, D.C.54.18. **–ος**, ον, *without ambition*, Eup. 234. 2. = ἀσπούδαστος 2, *Stoic.*3.38.

ἀσπράτουρα, ἡ, (*asper*) rough, i.e. *unworn, coin*, *OGI*484.25 (Pergam.); cf. κόλλυβος· *asperatura, Gloss.*

ἄσπρις, ἡ, *Turkey oak*, *Quercus Cerris*, Thphr.*HP*3.8.7.

ἄσπρος, α, ον, = Lat. *asper*, Ael.*NA*1.26. II. ἄ. γράμματα *invisible* writing, *Cat.Cod.Astr.*1.108 (the signf. *white* is very late); ἄσπρον, τό, *white of an egg*, [Gal.]14.560. III. name of an *ingredient of incense*, Aët.16.146,148.

ἄσσα, Ion. for ἅτινα, neut. pl. of ὅστις, Il.10.208, al., Hdt.1.47, al.; Att. **ἅττα** Pl.Com.49, etc. II. **ἄσσα**, Ion. for τινά, Att. **ἄττα**, *something, some*, Hom. only once, ὁπποῖ' ἄσσα *what sort*, Od.19.218; πόσ' ἄττα; Ar.*Ra.*173; δεῖν' ἄ. ib.925; οἷ' ἄττα βαΰζει Cratin. 6, etc.: with numerals, δύ' ἄττα ὀνόματα, τρία ἄττα γένη, Pl.*Sph.*255c, *Ly.*216d: added to a temporal Conj., πηνίκ' ἄττα..; Ar.*Av.*1514, etc. (ἄσσα (ἄττα) arises from false division of groups like ὁποῖά σσα where σσα = τι̯-α, neut. pl. of τις, cf. Megarian σά.)

ἀσσαριαῖος, α, ον, *at the rate of* 12 *asses per denarius per month*, τόκος *BMus.Inscr.*481*.66 (Ephesus, ii A.D.).

ἀσσάριον, τό, (Lat. *assarius* (sc. *nummus*)), D.H.9.27, *SIG*²869.5 (Calymna), *OGI*484.9, al. (Pergam., ii A.D.), Plu.*Cam.*13, *Ev.Matt.* 10.29. II. a sort of *valve*, Hero *Spir.*1.10.

ἀσσέως· ἐπὶ σοῦ, Hsch. (Fort. ἄος· ἕως, ⟨μ⟩έ⟨χρ⟩ις οὗ.)

ἀσσιδάριος, ὁ, = *essedarius*, Artem.2.32.

ἄσσιος· προκόλπιος, Hsch.

ἆσσον (Dor. **ἄσσιον** acc. to Eust.1643.32), Adv. Comp. of ἄγχι:—*nearer*, esp. of hostile approach, ἆσσον ἴτ' Il.1.567, al., cf. Hes.*Th.*748; τείχεος ἆ. ἴσαν Il.22.4, cf. Hdt.4.3, Ar.*Eq.*1306; simply of approach, γυναῖχ' ὁρῶ στείχουσαν ἡμῶν ἆ. S.*OC*312, cf. *El.*900; of a woman, ἥτις ἀνδρῶν ἆ. οὐκ ἐλήλυθεν Ar.*Eq.*1306; δίφρον ἆ. ἕλκεται πυρός Semon.7. 26: c. dat., S.*OC*722: with double Comp., ἕρποντι μᾶλλον ἆσσον Id.*Ant.*1210: Sup. ἄσσιστα A.*Fr.*6; ἄσιστα *IG*5(2).159.17 (Tegea), *Michel*1334 (Elis, iv B.C.). II. hence new Comp. **ἀσσοτέρω**, with or without gen., Od.19.506, 17.572; later Comp. Adj. **ἀσσότερος**, = ἐγγύτερος, Arat.878: Sup. Adv. ἀσσοτάτω *AP*9.430 (Crin.): Sup. Adj. ἀσσότατος ib.6.345 (Id.).

Ἀσσύριοι [ῠ], οἱ, *the Assyrians*, Hdt.1.193, al.:—**Ἀσσυρία**, Ion. –ίη (sc. γῆ), ἡ, *their country*, Id.2.17, etc.:—**Ἀσσύριος**, α, ον, as an Adj., Theoc.2.162, al.; later **Ἀσσυρικός**, ή, όν, St.Byz., al.

ἀσσύτεροι, = ἐπασσύτεροι, Opp.*C.*4.121,202; cf. **ἀσσυτία**· ἄλλα ἐπ' ἄλλοις, Hsch.

ᾄσσω, Att. contr. for ἀΐσσω.

ἀσταγανά· ἱμάς, Hsch.

ἀσταγής, ές, *not trickling*, ἀ. κρύσταλλος *hard-frozen* ice, dub. l. in S.*Fr.*149.4 (prob. εὐπαγή). II. *not merely trickling*, i.e. *gushing, in a stream*, A.R.3.805, Nic.*Th.*307.

ἀσταθής, ές, (ἵσταμαι) *unsteady, unstable*, κινήσεις Phld.*Ir.*p.26 W.; αὖραι *AP*10.74 (Paul. Sil.), cf. Nonn.*D.*8.140, al.; διάνοια Lxx 3*Ma.* 5.39.

ἀστάθμ-ευτος, ον, *not encamped*, App.*BC*2.74. **–ητος**, ον, *unsteady, unstable*, ἀστέρες, = πλανῆται, X.*Mem.*4.7.5; of persons, ὁ δῆμος –ότατον πρᾶγμα D.19.136, cf. Ar.*Av.*169, Pl.*Ly.*214d; of life, ἀ. αἰών E.*Or.*981 (lyr.); τὸ ἀ. τοῦ μέλλοντος *the uncertainty* of.., Th. 4.62; τῆς συμφορᾶς Id.3.59; τύχης –ότερον οὐδέν Ph.2.85. Adv. –τως D.Chr.4.122. **–ος**, ον, *unweighed, without record of weight*, *IG*1. 121.4, al., *Epigr.Gr.*805.

ἀσταίνει· δυσπαθεῖ, ἁμαρτάνει, μοχθεῖ, Hsch.

ἀστακός, ὁ, *the smooth lobster*, Philyll.13, Arist.*HA*526ᵃ11, 549ᵇ 14, Matro *Conv.*66, Archestr.*Fr.*24.1; ὁ ἐν τοῖς ποταμοῖς ἀ. *the* river *cray-fish*, Arist.*HA*530ᵃ28. II. *hollow of the ear*, Poll.2.85. (By assimilation from ὀστακός, the Att. form acc. to Ath.3.105b.)

ἀστακτ-ί, Adv. of sq., *not in drops*, i.e. *in floods*, S. (who has –ῑ in *OC*1646, –ῐ 1251), Pl.*Phd.*117c. **–ος**, ον, = ἀσταγής II, E.*IT*1242 (lyr.), Orph.*Fr.*47.

ἀστάλακτος [τᾰ], ον, *not damp*, ἀήρ Plu.*Crass.*4.

ἀστάλη, ἡ, *polypus in the nose*, Hsch. 2. = σκώληξ οὐρὰν ἔχων, Id.

ἀστᾰλής, ές, (στέλλομαι) *unarmed, unclad*, Call.*Fr.*266.

ἀσταλύζω, *weep and sob*, Hsch. (–ύχειν cod.).

ἀστάνδης, ου, ὁ, *courier*, Plu.*Alex.*18, 2.326f; cf. Armen. *astandel* 'wander'.

ἀστᾰσία, ἡ, *unsteadiness, inconstancy*, Man.1.19: pl., Vett.Val.38.3.

ἀστᾰσίαστος [ῐ], ον, *not torn by faction*, Ἀττική Th.1.2; στρατός App.*Hisp.*72; βίος Eus.Mynd.26. 2. *not liable to disturbance*, νομή *Sammelb.*5174 (iv A.D.), etc. II. of persons, *free from faction* or *party-spirit*, Lys.2.55, Pl.*R.*459e, etc.; of forms of government, Arist.*Pol.*1302ᵃ9. Adv. –τως D.S.17.54, Herm. *in Phdr.*p.186 A.: Comp., D.C.52.30: Sup. –ότατα Pl.*R.*520d.

ἀστᾰταίνω, = sq., Gal.19.493.

ἀστᾰτέω, *to be never at rest*, πόλοιο φορὰν..–έουσαν *App.Anth.*3.146. 4 (Theon); of the sea, Plu.*Crass.*17; βλέμμα ἀστατοῦν *Hippiatr.* 3. 2. *to be unsettled, to be a wanderer*, 1*Ep.Cor.*4.11; *to be inconstant*, περὶ τοὺς γάμους Vett.Val.116.30.

ἄστᾱτοι, οἱ, = Lat. *hastati*, Plb.6.23.1.

ἄστᾰτος, ον, (ἵσταμαι) *never standing still, unresting*, τὸ κύκλῳ σῶμα Arist.*Metaph.*1073ᵃ31; ἄ. τροχός Mesom.*Nem.*7. Adv. –τως, φορεῖσθαι Ph.1.181, cf. Vett.Val.27.1. 2. *unsteady, unstable*, τύχη Epicur.*Ep.*3 p.65 U., cf. Phld.*Rh.*1.166 S. (Sup.), Ph.1.230, al., Diog.Oen.18, Diogenian.Epicur.2.60, Plu.2.103f; of persons, ἄ. τὴν διάνοιαν Onos.3.3; ἄ. αἰών *IG*7.2543; θνητῶν βίος *Epigr.Gr.*699, cf. Ph.1.651; of a house, *ruinous*, *PLond.ined.*2194. 3. *uncertain*, θεωρία Plb.6.57.2. 4. Act., *making it impossible to stand*, πόνος, πάθος, Luc.*Ocyp.*36,71. II. *unweighed*, *IG*1.32 *B* 25, al., Nic.*Th.*602.

ἀστᾰφῐδίτης, ου, ὁ, fem. –ῖτις, ιδος, *of raisins*, ἀσταφιδῖτις ῥώξ bunch *of raisins*, *AP*9.226 (Zon.).

ἀστᾰφίς, ίδος, ἡ, sg. as collect. noun, *dried grapes, raisins*, *IG*5(1). 1.13 (Tegea, v B.C.), Hdt.2.40, Alex.127.4, etc.: pl., ἡ Ῥόδος ἀσταφίδας [παρέχει] Hermipp.63.16, cf. X.*An.*4.4.9, Arist.*HA*595ᵇ10; ἀσταφίδος οἶνος *raisin*-wine, Pl.*Lg.*845b: **ὀσταφίς**, v.l. ap.Phot. as in Cratin.121 (pl.), Nicopho 21; **σταφίς**, Hp.*Acut.*64, Theoc.27.9, etc. II. = σταφὶς ἀγρία, Ps.-Dsc.4.152, Gal.11.842, Plin.*HN*23.17. (ἀσταφίς is prob. by assimilation from ὀσταφίς; cf. ἀστακός.)

ἀστᾰφῠλῖνος, = σταφυλῖνος, Diocl.*Fr.*123.

ἀστάφῠλος [ᾰ], ον, *without grapes*, χῶρος Aus.*Ep.*12.24.

ἄστᾰχυς, υος, ὁ, (στάχυς with prothetic α) :—*ear of corn*, Il.2.148, Hdt.5.92.ζ', Call.*Cer.*20, etc.: metaph., βοστρύχων ἀστάχυες Philostr. *Im.*1.7, cf. Luc.*Charid.*3. II. *bandage*, Gal.18(1).813.

ἀστέγαστος, ον, *uncovered*, ἀγγεῖον Gal.17(2).153: of a ship, *undecked*, Antipho 5.22, cf. Apollod.*Poliorc.*185.10; *roofless*, *PGen.*11.7 (iv A.D.); διὰ τὸ ἀ. from their *having no shelter*, Th.7.87.

ἀστεγής, f.l. for ἀσταγής, δάκρυ *App.Anth.*3.198.

ἄστεγος, ον, (στέγη) *without roof, houseless*, Ps.-Phoc.24, Lxx *Is.* 58.7, App.*Hisp.*78; *unprotected, exposed*, Ph.1.574. II. (στέγω) Act., *not holding*: metaph., ἄ. χείλεσι *unable to keep* one's mouth *shut, given to prating*, Lxx *Pr.*10.8; στόμα ἄ. ib.26.28.

ἀστειεύομαι, = sq., Sch.Ar.*Ach.*1058, *Pax*370, Sch.Arat.956.

ἀστεΐζομαι, *write* or *talk wittily* or *eloquently*, Str.13.4.11, J.*Ap.*2. 9, Demetr.*Eloc.*149, Plu.*Marc.*21; *talk speciously*, Ph.2.123 :—Act. in St.Byz. s.v. ἄστυ.

ἀστειο-λογία, ἡ, *clever talking, wit*, Arist.*Rh.Al.*1436ᵃ20 (pl.), M.Ant.1.7. **–μελής**, ές, *with graceful limbs*, Heph.Astr.1. 1. **–ρρημονέω**· ἀστεΐζομαι, Zonar.

ἀστεῖος, α, ον, also ος, ον Diph.73: (ἄστυ):—*of the town* (but in the literal sense ἀστικός is used). II. *town-bred, polite*, Pl.*Phd.* 116d; opp. ἄγροικος, Plu.*Mar.*3; γένοιτ' ἀστεῖος οἰκῶν ἐν πόλει Alc. Com.26; *charming*, Isoc.2.34. 2. of thoughts and words, *refined, elegant, witty*, διάλεκτον ἀστείαν ὑποθηλυτέραν, opp. ἀνελεύθερον ὑπαγροικοτέραν, Ar.*Fr.*685; ἀστεῖόν τι λέξαι Id.*Ra.*901; ἀστεῖον λέγεις (where there is a play on the double sense, *witty* and *popular*) Id.*Nu.*204; ἀ. καὶ δημωφελεῖς οἱ λόγοι Pl.*Phdr.*227d; ἀστεῖον εἰπεῖν *Com.Anon.*248 Mein., cf. Axiop.1.14; ἀστειοτάτας ἐπινοίας Ar.*Eq.* 539; of persons, οἱ ἀ. *the wits*, Pl.*R.*452d; τὰ ἀ. *witty sayings, witticisms*, Arist.*Rh.*1411ᵇ21, al. Adv. –ως J.*AJ*12.4.4, Plu.2.123f, Luc.*Nigr.*13. 3. as a general word of praise, of things and persons, *pretty, charming*, βοσκήματε Ar.*Ach.*811; ἑορτή Pl.*Grg.* 447a; ἀ. καὶ εὐήθης Id.*R.*349b, cf. *Phdr.*242e, Hp.*Ep.*13; ἐστὶ γοῦν ἁπλῆ τις;—ἀστεία μὲν οὖν Anaxil.21; ἀστεῖον [ἐστι] ὅτι ἐρυθριᾷς it is *charming* to see you blush, Pl.*Ly.*204c; ἀστεῖον πάνυ εἰ.. Men. *Sam.*149. b. ironically, ἀ. κέρδος a *pretty* piece of luck, Ar.*Nu.* 1064; ἀστεῖος εἶ Diph.73. 4. of outward appearance, *pretty, graceful*, Lxx *Ex.*2.2, al.; οἱ μικροὶ ἀ. καὶ σύμμετροι, καλοὶ δ' οὔ Arist. *EN*1123ᵇ7; *handsome*, Lxx *Jd.*3.17 (of Eglon): in Comedy, of *dainty* dishes, κραμβίδιον, κρεῖσκον, Antiph.6, Alex.189. 5. *good* of its kind, αἷμα Hp.*Alim.*44; ἐλλέβορος Str.9.3.3; οἶνος Plu.2.620d; of persons, *good*, Ph.1.97, Plu.*Them.*5; ἀστεῖα *good qualities*, opp. φαῦλα, Demetr.*Eloc.*114. Adv. -είως *honourably*, πράττων Lxx 2*Ma.* 12.43, cf. Ph.1.244.

ἀστειοσύνη, ἡ, = sq., Lib.*Or.*11.154, Chor. in *Rev.Phil.*1.81.

ἀστειότης, ητος, ἡ, *prettiness, daintiness* of person, Vett.Val.161. 17; *politeness, wit*, μακαρισμὸς καὶ ἀ. Andronic.Rhod.p.570 M., cf. Lib.*Or.*11.270, Sch.Ar.*Pax* 370.

ἄστειπτος, ον, v. ἄστιπτος.

ἀστέ-ϊσμα, ατος, τό, *witticism*, Tz.*H.*4.780. **-ϊσμός**, ὁ, *wit*, D.H.*Dem.*54, Demetr.*Eloc.*128 (pl.), 130, Phld.*Rh.*1.181 S.: pl., *forms of wit*, Longin.34.2, Philostr.*VS*1.25.9; esp. of ironical self-depreciation, *mock-modesty*, Phld.*Acad.Ind.*p.52 M., Alex.*Fig.*1.18, Trypho *Trop.*24; = παράλειψις, Hdn.*Fig.*p.98 S.

ἄστεκτος, ον, (στέγω) *insufferable*, Hsch., A.*Fr.*224 ap.*AB*456 (Hsch. ἄστερκτα), Paul.Aeg.5.16, Dsc.*Ther.*13. Adv. -τως Hsch.

ἀστέλεφος, ὁ, *leathern case for a lyre*, Hsch.:—also **ἀστελοφοῦν**· δέρμα τὸ εἰς τὰ ἄκρα, Id.

ἀστελέχης, ες, *without main stem*, Thphr.*HP*1.3.1.

ἀστέλεχος· ὁ δακτύλιος, ἕδρα, Hsch.

ἀστέμβακτος, ον, = sq., Euph.123, Lyc.1117.

ἀστεμφής, ές, *unmoved, unshaken*, βουλή Il.2.344; βίη A.R.4. 1375; ἀστεμφὲς ἔχεσκε [τὸ σκῆπτρον] he held it *stiff*, Il.3.219; οὐδός Hes.*Th.*812; ἀ. οἴη νέκυς Opp.*H.*2.70. Adv., ὑμεῖς ἀστεμφέως ἐχέμεν you hold *fast!* Od.4.419, cf. 459; ἀστεμφῶς τὸν βίον διενήξατο Marin. *Procl.*15: neut. ἀστεμφές as Adv., *stiffly, starkly*, Mosch.4.113; νεφέλαι.. ἀ. μελανεῦσαι dark *without relief*, Arat.878. 2. of persons, *stiff*, ποιηταὶ σκληροὶ καὶ ἀ. Ar.*Fr.*579; ἀ. Τελαμών *unflinching*, Theoc.13.37; as pr.n. of a Titan, Emp.123. 3. metaph., of a trap, *relentless*, *AP*6.296 (Leon.); ζυγός, δεσμός, Opp.*H.*1.417, 2.84; νύξ *AP*9.424 (Duris).—Poet. word, also in late Prose, Agath.1.21. (Cf. στέμβω, στέμφυλον, Skt. *stabhnāti* 'supports', 'holds fast'.)

ἀστένακτος, ον, *without sigh* or *groan*, ἀ. κἀδάκρυτος S.*Tr.*1200, cf. 1074; ἄκλαυτος ἀ. E.*Alc.*173; ἀ. ἡμέρα a day *free from groans*, Id.*Hec.*691 (lyr.), cf. Pl.*Ax.*370d, *Mél.Nicole* 308 (Panticapaeum). Adv. -τως Plu.2.107a:—also **ἀστενακτί**, A.*Fr.*307, Ar.*Ec.*464.

ἀστέον, *one must sing*, Ar.*Nu.*1205, Pl.*R.*390e.

ἀστεπτος, ον, (στέφω) *uncrowned*, τίς ἄ. θεῶν; E.*Heracl.*440.

ἀστεργ-άνωρ [ᾱν], ορος, ὁ, ἡ, *without love of man, unwedded*, παρθενία, of Io, A.*Pr.*898 (lyr.). **-ής**, ές, *without love, implacable*, ὀργή S.*Aj.*776; ἀ. τι παθεῖν something *intolerable*, Id.*OT*229. II. *repellent*, Hp.*Gland.*16; *unyielding*, -έστερον ξύλον Id.*Fract.*16 (s.v.l.), cf. Ruf.ap.Orib.49.28.3.

ἀστερ-ιαῖος, α, ον, *like a star*, Cleom.1.11; *decorated with stars*, prob. in *PHamb.*10.44 (ii A.D.). **-ίας**, ου, ὁ, *starred*: hence, I. a fish, *Squalus stellaris*, Philyll.1.2, Arist.*HA*543^{a}17. II. a bird, 1. perh. *bittern*, *Ardea stellaris*, ib.609^{b}22. 2. a kind of *hawk*, ib.620^{a}18; = χρυσάετος, Ael.*NA*2.39. **-ίζω**, *arrange in constellations*, Hipparch.1.4.5 (Pass.), al.; *mark with stars*, Ptol.*Geog.*1. 23.3 (Pass.); *cast a nativity*, Vett.Val.187.15. **-ικός**, ή, όν, *planetary*, κινήματα *Theol.Ar.*37. **-ιος**, α, ον, also ος, ον, *starred, starry*, Arat.695; ἀ. ἅμαξα, = Ἄρκτος, Call.*Fr.*146; κύτος, of the sphere *of the fixed stars*, Vett.Val.172.32. 2. *of a star*, [σῶμα] Porph.*Chr.* 35; ὕλη Orph.*Fr.*353. II. ἀστέριον, τό, a kind of *spider*, Nic. *Th.*725. III. ἀστέριον, τό, name of a *plant*, Crateuas *Fr.*10; = κορωνόπους, Ps.-Dsc.2.130 (prob. for ἄστριον); = σφονδύλιον, Id.3. 76; = κάνναβις ἥμερος, ib.148; = ἀστὴρ Ἀττικός, Id.4.119. IV. ἀστέριον, τό, = ἀστήρ VI, Dsc.*Eup.*2.30. V. ἀστέριος λίθος *meteoric* stone, D.P.328. **-ίσκιον**, τό, Dim. of sq., *little star, boss, knob* on a helmet, Apollon.*Lex.* **-ίσκος**, ὁ, Dim. of ἀστήρ, *little star*, Call.*Iamb.*1.120, Hipparch.3.5.22 (pl.). 2. = ἀστερίσκιον, Eust. 424.5. II. *asterisk*, the mark ⋇ by which Gramm. distinguished fine passages in Mss., Id.599.34, etc.; also used as a metrical sign, Heph.*Poëm.*p.74 C. III. = ἀστὴρ Ἀττικός, *blue daisy*, Thphr.*HP* 4.12.2, Ps.-Dsc.4.119. IV. *capsule of the poppy*, Dsc.4.64. V. *small wheel with projections*, Hero *Aut.*24.5. VI. a *geometrical figure*, Id.*Stereom.*1.77. **-ισμός**, ὁ, *marking with stars*, Ptol.*Geog.* 1.22.4, Sch.Arat.205; *arrangement of constellations*, τῆς Ἀργοῦς Hipparch.1.8.1, cf. 2.1.12; *a starry ornament*, f.l. for foreg. in D.S.19. 34. II. = καταστερισμός, Herm.ap.Stob.1.49.44. **-ίτης** (sc. λίθος), ὁ, name of a *mythical precious stone*, Ptol.Heph.ap.Phot. p.153 B., Ps.-Democr.Alch.p.50 B.

ἄστερκτος, ον, = ἀστεργής, v. ἄστεκτος.

ἀστερο-βλής, βλῆτος, ὁ, ἡ, *star-flung*, κεραυνός *IG*14.641 i. **-δίνητος**, ον, (δινέω) *brought by the revolution of the stars*, Procl.*H.*1. 49. **-ειδής**, ές, *star-like*, Ph.1.20,633 (Sup.), Plu.2.933e. Adv. -δῶς Dsc.1.19. II. *starred, starry*, E.*Fr.*114 ap.Ar.*Th.*1067. **-εις**, εσσα, εν, = foreg. II, οὐρανός Il.4.44, *IG*9(1).882.15 (Corc.), etc. II. *like a star, sparkling*, θώρηξ Il.16.134; Ἡφαίστου δόμος 18.370. III. ἀ. πέδιλα, of the Senators' buskins which had *a half-moon* in front, *IG*14.1389 i 23. **-θεν**, Adv. *from the stars*, Arat.1013 (v.l. οὐρανόθεν). **-μαρμᾰρῠγή**, ἡ, *the brightness of the stars*, v.l. in Sch. Arat.328. **-νωτος**, ον, *with starry back*, οὐρανός Nonn.*D.*2.335.

ἀστεροόμμᾰτος, ον, *star-eyed*, epith. of night, Orph.*H.*34.13.

ἀστεροπ-ᾱγερέτας, α, ὁ, *lightning-compeller*, Cerc.4.25. **-αῖος**, ον, = ἀστεροπητής, Corn.*ND*9. **-ή**, ἡ, = στεροπή, ἀστραπή, *lightning*, Il.10.154 (v.l. for στεροπή), Pi.*N.*9.19, Ar.*Av.*1746, 1748 (anap.). **-ής**, ῆτος, ὁ, ἡ, *lightening*, κεραυνός *IG*14.641. **-ητής**, οῦ, ὁ, *lightener*, of Zeus, Il.1.580, Hes.*Th.*390, S.*Ph.*1198 (dact.).

ἀστερο-πληθής, ές, *full of stars*, Orac.ap.Eus.*PE*5.8. **-πληκτος**, ον, *struck 'sine fulmine'* (by a meteoric bolt), Seneca *QN*1.15.

ἀστεροπός, όν, = ἀστερωπός, Ζεύς Achae.2.3 (anap.).

ἀστερο-σκοπέω, *watch the stars*, S.E.*M.*5.68:—hence Subst. **-σκοπία**, ἡ, ib.80 (pl.). **-σκόπος**, ον, ὁ, *astronomer* or *astrologer*, Artem.2.69. **-φεγγής**, ές, *shining with stars*, αἰθήρ Orph.*H.*5.5; νύξ ib.3.3. **-φοιτος**, ον, *traversing the stars*, esp. of constellations, Ἠριδανός Nonn.*D.*23.298, al. II. *traversed by stars*, κύκλος Ὀλύμπου ib.32.10, al.

ἀστερόω, *turn into stars*, πέτρους ἠστερωκέναι *Placit.*2.13.3:—Pass., *to be marked by stars*, opp. εἶναι ἀνάστερα, Sch.Arat.273.

ἀστερόωνται, f.l. for ἀστερόεντες in Arat.548.

ἀστερ-ώδης, ες, = ἀστεροειδής, Ποταμός Sch.Arat.355. **-ωπός**, όν, *star-faced, star-like, bright-shining*, ὄμμα Λητῴας κόρης A.*Fr.*170; νυκτὸς ἀ. σέλας E.*Hipp.*851 (lyr.), cf. *Ph.*129 (lyr.). II. *star-eyed, starry*, αἰθήρ E.*Ion* 1078 (lyr.); ἀ. οὐρανοῦ δέμας Critias 25. 33 D. **-ωτός**, ή, όν, *starred*, φιάλη *IG*11(2).199 *B*8,42 (iii B.C.); πῖλος Sallust.4.

ἀστέφᾰν-ος, ον, *without crown, ungarlanded*, mostly in token of defeat, E.*Hipp.*1137 (lyr.); ἁμίλλας ἔθετ' ἀστεφάνους Id.*Andr.* 1021. **-ωτος**, ον, *uncrowned, forbidden to be crowned*, Sapph.78, Pl.*R.*613c, D.18.319; ἀ. ἐκ τῶν νόμων Aeschin.3.176. 2. *without the nuptial crown, unwedded*, *Epigr.Gr.*314.27.

ἀστεφής, ές, = ἀστέφανος, Man.6.517:—also **ἄστεφος**, ον, A.D. *Pron.*31.15.

ἀστή, ἡ, fem. of ἀστός, Hdt.1.173, al., Ar.*Th.*541, *BGU*1104.4 (i B.C.), etc.

ἄστηθι, = ἀν-στ-, Herod.8.1, cf. ἀνίστημι.

ἄστηλος, ον, *without tombstone*, *AP*7.479 (Theodorid.).

ἀστηνεῖ· ἀδυνατεῖ, Hsch., cf. sq.

ἄστηνος, ον, *miserable*, *BCH*29.410 (Rhenea, ii B.C.): heterocl. pl. ἀστῆνες Hsch.; expld. παρὰ τὸ μὴ στάσιν μηδ' οἴκησιν ἔχειν in *EM* 159.11, cf. Suid.

ἀστήρ, ὁ, gen. έρος: dat. pl. ἀστράσι Il.22.28,317 (Aristarch.; ἄστρασι Sch.Ven., Choerob.):—*star* (v. ἄστρον), ἀστέρ' ὀπωρινῷ Il. 5.5; οὔλιος ἀ. 11.62; Σείριος ἀ. Hes.*Op.*417; ἀ. Ἀρκτοῦρος *the chief star* in the constellation, ib.565, etc.; *shooting star* or *meteor*, Il.4. 75; οἱ διατρέχοντες ἀ. Ar.*Pax* 838; ᾄττοντας ὥσπερ ἀστέρας Pl.*R.* 621b, cf. Arist.*Mete.*341^{a}33, Plu.*Agis* 11. 2. *flame, light, fire*, E.*Hel.*1131 (lyr.). 3. ἀστὴρ πέτρινος *meteoric* stone, *Placit.*2.13. 9. II. metaph. of *illustrious* persons, etc., φανερώτατον ἀστέρ' Ἀθήνας E.*Hipp.*1122 (lyr.); Μουσάων ἀστέρα καὶ Χαρίτων *AP*7.1.8 (Alc. Mess.) III. *star-fish*, Hp.*Nat.Mul.*32, Arist.*HA*548^{a}7, *PA*681^b 9, etc. IV. name of a *bird*, perh. *goldfinch*, Dionys.*Av.*3.2. V. *blue daisy*, *Aster Amellus*, Nic.*Fr.*74.66, Dsc.4.119. VI. *Samian clay* used as sealing-wax, and in Medicine, Thphr.*Lap.*63, Dsc.5. 153, Gal.12.178, al. VII. architectural *ornament*, *IG*4.1484.83 (Epid.), *SIG*241 *B*111 (Delph., iv B.C.). VIII. *bandage*, Gal.18 (1).823. 2. name of various *remedies*, Id.12.761, al. IX. *birthmark in form of star*, Carcin.ap.Arist.*Po.*1454^{b}22: in Palmistry, a *mark* on the hand, τῷ ὑ'στοιχείῳ παραπλήσιον *Cat.Cod.Astr.*7.238.28. (Cf. Skt. *stár-* 'star', Lat. *stella* (from *stēr-la*), Goth. *stairnō*.)

ἀστήρει· σῖτος, Hsch.

ἀστηρίδιον, τό, Dim. of ἀστήρ, *ornament in shape of star*, *PHamb.* 10.44 (ii A.D.).

ἀστήρικτος, ον, *not supported by a staff*, *AP*6.203 (Lacon or Phil.); *unstable*, Longin.2.2, 2*Ep.Pet.*3.16, Gal.*UP*2.15, al.; ἀ. λογισμοῦ Vett.Val.242.3; *not remaining still*, of persons, Nonn.*D.*10.14, al.; of water, ib.32.8, al.

ᾄστης, ου, ὁ, (ᾄδω) *singer*, *Gloss.*

ἀστιάγγας· τὰς ὑποφυλλίδας τῶν βοτρύων, οἱ δὲ ἀκτῖνος αὐγάς, ἔνιοι **ἄστριγγας**, καὶ **ἄστριγας** ἄλλοι, *EM*159.38; cf. **ἄστιγγας**· αἶγας, ἢ ἄστριγγας, Hsch. (Cf. ἄστλιγξ, ὄστλιγξ.)

ἀστίαρχος, = ἀστύαρχος, *BGU*1024.

ἀστῐβής, ές, (στείβω) *untrodden*, τινί A.*Th.*859 (lyr.): hence, 2. *desert, pathless*, χῶρος S.*Aj.*657; ἀ. πόρος, of the sea, Arion 1.16; ὁδός *Hymn.Is.*149. 3. *not to be trodden, holy*, ἄλσος S.*OC*126; rare in Prose, as X.*Mem.*3.8.10. II. Act., *leaving no track*, τροχός Mesom.*Nem.*7.

ἀστίβητος [ῐ], ον, = foreg., Lyc.121, Procop.*Arc.*14; ἀ. οἶκοι· ἄδυτα, Hsch.:—also **ἄστῐβος**, ον, *AP*7.745 (Antip. Sid.).

ἀστῐγής, ές, *unpunctuated*, βιβλίον St.Byz. s. vv. Ἀνακτόριον, Βάβρας.

ἀστικός, ή, όν, (ἄστυ) *of a city* or *town*, opp. *country*, λεὼς ἀ. A. *Eu.*997; βωμοί Id.*Supp.*501; epith. of Hecate, *IG*9(2).575 (Larissa, v B.C.); τὰ ἀ. Διονύσια (= τὰ κατ' ἄστυ) Th.5.20; *home*, opp. ξενικός (*foreign*), A.*Supp.*618; ἀ. δίκαι suits *between citizens*, Lys.17.3; ἀ. δικαστήριον *IG*12(7).3.32 (Amorgos); ἀ. νόμοι *POxy.*706.9 (ii A.D.). 2. as Subst., = ἀστός, *TAM*2.377,886 (Xanthus). b. ἀστικοί, οἱ, = Lat. *cohortes urbanae*, D.C.56.32, 59.2; ἀστικόν, τό, Id.55.24. II. *fond of the town* or *town life*, D.55.11. 2. = ἀστεῖος, *polite*, ἀστικά, as Adv., opp. ἀγροίκως, Theoc.20.4.—In codd. often written ἀστυκός.

ἄστικτος, ον, *not marked with* στίγματα, *not tattooed*, τὸ ἄστικτον Hdt.5.6. II. χωρίον ἄ. an estate *not pledged* or *mortgaged* (those that were so being *marked by* στῆλαι or ὅροι), Lys.*Fr.*3 S., Men.1 D., Poll.3.85.

ἀστιλάζει· συμπεριπατεῖ, Hsch.

ἀστιξία, ἡ, *want of punctuation*, *An.Ox.*4.51.

ἄστιος, α, ον, = ἀστικός, δίκα *GDI*4976 (Crete), *IG*5(2).357.26 (Stymphalus, iii B.C.); πεντηκοστὴ ἡ ἀ. ib.11.287*A*9 (Delos, iii B.C.).

ἀστίοχος, ὁ, *stink-pot*, Hsch. **ἄστιππος**· ἱππέων ἑβδομήκοντα, Id.

ἄστιπτος, ον, = ἀστιβής, *untrodden*, ἀκτὴ.. βροτοῖς ἄ. S.*Ph*.2, v.l. ἄστειπτος, which is prob. in *OGI*606 (Syria).

ἀστίτης [ῑ], ου, ὁ, (ἄστυ) *townsman, citizen*, S.*Fr*.92; spelt **ἀστείτης** in *CIG*2134*b* 23.

ἀστλέγγιστος, ον, *not scraped clean*, *AP*6.298 (Leon.).

ἄστλιγξ, ιγγος, ἡ, = ὄστλιγξ, Philet.ap.Sch.A.R.1.1297, Hdn.Gr. 1.44.

ἄστοβος, ον, = ἀλοιδόρητος, Hsch.

ἀστοιχείωτος, ον, *ignorant of the first elements*, Ph.1.337.

ἄστοιχος, ον, *not in a row*, of the grains in an ear of wheat, Thphr. *HP*8.4.2.

ἀστολόγος, ὁ, title in Egypt, *Sammelb*.969.

ἄστολος, ον, (στέλλω) *ungirded*, χιτών S.*Fr*.872. **2.** of Charon's boat, A.*Th*.857 (lyr.) (ἄστονος cod. M).

ἀστομάχητος [ᾰ], ον, *without anger* (i.e. *not angered*), *PBaden* 35.17 (i A.D.), Alciphr.2.2. Adv. -τως *IG*14.2095.

ἀστόμιος, α, ον, = ἄστομος II, Nonn.*D*.7.244.

ἄστομ-ος, ον, *speechless*, S.*Fr*.76, Arr.*Epict*.2.24.26; ἄ. πεποιηκέναι reduce to *silence*, Luc.*Lex*.15. **2.** *with no mouth*, ἄ. καὶ ἄρρινες Str.2.1.9, cf. Plu.2.938c, 940b. **3.** *with no outlet*, λίμνη Str.7. 3.15. **II.** of horses, *hard-mouthed*, S.*El*.724, Plu.*Art*.9. **III.** of dogs, *soft-mouthed, unable to hold with the teeth*, X.*Cyn*.3.3. **IV.** of meat and drink, *unpalatable*, Hices.ap.Ath.7.323a, Dsc.1.110, al.: Comp., Sor.1.95. **V.** of metal, *soft, incapable of a fine edge*, Plu. *Lys*.17. **-ωτος**, ον, *with no orifice*, Sor.1.57, Orib.45.3.8, prob. in Gal.18(2).795. **II.** *unsharpened, untempered*, of metal, Hsch. s.v. ἄβαπτος.

ἀστονάχητος [ᾰ], ον, = sq., *IG*14.2111.

ἄστονος, ον, *without sighs*, πότος ἄ. a potion *to chase away sighs*, dub. in *Anacreont*.50.6, cf. Max.Tyr.3.9. **II.** (ἀ- intens.) = μεγαλόστονος, Hsch.

ἀστόξενος, ὁ, ἡ, *public guest of a city*, A.*Supp*.356.—Expld. by Ael. Dion.*Fr*.282, Hsch., as *a blood-relation, though a foreigner by birth*.

ἀστοργ-ία, ἡ, *want of natural affection*, Antipho*Fr*.73, Men.522, D.H.3.18. **-ος**, ον, *without natural affection*, ἄστοργος ψυχήν Aeschin.2.146; ὤστοργος *the heartless one*, Theoc.2.112, cf. *Lyr.Alex. Adesp*.6.9; ἄ. γυνή Theoc.17.43; ἄ. πρὸς τὰ ἔκγονα Clytus 1, cf. *IG* 12(5).14 (Ios); ἄ. θάνατος *cruel*, *AP*7.662 (Leon.), *IG*3.1374. **2.** *without attraction*, Plu.2.926f:—also **ἀστόργης** (sic) *An.Ox*.1.50.

ἀστορής, ές, *without bedding*, χαμεῦναι Nonn.*D*.16.93.

ἀστόριον· μέγα καὶ διακεχυμένον, Hsch.

ἀστός, ὁ, (ἄστυ) *townsman, citizen*, Il.11.242, Od.13.192, etc.; dist. from πολίτης, ἀστός being *one who has civil rights* only, πολίτης *one who has political rights* also, Arist.*Pol*.1278^{a}34; ἀ. πικρὸς πολίταις E. *Med*.223; οἱ ἀ. *the commons*, opp. οἱ ἀγαθοί, Pi.*P*.3.71, cf. Isoc.3.21; opp. ξένος, Pi.*O*.7.90, Hdt.2.160, 3.8; esp. at Athens, Lys.6.17, Pl. *Ap*.30a, Isoc. l.c., cf. S.*OT*817, *OC*13, etc.; opp. μέτοικος, ξένος, Pl. *R*.563a; in Egypt, *citizen of Alexandria* (cf. ἄστυ II.3), *PGnom*.38, al.—Fem. ἀστή, q.v., but Ἀστός fem. as epith. of Κόρη, *IG*12(5).225 (Paros, v B.C.). (ϝασστός and ϝαστός, *IG*9(1).333.14 (Locr., v B.C.), 9(2).1226 (Phalanna, v B.C.).)

ἀστόχ-αστος, ον, *not aimed*, D.H.14.10; *not aimed at, not considered*, πλήθους καὶ ποιότητος ἀστοχάστων Phld.*D*.3*Fr*.89. **2.** *hard to guess at*, Thphr.ap.Stob.4.11.16. **3.** Act., *missing the mark*, Phld.*Rh*.1.191 S. **-έω**, *miss the mark, miss*, τοῦ συμφέροντος *IG* 9(2).517.28 (letter of Philip V to Larissa); τινός Plb.5.107.2, al., Phld.*Rh*.1.219 S.; τοῦ μετρίου Plu.2.414f; ἀμφοῖν Luc.*Am*.22; *fail*, περί τινος Plb.3.21.10; περὶ τὴν πίστιν, τὴν ἀλήθειαν, 1*Ep.Ti*.6.21, 2. 2.18; ἔν τινι J.*BJ*2.8.12: abs., Alciphr.3.53.—Rare in poetry, ἠστόχηκέ μου *Lyr.Alex.Adesp*.4.21. **-ημα**, ατος, τό, *failure, fault*, Plu. 2.520b. **-ία**, ἡ, *missing the mark, failing*, Phld.*Vit*.p.41 J. (pl.), Plu.2.800a (pl.); ἀστοχίαι τῶν ἔργων *Cat.Cod.Astr*.2.162.6. **2.** *imprudence, thoughtlessness, error*, Plb.2.33.8, etc. **-ίζομαι**, = ἀστοχέω, S.*Fr*.442.4. **-ος**, ον, *missing the mark, aiming badly at*, τινός Pl.*Ti*.19e, *AP*9.370 (Tib. Ill.). **2.** abs., *aiming amiss, random*, οὐκ ἀστόχου διανοίας Arist.*HA*587^{a}9; κατηγορία *aimless, absurd*, Plb.5.49.4; of a person, Phld.*Ind.Sto*.32. Adv. -χως *amiss*, Alex.116.14, Plb.1.74.2, Phld.*Mort*.33.

ἀστρᾰβαλίζω, *make level*, *EM*159.59, Hsch. (-οβίζειν cod.).

ἄστραβδα (or -αβδά), παίζειν dub. sens. in Herod.3.64: perh. fr. ἀστράπτω, or *without turning* (ἀ- priv., στρέφω).

ἀστρᾰβ-εύω, *ride a mule*, Pl.Com.39. **-η**, ἡ, *mule's saddle, an easy padded saddle*, used by effeminate persons (Sch.D. l.c. infr.), ἐπ' ἀστράβης ἂν ὠχούμην Lys.24.11; ἐπ' ἀστράβης ὀχούμενος ἀργυρᾶς (v.l. ἐξ Ἀργούρας) D.21.133; τῶν ὑποζυγίων τὰ τριχώματα γίνεται λευκὰ ἐκ προστρίψεων τῆς ἀστράβης Arist.*Col*.interpol.post 798^{a}19; εὐτελῶς ἐπ' ἀστράβης Macho ap.Ath.13.582c; μαλακίζομαι ἐπ' ἀστράβης ὀχηθεὶς Luc.*Lex*.2: prov., σοφόν γ' ὁ βοῦς ἔφασκεν ἀστράβην ἰδών, *Com.Adesp*.563.—Expld. as εἶδος ἁμάξης in Hdn.Gr.1.308; as the *pommel* of a saddle, *EM*159.50, Hsch.; of the *mule* itself, Id., Harp., Eust.1625.40. **2.** Δημοσθένους ἀ., a kind of *surgical appliance*, Heliod.ap.Orib.49.4.34. **-ηλάτης** [λᾱ], ου, ὁ, *muleteer*, Luc.*Lex*.2, Poll.7.185. **-ηλος**, ὁ, = στράβηλος (with ἀ- euph.), a kind of *shell*, Agias 1, Dercyl.1. **-ής**, ές, = ἀστραφής, *not twisted, straight, steadfast*, Τροίας κίων (i.e. Hector) Pi.*O*.2.90; γέννες Hp.*Art*.31; τρίγωνον Pl.*Ti*.73b; τὸ σῶμα ποιεῖν ἀ. Arist.*Pol*.1336^{a}12; βάσεις *IG*7. 3073.104 (Lebad.); of timber, Thphr.*HP*3.9.2: Comp., ib.5.1.11: Sup., ib.5.3.5; *rigid, stiff*, ἀ. ἐντέταται Aret.*SA*1.6. Adv. -βῶς Ael.*NA*2.11. **-ίζω**, (ἀστράβη) *ride pillion*, καμήλους ἀστραβιζούσας A.*Supp*.285 (dub.). **-ιστήρ**, ῆρος, ὁ, *instrument used in levelling*, Hsch.

ἀστρᾰγάλ-ειος [γᾰ], α, ον, *covering the ankles*, = Lat. *talaris*, χιτών Aq.*Ge*.37.3. **-η**, ἡ, Ion. for ἀστράγαλος, Anacr.46, Herod.3.7, Ael.Dion.*Fr*.359. **II.** = ἡ τῆς ἴρεως ῥίζα, Hsch. **III.** = κακοήθης κύων, Id. **-ίζω**, *play with* ἀστράγαλοι, Pl.*Ly*.206e, *Alc*.1. 110b; ἀ. ἄρτοις Cratin.165, cf. Telecl.1.14. **-ῖνος**, ὁ, *goldfinch*, elsewh. ποικιλίς, Dionys.*Av*.3.2. **-ῖσις**, εως, ἡ, *playing with* ἀστράγαλοι, Arist.*Rh*.1371^{a}2 (pl.). **-ίσκος**, ὁ, Dim. of ἀστράγαλος, Roussel *Cultes Égyptiens* 218 (Delos, ii B.C.), Poll.6.99; name of a *surgical appliance*, *PMed.Lond*.2.14. **-ιστής**, οῦ, ὁ, *dice-player*; in pl., name of a comedy by Alex. Aet., Sch.Il.23.86 (Mein. for ἀστρολογισταί). **-ιστικός**, ή, όν, *of the dice*, βόλος Eust.1397.47. **-ῖτις**, ιδος, ἡ, = ἶρις Ἰλλυρική, Gal.12.422.

ἀστρᾰγᾰλόμαντις, εως, ὁ, *divining from* ἀστράγαλοι, Artem.2.69.

ἀστρᾰγᾰλος [ρᾰ], ὁ, (v. ὀστέον) *one of the vertebrae*, esp. of the neck, Il.14.466, Od.11.65, *AP*7.632 (Diod.); votive object, *IG*5 (2).125 (Tegea, ii A.D.). **II.** *ball of the ankle joint* (not to be confused with σφυρόν, Ruf.*Onom*.124), Hdt.3.129; in horses, X.*Eq*.1. 15; of various animals, Hp.*Int*.20, 30. **2.** οἱ μὲν πόδες ἀστράγαλοί τευ, as a compliment, i.e. *well-turned*, Theoc.10.36. **III.** *wrist*, Lxx *Da*.5.5, 24. **IV.** pl., ἀστράγαλοι *knucklebones* used as *dice* or *a game played with dice*, ἀμφ' ἀστραγάλοισι χολωθείς Il.23.88, cf. Hdt.1.94, Menecr.Com.1D.; ἀ. διάσειστοι Aeschin.1.59, cf. Men. 423; ἀ. μεμολιβδωμένοι loaded *dice*, Arist.*Pr*.913^{a}36, cf. Eust.1397. 34; later, *dice proper*, ἀντ' ἀστραγάλων κονδύλοισι παίζετε Pherecr. 43. **V.** ἡ ἐκ τῶν ἀστραγάλων μάστιξ scourge of *strung bones*, Luc. *Asin*.38; cf. ἀστραγαλωτός. **VI.** *moulding* in the capital of the Ionic column, *IG*1.322, Vitr.3.5.7. **VII.** *milk vetch*, *Orobus niger*, Dsc.4.61, Gal.11.841. **VIII.** *prism of wood*, Aen.Tact.31.17, al. **IX.** *ear-ring*, ξύλινοι ἀ. Anacr.21.4.

ἀστρᾰγᾰλ-ώδης, ες, *shaped like an* ἀστράγαλος, Tz.*H*.10.231. **-ωτός**, ή, όν, *made of* ἀστράγαλοι, μάστιξ Crates Com.35, Plu.2. 1127c; ἱμάς Posidon.9. **II.** -ωτή, ἡ, name of a *plant*, Philum. *Ven*.7.11; dub. in Harp.Astr. in *Cat.Cod.Astr*.8(3).150.26. **2.** (sc. στυπτηρία) a kind of *alum*, Gal.12.237.

ἀστραῖος, α, ον, (ἄστρον) *starry*, Orac.ap.Porph.ap.Eus.*PE*3.14, Nonn.*D*.1.191, al.

ἀστρακλεῖν· ἀδυνατεῖν, Hsch.

ἀστραλός, ὁ, = ψαρός (Thess.), Hsch. (Cf. Lat. *sturnus*, OHG. *stara*, OE. *stær*.)

ἀστρᾰπ-αῖος, α, ον, *of lightning*, ἄνεμος ἀ. a wind *with thunderstorms*, Arist.*Mete*.364^{b}30, cf. Thphr.*Sign*.37; τὰ ἀ. τῶν ὑδάτων *thunder*-showers, Plu.2.664c; Ζεὺς ἀ. Arist.*Mu*.401^{a}16, Corn.*ND*9, *IGRom*.3.17 (Bithyn.). **-ή**, ἡ, = ἀστεροπή, στεροπή, *flash of lightning, lightning*, βροντὴ καὶ ἀ. Hdt.3.86, cf. X.*HG*7.1.31, etc.; βροντὴ δ' ἐρράγη δι' ἀστραπῆς S.*Fr*.578, cf. Pl.*Ti*.68a, *Cra*.409c, Arist.*Mete*.369^b 6; personified, as subject of painting, Plin.*HN*35.96, Philostr.*Im*. 1.14: freq. in pl., *lightnings*, τὰς ἀ. τε καὶ κεραυνίους βολάς A.*Th*. 430; τᾶν πυρφόρων ἀστραπᾶν κράτη νέμων S.*OT*201 (lyr.). **2.** *light* of a lamp, A.*Fr*.386, *Ev.Luc*.11.36. **3.** metaph., ἀστραπήν τιν' ὀμμάτων *flashing* of the eyes, S.*Fr*.474; βλέπων ἀστραπάς Ar.*Ach*. 566; ἐκτυφλοῦν τιν' ἀστραπῇ [εἰμί] Antiph.195.4, cf. Ach.Tat.6.6.

ἀστρᾰπη-βολέω, *hurl lightnings*, Eust.1060.43. **-βόλος**, ον, (βάλλω) *hurling lightnings*, Id.1682.5. **-δόν**, Adv. *like lightning*, Aristobul.ap.Eus.*PE*8.10. **-φορέω**, *carry lightnings*, Ar.*Pax* 722. **-φόρος**, ον, *flashing*, πῦρ E.*Ba*.3.

ἀστράπιος [ᾰ], ον, = ἀστραπαῖος, Orph.*H*.15.9, 20.5.

ἀστρᾰπο-ειδής, ές, *like lightning, forked*, *Gloss*. **-κῠποδίωκτα**, prob. in *PMag.Lond*.1.46.20 for ἀστραποκυποδωκε. **-πληκτος**, ον, *lightning-stricken*, v.l. for ἀστερόπληκτος in Seneca *QN*1.15.

ἀστραπτικός, ή, όν, *lightening*, Sch.Il.1.580.

ἀστράπτω (cf. στράπτω), Ep. impf. ἀστράπτεσκον Mosch.2.86: fut. ἀστράψω Cratin.53, Nonn.*D*.33.376: aor. ἤστραψα Il.17.595, etc.:—*lighten, hurl lightnings*, freq. of omens sent by Zeus, ἀστράπτων ἐπιδέξι' Il.2.353; Κρονίδης ἐνδέξια σήματα φαίνων ἀστράπτει 9.237; ὡς δ' ὅτ' ἂν ἀστράπτῃ πόσις Ἥρης 10.5; ἀστράψας δὲ μάλα μεγάλ' ἔκτυπε 17.595; οὐλύμπιος ἤστραπτεν, ἐβρόντα Ar.*Ach*.531, cf. *V*. 626. **2.** impers., ἀστράπτει *it lightens*, ἤστραψε *it lightened*, οὐρανοῦ δ' ἄπο ἤστραψε S.*Fr*.578, cf. Arist.*Rh*.1392^{b}27. **II.** *flash* or *glance like lightning*, πᾶς γὰρ ἀστράπτει χαλινός S.*OC*1067 (lyr.); κατάχαλκον ἀ. πεδίον *gleams* with brass, E.*Ph*.111; so ἀ. χαλκῷ X. *Cyr*.6.4.1; of the face, εἶδον τὴν ὄψιν.. ἀστράπτουσαν Pl.*Phdr*.254b; ἀ. τοῖς ὄμμασι X.*Cyn*.6.15; of flowers, ἀνεμωνίδες ἀστράπτουσαι *bright*, Nic.*Fr*.74.64: c. acc. cogn., ἐξ ὀμμάτων δ' ἤστραπτε.. σέλας (sc. Τυφών) *flashed* flame from his eyes, A.*Pr*.358; ἵμερον ἀστράπτουσα κατ' ὄμματος *AP*12.161 (Asclep.), cf. Mosch. l.c.; ἤστραψε γλυκὺ κάλλος *AP*12.110 (Mel.). **2.** of persons, *to be brilliant, conspicuous*, ἔν τινι Opp.*C*.1.361, 2.23. **III.** trans., *consume with lightning*, dub. in Cratin.53. **2.** *illuminate*, τι Musae.276.

ἀστράρχη, ἡ, *queen of stars*, of the moon, Orph.*H*.9.10:—also **ἀστροάρχη**, Hdn.5.6.4.

ἀστρᾰτ-εία, ἡ, *exemption from service*, Ar.*Pax*526, Ph.2.373. **2.** *avoidance of service*, φεύγειν γραφὴν ἀστρατείας Ar.*Eq*.443; ἀστρατείας ἀλῶναι, ὀφλεῖν, Lys.14.7, And.1.74; γραφαὶ περὶ τῆς ἀ. Pl.Lg.943d; δίκη ἀστρατείας D.39.16. II. *she that stops an invasion*, of Artemis, Paus.3.25.3. **-ευσία**, ἡ, = foreg.1, Sammelb.4224.14. **-ευτος**, ον, *without service*: hence, 1. *exempt therefrom*, Lys.9.15. 2. *never having seen service*, Ar.V.1117, Aeschin.3.176; ἀ. καὶ λιποτάκτης Ph.1.144. Adv. -τως Poll.1.159.

ἀστρᾰτηγ-ησία, ἡ, *incapacity for command*, D.H.9.31. **-ητος**, ον, *never having been general*, Pl.Alc.2.142a. 2. *incapable of command, no general*, Cic.Att.7.13.1, cf. 8.16.1 (Sup.), Onos.33.5. Adv. ἀκόσμως καὶ -τως App.BC1.47, cf. Hierocl.p.17 A. II. *without a general*, J.BJ2.12.4. **-ία**, ἡ, *lack of a general*, Phryn.PSp.42 B.

ἀστρᾰφής, ές, = ἄστρεπτος I. 2, S.Fr.418; *fixed, immovable*, IG2.1054f20. II. = ἄστρεπτος II, πύλαι Epic.ap.Aristid.Or.49(25).4.

ἀστραφιστήρ, ῆρος, ὁ, dub. sens. in IG2.808d65; cf. ἀστραβιστήρ.

ἄστραψις, εως, ἡ, = ἀστραπή, Suid. s.v. μαρμαρυγή.

ἀστρεκίας· ἀστροφανίας, Hsch.

ἄστρεπτος, ον, *without turning the back*, Theoc.24.96. Adv. -τεί AP7.436 (Hegem.). 2. *unbending, rigid*, δόγμα ib.103 (Antag.), cf. 6.71 (Paul. Sil.); τὸ θεῖον Max.Tyr.11.3. II. *whence none return*, Ἅιδης Lyc.813.

ἀστρεφής, ές, = ἀστραφής, Hsch. s.v. ἄπολον. **ἀστρηνές**, = στρηνές, Id. **ἄστρητα**, τά, = τὰ ἐγγώνια τὰ ἐντὸς τοῦ δίφρου, Poll.1.143.

ἀστρίζω, (ἄστρις) = ἀστραγαλίζω, Poll.9.99.

ἀστρικός, ή, όν, *of* or *concerning the stars*, μαντεία Philostr.VA3.41; ἡ -κή *astronomy* or *astrology*, Tz.H.5.270; ἡ ἰδία τινὸς ἀ. (sc. μοῖρα or εἱμαρμένη) *destiny*, PMag.Leid.W.14.37; ἀ., ὁ, = ἀστρολόγος, Cat.Cod.Astr.8(4).174.

ἄστριον, τό, Dim. of ἀστήρ, *an architectural ornament*, IG4.1495.61. II. = ἀστερίτης λίθος, Plin.HN37.132, Isid.Etym.16.13.7. III. = κορωνόπους, Ps.-Dsc.2.130 (nisi leg. ἀστέριον).

ἄστρις, ιος, ἡ, = ἀστράγαλος, Call.Fr.238,239:—also **ἀστρῖχος**, ὁ, Antiph.92.

ἀστρο-άρχη, v. ἀστράρχη. **-βλέφᾰρος**, ον, *with starry eyes*, Orph.L.672 (s.v.l.). **-βλής**, ῆτος, ὁ, ἡ, *sun-scorched*, Arist.HA 602b22. **-βλησία**, ἡ, prob. l. for -βολησία (q.v.). **-βλητος**, ον, = ἀστροβλής, *sun-scorched*, Id.Juv.470a32, Thphr.HP4.14.7. **-βοᾶν**, f.l. for ἀστρόβολον, Hsch. **-βολέομαι**, Pass., *to be sun-scorched*, Thphr.HP4.14.2, etc.:—Act. in Porph.Plot.10. **-βολησία**, ἡ, *sun-scorch*, in plants, Thphr.CP5.9.4 (nisi leg. ἀστροβλησία). **-βόλητος**, ον, = ἀστροβλής, Hsch., v.l. in Thphr. for -βλητος (q.v.). **-βολία**, ἡ, = ἀστροβολησία, Id.CP5.9.2. **-βολίζομαι**, Pass., = ἀστροβολέομαι, Gloss. **-βολος**, ον, *lightning-like, swift*, Hsch. Adv. -λως Id. **-βρόντης**, ου, ὁ, *thundering from the stars*, epith. of Mithras, IG14.998. **-γείτων**, ον, gen. ονος, *near the stars*, κορυφαί A.Pr.721. **-δάμας** [δᾰ], αντος, ὁ, *subduing the stars*, PMag.Par.1.603. **-δίαιτος** [ῐ], ον, *living under the stars*, i.e. *in the open air*, Orph.H.11.5 codd. **-δίφης** [ῐ], ου, ὁ, = ἀστρονόμος, Herod.3.54. **-δώρητος**, ον, *endowed by the stars*, φύσις Vett.Val.221.22. **-ειδής**, ές, *starlike, starry*, Ph.1.485 (Sup.), Hierocl. in CA27p.483 M.; ἀ. περίοδος *like that of the stars*, Str.3.5.8. **-θεάμων** [ᾱ], ονος, ὁ, (θεάομαι) *observing the stars*, ἱστορία Dam.Pr.23; ἐπιστήμη Id.Isid.145. **-θεσία**, ἡ, *group of stars, constellation*, Ath.11.490f; *arrangement of planets*, Vett.Val.157.24. **-θετέω**, *class* or *group the stars* (in constellations), Str.1.1.6 (Pass.). **-θέτημα**, ατος, τό, *a group of stars, constellation*, Suid. s.v. ἀστήρ. **-θέτης**, ου, ὁ, *one who classes the stars*, Orph.H.64.2. **-θετος**, ον, *astronomical*, κανών AP7.683 (Pall.). **-θύτης** [ῠ], ου, ὁ, *star-worshipper*, D.L.Prooem.8, Sch.Pl.Alc.1.122a.

ἀστροΐτης, ου, ὁ, prob. for *astriotes*, a magical gem, Plin.HN37.133.

ἀστρο-κύων [ῠ], κύνος, ὁ, *the dog-star*, Horap.1.3. **-λάβος**, ὁ, *armillary sphere*, Ptol.Alm.9.2, al., Procl.Hyp.6; ἀ. στερεός Simp. in Cael.462.30:—also as Adj., ἀ. ὄργανον Ptol.Alm.9.9, al., Geog.1.2.2 (pl.); κύκλοι Id.Alm.5.1, 7.2. II. *planisphere*, Phlp. in Rh.Mus.6(1839).127. **-λογέω**, *study* or *practise astronomy*, Thphr.Sign.4, Sosip.1.15, Plb.9.20.5; τὰ -λογούμενα Cleom.2.1. **-λόγημα**, ατος, τό, *astronomy*, Tz.ad Lyc.363. **-λογία**, ἡ, *astronomy*, X.Mem.4.7.4, Isoc.11.23; a branch of mathematics, Arist.Ph.193b26, Metaph.989b33, cf. 997b35; γεωμετρία τε καὶ ἀ. Vit.Philonid.p.4 C.; ἀ. ναυτική Arist.APo.78b40. 2. later, *astrology*, S.E.M.5.1. **-λογικός**, ή, όν, *of* or *for astronomy*, ἐμπειρία, ἐπιστήμη, Arist.APr.46a19, APo.78b39; τὰ -κά Id.Cael.291b21. **-λόγος**, ὁ, *astronomer*, X.Mem.4.2.10, Epigr.ap.D.L.1.34. 2. later, *astrologer*, Epicur.Ep.2 p.40 U., LxxIs.47.13, SIG771.2 (Delph., i B.C.), S.E.M.5.2, etc. **-μαντεία**, ἡ, = sq., D.S.36.5. **-μαντική** (sc. τέχνη), ἡ, *astrology*, ibid., S.E.M.9.132. **-μαντις**, εως, ὁ, *astrologer*, Poll.7.188, Jul.Or.4.131a.

ἄστρον, τό, mostly in pl., *the stars*, Il.8.555, Od.12.312, A.Pr.458, Ag.4, etc.; τοῦ κατ' ἄστρα Ζηνός, = τοῦ ἐν οὐρανῷ, S.Tr.1106; ἄστρων εὐφρόνη, = εὐφρ. ἀστερόεσσα, Id.El.19: sg., like ἀστήρ, freq. of Sirius (in full, σήριον ἄστρον prob. l. in Alcm.23.63), Alc.39,40, X.Cyn.4.6, Thphr.CP6.10.9, al.; περὶ τὸ ἄ. in the *dog-days*, Hp.Epid.7.7; poet. of the sun, Pi.O.1.6, Pl.Def.411b: seldom of *any common star*, Gal.17(1).16, Sch.Arat.11; of the fixed stars, Arist.Cael.290a20; ἄστρα πλανητά, opp. ἀπλανῆ, Pl.Ti.38c; opp. ἐνδεδεμένα, Arist.Mete.346a2; opp. ἀστέρες, Herm.ap.Stob.1.21.9; ἐπὶ τοῖς ἄστροις at the times of *the stars'* rising or setting, Hp.Aër.10, Arist.HA568a18; ἄστροις σημαίνεσθαι, τεκμαίρεσθαι, guide oneself by *the stars*, Ael.NA2.7, 7.48; ἄστροις τὸ λοιπὸν ἐκμετρούμενος χθόνα knowing its place only by *the stars*, S.OT795: metaph., ἐχθροῖς ἄ. ὡς λάμψειν Id.El.66. II. of something *brilliant, admirable*, Ἀκροκόρινθον Ἑλλάδος ἄ. AP7.297 (Polystr.), cf. 9.400 (Pall.), APl.4.295; Σωκρατικῆς σοφίης ἄ. IG3.770a.

ἀστρονομ-έω, *study astronomy*, Ar.Nu.194, Pl.Tht.174a:—Med., D.L.1.34, Iamb.VP25.112:—Pass., ὡς νῦν ἀστρονομεῖται as *astronomy is* now *practised*, Pl.R.530c. **-ημα**, ατος, τό, *observation of the stars*, Timo 23. **-ία**, ἡ, *astronomy*, Hp.Aër.2, Ar.Nu.201, Pl.Smp.188b, etc.; title of a work ascribed to Hesiod, and Ptolemy's σύνταξις, Olymp. in Mete.68.20, al. **-ικός**, ή, όν, *skilled in astronomy*, Pl.R.530a, etc.; ἀστρονομικώτατον ἡμῶν Id.Ti.27a; τὰ -κά Thphr.Sign.1: Comp. -ώτερος Str.1.2.24. Adv. -κῶς Poll.4.16. II. of questions, *pertaining to astronomy*, Pl.Prt.315c. III. name of *ninth sign of* ἀποτελεσματογραφία, Paul.Al.M.4.

ἀστρο-νόμος, ὁ, (νέμω) *astronomer*, Pl.R.531a, etc.; ὁ ἀ. the *astronomer* par excellence, i.e. Ptolemy, Olymp. in Mete.188.33:—as Adj., Nic.Dam.p.3 D. **-πληγος**, ον, = ἀστροβλής, Gp.5.36.1. **-ποιέω** τι *make a constellation of* it, An.Ox.3.164. **-σκοπέω**, *observe the stars*, E.ap.Satyr.Vit.Eur.Fr.38 iii 12. **-σκοπία**, ἡ, *the study of the stars*, Herm. in Phdr.p.109 A. **-τέχνημα**, ατος, τό, *celestial globe*, Tz.H.5.282.

ἀστρούθιστος, ον, *not washed with* στρουθίον, Dsc.2.74.

ἀστρο-φαής or **-φάνής**, ές, *shining like a star*, Eumolp.ap.D.S.1.11. **-φεγγής**, ές, *shining with the light of heavenly bodies*, PMag.Par.1.2071. **-φόρος**, ον, (φέρω) *bearing stars*, Hymn.Is.23.

ἄστροφος, ον, (στρέφω) *without turning round* or *away, fixed*, ὄμματα A.Ch.99; ἀφέρπειν ἄ. go away *without turning back*, S.OC 490. 2. *without turning* or *twisting*, Pl.Plt.282d. II. *without strophe*, Heph.Poëm.5.

ἀστροχίτων [ῐ], ον, gen. ωνος, *star-clad*, of night, Orph.A.513, 1028, Nonn.D.40.408.

ἀστρώδης, ες, = ἀστροειδής, Lyd.Mens.4.73.

ἀστρῷος, α, ον (also ος, ον Sch.A.R.1.936), *starry*, οἶκος AP9.400 (Pall.); ἀ. ἀνάγκη the law *of the stars*, ib.505.14; ἀ. οὐρανοῦ διάθεσις Phlp. in Mete.117.20; ἀ. θεοί Procl. in Cra.p.49 P.; ψυχαί ib.p.87 P., Herm. in Phdr.p.130 A.; σώματα Alex.Aphr.Pr.1.116.

ἀστρωπός, όν, = ἀστερωπός, E.HF406 (lyr.).

ἀστρω-σία, ἡ, *practice of sleeping without bedding*, Pl.Lg.633c (pl.). **-τος**, ον, *without bed* or *bedding*, εὕδω Epich.35.14, cf. Pl.Smp.203d, Plt.272a. 2. *uncovered*, Id.Prt.321c: metaph., *bare*, πέδον E.HF52. 3. of a horse, *without trappings*, Arr.Tact.2.3, Suid.

ἄστυ, τό, Ep. and Ion. gen. εος (disyll. in Semon.7.74), Att. and Trag. εως (ἄστεος is never required by the metre, ἄστεως (trisyll.) is necessary in E.Or.761, Ph.842, El.246, and is the only form found in Att. Inscrr., as IG2.584.7, 2^2.463.76; it is a disyll. in E.El.298, Ba.840): pl., ἄστη Id.Supp.952; ἄστεα Hdt.1.5:—*town*, ἄ. μέγα Πριάμοιο Il.2.332, al.: with name in gen., Σουσίδος, Σούσων ἄ., A.Pers.119, 535; ἄ. Θήβης S.OC1372, Tr.1154, etc. 2. *lower town*, opp. *acropolis*, Hdt.1.176, al. II. in Attica, *town* (i.e. *Athens*), opp. ἀγρός (*country*), mostly without Art., στυγῶν μὲν ἄ. Ar.Ach.33; ἐξ ἄστεως νῦν εἰς ἀγρὸν χωρῶμεν Id.Fr.107; ἔγημα.. ἄγροικος ὢν ἐξ ἄστεως I married a *town* girl, Id.Nu.47; τῶν κατ' ἄστυ πραγμάτων Men.Georg.Fr.4: also with Art., πρὸς τὸ ἄ. Pl.R.327b, 328c, al. 2. *Athens*, opp. *Phalerum* or *Piraeus*, Id.Smp.172a, D.20.12, Arist.Pol.1303b12, al.; τὸ ἄστυ τῆς πόλεως, opp. *Piraeus*, Lycurg.18; ἄρχοντος ἐν ἄστει, opp. ἐν Σαλαμῖνι, IG2.594. 3. in Egypt, *Alexandria*, PHal.1.89 (iii B.C.), St.Byz. s.v. ἄστυ, etc. III. *town* in the material sense, opp. πόλις (*the civic body*), Il.17.144. IV. Adv. ἄστυδε (q.v.). (Ϝάστυ, cf. Ϝαστυόχος IG5(2).77 (Tegea): gen. Ϝάστιος ib.7.3170 (Orchom. Boeot.): but prob. not cogn. with Skt. *vásati* 'dwell', which has *e* in the root.)

ἀστῠ-άναξ [ᾰν], ακτος, ὁ, *lord of the city*, epith. of certain gods, A.Supp.1018 (lyr.): in Hom. only as pr. n., *Astyanax*, the son of Hector:—hence Adj. **Ἀστυανάκτειος**, α, ον, AP9.351 (Leon.). II. by an obscene pun, = ἄστυτος, Eust.849.54. III. name of a *fish*, Hsch. **-αρχος**, ὁ, title of *magistrate* in Alexandria, BGU1024^{v}8 (iv A.D.; ἀστί- Pap.). **-βοώτης**, ου, ὁ, (βοάω) *crying* or *calling through the city*, epith. of a herald, Il.24.701. (Prop. -βοήτης, Ion. contr. -βώτης, by 'distraction' -βοώτης.) **-γειτνιάω**, *to be neighbouring, adjacent*, τὰς -γειτνιώσας πόλεις CIG2820A 20 (Aphrodisias). **-γειτονέομαι** χθόνα *dwell in a neighbouring* land, A.Supp.286. **-γειτονικός**, ή, όν, *of* or *with neighbours*, πόλεμος Plu.2.87e. **-γείτων**, ον, gen. ονος, *near* or *bordering on a city*, σκοπαί A.Ag.309; πόλιες Hdt.6.99, cf. 9.122, E.Hipp.1161, Plu.Rom.23; πόλεμοι Arist.Pol.1330a18. 2. as Subst., *neighbour to the city, borderer*, Hdt.2.104, 5.66, Th.1.15, X.HG1.3.2., SIG633.10 (Milet., ii B.C.), etc.

ἄστῠδε, Adv. *into, to*, or *towards the city*, Il.18.255, Od.17.5, and in late Prose, as Alciphr.1.1.

ἀστῠ-δίκης [ῐ], ου, ὁ, = Lat. *praetor urbanus*, Lyd.Mens.1.19. **-δρομέομαι**, Pass., ἀστυδρομουμένα πόλις *filled with the turmoil of pursuers and pursued*, A.Th.221 (lyr.). **-θεμις**, ὁ, *just ruler of cities*, B.4.3.

ἀστυκός, v. ἀστικός.

ἀστυλάζει· λυπεῖ μετὰ κλαυθμοῦ, Hsch. **ἀστυλίς**· φυτόν, ὅθεν ὁ ἰξός, Id. **ἀστυλόν**· τὸ τραχὺ ἱμάτιον, Id.

ἄστῠλ-ος, ον, *without pillar* or *prop*, οἶκος AP7.648 (Leon.). **-ωτος**, ον, gloss on ἀνερμάτιστος, Sch.Ael.NA1.11.

ἀστῠ-νῖκος [ῠ] πόλις Athens *the victorious city*, A.Eu.915. **-νομέω**, *to be an* ἀστυνόμος, D.Prooem.55, OGI483.1 (Pergam.), IG11(4).

1145 (Delos). 2. at Rome, *to be praetor urbanus*, D.C.42.22. -νομία, ἡ, *the office of* ἀστυνόμος, Arist.*Pol.*1321^{b}23. 2. at Rome, *the city praetorship*, D.C.42.22. -νομικός, ή, όν, *of* or *for an* ἀστυνόμος or *his office*, Pl.*R.*425d, Arist.*Pol.*1264^{a}31; νόμος *PHal.*1.237 (iii B.C.). -νόμιον, τό, *the court of the* ἀστυνόμοι, Pl.*Lg.*918a. -νόμος, ὁ, (νέμω) *protecting the city*, θεοί A.*Ag.*88; ἀγλαΐαι ἀ. *public* festivals, Pi.*N.*9.31; ὀργαὶ ἀ. the feelings *of law-abiding* or *social life*, S.*Ant.* 355 (lyr.). II. as Subst., *a magistrate who had the care of the police, streets, and public buildings* at Athens, Is.1.15, D.24.112, Arist.*Ath.* 50.1, *SIG*313.17, *Com.Adesp.*25aD.: in other cities, as Tenos, *IG* 12(5).883.14; Iasos, *SIG*169.10; Rhodes, *IG*12(1).1; Pergamum, *OGI*483.7, etc., cf. Pl.*Lg.*759a, al. 2. = Lat. *praetor urbanus*, D.C. 53.2. -ξενοι, οἱ, *those who have no house in the city* (Tarent.), Hsch. -όχος, ον, (ἔχω) *protecting the city*, τεῖχος *AP*9.764 (Paul. Sil.); μέριμνα *APl.*4.36 (Agath.). (ϝαστ-, cf. ἄστυ fin.) -πολέω, *go up and down in a city, live in it, frequent the streets*, Theopomp. Hist.114a, Max.Tyr.8.1 and 9. -πολία, ἡ, *residence in a city*, Hierocl.p.62 A.

ἄστῠρον, τό, Dim. of ἄστυ, Call.*Fr.*19, *Aet.*3.1.74, *Hec.*1.1.6, Nic. *Al.*15.

ἀστῠσία, ἡ, *impotence*, D.C.79.16.

ἀστῠτίς, ίδος, ἡ, *lettuce*, used as an anti-aphrodisiac, Lycus ap.Ath. 2.69e, *Gp.*12.13.2.

ἄστῡτος, ον, (στύω) *impotent*, paratrag. for ἄστυλος in Xenarch.1.

ἀστύτριψ, ῖβος, ὁ, ἡ, (τρίβω) *always living in the city*, Critias 72 D., Philostr.*Im.*2.26.

ἀστῠφέλικτος, ον, *unshaken, undisturbed*, βασιλεία X.*Lac.*15.7; θεός Call.*Del.*26; Ἅιδης *Epigr.Gr.*540.3; ὕπνου χάριν *AP*9.764 (Paul. Sil.); σῶμα Orph.*Fr.*168.22; ἀσκηθὴς ἐν νευσὶ καὶ ἀ. ἐπ' αἴῃ *Sammelb.* 5829.3.

ἀστύφελος [ῠ], η, ον (ος, ον *AP*9.413 (Antiphil.)), *not rugged*, πατρίς Thgn.1044.

ἀστυφία, ἡ, = ἀστυσία, Anon.ap.*EM*197.53, *AB*456.

ἄστῡφος, ον, (στύφω) *not astringent*, Alex.Trall.2. II. *not over-dry*, Aët.7.102. III. *not mordanted*, *PHolm.*17.42.

ἀσυγγενής, ές, *not akin*, Hsch. (ἀξ-).

ἀσυγ-γνωμόνητος, ον, = sq., Phint.ap.Stob.4.23.61^a, Sch.A.*Pr.* 34. -γνώμων, ον, gen. ονος, *not pardoning, merciless*, D.21.100, Plu.2.59e: irreg. Sup. -έστατος Phint.ap.Stob.4.23.61. -γνωστος, ον, = foreg., Jul.*Ep.*184. II. *unpardonable*, Gal.1.13, Phalar. *Ep.*6, Him.*Ecl.*5.10, Lib.*Or.*59.144. Adv. -τως Phld.*Mort.*20.

ἀσύγγρᾰφος, ον, *without bond*, ἀσύγγραφα δανείζεσθαι D.S.1.79.

ἀσυγγύμναστος, ον, *unexercised*, Luc.*Par.*6.

ἀσυγκατα-θετέω, *withhold one's assent*, S.E.*M.*7.157. -θετος, ον, *withholding assent*, διάθεσις Chrysipp.*Stoic.*2.40; γνώμη Ph.1.287, cf. Aristocl.ap.Eus.*PE*14.18. Adv. -τως Chrysipp.*Stoic.*3.42, Ph. 1.78.

ἀσυγκέραστος, ον, *untempered*, φύσις *AP*9.180 (Pall.).

ἀσυγκίνητος [ῑ], ον, *without agitation*, Antyll.ap.Orib.6.21.16.

ἀσύγκλαστος, ον, *hard, pitiless*, πρὸς τοὺς ὁμοφύλους Phld.*Herc.* 1251.20.

ἀσύγκλειστος, ον, *not enclosed*, πλευραῖς Arist.*PA*688^{b}35.

ἀσύγκλωστος, ον, *not interwoven, disconnected, disjointed*, πράγματα Cic.*Att.*6.1.17, cf. Porph.*Abst.*3.18; λόγος Herm. *in Phdr.*p.187 A.; ἐξηγήσεις Porph.*Chr.*39; *incompatible*, συγκλώθειν τὰ ἀ. Phlp. *in Ph.* 34.14; πρὸς τὸ ἓν ἀ. καὶ ἀσύμβατος Dam.*Pr.*5.

ἀσυγκόλλητος, ον, *made in one piece*, Sch.Il.14.200.

ἀσυγκόμιστος, ον, *not gathered in*, καρπός X.*Cyr.*1.5.10.

ἀσύγκρᾱτος, ον, *incapable of blending, discordant*, δόξαι Plu.2.418d; δυνάμεις, of herbs, cj. ib.134d; φωνή Nicom.*Harm.*12.

ἀσύγκρῐτος, ον, *not comparable*, Thphr.*Fr.*89.7, Phld.*D.*1.15, *AP* 5.64; τοῖς ἄλλοις Plu.*Marc.*17; ἀσύγκριτος ἄνθρωπος ἀλόγῳ ζῴῳ Phld. *D.*1.11. 2. Adv. -τως *without the use of the comparative form*, D.T.635. 15. 2. *incomparable, surpassing*, θεός Ph.1.578, cf. Plu.*Dio* 47, *BGU*613.20 (ii A.D.), etc., *Ath.Mitt.*12.174 (Prusias); of remedies, Gal.14.112. Adv. -τως *incomparably*, Hierocl. *in CA*3 p.424 M., *CIG* 3493.14 (Thyatira). II. *antagonistic, of alien kind*, Plu.2.134d (but v. foreg.).

ἀσυγκρότητος, ον, v. ἀξυγκρότητος.

ἀσύγκτητος, ον, *not capable of being acquired with other things*, κάλλος ἀ. πρᾶγμα Secund.*Sent.*14.

ἀσύγχριστος, ον, *unanointed*, Antyll.ap.Orib.10.13.20.

ἀσύγχῡμος, ον, *not turned into syrup*, Orion s. v. χυλός.

ἀσύγχῠτος, ον, *not confused*, ἐπίνοιαι, δυνάμεις, Ph.1.6,434, cf. Plu. 2.735b, Procl.*Inst.*176; *not mingled together*, Arr.*Epict.*4.11.8. Adv. -τως *without confusion*, ib.8.20.

ἀσυγχώρητος, ον, *forbidden*, D.S.1.78; *not to be conceded* or *admitted*, Agatharch.8, S.E.*M.*7.380; *not duly authorized*, ἐπιγραφαί *SIG*793.8 (Cos, i A.D.).

ἀσύζευκτος, ον, *not paired*, Suid. s. v. ἀσυνδύαστος. Adv. -τως *AB*456.

ἀσύζῠγος, ον, *without exact correspondence*, Habron ap.A.D.*Synt.* 100.27. Adv. -γως Archig.ap.Gal.8.592,625. 2. *unique*, αἰτία Anon. *in Prm.* in *Rh.Mus.*47.617.

ἀσῡκοφάντητος, ον, *not plagued by informers*, Aeschin.3.216, Plu. 2.756d; ἑορτή *OGI*383.157 (Commagene, i B.C.); πενία ἀ. κτῆμα Secund.*Sent.*10; *free from misrepresentation*, Onos.*Praef.*10. II. *unexceptionable*, *BGU*1059.8 (Aug.), Luc.*Hist.Conscr.*59, *Salt.*81. III. Adv. -τως *without quibbling*, Phld.*Rh.*1.8 S., Plu.2.529d.

ἀσῡλ-αῖος, α, ον, *of an asylum*, θεός Plu.*Rom.*9. -εί or -ί, Adv. of ἄσυλος, *inviolably*, *IG*1.41, *Supp.Epigr.*1.362.23 (Samos), *SIG*110.10 (Rhodes), Theognost.*Can.*165.10. -ητος, ον, = ἄσυλος I, E.*Hel.*449, J.*AJ*19.1.1, D.C.75.14. -ία, ἡ, *inviolability*, i.e., 1. *safety to the person*, of suppliants, ἀ. βροτῶν A.*Supp.*610; of competitors at games, Plu.*Arat.*28; in Inscrr., as a privilege bestowed on one who has deserved well of the state, εἶμεν δὲ αὐτῷ ἀτέλειαν καὶ ἀ. καὶ κατὰ γᾶν καὶ κατὰ θάλασσαν *IG*7.11 (Megara), cf. 2.551.80, 5(1).1226 (Lacon.), etc. 2. *sanctity, inviolability* of character, ἀ. ἱερέως D.H.11.25. 3. of a place of refuge, *right of sanctuary*, Plb.4.74.2; ἀσυλίαν παρέχειν Plu.2.828d; freq. in Inscrr., ἀ. πόλεως καὶ χώρας *IG*12(5).1341 (Paros), etc. 4. *exemption from contributions*, Ph.2.250.

ἀσύλ-ληπτος, ον, *not conceiving*, Dsc.4.19; *preventing conception*, φάρμακον Aët.16.17. -ληψία, ἡ, *inability to conceive, barrenness*, Dsc.3.34, Aët.16.26.

ἀσυλλογ-ιστία, ἡ, *inconclusiveness, faultiness of logic*, Ps.-Alex. Aphr. *in SE*135.31. -ιστος, ον, *non-syllogistic, formally* or *materially invalid*, χρῆσις Arist.*APo.*91^{b}23, cf. *Rh.*1357^{b}24, Phld. *Rh.*2.24 S.; *irrelevant*, ἀ. πρὸς τὸ προκείμενον Anon. *in SE*16.33. 2. *unattainable by reasoning, incalculable*, Men.355.1, J.*AJ*4.7.1, al., Plu.2.24b, 580d. II. Act., *not reasoning justly, unreasoning*, Arist. *SE*167^{b}35, cf. Plb.12.3.2; ἀσυλλόγιστόν ἐστιν ἡ πονηρία Men.768: c. gen., *not rationalizing*, διάθεσις ἀ. τινῶν Chrysipp.*Stoic.*3.117; ἀ. τοῦ συμφέροντος *not calculating* it, J.*AJ*9.12.3; τοῦ χρησίμου Porph.*Abst.* 1.7. Adv. -τως, λέγειν Arist.*APo.*77^{b}40; ἀ. ἔχειν τινός Plu.*Caes.*59.

ἄσῡλος, ον, *safe from violence, inviolate*, ἐπεὶ πᾶν ἐστιν ἄ. Parm.8. 48; μενεῖς ἄ. E.*Med.*728; ἐκπεμπέτω ἄσυλον Pl.*Lg.*866d; of the persons of magistrates, D.H.7.45, 10.39; τὸ ἄ. *right of sanctuary*, *GDI*4940.13 (Allaria). 2. *not liable to reprisals* (cf. σῦλαι), *IG*9(1). 333 (Locr.). 3. c. gen., γάμων ἄ. *safe from* marriage, E.*Hel.* 61. II. of places, γῆν ἄ. παρασχεῖν make the land *a refuge*, Id. *Med.*387; ἱερὸν δ' ἄσυλον νενόμισται Plb.4.18.10, cf. *SIG*635.5, *BGU* 1053 ii 9 (i B.C.), etc.; ἄσυλον, τό, *sanctuary*, ib.304.28: metaph., νόμον τηρεῖν ἄ. *OGI*383.115 (Commagene, i B.C.); ἄ. γράμματα, στῆλαι, ib.8.110; so κόμην ἄ. φυλάξαι *uncut*, Philostr.*VA*4.16.

ἀσύλωτος [ῡ], ον, = foreg., πύργος *BSA*17.231 (Pamphyl.).

ἀσύμ-βᾰμα, ατος, τό, *not a* σύμβαμα or *full predicate*, Priscian.*Inst.* 18.1.4. -βᾰτος, Att. ἀξ-, ον, *not coming to terms*, τὸ ἀξ. Th.3.46; ἀ. ἐχθρός Ph.1.223; ἀντίθεσις ἀ. *irreconcilable*, Plu.2.946e, cf. Procl. *Inst.*28, Dam.*Pr.*5. Adv. -τως, ἔχειν to be *irreconcilable*, Ph.*Fr.*24 H., Plu.*Cic.*46: neut. pl. as Adv., ἀσύμβατα μνησικακοῦντες Ph.2. 520. 2. *not comparable, disparate*: εἰς ἕτερα ἀ. *incongruous* in other respects, Gal.5.540. 3. τραῦμα ἀ. wound *that will not close up, heal*, Aret.*CA*2.2. II. Act., *bringing no agreement*, κοινολογία Plb.15.9.1. -βίβαστος [ῐ], ον, *not to be brought into union, not to be reconciled* or *harmonized*, Eust.1658.40. -βλητος, Att. ἀξ-, ον, *not addible*, Arist.*Metaph.*1080^{b}9; *not comparable*, ib.1055^{a}7; ἀ. πρός τι or τινί, *incomparable with, far superior to*, Epicur.*Ep.*1p.31 U., *Fr.*556, cf. Plu.2.1125c. 2. *incommensurable*, Theo Sm.p.73 H.; *indeterminate*, μῆκος Gal.18(1).773. 3. of weights or measures, *not true according to the standard*, *IG*2.476.17. II. *not to be guessed, unintelligible*, ἀξύμβλητον ἀνθρώπῳ μαθεῖν S.*Tr.*694, cf. Ael.*NA*6. 60. III. *unsocial*, ἄπλατον ἀξ. S.*Fr.*387. -βολέω, *pay no contribution towards*, τινός Ach.Tat.8.17 (dub.). -βολος, ον, *without contribution* (cf. συμβολή), freq. in later Com.: I. of the dinner, δεῖπνον ἀ. *to which no one brings anything*, Alex.257.2, Amphis 39; δείπνων ἡδοναῖς ἀ. Timocl.8.10: metaph., ἀ. βίος *unsocial, solitary*, Plu.2.957a. II. of persons, *not contributing to* a feast, *not paying one's scot* or *share*, δεῖπνα δειπνεῖν ἀσύμβολον Aeschin.1.75, cf. Dromo 1.2; ἀ. κινεῖν ὀδόντας Timocl.10.4; τὸν ἀ. εὗρε γελοῖα λέγειν Ῥαδάμανθυς Anaxandr.10; τρέφειν τινὰ ἀ. Men.*Sam.*258, cf. Diph.73. 8; ἔστω ἀ. ἐν συνόδοις πάσαις *Michel* 998.44 (Delos); ἡδονὴ ἀ. Plu.2. 646b. Adv. -λως, δειπνεῖν Ath.4.162f (ἀσυμβόλῳ Kaib.). -μᾰχος, ον, *without allies*, E.*Antiop.*iv B 32 A. -μετρία, *incommensurability*, Arist.*Metaph.*1061^{b}1. II. *disproportion, want of proportion* or *harmony*, Pl.*Grg.*525a; πρός τι Arist.*Mete.*380^{a}32: in pl., αἱ τῶν πράτων δυναμίων ἀ. Ti.Locr.102b. -μετρος, Att. ἀξ-, ον, *incommensurable*, ταῖς μεγίσταις συμμετρίαις Pl.*Ti.*87d: abs., Arist.*Sens.* 439^{b}30, al., Pl.*Lg.*918b; ἀ. ἡ διάμετρος καὶ ἡ πλευρά Arist.*EN*1112^a 23. Adv. -ρως Dam.*Pr.*427. II. *disproportionate*, X.*Cyn.*2.7; ἀ. πρός τι *disproportionate* to it, Arist.*IA*708^{a}15; *ill-proportioned*, Id.*Po.*1461^{a}13; ὑπόμνημα *of excessive length*, Demetr.Lac.*Herc.* 1014.67 F.; κινήματα Phld.*Mort.*9. Adv. -ρως ib.8, Attic.ap.Eus. *PE*15.7. III. *unsuited*, πρὸς δημοκρατίαν Plu.*Per.*16, cf. *Them.* 22; τινί *Phoc.*3: c. inf., *not of fit size to..*, Arist.*GA*719^{b}12. -μικτος, ον, *incapable of blending*, στοιχεῖα D.H.*Comp.*22. -μνημόνευτος, ον, *not remembered in connexion*, Dsc.1*Praef.*3. -παγής, ές, *not compact*, Luc.*Anach.*24. -πάθεια [πᾰ], ἡ, *want of fellow-feeling*, S.E.*M.*5.44. -πᾰθής, ές, *without fellow-feeling* or *sympathy*, ἑαυτῷ Plu.*Cor.*21; πρός τινα Id.2.976c, cf. Phld.*Herc.*1251. 20, Plot.2.9.16, Procl.*Inst.*28; πρὸς τὸν λόγον Arr.*Epict.*2.9.21. Adv. -θῶς D.S.13.111, Porph.*Sent.*32. II. Medic., *unaffected* by an operation, Sor.2.60. III. Astrol., epith. of certain ζῴδια, *Cat. Cod.Astr.*1.135.13. Adv. -θῶς Vett.Val.146.24. -πάθητος [πᾰ], ον, = foreg. 1, *An.Ox.*2.340. -πέραντος, ον, *inconclusive*, Arist.*Ph.*186^a 25. -πέραστος, ον, *unfinished*, Sch.Pi.*I.*1 (Arg.). -περίφορος, ον, *unaccommodating*, Phld.*Ir.*p.54 W., Ptol.*Tetr.*159. -πλεκτος, ον, *unconnected*, Thphr.*CP*6.10.3. -πλήρωτος, ον, *not filled up*,

Dsc.1.70. **-πλοκος**, ον, *unconnected, absolute*, Ph.2.19. Adv. -κως *AB* 456. **-ποτος**, ον, *made of non-absorbent material*, κυθρίδιον Afric.ap.Olymp.Alch.p.75 B. **-πτωτος**, ον, *not falling in, full*, of face or body, Hp.*Hum*.4, Gal.11.25, al.; *not closing*, of the edges of a wound, ἀ. χείλη Antyll.ap.Orib.7.11.10; *not liable to collapse*, Anon.Lond.26.50. II. *not touching*, τῇ ψυχῇ Plu.*Lib.* 7. 2. esp. in Math., of lines or planes *which never meet*, e. g. parallel straight lines, Hero *Deff*.70; of lines *which do not cut* a curve, *non-secant*, ἀ. τῇ τομῇ αἱ ΓΔ, ΓΕ Apollon.Perg.*Con*.2.1, cf. 14; ἀσύμπτωτος (sc. γραμμή), ἡ, *asymptote*, of the hyperbola, ib.2.3, etc.; of the conchoid, Procl. *in Euc*.p.366 F. **-πώρωτος**, ον, (πωρόομαι) *not become callous*; of fractured bones *that have not united*, Dsc.1.112. **-φᾰνής**, ές, *dark*, ὑπόνομος Arist.*Mir*.836b19; *obscure*, Porph. *in Ptol*.181: Sup., Dam.*Pr*.38. Adv. -νῶς *obscurely*, Arg.4 Ar.*Ra*., Suid. **-φθαρτος**, ον, *without blending*, κρᾶσις Porph.*Gaur*. 10.6. **-φιλος**· ἀνόητος, ἄτιμος, Hsch., and **ἀσύμφηλος**, Cyr., Zonar., i. e. ἀσύφηλος (q. v.). **-φορος**, Att. **ἀξ-**, ον, *inconvenient, prejudicial*, φυτοῖσιν Hes.*Op*.782, cf. Hp.*Acut*.56, Antipho 2.1.10, Th.3.40; ἔς τι Id.1.32; πρός τι Id.2.91: Sup., E.*Tr*.491; ἀσυμφορώτατον ὑμῖν ἔθος εἰσάγειν D.19.2. Adv. -ρως, ἔχειν X.*HG*6.3.1; ζῆν πρὸς τὴν πολιτείαν Arist.*Pol*.1308b21. **-φυής**, ές, *not growing together*, μόρια *Placit*.5.19.5; τῇ κτίσει Hsch. **-φῦλος**, ον, *not akin, unlike*, Dsc.1 *Praef*.3, J.*AJ*11.6.5, Luc.*Hist.Conscr*.11; *incompatible, unsuitable*, Plu.2.709b, etc. Adv. -λως Sch.Il.9.643. **-φῦτος**, ον, *not growing together* or *uniting*, Hp.*de Arte* 10; *not able to unite*, Aret. *CA*1.7, Gal.10.336: generally, *detached*, *PLond*.1207.6 (i B.C.).

ἀσυμφων-έω, *to be out of harmony with*, παντὶ λόγῳ Plot.1.1.12. **-ία**, ἡ, *want of harmony, discord*, Pl.*Lg*.861a, Ph.1.5; *incoherence*, πολλῆς ἀσυμφωνίας ἔγεμεν ὁ λόγος Carneisc.*Herc*.1027.10. **-ος**, Att. **ἀξ-**, ον, *not harmonious*, Pl.*R*.402d; χορδῇ D.H. *Comp*.11. 2. metaph., *discordant, at variance*, ἐμαυτῷ Pl.*Grg*. 482c; ἕξεις Ocell.4.13; πρὸς ἀλλήλους *Act.Ap*.28.25, Arr.*An.Prooem*. (Comp.). Adv. -νως Pl.*Lg*.860c; τοῖς αὐτοῖς Arg.Str.1. II. *not speaking the same language*, πρὸς ἄλληλα Pl.*Plt*.262d, cf. *Lg*.777d; ἀ. ταῖς διαλέκτοις D.S.17.53.

ἀσυν-αίρετος, ον, Medic., *not contracted* or *shortened*, Paul.Aeg.6.107. II. Gramm., *uncontracted*, Eust.50.36. Adv. -τως Id.16.32. **-αίσθητος**, ον, *not perceptible*, Simp. *in Ph*.707.4. **-ἀκόλουθος**, Att. **ἀξ-**, ον, *without attendants*, Antiph.16. **-ακτος**, ον, *incompatible, incoherent, illogical*, Phld.*Sign*.14, Epict.*Ench*.44, S.E.*P*.2.137. **-άλειπτος** [ᾰλ], ον, (συναλείφω) *without synaloephe*, Hdn. Gr.2.912. Adv. -τως Eust.19.39, Sch.Ven.Il.3.150.

ἀσυνάλλ-ακτος, ον, *without intercourse*, Plu.2.416f; *unsociable*, D.H.1.41, 5.66. **-αξία**, ἡ, *lack of intercourse*, πρὸς ἀλλήλους *SIG* 684.14 (Dyme, ii B.C.), cf. Stob.2.7.25.

ἀσυν-άντητος, ον, *not to be met, unsocial*, Hsch. s. v. ἀξύμβλητον. **-απτος**, ον, *not joined*, Arist.*HA*516a30; *not connected*, συλλογισμοὶ ἀ. πρὸς ἀλλήλους Id.*APr*.42a21. **-αρθρος**, ον, Gramm., *without the article*, D.T.641.9, A.D.*Synt*.101.5, al. Adv. -ρως Sch.Il. 2.1. II. *inarticulate*, βοή prob. in *Corp.Herm*.1.4 (-ρως codd.). **-άρμοστος**, ον, *unfitting, unsuitable*, Plu.2.709b; τὸ ἀ. *incongruity*, S.E. *P*.1.43. **-άρτητος**, ον, *disconnected, incoherent*, D.H.*Th*.6, Gal.15.468, Sch.S.*OC*1560. II. in Metric, ἀσυνάρτητοι στίχοι verses *compounded of independent* κῶλα, Heph.15, Sch.Ar.*Ra*.1316, etc. **-δεξίαστος**, ον, *not entering into engagements*, Ptol.*Tetr*.166. **-δετος**, ον, *unconnected, loose*, X.*Cyn*.5.30, Apollod.*Poliorc*.169.8; *independent*, κίνησις Plu.2.386a: Astrol., of signs, Κριὸς πρὸς Σκορπίον ἀ. Gal. 19.333. II. of language, *without conjunctions*, Arist.*Int*.17a17; of style, Id.*Rh*.1413b29 (but ib.1407b38 ἄνευ μὲν συνδέσμου, μὴ ἀσύνδετα δέ without conjunction, but not *without connexion*); τὸ ἀ., in Rhet., *style without conjunctions*, Demetr.*Eloc*.268, cf. 192; σχῆμα Hermog.*Id*.2.1, al. Adv. -τως Philostr.*VS*1.16.4, Hermog.*Id*.1.9, Tib.*Fig*.40. **-δηλος**, ον, strengthd. for ἄδηλος, Plu.*Lyc*.28. **-δύαστος** [ῠ], ον, = ἀσύμπλοκος, Hsch.; = ἀσύζευκτος, Suid. **-εγκλῖτος**, ον, Gramm., *not undergoing enclisis at the same time*, Trypho *Fr*.5 V. **-είδητος**, ον, (σύνοιδα) *not privy to* a thing, ψυχαὶ ἀ. κακῶν Onos.4.2. Adv. -τως, τοῖς ἄλλοις Plu.2.214e, cf. *POxy*.123.16 (iii/iv A.D.). **-είκαστος**, ον, *not to be guessed, unintelligible*, Sch.S. *Tr*.694. **-έλευστος**, ον, *non-coagulating*, ἄτομοι Diog.Oen.20: Gramm., *not forming a compound*, A.D.*Pron*.45.24; *not entering into composition*, τὰ τοῦ τόνου Id.*Synt*.304.9. **-έμπτωτος**, ον, *not coinciding in form*, Eust.879.30, al. II. *not denoting coincidence in time*, A.D.*Synt*.210.14. **-έξωστος**, ον, *not to be dislodged*, of an athlete, *IG*14.1102, *CPHerm*.7 ii 3. **-έργητος**, ον, *not affording help*, Phld.*Oec*.p.67 J., *Vit*.p.24 J., Carneisc.*Herc*.1027.14. II. *unassisted*, Antyll.ap.Orib.10.30.8.

ἀσυν-εσία, Att. **ἀξ-**, ἡ, (ἀσύνετος) *want of understanding, stupidity*, E.*Ph*.1727 (lyr.), Th.1.122; opp. σύνεσις, Arist.*EN*1142b34 codd. **-ετέω**, *to be without understanding*, τὰ μέγιστα Hp.*Fract*.25, cf. Lxx *Ps*.118(119).158, Hsch. s. v. φελγύνει:—Aeol. **-έτημι**, *fail to understand*, τὰν ἀνέμων στάσιν Alc.18. **-ετίζομαι**, = foreg., Aq.*Je*.10.8.

ἀσυνετοποιός, όν, *nonsensical*, Sch.Ar.*Ra*.1286.

ἀσύνετος, Att. **ἀξ-**, ον, *void of understanding, witless*, Hp.*Fract*.31: Comp., Hdt.3.81, E.*Or*.493, Th.1.142; φρὴν ἀ. Ar.*Av*.456; τί τάδ' ἀσύνετα; what *folly* is this? E.*Hel*.352 (lyr.). Adv. -τως Plu.2.141b. 2. c. gen., *not able to understand*, λόγου Heraclit.1, cf. Plu.2.713b, Jul.*Or*.7.218b. II. *not to be understood, unintelligible*, E.*Ion* 1205, *Ph*.1731. Adv. -τως Hipparch.1.8.11.

ἀσυν-εχής, ές, *not continuous*; of winds, *variable*, Thphr.*Vent*. 11. **-ήθεια**, ἡ, *unfamiliarity*, Arist.*Metaph*.995a2, Thphr.*HP*9.17.2; ἀ. τοῦ δικολογεῖν *inexperience in*.., Arist.*Rh*.1368a21, cf. Plb. 15.32.7. **-ήθης**, ες, gen. εος, *unaccustomed*, χῶρος, τόπος, Emp. 118, Aen.Tact.16.19; τὰ ἀ. Hp.*Aph*.2.50; ἀσύνηθες τοῖς ζῴοις τὸ πίνειν Arist.*HA*606b26; φαντασία ἀ. πράγματος *Stoic*.3.98, al.; *not customary*, ὅπερ οὐκ ἀσύνηθες ὀνομάζειν Phld.*D*.3.2. II. of persons, *unaccustomed, inexperienced*, Hp.*Aph*.2.49, Plb.10.47.7. Adv. -θως Plu.2.678a. 2. *unfamiliar*, of persons, Arist.*EN*1126b26; ἐν ἀνδράσιν ἀ. amongst men *unknown to them*, D.H.8.44. **-ήμων**, ον, gen. ονος, *not comprehending*, A.*Ag*.1060. **-θεσία**, ἡ, *breach of covenant, transgression*, Lxx 2*Es*.9.2,4. II. *being uncompounded* or *uncombined*, A.D.*Pron*.32.10; opp. σύνθεσις, Phlp. *in Ph*.113.11. **-θετέω**, *break covenant, be faithless*, Lxx *Ps*.72(73).15, al.; opp. εὐσυνθετέω, Chrysipp.*Stoic*.2.63. **-θετος**, ον, (συντίθημι) *uncompounded*, Pl.*Phd*.78c, *Tht*.205c, Arist.*Pol*.1252a19; freq. in Gramm., as A.D.*Synt*.172.27, al.; ἀ. φωνή a word *standing alone*, Chrysipp.*Stoic*.2.50. Adv. -τως Eust.17.6. II. (συντίθεμαι) *bound by no covenant, faithless*, ὁ δῆμός ἐστιν πρᾶγμα τῶν πάντων ἀσυνθετώτατον D.19.136 (v.l. ἀσυνετ-), cf. *Ep.Rom*.1.31; *making no covenants*, ἀ. διατελοῦσι Phld.*Herc*.1251.19. **-θηκέω**, = ἀσυνθετέω, Sm.*Is*.63.8. **-θηκος**, ον, = ἀσύνθετος II, Onos.37.2. Adv. **-θηκεί**, *through breach of contract*, *POxy*.904.2 (v A.D.). **-νευστος**, ον, *non-convergent*; ἀ. σύννευσις, of curve and asymptote, Procl. *in Euc*. p.177 F. **-νεφής**, ές, *unclouded*, Sch.Pi.*O*.1.16; *not bringing clouds*, ἄνεμοι Thphr.*Vent*.11. **-νόμως**, Adv. *irregularly*, ἐπιπλέκεσθαι Vett.Val.119.4. **-νοος**, ον, contr. **-νους**, ουν, *thoughtless*, ἀργία Pl.*Sph*.267d. **-οπτος**, ον, *not easily perceived*, opp. εὐσύνοπτος, Aeschin.2.146, J.*BJ*7.6.1, Secund.*Sent*.1, 15.

ἀσύνορον· ἀσύμφωνον, Hsch.

ἀσυν-τακτικός, ή, όν, *against the rules of syntax*, Sch.E.*Hec*. 970. **-τακτος**, Att. **ἀξ-**, ον, *disorganized*, X.*Cyr*.8.1.45; of soldiers, *not in battle-order*, opp. συντεταγμένοι, X.*HG*7.1.16, J. *BJ*1.13.3, al.: c. dat., *not ranked on an equality with*.., Syrian. *in Metaph*.11.29. 2. *undisciplined, disorderly*, X.*Cyr*.7.5.21, D.13.15; στρατός Ph.2.120; πόλις Aen.Tact.3.1; ἀξ. ἀναρχία Th.6.72; ἡ πρόνοια τυφλόν τι κἀσύντακτον Nicostr.Com.19.5. Adv. -τως Plu. *Nic*.3. 3. *loosely put together, ill-proportioned*, σῶμα X.*Cyn*.3.3. 4. *ungrammatical, irregular*, Choerob. *in Theod*.2 p.18 H.; τὸ ἀ., a figure of speech, Ps.-Plu.*Vit.Hom*.41:—but of books, *not comprehended in a list*, D.L.9.47. 5. *not in the same order* or *class*, Dam.*Pr*.2. 6. Adv. -τως *without previous intimation* or *arrangement*, *UPZ* 61 (ii B.C.). II. Act., *not having composed a speech, without premeditation, unprepared*, Plu.2.6d. **-ταξία**, ἡ, *incapacity of entering into construction*, A.D.*Pron*.14.3, *Synt*.304.24; *irregularity*, Choerob. *in Theod*.2 p.18 H. II. *disorder, indiscipline*, App.*BC*2.20, *Gall*. 15. **-τᾰτος**, ον, (τείνω) v.l. for ἄτυτος in Xenarch.1. II. *without exertion*, περίπατος Antyll.ap.Orib.6.21.8. **-τέλεστος**, ον, *incomplete*, *IPE*1².32 *B*57 (Olbia, iii B.C.), D.S.4.12, Plu.2.1056d, *POxy*.707.30 (iii A.D.); *not executed*, *Annuario* 4/5.225 (Rhodes, ii B.C.). **-τελής**, ές, *not contributing, useless*, τοῖς κοινοῖς Them.*Or*.31.352c; πρός τι *Hippiatr.Praef*.2. Adv. ἀσυντελῶς, ἔχειν πρός τινας Sch.Pi.*O*.3. 81. II. = ἀσυντέλεστος, βίος M.Ant.3.8. **-τήρητος**, ον, *inaccurate*, παράδοσις Eust.300.43. **-τονος**, ον, *slack, lazy*. Adv., Sup. -ώτατα X.*Cyr*.4.2.31. **-τρητος**, ον, *imperforate*, Heliod.ap.Orib.44.23.59, Gal.19.438. **-τριπτος**, ον, *not easily rubbed* or *crushed*, Ph.*Bel*. 60.47. **-τροφον**, = βάκτος, Ps.-Dsc.4.37. **-τρόχαστος**, ον, *incompatible*, Simp. *in Cat*.380.25. **-ύπαρκτος**, ον, *incapable of coexisting*, A.D.*Conj*.221.8, Alex.Aphr.*Quaest*.97.28, S.E.*P*.2.202, Simp. *in Cat*.381.13.

ἀσυρής, ές, *lewd, filthy*, ἄνθρωπος Plb.4.4.5; βίος Id.18.55.7; λοιδορία Id.38.20.6; ἀπαιδευσία Lxx *Si*.23.13. Adv. -ρῶς Phld.*Rh*.1.348 S.

ἀσύρρηκτος, ον, *not burst* or *rent*, Gal.10.817.

ἀσυσκεύαστος, ον, *not arranged, not ready*, X.*Oec*.8.13.

ἀσυ-στασία, ἡ, *want of union, confusion*, Archig.ap.Gal.8.626. **-στᾰτέω**, *to be incapable of*, c. gen., A.D.*Conj*.228.14. **-στᾰτος**, Att. **ἀξ-**, ον, (συνίσταμαι) *not solidified*, γῆ ἀ. ὑπὸ βίας Pl.*Ti*.61a; *not cohesive*, ὕδωρ Plu.2.949b, etc.; τὸ ἀ. *want of cohesion*, ib.697a; γάλα ἀ. εἰς τυρόν *that will not curdle*, Aret.*CD*1.13. 2. *unformed*, ἔμβρυα Antyll.ap.Orib.6.31.5: metaph., *incoherent*, of Aeschylus, Ar.*Nu*.1367. 3. *that cannot be composed, incurable*, ἄλγος A.*Ag*. 1467 (lyr.). 4. *incapable of subsistence*, ἀ. καὶ ἀνύπαρκτος *Stoic*. 3.91; τὰ ἀ. Hermog.*Stat*.1. 5. Gramm., *irregular, inadmissible*, A.D.*Pron*.55.11, al. 6. *chaotic, confused*, Plu.2.1025a. 7. of self-evident propositions, *incapable of proof* (cf. σύστασις), Alex. Aphr. *in Top*.84.8. 8. of legal status, *not determined*, *POxy*.1680.11 (iii/iv A.D.). **-στᾰτόω**, *regard as* ἀσύστατος, τοὺς τὴν ἀστρονομίαν μὴ οἰομένους εἶναι τέχνην ἀλλ' ἐθέλοντας αὐτὴν ἀσυστατοῦν Sch. Ptol.*Tetr*.1.

ἀσύστροφος, ον, *not forming a solid mass*, Hp.*Gland*.13. II. of style, *not condensed*, D.H.*Din*.8. III. *slack, careless*, ἕξις, opp. εὐσύστροφος, Olymp. *in Grg*.p.258 J. IV. dub. sens., of the pulse, Archig.ap.Gal.8.650.

ἀσύφη, ἡ, a kind of κασία, *Peripl.M.Rubr*.12, Dsc.1.13 (v.l. ἀσυφήμων).

ἀσύφηλος [ῠ], ον, *headstrong*, or perh. *foolish*, ὥς μ' ἀσύφηλον ἐν Ἀργείοισιν ἔρεξεν ὡς εἴ τιν' ἀτίμητον μετανάστην Il.9.647; οὔ πω σεῦ ἄκουσα κακὸν ἔπος οὐδ' ἀσύφηλον 24.767, cf. Q.S.9.521: also in late Prose, as Eun.*VS* p.481 B. Adv. -λως *foolishly*, Dius ap.Stob.4.21.16.

ἀσφᾰγής, ές, *not to be sacrificed*, Ph.2.323.

ἀσφάδαστος [φᾱ], ον, *without convulsion* or *struggle*, esp. in dying, A.*Ag.*1293, S.*Aj.*833 (fort. –ᾳστος).

ἀσφάζει· ἀντέχεται, Hsch.

ἀσφᾰκέλιστος, ον, *not gangrened* or *mortified*, Hsch.

ἄσφακτος, ον, *unslaughtered*, E.*Ion* 228.

ἀσφάλαθος, v. ἀσπ–.

ἀσφάλαξ [φᾰ], ἄκος, ὁ, = ἀσπάλαξ, Babr.108.13, Str.15.1.44, Hdn. Gr.2.630.

ἀσφάλ-εια [φᾰ], gen. ας, Ion. ης, ἡ, (ἀσφαλής) *security against stumbling* or *falling*, ἀ. πρὸς τὸν πηλόν Th.3.22; *steadfastness, stability*, ἀσφαλείᾳ.. ἀνόρθωσον πόλιν raise up the city *so that it stand fast*, S.*OT* 51; κατασκευάζειν τὴν [τῆς πολιτείας] ἀ. Arist.*Pol.*1319b39. 2. *assurance from danger, personal safety*, A.*Supp.*495, etc.; τηρεῖν ἀ. ἐπιβουλῆς Antipho 2.2.8; ἀ. τῆς ἐπαναφορᾶς *precaution regarding* it, And.3.33, cf. Th.4.68, 8.4; ἡ ἰδία ἀ., opp. ὁ τῆς πόλεως κίνδυνος, Lys. 31.7; δεηθεὶς τῆς ἀ. ἔτυχε *safe-conduct*, Hdt.3.7; ἀ. διδόναι, παρέχειν, X.*HG* 2.2.2, *Cyr.*4.5.28: freq. with Preps., ἀσφαλείης εἵνεκεν Hdt.4. 33; ἀσφαλείας οὕνεκα Ar.*Av.*293; δι' ἀσφαλείας τὰς πόλεις οἰκεῖν Th. 1.17; τὸ σῶμ' ἐν ἀσφαλείᾳ καθιστάναι, καθεστάναι, Isoc.9.30, X.*Hier.* 2.10; κατ' ἀσφάλειαν *in safety*, Th.4.128; μετ' ἀσφαλείας Id.1.120, Pl. *Ti.*50b: pl., ἀσφάλειαι *seasons of safety*, Isoc.8.21. 3. *caution*, σῴζονται ὑπ' ἀσφαλείας Alciphr.1.10, cf. Heliod.(?)ap.Orib.46.11.27 and 14.4: in Lit. Crit., *circumspection*, Demetr.*Eloc.*287. 4. *assurance, certainty*, ἀ. πολλὴ μὴ ἂν ἐλθεῖν αὐτούς Th.2.11; ἀ. ἐργάζεσθαι τὴν γῆν *security* for agriculture, X.*Cyr.*7.4.5. 5. ἀ. λόγου *convincing nature, certainty* of an argument, Id.*Mem.*4.6.15, cf. *Ev.Luc.* 1.4. 6. as law-term, *security, bond*, Arr.*Epict.*2.13.7; *pledge*, *BGU* 1149.24 (i B.C.): in pl., = Lat. *cautiones*, Just.*Nov.*72.6. 7. Pythag. name for *eight*, *Theol.Ar.*56. **–ειος** (with collat. form –ιος, q.v.), ον, epith. of Poseidon, the *Securer*, Ar.*Ach.*682, Paus.3. 11.9, 7.21.7, Plu.*Thes.*36. **–ής,** ές, (σφάλλομαι, σφαλῆναι) *not liable to fall, immovable, steadfast*, in Hom. only once as Adj. (cf. infr. III), θεῶν ἕδος ἀ. αἰεί Od.6.42, cf. Hes.*Th.*128, Pi.*N.*6.3, Theoc.2.34, etc.; ἀσφαλῆ θεῶν νόμιμα S.*Ant.*454; *unshaken*, of purpose, ἀ. ὁ νοῦς Id. *Fr.*351. 2. of friends and the like, *unfailing, trusty*, οὐ γὰρ οἱ.. εὐρύνωτοι φῶτες ἀσφαλέστατοι Id.*Aj.*1251; ἀ. στρατηλάτης E.*Ph.*599, cf. Th.1.69: c. inf., φρονεῖν γὰρ οἱ ταχεῖς οὐκ ἀσφαλεῖς the hasty in counsel are not *safe*, S.*OT* 617, cf. Pl.*Sph.*231a; σῴζειν τὰ κοινὰ πράγματ' ἀσφαλέσταται E.*IT* 1062; of things, *sure, certain*, Th.4.108, etc. 3. *assured from danger, safe*, ἀ. αἰών Pi.*P.*3.86; ἀσφαλεῖ σὺν ἐξόδῳ S.*OC* 1288; ἀ. ὅρος X.*Lac.*12.1; ὁδὸς –εστέρα Id.*HG* 5.4.51; ἐν τῷ ἀσφαλεῖ *in safety*, Th.1.137, 8.39, cf. Pl.*Lg.*892e; ἐν ἀσφαλεῖ τοῦ μὴ παθεῖν X.*Cyr.*3.3.31; τοῦ λαλεῖν Men.*Sam.*25; ἐν –εστέρῳ, –εστάτῳ, X.*Cyr.*7.1.21, *An.*1.8.22; ἐν ἀ. βίου E.*Hipp.*785; μένειν ἐν τῷ ἀ. X. *An.*4.7.8; ἐξ ἀσφαλοῦς from *a place of safety*, Id.*Eq.Mag.*4.16; τοῦ ἀσφαλέος εἵνεκα Hdt.1.109; τὸ ἀ., = ἀσφάλεια, Th.6.55, etc.; μετὰ τοῦ αὐτῆς ἀ. with *no risk to* herself, Plot.4.8.7; ἀσφαλές [ἐστι], c. inf., *it is safe* to.., Hdt.3.75, E.*Ph.*891, Ar.*Av.*1489: abs., ἀλλ' οὐκ ἀσφαλές Pl.*Phlb.*61d, etc.; φεύγειν αὐτοῖς ἀσφαλέστερόν ἐστιν ἢ ἡμῖν X.*An.*3.2.19. 4. ἀ. ῥήτωρ a *convincing* speaker, Id.*Mem.*4. 6.15. 5. in Lit. Crit., *sound, not risky*, of language or rhythm, Demetr.*Eloc.*19, 41. Adv. –ῶς, ἐρεῖ ib.78. II. Subst. ἀσφαλές, τό, = ἀσφάλεια 6, *BGU* 984.14 (iv A.D.), etc. III. Ep. Adv. ἀσφαλέως, ἔχειν, μένειν, to be, remain *firm, steady*, Il.23.325, Od.17. 235: neut. ἀσφαλές as Adv., Il. (v. infr.); δρακεῖσ' ἀσφαλές Pi.*P.*2. 20; ἀ. ἀγορεύει *without faltering*, Od.8.171, Hes.*Th.*86; ἔμπεδον ἀσφαλέως Il.13.141, Od.13.86; ἔμπεδον ἀσφαλὲς αἰεί Il.15.683. Adv. ἀσφαλῶς (–έως) is used in all senses of the Adj., –έως βεβηκὼς ποσσί Archil.58.4; *in safety, with certainty*, S.*OT* 613; ἀ. βουλεύειν And.3. 34; ἀ. ἔχει Hdt.1.86: c. inf., Lys.27.6; ἀ. προσθεῖναι *as a precaution*, Alex.Aphr.*in Mete.*14.10: Comp. –έστερον Hdt.2.161, Pl.*Phd.*85d; but –εστέρως Hp.*Prorrh.*2.15, Th.4.71: Sup. –έστατα Hp.*Prorrh.* 2.23, Pl.*R.*467e.

ἀσφᾰλίζω Plb.18.30.3:—mostly in **Med.**, fut. –ιοῦμαι J.*BJ* 2.21.4, but –ίσομαι Id.*AJ* 13.5.11, and so D.S.20.24: pf. ἠσφάλισμαι Plb.5. 43.6: plpf. ἠσφάλιστο ib.7.12: aor. ἠσφαλισάμην Id.2.22.11; ἠσφαλίσθην J.*Vit.*62: some of these tenses are used in pass. sense (v. infr.):—*fortify*, τὸν τόπον Plb.18.30.3, etc.:—Pass., Id.1.42.7, 4.70.9, *Ev.Matt.*27.64. b. *secure*, *BGU* 829.9 (i A.D.). 2. more freq. in Med., *secure*, ἑαυτόν Epicur.*Fr.*215; τὰς εἰσβολάς, τὴν χώραν, etc., Plb.2.65.6, 4.60.5, etc.; τόπους Hero *Bel.*101.7; τὸν ὕσπληγγα *CIG* 2824 (Aphrodisias); *shut up, close*, πύλην Lxx *Ne.*3.15; ὀφθαλμοὶ ἠσφαλισμένοι, opp. ἀνεῳγμένοι, Polem.*Phgn.*55; τοὺς πόδας ἠσφαλίσατο εἰς τὸ ξύλον *made* them *fast*, *Act.Ap.*16.24. 3. *secure the person of, arrest*, τινά *PTeb.*283.19 (i B.C.), cf. *PRyl.*68.19 (i B.C., Pass.); *seize*, τὰ γενήματα ib.53.29 (ii B.C.). 4. Med., *certify*, ib. 2.77.40 (ii A.D.). II. Med., *secure oneself against, ward off*, τὰς καταφορὰς τῶν μαχαιρῶν Plb.6.23.4, cf. 9.3.3: abs., *safeguard oneself*, J.*AJ* 13.5.10, *POxy.*1033.13 (iv A.D.). 2. metaph. in Rhet., *safeguard* a risky metaphor, ἀ. τὰς μεταφορὰς Demetr.*Eloc.*85:—Pass., λέξις ἠσφαλισμένη τοῖς συνδέσμοις ib.193. (The word is βάρβαρον acc. to *AB* 456.)

'Ασφάλιος, = 'Ασφάλειος (q.v.), Opp.*H.*5.680, *IG* 5(1).559.14 (Amyclae), Aristid.*Or.*46(3).1, *BGU* 96.6 (iii A.D.).

ἀσφάλ-ισμα [φᾰ], ατος, τό, *pledge, security*, *BGU* 248.8 (i A.D.), 601.7 (ii A.D.). **–ιστός,** όν, *made secure*, Hdn.*Epim.*178.

ἀσφαλός, ὁ, name of a *bird*, Hsch. s.v. ἐνθύσκος.

ἀσφαλτίας, ου, ὁ, (ἀ- priv., σφάλλω) *not failing*, σφόνδυλος ἀ. *lowest vertebra*, Poll.2.179 (v.l. –ίτης).

ἀσφαλτίζω, *smell like asphalt*, Dsc.5.128.

ἀσφάλτιον, τό, = τρίφυλλον, *treacle clover, Psoralea bituminosa*, Dsc.3.109. 2. = πολύγονον ἄρρεν, Ps.-Dsc.4.4. 3. = πεντάφυλλον, ib.42.

ἀσφαλτίτης [ῑ], ου, ὁ, fem. **–ῖτις,** ιδος, *bituminous*, βῶλος Str.7.5.8; λίμνη 'Α. the Dead Sea, D.S.19.98, cf. J.*BJ* 1.33.5; πόα, = ἀσφάλτιον, Philum.ap.Orib.45.29.27, Archig.ap.Aët.5.84. II. v. ἀσφαλτίας.

ἀσφαλτόπισσα, ἡ, = πισσάσφαλτος, Lxx *Ex.*2.3.

ἄσφαλτος, ἡ (also ὁ, Gal.13.784), *asphalt, bitumen*, Hdt.1.179, 6.119, Theoc.16.100, Dsc.1.73; ἄ. ὀρυκτή Arist.*Mir.*842b15:—also **ἄσφαλτον,** τό, Hp.*Aër.*7, Ti.Locr.99c. II. a kind of *petroleum*, Dsc.1.99. III. *pitch*, Lxx *Ge.*6.14. (Ph.1.420 derives it from σφάλλω.)

ἀσφαλτοφόρος, ον, *producing bitumen*, λίμνη J.*AJ* 17.6.5.

ἀσφαλτ-όω, *smear with pitch*, Lxx *Ge.*6.14. **–ωδεύομαι,** *to be soaked in pitch*, Aët.2.73. **–ώδης,** ες, *full of* or *like asphalt*, Arist. *Sens.*444b33, Str.7.5.8, etc. **–ωσις,** εως, ἡ, gloss on πίσσωσις, Suid.

ἀσφαλών, ῶνος, ὁ, perh. *safe, cash-box*, *PGrenf.*1.14.8.

ἀσφᾰρᾰγέω, (ἀ- euph., σφαραγέω) *resound, clang*, of armed men, Theoc.17.94 (dub. l.).

ἀσφᾰρᾰγία, ἡ, *root-stock of asparagus*, Thphr.*HP* 6.4.2.

ἀσφάρᾰγος (A) [φᾱ], ὁ, = φάρυγξ, *throat, gullet*, Il.22.328, Plu.2. 698e, Q.S.11.82.

ἀσφάρᾰγος (B) [φᾰ], ὁ, *stone sperage, Asparagus acutifolius*, Cratin. 325, Amips.25, Antiph.301, Theopomp.Com.68, etc.; *the edible shoots thereof*, Thphr.6.4.2, Dsc.2.125, *AP* 11.325 (Autom.), Gal.6.641. II. *the shoots* of other plants, Nic.*Th.*883, etc.; κράμβης Diph.Siph.ap. Ath.2.62f; of ἄμπελος λευκή, Dsc.4.182. (ἀσφ- Attic, Phryn.89, *PS* p.41 B.: ἀσπ- in Antiph.301, Aristopho 16, and later writers, as Nic. l. c., Plb.34.8.5, etc.)

ἀσφᾰρᾰγωνία, ἡ, *wreath of asparagus*, Plu.2.138d.

ἄσφε, ἄσφι, Aeol. for σφέ, σφί, v. σφεῖς.

ἄσφηλοι· ἀσθενεῖς, σφηλὸν γὰρ τὸ ἰσχυρόν, Hsch.

ἀσφίγγωτος, ον, = sq., *Corp.Herm.*13.6 codd.

ἄσφιγκτος, ον, *not tightly bound, loose*, Gal.12.373, 18(2).627.

ἀσφοδέλινος, η, ον, *of asphodel*, ναῦς ἀ. a ship *built of asphodel stalks*, Luc.*VH* 2.26.

ἀσφόδελος, ὁ, *asphodel, Asphodelus ramosus*, Hes.*Op.*41, Arist. *HA* 627a8, Thphr.*HP* 1.10.7, 7.13.2, Crateuas *Fr.*5, Theoc.7.68, Dsc. 2.169, etc.; cf. σφοδελός. II. oxyt., as Adj., ἀσφοδελὸς λειμών the *asphodel* mead which the shades of heroes haunted, Od.11.539, 24. 13: generally, *flowery* mead, *h.Merc.*221, 344. (On the accent v. Hdn.Gr.1.160.)

ἀσφοδελώδης, ες, *like asphodel*, Thphr.*HP* 6.6.9.

ἀσφράγιστος [ᾰ], ον, *not sealed*, *Klio* 18.264 (Delph., iii B.C.), *SIG* 953.35 (Cnidus, ii B.C.), Harp. s.v. ἀσήμαντα, Horap.1.49; μόσχοι *PGnom.*183 (ii A.D.). II. *not assigned to a σφραγίς*, γῆ *BGU* 659 ii 9 (iii A.D.).

ἀσφυ-γμία, ἡ, = *pulsus defectio*, opp. ἀσφυξία, Cael.Aur.*CP* 1.2. **–κτέω,** *to be without pulsation*, Dsc.*Alex.Praef.*, Gal.7.194, al., Herod. Med. in *Rh.Mus.*58.71. **–κτος,** ον, (σφύζω) *without pulsation, lifeless*, Gal.2.647, *AP* 11.211 (Lucill.): metaph. of the mind, *without impulse, calm*, Plu.2.446d; *moderate*, ἂν ἰάσιμον ᾖ τὸ χεῖρον καὶ ἄ. ib. 500c. II. Act., *causing no violent pulsation*, ib.132e. **–ξία,** ἡ, *stopping of the pulse*, Aret.*SA* 2.11; *pulsus amputatio*, opp. ἀσφυγμία, Cael.Aur.*TP* 4.3.

ἀσχᾰδής, ές, (σχάζω) *not to be restrained*, A.*Fr.*418.

ἀσχᾰλάω, only pres. (exc. fut. –ήσω Thal.ap.D.L.1.44), 3 sg. ἀσχαλάᾳ Il.2.293; 3 pl. ἀσχαλόωσι 24.403; inf. ἀσχαλάαν 2.297; part. ἀσχαλόων 22.412; imper. ἀσχάλα Archil.66.6; inf. ἀσχαλᾶν E.*IA* 920:—more freq. **ἀσχάλλω,** once in Hom. ἀσχάλλῃς Od.2.193, cf. S.*OT* 937, E.*Or.*785, and so always in Prose, X.*Eq.*10.6, D.21.125, Onos.1.17, Eus.Mynd.6: impf. ἤσχαλλον Hes.*Fr.*76.3, Hdt.3.152, 9.117; imper. ἄσχαλλε Thgn.219: 3 sg. fut. ἀσχᾰλεῖ (prob. for –αλᾷ) A.*Pr.*764:—*to be distressed, grieved*, abs., ἀσχαλάαν παρὰ νηυσί Il.2. 297, cf. 22.412, etc.: the cause of distress is added by Hom. either in part., μένων ἀσχαλάᾳ Il.2.293, cf. Od.1.304; ἥν κε (sc. θωὴν) τίνων ἀσχάλλῃς 2.193: or in gen., ἀσχαλάᾳ δὲ πάϊς βίοτον κατεδόντων *is vexed because of*.., 19.159; κτήσιος ἀσχαλόων τήν οἱ κατέδουσιν 'Αχαιοί ib.534: later in dat., ἀ. τινί *at* a thing, Archil. l. c., A.*Pr.*764, E.*IA* 920; ἐπὶ τῷ διδόναι δίκην ἀσχάλλειν D. l. c., cf. Ph.2.521; πρός τι Longus 3.8: c. acc., θάνατον ἀ. πατρῷον E.*Or.*785.

ἀσχαλιάζω, = ἀσκωλιάζω II, Hsch.

ἄσχαστος, ον, *unshakable, firm*, λίθοι *IG* 7.3073.163 (Lebad.), cf. *BCH* 29.468 (Delos):—written **ἄσκαστος** *IG* 7.4255 (Oropus). II. *without a gap*, Eutoc. *in Archim.*3 p.94 H.

ἀσχέδωρος, ὁ, *wild boar*, in Magna Graecia, A.*Fr.*261, Sciras 1.

ἀσχέλιον· τραχύ (Cret.), Hsch.

ἄσχετος, Ep. also **ἀάσχετος,** ον, (σχεῖν) *not to be checked, ungovernable*, πένθος ἄσχετον οὐκ ἐπιεικτόν Il.16.549; ἀάσχετον ἵκετο πένθος 24.708; μένος ἄσχετοι υἷες 'Αχαιῶν *resistless* in might, Od.3. 104; μητρός τοι μένος ἐστὶν ἀάσχετον οὐδ' ἐπιεικτόν Il.5.892; κάκον ἄ. Alc.92; ὕβρις Epic. in *Arch.Pap.*7.6: in later Prose, ἄ. βοή Luc. *Dips.*9; ἄ. ὁρμή Aret.*SA* 2.12; of a person, *ungovernable, unmanageable*, γυνή *PMag.Par.*1.2071, cf. *PMag.Lond.*121.593. Adv. –τως Pl.*Cra.*415d: neut. ἄσχετον, –τα, as Adv., A.R.4.1738, 1087. 2. *not held together*, Phlp. *in Ph.*533.4. 3. *unrelated*, πρός τι Anon. *in*

Prm. (Rh.Mus.47.605), cf. Jul.Or.5.163b, Dam.Pr.3, al., Procl.in Cra.p.57 P., al.; ἀ. σχέσις Ps.-Alex.Aphr.in SE152.24; unqualified, ὕλη Dex.in Cat.51.21. Adv. -τως Procl.Inst.122, in Cra.p.70 P.

ἀσχημάτιστος [μᾰ], ον, without form or figure, Pl.Phdr.247c, Arist.Ph.191^{a}2. 2. that cannot be represented by a figure, Theol.Ar.11. 3. Astrol., not in aspect with other planets, Vett.Val.102.8, Anon.in Ptol.Tetr.104. II. not employing figures of speech, of orators, Plu.2.835b; φράσις D.H.Pomp.5, cf. Demetr.Eloc.67. Adv. -τως D.H.Rh.10.11.

ἀσχημ-ονέω, behave unseemly, disgrace oneself, E.Hec.407, Cratin.151, Pl.R.506d, etc.: c. acc. cogn., ἀ. ἄλλα ἄ.. D.22.53; ἀ. τὰ δεινότατα Id.60.25; μηδὲν ἀ. Arist.Pol.1273^{a}34, cf. EN1119^{a}30: c. part., Plu.2.178d:—Pass., πολλὰ ἀσχημονεῖται many unseemly things are done, D.H.2.26. **-όνησις**, εως, ἡ, = ἀσχημοσύνη, Sm.Ps.43(44).16. **-ος**, ον, late form for ἀσχήμων, Phld.Herc.1457.9 (Comp.), PRyl.144.18 (i A.D.), Polem.Phgn.13, Hippiatr.55: Sup. -όνατος D.L.2.88. Adv. -μως Sch.S.Aj.916. **-οσύνη**, ἡ, want of form, ἀ. καὶ ἀμορφία Arist.Ph.190^{b}15, cf. 188^{b}20, Simp.in Cael.129.26. 2. ungracefulness, Pl.Smp.196a, R.401a; awkwardness, Id.Tht.174c; disfigurement, τοῦ προσώπου, in playing on the flute, Arist.Pol.1341^{b}5. 3. ἀ. φέρει brings discredit, disgrace, Id.EN1126^{b}33. II. in moral sense, indecorum, obscene or disgraceful conduct, Ep.Rom.1.27: in pl., Ph.1.78, Vett.Val.61.31. III. euphem. for αἰδοῖον, Lxx Le.18.7, al.; for ἀπόπατος, ib.De.23.13(14). **-ων**, ον, gen. ονος, (σχῆμα) misshapen, ugly, Hp.Art.27, Procl.in Prm.p.624S. II. unseemly, shameful, E.Hel.299, Pl.Phlb.46a, Arist.Pol.1336^{b}14, etc. 2. of persons, ἀ. γενέσθαι to be indecorous, Hdt.7.160; ἀσχημονέστερος Arist.EN1127^{b}13. III. Adv. -νως J.BJ2.12.1, Phld.Sign.29: Sup. -έστατα very meanly, Pl.Lg.959d.

ἀσχῐδής, ές, (σχίζω) uncloven, undivided, ἰσχάδες Arist.Pr.930^{b}33; of animals, ἀσχιδῆ οἷον τὰ μώνυχα Id.HA499^{b}11, cf. PA642^{b}29; φύλλα Thphr.HP3.10.1.

ἀσχίον, τό, puff-ball, Lycoperdon giganteum, Thphr.HP1.6.9.

ἀσχιστόπους, ουν, gen. ποδος, not having cloven hoofs, Alex.Aphr.in Metaph.521.24.

ἄσχιστος, ον, uncloven, of solid-hoofed animals, opp. σχιζόπους, Arist.Metaph.1038^{a}14. 2. not curdled, γάλα Philum.ap.Orib.45.29.12. II. undivided, Pl.Ti.36d; πτερὸν ἄ. Arist.HA519^{a}28; δάκτυλοι ib.517^{a}32; φλέψ ib.513^{b}13; of logical division, Pl.Sph.221e. 2. indivisible by fission, Arist.Mete.385^{a}16, 386^{b}26, cf. Opp.C.2.528; not liable to split, Thphr.Ign.72.

ἀσχολ-έω, engage, occupy, τινά Luc.Zeux.7:—**Med.**, impf. ἠσχολεῖτο (v. infr.): fut. -ήσομαι M.Ant.12.2, Aristid.1.423J.; -ηθήσομαι Lxx Si.39.1: pf. ἠσχόλημαι D.C.71.10: aor. ἠσχολησάμην Gal.7.657, and -ήθην D.S.4.32, Luc.Macr.8:—to be occupied, busy, Alex.205, Men.999, Epicur.Fr.204, etc.; ἀσχολούμεθα ἵνα σχολάζωμεν Arist.EN1177^{b}4; περί or ἐπί τι, D.S.2.40, 17.94; πρός τινας Aristid.l.c., cf. 2.178J.: c. part., λαλῶν ἠσχολεῖτο Alex.261.12, etc.: c. acc. cogn., ἀ. ἀσχολίας ἀνωφελεῖς D.Chr.47.23; exercise a function, POxy.44.7,23 (i A.D.). II. Act. intr., in same sense as Med., Arist.Pol.1333^{a}41, 1338^{a}4, Philem.220; to be engaged in one's own business, Arist.Pol.1299^{b}33.—Not used in the best Att. **-ημα**, ατος, τό, business, engagement, Str.10.3.9 (pl.), Iamb.Protr.21.κβ' (pl.); performance of a public function, BGU8 ii 23 (iii A.D., pl.). **-ηματικός**, ή, όν, hard-working, Vett.Val.233.18. **-ία**, ἡ, occupation, business, engagement, πρᾶγμα ἀσχολίας ὑπέρτερον Pi.I.1.2, cf. Th.1.90, 8.72, Pl.Phd.58d; πρᾳότης καὶ ἀ. Lys.6.34; ἀ. καὶ ἀπραγμοσύνη D.21.141; opp. ἡσυχία, Th.1.70; ἐμοί τις ἀ. ἐστίν I have an engagement, Pl.Prt.335c; δι' ἀσχολίαν because of business, Eub.119.12; later, office, function, BGU1202.3 (i B.C.). II. want of time or leisure, ἀ. ἄγειν φιλοσοφίας πέρι to have no leisure for pursuing it, Pl.Phd.66d; ἀ. ἄγειν to be engaged or occupied, Id.Ap.39e; ἀ. ἔχειν πρός τι Plu.Comp.Sol.Publ.2; opp. σχολή, Arist.Pol.1333^{a}35; ἐν ἀσχολίᾳ λέγειν Pl.Tht.172d; ἀ. παρέχειν τινί cause one trouble, X.Cyr.4.3.12; μυρίας.. ἡμῖν παρέχει ἀσχολίας τὸ σῶμα Pl.Phd.66b: c. inf., hinder one from doing, X.Cyr.8.1.13; ἀ. μοι ἦν παρεῖναι I had no time, Antipho 6.12; πολλὴν ἀ. ἔχειν τοῦ ἐπιμεληθῆναι X.Mem.1.3.11; τοῦ (prob. for τῷ) εὐφραίνεσθαι πολλὰς ἀ. παρέχει Id.Cyr.8.7.12; ἀ. ἔχει τὸ μὴ [εἰς τὸ] πράττειν τὸ δεόμενον Id.HG6.1.16. **-ος**, ον, (σχολή) of persons, without leisure, engaged, busy, Pl.Lg.832b, D.3.27; ἄ. συγγόνου προσεδρίᾳ E.Or.93; ἄ. ἐς σοφίην busily engaged upon (or, with no leisure for).., Hdt.4.77; ἄ. περί τι busy about.., Plu.Tim.12; πρὸς τοῖς ἔργοις Arist.Pol.1305^{a}20: c. inf., having no time to.., Pi.P.8.29; ἄσχολοί εἰσιν ἐπιβουλεύειν Arist.Pol.1313^{b}20; ἄ. ὥστε μὴ ἐκκλησιάζειν ib.1318^{b}12. Adv. -λως, ἔχειν D.33.25; πρός τι Aristid.Or.23(42).61. II. of actions, etc., πάντα χρόνον ἄ. ποιεῖν fully occupied, Pl.Lg.831c; ἄ. πράξεις not leisured, Arist.EN1177^{b}8; κίνησις ἄ. unresting, Id.Cael.284^{a}31.

ἄσχυ, τό, inspissated juice of the fruit of the bird-cherry, Prunus Padus, Hdt.4.23.

ἄσω, = βλάπτω, coined by EM39.42.

ἀσώδης [ᾰ], ες, (ἄση) attended with nausea, ὀδύνη prob. in Hp.Art.19; suffering from nausea, Id.Acut.67; ἀ. στόμαχοι Dsc.1.17; surfeited, Plu.2.974b. Adv. -δως Gal.10.437. II. (ἄσις) slimy, muddy, A.Supp.31 (lyr.).

ἀσωμᾰτ-ία, ἡ, incorporeality, Porph.Abst.1.31, Iamb.Comm.Math.15,33, Procl.in Prm.p.686S. **-ος**, ον, disembodied, incorporeal, Pl.Phd.85e, al., Arist.Ph.209^{a}16, de An.404^{b}31, al., Epicur.Ep.1 p.22U., Stoic.2.117, etc.; σῶμα ἀσωματώτατον Arist.de An.409^{b}21: Comp. -ώτερος Id.Ph.215^{b}5. Adv. -τως Iamb.Myst.5.16, Procl.Inst.142, Dam.Pr.376. II. non-metallic, Maria ap.Zos.Alch.p.196B. III. in Law, not specified in the body of a document, PSI6.709.19. **-ότης**, ητος, ἡ, incorporeality, Ph.1.44,76. **-όω**, demetallize, Maria ap.Zos.Alch.p.196B. (Pass.).

ἄσωμος, ον, = ἀσώματος, EM161.40.

ἄσωστος, ον, (σῴζω) not to be saved, past recovery, ἄσωστά οἵ ἐστιν Ael.NA13.7, PFay.12.24 (ii B.C.). Adv. -τως, διατίθεσθαι, ἔχειν, Dsc.2.141, Gal.15.753.

ἀσωτ-εῖον, τό, abode of a prodigal, Stratt.51, Longus 4.17. **-εύω**, lead a profligate, spendthrift life, PSI1.41.12 (iv A.D.):—usu. Dep. **-εύομαι**, Arist.Pol.1316^{b}15, Babr.108.12, PFlor.99.7 (i/ii A.D.): pf. ἠσώτευμαι S.E.M.8.201. 2. c. acc., squander in riotous living, χρήματα Ael.VH5.9.

ἀσωτία, ἡ, prodigality, wastefulness, Pl.R.560e, Arist.EN1107^{b}10; τὴν ἀ. ὑγρότητα προσαγορεύουσιν Crobyl.4. 2. profligacy, Ep.Eph.5.18, al.: pl., ἐν ἀσωτίαις καὶ κραιπάλαις Hdn.2.5.1.

ἀσωτοδῐδάσκᾰλος, = ἀσωτίας διδάσκαλος, name of a play of Alexis, Ath.8.336d.

ἄσωτος, ον, (σῴζω) having no hope of safety, in desperate case, Arist.Pr.962^{b}5. Adv. -τως, ἔχειν to be past recovery, Plu.2.918d. II. in moral sense, abandoned, τᾶς ἀσώτου Σισυφιδᾶν γενεᾶς S.Aj.189 (lyr.); spendthrift, Pl.Lg.743b, Arist.EN1107^{b}12, 1120^{a}1, al.: Sup., D.C.67.6; profligate, Vett.Val.18.2. Adv. -τως Theopomp.Hist.217a, D.40.58, Ev.Luc.15.13: Comp. -ότερον D.C.62.27. III. Act., ἄσωτος γένει bringing destruction on the race, A.Ag.1597.

ἀσωφρόνως, Adv. = ἀσελγῶς, Sch.Ar.Pl.560.

ἀτα· ὦτα (Tarent.), Hsch.

ἀτᾰβῠρίτης [ῑ] ἄρτος, a kind of loaf, Sopat.9.

ἀτᾰγία, ἡ, absence of a ταγός (q.v.) in Thessaly, IG9(2).257.

ἀταής· ἀγύμναστος, Hsch. (fort. ἀτλής, cf. ἄτλας). **ἀταθήνιον**· χαλκός, ἔλυτρον, Id. **ἀται**· πληροῦται, Id. **ἄταιθα**· λαμυρά, Id.

ἀταῖος, = ὑοσκύαμος, Ps.-Dsc.4.68; cf. ἄτη.

ἀταισόν· ἀναδενδράς (Tyrrhen.), Hsch.

ἀτακτ-έω, of a soldier, to be undisciplined, opp. εὐτακτέω, X.Cyr.7.2.6, D.3.11; τοὺς ἀτακτοῦντας τῶν τριηράρχων IG2.809^{b}13:—Pass., πολλὰ γὰρ ἠτάκτητο αὐτοῖς J.AJ17.10.10: generally, neglect one's duty, fail to discharge obligation, PEleph.2.13 (iii B.C.), 2Ep.Thess.3.7, POxy.275.24 (i A.D.). 2. generally, lead a disorderly life, Lys.14.18, X.Oec.7.31: c. gen., τῆς πατρίου ἀγωγῆς to desert it, Plu.2.235b. 3. raise a riot or rebellion, OGI200.6 (iv A.D.). **-ημα**, ατος, τό, disorderly or contumacious act, irregularity, Stoic.3.136, OGI483.58 (Pergam., ii B.C.), Vett.Val.116.13. **-ος**, ον, not in battle-order, of troops, Hdt.6.93, Th.8.105 (Comp.). 2. not at one's post, Lycurg.39. II. undisciplined, disorderly, θόρυβος Th.8.10; ποιεῖν τὴν πολιτείαν ἀτακτοτέραν Arist.Pol.1319^{b}15; irregular, πυρετός Hp.Coac.26; οὐδὲν ἄ. τῶν φύσει Arist.Ph.252^{a}11; φθορὰ ἄ. casual, Id.HA556^{a}12; of sensual excess, irregular, inordinate, ἡδοναί, Ἀφροδίτη, Pl.Lg.660b, 840e; in Music, without rhythm, μελῳδίαι Aristid.Quint.1.13; Medic., irregular, σφυγμός Gal.8.458. 2. uncivilized, lawless, βίος Critias 25.1D. 3. Math., ἄτακτα προβλήματα indeterminate, not admitting of a definite solution, Procl.in Euc.p.220F.

B. Adv. -τως in an irregular, disorderly manner, of troops, ἀ. καὶ οὐδενὶ κόσμῳ προσπίπτοντες Th.3.108; ἀ. διώκειν Id.2.91; ἀτακτότερον προσπεσόντες Id.6.97, cf. X.Cyr.1.4.22, Hell.Oxy.6.4; ἀ. φέρεσθαι Isoc.1.32; οὐθὲν ἀ. θεῷ πράττεται Epicur.Ep.3 p.65U. 2. irregularly, of fevers, Hp.Epid.1.7; ζῆν Isoc.2.31. 3. Comp. ἀτακτοτέρως somewhat negligently, Demetr.Eloc.53.

ἀτᾰλαίπωρος, ον, not painstaking, οὕτως ἀ. τοῖς πολλοῖς ἡ ζήτησις τῆς ἀληθείας Th.1.20. Adv. -ρως, οὕτως αὐτοῖς ἡ ποίησις διέκειτο Ar.Fr.254; οὐκ ἀ. τινὰς χειροῦσθαι D.C.49.35; ἀ. διάγειν Ph.1.18; ἀ. ἀκούειν Simp.in Cael.143.16. II. of persons, not given to hard work, Hp.Aër.1; lazy, ἀνθρωπάρια Arr.Epict.1.29.55. 2. incapable of bearing fatigue, prob. in Hp.Aër.21. Adv. -ρως without incurring fatigue, Id.Acut.33. III. of stagnant water, sluggish, Ruf.ap.Orib.5.3.1:—also **-πώρητος**, ον, Poll.4.28; easy, Sor.2.11. Adv. -τως Hsch. s. v. ἀνοίκτως, Sch.E.Hec.204.

ἀτάλαντος [ᾰτᾰ], ον, (ἀ- copul., τάλαντον) equal in weight, equivalent to, like, ἀ. Ἄρηϊ Il.5.576; Διὶ μῆτιν ἀ. equal to Zeus in wisdom, 2.169, etc.: generally, like, ἀστέρι A.R.2.40. 2. in equipoise, Arat.22.

ἀτᾰλάφρων [ᾰτ], ον, gen. ονος, (φρονέω) tender-minded, of a child in arms, Il.6.400, Q.S.13.122:—also in form **ἀταλόφρων**, IG12(8).600.14 (Thasos).

ἀτάλλω [ᾰ], (ἀταλός) only in pres. and impf., skip in childish glee, gambol, ἄταλλε δὲ κήτε' ὑπ' αὐτοῦ Il.13.27, cf. Mosch.2.116, Philostr.Im.2.3. II. Act., bring up a child, rear, foster, Hom.Epigr.4.2; νέαν ψυχὴν ἀτάλλων S.Aj.559: metaph., ἐλπὶς ἀτάλλοισα καρδίαν Pi.Fr.214:—Pass., grow up, wax, h.Merc.400:—Act., intr. in this sense, ἐτρέφετ' ἀτάλλων [ᾰτ] Hes.Op.131.—Poet. and later Prose.

ἄταλμα [ᾰ], ατος, τό, frolic, Hsch. (pl.).

ἀτᾰλός [ᾰτ], ή, όν, tender, delicate, of youthful persons, as of maidens, Od.11.39; of fillies, Il.20.222; ἀταλὰ φρονέοντες of young, gay spirit, 18.567, cf. Hes.Th.989, h.Cer.24; μάτηρ E.El.699 (lyr.) (unless it = suckling her lamb); ἀ. χερσί, of the aged, tremulous, A.Pers.537 (anap.): c. dat., ἀταλὸς πατρί, i.e. subject, amenable to him, Pi.N.7.91. Adv. -λῶς Sch.Il.5.271: Sup. -ώτατα, παίζει IG1.492a.

ἀτᾰλό-φρων [ᾰτ], ονος, v. ἀταλάφρων. **-ψῡχος**, ον, *soft-hearted*, θηλύτεραι *AP*5.296 (Agath.).

ἀτάλυμνος [ᾰτᾰ], ὁ, = κοκκυμηλέα, Nic.*Al.*108.

ἀτᾰμίευτος, ον, *that cannot be stored*, Ph.2.113; *that cannot be regulated*, Arist.*GA*788ª34; *uncontrolled, inordinate*, J.*BJ*4.1.6. Adv. -τως, ὑπὸ θυμοῦ ἐπισπασθείς Plu.*Arat.*37. 2. *not needing to be husbanded*, Max.Tyr.3.9, al. II. Act., *not husbanding, prodigal, lavish*, χάριτες Ph.1.5: c. gen., ἡδονῶν Plu.2.12c. Adv. -τως, ταῖς ὀργαῖς χρώμενος Pl.*Lg.*867a; ἀ. πάντα χαρίζεσθαι Ph.2.274.

ἀταξία, Ion. -ίη, ἡ, *indiscipline*, prop. among soldiers, opp. εὐταξία, Hdt.6.11, Th.2.92, X.*HG*3.1.9, etc. 2. generally, *disorder, confusion*, ἀ. καὶ ἀκολασία Pl.*Cri.*53d; ἀμαθία καὶ ἀ. X.*Ath.*1.5; ἀ. καὶ ἀναρχία Arist.*Pol.*1302ᵇ28; εἰς τάξιν ἤγαγεν ἐκ τῆς ἀ. Pl.*Ti.*30a; ἀπὸ τύχης καὶ ἀ. Arist.*PA*641ᵇ23: in pl., ἀταξιῶν, opp. τῶν ἐν ταῖς κινήσεσι τάξεων, Pl.*Lg.*653e. 3. c. gen., διαίτης ἀ. *irregularity*, Hp.*Coac.*211; νόμων Aeschin.3.38.

ἀτάομαι [ᾰτ], Pass., (ἄτη) *suffer, be in distress*, in Trag. always in pres. part. ἀτώμενος S.*Aj.*384, *Ant.*17, 314, E.*Supp.*182, exc. ἀτώμεσθα S.*Aj.*269; ἀτασθῶσιν is dub. in Hes.*Cat.Oxy.*1358*Fr.*2.13. II. as law-term, αἴ τις ἀταθείη the *injured party*, *Leg.Gort.*4.29; but ὁ ἀταμένος the *loser* in a suit, ib.10.21; ἀϝατᾶται *suffers a penalty*, *IG* 5(1).1155 (Gythium):—Act., ἀτάω, aor. subj. 3 sg. ἀτάσῃ dub. in *Leg.Gort.*6.23, 43.

ἀτᾰπείνωτος, ον, *not humbled*, Zeno*Stoic.*1.53, Arr.*Epict.*4.6.8, Plu.*Cor.*21.

ἀταποῦ· χαλεπῆς, Hsch.

ἀτάρ [ᾰτᾰ], Ep. also **αὐτάρ** (q.v.); ἀϝυτάρ *IG*1.477:—Conj., *but, nevertheless*, marking a strong contrast; freq. in Hom. to introduce an objection or correction, Il.1.506, etc.; in form of a question, E.*Hec.* 258, X. ll. cc. infr., etc. it begins a sentence or clause, and, in apostrophe, is placed after the voc., Ἕκτορ, ἀ. που ἔφης *truly* thou didst say, Il.22.331; Ἕκτορ, ἀ. σύ μοί ἐσσι πατήρ..ἀλλ' ἄγε νῦν ἐλέαιρε 6. 429; γε is freq. added, with a word between, 16.573, E.*Med.*84: ἀ. sts. answers to μέν, more emphatic than δέ, Il.21.41, Od.3.298, Hdt. 6.133, al.; ἀεὶ μὲν δὴ..ἀτὰρ οὖν καὶ τότε Pl.*R.*367e, cf. *Prt.*335d, *Tht.* 172c; πῶς παισὶ μὲν πληθύεις ἀτὰρ..οὐ πέμπεις τινά; S.*Tr.*54, cf. Pl. *Sph.*225c: sts. after ἐπειδή, when it may be translated *then*, Il.12. 144; ἀτὰρ ἤδε is peculiar to Aret., *SD*1.9, al. 2. freq. in Pl. and Trag. to mark a rapid transition to another thought, A.*Pr.*343, S. *OT*1052, Pl.*Phdr.*227b, etc.; ἀτὰρ δή E.*Tr.*63 (also later, Eus.Mynd. 63). 3. without real contrast, μὰψ ἀτὰρ οὐ κατὰ κόσμον Il.2.214, cf. 3.268, 270, etc.—More freq. in Poetry (esp. Ep.) than in Prose, though found in Pl. ll. cc., *Tht.*142d, X.*Cyr.*1.6.9, *An.*4.6.14, etc.: also in Com., Cratin.188.

ἀτᾰρ-ακτέω, *keep calm*, Epicur.*Ep.*1 p.30 U., J.*AJ*15.10.3, S.E.*P.* 1.12. **-ακτοποιησία**, Ion. -ποιησίη, ἡ, *acting with perfect composure*, dub. in Hp.*Decent.*12. **-ακτος**, ον, *not disturbed, uniform*, περίοδοι Pl.*Ti.*47c. II. *not disturbed, without confusion, steady*, of soldiers, X.*Cyr.*2.1.31: generally, *quiet*, Id.*Eq.*7.10 (Sup.). Adv. Sup. -ότατα Id.*Eq.Mag.*2.1. III. *not excited, calm*, Arist.*HA* 630ᵇ12: Comp., M.Ant.4.24; of the sea, prob. in Arist.*Pr.*944ᵇ23. Adv. -τως, ζῆν Phld.*Herc.*1003. **-αξία**, Ion. -ίη, ἡ, *impassiveness, calmness*, Democr.ap.Stob.2.7.3ⁱ, Hp.*Ep.*12, Epicur.*Ep.*1 p.30 U., Phld.*Oec.*p.63 J., Cic.*Fam.*15.19.2, Hero *Bel.*71.2, Plu.2.101b, Plot. 1.4.1, etc.; prob. f.l. for ἀταξία in Hp.*Praec.*14. **-ᾰχος**, ον, = ἀτάρακτος, ἐν τοῖς φοβεροῖς Arist.*EN*1117ª31, cf. 1125ᵇ34, Epicur. *Sent.Vat.*79, Str.1.3.21, Onos.2.2, etc.; ἀτάραχον, τό, an *eyesalve*, Gal.12.786; of a will, *unchallengeable* *PMasp.*151.142 (vi A.D.). Adv. -χως *unconfusedly*, Epicur.*Ep.*1 p.14 U.; *calmly*, Hero*Bel.*72. 4, Phld.*Herc.*1003, D.S.17.54, J.*AJ*14.9.1, Archig.ap.Orib.46.26.1, Plu.*Fr.inc.*140: Comp. -ώτερον Arr.*Epict.*4.1.47. **-ᾰχώδης**, ες, *not liable to be disturbed*, Arist.*Div.Somn.*464ª14 (Comp.).

ἀτάρβακτος, ον, *unaffrighted*, γνώμα Pi.*P.*4.84; γυνά B.5.139; cf. ἀτάρμυκτος.

ἀταρβ-ής, ές, *fearless*, Il.13.299, Pi.*P.*5.51; ἀ. τῆς θέας *having no fear about* the sight, S.*Tr.*23; later of things, δοῦρας ἀ. *AP*6.97 (Antiphil.). 2. *causing no fear*, A.*Pr.*849. **-ητος**, ον, = foreg., ἐνὶ στήθεσσιν ἀ. νόος ἐστίν Il.3.63, cf. Hes.*Sc.*110, A.*Fr.*199: neut. pl. as Adv., ὕβρις ἀτάρβητα ὁρμᾶται stalks abroad *without fear*, S.*Aj.* 196. Adv. -τως Suid. II. *not dreaded*, κάματοι *IG*14.1003.2, cf. ib.7.96. **-ίζεται**· ἀτηρὸς φαίνεται, Hsch.

ἀταρβομάχας [μᾰ], α, ὁ, *fearing not the fray*, B.15.28.

Ἀταργατίς, gen. ῖδος, acc. ῖν (cf. Hdn.Gr.1.107, 2.761): dat. Ἀταργατεῖτι *IG*12(3).188 (Astypalaea): also gen. Ἀταργάτιος *BCH* 6.499 (Delos); dat. Ἀταργάτει *SIG*1135 (Delos), Ἀταργάτι *IG*12(3). 178 (Astypalaea):—*Atargatis*, a Syrian divinity, Mnaseas 32, Str.16. 1.27, Corn.*ND*6, etc.:—also **Ἀταργάτη**, *LW*1890, v.l. in Str.16.4. 27: **Ἀτταγάθη**, Hsch.

ἀτᾰρίχευτος [ῐ], ον, *not desiccated*, Arist.*Pr.*926ª35; *not salted*, Gal.12.321.

ἀτάρμυκτος, ον, *unblenching, unflinching*, ὄμμα Euph.124; φρενὸς οἶστρος Nic.*Al.*161.

ἀτάρνη· βρόχος, Hsch. (leg. ἀρτάνη).

ἀταρπῑτός, ἀταρπός, Ion. for ἀτρ- (qq.v.).

ἀταρτ-άομαι [ᾰτ], *hurt*, Hsch. **-ηρός**, όν, *mischievous, baneful*, ἀταρτηροῖς ἐπέεσσιν Il.1.223; of a person, Μέντορ ἀταρτηρέ Od.2.243; γενέθλη Hes.*Th.*610; στόμα Πόντου Theoc.22.28; of wild beasts, Q.S.4.223, 12.40.

ἄταρχον (ἀτάραχον cod., post ἀταρτηροῖς)· ἀχείμαστον, Hsch.; cf. τάρχη.

ἀτάρχῡτος, *unburied*, Ps.-Phoc.99, Lyc.1326; cf. ἀταρίχευτος.

ἀτασθᾰλία [ᾰτ], Ion. -ίη, ἡ, *presumptuous sin, recklessness, wickedness*, Hom., always in pl.; σφετέρῃσιν or σφῇσιν ἀτασθαλίῃσιν, Il.4.409, Od.1.34, al.; ἀτασθαλίαι δέ οἱ οἴῳ ἐχθραὶ ἔσαν 21.146; δι' ἀτασθαλίας ἔπαθον κακόν 23.67; ἀτασθαλίῃσι κακῇσιν 12.300:—after Hom. in sg., ἀτασθαλίῃ μέγα ῥέξαι, of the Titans, Hes.*Th.*209; εἵνεκ' ἀτασθαλίης τε καὶ ἠνορέης ὑπερόπλου ib.516; βασιλῆος ἀ. Pi.*Parth.*2*Fr.*1.31; οὐκ ἥρθη νοῦν ἐς ἀτασθαλίην Simon.111.4; ἀτασθαλίῃ χρησάμενον Hdt.2. 111: in later Prose, Alcid.ap.Arist.*Rh.*1406ª9, Luc.*Astr.*15; ἀ. ἡ εἰς τὸ θεῖον Arr.*An.*7.14.5; of an elephant, Id.*Ind.*13.13.

ἀτασθάλλω [ᾰτ], *to be insolent*, only in pres. part., μή τις..πλήξῃ ἀτασθάλλων Od.18.57; οὔ τις..γυναικῶν λήθει ἀτασθάλλουσα 19.88.

ἀτάσθᾰλος [ᾰτ], ον, *reckless, presumptuous, wicked*, of men, ἀνέρα..ἀ. ὀβριμοεργόν Il.22.418; ἀ. ἀνδρὶ ἔοικας Od.8.166, etc.; so in Hdt., ἄνδρα ἀνόσιόν τε καὶ ἀ. 8.109; ἀνὴρ δεινὸς καὶ ἀ. 9.116, cf. Him.*Ecl.*13.28, al. 2. of men's acts, words, etc., Τρωσὶν τῶν μένος αἰὲν ἀ. Il.13.634; λίην γὰρ ἀ. ὕβριν ἔχουσιν Od.16.86; ἄνδρες δραῖσιν ἀτάσθαλα Alc.*Supp.*27.11; λέγειν βάρβαρά τε καὶ ἀ. Hdt.7.35; ἔρδειν πολλὰ καὶ ἀ. Id.3.80; πρῆγμα ἀ. ποιήσαντες ib.49; ἀ. οὐδὲν ἔρεξας Theoc.22.131.—Ep., Aeol., and Ion. word, used for comic effect by Strato Com.1.38; also in later Prose, Luc.*Cont.*3, Arr.*An.*6.27.4, etc.—In *EM*261.56 also **ἀτασθάλεος**, ον.

ἀταύρωτος, ον, A.*Ag.*245, also η, ον Ar.*Lys.*217:—*unwedded, maiden*, A. l. c.; *chaste*, Ar. l. c., v. Scholl. ad locc., Poll.2.173.

ἀτᾰφία, ἡ, *want of burial*, J.*AJ*13.15.5, Luc.*Salt.*43, Plu.*Marc.*30.

ἄτᾰφος, ον, *unburied*, Hdt.9.27, S.*Ant.*29, *OC*1732 (lyr.), Th.2.50, etc. II. ἄ. πράξεις modes of *refusal of burial*, Pl.*Lg.*960b.

ἀτάω, v. ἀτάομαι.

ἅτε, properly acc. pl. neut. of ὅστε (as in Il.11.779, 22.127). I. *just as, as if, so as*, ἅ. σήριον ἄστρον prob. in Alcm.23.62, cf. Pi.*O.*1.2, *P.*4.30, Hdt.5.85, S.*Aj.*168 (lyr., s. v. l.); τιμᾶν τινα ἅ. ἱερόφαντιν Jul. *Or.*7.221c. II. causal, *inasmuch as, seeing that*, with part., ἅτε τὸν χρυσὸν ἔχων Hdt.1.154, cf. 102; Cratin.295, Ar.*Pax*623, Th.4.130, etc.: with gen. abs., ἅτε τῶν ὁδῶν φυλασσομένων Hdt.1.123, cf. Pl. *Smp.*223b, etc.:—with part. omitted, δίκτυα δοὺς [αὐτῷ] ἅτε θηρευτῇ [ὄντι] Hdt.1.123, etc.; ἅ. γένους προμάτωρ dub. in A.*Th.*140 (lyr.); ἅ. δή Hdt.1.171; ἅ. δὴ οὖν Pl.*Prt.*321b; ὡς ἅ. freq. in Olymp.*in Mete.*39.12, al.—Rare in Trag., and only in lyr.

ἆτε, Lacon. = ὡς, *IG*5(1).213.

ἀτεγκτος, ον, *not to be softened by water*, χαλκός Arist.*Mete.*385ᵇ 13; κηρός Plu.2.15d (s. v. l.). II. metaph., *not to be softened*, παρηγορήμασιν A.*Fr.*348: abs., *hard-hearted, relentless*, S.*OT*336, E.*HF*833, Ar.*Th.*1047, and in late Prose, D.H.5.8, J.*BJ*5.9.4, Plu. *TG*12, Luc.*DMeretr.*12.3, etc. Adv. -τως, πρὸς ἔρωτας ἔχειν Philostr. *Ep.*5.

ἀτειρής, ές, *not to be rubbed* or *worn away, indestructible*, in Hom. mostly of brass or iron, Il.5.292, al. II. metaph., *stubborn, unyielding*, αἰεί τοι κραδίη πέλεκυς ὥς ἐστιν ἀ. ib.3.60, cf. 15.697; [Hercules] μένος αἰὲν ἀ. Od.11.270; φωνή Il.13.45, 17.555; ὄμματα Emp.86; ἀτειρέσιν ἀκτίνεσσιν Id.84.6; ἀγαθόν Pi.*O.*2.36; of persons, κἂν μύθοισι καὶ ἐν προσόδοισιν ἀ. *stubborn*, Theoc.23.6; ἀτειρὴς οἴνῳ *AP*12.175 (Strat.); τὸ ἀτειρές *stubbornness*, Pl.*Cra.*395b; Pythag. etym. of τριάς, *Theol.Ar.*15.—In Archig.ap.Gal.8.87 **ἀτειρός**. Adv., Comp. -ότερον Gal.8.110, prob. in D.L.6.99.

ἀτείχιστος, ον, *unwalled, unfortified*, Th.1.2, 8.62, Lys.33.7: metaph., χάριν θανάτου πάντες ἄνθρωποι πόλιν ἀ. οἰκοῦμεν Epicur.*Sent. Vat.*31. Adv. -τως Sm.*Za.*2.4(8); ἀ. τετειχισμένοι, of Brahmans living in the open air, Philostr.*VA*3.15, 6.11. 2. *not walled off*, Th.1.64.

ἀτέκμαρτος, ον, *without distinctive mark, obscure, baffling*, χρηστήριον Hdt.5.92.γ'; μοῖρα A.*Pers.*910 (Sup.); ἐρημία *trackless*, Plu.*Luc.* 14; ἀτέκμαρτον προνοῆσαι *without mark* whereby to judge it, Pi.*P.* 10.63; ἀ. δέος Th.4.63, cf. Pl.*Lg.*638a. Adv. -τως, ἔχειν ὅτου ἕνεκά ἐστι X.*Mem.*1.4.4: neut. pl. as Adv., *bafflingly*, Pi.*O.*7.45. 2. of persons, *uncertain, inconsistent*, Ar.*Av.*170. II. *boundless, unlimited*, ὕδωρ Orph.*A.*1150: metaph., γαστήρ dub. in Opp.*H.*2.206.

ἀτέκμων, ονος, ἡ, (τεκεῖν) *childless, barren*, Man.4.584.

ἀτεκν-έω, *have no children*, v.l. in Hp.*Steril.*217, cf. Lxx *Ca.*4.2, *Ho.*9.12. **-ία**, ἡ, *childlessness, barrenness*, Arist.*Pol.*1265ᵇ10, Ph. 1.201, etc.: pl., Arist.*Pol.*1265ª41. **-ος**, ον, *without children, childless, barren*, Hes.*Op.*602, A.*Th.*828 (lyr.), S.*El.*164 (lyr.), Arist.*EN* 1099ᵇ4, *Tab.Heracl.*1.151, etc.; of animals and fishes, Arist.*HA*577ª 3, *GA*755ᵇ19: also c. gen., ἄ. ἀρσένων παίδων E.*Ba.*1305. Adv. -νως Sch.E.*Or.*206. II. in causal sense, λειχὴν ἄφυλλος ἄ. A.*Eu.*785. [ᾰτεκνος S. l. c., ᾰτεκνος A. and E. ll. cc.] **-όω**, *make childless*:—Pass., of the earth, *to be barren*, Lxx 4*Ki.*2.19. **-ωσις**, εως, ἡ, *barrenness*, Aq.*Ps.*34(35).12.

ἀτέλ-εια, Cret. ἀτέλεα *GDI*5040.22, ἡ:—*incompleteness, imperfection*, Arist.*Ph.*261ª36, *GA*758ᵇ20, *Mete.*380ª31, Thphr.*CP*4.13.1. II. *exemption from public burdens* (τέλη), ἀ. στρατιῆς καὶ φόρου Hdt.3. 67; ἔδοσαν Κροίσῳ..ἀτελείην καὶ προεδρίην Id.1.54, cf. 9.73, D.20.47; ἁπάντων ib.60; τοῦ ἄλλου (sc. φόρου) *IG*1.40; μετοικίου ib.2.121; στρατείας ib.551; ὧν ἂν εἰσάγῃ ἢ ἐξάγῃ *OGI*10.13; ἐς τὴν ἀ. to purchase *immunity*, *IG*2.570; ἀ. τινὸς ποιεῖν Alex.276.6; εὑρέσθαι, ἔχειν, enjoy *it*, D.20.1, 19: generally, τοιούτων πραγματειῶν ἀ. Isoc.12. 147; ἀ. ἐπικραίνειν confirm *immunity*, A.*Eu.*362; ἐξ ἀτελείας *without payment, gratis*, D.59.39, Philonid.1 D., Poll.4.46. **-ειος**, α, ον, =

ἀτελής, Phld.Rh.1.5S. —ειότης, ητος, ἡ, insufficiency, Zos.Alch. p.245B. —είωτος, ον, unfinished, incomplete, Arist.Fr.70, Sor.1.33: neut. pl. as Adv., Sch.Nic.Th.456 (v.l. -τως). —εσιούργητος, ον, not brought to an issue, ὠδῖνες Theol.Ar.55. —εστος, ον, without end, issue, or effect, unaccomplished, ἅλιον θεῖναι πόνον ἠδ' ἀ. Il.4.26, cf. 57,168, Od.2.273; σῖτον ἔδοντες μὰψ αὔτως ἀ. 16.111; τὰ δέ κεν θεὸς ἢ τελέσειεν ἤ κ' ἀτέλεστ' εἴη 8.571, cf. Tab.Defix.Aud.68b: rare in Prose, of prayers, not deserving of accomplishment, Antipho 1.22; ἀ. κῶνος truncated cone, Hero Stereom.1.16: neut. pl. as Adv., inconclusively, ἀ. λαλεῖν AP12.21 (Strat.). II. uninitiated in.., c. gen., βακχευμάτων E.Ba.40: metaph., ἀ. ἱερῶν καὶ μυστηρίων τῆς πολιτείας Plu.Flam.2: abs., ἀ. καὶ ἀμύητος Pl.Phd.69c, cf. Arist.Rh.1419a4, Phld.Acad.Ind.p.4M.; ἀ. τῷ θεῷ Ael.VH3.9; prob. unmarried, Tab. Defix.Aud.68a. III. = ἀτελής III, χώρα D.Prooem.55. IV. endless, eternal, Parm.8.4.

ἀτελεσφόρητος, ον, not brought to accomplishment, Sm.Jb.31.40.

ἀτελεύτ-ητος, ον, not brought to an end or issue, unaccomplished, ἀτελευτήτῳ ἐπὶ ἔργῳ Il.4.175, cf. 1.527. 2. without an end, interminable, Parm.8.32, Arist.Ph.204a5, Cael.273a5; everlasting, τὸ πᾶν Ocell.1.2, cf. Plu.2.114f, etc. II. of a person, impracticable, ἄτεγκτος κἀτελεύτητος S.OT336. —ος, ον, endless, eternal, ὕπνος A.Ag.1451 (lyr.).

ἀτελής, ές, without end, i.e., 1. not brought to an end or issue, unaccomplished, τῷ κε καὶ οὐκ ἀ. θάνατος μνηστῆρσι γένοιτο Od.17.546; εἰρήνη ἐγένετο ἀ. the peace was not brought about, X.HG4.8.15; τὰ μὲν λελεγμένα ἄρρητ' ἐγώ σοι κἀτελῆ φυλάξομαι unaccomplished, i.e. harmless, S.El.1012. 2. incomplete, unfinished, ἀτελῆ σοφίας καρπὸν δρέπειν Pi.Fr.209; ἀτελεῖ τῇ νίκῃ.. ἀνέστησαν Th.8.27; of a building, ib.40; without end or purpose, ἡ φύσις οὐθὲν.. ἀτελὲς ποιεῖ Arist.Pol.1256b21. 3. inchoate, imperfect, of growth, Hp.Art.41 (Comp.); ᾠὰ ἀ. Arist.GA733a2; ζῷα ib.774b5; πολῖται ἀ., of minors, Id.Pol.1275a17; ἀ. συλλογισμός Id.APr.24a13; ἀ. ποιεῖν τινά castrate, Luc.DSyr.20: Comp. -έστερος less highly developed, Phlp.in Ph.898.29. Adv. -λῶς incompletely, Arist.Pol.1275a13, dub. in Plu.2.472f. 4. never-ending, Δαναΐδων ὑδρεῖαι ἀ. Pl.Ax.371e. 5. indeterminate, Id.Phlb.24b; τὸ μὲν ἄπειρον ἀ. ἡ δὲ φύσις ἀεὶ ζητεῖ τέλος Arist.GA715b14, cf. Pol.1256b21. II. Act., not bringing to an end, not accomplishing one's purpose, ineffectual, ἀτελεῖ νόῳ Pi.N.3.42; of persons, ἀποπέμπειν τινὰ Pl.Smp.179d; ἀ. περὶ τὸ κρίνειν imperfectly fitted for.., Arist.Pol.1281b38; ἀ. εἴς τι Ph.2.417: c. inf., unable to do effectually, ἄκυρος καὶ ἀ. σῶσαι And.4.9; invalid, δίκα Michel 196 (Elis). 2. not giving accomplishment to a thing, μαντεύμασι Pi.P.5.62. III. (τέλος IV) free from tax or tribute, Hdt.2.168, 3.91, Lys.32.24: c. gen., ἀ. τῶν ἄλλων free from all other taxes, Hdt.1.192; καρπῶν ἀ. free from tithe on produce, Id.6.46; exempt, λητουργιῶν D.21.155; στρατείας ib.166, cf. IG2^2.1132.12, Arist.Pol.1270b4; τοῦ ἄλλου (sc. φόρου) IG1.40; μετοικίου ib.2.121. b. of things, untaxed, ἀ. τὸν σῖτον ἐξάγειν D.34.36; ὅσα οἱ νόμοι ἀ. πεποιήκασιν Id.42.18. 2. of sums, without deduction, nett, ὀβολὸς ἀ. an obol clear gain, X.Vect.4.14 sq.; τριάκοντα μνᾶς ἀτελεῖς ἐλάμβανε τοῦ ἐνιαυτοῦ D.27.9. 3. not costly, S.Fr.268, Amphis 29, Paus.Gr.Fr.305. IV. (τέλος V) uninitiated, c. gen., ἱερῶν h.Cer.481; ἀ. τῆς θέας Pl.Phdr.248b; prob. unmarried, Tab.Defix.Aud.68a: metaph., ἔρημον καὶ ἀ. φιλοσοφίαν λείπειν Pl.R.495c.

ἀτελώνητος, ον, untaxed, Zen.1.74, Hierocl.Facet.246, Just.Nov.106 Pr.

ἀτέμβιος· μεμψίμοιρος, EM163.32.

ἀτέμβω [ᾰ], only pres., maltreat, οὐ καλὸν ἀτέμβειν.. ξείνους Τηλεμάχου Od.20.294, 21.312; afflict, perplex, ἀτέμβει θυμὸν ἐνὶ στήθεσσιν Ἀχαιῶν 2.90:—Pass., c. gen., to be bereft or cheated of a thing, ἀτέμβονται νεότητος they have lost their youth, Il.23.445; ἀτεμβόμενός γε σιδήρου ib.834; μή τίς οἱ ἀτεμβόμενος κίοι ἴσης 11.705, cf. Od.9.42. II. Med. like Act., Q.S.5.147,173: c. dat., blame, be dissatisfied with, A.R.2.56, 3.99: c. inf., ἀτεμβόμενος τοῖον στόλον ἀμφιπένεσθαι Id.2.1199.

ἀτεν-ής, ές, stretched, strained, κισσός S.Ant.826 (lyr.); freq. of the eyes, staring, Arist.HA492a11; τὸ ἀ. τῆς ὄψεως καὶ ἄτεγκτον D.H.5.8; τὴν ὄψιν εἰς τὸ ἀ. ἀπερείδεσθαι intently, Luc.Icar.12. 2. intense, excessive, ὀργαί A.Ag.71 (lyr.); ὀδυρμοί Call.Fr.1.7P. 3. straight, direct, ἥκω δ' ἀτενὴς ἀπ' οἴκων straight from home, E.Fr.65. 4. of diseases, obstinate, ἰσχιάς prob. for ἀγεννής in Archig.ap.Aët.12.1. II. of men's minds and speech, intent, earnest, ἀτενεῖ.. νόῳ Hes.Th.661, Pi.N.7.88; ἁπλοῖ καὶ ἀ., of men, Pl.R.547e; ἀ. παρρησία E.Fr.737; ἀ. ψυχή Luc.Nigr.4. 2. unbending, stubborn, ἀ. ἀτεράμων τε Ar.V.730 (lyr.); ἀστένακτος καὶ ἀ. D.H.5.8: Comp., Phld. Lib.p.44O. III. Adv. ἀτενῶς, Ion. -έως Hp.Prorrh.1.24; ἀ. ἐμβλέπειν Agatharch.41; δυσπειθῶς καὶ ἀ. ἔχειν πρός τι to be obstinately averse to, Plu.Galb.25:—more freq. in neut., ἀτενὲς ἴκελοι exceeding like, Pi.P.2.77; ἀ. ἀπ' ἀοῦς from dawn onwards, Epich.124.1; καταμαθεῖν ἀ. Id.172.4; ἀ. τηρεῖν Diph.61; ἀ. βλέπειν Plb.18.53.9. —ίζω, look intently, gaze earnestly, τοῖς ὄμμασιν stare, Hp.Epid.7.10; εἴς τι Arist.Mete.343b12; πρός τι Id.Pr.959a24; of the eyes, ἀτενίζοντες αὐτῷ Ev.Luc.4.20, cf. Act.Ap.23.1, Placit.1.7; εἴς τι Plb.6.11.12, J.BJ5.12.3, S.E.P.1.75, etc.; εἴς τινα Act.Ap.6.15; εἰς τὸν θεόν Them. Or.4.51b; πρὸς τὸ ἐκείνου πρόσωπον Luc.Merc.Cond.11: abs., also of the eyes, Arist.Pr.957b18:—Pass., to be gazed upon, APl.4.204 (Praxit.). II. metaph. of the mind, ἀ. τὴν διάνοιαν πρός τι Arist. Ph.192a15; εἰς τὴν προαίρεσιν ἀτενίζοντα πράττειν Phld.Ir.p.96W.; to be obstinate, Lync.ap.Ath.7.313f. —ισις, εως, ἡ, straining of the eyesight, Paul.Aeg.6.21. —ισμός, ὁ, intent observation, Thphr. Vert.9. 2. fixed stare, τῶν ὀμμάτων, in apoplexy, Herod.Med.in Rh.Mus.58.80. —ιστός, ή, όν, that may be gazed at, Sch.Il.1.98.

ἄτερ [ᾰ], Ep., Ion., Trag. Prep. with gen., without, apart from, Hom.; κράτιστον Ἀχιλέος ἄ. Pi.N.7.27; ἄ. Ζηνός without his will, Il.15.292, cf. POxy.936.18 (iii A.D.); οὐ θεῶν ἄ. 'non sine dis', Pi.P.5.76; ἄ. μόχθου Democr.223; ἄ. πυρετοῦ καὶ ὀδύνης Hp.Prorrh.2.4. II. aloof, apart from, ἄ. ἥμενον ἄλλων Il.1.498; νόσφιν ἄ. τε κακῶν Hes.Op.91:—freq. in Trag., mostly after its case, A.Supp.377, etc.; but before it in Id.Pr.456, Supp.703 (lyr.), Ch.338 (lyr.), S.Ph.703 (lyr.), El.866:—also in late Prose, as Lxx 2Ma.12.15, D.H.3.10, Ev. Luc.22.6, Plu.Cat.Mi.5, Vett.Val.136.9, al. III. c. dat., ἄτερ ἄστρασιν Anub.87.

ἀτεραμν-ία [ᾰτ], Ion. -ίη, ἡ, harshness, hardness, ὑδάτων Hp.Aër.4. —ος, ον, unsoftened, hard, ὕδατα ib.1, Arist.GA767a34; πέτρα Theoc.10.7; ἀ. κοιλία costive, Hp.Aër.4; of food that will not cook, Plu.2.701c, Gal.17(2).157. II. metaph., stubborn, unfeeling, merciless, κῆρ Od.23.167; ὀργή A.Pr.192; βροντῆς μύκημ' ἀ. ib.1062. —ότης, ητος, ἡ, stubbornness; ἀ. πρὸς τὴν βλάστησιν slowness to germinate, Thphr.CP4.3.2. —ώδης, ες, not to be softened, ὕδατα Gal.17(2).187.

ἀτεράμων [ᾰτ] [ρᾰ], ον, gen. ονος, Att. for ἀτέραμνος, hard, tough, Μαραθωνομάχαι Ar.Ach.181, cf. Pl.Lg.853d, 880e, Eub.1 D.; hard to cook, Thphr.HP2.4.2, cf. 8.8.6, CP4.12.8.

ἀτεράτευτος [ρᾰ], ον, nowise prodigious or wonderful, Eust.918.5.

ἀτερέα· ὅρος, γοργόν (Cret.), Hsch. **ἀτέρεμνος**, ον, = ἀτέραμνος, Id. **ἀτερέψατο**· ἠθέτησεν, Id. **ἀτερήσιον**· ἀπρόμηθες, Id. (ἀρετή- cod.).

ἀτερηδόνιστος, ον, not worm-eaten, Dsc.1.16.

ἄτερθε [ᾰ], before a vowel -θεν, Aeol. ἄτερθα Hdn.Gr.2.192, = ἄτερ, Pi.O.9.78, etc.: c. gen., ἄ. πτερύγων A.Supp.783 (lyr.); λατρῶν ἄ. ib.1011; ἄ. τοῦδε S.Aj.645 (lyr.). II. as Adv., aloof, apart, Pi.P.5.96.

ἀτέριγε· χωρίς, Hsch.

ἀτερμ-άτιστος [μᾰ], ον, unbounded, ἐπιθυμία D.S.19.1, cf. Gal.19.472. II. = ἀβέβαιος, ἀθεμελίωτος, Hsch. —ων, ον, gen. ονος, without bound or end, αἰών Arist.Mu.401a16; ὕπνος Mosch.3.104; ἐνόπτρων ἀ. αὐγαί the mirror's countless rays, E.Hec.926; ἀ. πέπλος having no end or issue, inextricable, A.Eu.634.

ἀτεροῖον· τὸ ἑτέρωθεν καὶ χωρίς, Hsch.

ἀτερόπλευρος, ον, = ἑτερο–, SIG247 K^1.13 (Delph.).

ἀτερόπτιλλος, ον, Dor. = ἑτερόφθαλμος, IG4.951.34 and 72 (Epid.).

ἄτερος [ᾰ], Dor. etc. for ἕτερος, IG9(1).694.17 (Corc.); Aeol. ἄτερος Alc.41, al., etc.; τὸ ἄτερον, Megarian in Ar.Ach.813. 2. ἅτερος [ᾱ], Att. contr. for ὁ ἕτερος, Com.Adesp.14.23D., Pl.Lg.695b, etc.; also neut. θάτερον, gen. θατέρου, dat. θατέρῳ, θατέρᾳ, or with mark of crasis, θἀτέρου, etc.; but contr. forms when the Art. ends with a conson., are incorrect, as θάτερον τὸν τόπον Str.2.1.20, cf. Luc. DMort.26.1, Hist.Conscr.22: also nom. θάτερος Polem.Cyn.4; ὁ θάτερος Men.846; τὰ θάτερα Arist.Mu.397a2; ἅτερον for τὸν ἕτερον Luc. Pseudol.29. (sm-τερος; v. ἕτερος.)

ἀτέρπ-εια, Ion. -είη, -ίη, ἡ, = ἀτερψία, Democr.4,174, D.L.7.97. —ής, ές, unpleasing, joyless, λιμός Il.19.354; of the nether world, νέκυας καὶ ἀτερπέα χῶρον Od.11.94, etc.; πέτρης.. καὶ ἀτερπέϊ χώρῳ, of a rocky shore, 7.279; νούσων ἑσμός A.Supp.685 (lyr.), cf. Pr.31, Simon.37.6; λόγοι E.El.293; γῆρας Mosch.4.114; ἀτερπέστερον ἐς ἀκρόασιν less attractive to the ear, Th.1.22; ἦχοι ἀ., opp. ἐπιτερπεῖς, Phld.Po.994.23, cf. Mus.p.82K.; εἴ τις ὑπερβάλλοι τὸ μέτριον τὰ ἐπιτερπέστατα ἀτερπέστατα ἂν γίγνοιτο Democr.233, cf. Ph.1.396 (Sup.); of persons, ἀ. καὶ κακὸς ὀρχηστής Plu.Cor.25. Adv. -πῶς, οὐκ ἀ. ἱστορείσθω Gal.14.237; but ἀ. ζῆν without enjoyment, Plu.2.1100d. —νος, ον, = ἄγρυπνος, Stesich.78, Ibyc.52. —ος, ον, = ἀτερπής, Il.6.285 (dub. l.).

ἀτερψία, Ion. -ίη, ἡ, unpleasantness, Luc.Vit.Auct.14.

ἀτετόν· λευκόν, Hsch. **ἀτετῶς**· ἀφροντίστως, Id.

ἀτευκτ-έω, fail in gaining, τῆς πατρίου ἀγωγῆς Plu.2.235b; τῶν οἰκείων χρειῶν Phld.Ir.p.47W., cf. ib.p.9W., Herm.ap.Stob.1.49.44. II. Pass., to be unsuccessful, of an operation, Antyll.ap.Orib.45.25.6. —ος, ον, not gaining or obtaining, Max.Tyr.11.8, Hsch.

ἀτευξία, ἡ, not obtaining, privation, A.D.Synt.56.26, Dam. in AB 1345.

ἀτευχ-ής, ές, (τεῦχος) unequipped, unarmed, E.Andr.1119, AP9.320 (Leon.). —ητος, ον, = foreg., ib.543 (Phil.), Epic.Alex.Adesp.8.2.

ἄτεφρος, ον, epith. of δάφνη, PMag.Par.1.2582.

ἀτέχν-αστος, ον, artless, Them.Or.2.39d. —έω, to be ἄτεχνος, to be unskilful, Sch.Ar.Nu.296. —ής, ές, = ἄτεχνος, S.E.M.7.395, interpol. in Babr.75.4: Comp. -έστερος v.l. in Hp.Fract.16. —ία, ἡ, want of art or skill, Hp.Lex 4, Pl.Phd.90d, al., Arist.EN1140a21, Chrysipp.Stoic.2.269: pl., Simp. in Stoic.3.49. —ίτευτος [ῐ], ον, artless, simple, D.H.Lys.8:—hence Verb -ιτεύομαι, Hsch. s.v. ἐρρωπίζομεν. —ος, ον, without art, unskilful, Pl.Plt.274c; esp. ignorant of the rules or principles of art, opp. ἔντεχνος or τεχνίτης, unskilled, unprofessional, of persons, Id.Sph.219a, Gal.6.134, S.E.P.3.262; having no trade or profession, PFlor.4.14 (iv A.D.); unsystematic, διδασκαλία Anon.in SE67.31; of pursuits, ἄ. τριβή Pl.Phdr.260e, cf. 262c, Lg.938a; πίστεις ἄ. proofs not invented by the orator, Arist.Rh.1355b35, 1375a22; ἀποδείξεις Ph.1.355; αἰσχρὸν καὶ ἄ. not workmanlike, Hp.Fract.30; πῦρ uncreative, opp. τεχνικόν, Zeno Stoic.1.34; φαντασία ib.2.24.

ἀτέχνως, Adv. of ἄτεχνος, *without art, without rules of art, empirically*, X.*Mem*.3.11.7, Pl.*Grg*.501a. II. **ἀτεχνῶς** (with penult. short), Adv. of ἀτεχνής, *simply*, i.e. *really, absolutely*, freq. in Com., Pl., etc.; ἀ. ἥκω παρεσκευασμένος Ar.*Ach*.37, cf. *Nu*.408,1174, al.; καλὸν ἀ. *simply* beautiful, Id.*Av*.820; ἀ. γε παμπόνηρα Id.*Ra*.106; ῥύγχος ἀ. ἔσθ' ὑός *simply* a swine's snout, Pherecr.102; ἀ. μὲν οὖν σκύτη βλέπει Eup.282; ἀ. τὸ τοῦ Ὁμήρου ἐπεπόνθη Pl.*Smp*.198c; *bona fide, sincerely*, opp. κόμπου ἕνεκα, Philostr.*VA*6.20: freq. in comparisons, ἀ. ὥσπερ *just* like, Pl.*Phd*.90c, etc.; ἀ. οἷον Id.*Lg*.952e: with neg., οὐδ' ἂν διαλεχθείην γ' ἀ. would *just* not have spoken a word to him, Ar.*Nu*.425; ἀ. οὐδείς *simply* no one, Id.*Av*.605, cf. *Pl*. 362, Pl.*Plt*.288a.—On ἀτέχνως and -νῶς v. Sch.Ar.*Pl*.109.

ἀτέω [ᾰ], part. ἀτέων *demented, reckless*, c. gen., θεῶν *defying* the gods, Il.20.332 (Aristarch.); Μουσέων Call.*Fr*.537: abs., Hdt.7.223.

ἀτεώροχοι· ἄγαν αὐθάδεις, Hsch. (leg. ἀγέρωχοι).

ἄτη, ἡ, Dor. **ἄτα**, Aeol. **αὐάτα** (ἀϝ-), v. infr.:—*bewilderment, infatuation*, caused by *blindness* or *delusion* sent by the gods, mostly as the punishment of guilty rashness, τὸν δ' ἄτη φρένας εἷλε Il.16.805; Ζεῦ πάτερ, ἦ ῥά τιν' ἤδη.. βασιλήων τῇδ' ἄτῃ ἄασας 8.237; Ζεὺς καὶ Μοῖρα καὶ.. Ἐρινὺς.. φρεσὶν ἔμβαλον ἄγριον ἄτην 19.88 (so ἀλλ' ἐπεὶ ἀασάμην καί μευ φρένας ἐξέλετο Ζεύς ib.137); ἄτην δὲ μετέστενον ἣν Ἀφροδίτη δῶχ' ὅτε μ' ἤγαγε κεῖσε, says Helen, Od.4.261. 2. Ἄτη personified, *the goddess of mischief*, author of *rash actions*, πρέσβα Διὸς θυγάτηρ, Ἄτη, ἣ πάντας ἀᾶται Il.19.91, cf. 9.504, Hes. *Th*.230, Pl.*Smp*.195d; Ἄτης ἂν λειμῶνα Emp.121.4; coupled with Ἐρινύς, A.*Ag*.1433. II. of the consequences of such visitations, either, 1. Act., *reckless guilt* or *sin*, Ἀλεξάνδρου ἕνεκ' ἄτης Il.6.356: in pl., *deceptions*, 10.391: or, 2. Pass., *bane, ruin*, 24.480, Hdt.1.32; ἐγγύα, πάρα δ' ἄτα prov. in Thales ap.Stob.3.1.172: τὸ πῆμα τῆς ἄτης the anguish of the *doom*, S.*Aj*.363 (lyr.); ὕβρις γὰρ ἐξανθοῦσ' ἐκάρπωσε σταχὺν ἄτης A.*Pers*.822; Πειθὼ προβουλόπαις.. ἄτης Id.*Ag*.386 (lyr.): pl., Id.*Pers*.653 (lyr.), 1037 (lyr.), S.*Aj*.848, etc.; *strokes of fate*, ἀνδρείη τὰς ἄτας μικρὰς ἔρδει Democr.213. 3. Trag., of persons, *bane, pest*, δίκην ἄτης λαθραίου A.*Ag*.1230; δύ' ἄτα S.*Ant*.533. b. *ill-fated person*, A.*Ag*.1268 codd.—Not in Comedy (unless read for αὐτῆς, Ar.*Pax*605) nor in Att. Prose (exc. as pr. n. and in quotations of ἐγγύα, πάρα δ' ἄτα Cratin. Jun.12, Pl.*Chrm*.165a), but found in Arist.*VV*1251ᵇ20; κῆρας καὶ ἄτας D.H.8.61; τοιαύτας κακὰς ἄτας such *abominations*, of certain Epicurean expressions, Cleom.2.1. III. *fine, penalty*, or *sum lost* in a lawsuit, *Leg.Gort*.11.34, al. (From ἀάω, q.v.: orig. ἀϝάτη, Aeol. αὐάτα Alc.*Supp*.23.12, Pi.*P*.2.28, 3.24, *Lyr.Adesp*.123.) [ᾰ̄άτη, ᾱτη; ᾰτη is dub. in Archil.73.]

ἄτηκτος, ον, *not melted* or *to be melted* by fire, χιών Pl.*Phd*.106a; ἄ. πυρί Arist.*GA*762ᵃ31, cf. *Mete*.388ᵇ24. 2. *insoluble* in oil, Dsc. 5.160. II. metaph., *not to be softened* or *subdued*, νόμοις ἄτηκτοι Pl.*Lg*.853d.

ἀτημέλ-εια [ᾰτ], ἡ, *carelessness*, Plu.2.608f, Agath.5.13. **-έω**, *take no heed of, neglect*, pf. part. Pass. ἀτημελημένος f.l. in Procop. *Vand*.1.21 (for ἀπ-), cf. Sch.A.R.1.609. **-ής**, ές, *neglected*, κόμη Plu.*Ant*.18. II. of persons, *careless, neglectful*, χρημάτων E.*Fr*.184. Adv. -λῶς, ἔχειν τινός Plu.*Agis* 17; ἀτημελέως ἀλάλητο A.R.1.812 (v.l. -λέες). **-ητος**, ον, *unheeded, unnoticed*, X.*Cyr*.5.4.18, 8.1.14, and so prob. in A.*Ag*.891. Adv. -τως, ἔχειν to be *uncared for*, X.*Cyr*. 8.1.15. 2. *slovenly*, οὐκ ἀ. τοὺς κικίννους Alciphr.3.55; τὸ ἀ. τῶν τριχῶν Jul.*Mis*.365d. **-ία**, poet. -ίη, ἡ, = ἀτημέλεια, A.R.3.830.

ἀτηνεῖν· μοχθεῖν, Hsch. (leg. ἀστηνεῖν).

ἀτηρής [ᾱ], ές, = ἀτηρός, f.l. in Hp.*Aër*.24.

ἀτήρητος, ον, *unobserved, unnoticed*, Them.*Or*.23.294c.

ἀτηρία [ᾱ], ἡ, *mischief, evil*, Pl.Com.182, X.*Mem*.3.5.17 (v.l. ἀπειρία).

ἀτηρόγνωμος· *durus, Gloss*.

ἀτηρός [ᾱ], ά, όν, *blinded by* ἄτη, *hurried to ruin*, Thgn.433,634; φρήν S.*Fr*.264. II. *baneful, mischievous*, δύη A.*Pr*.746; τύχη Id. *Ag*.1483 (lyr.); κακόν E.*Andr*.353; ναυτιλίη *AP*9.23 (Antip.); τὸ ἀ. *bane, mischief*, A.*Eu*.1007 (anap.); μή τι ἀ. ποιέωσι [οἱ παῖδες] Democr. 279.—Once in Com., ἀτηρότατον κακόν an 'outrageous' nuisance, Ar.*V*.1299; and so Adv. -ῶς 'awfully' as a slang word, Phld.*Mus*. p.105 K.: in Pl.*Cra*.395b and c introduced only for an etym. purpose: also in later Prose, D.L.6.99.

Ἀτθίς, ίδος, ἡ, *Attic*, esp. (with or without γῆ) *Attica*, E.*IA*247 (lyr.) (unless -ίδας ναῦς be read); γῆς ἀπ' Ἀτθίδος Epin.1.6. 2. (sc. γλῶττα) *the Attic dialect*, Str.8.1.2. 3. (sc. ἱστορία) *history of Athens*, οἱ τὴν Ἀ. συγγράψαντες Id.9.1.6, cf. D.H.1.8, J.*Ap*.1.3. 4. *Athens*, written Ἀθθίς in *Pae.Delph*.8,14.

ἀτίετος [ῐ], ον, (τίω) *unhonoured*, A.*Eu*.385, 839 (both lyr.). II. Act., *not honouring* or *regarding*, φίλων E.*Ion* 701 (lyr.).

ἀτίζω [ᾰ], mostly in pres. part.; 2 and 3 sg., E.*Rh*.327, 253 (lyr.); inf., S.*OC*1153: fut. ἀτίσεις [ῐ] A.*Fr*.105: aor. subj. ἀτίσῃς [ῐ] Id. *Eu*.542 (lyr.); Ep. aor. ἄτισσα A.R.1.615:—Pass., Gal.18(2).642:—*not to honour, not to heed*, ὁ δὲ πρῶτον μὲν ἀτίζων ἔρχεται *unheeding*, Il. 20.166: c. acc., *slight, treat lightly*, θεοὺς ἀτίζων A.*Th*.441, cf. E.*Supp*. 19, Rhian.1.5: c. gen. rei, *deprive of honour* due, γεράων μιν ἄτισσαν A.R. l. c.—Never in early Prose; for Nic.*Al*.193 v. ἀτύζω.

ἀτῐθάσ-ευτος [θᾰ], ον, *untamable, wild*, Agatharch.74, Aesop.342, Plu.*Art*.25, 2.728a; κακία App.*BC*4.8; τοῦ νόμου τὸ λίαν ἀκριβὲς καὶ ἀ. Agath.4.21. **-ος**, ον, = foreg., dub. in Hdn.5.6.9; λύτται Ph. 1.20, al.

ἀτίθηνος [ῐ], ον, *without a nurse*, Man.4.368.

ἀτῑμᾰγελ-έω, (ἀγέλη) *forsake the herd, stray*, Arist.*HA*572ᵇ19, 611ᵃ 2, Theoc.9.5: metaph., *try to escape*, Luc.*Lex*.10. **-ης**, ου, Dor. **-ας**, α, ὁ, *despising the herd*, i.e. *straying, feeding alone*, S.*Fr*.1026, Theoc.25.132, *AP*6.255 (Eryc.).

ἀτῑμ-άζω, fut. -άσω A.*Eu*.917 (lyr.), Pl.*R*.465a, etc.: aor. ἠτίμασα S.*OC*49, Pl.*Euthd*.292e, etc.: pf. ἠτίμακα And.4.31, Pl.*Plt*. 266d:—Pass., pf. ἠτίμασμαι E.*Med*.20, Pl.*Smp*.219d, Ephor.*Fr*. 3.21 B.: aor. ἠτιμάσθην Pi.*Fr*.123.5, Pl.*Lg*.931b: fut. ἀτιμασθήσομαι A.*Ag*.1068, S.*OT*1081: (ἄτιμος):—*hold in no honour, esteem lightly*, c. acc., once in Il.9.450 ἀτιμάζεσκε δ' ἄκοιτιν; freq. in Od., τούσδε γ' ἀτιμάζει κατὰ δῆμον 6.283; οἶκον ἀτιμάζοντες ἔδουσιν 21.332, cf. 427; ἀ. τοκῆας Thgn.821: freq. in Trag., A.*Th*.1023, *Eu*.712, 917, al.; μή μ' ἀτιμάσας γένῃ Phryn.Trag.20 (= Id.Com.80), cf. D. 40.26, etc.; ἀ. καὶ κολάζειν, opp. ἐπαινεῖν καὶ τιμᾶν, X.*Cyr*.1.6.20; τὴν ἀνθρωπίνην ἀσθένειαν ἀ. Pl.*Phd*.107b, al.; *bring dishonour upon*, τὴν πόλιν And.4.31: c. acc. cogn., ἔπη ἃ ἀτιμάζεις πόλιν the words thou *speakest in dishonour of* the city, S.*OT*340:—Pass., *suffer dishonour, insult*, etc., πρός τινος Pi.*Fr*.123.5, Hdt.1.61; τινί S.*Aj*.1342; οὐκ ἀτιμασθήσομαι Id.*OT*1081, cf. D.21.74; τῷ γεγενημένῳ *put to shame by*.., Lys.2.27: c. neut. pl., ἀνάξι' ἠτιμασμένη E.*IA*943. 2. c. gen. rei, *treat as unworthy of*, μηδ' ἀτιμάσῃς λόγου (sc. ἐμέ) A.*Pr*. 783; μή μ' ἀτιμάσῃς ὧν σε προστρέπω φράσαι, = τούτων ἅ σε πρ. φρ., S.*OC*49, cf. *Ant*.22. 3. c. inf., ὦ θάνατε Παιάν, μή μ' ἀτιμάσῃς μολεῖν *do* not *deem* me *unworthy* of thy visit, A.*Fr*.255.1; μήτοι μ' ἀτιμάσῃς τὸ μὴ οὐ θανεῖν σὺν σοί *deem* me not *unworthy* to die, S.*Ant*. 544; but also οὐκ ἀτιμάσω θεοὺς προσειπεῖν *will* not *disdain* to.., E. *HF*608, cf. Pl.*La*.182c. II. in legal sense, *disfranchise*, ὑπὸ τῆς πόλεως ἠτιμασμένος Ephor. l. c.; at Rome, of the Censors, *punish with ignominia*, D.C.38.13. **-αλφέω**, *fail to fetch a price*, Hsch. **-ασμός**, ὁ, *dishonour*, Lxx *1Ma*.1.40 (v.l.), Aristeas 269. **-αστέος**, α, ον, *to be despised*, Hp.*Fract*.31, Pl.*Phdr*.266d, Jul.*Or*.6.198d. 2. ἀτιμαστέον *one must dishonour*, X.*Smp*.4.17, *Hippiatr.Praef*. **-αστήρ**, ῆρος, ὁ, *dishonourer*, A.*Th*.637. **-αστής**, οῦ, ὁ, = foreg., *Gloss*. **-αστός**, όν, *dishonoured*, γυναιξίν Mimn. 1.9. **-άω**, Ep. impf. ἀτίμων: fut. ἀτιμήσω: aor. ἠτίμησα: pf. ἠτίμηκα Gal.1.10:—Pass., aor. -ήθην Id.5.44:—used by Hom. for ἀτιμάζω, *dishonour, disdain*, σὲ δ' ἀτιμᾷ Od.16.307; ὃν τότ' ἀτίμα 21.99; τὸν πάντες ἀτίμων 23.28; τὸν Χρύσην ἠτίμασεν Il.1.11, cf. 94, al.; νῦν δέ σ' ἀτιμήσουσι 8.163, cf. Hes.*Op*.185; used once by Pi. in Dor. aor. ἠτίμᾱσα, *P*.9.80; once by S. in imper. ἀτίμα, *Aj*. 1129; ἀτιμῶσι v.l. for -οῦσι in X.*Ath*.1.14; also in later Ep., Call. *Dian*.260, Mosch.4.6, Nonn.*D*.17.313, al.; and in later Prose, Gal. l. c. **-ητεί**, Adv. *without a valuation*, *OGI*218.69 (Ilium, iii B.C.). **-ητέον**, *one must hold in disesteem*, συκοφάντας Isoc.15. 175. **-ητος**, ον, *unhonoured, despised*, ὡς εἴ τιν' ἀτίμητον μετανάστην Il.9.648; οὐκ ἀ. not *unrewarded*, X.*Hier*.9.10. II. (τιμή II) *not valued* or *estimated*, Is.3.35: esp. δίκη ἀ. a cause *in which the penalty is not assessed in court*, but fixed by law beforehand, D.21.90, Aeschin.3.210; opp. τιμητός (where the penalty is settled in court), D.27.67, cf. Poll.8.54,63, Harp. s.v.; Suid. erroneously reverses this explanation. 2. *invaluable, priceless*, Lxx *Wi*.7.9, Eust.781. 19. 3. *not assessed*, *IG*5(1).1433.45 (Messene); *not capable of being valued*, ἄγαλμα *Epigr.Gr*.805. **-ία**, Ion. -ίη, ἡ, *dishonour, disgrace*, ἀτιμίῃσιν ἰάλλειν Od.13.142, Pi.*O*.4.21, S.*El*.1035, etc.; ἐν ἀτιμίῃ τινὰ ἔχειν Hdt.3.3; ἀτιμίην προστιθέναι τινί Id.7.11; ὄνειδος καὶ ἀ. ἔχειν ib.231; ἀτιμίης κυρεῖν πρός τινος ib.158; θεῶν ἀ. *dishonour done to* the gods, E.*Heracl*.72, Pl.*Hipparch*.229c; οὐκ ἀτιμίᾳ σέθεν A.*Eu*.796: pl., ταῖς μεγίσταις κολάζειν ἀ. Pl.*Plt*.309a, cf. 310e, *R*. 492d, al.; ὕβρεις καὶ ἀτιμίας D.18.205, 21.23; *indignities*, Arist.*Pol*. 1336ᵇ11. 2. *deprivation of privileges*, A.*Eu*.394 (lyr.); esp. *of civic rights*, And.1.74, X.*Lac*.9.6, D.9.44; coupled with θάνατος and φυγή, *IG*1.27a74. II. of things, ἐσθημάτων ἀ., i.e. *sorry* garb, A.*Pers*.847; κόμη.. ἀτιμίας πλέως Cratin.9. [Ep. ἀτιμίη Hom. l.c., Tyrt.10.10.]

ἀτῑμο-πενθής, ές, *sorrowing for dishonour*, A.*Eu*.792 (lyr.).

ἄτῑμ-ος, ον, (τιμή I) *unhonoured, dishonoured*, Il.1.171; μετὰ πᾶσιν ἀτιμοτάτη θεός εἰμι ib.516; ἀτιμότερον δέ με θήσεις 16.90; ἀτιμότεροι, opp. λαχόντες τιμῆς, Thgn.1111; ἄ. μόρος *dishonourable*, A.*Th*.589; ἄτιμα δ' οὐκ ἐπραξάτην, i.e. they have met their deserts, Id.*Ag*.1443; ἄτιμος Ἀργείοισι *by* them, S.*Aj*.440; ἔκ γ' ἐμοῦ *by* me, Id.*OC*51. b. c. gen., ἄ. δωμάτων *without the honour of*.., *not deemed worthy of*.., A.*Ch*.409 (lyr.); πάντων ib.295; ἐκφορᾶς Id.*Th*.1029; χάρις οὐκ ἄ. πόνων no *unworthy* return for.., Id.*Ag*.354; ὧν μὲν ἱκόμην ἄτιμον ἐξέπεμψεν S.*OT*789. 2. *deprived of civic rights* (cf. ἀτιμία), ἄτιμα τὰ τέκνα γίνεται Hdt.1.173, cf. *IG*1.37, 9(1).334 (Locr.), etc.; opp. ἐπίτιμος, Ar.*Av*.766, *Ra*.692, And.1.80; ἄ. τὰ σώματα ib.74: c. gen., ib.75; ἄ. γερῶν *deprived of* privileges, Th.3.58; ἄ. τοῦ τεθνηκότος *debarred from all rights in* him, S.*El*.1214; ἄ. τοῦ συμβουλεύειν *deprived of the right of* advising, D.15.33; ἄ. τῆς πόλεως καθιστάναι τινά Lys.12.21; ἄ. εἶναι καθάπαξ D.21.32, Arist.*Ath*.22.8. 3. of things, *not honourable*, Hdt.5.6 (Sup.); ἄτιμον ποιεῖσθαί τι hold *in dishonour*, S.*Ant*. 78; ἄτιμα ποιεῖν ἔς τινα Hdt.2.141; ἄ. τοὔργον Ar.*Av*.166; ἕδρα ἀτιμοτέρα *less honourable*, X.*Cyr*.8.4.5; of parts of the body, τὸ τιμιώτερον καὶ τὸ ἀτιμότερον Arist.*PA*672ᵇ21; ἀ. σκεῦος D.S.17.66. II. (τιμή II) *without price* or value, τοῦ νῦν οἶκον ἄτιμον ἔδεις thou devourest his substance *without payment*, Od.16.431; *of little price, cheap*, opp. τίμιος, X.*Vect*.4.10. 2. *unavenged*, ἐκ θεῶν A.*Ag*.1279, cf. E.*Hipp*.1417. 3. *unpunished*, Pl.*Lg*.855c. III. Adv. -μως *dishonourably, ignominiously*, A.*Pr*.197,919, *Th*.1026, S.*OC*428, v.l. in Lys.32.17, etc.: Comp. -ότερον Pl.*Ep*.309b, D.S.1.67: Sup.

ἀτιμότατα Pl.*Lg.*728b. **-όω,** fut. -ώσω: aor. ἠτίμωσα A.*Supp.* 644 (lyr.), etc.: pf. ἠτίμωκα D.21.103:—**Pass.,** pf. ἠτίμωμαι E.*Hel.* 455, D.21.91: plpf. ἠτίμωτο Hdt.7.231, *IG*1.61*a*10: aor. -ώθην A. *Ch.*636 (lyr.), And.1.33, etc.: fut. ἀτιμωθήσομαι Isoc.5.64; ἠτιμώσομαι D.19.284:—*dishonour*, A.*Supp.*644:—Pass., *suffer dishonour* or *indignity*, Hdt.4.66, 7.231, A.*Ch.*636, E.*Hel.*455. **II.** *punish with* ἀτιμία 2, Ar.*Pax* 742, And.1.33, D.18.82, Arist.*Ath.*53.6 (Pass.); ἀτιμωθῆναι ἐπὶ αἰτίᾳ Lys.6.25; ἐκπεσόντα ἢ ἀτιμωθέντα Pl.*R.*553b.

ἀτῑμωρ-ητεί or **-τί,** Adv. of sq., *EM*664.37. **-ητος,** ον, *unavenged*, i.e., **I.** *unpunished*, ἀ. γίγνεσθαι to *escape punishment*, Hdt.2.100, Th.6.6, etc.; ἀ. ἁμαρτημάτων *unpunished for..*, Pl.*Lg.* 959c. Adv. -τως *with impunity*, ib.762d. **II.** *for whom no revenge has been taken*, Antipho 3.3.7; ἀτιμώρητον ἐὰν θάνατον Aeschin. 1.145. **III.** *undefended, unprotected*, Th.3.57.

ἀτίμωσις [τῐ], εως, ἡ, *dishonouring*, c. gen., τραπέζας A.*Ag.*702 (lyr.); πατρός Id.*Ch.*435 (lyr.). **II.** = *capitis deminutio*, J.*AJ*19.1.1.

ἀτίνακτος [ῐ], ον, *unshaken, immovable*, Opp.*H.*2.8, Nonn.*D.*10. 166, al.

ἀτῑσανδρέω· ἀτιμάζω ἄνδρα, Hsch.

ἀτῐτάλλω, aor. 1 ἀτίτηλα Il.24.60, *IG*14.2005:—**Med.,** aor. 1 ἀτιτήλατο Opp.*C.*1.271: (ἀταλός):—redupl. form of ἀτάλλω, *rear, tend*, θρέψα τε καὶ ἀτίτηλα Il. l. c.; παῖδα δὲ ὡς ἀτίταλλε Od.18.323; οἵ μ' ἐν σφοῖσι δόμοισιν ἐῢ τρέφον ἠδ' ἀτίταλλον Il.14.202, cf. 16.191, Hes.*Th.* 480, Pi.*N.*3.58; also of animals, τοὺς μὲν [ἵππους]..ἀτίταλλ' ἐπὶ φάτνῃ Il.5.271:—Pass., χῆν' ἥρπαξ' ἀτιταλλομένην ἐνὶ οἴκῳ Od.15.174. **2.** metaph., *cherish*, καί σε Κόως ἀτίταλλε Theoc.17.58: c. dat., καλοῖς Id.15.111; in bad sense, *beguile, cajole*, σκιράφοις ἀ. Hippon.86.—Poet. and late Prose, as Them.*Or.*20.234b.

ἀτῐτάλτας, α, ὁ, *foster-father*, *GDI*4978 (Gortyn).

ἀτίταν· ὁ μὴ ἔχων ἀποτῖσαι, Hsch. s. v. Τιτᾶνες.

ἀτῑτέω, = ἀτίω, D.P.1158: but **ἀτιτεῖν·** ἀδικεῖν, and **ἀτίται·** ἄδικοι, Hsch.

ἀτίτης [ῐ], ου, ὁ, (τίνω) *unpunished*, A.*Eu.*257 (lyr.). **II.** *unable to pay*, Hsch. **III.** (τίω) *unhonoured*, ἀτίται σαρκὶ παλαιᾷ A. *Ag.*72 (anap.). **IV.** v. foreg.

ἀτίτηστον· ἀπρόμηθες, Hsch.

ἄτῑτος, ον, (τίνω) *unavenged*, Il.13.414. **2.** *unpaid*, ποινή ib.14. 484 [where ῑ]. **3.** *not liable to penalty*, *IG*4.498 (Mycenae). **II.** (τίω) *unhonoured*, Menecr.Xanth.4.

ἀτίω [ῐ], = ἀτίζω, ἀτίει Thgn.621; ἀτίουσι Orph.*L.*62.

Ἀτλᾱγενής, ές, (γένος) *sprung from Atlas*, of the Pleiads, Hes.*Op.* 383.

Ἀτλαντικός, ή, όν, *of Atlas*, τέρμονες Ἀ. the pillars of Hercules, E.*Hipp.*3, 1053; τὸ Ἀ. πέλαγος Pl.*Ti.*24e, Arist.*Pr.*946a29; ἡ Ἀ. θάλασσα Id.*Mu.*392b22:—also **Ἀτλάντειος,** α, ον, Critias 18.5 D.:—fem. **Ἀτλαντίς,** ίδος, as Patron., Hes.*Th.*938; title of work by Hellanicus (also **Ἀτλαντιάς,** Harp. s. v. Ὁμηρίδαι); θάλασσα ἡ Ἀ. καλουμένη Hdt.1.202; ἡ Ἀ. νῆσος, a fabulous island in the far West, Pl.*Ti.*25a, Str.2.3.6.

Ἄτλας, αντος, ὁ, acc. also Ἄτλαν A.*Pr.*428 (lyr.), cf. Sch.: (ἀ- euph., and τλάς, v. *τλάω):—*Atlas*, Od.1.52: later, one of the Titans, Hes. *Th.*517, A.*Pr.*350, 428 (lyr.); αἱ δ' ἑπτ' Ἄτλαντος παῖδες Id.*Fr.*312. **II.** in hist. writers, *Mount Atlas* in West Africa, regarded as *the pillar of heaven*, Hdt.4.184, Str.17.3.2, etc.: pl., D.P.66. **2.** *the Atlantic Ocean*, Id.30. **3.** *axis* of the earth, Hsch. **III.** Ἄτλαντες, in Architecture, *colossal statues* as supports for the entablature (cf. τελαμῶνες), Moschio ap.Ath.5.208b, Vitr.6.7.6; κείονας Ἄτλαντάς τε *Epigr.Gr.*1072.7. **IV.** *seventh of the neck-vertebrae*, which supports the head, Poll.2.132. **V.** Pythag. name for *ten*, *Theol.Ar.*59. [ᾰτλ A.*Fr.* l. c.]

ἄτλας, αντος, ὁ, *not enduring* or *daring*, Hsch.; cf. ἀταής.

ἀτλησία· ἀμηχανία, ἀνυποστασία, Hsch.

ἀτλησίφρων [ῐ]· οὐδεμιᾶς τόλμης ἔννοιαν ἔχων, Hsch. (ἀτμ- cod.).

ἀτλητέω (Dor. **ἀτλᾱτέω,** Hsch.), *to be impatient, not to endure* or *submit to* a thing, S.*OT*515.

ἄτλητος, Dor. **ἄτλᾱτος,** ον, *not to be borne, insufferable*, πένθος, ἄχος, Il.9.3, 19.367, cf. Orac.ap.Hdt.5.56, Pi.*O.*6.38; ἀγγελία S.*Aj.* 223 (lyr.). **2.** *not to be dared*, ἄτλητα τλᾶσα A.*Ag.*408 (lyr.). **II.** Act., *incapable of bearing, impatient of*, c. gen., μόθων ἄ. *AP*9.321 (Antim.?). Adv. -τως, φέρειν Ael.*NA*16.28.

ἄτματα· καθάρματα, Hsch.

ἀτμενία, ἡ, (ἀτμήν) *slavery*, Man.6.59, *AP*9.764 (Paul. Sil.).

ἀτμένιος, ον, *toilsome, prepared with trouble*, Nic.*Al.*178, 426.

ἄτμενος, ὁ, = ἀτμήν, Archil.ap.Sch.Il.*Oxy.*1087, Call.*Fr.*538, Hsch., Eust.1750.62:—as Adj., ἄτμενον οἶτον Hsch.

ἀτμεύω, for ἀτμενεύω, *to be a slave*, Nic.*Al.*172.

ἀτμή, ἡ, = ἀτμός, ἀτμίς, Hes.*Th.*862.

ἀτμήν, ένος, ὁ, *slave, servant*, Call.*Aet.*1.1.19, Epic. in *Arch.Pap.* 7.4, *Et.Gen.*, Sch.Nic.*Al.*172, 426.

ἀτμησίφρων, v. ἀτλησίφρων.

ἄτμητος, ον, *not carved*, *IG*1.322; λίθοι Ph.2.253; *uncut*, ἔθειραι A.R.2.708; *unwounded*, S.*Fr.*124; *not laid waste, unravaged*, γῆ Th.1.82: and so metaph., ὑγίεια Gal.6.18; ἄμπελοι *unpruned*, Plu. *Num.*14; *unreaped*, Ph.2.390; λίβανος ἄ. *in lumps*, *PMag.Par.*1. 1991; ἀργυρεῖα ἄ. silver-mines *as yet unopened*, X.*Vect.*4.27; of animals, *entire*, Arist.*HA*632a9. **II.** *indivisible*, Pl.*Phdr.*277b, Arist.*EE* 1230a29, Ph.1.505, al., Iamb.*Comm.Math.*4. Adv. -τως Hero *Geom.* p.85 H. **III.** *that cannot be cut*, Arist.*Mete.*387a6, *Metaph.*1023a2.

ἀτμιάω, (ἀτμή) *steam, emit vapour*, Hp.*Morb.*4.49.

ἀτμῐδ-όομαι, Pass., *to be turned into vapour*, Arist.*Mete.*346b 25. **-οῦχος,** ον, (ἔχω) *containing vapour, damp*, Hsch. **-ώδης,** ες, *vaporous*, ἀναθυμίασις Arist.*Mete.*341b8 (Comp.), 360a9; ὁ βορέας ib.358a35; ἀήρ Id.*GA*786a12. **II.** *full of vapour*, γῆ Clidem.ap. Thphr.*CP*3.23.2.

ἀτμ-ίζω, pf. ἤτμικα Arist.*Pr.*930b36:—*smoke*, βωμὸς ἀτμίζων πυρί S.*Fr.*370; of water, *steam*, X.*An.*4.5.15: generally, *emit vapour*, of hot meat, ἥδιστον ἀ. Pherecr.108.15 codd. Ath. (ἀπατμ- edd.); of perspiration, interpol. post Hp.*Prog.*6; of fresh-burnt tiles, Arist.*Mete.* 383a24, cf. 388b32. **II.** *to be vaporized*, ib.349b23, 358b16, al. **-ίς,** ίδος (-ῖτος *PMag.Lond.*1.121.639), ἡ, = ἀτμός, Hdt.4.75, Pl.*Ti.*87a, Nicostr.15.5: properly, *moist vapour, steam*, opp. καπνός (but ἀτμὶς καπνοῦ Lxx *Jl.*2.30(3.3)), Arist.*Mete.*359b30, cf. 346b32, Ph.2.223, etc.; ἡ ἀ. συνίσταται εἰς ὕδωρ Arist.*Mete.*384a6. **II.** *sublimate* or *deposit* of colouring matter, *PHolm.*4.21. **III.** *poultice*, Crito ap. Gal.13.879. **IV.** = σπινθήρ, ἀπαύγασμα, Hsch. **-ιστός,** ή, όν, *capable of being turned into vapour*, Arist.*Mete.*387b8, dub. in Alex. Trall.*Febr.*5.

ἀτμοειδής, ές, = ἀτμιδώδης, S.E.*M.*7.119, Alex.Aphr.*Pr.*2.67. Adv. -δῶς Anon.Lond.22.19, Gal.*Nat.Fac.*1.16.

ἀτμός, ὁ, *steam, vapour*, A.*Eu.*138; ὅταν ἐκ γῆς ἀ. ἀνίῃ..ὑπὸ τοῦ ἡλίου Arist.*Pr.*862a4; Ἄραψ ἀ., of incense, *Pae.Delph.*11: in pl., *vapours*, A.*Fr.*205; *clouds* of steam, Jul.*Mis.*341d; esp. of *odours*, A.*Ag.*1311, Arist.*Pr.*908a21, Ph.1.96, al., Lib.*Or.*12.79 (pl.), etc.; distd. from ἀτμίς, as dry from moist, by Olymp. *in Mete.*165.25. [ᾱτμ A.*Fr.*205.]

ἀτμώδης, ες, = ἀτμιδώδης, Arist.*Mu.*394a14, Thphr.*CP*3.16.4. Adv. -δῶς Gal.*Nat.Fac.*3.7.

ἄτοιχος, ον, *unwalled*, E.*Ion*1133, D.C.74.4.

ἀτοκ-εῖον, τό, = *contraceptive*, *SIG*985.20 (Philadelphia, i B. C.). **-έω,** *not to bring forth, to be barren*, Ph.1.478. **-ί,** Adv. of ἄτοκος, D.C.58.21, *PTeb.*342.30 (ii A. D.), *BGU*725.23 (vii A. D.). **-ία,** ἡ, *unfruitfulness, barrenness*, Muson.*Fr.*15 A p.77 H. **-ιος,** ον, *causing barrenness*, Dsc.1.81; ἀτόκιον (sc. φάρμακον), τό, a *medicine for causing it*, Hp.*Mul.*1.76, Dsc.1.77. **II.** = λυχνὶς ἀγρία, Ps.-Dsc. 3.101. **-ος,** ον, *having never yet brought forth*, Hdt.5.41, E.*El.* 1127; ἄ. ὑπὸ νούσου *barren..*, Hp.*Aër.*3; δι' ἡλικίαν Pl.*Tht.*149c; of mules, Arist.*APr.*67a35. **II.** *not bearing interest*, χρήματα Pl.*Lg.* 921c, cf. D.53.12, *SIG*330.7 (Ilium), etc.: neut. pl. as Adv., *PAmh.* 2.50.10 (ii B. C.), al. **2.** *not paying interest*, Arist.*Oec.*1350a11.

ἀτολμ-έω, *to be* ἄτολμος, *be disheartened*, Hp.*Epid.*6.7.3: c. inf., *lack courage to..*, περαιτέρω προχωρῆσαι D.C.78.34:—also **-όω,** *AB* 407 (**ἀτολμάω,** Suid., is incorrect). **-ηρος,** ον, = ἄτολμος, Gal. 14.603 (Comp.). **-ητος,** Dor. **-ᾱτος,** ον, = ἄτλητος, *not to be endured, insufferable*, μόχθος Pi.*I.*8(7).11; of men, dub. in A.*Ag.* 375. **2.** *not to be dared*, οὐδὲν [τοῖς ποιηταῖς] ἀ. Aristid.*Or.*45(8). 2, cf. Gal.8.260; τῷ πλουσίῳ οὐδὲν ἀ. Him.*Ecl.*4.24. **-ία,** ἡ, *want of daring, cowardice*, E.*Fr.*364 (v.l. ἀνανδρία), Th.2.89, X.*HG*5.3.22, etc. **2.** *bashfulness*, D.61.20. **-ος,** ον, *daring nothing, cowardly*, Pi.*N.*11.32, Th.2.39 (Comp.), etc.; λῆμα..οὐκ ἄ. ἀλλ' ἕτοιμον Ar.*Nu.* 458; ἄ. καὶ μαλακός D.8.68, etc.; of women, ἄ. αἰχμά A.*Ch.*630 (lyr.); of things, ἄ. ἐπινόημα Jul.*Or.*2.75d: c. inf., ἄ. εἰμι..δῆσαι I have *not the heart* to bind, A.*Pr.*14. Adv. -μως Plb.3.103.3, Plu.2.47c: Comp. -ότερον *less boldly*, Gal.6.37.

ἄτομος, ον, *uncut, unmown*, λειμών S.*Tr.*200; ἄ. πώγωνος βάθη Ephipp.14.7; ἄ. λίβανος *in lumps*, Dsc.1.68.1; ἄτομον, τό, = ὑοσκύαμος, dub. in Ps.-Dsc.4.68 (cf. ἀταῖος). **2.** Gramm., of words, *not compound*, D.H.*Th.*22. **II.** *that cannot be cut, indivisible*, γραμμαί Arist.*Ph.*206a17, cf. *LI*968a1; μεγέθη Id.*Ph.*187a3; esp. of particles of matter, ἐτεῇ ἄτομα (sc. σώματα) καὶ κενόν Democr.9, 125, cf. Arist.*deAn.*404a2, *Metaph.*1039a10; in full, ἄ. σώματα Id. *Cael.*303a21, Epicur.*Nat.*14 *Fr.*5: sg., ἄτομόν ἐστι σῶμα στερεόν.. Id.p.129.24 U.; also ἀ. φύσεις Democr.ap.Diog.Oen.5, Epicur.*Ep.*1 p.7 U.; ἄτομοι, αἱ, ib.p.14 U., al., Phld.*Sign.*5, al., Alciphr.1.34. **2.** of Time, οὐχ οἷόν τε εἰς ἀ. χρόνους διαιρεῖσθαι τὸν χρόνον Arist.*Ph.*263b 27; κατ' ἄ. χρόνον Id.*Sens.*447b18; ἐν ἀτόμῳ in a *moment*, Id.*Ph.* 236a6, 1*Ep.Cor.*15.52; ἐν ἀ. ὀργῆς Sm.*Is.*54.8. **b.** metaph., *infinitely small*, διαφοραί Plu.*Phoc.*3. **III.** in Logic, *individual*, of terms, Pl.*Sph.*229d; of the εἶδος, Arist.*Metaph.*1034a8, *deAn.*414b 27. **2.** *individual*, Id.*APo.*96b11, al.: Subst. ἄτομον, τό, Id.*Cat.* 1b6, 3a38, *Metaph.*1058a18 (pl.), Plot.6.2.2, al. **3.** of the *summum genus*, πρὶν εἰς τὰ ἄ. ἐλθεῖν Arist.*Metaph.*994b21. Adv. ἀτόμως, ὑπάρχειν *immediately, without the intervention of a middle term*, Id. *APo.*79a33.

ἀτομόω, *leave undivided*, τὸν λόγον Olymp. *in Alc.*p.181 C.:—Pass., *to be individualized*, Simp. *in Ph.*255.28; *to be unified*, Id. *in deAn.* 217.36.

ἀτον-έω, *to be relaxed, exhausted*, Arist.*Pr.*945a17, Plu.*Cor.*25; ὁδοιπορίαις *Epigr.Gr.*613.4; στόμαχος ἀτονῶν Dsc.1.109: c. inf., *to be too weak to..*, D.L.4.14. **-ία,** ἡ, *slackness, enervation, debility*, Hp.*Aër.*20; *laziness*, Epicur.*Nat.*54 G.; ψυχῆς Plu.2.535d; ἀσθένεια καὶ ἀ. Luc.*Nigr.*36; ἰνῶν ἀ. καὶ τρόμος Phld.*Acad.Ind.*p.76 M.; as Stoic term, *lack of* τόνος (q. v.), Chrysipp.*Stoic.*3.120, 123, Arr.*Epict.* 2.15.4, etc.; in oratory, *lack of vigour* in delivery, Hermog.*Inv.*4. 3. **-ος,** ον, *not stretched, slack, relaxed*, of the limbs, Hp.*Aër.*3 (Comp.), 19; *lacking in elasticity*, of strands in torsion-engine, Ph. *Bel.*58.18; πνοαί D.S.1.41; σφυγμοί Aret.*SD*2.9; of fruit, *insipid*, Dsc. 1.112 (Comp.), al.; τὸ ἄ. τῆς γεύσεως v.l. ib.127; φωνεῖν ἄτονον Arist.*Phgn.*813b3: Medic., of the stomach, Ath.3.79f (Comp.), etc.:

c. inf., *too weak to*.., D.L.7.35; of oratorical style, D.H.*Dem.*20, cf. Hermog.*Id.*2.11 (Comp.), Eun.*VS* p.493B. (Comp.). Adv. -νως Plu. *Lyc.*18: Comp. -ώτερον J.*BJ*4.1.5; -ωτέρως Archig.ap.Orib.8.2.26. 2. as Stoic term, *lacking* τόνος (q. v.), σπέρμα Sphaer.*Stoic.*1.141; opp. εὔτονος, Chrysipp. ib.2.155, 3.121. **-όω,** *weaken*, Aq.*Ps.*68(69).24. **-ώδης,** ες, ἠτρία dub. in *AP*9.350 (Leon.).

ἀτόξ-ευτος, ον, *out of bow-shot*, πέτρα Plu.2.326e. **-ος,** ον, *without bow or arrow*, Luc.*DDeor.*19.1.

ἀτόπ-αστος, ον, *not to be guessed*, A.*Fr.*119. **-ημα,** ατος, τό, *absurdity*, S.E.*M.*1.80. 2. *strange sight* or *occurrence*, *POxy.*1557.6 (iii A. D.), al. 3. *offence*, *PTeb.*303.11 (ii A. D.), Procop.*Pers.*1.24. **-ηματοποιός,** ὁ, *one who commits absurdities* or *offences*, *Gloss.* **-ία,** ἡ, *being out of the way*, hence, 1. *absurdity*, Ar.*Ra.*1372; of persons, Id.*Ach.*349; *singularity*, Pl.*Smp.*215a; of sounds or words, *uncouthness*, D.H.*Comp.*12. 2. *extraordinary nature*, νοσήματος Th.2.51; τῶν τιμωριῶν Id.3.82; τοῦ πάθους Pl.*Phdr.*251d. 3. *logical absurdity*, S.E.*P.*3.240. 4. *wickedness, misdeed*, Lxx *Ju.*11.11: pl., Phld.*Vit.*p.34 J. **-ος,** ον, *out of place, out of the way*: hence, 1. *unwonted, extraordinary*, of symptoms, Hp.*Aph.*4.52: Comp., ibid.; ἄ. ἀδονά E.*IT*842 (lyr.), cf. Arist.*EN*1149^{a}15; ὄρνις Ar.*Av.*276; πόθος Id.*Ec.*956. 2. *strange, paradoxical*, δοῦλοι τῶν αἰεὶ ἀτόπων slaves to every new *paradox*, Th.3.38; ἄτοπόν τι πάσχειν And.4.34; τῶν -ωτάτων μέντἂν εἴη D.1.26; ἄτοπα τῆς σμικρολογίας *absurd* pettinesses, Pl.*Tht.*175a; ἄ. ἡδονῆς καὶ λύπης μεῖξις Id.*Phlb.*49a; ἄτοπόν ἐστι, c. inf., Pherecr.91, Eub.125; οὐδὲν ἄ. εἰ ἀποθάνοιμι Pl.*Grg.*521d, cf. Arist.*Cat.*11^{a}37, al., etc. b. of persons, Isoc.12.149; ἄ. παιδευτής Pl.*R.*493c; ἄ. καὶ δυσχερεῖς D.19.308; τὸν ἄτοπον φεύγειν ἀεί Men.203c; ἄ. φαγεῖν *given to strange* food, Philostr.*VA*3.55. 3. *unnatural, disgusting, foul*, πνεῦμα Th.2.49; *monstrous*, ἀτοπώτατον πρᾶγμα ἐξευρών Lys.3.7; later, *wicked, wrong*, Lxx *Jb.*27.6, *Ev.Luc.*23.41; of persons, opp. χρηστός, Phld.*Sign.*1; of things, *bad, harmful*, *Act.Ap.*28.6. Adv. -πως *in an unfavourable position*, κεῖσθαι, of planets, Vett.Val.63.12. 4. Adv. -πως *marvellously* or *absurdly*, Th.7.30, Pl.*Phd.*95b, al., Arist.*EN*1136^{a}12, etc.; ἀ. καθίζων, = ἀνυπόπτως, Eup.180. II. *non-spatial*, τῆς ἰδέας μενούσης ἐν ἀτόπῳ αὐτὸ τόπους γεννῆσαν Plot.6.5.8. Adv. -πως *non-spatially*, opp. τοπικῶς, Porph.*Sent.*33.

ἀτόρητος, ον, *not to be pierced, invulnerable*, Nonn.*D.*14.380.

ἀτόρνευτος, ον, *not turned in the lathe, not rounded*, *Gloss.*

ἀτόρῡ(νη)τος, ον, *not stirred with a ladle*, Orib.4.9.1.

ἆτος, ον, contr. for ἄατος.

ἀτρᾰγῳδ-ητος, ον, *not treated tragically*, Luc.*Merc.Cond.*19; τὸ ἀ. *absence of display* or *pomp*, Ph.2.76. **-ος,** ον, *untragical, unsuitable to tragedy*, ἀτραγῳδότατον τοῦτο.. Arist.*Po.*1452^{b}37, cf. Plu.2.519a. Adv. -δως *without noise* or *fuss*, M.Ant.1.16.3.

ἀτρακίς, ίδος, ἡ, name of a *spinous plant*, Gal.6.623.

ἀτράκτιον, τό, Dim. of ἄτρακτος, Epic. in *Arch.Pap.*7.9: pl. (written ἀτράκτεια), *POxy.*1740.2 (iii/iv A. D.).

ἀτρακτοειδής, ές, *spindle-shaped*, ῥαβδία Dsc.4.36.

ἄτρακτος, ὁ, and in Plu.2.271f, ἡ:—*spindle*, ἄτρακτον στρέφειν Hdt.5.12, cf. 4.34,162, Pl.*Plt.*281e, etc.; λίνου μεστὸν ἄ. Ar.*Ra.*1348 (lyr.); Ἀνάγκης ἄ. Pl.*R.*616c; τῶν Μοιρῶν Arist.*Mu.*401^{b}15, cf. *IG*12(7).447 (Amorgos). II. *arrow*, ἄ. τοξικός A.*Fr.*139; ἄ. alone, S.*Ph.*290, *Tr.*714. In this sense specially Lacon., Th.4.40. III. *upper part of a ship's mast*, Poll.1.91. IV. *spindle-shaped cautery*, Hp.*Int.*28, *Vid.Ac.*4. (Cf. ἀτρεκής, Lat. *torqueo*.)

ἀτρακτῦλίς or **ἀτρακτυλλίς,** ίδος, ἡ, *spindle-thistle*, used for making spindles, *Carthamus lanatus*, Arist.*HA*627^{a}8, Thphr.*HP*6.4.6, Theoc.4.52 (pl.), Dsc.3.93:—also **ἀτρακτύαλος** (leg. -τυλλος), Hsch.

ἀτρακτώδης, ες, *like a spindle*, Eust.1328.46.

ἀτρᾱνής, ές, Adv. -νῶς *not plainly*, Hsch. s.v. ἀσήμως.

ἀτράνωτος [ρᾱ], ον, *unexplained, not understood*, φόβος Diog.Oen.30.

ἀτράπεζος [ρᾰ], ον, (τράπεζα) *unsocial*, Man.4.563.

ἀτράπελος [ρᾰ], ον, = δυστράπελος, Sch.S.*Aj.*913, v.l. in Lxx *Jb.*39.9.

ἀτρᾰπ-ίζω, (ἀτραπός) *go through, traverse*, τὰς ἁρμονίας Pherecr.26. **-ῐτός,** ἡ, = sq., Od.13.195, A.R.4.123, etc.: metaph. of studies, Πλατώνειοι ἀ. *BCH*36.230 (Rhodes), cf. *AP*9.540:—also **ἀταρπῖτός** [ᾰτ], Od.17.234: **ἀτρᾰπητός,** *AB*460. **-ός,** Ep. **ἀταρπός,** as always in Hom., e. g. Il.17.743, ἡ:—*short cut*, or generally, *path*, Hom., Hdt.7.215, Ar.*Nu.*76, Th.4.36, etc.; ἀεὶ μίαν ἀ. πάντες βαδίζουσι [μύρμηκες] Arist.*HA*622^{b}25. 2. metaph., *walk of life*, ἡ πολιτικὴ ἀ. Pl.*Plt.*258c; μύθων Emp.24; ἱστορίης *IG*3.716; ἀ. μυρμηκος, v. μυρμηκιά.

ἀτραυμάτιστος, ον, *not caused by a wound*, πόνοι Luc.*Ocyp.*36, cf. Aët.7.9.

ἀτράφαξυς [ᾰτρᾰ], υος, ἡ, *orach*, *Atriplex rosea*, Hp.*Vict.*2.54, Thphr.*HP*7.1.2, al., Dsc.2.119, Gal.6.633. (The correct form is implied by the compound ψευδ-ατράφαξυς Ar.*Eq.*630, cf. *EM*565.17; other spellings are **ἀδράφαξυς** (ἀδρ- Eust.539.5) Thphr. l. c., **ἀνδράφαξυς** Dsc. l. c., Hp. l. c., **ἀτράφαξις** v.l. Dsc. l. c., Gal.11.843, cf. Hdn.Gr.1.539, 2.49, 467.)

ἀτρᾰφής, ές, (τρέφω) *wasting, atrophic*, Thphr.*CP*2.6.4.

ἀτράχηλος [ρᾰ], ον, *without neck*, of the crab, *AP*6.196 (Stat. Flacc.). II. *short-necked, bull-necked*, Teles p.55 H., Gal.5.383.

ἀτράχυντος [ρᾰ], Ion. **ἀτρήχ-,** ον, *without asperity*, Aret.*SD*2.12; ἔλαιον Id.*CA*1.10:—also **ἄτρᾱχυς,** υ, Eust.340.21.

ἀτρεής, ές, = ἄτρεστος: acc. ἀτρέα for ἀτρεέα, Euph.125; also, *not to be feared*, pl., ἀτρεῖς (for ἀτρεέες) ἀνάγκαι *IG*14.1389ii18.

Ἀτρείδης, ου, Ep. **Ἀτρεΐδης,** εω, Dor. **Ἀτρείδας,** α, *son of Atreus*, Hom., etc.

ἀτρέκ-εια, ἡ, Ion. -είη, also -ιη Man.3.229: (ἀτρεκής):—*precise truth, certainty*, Pi.*Fr.*213.4; τῶν ἡμεῖς ἀτρεκείην ἴδμεν Hdt.4.152, cf. 6.1; μαθεῖν..τὴν ἀ. ὅτι οὐκ αἱρέει learnt *for certain* that he is unable to take it, ib.82, cf. *IG*9(1).880 (Corc.): in pl., τὰς -ας τὰς λεγομένας Hp.*Prorrh.*2.3. II. Ἀτρέκεια personified, *Strict Justice*, Pi.*O.*10(11).13, E.*Fr.*91. **-έω,** *to be sure*, ἀτρεκήσασα ib.315. **-ής,** ές, *strict, precise, exact*, ἀλάθεια, καιρός, Pi.*N.*5.17, *P.*8.7; ἀριθμός Hdt.7.187; δίαιτα Hp.*Mochl.*42; βιότου ἀ. ἐπιτηδεύσεις *over-nice, precise*, E.*Hipp.*261; τὸ ἀ., = ἀτρέκεια, φράσαι, εἰπεῖν τὸ ἀ., Hdt.5.9, 7.60; τὸ -έστερον τούτων *more precise details*, Id.5.54; τὸ -έστατον Id.7.214; ἐγγὺς τοῦ -εστάτου ἥκειν Hp.*VM*12; rarely of persons, *exact, strict*, Ἑλλανοδίκας Pi.*O.*3.12. 2. *sure, certain*, ποδὶ ἀτρεκεῖ Id.*N.*3.41; ἀ. δόξα E.*Hipp.*1115 (lyr.). II. Hom. has only Adv. ἀτρεκέως (neut. as Adv., ἀτρεκὲς.. βαλών *accurately*, Il.5.208 (expld. as Adj. by Eust. ad loc.); δεκὰς ἀ. *precisely*, Od.16.245): mostly with the Verbs ἀγορεύειν, καταλέξαι, tell *truly, exactly*, Il.2.10, Od.1.169, etc.; ἀ. μαντεύσομαι 17.154; ἀ. ἔφρασεν *IG*3.716; ἀ. ὀλίγοι Thgn.636; freq. in Hdt., ἀ. εἰπεῖν 1.57, al.; εἰδέναι 1.209, al.; ἐπίστασθαι 3.130; ἐκμαθεῖν 7.10.η′; διακρῖναι 1.172; διασημῆναι 5.86; φαίνειν 2.49; ἀ. ἀριθμεῖσθαι Hp.*Prog.*20; ἀ. ὅμοιον *precisely* similar, Diog. Apoll.5. 2. ἀ. ἀποκαυλισθεῖσα broken *straight across*, opp. παραμηκέως, Hp.*Art.*14. 3. neut. as Adv. (cf. supr. II. 1), τὸ δ' ἀτρεκὲς ὄλβιος οὐδείς Thgn.167; ἐπ' ἀτρεκές *IG*9(1).880 (Corc.).—The word and its derivs. are rare in Trag. and not found in Att. Prose, ἀκριβής and its derivs. being used instead: freq. in Ion. Prose, esp. in Hp. and Aret., *SD*2.12, al., and in later Prose, cf. ἐπιστήμη καὶ γνώμη ἀ. Plb.1.4.9, ἀ. τριακάς Plu.*Rom.*12; ὁ σεν[ᾶ]τος ἀτρεκῶς γερουσίαν σημαίνει *strictly*, ib.13; οὐκ ἔφυγον δ' ἀτρεκῶς not *really*, *Epigr. Gr.*339.5; of persons, *truthful, accurate*, J.*BJ*3.8.9. (Cf. ἄτρακτος.)

ἀτρεκότης, ητος, ἡ, = ἀτρέκεια, Sch.E.*Hipp.*1114.

ἀτρέμ-ᾰ, (τρέμω) = ἀτρέμας, usually before a conson., once in Hom., αἰγίδα.. ἔχ' ἀ. Φοῖβος Il.15.318; proleptic, ἀτρέμ' ἀμπαύσας μεριμνᾶν B.5.7; μέν'.. ἀ. σοῖς ἐν δεμνίοις E.*Or.*258, cf. *Ba.*1072; ἔχ' ἀ. keep *still!* Ar.*Nu.*743, *Av.*1244, cf. Alciphr.3.2; elided before a vowel, Ar.*Ra.*339; ἀτρέμ' ἑστάναι Antipho 3.4.7 s. v. l. (but ἀτρέμας ἑστάναι 3.3.10); ἀ. διαπορεύεσθαι X.*Cyn.*5.31, cf. 9.5; freq. in Plu., μειδιάσας ἀ. *Per.*28, cf. *Alex.*46. b. *at leisure, at ease*, ἀ. σκοπούμενοι Pl.*Grg.*503d. 2. *fixedly*, i. e. *precisely, accurately*, χρονικοῖς ἀ. συντατομένοις Plu.*Them.*27. 3. *slightly*, Diocl.*Fr.*141. **-αῖος,** α, ον (ος, ον E.*Or.*147 (lyr.)), = ἀτρεμής, βοά a whisper, l. c.: neut. pl. as Adv., Id.*HF*1053 (lyr.); regul. Adv. -αίως Call.*Iamb.*1.241; οὐκ ἀτρεμαῖοι Hp.*Morb.Sacr.*15, cf. J.*AJ*15.7.5. **-αιότης,** ητος, ἡ, *calmness*, Hp.*Praec.*13. **-ᾱς,** Adv. *without trembling, without motion*, ἀ. ἑσταότα Il.13.438; ὀφθαλμοὶ δ' ὡς εἰ κέρα ἕστασαν ἠὲ σίδηρος ἀ. ἐν βλεφάροισι Od.19.212; ἀ. εὕδειν Il.14.352, Od.13.92; ἀ. ἧσο sit *still!* Il.2.200; ἀ. ἔχειν to keep *quiet*, Hdt.5.19, 8.16; ἀ. εἶχον τὸ στρατόπεδον Id.9.53; σφέας αὐτοὺς ib.54; ἀ. ἴθι E.*Or.*149 (lyr.); ἔχ' ἀ. Ar.*Av.*1200, Luc.*Herm.*41; ἀ. ἅπτεσθαί τινος *gently, softly*, E.*Hipp.*1358; ἀ. βαδίζειν, opp. ταχύ, D.37.55. **-εί,** Adv. of ἀτρεμής, ἀτρεμί Ar.*Nu.*261; ἀτρεμεί dub. in Alex.124.12. **-έω,** fut. -ήσω Plu.*Pomp.*58, App.*Syr.*2, etc.: aor. ἠτρέμησα v. l. in Hdt. (v. infr.), Hp.*Morb.Sacr.*14:—*not to tremble, to keep still* or *quiet*, ἵνα τοι τρίχες ἀτρεμέωσι Hes.*Op.*539; οὐδαμά κω ἠτρεμήσαμεν, of a restless people, Hdt.7.8.α′ (as v. l., cf. ἀτρεμίζω), etc.; of a state of health, *remain stationary*, Hp.*Aph.*1.3; ἀτρεμέει ἡ χολή Aret.*SD*1.15; of the patient, *endure*, ib.1.1; σχεδὸν οὐκ ἀναπνέων ἠτρέμει Luc.*Am.*16, al.; of water, *to be calm*, Antyll.ap.Orib.10.3.9:—ἀτρέμ' ἔσεσθαι shd. be read for inf. Med. ἀτρεμέεσθαι in Thgn.47.—Found in Arist.*Xen.*977^{b}17, but ἠρεμέω is the Att. equivalent. **-ής,** ές, *unmoved, calm*, ἦτορ Parm.1.29; θάλασσα Semon.7.37; φάσματα Pl.*Phdr.*250c; ὄμμα X.*Smp.*8.3: ἀτρεμές, τό, *calmness*, Id.*Ages.*6.7. Adv. -έως Thgn.978; ἀ. ἔχειν Hp.*Epid.*3.17.ε′. II. *stable, firm*, δόρυ Plb.6.25.9; ὁδοί Plu.*CG*7. **-ητον·** ἀσάλευτον, Hsch. **-ί,** v. ἀτρεμεί. **-ία,** ἡ, *keeping still*, ἀτρεμίαν ἔχειν X.*Cyr.*6.3.13, cf. Max.295; ἀ. λιμένων *AP*9.555.6 (Crin.); ἐν ἀτρεμίᾳ Cerc.5.7: pl., Arist.*HA*537^{a}4. 2. *intrepidity*, Pi.*N.*11.12. **-ίζω,** fut. -ιῶ Hdt.8.68.β′: aor. ἠτρέμισα Hp.*Morb.Sacr.*7:—*keep quiet*, Thgn.303: in Ion. Prose, mostly with neg., ἀσπίδος.. οὐδαμὰ ἀτρεμιζούσης never *being kept still*, Hdt.9.74; of restless, aggressive kings or nations, οὐκ ἀτρεμίζειν Id.1.185, 190; of people attacked, οὔτε αὐτοὺς οἰκὸς.. ἀτρεμιεῖν Id.8.68.β′; without a neg., γνώμην εἶχον ἀτρεμίζοντά σε μακαριστὸν εἶναι Id.7.18, cf. Hp.*Morb.Sacr.*14, *Vict.*1.10.—Not in good Att., exc. Antipho 2.4.9 (opp. νεωτερίζειν), cf. 3.4.4 and 5: also in later Prose, Ti.Locr.104b, D.C.43.35, Them.*Or.*26.317a, etc.

ἀτρεπί, = ἀτρεπτί, Hdn.*Epim.*256.

ἄτρεπτος, ον, *unchangeable*, opp. παθητός, οὐσία Chrysipp.*Stoic.*2.158; *unmoved, inflexible*, Arist.*Mu.*401^{b}19; *irreparable*, φόνος A.R.4.704; Μοῖρα *IG*9(2).317, cf. 14.1839; ἀτρέπτους κἀπαραιτήτους Phld.*D.*1.18; ἄ. τὸ πρόσωπον Luc.*VH*2.23; ἄ. πρὸς κινδύνους J.*BJ*7.8.7; πρὸς τὸ κακῶς ἀκούειν *indifferent* to ill-repute, *not caring*, Plu.*Alc.*13. Adv. -τως Ph.2.87, J.*BJ*7.9.1; *without hesitation*, D.S.34.2, Ael.*NA*17.17:—also **-πτί,** Hdn.*Epim.*256. II. Medic., of food, *undigested*, Aret.*SD*1.16, Gal.16.800.

ἄτρεστος, ον, (τρέω) *not trembling, fearless*, Trag., and Pl.*Cra.*395c:

c. gen., ἀ. μάχας *fearless of* fight, A.*Pr.*416 (lyr.); ἀ. ἐν μάχαις S.*Aj.* 365 (lyr.); ἀ. εὕδειν *securely*, Id.*OT*586. Adv. -τως A.*Supp.*240: neut. pl. ἄτρεστα as Adv., E.*Ion* 1198.

ἀτρεφής, v. ἀτραφής.

ἀτρεχής, ές, Dor. for ἀτρεκής, *Et.Gud.*91.56,611.20.

ἄτρητος, ον, *not perforated, without aperture*, Pl.*Plt.*279e, Arist. *HA*516a26; with *imperforate* anus, Ptol.*Tetr.*150; of a virgin, Procop.*Arc.*17. II. Act., *not making holes*, ζῷα interpol. in Arist. *HA*488a25.

ἀτρήχυντος, Ion. for ἀτρᾱχ- (q. v.).

ἀτριάκαστος, ον, *not belonging to a* τριακάς, Hsch.

ἀτρίακτος [ῐ], ον, *unconquered*, A.*Ch.*339.

ἀτρίαστος [ῐ], ον, *not admitting triplicity*, Dam.*Pr.*117.

ἀτρίβ-αστος [ῐ], ον, = sq., *not worn*, ἵππος ἀ. πρὸς τραχέα a horse *whose hoofs have not been worn off* on rough ground, X.*Eq.Mag.*8.3 (dub. l.). **-ής**, ές, *not rubbed*: hence, 1. of places, *not traversed, pathless*, Th.4.8,29, Ph.2.257, al.; of roads, *not worn* or *used*, X.*An.*4.2.8, App.*Hisp.*62: generally, *fresh, new*, X.*Mem.*4.3.13, cf. *Cyr.*8.7.22 (v. l. ἀκρ-). 2. of the neck, *not galled*, Pl.*Amat.* 134b; ἀ. ζεύγλης Babr.37.1. II. *not practised in*, πολεμικῶν ἀγώνων D.H.3.52. Adv. -βῶς Poll.5.145. **-os**, ον, = ἀτριβής II, ἀρετῆς dub.l. in Ph.1.325. **-ων**, ον, gen. ονος, poet. for ἀτριβής, *unskilled in*, λέσχης E.*Fr.*473.

ἀτρίζεται· πένεται (fort. πηνίζεται, cf. sq.), Hsch.

ἄτριον, τό, Dor. for ἤτριον, Theoc.18.33, *AP*15.27 (Simm.).

ἄτριπτος, ον, = ἀτριβής, χεῖρας ἀτρίπτους ἁπαλάς *not worn hard by work*, Od.21.151; of corn, *not threshed*, X.*Oec.*18.5; of bread, *not kneaded*, Arist.*Pr.*929a17; μᾶζα *not pounded*, Hp.*Vict.*2.40; ἀ. ἄκανθαι *trackless* thorns, Theoc.13.64; κέλευθοι ἀ. *untrodden* ways, Opp.*H.*4.68: metaph., ἀ. φρονήσεως ὁδοί Ph.1.316. 2. metaph., *unknown, strange*, Artem.4.63; of a problem, Simp.*in Ph.*520.23.

ἄτριστ-ος, ον, (τρίζω) *not crackling*, i.e. *stiff*, of tin, Zos.Alch. p.161 B.:—hence **-όω**, *make stiff*, Id.p.162 B.

ἀτρῐχέω, *not to be hairy*, Orib.10.15.2.

ἄτρῐχος, ον, = ἄθριξ, *without hair*, Call.*Dian.*77, Gal.4.572. 2. Subst., *serpent*, Hes.*Fr.*96.91. 3. *preventing the growth of hair*, Aët.1.19.

ἀτρῐχόσαρκος, ον, *smooth-skinned, not hairy*, Procl.*Par.Ptol.*202.

ἄτριψ, ῐβος, ὁ, = ἀτριβής II, Phryn.*PS* p.17 B.: c. gen., Suid.

ἀτριψία, ἡ, *inexperience, amateurishness*, Cic.*Att.*13.16.1.

ἀτρομ-έω, = ἀτρεμέω, Opp.*H.*3.355. **-ητος**, ον, = sq., B.12.123, *AP*6.256 (Antip.). **-ος**, ον, *fearless*, ἐν δέ τε θυμὸς στήθεσιν ἀ. ἐστι Il.16.163; μένος.. ἀ. 5.126, 17.157; σῶμα Orph.*Fr.*168.23; νεῦρα Aret.*CA*1.2; ἀ. ὕπνος *calm, undisturbed*, *AP*6.69 (Maced.). Adv. -μως Plu.2.474d, 475f.

ἀτροπάμπαις, παιδος, dub. sens. in *IG*5(1).278,279 (Sparta); cf. πρατοπάμπαις. (ἀτρο- perh. = ἀδρο- 'mature', cf. Βατρόμιος: Βαδρόμιος.)

ἀτροπ-ία, ἡ, *inflexibility*, κρέσσων τοι σοφίη.. ἀτροπίης Thgn.218; *rigour, cruelty*, ἀτροπίῃ A.R.4.387; ἀτροπίῃσι ib.1006. II. ἀτροπίη· ἀωρία, μεσονύκτιον, Hsch. **-ος**, ον, *not to be turned, unchangeable, eternal*, ὕπνος Theoc.3.49. 2. *inflexible, rigid*, Ἅιδης *AP*7.483; ἀρετή ib.10.74 (Paul. Sil.): pr. n., Ἄτροπος, ἡ, name of one of the Μοῖραι, Hes.*Th.*905, al., Pl.*Lg.*960c, Chrysipp.*Stoic.*2.264; ἀ. Κλωθώ *IG*3.1337: hence of the decrees of fate, ἄτροπα γραψάμεναι *Epigr. Gr.*153.4; ἀ. νόμος ib.288 (Cypr.). 3. *uncourteous, unseemly*, ἔπεα Pi.*N.*7.103. II. *not turned by the plough, untilled*, Call.*Del.*11.

ἀτροφ-έω, *have* or *get no food*, Ael.*NA*10.21, etc.; *waste away*, Arist.*Mu.*395b28, Plu.*Arat.*24; of trees, Thphr.*CP*5.9.9, cf. Plu. *Rom.*20; of fire, *have no fuel*, Ph.2.620. **-ής**, ές, = ἄτροφος I, Man.6.25. **-ία**, ἡ, *want of food* or *nourishment*, of trees, Thphr. *CP*5.9.9; φθινούσης ἀ. φλογός Plu.2.949a. 2. *atrophy*, Arist. *Pr.*888a10, Antyll.ap.Orib.6.21.7. 3. *starvation-diet*, καύσεις καὶ τομαὶ καὶ ἀ. Alex.Aphr.*in Top.*202.17. **-ος**, ον, *ill-fed*, X.*Mem.* 3.3.4; -ώτερος εἶναι Ael.*NA*12.20; *ill of atrophy, pining away*, Plu.2.912e. b. *non-viable*, of infants, Ptol.*Tetr.*127. 2. Act., *not nutritious*, Thphr.*CP*2.5.1, 2.6.4, Diph.Siph.ap.Ath.2.54a (Comp.); so prob. in Arist.*Mete.*384a25 (but possibly, *that will not curdle* (τρέφω I)). 3. ἄτροφος τυρός· ὁ πησσόμενος (Lacon.), Hsch.

ἀτρύγετος [ῡ], ον, later η, ον *IG*3.900:—*unharvested, barren*, freq. in Hom. as epith. of the sea, παρὰ θῖν' ἁλὸς ἀτρυγέτοιο Il.1.316, al.; πόντον ἐπ' ἀ. Od.2.370, al.; also δι' αἰθέρος ἀτρυγέτοιο Il.17.425, Hes. *Cat.Oxy.*1358.2.34, *h.Cer.*67,457: Ep. Adj., borrowed by S.*Fr.*476, Ar.*V.*1521, *Av.*1338 (all lyr.). 2. metaph., ἀ. νύξ, of death, *AP* 7.735 (Damag.). (Expld. as if from ἀ-priv., τρυγάω by Sch.Od.l.c., etc.: but = ἄτρυτος, *never worn out, unresting*, acc. to Hdn.Gr.2.284.)

ἀτρῠγ-ής, ές, (τρυγάω) *not gathered*, μέλι *AP*7.622 (Antiph.). **-ητος**, ον, = foreg., Arist.*Pr.*925b15; ἀ. γενήματα *PGnom.*233 (ii A.D.).

ἀτρυγηφάγου· πολυφάγου, Hsch.; cf. ὀτρυγηφάγος.

ἄτρῠγος, ον, (τρύξ) *without lees, clarified, pure*, οἶνος, opp. τρυγίας, Orac.ap.Arist.*Fr.*597; ἔλαιον Lxx *Ex.*27.20.

ἀτρύμων [ῡ], ον, gen. ονος, = ἄτρυτος, c. gen., ἀ. κακῶν *not worn out by* ills, A.*Th.*876 (lyr.).

ἀτρύνων· ἐγείρων, Hsch. (leg. ὀτρύνων).

ἀτρύπητος [ῡ], ον, = ἄτρητος, τὸ οὖς ἔχειν ἀ. Plu.*Cic.*26, 2.205b.

ἄτρῡτος, ον, *not worn, untiring, unwearied*, πούς A.*Eu.*403; *indefatigable*, φεῦ τῶν ἀ. οἷα κωτιλίζουσι Call.*Iamb.*1.277, cf. Plu.*Pomp.* 26; ironical in Herod.8.4. Adv. -τως, κάματον ἐκδέχεσθαι Ph.1.19; ὑπομένειν τι J.*AJ*11.5.8, cf. Jul.*Or.*7.226c, Orph.*Fr.*71. 2. of things, *unabating*: hence, *limitless*, πόνος Pi.*P.*4.178, Hdt.9.52; χρόνος B.8.80; χάος Id.5.27; κακά S.*Aj.*788; ἄλγεα Mosch.4.69; Ἰξίονος μοῖρα ἀΐδιος καὶ ἀ. Arist.*Cael.*284a35; τὸ ἀ. Id.*EN*1177b22; ἀνάγκαι Ph.2.434; Πόνος Chaerem.ap.Porph.*Abst.*4.8; of a road, *wearisome, never-ending*, Theoc.15.7; ὁδοιπορίαι Plu.*Caes.*17: Sup., Ph.1.418. 3. = ἀτρύγετος, αἰθήρ Corn.*ND*20.

Ἀτρῡτώνη, ἡ, *the Unwearied*, title of Pallas Athene, Il.2.157, Od. 4.762, etc. (Lengthd. form of ἀτρύτη, as Ἀϊδωνεύς of Ἅιδης.)

ἀτρύφερος [ῠ], ον, *not delicate* or *luxurious*, Eup.69; *plain, simple*, στολή Ceb.20; ὄψον Teles p.7 H.

ἀτρύφητος, ον, (τρῠφάω) = foreg., Plu.2.10b (s. v. l.); cf. ἀτύφωτος.

ἄτρῠφος, ον, = ἄθρυπτος, τυρός Alcm.34, cf. Hierocl.*in CA*17 p.458 M.

ἀτρώς, ῶτος, ὁ, ἡ, = ἄτρωτος, Choerob.*in Theod.*p.159 H.

ἀτρωσία, ἡ, *invulnerability*, Sch.A.R.1.57.

ἄτρωτος, ον, *unwounded*, κραδία Pi.*N.*11.10; ἀ. οὖθαρ ὑπὸ στύγους A.*Ch.*532; ἄτρωτον οὐ μεθῆκ' ἄν S.*OC*906, cf. Eub.107.4 (hex.), etc. II. *invulnerable*, παῖδες θεῶν Pi.*I.*3.18, cf. Acus.22 J., E.*Ph.* 594, Arist.*Rh.*1396b18; σιδήρῳ D.S.4.11, Nonn.*D.*2.452: metaph., ἀ. χρήμασιν Pl.*Smp.*219e; κακίας Philostr.*VA*1.11; πρὸς σώματος ὥραν Lib.*Or.*59.122. Adv. -τως, ἔχειν Ph.1.384 (s. v. l.). III. of capital, *intact*, *PLond.*2.483.81 (vii A.D.).

ἄττα (A), Att. for ἅσσα, (q. v.). II. ἄττα for ἅσσα, = ἅτινα, Pl.Com.49, etc.

ἄττα (B), a salutation used to elders, *father*, ἄττα γεραιέ Il.9.607, cf. Od.16.31, etc.; said to be Thess. by Eust.777.54. (From child-language.)

ἀτταβυγάς, a *bird* (perh. = ἀτταγᾶς), Hsch.

ἀττᾰγᾶς, ᾶ, ὁ, *francolin, Tetrao orientalis*, Alex.Mynd.ap.Ath.9.387f; πτερυγοποίκιλος, ποικίλος, Ar.*Av.*247, 761; a delicacy, Hippon.36.1, Ar.*Ach.*875, *Fr.*433: prov., τὸν πηλὸν ὥσπερ ἀ. τυρβάσεις βαδίζων Id.*V.*257.

ἀττᾰγεινός, ὁ, a *fish*, = σκεπινός, Dorio ap.Ath.7.322c.

ἀττᾰγήν, ῆνος, ὁ, = ἀτταγᾶς, Phoenicid.2.5, Arist.*HA*617b25, 633b1, Thphr.*Fr.*180. **-ηνάριον**, τό, Dim. of foreg., Gramm. in Gaisford *Choeroboscus* I p.43. **-ῆς**, έος, ὁ, = ἀτταγήν, Opp.*C.*2.405, 427.

ἀττάκης, ου, ὁ, a kind of *locust*, Lxx *Le.*11.22 (**ἀττακύς** Al. ibid.): —also **ἄττακος**, ὁ, Aristeas 145, Ph.1.85.

ἀτταλαγώσεται· μολυνθήσεται, Hsch.

ἀτταλασίξαι· ὀμόσαι, Hsch.; cf. ἀπαλασίξαι, ἀπαλοῖξαι.

Ἀττᾰλεῖον, τό, *meeting-place of* Ἀτταλισταί (q. v.), *CIG*3069. II. Ἀττάλεια, τά, festival at Delphi, *SIG*672.53.

ἀττάλη· φάρυξις (Phryg.), Hsch.

Ἀτταλιανόν, τό, kind of *garment*, *PGiss.*21.6 (ii A.D.).

ἀτταλίζομαι· πλανῶμαι (Sicel), Hsch.

Ἀτταλίς, ίδος, ἡ, φυλή tribe at Athens, *IG*2.444.

Ἀττᾰλισταί, οἱ, *guild of worshippers of Attalus*, *Michel* 1307 (ii B.C.).

ἀττάμιος, ον, Elean, = ἀζήμιος, *Michel* 1334 (iv B.C.).

ἄττανα· τήγανα, Hsch.:—hence **ἀττᾰνίτης**, ου, ὁ, a kind of *cake*, coupled with τηγανίτης, Hippon.36.3:—also **ἀττανίδες**, αἱ, Hsch.

ἀττάρᾰγος [τᾰ], ὁ, *crumb, morsel of bread*, Ath.14.646c: metaph., *the least crumb, bit*, οὐδ' ὅσον ἀττάραγόν τυ δεδοίκαμες Call.*Epigr.*47.9.

ἀττάρυμα· πόμα, σόφισμα Κρητικόν, Hsch. **ἄττασι**· ἀνάστηθι (Lacon.), Id.

ἀττᾰταῖ, a cry of pain or grief, S.*Ph.*790, etc.; doubled, Ar.*Ach.* 1190.

ἀττέλᾰβος, Ion. -εβος (both forms in Lxx *Na.*3.17 codd.), ὁ, *locust*, Hdt.4.172, Arist.*HA*550b32, 556a8, Thphr.*Fr.*174.3, Plu.2.636e:—also **ἀττελάβη**· ἀκρίδας, Hsch.

ἀττελεβόφθαλμος, ον, *with locust-eyes*, i.e. *with prominent, staring eyes*, Eub.107.10.

ἀττηγός, ὁ, *he-goat*, Ion. word, *SIG*589.51 (Magn. Mae., ii B.C.), Eust.1625.35. (*Attagus* Phryg. for *hircus* acc. to Arn.5.6.)

Ἄττης Ὕης, mystic formula recited by the priests of Cybele, D. 18.260, cf. *AB*207.

Ἀττίδεια [τῐ], τά, *festival of Attis*, *IG*2.622.10.

Ἀττῐκ-ηρῶς, Adv. *in Attic fashion*, Alex.213.4. **-ιανός**, ή, όν, *of Atticus*: ἀντίγραφα manuscripts *collected by A.*, *copied for A.*, or *written by A.*, Gal.*in Pl.Ti.*3, Harp. s. v. Ἀργᾶς. **-ίζω**, *side with the Athenians*, Th.3.62, X.*HG*1.6.13, *Hell.Oxy.*12.1. II. *speak Attic*, Eup.8.3 D., Pl.Com.168.1; opp. Ἑλληνίζω, Posidipp. 28. **-ισις**, εως, ἡ, *Attic style, Atticism*, Luc.*Lex.*14, Philostr. *VS*2.3. **-ισμός**, ὁ, *siding with Athens, loyalty to her*, Th.3.64, 4.133. II. = foreg., Alciphr.2.4: pl., ibid., cf. Cic.*Att.*4.19.1. **-ιστής**, οῦ, ὁ, *one who affects* or *collects Attic expressions*, Iamb. *VP*18.80, *EM*527.54, etc.; title of work by Moeris. **-ιστί**, Adv. *in the Attic dialect*, D.*Prooem.*8 (= Id.16.2, v. Ἀττικός III); Ἀ. λέγειν Antiph.97; λαλεῖν Alex.195. **-ίων**, a comic Dim., *little Athenian*, Ar.*Pax*214.

ἀττῐκοπέρδιξ, ῑκος, ὁ, *Attic partridge*, nickname of an actor, Ath. 3.115b.

Ἀττικός, ή, όν, *Attic, Athenian*, Sol.2, Alc.32, A.*Eu.*681, etc.; σφόδρ'.. Ἀττικάς *of* true *Attic breed*, Ar.*Lys.*56; Ἀ. πάροικος, prov. of a *troublesome* neighbour, Arist.*Rh.*1395a18. II. ἡ Ἀττική (sc. γῆ) *Attica*, Hdt.5.76, etc.; cf. Ἀτθίς. III. Gramm., Ἀττικοί, οἱ, *Attic writers*, Longin.34.2, Phryn.302, etc.; Ἀ. γράμματα the *Attic* alphabet, D.59.76, Paus.6.19.6; Ἀ. σχῆμα, use of nom. for voc., A.D.*Synt.*214.2; χρῆσις ib.59.20; –κόν, τό, *the Attic style*, Plu.2.79d: Comp. –ώτερος Cic.*Att.*1.13.5 (with play on the name *Atticus*): Sup., ib.15.1b.2. Adv. –κῶς D.16.2 codd., Luc.*Sol.*6: Comp. –ώτερον A.D.*Adv.*132.20. **IV.** Ἀττικόν, τό, *a remedy*, Hp.*Epid.*4.47.

Ἀττῐκ-ουργής, ές, *wrought in Attic fashion*, ῥήματα Men.1000. **–ωνικός**, ή, όν, comic alteration of Ἀττικός, after the form of Λακωνικός, Ar.*Pax* 215.

ἄττομαι, = διάζομαι, Hermipp.2.

ἄττω, Att. for ᾄσσω, ἀΐσσω.

ἀτυζηλός, ή, όν, *frightful*, δεῖμα A.R.2.1057.

ἀτύζομαι, in Hom., Lyr., Trag. only pres. and aor. part. Pass.:—*to be distraught from fear, bewildered*, ἀτυζομένους ὑπὸ καπνοῦ Il.8.183; ἀτυζομένω πεδίοιο *fleeing bewildered* o'er the plain, Il.6.38, cf. 18.7, Od.11.606: abs., ἀτύζονται, ἀτυζόμενος, Pi.*P.*1.13, *O.*8.39, B.12.116; *to be distraught with grief*, ἀτυζόμενος S.*El.*148 (lyr.), E.*Andr.*131, A.R.4.39: c. acc., *to be amazed at* a thing, ὄψιν ἀτυχθείς Il.6.468, cf. Tryph.685: c. inf., ἀτυζομένην ἀπολέσθαι *terrified* even to death, Il.22.474; ἀ. περὶ νύμφην *to be distressed* for..., *AP*7.528 (Theodorid.). **II.** in later Ep. Act. **ἀτύζω**, *strike with terror* or *amazement*, A.R.1.465: aor. opt. ἀτύξαι Theoc.1.56; ἠέρα παῦρον ἀτύζει *draws* short breaths, Nic.*Al.*193 (vv.ll. ἀτίζει, ἀλύξει).—Ep. Verb, used by Trag. only in lyr.

ἄτυκτος, ον, *undone*, οὐκέτι γὰρ δύναται τὸ τετυγμένον εἶναι ἄτυκτον Ps.-Phoc.56.

ἄτυλλα· ἀγκύλη, Hsch. (ἄττ– cod.). **ἀτυλόν**· μικρόν, ἀγενές, Id.

ἀτύλωτος [ῠ], ον, (ἀ– euph.) *made callous by labour, hardened*, ὦμοι Call.*Dian.*213 (Toup for ἀσύλωτοι). **II.** (ἀ– priv.) *that will not cicatrize*, Archig.ap.Gal.13.730.

ἀτύμβ-ευτος, ον, *without tomb*, θάνατος *AP*9.439 (Crin.); ὕβρις contemptuous *neglect of burial*, Onos.36.2; τάφος ἀ. burial *but not in a tomb*, Opp.*H.*5.346. **–ος**, ον, *without burial, without a tomb*, Luc.*Cont.*22. Adv. –βως prob. in *Anatolian Studies* p.118.

ἀτυπῆδες· κριθαὶ ἀπίτυροι, Hsch.

ἄτῠπ-ος, ον, *speaking inarticulately, stammering*, Gell.4.2.5 **II.** *conforming to no distinct type* (of illness), Gal.7.471 (Sup.). **–ωτος**, ον, *unformed, shapeless*, Ael.*NA*2.19, Plu.2.636c; ἀ. ψυχή *uninfluenced* by good or evil, *Stoic.*3.52. **2.** = ἄσκαλτος, Hsch.

ἀτῠράννευτος, ον, *not ruled by tyrants, free from tyrants*, Th.1.18, D.C.37.22, Chor.p.208 B.:—also **ἀτύραννος**, ον, Phryn.*PS*p.30 B.

ἀτύρωτος [ῡ], ον, *not curdled* or *coagulated*, Dsc.3.34, Orib.*Fr.*137.

ἀτῡφ-ία, ἡ, *freedom from arrogance*, Men.304, Plu.2.82b, Jul.*Or.*7.214b. **–ος**, ον, *not puffed up*, Pl.*Phdr.*230a, Timo 9.1; esp. of the Stoic sage, Cleanth.*Stoic.*1.127: Comp., Plu.*Alex.*45: Sup., D.L.4.37. Adv. –φως Plu.2.32d, M.Ant.1.16.4: Comp. –ότερον Hierocl. *in CA* 19 p.461 M.: Sup. –ότατα Ael.*Fr.*137:—also **ἀτῡφί**, dub. in *IG*14.2094. **–ωτος**, ον, = foreg., Plu.2.10b.

ἀτῠχ-έω, fut. –ήσω Ar.*Nu.*427, Eup.114: aor. ἠτύχησα Hdt.9.111, Antipho 4.2.6: pf. ἠτύχηκα D.20.53, Men.149, Philem.107: rarely in Pass. (v. infr.):—*to be unfortunate, fail, miscarry*, Ar.*Nu.*427, Th.1.32, etc.; opp. κατορθόω, Isoc.3.24, etc.; ἀ. ἔν τινι Id.12.105; πεζῇ Arist.*Pol.*1303ᵃ8; οἱ ἀτυχοῦντες, = οἱ ἀτυχεῖς, Antipho 2.4.9: euphem. for ἀτιμοῦσθαι, D.21.60. **2.** c. gen., *fail of* a thing, *fail in getting* it, τῆς ἀληθείας Pl.*Tht.*186c; τῶν δικαίων οὐδενός X.*HG*3.1.22: c. part., ἀ. κτώμενοι Th.2.62, cf. Men.*Epit.*470: c. inf., Vett.Val.358.30: c. acc., τὸ ἀγαθόν Eun.*VS*p.469 B. **3.** *fail in one's request, meet with a refusal*, Hdt.9.111; πρός τινα X.*Cyr.*1.3.14; παρὰ θεῶν.. ib.1.6.6; τι παρά τινος *IG*2.86; ἀ. τινός Eup.114:—Pass., τὰ ἀτυχηθέντα *mischances, failures*, D.18.212; τὰ ἠτυχημένα J.*AJ*16.8.6; ἠτύχητο ἡ μάχη D.H.*Isoc.*9.—Chiefly in Com. and Att. Prose, never in Trag. **–ημα**, ατος, τό, *misfortune, miscarriage*, Antipho 3.4.5 (v.l.), Timocl.6.18. **2.** *fault of ignorance, mistake*, D.23.70; opp. ἀδίκημα, ἁμάρτημα, Gorg.11, Arist.*Rh.*1374ᵇ6, *EN*1135ᵇ12: euphem., *crime*, ἀ. πρὸς τὸ δημόσιον Is.10.20, cf. Plb.12.14.2. **–ής**, ές, *unfortunate*, Antipho 2.2.1 (Sup.); οὐ γὰρ οὕτως ἄφρων οὐδ' ἀ. εἰμι D.3.21; euphem., ἀ. γενέσθαι 'get into trouble', Pl.*Lg.*905a: late acc. fem. ἀτυχήν *Annales du Service* 22.10 (i B.C./i A.D.). Adv. –χῶς Isoc.12.15: Sup. –έστατα Longin.33.5. **II.** *missing, without share in*, τινός Ael.*NA*11.31, Max.Tyr.20.5. **–ία**, ἡ, *ill-luck*, Amphis 3. **II.** = ἀτύχημα, *miscarriage, mishap*, Hp.*Fract.*25, Antipho 2.2.13, X.*Mem.*3.9.8 (pl.), Men.674; *defeat* in war, Aeschin.3.55. **2.** euphem. for ἀτιμία, D.21.59; for *crime*, Din.1.77, Plb.12.13.5, etc. **3.** of a person, ἀ. κοσμουμένα Axiop.4.5. **4.** *failure to obtain*, τινός Aret.*SD*1.5.

ἀτῶμαι, v. ἀτάω.

ἄτωρ· μελία (Egypt.), Hsch.

αὖ, Adv. of repeated action, *again, anew, afresh, once more*, Il.1.540, etc.: freq. after numerals, δεύτερον αὖ, τρίτον αὖ, etc., Hom.; τὸν δὲ πέμπτον αὖ λέγω A.*Th.*526, cf. *Ch.*1066 (lyr.); in a question, expressing impatience, τίς δὴ αὖ τοι..; Il.1.540. **II.** generally, *again*, i.e. *further, moreover*, ib.2.493, etc.; καὶ ἔτι γε αὖ Pl.*Tht.*192b. **2.** *on the other hand*, following δέ, τούτῳ μὲν .. τούτῳ δ' αὖ.. Il.4.417; also, *in turn*, οἳ δ' ἄρα ..Ἦλιδα δῖαν ἔναιον..τῶν αὖ τέσσαρες ἀρχοὶ ἔσαν ib.2.618; ἥξει γὰρ ἄλλος αὖ τιμάορος A.*Ag.*1280: hence = δέ, even when μέν precedes, Il.11.109, Od.4.211; freq. joined with δέ, ὃν δ' αὖ δήμου τ' ἄνδρα ἴδοι Il.2.198; ὦ πολλὰ μὲν τάλαινα πολλὰ δ' αὖ σοφή A.*Ag.*1295, cf. *Eu.*954 (lyr.); ὁ μὲν ἥμαρτε ὁ δ' αὖ..κατειργάσατο X.*Cyr.*4.6.4; οὐκ..οὐδ' αὖ S.*OT*1373, *El.*911, cf. Pl.*Tht.*160b: with τε, X.*Cyr.*1.1.1, Pl.*Prt.*326a, etc. **III.** in pleon. phrases, esp. in Trag. (v. αὖθις, ἔμπαλιν, πάλιν), μάλ' αὖ A.*Eu.*254, S.*El.*1410. **IV.** *on the contrary*, ἆρ' ὀρθῶς .. ἢ αὖ; Pl.*R.*468a. **V.** of Place, *backward*, only in the incorrect orthography αὖ ἔρυσαν, cf. αὐερύω.—Not placed first in a sentence. [ᾰυ before a vowel, Pl.Com.153.3, Archestr.ap.Ath.6.300e (both hex.).] (Cf. αὐτάρ, αὖτε, αὖτις, Lat. *aut*.)

αὖ αὖ, *bow wow*, of a dog, Ar.*V.*903.

Αὐαίνου λίθος *the Withering* stone, Ar.*Ra.*194.

αὐαίνω, Att. **αὑ–** (cf. ἀφ–, ἐπαφ-αυαίνω), impf. (καθ–)αύαινον Luc.*Am.*12: fut. αὐανῶ S.*El.*819: aor. ηὗηνα or αὔ– Hdt.4.172, inf. αὐῆναι Hp.*Mul.*1.84, part. αὐήνας Id.*Morb.*3.17:—Pass., impf. Ar.*Fr.*613: aor. ηὐάνθην or αὐ– (v. infr.), ἐξ– Hdt.4.151: fut. αὐανθήσομαι (cf. ἀφ–):—but also **Med.** αὐανοῦμαι in pass. sense, S.*Ph.*954: Mss. and editors differ with regard to the augm.: (v. αὔω):—*dry*, αὐανθέν (of a log of wood) Od.9.321; αὐ. ἰχθῦς πρὸς ἥλιον Hdt.1.200, 2.77, cf. 92, 4.172; αὐαίνεσθαι ὑπὸ τοῦ καύματος, διὰ ξηρότητα, X.*Oec.*16.14, 19.11, cf. *An.*2.3.16, etc. **2.** *wither*, Thphr.*HP*3.7.1 (Pass.): metaph., εὐνομίη αὐαίνει ἄτης ἄνθεα Sol.4.36; αὐανθεὶς πυθμήν A.*Ch.*260; αὐανῶ βίον I *shall waste* life *away, pine away*, S.*El.*819: αὐανοῦμαι I *shall wither away*, Id.*Ph.*954; ηὑαινόμην θεώμενος Ar.*Fr.*613. **II.** intr., *to be dry*, μήτε ὑγραὶ μήτε λίαν αὐαίνουσαι Hp.*Mul.*1.17.—The Act. is comparatively rare, esp. in Attic.

αὐᾰλέος, α, ον, (αὖος) *dry, parched, withered*, αὐ. χρὼς ὑπὸ καύματος Hes.*Op.*588; of hair, *rough*, dub. in Simon.37.9, cf. *AP*7.141 (Antiphil.); of plants, Orph.*A.*246; of the mouth, Call.*Cer.*6; of eyes, *sleepless*, *AP*5.279 (Agath.); αὐαλέῃ ἐνὶ κόγχῳ prob. in Timo 3.—Late in Prose, Aret.*SD*2.2, al. (αὑ– Call. l. c.)

αὔανσις, εως, ἡ, *drying up*, Arist.*Mete.*379ᵃ5, *GA*785ᵃ26; equivalent to γῆρας in plant-life, Id.*Resp.*478ᵇ28.

αὐαντή (sc. νόσος), ἡ, *wasting, atrophy*, Hp.*Morb.*2.66.

αὐαρά· τὰ Ποντικὰ κάρυα, Hsch.

Αὔασις, ἡ, = Ὄασις (q.v.), Str.2.5.33, al.

αὐασμός, ὁ, *drying, dryness*, Hp.*Hum.*4, *AB*462.

ἀυάτα, i.e. ἀϝάτα, Aeol. for ἄτη (q.v.).

αὐγάζω, fut. –άσω: aor. ηὔγᾰσα *AP*7.726 (Leon.):—**Pass.**, v. infr.: (αὐγή):—*view in the clearest light, see distinctly, discern*, S.*Ph.*217 (lyr.), *AP*9.221 (Marc. Arg.); τὸν ἴδιον νοῦν οἷα πρὸς κάτοπτρον Ph.2.156:—also in Med., Il.23.458, Hes.*Op.*478, A.R.1.155, Call.*Dian.*129, *AP*9.349 (Leon.); αἱ δὲ λῆς αὐγάσδεο *Carm.Pop.*18:—Pass., αὐγασθεῖσα *being mirrored* in the smooth water, dub. in S.*Fr.*598.6; simply, *appear*, Max.11, al., dub. in Orph.*Fr.*284. **II.** of the sun, *illumine*, τινά E.*Hec.*637 (lyr.):—Pass., Id.*Ba.*596 (lyr.). **2.** metaph., *enlighten*, 2*Ep.Cor.*4.4; *set in a clear light*, Ph.1.659, al. **III.** intr., *appear bright* or *white*, Lxx *Le.*13.25, al.; *shine*, *PMag.Par.*1.2558, 2.143.

αὔγαρος· ἄσωτος (Cypr.), Hsch.

αὔγ-ασμα, ατος, τό, *brightness, whiteness*, Lxx *Le.*13.38. **–ασμός**, ὁ, *radiance, flashing*, ἡλίου *Placit.*3.5.10. **–άστειρα**, ἡ, *light-giving*, of the moon, Orph.*H.*9.5.

αὐγεῖν· ἀλγεῖν, Hsch.

αὔγειον, τό, = ὠκιμοειδές, Ps.-Dsc.4.28.

αὐγέω, *to shine, glitter*, Lxx *Jb.*29.3.

αὐγή, ἡ, *light of the sun*, and in pl., *rays, beams*, πέπτατο δ' αὐ. ἠελίου Il.17.371, cf. Od.6.98, 12.176; ἠελίου ἴδεν αὐγάς, i.e. was born, Il.16.188; ὑπ' αὐγὰς ἠελίοιο, i.e. still alive, Od.11.498, 619; Διὸς αὐγάς Il.13.837; αὐγὰς ἐσιδεῖν see *the light*, i.e. to be alive, Thgn.426, cf. E.*Alc.*667; λεύσσειν A.*Pers.*710; βλέπειν E.*Andr.*935; ὑπ' αὐγὰς λεύσσειν or ἰδεῖν τι hold up to *the light* and look at, Id.*Hec.*1154, Pl.*Phdr.*268a, cf. Plb.10.3.1; ὑπ' αὐγὰς δεικνύναι τι Ar.*Th.*500 (πρὸς and ὑπ' αὐγήν, *in a full* and *in a side light*, Hp.*Off.*3); δυθμαὶ αὐγῶν *sun*-set, Pi.*I.*4(3).65; ξύνορθρον αὐγαῖς dawning with *the sun*, A.*Ag.*254 (lyr.); κλύζειν πρὸς αὐγάς rise surging towards *the sun*, ib.1182; λαμπροτάτη τῶν παρεουσέων αὐγέων brightest *light* available, Hp.*Fract.*3, cf. Arist.*PA*658ᵃ3, *Pr.*912ᵇ14, al.: metaph., βίου δύντος αὐγαί 'life's setting *sun*', A.*Ag.*1123 (lyr.); ἤδη γὰρ αὐγὴ τῆς ζόης ἀπήμβλυνται Herod.10.4. **2.** αὐγαὶ ἠελίοιο or αὐγαί alone, *the East*, D.P.84, 231. **3.** *dawn, day-break*, *Act.Ap.*20.11, *PLeid.W.*11.35. **4.** generally, *any bright light*, πυρὸς αὐγή Od.6.305, cf. Il.2.456; ἀρίζηλοι δέ οἱ αὐγαί, of lightning, 13.244; βροντῆς αὐ. S.*Ph.*1199 (lyr.); of a beacon, Il.18.211, A.*Ag.*9; λαμπάδος Cratin. post 150; distd. from φλόξ, Chrysipp.*Stoic.*2.186. **5.** of the eyes, ὀμμάτων αὐγαί S.*Aj.*70; αὐγαί alone, *the eyes*, E.*Andr.*1180 (lyr.), *Rh.*737: metaph., ἀνακλίναντας τὴν τῆς ψυχῆς αὐ. Pl.*R.*540a. **6.** *gleam, sheen*, of bright objects, αὐ. χαλκείη Il.13.341; χρυσὸς αὐγὰς ἔδειξεν Pi.*N.*4.83; ἀμβρόσιος αὐ. πέπλου E.*Med.*983 (lyr.); ἠλεκτροφαεῖς αὐ. Id.*Hipp.*741 (lyr.); αὐ. τῆς κρόκης Men.561; of gems, Philostr.*Im.*2.8.—Mostly poet., but freq. in Arist., chiefly in the sense of *sunlight*.

αὐγήεις, εσσα, εν, *bright-eyed, clear-sighted*, Nic.*Th.*34.

αὐγής, ές, f.l. for διαυγής, ὕδατα Alex.Aphr.*Pr.*1.116.

αὔγιον, τό, = ἰσάτις, dub. in Ps.-Dsc.2.184.

αὐγ-ίτης (sc. λίθος), ὁ, a *precious stone*, Plin.*HN*37.147:—fem. **–ῖτις**, ιδος, ἡ, = ἀναγαλλὶς ἡ Φοινικῆ, Ps.-Dsc.2.178.

αὐγοειδής, ές, *of the nature of light*, πνεῦμα, as the source of sight, *Stoic.*2.231; αἰσθητήριον, of the eye, Gal.*UP*8.6; *brilliant*, χρόα Plu.2.922d: metaph., ψυχή ib.565d; σῶμα, πνεῦμα, Iamb.*Myst.*5.10, 3.11; ὄχημα *luminous* vehicle, Procl. *in Ti.*2.81 D.: Comp., Ph.1.6: Sup., ib.504, al., Eus.Mynd.63. Adv. –δῶς dub. in Ph.2.487.

αὖγος, εος, τό, *the morning light, dawn*, Hsch. s.v. ἠώς.

Αὔγουστος, ὁ, *Augustus*, used as an Adj., = Gr. σεβαστός, Paus.

3.11.4, etc. :—hence **Αὐγούστειος**, ον, D.C.61.20: **Αὐγουστεῖον**, τό, *temple of Augustus*, Id.57.10: **Αὐγούστεια**, τά, *festival of A.*, *IG*3.129, 14.739:—**Αὐγουστάλιος**, ον, *Augustalis*, τὰ Αὐγουστάλια *ludi Augustales*, D.C.54.34; -άλιος, ὁ, *praefectus Augusti*, Lyd.*Mag.*2.3. II. the month *August*, Plu.*Num.*19.

Αὐγώ, *Daybeam*, name of a dog, X.*Cyn.*7.3.

αὐδάζομαι, Dep., (αὐδή) *cry out, speak*, αὐδάξασθαι φωνῇ ἀνθρωπηίῃ Hdt.2.55, cf. 5.51, Euph.48; τοῦτ' ἔπος ηὐδάσατο Call.*Aet.*3.1.21. 2. *name*, Opp.*H.*1.127:—Act., fut. αὐδάξω Lyc.892: aor. ηὔδαξα Id.360, dub. l. in *AP*6.218 (Alc.):—Pass., aor. αὐδαχθεῖσα Orph.*H.*27.9.

αὐδάω, impf. ηὔδων Il.3.203, Hdt.2.57, S.*OT*568, etc.: fut. αὐδήσω, Dor. -άσω [ᾱ] Pi.*O.*1.7, S.*OT*846; Dor. αὐδασοῦντι *APl.*4.120 (Archel. or Asclep.): aor. ηὔδησα, Dor. αὔδᾱσα Pi.*I.*6(5).42, etc.; part. αὐδήσας Il.10.47, Dor. αὐδάσαις Pi.*P.*4.61; Ion. 3 sg. αὐδήσασκε Il.5.786: pf. ηὔδηκα (ἀπ-) Hp.*Gland.*14:—Pass., impf. ηὐδώμην (v. infr.): aor. part. αὐδηθείς S.*Tr.*1106, Dor. αὐδαθείς E.*Med.*174 (lyr.): pf. ηὔδημαι Maiist.3: fut. αὐδηθήσομαι Lyc.630: Ep. pres. 3 pl. αὐδώωνται Opp.*H.*1.776:—also Med., **αὐδάομαι**, A.*Pr.*766, *Eu.*379, S.*Ph.*130: impf. ηὐδᾶτο Id.*Aj.*772: fut. αὐδήσομαι, Dor. αὐδάσομαι Pi.*O.*2.101: (αὐδή). I. c. acc. rei, 1. *utter sounds, speak*, Il.1.92, etc.; τόσον αὐδήσασχ' ὅσον ἄλλοι πεντήκοντα 5.786; ὡς δέ τις.. αὐδήσασκεν 17.420; αὐδᾶν κραυγήν *utter* a cry, E.*Ion*893 (lyr.). 2. *speak, say*, ὁμοκλήσας ἔπος ηὔδα Il.6.54; αὔδα ὅ τι φρονέεις 18.426; so οὐκ αὐδᾶν ἔσθ' ἃ μηδὲ δρᾶν καλόν S.*OT*1409; τί τινι Id.*OC*25:—Med., Id.*Ph.*130, 852 (lyr.):—Pass., ηὐδᾶτο γὰρ ταῦτα so '*twas said*, Id.*OT*731, cf. 527; ὡς ηὐδᾶτ' ἐκεῖ ib.940. 3. of oracles, *utter, proclaim*, ib. 392, etc.; οὕστινας κομπεῖς γάμους αὐδᾶν *speak out concerning them*, A.*Pr.*948. 4. αὐ. ἀγῶνα *sing of* a contest, Pi.*O.*1.7. 5. abs., *speak, utter*, of the statue of Memnon, *Epigr.Gr.*988 (Balbilla), al. II. c. acc. pers., 1. *speak to, address, accost*, ἀντίον αὐδᾶν τινά Il.3.203, al.; ἔπος τέ μιν ἀντίον ηὔδα 5.170; αὐδῶν δεινὰ πρόσπολον κακά E.*Hipp.*584; *call on* or *invoke* a god, Id.*HF*499, 1215. 2. c. acc. et inf., *bid, order* to do, αὐ. σε χαίρειν Pi.*P.*4.61, cf. S.*OC*1630; αὐ. σε μή.. *forbid*, A.*Th.*1048, etc.; αὐδῶ τινὶ ποιεῖν E.*IT*1226; αὐδῶ σιωπᾶν S.*OC*864; αὐδήσας χαίρειν *Epigr.Gr.*205.7 (Halic.); αὐδῶ καὖθις ἀπαυδῶ Ar.*Ra.*369:—Med., S.*Aj.*772. 3. *call by name*, λεὼς νιν Θετίδειον αὐδᾷ E.*Andr.*20:—Med., ὅν τε λέοντα αὐδάξαντο Nic.*Th.*464:—more freq. in Pass., αὐδῶμαι παῖς Ἀχιλλέως S.*Ph.*240; Ζηνὸς αὐδηθεὶς γόνος Id.*Tr.*1106; αὐδᾶσθαι νεκρόν Id.*Ph.*430; κάκιστ' αὐδώμενος most ill *reported of*, A.*Th.*678; ὁ παραμασήτης ἐν βροτοῖς αὐδώμενος Alex.236 (paratrag.). 4. *mean* such an one, E.*Hipp.*352.—Never in good Att. Prose.

αὐδή, Dor. **αὐδά**, ἡ, *human voice, speech* (but distd. fr. φωνή, *Stoic.*2.44), μέλιτος γλυκίων ῥέεν αὐ. Il.1.249. 2. generally, *sound* or *twang* of the bow-string, καλὸν ἄεισε χελιδόνι εἰκέλη αὐδήν Od.21.411; of a trumpet, E.*Rh.*989; of the τέττιξ, Hes.*Sc.*396; of the *sound* emitted by the statue of Memnon, *Epigr.Gr.*990.7 (Balbilla). II. *report, account*, ἔργων ἀΐοντες αὐδήν S.*OC*240 (lyr.), cf. E.*Supp.*600 (lyr.), *Hipp.*567. 2. *oracle*, Id.*IT*976. 3. *song, ode*, Pi.*N.*9.4. (Cf. Skt. *vadati* 'speaks', v. ἀείδω.)

αὐδήεις, εσσα, εν, *speaking with human voice*, ἀνθρώπων.. σχεδὸν αὐδηέντων Od.6.125; [Ἰνὼ] ἣ πρὶν μὲν ἔην βροτὸς αὐδήεσσα 5.334; of Achilles' horse, αὐδήεντα δ' ἔθηκε θεά Il.19.407; θνητοὶ αὐδήεντες, opp. ἀθάνατοι, Hes.*Th.*142b; of divinities, *using human speech*, of Calypso and Circe, Od.10.136, 11.8, 12.150, 449 (οὐδήεσσα or αὐλήεσσα Arist.*Fr.*171, Chamael.ap.Sch.Od.5.334); χθόνιαι θεαὶ αὐδήεσσαι A.R.4.1322; Ἀργοῦς.. αὐδῆεν (Hartung for αὔδασον) ξύλον A.*Fr.*20. 2. *vocal*, κόσμον αὐδάεντα λόγων Pi.*Fr.*194; αὐδάεις λόγος *rumour*, B.14.44; of the statue of Memnon, *Epigr.Gr.*1000, al.; opp. ἄναυδος, Epigr.ap.Paus.10.12.6. 3. *famous*, Hsch.

ἀϋδρ-ία, ἡ, = ἀνυδρία, Pl.*Lg.*844a, Thphr.*HP*8.6.6. **-ος**, ον, = ἄνυδρος, Id.*CP*2.4.10.

Αὐδυναῖος, ὁ (sc. μήν), name of month in Macedonia, Crete, etc., *Hemerolog.Flor.*; **Αὐδουν-**, *IG*12(3).254:—also **Αὐδν-**, **Αὐτναῖος**, *PPetr.*3 p.4, *PPar.*3, etc.

αὐειρόμεναι, v. ἀείρω. **αὐεκίζει**· σφακελίζει (Cypr.), Hsch.

αὐεοῦλλαι, = ἄελλαι, dub. in Alc.125.

αὖερος, v. αὐήρ.

αὐερύω, i. e. ἀϝ-ϝερύω, Ep. for ἀν-ϝερύω, = Att. ἀναρρύω: aor. αὐέρυσα:—*draw back* or *backwards*, τὰς [στήλας] οἵ γ' αὐέρυον *pulled* them *backwards*, Il.12.261; τόξον αὐερύοντα παρ' ὦμον 8.325: mostly abs., in sacrifice, *draw* the victim's head *back*, so as to cut its throat, αὐέρυσαν μὲν πρῶτα καὶ ἔσφαξαν 1.459, cf. Pi.*O.*13.81, Theoc.25.241, *AP*6.96 (Eryc.). II. of leeches, *suck*, Opp.*H.*2.603.

αὐετής, i. e. ἀ-ϝετής, ές, (ἀ- copul., ἔτος) = αὐτοετής, Hsch.

αὐῆλαι· αἶσαι, Hsch.

αὐήρ, i. e. ἀϝήρ, Aeol. for ἀήρ, Greg.Cor.p.612 S.; cf. **αὐερός**· σκιά, Hsch.

αὐηρός, ά, όν, = αὐαλέος, *AP*12.121 (Rhian.). **αὐήτω**· ἔπνεον, Hsch.

αὐθάγιος [ᾰ], α, ον, *absolutely holy*, θεός *PMag.Leid.W.*7.18.

αὐθάδ-εια [θᾰ], poet. and later Prose (*SIG*1243.27) **-ία**, ἡ, *wilfulness, stubbornness*, A.*Pr.*79, S.*OT*549, Ar.*Th.*704, Pl.R.590a, *BGU*1187.21 (i B. C.), *IG*7.2725.27 (Acraephia, ii A. D.), etc.; opp. εὐβουλία, A.*Pr.*1034; *surliness*, Thphr.*Char.*15.1; mean betw. ἀρέσκεια and σεμνότης, Arist.*EE*1221ª8; αὐθαδίαν αὐθαδίᾳ [ἐξελαύνειν] Antiph.300.4; ἡ αὐ. τῶν συνθηκῶν ὅτι οὐ μετὰ κοινῆς γνώμης αὐτὰς ἔπραξεν D.H.9.17. **-ης**, ες, *self-willed, stubborn*, ἦσάν τε αὐθαδέστεροι Hdt.6.92; τὰς ὀργὰς αὐ. Hp.*Aër.*24, cf. Arist.*Rh.*1367ª37; *surly*, Thphr.*Char.*15.1; αὐθάδη φρονῶν A.*Pr.*907; of a dog, X.*Cyn.*6.25. 2. metaph. of things, *remorseless*, σφηνὸς γνάθος αὐ. A.*Pr.*64. 3. Adv. -δως Ar.*Ra.*1020, *POxy.*1242.41: Comp. -έστερον Pl.*Ap.*34c; cf. αὐτώδης. (From αὐτο-άδης, cf. Arist.*MM*1192ᵇ33.) **-ιάζομαι** or **-ειάζομαι**, late form for sq., J.*BJ*5.3.4, Polem.*Call.*24, S.E.*P.*1.237, Procop.*Arc.*14, 15, Lib.*Decl.*15.47. **-ίζομαι**, aor. -ισάμενος Them.*Or.*34 p.467 D.:—*to be self-willed*, οὐκ αὐθαδιζόμενος Pl.*Ap.*34d; *to be puffed up, arrogant*, Them.*Or.*29.346b. **-ικός**, ή, όν, *like an* αὐθάδης, *self-willed*, Ar.*Lys.*1116. **-ισμα**, ατος, τό, *act of self-will, wilfulness*, A.*Pr.*964 (pl.). **-όστομος**, ον, *presumptuous of speech*, Ar.*Ra.*837.

αὐθ-αίμων, ον, gen. ονος, (αἷμα) *of the same blood, brother, sister, kinsman*, S.*Tr.*1041 (lyr.):—also **-αιμος**, ον, Id.*OC*1078, *AP*7.707 (Diosc.). **-αίρετος**, ον, *self-chosen, self-elected*, στρατηγοί X.*An.*5.7.29; στεφανηφόρος *voluntary*, i. e. undertaking the duty at one's own expense, *Ath.Mitt.*36.159 (Syros, ii A. D.), cf. *IG*12(5).660, 668; γυμνασίαρχος *OGI*583.8; συνήγορος *POxy.*1242.10. Adv. -τως *Inscr.Magn.*163.15, *PLond.*2.280.7 (i A. D.). II. *by free choice, of oneself*, E.*Supp.*931; αὐ. ἐξῆλθε 2*Ep.Cor.*8.17; *independent, free*, εὐβουλία Th.1.78; ἡ τοῦ τέλους ἔφεσις οὐκ αὐ. Arist.*EN*1114ᵇ6. III. of things, *due to one's own choice*, ὄλβος B.*Fr.*20; usu. of evils, *self-incurred*, πημοναί S.*OT*1231; οὐκ αὐθαίρετοι βροτοῖς ἔρωτες E.*Fr.*339; νόσοι.. αἱ μέν εἰσ' αὐ. ib.292.4; κίνδυνοι, δουλεία, Th.1.144, 6.40; θάνατος X.*HG*6.2.36; λῦπαι Men.634; δυστύχημα Id.618. Adv. -τως *of free choice*, Lxx 2*Ma.*6.19, al., Mitteis *Chr.*361 (iv A. D.); πείθεσθαί τινι Plu.*Pel.*24, *independently*, Luc.*Anach.*34.

αὖθε, Thess., = αὖθι, αὖθέ περ *IG*9(2).271 (Cierium).

αὐθ-έδραστος, ον, *self-established, self-supported*, Eustr. *in EN*347.13. **-έκαστος**, ον, *one who calls things by their right names, downright, blunt*, Arist.*EN*1127ª23, cf. Cleanth.*Stoic.*1.127; οὐκ ἔστ' ἀλώπηξ ἡ μὲν εἴρων.., ἡ δ' αὐ. Philem.89.7, cf. Posidipp.40; in later Prose, λόγος Phld.*Piet.*102 (Comp.), cf. Ph.2.51, Plu.*Cat.Ma.*6. Adv. -τως *bluntly*, Phld.*Sign.*32. 2. of style, *inartificial, plain*, D.H.*Comp.*22. 3. in bad sense, *self-willed* (αὐτάρεσκος, Hsch.; = ἀπαρέγκλητος, Suid.), αὐ. τὸν τρόπον, τῷ τρόπῳ, Men.843, *Sam.*205, cf. Luc.*Phal.*1.2, Plu.2.11e; οὐ γὰρ αὐθάδης οὐδὲ αὐ. ὁ σώφρων ἀνήρ ib.823a, cf. Phld.*Vit.*p.30 J. 4. *self-controlled*, ζῷον οὐ μονῆρες καὶ αὐ. ἀλλὰ κοινωνικὸν καὶ πολιτικόν Them.*Or.*34 p.446 D. Adv. -τως Plu.*Lys.*21. **-εκαστότης**, ητος, ἡ, *bluntness*, condemned by Phryn.330.

αὐθεντ-έω, *to have full power* or *authority over*, τινός 1*Ep.Ti.*2.12; πρός τινα *BGU*1208.37 (i B. C.): c. inf., Lyd.*Mag.*3.42. 2. *commit a murder*, Sch.A.*Eu.*42. **-ημα**· *auctoramentum*, *Gloss.* **-ης**, ου, ὁ, (cf. αὐτοέντης) *murderer*, Hdt.1.117, E.*Rh.*873, Th.3.58; τινός E.*HF*1359, A.R.2.754; *suicide*, Antipho 3.3.4, D.C.37.13: more loosely, *one of a murderer's family*, E.*Andr.*172. 2. *perpetrator, author*, πράξεως Plb.22.14.2; ἱεροσυλίας D.S.16.61: generally, *doer*, Alex.*Rh.*p.2 S.; *master*, δῆμος αὐθέντης χθονός E.*Supp.*442; voc. αὐθέντα ἥλιε *PMag.Leid.W.*6.46; condemned by Phryn.96. 3. as Adj., ὅμαιμος αὐ. φόνος, αὐ. θάνατοι, murder *by one of the same family*, A.*Eu.*212, *Ag.*1572 (lyr.). (For αὐτο-έντης, cf. συν-έντης, ἀνύω; root *sen-, sn̥-*.) **-ία**, ἡ, *absolute sway, authority*, *CIG*2701.9 (Mylasa), *PLips.*37.7 (iv A. D.), *Corp.Herm.*1.2, Zos.2.33. 2. *restriction*, Lxx 3*Ma.*2.29. 3. αὐθεντίᾳ ἀποκτεῖναι *with his own hand*, D.C.*Fr.*102.12. **-ίζω**, *take in hand*, *BGU*103.3. **-ικός**, ή, όν, *principal*, ἄνεμοι *Gp.*1.11.1. 2. *warranted, authentic*, χειρογραφία, ἀποχή, διαθήκη, *POxy.*260.20 (i A. D.), *Ostr.*1010, *BGU*326 ii 23 (ii A. D.); *original*, ἐπιστολαί *PHamb.*18 ii 6 (iii A. D.); ἐπιθύματα *PMag.Leid.W.*9.15; ὄνομα ib.14.25; *authoritative*, Ptol.*Tetr.*182. Adv. -κῶς, *loqui* make an *authoritative* statement, Cic.*Att.*9.14.2; αὐ. *nuntiabatur* ib.10.9.1: Comp. -ώτερον *with higher authority*, Ptol.*Tetr.*177. **-ρια**, ἡ, fem. of αὐθέντης, = κυρία, Keil-Premerstein *Zweiter Bericht* 142.

αὐθεύρετος, ον, *self-discovered*, Simp. *in Ph.*1250.14.

αὐθέψης, ου, ὁ, (ἕψω) Lat. *authepsa*, *self-boiler, urn*, Cic.*Rosc.Amer.*46.133, *Hist.Aug.Elag.*19.

αὐθημερ-εί or **-ί**, Adv. = αὐθημερόν, *Inscr.Prien.*28.17 (ii B. C.), *IG*2.471.71, 3.73, v.l. in Sch.Aeschin.1.128. **-ίζω**, *return on the same day*, Poll.1.64. **-ινός**, ή, όν, = sq., *ephemeral*, ποιηταί Cratin.306. 2. μίσθιος αὐ. *day*-labourer, Lxx *Jb.*7.1. 3. σοφὸς αὐ., = αὐτοσχέδιος, Eust.44.14. 4. = sq., Thphr.*Sign.*10. **-ος**, ον, *made* or *done on the very day*, αὐ. ἀναπλάσσεσθαι Hp.*Art.*37; λόγοι *extemporaneous* speeches, prob. f.l. for -ημερόν in Aeschin.3.208. 2. φάρμακον αὐ. curing *in one day*, Gal.12.755. II. Adv. **αὐθημερόν** (on the accent v. Hdn.Gr.1.491) *on the very day, on the same day, immediately*, A.*Pers.*456, Ar.*Ach.*522, al., Th.2.12, D.21.89:—also **αὐθήμερα** Hp.*Fract.*24, *Mochl.*42; Ion. **αὐτημερόν** Hdt.2.122, 6.139 (but αὐθ- in Hp.*Prog.*17, *Aph.*4.10); Locr. **αὐταμαρόν** *IG*9(1).334.33; Dor. **αὐθαμέραν** *SIG*559.57 (Megalop.); Cret. **αὐταμερίν** *GDI* 4999 (Gortyn).

αὖθι, Adv. shortd. for αὐτόθι, of Place, *on the spot, here, there*, Il.1.492, etc.; αὖθ' ἐπὶ τάφρῳ 11.48; ἐνθάδε κ' αὖθι μένων Od.5.208; ἐν Λακεδαίμονι αὖθι Il.3.244; αὖθι ἔχειν to keep him *there, as he is*, Od.4.416. 2. of Time, *forthwith, straightway*, Il.5.296, 6.281, etc.—Ep. word, borrowed by S.*Fr.*522; cf. αὐτόθι. 3. later, = αὖθις, Lyc.732, Call.*Dian.*241, *AP*9.343 (Arch.):—also **αὖθιν** (said to be Rhegian) acc. to Theognost.*Can.*161, 163.

αὐθιγενής, ές, *born on the spot, born in the country, native*, Μοῦσα B.2.11; θεός Hdt.4.180; ἔθνος D.H.1.9, cf. Luc.*Herm.*24; αὐ. ποταμοὶ Σκυθικοί the Scythian rivers *that rise in the country*, Hdt.4.48; τὸ ὕδωρ..αὐ. μὲν οὐκ ἔστι not *from a natural spring*, Id.2.149; δόκος E.*Fr*.472.5 (lyr.); οἶνος Anaxandr.41.71; αὐ. καὶ ἄκρατος ἀλλοτρίοις ἤθεσι βίος τῶν ἐνύδρων Plu.2.976a; αὐ. καὶ αὐτόχθων ἐλευθερία *IG*7.2713.38 (speech of Nero). 2. *genuine, sincere*, ἰάλεμος E.*Rh*.895 (lyr.).

αὐθίξας· κινήσας, Hsch.

αὖθις, Ep. and Ion. **αὖτις** (also in S.*Ichn*.227,229, *Fr*.599, cod. Laur. in Id.*OC*234 (lyr.), 1438, and Men.*Epit*.362, *Sam*.281,292), Adv., a lengthd. form of αὖ: I. of Place, *back, back again*, αὖτις ἰών Il.8.271, al.; ἂψ αὖτις ib.335; τὴν αὐτὴν ὁδὸν αὖτις 6.391; rare later, δευρὶ καὖθις ἐκεῖσε Ar.*Ra*.1077. II. of Time, *again, anew*, Il.4.222, etc.; freq. strengthd., ὕστερον αὖ. 1.27, cf. S.*Aj*.858; ἔτ' αὖ. Il.9.375; πάλιν αὖ. 5.257, S.*Fr*.487; αὖ. πάλιν Id.*OC*364, etc.; αὖ. αὖ πάλιν ib.1418 codd.; αὖ πάλιν αὖθις Ar.*Nu*.975; μάλ' αὖ. A.*Ch*.654,876, *Ag*.1345; βοᾶν αὖθις cry *encore!* X.*Smp*.9.4. 2. *in turn*, αὖθις ἐγὼ αὐτοὺς ἀνηρώτων Pl.*Chrm*.153d. 3. of future Time, *hereafter*, ταῦτα μεταφρασόμεσθα καὶ αὖ. Il.1.140, cf. A.*Ag*.317, S.*Aj*.1283, Antipho 5.94, Isoc.4.110; ὁ αὖ. χρόνος Pl.*Lg*.934a; οἱ αὖ. *posterity*, S.E.*M*.1.53. III. of sequence, *in turn*, A.*Th*.576, S.*OT*1403, Pl.*Ap*.24b; *on the other hand*, οὔτ' ἀβέλτερος οὔτ' αὖ. ἔμφρων Alex.245.8; sts. in apodosi for δέ, τοῦτο μέν ... τοῦτ' αὖθις.. S.*Ant*.167; πρῶτα μέν..αὖτις δέ.. Hdt.7.102.

αὐθϊτελής, ές, *decided on the spot*, δίκαι prob. in *OGI*7.4 (Cyme).

αὐθ-όμαιμος, strengthd. for ὅμαιμος, S.*OC*335, Lyc.222. **-ομολογέομαι**, *confess of oneself*, πρᾶγμα αὐθομολογούμενον a thing *that speaks for itself*, Luc.*Herm*.59 (dub. for αὖθις ὁμ.).

αὐθόρης· αὐτὸς βλέπων, Hsch. **αὐθορόν·** σύντομον, and **αὐθορίτους·** συντόμους, Id.; cf. αὐθωρός.

αὐθ-όρμητος, ον, *self-impelled*, Eustr.*in EN*33.29, Eust.1148.13. Adv. -τως Id.1370.23:—also **-ορμητικῶς** Sch.E.*Hec*.1227. **-ύπαρκτος**, ον, *self-subsistent*, Hsch. Adv. -τως Zonar. s.v. ἕνωσις. **-υπόστᾰτος**, ον, *self-substantial*, Jul.*Or*.4.139d, Iamb.ap.Stob.2.8.45, Procl.*in Prm*.p.610S. Adv. -τως Phlp.*in de An*.52.19. **-υπότακτος** (sc. χρόνος), ὁ, *the subjunctive aor. 2*, sts. also, *aor. 1*, Hdn.*Epim*.278, *AB*1086. Adv. -τως *in the subjunctive of this tense*, ibid. **-ωρός**, όν, *in that very hour*, ἀγώγιμον αὐθωρόν, of a spell, *taking immediate effect*, *PMag.Lond*.121.300. Adv. -ρόν *immediately*, Hp.*Mochl*.2, Str.3.5.7, *PFlor*.186.10 (iii A.D.), Eun.*VS*p.471B., Agath.3.9:—also **αὐθωρεί** or -ρί, Lxx *Da*.3.15, 3*Ma*.3.25, Cic.*Att*.2.13.1, Plu.2.512e.

αὐΐᾰχος [ῐ], ον, (i.e. ἀ-ϝίαχος) either, 1. (from ἀ- copul., ἰαχή) *joining in a shout*, or, 2. (from ἀν- or ἀ- priv.) *noiseless*, ἄβρομοι αὐΐαχοι Il.13.41, cf. Q.S.13.70:—ἀνίαχοι is v.l. in Il. l.c. and read by codd. in Q.S. l.c., cf. Hsch.

αὐίδετος, i.e. ἀ-ϝίδετος, ον, *unseen*, Hsch. **αὐκάν·** ἀλκάν (Cret.), Id. **αὐκήλως·** ἕως (Tyrrhen.), Id. **αὐκηρεσίη·** ἀφθάρτη, Id. **αὐκυών·** ἀλκ- (Cret.), Id.

αὐλά· πανδέκτης, Hsch.

αὐλαϝυδός, ὁ, later Boeot. for αὐλῳδός, *IG*7.3195 (Orchom. Boeot.).

αὐλαία, ἡ, (αὐλή) *curtain*, Hyp.*Fr*.139, Thphr.*Char*.5.9, Men.834, *Michel*832.26 (Samos, iv B.C.), Plu.*Alex*.49; esp. in the theatre, Men. l.c.; *hunting-net*, Plu.*Alex*.40: in pl., *screens* to protect a wall against missiles, Ph.*Bel*.95.34.

αὐλαῖος, α, ον, = αὔλειος, θύρα Lxx 2*Ma*.14.41:—as Subst., perh. *doorkeeper*, Baillet *Inscriptions des tombeaux des rois à Thèbes* 199.

αὐλᾰκ-εργάτης [γᾰ], ου, ὁ, (αὖλαξ) *tracing furrows*, *AP*9.742 (Phil. (?)). **-ίζω**:—Med., fut. -ίσομαι *PFlor*.326.10 (ii A.D.):—*trace furrows on, plough*, ἐδάφη *PFlor*. l.c.:—Pass., ib.331.7 (ii A.D.); αὐλακισμέναν ἀροῦν, prov. of doing work over again, Pratin.*Lyr*.3: metaph. of a shooting star *leaving a trail*, *Cat.Cod.Astr*.8(3).182.4. **-ιον**, τό, Dim. of αὖλαξ, Sch.D.T.p.196H. **-ισμός**, ὁ, *ploughing*, *PFlor*.354.3 (ii A.D.).

αὐλᾰκο-ειδής, ές, *furrow-like*, γραμμή Eust.598.34. **-εις**, εσσα, εν, *furrowed*, Max.506. **-τομέω**, *cut into furrows*, οὐσίαν S.E.*M*.9.40 (Pass.).

αὐλᾰκώδης, ες, *like a furrow*, φυτεία Eust.831.59.

αὖλαξ, ᾰκος, ἡ (also ὁ, *AP*9.274 (Phil.), Aret.*SD*2.13), also **ἄλοξ**, οκος (q.v.); **ὦλξ**, found only in acc. ὦλκα, ὦλκας; Dor. **ὦλαξ** *EM*625.38:—*furrow* made in ploughing, [βόε] ἱεμένω κατὰ ὦλκα hastening along *the furrow*, Il.13.707; κατὰ ὤλκας A.R.3.1054; εἰ ὦλκα διηνεκέα προταμοίμην Od.18.375; [βόε] ἐρίσαντε ἐν αὔλακι Hes.*Op*.439; ἰθεῖαν κ' αὔλακ' ἐλαύνοι ib.443; ὀρθὰς αὔλακας...ἤλαυνε Pi.*P*.4.227; ἀρότρῳ ἀναρρηγνύντες αὔλακας Hdt.2.14; αἰθέρος αὔλακα τέμνων Ar.*Av*.1400 (lyr.); ἐξ ἀλόκων ἐπετειᾶν A.*Ag*.1015; βαθεῖαν ἄλοκα διὰ φρενὸς καρπούμενος Id.*Th*.593; ἐν ἄλοκι Ar.*Av*.234 (lyr.). b. *furrow's breadth*, Thphr.*HP*8.8.7, *CP*4.12.1. 2. metaph., *wife*, σπείρειν τέκνων ἄλοκα E.*Ph*.18; αἱ πατρῷαι ἄλοκες thy father's *wife*, S.*OT*1211. 3. metaph., *furrow in the skin, gash, wound*, ὄνυχος ἄλοκι νεοτόμῳ A.*Ch*.25 (lyr.); δορὸς ἄλοκα E.*HF*164; of the line drawn by the stile in writing, ποίαν αὔλακα; Ar.*Th*.782 (anap.), cf. *AP*6.68 (Jul. Aegypt.). 4. *swathe*, Theoc.10.6. 5. αὖ. ὑδροφόρος aque-*duct*, *IG*14.453 (Catana). b. αὔλακας· κοίλους τόπους, Hsch.—Chiefly poet., never in good Att. Prose; Hom. only in acc. ὦλκα; αὖλαξ only is used by Pi. and Hdt., ἄλοξ only by Trag.; both αὖλαξ and ἄλοξ by Ar. (Cf. Lac. εὐλάκα 'plough', Lith. velkù, Slav. vlěką 'pull'.)

αὐλαρός· αὐλωρός, Hsch.

αὐλ-άρχης, ου, ὁ, *chief of the court, mayor of the palace*, Lxx 2*Ki*.8.18:—hence Subst. **-αρχία**, ἡ, ib.3*Ki*.3.1.

αὐλάχα· ἡ ὕννις, Hsch.

αὐλεία, ἡ, = αὐλαία, *IG*5(1).1390.35 (Andania, i B.C.).

αὔλειος, α, ον, sts. also ος, ον (cf. infr.):—*of* or *belonging to the court*, ἐπ' αὐλείῃσι θύρῃσι at the door *of the court*, i.e. the *outer* door, *house*-door, Od.11.239, cf. Pi.*N*.1.19, Hdt.6.69; αὔλειοι θύραι Sol.4.28; ἐπὶ προθύροις..οὐδοῦ ἐπ' αὐλείου Od.1.104; ἐκτὸς αὐ. πυλῶν S.*Ant*.18; πρὸς αὐλείοισιν ἑστηκὼς πύλαις E.*Hel*.438: sg., ἡ αὔλειος θύρα Lys.1.17, Pl.*Smp*.212c, Thphr.*Char*.28.3, Men.546; ἡ αὐλεία θύρα *IG*11(2).287*A*146 (Delos, iii B.C.), Thphr.*Char*.18.4; ἡ αὐλεία alone, Ar.*Pax*982, *Fr*.255, *SIG*[2]587.122; ἡ αὔλειος Plu.*Pomp*.46, 2.516f, Luc.*Tox*.17; αἱ αὔλειοι Plb.5.76.4.

αὐλείτης, ου, ὁ, = αὐλίτης, A.R.4.1487 codd.; for Boeot. αὐλειτάς v. αὐλητής.

αὐλέω, Boeot. part. αὐλίων *IG*7.3211,3212 (Orchom. Boeot.): (αὐλός):—*play on the flute*, Φρύγιον αὔλησεν μέλος Alcm.82, cf. Hdt.1.141, 2.60, Pl.*Prt*.327a: c. dat. pers., X.*Smp*.2.8, etc.; αὐ. ἔξοδον *play* a finale, Ar.*V*.582; αὐ. εἰρεσίαν, of the boatswain, Plu.*Alc*.32:—Pass., of tunes, *to be played on the flute*, ὁ Βακχεῖος ῥυθμὸς ηὐλεῖτο X.*Smp*.9.3; αὐλεῖται πᾶν μέλαθρον *is filled with music*, E.*IT*367. 2. of persons, *play to*, Philostr.*VA*2.34, cf. A.D.*Synt*.302.1:—mostly in Pass., *to be played to, hear music*, X.*An*.6.1.11, *Cyr*.4.5.7, Arist.*Pr*.917[b]19 (but possibly Med. as in Pl.*Lg*.791a), Thphr.*Char*.19.10, 20.10. II. generally, *play*, κέρατι Luc.*DDeor*.12.1, cf. Poll.4.74.

αὐλή, ἡ, *open court* before the house, *courtyard*, Il.4.433, 11.774, *SIG*1044.17 (Halic., iv/iii B.C.), etc. 2. *steading* for cattle, αὐλῆς ὑπεράλμενον Il.5.138, cf. Od.14.5. II. later, *court* or *quadrangle*, round which the house was built, Hdt.3.77, Ar.*V*.131, Pl.*Prt*.311a, etc. III. generally, *court, hall*, Ζηνὸς αὐ. Od.4.74, cf. Il.6.247; τὴν Διὸς αὐλήν A.*Pr*.122 (lyr.); αὐ. νεκύων E.*Alc*.260 (lyr.); *court* of a temple, ἱεροῦ *IG*2[2].1299.28 (Eleusis, iii B.C.), cf. ib.1126.35, Lxx *Ps*.83(84).3; *any dwelling, abode, chamber*, S.*Ant*.946 (lyr.), etc.; of a cave, Id.*Ph*.153 (lyr.); ἀγρόνομοι αὐλαί *homes* of dwellers in the wild, Id.*Ant*.786 (lyr.); later, *country-house*, D.H.6.50. IV. ἡ αὐλή *the Court*, αὐλὰς θεραπεύειν Men.897, Diph.97, *Com.Adesp*.145, cf. Plb.5.26.9; οἱ περὶ τὴν αὐλήν the *courtiers*, ib.36.1, cf. *OGI*735.4 (ii B.C.), *Inscr.Mus.Alex*.31; at Rome, Arr.*Epict*.1.10.3; ἡ βασίλειος αὐ. Hdn.3.11.7. (Wrongly expld. as τόπος διαπνεόμενος (cf. αὐλός) by Ath.5.189b.)

αὔλημα, ατος, τό, *piece of music for the flute*, Ar.*Ra*.1302, Pl.*Smp*.216c, al.

αὔληρα (i.e. ἄϝληρα, cf. ἄβληρα), τά, Dor. for εὔληρα (q.v.), Epich.178: sg. in Hsch.

αὔλ-ησις, εως, ἡ, *flute-playing*, Pl.*Prt*.327b,c, al., Arist.*Pol*.1341[a]25, etc. **-ητήρ**, ῆρος, ὁ, = αὐλητής, Hes.*Sc*.283,298, Archil.123, Thgn.825, Ar.*Fr*.566. **-ητηρία·** αὐλῶν θήκη, Hsch. **-ητήριον**, τό, a place at Tarentum, Id. **-ητής**, οῦ, ὁ, *flute-player*, Thgn.941, Hdt.1.141, 6.60, 129, Ar.*V*.581, And.1.12, Pl.*Prt*.327b, *OGI*51.62 (iii B.C.); Boeot. **αὐλειτάς** *IG*7.3195 (Orchom. Boeot.). II. kind of *wasp*, Hsch. III. αὐ. ὑπονόμων sanitary *engineer*, Procl.*Par.Ptol*.250. **-ήτης**, ου, ὁ, (αὐλή III), = αὐλίτης, Hsch. **-ητικός**, ή, όν, *of* or *for the flute*, Pl.*Ap*.27b; δάκτυλοι Pl.Com.211; κάλαμος *used for making flutes*, Thphr.*HP*4.10.1, Sch.Il.*Oxy*.221 ix 12; τέλος Plot.1.4.15: -κή (sc. τέχνη), ἡ, *flute-playing*, Pl.*Grg*.501e, Arist.*Po*.1447[a]15. Adv. -κῶς, δεῖ καρκινοῦν τοὺς δακτύλους Antiph.55.15, cf. Plu.2.404f. 2. *fitted for flute-playing*, ψυχή Pl.*Hp.Mi*.375b (Comp.). **-ήτρια**, ἡ, = αὐλητρίς, D.L.7.62. **-ητρίδιον**, τό, Dim. of sq., Theopomp.Hist.205, *Com.Adesp*.25.34D., D.L.7.13. **-ητρίς**, ίδος, ἡ, *flute-girl*, Simon.178, Ar.*Ach*.551, X.*HG*2.2.23, Pl.*Prt*.347d, *BCH*6.24 (Delos, ii B.C.), etc.

αὐλία· ἔπαυλις, ἡ ἡ μικρὰ αὐλή, *AB*463.

ἀϋλία [ῡ], ἡ, (ἄϋλος) *immateriality*, Hierocl.*in CA*26 p.479 M., Syrian.*in Metaph*.27.30, Nicom.*Ar*.1.3.

αὐλιάδες νύμφαι, (αὖλις) nymphs *protecting cattle-folds*, *APl*.4.291 (Anyte).

αὐλίδιον, τό, Dim. of αὐλή, *place of athletic exercises, ring*, Thphr.*Char*.5.9. II. (αὐλός) *small tube*, Alex.Trall.3.3.

αὐλιεῖον, τό, = αὔλιον II (nisi leg. αὔλειον), *Epigr.Gr*.1075.6 (Erythrae).

αὐλίζομαι, aor. 1 ηὐλισάμην always in Th., as 4.13, 6.7, cf. (κατ-) Plu.*Tim*.12; ηὐλίσθην always in X., as *An*.4.1.11, al.; both in Hdt., as 8.9 (ἐν-), 9.15: late fut. αὐλισθήσομαι Lxx *To*.6.10: pf. ηὔλισμαι Arr.*An*.3.29.7, J.*BJ*1.17.5:—*lie in the* αὐλή or *courtyard*, μυκηθμοῦ..βοῶν αὐλιζομενάων Od.12.265; κλαγγὴ..συῶν αὐλιζομενάων 14.412; *take up one's abode, lodge, live* in a place, ἐν ἄντρῳ, of sheep, Hdt.9.93; περὶ τὴν λίμνην, of birds, 3.110, cf. Arist.*HA*619[a]30; οἵοις ἐν πέπλοις αὐ. E.*El*.304; ἄδειπνος..ηὐλιζόμην *passed the night*, Eup.322; esp. as military term, *encamp, bivouac*, Hdt.8.9: Medic., of blood, *lodge* or *settle* in a place, Aret.*SA*2.2 (nisi leg. ἁλισθέν): metaph., τὸ ἑσπέρας αὐλισθήσεται κλαυθμός Lxx *Ps*.29(30).6. II. Act., *cause to dwell*, ib.*Je*.38(31).9, D.Chr.35.16.

αὐλικός, ή, όν, (αὐλή) *of the court, courtier-like*, κατὰ τὴν φύσιν Plb.23.5.4; αὐ. ἀγχίνοια 15.34.4; αὐ. βίος, opp. ὁ φιλόσοφος βίος, Phld.*Ind.Sto*.13: Comp., ἐξ αὐλικωτέρων γονέων Id.*Lib*.p.45 O.: as Subst., *courtier*, Plb.16.20.8, Plu.2.778b, *Demetr*.17. II. αὐλικούς· κιθαρῳδούς, Suid.

αὐλίκουροι· φύλακες, Hsch. **αὐλίξ·** φλέψ, Id. **αὐλίξαι·** στασιάσαι (leg. σταδ-), δραμεῖν, Id.

αὔλιον, τό, *country-house, cottage*, *h.Merc*.103; *fold, stable*, etc.,

E.*Cyc.*345,593, X.*HG*3.2.4, etc.: prov., βοῦς ἐν αὐλίῳ 'round peg in a square hole', Cratin.32. II. *chamber, cave, grotto*, ἀμφιτρῆς αὐ. S.*Ph.*19, cf. 954, al., *AP*6.334 (Leon.).

αὔλιος, α, ον, (αὐλή 1) *belonging to folds*, ἀστὴρ αὔλιος '*star that bids the shepherd fold*', A.R.4.1630, cf. Call.*Fr.*539; ὅταν αὐλίοις συρίζῃς, ὦ Πάν, τοῖς σοῖσιν ἐν ἄντροις dub. l. in E.*Ion* 500 (lyr.). II. αὔλιος θύρα dub. l. in Men.546; cf. αὐλία θύρα· πυλών, Hsch.

αὖλις, ιδος, ἡ, *tent* or *place for passing the night in*, αὖλιν ἔθεντο Il. 9.232; αὖλιν ἐσιέμεναι to go to *roost*, of birds, Od.22.470, cf. *h.Merc.* 71, E.*Cyc.*363, Call.*Dian.*87, Theoc.25.18, Arat.1027; αἰγινόμων *AP*6.221 (Leon.).

αὔλισις, εως, ἡ, = αὐλισμός, Ael.*NA*4.59.

αὐλίσκος, ὁ, (αὐλός 1.2) *small reed, pipe*, λιγύφθογγος Thgn.241; αὐλίσκων ὑπὸ λωτίνων cj. in Pi.*Parth.*2.14: prov., φυσᾷ οὐ σμικροῖσιν αὐλίσκοις makes a great bluster, S.*Fr.*768. II. generally, *small pipe* or *tube*, Arist.*Ath.*68.2, Plb.27.11.2, Mnesith.ap.Orib.8.38.3; *catheter*, Hp.*Morb.*1.6. III. = αἰδοῖον, Ptol.*Tetr.*187, Sch.Opp. *H.*1.582, Anon.*in Ptol.Tetr.*157. IV. *ear-ring* (Persian), Hsch.

αὔλ-ισμα, ατος, τό, = sq., Sch.Opp.*H.*3.5 (pl.). **-ισμός**, ὁ, *lodging*, Sm.*Is.*10.29: = διαννκτέρευσις, Hsch. **-ιστέον**, *one must fold* or *house* cattle, *Gp.*18.3.8. **-ιστήριον**, τό, *stall, steading*, Herm.ap.Stob.1.49.68, Aq.*Is.*10.29, Hsch. s.v. συοβαύβαλοι.

αὐλίτης [ῑ], ου, ὁ, (αὐλή III) *farm-servant*, S.*Fr.*502, A.R.4.1487; cf. αὐλείτης, αὐλήτης.

αὐλο-βόας, ὁ, ἡ, *sounding the flute, flute-playing*, *IG*3.82. **-δόκη**, ἡ, *flute-case*, *AP*5.205 (Leon.). **-θετέω**, *make flutes* or *pipes*, ib.6.120 (Leon.). **-θήκη**, ἡ, *flute-case*, Hsch.s.v. συρβηνεύς, Sch.Ar.*Th.* 1197. **-μᾰνέω**, *play the flute in mystic orgies*, D.S.36.4. **-μᾰνής**, ές, *flute-inspired*, Nonn.*D.*8.29. **-μελῳδία**, ἡ, *flute-* or *pipe-music*, Ps.-Callisth.1.46. **-ποιΐα**, ἡ, *flute-making*, Poll.7.153. **-ποιϊκή** (sc. τέχνη), ἡ, = foreg., Pl.*Euthd.*289c:—also **-ποιητική**, Asp.*in EN* 15.24: hence Adv. **-ητικῶς** Poll.7.153. **-ποιός**, ὁ, *flute-maker*, Pl.*R.*399d, 601d, Arist.*Pol.*1277ᵇ29, Dsc.2.75.

αὐλός, ὁ, *pipe, flute, clarionet*, Il.10.13, 18.495, *h.Merc.*452; Λύδιος Pi.*O.*5.19; Ἔλυμος, i.e. Φρύγιος (q.v.), S.*Fr.*398; Λίβυς E.*Alc.*347; αὐ. γυναικήιος, ἀνδρήιος, Hdt.1.17; αὐ. ἀνδρεῖοι, παιδικοί, παρθένιοι, Ath.4.176f, Poll.4.81; ὁ παρθένιος αὐ. τοῦ παιδικοῦ ὀξύτερος Arist. *HA*581ᵇ11; διδύμοις αὐλοῖσιν ἀεῖσαι Theoc.*Ep.*5.1; ἐμφυσᾶν εἰς αὐλούς D.S.3.59; αὐ. Ἐνυαλίου, i.e. *a trumpet*, *AP*6.151 (Tymn.); ὑπ' αὐλοῦ to the sound of *the flute*, Hdt. l. c.; πρὸς τὸν αὐ., ὑπὸ τὸν αὐ., X.*Smp.*6.3, etc.: pl., αὐλοὶ πηκτίδος *pipes* of the πηκτίς, *IG*4.53 (Aegina). 2. *hollow tube, pipe, groove*, περόνη τέτυκτο αὐλοῖσιν διδύμοισι the buckle was furnished with two *pipes* or *grooves* (into which the tongue fitted), Od.19.227; ἐγκέφαλος παρ' αὐλὸν ἀνέδραμε spirted up beside *the vizard* (cf. αὐλῶπις), or beside *the socket of the spear-head* into which the shaft fitted, Il.17.297; but in Od. 22.18 αὐλὸς παχύς means the *jet* of blood *through the tube* of the nostril; αὐλὸς ἐκ χαλκείου the smith's *bellows*, Hp.*Art.*47,77, cf. Th.4.100; *tube* of the clepsydra, Arist.*Pr.*914ᵇ14; βλέπειν δι' αὐλοῦ Id.*GA*780ᵇ19. 3. in animals, *blow-hole* of cetacea, Id.*HA*589ᵇ19, *PA*697ᵃ17; *funnel* of a cuttle-fish, Id.*HA*524ᵃ10; *conus arteriosus* in fishes, ib.507ᵃ10, *Resp.*478ᵇ8; *duct*, prob. in Id.*GC*322ᵃ 28. 4. *stadium* (cf. δίαυλος), Lyc.40. 5. *haulm* of grain, Sch. Theoc.10.46. 6. *cow-bane, Cicuta virosa*, Ps.-Plu.*Fluv.*10.3. 7. εἶδος ἀκολάστου σχήματος, *EM*170.28. II. *razor-shell*, = σωλήν (q.v.), Diph.Siph.ap.Ath.3.90d, Plin.*HN*32.103.

ἄῦλος [ῡ], ον, *immaterial*, dub. in Arist.*GC*322ᵃ28 (v. foreg. I. 3); ἀρετή Plu.2.440e; θεός ib.1085c; οὐσία Jul.*Or.*4.140c; τὸ ἄ. Hierocl. *in CA*26 p.481 M.: Comp. -ότερος, νοῦς Ph.1.61. Adv. -λως Plot.1. 3.6, Iamb.*Myst.*5.15, Simp.*in Cael.*441.4, etc. 2. v. ἄνυλος.

αὐλοστᾰτέω, *set up a farmstead*, *Schwyzer* 197.54,62 (Crete, iii B.C.).

ἀϋλότης, ητος, ἡ, *immateriality*, Plot.1.2.7.

αὐλο-τρύπης [ῠ], ου, ὁ, *flute-borer*, Stratt.3, Arist.*Pr.*919ᵇ7. **-τρῠπητικῶς**, Adv. *belonging to flute-boring*, Poll.7.153.

αὐλουρός, ὁ, *keeper of the court* or *fold*, Hsch.

αὐλῳδ-έω, *sing to the flute*, Sch.Ar.*Nu.*971. **-ία**, ἡ, *song to the flute*, Pl.*Lg.*700d, Plu.2.1132f. **-ικός**, ή, όν, *belonging to* αὐλῳδία, νόμοι ib.1132c, etc. **-ός**, ὁ, *one who sings to the flute*, *SIG*457.19 (Thespiae, iii B.C.), Plu.2.150a, Ath.14.621b; cf. αὐλαϝυδός.

αὐλωλάζειν· τὸ συρ⟨ίττ⟩ειν διὰ τῶν δακτύλων, Hsch.

αὐλών, ῶνος, ὁ, also ἡ S.*Fr.*549, Ar.*Av.*244, Carc.1, Philostr.*Im.* 2.6:—*hollow* between hills or banks, *defile, glen*, *h.Merc.*95, Hdt.7. 128,129, Ar. l. c. (lyr.); expld. as οἱ στενοὶ καὶ ἐπιμήκεις ποταμοί Sch. Il.*Oxy.*221 xiv 19. 2. *channel, trench*, A.*Fr.*167 A, Hdt.2.100,127, X.*An.*2.3.10. 3. *strait*, Μαιωτικός A.*Pr.*731; πόντιαι αὐ. sea-straits, *channels*, S.*Tr.*100 (lyr.). 4. *pipe, conduit*, Pl.*Ti.*79a; metaph. of *windpipe* or *duct*, Arist.*PA*664ᵃ27, Gal.*UP*4.14. 5. *furrow* in an elephant's hide, Aret.*SD*2.13.

Αὐλωνεύς, έως, ὁ, title of Dionysus, *IG*3.193.

αὐλωνιάς, άδος, ἡ, *glen-nymph*, Orph.*H.*51.7.

αὐλωνίζω, *live in an* αὐλών, Hsch.

αὐλωνίσκος, ὁ, Dim. of αὐλών, Thphr.*HP*9.7.1.

αὐλωνοειδής, ές, *full of valleys*, D.S.19.17; *in the shape of an* αὐλών, εἰσβολὴ νήσου Id.3.68.

αὐλωπίας, ου, ὁ (Dor. gen. ία Archestr.*Fr.*33), a large fish, similar to ἀνθίας, perh. *Serranus gigas*, Arist.*HA*570ᵇ19, Henioch.3.4, Ael. *NA*13.17; cf. αὐλωπός.

αὐλῶπις, ιδος, ἡ, (ὤψ) in Il. always epith. of τρυφάλεια, helmet *with a tube-like opening* between the cheek-pieces (acc. to Sch. *with a tube* (αὐλός) *to hold the* λόφος), Il.5.182, al.; λόγχη *with a socket* to hold the shaft, S.*Fr.*1027; περικεφαλαία *conical*, Ath.5.189c, cf. Hsch.

αὐλωπός, ὁ, = αὐλωπίας, Opp.*H.*1.256.

αὐλωτός, ή, όν, *furnished with pipes*, φιμοί A.*Fr.*326. II. *pipe-shaped*, Ath.Mech.24.3.

αὖμα· ἅλμα (Cret.), Hsch.

αὐνή, ἡ, prob. f.l. for Ἄχνη in Hecat.365 J.; cf. St.Byz. s. v. Ἴχναι.

αὐξάνιος [ᾰ], ον, (αὔξω, ἀνία) *increasing grief*, δάπεδον *JHS*34.18 (Xanthus).

αὐξάνω Pi.*Fr.*153, Hdt.7.16.α', A.*Pers.*756, E.*Supp.*233, *Fr.*362. 28, Pl.*Ti.*41d:—also **αὔξω** (poet. ἀέξω, q.v.) Thgn.823, Pi.*O.*5.4, Emp.37, S.*Tr.*117 (lyr.), Ar.*Ach.*227, X.*Smp.*7.4, Pl.*R.*573a, D. 3.26, etc. (so Att. Inscrr. and Ptolemaic Pap.; both forms in *NT*): impf. ηὔξανον only Ps.-E.*Fr.*1132.25; ηὖξον Hdt.9.31, etc.: fut. αὐξήσω Th.6.40, etc. (αὐξανῶ only in Lxx *Ge.*17.6, al.): aor. 1 ηὔξησα Sol. 11, X.*HG*7.1.24: pf. ηὔξηκα Pl.*Ti.*90b, X.*Hier.*2.15:—Pass., αὐξάνομαι Hdt.2.14, E.*Med.*918, Ar.*Av.*1065, Isoc.4.104, Pl.*Phd.*96c, D. 18.161; αὔξομαι Emp.26.2, Ar.*Ach.*227, Pl.*R.*328d, etc., impf. ηὔξετο Hes.*Th.*493, Hdt.3.39 (v. l. αὔξετο): pf. ηὔξημαι E.*IA*1248, Pl.*R.* 371e, Ion. αὐξ- Hdt.1.58: plpf. ηὔξητο Id.5.78: aor. ηὐξήθην Th.1.89, Pl.*Prt.*327c: fut. αὐξηθήσομαι D.56.48; αὐξήσομαι X.*Cyr.*6.1.12, Pl.*R.* 497a:—*increase*, not in Hom. (only ἀέξω), Pi.*Fr.*153, etc.; ὕβριν αὐ. Hdt.7.16.α'; ὄλβον A.*Pers.*756; opp. ἰσχναίνειν, Pl.*Plt.*293b; εἰς ἄπειρον αὐ. τι Id.*Lg.*910b; ἐπὶ τὸ ἔσχατον Id.*R.*573a; ἐπὶ πλεῖον ηὖξον τὴν μαγειρικὴν τέχνην Athenio1.16, etc. 2. *increase in power, strengthen*, αὐ. τὰ Ἑλλήνων *increase* their power, Hdt.8.30; νόμοισιν αὐ. πόλιν S.*Ant.*191, cf. X.*Mem.*3.7.2; *exalt by one's deeds, glorify*, πόλιν, πάτραν, Pi.*O.*5.4, *P.*8.38, cf. *IG*2².834, etc.; *exalt by praise, extol*, ἐπαινεῖν καὶ αὔξειν τινά Pl.*Ly.*206a; σέ γε.. καὶ τροφὸν καὶ ματέρ' αὔξειν *honour* thee *as*.., S.*OT*1092 (lyr.); of an orator, *amplify, exaggerate*, αὔξειν καὶ μειοῦν Arist.*Rh.*1403ᵃ17. 3. with an Adj., τρέφειν καὶ αὐ. τινὰ μέγαν *bring up* to manhood, Pl.*R.*565c; μείζω πόλιν αὐ. E.*IA*572 (lyr.); τὸν ὄγκον.. ἄπειρον αὐξήσει Pl.*R.*591d. 4. αὔξειν ἔμπυρα *to sacrifice*, Pi.*I.*4(3).62; cf. ἀέξω. 5. in Logic, = καταπυκνόω (q. v.), Arist.*APo.*79ᵃ30, al.; but ὁ αὐξόμενος λόγος, name of a *fallacy*, Plu.*Thes.*23, 2.559b. II. Pass., *grow, increase*, in size, number, strength, power, etc., Hes.*Th.*493, Pi.*P.*8.93, D.61.5, etc.; αὐ. ἐς πλῆθος, ἐς ὕψος, Hdt.1.58, 2.14; of a child, *grow up*, Id.5.92.ε'; ἐν γὰρ τοῖς πόνοισιν αὔξεται, of Theseus, E.*Supp.*323; ηὐξανόμην ἀκούων I *grew taller* as I heard, Ar.*V.*638; of the wind, *rise*, Hdt.7.188; ηὔξηται ἡ πόλις ὥστ' εἶναι τελέα Pl.*R.*371e. 2. with an Adj., αὔξεσθαι μέγας *wax* great, *grow* up, E.*Ba.*183; αὐ. μείζων A.*Supp.* 338, Pl.*Lg.*681a; αὐ. ἐλλόγιμος Id.*Prt.*327c; μέγας ἐκ μικροῦ.. ηὔξηται D.9.21. III. later, Act. intr., like Pass., ἡ σελήνη αὐξάνει Arist. *APo.*78ᵇ6, cf. *HA*620ᵃ21, Aristeas 208, D.S.4.64, *Ep.Col.*2.19, D. Chr.4.128, D.C.48.52, etc. IV. of Verbs, *take the augment*, both Act. and Pass., Hdn.*Epim.*280; αὔξουσα (sc. συλλαβή), ἡ, *augment*, ibid. (Cf. ἀέξω.)

αὔξ-η, ἡ, = αὔξησις, dub. l. in Hp.*Nat.Puer.*16, the form preferred by Pl.; σώματος αὐ. καὶ φθίσις *R.*521e; τὴν γένεσιν καὶ αὔξην καὶ τροφήν ib.509b, cf. Chrysipp.*Stoic.*2.157: also in pl., Pl.*Phlb.*42d. II. *dimension*, ἡ τῶν κύβων αὐ. Id.*R.*528b. **-ημα**, ατος, τό, = foreg., Hp.*Oct.*11, E.*Hyps.Fr.*3 ii 5 (lyr.). **-ηρός**, όν, dub. l. in Nic.*Al.* 588. **-ησία**, Ion. -ίη, ἡ, *the goddess of growth*, Hdt.5.82, *IG*5(1). 363 (I A.D.). **-ησις**, εως, ἡ, *growth, increase*, Hp.*VM*6; τῶν ἐχθρῶν Th.1.69, cf. Plu.*TG*13; κατὰ τὸ ποσόν Arist.*Metaph.*1069ᵇ 11; of the Delta, Hdt.2.13: in pl., *increments*, Pl.*R.*546b; *multiplications*, Ascl.*Tact.*2.7. 2. *amplification*, in Rhet., Arist.*Rh.*1368ᵃ 27, 1413ᵇ34; μετ' αὐξήσεως ἐξαγγέλλειν Plb.10.27.8, cf. D.H.*Th.*19 (pl.). 3. Gramm., *the augment*, *EM*338.47. **-ησίφως**, *increasing light*, epith. of a solar divinity, *PMag.Par.*1.601. **-ητέον**, *one must amplify, exaggerate*, Men.Rh.p.359 S. **-ητής**, οῦ, ὁ, *increaser*, Orph.*H.*11.11, 15.8. **-ητικός**, ή, όν, *growing, of growth*, ἡ αὐ. ζωή Arist.*EN*1098ᵃ1; ψυχή Id.*Juv.*469ᵃ26; αὐ. εἰς μῆκος Thphr. *HP*1.9.1. Adv. -κῶς, κινεῖσθαι Ph.1.492. II. Act., *promoting growth*, c. gen., σπληνός Hp.*Acut.*62; μεγέθους S.E.*M.*3.24: abs., τροφή Arist.*GA*745ᵃ3; -κόν, τό, Id.*Cael.*310ᵃ29. 2. metaph., *amplificatory*, in Rhet., Id.*Rh.*1368ᵃ10, Longin.11.2, etc. Adv. -κῶς Id.38. 2, Sch.Il.*Oxy.*221 ix 31. III. *productive*, Aq.*Is.*32.12. **-ητός**, όν, *that may be increased*, Arist.*Cael.*310ᵃ28. II. *increased*, ἀριθμός Antioch.Astr. in *Cat.Cod.Astr.*1.112.34.

αὖξι, *prosper!* in epitaphs, *Princeton Exp.Inscr.*568, al.; cf. αὐξίτω ib.159 (V A.D.).

αὐξί-δημος [ῐ], *increasing the people*, epith. of Hermes, Hsch. **-θᾰλής**, ές, (θάλλω) *promoting growth*, Orph.*H.*26.3. **-κερως**, ω, *with rising horns*, Archipp.11 (Dind.).

αὔξῐμος, ον, *promoting growth*, Hp.*Vict.*2.65 (Comp.), v.l. in Emp. 100.15, X.*Cyn.*7.3. II. intr., *growing*, Hp.*Art.*58, *Vict.*1.25, A. *Fr.*51, E.ap.*Lex.Sabb.*1.4, *Com.Adesp.*37 D.

αὔξις, εως, ἡ, = αὔξησις, Hsch.

αὐξίς, ίδος, ἡ, Byz. for κορδύλη or σκορδύλη, *young of the tunny*, Phryn.Com.56, Arist.*HA*571ᵃ17, Nic.*Al.*469.

αὐξί-τροφος [ῐ], ον, *promoting growth*, Orph.*H.*10.17, 51.13. **-φαής**, ές, *increasing light*, Man.5.174, *Cat.Cod.Astr.*8(4).217. **-φωνος**, ον, *strengthening the voice*, Philem.Lex. s. v. ἀλεξίκακος. **-φωτέω**, *increase in light, wax*, of the moon, Vett.Val.196.16, Paul Al.*M.*4. **-φωτία**, ἡ, *increase of light*, Lyd.*Mens.*4.71. **-φωτος**, ον, *waxing in light*, *EM*59.40.

αὐξο-βίος [ῐ], ον, *increasing in wealth*, Cat.Cod.Astr.8(4).119. **-μειόω**, *cause to wax and wane*, Ptol.*Alm*.6.7 :—Pass., αὐξομειουμένη Σελήνη Vett.Val.331.28. **-μείωσις**, εως, ἡ, *rise and fall of the tide*, Str.*Chr*.3.26 (pl.). II. *waxing and waning of the moon*, Ant. Diog.4 (pl.; also περὶ τοὺς οἰκείους ὀφθαλμούς ibid.), Ptol.*Alm*.2.1 (pl.); *variation in period*, ζῳδίων *Cat.Cod.Astr*.1.163.13. **-σέληνον**, τό, *increase of the moon, the waxing moon*, *AP*5.270 (Maced.).

αὐξύνω, aor. Pass. ηὐξύνθην, late form of αὐξάνω, Aesop.51.

Αὐξώ, οῦς, ἡ, (αὐξάνω) *goddess of growth*, called to witness in an Athenian citizen's oath, Paus.9.35.2, Poll.8.106.

αὔξω, v. αὐξάνω.

αὐόκωλος, ον, *withered of limb*, Semon.7.76 (prob. αὐτόκ-).

αὐονή (A), ἡ, (αὖος) *dryness, withering, drought*, Archil.125, A.*Eu*. 333 (lyr.), Herod.8.2.

αὐονή (B), ἡ, (αὔω B) *cry*, Semon.7.20.

αὖος, η, ον, Att. **αὗος**, α, ον, also ος, ον Arist.*Pr*.860ᵃ28, Philostr. *VS*1.21.1 :—*dry*, ξύλον *a pole*, Il.23.327; αὖα παλαί, περίκηλα, of timber, Od.5.240, cf. Pl.*Lg*.761c; αὔην καὶ διερὴν ἀρόων (sc. γῆν) Hes.*Op*.460; βόας αὔας shields of ox-hide, Il.12.137, cf. 17.493; so, of hippopotamus' hide, Hdt.2.71; τρύφος ἄρτου *stale*, *AP*6.105 (Apollonid.); *withered*, στέφανος Ar.*Eq*.534. 2. of sound, αὖον ἀϋτεῖν or αὔειν give *a dry, rasping* sound, κόρυθες δ' ἀμφ' αὖον ἀΰτευν Il.12.160; αὖον ἄϋσεν [θώρηξ] 13.441; αὖον δέ μοι οἶκος ἀϋτεῖ prob. in Epic.*Oxy*. 1794.8. 3. αὖον ἀπὸ χλωροῦ τάμνειν, i.e. to cut the nail from the quick, Hes.*Op*.743. 4. *drained dry, exhausted*, Alex.158, Theoc.8. 48 (Comp.), prob. in Ant.Lib.24.1. 5. *thirsty*, δίψῃ αὔη *IG*14.638 (Petelia), cf. *GDI*4959*a* (Eleutherna), Luc.*Luct*.8. 6. *trembling, shivering* (like a dry leaf), of the aged, Ar.*Lys*.385; esp. of fear, αὖός εἰμι τῷ δέει Men.*Epit*.480, cf. *Pk*.163, J.*BJ*1.19.5: abs., ib.6.4.2, Hld.1.12. 7. metaph., 'stony broke', *without money*, Luc.*Tox*. 16, *DMeretr*.14.1, Alciphr.3.70. 8. of lit. style, *dry*, ἰδέα λόγων Philostr.*VS*1.20.2. 9. αὔη ψυχὴ σοφωτάτη dub. in Heraclit.118. (Cf. Lith. *saũsas* 'dry', OE. *séar*.)

αὐότης, Att. **αὑότης**, ητος, ἡ, *dryness*, Arist.*HA*518ᵃ11.

ἀϋπν-έω, *to be sleepless*, Philostr.*Gym*.53 :—Med., ἀϋπνέομαι Phryn. *PS*p.9 B. **-ία**, ἡ, *sleeplessness*, Pl.*Lg*.807e, Max.Tyr.5.1; ἐν ὕπνῳ ἀ. Aret.*SD*2.6. **-ος**, ον, *sleepless, wakeful*, of persons, Od.9.404, 10.84, 19.591, A.*Pr*.32, E.*Or*.83, X.*Cyr*.2.4.26: Sup. -ότατος, τῶν στρατηγῶν D.C.72.8; ἔχειν ἀΰπνους ἄγρας, of fishermen, S.*Aj*.880; of the eye, ἄϋπνά τ' ὀμμάτων τέλη E.*Supp*.1137: metaph., *sleepless, never-resting*, ἄ. πηδάλια dub. in A.*Th*.206 (lyr.); κρῆναι S.*OC*685 (lyr.); ἀκταί E.*IT*423 (lyr.). Adv. -νως Sannyr.2 D. 2. of nights, *sleepless*, πολλὰς μὲν ἀΰπνους νύκτας ἴαυον Il.9.325, Od.19.340; also ὕπνος ἄ. a sleep *that is no sleep, from which one easily awakes*, S.*Ph*.848 (lyr.). **-οσύνη**, ἡ, = ἀϋπνία, Q.S.2.155.

αὔρα, Ion. **αὔρη**, ἡ, *breeze*, esp. *a cool breeze* from water (cf. Arist. *Mu*.394ᵇ13), or *the fresh air* of morning, once in Hom., αὔρη δ' ἐκ ποταμοῦ ψυχρὴ πνέει Od.5.469, cf. *h.Merc*.147, Hes.*Op*.670, etc.: rare in early Prose, αὔρας ἀποπνεούσας [ὁ Νεῖλος] μοῦνος οὐ παρέχεται Hdt. 2.19; αὔρα φέρουσα ἀπὸ χρηστῶν τόπων ὑγίειαν Pl.*R*.401c, cf. X.*HG* 6.2.29, *Smp*.2.25. 2. metaph., θυμιαμάτων αὖραι *the steam* of incense, Ar.*Av*.1717; ξανθαῖσιν αὔραις σῶμα πᾶν ἀγάλλεται, of a well-fried fish, Antiph.217.22; δεῖπνον ὄζον αὔρας Ἀττικῆς Dionys.Com. 2.40; αὔρη φιλοτησίη of the attractive influence of the female, Opp. *H*.4.114. 3. metaph., of *the changeful course of events*, μετάτροποι πνέουσιν αὖ. δόμων E.*El*.1148 (lyr.); πολέμου μετάτροπος αὖ. Ar.*Pax* 945; of a bodily *thrill*, E.*Hipp*.166; ψυχᾶς ἀδόλοις αὔραις guileless *movements* of soul, Id.*Supp*.1029 (lyr.), cf. 1048. 4. Αὖραι personified, Q.S.1.684, Orph.*A*.340. 5. *epileptic aura*, Gal.8.94, Alex. Trall.1.15. (Cf. ἀήρ (ἀϝέρ-), ἄελλα, ἄημι.)

αὔρηκτος, Aeol. for ἄ-ϝρηκτος, *unbroken*, Hdn.Gr.2.171, Eust.548. 31.

αὖρι, = ταχέως, *AB*464.

αὐρῐβάτης [βᾰ], ου, ὁ, (v. foreg.) *swift-striding*, A.*Fr*.280.

αὐρίγαμμος, ον, (*aurum*, γάμμα) *adorned with a golden* Γ, παραγαῦδαι Lyd.*Mag*.2.4.

αὐρίζω, *procrastinate*, Hsch., *EM*171.57; also, = ῥιγοῦν, ibid. (Cypr. acc. to Hsch.).

αὐρινός, ή, όν, *of the morrow*, *Gloss*.

αὔριον, Adv. *to-morrow*, Il.9.357, Od.1.272, etc.; αὔ. τηνικάδε *to-morrow* at this time, Pl.*Phd*.76b; ἐς or εἰς αὔ. *on the morrow*, Il.8. 538 (or *till morning*, Od.11.351), Nicoch.15, Anaxandr.4.4; *for the morrow*, καλέσαι ἐπὶ δεῖπνον εἰς αὔ. *IG*2².17, etc. 2. *presently, shortly*, φάγωμεν καὶ πίωμεν, αὔ. γὰρ ἀποθνήσκομεν 1*Ep.Cor*.15.32; opp. σήμερον, *Ev.Matt*.6.30. II. Subst., αὔ. ἣν ἀρετὴν διαείσεται *the morrow* will distinguish.., Il.8.535. III. ἡ αὔ. (sc. ἡμέρα) *the morrow*, S.*Tr*.945 (*OT*1090 is corrupt); τὴν αὔ. μέλλουσαν E.*Alc*. 784; ἡ αὔ. ἡμέρα X.*Oec*.11.6, Lys.26.6; also ἡ ἐς αὔ. ἡμέρα S.*OC*567; τὸ ἐς αὔριον Id.*Fr*.593.5; εἰς τὴν αὔ. Alex.241.3, *Act.Ap*.4.3; ἐπὶ τὴν αὔ. ib.5; ὁ αὔ. χρόνος E.*Hipp*.1117; ἡ Αὔ. personified by Simon.210 B.; δαίμονα τὸν Αὔριον Call.*Epigr*.16. (Cf. Lith. *aušrà* 'dawn', Skt. *usrás* 'of the dawn'; v. ἄγχαυρος, ἕως.)

αὐροι· λαγοί, ἢ σαῦροι, Hsch. (λόγοι ἴσαυροι cod.).

αὐροσχάς, άδος, ἡ, name of a *vine*, Ἰκαριωνείης Parth.*Fr*.17; also, = τὸ κατὰ βότρυν κλῆμα, Eratosth.37.

αὐροφόρητος, ον, *wind-borne*, Sch.Ar.*Ra*.1485.

αὐσαῖς· πνοαῖς, κραυγαῖς, Hsch.

αὐσαυτοῦ, τᾶς, τοῦ, Dor. for ἑαυτοῦ, τῆς, τοῦ, *IG*5(2).265.18 (Mantinea), *GDI*1696, al. (Delph.), 4959 (Eleutherna), *IG*4.840.3 (Calauria); cf. αὐς· αὐτός (Cret., Lacon.), Hsch.: Delph. αὐσωτόν, αὐσωτῶν, *GDI*1696, *SIG*703.11: Boeot. ἀσαυτῦ, = ἑαυτῷ, *IG*7.3303 (Chaeronea); cf. αὐταυτοῦ.

αὔσιος, = τηΰσιος, Ibyc.12; cf. αὔτως.

αὖσις, εως, ἡ, *drying*, *EM*170.44.

αὐσόν· ξηρόν, Hsch.

Αὐσονία, poet. -ίη, ἡ, *Italy*, *AP*14.121 (Metrod.): **Αὐσονίηθεν** *App.Anth*.2.712b.14 :—Adj. **Αὐσόνιος**, α, ον, *AP*7.343, al.: **Αὐσόνιοι**, οἱ, *Italians*, ib.363, al. :—also **Αὔσονες**, οἱ, Arist.*Pol*.1329ᵇ20, *IG*14.1374, Ael.*VH*9.16 (of the aborigines): fem. **Αὐσονίς**, ίδος, *IG* 14.2067, 2137.

αὖσος· ἄλσος (Cret.), Hsch.

αὐσταλέος, α, ον, Ep. **ἀϋσταλέος**, (αὔω A) *dried up, sunburnt*, Od. 19.327, Hes.*Sc*.265, Theoc.14.4, Call.*Cer*.16, A.R.2.200, etc.

αὐστήρ· μέτρου ὄνομα, Hsch.

αὐστηρία, ἡ, = αὐστηρότης, στρυφνότης καὶ αὐ. Thphr.*CP*6.12. 6. 2. metaph. of men, *austerity*, ἠθῶν Plb.4.21.1, *Cat.Cod.Astr*. 2.160.6, etc.; as a virtue, *Stoic*.3.66.

αὐστηρόπρακτος, ον, *austere in conduct*, Ptol.*Tetr*.159.

αὐστηρός, ά, όν, (αὔω) *harsh, rough, bitter*, ὕδωρ Pl.*Phlb*.61c, cf. *Ti*.65d; οἶνος αὐ., opp. γλυκύς, Hp.*Acut*.52, *Fract*.29, Arist.*Pr*.872ᵇ 35, 934ᵃ34; ὀσμή Id.*de An*.421ᵃ30; of country, *rugged*, τόποι *OGI* 168.57 (i B.C.): metaph., *harsh, crabbed*, ποιητής Pl.*R*.398a (Comp.); *severe, unadorned*, ἡ πραγματεία ἔχει αὐ. τι Plb.9.1.2, cf. D.H.*Dem*. 47; γυμνάδος αὐστηρὸν .. πόνον *severe*, *Epigr.Gr*.201. Adv. -ρῶς, κατεσκευάσθαι D.H.*Dem*.43. b. in moral sense, *rigorous, austere*, Arist.*EE*1240ᵃ2; τοῖς βίοις Plb.4.20.7 (Sup.), cf. Phld.*Hom*.p.23 O. (Comp.); αὐ. καὶ αὐθάδης D.H.6.27, cf. *Stoic*.3.162, Vett.Val.75.11; *strict, exacting*, *Ev.Luc*.19.21, *PTeb*.315.19 (ii A.D.); αὐστηρότερον, τό, *excessive rigour*, *BGU*140.18 (ii A.D.). Adv. -ρῶς Satyr.*Vit.Eur*. *Fr*.39 iv 19: Comp. -ότερον Lxx 2*Ma*.14.30.

αὐστηρότης, ητος, ἡ, *harshness, roughness*, X.*An*.5.4.29; οἴνου, opp. γλυκύτης, Pl.*Tht*.178c, Thphr.*HP*7.9.5. 2. metaph., *harshness, crabbedness*, τοῦ γήρως Pl.*Lg*.666b, cf. D.C.56.3.

αὐτ-άγγελος, ὁ, *carrying one's own message*, S.*Ph*.568; *bringing news of what oneself has seen*, Th.3.33: c. gen. rei, λόγων S.*OC*333; πάθους Plu.2.489e, cf. Arr.*An*.4.2.6, Max.Tyr.14.2, Nonn.*D*.8. 222. **-άγητος** [ᾰ], ον, (ἄγαμαι) = αὐθάδης, Anacr.142; *conceited*, Ion Trag.8. **-αγρεσία**, ἡ, *free choice*, ἐξ αὐταγρεσίης Call.*Fr*.120. 2. **-άγρετος**, ον, (ἀγρέω) poet. for αὐθαίρετος, *self-chosen, left to one's choice*, εἰ γάρ πως εἴη αὐτάγρετα πάντα βροτοῖσι Od.16.148; σοὶ δ' αὐτάγρετόν ἐστι δαήμεναι *h.Merc*.474. 2. *taken by one's own hands* or *exertions*, A.R.4.231. II. Act., *choosing freely*, Semon.1.19, Opp.*H*.5.588.

αὐτ-άγρευτος, ον, = αὐτόπλεκτος, Sch.Opp.*H*.4.449. **-άδελφος**, ον (η, ον Sch.E.*Hec*.944) *brother's* or *sister's*, αἷμα A.*Th*.718, *Eu*.89; αὐ. Ἰσμήνης κάρα S.*Ant*.1. II. Subst., *one's own brother* or *sister*, ib.503,696 :—later **-αδέλφη**, ἡ, Sch.E.*Ph*.135.

αὐταιώρητος, ον, *self-suspended*, Hsch.

αὐτάλεν· ἐσκίρτα, Hsch. **αὐτάλκης**· ζωμός, also = αὐτάρκης, Id.

αὐταμαρόν, αὐταμέριν, v. αὐθήμερος II.

αὐτ-ανδρί, Adv. of sq., Plb.3.81.11. **-ανδρος**, ον, (ἀνήρ) *together with the men, men and all*, ναῦς αὐτάνδρους ἀπέβαλον Plb.1.23.7, cf. Sosyl.p.31 B., A.R.3.582, Luc.*Bacch*.3, etc.; πόλεις αὐ. ἀνῃρῆσθαι D.H.7.60: hence αὐ. λαός the people, *every man of them*, J.*BJ*3.7. 31. **-ανέψιος**, ὁ, *own cousin*, A.*Supp*.984, E.*Heracl*.987, Pl.*Euthd*. 275b: Adj. αὐ. στόλος A.*Supp*.933 :—fem. **-ανεψία**, Lyc.811.

αὐτανίδας· αὖθις, πάλιν, Hsch. **αὐτάντας**· ὁ προεστώς τινος πράγματος καὶ αὐθεντῶν, Id.

αὐτάρ (ἀϝυτάρ *IG*1².1012), Conj. = ἀτάρ (Ep. and Cypr., *Inscr. Cypr*.57 H.) :—*but, besides, moreover*, prop. to introduce a contrast, Od.13.286, al.; also to mark a rapid succession of details, Il.2.406, al.; opp. μέν, Ἥφαιστος μέν.. αὐ. ἄρα Ζεύς.. ib.102 sq., cf. Od.19.512 sq.; αὐτάρ τοι *but nevertheless*, Il.15.45.—In an Epic reminiscence, Hermipp.63.17 (hex.). II. αὐτάρ· αὐτομάτη, ἑκουσία, Hsch.

αὐτᾰρέσκ-εια, ἡ, *self-satisfaction, self-indulgence*, Sm.*Ec*.6.9. **-έω**, *to be self-satisfied*, Tz.*H*.9.279. **-ος**, ον, *self-satisfied, self-willed*, Hsch. s.v. αὐθέκαστος :—also **αὐτάρεστος**, Id.

αὐτάρκ-εια, ἡ, *self-sufficiency, independence*, Democr.246, Hp.*Ep*. 17, Pl.*Phlb*.67a, Arist.*EN*1097ᵇ7, Epicur.*Ep*.3 p.63 U., etc.; αὐ. ζωῆς Arist.*Rh*.1360ᵇ15; κτήσεως Id.*Pol*.1256ᵇ32; ἡ τῆς τροφῆς αὐ. Id.*GA*776ᵇ8. II. concrete, *a sufficiency*, *PFlor*.242.8 (iii A.D.); *a competence*, Vett.Val.289.32. **-εσία**, ἡ, *sufficiency*, *Psalm.Solom*. 5.18. **-έω**, *supply with necessaries*, αὐτάρκησεν ἑαυτὸν ἐν ἐρήμῳ Lxx *De*.32.10. II. *to be sufficient*, Arist.*EE*1242ᵃ8, *PLips*.29.11 (iii A.D.). **-ης**, ες, (ἀρκέω) *sufficient in oneself, self-supporting, independent* of others, ἀνθρώπου σῶμα ἓν οὐδὲν αὔ. ἐστιν Hdt.1.32; αὐ. εἰς πάντα Pl.*Plt*.271d; εἰς εὐδαιμονίαν, of ἀρετή, Zeno *Stoic*.1.46; οὐκ αὐ. ἀλλὰ πολλῶν ἐνδεής Pl.*R*.369b; ὁ σοφὸς -έστατος Arist.*EN*1177ᵇ1, cf. Epicur.*Sent.Vat*.45; αὐτάρκη φρονεῖν E.*Fr*.29; νηδὺς αὐ. τέκνων *helping itself, acting instinctively*, A.*Ch*.757; αὐ. βοή a *self-reliant* shout, S.*OC*1057 (s.v.l.); πόλις αὐ. θέσιν κειμένη Th.1.37, cf. 2.36 (Sup.); οἰκία -έστερον ἑνός, πόλις δ' οἰκίας Arist.*Pol*.1261ᵇ11; τὸ τέλειον ἀγαθὸν αὐ. εἶναι δοκεῖ Id.*EN*1097ᵇ8; σῶμα αὐ. πρός τι *strong enough* for a thing, Th.2.51, cf. X.*Mem*.4.8.11: c. inf., *able of oneself* to do a thing, εἰ γὰρ αὐτάρκη τὰ ψηφίσματα ἦν ὑμᾶς ἀναγκάζειν κτλ. D.3.14, cf. X.*Cyr*.4.3.4. Adv. -κως, ἔχειν Arist.*Rh*.1362ᵃ27: Sup. -έστατα, ζῆν X.*Mem*.1.2.14. II. *sufficient* in quantity, ἀργύριον αὐ. εἰς σιτωνίαν Ph.2.69; ὕδωρ αὐ. τοῖς ποιμνίοις J.*AJ*2.11.2, cf. *PLond*.3.

1166.6 (i A.D.), *POxy*.729.19 (ii A.D.); ὄξους τὸ -έστατον Gal.13.1046. Adv. -κως *sufficiently*, *BGU*665.18 (i A.D.), Plot.3.3.3, *Theol.Ar*.45.

αὐταρχ-έω, *to be an absolute ruler*, Pi.*Pae*.4.37, D.C.44.2. **-ος**, ον, *autocratic*, ἰσχύς Id.61.7: as Subst., *IGRom*.4.1612 (Hypaepa).

αὐταύλης, ου, ὁ, *soloist on the flute*, condemned by Phryn.145.

αὐταυτόθεν, *of oneself*, Euryph.ap.Stob.1.6.19. **αὐταυτοῦ** or **-τῶ, αὐταυτῆς** (-τᾶς), Dor. for ἑαυτοῦ, ἑαυτῆς, πεπαίδευται γὰρ αὐταυτᾶς ὕπο Epich.172.7, cf. *IG*14.646 (Heraclea), Archyt.2, Philol.5, Axiop.1.15, Diotog.ap.Stob.4.7.62: acc., αὐταυτόν Ecphant.ap.Stob.4.7.64; αὐταυτόν *IG*4.156 (Aegina): as Adj., ταῖς **αὐταυταῖς** χερσίν Sophr.19 (-τᾶς Pors.):—also **αὐτοῦτα**, for ἑαυτοῦ, *IG*14.287, 288 (Segesta): pl., αὐτῶντα ib.316 (Thermae Himeraeae).

αὖτε, Adv., (αὖ, τε):—used by Hom. like αὖ, I. of Time, *again*, Il.1.202, 2.105,370, al.; freq. δὴ αὖτε 1.340, 2.225, and with crasis, δαὖτε Alcm.36, δηὖτε Archil.60, Sapph.40, Alc.19.1, Hippon.78. II. to mark Sequence or Transition, *again*, *furthermore*, ἕκτον δ' αὖτ' Ὀδυσῆα Il.2.407; Δαρδανίων αὖτ' ἦρχεν.. Αἰνείας ib.819, cf. 826, etc.; esp. in speeches, τὸν δ' αὖτε προσέειπε.. him *in turn* addressed.., 3.58, al.; ἀμφί μοι αὖτε ἄναχθ' ἑκαταβόλον ἀειδέτω φρήν Terp.2, cf. Ar.*Nu*.595; ἥδ' αὖθ' ἕρπει S.*Tr*.1009 (lyr.). 2. *on the other hand*, *on the contrary*, sts. opp. μέν (instead of δέ), Il.1.237, Od.22.6; coupled with δέ, *h.Cer*.137, A.*Pers*.183, *Th*.5, *Ag*.553.—Freq. in A., once in S., never in E.; not in Prose; Com. only in Dact. and Anap. in Epic reminiscences, Cratin.169, Ar.*Pax*1270, Metag.4.2 (prob.); νῦν αὖτε λεῴ προσέχετε τὸν νοῦν Ar.*V*.1015.

αὐτέγγυος, ον, *one's own security*, *PEdgar*30.21 (iii B.C.).

αὐτεῖ, Adv., Dor. for αὐτοῦ, Isyll.73, *IG*12(3).248.19 (Anaphe), A.D.*Synt*.238.9; Boeot. **αὐτῖ**, *Schwyzer*462 *A* 5 (Tanagra, iii B.C.).

αὐτ-έκμαγμα, ατος, τό, *one's very image*, Ar.*Th*.514. **-ενέργεια**, ἡ, *self-moving energy*, Eustr. *in EN*330.27: **αὐτοενέργεια**, Phlp. *in de An*.35.1. **-ενέργητος**, or **αὐτοεν-**, ον, *spontaneous*, ζωή Procl. *in Prm*.p.611 S. (αὐτ-), *in Alc*.p.18 C. (αὐτο-), *Theol.Plat*.6.22, Iamb.*Myst*.4.3. **-ενῐαυτός**, όν, *of the year*, *this year's*, γένη *BGU*1120.34 (i B.C.), al.; κόπρος *Gp*.2.21.10; οἶνος Orib.*Fr*.142: neut. as Adv., Epigr. in *Supp.Epigr*.2.431. **-εξούσιος**, ον, *in one's own power*, *free*, ποιῶν τὸ αὐ. Chrysipp.*Stoic*.2.284, cf. Diogenian.Epicur.3.61, Plot.1.4.8, Iamb.*Myst*.3.14; of persons, Muson.*Fr*.12 p.66 H., Arr.*Epict*.4.1.62, *PLips*.29.6 (iii A.D.); of captives, *freed unconditionally*, D.S.14.105; *absolute*, βασιλεία J.*AJ*15.7.10; δύναμις Plot.6.8.20; αὐ., τό, *freedom of choice*, Procl. *in Alc*.p.143 C., etc.; αὐ. ἀρχή Plot.3.2.10. Adv. -ως J.*BJ*5.13.5, Plot.6.8.20, Procl.*Theol.Plat*.6.16; cf. αὐτοεξούσιος. **-εξουσιότης**, ητος, ἡ, *free will*, v.l. in Lxx 4*Ma*.2.21: αὐτο- Eustr. *in EN*390.11. **-επάγγελτος**, ον, *offering of oneself*, *of one's free will*, αὐ. ἠθέλησε συμβαλέσθαι χρήματα Hdt.7.29; αὐ. ὑποστῆναι E.*HF*706; παρεῖναι, χωρεῖν, Th.1.33, 4.120; βοηθεῖν Isoc.1.25; ἐθέλονται D.18.68. Adv. -τως Ph.2.173. II. *self-invited*, dub. in Luc.*JTr*.37. **-έπαινος**, ον, *self-laudatory*, Sch.Il.*Oxy*.1087 i 17. **-επιβούλευτος**, ον, *self-destructive*, Ath.Mech.32.9, [Hero]*Poliorc*.p.269 W. **-επίβουλος**, ον, *plotting against oneself*, interpol. in Aesop.18; = αὐτοφονεύς, Hsch. **-επίσπαστος**, ον, *drawn on oneself*, *self-incurred*, Id. s.v. αὐθαιρέτῳ. **-επιστατέω**, *to be present oneself*, and Subst. **-επιστᾰσία**, ἡ, Sch.Theoc.7.6. **-επιστήμη**, ἡ, *absolute science*, Procl.*Theol.Plat*.4.14, Plot.5.8.4 (αὐτο-). **-επίστροφος**, ον, *returning upon oneself*, Olymp. *in Alc*.p.209 C. **-επιτάκτης**, ου, ὁ, *one who rules absolutely*, Pl.*Plt*.260e. **-επιτακτικός**, ή, όν, *belonging to absolute power*: -κή (sc. τέχνη), ἡ, ibid., etc. II. *ordaining by authority*, τῆς τριαδικῆς διαιρέσεως Dam.*Pr*.98. **-επίτακτος**, ον, *self-bidden*, *spontaneous*, Poll.1.156. **-επώνῠμος**, ον, *of the same surname with*, σοῦ πατρός E.*Ph*.769. **-ερέτης**, ου, ὁ, *one who rows himself*, i.e. rower and soldier at once, αὐ. καὶ μάχιμοι Th.1.10, cf. 3.18, 6.91. 2. *rowing one's own boat*, *AP*7.305 (Adaeus).

ἀῡτέω [ῡ], used by Hom. only in 3 pers. impf., and in Trag. (never in S.) only in pres. and impf.: ἠΰτησα Nonn.*D*.11.185, *Epigr.Gr*.995.7: (αὔω B):—*cry*, *shout*, μακρὸν ἄϋτει Il.20.50; καὶ μέγ' ἄϋτει 21.582; κληδὼν ἀϋτεῖ A.*Ag*.927: c. acc. cogn., τοιαῦτ' ἀϋτῶν Id.*Th*.384; ἀΰτει δ' ὀξὺ Id.*Pers*.1058 (lyr.); τί τινι E.*El*.757, etc. 2. c. acc. pers., *call to*, ἄϋτει πάντας ἀρίστους Il.11.258; ἀΰτευν Ἄρτεμιν E.*Hipp*.167 (lyr.); τί Ζῆν' ἀϋτεῖς; why call on Zeus? Ar.*Lys*.717: c. acc. pers. et inf., E.*Rh*.668. 3. c. acc. rei, *call for*, βοὰν ἀ. *call for* help, Id.*Hec*.1092 (lyr.). 4. *proclaim*, c. inf., Man.4.39,428.

ἀϋτή [ῡ], ἡ, (αὔω B) *cry*, *shout*, esp. *battle-shout*, *war-cry*, ἀϋτὴ δ' οὐρανὸν ἷκεν Il.2.153; ἀϋτή τε πτόλεμός τε 6.328; κίνδυνος ὀξείας ἀΰτᾶς Pi.*N*.9.35: generally, γλώσσης ἀϋτὴν Φωκίδος A.*Ch*.564; of the *blast* of the trumpet, Id.*Pers*.395; of the *creaking* of the axle, Parm.1.6. (ἀϝῡτά *IG*9(1).868 (Corc.).)

αὐτ-ήκοος, ον, (ἀκούω) *one who has himself heard*, *ear-witness*, αὐ. τινος γενέσθαι Th.1.133, Pl.*Lg*.658c. II. *hearing oneself*, i.e. *a law unto oneself*, Ph.2.2, al., Suid.; so, *self-acquired*, ἀρετή, ἐπιστήμη, Ph.1.371,354. **-ημαρ**, Adv. = αὐθημερόν, *on the self-same day*, Il.18.454, Od.3.311; *for that day*, Il.1.81. **-ημερόν**, Ion. for αὐθημερόν, Hdt.2.122.

αὐτίκᾰ [ῐ], Adv. *forthwith*, *at once*, *in a moment*, which notion is strengthd. by Hom. in αὐ. νῦν, μάλ' αὐ. *on the spot*, Od.10.111, al.: c. part., αὐτίκ' ἰόντι *immediately* on his going, 2.367; beginning a sentence, Sapph.*Supp*.20a.13: in Prose, αὐ. γενόμενος *as soon as* born, Hdt.2.146; αὐ. μάλα Id.7.103, *IG*1².39.47, Pl.*Prt*.318b; αὐ. δὴ μάλα *presently* (at the end of a sentence), D.21.19,23; αὐ. νυκτός Theoc.2.119. 2. *now*, *for the moment*, αὐ. καὶ μετέπειτα Od.14.403; ὁ μὲν αὐτίχ' ὁ δ' ἥξει A.*Ch*.1020; ἡδὺ μὲν γὰρ αὐ... ἐν δὲ χρόνῳ... E.*Andr*.781 (lyr.); Th. opposes τὸ αὐ. and ὁ μέλλων πόλεμος 1.36, cf. 2.41: with a Subst., τὴν μὲν αὐτίχ' ἡμέραν S.*OC*433; ὁ αὐ. φόβος *momentary* fear, Th.3.112, cf. 1.41,124. 3. in a slightly future sense, *immediately*, *presently*, αὐτίκ' ἀκούσεσθε D.19.17, cf. S.*Ph*.14, 1001, Ar.*Pl*.347, etc.; opp. νῦν, Pl.*Grg*.459c, *R*.420c; ἐμπέπτωκεν εἰς λόγους οὓς αὐ. μᾶλλον.. ἁρμόσει λέγειν D.18.42. II. *for example*, *to begin with*, Hp.*Epid*.1.25, *Acut*.16; αὐ. γὰρ ἄρχει διὰ τίν' ὁ Ζεύς; Ar.*Pl*.130, cf. *Av*.166,574, Pl.*Prt*.395e, *R*.340d, *Dialex*.2.2, al.; αὐ. δὴ μάλα *for example now*, D.25.29; *at any rate*, Plu.2.1137d. III. = αὖθις, Arat.880,1076 (but = εὐθέως, Sch.).

αὖτις, v. αὖθις: Cret. **αὖτιν** *Leg.Gort*.4.3.

αὐτίτης [ῑ], ου, ὁ, (αὐτός) *by oneself*, *alone*, Arist.*Fr*.668. II. as Subst., αὐτίτης (sc. οἶνος), ὁ, *home-made wine*, Telecl.9, Polyzel.1, Hp.*Morb*.3.14.

ἀϋτμενόπης (-πις cod.)· πεφυσημένος, πεπνευσμένος, Hsch.

ἀϋτμή, ἡ, (ἄημι) *breath*, εἰς ὅ κ' ἀ. ἐν στήθεσσι μένῃ Il.9.609; τεῖρε δ' ἀ. Ἡφαίστοιο *the fiery breath* of Hephaistos, 21.366; ὅσσον πυρὸς ἵκετ' ἀ. Od.16.290 (hence abs. for *heat*, 9.389): in pl., περισχίζοντο δ' ἀϋτμαὶ Ἡφαίστου Q.S.13.329; of bellows, εὔπρηστον ἀ. ἐξανιεῖσαι Il.18.471; ἀνέμων ἀμέγαρτον ἀϋτμήν Od.11.400. 2. *scent*, *fragrance*, με κνίσης ἀμφήλυθεν ἡδὺς ἀ. 12.369, cf. Il.14.174; θήρειος ἀ. *scent* of game, Opp.*C*.1.467.

ἀϋτμήν, ένος, ὁ, = ἀϋτμή, χέ' ἀϋτμένα Il.23.765; ἀνέμων ἐπ' ἀϋτμένα χεῦεν Od.3.289.

αὐτο-ᾰγᾰθός, ή, όν, *good in itself*, Plot.1.8.13: esp. in neut. **-ᾰγᾰθόν**, τό, *the ideal good*, *the Form of good*, Arist.*Metaph*.996^{a}28, Plot.6.6.10. **-ᾰγᾰθότης**, ητος, ἡ, *absolute goodness*, Procl.*Inst*.127. **-άδης** [ᾱ], etym. of αὐθάδης, Arist.*MM*1192^{b}33. **-άήρ**, έρος, ὁ, *air by itself*, Herm.ap.Stob.3.11.31. **-άληθές**, τό, *the true-in-itself*, Alex.Aphr. *in Metaph*.301.6. **-άληθῶς**, *in very truth*, Suid. s.v. αὐτό. **-άλφα, -βῆτα**, τό, *the very* ἄλφα, βῆτα, Arist.*Metaph*.1087^{a}9 (al. divisim). **-άνθρωπος**, ὁ, *the ideal man*, *the Form of man*, Id.*EN*1096^{a}35, *Metaph*.991^{a}29, etc. II. *a very man*, of a statue, Luc.*Philops*.18. **-άνῐσον**, τό, *inequality in the abstract*, Alex.Aphr. *in Metaph*.809.14. **-ανόσιον**, τό, *abstract impiety*, Procl. *in Prm*.p.773 S. **-απειρία**, ἡ, *infinity itself*, Id.*Inst*.92. **-άπειρος**, ον, *infinite in itself*, Plot.2.4.7. **-απλότης**, ητος, ἡ, *simplicity itself*, of a person, ὁ βασιλεὺς τὸν τρόπον ἦν αὐ. Anon.ap.Suid. s.v. **-αριθμός**, ὁ, *abstract number*, Alex.Aphr. *in Metaph*.109.17, al. **-αρχή**, ἡ, *ideal rule*, Epist.Gall. in Jul.*Ep*.455b. **-βᾰφής**, ές, *self-dipped*, Nonn.*D*.30.123. **-βῆτα**, τό, v. αὐτοάλφα. **-βλάβη** [ᾰ], ἡ, *very mischief*, Sch.rec.S.*El*.301. **-βλᾰβής**, ές, *self-harming*, Sch.A.*Th*.917. **-βοάω**, *bear testimony of oneself*, *AB*465, Suid. **-βοεί**, Adv. *by a mere shout*, *at the first shout*, αὐ. ἑλεῖν take *without a blow*, Th.2.81, 3.113, 8.62, etc.; αὐ. λαβεῖν κλέπτοντα, = ἐπ' αὐτοφώρῳ, *AB*465. **-βοήθητος**, ον, *self-supporting*, of an argument, Simp. *in Ph*.354.29. **-βόητος**, ον, *self-sounding*, ὄργανον Nonn.*D*.1.432. **-βορέας**, ου, ὁ, *a very Boreas*, Luc.*Tim*.54. **-βούλησις**, εως, ἡ, *the abstract will*, v.l. in Arist.*Top*.147^{a}8. **-βουλήτως**, *of one's own purpose*, Hsch. s.v. ἐθελοντής. **-βουλος**, ον, *self-willing*, *self-purposing*, A.*Th*.1058. **-βοῦς**, βοός, ὁ, *ideal ox*, Alex.Aphr. *in Metaph*.758.31. **-βρᾰδύτης**, ητος, ἡ, *ideal slowness*, Procl. *Hyp*.1.1. **-γᾰμος**, ον, = αὐτογόνος II, Nonn.*D*.40.405. **-γενέθλος**, ον, = sq., *Orac.Chald*.32; ἥλιος *Hymn.Mag*.4.24; κάνθαρος, of Kheper, *PMag.Par*.1.943. 2. *self-producing*, φύσις Nonn.*D*.41.52. **-γενέτωρ**, τορος, = foreg. 2, *PMag.Par*.2.1561, *PMag.Leid.W*.7.6. **-γενής**, ές, *self-produced*, δαίμων v.l. in Herm.ap.Stob.1.49.44, cf. Ph.1.618, Max.Tyr.16.6, Procl. *in Prm*.p.893 S., Orph.*Fr*.245.8. 2. αὐτογενές, τό, = νάρκισσος, Ps.-Dsc.4.158; ὀστοῦν αὐ., = κολοκυνθίς, ib.176. II. *sprung from the same stock*, *kindred*, A.*Supp*.8 (cj. Bamberger for αὐτογένητον). **-γένητος**, ον, *self-generated*, Simp. *in Ph*.824.16 (s.v.l.). **-γεννητικός**, ή, όν, *of itself productive of..*, Procl. *in Prm*.p.821 S. **-γέννητος**, ον, = αὐτογενής: αὐ. κοιμήματα μητρός a mother's intercourse *with her own child*, S.*Ant*.864. **-γεωργός**, f.l. for αὐτουργός, Ph.1.685. **-γῆ**, ἡ, *ideal earth*, *archetype of earth*, Plot.6.7.11, Herm.ap.Stob.3.11.31. **-γλῠφος**, ον, *self-engraved*, λίθος Ps.-Plu.*Fluv*.12.2. **-γλώχῑν**, ῑνος, ὁ, ἡ, *in one piece with the point*, οἰστός Hld.9.19. **-γνωμονέω**, *act of one's own judgement*, X.*HG*7.3.6. **-γνώμων**, ον, gen. ονος, *on one's own judgement*, *at one's own discretion*, κρίνειν αὐ., opp. κατὰ γράμματα, Arist.*Pol*.1270^{b}29, cf. 1272^{a}39. Adv. -όνως Plu.*Demetr*.6:—hence Subst. **-οσύνη**, ἡ, Zonar. **-γνῶσις**, εως, ἡ, *absolute knowledge*, Olymp. *in Phd*.p.100 N., Procl. *in Alc*.p.88 C. **-γνωτος**, ον, *self-determined*, *self-willed*, ὀργή S.*Ant*.875:—also **-γνωστος**, ον, *knowable in itself*, Simp. *in Ph*.1250.14, Dam.*Pr*.80. **-γονος**, ον, *self-produced*, Nonn.*D*.8.103, Syrian. *in Metaph*.187.9, Procl. *in Cra*.p.17 P. Adv. -νως Syrian. *in Metaph*.142.17, Procl. *in Prm*.p.897 S. II. Act., (-γόνος) *self-producing*, *breeding alone*, Nonn.*D*.9.229, Iamb.*Myst*.10.6. **-γραμμή**, ἡ, *line in itself*, Arist.*Metaph*.1036^{b}14, Plot.6.6.17. **-γρᾰφος**, ον, *written with one's own hand*, ἐπιστολαί D.H.5.7, Plu.*Sert*.27; τὸ αὐ. *one's own writing*, Id.2.1115c. **-γῠος**, ον, ἄροτρον αὐ. a plough *whose* γύης *is of one piece with the* ἔλυμα *and* ἱστοβοεύς, not fitted together (πηκτόν), Hes.*Op*.433, A.R.3.232, 1285. **-δᾰής**, ές, *self-taught*, ἀρετά Diagor.1; ὀρχήματα S.*Aj*.700 (lyr.). **-δάϊκτος** [ᾰ], ον, *self-slain*, *AP*9.293 (Phil.), Opp.*H*.2.349; *mutually slain*, A.*Th*.735 (lyr.). **-δαίμων**, ονος, ὁ, *arche-*

typal δαίμων, Plot.3.5.6. **-δαιτος**, ον, of a guest, *bringing his own share to a feast*, Lyc.480. **-δακής** μῆνις· μικρά, Hsch., cf. sq.

αὐτ-οδάξ, Adv. *with the very teeth*, γυναῖκες αὐτοδὰξ ὠργισμέναι women angered *even to biting*, Ar.*Lys.*687; τὸν αὐτοδὰξ τρόπον your *ferocious* temper, Id.*Pax* 607.

αὐτο-δεής, ές, *insufficient in itself*, dub. in *Corp.Herm.*10.10. **-δειπνος**, ον, = αὐτόδαιτος, Hsch. **-δεκα**, *just ten*, Th.5.20. **-δεκάς**, άδος, ἡ, *the series 1, 2, . . 10*, Plot.6.6.14. **-δερμος**, ον, *skin, bark and all*, Hsch. s.v. αὐτόφλοιον. **-δέσμητος**, ον, = αὐτάγρευτος, Sch.Opp.*H.*4.449. **-δεσποτεία**, ἡ, *absolute rule*, Procl. *in Prm.* p.736 S. **-δεσπότης**, ου, ὁ, *absolute master*, Eustr. *in EN*387.8. **-δέσποτος**, ον, *at one's own will, free*, Hierocl.*Prov.*ap.Phot. *Bibl.*p.172 B.; *absolute master*, παθῶν Lxx 4*Ma.*1.1. **-δετος**, ον, *self-bound*, Opp.*C.*2.376. **-δηλος**, ον, *self-evident*, A.*Th.*848 (lyr.). **-δημιούργητος**, ον, *self-made*, i.e. *in the natural state*, Hsch. s.v. αὐτόξυλον. **-διᾱκονία**, ἡ, *self-service*, Chrysipp.*Stoic.*3.177, Teles p.54 H. **-διᾱκονέω**, *serve oneself*, Eust.732.65. **-διάκονος** [ᾱ], ον, *serving oneself*, Str.16.4.26. **-δίδακτος** [ῐ], ον, *self-taught*, Od.22.347; αὐ. ἔσωθεν θυμός A.*Ag.*991 (lyr.); φιλοσοφία D.H. 5.12; of instinct, τὸ τῶν ὀργάνων αὐ. Gal.8.445. Adv. -τως *instinctively*, Id.19.175, cf. Alex.Aphr.*Pr.*1.14; *without instruction*, Phld. *Rh.*1.129 S. (dub.). **-διήγητος**, ον, *narrated in the first person*, opp. dialogue, D.L.9.111. **-διηγούμενος**, η, ον, *narrating in the first person*, ibid. **-δίκαιον** [ῐ], τό, *abstract right*, Aristid.2.182 J., Procl. *in Prm.*p.773 S., Dam.*Pr.*60. **-δῐκαιοσύνη**, ἡ, *very righteousness*, Plot.1.2.6, Herm. *in Phdr.*p.144 A. **-δῐκέω**, *to be* αὐτόδικος, Din. *Fr.*60.4, Poll.8.24. **-δῐκος**, ον, *with independent jurisdiction, with one's own courts*, Th.5.18, J.*AJ*19.2.2, *GDI*4985 (Gortyn).

αὐτόδῐον, Adv. *straightway*, Od.8.449.

αὐτο-διπλάσιον, τό, *the ideal double, its Form*, Arist.*Metaph.*990ᵇ32. **-δίπουν** [ῐ], ποδος, τό, *ideal biped*, Alex.Aphr. *in Metaph.*105.5. **-δοξα**, ἡ, *opinion in the abstract*, Arist.*Top.*162ᵃ30. **-δόξαστον**, τό, *the object of opinion in the abstract*, Suid. s.v. αὐτό. **-δορος**, ον, *hide and all*, Plu.2.694b. **-δουλεία**, ἡ, *absolute servitude*, Procl. *in Prm.*p.736 S. **-δρομέω**, *run of itself*, Dion.Byz.53. **-δρομος**, ον, *running* or *moving of itself*, Hp.*Hebd.*2. **-δῠάς**, άδος, ἡ, *the ideal number two*, Alex.Aphr. *in Metaph.*87.9, Phlp. *in de An.*77.8. **-δύνᾰμις** [ῠ], εως, ἡ, *abstract potentiality*, Procl.*Inst.*92. **-ε(θεί)ρας**· κόμας ἢ καὶ κόσμους, Hsch. **-ειδής**, ές, *true to its own* εἶδος, M.Ant.11.12 (s.v.l.), Olymp. *in Alc.*p.16 C. 2. *of ideal, abstract nature*, Dam.*Pr.*340. **-εἶδος**, τό, *abstract form*, read by Alex.Aphr. in Arist.*Metaph.*1087ᵃ6. **-έκαστος**, ον, = αὐθέκαστος, Arist.*Top.*162ᵃ27; τὸ αὐ. *the idea of each object*, Id.*EN*1096ᵃ35, cf. Dam.*Pr.*427. **-έκτᾰτος**, ον, (ἐκτείνω) *long by nature*, of syllables, Eust.943.59. **-ελαιουργός**, ὁ, dub. sens. in *PPetr.*3 p.169. **-ελέφας**, αντος, ὁ, *ideal elephant*, Alex.Aphr. *in Metaph.*761.30. **-έλικτος**, ον, *returning into itself*, κύκλος Nonn.*D.*33.272, al. **-έν**, τό, *abstract unity*, Alex.Aphr. *in Metaph.*87.9, al., Plot.5.3.12, 6.2.5, Procl. *in Prm.*p.547 S., *Inst.*2, al. **-ενάς**, άδος, ἡ, *ideal* ἑνάς, ib. 128. **-ενέργεια**, -ητος, v. αὐτεν-. **-εννεάς**, άδος, ἡ, *the ideal number nine*, Alex.Aphr. *in Metaph.*836.25. **-εντεί**, Adv. *with one's own hand*, D.C.58.24 (v.l. αὐτοεντία, as in *Fr.*13.2). **-έντης**, ου, ὁ, in S., = αὐθέντης, *a murderer*, *OT*107, *El.*272: also in late Prose, D.C. 58.15 (s.v.l.). **-εντία**, ἡ, = αὐθεντία, Id.*Fr.*13.2. **-εξάς**, άδος, ἡ, *ideal* ἑξάς, Sch.Arist.833ᵃ2. **-εξούσιος**, ον, *autonomous*, Anon. *in EN*139.17. Adv. -ίως ib.139.18. **-έπαινος**, ον, *praising oneself*, τὸ αὐ. Sch.Il.16.70. **-επιθῡμία**, ἡ, *the Form of desire*, v.l. in Arist.*Top.*147ᵃ8. **-επίπεδον**, τό, *ideal surface, plane in itself*, Alex. Aphr. *in Metaph.*128.3. **-επιστήμη**, ἡ, *abstract science*, Procl. *in Prm.*p.738 S. **-ετεί**, Adv. of -ετής, Theoc.28.13, Thphr.*CP*3.12.1. **-ετερότης**, ητος, ἡ, *abstract difference*, Plot.2.4.13, Dam.*Pr.*322. **-ετής**, ές, (ἔτος) *in* or *of the same year*, of trees, αὐτοετεῖς αὐαίνονται Thphr.*HP*3.7.1; ἔριφος J.*AJ*3.9.3. Adv. αὐτοετές *within the year*, Od.3.322, D.C.36.37; γεννᾶν Arist.*HA*562ᵇ12; *at one year old*, ὀχεύεσθαι ib.545ᵃ24. **-ετίτης**, ου, ὁ, f.l. for αὐτο-ετής, Gal.19.87. **-ζήμιος**, ον, *self-punished*, Hsch. s.v. αὐτόκαρνος. **-ζήτητος**, ον, *self-sought*, i.e. *unsought*, *EM*173.13. **-ζῷον**, τό, *animal in the abstract*, Arist.*Top.*137ᵇ11, Simp. *in Ph.*824.17, Dam.*Pr.*88. II. **-ζῳος**, ον, *self-existent*, ψυχή Herm. *in Phdr.*p.118 A., but usu. -ζως, ζων, *having life in itself*, Plot.3.8.8; πᾶσα ψυχὴ αὐ. ἐστι Procl.*Inst.*189, cf. Dam.*Pr.*80. **-ηδύ**, τό, *pleasure in the abstract*, v.l. in Arist. *Top.*147ᵃ8. **-ήλιος**, ὁ, *ideal sun*, Alex.Aphr. *in Metaph.*198.15. **-θαΐς**, ίδος, ἡ, *Thais herself*, Luc.*Rh.Pr.*12. **-θάνᾰτος** [θᾰ], ον, *dying by one's own hand*, Plu.2.293e.

αὐτόθε, v. αὐτόθεν.

αὐτο-θελεί, Adv. of sq., *voluntarily*, *AP*7.470 (Mel.). **-θελής**, ές, *of one's own will*, ib.9.79 (Leon.), 5.21 (Rufin.). Adv. -λῶς Eust. 771.20.

αὐτόθεν, before a conson. sts. **αὐτόθε**, Theoc.5.60, *Supp.Epigr.*2. 293 (Delph., iii/ii B.C.): Adv. I. of Place, = ἐξ αὐτοῦ τοῦ τόπου, *from the very spot*: freq. with a Prep., αὐ. ἐξ ἕδρης *straight* from his seat, without rising, Il.19.77; αὐ. ἐξ ἑδρέων Od.13.56, cf. 21.420; ἐκ τοῦ Ἄργους αὐ. Th.5.83; Ἄργεος ἐξ ἱεροῖο αὐ. Theoc.25.171: rare in Trag., σὺ δ' αὐ. μοι χαῖρε *from where you stand*, not coming nearer, S. *OC*1137; τῶν μὲν αὐ. τῶν δὲ ἀπὸ Στρυμόνος some *from the country* itself, others . ., Hdt.1.64; αὐ. παρασκευῇ ἐπιέναι with a force *raised on the spot*, Th.6.21; αὐ. πολεμοῦντα βιοτεύειν live *on the country*, Id.1.11; ὅπως αὐ. αὐτῷ τὰ σώματα καὶ τὴν γνώμην παρασκευάζοιντο X.*Ages.*1.28; οἱ αὐ. *the natives*, Th.2.25, 6.21, cf. 4.129; χρυσὸς αὐ. καθαρός *in its native state*, Plb.34.10.12; ἐνθένδ' αὐ. Ar.*Ach.*116; ὕδωρ αὐ. ποθὲν συλλειβόμενον Luc.*Alex.*13. 2. *from oneself*, *of one's own accord, spontaneously*, Demetr.*Eloc.*32; αὐ. εἰδέναι τι Dam. *Pr.*351. II. of Time, as we say *on the spot*, i.e. *at once, immediately*, Il.20.120, A.*Supp.*102, Hdt.8.64, Th.1.141; δῆλός ἐστιν αὐ. Ar.*Eq.*330, cf. *Ec.*246, Pl.*Grg.*470e; λέγετε αὐ. Id.*Smp.*213a. 2. *obviously*, αὐ. ἐκφανής *self*-evident, Cleom.1.8; αὐ. γνώριμος Muson. *Fr.*1 p.2 H.; αὐ. πρόδηλον S.E.*P.*2.164; αὐ. φαίνεσθαι Plu.2.930a; αὐ. ἐναργής Plot.5.5.1. 3. *hastily*, Plb.5.35.13, al., D.S.1.37. III. *merely, only*, dub. in Pl.*Sph.*220b, cf. Plu.2.631d, Luc.*Merc.Cond.*4.

αὐτό-θεος, ὁ, *very God*, Procl. *in Prm.*p.856 S., Eustr. *in EN*287.34. **-θεότης**, ητος, ἡ, *very Godhead*, Procl. *in Prm.*p.866 S. **-θερμος**, ον, *warm in itself*, Olymp. *in Phd.*p.226 N. **-θετος**, ον, *self-placed*, Sch.D.T.p.220 H. **-θηκτος**, ον, *self-sharpened*, epith. of cold-forged iron, A.*Fr.*356. **-θήρευτος**, ον, *self-caught* or *taken*, Sch.Opp.*H.*5.588.

αὐτόθῐ, Adv. = αὐτοῦ, *on the spot*, αὐτόθ' ἔασε κεῖσθαι Il.5.847, etc.; παρ' αὐ. (vv.ll. αὐτόφι, αὐτίκα) 23.147, cf. Hdt.1.93, 2.44, 56, al.: also in Com. and Att. Prose, Ar.*Eq.*119, Pherecr.84, Lys.23.11, Pl. *Prt.*314b, al. II. later of Time, *on the spot*, Luc.*Cal.*24.

αὐτοικος λεώς, prob. *a slave with his house*, *GDI*5533 e 6.

αὐτό-ϊππος, ὁ, *ideal horse*, Arist.*Metaph.*1040ᵇ33. **-ἴσον**, τό, *ideal equality*, Alex.Aphr. *in Metaph.*79.14, Procl. *in Prm.*p.676 S., Herm. *in Phdr.*p.121 A. **-ἰσότης**, ητος, ἡ, *abstract equality*, Procl. *in Prm.*p.676 S. **-κάβδᾰλος**, ον, *done carelessly, slovenly*, Arist. *Rh.*1415ᵇ38; αὐ. σκάφος a bark *built offhand*, Lyc.745. Adv. -λως *extempore*, περὶ εὐόγκων λέγειν Arist.*Rh.*1408ᵃ12. II. αὐτοκάβδαλοι, οἱ, *buffoons, improvisers*, Eup.200, Semus 20, Luc.*Lex.*10. **-κᾰκον**, τό, *evil in itself, radical evil*, Plot.1.8.8, Herm. *in Phdr.*p.156 A. 2. masc. -κακος, ὁ, *self-tormentor*, Theopomp.Com.20. **-καλές**· τὸ ἐπιτυχόν, συμβεβηκός, Hsch. **-καλλονή**, ἡ, *ideal, absolute beauty*, Procl.*Theol.Plat.*1.24; also **-καλλος**, τό, ib.5.14, Herm. *in Phdr.* p.157 A., Procl. *in Prm.*p.667 S. **-κᾰλον**, τό, *ideal beauty*, Aristid.2.182 J., Plot.1.8.13. **-καρνος**, ον, = αὐτοζήμιος, Hsch. **-καρπος**, ον, *self-fructifying*, *AB*464. **-κᾰσιγνήτη**, ἡ, *own sister*, Od.10.137, E.*Ph.*136 (lyr.), etc. **-κᾰσίγνητος**, ὁ, *own brother*, Il.2.706, al. **-κατάκρῐτος**, ον, *self-condemned*, *Ep.Tit.*3.11, Ph.2.652. **-κατασκεύαστος**, ον, *self-made, natural*, Sch.A.*Pr.*298, 301. **-κέλευθος**, ον, *going one's own road*, Tryph.314, *AP*9.362.5, Nonn.*D.*6.369: neut. pl. as Adv., ib.21.167. **-κέλευστος**, ον, *self-bidden*, i.e. *unbidden*, X.*An.*3.4.5, D.H.8.66, *AP*5.21 (Rufin.); προθυμία Ph.2.90, al. Adv. -τως Aristeas 92. **-κελής**, ές, = foreg., Hdt.9.5. **-κερας**, (κεράννυμι) *self-mixed*, Poll.6.24; used as Adv. acc. to Phryn.*PS* p.1 B. **-κέραστος**, *self-mixed*, i.e. *unmixed*, properly of light wines that need no water, dub., ibid. **-κερκίς**, ίδος, ἡ, *ideal shuttle*, Procl. *in Prm.*p.773 S. **-κῆρυξ**, ῡκος, ὁ, *self-heralded*, prob. in Phryn.*PS* p.5 B. **-κῑνέω**, *have the principle of motion in oneself*, f.l. in Procl.*Inst.*20, Serv. ad Virg.*Aen.*10.304. **-κῑνησία**, ἡ, = sq., Procl.*Inst.*20, Iamb.*Myst.*1.4, Dam.*Pr.*16, etc. **-κίνησις** [ῑ], εως, ἡ, *self-motion*, Syrian. *in Metaph.*45.26, etc.; ἔστιν ἡ ἐπιστήμη αὐ. Plot.6.2.18, cf. 6.6.6. **-κῑνητίζομαι**, *to be self-moved*, Dam.*Pr.*18. **-κίνητος** [ῑ], ον, *self-moved*, Arist.*Ph.*258ᵃ2, Plu. 2.952e, etc.; λογικὴ φύσις Ph.1.36, cf. Procl.*Inst.*14, Dam.*Pr.*78; of *live*-stock, πράγματα κινητά τε καὶ ἀκίνητα καὶ αὐ. *PMasp.*122.3 (vi A.D.), etc. Adv. -τως Procl.*Inst.*195, Olymp. *in Alc.*p.61 C. **-κλᾰδος**, ον, *branches and all*, Luc.*VH*1.40. **-κλητος**, ον, *self-called*, i.e. *uncalled, unbidden*, A.*Eu.*170 (lyr.), S.*Tr.*392, Pl. *Ep.*331b; συμβουλεῦσαι αὐ. Phld.*Ir.*p.46 W.; αὐ. ἐπίκουροι *natural* allies (of parents and children), Hierocl.p.57 A.; δῆμος εἰς τοὺς πολέμους αὐ. Him.*Ecl.*5.14; *personally invited*, Plu.2.707f. **-κμής**, ῆτος, ὁ, ἡ, (κάμνω) = αὐτοπόνητος, Opp.*H.*1.718. **-κομος**, ον, *with natural hair, shaggy*, λοφιά Ar.*Ra.*822. II. *leaves and all*, Luc.*VH*1.40. **-κρᾶνος**, ον, *self-accomplishing*, λόγος prob. in A.*Fr.*295. II. Pass., *self-accomplished, self-evident*, Hsch., *EM* 173.34. III. *monolith*, Hsch. **-κρας**, = αὐτοκέραστος, Poll. 6.24. **-κρᾱσία**, ἡ, = sq., *PTaur.*8.67. **-κράτεια** [ρᾰ], ἡ, *power over oneself*, Pl.*Def.*412d. **-κράτειρα** [ρᾰ], ἡ, fem. of αὐτοκράτωρ, Orph.*H.*70.8. **-κρᾰτής**, ές, *ruling by oneself, absolute, independent*, νοῦς Anaxag.12; τύχη Hp.*Loc.Hom.*46; φρήν E.*Andr.*482 (lyr.); ἀπειθής τε καὶ αὐ. Pl.*Ti.*91b; γένεσις οὐδεμία αὐ. ἐστιν Dam.*Pr.*394; τὸ αὐ. Plu.2.1026d. Adv. -κρατῶς Lyd. *Mag.*1.33. **-κράτητος** [ᾰ], ον, = αὐτάγρευτος, Sch.Opp.*H.*4.449. **-κρᾰτορεύω**, *to be* or *become Emperor*, D.C.69.4, *POxy.*33 ii 9 (ii A.D.). **-κρᾰτορία**, ἡ, *sovereignty*, of the Emperors, D.C. 67.12; also -εία, ἡ, *reign of an Emperor*, *PFlor.*56.13 (iii A.D.), etc. **-κρᾰτόρια**, τά, *festival in honour of the Emperor*, *IGRom.*3.682. **-κρᾰτορικός**, ή, όν, *of* or *for the Imperator*, ἐσθής D.H.8.59, cf. Gal.8.355, *BGU*970.23 (ii A.D.), etc. Adv. -κῶς *despotically*, Plu. *Ant.*15. **-κρᾰτορίς**, ίδος, ἡ, *the residence of a sovereign*, J.*AJ* 18.2.1. **-κρᾶτος**, ον, = αὐτοκέραστος, Ath.1.32f, Phryn.*PS* p.29 B. **-κράτωρ** [ᾰ], ορος, ὁ, ἡ, (κρᾰτέω) *one's own master*: hence, 1. of persons or states, *free, independent*, Th.4.63, *IG*12(9).189.44, etc.: of a youth *that has come of age*, X.*Mem.*2.1.21. 2. of ambassadors and commissioners, *possessing full powers, plenipotentiary*, αὐτοκράτορά τινα ἑλέσθαι Ar.*Pax* 359; αὐ. ἥκομεν Id.*Av.*1595; πρεσβευτής Lys.13.9; ξυγγραφεῖς Th.8.67; αὐ. βουλή And.1.15; ἀποδεῖξαι ἄνδρας ἀρχὴν αὐτοκράτορας, opp. a reference to the assembly, Th.5.27. 3. of rulers, *absolute*, στρατηγοί Id.6.72; ἄρχων X. *An.*6.1.21; ἀνυπεύθυνος καὶ αὐ. ἄρχειν Pl.*Lg.*875b, cf. *Plt.*299c; τὸ πᾶν αὐ. διαθεῖναι manage all *at their pleasure*, Th.1.126; ἦρχε τῶν ἀκολουθούντων αὐτὸς αὐτοκράτωρ, of Philip, D.18.235; μόναρχοι Arist.*Pol.* 1295ᵃ12; στρατηγία ib.1285ᵃ8 (dub.); νοῦς αὐ. (cf. αὐτοκρατής) Anaxag. ap.Pl.*Cra.*413c: hence, = Lat. *Dictator*, Plb.3.86.7, etc.; = *Imperator*, Plu.*Pomp.*8; of *the Emperor*, Id.*Galb.*1, etc. **4.** αὐ. λογισμός *peremptory* reasoning, Th.4.108. **II.** c. gen., *complete master of..*, πόλις οὐκ αὐ. οὖσα ἑαυτῆς Id.3.62; τῆς τύχης Id.4.64; τῆς αὐτοῦ πορείας Pl.*Plt.*274a; τῆς ἐπιορκίας αὐ. *having full liberty to* swear falsely, D.17.12: c. inf., αὐ. κολάσαι *having full power* to punish, Id. 59.80. **–κρής,** ές, = αὐτοκέραστος, Nic.*Al.*163. **–κρῖτος,** ον, (κρίνω) *self-interpreted*, κρίσεις ὀνείρων Artem.4.72. **·κτητος,** ον, *acquired* or *possessed by oneself*, χωρία *Test.Epict.*1.32. **–κτίστης,** ου, ὁ, *itself the creator*, Plu.*Nob.*12. **–κτῖτος,** ον, (κτίζω) *self-produced*, i.e. *made by nature*, *natural*, αὐτόκτιτ' ἄντρα A.*Pr.*303; αὐ. δόμους S.*Fr.*332. **–κτονέω,** *slay one another*, restored in S.*Ant.* 56 for the f.l. αὐτοκτενοῦντε. **–κτόνος,** ον, *self-slaying*, χεὶρ αὐ., of Medea, *who slew her own children*, E.*Med.*1254 (lyr.). Adv. –νως *with one's own hand*, A.*Ag.*1635. **2.** *slaying one another*, χέρες Id.*Th.*810; θάνατος αὐ. *mutual* death *by each other's hand*, ib.681; δῶρα αὐ. *AP*7.152 (Leont.). Adv. –νως A.*Th.*734 (lyr.). **–κῠβερνήτης,** ου, ὁ, *one who steers himself*, *AP*9.438 (Phil.). **–κυκλος,** ὁ, *the ideal circle*, *the Form of circle*, Them.*Or.*13.165a, Procl. *in Prm.* p.773S. **–κύλιστος** [ῠ], ον, *self-rolled* or *moved*, Opp.*H.*2.604, Nonn.*D.*2.434. **–κωλος,** 'skin and bone', *a mere skeleton*, prob. in Semon.7.76. **–κωπος,** ον, *with haft* and blade *in one*, βέλη αὐ., i.e. *swords*, A.*Ch.*163 (lyr.). **–λᾰβος,** ον, = foreg., Hsch. **–λάλητής,** οῦ, ὁ, *one who talks to himself*, Timo 50.

αὐτόλειον· λειτόν, Hsch.

αὐτο-λεξεί, Adv. *with the very words*, *in express words*, Ph.2. 597. **–λήκῠθος,** ὁ, *one who carries his own oil-flask*, *one who has no slave to do so*: hence, *wretchedly poor*, Antiph.16, Men.105; αὐ., οἱ, 'the Beggars', name of a club, D.54.14. **II.** *flatterer*, *parasite*, Luc.*Lex.*10, Plu.2.50c. **–ληπτον,** gloss on αὐτάγρετον, Apollon. *Lex.Hom.* **–λόχευτος,** ον, *self-engendered*, Nonn.*D.*4.427. **–λύκιον,** τό, *white hellebore*, *Hippiatr.*26. **–λῠρίζων** ὄνος an ass *that plays the lyre to himself*, prov. in Luc.*DMeretr.*14.4. **–λῠσις,** εως, ἡ, *couple* or *leash for hounds*, Hsch. **–μάθεια** [μᾰ], ἡ, *self-teaching* or *learning*, Plu.2.973e:—also **–μᾰθία,** Aristid.Quint.2.9. **–μᾰθής,** ές, *having learnt of oneself*, Ph.1.35, al., Plu.2.992a; τινός *self-taught*, of persons, *in* a thing, *AP*6.218 (Alc.); of that which is learnt, ἐπιστήμη Ph.1.164; *spontaneous*, συγγένειαν εἶναι μούσαις αὐτομαθῆ Phld.*Po.*2.47. Adv. –θῶς Philostr.*VS*1.15.2, Ph.1.62. **–μαρτῠς,** ῠρος, ὁ, ἡ, *oneself the witness*, i.e. *eyewitness*, A.*Ag.*989 (lyr.).

αὐτομᾰτ-εί or **–τί,** Adv. of –ματος, Nonn.*D.*4.153 (dub.). **–έω,** = αὐτοματίζω, Hsch. s.v. αὐτοφαρίζειν. **–ία,** ἡ, *the goddess of chance*, Plu.*Tim.*36, 2.542e, 816e. **–ίζω,** *act of oneself*, *act offhand* or *unadvisedly*, X.*Cyr.*4.5.21:—Pass., *to be done spontaneously* or *at random*, Plu.*Ages.*23, Procl. *in Ti.*1.297 D.; but ηὐτοματισμένη παράδοσις *haphazard*, Id.*Hyp.*7.35. Adv. ηὐτοματισμένως Id. *in Prm.* p.650S. **2.** *introduce the agency of chance*, of Anaxagoras, Simp. *in Ph.*327.27. **3.** of things, *happen of themselves*, *casually*, Hp. *Acut.*(*Sp.*)33; φήμη D.S.16.92:—Pass., *to be self-produced*, Ph.1. 441. **4.** of natural agencies, *act spontaneously*, ὥσπερ αὐτοματιζούσης τῆς φύσεως Arist.*GA*715ᵇ27, cf. D.H.*Comp.*20. **–ισμός,** ὁ, *that which happens of itself*, *chance*, Hp.*Acut.*(*Sp.*)57, Alcid.*Soph.* 25 (pl.), D.H.1.4, J.*AJ*10.11.7; κατ' αὐτοματισμόν Phleg.*Mir.*1.

αὐτομᾰτοποιητική (sc. τέχνη), ἡ, *art of making marionettes*, and τὰ αὐ. *treatise thereupon*, Hero *Aut.*1.1.

αὐτό-μᾰτος, η, ον, Hom. and Att.; ος, ον Hes.*Op.*103, Arist.*GA* 762ᵃ9, Philetaer.1 D., Hp.*Ep.*19 in *Hermes* 53.65. **1.** of persons, *acting of one's own will*, *of oneself*, αὐ. δέ οἱ ἦλθε Il.2.408; αὐ. φοιτῶσι Νοῦσοι Hes.*Op.*103; αὐ. ἥκω Ar.*Pl.*1190, cf. Th.6.91, D.S.2.25, etc. **2.** of inanimate things, *self-acting*, *spontaneous*, of the gates of Olympus, αὐτόμαται δὲ πύλαι μύκον οὐρανοῦ Il.5.749; of the tripods of Hephaistos, which ran of themselves, ὄφρα οἱ αὐτόματοι.. δυσαίατ' ἀγῶνα 18.376, cf. Pl.Com.188; ὅπλα.. αὐ. φανῆναι ἔξω προκείμενα τοῦ νηοῦ Hdt.8.37; τὰ αὐ. *marionettes*, Arist.*GA*734ᵇ10, Hero *Aut.* passim: generally, *spontaneous*, βίος Pl.*Plt.*271e; ἔπαινος Epicur. *Sent.Vat.*64. **3.** of natural agencies, ὁ ποταμὸς αὐ. ἐπελθών *of itself*, Hdt.2.14; of plants, *growing of themselves*, αὐ. ἐκ τῆς γῆς γίνεται Id.3.100; αὐ. φύεσθαι Id.2.94, Thphr.*Fr.*171.11; κύτισος αὐ. ἔρχεται Cratin.98.8: metaph., αὐτόματα πάντ' ἀγαθὰ.. πορίζεται Ar. *Ach.*976, cf. Cratin.160; of philosophers, αὐ. ἀναφύονται Pl.*Tht.* 180c. **4.** of events, *happening of themselves*, *without external agency*, αὐ. δεσμὰ διελύθη E.*Ba.*447; αὐ. θάνατος *natural* death, D. 18.205; κόποι αὐ. *not to be accounted for externally*, Hp.*Aph.*2.5; ἀπό τινος αἰτίας αὐτομάτης Pl.*Sph.*265c; *without visible cause*, *accidental*, opp. ἀπὸ πείρης, Hdt.7.9.γ'. **II.** αὐτόματον, τό, *accident*, τὸ αὐ. αἰτιᾶσθαι Lys.6.25; σε ταὐ. ἀποσέσωκε Men.*Epit.*568; διὰ τὸ αὐ. Arist.*Ph.*195ᵇ33; τὸ αὐ. ἀγαπῶντες Id.*Ath.*8.5; τῷ αὐ., opp. τέχνῃ, Id.*Metaph.*1070ᵃ7: most freq. in the form ἀπὸ τοῦ αὐτομάτου or ἀπὸ ταὐτομάτου, ἀποθανέειν ἀπὸ τοῦ αὐ. Hdt.2.66, cf. Th.2.77, Pl. *Ap.*38c, al., Arist.*Po.*1452ᵃ5, al., Men.*Pk.*31; ἐκ τοῦ αὐ. X.*An.*1. 3.13; τὸ Αὐ. personified, *Ath.Mitt.*35.458 (Pergam.); ταὐτόματόν ἐστιν ὡς ἔοικέ που θεός Men.291. **III.** Adv. –τως, = ἀπὸ ταὐτομάτου, v.l. in Hdt.2.180, Hp.*Fract.*43, Arist.*PA*640ᵃ27, al., Theoc.21. 27; *of itself*, κοχλίας αὐ. βαδίζων Plb.12.13.11:—also αὐτοματεί or –τί (q.v.). **–μάττιτα·** σπέρμα ἀνδρός, Hsch. **–μᾰχέω,** (μάχομαι) *fight for oneself*, *plead one's own cause*, in a law-court, Lys.*Fr.*102 S., Hsch., Suid. **–μέγεθος,** ους, τό, *abstract magnitude*, Procl. *in Prm.* pp.663, 676 S. **–μέλαθρος,** ον, *united with her abode*, of a Hamadryad, Nonn.*D.*48.519. **–μέλιννα,** ἡ, *a very Melinna*, *AP*6.353 (Noss.). **–μενίς,** ἡ, dub. sens. in *BGU*387 ii 4 (ii A.D.). **–μετάβλητος,** ον, *self-changed*, Dam.*Pr.*405. **–μετρος,** ον, *self-measured*, Simp. *in Ph.*767.2. **–μήκης,** ες, *self-lengthened*, i.e. *square*, of a number, opp. ἑτερομήκης, Iamb. *in Nic.*p.74 P. **–μῆκος,** ους, τό, *abstract length*, prob. in Arist.*Top.*143ᵇ24. **–μηνί,** Adv. *in the very month*, Attic.ap.Eus.*PE*15.4. **–μήνῡτος,** ον, *self-revealed* or *betrayed*, Phryn.*PS* p.51 B. **–μήτωρ,** ορος, ἡ, *very mother herself*, or *her mother's very child*, dub. in Semon.7.12. **–μοιρος,** ον, *with a single share*, S.*Fr.*250 (= μονόμοιρος, Hsch.).

αὐτομολ-έω, *desert*, Hdt.8.82, Ar.*Eq.*26, Th.3.77, etc.; αὐ. πρὸς τοὺς Πέρσας Hdt.1.127, etc.; ἐς αὐτούς Id.3.154, al.; ἐς Ἀθήνας ἐκ Περσέων ib.160; παρά τινος X.*An.*1.7.13; εἰς τοὺς πολεμίους αὐτομολήσας οἴχεσθαι And.1.44. **II.** metaph., αὐ. ἐν τῇ πολιτείᾳ *keep changing sides*, *rat*, Aeschin.3.75; αὐ. πρὸς τὴν ἐλευθερίαν D.S.2. 26. **III.** *come of one's own accord*, τὰ θηρία πρὸς τὰς παγίδας –μολήσει Lyd.*Ost.*39. **–ησις,** εως, ἡ, = sq., Ph.1.272; rejected by Thom.Mag.p.128 R. **–ία,** ἡ, *desertion*, Th.7.13, etc. **–ος,** ον, *going of oneself*, *without bidding*, Opp.*H.*3.360; *coming of oneself*, *AP* 5.21 (Rufin.):—but mostly, **2.** as Subst., *deserter*, Hdt.3.156, al., Th.4.118, al.; παρά τινος X.*An.*1.7.2; γυνὴ αὐ. Hdt.9.76. Adv. –λως *treacherously*, S.*Fr.*691.

αὐτομόλπως and **–πα·** ὁμοίως ἐκείνοις, Hsch.

αὐτό-μορφος, ον, *self-formed*, *natural*, E.*Fr.*125. **–νεκρος,** ον, *verily dead*, *a mere corpse*, Alciphr.3.7.

αὐτονομ-έομαι, Dep. c. aor. Pass. –ήθην Str.12.3.11:—*to be independent*, Th.1.144, D.4.4, etc. **–ία,** ἡ, of a state, *freedom to use its own laws*, *independence*, Th.3.46, X.*HG*5.1.36, Isoc.9.68, *IG*2². 34, etc. **2.** αὐ. ποιητική, poetic *licence*, Him.*Or.*1.1. **3.** *dogmatism*, Olymp. *in Mete.*151.21. **–ος,** ον, *living under one's own laws*, *independent*, of persons and states, Hdt.1.96, 8.140.α', Cratin. 15 D., etc.; freq. in Th., αὐ. ἐπὶ σφῶν αὐτῶν οἰκεῖν Id.2.63; ἀφιέναι αὐ. τινα Id.1.139; αὐ. ποιεῖν τινα Id.5.33; αὐ. ἀπό τινος X.*HG* 5.1.36, cf. *Lac.*3.1; πόλις.. ἐλευθέρα καὶ αὐ. *IG*3.481, al.; αὐ. πολιτεία Plu.*Rom.*27. **2.** generally, *of one's own free will*, ἀλλ' αὐ.. Ἀΐδην καταβήσει S.*Ant.*821 (lyr.). **3.** of animals, *feeding and ranging at will*, *AP*7.8 (Antip. Sid.).

αὐτο-νοέω, *think for oneself*, prob. in Meno *Iatr.*20.24. **–νοος,** ον, contr. **–νους,** ουν, of the Phaeacian ships, *instinct with sense*, Eust. 1153.32, with allusion to the nymph Autonoe. **–νους,** ὁ, *pure intellect*, Plot.3.2.16; νοῦ [ἕτερος] αὐτόνους Id.5.9.13. **–νυκτί,** Adv. = sq., J.*AJ*17.9.5. **–νῠχί** [ῐ] or **–χεί,** Adv., (νύξ) *that very night*, Il.8.197, Aristid.*Or.*48(24).16; *in the same night*, Arat.618, A.R.4. 1130. **II. αὐτ-ονῠχί,** (ὄνυξ) *with the nail*, *EM*173.57. **–νύχιος** [ῠ], ον, *nightly*, Hsch. s.v. ἔννυχος. **–νῠχίς** and **αὐτονῠχηδίς,** = αὐτονυχί 1, Theognost.*Can.*163.17. **–ξενεῖν** (–ξένειν cod.)· ἐν ἴσῳ τῷ προξενεῖν, Hsch. **–ξεστος,** ον, = αὐτοσχέδιος, Anon. *in Rh.*186. 2. **–ξῠλος,** ον, *of one piece of wood*, ἔκπωμα S.*Ph.*35, cf. *APl.*4.235 (Apollonid.), Str.11.4.3. **–ολον,** τό, *abstract totality*, Dam.*Pr.* 427. **–ολότης,** ητος, ἡ, = foreg., Procl.*Inst.*69. **–όμοιον,** τό, *abstract similarity*, Id. *in Prm.*p.588 S. **–ομοιότης,** ητος, ἡ, = foreg., Herm. *in Phdr.*p.151 A. **–όν,** ὄντος, τό, *self-existence*, Dam.*Pr.*28, Them. *in Ph.*9.29: pl., αὐτοόντα Procl.*Inst.*128. **–ουσία,** ἡ, *full* or *perfect being*, Plot.6.8.12. **–πᾰγής,** ές, (πήγνυμι) *compact of itself*, γῆ Ephor.108; *rough*, πέτροι Agatharch.32; θαλάμαι, of a swarm of bees in the air, *AP*9.404 (Antiphil.). **–πάθεια** [πᾰ], ἡ, *one's own experience*, ἐξ αὐ. διατίθεσθαι τοὺς λόγους Plb.3.108.2, cf. D.H.*Dem.* 22, Plu.*Lib.*1; = ἰδιοπάθεια, *primary affection*, Gal.8.78. **2.** Gramm., of words that are *reflexive*, opp. transitive, A.D.*Synt.*147. 21. **–πᾰθής,** ές, *speaking from one's own feeling* or *experience*. Adv. –θῶς Plb.3.12.1, Plu.*Cat.Mi.*54; *instinctively*, αὐ. φεύγομεν τὴν ἀλγηδόνα Epicur.*Fr.*66, etc. **II.** Gramm., of pronouns, *reflexive*, opp. ἀλλοπαθεῖς, A.D.*Pron.*44.11; of verbs, opp. μεταβατικά, *Synt.* 281.15. **–παίδευτος,** ον, *self-educated*, Anatolius in *Cat.Cod.Astr.* 8(3).188. **–παις,** παιδος, ὁ, ἡ, *the own child*, τῷ Διὸς αὐτόπαιδι S.*Tr.*826 (lyr.); prob. *a mere child*, Id.*Fr.*1029; dub. l. in *PPetr.* 3 p.110. **–πάμων** [ᾱ], ον, gen. ονος, (πέπᾱμαι) *sole heir*, Hsch. (αὐτόπομα cod.). **–παστοι** πύλαι· παστάδας ἔχουσαι, ποικίλαι, Id. **–πάτωρ** [ᾰ], ορος, ὁ, ἡ, *self-engendered*, φύσις Orph.*H.*10. 10, Iamb.*Myst.*8.2; of Zeus, Aristid.*Or.*43(1).9. **–πέδη,** *fetter*, dub. in Nonn.*D.*21.50. **–πεδον,** = αὐτοποδητί, Hsch. **–πειρος,** ον, *learnt by one's own experience*, Dam.*Isid.*121.

αὐτοπέλις· κλῖμαξ, Hsch.

αὐτο-περίγρᾰφος, ον, *self-circumscribed*, Dam.*Pr.*261, 273. **–πήμων,** ον, gen. ονος, *for one's own woes*, γόος A.*Th.*917 (lyr.). **–πήρίτης** [ῑ], ου, ὁ, *with only a wallet*, Menipp.*Ep.*tit. **–πιστος,** ον, *credible in itself*, ἀξιώματα Hero *Deff.*136.6, cf. Olymp. *in Phd.*p.225 N., Heliod. *in EN*117.36, Simp. *in Ph.*649.12; f.l. in Oenom.ap.Eus.*PE* 5.33. **–πλεκτος,** ον, *self-twined*, Opp.*H.*4.449. **–πληθος,** ους, τό, *abstract plurality*, Procl. *Theol.Plat.*3.21, Dam.*Pr.*202. **–ποδητί,** Adv. = sq., Luc.*Lex.*2. **–ποδί,** Adv. *on one's own feet*, *on foot*, D.C.50.5. **–ποδία,** ἡ, *use of one's own feet*, *walking*, αὐτοποδίᾳ κομισθῆναι D.C.44.8, cf. Stratt.5 D. **–ποιητικός,** ή, όν, opp. εἰδωλοποιϊκός, *making not a copy*, *but the thing itself*, Pl.*Sph.* 266a. **–ποίητος,** ον, = αὐτοπαγής, Sophr.13. **–ποιός,** όν, *self-produced*, i.e. *not planted by man*, *naturally grown*, of the Athenian olive, S.*OC*698 (lyr.); *made by one's own hand*, of votive offerings,

*IG*4.222 (Corinth). **-πόκιστος**, ον, = sq., Hsch. **-ποκος**, ον, *made of wool only, all wool*, ἱμάτιον *Com.Adesp.*854. **-πολις** πόλις *free, independent* state, Th.5.79. **-πολίτης** [ῑ], ου, ὁ, *citizen of a free state*, prob. in X.*HG*5.2.14. **-πόνητος**, ον, *self-wrought, natural*, ῥεῦμα μελισσῶν *AP*9.404(Antiphil.). **-πονος**, ον, = foreg., Nic.*Th*.23. **-πορος**, ον, *self-moving*, Nonn.*D*.1.308, 6.370. **-ποσόν**, τό, *abstract quantity*, Plot.4.3.2. **-πους**, ὁ, ἡ, -πουν, τό, gen. ποδος, *on foot, on one's own feet*, Luc.*Tim*.24. **-πρᾱγέω**, *act independently*, Str.8.3.30; *do one's own work*, Procl.*in R*.1.23K. **-πρᾱγία**, ἡ, *free, independent action*, Pl.*Def*.411e, Chrysipp.*Stoic*.3.176, Ph.2.51, Procl.*in Prm*.p.664S.; ἐξουσία αὐτοπραγίας *Stoic*.3.86. **-πραγμᾰτεύτως**, dub. l. (for ἀπραγμ-) in D.H.*Is*.16. **-πρακτος**, ον, *enjoying the privilege of collecting one's own taxes*, *PMasp*.19.3 (vi A.D.); αὐ. σχῆμα ib.2 iii 8, cf. *Cod.Theod*.11.22.4. **-πρεμνος**, ον, *together with the root, root and branch*, τὰ δ' ἀντιτείνοντ' αὐτόπρεμν' ἀπόλλυται (sc. δένδρα) S.*Ant*.714, cf. Antiph.231.7; ἀνασπᾶν αὐτοπρέμνοις τοῖς λόγοισιν Ar.*Ra*.903 (paratrag.); αὐ. τι νέμειν give *in absolute possession*, A.*Eu*.401. **-πρεπής**, v. αὐτοτροπήσας. **-προαίρετος**, ον, *self-chosen*, κακία Hierocl.*in CA*24 p.473 M., cf. Ps.-Plu.*Vit.Hom*.105. Adv. -τως, κολάζεσθαι Simp.*in Epict*.p.108 D. II. Act., *self-acting, acting of free will*, *Proll.Hermog*. in Rh.4.27 W.; τὸ αὐ. τε καὶ αὐτεξούσιον *free will*, Olymp.*in Grg*.p.264 J. **-προθύμως** [ῡ], Adv. *voluntarily*, *EM*173.8. **-πρόσωπος**, ον, *in one's own person, without a mask*, of an actor, Ath.10.452f, cf. Jul.*Mis*.367b; αὐ. φανῆναι Luc.*Pr.Im*.3; αὐ. ὁρᾶν τὸ κάλλος Id.*Tim*.27; λέγειν Id.*JTr*.29; *speaking in one's own person*, Sch.Il.*Oxy*.1086.64, al.; συγγράμματα αὐ. *in which the author speaks in his own person*, Ammon. *in Cat*.4.16; cf. αὐτοδιήγητος. Adv. -πως, θεσπίσαι Ph.2.208; εἰσάγειν τοὺς κωμῳδουμένους Hermog.*Stat*.11 (v.l. -πους); ὑποκρινόμενος Him.*Ecl*.2.21; ἀντεπιστεῖλαι *CPR*20 ii 5 (iii A.D.). **-πτερος**, ον, *with his own wings*, Aristid.*Or*.37(2).24.

αὐτοπτ-έω, *see with one's own eyes*, Paus.4.31.5, Hld.3.1; esp. *witness* a divine manifestation, Porph.ap.Eus.*PE*4.20:—Pass., φάσματα -ούμενα Marin.*Procl*.28. **-ης**, ου, ὁ, *seeing oneself, eyewitness*, Hdt.2.29, 3.115, al., Pl.*Lg*.900a, Euang.1.4, Din.3.15, D.22.22, etc.:—fem. **αὐτόπτις**, ἡ, Sch.Il.*Oxy*.1086.96. **-ικός**, ή, όν, *of an eyewitness*, πίστις Scymn.129; opp. λογικός, Gal.16.600. Adv. -κῶς Id.13.350. II. *concerned with a direct vision of divinity*, λεκανομαντ(ε)ία *PMag.Par*.1.221 (αὐθ-); αὐ. λεκάνης ἐνέργεια a *personal and active* power of dish-divination, Harp.Astr. in *Cat.Cod.Astr*.8(3).136.10; λόγος *PMag.Lond*.46.53, cf. 121.335; δεῖξις Iamb.*Myst*.2.6. **-ος**, ον, *self-revealed*, Jul.*Or*.7.221b, Suid.; ἐπ' αὐτόπτῳ, gloss on ἐπ' αὐτοφώρῳ, Hsch. II. = αὐτοπτικός II, *PMag.Lond*.121.319, 727, *PMag.Par*.1.162.

αὐτό-πτυκτος, *folded on itself*, φύλλα *Gloss*. **-πῡρ**, πῦρος, τό, *very fire*, Herm.ap.Stob.3.11.31. **-πῡρος**, ὁ, *of whole wheaten meal*, ἄρτος Alex.121, Gal.15.577, *PPetr*.3p.179; opp. σητάνειος, Plu.2.466d:—also **-πῡρίτης** [ῑ], ου, ὁ, Phryn.Com.38, Hp.*Int*.20, 22, Luc.*Pisc*.44. **-πώλης**, ου, ὁ, *selling one's own products*, Pl.*Plt*.260c; αὐ. περί τι Id.*Sph*.231d, cf. Sch.Ar.*Pl*.1155. **-πωλικός**, ή, όν, = foreg.: -κή (sc. τέχνη), ἡ, *trade of an* αὐτοπώλης, opp. ἐμπορική, καπηλική, Pl.*Sph*.223d, cf. 224e. **-ρέγμων**, ον, gen. ονος, (ῥέζω) *self-wrought*, πότμος A.*Fr*.117. **-ρήτωρ**, ορος, ὁ, *a self-made orator*, Eust.1301.32.

αὐτ-όροφος, ον, *self-covered, roofed* or *vaulted by nature*, πέτρα Opp.*H*.1.22; καλάμων σκηναί D.H.1.79; αὐ. στέγη a *natural* roof, Ael.*NA*16.17.

αὐτό-ρρεκτος, ον, *self-produced*, Opp.*C*.2.567, *H*.1.763. **-ρρῐζος**, ον, *together with the roots*, D.S.4.12: poet. **αὐτόρῐζος**, Babr.36.1. II. *self-rooted, self-founded*, ἑστία E.*Rh*.288. **-ρρῑφής**, ές, (ῥίπτω) *self-precipitated*, Sch.E.*Ph*.640. **-ρρῠτος**, ον, (ῥέω) *self-flowing, flowing unbidden*, *AP*9.669(Marian.); of resin, Gal.13.626: poet. **αὐτόρῠτος**, χρυσός Pi.*P*.12.17.

αὐτός (Cret. **ἀϝτός** *GDI*4976, al.), αὐτή, αὐτό (also αὐτόν *Leg.Gort*.3.4, al.), reflexive Pron., *self*:—in oblique cases used for the personal Pron., *him, her, it*:—with Art., ὁ αὐτός, ἡ αὐτή, τὸ αὐτό (also ταὐτόν), etc., *the very one, the same*.

I. *self, myself, thyself*, etc., acc. to the person of the Verb: freq. joined with ἐγώ, σύ, etc. (v. infr. 10), 1. *one's true self*, the *soul*, not the body, Od.11.602; reversely, *body*, not soul, Il.1.4; *oneself*, as opp. others who are less prominent, as king to subject, 6.18; Zeus to other gods, 8.4; bird to young, 2.317; man to wife and children, Od.14.265; warrior to horses, Il.2.466, or to weapons, 1.47; shepherd to herd, Od.9.167, cf. Il.1.51; Trojans to allies, 11.220; seamen to ships, 7.338: generally, whole to parts, ib.474; so later ἡ σίδη καὶ αὐτὴ καὶ τὰ φύλλα Thphr.*HP*4.10.7, cf. X.*Ath*.1.19, Pl.*Grg*.511e, etc.; αὐτή τε Μανδάνη καὶ τὸν υἱὸν ἔχουσα X.*Cyr*.1.3.1; αὐ. τε καὶ τὰ ποιήματα βουλόμενος ἐπιδεῖξαι Pl.*R*.398a: abs., *the Master*, as in the Pythag. phrase Αὐτὸς ἔφα, Lat. *Ipse dixit*; so τίς οὗτος..;—Αὐτός, i.e. Socrates, Ar.*Nu*.218; ἀναβόησον Αὐτόν ib.219; ἀνοιγέτω τις δώματ'· Αὐτὸς ἔρχεται *the Master*, Id.*Fr*.268, cf. Pl.*Prt*.314d, Thphr.*Char*.2.4, Men.*Sam*.41; αὐ. ἀϋτεῖ Theoc.24.50: neut., αὐτὸ σημανεῖ *the result* will show, E.*Ph*.623; αὐτὸ δηλώσει D.19.157; αὐτὸ δηλοῖ Pl.*Prt*.329b; αὐτὸ διδάξει ib.324a; esp. αὐτὸ δείξει Cratin.177, Pl.*Hp.Ma*.288b, cf. *Tht*.200e; in full, τάχ' αὐτὸ δείξει τοὔργον S.*Fr*.388; τοὔργον τάχ' αὐτὸ δείξει Ar.*Lys*.375; redupl., αὐτός θ' ὁ χρήσας αὐτὸς ἦν ὁ μαρτυρῶν A.*Eu*.798; of things, *the very*, ὑπὸ λόφον αὐτόν, i.e. *just, exactly* under.., Il.13.615; πρὸς αὐταῖς ταῖς θύραις *close* by the door, Lys.12.12; αὐτὸ τὸ δέον the *very* thing needed, X.*An*.4.7.7; αὐτὸ ὃ μάλιστα ἔδει ῥηθῆναι Pl.*R*.362d; αὐτὸ τὸ περίορθρον *the point* of dawn, Th.2.3; αὐτὰ τὰ ἐναντία the *very* opposite, X.*Mem*.4.5.7; αὐτὰ τὰ χρήσιμα καὶ ἀναγκαῖα D.H.*Th*.23; *even*, οὔ μοι μέλει ἄλγος οὔτ' αὐτῆς Ἑκάβης Il.6.451; εἴ περ ἂν αὐταὶ Μοῦσαι ἀείδοιεν 2.597.—In these senses αὐτός in Prose either precedes both the Art. and Subst., or follows both, e.g. αὐτὸς ὁ υἱός or ὁ υἱὸς αὐτός. The Art. is sts. omitted with proper names, or Nouns denoting individuals, αὐτὸς Μένων X.*An*.2.1.5; αὐτὸς βασιλεύς ib.1.7.11. 2. *of oneself, of one's own accord*, ἀλλά τις αὐ. ἴτω Il.17.254; σπεύδοντα καὶ αὐτὸν ὀτρύνεις 8.293; καταπαύσομεν· οἱ δὲ καὶ αὐτοὶ παυέσθων Od.2.168; ἥξει γὰρ αὐτά S.*OT*341; also, *in person*, τῶν πραγμάτων ὑμῖν.. αὐτοῖς ἀντιληπτέον D.1.2. 3. *by oneself* or *itself, alone*, αὐτός περ ἐών although *alone*, Il.8.99; αὐτὸς ἐγείναο παῖδ', i.e. *without a mother*, 5.880, cf. Hes.*Th*.924; ἀνακομισθῆναι αὐτὸν ἐς Φάληρον *by himself*, Hdt.5.85; αὐτοὶ γάρ ἐσμεν we are *by ourselves*, i.e. *among friends*, Ar.*Ach*.504, cf. *Th*.472, Pl.*Prm*.137b, Herod.6.70, Plu.2.755c, Luc.*DDeor*.10.2; αὐτοῖς τοῖς ἀνδράσι.. ἢ καὶ τοῖς ἄλλοις X.*An*.2.3.7; ἄνευ τοῦ σίτου τὸ ὄψον αὐτὸ ἐσθίειν Id.*Mem*.3.14.3; τὸν τρίβωνα ὃν αὐτὸν φορεῖ Thphr.*Char*.22.13 (prob.); αὐτὰ γάρ ἐστιν ταῦτα these *and no others*, Emp.21.13, al.: strengthd., αὐτὸς κτήσατο οἶος *himself* alone, Od.14.450; αὐτὸς μόνος, v. μόνος II; αὐτὸς καθ' αὑτόν, v. ἑαυτοῦ. 4. in Philosophy, *by* or *in itself*, of an abstract concept or idea, δίκαιον αὐτό Pl.*Phd*.65d; αὐτὸ τὸ ἕν Id.*Prm*.143a, al., cf. Arist.*Metaph*.997^{b}8: neut., αὐτό is freq. in this sense, attached to Nouns of all genders, οὐκ αὐτὸ δικαιοσύνην ἐπαινοῦντες ἀλλὰ τὰς ἀπ' αὐτῆς εὐδοκιμήσεις Pl.*R*.363a; less freq. with Art., τί ποτ' ἐστὶν αὐτὸ ἡ ἀρετή Id.*Prt*.360e; more fully, εἰ αὐτὸ τοῦτο πατέρα ἠρώτων, ἆρα ὁ πατὴρ ἐστὶ πατήρ τινος, ἢ οὔ; Id.*Smp*.199d; ἀδελφός, αὐτὸ τοῦτο ὅπερ ἔστιν *the ideal, abstract* brother, ibid.e: later, in compos., αὐτοαγαθόν, αὐτοάνθρωπος, etc. (q.v.), cf. Arist.*Metaph*.1040^{b}33; less freq. agreeing with the Subst., ἵνα αὐτὴ δικαιοσύνη πρὸς ἀδικίαν αὐτὴν κριθείη Pl.*R*.612c, etc.; doubled, ἐκ τῆς εἰκόνος μανθάνειν αὐτήν τε αὐτήν, εἰ καλῶς εἴκασται *its very self*, Id.*Cra*.439a. 5. in dat. with Subst., *in one, together*, ἀνόρουσεν αὐτῇ σὺν φόρμιγγι he sprang up lyre *in hand*, Il.9.194; αὐτῇ σὺν πήληκι κάρη helmet *and all*, 14.498, cf. Od.13.118; αὐτῷ σὺν ἄγγει E.*Ion*32, cf. *Hipp*.1213; also without σύν, αὐτῇ κεν γαίῃ ἐρύσαι Il.8.24: so freq. in Prose and Poetry, αὐτοῖς ἀνδράσι men *and all*, Hdt.6.93; αὐτοῖσι συμμάχοισι allies *and all*, A.*Pr*.223(lyr.); αὐτοῖς μελάθροις διακναιομένους E.*Med*.164: with Art., αὐτοῖσι τοῖσι ἱματίοισι ἀπ' ὧν ἔβαψε ἑωυτόν Hdt.2.47; αὐτοῖσι τοῖς πόρπαξι Ar.*Eq*.849, etc.; αὐτοῖς τοῖς ἵπποις κατακρημνισθῆναι X.*Cyr*.1.4.7. 6. added to ordinal Numbers, e.g. πέμπτος αὐτός *himself* the fifth, i.e. *himself* with four others, Th.1.46, cf. 8.35, X.*HG*2.2.17, *Apoc*.17.11, etc.:—αὐτός always being the chief person. 7. freq. coupled with οὗτος, τοῦτ' αὐτό ἐστι τὸ ζητηθέν Pl.*Plt*.267c, etc.; αὐτὸ τοῦτο μόνον Id.*Grg*.500b; also λεγόντων ἄλλο μὲν οὐδέν.. αὐτὰ δὲ τάδε Th.1.139; πόλεις ἄλλας τε καὶ αὐτὸ τοῦτο τὸ Βυζάντιον X.*An*.7.1.27; ταῦτα ἥκω αὐτὰ ἵνα.. Pl.*Prt*.310e. 8. καὶ αὐτός *himself* too, Od.7.73, 14.45, X.*An*.5.5.9, etc. 9. repeated in apodosi for emphasis, αὐτὸς ἐπαγγειλάμενος σώσειν.. αὐτὸς ἀπώλεσεν Lys.12.68, cf. A.*Fr*.350, X.*An*.3.2.4. 10. in connexion with the person. Pron., ἐγὼν αὐτός Od.2.194; σέθεν αὐτοῦ Il.23.312; νωΐτερον αὐτῶν 15.39 (always divisim in Hom.); folld. by an enclit. Pron., αὐτόν μιν Od.4.244; so αὐτόν γάρ σε δεῖ Προμηθέως A.*Pr*.86; also αὐτὸς ἔγωγε Pl.*Phd*.59b, etc.:—after Hom. in the oblique cases αὐτός coalesces with the Pron., ἐμαυτοῦ, σεαυτοῦ (these not in Alc. or Sapph., A.D.*Pron*.80.10 sqq.), ἑαυτοῦ, etc. (q.v.). b. with person. Pron. omitted, αὐτός.. ἧσθαι λιλαίομαι, for ἐγὼ αὐτός, Il.13.252; αὐτὸν ἐλέησον, for ἐμὲ αὐτόν, 24.503; αὐτῶν γὰρ ἀπωλόμεθ' ἀφραδίῃσιν Od.10.27; in 2.33 οἱ αὐτῷ is simply a strengthd. form of οἱ; and so in Att., when σὲ αὐτόν, ἐμοὶ αὐτῷ, etc., are read divisim, they are emphatic, not reflexive; in this case αὐτός generally precedes the person. Pron., cf. X.*Cyr*.6.2.25 with 6.1.14. c. with the reflexive ἑαυτοῦ, αὑτοῦ, etc., to add force and definiteness, αὐτὸς καθ' αὑτοῦ A.*Th*.406; αὐτοὶ ὑφ' αὑτῶν ib.194; αὐτοὶ καθ' αὑτούς X.*Mem*.3.5.4; αὐτὸ καθ' αὑτό Pl.*Tht*.201e; sts. between the Art. and reflex. Pron., τοῖς αὐτὸς αὑτοῦ πήμασιν βαρύνεται A.*Ag*.836, cf. *Pr*.762; τούς γ' αὐτὸς αὑτοῦ πολεμίους S.*Aj*.1132: also κατ' αὐτὺ (Boeot. for αὐτοί) αὐτῶν *IG*7.3172.121 (Orchom. Boeot.). d. αὐτοῦ, αὐτῶν with possess. Pron., πατρὸς κλέος ἠδ' ἐμὸν αὐτοῦ Il.6.446; θρῆνον.. ἐμὸν τὸν αὐτῆς A.*Ag*.1323; ἐχθρὸς ὢν τοῖς σοῖσιν αὐτοῦ S.*OT*416; τοῖς οἷσιν αὐτοῦ ib.1248; αὐτῶν σφετέρῃσιν ἀτασθαλίῃσιν Od.1.7; τοῖς ἡμετέροις αὐτῶν φίλοις X.*An*.7.1.29. e. αὐτὸς ἑαυτοῦ with Comp. and Sup. Adj., αὐτὸς ἑωυτοῦ ῥέει πολλῷ ὑποδεέστερος Hdt.2.25; τῇ εὐρυτάτῃ ἐστὶ αὐτὴ ἑωυτῆς Id.1.203. 11. αὐτός for ὁ αὐτός, *the same*, Il.12.225, Od.8.107, 16.138, Pi.*N*.5.1 (never in Trag.), and in later Prose, αὐταῖς ταῖς ἡμέραις *IG*14.966 (ii A.D.), cf. *Ev.Luc*.23.12. 12. Comp. αὐτότερος Epich.5: Sup. αὐτότατος *his very self*, Ar.*Pl*.83: neut. pl. αὐτότατα dub. in Phld.*Piet*.80. Adv., Comp. αὐτοτέρως Gal.18(2).431.

II. *he, she, it*, for the simple Pron. of 3 pers., only in oblique cases (exc. in later Gk., *Ev.Luc*.4.15, etc.), and rarely first in a sentence, Pl.*La*.194e, and later, *Ep.Eph*.2.10, etc.: rare in Ep., Il.12.204 (where Hdn. treated it as enclitic), and mostly emphatic, ib.14.457, Od.16.388; so in Trag., E.*Hel*.421: in Prose, to recall a Noun used earlier in the sentence, ἐγὼ μὲν οὖν βασιλέα.. οὐκ οἶδα ὅ τι δεῖ αὐτὸν ὀμόσαι X.*An*.2.4.7; πειράσομαι τῷ πάππῳ.. συμμαχεῖν αὐτῷ Id.*Cyr*.1.3.15; ἄνδρα δή.. εἰ ἀφίκοιτο εἰς τὴν πόλιν, προσκυνοῖμεν ἂν αὐτόν Pl.*R*.398a; after a Relative, ὃς κε θεοῖς ἐπιπείθηται.. ἔκλυον αὐτοῦ Il.1.218; οὓς μὴ εὕρισκον, κενοτάφιον αὐτοῖς ἐποίησαν X.*An*.6.

4.9, cf. 1.9.29; esp. where a second Verb requires a change of case in the Pron., οἳ ἂν ἐξελεγχθῶσι.. ὡς προδότας αὐτοὺς ὄντας τιμωρηθῆναι Id.*An.*2.5.27; ἐκεῖνοι οἷς οὐκ ἐχαρίζονθ' οἱ λέγοντες οὐδ' ἐφίλουν αὐτούς D.3.24; in subdivisions, ὅσοι..οἱ μὲν αὐτῶν.. X.*Cyr.*1.1.1, cf. Pl.*Chrm.*168e; later, pleonastically after a Relative, ὧν ὁ μὲν αὐτῶν Call.*Epigr.*43, cf. *Ev.Luc.*3.16, *Apoc.*7.2, etc.: in S.*Ph.*316 αὐτοῖς is emphatic 'in their own persons'.

III. with Art. ὁ αὐτός, ἡ αὐτή, τὸ αὐτό, and Att. contr. αὑτός, αὑτή, ταὐτό and ταὐτόν (as required by the metre, cf. S.*OT*734 with 325, and in Prose to avoid hiatus): gen. ταὐτοῦ, dat. ταὐτῷ, pl. neut. ταὐτά; Ion. ὡυτός, τὠυτό:—*the very one, the same*, rare in Hom., Il. 6.391, Od.7.55,326; ὁ αὐ. εἰμι τῇ γνώμῃ Th.3.38, cf. 5.75; ἐπὶ τὸ αὐ. αἱ γνῶμαι ἔφερον Id.1.79: c. dat., to denote sameness or agreement, esp. in Prose, τὠυτὸ ἂν ὑμῖν ἐπρήσσομεν Hdt.4.119; τὸν αὐτὸν χῶρον ἐκλιπὼν ἐμοί A.*Ch.*543; ὁ αὐτὸς τῷ λίθῳ *the same as* the stone, Pl. *Euthd.*298a; ἐν ταὐτῷ εἶναί τινι to be *in the place with..*, X.*An.*3.1.27; προσίεσθαί τινα ἐς ταὐτὸ ἑαυτῷ to have a person *meet* one, ib.30, cf. A.*Ch.*210; κατὰ ταὐτὰ τῷ Νείλῳ Hdt.2.20; τῇ αὐτῇ..καί Id.4.109; τὴν αὐτὴν διάνοιαν καὶ κατ' ἐκείνην ἡλικίαν Isoc.5.83; ὁ αὐτός.. ὥσπερ Pl.*Phd.*86a; ἐς ταὐτὸν ἀλλήλοις *face to face*, Jul.*Or.*2.52c. 2. in later Greek, *the said, the above-named*, Ἡρώδης ὁ αὐ. *PLille*23.8 (iii B.C.), etc.

IV. Adverbial phrases: 1. αὐτὸ μόνον *simply, merely*, Ph. 2.252, etc.; αὐ. μόνον ἐργάτης Luc.*Somn.*9; αὐ. μόνον τὸ ὄνομα τῆς φωνῆς A.D.*Synt.*22.20. 2. αὐτό as Adv., = ἄρτι, *Epigr.Gr.*540.1 (Thrace). 3. αὐτὸ τοῦτο as Adv., *PGrenf.*1.114 (ii B.C.), 2*Ep.Pet.* 1.5; τῆς αὐτὸ τοῦτο κινουμένης σφαίρας Iamb.*Comm.Math.*17. 4. with Preps., ἐπὶ τὸ αὐτό *added together, making a total*, *PLond.*2. 196.37 (ii A.D.); κατὰ τὸ αὐτό *together, at the same time*, *Act.Ap.*14. 1, etc.; but κατ' αὐτό *just then*, Hdn.1.12.3.

V. In Compos.: 1. *of* or *by oneself, self-..*, as in αὐτοδίδακτος, αὐτογνώμων, αὐτόματος: and so, *independently*, as in αὐτοκράτωρ, αὐτόνομος. 2. hence, *as a second self, very..*, *bodily*, as with proper names, Αὐτοθαΐς. 3. *in the abstract, the ideal*, v. supr. 1.4. 4. *precisely*, as in αὐτόδεκα. 5. rarely with reflex. sense of ἀλλήλων, as in αὐτοκτονέω. 6. *in one piece with, together with*, as in αὐτόκωπος, αὐτοχείλης, αὐτόπρεμνος, αὐτόρριζος. 7. *by itself*: hence, *only*, as in αὐτόξυλος, αὐτόποκος.—For αὑτοῦ, αὑτῷ, etc., v. the respective Arts.

αὑτός, v. sub αὐτός III.

αὐτοσανδᾰράκη [ρᾱ], ἡ, *very* σανδαράκη, οἷον τὸ χρῶμα γυναικός, αὐ. Alciphr.*Fr.*4.

αὐτοσαυτόν, Dor. = ἑαυτόν, *GDI*1749, al. (Delph.), *UPZ*1: gen. αὐτοσαυτοῦ *IG*2.550.5 (Delph.), 5(1).1432.28 (Messene, i B.C.), *Tab. Defix.*p.xxxi: gen. pl. αὐτοσαυτῶν *Tab.Heracl.*1.124.

αὐτόσε, Adv. *thither, to the very place*, ἀπιέναι v.l. in Hdt.3.124; καταβαίνειν Ar.*Lys.*873; αὐτομολεῖν Th.7.26, etc.; σφενδόνῃ οὐκ ἂν ἐφικοίμην αὐτόσ' Antiph.55.20.

αὐτοσί, emphatic form of αὐτός, *GDI*1339 (Dodona).

αὐτο-σίδηρος [ῐ], Dor. -ᾱρος, ον, *of sheer iron*, ἅμιλλα αὐ. 'with cold steel', E.*Hel.*356 (lyr.). **-σῖτος**, ον, *bringing one's own provisions*, Com. of a παράσιτος, Crobyl.1. **-σκᾰπᾰνεύς**, έως, ὁ, *very digger*, Alciphr.3.70. **-σκεύαστος**, ον, *self-made*, i.e. *natural*, Sch.Opp. *H.*1.22, Hsch. s.v. αὐτόστυλον. **-σκευος**, ον, = αὐτουργός II, Poll. 10.14; *artless*, φύσεως ἔρευθος αὐ. Aristaenet.2.21. **-σκωμμα**, ατος, τό, *essence of wit*, in pl., Alciphr.3.43. **-σμῑκρόν**, τό, *abstract smallness*, Procl.*in Prm.*p.676 S. **-σμῑκρότης**, ητος, ἡ, = foreg., ib.p.677 S. **-σοφία**, ἡ, *very wisdom*, Them.*Or.*6.73a. **-σοφος**, ον, *of, with native mother-wit*, Tz.*H.*8.437. **-σπορος**, ον, *self-sown*, A.*Fr.*196; *self-begotten*, Nonn.*D.*7.73, al.

αὐτόσσυτος, ον, *self-sped*, A.*Eu.*170 (lyr.), S.*Fr.*559.

αὐτο-στᾰδίη (sc. μάχη), ἡ, *stand-up fight, close fight*, Ep. word, used only in dat., ἔν γ' αὐτοσταδίῃ Il.13.325. **-στᾰσις**, εως, ἡ, *pure rest*, Plot.3.7.2, Procl.*in Prm.*p.793 S. **-στᾰτέω**, (ἵσταμαι) *to be independent, self-sufficient*, Ph.1.688. **-στᾰτος**, ον, *standing on its own base*, κανοῦν *IG*2.698 ii 17. **-στεγος**, ον, = αὐτόροφος, σπῆλυγξ Dionys.Trag.1. **-στέρῐφος**, ον, *strong in itself*, Hsch. **-στοιχος**, ον, *going by oneself, independent*, Anon.ap. Suid. s.v. **-στολος**, ον, *self-sent, going* or *acting of oneself*, S.*Ph.* 496, cf. *AP*7.585 (Jul.): metaph. of Leander swimming, νηῦς Musae. 255; αὐτόστολον ναυλοῦν to let a ship *by private contract*, *OGI*572. 41 (Myra). **-στονος**, ον, *lamenting for oneself*, γόος A.*Th.*916 (lyr.). **-στράτηγος** [ᾰ], ὁ, *general in independent command*, D.C. 44.4. **-στροφος**, ον, perh. *revolving*, ἐσχάρα *IG*2.816.9. **-στῦλον**· αὐτοσκεύαστον, Hsch. **-σύμμετρος**, ον, *ideally symmetrical*, Alex. Aphr.*in Metaph.*79.15. **-συμφῠής**, ές, f.l. for συμφυής, Porph. *Antr.*5. **-σύστᾰτος**, ον, *self-constituting*, Dam.*Pr.*89. **-σφᾰγής**, ές, *slain by oneself* or *by kinsmen*, both in S.*Aj.*841 (prob. spurious), cf. E.*Ph.*1316. **-σχεδά**, v. αὐτοσχεδόν. **-σχεδές**, τό, a kind of woman's *shoe*, Hsch.; cf. αὐτοσχιδής.

αὐτοσχεδι-άζω, aor. part. Pass. -ασθείς Stratt.4 D.: (αὐτοσχέδιος) :—*act* or *speak offhand, extemporize*, Pl.*Cra.*413d, *Mx.*235c, X. *Mem.*3.5.21. 2. c. acc., *extemporize*, τὰ δέοντα Th.1.138, cf. X.*HG* 5.2.32. II. mostly in bad sense, *act, speak*, or *think unadvisedly*, v.l. in Pl.*Euthd.*278e; αὐ. καὶ καινοτομεῖν περὶ τῶν θείων Id.*Euthphr.*5a, cf. *Ap.*20c, Isoc.9.41, D.61.43; περί τι Pl.*Euthphr.*16a, Arist.*Pol.*1326^{b}19; εἰς τὰ τῶν Ἑλλήνων σώματα Aeschin.3.158. **-ασμα**, ατος, τό, *work done offhand, impromptu, improvisation*, Arist.*Po.*1448^{b}23, Pl.Com.87. **-ασμός**, ὁ, *extemporaneous speaking*, Alcid.*Soph.* 18 (pl.). **-αστής**, οῦ, ὁ, *one who acts* or *speaks offhand*: and so, *raw hand, bungler*, opp. τεχνίτης, X.*Lac.*13.5. **-αστικός**, ή, όν, *extemporary*, Arist.*Po.*1449^{a}9:—also -αστός, όν, Alcid.*Soph.*16,17. **-ος**, α, ον, also ος, ον Plu.*Sull.*7:—*hand to hand*: used by Hom., in dat., αὐτοσχεδίῃ (sc. μάχῃ) *in close fight, in the mêlée*, αὐτοσχεδίῃ μεῖξαι χεῖράς τε μένος τε Il.15.510: acc. fem. as Adv., = αὐτοσχεδόν 1, Ἀντιφάτην δ'..πλῆξ' αὐτοσχεδίην 12.192, 17.294; αὐτοσχεδίην οὐτασμένος Od.11.536: also ἔς τ' αὐ. καὶ προμάχους ἰέναι Tyrt.11.12. II. *offhand, improvised, rough and ready*, ἐξ αὐτοσχεδίης πειρώμενος *h. Merc.*55; ποιήματα αὐ. D.H.2.34; μαντικὴ αὐ. Plu.*Sull.*7; τετρήρη ναυπηγεῖν αὐ. Arist.*Fr.*600; βωμός, τείχη, D.H.1.40, 3.67; μνῆμα Hld.2. 4; ναῦς Max.Tyr.12.2; of persons, αὐτοσχέδιος ὢν περὶ τὰς ἰσηγορίας Plu.2.642a; σοφιστής Ach.Tat.5.27; ἐκ τοῦ αὐτοσχεδίου εἰπεῖν D.C. 73.1; τὸ αὐ., opp. τὸ περιπτωτικόν, in Empiric medicine, Gal.1.66. Adv. -ίως, γεννηθῆναι Lxx *Wi.*2.2; οἰκοδομεῖσθαι Paus.6.24.3. 2. *ready to hand*, ὕλη Id.10.32.15; *wild, natural*, ἄνθη Lib.*Decl.*13.50.

αὐτο-σχεδόν, Adv. *near at hand, hand to hand*, in Hom. always of close fight, ξιφέεσσ' αὐ. οὐτάζοντο Il.7.273; δῄουν ἀλλήλους αὐ. 15.708; αὐ. ὡρμήθησαν 13.496, cf. Od.22.293:—once also αὐτοσχεδὰ δουρὶ..ἐπόρουσε Il.16.319; cf. αὐτοσχέδιος. 2. c. gen., *near, close to*, ἀλλήλων Arat.901. II. of Time, *on the spot, at once*, A.R. 1.12, 3.148. **-σχῐδής**, ές, *simply slit*: *simple*, ὑπόδημα Hermipp.18, cf. αὐτοσχεδές. **-σχολος**, ον, = ἑαυτῷ σχολάζων, Timo 50. **-σωκράτης** [ᾰ], ὁ, *the 'form' of Socrates*, Plot.5.7.1. **-σωμα**, ατος, τό, *abstract, ideal body*, Herm.*in Phdr.*p.151 A. **-σωφροσύνη**, ἡ, *abstract moderation* or *temperance*, ib.p.144 A. **-τᾱγος**, ον, *without a master, independent*, dub. in Hsch., cf. *EM*173. 47. **-τᾰχος**, ους, τό, *abstract velocity*, Procl.*Hyp.*1.1. **-τέγον**· ἀπηρτισμένον, πλῆρες, Hsch. **-τέλεια**, ἡ, *perfection, completeness*, Ocell.1.9. II. *complete sentence, proposition*, A.D.*Synt.*12.4, al.; αὐ. τοῦ λόγου ib.5.20. **-τέλειος**, ον, *self-complete, perfect*, Procl. *Inst.*78 (Comp.). **-τελειότης**, ητος, ἡ, *perfection*, Iamb.*Myst.*1. 15. **-τέλεστος**, ον, *self-accomplished, spontaneous*, Opp.*H.*1.763, *AP*1.19.6 (Claudian.), Nonn.*D.*43.233, al. **-τελής**, ές, *ending in itself, complete in itself*, ὁρισμός Arist.*Top.*102^{b}13, cf. Ocell.1.7; θεωρίαι αὐ. καὶ αὑτῶν ἕνεκα Arist.*Pol.*1325^{b}20; esp. in Gramm., λεκτόν *Stoic.*2.58; λόγος A.D.*Synt.*3.5, al.; ἀξίωμα S.E.*M.*8.79; διάνοια Hdn.*Fig.*p.93 S.; ῥῆμα *an intransitive* verb, A.D.*Synt.*116. 11; of unity, *Theol.Ar.*5, cf. Orph.*Fr.*247.10. Adv. -λῶς, opp. κατὰ συναφήν, *independently, separately*, Epicur.*Ep.*2 p.36 U. b. *perfect, complete, fully-grown*, Nonn.*D.*7.154, al. 2. *self-sufficing*, αὐ. καὶ ἀπροσδεᾶ φιλοσοφίας Plu.2.122e; of personal character, *independent*, προχείρου ἀ. εὐβούλου Phld.*Herc.*1457.5. 3. *absolute, with full powers*, στρατηγός Plu.2.754d, cf. D.C.52.22; αὐ. κρίνειν, opp. προανακρίνειν, Arist.*Ath.*3.5, cf. 53.2. 4. *final*, ψήφισμα *without appeal*, Hyp.*Eux.*15; δίκη Hsch., Suid.; διαλήψεις Plb.3.4.4; αὐ. πρὸς γνῶσιν καὶ σαφήνειαν ib.36.2; αἰτίαν Chrysipp.*Stoic.*2.292. Adv. -λῶς *at one's own discretion, arbitrarily*, οὐκ αὐ. ἀλλ' ἀκριβῶς Lys.*Fr.* 38, cf. Plb.3.29.3; ἂν αἱ φαντασίαι ποιῶσιν αὐ. τὰς συγκαταθέσεις Chrysipp.*Stoic.*2.291; αὐ. διαιτᾶν control, govern *absolutely*, Phld.*D.* 1.22. 5. *sufficing for oneself*: also, *supporting oneself*, ἱππεῖς Luc. *Tox.*54. 6. *entirely due to*, c. gen., νίκη τῶν ἡγουμένων Plb.5.12. 4. II. (τέλος IV) *taxing oneself, self-taxed*, Th.5.18, Stob.2.7. 3^{a}. **-τετράς**, άδος, ἡ, *abstract number four*, Phlp.*in de An.*77. 9. **-τεχνος**, ον, *self-instructed*, πρὸς ἴασιν Plu.2.991e.

αὐτότης, ητος, ἡ, *identity*, S.E.*M.*10.261, v.l. in Porph.*Sent.*39.

αὐτό-τμητος, ον, *self-severed*, Sch.Opp.*H.*2.349. **-τοκος**, ον, *young and all*, A.*Ag.*137: but, II. parox. αὐτοτόκος, ον, Act., *self-producing*, Nonn.*D.*8.81, etc. **-τρᾰγικὸς** πίθηκος *a very ape of tragedy*, D.18.242. **-τράπεζος** [ᾰ], ον, *eating at the same table with*, ἀθανάτοις Emp.147.1. **-τριάς**, άδος, ἡ, *the abstract number three*, Alex.Aphr.*in Metaph.*836.24, Phlp.*in de An.*77.9. **-τρίγωνον** [ῐ], τό, *the ideal triangle, the Form of triangle*, Arist.*GC*316^{a}12, Them.*Or.* 13.165a. **-τροπήσας**, in *h.Merc.*86 ὁδὸν αὐ., as if from αὐτοτροπέω, *to be like oneself*, i.e. *unique*, v.l. αὐτοπρεπὴς ὥς, in same sense. **-τροφος**, ον, = αὐτόσιτος, condemned by Phryn.179. **-τῠπος**, ον, *self-inflicted*, ὠτειλαί Opp.*H.*2.358.

αὐτοῦ, Dor. **αὐτῶ** and **αὐτεῖ**, Adv., prop. gen. of αὐτός:—*just there* or *just here*, Hom., etc.; ἐπίσχες αὐτοῦ stop *there!* Cratin.66:—freq. with the place added, αὐτοῦ ἐνὶ Τροίῃ, μέν' αὐτοῦ τῷδ' ἐνὶ χώρῳ, *here in* Troy, etc., Il.2.237, Od.10.271; αὐτοῦ ἔνθα Il.8.207; που αὐτοῦ ἀγρῶν somewhere *there* on the farm, Od.4.639; αὐτοῦ ὑπὲρ κεφαλῆς 8.68; αὐτοῦ περὶ τεῖχος A.*Ag.*452 (lyr.); αὐτοῦ ταύτῃ in this *very* place, *exactly* here, Hdt.1.214, 3.77, 4.135; αὐτοῦ τῇ περ ἔπεσε Id.1.30:—so that αὐτοῦ usu. precedes; but κεῖθι αὐτοῦ *h.Ap.*374; κατ' οἴκους αὐτοῦ Ar.*Pax*89; ἐνθάδ' αὐτοῦ Sol.36.11, Ar.*Pl.*1187; τοῖς ἐνθάδ' αὐτοῦ μὴ κατ' ἄστυ δημόταις S.*OC*78.

αὑτοῦ, Att. contr. for ἑαυτοῦ.

αὐτοϋγίεια, ἡ, *health in the abstract*, Alex.Aphr.*in Metaph.*79.12, Herm.*in Phdr.*p.151 A.

αὐτουδέτερος, ον, *absolutely neuter*, *An.Bachm.*2.302:—Subst. **-ότης**, -ητος, ἡ, ibid.

αὐτοΰδωρ, ατος, τό, *very water*, Herm.ap.Stob.3.11.31.

αὐτοΰπαρκτος, ον, = αὐθύπαρκτος, Hsch.

αὐτουργ-έω, *to be an* αὐτουργός, *work with one's own hand*, Hierocl. p.63 A., Luc.*DMar.*6.1; of the Creator, *to be his own workman*, Procl.*Theol.Plat.*5.17, cf. 18; *act directly*, Gal.18(1).780; esp. *farm one's own land*, *PTeb.*302.29 (i A.D.):—Pass., κτήματα -ούμενα *BGU* 475^{a}9 (ii A.D.). II. c. acc., *execute, fulfil of oneself*, τὰ ἐπὶ τῆς γῆς Arist.*Mu.*398^{a}5; τὴν μαντητὴν Luc.*Syr.D.*36; τὴν ἐπιβουλὴν Philostr.

*VS*1.21.4. **-ημα,** ατος, τό, *a piece of one's own work*, D.Chr.12.57: pl., ἴδια αὐ. *PMasp.*244 (vi A.D.). **-ητος,** ον, *self-wrought, rudely wrought*, *AP*6.33.5 (Maec.). **-ία,** ἡ, *working on oneself*, i.e. *self-murder* or *murder of kin*, A.*Eu.*336 (lyr., pl.). **II.** *personal labour*, opp. slave-labour, Plb.4.21.1, Plu.*Cat.Ma.*1, Porph.*Marc.*34. **2.** *farming oneself*, *PLips.*97 xxvii 10 (iv A.D.). **III.** *experience*, Plb.9.14.4. **-ικός,** ή, όν, *willing* or *able to work with one's own hand*, M.Ant.1.5; *industrious*, Muson.*Fr.*11 p.57 H. **II.** -κή (sc. τέχνη), ἡ, *art of making real things*, not semblances (εἴδωλα), Pl.*Sph.* 266d (dub.). **-ός,** όν, *self-working*, αὐτὸς αὐτουργῷ χερί S.*Ant.*52, cf. Aen.Tact.18.2; αὐ. βίος D.H.10.19. **2.** mostly Subst., *one who works his land himself* (not by slaves), *husbandman*, E.*Or.*920, Th.1.141, X.*Oec*.5.4, etc.: generally, *one who works for himself*, Pl. *R.*565a, Arist.*Rh.*1381^{a}24. **b.** metaph., αὐ. τῆς φιλοσοφίας *one that has worked at* philosophy *by himself*, without a teacher, X.*Smp.* 1.5; αὐ. τῆς ταλαιπωρίας *engaging in* hard service *oneself*, Plb.3.17.8: Sup., Jul.*ad Them.*264a. **II.** Pass., *self-wrought*, i.e. *rudely wrought*, D.H.*Dem.*39, *Comp.*19 (Comp.); *simple, native*, μέλος *AP* 9.264 (Apollonid. or Phil.). **-ότευκτος,** ον, = foreg. II, Lyc.747.

αὐτοῦτα, v. αὐταυτοῦ.

αὐτο-φάγος [ᾰ], ον, *self-devouring*, Hsch. s. v. αὐτόφορβος. **-φᾰής,** ές, = sq., Procl.*Phil.Chald.*p.1 J. (s. v. l.). **-φᾰνής,** ές, (φανῆναι) *self-appearing, personally appearing*, Iamb.*Myst.*2.4; *self-revealing*, Syrian. *in Metaph.*187.9; αὐ. τῆς οὐσίας θεωρία Procl. *in Alc.*p.9 C.

αὐτοφαρίζω· αὐτοματέω, Hsch.

αὐτόφι,-φιν, Ep. case-forms of αὐτός, in Hom. always with Prep., ἀπ' αὐτόφιν from *the very spot*, Il.11.44; so παρ' αὐτόφιν or -φι, 12.302, 13.42, etc.; ἐπ' αὐτόφιν on *the spot*, 19.255.

αὐτο-φίλαυτος [ῐ], ον, *wholly given to self-love*, J.*AJ*5.6.3. **-φλοιος,** ον, *with the bark on*, βάκτρον Theoc.25.208, cf. *Ep.*4.3, *AP*6.99 (Phil.). **-φονεύς,** gloss on αὐτεπίβουλος, Hsch. **-φόνευτος,** ον, *self-slain*, Sch.A.*Th.*735. **-φονία,** ἡ, = αὐτουργία I, ib.*Eu.*336 (pl.). **-φόνος,** ον, *murdering one's kin*, αὐτοφόνα κακά A.*Th.*850 (lyr.), *Ag.*1091 (lyr.); παλάμη *AP*7.149 (Leont.). Adv. -νως A.*Supp.*65 (lyr.). **2.** *suicidal*, Opp.*C.*2.480. **3.** *slaying with one's own hand*, ib.4.290. **-φόντης,** ου, ὁ, *murderer of kin*, E.*Med.*1269; prob. corrupt in S.*El.*272; στρῆνος Lyc.438. **-φορβος,** ον, (φέρβω) = αὐτοφάγος, A.*Fr.*114. **-φόρητος,** ον, *self-borne*, Nonn.*D.*10.150. **-φορτος,** ον, *travelling with one's own cargo*, S.*Fr.*251; dub. sense in *bearing one's own baggage*, A.*Ch.*675, Cratin.248. **II.** *cargo and all*, ὁλκάδες Plu.*Aem.*9, cf.2.467d. **-φρόνησις,** εως, ἡ, *absolute prudence*, Him. *Ecl.*32.12. **-φρων,** ον, gen. φρονος, = ὁμόφρων, Ion Trag.ap.*Lex. Sabb.* **-φῠής,** ές, *self-grown*, στρωμνὴ οἰκεία τε καὶ αὐ., of the fur of beasts, Pl.*Prt.*321a; *self-existent*, Critias 19.1 D. **2.** *self-grown, of home production*, ἀγαθά X.*Vect.*2.1; ὦ πόλι φίλη Κέκροπος, αὐτοφυὲς Ἀττική Ar.*Fr.*110. **3.** *natural*, opp. artificial, οὐδὸς Hes.*Th.*813; λιμήν Th.1.93; χρυσὸς αὐ. *native* gold, D.S.3.45; κύανος αὐ. Thphr. *Lap.*39; αὐ. λόφοι hills *in their natural state*, not quarried or mined, X.*Vect.*4.2; κορύναν αὐτοφυῆ *a natural growth*, Theoc.9.24; opp. χειροποίητος, Plb.9.27.4; opp. τὰ διὰ τέχνης, *wild, not cultivable*, Thphr.*CP*3.1.1; of a horse, τὸν αὐτοφυῆ (sc. δρόμον) διαπροχάζειν to have *natural* paces, X.*Eq.*7.11; αὐ. γηρύματα '*native wood*-notes *wild*', of birds, opp. language, Plu.2.973a; of style, *natural, simple*, D.H.*Din.*7; αὐ. αἴσθησις, opp. ἐπιστημονική, Phld.*Mus.*p.11 K., cf. p.63 K.: Comp. -έστερος *more natural*, of an explanation, Simp. *in Ph.*149.18. Adv. -φυῶς, ὅμοιον like *by nature*, opp. μιμητῆς, Pl. *Grg.*513b; αὐ. ἀγαθοί Id.*Lg.*642c. **4.** τὸ αὐ. *one's own nature*, Id. *R.*486e; *natural state*, opp. τὸ ἐπίκτητον, Arist.*Rh.*1365^{a}29. **II.** Act., *bearing, producing of itself*, γῆ αὐ. ὧν φέρει Philostr.*Im.*2.18. Adv. -φυῶς *spontaneously*, Syrian. *in Metaph.*123.22; αὐ. κινούμενοι Plot.6.5.1. **-φῠσις,** εως, ἡ, *abstract nature*, Phlp. *in de An.*99.16. **-φῠτος,** ον, *self-engendered*: hence, *arising naturally*, ἕλκεα Pi.*P.*3.47, cf. Antipho Trag.ap.*Lex.Sabb.*; *native*, ἀρετή D.C.44.37. **2.** *natural, primitive*, ἐργασία Arist.*Pol.*1256^{a}40. **-φωνία,** ἡ, *direct utterance*, title of work on oracles by Oenomaus, Jul.*Or.*7.209b. **-φωνος,** ον, *self-sounding*, χρησμὸς αὐ. an oracle *delivered by the god himself*, Luc.*Alex.*26. **-φώρᾱτος,** ον, *self-betrayed, self-revealed*, S.E.*M.*8.173. **-φωρία** (-φορία cod.)· τὸ ἐπὶ αὐτῇ φωρᾷ (φορᾷ cod.), Hsch. **-φωρος,** ον, (φώρ) *self-detected*, ἀμπλακήματα S.*Ant.*51. **II.** mostly in the phrase ἐπ' αὐτοφώρῳ λαμβάνειν to catch *in the act*, Lys.13.85, D.19.132; ἑλεῖν E.*Ion* 1214; ἐλέγχειν Lys.7.42: with pass. Verbs, ἐπ' αὐτοφώρῳ ἁλῶναι Hdt.6.72; εἰλῆφθαι Ar.*Pl.*455, Eup.181: hence, **2.** in a more general sense, *notoriously, manifestly*, ἐπιβουλεύοντας φανῆναι ἐπ' αὐ. Hdt. 6.137; ἐπ' αὐ. αὐτὸν ἐλέγξω Lys.13.30; τὸν θάνατόν τινος ἐπ. αὐ. μηχανωμένη Antipho 1.3; ἐπ' αὐ. καταλαμβάνειν τινὰ ἀμαθέστερον ὄντα Pl.*Ap.*22b, cf. *R.*359c; ἐπ' αὐ. εἴλημμαι πλουσιώτατος ὢν X. *Smp.*3.13; ἀξιῶ σε.. ἐπ' αὐ. ταὐτά μοι ἐπιδεῖξαι Lys.1.21; ἐπ' αὐ. κλέπται ὄντες ἐξελεγχόμενοι Aeschin.3.10. **-φως,** ωτος, τό, *very light*, ὁ ἥλιος αὐ. ἐστι καὶ πηγὴ φωτός Herm. *in Phdr.*p.118 A., cf. Dam. *Pr.*29, Aen.Gaz.*Thphr.*p.52 B. **-χάρακτος** [ᾰ], ον, *self-engraven* or *impressed*, of an image in a mirror, Nonn.*D.*5.599. **-χᾰρις,** ιτος, ἡ, *very grace*: αὐτοχάριτες Ἀττικαί *the essence of* Attic *graces*, Alciphr.3.43. **-χειλής,** ές, *with the natural rim*, i.e. in one piece, λήκυθοι S.*Fr.*138. **-χειρ,** χειρος, ὁ, ἡ, *with one's own hand, creative*, A.*Supp.*592 (lyr.); αὐ. λούειν, παίειν, κτείνειν, S.*Ant.*900, 1315, *Aj.* 57; τίνες ᾠκοδόμησαν;—ὄρνιθες αὐτόχειρες Ar.*Av.*1132 sq., cf. *Lys.* 269, Theopomp.Com.86, *Act.Ap.*27.19, etc.: c. gen., *very doer, perpetrator of* a thing, αὐ. τοῦδε τοῦ τάφου S.*Ant.*306; τῆς ἀσελγείας ταύτης D.21.60; αὐ. οὔτε τῶν ἀγαθῶν οὔτε τῶν κακῶν *men who accomplish* neither.., Isoc.5.150. **II.** abs., *one who kills himself, suicide*, S.*Ant.*1175; αὐ. ἑαυτῶν Arist.*Fr.*502; simply, *murderer*, S.*OT*231, D.21.116; αὐτὸν.. νομίζω αὐτόχειρά μου γεγενῆσθαι τούτοις τοῖς ἔργοις ib.106: c. gen., αὐ. καὶ φονεῖς τῶν πολιτῶν Isoc.4.111, cf. Men.*Sam.* 216; in full, τὸν αὐ. τοῦ φόνου S.*OT*266, cf. *El.*955, D.18.287. **III.** as Adj., *murderous*, esp. of murder *committed by one's own hand* or *by kinsmen*, αὐ. θάνατος, σφαγή, μοῖρα, E.*Ph.*880, *Or.*947, *Med.*1281 (lyr.); πληγέντες αὐτόχειρι σὺν μιάσματι, of brothers smitten by *mutual slaughter*, S.*Ant.*172; φόνος Pl.*R.*615c. **2.** αὐτόχειρα γράμματα *written with one's own hand, autograph*, D.C.59.4. **-χειρί,** Adv. of foreg., *with one's own hand*, Lycurg.122, Paus.7.16.6, Onos.33 tit.; dub. l. in E.*Or.*1040. **-χειρία,** ἡ, *murder perpetrated by one's own hand*, Pl.*Lg.*872b; δι' αὐτοχειρίας Nic.Dam.p.46 D. **II.** mostly in dat. αὐτοχειρίᾳ, Ion. -ίῃ, used adverbially, = αὐτοχειρί, mostly of slaughter, αὐ. κτείνειν Hdt.1.140; ἀπολέσαι Id.3.74, cf. 66: generally, αὐ. διελεῖν Id.1.123; διασπείρειν Id.3.13, cf. Ar.*Fr.*33 D.; λαβεῖν D.25.57; καὶ αὐ. καὶ κελεύων καὶ ψήφῳ [κτείνειν] Democr. 260. **-χειρίζω,** *do a thing* or *commit a murder with one's own hand*, Philist.60 ap.Poll.2.154, where the word is called παμμίαρον. **-χείριος,** α, ον, = αὐτόχειρ, Sch.E.*Med.*1269, A.D.*Pron.* 70.2. **-χειρος,** ον, = foreg., Hsch. Adv. -ρως, = αὐτοχειρί, Sch. E.*Or.*1040, v.l. in Hierocl.*Facet.*152. **-χειροτόνητος,** ον, *self-elected*, D.19 Arg.ii 9. **-χερί,** Adv. of αὐτόχειρ, poet. for αὐτοχειρί, Call.*Epigr.*22: c. gen., αὐτοχερὶ ποσίων ἐδάμησαν Man.3.200.

αὐτοχθηδόν· αὐτοποίητον, Hsch.

αὐτό-χθονος, ον, *country and all*, A.*Ag.*536. **-χθων,** ον, gen. ονος, *sprung from the land itself*; αὐτόχθονες, οἱ, *not settlers, of native stock*, Hdt.1.171, Th.6.2, etc.: c. gen., αὐ. Ἰταλίας D.H.1.10: esp. of the Athenians, E.*Ion* 29, al., *Fr.*360.8, Ar.*V.*1076, Isoc.4.24, 12.124. **II.** Adj., *indigenous, native*, τὰ μὲν δύο αὐτόχθονα τῶν ἐθνέων Hdt.4.197; αὐ. Αἰγύπτιοι *PGiss.*99.5 (ii A.D.); ἀρετή Lys.2.43; λάχανα τῶν αὐτοχθόνων Polioch.2.6; κόσμος Philod.Scarph. 127; *urbanitas, racy of the soil*, Cic.*Att.*7.2.3. **-χόλωτος,** ον, *their own enemy*, γένος ἀνθρώπων *AP*7.688 (Pall.). **-χορήγητος,** ον, *self-furnished*, Pl.*Ax.*371d. **-χόωνος,** ον, Ep. for αὐτοχόανος, -χωνος, *rudely cast, massive*, of a lump of iron used as a quoit, Il.23.826. **-χρημα,** Adv. *in very deed*, Ar.*Eq.*78, Luc.*Dem.Enc.*13, Procop.Gaz.*Ep.*58, Iamb.*Myst.*5.20; dub. in S.*Ichn.*38. **2.** *just, exactly*, Ael.*NA*2.44, Aristid.2.228 J. **II.** *straightway*, Jul.*Or.*6.181b. **-χρόϊνδον·** πρὸς τὸν χρῶτα, Hsch. **-χρονος,** ον, *being its own time*, οὔτε ἡ ψυχὴ ἔγχρονος ἀλλ' αὐ. Simp. *in Ph.*785.2. **-χροος,** ον, contr. -χρους, ουν, *with its own, natural colour*, Plu.2.270f. **2.** *of one and the same colour*, ib.330a. **-χρῡσος,** ον, *of very gold, precious*, Hsch. **-χῠτος,** ον, *poured out of itself, self-flowing*, θάλαμος Hes.*Fr.*96.102; ὕδωρ Aristid.*Or.*39(18).7,16, cf. Sch.Pi.*O.*7.12; γάλα Nonn.*D.*24.131. **-χωνον·** αὐτοχώνευτον, Hsch. **-χωρέω,** *absorb into oneself, partake of*, τοῦ ἀγνώστου Anon. *in Prm.* in *Rh.Mus.* 47.603 (dub.).

αὐτ-οψεί or **-ψί,** Adv. of αὔτοπτος, *with one's own eyes*, Jul.*Ep.*204, *PSI*3.238.11 (vi A.D.). **-οψία,** ἡ, *seeing with one's own eyes*, Dsc. *Praef.*5, *PTeb.*286.20 (ii A.D.), Luc.*Syr.D.*1; in Medic., as t.t. of the Empiric school, Gal.1.67; ἐπὶ τῆς αὐ. *SIG*827 *D* 4 (Delph., ii A.D.), cf. *POxy.*1272.19 (ii A.D.); ἐπὶ τὴν αὐ. ἐλθεῖν *IG*9(1).61.17. **II.** *supernatural manifestation, vision*, Procl. *in Alc.*p.92 C. (pl.), Iamb.*Myst.*2.4 (pl.), 7.3 (pl.); [δαίμων] κληθεὶς εἰς αὐ. Porph. *Plot.*10, cf. Dam.*Isid.*13 (pl.); opp. ὄνειρος, Ps.-Callisth.1.6; *magical operation* for the production of such a manifestation (αὐθ.), *PMag. Par.*1.950, *PMag.Leid.W.*16.38.

αὐτοψῡχή, ἡ, *absolute soul*, αὐ. καθαρά Herm. *in Phdr.*p.75 A., cf. Plot.5.9.13, Jul.*Ep.*89b (pl.).

αὐτ-ώδης, ες, Ion. for αὐθάδης, acc. to A.D.*Pron.*74.9, Hsch.: but Hdt.6.92 has αὐθαδέστεροι. **-ώλης,** ες, = αὐτόχειρ II, Hsch. **-ωνητής,** οῦ, ὁ, *one that buys for himself*, Din.*Fr.*89.11. **-ώρης,** ες, (ὄρνυμαι) *acting spontaneously*, of an oracle giving a response unquestioned, Call.*Fr.*264.

αὔτως, Adv.: **I.** *in this very manner, even so*, γυμνὸν ἐόντα αὔ. ὥς τε γυναῖκα unarmed *just as I am* like a woman, Il.22.125; *in the self-same way, likewise*, σὺν δ' αὔ. ἐγώ S.*Ant.*85, cf. Numen.ap.Ath. 7.328d; αὔ. ὅπωσπερ.. S.*Aj.*1179; αὔ., ὧδ' αὔ., ὥς μ' ὤλεσεν Id. *Tr.*1040 (lyr.); αὔ. ὡς.. Hes.*Th.*702, A.R.1.890: c. dat., γυναιξὶν αὔ. Anacr.21.14: hence ὡσαύτως (q.v.), in Hom. always ὡς δ' αὔτως, as in Pl.*Phd.*102e, X.*An.*5.6.9. **2.** in a contemptuous sense, *just so*, τίη σὺ κήδεαι αὔ. ἀνδρῶν; why take you *no better* care? v.l. for οὕτως in Il.6.55; οἴχεται αὔ. has gone off *just as he pleased*, Od.4.665: joined with words implying contempt, νήπιος αὔ. a *mere* child, Il.24.726, cf. 6.400; μὰψ αὔ. 20.348; ἀνεμώλιον αὔ. 21.474; αὔ. ἄχθος ἀρούρης Od.20.379, etc.; so, *in vain*, οὐκ αὔ. μυθήσομαι 14.151, cf. Il. 2.342, etc. **II.** in reference to the past, *just as before, as it was*, ἧσθαι, κεῖσθαι, Il.1.133, 18.338, Od.20.130; λευκὸν ἔτ' αὔ. still white *as when new*, Il.23.268; ἔτι κεῖται αὔ. ἐν κλισίῃσι *just as he was*, 24.413; καὶ αὔ. *still, unceasingly*, 1.520. (From αὐτός, hence αὔτως in Homer, cf. Il.23.268, Od.14.151 (from αὐτῇ with Aeol. psilosis acc. to Eust.235.5, al.); but αὕτως is usu. written in codd. of Trag. Gramm. were divided as to etym. and accent, cf. A.D.*Adv.*174.1, *EM*172.34, and distd. αὕτως 'likewise' from αὔτως 'in vain'. Dam. *Pr.*178 uses αὔτως, = *of itself* (from αὐτοῦ).)

αὔφην, Aeol. for αὐχήν, Jo.Gramm.*Comp.*3.16.

αὔφιτα, = ἄλφιτα, *Supp.Epigr.*1.414 (Gortyn, v/iv B.C.).

αὐχᾰλέος, α, ον, (αὔχη) *boastful*, Xenoph.3.5, Hsch.

αὐχάττειν· ἀναχωρεῖν, Hsch.; cf. ἀναχάζω.

αὐχεν-ίας, ου, ὁ, *bull-necked*, Gloss. **-ίζω**, (αὐχήν) *cut the throat of*.., S.*Aj*.298. 2. *seize by the throat*: metaph., κῆρες αὐ. ψυχήν Ph.1.654; λόγους παλαίσμασι ib.676:—Pass., 2.372. 3. *bind the neck with a ligature*, *Hippiatr*.10. **-ιον**, τό, Dim. of αὐχήν, *An. Ox*.2.356. II. = αὐχήν II. 5, Eust.1533.46. **-ιος**, α, ον, *belonging to the neck*, τένοντες αὐ. *neck*-sinews, Od.3.450, Pancrat.*Oxy*. 1085.29; χαίτη Opp.*C*.3.255; τρίχες Hld.10.28. 2. *stiff-necked, haughty*, γίγαντες *PMag.Par*.1.3058. II. a kind of *tunic*, Antiph. 315. **-ιστήρ**, ῆρος, ὁ, βρόχος αὐ. *halter*, Lyc.1100; *ligature for neck*, *Hippiatr*.10.

αὐχέω, chiefly pres. and impf. ηὔχουν, fut. αὐχήσω E.*Fr*.857, Luc. *DMort*.22.2, *AP*7.373 (Thall.): aor. ηὔχησα ib.6.283, 15.4, Apollod. 2.4.3: (αὔχη):—*boast, plume oneself*, ἐπί τινι on a thing, Batr.57, *AP*6.283; τινί E.*IA*412: with neut. Adj., τοσοῦτον αὐχεῖν Hdt.7.103; μέγ' αὐ. E.*Heracl*.353 (lyr.); μηδὲν τόδ' αὔχει Id.*Andr*.463; μεγάλα *Ep.Jac*.3.5: c. acc. objecti, *to boast of*, ἀστέρας *AP*7.373 (Thall.). II. c. acc. et inf., *boast* or *declare loudly* that.., αὐχέοντες κάλλιστα τιθέναι ἀγῶνα Hdt.2.160; ἀπεῶσθαι Th.2.39; σώσειν (σῶσαι codd.) E.*Andr*.311, cf. *Ba*.310: c. acc. only, αὐχῶ Σεβήραν *boast* (that I hold her), *IG*14.2001, cf. 3.172. 2. c. inf. fut., *say confidently, to be proudly confident* that, αὐχῶ γὰρ αὐχῶ τήνδε δωρεὰν ἐμοὶ δώσειν Δί' A.*Pr*.340, cf. 688 (lyr.), *Pers*.741, Cratin.1: with a neg., οὐ γάρ ποτ' ηὔχουν.. μεθέξειν I never *thought* that.., A.*Ag*.506, cf. *Eu*.561 (lyr.), E.*Heracl*.931. III. Med., αὐχήσασθαι· καυχήσασθαι, Hsch.—Never in S. (ἐπ-, ἐξ-αυχέω, *El*.65, *Ant*.390); rare in Com. and Prose.

αὔχη, ἡ, *boasting, pride*, κενεόφρονες αὖχαι Pi.*N*.11.29; αὐχάν· καύχησιν, Hsch.

αὐχ-ήεις, εσσα, εν, *braggart, proud*, Opp.*H*.2.677; [βοῦς] *AP*6. 114 (Simm.). **-ημα**, ατος, τό, *thing boasted of, object of pride, the pride, boast*, ⟨χθονός⟩ S.*OC*710 (lyr.); *cause for boasting, glory*, σὺ γάρ νιν εἰς τόδ' εἶσας αὐ. ib.713, cf. Th.7.75. II. = αὔχη, *boasting, self-confidence*, Id.2.62, 7.66; ὀπιθόμβροτον αὔ. δόξας Pi.*P*.1.92: in pl., ποῦ τὰ πρόσθεν αὐ.; Pl.*Ax*.365a. **-ημᾰτίας**, ου, ὁ, *boaster*, Sch. Luc.*Pr.Im*.10, Eust.537.42:—Adj. **-μᾰτικός**, ή, όν, Id.1967.9.

αὐχήν, ένος, ὁ, *neck, throat*, of men and beasts, Il.7.12, Hes.*Op*. 815, Arist.*HA*493^{a}5, *PA*691^{b}29: rarely, *gullet*, Nic.*Th*.350: in pl., of *one neck*, S.*Fr*.659.4, Orph.*L*.137, *AP*5.27 (Rufin.). 2. metaph., τὸν αὐ. ἱστάναι to be *high-spirited*, Philostr.*VA*7.23; αὐχένα ὑψηλὸν ἀποθέσθαι Vett.Val.261.16. II. metaph., *any narrow band* or *connexion* (*like a neck*): 1. *neck of land, isthmus*, Hdt.1.72, 6.37, X.*An*.6.4.3. 2. *narrow sea, strait*, of the Bosporus, Hdt.4.85, 118; αὐ. πόντου, of the Hellespont, A.*Pers*.72 (lyr.); of the point at which the Danube spreads from a single stream into several branches, Hdt.4.89. 3. *mountain-pass, defile*, Id.7.223. 4. *neck* of the thigh-bone, Hp.*Art*.55; *cervix uteri*, Id.*Steril*.230, Poll. 2.222 (but, *pars vaginalis*, Gal.*UP*14.3); *root* of the tongue, Ruf. *Onom*.57. 5. *handle of the steering-paddle* in a ship, Poll.1.90: in pl., Polyaen.3.11.14, Hld.5.28. 6. an architectural member, αὐχένες δρύινοι *SIG*²587.308. (Cf. αὔφην; ἄμφην Theoc.30.28.)

αὔχ-ησις, εως, ἡ, (αὐχέω) *boasting, exultation*, Th.6.16; cf. **αὐχῆτις** (sic)· σεμνότης, Hsch. **-ητής**, οῦ, ὁ, *boaster*, blamed by Poll. 9.146. **-ητικός**, ή, όν, = αὐχήεις, Sch.Pi.*O*.1.4. Adv. -ῶς Eust. 750.23.

αὐχμ-ᾰλέος, α, ον, = αὐχμηρός, Choeril.4.4, Epigr. in *POxy*.662 (Amynt.).

αὐχμέω, (αὐχμός) *to be squalid* or *unwashed*, αὐχμεῖς τε κακῶς καὶ ἀεικέα ἕσσαι Od.24.250, cf. Ar.*Nu*.442; *to be parched*, Pl.*R*.606d; αὐχμεῖ [φυτά] *dry up*, Thphr.*HP*4.10.7:—also **αὐχμάω**, part. αὐχμῶσαι interpol. in Hp.*Prog*.2; αὐχμώσης Arist.*Mete*.360^{b}11; αὐχμῶντες Thphr.*HP*8.10.4; αὐχμῶντα Plu.2.187d, Luc.*Vit.Auct*.7; αὐχμῶσαν Id.*Apol*.6, etc.; Ep. αὐχμώοντα Nonn.*D*.26.108, etc.—αὐχμέω is always used exc. in part. acc. to Phryn.*PS* p.10 B.; αὐχμᾷς is cited from Phryn.Com.76 by Poll.2.34; other forms are ambiguous, αὐχμῶν Ar.*Pl*.84, Anaxandr.34.6, Thphr.*Char*.26.5; αὐχμήσῃ Pl.*Phdr*. 251d, etc.

αὐχμή, ἡ, = αὐχμός, Q.S.9.372, Phryn.*PS* p.10 B.

αὐχμήεις, εσσα, εν, = αὐχμηρός, *h.Hom*.19.6.

αὐχμηρία, ἡ, = αὐχμός, *Cat.Cod.Astr*.2.161.1, 8(3).125.24.

αὐχμηρό-βῐος, ον, *squalid, sordid*, Pl.Com.16 D. **-κόμης**, ου, ὁ, *with squalid hair*, Anaxandr.41.9.

αὐχμηρός, ά, όν, *dry, without rain*, χειμών Hp.*Aph*.3.11, cf. *Aër*. 10; ἔτη Arist.*HA*605^{b}19; ἔαρ Id.*Pr*.860^{a}13; of places, *dry, parched*, τόποι Pl.*Lg*.761b (Sup.), cf. 2*Ep.Pet*.1.19; χωρία Thphr.*HP*9.11.10, etc.; καρποί D.S.2.53. b. *parching*, νόσοι Emp.121.3. 2. *dry, rough, squalid*, οὖδας E.*Alc*.947; σκληρὸς καὶ αὐ. Pl.*Smp*.203d; esp. of hair (cf. foreg.), S.*Fr*.475, E.*Or*.387, Theoc.25.225; βίος Luc.*Salt*. 1. Adv. -ρῶς, ἔχειν τοῦ προσώπου Philostr.*VA*4.10. 3. *miserable*, Man.2.169: c. gen., βιότοιο ib.454: irreg. Sup. αὐχμότατος dub. l. in Pl.Com.169.

αὐχμηρ-ότης, ητος, ἡ, *squalor*, metaph., Men.Rh.p.402 S. **-ώδης**, ες, = αὐχμηρός, Sch.Arist.25^{a}30.

αὐχμός, ὁ, *drought*, Emp.111.6, Hdt.2.13, 4.198, Hp.*Aph*.3.7: in pl., Th.1.23, Isoc.9.14, Plu.*Num*.13: metaph., ὥσπερ αὐχμός τις τῆς σοφίας *drought, dearth of*.., Pl.*Men*.70c; so perh. αὐχμὸς τῶν σκευαρίων Ar.*Pl*.839. 2. *effects of drought, squalor*, μεστὰς αὐχμοῦ τε καὶ κόνεως Pl.*R*.614d. 3. of style, *dryness, meagreness*, D.H.*Dem*. 44. 4. *thirst*, D.Chr.7.152. (Perh. akin to αὖος.)

αὐχμώδης, ες, *dry*, τὸ αὐ. *drought*, Hdt.1.142; ἔτη Arist.*HA* 602^{a}13; χώρα αὐχμωδεστέρα Thphr.*HP*8.1.6; *arid*, *CP*3.10.1; *squalid*, κόμη E.*Or*.223; σάρξ Plu.2.688d; of colour, *dull*, αἱματῖτις Thphr.*Lap*.37.

αὔχμωσις, εως, ἡ, *dirt, squalor*, of the hair, [Gal.]16.88.

αὖχος, ους, τό, = αὔχημα, Sch.A.*Pers*.871.

αὔω (A), *get a light, light a fire*, ἵνα μή ποθεν ἄλλοθεν αὔοι Od.5.490: —Med., *take fire*, Arat.1035.—Only poet. (Cf. ἐναύω, etc.; from αὐσγω, cf. ONorse *ausa* 'sprinkle', Lat. *haurio, haustum*.)

αὔω (B), fut. ἀΰσω E.*Ion* 1446: aor. ἤϋσα (v. infr.):—*cry out, shout, call aloud*, freq. in Hom., αὖε δ' Ἀθήνη Il.20.48, cf. Call.*Dian*.56 sq.; κέκλετ' ἀΰσας Il.4.508, cf. 6.66, etc.; μακρὸν ἄϋσε 5.101; ἤϋσε.. μέγα τε δεινόν τε ὄρθια 11.10; ἤϋσεν δὲ διαπρύσιον ib.275, etc.:—also in Trag., αὔειν λακάζειν A.*Th*.186; μηδὲν μέγ' ἀΰσῃς S.*El*.830 (lyr.); δεινὸν δ' ἀΰσας *OT*1260: c. acc. cogn., *utter*, στεναγμὸν.. ἀΰσατ' E. *Supp*.800 (lyr.); τίν' αὐδὰν ἀΰσω; Id.*Ion* 1446. 2. c. acc. pers., *call upon*, αὖε δ' ἑταίρους Il.11.461, 13.475, cf. Od.9.65, Theoc.13.58. 3. rarely of things, *ring*, καρφαλέον δέ οἱ ἀσπὶς.. ἄϋσεν Il.13.409 (v. sub αὖος 2); of the sea, *roar*, A.R.2.566. [In pres. and impf. αὐ- is a diphthong; in fut. and aor. a disyll. ἄϋσω, ἤϋσα.]

αὔω (C), = ἄω (A) II, ἰαύω, Nic.*Th*.263, 283.

αὔω, = ξηραίνω, Hdn.Gr.2.132.

αὔως, Aeol. for ἀώς, ἠώς, Sapph.*Oxy*.1787.1 + 2.18, al.

ἀφάβρωμα, ατος, τό, Megarian name of a *woman's garment*, Plu. 2.295b; cf. ἄβρωμα.

ἀφαγν-εύω, = sq., Plu.2.943c. **-ίζω**, fut. -ιῶ Lxx *Le*.14.52: aor. -ήγνισα Paus.2.31.8, Lxx *Le*.14.49:—Med., fut. -ιοῦμαι Hp. *Morb.Sacr*.1: aor. -ηγνισάμην E.*Alc*.1146:—Pass., fut. -αγνισθήσομαι Lxx *Nu*.19.19: aor. -ηγνίσθην ib.19.12:—*purify, consecrate*, χθόνα E. in *Gött.Nachr*.1922.9, Paus.2.31.8; πυρκαϊὴν χρὴ ἀφαγνίσαι .. οἴνῳ *Epigr.Gr*.1034.28 (Thrace):—Med., τοῖς νερτέροις θεοῖς E. *Alc*.1146, cf. Hsch., Suid. II. ἀφαγνίσας· ἀποδύσας, συλήσας, Hsch. **-ισμός**, ὁ, *purification*, Sch.E.*Alc*.98.

ἀφᾰδία, ἡ, (ἀφανδάνω) *enmity*, Eup.34:—also **ἀφάδιος** or **ἀφάδειος**, = ἐχθρός, Hdn.Gr.2.480.

ἄφᾰδος, ον, *displeasing, odious*, *EM*174.50.

ἀφαδρύνομαι, Pass., *mature, ripen*, Thphr.*CP*4.6.8.

ἀφάζει· ἀναδέχεται, Hsch.

Ἀφαία, ἡ, name of divinity in Aegina, *IG*4.1580; cf. Ἀφαία· ἡ Δίκτυννα, καὶ Ἄρτεμις, Hsch.

ἀφαιᾶσαι· ἀπαλγῆσαι, ἀπολειτουργῆσαι, καὶ ἀπολέσαι, Hsch.

ἀφαιλέω, Cret., = ἀφαιρέω (q.v.).

ἀφαίμαξις, εως, ἡ, *bleeding*, Archig.ap.Aët.8.76, *Hippiatr*.42.

ἀφαιμάσσω, Att. **-ττω**, *draw blood*, of leeches, Sor.2.11; *bleed*, *Hippiatr*.69.

ἄφαιμοι· ἀπόγονοι, εὐγενεῖς, Hsch.

ἀφαίρ-εμα, ατος, τό, *that which is taken away as the choice part*, Lxx *Ex*.35.21, *Nu*.18.27 sq., al., J.*AJ*14.10.12. 2. *tribute*, Lxx 1*Ma*.15.5. 3. *deduction*, *POxy*.1731.10 (ii A.D.). 4. *coarse grits made from* ζέα, Plin.*HN*18.112. **-εσις**, εως, ἡ, *taking away, carrying off, removal*, Pl.*Cri*.46c (pl.); *putting off*, τοῦ θνητοῦ Hierocl. *in CA*27 p.483 M.; opp. πρόσθεσις, Plu.*Lyc*.13 (pl.). 2. as law-term, *assertion of freedom of a reputed slave*, Hyp.*Fr*.23. 3. *amputation*, Archig.ap.Orib.47.13.4. II. in Logic, *abstraction*, ἐξ, δι' ἀφαιρέσεως, Arist.*Cael*.299^{a}16, *EN*1142^{a}18; esp. τὰ ἐξ ἀ. *mathematics*, Id.*APo*.81^{b}3, *Metaph*.1061^{a}29, al.; opp. ἐκ προσθέσεως, ib. 1077^{b}9; also τὰ ἐν ἀ. ὄντα Id. *de An*.429^{b}18, al.:—Cicero jokes on this term, *Att*.6.1.2. 2. Gramm., *removal* of initial letters, as in σῦς ὗς, Choerob. *in Theod*.1 p.148 H., cf. A.D.*Pron*.55.13, al.; also of medial letters, ib.93.13; of feet in verse, opp. πρόσθεσις, *POxy*. 220 iii 3. **-ετέον**, *one must take away*, Hp.*Aph*.1.10, Pl.*R*.361a; *one must exclude*, Id.*Plt*.291c; *one must take away in thought*, Thphr. *Metaph*.6. II. ἀφαιρετέος, έα, έον, *to be taken away, removed*, Pl. *R*.398e, cf. Jul.*Or*.8.249d. **-ετέω**, *pick off*, Ion Hist.1. **-έτης**, ου, ὁ, *one who deprives*, χρόνων Vett.Val.55.18, cf. Ptol.*Tetr*.189, Sch. Od.13.224, Suid. s.v. ἐξαίτης. **-ετικός**, ή, όν, *fit for taking away*, τινός A.D.*Adv*.165.12; χρόνος ἐλπίδος ἀ. Vett.Val.281.4; τὰ ἀ. τῶν βοηθημάτων *evacuant* remedies, prob. l. in Herod.Med. in *Rh.Mus*. 58.87. II. Astrol., *retrograde*, of planetary motion, Ptol.*Tetr*. 52, etc. **-έτις**, ιδος, ἡ, *one that takes away*, Μοῖραι ἀ. θνητοῖσιν ἀνάγκης Orph.*H*.59.18. **-ετός**, όν, *to be taken away, separable*, Pl.*Plt*.303e, Arr.*Epict*.3.24.3. 2. *deducted*, *PRev.Laws* 55.1 (iii B.C.). **-έω**, Ion. **ἀπαιρέω**, fut. -ήσω: pf. ἀφῄρηκα, Ion. ἀπαραίρηκα: aor. ἀφεῖλον, later inf. ἀφέλαι *GDI*4940.35 (Cret.); ἀφῄρησα Gal.11.121:—*take away from*:—Constr.: mostly ἀ. τί τινι, σῖτον μέν σφιν ἀφεῖλε *took* it *from* him, Od.14.455, cf. A.*Eu*.360 codd., etc. (but also, *relieve* one *of* a duty, X.*Cyr*.7.1.44): less freq. ἀ. τί τινος Ar.*Pax* 560, X.*Lac*.4.7; κῆρα χώρας A.*Th*.777 (lyr.); ἔκ τινος Id.*Eu*.444; also τινά τι prob. l. ib.360, S.*Ph*.933, v. infr. II. 1, III: c. gen., *take from*, τιμῆς οὔτ' ἀφελὼν οὔτ' ἐπορεξάμενος Sol.5.2; μηδὲν ἀφαιρῶμεν τοῦ ἀδίκου (*from* the unjust man) ἀπὸ τῆς ἀδικίας Pl.*R*.360e; τοῦ πλήθους *diminish* the number, X.*Vect*.4.4: c. acc. only, ἀπελὼν τὰ ἄχθεα *having taken* them *off*, Hdt.1.80; βασιλέων.. ὀργὰς ἀφῄρουν *took away*, E.*Med*.455, cf. Ar.*Pl*.22, *Ra*.518. 2. *set aside*, κρέα *SIG* 1044.41 (Halic., iv B.C.). b. *exclude, separate*, τὸ Ἑλληνικὸν ὡς ἓν ἀπὸ πάντων ἀφαιροῦντες χωρὶς Pl.*Plt*.262d; opp. προστιθέναι, Id. *Phd*.95e, etc. 3. Math., ἀ. ἀπὸ.. *subtract* from, Euc.*Ax*.3 (Pass.), etc.; of ratios, *divide out* from both sides of an equation, Apollon. Perg.1.41 (Pass.); *intercept*, in Pass., Procl.*Hyp*.2.27. 4. in

Logic, *abstract*, c. acc., Arist.*APo.*74^{a}37, al.: abs., Id.*Metaph.*1030^a 33. **II.** Med., fut. ἀφαιρήσομαι (in pass. sense, v.l. for ἀπαιρεθήσεσθαι, Hdt.5.35, cf. Antipho *Fr.*57), later ἀφελοῦμαι Timostr.5, Plb.3.29.7: aor. ἀφειλόμην, later ἀφειλάμην Ph.2.586, D.C.41.63, cf. Phryn.116: pf. ἀφῄρημαι (in med. sense) X.*Cyr.*7.5.79 (spelt ἀφείρ- *Sammelb.*4309 (iii B.C.)):—from Hom. downwds. more freq. than Act., *take away for oneself*; also in reciprocal sense, ἀφαιρεῖσθον τύχην ye *have received each* the fortune *of the other*, E.*El.*928:—Constr. like Act., ἀφαιρεῖσθαί τί τινι, as καὶ δή μοι γέρας.. ἀφαιρήσεσθαι ἀπειλεῖς Il.1.161; τί τινος 5.673,691, 9.335, Th.3.58, Lys.24.13, etc. (also τεύχεα.. ὤμοιϊν ἀφελέσθαι Il.13.510); τι πρός τινος E.*Tr.*1034; τι ἀπό τινος Ar.*V.*883; ἔκ τινος X.*Cyn.*12.9: c. dupl. acc. rei et pers., *bereave* or *deprive of*, μήτε σὺ τόνδ'.. ἀποαίρεο κούρην Il.1.275, cf. Hdt.1.71, 7.104; freq. in Att. and Trag., Lys. l.c., Th.8.74, D.20.46, etc.; τέκνα ἀ. τινά E.*Andr.*613, cf. Ar.*Ach.* 464: rarely c. acc. pers. et gen. rei, ἀ. τὰς κύνας τοῦ εὑρεῖν X.*Cyn.*6. 4; τῆς ἀρχῆς τινά Plu.*Ant.*60; τὴν Ἀμαζόνα τοῦ ζωστῆρος Paus.5.10. 9. **2.** c. acc. rei, ἀ. ψήφισμα *cancel* or *rescind*, And.2.24; ἀφελομένης τῆς νυκτὸς τὸ ἔργον *having broken off* the action, Th.4.134; ἕως κελαινῆς νυκτὸς ὄμμ' ἀφείλετο A.*Pers.*428: abs., μέχρι σκότος ἀφείλετο (sc. τὴν δίωξιν) X.*HG*1.2.16; ἀ. τὴν μνήμην πολλῶν ἀγαθῶν D.22. 13. **3.** folld. by μή c. inf., *prevent, hinder from* doing, τί μ' ἄνδρα .. ἀφείλου μὴ κτανεῖν; S.*Ph.*1303, cf. E.*Tr.*1146; κἄκτεινας, ἤ τις συμφορά σ' ἀφείλετο [μὴ κτεῖναι]; Id.*Andr.*913; c. inf. Pass., τὸν τὰ ὕστερον ἀφείλετο ἀδικήματα εὐεργέτην μὴ ὀνομασθῆναι Paus.8.52.2; c. inf. only, Pi.*I.*1.62: simply, *obstruct*, ἀρχήν Pl.*Lg.*958c. **4.** ἀ. τινὰ εἰς ἐλευθερίαν, Lat. *vindicare in libertatem, claim* as free, Pl.*Lg.* 914e, Isoc.12.97, D.58.19, cf. Lys.23.10, Aeschin.1.62. **III.** Pass., fut. -αιρεθήσομαι E.*Hel.*938; -ήσομαι Antipho *Fr.*57: pf. ἀφῄρημαι, Ion. ἀπαραίρημαι Hdt.7.159, etc.:—*to be robbed* or *deprived of* a thing, τι A.*Ch.*962 (lyr.), Hdt.3.137, etc.; τι πρός or ὑπό τινος, Id.1.70, 3.65, 7.159; ἀφῃρέθην τὰ ἐνέχυρα ὑπό τινος D.47.41; ἐκ χερῶν ἀφῃρέθην *had* them *taken* out of my hands, E.*Tr.*486: c. inf., ἀφῃρέθη Σκίρωνος ἀκτὰς ὄμμα τοὐμὸν εἰσορᾶν *was deprived of, hindered from* seeing them, Id.*Hipp.*1207: less freq. μηδὲν τοῦ ἐμοῦ ὄγκου ἀφαιρεθέντος ἀλλὰ σοῦ αὐξηθέντος Pl.*Tht.*155b. **2.** ὁ ἀφαιρεθείς, in Law, *the person from whom* a slave *has been claimed*, Id.*Lg.*915a. **-ημα**· ἀνάθημα, δῶρον, Hsch. **-ηματικῶς**, *abstractly*, interpol. in Phlp.*in APo.*242.24.

ἄφακες· εὐήθες, Hsch.

ἀφάκη [ἀφᾰ], ἡ, *tare, Vicia angustifolia*, Pherecr.188, Arist.*HA* 596^{a}25, Thphr.*HP*8.8.3, Dsc.2.148, etc.

ἀφάλλομαι, aor. inf. ἀφάλασθαι Ael.*VH*6.14; Ep. aor. part. ἀπάλμενος Bion *Fr.*10.15:—*spring off* or *down from*, πήδημα κοῦφον ἐκ νεὼς ἀφήλατο A.*Pers.*305; ἐπὶ τὴν κεφαλὴν.. ἀφήλατο *jumped off* on to his head, Ar.*Nu.*147; ἀφαλόμενος τοῦ ἵππου Plu.*Caes.*27, cf. Ael. l.c.; of a river, τῆς πέτρας πλεῖον ἢ στάδιον ἀ. τὴν καταφοράν Plb.10.48. 5. **2.** *jump, bound*, of a quick pulse, Ruf.*Syn.Puls.*7.5. **II.** *rebound, glance off*, ἀπὸ τῶν λείων Arist.*de An.*420^{a}22; πέτρου Nic. *Th.*906: abs., *AP*9.159; *to be reflected*, πῦρ ἀπὸ πυρός Plu.2.931b.

ἀφ-αλμός, ὁ, *springing off*, Antyll.ap.Orib.6.31 tit. **-αλσις**, εως, ἡ, *jumping exercise*, Aret.*CD*1.3, Philum.ap.Orib.45.29.37, Antyll.ib.6.31.1. **-αλτος**, ον, *springing off* or *back*, Hsch.

ἄφᾰλος, ον, *without* φάλος, κυνέη Il.10.258, *BGU*1190.3 (i B.C.?).

ἀφᾰμαρτάνω, aor. part. ἀφαμαρτήσαντος Orph.*A.*643; Ep. aor. ἀπήμβροτεν Il.15.521, 16.466,477, Pancrat.*Oxy.*1085.7:—*miss* one's mark, c. gen., καὶ τοῦ μέν ῥ' ἀφάμαρτεν Il.8.119, etc.; θηρός Pancrat. l.c.: also in Prose, X.*HG*6.1.15, D.14.13. **II.** *lose, be deprived of* what one has, σεῦ ἀφαμαρτούσῃ Il.6.411; φίλου ἀπὸ πατρὸς ἁμαρτών 22.505.

ἀφᾰμαρτοεπής, ές, = ἁμαρτοεπής, *talking at random*, Il.3.215.

Ἀφάμιος, ὁ (sc. μήν), name of month at Thronium, *Klio* 16.170; at Ambryssus, *GDI*2256.5.

Ἀφαμιῶται, ῶν, οἱ, name of *serfs* in Crete, like the Helots in Laconia, Str.15.1.34, Ath.6.263f (written Ἀμφ-); cf. ἀφημοῦντας, ἀφημιάστους.

ἀφαμμᾰτ-ίζω, *fasten off*, Antyll.ap.Orib.45.24.4:—hence **-ιστέον**, Sor.1.56.

ἀφάνα, = σκινδαψός, Suid. s.h.v.

ἀφανδάνω, Ion. aor. inf. ἀπαδεῖν Hdt.2.129:—*displease, not to please*, εἰ δ' ὑμῖν ὅδε μῦθος ἀφανδάνει Od.16.387; σοὶ τἄμ' ἀφανδάνοντ' ἔφυ S.*Ant.*501.

ἀφᾰν-εί, Adv. of ἀφανής, *invisibly, obscurely*, Hdn.*Epim.*255. **-εια**, ἡ, *obscurity, uncertainty*, τύχας Pi.*I.*4(3).49: metaph., ἀξιώματος ἀ. *want of illustrious* birth or rank, Th.2.37. **2.** *invisibility*, Dam. *Pr.*6. **II.** *disappearance, destruction*, A.*Ag.*384 (lyr.), Procl.*in Prm.*p.840 S.—The form **ἀφανία** is mentioned by A.D.*Synt.*341. 8. **-έω**, *fail to put in an appearance*, dub. in *PTeb.*43.22 (ii B.C.):—but **ἀφᾱνέω**, *thrash, beat*, Ar.*Eq.*394; cf. ἄφηναι· ἔκοψα, and ἀφῆναι· τὸ τὰς ἐπτισμένας κριθὰς ταῖς χερσὶ τρῖψαι, Hsch.; v. αἴνω. **-ής**, ές, (φαίνομαι) *unseen*, esp. of the nether world, Ταρτάρου πυθμὴν Pi.*Fr.*207, cf. A.*Th.*860 (lyr.); ἀ. κἠν Ἀΐδα δόμῳ φοιτάσῃς Sapph.68; χάσμα ἀ. a *blind* pit, Hdt.6.76; ἡ ἀ. θεός, of Persephone, S.*OC*1556 (lyr.); ὁ ἀ. πόλος, i.e. the south pole, Arist.*Cael.*285^{b}21, *Mu.*394^{b}31 (but ἀ. κόσμος *starless*, Vett.Val.6.22). **2.** ἀ. γίγνεσθαι, = ἀφανίζεσθαι, *disappear*, ὑπὸ γῆν Hdt.3.104, cf. E.*IT*757, Pl.*R.*360a; so ἀ. ἦν *disappeared*, Hdt.7.37, cf. X.*An.*1.4.7; of soldiers *missing* after a battle, Th.2.34; *runaway, absconded*, *PGen.*5.4 (ii A.D.). **b.** στήλας ἀ. ποιῆσαι *obliterate*, *SIG*38.38 (Teos). **3.** *unnoticed, secret*, ἀ. νόος ἀθανάτων Sol.17; ἀ. νεῦμα a *secret* sign, Th.1.134; ἀ. χωρίον *out of sight*, Id.4.29, cf. ib.67; ἀ. ξιφίδιον *concealed*, Id.8.69; δι' ἐπιστολῶν ἀφανῶν *secret* or *invisible* writings, Ph.*Bel.*102.29: c. part., ἀ. εἶναι ἀπιόντες depart *without being noticed*, X.*An.*4.2.4; ἀ. ὄντες ἠδίκουν Th.1.68; μαντικῇ χρώμενος οὐκ ἀ. ἦν he was *well known to* do .., X.*Mem.*1.1.2. **b.** *uncertain, doubtful*, ἀ. νοῦσοι Hdt.2.84; σὺν ἀφανεῖ λόγῳ on an *uncertain* charge, S.*OT*657 (lyr.); ἐν ἀφανεῖ λ. Antipho 5.59; μόρος S.*OC*1682 (lyr.); ὄνομα E.*Tr.*1322 (lyr.); ἐλπίς Th.5.103; πρόφασις ἀφανεστάτη λόγῳ Id.1.23; οὐκ ἀ. τεκμήρια X. *Ages.*6.1; μεθέντας τἀφανῆ, opp. τὸ πρὸς ποσί, S.*OT*131; ἀ. χάρις a favour *from an unknown hand*, D.19.240; ἐς ἀφανὲς τὸν μῦθον ἀνενείκας Hdt.2.23; μισῶ μὲν ὅστις τἀφανῆ περισκοπῶν S.*Fr.*737; τὰ ἀ. μεριμνᾶν Ar.*Fr.*672; ὑπὲρ τῶν ἀ. φανεροῖς μαρτυρίοις χρῆσθαι Arist. *EN*1104^{a}13; of what is *beyond the evidence of sense*, opp. φανερόν, ἁρμονίη ἀ. φανερῆς κρείττων Heraclit.54, cf. Phld.*Sign.*1, al.; τἀφανὲς διὰ τοῦ φαινομένου συλλογίζεσθαι Epicur.*Nat.*14.4; τὸ τῆς τύχης ἀ. οἷ προβήσεται E.*Alc.*785; τὸ ἀ. τοῦ κατορθώσειν Th.2.42; ἐν ἀφανεῖ ἔτι κεῖσθαι, ἐν τῷ ἀ. εἶναι, Id.1.42, 3.23; ἐν ἀ. κεκτῆσθαί τι *secretly*, Pl.*Lg.* 954e; ἐκ τοῦ ἀφανοῦς Th.1.51, 4.96, etc.; ἐξ ἀ. A.*Fr.*57.9, Ar.*Ra.* 1332: neut. pl. as Adv., E.*Hipp.*1289 (lyr.). Regul. Adv. ἀφανῶς Th. 3.43, etc.: Sup. -έστατα X.*HG*5.1.27. **4.** of persons and things, *unnoticed, obscure*, E.*Tr.*1244; also οὐ γὰρ ἀ. κρινεῖτε τὴν δίκην Th.3. 57; ἀ. καὶ ταπεινὴ φύσις D.61.35. **5.** ἀ. οὐσία *personal* property, as money, *which can be secreted and made away with* (cf. ἀφανίζω I.7), opp. φανερά (*real*), as land, Lys.32.4, cf. *BCH*27.219 (Crete); opp. ἐμφανής, *IG*12(2).15.8 (Mytil.), *SIG*554.17; but simply, *concealed*, ἀφανῆ καταστῆσαι τὴν οὐσίαν Lys.20.23: in lit. sense, ἀ. πλοῦτος Ar. *Ec.*602; πλοῦτος ἀ. ὃν σὺ κατορύξας ἔχεις Men.128.16. **-ίζω**, Att. fut. -ιῶ X.*An.*3.2.11, Pl.*Tht.*184a: pf. ἠφάνικα D.36.18:—*make unseen, hide*, νεφέλη.. ἠφάνισεν ἥλιον X.*An.*3.4.8; *hush up*, ἔργον Pl.*Smp.* 217e: hence, *lose sight of*, Eub.107.18; ἀ. τὸ συμφορώτατον *do away with, reject*, Hp.*VM*21 (v.l. for ἀφαιρέοντας); *make away with* a person, Hdt.3.126, X.*Mem.*1.2.53, Th.4.80; μή μ' ἀφανίσῃ λαβών Men. *Epit.*210:—Pass., τὴν γνώμην μηδὲν.. ἀφανισθεῖσαν in no part *concealed* or *suppressed*, Th.7.8. **2.** *do away with, remove*, ἄχος S. *OC*1712 (lyr.); τινὰ πόλεος *carry* one *off from* the city, E.*Ph.*1041 (lyr.); Μούσας ἀ. Ar.*Nu.*972; ἀ. αὑτὸν εἰς τὸν νεών *disappear* into the temple, Id.*Pl.*741. **3.** *destroy*, Ἀθήνας X.*An.*3.2.11, cf. Plb.1.81.6, Lxx *De.*7.2; ὅλως ἀ. ἱερά D.21.147, cf. *Epigr.Gr.*376.8 (Aezani). **4.** *obliterate* writing, Th.6.54; footsteps, X.*Cyn.*5.3, etc.; traces of bloodshed, Antipho 5.45; *spirit away* a witness, ib.52; *get rid of*, δίκην Ar.*Nu.*760. **5.** *secrete, steal*, X.*Oec.*14.2. **6.** *obscure, mar* one's good name, etc., πατρικὰς ἀρετάς, ἀξίωσιν, δόξαν, Th.7.69, 2.61: in good sense, ἀ. ἀγαθῷ κακόν *wipe out* ill deeds by good, ib.42; δύσκλειαν Id.3.58; τὰ χρώματα ἀ. ἐκ τοῦ σώματος, of the *wasting* effect of grief, Antiph.98; τρίχα βαφῇ ἀ. *disguise* it by dyeing, Ael.*VH*7.20; ἀ. τὰ πρόσωπα (cf. ἀπρόσωπος), of *artificial disfigurement*, *Ev.Matt.*6.16, cf. Lxx *Jl.*2.20, *Za.*7.14. **b.** *spoil*, οἶνον, ὕδωρ, Sor.1.90, Gal.9.645. **7.** *make away with* property, etc., ἀργύριον, ναυτικόν, ἀνθρώπους, Aeschin. 1.101, 3.222, D.28.12; ἀ. τὴν οὐσίαν Aeschin.1.103; but, *conceal the existence of*, ἐργαστήριον, οὐσίαν, D.27.26,44. **8.** *drain* a cup of wine, Eub.82. **9.** ἀφανίσαι· σκεπάσαι, προνομεῦσαι, Hsch. **II.** Pass., *disappear, be missing*, Hdt.4.8,124, S.*Ant.*255; of persons *buried* by a sand-storm, Hdt.3.26; or *lost* at sea, Th.8.38, X.*HG*1.6.33; ἀ. κατὰ τῆς θαλάσσης, of islands, Hdt.7.6; ὑποβρύχιος ἠφ. Plu.*Crass.*19; ἀ. ἐκ τῶν Θρηϊκίων Hdt.4.95; ἐξ ἀνθρώπων Lys.2.11; ἀ. εἰς ὕλην *disappear* into it, X.*Cyn.*10.23; καταγελασθὲν ἠφανίσθη was laughed down and *disappeared*, Th.3.83. **2.** *live retired*, X.*Ages.*9.1. **-ῐσις**, εως, ἡ, *getting rid of*, τῆς δίκης Ar.*Nu.*765; τῶν συνθηκῶν D.33.22; *destruction*, λόγων Pl.*Sph.*259e. **II.** (from Pass.) *disappearance*, Hdt.4. 15, Arist.*Pr.*953^{a}17, Epicur.*Ep.*2 p.52 U. **-ισμός**, ὁ, *extermination, destruction*, Plb.5.11.5; πόλεων D.S.15.48; σώματος καὶ ψυχῆς Plu.2.107d; ἀφανισμῷ ἀφανίζειν Lxx *De.*7.2. **II.** = foreg. II, Arist. *HA*580^{b}21, Luc.*Alex.*19; ἄστρων Thphr.*Sign.*2 (pl.), cf. Cleom.2.5; *occultation*, Theo Sm.p.137 H.; Περὶ ἀ. ἡλιακῶν, title of work by Eudoxus, on *occultations* of stars by the sun, Phld.*D.*1.21; τῆς σελήνης Plu.2.670c; ἐγγὺς ἀφανισμοῦ *Ep.Hebr.*8.13. **-ιστέος**, έα, έον, *to be suppressed*, [λόγος] Isoc.12.233. **-ιστής**, οῦ, ὁ, *destroyer*, dub. l. in Plu.2.828f, cf. Sch.A.*Th.*175, etc.; *scavenger*, *PLond.*2.387.9 (iii A.D.):—fem. **-ίστρια**, Sch.Opp.*H.*2.487:—hence **-ιστικός**, ή, όν, *causing to disappear*, τινός A.D.*Pron.*33.15; τριχῶν Archig.ap. Aët.6.63, cf. Crito ap.Gal.12.447; *destroying*, Sch.A.*Th.*145. Adv. -κῶς Sch.Il.21.220, al.

ἄφανος, ον, dub. sens., λίθος *PMag.Par.*2.195.

ἀφαντ-ᾰσίαστος, ον, *not manifested*, *Corp.Herm.*5.1, Olymp.*in Phd.*p.35 N. Adv. -τως Ascl.*in Metaph.*151.6, Olymp.*in Phd.*p.38 N. **-ᾰσίωτος**, ον, *unable to imagine* a thing, Plu.2.960d, *Cat. Cod.Astr.*7.215.7. **-αστος**, ον, *without* φαντασία, φύσις *Stoic.*2. 304, al.: c. gen., ψυχὴ ἀ. τοῦ ὄντος Ph.1.230. Adv. -τως, κινεῖσθαι, opp. ὁρμῇ καὶ φαντασίᾳ χρῆσθαι, Id.1.641, cf. Porph.*Gaur.*7.3. **2.** *without dreams*, Gal.16.221,525. **II.** *not sensibly presented*, εἶδος, of pure form, Syrian.*in Metaph.*92.5.

ἀφαντικά, τά, *derelict lands*, *Cod.Theod.*13.11.3, prob. in Lyd.*Mag.* 3.70; cf. *afanticius Cod.Theod.*5.11.9.

ἄφαντ-ος, ον, (φαίνομαι) *made invisible, blotted out*, ἀκήδεστοι καὶ ἄ. Il.6.60; ἄσπερμος γενεὴ καὶ ἄ. ὄληται 20.303, etc.; *hidden*, ἄ. ἕρμα A.*Ag.*1007 (lyr.); ἔφην' ἄφαντον φῶς S.*Ph.*297; ἄ. ἔπελες Pi.*O.*1.46; ἐκ βροτῶν ἄ. βῆναι S.*OT*832; ἀνὴρ ἄ. ἐκ.. στρατοῦ he has *disappeared*, A.*Ag.*624; ἄ. οἴχεσθαι ib.657, Jul.*Or.*2.59a; ἔρρειν S.*OT*560; ἀρθεῖσ' ἄ. E.*Hel.*606; ἐκ χερῶν Id.*Hipp.*827 (lyr.); ἴχνος πλαταν ἄ. *disappear-*

ing, A.*Ag*.695 (lyr.); *invisible*, νύξ Parm.9.3. 2. *in secret*, ἄφαντα βρέμειν Pi.*P*.11.30. 3. *obscure*, Id.*N*.8.34; θεοῖς δῆλος θνητοῖσι δ' ἄ. Epimenid.11.—Poet. and late Prose, ἄ. γενέσθαι D.S.3.60, 4.65, *Ev.Luc*.24.31; τὰ ἄφαντα φήναντες Aristid.1.260 J., cf. Sch.Arat. 899. **-όω**, *make* ἄφαντος, *hide*, Eust.882.45:—Pass., *disappear*, Sch.Arat.899; *evaporate*, Syn.Alch.p.67 B.; *to be sublimated*, Zos. Alch.p.163 B.

ἀφάπαξ [φᾰ], *once for all*, *PFlor*.158.10 (iii A.D.).

ἀφ-απτέον, *one must fasten*, Antyll.ap.Orib.45.24.10. **-άπτω**, aor. ἀφῆψα, imper. ἄφαψον Ph.*Bel*.65.37:—*fasten from* or *upon*, ἅμματα ἀπάψας *having tied* knots *on a string*, Hdt.4.98, cf. Hp.*Fist*.4:—Med., LXX *Pr*.3.3, al.:—Pass., *to be hung on*, *hang on*, pf. part. ἀπαμμένος (Ion. for ἀφημμ-) Hdt.2.121.δ'; ἀφημμένος ἐκ ποδεώνων Theoc. 22.52. 2. metaph. of argument, Gal.16.82.

ἄφᾰρ [ἄφ], poet. Adv. *straightway*, *forthwith*, in Hom. mostly at the beginning of a clause, with δέ following, ἄ. δ' ἤμυσε καρήατι Il.19. 405, cf. Od.2.95: without δέ, *thereupon*, *after that*, Il.11.418. 2. *suddenly*, *quickly*, ἄ. κεραοὶ τελέθουσι Od.4.85: strengthd., ἄ. αὐτίκα Il. 23.593; πέμπε δράκοντας ἄ. Pi.*N*.1.40, cf. 10.63, *Pae*.6.81, Emp.35. 6, 110.8.—Rare in Trag., A.*Pers*.469; ἄ. βέβακε S.*Tr*.133,529, cf. E. *IT* 1274 (lyr. exc. in A. l.c.): also in later Ep. as A.R.2.539, etc. 3. intens., *very*, Il.17.417, Od.2.169. II. in Thgn.716 as if Adj., *swift*, *fleet* (cf. ἀφάρτερος), παῖδες Βορέω τῶν ἄφαρ εἰσὶ πόδες.

ἄφαρβαν· ἐλεύθερον, Hsch.

ἀφαρεί, Adv. = ἄφαρ I. 2, *EM* 175.24, Hsch., Suid.

ἀφαρεύς, έως, ὁ, supposed *belly-fin of female tunny*, dub. in Arist. *HA* 543ᵃ13.

ἀφᾱρής, ές, *without* φᾶρος, *unclad*, *naked*, of the Χάριτες, Euph. 87; cf. ἄφᾱρος.

ἀφάρκη, ἡ, an evergreen tree, *hybrid arbutus*, *Arbutus hybrida*, Thphr.*HP* 1.9.3, 3.3.1.

ἀφαρκίδευτον· ἄγρευτον, ἀθυσίαστον, Hsch.

ἄφαρκτος, ον, v. ἄφρακτος.

ἀφαρμάκ-ευτος [μᾰ], ον, *without medicine*, *not physicked*, Hp.*Acut*. (*Sp*.)27; *without cosmetics*, ξανθίζειν ἀφαρμάκευτα Alciphr.*Fr*.5. 4. **-ος**, ον, *without medicinal properties*, Gal.6.650. II. *without bloom*, χρῶμα Eust.1416.2, Hsch. **-τος**, ον, *unanointed*, Nic. *Th*.115; *unpoisoned*, κύλιξ ἀ. Luc.*DMort*.7.2.

ἀφαρμόζω, Att. **-ττω**, *not to suit*, Oenom.ap.Eus.*PE* 5.24.

ἀφᾰρόζωμος [ἀφ], ὁ, *improvised*, 'hasty' *broth*, Eust.1191.13.

ἄφᾰρος, ον, = ἀφάρωτος, Call.*Fr*.183. II. **ἄφᾱρος**, ον, = ἀφαρής, Hsch.

ἀφαρπᾰγή· *abreptio*, *Gloss*.

ἀφαρπάζω, fut. Ep. -άξω, Att. -άσομαι:—Pass., pf. -ήρπασμαι X. *Cyn*.9.18: aor. 1 -ηρπάσθην Id.*HG* 5.4.17; -ηρπάγην *IPE* 1.26 (Olbia):—*tear off* or *from*, Ἕκτωρ δ' ὡρμήθη κόρυθα.. κρατὸς ἀφαρπάξαι Il. 13.189; *snatch away*, *steal from*, τί τινος Ar.*Eq*.1062: c. acc. only, *snatch eagerly*, S.*Tr*.548, E.*Ion* 1178; ἀ. τὸν στέφανον D.21.64; of death, *IG* 12(7).52.9 (Amorgos):—Pass., Lys.19.31; φωτὸς ἀφαρπασθείς, of one *dead*, *IG* 14.1386, cf. 12(7).400 (Amorgos).

ἀφάρτερος [ἄφ], α, ον, Comp. Adj. (from ἄφαρ) *more fleet*, τῶν δ' ἵπποι μὲν ἔασιν ἀφάρτεροι Il.23.311; cf. Dionys.Epic.ap.St.Byz. s.v. Κάσπειρος.

ἀφάρυμος· ἄτολμος, Hsch.

ἀφᾰ́ρωτος, ον, (φαρόω) *unploughed*, *untilled*, Call.*Fr*.82c.

ἀφᾰσία, ἡ, (ἄφατος) *speechlessness*, caused by fear or perplexity, ἔκπληξιν ἡμῖν ἀφασίαν τε προστιθεὶς E.*Hel*.549; ἀ. μ' ἔχει Id.*IA* 837, cf. Ar.*Th*.904; ἀ. ἡμᾶς λαμβάνει τί ποτε χρὴ λέγειν Pl.*Lg*.636e; εἰς ἀ. τινὰ ἐμβάλλειν Id.*Phlb*.21d; εἰς ἀ. ἐμβάλλειν πράγματος *inability to say anything* about it, S.E.*P*.2.211, cf. Dam.*Pr*.7.

ἀφάσσω, Ion., Ep., and late Prose, = ἀφάω, *feel*, Hp.*Nat.Mul*.11, etc.; ἄφασον αὐτοῦ τὰ ὦτα Hdt.3.69, cf. A.R.2.710, 4.428, v.l. in Call. *Fr*.317, cf. Musae.82, etc.; ὥσπερ ἐν σκότει ἀφάσσων *groping*, Dam. *Pr*.42, cf. Iamb.*Myst*.3.6, etc.:—Med., A.R.4.181:—Pass., Hp. *Morb*.2.30 and 41.

ἀφατέω, dub. sens. in *IG* 5(1).209.34.

ἀφατῆλες· μαστοί, θηλαί, Hsch.

ἄφᾰτος, ον, *not uttered* or *named*, *nameless*, ἄνδρες ὁμῶς ἄ. τε φατοί τε Hes.*Op*.3. 2. *unutterable*, *ineffable*, λόγος E.*Ion* 782 (lyr.); ἄ. μέλεα *monstrous*, Pi.*N*.1.47; κεφαλαί *AP* 6.112 (Pers.); ἄ. χρήματα *untold* sums, Hdt.7.190; ἄ. νέφος, κτύπος, S.*OT* 1314 (lyr.), *OC* 1464 (lyr.); ὀρνιθαρίων ἄφατον (Schw. for -των) πλῆθος Anaxandr.41.63; πώλων ἄφατον τάχος *IG* 14.2012.4 (Sulp. Max.); ἡδονή Phld.*D*.3.14; ὑπερβολὴ δυνάμεως Hermog.*Inv*.1.4; δύναμις Plot.4.8.6; ἄφατον ὡς.. *there's no saying* how.., i.e. *marvellously*, *immensely*, Ar.*Av*.428, *Lys*.198. Adv. -τως Dsc.1.13.

ἀφαυαίνω, aor. part. -ήνας Lyc.ap.Orib.8.25.8, *PHolm*.12.12, but inf. -ᾶναι Plot.4.4.32:—*starve*, *wither*, Thphr.*HP* 3.18.9:—Pass., ib. 4.2.11; *to be parched*, δίψῃ ἀφαυανθήσομαι Ar.*Ec*.146, cf. Arist.*Pr*. 896ᵃ14, Lyc.ap.Orib.8.25.17; ἵνα μὴ ζητῶν τὸν σύαγρον ἀφαυανθῇς Ath.9.401e. 2. *grill*, *roast*, Hld.2.19 (prob.), Porph.*Abst*.4.20. (Cf. ἀπαναίνω.)

ἀφαυρ-ός, ά, όν, *feeble*, *powerless*, ἠύτε παιδὸς ἀφαυροῦ Il.7.235, cf. Nic.*Th*.198; *dim*, Arat.256; almost always Comp. and Sup., σέο πολλὸν ἀφαυρότερος Il.7.457; ἵνα μή οἱ ἀφαυρότερον βέλος εἴη 12.458; οὔ μιν ἀφαυρότατος βάλ' Ἀχαιῶν 15.11, cf. Od.20.110, Hes.*Op*.586, Pi.*P*.4.272 (Comp.), Theoc.21.49 (Comp.); ἀνδρὸς γηρέντος πολλὸν -ότερος Xenoph.9, etc.; ῥείθρων ἀφαυροτέρην, of a bridge, *too weak to resist* the stream, *Epigr.Gr*.1078.6 (Adana): so in Prose, σιτία -ότερα *less nutritious*, Hp.*Mul*.1.67; [κενεὼν] -ότατόν ἐστι X.*Eq*.12. 8; Posit., Democr.285, Ti.Locr.102c, Arist.*EN* 1101ᵇ2, '*Hymn.Is*. 122. Adv. -ρῶς *AP* 6.267 (Diotim.): Comp. -ότερον, τροχάει Arat. 227. **-ότης**, ητος, ἡ, *feebleness*, τῶν αἰσθήσεων Anaxag.21. **-όω**, *make weak*, Erot. s.v. ἀμαλδύνεται (v.l. ἀμαυροῦται).

ἀφαύω, (αὔω) *dry up*, *parch*, v.l. for ἀφᾱνέω in Ar.*Eq*.394.

ἄφαψις, ἡ, dub. sens. in Gal.19.368.

ἀφάω, (ἀφή) Ep. Verb, *to handle*, θώρηκα καὶ ἀγκύλα τόξ' ἀφόωντα *rubbing and polishing* them, Il.6.322; ὠτειλὰς ἀφόωσιν Opp.*H*.5.329; ἀφόων θησαυρόν *AP* 11.366 (Maced.).

ἀφέγγ-εια, ἡ, *want of light*, Max.Tyr.40.4. **-ής**, ές, *without light*, φῶς ἀ. a light *that is no light* (i.e. to the blind), S.*OC* 1549; νυκτὸς ἀφεγγὲς βλέφαρον, of the moon, E.*Ph*.543; simply, *dark*, σπῆλυγξ Opp.*C*.3.324; ὁμίχλη *AP* 9.675; δηϊοτής a *night* battle, Nonn. *D*.24.165; Ἀΐδα.. τὸν ἀφεγγέα χῶρον *Epigr.Gr*.372.13 (Cotiaeum), cf. D.H.8.52. 2. *not visible to the eye*, ὀδμά A.*Pr*.115. 3. metaph., εἴ τι.. τυγχάνεις ἀφεγγὲς φέρων something *ill-starred*, *unlucky*, S.*OC* 1481 (lyr.). 4. *obscure*, ἔκδοσις Olymp.Alch.p.70 B.

ἀφέδιτος (prob. ἀφείδ-, cf. φειδίτια) ἡμέρα day *when no sacrifice is offered*, at Sparta, Hsch. (leg. ⟨οὐ⟩ θύουσιν).

ἀφεδνήν· ἀναιδῆ, Hsch.

ἀφεδρ-εία, ἡ, *menstruation*, Dam.ap.Suid. s.v. διαγνώμων. **-εύω**, = ἐπὶ δίφρῳ καθίσαι, Hsch.

ἀφεδρῆ· ἀποπνίγῃ, Hsch.

ἀφεδριατεύοντες, οἱ, title of *Boeotian magistracy*, *IG* 7.3207 (Orchom. Boeot.), al.

ἄφεδρος, ἡ, *menses muliebres*, LXX *Le*.15.19, al., Dsc.2.75, Gal.14. 208. II. Εἰλειθυίας ἄ. *exudation from* silver fir, Thphr.*HP* 5.9.8.

ἀφεδρών, ῶνος, ὁ, (ἕδρα) *privy*, *OGI* 483.220 (Pergam.), *Ev.Matt*. 15.17.

ἀφειδ-έω, *to be unsparing*, *lavish of*, ψυχῆς S.*El*.980; τοῦ βίου Th. 2.43; σφῶν αὐτῶν ib.51; τῶν σωμάτων Lys.2.25: abs., ἀφειδήσαντες [πόνου, or the like] *ungrudgingly*, Hp.*Art*.37; *recklessly*, E.*IT* 1354. II. *take no care for*, *neglect*, εἴ τις τοῦδ' ἀφειδήσοι πόνου S.*Ant*. 414 (s.v.l.); *reck not of*, μαινομένης θαλάσσης Musae.303; βασιλῆος, ἀέθλων, τοκήων A.R.2.98 (ἀκήδησαν Choerob.), 869, 3.630; Ἀφροδίτης Nonn.*D*.8.217: also in Prose, Str.1.2.6. **-ής**, ές, (φείδομαι) *not sparing of*, νεῶν καὶ πεισμάτων A.*Ag*.195 (lyr.); ἀ. δείματος *lightly regarding* it, A.R.4.1252; ἀ. πρὸς τὸν ἔρωτα Call.*Epigr*.47.7: Sup. -έστατοι, τῶν ἀγαθῶν D.Chr.1.24. 2. of things, ἀ. ὁ κατάπλους καθεστήκει the landing was made *without regard to cost* or *risk*, Th.4.26; *not spared*, *lavishly bestowed*, χρυσός Call.*Cer*.128; δῶρα *AP* 11.59 (Maced.). II. Adv. -δῶς, Aeol. and Ion. -δέως Alc.34, Hdt.1. 163, al., Ep. -δείως A.R.3.897:—*freely*, *lavishly*, Alc. l.c.; διδόναι Hdt. l.c., D.18.88; ἀ. ἀπιέναι τὰ τοξεύματα Hdt.9.61: Comp. -έστερον, ταῖς λέξεσι χρῆσθαι Hermog.*Id*.2.11; *unsparingly*, ὁρμῆσαι πρὸς τὸν πόλεμον D.11.2. 2. *without mercy*, κατακόψαι Hdt.1.207; φονεύειν Id.9.39; χρώμενον Democr.159; κολαζόντων ἀφειδέστερον ἢ ὡς δεσπόται, -έστατα τιμωρεῖν, X.*Cyr*.4.2.47, *An*.1.9.13; ἀ. ἔχειν ἑαυτῶν Arist. *Pol*.1315ᵃ29, cf. Paus.4.4.8. **-ία**, ἡ, *generosity*, *liberality*, Pl.*Def*. 412c, Plu.2.762d. 2. *unsparing treatment*, σώματος *Ep.Col*.2.23.

ἀφείδιτος, v. ἀφέδιτος.

ἀφείργω, = ἀπείργω (q.v.), pf. part. Pass. ἀφειργμένη Ael.*NA* 12.21.

ἀφεκάς [ᾱς], Adv. *far away*, Nic.*Th*.674.

ἀφεκτ-έον, (ἀπέχομαι) *one must abstain from*, τινός X.*Mem*.1.2. 34; τροφῆς Porph.*Abst*.1.38, etc.; *one must leave alone*, τινός Gal. 17(2).359: so in pl. **-τέα**, Ar.*Lys*.124; cf. ἀποσχετέον. **-ικός**, ή, όν, (ἀπέχομαι) *abstemious*, Arr.*Epict*.2.22.20; τὸ ἀ. Porph.*Abst*. 3.26: c. gen., ib.3.1.

ἀφελγύνουσα· κακοῦσα, Hsch.

ἀφέλ-εια, Ion. **-είη**, ἡ, *simplicity*, Hp.*Decent*.3, Antiph.163.8; περὶ τὴν δίαιταν Plb.6.48.3; of style, Ath.15.693f, Hermog.*Id*.1.1, al.; opp. σφοδρότης, ib.11; of terminology, Gal.10.269. **-έον**· συνηγμένον, κοινόν, Hsch. **-ής**, ές, (φελλεύς) *without a stone*, *even*, *smooth*, διὰ τῶν ἀφελῶν πεδίων Ar.*Eq*.527. II. *artless*, *simple*, of persons, S.*Fr*.723, D.*Ep*.4.11, Luc.*DDeor*.4.3; εὔκολος καὶ ἀ. Plu.*Cat. Ma*.6; ἀφελέστατοι τῶν πρότερον Phylarch.43; *frater* ἀφελέστατος Cic.*Att*.1.18.1; ἀ. κατὰ τὴν ἐσθῆτα Plb.11.10.3; also ἀ. ἐντεύξεις Id. 18.49.4; ἀ. ψυχή *simple*, in good sense, *IG* 14.1839. Adv. -λῶς, ἔχειν Plb.38.7.4; μετρίως καὶ ἀ. οἰκεῖν Plu.*Pomp*.40; *naively*, Cic.*QF* 1.2.3 (prob.); πολλὰ ἀ. πιστεύσας ἀπώλεσεν Vett.Val.168.23. b. in bad sense, *bold*, *brazen*, *AP* 5.41 (Rufin.). Adv. -λῶς, παίζουσα dub. l. in Thgn.1211; κατηγορίαν ποιήσασθαι Aristid.2.116 J. 2. Rhet., *simple*, *not intricate* or *involved*, opp. ἐν κώλοις, περίοδος Arist. *Rh*.1409ᵇ16: generally, of style, *affecting simplicity* or *artlessness*, τὸ ἀ. D.H.*Comp*.22; λέξις λιτὴ καὶ ἀ. Id.*Dem*.2; φράσις ἰσχνὴ καὶ ἀ. Id.*Pomp*.2; λέξις ἀ. καὶ ἄθρυπτος Plu.*Lyc*.21; ἀφέλεια -εστέρα Hermog.*Id*.2.12. Adv. -λῶς, γράφειν ib.10.

ἀφελκόω, *make an incision*, *tap* a tree, Thphr.*HP* 9.1.5, 9.2.1 (Pass.):—Pass., *to be ulcerated*, f.l. in Hp.*Epid*.4.41, Arist.*Pr*.889ᵇ 13; *to be abraded*, Thphr.*CP* 5.5.2.

ἀφέλκ-ῠσις, εως, ἡ, *dragging away*, *Gloss*. **-υστέον**, *one must draw off*, Antyll.ap.Orib.7.21.7. **-ω**, Ion. ἀπέλκω, fut. ἀφέλξω E. *Hec*.142 (lyr.): aor. ἀφείλκῠσα (v. infr.): pf. ἀφείλκῠκα M.Ant.3.6:—*drag away*, ἱκέτας ἐκ τοῦ ἱροῦ Hdt.3.48, cf. S.*OC* 844, E.*Heracl*.113; πῶλον ἀπὸ μαστῶν Id.*Hec*.142 (lyr.); τινὰς ἀπὸ τέκνων καὶ γονέων καὶ γυναικῶν Lys.12.96; *drag* a speaker *from* the βῆμα, Pl.*Prt*.319c; ἀ. τὰς τριήρεις *drag* or *tow* ships *away*, Th.2.93, cf. 7.53,74; *draw aside*, *divert*, ἐπὶ τὰ ἡδέα X.*Mem*.4.5.6; τὸ δέρμα ἀ. *to draw* it *off*, Hp.*Art*.

11:—Pass., ibid. II. *draw off* liquor, κάδων πώματα Archil.4; θρόμβους οὓς ἀφείλκυσας φόνου A.*Eu.*184. 2. Med., τοῦ δόρατος ἀφελκύσωμαι τοὔλυτρον *let me draw off* the sheath *from..*, Ar.*Ach.*1120.

ἀφέλκωσις, εως, ἡ, *abrasion of plant-stem*, Thphr.*CP*5.5.3.

ἀφελληνίζω, *hellenize*, i.e. *civilize thoroughly*, τὴν βάρβαρον Ph.2.567:—Pass., aor. -ηλλήνισθη D.Chr.37.26.

ἀφελλίαι· μέλανος ἀλφός, Hsch. **ἄφελμα**· τὸ κάλλυντρον, Id.; cf. ὄφελμα.

ἀφελόζωος, ον, *living simply*, *PMag.Par.*1.1371.

ἀφελότης, ητος, ἡ, *simplicity*, *unworldliness*, *Act.Ap.*2.46, Vett. Val.240.15.

ἀφελπίζω, = ἀπελπ-, *IG*14.966 (Pass.).

ἄφεμα, ατος, τό, *that which is let go*: *remission of tribute* or *taxation*, Lxx 1*Ma.*10.28 (pl.), al., *PTeb.*226 (ii B.C.), *PFlor.*379.37 (ii A.D.).

ἀφενάκιστος [νᾰ], ον, *free from cajolery*, *straightforward*, Ph.1.564.

ἄφενος, εος, τό, *revenue*, *riches*, *wealth*, *abundance*, ἄφενος καὶ πλοῦτον ἀφύξειν Il.1.171, cf. 23.299, Thgn.30; μύρμηκος Crates Theb.10.7; of the *wealth* of the gods, Hes.*Th.*112: masc. acc. ἄφενον v.l. in Id. *Op.*24: gen. οιο Call.*Jov.*96, *AP*9.234 (Crin.); cf. ἄφνος.

ἄφεος· ἄφωνος, Hsch.

ἄφεξις, εως, ἡ, (ἀπέχομαι) *abstinence*, τινός *from* a thing, Aret.*CD*1.2.

ἀφέργω, = ἀπείργω, *keep off*, *withhold*, *Tab.Heracl.*1.131.

ἀφερεπον-ία, ἡ, *incapacity for bearing labour*, Eust.222.28. **-ος**, ον, *incapable of labour*, Vett.Val.77.1, 150.27, Ptol.*Tetr.*156, Sch.A.R. 1.269. Adv. -νως *carelessly*, Simp.*in Ph.*43.4.

ἀφέριστα· ἄχρηστα, Hsch.

ἄφερκτος, ον, (ἀφείργω) *shut out from*, A.*Ch.*446 (lyr.).

ἀφερμηνεύω, *interpret*, *expound*, τὸ λεχθὲν παρ' αὐτῶν ἀ. Pl.*Sph.* 246e: abs., ὡς σὺ κατ' Αἴγυπτον ἀ. Id.*Lg.*660c; *translate*, Plu.*Rom.*21.

ἄφερνος, ον, *dowerless*, Hsch. s.v. ἄεδνον.

ἀφερπετόομαι, Pass., *become a reptile*, prob. in Herm.ap.Stob.1. 49.69.

ἀφερπυλλόομαι, Pass., *change into* ἕρπυλλος, Thphr.*CP*5.7.2.

ἀφέρπω, *to creep off*, *steal away*, S.*Tr.*813, *OC*490: generally, *go away*, *retire*, Id.*Aj.*1161, Theoc.4.29, Herod.6.98; *die*, Pempel.ap. Stob.4.25.52.

ἀφέρτεροι· ἥσσονες, Hsch.; but ἀφερτέρους· πολὺ φερτέρους, ταχυτέρους, Id.; cf. ἀφάρτερος.

ἄφερτος, ον, *insufferable*, *intolerable*, A.*Ag.*386 (lyr.), al.; κακόν Id.*Eu.*146 (lyr.).

ἀφέσιμος ἡμέρα *holiday*, Arist.*Ath.*43.3, Aristid.*Or.*50(26).98:—also of persons, *released from payment*, *PTeb.*224 (ii B.C.).

Ἀφέσιος, ὁ, *Releaser*, epith. of Zeus, Arr.ap.*EM*176.32, Paus.1.44.9.

ἄφεσις, εως, ἡ, (ἀφίημι) *letting go*, *release*, περὶ τῆς τῶν πλοίων ἀφέσεως Philipp.ap.D.18.77, cf. Pl.*Plt.*273c; καρπῶν *PAmh.*2.43.9 (ii B.C.); γῆ ἐν ἀφέσει land *in private hands*, opp. βασιλική, *PTeb.* 5.37 (ii B.C.), etc. b. of persons, *dismissal*: in ritual, λαοῖς ἄ. Apul.*Met.*11.17; *release*, Plb.1.79.12, *IG*2.314.21, *Ev.Luc.*4.18. 2. c. gen., ἀ. φόνου *quittance from* murder, Pl.*Lg.*869d: so abs., Hermog.*Stat.*8; *discharge from* a bond, D.33.3; ἄ. ἐναντίον μαρτύρων ποιήσασθαι Id.45.41; opp. ἀπόδοσις χρημάτων, Isoc.17.29; *exemption from attendance*, *leave of absence*, Arist.*Ath.*30.6; ἀ. τῆς στρατείας *exemption from* service, Plu.*Ages.*24; *remission* of a debt, ταλάντου *Michel* 1340*B*7 (Cnidus, ii B.C.); χρημάτων *IPE*1^2.32*B*70 (Olbia, iii B.C.); sc. καταδίκης, *Inscr.Magn.*93*c*16. b. *forgiveness*, *Ev. Marc.*3.29; ἁμαρτιῶν *Ev.Matt.*26.28. 3. *relaxation*, *exhaustion*, Hp.*Epid.*3.6. 4. *divorce*, τινὶ πέμπειν Plu.*Pomp.*42. 5. *starting* of horses in a race, ἵππων ἄ. ποιεῖν D.S.4.73: hence, *starting-post* itself, ἰσώσας τἀφέσει (Musgr. for τῇ φύσει) τὰ τέρματα having made the winning-post one with the *starting-post*, i.e. having completed the δίαυλος and come back to the *starting-post*, dub. cj. in S.*El.*686, cf. Paus.5.15.5, 6.20.9: metaph., *the first start*, *beginning* of anything, Man.3.405, etc. 6. *discharge*, *emission*, ὕδατος Arist.*PA* 697^{a}24; βέλους D.S.17.41; τοῦ θορου, τοῦ ᾠοῦ Arist.*GA*756^{a}12; τοῦ κυήματος Id.*HA*608^{a}1; *the dropping* of a foal, ib.576^{a}25. b. *discharge*, *release* of an engine, Ph.*Bel.*58.24. 7. = ἀφεσμός, Arist.*HA* 625^{a}20 (pl.). 8. *release*, ὕδατος *PPetr.*2 p.34 (iii B.C.): hence, in concrete sense, *conduit*, *sluice*, ib.3 p.88, *PFlor.*388.44 (iii A.D.): pl., ἀφέσεις θαλάσσης *channels*, Lxx 2*Ki.*22.16. 9. Astrol., *reckoning of the vital quadrant*, Ptol.*Tetr.*127, cf. Vett.Val.136.2 (but ἀπὸ Λέοντος τὴν ἄφεσιν ποιούμενοι, simply, *starting from..*, Id.31.8).

ἀφεσμός, ὁ, *swarm of bees*, Arist.*HA*629^{a}9.

ἀφεσοφῠλᾰκία, ἡ, *supervision of sluices* (cf. ἄφεσις 8), *PStrassb.* 55.8 (ii A.D.).

ἀφεσταίη, 3 sg. opt. pf. of ἀφίστημι.

ἀφεστήξω, Att. intr. fut. from ἀφέστηκα, I *shall be absent*, *away from*, τινός Pl.*R.*587b; I *shall desert*, X.*An.*2.4.5.

ἀφεστήρ, ῆρος, ὁ, at Cnidus, *president of the* βουλή, *GDI*3505.19, Plu.2.292a.

ἀφεστής· ἀγαθός, Hsch.

ἀφεστίᾱσις, εως, ἡ, *feasting*, Sch.Pl.*Ti.*17b.

ἀφέστιος, ον, *far from hearth and home*, dub. l. in Lxx *Si.*37.11.

ἀφέταιρος, ον, *friendless*, Theopomp.Hist.308; cf. ἀπέταιρος.

ἀφετ-έον, *one must dismiss*, τὴν σκέψιν, τὸ νῦν λεχθέν, etc., Pl.*R.* 376d, *Phdr.*260a, al. 2. ἀφετέος, έα, έον, *to be let go*, *dismissed*, Id.*Euthphr.*15d, Phld.*Mus.*p.89 K. **-εύω**, Astrol., *to be* ἀφέτης I. 2, *Cat.Cod.Astr.*8(4).236. **-ήρ**, ῆρος, ὁ, = ἀφετήριον, *starting-point*, Iamb.*Protr.*21.λη'. **-ήριος**, α, ον, (ἀφίημι) *for letting go*, ἀ. ὄργανα engines *for throwing stones*, etc., J.*BJ*3.5.2, cf. 5.6.3. 2. ἀφετηρία (sc. γραμμή), ἡ, *starting-point of a race*, *CIG*2758 iii *D*7 (Aphrodisias), Sch.Ar.*Eq.*1156: hence ἀ. Διόσκουροι, whose statues adorned the race-course, Paus.3.14.7; ἀ. ἕρμα *AP*9.319 (Philox.): metaph., ἀφετήριον πρὸς μάθησιν S.E.*M.*1.41; ἀ. ἡ ῥητορική Phld.*Rh.*1.223 S. 3. ἀφετηρία· ἀρχή, ἡγεμονία, Hsch. 4. ἀφετήριον (sc. πλοίων), τό, *outlet of a harbour*, Str.11.2.4. 5. *gate* of a sluice, *PLond.*3.1177. 291 (ii A.D.). **-ης**, ου, ὁ, (ἀφίημι) *one who lets off a military engine*, Plb.4.56.3. b. *teacher of ballistic*, *IG*2.465.22. c. *starter* in races, *POxy.*152.1 (vii A.D.). 2. Astrol., *prorogator*, heavenly body which determines the vital quadrant, Ptol.*Tetr.*131. II. Pass., *a freed-slave* among the Spartans, Myro 2. **-ικός**, ή, όν, *determining the vital quadrant*, τόποι Ptol.*Tetr.*127. **-ις**, ιδος, ἡ, fem. of ἀφέτης I. 2, ib.133. **-ος**, ον, (ἀφίημι) *let loose*, *ranging at large*, esp. of sacred flocks that *were free from work*, ἄ. ἀλᾶσθαι γῆς ἐπ' ἐσχάτοις ὅροις A.*Pr.*666; ἀφέτων ὄντων ταύρων ἐν τῷ..ἱερῷ Pl. *Criti.*119d; νέμονται ὥσπερ ἄφετοι Id.*Prt.*320a, cf. *R.*498c, Isoc.5. 127, Call.*Del.*36. II. of persons, *dedicated*, *free from worldly business*, E.*Ion*822, Plu.2.768b; [γένη] ἀπόλυτα καὶ ἄ. Iamb.*Myst.*1.8; ἄ. παντὸς τοῦ δεινοῦ Max.Tyr.3.9. 2. of things, ἄ. ἡμέραι *holidays*, Poll.1.36; νομὴ ἄ. *free* range, of horses, Plu.*Lys.*20; ὁρμαί Ph.2.380, cf. Plu.2.12a; δρόμοι Id.*Cleom.*34; ἐξουσία τοῦ λέγειν Phld.*Herc.*862. 10; κακουργίαι Id.*Piet.*21; τὸ ἄ. τῆς κόμης Luc.*Dom.*7; τοῦ λόγου Hermog.*Id.*1.6. Adv. -τως, ὁρμᾶν *freely*, Ph.1.135, cf. Dam.*Pr.*307; ἀπολαύει Phld.*D.*3 *Fr.*89. 3. of style, *rambling*, *prolix*, Luc.*Tox.* 56. III. Ἀφέται, pr. n., the place *whence* the Argonauts *loosed* their ship, Hdt.7.193.

ἄφευκτος, ον, *fixed*, *fast*, of gilding or silvering, Zos.Alch.p.157 B.:—hence **ἀφευκτότης**, ητος, ἡ, *incapacity for sublimation*, Olymp. Alch.p.77 B., and **ἀφευξία**, ἡ, ibid.

ἀφεύρεμα, ατος, τό, *deficiency*, *UPZ*112, *PTeb.*8.23 (iii B.C.), *BGU* 1118.14 (ii B.C.); *loss* on resale, *PPetr.*3 p.232 (iii B.C.).

ἀφευρίσκω, pf. ἀφεύρηκα, *to be deficient*, *PTeb.*8.19 (iii B.C.).

ἀφεύς· ἀδύνατος, Hsch.

ἀφεύω, aor. 1 ἄφευσα Semon. (v. infr.), Ar.*Th.*590: pf. part. Pass. ἠφευμένος A.*Fr.*310: aor. part. ἀφευθείς Suid.:—*singe off*, ἀφεύων τὴν..τρίχα Ar.*Ec.*13: abs., *singe clear of hair*, Id.*Th.*216, al.:—Pass., καλῶς ἠφευμένος ὁ χοῖρος well *singed*, A. l.c. 2. *toast*, *roast*, κρέα Semon.24; φασήλους Ar.*Pax*1144.

ἀφέψᾰλος, ον, *without a spark of fire*, Hsch.

ἀφεψ-εῖν· βάπτειν τρίχα, Hsch. **-ημα**, ατος, τό, *decoction*, Dsc. 2.107, Lyc.ap.Orib.8.25.2, Ruf.ib.7.26.67, Gal.13.9. **-ησις**, εως, ἡ, = ἄφεψις, *PPetr.*3 p.315, Sch.Lyc.156.

ἀφεψιάομαι, *retire from intercourse*, ἀφεψιασάμην, = ἀφωμίλησα, S. *Fr.*138; v. ἑψία.

ἄφεψις, εως, ἡ, *boiled down pitch*, Thphr.*HP*9.2.5.

ἀφέψω (later -άω, part. -ῶντες Olymp.*in Mete.*164.35), Ion. **ἀπέψω**:—*purify* or *refine by boiling off* the refuse, *boil down*, καρπόν Hdt. 2.94; τι εἰς τὸ τρίτον Dsc.5.6; esp. *free of dross*, *refine*, χρυσίον καθαρώτατον ἀπεψήσας Id.4.166; τὸν Δῆμον ἀφεψήσας..καλὸν ἐξ αἰσχροῦ πεποίηκα Ar.*Eq.*1321, cf. 1336:—Pass., ὕδωρ ἀπεψημένον Hdt. 1.188, cf. Hp.*Aër.*8, Dsc.2.107. 2. *boil off*, τοῦ ὕδατος μέρος τι Arist.*Mete.*359^{a}30:—Pass., ἀφέψεται τὸ ἁλμυρὸν Id.*Pr.*933^{b}15; τοῦ ὀγδόου μόνον ἀφεψηθέντος Plb.34.10.12; cf. ἄπεφθος.

ἀφέωνται, v. ἀφίημι.

ἀφή, ἡ, (ἅπτω) *lighting*, *kindling*, περὶ λύχνων ἁφάς about lamp-*lighting* time, Hdt.7.215, cf. *PTeb.*88.12 (ii B.C.), D.H.11.33, D.S.19. 31, Ath.12.526c. II. (ἅπτομαι) *touch*, ἐπώνυμον δὲ τῶν Διὸς γέννημ' ἁφῶν (Wieseler for γεννημάτων) τέξεις..Ἔπαφον A.*Pr.*850. 2. *sense of touch*, Pl.*R.*523e, cf. Arist.*EN*1118^{b}1, *de An.*424^{a}12; ἀκριβεστάτην ..τῶν αἰσθήσεων τὴν ἁφήν Id.*HA*494^{b}16; ἡ ἁφὴ ἐν ταῖς αἰσθήσεσι παρέσπαρται Luc.*Salt.*70. 3. *touch of the harp-strings*, metaph., ἐμμελοῦς ἁφῆς καὶ κρούσεως Plu.*Per.*15; οὐχὶ συμφώνους ἁφάς Damox. 2.42. 4. *grip*, in wrestling, etc., ἁφὴν ἐνδιδόναι αὑτοῦ Plu.2.86f: metaph., τοῖς ἀθληταῖς τῆς λέξεως ἰσχυρὰς τὰς ἁ. προσεῖναι δεῖ καὶ ἀφύκτους τὰς λαβάς D.H.*Dem.*18; ἁφὰς ἔχει καὶ τόνους ἰσχυροὺς Id.*Lys.* 13; ἁ. εἶχεν ἡ συνδιαίτησις ἄφυκτον, of Cleopatra, Plu.*Ant.*27. 5. *sand sprinkled over wrestlers*, *to enable them to get a grip of one another*, Arr.*Epict.*3.15.4; ἁφῇ πηλώσασθαι *IG*4.955 (Epid., ii A.D.). 6. Math., *contact* of surfaces, etc., Arist.*Ph.*227^{a}17, *Metaph.*1014^{b}22, al.; *point of contact*, Euc.*Phaen.*p.16 M., al.; *of intersection*, Papp. 988.9, cf. Alex.Aphr.*in Top.*24.16. 7. in pl., *stripes*, *strokes*, Lxx 2*Ki.*7.14, al. 8. *infection*, esp. of *leprosy*, ib.*Le.*13.6, al.: generally, *plague*, Aq.*Ge.*12.17, Aq., Sm.*Ex.*11.1. III. *junction*, *point of contact* in the body, Arist.*GC*326^{b}12, 327^{a}12; *ligament*, *Ep. Eph.*4.16, *Ep.Col.*2.19.

ἀφηβάω, *to be past the prime of life*, ἀφηβηκώς Lib.*Decl.*23.59; τὴν ἀκμὴν τῶν παθῶν ἀφηβῶντες Ph.1.516; ἀφηβηκότες κλάδοι Poll.1.236: pf. part. Pass., Id.2.10,18.

ἀφηγ-έομαι, Ion. ἀπηγ-, *lead the way from* a point, and so generally, *lead the way*, *go first*, Pl.*Lg.*760d, etc.; οἱ ἀφηγούμενοι *the van*, X.*HG*4.8.37; ἀ. τῆς ἀποικίας, τῆς ἀγέλης, *to be leader of..*, Arist.*Fr.* 514, *Mir.*831^{a}22; πρεσβείας Str.1.3.1; τῆς σχολῆς D.L.4.14; τῆς Ἀκαδημείας Phld.*Acad.Ind.*p.57 M.; ζῴων Porph.*Abst.*2.38; οὐκ ἀφηγησαμένῳ δὴ τὸ τέλος ἐγένετο died without ever *taking up his command*, Phld.*Acad.Ind.*p.61 M. II. *tell*, *relate*, Hdt.1.24, al., E.*Supp.* 186; *assert*, Aret.*CA*2.7:—pf. in pass. sense, ἀπήγηταί μοί τι Hdt. 5.62; τὸ ἀπηγημένον *what has been told*, Id.1.207, cf. 9.26. **-ημα**, Ion. ἀπήγ-, ατος, τό, *tale*, *narrative*, Hdt.2.3. II. *guiding*, *leading*, Lxx 4*Ma.*14.6. **-ημᾰτικός**, ή, όν, *narrative*, λόγος Hermog.*Id.*1.

10; σχήματα Aristid.*Rh.*1 p.500 S., cf. D.H.*Rh.*1.8. Adv. -κῶς Hermog.*Id.*1.1, Procl.*in Prm.*p.477 S. **-ημων,** ονος, ὁ, = ἀφηγητής, Hsch. (prob. should be ἀφηγεμών). **-ησις,** εως, Ion. **ἀπήγ-,** ιος, ἡ, *narration*, ἀξιωτάτη ἀπηγήσιος worth *telling*, Hdt.2.70; οὐκ ἀξίως ἀ. in a way not fit *to be told*, Id.3.125; ἱστορίας D.H.2.7; πραγμάτων J.*BJ*1.11.4, cf. Arr.*An.Prooem.*2, Luc.*Hist.Conscr.*30, Aristid.1.154 J., Hermog.*Id.*1.1, al.; *report*, *SIG*578.54 (Teos, ii B.C.). **-ητέον,** *one must explain*, Porph.*Chr.*94. **-ητήρ,** ῆρος, ὁ, *guide*, κελεύθου *AP*14.114 (-ήτορα cod.). **-ητής,** οῦ, ὁ, = foreg., Hsch. **-ητικός,** ή, όν, *tending to make*, Vett.Val.15.27. **-οῦσα·** μεταστρέφουσα, Hsch.

ἀφηδύνω, (ἡδύς) *sweeten*, Luc.*Am.*3; τὰς ἀκοάς Ph.1.353:—Pass., τὸ ἦθος Plu.*Dio* 17.

ἀφηθέω, *filter off*, Thphr.*Lap.*56.

ἀφηκές· εὐήθες, Hsch.

ἀφήκω, *arrive at* or *have arrived*, οἷ πάντα δεῖ ἀφήκειν Pl.*R.*530e; ἐς θεούς D.C.52.4; ἐς πρῖσιν ἀ. *is a case* for operation, Hp.*VC*9. II. *depart*, πολὺ ἀπό τινων D.C.41.8.

ἀφηλῐκιότης, ητος, ἡ, *childhood*, *nonage*, Eust.1282.24, *PLond.*1.113(1).18 (vi A.D.). **ἀφήλῐκος,** ον, = sq., *PMasp.*6.2 (vi A.D.).

ἀφῆλιξ, Ion. **ἀπῆλιξ,** ῐκος, ὁ, ἡ, *beyond youth*, *elderly*, ἀνὴρ ἀπηλικέστερος Hdt.3.14, cf. Hp.*Mul.*2.120, Alciphr.1.6; ἀφηλικεστάτην Pherecr.206: acc. to Phryn.*PS* p.1 B., only in Comp. and Sup.; but Posit. in *h.Cer.*140, Cratin.369, Phryn.Com.67 (who used it of *young* persons, cf. ἀφηλικεστέραν· νεωτέραν, Hsch., and so later Aristobul.Jud.ap.Eus.*PE*8.10). II. *minor*, *infant*, in law, *POxy.*487.5.

ἀφηλῐώτης, ου, ὁ, = ἀπηλιώτης (q.v.), *IG*14.1308, Apion ap.J.*Ap.*2.2:—hence Adj. **ἀφηλῐωτικός,** ή, όν, Ptol.*Geog.*1.11, Gem.2.11.

ἀφηλόω, (ἧλος) *detach*, in Pass., *Stud.Pal.*22.54.16 (ii A.D.); τοῦ σώματος Porph.*Abst.*1.57:—hence Subst. **ἀφήλωσις,** εως, ἡ, *Gloss.*

ἄφημαι, *sit apart*: part. ἀφήμενος Il.15.106.

ἀφημερεύω, *to be absent for a day*, μήτ' ἀ. μήτ' ἀποκοιτεῖν Decr.ap. D.18.37, cf. *PHib.*148 (iii B.C.), etc.

ἀφημερινός, ή, όν, *daily*, Alex.Aphr.*Pr.*1.83; πυρετός *POxy.*1151.36 (v A.D.). **ἀφήμερος,** ον, *absent for a day*, *PGiss.*2.27 (ii B.C.), *PTeb.*104.28 (i B.C.), etc. **ἀφημιάστους·** ἀγροικίας, Hsch.

ἀφημιζεσθαι· ἀθερίζεσθαι, Hsch.

ἀφήμιστος, ον, = sq., Vett.Val.104.22.

ἄφημος, ον, and **ἀφήμων,** ον, (φήμη) *unknown*, Hsch.: also Adv. ἀφήμως· ἐν κόσμῳ, ἡσυχῇ, Id., cf. *h.Ap.*171 ap.Th.3.104.

ἀφημοῦντας· ἀγροίκους, Hsch.; cf. ἀφημιάστους.

ἀφηνα, ἀφῆναι, v. ἀφάνεω.

ἀφηνῐ-άζω, (ἡνία) *refuse to obey the reins*, Ph.1.85, Luc.*DDeor.*25.1; of persons, *turn restive*, *rebel*, Ph.1.125, al., Str.17.3.25, Hdn.1.4.5: c. gen., *rebel against*, συντάγματος J.*BJ*4.7.1, cf. Luc.*Bis Acc.*20. II. Med. or Pass., ἀφηνιάζετο· ἐχωρίζετο, Hsch. **-ᾰσις,** εως, ἡ, = sq., Hierocl.*in CA*16 p.456 M. **-ασμός,** ὁ, *refusal to obey the reins*, Ph.1.311 (pl.): metaph., *rebellion*, ib.171, al. **-αστής,** οῦ, ὁ, *refusing the reins*, ἵππος ib.114; *rebellious*, ib.337, al.

ἀφηράαν· μακράν, Hsch.

ἀφηρωΐζω, aor. -ηρώϊξα, (ἥρως) *canonize as a hero*, *IG*12(3).864, al. (Thera).

ἀφῆς· ἀδύνατος, ἄλαλος (ἄλλος cod.), Hsch., cf. ἀφεύς; perh. to be read in Call.*Hec.*1.2.3.

ἀφήσασθαι· ἅψασθαι, Hsch.

ἀφησῠχάζω, *settle down*, *be quiet*, Hp.*Ep.*12, Plb.2.64.5, *CPR*232.4 (ii/iii A.D.). II. c. acc., *pass over in silence*, Ph.2.3.

ἀφητορεία· μαντεία, Hsch.

ἀφήτωρ, ορος, ὁ, (ἀφίημι) *archer*, epith. of Apollo, Il.9.404:—the Sch. gives an alternative expl., *prophet* (from ἀ- copul., and φημί), cf. Orac. in *App.Anth.*6.149.7; cf. ὁμοφήτωρ.

ἄφθα (A), ἡ, (ἅπτω) *an infantile disease*, *thrush*, mostly in pl., ἄφθαι Hp.*Aph.*3.24.

ἄφθα (B), or **ἆφθα,** ἡ, = νάφθα, Ph.*Bel.*94.9: **ἄφθας,** α, ὁ, Str.*Chr.*16.8.

ἀφθαρ-σία, ἡ, *incorruption*, *immortality*, Epicur.*Ep.*1 p.28 U., Phld.*D.*3.9, al., Lxx *Wi.*2.23, Ph.1.37, al., *Ep.Rom.*2.7, Simp.*in Cael.*298.16, etc. II. *integrity*, *sincerity*, *Ep.Eph.*6.24. **-τος,** ον, *uncorrupted*, *undecaying*, Ph.*Bel.*67.37. II. *incorruptible*, Epicur.*Ep.*1 p.29 U., al., Phld.*D.*3 *Fr.*88b, al., Diog.Oen.63, al. 2. *eternal*, Arist.*APo.*85b18, *Cael.*270a21; *immortal*, πνεῦμα Lxx *Wi.*12.1; τὸ πᾶν Ocell.1.10, D.S.1.6; ψυχαί D.H.8.62; θεός *Ep.Rom.*1.23; γένος Ph.1.689; οἱ νεκροὶ ἐγερθήσονται ἄ. 1 *Ep.Cor.*15.52; of poems, Μοῦσαι *Epigr.Gr.*226.5 (Teos). Adv. -τως, τιμᾶν ib.919.10 (Lycia).

ἄφθας, v. ἄφθα (B).

ἀφθάστως, Adv., gloss on ἀκιχήτως, Sch.Il.17.75.

ἀφθάω, *suffer from* ἄφθαι, Hp.*Nat.Mul.*60, al.

ἀφθεγγής, ές, *speechless*, *AB*473.

ἀφθεγκ-τέω, *to be speechless*, Poll.5.146. **-τί,** Adv. of sq., *without speech*, ib.147. **-τος,** ον, = ἄφθογγος, *voiceless*, μηνυτήρ A.*Eu.*245; στόμα (of a pen) *AP*9.162; ἀστράγαλοι ib.7.427.14 (Antip. Sid.). 2. of places, etc., *where none may speak*, τῷδ' ἐν ἀφθέγκτῳ νάπει S.*OC*156 (lyr.). II. Pass., *unspeakable*, *unutterable*, B.*Fr.*2.2, Pl.*Sph.*238c. Adv. -τως Iamb.*Myst.*7.4.

ἄφθησις, εως, ἡ, = ἄφθα (A), *Hippiatr.*61.

ἀφθιβόρος, *one who eats greedily*, Hsch.

ἀφθῐτό-μητις, ιος, ὁ, *of immortal counsel*, Orph.*Fr.*66. **-μῖσος,** ον, *of undying hatred*, Man.4.234.

ἄφθῐτος, ον, (φθίνω) *not liable to perish*, *undecaying*, *imperishable*, freq. in Hom. (mostly in Il.) and Trag.: 1. of things, σκῆπτρον πατρώϊον ἄ. αἰεί Il.2.46; χρυσέη ἴτυς ἄ. 5.724; καλὸν θρόνον ἄ. αἰεί 14.238; Ἡφαίστου δόμος 18.370; ἄ. ἄμπελοι Od.9.133; ἄντρον Pi.*I.*8(7).41; πυρὸς φέγγος A.*Ch.*1037; Γᾶ S.*Ant.*339 (lyr.). 2. of persons, *immortal*, of the gods, *h.Merc.*326; Στύξ Hes.*Th.*389, 397; of Tantalus, Pi.*O.*1.63; ἄ. ὑμνοπόλος, of Anacreon, Simon.184; ἀφθίτους θεῖναι βροτούς A.*Eu.*724; γέννας ἀφθίτου λαχόντες S.*Fr.*278. 3. of men's thoughts, etc., Ζεὺς ἄφθιτα μήδεα εἰδώς Il.24.88, Hes.*Th.*545; κλέος ἄ. Il.9.413; ἄ. ὄπις *unceasing* care, Pi.*P.*8.72 (v.l. ἄφθονος); ἄ. γνῶμαι *unchanging*, *unchangeable*, S.*Fr.*414; ἄφθιτα μηδομένοισι Ar.*Av.*689.—Poet. and later Prose, δόξα Plu.2.723e; prob. in Arist.*Cael.*270a26.

ἀφθογγία, ἡ, *speechlessness*, λίθου Callistr.*Stat.*9.

ἄφθογγος, ον, *voiceless*, *speechless*, *h.Cer.*198, Hdt.1.116; φόβῳ ἄ. A.*Pers.*206; ἄ. εἶναι remain *silent*, Id.*Eu.*448; ἄ. ἄγγελος a beacon-fire, Thgn.549; ἀφθόγγῳ φθεγγομένα στόματι, of an epitaph, *Epigr. Gr.*234.4 (Smyrna). 2. ἄφθογγα (sc. γράμματα) *mutes*, Pl.*Phlb.*18c, *Cra.*424c. II. Pass., = ἄφατος, *not to be spoken of*, γάμοι S.*Fr.*618 (dub.).

ἀφθόν-ητος, ον, *unenvied*, A.*Ag.*939; *beyond the reach of envy*, αἶνος Pi.*O.*10(11).7. II. Act., *bearing no grudge against*, τινί ib.13.25. Adv. -τως Eust.823.8. 2. *bountiful*, *BGU*984.27 (iv A.D.). **-ία,** ἡ, *freedom from envy* or *grudging*, *liberality*, πᾶσαν προθυμίαν καὶ ἀφθονίαν εἴχομεν ἀλλήλους διδάσκειν Pl.*Prt.*327b. II. of things, *plenty*, *abundance*, Pi.*N.*3.9; τῶν ὠφελούντων Pl.*Ap.*24e, cf. 23c; κακῶν Men.589; ἀφθονίας οὔσης ὀργίζεσθαι *abundance of matter* for.., Lys.12.2; ἀ. ἦν καταπίνειν Telecl.1.10; τοσαύτην ἀ. κατηγοριῶν D.21.102; εἰς ἀ. in *abundance*, X.*An.*7.1.33; opp. ἀφορία, Id.*Smp.*4.55: pl., καρπῶν ἀφθονίῃσι Emp.78. III. = κακία, Hsch. **-ος,** ον, *without envy*: hence, I. Act., *free from envy*, Pi.*O.*6.7; ἄνδρα τύραννον ἄ. ἔδει εἶναι Hdt.3.80, cf. Pl.*R.*500a. Adv. -νως Id.*Lg.*731a. 2. *ungrudging*, *bounteous*, of earth, ἄφθονε δαῖμον *h.Hom.*30.16; ἀφθόνῳ μένει, ἀφθόνῳ χερί, A.*Ag.*305, E.*Med.*612; ἀ. λειμῶνες Pl.*Sph.*222a, cf. *Ax.*371c. II. more freq. (esp. in Prose) *not grudged*, *plentiful*, ἄ. πάντα παρέσται *h.Ap.*536; καρπὸν πολλόν τε καὶ ἄ. Hes.*Op.*118; πλοῦτος Sol.33.5; χρυσὸς ἄ. Hdt.6.132, cf. 7.83; χώρῃ..ἄ. λίην Id.2.6; ἄ. βίοτος A.*Fr.*196; πόλιν ἀφθονεστάτην χρήμασιν Eup.307; χώρα πολλὴ καὶ ἄ. X.*An.*5.6.25; ἄφθονα καὶ πολλὰ ἔχων εἰπεῖν Aeschin.3.203; λόγοι ἄ. D.21.136; ἐν ἀφθόνοις βιοτεύειν to live in *plenty*, X.*An.*3.2.25; ἐν ἀφθόνοις τραφείς D.18.256; τὸ χαίρειν ἄφθονον εἰπών *IG*12(7).445 (Amorgos). 2. *unenvied*, *provoking no envy*, ὄλβος A.*Ag.*471 (lyr.). III. irreg. Comp. -έστερος Pi.*O.*2.104, A.*Fr.*72, Pl.*R.*460b: Sup. -έστατος Eup. l. c.; regul. forms -ώτερος, -ώτατος, X.*An.*7.6.28, *Cyr.*5.4.40, etc. IV. Adv., πάντα δ' ἀφθόνως πάρα Sol.38; ἀ. ἔχειν τινός to have *enough* of it, Pl.*Grg.*494c; ἀ. διδόναι Arist.*Pol.*1314b4; πολλά με διδάσκεις ἀ. Philem.154; ξένων καὶ ἐντοπίων ἀ. ζήσας *IG*5(2).491 (Megalop., ii/iii A.D.).

ἀφθορία, ἡ, *incorruption*, prob. l. for ἀδιαφθορία in *Ep.Tit.*2.7, cf. Them.*in Ph.*82.22.

ἄφθορος, ον, *uncorrupt*, of young persons, Artem.5.95; κούρη *AP*9.229 (Marc. Arg.), cf. Lxx *Es.*2.3, D.S.4.7; παῖς Sor.1.81; of a man, *IG*14.2088. II. *pure*, *unadulterated*, γάλα *BGU*1107.7 (i B.C.), al.

ἀφθώδης, ες, *suffering from* ἄφθαι, στόματα Hp.*Epid.*3.3.

ἀφία, ἡ, *lesser celandine*, *Ranunculus Ficaria*, Thphr.*HP*7.7.3.

ἀφίας· βωμός, Hsch.

ἀφιδρόω, *sweat off*, *get rid of* a thing *by sweating*, Hp.*Epid.*7.58, Arist.*Pr.*868a37, *Com.Adesp.*3 D.:—Pass., *exude*, ἀπό τινος Dsc.5.1.

ἀφίδρ-ῠμα, ατος, τό, *thing set up*, esp. *image* of the gods (cf. Suid. s.v.), *IG*2².1046.13, *Inscr.Prien.*112.115, D.H.2.22, Str.12.5.3, Plu.*Num.*8, etc.; χρυσοῦς μόσχος, τὸ Αἰγυπτίων ἀ. Ph.1.256. 2. *shrine*, *temple*, Cic.*Att.*13.29.1(2), Str.6.2.5, 16.4.4. II. *copy taken from such image* or *shrine*, D.S.15.49; ἱερὸν Ἀσκληπιοῦ ἀ. τοῦ ἐν Τρίκκῃ Str.8.4.4. **-ῡσις,** εως, ἡ, *setting up* a statue, Id.8.7.2, Plu.2.1136a. **-υσμα·** ἱερόν, Hsch. **-ύω,** *remove to another settlement*, *transport*, in Med., πατρίδος θεοί μ' ἀφιδρύσαντο γῆς ἐς βάρβαρ' ἤθη E.*Hel.*273:—Pass., *to be transferred*, of a cult, ἀφιδρυθῆναι ἐκ Κρήτης D.S.4.79. II. *make statues* or *temples after a model*, Δήλιον τὸ ἱερὸν Ἀπόλλωνος ἐκ Δήλου -υμένον Str.9.2.7, cf. 12.3.32. III. simply, = ἱδρύω, *set up*, in Pass., Harp. s.v. Πάνδημος, Jul.*Or.*1.29d, *APl.*4.260 (in later form of aor. -ύνθην). [ῠ in pres., ῡ in fut., aor. 1, pf. Pass.]

ἀφίδρ-ωσις [φῐ], εως, ἡ, *sweating off*, Arist.*Pr.*867a13 (pl.), Thphr.*Sud.*22 (pl.), Sor.2.46 (pl.). **-ωτήριον,** τό, *natural vapour-bath*, Herod.Med.ap.Orib.10.40.1 (pl.).

ἀφῐερ-ισμένα· περικεκαθαρμένα, Hsch. **-όω,** *hallow*, *consecrate*, τῷ Κρόνῳ Ath.3.110b, cf. D.S.1.90 (Pass.), Plu.2.271a; πόλιν τῇ Λητῷ καὶ τῷ Ἀπόλλωνι *OGI*746.2 (Xanthus, ii B.C.). II. Pass., ταῦτ' ἀφιερώμεθα *I have had these expiatory rites performed*, A.*Eu.*451. **-ωσις,** εως, ἡ, *hallowing*, *dedication*, D.S.1.90, Plu.*Publ.*15; χρημάτων *BMus.Inscr.*481*.386 (Ephesus, ii A.D.).

ἀφιζάνω, *rise from one's seat*, Suid.:—also **ἀφίζω,** Hsch.

ἀφίημι, 2 sg. ἀφίης Pl.*Phlb.*50d, etc., 3 sg. ἀφίησι, also ἀφιεῖ, Ion. ἀπιεῖ Hdt.2.96, 1 pl. ἀφίεμεν Ar.*Nu.*1426; imper. ἀφίει Id.*V.*428; impf. ἀφίειν, with double augm. ἠφίειν Pl.*Euthd.*293a; 3 sg. ἀφίει Il.1.25, *IG*2².777.15, D.6.20, Ion. ἀπίει Hdt.4.157, ἠφίει Th.2.49, Pl.*Ly.*222b, ἤφιε *Ev.Marc.*11.16; 2 pl. ἀφίετε D.23.188; 3 pl. ἀφίεσαν

E.*Heracl.*821, Th.2.76, D.21.79, etc., ἠφίεσαν X.*HG*4.6.11, ἠφίουν Is. 6.40 (dub.): fut. ἀφήσω Il.2.263, etc., Ion. ἀπ- Hdt.7.193: pf. ἀφεῖκα X.*An.*2.3.13, D.56.26: aor. 1 ἀφῆκα, Ion. ἀπ-, Ep. ἀφέηκα, used in ind. only, Il.23.841, etc.: aor. 2 ind. only in dual and pl., ἀφέτην, ἀφεῖμεν, ἀφεῖτε or ἄφετε, ἀφεῖσαν or ἄφεσαν; imper. ἄφες, subj. ἀφῶ, opt. ἀφείην (2 pl. ἀφεῖτε Th.1.139), inf. ἀφεῖναι, part. ἀφείς:—**Med.**, ἀφίεμαι, Ion. ἀπίεμαι, Hdt.3.101, Th.2.60, etc.: impf. 3 sg. ἀφίετο Od.23.240, D.25.47: fut. ἀφήσομαι E.*Hel.*1629: aor. 2 ἀφείμην X.*Hier.*7.11; imper. ἀφοῦ, ἄφεσθε, S.*OT*1521, Ar.*Ec.*509; inf. -έσθαι Isoc.6.83, part. -έμενος Pl.*R.*354b; Arc. inf. ἀφεῶσθαι *SIG*306.19 (Tegea, iv B.C.):—**Pass.**, pf. ἀφεῖμαι S.*Ant.*1165, Pl.*Lg.*635a; inf. ἀφεῖσθαι *SIG*577.77 (Milet., iii/ii B.C.): plpf. 2 sg. ἀφεῖσο Men.*Epit.*572: rarer pf. 3 pl. ἀφέωνται *Ev.Jo.*20.23, imper. ἀφεώσθω *IG*5(2).6.14: aor. ἀφείθην E.*Ph.*1377, ἀφέθην Batr.87, Ion. ἀπείθην Hdt.6.112; later Aeol. inf. ἀφέθην *Milet.*3 No.152.34 (ii B.C.): fut. ἀφεθήσομαι Pl.*R.*472a, etc. [ῑ mostly in Ep. (except in augm. tenses): ῐ always in Att. Hom. also has ἀφῑετε, metri gr., Od.7.126]:—*send forth, discharge*, of missiles, ἔγχος, δίσκον ἀφῆκεν, Il.10.372, 23.432; ἀφῆκ' ἀργῆτα κεραυνόν 8.133; ἀπῆκε βέλος Hdt.9.18, etc.: hence in various senses, ἀ. ἑαυτὸν ἐπί τι *throw oneself* upon, *give oneself up* to it, Pl.*R.*373d; ἀ. αὑτὸν εἰς τὴν πολιτείαν Plu.*Alc.*13; ἀ. γλῶσσαν *let loose* one's tongue, *make* utterance, Hdt.2.15, E.*Hipp.*991; ἀ. φθογγήν ib.418; ἔπος S.*OC*731; φωνάς D.18.218; γόους E.*El.*59 (v. infr. II. 2); ἀρὰς ἀφῆκας παιδί Id.*Hipp.*1324; ἀ. θυμὸν ἔς τινας *give vent to*.. (v. infr. II. 2), S.*Ant.*1088; ὀργὴν εἴς τινα *vent* upon.., D.22.58; ἀ. δάκρυα *shed* tears, Aeschin.3.153; ἀ. παντοδαπὰ χρώματα *change* colour in all ways, Pl.*Ly.*222b; freq. of liquids, etc., *emit*, ἀ. τὸ ὑγρόν, τὸν θολόν, τὸ σπέρμα, etc., Arist.*HA*487^{a}18, 524^{a}12, 489^{a}9; ἀ. τὸ ᾠόν, τὸ κύημα, ib.568^{b}30, ^{a}22; of plants, ἄνθος ἀφιεῖσαι *putting forth*, Od.7.126, cf. Thphr.*HP*7.7.3; of a spider, ἀ. ἀράχνιον Arist.*HA*555^{b}5; ἱδρῶτα Plu.*Mar.*26; *put forth, produce*, καρπόν Thphr.*HP*3.4.5; φύλλον ib. 6.5.1 (but ἀ. σπέρμα *leave* issue, *Ev.Marc.*12.22):—Pass., *to be emitted*, Il.4.77 (tm.); of troops, *to be let go, launched* against the enemy, Hdt.6.112. 2. *let fall* from one's grasp, Il.12.221; opp. κατέχω, Plu.2.508d; πόντιον ἀ. τινά E.*Hec.*797. 3. *give up* or *hand over to*, τὴν Ἰωνίην τοῖσι βαρβάροισι Hdt.9.106; ἐχθροῖς αἶαν A.*Th.*306; ἀ. τινὰ δημόσια εἶναι Th.2.13:—Pass., ἡ Ἀττικὴ ἀπεῖτο ἤδη Hdt.8.49. II. *send away*, 1. of persons, κακῶς ἀφίει Il.1.25; αὐτὸν δὲ κλαίοντα.. ἀφήσω 2.263. b. *let go, loose, set free*, ζωόν τινα ἀ. 20.464; *let loose*, βοῦς Hdt.4.69; περιστεράς Alex.62.3; ἀ. Αἴγιναν αὐτόνομον Th.1.139; ἀ. ἐλεύθερον, ἀζήμιον, Pl.*R.*591a, *Lg.*765c; τινὰς ἀφορολογήτους Plb.18.46.5; ἀφέντ' ἐᾶν τινα S.*Aj.*754, cf. E.*Fr.*463; ἐς οἴκους, ἐκ γῆς, S.*OT*320, E.*IT*739: c. acc. pers. et gen. rei, *release from* a thing, ἀποικίης Hdt.4.157: in legal sense, *acquit of* a charge or engagement, φόνου τινα D.37.59 (abs., ἐὰν αἰδέσηται καὶ ἀφῇ ibid.); συναλλαγμάτων Id.33.12: c. acc. only, *acquit*, Antipho 2.1.2, etc. (v. infr. 2 c):—Pass., κινδύνου ἀφιέμενοι Th.4.106; τοὺς γέροντας τοὺς ἀφειμένους *released* from duty, Arist.*Pol.*1275^{a}15; ἐγκλημάτων ἀφεῖσο Men.*Epit.*572. c. *let go, dissolve, disband*, of an army or fleet, Hdt.1.77, etc.; *dismiss*, δικαστήρια (opp. λύειν ἐκκλησίαν) Ar.*V.*595. d. *put away, divorce*, γυναῖκα Hdt.5.39; ἀ. γάμους *break off* a marriage, E.*Andr.*973; ἀ. τὸν υἱόν *disown* him, Arist.*EN*1163^{b}22 (but with metaph. from *releasing* a debtor). e. *dedicate*, τὰ νεογνὰ τῷ θεῷ X.*Cyn.*5.14; ἱερὸν.. ἄβατον ἀφεῖτο Pl.*Criti.*116c. 2. of things, *get rid of*, ἀφέτην πολυκαγκέα δίψαν Il.11.642; ἀφίει μένος [ἔγχεος] *slackened* its force, 13.444; ἀ. ὀργὴν *put away* wrath (v. supr. I. 1), A.*Pr.*317; ὀργήν τινι Arr.*An.*1.10.6; γόους (v. supr. I. 1) E.*Or.*1022; νόσημα Hp.*Prorrh.*2.39; ἀ. πνεῦμα, ψυχήν, *give up* the ghost, E.*Hec.*571, *Or.*1171: in Prose, *give up, leave off*, μόχθον Hdt.1.206; ξυμμαχίαν, σπονδάς, Th.5.78, 115, etc.:—Med., ἀ. τὸ προλέγειν D.S.19.1. b. ἀ. πλοῖον ἐς.. *loose* ship for a place, Hdt.5.42. c. in legal sense (v. supr. 1 b), c. dat. pers. et acc. rei, ἀ. τινὶ αἰτίην *remit* him a charge, Id.6.30; τὰς ἁμαρτάδας Id.8.140.β', cf. *Ev.Matt.*6.12, al.; τὰς δίκας.. ἀφίεσαν τοῖς ἐπιτρόποις D.21.79; ἀ. τινὶ εἰς ἐλευθερίαν χιλίας δραχμάς Id.59.30, cf. *IG*2^2.43 *A* 27; ἀ. πληγάς τινι *excuse* him a flogging, Ar.*Nu.*1426; ἀ. ὅρκον Jusj. in Lexap.And.1.98; φόρον Plb.21.24.8 (Pass.); δάνειόν τινι *Ev.Matt.*18.27. III. *leave alone, pass by*, Hdt.3.95, etc.; *neglect*, τὰ θεῖα S.*OC*1537; τὸν καιρόν D.1.8; λέκτρων εὐνάς A.*Pers.*544: folld. by a predicate, ἀφύλακτον ἀ. τὴν ἑωυτῶν *leave* unguarded, Hdt.8.70; ἄτιμον, ἔρημον ἀ. τινά, S.*OC*1279, *Ant.*887; ἀ. τινὰς ὀρφανοὺς *Ev.Jo.*14.18; ἀ. τι ἀόριστον Arist.*Pol.*1265^{a}39; *leave*, περὶ κινήσεως, ὅθεν ὑπάρχει, τοῖς ἄλλοις ἀφεῖσαν Id.*Metaph.*985^{b}20, cf. 987^{b}14:—Pass., esp. in pf. imper., ἀφείσθω ἐπὶ τοῦ παρόντος *missum fiat*, Id.*EN*1166^{a}34, cf. *Pol.*1286^{a}5, 1289^{b}12. 2. c. acc. et inf., ἀ. τὸ πλοῖον φέρεσθαι *let* the boat be carried away, Hdt.1.194; μὴ ἀφεῖναί με ἐπὶ ξένης ἀδιαφορηθῆναι *PLond.*2.144.14 (i A.D.). IV. c. acc. pers. et inf., *suffer, permit* one to do a thing, ἀ. τινὰ ἀποπλέειν Hdt.3.25, cf. 6.62, al., etc.: with inf. understood, ἡνίκα προῖκ' ἀφιᾶσιν (sc. θεᾶσθαι) οἱ θεατρῶναι Thphr.*Char.*30.6: c. subj., ἄφες ἐκβάλω *Ev.Matt.*7.4, cf. Arr.*Epict.*1.9.15; ἄφες ἐγὼ θρηνήσω *POxy.*413.184 (i A.D.); ἄφες ἵνα.. Arr.*Epict.*4.13.19; οὐκ ἤφιεν ἵνα... *Ev.Marc.*11.16:—Pass., ἀφείθη σχολάζειν Arist.*Metaph.*981^{b}24. V. seemingly intr. (sc. στρατόν, ναῦς, etc.), *break up, march, sail*, etc., Hdt.7.193; ἀ. ἐς τὸ πέλαγος Th.7.19; cf. II. 2 b. 2. c. inf., *give up* doing, ἀφεὶς σκοπεῖν τὰ δίκαια Diph.94.

B. Med., *send forth from oneself*, much like Act.; θορήν Hdt.3.101. 2. *loose* something *of one's own from*, δειρῆς δ' οὔ πω.. ἀφίετο πήχεε λευκώ she *loosed* not *her* arms *from off* my neck, Od.23.240. 3. freq. in Att. c. gen. only, τέκνων ἀφοῦ *let go of* the children! S.*OT*1521; τοῦ κοινοῦ τῆς σωτηρίας ἀ. Th.2.60; λόγων Pl.*Grg.*458c, Aeschin.1.178; μὴ ἀφίεσο τοῦ Θεαιτήτου, ἀλλ' ἐρώτα Pl.*Tht.*146b, etc.; ἀφεῖσθαι τοῦ δικαίου τούτου D.37.1; ἀφέμενος τῆς ἰαμβικῆς ἰδέας Arist.*Po.*1449^{b}8.

ἀφῑκάνω [ᾰ], Ep. = ἀφικνέομαι, only pres. and impf., *arrive at*, mostly c. acc., Od.14.159, al.; πρὸς τεῖχος.. ἀφικάνει Il.6.388: c. gen., A.R.1.177.

ἀφικλῶντο (fort. ἀφικμ-, cf. ἰκμάω)· ἀπεσείοντο ἢ ἀποελῶντο (fort. ἀπηλοῶντο), Hsch.

ἀφικνέομαι, Ion. ἀπ- Hdt.2.28, al.: impf. ἀφικνεῖτο Th.3.33: fut. ἀφίξομαι Il.18.270, etc., Ion. 2 sg. ἀπίξεαι Hdt.2.29, 3 sg. ἀπίξεται Theoc.29.13: pf. ἀφῖγμαι Od.6.297, Att. 2 sg. ἀφῖξαι A.*Pr.*305, 3 sg. ἀφῖκται S.*OC*794: plpf. ἀφῖκτο ib.1590, Ion. 3 pl. ἀπίκατο Hdt.8.6: aor. ἀφῑκόμην Il.18.395, etc.; inf. ἀφικέσθαι; Dor. imper. ἀφίκευσο Theoc.11.42: aor. 1 part. ἀφιξάμενος *Epigr.Gr.*981.9 (Philae):—*arrive at, come to, reach*: Constr., in Hom., Pi., and Trag. mostly c. acc. loci, Il.13.645, Pi.*P.*5.29, A.*Pers.*15, etc.; ὅνδε δόμονδε Hes.*Sc.*38: in Hom. also c. acc. pers., μνηστῆρας ἀ. *came up to* them, Od.1.332, cf. 11.122, etc.; ὅτε μ' ἄλγος ἀφίκετο *came to* me, Il.18.395; similarly, τοῦτον νῦν ἀφίκεσθε *come up to* this throw! Od.8.202; freq. also with Preps., ἀ. ἐς.. Il.24.431, Od.4.255, etc.; less freq. ἐπί.. Il.10.281, 22.208; still more rarely κατά.., ποτί.., 13.329, Od.6.297; ἀ. πρὸς τέλος γόων S.*OC*1622; ἐπὶ τῶν νήσων X.*HG*5.1.2; ἄχρι τοῦ μὴ πεινῆν ἀ. Id.*Smp.*4.37; θανάτου τοὔτ' ἐγγυτάτω τοὔπος ἀφῖκται S.*Ant.*934; παρά τινος ἀ. Id.*OT*935, etc.: abs., *arrive*, ὁπποίης ἐπὶ νηὸς ἀφίκεο Od.1.171; ὅταν ἀ. ὥρη Thgn.723; σῖτος ἀφικνούμενος D.20.31; ὁ ἀφικνούμενος *the stranger, newcomer*, *IG*1^2.118.11:—Phrases: 1. ἀ. ἐπὶ or εἰς πάντα, *to try* every means, S.*OT*265, E.*Hipp.*284; ἀ. ἐς πᾶσαν βάσανον Hdt.8.110; ἐς διάπειράν τινος ἀ. Id.2.28,77; ἐπὶ τὸ τέμνειν μῦς ἀ. Gal.2.230. 2. *come into* a certain condition, ἀ. ἐς πᾶν κακοῦ Hdt.7.118; ἐς ἀπορίην πολλήν Id.1.79; ἐς τοσοῦτο τύχης, ἐς τοῦτο δυστυχίας, *come into* such a.., ib.124, Th.7.86; ἐς ὀλίγον ἀ. νικηθῆναι *come* within little of being conquered, Id.4.129; εἰς τὸ ἴσον ἀ. τινί *attain* equality with.., X.*Cyr.*1.4.5; εἰς ὀργήν Men.*Pk.*44; ellipt., ἐς ἀνδρ' ἀφίκου *reachedst* man's estate, E.*Ion* 322. 3. of intercourse with others, ἀ. τινὶ ἐς λόγους *hold* converse with one, Hdt.2.28; ἐς ἔχθεα, ἐς ἔριν ἀ. τινί, Id.3.82, E.*IA*319; διὰ μάχης, δι' ἔχθρας ἀ. τινί, Hdt.1.169, E.*Hipp.*1164; διὰ λόγων ἐμαυτῇ Id.*Med.*872. b. less freq. c. dat. pers., ἀ. τινί *come at* his *call*, Pi.*O.*9.67, Hdt.5.24, Th.4.85. 4. εἰς τόξευμα ἀ. *come* within shot, X.*Cyr.*1.4.23, etc. 5. of things, ἐς ὀξὺ ἀ. dub. l. for ἀπηγμένα, -μένας in Hdt.2.28, 7.64; ὁ λόγος εἰς ταὐτὸν ἀ. Arist.*EN*1097^{a}24, cf. 1167^{a}12, al. II. the sense of *return* is sts. implied in the context, but is not inherent in the word, as Od.10.420, Pi.*P.*8.54, E.*El.*6, Pl.*Chrm.*153a.

ἀφικτός and **ἀφικτρός**, *impure*, Hsch.

ἀφίκτωρ, ορος, ὁ, = ἱκέτης, A.*Supp.*241. 2. Ζεὺς ἀφίκτωρ, = ἱκέσιος, ib.1.

ἀφίκω, = ἀφικνέομαι, *extend, reach*, Hp.*Epid.*5.26.

ἀφῐλ-άγᾰθος [ᾰγ], ον, *not loving the good*, 2*Ep.Ti.*3.3. **-ανθρωπία**, ἡ, *lack of human feeling*, Arist.*VV*1251^{b}3, Phld.*Oec.*p.68 J. **-άνθρωπος**, ον, *not loving men*, Plu.2.1098d, Lib.*Decl.*51.10. **-αργῠρία**, ἡ, *freedom from avarice*, Hp.*Decent.*5, Onos.1.8, D.S.9.12. **-άργῠρος**, ον, *not loving money*, *Inscr.Prien.*137.5 (ii B.C.), D.S.9.11, 1*Ep.Ti.*3.3, *Ep.Hebr.*13.5, Sor.1.4, *POxy.*33 ii 11 (ii A.D.). Adv. -ρως *IG*2^2.1343.25 (i B.C.), *SIG*708.17 (Istropolis, ii B.C.).

ἀφῐλᾰρ-όω, *brighten, cheer*, Phld.*Mus.*p.84 K. **-ύνω**, = foreg., in Pass., *have a cheerful expression*, *Stoic.*3.43.

ἀφῐλάσκομαι, *appease*, θυμόν Pl.*Lg.*873a; ἀφειλαξόμενον (sc. the gods) Polystr.p.9 W.

ἀφίλ-αυτος [ῐ], ον, *not showing self-love*, Plu.2.542b. **-έχθρως**, Adv. *with no disposition towards enmity*, Sch.Od.8.77. **-ήδονος**, ον, *not liking sensuality*, Ph.2.458, M.Ant.5.5.

ἀφίλης· καθαρός, ὑγιής, ὁλόκληρος, Hsch.

ἀφίλ-ητος [ῐ], ον, *unloved*, S.*OC*1702 (lyr.), Phld.*D.*1.1. **-ία**, ἡ, *want of friends*, Arist.*EN*1115^{a}11, *Rh.*1386^{a}9, Phld.*Oec.*p.67 J., Plu.*Sol.*7. **-ίωτος**, ον, *not to be made a friend of* or *reconciled*, Hsch. s.v. ἀσύμβατον.

ἀφῐλο-δοξέω, *to be free from ambition*, prob. in Phld.*Vit.*p.7 J. **-δοξος**, ον, *free from conceit* or *ambition*, Id.*Rh.*2.273 S., *Lib.*p.42 O.; τὸ ἀ. Cic.*Att.*2.17.2, Ph.2.458.

ἀφῐλοικτίρμων, ον, gen. ονος, *unmerciful*, Hsch.

ἀφῐλο-κάλητος [κᾰ], ον, *without adornment*, δόμος Procl. ad Hes. *Op.*746, cf. Eust.669.41. **-κᾰλία**, ἡ, *character of the* ἀφιλόκαλος, Ath. 1.3a (cf. Eup.366). **-κᾰ⟨λοκᾰ⟩γᾰθία**, ἡ, *dishonesty*, *POxy.*33 ii 13 (ii A.D.). **-κᾰλος**, ον, *without love for beauty* or *honour*, Plu.2.672e, Gal.5.39. **-λογος**, ον, *without love for learning literature*, Plu.2.673a. **-νείκητος**, ον, = sq., Hdn.*Epim.*177. **-νεικος**, ον, *not fond of strife*, Arist.*VV*1250^{a}43, 1251^{a}15, Andronic.Rhod.p.575 M., Ph.2.5; ἡγεμονία ib.555. Adv. -κως, παραχωρεῖν τινός τινι Plb.21.20.1, cf. Ph.1.324, al., Luc.*Symp.*37. **-ξενος**, ον, *inhospitable*, Eust.1733.20. **-πλουτία**, ἡ, *contempt for wealth*, Plu.*Comp.Lys.Sull.*3. **-πονος**, ον, *disliking work*, Plb.12.27.4 (Comp.). **-πρωτία**, ἡ, *want of ambition*, Men.Prot.p.90 D.

ἄφῐλος, ον, of persons, *friendless*, A.*Ch.*295, S.*El.*819, Pl.*Lg.*730c, *R.*580a; ἄ. ἔρημον ἄπολιν S.*Ph.*1018; ἄκλαυτος ἄ. Id.*Ant.*876 (lyr.): c. gen., ἄ. φίλων E.*Hel.*524 (lyr.); τὸ ἄ. Ph.2.662. II. of persons and things, *unfriendly, hateful*, A.*Th.*522, S.*OC*186; ἄφιλα παρ' ἀφίλοις ἔπεσε..'Ατρείδαις Id.*Aj.*620; λίαν ἄφιλον φαίνεται Arist. *EN*1101ᵃ23; *unsociable*, γῆρας S.*OC*1237: perh., c. gen., *hostile to*, ἀσφαλείας Phld.*Lib.*p.36 O.; τὸ λαθραιοπραγεῖν -ώτατον ib.p.20 O., cf. Carneisc.*Herc.*1027.16. Adv. -λως *in unfriendly manner*, A.*Ag.* 805.

ἀφῐλο-σόφητος, ον, *not versed in philosophy*, ὄχλος D.H.2.20, Phld.*Herc.*1005.11. II. *without philosophical significance*, Arg. Sch.Od.1. **-σοφία**, ἡ, *contempt for philosophy*, Pl.*Def.*415e. **-σοφος**, ον, of persons, *without taste for philosophy*, Id.*Sph.*259e, Ph. *Fr.*35 H.; γένος Pl.*Ti.*73a; συγγραφεύς *unphilosophical*, Plb.12.25.6. 2. of conditions, *unphilosophic*, δίαιτα Pl.*Phdr.*256c; ἀ. τήρησις S.E.*M.*11.165. **-στάχυος** [τᾰ], ον, *without ears of corn, starving*, πενία *AP*6.40.8 (Maced.). **-στοργία**, ἡ, *absence of natural affection*, implied in punning phrase of Timagenes, ἡ πρὸς τὰ ἔκγονα φιλοστοργία (ἔκγον' ἀ.) Plu.2.634f. **-στοργος**, ον, *without natural affection*, ib.140d. **-τῑμία**, ἡ, *want of due ambition*, Arist.*EN* 1125ᵇ22. **-τῑμος**, ον, *lacking in ambition*, Is.7.35, Lycurg.69, Arist.*EN*1107ᵇ29: Sup., Plb.6.48.8; βίος ἀ. εἰς δόξαν *Inscr.Prien.* 112.11, cf. Eun.*VS*p.491 B. Adv. -μως Plb.12.23.8; πρὸς πολίτας ζῆν Plu.2.525d; but also, *without fear or favour, impartial*, *IG*9(2). 517.34 (Epist. Philipp.). 2. simply, *indifferent*, πρὸς κάλλος J. *AJ*2.9.6. Adv. -μως *lukewarmly*, *PPetr.*2 p.5. II. of things, *not honourable, paltry*, ἡ ἀπὸ μικρῶν δόξα ἀ. Plu.2.35a. **-χρημᾰτία**, ἡ, *contempt for riches*, Plu.*Comp.Ag.Gracch.*1, Socr.*Ep.*5.2:—hence Adj. **-ᾰτος**, ον, Ph.2.458, Eun.*Hist.*p.243 D. **-ψῡχος**, ον, *not cowardly*, prob. in Plu.2.761c.

ἀφῑμᾰτόω, (ἱμάτιον) *strip of clothing*, Suid.

ἀφίμωσις, εως, ἡ, an operation connected with the manufacture of vegetable oils, *PPetr.*3p.315.

ἄφῑξις, εως, Ion. **ἄπιξις**, ιος, ἡ: (ἀφικνέομαι):—*arrival*, Hdt.1.69, al.; τὴν ἀπὸ Κορίνθου ἄ. *arrival* from C., Id.5.92.ζ; ἐς Θήβας Id.9. 17; ἄ. ἐπὶ Σαρπηδονίης ἄκρης ποιεῖσθαι Id.7.58; μέρος αὐτῆς ἀπίξιος παρὰ τὸν μάγον her turn *for going in* to him, Id.3.69, cf. Pl.*Ep.*337e, Aristeas 173, J.*Ap.*1.18, etc.; ἄ. εἰς τοὺς πολεμίους ποιησάμενος D.5.8; ἄ. εἰς Κύπρον Isoc.9.53; ἡ ἐνθάδε ἄ. Hdt.3.145, Lys.2.26; ἡ οἴκαδε ἄ. *home again*, D.*Ep.*1.2, 3.39. 2. *departure*, J.*AJ*2.2.4, *Act.Ap.*20. 29. II. = ἱκεσία, A.*Supp.*483.

ἀφιππ-άζομαι, aor. -ασάμην Hld.7.29, etc.:—*ride off* or *away*, Plb. 29.6.18, Str.7.2.1, J.*AJ*14.13.5, Plu.*Aem.*19, Luc.*Tox.*50. **-εύω**, *ride off, away*, or *back*, X.*An.*1.5.12, D.S.2.19, Plu.*Arat.*40:—also Med., Hld.4.18. **-ία**, ἡ, *awkwardness in riding*, X.*Eq.Mag.*8. 13.

ἀφιππο-δρομά, ἡ, *contest of riders who dismounted while racing*, *IG* 9(2).527 (Larissa). **-λαμπάς**, άδος, ἡ, *torch-race on horseback*, ib. 531 (ibid.).

ἄφιππος, ον, *unsuited for cavalry*, Καρία X.*HG*3.4.12, cf. Plu.*Ant.* 47. II. of persons, *unused to riding*, opp. ἱππικός, Aeschin.Socr. *Oxy.*1608 *Fr.*1.15; *ignorant of horsemanship*, Pl.*Prt.*350a, *R.*335c, Luc.*Nav.*30. 2. *without cavalry*, Polyaen.4.6.6.

ἀφιπποτοξότης, v. ἀμφιπποτ-.

ἀφίπτᾰμαι, = ἀποπέτομαι, *fly away*, E.*IA*1608, Luc.*Somn.*16, Lib. *Decl.*51.15, Aët.7.103.

ἀφιστάνω, later form of ἀφίστημι, *CPR*5.14 (ii A.D.), Dsc.3.87, Luc.*Sol.*7:—Pass., ἀφιστάνομαι *renounce*, τινί τινος *PRyl.*117.22 (iii A.D.):—also **ἀφιστάω**, Ath.1.9b, Lib.*Decl.*51.14; opt. ἀφιστῴην dub. in X.*Smp.*2.20 (v. sq. A. II), cf. Luc.*Sol.*7.

ἀφίστημι: A. causal in pres. and impf., in fut. ἀποστήσω, and aor. 1 ἀπέστησα, as also in aor. 1 Med. (v. infr.):—*put away, remove, keep out of the way*, τὸ ἀσθενέστατον τοῦ στρατεύματος X.*HG*7.5.23; ἄχος A.*Ch.*416 (lyr.); of diseases, Dsc.2.96, Gal.13. 846; τὰ συγκείμενα ἀ. ἀπ' ἀλλήλων Pl.*Plt.*282b; ἀ. τῆς ἐλάας τὸν φλοιόν Thphr.*CP*3.3.2; ἀ. τινὰ λόγου *hinder from*.., E.*IT*912; ἀ. τὰς τῶν πολεμίων ἐπιβουλάς *frustrate* them, Th.1.93; ἀ. τὸν ἄρχοντα *depose* him, X.*HG*7.1.45:—aor. Med., 'Αργείων δόρυ πυλῶν ἀπεστήσασθε *removed* it *from your own* gates, E.*Ph.*1087:—in Hdt.9.23 ἀποστήσαντες, = ἀποστάντες, *having retired*. 2. *cause to revolt*, of allies, Id.8.19, Ar.*Eq.*238, Th.1.81; τινὰ ἀπό τινος Hdt.1.76,154, etc.; τινά τινος And.3.22. 3. in geom. constructions, *cut off*, Procl.*Hyp.* 6.7. II. *weigh out*, X.*Smp.*2.20; ἀποστησάτωσαν τὰ χρυσία *IG*7. 303.19 (Oropus); *pay*, δραχμὰς η' ἀργυρίου *UPZ*93.2 (ii B.C.): also in aor. 1 Med., μὴ..ἀποστήσωνται 'Αχαιοὶ χρεῖος lest they *weigh out* (i.e. *pay in full*) the debt, Il.13.745, cf. *IG*1².91.20, al.:—in strict sense of Med., ἀποστήσασθαι τὸν χαλκόν *to have* the brass *weighed out to one*, D.49.52.—Hom. has it trans. only in l.c. III. Med., *give a final decision* (or *break up, dismiss* the assembly), ῥήτρα ap.Plu. *Lyc.*6.

B. intr., in Pass., as also in aor. 2 ἀπέστην, imper. ἀπόστηθι Ar. *Th.*627, ἀπόστα Men.375: pf. ἀφέστηκα in pres. sense, sync. in pl. ἀφέστᾰμεν, -στᾰτε, -στᾶσι, as in inf. ἀφεστάναι, part. ἀφεστώς, -ῶσα, -ός or -ώς: plpf. ἀφεστήκειν, Att. -κη Pl.*Tht.*208e: fut. Med. ἀποστήσομαι E.*Hec.*1054, Th.5.64, etc. (while aor. 1 Med. is causal (v. supr.)): for fut. ἀφεστήξω v. h. v.:—*stand away* or *aloof from, keep far from*, ὅσσον δὲ τροχοῦ ἵππος ἀφίσταται Il.23.517; οὐ μέν κ' ἄλλη γ' ὧδε γυνὴ..ἀνδρὸς ἀφεσταίη Od.23.101; ἀποστᾶσ' ἐκποδών E.*Hel.*1023; ἐς ἄλλο σχῆμ' ἀ. βίου Id.*Med.*1039; ἀποσταθῶμεν πράγματος τελουμένου A.*Ch.*872; ὡς γραφεὺς (or βραβεὺς) ἀποσταθείς E.*Hec.*807; μακρὰν τόποις καὶ χρόνοις ἀ. D.S.13.22: hence in various relations, ἀφεστάναι φρενῶν *lose* one's wits, S.*Ph.*865; φύσεος Ar.*V.*1457 (lyr.); οὐδενὸς ἀποστήσονται ὅσα ἂν δίκαια λέγητε *depart from, object to* right proposals, Th.4.118; ἀ. φόνου E.*Or.*1544; ἀ. ἀρχῆς *to be deposed from* office, Pl.*Lg.*928d; simply, *resign*, *SIG*527.105 (Crete, iii B.C.); ἀ. τῶν πραγμάτων, τῆς πολιτείας, etc., *withdraw from* business, politics, *have done with* it, D.10.1, 18.308, etc.; ἔργων ἢ πόνων ἢ κινδύνων *shun* them, Isoc.4.83, cf. X.*HG*7.5.19, etc.; ὧν εἷλεν ἀποστάς *giving up all claim to* what he had won (at law), D.21.181; τῶν αὐτῆς Id.19.147, cf. 35.4; ἀφίστασθαι τῶν τοῦ ἀδελφοῦ ib.44; οὐδενὸς τῶν ἀνηκόντων τῇ πόλει *Inscr.Magn.*53.65; τὴν πολιτείαν.. τὴν ἀφεστηκυῖαν τοῦ μέσου πλεῖον further *removed from*.., Arist.*Pol.* 1296ᵇ8; ἀποστὰς τῶν πατρῴων Luc.*DMort.*12.3; ἀ. ἐκ Σικελίας *withdraw* from the island, *give up* the expedition, Th.7.28; *retire*, ἐς 'Ιθώμην Id.1.101: rarely c. acc., *avoid, shrink from*, τὸν ἥλιον X.*Cyn.* 3.3; τὸν πόλεμον Id.*An.*2.5.7; τινάς E.*Fr.*1006; πυγμήν Philostr. *Gym.*20 (prob. cj.). 2. in Prose, ἀ. ἀπό τινος *revolt* from.., Hdt. 1.95,130, etc.; τινός Id.2.113; οὐκ ἀποστήσομαι ἀπὸ τοῦ δήμου 'Αθηναίων *IG*1².39.21; but 'Αθηναίων τοῦ πλήθους ib.10.22; also ἀ. εἰς or πρός τινας, Hdt.2.30,162, cf. X.*An.*1.6.7; ἐς δημοκρατίαν ἀ. Th.8.90: abs., *revolt*, Hdt.1.102, etc.; ὑπό τινος at his instigation, Th.8.35 (ἀπό codd.). 3. ἀ. τινί *make way for* another, *give way to* him, E. *Hec.*1054, D.8.37. 4. c. gen., *shrink from*, τῶν κινδύνων Isoc.9. 29: also c. inf., *shrink from* doing, ἀπέστην τοῦτ' ἐρωτῆσαι σαφῶς E. *Hel.*536. 5. abs., *stand aloof, recoil* from fear, horror, etc., τίπτε καταπτώσσοντες ἀφέστατε; Il.4.340; πολλὸν ἀφεσταότες 17.375; παλίνορσος ἀπέστη 3.33, Pi.*O.*1.52, *P.*4.145; ἐγὼ οὐδέν τι μᾶλλον ἀ. Pl.*Tht.*169b, cf. D.19.45, etc.; *desist*, μὴ νῦν -ώμεθα Pl.*Lg.*960e; δοῦλος ἀφεστὼς *a runaway*, Lys.23.7. 6. Medic., ἀφίσταται, = ἀπόστασις γίγνεται, εἰς ἄρθρα Hp.*Aph.*4.74; ἀ. ὀστέον *exfoliates*, ib. 6.45; also ἀ. ἀπὸ τῶν ὀστῶν Pl.*Ti.*84a; τὸ δέρμα ἀ. X.*Eq.*1.5; also, *project, stand out*, ὦτα ἀφεστηκότα *PLond.*3.1209.12 (i B.C.). b. *to be separated* by the formation of an abscess, Gal.11.116, al. (also in Act., τὸ πύον ἀφίστησι 7.715).

ἀφιστορέω, *observe from* a place, τινὰ ἀπὸ τοῦ ὄρους Philostr.*Im.*2. 18; *explore, visit for information*, Id.*VA*1.27.

ἀφλάσαι· ἀπολέσαι, Hsch.

ἄφλαστον, τό, *curved poop of a ship* with its ornaments, Il.15.717, Asclep.Tragil.31 J., Sch.A.R.1.1089: in pl., of a single ship, Hdt. 6.114.

ἄφλεβος, ον, (φλέψ) *without veins*, Thphr.*HP*1.5.3; *without visible veins*, Gal.18(1).598:—Eust.54.16 has **ἀφλεβής**, ές.

ἀφλεγ-ής, ές, *not burnt* or *burning*, Nonn.*D.*40.475, 45.100. **-μαντος**, ον, *free from inflammation*, Hp.*Acut.*46, *Fract.*31; *not liable to it*, Arist.*Pr.*863ᵃ15; ἐπίδεσις -οτάτη *least inflammatory*, Gal. 10.451. Adv. -τως *without causing inflammation*, Aët.15.14. 2. *relieving* or *checking inflammation*, παντὸς τραύματος Thphr.*Od.*35, cf. Heliod.ap.Orib.46.8.1, Dsc.1.73. 3. of food, *not heating*, τράπεζαι Ion Lyr. in *PLG*2.257. II. *without phlegm*, πύον Hp.*Coac.* 396.

ἄφλεκτος, ον, (φλέγω) *unburnt, unconsumed by fire*, πέλανοι E. *Hel.*1334; πεῦκαι *Epigr.Gr.*241 a1 (Smyrna); *uncooked by fire*, ἄφλεκτα ἔδοντες A.R.1.1074.

ἀφλετῆρες· μαστοί, θηλαί, Hsch.; cf. ἀφατῆλες.

ἀφλόγ-ιστος, ον, *not inflammable*, Arist.*Mete.*387ᵇ18. **-ος**, ον, (φλόξ) *without flame* or *fire*, Lyc.36.

ἄφλοιος, ον, *without integument* or *bark*, Thphr.*HP*7.9.4, *Carm. Pop.*33, Epigr.ap.Plu.*Flam.*9, Ath.Med.ap.Orib.1.11.1.

ἄφλοισβος, ον, *without rushing noise*, Nonn.*D.*1.89, al.

ἀφλοισμός, ὁ, *foaming at the mouth*, ἀφλοισμὸς δὲ περὶ στόμα γίγνετο, of an angry man, Il.15.607, cf. Euph.51.4. (Cf. πεφλοιδέναι, ἔφλιδεν, Hsch.)

ἀφλοῦς· ἀφλοῖο, Hsch. (fort. ἄφλους· ἄφλοιος).

ἀφλύᾱρος [ῠ], ον, *not chattering idly*, M.Ant.5.5.

ἀφλυκταίνωτος, ον, *free from blisters*, Dsc.5.156.

ἀφνειός, όν, also ή, όν Hes.*Fr.*134.2, Pi.*O.*7.1, A.R.1.57, etc.: (ἄφενος):—*rich, wealthy*, Il.2.825, etc.; *in* a thing, c. gen., ἀφνειὸς βιότοιο 5.544; χρυσοῖό τε ἐσθῆτός τε Od.1.165 (Comp.): c. acc., φρένας ἀφνειός Hes.*Op.*455: c. dat., ἀ. ἀρούραις, μήλοις, Theoc.24.108, 25. 119; *abundant*, ἄγρη Opp.*H.*3.648; δάκρυα Nonn.*D.*2.156; 'Α., title of Ares in Arcadia, Paus.8.44.7: irreg. Sup. -έστατος Antim. 73: regul. Comp. and Sup., Od. l.c., Il.20.220:—also **ἀφνεός**, ά, όν, Thgn.188,559, and generally in Lyr. and Trag., Pi.*O.*1.10, al., B.1.62, al., A.*Pers.*3 (anap.), *Fr.*96, S.*El.*457 (Comp.). [ᾰφν in Hom.; ᾰφν A.; ᾰφνεώτερος in S. l.c.: Thgn. has ᾰ in ll. cc.]

ἀφνήμων, ον, gen. ονος, = ἀφνεός, Antim.67.

ἀφνιδία· ἀφνίδαν, ἄφνω, and **ἀφνός**· ἐξαίφνης, Hsch.

ἄφνος, εος, τό, = ἄφενος, Pi.*Fr.*219.

ἀφνύει· ἀφνύνει, ὀλβίζει, Hsch.

ἄφνω, Adv. *unawares, of a sudden*, A.*Fr.*195, E.*Med.*1205, *Alc.* 420, Eup.268, etc.: in Prose, Th.4.104, 7.37, D.21.41, *Act.Ap.*2.2, etc.:—also **ἄφνως**, *Epigr.Gr.*468.

ἀφοβ-έω, *to be fearless*, Sch.Opp.*H.*3.355. **-ητος**, ον, *without fear of*, Δίκας S.*OT*885 (lyr.): abs., *fearless*, *AP*9.59 (Antip.). **-ία**, ἡ, *fearlessness*, Pl.*Lg.*649a sq., Arist.*EN*1107ᵇ1, Plu.*Cleom.*9, Onos. 13.3.

ἀφοβοποιός, όν, *removing fear, calming*, Sch.A.*Pr.*849.

ἄφοβος, ον, *without fear*, and so: 1. *fearless, intrepid*, Pi.*I.*5(4). 40, S.*OC*1325, etc.; πρὸς ἐρημίαν, περὶ τοῦ μέλλοντος, Plu.*Lyc.*16, *Galb.*23: c. gen., *having no fear of*, τῶν ἀρχόντων D.Chr.2.52; τὸ ἄφοβον, = ἀφοβία, Pl.*La.*197b. Adv. -βως X.*Hier.*7.10, Pl.*Lg.* 682c, *PTeb.*24.74 (ii B.C.). 2. *causing no fear, free from fear*, A.

*Pr.*902; λόγος οὐκ ἄ. εἰπεῖν Pl.*Lg.*797a. 3. ἄ. θῆρες, in S.*Aj.*366, is an oxymoron, beasts *which fear not men* or *which no one fears, tame* beasts, *cattle.*

ἀφοβόσπλαγχνος, ον, *fearless of heart*, Ar.*Ra.*496.

ἀφόδ-ευμα, ατος, τό, *excrement*, Dsc.*Eup.*1.89, *Gp.*12.11, Aesop. 400: in pl., Sch.Ar.*Pl.*1185 (also **-ήματα** ib.1184). II. ἀ. κροκοδείλου, = Αἰθιοπικόν, *ajowan*, *PMag.Leid.V.*12.30, *W.*6.27. **-ευσις**, εως, ἡ, *voiding of excrement*, Erot. s. v. ἀπόπατοι (pl.). **-ευτήριον**, τό, *night-stool*, Sch.Ar.*Pl.*1184. **-ευτικὸς** δίφρος *night-stool*, Gal. 19.104. **-εύω**, *go to stool, discharge excrement*, Hp.*Fist.*9, Pl.Com. 5, Arist.*HA*627^{a}10, al.

ἀφόδιοι· ἐχθροί, Hsch.; cf. ἀφάδιος.

ἄφοδος, Ion. **ἄποδος**, ἡ (ὁ, v. infr. II), *going away, departure*, Hdt. 5.19, 9.55, X.*An.*6.4.13, etc.; *departure out of life, death*, Hierocl. p.58 A., Plot.4.3.25. 2. *going* or *coming back, return*, Hdt.4.97; *retreat*, X.*HG*6.5.20, *An.*5.2.21; ἄ. λείπειν τινί ib.4.2.11. II. *privy*, Hp.*Fract.*16, Ar.*Ec.*1059, Antiph.40.5. 2. *excrement*, Hp. *Acut.*30, al., Arist.*Mir.*830^{a}22 (masc.), Dsc.2.80, Artem.2.26. 3. in pl., *seminal ducts*, Aret.*CD*2.5.

ἀφοίβαντος, ον, *uncleansed, unclean*, A.*Eu.*237, *Fr.*148.

ἀφοιδεῖν· μὴ φροντίζειν, Hsch. (leg. ἀφειδεῖν).

ἀφοίνικτος, ον, *unreddened*, Ach.Tat.3.7.

ἀφοίνους· ἀφόνους, ὑγιεῖς, Hsch.

ἀφοίτητος, ον, *untrodden, inaccessible*, Opp.*H.*2.527.

ἀφολίδωτος [ῐ], ον, *not sheathed in scales*, Porph.*Abst.*4.14.

ἀφ-ολκή, ἡ, *evacuation, depletion*, Archig.ap.Orib.8.1.38. **-ολκος**, ον, (ὁλκή) *not having weight*, δραχμῇ ἀφολκότερον *too light* by a drachm, Str.15.3.22.

ἀφομῑλέω, *avoid, escape, a comitatu* Cic.*Fam.*16.17.2; cf. Hsch. s. v. ἀφεψιασάμην.

ἀφόμοι-ος, ον, *unlike*, Dsc.5.102:—but, 2. *likened, made like*, in Subst. **ἀφόμοιον**, τό, *copy*, Lxx *Si.Prol.*21. **-όω**, *make like*, τινί τι X.*Eq.*9.9; τοῖς γράμμασι τὰ ἔργα Pl.*Cra.*427c; μαινομένοις.. ἀ. αὑτούς Id.*R.*396a; [τῶν θεῶν] τὰ εἴδη ἑαυτοῖς ἀ. οἱ ἄνθρωποι Arist. *Pol.*1252^{b}27:—also in Med. or Pass., *become* or *be made like*, τινί Pl. *R.*396b, al.; πρός τι Id.*Sph.*240a, etc. II. *compare*, τινί τι Id. *R.*517b, 564b. III. c. acc. rei, *portray*, of painters, X.*Mem.*3. 10.2: abs., *make a copy*, Pl.*Cra.*424d. **-ωμα**, ατος, τό, *resemblance, copy*, Id.*R.*395b. **-ωμᾰτικός**, ή, όν, *assimilative*, θεοί Procl.*Theol.Plat.*6.3, cf. Lyd.*Mens.*1.15. Adv. -κῶς Procl. *in Alc.* p.52 C. **-ωσις**, εως, ἡ, *making like, comparison*, τὰς ἀ. ποιεῖσθαι Plu.2.988d, Iamb.*Myst.*1.11; *representation of..*, ἐπ' ἀφομοιώσει τῶν ἐμφάσεων Phld.*Po.*2.24. **-ωτέον**, *one must compare*, Thphr.*HP*1. 1.5. **-ωτικός**, ή, όν, *assimilative*, δύναμις Procl. *in Prm.*p.565 S.; διακόσμησις, θεοί, Dam.*Pr.*338, 340, Iamb.*Myst.*5.11.

ἀφοπλ-ίζω, *disarm*, τινά D.S.11.35, *APl.*4.171 (Leon.), Luc. *DDeor.*19.1:—Pass., D.S.14.64:—Med., ἀφοπλίζεσθαι ἔντεα *put off one's* armour, Il.23.26:—Pass. (in Lacon. form ἀφοπλίττονται), *to be discharged from service*, Hsch. **-ισμός**, ὁ, *disarming*, *Cod.Just.* 12.40.12. **-ιστής**, οῦ, ὁ, *one who disarms*, Just.*Nov.*8.12.

ἀφορ-άω, Ion. **-έω**, fut. ἀπόψομαι: aor. ἀπεῖδον:—*look away from* all others at one, *have in view*, Hdt.8.37; *look at*, τι Lycurg.17; of a distant object, D.*Ep.*2.20; πρός τι Th.7.71; τι πρός τι *compare*, Pl. *R.*585a; ἀ. ὅθεν.. *look to the point* whence.., ib.584d; εἴς τι or τινα, Plu.*Lyc.*7, Luc.*Philops.*30; εἰς τὸν θεόν Arr.*Epict.*2.19.29; εἰς τὸν Ἰησοῦν *Ep.Hebr.*12.2: hence, *obey*, Nic.Dam.p.22 D.; ἐπί τινα Plu.*Cat. Mi.*52; πρός τινα Id.*Cat.Ma.*19, Arr.*Epict.*3.24.16:—in Med., Ar.*Nu.* 281. b. of Places, *look towards*, εἰς βόρειον ὠκεανόν App.*Praef.*3, cf. Philostr.*Im.Prooem.* 2. *to view from a place*, ἀπὸ δενδρέου Hdt.4.22; πόρρωθεν ἀπιδών Timocl.21.6. II. rarely, *look away, have the back turned*, prob. in Thphr.*HP*4.16.6; ἀφορῶντας παίειν X.*Cyr.*7.1. 36. **-ᾱσις**, εως, ἡ, *looking away*, ἡ εἰς τὸ πλῆθος ἀ. Procl. *in Alc.* p.251 C.

ἀφόρδιον, τό, *excrement*, γαστρός Nic.*Th.*692, *Al.*140.

ἀφορέω, (ἄφορος) *to be barren*, Xenag.ap.Macrob.*Sat.*5.19.30, f.l. for ἀφοράω in Thphr.*HP*4.16.6, cf. Ph.2.249; *dry up*, of a river, Id. 1.690.

ἀφόρητος, ον, *unendurable*, κρυμός Hdt.4.28; χειμῶνος χρῆμα ἀφόρητον Id.7.188; μεγέθει βοῆς ἀφόρητοι Th.4.126; οὐκ ἔστιν.. οὐδὲν τῆς ὕβρεως -ότερον D.21.46; ἀ. κακόν Arist.*EN*1126^{a}13, cf. Epicur. *Fr.*447, Phld.*Lib.*p.17 O.; *irresistible*, Jul.*Or.*1.28d. Adv. -τως Poll. 3.130. II. *not worn, new*, censured by Luc.*Lex.*9, Ath.3.98a.

ἀφορητότης· *intolerabilitas*, *Gloss.*

ἀφορία, ἡ, (ἄφορος) *not bearing*:—hence, 1. c. gen. objecti, *non-production, dearth*, καρπῶν -ίαι X.*Vect.*4.9; πίττης Thphr.*HP*9. 2.4; παίδων Pl.*Lg.*740c (pl.); ἀρετῆς Ph.1.430: abs., *dearth*, αἱ ἀ. γίγνονται Antipho 2.1.10, cf. Lycurg.84, Arist.*Mete.*351^{b}14 (pl.). 2. in subj. sense, *barrenness, sterility*, ἀ. ψυχῆς τε καὶ σωμάτων Pl.*R.* 546a; ψυχῶν κρειττόνων εὐφορίαι ἢ ἀ. Chrysipp.*Stoic.*2.337; φρενῶν X.*Smp.*4.55.

ἀφορ-ίζω, *mark off by boundaries*, ἐξελόντας [τὸ ὄρος] τῷ θεῷ καὶ ἀφορίσαντας Hyp.*Eux.*16; οὐσία ἀφωρισμένη property *marked out by boundary-pillars*, D.49.61:—Med., *mark off for oneself, appropriate to oneself*, χώραν ὅτι πλείστην Isoc.5.120: metaph., ἀ. τιμάς E.*Alc.*31:—Pass., ἡ ὑπό τινος ἀφορισθεῖσα χώρα Isoc.4.36. b. *border on*, τοὺς ὅρους -ίζοντας τὸν Ἀσωπόν Pl.*Criti.*110e. 2. *determine, define*, Id.*Sph.*240c:—also Med., περὶ φύσεως ἀφοριζόμενοι Epicr.11.13:—Pass., χρόνος ἀφωρισμένος a *determinate* time, Pl.*Lg.*785b; ὅροι -ισμένοι *well-defined*, Id.*Criti.*110d; ἀφωρισμένα *definite cases*, Arist. *Rh.*1354^{b}8: part. ἀφορίσας *definitely*, D.25.29. 3. *separate, distinguish*, Antipho Soph.*Oxy.*1364.290 (Pass.); *exclude*, Pl.*R.*501d, al., ἀ. χωρίς Arist.*Pol.*1331^{a}27; ἀ. τί τινος Pl.*Hp.Ma.*298d; ἱππέων ἕδρας ἀπὸ τῶν ἄλλων D.C.36.42:—Med., Pl.*Lg.*644a, *Chrm.*173e; τι ἀπό τινος Id.*Sph.*227c:—Pass., ἀφορίζεσθαι ἀπό τινος Id.*Smp.*205c: abs., ἀγνοίας ἀφωρισμένον εἶδος *distinct* species, Id.*Sph.*229c; ἐπιστήμη ἀφωρισμένη Arist.*Rh.*1354^{a}3. 4. *bring to an end, finish*, βίβλους Plb.2.71.10:—Med., λόγον Isoc.15.58. 5. *grant as a special gift*, τᾷ κάλλος ἀφώρισε Κύπρις *Epigr.Gr.*244.3 (Cyzicus). II. c. acc. pers., 1. *banish*, καί μ' ἀπὸ γᾶς ὥρισε E.*Hec.*940 (lyr.). 2. *separate*, *Act.Ap.*19.9, etc.:—Pass., ἱερέων γένος ἀπὸ τῶν ἄλλων -ισμένον Pl.*Ti.*24a; ἔκ τινων ἀφωρισμένων from *a definite class* of persons, Arist.*Pol.*1292^{b}4; ἀφωρισμένος τέχνην *having a definite* art *assigned one*, Pl.*Sph.*231e. b. *set apart* for rejection, *cast out, excommunicate*, *Ev.Luc.*6.22. c. *set apart for* some office, *appoint, ordain*, *Act.Ap.*13.2, *Ep.Rom.*1.1 (Pass.), *Ep.Gal.*1.15. d. Pass., ἀρχὴ ἀφωρισμένη πρὸς τὰς θυσίας Arist.*Pol.*1322^{b}26; of a treatise, *to be devoted to*, c. dat., Olymp. *in Mete.*9.15. **-ιος**· θρασύς, ἄπιστος, Hsch. **-ῐσις**, εως, ἡ, = sq., *Gloss.* **-ισμα**, ατος, τό, *that which is set apart*: *the wave-offering*, Lxx *Ex.*29.24, al. **-ισμός**, ὁ, *delimitation, assignment of boundaries*, *SIG*827 *F*7; γῆς *PFreib.*11.7 (iv A.D.); θέσεως Simp. *in Ph.*626.20. II. *separation, distinction*, Thphr.*CP*3.14.2; ἀπὸ τοῦ λαοῦ Thd.*Is.*56.3: hence, *banishment*, = Lat. *relegatio*, Lyd.*Mag.* 3.17 (pl.), *Ost.*9c (pl.). 2. *determination*, Arist.*Cat.*3^{b}22. 3. *attainment of definiteness*, Thphr.*Metaph.*28; *distinctive character* or *feature*, Alex.Aphr. *in Top.*74.14. 4. *pithy sentence, aphorism* (such as those of Hp.), Critias 39 D., Ph.1.636, Hermog.*Id.*1.6. 5. *fixed rule*, Thphr.*HP*9.2.1. **-ιστέον**, *one must reject*, Arist.*EN* 1097^{b}34. II. *one must define* or *assign*, Ph.*Bel.*92.49, Iamb.*Myst.* 2.1, Dam.*Pr.*448; *one must separate*, τί τινος Gal.9.379, cf. Plot.6.3. 1. **-ιστικός**, ή, όν, *delimiting*, Simp. *in Ph.*541.4, al.; *separative*, Sch.Luc.*Nav.*1; *aphoristic*, διδασκαλία Gal.11.802. Adv. -κῶς ibid.; *pithily, sententiously*, D.H.*Is.*7.

ἀφορμ-άω, Dor. part. dat. ἀφορμίοντι (-ιῶντι codd.) Archyt.ap. D.L.3.22:—*make to start from* a place:—Pass., *start, depart*, ναῦφιν Il.2.794, cf. Od.2.375, 4.748, Sapph.*Supp.*6.7, etc.: c. gen., *from* a place, οἷον ἄρ' ὁδοῦ τέλος Ἄργους ἀφωρμήθημεν S.*OC*1401; δόμων E. *Or.*844; ἐκ Κεγχρειῶν Th.8.10; *to* a place, δεῦρο Ar.*Nu.*607. II. intr. in Act. in same sense as Pass., ἀ. χθονός E.*Rh.*98; ἐκ δόμων Id. *Tr.*939, cf. Th.4.78; οἴκαδε Aeschin.2.40; εἰς Λιβύην Plb.1.39.1; of lightning, *to break forth*, S.*OC*1470 (lyr.): c. acc. cogn., τί τήνδ'.. ἀφορμᾷς πεῖραν; Id.*Aj.*290. 2. *feel aversion*, opp. ὁρμάω, Arr.*Epict.* 1.4.14, Simp. *in Epict.*p.22 D. **-ή**, ἡ, *starting-point*, esp. in war, *base of operations*, ἀναχώρησίς τε καὶ ἀ. Th.1.90, cf. Plb.1.41.6, etc.; *place of safety*, E.*Med.*342. 2. generally, *starting-point, origin, occasion* or *pretext*, ἀφορμαὶ λόγων Id.*Hec.*1239, *Ph.*199; ἀφορμὴν παρέχειν D.18.156; δεδωκέναι Id.21.98, cf. 2*Ep.Cor.*5.12; λαβεῖν ἀ. Isoc.4.61, *Ep.Rom.*7.8; εὑρεῖν *BGU*615.6 (ii A.D.), 923.22 (i/ii A.D.); ἵνα ἀ. γένοιτο τιμῆς *Inscr.Prien.*105.16 (i B.C.); ἀ. καὶ πρόφασις Plb. 2.52.3; *occasion, origin* of an illness, Hp.*Epid.*2.1.11, Sor.1.29; εἰ δέ τις οἴεται μικρὰν ἀ. εἶναι σιτηρέσιον τοῖς στρατευομένοις ὑπάρχειν a small *inducement*, D.4.29; τὸ γὰρ εὖ πράττειν παρὰ τὴν ἀξίαν ἀ. τοῦ κακῶς φρονεῖν Id.1.23; *instigation, incitement*, *POxy.*237 vii 21 (ii A.D.). 3. *means with which one begins* a thing, *resources*, ἀ. τοῦ βίου Lys.24.24; εἰς τὸν βίον X.*Mem.*3.12.4; τίνας εἶχεν ἀφορμὰς ἡ πόλις; D.18.233; ἀφελεῖν τὴν ἀ. δι' ἣν ὑβρίζει Id.21.98; πίστις ἀ. μεγίστη πρὸς χρηματισμόν good faith is the best *asset* for business, Id.36.44, cf. 11.16; ἀ. ἐπί.. Id.3.33; esp. *means of war*, And.1.109; ἀ. εἰς ξένους χιλίους *means for levying* 1000 mercenaries, X.*HG*4.8.33; ἀ. ἔργων *means for undertaking..*, Id.*Mem.*2.7.11, cf. 3.5.11; πρὸς ἀφορμὴν ἐμπορίας ἢ γεωργίας Arist.*Pol.*1320^{a}39; πάντων ἀ. τῶν καλῶν Philem.110. 4. *capital* of a banker, etc., Lys.*Fr.*1.2, X.*Mem.*2.7.12, Lycurg.26, D.14. 30, 36.11; ἀφορμῆς δίκη suit for *restitution of capital*, Arg.D.36. 5. Rhet., *food for argument, material, subject*, ὑποθέσεις καὶ ἀφορμαὶ λόγων Luc.*Rh.Pr.*18, cf. Men.Rh.p.334 S., Aps.p.264 H. 6. *aptitude, inclination*, εἰς φιλανθρωπίαν Phld.*Ir.*p.53 W. (pl.). II. Stoic term for *repulsion* (opp. ὁρμή), Chrysipp.*Stoic.*3.42, cf. 40, Simp. *in Epict.*p.22 D. III. *release* of water from sluice, *PAmh.*2.143. 17 (iv A.D.). **-ητικός**, ή, όν, (cf. foreg. II) *of repulsion*, δύναμις, opp. ὁρμητικός, Arr.*Epict.*1.1.12. **-ίζομαι**, Med., *loose one's* ships *from harbour*, ναῦς E.*IT*18.

ἀφόρμικτος, ον, *without the lyre*, of melancholy music, A.*Eu.*332 (lyr.).

ἄφορμος, ον, = ἀφορμηθείς, *moving off from, departing from*, αὖθις ἄφορμος ἐμᾶς χθονὸς S.*OC*234.

ἀφορολογ-ησία, ἡ, *exemption from tribute*, *BCH*10.300 (Alabanda, ii B.C.). **-ητος**, ον, *not subjected to tribute*, *IG*2^{2}.1009.41, *GDI*5160. 10 (Cret.), *OGI*223 (Erythrae, iii B.C.), Plb.4.25.7, Lxx 1*Es.*4.50, Plu. *Flam.*10.

ἄφορος, ον, *not bearing, barren*, δένδρεα Hdt.2.156; γῆ X.*Oec.*20. 3; of females, *barren*, περὶ ἀφόρων Hp.*Steril.* tit. 2. *causing barrenness*, σταλαγμός A.*Eu.*784 (lyr.); νοῦσος Hp.*Mul.*1.38; χρόνος ib.6. II. *exempt from tribute*, ἄ. καὶ ἀτελής Str.15.1.39, cf. *BGU* 889.24 (ii A.D.). III. Pass., *not to be borne*, νόσημα v.l. for ἄπορος in Hp.*VM*8.

ἄφορτος, ον, opp. φορτικός (q.v.), πολιτικὸς καὶ ἄ. καὶ εὐγνώμων Antip.*Stoic.*3.254. Adv. -τως, φέρειν bear *easily*, Teles p.15 H. II. at Sparta, *not having undergone the Lycurgean training*, Hsch.

ἀφόρυκτος, ον, *unspotted, unstained*, *AP*9.323 (Antip.).

ἄφος· τραγάκανθα, Hsch.

ἀφόσι-ος, α, ον, *unholy*, ἀσεβήματα *Annales du Service* 19.40 (i B.C.). **-όω,** Ion. **ἀποσ-,** *purify from guilt* or *pollution*, τὴν πόλιν Pl.*Lg.*873b; σεαυτόν Id.*Euthphr.*4c; πόλιν τὰ πρὸς τοὺς θεοὺς Aeschin.3.120. 2. *dedicate, devote*, κόρας ἑταιρισμῷ Clearch.6. 3. *establish, consecrate*, θυσίας *OGI* 383.202. II. Med., *satisfy one's conscience*, Pl.*Phd.*60e; *make atonement* or *expiation*, Id.*Phdr.*242c; ἀποσιοῦσθαι τῇ θεῷ Hdt.1.199; ἀ. ὑπὲρ αὐτοῦ Pl.*Lg.*874a. 2. c. acc. rei, *acquit oneself of* an obligation, ἀποσιεύμενος τὴν ἐξόρκωσιν *quit oneself conscientiously of* one's oath, Hdt.4.154; ἀ. λόγιον *quitting oneself of the orders of* an oracle, ib.203; τὰ πρὸς τοὺς θεοὺς Jul.*Mis.* 361b. b. *avert* a curse or the consequence of crime, ἄγος Plu.*Cam.*18, cf. *Alc.*33, al.; διαβολάς D.H.4.79; τὴν ἀσθένειαν τῆς φύσεως Sallust.18 (prob. l.). c. *do* a thing *for form's sake*, i.e. *do* it *perfunctorily*, οὐδ' ἀφοσιούμενος ἀλλ' ὡς οἷόν τ' ἄριστα παρασκευαζόμενος Is.7.38; ἀ. περί τινος Pl.*Lg.*752d, cf. *Ep.*331b; προβολήν Plu.*Per.*10. d. *allege as an excuse*, τὴν ἀνάγκην Id.*Them.*24. e. *eschew on religious grounds, hold in abomination*, κρόμυον, κυάμους, Id.2.353f, 286d: abs., *Ant.*28. III. Pass., ἀφωσιωμέναι· ἀνόσιαι, ἄποθεν τοῦ ὁσίου γεγενημέναι, S.*Fr.*253. **-ωμα,** ατος, τό, *act of purification, expiation*, Hsch. **-ωσις,** εως, ἡ, *purification, expiation*, D.H.2.52: pl., Plu.2.302b; defined as ὁσιότητος παραλελειμμένης ἀποπλήρωσις Herm.*in Phdr.*p.94A. 2. *doing as matter of form*, ἀφοσιώσεως ἕνεκεν for *form's* sake, Plu.*Eum.*12; τιμῆς ἀ. *outward, formal* respect, Id.*Tim.*39; κατὰ ἀφοσίωσιν Dam.*Pr.*171.

ἀφουλωτικός, ή, όν, *causing to scar over*, Paul.Aeg.6.5.

ἄφρα, ἡ, a kind of *plaster*, Aët.15.14.

ἀφρᾰδ-έω, only in pres., *to be senseless, behave thoughtlessly*, σοὶ.. μαχήσομαι ἀφραδέοντι Il.9.32; αἰεὶ γάρ τε νεώτεροι ἀφραδέουσι Od.7.294. **-ής,** ές, (φράζομαι) *insensate, reckless*, μνηστῆρες ib.2.282, cf. Nonn.*D.*5.349; of the dead, *without sense, senseless*, Od.11.476. Adv. ἀφραδέως *senselessly, recklessly*, Il.3.436, etc. **-ία,** Ion. **-ίη,** ἡ, *folly, thoughtlessness*, in Hom. always in dat. pl., ἀνέρος ἀφραδίῃσι Il.5.649; ποιμένος ἀφραδίῃσι 16.354; exc. δι' ἀφραδίας Od.19.523, and ἀφραδίῃ πολέμοιο Il.2.368.—Ep. word, ἀφροσύνη being used for it in Prose; ἀφραδίῃσι in a mock heroic line, Ar.*Pax* 1064 (hex.). **-μων,** in Trag. **ἀφράσμων,** ον, gen. ονος, = ἀφραδής, c. inf., ἀφράδμονες προγνώμεναι *without sense* to foresee, *h.Cer.*256; γυναικὸς ὡς ἀφράσμονος A.*Ag.*1401, cf. S.*Fr.*613. Adv. ἀφρασμόνως A.*Pers.*417.—Only poet.

ἀφράζω, = sq., cited from Hp. by Gal.19.87; cf. ἀφράσει· ἀσυνετεῖ, Hsch.

ἀφραίνω, (ἄφρων) *to be foolish*, Il.2.258, 7.109, Od.20.360, Phoc.5.—Poet. and Hp.*Gland.*12; later as a philosophic term, Chrysipp.*Stoic.*3.166, Plu.2.1037d, S.E.*M.*11.94, Plot.5.8.3.

ἄφρακτος, ον, old Att. **ἄφαρκτος** (though this form has generally been altered by the copyists), *unfenced, unfortified, unguarded*, οἴκησις, στρατόπεδον, Th.1.6, 117: c. gen., ἀ. φίλων *by* friends, S.*Aj.*910 (lyr.); of ships, *not decked*, *IG* 12(1).44 (Rhodes); of horses, opp. πεφραγμένοι, Arr.*Tact.*2.5. 2. *not obstructed*, Gal.17(1).598. 3. *not to be kept in, irrepressible*, σταγόνες A.*Ch.*186 (with v.l. ἄφραστοι). II. *unguarded, off one's guard*, ηὑρέθην E.*Hipp.*657; ληφθήσεσθε Th.6.33, cf. Ar.*Th.*581; πρός τινα Th.3.39.

ἀφράσμων, v. ἀφράδμων.

ἄφραστ-ος, ον, (φράζω) *unutterable, marvellous*, ἄ. ἠδ' ἀνόητα *h.Merc.*80; οὐδὲν -ότερον πέλεται νόου ἀνθρώποισιν Hom.*Epigr.*5.2; πέδη S.*Tr.*1057; *inexpressible*, μέριμνα A.*Pers.*165 codd.; *too wonderful for words*, φάτις S.*Tr.*694. II. (φράζομαι) *not perceived, unseen*, *h.Merc.*353; *not to be observed, known*, or *guessed*, A.*Supp.*95 (lyr.); *incomprehensible*, Orph.*L.*46; κατακρύπτει ἐς τὸ -ότατόν οἱ ἐφαίνετο εἶναι [χωρίον] the place *least likely to be thought of*, Hdt.5.92.δ'; *unforeseen*, A.R.2.824. Adv. -τως *beyond thought*, S.*El.*1262 (lyr.). III. Act., of persons, *beside themselves*, Nic.*Th.*776. 2. *giving no sign*, Nonn.*D.*9.134, 22.82. **-ύς,** ύος, ἡ, Ion. for ἀφραδία, Call.*Fr.anon.*9 (pl.).

ἀφρατίας· ἰσχυρός (Cret.), Hsch.

ἄφρατον, τό, Lat. *aphratum, soufflé, mousse*, Isid.*Etym.*20.2.29, Alex.Trall.*Febr.*3, Steph.*in Hp.*1.87 D.

***Ἄφραττος·** ἡ Ἑκάτη (Tarent.), Hsch.

ἄφρενος, ον, = ἄφρων, dub. l. in Beros.1.3.

ἀφρέω, (ἀφρός) *foam*, Hp.*Morb.Sacr.*7, etc. II. c. acc., *befoam, cover with foam*, ἵπποι ἄφρεον στήθεα (disyll.) Il.11.282.

ἀφρηλόγος, ον, poet. for ἀφρολόγος (which does not occur), *gathering froth, skimming*, λίπους *AP* 6.101 (Phil.).

ἀφρηστής, οῦ, ὁ, *foamer*, of a dolphin, *AP* 7.214 (Arch.).

ἀφρήτωρ, ὁ, Ion. for ἀφράτωρ, *without brotherhood* (φρήτρη), i.e. *bound by no social tie*, Il.9.63.

ἀφρ-ιάω, poet. for ἀφρέω, Opp.*H.*1.772, Porph.ap.Eus.*PE* 3.11. **-ίζω,** = ἀφρέω, *foam*, S.*El.*719, Hp.*Mul.*2.123, Thphr.*CP* 6.1.5; of a wine-cup, Antiph.174.6, Alex.119.3.

ἀφρικτί, Adv., (φρίσσω) *without shuddering*, Call.*Dian.*65.

ἀφρῖνον· τάλαρον τῶν ἑλκυσμάτων τῶν ἐρίων, Hsch.

ἀφριόεις, εσσα, εν, (ἀφρός) *foamy*, γένειον *AP* 7.531 (Antip.Thess.); γάλακτος τεῦχος Nic.*Al.*206, cf. *Hymn.Is.*164.

***Ἄφριος,** ὁ, epith. of Zeus in Thessaly, Ἀρχ.Ἐφ.1913.219: also, name of month, *IG* 9(2).206 iii c, al.

ἀφρίους· αἰθέρας, Hsch. **ἀφρίς·** μύρτον, Id.

ἀφρισμός, ὁ, (ἀφρίζω) *foaming*, Archig.ap.Philum.*Ven.*14.3, Paul.Aeg.3.13, Sch.Il.9.539.

ἄφρισσα, ἡ, a plant, = ἀσκληπιάς, Apul.*Herb.*15.

ἀφριστής, οῦ, ὁ, *foamer*, Sch.Il.1.535.

ἀφρῖτις, ιδος, ἡ, = ἀφρός III, Arist.*Fr.*309, Ath.7.325b, Opp.*H.*1.776.

ἀφρό-γᾰλα, ακτος, τό, *frothed milk*, Gal.10.468. **-γένεια,** ἡ, *foam-born, Aphrodite*, Mosch.2.71, Coluth.167; the planet *Venus*, Max.402, Doroth.ap.*Cat.Cod.Astr.*2.82.2: **ἀφρογενής,** ές, = foreg., Ἀφροδίτην ἀφρογενῆ Orph.*Fr.*183, cf. *APl.*4.211 (Stat. Flacc.); the planet *Venus*, Doroth.ap.Heph.Astr.1.6.

Ἀφροδίσ-ια [δῐ], τά, v. Ἀφροδίσιος. **-ιάζω,** *have sexual intercourse*:—Act., of the man, Hp.*Vict.*3.73, al., Pl.*R.*426a, X.*Mem.*1.3.14, etc.:—Pass., of the woman, Id.*Hier.*3.4, Arist.*HA* 581^{b}17, etc. **-ιακός,** ή, όν, *sexual*, τέρψεις D.S.2.23; [λίθος] a precious stone *with aphrodisiac properties*, Plin.*HN* 37.148; ἔλαιον *POxy.*1293.5 (ii A.D.). **-ιάς,** άδος, ἡ, *sacred to Aphrodite*, name of an island, Hdt.4.169. II. = ἄκορος, Apul.*Herb.*6. **-ιασμός,** ὁ, *sexual intercourse, lustfulness*, Hp.*Aph.*6.30, Arist.*GA* 725^{b}17 (pl.). **-ιαστής,** οῦ, ὁ, *voluptuary*, Polem.*Phgn.*14. 2. *lessee of public brothel*, *POxy.*511.3. 3. in pl., *worshippers of Aphrodite*, at Rhodes, *IG* 12(1).162. **-ιαστικός,** ή, όν, = ἀφροδισιακός, χάρις Arist.*Pol.*1311^{b}16; συνδυασμοί Gal.1.339. 2. of men and animals, *lecherous, salacious*, Arist.*HA* 488^{b}4, Gal.1.624. II. *aphrodisiac*, ἐδέσματα Arist.*Pr.*954^{a}3, cf. Gal.14.241. **-ιος,** α, ον, also ος, ον D.H.2.24, Luc.*Am.*12, Ael.*NA* 1.2:—*belonging to the goddess of love*, ἔργον Semon.7.48; ἄγρα S.*Fr.*166; ὅρκος Pl.*Smp.*183b; ἀθύρματα Crates Com.2 D.; λόγος Pl.Com.2 D.; κῆπος Archipp.2 D.; ὑμέναιον Pherecr.12 D. II. Ἀφροδίσια, τά, *sexual pleasures*, Hp.*Mochl.*36, freq. in Pl., as *Phd.*81b, al.; τέρπν' ἄνθε' Ἀ. Pi.*N.*7.53; τὰ τῶν ὡραίων Ἀ. X.*Mem.*2.6.22; ἔργα Ἀ. Hp.*Jusj.*:—also as concrete, = *amasius*, X.*Mem.*1.3.8. 2. *festival of Aphrodite*, Ἀ. ἄγειν Id.*HG* 5.4.4, Alex.253.1. 3. *pudenda*, Luc.*Nigr.*16. III. Ἀφροδίσιον, τό, *temple of Aphrodite*, X.*HG* 5.4.58, *GDI* 5075.70 (Crete); *her statue*, Plu.*Thes.*21, *PPetr.*3 p.113. 2. in pl., *brothels*, *PTeb.*6.29 (ii B.C.). IV. Ἀφροδίσιος, ὁ (sc. μήν), name of a month in Cyprus, Porph.*Abst.*2.54, etc. **-ιών,** ῶνος, ὁ (sc. μήν), name of a month at Demetrias, *SIG* 1157.52.

Ἀφροδῑτ-ᾰρίδιον [ῐδ], τό, 'darling', Pl.Com.3 D. **-άριον,** τό, name of an *eyesalve*, Gal.12.752. II. name of a *horse-medicine*, *Hippiatr.*129.

Ἀφροδίτη [ῑ], ἡ, (ἀφρός) *Aphrodite*, *h.Hom.*5, Hes.*Th.*195; διὰ τὴν τοῦ ἀφροῦ γένεσιν Ἀφροδίτη ἐκλήθη Pl.*Cra.*406c. II. as Appellat., *sexual love, pleasure*, Od.22.444; ὑπ' Ἀπόλλωνι ψαύειν Ἀφροδίτας Pi.*O.*6.35; ἔργα Ἀφροδίτης *h.Ven.*1,9, etc.; μὰ τὴν Ἀ., νὴ τὴν Ἀ., a woman's form of oath, Ar.*Lys.*208, *Ec.*189, etc. 2. generally, *vehement longing* or *desire*, E.*IA* 1264; Ἀ. τιν' ἡδεῖαν κακῶν *enjoyment*, Id.*Ph.*399. 3. *beauty, grace, charm*, ἔρρει πᾶσ' Ἀ. A.*Ag.*419 (lyr.); τοιαύτην Ἀ. ἐπὶ τῇ γλώττῃ.. ἔχει Luc.*Scyth.*11; πολλὴν Ἀ. τῷ λόγῳ περιτιθέναι D.H.*Comp.*3. III. ὁ τᾶς Ἀφροδίτας [ἀστήρ] *the planet Venus*, Ti.Locr.97a, cf. Pl.*Epin.*987b, Arist.*Metaph.*1073^{b}31, etc. IV. Pythag. name for *five*, *Theol.Ar.*31. V. *seedtime*, Orph.*Fr.*33. VI. name of various *plasters*, Aët.12.48, 15.15.

ἀφρό-κομος, ον, lit. *foam-haired*, but always metaph., ῥαθάμιγξ Musae.262, Nonn.*D.*2.618; στόματα ib.46.161. **-λιτρον,** τό, Att. for ἀφρόνιτρον (q.v.).

ἀφρον-εύομαι, = ἀφρονέω, Lxx *Je.*10.21, Sm.*Jb.*1.22. **-ευσις,** εως, ἡ, *playing the fool*, opp. φρονίμευσις, *Stoic.*3.25. **-έω,** (ἄφρων) *to be silly, act foolishly*, Il.15.104, *AP* 10.66 (Agath.); τὸ ἀφρονεῖν Ceb.41. 2. trans., *make foolish* or *vain*, f.l. in Aq.2 *Ki.*15.31. **-η,** ἡ, = ἀφροσύνη, *AB* 472. **-ησις,** εως, ἡ, = foreg., J.*AJ* 19.1.14 (dub.). **-ίζω,** *make foolish*, prob. in Aq.2 *Ki.*15.31. **-ικός,** ή, όν, = ἄφρων, Sch.Luc.*Bis Acc.*22.

ἀφρόνιτρον, Att. **ἀφρόλιτρον** (the two distd. by Gal. l.c., cf. *Gp.*2.28), τό, a form of *native sodium carbonate* (cf. νίτρον), distd. by Gal.12.212 from the finer ἄνθος νίτρου, cf. Herod.Med.ap.Orib.6.20.5: in Hp. and correct Greek divisim ἀφρὸς νίτρου: hence ἀφρόνιτρον is condemned by Phryn.272.

ἄφροντ-ις, ιδος, ὁ, ἡ, *free from care, careless*, c. gen., ἄ. τοῦ θανεῖν E.*Fr.*958; τῶν καθηκόντων Plu.2.45d; περί τινος Luc.*Dem.Enc.*25: abs., δίαιτα Plu.2.792b (in acc. ἄφροντιν), cf. Max.Tyr.3.9: Comp. -έστερος Steph.*in Hp.*1.263 D. **-ιστέω,** *to be heedless*, Pl.*Lg.*917c. 2. *have no care of, pay no heed to*, ἀρχόντων ib.885a, v.l. in X.*An.*5.4.20, cf. Plb.9.13.1; περί τινος Hp.*Praec.*7 (dub.); ὑπὲρ τῆς βασιλείας Philostr.*VA* 1.38. **-ιστητέον,** *one must disregard*, c. gen., Plb.9.16.5. **-ιστί,** Adv. of -ιστος, *thoughtlessly*, Ath.14.632d. **-ιστία,** ἡ, *heedlessness*, τοῦ συμμέτρου Them.*Or.*15.186c; τοῦ βίου Porph.*Plot.*7. II. in pass. sense, *being unheeded*, ὑπ' ἀνθρώπων Phld.*Mort.*36. **-ιστος,** ον, *thoughtless, heedless*, X.*Smp.*6.6; Ἔρως Theoc.10.20; ἐς τὸ ἀ. ἐπαίρεσθαι D.C.47.11. Adv. -τως *without taking thought, inconsiderately*, S.*Tr.*366, Timo 67.3; ἀ. ἔχειν to be *heedless*, X.*Cyr.*1.6.42; πρὸς τὸ μέλλον Plb.3.79.2; euphem. for ἄφρων εἶναι, S.*Aj.*355. 2. *without causing anxiety*, Ruf.ap.Orib.45.30.20. II. Pass., *unthought of, unexpected*, ἐμοὶ δ' ἀγὼν ὅδ' οὐκ ἀ.. ἦλθε A.*Ag.*1377.

ἀφρόομαι, Pass., *become frothy*, *Theol.Ar.*40.

ἀφρός, ὁ, *foam*, of the sea, ῥόος Ὠκεανοῖο ἀφρῷ μορμύρων Il.18.403, etc.; of a river, 5.599. 2. of persons and animals, *foam, slaver, froth*, περί τ' ἀ. ὀδόντας γίγνεται 20.168; ἀ. περὶ στόμα Hp.*Aph.*2.43, cf. *Ev.Luc.*9.39; μέλαν' ἀπ' ἀνθρώπων ἀφρόν *frothy blood*, A.*Eu.*183, cf. *Fr.*372; θρομβώδεις ἀφροί S.*Tr.*702; βακχίου παλαιγενοῦς ἀφρῷ, of wine, Antiph.237; κύλικα.. ἀφρῷ ζέουσαν Theophil.2. II.

ἀφρὸς νίτρου, = ἀφρόνιτρον, Hp.*Mul.*1.75; ἀ. alone, Arist.*Col.*794a20. 2. ἀ. αἵματος, = σπέρμα, Diog.Apoll.A 24 D. III. a kind of ἀφύη, Arist.*HA*569a29, b28, Ath.7.325b; Ionic, acc. to Archestr. *Fr.*9.2, but cf. Hsch. s. v. ἀφύων τιμή. (*m̥bhrós*, cf. Skt. *abhrám* 'cloud', Lat. *imber*.)

ἀφροσέληνος, ὁ, = σεληνίτης, Ps.-Democr.ap.Zos.Alch.p.122 B., Dsc.5.141.

ἀφροσῐβόμβαξ, ακος, ὁ, *puffing, bustling fellow*, Timo 29.

ἀφρόσκορδον, τό, *African* σκόροδον, i. e. *Cyprian garlic, Allium sativum*, Colum.11.3.20.

ἀφροσύνη, ἡ, (ἄφρων) *folly, thoughtlessness*, freq. in pl., παῖδας καταπαυέμεν ἀφροσυνάων Od.24.457, cf. 16.278: in sg., οὐδέ τί σε χρὴ ταύτης ἀφροσύνης Il.7.110, cf. Democr.254, Hdt.3.146, 9.82; κοῦφαι ἀ. S.*OC*1230 (lyr.); καταφρόνησιν ἢ .. ἀ. μετωνόμασται Th.1.122; opp. σωφροσύνη and σοφία, Pl.*Prt.*332e; συμβαίνει ἡ ἀ. μετὰ ἀκρασίας ἀρετή Arist.*EN*1146a27.

ἀφροτόκος, ον, *producing foam, foaming*, Nonn.*D.*45.156.

ἀφρουρ-έω, *leave unguarded*, τὰ οἴκοι Str.15.1.53. **-ητος**, ον, *unguarded*, Pl.*Lg.*760a, Plu.2.340f; *ungarrisoned*, Plb.4.25.7, al., Plu.*Flam.*10: metaph., Gal.18(1).321. **-ος**, ον, *off one's guard*, Pl.*Phdr.*256c; ἄ. καὶ ἄνοπλοι Plu.*Demetr.*32. 2. *free from military duty*, Arist.*Pol.*1270b4.

ἀφροφυής, ές, *foamy*, of a lettuce, from its milky juice, *AP*9.412 (Phld.).

ἄφρυκτος, ον, *unroasted*, κριθαί Poll.6.77, Harp.s.v. προκώνια, Gal.11.807, etc.

'Αφρώ, οῦς, ἡ, = 'Αφροδίτη, Nic.*Al.*406.

ἀφρώδης, ες, *foamy*, αἷμα Diog.Apoll.6, Hp.*Aph.*5.13, cf. *Acut.*53; στόματος ἀ. πέλανος E.*Or.*220; ὄμβρος Tim.*Pers.*71 (dub.); γένος Pl.*Ti.*60b; σπέρματα Corn.*ND*24. II. μήκων ἀ. *frothy* poppy, *Silene inflata*, Dsc.4.66; = πέπλος, ib.167 (but, = πεπλίς, Plin.*HN*27.119); = χαμαισύκη, Ps.-Dsc.4.169.

ἄφρων, ον, gen. ονος, (φρήν) *senseless*, of statues, X.*Mem.*1.4.4:— and so, *crazed, frantic*, ἄφρονα κούρην Il.5.875, cf. 761, A.*Eu.*377 (lyr.); *silly, foolish*, Il.3.220, Hes.*Op.*[210], S.*El.*941, etc.; φρένας ἄ. Il.4.104; τὸ ἄ., = ἀφροσύνη, Th.5.105, X.*Mem.*1.2.55; τῷ φρονίμῳ τῆς γνώμης παύοντες τὸ ἄ. ⟨τῆς ῥώμης⟩ Gorg.*Fr.*6; ἐξ ἄφρονος σώφρων γεγένηται X.*Cyr.*3.1.17: Comp. -έστερος Pl.*Cra.*392c: Sup. -έστατος X.*Mem.*2.1.5. Adv. -νως *senselessly*, S.*Aj.*766, X.*HG*5.1.19; opp. νοῦν ἐχόντως, Isoc.5.7: Comp. -εστέρως Pl.*La.*193c; -έστερον Jul.*Or.*7.224d. 2. ἄφρων, = κώνειον, Ps.-Dsc.4.78.

ἀφυβρίζω, *work off youthful passion, sow one's wild oats*, Men.377. 2. of wine, *to be done fermenting*, Alex.45.4. II. *give a loose rein* to passion, *indulge freely*, εἰς τρυφάς Plu.*Demetr.*19; ἀ. ἔς τινα *vent* upon .., Agath.1.20, 4.19.

ἀφῠγής, ές, (φυγεῖν) *without strength to flee*, Timo 72.1.

ἀφῠγι-άζω, *cure, heal*, Archig.ap.Gal.12.821, Philum.*Ven.*5.3, 17.5 (Pass.), Iamb.*VP*25.114, Paul.Aeg.5.4. **-ασμός**, ὁ, *healing*, Iamb.*VP*15.64 (pl.).

ἀφυγραίνω, *moisten*, Arist.*HA*637b29 (Pass.).

ἀφύδιον [ῠ], τό, Dim. of ἀφύη, Ar.*Fr.*507.

ἀφυδραίνω, *wash clean*:—Med., *wash oneself, bathe*, καθαραῖς δρόσοις E.*Ion* 97 (lyr.).

ἄφυδρος, ον, *without water*, dub. in Hp.*Aër.*13.

ἄφυζα, *unfleeing*, of the lion, Hes.*Fr.*235.

ἄφυζε· ἀπόλαβε, Hsch.

ἀφύη [ῠ], ἡ (gen. pl. ἀφύων, not ἀφυῶν, Hdn.Gr.1.425.13), *small fry* of various fishes (cf. ἀφρός III), Epich.60,89,124, Ar.*Ach.*640, Hices.ap.Ath.7.285b; = μεμβράς, Hsch.; nickname of ἑταίρα, Ath.13.586b: prov., ἀφύα πῦρ or εἶδε πῦρ ἀ. 'no sooner said than done', Zen.2.32, Eust.1150.40.—Not used in sg. by Att., acc. to Hsch. s. v. ἀφύων τιμή.

ἀφῠής, ές, acc. ἀφυῆ S.*Ph.*1014 codd.: (φυή) :—*without natural talent, not clever, dull*, opp. εὐφυής, πρός τι Pl.*R.*455b; οὐκ ἀ. *no fool*, Id.*Lg.*832a; ἀ. πρὸς ταύτην τὴν σκέψιν *wanting wit* for it, Id.*Phd.*96c; ἐς μάθησιν Democr.85, cf. *AP*14.62. 2. in good sense, *simple, unschooled*, S. l. c. II. *naturally unsuited*, οὐκ ἀ. πρὸς τὸ φιλοκερδεῖν X.*Cyr.*1.6.32; of places, ταῖς δυνάμεσι Plb.1.30.7; πρός τι Id.4.38.1 (Sup.). Adv. ἀφυῶς, διακεῖσθαι πρός τι Id.1.88.11; ἀ. ἔχειν πρός τι Arist.*IA*710a5, Plu.*Aem.*2: Comp. -έστερον Anon.Rhythm.*Oxy.*9. iii 11. III. = δυσφυής (as etym. of ἀφύη), Ath.7.324d.

ἀφῠΐα, ἡ, *want of natural power* or *faculty*, τῆς κάμψεως Arist.*PA*659a29; φωνητηρίων ὀργάνων Str.14.2.28; ψυχῆς Plu.2.104c; ἀ. πρὸς τὸ ἡδέως ζῆν *natural unfitness* for .., ib.1088b; in pl., ἀφυΐαι, opp. εὐφυΐαι, Porph.*Abst.*3.8, cf. Colot.*in Euthd.*2. (Written ἀφύεια in Colot. l. c., Epicur.*Nat.Herc.*1420.)

ἄφῡκος, ον, *without cosmetics*, Hsch.

ἄφυκτος, ον, (φεύγω) *not to be shunned*, δῶρα θεῶν Sol.13.64; *from which none escape*, θάνατος Simon.39.3; χείρ, γυιοπέδαι, Pi.*I.*8(7).65, *P.*2.41; θεῶν ὄμμα A.*Pr.*903; κακῶν τρικυμία ib.1016; ἄ. κύνες, of the Erinyes, S.*El.*1388; of an arrow, *unerring*, Id.*Ph.*105, *Tr.*265, E.*Med.*634 (lyr.); λαβή Nicoch.3 D.; of a question, *admitting no escape, inevitable*, Pl.*Tht.*165b; λόγος Aeschin.3.17; ἄφυκτα ἐρωτᾶν Pl.*Euthd.*276e; λόγοι ἄ. Ar.*Eq.*757: Comp. -ότερος Hp.*Acut.*(*Sp.*) 10. Adv. -τως Lyc.493, etc. II. Act., *unable to escape*, μέσον λαβὼν ἄ. Ar.*Nu.*1047; dub. l. in A.*Supp.*784 (lyr.). Adv. -τως Lxx 3*Ma.*7.9: Comp. ἀφυκτοτέρως ἂν διακέοιντο Aen.Tact.16.12.—In codd. freq. written ἄφευκτος, Philem.115.4, Plu.*Lys.*29; ἄφευκτος ἀνάγκη *IG*14.803 (Naples).

ἀφ-ῠλακτέω (A), *bark out*, λόγοι ἀφυλακτούμενοι Luc.*Am.*17.

ἀ-φῠλακτέω (B), *to be off one's guard*, X.*An.*7.8.20, *Eq.Mag.*5.15: c. gen., *to be careless about*, Id.*Cyr.*1.6.5:—Pass., *to be ill-guarded*, Plb.5.73.10, cf. Onos.42.15.

ἀφύλ-ακτος [ῠ], ον, (φυλάσσω) *unguarded, unwatched*, ἀφέντες τὴν ἑωυτῶν ἀφύλακτον Hdt.8.70, cf. Th.2.13,93; ἀ. ἡ τήρησις *no* watching is *sufficient*, E.*Fr.*162. II. (φυλάσσομαι) *unguarded, off one's guard*, ἀφυλάκτῳ τινὶ ἐπιπεσεῖν, ἐπιγενέσθαι, Hdt.9.116, Th.7.32; πρὸς τὸ ἀδικεῖσθαι Arist.*Rh.*1372a19; ἀφύλακτον εὕδειν εὐφρόνην sleep *securely* through the night, A.*Ag.*337; ἀ. τινα λαμβάνειν catch one *off his guard*, X.*Cyr.*1.6.37; ἵνα .. ἀ. ληφθῇ D.4.18; τὸ ἀ. *want of precaution*, Th.3.30: Comp. -ότερος J.*AJ*5.7.4: Sup. -ότατος, νυκτὸς ὥρα D.H.2.38. Adv. -τως X.*HG*4.1.17; διακεῖσθαι Plb.4.36.4; ὁμιλεῖν Phld.*Ir.*p.30 W.; ῥαθύμως καὶ ἀ. D.H.9.19: Comp. -ότερον ἔχειν Paus.7.16.2. 2. of things, *against which no precautions are* or *can be used, not guarded against*, Arist.*Rh.*1372a24; *inevitable*, τύχη D.H.9.25; τὸ πεπρωμένον Plu.*Caes.*63; 'Ερινύς *Epigr.Gr.*218.7; ἀκωκή *IG*12(7).115.7 (Amorgos); βέλος *APl.*4.211 (Stat. Flacc.); 'Ερως ib.198 (Maec.). **-ακτηρίαστος**, ον, *not protected by a phylactery*, *PMag.Par.*1.2507. **-αξία**, ἡ, *carelessness in watching*, X.*Oec.*4.10; *negligence*, Antipho 3.4.7; *absence of guards*, X.*Hier.*6.4, D.C.55.15.

ἀφῠλ-ίζω, *strain off*, *AP*6.191.5 (Corn. Long.), f. l. in Dsc.2.76.8. **-ισμα**, ατος, τό, *whey*, Hsch. s. v. ὀρὸς γάλακτος. **-ισμός**, ὁ, *cleaning out*, or (ὕλη) *clearing of brushwood*, χωμάτων *PColumbia Inv.*56.

ἀφυλλάκανθος [λᾰ], ον, *without prickles on the leaves*, Thphr.*HP*6.4.8.

ἀφυλλ-άνθης, ες, *with no ray-florets*, ἄνθεμον *wild chamomile, Matricaria Chamomilla*, var. *eradiata*, Thphr.*HP*7.8.3. **-ος**, ον, *leafless*, Il.2.425, Thphr.*HP*1.14.3, Plu.2.648f; *stripped of leaves*, στέφανος Xenarch.13; ἀ. στόματος λιταί prayers *not seconded by the suppliant's olive-branch*, E.*Or.*383. II. Act., *stripping off the leaves, blighting*, λειχήν A.*Eu.*785 (lyr.). **-ωτος**, ον, *bare of foliage, treeless*, πέτρα S.*Fr.*299.

ἄφῡλος, ον, *without a tribe*, Max.Tyr.21.4, prob. in *EM*178.39.

ἀφύξιμος, ον, (ἀφύσσω) κυάθῳ τρὶς ἀ. οἴνην thrice *drawn* into the cyathus, i. e. 3 cyathi, Nic.*Th.*603.

ἄφυξις, εως, ἡ, (ἀφύσσω) *drawing out, ladling*, dub. in Hsch., Cyr.

ἀφυπν-ίζω, *awaken from sleep*, E.*Rh.*25, Plu.*Nic.*9, Longus 1.25, etc.:—Pass., *wake up, keep awake*, Cratin.306 (lyr.), Pherecr.191 (lyr.): intr. in Act., Philostr.*VA*2.36. **-ισμός**, ὁ, *keeping awake*, Eust.1297.31. **-όω**, *awake from sleep*, *AP*9.517 (Antip. Thess.), Ant.Diog.9. II. *fall asleep*, *Ev.Luc.*8.23, Paul.Aeg.1.98:—Med., Hld.9.12 (v.l. ὑφυπν-). **-ώττω**, = ἀφυπνόω II, Sch.Pi.*I.*7(6).23.

ἀφύρᾱτος [ῠ], Ion. -ητος, ον, *not kneaded*, Hp.*VM*14.

ἀφυρεῖν· ἀκαθαρσία, Hsch.

ἄφυρτος, ον, *unmixed*. Adv. -τως Nic.Dam.p.144 D.

ἀφυσγετός (ἀφύσγετος Tyrannio ap.Sch.Il.11.495), ὁ, *mud and rubbish* which a stream carries with it, Il.11.495, Opp.*H.*1.779. II. as Adj., *filthy*, ὕδρωψ Nic.*Al.*342. 2. (ἀφύσσω) *abundant*, νέκταρ ib.584.

ἀφύσητος [ῡ], ον, *not inflated*, ἀσκός Hp.*Art.*47,77.

ἀφύσικος [ῠ], *unphilosophical, unscientific*, Arist.ap.S.E.*M.*10.46. 2. *contrary to the laws of nature*, ib.250.

ἀφύσιμος, = ἀρύσιμος, Sch.Nic.*Al.*584.

ἀφῠσιολόγ-ητος, ον, *not to be explained by science*, Epicur.*Fr.*141, 200. II. *without knowledge of natural laws*, in Adv. -τως, φαντάζεσθαι prob. in M.Ant.10.9. **-ος**, ον, *not versed in natural philosophy*, prob. l. in Id.9.41.

ἀφυσμός, ὁ, *drawing off*, of liquids, Suid.

ἄφῡσος, ον, (φῦσα) *without flatulence*, Hp.*Hum.*3. 2. *causing no flatulence*, Diocl.*Fr.*128, Gal.6.540. 3. *expelling flatus*, Ruf.*Fr.*1, Gal.12.101.

ἀφύσσα, ἡ, = κοτύλη, (Tarent.), Hsch.

ἀφύσσω, Ep. impf. ἄφυσσον Call.*Cer.*70: fut. ἀφύξω, Dor. -ξῶ Theoc.7.65: aor. ἤφῠσα Od.9.165, Ep. ἄφυσσα 2.379, E.*IA*1051 (lyr.), imper. ἄφυσσον Od.2.349:—**Med.**, aor. ἠφῠσάμην, Ep. ἀφύσσατο Il.16.230:—*draw* liquids, esp. from a larger vessel with a smaller, νέκταρ ἀπὸ κρητῆρος ἀφύσσων Il.1.598, cf. Od.9.9; οἶνον ἐν ἀμφιφορεῦσιν ἠφύσαμεν 9.165; εἰς ἄγγε' ἀφύσσαι δῶρα Διωνύσου Hes.*Op.*613:—Pass., πίθων ἠφύσσετο οἶνος *was drawn from* the wine-jars, Od.23.305: metaph., ἄφενος καὶ πλοῦτον ἀφύξειν *draw full draughts of* wealth, i. e. *heap it up*, τινί for another, Il.1.171; ἀ. νέκταρ ἐρώτων *AP*5.225 (Paul. Sil.). 2. *sound, probe*, ἰητὴρ ἕλκος ἀ. Opp.*H.*2.597. II. Med., *draw for oneself, help oneself to*, οἶνον ἀφυσσόμενος Il.23.220; ἀπὸ Κηφισοῦ ῥοὰς .. ἀφυσσαμέναν, of Aphrodite, E.*Med.*836 (lyr.); φύλλα ἠφυσάμην I *heaped me up* a bed of leaves, Od.7.286, cf. 5.482: metaph., αἰῶνος σπειρήματ' ἀφυσσάμενος *App.Anth.*3.186.—Trag. only in E. l. c. and *IA*1051.

ἀφύστα· κοτύλη, στάμνος, Hsch.

ἀφυστερέω, *come too late, be behindhand*, Plb.1.52.8, 21.22.2, D.H.10.26; ἐὰν ἀφυστερῇ τὸ βαλανεῖον καύμασι *PLond.*3.1166.13 (i A.D.). II. *withhold*, Lxx *Ne.*9.20.

ἀφύτευτος [ῠ], ον, *not planted*, χῶρος X.*Oec.*20.22.

ἄφυτρις· ἀρύταινα (ἄρπαινα cod.), Hsch. (leg. ἀρυστρίς).

ἀφύω, *to become white* or *bleached*, Hp.*Int.*40.

ἀφυώδης, ες, *whitish, like an* ἀφύη, χρῶμα Hp.*Mul.*2.110,116.

ἄφωκτος, ον, *not roasted*, Dieuch.ap.Orib.4.7.21, Gal.12.619.

ἀφώλιος, = ἀποφώλιος, Theognost.*Can.*57.

ἀφων-έω, *to be speechless*, Hp.*Epid*.1.26.ιγ'. **-ητέω**, = foreg., Sch.A.*Ag*.241. **-ητος**, ον, *unspeakable, unutterable*, ἄχος Pi. *P*.4.237. II. *voiceless, speechless*, παρέσχε φωνὴν τοῖς ἀ. S.*OC* 1283. **-ία**, Ion. **-ίη**, ἡ, *speechlessness*, Hp.*Epid*.3.17.γ', Pl.*Smp*. 198c. II. *mispronunciation*, Philostr.*VA*6.36. **-ος**, ον, (φωνή) *voiceless, dumb*, Thgn.669, Hdt.1.85, D.18.191; ῥήτωρ Antiph.196. 14; κακὸν ἄ. *Com.Adesp*.8 D.; stronger than ἄναυδος (q.v.), Hp.*Epid*. 3.17.γ'; εἴδωλα 1*Ep.Cor*.12.2; *unable to speak*, of a child, Sapph.118: c.gen., ἄ. τῆσδε τῆς ἀρᾶς *unable to utter* it, S.*OC*865. Adv. -νως ib.131 (lyr.): neut. pl. as Adv., ἄφωνα σημανοῦσιν.. ὡς.. A.*Pers*.819. 2. *with a poor voice*, τραγῳδός D.T.631.21. 3. *intestate*, *Tab.Heracl*.1. 151. 4. ἄφωνα (sc. γράμματα, στοιχεῖα) *consonants*, ἄ. καὶ φωνοῦντα (fort. ἄ. φωνήεντα) E.*Fr*.578.2; τοῖς ἄλλοις φωνήεσί τε καὶ ἄ. Pl.*Cra*.393e; τὸ σῖγμα τῶν ἀ. ἐστί Id.*Tht*.203b: but esp. of *mutes*, τὰ ἄφθογγα καὶ ἄ. Id.*Phlb*.18c, cf. *Cra*.424c; opp. ἡμίφωνα, Arist. *Po*.1456ᵇ28, cf. Phld.*Po*.2.16, *Herc*.994.28, D.H.*Comp*.14, D.T.631. 20, S.E.*M*.1.102.

ἀφωντεύς, fem. **ἀφώντισσα**, title of doubtful meaning, *BGU*1249 (ii B.C.).

ἀφώρατος, ον, *not detected*, Oenom.ap.Eus.*PE*5.20. Adv. -τως Ph.2.521.

ἀφωρισμένως, (ἀφορίζω) *definitively*, Arist.*Cat*.12ᵇ39; *separately, specially*, Plu.2.466a, Aristid.Quint.1.21, Artem.4.84, etc.

ἄφως, ωτος, *without light*, Eust.968.48.

ἀφώτιστος, ον, *dark, obscure*, J.*AJ*13.11.2, Arr.*Epict*.1.14.10, Plu. 2.931c, Onos.10.13, S.E.*M*.10.164, Orph.*Fr*.272, etc.; ἀ. τοῦ ἡλίου *unlit by* the sun, Gem.11.3: metaph., ψυχή Ph.1.638; φῶς Anon.*in Prm*. in *Rh.Mus*.47.608; σελήνη Nonn.*D*.6.91; *unenlightened*, Plot. 1.2.4.

ἀχά, ἡ, v. sub ἠχέω, ἰαχή.

Ἀχαία, Ion. **Ἀχαιΐη**, ἡ, epith. of Demeter in Attica, Hdt.5.61; also in Boeotia, Plu.2.378e; Ἀχέα at Thespiae, *IG*7.1867. II. **ἀχαιά**, ἡ, = ἔριθος, Philet.ap.Gramm. post Orionem p.185 S. (Acc. to Hsch. from ἄχος *grief* for the loss of her daughter: also **Ἀχηρώ** Id.) **Ἀχαΐα**, v. Ἀχαιός.

ἀχαίας· λύπας, Hsch. **ἀχαΐζειν**· ἑλληνίζειν, Id.

Ἀχαιικός, ή, όν, (Ἀχαιός) *of* or *for the Achaians, Achaian*, A.*Ag*. 185, 624, E.*Tr*.236, al.

Ἀχαιΐς, ΐδος, ἡ, *the Achaian land*, with or without γαῖα, Il.1.254, 3.75, etc. 2. (sc. γυνή) *Achaian woman*, Ἀχαιΐδες οὐκέτ' Ἀχαιοί 2.235, etc.:—also **Ἀχαιϊάς**, άδος, 5.424, etc.

ἀχαιμενίς, ίδος, ἡ, = πόλιον, Ps.-Dsc.3.110. II. = *Euphorbia antiquorum*, Plin.*HN*24.161.

ἀχαίνει· σαίνει, παίζει, κολακεύει, Hsch.

ἀχαίνη, ἡ, a kind of *large loaf*, baked by the women at the Thesmophoria, Semus 13.

ἀχαΐνης [ῐ] ἔλαφος *brocket, two-year* stag, Arist.*HA*611ᵇ18: gen. ἀχαΐνεω *AP*6.165 (Phal.):—also fem. ἀχαΐνη Arist.*HA*506ᵃ24; also ἀχαΐνη *deer*, Babr.95.87; poet. ἀχαιϊνέη A.R.4.175, Opp.*C*.2.426.

ἀχαιόμαντις, εως, ὁ, title of diviner in Cyprus, Hsch.

Ἀχαιός, ά, όν, *Achaean*, Hom., etc.: hence as Subst., 1. Ἀχαιοί, οἱ, *the Achaeans*, in Hom. for the *Greeks* generally, Il.2.235, etc. 2. **Ἀχαΐα**, ἡ, *Achaia* in Peloponnese, Th., etc.; under the Romans, *the province of Greece*.

ἄχαιος, perh. = ἀχήν, *IG*3.1385.

Ἀχαϊστί, = *Graeco ritu*, Orac.ap.Phleg.*Mir*.10.

ἀχᾰλέπως, Adv. *without difficulty*, Ph.*Bel*.92.15.

ἀχάλῑν-ος [χᾰ], ον, *unbridled*, στόματα E.*Ba*.386 (lyr.), cf. *HF*382 (lyr.), Ar.*Ra*.838, Pl.*Lg*.701c; ἀχάλινα λέγειν *APl*.4.223; ἀ. ὑπ' ἀργύρου, i.e. *uncorrupted* by bribes, *IG*9(1).270 (Atalante): neut. pl. as Adv., E.*HF* l.c. **-ωτος** ον, *unbridled*, ἵππος X.*Eq*.5.3, D.H.9.65, Ph.1.313; στόματα *AP*11.177 (Lucill.); ἀνάγκαι Orph.*H*.55.13.

ἀχάλιον, τό, = σιδηρῖτις, = ἀλθαία, *Hippiatr*.11.

ἀχάλκ-εος, ον, *without a* χαλκοῦς, *penniless*, ἀ. οὐδός (with a pun on χάλκεος οὐδός) *AP*11.403 (Lucill.). **-ευτος**, ον, *not forged of metal*, πέδαι A.*Ch*.493, Critias 20 D.; τρύπανα S.*Fr*.708. **-έω**, (χαλκοῦς) *to be penniless*, *AP*11.154 (Lucill.). **-ής**, ές, *without brass*, ὁπλαί Tryph.87. **-ος**, ον, *without brass*, ἄχαλκος ἀσπίδων, i.e. ἄνευ ἀσπίδων χαλκείων S.*OT*191 (lyr.). **-ωτος**, ον, lit. *not brazened*: *without money*, κυνοῦχος *AP*6.298 (Leon.).

ἀχανά· κλήματα, Hsch.

ἀχανδής, ές, dub. in *Anacreont*.56.35.

ἀχάνεια [χᾰ], ἡ, (ἀχᾰνής II) *immensity, infinite expanse*, τοῦ ὀπίσω καὶ πρόσω αἰῶνος M.Ant.12.7; *infinite void*, Syrian.*in Metaph*.60.5; εἰς ἀ. λήγειν Olymp.*in Mete*.82.22; ἡ τοῦ ἀπείρου ἀστάθμητος ἀ. Dam. *Pr*.53. 2. Medic., *wide opening, cavity*, Heliod.(?)ap.Orib.46.19. 12, Paul.Aeg.6.107.

ἀχάνη, ἡ, name of a *Persian* (also, *Boeotian*, Arist.*Fr*.566) *measure*, = 45 μέδιμνοι, Ar.*Ach*.108, 109. 2. *chest, box*, Phanod.25, Plu. *Arat*.6. [ἄχᾱ Ar.*Ach*. ll. cc.]

ἀχᾰνής, ές, (χάσκω, χανεῖν) *not opening the mouth*, of one mute with astonishment, Hegesipp.Com.1.25, Plb.7.17.5, Luc.*Icar*.23, Alciphr. 3.20; also δι' ἀχανοῦς through *a narrow opening*, Thphr.*Vent*.29. II. *yawning*, κρημνός Timae.28; χάσμα *AP*9.423 (Bianor), J.*AJ*7.10.2; *without a lid*, Hero *Aut*.28.4; *wide-mouthed*, τεῦχος Diocl.ap.Orib. 5.4.2, cf. Antyll.ib.44.8.12; *open*, ἀ. καὶ ἀνώροφος νεώς D.C.37.17; *open, unoccupied*, of building land, *POxy*.1702.3 (iii A.D.); χάσμα Parm.1.18; σκότος Lxx *Wi*.19.17, cf. Lyr.Anon.*in PFay*.2 ii 20; τὸ ἀχανὲς *the yawning gulf*, Arist.*Mete*.367ᵃ19; ἡ ἀ. χώρα Ph.1.7; ἀχανές· τὸ μὴ ἔχον στέγην.. ἐπὶ τοῦ λαβυρίνθου, S.*Fr*.1030; ὄψει πάντα ἀχανῆ *PMag.Par*.1.1107. 2. generally, *vast, immense*, στράτευμα Plu. 2.866b; πέλαγος Id.*Cic*.6, Jul.*Or*.4.142c.

ἀχανόωσαν· ἐπιθυμοῦσαν, Hsch.; cf. ἰχανάω.

ἀχάντιον, τό, Ion. for ἀκάνθιον, Greg.Cor.pp.414, 649 S.

ἀχάρακτος [χᾰ], ον, *not marked* or *branded*, κάμηλος *BGU*13.8 (iii A.D.); *not stamped*, *Ath.Mitt*.33.384 (Pergam.); of ships, *without emblem* or *figurehead*, *PLille*22.6; *not graven* or *cut*, Nonn.*D*. 13.84; *that cannot be cut*, σιδήρῳ γυῖα ἀ. ib.16.158, cf. 26.242.

ἀχᾰράκωτος [ρᾰ], ον, *not palisaded*, Plb.10.11.2, Plu.*Mar*.20: metaph., *defenceless, friendless*, Philostr.*VA*5.35. Adv. -τως, αὐλίσασθαι App.*BC*3.70.

ἀχαρές· λυπηρόν, Hsch.

ἀχᾰριότης, ητος, ἡ, *awkwardness, stupidity*, with a play on the name Χαριμόρτης, dub. in Plb.18.55.2.

ἄχᾰρις, ὁ, ἡ, ἄχαρι, τό, gen. ιτος, dat. ἀχάρι Hdt.1.41 codd.:—*without grace* or *charm*, συμπόσιον γίνεται οὐκ ἄχαρι Thgn.496, cf. 1236; of an immature girl, Sapph.34. 2. *unpleasant, disagreeable*, οὐδὲν ἄ. πείσεται Hdt.2.141, cf. 6.9; πρός τινος 8.143; οὐδὲν ἄ. παριδεῖν τινι 1.38, 108; ἐνδιδόναι οὐδὲν ἄ. 7.52; esp. as euphem. for a *grievous* calamity, ἄ. συμφορή 1.41, 7.190; τὸ τέλος σφι ἐγένετο ἄ. 8.13; [βίος] οὐκ ἄ. εἰς τὴν τριβήν Ar.*Av*.156. II. *ungracious, thankless*, ἄ. τιμή a *thankless* office, Hdt.7.36; χάρις ἄχαρις *graceless* grace, *thankless* favour, A.*Pr*.545 (lyr.), *Ag*.1545 (lyr.); κακῆς γυναικὸς χάριν ἄχαριν ἀπώλετο E.*IT*566.

ἀχᾰριστ-έω, *show ingratitude*, Antipho Soph.54, Phld.*Herc*.1251. 17, *Hom*.p.59 O.; πρὸς τοὺς φίλους X.*Mem*.2.2.2; τινί *Vit.Philonid*. p.13 C., Plu.*Phoc*.36; τινί τινος D.H.7.60. 2. *disoblige*, τοῖς κακοῖς καὶ νοσώδεσιν ἀ. Pl.*Smp*.186c, cf. *SIG*495.159 (iii B.C.), Luc.*DMar*. 9.2, Nic.Dam.p.5 D. 3. Pass., *to be treated ungratefully*, Plb.22. 11.8, Corn.*ND*16, J.*BJ*2.16.4, Plu.*Cam*.13, Just.*Nov*.98 *Pr*.; ὑπό τινος Plu.*Mar*.28. **-ία**, ἡ, *ingratitude*, X.*Cyr*.1.2.7; εἰς ἀ. ἄγειν D.18. 316: in pl., ἀχαριστίαι πρὸς ἀνθρώπους Phld.*Herc*.1251.10; ὀλιγωρίας καὶ ἀ. ib.1457.9. 2. *ungraciousness*, ἀρρυθμία καὶ ἀ. Pl.*R*.411e. **-ος**, ον, (χαρίζομαι) *ungracious, unpleasant*, οὐκ ἀχάριστα μεθ' ἡμῖν ταῦτ' ἀγορεύεις Od.8.236: irreg. Comp., δόρπου ἀχαρίστερον (for -ιστότερον) 20.392; *without grace* or *charm*, οὐκ ἀχάριστα λέγειν X.*An*.2.1.13; φωνή Epicur.*Sent.Vat*.75; -ότερον ἐπιμέλημα a *more thankless* business, X.*Oec*.7.37; ἀ. ἐξέτασις D.H.*Pomp*.1. II. of persons, *ungracious, unfavourable*, Thgn.841 (-τως Bgk.), Phld.*Ir*.p.60 W. 2. *ungrateful, thankless*, Hdt.1.90, X.*Cyr*.1.2.7, Crates Theb. 19, etc.; δῆμος Hdt.5.91; προδότας E.*Ion*880 (lyr.), cf. *Med*.659 (lyr.); ἀ. πρὸς τοὺς γονέας X.*Mem*.2.2.14; τινί E.*Hec*.138 (lyr.); σπείρων εἰς ἀχάριστα sowing in *thankless soil*, *IG*14.2012 (Sulp. Max.). Adv. -τως, ἀποπέμψασθαι εὐεργέτας X.*An*.7.7.23, cf. Lys.30.6. 3. Pass., *unrequited*, ἀ. εἶναι τὰ ἀνηλωμένα Lys.21.12. Adv. οὐκ ἂν ἀχαρίστως μοι ἔχοι πρός τινος *thanks* would not be *refused* me by.., X. *An*.2.3.18. 4. Adv. -τως *with a bad grace, with an ill will*, ἀ. ἕπεσθαι follow *sulkily*, Id.*Cyr*.7.4.14; τὰς χάριτας ἀ. χαρίζεσθαι Isoc.1. 31. 5. ἀχάριστον, τό, *antidote*, *PGrenf*.1.52.1, 12 (iii A.D.), Marcell. Empir.20: also ἀχάριστος, ἡ, Alex.Trall.*Febr*.7. b. name of an *eyesalve*, Cels.6.6.7, Gal.12.749.

ἀχάρῑτος [χᾰ], ον, = foreg., *unseemly*, Plu.*Sol*.20; euphem., παθήματα ἀ. ἐόντα μαθήματα γέγονε Hdt.1.207. Adv. οὐκ -τως ἔφη Ath.7. 281c, cf. Hermog.*Id*.2.11, D.C.66.9. 2. *ungrateful, thankless*, δῆμον εἶναι συνοίκημα ἀχαριτώτατον Hdt.7.156; χάρις ἀ. A.*Ch*.42 (lyr., Elmsl.), E.*Ph*.1757 (lyr.).

Ἀχαρναί, ῶν, αἱ, *Acharnae*, a famous deme of Attica, Th.2.19 sq.:—**Ἀχαρνεύς**, έως, ὁ, *inhabitant of Acharnae*, pl. Ἀχαρνῆς, title of play by Ar.: poet. **Ἀχαρνηΐδαι** Ar.*Ach*.322:—Adj. **Ἀχαρνικός**, ή, όν, ib. 180; Ἀ. κισσός, = κορυμβίας, Thphr.*HP*3.18.6:—also **Ἀχαρνίτης**, ου, ὁ, κισσός *AP*7.21 (Simm.):—Adv. **Ἀχαρνῆσι** *at Acharnae*, Luc.*Icar*. 18: **Ἀχαρνῆθεν** *from Acharnae*, Anaxandr.41.18.

ἀχαρνώς, ώ, ὁ, = ὀρφώς, a *sea-fish*, prob. *bass*, Callias Com.3: **ἄχαρνος** in Ath.3.286b: **ἀχάρνας** Arist.*HA*602ᵃ12; gen. ἀχάρνου ib. 591ᵇ1:—also **ἀχάρνα** and **ἄχερνα**, names of *fish* in Hsch.

ἀχάσμητος, ον, *without hiatus*, Eust.919.35.

ἀχάτης [ᾰχᾱ], ου, ὁ, *agate*, Thphr.*Lap*.31, J.*AJ*3.7.5, D.P.1075, Nonn.*D*.5.170.

ἀχεδών, Dor. for ἠχεδών, f.l. in Mosch.3.54.

ἄχει or **ἄχι**, τό, *reed-grass*, Lxx *Ge*.41.2, al.; used for *lamp-wick*, *PMag.Par*.1.1091, 1101. (Egyptian word.)

ἀχείμ-αντος, ον, *not stormy*, βλήχρων ἀνέμων ἀ. πνόαι Alc.16; *not vexed by storms*, Μέμφις B.*Fr*.22:—also **-αστος**, ον, θάλασσα J.*AJ* 3.5.3: **-ᾰτος**, ον, A.*Supp*.136 (lyr.): **-ερος**, ον, Arat.1121: **-ων**, ον, gen. ονος, Nonn.*D*.1.142.

ἄχειρ, ρος, *without hands*, ἄποδα καὶ ἄ. [ζῷα] Arist.*HA*515ᵇ24; ἄ. καὶ ἄποδας [Ἑρμᾶς] Plu.2.797f, cf. Corn.*ND*16; τὰ ἄ. *hinder parts*, X. *Cyr*.3.3.45.

ἀχειρ-ἀγώγητος, ον, *untamed*, Ph.1.680. **-άπτητος**, ον, *not touched by hand*, Iamb.*VP*29.157. **-ής**, ές, = ἄχειρ, καρκίνοι Batr. 298: metaph., = ἀχρεῖος, Hsch. II. *not made with hands*, ἄγαλμα B.9.11. **-ία**, ἡ, *want of hands*: hence, *awkwardness*, Hp.*Morb*. 1.1, Apollon.Cit.1. **-ίδωτος** [ρῐ], ον, *without sleeves*, *Dialex*.2.9, Sch.Luc.*Vit.Auct*.7.

ἀχειρο-ποίητος, ον, *not made by hands*, of buildings and statues, *Ev.Marc*.14.58, 2*Ep.Cor*.5.1; ἀ. περιτομή, i.e. *spiritual*, *Ep.Col*.2. 11. **-τόνητος**, ον, *not elected*, D.19 Arg. ii 13. II. *not granted by vote*, τιμή Max.Tyr.12.5.

ἀχειρούργητος, ον, = sq., Poll.2.154.

ἀχείρωτος, ον, *untamed, unconquered*, Th.6.10, D.S.5.15. II. ἀ. φύτευμα, of the olive, *not planted by man's hand*, S.*OC*698 (lyr.).

ἀχέλιον· τὸ λεπτομερές, Hsch. **ἀχέλουρις**· ποίμνη τις (Tarent.), Id.

Ἀχελωΐδες (sc. νῆσοι), αἱ, *islands at the mouth of the Achelous*, A. *Pers.*869 (lyr.).

Ἀχελῷος, poet. **Ἀχελώϊος**, ὁ, *Achelous*, name of several rivers, Il.21.194, 24.616, Hes.*Th.*340, Str.9.5.10, etc. II. in Poets, *any stream*: generally, *water*, S.*Fr.*5, E.*Ba.*625, Ar.*Fr.*351, Achae.9, Ephor.27.

ἄχερδος [ᾰ], ἡ (less freq. ὁ, Theoc.24.90), *wild pear, Pyrus amygdaliformis*, Od.14.10, S.*OC*1596, Pherecyd.33 J., Theoc. l.c.; ἀ. τῆς ἀκραχολωτάτης Pherecr.164: special kind at Ceos, Arist.*Mir.*845^{a}15.

Ἀχερδούσιος, *inhabitant of the deme* Ἀχερδοῦς: hence with play on ἄχερδος, *Crabby*, μοχθηρὸς ὢν καὶ τὴν γνώμην Ἀχερδούσιος *Com. Adesp.*1277; cf. ἀχραδούσιος.

ἄχερλα, v. ἀχαρνώς.

Ἀχερόντειος, α, ον, *of Acheron*, ναῦς Call.*Hec.*31.3:—also **Ἀχερόντιος**, E.*Alc.*443 (lyr.), Ar.*Ra.*471:—fem. **Ἀχεροντιάς**, άδος, νύξ *AP*5.240 (Paul. Sil.): and **Ἀχερούσιος**, α, ον (also ος, ον A.*Ag.*1160), Th.1.46:—fem. **Ἀχερουσιάς**, άδος, X.*An.*6.2.2, Pl.*Phd.*113a.

ἀχερωΐς, ΐδος, ἡ, *white poplar, Populus alba*, elsewh. λευκή, Il.13.389, A.R.4.1476. (Expld. with ref. to Ἀχέρων, from the legend that it had been brought from the nether world by Hercules, Paus.5.14.2.) II. Ἀχερωΐδες ὄχθαι *of* the river *Acheron* in Asia Minor, Nic.*Al.*13.

Ἀχέρων, οντος, ὁ, *Acheron*, river in the nether world, Od.10.513, etc.; of other rivers, Th.1.46, Str.6.1.5, etc.

ἀχέτας or **ἀχέτᾱ**, Dor. and Att. for ἠχέτης (q. v.).

ἀχεύω and **ἀχέω** (A) [ᾰ], Ep. Verbs used in pres. part., *grieving, mourning*, ὀδυρόμενος καὶ ἀχεύων Il.9.612, Od.2.23; κεῖτ' ἀχέων Il.2.724; ἀχέουσά περ ἔμπης Od.15.361, cf. Sapph.*Supp.*1.11: c. acc., κῆρ ἀχέων *grieving in* heart, Il.5.399; θυμὸν ἀχεύων ib.869, 18.461, Hes.*Op.*399: c. neut. Adj., πυκινὸν περ ἀχεύων Od.11.88; μέγ' ἀχεύων 16.139: c. gen. causae, τῆς ἀχέων *sorrowing for* her, Il.2.694, 18.446; Ὀδυσσῆος μέγ' ἀχεύων Od.16.139; so ἕνεκ' ἀλλοτρίων ἀχέων Il.20.298; τοῦγ' εἵνεκα θυμὸν ἀχεύων Od.21.318; later ἐπὶ σφετέροις ἀχέουσα παισί A.R.3.643. II. other forms (chiefly Ep.): 1. in causal sense, *vex, annoy*, redupl. aor. 2 **ἤκᾰχε** (but part. ἀκαχών intr., *grieving*, Hes.*Th.*868): hence redupl. pres. **ἀκᾰχίζω**, fut. ἀκαχήσω, aor. 1 ἀκάχησα: c. acc. pers., μέγα δ' ἤκαχε λαόν Il.16.822, cf. Od.16.427; ἐμὲ μεγάλως ἀκαχίζεις ib.432; θανὼν ἀκάχησε τοκῆας by his death, Il.23.223; ἕ μάλιστα ἤκαχ' ἀποφθιμένη Od.15.357; ἀκαχήσεις μηλοβοτῆρας *h.Merc.*286. 2. Pass., **ἄχομαι, ἄχνῠμαι, ἀκᾰχίζομαι**, imper. ἀκαχίζεο, -ίζευ, Il.6.486, Od.11.486: pf. ἀκάχημαι 8.314, Ep. 3 pl. ἀκηχέδαται (with v. l. ἀκηχέαται) Il.17.637; imper. ἀκάχησο A.R.4.1324; inf. ἀκάχησθαι Il.19.335; part. ἀκαχήμενος (accent. as a pres.) ib.312, Ep. also ἀκηχέμενος 5.364, 18.29: plpf. ἀκαχήατο 12.179: aor. 2, 3 pl. ἀκάχοντο Od.16.342; opt. ἀκαχοίμην, -οιτο, -οίμεθα, 1.236, Il.13.344, 16.16, etc.:—in later Ep. pres. ἀκάχονται, impf. ἀκάχοντο, Q.S.3.224, 5.652:—Constr.: abs., ἄχομαι Od.18.256, 19.129; ἄχνυνται Il.18.62; ἀχνύμενος, like ἀχέων or ἀχεύων, 1.103, 241, etc.; ἀχνυμένη κραδίῃ 24.584; ἀχνύμενος κῆρ 7.428, 431, etc.; ἀκαχήμενος ἦτορ Od.9.62, etc.; θυμὸν ἀκηχέμεναι Il.18.29; ἀκαχήατο θυμόν 12.179: less freq. c. dat., ἀκαχίζεο θυμῷ 6.486; also κῆρ ἄχνυται ἐν θυμῷ, ἄχνυτο.. θυμὸς ἐνὶ στήθεσσιν 6.524, 14.38: c. gen. causae, *grieve for*, sts. with a part., ἀχνύμενός περ ἑταίρου, υἷος ἑοῖο, etc., 8.125, 24.550, etc.; σεῖο.. ἀχνύμεθα φθιμένοιο Od.11.558, cf. 14.376, Il.16.16; less freq. c. dat., οὔ κε θανόντι περ ὧδ' ἀκαχοίμην Od.1.236; ἀχνυμένη περὶ παιδί *h.Cer.*77: later c. acc., *lament*, τὸ δ' ἄχνυμαι Pi.*P.*7.16; ἀχνύμενος μόρον Ἀντιγόνης S.*Ant.*627: with part., δρόων ἀκάχημαι Od.8.314, cf. Il.17.637; μή τι θανὼν ἀκαχίζευ Od.11.486, cf. Il.6.486.—Once in Trag., S. l.c.; never in Prose.

ἀχέω (B) [ᾰ], poet. form for ἰαχέω, *utter*, *h.Cer.*479, prob. l. in *h.Hom.*19.18; ἣν ἄτην ἀχέων Hes.*Sc.*93 codd.; ὕμνον ἀχέων Ion Trag.39: fut. ἀχήσεται *Trag. Adesp.*237.

ἀχέω (C) [ᾱ], Dor. for ἠχέω (q. v.).

ἄχηλος, ον, *with undivided hoof*, Gal.2.431.

ἀχήλωτος, ον, *not barbed*, Ph.*Bel.*73.43, 75.35.

ἀχήν [ᾱ], ὁ, ἡ, Dor., = ἠχήν (q. v.), *poor, needy*, Theoc.16.33: dat. pl. ἀχήνεσσιν Epigr. in *BCH*11.161 (Lagina).

ἀχηνεῖς· κενοί, Hsch.

ἀχηνία [ᾰ], ἡ, *need, want*, χρημάτων A.*Ch.*301; φίλων ἀχηνίᾳ Ar.*Fr.*20, cf. 1 D.; ὀμμάτων ἐν ἀχηνίαις in the eyes' *blank gaze*, A.*Ag.*418 (lyr.).

ἀχηρής, v. l. for ἀχθηρής, Suid.

ἄχηρον· ἀκρίδα (Cret.), Hsch. **Ἀχηρώ**, v. Ἀχαία. **ἀχητεῖς**· ἀζήτητοι, ἀσύνετοι, ἄποροι, Id.

Ἀχθεία· ἡ Δημήτηρ, μυστικῶς, Hsch.

ἀχθ-εινός, ή, όν, (ἄχθος) *burdensome, oppressive*, of persons, E. *Hipp.*94; of things, Id.*Hec.*1240; τὸ -ότατον τοῦ βίου X.*Mem.*4.8.1; βοοκτασία, i.e. *that cost* the slayer *dear*, *AP*6.263 (Leon.). Adv. -νῶς *unwillingly*, οὐκ ἀ. ὁρᾶν τι X.*HG*4.8.27. II. *laborious*, βόες *IG*14.2012.16 (Sulp. Max.). **-έω**, *load*, in aor. part. ἀχθήσας, Hsch. **-ηδών**, όνος, ἡ, *weight, burden*, ἀ. κακοῦ A.*Pr.*26. 2. metaph., *vexation, annoyance*, Th.2.37, Pl.*Lg.*734a; ἐρέσθαι τινὰ δι' ἀχθηδόνα for the sake of *teasing*, Th.4.40; μὴ πρὸς ἀχθηδόνα μου ἀκούσῃς Luc.*Tox.*9. **-ήεις**, εσσα, εν, *grievous*, κάματος Marc. Sid.96. **-ήμων**, ον, gen. ονος, *suffering*, Man.4.501. **-ηρής**, ές, = sq., Hsch. **-ηρός**, όν, *grievous*, dub. l. in Antiph.94. **-ηφορέω**, v.l. for ἀχθοφορέω, D.H.4.81, Ph.2.604, D.C.72.12:—so **ἀχθηφόρος**, for -οφόρος, Id.62.6. **-ίζω**, *load*, Ἄραψ κάμηλον ἀχθίσας Babr.8.1.

ἄχθομαι, Pass.: fut. Med. ἀχθέσομαι Ar.*Nu.*865, 1441, *Av.*84, Pl.*R.*603e, *Hp.Ma.*292e; Pass., ἀχθεσθήσομαι And.3.21, Pl.*Grg.*506c, v.l. in X.*Cyr.*8.4.10, (συν-) Aeschin.3.242: pf. ἤχθημαι Lyc. 827: aor. ἠχθέσθην Hdt.2.103, A.*Pr.*392, Th.6.15, Isoc.12.17:—*to be loaded*, ὅτε δὴ κοίλη νηῦς ἤχθετο Od.15.457: c. gen., τράπεζα τυροῦ καὶ μέλιτος πίονος ἀχθομένη Xenoph.1.10: c. dat., ἐλάτην.. ἀχθομένην ὄζοις A.R.1.1191. II. mostly of mental oppression, *to be vexed, grieved*:—Constr.: abs., ἤχθετο γὰρ κῆρ Il.11.274, cf. A.*Pr.*392; ὅτῳ μὴ ἀχθομένῳ εἴη (constr. like ἀσμένῳ, βουλομένῳ ἐστί) X.*Cyr.*4.5.21; ἀχθομένην ὀδύνῃσι Il.5.354; ἄ. τινί *at* a thing, or *with* a person, Hdt. 2.103, 3.1, al., Ar.*Ach.*62, *Pax* 119, Th.6.28, etc.; μοι μὴ ἄχθεσθε λέγοντι τἀληθῆ Pl.*Ap.*31e, cf. *Men.*99e: with Preps., ἐπί τινι X.*HG* 7.1.32, etc.; ἐφ' ἑκάστου Pl.*Prm.*130a; περὶ τῶν νεῶν Hdt.8.99; ὑπέρ τινος Ar.*Lys.*10, Pl.*Ap.*23e; διά τινα Isoc.12.17: also c. acc., λίην ἄχθομαι ἕλκος Il.5.361: c. neut. Adj., τοῦτο X.*An.*3.2.20; μεῖζον Pl. *Smp.*216c: c. gen., τῆς οἰκίας Plu.*Publ.*10: c. part., either of subject, οὐκ ἄχθομαί σ' ἰδών τε καὶ λαβὼν φίλον S.*Ph.*671, cf. Ar.*Pl.*234, Th.1.92, X.*Cyr.*3.3.20, Pl.*Prt.*342c, etc.; or of object, ἤχθετο δαμναμένους *at* their being conquered, Il.13.352; Ἀρίσταρχον στρατηγοῦντ' ἄ. Eup.43: but the part. of the object is also put in gen., οὐδὲν ἤχθετο αὐτῶν πολεμούντων he *had* no *objection to*.., X.*An.*1.1.8, cf. Th.1.95: folld. by a relat. clause, ἄ. εἰ.., or ἤν.., E.*IA*1413, Th.8.109, Pl.*Hp.Ma.*292e; less freq. ἄ. ὅτι.. Ar.*Pl.*899, X.*Cyr.*3.3.13, Pl.*R.*549c.

ἄχθος, εος, τό, *burden, load*, Il.12.452, Hes.*Op.*692, Tyrt.6, etc.; ἄχθεα δυνατώτεραι φέρειν, of camels, Hdt.3.102, cf. 1.80, Ar.*Ra.*9, Th.4.115; ἄ. οὐκ εὐάγκαλον A.*Pr.*352; ἄ. ἀρούρης *cumberers* of the ground, Il.18.104, Od.20.379, etc.; περισσὸν ἄ. γυναικῶν *plague* of women, S.*El.*1241 (lyr.); γῆς ἄλλως ἄχθη Pl.*Tht.*176d; ἄ. μυρία γαίης *pests*, Nic.*Th.*9: but φίλτατον ἄχθος, of a corpse, E.*Rh.*379 (lyr.): metaph., δίδυμον ἄ. double *burden* of praise, Pi.*N.*6.57. II. *load of grief*, χάρμα καὶ ἄ. Hes.*Sc.*400; ἀπὸ φροντίδος ἄ.. βαλεῖν A. *Ag.*166; λύπης ἄ. S.*El.*120 (lyr.), cf. *Ant.*1172; φέρειν ἄχθη κακῶν E.*IT*710; ἄ. φέρειν bring or cause *sorrow*, X.*Ep.*1.

ἀχθο-φορέω, *bear burdens*, Plb.4.32.7, Plu.*Mar.*13; *to be loaded*, ἡ κοιλία Hp.*Acut.*28. 2. *bear as a burden*, νέκυν *AP*7.468 (Mel.); κριόν *IG*14.1301; ὄστρακον *APl.*4.333 (Antiphil.). **-φορία**, ἡ, *bearing of burdens*, βαρῶν Plu.2.113cd (pl.), cf. Luc.*Asin.*19; μυρμήκων M.Ant.7.3; *any heavy pressure*, Hp.*Art.*63. **-φόρος**, ον, *bearing burdens*, κτήνεα Hdt.7.187; ὑποζύγια D.H.1.85; μύρμηκες Ael.*NA* 2.25. II. as Subst., *porter*, Gell.5.3.2, Luc.*Herod.*5.

ἄχι, v. ἄχει.

ἀχίαστος [ῐ], ον, *not arranged chiastically*, περίοδος Sch.Isoc.8.102. Adv. -τως Jo.Sic. in Rh.6.343 W.

Ἀχίλλειος, α, ον, *of Achilles*, E.*Tr.*39, etc.; poet. Ἀχιλλέϊος Theoc. 29.34: Ion. **Ἀχιλλήϊος** Hdt.4.55, 76; used in lyr. by S.*Fr.*152:—fem. **Ἀχιλληΐς** (v. infr.), also **Ἀχιλλεῖτις**, ιδος, D.L.1.74. II. Ἀχίλλειαι κριθαί, a *fine* kind of barley, Ath.3.114f; also κριθαὶ Ἀχιλληΐδες Hp.*Morb.*3.17; κριθὴ Ἀχιλληΐς Thphr.*HP*8.10.2; Ἀ. μᾶζαι cakes *of fine barley*, Pherecr.130.4; Ἀχιλλείων ἀπομάττεσθαι (v. sub ἀπομάσσω) Ar.*Eq.*819; Ἀχίλλειον, τό, a *cake of this sort*, Eust.1414. 33. 2. Ἀ. (sc. σπόγγος), ὁ, *fine* kind of *sponge*, used as padding for the inside of helmets, greaves, etc., Arist.*HA*548^{b}1 and 20. 3. Ἀχίλλειος, ὁ, = μυριόφυλλον, Ps.-Dsc.4.114. b. *Achilles woundwort*, Crateuas *Fr.*3, Dsc.4.36, Plin.*HN*25.42.

Ἀχιλλεύς, Ep. also **Ἀχιλεύς**, gen. Ἀχιλλέως (either quadrisyll. or trisyll., as the metre requires, cf. S.*Ph.*4, 50 with 57, 364): acc. Ἀχιλλέᾱ ib.331, 358, voc. Ἀχιλλεῦ: Ep. gen. Ἀχιλλῆος, etc.:—*Achilles*. II. the fallacy vulgarly called '*Achilles* and the Tortoise', invented by Zeno of Elea, Arist.*Ph.*239^{b}14, D.L.9.29.

ἄχῑλος, ον, *without grass*, or (with ἀ- intens.) *rich in grass*, both senses in Hsch. s.v. ἄχειλον.

ἀχῐόνιστος, ον, *not snowed upon*, Sch.Od.6.44.

ἀχίτων [ῐ], ον, gen. ωνος, *without tunic*, i.e. wearing the ἱμάτιον only, of Socrates, X.*Mem.*1.6.2; of Agesilaus, Ael.*VH*7.13, Plu.2.210b, cf. 276c; of Cleanthes the Stoic, D.L.7.169; of Gelon, ἀ. ἐν ἱματίῳ D.S.11.26.

ἀχλαιν-ία, ἡ, (χλαῖνα) *want of a cloak* or *mantle*, E.*Hel.*1282. **-ος**, ον, *without cloak* or *mantle*, Simon.167.3, Call.*Dian.*115, Lyc.763; βίος ib.635.

ἄχλαξ· κάχληξ, Suid.

ἀχλάς, άδος, ἡ, late form of ἀχράς (q.v.), Sch.Theoc.1.134.

ἄχλοος, ον, contr. **ἄχλους**, ουν, (χλόα) *without herbage*, E.*Hel.* 1327 (lyr.). II. *sere, withered*, Opp.*H.*2.496. III. *discoloured*, Hp.*Coac.*596.

ἀχλυδιᾶν· θρύπτεσθαι, Hsch.

ἀχλύμενος· λυπούμενος, Hsch. (leg. ἀχν-).

ἀχλύνω, = ἀχλύω II, Q.S.2.550 (Pass.).

ἀχλῠό-εις, εσσα, εν, *dark, gloomy, dismal*, δεσμός Epigr.ap.Hdt. 5.77; *darkened*, καπνῷ ἀ. αἰθὴρ πέλεν A.R.4.927, cf. Arat.908, Nonn. *D.*9.65, al.; of colour, ἰχώρ Opp.*H.*3.163; *cloudy*, of urine, Ruf.*Fr.* 79.26. 2. *secret*, γάμος Musae.3. **-πεζα**, ἡ, *fringed* or *bordered with gloom*, ἠώς Tryph.210.

ἀχλυόω, *darken, make dim*, Aret.*CD*1.3 :—Pass., *become gloomy, grow dark*, Thphr.*Vent.*35 ; *become dim*, Syn.Alch.p.58 B.

ἀχλύς, ύος, ἡ, (acc. **ἀχλύα** Orph.*A.*341) *mist*, Od.20.357 ; elsewh. in Hom. of *a mist over the eyes*, as of one dying, κατὰ δ' ὀφθαλμῶν κέχυτ' ἀ. Il.5.696 ; as result of ulceration, ἀχλύες Hp.*Prorrh.*2.20, cf. Thphr.*HP*7.6.2, Dsc.2.78 (pl.), Aët.7.27 ; or in emotion, Ἔρως πολλὴν κατ' ἀχλὺν ὀμμάτων ἔχευεν Archil.103 ; of drunkenness, πρὸς ὄμμ' ἀ. ἀμβλωπὸς ἐφίζει Critias 6.11 D. ; of one whom a god deprives of the power of seeing and knowing others, κατ' ὀφθαλμῶν χέεν ἀχλύν Il.20.321 ; ἀπ' ὀφθαλμῶν σκέδασ' ἀχλύν ib.341, cf. 5.127, 15.668 :— personified as *Sorrow*, πὰρ δ' Ἀχλὺς εἱστήκει ἐπισμυγερή τε καὶ αἰνή, χλωρή, αὐσταλέη Hes.*Sc.*264. 2. metaph., δνοφεράν τιν' ἀχλὺν . . αὐδᾶται A.*Eu.*379 (lyr.), cf. *Pers.*668 (lyr.) ; ἀχλὺν ἀπὸ τῆς ψυχῆς ἀφελεῖν D.C.38.19 ; διάνοια ἀχλύος γέμουσα Plu.2.42c. 3. ἀ. ὑγρή liquid emitted by cuttlefish, Opp.*H.*3.158.—Mostly poet., but used by Hp. (v. supr.) and Arist.*Mete.*367ᵇ17, 373ᵇ12 (pl.) : also in later Prose, Plb.34.11.15, Str.6.2.8, and v. supr. 2. [ῡ in nom. and acc. sg., Hom., Hes. : ῠ in later poets.]

ἄχλυσις, εως, ἡ, *dimming, clouding*, Syn.Alch.p.58 B.

ἀχλύω, aor. 1 ἤχλῡσα, *to be* or *grow dark*, ἤχλυσε δὲ πόντος ὑπ' αὐτῆς (sc. νεφέλης) Od.12.406 ; ὄμματα δ' αὔτως ἤχλυσαν A.R.3.963. II. trans., *darken*, Q.S.1.598, Nonn.*D.*4.368, Pancrat.*Oxy.*1085.12.

ἀχλῠώδης, ες, *hazy, misty*, νότοι Hp.*Aph.*3.5, Arist.*Mete.*367ᵃ20 ; ἀέρες Str.17.3.8 ; ἡμέρα App.*Syr.*33 ; κορυφή D.Chr.1.68 ; *dim*, of sight, ὄψις -εστέρα Gal.16.224 ; *dark*, of complexion or appearance, Aret.*CA*2.4, *SD*2.13.

ἀχνάζω, Aeol. **ἀχνάσδημι**, (ἄχος) *to be miserable*, Alc.81.

ἄχνη, Dor. **ἄχνα**, ἡ, *anything that comes off the surface* : I. of liquids, *foam, froth*, in Hom. of the sea, Od.12.238, al. ; ἁλὸς ἄ. 5.403, cf. Tim.*Pers.*95, A.R.2.570 ; θοὴν ἀπερεύγεται ἄχνην, of a river, D.P.693 : Medic., *exudation*, Hp.*Int.*1 ; οἰνωπὸς ἄ. *froth* of wine, E.*Or.*115 ; ἄχνα οὐρανία *dew* of heaven, S.*OC*681 (lyr.) ; δακρύων ἄχνα *dewy* tears, Id.*Tr.*848 (lyr.) ; also ἄχνη πυρός, i.e. smoke, A.*Fr.*336. II. of solids, *chaff*, in pl., ὡς δ' ἄνεμος ἄχνας φορέει Il.5.499 ; καρπόν τε καὶ ἄχνας ib.501 ; *down* on the quince, μῆλον λεπτῇ πεποκωμένον ἄ. *AP*6.102 (Phil.) ; ἄχνη ἡ ἀφ' ἡμιτυβίου *fluff, shreds*, used for *lint*, Hp.*Art.*37 ; ὀθονίου Id.*Mochl.*2 ; ἄ. Λυδῆς κερκίδος, of *fine-spun* fabrics, S.*Fr.*45 ; ἄ. χαλκίτιδος metallic *dust*, Plu.2.659c, cf. Orph.*L.*455 ; ἄχναι *wall-decorations*, dub. in Aret.*CA*1.1 (*stramina* Cael. Aur.). III. ἄχνην in acc., as Adv., *morsel, the least bit*, ἣν δ' οὖν καταμύσῃ κἂν ἄχνην Ar.*V.*92. IV. πυρὸς ἄ., = χαμελαία, Dsc.4.171 ; = θυμελαία, ib.172. V. ἄχναν· τὴν οἴκησιν, Hsch.

ἀχνηκώς, v. ἄγω. **ἄχνημος**· νῆστις, Hsch. **ἀχνητόν**· δαψιλές, κτλ., Id.

ἄχνοος, ον, contr. **ἄχνους**, ουν, *without down*, Ἑρμῆς *AP*6.259 (Phil.), cf. 242 (Crin.), Q.S.4.431, Nonn.*D.*10.180 : metaplast. acc. pl. ἄχνοας Man.1.126.

ἀχνοῦχος, ὁ, dub. sens. in *PMag.Leid.W.*8.21 (perh. 'Lord of the Foam').

ἄχνυλα· κάρυα (Cret.), Hsch.

ἄχνυμαι, v. ἀχεύω, ἀχέω.

ἀχνύς, ύος, ἡ, = ἄχος, Call.*Fr.anon.*79.

ἀχνώδης, ες, *like, of the nature of* ἄχνη, Hsch.

ἄχολος, ον, *lacking gall*, Hp.*Prorrh.*1.98 ; *lacking a gall-bladder*, ἧπαρ ἄ. Arist.*HA*506ᵇ2 ; τὰ μώνυχα ἄ. Id.*PA*677ᵃ33 ; *deficient in bile* (with allusion to signf. 2), Plot.4.4.28. 2. metaph., πόλιος τᾶς ἀχόλω Alc.37 A, cf. Plu.*Daed.*2. II. Act., *allaying bile* or *anger*, φάρμακον . . νηπενθές τ' ἄχολόν τε Od.4.221.

ἄχομαι, v. ἀχεύω, ἀχέω.

ἄχονδρος, ον, *without cartilage*, Arist.*Spir.*484ᵃ29.

ἄχορα· τὰ πίτυρα, ἔνιοι δὲ κρανίον, Hsch.

ἄχορδος, ον, *without strings*, μέλος Poet.ap.Arist.*Rh.*1408ᵃ6 : φόρμιγξ ἄ., metaph. of a bow, Thgn.Trag.1 (= *Lyr.Adesp.*127).

ἀχόρευτος, ον, *not trained in the dance* or *chorus*, Pl.*Lg.*654a ; *not joining in the dance*, Nonn.*D.*44.125, al. II. *not attended with the dance*, γάμος Musae.274 ; esp. in bad sense, *ill suiting it, joyless*, ὀνείδη S.*El.*1069 (lyr.) ; ἆται E.*Tr.*121 (lyr.) ; φάρμα Telest.1.8.

ἀχορηγ-ησία, ἡ, *want of supplies*, Plb.5.28.4, 28.8.6. **-ητος**, ον, *without supplies*, *IG*1².187, Arist.*EN*1099ᵃ33 ; ἀ. τῶν ἀναγκαίων Id.*Pol.*1288ᵇ32.

ἄχορος, ον, *without the dance*, epith. of Ares, to mark the horrors of war, A.*Supp.*681 (lyr.) ; of death, μοῖρ' . . ἄλυρος, ἄ. S.*OC*1222 (lyr.) ; ἄ. στοναχαί v.l. in E.*Andr.*1037 (lyr.).

ἀχόρτ-αστος, ον, *unfed, starving*, τύχη Men.690, Sm.*Ps.*58(59).16 ; = ἄπληστος, Hsch. :—hence Subst. **-ασία**, ἡ, *ravenous hunger*, Sm.*De.*28.20.

ἄχος [ᾰ], εος, τό, *pain, distress*, in Hom. always of mind, ἄχος αἰνόν, ἄλαστον, ἄτλητον, ὀξύ, Il.4.169, al. ; ἄχεος νεφέλη μέλαινα 17.591 ; ἄχε' ἄκριτα 3.412 ; τὸν δ' εἷλεν ἄχος κραδίαν B.10.85 ; also of physical ills, Pi.*P.*3.50 (pl.) ; δειμάτων ἄχη A.*Ch.*586 (lyr.) ; ἀκοῦ δ' ἄχος, with a play on the words, S.*Tr.*1035 ; οὐράνι' ἄχη A.*Pers.*573 (lyr.) ; ἐμοὶ δ' ἄχε', ἄχεα κατέλιπε Ar.*Ra.*1353 (paratrag.), cf. 1531 (hex.).—Rare in Prose, ἡ παῖς ἀπήγξατο ὑπὸ ἄχεος Hdt.2.131 ; ἄ. αὐτὸν ἔλαβεν X.*Cyr.*5.5.6, cf. Plu.*Cor.*20.

ἆχος, Dor. for ἦχος.

ἀχράαντος [ρᾱ], ον, poet. for ἄχραντος (q.v.), Call.*Ap.*111.

ἀχραδῆναι· ζῷά τινα ξυλοφάγα, Hsch.

ἀχράδινος [ρᾰ], η, ον, *of the* ἀχράς, ξύλον Dsc.*Alex.*23.

Ἀχρᾰδούσιος, formed from ἀχράς, as if the name of a δῆμος, *Crabby*, Ar.*Ec.*362 ; cf. Ἀχερδούσιος.

ἀχραής, ές, gen. έος, = sq., Nic.*Th.*846 ; ψυχρὸν ἀ. *pure* cold water, *AP*9.314 (Anyte).

ἀχράνής, ές, = sq., Hsch.

ἄχραντος, ον, *undefiled, immaculate*, E.*IA*1574, A.R.4.1025 ; μίτρη Mosch.2.73 : c. gen., ἡδονῶν M.Ant.3.4 ; ἐμψύχου βρώσεως Philostr.*VA*6.11 ; αἵματος Opp.*H.*2.648 : metaph., τεκμήριον καθαρὸν καὶ ἄ. Pl.*Alc.*1.113e ; ἄ. ἰδέα Luc.*Dem.Enc.*13, cf. *Am.*22 ; οἰκειότητες Jul. *Or.*1.9c ; τὸ ἄ. δικαστήριον, freq. in Pap., as *POxy.*59.10 (iii A.D.) ; ἄ. πυρί, of a cup, Ion Trag.1, cf. Theoc.1.60. Adv. -τως Iamb.*Myst.*5.9, Procl. *in Alc.*p.32 C.

ἀχράς, άδος, ἡ, a kind of *wild pear*, *Pyrus amygdaliformis*, Teleclid.32, Ar.*Ec.*355, Dsc.1.116 ; used for the tree as well as the fruit, cf. Arist.*HA*627ᵇ17 with 595ᵃ29, Thphr.*HP*1.4.1 with *CP*2.8.2 ; cf. ἄχερδος.

ἄχρατοι· οἱ πολέμιοι, Hsch. **ἀχρέα**· βλάσφημον, κτλ., Id.

ἀχρεία, ἡ, *rubbish*, Sch.E.*Hec.*159.

ἀχρειόγελως, ων, *untimely-laughing*, epith. of the Athenians, Cratin.323, cf. *AB*475.

ἀχρειοποιός, όν, *rendering useless*, Eust.217.38.

ἀχρεῖος (Att. ἄχρειος acc. to Hdn.Gr.1.136), ον, also α, ον *IG*7.303.10 (Oropus), Dsc.4.5, Polem.*Phgn.*69 : Ion. **ἀχρήϊος** :—*useless, unprofitable*, ἀχρήϊος ἀνήρ Hes.*Op.*297 ; ἐπέων νομός ib.403 ; δέμας A.*Pr.*365, cf. Hp.*Int.*39 ; οἰκητήρ S.*OC*627 ; opp. εὐγενής, Id.*Fr.*667 ; ἐρινὸς ἀ. ὢν ἐς βρῶσιν ib.181 ; ἀ. κοὐ σοφός E.*Med.*299 ; δοῦλος *Ev.Matt.*25.30 ; οὐκ ἀπράγμονα ἀλλ' ἀχρεῖον νομίζομεν Th.2.40 ; λόγον ἀχρεῖον ἀπέρριψαν Ant.Lib.11.3 : Comp. -ότερος, ὄρνιθες Chrysipp.*Stoic.*3.195 : c. inf., *unfit* to do, ἀ. πράττειν τι Pl.*R.*371c : c. dat., ἀ. τοῖς σώμασι Agatharch.*Fr.Hist.*3, cf. Them.*Or.*26.326a. 2. esp. *unfit for war*, ἀ. ὅμιλος Hdt.3.81 ; τὸ ἀ. τοῦ στρατοῦ *the unserviceable part* of an army, Id.1.191 ; οἱ ἀχρειότατοι Th.1.93, 2.6, cf. X.*HG*7.2.18 ; τὸ ἀ. τῆς ἡλικίας Th.2.44. Adv. -είως, ἔχειν πρὸς ναυμαχίαν App.*BC*5.84. II. neut. ἀχρεῖον, as Adv., twice in Hom., ἀχρεῖον ἰδών giving a *helpless* look, looking *foolish*, of Thersites after being beaten, Il.2.269 ; ἀχρεῖον δ' ἐγέλασσε laughed *without cause*, made a *forced* laugh, of Penelope trying to disguise her feelings, Od.18.163 ; ἀχρεῖον κλάζειν bark *without need* or *cause*, Theoc.25.72. III. Adv. ἀχρείως γέλασόν με (cf. ἀχρειόγελως) *APl.*4.86, cf. Them.*Or.*33.367b : neut. pl. as Adv. ἀχρεῖ' ἀσπαίροντος *helplessly*, Euph.44.

ἀχρει-οσύνη, ἡ, = sq., *Gloss.* **-ότης**, ητος, ἡ, *unprofitableness, worthlessness*, Lxx *To.*4.13. **-όω** or **-χρεόω** (*OGI*573.16), pf. ἠχρείωκα :—*render useless, disable, damage*, Dicaearch.2.3, Plb.3.64.8, Lxx *Da.*4.11, *OGI* l.c. :—Pass., ἀχρεῶσθαι *SIG*569.31 (Crete, iii B.C.), cf. Plb.1.14.6, *BCH*35.286 (Delos, ii B.C.) ; *to be corrupted*, Lxx *Ps.*13(14).3 ; δι' ἀπειρίαν ἠχρειώθησαν Apollon.Cit.1.1.

ἀχρεοκόπητος, ον, *free from debt*, i.e. *undiminished*, δύναμις *PMag. Par.*1.527.

ἄχρεος, ον, = ἀχρεῖος, Epic. in *Arch.Pap.*7.10, Tryph.125.

ἀχρήεις, εσσα, εν, = ἀχρεῖος, v.l. in Man.4.76 :—also **ἀχρήϊστος**, ον, Musae.328, Nonn.*D.*24.266. **ἀχρήϊος**, ον, Ion. for ἀχρεῖος.

ἀχρημ-ᾰτέω, *to be without money*, Hsch. s.v. πένεται. **-ᾰτία**, ἡ, *want of money*, Th.1.11, D.H.7.24, Eus.Mynd.7. **-άτιστος** [μᾰ], ον, ἡμέρα ἀ. a day *on which no public business was done*, Plu.2.273e, cf. Sch.Luc.*Tim.*43. II. *disused*, φρέαρ *PMag.Lond.*46.345. III. dub. sens. in *Sammelb.*2276. IV. Astrol., *unprofitable, bringing no advantage*, τόποι Antioch.Astr. in *Cat.Cod.Astr.*8(3).106 ; of planets, Vett.Val.5.8. **-ᾰτος**, ον, *without money* or *means*, Hdt.1.89, Timocl.9.7 ; ἀ. τὴν πόλιν ποιεῖν Arist.*Pol.*1271ᵇ16 ; μήτ' ἀχρημάτοισι λάμπειν φῶς *on the poor*, A.*Pers.*167. **-ονέω**, *to be in want of money*, Poll.6.196. **-οσύνη**, ἡ, *want of money*, Od.17.502, Thgn.156. **-ων**, ον, gen. ονος, *poor, needy*, Sol.13.41, Pi.*Fr.*218 ; once in Trag., E.*Med.*461.

ἀχρησ-τία, ἡ, (χράομαι) *disuse, non-user*, Anon. *in Rh.*17.37. **-ιμος**, ον, *useless*, ἐν ἀ. διαθέσει *CPHerm.*119ʳiv9 (iii A.D.), cf. Sopat. in Rh. 8.10 W., *Hippiatr.*14. **-ιμότης**, ητος, ἡ, *uselessness*, *Gloss.* **-τεύω**, Gramm., *not to be in use*, Sch.D.T.p.195 H. **-τέω**, *to be useless*, S.E.*M.*1.259. **-τία**, Ion. -τίη, ἡ, *uselessness, unfitness*, Hp.*Praec.*9, Pl.*R.*489b, *AP*15.38 (Comet.), Them.*Or.*26.326a. II. *nonusance* of a thing, Pl.*R.*333d, Plu.2.135c. **-τολογέω**, *to speak unprofitably* or *amiss*, *EM*463.25. **-τος**, ον, *useless, unprofitable*, μετάνοια Batr.70 ; νέες Hdt.1.166 ; ἀ. ὁ ὀφθαλμὸς γίνεται Hp.*Prorrh.*2.19 ; οὐκ ἀ. ἦδ' ἡ ἄνοια Th.6.16 ; χρεομένῳ ἄχρηστα *useless* if you try to use them, Hp.*Art.*14 ; πεσεῖν ἄ. θέσφατον *without effect*, E.*IT*121 ; ἀ. ἐς πόλεμον Hdt.8.142, Lycurg.53 ; πρός τι Arist.*HA*560ᵇ14 : c. gen. rei, ἄ. τῶν ἔργων Id.*Oec.*1345ᵃ35 ; ἄ. τινι *useless* to a person, Hdt.1.80, cf. X.*Oec.*8.4 (Sup.) ; τῇ πόλει E.*Heracl.*4 ; τὸ διηπορηκέναι οὐκ ἄ. Arist.*Cat.*8ᵇ24. 2. = ἀχρεῖος (which it almost superseded in the Oratt. and later Greek), *useless, do-nothing*, D.19.135 (Comp.), etc. ; ἄ. πολῖται Is.7.37 ; σοφισταί prob. l. in Lys.33.3 ; *non-effective, unwarlike*, Eun.Hist.p.239 D. ; so (with a pun—*not having received an oracle*) Ath.3.98c. Adv. -τως, ἔχειν πρός τι D.61.43. II. *unkind, cruel*, θεοί Hdt.8.111 ; λόγος Id.9.111. III. Act., *making no use of*, c. dat., ξυνέσει τ' ἄχρηστον τῇ φύσει τε λείπεται E.*Tr.*672. IV. *not used*, i.e. *new*, ἱμάτια Luc.*Lex.*9, Ath.3.97e. 2. *obsolete*, Eust.118.25, Sch.rec.S.*El.*132. 3. *not to be used, unseemly*, *EM*463.26. **-τόω**, *make useless*, Horap.1.50 ; *corrupt*, τὴν Ἑλλάδα φωνήν Eust.367.40.

ἄχρι and **ἄχρις** (v. sub fin.) : I. Adv. *to the uttermost*, τένοντε καὶ ὀστέα λᾶας ἀναιδὴς ἄχρις ἀπηλοίησεν Il.4.522 ; ἀπὸ δ' ὀστέον ἄχρις ἄραξε 16.324, cf. 17.599. **2.** after Hom., before Preps., ἄχρι εἰς Κοτύωρα X.*An*.5.5.4 ; ἄ. ἐς ποταμόν *Tab.Heracl*.1.17 ; ἄχρι πρὸς τὸν σκοπόν, πρὸς τὴν πόλιν, Luc.*Nigr*.36, *Herm*.24 ; ἄχρις ἐπ' ἄκνηστιν A.R.4.1403 ; ἐπ' ὀστέον *IG*12(7).115.9 (Amorgos) ; ἄχρι ἐπὶ πολὺ τῶν πλευρῶν Thphr.*Char*.19.3 ; ἄχρις ἐς ἠῶ Q.S.6.177 ; ἄχρι ὑπὸ τὴν πυγήν Luc.*DMort*.27.4 : less freq. after the Noun, ἐς τέλος ἄχρις Q.S.2.617, cf. Nonn.*D*.5.153, etc. : rarely c. acc., ἄχρι.. θρόνον ἦλθεν *IG*14.2012 (Sulp. Max.) : with an Adv., ἄχρι πόρρω *still* farther, Luc.*Am*.12 ; ἄχρι δεῦρο S.E.*M*.8.401. **II.** Prep. with gen., *even to, as far as,* **1.** of Time, *until*, ἄχρι μάλα κνέφαος *until* deep in the night, Od.18.370 ; ἄχρι τῆς τήμερον ἡμέρας D.9.28 ; ἀπὸ τῆς ἀρχῆς ἄχρι τῆς τελευτῆς Id.18.179 ; ἄχρι γήρως Apollod.Com.2 ; ἄχρι δὲ τούτου *until* then, Sol.13.35 ; ἄχρι τοῦ νῦν Timostr.1, *Ep.Rom*.8.22 ; ἄχρι νῦν Luc. *Tim*.39, Lxx *Ge*.44.28 ; ἄχρι παντός *continually*, Plu.*Cic*.6. **2.** of Space, *as far as, even to*, ἄχρι τῆς ἐσόδου τοῦ ἱροῦ Hdt.2.138 (who elsewh. has μέχρι) ; ἄ. τῆς ὁδοῦ *IG*1^{2}.893 ; ἄ. τῆς πυλίδος *SIG*^{2}587.25 ; ἄ. τοῦ Πειραιῶς D.18.301 ; ἔδακνεν ἄχρι τῆς καρδίας *Com.Adesp*.475 ; ἄχρις ἥπατος Ti.Locr.101a, cf. 100e ; ἄχρι τῆς πόλεως D.H.2.43 ; ἄ. τοῦ δεῦρο Gal.10.676 : after its case, ἰνίου ἄχρις Euph.41. **3.** of Measure or Degree, ἄχρι τούτου *up to* this point, D.23.122 ; ἄχρι τοῦ μὴ πεινῆν X.*Smp*.4.37 ; ἄχρι τοῦ θορυβῆσαι D.8.77 ; ἄ. θανάτου *Act.Ap*.22.4 ; ἄχρι τῆς πρὸς τὸν πλησίον δοξοκοπίας Polystr.p.19 W. **III.** as Conj., ἄχρι, ἄχρις with or without οὗ, **1.** of Time, *until, so long as*, ἄχρι οὗ ὅδε ὁ λόγος ἐγράφετο X.*HG*6.4.37 ; ἄχρις ὅτου *Epigr.Gr*.314.24 (Smyrna) ; ἄχρι οὗ ἄν or ἄχρι ἄν with Subj., ἄχρι ἂν σχολάσῃ *till* he should be at leisure, X.*An*.2.3.2 ; ἄχρις οὗ ἂν δοκέῃ Hp.*Fist*.3 ; ἄχρις ἂν αἱ ἡμέραι παρέλθωσιν Id.*Int*.40 ; ἄχρι ἂν ἔχῃ τὸ ἴδιον ἐντελές [ἡ ἱστορία] Luc.*Hist.Conscr*.9 : without ἄν, ἄχρις ῥεύσῃ Bion 1.47 ; ἄχρι οὗ τελευτήσῃ (v.l. –σει) Hdt.1.117 ; ἄχρι οὗ ἐπιλάμψῃ Plu.*Aem*.17 ; ἄχρι ἄν, c. inf., Epist. Mithr. in *SIG*741.37 : c. inf. only, ἄχρις ἱκέσθαι ὀστέον Q.S.4.361. **2.** of Space, *so far as*, διώξας, ἄχρι οὗ ἀσφαλὲς ᾤετο εἶναι X.*Cyr*.5.4.16 : c. subj., αὐξάνεται εἰς μῆκος, ἄχρι οὗ δὴ ἐφίκηται τοῦ ἡλίου Thphr.*HP*5.1.8 ; cf. μέχρι throughout. —Ep. poets use ἄχρι or ἄχρις, as the metre requires : in Ion. μέχρι is preferred (v. supr.) : but ἄχρι, –ις are more common in Hom. than μέχρι : the only Att. forms are ἄχρι, μέχρι, before both consonants and vowels, cf. Phryn.6, Moer.34 ; and so in Att. Inscrr. (where it is somewhat less freq. than μέχρι) : ἄχρι ἄν with hiatus in *IG*2.2729, Hegesipp.Com.1.26 ; but ἄχρις Men.*Sam*.179.—Never in Trag. (ἄχρι, = m̥-χρι, cf. μέχρι.)

ἀχρισατέες· ἀληθές, Hsch.

ἀχροέω and **ἀχροιέω**, (ἄχροος) *to be colourless* : *to be discoloured, ill-coloured*, Hp.*Fract*.25, Sor.2.43.

ἄχροια, ἡ, *absence of colour*, Plot.2.4.10. **2.** *loss of colour, paleness*, Hp.*Prorrh*.2.24, Arist.*Pr*.967^{a}8 ; opp. εὐχροια, Thphr.*Sud*.39. **II.** (ἀ- copul.) *likeness in colour*, Hsch.

ἄχρονος, ον, *without time, instantaneous*, Gal.7.448 ; ἡ ἄ. φύσις Dam.*Pr*.404 ; *short-lived*, of infants, Ptol.*Tetr*.125, cf. *Placit*.5.18.6. **2.** *independent of time*, S.E.*M*.10.225 ; *non-temporal*, ἄ. πᾶσα ἡ νόησις Plot.4.4.1. Adv. –νως *timelessly*, Alex.Aphr. *in Mete*.129.5, *in Sens*.135.14, Procl.*Inst*.124, Herm. *in Phdr*.p.159 A. ; *instantaneously*, Ph.1.571, al., Them.*Or*.15.196b.

ἀχρονοτριβής, ές, *not wasting time*, Hsch.

ἄχροος, ον, contr. **ἄχρους**, ουν, *colourless*, Arist. *de An*.418^{b}27, Nic.*Th*.236, Ocell.2.3, Plot.2.4.12. **II.** *ill-complexioned, pallid*, opp. εὔχροος, Hp.*Aër*.6, *VC*19, Arist.*Pr*.966^{b}35, al. : Comp. ἀχρούστερος Hp.*Prorrh*.2.4, Arist.*HA*584^{a}14 : also –οώτερος Hp.*Vict*.2.63. **2.** ἄχροοι· πυρραὶ ἡμίονοι, Hsch. ; also ἄχροον· πονηρόν· Λάκωνες νόθον, Id.

ἄχρυσος, ον, *without gold*, ἄ. καὶ ἀνάργυροι Pl.*Lg*.679b, cf. Ath.6.231e.

ἀχρωμ-άτιστος [μᾰ], ον, *uncoloured*, Arist.*Mete*.371^{b}9, 377^{b}1, Thphr.*Od*.31. Adv. –τως [Lib.]*Decl*.30.5. **–ᾰτος**, ον, *colourless*, Pl.*Phdr*.247c, Plu.2.97b, etc. **2.** *unblushing, shameless*, Suid. s.v. ἄχρωμος. **–ος**, ον, = foreg. 2, Hp.*Epid*.7.122, Artem.4.44 : Comp., οὐδὲν –ότερον Hierocl.*Facet*.203 :—hence Subst. **ἀχρωμία**, ἡ, *Gloss*.

ἄχρως, ων, gen. ω, = ἄχροος, Hp.*Epid*.7.85, Pl.*Chrm*.168d, Arist.*Metaph*.989^{b}9.

ἄχρωστος, ον, (χρώζω) *untouched*, ἄ. γόνατα χερῶν ἐμῶν E.*Hel*.831. **II.** *uncoloured, colourless*, Democr.ap.Plu.2.1111a.

ἀχρώτιστος, ον, = ἀχρωμάτιστος, σαμψοῦχον *PMag.Par*.1.3010, cf. *PMag.Berol*.1.7 (–τως Pap.).

ἄχυ, Hebr. *āḥū, quill-cassia*, Dsc.1.13.

ἀχῡλ-ία, ἡ, *insipidity*, Diocl.*Fr*.138 (pl.). **–ος**, ον, *without juice, insipid*, Thphr.*CP*6.19.4, Xenocr.18, Diocl.*Fr*.138 : Comp., Ath.Med. ap.Orib.1.2.14. **–ωτος**, ον, *not converted into chyle*, διαχωρήματα Gal.7.446, cf. 6.575.

ἄχῡμ-ος, ον, *without flavour*, Arist.*Metaph*.989^{b}10, *Sens*.443^{a}11, Xenocr.45 ; *tasteless*, of water, Thphr.*CP*6.3.1. **–ωτος**, ον, = foreg., Gal.1.584, Suid.

ἀχύνετος [ῡ], ον, (χέω, χύνω) *far-spread, copious*, ὕδωρ Nic.*Al*.174.

ἀχύνωψ, = κύνωψ (q.v.), *fleawort, Plantago Psyllium*, Thphr.*HP*7.11.2, Plin.*HN*21.89, 101.

ἀχῠρ-ᾰγωγός [ᾰχ], όν, *for the conveyance of chaff*, prob. for ἀγυρατωγά, Hsch. s.v. σαργάναι. **–άριος**, ὁ, = ἀχυροπράκτωρ, *Theb.Ostr*.106. **–ηγέω**, *carry chaff*, *BGU*698.22 (ii A.D.), 14 iii 17 (iii A.D.). **–ικὸν** τέλος tax *on chaff*, *Sammelb*.1092. **–ινος**, η, ον, *fed by chaff*, φλόξ Plu.2.658d. **–ιος**, ὁ, = ἀχυρός, *Tab.Heracl*.1.139 sq. **–ῖτις**, ιδος, ἡ, *of chaff*, dub. in *AP*9.438.5 (Phil.). **–μιά**, ἡ, *heap of chaff*, Il.5.502, *AP*9.384.15. **–μιος**, α, ον, *consisting mainly of chaff*, ἀμητός Arat.1097. **–μός**, οῦ, ὁ, v. ἀχυρός.

ἀχῠρο-βολών [ᾰ], ῶνος, ὁ, *barn for chaff*, *PHamb*.23.18 (vi A.D.), Ael.Dion.*Fr*.88. **–δόκη**, ἡ, *chaff-holder*, X.*Oec*.18.7. **–θήκη**, ἡ, = foreg., *PLond*.5.1768 (vi A.D.), *PMasp*.279.18 (vi A.D.), Sch.Il.5.202.

ἄχῠρον [ᾰ], τό, mostly in pl. ἄχυρα, *chaff, bran, husks* left after threshing or grinding, Hdt.4.72, Pherecr.161, Antiph.226.2, X.*Oec*.18.1 ; ἐν τοῖς ἀ. κυλινδομένην Hermipp.47 : sg., Thphr.*HP*8.4.1, *Ev.Matt*.3.12, etc. : prov., ὄνος εἰς ἄχυρα 'pig in clover', of unexpected good fortune, Philem.188, cf. Ar.*Fr*.76 : metaph., ἄχυρα τῶν ἀστῶν, of μέτοικοι, Id.*Ach*.508 ; ἄχυρα ἀπὸ τοῦ τοίχου ἀποσπᾶν, of dying persons, Hp.*Prog*.4. **II.** in pl., ἄ. χρυσοχοϊκά *slag* from gold-smelting, *PHolm*.5.7.

ἀχῠρο-πᾰροχία [ᾰχ], ἡ, *supply of chaff*, *Arch.Pap*.4.116 (iii A.D.). **–πράκτωρ**, ορος, ὁ, *collector of chaff* (or *of the tax thereon*), *Ostr*.1012 (ii A.D.).

ἀχῠρός or **ἄχῡρος** [ᾰ], ὁ, *chaff-heap*, Eup.299, Ar.*Fr*.10 D., Pl.Com.6, and in the best Mss. of Ar.*V*.1310 : but ἀχυρμός should be read.

ἀχῠρότριψ [ᾰ], ῐβος, ὁ, ἡ, *threshing out the husks*, τρίβολοι *AP*6.104 (Phil.).

ἀχῠρόω [ᾰ], *mix chaff* or *straw* with mud, Thphr.*HP*4.8.8 :—Pass., μᾶζαν ἠχυρωμένην *mixed with chaff*, Polioch.2 ; πηλὸς ἠχ. *IG*2^{2}.463.18 ; ἠχ. ἀμόργῳ Ph.*Bel*.86.44 ; *to be strewn with straw*, of the orchestra, Arist.*Pr*.901^{b}30. **–ώδης**, ες, *like chaff, chaffy*, ib.928^{a}20 (Sup.) ; θρίσσαι Hices.ap.Ath.7.328c ; of an eruption, f. l. in Hp.*Liqu*.6. **II.** ἀχυρῶδες, = ἄχυρον, Dsc.2.93. **–ών**, ῶνος, ὁ, *storehouse for chaff*, *IG*11(2).287*A*149, al. (Delos, iii B.C.), *Gp*.6.2.8. **–ωσις**, εως, ἡ, *mixing of chaff with mud* or *straw*, compared with the swallow's nest-building, Arist.*HA*612^{b}22.

ἀχύτλωτος, ον, *unbathed, unanointed*, Nonn.*D*.9.25.

ἄχῠτος, ον, *insoluble*, τὰ ἀ. Gal.17(2).45.

***ἄχω**, v. ἀχέω. **ἀχώ**, ἡ, Dor. for ἠχώ.

ἀχώνευτος, ον, = ἄκαυστος, Hsch.

ἄχωρ [ᾰ], ορος, ὁ, *scurf, dandriff*, Ar.*Fr*.410, etc. (ἀχώρ, ῶρος, in Alex.Trall.1.8, Paul.Aeg.3.3, Dsc.1.33, al., cf. Phryn.*PS*p.8 B., *AB*475, after the analogy of ἰχώρ, ῶρος, but ἄχωρ acc. to Hdn.Gr.2.937.)

ἀχωρέω or **ἀχωριάω** [ᾰ], *suffer from* ἄχωρ, in part. ἀχωροῦντας or –ιῶντας, prob. cj. for ἰχωρροοῦντας in Paul.Aeg.3.3.

ἀχώρητος· ὁ μὴ χωρούμενος, Hsch.

ἀχωριστ-έω, *to be inseparable*, Phld.*D*.3.9. **–ία**, ἡ, *inseparability*, Id.*Mus*.p.94 K. **–ος**, ον, (χωρίζω) *not parted, undivided*, Pl.*R*.524c ; *inseparable*, Arist.*EN*1102^{a}30, *de An*.427^{a}2 ; ἀρετὴ ἀ. ἡδονῆς Epicur.*Fr*.506, cf. *Ep*.3 p.64 U., Gal.16.521, al. Adv. –τως Phld.*Sign*.20. **II.** (χῶρος) *without a place assigned one*, X.*Lac*.9.5.

ἄχωρος, ον, *without resting-place, homeless*, Ael.*Fr*.77 ; εἴ τι μέλλει ἐργάζεσθαι, ἀνόνητα γένοιτο καὶ ἄχωρα *Tab.Defix*.97.11, cf. 96.17.

ἀχωρώδης [ᾰ], ες, *like* ἄχωρ, ἐξανθήματα Aët.8.15, v.l. in Hp.*Liqu*.6.

ἄχωστος, ον, *not heaped up*, Hld.9.3.

ἄψ, Adv. of Place, (ἀπό, Lat. *abs*) *backwards, back again*, freq. in Hom., mostly with Verbs of motion, freq. before ἐς, ἀπό, ἐκ, ἂ. ἐς Ὄλυμπον ἵκεσθον Il.8.456, cf. 10.211, etc. ; with trans. Verbs, ἂ. ἐς κουλεὸν ὦσε 1.220, cf. 15.418 ; ἂ. ἐπὶ νῆας ἔεργε 16.395 ; ἂ. ἵππους στρέψαι 13.396, cf. 18.224. **2.** of actions, *again, in return*, ἂ. διδόναι Il.22.277 ; ἂ. ἀφελέσθαι 16.54 ; ἂ. ἀπολύειν 6.427 ; ἂ. ἀρέσαι 9.120 ; ἂ. τέτατο ὑσμίνη 17.543 ; ἂ. ἐπιμισγομένων 5.505 ; [ἂψ ἀπαγγ]εῖλαι prob. in Epich.99 ; ἂ. λαμβάνειν, = ἀναλαμβάνειν, Theoc.25.65 : pleon., ἂ. αὖτις *yet* again, Il.8.335, 15.364 ; ἂ. πάλιν 18.280.

ἀψάκειν or **ἀψακεῖν·** ἀποτυχεῖν, Hsch.

ἀψαλᾷ· ἀψοφητὶ πορεύεται, Hsch., Cyr., Zonar.

ἀψάλακτος [ψᾰ], ον, *untouched, unhandled*, S.*Fr*.550. **2.** *scot-free*, Crates Com.46, Ar.*Lys*.275.

ἀψάμαθος and **ἄψαμμος**, ον, *without sand, not sandy*, Hsch.

ἀψαυστ-έω, *leave untouched*, σώμασι App.*Gall*.14 :—Pass., Poll.1.9. **–ί**, Adv. of ἄψαυστος, *without touching*, Plu.2.665f. **–ία**, ἡ, *want of contact*, Iamb. *in Nic*.p.57 P. **–ος**, ον, *untouched*, Hdt.8.41, Thphr.*HP*5.5.6, Ph.2.14 ; *not to be touched, sacred*, Th.4.97 ; χρήματα App.*BC*2.41. **II.** Act., *not touching*, c. gen., ἄ. ἔγχους S.*OT*969 ; ἄ. τέκνων, of persons dying young, *Epigr.Gr*.241.2 (Smyrna).

ἀψεγής, ές, *blameless*, S.*El*.497 (lyr.). Adv. ἀψεγέως A.R.2.1022.

ἄψεκτος, ον, = foreg., Thgn.799 ; *not disapproved*, Gal.17(2).184.

ἀψελές· ὑγιές, Hsch. **ἄψερον**, = ὕστερον, πάλιν, Alc.*Supp*.26.11, Hsch., Zonar.

ἀψεύδ-εια, ἡ, *truthfulness*, Corinn.*Supp*.2.70, Pl.*R*.485c, Iamb.*Protr*.20 ; *reliability*, of times and seasons, Arist.*Mu*.397^{a}11 : –ία, Ph.*Fr*.110 H., Them.*Or*.21.257c. **–έω**, *not to lie, to speak truth*, πρός τινα S.*Tr*.469, Aeschin.2.95 : abs., Ar.*Fr*.751 ; *not to err*, Pl.*Tht*.199b ; περί τι Arist.*SE*165^{a}25. **II.** *observe faithfully*, *IG*5(2).343.38, 57 (Orchom. Arc., iv B.C.). **–ής**, ές, *without deceit, truthful*, esp. of oracles and the like, Hes.*Th*.233, Hdt.1.49, 2.152 (Sup.), al. ; μάντις ἀ., of Apollo, A.*Ch*.559, cf. *Fr*.350.5, Cratin.29 D. (Sup.) ; θεός *Ep.Tit*.1.2 ; ἀψευδεῖ τέχνῃ, of augury, A.*Th*.26 ; ἦθος E.*Supp*.869 ; *unerring*, Pl.*Tht*.160d, etc. ; μάρτυς –έστατος Ph.2.341. **2.** of things, *uncorrupt*, *pure from all deceit*, ἀ. πρὸς ἄκμονι χάλκευε γλῶσσαν Pi.*P*.1.86. 3. ἀψευδής, = κώνειον, Ps.-Dsc.4.78. II. Adv. -δέως, Att. -δῶς, *really and truly*, οἱ ἀ. ἄριστοι Hdt.9.58, cf. Ph.1.19, al., Iamb.*Myst*.2.2: Sup. -έστατα, ἐρεῖν Ph.1.34.

ἀψευδόμαντις, *of no false diviner*, τέχνη Nicoch.ap.*Lex.Sabb.*

ἀψευστ-έω, later form of ἀψευδέω, Plb.3.111.8; πρός τινα Phalar. *Ep*.123. **-ος**, ον, later form of ἀψευδής, Ph.*Fr*.51 H.; νόμος Plu. *Art*.28; *unfeigned*, πένθος *AP*7.638.6 (Crin.). Adv. -τως *PMag. Lond*.121.248.

ἀψεφ-έω, *neglect*, Hsch. **-ής**, ές, (ψέφω) = ἀφρόντιστος, *free from care*, S.*Fr*.692.

ἄψηκτος, ον, (ψήχω) *untanned*, κόθορνος Ar.*Lys*.658; *uncombed*, χαῖται A.R.3.50.

ἀψηλάφητος [λᾰ], ον, *not tried* or *tested*, Plb.8.19.5. II. *untouched*, Hsch.; gloss on ἄψαυστος, Id.

ἄψητος· ἀνυπότακτος, Hsch.

ἀψήφιστος, ον, *not having voted*, Ar.*V*.752. II. *not voted for, unwelcome*, πενία ἀ. οὐσία Secund.*Sent*.10.

ἄψηφος, ον, *without a stone*, δακτύλιος Artem.2.5. II. = πολύ, μέγα, ἰσχυρόν, Hsch.

ἀψηφοφόρητος, ον, *not having yet voted*, Plb.6.14.7.

ἀψίαι· ἑορταί (Lacon.), Hsch.

ἀψῖδο-ειδής, ές, *arched, vaulted*, D.C.68.25; *wheel-shaped*, Eudox. *Ars* 19.13. **-ομαι**, Pass., *to be tied in a circle* or *curve*, δικτύοις μόλυβδον ἡψιδωμένον *AP*6.90 (Phil.).

ἀψῖδωτός, όν, *vaulted*, *Gloss*. 2. *with tyres*, τροχός *Edict.Diocl.* 15.32.

ἀψῐ-κάρδιος, ον, (ἅπτομαι) *heart-touching*, M.Ant.9.3. **-κορία**, ἡ, *rapid satiety*, Plb.14.1.4, Plu.2.504d, Andronic.Rhod.p.572 M.; *fickleness*, δίχα ὕβρεως καὶ ἀ. *PLond*.5.1711 (vi A.D.). **-κορος**, ον, *quickly sated*: hence, *fickle*, Pl.*Ax*.369a; ἀ. πρὸς τὰς ἐπιθυμίας οἱ νέοι Arist.*Rh*.1389^a6, cf. D.Chr.32.28, Ph.2.312, al.; ποικιλώτατος καὶ ἀ. βίος Posidon.41: τὸ ἀ., = ἀψικορία, Plu.*Cor*.4, Luc.*Cal*.21. Adv. -ρως Ph.1.214, Hsch. II. Act., *quickly sating*, χάρις Plu.2.20b; λόγος ib.7b.

ἄψιλον· ἄπτερον ἢ πολύπτερον, Hsch.

ἀψι-μᾰχέω, *skirmish with an enemy*, Hyp.*Fr*.131, Plb.18.8.4, D.S. 11.52; *entice* or *lead on to fight*, Plu.*Crass*.10, *Dio* 39. **-μᾰχία**, ἡ, *skirmishing*, D.S.20.29, Plu.*Brut*.39, al.: metaph., *altercation*, ῥητόρων Aeschin.2.176, cf. Hyp(?).*Oxy*.1607.11 26, Plb.5.49.5, Plu.*Lyc*.2, *PPetr*.3 p.104: pl., ἀ. χειρῶν *personal encounters*, D.H.6.22; λόγων τε καὶ ἔργων ib.34. **-μᾰχικός**, ή, όν, = sq., *Gloss*. **-μᾰχος**, ον, = φιλοκίνδυνος, Alex.Aphr.*de An*.185.26. Adv. -χως *provocatively*, D.H.6.59. **-μῖσία**, ἡ, (μῖσος) *trivial and transient enmity*, Hsch., Suid.

ἀψινθ-ᾶτον, τό, *draught of wormwood*, Aët.3.69, Alex.Trall.1.15: —also **ἀψινθάτιον** (leg. -ιᾶτον) *PLond*.3.1259.32 (iv A.D.). **-ινος**, η, ον, *flavoured with wormwood*, ἔλαιον Alex.Trall.1.15. **-ιον**, τό, *wormwood, Artemisia Absinthium*, Hp.*Morb*.3.11, *Mul*.1.74, X.*An*. 1.5.1, Thphr.*HP*1.12.1, Dsc.3.23; ἀψινθίῳ κατέπασας Ἀττικὸν μέλι Men.708:—also **ἄψινθος**, ἡ, Aret.*CD*1.13, but ὁ, *Apoc*.8.11; and **ἀψινθία**, ἡ, Alex.Trall.1.10. II. ἀψίνθιον, = ἀβρότονον, Ps.-Dsc.3. 24. 2. = *Artemisia monosperma*, Aq.*Pr*.5.4. 3. ἀ. θαλάσσιον, = σέριφον, Dsc.3.23. **-ίτης** [ῑ] οἶνος wine *prepared with wormwood*, ibid.

ἀψίον· τὸ πρόσωπον, Hsch. **ἀψίορ**· μέγα, πλατύ, πολύ, ἰσχυρόν, Id.

ἀψίς, Ep. and Ion. **ἁψίς**, ῖδος, ἡ, (ἅπτω) *loop, mesh*, such as form a net, ἀψῖσι λίνου Il.5.487; ἀψῖδες *nets*, A.R.3.138, Opp.*H*.4.146. 2. *felloe* of a wheel, Hes.*Op*.426, Lyr. in *PLG*3.740; the *wheel* itself, Hdt.4.72, E.*Hipp*.1233; κύκλος ἀψῖδος the potter's *wheel*, *APl*.4.191 (Nicaenet.). 3. in Archit., *dowel-pin*, *IG*11(2).161 *A* 70 (Delos, iii B.C.). 4. *disk*, τὴν ἡμερίαν ἀψῖδα, of the sun, E.*Ion* 88; *segment* cut off by rainbow, Arist.*Mete*.371^b28, cf. Poet.ap.Plu.2.103f. 5. *arch* or *vault* (cf. ψαλίς II), ἐπὶ τὴν ὑπουράνιον ἀψῖδα Pl.*Phdr*.247b, cf. Suid. s.v. αἰθεροβατεῖν, *Epigr.Gr*.1078 (Adana), *IGRom*.3.975, *PMag. Lond*.46.41; κατὰ τὴν ἀψῖδα ποτώμενος Luc.*BisAcc*.33; *triumphal arch*, D.C.53.22,26, etc.: metaph., κάμπτειν ἐπῶν ἀψῖδας Ar.*Th*. 53. b. σελάνας ἐς δεκάταν ἀψῖδα in the moon's tenth *orbit*, i.e. the tenth month, *Hymn.Is*.38. c. ἡ ἀνωτάτω ἀ. θεάτρου uppermost *tier*, D.C.61.17. (ἀψῖδα in late Poets, *Epigr.Gr*.440.9, 445.4.)

ἄψις, εως, Ion. ιος, ἡ, (ἅπτομαι) *touching*, Hp.*Epid*.7.5; *contact*, Pl. *Prm*.149a, Arist.*HA*621^a11: pl., Pl.*Prm*.149c. 2. metaph., ἄ. φρενῶν *distraction of mind*, Hp.*Acut*.52.

ἄψογος, ον, *blameless*, *Sammelb*.625, Poll.3.139. Adv. -γως Eust. 19.17.

ἄψοος· θηρίον τι κατεσθίον ἀμπέλους, Hsch.

ἀψόρροος, ον, contr. -ρρους, ουν, (ἄψ, ῥέω) *back-flowing, refluent*, Homeric epith. of Ocean, regarded as a stream *encircling* the earth and *flowing back* into itself, Il.18.399, Od.20.65.

ἄψορρος, ον, *going back, backwards*, ἄψορροι κίομεν Il.21.456; ἄψορροι προτὶ Ἴλιον ἀπονέοντο 3.313; ἐκ δόμων ἄ... περᾷ S.*Ant*.386, cf. *OT*431: mostly in neut. ἄψορρον as Adv., *backward, back again*, ἄψορρον.. ἔβη Il.7.413; ἄ. οἱ θυμὸς ἀγέρθη 4.152; ἄ. προσέφην Od.9. 282; ἄψορρον ἥξεις A.*Pr*.1021, cf. S.*El*.53; ὦ παῖδες, οὐκ ἄψορρον (sc. ἄπιτε); ib.1430; οὐκ ἄ. ἐκνεμῇ πόδα; Id.*Aj*.369 (lyr.). (For ἄψ-ορσος, cf. παλίν-ορσος.)

ἄψος, εος, τό, (ἅπτω) *juncture, joint*, λύθεν δέ οἱ ἄψεα πάντα all *his joints* were relaxed [by sleep], Od.4.794, cf. Nic.*Al*.541; ἄψεα δεσμοῦ Opp.*H*.3.538: in pl., *limbs*, *AP*5.217 (Agath.), al.

ἀψοφ-ητί or -ητεί, Adv. of sq., Pl.*Tht*.144b, D.25.90, Arist.*HA* 533^b32, Men.298, Ph.1.643; λέξις ὥσπερ ἔλαιον ἀ. ῥέουσα D.H.*Dem*. 20. **-ητος**, ον, (ψοφέω) *noiseless*, c. gen., ἀ. κωκυμάτων *without sound* of.., S.*Aj*.321. **-ία**, ἡ, *noiselessness*, Arist.*Ph*.244^b17, Plot.2.1.6. **-ος**, ον, = ἀψόφητος, S.*Tr*.967 (lyr.), E.*Tr*.887, *Com. Adesp*.1310, Arist.*de An*.420^a7. Adv. -φως and -φέως *EM*183.22.

ἀψυδρακίωτος, ον, *without pustules* or *pimples*, σῶμα Dsc.2.72.

ἀψῠθής, ές, = ἀψευδής, Hsch.

ἄψυκτος, ον, *not capable of being cooled*, Pl.*Phd*.106a.

ἀψῡχ-ἄγώγητος, ον, *not rejoicing the heart*, Plb.9.1.5. Adv. -τως *without being comforted*, Jul.*Or*.8.252a. **-εί**, Adv. of ἄψυχος, Hdn. *Epim*.257. **-έω**, *swoon*, Hp.*Morb*.2.5, *Epid*.7.1. **-ία**, Ion. -ίη, ἡ, *swooning, syncope*, Id.*VM*10, *Coac*.222. II. *want of spirit, faint-heartedness*, A.*Th*.259,383, E.*Alc*.642, etc. **-οποιός**, όν, *making lifeless* or *faint*, Eust.611.5. **-ος**, ον, *lifeless, inanimate*, πόθῳ Archil.84; μνημεῖ' ἄψυχ' ἐμψύχων Simon.106.4, cf. E.*Fr*.655, *Tr*. 623; λωτὸς ἄ. ἔμπνουν ἀνίει Μοῦσαν Sopat.10; ἃ -ότατα τῶν ὀστῶν *with least life* or *sensation*, Pl.*Ti*.74e, cf. Arist.*de An*.413^a21, etc.; ἄ. θεοί, of statues, Timae.127. 2. ἄ. βορὰ *non-animal* food, E.*Hipp*. 952. II. *spiritless, faint-hearted*, κάκη A.*Th*.192; ἀνὴρ *Trag. Adesp*.337: ἀψυχότεραι αἱ θήλειαι [ἐλέφαντες] Arist.*HA*610^a21; of style, *lifeless*, D.H.*Dem*.20. Adv. -χως Poll.2.227. III. *materialistic*, λόγος Porph.*Gaur*.14.4 (Comp.).

ἄω (A), = ἄημι (q.v.), *blow*, only in impf. ἄεν, A.R.1.605, 2. 1228. II. = αὔω, ἰαύω, *sleep*, only in aor., ἐνὶ κοίτῃ ἄεσα Od.19. 342; νύκτα μὲν ἀέσαμεν 3.151; ἔνθα δὲ νύκτ' ἄεσαν ib.490; contr., νύκτ' ἄσαμεν 16.367.

ἄω (B), *hurt*, contr. from ἀάω (q.v.); cf. ἄτη.

ἄω (C), Ep. inf. ἄμεναι: fut. ἄσω Il.11.818: aor. 1 subj. ἄσω 18.281, inf. ἆσαι (v. infr.): aor. 2 subj. 1 pl. ἕωμεν 19.402:—Med., Ep. 3 sg. ἄαται Hes.*Sc*.101; cf. ἆται· πληροῦται, Hsch.: fut. ἄσομαι Il.24.717: aor. ἀσάμην 19.307:—*satiate*, αἵματος ἆσαι Ἄρηα *to give* him *his fill of* blood, 5.289: but, II. mostly intr., *take one's fill of* a thing, ἱεμένη χροὸς ἄμεναι 21.70; λιλαιομένη χροὸς ἆσαι ib.168, cf. 15.317; γόοιο μὲν ἔστι καὶ ἆσαι 23.157:—Med., ἄσεσθε κλαυθμοῖο 24.717; ποτῆτος ἄσασθαι φίλον ἦτορ 19.307. (Root *sā*: *sə*, cf. ἄ-ατος, ἄ-δην.)

ἀῶ· ὑγεία, ἡμέρα, Hsch.

ἀώδης, ες, (ὄζω) *without smell*, Thphr.*Od*.18, Plu.2.1014f.

ἀωδῠνεῖν, *to be free from pain*, Hsch.

ἀῶθεν, Adv., Dor. for ἠῶθεν, Theoc.15.132.

ἀωΐλιον, τό, Egyptian measure of capacity, = 2 *cubic* πήχεις, *PPetr*. 2 p.14, al. (iii B.C.):—also **αὐωΐλιον**, ib.p.118.

ἀώιος, for ἠῷος, ἀστήρ Ion Lyr.10, prob. in B.*Fr*.3.11.

ἀώλυπον· τὸ οὐκ ἀπολλύμενον, Hsch.

ᾀών, ᾀόνος, ἡ, Dor. for ἠϊών, v.l. in Mosch.3.122.

ἀών [ᾱ], όνος, ὁ, a kind of *fish*, Epich.63. II. a kind of *garment*, *PAmh*.2.3 *a* ii 21 (iii A.D., pl.).

ἄωρ, ὁ, v. ἄορ.

ἀωρέω, *to be careless* (ἀ- priv., ὤρα), Hsch., Suid.:—also, = φυλάττειν (ἀ- intens.), Hsch.

ἀωρί (-εί *PFay*.19.2 (ii A.D.)), Adv. of ἄωρος, *at an untimely hour, too early*, Heraclid.Com.1.2, Luc.*BisAcc*.1, *AP*12.116; ἀ. θανάτῳ ἀπέθανεν Ar.*Fr*.663 cod.; νυκτὸς ἀωρί *at dead of* night, Theoc.11.40, 24.38; ἀωρὶ τῶν νυκτῶν Antipho 2.1.4, 2.4.5; ἀωρὶ νύκτωρ (v.l. νυκτῶν) Ar.*Ec*.741, Phalar.*Ep*.141.2.

ἀωρία, ἡ, *wrong time*: hence, *untimely fate* or *death*, Hld.10.16; but ἀωρίη *old age*, Herod.3.29; *bad condition*, πραγμάτων Procop. *Arc*.14: pl., ἀωρίαι *bad seasons*, Plu.2.371b; ἀωρία *midnight, dead of night*, Pherecr.6 D., Ael.*Fr*.81; in full, ἦν ἀ. τῆς νυκτὸς μεσούσης Alciphr.3.47: metaph., ἀωρίη τοῦ πρήγματος Aret.*CD*1.4; *darkness* (figure of *calamity*), prob. in Lxx *Is*.59.9: acc. as Adv., ἀωρίαν ἥκειν to have come *too late*, Ar.*Ach*.23; ποῦ βαδίζεις ἀωρίᾳ; whither *so late*? Luc.*Asin*.24.

ἀωρῐλουστής, οῦ, ὁ, *an early bather*, better written divisim in M.Ant.1.16.8.

ἀώριος, α, ον, = ἄωρος (A), Thphr.*CP*2.2.2, Arat.1076, *AP*7.600 (Jul. Aegypt.); ἀϝώριος *IG*1^2.980: nom. pl. fem. ἀώριαι Ἐφ.Ἀρχ.1911. 59 (Peraea, iv B.C.).

ἀωρο-βόρος, ον, *devouring those who die untimely*, *PMag.Par*.1. 2867. **-θάνᾰτος** [θᾰ], ον, *untimely dead*, Ar.*Fr*.663 (cj. Dind. for ἀωρὶ θαν., cf. Phryn.*PS* p.42 B.). **-θανής**, ές, = foreg., *CIG*3846*q* (Aezani), Calder *Philadelphia and Montanism* 35. **-λειος**, ον, *unnaturally smooth*, esp. men who by pulling out their beards tried to make themselves look young, Cratin.10; of a youth, *beardless*, Ael.*NA*13.27. **-μορος**, ον, *dying untimely*, *IG*12(8).444 (Thasos). **-νυκτος**, ον, *at midnight*, ἀ. ἀμβόαμα ἔλακε A.*Ch*.34 (lyr.).

ἄωρος (A), ον, (ὥρα) *untimely, unseasonable*, χειμών, τύχαι, A.*Pers*. 496, *Eu*.956 (lyr.); θάνατος E.*Or*.1030; τελευτή Antipho 3.1.2; ξυνουσίη Aret.*CD*1.4 (but ἄ. γάμος *too late*, D.H.4.7); πένθος Lxx *Wi*. 14.15; μετὰ μάχην ἱκετεύειν ἄωρον ἐδόκει J.*BJ*5.11.1; ἄ. θανεῖν E.*Alc*. 168, cf. Hdt.2.79; οἱ ἄ. those *who die untimely*, Apollod.Com.4, cf. Philostr.*VA*6.4; esp. of those dying *unmarried*, *PMag.Par*.1.342, cf. 2725; in Epitaphs, ὤλετ' ἄ. *IG*1^2.977: Sup. ἀωρώτατε (sic) *Sammelb*. 1420; ἕνεκα χρόνου πάντες ἐσμὲν ἄ. *unripe* (for death), Metrod.52; ἀώροις περιπέσοιτο συμφοραῖς *Epigr.Gr*.376 (Aezani): Comp. γήρως ἀωρότερα πράττειν things *unbecoming* old age, Plu.*Sull*.2. 2. *unripe*, of fruit, Dsc.1.126, Lxx *Wi*.4.5; of fish, *out of season*, opp. ὥριμος, Nicom.Com.1.21: metaph., ἄωρος πρὸς γάμον Plu.*Lyc*.15; ἄ. ὥρα Id.

*Comp.Thes.Rom.*6. 3. *without youthful freshness, ugly,* Eup.69, X.*Mem.*1.3.14 (Sup.), Pl.*R.*574c. Adv. -ρως J.*AJ*4.8.19.

ἄωρος (B), ον, of the πλεκτάναι or polypus-like legs of Scylla, τῆς ἤ τοι πόδες εἰσὶ δυώδεκα πάντες ἄωροι Od.12.89; one of the Sch. expld. it as κρεμαστοί, ἀπὸ τοῦ αἰωρῶ, but more prob. = ἄκωλοι, as Sch.HQ, from Ion. ὤρη B. II. ἄωροι πόδες *fore*-feet, οὐ τοὺς ἀώρους εἶπά σοι.. πόδας πρίασθαι; σὺ δὲ φέρεις ὀπισθίους Philem.145.

ἄωρος (C), contr. **ὦρος,** ὁ, *sleep,* Sapph.57; ἤλασ' ἄωρον prob. for ἤλασας ὦρον in Call.*Fr.*150.

ἀωροσύνη, ἡ, *untimeliness, immaturity,* dub. in *Epigr.Gr.*414.

ἀωρότοκος, ον, *laid prematurely,* of soft-shelled eggs, *Hippiatr.*22.

ἄωρτο, Ep. plpf. Pass. of ἀείρω.

ἄως, Boeot., = ἕως, *IG*7.2228.

Ἀώς, ἡ, Dor. for Ἠώς, Ἕως; ἐπ' ἀϝῶ c. gen., *to east of, Mnemos.* 42.332 (Argos, iv B.C.).

Ἀωσφόρος, ὁ, = Ἑωσφόρος (q. v.).

ἀωτ-έω [ᾰ], *sleep,* Ep. Verb, only pres., τί πάννυχον ὕπνον ἀωτεῖς; Il.10.159; μηκέτι νῦν εὕδοντες ἀωτεῖτε γλυκὺν ὕπνον Od.10.548: abs., Simon.37.5:—in Hsch., **ἀωτεύειν·** ἀπανθίζεσθαι (also ἀωτεῖτε· ἀπανθίζετε τὸν ὕπνον), but expld. by ὑφαίνειν, *AB*476, cf. Suid. s. v. ἀωτεμεῖν (sic); perh. to be read (in signf. *sleep*) in B.8.13 for ἀσαγεύω. **-ίζομαι,** *cull the choicest* or *best;* v. λωτίζομαι.

ἄωτον [ᾰ], τό, and **ἄωτος,** ὁ, *the choicest, the flower of its kind:* in Hom. mostly of the *finest wool,* οἰὸς ἄωτον Il.13.599,716, Od.1.443; without οἰός (which must be supplied from the context), *flock, down,* 9.434; once of the *finest linen,* λίνοιό τε λεπτὸν ἄωτον Il.9.661; of the golden fleece, χρύσεον ἄωτον A.R.4.176, cf. Orph.*A.*1336; ἄκρον ἄωτον [ὕδατος], of *pure* water, Call.*Ap.*112; of the *foam* on a wave, κύματος ἄκρῳ ἀ. Id.*Hec.*1.4.3; μέλιτος ἄ. γλυκύς Pi.*Pae.*6.59: freq. in Pi., ἄ. ζωᾶς *the prime* or *flower* of life, Id.*I.*5(4).12; ἄ. στεφάνων *the fairest* of.., ib.6(5).4, cf. *O.*5.1; Χαρίτων ἄ. their *fairest gift,* Id.*I.* 8(7).16; σοφίας ἄκρος ἄ. the *choicest gift* of minstrel's art, ib.7(6).18; ἄ. γλώσσας, i. e. a song, ib.1.51; ὕμνων Id.*P.*10.53; δίκας ἄ. Id.*N.*3. 29; Ἀφροδίτας.. ἄωτον A.*Supp.*666 (lyr.): rarely in pl., στεφάνων ἄωτοι Pi.*O.*9.19; ἡρώων ἄωτοι Id.*N.*8.9; ῥόδων ἄωτοι Simon.148: in Epitaphs, θνήσκω... ἀκμᾶς ἐν ἀώτῳ *in the flower* of youth, *IG*3.1328; τὸν.. ἄωτον τοῦ δήμου *CIG*2804, cf. *Epigr.Gr.*455. II. *that which gives honour and glory* to a thing, ἄ. ἵππων *a song in praise of* horses, Pi.*O.*3.4; χειρῶν ἄ. ἐπίνικον Id.*O.*8.75.—The gender is indeterminate in Hom. and A.; Pi. always has ἄωτος, and so Theoc.13.27; A.R. and later Ep. ἄωτον (Opp.*C.*4.154, οἰὸς ἄωτα in pl.).

ἄωτος, ον, (οὖς) *without ears,* Plu.2.963b; of vessels, *without lugs,* Philet.ap.Ath.11.783a, dub. in Call.*Fr.*115, cf. Aët.1.138.

B

B β, βῆτα, indecl., second letter of the Gr. alphabet: hence as numeral, β' = δύο and δεύτερος, but ͵β = 2,000. II. to represent ϝ, freq. in Hsch., esp. in Lacon. words, cf. βείκατι, etc.

βᾶ, shortd. form of βασιλεῦ, *king!* A.*Supp.*892 (lyr.). II. an exclam. *baa!* (with ref. to the *baaing* of a lamb), Hermipp.19.

βαβάζω, *speak inarticulately,* or *shout,* Hsch.; but aor. inf. βαβάξαι *dance,* Id. (Cf. βαβάκτης.)

βαβαί, exclam. of surprise or amazement, *bless me!* E.*Cyc.*156, Ar.*Av.*272, etc.; doubled, *hurrah!* Achae.28, cf. Chrysipp.*Stoic.*3. 178; οὐχὶ τῶν μετρίων, ἀλλὰ τῶν βαβαὶ βαβαί, to denote persons *extravagant* in their expressions, Alex.206: c. gen., βαβαὶ τοῦ λόγου *bless me* what an argument! Pl.*Phlb.*23b, cf. Jul.*Caes.*309b, etc. (On the accent, cf. Hdn.Gr.1.502; βαβαῖ cod. B in Pl. l.c.)

βαβαιάξ, strengthd. for βαβαί, Ar.*Ach.*64, al.; βαβαὶ βαβαιάξ Id. *Pax*248.

βάβακα· τὸν γάλλον, Hsch.

βαβάκινος· χύτρας εἶδος, Hsch.

βάβακοι, in Elis, = τέττιγες; in Pontus, = βάτραχοι, Hsch.

βαβάκτης, *reveller,* of Pan, Cratin.321, cf. Eust.1431.46; of Dionysus, Corn.*ND*30; expld. by ὀρχηστής, *EM*183.45, Hsch.

βάβαλον· αἰδοῖον, Hsch.: also βάβαλον· κραύγασον (Lacon.), Id.

βάβαξ, ακος, ὁ, *chatterer,* Archil.33, Lyc.472.

βαβέλιος, Pamph., = ἀέλιος, ἥλιος, Eust.1654.20.

βαβήρ· ὁ Ἄρης, Hsch.

βαβίζω or **-ύζω,** = βαΰζω, Zenod.ap.Ammon.p.231 V.

βάβιον, τό, Syrian word for *child,* Dam.*Isid.*76.

βαβράζω, *chatter, chirp,* of the grasshopper, Anan.5.6.

βάβρηκες, οἱ, *gums,* or *food in the teeth,* Hsch. **βαβρήν,** *lees of olive-oil* (Maced.), Id. **βαβύας,** ὁ, *mud,* Id.:—also **βαβύλυς,** Suid.

βαβυκώς, = πελεκάν, Philet.ap.Hsch.

Βᾰβῠλών, ῶνος, ἡ, *Babylon,* Alc.*Supp.*16.10, etc.:—**Βᾰβῠλώνιοι,** οἱ, *Babylonians,* Hdt.1.77, etc., and **Βᾰβῠλωνία,** ἡ, *Babylonia,* Arist. *Oec.*1352ᵇ27:—also **Βᾰβῠλωνεύς,** έως, ὁ, St.Byz.; fem. **Βᾰβῠλωνίς,** ίδος, Nonn.*D.*40.303:—Adj. **Βᾰβῠλώνιος,** α, ον, Hdt.1.106, etc.; ος, ον, Arr.*An.*6.29.6; or **Βᾰβῠλωνιακός,** ή, όν, Alex.308.

βαβύρας· πίων, Cyr.

βαβύρτας· ὁ παράμωρος, Hsch. (Cf. Lat. *baburrus.*)

βαγαῖος· μάταιος, Hsch. II. title of Zeus in Phrygia, Id. (Cf. Slav. *bogŭ* 'god'.)

βαγαρόν· χλιαρόν (Lacon.), Hsch. **βαγεῖ·** εἰσελθοῦσαι, Id. **βάγιον·** μέγα, Id., Suid.

βάγμα, ατος, τό, (βάζω) *speech,* A.*Pers.*637 (lyr., pl.).

βάγος· κλάσμα ἄρτου, Hsch.

βαγός· βασιλεύς, καὶ στρατηγός (i. e. Lacon., = ἀγός), Hsch.

βαγώας, ὁ, Lat. *Bagoas* and *Bagōus,* Persian word, said to be = εὐνοῦχος, as pr. n. in Str.15.3.24, etc.

βαδάς· κίναιδος, Amerias ap.Hsch. **βαδελεγεῖ·** ἀμέλγει, Id. (βαδέλγει Cyr., alii alia).

βαδδίν· βύσσινον ἔνδυμα ἐξαίρετον, Hsch.

βάδην [ᾰ], Adv., (βαίνω) *step by step,* β. ἀπιόντος Il.13.516; ἀράχνος ὡς β. A.*Supp.*887; *in marching step,* ἦγε β. Hdt.9.57; ἡγοῦ β. Ar.*Lys.*254; β. ταχὺ ἐφέπεσθαι *at quick march,* opp. δρόμῳ θεῖν, X.*An.*4.6.25; θᾶττον ἢ β. Id.*HG*5.4.53, Men.837, Aristaenet.2.14; β. ὑποχωρεῖν Arist.*HA*629ᵇ14. 2. *gradually, more and more,* πεινῆν Ar.*Ach.*535. II. *on foot,* opp. ἐφ' ἵππων, ἐπὶ ναῶν, A.*Pers.* 19 (anap.); opp. ἐπ' ἀπήνης, App.*Gall.*1.

βᾰδίζω, Att. fut. βαδιοῦμαι Ar.*Th.*617, *Pl.*495, Pl.*Smp.*190d, etc.; later βαδίσομαι Gal.*UP*12.10, and βαδιῶ Nicol.*Prog.*p.69 F., Ael.*Tact.* 36.4, (δια-) Luc.*Dem.Enc.*1; βαδίσω D.Chr.10.8: aor. ἐβάδισα Hp.*Int.* 44, Pl.*Erx.*392b, Arr.*An.*7.3.3, etc.: pf. βεβάδικα Arist.*Metaph.*1048ᵇ 31, J.*Ap.*2.39:—Med., imper. βαδίζου Cratin.391:—*walk,* ἐπιστροφάδην δ' ἐβάδιζεν *h.Merc.*210; β. ἀρρύθμως Alex.263; opp. τρέχω, X.*Cyr.* 2.3.10, etc.; of horsemen, interpol. in Id.*An.*6.3.19; ἐπὶ κτήνους β. D.Chr.34.5; *go by land,* opp. πλέω, D.19.164,181; also of *sailing,* X. *Oec.*16.7; of a ship, Lxx *Jn.*1.3; *march,* of armies, Ael.*Tact.* l.c.; of certain animals, κατὰ σκέλη β., v. σκέλος 1: c. acc. cogn., βάδον β. Ar.*Av.*42; ὁδόν Hp. l.c., X.*Mem.*2.1.11; ἀεὶ μίαν ἀτραπόν Arist.*HA* 622ᵇ25; ὁδῷ β. Luc.*Tim.*5; βάδιζε *go!* Men.*Epit.*159, *Sam.*43. 2. *go about,* βῆ βῆ λέγων β. Cratin.43, al.; κατὰ ζυγά in pairs, Arist.*HA* 544ᵃ5. 3. generally, *go, proceed,* Antipho 5.24; ἐπ' οἰκίας β. *enter* houses, D.18.132, cf. Test.ap.eund.21.121; β. ἐπί τινα ψευδοκλητείας *proceed* against him for.., D.53.15; εἰς τὸ πολίτευμα, εἰς τὰς ἀρχάς, εἰς τὰ ἀρχεῖα, Arist.*Pol.*1293ᵃ24, 1298ᵃ15, 1299ᵃ36; β. εἰς τὰ πατρῷα *enter* on one's patrimony, Is.3.62; *proceed* (in argument), πρὸς τὰ κατηγορήματα D.18.263, cf. Arist.*APo.*97ᵃ5; εἰς ἄπειρον β., of an infinite *process, Metaph.*1000ᵇ28; ὀμόσε τῇ φήμῃ β. Plu.*Thes.*10. 4. of things, αἱ τιμαὶ ἐπ' ἔλαττον ἐβάδιζον prices *were getting* lower, D. 56.9; τὸ πρᾶγμα πορρωτέρω β. Id.23.203.—Very rare in Poets: [ἥλιος] β. τὸν ἐνιαύσιον κύκλον E.*Ph.*544.

βάδιλλος, ὁ, = Lat. *batillus, shovel,* β. σιδηροῦς *POxy.*521.13 (ii A.D.).

βάδιον, τό, Dim. of βάδος or βάτος, a measure, = 50 ξέσται, *PBaden* 43.10 (iii A.D.), *POxy.*1658.4 (iv A.D.).

βάδ-ῐσις [ᾰ], εως, ἡ, *walking, going,* Ar.*Pl.*334; βαδίσει χρῆσθαι Hp.*Aër.*15; of hares, τεχνάζειν τῇ β. X.*Cyn.*8.3; opp. πτῆσις, ἅλσις, Arist.*EN*1174ᵃ31. **-ισμα,** ατος, τό, *walk, gait,* X.*Ap.*27, D.37. 55: pl., Luc.*Herm.*18; ἐλθὼν ἐν ἠρεμαίῳ β. Palaeph.31. **-ισμᾰτίας,** ου, ὁ, *a good walker,* Cratin.392. **-ισμός,** ὁ, = βάδισις, Pl. *Chrm.*160c. **-ιστέον,** *one must walk* or *go,* σοὶ β. πάρος S.*El.* 1502, Str.17.1.54; *one must proceed,* ἐπὶ τὸ καθόλου Arist.*EN*1180ᵇ21: pl., βαδιστέα Ar.*Ach.*394. **-ιστηλάτης** [λᾰ], ὁ, *driver of riding-donkeys, PTeb.*262 (ii B.C.), *POxy.*1514.2 (iii A.D.), etc. **-ιστής,** οῦ, ὁ, *goer,* ταχὺς β. a quick *runner,* E.*Med.*1182; ἵππος β. Hsch. s. v. κάλπις: ὄνος β. *riding*-donkey, *PGrenf.*2.14ᵇ5 (iii B.C.); β. alone, = ὄνος, *PFlor.*376.23 (iii A.D.). **-ιστικός,** ή, όν, *good at walking,* Ar.*Ra.*128, Thphr.*Fr.*180; *able to walk,* Simp.*in Ph.*887.17; τὸ β. *that which is capable of walking,* Arist.*Int.*21ᵇ16; ποὺς.. ὄργανον β. Gal.*UP*2.9. Adv. -κῶς Porph.*Gaur.*1.3. II. *for riding animals,* στάβλον *POxy.*146.1 (vi A.D.). **-ιστός,** ή, όν, *that can be passed on foot,* Arr.*Ind.*43.10:—but **βάδιστοι·** βαδύτατοι, Hsch. (i. e. ἡδ-).

βάδομαι· ἀγαπῶ, Hsch. (For ἥδομαι.)

βάδος, ὁ, *walk,* βάδον βαδίζειν, coined by Ar.*Av.*42. II. v. βάτος.

Βαδρόμιος, Βαδρομιών, v. Βοηδρόμιος, Βοηδρομιών.

βαδύς (i. e. ϝαδύς), Elean for ἡδύς, Pherecyd.*Fr.*79 J., Paus.5.3.2, cf. **βάδηδοι·** ἠχεῖοι (leg. βαδύ· ἡδύ· Ἠλεῖοι), Hsch.

βάζω, poet. Verb, used chiefly in pres. and impf.: aor. ἔβαξα Hsch.: pf. Pass. (v. infr.):—*speak, say,* ἄρτια βάζειν Il.14.92, al.; ἀνεμώλια β. Od.4.837; πεπνυμένα βάζεις Il.9.58; οἵ τ' εὖ μὲν βάζουσι κακῶς δ' ὄπιθεν φρονέουσιν Od.18.168; νήπια β. Pi.*Fr.*157; ἐβληχημένα β. *AP*7.636 (Crin.): c. dupl. acc., ταῦτά μ' ἀγειρόμενοι θάμ' ἐβάζετε Il.16.207, cf. E.*Hipp.*119; πολλὰ κακῶς β. ἑστίαν Ἀτρειδᾶν Id. *Rh.*719 (lyr.); καθεύδουσιν μάτην ἄκραντα β. A.*Ch.*882: c. dat. modi, χαλεποῖς βάζοντες ἔπεσσι *address* with sharp words, Hes.*Op.*186; κακοῖσι β. πολλὰ Τυδέως βίαν A.*Th.*571; ὑπέραυχα β. ἐπὶ πτόλει ib. 483; εἴ τι μὴ ψεῦδος ἡ παροιμίη βάζει Herod.2.102; Διονύσῳ ὄργια βάζων *IG*14.1642:—Pass., ἔπος.. βέβακται a word *has been spoken,* Od.8.408. (Cf. βάξις, βάσκειν (for βάκ-σκειν), ἀβακής.)

βαθακίζων· κακῶς ἕρπων, Hsch. **βαθάλη·** κρήνη, Amerias ap. eund. **βαθανίαν·** νεοσσιάν (Cret.), Hsch. **βαθάρα·** πυκλιή (Maced.), πυρλός (Athaman.), Id.

βαθίων, βάθιστος, Comp. and Sup. of βαθύς.

βαθμ-ηδόν, Adv., (βαθμός) *by steps,* Gal.18(1).793, Ath.1.1c. **-ίς,** ἡ, gen. ίδος Pi.*N.*5.1, ῖδος *AP*7.428.4 (Mel.):—*step* or *threshold,* ἀκρᾶν βαθμίδων ἄπο Pi.*P.*5.7, cf. *J.AJ*15.11.5; cf. βασμίς. II. *base, pedestal,* Pi.*N.*5.1. 2. *socket,* Hp.*Fract.*2: generally, *hollow* in a joint, ib.37. **-οειδής,** ές, *like steps,* Democr.155, Zos.Alch. p.176 B. **-ός** or **βασμός,** ὁ, (βαίνω) *step, threshold,* Lxx 1*Ki.*5.5,

[S.]*Fr.*1127; *degree* on the dial, Lxx 4*Ki.*20.9 sq.; *fifteen degrees* of the zodiac, Vett.Val.31.2; *interval* in a musical scale, Iamb.*VP*26. 120. 2. *rung* of a ladder, Luc.*Trag.*221. 3. *base* or *plinth* of a tower, *GDI*5524.10 (Cyzicus). II. metaph., *step, degree* in rank (οἱ β. κλίμακος προκοπὴν σημαίνουσι Artem.2.42), 1*Ep.Ti.*3.13, Procop.*Arc.*24, Lyd.*Mag.*2.8, al.; οἱ τᾶς ἀξίας βάσμοι *IG*12(2).243. 16 (Mytil.); simply, *degree*, τολμημάτων βαθμοί J.*BJ*4.3.10; ὥσπερ ἡδονῆς κλίμακα συμπηξάμενος ἔρως πρῶτον ἔχει β. ὄψεως Luc.*Am.*53; *step* in an argument, Simp.*in Cael.*718.35; of a genealogy, ἀπωτέρω δυοῖν β. two *steps* farther back, i.e. farther back than one's grandfather, D.Chr.41.6. III. *tax paid on stairs*, *POxy.*574 (ii A.D.): acc. to Phryn.296, Moer.97, βαθμός is Ion., βασμός Att., but βασμός occurs *GDI*5524.10 (Cyzic.), *Jahresh.*3.55 (Scepsis). **-ώδης**, expl. of βαλβιδώδης, Bacch.ap.Erot.*Fr.*42.

βᾱθόημι, Aeol., = βοηθέω, impf. ἐβαθόη *IG*12(2).645.21 (Nesus); dat. part. βαθόεντι ib.526.27 (Eresus).

βάθος [ᾰ], εος, τό, (βαθύς) *depth* or *height*, acc. as measured up or down, Ταρτάρου βάθη A.*Pr.*1029; αἰθέρος βάθος E.*Med.*1297, cf. Ar. *Av.*1715; βάθους μετέχειν to be a solid, possessing *depth* as well as length and breadth, Pl.*R.*528b; εἴτ' ἐν βάθεσιν εἴτ' ἐν τάχεσιν Id.*Plt.* 299e; βάθους αὔξη Id.*R.*528d; opp. μῆκος, πλάτος, Arist.*Ph.*209a5; μεγέθους τὸ ἐπὶ τρία [συνεχὲς] β. Id.*Metaph.*1020a12: with Preps., ἐκ βάθεος *in depth*, Hdt.1.186; ἐκ βάθους *through and through*, Plot. 5.8.10; εἰς βάθος Arist.*Mete.*386a23, al.; ἐν βάθει Id.*Sens.*440a14, etc.; κατὰ βάθους Id.*Mete.*339b12; κατὰ βάθος *in a descending scale*, metaph. of causation, Dam.*Pr.*95: freq. in military sense, *depth* of a line of battle, X.*HG*3.4.13, etc.; ἐπὶ βάθος τάσσεσθαι *in depth of line*, Th.5.68; ἐς β. ἐκτάξαι Arr.*An.*1.2.4; β. τριχῶν, of *long thick* hair, Hdt.5.9; ἄτομα πώγωνος βάθη Ephipp.14.7; *interior* of a country, Str.3.3.7, al.; *depth*, of perspective in a picture, Procop.Gaz.*Ecphr.* p.157B.: pl., βάθη *depths*, Pl.*Ti.*44d, etc.; *deep water*, opp. shallows near shore, Lxx *Ps.*68(69).2, al., *Ev.Luc.*5.4; ἐν τοῖς βάθεσιν Arist. *HA*599b9. b. Astron., = ταπείνωμα, Vett.Val.241.26. 2. metaph., κακῶν ὁρῶν β. A.*Pers.*465; ἡ μακροῦ πλούτου βάθει S.*Aj.*130, cf. *Ep.Rom.*11.33; β. ἡγεμονίας Plu.*Pomp.*53; *depth of mind*, β. τι ἔχειν γενναῖον, of Parmenides, Pl.*Tht.*184a; ἐν βάθει πόσιος *deep* in drink, Theoc.14.29; β. καρδίας ἀνθρώπου Lxx *Ju.*8.14; τὰ β. τοῦ θεοῦ, τοῦ Σατανᾶ, 1*Ep.Cor.*2.10, *Apoc.*2.24. 3. of lit. style, *bathos*, ὕψους ἢ β. Longin.2.1. (Substituted for βένθος under the influence of βαθύς.)

βάθρα, ἡ, = βαθμός, Ar.*Fr.*513, cf. Poll.10.47, *Sammelb.*402 (iii A.D.), Lyd.*Mag.*1.3; = βάσις, *Et.Gud.*: = ἀποβάθρα, dub. in Plu.2. 347b.

βαθράδιον, τό, Dim. of βάθρον, Ar.*Fr.*514 codd. Poll.(10.47): leg. βαθρίδιον.

βάθρακος, v. βάτραχος.

βαθρεία, ἡ, = βάθρον, A.*Supp.*860 (dub. l.).

βαθρίδιον, v. βαθράδιον.

βαθρικόν, τό, *base*, *IGRom.*4.835 (Hierapolis); *stairway*, *Rev.Ét. Gr.*19.265 (Aphrodisias).

βαθρίον, τό, Dim. of βάθρον, Suid. s.v. κλινίς:—also **βαθρεῖον**, τό, Cumont *Études Syriennes* 336 (Cyrrhus, pl.).

βάθρον, τό, (βαίνω) *that on which anything steps* or *stands*, hence, 1. *base, pedestal*, τὸ β. καὶ ὁ θρόνος Hdt.1.183; of a statue, Id.5.85, X.*Eq.*1.1; δαιμόνων ἱδρύματα.. ἐξανέστρεπται βάθρων A. *Pers.*812; *throne*, ὑψηλὸν Δίκας β. S.*Ant.*854. 2. *stage, scaffold*, Hdt.7.23. 3. generally, *solid base*, ἀμφιρύτου Σαλαμῖνος β. S.*Aj.* 135 (anap.), cf. *Ph.*1000, *OC*1662; ὦ πατρῷον ἑστίας β., i.e. *house* of my father, Id.*Aj.*860: metaph., Εὐνομία βάθρον πολίων Pi.*O.*13. 6: pl., *foundations*, Ἴλιον.. ἐξαναστήσας βάθρα E.*Supp.*1198; ἐν βάθροις εἶναι stand *firm*, Id.*Tr.*47; ἐκ βάθρων ἀνῃρῆσθαι *utterly*, Id. *El.*608, cf. D.H.8.1, Lyc.770, *AP*9.97 (Alph.). 4. *step*, S.*OC* 1591; *rung of a ladder*, E.*Ph.*1179. 5. *bench, seat*, S.*OT*142, *OC* 101, Phryn.Com.3.5; τὰ β., of a lecture-room or school, Pl.*Prt.*315c, 325e, etc.; τὰ βάθρα σπογγίζων D.18.258; *seats* in the council-chamber, Lys.13.37. 6. β. Ἱπποκράτους *machine for reducing dislocation*, Ruf.ap.Orib.49.26. 7. metaph., πόνους ἀφῖγμαι κἀπὶ κινδύνου βάθρα *the verge* of danger, E.*Cyc.*352.

βάθρωσις, εως, ἡ, *stand* in the Delphic stadium, *BCH*23.567.

βᾰθῠ-αγκής, ές, *with deep dells*, Ἄλπεις *AP*9.283 (Crin.); τὰ β. Thphr.*HP*3.11.4. **-αίδοιος**, ον, *mentulatus*, of Priapus, *EM*2.24, Sch.Lyc.831. **-βουλος**, ον, *deep-counselling*, φροντὶς A.*Pers.*142 (lyr.). **-γειος**, ον, Call.*Ap.*65, Thphr.*HP*4.11.9, Str.6.3.5, D.S. 20.109: Sup., Ph.1.332, al.: Ion. **-γαιος** Hdt.4.23; Att. **-γεως**, ων, Thphr.*CP*2.4.10:—*with deep soil, productive*, ll. cc. **-γένειος**, ον, *with deep, full beard*, Poll.2.88, Jul.*Mis.*349c. **-γηρως**, ων, gen. ω, *in great old age*, S.E.*M.*6.13; *decrepit*, *AP*6.247.7 (Phil.). **-γλωσσος**, ον, *of unintelligible speech*, λαός Lxx *Es.*3.5: but expld. by ἐλλόγιμος, Hsch., Suid. **-γνώμων**, ον, gen. ονος, *of profound wisdom*, Ἀληθίη Babr.126.5, cf. Eun.*VS* p.481B., *Hist.*p.254D. **-δείελος**, ον, *steeped in sunshine*, πόλις B.1.29; cf. εὐδείελος. **-δενδρος**, ον, *deep-wooded*, *Lyr.Adesp.*96; Ἑλικών *Pae.Delph.*1. **-δίνης** [ῑ], ου, ὁ, *deep-eddying*, ποταμός Il.20.73, etc.; ὠκεανός Hes.*Op.*171:—also **-δῑνήεις**, εσσα, εν, Il.21.15: **-δίνης**, ες, Dem.Bith.4.4: **-δῑνήτης**, Doroth.11. **-δοξος**, ον, *far-famed, illustrious*, Pi.*P.*1.66, *Pae.* 2.58. **-εργέω**, *plough deep*, *Gp.*2.23.14 (Pass.). **-ζωνος**, ον, *deep-girded* (cf. βαθύκολπος), βαθυζώνους τε γυναῖκας Il.9.594, Od.3.154; βαρβάρων γυναικῶν τὸ ἐπίθετον Sch.Od. l. c.; βαθυζώνων.. Περσίδων A.*Pers.*155 (lyr.); but epith. of Leto, B.10.16, Pi.*Fr.*89; Χάριτες Id.*P.*9.2, B.5.9; [Μοῦσαι] Pi.*I.*6(5).74; νύμφα βαθύζωνε S.*Ichn.*237 (lyr.).—Not in E. **-θριξ**, τρῐχος, ὁ, ἡ, *with thick, long mane*, Opp.*C.*1.314; of sheep, *with thick* or *long wool*, *h.Ap.*412. **-καμπής**, ές, *strongly curved*, *AP*6.306 (Ariston). **-κάρδιος**, ον, *of profound mind*, Procl.*Par.Ptol.*222. **-καρπος**, ον, *rich in fruits*, εἰρήνη *IG*3.170. **-κήτης** πόντος *deep yawning* sea, Thgn.175; cf. μεγακήτης. **-κλεής**, ές, = βαθύδοξος, *AP*9.575 (Phil.). **-κληρος**, ον, *with rich lands*, of persons, Hom.*Epigr.*16. II. *very rich*, of land, Coluth.218, Man.3.239. **-κνήμῑς**, ῑδος, *wearing high greaves*, Q.S.1.55. **-κνημος**, ον, *with high mountain-spurs*, Πλαταιαί Nonn.*D.*4.336. **-κολπος**, ον, *with dress falling in deep folds* (cf. βαθύζωνος), epith. of Trojan women, Il.18.122,339,24. 215; of Nymphs, *h.Cer.*5, *Ven.*257; Muses, Pi.*P.*1.12; παρθένος (of Aegina) Id.*Pae.*6.135: hence, *with deep, full breasts*, ἐκ β. στηθέων A.*Th.*864 (lyr.): metaph. of the earth, *deep-bosomed*, Pi.*P.*9. 101. 2. simply, *very deep*, χειή Nonn.*D.*12.327; *with deep foundations*, ib.40.534; *set deep*, ὀχῆα ib.21.94. 3. = ἀρχαία, παλαιά, κοίλη, Hsch. **-κόμης**, ου, *with thick hair*, Poll.2.24. **-κομος**, ον, *with thick leaves*, ὄρεα β. *covered with thick forests*, Ar.*Fr.*698 (lyr.). **-κρημνος**, ον, *with high cliffs*, ἅλς Pi.*I.*4(3).56; β. ἀκταί *deep and rugged* banks, Id.*N.*9.40; Συήνη D.P.244, cf. 618. **-κρήπῑς**, ῖδος, ὁ, ἡ, *with deep foundations*, Ἄβυδος Musae.229. **-κτέᾰνος**, ον, *with great possessions, wealthy*, Μῆδοι *Eleg.Alex.Adesp.*2.13; τύχη *AP*10.74 (Paul. Sil.); ῥέεθρον Nonn.*D.*12.126. **-κύμων** [ῡ], ον, gen. ονος, *deep in waves*, ὄχθαι Musae.189; φωνή, of Oceanus, Nonn. *D.*23.320, cf. Antioch.Astr. in *Cat.Cod.Astr.*1.110. **-λειμος**, ον, = sq., Il.9.151,293. **-λείμων**, ον, gen. ονος, *surrounded by rich meadows*, πέτρα β., i.e. Cirrha, where the land was forbidden to be ploughed, Pi.*P.*10.15. **-λήϊος**, ον, *with deep crop, very fruitful*, τέμενος, v. l. for βασιλήϊον in Il.18.550, cf. A.R.1.830, *AP*9.110 (Alph.). **-μαλλος**, ον, *thick-fleeced*, Pi.*P.*4.161, App.*Mith.* 103. **-μητᾱ**, ὁ, Aeol. for βαθυμήτης, *deep-counselling*, Pi.*N.* 3.53. **-νοος**, ον, contr. **-νους**, ουν, *of deep mind*, Νέστωρ [Arist.] *Pepl.*9.

βᾰθύνω:—Pass., plpf. βεβάθυστο Nonn.*D.*39.305: (βαθύς):—*deepen, hollow out*, βάθυνε δὲ χῶρον ἅπαντα, of a torrent, Il.23.421; ἔσκαψε καὶ ἐβάθυνε dug and *dug deep*, *Ev.Luc.*6.48; ἐβάθυνε πέδον ταρσῷ, of a dog, Nonn.*D.*47.239: metaph., ὁ λιμὸς βαθύνει ἑαυτόν J. *BJ*5.12.3: esp. as military term, *deepen*, τὴν φάλαγγα X.*Cyr.*6.3.23, 8.5.15, cf. Arr.*Tact.*25.11:—Pass., *become deep, be deepened*, λίμνη β. Thphr.*HP*4.11.3; κρημνὸς βαθύνεται εἰς ἀπορρῶγα J.*BJ*1.21.3; νάσως βαθυνομένας ἀπὸ ῥιζᾶν, of Delos, *Hymn.Is.*160; τὸ βαθυνόμενον τῆς ῥηγμῖνος Agath.2.2; of a deep wound, Nonn.*D.*39.305; βαθυνομέναις χερσί *in* or *with the hollowed* hands, ib.11.180. 2. Math., *add a third dimension*, β. τὰ ἐπίπεδα Procl.*in R.*2.52K., cf. *in Ti.*1. 146D.:—Pass., κυκλικῶς βαθυνθέντες Simp.*in Ph.*59.17. II. intr., *sink deep*, Ph.1.248, 2.402; *sink, crumble*, Apollod.*Poliorc.*157. 8. 2. metaph., *go deeply into a subject*, βαθύνας θεωρῆσαι Procl.*in Prm.*p.622S.

βᾰθύ-ξῠλος, ον, *with deep wood*, ὕλης ἐν βαθυξύλῳ φόβῃ E.*Ba.*1138; β. δρυμοί Arist.*Mu.*392b18. 2. *built high with wood*, [πυρά] B.12. 169. b. *deeply carved*, γλυφαί, of coffered ceilings, J.*AJ*15.11. 5. **-ορυγή**, ἡ, *deep excavation*, *PHal.*1.81 (iii B.C.). **-πεδος**, ον, *with deep plain, lying low* (between hills), of Nemea, Pi.*N.*3.18 (prob. for -πεδίῳ). **-πελμος**, ον, (πέλμα) *thick-soled*, εὔμαρις *AP* 7.413 (Antip.). **-πεπλος**, ον, *with long robe*, Q.S.13.552. **-πικρος**, ον, *intensely bitter*, ἀψίνθιον Ps.-Dsc.3.23. **-πλεκής**, ές, *close-knit*, Opp.*H.*4.638. **-πλευρος**, ον, *deep-flanked*, *Gp.*17.2. 1. **-πλήξ**, ῆγος, ὁ, ἡ, *deep-striking*, σκορπίος Nic.*Fr.*31. **-πλόκᾰμος**, ον, *with thick hair*, B.10.8 (prob.), A.R.1.742, Mosch.2.101, Orph. *Fr.*114. **-πλοκος**, ον, (πλέκω) *deeply involved*, in Comp. -ώτερα πρὸς ἀπιστίαν Eun.*Hist.*p.259D. **-πλοος**, ον, *going deep in the water*, ναῦς prob. in D.S.3.40. **-πλούσιος**, ον, = sq., Poll.3. 109. **-πλουτος**, ον, *exceeding rich*, ζωά B.3.82; χθών A.*Supp.*554 (lyr.); Εἰρήνα E.*Fr.*453, copied by Ar.*Fr.*109; of persons, Ph.1.635, Alciphr.3.10; β. κατασκευαὶ οἰκιῶν D.H.20.4. **-πόλεμος**, ον, *plunged deep in war*, Pi.*P.*2.1. **-πόνηρος**, ον, *deeply depraved*, Ptol.*Tetr.*159, Vett.Val.104.4. **-πορος**, ον, *causing heavy going*, πεδίον, cj. for βαθύτερον in Plu.*Eum.*16. **-πτερος**, ον, *deep-winged*, Epic. in *Arch.Pap.*7 p.4. **-πύθμην**, ὁ, ἡ, gen. ενος, *with deep foundations*, *AB*1339, *EM*696.35. **-πώγων**, ον, gen. ωνος, *with thick beard*, D.S.34.1, Plu.2.710b, Luc.*JTrag.*26. **-ρρείτης**, ου, ὁ, (ῥέω), = βαθύρροος, Ep. gen. βαθυρρείταο Il.21.195, Hes.*Th.* 265. **-ρρείων**, ον, gen. οντος, = βαθύρροος, A.R.2.659,795. **-ρρηγαλῆ**, ἰκτῖνος (Lydian), Hsch. **-ρρηνος**, ον, (ῥήν) *with thick wool*, τάπης *AP*6.250 (Antiphil.). **-ρρῐζία**, ἡ, *depth of root*, Thphr.*HP*1. 7.1. **-ρριζος**, ον, *deep-rooted*, δρῦς S.*Tr.*1195, cf. A.R.1.1199, Q.S. 4.202; πέτρα, i.e. *lofty*, *Trag.Adesp.*203: Comp. -ριζότερος Thphr. *HP*1.7.2. **-ρροος**, ον, contr. **-ρους**, ουν, *deep-flowing*, Ὠκεανός Il. 7.422, cf. Hes.*Cat.Oxy.*1358.2.23, etc.; β. ποταμὸν Εὔηνον S.*Tr.*559. [βᾰθῠρους Poet.*de herb.*118.] **-ρρωχμος**, ον, (ῥωχμή) *with deep clefts*, Q.S.1.687.

βᾰθύς, βαθεῖα Ion. βαθέᾰ, βαθύ; fem. βαθύς Call.*Del.*37, Eratosth. 8; gen. βαθέος, βαθείας Ion. βαθέης: dat. βαθεῖ, βαθείῃ Ion. βαθέῃ: Comp. βαθύτερος, poet. βαθίων [ῑ Att., ĭ Theoc.5.43], Dor. βάσσων (q.v.): Sup. βαθύτατος, poet. βάθιστος:—*deep* or *high*, acc. to one's position, Hom., etc.; βαθείης ἐξάλλεται αὐλῆς a court *within a high fence*, Il.5.142, cf. Od.9.239; ἠϊόνος προπάροιθε βαθείης *the deep*, i.e. *wide*, shore, Il.2.92; τάφρος 7.341, al.; κρατήρ S.*Fr.*563; κύλικες Id.

*Aj.*1200 (lyr.); βαθὺ πτῶμα a fall *from a high rock*, A.*Supp.*796; πλευρὰ βαθυτάτη (vulg. βαρυτάτη), of an athlete, Ar.*V.*1193; of a line of battle, βαθύτεραι φάλαγγες X.*Lac.*11.6, cf. *HG*2.4.34; β. τομή, πληγή, a *deep* cut, Plu.2.131a, Luc.*Nigr.*35. 2. *deep* or *thick* in substance, of a mist, ἠέρα βαθεῖαν Il.21.7, cf. Od.9.144; of sand, ἀμάθοιο βαθείης Il.5.587; ἐπὶ θῖνα βαθύν Theoc.22.32; of ploughed land, νειοῖο βαθείης Il.10.353; β. γῆ, opp. to stony ground, E.*Andr.*637, Thphr.*CP*1.18.1; of luxuriant growth, *deep, thick*, of woods, etc., βαθείης τάρφεσιν ὕλης Il.5.555; βαθείης ἐκ ξυλόχοιο 11.415; βαθὺ λήϊον 2.147, Thgn.107; τοῦ λητου τὸ. . βαθύτατον Hdt.5.92.ζ'; λειμών A.*Pr.*652; σῖτος X.*HG*3.2.17; χλόα E.*Hipp.*1139 (lyr.); χαίτη, τρίχες, πώγων, Semon.7.66, X.*Cyn.*4.8, Luc.*Pisc.*41. b. *deep*, of colour, *PHolm.*21.9: Comp., Ael.*VH*6.6, Lyd.*Mag.*2.13, πορφύριον -ύτερον *PLond.*3.899.4 (ii A.D.). 3. of quality, *strong, violent*, βαθείῃ λαίλαπι Il.11.306. b. generally, *copious, abundant*, β. κλᾶρος Pi.*O.*13.62; β. ἀνήρ *a rich* man, X.*Oec.*11.10; β. οἶκος Call. *Cer.*113; β. πλοῦτος Ael.*VH*3.18, Jul.*Or.*2.82b; β. χρέος *deep* debt, Pi.*O.*10(11).8; στεφάνων β. τέρψις S.*Aj.*1200 (lyr.); β. κλέος Pi.*O.*7.53; κίνδυνος Id.*P.*4.207; β. ὕπνος *deep* sleep, Theoc.8.65, *AP*7.170, cf. Luc.*DMar.*2.3; εἰρήνη Id.*Tox.*36; σιωπή App.*Mith.*99, *BC*4.109 (Sup.). 4. of the mind, ἄχος ὀξὺ κατὰ φρένα τύψε β. in the *depths* of his soul, Il.19.125; but also, *profound*, φρήν Pi.*N.*4.8; φροντίς A. *Supp.*407; μέριμνα Pi.*O.*2.60; βαθεῖαν ἄλοκα διὰ φρενὸς καρπούμενος A.*Th.*593; μουσικὴ πρᾶγμ' ἐστὶ β. Eup.336; βαθύτερα ἤθη *more sedate* natures, Pl.*Lg.*930a (but, *more recondite*, i.e. *civilized*, manners, Hdt.4.95): of persons, *deep, wise*, β. τῇ φύσει στρατηγός Posidipp. 27.4; ταῖς ψυχαῖς Plb.6.24.9; also, *deep, crafty*, Men.1001; ἦθος Ph. 2.468. 5. of time, β. ὄρθρος *dim* twilight, Ar.*V.*216, Pl.*Cri.* 43a, etc.; β. νύξ *a late hour* in the night, Luc.*Asin.*34; περὶ ἑσπέραν β. Plu.2.179e, cf. Paus.4.18.3; βαθὺ τῆς ἡλικίας Ar.*Nu.*514; β. γῆρας cj. in *AP*7.163 (Leon.), cf. Eun.*VS*p.457 B., al.; β. ὥρα ἔτους Charito 1.7. II. Adv. -έως Theoc.8.66; *profoundly*, Procl.*in Prm.*p.475 S.: Sup. βαθύτατα, γηρῶν Ael.*VH*2.36. (βαθύς, cf. βένθος.)

βαθύσαρκος [ῠ], ον, *fleshy*: τὰ β. *Hippiatr.*71,72.

βαθύσικος, ὁ, kind of *cheese*, Gal.6.697 (Lat. *vatusicus*).

βᾰθύ-σκαρθμος, ον, (σκαίρω) *high-leaping*, Nonn.*D.*10.238. **-σκᾰφής**, ές, *deep-dug*, S.*El.*435. **-σκῐος**, ον, *deep-shaded, dark*, πέτρης κευθμῶνα *h.Merc.*229, cf. Theoc.4.19; ὗλαι Babr.92.2; οἰκίαι Ath. Med.ap.Orib.*inc.*23.18. II. Act., *throwing a deep shade*, ἀστήρ Musae.111. **-σκόπελος**, ον, *with high cliffs*, Orph.*A.*638, Q.S. 1.316. **-σκοτος**, ον, *murky*, θύελλα Tz.*H.*10.294.

βάθυσμα [ᾰ], ατος, τό, *deep place*, λίμνης Thphr.*HP*4.11.8.

βᾰθυ-σμῆριγξ, ιγγος, ὁ, ἡ, *thick-haired*, Nonn.*D.*1.528. **-σοφός**, gloss on γλαφυρός, *EM*233.44. **-σπῆλυγξ**, υγγος, ὁ, ἡ, *with deep caves*, Nonn.*D.*40.260. **-σπορος**, ον, *deep-sown, fruitful*, E.*Ph.* 648 (lyr.). 2. -σπόρος, = βαθεῖαν σπείρων γῆν, Hsch. **-στερνος**, ον, *deep-chested*, λέων Pi.*I.*3.12; β. αἶα *deep-bosomed* earth, Cypr. *Fr.*1; χθών Pi.*N.*9.25; πόντος Orph.*H.*17.3. **-στολέω**, *wear long flowing robes*, Str.11.14.12. **-στολμος**, ον, *with deep, full robe*, prob. cj. in *AP*7.413 (Antip.). **-στομος**, ον, *deep-mouthed, deep*, σπήλαια Str.16.2.20. II. *cutting deep*, βουπλήξ Q.S.1. 337. **-στρωτος**, ον, *deep-strewn, well-covered*, λέκτρα Musae.266; κοίτη Babr.32.7. **-σχῖνος**, ον, *deep-grown with σχῖνος*, *AP*9.744 (Leon.). **-σχοινος**, ον, *deep-grown with rushes*, Ἀσωπός Il.4. 383; χλόη Babr.46.2. **-τέρμων**, ον, gen. ονος, *deep, large*, ναῦς Opp.*C.*2.87.

βᾰθύτης, ητος, ἡ, = βάθος, *depth*, Luc.*Icar.*5: metaph. of character, Phld.*Ir.*p.60 W.; of mental *profundity*, Cic.*Att.*4.6.3, al.

βᾰθύ-τῖμος [ῠ], v. βαρύτιμος. **-τομέω**, *cut deeply*, τὸν μαστόν Leonid.ap.Aët.16.44. **-ϋδρος**, ον, *with deep water*, Sch.Il.16. 3. **-ϋπνος**, ον, *in deep sleep*, Nic.*Th.*394. **-φροσύνη**, ἡ, *profundity of mind*, *Cat.Cod.Astr.*2.161.5. **-φρων**, ον, gen. ονος, = βαθύβουλος, Sol.33.1; Μοῖραι Pi.*N.*7.1. **-φυλλος**, ον, *thick-leafed, leafy*, Mosch.*Fr.*1.11. **-φωνος**, ον, *of deep*, i.e. *hollow, voice*, Lxx *Is.*33.19. **-χάϊος** or **-χαῖος**, ον, *of old nobility*, A.*Supp.*858 (lyr.); cf. χάϊος. **-χαιτήεις**, εσσα, εν, = sq., A.*Eleg.*4. **-χαίτης**, ου, ὁ, *with thick long hair*, Hes.*Th.*977, Ph.2.479; Ἄδωνις Orph.*H.* 56.7. **-χεύμων**, ον, gen. ονος, (χεῦμα) = βαθυκύμων, Procl.*H.*3. 6. **-χθων**, ον, gen. ονος, = βαθύγειος, αἶα A.*Th.*306 (lyr.). **-χρήμων**, ον, gen. ονος, = βαθύπλουτος, Man.4.66. **-χροος**, ον, contr. **-χρους**, ουν, *deep-coloured*, Dsc.5.94.

βαΐα, ἡ, *nurse*, Str.*Chr.*5.39.

βαΐβυξ, υκος, ὁ, = πελεκάν, Hdn.Gr.2.741, Philet.ap.Hsch.

βαίδειον· ἕτοιμον (Elean), Hsch. **βαιδυμήν**· ἀροτριᾶν (Boeot.), Id.:—also **βαιτρεύειν**, Id. **βαίεσσα**· βότρυς, Id. **βαῖκαν**· κρῆτες, Id. **βαίκυλος**· προβατώδης, Id. **βαιμάζειν**· βασιλεύειν, ἢ βαστάζειν, Id.

βαϊνός, όν, (βάϊς) *of palm-leaves*, Sm.*Ge.*40.16: **βαϊνή**, ἡ, *palm-rod*, Lxx 1*Ma.*13.37.

βαίνω (inf. βαίμεναι Hsch.), fut. βήσομαι Il.2.339, etc., Dor. βασεῦμαι Theoc.2.8, etc.: pf. βέβηκα Il.15.90, etc., Dor. βέβᾱκα Pi.*I.*4(3). 41, etc., with shortd. forms βεβάᾱσι Il.2.134, contr. βεβᾶσι A.*Pers.* 1002 (lyr.), *Eu.*76, etc.; subj. βεβῶσι (ἐμ-) Pl.*Phdr.*252e; inf. βεβάμεν Il.17.359, βεβάναι E.*Heracl.*610 (lyr.); part. βεβαώς, -υῖα Il.14. 477, Hom.*Epigr.*15.10, contr. βεβώς: plpf. ἐβεβήκειν Il.11.296, etc., Ep. βεβήκειν 6.495; sync. 3 pl. βέβασαν 17.286, etc.: aor. 2 ἔβην Il. 17.112, etc., Dor. ἔβᾱν Pi.*O.*13.97, etc.; Ep. 3 sg. βῆ Il.13.297, Ep. 3 dual βάτην [ᾰ] 1.327, 3 pl. ἔβαν A.*Pers.*18 (lyr.), (κατ-) S.*Tr.*504 (lyr.), Ep. βάν Il.20.32; imper. βῆθι, Dor. βᾶθι S.*Ph.*1196 (lyr.); βᾶ in compds. ἔμβα, κατάβα, etc., 2 pl. βᾶτε A.*Supp.*191, *Eu.*1033 (lyr.); subj. βῶ, Ep. 3 sg. βήῃ (ὑπερ-) Il.9.501, βήω 6.113, ἐμ-βέῃ *GDI*5075. 4 (Cret.), Dor. βᾶμες (for βῶμεν) Theoc.15.22; opt. βαίην; inf. βῆναι (Att. Prose only in compds.), Ep. βήμεναι Od.19.296, Dor. βᾶμεν Pi.*P.*4.39; part. βάς βᾶσα βάν, Dor. pl. ἐκ-βῶντας Th.5.77:— **Med.**, Ep. aor. 1 ἐβήσετο (ἀπ-) Il.1.428:—**Pass.**, pres. (v. infr. A.II.1): in compds., aor. ἀν-, παρ-, ξυν-εβάθην, X.*Eq.*3.4, Th.3.67, 4.30; later παρ-εβάνθην D.C.48.2, al.; ἀνα-, παρα-, ξυμ-βέβᾰμαι, X.*Eq.Mag.*1.4, Th.1.123, 8.98; παρα-βέβασμαι D.17.12: fut. παρα-βαθήσομαι Sch.E. *Hec.*802.—For the Act. fut. and aor. 1, v. infr. B; for pres. part. βιβάς, v. βίβημι.—In correct Att. Prose the pres. βαίνω is almost the only tense in use; but in compds. Prose writers used all tenses freely.

A. in the above tenses, I. intr., *walk, step*, prop. of motion *on foot*, ποσὶ βήσετο Il.5.745, etc.; but also of all motion *on ground*, the direction being commonly determined by a Prep.:—the kind of motion is often marked by a part., βῆ φεύγων, βῆ ἀΐξασα, Il.2.665, 4. 74: c. part. fut., denoting purpose, βῆ ῥ' Ἶσον. . ἐξεναρίξων *he went to* slay, Il.11.101: with neut. Adj. as Adv., σαῦλα ποσὶν β. *h.Merc.*28; ἁβρὸν β. παλλεύκῳ ποδί E.*Med.*1164, cf. 830 (lyr.); ἴσα or ὁμοίως β. τινί, D.19.314, X.*Eq.*1.3; ἐν ποικίλοις β. A.*Ag.*936, cf. 924; *march* or *dance*, μετὰ ῥυθμοῦ, ἐν ῥυθμῷ, Th.5.70, Pl.*Lg.*670b: freq. c. inf. in Hom., βῆ δ' ἰέναι *set out* to go, *went* his way, Il.4.199, etc.; βῆ δ' ἴμεν 5.167, etc.; βῆ δὲ θέειν *started* to run, 2.183, etc.; βῆ δ' ἐλάαν 13.27: c. acc. loci, νέας Od.3.162, cf. S.*OT*153 (lyr.), *OC*378; ἐπὶ νηὸς ἔβαινεν *was going* on board ship, Od.11.534; but ἐν δὲ ἑκάστῃ [νηΐ]. . ἑκατὸν καὶ εἴκοσι βαῖνον *were on board*, Il.2.510; ἐφ' ἵππων βάντες *having mounted* the chariot, 18.532; ἐπὶ πώλου βεβῶσα *mounted* on. ., S.*OC*313; ἐς δίφρον Il.5.364; ἐς ἅρματα E.*El.*320; βαίνειν δι' αἵματος *wade* in blood, Id.*Ph.* 20. 2. in pf., *stand* or *be* in a place, χῶρος ἐν ᾧ βεβήκαμεν S.*OC*52; βεβηκὼς σφόδρα firmly *poised* (opp. κρεμάμενος) Pl.*Ti.*62c; β. μάχη *steady* fight, Plu.*Phil.*9: freq. almost, = εἰμί (*sum*), εὖ βεβηκώς *on a good footing*, well *established, prosperous*, [θεοὶ] εὖ βεβηκότας ὑπτίους κλίνουσ' Archil.56.3; τυραννίδα εὖ βεβηκυῖαν Hdt.7.164, cf. S.*El.*979; εὖ βίου βεβηκότα prob. for ἐν βίῳ βεβιωκότα Nicom.Com.2; ἀσφαλέως βεβηκὼς ποσσί Archil.58.4; ἐπισφαλῶς βεβ. Lxx *Wi.*4.4; ἄγαλμα βεβηκὸς ἄνω τὰ κάτω δὲ κεχηνός Eub.107.23; οἱ ἐν τέλει ἐόντες, βεβῶτες, they who *are* in office, Hdt.9.106, S.*Ant.*67; τοῦτον οὐχ ὁρῇς ὅκως βέβη-[κεν] ἀνδριάντα; Herod.4.36; [λίθους] ἐν ταῖς ἰδίαις χώραις βεβηκότας *IG*7.3073.163 (Lebad.); ἐν κακοῖς βεβ. S.*El.*1057; μοῖρα οὐκ ἐν ἐσθλᾷ β. ib.1095 (lyr.); βοῦς, κλεὶς ἐπὶ γλώσσῃ βέβηκεν, v. βοῦς IV, κλείς 4; φρόνει βεβὼς ἐπὶ ξυροῦ τύχης S.*Ant.*996. b. Geom. of figures, *stand* on a base, ἐπί τινος Arist.*IA*709ᵃ24, cf. Apollon.Perg.*Con.*3.3; πυραμὶς ἐπὶ τετραγώνου βεβηκυῖα Hero *Ster.*1.31; of an angle, *stand* on an arc, ἐπί τινος, πρός τινι, Euc.3*Def.*9, cf. 16.26. c. βεβηκὼς ῥυθμός *stately* rhythm, Syrian.*in Hermog.*1 p.69 R.; ἀνάπαυσις ib.p.18 R. 3. *go away, depart*, ἐν νηυσὶ φίλην ἐς πατρίδ' Il.12.16; ἔβαν ἄγοντες, ἔβαν φέρουσαι, *have gone* and taken away, 1.391, 2.302; ἄφαρ βέβακεν S.*Tr.* 134; θανάσιμος βέβηκεν Id.*OT*959, cf. 832; βεβᾶσι φροῦδοι E.*IT*1289; βέβηκα euphem. for τέθνηκα, A.*Pers.*1002 (lyr.); of things, ἐννέα ἐνιαυτοὶ βεβάασι nine years *have come and gone*, Il.2.134; πῇ ὅρκια βήσεται; ib.339, cf. 8.229. 4. *come*, τίπτε βέβηκας; 15.90; *arrive*, S.*OT*81, *Aj.*921. 5. *go on, advance*, ἐς τόδε τόλμης, ἐς τοσοῦτον ἐλπίδων, Id. *OT*125, 772; ἐπ' ἔσχατα Id.*OC*217 (lyr.). 6. c. part. as periphr. for fut., βαίνω καταγγέλλων *PMag.Par.*1.2474. II. c. acc., *mount*, Hom. only in aor. Med. βήσασθαι δίφρον Il.3.262, Od.3.481: in Act. (fut. part. Med. βησόμενος Them.*Or.*21.248b), of the male, *mount, cover*, Pl.*Phdr.*250e, Achae.28, Arist.*HA*575ᵃ13, etc.:—in Pass., ἵπποι βαινόμεναι *brood* mares, Hdt.1.192. 2. c. acc. cogn., β. Δωρίαν κέλευθον ὕμνων Pi.*Fr.*191; Καλλαβίδας Eup.163; ἔβα ῥόον *went down* stream, i.e. *died*, Theoc.1.140. b. metaph. of metre, *scan*, D.H.*Comp.*21 (Pass.), Aristid.Quint.1.23, 24, etc.; βαίνεται τὸ ἔπος *is scanned*, Arist.*Metaph.*1093ᵃ30. 3. χρέος ἔβα με debts *came on* me, Ar.*Nu.*30; ὀδύνα μ' ὀδύνα βαίνει E.*Hipp.*1371 (lyr.). 4. Poet. with acc. of the instrument of motion, βαίνειν πόδα E.*El.*94, 1173 (lyr.). 5. βαίνειν· φιλεῖν, κολακεύειν, Hsch.

B. Causal, in fut. βήσω, (ἐπι-) Il.8.197, (εἰσ-) E.*IT*742: aor. 1 ἔβησα:—*make to go*, φῶτας βῆσεν ἀφ' ἵππων *he made* them *dismount*, Il.16.810; ἀμφοτέρους ἐξ ἵππων βῆσε κακῶς *he brought* them *down* from the chariot in sorry plight, 5.164; ὄφρα βάσομεν ὄκχον Pi.*O.* 6.24.—Rare in Trag. (exc. in compds.), E.*Med.*209 (lyr.).—The simple Verb is uncommon in later Gr. (For βάμ-yω, cf. Lat. *venio*, Skt. *gamyáte*; βάσκω corresponds to Skt. *gácchati* (*gᵘm̥-sk-*); root *gᵘem-* in OHG. *quëman* 'come'; ἔβην, βήσομαι fr. root *gᵘā-*, Skt. *jigāti*, aor. *ágāt*.)

βαΐον, τό, = βάϊς, *Ev.Jo.*12.13; for gen. pl. βαΐων v. βάϊς. II. *measuring-rod*, β. δικαίῳ ἐξαπήχει *PFlor.*37.3 (v/vi A.D.), cf. *BGU* 1094.12 (vi A.D.).

βαιός, ά, όν, *little, small*, βαιὰ ποικίλλειν ἐν μακροῖσιν κτεάνων Pi.*P.* 9.77; β. νῆσος A.*Pers.*448; μέρος β. ἔχειν Id.*Ag.*1574 (lyr.); ὄλβος prob. in E.*Fr.*825; γλῶττα Ar.*Nu.*1013; μαλλὸς εἰρίων Herod.8.12; *scanty*, and of number, *few*, σῦκα βαιά Anan.3, cf. Hp.*Lex*1; βαιά γ' ὡς ἀπὸ πολλῶν A.*Pers.*1023 (lyr.); β. κύλιξ a *scanty* cup, i.e. one only, S.*Fr.*42, Lyc.*Fr.*3; ῥάκη β. *a few, paltry*, S.*Ph.*274; εἶπε πρός με βαιά *few words*, Id.*Aj.*292; but βαιὰν. . λόγων φάμαν *low-spoken*, Id.*Ph.*845 (lyr.); ἥσθην δὲ βαιά, πάνυ δὲ βαιά, τέτταρα Ar. *Ach.*2; ἐχώρει βαιὸς he was going *with scanty escort*, i.e. *alone*, S. *OT*750; of condition, *mean, humble*, βαιοί, opp. οἱ μεγάλοι, Id.*Aj.*

160 (anap.); ἐκ κάρτα βαιῶν γνωτὸς ἂν γένοιτ' ἀνήρ from *a low condition*, Id.*Fr.*282; οὐχὶ βαιὰ τἀνθυμήματα Id.*OC*1199; βαιᾷ τῇδ' ὑπὸ στέγῃ Id.*Ph.*286; of time, *short*, Sol.10, S.*Tr.*44; βαιῆς ἄπο from *infancy* (of a girl), *IG*14.1892: neut. βαιόν as Adv., *a little*, S.*Aj.* 90, *Ph.*20: of time, Id.*OC*1653, *Tr.*335: pl., βαιά, φρονήσει τύχη μάχεται Democr.119; κατὰ βαιόν *by little and little*, D.P.622: Comp. βαιότερος, opp. μείζων, Parm.8.45, cf. Opp.*C.*3.86: Sup. -ότατος *AP*9.438 (Phil.).—Poet., Ion., and later Prose, as Phld.*Rh.*1.195, 244 S., Id.*Ir.*p.95 W.

βαϊο-φορέω, *bear a palm-leaf*, of a priest, *PTeb.*294.10 (ii A.D.): **-φορία**, ἡ, ib.295.11 (ii A.D.).

βαιόχρονος, ον, *brief*, [βίος] *Inscr.Prien.*287 (i B.C.).

βάϊς, ἡ, acc. βάϊν Horap.1.3:—*palm-leaf* (Coptic *bai*), Chaerem. ap.Porph.*Abst.*4.7, *PMag.Leid.V.*7.16, *PLond.*1.131^{r}384 (i A.D.), etc.; gen. pl. βαΐων *PMag.Leid.V.*7.17, Lxx 1 *Ma.*13.51.

βαισήνης· παρ' Ἰνδοῖς τὸ στρατόπεδον, Hsch. **βαίσηνος**· ὁ στρατός, Id. **βαισσόν**· βάθος, Id. **βαιτάς**, άδος, ἡ, = εὐτελὴς γυνή, Id.

βαίτη, ἡ, Dor. **βαίτα** Sophr.38:—*shepherd's* or *peasant's coat of skins*, Hdt.4.64, Theoc.3.25, *IG*5(2).268.48 (Mantinea, circ. i A.D.); τὴν β. θάλπουσαν εὖ δεῖ καὶ ῥάπτειν 'one good turn deserves another', Herod.7.128. II. *tent of skins*, S.*Fr.*1031. III. **βαίτης**, ου, ὁ, *warmed hall*, *Inscr.Magn.*179.12,15, *IG*5(2).268.48 (Mantinea, i B.C.). (Thracian word; Goth. *paida* 'garment'.)

βαίτιον, τό, = δίκταμνος, Ps.-Dsc.3.32, Hsch.

βαιτοφόρος, ον, (βαίτη) *wearing a coat of skin*, prob. for βαττ– in D.S.*Fr.*29.

βαιτρεύειν, v. βαιδυμῆν.

βαίτῠλος, ὁ, *meteoric stone*, held sacred, because it fell from heaven, Dam.*Isid.*94,203; of the stone swallowed by Kronos, Hsch.

βαῖτυξ, υγος, ἡ, *leech*, Hsch., *AB*1199. **βαιτῶνα**· τὸν εὐτελῆ ἄνδρα, Hsch.

βαιῶμφαι· αἱ αἶγες, ἐν ἱερατικοῖς, Hsch., Suid.

βαιών, όνος, ὁ, = βλέννος, Epich.64: prov., μή μοι β.· κακὸς ἰχθύς Ath.7.288a. II. at Alexandria, *a measure*, Hsch.

Βαιῶτις, ἡ, title of Aphrodite at Syracuse, Hsch.

βακάϊον· μέτρον τι, Hsch.

βάκανον, τό, *cabbage*, *PFay.*117.12 (pl.); also, *cabbage-seed*, Aët. 10.2, Alex.Trall.9.1, Paul.Aeg.7.11.42.

βάκηλος [ᾰ], ὁ, *eunuch in the service of Cybele*, *Gallus*, Luc.*Eun.*8, *Sat.*12. II. *womanish*, Antiph.113, Men.477, Teles p.24 H., Zen.2.62.

βακίας· πηλός (Tarent.), *EM*186.1.

Βᾰκίζω, *prophesy like Bacis*, Ar.*Pax*1072.

Βακίνθιος, v. Ὑακίνθιος.

Βᾰκίς, ίδος, ὁ, Boeotian prophet, Hdt.8.20,77, al.; acc. Βάκιν Ar. *Pax*1071; others are mentioned in Sch.Ar. l.c.: hence in pl., Βακίδες, οἱ, *soothsayers*, Arist.*Pr.*954^{a}36.

βάκκαρ, τό, = ἄσαρον, Plin.*HN*21.29,30.

βάκκᾰρις, ἡ, gen. ιδος, dat. ιδι Ar.*Fr.*319, Magnes 3, but βακκάρῑ Semon.16, Hippon.41: acc. -ιν Hp.*Nat.Mul.*6: pl., βακκάρεις A.*Fr.* 14, Ion Trag.24:—*unguent* made from ἄσαρον, ll.cc. (Lydian word, Sch.A.*Pers.*42: one kind, = μύρον Λύδιον, Hsch.)

βάκλον, τό, = Lat. *baculum*, *stick*, *cudgel*, Aesop.188, Sch.Ar.*Pl.* 476 (pl.): pl., βάκυλα, = Lat. *fasces*, Plu.*Rom.*26:—hence **βακλίζω**, *cudgel*, *PMasp.*5.18 (vi A.D.).

βακνίδες· εἶδος ὑποδημάτων, Hsch. **βάκοα**· βάθρον, Id. **βακοίας**· πηλός, Id. **βακόν**· πεσόν (Cret.), Id. **βάκται**· ἰσχυροί, Id.

βακταρικροῦσα, barbarous word in Ar.*Av.*1629.

βακτηρ-εύω, = βακτρεύω, Suid. **-ία**, ἡ, *staff*, *cane*, Ar.*Ach.*682, Th.8.84, Lys.24.12, X.*Eq.*11.4, etc.; συκίνη β., = σ. ἐπικουρία (q.v.), Alciphr.1.39, Macar.7.83. II. *wand*, as a badge of office, carried by δικασταί, D.18.210; ὁ λαβὼν τὴν β. βαδίζει εἰς τὸ δικαστήριον τὸ ὁμόχρων τῇ β. Arist.*Ath.*65.2. (Cf. Lat. *baculum*, *imbēcillus*, OIr. *bacc* 'crook, curved stick'.) **-ίδιον**, τό, Dim. of βακτηρία, Hsch. s.v. κάλιον. **-ιον**, τό, Dim. of βακτηρία, Ar.*Ach.*448, Men.*Sam.* 232. **-ίς**, ίδος, ἡ, = βακτηρία, prob. in Achae.21.

Βάκτρα, τά, *Balkh*, Hdt.9.113, Arist.*Mir.*833^{b}14, Str.11.8.9: the people were **Βάκτριοι**, Hdt.3.102; or **Βακτριανοί**, Str. l.c.; cf. Βακτριανή, ἡ, Id.11.9.2:—the Bactrian camels were famous, Arist. *HA*498^{b}8.

βάκτρ-ευμα, ατος, τό, *a staff*, βακτρεύμασι τυφλοῦ ποδός *by support lent to . .*, E.*Ph.*1539 (lyr.). **-εύω**, *support as a staff*, ἀλαὸν πόδα, of Antigone, Arg.metr.S.*OC.* **-ιασμός**, ὁ, f.l. in Poll.4.101 for μακτρισμός.

βάκτρον, τό (cf. βακτηρία), *stick*, *cudgel*, A.*Ag.*202, *Ch.*362, E.*Ph.* 1719 (all lyr.), Theoc.25.207: metaph., τοκέων β. prob. in *Epigr.Gr.* 257.2 (Cyprus).

βακτρο-προσαίτης, ου, ὁ, *going about begging with a staff*, epith. of a Cynic, *AP*11.410 (Lucill.). **-φόρας**, ου, ὁ, *the staff-bearer*, epith. of Diogenes the Cynic, Cerc.1.2.

βάκχαρ, τό, = ἄσαρον, Ps.-Dsc.1.10; cf. βάκκαρ. **βάκχαρι**, τό, *unguent* prepared therefrom, Aret.*CA*2.10.

βάκχᾰρις, ἡ, *sowbread*, *Cyclamen hederaefolium*, Cephisod.3, Dsc. 3.44.

Βακχᾶς, ὁ, = Βακχευτής, S.*Fr.*674.

Βακχάω, *to be in Bacchic frenzy*, *to rave*, A.*Th.*498.

Βακχέβακχον ᾆσαι sing *the song* (to Bacchus) beginning with Βάκχε Βάκχε! Ar.*Eq.*408.

Βακχ-εία, ἡ, *Bacchic frenzy*, *revelry*, Βακχείας καλῆς A.*Ch.*698, cf. E.*Ba.*232, Arist.*Pol.*1342^{b}4; ἡδονῇ δοὺς ἔς τε Β. πεσών (prob. for -εῖον) E.*Ph.*21; τῆς φιλοσόφου μανίας τε καὶ Βακχείας the madness and *frenzy* of philosophy, Pl.*Smp.*218b: in pl., *Bacchic orgies*, E.*Ba.* 218,1293. **-ειακός**, ή, όν, = Βακχεῖος II.3, μέτρον Heph.13.1, al. **-εῖον**, τό, *Bacchic revelry*, Ar.*Lys.*1: pl., Id.*Ra.*357; Βάκχια, dub. l. in E.*Ba.*126. 2. *congregation of Bacchic worshippers*, *IG*7.107 (Megara, ii A.D.), *Archives des Missions* 1876.150 (Perinthus). b. = τελεστήριον, νάρθηξ, Hsch. **-ειος** or **Βακχεῖος**, α, ον, also **Βάκχιος**, α, ον (to suit the metre), fem. ος Luc.*Ocyp.*171:—*of* or *belonging to Bacchus* and *his rites*, βότρυς S.*Fr.*255.2; νόμος E.*Hec.*686 (lyr.); ῥυθμός X.*Smp.*9.3, etc.: hence, *frenzied*, *rapt*, Β. Διόνυσος *h.Hom.*19.46, cf. Hdt.4.79; ὁ Β. θεός S.*OT*1105 (lyr.); Βάκχειε δέσποτ' Ar.*Th.*988 (lyr.), cf. *IG*4.558.20 (Argos), etc.; τὸν Β. ἄνακτα, of Aeschylus, Ar.*Ra.*1259. II. as Subst., Βάκχιος, ὁ, = Βάκχος, S.*Ant.*154 (lyr.), E.*Cyc.*9:—also, = οἶνος, Id.*IT*953, *Cyc.*519, Antiph. 237. 2. **Βάκχια** or **-εία**, τά, v. Βακχεῖον. 3. Βακχεῖος (sc. πούς), ὁ, *the bacchius*, *a metrical foot of three syllables*, ‒ ‒ ◡, D.H.*Comp.*17 (opp. ὑποβ. ◡ ‒ ‒); but later ◡ ‒ ‒, Heph.3 (opp. παλιμβ. ‒ ‒ ◡), etc.; also β. ἀπὸ τροχαίου (‒ ◡ ◡ ‒), ἀπ' ἰάμβου (◡ ‒ ‒ ◡), Aristid.Quint. 1.17, cf. Anon.Rhythm.*Oxy.*9 iii 12; = ◡ ◡ ‒ ‒, Bacch.*Harm.* 101. **-ειοχόρειος** (sc. πούς), ὁ, the foot ‒ ‒ ◡ ‒ ◡, Diom.p.482 K. **-ευμα**, ατος, τό, in pl., *Bacchic revelries*, E.*Ba.*40,317, Plu.*TG* 10. **-εύς**, έως, ὁ, = Βάκχος, A.*Fr.*341, S.*Ant.*1121, E.*Ba.*145, etc. (only in lyr.), Orph.*H.*45.2, *APl.*4.156, *SIG*1014.147 (Erythrae), 1024.27 (Myconos). **-εύσιμος**, ον, *Bacchanalian*, *frenzied*, E.*Ba.* 298. **-ευσις**, εως, ἡ, *Bacchic revelry*, ib.357. **-ευτής**, οῦ, ὁ, *a Bacchanal*, *any one full of Bacchic frenzy* or *of wine*, Orph.*H.*11.21, 47.6; β. θεός *APl.*4.290 (Antip.):—fem. **-εύτρια** *AB*225, Hsch. s.v. Βάκχου Διώνης. II. as Adj., β. ῥυθμός *AP*11.64.2 (Agath.). **-ευτικός**, ή, όν, *disposed to Bacchic revels*, Arist.*Pol.*1342^{b}26. **-εύτωρ**, ορος, ὁ, = Βακχευτής, *CIG*38, *AP*9.524. **-εύω**, *celebrate the mysteries of Bacchus*, Hdt.4.79. 2. *speak* or *act like one frenzy-stricken*, S.*Ant.* 136 (lyr.), E.*Ion*1204, etc.: also of places, β. στέγη A.*Fr.*58, cf. E. *IT*1243 (lyr.). II. causal, *inspire with frenzy*, αὗταί σε βακχεύουσι συγγενῆ φόνον; E.*Or.*411, cf. *HF*966:—Pass., Id.*Or.*835; φιλοσοφία εὖ μάλα βεβακχ. *full of mysticism*, Plu.2.580c. 2. *initiate in the Bacchic mysteries*, in Pass., *Schwyzer*792 (Cyme, v B.C.).

Βακχέχορος, ον, *leading the Bacchic dance*, Διώνυσος Orph.*H.*57.3, 75.1.

Βάκχη, ἡ, *Bacchante*, A.*Eu.*25, S.*Ant.*1122 (lyr.), Ar.*Nu.*605, Pl. *Ion*534a, etc.: generally, Βάκχη Ἅιδου *frantic handmaid* of Hades, E.*Hec.*1077; β. νεκύων Id.*Ph.*1489 (lyr.). II. a kind of *pear*, Nic. *Al.*354, *Th.*513.

Βακχ-ιάζω, = Βακχεύω I, E.*Cyc.*204; = βακχεύω II, Id.*Ba.*931, Philod.Scarph.14. **-ιακός**, ή, όν, = Βάκχιος, νύκτες Orph.*H.*79. 9. **-ιάς**, άδος, ἡ, poet. fem. of Βάκχειος, ὀπώρη *AP*6.72 (Agath.), Nonn.12.296, al. **-[ια]στής**, οῦ, Dor. **-τάς**, ὁ, *Bacchic reveller*, Philod.Scarph.144. **-ικός**, ή, όν, = Βάκχειος, Arist.*Pr.*922^{b}22; ἔπη D.S.1.11; -κόν, τό, Str.10.3.10: Sup. -ώτατος Luc.*Bis Acc.*9. Adv. -κῶς Str.15.1.8: Comp. -ώτερον Duris 24. **-ιος**, α, ον, = Βάκχειος (q.v.). **-ιόω**, *fill with the divine presence*, βεβακχιωμένην . . Νῦσαν S. *Fr.*959. **-ίς**, ίδος, ἡ, = Βάκχη, Νύμφαι Id.*Ant.*1129. **-ισταί**, οἱ, *worshippers of Bacchus*, *IG*12(3).1296 (Thera). **-ιών**, ῶνος, ὁ, name of a month at Myconos, *SIG*1024.26. **-ιώτης**, ου, ὁ, = Βακχευτής, S.*OC*678 (lyr.).

βακχόαν· βόθρον (Aeol.), Hsch.; cf. βάκοα, βακοίας.

Βάκχος, ὁ, *Bacchus*, name of Dionysus, first in S.*OT*211 (lyr.), cf. E.*Hipp.*560 (lyr.), al., Limen.19, Theoc.*Epigr.*18.3, etc. 2. Ζεὺς Β. *Epigr.Gr.*1035.22. II. *wine*, E.*IA*1061 (lyr.), etc. III. *Bacchanal*, Heraclit.14, E.*Ba.*491: generally, *any one inspired*, *frantic*, Ἅιδου Βάκχος Id.*HF*1119; πολλοὶ μὲν ναρθηκοφόροι, Β. δέ τε παῦροι Orph.*Fr.*5. 2. *branch* carried by initiates, Xenoph.17. IV. a kind of *grey mullet*, Hices.ap.Ath.7.306e; = ὀνίσκος II, Dorio ap. Ath.3.118c, cf. Xenocr.1. V. *garland*, βάκχοισιν κεφαλὰς περιάνθεσιν ἐστέψαντο Nic.*Fr.*130. VI. = κλαυθμός (Phoenician), Hsch.

βακχούρια, τά, Hebr. word in Lxx, = πρωτογεννήματα, *Ne.*13.31.

βάκχῠλος, ὁ, *bread baked in hot ashes*, Elean word, Nic.*Fr.*121.

Βακχ-ώδης, ες, (Βάκχος) *filled with the spirit of Bacchus*, Arr.*Ind.* 8.1 (Sup.). **-ων**, ωνος, ὁ, Dim. of Βακχυλίδης, Sch.D.T.p.227 H.

βάλαγρος, ὁ, a fresh-water fish, prob. a kind of *carp*, Arist.*HA* 538^{a}15.

βάλαικες· δεσμωτήριον, καὶ **βαλαικάκες**, Hsch.:—also **βάλεκες**, Id., and **βάλακες**, **βαλάδες**, Cyr.

βαλαιόν· μέγα, πολύ, οἱ δὲ ταχύ, Hsch.

βαλακρός, Maced. = φαλ–, Plu.2.292e.

βᾰλᾰν-άγρα, ἡ, *key* or *hook for pulling out the* βάλανος II.4, Hdt. 3.155, X.*HG*5.2.29, Aen.Tact.18.9: in pl., = βάλανος II.4, Plb.7.16.5, Them.*Or.*26.315d. **-άριον**, τό, *bath-towel* (or *-bag*), *PAmh.*2.126. 45 (ii A.D.), *POxy.*921.18 (iii A.D.). **-ειόμφᾰλος**, ον, *with a boss like the valve of a bath*, φιάλη β. a cup *with a round bottom*, Cratin. 50. **-εῖον**, τό, *bath*, *bathing-room*, Ar.*Nu.*837,1054, etc.; β. δημόσιον *BGU*1130.9 (i B.C.): more freq. in pl., Ar.*Nu.*991, *Eq.*1401, etc. 2. *bath* taken, Aristo *Stoic.*1.88, Gal.11.46.—Prose word for poet. λουτρά. **-είτης**, ου, ὁ, = sq., Plb.30.29.4. **-εύς**, έως, ὁ, *bath-man*, Ar.*Eq.*1403, *Ra.*710, Pl.*R.*344d, etc.: prov., βαλανεὺς ἐπὶ τῶν πολυπραγμόνων Diogenian.3.64. **-ευτής**, οῦ, ὁ, = βαλανεύς,

*PSI*5.584 (iii B.C.), *PTeb.*401.24 (i A.D.), etc. :—fem. **-εύτρια,** Poll 7.166, Lib.*Decl.*26.19. **-ευτικός,** ή, όν, *of* or *for baths,* ἔλαιον *PTeb.*117.61 (i B.C.); κονία *Gp.*10.29.4; ἡ -κή (sc. τέχνη), Pl.*Sph.* 227a. **-εύω,** *heat the bath,* Ar.*Lys.*337; but β. ἑαυτῷ *to be* one's own *bath-man,* Id.*Pax* 1103; *drench like a bath-man,* οἴνῳ κατὰ τοῦ κεράμου β. Pherecr.130.6:—Pass., Timocl.2 (dub.). 2. *bawl, shout,* Hsch. **-ηρός,** ά, όν, (βάλανος) *of the acorn type,* Thphr.*HP*1.11.3.

βᾰλᾰνη-φᾰγέω, *live on acorns,* App.*BC*1.50. **-φᾰγία,** ἡ, *a living on acorns,* Ph.2.409. **-φάγος** [φᾰ], ον, *acorn-eating,* esp. of Arcadians, Alc.(?).91, Orac.ap.Hdt.1.66, Plu.*Cor.*3, Nonn.*D.*13.287, Them.*Or.*26.316c. **-φόρος,** ον, *bearing dates,* φοίνικες Hdt.1.193.

βᾰλᾰν-ίδιον, τό, *small bathing-establishment,* δημόσιον β. *POxy.* 1430.13 (iv A.D.). **-ίζω** δρῦν, *shake acorns from* the oak, hence as prov. answer to beggars, ἄλλην δρῦν βαλάνιζε *AP*11.417, Zen. 2.41, etc. II. (βάλανος II.6) β. τινά *administer a suppository to* him, Hp.ap.Poll.10.150. **-ικός,** ή, όν, *of* or *for the bath*: τὸ β., = ἐπίλουτρον, Sch.Luc.*Lex.*2. **-ῖνος,** η, ον, *made of* βάλανος, β. ἔλαιον oil *of zukkum,* Thphr.*Od.*29, Dsc.1.34, cf. 19. 2. *of the colour of* β., *POxy.*265.3 (i A.D.). **-ιον,** τό, *decoction of acorns,* used as a restorative after drunkenness, Nicoch.15. 2. = βάλανος II.6, Hp. *Mul.*1.92, Ruf.ap.Orib.8.39, Dsc.4.176. **-ίς,** ίδος, ἡ, *pessary,* Hp.*Mul.*2.155, *Steril.*221. 2. *peg, stopper, PLond.*3.1177.178 (ii A.D.). II. = βαλάνισσα, Suid. **-ισις,** εως, ἡ, = sq., *Gloss.* **-ισμός,** ὁ, *administration of a suppository,* Aët.8.49, Cael. Aur.*TP*4.7.105. **-ισσα,** ἡ, fem. of βαλανεύς, *bathing-woman, AP*5.81. **-ιστέον,** *one must administer a suppository,* Archig.ap. Aët.9.27, Paul.Aeg.2.98. **-ιστής,** οῦ, ὁ, *one who collects acorns,* Zen.2.41. **-ίτης** [ῑ], ου, ὁ, *acorn-shaped,* β. λίθος a precious stone, Plin.*HN*37.149. II. β. βίος *of those who live on acorns,* Eust. 1859.47. **-ῖτις,** ιδος, ἡ, a sort of *sweet chestnut,* Plin.*HN*15.93.

βᾰλᾰνο-δόκη, ἡ, (δέχομαι) *socket in a door-post to receive the* βάλανος (II.4), Aen.Tact.18.3, al. **-ειδής,** ές, *like an acorn,* Dsc.5. 137. **-κάστᾰνον,** τό, *chestnut,* prob. for βολβο-, Alex.Trall.5.6.

βάλᾰνος [βᾰ], ἡ, *acorn,* Od.10.242, 13.409, Arist.*HA*603^{b}31, Thphr.*HP*3.8.3: *any similar fruit, date,* Hdt.1.193, X.*An.*2.3.15, Arr.*Ind.*11.8; Διὸς β. v. Διοσβάλανος; β. μυρεψική *bān, Balanites aegyptiaca,* Dsc.4.157, cf. Thphr.*HP*4.2.1. 2. *tree which bears* βάλανοι, ib.6, Plb.34.8.1, Lxx *Ge.*35.8. II. from similarity of shape, 1. a sea shell-fish, *barnacle,* Arist.*HA*535^{a}24, 547^{b}22, Xenocr.ap.Orib.2.58.50. 2. *glans penis,* Arist.*HA*493^{a}27, Ar.*Lys.* 413, Gal.10.381. 3. *air-vessel* of a seaweed, *bladder-wrack, Fucus vesiculosus,* Thphr.*HP*4.6.9. 4. *iron peg, bolt-pin,* Ar.*V.*200, Th.2. 4, Aen.Tact.18.1, al. 5. *fastening for necklaces,* Ar.*Lys.*410. 6. Medic., *suppository,* Hp.*Epid.*1.26.α′, Aret.*CA*1.1. b. *pledget, pessary,* Hp.*Mul.*1.84. 7. *ballot-ball,* Arist.*Ath.*63.2. (Lat. *glans,* Slav. *želądĭ,* Lith. *gìlė.*)

βᾰλᾰνο-φᾰγέω, = βαλανηφαγέω, Sch.Od.19.163. **-φάγος** [φᾰ], = βαλανηφάγος, *EM*790.36.

βᾰλᾰνόω, *fasten with a* βάλανος (II.4), βεβαλάνωκε τὴν θύραν Ar.*Ec.* 361:—Pass., *to be shut close, secured,* Id.*Av.*1159: metaph. in pf. part. Pass., *constipated,* Id.*Ec.*370.

βαλαντίδιον, βαλάντιον, βαλαντιοτομέω, -τόμος, v. βαλλ-.

βᾰλαντιοκλέπτης, ου, ὁ, *cutpurse,* Phryn.201 (who condemns the form βαλαντο-).

βᾰλᾰν-ώδης, ες, *acorn-like,* Thphr.*CP*4.3.4, *HP*3.16.1. **-ω[σις],** εως, ἡ, *right of gathering acorns,* prob. in *IG*5(2).456 (Megalopolis). **-ωτός,** ή, όν, (βαλανόω) *fastened with a* βάλανος (II.4), ὀχεύς Parm.1.16; θύρα X.*Oec.*9.5. II. *adorned with acorns,* φιάλη Ath.11.502b.

βάλαρες· οἱ βλαισοί, **βαλάρα** γὰρ γυνὴ παρὰ Βοιωτοῖς, Hsch.

βάλαρις, = βρύον θαλάσσιον, Ps.-Dsc.4.98. 2. = βοτάνη τρίφυλλος, Hsch. 3. (βάλλ-), = λυχνὶς στεφανωματική, Ps.-Dsc.3.100.

βαλαρός, ὁ, Corsican word for φυγάς, Paus.10.17.9.

βαλάσαι· ἀγοράσαι, Hsch.

βαλαύστιον, τό, *flower of the wild pomegranate,* Dsc.1.111, Gal.11. 847:—hence Adj. **βαλαύστινος,** *PSI*4.333.8 (iii B.C.). **βαλαυστιουργός,** ὁ, *dyer* (?), dub. in Alciphr.1.2.

βαλαύστρινος, η, ον, *of the colour of pomegranate flowers, Stud.Pal.* 20.41 (ii A.D.).

βαλβῑδοῦχος, ὁ, *judge* in races, Hsch.

βαλβῑδώδης, ες, *with cavities* or *grooves,* Hp.*Mochl.*1.

βαλβίς, ῖδος, ἡ, prop. *rope drawn across the race-course at the starting and finishing-point*: mostly in pl., *posts to which this rope was attached,* Ar.*Eq.*1159: so in sg., *turning-post,* νῆσος β. ξεστῇ εἴκασται Philostr.*VA*5.5: also, *platform from which the quoit was thrown,* Id.*Im.*1.24: hence, *any starting-point,* Antipho Soph.69; βαλβίδων ἄπο E.*HF*867, cf. Ar.*V.*548: metaph., ἕρπε πρὸς βαλβῖδα λυπρὰν βίου E.*Med.*1245; ἐκ β. εἰς τέρμα Them.*Or.*13.177d; β. λόγου βέβληται Philostr.*VS*2.20.3; βιβλίου *AP*4.3b.75 (Agath.); but, *edge,* ib.39. II. since *the starting-point* was also *the goal,* βαλβῖδες was used for *any point to be gained,* as *the battlements* (by one scaling a wall), S.*Ant.*131 (lyr.), cf. Lyc.287, Opp.*C.*1.513. III. = κοιλότης παραμήκης, Gal.19.87; v. foreg.

βάλε, *O that! would God!* c. opt., Alcm.26, Call.*Hec.*26.2; cf. ἄβαλε.

βάλερος or **βαλῖνος,** ὁ, kind of *carp,* Arist.*HA*568^{b}27:—also **βαλλιρός,** ib.602^{b}26; cf. βάλαγρος.

βαλήν, ὁ, v. βαλλήν.

Βάληος, epith. of Zeus in Bithynia, *Ath.Mitt.*19.373.

βαλία· ὀφθαλμία, καὶ τὸν **βάλιον** πηρόν (Cret.), Hsch.

βαλιδικός, ή, όν, epith. of a kind of *nut,* κάρυα βαλιδικά *PPetr.*3 p.332.

βαλικιώτης (ϝαλ-), Cret. for ἡλικιώτης, Hsch. **βαλῖνος,** v. βάλερος.

βᾰλιός, ά, όν, *spotted, dappled,* ἔλαφος, λύγκες, E.*Hec.*90, *Alc.*579 (both lyr.); πέρδιξ *AP*7.203 (Simm.). 2. parox., Βαλίος, as name of one of Achilles' horses, *Piebald, Dapple,* Il.16.149, al., cf. E.*IA* 222. II. *swift,* Opp.*C.*2.314, Tryph.84, Nonn.*D.*9.156, al.

βαλίς, = σίκυς ἄγριος, Ps.-Dsc.4.150.

βαλιῶται· πρόγονοι, Hsch. **βάλλαι·** βαθμοί (Cypr.), Id. (Aeol. = βηλός).

βαλλαντιατόμος, v. βαλλαντιοτόμος.

βαλλαντίδιον [ῐ], τό, Dim. of sq., to be read for βαλ- in Eup.23, Hld.2.30.

βαλλάντιον, τό, *bag, pouch, purse,* [Simon.]178, Epich.10 (βαλ-), Ar.*Eq.*707, al., Thphr.*Char.*17.5; παῖς ἐκ βαλλαντίου a supposititious child, Teleclid.41. II. *javelin* (as if from βάλλω), a pun in Dionys. ap.Ath.3.98d. (The spelling βαλλ- is better attested than that with βαλ-, cf. Phld.*Rh.*1.354S., etc.; cf. βαλλαντιοτομέω, -τόμος.)

βαλλαντιο-τομέω, *cut purses,* Pl.*R.*575b, X.*Mem.*1.2.62 (βαλ-). **-τόμος,** ὁ, *cutpurse, footpad,* Ecphantid.4, Teleclid.15, Aeschin.3. 207, v. l. in Pl.*R.*552d (leg. βαλλαντιᾱτόμοι (βαλ- codd. AF)); τοῖσι βαλλαντιοτόμοις, prob. for τοῖς βαλαντιοτόμοις, Ar.*Ra.*772.

βαλλαχράδαι, οἱ, *pear-throwers, nickname among boys at Argos,* Plu.2.303a.

βάλλεκα· ψῆφον, Hsch. **βαλλήιαι·** οἱ ἀκροβολισμοί, Id.

βαλλήν, ὁ (not βαλήν Hdn.Gr.2.923), *king,* A.*Pers.*657, S.*Fr.*515.—Prob. Phrygian word acc. to Hsch., but Thurian acc. to Hermesianax Hist.ap.Ps.-Plu.*Fluv.*12.4: **βαλληναῖον** ὄρος, = βασιλικόν (in Phrygia) and **βαλλήν,** a fabulous precious stone, Ps.-Plu.*Fluv.*12. 3,4.

Βαλλήνᾰδε βλέπειν, a pun between βάλλω and the Attic deme Παλλήνη, Ar.*Ach.*234.

βαλλητύς, ύος, ἡ, *throwing,* Ath.9.406d, 407c; festival of Demeter at Athens with a sham fight, Hsch.

βαλλίζω, *dance, jump about,* in Sicily and Magna Graecia, Epich. 79, Sophr.11,12, Ath.8.362bsq.

βαλλίον, τό, = φαλλός, Herod.6.69. **βαλλιρός,** ὁ, v. βάλερος.

βάλλις, εως, ἡ, *plant* with wonderful medicinal properties, Xanth. 16.

βαλλισμός, ὁ, *jumping about, dancing,* Alex.107, Ath.8.362b.

Βαλλιστής, οῦ, ὁ, a constellation, *Cat.Cod.Astr.*7.204.14.

βαλλίστρα, ἡ, *catapult, engine of war,* Procop.*Goth.*1.22, al., Steph. *in Hp.*2.384D.

βάλλω, fut. βᾰλῶ (in Att. Prose only in compds.), Ion. βαλέω Il. 8.403, βαλλήσω Ar.*V.*222, 1491: aor. 2 ἔβᾰλον, Ion. προ-βάλεσκε Od. 5.331; later aor. 1 ἔβαλα Lxx 3*Ki.*6.1 (5.18); Ep. and Ion. inf. βαλέειν Il.2.414, al., Hdt.2.111, al., but βαλεῖν Il.13.387, 14.424; opt. βλείης in Epich.219, part. βλείς Id.176, as if from ἔβλην (v. συμβάλλω): pf. βέβληκα: plpf. ἐβεβλήκειν, Ep. βεβλήκειν Il.5.661:—Med., Ion. impf. βαλλέσκετο Hdt.9.74: fut. βᾰλοῦμαι (προ-) Ar.*Ra.*201, (ἐπι-) Th.6.40, etc., Ep. βαλεῦμαι (ἀμφι-) Od.22.103: aor. 2 ἐβᾰλόμην, Ion. imper. βαλεῦ Hdt.8.68.γ′, used mostly in compds.:—**Pass.,** fut. βληθήσομαι X.*HG*7.5.11, (δια-) E.*Hec.*863; also βεβλήσομαι Id. *Or.*271, Hld.2.13, (δια-) D.16.2; part. δια-βεβλησόμενος Philostr. *VA*6.13 (Ep. fut. ξυμ-βλήσομαι, v. συμβάλλω): aor. ἐβλήθην Hdt.1. 34, Th.8.84, etc.: Hom. also has an Ep. aor. Pass., ἔβλητο Il.11. 675, ξύμβλητο 14.39; subj. βλήεται Od.17.472; opt. βλῇο or βλεῖο Il.13.288; inf. βλῆσθαι 4.115; part. βλήμενος 15.495: pf. βέβλημαι, Ion. 3 pl. βεβλήαται 11.657 (but 3 sg. *h.Ap.*20), opt. δια-βεβλῇσθε And.2.24: plpf. ἐβεβλήμην (περι-) X.*HG*7.4.22, (ἐξ-) Isoc.18.17; Ion. 3 pl. περι-εβεβλέατο Hdt.6.25.—Ep. pf. βεβόλημαι in special sense, v. βολέω.

A. Act., *throw*: I. with acc. of person or thing aimed at, *throw so as to hit, hit* with a missile, freq. opp. *striking* with a weapon in the hand, βλήμενος ἠὲ τυπείς Il.15.495; τὸν βάλεν, οὐδ' ἀφάμαρτε 11.350, cf. 4.473, al.; so even in ἐγγύθεν ἐλθὼν βεβλήκει.. δουρί 5.73; and δουρὶ ὤμων μεσσηγὺς σχεδόθεν βάλε 16.807; but later opp. τοξεύειν, D.9.17, X.*An.*4.2.12; ἐκ χειρὸς β. ib.3.3.15: c. dat. instrumenti, β. τινὰ δουρί, πέτρῳ, κεραυνῷ, etc., Il.13.518, 20.288, Od.5. 128, etc.: βλήμενος ἢ ἰῷ ἢ ἔγχεϊ Il.8.514: c. dupl. acc. pers. et partis, μιν βάλε μηρὸν ὀϊστῷ 11.583: c. acc. partis only, 5.19, 657; so τὸν δ' Ὀδυσεὺς κατὰ λαιμὸν.. βάλεν ἰῷ Od.22.15; δουρὶ βαλὼν πρὸς στῆθος Il. 11.144: c. acc. cogn., ἕλκος.., τό μιν βάλε Πάνδαρος ἰῷ 5.795; also βάλε Τυδεΐδαο κατ' ἀσπίδα *smote upon* it, ib.281. 2. less freq. of things, ἡνίοχον κονίης ῥαθάμιγγες ἔβαλλον 23.502; of drops of blood, 11.536, cf. A.*Ag.*1390: metaph., κηλὶς ἔβαλέ νιν μητροκτόνος E.*IT* 1200, cf. *HF*1219; of the sun, ἀκτῖσιν ἔβαλλεν [θάμνους] Od.5.479; ἔβαλλε.. οὐρανὸν Ἠώς A.R.4.885 (so Pass., σελήνη.. δι' εὐτρήτων βαλλομένη θυρίδων *AP*5.122 (Phld.)); *strike* the senses, of sound, ἵππων ὠκυπόδων ἀμφὶ κτύπος οὔατα βάλλει Il.10.535, cf. S.*Ant.*1188, *Ph.*205 (lyr.); of smell, ὀσμὴ β. τινά Id.*Ant.*412; τάχ' ἄν πέμφιξ σε βροντῆς καὶ δυσοσμίας β. Id.*Fr.*538. 3. metaph., β. τινὰ κακοῖς, φθόνῳ, ψόγῳ, *smite* with reproaches, etc., Id.*Aj.*1244, E.*El.*902, Ar. *Th.*895; στεφάνοις β. τινά Pi.*P.*8.57 (hence metaph., *praise,* Id.*O.*2. 98); φθόνος βάλλει A.*Ag.*947; φίλημα βάλλει τὴν καρδίαν Ach.Tat. 2.37. II. with acc. of the weapon thrown, *cast, hurl,* of missiles, rare in Hom., βαλὼν βέλος Od.9.495; χαλκὸν ἐνὶ στήθεσσι βαλών Il.5.

346, cf. Od.20.62; ἐν νηυσὶν..πῦρ β. Il.13.629: c. dat., of the weapon, *throw* or *shoot with* a thing, οἱ δ' ἄρα χερμαδίοισι..βάλλον 12.155; βέλεσι Od.16.277: in Prose abs., β. ἐπί τινα *throw* at one, Th.8.75; ἐπὶ σκοπόν X.*Cyr*.1.6.29; ἐπίσκοπα Luc.*Am*.16; alone, οἱ ψιλοὶ βάλλοντες εἶργον Th.4.33: c. gen., βάλλοντα τοῦ σκοποῦ *hitting* the mark, Pl.*Sis*.391a. 2. generally of anything thrown, εἰς ἅλα λύματ' ἔβαλλον Il.1.314; τὰ μὲν ἐν πυρὶ βάλλε Od.14.429; [νῆα] β. ποτὶ πέτρας 12.71; εὐνὰς β. *throw out* the anchor-stones, 9.137; β. σπόρον *cast* the seed, Theoc.25.26; β. κόπρον *POxy*.934.9 (iii A.D.): hence β. ἀρούρας *manure*, *PFay*.118.21 (ii A.D.): metaph., ὕπνον..ἐπὶ βλεφάροις β. Od.1.364; β. σκότον ὄμμασι E.*Ph*.1535 (lyr.); β. λύπην τινί S.*Ph*.67. b. of persons, β. τινὰ ἐν κονίῃσιν, ἐν δαπέδῳ, Il.8.156, Od.22.188; γῆς ἔξω β. S.*OT*622; β. τινὰ ἄθαπτον Id.*Aj*.1333; ἄτιμον Id.*Ph*.1028:—Pass., ὑπὸ χλαίνῃ βεβλημένος *AP*5.164 (Mel.); βεβλημένος *on a sick-bed*, *Ev.Matt*.8.14: then metaph., ἐς κακὸν β. τινά Od.12.221; ὅς με μετ'..ἔριδας καὶ νείκεα β. Il.2.376; β. τινὰ ἐς ἔχθραν, ἐς φόβον, A.*Pr*.390, E.*Tr*.1058; also ἐν αἰτίᾳ or αἰτίᾳ β. τινά, S.*OT*657, *Tr*.940 (but in E.*Tr*.305 β. αἰτίαν ἔς τινα); κινδύνῳ β. τινά A.*Th*.1053. 3. *let fall*, ἑτέρωσε κάρη βάλεν Il.8.306, cf. 23.697; β. ἀπὸ δάκρυ παρειῶν Od.4.198, cf. 114; κατὰ βλεφάρων β. δάκρυα Thgn.1206; κατ' ὄσσων E.*Hipp*.1396; αἵματος πέμφιγα πρὸς πέδῳ β. A.*Fr*.183; β. τοὺς ὀδόντας *cast, shed* them, Arist.*HA*501^{b}2, etc.; so βάλλειν alone, ib.576^{a}4; βοῦς βεβληκώς *SIG*958.7 (Ceos). 4. of the eyes, ἑτέρωσε βάλ' ὄμματα *cast* them, Od.16.179; ὄμματα πρὸς γῆν E.*Ion* 582; πρόσωπον εἰς γῆν Id.*Or*.958: intr., ὀφθαλμὸς πρὸς τὸ φῶς βαλών *aiming at*.., Plot.2.4.5; βαλὼν πρὸς αὐτό *directing one's gaze* at.., Id.3.8.10. 5. of animals, *push forward* or *in front*, τοὺς σοὺς [ἵππους] πρόσθε βαλών Il.23.572; πλήθει πρόσθε βαλόντες (sc. ἵππους) ib.639; βάλλε κάτωθε τὰ μοσχία Theoc.4.44: metaph., β. ψυχὰν ποτὶ κέρδεα Bion *Fr*.5.12. 6. in a looser sense, *put, place*, with or without a notion of haste, τὼ μὲν..βαλέτην ἐν χερσὶν ἑταίρων Il.5.574, cf. 17.40, 21.104; μῆλα..ἐν νηΐ β. Od.9.470; ἐπὶ γᾶν ἴχνος ποδὸς β. E.*Rh*.721 (lyr.); φάσγανον ἐπ' αὐχένος β. Id.*Or*.51; τοὺς δακτύλους εἰς τὰ ὦτα *Ev.Marc*.7.33; β. πλίνθους *lay* bricks, *Edict.Diocl*.7.15; *pour*, οἶνον εἰς ἀσκούς *Ev.Matt*.9.17; εἰς πίθον Arr.*Epict*.4.13.12, cf. Dsc.1.71.5 (v.l. for ἐμβ.): metaph., ἐν στήθεσσι μένος βάλε ποιμένι λαῶν Il.5.513; ὅπως..φιλότητα μετ' ἀμφοτέροισι βάλωμεν *may put* friendship between them, 4.16; μαντεύσομαι ὡς ἐνὶ θυμῷ ἀθάνατοι βάλλουσι Od.1.201; ἐν καρδίᾳ β. Pi.*O*.13.16; but also θυμῷ, ἐς θυμὸν β., *lay* to heart, A.*Pr*.706, S.*OT*975. b. esp. of *putting round*, ἀμφ' ὀχέεσσι θοῶς βάλε καμπύλα κύκλα Il.5.722; of clothes or arms, ἀμφὶ δ' Ἀθήνη ὤμοις..βάλ' αἰγίδα 18.204; *put on*, φαιὰ ἱμάτια Plb.30.4.5. c. *place* money *on deposit*, ἀργύριον τοῖς τραπεζίταις *Ev.Matt*.25.27. d. *pay*, *PLond*.3.1177 (ii A.D.), *POxy*.1448.5 (iv A.D.). 7. of dice, *throw*, τρὶς ἓξ βαλεῖν A.*Ag*.33, cf. Pl.*Lg*.968e; ἄλλα βλήματ' ἐν κύβοις βαλεῖν E.*Supp*.330: so prob. ψῆφος βαλοῦσα, abs., *by its throw*, A.*Eu*.751: metaph., εὖ or καλῶς βάλλειν *to be lucky, successful*, Phld.*Ir*.p.51 W., *Rh*.1.10 S. III. intr., *fall*, ποταμὸς Μινυήϊος εἰς ἅλα βάλλων Il.11.722, cf. A.R.2.744, etc.; ἄνεμος κατ' αὐτῆς (sc. νεώς) ἔβαλε *Act.Ap*.27.14; [ἵππους] περὶ τέρμα βαλούσας *having run* round the post, Il.23.462; ἐγὼ δὲ..τάχ' ἐν πέδῳ βαλῶ (sc. ἐμαυτήν) A.*Ag*.1172 (lyr.); λίμνηθεν ὅτ' εἰς ἁλὸς οἶδμα βάλητε *arrive* at.., A.R.4.1579; εἴσω β. *enter* a river's mouth, Orac. ap.D.S.8.23; βαλὼν κάθευδε *lie down and* sleep, Arr.*Epict*.2.20.10; τί οὖν, οὐ ῥέγκω βαλών; ib.4.10.29; βαλὼν ἐπὶ τῆς στιβάδος ἐπεχείρει καθεύδειν Anon.ap.*POxy*.1368.51; cf. A. II.4. 2. in familiar language, βάλλ' ἐς κόρακας *away with you! be hanged!* Ar.*V*.835, etc.; βάλλ' ἐς μακαρίαν Pl.*Hp.Ma*.293a, cf. Men.*Epit*.389.

B. Med., *put for oneself*, ὡς ἐνὶ θυμῷ βάλλεαι that thou *may'st lay it* to heart, Il.20.196, cf. Od.12.218; σὺ δ' ἐνὶ φρεσὶ βάλλεο σῇσιν Hes.*Op*.107; εἰ μὲν δὴ νόστον γε μετὰ φρεσὶ..βάλλεαι Il.9.435; ἐς θυμὸν βαλέσθαι τι Hdt.1.84, etc.; εἰς or ἐπὶ νοῦν, εἰς μνήμην, Plu.*Thes*.24, Jul.*Or*.2.58a, etc. (v. supr. A. II.6); ἐπ' ἑωυτῶν βαλόμενοι *on their own responsibility*, Hdt.4.160, cf. 3.71, al.; ἑτέρως ἐβάλοντο θεοί, v.l. for ἐβόλοντο in Od.1.234; θεοὶ δ' ἑτέρωσε βάλοντο Q.S.1.610. 2. τόξα or ξίφος ἀμφ' ὤμοισιν βάλλεσθαι *throw about one's* shoulder, Il.10.333, 19.372, etc.; ἐπὶ κάρα στέφη β. E.*IA*1513 (lyr.). 3. ἐς γαστέρα βάλλεσθαι γόνον *conceive*, Hdt.3.28. 4. *lay as foundation*, κρηπῖδα βαλέσθαι Pi.*P*.7.3, cf. 4.138, Luc.*Hipp*.4; also, *lay the foundations of, begin to form*, οἰκοδομίας Pl.*Lg*.779b; χάρακα Plb.3.105.10, Poll.8.161; simply, *build*, ἱερὸν περί τι Philostr.*VA*4.13; β. ἄγκυραν *cast* anchor, Hdt.9.74, etc.; καθάπερ ἐξ ἀγκυρῶν βαλλόμενος ψυχῆς δεσμούς Pl.*Ti*.73d. II. rarely, χρόα βάλλεσθαι λουτροῖς *dash oneself* with water, *bathe*, *h.Cer*.50 (but λουτρὰ ἐπὶ χροῒ βαλεῖν E.*Or*.303). (Arc. -δέλλω in ἐσ-δέλλοντες, = ἐκ-βάλλοντες, *IG*5(2).6.49: ζέλλειν· βάλλειν, Hsch. Root $g^{w}el$- 'throw', Skt. *galati* 'trickle', OHG. *quellan* 'spurt up', Lith. *gulēti* 'lie'.)

βαλλωτή, ἡ, *black horehound, Ballota nigra*, Dsc.3.103.

βαλμός, ὁ, = στῆθος, Hsch., Suid. **βαλοιτήσειρον**· παρὰ τὸ διεστραμμένον εἶναι τοὺς πόδας, Hsch.

βαλός, ὁ, Dor. for βηλός (q.v.).

βαλσᾰμ-έλαιον, τό, = σίλφιον, Sch.Ar.*Pl*.926. **-ίνη**, ἡ, = βούφθαλμον, Ps.-Dsc.3.139; *balsaminum*, = ὀποβάλσαμον, Plin.*HN*23.92. **-ον**, τό, *balsam-tree, Balsamodendron Opobalsamum*, Thphr.*HP*9.6.1, Dsc.1.19; ξύλα βαλσάμου *BGU*953.6 (iii/iv A.D.). 2. the fragrant oil of this tree, *Mecca balsam*, Arist.*Fr*.110, Thphr.*HP*9.4.1, *POxy*.1052 (βαρσ-, iv A.D.). II. *an aromatic herb, costmary, Chrysanthemum Balsamita*, *Gp*.11.27 tit.—Prob. Semitic. [βάλσᾰμον in Nic.*Th*.947, but ᾰ in Androm.ap.Gal.14.39, and Damocr.ap.Gal.14.97, as in *balsămum* in Lat. Poets.] **-ῶδες**, τό, a *bark* like cassia, Plin.*HN*12.97.

βαλώστιον, τό, = βαλαύστιον, *PSI*5.489 (iii B.C.).

βάμβα, = βάμμα (Syrac.), Hsch.

βαμβαίνω, onomatop. word, *chatter with the teeth*, Il.10.375; *stammer*, Bion *Fr*.6.9, *AP*5.272 (Agath.), Procop.*Arc.Praef*.:—so also **βαμβᾰκύζω**, *chatter with cold*, Hippon.17:—also **βαμβᾰλύζω**, Phryn.*PS*p.54 B., Hsch.; possibly to be restored (for βομβυλιάζω) in Arist.*Pr*.949^{a}13.

βαμβᾰκ-εία, -κεύτρια, ἡ, = φαρμακεία, -κεύτρια, Hsch.: **βάμβᾰκος**, ὁ, = φαρμακός (Cilic.), *AB*85.

βαμβάκιον [ᾰ], τό, *cotton*, Suid. s.v. πάμβαξ.

βαμβᾰκοειδής, ές, *like cotton*, v.l. for βομβυκ-, Dsc.3.16.

βαμβάκτης, ου, ὁ, *highway, causeway*, Cyr.Dresd.

βάμβαλα· χειμερινὰ ἱμάτια, Hsch.: in sg. also, = τὸ αἰδοῖον (Phryg.), Id. **βαμβάλειν**· τρέμειν, ψοφεῖν τοῖς χείλεσι, Id.

βαμβᾰλύζω, v. βαμβαίνω.

βαμβρᾰδών, όνος, ἡ, = βεμβράς, Epich.60, Sophr.65.

βαμβράσσει· ὀργίζεται, and **βαμβρασμός**· καχλασμός, Cyr.Dresd.

βᾶμες, Dor. for βῶμεν, 1 pl. subj. aor. 2 of βαίνω, Theoc.15.22.

βάμμα, ατος, τό, (βάπτω) *that in which a thing is dipped, dye*, Pl.*Lg*.956a; βάμμα Σαρδιανικόν, Κυζικηνικόν, v. βάπτω I.2: in pl., διάφορα β. *POxy*.914.7 (v A.D.); β. λευκώματος a whitish *tinge*, Arist.*Phgn*.813^{a}28. II. *sauce*, Nic.*Th*.622, cf. Hsch. s.v. βάμβα. III. = ὄα, *AB*362.

βάν [ᾰ], Ep. for ἔβαν, ἔβησαν, 3 pl. aor. 2 of βαίνω.

βᾰνά, Boeot. for γυνή, Corinn.21: pl., βανῆκες, Hsch.

βᾰναυσ-ία, ἡ, *handicraft*, Hdt.2.165, Pl.*R*.590c, etc. II. *the habits of a mere artisan, vulgarity, bad taste*, Arist.*EN*1107^{b}19, *Pol*.1317^{b}41, *UPZ*62.3 (ii B.C.). 2. *quackery, charlatanism*, Hp.*Morb.Sacr*.18. **-ικός**, ή, όν, *of* or *for artisans*: τέχνη β. *handicraft*, X.*Smp*.3.4, *Oec*.4.2; τὸ β. Arist.*Pol*.1321^{a}6.

βάναυσος [ᾰ], ον, (for βαύναυσος, from βαῦνος, αὔω acc. to *EM*187.40, cf. βαναυσία· πᾶσα τέχνη διὰ πυρός, Hsch.; βαναύσων seems to be f.l. for βαύνων in Heraclit.*All*.69):—epith. of the class of handicraftsmen or artisans, τὸ β., = τὸ περὶ τὰς τέχνας ὧν ἄνευ πόλιν ἀδύνατον οἰκεῖσθαι Arist.*Pol*.1291^{a}1, etc.; ὁ β. δῆμος, opp. ὁ γεωργικός, ὁ ἀγοραῖος, ib.1289^{b}33: as Subst., *artisan*, ib.1277^{b}35; ἡ βελτίστη πόλις οὐ ποιήσει β. πολίτην ib.1278^{a}8; τὸ β., = οἱ βάναυσοι, ib.1329^{a}20. II. τέχνη β. a *mechanical* art, *handicraft*, S.*Aj*.1121, Pl.*Tht*.176c (pl.); β. ἔργον Arist.*Pol*.1337^{b}8; βαναυσόταται τῶν ἐργασιῶν ib.1258^{b}37; β. βίον ζῆν *a mere mechanic's* life, ib.1278^{a}21, 1328^{b}39; β. πόνοι Plu.*Num*.14: hence, 2. *vulgar, in bad taste*, Arist.*EN*1123^{a}19, Pl.*Ep*.334b; of persons, Axiop.1.4. Adv. -σως, προσβλέπειν *unworthily, meanly*, Phld.*D*.1.11. 3. later, *fastidious*, *AP*11.326 (Autom.), 12.237 (Strat.).

βᾰναυσοτεχνέω, = sq., Str.16.4.25.

βᾰναυσουργ-έω, *follow a mere mechanical art*, Poll.7.6. **-ία**, ἡ, *handicraft*, Plu.*Marcell*.14. **-ός**, ὁ, *handicraftsman*, Poll.7.6.

βανθῶσαι· σκοτοδινιάσαι, Hsch. **βάνισος**· εἶδος θυμιάματος, Id. **βανκόν**· μωρόν, Id. **βάννας**· βασιλεύς (Ital.), Id. **βανvάται**· αἱ λοξοὶ ὁδοί (Tarent.); also **βάνvατροι**, Id. **βάννεια** and **βάννιμα**, τά, = ἄρνεια, Id. **βανοί**· τέχναι, Id. **βανόν**· λεπτόν, Id. **βάνος**· κλάσμα, μωρός, καὶ τυφλός, Id. **βανούς**· ὄρη στρογγύλα, Id. **βανύσει**· μωραίνει, ἐπιμαίνεται, Id.

βανωτός, ὁ, a kind of *vase* used as a measure, *PSI*4.428.12 (iii B.C.), 5.535.23 (iii B.C.), Callix.2:—Dim. **βανώτιον**, τό, *PSI*4.428.22 (iii B.C.).

βάξις, εως, ἡ, (βάζω) poet. Noun, *saying*, esp. *an oracular saying, inspired utterance*, κλύειν εὐηκέα β. Emp.112.11; ἐναργὴς β. ἦλθεν Ἰνάχῳ A.*Pr*.663; θεσφάτων β. S.*Tr*.87. 2. *report, rumour*, μιν..β. ἔχει χαλεπή Mimn.15; β. ἀργαλέη Id.16; θεῶν ἐποπίζεο μῆνιν βάξιν τ' ἀνθρώπων Thgn.1298; β. ἀλγεινήν, β. καλὴν λαβεῖν, S.*Aj*.494, *El*.1006; σπείρειν ματαίαν β. ἐς πᾶσαν πόλιν ib.642, cf. 638; διὰ δὲ πόλεως ἔρχεται β. E.*Hel*.224 (lyr.); ὀξεῖα γάρ σου β...διῆλθ' Ἀχαιούς *a report concerning* thee, S.*Aj*.998; ἁλώσιμος β. *tidings* of the capture, A.*Ag*.10; θανόντος β. ἀνδρός E.*Hel*.351 (lyr.); so τήν τ' ἀμφὶ Θησέως β. Id.*Supp*.642. II. *voice*, *Epigr.Gr*.989.2.

βᾶξον (i.e. ϝᾶξον)· κατᾶξον (Lacon.), Hsch.

βαπαίνει· παρακαλεῖ, Hsch.

βάπτης, ου, ὁ, *dipper, bather*: in pl. of those who celebrated the mysteries of Cotytto; title of play by Eupolis, cf. Luc.*Ind*.27, Sch. Juv.2.91.

βαπτ-ίζω, *dip, plunge*, ξίφος εἰς σφαγὴν J.*BJ*2.18.4; σπάθιον εἰς τὸ ἔμβρυον Sor.2.63:—Pass., of a trephine, Gal.10.447; βάπτισον σεαυτὸν εἰς θάλασσαν Plu.2.166a; β. Διόνυσον πρὸς τὴν θάλασσαν ib.914d:—in Pass., *to be drowned*, Epict.*Gnom*.47; of ships, *sink* or *disable* them, Plb.1.51.6, 16.6.2 (Pass.); ἐβάπτισαν τὴν πόλιν *flooded* the city, metaph., of the crowds who flocked into Jerusalem at the time of the siege, J.*BJ*4.3.3; β. τινὰ εἰσφοραῖς D.S.1.73; β. τινὰ ὕπνῳ *AP*11.49 (Even.); ὕπνῳ βεβαπτισμένος Archig. and Posidon.ap.Aët.6.3:—Pass., ὡς ἐκ τοῦ βεβαπτίσθαι ἀναπνέουσι Hp.*Epid*.5.63; *to be drenched*, Eub.68: metaph., βεβαπτισμένοι *soaked in wine*, Pl.*Smp*.176b; ὀφλήμασι βεβ. *over head and ears* in debt, Plu.*Galb*.21; γνοὺς βαπτιζόμενον τὸ μειράκιον seeing that he was *getting into deep water*, Pl.*Euthd*.277d; β. εἰς ἀναισθησίαν καὶ ὕπνον J.*AJ*10.9.4; ὁ τῷ θυμῷ βεβαπτισμένος καταδύεται Ach.Tat.6.19; ψυχὴ βεβαπτισμένη λύπῃ Lib.*Or*.64.115. 2. *draw wine by dipping* the cup in the bowl, Aristopho 14.5; φιάλαις β. ἐκ..κρατήρων Plu.*Alex*.67. 3. *baptize*, τινά Ev.Marc.1.4; ἐν ὕδατι εἰς μετάνοιαν Ev.Matt.3.11:—Pass., βαπτισθήτω ἕκαστος εἰς ἄφεσιν ἁμαρτιῶν Act.Ap.2.38; εἰς Χριστόν Ep.Rom.6.3, etc.:—Med., *dip oneself*, Lxx 4Ki.5.14; *get oneself baptized*, Act.Ap.22.16, 1Ep.Cor.10.2:—Pass., *perform ablutions*, Ev.Luc.11.38. **-ικός**, ή, όν, *for dyeing*, χρώματα Sch.Lyc.1138. II. *suited for gilding* or *silvering*, opp. σμηκτικός, Ps.-Democr.Alch.p.47 B.: Comp., *more suited for a wash*, Zos.Alch.p.129 B. **-ῐσις**, εως, ἡ, *dipping*: *baptism*, J.AJ18.5.2. **-ισμα**, ατος, τό, *baptism*, Ev.Matt.3.7, etc.; β. εἰς τὸν θάνατον Ep.Rom.6.4. **-ισμός**, ὁ, *dipping in water, immersion*, Ev.Marc.7.4, Ep.Hebr.9.10, Antyll.ap.Orib.10.3.9. 2. metaph., εἰς κακίας β. οἰχήσεται Theol.Ar.30. 3. *lethargic sleep*, Archig. and Posidon.ap.Aët.6.3. 4. *baptism*, J.AJ18.5.2. **-ιστήριον**, τό, *swimming-bath*, Plin.Ep.2.17.11. **-ιστής**, οῦ, ὁ, *one that dips*: *baptizer*, ὁ β. *the Baptist*, Ev.Matt.3.1, cf. J.AJ18.5.2, etc.: metaph. of the Passion, Ev.Luc.12.50. **-ός**, ή, όν, *dipped, dyed*, D.S.5.30; *bright-coloured*, ὄρνις Ar.Av.287; ἱμάτια Id.Pl.530; τὰ βάπτ' ἔχοντες *dyed*, i.e. *black*, garments, Hegesipp.1.13, cf. Plu.Ages.30. 2. *for dyeing*, χρώματα Pl.Lg.847c. II. of water, *drawn by dipping vessels*, E.Hipp.123 (lyr.). **-ρια**, ἡ, fem. of βάπτης, Eup.401.

βάπτω, fut. βάψω (ἐμ-) Ar.Pax959: aor. ἔβαψα S.Aj.95, etc.:—Med., fut. βάψομαι Ar.Lys.51: aor. ἐβαψάμην Arat.951, AP9.326 (Leon.):—**Pass.**, fut. βαφήσομαι Lxx Le.11.32, M.Ant.8.51: aor. ἐβάφθην AP6.254 (Myrin.), (ἀπ-) Ar.Fr.416; in Att. generally ἐβάφην [ᾰ] Pl.R.429e, etc.: pf. βέβαμμαι Hdt.7.67, Ar.Pax1176. I. trans., *dip*, ὡς δ' ὅτ' ἀνὴρ χαλκεὺς πέλεκυν .. εἰν ὕδατι ψυχρῷ βάπτῃ (so as to temper the red-hot steel) Od.9.392; β. εἰς ὕδωρ Pl.Ti.73e, cf. Emp.100.11; τάρια θερμῷ Ar.Ec.216; εἰς μέλι, εἰς κηρόν, Arist.HA605a29, de An.435a2:—Pass., βαπτόμενος σίδηρος iron *in process of being tempered*, Plu.2.136a; and of coral, *become hard*, Dsc.5.121 (s.v.l.). b. of slaughter in Trag., ἐν σφαγαῖσι βάψασα ξίφος A.Pr.863; ἔβαψας ἔγχος εὖ πρὸς Ἀργείων στρατῷ; S.Aj.95; φάσγανον εἴσω σαρκὸς ἔβαψεν E.Ph.1578 (lyr.); in later Prose, εἰς τὰ πλευρὰ β. τὴν αἰχμὴν D.H.5.15; β. τὸν δάκτυλον ἀπὸ τοῦ αἵματος Lxx Le.4.17. c. also, *dip in poison*, ἔβαψεν ἰοὺς S.Tr.574; χιτῶνα τόνδ' ἔβαψα ib.580. 2. *dye*, ἔβαψεν .. ξίφος the sword *dyed* [the robe] *red*, A.Ch.1011; β. τὰ κάλλη *dye* the beautiful cloths, Eup.333; β. ἔρια ὥστ' εἶναι ἁλουργά Pl.R.429d; εἵματα βεβαμμένα Hdt.7.67; τρίχας βάπτειν AP11.68 (Lucill.): abs. in Med., *dye the hair*, Men.363.4, Nicol.Com.1.33; *glaze* earthen vessels, Ath.11.480e; of *gilding* and *silvering*, Ps.-Democr.Alch.p.46 B.: Com., βάπτειν τινὰ βάμμα Σαρδιανικόν *dye* one in the [red] dye of Sardes, i.e. give him a bloody coxcomb, Ar.Ach.112; but βέβαπται β. Κυζικηνικόν *he has been dyed in* the dye of Cyzicus, i.e. is an arrant coward, Id.Pax1176 (v. Sch.). 3. *draw* water *by dipping* a vessel, ἀνθ' ὕδατος τᾷ κάλπιδι κηρία βάψαι Theoc.5.127; ἀρύταιναν .. ἐκ μέσου βάψασα τοῦ λέβητος ζέοντος ὕδατος *draw* water *by dipping* the bucket, Antiph.25, cf. Thphr.Char.9.8; βάψασα ποντίας ἁλὸς (sc. τὸ τεῦχος) *having dipped* it *so as to draw* water from the sea, E.Hec.610. 4. *baptize*, Arr.Epict.2.9.20 (Pass.). II. intr., ναῦς ἔβαψεν the ship *dipped, sank*, E.Or.707; β. εἰς ψυχρὸν [αἱ ἐγχέλυς] Arist.HA592a18; εἰ δ' ὁ μὲν (sc. ἥλιος) ἀνέφελος βάπτοι ῥόου ἑσπερίοιο Arat.858 (ῥόον Sch.): c. acc., νῆα .. βάπτουσαν ἤδη κῦμα κυρτόν *dipping into* .., Babr.71.2:—also Med., ποταμοῖο ἐβάψατο Arat.951. 2. βάψας (sc. τὴν κώπην) Ar.Fr.225. (Cf. ONorse *kuefia* 'dip'.)

βάρα· νόσημά τι καρηβαρικόν, ἢ θρέμματα (Lacon.), Hsch.

βᾰραγχιάω, βᾰράγχια, = βραγχ-, Hdn.Gr.2.481, Hsch.

βάραγχος [βᾰ], ὁ, = βράγχος, Hippon.106.

βάραθρον [βᾰ], Ep. and Ion. **βέρεθρον** (q.v., cf. ζέρεθρον), shortd. **βέθρον** (q.v.), τό, *gulf, pit*, Arist.Pr.947a19; esp. at Athens, *a cleft* into which criminals were thrown, Hdt.7.133, Ar.Nu.1450, Com.Adesp.24.10 D., Pl.Grg.516c, AB219, Sch.Ar.Pl.431. 2. metaph., ἐν τῷ β. χειμάζειν D.8.45; *ruin, perdition*, Luc.Am.5, etc.; name of a courtesan, Theophil.Com.11. II. a woman's *ornament*, Ar.Fr.320.8. III. = βράθυ, f.l. for βόρατον, Dsc.1.76. (Root g^{w}er 'devour', cf. βορά.)

βάραθρος [βᾰ], ὁ, *one that ought to be thrown into the pit*, Luc.Pseudol.17 (but perh. neut.).

βᾰραθρώδης, ες, *like a pit* or *gulf*, Str.13.1.67, Plu.Lyc.16; β. πέλαγος *abysmal*, of a dangerous sea, Ph.2.514; *precipitous*, of a road, Str.5.1.11: metaph., θολερὸς καὶ β. βίος Ph.1.322; of a person, τὴν ψυχὴν ἄδικος καὶ β. Agath.2.23.

βαρακινῆσιν· ἀκάνθαις, σκόλοψι, Hsch. **βαρακίς**· γλαύκινον ἱμάτιον, Id.

βάρακος, a kind of *fish*, Hsch.; also = βάτραχος, Id.

βάραξ, ακος, ὁ, a kind of *cake*, Epil.3; cf. βήρηξ.

βάρβαξ or **βάραξ**, a Libyan bird, Hsch.

βαρβάρα, ἡ, a kind of *plaster*, Alex.Trall.5.5.

βαρβᾰρ-ίζω, *behave* or *speak like a barbarian*, Hdt.2.57, Philostr.VA1.21, Arr.An.7.6.5; *speak broken Greek, speak gibberish*, Pl.Tht.175d codd. (sed leg. βατταρίζων); βαρβαριζόντων ἑτεροφώνων Phld.Po.994.6; *violate the laws of speech, commit barbarisms*, τῇ λέξει β. Arist.SE165b21, cf. Plb.39.1.7, Str.14.2.28, Luc.Rh.Pr.17, 23, etc.; distd. from σολοικίζω, Phld.Rh.1.154 S. 2. trans., '*murder*', *mangle*, τὴν Ῥωμαίων φωνὴν Luc.Merc.Cond.24. II. *side with the barbarians*, i.e. *the Persians*, X.HG5.2.35, Max.Tyr.4.2. **-ίκιον**, τό, name of a *foreign garment*, POxy.1684.5, 9 (iv A.D.). **-ικός**, ή, όν, *barbaric, non-Greek*, χείρ Simon.136; ψυκτήρ OGI214.47 (Didyma, Seleucus I); τὸ β., = οἱ βάρβαροι, Th.1.6, 7.29; τὰ β. ἔθνη Arist.Pol.1257a25, etc.; νόμιμα β. *leges barbarorum*, name of a treatise by Arist.; νόμοι λίαν ἁπλοῖ καὶ β. Pol.1268b40; esp. of the Persians, X.An.1.5.6; ἐς τὸ β. *in barbaric fashion*, Luc.DMort.27.3; β. ἐπιδρομή inroad *of barbarians*, PMasp.321.5 (vi A.D.); ἐς τὸ βαρβαρικώτερον *more in the Persian fashion*, Arr.An.4.8.2: Sup. -ώτατος Sch.Th.7.29. Adv., ἐβόα καὶ -κῶς καὶ Ἑλληνικῶς, i.e. both *in Persian* and Greek, X.An.1.8.1, cf. Phld.Lib.p.13 O.; κεκλημένον β. *in the language of the country*, Arist.Mir.846a32; *in foreign fashion*, App.Hisp.72. II. *barbarous, violent*, πένθη Plu.2.114e. Adv. -κῶς *barbarously*, ὠμῶς καὶ β. Id.Dio35: Comp. -ώτερον Id.Alex.2. **-ισμός**, ὁ, *use of a foreign tongue* or *of one's own tongue amiss, barbarism*, Arist.Po.1458a26, Diog.Bab.Stoic.3.214, Ph.1.124, Plu.2.731e; μιᾶς λέξεως κακία ὁ β., ἐπιπλοκῆς δὲ λέξεων ἀκαταλλήλων ὁ σολοικισμός A.D.Synt.198.7. **-ιστί**, Adv. *in barbarous fashion*, Plu.2.336c. II. *in barbarian* or *foreign language*, κεκράξονται β. Ar.Fr.79; ἀξύνετα βαρβαριστὶ παρακαλούντων App.Mith.50, cf. A.D.Adv.162.5.

βαρβᾰρό-γλωσσος, ον, = βαρβαρόφωνος, Sch.Lyc.276. **-κτόνος**, ον, *slaughtering barbarians*, Thom.Mag.p.141 R.

βάρβᾰρος, ον, *barbarous*, i.e. *non-Greek, foreign*, not in Hom. (but cf. βαρβαρόφωνος); β. ψυχαί Heraclit.107; esp. as Subst. βάρβαροι, οἱ, originally *all non-Greek-speaking peoples*, then specially of the Medes and Persians, A.Pers.255, Hdt.1.58, etc.: generally, opp. Ἕλληνες, Pl.Plt.262d, cf. Th.1.3, Arist.Pol.1252b5, Str.14.2.28; βαρβάρων Ἕλληνας ἄρχειν εἰκός E.IA1400; β. καὶ δοῦλον ταὐτὸ φύσει Arist.Pol.1252b9; οἱ β. δουλικώτεροι τὰ ἤθη φύσει τῶν Ἑλλήνων ib.1285a20; β. πόλεμον war *with the barbarians*, Th.2.36 codd.; ἡ βάρβαρος (sc. γῆ), opp. αἱ Ἑλληνίδες πόλεις, Th.2.97, cf. A.Pers.187, X.An.5.5.16. Adv. -ρως, opp. Ἑλληνικῶς, Porph.Abst.3.3. 2. esp. of language, φωνὴ β. A.Ag.1051, Pl.Prt.341c; γλῶσσα β. S.Aj.1263, cf. Hdt.2.57, Str. l.c. supr., etc.; συγγραφαί Hippias 6 D.; of birds, Ar.Av.199. Adv., βαρβάρως ὠνόμασται have *foreign* names, Str.10.3.17. 3. Gramm., of *bad Greek*, Gell.5.20.5; τὸ β., of style, opp. Ἑλληνικόν, S.E.M.1.64. II. after the Persian war, *brutal, rude*, ἀμαθὴς καὶ β. Ar.Nu.492; τὸ τῆς φύσεως β. καὶ θεοῖς ἐχθρόν D.21.150; σκαιὸς καὶ β. τὸν τρόπον Id.26.17; β. ἀνηλεής τε Men.Epit.477: Comp. -ώτερος X.Eph.2.4: Sup., πάντων βαρβαρώτατος θεῶν Ar.Av.1573, cf. Th.8.98, X.An.5.4.34. III. used by Jews of *Greeks*, Lxx 2Ma.2.21. IV. name for various *plasters*, Androm. and Heras ap.Gal.13.555. (Onomatopœic acc. to Str.14.2.28.)

βαρβᾰρο-στομία, ἡ, (στόμα) *barbarous way of speaking*, Str.14.2.28. **-της**, ητος, ἡ, *nature* or *conduct of a* βάρβαρος, Tz.H.9.972, Sch.E.Hec.1129. **-φωνέω**, *speak Greek barbarously*, Str.14.2.28. **-φωνος**, ον, *speaking a foreign tongue*, Κᾶρες Il.2.867; of the Persians, Orac.ap.Hdt.8.20, 9.43. II. *speaking bad Greek*, Str.14.2.28.

βαρβᾰρ-όω, *make barbarous*: only used in Pass., *to become barbarous*, E.Or.485, Antipho Soph.Oxy.1364.274; οἱ βαρβαρωθέντες τόποι PLond.5.1674.22 (vi A.D.); κακῷ κλάζοντας οἴστρῳ καὶ βεβαρβαρωμένῳ *unintelligible*, of birds, S.Ant.1002. **-ώδης**, ες, *barbaric*, Sch.Ar.Pax752: Comp., Tz.H.4.601.

βάρβῑλος, ἡ, *seedling peach-tree*, Gp.10.13.5 (v.l. βράβιλος).

βαρβῐτ-ίζω, *play on the barbiton*, Ar.Fr.752. **-ιστής**, οῦ, ὁ, *player on the barbiton*, name of play by Magnes, Sch.Ar.Eq.519. **-ος**, ἡ or ὁ, *musical instrument of many strings* (πολύχορδος Theoc.16.45), invented by Terpander, Pi.Fr.125; freq. used for *the lyre*, Anacr.143, B.Scol.Oxy.1361.1.1, E.Cyc.40, Ar.Th.137, etc.: fem. in Anacreont.23.3, but masc. in 14.34: in earlier Poets the gender is not determined:—later **βάρβῐτον**, τό, as in Latin, Neanth.5, D.H.7.72, Ath.4.175e, etc. (Prob. a foreign word, Str.10.3.17.) **-ῳδός**, όν, *singing to the barbiton*, Luc.Lex.14.

βαρβός, ὁ, = μύστρον, Ar.Fr.341.

βαρδῆν· τὸ βιάζεσθαι γυναῖκας (Ambrac.), Hsch.; cf. **βαρδίσαγνος**· ὁ τὰς γυναῖκας βιαζόμενος, Suid., Zonar.

βάρδιστος, η, ον, poet. for βράδιστος, Sup. of βραδύς, Il.23.310, Theoc.15.104, Doroth.(?)ap.Heph.Astr.3.30: Comp. βαρδύτερος Theoc.29.30.

βάρδοι, οἱ, *poets of the Celts, bards*, Posidon.23, D.S.5.31, Str.4.4.4. II. βάρδος, ὁ, *sumpter animal*, BGU276.11 (iii A.D.).

βαρδύνω, = βραδύνω, Babr.110.4.

βαρέω, Aeol. **βορ-**, v. infr., fut. -ήσω Luc.DMort.10.4: pf. βεβάρηκα D.C.78.17:—Pass., v. infr.:—*weigh down, depress*, βαρήσει ταῦτα τὸ πορθμεῖον Luc. l.c. (censured, Id.Sol.7); τὴν τῆς δίκης ῥοπὴν β. Procop.Arc.14; ὅταν τὰ πράγματα βαρῇ τοὺς ἀντιδίκους Hermog.Inv.2.7; ἵνα μὴ τὴν πόλιν βαρῶμεν IG14.830.15 (Puteoli), cf. POxy.1159.2 (iii A.D.); τὸ ἔθνος ἐβάρει ταῖς εἰσφοραῖς J.BJ2.14.1, cf. D.C. l.c.:—Pass., κῆρ .. βόρηται Sapph.Supp.25.17; β. διά τινα Diog.Oen.64, cf. POxy.525.3 (ii A.D.); β. τῷ ἐκφορίῳ PGiss.6.7 (ii A.D.): c. acc., *to be indignant at*, αὐτῶν τὴν εὐγένειαν Hdn.8.8.1; οὓς βαροῦνται M.Ant.8.44. 2. *charge* an account, POxy.126.8 (vi A.D.). II. intr. in Ep. pf. part. βεβαρηώς *weighed down, heavy*, οἴνῳ βεβαρηότες Od.3.139, cf. 19.122:—later, pf. part. Pass. βεβαρημένος, μεθυσθεὶς τοῦ νέκταρος β. ηὗδεν Pl.Smp.203b; οἴνῳ β. Ph.1.373; τοὺς ὀφθαλμοὺς β. ὑπ' οἴνου ib.377; ὠδίνεσσιν Theoc.17.61; ὕπνῳ AP7.290 (Stat. Flacc.), Gp.13.1.8, Ev.Luc.9.32 (without ὕπνῳ Ev.Matt.26.43); β. τὰ πρόσωπα πένθει Plu.Aem.34; τὰ σώματα πλησμονῇ β. Id.Mar.19; γυνὴ πολλοῖς ἔτεσι β. PTeb.327.25 (ii A.D.); οἷον βεβαρημένος as though *pregnant*, Plot.3.8.8:—Pass., pres. βαρέεται Hp.Morb.4.49: aor. ἐβαρήθην Parth.9.8: pf. βεβάρηται Placit.3.12.2.

βάρηκες, *gums, cheeks*, or *particles of food adhering to the teeth*; also, = τολύπη, EM188.37.

βάρ-ημα [βᾰ], ατος, τό, *burden, load*, v.l. in D.H.10.16. **-ησις**, εως, ἡ, *pressure, oppression*, Iamb.*Protr.*21.κε′: pl., *SIG*888.141 (Thrace, iii A.D.).

βᾱρίβας [ῐ], ὁ, *one that goes in a boat*, S.*Fr.*517.

βαρίη, ἡ, = βάρος, τοῦ ἠέρος Aret.*SD*1.11 (sed leg. ἀπορίη).

βαρινακέδα· τὸν δούριον ἵππον, Hsch.

βαρῖνος, ὁ, v.l. for βάλαγρος (q.v.).

βάριον· πρόβατον and **βάριχοι**· ἄρνες (Lacon.), Hsch. (β for ϝ, cf. ἀρήν, ἄριχα.)

βᾶρις, ιδος (also -εως J.*AJ*14.16.2, cf.*Et.Gud.*, *AB*84), Ion. ιος, ἡ: acc. βᾶριν J.*AJ*10.11.7, Iamb.*Myst.*6.5; dat. βάρει J.*AJ*11.4.6: pl. βάρεις Lxx 2*Ch.*36.19, al., Ion. βάριες Hdt.2.41; gen. βαρέων Lxx*Ps.* 44(45).8; poet. dat. pl. βαρίδεσσι A.*Pers.*553 (lyr.):—*flat-bottomed boat*, used in Egypt, Id.*Supp.*874 (lyr.), Hdt.2.41, 96, 179, *PHib.*100. 13 (iii B.C.), Procop.*Aed.*1.6; βάρβαροι βάριδες E.*IA*297 (lyr.); of Odysseus' *raft*, Lyc.747. 2. later, *large house, tower*, Lxx *Ps.* 44(45).8, *Da.*8.2, al., J. ll. cc., Kalinka *Antike Denkmäler in Bulgarien* 142 (Apollonia, ii A.D.); λέγεται β. ἡ οἰκία, ὡς Ποσείδιππος, καὶ ἡ συνοικία ὡς Ἔφορος St.Byz. (Egyptian word.)

βαρισίκται· οἱ μὴ γεννῶντες, Hsch.

βαρίτης [ῑ], ου, ὁ, a *bird*, Dionys.*Av.*3.2.

βάριχοι, v. βάριον. **βαρκάζω**· βαρβαρίζω, *EM*188.43. **βάρκαλις**, v. βώκκαλις. **βαρκίων**, name of an *Egyptian plant*, Hsch. **βαρμίγκαλλος**· ὑπέρκαλλος, Id.

βάρμος, ὁ, = βάρβιτος, Alc.*Supp.*23.4, Phillis ap.Ath.14.636c:—also **βάρωμος**, Euph.*Fr.Hist.*8.

βάρνακα· ἄγρια λάχανα δύσπλυτα, *EM*291.46 (cf. βράκανα).

βάρνᾰμαι, = μάρναμαι, *IG*1².943, 9(1).868 (Corc.).

βάρος [ᾰ], ους, Ion. εος, τό, *weight*, Hdt.2.73, etc. **II.** *a weight, burden, load*, τέκνων A.*Ch.*1000, etc.; β. περισσὸν γῆς S.*Fr.*945: pl., βάρη *weights*, Arist.*Mech.*850ᵃ30. **III.** *oppressiveness*, τὸ τῆς ὀσμῆς ἀφόρητον β. Lxx 2*Ma.*9.10; βάρος φέρειν to give *trouble*, τινί *POxy.*1062.14 (ii A.D.). **IV.** *heaviness, torpor*, β. ναρκῶδες Plu. 2.345b; σπληνὸς βάρεα Hp.*Acut.*(*Sp.*)4; βάρη καὶ δυσαρεστήματα perh. *feeling of oppression*, Antyll.ap.Stob.4.37.15. **V.** metaph., *heavy weight*, σιγῆς β. S.*Ant.*1256; βάρος πημονῆς, συμφορᾶς, Id.*El.* 939, *Tr.*325; χρὴ τοῦ βάρους μεταδιδόναι τοῖς φίλοις X.*Mem.*2.7.1; ὥσπερ βάρους μεταλαμβάνειν Arist.*EN*1171ᵃ31; τὰ β. ὅσα ψυχὴν καθέλκοι Ph.2.674: hence alone, *grief, misery*, A.*Pers.*946 (lyr., pl.), S. *OC*409; κεφαλῆς πόνος καὶ β. Arist.*HA*603ᵇ8; τὸ β. ἔχειν Id.*EN* 1126ᵃ23; ἐν συνοχαῖς καὶ βάρεσι Vett.Val.292.6; of *oppressive* demands, β. τῶν ἐπιταγμάτων, τῶν φόρων, Plb.1.31.5, 1.67.1; τῆς λειτουργίας *BGU*159.5 (iii A.D.); οὐκέτι δυνάμεθα φέρειν τὰ β. *SIG*888. 67 (Thrace, iii A.D.); κουφίσαι τὰ β. *PGiss.*7.13 (ii A.D.). **VI.** in good sense, *abundance*, πλούτου, ὄλβου, E.*El.*1287, *IT*416; αἰώνιον β. δόξης 2*Ep.Cor.*4.17; *strength*, στρατοπέδων Plb.1.16.4; β. τῆς ὑλακῆς *violence* of.., Alciphr.3.18. **VII.** *weight, influence*, Plb.4.32.7, D.S.19.70, Plu.*Per.*37, etc.; *gravity, dignity* of character, Id.2.522e; opp. χάρις, Id.*Demetr.*2. **VIII.** Gramm., *stress* of accent, A.D. *Synt.*98.1. **IX.** in Music, = βαρύτης, *low pitch*, Aristid.Quint.1.11.

βᾶρος, ὁ, or **βᾶρον**, τό, a kind of *spice*, Mnesim.4.62.

βᾰρουλκός (sc. μηχανή), ἡ, *lifting-screw*, invented by Archimedes, Papp.1060, al., prob. in Vitr.10.1.1.

βάρπυργος· πορμεῖο περὶ ἀμφωδῶν, Hsch. **βαρραχεῖν**· ἠχεῖν, σκιρτᾶν, Id. **βαρρεῖ**· ἀπολεῖ, Id.

βαρύ, τό, *perfume* used in incense, *AB*225.

βᾰρῠ-ᾱής, ές, *breathing hard*, ὕπνος Opp.*C.*3.421. **II.** *strong-smelling*, Nic.*Th.*43. **-αλγής**, ές, *grievously suffering*, Orph.*H.* 69.7. **II.** = sq., νοῦσος *Epigr.Gr.*228 (Ephesus), 803 (Delos). **-άλγητος**, ον, *very grievous*, neut. pl., -άλγητα καγχάζειν S.*Aj.*199 (lyr.). **-αρον**· ἰσχυρόν, στερέμνιον, Hsch. **-ᾱχής**, ές, Dor. for βαρυηχής, ταῦροι *bellowing*, B.15.18; Ὠκεανός, βρονταί, Ar.*Nu.*278, *Av.* 1750; μέλισσαι *Lyr.Alex.Adesp.*7.15. **II.** *awakening sore lament*, S.*OC*1561, Sch. (al. βαρυαχεῖ). **-αχθής**, ές, *very heavy*, τὸ κατὰ γαστρὸς β. Sor.1.55; *very burdensome*, Nonn.*D.*40.155. **-βάμων** [ᾱμ], ον, gen. ονος, *slowly moving*, φλόξ Man.4.318. **-βόας**, ου, ὁ, *heavy-sounding*, πορθμὸς Ἀχέροντος Pi.*Fr.*143.2. **-βρεμέτης**, ου, ὁ, *loud-thundering*, Ζεύς S.*Ant.*1117:—also **-βρομήτης** πέτρος prob. in *AP*7.394 (Phil.):—fem. **-βρεμέτειρα** Orph.*H.*10. 25. **-βρομος**, ον, *loud-roaring*, βαρύβρομα θωύσσοντες Hom.*Fr.* 25; πέλαγος B.16.76; Trag. only in lyr., βρονταί, κῦμα, E.*Ph.*183, *Hel.*1305; ἀκταί Id.*Hyps.Fr.*41.80; *loud-sounding*, αὐλός, τύμπανα, Id. *Hel.*1351, *Ba.*156, cf. Ar.*Nu.*313; β. ἁρμονία Αἰολίς Lasus 1. **-βρώς**, ὁ, ἡ, gen. βρῶτος, *gnawing, corroding*, στόνος S.*Ph.*695 (lyr.). **-γδουπος**, ον, *loud-thundering, loud-roaring*, Ζεύς Pi.*O.*8.44; ἄνεμοι Id. *P.*4.210, cf. *AP*9.674; ἔρωτες Ion Lyr.9.3. **-γέτας**· ἀλαζών, *EM*206.23, cf. Hsch. **-γλωσσος**, ον, *grievous of tongue*, v.l. for βαθυ-, Lxx *Ez.*3.5. **-γουνος**, ον, *heavy-kneed, lazy*, Call.*Del.* 78, Coluth.121:—also **-γούνατος** Theoc.18.10. **-γυιος**, ον, *weighing down the limbs, wearisome*, κέλευθα Opp.*H.*5.63; νοῦσος *AP*6.190.9 (Gaet.). **-δαιμονέω**, *to be grievously unlucky*, Ar.*Eq.* 558. **-δαιμονία**, ἡ, *grievous ill-luck*, Antipho 2.2.2. **II.** *surliness, churlishness*, Lys.4.9, Ph.1.487, 558. **-δαίμων**, ον, gen. ονος, *pressed by a heavy fate, luckless*, πόλις Alc.37 A, cf. E.*Alc.*865, Ar.*Ec.* 1102, *Cat.Cod.Astr.*2.162.30. **-δάκρυος**, ον, = sq., Nonn.*D.*40. 194. **-δακρυς**, υ, *weeping grievously*, ἀηδών *AP*9.262 (Phil.).

βαρυδάνιν, βαρύδαν (leg. βαρίβαν ἢ βαριβάν)· τὸν ναυσιβάτην, Hsch.

βαρύ-δεσμος [ῠ], ον, *loaded with chains*, Nonn.*D.*25.140, al. **-δῐκος**, ον, *taking heavy vengeance*, ποινά A.*Ch.*936.

βᾰρύδιον, Dim. of βάρος, *small weight*, f.l. for βαρύλλιον, Hero *Spir.*2.4.

βᾰρῠ-δότειρα, ἡ, *giver of ill gifts*, Μοῖρα A.*Th.*977. **-δουπος**, ον, = βαρύγδουπος (q.v.), Mosch.2.120; θρῆνος *Epigr.Gr.*344.13. **-δρόμου**· μεγαλοφώνου, Hsch. (fort. βαρυβρ-). **-εγκέφᾰλος**, ὁ, *heavy-headed*, Epicur.*Fr.*237. **-εργέω**, *plough deep*, *Gp.*2.23.14 (Pass.). **-εργής**, ές, *strongly influenced*, ἐς τὰ τοιαῦτα App.*BC*1.83.

βαρύες· δένδρα, Hsch.

βᾰρύ-ζηλος, ον, *exceeding jealous* or *envious*, Lyc.57; Ἔρως *AP* 5.242 (Maced.). **-ηκοέω**, *to be hard of hearing*, Hp.*Morb.*2. 4. **-ηκοΐα**, ἡ, *hardness of hearing*, Id.*Aph.*3.17. **-ήκοος**, ον, (ἀκούω) *hard of hearing*, Aret.*SD*1.4, Poll.2.81. **II.** Act., *impairing the hearing*, νόσοι Hp.*Aph.*3.5, cf. Ph.2.99, S.E.*M.*6.49. **-ηχής**, ές, *deep-voiced*, ταῖς φωναῖς D.S.5.31, cf. Opp.*H.*4.317; *deep-roaring*, θάλασσα Orph.*Fr.*168.28; θόρυβος Lxx 3*Ma.*5.48. **-ηχος**, ον, = foreg., *AB*225: Sup. -ηχότατος Agath.5.8. **-θροος**, ον, *deep-* or *loud-sounding*, Mosch.2.123. **-θῡμέω**, *to be weighed down*: *to be melancholy* or *indignant*, Lxx*Nu.*15.16, App.*BC*2.20; ἐπί τινι D.S. 20.41:—Med., Plu.*Sull.*6. **-θῡμία**, ἡ, *sullenness*, Arist.*VV*1251ᵃ 4, Andronic.Rhod.p.570 M.; *heaviness of heart, depression*, J.*AJ*16. 10.5, Plu.*Mar.*40: pl., Id.2.477e. **-θῡμος**, ον, *heavy in spirit*: *indignant, sullen*, ὀργή E.*Med.*176, cf. Call.*Cer.*81, etc.; opp. ὀξύθυμος, Plu.2.13e: Sup., Phld.*Ir.*p.64 W. Adv. -μως, ἔχειν Alciphr. 2.3; rejected by Poll.3.99.

βᾰρύθω [ῡ], *to be weighed down*, βαρύθει δέ μοι ὦμος ὑπ' αὐτοῦ [τοῦ ἕλκεος] Il.16.519; βαρύθει δέ θ' ὑπ' αὐτῆς (sc. ὕβρεως) Hes.*Op.*215; καμάτῳ A.R.2.47; ὑπὸ κύματος Nic.*Th.*135. 2. abs., *to be heavy*, στάλα *AP*7.481 (Philet.); βαρύθεσκε.. γυῖα A.R.1.43:—Pass., Max. 212, Q.S.13.6.

βαρύκα· αἰδοῖον (Tarent.), Hsch. **βαρύκαν**· σφῦραν, Id.

βᾰρῠ-κάρδιος, ον, *heavy, slow of heart*, Lxx*Ps.*4.2. **-καρπέω**, *bear a heavy crop of fruit*, *Aegyptus* 5.129 (ii B.C.). **-κέφᾰλος**, ον, *large-* or *heavy-headed*, of dogs, Arr.*Cyn.*4.4. **II.** metaph., *top-heavy*, Vitr.3.3.5. **-κομπος**, ον, *loud-roaring*, λέοντες Pi.*P.* 5.57. **-κοτος**, ον, *heavy in wrath*, A.*Eu.*780 (lyr.). **-κτῠπος**, ον, *heavy-sounding, loud-thundering*, epith. of Zeus, *h.Cer.*3, Hes. *Op.*79; of Poseidon, Id.*Th.*818, Pi.*O.*1.72, *Pae.*4.41; also of the sea, *AP*9.753 (Claudian). **-λαῖλαψ**, ᾰπος, ὁ, ἡ, *loud-storming*, αὖραι ib.247 (Phil.).

βᾰρύλλιον, τό, Dim. of βάρος: *instrument to find the weight of liquids*, Hero *Spir.*1.39, al.

βᾰρύ-λογος [ῠ], ον, *vented in bitter words*, ἔχθεα Pi.*P.*2.55; *offensive*, of certain Stoic tenets, Phld.*Sto.Herc.*339.12. **-λῡπος**, ον, *very sad*, Plu.2.114f (Sup.). **-μαστος**, ον, *with large, heavy breasts*, Str.17.3.4. **-μελής**, ές, (μέλος) *with heavy limbs*, Sch.Opp.*H.* 1.360. **-μηνιάω**, *to be exceedingly wrathful*, Hld.1.15. **-μήνιος**, ον, Dor. **-μάνιος**, = sq., ἥρως Theoc.15.138. **-μηνις**, ι, *heavy in wrath, exceeding wrathful*, δαίμων A.*Ag.*1482; ἡ β. Κλωθώ *IG*14.1466; of persons, Ph.2.94, al., Hld.7.20: βαρύμηνι, τό, Ph.2.108. **-μηνος**, ον, = foreg., πρόσωπα Doroth.(?)ap.Heph.Astr.3.4. **-μισθος**, ον, *largely paid, grasping*, *AP*5.1. **-μοχθος**, ον, *toilsome*, γραμματική *AP*10.97 (Pall.); *painful*, οἶστρος Nonn.*D.*42.170. **II.** *hard-working*, κύων ib.5.469; epith. of Heracles, *APl.*4.102.

βᾰρῠμωροκάρδιος, ον, *stubborn and foolish*, Sm.*Pr.*14.14.

βάρυν-σις [ᾰ], εως, ἡ, *oppression, annoyance*, Artem.1.17. **II.** *weighing down*, Plot.4.3.15. **-τέον**, *one must mark with the grave accent*, Sch.Il.14.264. **II.** *one must bear hardly*, D.Chr.7. 115. **-τικός**, ή, όν, *weighing down*, Arist.*Cael.*310ᵃ32. **II.** *retracting the accent*, Αἰολεῖς *EM*548.19, *AB*663. **-ω**, Pi.*P.*1. 84, Pl.*Phdr.*247b: impf., Od.5.321: fut. -ῠνῶ X.*Ap.*9: aor. ἐβάρῡνα Plu.2.127c, etc.:—**Pass.**, pres., Il.19.165, etc.: fut. βαρυνθήσομαι S.*Fr.*697, Plb.5.94.9, Lxx *Si.*3.26: aor. ἐβαρύνθην Il.20.480, etc.: pf. βεβάρυμμαι Hp.*Ep.*17, Arist.*Phgn.* (v. infr.), Lxx *Na.*2.9 (10): (βαρύς):—*weigh down, oppress, depress*, εἵματα γὰρ β' ἐβάρυνε Od.5.321; βάρυνε δέ μιν δόρυ μακρὸν ἑλκόμενον Il.5.664, etc.; ἤν σε βαρύνῃ δίψος Epigr.ap.Sotion.p.39 W.:—Pass., λάθρῃ γυῖα βαρύνεται *he is heavy*, i.e. *weary*, in limb, Il.19.165; χεῖρα βαρυνθεὶς *disabled* in hand, 20.480; βεβαρύνθαι *to be oppressed* by surfeit, etc., Arist.*Phgn.*810ᵇ22, cf. *HA*582ᵇ8, Ph.1.38; ὑπὸ κόπου D.H.1.39; βαρύνεσθαι τὴν γαστέρα *to be pregnant*, Luc.*Merc.Cond.*34, cf. X.*Mem.* 2.2.5; τόκοις E.*IT*1228; β. alone, Nonn.*D.*26.270; βαρύνεταί τινι τὸ σκέλος Ar.*Ach.*220, cf. Pl.*Phd.*117e; ὄμμα β., of one dying, E. *Alc.*385; βαρυνόμεν' ἔνθα καὶ ἔνθα ἐκ παθέων Timo 9; also ὁ αὐταῖς ἐβαρύνθη *weighed upon* them, Plot.4.3.15. 2. metaph., *oppress, weary*, ἀστῶν ἀκοὰ κρύφιον θυμὸν β. Pi.*P.*1.84; τοὺς δικαστὰς X.*Ap.*9; of cold, Arist.*Somn.Vig.*456ᵇ26; *make more grievous*, ἀνίαν Ph.2.425:—Pass., *to be oppressed, distressed*, Simon.184.5, Pi.*N.*7.43, S.*El.*820, Th.8.1; πήμασιν *by* calamities, A.*Ag.*836, cf. 189 (lyr.); χόλῳ S.*Aj.* 41; κακῇ ὀσμῇ Id.*Ph.*890; ὀσμῆς Id.*Fr.*697; ξυντυχίᾳ Cratin.166; διά τι Th.5.7; ὑπό τινων Nic.Dam.p.38 D.; ἐβαρύνθη ἡ καρδία *was made stubborn, was hardened*, Lxx*Ex.*8.15(11), al.; also c. acc., τὰ λυπηρὰ τῆς τύχης D.H.4.14; γῆρας J.*BJ*1.32.2, cf. Plu.*Cor.*31, D.Chr.43.6; τινά Id.40.1, Plu.*Thes.*32, *POxy.*298.26 (i A.D.); τὸν πλοῦτον *to be overloaded with*, Eun.*Hist.*p.248 D. **II.** *mark with the grave accent*, Hdn.Gr.1.18, A.D.*Synt.*120.4, Ath.2.52f.—βαρύνω I is replaced by βαρέω in later Greek.

βᾰρύ-νωτος [ῠ], ον, *with heavy back*, κόγχαι Emp.76. **-οδμία**, ἡ, *oppressiveness of smell*, Aret.*SA*1.5. **-οδμος**, ον, *of oppressive smell*, Nic.*Th.*51, cf. Aret.*CA*1.6. **-οζος**, ον, (ὄζω) = foreg., Dsc.5.

106. **-ολκός**, = βαρουλκός, ἡ β. Tz.*H.*2.155. **-όπᾶς**, ὁ, (ὄψ) *loud-voiced*, of Zeus, in acc. -ᾶν, Pi.*P.*6.24. **-όργητος**, ον, *exceeding angry*, Πιερίδες *AP*5.106 (Phld.). **-οσμος**, ον, = βαρύοδμος, Arist.*Mir.* 831b24, Sor.2.29: Comp., Dsc.3.121. II. metaph., 'in bad odour', *PSI*2.158.25. **-πᾰθέω**, *to be much annoyed*, Plu.2.167f (v.l.). **-πάλᾰμος** [πᾰ], ον, *heavy-handed*, χόλος Pi.*P.*11.23. **-πένθεια**, ἡ, *heavy, deep affliction*, Plu.2.118b. **-πενθής**, ές, = sq., Ph.2.269, *IG*12(5).675.6 (Syros), Orph.*Fr.*32c:—a fem. form **-πενθάς** *Epigr. Gr.*367 (Cotiaeum). II. *causing grievous woe*, μάχαι B.13.12; τόξα *APl.*4.134 (Mel.). **-πένθητος**, ον, *mourning heavily*, *AP*7.743 (Antip.). **-πεσής**, ές, *heavy-falling*, πούς A.*Eu.*369 (lyr.). **-πήμων**, Dor. **-πάμων**, ον, gen. ονος, *miserable*, *Hymn.Is.*44, Suid. **-πλουτος**, ον, *very wealthy*, Nic.Dam.p.144 D. **-πνείων**, οντος, *blowing fiercely*, ἀῆται Musae.216, 309. **-πνοια**, ἡ, *laboured breathing*, Sor.2.26. **-πνοος**, ον, = βαρυαής II, Nic.*Th.*76, *Al.*338. **-ποτμος**, ον, = βαρυδαίμων, of persons, S.*Ph.*1096 (lyr.); of sufferings, *grievous*, Id.*OC*1449 (lyr.): Comp. -ότερος Plu2.989e: Sup. -ότατος Id.*TG*5, Ph.1.637; but ξυμφορᾶς βαρυποτμωτάτας (metri gr.) E.*Ph.* 1345 (lyr.). **-πους**, ὁ, ἡ, πουν, τό, gen. ποδος, of a club, *heavy at the end*, *APl.*4.104 (Phil.). **-πρεπής**, ές, = μεγαλοπρεπής, εὐωχία Anon.ap.Suid. **-πυκνος**, ον, *in the lower part of the* πυκνόν (q.v.), φθόγγοι Aristid.Quint.3.10, Cleonid.*Harm.*4, etc. **-ρρήμων**, ον, gen. ονος, *using heavy words*, Sch.Ar.*Ra.*863.

βᾰρύς, εῖα, ύ, poet. gen. pl. fem. βαρεᾶν dub. in A.*Eu.*932 (anap.): Comp. βαρύτερος, Sup. βαρύτατος:—*heavy in weight*, β. ἀείρεσθαι, opp. κοῦφος, Hdt.4.150, cf. Pl.*Tht.*152d, Arist.*Cael.*310b25, etc.: in Hom. mostly with collat. notion of *strength and force*, χεῖρα βαρεῖαν Il.1.219, cf. 89; ἀκμᾷ βαρύς Pi.*I.*4(3).51; β. τὸ σῶμα App.*Mac.*14; of athletes, Philostr.*Gym.*31; ὀφρύς *bushy*, ib.48; but also, *heavy with age, infirmity* or *suffering*, νόσῳ S.*Tr.*235; σὺν γήρᾳ Id.*OT*17; ἐν γήρᾳ Id. *Aj.*1017; ὑπὸ γήρως Ael.*VH*9.1; ὑπὸ τῆς μέθης Plu.2.596a; *pregnant*, *PGoodsp.Cair.*15.15 (iv A.D.); β. βάσις *heavy, slow*, S.*Tr.*966; τυπάδι βαρείᾳ Id.*Fr.*844. Adv. κοῦφον βαρέως Pl.*Tht.*189d. 2. *heavy to bear, grievous*, ἄτη, ἔρις, κακότης, Il.2.111, 20.55, 10.72; Κλῶθες Od.7.197; κῆρες Il.21.548; β. κὴρ τὸ μὴ πιθέσθαι A.*Ag.*206 (lyr.); βαρὺ or βαρέα στενάχειν *sob heavily*, Od.8.95,534, Il.8.334, etc.: in Trag. and Prose, *burdensome, grievous, oppressive*, β. ξυμφορά, τύχαι, καταλλαγαί, etc., A.*Pers.*1044 (lyr.), *Th.*332 (lyr.), 767 (lyr.), etc.; ἡδονή S.*OC*1204; ἀγγελία β. ἦν ἐν τοῖς βαρύτατ' ἂν ἐνέγκαιμι Pl.*Cri.*43c; πόλεμος D.18.241; βαρὺ κοὐχὶ δίκαιον Id.21.66; νόσος *causing disgust*, S.*Ph.*1330; αὐδά, ἠχώ, ib.208 (lyr.), E.*Hipp.*791; *unwholesome*, χωρίον X.*Mem.*3.6.12; πλησμονή Id.*Cyn.*7.4; *indigestible*, Ath.3.115e; β. νότος Paus.10.17.11. Adv. -έως, φέρειν τι *take a thing ill, suffer it impatiently*, Hdt.5.19; β. φέρειν ἐπί τινι Plb.15.1.1 (but β. φέρειν *bear with dignity*, D.S.26.3); β. ἔχειν, c. part., Arist.*Rh.Al.* 1424b5; πρός τι Id.*Pol.*1311b9; τοῖς λογίοις Arg.E.*Heracl.*: Comp. βαρυτέρως τινὶ ἐναντιωθῆναι Lxx 3*Ma.*3.1; βαρέως ἀκούειν *hear with disgust*, X.*An.*2.1.9. 3. *violent*, ὀργή S.*Ph.*368; μῆνις Id.*OC*1328; ἀπέχθειαι Pl.*Ap.*23a (Sup.); θυμός Theoc.1.96. 4. *weighty, grave*, ἐπιστολαί 2*Ep.Cor.*10.10; αἰτιώματα *Act.Ap.*25.7; τὰ βαρύτερα τοῦ νόμου *Ev.Matt.*23.23; *ample*, βαρυτάτην εὐδαιμονίαν τοῖς ἀρχομένοις παρέχειν Hdn.2.14.3. II. of persons, *severe, stern*, β. ἐπιτιμητής A. *Pr.*77; εὔθυνος Id.*Pers.*828, cf. S.*OT*546; Κύπρι βαρεῖα Theoc.1.100; *wearisome, troublesome*, E.*Supp.*894, Pl.*Tht.*210c, etc.; ξύνοικος A. *Supp.*415, S.*Fr.*753; γείτονες Plb.1.10.6. 2. *overbearing*, σεμνότεροι ἢ βαρύτεροι Arist.*Rh.*1391a27 (but σεμνὸς καὶ β. Str.14.1.42); ὑπερήφανοι καὶ β. Plu.2.279c; *important, powerful*, πόλις Plb.1.17.5, etc. 3. of soldiers, *heavy-armed*, X.*Cyr.*5.3.37 (s.v.l.); of the ὁπλίτης Pl.*Lg.*833b (Comp.); τὰ β. τῶν ὅπλων Plb.1.76.3. 4. *difficult*, ὅρκος γὰρ οὐδεὶς ἀνδρὶ φηλήτῃ β. S.*Fr.*933. III. of impressions on the senses, 1. of sound, *strong, deep, bass*, opp. to ὀξύς, Od.9.257, S.*Ph.*208, Pl.*Prt.*332c, Arist.*EN*1125a14, etc.; βαρὺ ἀμβόασον A.*Pers.* 572 (lyr.); φθέγγονται βαρύτατον ἀνθρώπων Hp.*Aër.*15; βαρύτατα ὑπακούειν, of diseases, Id.*Prorrh.*2.39; πενθεῖν Ael.*VH*12.1; esp. of musical pitch, *low*, opp. ὀξύς, βαρυτάτη χορδή Pl.*Phdr.*268e; ἆχος, φωνά, Archyt.1, cf. Arist.*EE*1235a28, Aristox.*Harm.*p.3 M.; of accent, *grave*, ἀντὶ ὀξείας τῆς μέσης συλλαβῆς βαρεῖαν ἐφθεγξάμεθα Pl. *Cra.*399b; ὀξείᾳ καὶ βαρείᾳ καὶ μέσῃ φωνῇ Arist.*Rh.*1403b30, etc.: hence ἡ βαρεῖα (sc. προσῳδία) *accentus gravis*, D.T.630.1, etc.; β. τάσις D.H.*Comp.*11, A.D.*Synt.*307.13; β. τόνος D.T.674.13, cf. A.D.*Pron.* 36.5; β. συλλαβή *unaccented*, Id.*Synt.*100.8, al. Adv. βαρέως *with the accent thrown back*, Id.*Pron.*51.1, Ath.2.53b: Comp. -ύτερον, opp. ὀξύτερον (οὐ opp. οὔ), Arist.*SE*178a3 (but, *on a lower note*, αὐλεῖν Id.*GA* 788a22). 2. of smell, *strong, offensive*, Hdt.6.119. 3. Adv. βαρέως *slowly*, ἐπισπᾶσθαι Hero *Aut.*26.6. (g^ur̥r-u- from g^ur̥-u-, Skt. *gurús* 'heavy', Lat. *gravis* (from fem. g^urəwī-), Goth. *kaúrus* 'heavy'.)

βᾰρύ-σαρκος, ον, = βαθύσαρκος, *Hippiatr.*30 (s.v.l.). **-σίδηρος** [ῑ], ον, *heavy with iron*, Plu.*Aem.*18. **-σκελής**, ές, *heavy in the legs, slow*, *Trag.Adesp.*250. **-σκίπων** [ῐ], ον, gen. ωνος, *with a heavy club*, Call.*Fr.*120. **-σμάρᾰγος** [σμᾰ], ον, = βαρύκτυπος, Nonn.*D.*1.156. **-σπλαγχνος**, ον, *ill-tempered*, Ph.2. 269. **-σταθμέω**, *weigh heavy*, Ps.-Dsc.1.26. **-σταθμος**, ον, *weighing heavy*, Ar.*Ra.*1397, Canthar.2, Arist.*EN*1142a22; νόμισμα Plu.*Lys.*17. **-στένακτος**, ον, = βαρύστονος, Sch.Opp.*H.*5. 152. **-στενάχων** [νᾰ], ουσα, *sobbing heavily*, better written βαρὺ στ- divisim, Il.1.364, etc. **-στομος**, ον, *heavy in pronunciation*, of the first syllable of σκῆπτρον, Phld.*Po.*2.14 (dub.). 2. *of heavy*, i.e. *abusive, mouth*, Nonn.*D.*48.420. 3. of a weapon, *cutting deeply*, Opp.*H.*4.481. **-στονος**, ον, *groaning heavily*, τοῖς βαρυστόνοις ἐπικαλουμένοις .. ὑποκριταῖς nicknamed *the bellowers*, D.18.262, cf. Epicur.*Fr.*114, 237; *resounding*, λίθος *AP*9.246 (Marc. Arg.). Adv. -νως A.*Eu.*794. II. of things, *heavily lamented, grievous*, S.*OT* 1233, Orac.ap.Paus.10.9.11. **-σύμφορος**, ον, *weighed down by ill-luck*, in Sup. -ώτατος Hdt.1.45, App.*Mac.*19. Adv. -ώτατα D.C.78. 41. 2. Act., *calamitous*, πόλεμος Them.*Or.*15.184c (Sup.). **-σφάρᾰγος** [φᾰ], ον, = βαρυσμάραγος, *loud-thundering*, of Ζεύς, Pi.*I.*8(7). 23. **-σωμος**, ον, *heavy in body*, Sch.Pi.*N.*8.41. **-τάλαντος** [τᾰ], ον, = *weighing heavily*, Zonar. s.v. ὁλκός. **-ταρβής**, ές, *terrifying*, εἰκών A.*Fr.*57.11. **-τελής**, ές, *heavily taxed*, *PLond.*5.1674. 33 (vi A.D.).

βᾰρύτης [ῠ], ητος, ἡ, (βαρύς) *weight, heaviness*, νεῶν Th.7.62, cf. Plb.1.51.9; opp. κουφότης, Thphr.*HP*5.3.1; *heaviness* of limb, β. ναρκώδης Plu.2.978c; of digestion, ἀπεψία καὶ β. ib.128b. II. of men, *troublesomeness, importunity*, ἀηδίαι καὶ βαρύτητες Isoc.12.31; *disagreeableness*, D.18.35, Plu.*Cor.*30, al.; β. φρονήματος Id.*Cat.Mi.* 57. 2. *arrogance*, Arist.*Rh.*1391a28; *gravity*, τοῦ ἤθους Plu. *Fab.*1 codd. III. of sound, *depth, low pitch*, opp. ὀξύτης, Pl.*Prt.* 316a, Arist.*GA*778a19, *de An.*422b30, Aristox.*Harm.*p.3 M., D.H. *Comp.*11, etc.; *the grave accent*, opp. ὀξύτης, Arist.*Po.*1456b33; *absence of accent*, A.D.*Pron.*38.15, al. IV. Rhet., *adoption of an injured tone*, Aps.p.331 H.

βᾰρῠ-τῑμέω, *raise the price of goods*, *EM*759.5, Suid. s.v. τιμουλκέω. **-τῑμος**, ον, *punishing severely*, of the gods below, A.*Supp.* 24. II. *very costly*, Str.17.1.13, *Ev.Matt.*26.7. III. *selling dearly*, Hld.2.30 (s.v.l.). **-τλητος**, Dor. **-τλᾶτος**, ον, *bearing heavy weight*, dub. in Naumach.ap.Stob.4.22.32; *unfortunate*, Ἀττικὴ β. *AP*7.343. II. Pass., *ill to bear*, συμφορά B.13.4; ὀδύναι *APl.*4.245 (Leont.). **-τονέω**, *pronounce with the grave accent*, D.H.2.58: abs., *use the grave accent*, Cleonid.*Harm.*12. **-τόνησις**, εως, ἡ, *grave accentuation*, Eust.70.45. **-τονητέος**, α, ον, *to be marked with the grave accent*, Sch.Ar.*Ra.*864, al. **-τονος**, ον, (τόνος) *deep-sounding*, β. φωνεῖν, of dogs, Arist.*Phgn.*813b2; so prob. β. στῆθος X.*Cyn.*5. 30; *deep*, of musical notes, Bacch.*Harm.*32. 2. Gramm., of enclitics, *unaccented*, A.D.*Pron.*35.25; of words, *not oxytone*, ib.38. 12, D.T.674.18, etc. Adv. -νως *POxy.*1012 *Fr.*16.16, Eust.41.3, Moer.109. **-ϋπνος**, ον, *sleeping heavily*, Nonn.*D.*48.765. **-φθέγκτης**, ου, ὁ, = sq., λέων Pi.*Fr.*239. **-φθογγος**, ον, *loud-roaring*, λέων *h.Ven.*159, B.8.9; *deep-lowing*, of cows, Arist.*GA*787a33; β. νευρά *loud-twanging* bowstring, Pi.*I.*6(5).34; *deep-toned*, αὐλοί *AP*6. 51. **-φθονος**, ον, *heavy with envy*, χείρ *Epigr.Gr.*376a (Aezani), al. **-φλοισβος**, ον, *loud-roaring*, γενέθλη Procl.*H.*1.20. **-φορτος**, ον, *heavy-burdened*, i.e. *pregnant*, Nonn.*D.*48.769. **-φροσύνη**, ἡ, *melancholy*, Plu.2.710f (pl.), *Fr.inc.*146; *indignation*, Id.*Cor.*21, Porph.ap.Stob.1.49.60 (prob.). **-φρων**, ον, gen. ονος, (φρήν) *heavy of mind, melancholy, gloomy*, συντυχίαι *Lyr.Adesp.*140.8; Αἰήτης A.R.4.731; *savage*, ταῦρος Lyc.464; *cruel*, δαίμων Opp.*H.*4. 174. 2. *weighty of purpose, grave-minded*, Theoc.25.110. **-φωνέω**, *utter low-pitched sounds*, Arist.*Pr.*900b13. **-φωνία**, Ion. **-ίη**, ἡ, *deepness of voice, a bass voice*, Hp.*Aër.*8, Alex.311, Arist.*GA*786b 35. **-φωνος**, ον, *with a deep, bass voice*, opp. ὀξύφωνος, Hp.*Aër.* 6, Arist.*GA*786b7, etc. **-χειλος**, ον, *thick-lipped*, *APl.*2.20 (Ammian.). **-χείμων**, ον, gen. ωνος, *with heavy storms*, Theognost.*Can.* 460. **-χορδος**, ον, *deep-toned*, φθόγγος *AP*12.187 (Strat.). **-χρους**, ουν, *deep-coloured*, v.l. for βαθυ-, Dsc.5.94. **-ψῡχος**, ον, *heavy of soul, dejected*, S.*Aj.*319, *Cat.Cod.Astr.*7.198. **-ώδης**, ες, (ὄζω) = βαρύοδμος, Nic.*Th.*895. **-ώδῠνος**, ον, (ὀδύνη) *suffering grievous pangs*, Nonn.*D.*47.163. 2. *causing grievous pangs*, ib.48.808. **-ωπέω**, *to be dim-sighted*, Lxx *Ge.*48.10.

βασά· αἰσχύνη· ὃ ἐστι δρῦς, Hsch. **βασαγεῖ**· ἀλεσχοῖ, Id.

βασαγίκορος, = ὁ θᾶσσον συνουσιάζων, Hippon.107.

βᾰσᾰν-αστρᾰγάλη [γᾰ], Dor. -α, ἡ, *plague of the joints*, of the gout, in voc., Luc.*Trag.*199. **-εύω**, = -ίζω, Hsch. (Pass.). **-ηδόν**, Adv. *by means of torture*, Man.4.197. **-ίζω**, Att. fut. -ιῶ Ar.*Ra.* 802, 1121, *Ec.*748: aor. ἐβασάνισα, subj. βασανίσω v.l. in Id.*Ra.*618 cod.R:—**Pass.**, aor. ἐβασανίσθην: pf. βεβασάνισμαι:—*rub upon the touch-stone* (βάσανος), χρυσόν Pl.*Grg.*486d: hence, *put to the test, prove*, Arist.*GA*747a3 (Pass.), etc.; *investigate scientifically*, Hp.*Aër.*3; of the instances used in inductive inference, ἀπὸ τῶν πανταχόθεν βεβασανισμένων [μεταβαίνομεν] Phld.*Sign.*29. II. of persons, *examine closely, cross-question*, Hdt.1.116, 2.151, Ar.*Ach.*110, *Ra.*802, etc.; βεβασανισμένος εἰς δικαιοσύνην *having* his love of justice *put to the test*, Pl.*R.*361c, cf. 413e, *Smp.*184a; ὑπὸ δακρύων βασανίζεσθαι, i.e. *to be convicted* of being painted by tears (washing off the cosmetic), X.*Oec.*10.8. 2. *question by applying torture, torture, rack* (v. βάσανος III), Ar.*Ra.*616, 618; [δούλους] πάντας παραδίδωμι βασανίσαι Antipho 2.4.8, cf. 5.36:—Pass., *to be put to the torture*, Th.7.86, Lys.4. 14, Arist.*Rh.Al.*1443b31; αἰωνίοις ἀμοιβαῖς βασανισθησόμενοι πρὸς τῶν θεῶν Phld.*D.*1.19; *to be tortured* by disease (censured by Luc.*Sol.*6), *Ev.Matt.*8.6; ὑπὸ τῶν κυμάτων ib.14.24; of animals, Philostr.*VA* 1.38: metaph. of the earth, ib.6.10. 3. metaph. of style, *strain*, Longin.10.6; βεβασανισμένος *forced, unnatural*, D.H.*Th.*55. **-ισμός**, ὁ, *torture*: ὁ γὰρ Κορίνθιος (sc. οἶνος) β. ἐστι Alex.290, cf. *Apoc.*9. 5. **-ιστέος**, α, ον, *to be proved* or *tested under suffering*, Ar.*Lys.* 478, Pl.*R.*540a. II. βασανιστέον *one must put to the test, prove*, τινά ib.503d, Max.Tyr.24.4, Gal.17(1).337, Jul.*Or.*7.226a, Them. *Or.*23.287c; *one must put to the torture*, D.29.35. **-ιστήριον**, τό, *question-chamber*, Theopomp.Com.63, Polyaen.8.62, Phalar.*Ep.*82, 115; of the stocks, Sm.*Je.*20.2. II. in pl., *instruments of torture*,

Plu.2.315d, Charito 4.2, Them.*Or.*13.175c. **III.** *touchstone, test,* χρυσοῦ, πορφύρας ib.21.247b: metaph., ib.248a. **-ιστήριος,** ον, *of* or *for torture,* ὄργανα J.*BJ*2.8.10. **-ιστής,** οῦ, ὁ, *examiner, questioner, torturer,* Antipho 5.32, D.37.40, Plu.2.498d; *gaoler, Ev. Matt.*18.34. **II.** *one who tests,* Them.*Or.*21.247c:—fem. **-ίστρια,** *examiner,* ἐπῶν Ar.*Ra.*826. **-ιστικός,** ή, όν, *given to* or *for torturing,* Vett.Val.78.15, *AB*306, *EM*769.11. **2.** *for testing,* Them. *Or.*21.247c. **-ίτης** λίθος, = sq., Hsch. **-ος,** ἡ, *touchstone,* on which pure gold leaves a yellow streak, ἐς βάσανον δ' ἐλθὼν παρατρίβομαι ὥστε μολύβδῳ χρυσός Thgn.417; χρυσὸν τριβόμενον βασάνῳ Id.450, cf. 1105; παρατρίβεσθαι πρὸς τὰς β. Arist.*Col.*793^b1, cf. *HA* 597^b2: metaph., β. τοῦ ἀρώματος (sc. τοῦ κινναμώμου) τὴν αἶγα εἶναι Philostr.*VA*3.4. **II.** *the use of this as a test,* χρυσὸς ἐν β. πρέπει Pi.*P.*10.67: generally, *test, trial of genuineness,* οὐκ ἔστιν μείζων β. χρόνου [Simon.]175.1; δόμεν τι βασάνῳ ἐς ἔλεγχον Pi.*N.*8.20; σοφὸς ὤφθη βασάνῳ θ' ἁδύπολις S.*OT*510 (lyr.), cf. 494; βάσανον λαμβάνειν περί τινος Pl.*Lg.*648b; εἰς β. εἶ χερῶν wilt come to *a trial* of strength, S. *OC*835; πλοῦτος β. ἀνθρώπου τρόπων Antiph.232.5; [νόσου] ἔσχ' ἐπὶ σοὶ βάσανον had *experienced* it in you, i. e. you had had it first, *IG*14. 1320; βάσανον ὑποκείσονται will be subjected to *a test,* of candidates, *POxy.*58.25 (iii A.D.). **III.** *inquiry by torture,* ἐς πᾶσαν β. ἀπικνέεσθαι Hdt.8.110; εἰς β. αἰτεῖν Herod.2.88; ἐξετάσαι διὰ βασάνων *SIG*780.12 (Astypalaea, Aug.); esp. at Athens, used to extort evidence from slaves, εἰς β. δέχεσθαι Antipho 1.12; εἰς β. παραδοῦναι Is.8.17; ἐκ βασάνων εἰπεῖν ib.12: in pl., *confession upon torture,* D. 53.24, Hyp.*Fr.*5, Arist.*Rh.*1355^b37. **2.** *agony* of battle, ἡ κατὰ τὸ ἔργον β. S.E.*M.*6.24; *tortures* of disease, *Ev.Matt.*4.24; cf. ἐπάγρυπνος β. Vett.Val.211.28; also ψυχικαί Id.182.19; *torments* of hell, *Ev.Luc.*16.23. **3.** *trespass-offering,* Lxx 1*Ki.*6.17.—Oriental word.

βᾰσείδιον, τό, Dim. of βάσις, *BGU*781 iii 6 (i A.D.).

βασίαρξ, dub. in *BGU*630 i 22 (ii A.D.).

βᾰσίλ-εια [ῐ], ἡ, βασιλέα Pi.*N.*1.39: fem. of βασιλεύς:—*queen, princess,* Od.4.770, A.*Ag.*84 (lyr.), Hdt.1.11, etc.; of goddesses, Κύπρις β. Emp.128.3, cf. *Hymn.Is.*1, etc.; β. θεά Ar.*Pax* 974; β. γύναι A.*Pers.*623 (lyr.), E.*El.*988 (lyr.). **-εία,** Ion. **-ηΐη,** ἡ, *kingdom, dominion,* Hdt.1.11, etc.; παιδὸς ἡ β. Heraclit.52; *hereditary monarchy,* opp. τυραννίς, ἐπὶ ῥητοῖς γέρασι πατρικαὶ β. Th.1.13; βασιλείας εἴδη τέτταρα Arist.*Pol.*1285^b20; ἡ πρώτη πολιτεία μετὰ τὰς β. after *the age of monarchies,* ib.1297^b17: metaph., ἐποίησεν ἡμᾶς β. *Apoc.*1.6; β. τῶν οὐρανῶν *Ev.Matt.*3.2; τοῦ θεοῦ ib.6.33, etc. **2.** *kingly office,* β. καὶ στρατηγία Arist.*Pol.*1273^a37. **3.** at Athens, *the office of the archon* βασιλεύς, Paus.1.3.1. **4.** Pass., *being ruled by a king,* τῆς ὑπ' ἐκείνου βασιλείας Isoc.9.43. **II.** *diadem,* D.S.1.47, *OGI*90.43 (Rosetta). **III.** *reign,* ib.331.40 (Pergam.), D.S.17.1, *POxy.*1257.7 (iii A.D.); so αἱ β. *the reigns of the Kings,* title of book of *VT*; *accession to the throne, BGU*646.12 (ii A.D.). **IV.** concrete, *His Majesty,* Lxx 4*Ki.*11.1, 1*Ma.*6.47. **-ειάω,** Desid., *aim at royalty, Com.Adesp.*958, J.*BJ Praef.*2, 1.4.1. **-είδης,** ου, ὁ, *prince,* τῶν δέκα βασιλειδῶν Pl.*Criti.*116c. **-είδιον,** τό, Dim. of βασιλεύς, *tiny king,* Plu.*Ages.*2. **-ειον,** Ion. **-ήϊον,** τό, *kingly dwelling, palace,* X.*Cyr.*2.4.3, etc.; more common in pl., Hdt.1.30, 178, Arist.*Oec.*1352^a11, etc. **b.** *seat of empire, capital,* Plb.3.15.3, D.S.19.18, Str.1.2.25. **2.** *royal treasury,* Hdt.2.149: pl., Isoc. 3.31. **II.** *tiara, diadem,* Lxx 2*Ki.*1.10, Roussel *Cultes Égyptiens* 233 (Delos, ii B.C.), *OGI*90.45 (Rosetta), Plu.2.358d, Porph.ap.Eus. *PE*3.11, Horap.1.15: metaph., τὸ β. τῆς εὐπρεπείας *diadem* of beauty, Lxx *Wi.*5.16. **III.** = ἄλιμος, Ps.-Dsc.1.91; = λευκόϊον, Id.3. 123. **IV.** Βασίλεια, τά, *festival of Zeus Basileus,* in Boeotia, *IG*7. 552, Sch.Pi.*O.*7.153, *IG*12(1).78; at Olbia, *IPE*1.105. **-ειος,** ον, also α, ον A.*Pers.*589, $IG1^2$.115; Ion. and Aeol. **-ήϊος,** η, ον, also **-ῆος** Melinno ap.Stob.3.7.12, *Hymn.Is.*138:—*royal,* δεινὸν δὲ γένος βασιλήϊόν ἐστι κτείνειν Od.16.401; ὁ β. θρόνος Hdt.1.14, etc.; used by Trag. in lyr., β. οἶκοι, μέλαθρα, A.*Ag.*157, *Ch.*343; ἰσχύς, τιάρα, Id.*Pers.*589, 661; νόστος ὁ β. *the king's* return, ib.8; τοῖς β. νόμοις S.*Ant.*382; cf. πῆχυς. **2.** *of the archon* βασιλεύς, ἡ β. στοά $IG1^2$. 115, Arist.*Ath.*7.1, Paus.1.3.1 (also of the *basilica* of Herod at Jerusalem, J.*AJ*15.11.5). **3.** 'royal', i. e. *choice,* μύρον Sapph.*Supp.*23. 19, Crates Com.2; cf. βασίλεια· γένος ἰσχάδων, Hsch. **4.** Ἄρτεμις βασιληΐη, divinity in Thrace, Hdt.4.33.

βᾰσῐλ-εύς, ὁ, gen. έως, Ep. ῆος, Cypr. ῆϝος *Inscr.Cypr.*104, 135 H.: acc. βασιλέα, contr. -ῆ Orac.ap.Hdt.7.220, E.*Fr.*781.24 (lyr.): nom. pl. βασιλεῖς, Aeol. -ηες Sapph.*Supp.*6.4, *IG*12(2).6 (Mytil.), -ειες ib. 646*a*45, al., Ep. -ῆες, old Att. -ῆς S.*Aj.*188, 960 (both lyr.), cf. Hdn. Gr.1.430: acc. pl. βασιλέας $IG1^2$.115, later βασιλεῖς ib.2.243, etc.:—*king, chief,* Hom., etc.: freq. with collat. sense of *captain* or *judge,* Hes. *Op.*202; διοτρεφέες β. Il.2.445, etc.; θεῖοι Od.4.691, etc.; later, *hereditary king,* opp. τύραννος, Arist.*EN*1160^b3, etc.; but also of tyrants, as Hiero, Pi.*O.*1.23; of Gelo, Hdt.7.161; of Pisistratus, Eup.123, cf. Sch. Ar.*Ach.*61: joined with a Subst., βασιλεὺς ἀνήρ Il.3.170, etc.; ἀνὴρ β. Hdt.1.90; ἄναξ β. lord *king,* A.*Pers.*5, cf. B.17.1: c. gen., β. νεῶν A. *Ag.*114 (anap.); οἰωνῶν β., of the eagle, ibid., Pi.*O.*13.21: Comp. βασιλεύτερος *more kingly,* Il.9.160, 392, Od.15.533, Tyrt.12.7: Sup. βασιλεύτατος Il.9.69. **b.** of the gods, Ζεὺς θεῶν β. Hes.*Th.*886, cf. Pi.*O.*7.34, Emp.128.2, etc. (in this sense Hom. uses ἄναξ); as cult title of Zeus, *IG*7.3073.90 (Lebad.), *SIG*1014.110 (Erythrae), etc. (but Ζεὺς β., = Ahuramazda, X.*Cyr.*3.3.21, al., Arr.*An.*4.20.3); ὁ μέγας β., of *God,* Lxx *Ps.*47(48).2, Ph.2.107: Sup. βασιλεύτατοι τῶν θεῶν Max.Tyr.29.5. **2.** as a title of rank, *prince,* β. εἰσὶ καὶ ἄλλοι πολλοὶ ἐν.. Ἰθάκῃ Od.1.394, cf. 8.390, etc.; of Cyrus, X.*Oec.* 4.16. **b.** *descendant of a royal house,* esp. in Ionia, Arist.*Ath.* 41.3; βασιλέων οἶκοι 'estates *of the royal house*', name of a district in Chios, Ἀθηνᾶ 20.168. **3.** generally, *lord, master,* Il.18.556, Pi.*O.*6.47. **4.** metaph., πόλεμος πάντων β. Heraclit.53; νόμος ὁ πάντων β. Pi.*Fr.*169. **II.** at Athens, *the second of the nine Archons,* $IG1^2$.76, al., Antipho 6.38, Lys.6.4, Arist.*Pol.*1285^b17, *Ath.* 57, etc.; ἡ τοῦ β. στοά Pl.*Euthphr.*2a. **2.** title of magistrates in other Greek states, as βασιλᾶες at Elis, *GDI*1152, cf. *IG*12(2).6 (Mytil.), etc., Arist.*Pol.*1322^b29. **3.** at Rome, β. τῶν ἱερῶν, = *rex sacrorum,* D.H.5.1, cf. D.C.54.27. **III.** after the Persian war (without Art.), *the king of Persia,* Hdt.7.174, al.; ἄναξ Ξέρξης β. A.*Pers.*5, cf. 144, Ar.*Ach.*61, Th.8.48, $IG2^2$.141 (βασιλῆς βασιλέως ὕπογοι μεγάλου, of the Satraps, A.*Pers.*24, cf. 44, S.E.*M.*2.22); less freq. ὁ βασιλεύς Hdt.1.132, 137, Arist.*Pol.*1304^b13; β. ὁ μέγας Hdt. 1.188. **2.** of Alexander and his successors, usually with Art., $IG2^2$.641, 687, Men.293, 340 (pl.); Σέλευκος Antiph.187; Ἀντίγονος Alex.111; Πτολεμαῖος Id.244; Ὀσυμανδύας βασιλεὺς βασιλέων D.S. 1.47; title used by Parthian *kings,* Plu.*Pomp.*38, D.C.37.6, etc.; by Antony, Plu.*Ant.*54; of *God, Apoc.*17.14, 19.16. **3.** of the Roman *emperors, AP*10.25 (Antip. Thess.); β. Ῥωμαίων *BGU*588. 10 (i A.D.), etc., cf. 1*Ep.Ti.*2.2, J.*AJ*14.15.14; β. αὐτοκράτωρ *IG*3. 13 (Hadrian), Hdn.1.6.5; without Art., Paus.10.32.19. **IV.** of any *great man,* πένησί τε καὶ βασιλεῦσιν Ps.-Phoc.113. **2.** *first* or *most distinguished of any class,* Ἡρώδην τὸν β. τῶν λόγων Philostr. *VS*2.10.1, cf. Luc.*Rh.Pr.*11; *winner* at a game, Poll.9.106, Sch.Pl. *Tht.*146a; Stoic *sage,* μόνος β. Luc.*Herm.*16; βασιλέως ἐγκέφαλος 'morsel fit for a king', Clearch.5; β. σῦκα, name of a *choice* kind, Philem.Lex.ap.Ath.3.76f., cf. Poll.6.81. **V.** = συμποσίαρχος, Plu.2.622a, Luc.*Sat.*4. **VI.** *wren,* Arist.*HA*592^b27. **VII.** *queen-bee,* ib.623^b9, *GA*759^a20, etc. (The form βασιλέα is scanned ⏑ ⏑ – in Pi.*N.*1.39; codd. βασίλεια.) **-εύτός,** ή, όν, *suited for monarchical rule,* Arist.*Pol.*1288^a8. **-εύτωρ,** ορος, ὁ, = βασιλεύς, Antim.5. **-εύω,** *to be king, rule, reign,* οὐ μέν πως πάντες βασιλεύσομεν ἐνθάδ' Ἀχαιοί Il.2.203; ἶσον ἐμοὶ βασίλευε 9.616; ἐν ὑμῖν.. βασίλευε *was king* among you, Od.2.47; ὄφρ' Ἰθάκης κατὰ δῆμον.. βασιλεύοι 22.52; also of a woman, ἡ βασίλευεν ὑπὸ Πλάκῳ *reigned as queen,* Il.6.425; ἡ δὲ Πύλου βασίλευε Od.11.285: in aor., *to have become king,* Hdt.2.2: c. gen., *to be king of, rule over,* ἐν.. Ἰθάκῃ βασιλεύσει Ἀχαιῶν Od.1.401, etc.; βασιλεύοντος βασιλέων Ἀρσάκου *PAvrom.*1 *A* 1: c. dat., *to be king among,* Γιγάντεσσιν βασίλευεν Od. 7.59; later β. ἐπὶ τὰς δύο βασιλείας Lxx 1*Ma.*1.16:—Pass., *to be governed by a king,* Pl.*R.*576d,e, al., Arist.*Pol.*1284^b39, etc.: c. acc. cogn., βασιλείαν πασῶν δικαιοτάτην βασιλεύεσθαι Pl.*Lg.*680e: generally, *to be governed* or *administered,* Pi.*P.*4.106, etc.; ὑπὸ νόμου Lys. 2.19: hence, *submit to the king,* Plu.*Sull.*12. **b.** *to be* ἄρχων *β.* at Athens, Isoc.18.5, $IG1^2$.776, al.; of other magistrates, *SIG*709 (Chersonesus), 1054 (Samothrace). **c.** later ἡ βασιλεύουσα πόλις the *imperial* city, of Rome, Ath.3.98c, cf. *CPHerm.*125 ii 3. **2.** *enjoy as master,* τῷ χρυσῷ β. Theoc.21.60 codd. **3.** abs., *live royally,* β. ἐν πενίᾳ Plu.2.101d, cf. 1*Ep.Cor.*4.8. **II.** causal, *appoint as king,* τινά Lxx *Jd.*9.6; but β. τινὶ βασιλέα *make* them *a king,* ib.1*Ki.*8.22, 12.1. **-η,** ἡ, = βασίλειᾰ, *queen, princess,* S.*Fr.*310, cf. Hdn.Gr.1. 275. **2.** a divinity, worshipped with Neleus and Codrus at Athens, $IG1^2$.94, Pl.*Chrm.*153a. **-ηΐη, -ήϊος,** Ion. for βασιλεία, -λειος. **-ηΐς,** ΐδος, ἡ, pecul. fem. of βασίλειος, *royal,* τιμή Il.6.193, Hes.*Th.*462, E.*Hipp.*1280 (lyr.). **2.** = βασίλειᾰ, *a queen,* Man.1. 283, *Epigr.Gr.*989.3 (Memnon). **-ίζω,** *to be of the king's party,* Plu. *Flam.*16: also, c. acc., ἐγώ εἰμι ὁ βασιλίζων τὸν τόπον εἰς ὀνόματι (sic) Μωυσ[ῆ] *Stud.Pont.*3 No.10*g* (Amisus):—Med., *affect, assume the state of a king,* App.*BC*3.18; so in Act., J.*AJ*1.10.4. **-ικός,** ή, όν, *royal, kingly,* ποιέεις οὐδαμῶς -κά Hdt.2.173; β. γένος A.*Pr.*869; β. [μοναρχία] Pl.*Plt.*291e; opp. τυραννικός, Arist.*Pol.*1285^b3; βασιλικοὶ ἀπέβησαν proved themselves *truly kingly,* Plb.8.10.10; βασιλικὸν [ἐστι] πράττειν μὲν εὖ, κακῶς δ' ἀκούειν Arr.*Epict.*4.6.20; ἦθος β. X. *Oec.*21.10; τὸ β. Id.*Cyr.*1.3.18: βασιλική (sc. τέχνη), ἡ, *art of ruling,* Andronic.Rhod.p.574 M.: Comp. -ώτερος Herm.ap.Stob.1.49.45, Jul.*Or.*2.54d: Sup. βασιλικώτατος καὶ ἄρχειν ἀξιώτατος X.*An.*1.9.1, cf. Isoc.2.29; -ωτάτη χάρις Plu.*Alex.*21. Adv. -κῶς, παρών *as a king, with kingly authority,* X.*Cyr.*1.4.14; β. ἄρχειν Arist.*Pol.*1259^b 1. **2.** *of* or *belonging to a king,* οἱ β. *the king's friends* or *officers,* Plb.8.12.10; ἐγκλήματα β. charges *of high-treason,* Id.25.3.1; ὀφειλήματα β. debts *to the king,* ib.3; β. πρόσοδοι *PPetr.*3 p.56; γραμματεύς (cf. II. 1) Wilcken *Chr.*233.2 (ii B.C.), etc.; γεωργοί *PTeb.*5. 200 (ii B.C.), etc.; ὁδὸς β. the *king's* highway, Lxx *Nu.*20.17, *PPetr.*3 p.65 (iii B.C.); μὴ εἶναι β. ἀτραπὸν ἐπὶ γεωμετρίαν no *royal* road, Euc. ap.Procl.*in Euc.*p.68 F.; β. νόμος *OGI*483.1, *Ep.Jac.*2.8; αἱ β. βίβλοι the books *of Kings,* Ph.1.427. **3.** *choice* (cf. βασίλειος 3), μίνδαξ Amphis 27. **4.** κάρυα β. *walnuts,* Dsc.1.125; καρύαι *PSI*4.428. 65 (iii B.C.). **b.** β. κύμινον, = ἄμι, Dsc.3.62. **II.** as Subst., **1.** βασιλικός (sc. γραμματεύς), ὁ, official in Egyptian νομοί, *POxy.*1219. 15 (iii A.D.). **b.** (sc. οἶκος) *basilica, CIG*2782.25 (Aphrodisias). **c.** (sc. ὄρνις) = ἀκαλανθίς, Sch.Ar.*Pax* 1078. **d.** (sc. ἀστήρ) = βασιλίσκος v, *Cat.Cod.Astr.*7.201.23. **2.** βασιλικὴ στοά *hall* divided into aisles by columns, *IG*12(3).326.18 (Thera), Str.5.3.8 (pl.); β. alone, *OGI*511.15 (Aezani), Lat. *basilica,* Vitr.5.1.4, 6.3.9, cf. Plu.*Publ.*15, *Cat.Mi.*5, App.*BC*2.26. **3.** βασιλικόν (sc. ταμιεῖον), τό, *treasury,* εἰς τὸ β. ἀπομετρῆσαι, τελεῖν, *PSI*4.344.17 (iii B.C.), D.S.2.40, etc.; ὀφείλειν *PRev.Laws* 5.1, al.; *royal bank, OGI*90.29 (Rosetta),

*PRein.*13.19,al., *BGU*830.18 (i A.D.). **b.** (sc. δῶμα) *palace*, D.C. 60.4. **c.** (sc. πρόσταγμα) *royal decree*, Lxx *Es.*1.19. **d.** (sc. φάρμακον) name for various remedies, = τετραφάρμακον, Gal.12.601; of other compounds, ibid.; *a plaster*, Id.13.184; *an eyesalve*, Id.12.782 (also -κός, ὁ, *a bandage*, Id.18(1).777). **e.** (sc. φυτόν) *basil, Ocimum basilicum*, Suid. **f.** βασιλικά, τά, *communications received from kings*, *SIG*333.23 (Samos), 426.26 (Teos); also, *interests* or *revenues of the crown*, *PRev.Laws*15.4 (iii B.C.), *PTeb.*5.256 (ii B.C.), Lxx 1*Ma.*10.43; *prerogatives*, ib.15.8.

βασῑλῑναῦ, barbarism for βασίλιννα (i.e. βασίλειἄ), Ar.*Av.*1678.

βᾰσῐλ-ίνδα, Adv., ἡ β. παιδιά 'king of the castle', a game, Poll.9.110, *AB*1353. **-ιννα,** v. βασίλισσα. **-ίς,** ίδος, ἡ, = βασίλειἄ, *queen, princess*, S.*Ant.*941 (dub. l.), E.*Hec.*552; β. νύμφη, γυνή, E.*Med.*1003, *Hipp.*778: in Prose, β. γυναικῶν Pl.*Lg.*694e, cf. Plu.*Alex.*21; of a Roman Imperial *princess*, Philostr.*VA*1.3. **b.** = βασίλισσα 2, Eust. 1425.42. **2.** as Adj., *royal*, ἑστία, εὐναί, E.*Rh.*718, *IA*1307 (lyr.); of cities, β. Ῥώμη *IG*14.830 (Puteoli); β. πόλις, of Rome, Gal.14.796; of Constantinople, *OGI*521.22 (Abydos), Them.*Or.*11.144a, Agath.1.4, etc.; so β. alone, Lyd.*Mag.*2.14; also β. χώρα, = Rome, Vett.Val.226.14. **b.** metaph., καρδίη β. Hp.*Nat.Hom.*6. **II.** *kingdom*, D.S.29.22. **-ίσκος,** ὁ, Dim. of βασιλεύς, *princelet, chieftain*, Plb.3.44.5, *OGI*200.18 (Axum); also, = βασιλείδιον, Ath.13.566a. **II.** *kind of serpent, basilisk*, perh. *Egyptian cobra*, Hp.*Ep.*19 (*Hermes* 53.65), Lxx *Ps.*90(91).13, al., Hld.3.8, Artem.4.56, Horap.1.1, Democr.[300], Plin.8.78. **III.** *wren*, Aesop.ap.Plu.2.806e, Ruf.*Fr.*117, Artem.4.56; *gold-crest*, Philagr.ap.Aët.11.11. **IV.** *sea-fish*, Opp.*H.*1.129, Marc.Sid.26. **V.** *the star α Leonis, Regulus*, Gem.3.5, Heph.Astr.2.18, etc. **VI.** kind of *shoe*, Poll.7.85. **-ισσα,** ἡ, = βασίλειἄ, *queen*, Alc.Com.6, X.*Oec.*9.15, Philem.16.1, Arist.*Fr.*179, *Supp.Epigr.*1.366.34 (Samos, iii B.C.), Theoc.15.24, *IG*2.614*b*; ἡ β. τῶν μελισσῶν Arr.*Epict.*3.22.99; condemned by Phryn.202, but cf. Ael.Dion.*Fr.*91. **2.** *wife of the ἄρχων βασιλεύς at Athens*, Poll.8.90:—also **βασίλιννα,** D.59.74, Men.907. **3.** the *Roman Empress*, Hdn.1.7.4, etc. **4.** = βασιλεύς VI, *PMag.Leid.V.*1.31. **-ισταί,** οἱ, guild of worshippers of Ptolemy Euergetes II, *OGI*130.6, *IG*12(3).443 (Thera).

βάσῐμος [ᾰ], ον, (βαίνω) *passable, accessible*, D.S.5.44,al. (dub. sens. in Tim.*Pers.*65); τόποι S.E.*M.*1.78: metaph. of a rhetorical τόπος, D.25.76, cf. D.S.23.15,al.; χρόνος ἱστορίᾳ β. Plu.*Thes.*1. **II.** *fixed, stable*, Eustr. *in EN*98.3.

βάσις [ᾰ], εως, ἡ, (βαίνω) *stepping, step*, and collectively, *steps*, A.*Eu.*36, S.*Aj.*8, etc.: metaph., ἡσύχῳ φρενῶν βάσει A.*Ch.*452 (lyr.); οὐκ ἔχων β. *power to step*, S.*Ph.*691 (lyr.); τροχῶν βάσεις the *rolling* of the wheels, the *rolling* wheels, Id.*El.*718; ἀρβύλης β. the *print* of the sandal, E.*El.*532; ποίμναις τήνδ' ἐπεμπίπτει βάσιν S.*Aj.*42. **2.** *measured step* or *movement*, β. χορείας Ar.*Th.*968, cf. Pi.*P.*1.2: hence, *rhythmical* or *metrical movement*, Pl.*R.*399e, *Lg.*670d: in Rhet., *rhythmical close* of a sentence, Hermog.*Id.*1.6,al.; *clause forming transition from* πρότασις *to* ἀπόδοσις, Id.*Inv.*1.5: and in Metric, *metrical unit, monometer*, Arist.*Pol.*1263ᵇ35, *Metaph.*1087ᵇ36, Heph.11, Longin.*Proll.Heph.*3, Mar.Vict.p.47.3 K., etc. **3.** *order, sequence*, θέσις καὶ β. Epicur.*Ep.*1 p.10 U. **II.** *that with which one steps, a foot*, Pl.*Ti.*92a, Arist.*GA*750ᵃ4; ποδῶν β. E.*Hec.*837; θηλύπους β. their women's *feet*, Id.*IA*421; β. δίχηλος, of the ostrich, D.S.3.28.3: abs., αἱ βάσεις Ph.1.226, *Act.Ap.*3.7; σφίγξ εἶχε β. λέοντος Apollod.3.5.8; *leg*, Id.1.3.5; βάσεων ἀποκοπαί Diog.Oen.39. **III.** *that whereon one stands, base, pedestal*, [κρατῆρος] Alex.119; of statues, *OGI*705.6, etc.; τρία ἔργα.. ἐπὶ μιᾶς β. Str.14.1.14, cf. Luc.*Philops.*19; λεβήτων Plb.5.88.5; of an engine, Hero *Bel.*88.1, al.; of a column, *PLond.*3.755ᵛ6 (iv A.D.): Medic., τοῦ ἐγκεφάλου Herophil.ap.*Placit.*4.5.4, cf. Plu.*Per.*6; τραχήλου Id.*Pyrrh.*34; κοῖλαι βλεφάρων ἰοτυπεῖς βάσιες *AP*5.86 (Rufin.); αἱ ἐν ὀφθαλμοῖς β. Sor.1.27, cf. Archig.ap.Aët.16.101(91); of the heart, Gal.*UP*6.13; ἐπανόρθωσις τὴν τοῦ κενουμένου βάσιν ἀναπληροῦσα Id.1.474; *foundation, basement*, ῥίζα πάντων καὶ β. ἁ γᾶ ἐρήρεισται Ti.Locr.97e; so, of the soil, πεδίων σπορίμα β. *Hymn.Is.*162. **2.** Geom., *base* of a solid or plane figure, Pl.*Ti.*55b, Arist.*APr.*41ᵇ15,al.; [κώνου] Democr.155; πυραμίδος Speus.ap.*Theol.Ar.*63. **IV.** *position, fixedness*, opp. φορά, etym. of βέβαιος, Pl.*Cra.*437a. **V.** Astrol., = ὡροσκόπος, Vett.Val.88.6, Paul.Al.*T.*2, *Cat.Cod.Astr.*8(4).132.

βάσκα· μακέλη, Hsch.; cf. μάσκη.

βασκ-αίνω, fut. -ᾰνῶ Lxx *De.*28.56: aor. ἐβάσκηνα Philostr. (v. infr.), -ᾱνα Arist.*Pr.*926ᵇ24:—Pass., aor. ἐβασκάνθην (v. infr.):—*bewitch* by the evil eye, etc., Arist. l.c., Lxx *De.*28.56: metaph., *Ep.Gal.*3.1; ἐβάσκηνε πάντα.. τύχη Hdn.2.4.5:—Pass., ὡς μὴ βασκανθῶσι Arist.*Fr.*347; ὡς μὴ βασκανθῶ τρὶς ἔπτυσα Theoc.6.39. **II.** c. acc., *malign, disparage*, Pherecr.174, D.8.19; ἄν τι δύσκολον συμβαίνῃ τοῦτο βασκαίνει Id.18.189; εἰσίν τινες.. οὓς τὸ βασκαίνειν τρέφει Dionys.Com.11:—Pass., ὑπὸ τῶν ἀντιτέχνων βασκανθῆναι Str.14.2.7. **2.** c. dat., *envy, grudge*, D.20.24, etc.; τινί τινος *grudge* one a thing, D.Chr.78.37, Philostr.*VA*6.12; τινὶ ἐπί τινι D.Chr.78.25: abs., Luc.*Nav.*17: τινός *keep to oneself*, Id.*Philops.*35. **3.** c. acc. et inf., μὴ βασκήνας γελάσαι καὶ ἄλλον Ael.*VH*14.20. **-ᾰνία,** ἡ, *malign influence, witchery*, Pl.*Phd.*95b; β. φαυλότητος ἀμαυροῖ τὸ καλόν Lxx *Wi.*4.12; βασκανίας φάρμακον τὸ πήγανον Arist.*Pr.*926ᵇ20. **2.** *malignity*, ἀγνωμοσύνη καὶ β. D.18.252; ὄχλος καὶ β. Id.19.24: pl., Lxx 4*Ma.*2.15. **3.** *jealousy*, ᾕεισεν κρέσσονα βασκανίης Call.*Epigr.*23, cf. Ph.2.81,al. **-άνιον** [ᾰ], τό, *charm, amulet*, Ar.*Fr.*592, Str.16.4.17, cf. Phryn.68. **II.** in pl., *malign influences*, Ἀΐδεω β. *Epigr.Gr.*381 (Aezani). **-ᾰνος,** ὁ, *one who bewitches, sorcerer*, as a term of abuse, D.21.209, Men.*Pk.*279, Str.14.2.7; β. καὶ φθοροποιός St.Byz. s.v. Θίβα. **2.** *slanderer*, D.18.132, Vett.Val.358.5. **II.** Adj. βάσκανος, ον, *slanderous, malicious*, Ar.*Eq.*103, *Pl.*571; ὁ συκοφάντης πανταχόθεν βάσκανον D.18.242, cf. Str.14.1.22; δύσκολος καὶ β. Plu.*Fab.*26; β. πρᾶγμα... ποιοῦντες D.18.317; β. ἔσσ', Ἀΐδα Erinna 6.3; κώμων β. ἐστι λίθος *AP*9.756 (Aemil.); μ' ὁ β. ἥρπασε δαίμων *Epigr.Gr.*345; freq. in sepulchral inscriptions, *IG*14.1362, etc.: Sup. -ώτατος *Com.Adesp.*359. Adv. -νως J.*AJ*11.4.9, Porph.*VP*53. **2.** β. ὀφθαλμός *evil* eye, Plu.2.680c, cf. Alciphr.1.15. **-αντικός,** ή, όν, *envious*, φθονητικὴ καὶ β. ἕξις Plu.2.682d, cf. Phld.*Vit.*p.42 J.

βασκᾰρίζειν (i.e. ϝασκ-)· ⟨ἀ⟩σκαρίζειν (Cret.), Hsch.

βασκάς (or -ᾶς), άδος, ἡ, a kind of *duck*, Ar.*Av.*885; cf. βοσκάς, φασκάς.

βασκαύλης, ου, ὁ, perh. = Lat. *vasculum*, *POxy.*109.22 (iii/iv A.D.).

βάσκειν· λέγειν, κακολογεῖν, καὶ ἀνίστασθαι, Hsch.; cf. βάζω.

βασκευταί· φασκίδες, ἀγκάλαι, Id.:—also **βάσκιοι·** δεσμαὶ φρύγανων, Id. **βάσκιλλος·** κίσσα, Id. **βάσκον·** χῶρον, Id.

βασκοσύνη, ἡ, poet. for βασκανία, Poet. *de herb.*51,131, *PMag.Lond.*122.34, *PMag.Par.*1.1400.

βάσκω (akin to βαίνω), only imper., βάσκ' ἴθι *speed thee! away!* Il.2.8, etc.; βάσκετ', ἐπείγετε Ar.*Th.*783; but βάσκε *come!* A.*Pers.*663,671 (both lyr.); βάσκ', ἄλαστε *Mim.Oxy.*413.60. (βάσκου· πορεύου is prob. f.l. in Hsch.)

βασμιαῖος λίθος *flat* block *used as a base*, Haussoullier *Milet* p.172, *Rev.Phil.*43.188.

βασμίς, βασμός, v. βαθμ-. **βᾶσσα,** ἡ, Dor., = βῆσσα:—hence **βᾱσσαίας·** τὰς ἐν βήσσῃ γεγονυίας, Hsch.

βασσάρ-α [ᾰρ], ἡ, = ἀλώπηξ, *fox*, Sch.Lyc.771 (Cyren. acc. to Hsch.). **II.** *dress of Thracian bacchanals*, made of *fox*-skins, *AB* 222, Hsch. **2.** *Thracian bacchanal*, in pl., title of play by A., Sch.Ar.*Th.*142, cf. Callix.2. **3.** *impudent woman, courtesan*, Lyc.771, 1393. **-εύς,** έως, ὁ, name of Bacchus, Corn.*ND*30, Hor.*Od.*1.18.11. **-έω,** = Βακχεύω, v. ἀναβασσαρέω. **-ικός,** ή, όν, = βακχικός, θίασος *AP*6.165 (Phalaec.): βασσαρικά, τά, = Διονυσιακά, Soterich.ap.Suid. **-ιον,** τό, Dim. of βασσάρα I, *little fox*, Hdt.4.192. **-ίς,** ίδος, ἡ, = βασσάρα I, Hsch. s.v. ψυῖαι. **II.** = βασσάρα II. 2, Anacr.55, *AP*6.74 (Agath.). **-ος,** ὁ, = Βασσαρεύς, Orph.*H.*45.2. **II.** = βασσάρα I, *EM*191.1.

βάσσος, εος, τό, = βασσάρα, *EM*191.1.

βάσσων, ον, gen. ονος, Dor. Comp. of βαθύς, Epich.188. **2.** *baggage-train*, Petr.Patr.p.434 D.

βαστά· ὑποδήματα (Ital.), Hsch.

βαστᾰγ-άριος, ὁ, *transport-worker*, *Stud.Pal.*20.82.5 (iv A.D.). **-ή,** ἡ, *transport*, τῶν ἀναγκαίων Lyd.*Mag.*1.13.

βαστάγιον, τό, *baldric*, Eust.828.35.

βάσταγμα, ατος, τό, *that which is borne, burden*, E.*Supp.*767, Plb.36.6.7, Plu.2.59b, etc.; εἶναι βαρὺ β. βασιλείαν J.*AJ*19.9.2.

βαστάζω, Od.11.594, etc.: fut. -άσω A.*Pr.*1019, S.*Aj.*920; late -άξω Ps.-Callisth.1.45, etc.: aor. ἐβάστασα Od.21.405, Ar.*Th.*437 (lyr.), etc.; late ἐβάσταξα *PFay.*122, Lxx *Si.*6.25, J.*AJ*3.8.7, Epigr.ap.Stob.1.49.52:—Pass., fut. βασταχθήσομαι Ps.-Callisth.1.42: aor. ἐβαστάχθην Nic.Dam.p.114 D., D.L.4.59, Ath.15.693e: aor. 2 βασταγῆναι Artem.2.68: pf. βεβάσταγμαι (ἐμ-) Luc.*Ocyp.*14:—*lift up, raise*, λᾶαν βαστάζοντα... ἀμφοτέρῃσι Od.11.594; ἐπεὶ μέγα τόξον ἐβάστασε 21.405; πεπτῶτα β. τινά S.*Aj.*827, etc.; *lift* a veil, Id.*El.*1470:—Pass., of sluice-gates, *PRyl.*81.6 (ii A.D.). **2.** metaph., *lift up, exalt, ennoble*, Pi.*O.*12.19; β. τινὰ χαρίτεσσιν Id.*I.*3.8. **II.** *bear, carry*, A.*Pr.*1019, etc.; χεροῖν β. τινά S.*El.*1129, cf. 1216; δόρυ Hermipp.46.2 (anap.), Theoc.16.78; ὅπλα Men.*Epit.*107. **2.** *hold in one's hands*, S.*El.*905; χεροῖν Id.*Ph.*657, cf. 1127 (lyr.); of books, συνεχῶς β. Epicur.*Ep.*2 p.35 U.:—in Pass., *to be popular*, Arist.*Rh.*1413ᵇ12. **3.** β. ἐν γνώμῃ *bear* in mind, *consider, weigh*, A.*Pr.*888; φρενί Ar.*Th.*437 (lyr.); β. προβούλευμα *deliberate on*.., Eup.73; βαστάσας αἱρήσομαι *on consideration*, Id.303. **4.** *bear, endure*, οὐκέτι βαστάζω τὴν σεῖο διαζυγίην *AP*5.8 (Rufin.). **5.** *produce, yield*, of land, *PGiss.*6 iii 8 (ii A.D.). **III.** *carry off, take away*, *Ev.Jo.*20.15; *steal*, Plb.32.15.4, J.*AJ*1.19.9, D.L.4.59, Luc.*Asin.*16, *PTeb.*330.7 (ii A.D.), perh. also in *Ev.Jo.*12.6, Ath.2.46f (Pass.). **2.** in Pass., *to be sublimated*, Zos.Alch.p.198 B. **IV.** in Trag., *touch*, χέρα ἄνακτος... τῇδε β. χερί A.*Ag.*35; *embrace*, σῶμα S.*OC*1105.—Not in Att. Prose: Pass. first in Plb.

βάστακες· πλούσιοι καὶ εὐγενεῖς (Boeot.), *EM*191.12.

βαστακ-τέον, *one must bear*, Sch.E.*Or.*769. **II.** Adj. **βαστακτέος,** α, ον, *to be borne* or *carried*, Sch.Ar.*Ach.*258. **-τής,** οῦ, ὁ, *bearer, porter*, *Gloss.* **-τικός,** ή, όν, *fit for bearing*: Adv. -κῶς, gloss on ἀέρδην, Sch.A.*Ag.*240. **-τός,** ή, όν, *borne*, *AP*12.52 (Mel.).

βάσταχας· τοὺς τραχήλους (Boeot.), and **βασταχάζει·** τραχηλίζει, Hsch. (βαστρ- cod.):—also **βάστραχες,** Boeot., = οἱ τράχηλοι, and **βαστραχαλίσαι,** = τραχηλιάσαι, *EM*191.11.

βαστέρνιον, τό, Lat. *basterna*, *closed litter*, *Cod.Just.*8.10.12, *Cat.Cod.Astr.*1.103:—hence **βαστερνάριοι,** οἱ, *litter-bearers*, *IG*3.1433.7.

βασυνίας (sc. πλακοῦς), ὁ, a kind of *cake*, Semus 3.

βαταίνει· καλεῖ, Hsch. **βαταῖς·** πορφυρίσιν, ἢ ὁδοί, Id.

βᾰτᾰλίζομαι, *live like a* βάταλος, Theano *Ep.*1.3:—later in Act., β. τὰ ὀπίσθια *wriggle*, of a horse, *Hippiatr.*30.

βάτᾰλος [βᾰ], ὁ, = πρωκτός, Eup.82; cf. βάτας, βατέω. II. *stammerer* (cf. βατταρίζω), a nickname given to Demosthenes, Aeschin. 2.99, cf. D.18.180. (Codd. vary between βάταλος and βάτταλος: Βάτταλος is pr. n. in Hedyl.ap.Ath.4.167d.)

βᾰτάνη [τᾰ], ἡ, = πατάνη, Matro *Conv.*85:—Dim. **βᾰτάνιον**, τό, Antiph.95, Eub.38, Alex.24,172.18, *POxy.*739.9 (i A.D.), Bilabel Ὀψαρτ.p.18, Zos.Alch.p.222 B. (Sicel word for λοπάδια, Hsch.)

βάτας· ὁ καταφερής (Tarent.), Hsch. (Fort. βατᾶς, = βάταλος.)

βᾰτε, Dor. imper. aor. 2 of βαίνω.

βᾰτεία, ἡ (scanned –εῖα), *bush, thicket*, Pi.*O.*6.54.

βάτελλα, ἡ, = Lat. *patella*, *POxy.*741.18 (ii A.D.):—Dim. **βατέλλιον**, τό, *Ostr.*1218, *POxy.*1657.5 (iii A.D.).

βᾰτεύω, perh. *trample, damage*, τὰ βεβατ[ευ]μένα *BGU*45.21 (iii A.D.).

βᾰτ-έω, (βαίνω) *cover*, τὰς χιμάρας ἐβάτευν *AP*9.317:—Pass., of she-goats, οἷα βατεῦνται Theoc.1.87. II. at Delphi, = πατέω, Plu. 2.292e. **–ήρ**, ῆρος, ὁ, *that on which one treads, threshold*, ἐπ' αὐτὸν ἥκεις τὸν β. τῆς θύρας, prov. of those who 'come to the point', 'hit the nail on the head', Amips.26; *base* of a statue, *IG*11(2).147.18 (Delos, iv B.C.), Ἀρχ.Ἐφ.1913.7 (Nisyros, iii B.C.). 2. *place from which one jumps*, *AB*224, Hsch., Eust.1404.56. 3. = βακτηρία, Nic.*Th.*377. 4. *bridge* of a lyre, Nicom.*Harm.*6; also, *part of flute*, ib.10. 5. *one who walks*, Hsch. **–ηρία**, Ion. **–ίη**, ἡ, = βακτηρία, Herod.8.60. **–ήριον** λέχος (cf. βάτης), = ὀχεία, Ps.-Phoc.188. **–ηρίς**, ίδος, ἡ, κλῖμαξ β. a *mounting* ladder, *AP*7.365 (Zon. or Diod.). **–ῆρος**· ἐξ ἐχίνου σφάκελος, Hsch. **–ης**, ου, ὁ, *one that treads* or *covers*, expld. by πίθηκος, ἀναβάτης, Id.

βᾰτιάκη [ᾰκ], ἡ, a kind of *cup*, Diph.80; β. χρυσαῖ, χαλκαῖ, Alexandr.Epist.ap.Ath.11.784a, Arist.*Mir.*834^{a}4, *IG*11(2).137 (Delos, iv B.C.):—Dim. **βᾰτιάκιον**, τό, dub. in Philem.87, cf. *IG*11.199*B*8 (Delos, iii B.C.).

βᾰτῐδοσκόπος, ον, *looking after skates, greedy for them*, Ar.*Pax* 811.

βάτινον, τό, *fruit of* βάτος, *blackberry*, Gal.6.589, 12.920.

βάτιον, τό, Dim. of βάτος (A), Salaminian name for *mulberry*, Parth.ap.Ath.2.51f.

βᾰτίς, ίδος, ἡ, a flat fish, perh. *skate* or *ray*, Epich.59.1, 90.1, Ar. *V.*510, Hermipp.45.2, Arist.*HA*565^{a}22, al. II. *bird that frequents bushes*, possibly *stone-chat*, ib.592^{b}17. III. *samphire, Crithmum maritimum*, Plin.21.86, 174, Colum.12.7.

βάτνος· αὐλός (Messen.), Hsch.

βᾰτοδρόπος, ον, *pulling up brambles*, *h.Merc.*190.

βᾰτόεις, εσσα, εν, (βάτος A) *thorny*, Nic.*Al.*267.

βάτον [ᾰ], τό, *blackberry*, D.S.1.34.

βάτος (A) [ᾰ], ἡ, *bramble, Rubus ulmifolius*, Od.24.230, Aen.Tact.28.6, Theoc.1.132; ὁ, Hp.*Mul.*2.112, Ar.*Fr.*754 (Att. acc. to Moeris), Thphr.*HP*1.5.3, Lxx *Ex.*3.2: whence ἐπὶ τοῦ (v.l. τῆς) βάτου in *Ev.Marc.*12.26: fem., Dsc.4.37, *Ev.Luc.*20.37. II. β. Ἰδαία *raspberry, Rubus Idaeus*, Dsc.4.38; = β. ὀρθοφυής Thphr.*HP*3.18.4. III. β. Μοσυλῖτις, a kind of *cassia*, Dsc.1.13. IV. = ἑλένιον, *elecampane*, Ps.-Dsc.1.28.

βάτος (B), ὁ, a *fish*, a kind of *skate*, Epich.59.2, 90.2, Arist.*HA* 489^{b}6, al.

βάτος (C), ὁ, the Hebrew liquid measure *bath*, = Egypt. ἀρτάβη or Att. μετρητής, Lxx 2*Es.*7.22, *Ev.Luc.*16.6, J.*AJ*8.2.9:—also **βάδος**, v.l. in Lxx l.c., Hsch.

βᾰτός, ή, όν, (βαίνω) *passable, accessible*, τοῖς ὑποζυγίοις X.*An.* 4.6.17, cf. Men.924, Arr.*An.*4.21.3, Nonn.*D.*1.54, al.; = βέβηλος, opp. ἄβατος, Porph.*Abst.*4.11: metaph., *permissible*, Just.*Nov.*30.8 *Intr.* II. Act., *speeding*, ποὺς Nonn.*D.*2.96, 18.55.

βᾰτρᾰχ-ειος [ρᾰ], ον, (βάτραχος) *of* or *belonging to a frog*: βατράχεια (sc. χρώματα) *frog-colour, pale-green*, Ar.*Eq.*523:—also **βατράχεος**, α, ον, Nic.*Fr.*85.5. **–ίδιον**, τό, Dim. of βάτραχος, Plu.*Nob.* 21. **–ίζω**, *to be* or *move like a frog*, *Hippiatr.*26. **–ιον**, τό, *Ranunculus*, Hp.*Nat.Mul.*32, Dsc.2.175 (who incl. *R. asiaticus, garden r.*, β. χρυσάνθεμον *Gp.*2.6.30, and *R. sardous, hairy crowfoot*, cf. Dsc.*Alex.*14). II. = βάτραχος I, Paus.9.21.1. III. = βάτραχος III, Ptol.*Phas.* p.27 H., al. IV. *malachite*, Syn.Alch. p.64 B. **–ιοῦν**, τό, *a court of law* at Athens, so called from its colour (cf. Φοινικιοῦν), Paus.1.28.8:—Adj. **βᾰτρᾰχε(ι)οῦς** *IG*2. 758*B* ii 23. **–ίς**, ίδος, ἡ, *frog-green garment*, Ar.*Eq.*1406, *IG*2. 754.16, D.C.59.14. 2. = βατράχιον I, Alex.Trall.3.6: but, II. **βᾰτρᾰχίς**, ῖδος, Dim. of βάτραχος, Nic.*Th.*416. **–ίσκοι**, οἱ, *part of the* κιθάρα, Hsch. **–ίτης** λίθος, ὁ, *a frog-green* stone, Plin.37. 149.

βᾰτρᾰχομῠομᾰχία, ἡ, *battle of the frogs and mice*, title of mock-epic poem ascribed to Homer, cf. Plu.2.873f.

βάτρᾰχος [βᾰ], ὁ, *frog*, Batr.6, 18, 59, al., Hdt.4.131, etc.: prov., ὕδωρ πίνειν βάτραχος *a very frog* to drink, Aristopho 10.3; βατράχοις οἰνοχοεῖν, of those who give what is not wanted, Pherecr.70.5; μέλει μοι τῶν τοιούτων ἧττον ἢ τῶν ἐν τοῖς τέλμασι β. Jul.*Mis.*358a; χλωρὸς β., of the tree-*frog*, Thphr.*Sign.*15. II. = ἁλιεύς, a kind of *fish, fishing-frog* or *sea-angler, Lophius piscatorius*, Arist.*GA*749^{a}23, Ael. *NA*13.5. III. *frog of a horse's hoof*, *Gp.*16.1.9, *Hippiatr.*8: hence Astron., of the star β Centauri, Ptol.*Alm.*8.1. IV. ἐσχάρας εἶδος, Hsch. V. *swelling under the tongue*, Aët.8.39.—Dial. forms are cited by Gramm., 1. Ion. βάθρακος, cited from Hdt. (prob. 4.131) by Sch.Il.4.243, Eust.1570.11, and found in *PLond.*1.124.31 (iv/v A.D.); Ion. also βότραχος Hp.ap.Gal.19, βρόταχος Xenoph.40 (as pr. n., *GDI*5577, 5592). 2. βράταχος Hsch. (as pr. n., *GDI*5727*d* 29). 3. Cypr. βρούχετος Hsch. 4. Phoc. βριαγχόνη Id. 5. Pontic βάβακος Id. Cf. βύρθακος, βρύτιχος.

βάτταλος, ὁ, v. βάταλος.

βαττᾰρ-ίζω, onomatop. word, *stammer*, Hippon.108, Pl.*Tht.*175d (prob. l.), Cic.*Att.*6.5.1, Luc.*JTr.*27. **–ισμός**, ὁ, *stuttering*, Phld. *Rh.*2.136 S., Porph.*Hist.Phil.Fr.*11; also, *twittering* of swallows, Eust.1914.32. **–ιστής**, οῦ, ὁ, *stutterer*, Hsch.

βάττικες· γυναῖκες (Boeot.), Hsch.

βαττο-λογέω, = βατταρίζω, *speak stammeringly, say the same thing over and over again*, *Ev.Matt.*6.7, Simp.*in Epict.*p.91 D. **–λογία**· ἀργολογία, ἀκαιρολογία, Hsch. (βατο– cod.).

βάττος, ὁ, *stammerer, lisper*, Hsch.

βατύλη, ἡ, *she-dwarf*, dub. name of a play by Theopompus, Sch. Ar.*Pl.*1012.

βᾰτώδης, ες, *thorny*, Str.4.3.5. 2. *like a blackberry*, τὸ μόρον τὸ β. Phan.Hist.33. II. *overgrown with thorns*, Plb.2.28.8.

βαύ, βαύ, *bow, wow*, imit. of a dog's bark, *Com.Adesp.*1304.

βαῦ, a kind of *flower*, Hsch.

βαυβᾰλίζω, = βαυκαλάω, Alex.229 (βαβ– cod. Hsch.).

βαυβάω, *sleep*, E.*Fr.*694, *Trag.Adesp.*165, Canthar.3. II. Act., *lull to sleep*, Hsch.

βαύβυκες· πελεκᾶνες, Hsch.

βαυβώ, ἡ, = κοιλία, Emp.153.

βαυβών, ῶνος, ὁ, = ὄλισβος, Herod.6.19.

βᾰΰζω (βαΰζω disyll. Lyc.1453 is f.l. for βάζω), Dor. **βαΰσδω**, onomatop. word, *cry* βαύ βαύ, *bark*, Theoc.6.10; of angry persons, *snarl, yelp*, παῦσαι βαΰζων Ar.*Th.*173, cf. 895; τάδε σιγά τις βαΰζει thus they *snarl* in secret, A.*Ag.*449 (lyr.); οἷ' ἄττα β. Cratin.6. II. trans., *shriek aloud for*, τινά A.*Pers.*13; of dogs, *bark at*, τινά Heraclit.97 codd.

βαϋθεῖ· μασᾶται, Hsch.

βαυκᾰλ-άω, *lull to sleep*, Crates *Ep.*33, Luc.*Lex.*11 (wrongly said to be Att. by Moer.102): metaph., *nurse, look after*, Aret.*SD*2. 11. **–η**, ἡ, *cradle*, Sor.1.106, 109. **–ημα**, ατος, τό, *lullaby*, Socr. *Ep.*27. **–ησις**, εως, ἡ, *lulling* a child to sleep, Ruf.ap.Orib.*inc.*20. 26, Crat.*Ep.*33. **–ίζω**, = βαυκαλάω, *AB*85, Hsch. **–ιον**, τό, *narrow-necked vessel, that gurgles when water is poured in* or *out*, *POxy.*936.6 (iii A.D.), Olymp.*in Mete.*93.6: pl., Alex.Aphr.*Pr.*1.94 (καυκ– codd.). **–ις**, ιδος, ἡ, *vessel for cooling wine* or *water in*, elsewh. ψυκτήρ, *AP*11.244; β. ἡ τετράκυκλος Sopat.24.—Alexandr. word acc. to Ath.11.784b; on the accent cf. Hdn.Gr.1.90.

βαύκαλον· μαλακιζόμενον, τρυφερόν, καὶ ὡραϊστόν, *EM*192.20.

βαυκανήσεται· βοήσεται, Hsch. (For βυκ–.)

βαυκίδες, αἱ, a kind of *woman's shoes*, Ar.*Fr.*342, Alex.98.7, Herod. 7.58.

βαυκ-ίζω, (βαυκός) *to play the prude*, *AB*225:—Med., Alex.222.9, Hsch. **–ισμα**, ατος, τό, *coyness, affectation*, *AB*225 (pl.), Hsch. (pl.). **–ισμός**, ὁ, kind of *dance*, Poll.4.100, Hsch.

βαυκοπᾰνοῦργος, ὁ, *humbug*, Arist.*EN*1127^{b}27.

βαυκός, ή, όν, *prudish, affected*, Arar.9.

βαῦνος or **βαυνός**, ὁ, *furnace, forge*, Eratosth.24, Max.Tyr.22.3, Asp.*in EN*104.23; also, = χυτρόπους, Poll.10.100:—in Hsch. also **βαύνη**, ἡ.

βαυρία, ἡ, = οἰκία, Messapian word, *EM*389.25.

βαυριόθεν (cf. foreg.), = οἴκοθεν, Cleon Sic.2.

βᾰϋστικός, ή, όν, *inclined to bark*, Sch.Opp.*H.*1.721.

βαφά· ζωμός (Lacon.), Hsch.

βᾰφ-εῖον, τό, *dyer's house* or *workshop*, Str.16.2.23, *PLond.*2.371.3 (i A.D.). **–εύς**, έως, ὁ, (βάπτω) *a dyer*, Pl.*R.*429d, Diph.72, Plu. *Per.*12, etc.; the βαφεῖς formed a guild at Thyatira, *IGRom.*4.1265; also in the νομὸς Ἀρσινοΐτης, *PTeb.*287.3 (ii A.D.). II. *gilder*, Zos.Alch.p.154 B. **–ή**, ἡ, *dipping* of red-hot iron in water, S.*Aj.* 651: hence, *temper* or *edge* of a blade or tool *produced thereby*, τὴν β. ἀφιᾶσιν ὥσπερ ὁ σίδηρος εἰρήνην ἄγοντες Arist.*Pol.*1334^{a}8, cf. Plu.*Alex.* 32, *Pyrrh.*24; τὰ σιδήρια τὴν β. ἀνίησι *lose their edge*, Thphr.*HP*5.3.3, cf. *CP*1.22.6; χαλκοῦ βαφαί prob. poet. for σιδήρου β. in A.*Ag.*612 (v. Sch. ad loc., but cf. βάψις): metaph., *temper*, τῆς ἀνδρείας οἷον β. τις ὁ θυμός ἐστι καὶ στόμωμα Plu.2.988d; of wine, ib.650b. II. *dye*, Thphr.*HP*4.6.5; πορφυρᾷ β. A.*Pers.*317 (metaph. of blood), cf. Pl.*R.* 430a; κρόκου βαφάς the saffron-*dyed robe*, A.*Ag.*239 (lyr.); βαφαὶ ὕδρας *the arrows dipped* in the hydra's blood, E.*HF*1188 (lyr.); χελλέων β. Philostr.*Ep.*22: metaph., β. τυραννίδος Plu.2.779c. III. *enamelling*, χαλκοῦ . . βαφῇ κυάνου στίλβοντος ib.395b. 2. *gilding, silvering*, αἱ δύο β. Zos.Alch.p.168 B., cf. p.208 B. IV. *infection*, Aret.*CD*2.13. **–ικός**, ή, όν, *fit for dyeing*, κόκκος Dsc.*Eup.*1.37; βοτάνη Luc.*Alex.*12: **–κή** (sc. τέχνη), ἡ, *art of dyeing*, Ph.1.353, Plu.2.228b, *PRyl.*98.2 (ii A.D.). II. βίβλοι βαφικαί, in Alchemy, books *on gilding and silvering*, Ps.-Democr.ap.Syn.Alch.p.57 B.; καῦσις β. Zos.Alch.p.208 B. III. βαφικόν, τό, form of ἰνδικόν, Dsc.5.92. **–ιον**· ὀξύβαφον (Tarent.), Hsch. **–ισ⟨σ⟩α**, ἡ, *female dyer*(?), *Sammelb.*1957.

βάχθει· τέλμα ὕδατος, ἢ βάθος, Hsch.

βάψιμος, ον, *to be dyed*, Lysis ap.Iamb.*VP*17.76.

βάψις, εως, ἡ, *dipping, tempering*, χαλκοῦ καὶ σιδήρου Antipho Soph. 40. II. *a dye*, Perict.ap.Stob.4.28.19.

βάω, = βαίνω, only in compds.

βδᾰλεύς, έως, ὁ, *milk-pail*, Sch.Luc.*Hes.*4.

βδάλλω, aor. part. βδάλας Alciphr.3.16: aor. opt. Med., βδήλαιο

Nic.*Al.*262 :—*milk* cows, πολὺ βδάλλων *milking* many kine, rich in kine, Pl.*Tht.*174d ; β. τινά ibid.; ὁ βδάλλων *the milker*, Arist.*HA* 522ᵇ17 ; β. γάλα Procop.*Aed.*3.6 :—Med., *yield*, of the cow, βοΐδια .. ὧν ἕκαστον βδάλλεται γάλα πολύ Arist.*HA*522ᵇ15 ; βόες βδάλλονται ἑκάστη ἀμφορέα ib.16 : also in sense of Act., νέον γλάγος Nic.l.c. II. *suck*, Arist.*GA*746ᵃ20, cf. Gal.7.130 :—Pass., Arist.*HA*522ᵃ5,20.

βδαλοί· ῥαφίδες θαλάσσιαι, καὶ φλέβες κρισσώδεις, Hsch.

βδάλσις, εως, ἡ, *suction*, Gal.7.131, Aët.9.19.

βδαροί· δρύες, δένδρα, Hsch.

βδέλλ-ᾰ, ἡ, (βδάλλω) *leech*, Hdt.2.68, Arist.*IA*709ᵃ29, Theoc.2.56, Nic.*Al.*500, Lxx*Pr.*24.50 (30.15): metaph., β. σπιλάδων, of a fisherman, *AP*6.193 (Flacc.). 2. *lamprey*, Str.17.3.4. II. = βδέλλιον, J.*AJ*3.1.6, *Peripl.M.Rubr.*37, al., *Edict.Diocl.*32.54, Damocr.ap. Gal.14.129, *PMag.Berol.*1.286, *PMag.Leid.V.*12.24. **-άζεται·** ἀμέλγεται, Erot. (perh. v.l. for ἐκθηλάζεται Hp.*Mul.*1.73). **-ίζω,** *bleed with leeches*, in Pass., Antyll.ap.Orib.7.21.3, Gal.11.317.

βδέλλιον, τό, the aromatic gum obtained from *Balsamodendrum africanum* and *B. Mukul*, Dsc.1.67, Damocr.ap.Gal.14.118, Plin. *HN*12.35, Aq., Sm., Thd.*Ge.*2.12. (Semitic word.)

βδελλιστέον, *one must apply leeches*, Herod.Med.in *Rh.Mus.*58. 113.

βδελλολάρυγξ [ᾰ], υγγος, ὁ, *leech-throat*, name for *a greedy parasite*, Cratin.44.

βδέλλων· τρέμων ἢ βδέων, Hsch.; cf. **βδέλεσθαι·** κοιλιολυτεῖν, Id.

βδέλυγ-μα, ατος, τό, *abomination*, τοῖς Αἰγ. πᾶς ποιμὴν β. Lxx*Ge.* 43.32, etc.; β. τῶν ἐρημώσεων, ἐρημώσεως, of an idol, ib.*Da.*9.27, 1*Ma.* 1.54, cf. *Ev.Matt.*24.15. **-μία,** ἡ, *nausea, sickness*, Cratin.251, X. *Mem.*3.11.13. 2. *filth, nastiness*, Hp.*Fist.*1. **-μός,** ὁ, *abomination*, Lxx1*Ki.*25.31, *Na.*3.6.

βδελυκ-τός, ή, όν, *disgusting, abominable*, Lxx*Pr.*17.15, *Ep.Tit.*1. 16, Ph.2.261. **-τροπος,** ον, = foreg., A.*Eu.*52.

βδελῠρ-εύομαι, *behave in a beastly manner*, D.17.11. **-ία,** ἡ, *beastly, coarse*, or *objectionable behaviour*, And.1.122, Is.8.42 (pl.), D. 22.52, Aeschin.1.105, Thphr.*Char.*11, Plu.*Caes.*9. 2. *disgust, nausea*, Hp.*Int.*26, Jul.*Or.*6.190d. **-ός,** ά, όν, *disgusting, loathsome, blackguardly*, Ar.*Ra.*465, Pl.*R.*338d, Thphr.*Char.*11; θεοῖς ἐχθρὸς καὶ β. D.21.197; θρασὺς καὶ β. Plu.2.10c: Comp. -ότερα, πολιτεία Jul.*Or.* 7.210c: Sup. -ώτατος D.19.206,208. Adv. -ρῶς Ph.1.209. II. of things, *disgusting*, Gal.12.291; τὸ β. Alex.Trall.4.1. III. βδελυρά, = χαμελαία, Ps.-Dsc.4.171.

βδελύσσομαι, Att. **-ττομαι,** fut. -ύξομαι Hp.*Mul.*1.39,41 (Act. βδελύξειν wrongly cited by Erot.): aor. ἐβδελύχθην Ar.*V.*792, Plu. *Alex.*57, etc.; later ἐβδελυξάμην Lxx*Ge.*26.29, al., J.*BJ*6.2.10, Jul. *Or.*7.210d :—*feel a loathing for food*, Hp. ll. cc.; *to be sick*, Ar.*V.* 792. 2. c. acc., *feel a loathing at*, Id.*Ach.*586, Lxx l. c., al., Plu. *Alex.*57; β. [τραγῳδίας] Jul. l. c.; ὠμοφαγίαν ib.6.193c : β. ἀπό τινων Lxx*Ex.*1.12. II. later causal, in Act., *cause to stink, make loathsome* or *abominable*, fut. -ύξω Lxx*Le.*20.25 : aor. ἐβδέλυξα ib.*Ex.* 5.21 :—Med. and Pass., *to be loathsome*, fut. -υχθήσομαι ib.*Si.*20.8 : aor. -ύχθην ib.*Ps.*13(14).1 : pf. ἐβδέλυγμαι ib.*Pr.*8.7 ; οἱ ἐβδελυγμένοι *the abominable* (in ref. to the use of βδέλυγμα as *an idol*), *Apoc.* 21.8 :—this pf. in causal sense, Lxx*Pr.*28.9. (Cf. βδέω.)

βδελυχρός, ά, όν, Dor. for βδελυρός, Epich.63.

βδέννυμαι· ἐκκενοῦμαι τὴν κοιλίαν, Suid.; **βδένεσθαι** (sic), Hsch.

βδέσμα, ατος, τό, (βδέω) *stench, Gloss.*

Βδεῦ, (βδέω) comic parody on Ζεῦ, ὦ Βδεῦ δέσποτα *Com.Adesp.*28.

βδέω, poet. aor. βδέσα *AP*11.242 (Nicarch.); later ἔβδευσα Hierocl. *Facet.*233, al. :—*break wind*, Ar.*Pl.*693, *Pax*151, etc.: c. acc. cogn., οὐ λιβανωτὸν βδέω Id.*Pl.*703 :—Med. or Pass., Id.*Eq.*900. 2. of the cockroach, σίλφης κατοικιδίου τῆς βδεούσης τὸ στέαρ Archig.ap. Aët.8.35, cf. Gal.12.861. (Onomatopoeic word: root *bzd*, cf. Czech *bzdíti*, Slov. *pezdēti*, Lat. *pēdo*.)

βδόλος, ὁ, *stench, stink*, *Com.Adesp.*781.

βδύλλω, *to be in deadly fear of*, τινάς Ar.*Lys.*354, cf. *Eq.*224, Luc. *Lex.*10.

βέβαιος, ον (so always in Th., Pl.), also α, ον (v. infr.) : (βαίνω) :— *firm, steady*, κρύσταλλος Th.3.23 ; ὄχημα Pl.*Phd.*85d (Comp.); γῆ β. *terra firma*, Arr.*An.*2.21.5 ; *steadfast, durable*, ὁμιλία .. πιστὴ καὶ βέβαιος S.*Ph.*71 ; ἀρετῆς βέβαιαι .. αἱ κτήσεις μόνης Id.*Fr.*194 ; ψῆφος βεβαία E.*El.*1263 ; τὴν χάριν βέβαιον ἔχειν Th.1.32 ; οὐδέπω βέβαιος ἦν ἡ σωτηρία And.1.53 ; εἰρήνην βεβαίαν ἀγαγεῖν Isoc.4.173 ; φιλία βέβαιος Pl.*Smp.*182c ; βεβαίου τε καὶ καθαρᾶς ἡδονῆς γενέσθαι Id.*R.* 586a ; δόξαι καὶ πίστεις βέβαιοι καὶ ἀληθεῖς Id.*Ti.*37b, etc. b. *sure, certain*, τέκμαρ A.*Pr.*456 ; ἄκεα Id.*Eu.*506 (lyr.) ; τοξεύματα S.*Ant.*1086 ; πύλας β. παρέχειν make *safe, secure*, Th.4.67 ; βεβαιότερος κίνδυνος a *surer* game, Id.3.39 : Sup. -ότατος Id.1.124 ; βέβαιόν ἐστί τινι ὅτι .. D.H.3.35 ; τὰ παρ' ἀνθρώπων αὐτῷ β. ἦν ibid.; but β. παρέχειν τὰν ὠνάν *confirm, guarantee*, *GDI*1867, al. (Delph.); μένειν κυρίαν καὶ β. .. συγχώρησιν *BGU*1058.47 (i B.C.). 2. of persons, etc., *steadfast, constant*, φίλος A.*Pr.*299 (Comp.), cf. Th.5.43, etc.: c. inf., βεβαιότεροι μηδὲν νεωτεριεῖν *more certain* to make no change, Th.3.11. 3. τὸ β. *certainty*, Hdt.7.50, cf. Pl.*Phlb.*59c, etc.; but τὸ β. τῆς διανοίας *firmness, resolution*, Th.2.89. b. *security, guarantee*, τὸ δημόσιον β. *IG*1².189. II. Adv. -ως A.*Ag.*15 ; β. κληστόν Th.2.17 ; β. οἰκεῖσθαι Id.1.2 ; ἔχειν, γνῶναι, δημοκρατεῖσθαι, D.8.41,39, 10.4 : Comp. -ότερον, οἰκεῖν Th.1.8 ; -οτέρως Isoc.8.60, Porph.*Abst.*1.11 : Sup. -ότατα Th.6.91.

βεβαιότης, ητος, ἡ, *steadfastness, stability*, τῆς οὐσίας Pl.*Cra.*386a ; μετὰ ἡσυχίας καὶ βεβαιότητος ζῆν Id.*R.*503c, cf. *Lg.*735a, 790b, Arist. *EN*1100ᵇ12. 2. *assurance, certainty*, Pl.*Phdr.*277d ; *security, safety*, βεβαιότητος ἕνεκα Th.4.66 ; β. καὶ ἀσφάλεια Plu.*Fab.*19.

βεβαιότροπος, ον, *firm, resolute*, Dam.*Isid.*16.

βεβαι-όω, *confirm, establish, make good*, τοῖς δικασταῖς τὴν δόξαν Pl.*Cri.*53b ; δωρεὰν Is.1.18 ; εἴτε δεξιὰς δοῖεν ἐβεβαίουν X.*Cyr.*8.8.2, etc.; ἔργῳ βεβαιούμενα, opp. ἀκοῇ λεγόμενα, Th.1.23 ; β. λόγον *make good* one's word, Lys.20.32 ; β. τὴν πρᾶξιν X.*An.*7.6.17 ; *treat as valid*, τὰς αὐτῶν αἰσθήσεις Metrod.1, cf. Epicur.*Sent.*24 ; β. τινί τι *secure* one *the possession of* a thing, οὐδ' ἡμῖν αὐτοῖς βεβαιοῦμεν [τὴν ἐλευθερίαν] Th.1.122 ; τοῖς θεοῖς βεβαιοῦντες τοὺς νόμους οὓς ἐψηφίσασθε Lys.6.29, cf. D.21.30 ; τὴν ἀρχήν τινι Plu.*Sull.*22 ; τὸν λόγον *Ev.Marc.*16.20 :—Med., *establish for oneself, secure*, σφᾶς αὐτοὺς Th. 1.33 ; τὴν ἀρχήν, τὴν φιλίαν τινός, Id.6.10,78 ; β. τινάς *confirm* them *in one's interest*, ib.34 ; βασιλείαν Paus.3.11.4 ; τὰ περὶ τῆς βοηθείας Plb.2.51.5. 2. Med., *secure one's ground* in argument, Pl.*Tht.* 169e ; *confirm* oneself in an opinion, Id.*Grg.*489a, *Prt.*348d. 3. *guarantee the validity of* a purchase, *warrant* the purchaser's title, β. τινὶ τὸ βαλανεῖον Is.5.23, cf. Din.1.42, D.37.12, *SIG*46.4 (Halic., v B.C.) ; τὴν μίσθωσιν *BGU*1119.47 (i B.C.) : generally, β. τοὺς κανόνας Arr.*Epict.*2.11.24. II. intr., *determine, show itself positively*, τοῖσιν ἐνδοιαστῶς ἔχουσι .. ἐβεβαίωσε [ἡ νοῦσος] Hp.*Epid.*1. 2. **-ωμα,** ατος, τό, *confirmation, proof*, J.*AJ*2.12.4, 17.1. 1. **-ωσις,** εως, ἡ, *confirmation*, β. γνώμης Th.1.140, cf. 4.87, Demetr. Lac.*Herc.*1012.38F., Ph.1.486, al., D.H.*Rh.*10.18, Hermog.*Prog.* 5 ; εἰς β. in *perpetuity*, ἡ γῆ οὐ πραθήσεται εἰς β. Lxx*Le.*25.23. 2. legal *warranty*, Aeschin.3.249 (pl.), *PTeb.*311.27 (ii A.D.), etc.; βεβαιώσεως δίκη Poll.8.34. **-ωτέον,** *one must confirm*, ὅρκους Ph.2.272 ; ὑπόσχεσιν Id.1.23. **-ωτήρ,** ῆρος, ὁ, = sq. 2, *GDI*1684 (Delph.), al. **-ωτής,** οῦ, ὁ, *one who gives assurance of* a thing, *authority*, ἀμφισβητουμένων Plb.4.40.3 (pl.) ; ἱστορίας D.H.1.28, cf. 3.67, al.; *confirmatory*, λόγοι Phld.*Sign.*29. 2. legal *surety*, τοῦ μόνιμον τὴν ὁμόνοιαν γενέσθαι Plb.2.40.2 ; β. τῆς πίστεως παρέχεσθαι Plu. *Flam.*4 ; *warrantor* in sales, *SIG*²832 (Amphipolis), etc. **-ωτικός,** ή, όν, *confirmatory*, Epict.*Ench.*52, S.E.*P.*1.169, etc. II. **-κόν,** τό, *tax paid to the Government as warrantor of sales*, *BGU*156.9 (iii A.D.). **-ώτρια,** ἡ, fem. of βεβαιωτής, ib.994 iii 7 (ii B.C.), *PStrassb.* 88.29 (ii B.C.), etc.

βεβάμεν, v. βαίνω. **βεβᾰρηώς,** v. βαρέω. **βέβᾰσαν,** v. βαίνω.

βεβᾰσᾰνισμένως, Adv. *with severe scrutiny*, Poll.6.150.

βέβασις· τὸ εὐζόμενον, Hsch.

βέβηλ-ος, ον, Dor. **βέβᾱλος** *IG*3.3845, Ps.-Lysisap.Iamb.*VP*17. 75 : (βαίνω, βηλός) :—*allowable to be trodden*, prob. of ground (opp. ἱερός, D.H.7.8) ; καὶ πῶς β. ἄλσος ἂν ῥύοιτό με ; A.*Supp.*509 ; ἢ πρὸς βεβήλοις ἢ πρὸς ἄλσεσιν θεῶν either on *profane ground* or .., S.*OC*10 ; ἔς τε τἄβατα καὶ πρὸς βέβηλα Id.*Fr.*88 : hence generally, *permitted*, καὶ βέβηλα καὶ κεκρυμμένα λόγια *public, current*, E.*Heracl.*404 ; ἐν βεβήλῳ Th.4.97 ; βέβηλα *permitted meats*, Ath.2.65f. II. of persons, *unhallowed*, = ἀμύητος, S.*Fr.*154, Orph.*Fr.*245 ; *impure*, E.*Fr.*648 ; β. τε καὶ ἄγροικος Pl.*Smp.*218b ; β. καὶ ἀνόσια ἐνθυμήματα Ph.2.165 : c. gen., *uninitiated*, τελετῆς *AP*9.298 (Antiphil.) ; ἀποδεικτικῆς μεθόδου Gal.*UP*12.6. Adv. -λως Ph.1.523. **-όω,** *profane*, τὸ σάββατον Lxx*Ex.*31.14, *Ev.Matt.*12.5 ; τὰ ἀνθρώπινα Jul.*Or.*7.228d. 2. *pollute, defile*, τινά Lxx*Le.*21.9, Hld.2.25. **-ωσις,** εως, ἡ, *profanation*, Lxx*Le.*21.4, Ph.1.523.

βεβῐασμένως, Adv. *of necessity*, D.S.3.25 ; *with effort*, Marcellin. *Puls.*311.

βέβλειν and **βέβλεσθαι,** = μέλλειν, Hsch.

βεβολήατο, βεβολημένος, v. βάλλω.

βεβουλευμένως, Adv. *advisedly, designedly*, D.21.41.

βεβράδα· ἀθερίνην, Hsch. **βεβράξαντα·** συντόνως κεκραγότα, Id. **βέβρηκες·** τὸ ἔνδον τῶν σιαγόνων μέρος, Id. **βέβροξ·** ἀγαθός, χρηστός, καλός, Id.

βεβρός, ά, όν, *stupid, doting*, δεσπότεω βεβροῦ Hippon.64 ; also **βεμβρός,** Hsch.

βέβρῡχε, v. βρύχω. **βεβρώθοις,** v. βιβρώσκω.

βεβυκῶσθαι (βεβηκ- codd.)· πεπρῆσθαι (Thess.), Hsch.; cf. βύκτης. **βεβυλλῶσθαι·** βεβύσθαι, Id.

βεβώς, βεβῶσα, v. βαίνω.

βέδυ, τό, Phryg., = ἀήρ, Philyll.20 ; also, = ὕδωρ, Orph.*Fr.*219.

βέῃ, v. βέομαι.

βέθρον, τό, contr. from βέρεθρον, Euph.148, Crates ap.*EM*194. 22.

βειέλοπες· ἱμάντες, used as crowns for victors at Sparta, Hsch. **βεικάδες,** *the skins of animals which die naturally* (Lacon.), Id. **βεικάσθων·** κατ' ὀλίγον προβάς, Id. (leg. βιβάσθων). **βείκατι** (β = ϝ), = εἴκοσι (Lacon.), Id. **βείκηλα·** νωχελῆ, ἀχρεῖα (Lacon.), Id. **βειλαρμόστας, βειλάρχας,** = ϝιλ- (Tarent.), Id. **βείλομαι,** Boeot., = βούλομαι (q. v.). **βείομαι, βείω,** v. sub βέομαι. **βείρακες·** ἱέρακες, Hsch. **βειρακή·** ἡ ἁρπακτική, Id. **βεῖριξ·** ἔλαφος, Id. **βειρόν·** δασύ, Id.

βεκκεσέληνος, ον, (βέκος, cf. προσέληνος, and v. Hdt.2.2) = ἀρχαῖος, *superannuated, doting*, coined by Ar.*Nu.*398, cf. Plu.2.881a.

βέκος or **βεκός,** τό, gen. βέκους Aristid.2.3 J. :—*bread*, Phryg. acc. to Hdt.2.2, cf. *Jahresh.*8 *Beibl.*95 ; but Κυπρίων β. Hippon.82.

βεκῶς· μακρόθεν, Hsch. (ϝεκάς).

βέλα· ἥλιος καὶ αὐγή (Lacon.), Hsch. :—also **βελλάσεται·** ἡλιωθήσεται, Id. **βελάς·** εἴρων καὶ καταγελαστής, Id.

βελεηφόρος, ον, *bearing darts*, *AP*14.111.

βέλεκκοι, οἱ, = ὄσπρια, Ar.*Fr.*755.

βέλεμνον, τό, poet. for βέλος, *dart, javelin*, Il. only in pl., πικρὰ β. 22.206: later in sg., ἀμφιτόμῳ β. A.*Ag.*1496 (lyr.), cf. 1520, Theoc. 11.16; poet., of *hail-stones*, Orph.*L.*597.

βελενκώθιον, τό, *basket* (?), *PFay.*118.20 (ii A.D.).

βελεσσιχάρης, ές, *joying in darts*, of Apollo, *AP*9.525.3.

βελικός, ή, όν, *of* or *belonging to projectiles*: βελικά, τά, work by Agesistratus, Ath.Mech.8.6.

βελίτης [ῑ] κάλαμος reed used *for making darts*, *Gp.*2.6.23.

βέλλαι· ῥαφίδες θαλάσσιαι, Hsch. **βέλλιον**· ἀτυχές (Cret.), Id. **βέλλιρ**· τρυφάλεια (Lacon.), Id. **βέλλομαι**, v. βούλομαι. **βελλούνης**· τριόρχης, Id.

βελοθήκη, ἡ, *quiver*, Lib.*Decl.*30.9.

βελόνη, ἡ, (βέλος) *needle*, Batr.130, Eup.259, Arist.*Cael.*313ᵃ19; βελόνας διείρειν Aeschin.3.166. **II.** *pipe-fish, Syngnathus*, Arist. *HA*567ᵇ23; *garfish, Belone acus*, ib.506ᵇ10, Dorio ap.Ath.7.319d; but prob. f.l. for βάλανος, Archipp.24.

βελονίς, ίδος, ἡ, Dim. of foreg., *little needle*, Hermipp.49. **II.** a little *fish*, Sch.Opp.*H.*3.577.

βελονο-ειδής, ές, *needle-shaped*, σχήματα Thphr.*Sens.*77; β. ἔκφυσις *styloid* process of the temporal bone, Gal.*UP*7.19, al. **-θήκη**, ἡ, *needle-case*, Sch.Ar.*Pl.*175. **-ποικίλτης**, ου, ὁ, *embroiderer*, Hsch. **-πώλης**, ου, ὁ, *needle-seller*, Critias 70 D., Ar.*Pl.*175:—fem. **-πωλις**, ιδος, Poll.7.197.

βελο-ποιΐα, ἡ, *manufacture of missiles*, Hero *Bel.*72.6, Poll.7.156:—also **-ποιϊκή** (sc. τέχνη), ἡ, Hero *Bel.*74.11. **-ποιός**, όν, *making missiles*, Ph.*Bel.*58.50, Poll.7.156.

βέλος, εος, τό, *missile*, esp. *arrow, dart*, freq. in Hom.; of the piece of rock *hurled* by the Cyclops, πόντονδε βαλὼν β. Od.9.495; of an ox's leg *thrown* by one of the suitors at Ulysses, 20.305; of a stool, 17.464; ὑπὲκ βελέων out *of the reach of darts*, out *of shot*, Il.4.465; ἐκ βελέων 11.163; ἔξω βελῶν X.*Cyr.*3.3.69, etc.; ἔξω βέλους Arr.*An.*2.27.1, Luc.*Hist.Conscr.*4; opp. ἐντὸς βέλους, D.S.20.6, Arr.*An.*1.2.5; εἴσω β. παρελθεῖν ib.1.6.8. **2.** used of *any weapon*, as a *sword*, Ar.*Ach.*345, cf. S.*Aj.*658; an *axe*, E.*El.*1159; *the sting of* a scorpion, A.*Fr.*169; of the gad-fly, Id.*Supp.*556. **3.** ἀγανὰ βέλεα of Apollo, Il.24.759, Od.3.280, and of Artemis, ib.5.124, denote *sudden, easy death* of men and women respectively; βέλος ὀξύ, of Ilithyia, *pangs* of childbirth, Il.11.269, cf. Theoc.27.29. **4.** after Hom. of *anything swift-darting*, Διὸς βέλη *the bolts* of Zeus, lightnings, Pi.*N.*10.8, cf. Hdt.4.79, etc.; Ζηνὸς ἄγρυπνον β. A.*Pr.*360; πύρπνουν β. ib.917; βέλεσι πυρπνόου ζάλης, of a storm, ib.373; πάγων δύσομβρα β. S.*Ant.*358: metaph., ὀμμάτων β. *glance* of the eye, A.*Ag.*742; φίλοικτον β. a piteous *glance*, ib.241 (lyr.); ἱμέρου β. the *shaft* of love, Id.*Pr.*649; θυμοῦ βέλη S.*OT*893 (s.v.l.); of arguments, πᾶν τετόξευται β. A.*Eu.*679, cf. Pl.*Phlb.*23b; β. τὰ ἀπὸ τοῦ στόματος, of invective, Lib.*Or.*51.8; of *mental anguish* or *fear*, ἄτλατον β. Pi.*N.*1.48 (v.l. δέος); ὁ φθόνος αὐτὸς ἑαυτὸν ἑοῖς βελέεσσι δαμάζει *AP*10.111. **5.** *engine of war*, Ph.*Bel.*82.8: pl., *artillery*, ib.97.10. (Cf. βάλλω, Lith. *gélti* 'sting', *gėlà* 'sharp pain', OHG. *quelan* 'feel sharp pain'. Root *gʷel-* 'pierce', cf. δέλλιθες.)

βελο-στάσία, ἡ, *range* or *battery of warlike engines*, Ath.Mech.22.11. **-στάσις**, εως, ἡ, = foreg., Plb.9.41.8, Ph.*Bel.*81.17, D.S.20.85. **-σφενδόνη**, ἡ, *dart wrapped with pitch and tow, and thrown while on fire from an engine*, Plu.*Sull.*18.

βελουλκ-έω, *draw out darts*, αὐτὸς ἑαυτὸν βελουλκεῖ *extracts the weapon* (i.e. *hook*) *from* itself, Plu.2.977b. **-ητέον**, *one must draw out darts*, Paul.Aeg.6.88. **-ία**, ἡ, *drawing out of darts*, Eust.464.41 (pl.). **-ικός**, ή, όν, *of* or *for* βελουλκία, Paul.Aeg.6.88. **-ός**, ὁ, *instrument for drawing out darts*, ibid. **II.** = δίκταμνος, Ps.-Dsc.3.32.

βελοφόροι, οἱ, = Lat. *sagittarii*, Lyd.*Mag.*1.46.

βέλτ-ερος, α, ον, = βελτίων, poet. Comp. of ἀγαθός, *better, more excellent*, Hom. only in neut., βέλτερόν [ἐστι] *it is better*, c. inf., Il.15.511, 21.485: c. dat. pers. et inf., Od.17.18; βέλτερον εἰ.. 6.282, cf. Thgn.92, A.*Th.*337, etc.: Sup. **βέλτατος**, η, ον, Id.*Eu.*487, *Supp.*1054. **-ιότης**, ητος, ἡ, *superiority*, Sch.Pi.*O.*1.5. **-ιόω**, *improve*, Ph.1.202, al., *Stud.Pal.*1.7 ii 20 (V A.D.), etc.:—Pass., Ph.1.169, al., Plu.2.85c, *SIG*888.5 (Thrace, iii A.D.), Antyll.ap.Orib.10.23.18, etc.; οὔτε βελτιοῦσι τὴν αἰτίαν τῶν παθῶν *give* no *better reason for*, Posidon.ap.Gal.5.469. **-ιστος**, η, ον, Dor. βέντ-, Sup. of ἀγαθός, *best, most excellent*, β. ἀνὴρ γενέσθαι περὶ τὸν δῆμον Ar.*Eq.*765; ὦ βέλτιστε or β., a common mode of address, *my dear friend*, Id.*Pl.*1172, Antiph.289, Pl.*R.*337e, etc.; ὦ βέλτιστε σύ Eub.106; ὦ β. ἀνδρῶν Pl.*Grg.*515a; ὦ ἄριστε καὶ β. Id.*Lg.*902a; βέντισθ' οὗτος Theoc.5.76; ὑπὲρ τὸ β. A.*Ag.*378; οἱ β. or τὸ β. *the aristocracy*, X.*HG*5.2.6, *Cyr.*8.1.16, *Ath.*1.5, etc.; τὸ β., in Philos., *the highest good*, Pl.*Phd.*99a,b, Epict.*Ench.*51, etc.; τὰ β. βουλεύειν Th.4.68; οὐκ ἀπὸ τοῦ β. ἀναστρέφεσθαι *SIG*593.7 (ii B.C.), *PTeb.*282.8 (ii A.D.). Adv. βέλτιστα X.*Oec.*7.29, etc.; βελτίστως Simp.*in Cael.*419.25. **-ίων**, ον, gen. ονος, Comp. of ἀγαθός, *better* (not in Hom.), βέλτιόν [ἐστι] *it is fitting, convenient*, Arist.*Pol.*1264ᵇ28; μανθάνειν βελτίονα [S.]*Fr.*1120.5; ἐπὶ τὸ β. χωρεῖν *improve, advance*, Th.7.50; ἐπὶ τὸ β. ἐλθεῖν Din.1.65; ἄγειν ib.29; τὰ βελτίω προσδοκᾶν ἀεί Apollod.Com.9. Adv. βελτιόνως, ἔχειν Hp.*Mul.*1.2, cf. Pl.*R.*484a. [ῑ Att., but βέλτῐον Mimn.2.10.] **-ίωσις**, εως, ἡ, *improvement*, Ph.1.30, al., Plu.2.702c, S.E.*M.*7.23; *putting in repair*, *PMasp.*97.69 (vi A.D.). **-ιώτερος**, α, ον, = βελτίων, prob. in Telesill.6.

βελτός· βλητός, Hsch. **βέλφιν**, Aeol., = δελφίς, *EM*200.24.

Βελφός, -οί, Boeot. and Aeol. for Δελφ-.

βεμβεύει· δινεύει, Hsch. **βεμβίδιον**, a small *fish*, Id. (leg. βεμβρ-, cf. βεμβράς).

βεμβῐκ-ιάω, (βέμβιξ) *spin like a top*, Ar.*Av.*1465. **-ίζω**, *set a-spinning*, ἑαυτούς Id.*V.*1517. **-ώδης**, ες, *like a top*, Ath.11.496a.

βέμβιξ, ῑκος, ἡ, *whipping-top*, Ar.*Av.*1461, Call.*Epigr.*1.9. **II.** *whirlpool*, Opp.*H.*5.222. **III.** *cyclone*, Hsch. **IV.** *buzzing insect*, Nic.*Al.*183, *Th.*806, Parmeno 4.

βέμβλετο, v.l. for μέμβλετο in Il.21.516, Sch.Il.*Oxy.*221 xi 35: βεμόλετο (sic) Hsch., who also gives **βέμβλωκα** for μεμβλ-.

βεμβράς, άδος, ἡ, = μεμβράς, Aristomen.7, Numen.ap.Ath.7.287c:—Dim. **βεμβ⟨ρ⟩ίδιον**, Hsch.

βεμβρᾰφύη [ῠ], ἡ, *a dish of* μεμβράδες *and* ἀφύαι, Aristonym.2.

βεμβρεῖ· δινεύει, Hsch. **βεμβρός**, v. βεβρός. **βεμεῖ**· δονεῖ, Id. **βεμόλετο**, v. βέμβλετο. **βεμόριξ** (prob. for βέμβριξ), = βέμβιξ, Id.

Βενδῖς, ῖδος, ἡ, acc. Βενδῖν (not Βένδις, ιδος, Hdn.Gr.1.107):—*Bendis, the Thracian Artemis*, worshipped under this name at the Piraeus, Hippon.120, *IG*1².310, Luc.*JTr.*8, Orph.*Fr.*200:—hence **Βενδίδ-ειον**, τό, *temple of Bendis*, X.*HG*2.4.11: **-εια**, τά, *her festival*, Pl.*R.*354a, *IG*2.741 (written -εα): **-ειος**, ὁ (sc. μήν), name of month in Bithynia, *Hemerolog.Flor.*

Βενετιανός, ὁ, *a favourer of the blues*, M.Ant.1.5, *IG*14.1503.

βένετος, ον, = καλλάϊνος, *blue*, Lyd.*Mens.*4.30: esp. of *the blue faction* in the Circus, *Tab.Defix.Aud.*166.38 (Rome, iv/v A.D.), Lyd. l.c., Procop.*Pers.*1.24: Adj. **Βενέτειος**, ον, *of the* Βένετοι, στοά ibid.

βένθος, εος, τό, poet., = βάθος, *depth* of the sea, κατὰ βένθος ἁλὸς Il.18.38,49; ἁλὸς βένθοσδε Od.4.780, 8.51: in pl., ὅστε θαλάσσης πάσης βένθεα οἶδεν 1.53; ἐν βένθεσσιν ἁλὸς Il.1.358; βένθεσι λίμνης 13.21, 32; also βαθείης βένθεσιν ὕλης Od.17.316: metaph., βένθεϊ σῆς κραδίης *AP*5.273 (Paul. Sil.).—Used also by Emp.35.3, al., Pi.*O.*7.57, and in lyr., E.*Fr.*304, Ar.*Ra.*666. (Cf. βαθύς.)

βέντιστος, α, ον, v. βέλτιστος.

βέομαι and **βείομαι**, Homeric subj. used as fut., I *shall live*, οὔ τι Διὸς βέομαι φρεσίν Il.15.194; οὐδ' αὐτὸς δηρὸν βέῃ 16.852, cf. 24.131; τί νυ βείομαι αἰνὰ παθοῦσα; 22.431. (Cf. βιόμεσθα, βίονται (v. βιόω), whence βίομαι, βίε' should perh. be restored in Hom.)

Βερβεία, title of Aphrodite in Cyprus, Eriph.2.13.

βέρβερι, εος, τό, *pearl-mussel*, foreign word, Androsth.ap.Ath.3.93b.

βερβερίζω, = βατταρίζω, in later Greek, *EM*191.35.

βερβέριον, τό, *shabby garment*, Anacr.21.3.

βερβίνια, τά, *pegs for hanging up vases*, Hermipp. in Gloss.*Oxy.*1801.57, Hsch.

βεργαΐζω, *romance*, St.Byz. s.v. Βέργη: **βεργαῖος** ὕθλος Alex. in Gloss.*Oxy.*1801.50; β. διήγημα Str.2.3.5 (Antiphanes of Berga in Thrace was proverbial for his 'tall' stories).

βέρεδος, ὁ, = Lat. *veredus, post-horse*, Procop.*Pers.*2.20:—hence **βερεδάριος**, ὁ, Id.*Aed.*5.3:—also written **βερηδάριος**, τί ἐστι ναύτης; θαλάσσης β. Secund.*Sent.*18.

βέρεθρον, Ep. and Ion. for βάραθρον, Il.8.14, Pherecyd.51(b) J., Epic. in *Arch.Pap.*7 p.7; of the *underground course* of a river, Thphr. *HP*3.1.2, 5.4.6, Posidon.55.

βερεκύνδαι· δαίμονές τινες, Hsch.

Βερέκυντες, οἱ, a Phrygian people, Str.10.3.12, 12.8.21: acc. sg. Βερέκυντα A.*Fr.*158; Βερέκυντα βρόμον, of the *Phrygian* flute, S.*Fr.*513:—also **Βερέκυνται**, Hsch.:—Adj. **Βερεκύνθιος**, α, ον, *Phrygian, devoted to Cybele*, Call.*Dian.*246; **Βερεκύντιος**, Hsch.

Βερεκυντίας, ὁ, = ἀπηλιώτης (Pontic word), Thphr.*Vent.*62.

Βερενίκη [ῑ], ἡ, Macedon. form for Φερενίκη, freq. pr. n. in the time of the Ptolemies:—also **Βερνίκη** *Act.Ap.*25.13: **Βερενίκης** πλόκαμος, a *constellation*, Gem.3.8, etc.; also, a *throw of the dice*, Hsch.:—hence **βερενίκιον**, τό, a *plant*, Hsch.; also, *nitre* of the best quality, Gal.13.568:—Dim. **βερενικάριον** or **βερνικάριον** νίτρον, Orib.*Fr.*107, Aët.6.54:—**βερενικίδες**, αἱ, women's *shoes*, Hsch.

Βερέσχεθοι, οἱ, *the Powers of Folly*, Ar.*Eq.*635; βερέσχετοι Gloss. *Oxy.*1801.

βερίκοκκον, τό, *apricot*, *Gp.*10.73.2:—Dim. **βερικόκκιον** ib.3.1.4, Artem.1.73; β. μῆλον Herod.Med. in *Rh.Mus.*58.100. (Lat. *praecoqua.*)

βέρκιος· ἔλαφος (Lacon.), Hsch. **βερκνίς**· ἀκρίς, Id. (cf. βρεῦκος). **βερνώμεθα**· κληρωσώμεθα (Lacon.), and **βερρέαι**· κληρῶσαι (prob. = μείρεαι), Id. **βέρρης**, ου, ὁ, = δραπέτης, *a fugitive*; and **βερρεύω**, = δραπετεύω, Id. **βερρόν**, = βειρόν, Id. **βερωνετῶν**· ἀλλὰ ἀνετῶν, Id. **βέσκεροι**· ἄρτοι (Lacon.), Id. **βεσόν**· ἔθος, Id. (prob. Lacon. = ϝέθος). **βεστικός**· ὁ τῶν ἐσθήτων ἔμπειρος cj. in Id. s. v. βεσόν. (Cf. *vestis.*)

βεστίον, τό, *clothing*, *PLond.*5.1654 (iv A.D.).

βέστον and **βέττον**, = ἱμάτιον, Diogenian.ap.*EM*195.45.

βεττονική, ἡ, = βρεττανική, interpol. post Dsc.4.2 (p.170 Wellm.). **2.** *Paul's betony, Sideritis purpurea*, Paul.Aeg.7.3. **3.** = κέστρος (q.v.), ibid.

βεῦδος, εος, τό, *woman's dress*, Sapph.155, Call.*Fr.*155, Nicaenet.(?) ap.Parth.11.4 (pl.). **II.** = ἄγαλμα, at Hermione, *EM*195.52.

βέφῡρα, Boeot. for γέφυρα, Stratt.47.5.

βῆ βῆ, *baa*, the cry of sheep, βῆ βῆ λέγων βαδίζει Cratin.43, cf. Ar. *Fr.*642, Varro *RR*2.1:—hence **βηβήν**· πρόβατον, and **βήζει**· φωνεῖ, Hsch.

βῆγμα, ατος, τό, (βήσσω) *expectoration, phlegm*, Hp.*Morb.*2.47.

βήθυλος· εἶδος ὀρνέου, *EM*196.54. **βῆκα**· ἀναδενδράς, Hsch. **βήκη**· χίμαιρα, Id.

βηκία, τά, = πρόβατα, Hp.ap.Gal.19.88: but **βηκία** and **βηκίον** (which = ἐλελίσφακος, Ps.-Dsc.3.33, and = ψευδοδίκταμνος, ib.32), = βήχιον, Erot., Ps.-Dsc.3.112. **βηκώνιον**· εἶδος βοτάνης, Hsch. (leg. μηκ–).

βηλά, ῶν, τά, = πέδιλα, Panyas.23.

βῆλημα (i.e. ϝηλ–), ατος, τό, = κώλυμα, φράγμα ἐν ποταμῷ (Lacon.), Hsch., cf. *IG*5(1).1390.104 (Andania).

βηλήσσει· βληχᾶται, Hsch.

βηλόθῠρον, τό, *door-curtain, portière*, Sch.Ar.*Ra*.969.

βήλομαι, v. βούλομαι.

βηλός, Dor. **βᾱλός** (also used in Trag., *AB*224), ὁ: (βαίνω):—*threshold*, Il.1.591, A.*Ch*.571, Porph.*Antr*.14; β. ἀστερόεις Q.S.13.483.

βῆμα, Aeol. and Dor. **βᾶμα**, ατος, τό, (βαίνω) *step, pace*, *h.Merc*.222, 345, Pi.*P*.3.43, A.*Ch*.799 (lyr.); σπουδῇ.. βημάτων πορεύεται E.*Andr*. 880; τοσόνδε β. διαβεβηκώς Ar.*Eq*.73; *footfall*, ἐρατὸν βᾶμα Sapph. *Supp*.5.17; Διὸς εὔφρονι βήματι μολεῖν *to journey under the kindly guidance* of Zeus, S.*El*.163 (lyr.); *gait*, β. οὐκ ὀρθὸν *Hippiatr*.27. 2. *step*, as a measure of length, = 10 παλαισταί, about 2½ feet, Hero *Deff*. 131. 3. metaph., *step*, '*moment*', πρόοδος ἐν τρισὶ β. διισταμένη Dam.*Pr*.258. II. = βάθρον, *step, seat*, S.*OC*193 (lyr.). 2. *raised place* or *tribune* to speak from in a public assembly, etc., Th.2.34, Lxx *Ne*.8.4, etc.; in the Pnyx at Athens, ἐπὶ τὸ β. ἀναβῆναι enter *public life*, D.18.66; αἱ ἀπὸ τοῦ β. ἐλπίδες Id.4.45; also in the law-courts, Id.48.31, Aeschin.3.207; of a suppliant, ἐπὶ τοῦ β. καθεδούμενον Ar.*Pl*.382; in the βουλευτήριον, Antipho 6.40. b. *tribunal* of a magistrate, τοῦ ἡγεμόνος β. *PTeb*.434 (ii A.D.). 3. = θυμέλη, Poll.4.123; β. θεήτρου *IG*3.239. 4. *base, pedestal*, *OGI*219.36 (Ilium, iii B.C.), 299.15 (Pergam., ii B.C.).

βῆμα· πρόβατα, Hsch.

βημᾰτ-ίζω, (Act. only in Hsch.) *measure by paces*, Plb.3.39.8 (Pass.); ὁδὸς βεβηματισμένη κατὰ μίλιον Str.7.7.4:—Med., ὄμματι βηματίσαισθε τὸν ἀέρα Dionys.Eleg.3.5. II. *step, walk*, Aesop. 322b. **–ιστής**, οῦ, ὁ, *one who measures by paces*, Ath.10.442c. II. *quartermaster*, *SIG*303 (Olympia, iv B.C.).

βήμεναι, v. βαίνω. **βηνῶσα**· ἡ φωνὴ τῶν προβάτων, Hsch.

βήξ, βηχός, *cough*, ὁ, Th.2.49; ἡ, Hp.*Prog*.14, Phryn.Com.60, Arist.*de An*.420b33, Thphr.*HP*3.18.3.

βηράνθεμον (i.e. ϝηρ–)· νάρκισσος, Hsch.

βήρβη· κωδύα (–δία cod.) μήκωνος, Hsch.

βήρηξ, ηκος, ὁ, a kind of *loaf*, Ar. in Gloss.*Oxy*.1801.59 (pl.), Ath.3.114f, *AB*226, Hsch. (who also has **βήραξ**); cf. βάραξ, πάραξ.

βηρίδες, = ἐμβίδες, Hsch. **βηρίχαλκον**· μάρα[ν]θον (Lacon.), Id.

βηρύλλιος, = ἀείζωον τὸ μέγα, Ps.-Dsc.4.88. 2. = ἀνεμώνη ἡ Φοινική, Osthanes ap.eund.2.176; cf. Hsch. s. v. βήρυλλος.

βήρυλλος, ἡ, *gem of sea-green colour, beryl*, Lxx *To*.13.17, D.P. 1012, Tryph.70, *PHolm*.8.10, al.; Ἰνδὴ β. *AP*9.544 (Adaeus); β. λίθος Luc.*VH*2.11:—Dim. **βηρύλλιον**, τό, Lxx *Ex*.28.20, D.S.2.52.

βηρυσσεύειν· σπείρειν (perh. σπειρᾶν), Hsch.; cf. μηρύειν.

βῆρυς· ἰχθύς, Hsch.; cf. μῆρυξ.

βήσαλον (or βισ–), τό, *brick*, Alex.Trall.9.2:—hence **βησαλικόν**, τό, *brick-work*, Hero *Stereom*.1.76.

βησασᾶ, usu. indecl., but acc. βησασᾶν v.l. in Dsc.3.46:—*Syrian rue*, Antyll.ap.Orib.10.23.26, etc.: **βησάς**, ἡ, *PMag.Par*.1.800.

βήσετο, v. βαίνω. **βησίον**, v. βησσίον.

βῆσσα, Dor. **βᾶσσα**, ἡ, poet. Noun, *wooded combe, glen*, in Hom. mostly οὔρεος ἐν βήσσῃς in the mountain *glens*, Il.3.34, al.; ἐν καλῇ βήσσῃ 18.588, cf. Od.19.435; κοίλη δ' ὑποδέδρομε βῆσσα τρηχεῖα *h.Ap*.284: pl. for sg., ἐν βήσσῃσι Od.10.210: used also by Pi., twice by S. (lyr.), *OC*673, *Aj*.197, and Arist.*HA*618b24. II. *drinking-cup* at Alexandria, broader below and narrower above, Ath.11.784b.

βησσήεις, εσσα, εν, *of* or *like a glen, woody*, ἄγκεα, δρία, Hes.*Op*. 389,530; οὔρεα D.P.1183; νομός Coluth.41.

βησσίον, τό, *cup*, *PHolm*.16.3, Hsch., prob. in *PMag.Par*.1.750: **βησίον** *Stud.Pal*.20.67 (ii/iii A.D.).

βήσσω, Att. –ττω, fut. βήξω Hp.*Mul*.1.41: aor. ἔβηξα Hdt.6.107, Hp.*Prog*.8: (βήξ):—*cough*, ll.cc., Ar.*Ec*.56, etc.:—Med. in act. sense, Hp.*Morb*.2.52:—Pass., τὰ βησσόμενα Id.*Epid*.1.3.

βῆτα, τό, indecl., *the letter* β, Pl.*Cra*.393e, Arist.*Metaph*.1087a8, *AP*11.437 (Arat.), Luc.*Herm*.40, etc. (Aram. *bēthā'*.)

βηταρμός, ὁ, *dance*, β. ἐνόπλιον ὠρχήσαντο A.R.1.1135.

βητάρμων, ονος, ὁ, *dancer*, in pl., Od.8.250,383, Man.2.335:—later, as Adj., καπνός Nonn.*D*.36.297; κάπρος ib.22.44. (βαίνω, ἀραρίσκω.)

βηχία, ἡ (or **βηχίας**, ὁ), (βήξ) *hoarseness*, Nicom.*Harm*.11, *Exc*. 4 (pl.), Menipp.*Ep*.

βηχικός, ή, όν, *suffering from cough*, γραίη f.l. in Hp.*Epid*.7. 105. 2. *good for a cough*, φάρμακα Gal.11.769, al., cf. Alex.Trall.5.

βήχιον, τό, *colt's-foot, Tussilago Farfara*, used to allay cough, Hp. *Art*.63, Dsc.3.112. II. *slight cough*, Id.*Eup*.2.31.

βηχώδης, ες, *coughing*, Hp.*Epid*.1.3. 2. *accompanied by, productive of coughing*, κατάρροοι Id.*Aph*.2.31, cf. Id.*Art*.49 (Comp.).

βία, Ion. **βίη** [ῐ], ἡ: Ep. dat. βίηφι Od.6.6:—*bodily strength, force*, Hom., etc.; χειρῶν βία B.10.91:—in Hom., periphr. of strong men, βίη Ἡρακληείη Il.2.658, where the part. masc. πέρσας follows, cf. 11.690; βίη Ἐτεοκληείη, Ἰφικλείη, 4.386, Od.11.290, etc.; βίη Διομήδεος Il.5.781; also ἶς.. βίης Ἡρακληείης Hes.*Th*.332: so in Lyr. and Trag., Πέλοπος βία B.5.181; Τυδέως βία, Πολυνείκους β., A.*Th*. 571,577; φίλτατ' Αἰγίσθου β. Id.*Ch*.893; θήρειος β., = Κένταυροι, S. *Tr*.1059. 2. personified, Κράτος Βία τε A.*Pr*.12. 3. of the mind, οὐκ ἔστι βίη φρεσίν Il.3.45. b. of an argument, βίαν οὐκ ἔχειν πρὸς ⟨τὸ⟩ ἀποδεῖξαι Phld.*Sign*.9. II. *act of violence*, ὕβρις τε βίη τε Od.15.329: mostly in pl., κείνων γε βίας ἀποτείσεαι 11.117; βίας ὑποδέγμενος ἀνδρῶν 16.189; βίαι ἀνέμων Il.16.213. 2. βίᾳ τινός *against* one's *will, in spite of* him, A.*Th*.746 (lyr.), S.*Ant*.79, Th.1. 43, etc.; β. φρενῶν A.*Th*.612; β. καρδίας Id.*Supp*.798; β. alone as Adv., *perforce*, Od.15.231, B.17.10, A.*Pr*.74, al.; βίῃ ἐπειρᾶτο Hdt. 6.5; opp. κατὰ φύσιν, Arist.*Ph*.215a1; also πρὸς βίαν τινός A.*Eu*.5; πρὸς βίαν ἄγειν τινά Id.*Pr*.210, cf. S.*OT*805, Eup.8.10D., Ar.*V*.443, etc.; opp. ἑκών, Pl.*Phdr*.236d; ἐκ βίας S.*Ph*.563, al., Herod.5.58; ὑπὸ βίης Hdt.6.107; ἀπὸ βίας D.S.20.51; of Zeus, εὐμενεῖ βίᾳ κτίσας A.*Supp*.1068 (lyr.). 3. in Att. law, *rape*, βίας δίκη Sch.Pl.*R*.464e; βίᾳ αἰσχύνεσθαί τινα Lys.1.32. 4. = Lat. *vis*, βίας γραφή D.C.37. 31, cf. 33; μαρτύρομαι τὴν βίαν *POxy*.1120.11 (iii A.D.). (Cf. Skt. *jyā jiyā* 'preponderating power', *jināti* 'oppress'.)

βῐάζω, *constrain*, Act. once in Hom., ἦ μάλα δή με βιάζετε Od.12. 297; ἐβίασε τὴν γυναῖκά μου Alc.Com.29: abs., εἰ πάνυ ἐβίαζον if *they used force*, Hp.*Epid*.2.24; cf. infr.I.2:—Pass., fut. βιασθήσομαι Paus. 6.5.9: aor. ἐβιάσθην, pf. βεβίασμαι (v. infr.):—*to be hard pressed* or *overpowered*, βελέεσσι βιάζεται Il.11.589; βιάζετο γὰρ βελ. 15.727; βιασθέντες λύᾳ Pi.*N*.9.14; νόσῳ Ar.*Fr*.20 (= *Trag.Adesp*.70); *to be forced* or *constrained* to do, c. inf., Id.*Th*.890: c. acc. cogn., βιάζομαι τάδε S.*Ant*.66, cf. 1073; βιασθεὶς Id.*El*.575; ἐπεὶ ἐβιάσθη Th.4. 44; ὑπό τινος Id.1.2; opp. ἀδικεῖσθαι, ib.77; βιασθεὶς ἄκων ἔπραξεν D.6.16; ἵνα ἢ συγχωρήσωσιν.. ἢ βιασθῶσιν Id.18.175; βιαζόμενος ὑπό τινος ἐξήμαρτεν Antipho 4.4.5; βεβιασμένοι *forcibly made slaves*, X.*Hier*.2.12; πόλεις βεβ. Id.*HG*5.2.23; βιαζόμενος ὑπὸ τῆς παρούσης ἀπορίας Th.7.67; τὸ βιασθέν *those who are forced*, Arist.*Pol*.1255a 11; of things, τοὔνειδος ὀργῇ βιασθὲν *forced from one* by anger, S.*OT* 524; τὸ βεβιασμένον *forced* to fit a hypothesis, Arist.*Metaph*.1082b2; βεβ. σχήματα *forced* figures of speech, D.H.*Th*.33, cf. Porph.*Antr*. 36. 2. Act., *make good, suffice to discharge* a debt, *PFlor*.56. 13. II. more freq. βιάζομαι, aor. Med. ἐβιασάμην, pf. βεβίασμαι D.19.206, Men.*Sam*.63, D.C.46.45:—*overpower by force, press hard*, ἦ μάλα δή σε βιάζει ὠκὺς Ἀχιλλεύς Il.22.229, etc.; β. τοὺς πολεμίους *dislodge* them, X.*An*.1.4.5; β. νόμους *to do* them *violence*, Th. 8.53; βιασάμενος ταῦτα πάντα *having broken through* all these restraints, Lys.6.52; β. γυναῖκα *force* her, Ar.*Pl*.1092; opp. πείθειν, Lys.1.32; β. αὑτόν *lay violent hands on* oneself, Pl.*Phd*.61c,d; β. τινά, c. inf., *force* one to do, X.*An*.1.3.1; τί με βιάζεσθε λέγειν; Arist. *Fr*.44: with inf. omitted, β. τὰ σφάγια *force* the victims [*to be favourable*], Hdt.9.41; β. ἄστρα Theoc.22.9: c. dupl. acc., αὐδῶ πόλιν σε μὴ β. τόδε A.*Th*.1047. 2. c. acc. rei, *carry by force*, βιάσασθαι τὸν ἔκπλουν *force* an exit, Th.7.72; τὴν ἀπόβασιν Id.4.11: c. acc. neut., And.4.17, X.*HG*5.3.12. 3. abs., *act with violence, use force*, A.*Pr*. 1010, *Ag*.1509 (lyr.), S.*Aj*.1160, etc.; πρὸς τὸ λαμπρὸν ὁ φθόνος βιάζεται *Trag.Adesp*.547.12; opp. δικάζομαι, Th.1.77; β. διὰ φυλάκων *force one's way*, Id.7.83; β. ἐς τὸ ἔξω, β. εἴσω, ib.69, X.*Cyr*.3.3.69; δρόμῳ β. Th.1.63: c. inf., β. πρὸς τὸν λόφον ἐλθεῖν Id.7.79; βιαζόμενοι βλάπτειν *using every effort* to hurt me, Lys.9.16; but βιαζόμενοι μὴ ἀποδιδόναι refusing *with violence* to repay, X.*HG*5.3.12: esp. in part., ἵνα βιασάμενοι ἐκπλεύσωσι may sail out *by forcing their way*, Th.7.67; συνεξέρχονται βιασάμενοι X.*An*.7.8.11; ἐπὶ μᾶλλον ἔτι β. (of a famine) *grow worse and worse*, Hdt.1.94. 4. *contend* or *argue vehemently*, c. inf., Pl.*Sph*.246b; β. τὸ μὴ ὂν ὥς ἐστι κατά τι ib. 241d: abs., *persist in assertion*, D.21.205.

βιαιοελπίου, dub. in *PPetr*.3p.317.

βῐαιο-θᾰνᾰσία, ἡ, *violent death*, Vett.Val.94.1, Paul.Al.*N*.2. **–θᾰνᾰτέω**, *die a violent death*, Vett.Val.67.8, Ps.-Plu.*Fluv*.7.3. **–θάνᾰτος** [θᾰ], ον, *dying a violent death*, most freq. of *suicides*, Vett.Val.74. 29, Paul.Al.*M*.2, Olymp.*in Phd*.p.243N., *PMag.Par*.1.1950, Suid. s. v. κυνήγιον.—Freq. written βιοθάνατος. **–κλώψ**, ῶπος, ὁ, (κλέπτω) *stealing forcibly*, Lyc.548. **–μάχος** (cod. Pal. –μάχας) [ᾰ], ὁ, *fighting violently*, *AP*6.129 (Leon.). **–μᾰχέω**, *fight at close quarters*, of ships, opp. ταχυναυτεῖν, Plb.1.27.12: generally, Id.5. 84.2, Phld.*Rh*.1.195S.

βίαιος [ῐ], α, ον, also ος, ον Pl.*R*.399a, Philostr.*VA*1.33: (βία):—*forcible, violent*: Adj. once in Hom., ἔρδειν ἔργα βίαια Od.2.236, Adv. twice, *by force, perforce*, κατέδουσι βιαίως οἶκον Ὀδυσσῆος 2.237; γυναιξὶ παρευνάζεσθε βιαίως 22.37: freq. in all writers, ἔργα β. Thgn. 1343; νόμος ἄγει δικαιῶν τὸ βιαιότατον Pi.*Fr*.169; of persons, βιαιότατος τῶν πολιτῶν Th.3.36; χρόνος καταψήχει καὶ τὰ βιαιότατα Simon. 176; β. θάνατος a *violent* death, Hdt.7.170, Pl.*R*.566b, etc.; β. νόσος S.*Ant*.1140 (lyr.); β. ἄνεμος Arist.*Mete*.370b9; ἐπάρδευσις Epicur.*Ep*. 2p.44U. (Comp.); ὁ πόλεμος β. διδάσκαλος teaches *by violence*, Th. 3.82; δίκη βιαίων an action *for forcible rescue*, Harp.; τοῖς β. or τῶν βιαίων ἔνοχος, Lys.23.12, Pl.*Lg*.914e; βιαίων [ἐγκαλεῖ] D.37.33; τὰ [περὶ] τῶν βιαίων ibid.; συναλλάγματα β., λαθραῖα, *obligationes ex delicto*, Arist.*EN*1131a8; κλοπαῖα καὶ β. Pl.*Lg*.934c. Adv. βιαίως, ἀποθανεῖν Antipho 1.26; β. σέλμα σεμνὸν ἡμένων *in their irresistible might*, A.*Ag*.182 (lyr.); χαλεπῶς καὶ β. by struggling and *forcing their way*, Th.3.23; *firmly*, σχεδίας β. ζεύξαντες Plb.3.46.1: neut. pl. as Adv., A.*Supp*.821 (lyr.); πρὸς τὸ β. Id.*Ag*.130; ἐκ τοῦ βιαιοτάτου D.H.10. 36. 2. esp. of magic, β. τέχνη Philostr.*VA*1.33. Adv. βιαίως, σοφὸς *a wizard*, ib.1.2. II. Pass., *forced, constrained*, opp. ἑκούσιος, πράξεις Pl.*R*.603c; β. κίνησις, = παρὰ φύσιν κ., Arist.*Ph*.254a9, cf. Pl.*Ti*.64d; τὸ β., = οὗ ἔξωθεν ἡ ἀρχὴ μηδὲν συμβαλλομένου τοῦ βιασθέντος Arist.*EN*1110b15; ἡ β. τροφή, of the diet of athletes, Id.

Pol.1338b41 ; πόνοι μὴ β. ib.1335b9 ; ὁ χρηματιστὴς (sc. βίος) β. τίς ἐστιν, Id.EN1096a6 ; βιαιότερος λόγος Jul.Or.6.191d. Adv. -ως, = παρὰ φύσιν, κινεῖσθαι Arist.Ph.253b34 : Comp. -οτέρως Gal.17(1).19. 2. = βιαιοθάνατος, PMag.Par.1.332.

βῐαιότης, ητος, ἡ, *violence*, β. καὶ παρανομία Antipho 5.8, And.4.10, cf. Lys.23.11.

βῐ-αρκής, ές, (βίος II, ἀρκέω) *supplying the necessaries of life*, AP6.179 (Arch.). 2. *life-giving*, Nonn.D.17.370. **-αρχος**, ὁ, (βίος II, ἄρχω) *commissary-general*, Lyd.Mag.1.48, al., BGU316.4 (iv A. D.).

βῐασ-μός, ὁ, *violence*, Aen.Tact.24.15, Eup.64 ; *rape*, παρθένου Men.Epit.236, cf. Satyr.Vit.Eur.Fr.39viii8 (pl.) ; ἁρπαγὴ καὶ β. Plu.2.755d, cf. D.H.1.77. II. Medic., = τεινεσμός, interp. in Dsc.3.94. **-τέον**, *one must do violence to*, τύχην E.Rh.584 ; ἀλόγως β. Phld.Oec.p.56 J. **-τήρ**, ῆρος, ὁ, = sq., prob. in Gorg.Hel.12. **-τής**, οῦ, ὁ, = βιατάς, Ev.Matt.11.12. **-τικός**, ή, όν, *forcible, violent*, νόμος Pl.Lg.921e, Arist.MA703a22 : Comp., ἀνάγκη Ph.2.395 : Sup., φίλτρον ib.28 ; *cogent*, τὸ β. [τοῦ λογικοῦ] Jul.Or.7.216a. Adv. -κῶς *violently*, EM197.11 : of a *forced* construction, Sch.Philostr. Her.p.484 B. : Comp. -ώτερον, ἐπιτάττειν S.E.M.6.7 : also, *cogently*, ἀποδείκνυται Gal.5.480. **-τός**, ή, όν, *violent*, πράγματα Chor. in Lib.4.793 Reiske.

βῐᾱτάς, α, ὁ, *forceful, mighty*, Pi.Pae.6.84, al. ; σοφοὶ καὶ χερσὶ βιαταί Id.P.1.42 ; β. νόος Id.O.9.75 ; of wine, *potent*, Id.N.9.51 ; Ἄρης AP7.492 (Anyte).

βιάτωρ· κυάθιον μικρόν, κοχλιάριον, Hsch.

βῐάω, Ep. form of βιάζω, *constrain*, Act. only in the pf., ἄχος, χρειὼ βεβίηκεν Ἀχαιούς, Il.10.145,172, 16.22 :—Pass., *to be forcibly driven*, of fire, ἀνέμῳ βιώμενον Hdt.1.19 ; πῦρ βεβιημένον AP9.546 (Antiphil.) ; θανάτῳ βιηθείς Hdt.7.83, cf. Hp.Mul.1.40 : fut., οὐ βιήσεται (in pass. sense) *will not yield to force*, ib.2.132 ; βιωομένη (v.l. βιαζ-) Mosch.2.13. II. freq. as Dep. (pres. imper. βιάσθω Parm.1.34, fut. βιήσεται Emp.4.6) in act. sense, οἵ κεῖνον βιόωνται Od.11.503, cf. 23.9, Pl.Ti.63c ; ὡς εἴ ἑ βιῴατο (opt.) .. Τρῶες *should press* him *hard*, Il.11.467 ; βιήσατο κῦμ' ἐπὶ χέρσον it *forced* me upon.., Od.7.278 ; ψεύδεσσι βιησάμενος over-reaching, Il.23.576 ; τότε νῶϊ βιήσατο μισθὸν ἅπαντα *wronged us, deprived us of* our wages, 21.451 ; τὸ δοκεῖν καὶ τὰν ἀλάθειαν βιᾶται Simon.76, cf. Pi.N.8.34, B.12.200 ; *force, ravish*, παρθένον Hdt.4.43 ; *drive* or *urge on*, βιᾶται δ' ἁ τάλαινα πειθώ A.Ag.385 (lyr.).

βιβ-άζω, fut. βιβάσω, Att. βιβῶ, with part. βιβῶν S.OC381, (δια-) Pl.Lg.900c, D.23.157, (ἐμ-) X.An.5.7.8, (προσ-) Ar.Av.426, Pl. Phdr.229e (but διαβιβάσοντες codd. in X.An.4.8.8, 5.2.10) : aor. ἐβίβασα (ἀν-) Id.HG4.5.3, (ἀπ-) Pl.Grg.511e :—Med., pres. (ἀνα-) Th.7.33 : fut. βιβάσομαι, Att. βιβῶμαι (ἀνα-) Amips.30, Aeschin.2.146, D.19.310, but ἀναβιβάσομαι codd. in And.1.148, Lys.18.24 : aor. ἐβιβασάμην (ἀν-) Th.7.35, Lys.20.34, etc. :—Pass., fut. βιβασθήσομαι (δια-) D.S.13.81 : aor. βιβασθείς Arist.HA577a30 : pf. βεβίβασται (συμ-) S.E.M.7.283 :—causal of βαίνω, mostly used in compds., *cause to mount, exalt*, πρὸς οὐρανὸν βιβῶν S.OC381 : simply, *cause to go*, μή με τᾶσδ' ἐξ ὁδοῦ βίβαζε Id.Ichn.368. II. of animals, *put the female to the male*, Alc.Com.18, Arist.HA573b7 ; also of the male, Horap.1.48 :—Pass., of the female, Arist.HA577a29, Lxx Le.18.23. **-άσθω**, = βιβάω, only in part., μακρὰ βιβάσθων *long-striding*, Il.13.809, 16.534. **-ᾰσις**, εως, ἡ, *a Spartan dance*, Poll.4.102. II. = ὀχεία, *Gloss*. III. = κοίτη, στιβάς, Hsch. **-αστής**, οῦ, ὁ, *stallion*, *Gloss*. **-άω**, poet. collat. form of βαίνω, *stride*, πέλωρα βιβᾷ he *takes* huge *strides*, h.Merc.225 ; ἐβίβασκε, Ion. impf., h.Ap.133 : elsewh. only part., μακρὰ βιβῶντα (βιβάντα Aristarch.), μακρὰ βιβῶσα, Il.3.22, Od.11.539 ; κοῦφα βιβῶν lightly *stepping*, Pi.O.14.17. **-ημι**, poet. collat. form of βαίνω, *to stride*, used by Hom. only in part., μακρὰ βιβάς Il.7.213, al. ; ὕψι βιβάντα 13.371, al. (v. foreg.) : Dor. 3 sg. βίβαντι Epigr.Lacon.ap. Poll.4.102.

βιβλ-, βυβλ-, v. βύβλος.

βιβλ-αρίδιον, τό, Dim. of βίβλος, *small roll*, Apoc.10.2. **-άριον**, τό, = foreg., PLille 1.7.7 (iii B.C.), AP11.78 (Lucill.).

βιβλιαγράφος, v. βιβλιογράφος.

βιβλι-αίγισθος, Ἀνδρέας ὁ ἰατρὸς ἐπεκλήθη ὑπὸ Ἐρατοσθένους ὅτι λάθρα αὐτοῦ τὰ βιβλία μετέγραψε EM198.20. **-ακός**, ή, όν, *versed in books*, Phld.Ir.p.90 W. (βυβλ-) ; ἐν ἱστορίᾳ βιβλιακώτατος Plu. Rom.12 ; *pedantic*, χαρακῖται Timo 12 ; ἕξις Plb.12.25h.3. 2. *of a book*, σελίδες AP7.594 (Jul.) ; *in* or *of books*, συντάξεις Chaerem. ap.Porph.Abst.4.7. **-αρίδιον**, τό, = βιβλαρίδιον, Gal.16.5. **-άριον**, τό, = βιβλάριον, Antisth.ap.D.L.6.3.

βιβλιαφόρος, ον, *letter-carrier*, Plb.4.22.2, D.S.2.26 : **βυβλιοφόρος** PHal.7.6 (iii B.C.).

βιβλιδάριον, τό, = βιβλάριον, Ar.Fr.756, Agatharch.111.

βιβλίδιον [ῐδ], τό, Dim. of βιβλίον, D.56.1, Plb.23.2.5 (βυβλ-), SIG663.20 (Delos, iii/ii B.C.), AP12.208 (Strat.), Antiph.162 : **βιβλείδιον**, τό, *petition*, Lat. *libellus*, POxy.1032.4 (ii A.D.), etc. ; ἐπὶ βιβλειδίων, = Lat. *a libellis*, IG14.1072 :—written **βυβλείδιον** Demetr. Lac.Herc.1012.35 F., 1013.12 F.

βίβλινος, η, ον, *made of* βίβλος (βύβλος), BGU544.4 (ii A.D.).

βιβλιο-γρᾰφία, ἡ, *writing of books*, Dsc.1.85, D.L.7.36. **-γράφος** [ᾰ], ὁ, *writer of books, scribe*, Antiph.197, Lib.Ep.263 :—also **βιβλιᾰγράφος** (correct form acc. to Phryn.67), Cratin.249, Luc.Ind.24. **-θήκη**, ἡ, *book-case*, Cratin.Jun.11 (βυβλ-). 2. *library, collection of books*, Plb.12.27.4, Lxx Es.2.23, Posidon.41, Phld.Sto. Herc.339.13 (βυβλ-), Str.13.1.54, al., J.AJ12.2.1 ; β. ἔμψυχος, of Longinus, Eun.VSp.456 B. 3. *record-office, registry*, PTeb.389.18 (ii A.D.) ; β. ἐγκτήσεων BGU76.1 (ii/iii A.D.) ; β. δημοσίων [λόγων] PRyl.291.1 (iii A.D.). 4. *compilation* from various sources, title of works by Apollod. and D.S. **-κάπηλος** [ᾰ], ὁ, *dealer in books*, Luc.Ind.4,24. **-λάθας** [λᾱ], α, ὁ, (λήθη) *book-forgetting*, nickname of Didymus the Gramm., who had written so many books (3,500) that he could not remember them, Demetr.Troez.ap.Ath.4.139c. **-μᾰχέω**, *present a counter-petition*, POxy.68.33 (ii A.D.).

βιβλίον or **βυβλίον**, τό, *strip of* βύβλος, Thphr.HP4.8.4 : hence, *paper, document*, Hdt.1.123, 3.128, Ar.Av.974, etc. ; τὸ β. τοῦ ψηφίσματος IG2².1.61 ; β. ἀποστασίου *notice* of divorce, Ev.Matt.19.7. 2. = βιβλίδιον, *petition* to the Government, = Lat. *libellus*, BGU422 (ii A.D.), POxy.86.16 (iv A.D.), etc. 3. = δέλτος, *tablet*, Lxx To.7.14. II. *book*, Eup.304, Theognet.1.8, Pl.Ap.26d, etc. ; μέγα β. ἴσον τῷ μεγάλῳ κακῷ Call.Fr.359. 2. *book* as the division of a work, ἐν τῷ πρώτῳ β. Dsc.2 Praef., Ph.1.329, etc. 3. τὰ β. *place in which books are kept, library*, ἀνεθήκατε εἰς τὰ β. D.Chr.37.8. 4. τὰ β. τὰ ἅγια the sacred *books* or *Scriptures*, Lxx 1 Ma.12.9 ; τὰ β. τοῦ νόμου ib.1.56.

βιβλιο-πωλεῖον, τό, *bookseller's shop*, Ath.1.1e, Gal.Lib.Propr.1. **-πώλης**, ου, ὁ, *bookseller*, Theopomp.Com.77, Nicoph.19.4, Aristomen.9, Arist.Fr.140. **-φόριον**, τό, *book-* or *letter-case*, AB 314. **-φῠλᾰκέω**, *to be a librarian*, PBodl.ined. (MS. Gr. Class. d 86 P r 9). **-φῠλᾰκία**, ἡ, *office of* βιβλιοφύλαξ, PRyl.374.8 (i/ii A.D.). **-φῠλάκιον** [ᾰ], τό, *place to keep books in*, τὰ βασιλικὰ β. the royal *archives*, Lxx 1 Es.6.21,23, PTeb.318.23 (ii A.D.). **-φύλαξ** [ῠ], ακος, ὁ, *keeper of archives*, ib.112 Intr.10 (ii B.C.), PFay.31.3 (ii A.D.) : **βυβλ-** Milet.6.36 (Didyma), POxy.483.32, CPR1.18.41 (ii A.D.).

βιβλίς, ίδος, ἡ, = βιβλίον, EM197.30. II. pl., *cords of* βίβλος, ibid.

βιβλοπώλης, = βιβλιο-, Phryn.PSp.52 B. **βίβλος**, ἡ, v. βύβλος.

βιβρώσκω, Babr.108.9, (cf. βρώζω, βορά) : βρώσομαι Philostr.VA3.40 : aor. ἔβρωσα (ἀν-) Nic.Th.134 ; inf. βρῶξαι (κατα-) Epic. in Arch. Pap.7.5 : Ep. aor. 2 ἔβρων Call.Jov.49, (κατ-) h.Ap.127 : pf. βέβρωκα Il.22.94, Eup.68 ; sync. part. βεβρώς, ῶτος, S.Ant.1022 ; opt. βεβρώθοις, as if from pf. βέβρωθα, Il.4.35 :—Pass., pres., Hp.Aff.4 : fut. βρωθήσομαι Lyc.1421, S.E.P.3.227 ; βεβρώσομαι Od.2.203 : aor ἐβρώθην Hp.Acut.37, etc., (κατ-) Hdt.3.16 : pf. βέβρωμαι A.Ag.1097 (lyr.), (δια-) Pl.Ti.83a, (κατα-) SIG²587.310 : plpf. ἐβέβρωτο Hp.Epid.4.19. —In Ion. Prose and Lxx βέβρωκα ἐβρώθην βέβρωμαι take the place of Att. ἐδήδοκα ἠδέσθην ἐδήδεσμαι :—*eat, eat up*, βεβρωκὼς κακὰ φάρμακ' Il.22.94, etc. ; οὐδὲν βεβρ. Eup.68 : c. gen., *eat of* a thing, [λέων] βεβρωκὼς βοὸς Od.22.403 ; τῶν μελῶν βεβρωκότες Ar.V.463 ; κρειῶν τε καὶ αἵματος Theoc.25.224 : abs., βεβρωκώς, opp. πεινῶν, Arist.HA 629b9 ; β. καὶ πεπωκώς Id.Fr.232, cf. Plb.3.72.6, Ev.Jo.6.13 :—Pass., *to be eaten*, Hp.Acut.37 ; of teeth, *decay*, Id.Epid.4.19 ; χρήματα δ' αὖτε κακῶς βεβρώσεται *will be devoured*, Od.2.203 ; βεβρωμένοι ἄρτοι *mouldy* bread, Lxx Jo.9.12 ; ῥίζα βεβρ. *worm-eaten*, Dsc.3.9 ; *to be bitten*, ὑπὸ τῶν κροκοδείλων Gal.14.246.

βίδην, εἶδος, κροῦμα· ἄλλοι βίθυν, S.Fr.60 (ap.Hsch.) ; cf. βυδοί.

βιδιαῖοι, οἱ, *officers* at Sparta, whose duties were connected with the charge of the ephebi, five in number, acc. to Paus.3.11.2 ; but six in Inscrr. :—written **βίδεοι** IG5(1).32 B, al., **βίδυοι** ib.41 : sg. **βίδυιος** ib.1498.13 (Messenia, ii B.C.). (For ϝίδυιοι, i. e. *overseers*.)

βιζάριον, τό, *she-camel* or *suckling camel*, PLond.ined.1821.

βιζῆαι· κοῖται, στιβάδες, Hsch.

βῑημάχος [ᾰ], ον, = βιαιομάχας, Ἔρως AP5.292.1 (Paul. Sil.) ; βασιλεύς ib.4.3b.2 (Agath.).

βίθυν, v. βίδην.

Βῑθῡνι-άρχης, ου, ὁ, *President of the Provincial Council of Bithynia*, OGI528.10 (Prusias), al. : **-αρχία**, ἡ, *his office*, Dig.27.1.6.14, IGRom. 3.1427 (Βειθ-).

βῖκας· σφίγγας, Hsch.

βῑκίον, τό, Dim. of βῖκος, v.l. in Dsc.2.78 ; β. ὑέλινον Gp.10.69.1 :—also **βῑκίδιον**, Suid.

βῑκίον, τό, *vetch*, *Vicia sativa*, Gal.6.550 :—also **βικία**, ἡ, Edict. Diocl.17.6, Gp.3.6.7 :—hence Adj. βίκειος, χόρτος Hippiatr.104.

βῖκος, ὁ, *jar* or *cask*, Hdt.1.194, X.An.1.9.25, PHal.7.5 (iii B.C.), PHib.1.49 (iii B.C.), Lxx Je.19.1, etc. 2. *drinking-bowl*, Pollux Par.ap.Ath.11.784d. 3. *a measure*, BGU1112.15 (i A.D.), PTeb.472 (ii A.D.). [ῐ, v. Ephipp.8.2, Archestr.Fr.38.2.]

βῑκόστομον, τό, *opening of a receiving vessel*, of a still, Zos.Alch. p.224 B.

βιλίσκος, vulg., = ὀβελίσκος, PLond.2.329.

βιλλαρικός, ή, όν, perh. = Lat. *villaticus*, POxy.1026.12 (v A.D.).

βιλλᾶς, dub. sens. in Hdn.Gr.1.55. **βιλλίν**· τὸ αἰδοῖον, ib.158. **βίλλος**, = foreg., ibid. **βιμβικίζεται**· περικρούεται, Hsch. **βίμβλινος**, = βίβλινος, Id.

βῑνέω, *inire, coïre*, of illicit intercourse, opp. ὀπυίω, Sol.ap. Hsch., Ar.Ra.740 : c. acc. pers., Id.Av.560, etc. :—Med., Ion. impf. βινεσκόμην Id.Eq.1242 :—Pass., of the woman, Eup.351.2, Philetaer.9.4.

βῑνητιάω, Desiderat. of βινέω, *coïre cupio*, of the woman, Ar.Lys.715, Macho ap.Ath.13.583c ; of the man, Luc.Pseudol.27.

βῐο-γρᾰφία, ἡ, *biography*, Dam.Isid.8. **-δότης**, ου, ὁ, *giver of livelihood*, θεός Pl.Lg.921a. **-δωρος**, ον, *life-giving*, ἀμαχανίας ἄκος Pi.Pae.3.26 ; νύμφαις.. ποταμοῦ παισὶν β. A.Fr.168 (hex.) ; αἶα S.Ph.1162 (lyr.) : in late Prose, γῆ Artem.2.39. **-δώτης**, ου, ὁ, = βιοδότης, of Apollo, AP9.525.3 ; voc. βιοδῶτα IG14.1015 :—fem. **-δῶτις**, ιδος, Orph.H.29.3. **-δώτωρ**, ορος, ὁ, = foreg., ib.73.2, IG3.

239. 2. *furnishing a livelihood*, [ναῦς] *AP*7.585 (Jul.). **-ζῠγής**, ές, *linking lives together*, ὑμέναιοι Nonn.*D*.33.179. **-θάλμιος**, ον, (θάλλω) *strong, hale*, *h.Ven*.189. **-θᾰνᾰσία**, = βιαιο–, Ptol.*Tetr*. 85. **-θάνᾰτος** [θᾰ], = βιαιο–, *PMag.Par*.1.1950. **-θρέμμων**, ον, gen. ονος, *life-supporting*, πάντων Ar.*Nu*.570 (lyr.); φῦλα Orph.*H*.34.19. **-θρέπτειρα**, ἡ, fem. of foreg., ib.27.13. **-κλώστειρα**, ἡ, *spinning the thread of life*, of Fate, *Arch.Pap*.1.221 (ii B.C.). **-κουρος**, ὁ, (*via*, *curo*), = IIIvir *viarum curandarum*, *IGRom*.4.1307 (Lydia). **-κωλύτης** [ῡ], ου, ὁ, *an officer to suppress violence* or *lawlessness*, Just.*Nov*.8.12, al. **-λογέομαι**, Pass., *to be sketched from life*, esp. *common life*, τὰ βιολογούμενα Longin.9.15. **-λογικός**, ή, όν, *of a* βιολόγος, κωμῳδίαι, = μῖμοι, Suid. s.v. Φιλιστίων. **-λόγος**, ὁ, *one who represents to the life*, *player*, *IG*14.2342, *POxy*.1025.7 (iii A.D.). **-μήχᾰνος**, ον, *clever at getting a living*, Antipho Soph.41; of birds, Arist.*HA*616^{b}17, al. **-μορος**, ον, = βιαιοθάνατος, *PMag.Par*.1.1400. **-πλαγκτος**, ον, = sq., τύχη Nonn.*D*.3.356. **-πλᾰνής**, ές, *wandering to get one's living*, *a beggar*, βιοπλανές (poet. nom. pl. for -πλανέες) Call.*Fr*.497: neut. sg. βιόπλανες Hdn.Gr.ap.*Et.Gen*., A.D.*Pron*.93.8. **-πονητικός**, ή, όν, = sq., Hippodam.ap.Stob.4.1.94. **-πόνος**, ον, *living by labour*, ib.93. **-πρᾶγος**, ον, *prosperous, successful*, Astramps. *Orac*.85, al. **-πρᾶτος**, ὁ, *ne'er-do-weel*, *POxy*.1477.14 (iii/iv A.D.).

βιορρός· δουλεία, Hsch. (fort. εἴρερος).

βίος [ῐ], ὁ, *life*, i.e. not animal life (ζωή), but *mode of life* (cf. εἰ χρόνον τις λέγοι ψυχῆς ἐν κινήσει μεταβατικῇ ἐξ ἄλλου εἰς ἄλλον βίον ζωὴν εἶναι Plot.3.7.11), *manner of living* (mostly therefore of men, v. Ammon. p.32 V.; but also of animals, διεχώριζον ζῴων τε βίον δένδρων τε φύσιν Epicr.11.14, cf. X.*Mem*.3.11.6, etc.; also ζῆν φυτοῦ βίον Arist.*GA*736^{b}13); ζώεις δ' ἀγαθὸν βίον Od.15.491; ἐμὸν βίον ἀμφιπολεύειν 18.254; αἰῶνα βίοιο Hes.*Fr*.161; τὸν μακρὸν τείνειν βίον A.*Pr*.537 (lyr.); ὁ καθ' ἡμέραν β. S.*OC*1364; βίον διαγαγεῖν Ar.*Pax*439; τελεῖν S.*Ant*.1114; διατελεῖν Isoc.6.45; διέρχεσθαι βίου τέλος dub. in Pi.*I*.4(3).5; τελευτᾶν Isoc.4.84; ὑπ' ἄλλου τελευτῆσαι β. Pl.*Lg*.870e; ἐπειδὰν τοῦ ἀνθρωπίνου βίου τελευτήσω X.*Cyr*.8.7.17; τέρμα βίου περᾶν S.*OT*1530; ὁδὸς βίου Isoc.1.5, cf. X.*Mem*.2.1.21; διὰ βίου Arist.*Pol*.1272^{a}37; prov., ὁ ἐπὶ Κρόνου βίος 'the Golden Age', Id.*Ath*.16.7; so Ταρτησσοῦ β. Him.*Ecl*.10.11; β. ζωῆς Pl.*Epin*.982a (cf. βιοτή); ζῆν θαλάττιον β. Antiph.100; ἀμέριμνον ζῆν β. Philem.92.8; λαγὼ β. ζῆν δεδιὼς καὶ τρέμων D.18.263; σκληρὸς τῷ β. Men.*Georg*.66: rarely in pl., Alex.116.6 and 11, Men.855; τίνες καὶ πόσοι εἰσὶ β.; Pl.*Lg*.733d, cf. Arist.*EN*1095^{b}15, *Pol*.1256^{a}20. 2. in Poets sts. = ζωή, βίον ἐκπνέων A.*Ag*.1517 (lyr.); ἀποψύχειν S.*Aj*.1031; φείδεσθαι βίου Id.*Ph*.749; νοσφίζειν τινὰ βίου ib.1427, etc. 3. *lifetime*, ἐς τὸν ἅπαντα ἀνθρώπων β. Hdt.6.109; τῶν ἐπὶ τοῦ σοῦ β. γεγονότων λόγων Pl.*Phdr*. 242a, cf. *PMagd*.18.7 (iii B.C.), etc. II. *livelihood, means of living* (in Hom. βίοτος), βίος ἐπηετανός Hes.*Op*.31, Pi.*N*.6.10; τὸν βίον κτᾶσθαι, ποιεῖσθαι, ἔχειν ἀπό τινος, to make one's *living* off, to *live* by a thing, Hdt.8.106, Th.1.5, X.*Oec*.6.11; ἀπεστέρηκας τὸν βίον τὰ τόξ' ἑλών S.*Ph*.931, cf. 933, 1282; κτᾶσθαι πλοῦτον καὶ βίον τέκνοις E.*Supp*.450; πλεῖον' ἐκμοχθεῖν β. ib.451; β. πολύς ib.861; ὀλίγος Ar.*Pl*.751; βίον κεκτημένος Philem.99.4; ὁ ἴδιος β. private *property*, *AJA*17.29 (i B.C.), cf. *SIG*762.40, Iamb.*VP*30.170; β. Δημήτριος, = *corn*, A.*Fr*.44. III. *the world we live in*, 'the world', οἱ ἀπὸ τοῦ β., opp. *the philosophers*, S.E.*M*.11.49; simply ὁ βίος Id.*P*.1.211; ὁ β. ὁ κοινός ib.237; μυθικὰς ὑποθέσεις ὧν μεστὸς ὁ β. ἐστί Ph.1.226; ἐκκαθαίρειν τὸν β., of Hercules, Luc.*DDeor*.13.1; τὸν βίον μιμούμενοι, of comic poets, Sch.Heph.p.115 C.; also, 'the public', ἵνα ὁ β. εἰδῇ τίνα δεῖ μετακαλεῖσθαι Sor.1.4. IV. *settled life*, almost, = *abode*, ἐν τῇ Θρᾳκίᾳ νήσῳ βίους ἱδρύσαντο D.H.1.68, cf. 72. V. *a life, biography*, as those of Plu., *Thes*.1, cf. Ph.2.180. VI. *caste*, διεῖλε τὸ πλῆθος εἰς τέτταρας β. Str.8.7.1. VII. *wine made from partly dried unripe grapes*, Plin.*HN*14.77. VIII. Astrol., *the second region*, Paul.Al.*L*.2. (Cf. Skt. *jīvás* 'alive', *jīvati* 'live', Lat. *vīvus*, etc.)

βιός, ὁ, *bow*, = τόξον, Il.1.49, Heraclit.48, etc. (Ambracian acc. to *AB*1095. Cf. Vedic *jiyā́* 'bow-string', Lith. *gijà* 'thread'.)

βιόσσαο· τὸ ζῆν ἔδωκας, βιῶσαι ἐποίησας, Hsch. (i.e. ἐβιώσαο).

βῐοσσόος, ον, *life-supporting* or *-preserving*, Nonn.*D*.33.109, 41.333, al.

βῐοστερής, ές, *reft of the means of life*, S.*OC*747.

βῐοτεία, ἡ, *way of life*, X.*Oec*.6.10, Plb.6.7.5.

βῐο-τελής, ές, dub. sens., *EM*198.11. **-τέρμων**, ον, gen. ονος, *marking the beginning of life*, ὥρη Man.4.77. II. *lasting till the close of life*, πλοῦτος Antioch.Astr. in *Cat.Cod.Astr*.1.110.

βῐότ-ευμα, ατος, τό, *manner of life*, Socr.*Ep*.29. **-εύω**, *live*, Pi.*N*.4.6; ἀβίωτον χρόνον β. E.*Alc*.243 (lyr.); β. ἀκρατῶς Arist.*EN*1114^{a}16; φαιδρῶς X.*Cyr*.4.6.6. 2. *get food*, αὐτόθεν πολεμοῦντα Th.1.11; *live* by or off a thing, ἀπὸ πολέμου X.*Cyr*.3.2.25; ἀπὸ τῶν ἀκανθῶν Arist.*HA*610^{a}5. 3. *reside*, ἐς θάλασσαν Aret.*CD*1.2; ἐν χώρῃσι θερμῇσι ib.4. **-ή**, ἡ, = βίοτος, βίος, Od.4.565, Phoc.10; ἑκατονταετὴς β. Pi.*P*.4.282: Trag. in lyr., A.*Pers*.853, S.*Ph*.690, E.*Andr*.785; rare in Prose, Hdt.7.47, Democr.200, 297, X.*Cyr*.7.2.27, Ael.*NA*2.23: metaph. of foods, τὰ ἀσθενέστερα σιτία ὀλιγοχρόνιον β. ἔχει Hp.*Epid*.6.5.14. II. *living, sustenance*, S.*Ph*.164, 1159, Ar.*V*.1452 (lyr.). **-ης**, ητος, ἡ, = foreg., *h.Hom*.8.10, *IG*14.1449. **-ήσιος**, ον, *supporting life*, ὦνος A.R.2.1006; ναυτιλίη β. voyage *of life*, *AP*9.208; ἴχνος ὅπου λήγει β. Benndorf-Niemann *Reisen in Lykien u. Karien* p.79. **-ιον**, τό, Dim. of βίοτος, *scant living*, Ar.*Pl*. 1165. **-ος**, ὁ, Ep., = βίος I, *life*, βιότοιο τελευτή Il.7.104, cf. Emp. 15.2, A.*Pers*.360, al. II. = βίος II, *means of living, substance*, ναῖε δὲ δῶμα ἀφνειὸν βιότοιο Il.14.122; β. κατακείρετε πολλόν Od.4.686; γύαι φέρουσι β. ἄφθονον βροτοῖς A.*Fr*.196; βιότου κτῆσις Ar.*Av*.718, cf. *Ec*.669:—in late Prose, *PLond*.5.1889 (vi A.D.). III. = βίος III, *the world, mankind*, μνήμη βιότου παρέδωκεν *Epigr.Gr*.319 (Philadelphia).

βῐοτοσκόπος, ον, *of* or *for casting a nativity*, ὥρη Man.4.572.

βῐο-τρόφος, ον, *life-sustaining*, πνοή Aenigm. in *App.Anth*.7.69. **-φειδής**, ές, *penurious*, *AP*6.251 (Phil.). **-φθορία**, ἡ, *destruction of life*, Orph.*H*.73.8. **-φθόρος**, ον, *destructive of life*, χρυσός Ps.-Phoc.44.

βῐόω, βιοῖ Arist.*HA*558^{a}20; βιοῦσι Democr.200, Arist.*HA*576^{b}2; βιοῦν E.*Fr*.238, etc.; part. βιοῦντες Arist.*HA*566^{b}24; subj. βιῶσι Emp.15.2: impf. ἐβίουν Hp.*Epid*.5.48: fut. βιώσομαι E.*Alc*. 784, Ar.*Eq*.699, Pl.*R*.344e, Men.*Pk*.399; later βιώσω Id.*Mon*.270, App.*BC*4.119: aor. 1 ἐβίωσα Hdt.1.163, Pl.*Phd*.113d, X.*Oec*.4.18, Arist.*HA*585^{a}21; but in earlier writers aor. 2 is more used, ἐβίων Isoc.9.71, Is.3.1 codd.; 3 sg. imper. βιώτω Il.8.429; subj. βιῶ Pl.*Lg*.872c; opt. βιῴην Id.*Ti*.89c, v.l. for βιοίη in Id.*Grg*.512e; inf. βιῶναι Il.10.174, Aeschin.3.174, etc.; part. βιούς Hdt.9.10, Th.2.53, al.: pf. βεβίωκα Isoc.15.27 and 28, Pl.*Phd*.113d, etc.:—**Med.**, βιόομαι Hdt.2.177, Arist.*EN*1180^{a}17: for aor. Med. v. βιώσκομαι:—Pass., fut. βιωθήσομαι M.Ant.9.30: pf. βεβίωμαι (v. infr.).—In early writers pres. and impf. are mostly supplied by ζάω: Hom. has only aor. 2:—*live, pass one's life* (opp. ζάω, *live, exist*), βέλτερον ἢ ἀπολέσθαι ἕνα χρόνον ἠὲ βιῶναι Il.15.511, cf. 10.174; ἄλλος μὲν ἀποφθίσθω, ἄλλος δὲ βιώτω 8.429; βίον βιοῦν Pl.*La*.188a, etc.; β. παρανόμως, μετρίως, ἐνδόξως, D.22.24, Lys.16.3, Plu.2.145f: with neut. Pron., ἀπ' αὐτῶν ὧν αὐτὸς βεβίωκεν ἄρξομαι.. from the very *actions of* his own *life*, D.18.130:—Pass., τὰ σοὶ κἀμοὶ βεβιωμένα *the actions of* our *life*, ib.265, cf. Isoc.15.7, Lys.16.1; τὰ πεπραγμένα καὶ βεβ. D.22.53; τοιούτων ὄντων ἃ τῷ βδελυρῷ τούτῳ..βεβίωται Id.21.151; ἐπιτηδευμάτων οἷα τούτῳ βεβίωται Id.22.78; ὅ γε βεβιωμένος [βίος] Id.19.200; impers., βεβίωταί [μοι] *I have lived*, Lat. *vixi*, Cic.*Att*.12.2.2, 14.21.3:—Med. in act. sense, Hdt.2.177, Arist.*EN*1180^{a}17. 2. *survive*, ἐβίω καυθείς Hp.*Epid*.5.16.—βιόμεσθα (as if from βίομαι) is found *h.Ap*.528 and 3 pl. βίονται Orac.ap.Phleg.*Mir*.2, cf. βέομαι.

βιόωνται, -το, v. βιάω.

βιπίννιον, τό, Dim. of Lat. *bipennis*, *Edict.Diocl*. in *IG*5(1).1406.9 (Asine).

βιπτάζω, for βαπτίζω, Epich.175, Sophr.114.

βίρρη· πυράγρα, οἱ δὲ δρέπανον, Hsch. **βίρροξ**· δασύ (Maced.), Id.

βίρρος, ὁ, Lat. *birrus*, a kind of *cloak*, Artem.2.3, *PGiss*.76.4 (ii A.D.), *Edict.Diocl*.19.26, al., Hierocl.*Facet*.99, Suid. (Cf. βύρρος.)

βιρρωθῆναι· ταπεινωθῆναι, Hsch.

βίσβη, ἡ, *pruning-hook* (Messap.), Hsch.:—hence **Βισβαῖα**, τά, a festival, = κλαδευτήρια, Id.

βίσκαρις· εἶδος βοτάνης, Hsch.

βιστάκιον, τό, = πιστ., Posidon.6, v.l. in Nic.*Th*.891, acc. to Ath. 14.649d.

βίσταξ· βασιλεύς (Pers.), Hsch. **βιστήνη**· καρδία, Id.

βίσχυν, Adv. = σφόδρα ὀλίγον (Lacon.), Hsch., cf. Hdn.Gr.1. 509.

βίσων [ῐ], ωνος, ὁ, *bison*, Paus.10.13.1, Opp.*C*.2.160.

βίτος, ὁ, *tyre*, *Edict.Diocl*.15.31a:—hence **βιτωτός**, ή, όν, *with tyres*, τροχοί ib.34; σαράγαρα, καροῦχον β., *with tyred wheels*, ib.36, 37.

βίττακος, ου, ὁ, = ψίττακος, Eub.123, Ctes.*Fr*.57.3.

βίῳ, βιῴην, βιῶναι, βιώτω, v. βιόω. **βιῴατο**, v. βιάω.

βιώλεθρος, ον, *destructive of life*, Hdn.*Epim*.203, Zonar.

βιώνης, ου, ὁ, (ὠνέομαι) *one who buys food* on the public account, Hsch., Suid.

βίωρ (i.e. ϝίωρ)· ἴσως (Lacon.), Hsch.

βιώσιμος, ον, (βιόω) *to be lived*, χρόνος E.*Alc*.650; αἱ β. ἡμέραι Lib.*Decl*.2.34; esp. οὐ βιώσιμόν ἐστί τινι 'tis not *meet* for him to *live*, Hdt. 1.45; τί γὰρ μόνῃ μοι τῆσδ' ἄτερ β.; S.*Ant*.566; οὐκ ἂν ἦν βιώσιμα ἀνθρώποισι Hdt.3.109. 2. *likely to live*, Thphr.*HP*9.12.1, Arr.*An*. 2.4.8.

βίωσις, εως, ἡ, *way of life*, Lxx *Si.prol*.12, *Act.Ap*.26.4: in a Jewish Inscr., ἐνάρετος β. *IGRom*.4.655 (Acmonia, i A.D.); ἐν μιᾷ β. μετ' ἀλλήλων *PMasp*.158.26 (vi A.D.).

βῐ-ώσκομαι, causal of βιόω, *quicken, make* or *keep alive*, once in Hom. in aor., σὺ γάρ μ' ἐβιώσαο, κούρη Od.8.468; cf. βιόσσαο: the pres. occurs in the compd. ἀναβιώσκομαι. II. later in pass. sense, *revive*, ἕτεροι τόποι βιώσκονται Arist.*Mete*.351^{a}35; simply, *live*, βιωσαμένῳ *IG*14.2100; βιώσκεσθαι Arr.*Ind*.9. **-ωτέον**, *one must live*, Pl.*Grg*.500d, Lib.*Decl*.35.15. **-ωτικός**, ή, όν, *fit for life, lively*, τὴν διάνοιαν β. καὶ εὐμήχανος, = βιομήχανος, Arist.*HA*616^{b}27; acc. to Phryn.332 (who condemns the word), = χρήσιμος ἐν τῷ βίῳ, as in Sotad.6.12. II. *of* or *pertaining to life*, Plb.4.73.8, D.S.2.29, Ph. 2.159; χάριτες Plu.2.142b; ἀηδίαι Artem.2.30; ἡ -κή (sc. τέχνη) M.Ant.7.61; τὰ β. κριτήρια, opp. λογικά, S.E.*P*.2.15; μέριμναι β. *Ev.Luc*.21.34; β. φροντίς Iamb.*Protr*.21.α'; β. σύμβολα *business* documents, *PTeb*.52.9 (ii B.C.); β. θρησκεία *popular* superstition (cf. βίος III), Sor.1.4; ὁ β. νόμος Arr.*Epict*.1.26 tit.; τὰ β. ib.3, cf. Plu.2. 679d. Adv. -κῶς *in the tone of common life*, D.T.629; *in popular language*, Gal.10.269. 2. βιωτικά, τά, *victuals*, *PRyl*.125.11 (i A.D.); ἡ β. ἀγορά *BCH*44.74 (Lagina). **-ωτός**, όν, *to be lived, worth living*, mostly with neg., ἔμοιγ' ὁ μέλλων βίος οὐ β. S.*OC*1692 (lyr.), cf. Ar.*Pl*.197 (dub.), Pl.*Ap*.38a; οὐ βιωτὸν οὐδ' ἀνασχετόν Antiph.190.

10; οὐκ ἦν μοι β. τοῦτο ποιήσαντι D.21.120; ἆρ' οὖν β. ἡμῖν ἐστιν μετὰ μοχθηροῦ σώματος Pl.*Cri.*47e. **-ωφελής**, ές, *useful for life*, Ph.2. 88, al., Luc.*Am.*51; of persons, Ptol.*Tetr.*183: Comp., Ph.2.633: Sup., ib.480, Agath.1.7. Adv. -λῶς S.E.*M.*1.279.

βλᾰβεραυγής, ές, *baneful-gleaming*, Man.4.309.

βλᾰβερός, ά, όν, *harmful*, β. τὸ θύρηφιν Hes.*Op.*365 (= *h.Merc.*36); opp. συμφέρον, Democr.237; opp. ὠφέλιμος, X.*Cyr.*8.8.14; β. καὶ ζημιώδες Pl.*Cra.*417d. Adv. -ρῶς Id.*Phdr.*243c; opp. ὠφελίμως, Id. *Chrm.*164c, cf. Plu.2.599b.

βλάβ-η [ᾰ], ἡ, (v. βλάπτω) *harm, damage*, A.*Pr.*763, *IG*1².18, etc.; πεπονθέναι.. ἐς βλάβην φέρον S.*OT*517; τίς β.; c. inf., Id.*OC*1187; οἷς ἦν ἐν β. τειχισθέν Th.5.52; προσκαλοῦμαί σε..βλάβης τῶν φορτίων Ar.*V.*1407; β. θεοῦ *mischief from* a god, E.*Ion*520, cf. S.*Ant.*1104; of a person, ἡ πᾶσα β. who is naught but *mischief*, Id.*El.*301, cf. 784, *Ph.*622: pl., ἐν ὄμμασιν βλάβας ἔχω A.*Ag.*889, cf. *Eu.*799; αἱματηρὰς θηγάνας, σπλάγχνων βλάβας νέων ib.859. 2. βλάβης δίκη an action *for damage done*, D.21.25; β. τετραπόδων *damage done by* cattle, Plu. *Sol.*24; β. τῶν θηρίων Id.2.642b (pl.); οἰκῆος καὶ δούλης τὴν β. εἶναι ὀφείλειν Sol.ap.Lys.10.19; οἱ περὶ τῆς β. νόμοι.. ἁπλοῦν τὸ βλάβος κελεύουσιν ἐκτίνειν D.21.43; διπλῆν τὴν β. ὀφείλειν (ὀφλεῖν Meier) Din.1.60, cf. *Foed.Delph.Pell.*1 *B* 7. **-όεις**, εσσα, εν, = βλαβερός, Nic.*Al.*186. **-ομαι**, = βλάπτομαι, only 3 sg., βλάβεται δέ τε γούνατ' ἰόντι Il.19.166; *stumble, hesitate*, of a speaker, ib.82; of a bowstring, *Anacreont.*31.26. **-ος**, gen. εος, contr. ους, τό, = βλάβη, Hdt.1. 9, E.*Heracl.*255, *Ion*998, Ar.*Ra.*1151, Antipho 5.91, Pl.*Lg.*843c, *Foed.Delph.Pell.* 2 *A* 12, Arist.*Pol.*1328ᵃ14, *PRyl.*126.19 (i A.D.); distd. from βλάβη, D.21.43 (v. βλάβη 2). (More Attic than βλάβη acc. to Moer.103.)

βλαβύρει· πτερύσσεται, Hsch. **βλαβυρία**· εἰκαιολογία, Id. **βλαβύσσειν**· βλάπτεσθαι, Id. **βλαγίς**· κηλίς (Lacon.), Id. **βλαδάν**· νωθρῶς, Id.

βλᾰδᾰρός, ά, όν, = πλαδαρός, *flaccid*, cj. in Gal.19.88:—Hsch. has **βλᾰδός** and **βλᾰδύς** (which is prob. in Hp.*Aër.*20). (With βλαδύς cf. Skt. *mṛdús* 'soft', Lat. *mollis*; cf. μέλδομαι, ἀμαλδύνω.)

βλάζειν· μωραίνειν, Hsch. **βλάθρον**, = βλῆχνον, Id. **βλαί**· βλητή (leg. βληχή) (Lacon.), Id. **βλαῖκος**· ὁ δαλός, κλάδος, ὄζος, *EM*199.31.

βλαισ-όομαι, Pass., *to be crooked*, pf. ἐβλαίσωται Arist.*HA*498ᵃ21; but βεβλ- Id.*IA*713ᵇ4, Gal.18(1).677. **-ός**, ή, όν, *bent, distorted*: hence, *splay-footed*, Hp.*Art.*53, cf. 82 (Comp.); ἐς τὸ β. ῥέπων ib.62, cf. Gal.18(1).674, al.; οἱ β. τῶν ἀνθρώπων X.*Eq.*1.3; also, *bandy*, β. καρκίνοι Batr.297, cf. Arist.*HA*526ᵃ23; τὰ β. τῶν ὀπισθίων *the hollow* of the hind-leg in which bees carry the pollen, ib.624ᵇ2: generally, *twisted, crooked*, πλατάνιστος *AP*4.1.17 (Mel.); κισσός ib.7.21 (Simm.). **-ότης**, ητος, ἡ, *crookedness, curvature*, τῶν σκελῶν Arist. *IA*713ᵇ9; *curliness*, τῶν τριχῶν Id.*Pr.*909ᵃ31. **-ώδης**, ες, = βλαισός, Gal.6.328. **-ωσις**, εως, ἡ, = βλαισότης, Gal.*UP*3.9. II. metaph., *retorting of a dilemma* on its proposer, Arist.*Rh.*1399ᵃ26.

βλαιτόνους· ὁ βλαισόπους, *EM*199.32.

βλᾰκ-εία (-ία, Hsch.), ἡ, (βλάξ) *slackness*, X.*Cyr.*2.2.25, 7.5. 84; *stupidity*, Pl.*Euthd.*287e, Phld.*Mus.*p.56 K., Hierocl.*in CA*17 p.457 M.; τὸ τῆς β. πεδίον Luc.*VH*2.33. **-εννόμιον** τέλος tax paid by astrologers at Alexandria (because *fools* consult them), *EM* 199.11. **-ευμα**, ατος, τό, *stupid trick*, Eust.1405.33. **-εύω**, *to be slack, lazy*, X.*An.*2.3.11, 5.8.15, Phld.*Hom.*p.39 O., etc.; ἐν τῇ κατατάσει Hp.*Fract.*17; β. καὶ ἀποδειλιᾶν D.H.9.31:—Med. (which is cited from X. by Eust.1405.32), = τρυφάω, Hld.7.27; but Act. in this sense, Procop.*Arc.*9. II. c. acc., *lose* or *waste through laziness*, Luc.*Ep.Sat.*26. **-ίας**· ἰχθύς ποιός, Hsch. **-ικός**, ή, όν, (βλάξ) *stupid*, Pl.*R.*432d, X.*Oec.*8.17, etc.; *lazy, sluggish*, δειλὰ καὶ β. Pl.*Plt.* 307c; β. τὸ ἦθος Arist.*HA*618ᵇ5. Adv. -κῶς Ar.*Av.*1323. **-ότης**, ητος, ἡ, = βλακεία, Steph.*in Hp.*1.63,97 D. **-ώδης**, ες, *lazy*, X. *Eq.*9.1 (Comp.); βλακῶδες βαίνειν καὶ θρύπτεσθαι walk *mincingly*, of a coxcomb, Hld.4.7. Adv. -δῶς *indolently, stolidly*, Poll.3.123: Comp. -έστερον ibid.

βλάμμα, ατος, τό, = βλάβη, opp. ὠφέλημα, Chrysipp.*Stoic.*3.71 (pl.), Phld.*Rh.*1.215 S. (pl.); expl. of σίνος, Gal.18(2).445.

βλάνος· τυφλώδης, Hsch.

βλάξ, βλᾱκός, ὁ, ἡ, *stolid, stupid*, Pl.*Grg.*488a; β. καὶ ἠλίθιος X.*Cyr.* 1.4.12; β. καὶ ἄφρων Arist.*EE*1247ᵃ18; θεὸς κολάζει τοὺς βλᾶκας X. *Oec.*8.16, cf. Plb.16.22.5; β. ἄνθρωπος Heraclit.87: usually of persons, but β. ἵππος, opp. θυμοειδής, X.*Eq.*9.12: Comp. βλακότερος or -ώτερος Id.*Mem.*4.2.40: Sup. βλακότατος or -ώτατος (but -ίστατος ap.Ath.) ib.3.13.4. II. name of a *fish*, ὃς ἐν τῷ συνουσιάζειν δυσαπολύτως ἔχει, Erot. s.v. βλακεύειν. (Perh. βλᾱ- < μλᾱ-, cf. Skt. *mlāyati* 'become soft', μαλακός: Hsch., ἀπό τινος ἰχθύος δασώδους (leg. δυσώδους).)

βλαπτ-ήριος, ον, = sq., Opp.*H.*2.456. **-ικός**, ή, όν, *hurtful, mischievous*, δυνάμεις Ph.1.14, cf. S.E.*M.*6.4, etc.: c. gen., ἀνθρώπων Str.15.1.45, cf. Phld.*Piet.*99,100. Adv. -κῶς Arr.*Epict.*3.23.4, Ptol. *Tetr.*168.

βλάπτω, fut. -ψω E.*Heracl.*704, etc.: aor. ἔβλαψα, Ep. βλάψε Il.23. 774: aor. 2 ἔβλαβον Q.S.5.509: pf. βέβλᾰφα D.19.180, Plb.12.26.2, ἔβλαφα (κατ-) *IG*7.303.51 (Oropus):—Pass., fut. βλᾰβήσομαι Isoc.1. 25, Pl.*Men.*77e, *Grg.*475d, *Hp.Mi.*373a; βεβλάψομαι Hp.*Acut.*16: also fut. Med. βλάψομαι (in pass. signf.) Th.1.81, 6.64: aor. 1 ἐβλάφθην Il.16.331, etc.: aor. 2 ἐβλάβην [ᾰ], 3 pl. ἔβλαβεν, βλάβεν, 23.461, 545, part. βλᾰβείς A.*Ag.*120 (lyr.) (aor. Med. βλάψαντο only in Q.S.5. 466): pf. βέβλαμμαι Il.16.660, etc.:—*disable, hinder*, μή τιν' ἑταίρων βλάπτοι ἐλαυνόντων Od.13.22; βλάψας δέ μοι ἵππους Il.23.571; β. πόδας *disable* the feet for running, *lame* them, ib.782:—Pass., ζωὸν ἕλε βλαφθέντα κατὰ κλόνον *entangled* in the mêlée, 16.331; ὄζῳ ἔνι βλαφθέντε μυρικίνῳ [the horses] *caught* in a branch, 6.39; βλάβεν ἅρματα καὶ ταχέ' ἵππω chariots and horses *were stopped*, 23.545; Διόθεν βλαφθέντα βέλεμνα *stopped, baffled* by Zeus, 15.489, cf. 484; βεβλαμμένος ἦτορ *stopped* in his life (s.v.l.), 16.660. 2. c. gen., *hinder from*, τόν γε θεοὶ βλάπτουσι κελεύθου Od.1.195; οὐδέ τις αὐτὸν βλάπτειν οὔτ' αἰδοῦς οὔτε δίκης ἐθέλει Tyrt.12.40 (repeated in Thgn. 938):—Pass., βλαβέντα λοισθίων δρόμων *arrested in* its last course, A.*Ag.*120 (lyr.). II. of the mind, *distract, pervert, mislead*, of the gods, τὸν δέ τις ἀθανάτων βλάψε φρένας Od.14.178, cf. *Trag.Adesp.* 455: c. acc. pers., Il.22.15, Od.23.14; so of Ate, φθάνει δέ τε πᾶσαν ἐπ' αἶαν βλάπτουσ' ἀνθρώπους Il.9.507; also of wine, Od.21.294; βλαφθείς, Lat. *mente captus*, Il.9.512: so c. gen., ἢ τε [Περσεφόνη].. βλάπτουσα νόοιο Thgn.705; νόου βεβλαμμένος ἐσθλοῦ Id.223. III. after Hom., *damage, hurt*, οἷσι μὴ βλάψῃ θεός (sc. τὰ τέκνα) A.*Eu.* 661, etc.: with neut. Adj., πλείω β. τινά Th.6.33; μείζω Pl.*Ap.*30c; ἄλλο τι X.*HG*1.1.22, etc.:—Pass., μεγάλα βεβλάφθαι Id.*Cyr.*5.3.30; βεβλαμμένος τὸν ὀφθαλμόν *PStrassb.*52.2 (ii A.D.), etc.: c. acc. cogn., β. τοὺς βίους μείζους βλάβας *do* greater *mischiefs to*.., Posidipp.12.4: c. dupl. acc., β. τὴν πόλιν τοὺς ὑπολοίπους *rob* her of.., App.*BC*2.131:—Pass., τοσούσδε βλαβῆναι τὴν πόλιν *lose* them, Id.*Hann.*28; τὸ βλαβέν, = βλάβη, Pl.*Lg.*933e. 2. c. acc. rei, β. λόγον *mar* the prophecy, Pi.*P.*9.94; τοὺς ὅρκους *violate* them, Arist.*Fr.*148. (βλαπ- < μλαπ- (*mlq*), cf. Skt. *marcáyati* 'injure', *mṛktás* 'wounded', Lat. *mulco* 'maltreat'.)

βλάσαμον, τό, metath. for βάλσαμον, v.l. in Nic.*Al.*64.

βλάσκει· λέγει, καπνίζει, Hsch. **βλασκίας**, ὁ, a *fish*, Id. **βλαστά**· πλαταγώνια (Sicel), Id. **βλαστάζειν**· βλιμάζειν, Id.

βλαστάνω, S.*OC*611, etc. (later **βλαστέω**, Thphr.*CP*2.17.4 (interpol. in A.*Ch.*589, corrupt in Pass. -ουμένη S.*Fr.*255.7)); Ion. impf. βλαστάνεσκε (v.l. βλάστεσκεν) Id.*Fr.*546: fut. βλαστήσω Thphr.*HP* 2.7.2, βλαστήσομαι Alex.Trall.12: aor. 2 ἔβλαστον S.*Fr.*341, etc.: aor. 1 ἐβλάστησα Emp.21.10, Hp.*Nat.Puer.*26, etc. (not in Att.): pf. βεβλάστηκα Id.*Oss.*12, Hellanic.1 (b) J., Plu.2.684c; ἐβλάστηκα E.*IA* 594 (lyr.), Eup.329: plpf. ἐβεβλαστήκει Th.3.26:—*bud, sprout, grow*, prop. of plants, A.*Th.*594, S.*OC*697 (lyr.), Th. l. c., Ar.*Nu.*1124, etc.; ἡ βλαστὸς οὐκ ἔβλαστεν; S.*Fr.*341; εἰς ἴα σου.., καὶ ἐς κρίνα βλαστήσειεν ὀστέα *IG*14.607 (Carales). 2. metaph. in Poets, *shoot forth, come to light*, βλάστε νᾶσος ἐξ ἁλός, of Rhodes, Pi.*O.*7.69; of children, *to be born*, Id.*N.*8.7; ἀνθρώπου φύσιν βλαστών *born* in man's nature, S. *Aj.*761, cf. *OT*1376, *El.*440; ἄργυρος κακὸν νόμισμ' ἔβλαστε Id.*Ant.* 296; β. δ' ἀπιστία Id.*OC*611; μέγιστ' ἔβλαστε νόμιμα Id.*El.*1095 (lyr.); not common in Prose, Th. l. c., Pl.*R.*498b, *Phdr.*251b, Iamb. *Myst.*3.28. II. causal, *make to grow, produce, propagate*, in pres., Hp.*Alim.*54: metaph., β. χάριτες εὔνοιαν Aristeas 230: mostly aor. 1 ἐβλάστησα A.R.1.1131; θεὸς.. ἄμπελον ἐβλάστησεν Nonn.*D.*36.356, cf. Lxx *Ge.*1.11, *Nu.*17.8:—Pass., βλαστηθείς Ph.1.667.

βλασταρίζουσα· ἐπικροτοῦσα, Hsch. **βλαστάριον**· ἕλιξ ἀμπέλου, *EM*330.30.

βλαστ-άω, late form of βλαστάνω, trans., *bring forth*, Lxx *Ec.*2.6: intr., Sch.Pi.*P.*4.113. **-εῖον**, τό, = βλάστη, Nic.*Al.*609 (pl.). **-η**, ἡ, = βλαστός, S.*Ichn.*276, Pl.*Lg.*765e, etc.; πετραία β. the *growth* of stone, S.*Ant.*827 (lyr.). II. of children, βλάσται γενέθλιοι πατρός *birth from* a father, Id.*OC*972; παιδὸς βλάσται Id.*OT*717, cf. *Tr.*382, *Trag.Adesp.*373. **-ημα**, ατος, τό, = βλάστη I, κισσίνοις β. E.*Ba.* 177, cf. Isoc.1.52, Thphr.*HP*1.1.9, *PLond.*1.131ʳ ix 191 (i A.D.). II. metaph., *offspring, offshoot*, μητρὸς β. A.*Th.*533; τέκνων γλυκερὸν β. E.*Med.*1099 (lyr.), cf. *IG*12(7).496.3 (Amorgos), etc.; also of animals, E.*Cyc.*206; ὦ χρυσέ β. χθονός *Trag.Adesp.*129.1: also in late Prose, Jul.*Or.*7.232d. III. *excrescence*, Hp.*Hum.*1; *eruption* on the skin, Aret.*CD*1.2. **-ημός**, ὁ, *growth*, βλαστημὸν ἀλδαίνοντα σώματος πολύν A.*Th.*12, cf. *Supp.*318. **-ήμων**, ον, gen. ονος, = βλαστικός, Nic.*Al.*548. **-ησις**, εως, ἡ, *budding, sprouting*, Arist.*HA*564ᵇ2, Thphr.*HP*3.5.4 (pl.). **-ητικός**, ή, όν, *in active growth, sprouting*, Id.*CP*1.11.4; β. ὧραι *sprouting* season, Id.*Od.*63. **-ικός**, ή, όν, *budding, sprouting*, Id.*HP*3.12.8: Sup., dub. in Id.*CP*1.13.10; *furthering growth*, ὥρα *Gp.*9.9.3 (Comp.); κίνησις Herm.ap.Stob.1. 41.7.

βλαστο-δρεπής, ές, *plucked as young shoots*, prob. in Nic.*Fr.*74. 20. **-κοπέω**, *cut off young shoots*, in Pass., ὅταν ὑπὸ πνευμάτων -ηθῇ Thphr.*HP*4.14.6, cf. *CP*5.9.13. **-λογέω**, *pick off young shoots*, ib.3.16.1, Gal.6.619, *PLond.*1.131ʳ xxiii 507 (i A.D.):—Subst. **-λογία**, ἡ, Thphr. l. c., *POxy.*1631.13.

βλαστόν, τό, = sq., Nic.*Fr.*74.52.

βλαστός, ὁ, *shoot*, Hdt.6.37, 8.55, Thphr.*HP*3.6.3, Arist.*Col.*795ᵃ 4, *GA*731ᵃ9, *POxy.*1692.20; *bud*, Thphr.*HP*1.8.4, *CP*1.11.4; *embryo, germ*, Id.*HP*8.2.2; ὁ τοῦ β. καιρός, i.e. Spring, D.S.17.82. 2. *blossom*, β. κρίνου Lxx 3*Ki.*7.24. II. *offspring*, S.*Fr.*341, *Epigr. Gr.*224 (Samos).

βλαστοφυέω, *put forth shoots*, prob. cj. in Thphr.*CP*1.11.7.

βλαστόω, = βλαστὸν παρατίθημι, *An.Ox.*1.96.

βλασφημ-έω, pf. βεβλασφήμηκα D.18.10:—*speak profanely of sacred things*, εἰς θεοὺς Pl.*R.*381e; *offer rash prayers*, Id.*Alc.*2.149c; β. κατά τινος *utter imprecations* against, Aeschin.1.180. 2. *speak ill* or *to the prejudice of* one, *slander*, περὶ τῆς ἐμῆς διατριβῆς Isoc.15.2, cf. D. l. c., ib.82; β. κατά τινος Isoc.12.65, cf. Arist.*Fr.*44; ὅσα εἰς ἡμᾶς ἐβλασφήμησαν D.51.3; β. τινά Babr.71.6, *Ev.Luc.*23.39, etc.:

abs., Phld.*Lib.*p.8 O.:—Pass., *to have evil spoken of one*, βεβλασφημημένους Id.*Vit.*p.12 J., cf. 1*Ep.Cor.*10.30. 3. *speak impiously* or *irreverently of God, blaspheme*, εἰς τὸν Κύριον Lxx *Da.*3.29(96); εἰς τὸ πνεῦμα τὸ ἅγιον *Ev.Marc.*3.29; εἰς τὰ θεῖα Vett.Val.58.12; τοὺς θεούς Id.67.20: abs., Lxx 2*Ma.*10.34, al., *Ev.Matt.*9.3. **-ία**, ἡ, *word of evil omen, profane speech*, D.25.26; βλασφημίαν ἐφθέγξατο, at a sacrifice, E.*Ion* 1189; εἴ τις παραστὰς τοῖς βωμοῖς βλασφημοῖ β. πᾶσαν Pl.*Lg.*800c; πᾶσαν β. ἱερῶν καταχέουσι ib.d. 2. *defamation, slander*, Democr.177, D.10.36, 18.95; β. ποιεῖσθαι εἴς τινα Aeschin. 1.167, cf. *Ep.Eph.*4.31; ὅλας ἁμάξας βλασφημιῶν whole cart-loads *of abuse*, Luc.*Eun.*2. 3. *irreverent speech against God, blasphemy*, ἡ εἰς τὸ θεῖον β. Men.715: in pl., Lxx *Ez.*35.12, al.; τοῦ Πνεύματος *against..*, *Ev.Matt.*12.31; πρὸς τὸν θεόν *Apoc.*13.6. **-ος**, ον, *speaking ill-omened words, evil-speaking*, Arist.*Rh.*1398ᵇ11: c. gen., *against..*, Plu.2.1100d, etc. 2. of words, *slanderous, libellous*, δέδοικα μὴ βλάσφημον μὲν εἰπεῖν ἀληθὲς δ' ᾖ D.9.1, cf. Luc.*Alex.*4 (Sup.). Adv. -μως Philostr.*VA*4.19, App.*BC*2.126. 3. *blasphemous*, ἔθνη Lxx 2*Ma.*10.4; ῥήματα *Act.Ap.*6.11; λαλεῖν βλάσφημα *Apoc.*13.5: Subst., *blasphemer*, Lxx 2*Ma.*9.28, 1*Ep.Ti.*1.13, etc.

βλάττα, ἡ, Lat. *blatta, purple*, *Edict.Diocl.*24.2:—Dim. **βλαττίον**, τό, Lyd.*Mens.*1.21.

βλάτταν· χόρτος, ἢ λάχανον, Hsch. **βλαττοῖ**· παιδαριεύεται, Id. **βλαῦδες**· ἐμβάδες, Id.

βλαύτ-η, ἡ, *slipper*, Hermipp.47.4, Lysipp.2, Herod.7.58: mostly in pl., βλαύτας σύρων Anaxil.18.2; β. ὑποδεδεμένος Pl.*Smp.* 174a. **-ίον**, τό, Dim. of foreg., Ar.*Eq.*889, Aristodem.8, *AP*6. 293 (Leon.); **βλαύρια** in Hsch., Cyr. **-όω**, *beat with slippers*, Hsch.; also, = ὑποδέω, Id.

βλαχάν· ὁ βάτραχος, Hsch.

βλάχνον, τό, = βλῆχνον, Phan.Hist.25, Sch.Nic.*Th.*39:—also **βλάθρον** and **βλάχρον**, Hsch.

βλάψις, εως, ἡ, *harming, damage*, Pl.*Lg.*932e (pl.).

βλαψί-τάφος [ῐ], ον, *violating the grave*, ἀτασθαλίη *IG*14.934.4. **-φρων**, ον, gen. ονος, (φρήν) *maddening*, φάρμακα Euph.14.2; ἄτη Tryph.411, cf. Orph.*H.*77.3, etc. II. = φρενοβλαβής, A.*Th.*725.

βλεαίρει (Boeot. for ἐλεαίρει)· οἰκτείρει, Hsch. (βλεερεῖ cod.).

βλέθρα, = πλέθρα, *BCH*9.382 (Thespiae, iii B.C.).

βλεθράνασιν· ἰχθῦν, Hsch. **βλεῖ**, = βλίσσει, v.l. in Id. **βλείης**, **βλεῖο**, v. βάλλω. **βλεκέμυξος**· βλακώδης, Id. **βλέκυξ**, v. βλέτυγες.

βλεμεαίνω, *exult*, σθένεϊ βλεμεαίνων, of a lion, Il.12.42; of Hector, 8.337; cf. ἀβλεμής.

βλέμμα, ατος, τό, *look, glance*, E.*HF*306, Ar.*Pl.*1022, D.21.72, Antiph.235, 2*Ep.Pet.*2.8, *POxy.*471.60 (ii A.D.); *eyesight*, *AP*9.159; βλεμμάτων βολή A.*Fr.*242.

βλέννα, ἡ, = μύξα, *mucous discharge*, Hp.*Mul.*1.58 (pl.); of the humour '*phlegm*', Prodic.4, etc.

βλέννος, ους, τό, *slime*, Arist.*HA*591ᵃ28. II. β., ὁ, *fish* allied to κωβιός, βαιών, Sophr.43, Opp.*H.*1.109.

βλεννός, ή, όν, *drivelling*, Epich.119, Sophr.51.

βλεννώδης, ες, *slimy, mucous*, Hp.*Morb.*2.12, Arist.*HA*591ᵃ26.

βλέορον (prob. βλέθρον, cf. βέρεθρον, βέθρον)· βάθος, δεσμωτήριον, Hsch. **βλεπάζοντες**· βλέποντες, Id.

βλεπεδαίμων, ον, gen. ονος, *ghostlike*, *Com.Adesp.*85; a nickname of the Socratics, Paus.Gr.*Fr.*209.

βλεπετύζει· σκαρδαμύττει, βλέπει, Hsch.

βλέπησις, εως, ἡ, *look, glance*, Ar.*Fr.*757; πρὸς βλέπησιν *by eye*, βάπτειν *PHolm.*16.33.

βλέπος, ους, τό, = βλέμμα, *look*, Ἀττικὸν β. Ar.*Nu.*1176, cf. Theoc. 23.12.

βλεπτ-έον, *one must look*, εἴς τι Pl.*Lg.*965d, Arist.*APr.*44ᵃ36, etc. **-ικός**, ή, όν, *of* or *for sight*, αἴσθησις *App.Anth.*3.158; *sharp-seeing*, Hdn.*Epim.*101 (Sup.). **-ός**, ή, όν, *to be seen*, S.*OT*1337.

βλέπω, Sol.11.8, etc.: impf. ἔβλεπον Batr.67: fut. βλέψομαι D. 25.98, Dor. inf. βλεψεῖσθαι *IG*4.951.75 (Epid.), later βλέψω Lxx *Is.* 6.9, Aristid.2.46 J., etc.: aor. ἔβλεψα (v. infr.): pf. βέβλεφα (ἀπο-) Antip.*Stoic.*3.254 (codd. Stob.); βέβλοφα (ἐμ-) *PLond.*1.42.21 (ii B.C.):—Pass., aor. ἐβλέφθην (προσ-) Plu.2.68of: pf. βέβλεμμαι to be supplied in Ath.10.409c, cf. Eust.1401.16:—chiefly in pres. and aor. Act. in early writers: Med. (exc. fut.) and Pass. only late:—*see, have the power of sight* (dist. fr. ὁρῶ *perceive, be aware of*, cf. Plot.6.7.37), opp. τυφλὸς εἰμι, S.*OT*302, cf. 348, *OC*73, Ar. *Pl.*15, etc.; βλέποντες ἔβλεπον μάτην A.*Pr.*447; βλέποντας ἀθλιωτάτους Alex.234; μὴ βλέπων ὁ μάντις ᾖ lest he *see too clearly*, S.*OT*747; ὁ βλέπων *the seer*, Hebraism in Lxx 1*Ki.*9.9; ὀλίγον βλέπων *short-sighted*, *POxy.*39.9 (i A.D.). II. *look*, βλέφ' ὧδε S.*Tr.*402; ἐπὶ ἐμοί Id.*Aj.*345 (s.v.l.); εἴς τι A.*Pers.*802; ἐπί τι Th.7.71; εἰς τὰ τούτων πρόσωπα D.18.283; πῶς βλέπων; with what *face*? S.*Ph.*110; ὄμμασιν ποίοις β.; Id.*OT*1371; β. ἅμα πρόσσω καὶ ὀπίσσω Pl.*Cra.*428d: with Adv., φιλοφρόνως, ἐχθρῶς β. πρός τινας, X.*Mem.*3.10.4, *Smp.*4.58: freq. folld. by noun in acc., φόβον β. *look* terror, i.e. to *look* terrible, Θυιὰς ὣς φόβον βλέπων A.*Th.*498; Com., ἔβλεψε νᾶπυ *looked* mustard, Ar.*Eq.*631; ἀνδρεῖον.. καὶ βλέποντ' ὀρίγανον Id.*Ra.*603; βλεπόντων κάρδαμα Id.*V.*455; πυρρίχην βλέπων *looking like* a war-dancer, Id.*Av.* 1169; αἴκειαν βλέπων *looking like* one disgraced, ib.1671; σκύτη β., of a slave, Eup.282, Ar.*V.*643; β. ἀπιστίαν Eup.309: also folld. by Adj., μέγα β. dub. in Semon.19; φθονερὰ β. Pi.*N.*4.39; γλίσχρον β. Euphro 10.16, cf. Men.*Epit.*479, Jul.*Caes.*309c: by inf., ἁρπάζειν β. Men.*Epit.*181; ὀρχεῖσθαι μόνον β. Alex.97: by part. neut., τί φροντικὸς βλέπεις; E.*Alc.*773. 2. β. ἐς *look* to, *rely* on, εἰς ἔργον οὐδὲν γιγνόμενον βλέπετε Sol.11.8; ἐς θεοὺς S.*Ant.*923; οὐκέτ' ἔστιν εἰς ὅ τι βλέπω Id.*Aj.*514; ἐς σε δὴ βλέπω, ὅπως.. in the hope that.., Id.*El.*954: metaph. also, *have regard* to, ἡ πολιτεία β. εἰς πλοῦτον Arist.*Pol.*1293ᵇ14; of aspects, οἰκίαι πρὸς μεσημβρίαν βλέπουσαι.., X.*Mem.*3.8.9; πέτρα βλέπουσα πρὸς νότον Str.4.1.4; κάτω γὰρ οἱ ὀδόντες βλέπουσι Arist.*HA*502ᵃ1; ὅταν τὸ οὖθαρ βλέπῃ κάτω ib.523ᵃ 2. 3. *look longingly, expect, propose*, c. inf., Ar.*Ach.*376, *V.* 847. 4. *look to* a thing, *beware*, ἀπό τινος *Ev.Marc.*8.15; τι *Ep. Phil.*3.2: c. acc. pers., β. ἑαυτοὺς *Ev.Marc.*13.9; βλέπε σα(υ)τὸν ἀπὸ τῶν Ἰουδαίων *BGU*1079.24 (i A.D.); β. ἵνα.. 1*Ep.Cor.*16.10; β. ἑαυτοὺς ἵνα μὴ.. 2*Ep.Jo.*8; βλέπετε τί ἀκούετε *Ev.Marc.*4.24. III. trans., *see, behold*, c. acc., S.*Aj.*1042, etc.; ἐξ αὑτοῦ βλεπόμενον *self-evident*, S.E.*M.*1.184; τὰ βλεπόμενα *the visible universe*, Lxx *Wi.*13. 7. 2. ζῇ τε καὶ β. φάος *sees* the light of day, A.*Pers.*299, cf. E.*Hel.* 60; νόστιμον β. φάος A.*Pers.*261; βλέποντα νῦν μὲν ὀρθ' ἔπειτα δὲ σκότον (i.e. being blind) S.*OT*419: hence, without φάος, *to be alive*, ζῶντα καὶ βλέποντα A.*Ag.*677; βλέποντα κἀμπνέοντα S.*Ph.*883, cf. 1349, *Aj.*962; of things, ἀληθῆ καὶ βλέποντα *actually existing*, A.*Ch.* 844. 3. *look for*, μεῖζόν τι β. Pl.*Chrm.*172c. 4. Astrol. of signs equidistant from the tropical points, *to be in aspect*, β. ἄλληλα Ptol.*Tetr.*36, Heph.Astr.1.9. (βλέφαρα occurs in Hom., but not βλέπω exc. in Batr. l. c.)

βλέτενον· βλιτώδη (βλητ- cod.), Hsch. **βλέτυγες**· φλυαρίαι: also **βλέκυγες**, Id.:—sg. **βλέκυξ**, Hdn.Gr.2.482. **βλέτυες**· αἱ βδέλλαι, Hsch.

βλεφἄρ-ίζω, *wink*, Sch.Ar.*Eq.*292. **-ικός**, ή, όν, *of* or *for the eyelids*, *collyria* Cael.Aur.*TP*4.2.17. **-ίς**, ίδος, ἡ, *eyelash*, Ar.*Ec.* 402: mostly in pl., Id.*Eq.*373, X.*Mem.*1.4.6, Arist.*PA*658ᵃ11. II. = βλέφαρον, *eyelid*, Id.*HA*504ᵃ29. **-ῖτις**, ιδος, ἡ, *of* or *on the eyelids*, τρίχες Paul.Aeg.6.13.

βλεφἄροκάτοχος, ον, *holding the eyelid*, μυδίον Paul.Aeg.6.8.

βλέφἄρον, Dor. **γλέφἄρον**, τό:—mostly in pl. (as always in Hom.), *eyelids*, βλέφαρ' ἀμφὶ καὶ ὀφρύας Od.9.389, al.; of sleep, φίλα βλέφαρ' ἀμφικαλύψας 5.493; ὕπνος ἀπὸ βλεφάροιϊν (dual) Il.10.187; ὕπνον ἐπὶ βλεφάροισιν ἔχευεν Od.20.54, al.; παῦρον ἐπὶ γλεφάροις ὕπνον ἀναλίσκοισα Pi.*P.*9.24; γλεφάρων ἁδὺ κλαΐστρον ib.1.8; βλέφαρα κέκλῃται S.*Fr.*711; β. συμβαλεῖν, κοιμᾶν ὕπνῳ, A.*Ag.*15, *Th.* 3; of weeping, δάκρυ χαμαὶ βάλεν ἐκ βλεφάροιϊν Od.17.490, cf. 23. 33; of death, λύειν β. S.*Ant.*1302: in Prose, Antipho Soph.81a, Pl. *Ti.*45d, *PPetr.*3 p.23 (iii B.C.): rarely in sg., E.*Or.*302; β. τὸ ἄνω καὶ κάτω Arist.*HA*491ᵇ19, cf. *PA*657ᵇ14. II. in pl., *eyes*, βλεφάρων κυανεάων Hes.*Sc.*7 (where the fem. Adj. points to a nom. ἡ βλέφαρος); freq. in Trag., σκοτώσω β. καὶ δεδορκότα S.*Aj.*85, cf. *Tr.* 107 (lyr.): in sg., of the sun, ἁμέρας β. Id.*Ant.*104 (lyr.); of the curtain of darkness at nightfall, νυκτὸς ἀφεγγὲς β. E.*Ph.*543.

βλεφἄρό-ξυστον, τό, *an instrument for trimming the eyelids*, Paul. Aeg.3.22.12. **-σπάξ**, *arching the eyebrows*, Hdn.Gr.1.43. **-τόμον**, τό, surgical instrument, *Hermes*38.280.

βλεψίας, ου, ὁ, a *fish*, = κεφαλῖνος, Dorio ap.Ath.7.306f.

βλέψις, εως, ἡ, *act of sight*, τὸ βλεπόμενον τὸ ὄν, οὐχ ἡ β. Plot.6.2. 8. II. *sight* (i.e. *thing seen*), πρὸς τὴν βλέψιν ἀναφλεχθείς Plu. *Pel.*32. III. metaph., *contemplation, consideration*, συμφερόντων Epicur.*Ep.*3 p.63 U.

βλήδην, Adv. *by throwing, hurling*, Hsch. **βλήεται**, v. βάλλω.

βλῆθα, v. βλῆμα 4.

βληθρήν· τραχεῖαν, οἱ δὲ (ἁ)παλήν, Hsch.

βλῆμα, ατος, τό, (βάλλω) *throw, cast*, of dice, ἄλλα βλήματ' ἐν κύβοις βαλεῖν E.*Supp.*330; of a missile, D.H.10.16; of *the missile* itself, Ph.2.431, Max.Tyr.9.8 (pl.). 2. *shot, wound*, Hdt.3.35, Hp.*Prorrh.*2.14 (pl.). 3. *coverlet*, *AP*7.413 (Antip.). 4. = ἄρτος ἐντεθρυμμένος καὶ θερμός, Seleuc.ap.Ath.3.114d (**βλῆθα** in Hsch.).

βλήμενος, v. sub βάλλω. **βλῆναι**· ἀληθεῖς, Hsch.

βλῆραι· αἱ κνίδαι, ἄλλοι χόρτον, οἱ δὲ τῶν ὀσπρίων τὴν καλάμην, Hsch.

βλής, ητός, ὁ, ἡ, *thrown*, prob. f.l. for ἀβλής, Call.*Fr.anon.*341.

βλῆσθαι, v. βάλλω. **βλήσσα⟨ν⟩**· βότρυν ἡμιπέ⟨πε⟩ιρον, Hsch. **βλήσσανον**· φυτὸν σχίνῳ ὅμοιον, Id. **βληστάς**· ὁ χερσαῖος σκορπίος, Id.

βληστρ-ίζω, *toss about*, ἑαυτὸν β., as a sick person on his bed, Hp. *Morb.*3.7; βληστρίζοντες ἐμὴν φροντίδ' ἀν' Ἑλλάδα γῆν Xenoph.8.2: metaph., ἐμαυτὸν πόλιν ἐκ πόλεως φέρων ἐβλήστριζον Id.45:—Pass., = βληστρίζειν ἑαυτόν, Aret.*CA*1.1. **-ισμός**, ὁ, *tossing, restlessness*, Hp.*Epid.*1.26.β'.

βλήτ-ειρα, ἡ, *thrower, darter*, ὀϊστῶν Alex.Aet.4.5. **-έον**, *one must throw* or *put*, *Ev.Marc.*2.22. **-ίεῖ**· καταβαλεῖ, νικήσει, Hsch. **-ικόν**, τό, = βλητόν (v. βλητός 2), Thphr.*Fr.*178. II. *striking*, β. ζῷα, opp. δάκετα (*biting*), prob. for βλητά in Ael.*NA*3.32.

βλῆτο, v. βάλλω. **βλῆτον**, v. βλίτον.

βλητ-ός, ή, όν, (βάλλω) *stricken, palsy-stricken*, Hp.*Acut.*17, *Coac.* 394; *smitten by disease*, λεχωΐδες Call.*Dian.*127, cf. *Cer.*102. 2. v. βλητικόν. **-ρον**, τό, *fastening*: *band* or *hoop*, ξυστὸν κολλητὸν βλήτροισι Il.15.678. II. = βλῆχνον, Nic.*Th.*39 (gen. sg., v.l. βλίτρου; Sch. gives nom. βλῆτρος). **-ρώσας**· ἐμβαλών, Hsch.

βληχ-άζω, = sq., Autocr.3. **-χάομαι**, aor. ἐβληχησάμην *AP* 7.657 (Leon.), Longus 3.13:—*bleat*, of sheep and goats, προβατίων βληχωμένων Ar.*Pax* 535, *Fr.*387.5; βληχώμενοι προβατίων αἰγῶν τε..μέλη Id.*Pl.*293; of infants, τὰ δὲ συγκύψανθ' ἅμα βληχᾶται Id.*V.* 570: metaph. of men, c. acc. cogn., πάταγον Porph.*Chr.*35; βληχοῖντο (as if from βληχέομαι) is v.l. for βληχῷντο in Theoc.16. 92. **-άς,** άδος, ἡ, *bleater,* ὄϊας περὶ β. Opp.*C.*1.145. **-ή,** Dor. **βλᾱχά,** ἡ, *bleating,* οἰῶν Od.12.266; of lambs, E.*Cyc.*48 (lyr., pl.); *wailing* of infants, A.*Th.*348 (lyr., pl.). (Onomatop.) **-ηθμός,** ὁ, = foreg., Ael.*NA*5.51, Nonn.*D.*14.157. **-ημα,** ατος, τό, = βληχή, Hsch. (pl.): sg., = μωρός, προβατώδης, Id. **-ητά,** ῶν, τά, *bleaters,* i. e. *sheep,* Ael.*NA*2.54; β. τέκνα *sheepish* lads, Eup.103.

βλῆχνον, τό (v. l. **βλῆχρον,** as in Sch.Theoc.3.14, Cyr. (βλῆχρα Hsch.)), = πτέρις, *male fern, Aspidium Filix-mas,* Dsc.4.184.

βληχρός, ά, όν, *faint, gentle,* ἄνεμοι Alc.16; of the rivers of hell, *dull, sluggish,* Pi.*Fr.*130; πελάγη A.R.4.152; *gentle,* opp. ἀκράχολος, Phld.*Lib.*p.44 O.; β. πυρετοί *slight,* Hp.*Aph.*5.64, cf. Plu.*Per.*38; β. σφυγμοί Hp.*Mul.*1.37; νοῦσος -οτέρη ib.36; ὕπνου β. ὄνειαρ Q.S. 2.182. Adv. -ρῶς *slightly,* Hp.*Mul.*2.203; *weakly,* β. εἶχον καὶ οὐκ ἰσχυρῶς Ctes.*Fr.*29.42: Comp. -ότερον Hp.*Morb.*2.61. **2.** metaph., *slight, small,* β. ἀπ' ἀρχᾶς B.10.65; χάριν οὐ β. Id.12.227.—Not in Hom. (who has ἀβληχρός), nor in Att.; η in all dialects.

βλῆχρος, ἡ, = γλήχων, Thphr.*CP*1.7.4, Ps.-Dsc.3.31.

βλῆχρον, v. βλῆχνον.

βληχώδης, ες, *bleating, sheepish,* Babr.93.5.

βλήχων, ἡ (later ὁ, *Gp.*8.7), gen. ωνος, also **βληχώ,** gen. οῦς; Ion. **γλήχων, -ώ,** Dor. **γλάχων, -ώ** (on the forms see Phryn.*PS* p.53 B., Sch.Ar.*Pax* 711), dat. γλήχωνι *h.Cer.*209; βληχοῖ Thphr.*HP* 9.16.1: gen. γληχοῦς Hp.*Morb.*3.17; γλάχωνος Boeot.ap.Ar.*Ach.* 869: acc. γλάχωνα ib.861, Theoc.5.56; γλήχωνα Herod.9.13; γλαχώ Ar.*Ach.*874; βληχώ Id.*Lys.*89:—*pennyroyal, Mentha Pulegium,* ll. cc., Dsc.3.31, etc.

βληχωνίας, ου, ὁ, *prepared with pennyroyal,* κυκεών Ar.*Pax* 712.

βληχώνιον, τό, = βλήχων, Sch.Theoc.5.56.

βλιαρόν· ἀβλεβές, Hsch.: βλιαρόν· λαῦρον, *EM*201.41. **βλιβρόν·** λαγ⟨α⟩ρόν, Hsch. **βλίδες·** ψεκάδες, Id. **βλίζω,** = βλίττω, Id. s.v. βλεῖ, cf. *EM*200.33. **βλιηχῶδες·** βλιχανῶδες (βλιχῶνες cod.), Hsch. **βλίκανος,** ὁ, = βάτραχος, Hsch., *EM*201. 42:—also **βλίχας,** Hsch.: **βλίκαρος,** Suid. **βλικάς** or **βλίκας,** *fig-leaf,* Hsch., *EM*201.41.

βλῑμ-άζω, Lacon. **-άττω,** *feel* hens to see if they are fat, Ar.*Av.* 530: hence sens. obsc., Cratin.302, Ar.*Lys.*1164, S.*Fr.*484:—Pass., *to be squeezed,* Hp.*Epid.*5.1. **2.** *handle, treat,* β. τοὺς ἀξίους ἐπιεικέστερον Aristeas 188. **II.** = βλίττω, *EM*200.47. **-ᾰσις,** εως, ἡ, *lewd handling,* Hsch.

βλίμη· προπηλακισμός, ὕβρις, Hsch., *EM*201.40. **βλινόν·** δαλόν, Hsch. **βλίξ·** συνεχῶς, Id. **βλίσσω,** v. βλίττω.

βλιστηρίς, ίδος, ἡ, (βλίττω) *honey-taking,* χείρ *AP*9.226 (Zon.).

βλιτάς, άδος, ἡ, *worthless woman,* Men.955.

βλιτάχεα, τά, = κογχύλια or σελάχια, Epich.193: but **βλίταχος·** βάτραχος, Hsch.

βλῐτο-μάμμας or **-μάμας,** ου, ὁ, *booby,* Ar.*Nu.*1001, cf. Phryn. *PS* p.55 B.

βλίτον, τό, *blite, Amaranthus Blitum,* Hp.*Vict.*2.54, 3.75:—written **βλῆτον** Id.*Aff.*41, Thphr.*HP*1.14.2, Dsc.2.117: in pl., Theopomp.Com.62, Diph.14.

βλίττω, aor. ἔβλῐσα Pl.*R.*564e:—*cut out the comb of bees, take the honey,* l. c.; σφηκιὰν β. S.*Fr.*778: metaph., β. τὸν δῆμον *rob* the people *of their honey,* Ar.*Eq.*794, cf. *Lys.*475:—Pass., πλεῖστον δὴ.. τοῖς κηφῆσι μέλι βλίττεται prob. in Pl. l. c.; β. τὰ σμήνη the hives *have their honey taken,* Arist.*HA*554ᵃ15, cf. 627ᵇ2. **II.** βλίσσειν· = μαλάσσειν, Erot.*Fr.*16. (For μλίτ-yω, cf. μέλι.)

βλίτυρι, τό, *twang of a harp-string*: hence of a *meaningless sound,* S.E.*M.*8.133, D.L.7.57, Artem.4.2, Gal.8.662.

βλιτυρίζομαι, Pass., *sound like a harp-string,* coined by Gal.8.662.

βλίτυρον ἐστὶ φυτὸν ἢ φάρμακον, ἢ χορδῆς μίμημα, *EM*201.43.

βλίτωνας· τοὺς εὐήθεις, Hsch.

βλῐχ-ᾰνώδης, ες, of fish, *clammy,* Diph.17.15. **-ώδης,** ες, *clammy, sticky,* of wounds or ulcers, Hp.*VC*19 ap.Erot. (γλισχρῶδες codd.), cf. Archig.ap.Orib.46.23.3.

βλοσέμεν· σκοτωθῆναι, Hsch.

βλοσῠρόμμᾰτος, ον, *grim-eyed,* prob. in Cerc.*Oxy.*1082 *Fr.*28.

βλοσῠρός, ά, όν, also ός, όν v.l. in Hes.*Sc.*250:—*hairy, shaggy, bristling,* μειδιόων βλοσυροῖσι προσώπασι Il.7.212; τὼ δέ οἱ ὄσσε λαμπέσθην βλοσυρῇσιν ὑπ' ὀφρύσιν 15.608, cf. Hes.*Sc.*147; of lions, ib. 175; of the Κῆρες, ib.250; ἡ δὲ συὸς βλοσυρῆς, to describe a woman, Phoc.3.3; β. χαίτη *Lyr.Alex.Adesp.*11.4; ἄρκτοι, φώκη, Opp.*H.*2.247, 5.38; πορδαλίων βλοσυρὰς δύσαντο καλύπτρας Nonn.*D.*14.131; later, *grim, fearful,* ἄγος A.*Eu.*167 (lyr.); ἄκρη A.R.2.740; κύματα *AP*9. 84 (Antiphan.), cf. 278 (Bianor); φάσματα ἀρχαγγέλων Iamb.*Myst.*2. 3. **2.** *virile, burly,* γενναίους τε καὶ β. τὰ ἤθη Pl.*R.*535b; β. γε τὴν ψυχὴν ἔχεις Nicostr.35; of a woman, μαῖα γενναία καὶ β. *masculine,* Pl.*Tht.*149a; βλοσυρωτάτη τὸ εἶδος, of Boudicca, D.C.62.2; also, *coarse,* πίττα Thphr.*HP*9.2.3 (Comp.), cf. *CP*6.12.5 (Comp.). **3.** *solemn, dignified,* σεμνὸν καὶ β. δρᾶν Ael.*VH*12.21; of persons, σεμνὴ καὶ β. Aristaenet.1.7, cf. Him.*Or.*23.12. Adv. -ῶς Hld.10.27.

βλοσῠρό-της, ητος, ἡ, *grimness,* Eust.1194.46. **-φρων,** ον, gen. ονος, *savage-minded,* A.*Supp.*833 (lyr.).

βλοσῠρ-ώπης, ου, ὁ, later masc. of sq., Opp.*C.*1.144. **-ῶπις,** ιδος, ἡ, (ὤψ) *grim-looking,* Γοργώ Il.11.36. **-ωπός,** όν, later form of foreg., D.P.123.

βλόχον, = βδέλλιον, Dsc.1.67. **βλύδιον·** ὑγρόν, ζέον, Hsch.

βλύζω, aor. ἔβλῠσα A.R.4.1446, Q.S.1.242, *AP*7.352, etc.; poet. opt. βλύσσειε *AP*11.58 (Maced.): aor. Pass. ἐβλύσθη Orac.ap.Eus.*PE* 5.16:—*bubble, gush forth,* of liquids, A.R. l. c., Orac. in Paus.5.7.3; ἐκ πηγῆς Philostr.*VA*3.45: c. dat., β. Λυαίῳ *with* wine, *AP*11.58 (Maced.): c. acc. cogn., μέθυ β. *spout* wine: metaph. of Anacreon, ib. 7.27 (Antip. Sid.); ὕδωρ Orph.*A.*599, cf. Nonn.*D.*17.125, al.; χρυσίον Lyd.*Mag.*3.45: metaph., αἰσχρὰ καθ' ἡμετέρης ἔβλυσε παρθενίης *AP* 7.352.

βλύσις [ῠ], εως, ἡ, *bubbling up, AP*9.819:—also **βλύσμα,** ατος, τό, Hdn.*Epim.*11: **βλυσμός,** ὁ, *Gloss.*

βλυστάνω, = sq., Procl.*in Cra.*p.80 P., Mich.*in PN*51.1, *Et.Gud.*

βλυχάζω, = μολύνω, in pf. part. Pass., Hsch.

βλύω, = βλύζω, c. dat., φόνῳ βλύουσαι Lyc.301: c. acc., δέμας οἱ ἔβλυεν ὕδωρ Nonn.*D.*19.287: c. gen., παρ' ὄρει θερμῶν ὑδάτων βλύοντι *OGI*199.11. [ῡ between two long syll. in Ep., ἀνα-βλύεσκε A.R. 3.223, cf. 4.1417.]

βλωθρός, ά, όν, *tall,* πίτυς β. Il.13.390; β. ὄγχνη Od.24.234, cf. A.R.4.1476, Q.S.8.204; βλωθρὴ ἐπὶ ποίῃ Arat.1089. (Perh. cf. Skt. *mūrdhá* 'head', OE. *molda* 'head'.)

βλωμ-ός, ὁ, = ψωμός, *morsel* of bread, Call.*Fr.*240; cf. ὀκτάβλωμος:—Dim. **-ίδιον,** τό, Eust.1817.55: **βλωμιαῖοι** ἄρτοι prob. l. in Philem.Gloss.ap.Ath.3.114e. **II.** βλωμοί· στραβοί, Hsch.

βλωρός, ὁ, *fig-leaf,* Hsch.

βλῶσις, εως, ἡ, *arrival, presence,* Hsch. **II.** *seat,* δίφρου β. *Trag.Adesp.*150.

βλώσκω, Nic.*Th.*450, (κατα-, προ-) Od.16.466, 21.239: fut. μολοῦμαι A.*Pr.*689 (lyr.), S.*OC*1742 (lyr.): aor. 2 ἔμολον Pi.*O.*14.18, etc., Ep. μόλον (ἐκ-, προ-) Il.11.604, Od.15.468, freq. in Trag., also Dor. (as aor. of pres. ἕρπω 'go') *IG*4.952.14 (Epid.), *SIG*558.26 (Ithaca), and sts. in Prose, X.*An.*7.1.33, Plb.30.9.5, Plu.*Cleom.*38; imper. μόλε Cratin.111: pf. μέμβλωκα Od.17.190, E.*Rh.*629; part. -κώς Call.*Aet.*1.1.7 (cf. βέβλωκεν· ἠρεμεῖ, φύεται, Hsch.): later fut. βλώξω (κατα-) Lyc.1068: aor. 1 ἔβλωξα Id.448, 1327: aor. 2 ἔβλω· ᾤχετο, Hsch., cf. μολέω:—*go* or *come,* mostly Poet. in aor. 2, δεῦρο μολόντες Od.3.44; μολοῦσα ποτὶ μέγαρ' Il.6.286; of Time, πρὶν δωδεκάτη μόλῃ ἠώς 24.781; μέμβλωκε μάλιστα ἦμαρ *has passed,* Od.17.190; ὅτε τὸ κύριον μόλῃ A.*Ag.*766 (lyr.): freq. with Preps., μολεῖν εἰς οἴκους, ἐπὶ δόμον, S.*OT*1010, E.*Or.*176 (lyr.); πρὸς χθόνα S.*Ph.*479; ἀπὸ Στρυμόνος, ἐκ Διός, A.*Ag.*192 (lyr.), *Pr.*667; κατὰ γαίας E.*Alc.*107 (lyr.): c. acc. only, ἔμολεν Ἥρας λαόν Pi.*N.*10.36; γῆν μολόντες Ἑλλάδα A. *Pers.*809, cf. *Ag.*968, *Supp.*239, S.*Ph.*1332, E.*Rh.*289; πρὶν φάος μολεῖν χθόνα ib.223; ἥβης τέλος μ. Id.*Med.*921, cf. *IT*1421: c. dat. pers., μηδέ μοι..θάνατος μόλοι Sol.21, cf. S.*OC*70, *Ant.*233, etc.; δι' ἔχθρας μ. τινί, διὰ μάχης μολεῖν τινί, E.*Ph.*479, *IA*1392; εἰς ὕποπτα μ. τινί, = ὑποπτεύειν τινά, Id.*El.*345.—Rare in Prose (v. supr.); used by Ar. only in lyr. (*Av.*404, *Th.*1146, 1155, al.), or in the mouth of a Laconian, Id.*Lys.*984, cf. Plu.2.220e, 225d (both from *Apophth.Lac.*).

βόα, ἡ, a *fish,* = σάλπη, Pancrat.ap.Ath.7.321f.

βο-ᾱγός, ὁ, v. βουαγός:—hence **-ᾱγίδης,** ου, ὁ, of Heracles, Lyc. 652. **-άγριον,** τό, *shield of wild bull's hide,* Il.12.22, Od.16. 296, *AP*9.323 (Antip.). **-αγρος,** ὁ, (βοῦς) *wild bull,* Philostr. *VA*6.24.

βοαδεῖ· ὀκνεῖ, Hsch.

βοᾱθόος, Dor. for βοηθόος (q. v.); name of a Delphic month, *SIG* 672.78.

βόᾱμα, ατος, τό, (βοάω) Dor for βόημα (which occurs in D.C.51. 17), *shriek, cry,* χαμαιπετὲς β. A.*Ag.*920; *loud strain,* τηλέπορόν τι β. λύρας *Lyr.Adesp.*102.

βο-άνθεμον, τό, = βούφθαλμον, Hp.*Mul.*1.78, Nic.*Fr.*74.38. **-άνθρωπος,** ὁ, *bull-man,* of the Minotaur, Tz.*H.*1.489.

βόαξ, ᾱκος, ὁ, Ion. **βόηξ,** contr. **βῶξ,** Diph.Siph.ap.Ath.8.356a, Arist.*HA*610ᵇ4, *Gp.*20.7.1:—a *grunting fish,* sacred to Hermes, called from the sound it makes, *Box boops,* Epich.29, Ar.*Fr.*475, Numen.ap.Ath.7.286f, Speus.ibid.; cf. βόωψ.

βοάριος, α, ον, = Lat. *boarius*: ἀγορὰ βοαρία, = *forum boarium* at Rome, D.H.1.40, cf. D.C.78.25.

βο-αρμία, ἡ, (ἀραρίσκω) *ox-yoker,* epith. of Athena, Lyc.520. **-αρχος,** ον, *beginning with an ox,* of a sacrifice in which an ox is the first victim, τρίττοα *IG*1².5 (v B. C.). **-ᾱτις,** ιδος, ἡ, v. βοητής. **-αύλιον,** τό, Dim. of sq., Epic. in *Arch.Pap.*7.7, Orph.*A.*438. **-αυλος,** ὁ, (βοῦς, αὐλή) *ox-stall,* Theoc.25.108:—also **-αυλον,** τό, A.R.3. 1290.

βοάω, Ep. 3 sg. βοάᾳ, 3 pl. βοόωσιν, part. βοόων, Il.14.394, 17.265, 15. 687: Ion. impf. βοάασκε A.R.2.588: fut. βοήσομαι Th.7.48, etc.; Dor. βοάσομαι Ar.*Nu.*1154 (lyr.); later βοήσω A.R.3.792, *AP*7.32 (Jul.), etc. (βοάσω E.*Ion* 1447 (lyr.) is aor. subj.): aor. ἐβόησα Il.11.15, S.*Tr.* 772, etc.; Ep. βόησα Il.23.847; Dor. βόασα B.16.14; Ion. ἔβωσα Il.12. 337, Hdt.1.146, Hippon.1, Herod.3.23; sts. in Com., Cratin.396, Ar. *Pax* 1155: pf. βεβόηκα Philostr.*VS*2.1.11:—**Med.,** βοώμενος Ar.*V.* 1228 (perh. Pass.): Ep. aor. βοήσατο Q.S.10.465, Ion. ἐβώσατο Theoc. 17.60; part. βοησάμενος Ant.Lib.25.3:—**Pass.,** Ion. aor. ἐβώσθην Hdt.6.131: pf. βεβόημαι *AP*7.138 (Aceratus), Ion. part. βεβωμένος Hdt.3.39: plpf. ἐβεβόητο Paus.6.11.3:—*cry aloud, shout,* ὀξὺ βοήσας Il.17.89; ὅσσον τε γέγωνε βοήσας Od.6.294; πᾶσα γὰρ πόλις βοᾷ A. *Ag.*1106 (lyr.); ὡς δράκων β. Id.*Th.*381; β. γραμμάτων ἐν ξυλλαβαῖς ib.468; οἱ βοησόμενοι *men ready to shout* (in the ἐκκλησία), D.13. 20; ὁ δῆμος ἐβόησεν.., of acclamations, *POxy.*41.19 (iii/iv A. D.), cf. Charito 1.1, al., *IG*12(9).906 (Chalcis, iii A. D.). **2.** of things, *roar, howl*, as the wind and waves, οὔτε.. κῦμα τόσον βοάᾳ ποτὶ χέρσον Il.14.394; *resound, echo*, ἀμφὶ δέ τ' ἄκραι ἠϊόνες βοόωσιν 17.265; βοᾷ δὲ πόντιος κλύδων A.*Pr.*431 (lyr.), etc.; βοᾷ δ' ἐν ὠσὶ κέλαδος *rings*, Id.*Pers.*605; τὸ πρᾶγμα φανερόν ἐστιν, αὐτὸ γὰρ βοᾷ it *proclaims* itself, Ar.*V.*921; φαίνεται αὐτὰ τὰ στοιχεῖα βοῶν ὡς ἑλκόμενα Arist.*Metaph.*1091ᵃ10. II. c. acc. pers., *call to one, call on*, Pi.*P.*6.36, E.*Med.*205 (lyr.), Hdt.8.92, X.*Cyr.*7.2.5, Herod.4.41:—Med. βοησάμενοι δαίμονας Ant.Lib.l.c. 2. c. acc., *call for, shout out for*, S.*Tr.*772; β. τὴν βοήθειαν *Hell.Oxy.*10.2. 3. c. acc. cogn., β. βοάν Ar.*Nu.*1153 (lyr.); β. μέλος, ἰωάν, S.*Aj.*976, *Ph.*216 (lyr.); β. λοιγόν A.*Ch.*402 (lyr.); ἄλγος E.*Tr.*1310 (lyr.): c. dupl. acc., βοάσαθ' ὑμέναιον ἀοιδαῖς ἰαχαῖς τε νύμφαν *sound aloud* the bridal hymn in honour of the bride, ib.335 (lyr.); ἔλεγον ἰήϊον ἐβόα κίθαρις E.*Hyps.* *Fr.*3(1).iii 10. 4. *noise abroad, celebrate*, ἡ ῥάφανος ἣν ἐβοᾶτε Alex.15.7; πρήγματα βεβωμένα ἀνὰ Ἰωνίην Hdt.3.39; ἐβώσθησαν ἀνὰ τὴν Ἑλλάδα Id.6.131; οἱ βοηθέντες ἐπὶ χρήμασι Lib.*Or.*59.155; βεβοῆσθαι ἀπὸ τοῦ Μαραθῶνος, ἐκ τῶν ἀδικημάτων, Id.*Decl.*11.18, 5.53. 5. c. inf., *cry aloud* or *command in a loud voice* to do a thing, S.*OT*1287, E.*Andr.*297 (lyr.); βοᾶν τινι ἄγειν X.*An.*1.8.12; ἐβόων ἀλλήλοις μὴ θεῖν ib.19; also, *cry aloud* that.., Epicrat.11.31 (anap.); β. ὅτι.. X.*An.*1.8.1, Antiph.125.5. 6. Pass., *to be filled with sound*, πᾶσαν δὲ χρὴ γαῖαν βοᾶσθαι ὑμνῳδίαις E.*Hel.*1434; *to be deafened*, Ar.*V.*1228. (Cf. βοή.)

βοει-ακός, ή, όν, = sq., *EM*254.44. **-κός**, ή, όν, (βοῦς) = βόειος, *of* or *for oxen*, ζεύγη β. wagons *drawn by oxen*, Th.4.128, X.*An.*7.5.2, cf. Ar.*Fr.*109; κρέας β. Poll.6.55:—the form **βοϊκός**, freq. in codd. as in D.H.8.87, is censured by Hdn.Gr.2.416, but cf. ἱερεῖον βοϊκόν *Milet.*1(7).203a (i B.C.); θυσία βοϊκή *Inscr.Prien.*112.109 (i B.C.); βοϊκά, = *oxen*, *GDI*1158 (Elis); β. κτήνη *BGU*1189.12 (i A.D.). **-ος**, α, ον, Ep. and Ion. **βόεος**, η, ον (βόϝεον *Glotta*4.201 (Apulian vase) is dub.): (βοῦς):—*of an ox* or *oxen*, esp. *of ox-hide*, δέρμα βόειον Od.14.24; βοέοισιν ἱμᾶσιν Il.23.324; βοείας ἀσπίδας 5.452; βόεα κρέα Hdt.2.37,168; τὰ β. κρέα Pl.*R.*338c; γάλα β. E.*Cyc.*218, Arist.*HA*521ᵇ33, Dsc.4.83, Porph.*Abst.*4.17; ποδὶ βοείῳ τὸν θεὸν ἐλθεῖν, of Dionysus, Plu.2.364f: metaph., β. ῥήματα *bull*-words, Ar.*Ra.*924. II. **βοείη** or **βοέη** (sc. δορή), ἡ, *ox-hide*, ἀδέψητον βοέην Od.20.2,142; βοὸς μεγάλοιο βοείην Il.17.389; *ox-hide shield*, βοέης εἰλυμένω ὤμους αὔησι στερεῇσι ib.492; βοῶν τ' εὖ ποιητάων (contr. for βοέων) 16.636. 2. = βοεύς, λύσαντε βοείας *h.Ap.*487, cf. 503 (s.v.l.).

βοεύς, έως, ὁ, *rope of ox-hide*, ἐϋστρέπτοισι βοεῦσι Od.2.426.

βοή, Dor. **βοά**, ἡ, *loud cry, shout*, in Hom. mostly *battle-cry*, βοὴν ἀγαθός Il.2.408, al.; βοᾶς δ' ἔτι μηδ' ὄνομ' εἴη let there be not even the name of *war*, Theoc.16.97; later of prayer, Ἑλληνικὸν νόμισμα θυστάδος β. A.*Th.*269; κακοφάτιδα β. *cry* of mourning, Id.*Pers.*936 (lyr.); β. καὶ οἶκτος And.1.48; κραυγὴ καὶ β. D.54.9; also, *song* of joy, ἴτω ξύναυλος βοὰ χαρᾷ E.*El.*879 (lyr.), cf. Pi.*N.*3.67, Ar.*Ra.*212; of oracles, ἀείδουσα.. βοὰς ἃς ἂν Ἀπόλλων κελαδήσῃ E.*Ion* 92 (lyr.); *shout, murmur* of a crowd, Pl.*Lg.*700c (pl.); θόρυβος καὶ β. Id.*Ti.*70e; of things, *roar* of the sea, Od.24.48; *sound* of musical instruments, αὐλοὶ φόρμιγγές τε βοὴν ἔχον Il.18.495, cf. Pi.*O.*3.8, *P.*10.39 (pl.); β. σάλπιγγος A.*Th.*394; *cry* of birds, S.*Ant.*1021; θηρίων β. E.*Ba.*1085; βοὴν θωΰσσειν, ἀϋτεῖν, S.*Aj.*335, E.*Hec.*1092 (lyr.); ἐφθέγξατο βοή τις Id.*IT*1386; βοάσομαι τὰν ὑπέρτονον βοάν Phryn.Com.46 (lyr.); βοὴν ἱστάναι Antiph.196.2; ὅσον καὶ ἀπὸ βοῆς ἕνεκα as far as *sound* went, only in appearance, Th.8.92, cf. X.*HG*2.4.31. II. = βοήθεια, *aid called for, succour*, A.*Supp.*730, *Ag.*1349, S.*OC*1057 (lyr.). (*gʷoᵘā*, cf. Skt. *jō-guvē* (intensive of *gávatē*) 'proclaim aloud'.)

βοηγενής, ές, *born of an ox*, of bees, *AP*9.363.13 (Mel.).

βο-ήγια, τά, festival at Miletus, *SIG*577.71 (written **βοιη-**); but **-ηγία**, ἡ, a form of *contest*, perh., = ταυροκαθαψία, *Michel* 838 (Didyma). **-ηγοί**, οἱ, *ox-drivers* in a procession, dub. in *Inscr.Prien.*112.108 (i B.C.).

βοηδόν, Adv. *like oxen*, πίνειν Agatharch.38.

βοηδρομ-έω, Dor. **βοᾱ-**, *run to a cry for aid, haste to help*, πρὸς δόμους E.*Or.*1356; ἐπ' ἐσχάραν Id.*Heracl.*121; πρὸς τὸ νικώμενον Plu.*Sert.*19; σὺν ἵπποις, Ἀρχ.Δελτ.1.57 (Thermon). 2. *run with a cry*, App.*Hann.*42: c. inf., τύραννον ἀνελεῖν Id.*BC*2.119. **-ια**, ων, τά, *games in memory of the succour given* by Theseus against the Amazons, Plu.*Thes.*27; B. πέμπειν lead a procession *at the B.*, D.3.31. **-ίη**, ἡ, *helping, aiding*, Max.381 (pl.). **-ιος**, ον, = βοηδρόμος, of Apollo, Call.*Ap.*69, Paus.9.17.2. II. Dor. **Βαδρόμιος** (sc. μήν), name of month at Rhodes, *SIG*644.19 (ii B.C.), etc. **-ιών**, ῶνος, ὁ, name of a month at Athens, etc., D.3.5, Arist.*HA*578ᵇ13, *SIG*282.18 (Priene, iv B.C.), etc. (Written Βοι- *IG*2².657, al.) **-ος**, ον, *giving succour*, E.*Ph.*1432; β. ποδί Id.*Or.*1290 (lyr.).

βοήθ-αρχος, ὁ, *captain of auxiliaries*, name of a Carthaginian officer, Plb.1.79.2, App.*Pun.*70. **-εια**, ἡ (Dor. **βοάθοια** *SIG*421.36 (Thermon)), *help, aid*, Th.2.22, etc.; β. τῷ λόγῳ πρός τινα Pl.*Prm.*128c; ἡ ὑπὲρ τῶν δικαίων β. D.56.15; βοήθειαν ἔχειν πρὸς ὑγίειαν, πρὸς τὴν ἑκάστου ὑπερβολὴν μηχανᾶσθαι, Arist.*PA*651ᵇ1, 652ᵃ32: nom.sg., as exclamation '*help!*', Plb.13.8.5: pl., Gorg.*Pal.*33, D.18.302, Arist.*Rh.*1383ᵃ29; αἱ πρὸς εὔπλοιαν β. Ph.2.46, cf. *Act.Ap.*27.17. 2. *medical aid, cure*, κίνδυνος ἰσχυρότερος πάσης β. Plu.*Alex.*19. II. *force of auxiliaries*, ἡ παρὰ Διονυσίου β. X.*HG*7.1.20; νεῶν β. Th.4.8: opp. regular forces, D.4.32. **-έω** (sts. written βοιηθέω, *IG*2².237 (iv B.C.), *BGU*1007.12 (iii B.C.)), Ion. **βωθέω**, only Hsch. βωθέοντες, not in Hdt. (but cf. Eust.812.59) or Hp., cf. βοηθήσω *Michel* 12.15 (Erythrae, iv B.C.); Dor. **βοᾱθοέω** *SIG*421.27 (Thermon); Aeol. **βᾱθόημι** (q.v.):—Med., fut. -ήσομαι Lib.*Or.*1.128:—*come to aid, succour, assist, aid*, c. dat., τῇ σφετέρῃ Hdt.1.82; τοῖσιν ἠδικημένοις E.*IA*79; πρὸς τοὺς αὐτῶν ψιλοὺς X.*HG*1.2.3; τινὶ ἀντία τινός Hdt.5.99; τινὶ πρὸς τὸ ἄναντες X.*HG*4.8.38; ναυσὶ β. τινὶ πολιορκουμένῳ ib.1.6.22; β. τοῖς φίλοις τὰ δίκαια Id.*Mem.*2.6.25; β. τοῖς τῶν προγόνων ἀτυχήμασιν Aeschin.3.169; β. τῷ λόγῳ Pl.*Phd.*88e; β. τῷ θεῷ *maintain* his *rights*, Epist.Philipp.ap.D.18.157; β. τοῖς νόμοις Aeschin.1.33: c. dat. et acc., πατρὶ βοηθῶν θάνατον Pl.*Lg.*874c; of a physician, β. τῷ θερμῷ ἐπὶ τὸ ψυχρόν Hp.*VM*13: abs., Plu.*Alex.*19. 2. abs., *come to the rescue*, Hdt.1.30, 7.158, A.*Supp.*613, etc.; β. παρά τινα Hdt.9.57; ἐπί τινα *against* one, Id.1.62, 4.125, Th.1.126, etc.; β. ἐς.. Hdt.6.103; ἐπὶ.. Th.3.97, 4.72; ἐπὶ τὰς ναῦς Id.8.11; ἐκεῖσε D.4.41; β. πρός τι *contribute* to an object, v.l. in Arist.*EN*1155ᵃ14, cf. *Metaph.*1079ᵇ16, or *keep* it *off*, Id.*Resp.*474ᵇ24, *HA*621ᵃ13; χρήμασι *with* money, Id.*EN*1130ᵃ19: Medic., βοηθεῖ πρὸς τὸ κώνειον it *is an antidote* to.., Thphr.*HP*9.20.1; freq. in Dsc. as β. τοῖς φαγοῦσι 4.83. 3. Pass., *to be assisted, receive help*, παρά τινος Arist.*Rh.*1383ᵇ28; βοηθήσομαι LxxDa.11.34, but βοηθηθήσομαι *Is.*44.2; ἐβοήθην ib.10.3, 2*Ch.*26.15 (v.l. ἐβοηθήθην); ἵν' ὦ βεβοηθημένη *PRyl.*122.12 (ii A.D.); esp. of patients, *derive benefit*, Dsc.4.82, Plu.2.687f: impers., ἐμοὶ βεβοήθηται τῷ τεθνεῶτι Antipho 1.31; ταύτῃ μοι βεβοηθημένον ἐγεγόνει φιλοσοφίᾳ Pl.*Ep.*347e. **-ημα**, ατος, τό, *resource*, Arist.*Rh.*1405ᵃ7 (pl.); *assistance*, πρὸς τὴν μάχην Plb.1.22.3: in pl., *succours*, τὰ -ματα τοῦ συγγράμματος Diog.Oen.2. 2. *remedy*, Hp.*VM*13, D.S.1.25, Dsc.4.83, S.E.*P.*3.280. **-ημᾰτικός**, ή, όν, = βοηθητικός, Dsc.*Alex.Praef.*, Gal.19.395. **-ήσιμος**, ον, *curable*, Thphr.*HP*9.16.7. **-ησις**, εως, ἡ, *aid, succour*, Hp.*Praec.*8, dub. in Aen.Tact.16.4; πρὸς τὴν τῆς ὑγιείας β. Alex.Aphr. *in Sens.*98.22. **-ητέον**, *one must help*, X.*HG*6.5.10, D.1.17, etc. II. Adj. -ητέος, α, ον, Jul.*Or.*7.229a. **-ητικός**, ή, όν, *ready* or *able to help, serviceable*, τινί Arist.*Rh.*1374ᵃ24; τοῖς πένησι Plu.*Sol.*29; τῶν δεομένων Diotog.ap.Stob.4.7.62; πρός τι so as to *keep it off*, Arist.*Pol.*1267ᵃ16; or towards *promoting it*, Id.*HA*515ᵇ9: Comp. -ώτερον, τὸ ἄρρεν τοῦ θήλεος ib.608ᵇ15: Sup. -ώτατος Iamb.*VP*25.111. **-όος**, Dor. **βοᾱ-**, ον, (βοή, θέω, cf. βοη-δρόμος) *hasting to the cry for help* or *the call to arms*, Il.13.477; β. ἅρμα a chariot *hasting to the battle*, 17.481. II. *aiding, helping*, Pi.*N.*7.33, B.*Fr.*34:—Subst., *helper*, prob. Id.12.103, Theoc.22.23, Call.*Del.*27:—in Prose **βοηθός**, όν, *assisting, auxiliary*, νῆες Th.1.45: c. dat., ὁ τοῖς νόμοις β. Lys.*Fr.*53.1; freq. as Subst., *assistant*, Hdt.5.77, 6.100, Antipho 1.2, Pl.*R.*566b, al.; τῆς ἐπιτροπῆς *BGU*1047 iii 11 (ii A.D.); τοῦ στρατηγοῦ *POxy.*1469.10 (iii A.D.), etc. **-οῦρα**, ἡ, (with Lat. termination *-ura*) = βοήθεια, Lyd.*Mag.*3.6,13.

βοηλ-ᾰσία, ἡ, *driving of oxen, cattle-lifting*, Il.11.672. II. *place where cattle are pastured, cattle-run*, *AP*7.626. III. *struggle with a bull*, Hld.10.31. **-ᾰτέω**, *drive away oxen*, Ar.*Fr.*758: generally, *urge on*, οὓς ἡ Κλεάνθους μωρία βοηλατεῖ Sosith.4; possibly, *drive with shouts*, Opp.*C.*4.64. 2. *tend oxen*, Lyc.816, Plu.*Phil.*4. **-άτης** [ᾰ], ου, ὁ, fem. **-άτις**, ιδος, ἡ: (βοῦς, ἐλαύνω):—*one that drives away oxen, cattle-lifter*, S.*Ichn.*117, *AP*11.176 (Lucill.). II. *ox-driving*, ῥάβδος *APl.*4.200 (Mosch.); *ox-tormenting*, μύωψ A.*Supp.*307. III. *cattle-driver*, Lys.7.19, Pl.*Plt.*261d, *PLond.*3.1177.112 (ii A.D.). IV. β. διθύραμβος the dithyramb *which gains a bull for the prize*, Pi.*O.*13.19. **-ᾰτικός**, ή, όν, *of* or *for cattle-driving*: -κή (sc. τέχνη), ἡ, *the herdsman's* art, Pl.*Euthphr.*13c.

βόημα, v. βόαμα.

βοηνόμος, ὁ, ἡ, *tending oxen*, Theoc.20.41.

βόηξ, v. βόαξ.

βο-ήροτος, ον, *ploughed by oxen*, Nic.*Fr.*43. **-ησις**, εως, ἡ, = βοή, *cry, shout for assistance*, Thd., Quint.*Ps.*21(22).2. **-ητής**, οῦ, ὁ, *clamorous*, Hp.*Ep.*19, prob.l. in *Morb.Sacr.*15, cf. Hsch. s.v. ἠπύτα: Dor. fem., **βοᾶτις** αὐδά A.*Pers.*575 (lyr.). **-ητικός**, ή, όν, gloss on foreg., Sch.A. l.c. **-ητός**, ή, όν, *shouted* or *sung aloud*, θρήνοισι βοητὸν ὑμήναον *Epigr.Gr.*418.7 (Cyrene). **-ητύς**, ύος, ἡ, Ep. for βόησις, Od.1.369.

βοθρ-εύω, *dig a trench* or *pit*, *Gp.*9.6.2:—also **-έω**, Nonn.*D.*47.69, and **-ίζω**, Heliod.ap.Orib.46.22.16. **-ίον**, τό, Dim. of βόθρος, *small trench*, to set plants in, *Gp.*8.18.2, Alciphr.3.13. II. *small ulcer*, Hp.*Liqu.*6. 2. in pl., *sockets* of the teeth, Gal.2.754.

βοθροειδής, ές, '*pitting*' on pressure, of tumours, Hp.*Mul.*2.118.

βόθρ-ος, ὁ, *hole, trench*, or *pit dug in the ground*, βόθρον ὀρύξαι Od.10.517; βόθρου τ' ἐξέστρεψε [τὴν ἐλαίαν] Il.17.58; *trough*, Od.6.92: generally, *hollow*, X.*An.*4.5.6; *grave*, *IG*14.238 (Acrae); ritual *pit* for offerings to ὑποχθόνιοι θεοί, β. καὶ μέγαρα Porph.*Antr.*6. **-όω**, = βοθρεύω, Gal.8.951 (Pass.); of caries, Heliod.ap.Orib.46.22.1; of a tumor '*pitting*' on pressure, Aët.15.1.

βοθύν-ιον [ῠ], τό, Dim. of sq., '*fossette*', Zos.Alch.p.222 B. **-ος**, ὁ, = βόθρος, Cratin.210, X.*Oec.*19.3, *BGU*1122.17 (i B.C.). II. a meteorological phenomenon, Arist.*Mete.*342ᵃ36, *Mu.*392ᵇ4. **-ωτής**, οῦ, ὁ, *ditcher*, Aq.4*Ki.*25.12.

βοιδ-άριον, τό, Dim. of βοῦς, Ar.*Av.*585, *Fr.*82. **-ης**, ου, ὁ, *like an ox, quiet, stupid*, Men.1002. **-ιον**, τό, Dim. of βοῦς, Ar.*Ach.*1036, Arist.*HA*522ᵇ14, *PSI*1.84 (iv/v A.D.):—also **βοΐδιον**, *AP*7.169; **βούδιον** (rejected by Phryn.69), Hermipp.35.2, *PFlor.*150.2 (iii A.D.).

βοικεῖ· γαμίσκει, Theognost.*Can.*19.4. **βοικία**· ἡ θεράπαινα, *AB*1354. 2. = ϝοικία, γὰρ καὶ βοικίαρ ἔγκτησιν *Schwyzer* 425.24 (Elis, iii/ii B.C.).

βοϊκός, v. βοεικός. Adv. -κῶς Porph.*Abst.*3.3.

βόϊνος, η, ον, = βόειος, *Gloss.*; β. σάλπιγξ *having* βοὸς προτομή *as mouthpiece*, Eust.1139.58.

βοιόν, τό, *cycle of fifty years*, Hdn.Gr.1.376.

βοϊστί, Adv. *in ox-language*, λαλεῖν Porph.*VP*24.

Βοιωτ-άρχης, ου, ὁ, *Boeotarch*, one of the chief magistrates of the Boeotian league, Hdt.9.15, Th.4.91, *Hell.Oxy.*11.3, etc.:—also **-αρχος**, X.*HG*3.4.4: hence **-αρχέω**, *to be a Boeotarch*, Th.4.91, D.59.99. **-αρχία**, ἡ, *office of Boeotarch*, Ael.*VH*13.42, Plu.*Pel.*25: pl., Id.2.785c.

Βοιωτ-ιάζω, τῇ φωνῇ *speak Boeotian*, X.*An.*3.1.26, *Com.Adesp.*677. II. *side with the Boeotians*, in politics, etc., X.*HG*5.4.34, Aeschin.3.139:—also **-ίζω**, Plu.2.575d codd. **-ίδιον** [τῐ], τό, Dim. of Βοιώτιος, Ar.*Ach.*872.

Βοιωτιουργής, ές, (ἔργον) *of Boeotian work*, κράνος X.*Eq.*12.3.

Βοιωτός, ὁ, *a Boeotian*, Il.2.494, etc.:—**Βοιωτία**, ἡ, *Boeotia*, so called from its *cattle-pastures*:—Adj. **Βοιώτ-ιος**, α, ον, *Boeotian*, Hes.*Fr.*132, etc.; with a notion of *gluttonous*, οὕτω σφόδρ' ἐστὶ τοὺς τρόπους B. Eub.39, cf. 34; εἰμὶ γὰρ B. πολλὰ.. ἐσθίων Mnesim.2; ὀξύπεινον ἄνδρα καὶ B. Demonic.1; and of *dull, stupid*, Plu.2.995e: prov., ὗς Βοιωτία Pi.*O.*6.90, cf. *Fr.*83; also B. νόμος, melody used in κιθαρῳδία, S.*Fr.*966, Plu.2.1132d; Βοιώτιον μέλος Sch.Ar.*Ach.*13:—also **-ικός**, ή, όν, πόλεμος D.S.14.81, Plu.*Lys.*27, and **-ιακός**, ή, όν, *IG*11.161*B*122 (Delos, iii B.C.), Str.9.2.11. Adv. **-ιακῶς** (v.l. -ικῶς) ibid.; Βοιωτιακά, τά, title of work by Hellanicus, Sch.Il.2.494:—fem. **Βοιωτίς**, ίδος, X.*HG*5.1.36.

Βοκόπια or **Βουκόπια**, τά, festival at Lindus, *IG*12(1).792, al.

βολαῖος, α, ον, (βολή) *violent*, θύννος *Trag.Adesp.*391, cf. Eust.1404.52.

βολαυγέω, Astrol., = ἀκτινοβολέω, τινὰ ἀκτῖσι or ἐν ἀκτίνεσσι, Man.4.272,431.

βόλβα, ἡ, = Lat. *vulva*, *AP*11.410 (Lucill.).

βολβ-άριον, τό, Dim. of βολβός, Epict.*Ench.*7. **-ίδιον**, τό, *small cuttle-fish*, with a strong smell, Hp.*Mul.*2.133: **-ίτιον**, Gal.19.89.

βόλβιθος, ὁ, v. βόλιτον.

βολβ-ίνη, ἡ, *star-flower, Ornithogalum umbellatum*, Thphr.*HP*7.3.9, Matro *Fr.*2.3. **-ίον**, τό, Dim. of βολβός, Hp.*Mul.*2.196. **-ίσκος**, ὁ, *AP*11.35 (Phld.). **-ιτίνη** (prob. l. for βολβοτύνη), ἡ, = βολβίδιον, Arist. and Speus.ap.Ath.7.318e:—also **-ιτίς**, ίδος, ἡ, Epich.61.

βόλβῖτον, τό, or **βόλβῖτος**, ὁ, Thphr.*HP*5.5.3, Dsc.2.167, Archig.ap.Gal.12.173, worse forms of βόλιτον, -τος, acc. to Phryn.335.

βολβο-ειδής, ές, *bulb-like, bulb-shaped*, Dsc.2.144, Aët.12.63. **-κάστᾰνον**, τό, *earth-nut*, = βούνιον, Alex.Trall.5.6.

βολβός, ὁ, *purse-tassels, Muscari comosum*, Ar.*Ec.*1092, Pl.*R.*372c, Arist.*Pr.*926a6, Thphr.*HP*7.13.8, Theoc.14.17, Dsc.2.170: freq. in Com., Pl.Com.173.9, etc.; identified with ὕδνον by Sch.Ar.*Nu.*188; also of other bulbous plants, β. ἐμετικός, = *Narcissus Tazetta*, Dsc.4.156; β. ἄγριος, = κολχικόν, ib.4.83; β. ἐριοφόρος, = *Scilla hyacinthoides*, Thphr.*HP*7.13.8 (an Indian kind, perh. *Euodendron anfractuosum*, Phan.Hist.28); β., = νάρκισσος, Ps.-Dsc.4.158; = ἡμεροκαλλές, Id.3.122; βολβοί perh. = *eyes* on root-stock of κάλαμος, Dsc.1.85.

βολβοτύνη, v. βολβιτίνη.

βολβοφάκῆ, ἡ, *soup of bulbs and lentils*, *Com.Adesp.*367,368, Ath.13.584d.

βολβώδης, ες, *bulbous*, Thphr.*HP*7.13.9.

βολβωρῠχέω, *dig* βολβοί, *Com.Adesp.*959.

βολετισμός, ὁ, *angling*, Orac. in *Ath.Mitt.*25.399 (Aezani).

βολέω, = βάλλω, *Theol.Ar.*37, Eust.1405.4; in early writers Ep. pf. Pass. βεβόλημαι *to be stricken* with grief and the like, ἄχεϊ.. βεβολημένος ἦτορ Il.9.9, cf. Od.10.247; πένθεϊ.. βεβολήατο πάντες Il.9.3; ἀμηχανίῃ βεβόλησαι A.R.4.1318; ἀμφασίῃ βεβόλητο Q.S.7.726. II. in literal sense, μήτηρ ἀμφ' αὐτὸν βεβολημένη *falling* about his neck, A.R.1.262; Βοώτης.. ἀντέλλει βεβολημένος Ἀρκτούροιο *dominated by* Arcturus, Arat.609.

βολεών, ῶνος, ὁ, *dunghill*, Din.ap.Harp., Philem.221 codd., Nic. ap.Harp., Eust.1404 fin.

βολή, ἡ, *throw*: 1. *stroke* or *wound* of a missile (opp. πληγή, of sword or pike), Od.17.283, cf. 24.161; β. πέτρων E.*Or.*59; λίθων Phld.*Ir.*p.31 W. (pl.); μέχρι λίθου καὶ ἀκοντίου βολῆς Th.5.65; β. ἔρωτος *shafts of love*, *AP*12.160; βολαῖς.. σφόγγος ὤλεσεν γραφήν by its *stroke* or *touch*, A.*Ag.*1329; *swing* of ἁλτῆρες, Antyll.ap.Orib.6.34.1. 2. κύβων βολαί *throws* or *casts* of dice, S.*Fr.*429. 3. metaph., β. ὀφθαλμῶν *quick glances*, Od.4.150; κάτω.. βλεμμάτων ῥέπει β. A.*Fr.*242, cf. Philostr.*VS*2.27.5. 4. β. κεραύνιοι thunderbolts, A.*Th.*430; βολαὶ ἡλίου sun-beams, S.*Aj.*877, cf. E.*Ion* 1134; χρυσοῦ.. βολαῖς *with* golden *rays*, of a statue, *IG*14.1026 (iii A.D.); βολαὶ χιόνος *radiance*, E.*Ba.*662; τὰς ψυχὰς οἷον βολὰς εἶναι λέγουσιν Plot.6.4.3. 5. βολαί, = ὠδῖνες, Procop.*Goth.*4.22. 6. *payment*, ἀποδώσω ἐπὶ βολαῖς δυσίν *Stud.Pal.*20.139 (vi A.D.).

βολίδιον, τό, Dim. of βολίς 2, Olymp. *in Mete.*298.33.

βολίζη, ἡ, *female slave*, Cretan word in Seleuc.ap.Ath.6.267c.

βολίζω, (βολίς) *heave the lead, take soundings*, *Act.Ap.*27.28, Eust.563.30:—Pass., *sink in water*, *Gp.*6.17.

βόλῖμοι δίκαι, = ἀναβόλιμοι δ., *deferred, adjourned* suits, Ἀρχ.Ἐφ.1911.133 (Gonni): **βόλῖμον**, τό, *period of delay*, *BCH*37.204 (Chios): hence **βολῖμοδῐκασταί**, οἱ, *judges who try* β. δίκαι, Ἀρχ.Ἐφ.1911.129 (Gonni).

βόλιμος, = μόλιβος, *SIG*241.28 (Delph., iv B.C.), *IG*4.1484.275 (Epid., iv B.C.): Syracusan acc. to *EM*204.40.

βόλινθος, ὁ, perh. = βόνασος, Arist.*Mir.*830a7.

βόλιον, τό, *counter* used in the game of πεττοί, Hsch., *EM*666.16, Eust.1396.59. II. = πόλιον, Ps.-Dsc.3.110.

βολίς, ίδος, ἡ, *missile, javelin*, Plu.*Demetr.*3. 2. *sounding-lead*, Sch.Il.24.80. 3. ἀστραπῶν βολίδες *flashes* of lightning, Lxx *Wi.*5.21; ἀστραπὴ βολίς (sic) ib.*Za.*9.14. 4. *cast of the dice*, *AP*9.767 (Agath.). b. *die*, ib.768 (Id.).

βολιστικός, ή, όν, (βόλος) *to be caught by the casting-net*, Plu.2.977f.

βολίτ-αινα [ῐ], ἡ, = βολβίδιον, Arist.*HA*525a19, 621b17; cf. ὄζολις. **-ινος**, η, ον, *of cow-dung*, Ar.*Ra.*295; σκέλος Cratin.*inc.*17 Mein. **-ον**, τό (**βόλῖτος**, ὁ, acc. to Sch.Ar.*Ra.*295:—also **βόλβιθος**, ὁ, *PMag.Par.*1.1439), *cow-dung*, mostly in pl., Cratin.39, Ar.*Ach.*1026, *Eq.*658: prov., βολίτου δίκη vexatious action, Sch.Ar.*Eq.*658.

βόλλα, Aeol. for βουλή, Plu.2.288b, *IG*12(2).6.38, etc.:—**βόλλαος**, = βουλαῖος, ib.68.8:—**βολλεύω**, for βουλεύω, ib.6.34.

βόλλομαι, Aeol., = βούλομαι, Sapph.*Supp.*5.17, Theoc.28.15.

βολλωτός, ή, όν, (Lat. *bulla*) *possessing knobs*, περονείδων ζεῦγος βολλωτῶν *CPR*12.4 (i A.D.).

βολοί, οἱ, shortening of ὀβολοί, Amphis 30.12, Hsch.

βολοκτῠπία, ἡ, *rattling of dice*, *AP*9.767 (Agath.).

βόλομαι, Ep., Ion. (*IG*12(9).189.31 (Eretria, iv B.C.)), Arc. (ib.5(2).3.9 (Tegea, iv B.C.)), = βούλομαι, Τρωσὶν δὴ βόλεται δοῦναι κράτος Il.11.319; εἰ.. βόλεσθε αὐτόν τε ζώειν κτλ. Od.16.387; νῦν δ' ἑτέρως ἐβόλοντο θεοί (vulg. ἐβάλοντο) 1.234, cf. A.R.1.262; εἴ τι βόλεστε (2 pl.) *SIG*1259.5 (iv B.C.).

βόλος, ὁ, *throw with a casting-net*, Orac.ap.Hdt.1.62; μέγα δίκτυον ἐς β. ἕλκει draws it back for *a cast*, Theoc.1.40: metaph., εἰς β. καθίστασθαι, ἔρχεσθαι, fall within *the cast* of the net, E.*Ba.*848, *Rh.*730. b. *net*, Herod.7.75, Ael.*NA*8.3; for birds, *AP*6.184 (Zos.). 2. *thing caught*, ἰχθύων β. *draught, catch*, of fishes, A.*Pers.*424, Plu.2.91c; βόλον ἀνσπάσασθαι land one's *catch*, E.*El.*582. II. *casting of teeth*, Arist.*HA*576b13 (pl.), *GA*748b9; καταμαθεῖν τὸν β. examine a horse's *teeth*, Hierocl.*Facet.*37. III. *cast of dice*, Poll.7.204, Plaut.*Rud.*360. IV. βόλος· θύρα, πηλός (i.e. βῶλος), Hsch.

βόλυβδος, ὁ, = μόλυβδος, *Tab.Defix.*107 (iv B.C.).

βόλυνθον, τό, = βόλιτον, Hsch.

βομβάζω, *jeer at*, Suid.

βομβάξ, interjection, *prodigious!* Ar.*Th.*45; intensified, **βομβᾰλοβομβάξ**, ib.48.

βομβαύλιος, ὁ, (βομβέω, αὐλός) comic compd. for ἀσκαύλης, *bagpiper*, with play on βομβυλιός, Ar.*Ach.*866.

βομβ-έω, (βόμβος) *make a booming noise*; in Hom. always of falling bodies, τρυφάλεια χαμαὶ βόμβησε πεσοῦσα Il.13.530; αἰχμὴ χαλκείη χαμάδις βόμβ. πεσ. 16.118, cf. Od.18.397; βόμβησαν.. κατὰ ῥόον the oars *fell with a loud noise*.., 12.204; βόμβησεν δὲ λίθος the stone *flew humming* through the air, 8.190; of the sea, *roar*, Simon.1; of thunder, *roll, rumble*, Nonn.*D.*1.301; *hum*, of bees, etc., Arist.*HA*535b6, 627a24, Theoc.3.13, Pl.*R.*564d; βομβεῖ δὲ νεκρῶν σμῆνος S.*Fr.*879; of mosquitoes, *buzz*, Ar.*Pl.*538; of birds, λιγυρὸν βομβεῦσιν ἀκανθίδες *AP*5.291 (Agath.): generally of sound, *buzz in one's ears*, Pl.*Cri.*54d; but ὦτα βομβεῖ μοι Luc.*DMeretr.*9.2: c. dat. instr., κόχλῳ β. Nonn.*D.*36.93. **-ηδόν**, Adv. *buzzing, with a hum*, A.R.2.133, Luc.*Pisc.*42. **-ήεις**, εσσα, εν, = βομβητικός, *APl.*4.74; κῦμα Nonn.*D.*3.32. **-ησις**, εως, ἡ, *buzzing*: *buzzing crowd*, Lxx *Ba.*2.29. **-ητής**, οῦ, ὁ, *buzzing*, ἑσμός *AP*6.236 (Phil.):—fem. **-ήτρια**, Νύμφαι Orph.*H.*51.9. **-ητικός**, ή, όν, *humming*, Eust.945.23:—also **-ικός**, ή, όν, τὸ τῶν θρήνων β. Sch. metr.Pi.*O.*1.

βομβοία· κολυμβὰς ἐλαία (Cypr.), Hsch.: **βομβοιλαδόνας**· ἐνιαυτούς, Id.

βόμβος, ὁ, *booming, humming*, Pl.*Prt.*316a, Arist.*Resp.*475a16; β. ἀνέμου κατιόντος its *booming sound*, Hld.5.27; of thunder, Epicur.*Ep.*2 p.46 U.; *buzzing in the ears*, Hp.*Coac.*189; *rumbling in the intestines*, Gal.7.241:—**βόμβο**, τό, barbarism in Ar.*Th.*1176. (Onomatop.)

βομβόχυλον, = μανδραγόρας, Dsc.4.75.

βομβρύζων· τονθορύζων, βοῶν, Hsch. **βομβρυνάζειν**· βρενθύεσθαι, Id.

βομβῡκ-ίας κάλαμος reed *used for making deep-toned flutes* (cf. βόμβυξ II), Thphr.*HP*4.11.3. **-ινος**, η, ον, *silken*, ἱμάτια Lib.*Decl.*33.6; σινδών Ps.-Callisth.3.28.

βομβύκιον [ῡ], τό, species of *mason-bee, Chalicodoma muraria*, Arist.*HA*555a13 (v.l. βομβυκοειδῶν). 2. *small buzzing insect*, Sch. Ar.*Nu.*158. II. *cocoon of silk-worm*, Arist.*HA*551b14.

βομβῡκοειδής, ές, *like silk*, ὑφή Dsc.3.16.

βομβῠλεύματα, τά, *kickshaws*, *Com.Adesp.*960.

βομβύλη, ἡ, = λήκυθος, Hsch., Sch.A.R.2.569.

Βομβυλία, ἡ, title of Athena in Boeotia, Hsch.

βομβῠλι-άζω, (βομβέω) = βορβορύζω, Arist.*Pr.*949a13 (v.l. -ίζουσιν). **-ον**, τό, = βολβίδιον, Gal.19.89. **-ός** or **-ύλιος**, ὁ, *buzzing insect*: *humble-bee*, Ar.*V.*107, Isoc.10.12, Arist.*HA*623b12, 629a29; *gnat, mosquito*, Hsch. 2. *cocoon of the silk-worm* (v.l. βομβυλίς), Arist.*HA*551b12. II. *narrow-necked vessel* that *gurgles* in pouring, Hp.*Morb.*3.16, *IG*11(2).154*A*68 (Delos, iii B.C.), Socr.ap.Ath.11.784d, Luc.*Lex.*7. (On the accent v. Hdn.Gr.1.116, al.)

βομβῠλίς, ίδος, ἡ, = πομφόλυξ, Hsch. II. cf. βομβυλιός I. 2.

βόμβυξ, ῡκος, ὁ, *silk-worm*, Arist.*HA* ap.Ath.7.352f. b. insect like a wasp, Hsch. 2. *silk garment*, Alciphr.1.39. II. *deep-toned flute*, A.*Fr*.57.3, Arist.*Aud*.800ᵇ25, Poll.4.82, Plu.2.713a. 2. *cap of a flute*, Poll.4.70. 3. *lowest note* on the flute, Arist.*Metaph*. 1093ᵇ3:—hence Comp. **βομβυκέστερος**, *deeper in tone*, Nicom.*Harm*. 11. III. Lacon., = στάμνος, Hsch., *AB*1354.

βομβώδης, ες, = βομβητικός, Ael.*NA*6.37; of intestinal flatus, Gal.7.241.

βομβών, ῶνος, ὁ, late form for βουβών, Moeris94, Hdn.Gr.1.23, 2.483.

βόνασος or **βόνασσος**, ὁ, *European bison, aurochs, Bos bonasus*, Arist.*HA*498ᵇ31, 630ᵃ18, *PA*663ᵃ14, Str.15.1.69.

βοο-βοσκός, ὁ, *herdsman*, Suid. **-γληνος**, ον, *ox-eyed*, Nonn.*D*.7.260. **-δμητήρ**, ῆρος, ὁ, (δαμάω) *slaying oxen*, λέοντε Q.S.1.524, cf. 587. **-ζύγιον** [ῠ], τό, *ox-yoke*, Lxx *Si*.26.7. **-θύτης** [ῠ], ου, ὁ, *slayer of oxen*, Suid. **-κλεψ**, contr. **βοῦκλεψ**, ὁ, *stealer of oxen*, S.*Fr*.318. **-κλόπος**, ον, *ox-stealing*, Orph.*A*.1057, Nonn.*D*.1.337; cf. βουκλόπος. **-κραιρος**, ον, *ox-horned*, ib.13.314. **-κτᾰσία**, ἡ, (κτείνω) *slaying of oxen*, A.R.4.1724(pl.). **-κτῐτος**, ον, (κτίζω) of Thebes, *founded where the heifer lay*, Nonn.*D*.25.415. **-νόμος**, ὁ, *herdsman*, Cyr., Suid. **-πρόσωπος**, ον, *ox-faced*, Porph.*Abst*.3.16 codd. **-ρραίστης**, ου, ὁ, *slayer of oxen*, Tryph.361. **-σκόπος**, ον, *looking after oxen*, Nonn.*D*.31.225 (**βόοσκος**, Hsch. may be f.l. for this word). **-σσόος**, ον, (σεύω) *driving oxen wild*, of the gadfly, Nonn.*D*.11.191: contr., βουσσόον ὅν τε μύωπα..καλέουσιν Call.*Fr*.46, cf. Cerc.8.2. II. *ox-driving*, κέντρα Q.S.5.64, cf. Nonn.*D*.11.149, al. 2. = βοηλάτης I, epith. of Hermes, ib.4.31. **-στάσιον** [ᾰ], τό, = sq., *Stud.Pal*.20.74 (iii A.D.). **-στᾰσις**, εως, ἡ, = βούστασις, Call.*Del*.102. **-στικτος**, ον, dub. sens., θυηλή (of an offering *of bull's blood*) Nonn.*D*.5.281. **-στολος**, ον, *riding on a bull*, νύμφη, of Europa, ib.1.66. **-σφᾰγία**, Ion. -ίη, ἡ, *slaughter of oxen*, *APl*.4.101. **-τρόφος**, ον, = βουτρ-, D.P.558, Nonn.*D*.14.377, *PLond*.5.1654 (iv A.D.).

βοόω, *change into an ox*, Eust.70.28.

βορά, ἡ, *food*, prop. of carnivorous beasts, ποντίοις δάκεσι δὸς βοράν A.*Pr*.583 (lyr.), cf. *Ch*.530; θηρσὶν ἄθλιον β. E.*Ph*.1603, cf. S.*Ant*.30; κυνὸς β. Ar.*Eq*.416; ὁ λέων..[χαίρει] ὅτι β. ἕξει Arist.*EN*1118ᵃ23; of cannibal feasts, Hdt.1.119; κρεῶν .. οἰκείας βορᾶς of their own flesh *served as food*, of the children of Thyestes, A.*Ag*.1220, cf. 1597; βορᾶς τοῦ..Οἰδίπου γόνου *food* torn from the body of the son of Oedipus, S.*Ant*.1017, cf. 1040; βορᾷ χαίρουσιν ἀνθρωποκτόνῳ; E.*Cyc*.127; οὐ γὰρ ἐν γαστρὸς β. τὸ χρηστὸν εἶναι in *gluttony*, Id.*Supp*.865: less freq. of simple *food*, Pi.*Fr*.124.5, A.*Pers*.490, S.*Ph*.274, etc. (βορρά is prob. f.l. for φορβά in *AP*3.14.) (Cf. βιβρώσκω: gʷerə-, cf. Skt. *-gara-* in compds. (cf. δημο-βόρος, Lat. *carni-vorus*) 'devouring', *giráti* 'swallow', Lat. *vorare*, Lith. *gérti* 'drink', etc.)

βοράζω, = τρέφω, *EM*205.6 (but -ᾴζω, 737.21).

βόρασσος, ὁ, *growing spadix of the date with immature fruit*, Dsc.1.109.

βόρατον, τό, *juniper, Juniperus foetidissima*, D.S.2.49. II. = βράθυ, Dsc.1.76.

βοράω, *eat*, *EM*216.14.

βορβορ-ίζω, (βόρβορος) *to be like mud*, ἐν γεύσει Dsc.5.75. II. βορβορίζει· γογγύζει, μολύνει (Cypr.), Hsch. **-ισμός**, ὁ, = βορβορυγμός, Cael.Aur.*CP*3.20.194. **-ῖται**, οἱ, name of a guild at Thera, *IG*12(3).6.

βορβορό-θῡμος, ον, *muddy-minded*, Ar.*Pax*753. **-κοίτης**, ου, ὁ, *Mudcoucher*, name of a frog, Batr.230.

βορβορόπη, ἡ, *filthily lewd*, Hippon.110.

βόρβορος, ὁ, *mire, filth*, Asius 1, Heraclit.13, A.*Eu*.694, Ar.*V*.259, Pl.*Phd*.69c, Lxx *Je*.45.6, 2*Ep.Pet*.2.22, etc.: distd. fr. πηλός *clay, moist earth*, Luc.*Prom.Es* 1; *sewer*, Hsch.: metaph., *foul abuse*, τοσοῦτον β. κατήντλησάς μου Luc.*Lex*.17.

βορβορο-τάραξις, ὁ, *mud-stirrer*, Ar.*Eq*.309. **-φόρβα**, ἡ, fem. Adj. *feeding on filth*, *PMag.Par*.1.1402.

βορβορ-όω, *make muddy*, Arist.*GA*763ᵃ29 (Pass.). **-ῠγή**, ἡ, = sq., Hsch. **-υγμός**, ὁ, *intestinal rumbling*, Hp.*Prog*.11; *belching*, Suid. **-ώδης**, ες, *miry, filthy*, πηλὸς -έστερος Pl.*Phd*.111d; ἰλύς Arist.*HA*547ᵇ20; θάλαττα Men.25; of pus or pitch, *turbid*, Hp.*Aph*.7.44, Thphr.*HP*9.2.3: metaph., βίος Ph.1.322. **-ωπόν**· αἰσχρόν, βορβόρῳ ἐμφερές, Hsch. **-ωσις**, εως, ἡ, = βορβορυγμός, Archig.ap.Aët.9.40.

βορβύλα, ἡ, a *cake* made of poppy and sesame, Hsch. **βορδών**, ῶνος, ὁ, = βουρδών, Philagr.ap.Aët.12.51.

Βορεάδης, ου, ὁ, *son of Boreas*, D.S.4.44; Ep. **Βορηϊάδης** *AP*9.550 (Antip.).

Βορέας, ου, ὁ; Aeol. **Βορίαις** Alc.*Supp*.7.13; Ion. **Βορέης** Hom., or **Βορῆς**, έω, Hdt.7.189; Att. **Βορρᾶς**, ᾶ, Cratin.207, Th.6.2, al., Pl.*Criti*.112b, *PPetr*.1.21.11 (iii B.C.), *Ev.Luc*.13.29, etc.; but gen. Βορέου *IG*1².373.29:—*north wind*, personified as *Boreas*, Od.5.296, etc.: generally, opp. νότος, Β. καὶ ἀπαρκτίας Arist.*Mete*.363ᵇ14, cf. *Mu*.394ᵇ20 (pl.), *HA*612ᵇ5 (pl.); Β. πνέουσιν ὀρνιθίαι *PHib*.1.27.59 (iii B.C.). 2. *the north*, πρὸς Βορέην (v.l. -ρῆν) ἄνεμον towards *the north*, Hdt.2.101; πρὸς Βορέαν τοῦ ὄρους Th.2.96, cf. 6.2; Βορρᾷ *to the north*, *BGU*1127.12 (i B.C.), etc.; cf. Βορέην· τὴν φῦσαν, Hsch.

Βορεάς, poet. **Βορειάς** and **Βορηϊάς**, άδος, ἡ, *Boread, daughter of Boreas*, S.*Ant*.985 (lyr.), Orph.*A*.738:—also **Βορηΐς**, ΐδος, Nonn.*D*.33.211. II. as fem. Adj., *northern*, πνοαί A.*Fr*.195.

Βορε-ασμός, ὁ, *festival of Boreas* at Athens, Hsch. (pl.). **-ηθεν**, Adv. *from the north*, D.P.79. **-ηνδε**, Adv. *northwards*, Id.137. **-ῆτις**, ιδος, ἡ, fem. of Βόρειος, Id.243.

βορειαῖος, α, ον, = βόρειος, *APl*.4.230 (Leon.).

βορεινός, ή, όν, = βόρειος, A.D.*Synt*.94.15, *CPHerm*.28.13 (iii A.D.):—also **βορινός**, ή, όν, *POxy*.498.8 (ii A.D.): **βορρινός**, ή, όν, ib.243.21 (i A.D.), etc.

Βορειόθεν, poet. for Βορέηθεν, Nonn.*D*.6.127.

βορεῖον· γαστὴρ ἐσκευασμένη πως, Hsch.

βόρειος, α, ον, also ος, ον S.*OC*1240 (lyr.): Ion. **βορήϊος**, η, ον:—*from the quarter of the north wind, northern*, opp. νότιος, θάλασσα Hdt.4.37, 6.31; β. ἀκτά *exposed to the north*, S. l. c.; τὸ β. τεῖχος Ar.*Fr*.556, And.3.5, Pl.*R*.439e; τῆς Πλειάδος βορείου γενομένης having appeared *in the north*, Arist.*HA*542ᵇ11. 2. *of the north wind*, β. χειμών a winter *during which northerly winds prevail*, Hp.*Aph*.3.11, Arist.*Pr*.859ᵇ21; ἔαρ ib.860ᵃ13; βόρεια, τά, *northerly winds*, ib.944ᵃ1, etc. (rarely in sg., Ar.*V*.265; ὅταν ᾖ βόρειον X.*Cyn*.8.1); βορείοις *in the time of northerly winds*, Arist.*HA*574ᵃ1, al.; βορείων ὄντων ib.592ᵃ14: Comp. -ότερος Arat.247, Alex.Aphr.*in Metaph*.446.34: Sup. -ότατος Man.4.241. II. βόρειον, = ἑλλεβορίνη, Ps.-Dsc.4.108; βόρειος, = ἀείζωον τὸ μέγα, ib.88.

βορεύς, ὁ, = βορέας, in oblique cases βορῆος, -ῆι, -ῆα, Arat.430, 829, 882, etc.: nom. pl. βορεῖς Alciphr.1.1.

βορεύω, *blow from the north*, χειμῶνος βορεύοντος Thphr.*Sign*.53.

βορηά· βοτάνη πᾶσα (fort. ποιά), Hsch.

Βορηϊάς, βορήϊος, Βορῆς, v. Βορεάς, βόρειος, Βορέας.

βορθαγορίσκεα· τὰ χοίρεια κρέα: and **βορθαγορίσκοι**· μικροὶ χοῖροι (Lacon.), Hsch.; cf. ὀρθαγορίσκος.

Βορθεία, ἡ, = Ὀρθία, title of Artemis, *IG*5(1).864, al.

βορι-αῖος, α, ον, = βόρειος, Phlp.*in Ph*.894.19:—also **-ακός**, *IG Rom*.4.1603 (Chondriae).

βόρμαξ, = μύρμηξ, also **βύρμαξ**, Hsch.

βόρμος, ὁ, = βρόμος, Dieuch.ap.Orib.4.7.20, *EM*205.3, Hsch.

βοροποιός, όν, (ποιέω) *inducing appetite*, Eust.1538.30.

βορός (A), ά, όν, (βορά) *gluttonous*, Ar.*Pax* 38, Arist.*Phgn*.810ᵇ18: Sup., Mnesith.ap.Orib.21.7.7, Luc.*Tim*.46. Adv. -ῶς Ath.5.186c. II. *inducing appetite*, Asclepiad.ap.Eust.1538.30.

βορός (B), οῦ, ὁ (for ϝορός), *juice of pressed grapes* (Lacon.), Hsch.

βορράζων· ψοφῶν, Hsch.

Βορρ-ᾶθεν, = Βορέηθεν, Thphr.*Sign*.11, *IG*2².1241, al., Hp.*Vict*.2.37. **-αῖος**, α, ον, also ος, ον *AP*9.561 (Phil.), = βόρειος, A.*Th*.527, *AP*6.245 (Diod.), etc. **-απηλιώτης**, ου, ὁ, *north-east wind*, Ptol.*Tetr*.67:—Adj. **-απηλιωτικός**, ή, όν, *north-eastern*, ibid. **-ᾶς**, ᾶ, ὁ, v. Βορέας.

βορρό-λιψ, λῖβος, ὁ, *north-west wind*, *PMag.Par*.1.1646, Ptol.*Tetr*.60:—hence Adj. **-λῐβῠκός**, ή, όν, *north-western*, ib.39.

βορσόν· σταυρόν (Elean), Hsch. **βόρταχος**· βάτραχος, Id.

βόρυβος, = ὄροβος, *Ostr.Strassb*.606 (i/ii A.D.).

βόρυες, οἱ, = ὄρυες, Hdt.4.192.

Βορυσθέν-ης, ους, ὁ, *Borysthenes, Dniepr*, Hdt.4.18:—hence **-είτης** or **-ίτης**, ου, Ion. **-εΐτης**, εω, ὁ, *an inhabitant of its banks*, Hdt.4.17, Men.883, etc.

βόσις, εως, ἡ, (βόσκω) *food, fodder*, ἰχθῦσι Il.19.268; οἰωνοῖς καὶ θηρσί Q.S.1.329; β. καὶ τροφή Porph.*Antr*.15.

βοσκ-άδιος [ᾰ], α, ον, *foddered, fatted*, χήν Nic.*Al*.228. **-άς**, άδος, ἡ, *feeding, fed*, νηδύς Id.*Th*.782; ὀρταλίς Id.*Al*.293. 2. of birds *which feed themselves, not artificially fed*, Aët.9.30 (cf. βοσκός). II. as Subst., kind of *duck*, perh. *teal, Anas crecca*, Arist.*HA*593ᵇ17, Alex.Mynd.ap.Ath.9.395d. **-εύς**, ῶνος, ὁ, *feeder*, Hsch. **-ή**, ἡ, *fodder, food, pasturage*, A.*Eu*.266 (lyr.); πέτεσθαι ἐπὶ βοσκήν Arist.*HA*624ᵃ27, cf. *PLond*.5.1692 (vi A.D.): pl., μήλων τε βοσκάς A.*Fr*.44.5, cf. E.*Hel*.1331 (lyr.). **-ημα**, ατος, τό, *that which is fed* or *fatted*: in pl., *fatted beasts, cattle*, S.*Tr*.762, E.*Ba*.677, X.*HG*4.6.6; of sheep, E.*Alc*.576 (lyr.), *El*.494; ἐμῆς χερὸς β., of horses, Id.*Hipp*.1356 (lyr.); of dogs, X.*Cyr*.8.1.9; ζῆν ἀπὸ βοσκημάτων Arist.*Pol*.1319ᵃ20: dual, of a couple of pigs, Ar.*Ach*.811: sg., of *a single beast*, ἄκανθα ποντίου β. A.*Fr*.275.3; ἐν τρόπῳ βοσκήματος πιαινόμενον ζῆν Pl.*Lg*.807a; opp. θηρίον, Arist.*MM*1204ᵃ38, Str.16.4.16. II. *food*, β. πημονῆς A.*Supp*.620, cf. S.*El*.364, Ar.*Ra*.892; ἀναίματον β. δαιμόνων *prey* drained of blood by the Erinyes, A.*Eu*.302. **-ημᾰτώδης**, ες, *brutish, bestial*, θηριώδες καὶ β. Str.5.2.7, cf. Ocell.4.14, M.Ant.4.28; ἀναίσθητος καὶ β. Aristid.Quint.2.6: coupled with ζῳώδης, Iamb.*Protr*.21.ιε'; β. ἔννοιαι Procl.*in Cra*.p.68 P. **-ησις**, εως, ἡ, *feeding, pasture*, Sm.*Ec*.1.14, Hierocl.*Facet*.47. **-ητέον**, *one must feed*, τὸν πατέρα Ar.*Av*.1359. **-ήτωρ**, ορος, ὁ, *herdsman*, *EM*205.52, Sch.Il.12.302.

βοσκός, ὁ, *herdsman*, Aesop.316, interpol. in *AP*7.703 (Myrin.); β. προβάτων *shepherd*, interpol. in Dsc.4.119. II. as Adj., *feeding itself* (= Lat. *agrestis, non pastus*), φασιανός, χήν, *Edict.Diocl*.4.18 (variant for ἄγριος), 22; cf. βοσκάς.

βόσκω, impf. ἔβοσκον, Ep. βόσκε Il.15.548: fut. -ήσω Od.17.559, Ar.*Ec*.590: aor. ἐβόσκησα *Gp*.18.7: pf. βεβόσκηκα *PMag*.6.13 (iii B.C.):—Pass. and Med. (v. infr. II); Ion. impf. βοσκέσκοντο Od.12.355: fut. βοσκήσομαι Sarap. in Plu.2.398d, Dor. βοσκησεῦμαι Theoc.5.103: aor. ἐβοσκήθην Nic.*Th*.34, Babr.89.7. I. prop. of herdsmen, *feed, tend*, αἰπόλια Od.14.102; ταῶς Stratt.27; ὁ βόσκων *the feeder*, Arist.*HA*540ᵃ18. 2. generally, *feed, nourish*, βόσκει γαῖα

..ἀνθρώπους Od.11.365, cf. 14.325; γαστέρα βοσκήσεις 17.559; πάντα βόσκουσαν φλόγα..Ἡλίου S.*OT*1425; *maintain, keep*, ἐπικούρους Hdt.6.39; ναυτικόν Th.7.48; γυναῖκας Ar.*Lys*.260; οἰκέτας ib.1204, Herod.7.44: metaph., β. νόσον S.*Ph*.313; πράγματα β. troubles, i.e. children, Ar.*V*.313. **II.** Pass., of cattle, *feed, graze*, Od.21.49, etc.; ξύλοχον κάτα Il.5.162: c. acc., *feed on*, ποίην *h.Merc*.27,232, cf. A.*Ag*.118 (lyr.), Arist.*HA*$591^{a}16$,al.; τινί A.*Th*.244. **2.** metaph., *to be fed* or *nurtured*, ἰυγμοῖσι Id.*Ch*.26 (lyr.); κούφοις πνεύμασιν S.*Aj*. 558; ἐλπίσιν E.*Ba*.617; β. τινί or περί τι *run riot in* a thing, *AP* 5.271 (Paul. Sil.), prob. in 285 (Id.). ($g^{u}\bar{o}$, cf. Lith. *guotas* 'herd'.)

βόσμορον, τό, an Indian *millet, ragi, Eleusine coracana*, Str.15.1.13 and 18:—also **βόσμορος**, ὁ, *Peripl.M.Rubr*.14,41.

Βόσπορ-ος, ὁ, (βοὸς πόρος Opp.*H*.1.617) wrongly expld. by the Greeks as *Ox-ford*, name of several straits, β. Κιμμέριος, Θρᾴκιος, Hdt.4.12,83, etc. (also applied to the Hellespont by A.*Pers*.723, 746, S.*Aj*.884, Sch.adll.cc.):—Adj. **-ειος**, ον, S.*Fr*.707: **-ιος**, α, ον, Id.*Aj*.l.c.: **-εῖον**, τό, name of a temple, Decr.Byz.ap.D.18.91: **-ίτης** [ῑ], ου, ὁ, *dweller on the Bosporus*, S.*Fr*.503: **-ᾱνός** or **-ηνός**, ὁ, *inhabitant of the kingdom of Bosporus*, Str.7.4.7, 11.2.10, 16.2.39.

βοστρῠχ-ηδόν, Adv. *curly, like curls*, Luc.*Hist.Conscr*.19, *Philops*. 22. **-ιδῆ**· πολυκαμπῆ, Hsch. **-ίζω**, *curl* hair, Anaxil.42; ἄρρενες βεβοστρυχισμένοι D.H.7.9: metaph., *dress out*, διαλόγους κτενίζειν καὶ β. Id.*Comp*.25. **-ιον**, τό, Dim. of βόστρυχος, *AP* 11.66 (Antiphil.):—*vine-tendril*, Arist.*HA*$549^{b}33$, cf. $544^{a}9$: in pl., = στέμφυλα, *pressed grapes*, Hsch. **-ίτης** [ῑ], οἶνος wine *made from pressed grapes*, Aët.15.21.

βοστρῠχο-ειδής, ές, *curly*, Adv. **-δῶς** Gal.2.900:—the Adj. may perh. be read in Hsch. for **βοστρυχιδῆ** and **βοστρυχῆνδες**. **-ομαι**, *to be curled*, Ach.Tat.1.19.

βόστρῠχ-ος, ὁ, heterocl. pl. βόστρυχα in *AP*5.259 (Paul. Sil.), 6.71 (Id.): acc. pl. βόστρυχας Dionys.*Av*.2.7:—*curl, lock of hair*, Archil. 58, A.*Ch*.178, Ar.*Nu*.536, etc.: in sg. collectively, *hair*, ἀμπέτασον β. ὤμοις E.*Hipp*.202 (lyr.). **2.** poet., *anything twisted* or *wreathed*, πυρὸς ἀμφήκης β. *thunderbolt*, A.*Pr*.1044: in pl., *tendrils*, Philostr. *VA*3.4. **3.** metaph., *ornament*, τῆς ἠπείρου, of Smyrna, Aristid. *Or*.18(20).9; of Nicomedia, Lib.*Or*.61.12; ἑστίας χρυσοῦς β., of a son, Him.*Or*.23.7. **II.** *winged insect*, perh. *male of the glow-worm*, Arist.*HA*$551^{b}26$. **2.** in pl., *sea-weed*, Dionys.*Av*. l.c. **-ώδης**, ες, *curly*, γενειάς Philostr.*VS*2.5.1.

βοτάμια, τά, (βόσκω) *pastures*, dub. in Th.5.53.

βοτάνη [ᾰ], ἡ, (βόσκω) *pasture*, Il.13.493, Pl.*Prt*.321b, etc.; ἐκ βοτάνης ἀνιόντα Theoc.25.87; ἐν β. Id.28.12; ἔγρονται ἐς βοτάναν E.*Fr*.773.29; β. ἁ λέοντος the lion's *pasture*, i.e. Nemea, Pi.*N*.6.42: metaph., ὥσπερ ἐν κακῇ β. τρεφόμενοι Pl.*R*.401c. **2.** *fodder*, Od. 10.411. **3.** *herb*, Thphr.*HP*4.4.13, Dsc.1 *Praef*.1 (pl.), etc. **4.** in pl., *plants*, as material for making clothes, opp. δοραί, Diog.Oen. 10. **5.** *weeds*, Thphr.*HP*2.7.5, *POxy*.729.22 (ii A.D.): in pl., *Gp*. 2.46.2. **6.** ἱερὰ β., = περιστερεών, Dsc.4.60.

βοτάνη-θεν [ᾰ], Adv. *from the pasture*, Opp.*H*.4.393. **-φάγος** [φᾰ], ον, *herbivorous*, ib.3.424. **-φόρος**, ον, *herb-bearing*, Nonn. *D*.25.526.

βοτᾰν-ίδιον, τό, Dim. of βοτάνη, Sch.Pi.*N*.6.71. **-ίζω**, *root up weeds*, Thphr.*CP*3.20.9, *PLond*.1.131^{r}ii 42 (i A.D.), *Gp*.3.3.13:—Pass., ib.2.24.3. **-ικός**, ή, όν, *of herbs*, φάρμακα Plu.2.663c; ἡ β. παράδοσις the science *of herbal remedies*, Dsc.1 *Praef*.1:—τὰ -κά Id.2 *Praef*.; β. ἰατρὸς *herbalist*, Gal.*Thras*.24; -κοί, οἱ, *herb-gatherers*, Id.14.9. **-ιον**, τό, Dim. of βοτάνη, Thphr.*CP*2.17.3, Dsc.2.156: pl., Antiph.142.3 (s.v.l.). **2.** β. Ἑρμοῦ, = λινόζωστις, Dsc.4. 189. **-ισμός**, ὁ, *weeding*, *Gp*.2.24 tit., *BGU*197.17 (i A.D.), *PFlor*. 20.22 (ii A.D.).

βοτᾰνο-λογέω, *gather herbs*, Hp.*Ep*.16. **II.** *root up weeds*, *PGiss*.56.11 (vi A.D.). **-λογία**, ἡ, *weeding*, *POxy*.1631.26 (iii A.D.). **-λόγος**, ὁ, *gatherer of herbs*, Zonar.

βοτᾰνώδης, ες, *herbaceous*, Ath.2.62d: Comp., Dsc.4.173. **2.** *rich in herbs*, *Gp*.2.46.2.

βότειος, α, ον, (βοτόν) *of a sheep*, κώδια *PFay*.107.4.

βοτέω, = βόσκω, Ep. pres. part. βοτείων Call.*Fr*.7.5 P., cf. Hsch.:—Pass., Nic.*Th*.394.

βοτ-ήρ, ῆρος, ὁ, (βόσκω) *herdsman*, Od.15.504; οἰωνῶν β. *a soothsayer*, A.*Th*.24; κύων β. *herdsman's* dog, S.*Aj*.297: in later Prose, D.H.2.2, Plu.*Rom*.7, al.:—fem. **βότειρα**, epith. of Demeter, Eust. 1723.14. **-ηρικός**, ή, όν, *of* or *for a herdsman*, ἑορτή Plu.*Rom*.12; κύπελλα *AP*6.170 (Thyill.).

βότης, ου, ὁ, = βούτης, *EM*218.42.

βότις, ιος, ἡ (?), a *fish* or *plant* (dub.), Sophr.64:—βοτίς· βόλτιον, Hsch.

βοτόν, τό, (βόσκω) *beast*, A.*Ag*.1415, S.*Tr*.690: mostly in pl., *grazing beasts*, Il.18.521, S.*Aj*.145 (lyr.), etc.; opp. θηρία, Pl.*Mx*. 237d; but also of birds, Ar.*Nu*.1427; of the ostrich, Opp.*H*.4.630.

βότρᾰχος, v. βάτραχος.

βοτρεύς, έως, ὁ, *vintager*, *PLond*.2.189.58 (ii A.D.).

βοτρ-ύδιον [ῠ], τό, Dim. of βότρυς, *small cluster*, Alex.172.13, Dsc. 1.21, al., Longus 2.13. **II.** *an ear-ring of this pattern*, *Com.Adesp*. 962, Hsch. **-ῠδόν**, Adv. *like a bunch of grapes*: *in clusters*, β. πέτονται, of bees, Il.2.89, cf. *Gp*.15.2.29, Him.*Or*.28.1; τίκτει [ὁ πολύπους] ᾠὰ β. Arist.*Fr*.334, cf. Opp.*H*.1.550; τὰ ἄνθη πέφυκεν β. Thphr.*HP*3.16.4: metaph. of a crowd, Luc.*Pisc*.42.

βοτρῠ-ηρός, ά, όν, *of the grape kind*, Thphr.*HP*1.11.5. **-ηφόρος**, ον, *grape-bearing*, ἄμπελος Ph.1.681. **-ῖος**, α, ον, *of grapes*, φυτόν *AP*6.168 (Paul. Sil.). **-ίτης** [ῑ] (sc. λίθος), ου, ὁ, *calamine*, Dsc. 5.74:—also fem. **-ῖτις**, ιδος, ἡ, Plin.*HN*34.101, Gal.12.220.

βοτρυμός· τρυγητός, Hsch.

βοτρῠό-δωρος, ον, *grape-producing*, Ar.*Pax* 520 (paratragoed.). **-ειδής**, ές, *like a bunch of grapes*, Dsc.4.189. Adv. **-δῶς** Orib.45.18. 23. **-εις**, εσσα, εν, *full of grapes, clustering*, οἰνάς Ion Eleg.1.4; κισσός *AP*9.363.12 (Mel.); πλοχμοί A.R.2.677; δένδρεα *IG*14.1389 ii 10. **-κοσμος**, ον, *decked with grapes*, Orph.*H*.52.11.

βότρῠον, τό, *cluster of berries*, Thphr.*HP*3.7.3; βότρυς, dub. in Luc.*Bacch*.2. **II.** = θλάσπι, Ps.-Dsc.2.156. **III.** a kind of *medicine*, Plin.*HN*28.44.

βοτρῠόομαι, of vines, *form clusters*, Thphr.*CP*1.18.4.

βοτρῠό-παις, παιδος, ὁ, ἡ, *grape-born, child of the grape*, χάρις *AP* 11.33 (Phil.). **2.** Act., *bearing grapes*, ἄμπελος Theoc.*Ep*.4. 8. **-στᾰγής**, ές, *dripping with grapes*, Archestr.*Fr*.60.3. **-στέφᾰνος**, ον, *grape-crowned*, of a vine-bearing district, Archyt.Amph.1; κωμῳδία dub. in *IG*3.3688. **-φορέω**, *bear grapes*, Ph.2.54. **-χαίτης**, ου, ὁ, *with clustering hair*, *AP*9.524.

βότρυς, υος, ὁ (heterocl. pl. βότρυα, τά, Euph.149), *bunch of grapes*, μέλανες δ' ἀνὰ βότρυες ἦσαν Il.18.562, etc.: pl., *grapes*, Hp.*Vict*.2.55: prov., βότρυς πρὸς βότρυν πεπαίνεται Jul.*Or*.7.225b. **2.** = sq.1, βότρυς κόμης *AP*5.286 (Agath.), cf. Nonn.*D*.1.528, etc. **3.** *clustered ear-ring*, Ar.*Fr*.320.10. **II.** = ἀμβροσία and ἀρτεμισία, Dsc.3. 114. **2.** *oak of Jerusalem, Chenopodium Botrys*, ib.115. **III.** *the Pleiades*, Sch.Il.18.486.

βότρῠχος, ὁ, = βόστρυχος, Pherecr.189, cj.in E.*Or*.1267 (lyr.). **II.** *peduncle of bunch of grapes*, Gal.6.577.

βοτρῠχώδης, ες, restored metri gr. for βοστρυχώδης, E.*Ph*.1485 (lyr.).

βοτρῠώδης, ες, = βοτρυοειδής, E.*Ba*.12, Thphr.*HP*3.13.6, al.

βου-, prefix used in compos. (cf. βουγάϊος, etc.), *huge, monstrous*. (From βοῦς, cf. ἱππο-.)

βοῦα, ἡ, = ἀγέλη παίδων, at Sparta, Hsch.

βουαγετόν· ὑπὸ βοῶν εἱλκυσμένον ξύλον (Lacon.), Hsch. **βουᾱγόρ**, ὁ, (ἄγω) Lacon., *leader of a* βοῦα at Sparta, Id., *IG*5(1).257, al.:—also **βοαγόρ**, ib.292:—**βουᾱγός, βοᾱγός**, ib.283,523. **βουάκραι**, *palms* (Lacon.), Hsch. **βουάρχη**, gloss on βούπρωρος, Id.

βουβάλειος [ᾰ], α, ον, *of an antelope*, κέρας Hdn.Gr.2.438.

βουβάλια [βᾰ], ων, τά, a kind of *bracelets*, Nicostr.33, Diph.59, Lib. *Decl*.32.30, cf. *EM*206.16; Ἐρωτίων καὶ βουβαλίων ζεῦγος *IG*11(2). 161*B*118 (Delos, iii B.C.). **II.** sg., **βουβάλιον**, τό, = σίκυς ἄγριος, Ps.-Dsc.4.150, Hp.ap.Hsch. (but in masc. form **βουβάλιος**, ὁ, Id.ap. Gal.19.89).

βούβᾰλις, ιος, ἡ, an African *antelope, Bubalis mauretanica*, Hdt.4. 192, A.*Fr*.330: gen. βουβαλίδος Arist.*HA*$515^{b}34$: gen. pl. -ίδων D.C. 48.23: also an Indian species, Ael.*NA*13.25. (On the accent v. Hdn.Gr.1.90: -ίς, Hsch.)

βούβᾰλος, ὁ, = foreg., Arist.*PA*$663^{a}11$, Plb.12.3.5, D.S.2.51, Str. 17.3.4, Ph.2.353, J.*AJ*8.2.4, Opp.*C*.2.300. **II.** = ἀστράγαλος, Hsch. **III.** *buffalo*, Agath.1.4.

βουβάρας, = μέγας καὶ ἀναίσθητος, Hdn.Gr.1.57; cf. βουβάραι· μεγάλαι, Hsch.: also expld. as = μεγαλοναύτης (cf. βᾶρις), Id., cf. *EM* 206.18:—**βούβαρις**, Philist.56 (-βάρτις cod. Hsch.).

Βούβαστ-ις, ιος, ἡ, Egyptian divinity, Hdt.2.137, etc.:—hence **Βουβαστεία**, ἡ, Pythag. name for *five*, *Theol.Ar*.31. **-εῖον**, τό, *temple of Bubastis*, *BGU*820.18: **-ια**, τά, *festival of B.*, *OGI*56.37 (Canopus), *IG*9(1).86 (Phocis).

βούβαστις, ὁ, *groin*, Aët.4.21:—hence **βουβαστικά**, τά, *remedies for sores in the groin*, ibid.

βουβαυκαλόσαυλος, com. compd., prob. in Anaxandr.41.5.

βούβελα· κρέα βόεια, Hsch.

βου-βῆτις, ιος, ἡ, *stream for watering cattle*, *Tab.Heracl*.2.13. **-βόσιον**, τό, (βόσκω) *cattle-pasture*, Call.*Ap*.49, Arat.1120: in pl., *grazing*, Str.12.4.7. **-βίλιξ**· σιταποχία, Hsch. **-βοσις**, εως, ἡ, (βόσκω) = βούβρωστις, *EM*206.24. **-βότης**, ου, ὁ, *giving pasture to cattle*, πρῶνες Pi.*N*.4.52. **2.** as Subst., *herdsman*, Id.*I*.6(5). 32. **-βοτος**, ον, *grazed by cattle*, Od.13.246, *AP*6.114 (Simm. or Phil.). **-βρωστις**, εως, ἡ, *ravenous appetite*, Opp.*H*.2.208, Call. *Cer*.103, *AP*11.379 (Agath.): *famine*, *Epigr.Gr*.793.3: in Hom. only metaph., *grinding poverty* or *misery*, Il.24.532 (but expld. by Sch. as = οἶστρος).

βουβών, ῶνος, ὁ, *groin*, Il.4.492, etc.; κοινὸν μέρος..μηροῦ καὶ ἦτρου β. Arist.*HA*$493^{b}9$: in pl., μέχρι βουβώνων Pherecr.23, cf. Luc.*Tim*. 56. **2.** in pl., *glands*, Hp.*Epid*.2.2.24. **3.** *swollen gland*, Id. *Aph*.4.55, Arist.*Pr*.$883^{b}21$, Men.*Georg*.51, J.*Ap*.2.2. **II.** = Lat. *bubo, owl*, Id.*AJ*18.6.7, 19.8.2.

βουβων-ιακός, ή, όν, *for the groin*, of a bandage, Sor.*Fasc*.12.514C. (also **-ικός**). **-ιασκόπος**, ὁ, *one who treats* βουβῶνες *by magic*, Hsch., *EM*206.25. **-ιάω**, *suffer from swollen groins*, Ar.*V*.277, Call.Com.26, J.*Ap*.2.2: c. acc., τὼ νεφρὼ Ar.*Ra*.1280:—hence Subst. **-ίᾱσις**, εως, ἡ, Gal.19.566. **-ιον**, τό, = ἀστὴρ Ἀττικός, Dsc.4.119. **-ίσκος**, ὁ, *bandage for the groin*, Heliod.ap.Orib.48. 55 tit.

βουβωνο-ειδής, ές, *like a* βουβών, Poll.4.198. **-κήλη**, ἡ, *inguinal hernia*, Heliod.ap.Orib.48.57.5, Gal.7.730:—hence Adj. **-κηλικός**, ή, όν, *suffering from it*, Aët.4.26, Paul.Aeg.6.66. **-ομαι**, Pass., *swell to a* βουβών, Hp.*Gland*.8. **-φύλαξ** [ῠ], ακος, ὁ, *truss for hernia*, Heliod.ap.Orib.48.57 tit.

βουβωνώδης, ες, = βουβωνοειδής, Ruf.ap.Orib.44.17.3.

βου-γάϊος [ᾰ], ὁ, (γαίω) *bully, braggart*, only voc. as term of reproach, Il.13.824, Od.18.79; applied to those who lived on milk in Dulichion and Same, Nic.*Fr.*131. **-γενής**, ές, = βοηγενής, Emp.61.2, Call.*Fr.*230; of bees, Philet.22, *AP*9.548 (Bianor); Διόνυσος Plu.2.364f: metaph. of souls, Porph.*Antr.*18. **-γλωσσον**, τό (masc. form *buglossos* Plin.*HN*25.81), *bugloss, Anchusa italica*, Dsc.4.127, Opp.*H.*1.99. **2.** β. μέγα, = κρίσσιον, Ps.-Dsc.4.118. **3.** a surgical instrument, perh. *tongue-depressor*, *Hermes* 38.280. **-γλωσσος**, Att. -ττος, ὁ (Matro *Conv.*77) and ἡ (Archestr.*Fr.*32.2), a fish, *sole*, Epich.65, Xenarch.8.4, Speus.ap.Ath.7.329f, Dorio ib.330a; classed with σελάχη, Arist.*Fr.*280. **-γονής**, ές, *born of an ox*, of bees, *Gp.*15.2.14; βουγονή (nom.) ibid. tit. is perh. f.l. for βουγονῆ:—also **-γονία**, title of poem by Eumelus, Varro *RR* 2.5.5.

βου-δάκη· ἡ βούπρηστις, Hsch. **-δεψήϊον**, τό, *tannery*, Id.

βούδιον, τό, v. βοΐδιον.

βου-δόκος, ον, *receiving oxen*, ἐχῖνος (i.e. λέβης) Call.*Fr.*250b. **-δόρος**, ον, (δέρω) *flaying oxen, galling*, Hes.*Op.*504 (βούδορα codd., βουδόρα Sch.T.Il.17.550, cf. Eust.1117.53). **II.** *for flaying*, μάχαιρα Babr.97.7: as Subst., Hsch., prob. in Tim.*Pers.*28. **2.** prov., β. νόμῳ of those who deserve flaying, Diogenian.3.66. **-δύτης** [ῠ], ου, ὁ, a bird, perh. *wagtail*, Dionys.*Av.*3.2.

Βου-ζύγης [ῠ], ὁ, epith. of an Attic hero *who first yoked oxen*, Arist.*Fr.*386, Hsch.; Heracles, acc. to Suid. **2.** *keeper of bullocks* at Eleusis, *IG*3.71; ἱερεὺς Β. ib.3.294, cf. Eup.96,97. **-ζύγιος** [ῠ] (sc. ἄροτος), ὁ, *ritual ploughing*, at Athens, Plu.2.144b:—also Βουζύγια, τά, Ph.2.630. **-θερής**, ές, *affording summer-pasture*, λειμών S.*Tr.*188. **-θήλεια**, ἡ, = δάμαλις, *Gp.*17.2 tit. (pl.). **-θοίνης**, ου, ὁ, *beef-eater*, epith. of Hercules, *APl.*4.123, Eust.962.7. **-θόρος**, ον, *vaccas iniens*, ταῦρος A.*Supp.*301. **-θορος**, = βουθερής, Hsch. s.h.v. **-θουτον**, τό, a plant, = ἀμέμαρον (Lacon.), Hsch. **-θυσία**, Ion. -ίη, ἡ, *sacrifice of oxen*, *IG*14.830 (Puteoli), *AP*7.119, Porph.*Abst.*2.55; Ἥρας in her honour, Pi.*N.*10.23: in pl., Id.*O.*5.6, D.C.46.40. **-θύσιον** [ῠ], τό, = foreg., Sch.A.R.1.516. **-θυτέω**, *slay* or *sacrifice oxen*, S.*OC*888, E.*El.*785, Jul.*Mis.*362c, etc.: also in later Prose, Plb.32.15.2, D.C.42.28, al.: generally, *sacrifice, slaughter*, β. ὗν καὶ τράγον καὶ κριόν Ar.*Pl.*819; τὰς θυσίας τὰς καθηκούσας *IG*2.594.5; τῷ Ἀπόλλωνι ib.12(7).389.16, cf. *POxy.*1021.16 (i A.D.). **-θύτης** [ῠ], ου, ὁ, name given to Pythagoras, Procl.*in Euc.*p.426 F. **-θυτος**, ον, *of* or *belonging to sacrifices*, esp. *of oxen*, τιμαί A.*Supp.*706 (lyr.); ἡδονή E.*Ion*664; *accompanied by sacrifices*, ἑορταί B.3.15. **2.** *on which oxen are offered, sacrificial*, ἑστία S.*OC* 1495 (lyr.); ἐσχάρα Ar.*Av.*1232; ἦμαρ, ἀμέρα, A.*Ch.*261, E.*Hel.* 1474 (lyr.). **-θώνης**· βούχειλος, Hsch.

βουκαῖος, ὁ, (βοῦκος) *cowherd*, Nic.*Th.*5. **II.** *one who ploughs with oxen*, Theoc.10.1,57 (prob. a pr. n.), Nic.*Fr.*90.

βουκᾰνάω, βουκᾰνισμός, v. sub βυκ-.

βουκανή, = ἀνεμώνη (Cypr.), Hsch.

βου-κάπη [ᾰ], ἡ, *ox-stall*, Hsch. **-κάπηλος** [ᾰ], ου, ὁ, *cattle-dealer*, Poll.7.185.

βουκαρδία, ἡ, a *gem*, Plin.*HN*37.150.

Βουκάτιος, ὁ, a month in west central Greece, *SIG*241.105 (Delph.), *IG*7.1777 (Thespiae), etc.: **Βουκάτια**, τά, festival held therein, *SIG*²438.42, al. (Delph.).

βούκελλα, ἡ, = Lat. *bucella, small loaf*, *PFlor.*74.13 (ii A.D.).

βου-κέντης, ου, ὁ, *goader of oxen, ox-driver*, Diogenian.7.86. **-κεντρον**, τό, *ox-goad*, Lxx *Ec.*12.11. **-κέραος**, ον, = βούκερως, Nonn.*D.*14.319. **-κερας**, αος (also βούκερον, τό, *Hippiatr.*117, dat. -ῳ Thphr.*HP*8.8.5), τό, = τῆλις, ll. cc., Nic.*Al.*424. **-κερως**, ων, gen. ω, *horned like an ox* or *cow*, ἄγαλμα Hdt.2.41; β. παρθένος, of Io, A.*Pr.*588 (lyr.); Ἴακχος S.*Fr.*959. **II.** = foreg., Dsc.2.102. **-κεφάλας**, α, ὁ, the horse of Alexander the Great, Str.15.1.29, Plu.*Alex.*61, Arr.*An.*5.14.4.

βουκεφάλιον [ᾰ], τό, *ox-head*, used as an ornament, Lys.*Fr.*34, *SIG*695.71 (Magn. Mae.); β. χρυσᾶ *SIG*²588.199 (Delos, ii B.C.).

βουκέφᾰλος, ον, *bull-headed*, epith. of Thessalian horses, τὸν βουκέφαλον καὶ κοππατίαν Ar.*Fr.*42, cf. 41. **2.** = τρίβολος, Ps.-Dsc.4.15. **3.** βουκέφαλον, τό, = foreg., *IG*2.736 B 11, *Chron.Lind.*C.114.

βουκῐνίζω, *blow the trumpet*, στρόμβοις S.E.*M.*6.24:—also **βῡκᾰνίζω** or -ῐνίζω, Eust.1321.33, etc.: **βουκῐνάτωρ**, ὁ, = Lat. *buccinātor*, Lyd.*Mag.*1.46, etc.; cf. βυκάνη.

βουκλόπος, = βοοκλόπος, θεός Porph.*Antr.*18.

βουκολ-εῖον, τό, *residence of the* ἄρχων βασιλεύς at Athens, Arist.*Ath.*3.5. **-έω**, *tend cattle*, ἕλικας βοῦς βουκολέεσκες (Ep. impf.) Il.21.448, etc.: abs., Parth.4.1, Luc.*DDeor.*3:—Med., βουκολεῖσθαι αἶγας Eup.18:—Pass., of cattle, *graze*, ἕλος κάτα βουκολέοντο, of horses, Il.20.221, cf. Ar.*Pax* 153: metaph. of meteors, *range through the sky*, Call.*Del.*176. **b.** c. acc. rei, *graze on*, Τρηχινίδα Euph.114. **2.** of persons, βουκολεῖς Σαβάζιον *you tend, serve him* (with allusion to his *tauriform* worship), Ar.*V.*10:—Med., μὴ πρόκαμνε τόνδε βουκολούμενος πόνον *ruminating, pondering*, A.*Eu.*78. **II.** metaph., *cheat, beguile*, πάθος Id.*Ag.*669; τὸ δήμιον Ar.*Ec.*81, cf. Men.*Sam.*251; αἱ τίτθαι τοὺς παῖδας διὰ μυθολογίας βουκολοῦσιν Max.Tyr.10.3; β. λύπην Babr.19.7; ἀλλοτρίοις κόσμοις τὸ τῆς φύσεως ἀπρεπὲς β. Luc.*Am.*38:—Med., ἐλπίσι βουκολοῦμαι *I feed myself* on hopes, *cheat myself* with them, Alciphr.3.5, cf. Luc.*Trag.*29; ἐπιθυμίαις Id.*Am.*2:—Pass., *Stoic.*3.147; βουκολεῖσθαι ὑπὸ ἐνυπνίων Porph.*Marc.*6. **-ημα**, ατος, τό, *beguilement*, τῆς λύπης Babr.136.9. **-ησις**, εως, ἡ, *tending of cattle*, Plu.2.802e. **-ητής**, οῦ, ὁ, *deceiver*, Hsch. **-ία**, ἡ, *herd of cattle*, *h.Merc.*498, Hes.*Th.*445, Hdt.1.114. **II.** *tending of cattle*, A.R.1.627 (pl.). **III.** perh. = βουκολεῖον, Crates Gramm.ap.Ath.6.235c. **IV.** = κακολογία, Hsch. **-ιάζομαι, -ιάσδομαι**, fut. -αξεῦμαι:—*sing* or *write pastorals*, Theoc.5.44, al., Mosch.3.120. **-ιασμός**, ὁ, *singing of pastorals*, Ath.14.619a (v.l. -ισμός). **-ιαστής**, οῦ, ὁ, *pastoral poet*, Theoc.5.68. **-ίζω**, = βουκολιάζομαι, Eust.1416.39. **-ικός**, ή, όν, *rustic, pastoral*, ἀοιδά Theoc.1.64,70, etc.; τὰ β. *pastoral poetry*, Hermog.*Id.*2.3. **2.** β. μέτρον metre *used by pastoral poets*, Plu.*Metr.*2; τομή '*bucolic*' caesura, ib.3. **II.** βουκολικός, ὁ, official in cult of Dionysus, *IG*2².1368.123. **2.** *bucolicon*, = πάνακες Ἀσκληπίειον, Plin.*HN*25.31. **-ίνη**, = κίγκλος, Hsch. **-ιον**, τό, *herd of cattle*, Hdt.1.126, X.*HG*4.6.6, Theoc.8.39, 25.13, etc. **2.** τὰ β. *district* of lower Egypt, *inhabited by shepherds*, Hld.1.5, *BGU*625.6 (ii/iii A.D.), etc. **II.** *means of beguiling*, πενίης *AP*9.150 (Antip.), = ib.255 (Phil.); but with play on I. **-ίς** (sc. γῆ), ίδος, ἡ, *cattle-pasture*, D.H.1.37; β. πόα ib.39. **-ίσκος**, ὁ, a kind of *bandage*, Gal.18(1).777. **-ος**, ὁ, *tending kine*, βουκόλοι ἄνδρες, ἀγροιῶται, Il.13.571, Od.11.292, al.; β. δοῦλος Pl.*Ion* 540c; ποιμὴν αἰπόλος.. καὶ β. Cratin.281: also abs., Hdt.1.110, *PGoodsp.Cair.*30 ix 1 (ii A.D.), etc.; βέλει βουκόλου πτερόεντος, i.e. the gadfly, A.*Supp.*557 (lyr.); β. ἵππων Ael.*NA*12.44. **II.** *worshipper of Dionysos in bull-form*, in pl., title of play by Cratinus, cf. E.*Fr.*203, *IG*12(9).262 (Eretria, i B.C.), *IGRom.*4.386 (Pergam.), Luc.*Salt.*79, Hsch. s.v. πυρπερέγχει. **2.** β. τοῦ Ὀσοράπι *devotee* of Sarapis, *UPZ*57.7. (βοῦς, q^uel-, cf. Lat. *colo*: in these words βωκολ- is found as v.l. for βουκολ- in some codd. of Theoc.)

βουκονιστήριον, τό, *bullring*, *IGRom.*3.484 (Oenoanda, ii A.D.).

βουκόπια, τά, v. βοκόπια.

βουκόπος, gloss on βουπλήξ, Hsch.

βου-κόρυζα, ης, ἡ, *severe cold in the head*, Men.1003. **-κόρυζος**, ον, *stupid* and *drivelling*, Hsch.

βοῦκος, Dor. **βῶκος** (v.l.), ὁ, = βουκαῖος, Theoc.10.38. (Perh. a pr. n.)

βου-κράνιον [ᾱ], τό, *ox-head*, *EM*207.55. **II.** = ἄμπελος μέλαινα, Ps.-Dsc.4.183. **2.** = ἀντίρρινον, ib.130, Gal.19.82. **III.** *machine for reducing dislocations*, Orib.49.4.74. **-κρᾱνος**, ον, *bull-headed*, Emp.61.3, Call.*Fr.*203, Plu.2.358d. **II.** βούκρᾱνον, τό, *ox-head*, Gem.3.3. **-κρῑος**, ὁ, *ox-ram*, fabulous monster, Ps.-Callisth.3.17.

βούκτησις· φυσητική, Hsch.; cf. βύκτης.

βουλαῖος, α, ον, (βουλή) *of the council*, epith. of certain gods as having statues in the Council Chamber (Ἑστία βουλαία· ἡ ἐν τῇ βουλῇ ἱδρυμένη, Harp.), τὴν Ἑστίαν ἐπώμοσε τὴν β. Aeschin.2.45; of Zeus and Athena, Antipho 6.45, cf. *IG*3.272, *SIG*1011.6 (Chalcedon), Corn.*ND*9, Plu.2.789d; of Artemis, *IG*2².916, al.; Themis, Plu.2.802b; θεοὶ β., name of thirty stars, D.S.2.30; of a man, θεῶν βουλαῖος ἀνάκτων, = imperatorum divorum *consiliarius*, *IG*4.1475 (Epidaurus). **II.** Subst. **βουλαία**, ἡ, = βουλεία, *Milet.*7.71; but **βουλαῖα**· τὰ βεβουλευμένα, and **βούλεον** (sic)· βούλευμα, Hsch.

βούλακα· βόλου ὄνομα, i.e. throw at dice, Hsch.

βουλάπαθον, τό, Lat. *bulapathum, Rumex scutatus*, Plin.*HN*20.235.

βουλαπτεροῦν, etym. of βλαβερόν (βουλόμενον ἅπτειν ῥοῦν), Pl.*Cra.*417e.

βουλαρχ-έω, *to be a* βούλαρχος, *IG*9(1).65 (Daulis), 226 (Drymaea), Arist.*Pol.*1295ᵇ12. **-ία**, ἡ, *office of* βούλαρχος, *IG*9(1).228 (Drymaea), 12(2).484.7 (Mytilene). **-ος**, ὁ, *president of the senate*, as at Thyateira, *IGRom.*4.1230; at Amorgos, *IG*12(7).287, cf. *Milet.*3.230, 7.70. **II.** *adviser of a plan*, A.*Supp.*11,970.

βουλᾱφόρος, Dor. for βουληφ-.

βουλαχ-εύς, έως, ὁ, (perh. βοῦς, λαγχάνω) dub. sens. in *Milet.*1(7).p.323 (Didyma). **-έω**, *to be* βουλαχεύς, ib.3(2) Nos.168,171.

βουλ-εία, ἡ, (βουλεύω) *office of councillor*, Ar.*Th.*809, X.*HG*2.3.38, Din.*Fr.*89.12; *membership of the Senate* at Rome, D.C.37.30, al.; of local βουλαί, *POxy.*1406.8 (iii A.D.). **-εῖον**, τό, = βουλευτήριον, *SIG*1011 (Chalcedon), 614.34 (Delph., ii B.C.), Ps.-Hdt.*Vit.Hom.*12. **-εκκλησία**, ἡ, *joint session of* βουλή *and* ἐκκλησία, *Inscr.Prien.*246.9 (iii A.D.) (pl.). **-ευμα**, ατος, τό, *resolution, purpose*, A.*Pr.*171 (lyr.), 619, Ar.*Av.*993, etc.: freq. in pl., Pi.*N.*5.28, Hdt.3.80, S.*OT*45, A.*Th.*594, Pl.*R.*334a, D.18.296: prov., τοῖς οἰκείοις β. ἁλίσκεσθαι '*to be hoist with one's own petard*', Lib.*Or.*59.20. **II.** *sitting of a* βουλή, φοιτᾶν εἰς τὰ β. Philostr.*Her.*19.6. **-ευμάτιον**, τό, Dim. of foreg., Ar.*Eq.*100. **-εύς**, έως, ὁ, *Counsellor*, title of Zeus, *SIG*1024.17 (Myconos). **-ευσις**, εως, ἡ, *deliberation*, Arist.*EN*1112ᵇ22. **II.** as Att. law-term, **1.** *conspiracy* against life, Arist.*Ath.*57.3; against property, Hyp.*Ath.*18. **2.** *wrongful retention on the list of state debtors of the name of one who has paid his debt*, D.25.28 and 73, Arist.*Ath.*59.3. **-ευτέον**, *one must take counsel*, ὅπως.. A.*Ag.*847; τί χρὴ δρᾶν S.*El.*16; περί τινος Isoc.6.90: pl., βουλευτέα Th.7.60. **-ευτήρ**, ῆρος, ὁ, = βουλευτής, Hsch. s.v. μάστροι. **-ευτήριον**, τό, *council-chamber*, seat of a βουλή, Hdt.1.170, A.*Eu.*570,684, E.*Andr.*1097, And.1.36, D.18.169, Pl.*Grg.*452e, *Michel* 1203 (Iasos), etc.; = Lat. *curia*, Plu.*Cic.*31, Hdn.5.5.7. **II.** *Council, Senate*, D.H.2.12; of local βουλαί, *PLond.*2.408.14 (iv A.D.), etc.; of individuals, δόλια βουλευτήρια treacherous *counsellor*, E.*Andr.*446; ῥυσὰ β. Theopomp.Com.75 (paratrag.). **-ευτήριος**, ον, *giving advice*, κακῶν τ' Ἀδράστῳ τῶνδε βουλευτήριον A.*Th.*575. **-ευτής**, οῦ, ὁ, *councillor, senator*, Il.6.114, Hdt.9.5, Pl.*Ap.*25a, etc.; at Athens, *one of the* 500, Antipho 6.45, And.1.43, Ar.*Th.*808; at Rome, *senator*, D.H.2.12, Plu.*Rom.*13, etc. 2. *plotter, contriver*, θανάτου, πληγῆς, Antipho 4.3.4. **-ευτικός**, ή, όν, *of* or *for the council*, β. ὅρκος oath *taken by the councillors*, X.*Mem*.1.1.18; νόμοι ap.D.24.20; β. τιμαί *CIG*1716 (Delph.); ἀρχὴ β. right *to sit in the* βουλή, Arist.*Pol*.1275^{b}19; of the Roman Senate, τίμημα, ἐσθής, D.C.54.17, 40.46; -κά, τά, *funds at the disposal of a council*, *POxy*.1416.3 (iii A.D.). 2. *able to advise* or *deliberate*, ὁ β., opp. ὁ πολεμικός, Pl.*R*.434b, cf. 441a, Arist.*EN*1140^{a}31, 1152^{a}19; τὸ β. *the deliberative faculty*, Id.*Pol*.1260^{a}12. II. Subst., -κόν, τό, in the Athen. theatre, *seats reserved for the Council*, Ar.*Av*.794, Hsch. 2. the *deliberative and judicial element* in the state, Arist.*Pol*.1329^{a}31; at Rome, *senatorial order*, Plu.*Rom*.13. **-ευτις**, ιδος, ἡ, fem. of βουλευτής, A.*Fr*.172 (= Pl.Com.88). **-ευτός**, ή, όν, *devised, plotted*, A.*Ch*.494. II. *matter for deliberation*, Arist.*EN*1113^{a}2, etc. III. βουλευτός, = βουλευτής, Hsch. **-εύω**, Il.2.379, etc., aor. ἐβούλευσα Od.5.23, etc., Ep. βούλ- Il.14.464: pf. βεβούλευκα S.*OT*701:—Med. and Pass., v. infr.: (βουλή):—*take counsel, deliberate*, in past tenses, *determine* or *resolve after deliberation*: 1. abs., ὣς βουλεύσαντε Il. 1.531; βουλευέμεν ἠδὲ μάχεσθαι *in council* or in battle, Od.14.491; β. ὅπως ὄχ' ἄριστα γένοιτο 9.420, cf. 11.229; δυσμενέεσσι φόνον πέρι β. 16.234; ἔς γε μίαν βουλεύσομεν (sc. βουλήν) we *shall agree* to one plan, Il.2.379; θυμῷ β. Od.12.58; β. περί τινος Hdt.1.120, Th.3.28, 5.116: in Prose, chiefly Med. in this sense, v. infr. B. 2. c. acc. rei, *deliberate on, plan, devise*, β. βουλάς Il.24.652, al.; οὐ . . τοῦτον μὲν ἐβούλευσας νόον αὐτή; Od.5.23; ὁδόν 1.444; φύξιν Il.10.311, 398; κέρδεα Od.23. 217; ψεύδεα 14.296: c. dat. pers., τῷ γάρ ῥα θεοὶ βούλευσαν ὄλεθρον Il. 14.464, cf. Hdt.9.110; θάνατόν τινι Pl.*Lg*.872a; β. πῆμά τινι Od.5.179, etc.; κέλευθον A.*Pers*.758; ποινάς Id.*Ag*.1223; νεώτερα β. περί τινος Hdt.1.210:—Pass. (with fut. Med., A.*Th*.198), aor. ἐβουλεύθην Hdt. 7.157, Th.1.120, Pl.*R*.442b: pf. βεβούλευμαι (usu. in med. sense, v. infr. B):—*to be determined* or *planned*, ψῆφος κατ' αὐτῶν βουλεύσεται A. l.c.; βεβούλευται τάδε Id.*Pr*.998, cf. Hdt.7.10.δ'; τὰ βεβουλευμένα, = βουλεύματα, Id.4.128; τὰ βουλευόμενα X.*Cyr*.6.2.2; πῶς σφῷν βεβούλευται Pl.*Euthd*.274a. 3. c. inf., *take counsel, resolve* to do, τὸν μὲν ἐγὼ βούλευσα . . οὐτάμεναι Od.9.299, cf. Hdt.1.73, 6.52, 61, etc.:—Pass., τοῖσι ἐβεβούλευτο τὸ παιδίον προσουδίσαι Id.5.92.γ'. II. *give counsel*, τὰ λῷστα β. A.*Pr*.206; β. δυνατός Pl.*Lg*.694b: c. dat. pers., *advise*, ἵνα σφίσι βουλεύησθα Il.9.99, cf. A.*Eu*.697. III. *sit in council*, of the Spartan γέροντες, Hdt.6.57; *to be a member of a* βουλή, Arist.*Pol*.1282^{a}30; esp. *of the Council of* 500 at Athens, Antipho 6.45, And.1.75, X.*Mem*.1.1.18, Arist.*Ath*.62.3; ἡ βουλὴ ἡ βουλεύουσα Lys.13.19; βουλὴν β. *to be a member of the* β., ib.20; βουλεύειν λαχών Pl.*Grg*.473e.

B. Med., fut. -εύσομαι A.*Ag*.846, *Ch*.718, Th.1.43, Pl.*Smp*. 174d: aor. ἐβουλευσάμην S.*OT*537, etc.; Ep. βουλ- Il.2.114; ἐβουλεύθην D.H.15.7: pf. βεβούλευμαι Hdt.3.134, S.*El*.385, Th.1.69, E.*Supp*.248, Pl.*Chrm*.176c (also in pass. sense, v. supr.):—more freq. in Att. Prose than Act., 1. abs., *take counsel with oneself, deliberate*, Hdt.7.10.δ', Arist.*EN*1112^{b}11, 20; παραχρῆμα οὐδὲ -σάμενος D.37.13; ἅμα τινί Hdt.8.101; περὶ τοῦ μέλλοντος τῶν οἰκείων Th.3.44, cf. Pl.*Phdr*.231a; περί τι Id.*R*.604c; ὑπέρ τινος ib.428d; πρὸς τὴν γεγενημένην ξυμφοράν Th.7.47: c. acc. cogn., β. βούλευμα And.3.29; βουλήν Pl.*Plt*.298b, etc.; ἴσον τι ἢ δίκαιον Th.2.44:—also like Act., *take counsel*, πρός τινας Lxx 4*Ki*.6.8. 2. *act as member of council*, and so *originate measures*, β. καὶ κρίνειν Arist.*Pol*.1281^{b}31; τὸ βουλευόμενον ib.1291^{a}28. 3. c. acc. rei, *determine with oneself, resolve on*, κακὴν ἀπάτην βουλεύσατο Il.2.114 (Med. here only in Hom.); ἀλλοῖόν τι περί τινος Hdt.5.40, cf. Pl.*Ap*.32c. 4. c. inf., *resolve* to do, Hdt.3.134, Pl.*Chrm*.176c. 5. rarely folld. by Relat., β. ὅ τι ποιήσεις ibid.; β. ὅπως . . with subj., X.*Cyr*.1.4.13; β. πῶς τις, c. fut., Id.*An*.3.4.40; πῶς καὶ τί πρακτέον εἴη Plb.1.33.3; ἵνα *Ev.Jo*.12.10.

βουλεψίη, dub. sens. of the Amazons, Xanth.ap.Hsch.

βουλή, ἡ, Dor. **βωλά** Decr.Byz.ap.D.18.90, Aeol. **βόλλα** *Schwyzer* 623.1 (ii B.C.), Plu.2.288b: acc. pl. βουλᾱ́ς Hes.*Th*.534: (βούλομαι):—*will, determination*, esp. of the gods, Il.1.5, etc. 2. *counsel, design*, βουλὰς βουλεύουσι Il.24.652, etc.: generally, *counsel, advice*, opp. μάχεσθαι, Il.1.258, cf. 2.202, etc.; κακὴ β. Hes.*Op*.266; πρᾶτος . . καὶ βουλᾷ καὶ χερσὶν ἐς Ἄρεα *IG*9(1).658 (Ithaca); νυκτὶ βουλὴν διδόναι Hdt.7.12 (but ἐν νυκτὶ β. διδοὺς ἐμαυτῷ Men.*Epit*.35); ἐν β. ἔχειν τὰ γενόμενα Hdt.3.78; β. ποιεῖσθαι, = βουλεύεσθαι, Id.6.101, etc.; β. διδόναι X. *Cyr*.7.2.26; β. προτιθέναι περί τινος D.18.192; β. ἄγειν Polyaen.7. 39; ἐν βουλῇ γενέσθαι πότερον . . D.H.2.44; τούτοις οὐκ ἔστι κοινὴ β. they have no common *ground of argument*, Pl.*Cri*.49d; βουλῆς ὀρθότης ἡ εὐβουλία Arist.*EN*1142^{b}16: in pl., *counsels*, A.*Pr*.221, *Th*. 842 (lyr.); ἐν βουλαῖς ἄριστος, ἐν βουλαῖσι κράτιστος, *Epigr.Gr*.854, *IG*3.716. 3. *deliberation*, Arist.*EN*1112^{a}19, D.9.46. 4. *decree*, β. εἰσηγεῖσθαι And.1.61; β. ἄκυρον θεῖναι Id.2.28. II. *Council of elders, Senate*, βουλὴν ἷζε γερόντων Il.2.53, cf. Od.3.127, A.*Ag*.884; esp. at Athens, *Council* or *Senate of* 500 created by Cleisthenes, Hdt.9.5, Ar.*V*.590, Antipho 6.40, etc.; commonly called ἡ β. (or ἡ β. οἱ πεντακόσιοι Aeschin.3.20, to distinguish it from ἡ β. ἡ ἐν Ἀρείῳ πάγῳ ibid.; also β. ἀπὸ κυάμου Th.8.66); in other states, as at Argos, Hdt.7.149; at Thebes, X.*HG*5.2.29; of the Roman *Senate*, D.H.6.69, etc.; of local *senates*, *POxy*.58.14 (iii A.D.), etc.; βουλῆς εἶναι to be *of the Council, a member of it*, Th.3.70 (whence Sch. and Suid. made a Subst. **βουλής**, ὁ); ἀνὴρ βουλῆς τῆς Ῥωμαίων Paus.5. 20.8; ἄνδρα ἐκ τῆς βουλῆς Id.7.11.1.

βουλ-ηγορέω, *speak in the Senate*, App.*BC*3.51. **-ηγορία**, ἡ, *speech in the Senate*, Poll.4.26. **-ηγόρος**, ὁ, *one who speaks in the Senate*, ib.25. **-ήεις**, εσσα, εν, *of good counsel, sage*, Sol.33. 1. **-ημα**, ατος, τό, *purpose*, Gorg.*Hel*.6 (pl.), Ar.*Av*.993, Isoc.3.15, D.18.49 (pl.); *intent*, τοῦ νομοθέτου Pl.*Lg*.769d, 802c (pl.), al.; τὸ β. τῆς κρίσεως *intention* to judge, Id.*Phlb*.41e: pl., βουλήμασι Μοίρης *IG* 12(7).303. 2. *meaning*, οὐδεὶς σαφῶς παρέδωκε τὸ β. Ael.*Tact*.18.1; τὸ β. τοῦ ποιητοῦ Hipparch.1.4.9, al. 3. *intention of a testator*, *BGU* 361 ii 23 (ii A.D.): hence, *will, testament*, *POxy*.907.1 (iii A.D.), *PLips*. 29.7 (iii A.D.). II. *express will, consent*, τῆς συγκλήτου Plb.6.15. 4. **-ημάτιον**, τό, Dim. of foreg. I. 3, *will, testament*, *PMasp*.151. 304 (vi A.D.). **-ησις**, εως, ἡ, *willing*, Arist.*de An*.433^{a}23; β. ἀγαθοῦ ὄρεξις Id.*Top*.146^{b}5, cf. *EN*1111^{b}19; τῶν ἀδυνάτων, τοῦ τέλους, ib. 1111^{b}22, 1113^{a}15; *purpose*, πράσσειν β. E.*HF*1305; *wish, desire*, Th.3. 39, Pl.*Grg*.509d, etc.; βούλησιν ἐλπίζει entertains a hope and *purpose*, Th.6.78; κατὰ τὴν β. Pl.*Cra*.420d, al.; παρὰ τὴν β. ibid., Arist.*EN* 1136^{b}24: pl., Pl.*Lg*.688b, Arist.*Rh*.1378^{b}18; of the gods, Polystr. p.10 W. II. *purpose* or *meaning* of a poem, Pl.*Prt*.344b; *signification* of a word, Id.*Cra*.421b. III. *will, testament*, β. ἔγγραφος *PLips*.33 ii 10 (iv A.D.). **-ητέος**, α, ον, *to be wished for*, τὸ β. Arist. *MM*1208^{b}38. 2. βουλητέον, *one must wish for*, Id.*Rh.Al*.1420^b 23. **-ητός**, ή, όν, *that is* or *should be willed*, οὔτε χρήσιμον οὔτε β. Phld.*Rh*.1.185 S.: τὸ β. *object of desire* or *will*, Pl.*Lg*.733d, Arist.*EN* 1113^{a}17. Adv. -τῶς Procl.*in Prm*.p.752 S.

βουληφόρος, ον, *counselling, advising*, in Il. a constant epith. of princes and leaders, β. ἄνδρα 2.24, al.; title of Artemis, *SIG*^{2}660.3 (Milet.): also c. gen., β. Ἀχαιῶν, Τρώων, Il.24.651, 5.180; in Od.9.112 οὔτ' ἀγοραὶ β. οὔτε θέμιστες, cf. Pi.*O*.12.5: in later Prose, = βουλευτής, οἱ τοῦ μιάσματος β. Agath.3.5. Adv. -ρως *like a counsellor*, Men.123.

βουλῑμ-ία, ἡ, *ravenous hunger*, Timocl.13.3, Arist.*Pr*.887^{b}39. **-ῐᾱσις**, εως, ἡ, *suffering from* βουλιμία, Plu.2.695d. **-ιάω**, *suffer from* βουλιμία, Ar.*Pl*.873, X.*An*.4.5.7, Arist.*Pr*.887^{b}38, Erasistr. ap.Gell.16.3.10, Plu.*Brut*.25. **-ος**, ὁ, = βουλιμία, Id.2.693f, Erasistr.ap.Gell.16.3.9, Sor.2.4, etc.; β. ἐσθ' ἄνθρωπος Alex.135. 17. **-ώδης**, ες, *of the nature of* βούλιμος, Herod.Med.ap.Orib.5. 30.15 (also **-ιώδης**, Gal.13.122). **-ώττω**, = βουλιμιάω, Suid.

βούλιος, ον, (βουλή) = βουλευτικός I. 2, *sage*, A.*Ch*.672 (in Comp. -ώτερος), prob. (for δούλιος) in Id.*Supp*.599 (lyr.).

βούλλα, ἡ, *tin*, *PHolm*.2.4, *PLeid*.X.6.

βουλο-γρᾰφία, ἡ, *registration of senatorial decrees*, *CIG*4015 (Ancyra):—hence **-γρᾰφέω**, *Ostr*.1549. **-κοπίδης**, ου, ὁ, Com. name, on analogy of δημοκόπος, *AB*221.3.

βούλομαι (Ep. also **βόλομαι**, q.v.), Dor. **βώλ-** (q.v.), Aeol. **βόλλ-** (v. βόλομαι), Thess. **βέλλ-** *IG*9(2).517.20, Boeot. **βείλ-** ib.7.3080, **βήλ-** *SIG*1185.18 (Tanagra, iii B.C.), Locr. and Delph. **δείλ-** *IG*9(1). 334.3, *GDI*2034.10, Coan, etc. **δήλ-** (q.v.), Ion. 2 sg. βούλεαι Od.18. 364, Hdt.1.11: impf. ἐβουλόμην Il.11.79, etc.; ἠβουλόμην E.*Hel*.752, D.1.15, etc.; Ion. 3 pl. ἐβουλέατο codd. in Hdt.1.4, 3.143: fut. βουλήσομαι A.*Pr*.867, S.*OT*1077, etc.; later fut. βουληθήσομαι v.l. in Aristid.*Or*.48(24).8, Gal.13.636: aor. ἐβουλήθην, also ἠβ- (v. infr.), βουληθείς S.*OC*732, *IG*2^2.1236, etc., but Ep. aor. subj. 3 sg. βούλεται (from *βόλσ-ε-ται) Il.1.67: pf. βεβούλημαι D.18.2; also βέβουλα (προ-) Il.1.113 (ἐβέβουλε dub. in Epigr. in *Berl.Sitzb*.1894.907):—forms with augm. ἠ- are found in Att. Inscrr. from 300 B.C. onwards, as *IG*2^2.657, al., and occur frequently in Mss. as ἠβούλοντο v.l. in Th. 2.2, 6.79, ἠβούλου Hyp.*Lyc*.11; said to be Ionic in *An.Ox*.2.374.—An Act. βούλητε (= βούλησθε) Mitteis *Chr*.361.10 (iv A.D.):—*will, wish, be willing*, Hom., etc.: usu. implying choice or preference (cf. IV) opp. ἐθέλω 'consent', εἰ βούλει, ἐγὼ ἐθέλω Pl.*Grg*.522e, cf. *R*. 347b, 437b; ἐὰν βούλῃ σύ . . ἐὰν θεὸς ἐθέλῃ Id.*Alc*.1.135d; ἄν οἵ τε θεοὶ θέλωσι καὶ ὑμεῖς βούλησθε D.2.20; οὔτ' ἀκούειν ἤθελετ' οὔτε πιστεύειν ἐβούλεσθε Id.19.23; but ἐθέλω is also used = 'wish', λέξαι θέλω σοι, πρὶν θανεῖν, ἃ βούλομαι, E.*Alc*.281 (so ἐθέλω εἰπεῖν Pl.*Prt*.309b, but φράσαι τι βούλομαι Ar.*Pl*.1090): Hom. uses βούλομαι for ἐθέλω in the case of the gods, for with them *wish* is *will*: ἐθέλω is more general, and is sts. used where βούλομαι might have stood, e.g. Il. 7.182.—Construct.: mostly c. inf., Τρώεσσιν ἐβούλετο κῦδος ὀρέξαι 11.79, etc.; sts. c. inf. fut., Thgn.184; c. acc. et inf., Od.4.353, and freq. in Prose: when βούλομαι is folld. by acc. only, an inf. may generally be supplied, as καί κε τὸ βουλοίμην (sc. γενέσθαι) Od.20. 316; ἔτυχεν ὧν ἐβούλετο (sc. τυχεῖν) Antiph.18.6; πλακοῦντα β. (sc. σε λέγειν) Id.52.11; καὶ εἰ μάλα βούλεται ἄλλῃ [Ποσειδάων] (sc. τοῦτο γενέσθαι) Il.15.51; so εἰς τὸ βαλανεῖον βούλομαι (sc. ἰέναι) Ar.*Ra*. 1279; βουλοίμην ἄν (sc. τόδε γενέσθαι) Pl.*Euthphr*.3a. 2. in Hom. of gods, c. acc. rei et dat. pers., Τρώεσσιν . . ἐβούλετο νίκην he *willed* victory to the Trojans, Il.7.21, cf. 23.682: later c. acc., τὸ βουλόμενον τὴν πολιτείαν πλῆθος *that supports* the constitution, Arist.*Pol*.1309^b 17. II. Att. usages: 1. βούλει or βούλεσθε folld. by Verb in subj., βούλει λάβωμαι; *would you have* me take hold? S.*Ph*.761; βούλει φράσω; Ar.*Eq*.36, cf. Pl.*Phd*.79a, *R*.596a; ποῦ δὴ βούλει ἀναγνῶμεν; Id.*Phdr*.228e. 2. εἰ βούλει *if you please*, S.*Ant*.1168, X.*An*.3.4. 41; also εἰ δὲ βούλει, ἐὰν δὲ βούλῃ, to express a concession, or *if you like*, Pl.*Smp*.201a, etc.; εἰ μὲν β., φρονήσει, εἰ δὲ β., ἰσχύι Id.*R*. 432a. 3. ὁ βουλόμενος *any one who likes*, Hdt.1.54, Th.1.26, etc.; ἔδωκεν ἅπαντι τῷ βουλομένῳ D.21.45; ὁ β. the 'common informer', Ar. *Pl*.918 (whence, in jest, βούλομαι ib.908); ὅστις βούλει who or which ever *you like*, Pl.*Grg*.517b, *Cra*.432a. 4. βουλομένῳ μοί ἐστι, c. inf., it is *according to* my *wish* that . ., Th.2.3; εἰ σοὶ β. ἐστὶν ἀποκρίνεσθαι Pl.*Grg*.448d; also τὰ θεῶν οὕτω βουλόμεν' ἔσται E.*IA*33; τὸ κείνου βουλόμενον his *wish*, ib.1270; but with pass. sense, τὸ β. the *object of desire*, Luc.*Am*.37, Plu.*Art*.28. 5. τί βουλόμενος; *with* what *purpose?* Pl.*Phd.*63a, D.18.172; τί βουληθεὶς πάρει; S.*El.*1100. III. *mean*, Pl.*R.*362e, 590e, etc.; τί ἡμῖν βούλεται οὗτος ὁ μῦθος; (folld. by β. λέγειν ὡς..) Id.*Tht.*156c; τί β. σημαίνειν τὸ τέρας D.H.4.59; βούλεται εἶναι *professes* or *pretends* to be, Pl.*R.*595c; β. τὸ ὄνομα ἐπικεῖσθαι Id.*Cra.*412c; freq. in Arist., τὸ ἀκούσιον βούλεται λέγεσθαι οὐκ εἰ.. *EN*1110^{b}30; β. ἄσωτος εἶναι ὁ ἕν τι κακὸν ἔχων ib.1119^{b}34; β. ὁ πρᾶος ἀτάραχος εἶναι ib.1125^{b}33; *tend* to be, ἡ τοῦ ὕδατος φύσις β. εἶναι ἄχυμος Id.*Sens.*441^{a}3; β. ἤδη τότε εἶναι πόλις ὅταν.. Id.*Pol.*1261^{b}12, cf. 1293^{b}40; ἡ φύσις β. μὲν τοῦτο ποιεῖν πολλάκις, οὐ μέντοι δύναται ib. 1255^{b}3, cf. *GA*778^{a}4, al. 2. *to be wont*, X.*An.*6.3.18. IV. folld. by ἤ.., *prefer*, for βούλομαι μᾶλλον (which is more usu. in Prose), βούλομ' ἐγὼ λαὸν σόον ἔμμεναι ἢ ἀπολέσθαι *I had rather..*, Il.1.117, cf. 23.594, Od.3.232, 11.489, 12.350; β. τὸ μέν τι εὐτυχέειν.. ἢ εὐτυχέειν τὰ πάντα Hdt.3.40; β. παρθενεύεσθαι πλέω χρόνον ἢ πατρὸς ἐστερῆσθαι (for πολὺν χρόνον, μᾶλλον ἤ..) ib.124, cf. E.*Andr.* 351; less freq. without ἤ.., πολὺ βούλομαι αὐτὴν οἴκοι ἔχειν I much *prefer..*, Il.1.112, cf. Od.15.88. (*gᵘel-gᵘol-*, cf. the dialectic forms.)

βουλόμᾰχος, ον, *strife-desiring*, Ar.*Pax* 1293 (hex.).

βου-λύσιος [ῡ] ὥρα the time *for unyoking*, Arat.825. **-λῦσις**, εως, ἡ, = sq., only in Cic.*Att.*15.27.3. **-λῦτός** (sc. καιρός), ὁ, *time for unyoking oxen* (*early afternoon*, Hld.2.19, cf. Eust.1614.44, but *evening*, Ael.*NA*13.1, cf. Philostr.*Her.*19.20), Ar.*Av.*1500, A.R.3.1342, Luc.*Cat.*1, etc.; ὑπὸ.. ἀστέρα βουλυτοῖο *IG*14.2012.15 (Sulp. Max.):—Hom. only in Adv. **βουλῡτόνδε**, Il.16.779, Od.9.58. **-μᾰνές**, τό, a *plant*, Hsch. **-μασθος** or **-μαστος** (so in *PSI*4.429 (iii A.D.)) (sc. ἄμπελος), ἡ, *vine bearing large grapes*, Virg.*G.*2.102, Plin. *HN*14.15, Macr.*Sat.*3.20.7. **-μελία**, ἡ, *ash*, *Fraxinus excelsior*, Thphr.*HP*3.11.4, 4.8.2 (v.l. **βουμέλιος**, ὁ). **-μέτρης**, ου, ὁ, *official in charge of sacrifices* (Aetol.), Hsch. **-μολγός**, ὁ, (ἀμέλγω) *cow-milking*, *AP*6.255 (Eryc.). **-μῡκοι**, οἱ, *loud bellowings*, a kind of subterranean noise, Arist.*Pr.*937^{b}39; in Hsch. βούμῡκαι.

βουναία, ἡ, epith. of Hera, because her temple stood on a βουνός, Paus.2.4.7.

βουνιάς, άδος, ἡ, *French turnip*, *Brassica Napus*, Agatharch.51, Nic.*Fr.*70.3, J.*AJ*3.7.6, Dsc.2.111.

βουνίζω, (βουνός) *heap up*, *pile up*, Lxx *Ru.*2.14,16.

βούνιον, τό, *earth-nut*, *Bunium ferulaceum*, Dsc.4.123. 2. = περιστερεών, Ps.-Dsc.4.59. II. Dim. of βουνός I, *hill*, *Inscr.Prien.* 42.41 (ii B.C.).

βοῦνις, ιδος, ἡ, *hilly*, Ἀπίαν βοῦνιν A.*Supp.*117 (lyr.); voc. ἰὼ γᾶ βοῦνι, πάνδικον σέβας (prob. for βουνῖτι ἔνδικον) ib.776 (lyr.).

βουνίτης [ῑ], ου, ὁ, *dweller on the hills*, of Pan, *AP*6.106 (Zon.). II. cf. βωνίτης.

βουνο-βᾰτέω, *walk on* or *mount hills*, πρῶνας *AP*6.218 (Alc.). **-ειδής**, ές, *hill-like*, *hilly*, D.S.5.40, Str.11.8.4, Plu.*Thes.*36, etc.

βου-νομέω, *pasture cattle*, Str.13.1.7. **-νομία**, ἡ, *pasturage*, Pi. *Pae.*3.27. **-νομος**, ον, *grazed by cattle*, of pastures, A.*Fr.*249, S. *El.*181 (lyr.). 2. ἀγέλαι βουνόμοι (parox.) herds *of grazing oxen*, Id.*OT*26.

βουνός, ὁ, *hill*, *mound*, Cyrenaic word, acc. to Hdt.4.199; freq. in Syracusan poets, acc. to Phryn.333, cf. Philem.49,142, Lxx *Ex.* 17.9, al., Plb.3.83.1, *Schwyzer* 289.168 (Rhodian, ii B.C.), Str.3.2.9, *BGU*1129.14 (i B.C.), etc. 2. *heap* of stones, etc., Lxx *Ge.*31.46; σίτου *PFlor.*58.12. II. *clot* of blood, Cyr. s.v. θρόμβος, cf. Hsch. s.v. θρόμβοι. III. *altar*, Hsch. IV. = στιβάς (Cypr.), Id. (Barbarous word acc. to Ael.Dion.*Fr.*93.)

βουνώδης, ες, = βουνοειδής, *hilly*, Plb.2.15.8, etc.; θίς Plu.*Crass.* 25.

βούπαις, αιδος, ὁ, *big boy*, Ar.*V.*1206, Eup.402, A.R.1.760, *BCH* 47.85 (Philippi), Agath.2.14 (pl.). II. *child of the ox*, = βουγενής, of bees, in allusion to their fabulous origin, *AP*7.36 (Eryc.). III. a *fish* (nisi leg. ἰσχυρός), Hsch. IV. = βουκόλος, Suid.

βουπάλινα, τά, prob. = βουβάλια (v. βουβάλιον), *SIG*^{2}588.171 (Delos, ii B.C.):—also **βουπαλίδες**· περισκελίδες, Hsch.

βούπᾰλις, εως, ὁ, ἡ, (πάλη) *wrestling like a bull*, i.e. *hard-struggling*, ἀεθλοσύνη *APl.*4.67.

βου-πάμων [ᾰ], ον, gen. ονος, (πάομαι) *rich in cattle*, *AP*6.263 (Leon.), 7.740 (Id.). **-πεινα**, ἡ, = βουλιμία, Lyc.581, Call.*Fr.*7.11 P. **-πελάτης** [ᾰ], ου, ὁ, *herdsman*, A.R.4.1342, Nic.*Al.*39, Opp.*C.*1.534, Androm.ap.Gal.14.37. **-πλᾰνόκτιστος**, ον, (βοῦς, πλάνη, κτίζω) *founded by the wandering cow*, of Troy, λόφος Lyc.29. **-πλάστης**, ου, ὁ, *cow-modeller*, of the sculptor Myron, *AP*9.734 (Diosc.). **-πλευρος**, ἡ, (cf. Sch.Nic.l.c.) *bishop's weed*, *Ammi majus*, Nic.*Th.*585. **-πληθής**, ές, *full of oxen*, Euph.52. **-πληκτρος**, ον, *goading oxen*, ἄκαινα *AP*6.41 (Agath.). **-πλήξ**, ῆγος, ὁ (also ἡ, Ps.-Luc.*Philopatr.*4, *EM*371.40), *ox-goad*, θεινόμεναι βουπλῆγι (gender undetermined) Il. 6.135. 2. *axe for felling an ox*, *AP*9.352 (Leon.), Timo 4.1, Q.S.1. 159. **-ποίητος**, ον, = βούπαις II, *AP*12.249 (Strat.). **-ποίμην**, ενος, ὁ, *herdsman*, ib.7.622 (Antiphil.). **-πόλος**, ον, *tending oxen*, Hsch.; cf. βουκόλος. **-πομπός**, όν, *celebrated with a procession of oxen*, ἑορτή Pi.*Fr.*193. **-πόρος**, ον, (πείρω) *ox-piercing*, β. ὀβελός a spit *large enough for a whole ox*, Hdt.2.135, cf. E.*Cyc.*302; ἀμφώβολοι σφαγῆς.. βουπόροι spits *fit to pierce an ox's* throat, Id.*Andr.*1134; β. ὀβελίσκος X.*An.*7.8.14. **-πρηόνες**, *great precipices*, Hsch. **-πρηστις**, ιδος or εως, ἡ, (πρήθω) *poisonous beetle*, which being eaten by cattle in the grass causes them to swell up and die, Hp.*Nat.Mul.* 32, Arist.*Fr.*376, Nic.*Al.*346, Dsc.2.61. II. *hare's ear*, *Bupleurum protractum*, Thphr.*HP*7.7.3. **-πρόσωπος**, ον, *with the face of an ox* or *cow*, Porph.*Abst.*3.16 (βοο- codd.), Lyd.*Mens.*4.46, Phlp. *in GA*185.11. **-πρῳρος**, ον, (πρῷρα) *with the forehead* or *face of an ox*, S.*Tr.*13 (ap.Str.10.2.19; Laur. Ms. βούκρανος); β. πρόσωπα Philostr. Jun.*Im.*4. II. β. ἑκατόμβη offering of 100 sheep *and one ox*, *SIG*604.8 (Delph., ii B.C.), Plu.2.668c, Hsch.; β. θυσία *Delph.*3(2). 66; ἔπεμψαν Κεῖοι δωδεκηΐδα β. ταῦρον Dürrbach *Choix d'Inscriptions de Délos* p.183 (ii A.D.). **-πρως**· ἀσθένεια, Hsch.

βούπτινον, = τρίφυλλον, Hsch.

βουργάριος, ὁ, = Lat. *burgarius*, *SIG*880.52 (Thrace).

βουρδών, ῶνος, ὁ, = βορδών, *mule*, *IG*5(1).1115*B*137, *Edict.Diocl.* 14.10, *PLips.*87.1 (iv A.D.):—hence **βουρδωνάριος**, ὁ, *muleteer*, *Edict. Diocl.*7.17, Sch.Ar.*Th.*498: **βουρδωνάριον**, τό, Dim. of βουρδών, *PRyl.*238.11 (iii A.D.).

βουρικυπάρισσος· ἄμπελος (Perga), Hsch.

βούρινον, τό, = κυνοκεφάλιον, Ps.-Apul.*Herb.*86.

βουριχάλλιον, τό, senator's *ox-cart*, Lyd.*Mag.*1.18.

βούρυγχος, ὁ, a large *fish*, Hsch. **βούρυτος**, ὁ, *mighty river*, Id.

βοῦς, Dor. **βῶς** Theoc.9.7, *GDI*5005.5 (Gortyn), ὁ and ἡ: gen. βοός (written βοιός *GDI* iv p.883 No.62 (Erythrae)), poet. also βοῦ A. *Fr.*421, S.*Fr.*280: acc. βοῦν *IG*1^2.45*A* 11, etc., βῶν Il.7.238 and Dor., *IG*4.914.18, al. (Epid.), *SIG*56.16 (Argos), Theoc.27.64, Ion. and poet. also βόα Pherecyd.162 J., *AP*9.255 (Phil.): dual βόε Hes.*Op.* 436: pl., nom. βόες, rarely contr. βοῦς Ar.*Fr.*760, Plu.*Aem.*33, etc.: gen. βοῶν, contr. βῶν Hes.*Th.*983; Boeot. βουῶν *IG*7.3171.45: dat. βουσί, Ep. βόεσσι, βοσί *AP*7.622 (Antiphil.); Boeot. βούεσσι *IG*7.3171. 38: acc. βόας Il.5.556, al., βοῦς 1.154, al., S.*Aj.*175 (lyr.), and Att., Antiph.172.5, etc. (but later βόας *Ev.Jo.*2.14, *POxy.*729.16 (ii A.D.), etc.):—*bullock*, *bull*, *ox*, or *cow*, in pl. *cattle*, commonly fem.: to mark the male Hom. adds a word, β. ἄρσην Il.20.495; or ταῦρος β. 17.389; as a measure of value, βοὸς ἄξιον 23.885, cf. 7.474 and v. ἀλφεσίβοιος, ἑκατόμβοιος. b. βοῦς ἄγριος *buffalo*, Arist.*HA*499^{a}4. c. βοῦς ἐν Συρίᾳ *zebu*, ib.606^{a}15; β. ἐν Παιονίᾳ, perh. *urus*, Id.*Mir.*842^b 33. d. βοὸς ὄμμα, = βούφθαλμος, *AP*4.1.52 (Mel.). 2. metaph. of any *dam* or *mother*, μία β. Κρηθεῖ τε μάτηρ καὶ Σαλμωνεῖ Pi.*P.*4.142; ἄπεχε τῆς β. τὸν ταῦρον A.*Ag.*1125. II. = βοείη or βοέη (always fem.), *ox-hide shield*, νωμῆσαι βῶν Il.7.238; τυκτῇσι βόεσσιν 12.105; βόας αὔας ib.137; γέρρα λευκῶν β. X.*An.*5.4. 12. III. a *fish*, perh. *Notidanus griseus*, Arist.*HA*540^{b}17, *Fr.* 280. 2. a fish of the Nile, Str.17.2.4. IV. ἕβδομος β. *crescent loaf*, Clidem.16. V. *seam*, Poll.7.65. VI. *the constellation Taurus*, Max.162. VII. = μάστιξ, Hsch. VIII. prov., β. ἐπὶ γλώσσης ἐπιβαίνων Thgn.815; βοῦς ἐπὶ γλώσσῃ βέβηκε A.*Ag.*36; of people who keep silence from some weighty reason, τὸν βοῦν ἐπιτίθημι τῇ γλώττῃ Jul.*Or.*7.218a; βοῦς ἐμβαίνει μέγας Strattis 67 (wrongly expld. by Zen.2.70, etc., of bribery with coins bearing type of ox); β. ἐν πόλει 'bull in a china-shop', Diogenian.3.67; β. ἐν αὐλίῳ, of a useless person, Cratin.32; β. λύρας 'pearls before swine', Macho ap.Ath.8.349c. (βοῦς (from βωὺς, Skt. *gaús*) acc. βῶν (Skt. *gā́m*) are old forms: stem βωϝ- βοϝ-, cf. Lat. (Umbr.) *bos*, etc.)

Βούσβατον· τὴν Ἄρτεμιν (Thracian), Hsch.

βουσέλῑνον, τό, = σμύρνιον, Plin.*HN*20.118, Archig.ap.Gal.12. 406.

βουσή· δούλη, Hsch. **βουσία**· γογγυλίδι ὅμοιον (Thess.), Id.

βουσκᾰφέω, *undermine*, Lyc.434.

βουσκητήριον· εἰς εὐρύνην· εἴρηται κακοσχόλως ἐπὶ τοῦ γυναικείου αἰδοίου, Hsch.

βου-σόη, Lacon. **βουὄα**, ἡ, *herd*, *EM*208.6, 391.19. **-σόος**, v. βοοσσόος.

βουσός, ἡ, *pasture for oxen*, *Schwyzer* 664.15 (Orchom. Arc., iv B.C.).

βούσταθμον, τό, *ox-stall*, E.*Hel.*29, *IA*76, Lyc.92 (pl.): in masc. form, ἀμφὶ βουστάθμους E.*Hel.*359 (lyr.):—as Adj., βουστάθμου κάπης S.*Ichn.*8.

βου-στάνη· βοοστασία, Hsch.: also, = μάστιξ or πληγή, Id. **-στάς**, άδος, ἡ, *where oxen are stalled*, αὐλαί S.*Fr.*321. **-στᾰσία**, ἡ, = βούσταθμον, Luc.*Alex.*1. **-στάσιον** [ᾰ], τό, = foreg., *PFlor.* 50.60 (iii A.D.), *Gp.*2.27.2, Olymp. *in Mete.*113.22. **-στᾰσις**, εως, ἡ, = foreg., A.*Pr.*653 (pl.), *IG*11(2).145.19 (Delos, iv B.C.), D.H.1. 79. **-στροφηδόν**, Adv. *turning like oxen in ploughing*; of writing from left to right and right to left alternately, Euph.ap.Harp. ὁ κάτωθεν νόμος, Paus.5.17.6, Hsch. **-στροφος**, ον, *ploughed by oxen*, Lyc.1438; but, II. parox. **-στρόφος**, ον, *ox-guiding*, δεσμά *AP*6.104 (Phil.); *ox-tormenting*, μύωψ ib.95 (Antiphil.). **-σῡκον**, τό, (βου-) *a large*, *coarse fig*, Hsch., cf. Varro *RR*2.5.4. **-σφᾰγέω**, *slaughter oxen*, E.*El.*627.

βούτᾰλις, ἡ, = ἀηδών, Aesop.85 (v.l. βώτ-). **βουτάνη**, *part of ship to which rudder was fastened*, Hsch.; also expld. as = μάστιξ, or μάχη, ἀηδία, Id.

βούταρος· ὁ παχύς, Hsch. **βουτελέστην**· θύτην, Id.

βούτης, ου, Dor. **βούτας** α, ὁ, (βοῦς) *herdsman*, A.*Pr.*568 (lyr.), E.*Andr.*280 (lyr.), Theoc.1.80, *AP*6.255 (Eryc.), etc.:—as Adj., β. φόνος the slaughter *of kine*, E.*Hipp.*537. II. = ὀρίγανος (Cydonia), Hsch.

βούτῑμος, ον, *worth an ox*, Hsch., *EM*207.5.

βοῦτις or **βοῦττις**, ἡ, *vessel in the shape of the frustum of a cone*, Hero *Stereom.*2.9; βούτη ib.1.52, Aët.3.133:—Dim. **βούτιον** *Hippiatr.*34.

βού-τομον, τό, or **-τομος**, ὁ, (τέμνω) *sedge*, *Carex riparia*, Ar.*Av.* 662, Theoc.13.35: masc., Thphr.*HP*1.10.5: neut., ib.4.10.4, Theoc.

l.c., *Gp.*2.6.28, Lxx *Jb.*8.11. **-τόρος**, ον, = βουπόρος, Suid.: βούτορον ψάκαστρον· νιφάδ' ὑετοῦ, Hsch.

βουτόων· ὁδόν, ἀτραπόν, Hsch. (fort. βουδον, cf. βουσόη).

Βουτράγιος, ὁ (sc. μήν), name of month at Melitaea, *IG*9(2).206 i b 19.

βού-τρᾰγος, ὁ, *ox-goat*, fabulous animal, Philostr.*VA*6.24. **-τρᾰγοταυράνθρωπος**, ὁ, *a compound of ox, goat, bull, and man*, Tz.*H.*7.484. **-τροφία**, ἡ, *feeding of cattle*, Agatharch.7. **-τρόφος**, ον, *ox-feeding*: ὁ βουτρόφος, = βούτης, Poll.1.249, *EM*209.54; cf. βοοτρόφος. **-τρωκτον**, τό, = ὄροβος, Hsch. **-τύπος** [ῠ], ὁ, *ox-butcher, slaughterer*, A.R.2.91, 4.468; esp. of the priest at the Dipolia (cf. βουφόνια), *IG*1².839, 3.1163.2, Clidem.17, Porph.*Abst.*2.30. 2. = οἶστρος, *gadfly*, Opp.*H.*2.529; but = ἐμπίς, Hsch. **-τύρινος** [ῡ], η, ον, *of butter*, μύρον Dsc.1.54. **-τῡρον**, τό, *butter*, τὸ πῖον τοῦ γάλακτος Hp.*Morb.*4.51, cf. Arist.*Fr.*636, Plu.2.1109b, Lxx *Ge.*18.8, Sor.1.86, Dsc.2.72, *Edict.Diocl.*4.50:—also **βούτῡρος**, ὁ, Gal.13.527. II. a *plant*, Hsch.; ὄζει ὁ τόπος β. Ath.9.395a. **-τῡροφάγος** [ᾰ], ον, ὁ, *butter-eater*, Anaxandr.41.8 (prob.). **-φάγος** [ᾰ], ον, *ox-eating*, Simon.179.4, *AP*7.426 (Antip. Sid.); of Hercules, Luc.*Am.*4, Porph.*Abst.*1.22, cf. *AP*9.59 (Antip.): expld. by πολυφάγος, Hsch.

βουφάρας· γεφύρας, Hsch.

βούφαρον· τὴν εὐάροτον γῆν· φάρος γὰρ ἡ ἄροσις· καὶ ἐπίθετον βοός, Hsch.

βούφθαλμον, τό, (βοῦς, ὀφθαλμός) *ox-eye*, *Anacyclus radiatus*, Dsc.3.139, Nic.*Fr.*74.59. 2. = χρυσάνθεμον, Ps.-Dsc.4.58; = ἀείζωον, Dsc.4.88; = βοάνθεμον, Gal.19.87.

βούφθαλμος, ὁ, a *fish*, Marc.Sid.8.

βουφον-έω, *slaughter oxen*, Il.7.466. **-ια** (sc. ἱερά), τά, at Athens, ceremony at the Dipolia, at which *an ox was slain*, Ar.*Nu.*985, Androt.13, Paus.1.28.11, Ael.*VH*8.3. **-ιών**, ῶνος, ὁ, month at Delos, *IG*11.203 *A*32, 52 (iii B.C.); at Tenos, ib.12(5).824. **-ος**, ον, *ox-slaying*, *h.Merc.*436; θεράπων Simon.172.4; πελέκεις D.S.4.12:—as Subst., *priest*, Paus.1.28.10. II. *at* or *for which steers are slain*, θοῖναι A.*Pr.*531 (lyr.).

βουφορβ-έω, *tend cattle*, E.*Alc.*8. **-ια**, τά, *herd of oxen*, ib.1031, *IT*301. **-ός**, όν (fem. -φορβή, of Persephone, *Hymn.Mag.*3.26), *ox-feeding*:—as Subst., *herdsman*, E.*IT*237, Pl.*Plt.*268a.

βού-φορτος, ον, = πολύφορτος, *AP*6.222 (Theodorid.). **-χανδής**, ές, (χανδάνω) *holding an ox*, λέβης ib.153 (Anyte); expld. by πολυχώρητος, Hsch. **-χῑλος**, ον, *rich in fodder*, λειμών A.*Supp.*540 (lyr.); Ἀρκαδίη *AP*6.108 (Myrin.). **-χρώς** τις· ἰσχυρός, ἢ ἴξηρος, Hsch.

βούχωμα· φρόνημα, Hsch.

βοώδης, ες, *ox-like*, Adam.2.37; *stupid*, Apollon.*Lex.* s.v. βουγάϊε.

βοών, ῶνος, ὁ, *cow-house, byre*, *Tab.Heracl.*1.139, Phryn.*PS* p.52 B.

βοῶνα· ὁδόν, and **βοῶνας**· ἀγροικίας, Hsch.

βο-ωνέω, *buy oxen*, *IG*2.163.17. **-ώνης**, ου, ὁ, (ὠνέομαι) at Athens, *an officer who bought oxen for the sacrifices*, D.21.171, *IG*2.163.18. **-ώνητος**, ον, *purchased with an ox*, Hsch.; τὰ β., name of a place in Sparta, Paus.3.12.1. **-ωνία**, ἡ, *purchase of oxen*, *IG*2.741ᵃ8. II. βοωνία· αὔλιος θύρα (Cret.), Hsch. **-ῶπις**, ιδος, ἡ, (ὤψ) *ox-eyed*, i.e. *having large, full eyes*, βοῶπις πότνια Ἥρη Il.1.551, al., cf. Eup.403; of Artemis, B.10.99; Amphitrite, Id.16.110; Harmonia, Pi.*P.*3.91; of women, Il.3.144, 7.10, 18.40:—masc. **βοώπης** Eust.768.43. II. (ὄψ) = μεγαλόφωνος, Hsch. **-ωτέω**, *plough*, Hes.*Op.*391. **-ώτης**, ου, ὁ, *ploughman*, Lyc.268, Babr.52.3, *APl.*4.333 (Antiphil.). II. the constellation *Boötes*, Arat.92; but prob. = the star Ἀρκτοῦρος in Od.5.272. **-ωτία**, ἡ, *arable land* or *ploughing*, Crito Hist.3. **-ωψ**, ωπος, ὁ, small *fish* with large eyes, Ar.Byz.ap.Ath.7.287a. (Expld. as more correct than βό-ωξ, βῶξ (q.v.).)

βρά· ἀδελφοί (Elean), Hsch.

βρᾶ, Aeol. for βράδιον (i.e. ϝράδιον), A.D.*Adv.*163.21, Hdn.Gr.2.214.

βρᾰβ-εία, ἡ, *office of* βραβεύς: generally, *arbitration, judgement*, ὅπως κλύοιμί σου κοινὰς βραβείας E.*Ph.*450, cf. Lyc.1154. **-εῖον**, Ep. **-ήϊον**, τό, *prize in the games*, Men.*Mon.*653, 1 *Ep.Cor.*9.24, Plu.2.742c, Opp.*C.*4.197. II. *wand, baton* given as a prize, τιμηθεὶς χρυσείῳ β. *CIG*3674 (Cyzicus, ii A.D.), cf. *IG*14.748 (Naples). **-ευμα**, ατος, τό, *judge's award*, S.*Fr.*317. **-εύς**, έως, ὁ, Att. pl. βραβῆς: acc. sg. βραβῆ (v. infr.):—*judge at the games*, S.*El.*690, 709, Pl.*Lg.*949a: generally, *judge, arbitrator, umpire*, δίκης E.*Or.*1650; λόγου Id.*Med.*274, etc.; Ἀΐδην κοινὸν ἔθεντο βραβῆ Epigr.ap.D.18.289. 2. generally, *chief, leader*, μυρίας ἵππου β. A.*Pers.*302; φιλόμαχοι β. Id.*Ag.*230 (lyr.); *author*, μόχθων τῶν ἐν Ἰλίῳ, of Helen, E.*Hel.*703. **-ευτής**, οῦ, ὁ, = βραβεύς, Is.9.35, *POxy.*1050.11 (ii/iii A.D.); β. τῶν λόγων Pl.*Prt.*338b; β. τοῦ δικαίου ὁ δικαστής Arist.*Rh.*1376ᵇ20, cf. Ph.2.346, al.; αἱρεῖσθαί τινα β. Plu.*Cat.Mi.*44. II. *official of a religious confraternity*, Buresch *Aus Lydien* 10, Ramsay *Eastern Provinces* 320. **-εύω**, *act as judge* or *umpire*, ἐν τῇ κληρώσει τὴν τύχην βραβεύσειν Isoc.7.23; ὀρθῶς β. Axiop.2.7; *preside* at an election, Plu.*Cat.Mi.*44. II. c. acc., *arbitrate, decide on*, τὰ τῶν ἄλλων δίκαια D.3.27, cf. Arist.*Ath.*9.2; κρίσεις Plu.*Cic.*35; δικαστήριον ib.9; ἅμιλλαν Id.2.960a, etc.: c. acc. et dat., ἀγῶνα ἰσχυρὸν ἐβράβευσεν αὐτῷ Lxx *Wi.*10.12; προσήκει βασιλεῖ τὰ δίκαια β. τοῖς ὑπηκόοις Muson.8 p.33 H.:—Pass., βραβευθήσεται τὰ τοῦ πολέμου τῷ νενικηκότι J.*AJ*6.9.1; τὰ παρά τινι βραβευόμενα Isoc.5.70; συνέβη..τὴν κρίσιν βραβευθῆναι *SIG*685.37 (Cret.). 2. *direct, control*, *Michel*163.10 (Delos), *AP*12.56 (Mel.); νοῦς β. πάντα Ph.1.94:—Pass., Plb.6.4.3, Plu.*Pel.*13; πάντων ὑπὸ τοῦ δαιμονίου -ομένων Phld.*Herc.*1251.7.

βραβύλη, = ἀνεμώνη ἡ φοινική, Ps.-Dsc.2.176.

βράβῠλον, τό, *sloe*, *Prunus spinosa*, Theoc.7.146 (wrongly expld. by Sch. as *damson*), 12.3, Antyll.ap.Orib.10.20.4, Gal.6.621. II. = κοκκύμηλον (q.v.), Seleuc.ap.Ath.2.50a, Clearch.82.

βράβῠλος, ἡ, *the tree which bears* βράβυλα, Aret.*CA*2.2, *Gp.*10.39. II. = βράβυλον, *AP*9.377 (Pall.). III. *seedling peach*, *Gp.*10.13.5. (The forms βράβιλος, βράβηλος are found in codd. of *Gp.* and *AP*, βράβηλον *EM*211.3, βράβιλον codd. of Theoc. and Ath.)

βράγος, = βράχος (B), Hsch.

βραγχ-ᾰλέος, α, ον, (βράγχος) *hoarse*, Hp.*Acut.*(*Sp.*)55. **-άω**, *to have a sore throat*, Arist.*HA*603ᵇ13, D.C.63.26, Porph.*Abst.*3.7. **-εία**, ἡ, = βράγχος I.1, Hsch. **-η**, ἡ, = βράγχος I.2, Xenocr.52. **-ιάζοισθε**· πνίγοισθε, Hsch. **-ιάω**, = βραγχάω, Arist.*Pr.*901ᵇ5, *Aud.*804ᵃ18, Lxx *Ps.*68(69).3; condemned by Phot. s.v. λιθῶντας. **-ιοειδής**, ές, = βραγχοειδής, Arist.*HA*526ᵇ20. **-ιον**, τό, *fin*, dub. in Arion 1.4 (βράγχιοι codd. Ael.). II. in pl., *gills of fishes*, Arist.*HA*589ᵇ19, *PA*696ᵇ1, Theoc.11.54 (sg., Ael.*NA*16.12). III. = βρόγχιον, βρόγχος, dub.l. in Arist.*Spir.*483ᵃ22, cf. *HA*603ᵃ32. IV. *hull* of a ship, Hsch. **-ιώδης**, ες, = βραγχοειδής, Arist.*HA*526ᵃ26.

βραγχοειδής, ές, *like fishes' gills*, Arist.*PA*684ᵃ20.

βράγχος, ὁ, *hoarseness* or *sore throat causing hoarseness*, Hp.*VM*19 (pl.), al., Th.2.49: pl., Arist.*Pr.*860ᵃ30, 37. 2. a *disease* in swine (either *anthrax* or *foot-and-mouth disease*), Id.*HA*603ᵃ31. II. βράγχος, τό, in pl., = βράγχια, Opp.*H.*1.160; but βράγχος, ὁ, in Ptol.*Alm.*8.1.

βραγχός, ή, όν, *hoarse*, βραγχὰ λαρυγγιόων *AP*11.382.2 (Agath.).

βραγχώδης, ες, *subject to hoarseness*, Hp.*Aër.*6, *Epid.*1.1. Adv. -δῶς Gal.13.4. 2. *causing it*, ὕδατα -έστατα Hp.*Aër.*7.

βρᾰδᾰνίζω (= ϝραδ-)· ῥιπίζω, τινάσσω (Aeol.), Hsch.

βράδινος [ᾰ], α, ον, Aeol. for ῥαδινός, Sapph.90, 104.

βράδιον, Aeol., = ϝράδιον, *EM*210.43.

βράδος [ᾰ], εος, τό, = βραδυτής, X.*Eq.*11.12, Epicur.*Ep.*1 p.10 U.

βρᾰδῠ-ανάφορος, ον, *slow-rising*, τὰ β. τῶν ζῳδίων Anon. *in Ptol.Tetr.*114. **-βάμων** [ᾱ], ον, gen. ονος, *slow-walking*, Arist.*Phgn.*813ᵃ3. **-βουλία**, ἡ, *slowness of counsel*, Ph.2.662. **-γάμος**, ον, *late in marrying*, Ptol.*Tetr.*183. **-γενής**, ές, *late born*, Sch. Lyc.1276. **-γλωσσος**, Att. **-ττος**, ον, *slow of tongue*, Lxx *Ex.*4.10, *Cat.Cod.Astr.*2.167, Ps.-Luc.*Philopatr.*13. **-δῑνής**, ές, *slow-eddying* or *whirling*, Nonn.*D.*37.482. **-ήκοος**, ον, (ἀκούω) *slow of hearing*, *EM*430.28. **-θάνᾰτος** [θᾰ], ον, *dying slowly*, Gal.16.631. **-καρπος**, ον, *late-fruiting*, Thphr.*CP*5.17.6. **-κατάφορος**, ον, *slow in setting*, ζῴδια Sch.Ptol.*Tetr.*114. **-κίνητος** [ῑ], ον, *slow-moving*, Gal.5.318, Adam.1.7: Comp. -τότερος Phlp. *in Ph.*680.31: Subst. **-κῑνησία**, ἡ, Aristid.Quint.2.9, Diog.Oen.71. **-κρίσῐμος** [ρῐ], ον, *slow in reaching a crisis*, Herod.Med. in *Rh.Mus.*58.95. **-λογία**, ἡ, *slowness of speech*, Poll.2.121:—Adj. **-λόγος**, ον, Sch.Ven.Il.3.155. **-μᾰθής**, ές, *slow in learning*, Hsch. s.v. ὀψιμαθής:—Subst. **-μᾰθία**, ἡ, Zonar. **-νοια**, ἡ, *slowness of understanding*, D.L.7.93. **-νοος**, ον, contr. **-νους**, ουν, *slow of understanding*, Dam.*Isid.*81.

βρᾰδύνω, fut. -ῠνῶ Lxx *De.*7.10: aor. ἐβράδῡνα Luc.*Cont.*1, App.*BC*1.69: plpf. ἐβεβραδύκειν Luc.*Symp.*20: (βραδύς): I. trans., *make slow, delay*, Lxx *Is.*46.13:—Pass., *to be delayed*, τἀπὸ σοῦ βραδύνεται S.*OC*1628; ἡ δ' ὁδὸς βραδύνεται Id.*El.*1501. II. intr., *loiter, delay*, εἰ βραδύνοιμεν βοῇ A.*Supp.*730 (so in Med., χεῖρα δ' οὐ βραδύνεται..ἁρπάσαι δόρυ Id.*Th.*623); μὴ βράδυνε S.*Ph.*1400; σπεύδων..βραδύνω Pl.*R.*528d: c. inf., Polyaen.1.48.4; βραδύνει σοι τοῦτο; *are you slow, slack in this?* Philostr.*Im.*1.6.

βρᾰδῠ-πειθής, ές, (πείθομαι) *slow to be persuaded*, *AP*5.286 (Agath.). II. *reluctant*, Nonn.*D.*4.313. **-πεπτέω**, *digest slowly*, Dsc.5.39. **-πεπτος**, ον, *slow of digestion*, v.l. in Gal.6.770 (Comp.). **-πεψία**, ἡ, *slowness of digestion*, Sor.1.51, Dsc.5.38 (pl.), Gal.7.62. **-πλοέω**, *sail slowly*, *Act.Ap.*27.7, Artem.4.30, *AB*225. **-πνοος**, ον, *breathing slowly*, Aret.*SD*1.10. **-πορέω**, *proceed slowly*, of the sun, *Placit.*5.18.1. **-πόρος**, ον, *slow-passing*, of food, Hp.*Acut.*62, Ruf.ap.Orib.5.3.4, Philagr.ib.5.19.4; of humours, Gal.7.341: generally, *slow*, ὅρασις Plu.2.626a; β. πέλαγος *slow to pass*, ib.941b. **-πους**, ὁ, ἡ, πουν, τό, gen. ποδος, *slow of foot, slow*, ἤλυσις E.*Hec.*66 (anap.); ὄνος *AP*9.301 (Secund.), cf. 310 (Antiphil.); βουλή ib.10.37 (Luc.).

βρᾰδύς, εῖα, ύ: Comp. βραδύτερος Th.4.8; metath. βαρδύτερος Theoc.29.30; βραδίων Artem.1.70: Sup. βραδύτατος Ar.*Fr.*357, also βράδιστος (metath. βάρδιστος Il.23.310, 530, Doroth(?).ap.Heph.*Astr.*3.30) Aret.*SD*1.6, βραδίστατος Ael.*Fr.*325:—*slow*, κιχάνει τοι β. ὠκύν Od.8.329, etc.: c. inf., ἀλλά τοι ἵπποι βάρδιστοι θείειν *slowest* at running, Il.23.310; β. λέγειν E.*HF*237, etc.; τὸ β. *delay*, Pl.*Lg.*766e. Adv. βραδέως, χωρεῖν Th.5.70; θεῖν Pl.*Prt.*336a, etc.: Comp. -ύτερον Hp.*Prog.*22, Pl.*Tht.*190a; βραδυτέρως Aen.Tact.16.12; βράδιον Hes.*Op.*528, Sor.1.117 (condemned by Luc.*Sol.*7): Sup. -ύτατα Pl.*Ti.*39b. 2. of the mind, *dull, sluggish*, ἐπιλήσμων καὶ β. Ar.*Nu.*129; opp. ἀγχίνους, Pl.*Phdr.*239a; βράδιστοι τὴν γνώμην Aret. l.c.: c. inf., προνοῆσαι βραδεῖς Th.3.38; τὸ β. καὶ μέλλον *slowness* and deliberation, Th.1.84. Adv. βραδέως, βουλεύεσθαι ib.78; β. ὀλίγην ὀργὴν ποιεῖσθαι Pl.*Phdr.*233c. 3. in Egypt, of illiterates, βραδέως, βραδύτερον γράφειν, *PTeb.*316.101 (i A.D.), *PRyl.*173.13 (i A.D.); also βραδέα γράφουσα *BGU*446.19 (ii A.D.). II. of Time, *tardy, late*, σὺν χρόνῳ β. μολών S.*Tr.*395, cf. Th.7.43; βραδεῖαν.. ὁδὸν πέμπων S.*Aj.*738. Adv., ἕως βραδέως ἦν τῆς ἡμέρας D.L.2.139: neut. as Adv., ὀψὲ καὶ βραδὺ τῆς ἡλικίας Hld.2.29; βράδιον ἀπογαλακτίζειν Sor. l. c.

βρᾰδῠ-σῑτέω, *eat late in the day*, Alex.Trall.7.6:—Subst. **-σῑτία**, ἡ, Id.1.15, 11.1. **-σκελής**, ές, *slow of leg*, Ἥφαιστε *AP*6.101 (Phil.).

βρᾰδυσμός, ὁ, *making slow*, Sch.E.*Or.*426.

βρᾰδῠτεκνία, ἡ, *lateness in having offspring*, *Cat.Cod.Astr.*2.163.

βρᾰδυτής, ῆτος, ἡ, *slowness, sluggishness*, βραδυτῆτί τε νωχελίῃ τε Il.19.411; so of persons, S.*Ant.*932 (anap.), Th.1.71, 5.75, Pl.*Phd.*109d, Thphr.*Char.*14.1: in pl., Isoc.4.141, D.18.246: lit. *slowness*, opp. τάχος, Pl.*Ti.*39b, cf. Arist.*Ph.*228^{b}29.

βρᾰδῠ-τόκος, ον, *slow in bringing to birth*, Arist.*Pr.*891^{b}28 (Comp.). **-χρόνιος**, ον, *late*, Sch.Il.2.325.

βράδων· ἀδύνατος, Hsch.

βράζω, *boil, froth up, ferment*, Call.Hist.3, Hld.5.16, Alex.Aphr. *Pr.*1.104. II. *growl*, of bears, Poll.5.88; of elephants, Juba ap. Poll. l. c.; but βράζειν· τὸ ἡσυχῇ ὀδύρεσθαι, Hsch.

βράθυ, υος, τό, *savin, Juniperus Sabina*, Dsc.1.76; also, = *J. foetidissima*, ibid. (Aram. berāt 'cypress'.)

βράκαι, ῶν, αἱ, Lat. *braccae, breeches, trews, worn by the Gauls*, D.S.5.30 (**βράκες** (sic)· ἀναξυρίδες, Hsch.):—Dim. **βράκια**, τά, Sch.Ar.*V.*1082, *PGiss.*80.6 (iv A.D.), *IG*5(1).1406.23 (Edict. Diocl., Asine):—hence **βρακάριος**, ὁ, *breeches-maker*, ib.18, cf. *POxy.*1341 (iv A.D.):—but **βρακαρίαι**, αἱ, *breeches*, *PGiss.*90.6 (ii A.D.).

βράκαλον· ῥόπαλον, Hsch.

βράκανα, τά, *wild herbs*, Pherecr.13, Luc.*Lex.*2, Hsch.

βρακεῖν, βρακείς, Aeol., = συνιέναι, συνείς, Hsch.

βρακέλλαι, αἱ, = βράκαι, *BGU*814.29 (iii A.D.).

βράκετ(ρ)ον, τό, *pruning-hook*, Hsch.; also = πλῆθος, Id.

βράκια, τά, = βράκαι, *PGen.*80.6 (iv A.D.).

βρακίας· τραχεῖς τόπους, Hsch. (fort. βραχ-, cf. ῥαχία).

βράκος (i. e. *ϝ*ράκος), εος, τό, *long robe*, Sapph.70; ὑδάτινα β. Theoc.28.11. II. = κάλαμος, Hsch.

βράπτω, aor. inf. βράψαι, = μάρπτω, Hsch. (βράξαι is f.l. for βράψαι).

βράσις [ᾰ], εως, ἡ, *boiling*, of water, Orib.5.33.3.

βράσμα, ατος, τό, *boiling*, μέχρι βρασμάτων ἑπτά Aët.6.80. II. v. l. for βρέγμα, Dsc.2.159. III. *shaking motion*, Herod.Med. in *Rh.Mus.*58.81.

βρασμᾰτίας, ου, ὁ, = βράστης, opp. σεισματίας, Posidon.ap.D.L.7.154, Amm.Marc.17.7.13 (pl.), Heraclit.*All.*38.

βρασμός, ὁ, *boiling up*, Aët.1.130, Hld.5.17; *fermentation*, τῆς ὕλης Corn.*ND*3: hence, *agitation, shaking*, γῆς Arist.ap.Ar.Did.*Fr.*13 (pl.), Orph.*H.*47.3 (pl.), Sor.1.65; *shivering* as if from cold, ib.80, Aret.*SD*2.3; *rigor*, Gal.7.607. 2. metaph., τοῦ πάθους, τῶν παθῶν, Ph.1.306, 238. II. = βράστης, J.*BJ*1.19.4, D.C.68.24, Phlp. *in Mete.*7.23, Agath.5.3; of a tidal wave, Id.2.16.

βρασσιότροχος· κεραμικὸς ὁ μὴ ἐρρωγώς, Hsch.

βράσσω, Att. -ττω, aor. ἔβρᾰσα Hp.*Ep.*23, etc.:—**Pass.**, aor. ἐβράσθην Aret.*SA*1.5: pf. βέβρασμαι (v. infr.):—*shake violently, throw up*, of the sea, σκολόπενδραν.. ἔβρασ' ἐπὶ σκοπέλους *AP*6.222 (Theodorid.); τὸν πρέσβυν.. ἔβρασε.. εἰς ἠϊόνα ib.7.294 (Tull.Laur.):—Pass., ὀστέα.. βέβρασται.. τῇδε παρ' ἠϊόνι ib.288 (Antip.), cf. Opp.*H.*1.779; *boil*, of surf, A.R.2.323, Opp.*H.*3.476; β. ὑπὸ γέλωτος *shake* with laughter, Luc.*Eun.*12. 2. *winnow* grain, Ar.*Fr.*271, Pl.*Sph.*226b. 3. abs., = βράζω, *boil*, interpol. in *Gp.*7.15.20; dub. sens. in Hp. l. c. 4. βράττειν· πληθύνειν, βαρύνειν, Hsch.

βράσσων, ον, Homeric Comp. of βραχύς (q. v.).

βραστέον, *one must winnow*, *Gp.*3.7.1.

βραστήρ, ῆρος, ὁ, *winnowing-fan*, *Gloss.*

βράστης, ου, ὁ, (βράσσω) of an earthquake, *upheaving the earth vertically*, Arist.*Mu.*396^{a}3.

βραστικός, ή, όν, f.l. for βλαστικός, Herm.ap.Stob.1.41.7.

βρατάναν· τορύνην (Elean), Hsch. **βρατάνει**· ῥαΐζει ἀπὸ νόσου (Elean), Id. **βράταχος**, v. βάτραχος.

βραυκᾰνάομαι, v.l. for βρυχανάομαι, Nic.*Al.*221; *cry*, of infants, Hsch.

βραύκη, = ἀκρίς, Hsch.: **βραῦκος**, = μικρὰ ἀκρίς (Cret.), *AB*223; cf. βρεῦκος. **βραύλα**· φθείρ, Hsch. **βραῦλον**· κοῖλον, Id. **βραῦνα**· κήλη, κύστις, ἐντεροκήλη, Id. **βραυνία**· κοιλώματα γῆς, Id. **βραυῶσα**· κεκραγυῖα, Id.

βράχαλον· χρεμετισμόν, Hsch.

βράχεα, τά, as if from a nom. βράχος, τό (or **βραχέα**, neut. pl. of βραχύς, Arist.*HA*568^{b}28):—*shallows*, Hdt.2.102, 4.179, Th.2.91, Plb.1.39.3, etc.: sg. only late, Procop.*Pers.*1.19, *Goth.*1.1.

βρᾰχεῖν, aor. with no pres. in use, inf. only in Hsch., elsewh. in 3 sg. ἔβραχε or βράχε:—onomatop. Verb, *rattle, clash, ring*, mostly of arms and armour, δεινὸν ἔβραχε χαλκός Il.4.420; βράχε τεύχεα χαλκῷ 12.396, Hes.*Sc.*423, etc.; βράχε δ' εὐρεῖα χθών (with the din of battle) Il.21.387; μέγας ἔβραχεν αἰθήρ A.R.4.642; of a torrent, *roar*, βράχε δ' αἰπὰ ῥέεθρα Il.21.9; ἔβραχε δ' ἅλμη Q.S.14.527; *creak*, μέγα δ' ἔβραχε φήγινος ἄξων Il.5.838; *shriek* or *roar* with pain, ὁ δ' ἔβραχε χάλκεος Ἄρης ib.859; ὁ δ' ἔβραχε θυμὸν ἀΐσθων (of a wounded horse) 16.468; *shout* a command, c. inf., A.R.2.573.

βρᾰχείς, εῖσα, έν, v. βρέχω.

βρᾰχῑάλιον, τό, *bracelet*, Sm., Th.2 *Ki.*1.10:—also **-άριον**, τό, Aq. ibid., and **βραχιόλιον**, τό, Alex.Trall.1.15.

βρᾰχ-ῑόνιον, τό, = sq., Roussel *Cultes Égyptiens* 235 (Delos, ii B.C.), Poll.5.99. **-ῑονιστήρ**, ῆρος, ὁ, *armlet*, Plu.*Rom.*17, Tz.*H.*13.48. **-ίων** [ῑ], ονος, ὁ, *arm* (opp. πῆχυς, Pl.*Ti.*75a, but = πῆχυς, Arist.*MA*698^{b}2), Il.13.529, Hdt.5.12, X.*Eq.*12.5, Arist.*HA*493^{b}26, etc.; πρυμνὸς βραχίων *the shoulder*, Il.13.532, 16.323; also, *shoulder of beasts*, ib.594^{b}13:—Poet. as a symbol of strength, ἐκ βραχιόνων by *force of arm*, E.*Supp.*478.

βρᾰχίων [Ion. ῐ, Att. ῑ], **βράχιστος**, Comp. and Sup. of βραχύς.

βραχμάζουσαι· χρεμετίζουσαι, Hsch.

Βραχμᾶνες, οἱ, *Brahmans*, D.Chr.49.7, Luc.*Fug.*6, etc.

βράχος (A) [ᾰ], ὁ, prob. f. l. for βάτραχος, Ephipp.13.

βράχος (B), εος, τό, v. βράχεα.

βρᾰχῠ-βάμων [ᾱ], ον, gen. ονος, *taking short steps*, Arist.*Phgn.*813^{a}5. **-βῐος**, ον, *short-lived*, Pl.*R.*546a, Arist.*HA*494^{a}1, etc.: Comp., Hp.*Art.*41, Arist.*HA*501^{b}23; of plants, Thphr.*HP*4.13.1 (= χειλιδόνιον μέγα, Ps.-Dsc.2.180): Sup. -ώτατος Str.16.4.12. **-βῐότης**, ητος, ἡ, *shortness of life*, Arist.*Pr.*964^{a}35 (he also wrote περὶ μακρο- καὶ βραχυβιότητος); of plants, Thphr.*HP*4.13.1. **-βλᾰβής**, ές, *harming slightly*, Luc.*Trag.*323. **-βωλος**, ον, *with small* or *few clods*, β. χέρσος a *small* spot of ground, *AP*6.238 (Apollonid.): Ἴκος ib.7.2 (Antip. Sid.). **-γνώμων**, ον, gen. ονος, *of small understanding*, X.*Eq.Mag.*4.18 (Comp.). **-γρᾰφέω**, *write with a short syllable*, Tz.*H.*8.701. **-δάκτῠλος**, ον, *short-fingered*, Polem.*Phgn.*86. **-δρομος**, ον, *running a short way*, X.*Cyn.*5.21 (Sup.). **-έπεια**, ἡ, *laconic style*, dub. l. in Rutil.2.8. **-ῆλιξ**, -ῐκος, *youthful*, Eust.1554.2. **-θάλασσος** [θᾰ], ον, gloss on εὔφαλον (sic, i. e. ἔφαλον), Hsch. **-κατάληκτος**, ον, *ending in a short syllable*, A.D.*Pron.*50.24, Arc.192.20. Adv. -τως f. l. for -παραλήκτως (q. v.), Sch.Ar.*Pl.*1057, = Suid. s. v. παιδιά. II. β. μέτρον, *short by a foot*, Heph.4.4, Aristid.Quint.1.23:—hence **-καταληκτέω**, *to end so*, Sch.Ar.*Ra.*317:—Subst. **-καταληξία**, ἡ, *such an ending*, Heph.*Poëm.*5. **-κέφᾰλος**, ὁ, a *fish*, Xenocr.19. **-κίνητος** [ῑ], ον, *accompanied by slight motion*, ἐνέργεια Porph.*Gaur.*1.3. **-κομέω**, *wear short hair*, Str.11.11.8. **-κωλία**, ἡ, *use of short members*, Hermog.*Id.*1.12. **-κωλος**, ον, *with short strings*, of slings, Str.3.5.1. II. *consisting of short clauses*, περίοδοι Arist.*Rh.*1409^{b}31. **-λογέω**, *to be brief in speech*, Id.*Rh.Al.*1434^{b}10, Plu.2.193d, Demetr.*Eloc.*242; ὧδε ἐβραχυλόγησε, introducing a quotation, Philostr.*VA*4.33. **λόγημα**, ατος, τό, *pithy saying*, Tz.*H.*5.317. **-λογητέον**, *one must be brief in speech*, Arist.*Rh.Al.*1441^{a}18. **-λογία**, ἡ, *brevity in speech* or *writing*, Hp.*Decent.*12, Pl.*Grg.*449c; β. τις Λακωνική Id.*Prt.*343b, etc.; ἡ Πιττακοῦ β. Plu.2.153e, cf. Demetr.*Eloc.*243 (pl.); opp. μῆκος, Pl.*Lg.*887b. **-λογος**, ον, *short in speech, of few words*, Id.*Grg.*449c (Comp.), etc.; of the Spartans, Id.*Lg.*641e, Demetr.*Eloc.*7, etc. Adv. -γως Poll.4.24.

βρᾰχῠλός, = μικρός, dub. in Hsch.

βρᾰχῠ-μέρεια, ἡ, *aggregate of small elements*, νεφελοειδής, the 'Milky Way', Gem.5.68. **-μετρος**, ον, *short in measurement*, Aristeas 55. **-μογής**, ές, *losing one's breath rapidly*, Hp.*Epid.*2.2.24. **-μῡθία**, ἡ, = βραχυλογία, Suid.

βρᾰχύνω, *abridge, shorten*, i. e. *to be a sign of a brief attack*, Hp.*Aph.*1.12; *use as short*, συλλαβήν Pl.*Per.*4:—Pass., opp. μηκύνομαι, Luc.*Hist.Conscr.*55; -όμενον φωνῆεν Heph.1.1, D.T.633.

βρᾰχῠ-νωτος [ῠ], ον, *short-backed*, Orac.ap.Str.6.1.12, Ruf.ap.Orib.7.26.9; στέρνον χθονὸς dub. in Pi.*Pae.*4.14. **-όνειρος**, ον, *with short* or *few dreams*, ὕπνος Pl.*Ti.*45e; φαντασίαι Plu.2.686b. **-παραλήκτως**, Adv. *with short penult.*, Sch.Ar.*Pl.*253. **-πνοέω**, *to be short of breath*, Antyll.ap.Orib.6.21.9. **-πνοια**, ἡ, *shortness of breath*, Gal.7.836. **-πνοος**, ον, contr. **-πνους**, ουν, *short of breath*, Hp.*Epid.*3.17.ιε'. **-πόρος**, ον, *with a short orbit*, of a cycle of births, Pl.*R.*546a; οἱ β. ὄρνιθες *of short flight*, Philostr.*VA*3.48: Comp., *completing an orbit in shorter time*, Procl.*Hyp.*1.24. 2. *with narrow passage*, εἴσπλους Plu.*Mar.*15 (dub. l.). **-πότης**, ου, ὁ, *one that drinks little*, Hp.*Prorrh.*1.16. **-πότος**, ον, *drinking little*, Gal.17(1).755. **-πτερος**, ον, *short-winged*, Arist.*PA*644^{a}20. **-πτολις**, εως, ἡ, *little city*, Lyc.911:—also **-πολις**, Adj. *belonging to a small city*, Νιρεύς Eust.317.29. **-ρρεπής**, ές, *short in weight*: Comp. -έστερον *a smaller weight*, Damocr.ap.Gal.13.1004. **-ρρήμων**, ον, gen. ονος, (ῥῆμα) *brief of speech*, Them.*Or.*26.315a. **-ρρῐζία**, ἡ, *shortness of root*, Thphr.*CP*3.7.2. **-ρρῐζος**, ον, *with a short root*, ib.1.

βρᾰχύς, εῖα (Ion. έα Hdt.5.49), ύ, dat. pl. βραχέοις *JHS*33.317 (Thess.): Comp. βραχύτερος, βραχίων (cf. βράσσων): Sup. βραχύτατος, βράχιστος:—*short*, 1. of Space and Time, β. οἶμος, ὁδός, Pi.*P.*4.248, Pl.*Lg.*718e, etc.; [αἰών] prob. in B.3.74; βίος Hdt.7.46; καιρός Call.*Ep.*9; χρόνος A.*Pr.*939, *Pers.*713, etc.; μῦθος, λόγος, Id.*Pr.*505, v. l. in *Pers.*713; ἐν βραχεῖ (Ion. βραχέϊ) *in a short time*, Hdt.5.24, Pl.*Smp.*217a codd.; διὰ βραχέος Th.2.83; μακρὰν συνήθειαν βραχεῖ λῦσαι χρόνῳ Men.726; βραχὺ τηδὶ μεταστῶμεν *for a moment*, Id.*Georg.*32; of distance, β. ἀπόδοσις *short return* in ball-play, Antiph.234.6; ἐπὶ βραχὺ ἐξικνεῖσθαι X.*An.*3.3.17; πρὸ βραχέος Iamb.*VP*25.112: Comp., ἡ φάλαγξ -υτέρα ἐγένετο ἀναδιπλουμένη X.*Cyr.*7.5.5; τάξιν -υτέραν ἢ πρόσθεν, βαθυτέραν δὲ ποιήσαντες Plb.1.33.10; βραχύτερα τοξεύειν X.*An.*3.3.7. Adv. βραχέως, [πολέμους] ἐπ' ἀλλήλους ἐπιφέρειν *scantily, seldom*, Th.1.141. 2. of Size, *short, small*, μορφάν β. Pi.*I.*4(3).53; βραχὺς ἐξικέσθαι θεῶν ἕδραν *too puny* to reach.., ib.7(6).44; β. τεῦχος S.*El.*1113, cf. 757; β. τεῖχος a *low* wall, Th.7.29; βραχύ μοι στόμα πάντ' ἀναγήσασθαι my mouth is *too small* to.., Pi.*N.*10.19; κατὰ β. προϊών *little by little*, Th.1.64, cf. Pl. *Sph.*241c; παρὰ βραχύ *scarcely, hardly*, φυγεῖν Alciphr.3.5; βραχύ τι λωφᾶν ἀπὸ νόσου καὶ πολέμου Th.6.12; ἁλὸς βραχύ *a small quantity* of salt, Bilabel'Οψαρτ.p.11. 3. of Number, *few*, ἐν βραχεῖ in *few words*, Pi.*P.*1.82, S.*El.*673; ἐν βραχίστοις Pi.*I.*6(5).59; ἐν βραχυτέροις Pl.*Grg.*449c; so διὰ βραχέων in *few words*, Id.*Prt.*336a; ὡς ἂν δύνωμαι διὰ βραχυτάτων D.27.3, Lys.16.9, cf. Pl.*Grg.*449c; ὡς ἐν βραχυτάτοις Antipho 1.18. Adv. βραχέως, ἀπολογεῖσθαι *briefly, in few words*, X.*HG*1.7.5. 4. of Value or Importance, of persons, *humble, insignificant*, S.*OC*880; τὸν μὲν ἀφ' ὑψηλῶν βραχὺν ᾤκισε E. *Heracl.*613; β. τὴν διάνοιαν J.*AJ*12.4.1; of things, *petty, trifling*, ἀρχὴ β. ἐλπίδος S.*OT*121; χάρις Id.*Tr.*1217; πρόφασις E.*IA*1180; β. τις ἀσάφεια a *slight* obscurity, Gal.18(1).304; λυπεῖν τινὰ βραχύ, opp. μέγ' εὑρεῖν κέρδος, S.*El.*1304; οὐ περὶ βραχέων βουλεύεσθαι Th. 1.78, cf. 140; β. καὶ οὐδενὸς ἄξιον Id.8.76; β. κέρδους ἕνεκα Lys.7.17; οὐσία Is.10.25: neut. as Adv., βραχὺ φροντίζειν τινός think *lightly* of, D.17.4. 5. *short*, of vowels or syllables, Arist.*Cat.*4^{b}34, *Rh.* 1409^{a}18, *Po.*1458^{a}15, Heph.1.1, D.T.631, etc.; ἡ β. προσῳδία the sign ᵕ, S.E.*M.*1.113. (Cf. Avest. *mərəzu-* 'short', Goth. *gamaurgjan* 'shorten', Lat. *brevis*.)

βρᾰχύ-σημος [ῠ], ον, in Comp., *containing fewer time-units*, πούς Aristid.Quint.1.24. **-σίδηρος** [ῐ], Dor. **-σίδᾱρος**, ον, ἄκων β. a dart *with a short, small head*, Pi.*N.*3.45. **-σκελής**, ές, *short-legged*, S.*Ichn.*297, Arist.*PA*692^{b}5, *IA*714^{a}13, Gal.*UP*3.3, *Gp.*19. 6.2. **-σκῐος**, ον, *with a short shadow*, Ach.Tat.*Intr.Arat.* 31. **-στελέχης**, ες, *with a short stem*, Thphr.*HP*4.6.10. **-στῐχος**, ον, *of few verses*, Eust.ad D.P.1039. **-στομία**, ἡ, *smallness of mouth*, Eust.767.16. **-στομος**, ον, *with narrow mouth*, λιμήν Str.14.1.24; ἀγγεῖα Plu.2.47e. **-συλλᾰβία**, Ep. -ίη, ἡ, *fewness of syllables, brevity*, Call.*Ep.*10. **-σύλλᾰβος**, ον, *of short syllables*, D.H.*Comp.*17, Longin.41.3; χρόνος, *occupied by a 'short'*, Bacch. *Harm.*94. 2. of the pulse, *with rapid rhythm*, Ruf.*Syn.Puls.* 4.4. **-σύμβολος**, ον, *bringing a small contribution*, *AP*9.229 (Marc. Arg.). **-σώμᾰτος**, ον, *short of body*, Plu.*Fr.inc.* 149. **-τελής**, ές, *ending shortly, brief*, Lxx *Wi.*15.9.

βρᾰχύτης [ῠ], ητος, ἡ, *shortness*, opp. μῆκος, Pl.*Plt.*283c; μελέτης βραχύτητι with *shortness* of practice, Th.1.138; *narrowness, deficiency*, μετὰ βραχύτητος γνώμης Id.3.42. 2. *smallness*, τοῦ βάθους Arist.*Mete.*354^{a}18. 3. *shortness* of a syllable, in prosody, Pl.*R.*400c (pl.), Arist.*Po.*1456^{b}32, Plu.2.947e, S.E.*M.*1.100. 4. *scantiness*, τῶν ὄντων Lib.*Or.*62.59. 5. *shallowness*, θαλάττης Scyl. 112. 6. Rhet., *use of a condensed* or *allusive expression*, Trypho *Trop.*p.202 S.

βρᾰχῠ-τομέω, *prune close*, Thphr.*CP*3.14.2, *Gp.*5.32. **-τομος**, ον, *cut short, clipped*, Thphr.*CP*3.2.3. **-τονέω**, *have a short* τόνος (q.v.), of torsion-engines, Ph.*Bel.*53.30. **-τονος**, ον, *with a short* τόνος (q.v.), of torsion-engines, ib.53.34, Plu.*Marc.*15. **-τράχηλος** [τρᾰ], ον, *short-necked*, Pl.*Phdr.*253e, Arist.*HA*597^{b}26. **-ϋπνος**, ον, *of short* or *little sleep*, Id.*Somn.*454^{b}19, *HA*537^{a}2. **-φεγγίτης** [ῐ], ου, ὁ, *giving a feeble light*, λύχνος *AP*6.251(Phil.). **-φυλλος**, ον, *with few leaves*, δένδρον ib.9.612. **-φωνία**, ἡ, *smallness, weakness of voice*, Polyaen.1.21.2. **-χειρ**, ὁ, ἡ, gen. χειρος, *short-handed*, opp. μακρόχειρ, Eust.610.32. **-χρόνιος**, ον, *of brief duration*, γένος Pl. *Ti.*75c(Comp.); τὸ β. τοῦ βίου Plu.2.107a. **-ωτος**, ον, (οὖς) *with short handles*, κώθων Henioch.1.

βραχώδης· τραχύς, Hsch. (Cf. ῥαχίς.)

βρέβιον, τό, (Lat. *brevis*) *list, inventory*, *IG*12(9).907.15 (Chalcis, iv A.D.), *Cod.Just.*4.21.22 (pl.); βρέουιον *PLond.*2.414.9 (iv A.D.).

βρέγκος, ὁ, a sobriquet of doubtful meaning, Φίλιππος ὁ β. Herod. 2.73. (Perh. βρεῦκος should be read.)

βρέγμα, ατος, τό, *front part of the head*, Batr.228, Hp.*VC*2, Stratt.34, Arist.*HA*491^{a}31, al., *PA*653^{a}35, Herod.4.51, 8.9, etc.:—also **βρεγμός** *EM*212.14; βρέχμα, βρεχμός, βροχμός (q.v.) (prob. from βρέχω, because this part of the bone is longest in hardening, Hp. l.c., Arist. *GA*744^{a}24). 2. in pl., *parietal bones*, Gal.17(2).3. 3. *substance found in peppercorns*, Dsc.2.159. II. = ἀπόβρεγμα, *infusion, extract*, D.S.3.32. III. *drenching* with rain, Erot. s.v. ὕσματα (pl.).

βρεκάριος, = βρακ-, *PLond.ined.*2176 (vi A.D.).

βρεκεκεκέξ, formed to imitate *the croaking of frogs*, Ar.*Ra.*209 sqq.

βρέκται· φυσσῆται, Hsch.

βρεκτέον, *one must soak*, *Gp.*3.8.

βρεκτός, ή, όν, *soaked*, *Hippiatr.*129.

βρέλλιον, τό, perh. f.l. for βδέλλιον, *POxy.*1142.3 (iii A.D.).

βρέμβος· ἔμβρυον, Hsch. **βρεμεαίνων**· ἠχῶν, Id.

βρέμω, only pres. and impf. (aor. ἔβραμεν, vv.ll. ἔβραχεν, ἔβρεμεν, Call.*Del.*140):—*roar*, [κῦμα] ῥηγνύμενον μεγάλα βρέμει Il.4.425; δυσάνεμοι βρέμουσιν ἀκταί S.*Ant.*592 (lyr.):—Med., αἰγιαλῷ μεγάλῳ βρέμεται Il.2.210; of wind, μέγα βρέμεται χαλεπαίνων 14.399, cf. S.*Ant.*592 (lyr.), Ar.*Th.*998 (lyr.). II. after Hom., of arms, *clash, ring*, E.*Heracl.*832; of men, *clamour, rage*, β. ἐν αἰχμαῖς A. *Pr.*424 (lyr.), cf. *Th.*378; πολλοῖς μὲν ἵπποις, μυρίοις δ' ὅπλοις β. E.*Ph.*113; δεινὰ β. τινί *against* one, Id.*HF*962; of a mob, A.*Eu.* 978 (lyr.); *murmur, grumble*, ὁ χαμηλὰ πνέων ἄφαντον β. Pi.*P.*11. 30; *wail*, in Med., βλαχαὶ βρέμονται A.*Th.*350 (lyr.); but also of music, λύρα βρέμεται καὶ ἀοιδά Pi.*N.*11.7; λιγὺ λωτὸς βρέμων *Pae. Delph.*12; φθέγμα μηχανῇ βρέμον S.*Ichn.*278: c. acc., λωτὸς ὅταν ἱερὰ παίγματα βρέμῃ E.*Ba.*161 (lyr.). (*mrem-*, cf. Skt. *mármaras* 'noisy', Lat. *murmur*, Gk. μορμύρω, Lat. *fremo*, etc.)

Βρέμων, *Roarer*, name of a dog, X.*Cyn.*7.5.

βρεναίαται· δυσχεραίνει, προσποιεῖται, Hsch. **βρένδος**, = ἔλαφος, Id., *EM*212.47.

βρένθειος, α, ον, *costly*, μύρον Sapph.*Supp.*23.19; without μύρον, Pherecr.101.2.

βρενθινά (**βρενθία** Diogenian.ap.*EM*212.45), τά, roots used by women to make face-paint, Hsch.; cf. β(ρ)ενθινῷ· ἀνθινῷ, Id.

βρένθις, Cypr., = θρίδαξ, Nic.*Fr.*120 (-θιξ Hsch.).

βρένθον, τό, = βρένθειον μύρον, Hsch.

βρένθος, ὁ, an unknown *water-bird*, Arist.*HA*609^{a}23, Ael.*NA*5. 48, but in Arist.*HA*615^{a}16 (with v.l. βρίνθος) some kind of *singing-bird* (= κόσσυφος, Hsch.). II. *haughty carriage, arrogance*, Ath. 13.611e. III. *tomb*, Hsch.

βρενθύομαι [ῠ] (-ύνομαι *AP*11.305 (Pall.)), only pres. and impf., *bear oneself haughtily, hold one's head high, swagger*, ὑπὸ φρονήματος Ar.*Pax* 26, cf. *Nu.*362, Pl.*Smp.*221b, Luc.*DMort.*10.8; πρός τινα Ar. *Lys.*887; β. τι πρὸς αὐτόν Luc.*Tim.*54; β. ἐπί τινι *plume oneself* on.., Ath.14.625b; ἐβρενθύετο Lib.*Or.*56.17, Agath.1.14; also, *take umbrage*, β. καὶ ἀγανακτῶν Ael.*NA*5.36. (Either from βρένθος II or from βρένθειος, as Phld.*Vit.*p.37 J., Sch.Ar.*Lys.*887.)

βρένθυς, υος, ἡ, *perfume of* βρένθειον μύρον, Phld.*Vit.*p.37 J.

βρενταί· βρονταί, Hsch. **βρέουιον**, v. βρέβιον.

βρέντιον, Messap., = *stag's head*, Str.6.3.6; cf. βρένδος.

βρέξις, εως, ἡ, (βρέχω) = βροχή, *a wetting*, X.*Eq.*5.9.

Βρετᾰνικός or **Βρεττᾰνικός**, ή, όν, *British*, νῆσοι Arist.*Mu.*393^b 12. II. βρεττανική, ἡ, *scurvy-grass*, *Cochlearia anglica*, Dsc.4.2, Damocr.ap.Gal.14.197 (*herba Britannica*, Plin.*HN*25.20,99). 2. = ἅλιμος, Ps.-Dsc.1.91.

βρέτας, τό, gen. βρέτεος, dat. βρέτει A.*Eu.*259 (lyr.): pl., nom. and acc. βρέτεα Id.*Supp.*463, but βρέτη Id.*Th.*95 (lyr.), 185, etc.; gen. βρετέων ib.97 (lyr.), *Supp.*429 (lyr.); Ep. dat. βρετάεσσιν Nic. *Fr.*74.68:—*wooden image* of a god, A.*Eu.*80, al., E.*Alc.*974 (lyr.), Ar.*Eq.*31, etc.; of a man, *IG*7.118 (Megara): in Prose, Str.8.7.2, Jul.*Or.*1.29d. 2. *mere image*, of a *blockhead*, Anaxandr.11.

βρέττανα· φοβερά, Hsch.

Βρέττιος, α, ον, *Bruttian*, γλῶσσα Β., i.e. *barbarous*, Ar.*Fr.*629 (dub.); Β., ὁ, = δραπέτης, D.S.16.15; Βρεττία· μέλαινα πίσσα, *AB* 223.

βρεῦκος, v. βροῦκος.

βρεφικός, ή, όν, *infantile*, Ph.2.84, Eust.767.16.

βρεφόθεν, Adv. *from a child*, Eust.14.20, etc.

βρεφο-κομέω, *nurse children*, Eust.565.40. **-κτόνος**, ον, *child-murdering*, Lyc.229.

βρέφος, εος, τό, *babe in the womb, foetus*, β. ἡμίονον κυέουσαν, of a mare, Il.23.266, cf. Chrysipp.*Stoic.*2.222. II. *new-born babe*, Simon.37.15, Pi.*O.*6.33, A.*Ag.*1096 (lyr.); νέον β. E.*Ba.*289 [not in S.]: in later Prose, Lxx *Si.*19.11, *BGU*1104.24 (i B.C.), etc.; of beasts, *foal, whelp, cub*, etc., Hdt.3.153, Phylarch.36, Ael.*NA*3.8, Opp.*H.*5.464, etc.; *nestling*, Horap.2.99; ἐκ βρέφεος from *babyhood*, *AP*9.567 (Antip.); ἀπὸ β. 2*Ep.Ti.*3.15. (Cf. Slav. *žrěbę* 'foal'.)

βρεφοτροφέω, *rear infants*, Tz.*H.*9.513.

βρεφ-όω, *form into a foetus, engender*, Eust.1535.44:—Pass., *Theol.Ar.*6. **-ύλλιον**, τό, Dim. of βρέφος, Luc.*Fug.*19, Eust. 565.50. **-ώδης**, ες, *childish*, Ph.1.394, Diog.Oen.9, Procl.*Par. Ptol.*284.

βρέχ-μα, ατος, τό, = βρέγμα, Alciphr.3.5. **-μός**, ὁ, = foreg. 1, Il.5.586, Nic.*Th.*219, Q.S.13.155.

βρέχω, fut. -ξω Lxx *Am.*4.7, al., (ἀπο-) Gal.6.591, etc.: aor. ἔβρεξα Hp.*Mul.*1.78, Pl.*Phdr.*254c, X.*An.*4.3.12, etc.:—**Pass.**, fut. βρᾰχήσομαι Lxx *Is.*34.3: aor. ἐβρέχθην E.*El.*326, X.*An.*1.4. 17, etc.: aor. 2 ἐβράχην [ᾰ] Hp.*Mul.*1.80, Arist.*Pr.*906^{b}26, Sotion p.190 W., Gal.6.270, *Anacreont.*31.26; but ἐβρέχην *PGiss.*160^{v}12 (ii A.D.), Wilcken *Chr.*341.6 (ii A.D.): pf. βέβρεγμαι Pi.*O.*6.55, Hp.*Acut.*(*Sp.*)47:—*wet*, of persons walking through water, τὸ γόνυ Hdt.1.189; τοὺς πόδας Pl.*Phdr.*229a; *steep* in water, Hp.*VM* 3; ἐν οἴνῳ Id.*Fract.*29; β. χρυσέαις νιφάδεσσι πόλιν *shower* wealth upon it, Pi.*O.*7.34; δακρύοισιν ἔβρεξαν ὅλον τάφον *IG*14.1422; β. ἐν δάκρυσι τὴν στρωμνήν Lxx *Ps.*6.7, cf. 77(78).27:—Pass., *get wet*, βρεχόμενοι πρὸς τὸν ὀμφαλόν X.*An.*4.5.2; βρέχεσθαι ἐν ὕδατι *to be bathed* in sweat or *drench themselves*, Hdt.3.104 (so ἱδρῶτι β. τὴν ψυχήν Pl.*Phdr.*254c); βεβρεγμένος *filled with water*, opp. διερός, Arist.*GC*330^{a}17; of sponges, Id.*Mete.*386^{b}5; ἄλφιτα β. ἐν ὕδατι Hp.*Mul.*2.110; *to be rained upon*, Plb.16.12.3; ὄμβροις Str. 15.1.13; esp. in Egypt of the inundation of the Nile, τὰ βρεχέντα πεδία *PFlor.*331.6 (ii A.D.); ἡ βεβρεγμένη (sc. γῆ) *PTeb.*71.2 (ii B.C.), *OGI*669.57 (i A.D.); γῆ οὐ βρεχομένη Lxx *Ez.*22.24:—but also intr. in Act., *to be inundated*, *PPetr.*3 p.119 (iii B.C.), *PTeb.*106.19 (ii B.C.): metaph., ἀκτῖσι βεβρεγμένος *steeped, bathed in* light, Pi.*O.* 6.55; σιγᾷ βρέχεσθαι Id.*Fr.*240; of hard drinkers, μέθῃ βρεχθείς E.*El.*326; βεβρεγμένος *tipsy*, Eub.126. II. *rain, send rain*, *Ev. Matt.*5.45; Ζεὺς ἔβρεχε *POxy.*1482.6 (ii A.D.): c. acc., ἔβρεξε Κύριος χάλαζαν Lxx *Ex.*9.23; θεῖον ib.*Ge.*19.24, cf. *Ev.Luc.*17.29; ἄρτους Al.*Ex.*16.4. 2. impers., βρέχει *it rains*, Telecl.54, *Ep.Jac.*5.17; ὅταν βρέχῃ Arr.*Epict.*1.6.26; also ἵνα ὑετὸς βρέχῃ *Apoc.*11.6.

βρῆγμα, ατος, τό, and **βρήσσω**, variants for βῆγμα, βήσσω, Gal.19. 89, Hp.ap.*AB*223, Hsch.

Βρησαγενής, title of Dionysus, *IG*12(2).478.2:—also **Βρησσαῖος** Hsch.; and **Βρησεύς** *CIG*3160 (Smyrna); cf. Βρισεύς.

βρήσσω, *bleat*, Hsch.

βρητός· ἀλεκτρυὼν ἐνιαύσιος, Hsch.

βρῖ, = βριθύ (for βριθέως), A.D.*Adv.*157.13, Hsch.; = βριαρόν, Hes.*Fr.*236.

βρία, ἡ, = πόλις (Thracian), Str.7.6.1; but, = κώμη, Hsch.

βριαγχόνη, v. βάτραχος.

Βρίακχος, ἡ, = Βάκχη, S.*Fr.*779 (expld. by βριαρῶς ἰακχάζουσα, Hsch., *EM*213.26): name of a Satyr on vases, Berlin 2256, BMus. E.253.

Βρῐάρεως [ᾰ], ὁ, gen. Βριάρηο Ibyc.45, (βριᾰρός) a hundred-handed giant, *Aegaeon*, Il.1.403, Hes.*Th.*714: Βριάρεω στῆλαι, older name for the Pillars of Hercules, Arist.*Fr.*678; cf. ὄβριμος. (-ρεως is monosyll. in Ep.)

βρῐᾰρός, ά, όν, Ion. **βριερός**, ή, όν, Ep. Adj. *strong*, κόρυς, τρυφάλεια, Il.16.413, 19.381, cf. Coluth.30; δέμας Tryph.19; ῥίζα Nic.*Th.*659; δόμος Οὐλύμποιο Orph.*Fr.*248; of persons, Nonn.*D.*28.172, al.; στρατιή *Epigr.Gr.*448; λέων *IG*14.1293*C*.

βρῐᾰρότης, ητος, ἡ, *strength, might*, Eust.1289.14.

βρῐᾰρόχειρ, ειρος, ὁ, ἡ, *strong-handed*, Eust.586.2.

βρῐάω, (βρῖ) *make strong and mighty*, Hes.*Th.*447. II. intr., *to be strong*, βριάων Opp.*H.*5.96: in both senses, [Ζεὺς] ῥέα μὲν γὰρ βριάει, ῥέα δὲ βριάοντα χαλέπτει Hes.*Op.*5.

βρίγκα· μικρόν (Cypr.), Hsch.

βρίγκος, ὁ, a *sea-fish*, Ephipp.12.3, Mnesim.4.38.

βριγκώμενον· ὀργιζόμενον, θυμούμενον, Hsch. (leg. βριμώμενον).

βριγχός, όν, of taste, between δριμύς (*pungent*) and στρυφνός (*astringent*), Apollon.ap.Lyd.*Mens.*4.125.

βριερός, v. βριαρός.

βρίζα, ἡ, *rye, Secale cereale*, in Thrace and Macedonia, Gal.6.514. (Probably a Thracian word, cognate with Lith. *rugiai* 'rye', Engl. *rye*, etc.) II. Aeol. for ῥίζα, A.D.*Adv.*157.20, Greg.Cor.p.576 S.

βρίζω, aor. ἔβριξα E.*Rh.*826 (lyr.):—Pass., aor. βρισθείς· ὑπνώσας, Hsch.:—poet. Verb, *to be sleepy, nod*, οὐκ ἂν βρίζοντα ἴδοις Ἀγαμέμνονα Il.4.223; *slumber*, βρίζων A.*Ch.*897; δόξαν.. βριζούσης φρενός Id.*Ag.*275: metaph. of guilt, βρίζει γὰρ αἷμα Id.*Eu.*280. II. βρίζει· ἐσθίει, πιέζει, κύει, Hsch.

βριζώ, οῦς, ἡ, = ἐνυπνιόμαντις, Semus 5.

βρῐήπὕος, ον, (ἀπύω) *loud-shouting*, of Ares, Il.13.521.

βρίηρον· μεγάλως κεχαρισμένον, Hsch. (Cf. ἦρα.)

βρῖθος, εος, τό, *weight*, Hp.*Mul.*1.48, E.*Tr.*1050, Plu.*Marc.*15; τῶν ἀτυχημάτων τὰ μὲν ἔχει τι β. καὶ ῥοπὴν πρὸς τὸν βίον Arist.*EN* 1101ᵃ29.

βρῑθοσύνη, ἡ, *weight*, Il.5.839, 12.460, Nonn.*D.*1.298.

βρῑθύ-κερως, ων, gen. ω, *with heavy horns*, Opp.*H.*2.290. **-νοος**, ον, *grave-minded, thoughtful*, *AP*9.525.3.

βρῑθύς, εῖα, ύ, *heavy*, ἔγχος Il.5.746, etc.; once in Trag., βριθύτερος A.*Ag.*200 (lyr.), cf. Id.*Eleg.*5, Q.S.3.540 (Comp.).

βρίθω [ῑ], Ep. subj. βρίθῃσι Od.19.112: Ep. impf. βρῖθον 9.219: fut. βρίσω B.9.47, Ep. inf. -έμεν *h.Cer.*456: aor. ἔβρισα Il.12.346, etc.: pf. βέβρῑθα 16.384, Hp.*Mul.*2.133, E.*El.*305: plpf. βεβρίθει Od. 16.474:—Pass. (v. infr.):—poet. Verb (also in later Prose, v. infr.), *to be heavy* or *weighed down with*, c. dat., σταφυλῇσι βρίθουσαν ἀλωήν Il.18.561; βρίθῃσι δὲ δένδρεα καρπῷ Od.19.112, cf. 16.474; ὑπὸ λαίλαπι.. βέβριθε χθών (sc. ὕδατι) Il.16.384; βότρυσι, καρποῖς, Jul.*Or.*3. 113a, 7.230d: metaph., ἀλάστωρ ξίφεσι βρίθων E.*Ph.*1557 (lyr.); ὄλβῳ β. Id.*Tr.*216 (lyr.); πίνῳ.. βέβριθα Id.*El.*305; κάτω β. περὶ τὴν ὕλην Iamb.*Myst.*5.11. 2. c. gen., *to be laden with* or *full of*, τράπεζαι σίτου καὶ κρειῶν ἠδ' οἴνου βεβρίθασι Od.15.334; πάντα δ' ἐρίθων ἀραχνᾶν βρίθει S.*Fr.*286; πεδιὰς βρίθουσα ζῴων καὶ φυτῶν Ph.2.217. 3. c. acc., βούβρωστις φόνον βρίθουσα *Epigr.Gr.*793.4. 4. abs., *to be heavy*, ἔρις.. βεβριθυῖα (= βαρεῖα) Il.21.385; εὔχεσθαι.. βρίθειν Δημήτερος ἱερὸν ἀκτήν Hes.*Op.*466; so in Hp. and later Prose, ᾗ ἂν.. βρίσῃ wherein *the weight is thrown*, Hp.*Flat.*10; βεβρίθασιν οἱ τιτθοί *are loaded*, Id.*Mul.*2.133, cf. Ph.1.330, etc.; ἐς γόνατα ἡ κεφαλὴ β. Philostr.*Im.*1.18: but rare in Att., βρίθει ὁ ἵππος *bows* or *sinks*, Pl. *Phdr.*247b; ὅταν βρίσῃ [ὁ κύκλος] ἐπὶ θάτερον μέρος *inclines* to one side, Arist.*Pr.*915ᵇ3: metaph., πᾷ τύχα βρίσει how Fortune *will incline the scales*, B.9.47. II. of men, *outweigh, prevail*, ἐέδνοισι βρίσας Od.6.159: abs., *have the preponderance in fight, prevail*, ὧδε γὰρ ἔβρισαν Λυκίων ἀγοί Il.12.346; τῇ δὲ γὰρ ἔβρισαν.. Ἕκτωρ Αἰνείας τε 17.512; βρίσαντες ἔβησαν charged *with their might*, ib.233; later εὐδοξίᾳ β. *to be mighty* in.., Pi.*N.*3.40; εἰ.. χειρὶ βρίθεις ἢ πλούτου βάθει S.*Aj.*130. III. trans., *weigh down, load*, ὅσπερ Κινύραν ἔβρισε πλούτῳ Pi.*N.*8.18; τάλαντα βρίσας A.*Pers.*346. 2. Pass., *to be laden*, μήκων καρπῷ βριθομένη *laden* with fruit, Il.8.307; μόροισι βρίθεται [ἡ βάτος] A.*Fr.*116; τῷ δ' οὐ βρίθεται [ἡ τράπεζα]; E.*Fr.*467; ἐβρίθοντο αἰόνες [σώμασι] Tim.*Pers.*108; πλοῦτον χρυσῷ καὶ ἀργύρῳ -όμενον Jul.*Or.*2.86b: c. gen., πέτηλα βριθόμενα σταχύων Hes.*Sc.*290; συμποσίων.. βρίθοντ' ἀγυιαί B.*Fr.*3.12; βριθομένης ἀγαθῶν τραπέζης Pherecr.190 (hex.); βριθομένη χαρίτων *AP*5.193 (Posidipp. or Asclep.): abs., ἄξονες βριθόμενοι A.*Th.*153 (lyr.). (Cf. βρῖ.)

βρίκελος, ὁ, a name of a *tragic mask*, Cratin.205, acc. to Did.ap. Hsch. also expld. as = ἱστοπόδης or βάρβαρος (βριξὶν (leg. βρύξιν) ἴκελα· οὕτω δὲ ἔλεγον τοὺς βαρβάρους Paus.Gr.*Fr.*95).

βρικίννη· εἶδος βοτάνης, Hsch.

βρικίσματα, τά, name of a Phrygian *dance*, Hsch.

βρικόν· ὄνον (Cyren.), Hsch.: **βρικοί**· πονηροί, Id.

βρῑμ-άζω, *roar like a lion*, Suid., Hsch.: c. acc., *roar against*, *PMag.Par.*1.2247 (s.v.l.); also, = ὀργᾶν ἐς συνουσίαν (Cypr.), Hsch. **-αίνω**, = βριμάομαι, *EM*213.45: also in Med., Hsch. **-άομαι**, *snort with anger, to be indignant*, εἰ σὺ βριμήσαιο Ar.*Eq.*855, cf. Phld.*Ir.*p.49 W.:—Act. in Hsch. **-η**, ἡ, *strength, might*, *h.Hom.* 28.10, A.R.4.1677. II. = ἀπειλή, Hsch. 2. *bellowing, roaring*, βρίμας ταυρείους ἀφιεὶς χαροποῦ τε λέοντος prob. in Orph.*Fr.* 79. III. = γυναικεία ἀρρητοποιΐα, Hsch. **-ημα**, ατος, τό, = βρίμη, prob.l. *APl.*4.103 (Gem.), cf. Hsch. **-όομαι**, = βριμάομαι, ἐβριμοῦτο τῷ Κύρῳ *was indignant with* Cyrus, X.*Cyr.*4.5.9 (expld. by ἀπειλεῖ Ael.Dion.*Fr.*95): abs., Ph.1.681. **-ός**· μέγας, χαλεπός, Hsch. **-ώ**, οῦς, ἡ, epith. of Hecate and Persephone, *the Terrible one*, A.R.3.861, Orph.*Fr.*31, Luc.*Nec.*20. **-ώδης**, ες, *grim, stern*, dub. in Herm.ap.Stob.1.49.45 (Comp.). **-ωσις**, εως, ἡ, *indignation*, Phld.*Ir.*p.26 W.: pl., ib.p.52 W.

βρινδεῖν· θυμοῦσθαι, ἐρεθίζειν, Hsch. **βρίννια**, τά, *lamb's flesh*, Id. **βρίξ**· θριδακίνη, καὶ εἶδος ἄνθους, οἱ δὲ περιστερεῶνα, Id.

βρῖσ-αρμᾰτος, ον, (βρίθω) *chariot-pressing*, epith. of Ares, Hes.*Sc.* 441, *h.Hom.*8.1: [Θῆβαι] Pi.*Dith.Oxy.*1604 *Fr.*1 ii 26. **-αύχην**, ενος, *neck-pressing*, i.e. *heavy*, Hsch. s.v. ὁ β.

Βρῑσεύς, έως, ὁ, title of Dionysus at Smyrna, *SIG*851 (written Βρεισ–, ii A.D.), Aristid.*Or.*41(4).5, Macr.*Sat.*1.18.9; cf. Βρησαγενής.

βρῑσόμᾰχος, ον, *prevailing in fight*, *EM*668.55.

Βρῑτόμαρτις, ἡ, acc. -ιν *SIG*527.29 (Dreros, iii B.C.; where B. is distd. fr. Artemis), name of Artemis in Crete, = *virgo dulcis*, acc. to Solin.11.8 (but a nymph in Call.*Dian.*190): gen. -εως, Str.10.4.14; -ιδος, *EM*214.23:—hence **Βρῑτομάρτια**, τά, festival at Delos, *IG*11 (2).145.34. (Derived from **βρίτον**, = ἀγαθόν, acc. to *EM*214.29.)

βρίτος· ἔτος, Hsch. **βριτύ**· γλυκύ (Cret.), Id.

βρογχ-εῖον, τό, *bronchial cartilage*, S.E.*M.*8.252. **-ία**, Ion. -ίη, ἡ, imaginary *system of ducts* connecting heart with liver, Hp.*Anat.* 1. **-ια**, ων, τά, *bronchial tubes*, Id.*Acut.*17, Ruf.*Anat.*25,27, cj. in Arist.*HA*603ᵃ32: later in sg., Aret.*SD*1.10. 2. *cartilaginous rings of the trachea*, Gal.*UP*7.7: in sg., *one such ring*, Id.8.2. 3. *gills* of fish, Id.5.199. 4. *tubes passing through the ethmoid bone*, Hp.*Carn.*16. **-ιάζω**, *gulp down*, Hsch.

βρογχο-κήλη, ἡ, *tumour in the throat*, Sor.1.69, Gal.19.443, Aët. 15.6, Vett.Val.110.5. **-κηλικός**, όν, *suffering from* βρογχοκήλη, interpol. in Dsc.4.119. **-παράταξις**, εως, ἡ, *competition in gluttony*, Ath.7.298e.

βρόγχος, ὁ, *trachea, windpipe*, Hp.*Epid.*5.68, Arist.*Pr.*900ᵃ13, Gal.*UP*7.11, etc. 2. generally, *throat*, Hp.*Aph.*6.37, Aret.*SA*1. 6. II. *gulp, draught*, ψυχροῦ Apollon.ap.Arr.*Epict.*3.12.17. III. = βάτραχος, Hsch.

βρογχωτήρ, ῆρος, ὁ, *neck-hole in a garment*, J.*AJ*3.7.2.

βροδοδάκτυλος, ον, = ῥοδο–, *rosy-fingered*, μήνα (leg. σελάννα) Sapph.*Supp.*25.8.

βρόδον, i.e. ϝρ–, Aeol. for ῥόδον, Sapph.68.2, *Supp.*25.13, A.D. *Adv.*157.20.

βροδόπᾱχυς, = ῥοδόπηχυς, Sapph.65.

βρόκος, = βροῦκος, Hsch. II. = sq., in later Greek, Id.

βρόκων, ὁ, *boorish person*, Hsch.

βρομέω, = βρέμω, only used in pres. and impf. (exc. fut. βρομήσω *EM*214.36); of flies, *buzz*, Il.16.642; of wind, *roar*, θύελλαι β. A.R. 4.787, cf. Nic.*Al.*596; of boiling broth, Id.*Fr.*68.5; also ἶσα Διὶ βρομέει, of a proud person, Rhian.1.13.

βρομι-άζομαι, = Βακχεύω, from Βρόμιος, *AP*9.774 (Glauc.). **-άς**, άδος, ἡ, fem. of sq. II, θοίνα Pi.*Dith.Oxy.*1604 *Fr.*1 i 11; πηγή Antiph. 52.12. II. *large cup*, Ath.11.784d. **-ος**, α, ον, (βρόμος) *sounding*, φόρμιγξ Pi.*N.*9.8; *noisy, boisterous*, whence, II. **Βρόμιος**, ὁ, as a name of *Bacchus*, Id.*Fr.*75.10, A.*Eu.*24, E.*Ph.*649 (lyr.), al., Telecl. 55; ὦ Διόνυσε Β. Ar.*Th.*991; Βρομίου πῶμα, i.e. wine, E.*Cyc.*123; ποδαπὸς ὁ Βρόμιος; whence comes the *wine*? Alex.230.3, cf. *APl.*4. 309, *AP*9.368 (Jul. Imp., with play on βρόμος (B)). 2. Adj. Βρόμιος, α, ον, *Bacchic*, E.*HF*893 (lyr.), etc.; Β. χάρις, of the Dionysia, Ar.*Nu.*311:—also **Βρομιώδης**, ες, *Bacchic*, πηλός, of a drinking-cup, *AP*11.27 (Maced.): fem. **Βρομιῶτις**, ιδος, ἡ, Opp.*C.*4.340: as Subst., *Bacchante*, ib.300. III. βρόμιον, τό, name of a *plaster*, Orib.*Fr.*90.

βρόμος (A), ὁ, (βρέμω) *any loud noise*, as the *crackling* of fire, Il.14. 396, Thphr.*Fr.*165; *roaring* of thunder, Pi.*O.*2.27; of a storm, A. *Th.*213 (lyr.), *Fr.*195 codd.; of the drum, [Simon.]179.7; of horses, A.*Th.*476; ἐλάφῳ β. *belling*, Alc.97 (cf. *POxy.*1789.29); of the flute, *h.Merc.*452, cf. S.*Fr.*513: hence, *rage, fury*, E.*HF*1212:—rare in Prose, βρόμοι καὶ ὀλολυγμοί Epicur.*Fr.*143; of thunder, earthquake, or sea, Arist.*Mu.* 395ᵃ13, 396ᵃ12, *Mir.*843ᵃ8; of a volcano, Id. *Fr.*634. II. τόπος εἰς ὃν ἔλαφοι οὐροῦσι καὶ ἀφοδεύουσι, Hsch.

βρόμος (B), also **βόρμος** (Dieuch.ap.Orib.4.7.20, Hsch.), ὁ, *oats, Avena sativa*, Hp.*Vict.*2.43, Dsc.2.94, Polem.Hist.88. 2. *wild oats, Avena barbata*, Thphr.*HP*8.9.2, Ps.-Dsc.4.137: also, = αἰγίλωψ, ibid.

βρομώδης, freq. f.l. for βρωμ– (q.v.), Ath.3.88a, Plu.2.792b, etc.

βροντ-ᾰγωγός, *bringing thunder*, *PMag.Par.*1.182. **-άζω**, = βροντῶ, ib.1039, Hsch. **-αῖος**, α, ον, *thundering*, Ζεύς Arist.*Mu.* 401ᵃ17, Orph.*H.*15.9; ὕδωρ β. thunder-*rain*, Hp.*Epid.*6.4.17. **-άω**, *thunder*, Ζεὺς δ' ἄμυδις βρόντησε Od.14.305, cf. Il.8.133; βροντᾶν οὐκ ἐμὸν ἀλλὰ Διός Call.*Fr.*490; so Βροντῶν, title of Zeus in Phrygia, *JHS*5.258, etc. (but βροντῶν θεός, = *Jupiter Tonans*, *IG*14.982, cf.

D.C.54.4) : metaph. of Pericles, Ar.*Ach.*531, cf. *V.*624 ; of a seller asking too high a price, Herod.7.65. **2.** impers., χειμέρια βροντᾷ *it thunders*, Ar.*Fr.*46 ; βροντήσαντος *if it thunders*, Arist.*HA*610^{b}35. **II.** Pass., *to be thunderstruck*, Id.*Div.Somn.*463^{a}13. **-εῖον,** τό, *engine for making stage-thunder*, Poll.4.130. **-ή,** ἡ, *thunder*, Διὸς μεγάλοιο κεραυνὸν δεινήν τε β. Il.21.199; ὑπὸ βροντῆς πατρὸς Διός 13.796 ; Ζηνός τε βροντῇ Od.20.121 ; ἀστραπὴ καὶ β. Hdt.3.86 ; β. στεροπῇ τε A.*Supp.*34 (anap.) ; β. καὶ κεραυνίᾳ φλογί Id.*Pr.*1017 ; βροντῆς μύκημα ib.1062 (anap.), cf. 1083 (anap.) ; β. δ' ἐρράγη δι' ἀστραπῆς S.*Fr.*578, etc. : in pl., Id.*OC*1514, X.*HG*1.6.28, Thphr. *Sign.*21, etc. ; χθόνιαι β. Ar.*Av.*1745 : metaph., τούτου τὰς β. οἶδ' ὅτι δείσεις Lib.*Ep.*98.4. **II.** *the state of one struck with thunder, astonishment*, ἐπεάν σφι θεὸς ἐμβάλῃ β. Hdt.7.10.ε'. (βρομτᾶ, cf. βρέμω.) **-ημα,** ατος, τό, *thunder-clap*, A.*Pr.*993. **II.** = ἐμβρόντητος, Hsch. **-ης,** ου, ὁ, *Thunderer*, one of the three Cyclopes, Hes.*Th.*140. **-ησικέραυνος,** ον, *sending thunder and lightning*, Νεφέλαι Ar.*Nu.*265 (anap.). **-ήσιος** Ζεύς, = *Jupiter Tonans*, *Mon.Anc.Gr.*18.21. **-ητικός,** *thundering*, epith. of Ζεύς, Eust. 141.27.

βροντο-κεραυνοπάτωρ [ᾰ], ορος, ὁ, *father of the thunderbolt*, epith. of Kronos, *PMag.Par.*1.3102. **-ποιός,** όν, *thunder-making*, Vett. Val.6.24, Ps.-Luc.*Philopatr.*4,24. **-σκοπία,** ἡ, *divination from thunder*, Lyd.*Ost.*27 tit., al.

βροντώδης, ες, *like thunder, thundering*, κτύποι Agath.5.8, cf. Lyd. *Ost.*42, al., Sch.Ar.*Ra.*826. **II.** *charged with thunder*, Vett.Val. 14.17, Ptol.*Tetr.*94.

βρόξαι, v. *βρόχω.

βρόσσων, Aeol., = βράσσων, Hsch.

βρότᾰχος, ὁ, Ion. for βάτραχος (q.v.), Xenoph.40.

βρότειος, ον, also α, ον Archil.15, Emp.2.9, E.*Hipp.*19, *Supp.*777 :— poet. Adj. *mortal, human*, A.*Pr.*116 (lyr.), etc. ; β. μῆτις Emp. l. c. ; β. γένος E.*Fr.*898.13 ; ψυχὴν βροτείαν Id.*Supp.*777 ; β. πόνοι *of mortals*, Alex.240.9 :—in Hom. only **βρότεος,** η, ον, φωνή Od.19.545 ; εὐνή *h.Ven.*47 ; also in Pi.*O.*9.34, Emp.100.17, A.*Eu.*171 (lyr.).

βροτήσιος, α, ον, = foreg., ἔργα Hes.*Op.*773 ; ἀνήρ Pi.*P.*5.3 ; δέμας Id.*Pae.*6.79 ; μορφή E.*Ba.*4, *Or.*271 ; φθογγή Lyc.1321 : in late Prose, β. γένος *PMasp.*151.18 (vi A. D.).

βροτο-βάμων [ᾱ], ον, gen. ονος, *trampling on men*, *AP*15.21 (Theoc.). **-γηρυς,** υ, *with human voice*, ψιττακός ib.9.562 (Crin.). **-δαίμων,** ὁ, = ἡμίθεος, Hsch. **-ειδής,** ές, *like a man*, δείκηλον Man.6.446. **-εις,** εσσα, εν, (βρότος) *gory*, ἔναρα Il.6. 480, etc. ; ἀνδράγρια 14.509. **II.** = βρότειος, Nonn.*D.*47.431 (s. v. l.). **-κέρτης,** ου, ὁ, (κείρω) *man-shaver*, pedantic word for *barber*, Alexarch.ap.Heraclid.Lemb.5. **-κλώστειρα,** ἡ, *weaving the destiny of mortals*, κόσμοιο χορείη Man.4.11. **-κτονέω,** *murder men*, A.*Eu.*421. **-κτόνος,** ον, *man-slaying, homicidal*, θυσίαι E. *IT*384 (lyr.) ; κράνεια *AP*6.123 (Anyte) : Ἄρης Orph.*H.*65.2 ; οὐ τὴν Οἰδιπόδαο βροτοκτόνον his *murderess*, i. e. the Sphinx, *Epigr.Gr.* 1015. **-λοιγός,** όν, *plague of man, bane of men*, Ἄρης Il.5.31, al., Od.8.115 ; of Apollo, *Epigr.Gr.*1034.29 ; once in Trag., A.*Supp.* 665 (lyr.) ; ἔρως *AP*5.179 (Mel.).

βροτόομαι, Pass., (βρότος) *to be stained with gore*, βεβροτωμένα τεύχεα Od.11.41, Q.S.1.717 ; δράκων κάρα βεβρ. Stesich.42.

βροτόπους ἵππος horse *with human feet*, coin-legend in Head *Historia Numorum* p.517 (Nicaea).

βροτός, ὁ, poet. Noun, *mortal man*, opp. ἀθάνατος or θεός, in Hom. usu. Subst., οἷοι νῦν βροτοί εἰσι Il.5.304, al. ; βροτὸς εἰς θεὸν E. *Andr.*1196 (lyr.) ; λόγος τις Ζῆνα μιχθῆναι βροτῷ A.*Supp.*295 ; θεοῦ δὲ πληγὴν οὐχ ὑπερπηδᾷ βροτός S.*Fr.*961 ; βροτοί, opp. νεκροί, Id.*Ant.* 850 (lyr.) ; but β. ἀνήρ Il.5.361 ; and so β. ἔθνος Pi.*P.*10.28 : as fem., β. αὐδήεσσα Od.5.334 ; β. οὖσαν *AP*9.89 (Phil.) ; but βροταί· γυναῖκες, Hsch. (s. v. l.) : freq. in gen. pl., after πολλοί B.1.42, S.*OT* 981, etc. ; after τίς ib.437, etc. ; βροτοί never takes the Art. in Trag. and Com., exc. when an Adj. or Pron. is added, τῶν πολυπόνων β. E.*Or.*175 ; ἡμεῖς οἱ β. Ar.*Eq.*601, *Pax* 849, cf. Sannyr.1 ; οἱ ταλαίπωροι β. Alex.66 ; οἱ πάντες β. Men.538.8.—Rare in Prose, Pl. *R.*566d, Arist.*Top.*133^{a}31, 149^{a}7. **II.** of the *dead*, A.*Ch.*129 (v.l. νεκροῖς Sch.). (From *μροτός (cf. ἄ-μβροτος, μορτός), Skt. *mṛtás* 'dead', Lat. *morior*, etc.)

βρότος, ὁ, *blood that has run from a wound, gore*, in Il. always αἱματόεις, 7.425, al. ; μέλας Od.24.189.

βροτο-σκόπος, ον, *taking note of man*, Ἐρινύες A.*Eu.*499 (lyr.). **-σσόος,** ον, (σαόω, σῴζω) *man-saving*, Orph.*L.*756. **-στόνος** κλύδων dub. in E.*Fr.*669. **-στῠγής,** ές, *hated by men*, Γοργόνες A.*Pr.*799 ; δνόφοι Id.*Ch.*51 (lyr.). **-φεγγής,** ές, *giving light to men*, αἴγλη *AP*9.399. **-φηλος,** ον, *deceiving men*, Hsch. **-φθόρος,** ον, *man-destroying*, A.*Eu.*787 (lyr.), *Supp.*264, etc. **II.** σκῦλα βροτοφθόρα *of slain men*, E.*Fr.*266.

βροτωφελής, ές, *helpful to men*, μελέτα B.12.191.

βροῦ, v. βρῦν.

βροῦκος, ὁ, *locust*, or its *wingless larva* (Ionic acc. to Hsch.), Thphr.*Fr.*174.4 ; **βροῦχος** Lxx *Le.*11.22, al., Ph.1.85, Lyd.*Ost.*56 ; collective in sg., Heph.Astr.1.20 ; Cypr. **βροῦκα,** Hsch. ; **βρεῦκος** (Cret. acc. to Hsch.), prob. as sobriquet in Herod.2.73.

βρουλλοκύπερος, ἡ, a kind of κύπερος, Aët.1.132.

βρουλός· πονηρός, Hsch. **βροῦνος·** ἐνεὸς ἢ μαινόμενος, Id. **βρούξ·** τράχηλος, βρόγχος, Id. **βρούτιδες·** γυναῖκες οὕτω καλούμεναι, Cyr., Suid. **βροῦτος,** = βρῦτος, Hsch. **βροῦχαλ·** θερμός, Id. **βρούχετος·** βάρβαρος : also, = βάτραχος (Cypr.), Id.

βροχετός, ὁ, (βρέχω) *wetting, rain*, *AP*6.21.3.

βροχή, ἡ, (βρέχω) *rain*, Democr.14.8, Lxx *Ps.*67(68).10, *Ev.Matt.* 7.25, Ph.1.48, *Gp.*2.39.7. **II.** *moistening*, Dsc.1.49, Philagr.ap. Orib.5.32.1, Mnesith.ib.8.35.11 ; *steeping*, in brewing, *PTeb.*401.27 (i A. D.). **III.** *inundation* of the Nile, in pl., *POxy.*280.5 (i A. D.), Heph.Astr.1.23. **2.** *irrigation*, Thphr.*HP*9.6.3, *PPetr.*3 p.119 (iii B. C.).

βροχθίζω, *take a mouthful*, Arist.*Pr.*948^{a}5. **II.** *clear the throat*, τινί with . . , Clearch.Com.2. **III.** *give to drink*, Aq.*Ge.*24.17.

βρόχθος, ὁ, *throat*, Theoc.3.54. **II.** *throatful* (as vomited), Hp.*Morb.*2.69,74. **2.** *draught* (that which can be swallowed at a gulp, Sch.Nic.*Th.*366), *AP*11.298, Phld.*Mort.*33.

βροχθώδης, ες, *shallow* (acc. to Sch., cf. βρόχθος II. 2), λίμνη Nic. *Th.*366 ; τόπος τοῦ Νείλου *EM*206.28.

βροχίζω, *hang, strangle*, ἑαυτόν *POxy.*850.6 ; cf. Hsch. s. v. ἀλαῶν : —Pass., *to be ligatured*, Gal.4.679.

βροχικός, ή, όν, *rainy*, ζῴδια *Cat.Cod.Astr.*1.133.21,31.

βρόχιον, τό, *pot*, μέλανος *POxy.*326 (i A. D.).

βροχίς, ίδος, ἡ, Dim. of βρόχος, Opp.*H.*3.595 ; of a spider's *web*, *AP*9.372 (pl.). **II.** (βρέχω) *ink-horn*, ib.6.295 (Phan.). **III.** a measure of length, *IG*12(3).1232.10 (Melos).

βροχ-μός, = βρέγμα, Hsch. ; from βρέχω, *EM*285.16. **-μώδης,** ες, *damp*, Democr.133.

βρόχος, ὁ, *noose, slip-knot*, Od.11.278, 22.472, Hdt.4.60, Democr. 134, S.*Ant.*1222, etc. ; *snare for birds*, Ar.*Av.*527 ; θηρῶν β. E.*Hel.* 1169 ; ἁλοὺς βρόχων πλεκταῖς ἀνάγκαις Xenarch.1.8 ; *mesh* of a net, X.*Cyn.*2.5, etc. : metaph., β. ἀρκύων ξιφηφόροι E.*HF*729 ; ὡς ἂν ληφθῶσιν ἐν ταὐτῷ βρόχῳ A.*Ch.*557 ; ἐν βρόχῳ τὸν τράχηλον ἔχων νομοθετεῖν 'with *a halter* round one's neck', D.24.139. (βρόκχον shd. be written in Thgn.1099.)

βρόχυς, Thess. and Aeol., = βραχύς, Sapph.2.7, *IG*9(2).460.13 (as pr.n. Βρόχυς) ; cf. βρόσσων.

***βρόχω,** *gulp down*, only aor. 1 ἔβροξα *AP*9.1 (Polyaen.), subj. βρόξῃ (βρώξῃ codd.) ib.11.271, inf. βρόξαι· ῥοφῆσαι, Hsch. : used by Hom. only in compds., **1.** ἀναβρόξαι, *swallow again, suck down again*, ἀλλ' ὅτ' ἀναβρόξειε . . ἁλμυρὸν ὕδωρ, opp. ὅτ' ἐξεμέσειε, of Charybdis, Od.12.240 ; πάντας ἀναβρόξασα A.R.4.826 ; ἅλις ἀναβέβροχεν (Zenod., -βέβρυχεν vulg.) ὕδωρ *has drunk up* water enough, Il.17.54 :—Pass., ὕδωρ ἀπολέσκετ' ἀναβροχέν Od.11.586. **2.** καταβρόξαι *gulp down* (καταβρόξαι· καταπιεῖν, Hsch.), ὃς τὸ καταβρόξειε whoever *swallowed* the potion, Od.4.222 : aor. part. Pass. καταβροχθείς Lyc.55 : misspelt κατα-βρώξῃ Id.742, -βρώξειε D.P.604, -βρώξας A.R.2.271.

βροχωτός, όν, *formed by a noose*, ἀγχόνη Neophr.3.2. **2.** *twisted, corded*, of chain-work, β. ἔργον Aq., Sm.*Ex.*28.15.

βρῦ, v. βρῦν.

βρύα, ἡ, = μυρίκη, Plin.*HN*13.116.

βρῠ-άζω, fut. βρυάσομαι Hsch., aor. ἀν-εβρύαξα Ar.*Eq.*602, otherwise only pres. and impf. :—*swell, teem*, καρποῖσι β. Orph.*H.*53.10, cf. 33.7 ; ὁπόταν γε [Ζεὺς] βρυάζων οἶκον ἐσέλθῃ ib.73.4 ; of a lioness, *to be pregnant*, A.*Fr.*491 ; *bubble up*, δέπας ἀφρῷ βρυάζον Tim.*Fr.*7 : metaph., *wax wanton*, A.*Supp.*878 ; ἁ λίθος οἶδε βρυάζειν *AP*9.756 (Aemil.) : c. dat., *revel in*, Epicur.*Fr.*181 ; χαίρειν καὶ β. prob. l. Id. *Fr.*600, cf. 605 ; αἱ γυναῖκες ἐβρύαζον ταῖς Δωρίαις στολαῖς Duris 50 ; τοῦ ποτοῦ λαμπρῶς ἤδη -οντος Hld.5.16.

βρύαθ⟨μ⟩ον· βρυασμόν, Hsch., cf. *Hymn.Is.*89 (dub. sens.).

βρυάκτης, ου, ὁ, of Pan, *the jolly god*, Poet.ap.Stob.1.1.30.

βρῠᾰλ-ιγμός, ὁ, *noise*, Hsch. **-ίζων·** διαρρήσσων, Id. **-ίκτης** or **βρυαλλίκτης,** ου, ὁ, *one who performs in a kind of war-dance*, Stesich.79, Ibyc.53.

βρυανιῶν (-ίων cod.)· μετεωριζόμενος καὶ κορων⟨ι⟩ῶν, Hsch.

βρύας, ου, ὁ, v. βύας.

βρυασμός, ὁ, *voluptuousness*, Plu.2.1107a. **β⟨ρ⟩υατά·** βεβυσμένα αὔτη, Hsch.

βρύγ-δην, Adv., (βρύκω) properly, *with clenched teeth* : of a polypus, *tightly*, *AP*9.14 (Antiphil.). **-μα,** ατος, τό, *a bite, gnawing*, Nic.*Th.*483. **-μός,** ὁ, *biting*, ib.716 (pl., v.l. βρυχμός) ; *gobbling*, Eup.347 ; *chattering, shivering*, Hp.*Vict.*3.84, *Steril.*214, Euryphon ap.Gal.17(1).888 ; β. ὀδόντων *gnashing* of teeth, *Ev.Matt.*8.12, al. **II.** *roaring* of a lion, Lxx *Pr.*19.12.

βρυγκός· ἄφωνος, νεκρός, Hsch. **βρυγχός,** = βρόχος, Id. **βρυδαλίχα,** ἡ, *female mask* ; also, *lewd woman* (Lacon.), Id.

βρύζω, dub. sens. in Archil.32.2. **II.** Pass., ἐβρύσθη· ἔπεσεν, Hsch. (Cf. Lith. *griúti* 'collapse'.)

βρύθακες, *silken tunics*, Hsch. **βρύκαι·** αἱ ἱεραί (leg. βρύκαιναι· ἱεραί) (Dorian), Id. **βρῡκᾰνάομαι,** = βρυχ-, Id. **βρυκεδανός·** πολυφάγος, οἱ δὲ μακρός, Id. **βρυκετός,** = βρυγμός, Id. **βρύκος·** κῆρυξ (cf. βρόυχος), οἱ δὲ βάρβαρος (cf. βρούχετος), οἱ δὲ ἀττέλεβος (cf. βροῦκος), Id. **βρυκταία,** a kind of *plant*, Id.

βρύκω or **βρύχω** [ῡ] (the former Att. acc. to Moer. and Ammon. ; the distn. βρύκω *bite*, βρύχω *gnash* does not hold good), mostly pres. : fut. βρύξω Hp.*Mul.*1.2, Lyc.678 : aor. ἔβρυξα Hp. *Epid.*5.86, Nic.*Th.*207, al., *AP*7.624 (Diod.), (ἐπ-) Archipp.35 : aor. 2 ἔβρῠχε *AP*9.252 (late, perh. impf.) : for βέβρῡχα, v. βρυχάομαι :—Pass., v. infr. :—*eat greedily, gobble*, γνάθος ἱππείη βρύκει *champs* the bit, Hom.*Epigr.*14.13 ; ἑφθὰ καὶ ὀπτὰ [κρέα] . . βρύκειν E. *Cyc.*358, cf. 372 ; πρὸς ταῦτα βρύκετ' Ar.*Pax* 1315 ; *bite*, βρύκουσ' ἀπέδεσθαι . . τοὺς δακτύλους *biting*, Id.*Av.*26 ; of smoke, ὀδὰξ ἔβρυκε τὰς λήμας ἐμοῦ Id.Lys.301; later, simply, devour, consume, Nic.Al. 489, al.; βρύξας, of the sea, is perh. f.l. for βρόξας in AP7.624 (Diod.): metaph., tear in pieces, devour, of a gnawing disease, βρύκει S.Tr.987 (lyr.); βρύκει γὰρ ἅπαν τὸ παρόν Cratin.58; τὰ πατρῷα βρύκει Diph. 43.27:—Pass., ἀπόλωλα, τέκνον, βρύκομαι S.Ph.745; βρυχθεὶς ἁλὶ AP9.267 (Phil.). II. gnash or grind the teeth, τοὺς ὀδόντας βρύχει Hp.Mul.1.7, etc., cf. AP15.51 (Arch.); τὸ στόμα β. Babr.95.45; β. τοὺς ὀδόντας ἐπί τινα Act.Ap.7.54; also βρύχει alone, Hp.Mul.2.120; also intr., οἱ ὀδόντες βρύχουσι ib.1.36; βρῦκον στόμα Nic.Al.226, cf. Th.207, al.:—Med., βρύχονται Hp.Morb.Sacr.1 (prob.).

βρυλλιχίζειν, wear a female mask, Hsch.; also, = ἀκταίνειν, Id.:—Subst. **-ιστής**, cf. βρυδαλίχα.

βρύλλω, cry for drink, of children (cf. βρῦν), Ar.Eq.1126, cf. Sch. II. βρύλλων· ὑποπίνων, Hsch.

βρύματα· μηρύματα, Hsch. (μυρήμ- cod.).

βρῦν εἰπεῖν cry for drink, of children, Ar.Nu.1382:—also **βρῦ** or **βροῦ**, Phryn.PS p.55 B., AB85 (βροῦς Hsch.).

βρυνχόν· κιθάραν (Thracian), Hsch.

***βρύξ**, in acc. βρύχα, depth of the sea, Opp.H.2.588: gen. βρυχός prob. l. in Orph.A.1066.

βρῠόεις, εσσα, εν, weedy, ποταμός Nic.Th.208. II. flourishing, Id.Al.371,478.

βρύον [ῠ], τό, (βρύω) oyster-green, Ulva Lactuca, β. θαλάσσιον Hp.Mul.1.53, cf. Arist.HA591^{b}12, Dsc.4.98: pl., Plu.Caes.52; β. alone, Nic.Th.792; also, a marsh-plant, ib.415. II. tree-moss, Usnea barbata, Theoc.21.7, Dsc.1.21. III. liverwort, Marchantia polymorpha, Id.4.53. IV. clustering male blossom of the hazel, Arist.HA624^{a}34: generally, catkin, Thphr.HP3.7.3, Nic.Th.71,898. V. = καυκαλίς, Democr.ap.Ps.-Dsc.2.139.

βρῠόομαι, aor. ἐβρυώθην, Pass., to be grown over with βρύον, Arist.Col.791^{b}26, 792^{a}1.

βρῠοφόρος, ον, catkin-bearing, Thphr.CP2.11.4.

βρύοχον· κήρυκα, Hsch. **βρύσδην**· χύδην, Id. (cod. βρύγδην).

βρύσις [ῠ], εως, ἡ, bubbling up, Suid., Eust.1095.16: **βρυσμός**, ὁ, Arc.58.24.

βρύσσος, Att. **-ττος**, ὁ, a kind of sea-urchin, Arist.HA530^{b}5, Hsch.

βρύσται· κρημνοί, also as place-name, Hsch.

Βρῡσωνοθρᾰσῠμᾰχειοληψῐκέρμᾰτος, ον, taking coin like Bryso and Thrasymachus, Ephipp.14.3.

βρύτανα, = βύτανα, Hdn.Gr.2.484.

βρῠτανεῖον, **-εύω**, v. πρυτ-.

βρύτεα or **βρύτια** (so prob. in Cerc.4.34 [ῡ]), τά, = στέμφυλα, refuse of olives or grapes after pressing, Ath.2.56d, Hdn.Gr.2.484 (also expld. as εἶδος σκορόδου, Hsch.): metaph., τὰ δ' ἔσχατα β. Μυσῶν Cerc.l.c.; τὸ τῶν βρυτέων πόμα Aret.SA1.9, SD2.9.

βρύτηρ (i.e. ϝρύ-), ηρος, ὁ, Aeol. for ῥυτήρ, A.D.Adv.157.20; = ῥόμβος, EM706.31.

βρυτιγγοί· χιτῶνες, Hsch.

βρῦτ-ικός, ή, όν, drunken with beer, Antiph.45 (codd. Ath.). **-ινος**, η, ον, of or for βρῦτον, Cratin.96 (παρὰ προσδοκίαν for βύσσινος).

βρυτίς, = ῥυτίς, EM214.32.

βρύτιχοι· βάτραχοι μικροὶ ἔχοντες οὐράς, Hsch.

βρυτονία· ῥίζα τις, Hsch.

βρύτον· ζῷον ὅμοιον κανθάρῳ, Hsch. s.v. βρυτίνη.

βρῦτος, ὁ (S.Fr.610), **βρῦτον**, τό (Ath.10.447c), elsewh. the gender is dub.:—fermented liquor made from barley, beer, Archil.32, Hecat.154 J., Hellanic.66 J., A.Fr.124.

βρύττειν· ἐσθίειν, Hsch.; also, = πυρέττειν, EM216.25; = ὀρύττειν, Lex.Rhet.ib.28. **βρύττιον**· πόμα ἐκ κριθῆς, Hsch.

βρυχάνα, = βυκάνη, Hsch.

βρῡχᾰνάομαι, rarer form of sq., Nic.Al.221.

βρῡχ-άομαι, aor. ἐβρυχησάμην, Ep. βρυχ- A.R.4.19, Max.Tyr. 31.3, D.C.68.24, (ἀν-) Pl.Phd.117d; also ἐβρυχήθην (v. infr.): Ep. pf. βέβρῡχα Od.5.412, al.: plpf. ἐβεβρύχει 12.242:—onomatop. Verb, roar, bellow, prop. of lions, acc. to Hsch. and Ammon.; of a bull, ταῦρος ὣς βρυχώμενος S.Aj.322, cf. Ar.Ra.823; of wild beasts, δεινὸν δ' ἐβρυχῶντο Theoc.25.137; of the elephant, Plu.Pyrrh.33: in Il. mostly of the death-cry of wounded men, κεῖτο τανυσθείς, βεβρυχώς 13.393; so βρυχώμενον σπασμοῖσι, of Hercules, S.Tr.805, cf. 904; βέβρυχα κλαίων ib.1072; δεινὰ βρυχηθεὶς Id.OT1265; later, of an infant's wail, Men.1004; κλαίων καὶ β. Alciphr.1.35; also of the roaring of waves, ἀμφὶ δὲ κῦμα βέβρυχεν ῥόθιον Od.5.412, cf. Il.17.264; ἀμφὶ δὲ πέτρη δεινὸν βεβρύχει Od.12.242, cf. Aristid.Or.17(15).14; βρυχομένη (as if from βρύχομαι) is required by the metre in Q.S.14.484, cf. βρύχεται· μαίνεται, Hsch.; but βρυχῶνται, -ώμενος shd. be read in Hp.Morb.Sacr.1, Luc.DMar.1.4. **-ετός**, ὁ, (βρύχω) chattering of teeth, ague, Hsch. **-ή**, ἡ, (βρύχω) gnashing of teeth, ὀδόντων A.R.2.83, Q.S.5.392. II. (βρυχάομαι) bellowing, Opp.H.2.530. **-ηδόν**, Adv., (βρύχω) with gnashing of teeth, AP9.371. II. (βρυχάομαι) with bellowing, A.R.3.1374, Nonn.D.29.311. **-ηθμός**, ὁ, roaring, of the sea or a river, Arist.Mir.843^{a}22, Opp.C.4.171 (pl.); λέοντος Max.Tyr.31.3, cf. Aesop.226. 2. (βρύχω) gnashing of teeth, lamentation, Men.Epit.472. **-ημα**, ατος, τό, roar, roaring, λέοντος APl.4.94 (Arch.), cf. Opp.C.3.36; improperly of sheep (cf. βληχάομαι), A.Fr.158 (pl.); of men, Plu.Mar.20, Alex.51. **-ητήρ**, ῆρος, ὁ, roarer, of the constellation Leo, Doroth.ap.Heph.Astr.3.36. **-ητής**, οῦ, ὁ, roaring, β. χόλος AP6.57 (Paul.Sil.). **-ητικός**, ή, όν, roaring, bellowing, Tz.ad Lyc.739.

βρυχιάω, chatter (?), of a defect of speech, Cat.Cod.Astr.2.167.

βρύχιος [ῠ], α, ον, also ος, ον A.Pers.397: (*βρύξ):—from the depths of the sea, deep, ἅλμη A.l.c., Tim.Pers.96; ἅλς A.R.1.1310; βρυχία ἠχὼ βροντῆς the sound of thunder from the deep, A.Pr.1082 (lyr.): metaph., βρύχιον ὑποστένειν heave a deep sigh, Hld.6.9.

βρυχίς· κλῆμα, Hsch.

βρυχμή, ἡ, f.l. for βρυχή, Q.S.4.241. **βρυχμός**, v. βρυγμός.

βρυχός, = βρύκος, Hsch. **βρύχω**, v. βρύκω; but **βρύχομαι**, v. βρυχάομαι.

βρύω [ῠ], mostly pres.: impf., Pherecyd.Syr.ap.D.L.1.122, Nicaenet.7: aor. part. βρύσας Procop. (v. infr.):—to be full to bursting: 1. c. dat., swell or teem with, esp. of plants, ἔρνος... βρύει ἄνθεϊ λευκῷ swells with white bloom, Il.17.56, cf. E.Ba.107 (lyr.); κισσῷ κάρα βρύουσαν Eub.56.6; ἰούλῳ, θριξί, κόμαις, Philostr.Her.2.2, Alciphr.3.31, Luc.Am.12; γῆ φυτοῖς βρύουσα Arist.Mu.392^{b}15; also βρύει ἱερὰ βουθύτοις ἑορταῖς B.3.15: metaph., βίος.. βρύων μελίτταις καὶ προβάτοις κτλ. Ar.Nu.45; of men, β. δόξᾳ B.12.179; παμμάχῳ θράσει βρύων A.Ag.169 (lyr.); ἀγαθοῖσι βρύοις Id.Supp.966 (anap.); μαντικῇ β. τέχνῃ Id.Fr.350.6; ἄλλων ἰατρὸς αὐτὸς ἕλκεσι βρύων E.Fr.1086; β. ἄνθεσιν ἥβας Tim.Pers.221; βρύουσαν ἀοιδὰν σοφίᾳ Lyr.Alex.Adesp.20.4; ἐμπόριον πλούτῳ βρύον Jul.Or.2.71d. 2. c. gen., to be full of, χῶρος.. βρύων δάφνης ἐλαίας ἀμπέλου S.OC16; βρύοντα στέφανον μύρτων Ar.Ra.329 (lyr.); στεφάνων δόμος ἔβρυεν prob. l. in Nicaenet. l.c.; τράπεζαν.. κόσμου βρύουσαν Alex.86.3; καρπόν.. βρύειν σμαράγδου λίθου Philostr.VA5.5; τόπος β. ὕλης J.AJ13.3.1; φθειρῶν ἔβρυον πᾶς Pherecyd.Syr.l.c.: metaph., νόσου β. A.Ch.70. 3. abs., abound, grow luxuriantly, S.El.422; of the earth, teem with produce, X.Cyn.5.12, cf. Philostr.VA3.56; of water, burst forth, ὕδωρ βρύσαν ἐξ ὑπονόμων Procop.Arc.19. 4. c. acc. cogn., burst forth with, gush with, γλυκύ, πικρὸν [ὕδωρ] Ep.Jac.3.11; τὴν γῆν τὰ οἰκεῖα βρύειν φησὶν ἀγαθά Ael.Fr.25; causal, Ὧραι β. λειμῶνας Him.Or.1.19; ῥόδα Anacreont.44.2.—Poet. and later Prose.

βρῠώδης, ες, full of seaweed, Arist.HA543^{b}1; τὰ β., = seaweed, Gp.2.22.2; of a ship, β. ἐπιπάγους προσάγεσθαι Plu.2.641e. 2. 'mossy', flabby, σὰρξ πλαδαρὸς καὶ β. Alex.Aphr.Pr.2.62, cf. Gal.10.195, Sor.1.82,95. II. catkin-like, ἄνθος Dsc.1.87, 4.181. III. = δυσώδης, Hsch.

βρῠ-ώνη, ἡ, = ἄμπελος μέλαινα, Nic.Th.939:—also **-ωνίς**, ίδος, ἡ, ib.858; cf. sq. **-ωνία**, ἡ, prop. = ἄμπελος μέλαινα, Dsc.4.183; also, = ἄμπελος λευκή, bryony, ib.182, cf. Gal.11.827; β. ἀγρία, = χαμαίπιτυς, Ps.-Dsc.3.158; β., = φύλλον, ib.125. **-ωνιάς**, άδος, ἡ, = foreg., Colum.10.250.

βρώζω, = βιβρώσκω, Herod.7.63.

βρῶμα, ατος, τό, (βιβρώσκω) that which is eaten, food, meat, Hp.VM6, Th.4.26, al.: metaph., Ar.Fr.333: freq. in pl., Hp.VM3, Antiph.246, Pl.Criti.115b, etc.; opp. ὄψα, Sosip.1.30. II. cavity in a tooth, Hp.Epid.4.25, Dsc.1.105, Archig.ap.Gal.12.859. 2. moth-eating, in pl., Lxx Ep.Je.12. III. pl., filth, ordure, prob. in Ev.Marc.7.19; cf. βρῶμος (B).

βρωμάομαι, (βρέμω) bray, βρωμησάμενος Ar.V.618; bellow, of the stag or hart, Arist.HA579^{a}1. III. suffer hunger, Hsch. (also aor. Act.).

βρωμᾰτίζω, give to eat, Aq.De.8.3.

βρωμάτιον, τό, Dim. of βρῶμα, Ath.3.111a.

βρωμᾰτομιξᾰπάτη [πᾰ], ἡ, the false pleasure of eating made dishes, AP9.642 (Agath.).

βρωμ-έω, (βρῶμος) smell rank, Al.Ex.7.18. **-η**, ἡ, (βιβρώσκω) = βρῶμα, Od.10.460, Nic.Al.499, A.R.3.1058, Opp.C.2.352. **-ήεις**, εσσα, εν, (βρωμάομαι) brayer, i.e. ass, Nic.Al.409,486. **-ησις**, εως, ἡ, braying of an ass, Ael.NA3.7, Poll.5.88. **-ηστής**, οῦ, ὁ, = sq., EM215.57; also, = χορτοφάγος, ibid. **-ητής**, οῦ, ὁ, brayer, i.e. ass, Nic.Fr.74.30. **-ήτωρ**, ορος, ὁ, = foreg., Id.Th.357.

βρωμολόγος, ον, foul-mouthed, Luc.Pseudol.24.

βρῶμος (A), ὁ, (βιβρώσκω) = βρῶμα, Arat.1021.

βρῶμος (B), ὁ, stink, noisome smell, Lxx Jb.6.7, al., Gal.7.214, Sch.Nic.Al.519, Dsc.Alex.Praef. (Condemned by Phryn.133; βρόμος is freq. f.l.)

βρωμώδης, ες, stinking, foul-smelling, Str.5.4.6, Diph.Siph.ap.Ath.8.355f, Diocl.Fr.138, Dsc.1.7, etc.; cf. βρομώδης.

βρωσείω, Desiderat. of βιβρώσκω, to be hungry, Call.Fr.435.

βρώσιμος, ον, eatable, A.Pr.479, Diph.13, Lxx Le.19.23, Ev.Luc.24.41; ἃ καὶ κυσὶν πεινῶσιν οὐχὶ βρώσιμα Trag.Adesp.118.4.

βρῶσις, εως, ἡ, Ep. **-ιος** Hes.Th.797: (βιβρώσκω):—meat, opp. πόσις, Od.15.490, cf. Hp.Acut.28, X.Mem.1.3.15, Pl.Lg.783c: in pl., opp. πόσεις, Democr.235; β. ἀναγκαία Th.2.70. 2. pasture, προβάτων PLips.118.15 (ii A.D.). II. eating, παίδων Pl.R.619c; ἐρινὸς ἀχρεῖος ὢν ἐς βρῶσιν S.Fr.181. 2. taste, flavour, Nic.Al.377. 3. corrosion, rust, Ev.Matt.6.19; decay, Gal.6.422 (pl.), 12.879.

βρωστήρ, ῆρος, ὁ, moth, Aq.Ho.5.12; cf. βρωτήρ.

βρω-τέος, α, ον, to be eaten, Luc.Par.9, Porph.Abst.2.10. 2. βρωτέον one must eat, Muson.Fr.18 B p.105 H.; ἀνθρώποις β. ταῦτα Porph.Abst.2.4. **-τήρ**, ῆρος, ὁ, eating, βρωτῆρας αἰχμάς A.Eu.803; ὀδόντες Nic.Al.421; ἱππάκης βρωτῆρες.. Σκύθαι A.Fr.198: as Subst. in pl., of insects, etc., Orph.L.599; moth, Aq.Is.50.9. **-τικός**, ή, όν, inclined to eat, voracious, Arist.GA745^{a}29, PA682^{a}17 (Comp.), Fr.231 (Sup.), Plu.2.352f (Comp.). Adv. -κῶς, ἔχειν EM485.17, Eust.966.4, etc. II. promoting this inclination, δυνάμεις dub. l. in Chrysipp.Stoic.3.199 (ἐρωτικαί Coraes). III. gnawing, ἄλγημα Hp.*Epid.*7.52. **-τός**, ή, όν, *to be eaten*, Archestr.*Fr.*28; φάρμακον, opp. ποτόν, Porph.*Abst.*1.27. II. βρωτόν, τό (τὸν β. *Bull.Soc.Alex.*6.45), *meat*, opp. ποτόν, X.*Mem.*2.1.1; βρωτοῖσι καὶ ποτοῖσι E.*Supp.*1110, cf. Lxx 1*Es.*5.54, Aristeas 128, *PSI*1.64.21 (ii A.D.). **-τύς**, ἡ, Ion. for βρῶσις, *eating*, acc. βρωτὺν Il.19.205, Od. 18.407: gen. βρωτύος Philox.2.38. II. *food*, *AP*11.371 (Pall.).

βῦ, exclamation of admiration, *EM*216.55.

βύας, ου, ὁ, *eagle-owl*, *Strix bubo*, Arist.*HA*592ᵇ9 (v.l. βρύας); βύας ἔβυξε *an owl* hooted, D.C.56.29, 72.24. (Onomatop.)

βυβλάριον, τό, Dim. of βύβλος, *PLille*7.7 (pl.); βιβλ–, *AP*11.78 (Lucill.).

βυβλείδιον, v. βιβλίδιον.

βυβλία, ἡ, *papyrus-bed*, *Tab.Heracl.*1.58; cf. βύβλινος.

βυβλῐνοπέδῐλος, ον, *with sandals of* βύβλος, Anon.ap.Eust.1913.44.

βύβλινος, η, ον, *made of* βύβλος (of various kinds), ὅπλον νεὸς ἀμφιελίσσης βύβλινον Od.21.391, cf. Hdt.7.25,36; ὑποδήματα, ἱστία, Id.2.37,96; τεύχη *Inscr.Prien.*114.11 (i B.C.); ἐπιστολαί Lxx *Is.*18.2 (βιβλ–); μασχάλα *papyrus*-marsh, *Tab.Heracl.*1.92; ζυγίδες *BGU* 544.4 (βιβλ–, ii A.D.).

βυβλιοθήκη, v. βιβλ–.

βύβλιοι· τάφων φύλακες (Cypr.), Hsch.

βύβλος and **βίβλος** (v. sub fin.), ἡ, *the Egyptian papyrus*, *Cyperus Papyrus*, Hdt.2.92, A.*Supp.*761, Str.17.1.15: in pl., *stalks of papyrus*, *PTeb.*308.7 (ii A.D.). 2. *rind* enclosing the pith of this plant, Thphr.*HP*4.8.4, etc.: generally, *bark*, φελλῶν καὶ βύβλων Pl.*Plt.* 288e, cf. Hdt.2.96, Plot.2.7.2. b. in pl., *slices of the pith* used as writing-material, Hdt.5.58, Hermipp.63.13: sg., *strip of* β., βύβλον εὐρύναντες ἀντὶ διαδήματος Ph.2.522. 3. *roll* of papyrus, *book*, Hdt.2.100, A.*Supp.*947, etc.: heterocl. pl., βύβλα, τά, *AP*9.98 (Stat. Flacc.); esp. of sacred or magical *writings*, βίβλων ὅμαδον Μουσαίου καὶ Ὀρφέως Pl.*R.*364e, cf. D.18.259, *Act.Ap.*19.19, *PPar.*19.1 (ii A.D.); ἱεραὶ β. *OGI*56.70 (Canopus, iii B.C.); β. ἱερατική *PTeb.*291.43 (ii A.D.); so of the Scriptures, ἡ β. γενέσεως οὐρανοῦ καὶ γῆς Lxx *Ge.*2.4, etc.; ἡ β. *the Sacred Writings*, Aristeas 316; β. Μωυσέως, ψαλμῶν, προφητῶν, *Ev.Marc.*12.26, *Act.Ap.*1.20, 7.42; β. ζωῆς *Ep. Phil.*4.3: pl., of magical *books*, *Act.Ap.*19.19. 4. a *division* of a book, Plb.4.87.12, D.S.1.4, etc.; αἱ β. the nine *books* of Hdt., Luc. *Herod.*1. II. β. στεφανωτρίς *flowering head of papyrus*, Theopomp.Hist.22c, Plu.*Ages.*36. [ῡ, A.*Supp.*761.] (βύβλος, βύβλινος, βυβλίον, etc., are the original forms: βιβλ– seems to have arisen in Attic by assimilation in βιβλίον, and is found in earlier Attic Inscrr., cf. *IG*2.1*b*, etc., and prevails in Ptolemaic papyri; Inscrr. vary, βυβλία *Test.Epict.*8.32 (iii/ii B.C.); βιβλία *IG*5(1).1390.12 (Andania, i B.C.); in Roman times βυβλ– was restored.)

βυβός, ή, όν, = μεστός, πλήρης, μέγας, Sophr.115.

βυδοί· οἱ μουσικοί, ἢ κρουμά τι, Hsch.; cf. βίδη.

βῦζα, ἡ, = βύας, Nic.*Fr.*55.

βυζαντία· εἶδος ὁρμιᾶς, Hsch.

βύζην, Adv. *close pressed*, *closely*, β. κλείειν Th.4.8, cf. Arr.*An.*2.20.8, App.*Pun.*123, etc.; β. ὠστιζόμενοι Luc.*Lex.*4; τὰ β. συνεστηκότα στίφη Ph.2.382. II. = ἀθρόως (cf. Erot.), Hp.*Nat.Puer.*15, *Mul.*1.5.

βυζόν· πυκνόν, συνετόν, γαῦρον δὲ καὶ μέγα, Hsch.

βύζω (A), (βύω) *to be frequent*, ἡ πτύσις βύζεται Aret.*SA*2.2; cf. foreg., and βύζαντες· πλήθοντες, Hsch.

βύζω (B), *hoot*, βύας ἔβυξε D.C.56.29, 72.24.

βύθαλον· βύσμα, Hsch.

βῦθ-άω, (βυθός) *strike deep*, ῥίζα βυθόωσα Nic.*Th.*505. **-ίζω**, *sink* a ship, S.*Fr.*552; μίαν πεντήρη ἐβύθισαν Plb.2.10.5; *let down*, ἀγκύρας Them.*in Ph.*133.20; *bury*, *plunge*, ἑρπετὸν. . ἐν μυχῷ τοῦ πηλοῦ Luc.*Alex.*13:—Pass., of a ship, etc., *sink*, D.S.11.18, Babr. 117.1, Plu.*Caes.*49, D.Chr.63.3; of a person, *to be plunged into the sea*, Plu.2.831d. II. *overwhelm*, *submerge*, of a flood, οἰκίας Plu. 2.306f:—Pass., Id.*Daed.*7. III. metaph., β. ἀνθρώπους εἰς ὄλεθρον 1*Ep.Ti.*6.9:—Pass., *to be ruined*, τοὺς διὰ φιλοκερδίαν βυθιζομένους Phld.*Mort.*33; τὸ νῆφον ὑπὸ τοῦ πάθους βυθίζεται Alciphr.1.13; νοῦς βυθισθεὶς θυμῷ ἢ ἐπιθυμίᾳ Simp.*in Ph.*273.11, cf. Hld.7.12. **-ιος**, α, ον, also ος, ον Gal.2.634:—*in the deep*, *sunken*, Luc.*DMar.*3.1; κρηπῖδας β. πηξαμένη *AP*9.791 (Apollonid.); ἐκ β. ἰλύος from the mud *of the deep*, *Hymn.Is.*71. II. *in* or *of the sea*, τὰ β. (sc. ζῷα) *water-animals*, *AP*6.182 (Alex. Magn.); β. Κρονίδης *Poseidon*, Luc.*Epigr.*34; τέχνη *fishery*, Opp.*H.*3.15. III. metaph., *deep*, βύθιόν τι καὶ δεινὸν φθέγγεσθαι Plu.*Crass.*23; β. διάνοια Ph.1.194 (but ἕως ἂν λογισμὸς β. οἴχηται vanishes *in the deep*, ib.639, cf. Nonn.*D.*2.55); *abysmal*, Dam.*Pr.*106. **-ισμός**, ὁ, *sinking*, *submersion*, Hld.9.8. **-ῖτις**, ιδος, pecul. fem. of βύθιος, ψάμμος *AP*9.290 (Phil.). **-μός**· ἄντρον, πυθμήν, καὶ **βυθμήν**, Hsch.

βῠθοκῡμᾰτοδρόμος, ον, *traversing the depths of the sea*, ναῦται *Lyr. Alex.Adesp.*32.1.

βῠθός, ὁ, *the depth*, esp. of the sea, A.*Pr.*432 (lyr.), 2*Ep.Cor.*11.25. b. generally, συνιζάνειν εἰς β. sink to the *bottom*, Thphr.*Od.*29: metaph., ἐξ οὐρίων δραμοῦσαν ἐς βυθὸν πεσεῖν S.*Aj.*1083; ἀνακουφίσαι κάρα βυθῶν Id.*OT*24; ἐκ βυθοῦ κηκῖον αἷμα from the *deep wound*, Id. *Ph.*783; καταφέρεσθαι εἰς β. Arist.*HA*619ᵃ7, etc.; τὴν ἀναφορὰν ποιησάμενος ἐκ τοῦ β. ib.622ᵇ7; ἐν τῷ β. τῆς θαλάττης ib.537ᵃ8: metaph., ἐν βυθῷ ἀτεχνίης in the *depth* of.., Hp.*Praec.*7; ἐν β. ἡ ἀλήθεια Democr.117; εἴς τινα β. φλυαρίας ἐμπεσών Pl.*Prm.*130d; ἀθεότητος Plu.2.757c; ὑπέρκοσμος β. *abyss*, Dam.*Pr.*106,205.

βῡθο-τᾰραξοκίνησε [ῐ] (sic, voc.), *stirring the deep to movement*, *PMag.Par.*1.184. **-τρεφής**, ές, *living in the deep*, Lxx 3*Ma.*6.8.

βῡκᾰν-άω or **βουκᾰνάω**, *blow the trumpet*, Plb.6.35.12. **-η**, ἡ, *spiral trumpet*, *horn*, Id.15.12.2, al., D.H.2.8. (From Lat. *bū-cĭna*.) **-ημα**, ατος, τό, *sound of the trumpet*, App.*Pun.*21. **-ητής**, οῦ, ὁ, *trumpeter*, Plb.2.29.6, App.*Hann.*41. **-ισμός**, ὁ, *deep note*, *bourdon*, Nicom.*Exc.*4 (**βουκανισμός** Ptol.*Harm.*1.4). **-ιστής**, οῦ, ὁ, = βυκανητής, Plb.30.22.11, D.H.4.18.

βυκήης· ὑπνηλός, Hsch. **βυκνισταί**· εἰκασταί, Id. **βυκός**· δασμοφόρος, Id. **βυκτά**· σχέτλια, δείλαια, Id.

βύκτης, ου, ὁ, *swelling*, *blustering*, βυκτάων ἀνέμων Od.10.20. II. Subst., *hurricane*, Lyc.738,756.

βυλλά· βεβυσμένα, Hsch.:—hence **βυλλόω**, *stuff*, pf. Pass. βεβυλλῶσθαι, Id. **βυλλίχαι**, *dances at Sparta*, and **βυλλίχης**, *dancer*, Id. **βυλλιχίδες**· ῥαχίδες, Id. **βυνεύς**· σκεύασμά τι κρίθινον, Id.

βῡνέω, = βύω, χρυσίῳ.. ἐβύνουν τὸ στόμα Ar.*Pax*645.

βύνη, ἡ, *malt for brewing*, *PHolm.*15.33, *PLeid.X.*22, Aët.10.29. II. = πεύκη, Hsch.

Βύνη [ῠ], ἡ, an old name of *the sea-goddess Ino* or *Leucothea*, Lyc. 107: hence, *the sea itself*, Euph.127.

βύνητος, ὁ, an Egyptian *garment*, Hdn.Gr.1.219.

βύνις, εως, dub. sens. in *PMag.Leid.V.*13.10,17.

βυννεῖν, *hold in the mouth*, Hsch.

βῡνοκ[οπία], ἡ, *preparation of malt*, prob. in *PTeb.*401.30 (i A.D.).

βύξ· βυθός, Hsch. (Fort. βρύξ.)

βύπτειν· βαπτίζειν, Hsch. **βύρθακος**· βάτραχος, Id. **βυρικόμενος**· πνιγόμενος, τραχηλιζόμενος, Id. **βυριόθεν**, = βαυρ–, q.v., Id.: **βύριον**· οἴκημα, Id. **βύρμακας**· μύρμηκας, Id. **βυρμός**· σταθμός, Id. **βυρρός**, = κάνθαρος (Tyrrhen.), Id. II. = βίρρος, *BGU*814.8 (iii A.D.).

βύρσα, ἡ, *skin stripped off*, *hide* (prop. ox-hide, β. καὶ ἄλλα δέρματα Hdt.3.110), Batr.127, Arist.*HA*531ᵃ11, etc.; βύρσης ὄζειν smell *of leather*, Ar.*Eq.*892; βύρσης κτύπος *of the drum*, E.*Ba.*513; *wineskin*, Luc.*Lex.*6, Aristid.*Or.*26(14).18. 2. *skin* of a live animal, Theoc.25.238. 3. in contempt, of the human *skin*, ἡ κακὴ β. Herod.3.80. 4. *screen* or perh. *sail*, Luc.*Nav.*4.

βυρσ-αίετος, ὁ, *leather-eagle*, com. name of Cleon the tanner, Ar. *Eq.*197. **-άτονος**, = βυρσότονος, Hsch. **-εῖον**, τό, *tan-pit*, Sch.Ar.*Ach.*724. **-εύς**, έως, ὁ, later word for βυρσοδέψης, Artem. 4.56, *Act.Ap.*9.43, *PFay.*121.15 (ii A.D.); guild of βυρσεῖς at Thyatira, *IGRom.*4.1216. **-εύω**, *dress hides*, *tan*, Hsch. s.v. σκυλοδέψιος. **-ικός**, ή, όν, *of hides* or *leather*, δυσωδία *Gp.*6.2.7. II. *used by tanners*, ῥοῦς *Hippiatr.*35. **-ιμώλους**· βυρσοδεψίμους, Hsch. **-ίνη**, ἡ, *leathern thong*, Ar.*Eq.*59,449 (with a play on μυρσίνη). **-ινος**, η, ον, *leathern*, πλοιάρια D.C.48.19. **-ίς**, ίδος, ἡ, Dim. of βύρσα, Hsch.

βυρσοδεψ-εῖον, τό, = βυρσεῖον, *EM*187.17. **-έω**, *dress* or *tan hides*, Ar.*Pl.*167, Artem.1.51. **-ης**, ου, ὁ, (δέψω) *tanner*, Ar.*Eq.*44, Pl.*Smp.*221e, Herod.6.88, *PPetr.*3 p.78 (iii B.C.), Artem.2.20. **-ησις**, εως, ἡ, *tanning*, Eust.887.24. **-ικός**, ή, όν, *of* or *for tanning*, Hp.*Mul.*1.78, Thphr.*CP*3.9.3: hence -ική, ἡ, *art of tanning*, Socr.*Ep.*14.2. **-ιμος**, v. βυρσιμώλους. **-ιον**, τό, *tan-pit*, *IG*14.352 i 71 (Halaesa).

βυρσό-καπηπος, ὁ, dub. sens. (fort. -κάπηλος), sobriquet of Cleon, *Com.Adesp.*61. **-πᾰγής**, ές, (πήγνυμι) *made of hides*, ῥόπτρα Plu. *Crass.*23. **-παφλᾰγών**, όνος, ὁ, *leather-Paphlagonian*, nickname of Cleon, Ar.*Eq.*47. **-ποιός**, όν, *tanning hides*, Din.*Fr.*89.19. **-πώλης**, ου, ὁ, *leather-seller*, Ar.*Eq.*136. **-τενής**, ές, = βυρσότονος, τύμπανα E.*Hel.*1347 (lyr.). **-τομέω**, *cut leather*, Poll. 7.81. **-τόμος**, ον, (τέμνω) *leather-cutting*, Man.4.320, Hsch. s.v. ῥινοτόρος. **-τονος**, ον, *with skin stretched over it*, β. κύκλωμα, = τύμπανον, E.*Ba.*124 (lyr.).

βυρσ-όω, *cover with skins* or *leather*, Ath.Mech.12.10, al. **-ώδης**, ες, lit. *leathery*; of the pulse, *hard*, Gal.8.456 (Comp.).

βύρτη· λύρα, Hsch.

βῡσαύχην, ενος, ὁ, ἡ, (βύω) *short-necked*, Ar.*Fr.*725 (v.l. for μεσαύχ–), Xenarch.1.4.

Βύσιος, ὁ, a Delphic month, *IG*2².1126.45, Plu.2.292e, etc.

βύσμα, ατος, τό, (βύω) *plug*, *bung*, Hp.*Mul.*2.114 (pl.), Ar.*Fr.* 299; Στίλπωνος βύσματα Stilpo's *stoppers*, i.e. arguments with which he stopped his opponents' mouths, Diph.23.

βύσσα, ἡ, = βυσσός, Opp.*H.*1.453. II. a *bird*, Ant.Lib.15.

βύσσαλοι· βόθροι, and **βυσσαλεύω**, *sink to the bottom*, Hsch.

βύσσινος, η, ον, *made of* βύσσος, σινδὼν β. *fine linen* bandage, used for mummy-cloths, Hdt.2.86; for wounds, Id.7.181; πέπλοι A.*Pers.* 125 (lyr.), E.*Ba.*821; φάρος S.*Fr.*373; ὀθόνια β. *OGI*90.17 (Rosetta), *PStrassb.*91.16 (i B.C.), Aristeas 320; β. περιβόλαια *PStrassb.*91.9 (i B.C.); βύσσινον, τό, Lxx *Es.*1.6 (pl.), al., *Apoc.*19.8; ὀθόνια καὶ βύσσινα *PHolm.*15.26. II. = πορφυροῦς, Hsch.

βυσσοβαρῆ· μεγάλα, and **βυσσοφαρεῖ**· μεγαλοφαρεῖ, Hsch.

βυσσοδομεύω, (δομέω) *build in the deep*: hence, *brood over* a thing *in the depth of one's soul*, *ponder deeply*; Hom. only in Od., always in bad sense, κακὰ φρεσὶ βυσσοδομεύων 17.66, al.; μύθους β. 4.676; δόλον φρεσὶ β. Hes.*Sc.*30: also in late Prose, ὀργὴν β. Luc.*Cal.*24; τὰ βυσσοδομευόμενα *secret designs*, Hld.7.11:—also **-δομέω**, Eust. 1513.46, Suid.

βυσσόθεν, Adv. *from the bottom* of the sea, S.*Ant.*590; of a river, Call.*Del.*127; κινήσασα β. γνώμην Babr.95.49, cf. Eratosth.*Fr.*36.4:

metaph., *fundamentally*, Plot.6.5.12; *from the depths of the heart*, β. οἰμωγή Opp.*H*.4.17.

βυσσομέτρης, ου, ὁ, *measuring the deeps*, epith. of a fisherman, *AP*6.193 (Stat. Flacc.).

βυσσός, ὁ, = βυθός, *depth of the sea*, Il.24.80, Hdt.2.28,96, Arist. *HA*547b15.

βύσσος, ἡ, *flax*, and *the linen made from it*, Emp.93, Theoc.2.73, etc.; used of *perennial flax, Linum angustifolium*, grown in Elis, Paus.6.26.6, and of *Linum usitatissimum*, = λίνον Ἑβραίων, Id.5.5.2; also, in later writers, of *Indian cotton, Gossypium herbaceum*, Poll. 7.76, Philostr.*VA*2.20; and of *silk*, τὰ Σηρικὰ ἔκ τινων φλοιῶν ξαινομένης βύσσου Str.15.1.20.

βυσσ-ουργός, ὁ, *byssus-weaver*, *PTeb*.5.239 (ii B.C.):—hence **-ουργικός**, ή, όν, ἐργαλεῖα ib.243. **-οφαρεῖ**, v. βυσσοβαρῆ. **-όφρων**, ον, gen. ονος, (φρήν) = βαθύφρων, *deep-thinking*, Ἐρινύς A.*Ch*.651 (lyr.). **-ωμα**, ατος, τό, *net woven of* βύσσος, *AP*6.33 (Maec.).

βύσταξ, ακος, ὁ, = μύσταξ, Antiph.44.4.

βυστίχοις· τοῖς ἐν θαλάττῃ βρόχοις, Hsch.

βύστρα, ἡ, = βύσμα, Antiph.180.

βύτανα· κόνδυλοι, Hsch. **βύτθαν**· τὸν ψᾶρα, Id. (fort. ψῆνα). **βυτθόν**· πλῆθος, Id. **βυτίνη**, ἡ, = πυτίνη (Tarent.); also, = ἀμίς, Id. **βύττος**· γυναικὸς αἰδοῖον, Id.

βύω Arist.*HA*632a18: fut. βύσω [ῡ] Thales ap.D.L.1.35, (ἐπι-) Cratin.186.4, (προ-) Ar.*V*.250: aor. ἔβῡσα Hp.*Morb*.3.14, (ἐπι-) Ar. *Pl*.379:—**Med.**, only in compds.:—**Pass.**, aor. ἐβύσθην (παρ-) Luc. *Deor.Conc*.10: pf. βέβυσμαι, the tense chiefly in use (v. infr.):—*stuff*, 1. c. gen. rei, *stuff full of*, only in Pass., νήματος βεβυσμένος *stuffed full of* spun-work or spinning, Od.4.134; τὸ στόμα ἐβέβυστο (sc. χρυσοῦ) Hdt.6.125; ἀνάγκης βεβυσμένος οἶκος Nonn.*D*.9.298. 2. c. dat. rei, *stop* or *plug with*, βύσας τὴν ἕδρην σπόγγῳ Hp. l. c., cf. Arist. l. c.:—Pass., σπογγίῳ βεβυσμένος Ar.*Ach*.463; κηρίῳ Id.*Th*. 506; ῥαφάνοις τὴν ἕδραν βεβ. Alciphr.3.62; ἵππος ἀριστήεσσι βεβ. Tryph.308; ἀφραδίῃ τε βέβυστο [πόλις] Id.450. 3. abs., βεβυσμένος τὴν ῥῖνα *having* one's nose *stopped*, Hegesipp.1.26; βεβ. τὰ ὦτα *deaf*, Luc.*Cat*.5; εἶμα βεβ. a *close, thick-woven* robe, Hp.*Mul*.1. 1. 4. *stow* or *tuck away*, τι ὑπὸ τῇ πτέρυγι Ael.*NA*11.18. (Root βυσ-, cf. βύζην (<*βυσ-δην), βύσ-τρα; cf. ζέβυται· σέσακται, Hsch.)

βυωτήν· τὴν ἄρσιν, Hsch. **βῶ**· βοῦν, Id., cf. Sch.Il.7.238.

βωβός, ή, όν, *dumb*, ἐκ γενετῆς κωφοὶ καὶ β. Plu.*Fr.inc*.149, cf. Phlp.*in GA*223.32; also, = πηρός, χωλός, Hsch.

βωβύζειν· σαλπίζειν, Hsch. **βώδιον**, τό, = βοΐδιον, Id. **βωθέω**, Ion. contr. for βοηθέω, v.l. in Hdt.8.47.

βωθύζειν· βοᾶν, θωΰσσειν, Hsch. **βωκάριν**, prob. f.l. for σωκάριον, *Gp*.20.42. **βώκαρος**, = ἔαρ (Troezen.), *EM*217.40.

βώκκαλις, ιδος, ἡ, an Indian *bird*, Ael.*NA*13.25.

βωκολ-ιάσδω, **-ιαστής**, **-ικός**, **-ος**, Dor. for βουκ-. **βῶκος**, ὁ, Dor. for βοῦκος. **II.** βωκός· τρυφερὸς χιτών, Hsch. (fort. βράκος).

βωλά, Dor. for βουλή, *SIG*261.15 (Argos, iv B.C.), Decr.Byz.ap. D.18.90, etc.

βωλάζω, in pf. part. Pass. βεβωλασμένα πεδία *cloddy*, Onos.10.4.

βωλ-άκιον [ᾰ], τό, *loamy soil*, Hsch., Zonar. **-άκιος** [ᾰ], α, ον, *lumpy, loamy*, opp. dry sandy soil, γῆ Pi.*P*.4.228. **-αξ**, ᾰκος, ἡ, = βῶλος, ib.37, Theoc.17.80, A.R.3.1334. **-άριον**, τό, Dim. of βῶλος, Str.16.4.18; λιβανωτοῦ M.Ant.4.15; Ἄθως β. τοῦ κόσμου Id. 6.36; ἁλός Aët.2.3. **-ηδόν**, Adv. *clod-like*, Dsc.5.106.

βωληνή (sc. ἄμπελος), ἡ, a kind of *vine* grown in Bithynia, *Gp*. 5.17.5.

βωλητάρια· πινάκια *mushroom-shaped* dishes, *BGU*781 iii 8 (ii A.D.).

βωλήτης, = βωλίτης, Ath.3.113e:—hence **βωλητῖνος** ἄρτος a loaf *of this shape*, ibid.

βωλήτιον, τό, *saucepan*, *POxy*.1657.4 (iii A.D.).

βώλινος, η, ον, *made of clay*, i.e. *of brick*, Hsch.

βωλίον, τό, Dim. of βῶλος, Ar.*V*.203, Arist.*Mir*.833b14.

βωλίς, ἡ, *cake* used in sacrifices, Hsch.

βωλίτης [ῑ], ου, ὁ, *terrestrial fungus*, Lat. *boletus*, *Gp*.12.17.8, Gal. 6.655. **II.** *root of* λυχνίς, Plin.*HN*21.171.

βωλο-ειδής, ές, *cloddy, lumpy*, Thphr.*Ign*.65, Erot. s.v. μώλυζα. Adv. -δῶς Dsc.1.73. **-κοπέω**, *break clods of earth*, Ar.*Fr*.761, Hp. *Ep*.17, Ael.*Ep*.19, *PLond*.1.131r iii 50 (i A.D.): pf. βεβωλοκόπηκα Ar.*Fr*.57 D.: metaph. in mal. part., Ἀρχ.Δελτ.2 *App*.47 (Thyrrheum). **-κόπος**, ον, *clod-breaking*, Cratin.5. **-κρῖθον**, τό, *barley-cake* for fodder, *PLond.ined*.2360 (iii B.C.). **-λογέω**, *sift out earth* from corn, *POxy*.708.7 (Pass., ii A.D.).

βώλομαι, Cret. for βούλομαι, *GDI*5042.16 (iii B.C.).

βωλόναι, αἱ, *mounds, barrows*, S.*Fr*.1035.

βωλο-ποιέω, *make into clods*, f.l. in Hp.*Ep*.17. **-πῡρος**, ὁ, *wheat-cake* for fodder, Wilcken *Chr*.198 (iii B.C.), *PLond.ined*.2360 (iii B.C.).

βωλόρυχα (βῶλος, ὀρύσσω)· τὴν σῦν (Lacon.), Hsch.

βῶλος, ἡ, less freq. ὁ (v. sub fin.), *lump, clod of earth*, εἴκοι δ' ὑπὸ βῶλος ἀρότρῳ Od.18.374; ὑγρὰς ἀρούρας β. S.*Aj*.1286; ὡς βαλῶ ταύτῃ τῇ βώλῳ X.*Cyr*.8.3.27; β. ἀνιστάναι Plu.*Rom*.11; βῶλος ἄρουραν, prov. 'carrying coals to Newcastle', Zen.2.74; esp. of *earth* fraudulently mixed with corn, *POxy*.708.8 (ii A.D.); cf. ἄβωλος. 2. in Poets, *land, soil*, βαθεῖαν β. ἀροῦντες Mosch.4.37, cf. *AP*9.561 (Phil.), etc.; Λίβυσσα κρύψει β. Ἀννίβου δέμας Orac.ap.Plu.*Flam*.20, cf. Jul.*Or*.3.125b. 3. generally, *lump*, as of gold, *nugget*, Arist. *Mir*.833b11, Str.3.2.8; χρυσέα βῶλος, of the sun, E.*Fr*.783, cf. *Or*.984 (lyr.); β. μολίβδου D.S.3.14. 4. = βωλίτης, Sch.Nic.*Al*.526. 5. = σπαργάνιον, Ps.-Dsc.4.21 (v.l.). (Fem. acc. to Phryn.37, Moer. 95; masc. in Arist. l. c., D.C.40.47, *PHolm*.2.31, etc.)

βωλο-στροφέω, *turn up clods in ploughing*, *Gp*.2.23.14 (Pass.), Eust.581.16:—hence **-στροφητέος**, α, ον, also **-στροφία**, ἡ, *turning up of clods*, and **-στρόφιον**, τό, *dibble*, Gloss. **-τόμος**, ον, *clod-breaking*, μύρμηκες *AP*9.438 (Phil.).

βωλ-ώδης, ες, = βωλοειδής, Thphr.*Lap*.42, *PHolm*.24.38. **-ωσις**, εως, ἡ, *formation of lumps*, *PHolm*.8.3.

βωμαίνω, aor. ἐβώμηνα, *swear*, Hsch.

βωμάκευμα [μᾰ], ατος, τό, = βωμολόχευμα, Apollod.Cyren.ap.Sch. Pl.*R*.606c (pl.), *EM*218.7.

βώμαξ, ᾱκος, ὁ, ἡ, = βωμολόχος, Agath.2.30, *EM*199.2, Suid. **II.** **βῶμαξ**, ᾰκος, ἡ, Dim. of βωμός, *AB*85. **βώμενος**· βωμός, Hsch.

βώμευσις, εως, ἡ, *erection of an altar*, Hsch.

βωμιαῖος, α, ον, = sq., S.*Fr*.38.

βωμικός, ή, όν, = βώμιος, *BCH*2.600 (Cibyra).

βωμίνας· ἀναβάσεις, Hsch.

βώμιος, ον, also α, ον, v. infr.: (βωμός):—*of an altar*, ἀκτὰν πάρα βώμιον S.*OT*183 (lyr.); βώμιοι ἐσχάραι E.*Ph*.274; β. ἕδρη Orph.*A*. 992. 2. of a suppliant, βωμία ἐφημένη *at the altar*, E.*Supp*.93, cf. S.*Ant*.1301; ἀμφὶ βωμίους λιτάς E.*Ph*.1749 (lyr.).

Βώμιος, ὁ, name of a Lamian month, *IG*9(2).71.3, al.

βωμ-ίς, ίδος, ἡ, Dim. of βωμός, *step*, Hdt.2.125. **-ισκάριον**, τό, Dim. of βωμός, *IG*14.1030:—also **-ίσκιον**, τό, *BGU*162.12 (ii/iii A.D.). **-ίσκος**, ὁ, Dim. of βωμός, *altar-shaped vessel*, Hero *Spir*. 1.38, al. 2. *bandage*, Gal.18(1).823. 3. Arith., *solid* or *solid number* with all its dimensions unequal bounded by rectangles and trapezia, Hero *Deff*.114, Theo Sm.p.41 H., Nicom.*Ar*.2.16, Syrian. *in Metaph*.143.7, al. b. Geom., *plane figure* resembling the solid β. in appearance, Papp.878. 4. name of a *constellation*, Ptol.*Alm*. 8.1. 5. *base* of molar teeth, Poll.2.93. **-ίστρια**, ἡ, *priestess*, Nic.*Al*.217. **-ῖτις** (sc. γῆ), ιδος, ἡ, *consecrated* land, *Inscr.Perg*. 157*D*17.

βωμοειδής, ές, *like an altar*, Plu.*Them*.32.

βωμολόχ-ευμα, ατος, τό, only in pl., *ribald jests*, Ar.*Eq*.902, *Pax* 748. **-εύομαι**, *play the buffoon, indulge in ribaldry*, Ar.*Fr*.166; opp. σεμνύνομαι, Isoc.7.49; *play low tricks*, in Music, Ar.*Nu*.969, Phld.*Mus*.p.94 K.:—Act. in Hsch. s.v. Λέσβιος ᾠδός, Suid. **-έω**, *beg*, Poll.3.111. 2. = foreg., Plu.2.407c. **-ία**, ἡ, *mendicancy*, Poll. 3.111. 2. *coarse jesting, buffoonery, ribaldry*, Pl.*R*.606c, Arist. *EN*1108a24, Plu.*Lyc*.12, etc. **-ικός**, ή, όν, *inclined to ribaldry*, Luc.*Herm*.58, Gal.6.228, al. Adv. -κῶς (Lat. *-ice*), Id.*Subf.Emp*. 11. **-ος**, ον, (λοχάω) prop. *one that waited about the altars, to beg or steal some of the meat offered thereon*, ἵνα μὴ πρὸς τοῖσι βωμοῖς ἀεὶ λοχῶντες βωμολόχοι καλώμεθα Pherecr.141; β. ἱερεῖς Man.5.119; expld. by ἱερόσυλος, Hsch., *Et.Gud*. 2. metaph., *ribald, coarse*, β. ξυνήγορος Ar.*Eq*.1358, cf. *Ra*.1085,1521, al., Arist.*EN*1108a25, *Rh*.1419b9, Luc.*Merc.Cond*.24, etc.; β. κόλαξ *AP*11.323 (Pall.): Sup. -ώτατος Phld.*Mus*.p.77 K.; βωμολόχον τι ἐξευρεῖν invent some *ribald trick*, Ar.*Eq*.1194; β. ἔπεσιν χαίρει Id.*Ra*.358; τὸ β., = βωμολοχία, Plu.2.68a sq. Adv. -χως Procop.*Arc*.9, Olymp.*in Phd*. p.70 N. 3. small *jackdaw*, Arist.*HA*617b18.

βωμονίκης [ῑ], ου, ὁ, at Sparta, *the lad who won the prize for the endurance of the voluntary whipping at the altar of* Artemis Orthia, *IG* 5(1).554, al.:—hence **-νικέω**, ib.654.

βωμός, ὁ, (βαίνω) *raised platform, stand*, for chariots, Il.8.441; *base* of a statue, Od.7.100: but, 2. mostly, *altar with a base*, ἱερὸς β. Il.2.305, etc.; πρὸς βωμῷ σφαγείς A.*Eu*.305; βωμὸς ἀρῆς φυγάσιν ῥῦμα Id.*Supp*.84 (lyr.); βωμῶν ἀπείργειν τινά Id.*Ch*.293; ἀγυιεὺς β. S.*Fr*.370; of suppliants, ποτὶ βωμὸν ἵζεσθαι Od.22.334; βωμοῖσι προσῆσθαι, προσπεσόντα βωμῷ καθῆσθαι, S.*OT*16, *OC*1158; βωμὸν ἵζειν E.*Ion*1314: also in Prose, β. ἱδρύσασθαι Hdt.3.142, cf. Pl.*Prt*.322a; ἱζόμενοι ἐπὶ τὸν β. Hdt.6.108; ἐπὶ βωμῶν καθέζεσθαι Lys.2.11. 3. later, *tomb, cairn*, *Epigr.Gr*.319. 4. title of poems by Dosiades and Besantinus, *AP*15.26 and 25, cf. Luc.*Lex*.25. 5. *altar-shaped cake*, *IG*2.1651*B,C*, Poll.6.76. 6. Ζεὺς Βωμός, prob. a Syrian god, *Hermes*37.118 (Syria). 7. *central fire* in the system of Philolaus, acc. to *Placit*.2.7.7. 8. in pl., = ἔμβολοι, Hsch.

βωμόσπειρον, τό, *round base* or *torus* of a column *placed upon a square plinth*, *CIG*2782.31 (Aphrodisias), *Rev.Phil*.44.73 (Lydia).

βῶν, v. βοῦς.

βώνημα· εἴρημα (Lacon.), Hsch.

βωνίτης, ου, Dor. **-τας**, ὁ, = βουκόλος, Call.*Fr*.157, Choerob. in *An.Ox*.1.184, Hsch.; but βουνιτῆσι· τοῖς βουκόλοις, Suid.

βῶξ, βωκός, ὁ, contr. for βόαξ (q.v.).

βωρεύς, εως, ὁ, *pickled mullet*, Xenocr.76:—Dim. **βωρίδιον**, τό, Id. 78.

Βωρθία· Ὀρθία (q.v.), Hsch.; cf. Βορθεία.

βώριμος or **βῶρμος**, name of a Mariandynian *dirge*, Poll.4.54.

βῶροι· ὀφθαλμοί, Hsch.

βῶς, v. βοῦς.

βωσαρή, Indian name for an *elephant*, *Peripl.M.Rubr*.62.

βώσας, **βῶσον**, v. sub βοάω. **βώσεσθε**, poet. for βιώσεσθε, A.R.1.685.

βωσιδία, ἡ, = sq., *Sammelb*.1160.4.

βωσίον, τό, dub. sens. of a *household utensil*, β. χαλκοῦν *Stud.Pal*. 20.67 (ii/iii A.D.).

βωστήρ, ῆρος, ὁ, = βοτήρ, Hsch.

βωστρέω, *call on*, esp. *call to aid*, βωστρεῖν δὲ Κραταιΐν Od.12.124, cf. Ar.*Pax* 1146, al., Theoc.5.64; *cry after*, ἁ Κύπρις τὸν Ἔρωτα.. ἐβώστρει Mosch.1.1; β. τινὶ ποιεῖν τι Opp.*C*.4.293: abs., τὰ δ' ἐσίγα, τὰ δ' ἐβώστρει, of birds, *Lyr.Alex.Adesp*.7.8. (Formed from βοάω, cf. ἐλαστρέω, καλιστρέω.)

βωτάριον, *vessel for slow heating*, Zos.Alch.p.165 B.; cf. βοῦτις.

βωτάζειν· βάλλειν, Hsch. **βωτῆρες**, gloss on βώτορες, Id.

βωτῐάνειρα [ᾰν], ἡ, (βόσκω) *man-feeding, nurse of heroes*, epith. of fruitful countries, Il.1.155; χθών *h.Ap*.363, Hes.*Cat.Oxy*.1369 *Fr*. 1.16. **βωτίον**· σταμνίον, Hsch.

βώτωρ, ορος, ὁ, = βοτήρ, Il.12.302; βώτορες ἄνδρες Od.14.102, *AP* 6.262 (Leon.).

βώχ· βοτάνης εἶδος, Hsch.

Γ

Γ γ, third letter in Gr. alphabet; as Numeral γ' = *three, third, thrice*: also, with pr. n., Βάσσος γ' *B., son and grandson of B.*, *IGRom*.4.1587 (ii A.D.), etc.: but ͵γ = 3,000. **II.** written for ϝ, freq. in Hsch., as γανδάνειν· ἀρέσκειν, etc.

γᾰ, Dor. for γε, Ar.*Ach*.775, etc.; cf. ἔγωγα, τύγα.

γᾶ, Dor. and Aeol. for γῆ.

γαβαθόν· τρύβλιον, Hsch.; cf. ζάβατος. **γαβαλάν**· ἐγκέφαλον ἢ κεφαλή, Id. **γάβενα**· ὀξυβάφια ἤτοι τρύβλια, Id. **γαβεργόρ** (= γαϝεργός), *labourer* (Lacon.), Id.

Γᾰγάτης (sc. λίθος), ου, ὁ, *lignite*, Orph.*L*.474, Plin.*HN*36.141, Dsc.5.128, Gal.12.203, *Gp*.15.1.32. **2.** *jet*, Solin.22.11. **II.** = ἀστράγαλος, cj. in Ps.-Dsc.4.61. (From Γάγας or Γάγγαι, a town and river in Lycia.)

γαγγαίνειν· τὸ μετὰ γέλωτος προσπαίζειν, Hsch.

γαγγᾰλ-ιάω, = -ίζεσθαι, Hsch. **-ίζω**, later form of Att. γαργαλίζω, Phryn.77, *Anacreont*.5.7 (but the contrary is stated in Phryn. *PS* p.56 B.). **-ίδες**· γελασῖνοι, Hsch. **-ος**, ὁ, *fickle person*, Id.

γαγγᾰμ-εύς, έως, ὁ, *fisher*, Hsch. **-ευτής**, οῦ, ὁ, = foreg., prob. in *EM*219.25. **-ον**, τό, *small round net*, esp. for oyster-catching, Opp.*H*.3.81: metaph., μέγα δουλείας γ. A.*Ag*.361 (anap.): —also **γαγγάμη**, ἡ, Str.7.3.18. **2.** *umbilical region*, Poll.2.169 (γαγγαμών is f.l.). **-ουλκός**, όν, (ἕλκω) *dragging an oyster-net*, *EM*219.23.

Γαγγητικός, ή, όν, *from the Ganges*, νάρδος, a fragrant medicinal grass, = *Cymbopogon Iwarancusa*, *Peripl.M.Rubr*.63; σινδόνες ibid.

γαγγίας ἢ **γαγγαλίας** (leg. γαγγαλίδας)· οἱ μὲν γελασῖνον, οἱ δὲ τὴν τῶν νεύρων (ἐρίων cod.) συστροφήν, ἄλλοι ὑποστάθμην, Hsch.

Γαγγῖτις or **Γαγγῆτις** λίθος, = Γαγάτης, Str.16.1.24: also Γ. νάρδος, = Γαγγητικὴ νάρδος, Dsc.1.7, Damocr.ap.Gal.13.1057.

γαγγλίον, τό, *encysted tumour on a tendon* or *aponeurosis*, Philagr. ap.Aët.15.9 (Ἀθηνᾶ 21.29), Heras ap.Gal.13.815, etc.; also on the head, Paul.Aeg.6.39; the nerve-knots now called *ganglia* are compared to such a tumour, Gal.*UP*16.5.

γαγγλιώδης, ες, *of the ganglion kind*, Hp.*Art*.40:—also **γαγγλιοειδής**, ές, Hsch.

γάγγραιν-α, ἡ, (γράω?) *gangrene*, Hp.*Mochl*.33, 2*Ep.Ti*.2.17, Dsc.1.61, Plu.2.65d, Gal.18(1).687. **-ικός**, ή, όν, *gangrenous*, νομαί Dsc.2.107: -κά, τά, Id.4.93. Adv. -κῶς Heliod.(?)ap.Orib. 47.16.1. **-όομαι**, Pass., *become gangrenous*, Hp.*Art*.63, Gal.18 (1).156. **-ώδης**, ες, *of the gangrene kind*, Hp.*Epid*.7.110, Gal. 11.818. **-ωμα**, τό, = sq., Pall.*Febr*.7. **-ωσις**, εως, ἡ, *becoming gangrenous*: *gangrenous affection*, φλεβῶν Hp.*Fract*.11 (pl.), *Mochl*. 30 (pl.), Aret.*SA*2.10 (pl.).

Γάδαρα [ᾰ], ων, τά, a town in Palestine, Str.16.2.29:—**Γᾰδᾰρεύς** or **Γᾰδᾰρηνός**, ὁ, an inhabitant, *Ev.Matt*.8.28:—**Γᾰδᾰρίς** (sc. γῆ), ἡ, the country, Str. l.c.

γάδαρος, = γαϊδάριον, Diogenian.5.36.

γαδεῖν, γάδεσθαι, = ϝαδ- (ϝηδ-), Hsch.:—also **γαδεδᾶν**· χαίρειν, and **γαδεῶ**· χαρά, Id.

Γάδειρα [ᾰ], ων, τά, *Cadiz*, Pi.*N*.4.69, etc.; Ion. **Γήδειρα** Hdt.4.8: **Γᾰδειρίτης** [ῑ], **Γᾰδειρεύς**, ὁ, *a man of Cadiz*, St.Byz.:—Adj. **Γᾰδειρικός**, ή, όν, τάριχος Eup.186, Pl.*Criti*.114b; or **Γᾰδειραῖος**, α, ον, as Γ. πορθμός the Straits *of Gibraltar*, Plu.*Sert*.8. Adv. **Γᾰδειρόθεν** *AP* 14.121 (Metrod.), Euthyd.ap.Ath.3.116c.

Γᾰδειτάνα, ἡ, *woman of Cadiz, courtesan*, *PGrenf*.1.53.28 (iv A.D.: γαειτ- Pap.).

γαδή· κίβωτος, Hsch.

γάδιξ(ις)· ὁμολογία, Hsch. (ϝαδ-). **γᾶδος**· γάλα, ἄλλοι ὄξος, Id.

γάδος, a *fish*, = ὄνος, Dorio ap.Ath.7.315f. **II.** = γάνδος (q.v.).

γαεών, ῶνος, ὁ, v. γαιών.

γάζα [γᾰ], ἡ, *treasure*, Thphr.*HP*8.11.5, *OGI*54.22 (iii B.C.), Epigr. ap.Str.14.1.39, Lxx 2*Es*.5.17, *Act.Ap*.8.27, etc.; ἐκ τῆς βασιλικῆς γ. D.S.17.35. **II.** *large sum of money*, Plb.11.34.12. (Persian word.)

γάζας, a *fish*, Hsch.

Γαζίτιον, τό, *Gaza measure*, *POxy*.1924.8 (v/vi A.D.).

γᾱζο-φῠλᾰκέω, *to be a treasurer*, D.S.17.74. **-φῠλάκιον** [λᾰ], τό, *treasury*, *OGI*225.16 (Didyma, iii B.C.), Lxx 4*Ki*.23.11, Str.7.6.1, *Ev.Luc*.21.1, al. **-φύλαξ** [ῠ], ᾰκος, ὁ, *treasurer*, Phylarch.29, Lxx 1*Ch*.28.1, Str.16.2.40, J.*AJ*11.1.3, Plu.*Demetr*.25; written γαζζο-, *Syria* 5.347 (Dura).

γάθευδον· ἐκ γῆς ῥέον, Hsch.

γᾱθέω, γάθω, Dor. for γηθέω, γήθω. **γαθία**· ἀλλαντία, Hsch.

γαῖα, ἡ, gen. γαίης Hom. (and Antiph., v. infr.), Trag. γαίας, dat. γαίᾳ A.*Pers*.618, S.*Aj*.659, E.*Med*.736, etc., acc. γαῖαν: nom. γαίη only in late Poets, *IG*14.1935, etc.; Dor. γαῖα ib.803 (Naples): pl. γαῖαι Od. (v. infr.), Lxx 4*Ki*.18.35, al.:—poet. for γῆ, *land, country*, φίλην ἐς πατρίδα γαῖαν to one's dear father*land*, Il.2.140, al.; γαῖάν τε τεὴν δῆμόν τε Od.8.555: pl., οὐδέ τις ἄλλη φαίνετο γαιάων 12.404, D.P.882. **2.** *earth*, χυτὴ γ. *earth* thrown up to form a cairn, Il.23. 256; ὦ γ. κεραμί, of potters' *earth*, Eub.43, cf. Sannyr.4; κύτος πλαστὸν ἐκ γαίης Antiph.52.3; the forms γαιῶν, γαίαις, γαίας in codd. of Lxx are written for γεῶν, etc. **3.** *earth*, as an element, ὑμεῖς.. ὕδωρ καὶ γ. γένοισθε Il.7.99; ἐμοῦ θανόντος γ. μειχθήτω πυρί *Trag. Adesp*.513; γαίης καὶ ὕδατος ἐκγενόμεσθα Xenoph.33, cf. Emp.17.18, 109.1, etc. **II.** *the earth*, Theoc.18.20: elsewh. Γαῖα, as pr. n., *Earth*, Hes.*Th*.45, A.*Eu*.2, etc. (The usu. form in Hom.; used in Trag. metri gr. and by Com. in paratrag., v. supr.)

γαιάδας· ὁ δῆμος (Lacon.), Hsch. **γαιᾶται**· κερτομεῖ, Id. (leg. γλιᾶται).

γαϊδάριον, τό, *donkey*, *PAmh*.2.153 (vi/vii A.D.). (Arabic word.)

γαιη-γενής, ές, poet. for γηγενής, A.R.3.1186. **-θεν**, Adv. *from the land*, Opp.*H*.1.39. **2.** *out of the earth*, ἐκφύεται γ. Orac. ap.Eus.*PE*6.2 (*App.Anth*.6.113); *from the earth*, ἀναστήσαντες Orac. ib.5.9 (*App.Anth*.6.162). **-ῐος**, α, ον, *sprung from Gaia* or *Earth*, Τιτυόν, Γαιήϊον υἱόν Od.7.324, cf. *AP*14.23. **II.** *earthly*, βίου βροτέου γ. δεσμά Nonn.*D*.37.4; μελέων γ. ἄχθος *Eranos* 13.88. **-οχος** (also **-οῦχος**, Hsch.), Dor. **γαιάοχος**, ον, **γαιάϝοχος** *IG*5(1).213 (Sparta, v B.C.):—epith. of Poseidon, *earth-moving, earth-carrying*, Il.13.43, al., A.*Th*.310 (lyr.), cf. S.*OC*1072 (lyr.): **Γαιάοχος**, abs., Il. 13.125, Pi.*O*.13.81, and so Γαιάϝοχος (v. supr.): also in pl., Γαάοχοι, name of a contest, *IG*5(1).296.11 (Sparta). **2.** ὠκεανὸς γ. *App. Anth*.3.209. **II.** *protecting the country*, γαιάοχε παγκρατὲς Ζεῦ A.*Supp*.816 (lyr.); γαιάοχόν τ' Ἄρτεμιν S.*OT*160 (lyr.). **2.** = ἠπειρώτης, Hsch. (In signf. I from γαῖα and ϝεχ-: ϝοχ-, cf. ὄχεα, Lat. *veho*, Skt. *váhati*, Germ. *be-wegen*, etc. In signf. II from ἔχω (q.v.).) **-φάγος** [ᾰ], ον, *earth-eating*, of worms, Numen.ap.Ath. 7.305a; cf. γαφάγας.

γαιθυλα (δ supra scr.)· ἀμπελόπρασα, Hsch.; cf. γηθυλλίς.

γαϊκός, ή, όν, *concerning land*, κρίμα *SIG*421.44 (Thermon, iii B.C.).

γαίνεται· ἀνύει, Hsch.

γαΐνος, Dor. = γήϊνος (q.v.).

γαιο-γράφος [ᾰ], ὁ, = γεωγράφος, Hsch. **-δότης**, f.l. for γεωδαίτης in Call.*Fr*.158. **-μέτρης**, ου, ὁ, = γεωμ-, Man.4.210. **-νόμος**, ον, *dwelling in the land*: *inhabitant*, A.*Supp*.54 (anap.).

γάϊος [ᾱ], α, ον, Dor. for γήϊος, *on land*, A.*Supp*.826 (lyr.); *earthy*, γ. κόνις Id.*Th*.736; *of the land*, κόγχοι Epich.42.9; παῖς γ. child *of earth*, *terrae filius*, of a slave, prob. in *IG*14.1432 (cf. γάϊος παρὰ Ἰταλιώταις καὶ Ταραντίνοις ὁ μίσθιος Eust.188.30, cf. *EM*223.24); ἄνεμος a *land* wind, Hsch.; also, = ἐργάτης βοῦς, Id., *EM* l.c. **II.** τὸν γάϊον, = καταχθόνιον, prob. in A.*Supp*.156 (lyr.).

γαιός· μακροκέντης ἢ κόντος ἢ κολοβός, Cyr., cf. Hsch.

γαιο-φάγος [ᾰ], ον, = γαιηφάγος, Nic.*Th*.784. **-φανής**, ές, *earth-coloured*, in Comp., Archig.ap.Orib.8.2.4 (v.l. γεω-); τὸ γ. *the earthy appearance* of the moon, *Placit*.2.30.1 codd.

γαιόω, *make land, make solid*, Tz.*H*.1.907, al.

γαῖσος, ὁ (or **γαῖσον**, τό, Ph.*Bel*.99.16, cf. *AB*88), a sort of *javelin*, Lxx *Jo*.8.18, *Ju*.9.7, Plb.6.39.3, 18.18.4, *PTeb*.230 (ii B.C.), D.S.13. 57:—hence prob. Celtic pr. n. **Γαισάται** or **-οι**, οἱ, expld. by Plb. as *mercenaries*, 2.22.1. (Iberian word acc. to Ath.6.273f.)

γαῖται· γεωργοί, Hsch., *EM*223.29.

γαϊτανά, τά, *aseptic ligaments* made in Gaul, Gal.10.942, Marcell. Empir.8.27.

γαίω, impf. γαίεσκον Hsch.:—*rejoice, exult*, Hom. only in Il., in phrase, κύδεϊ γαίων Il.1.405, 5.906, 8.51; [Σφαῖρος] μονίῃ γαίων Emp. 27.4. (γάϝ-yω, v. γάνυμαι.)

γαιώδης, f.l. for γεώδης in Plb.2.15.8.

γαιών, ῶνος, ὁ, *heap of earth, boundary-heap*, *Tab.Heracl*.1.136: **γαεών** *IG*14.352 ii 83 (Halaesa, pl.).

γάκα· ἡδέως, **γακεῖαι**· γλυκεῖαι, **γάκου**· ἡδύ, γλυκύ, **γακούδια**· ἡδύσματα, and **γακουπώνης**· ἡδυπότης, Hsch. **γᾱκίνας** [ῑ], ὁ, *earthquake*, Id., Eust.890.38:—also **γᾱκῖνίας**, ὁ, Hsch., and **γάκῑνος**, ὁ, Att. acc. to *EM*219.41. **γακτός**· κλάσμα, Hsch. (ϝακ-, cf. ϝάγ-νυμι.)

γάλα [⏑⏑], τό, gen. γάλακτος (also γάλακος, dat. γάλακι Call.*Hec*. 1.4.4, prob. in Pherecr.108.18, cf. *An.Ox*.4.338), also τοῦ γάλα indecl., Pl.Com.238: dat. pl. γάλαξι Pl.*Lg*.887d. (For γλακτ-, cf. Lat. *lac* for *glact*):—*milk*, ἀμελγόμενοι γ. λευκόν Il.4.434, cf. Od.4.88, etc.; εὔποτον γ., εὐτραφὲς γ., A.*Pers*.611, *Ch*.898; ἐν γάλακτι ὤν, τεθραμμένη, at *the breast*, E.*HF*1266, Pl.*Ti*.81c; ἐν γάλαξι τρέφεσθαι Id.*Lg*. l.c. (so metaph., ἐν σπαργάνοις καὶ γάλαξιν εἶναι, of art, Ael.*VH* 8.8); διδόναι γάλα X.*Cyn*.7.4; ἐμπλῆσαι γάλακτος to fill full of *milk*, Theoc.24.3: metaph., οἶνος, Ἀφροδίτης γ. Ar.*Fr*.596. **2.** ὀρνίθων γ. (ὄρνιθος γάλα, = ὀρνιθόγαλον, Nic.*Fr*.71.5, Dsc.2.144), prov. of rare and dainty things, Ar.*V*.508, *Av*.734, Men.936; τὸ λεγόμενον, σπανιώτατον πάρεστιν ὀρνίθων γ. Mnesim.9, cf. Ach.Tat.*Intr.Arat*. 4 (expld. by Anaxag.22 as *white of egg*, cf. Sch.Luc.*Merc.Cond*. 13). **3.** ἀγαθὸν γ. a good *wet-nurse*, Call.*Ep*.51; οὐδ' εἰ γ. λαγοῦ εἶχον . . καὶ ταῶς, κατήσθιον Alex.123. II. *milky sap* of plants, Thphr.*HP*6.3.4, etc. III. *the milky way*, Parm.11, Arist.*Mete.* 345^{a}12, Arat.476; but ὁ τοῦ γάλακτος κύκλος Euc.*Phaen.*p.4 M., Gem.5.69.

γάλαγγα, *galingale, Alpinia officinarum*, Aët.1.131.

γᾰλᾰθηνός, ή, όν, *sucking, young, tender*, νεβροί Od.4.336, cf. Anacr.51; τέκος Simon.52; ἄρνες Theoc.18.41, J.*AJ*6.2.2; γαλαθηνά (sc. πρόβατα) Hdt.1.183; (sc. χοιρία) opp. τέλεια, Pherecr.44, cf. Hp.*Aff.*43, *SIG*1015.32 (Halic., written γαλαθεινός); ἀρνῶν καὶ χοίρων Crates Com.1; ὗς Pherecr.28, cf. Arist.*HA*603^{b}25; βρέφη Clearch.17, cf. Theoc.24.31. (γάλα, θῆσθαι.)

γαλαίριον, τό, and **γαλάτιον**, τό, = γάλιον, Dsc.4.95.

γαλακοθρέμμων, ον, gen. ονος, (τρέφω) *milk-fed*, prob. in Antiph. 52.4 for γαλακτο-. **γαλακόχρως**, = γαλακτόχρως, nom. pl. -χροες Opp.*C.*3.478.

γαλακτηφόρος, ον, = γαλακτο-, *BCH*37.97 (ii/iii A. D.).

γᾰλακτ-ίας, ου, ὁ, with and without κύκλος, = γαλαξίας, Ptol.*Alm.* 8.2. **-ιάω**, *give no milk*, Poll.3.50; but γαλακτιῶντες· γάλακτος μεστοί, Hsch. **-ίζω**, *to be milky in appearance*, Dsc.2.144,175. 2. *form a milky way*, Phlp. *in Mete.*117.20. **-ινος**, η, ον, *milk-white*, στήθεα *AP*5.192 (Diosc.); χιτών *POxy.*267.7 (i A. D.); *milky*, χρώματα *PHolm.*24.31; v.l. for γαλακτίζον, Dsc.2.175. **-ιον**, τό, Dim. of γάλα, M.Ant.5.4: in pl., *fancy bread made with milk*, Alciphr.*Fr.* 6.10. **-ὶς** πέτρα, = -ίτης, Orph.*L.*201. II. γαλακτίς, ίδος, ἡ, = τιθύμαλλος, Aët.1.397. **-ισμός**, ὁ, *suckling*, παιδίου Mnesith.Cyz. ap.Orib.*inc.*15.17. **-ίτης** [ῑ] λίθος, stone *which makes water milky*, Dsc.5.132. II. γαλακτίτης, = γαλακτίς II, *Gloss.*

γᾰλακτο-δόχος, ον, *receiving, holding milk*, Sch.Theoc.1.25. **-ειδής**, ές, *like milk, milk-white*, χρῶμα *Placit.*3.1.4. **-θρέμμων**, v. γαλακοθρ-. **-κόμος**· ποιμήν, Hsch. **-κράς**, gen. -κρᾶτος, *mixed with milk*, Hdn.Gr.1.51, 2.759.

γᾰλακτόομαι, Pass., *become milk* or *milky*, Thphr.*CP*1.7.3, Dsc. 3.48; τῇ χροίᾳ Antyll.ap.Orib.4.11.6, cf. Plu.2.968a.

γᾰλακτο-πᾰγής, ές, *like curdled milk*, χρώς *AP*5.59 (Rufin.); ἄρνα ib.12.204 (Strat.). **-ποιέω**, *convert into sap*, Tz. ad Hes.*Op.* 72. **-ποιητικός**, ή, όν, *milk-producing*, βοτάνη *EM*232.37. **-ποιΐα**, ἡ, *production of milk*, Sch.Vat.Nic.*Th.*944. **-ποσία**, ἡ, *drinking of milk*, Hp.*Int.*16. **-ποτέω**, *drink milk*, Id.*Morb.*2.51, *Int.* 16, Thphr.*HP*9.15.4, Str.17.3.8. (Written -πωτέω by Ammon. p.111 V.) **-πότης**, ου, ὁ, *milk-drinker*, Hdt.1.216, 4.186, E.*El.*169 (lyr.). **-πώλης**, ου, ὁ, *milkseller*, *Gloss.* **-ρῠτος**, ον, *flowing with milk*, κρῆναι *Lyr.Alex.Adesp.*37.11. **-τροφέω**, *nourish with milk*, Lxx 4*Ma.*13.21, Ph.2.82 (Pass.), *PTeb.*399.4 (ii A. D.). **-τρόφησις**, εως, ἡ, *nourishment with milk*, Sch.rec.S.*Aj.*506. **-τροφία**, ἡ, = foreg., Lxx 4*Ma.*16.7, Ph.2.83, *BGU*297.14 (i A. D.).

γᾰλακτ-ουργέω, *make of milk*, as cheese, Poll.1.251. II. *make milk*, as a nursing woman, Sor.2.5. **-ουργός**, όν, *making milk-dishes*, Parmenion ap.Ath.13.608a. **-ουχέω**, *have* or *suck milk*, Poll.3.50; γαλακτουχούσης prob. in Plu.2.640f (γαλακτούσης codd.). **-οῦχος**, ον, (ἔχω) *having* or *sucking milk*, Poll.3.50.

γᾰλακτο-φᾰγέω, *live on milk*, Philostr.*VS*2.1.7. **φάγος** [φᾰ], ον, *milk-fed*, Str.7.4.6, S.E.*P.*1.56. **-φορία**, ἡ, *giving milk*, *BGU* 297.14 (i A. D.). **-φόρος**, ον, *giving milk*, *PLond.*1.3.22 (ii B. C.), J.*BJ*3.3.4, Opp.*C.*1.443; of food, *causing an abundant flow of milk*, Sch.Nic.*Th.*553. **-χρως**, ωτος, ὁ, ἡ, *milk-coloured*, Philyll.4, Nausicr.2: neut. pl., γαλακτόχροα Dsc.3.47: nom. pl. γαλακτόχροες in Opp.*C.*3.478 is f.l. for γαλακόχροες.

γᾰλακτ-ώδης, ες, = γαλακτοειδής, ὑγρότης Arist.*HA*540^{b}32; γ. τροφή Id.*PA*692^{a}15; χυμός Thphr.*CP*6.4.1. 2. *milk-warm, tepid*, Herod.Med.ap.Orib.5.30.38, Antyll.ib.9.23.9, Alex.Trall.*Febr.* 4. 3. *mixed with milk*, οἶνος Hp.*Epid.*7.101. **-ωσις**, εως, ἡ, *changing into milk*, Thphr.*CP*4.4.7.

γᾰλ-άνα, -ανός, Dor. for -ήνη, -ηνός. **γαλαός**, v. γάλις.

γάλαξ, ακος, ἡ, a kind of *shell-fish*, prob. *Mactra lactea*, Arist.*HA* 528^{a}23.

γαλαξ-αῖος, α, ον, *milky, milk-white*, Nonn.*D.*6.338, al. **-ήεις**, εσσα, εν, = foreg., ῥέεθρα v.l. ib.22.18. **-ια**, τά, *festival at Athens* in honour of Cybele, *at which a kind of milk-frumenty* (**γαλαξία**, ἡ) *was eaten*, *IG*2^2.1011.13, Thphr.*Char.*21.11, Hsch. **-ίας**, ου, ὁ: 1. (sc. κύκλος) *the milky way*, D.S.5.23, Luc.*VH*1.16, Man.2. 116, etc.; in full, γ. κύκλος *Placit.*2.7.1, Sallust.4. II. (sc. λίθος) = λίθος μόροχθος, *tailor's chalk*, Dsc.5.134. III. = γαλεός I, Gal.6. 727 (v.l. γαλεξ-). **-ιών**, ῶνος, ὁ, name of a Delian month, *IG*11 (2).203 *A* 31, al. (Delos, iii B. C.).

γαλαρίας, ου, ὁ, = ὀνίσκος, Hsch.

γάλας· γῆ (Cypr.), Euclus ap.Hsch.: **γαλάσιον**· ἐνηρόσιον, Hsch.

Γάλαται [λᾰ], οἱ, = Κελτοί (but Κελτοὶ καὶ Γ. Arist.*Fr.*35), Plb.1.6. 2, etc.: fem. sg. **Γαλάτισσα**, *GDI*2154.7 (Delph., ii B. C.):—Adj. **Γᾰλᾰτικός**, ή, όν, πέλαγος Arist.*Mu.*393^{a}27; χώρα *Act.Ap.*16.6; ἔργα βάρβαρα καὶ Γ. Plu.2.1049b. Adv. -κῶς, ἐνεσκευασμένος Id. *Oth.*6.

Γᾰλᾰτάρχης, ου, ὁ, *president of the provincial council of Galatia*, *OGI*547.11 (Ancyra), etc.

γαλάτιον, v. γαλαίριον. **γαλατμόν**· λάχανον ἄγριον, Hsch.

γάλβινα χρώματα, (Lat. *galbus*) *greenish-yellow* shades of colour, *PHolm.*25.2.

γαλεάγκων, v.l. for γαλιάγκων (q.v.).

γᾰλεάγρα, ἡ, *weasel-trap* or *weasel-cage*, Hyp.*Fr.*34, 239: metaph., πλοῖον ἀνεφγμένη γ. Secund.*Sent.*17: generally, *cage for beasts*, Lxx *Ez.*19.9, cf. Hierocl.p.59 A.; θηρίων Str.6.2.6; used for prisoners, Plu.*Phoc.*33, App.*Pun.*4.

γαλέαγρος· *furo* (cod. *suro*), *Gloss.*

γαλέη, contr. **γαλῆ**, ῆς, ἡ, a name given to various animals of the *weasel* kind, *weasel, marten, polecat* or *foumart*, Batr.9, al., Ar.*Ach.* 255, *Pl.*693, Arist.*HA*609^{a}17, al.; εἰ διάξειεν γαλῆ (a bad omen) Ar.*Ec.*792, cf. Thphr.*Char.*16.3: prov., θύρα δι' ἧς γαλῆ . . οὐκ εἰσέρχεται Apollod.Car.6. 2. γ. ἀγρία wild *ferret* (found in Africa and Spain, Hdt.4.192), Arist.*HA*580^{b}26, Ruf.*Fr.*79, Str.3.2.6; γ. Ταρτησσία Hdt. l. c., Diogenian.3.71. 3. γ. ἐνοικίδιος tame *weasel*, Plu.2.446e; γ. κατοικίδιος Philum.*Ven.*33.1, Dsc.2.25. 4. prov., γαλῆν ἔχεις, of bad luck, Diogenian.3.84; γαλῇ χιτώνιον κροκωτόν, of 'pearls before swine', Stratt.71, Zen.2.93; γαλῇ στέαρ, = βατράχῳ ὕδωρ (q. v.), Diogenian.3.83. II. a small *fish*, distd. from γαλεός by Ael.*NA*15.11. (From γαλεγᾱ, Adj. from *γαλις, cf. Skt. *girikā* 'mouse', Lat. *glīs.*)

γᾰλεό-βδολον, τό, = γαλήοψις, Dsc.4.94. **-ειδής**, ές, (γαλεός I) *of the shark kind*, οἱ γ. Arist.*HA*565^{a}20:—more usu. **-ώδης** ib.505^a 5, al.

γᾰλεός, ὁ, *dog-fish* or small *shark*, Pl.Com.137, Arist.*HA*489^{b}6; γ. νεβρίας, *Scyllium stellare*, ib.565^{a}26; γ. ἀστερίας ib.543^{a}17, cf. Philyll. 1; γ. λεῖος, *Mustela laevis*, Arist.*HA*565^{b}2. II. = γαλέη I. 3, οἱ ἐνοικάδιοι γ. Aret.*CD*1.4.

γᾰλερός, ά, όν, = γαληνός, *cheerful*, Hsch., *AB*229. Adv. -ρῶς cj. in *AP*12.50 (Asclep.).

γαλερωπός, όν, *with cheerful, happy face*, *AB*229.

γαλεώδης, v. γαλεοειδής.

γαλεώνυμος, ὁ, = γαλεός I, Philotim.ap.Gal.6.726.

γᾰλεώτης, ου, ὁ, *gecko lizard*, Ar.*Nu.*173, Arist.*Fr.*370. II. *sword-fish*, = ξιφίας, Plb.34.2.12, Str.1.2.15. III. *weasel*, Luc. *VH*1.35; γ. γέρων (transl. by *colore mustelino*, Ter.*Eun.*4.4.21) Men.188.

γαλῆ, ἡ, contr. for γαλέη (q.v.).

γάλη· ἐξέδρας εἶδος, καὶ ἐν ᾗ (leg. γαλῇ) γαλέα τὸ ζῷον, Hsch.

γᾰλην-αίη, ἡ, Ep. for γαλήνη, A.R.1.1156. **-αῖος**, α, ον, = γαληνός, *AP*10.21 (Phld.); ὀπωπαί *Epigr.Gr.*403.2 (Sebastopolis). Adv. -αίως Sch.Od.7.319. **-ειᾰ**, Dor. **γᾰλάνειᾰ**, ἡ, = γαλήνη, E.*IA* 546 (lyr.), *HF*402 (lyr.), *Hyps.Fr.*3iii4 (lyr.). **-η**, ἡ, *stillness of the sea, calm* (γ. μὲν ἐν θαλάσσῃ νηνεμία δ' ἐν ἀέρι Arist.*Top.*108^b 25, but cf. Od.5.452, 12.168), Hom. only in Od., λευκὴ δ' ἦν ἀμφὶ γαλήνη 10.94; οἱ δ' ἐλόωσι γαλήνην will sail the *calm sea*, 7.319; *stillness* of deep waters, Coluth.360; νηνεμίας τε καὶ γ. Pl.*Tht.*153c; ἐν ταῖς γ. καὶ εὐδίαις Arist.*HA*533^{b}30: metaph. of the mind, *calmness, serenity*, φρόνημα νηνέμου γαλάνας A.*Ag.*740 (lyr.); ἐν γαλήνῃ in *calm, quiet*, S.*El.*899; γ. ἐν τῇ ψυχῇ Pl.*Lg.*791a. II. *lead sulphide, galena*, Plin.*HN*33.95, 34.159. III. name of an *antidote*, Androm.ap.Gal.14.32. (Aeol. γελήνη (sic) acc. to Jo.Gramm.*Comp.* 3.1; perh. akin to γελάω.) **-ής**, ές, = γαληνός, Arist.*Phgn.*811^b 38. **-ιάζω**, = sq., Hp.*Vict.*2, Ph.1.276, Them.*Or.*1.17a:—**Pass.**, aor. γαληνιασθῆναι Simp.*in Epict.*p.20 D. **-ιάω**, *to be calm, find peace*, χαίρει καὶ γ. Epicur.*Fr.*425, cf. Opp.*C.*1.115, Them.*Or.*15. 195a; Ep. part. γαληνιόων, -ωσα, *AP*9.208, 5.34.7 (Rufin.). **-ίδιον**, Dim. of γαλήνη, *Gloss.* **-ίζω**, *calm, still*, esp. waves or winds, Hp.*Vict.*3.71, E.*Fr.*1079. 2. intr., *become calm*, prob. in Hp. *Morb.Sacr.*13; *to be calm* or *tranquil*, Alex.178.6, Ph.1.354; τὸ γαληνίζον τῆς θαλάττης Arist.*Pr.*936^{a}5:—so in Med., Xenocr.ap. Orib.2.58.98. **-ιος**, ον, = γαληνός, Luc.*Halc.*2. **-ισμός**, ὁ, *calming*, Epicur.*Ep.*1 p.32 U.; *calming* of the conscience, Arist. *Ep.*5.

γᾰληνοβάτης [βᾰ], ου, ὁ, in pl., epith. of demons, *PMag.Par.*1. 1364.

γαληνός, όν (ή, όν *Cat.Cod.Astr.*1.136), *calm*, esp. of the sea, γαλήν' ὁρῶ (neut. pl.) I see *a calm*, E.*Or.*279; of persons, *gentle*, Id. *IT*345; γ. προσφθέγματα Id.*Hec.*1160; γαληνὴ ἕξις μετώπου Arist. *Phgn.*812^{a}1; βίος Pl.*Ax.*370d, Ph.1.411; τὸ γ. Them.*Or.*34 p.459 D.; as title, γαληνότατος δεσπότης *PGrenf.*1.60.16 (vi A. D.). Adv. -νῶς D.L.9.45: Comp. -νότερον J.*BJ*1.28.2.

γᾰληνότης, ητος, ἡ, = γαλήνη, S.E.*P.*1.10.

γᾰληνώδης, ες, *calm*, Sch.A.*Pr.*139.

γαληόψις, εως, ἡ, *brownwort, Scrofularia peregrina*, Dsc.4.94.

γαληρός, = γαλερός, Hsch. **γαληψός**, a *plant*, Id., *AB* 230. **γάλι**· ἱκανόν, Hsch.

γαλία· εἶδος πλοίου λῃστρικοῦ, *EM*502.44.

γαλιάγκων, ωνος, ὁ, *weasel-armed*, i.e. *short-armed*, Hp.*Art.*12, al.:—more correctly written γαλεάγκων in Arist.*Phgn.*808^{a}31, 813^a 12, Plu.2.520c.

γαλίαι· οἱ ὀνίσκοι, Hsch.

γαλιάω, = ἀκολασταίνω, *Com.Adesp.*967.

γᾰλῐδεύς, έως, ὁ, *a young weasel*, Cratin.265.

γάλινθοι (or **γέλινθοι**)· ἐρέβινθοι, Hsch.

γᾰλῐοβρᾰχίων [χῐ], ονος, ὁ, = γαλιάγκων, coined by Gal.19.9c.

γάλιον, τό, *bedstraw, Galium verum*, Dsc.4.95 (expld. by Dsc. from γάλα because used in place of rennet).

γάλις· γαλαός, Hsch.

γαλλάζω, *practise cult of Cybele*, *Schwyzer*633.12 (Eresus, ii/i B. C.).

γαλλαῖος, α, ον, *of a* Γάλλος, γ. Κυβέλης ὀλόλυγμα Rhian.67.

γαλλερίας, ου, ὁ, = ὀνίσκος, Dorio ap.Ath.7.315f.

γάλλι, τό, = δρῶπαξ, Aët.3.180.

γάλλια· ἔντερα, Hsch.

γαλλῐαμβικὸν μέτρον, variety of Ion. metre used in cult of Cybele, Heph.12.3.

γαλλιάριος, ὁ, *footpad, cutpurse*, *PLips.*40ii 10 (iv A.D.).

γαλλικός, ή, όν, perh. *gelded*, *POxy.*1836 (v/vi A.D.).

γαλλιστὶ τεμεῖν, prov. 'cut the Gordian knot', Macar.2.92.

γαλλιώτας, = γαλεώτης I (Lacon.), Hsch. **γάλλοι**· ἧλοι, Id. (Aeol. ϝάλλοι).

γαλλομᾰνής, ές, *frenzied like a* Γάλλος, Man.4.221.

Γάλλος, ὁ, *priest of Cybele*, *Schwyzer*633.11 (Eresus, ii/i B.C.), Arr. *Epict.*2.20.17, *AP*6.234 (Eryc.), 220 (Diosc.):—fem. form **Γαλλαί** *Lyr.Adesp.*121. II. *eunuch*, J.*AJ*4.8.40, *PGnom.*244, D.L.4.43.

γάλμινος, misspelling for γάλβινος, *Sammelb.*2251.

γᾰλ-ουργέω, *make of milk*, Poll.1.251. **-ουχέω**, *suckle*, Sor.1.88, J.*AJ*2.9.5, A.D.*Synt.*278.1 codd., Sm.1*Ki.*6.7: **-ουχία**, *suckling*, *Gp.*16.21.7: **-οῦχος**, ὁ, *wet-nurse*, Sor.1.89, Paul.Aeg.3.13. (Later forms for γαλακτ-.)

γάλοως [ᾰ], ἡ, gen. γάλοω, dat. sg. and nom. pl. γαλόῳ Il.3.122, 22.473: Att. **γάλως**, gen. γάλω Hdn.Gr.2.236 (also gen. γάλωτος acc. to *EM*220.18):—*husband's sister* or *brother's wife*, *sister-in-law*, Il.6.378, al. (Cf. Lat. *glōs*, Phryg. **γέλαρος**· ἀδελφοῦ γυνή, Hsch.)

γαλωνές· χρῶμα ἵππων τὸ ὀνοειδές, *EM*220.32.

γαμάλη· κάμηλος (Chald.), Hsch.

γαμβρά, ἡ, fem. of γαμβρός, *sister-in-law*, *BGU*827.29 (ii A.D.), *PLond.*2.403 (iv A.D.).

γαμβρεύω, *form connexions by marriage*, πρός τινας Lxx*De.*7.3; τισί 2*Es.*9.14:—Med., *marry*, v.l. ib.*Ge.*38.8:—Pass., *to be connected by marriage*, τινί J.*AJ*14.12.1.

γάμβριον· τρύβλιον, Hsch. **γάμβρια**· δῶρα ἢ δεῖπνα γαμβροῦ, Id.

γαμβρο-κτόνος, ον, *bridegroom-slaying*, Lyc.161. **-ποιέω**, *make a son-in-law of*, Tz.*H.*10.433.

γαμβρός, ὁ, *connexion by marriage*, Pi.*N.*5.37, A.*Ag.*708 (pl.): hence, I. *son-in-law*, Il.6.249, Hdt.5.30,67, Democr.272, E.*Ph.*427, etc. II. *brother-in-law*, i.e. *sister's husband*, Il.5.474, 13.464, Hdt.1.73, etc.; or, *wife's brother*, S.*OT*70. III. = πενθερός, *father-in-law*, E.*Hipp.*635, *Andr.*641, Lxx*Ex.*3.1. IV. Dor. and Aeol., *bridegroom*, *wooer*, Sapph.103, Pi.*P.*9.116, Theoc.18.49, 15.129, Arat.248. (Cf. Skt. *jārá-* (from *ǵn̥ro-*) 'lover'.)

γαμβροτιδεύς, έως, ὁ, *son of a* γαμβρός, Iamb.*Protr.*21.κζʹ.

γάμελα, τά, *offerings made on the occasion of a marriage*, *Michel* 995*B*36 (Delph., v B.C.).

γᾶμεν, Dor. for ἔγημεν, aor. I of γαμέω, Pi.*P.*3.91, Theoc.8.93.

γᾰμετ-ή, ἡ, fem. of sq., *married woman*, *wife*, opp. concubine, [γυναῖκα] κτητήν, οὐ γαμετήν Hes.*Op.*406, cf. Pl.*Lg.*841d, Lys.1.31 (pl.), Men.*Pk.*237, *PTeb.*104.17 (i B.C.), etc.; γαμετῇ ἀλόχῳ *Epigr. Gr.*310 (Smyrna); so γαμετή alone, A.*Supp.*165 (lyr.), Arist.*Fr.*144, *POxy.*795.4 (i A.D.); τέκνα καὶ γαμετάς Phld.*Ir.*p.53W., cf. *Herc.*1457.10, al. **-ης**, ου, ὁ, *husband*, *spouse*, A.*Pr.*897 (lyr.), E.*Tr.*311 (lyr.), Euph.107.3; poet. word used by X.*Cyr.*4.6.3, and late, *PLond.*5.1711.53 (vi A.D.); Dor. gen. γαμέτα E.*Supp.*998 (lyr.):—fem. **γᾰμέτις**, ιδος, *a wife*, dub. in *AP*5.179 (Mel.), cf. *IPE*2.298.10 (Panticapaeum).

γᾱμετρία, = γεωμετρία, Archyt.1, Perict.ap.Stob.3.1.121:—so **γᾱμέτρας**, for γεωμέτρης, *Tab.Heracl.*1.187; **γᾱμετρικός** Archyt.2.

γᾰμέω, fut. γαμέω Il.9.388,391, contr. γαμῶ A.*Pr.*764, S.*OT*1500, *Ant.*750, E.*Or.*1655, X.*Cyr.*5.2.12, etc.; later γαμήσω Plu.2.386c, Luc.*Rh.Pr.*8 (for γαμήσεις *Tim.*52 leg. γαμησείεις): aor. I ἔγημα Il.14.121, etc.; later ἐγάμησα Lxx*Es.*10.3, *Ev.Marc.*6.17, Luc.*DDeor.*5.4, etc. (cf. infr. II. 2): pf. γεγάμηκα Ar.*Lys.*595, Pl.*Lg.*877e: plpf. ἐγεγαμήκει Th.1.126:—Med., fut. Ep. γαμέσσεται Il.9.394 codd., Att. γαμοῦμαι E.*Ph.*1673, Ar.*Th.*900, later γαμήσομαι Plu.*Art.*26, etc.: aor. ἐγημάμην Od.16.392, Anacr.86, Is.5.5, etc.:—**Pass.**, fut. γαμηθήσομαι J.*AJ*6.13.8, Ant.Lib.1.2, D.C.58.3, Hld.5.30, etc.: aor. ἐγαμήθην D.H.11.34, Str.10.4.20, etc.: poet. shortd. γαμεθεῖσα v.l. in Theoc.8.91, cf. Eust.758.52: pf. γεγάμημαι X.*An.*4.5.24, D.36.32: plpf. ἐγεγάμητο App.*BC*4.23: (γάμος):—*marry*, i.e. *take to wife*, of the man, Ἀδρήστοιο δ' ἔγημε θυγατρῶν one of his daughters, Il.14.121; ἔνθα δ' ἔγημε γυναῖκα Od.15.241; γ. γυναῖκα ἐς οἰκία, like ἄγεσθαι, Hdt.4.78: c. acc. cogn., γάμον γαμεῖν A.*Pr.*764,909; τὸν Ἑλένης γάμον..γήμας E.*IA*467; γῆμαι λέκτρα βασιλέως the king's daughter, Id.*Med.*594: rarely c. dupl. acc., γάμους τοὺς πρώτους ἐγάμεε Κύρου δύο θυγατέρας (for πρῶτον ἐγάμεε.. θυγατέρας) Hdt.3.88, cf. E.*Tr.*357; also γάμῳ γ. *marry* in lawful wedlock, D.39.26; ἐκ κακοῦ, ἐξ ἀγαθοῦ γῆμαι, *marry a wife* of mean or noble stock, Thgn.189,190; ἐκ μειόνων X.*Hier.*1.28; ἐκ γενναίων E.*Andr.*1279; παρά τινος ib.975, Pl.*Plt.*310c; ἐπὶ θυγατρὶ γ. ἄλλην γυναῖκα set a stepmother over one's daughter, Hdt.4.154, cf. E.*Alc.*372; ἐπὶ δέκα ταλάντοις τινὰ γαμεῖν *marry a wife* with a dowry of ten talents, And.4.13. 2. of mere sexual intercourse, *take for a paramour*, Od.1.36, Luc.*Asin.*32; γ. βιαίως σκότιον λέχος E.*Tr.*44. 3. later of the woman, ἐὰν γαμήσῃ ἄλλον *Ev.Marc.*10.12: abs., 1*Ep.Cor.*7.28. II. Med., *give oneself* or *one's child in marriage*: 1. of the woman, *give herself in marriage*, i.e. *wed*, c. dat., γαμέεσθαι τῷ ὅτεῳ τε πατὴρ κέλεται Od.2.113; γημαμένη ᾧ υἱϊ· ὁ δ' ὃν πατέρ' ἐξεναρίξας γῆμεν 11.273: abs., Hdt.4.117; σοὶ μὲν γαμεῖσθαι μόρσιμον, γαμεῖν δ' ἐμοί A.*Fr.*13; εἰς τύραννʼ ἐγημάμην I *married* into a royal house, E.*Tr.*474; γήματο δ' εἰς Μαραθῶνα, i.e. she *married* Herodes of Marathon, *IG*14.1389 i 5 (ἥν τ' ἐγήματο is f.l. for ἥ τ' ἐγ. in E.*Med.*262): ironically of a henpecked husband, κεῖνος οὐκ ἔγημεν ἀλλ' ἐγήματο Anacr.86; so Medea to Jason, μῶν γαμοῦσα..σέ; did I *marry* you? E.*Med.*606; ἐγημάμην, of a man marrying a rich wife, Antiph.46; γαμεῖται ἕκαστος (sens. obsc.) Luc.*VH*1.22; ὁ γαμηθεὶς ὡς παρθένος κἄπειτα γενόμενος ἀνήρ Phld.*Sign.*2; incorrectly, in later writers, γημάμενος Apollod.3.12.6, cf. Q.S.1.728. 2. of parents, *get their children married*, *betroth* them, *get a wife for the son*, Πηλεύς θήν μοι ἔπειτα γυναῖκα γαμέσσεται αὐτός (where Aristarch. γε μάσσεται *will seek* or *make suit* for) Il.9.394:—Act. aor. I ἐγάμησα in this sense, Men.885. III. Pass., *to be taken to wife*: hence, *marry a husband*, ll.cc. ad init., *PGrenf.*2.76.11 (iv A.D.), etc.; rarely in correct authors, Poll.3.45.

γᾰμήγῠρις, εως, ἡ, *enrolment of youths in* φρατρίαι, *EM*221.4.

γᾰμήλ-ευμα, τό, = γάμος, A.*Ch.*624 (lyr.). **-ιος**, ον, *of* or *for a wedding*, *bridal*, *nuptial*, κοίτη Id.*Supp.*805 (lyr.); τέλος Id.*Eu.*835; χοαί Id.*Ch.*487; λέκτρα Id.*Fr.*242; εὐνή E.*Med.*673; οὐχ ἧψαν φῶς τὸ γ. *Epigr.Gr.*256.7 (Cyprus); ζυγὸν γ. *IG*14.2125; of divinities, *presiding over marriage*, Ath.5.185b, Poll.1.24; Ἀφροδίτα E.*Fr.*781.17 (lyr.). II. as Subst., γαμήλιος (sc. πλακοῦς), ὁ, *bride-cake*, Philetaer.13.5. 2. γαμηλία (sc. θυσία), ἡ, *wedding-feast*, γαμηλίαν εἰσφέρειν τοῖς φράτερσι contribute *the wedding-feast* for one's clansmen, D.57.69; τοῖς φ. ὑπέρ τινος ib.43, cf. Is.3.79: abs., ib.76. **-ιών**, ῶνος, ὁ, the seventh month of the Attic year, *IG*1².6.80, Arist.*Mete.*343^{b}5, Thphr.*HP*7.1.2, etc. (from γαμέω, because *it was the fashionable time for weddings*).

γᾰμ-ησείω, Desiderat. of γαμέω, *wish to marry*, Alciphr.1.13, 3.37. **-ήσιμος**, η, ον, *marriageable*, *Gloss.* **-ητέον**, *one must marry*, Plu.*Demetr.*14 (parody of E.*Ph.*395), Arr.*Epict.*3.7.19, Hermog.*Prog.*11. **-ητικῶς**, Adv. *with an inclination for marriage*, Hsch. s.v. γαμησείειν. **-ίζω**, *give* a daughter *in marriage*, A.D.*Synt.*280.11, 1*Ep.Cor.*7.38. **-ικός**, ή, όν, *of* or *for marriage*, νόμοι Pl.*Lg.*721a; γ. ὁμιλία *connubial* intercourse, Arist.*Pol.*1334^{b}32; γ. ὑμέναιος Pherecr.12D.; γ. ὕμνος a *bridal* song, Hippoloch.ap.Ath.4.130a, Porph.*Marc.*2; συγγραφὴ *POxy.*1473.25 (iii A.D.); τὰ γ. *bridal*, *wedding*, Th.2.15; *questions of marriage-rights*, Id.6.6, cf. Arist.*Pol.*1304^{a}14. Adv. -κῶς ἑστιᾶν feast *as at a wedding*, Id.*EN*1123^{a}22. 2. γαμικόν, τό, *marriage-contract*, *POxy.*903.17 (iv A.D.). II. of persons, *of marriageable age*, *Epigr.Gr.*288.7 (Cyprus): pr. n. in *IG*14.496.

Γαμίλιος, ου, ὁ (sc. μήν), name of month in Epirus, *GDI*1339 (Dodona).

γάμ-ιος [ᾰ], α, ον, = γαμήλιος, μέλος Mosch.2.124; εὐνή Opp.*C.*3.149, cf. Nonn.*D.*1.69, al.; γαμίης ἐλπίδος ἐστέρεσεν *IG*12(8).600 (Thasos). **-ίσκω**, = γαμίζω, Callicrat.ap.Stob.4.28.18:—Med. (or Pass.) in Arist.*Pol.*1335^{a}20; ἀνδρί, of a woman, *PLond.*5.1708 (vi A.D.):—Pass., *Ev.Marc.*12.25.

γάμμα, τό, indecl., *the letter* γ, X.*Cyr.*7.1.5, *Oec.*19.9, etc.:—also **γέμμα** Democr.19. (Aram. *gamlā* 'camel'.)

γαμμᾰτίσκιον, τό, Dim. of γάμμα, *ornament on official dress*, Lyd.*Mag.*2.4.

γαμμοειδής, ές, *shaped like a* Γ, οἰκία *BGU*1037.8 (i A.D.); of the top of the thigh-bone, Heliod.ap.Orib.49.13.3, cf. Hero*Spir.*1.28. Adv. -δῶς Nicom.*Ar.*1.19.

γᾰμο-δαίσια (sc. ἱερά), τά, *wedding*, Ael.*NA*12.34. **-κλοπέω**, *have illicit intercourse*, Ps.-Phoc.3. **-κλόπος**, ον, (κλέπτω) *adulterous*, *AP*9.475, Tryph.45, Nonn.*D.*3.377, al. **-ποιΐα**, ἡ, *celebration of a wedding*, Ath.5.180c.

γᾰμόρος, ὁ, Dor. for γημόρος (q.v.).

γάμος [ᾰ], ὁ, *wedding*, Il.5.429, al.; γάμοι εἰλαπίναι τε 18.491; γάμον τεύχειν furnish forth *a wedding*, Od.1.277; γ. δαινύναι 4.3; ἀρτύειν ib.770; γάμον ποιεῖν Herod.7.86, *Test.Epict.*2.19: pl., γάμους διττοὺς ἑστιᾶν Is.8.9; of a single wedding, οἰκοσίτους τοὺς γ. ποιεῖσθαι Men.450; γάμους ποιεῖν D.30.21, *Ev.Matt.*22.2; ἐπιτελεῖν γ. τῆς θυγατρὸς Arist.*Fr.*549, cf. D.S.13.84; οἱ κεκλημένοι εἰς τοὺς γ. Diph.17.2; ἐν τοῖς γ. ἄκλητος εἰσδεδυκέναι Apollod.Car.24. II. *marriage*, *wedlock*, Il.13.382, etc.; ἄγειν [γυναῖκα] ἐπὶ γάμῳ X.*An.*2.4.8; ἀγαγέσθαι τινὰ πρὸς γάμον Plu.*Cat.Ma.*24; τὸν Οἰνέως γ. the *marriage* granted by O., S.*Tr.*792; γ. θεῶν τινος E.*Tr.*979, cf. *IT*25; εἰς γ. τινὸς ἐλθεῖν Id.*IA*1044 (lyr.); more freq. in pl., A.*Pr.*558 (lyr.), 739 (lyr.), *Ag.*1156 (lyr.), etc.; cf. γαμέω I: also τοῖς μεθημερινοῖς γάμοις, i.e. *prostitution*, D.18.129; Πανὸς ἀναβοᾷ γάμους, i.e. *rape*, E.*Hel.*190 (lyr.); of *unlawful wedlock*, as of Paris and Helen, Id.*Tr.*932; γάμοι ἄρρενες Luc.*VH*1.22; γ. ἀνδρεῖοι Procop.*Arc.*16.23:—E.*Andr.*103, X.*Cyr.*8.4.19, do not establish the sense of *a wife*; for E.*Tr.*357, v. γαμέω I.1. III. ἱερὸς γ. *ritual marriage*, Men.320, Hsch., *EM*468.56; as a nickname, Anaxandr.34.2; name of play by Alc.Com. IV. Pythag. name for *three*, *Theol.Ar.*16; for *five*, Plu.2.388c; for *six*, Theo Sm.p.102H., *Theol.Ar.*33. V. Γάμος personified, Philox.13, Lib.*Or.*5.27. VI. name of month at Epidaurus, *IG*4.1485,1492. (Perh. akin to Skt. *jāmis* 'brother or sister', Lat. *geminus*.)

γᾰμο-στολέω, *furnish forth a wedding*, Sch.Pi.*N.*3.97. **-στολικός**, ή, όν, *determining marriage*, Vett.Val.119.8; τόπος *Cat.Cod. Astr.*5(1).203. **-στόλος**, ον, *preparing a wedding*, epith. of Hera and Aphrodite, Pisand.ap.Sch.E.*Ph.*1760, *Epic.Alex.Adesp.*9iii 5, Orph.*H.*55.8, *AP*6.207 (Arch.); Ὑμέναιος ib.7.188 (Ant. Thall.); νύξ Musae.282. 2. Astrol., name for the seventh house of the horoscope, Paul.Al.*M.*2. **-τελεῖν**· γάμους ἐπιτελεῖν, Hsch.

γαμφαί, αἱ, = sq., Lyc.152.

γαμφηλαί, ῶν, αἱ, *jaws* of animals, as of the lion, Il.16.489; of the horse, 19.394; of Typhon, A.*Pr.*357; *bill* or *beak* of birds, E.*Ion*

159 (lyr.), cf. Ps.-Orac. in Ar.*Eq.*198: as Adj., ὑπὸ γαμφηλῇσιν ὀδοῦσιν (sic) Man.5.187 (s.v.l.): once in sg., γαμφηλή· ἡ γνάθος ἢ σιαγών, *EM*221.13.

γαμψ-ός, ή, όν, *curved, crooked,* of the uterine κόλποι, Hp.*Nat.Puer.* 31; κέρατα Arist.*HA*630a31; ῥύγχος Id.*PA*662b2; ὄνυχες ib.662b5 (Comp.); ἅρπαι Lyc.358. **2.** of birds of prey, = γαμψῶνυξ, Ar. *Nu.*337 (anap.). **-ότης**, ητος, ἡ, *crookedness,* of talons, Arist. *HA*619b9. **-όω**, *make curved*: only used in Pass., *to be* or *become so*, ib.619a17. **-ωλή**, ἡ, = γαμψότης, Hsch., *AB*1356. **-ῶνυξ**, ῠχος, ὁ, ἡ, (ὄνυξ) *with crooked talons,* of birds of prey, αἰγυπιοὶ γαμψώνυχες Il.16.428, Od.22.302; οἰωνοί A.*Pr.*488; τὰν γ. παρθένον, of the Sphinx, S.*OT*1199 (lyr.); γ. ἅρπη Nonn.*D.*12.336, etc.:—also **-ώνυχος**, ον, Arist.*HA*563b20, *GA*750a11, Plu.2.727c; τὸ γ. Plot. 6.7.9, Iamb.*Protr.*21.ιθ΄: pl., γαμψώνυχοι ἀσταφίδες Epich.30; τὰ γ., of beasts of prey, Arist.*HA*517b1, cf. 503a30.

γαμψωνῠχοπαντοφῐλάρπᾰσος, ον, *snatcher of everything with curved talons,* Lyr. in *Philol.*80.336.

γᾶν· ἀγγεῖον σκύφῳ παραπλήσιον, Hsch.

γάνα (A) [ᾰ], Dor., esp. Sicil., for γυνή, Greg.Cor.p.345 S.

γάνα (B)· χέρσος, γῆ, Hsch. **γανάεις**, cf. sq. II. 2.

γαναπέας· τελείας, and **γαναπέα**· πελία, Cyr. **γανάσσας**· καλῶς, Hsch. **γαναυγέας**· τέλειος ἐν τῷ ὁρᾶν, Id.

γᾰνάω, (γάνος) *glitter, gleam,* of metals; Hom. always in Ep. part., θώρηκες λαμπρὸν γανόωντες Il.13.265; κόρυθες λαμπρὸν γανόωσαι 19.359: hence, *look fresh and smiling,* πρασιαὶ.. ἐπηετανὸν γανόωσαι, of garden-beds, Od.7.128; νάρκισσον.. γανόωντα *h.Cer.*10; χαλκῷ γανάοντας ἐφήβους *Mus.Belg.*16.70 (Attica, ii A.D.); ὀφθαλμοὶ γανόωντες, in phthisis, Aret.*SD*1.8. **2.** *exult, rejoice,* Opp.*H.*1. 659. **II.** trans., *make bright,* Arat.190; cf. γανάσσαι· σμῆξαι, ἡδῦναι, Hsch. **2.** γανάοντες *glorifying,* Herm. for γανάεντες, A. *Supp.*1019 (lyr.).

γανδάνειν· ἀρέσκειν, Hsch. **γανδάω**· λάμπω, Id. **γάνδιον**· κιβώτιον, Id. **γάνδος**· ὁ πολλὰ εἰδὼς καὶ πανοῦργος· τινὲς δὲ **γάδος**, Id. **γάνδομα**· πυροί, ἄλευρα, Id. **γάνεα**· κήπους, Id. (κόπους cod.). **γανεῖν**· λευκαίνειν, Id., *EM*223.44. **γανῖται**· δάπανοι, ἄσωτοι, Hsch. (cf. Lat. *ganeo*).

γάννος, = γλάνος (Ephes.), Phlp.*in GA*149.20.

γάννυα, perh. = γάνεα, Orph.*Fr.*47.5.

γάνος (A) [ᾰ], εος, τό, (γαίω, cf. γάνυμαι) *brightness, sheen,* Sapph. 127(?), *Supp.*9.2. **2.** *gladness, joy, pride,* λάφυρα.. ἀρχαῖον γάνος A.*Ag.*579. **3.** of water and wine, from their *quickening* and *refreshing* qualities, χαίρουσαν οὐδὲν ἧσσον ἢ διοσδότῳ γάνει σπορητὸς (Pors. for Διὸς νότῳ γᾶν εἰ), i.e. rain, ib.1392; κρηναῖον γ. Id.*Pers.* 483; γ. ἀμπέλου, βότρυος, ib.615, E.*Ba.*261,383 (lyr.); also of honey, γ. μελίσσης Id.*IT*634: abs., *water,* Lyc.1365; Ἀσωποῦ γ. E.*Supp.* 1150 (lyr.). **4.** of a divine being, παγκρατὲς γ. *Hymn.Curet.*3.

γάνος (B)· παράδεισος (Cypr.), *EM*223.48, cf. γάνεα; dub. in *Ber. Sächs.Gesellsch.*1908.5 (Cypr.), *IG*12(2).58.17 (Mytilene). (Hebr. *gan* 'garden'.)

γᾰνόω, *make bright, polish,* Plu.2.74e: metaph., τὰ πράγματα τοῖς εὐπροσωποτάτοις τῶν ἐπιθέτων ib.683e:—metaph. in Pass., ἀληθείας φωτὶ γεγανωμένα Dam.*Pr.*33, cf. 26; ἀὴρ.. ζοφερὸς καὶ οἷον γεγανωμένος Agath.5.3; ἑοῖς ἐγάνωσεν ἰάκχοις *glorified,* *Epigr.Gr.*985 (Philae); *make glad, delight,* τὴν ψυχήν Ph.1.121:—Pass., *to be made glad, exult,* ταῦθ' ὡς ἐγανώθην Ar.*Ach.*7, Ph. l.c., al.:—esp. pf. part. Pass. γεγανωμένος *bright,* χλανίς Phld.*Vit.*p.21 J.; *glad-looking,* στίλβων καὶ γεγανωμένος Anacr.13A; γεγ. ὑπὸ τῆς ᾠδῆς, *under the glamour* of song, Pl.*R.*411a, cf. Phld.*Mort.*13, Plu.2.42c; γεγ. καὶ ἀνθηρός, of oratorical style, Id.*TG*2. **II.** *tin, lacker,* ἀγγεῖον γεγανωμένον Crito ap.Gal.12.490; γ. τῷ κασσιτέρῳ Aët.12.55, cf. Eust.1188.61.

γάνῠμαι [ᾰ], mostly pres.; impf. ἐγάνυντο Q.S.5.652; ἐγάνυτο Jul.*Or.*1.8c: Ep. fut. γανύσσομαι Il.14.504: pf. part. γεγανυμένος *Anacreont.*35.3, Them.*Or.*13.177a: plpf. ἐγεγάνυσο ib.20.240d, al.:—*brighten up, be glad* or *happy,* γάνυται φρένα he *is glad* at heart, Il.13.493: c. dat., δάμαρ ἀνδρὶ φίλῳ ἐλθόντι γανύσσεται 14.504, cf. 20.405, Od.12.43, Ar.*V.*612; γ. ἐπί τινι E.*IT*1239 (lyr.); τινός A. *Eu.*970 (lyr.), cf. E.*Cyc.*504 (lyr.); ὑπὸ τοῦ λόγου Pl.*Phdr.*234d.—Freq. in later Prose, Ph.1.36,56, Plu.2.1098f, Polyaen.1.18, Jul. *Or.*1.40b, al., Them. ll.cc.; ᾄδων καὶ γανύμενος Aristid.*Or.*50(26). 40; freq. written γανν- in codd. (γα-ν-υ- from root γαυ-, cf. γαίω, γαῦρος.)

γανύματα· ἀρτύματα, *AB*230 (γανύρμ- Hsch.). **γανυρόν**· λευκόν, ἡδύ, ἱλαρόν, Hsch.:—also **γανερόν**, *EM*223.46.

γᾰνύσκομαι, Dep., = γάνυμαι, Them.*Or.*2.26d, 21.254c: c. gen., γ. τοῦ τόπου Socr.*Ep.*18.

γανυτελεῖν· γανοπετεῖν, ἡδύσματα ποιεῖν, Hsch.

γᾰν-ώδης, ες, *bright*: of ground, *rich,* Thphr.*HP*6.5.4. **-ωμα**, ατος, τό, = γάνος, *brightness, brilliance,* prob. in *IG*4.1484.97 (Epid., iv B.C.), Plu.2.48d, 50a. **II.** *joy, gladness,* Ph.1.335, al. **III.** *lacker,* ἔστω τὸ γ. τοῦ χαλκοῦ μόλιβδος Aët.6.58. **2.** metaph. of internal *membranes* or *coats,* τὸ γ. τῶν ἐντέρων Alex.Trall.9.3, cf. Sever.*Clyst.*p.34 D. **-ωσις**, εως, ἡ, *polishing* (with oil or wax), ἀγάλματος Plu.2.287c, cf. Vitr.7.9.4; *varnishing, lackering,* Aq.*Am.* 7.7. **2.** metaph., *making glad, brightening,* Phld.*Mus.*p.30 K. **-ωτής**, οῦ, ὁ, *tinsmith,* Gloss. **-ωτός**, ή, όν, *tinned, polished, lackered,* ἀγγεῖον Aët.12.1.

γᾱοδίκαι [ῐ], οἱ, *arbitrators in territorial dispute,* *SIG*421.45 (Thermon, iii B.C.).

γᾱοργέω, Thess., = γεωργέω, *IG*9(2).1229.16 (Phalanna).

γάπεδον, τό, Dor. for γήπεδον, *IG*4.823.58 (Troezen).

γαπελεῖν· ἀμελεῖν, Hsch. **γάπος**· ὄχημα (Tyrrhen.), Id.

γάποτος [ᾱ], ον, *to be drunk up by Earth,* γ. χύσις, γ. χοαί, γ. τιμαί, of libations, A.*Ch.*97,164, *Pers.*621.

γάπτωμα (sic), prob. γναμπτ-, *curvature,* *BCH*23.178 (Pisid.).

γάρ (γε, ἄρα), causal Conj., used alone or with other Particles.

I. introducing the reason or cause of what precedes, *for,* τῷ γὰρ ἐπὶ φρεσὶ θῆκε θεὰ λευκώλενος Ἥρη· κήδετο γ. Δαναῶν Il.1.56, etc.; but freq. in expl. of that wh. is implied in the preceding clause, πολλάων πολίων κατέλυσε κάρηνα.. τοῦ γὰρ κράτος ἐστὶ μέγιστον 2. 118, etc.: hence, **b.** in simple explanations, esp. after a Pronoun or demonstr. Adj., ἀλλὰ τόδ' αἰνὸν ἄχος κραδίην καὶ θυμὸν ἱκάνει· Ἕκτωρ γ. ποτε φήσει 8.148, cf. Od.2.163; ὃ δὲ δεινότατον.. ὁ Ζεὺς γ... Ar.*Av.*514; ὃ δὲ πάντων ἀδικώτατον ἔδοξε· τῶν γὰρ προγεγραμμένων ἠτίμωσε καὶ υἱούς Plu.*Sull.*31; freq. in introducing proofs or examples, μαρτύριον δέ· Δήλου γ. καθαιρομένης.. Th.1.8; τεκμήριον δέ· οὔτε γ. Λακεδαιμόνιοι.. Id.2.39, cf. D.20.10, etc.; in full, τεκμήριον δὲ τούτου τόδε· αἱ μὲν γ... Hdt.2.58; παράδειγμα τόδε τοῦ λόγου· ἐκ γ... Th.1.2; δηλοῖ δέ μοι τόδε· πρὸ γ... ib.3. **c.** to introduce a detailed description or narration already alluded to, ὅμως δὲ λεκτέα ἃ γιγνώσκω· ἔχει γ. [ἡ χώρα] πεδία κάλλιστα.. X.*An.* 5.6.6, etc. **d.** in answers to questions or statements challenging assent or denial, *yes,.., no,..,* οὔκουν.. ἀνάγκη ἐστί;—ἀνάγκη γ. οὖν, ἔφη, *ay doubtless* it is necessary, X.*Cyr.*2.1.7, cf. §§ 4 and 13; indicating assent, ἔχει γ. Pl.*Phdr.*268a; ἱκανὸς γ., ἔφη, συμβαίνει γ., ἔφη, Id.*R.*502b,c, cf. *Ap.*41a, etc.; οὔκουν δὴ τό γ' εἰκός.—οὐ γ.· Id.*Phdr.* 276c. **2.** by inversion, preceding the fact explained, *since, as,* Ἀτρεΐδη, πολλοὶ γ. τεθνᾶσιν Ἀχαιοί.. τῷ σε χρὴ πόλεμον παῦσαι Il.7.328; χρόνου δὲ οὐ πολλοῦ διελθόντος (χρῆν γ. Κανδαύλῃ γενέσθαι κακῶς) ἔλεγε πρὸς τὸν Γύγην τοιάδε, Γύγη, οὐ γ. σε δοκέω πείθεσθαι.. (ὦτα γ. τυγχάνει κτλ.), ποίει ὅκως.. Hdt.1.8, cf. 6.102, al.; εἶεν, σὺ γ. τούτων ἐπιστήμων, τί χρὴ ποιεῖν; Pl.*Phd.*117a; the principal proposition is sts. **b.** blended with the causal one, τῇ δὲ κακῶς γ. ἔδεε γενέσθαι εἶπε, i.e. ἡ δέ (κακῶς γ. οἱ ἔδεε γενέσθαι) εἶπε Hdt. 9.109, cf. 1.24, 4.149, 200, Th.1.72, 8.30. **c.** attached to the hypothet. Particle instead of being joined to the apodosis, οὐδ' εἰ γ. ἦν τὸ πρᾶγμα μὴ θεήλατον, ἀκάθαρτον ὑμᾶς εἰκὸς ἦν οὕτως ἐᾶν, i.e. οὐδὲ γ. εἰ ἦν.., S.*OT*255. **d.** repeated, οὐ γ. οὖν σιγήσομαι· ἔτικτε γ... Id.*OC*980, cf. *Ant.*659 sq., 1255. **3.** in elliptical phrases, where that of which γάρ gives the reason is omitted, and must be supplied, **a.** freq. in Trag. dialogue and Pl., when *yes* or *no* may be supplied from the context, καὶ δῆτ' ἐτόλμας τούσδ' ὑπερβαίνειν νόμους;—οὐ γ. τί μοι Ζεὺς ἦν ὁ κηρύξας τάδε [yes], *for* it was not Zeus, etc., S.*Ant.*450, cf. *OT*102, etc.; καλῶς γὰρ αὐτὸς ἠγώνισαι Pl. *Smp.*194a; freq. in phrase ἔστι γ. οὕτω [yes], *for* so it is, i.e. yes certainly: λέγεταί τι καινόν; γένοιτο γ. ἄν τι καινότερον ἤ..; [why,] could there be..? D.4.10; with negs., Ar.*Ra.*262 τούτῳ γ. οὐ νικήσετε [do so], *yet* shall ye never prevail by this means: for ἀλλὰ γ., v. infr. II. 1. **b.** to confirm or strengthen something said, οἶδ' οὐκέτ' εἰσί· τοῦτο γάρ σε δήξεται [I say this], *for* it will sting thee, E. *Med.*1370: after an Exclamation, ὦ πόποι· ἀνάριθμα γ. φέρω πήματα S.*OT*168 (lyr.), cf. E.*Hel.*857. **c.** in conditional propositions, where the condition is omitted, *else,* οὐ γ. ἄν με ἔπεμπον πάλιν (sc. εἰ μὴ ἐπίστευον) X.*An.*7.6.33; γίνεται γ. ἡ κοινωνία συμμαχία *for in that case,* Arist.*Pol.*1280b8. **4.** in abrupt questions, *why, what,* τίς γ. σε θεῶν ἐμοὶ ἄγγελον ἧκεν; *why* who hath sent thee? Il.18.182; πῶς γ. νῦν.. εὕδουσι; 10.424; πατροκτονοῦσα γ. ξυνοικήσεις ἐμοί; *what,* wilt thou..? A.*Ch.*909: generally, after interrog. Particles, ἦ γ...; *what,* was it..? S.*OT*1000,1039, etc.; τί γ.; *quid enim?* i.e. it must be so, Id.*OC*539,542,547, etc.; τί γ. δή ποτε; D.21.44; also πῶς γ.; πῶς γ. οὔ;, v. πῶς. **5.** to strengthen a wish, c. opt., κακῶς γ. ἐξόλοιο *O that* you might perish! E.*Cyc.*261; cf. αἴ, εἰ, εἴθε, πῶς. **II.** joined with other Particles: **1.** ἀλλὰ γ. where γάρ gives the reason of a clause to be supplied between ἀλλά and itself, as ἀλλ' ἐν γὰρ Τρώων πεδίῳ.. but [*far otherwise*], *for..*, Il.15.739; ἀλλὰ γὰρ ἤκουσ' αὐδ' ἐπὶ πρᾶγος πικρόν but [*hush*], *for..*, A.*Th.*861; ἀλλ' οὐ γ. σ' ἐθέλω.. but [*look out*] *for*, Il.7.242; in full, ἀλλ' οὐ γάρ σφιν ἐφαίνετο κέρδιον εἶναι μαίεσθαι προτέρω, τοὶ μὲν πάλιν αὖτις ἔβαινον Od.14.355; ἀλλ', οὐ γ. ἔπειθε, διδοῖ τὸ φᾶρος Hdt.9.109. **2.** γ. ἄρα *for* indeed, Pl.*Prt.*315d, *Smp.*205b. **3.** γ. δή *for* of course, *for* you know, Il.2.301, 23.607, Hdt.1.34,114, etc.; φάμεν γ. δή *yes* certainly we say so, Pl.*Tht.*187e, cf. 164d; οὐ γ. δή S.*Ant.*46, etc. **4.** γ. νυ Od.14.359. **5.** γ. οὖν *for* indeed, to confirm or explain, Il.15.232, Hdt.5.34, S.*Ant.*489,771, etc.; φησὶ γ. οὖν *yes* of course he says so, Pl.*Tht.*170a; γ. οὖν δή Id.*Prm.*148c, etc.; οὐ γ. οὖν ib.134b; cf. τοιγαροῦν. **6.** γ. που *for* I suppose, esp. with negs., Id.*R.*381c, *Phd.*62d, etc.; οὐ γ. δήπου Id.*Prt.*309c. **7.** γ. ῥα, = γὰρ ἄρα, Il.1.113, al. **8.** γ. τε, 23.156; also τε γ. D.19.159, Arist.*Pol.*1333a2, al. **9.** γ. τοι *for* surely.., E.*Hel.*93, *Supp.*564, etc.; οὐ γ. τοι Od.21.172, etc.; cf. τοιγάρτοι.

B. Position: γάρ prop. stands after the first word in a clause, but in Poets it freq. stands third or fourth, when the preceding words are closely connected, as ὁ μὲν γὰρ.. S.*Aj.*764; χὴ ναῦς γὰρ.. Id.*Ph.*527; τό τ' εἰκαθεῖν γὰρ.. Id.*Ant.*1096; τὸ μὴ θέμις γὰρ.. A.*Ch.*641, cf. 753: also in Prose, τὸ κατ' ἀξίαν γὰρ.. Arist. *EN*1163b11: sts. for metrical reasons, where there is no such connexion, as third (A.*Ag.*222,729, S.*Ph.*219 (all lyr.)), fourth (Ar.*Av.*1545); in later Com. fifth (Men.462.2); sixth (Antiph.26. 22); seventh (Men.*Epit.*531, *Pk.*170, Athenio 1.5); once sixth in S., καιρὸς καὶ πλοῦς ὅδ' ἐπείγει γὰρ κατὰ πρύμναν *Ph.*1451. 2. inserted before the demonstr. -ί, as νυνγαρί for νυνὶ γάρ; cf. νυνί.

C. Quantity: γάρ is sts. long in Hom. metri gr., θήσειν γὰρ ἔτ' ἔμελλεν Il.2.39; φωνῆς γὰρ ἤκουσα *h.Cer.*57.—In Att. always short: Ar.*Eq.*366, *V.*217, *Lys.*20 are corrupt.

γάραβος· ὀλολυγών, Hsch.

γᾰράριον, τό, *jar for* γάρος, *BGU*781 iii 7 (i A. D.), etc.

γάργα· αἴγειρος, Hsch.

γαργαίρω, (γάργαρα) *swarm with*, ἀνδρῶν ἀρίστων πᾶσα γ. πόλις Cratin.290, cf. Ar.*Fr.*359; ἀργυρωμάτων ἐγάργαιρεν ἁ οἰκία Sophr.30 (ἐμάρμαιρεν codd. Ath.): c. dat., πόντος ἐγάργαιρε σώμασιν Tim.*Pers.* 107.

γάργαλα, = γάργαρα, Hsch.

γαργάλη, ἡ, = ἐρεθισμός, Erot. s. v. γαργαλισμός.

γαργαλής, ές, prob. f.l. for δυσγαργ-, Ael.*NA*16.9.

γαργᾰλ-ίζω, *tickle, titillate*, Pl.*Phlb.*47a, Epicur.*Fr.*411; αὐτὸς αὑτὸν οὐδεὶς γ. Arist.*Pr.*965^{a}11:—Pass., γαργαλίζεσθαι μόνον ἄνθρωπον Id.*PA*673^{a}6, cf. *EN*1150^{b}22: also, generally, *feel tickling* or *irritation*, Pl.*Phdr.*251c. 2. metaph., τὰ τὰς αἰσθήσεις γαργαλίζοντα ἡδέα Phld.*Mus.*p.33 K., cf. Ph.2.352; τὰ ὦτα γ. Aristid.*Or.*34(50). 16, cf. Luc.*Cal.*21; also of pain, ἀλγηδὼν -ουσα Plu.2.1088a:—Pass., γαργαλιζομένου τοῦ σώματος Plot.6.7.34. **-ισμός**, ὁ, *tickling* (γέλως διὰ κινήσεως τοῦ μορίου τοῦ περὶ τὴν μασχάλην Arist.*PA*673^{a}8), Hp. *Alim.*26, Pl.*Smp.*189a (pl.), *Phdr.*253e, Epicur.*Fr.*412 (pl.); ἐν τῷ σώματι διέδραμε γ. Hegesipp.1.16; ἡδονὴ γαργαλισμοῦ ἐφίεται Ph.1. 118, cf. 212 (pl.), Plu.2.765c: **γάργαλος**, ὁ (more Att. acc. to Moer., cf. Ar. *Th.*133), and **γαργάλη**, ἡ, are cited by Erot. s. v. γαργαλισμός, fr. Ar.*Fr.*175 and Diph.25.

γάργανον, τό, v. τάργανον.

γάργᾰρα, τά, *heaps, lots, plenty*, ἀνδρῶν Aristomen.1; ἀνθρώπων Alc.Com.19.

γαργᾰρεών, ῶνος, ὁ, *uvula*, Hp.*Prog.*[23], Arist.*Resp.*474^{a}20; γ. ἀνεσπασμένος Hp.*Epid.*3.1.ς′, cf. Gal.*UP*7.5. 2. *a morbid condition thereof*, = σταφυλή, Hp.*Aff.*4. 3. *trachea*, Arist.*HA*492^{b}11.

γαργαρής· θόρυβος, Hsch.

γαργᾰρ-ίζω, *gargle*, Sch.Il.8.48 (but f.l. for γαργαλ- in Gal.11. 352). **-ισμός**, ὁ, *gargling*, Alex.Trall.5.4. **-ιστέον**, *one must gargle*, Orib.*Fr.*19.

γαργάρται· λίθοι αὐτοφυεῖς, Hsch. **γάργασις**· γαργάλη ὑποσταθμοῦ, Id.

γᾰρέλαιον, τό, *paste made of* γάρος *and oil*, Gal.6.716.

γᾰρηρόν, τό, *pot of* γάρος, *POxy.*1299.8 (iv A. D.), etc.

γαρῖνος, ὁ, an unknown *fish*, Marcell.Sid.37.

γάριον [ᾰ], τό, Dim. of γάρος, Arr.*Epict.*2.20.29, *POxy.*1759.9 (ii A. D.).

γᾰρίσκος, ὁ, an unknown *fish*, Marcell.Sid.33.

γᾰρῑτικός, ή, όν, *made to hold* γάρος, βῖκος *PSI*5.535.36 (iii B. C.).

γάρκα, ἡ, *rod* (Maced.), Hsch.

γάρκον, τό, *axle-pin*, *EM*221.45: **γάρνον**, Poll.1.145, Hsch.

γᾰροπώλης, ὁ, *seller of* γάρος, *PBaden* 42.9 (ii A. D.), *Gloss.*

γάρος [ᾰ], ὁ, a kind of *sauce* or *paste, made of brine and small fish*, τὸν ἰχθύων γ. A.*Fr.*211; ταριχηρὸς γ. S.*Fr.*606, cf. Cratin.280, Pherecr.173, Pl.Com.198, Alciphr.1.18; of the *fish* itself, Ruf. *Podagr.*10 (Lat. version):—also **γάρον**, τό, Str.3.4.6, and **γάρος**, ους, τό, *POxy.*937.27 (iii A. D.).

γᾱρότας, α, ὁ, (γῆ, ἀρόω) Sicilian for a *bullock*, Athanis 1, = Dionys. Trag.12.

γάρρα· ῥάβδος, Hsch. **γάρρης**· ἄρρης (i.e. ϝάρρης, = ἄρρην), Id. **γαρρίαι**· γάμοι, Id. **γαρριώμεθα**· λοιδορούμεθα, Id. **γάρσανα**· φρύγανα (Cret.), Id. **γάσος**, ὁ, *cheat, rogue*, Id.

γάσσα, ἡ, acc. to Hsch., = ἡδονή. (Perh. akin to γηθέω.)

γαστερο-πλήξ, πλῆγος, ὁ, *glutton*, Eust.1837.39. **-χειρ**, χειρος, ὁ, ἡ, = γαστρόχειρ (q. v.), Str.8.6.11.

γαστήρ, ἡ, gen. έρος, γαστρός: dat. -έρι, γαστρί (the longer forms in Ep., Lyr., and once in Trag., E.*Cyc.*220): dat. pl. γαστῆρσι Hp. *Morb.*4.54, γαστράσι D.C.54.22:—*paunch, belly*, Il.13.372, etc.; γ. ἀσπίδος *the hollow* of a shield, Tyrt.11.24; *belly* or *wide part* of a bottle, Cratin.190. 2. *the belly*, as craving food, κέλεται δέ ἑ γ. Od.6. 133; βόσκειν ἣν γαστέρ' 17.228; γαστέρι δ' οὔ πως ἔστι νέκυν πενθῆσαι, i.e. by fasting, Il.19.225; ἐν γαστρὸς ἀνάγκαις A.*Ag.*726 (lyr.); to express *gluttony*, γαστέρες οἶον Hes.*Th.*26; γ. ἀργαί Epimenid.1; ἐγκράτεια γαστρὸς καὶ ποτοῦ X.*Cyr.*1.2.8, cf. *Oec.*9.11; γαστρὸς ἐγκρατής master of *his belly*, Id.*Mem.*1.2.1; opp. γαστρὸς ἥττων, ib.1.5. 1; γαστρὶ δουλεύειν, χαρίζεσθαι, to be the slave of *his belly*, ib.1.6.8, 2. 1.2; γ. δελεάζεσθαι ib.2.1.4; τῇ γ. μετρεῖν τὴν εὐδαιμονίαν D.18.296; τᾶς γαστρὸς φείδεσθαι, com. of one who has nothing to eat, Theoc. 21.41. 3. *paunch stuffed with mincemeat, sausage, haggis*, Od.18.44, 118, 20.25, Ar.*Nu.*409. II. *womb*, ὅντινα γαστέρι μήτηρ .. φέροι Il.6.58; ἐκ γαστρός from *the womb*, from *infancy*, Thgn.305; ἐν γαστρὶ ἔχουσα big with child, Hdt.3.32; ὃν ἔχουσαν ἐν γ. *PFlor.*130.3 (iii A. D.); ἐν γ. φέρουσα Pl.*Lg.*792e; ἐν γ. λαβεῖν *conceive*, Arist.*HA* 632^{a}28, *AP*11.18 (Nicarch.), Lxx *Ge.*30.41, al.; συλλαμβάνειν v.l. ib.*Ge.*25.21, cf. *Ev.Luc.*1.31; ἐς γ. βάλλεσθαι Hdt.3.28; κατὰ γαστρὸς ἔχειν Vett.Val.193.33; φέρειν *Gp.*16.1.3; also γυνὴ ἑπτὰ ἤδη γαστέρας δυστοκοῦσα Philostr.*VA*3.39. (Perh. for γραστήρ, cf. γράω.)

γάστρα, Ion. -τρη, ἡ, *the lower part* of a vessel *bulging out like a paunch*, τρίποδος Il.18.348, Callix.2, Hero *Spir.*2.16; *hull* of a ship, Sch.Th.1.50. II. a *vase with such a belly*, Aen.Tact.4.2 (prob. l.), *PSI*4.420.25 (iii B. C.), *IG*12(3).174.26 (Astypalaea), *J.BJ* 2.14.5, Dsc.5.88, *Gp.*14.8.2, etc. III. *architectural member* of similar shape, *Milet.*7.59, *BCH*29.460 (Delos). IV. = γαστήρ I, dub. in Eratosth.18. V. *back of the thigh*, Hsch. (pl.). VI. = γογγυλὶς ἢ κράμβη, Id.

γαστραία, ἡ, a kind of *turnip*, Lacon. word, Hsch.; restored in Ath.9.369a for γαστέρας or γαστέας.

γαστρᾰφέτης, ου, ὁ, *stomach-bow*, Hero *Bel.*81.2.

γαστρήσιος, = *castrensis*, *Edict.Diocl.*3.8 (Aegina).

γαστρίαν· στρόφον ἢ διάνοιαν, Hsch.

γαστρίδιον, τό, Dim. of γαστήρ, γαστρίον, Ar.*Nu.*392.

γαστρίδουλος [ῐ], ὁ, *a slave to one's belly*, D.S.8.18.

γαστρίζω, (γάστρις) *punch* a man *in the belly*, Ar.*Eq.*273 (Pass.), 454, *V.*1529. II. *stuff, gorge*, τὸν παιδαγωγόν D.Chr.66.11, cf. Luc. *DMeretr.*10.4 (Phryn.76 is incorrect):—Pass., *to be stuffed full, eat gluttonously*, Theopomp.Hist.187, Men.*Pk.*98, Posidon.18, Luc.*Rh. Pr.*24, Alciphr.3.45; ἱκανῶς γεγαστρίσμεθα Ath.3.96f. III. γαστρίζων σφυγμός, term invented by Archig., Gal.8.665.

γαστρῐ-μαργέω, *to be gluttonous*, Ph.2.22. **-μαργία**, ἡ, *gluttony*, Hp.*Int.*6, Pl.*Phd.*81e (pl.), Eus.Mynd.9, Andronic.Rhod.p.572 M.; pl., Luc.*Am.*42. **-μαργος**, ον, *gluttonous* (cf. λαίμαργος), Pi.*O.* 1.52, Arist.*EN*1118^{b}19, Xanth.12, Cerc.16.2, Nic.Dam.p.22 D., etc.: Sup. -ότατα, θηρία Ph.2.22.

γαστρίον, τό, Dim. of γαστήρ, *paunch*, *SIG*1002.9 (Milet., v/iv B. C.); *sausage*, Archestr.*Fr.*47, *Com.Adesp.*394, *Milet.*6.21 (v B. C.). 2. *cake*, made with σήσαμον (Cret.), *EM*221.45. 3. Dim. of γάστρα II, Herm. *in Phdr.*p.202 A.

γάστρις, ιδος or εως, ὁ, ἡ, *pot-bellied*, πίθος Ael.*NA*14.26: as Subst., = γάστρα, *IG*11(2).154 *A* 69 (Delos, iii B. C.). 2. as Subst., *glutton*, Ar.*Av.*1604, *Th.*816, Jul.*Or.*5.176c: Comp. γαστρίστερος *more of a glutton*, Pl.Com.195: as Adj., γάστρις ἡδονή Ph.1.261. 3. *affected with tapeworm*, Hsch. II. *cake*, made in Crete, Chrysipp. Tyan.ap.Ath.14.647f.

γαστρισμός, ὁ, *gluttonous eating*, Sophil.6.

γαστρο-βᾰρής, ές, *heavy with child*, *AP*5.53 (Diosc.). **-βόρος**, ον, = γαστρίμαργος, Poll.2.168, 175. **-ειδής**, ές, *paunchlike, round*, ναῦς Plu.*Per.*26: in Eust.1684.28 **-οίδης** (leg. γαστροίδης).

γαστροιΐς, ΐδος, ἡ, = foreg., Pherecr.143.5 (pl.).

γαστρο-κνήμη, *calf of the leg*, Gal.14.708, v.l. in Hp.*Off.*9:—also **-κνημία**, Ion. -ίη, ἡ, Hp.*Art.*60, Arist.*HA*494^{a}7, *BGU*183.3 (i A. D.), Luc.*VH*1.22, Gal.2.316; and **-κνήμιον**, τό, Poll.2.190, *PFay.*90.8 (iii A. D.). **-λογία**, ἡ, the Greek *Almanach des Gourmands*, written by Archestratus, Ath.3.104b, 7.278b; also cited by the title of ἡ γαστρονομία, Id.1.4e, 2.56c. **-μαντεύομαι**, *divine by the belly*, Alciphr.2.4, 15. **-νομία**, v. γαστρολογία. **-πίων** [ῑ], ονος, ὁ, ἡ, *a pot-bellied person*, D.C.65.20.

γαστρ-όπτης, ου, ὁ, *vessel for cooking sausages*, *Demioprat.*ap. Poll.10.105:—fem. **-οπτίς** *IG*11(2).161 *B* 128 (Delos, iii B. C.), but **γαστροποτίς** ib.199 *B* 79.

γαστρο-ρρᾰφία, ἡ, (ῥάπτω) *sewing up of a belly-wound*, Scrib. Larg.206, Gal.10.416, Antyll.ap.Orib.44.23.46. **-ρροια**, ἡ, *diarrhoea*, Lyd.*Ost.*33, Steph. *in Hp.*1.87 D. **-τόμος**, ον, *opening bellies*, for embalming, Man.4.267. **-φορέω**, *bear in the belly*, of a bottle, *AP*9.232 (Phil.). **-φόρος**, ὁ, *bearer of* γάστρα II, *PLond.*1821. **-χάρυβδις** [χᾰ], ιος, ὁ, ἡ, *with a gulf of a belly*, Cratin.397. **-χειρ**, χειρος, ὁ, ἡ, *living by one's hands*, written γαστερόχειρ in Str.8.6.11, *EM*221; cf. χειρογάστωρ, ἐγχειρογάστωρ.

γαστρώδης, ες, = γαστροειδής, *pot-bellied*, Ar.*Pl.*560: generally, *convex, bulging*, Hp.*Medic.*7, Gal.19.120.

γάστρων, ωνος, ὁ, = γάστρις, *pot-belly*, Alc.37 B, Ar.*Ra.*200, Ph. 1.686.

γατειλαί (γατάλαι cod.)· οὐλαί, Hsch.; cf. ὠτειλή.

γᾱτόμος, ον, Dor. for γή-τομος, *cleaving the ground*, δίκελλα A.*Fr.* 196, cf. *AP*6.95 (Antiphil.), Hsch. s. v. τμήγας.

γαυλικός, ή, όν, *of* or *for a* γαῦλος II, χρήματα γ. *its* cargo, X.*An.*5. 8.1 (v.l. γαυλιτικά).

γαυλίς, ίδος, ἡ, = sq., Opp.*C.*1.126.

γαυλός, ὁ, *milk-pail*, Od.9.223, *AP*6.35 (Leon.); *water-bucket*, Hdt.6.119; *machine for raising water*, *IG*11.146 *A* 29 (Delos): generally, *any round vessel, beehive*, *AP*9.404 (Antiphil.); *drinking-bowl*, Antiph.224.5, Theoc.5.104, Longus 3.4. 2. = ὁ ἐξ ἀλλοτρίων ζῶν, Hsch., Cyr.; also, = εὐεξαπάτητος, Id. II. **γαῦλος** (on the accent cf. Hdn.Gr.1.156, Eust.1625.3), ὁ, *round-built Phoenician merchant vessel*, opp. μακρὰ ναῦς, γαύλοισιν ἐν Φοινικικοῖς Epich.54, cf. Hdt.3.136, 137, Ar.*Av.*602, Call.*Sos.*9.7, etc.

γαυνάκη, ἡ (in Lat. form *gaunaca*), and **γαυνάκης**, ὁ, *PSI*4.340. 22 (iii B. C.); = καυνάκης, *Gloss.*:—Dim. **γαυνάκιον** *PAmh.*2.144.22 (v A. D.).

γαύρηξ, ηκος, ὁ, (γαῦρος) *a braggart*, Alc.37 B, cf. Hsch. s. v.

γαυρ-ίᾱμα, ατος, τό, *arrogance, exultation*, Lxx *Ju.*10.8, Phld. *Mort.*18, Plu.*Aem.*27, etc. **-ιάω**, mostly pres. Act. and Med., aor. 1 ἐγαυρίασα Lxx *Ju.*9.7:—*bear* oneself *proudly, prance*, prop. of horses, γαυριῶντες Plu.*Lyc.*22:—Med., φυσῶντα καὶ γαυριώμενον X.*Eq.*10.16; *to be splendid*, γαυριῶσαι .. τράπεζαι Cratin.301; *to be luxuriant*, ἡ γῆ θάλλει καὶ γ. Jul.*Or.*4.155c; of persons, Phld.*Vit.* p.27 J., Ph.1.152, al.: c. dat., *pride oneself on* a thing, εἰ ταύτῃ [τῇ ἥττῃ] γαυριᾷς D.18.244; so ἐπὶ σφισι γαυριώωντες (Meineke -όωντο) Theoc.25.133, cf. Plu.*Lyc.*30, Palaeph.1.8, Anon.*Oxy.*220 iii 3.

γαῦρ-ος, ον, *exulting in*, βοστρύχοισι Archil.58; ὄλβῳ E.*Supp.* 862: abs., *haughty, disdainful*, Id.*Fr.*788, Ar.*Ra.*282; γ. καὶ μετέωρος Luc.*Nigr.*5, cf. Jul.*Caes.*319d; in good sense, *splendid*, D.Chr. 67.5 (Comp.), D.C.68.31; epith. of ἔφηβοι, *IG*7.544,545 (Tanagra); also, *skittish*, μόσχω γαυροτέρα Theoc.11.21: τὸ γ., = γαυρότης, τὸ γ. ἐν φρεσὶν κεκτημένοι E.*Supp.*217; τὰ γαῦρα Babr.43.6. Adv. Sup. γαυρότατα, εἰπεῖν Max.Tyr.7.7. (Cf. γαίω.) -ότης, ητος, ἡ, *exultation*, Plu.*Marc.*6; of a horse or ass, Id.*Pel.*22, *Mar.*38. -όω, *make proud*, only aor. ἐγαύρωσα Plu.*Cor.*15, D.C.55.6 (unless γαυρῶν 'overriding' (of χρόνος) is to be read in E.*Fr.*52.8): elsewh. Pass. **γαυρόομαι**, = γαυριάω, *exult*, στῆ δὲ παρὰ λίμνην γαυρούμενος Batr. 262a; λέων γαυρούμενος Ph.2.125: c. dat., *pride oneself on*, μὴ γαυροῦ σοφίῃ Ps.-Phoc.53; πλούτῳ γαυρωθείς *PFlor.*367.11 (iii A.D.); ξανθοῖς βοστρύχοις γαυρούμενος E.*Or.*1532, cf. *Ba.*1144; ἐπὶ τῷ ἔργῳ γαυροῦνται X.*Hier.*2.15: impf. ἐγαυρούμην Babr.43.15, D.C.53.27: fut. -ωθήσομαι Lxx *Nu.*23.24 (v.l. γαυρι-): aor. ἐγαυρώθην *PFlor.*367.11 (iii A.D.), D.C.48.20: pf. γεγαύρωμαι Lxx *Wi.*6.2. -ωμα, ατος, τό, *subject for boasting*, E.*Tr.*1250, Aristid.*Or.*28(49).124.

γαυσάδας· ψευδής, Hsch. **γαυσαλίτης**, an Indian *bird*, Id.

γαύσᾰπος, ὁ, = Lat. *gausăpa*, Str.5.1.12: **γαυσάπης**, Varr.ap. Prisc.*Inst.*7.56.

γαυσόομαι, *to be bent*, pf. Pass. γεγαύσωται Sor.*Fract.*19:—Act., γαυσῶσαι, Hsch.

γαυσός, ή, όν, or **γαῦσος**, η, ον (accent uncertain, Gal.18(2).518; codd. of Hp. have γαῦσος but γαυσοί), *crooked, bent outwards*, μηρός Hp.*Fract.*20, *Art.*77.

γᾱφάγας, α, ὁ, Dor. word (Syrac., *EM*221.49), *earthworm*, Hsch., *AB*230.

γάφυτον· γηγενές, Hsch.

γδοῦπος, γδουπέω, poet. forms for **δοῦπος, δουπέω** (esp. in compds., e.g. ἐρίγδουπος, ἐριγδουπέω), ἐπὶ δ' ἐγδούπησαν Il.11.45.

γε, Dor. and Boeot. **γα**, enclitic Particle, giving emphasis to the word or words which it follows.

I. with single words, *at least, at any rate*, but often only to be rendered by italics in writing, or emphasis in pronunciation: τὸ γὰρ.. σιδήρου γε κράτος ἐστίν such is the power of *iron*, Od.9.393; εἴ που πτωχῶν γε θεοὶ.. εἰσίν if the poor *have* any gods to care for them, 17.475; μάλιστά γε 4.366; ὅ γ' ἐνθάδε λεώς *at any rate* the people here, S.*OC*42, etc.: with negs., οὐ δύο γε not *even* two, Il.5.303, 20.286; οὔκουν φθόγγος γε not *the least* sound, E.*IA*9. 2. with Pronouns: with Pron. of 1st Pers. so closely joined, that the accent is changed, in ἔγωγε, ἔμοιγε (also ἔγωγα Lacon., but ἐγώνγα, ἱώνγα Boeot.): in Hom. freq. with Art. used as Pron., v. ὅ γε: with demonstr. Pronouns, κεῖνός γε, τοῦτό γε, etc.: in Com. coalescing with -ί final, αὑτηγί Ar.*Ach.*784; τουτογί, ταυταγί, etc., Id.*V.*781, *Pax* 1057, etc. (but ἐνγεταυθί *Th.*646): after possess. Pronouns, ἐμόν γε θυμόν Il.20.425, etc.: freq. after relat. Pronouns, ὅς γε, οἵ γε, etc., οἵ γέ σου καθύβρισαν S.*Ph.*1364; ὅς γ' ἐξέλυσας δασμόν Id. *OT*35, etc.; ὅσον γε χρῄζεις *even* as much as.., ib.365; οἷόν γέ μοι φαίνεται Pl.*R.*329a: rarely with interrog. Pronouns, τίνα γε.. εἶπας; E.*Tr.*241; ποίου γε τούτου πλὴν γ' Ὀδυσσέως ἐρεῖς; S.*Ph.*441. 3. after Conjunctions, to emphasize the modification or condition introduced by the subjoined clause, πρίν γε, before *at least*, sts. repeated, οὐ μὲν.. ὀΐω πρίν γ' ἀποπαύσεσθαι, πρίν γε.. αἵματος ἆσαι Ἄρηα Il.5.288, cf. Od.2.127; πρὶν ἄν γε or πρίν γ' ἄν, Ar.*Eq.*961, *Ra.*78, etc.; ὅτε γε Pl.*Phd.*84e; ὁπότε γε S.*OC*1699; ἐπεί γε X.*An.*1.3.9; ἐπειδή γε Th.6.18; ὅπου γε X.*Cyr.*2.3.11; εἴ γε, ἐάν γε, if *that is to say*, if *really*, Th.6.18, Pl.*Phdr.*253c; also simply to lay stress on the condition, κἄν γε μὴ λέγω and *if* I do not.., Ar.*Ach.*317; εἴπερ γε if *at any rate*, Hdt.7.16.γ', 143, etc.; ὥστε γε (v.l. ὥς γε), with inf., so far *at least* as to.., Pl.*Phdr.*230b; ὥς γ' ἐμοὶ χρῆσθαι κριτῇ E.*Alc.*801; ὥς γε or ὥσπερ γε as *at least*, S.*Ant.*570, *OT*715, etc.:—γε may follow τε, when τε is closely attached to the preceding word, ὡς οἷόν τέ γε μάλιστα X.*Mem.*4.5.2, Pl.*R.*412b; ἐάντε γε Id.*Plt.*293d; οἵ τέ γε Id.*Grg.*454e:—for its use in opposed or disjunctive clauses, v. infr. II. 3. 4. after other Particles, καὶ μὴν.. γε, οὐ μὴν.. γε, with words intervening, X.*Mem.*1.4.12, E.*Alc.*518, etc.; after ἄν in apodosi, when preceded by οὐ or καί, Id.*Ph.*1215, *Or.*784; ἄταρ.. γε but *yet*, Ar.*Ach.*448; καίτοι γε, v. καίτοι; ἀλλά γε (without intervening words) is f.l. in Pl.*Hp.Ma.*287b (leg. ἀλλ' ἄγε), *R.*331b (ἀλλὰ γε ἓν codd., ἀλλὰ ἕν γε Stob.); ἀλλά γε δή dub. in Id.*Phdr.*262a; later, Plu.2.394c, Ael.*NA*10.49 codd.: but, 5. when preceding other Particles, γε commonly refers to the preceding word, while the Particle retains its own force: but sts. modifies the sense of the following Particle, γε μήν *nevertheless*, πάντως γε μήν Ar.*Eq.*232, cf. E.*El.*754, X., etc.; Ep. and Ion. γε μέν Il.2.703, Od.4.195, Hdt.7.152; γε μὲν δή A.*Ag.*661, S.*Tr.*484; γε μέντοι Pl.*Tht.*164a, X.*An.*2.3.9, etc.: γε δή freq. strengthens an assertion, A.*Pr.*42, Th.2.62, etc.; οἰόμεθά γε δή Pl.*Euthd.*275a (cf. also II. 1); γέ τοι, implying that the assertion is *the least* that one can say, Ar.*V.*934, *Pl.*424,1041, etc.; γέ τοι Pl. *Grg.*447b; γέ τοι δή S.*OT*1171, Pl.*Phdr.*264b; γέ τοί που Id.*Lg.*888e; γε δήπου Id.*Phd.*94a, etc.; γέ που *at all events, any how*, Ar. *Ach.*896, Pl.*R.*607d, 478a, etc.; for γε οὖν, v. γοῦν. II. exercising an influence over the whole clause: 1. epexegetic, *namely, that is*, Διός γε διδόντος *that is* if God grant it, Od.1.390; κλῦθι, Ποσείδαον.., εἰ ἐτεόν γε σός εἰμι if *indeed* I am really thine, 9.529: hence to limit, strengthen or amplify a general assertion, ἀνὴρ.. ὅστις πινυτός γε any man—*at least* any wise man, 1.229; freq. preceded by καί, usu. with words intervening, ἦ μὴν κελεύσω κἀπιθωΰξω γε πρός *ay and* besides that.., A.*Pr.*73; παρῆσάν τινες καὶ πολλοί γε some, *ay and* a great many, Pl.*Phd.*58d; καὶ γελοίως γε Id.*R.*531a; freq. with the last term in an enumeration, ταύτῃ ἄρα.. πρακτέον καὶ γυμναστέον καὶ ἐδεστέον γε καὶ ποτέον Id.*Cri.*47b; ὄψεις τε καὶ ἀκοαὶ καὶ.. καὶ ἡδοναί γε δή Id.*Tht.*156b; repeated, συνήγαγόν μοι καί γε ἀργύριον καί γε χρυσίον Lxx *Ec.*2.8; rarely without intervening words, καί γε ὁ θάνατος διὰ τὴν μοίρην ἔλαχεν Hp.*Septim.*9, cf. Lys.11.7 codd.; καί γε.. ἐκχεῶ *Act.Ap.*2.18: hence, 2. in dialogue, in answers where something is added to the statement of the previous speaker, as ἔπεμψέ τίς σοι.. κρέα; Answ. καλῶς γε ποιῶν *yes and* quite right too, Ar.*Ach.*1049; κενὸν τόδ' ἄγγος, ἢ στέγει τι; Answ. σά γ' ἔνδυτα.. *yes indeed*, your clothes, E.*Ion*1412; οὕτω γὰρ ἂν μάλιστα δηχθείη πόσις. Answ. σὺ δ' ἂν γένοιο γ' ἀθλιωτάτη γυνή *yes truly*, and you.., Id.*Med.*817, cf. S.*OT*680, etc.; πάνυ γε *yes* certainly, Pl.*Euthphr.*8e, etc.; οὕτω γέ πως *yes* somehow so, Id.*Tht.*165c; sts. preceded by καί, καὶ οὐδέν γ' ἄτοπον *yes* and no wonder, ib.142b, cf. d, 147e; sts. ironically, εὖ γε κηδεύεις πόλιν E.*IT*1212. 3. to heighten a contrast or opposition, a. after conditional clauses, εἰ μὲν δὴ σύ γ'.., τῷ κε Ποσειδάων γε.. if *you* do so, then *at all events* Poseidon will.., Il.15.49 sq.; ἐπεὶ πρὸς τοῦτο σιωπᾶν ἥδιόν σοι.. τόδε γε εἰπέ *at any rate* tell me this, X.*Cyr.*5.5.20; εἰ μὴ τὸ ὅλον, μέρος γ' ἐπιβάλλει D.18.272:—sts. in the protasis, εἰ γὰρ μὴ ἑκόντες γε.. ἀλλ' ἀέκοντας.. Hdt.4.120. b. in disjunctive sentences to emphasize an alternative, ἤτοι κεῖνόν γε.. δεῖ ἀπόλλυσθαι ἢ σέ.. Id.1.11; ἤτοι κρίνομέν γε ἢ ἐνθυμούμεθα ὀρθῶς τὰ πράγματα Th.2.40; πατὴρ δ' ἐμὸς.. ζώει ὅ γ' ἢ τέθνηκε Od.2.131, cf. Il.10.504: also in the second clause, εἰπέ μοι, ἠὲ ἑκὼν ὑποδάμνασαι ἤ σέ γε λαοὶ ἐχθαίρουσι Od.3.214, cf. Hdt.7.10.δ', S.*OT*1098 sq. 4. in exclamations, etc., ὥς γε μὴ ποτ' ὤφελον λιπεῖν dub. in E.*IA*70, cf. S.*OC*977, *Ph.*1003, Ar.*Ach.*93,836, etc.; in oaths, οὔτοι μὰ τὴν Δήμητρά γ' v.l. in Ar.*Eq.*698; μὰ τὸν Ποσειδῶ γ' οὐδέποτ' Id.*Ec.*748; καὶ ναὶ μὰ Δία γε X.*Ap.*20; καὶ νὴ Δία γε Ar.*Eq.*1350, D.Chr.17.4, Luc. *Merc.Cond.*28, Lib.*Or.*11.59, etc.: with words intervening, καὶ νὴ Δί', ὦ ἄνδρες Ἀθηναῖοι, ἕτεροί γε.. D.13.16; νὴ Δία, ὦ Ἀθηναῖοι, ὥρα γε ὑμῖν X.*HG*7.1.37; merely in strong assertions, τίς ἂν φιλέοντι μάχοιτο; ἄφρων δὴ κεῖνός γε.. Od.8.209, etc. 5. implying concession, εἰμί γε *well then* I will go (in apodosi), E.*HF*861; δρᾶ γ' εἴ τι δράσεις Id.*IA*817, cf. *Andr.*239. III. γε freq. repeated in protasis and apodosis, as πρίν γε.., πρίν γε, v. supr. I. 3; εἰ μή γε.. τινὶ μείζονι, τῇ γε παρούσῃ ἀτιμίᾳ Lys.31.29; even in the same clause, οὐδέν γ' ἄλλο πλήν γε καρκίνους Ar.*V.*1507, cf. Hdt.1.187, E.*Ph.*554, Pl.*R.*335b, *Grg.*502a. IV. Position: γε normally follows the word which it limits; but is freq. placed immediately after the Article, as ὅ γε πόλεμος Th.1.66, etc.; or the Prep., κατά γε τὸν σὸν λόγον X.*Cyr.*3.1.15; ἔν γε ταῖς Θήβαις S.*OT*1380; or δέ, νῦν δέ γε Pl.*Tht.*144e; τὸ δέ γε ib.164b; δοῖμεν δέ γέ που ἂν Id.*R.*607d, cf. *Phd.*94a, etc.; freq. in retorts, ἁμές ποκ' ἦμες ἄλκιμοι νεανίαι. Answ. ἁμὲς δέ γ' εἰμές *Carm.Pop.*18; οὐκ οἶδ' ὅτι λέγεις. Answ. ἡ γραῦς δέ γε οἶδ', ὡς ἔγῳμαι Men.*Epit.*577, cf. A.*Th.*1031, etc.

γέα, v. γῆ. **γέαρ·** ἔαρ, Hsch. (γ = ϝ). **γέβους·** ζυγά, Id. **γέβουτον·** ψόφον, Id. **γεγάᾱτε, γεγάᾱσι**, v. γίγνομαι. **γεγάθει**, v. sub γηθέω.

γεγάκειν [ᾰ], Dor. for γεγακέναι, = γεγονέναι, Pi.*O.*6.49.

γεγάλημαι· γεγαλήνισμαι, διακέχυται, Hsch. **γεγάμεν, γεγαώς**, v. γίγνομαι. **γέγγει·** βρέχει, Id. (leg. τέγγει).

γέγειος, ον, *earth-born*, ἄνθεα Call.*Fr.*252b: hence, *ancient*, Hecat. 362J.; λόγος Call.*Fr.*252: Comp. -ότερον ib.103.

γεγηθότως, Adv. pf. of γηθέω, *with joy*, Hld.7.5, Ph.2.295.

γέγλανται· κεκοίλανται, Hsch.; cf. γλάφω. **γεγλύπωνται·** ἀντεγκλείονται, Id. **γεγριφώς·** ὁ ταῖς χερσὶν ἀλοῶν, Id.

γεγυμνωμένως, *defencelessly*, J.*Ap.*1.22. **γεγυναικωμένα·** πέμματά τινα, Hsch.

γέγων-α, Ep. pf. with pres. and past signf., used by Hom. in 3 sg. γέγωνε and part. γεγωνώς Il.11.275, al.: 3 sg. plpf. (with impf. signf.) ἐγεγώνειν 22.34, 23.425, Od.21.368: later, imper. γέγωνε A.*Pr.*195, S.*Ph.*238, E.*Or.*1220; subj. γεγώνω S.*OC*213; part. γεγωνώς Arist.*Pr.*904^{b}35, cf. γεγωνός:—from pres. ***γεγώνω** Hom. has inf. γεγωνέμεν Il.8.223, 11.6, 3 sg. impf. ἐγέγωνεν (v.l. γέγωνεν) 14.469:—from pres. ***γεγωνέω** come inf. γεγωνεῖν 12.337, Pi.*P.*9.3, A.*Pr.*523, Pl.*Hp.Ma.*292d: impf. ἐγεγώνευν Od.17.161, γεγώνευν 9.47: after Hom., 3 sg. γεγωνεῖ Arist.*deAn.*420^{a}1, *Pr.*917^{b}21: impf. -είτω X.*Cyn.*6.24; part. γεγωνέοντες *Michel*1383*B* (Chios): fut. γεγωνήσω E.*Ion*696 (lyr.): aor. inf. γεγωνῆσαι A.*Pr.*990, part. -ήσας D.C.68.3; cf. γεγωνητέον, γεγωνίσκω:—*shout so as to make oneself heard*, κώκυσεν.. γέγωνέ τε πᾶν κατὰ ἄστυ Il.24.703; ἐβόησε, γέγωνέ τε πᾶσι θεοῖσι Od.8.305: in pres. sense, ὅσσον τε γέγωνε βοήσας as far as [a man] *can make himself heard* by shouting, Od.6.294 (also in past sense, 5.400, al.); οὔ πώς οἱ ἔην βώσαντι γεγωνεῖν Il.12.337; ἀδηνέως γεγωνέοντες *Michel* l.c.; *make one's voice carry*, πολλῷ πλέον γεγωνεῖν (Cobet for ἢ ἀγνοεῖν) ἔστι νύκτωρ ἢ μεθ' ἡμέραν Antipho 5.44; πορρωτέρω ὁ αὐτὸς τῇ αὐτῇ φωνῇ γεγωνεῖ μετ' ἄλλων ᾄδων καὶ βοῶν ἢ μόνος Arist.*Pr.*917^{b}21: c. dat. pers., *cry out to*, ἐγεγώνει.. Πουλυδάμαντι Il.14.469, etc.; θεοῖσι μετ' ἀθανάτοισι γεγώνευν Od.12.370; *make oneself heard by* a person, οὐδέν σοι μᾶλλον γεγωνεῖν δύναμαι ἢ εἴ μοι παρεκάθησο λίθος Pl.*Hp.Ma.*292d. b. *speak articulately*, opp. to mere sound, ὁ ἀὴρ οὐ γεγωνεῖ Arist. *de An.*420^{a}1; οὐ δύναται γεγωνεῖν.. ἀλλὰ μόνον φωνοῦσιν Id.*Aud.*804^{b}24. 2. c. acc. pers., *sing, celebrate*, Pi.*P.*9.3. 3. c. acc. rei, *tell out, proclaim*, A.*Pr.*523, al.; τινί τι ib.195,784, S.*Ph.*238; τινί τι ἐς οὖς γ. E.*Ion*696; τὰ γεγωνᾱμένα the *proclamation*, *IG*5(1).1111.12 (Geronthrae); also οὐκ ἔχω.. γεγωνεῖν ὅπα I cannot *tell* where [it is], E.*Hipp.*586 codd.—For part. γεγωνώς as Adj., v. γεγωνός 2. -αί· ὁμιλίαι, Hsch. **-ησις**, εως, ἡ, *loud talking, hallooing*, Plu.2.722f (pl.). **-ητέον**, *one must proclaim*, Pi.*O*.2.6. **-ίσκω**, lengthd. pres. for γέγωνα, *cry aloud, shout*, ὡς ἐπὶ πλεῖστον Th.7.76: impf. ἐγεγώνισκον D.C.56.14. 2. c. acc. rei, *tell out, proclaim*, A.*Pr.* 627, E.*El.*809.

γεγωνοκώμη, ἡ, *filling the village with clamour*, *Com.Adesp.*1354.

γεγωνός, όν, Adj. (from part. γεγωνώς, as ἀραρός, όν, from ἀραρώς) *loud-sounding, sonorous*, πέμπει γεγωνὰ..ἔπη A.*Th.*443; ὄντα δ' ἄφωνα βοὴν ἵστησι γεγωνόν Antiph.196.2; *loud of voice*, ἀνήρ *AP*7.428.15 (Mel.): in later Prose, φωνή D.H.8.56, Ph.1.348, Corn.*ND* 16; λόγος Ph.1.95, al.; οὐ λόγῳ γ. ἀλλὰ τῇ ψυχῇ ἐκτείνασιν ἑαυτοὺς εἰς εὐχήν Plot.5.1.6: Comp. γεγωνότερος, κύκνων *AP*9.92 (Antip. Thess.), cf. D.H.5.24, Hld.10.32; γ. φθέγγεσθαι Ath.14.622e, etc. 2. γεγωνός as neut., γ. μέλος Ael.*VH*2.44; γεγωνὸς ἀναβοᾶν Luc.*Gall.*1; φθέγγεσθαι Philostr.*VA*5.9, cf. *Her.*2.2; τὸ γ. τῆς ὀγκήσεως Corn.*ND*21: also masc. and fem. as Adj., γεγωνότος λόγου Ph.1.133; πλήξεις γεγωνυίας *resounding* blows, ib.123. 3. Adv. Comp. γεγωνότερον ἐκβοήσας J.*AJ*4.3.2, cf. Porph.*Chr.*23.

γεγώς, ὦσα, ώς, v. γίγνομαι.

γέεννα, ης, ἡ, Hebr. *gê-hinnôm*, the *valley of Hinnom*, which represented *the place of future punishment*, *Ev.Matt.*5.22, al.

γέη, ἡ, = γῆ, Orac.ap.Eus.*PE*4.9: **γέηθεν**, *from the earth*, Orac.ib. 5.9.

γεη-πόνος, -πονικός, -πονία, ἡ, v. γεωπ-.

γεήοχος, ὁ, = γαιήοχος, v.l. in Hes.*Th.*15.

γεηρός, όν, (γέα) *of earth, earthy*, Arist.*GA*743^{a}12, etc.; γ. καὶ πετρώδη Pl.*R.*612a, cf. Hp.*Aër.*7; τὸ γ., opp. τὸ οὐράνιον, Them.*Or.* 32.359a.

γειᾰρότης, ου, ὁ, *plougher of earth*, *AP*9.23 (Antip.), *APl.*4.94 (Arch.), etc.; of oxen, *Epigr.Gr.*793 (Phrygia, ii A.D.).

γειδάριον, τό, = γαϊδάριον, *BGU*377.

γεῖθρον· ἔνδυμα, Hsch.

γεϊκός, ή, όν, *of land*, γ. πόδες, in land-surveying, Hero *Geom.*23. 67, al.

γείνομαι (γέν-yομαι, cf. γί-γν-ομαι): I. as Pass., only pres. and impf., *to be born*, cf. γίγνομαι (which is a constant v.l. in Hom.), γεινομένῳ *at one's birth*, Il.20.128, 24.210, Od.4.208, cf. Hes.*Th.*82, Alc.*Supp.*14: impf. γεινόμεθ' Il.22.477, Hes.*Sc.*88. II. as Med., aor. 1 ἐγεινάμην (Aeol. 3 sg. γένντατ' Alc.*Supp.*8.13), in causal sense, *beget*, ἐγείναο παῖδ' ἀΐδηλον Il.5.880, cf. S.*Aj.*1172, etc.; more freq. of the mother, *bring forth*, θεὰ δέ σε γείνατο μήτηρ Il.1.280, cf. 6.26, Od.6.25, etc.; οἱ γεινάμενοι the *parents*, Hdt.1.120, X.*Ap.*20; ὁ γεινάμενος the *father*, Ph.2.171; ἡ γειναμένη the *mother*, Hdt.4.10, 6.52, E.*Tr.*825 (lyr.); αἱ γ. *women in childbed*, Arist.*HA*582^{b}15; μήτηρ ἥ μ' ἐγείνατο she who *bare* me, A.*Eu.*736, cf. *Fr.*175, *Supp.*581 (lyr.), S. *OT*1020; πατρὶς ἥ μ' ἐγείνατο E.*Ph.*996. 2. of Zeus, *bring into life*, οὐκ ἐλεαίρεις ἄνδρας, ἐπὴν δὴ γείνεαι αὐτός Od.20.202. 3. metaph., ἐγείνατο μόρον αὐτῷ A.*Th.*751 (lyr.). III. aor. 1, in later Poets, in pass. sense, = ἐγενόμην, Call.*Cer.*58. (Sts. written by itacism for γίνομαι, as *IG*2^2.786.7 (iii B.C.).)

γειόθεν, Adv. = γῆθεν, Call.*Fr.*35c, A.D.*Adv.*188.19.

γειο-κόμος, ον, *cultivating land*, Hsch. **-μόρος**, = γεωμόρος, A.R.3.1387, *AP*9.438 (Phil.), D.P.190. **-πόνος**, = γεωπόνος, *AP*6.41 (Agath.), Nonn.*D.*42.329, etc. **-τόμος**, = γητόμος, A.R. 1.687, Opp.*C.*1.137, Nonn.*D.*21.97, al. **-φόρος**, ον, *earth-bearing*, σκαφίδες *AP*6.297 (Phan.).

γεῖσα, ἡ, = γεῖσον, *AB*227.

γεισήπους, ποδος, ὁ, *projecting end of rafter*, *IG*2^2.463.51:—hence **γεισηπόδισμα**, ατος, τό, ib.114: the spellings **γεισίποδες** (Poll.1.81, *AB*227), **γεισιπόδ-ισμα** and **-ίζω** (*support the cornice*, Is.*Fr.*113) are less correct.

γείσιον, τό, Dim. of γεῖσον, *low parapet*, J.*BJ*5.5.6.

γεισόλογχος, ον, *with a cornice of spear-heads*, γ. ὄγκωμα ὀδόντων, metaph. of thole-pins, prob. in Tim.*Pers.*4.

γεῖσ-ον (in codd. freq. written **γεῖσσον**), τό, *projecting part of the roof, cornice*, *IG*2^2.463.51, Thphr.*Sign.*18 (pl.), Demetr.*Eloc.*108 (pl.): in pl., of the stones composing it, *IG*1^2.372.152; γ. καταιέτια ib.2. 1054.39. 2. *coping* of a wall, E.*Or.*1570, 1620, *Ph.*1158, 1180. 3. metaph., *hem* or *border of a garment*, Ar.*Fr.*762; γεῖσα ὀφρύων Poll. 2.49. **-ος**, ους, τό, = foreg., Lxx *Ez.*43.17: pl., γείση *BCH*35.76 (ii B.C.); dat. pl. γείσεσι *OGI*483.127 (Pergam., ii B.C.):—also γεῖσος, ὁ, *Gloss.* (Carian word, acc. to St.Byz. s.v. Μονόγισσα.) **-όω**, *protect with a* γεῖσον, *EM*229.40. **-ωμα**, ατος, τό, *pent-house*, Poll.1.76. **-ωσις**, εως, ἡ, *eaves*, Hsch., *EM*229.41.

γείταινα, ἡ, fem. of γείτων, as τέκταινα of τέκτων, *AB*1199.

γείτη· βάμματα ἐξ ἐρίων, Hsch.

γειτνέω, = γειτνιάω, *BGU*775.15 (iii A.D.).

γειτνί-α, ἡ, = γειτονία I, Hp.*Ep.*23, *OGI*383.98 (Commagene): in pl., *adjoining areas*, *PTeb.*14.10 (ii B.C.), *PAvrom.*2 *A* 8 (i B.C.), *PAmh.*2.68.4 (i A.D.), etc. **-άζω**, = γειτνιάω, Aesop.75. **-ακός**, ή, όν, *neighbouring*, J.*AJ*2.14.6. **-ᾱμα**, ατος, τό, gloss on γειτόνημα, Hsch. **-ᾱσις**, εως, ἡ, = γειτονία, *neighbourhood, proximity*, Arist.*PA*672^{b}28, etc. 2. *a neighbourhood, district*, *OGI*483.28, 32 (Pergam., ii B.C.), Ph.2.475 (pl.), Plu.*Cor.*24; βαρβαρικαὶ γ. Id. *Per.*19. II. *proximity, resemblance*, κατὰ τὴν γ. καὶ ὁμοιότητα Arist.*EE*1232^{a}21, cf. *Pol.*1257^{a}2, J.*AJ*12.2.9. **-άω**, pres. (3 sg. impf. ἐγειτνία S.*Ichn.*232, and v. sub fin.), *to be a neighbour, be adjacent*, Ar.*Ec.*327, D.55.3, *PTeb.*105.19 (ii B.C.), Plb.6.33.10, Jul. *Or.*5.168a, etc.:—chiefly in Prose, but Ep. part., γειτνιόωσαν πόντῳ *IG*14.889 (Sinuessa). II. *border on, resemble*, γ. τῇ πολιτείᾳ Arist. *Pol.*1295^{a}33; [τῷ καλῷ] Id.*Rh.*1367^{b}12; νόσος γειτνιῶσα θανάτῳ Ph.2.548; τινὶ κακῷ Metrod.*Herc.*831.3: later fut. -άσω Gal.3.690: aor. ἐγειτνίᾱσα Ps.-Luc.*Philopatr.*1. **-ος**, α, ον, *neighbouring, adjacent*, *BGU*94.

γειτον-εία, ἡ, = γειτονία, *IG*5(2).443.13 (Megalop., ii/i B.C.), Plot. 5.8.7; *nearness*, Phld.*D.*3.9. **-εύω**, = sq., c. dat., X.*Vect.*1.8, Str. 3.3.8, al.: abs., Id.4.6.8, al., Phld.*Ir.*p.48 W., etc.:—Med., τὸ ἄλλο ἥμισυ τοῦ σώματος γειτονεύεται ταύτῃ τῇ ἴξει Hp.*Fract.*18. **-έω**, = γειτνιάω, c. dat., A.*Pers.*311, *Supp.*780 (lyr.), v.l. in S.*OC*1525, *SIG* 685.38 (ii B.C.), Procop.*Aed.*4.1; γειτονεῦσ' ἀποπνίγεις Call.*Iamb.*1. 300: metaph., τὸ σῶμα γειτονήσαν μετέλαβεν αὐτῆς (sc. ψυχῆς) Plot.3. 9.2, cf. 1.2.5. **-ημα**, ατος, τό, *neighbourhood, neighbouring place*, Alcm.116; ἁλμυρὸν καὶ πικρὸν γ. Pl.*Lg.*705a, cf. Ael.*Ep.*13, Procop. *Aed.*1.11, al., Agath.3.6; τῆς καρδίης καίριον γ. ὁ στόμαχος Aret. *CA*2.3, cf. *CD*2.6; *proximity*, τὸ ψυχῆς πρὸς τὸ ἄνω γ. Plot.5.1. 3. **-ησις**, εως, ἡ, = sq., Luc.*Symp.*33, Plot.1.2.5. **-ία**, ἡ, *neighbourship*, πικρὰ γ. Pl.*Lg.*843c, cf. Arist.*Rh.*1395^{b}9; *neighbouring region*, Plot.4.4.19. 2. *quarter, ward*, in a city, J.*BJ*7.4.1:— hence **-ίαρχος**, ὁ, *chief official of a ward*, Hsch. s.v. ῥεγεονάριος. **-ιάω**, = γειτνιάω, Theopomp.Hist.253.

γειτο-σύνη, ἡ, = γειτονία, Str.13.1.22. **-συνος**, ον, *neighbouring*, *AP*9.407 (Antip.).

γείτων, ονος, ὁ, ἡ, *neighbour, borderer*, γείτονες ἠδὲ ἔται Μενελάου Od.4.16, cf. 9.48, Hes.*Op.*346, etc.; opp. σύνοικος, Pl.*Lg.*696b; γ. τινός E.*IT*1451, X.*An.*3.2.4; τινί ib.2.3.18; ἐκ τῶν γ. or ἐκ γειτόνων *from* or *in the neighbourhood*, Ar.*Pl.*435, etc.; οἷον ἐκ γ. φωνὴν θηρευόμενοι Pl.*R.*531a; λύχνον ἐκ τῶν γ. ἐνάψασθαι Lys.1.14; ἐκ γ. τῆς πατρίδος μετοικεῖν Lycurg.21, cf. Str.10.4.12; rarely ἀπὸ γ. D.S.13. 84; ἐν γειτόνων (sc. οἴκοις) οἰκεῖν Men.*Pk.*27, Luc.*Philops.*25, etc.; τὸ χωρίον τὸ ἐν γ. D.53.10: metaph., ἐν γ. εἶναι to be *of like kind*, Luc.*Icar.*8: prov., μέγα γείτονι γείτων Alcm.50, cf. Pi.*N.*7.87. II. as Adj., *neighbouring, bordering*, πόλις, πόντος, Id.*P.*1.32, *N.*9.43; χώρα, πύλαι, ῥοαί, A.*Pers.*67 (lyr.), *Th.*486, S.*Aj.*418 (lyr.): c. dat., Ἀθήναις γ. πόλις E.*Ion*294; νεκροῖσι γ. θᾶκοι Id.*HF*1097; also in Prose, ἡ γ. πόλις Pl.*Lg.*877b; οἱ γ. βάρβαροι Jul.*Or.*2.72c: neut. γεῖτον Hsch.: neut. pl. γείτω *IG*2.814^a*B* 36. III. **γίτονας** (sic)· τὰ δύο αἰδοῖα, Hsch.

γειωπείνης, ὁ, = γεωπείνης, Hdn.*Epim.*15.

γειώρας, ου, ὁ, *sojourner*, Lxx *Is.*14.1, Ph.1.417. 2. *proselyte*, Hsch.

γεκαθά· ἑκοῦσα, Hsch. (Prob. Cret. ϝέκαθθα < ϝεκητ-yă.) **γέκαλον** (i.e. ϝέκηλον)· ἥσυχον, Id. **γεκᾶσα** (γ = ϝ)· ἑκοῦσα, Id. **γελαιώς**· ὁ γέλως, Id. **γέλαν**· αὐγὴν ἡλίου, Id. (ϝελ-, cf. εἵλη); cf. γελεῖν. **γελανδρόν**· ψυχρόν, Id.

γελᾱνής, ές, (γελάω) *cheerful*, καρδία, θυμός, Pi.*O.*5.2, *P.*4.181.

γέλανοι, οἱ, *an inferior breed of horses*, Hsch.

γελᾰνόω, *brighten, cheer*: hence, *calm*, θυμόν B.5.80.

γελαρής· γαλήνη (Lacon.), Hsch. **γελαρίης**, = γαλλερίας, Euthyd.ap.Ath.7.315f. **γέλαρος**, v. γαλόως. **γέλας**· ναύτας, Hsch.

γελᾰσ-είω, Desiderat. of γελάω, *to be ready to laugh*, Pl.*Phd.* 64b. **-ιμος**, ον, *laughable*, Stratt.72, Luc.*Somn.*5: less correct than γέλοιος, Phryn.206. **-ῖνος**, ὁ, *laugher*, of Democritus, Ael. *VH*4.20: fem. γελασίνη Anaxandr.25. II. οἱ γ. (sc. ὀδόντες) *the grinners*, i.e. *the front teeth*, which show when one laughs, Poll.2. 91. 2. mostly pl., *dimples*, which appear in the cheeks when persons laugh, Mart.7.25 (sg.), Choerob.in *An.Ox.*2.188; also of *dimples in the hinder parts*, Alciphr.1.39, *AP*5.34 (Rufin.). **-ις**, εως, ἡ, *laughing*, *EM*801.13. **-κω**, = γελάω, *AP*7.621. **-μα**, ατος, τό, *smile*, κυμάτων ἀνήριθμον γέλασμα A.*Pr.*90. II. *cause of laughter*, γῆρας πολυχρόνιον γ. Secund.*Sent.*12. **-τής**, οῦ, ὁ, *laugher, sneerer*, S.*OT*1422:—fem. **-τρια**, Sch.Ar.*Th.*1068. **-τικός**, ή, όν, *able to laugh*, S.E.*P.*2.211, Simp.*in Ph.*104.27; τό γ. Antig.*Mir.* 175, Iamb.*Protr.*21.κς'; ἄνθρωπος γελαστικόν Luc.*Vit.Auct.*26. Adv. -κῶς Suid. **-τός**, ή, όν, *laughable*, ἔργα Od.8.307; of persons, Babr.45.12. **-τύς**, ύος, ἡ, Ion. for γέλως, Call.*Del.*324.

γελάω, Ep. **γελόω** Od.21.105, Aeol. **γέλαιμι** Hdn.Gr.2.463, al.; Ep. part. γελόωντες Od.18.40, γελώοντες, -ώωντες, or -οίωντες ib.111, cf. 20.390; Ep. impf. γελώων or -οίων 20.347; Dor. part. γελᾶσα, 3 pl. γελᾶντι, Theoc.1.36, 90; Aeol. γελαίσας Sapph.2.5: Att. fut. γελάσομαι Pl.*Phdr.*252b, X.*Smp.*1.16, etc.; later γελάσω *AP*5.178 (Mel.), 11.29 (Autom.), *Anacreont.*38.8, etc.: aor. ἐγέλᾰσα E.*IT*276, etc.; Ep. ἐγέλασσα Il.15.101; Dor. ἐγέλαξα Theoc.20.1, v.l. ib.7.42; 3 pl. γέλαν for ἐγέλασαν Poet.ap.*EM*255.6:—Pass., fut. -ασθήσομαι D.L.1.78, Luc.*Am.*2: aor. ἐγελάσθην D.2.19, (κατ-) Th.3.83, Pl. *Euthphr.*3c, etc.: pf. γεγέλασται (κατα-) Luc.*DMort.*1.1. I. abs., *laugh*, ἁπαλὸν γελάσαι Od.14.465; ἀχρεῖον γ. 18.163; γναθμοῖσι γελοίων ἀλλοτρίοισιν 20.347; δακρυόεν γ. Il.6.484; μηδὲν ἴλεων γ. S.*Aj.* 1011; ἡ δ' ἐγέλασσε χείλεσιν, of feigned laughter, Il.15.101; ἐγέλασσε δέ οἱ φίλον ἦτορ his heart *laughed* within him, 21.389; γελῶ ὁρῶν Hdt.4.36:—Pass., εἵνεκα τοῦ γελασθῆναι for the sake of *a laugh being raised*, D.2.19. 2. of things, γέλασσε δὲ πᾶσα περὶ χθὼν Il. 19.362; γαῖά τε πᾶσ' ἐγέλασσε *h.Cer.*14; γελᾷ δέ τε δώματα πατρός Hes.*Th.*40; γελῶντα ὕδατη *Lyr.Alex.Adesp.*32.4. II. *laugh* at, ἐπ' αὐτῷ ἡδὺ γέλασσαν Il.2.270, 23.784; ἐπ' ἀλλήλοισι γελῶσιν Thgn. 1113; γελᾷ δὲ δαίμων ἐπ' ἀνδρὶ θερμῷ *laughs scornfully* at.., A.*Eu.* 560 (lyr.); ἐπί τινι at a thing, X.*Mem.*4.2.5, Pl.*Phlb.*50a: freq. c. dat., γελᾷ δὲ τοῖσδε..ἄχεσιν πολὺν γέλωτα S.*Aj.*957 (lyr.), cf. 1043, Ar. *Nu.*560; ἐγέλασα ψολοκομπίαις *was amused* at them, Id.*Eq.*696;

ὅταν ποτ' ἀνθρώποισιν ἡ τύχη γελᾷ Philem.110; εἰς ἐχθροὺς γ. S. *Aj.*79; ἐν κακοῖσι τοῖς ἐμοῖς A.*Ch.*222: rarely c. gen. pers., γελᾷ μου S.*Ph.*1125 (lyr.), cf. Pl.*Tht.*175b, Luc.*Dem.Enc.*16, Procop.*Goth.*4. 28 (v.l.). **2.** c. acc., *deride*, τινά Theoc.20.1; ἢ τόδε γελᾶτε, εἰ..; X.*Smp.*2.19; τί δὲ τοῦτ' ἐγέλασας ἐτεόν; *what is this you are laughing at?* Ar.*Nu.*820:—Pass., *to be derided*, A.*Eu.*789 (lyr.), S.*Ant.* 839 (lyr.); πρός τινος Id.*Ph.*1023; παρά τινος Id.*OC*1423.

γέλγει· βαπτίζει, χρωματίζει, Hsch.

γέλγη, έων, τά, = ῥῶπος, *frippery*: *the market where they are sold*, Eup.304, Luc.*Lex.*3. (γέλγη, ἡ, Ael.Dion.*Fr.*295, is prob. an error due to Eust.)

γελγηθεύειν· ἀπατηλογεῖν, Hsch. **γέλγια·** πήνη, σπάθη, κουράλια, Id.

γελγῖδόομαι, Pass., *form a compound bulb*, of garlic, Thphr.*HP* 7.4.11.

γέλγις, ἡ, gen. γέλγῖθος, also γέλγιος and -ιδος (in codd. freq. with false accent γελγίς, γελγῖθος, etc., but cf. Hdn.Gr.1.87): pl. γέλγεις Thphr.*HP*7.4.11, *CP*1.4.5:—*head of garlic*, and in pl., the *cloves* which compose it, ἡ γέλγις διαιρεῖται εἰς τὰς γέλγεις Id.*HP*7.4.12, cf. Hp.*Nat.Mul.*77; πότιμοι γέλγιθες *AP*6.232 (Crin.).

γελγο-πωλέω, *sell garlic*, Hermipp.13. **II.** *sell* γέλγη, Hsch. **-πώλης,** ου, ὁ, *dealer in garlic*, Poll.7.198:—fem. **-πωλις,** ιδος, Cratin.48.

γέλεα· τέλεα, Hsch. **γελεῖν·** λάμπειν, ἀνθεῖν, Id. **γέλενος·** ἀσφόδελος, νάρκισσος, Id.

Γελέοντες, οἱ, one of the four Ionic tribes, Plu.*Sol.*23, *CIG*3078 (Teos), 3664 (Cyzicus), etc.: **Γελέων,** οντος, ὁ, epith. of Zeus, *IG*2². 1072.

γελίκη· ἕλιξ, Hsch. **γέλιν·** ὀρκιᾶν (leg. ὀρμιάν), Id. **γέλινθοι·** ἐρέβινθοι, Id. **γέλλαι·** τῖλαι (cf. Lat. *vello*), Id. **γελλίζειν·** γαργαλίζειν, Id. **γελλίξαι** (Aeol. for ϝειλίξαι)· συνειλῆσαι, Id. (In the above lemmata, exc. γελλίζειν, γ stands for ϝ.)

Γελλώ, οῦς, Aeol. **Γέλλω,** ως, ἡ, a kind of *vampire* or *goblin*, supposed to carry off young children, Sapph.47.

γελοδυτία· ἡλιοδυσία, Hsch.; cf. γέλαν.

γελοι-άζω, only pres., *jest*, Lxx *Ge.*19.14, Aristarch.ap.Ath.2.39e, Plu.2.231c, Arr.*Epict.*3.16.4, Jul.*Caes.*306b, Procop.*Arc.*9. **-ασμός,** ὁ, *jesting*, Lxx *Je.*31(48).27. **-αστής,** οῦ, ὁ, *jester, buffoon*, Ptol. Megalop.2, Lxx *Jb.*31.5, Poll.5.128, prob. in Luc.*Merc.Cond.* 4. **-αστικός,** ή, όν, *mirth-provoking*, Eust.1837.8. **-άω,** Ep. for γελάω, in aor. part. γελοιήσασα *h.Ven.*49.

γελοιομελέω, *write comic songs*, *AP*7.719 (Leon.).

γέλοιος or **γελοῖος,** α, ον, *mirth-provoking, amusing*, once in Hom., Il.2.215 (in Ep. form γελοίϊος); χρῆμα Archil.79, cf. Hdt.8.25; Αἰσώπου τι γ. Ar.*V.*566, cf. 1259; γελοῖα *jests*, Thgn.311; γέλοια λέγειν Anaxandr.10, Alex.183; opp. σπουδαῖος, X.*Cyr.*2.3.1, Pl.*Lg.* 816d; τοῦ ἀληθοῦς ἕνεκα, οὐ τοῦ γ. Id.*Smp.*215a; τὸ γ. the *comic*, Arist.*Po.*1449ᵃ34, al.; τὰ γ. ἡδέα Id.*Rh.*1371ᵇ35; of persons, *facetious*, μισῶ γελοίους E.*Fr.*492; ἡδὺς καὶ γ. Aeschin.1.126; γ. ἐστι καὶ βούλεται Pl.*Smp.*213c. Adv. -οίως Id.*Cri.*53d. **II.** *ludicrous, absurd*, Ζεὺς γ. ὀμνύμενος τοῖς εἰδόσιν Ar.*Nu.*1241; γ. ἔσομαι αὐτοσχεδιάζων Pl.*Phdr.*236d; γ. ἰατρός, διδάσκαλος, Id.*Prt.*340e, *R.* 392d; ἐπὶ τὸ -ότερον ὅμοιος a *caricature*, Arist.*Top.*117ᵇ17, cf. *Po.* 1449ᵃ36; of arguments, etc., *paradoxical*, Pl.*Prt.*355a, *Tht.*158e, etc. Adv. -οίως, ἔχειν Id.*R.*528d, cf. Arist.*Mete.*362ᵇ12.—In *Smp.*189b, Pl. confines γ. to signf. 1, γ. εἰπεῖν ἀλλὰ μὴ καταγέλαστα. (Att. γέλοιος A.D.*Pron.*50.5, but γελοῖος Ael.Dion.*Fr.*101, and so cod. R in Ar.*Ach.*1058, *Nu.*1241. Some Gramm. expl. γέλοιος, = γέλωτος ἄξιος, γελοῖος, = γελωτοποιός, Ammon.p.38V., *EM*224.43; others reversely, *Et.Gud.*, etc.: Suid. gives both views. Phlp.ap.Eust. 906.53 wrote γελοιός, = γελωτοποιός.)

γελοιότης, ητος, ἡ, *absurdity*, Ath.11.497f.

γελοιώδης, ες, = γέλοιος II, Porph.*Chr.*55, Procop.*Arc.*23, *Goth.* 4.21, Sch.Ar.*V.*564. Adv. -δῶς Id.*Pl.*681, Hsch. s.v. ἀστείως.

γελοίων, γελοίωντες, γελόω, γελόωντες, v. sub γελάω.

γέλουτρον· ἔλυτρον, Hsch. (ϝελ-).

γελοωμῑλία, ἡ, *fellowship in laughing*, *AP*9.573 (Ammian.).

γελσόν· ἀτυχές, Hsch. **γελυνμάξαι·** γελοιάσαι, Id.

Γελχάνος (i.e. ϝελχ-), title of Zeus in Crete, Hsch.

γέλως, Aeol. **γέλος,** ὁ, gen. γέλωτος, Att. γέλω: dat. γέλωτι, Ep. γέλω or γέλῳ Od.18.100: acc. γέλωτα, poet. (and late Prose, Polyaen.1.34.2, f.l. in Palaeph.30) γέλων, v. infr. (acc. γέλω is v.l. in Od.18.350, cf. infr.): gen. pl. γελώτων Pl.*Lg.*732c: dat. γελώτων Ph. 2.167, *PGiss.*1.3.6 (ii A.D.): (γελάω):—*laughter*, γέλῳ ἔκθανον Od. 18.100; γέλω.. παρέχουσαι 20.8; ἄσβεστον γέλω (v.l. γέλον) ὦρσεν ib.346; ἄσβεστος δ' ἄρ' ἐνῶρτο γέλως.. θεοῖσι Il.1.599; γέλων δ' ἑτάροισιν ἔτευχε Od.18.350; γέλων δ' ἔθηκε συνδείπνοις E.*Ion*1172; γέλωτα ποιεῖν, μηχανᾶσθαι, κινεῖν, X.*Cyr.*2.2.11 and 14, *Smp.*1.14; παρασκευάζειν Pl.*Lg.*669d; γέλων ξυντιθέναι, γέλωτα ἄγειν, S.*Aj.*303,382; γ. ἔχει τινά Od.8.344; γ. ἂν γίγνοιτο Pl.*Plt.*295e; γέλωτος καταρραγέντος Ath.5.211c (so in Act., πολλοὺς κατέρρηξεν ἡμῶν γέλωτας Hippoloch.ib.130c); κατασχεῖν γέλωτα X.*Cyr.*2.2.5, etc.; οὐ γέλωτα δεῖ σ' ὀφλεῖν E.*Med.*404, cf. Ar.*Fr.*898; ἐπὶ γέλωτι to provoke *laughter*, Hdt.9.82, Ar.*Ra.*405; γέλωτος ἄξια *ridiculous*, E.*Heracl.*507; ἅμα or σὺν γέλωτι, Pl.*Lg.*789d, X.*An.*1.2.18; μετὰ γέλωτος Antiph.144.6; ἐν γέλωτι προφέρειν in *joke*, Plu.2.124d; πολὺς γ. loud *laughter*, X.*Cyr.* 2.3.18, etc. (πλατὺς γ., which Thom.Mag.p.293R. recommends, is not classical); μέγιστος, ἰσχυρὸς γ., Pl.*Plt.*l.c., *R.*388e; Σαρδόνιος γ. (v. Σαρδόνιος); Αἰάντειος γ. a maniac's *laugh*, Diogenian.1.17. **2.** metaph. of waves, = γέλασμα, Opp.*H.*4.334. **II.** *occasion of laughter, food for laughter*, γ. γίγνομαί τινι S.*OC*902; ταῦτ' οὐ γ. κλύειν ἐμοῦ; E.*Ion*528; γέλωτά τινα τίθεσθαι Hdt.3.29, 7.209; ἀποδεῖξαι Pl.*Tht.* 166a; εἰς γ. τρέπειν, ἐμβάλλειν, Th.6.35, D.10.75; ἐν γέλωτι ποιεῖσθαί τι Luc.*Hist.Conscr.*32, etc.; γ. ἔσθ' ὡς χρώμεθα τοῖς πράγμασι D.4.25; ὅσα γὰρ.., πλείων ἐστὶ γ. τοῦ μηδενὸς Id.14.26. **III.** *dimple* in the hinder parts, Luc.*Am.*14.

γελωτῖνος· καταγέλαστος, Hsch.

γελωτο-ποιέω, *to create, make laughter*, esp. by buffoonery, X.*Smp.* 3.11, Pl.*R.*606c, Hyp.*Phil.*2. **-ποιΐα,** ἡ, *buffoonery*, X.*Smp.*4.50, Luc.*Salt.*68, Procop.*Arc.*15. **-ποιῐκῶς,** Adv. *ridiculously*, Poll.9. 149. **-ποιός,** όν, *exciting laughter, ridiculous*, A.*Fr.*180.2; βωμολοχίαι Procop.*Arc.*9. **II.** as Subst., *jester, buffoon*, X.*An.*7.3.33, *Smp.*1.11, Pl.*R.*620c. **2.** = βατράχιον II (because it produced a wry face), Ps.-Dsc.2.175. **-φυή,** ἡ, = foreg. II. 2, Apul.*Herb.* 8. **-φυλλίς,** ίδος, ἡ, *Indian hemp, Cannabis sativa*, Plin.*HN*24.164.

γελωτός, ή, όν, prob. f.l. for γελοῖος, Olymp. *in Alc.*p.10C.

γελώων, γελώωντες, v. γελάω.

γεμ-ίζω, (γέμω) *fill full of, load, freight* or *charge with*, prop. of a ship, τινός Th.7.53, X.*HG*6.2.25, etc.; γεμίσας τὴν ναῦν ξύλων Test. ap.D.21.168; ναῦν σίτου D.34.36; θηρίων τὰς ναῦς Plb.1.18.8; τραπέζας θοίνης *OGI*383.146 (Commagene); of animals, *load*, κτήνη *PFay.*117.14 (ii A.D.), cf. *PTeb.*419.17 (iii A.D.): c. dupl. acc., *PFlor.* 195.4 (iii A.D.); σποδοῦ γ. λέβητας *charging* them *with* ashes, A.*Ag.* 443; γεμίσω σε *let me fill* you, addressed to a cup, Theopomp.Com. 32; αὐτόν *stuff, gorge*, Men.*Pk.*296; τὴν κοιλίαν ἀπό τινος v.l. in *Ev. Luc.*15.16:—Med., D.20.31; ἐγεμιζόμην ἀνθρωπείου τροφῆς Luc. *Asin.*46:—Pass., metaph. of the Cyclops, E.*Cyc.*505 (lyr.); of bees, γεμισθεῖσαι ἀποπέτονται Arist.*HA*624ᵇ2: c. gen., γ. ἀλαζονείας, εὐσεβείας, Ph.2.186,357. **II.** later, c. acc. rei, γεμίζειν ὕδωρ (sc. τὴν ὑδρίαν) *to fill* it *full of* water, Paus.3.13.3:—Pass., οἶνον, πῦρ γεμισθείς, *AP*12.85 (Mel.). **-ισμα,** ατος, τό, gloss on γέμος, Hsch. **-ιστός,** ή, όν, *laden, full*, Ath.9.381a.

γέμμα, Ion., = γάμμα, Democr.19.

γέμματα· ἱμάτια, Hsch. (ϝέμμ-, cf. εἷμα).

γέμος, ους, τό, *load*, σπλάγχν', ἐποίκτιστον γέμος A.*Ag.*1221.

γεμόω, = γεμίζω, *PRein.*53.4 (iii A.D.).

γεμπός· κοῖλος, Hsch. **γεμπύλος,** ὁ, = πηλαμύς, Id.

γέμω, used only in pres. and impf., *to be full*, prop. of a ship, Hdt. 8.118, X.*HG*5.1.21: generally, πάντα γ. Jul.*Mis.*368c. **b.** = κύειν, Hsch. **2.** c. gen. rei, *to be full of*, πλοῖα γέμοντα χρημάτων Th.7. 25; λιμὴν ἔγεμεν πλοίων Pl.*Criti.*117e; κώμας πολλῶν καὶ ἀγαθῶν γεμούσας X.*An.*4.6.27; of animals, *to be laden*, ὄνοι γέμοντες οἴνου καὶ βρωμάτων Posidon.5: metaph., κόμπος τῆς ἀληθείας γ. A.*Ag.*613, cf. S.*OT*4; γέμω κακῶν δή E.*HF*1245; γ. θρασύτητος Pl.*Lg.*649d; ἀσυμμετρίας καὶ αἰσχρότητος γέμουσα ψυχή Id.*Grg.*525a; πικρίας Phld. *Ir.*p.56 W.: c. dat., *to be filled with*, ἰτρίοισι, πέμμασι, Archipp.9, Antiph.174.2; γῆν πυρὸς γέμουσαν ῥεύμασιν Carc.5; γ. ἐξ ἁρπαγῆς *Ev.Matt.*23.25.

γεναρχ-έω, *to be the ancestor of the human race*, ὁ γεναρχῶν ἄνθρωπος (of the Gnostic πρωτάνθρωπος) Iamb.*Myst.*10.5. **-ης,** ου, ὁ, *founder* or *first ancestor of a family*, Call.*Fr.*36, Lyc.1307; of Julius Caesar, Ph.2.528; of Abraham, Id.1.513; epith. of Heracles, *IG* 5(1).497 (Sparta), al. **II.** *ruler of created beings*, γενάρχα τῆς γενεσιουργίας *Corp.Herm.*13.21, cf. Orph.*H.*13.8.

γενεά, ᾶς, Ion. **γενεή,** ῆς, ἡ, Ep. dat. γενεῆφι Il.14.112: (γενέσθαι): **I.** of the persons in a family, **1.** *race, family*, Πριάμου γ. Il.20.306, cf. Od.1.222, 16.117; γενεήν τε τόκον τε Il.15.141; ἴδμεν.. γενεήν, ἴδμεν δὲ τοκῆας 20.203, cf. 214; γενεῇ ὑπέρτερος higher *by birth* or *blood*, 11.786 (but *younger* in Archil.ap.Sch.ad l.); ταύτης εἶναι γ. καὶ αἵματος *of* this *race* and blood, Il.6.211; πατρόθεν ἐκ γενεῆς ὀνομάζειν 10.68; γενεῇ *by birthright*, Od.1.387; Αἰτωλὸς γενεήν *by descent*, Il.23.471; γενεὴν Διός 21.187; γενεὴ ἔκ τινος *descent* from.., ib.157; γενεὴν ἀπὸ Θρηίκης Hdt.2.134; of horses, *breed, stock*, Il.5.265, 268: pl., χρήματα καὶ γενεάς *families*, Plu.*Tim.*34; γενεὰν ποιεῖσθαι to have *issue*, *GDI*1798 (Delph.); πατριὰ καὶ γ., = φρατρία καὶ γένος, ib.1152 (Elis): hence, *tribe, nation*, Περσῶν γ., Τυρρηνῶν γ., A.*Pers.* 912 (lyr.), *Eleg.*2:—rare in Prose, τίς ὢν γενεάν; X.*Cyr.*1.1.6; καὶ αὐτὸν καὶ τὰν γ. ἀπολέσθαι *SIG*306.8 (Tegea, iv B.C.). **2.** *race, generation*, οἵηπερ φύλλων γ. τοιήδε καὶ ἀνδρῶν Il.6.146; δύο γ. μερόπων ἀνθρώπων 1.250, etc., cf. Hdt.2.142, Th.1.14, Heraclit.ap.Plu.2.415e (but, = μήν, Id.ap.Lyd.*Mens.*3.14); ἀστὴν ἐξ ἀστῶν ἀμφοτέρων ἐπὶ τρεῖς γ. γεγενημένην *SIG*1015.6 (Halic.); *age*, γ. ἀνθρωπηίη the historical, opp. to the mythical, *age*, Hdt.3.122; ἐπὶ τῆς ἡμετέρας γ. D.H.3. 15. **3.** *offspring*, Il.21.191, Orac.ap.Hdt.6.86, S.*Aj.*189 (lyr.); of a single person, Τυροῦς γ. (i.e. Pelias) Pi.*P.*4.136, cf. *I.*8(7).71. **4.** metaph., *class, kind*, τὸ σύμμετρον καὶ καλὸν καὶ ὁπόσα τῆς γ. ταύτης ἐστίν Pl.*Phlb.*66b; ταύτης τοι γενεᾶς ὁ νοῦς οὗτος Plot.5.1.7. **II.** of Time or Place, **1.** *birthplace*, γ. ἐπὶ λίμνῃ Γυγαίῃ Il.20.390, cf. Od.1.407; of an eagle's *eyrie*, 15.175. **2.** *age, time of life*, γενεῆφι νεώτατος Il.14.112; γενεῇ πρεσβύτατος, προγενέστερος, ὁπλότερος, 6.24, 9.161, Od.19.184. **3.** after Hom., *time of birth*, ἐκ γενεῆς Hdt.3.33, 4.23; ἀπὸ γ. X.*Cyr.*1.2.8.

γενεᾱλογ-έω, Ion. **γενεη-,** *trace a pedigree*, γ. γένεσιν Hdt.2.146; γ. ἑωυτὸν *draw out* one's pedigree, ib.143; γ. τὴν συγγένειαν X.*Smp.* 4.51; γ. τινά τινος Plu.2.894b; γ. τινὰ γενέσθαι, εἶναι.., Id.*Lyc.*1, Paus.5.14.9; περί τινος Luc.*Salt.*7: abs., οἱ -λογοῦντες Isoc.15.180, Thphr.*Char.*28.2:—Pass., Hp.*Sept.*4; ταῦτα μέν νυν γεγενεηλόγηται Hdt.6.54; τὰ νυνδὴ γενεαλογηθέντα Pl.*Ti.*23b; γενεαλογούμενος ἐκ τινος *Ep.Hebr.*7.6; ἐγενεαλογήθη (impers.) *the genealogy was reckoned*, Lxx 1*Ch.*5.1. **-ημα,** ατος, τό, *pedigree*, Eust.18.29. **-ία,** ἡ, *tracing a pedigree*, Pl.*Cra.*396c, al.: in pl., Isoc.11.8; title of work by Hecataeus; γ. καὶ μῦθοι Plb.9.2.1, cf. 1*Ep.Ti.*1.4, Jul.*Or.*7.205c. **-ικός,** ή, όν, *genealogical*, Plb.9.1.4, Ph.2.141, S.E.*M.*1.253. **-ος,** ὁ, *genealogist*, D.H.1.13, D.L.1.115.

γενεάρχ-ης, ου, ὁ, = ἄρχων τοῦ γένους, *IG*3.1278, cf. *OGI*531 (Bith.); = γενάρχης (which is freq. v.l.), Apollod.2.1.4, Heraclit. *All.*22, Jul.*Ep.*89, etc.; πόλεως γ. *chief, sheikh*, *CRAcad.Inscr.*1924.28 (Dura). **-ικός,** ή, όν, *patrimonial*, χωρία Just.*Edict.*3.1.1.

γενεῆθεν, Adv. *from birth, by descent*, Arat.260; ἄγραυλοι γ. *AP* 7.445 (Pers.).

γενέθλ-η, Dor. **-θλα,** ἡ: I. of persons, *race, stock, family*, c. gen. pers., Παιήονός εἰσι γενέθλης Od.4.232, cf. 13.130; σῆς ἐξ αἵματός εἰσι γενέθλης of thy *race* by blood, Il.19.111; γενέθλην *by birth* or *origin*, ἦν δὲ γ. Ἴκιος Call.*Aet.*1.1.7; of horses, *breed, stock*, Il.5.270; θηρῶν γ. *h.Hom.*27.10; τῶν ἀλιθίων ἀπείρων [ἐστὶ] γενέθλα Simon.5.6. 2. *offspring*, *h.Ap.*136, S.*El.*129 (lyr.), 226 (lyr.), etc. 3. *birth*, γενέθλας ἀρχά *Hymn.Is.*36. II. *birthplace*, ὅθι ἀργύρου ἐστὶ γ. Il.2.857. 2. *generation, age*, οὔ τι παλαιόν, ἐφ' ἡμετέρῃ δὲ γενέθλῃ Opp.*H.*5.459. 3. *time of birth*, ἐκ γενέθλης D.P.1044. **-ήϊος,** ον, = γενέθλιος, Orac.ap.Eus.*PE*6.2. **-ια,** τά, v. γενέθλιος. **-ιάζω,** *keep a birthday*, App.*BC*4.134. **-ιακός,** ή, όν, *belonging to a birthday*, ὧραι *AP*6.321 (Leon.); ἡμέρα Vett.Val.26.14, al., cf. Ph.2.529. II. = γενεθλιαλόγος, Gal.15.441, cf. Gell.14.1.1.

γενεθλιαλογ-έω, *cast nativities, practise astrology*, Str.16.1.6:—Med., *Cat.Cod.Astr.*1.170. **-ία,** ἡ, *casting of nativities, astrology*, J.*AJ*18.6.9, Ptol.*Tetr.*7, Iamb.*Myst.*9.1, Hierocl.*Prov.*ap.Phot. p.172 B. **-ικός,** ή, όν, *of* or *for nativity-casting*, Ptol.*Tetr.*54: ἡ -κή (sub. τέχνη), = foreg., Ph.1.464. **-ος,** ὁ, *caster of nativities*, Ptol.*Tetr.*13, Hierocl.*Prov.*ap.Phot.p.172 B., Iamb.*Myst.*1.18.

γενεθλίδιος, ον, = γενέθλιος, δῶρα *AP*6.325 (Leon.), cf. 243 (Diod.).

γενεθλιολόγος, = γενεθλιαλ-, Hsch. s.v. ἀστρολόγος.

γενέθλιος, ον, also α, ον Lyc.1194:—*of* or *belonging to one's birth*, γ. δόσις a *birthday* gift, A.*Eu.*7; ἡ γενέθλιος ἡμέρα *birthday*, Epicur. *Fr.*217, *OGI*111.29 (ii B.C.), etc.; γενεθλία ἡμέρα ib.222.6 (iii B.C.): pl., ib.493.20 (ii A.D.); τῇ γενεθλίᾳ *POxy.*494.24 (ii A.D.); and ἡ γενέθλιος, without ἡμέρα, *CIG*3957*b*, Luc.*Dem.Enc.*2; γενέθλιον ἦμαρ *AP*6.261 (Crin.); also ἀγὼν γ. τοῦ θεάτρου *to celebrate a birthday*, *CIG* 4342*d* (Aspendus); τὰ γ. *birthday feast*, *SIG*463.11; γ. θύειν offer *birthday offerings*, E.*Ion* 653, Pl.*Alc.*1.121c; ἑστιᾶν Luc.*Herm.*11, cf. *BGU*362 x 9 (iii A.D.), etc. II. *of one's race* or *family*, esp. of tutelary gods, Ζεὺς γ. Pi.*O.*8.16, *P.*4.167; γ. δαίμων Id.*O.*13.105; γ. θεοί A.*Th.*639 (but in Pl.*Lg.*729c, 879d, *presiding over generation*, and in D.H.1.67, = *Penates*); αἷμα γ. *kindred* blood, E.*Or.*89; γ. ἀραί a *parent's* curse, A.*Ch.*912. III. *giving birth, generative*, γενέθλιος ἀκτίνων πατήρ, i.e. the Sun, Pi.*O.*7.70; γ. πόρος thy *natal* stream, A.*Eu.*293; βλάσται γ. S.*OC*972; ἀνέλυσα γενέθλιον . . [δελφύν], of her first child, *Hymn.Is.*17.

γενεθλίωμα, ατος, τό, = γενέθλη, Iamb.ap.Sch.Hes.*Th.*459.

γένεθλον, τό, = γενέθλη, *race, descent*, A.*Supp.*290. 2. *offspring*, Id.*Ag.*784 (lyr.), 914, etc.; γ. Οἰταίου πατρός S.*Ph.*453; τὰ θνητῶν γ. the *sons* of men, Id.*OT*1425.

γενει-άζω, Dor. **-άσδω,** (γένειον) *get a beard, come to man's estate*, D.H.1.76, *AP*12.12 (Flacc.); ἄρτι γενειάσδων Theoc.11.9, cf. *CIG* 3715 (Apamea Bith.): pf. γεγενείακα Philem.15. **-άς,** άδος, ἡ, *beard*, κυάνεαι . . γενειάδες ἀμφὶ γένειον (pl. for sg.) Od.16.176; δάσκιον γενειάδα A.*Pers.*316, cf. S.*Tr.*13, Theoc.2.78; πρός ⟨σε⟩ γενειάδος . . ἅπτομαι E.*Supp.*277. 2. pl., *cheeks*, E.*Ion* 1460, *Ph.* 1381, *IT*1366; of horses, χαλινὰ γενειάσιν ἀφρίζοντες δάπτον Q.S.4.548. II. *bandage for the chin*, Heliod.ap.Orib.48.20.9, Gal.18(1).786. **-ᾱσις,** εως, ἡ, *growth of the beard*, in pl., Plot.4.3.13. **-άσκω,** *begin to get a beard*, Pl.*Smp.*181d, X.*Cyr.*4.6.5; ἄρτι γενειάσκων *IG*3.1314. **-αστήρ,** ῆρος, ὁ, *chin-strap* of a bridle, Poll. 1.147. **-άτης** [ᾱ], Ep. and Ion. **-ήτης,** ου, ὁ, *bearded*, Theoc. 17.33, Luc.*BisAcc.*28, Jul.*Or.*4.131a, Call.*Dian.*90:—fem. **-ᾶτις,** τρίγλα Sophr.31; Ion. γενειῆτις τρίγλη Eratosth.12. **-άω,** = γενειάζω, *grow a beard, get a beard*, ἐπὴν δὴ παῖδα γενειήσαντα ἴδηαι Od.18.269, cf. 176, Hp.*Nat.Puer.*20, X.*An.*2.6.28, etc.; εἰς ἄνδρα γενειῶν Theoc.14.28. 2. *have a beard*, Ar.*Ec.*145, Pl.*Plt.*270e, Arist.*GA*746^{b}24, D.C.68.15. **-όλης,** ου, ὁ, = γενειάτης, Hdn.Gr. 2.638. **-ον,** τό, (γένυς) *part covered by the beard, chin*, Od.16.176; πολιὸν γ. Il.22.74; esp. in supplication, ἔλλαβε χειρὶ γενείου 8.371; γ. χειρὶ παχείῃ ἀψάμενος 10.454; γενείου λευκήρη τρίχα A.*Pers.*1056 (lyr.), cf. *Th.*666, Hdt.2.36: in pl., S.*OT*1277, Plu.*Ant.*1; κείρασθαι τὰ γ. Id.*Cat.Mi.*53: prov. of a lean animal, οὐδὲν ἄλλο πλὴν γ. τε καὶ κέρατα nothing but *chin* and horns, Ar.*Av.*902. 2. *beard*, Hdt.6.117: pl., Theoc.6.36, J.*AJ*11.5.3, Paus.2.10.3, TheoSm.p.104 H. b. a lion's *mane*, Luc.*Cyn.*14. 3. *chaps*, Arist.*HA*518^{b}17; *jaws*, *AP*7.531 (Antip.Thess.). 4. pl., *teeth* of a saw, Nic.*Th.*53. 5. dub. sens. in *IG*11(2).165.11, 28 (Delos, iii B.C.).

γενειοσυλλεκτάδαι, οἱ, *beard-gatherers*, Ath.4.157b.

γενεός· εἶδός τι πελέκεος, Hsch.

γενεσιακός, ή, όν, = γενεθλ-, ἡμέρα Vett.Val.19.27.

γενεσιᾱλόγος (**-ολόγος,** *Gloss.*), ὁ, = γενεθλιαλόγος, Ach.Tat.*Intr. Arat.*23, v.l. in Artem.2.69.

γενεσι-άρχης, ου, ὁ, *creator*, τοῦ κάλλους Lxx *Wi.*13.3; of the Sun, Jul.Astr. in *Cat.Cod.Astr.*1.136.2. **-αρχικός,** ή, ον, = γενεαρχικός, χωρία Just.*Nov.*21.2. **-ος,** ον, = γενέθλιος, θεός Plu.2.402a; epith. of Posidon, Paus.2.38.4. II. Γενέσιον, τό, shrine of Posidon Γ., Paus.l.c. III. γενέσια, τά, *day kept in memory of the birthday of the dead*, Hdt.4.26, cf. Ammon.p.36 V., Phryn.83; to be distinguished from γενέθλια *birthday-feast*, though used for it in Pl.*Lg.*784d (s.v.l.) and later Gk., *POxy.*736.56 (i B.C./i A.D.), *PFay.*114.20 (i/ii A.D.), etc., Alciphr.3.18 and 55, *Ev.Matt.*14.6, *Ev.Marc.*6.21, D.C.47.18; so ἡ γ. ἡμέρα, = ἡ γενέθλιος, *CIG*2883*c* (Branchidae); ἡ γ. alone, *OGI*583.14 (Cyprus); τῇ τοῦ Σεβαστοῦ ἐμμήνῳ γ. *IGRom.*4.353*b* (Pergam., ii A.D.). **-ουργέω,** *bring into being*, μυριάδας ψυχῶν Herm.ap.Stob.1.49.44. **-ουργία,** ἡ, *generation*, *Corp.Herm.*13.21, Iamb.*Comm.Math.*9; τοῦ κόσμου Id. *Myst.*1.11. **-ουργός,** όν, *concerned with* or *incident to generation*, φύσις ibid.; δαίμονες ib.2.7; παθήματα Id.*VP*32.228; ἀστήρ Porph.ap.Eus.*PE*3.11; ὁρμαί Procl. *in Cra.*p.105 P.; δυνάμεις Id.*Inst.* 209; θεοί Dam.*Pr.*381, al.; τὸ γ. ib.349:—Subst. γ., ὁ, *author of existence*, c. gen., Lxx *Wi.*13.5; τῆς παλιγγενεσίας *Corp.Herm.*13.4; *fashioner, creator*, Herm.ap.Stob.1.49.44; παντὸς κόσμου Jul.*Gal.* 100c.

γένεσις, εως, ἡ, (γένεσθαι) *origin, source*, Ὠκεανόν τε θεῶν γένεσιν Il.14.201; Ὠκεανοῦ, ὅς περ γ. πάντεσσι τέτυκται ib.246, cf. Pl.*Tht.* 180d; *beginning*, in dual, τοῖν γενεσέοιν ἡ ἑτέρα Id.*Phd.*71e. II. *manner of birth*, Hdt.1.204, 6.69, etc.; *race, descent*, Id.2.146; πατρὸς οὖσα γένεσιν Εὐρύτου S.*Tr.*380; κατὰ γένεσιν, opp. καθ' υἱοθεσίαν, *IG*12(1).181 (Rhodes). 2. Astrol., *nativity, geniture*, *AP* 11.164 (Lucill.), 183 (Id.), *Epigr.Gr.*314.21 (Smyrna), *PLond.*1.98^{r}60 (i A.D.), Vett.Val.216.6: hence, *lot, fortune*, Astramps.*Orac.* 16.8, 23.7. III. *production, generation, coming into being*, opp. ὄλεθρος, Parm.8.21; more usu. opp. φθορά, Pl.*Phlb.*55a, etc.; περὶ γενέσεως καὶ φθορᾶς, title of work by Arist.: generally, *formation*, πύου Hp.*Aph.*2.47; *origination, making*, ἱματίων, περὶ τὰ ἀμφιέσματα, Pl. *Plt.*281b,e; γ. καὶ οὐσία δικαιοσύνης Id.*R.*359a. 2. = τὸ γίγνεσθαι, *becoming*, opp. οὐσία, ib.525b, *Ti.*29c, Procl.*Inst.*45, al. IV. concrete, *creation*, i.e. *all created things*, Pl.*Phdr.*245e; γ. καὶ κόσμος Id. *Ti.*29e, freq. in Ph., as 1.3, al., cf. Plot.6.3.2, etc. V. *race, kind* or *sort* of animals, Pl.*Plt.*265b, etc.; *family*, δίδυμος γ. of the Spartan kings, Id.*Lg.*691d. VI. *generation, age*, Id.*Phdr.*252d: pl., Id. *Plt.*310d; κατὰ περίστασιν τῆς γ. according to the circumstances of his *time*, Porph.*Sent.*32. VII. παιδοπόρος γ. *genitalia muliebria*, *AP*9.311 (Phil.). VIII. Math., *generation* of a figure, Papp.234.4, al. b. *origin* of a spiral, Id.272.7; ἡ ἐν γ. εὐθεῖα the *initial* line, Id.286.22.

Γενεσιών, ῶνος, ὁ (sc. μήν), name of month at Magnesia on the Maeander, *Inscr.Magn.*116.

γενέτ-ειρα, fem. of γενετήρ, *mother*, Pi.*N.*7.2, *CIG*4132 (Galatia); late Prose, τροφὸς πάντων καὶ γ. ἡ γῆ Artem.1.79; ἀλήθεια γ. Plot.5.8.4. II. *daughter*, Euph.84.4. **-ή,** ἡ, = γενεά II. 3, ἐκ γενετῆς from *the hour of birth*, Il.24.535, Od.18.6; εὐθὺς ἐκ γ. Arist.*EN*1144^{b}6; opp. δι' ἔθος, ib.1154^{a}33; later ἀπὸ γενετῆς Iamb.*VP*30.171. **-ήρ,** ῆρος, ὁ, = γενέτης, *Epic.Alex.Adesp.*3.10, Arist.*Mu.*397^{a}4, *IG*3.716, Coluth.373, Tryph.294: in pl., *parents*, *IG*7.2543, Nonn.*D.*4.61, al. **-ης,** ου, ὁ, *begetter, ancestor*, E.*Or.*1011 (anap.), Call.*Epigr.* 23.2; *father*, *IG*3.1335, 12(7).115 (Amorgos); γενέται καὶ πατρὶς ἔχουσιν ὀστέα, i.e. *the tomb of my fathers*, *BMus.Inscr.*2.179, al.: in pl., *parents*, *IG*4.682 (Hermione): generally, *author*, *Epigr.Gr.*979.4 (Philae). 2. *son*, ὁ Διὸς γ. S.*OT*472; ὁ ἐμὸς γ. E.*Ion*916 (lyr.). II. as Adj., = γενέθλιος, θεοί A.*Supp.*77 (lyr.), E.*Ion* 1130. 2. *produced*, ὁ Νεῖλος θέρει γ. Olymp. *in Mete.*94.9. **-ήσιος,** ον, *sexual*, ὁρμή *AP*15.12.12 (Leo Phil.). **-ικός,** ή, όν:—fem. -κή (sc. πτῶσις), ἡ, *genitive case*, Sch.D.P.449. **-ιος,** ὁ (sc. μήν), name of month at Halos, *IG*9(2).109*a*74. **-ις,** ἡ, fem. of γενέτης, Lxx *Wi.*7.12: acc. -τιν Aglaïas 10.

Γενετυλλίς, ίδος, ἡ, *goddess of one's birth-hour*, Ar.*Nu.*52: in pl., Id.*Th.*130, Luc.*Pseudol.*11.

γενέτωρ, ορος, ὁ, = γενέτης, πόντος γ. νεφέων ἀνέμων τε Xenoph. 30.5, cf. Hdt.8.137; γ. πατήρ E.*Ion*136 (lyr.), cf. *IG*5(1).540 (Lacon.), 14.1565, Arist.*Mu.*397^{b}21, 399^{a}31; Ἀπόλλων ὁ γ. Id.*Fr.*489; Ἀδριανῷ γενέτορι *IGRom.*4.562 (Aezani).

γενή, ἡ, poet. for γενεά, Call.*Fr.*241, Herod.2.1, 4.84.

γενῆΐς, -ΐδος, Att. **γενῄς,** ῆδος, ἡ, *pickaxe, mattock*, S.*Ant.*249.

γένημα, ατος, τό, *produce*, of the fruits of the earth (cf. γέννημα), *PRev.Laws* 24.15, al. (iii B.C.), Lxx *Ge.*40.17, al.; γ. τῆς ἀμπέλου *Ev. Marc.*14.25: pl., τοῦ ἐνεστῶτος ἔτους *OGI*262.9 (Syria), cf. *BGU* 188.9 (ii A.D.), *POxy.*277.6 (i B.C.); γ. καὶ ἐπιγενήματα *PRyl.*154.22 (i A.D.), etc. **γενημάτιον,** τό, Dim. of foreg., *PEdgar*41.9.

γενημᾰτο-γρᾰφέω, *sequester produce of land* for non-payment of taxes, in Pass., *PFay.*23.14, 26.8, al., *BGU*291, 599. **-γρᾰφία,** ἡ, *sequestration*, prob. in Wilcken *Chr.*363 (ii A.D.). **-φύλαξ** [ῠ], ακος, ὁ, *custodian of crops*, *PMagd.*1.10 (iii B.C.), etc.:—hence **-φῠλᾰκέω,** τὸν σπόρον *PTeb.ined.*, and **-φῠλᾰκία,** ἡ, *PTeb.*27.4 (pl.), al. (ii B.C.), *PRyl.*90.50 (iii A.D.).

γενητικός, v.l. for γενν-, Arist.*Top.*124^{a}24.

γενητός, ή, όν, (γενέσθαι) *originated* or *originable*, Arist.*Cael.*280^b 15 sqq., v.l. in Pl.*Ti.*28b,c, cf. Ph.1.3, al. (Freq. confused with γεννητός in codd.)

γενιάς· ἔκγονος, Hsch.

γενικός, ή, όν, *belonging to* or *connected with the* γένος, Arist.*Top.* 102^{a}36; ἡ διαφορὰ γ. ib.101^{b}18; *generic*, Chrysipp.*Stoic.*2.28, Phld. *Sign.*18, 19, etc.: Comp., *Stoic.*2.117, Ptol.*Phas.*p.5 H.: Sup., Diog. Bab.*Stoic.*3.214, *BGU*282.19 (ii A.D.), etc. Adv. -κῶς M.Ant.8.55,

Plot.6.1.9, Iamb. *in Nic.*p.22 P., etc. 2. *principal, typical,* ὀρχήσεις Luc.*Salt.*34(Comp.), cf. 22 (Sup.). II. *consisting of families,* φυλαί D.H.4.14, etc.; *of the family,* νόμος *CIG*3467.54 (Sardis), cf. 2712 (Mylasa). III. *sexual,* ἁμάρτημα Hdn.6.1.5 (dub.). IV. *in kind,* opp. ἀργυρικός, λόγος *PFlor.*77.7 (iii A.D.). V. Gramm., ἡ γενική (sc. πτῶσις) *genitive case, Stoic.*2.59, D.T.636, etc.

γενισμός, ὁ, *arrangement according to* γένη, *classification of rents according to* (1) *hypothetical estimate* and (2) *actual method of collection, PTeb.*67.5, al. (ii B.C.).

γέννᾰ Emp.17.27, 22.9, A.*Pr.*853 (but γέννᾱ in lyr. passages of E., as *Hec.*159), ης, ἡ:—poet. for γένος, *descent, birth, origin,* γέννᾳ μεγαλυνομένων A.*Pr.*892, cf. *Ag.*760 (lyr.). 2. *origin,* [τοῦ ὄντος] Parm. 8.6; διέχειν γέννῃ τε κρήσει τε Emp.22.7; γῆ γ. πάντων Secund. *Sent.*15; *production,* πύου Aret.*SD*1.14; ὑγρῶν ib.15. II. *offspring, son,* Pi.*O.*7.23; θνᾴσκοντα γέννας ἄτερ A.*Th.*748; λαγίνα γ. Id.*Ag.*119; *generation,* πέμπτη δ' ἀπ' αὐτοῦ γέννα Id.*Pr.*853, cf. 774. 2. *race, family,* οὐρανία γ. ib.165; ἀρσένων γ. E.*Med.*428 (lyr.): rare in Prose, ἡ τοῦ πέρατος γ. Pl.*Phlb.*25d, cf. Is.*Fr.* 136. 3. *creation, creature, PMag.Leid.V.*7.14. 4. personified, *Creative Force,* ib.*W.*5.3. III. of the Moon, *coming forth,* Ach.Tat.*Intr.Arat.*21, Sch.Arat.735, Paul.Al.*G.*4. **-άδας** [νᾰ], ου, ὁ, (Dor. word) *noble, generous,* χρηστὸς καὶ γ. Ar.*Ra.*179; γ. καὶ πρᾷος Pl.*Phdr.*243c, cf. Arist.*EN*1100b32; *highly bred,* ἐπὶ τῶν γενναδῶν ἵππων Polem.*Phgn.*78; *notable,* c. inf., Luc.*Hist.Conscr.* 33. **-αιάζω,** *to be brave,* Sch.E.*Hipp.*206:—also **-αΐζομαι,** Suid. s.v. τὴν λεοντῆν ἐνδύου. **-αιοπρεπής,** ές, *befitting a noble*: only in Adv. -πῶς Ar.*Pax*988. **-αῖος,** α, ον, also ος, ον E.*Hec.*592: (γέννα):—*true to one's birth or descent* (εὐγενὲς μέν ἐστι τὸ ἐξ ἀγαθοῦ γένους, γενναῖον δὲ τὸ μὴ ἐξιστάμενον ἐκ τῆς αὐτοῦ φύσεως Arist.*HA*488b19, cf. *Rh.*1390b22), οὔ μοι γενναῖον ἀλυσκάζοντι μάχεσθαι Il.5.253 (nowhere else in Hom.); γενναῖόν δέ σοι ταχέως ὑπακούειν Ar.*Fr.*28 D.: hence, I. of persons, *high-born, noble,* Archil.107, etc.; τέκνα Hdt.1.173; ὦ γονῇ γενναῖε S.*OT*1469; ἐσθλοὺς ἔκ τε γενναίων γεγῶτας Id.*Fr.*107.3; γενναῖός τις ἑπτὰ πάππους ἔχων ἀποφῆναι Pl.*Tht.*174e; οἱ γ., opp. οἱ ἀγεννεῖς, Arist.*Pol.* 1296b22; so of animals, *well-bred,* σκύλαξ Pl.*R.*375a, X.*Cyr.*1.4.15; opp. ἀγεννής, Arist.*HA*558b16. 2. *noble in mind, high-minded,* Hdt.3.140 (Sup.), S.*El.*129 (lyr.), etc.; τὸ γ.,=γενναιότης, Id.*OC* 569; of actions, *noble,* Hdt.1.37; λῆμα γ. Pi.*P.*8.44; τλάσας τὸ γ. S. *OC*1640, cf. E.*Alc.*624; γ. ἔπος, λόγοι, πόνοι, S.*Ph.*1402, E.*Heracl.* 537, *HF*357 (lyr.). 3. as a form of polite speech, γενναῖος εἶ *you are very good,* Ar.*Th.*220. b. ὦ γενναῖε, common form of address in Pl., as *Grg.*494e, cf. S.*Ph.*801; ironical, D.H.7.46. II. of things, *good of their kind, excellent,* μέλος A.*Fr.*281.5; σταφυλή, σῦκα, Pl. *Lg.*844e; γενναίου.. ἄξιον οὐθενός of no *great* use, Ath.Mech.31.2; ironical, γένει γ. σοφιστική Pl.*Sph.*231b (cf. I. 1), etc.; *genuine, intense,* δύη S.*Aj.*938, etc.; *violent,* σεισμός Philostr.*VA*6.38; θάλπη Jul.*Or.* 2.101d. b. γενναῖον· τὸ τῆς γενέσεως ἀρχηγόν, Hsch. III. Adv. -αίως *nobly,* Hdt.7.139, Th.2.41, Pl.*La.*196b, Men.672; ὅρκος, πῆγμα γ. παγέν A.*Ag.*1198; ironical, μάλα γ. ἐπιλαθόμενον ὢν εὖ πάθοι Jul.*Or.*3.125c: Comp. -οτέρως Pl.*Tht.*166c, Ps.-Callisth.1.38: Sup. -ότατα E.*Cyc.*657 (lyr.). 2. irreg. Sup. γενναιέστατος Dinol. 10. **-αιότης,** ητος, ἡ, *the character of a* γενναῖος, *nobility,* E.*Ph.* 1680, Th.3.82; of land, *fertility,* X.*Cyr.*8.3.38, Plb.3.44.8; *noble birth,* J.*AJ*19.3.1; *high spirit,* of colts, Max.Tyr.7.8. **-ας,** ὁ, *mother's brother, uncle,* Hsch. **-άω,** fut. Med. γεννήσομαι in pass. sense, D.S.19.2 (but -ηθήσομαι Id.4.9): (γέννα):—causal of γίγνομαι (cf. γείνομαι), mostly of the father, *beget,* ὁ γεννήσας πατήρ S.*El.*1412; οἱ γεννήσαντές σε *your parents,* X.*Mem.*2.1.27; τὸ γεννώμενον ἔκ τινος Hdt.1.108, etc.; ὅθεν γεγενναμένοι *sprung,* Pi.*P.*5.74; of the mother, *bring forth, bear,* A.*Supp.*48, Arist.*GA*716a22, X. *Lac.*1.3, etc.:—Med., *produce from oneself, create,* Pl.*Ti.*34b, *Mx.* 238a. 2. *produce, grow, get,* κἂν σῶμα γεννήσῃ μέγα S.*Aj.*1077. 3. metaph., *engender, produce,* λήθη τῶν ἰδίων κακῶν θρασύτητα γεννᾷ Democr.196; παντοίαν ἀρετήν Pl.*Smp.*209e; διανοήματά τε καὶ δόξας Id.*R.*496a, etc.; γεννῶσι τὸν οὐρανὸν [οἱ φιλόσοφοι] *call it into existence,* Arist.*Cael.*283b31; ὁ ἐξ ἀσωμάτου γεννῶν λόγος ib.305a16, cf. Plot.6.6.9; of numbers, *produce* a total, Ph.1.347. **-ῆεις,** εσσα, εν, *generative,* μήδεα Emp.29.2. **-ημα,** ατος, τό, *that which is produced* or *born, child,* S.*Tr.*315; παίδων τῶν σῶν νέατον γ. Id. *Ant.*627; τῶν Λαΐου.. τις ἦν γεννημάτων Id.*OT*1167: generally, any *product* or *work,* Pl.*R.*597e, etc.: in pl., *fruits* of the earth, Plb.1.71.1, etc.; τῶν στοιχείων Phld.*Sign.*37. 2. *breeding,* δηλοῖ τὸ γ. ὠμὸν (sc. ὄν)..παιδός S.*Ant.*471. II. Act., *begetting,* A.*Pr.* 850 (pl., s.v.l.). 2. *producing,* Pl.*Sph.*266d. **-ημᾰτίζω,** *produce offspring,* Aq.*Is.*55.10, al. **-ημᾰτικός,** ή, όν,=γεννητικός, J.*BJ*4. 8.3. **-ησιουργός,**=γενεσιουργός, Hsch. **-ησις,** Dor. **-ᾱσις,** εως, ἡ, *engendering, producing,* E.*IA*1065 (lyr., codd.); γ. καὶ τόκος Pl.*Smp.*206e; *birth, IG*2².1368.130, v.l. in *Ev.Luc.*1.14. 2. *production,* ἀγαθῶν Arist.*Pol.*1332a18 (pl.). **-ήτειρα,** ἡ, fem. of γεννητήρ, Pl.*Cra.*410c. **-ητέον,** *one must produce, grow,* Gal.10. 198. **-ητήρ,** ῆρος, ὁ,=sq. I, *App.Anth.*6.128. **-ητής,** οῦ, ὁ, *begetter, parent,* S.*OT*1015, *Fr.*752, Pl.*Cri.*51e, *Lg.*717e; τῶν πράξεων ὥσπερ καὶ τέκνων Arist.*EN*1113b18: generally, *producer,* Plot.3.3.3. II. **γεννῆται,** οἱ, (γέννα) at Athens, *members of* γένη, Pl.*Lg.*878d, Philoch.94; εἰς τοὺς γ. ἐγγράφειν, ἄγειν, Is.7. 13, 15, cf. Arist.*Ath.Fr.*3, *IG*2².1229.5; Ἀπόλλωνος Πατρῴου καὶ Διὸς Ἑρκείου γ. D.57.67. **-ητικός,** ή, όν, *generative, productive,* ἡ πρᾶξις ἡ γ. Arist.*HA*539b21; ψυχὴ γ. Id.*de An.*416b25: c. gen., *generative* or *productive of..,* τινός Epicur.*Ep.*1 p.11 U., Arist.*GA*726b21, etc.; ὕλην σπέρματος -κήν Epicur.*Nat.Herc.*908.1. 2. of men or animals, *able to procreate,* Arist.*HA*544b26, *de An.*432b24. **-ητός,** ή, όν, *begotten,* υἱὸς γ., opp. ποιητός, Pl.*Lg.*923e; *mortal,* Luc.*Icar.*2; γεννητοὶ γυναικῶν *born of* women, *Ev.Matt.*11.11, *Ev.Luc.*7.28. II. *generable,* opp. φθαρτός, Arist.*Metaph.*1027a29 (v.l.); ὕλη γ. matter *for generation,* ib.1042b6. Adv. -τῶς *by means of generation,* Iamb. *Myst.*1.18. **-ήτρια,** ἡ,=γεννήτειρα, δικῶν Phryn.*PS*p.62 B. **-ήτωρ,** Dor. **-άτωρ,** ορος, ὁ,=γενέτωρ, Ζεύς A.*Supp.*206, E.*Hipp.*683, Jul.*Or.*2.51d, v.l. in Arist.*Mu.*397b21; γ. καὶ ἑστιοῦχον Pl.*Lg.*878a: pl., ib.869a; θεῷ γεννήτορι πάντων *IG*3.636: metaph. of numbers, ἐὰν πυθμενικοὶ ὦσιν οἱ γ. Iamb. *in Nic.*p.56 P., al. **-ικός,** ή, όν,= γενναῖος, *noble,* Ar.*Eq.*457 (Sup.), Pl.*Phdr.*279a (Comp.); γ. καὶ κοσμία γύναι Men.*Georg.*42; of things, λεπαστή Antiph.45; δεῖπνον Alciphr.3.5. Adv. -ῶς Ar.*Lys.*1070, Antiph.192, Luc.*Somn.*7, Max.Tyr.31.1; *vigorously, drastically,* of the action of medicines, Gal.11.864, al.

γεννοδότειρα, ἡ, *the giver of heirs,* Ἀφροδίτη Orph.*H.*55.12.

γεννόν· ἀρχαῖον, Hsch. (perh. for ἔνον); also,=κοῖλον, Id. **γέννου·** καὶ λάβε (cf. γέντο) καὶ κάθιζε (Cypr.), Id.

γένος, εος or ους, τό, *race, stock, kin,* ἀμφοτέροισιν ὁμὸν γ. ἠδ' ἴα πάτρη Il.13.354; αἷμά τε καὶ γ. Od.8.583; ὑμετέρου δ' οὐκ ἔστι γένεος βασιλεύτερον 15.533; γένος πατέρων αἰσχυνέμεν Il.6.209; γ. ἀπόλωλε τοκήων Od.4.62; ὅθι τοι γένος ἐστὶ καὶ αὐτῇ 6.35: freq. abs. in acc., ἐξ Ἰθάκης γένος εἰμί from Ithaca I am *by race,* 15.267, cf. Il. 5.544, 896, S.*Ph.*239, etc.; in Att. freq. with the Art., ποδαπὸς τὸ γένος εἶ; Ar.*Pax*186, cf. Pl.*Sph.*216a: so in dat., γένει πολῖται D.23.24; γένει υἱός, opp. an adopted son, Id.44.2; οἱ ἐν γένει,= συγγενεῖς, S.*OT*1430; οἱ ἔξω γένους Id.*Ant.*660; οὐδὲν ἐν γένει Id. *OT*1016; γένει προσήκειν τινί X.*An.*1.6.1; γένει ἀπωτέρω εἶναι D. 44.13: in gen., γένους εἶναί τινος to be of his *race,* ἄναγνος καὶ γένους τοῦ Λαΐου S.*OT*1383, cf. X.*HG*4.2.9; ἐγγυτέρω, ἐγγύτατα γένους, nearer, next *of kin,* Is.8.33, A.*Supp.*388. 2. *direct descent,* opp. *collateral relationship,* γένος γάρ, ἀλλ' οὐχὶ συγγένεια Is.8.33; αἱ κατὰ γένος βασιλεῖαι *hereditary* monarchies, Arist.*Pol.*1285a16, 1313a 10. II. *offspring,* even of *a single descendant,* σὸν γ. Il.19.124, 21.186; ἡ δ' ἄρ' ἔην θεῖον γ. οὐδ' ἀνθρώπων 6.180; ἀμὸν Οἰδίπου γ. A. *Th.*654; Διὸς γ., of Bacchus, S.*Ant.*1117 (lyr.); Τέκμησσα, δύσμορον γ. Id.*Aj.*784. 2. collectively, *offspring, posterity,* ἐκεῖνοι καὶ τὸ γ. τὸ ἀπ' ἐκείνων Th.1.126; ἐξώλη ποιεῖν αὐτὸν καὶ γ. καὶ οἰκίαν D.19. 71. III. generally, *race,* of beings, θεῶν Ar.*Th.*960; ἡμιθέων γ. ἀνδρῶν Il.12.23; ἡμιόνων, βοῶν γ., Il.2.852, Od.20.212; ἵππειον γ., i.e. *mules,* S.*Ant.*342; ἰχθύων πλωτὸν γ. Id.*Fr.*941.9. b. *clan, house, family,* Hdt.1.125, etc.; Φρὺξ μὲν γενεῇ, γένεος δὲ τοῦ βασιληΐου ib.35; τοὺς ἀπὸ γένους men *of noble family,* Plu.*Rom.*21; ἱερεὺς κατὰ γ. *IG* 5(1).497, al.; also ἱέρεια ἀπὸ γένους, διὰ γένους, ib.607.29, 602; esp. at Athens and elsewhere as a subdivision of the φρατρία, Arist.*Ath. Fr.*3, Pl.*Alc.*1.120e, etc.; = Lat. *gens,* D.S.4.21, Plu.*Num.*1. c. *tribe,* as a subdivision of ἔθνος, Hdt.1.56, 101. d. *caste,* Id.2.164. e. of animals, *breed,* Id.4.29. 2. *age, generation,* Od.3.245; γ. χρύσεον, etc., Hes.*Op.*109: hence, *age, time of life,* γένει ὕστερος Il.3. 215, cf. Arist.*Rh.*1408a27. IV. *sex,* Epich.172.1, Pl.*Smp.*189d; *gender,* Arist.*Rh.*1407b7, Diog.Bab.*Stoic.*3.214, etc. V. *class, sort, kind,* τὰ γ. τῶν κυνῶν ἐστι δισσά X.*Cyn.*3.1; τὸ φιλόσοφον γ. Pl. *R.*501e; τὸ τῶν γεωργῶν [γ.] Id.*Ti.*17c, cf. *R.* 434b, Arist.*Pol.*1329a 27; τῶν ἰχθυοπωλῶν γ. Xenarch.7.4; τὸ τῶν παρασίτων γ. Nicol. Com.1.1, etc. 2. in Logic, opp. εἶδος (species), Pl.*Prm.*129c, al., Arist.*Top.*102a31, 102b12, al.; τὰ γ. εἰς εἴδη πλείω καὶ διαφέροντα διαιρεῖται Id.*Metaph.*1059b36. 3. in the animal kingdom, τὰ μέγιστα γ.,= the modern *Classes,* such as birds, fishes, Id.*HA*490b7, cf. 505b26; so in the vegetable kingdom, γένη τὰ μέγιστα,= σιτώδη, χεδροπά and ἀνώνυμα, Thphr.*HP*8.1.1. b. *genus,* τὸ τῶν καρκίνων γ., τὸ τῶν περιστερῶν γ., etc., Arist.*HA*487b17, 488a4; τῶν δένδρων καὶ τῶν φυτῶν εἴδη πλείω τυγχάνει καθ' ἕκαστον γένος Thphr.*HP*1.14.3; τοῦ αὐτοῦ γένους [πίτυς] καὶ πεύκη Dsc.1.69, al. c. γένος τι *a species* of plant, Thphr.*HP*4.8.13; so later, γένη,= *crops,* ἄλλοις γένεσι τοῖς πρὸς πυρὸν διοικουμένοις *PTeb.*66.43, al. (ii B.C.); οἷς ἐὰν αἱρῶμαι γένεσι πλὴν κνήκου *PAmh.*2.91.15 (ii A.D.); *produce, POxy.*727.20 (ii A.D.); *materials,* ib.54.16 (iii A.D.); ἐν γένεσιν in *kind,* opp. ἐν ἀργυρίῳ, *PFay.*21.10 (ii A.D.). 4. τὰ γ. the *elements,* Pl.*Ti.*54b. (Cf. Skt. *jánas,* gen. *jánasas*; Lat. *genus, –eris,* v. γίγνομαι.)

γενούστης, ου, ὁ, misread for γένους τῆς in Pl.*Phlb.*30d, cf. Hsch.

γέντα, τά,= ἔντερα, Call.*Fr.*309, Nic.*Al.*62, 557; = κρέα, σπλάγχνα, Hsch.

γεντιᾱνή, ἡ, *gentian,* Hp.*Ep.*19, Dsc.3.3. [-ᾱνή Damocr.ap.Gal. 13.822, 14.97, but -ᾰνή ib.14.123.]

γεντιὰς ῥίζα,= foreg., Androm.ap.Gal.14.41. 2.= γλυκύρριζα, Dsc.3.5; = κενταύρειον τὸ μέγα ib.6.

γέντιμος· ἄκρον τοῦ ἁλιευτικοῦ καλάμου, Hsch.; cf. γέρσυμον. **γέντινοι·** οἰκεῖοι, and **γέντινος·** ὕπνος, Id.

γέντο, *he grasped,* = ἔλαβεν, 3 sg. of Verb found only in this form, Il.8.43, al. (Cf. ἀπόγεμε· ἄφελκε, and ὕγγεμος· συλλαβή (Cypr.), Hsch.) II. shortd. form for ἐγένετο, v. γίγνομαι.

γένυξ· πέλεκυς, Hsch.

γένῡς, υος, ἡ, dat. γένυι Pi.*O.*13.85: pl., gen. γενύων *P.*4.225 (disyll.), A.*Th.*122 (lyr.): dat. γένυσι S.*Ant.*121 (lyr.), Ep. γένυσσι Il.11.416, γενύεσσι Nic. (v. infr.): acc. γένυας, contr. γένῡς:—*jaw,* πυκνὰς τε γένυς εὐανθέϊ λάχνῃ Od.11.320; ἡ ἄνω γ., ἡ κάτωθεν, Arist.*HA*492b 23, sq.: pl., γένυες *both jaws, the mouth with the teeth,* Il.23.688, 11.

416, Pi.*P*.4.225, S.*Ant*.121 : in sg., Thgn.1327, E.*Ph*.1380, al.: generally, *side of the face, cheek*, φίλον φίλημα παρὰ γένυν τιθέντα E. *Supp*.1154. II. *edge of an axe, axe*, S.*Ph*.1205 (lyr.), *El*.196 (lyr.); of a fishing-hook, Opp.*H*.3.539; πυράγρης Nic.*Al*.50 (pl.). (Cf. Skr. *hanus*, Lat. *gena*, etc.) [ῠ twice in E., *El*.1214 (lyr.), *Fr*. 530.6.]

γεο-ειδής, ές, = γεώδης, Ti.Locr.101a, Arist.*GA*731b13, *HA*555b 28. **-θαλπής**, ές, *earth-cherishing*, *CIG*3769 (Nicomedia). **-κτείτης**, ου, = γεωμόρος (?) (add.), ib.3695*b* (Mysia).

γεόομαι, Pass., *to become earth*, D.S.3.40.

γεοῦχος, ὁ, *landowner*, Agatharch.95, *PAmh*.88.30 (ii A. D.), *POxy*.910.16, etc. (γαιοῦχος Paul.Al.*N*.2): hence **γεουχέω** *PFay*.23. 6, *BGU*18.19 (ii A. D.), etc.; **γεουχικός**, ή, όν, *POxy*.1638.15 (iii A. D.).

γέραδος· αἰγιαλός, Hsch.; cf. χέραδος. **γεράζω**, *honour*, *EM* 8.5, 227.43:—Pass., Hsch.

γεραίομαι, dub. l. in Nic.*Al*.396.

γεραιός, ά, όν, (γέρων, γῆρας) = γηραιός, *old*: in Hom. (who never has γηραιός) always of men, with notion of dignity (v. infr.), cf. Pi. *N*.4.89; ὁ γεραιός that *reverend sire*, Il.1.35, etc.; γεραιέ 10.164, etc.; but γεραιάς (acc. pl. fem.) 6.87 (cf. 270,287) is f.l. for γεραίρας, v. γεραρός: Comp. γεραίτερος Od.3.24, A.*Eu*.848, Hdt.6.52; γονῇ πεφυκὼς γ. (-τέρᾳ codd.) S.*OC*1294; freq. in political sense, οἱ γ. *the elders, senators*, X.*Cyr*.1.5.5, Pl.*Lg*.952a, *IG*14.2445 (Massilia): Sup. γεραίτατος Ar.*Ach*.286, Pl.*Lg*.855e, etc.; rarely, = πρεσβύτατος, *eldest*, Theoc.15.139. II. of things, *ancient*, πόλις A.*Ag*.710 (lyr.); χείρ E.*Hec*.64 (lyr.). (γεραϊός Tyrt.10.20, E.*HF*446 (lyr.); cf. γεραός.)

γεραιότης, ητος, ἡ, *advanced age*, *PMasp*.279.26 (vi A. D.), etc.

γεραιό-φλοιος, ον, *with old, wrinkled skin*, σῦκα *AP*6.102 (Phil.). **-φρων**, ονος, ὁ, ἡ, (φρήν) *old of mind, sage*, A.*Supp*.361 (lyr., Burges for γεραφρόνων).

γέραιρα, ἡ, v. γεραρός. **γεραιράδες** or **γεραράδες**, αἱ, = γεραραί, *AB*228; priestesses of Athena at Argos, ib.231.10; γερηράδες, Hsch.

γεραίρω, Ep. impf. γέραιρον Il.7.321: fut. γερᾰρῶ Jusj.ap.D.59. 78, *Epigr.Gr*.992 (Balbilla): aor. 1 ἐγέρηρα *CIG*2936 (Tralles), *APl*. 4.183.7, Orph.*A*.507, γέρηρα *IG*4.1475 (Epid.); ἐγέρᾱρα Pi.*O*.5.5, *N*.5.8: (γεραρός):—*honour, reward* with a gift, νώτοισιν δ' Αἴαντα διηνεκέεσσι γέραιρεν Il.7.321, cf. Od.14.437,441, etc.: generally, *honour*, τινά Pi.*O*.3.2: c. dat. modi, βωμοὺς ἑορταῖς ib.5.5; τινὰ ἐπινικίοις B.2.8; γένος θεῶν γ. φωνῇ Ar.*Th*.961 (lyr.); δώροις καὶ ἀρχαῖς καὶ ἕδραις καὶ πάσαις τιμαῖς X.*Cyr*.8.1.39; στεφάνοις τοὺς νικῶντας Id. *HG*1.7.33; δν..ἐπεστεφάνωσε γεραίρων *IG*3.713:—Pass., τίμιος γεραίρεται E.*Supp*.553; τιμαῖς X.*Cyr*.8.8.4. 2. γεραίρει· τέρπει, Hsch.:—Pass., γεραιρόμενα μυίοισι prob. in Nic.*Al*.396. 3. reversely, γ. τινί τι *present as an honorary gift*, τὰ Ἰοβάκχεια τῷ Διονύσῳ Jusj.ap.D. l.c. II. *celebrate*, τὰ πάθεα τραγικοῖσι χοροῖσι Hdt. 5.67; χορείαις θυσίαν Pl.*Lg*.799a, cf. *Epin*.980b.—Not in early Prose, exc. Hdt., X., and Pl.: in later Prose, Ph.1.186, Arr.*Ind*.8.5 (Pass.), Porph.*Abst*.2.16, etc.

Γεραίστιος, v. Γεράστιος.

γεραίτερος, γεραίτατος, Comp. and Sup. of γεραιός (q.v.).

γερᾰλέος, = γηρ-, Hsch.

γεράνδρῡον, τό, (δρῦς) *an old tree* or *stump*, Ph.2.437, Plu.2.796b, etc.: hence of an old person, Aristaen.2.1: heterocl. pl., γεράνδρυες, Hsch. 2. as Adj., *old, withered*, Thphr.*HP*2.7.2, A.R.1. 1118, Jul.*Ep*.98; γ. πρέμνα Dsc.4.186. (ῡ A.R. l.c., ῠ *AP*9.233 (Eryc.).)

γεράν-ειον [ᾰ], τό, a kind of *truffle*, Eust.1017.19; = ὕδνον, Thphr. *HP*1.6.9, ap.Ath.2.62a (om.codd. Thphr.); but dist. from ὕ. ib.1.6.5, ap.Ath.2.61f. **-ίας**, ου, ὁ, (γέρανος) *crane-necked, long-necked*, Phryn.*PS*p.55 B. **-ίζω**, *utter the crane's note*, *Gloss*. **-ιον**, τό, (γέρᾰνος) *Geranium tuberosum*, a plant, Dsc.3.116; ἕτερον γ. *crane's-bill, Erodium malacoides*, ibid.; also **γεράνιος**, Hsch. (but ἡ γεράνιος a *plaster*, Aët.15.15). II. substance used in Alchemy, Pelag.Alch.p.256 B. **-ίς**, ίδος, ἡ, a kind of *surgical bandage*, Heliod.ap.Orib.48.47 tit., Gal.18(1).814. **-ίτης** (sc. λίθος), ου, ὁ, *a precious stone*, Plin.37.187. [ῑ]

γερᾰνο-βοσία, ἡ, = sq., Poll.9.16. **-βωτία**, ἡ, *feeding of cranes*, Pl.*Plt*.264c (pl.). **-γέρων**, = γεράνιον, Ps.-Dsc.3.116. **-μᾰχία**, ἡ, *battle with cranes*, Ὁμηρικὴ τῶν Πυγμαίων γ. Str.2.1.9. **-πόδιον**, = λυχνίς, Ps.-Dsc.3.100.

γέρᾰνος, ἡ, also ὁ, Thphr.*Sign*.38:—*crane, Grus cinerea*, Il.3.3, Hes.*Op*.448, Alc.*Supp*.9, Ar.*Av*.710, Arist.*HA*614b18, al. II. *crane for lifting weights*, esp. used in the theatre, Poll.4.130. 2. *quern*, Hsch. III. *dance resembling the movements of the crane*, Luc.*Salt*.34, Plu.*Thes*.21, Poll.4.101. IV. (masc.) a *fish*, Ael. *NA*15.9. V. = ὄμβρος (Cyren.), *EM*227.51. (Cf. OHG. *chranuh*, OE. *cran* 'crane', Lith. *garnỹs* 'stork', etc.)

γερᾰνουλκός, ὁ, *leader of the dance called* γέρανος at Delos, Hsch.

γερᾰνόφθαλμος, ον, *crane-eyed*, Sch.Opp.*H*.1.386.

γερᾰνώδης, ες, *crane-like*, τράχηλος Phryn.*PS*p.55 B.

γερᾰός, ή, όν, = γεραιός, S.*OC*200, Tim.*Pers*.227, Nic.*Fr*.74.71, *IG*3.779.

γεραόχος, ον, *holder of privilege*, gloss on ἀγέρωχος, Sch.Il.10.430.

γερᾰρός, ά, όν, *of reverend bearing, majestic*, Il.3.170; γεραρώτερος ἦεν Ὀδυσσεύς ib.211; γεραρὴ τράπεζα a table *of honour*, Xenoph.1.9; γεραραῖς χερσί *IG*14.818; ἀνὴρ γ. τὸ εἶδος Plu.*Alex*.26; τὸ γ. τοῦ ἤθους M.Ant.1.15. Adv. -ρῶς, μέλπουσιν *AP*9.692. 2. later, = γεραιός, A.*Ag*.722 (lyr.); γ. τοκῆες *IG*3.1335, Q.S.9.90. 3. γεραραί, αἱ, *elders*, A.*Supp*.667 (lyr.); but γεραραί *priestesses of Dionysus* is f. l. for **γέραιραι** in D.59.73, al.; cf. Μητρὸς...πρόπολος σεμνή τε γέραιρα *IG*2.2116, and γεραίρας (acc. pl.) is prob. l. in Il.6.270, cf. 87,287 (cf. Sch. BT); cf. *EM*227.35. (γέραιρα old fem. of γεραρός; cf. χίμαιρα: χίμαρος.)

γέρᾰς, αος (in Prose -ως X.*Ag*.1.5, Luc.*Tyr*.9), τό: nom. pl. γέρᾰ, apoc. for γέραα, Il.2.237, 9.334, Od.4.66; γέρᾱ E.*Ph*.874; γέρεα Hdt.2.168, *SIG*1037 (Milet.); γέρη ib.1025 (Cos); γέρᾱτα *IG*14. 1389 i 29: gen. pl. γερῶν Th.3.58, etc.; Ep. dat. γεράεσσι Hes.*Th*. 449, Theoc.17.109:—*gift of honour*, μοῖραν καὶ γ. ἐσθλὸν ἔχων Od.11. 534; τὸ γὰρ γ. ἐστὶ θανόντων *the last honours* of the dead, Il.16.457; *privilege, prerogative* conferred on kings or nobles, γ. θ' ὅ τι δῆμος ἔδωκεν Od.7.150, cf. Il.20.182; τὰς ἀγγελίας ἐσφέρειν ἐδίδου γ. Hdt. 1.114, etc.; πρότερον δὲ ἦσαν ἐπὶ ῥητοῖς γέρασι πατρικαὶ βασιλεῖαι Th. 1.13; τιμαὶ καὶ ἔπαινοι καὶ γ. Pl.*R*.516c; γ. καὶ ἆθλα ib.460b; freq. of priests (cf. 3), Aeschin.3.18; δαίμοσιν νέμει γέρα ἄλλοισιν ἄλλα A.*Pr*.231; so later, γ. ἀλειτουργησίας *PFlor*.382.3 (iii A. D.). 2. generally, *gift, present*, Od.20.297, etc. 3. esp. *perquisite* received by priests at sacrifices, τὰ δέρματα καὶ τὰ ἄλλα γέρεα *SIG*1037 (Milet., iv/iii B. C.); γέρη λαμβάνει τὸ δέρμα καὶ τὸ σκέλος ib.1025.22 (Cos, iv/iii B. C.); ὁ πριάμενος τῶν γερῶν λήψεται τὰς γενομένας καρπείας *PEleph*.14.13 (iii B. C.). 4. *reward*, *POxy*.1408.16 (iii A. D.). (If akin to γέρων, prop. *privilege of age*.)

γεράσμιος, ον, (γέρας) *honouring*, *h.Merc*.122. II. = γεραρός, *honoured*, E.*Ph*.923; μάντις Nic.*Th*.613; *aged*, ὄσσων E.*Supp*.95.

Γεράστιος, ὁ, *a month* at Sparta and Cos, Th.4.119, *SIG*1012.15; at Troezen and Calaurea (in form Γεραίστ-), Caryst.13, *SIG*993.

γεραστός, ή, όν, *honoured*, *EM*227.43.

γερασφόρος, ον, *winning honour*, Pi.*P*.2.43.

γεράτης, name of a breed of horses, *POxy*.922.7 (vi/vii A. D.).

γεργαθός, = γυργ-, *POxy*.741.5 (ii A. D.). **γέργανα** (i. e. ϝεργ-)· ἐργαλεῖα, Hsch.

γέργερα· πολλά, Hsch. (γέργενα cod., cf. Varr.*LL*5.11).

γεργέριμος (sc. ἐλαία), = δρυπεπής, Call.*Fr*.50, cf. Suid., Hsch.; also of figs, Didym.ap.Ath.2.56d.

γεργέρινος, = γεργῖνος, Hsch. **γέργερος**· βρόγχος, Id.; cf. γαργαρεών. **γεργέροψ**· ζῷον, Id. (γεργέλ- cod.). **γεργῖνος**, ὁ, = διάβολος, Id. **γέργυπες**· νεκροί, Id.

γέργυρα, v. γόργυρα.

γερδιοραβδιστής, ὁ, *worker who beat the web* in a weaving-shed, *PTeb*.305.5 (ii A. D.).

γερδιός or **γέρδιος**, ὁ, *weaver*, Hsch., *Rev.Épigr*.1.146, *PTeb*.116. 48 (ii B. C.), *POxy*.39.8 (i A. D.), etc.:—also **γέρδις**, *BGU*426.19, etc.:—fem. **γερδία**, *Edict.Diocl*.20.12, **γερδίαινα**, *BGU*617.4 (but **γέρδιος**, ἡ, *EM*228.40):—Adj. **γερδιακός**, ή, όν, τέχνη *PGrenf*.2.59. 10; ἱστός *POxy*.646: **-κόν** (sc. τέλος), τό, *tax on weaving*, ib.288.2 (i A. D.).

γερδιών, ῶνος, ὁ, *weaving-shed*, *PFlor*.50.70 (iii A. D.).

γερδοποιόν, τό, = *textrinum*, *Gloss*.

γερεᾱφόρος, *one who enjoys perquisites*, title of priest at Cos (cf. γέρας 3), γ. βασιλέων *SIG*1025.21.

γέρην, ἡ, fem. of γέρανος, Ael.Dion.*Fr*.104, Hsch.; also, = ἔντιμος, Id.

Γερήνιος, ὁ, Homeric epith. of Nestor, Γερήνιος ἱππότα Νέστωρ, *from Gerena* or *Gerenon*, a city of Messenia; ξεῖνος ἐὼν...παρ' ἱπποδάμοισι Γερήνοις Hes.*Fr*.15.3.

γερη-φορία, ἡ, *enjoyment of privileges*, D.H.2.10 (pl.). **-φόρος**, = γερεαφόρος, *BCH*12.282 (Myndos).

γερθυρέον· ἱλαρόν, Hsch. **γέρινθοι**· ἐρέβινθοι, Id.

γεροάκται· δήμαρχοι (Lacon.), Hsch. (for γερω'ιακταί, = γερουσιασταί).

γεροῖα, τά, *tales of old time*, Corinn.20: as title of poems by her, Ant.Lib.25 (prob.).

γεροίταν· πάππον (Cypr.), Hsch.; cf. **γέρυς, γερύτας**, = γέρων, Id.

γεροντ-ᾰγωγέω, (ἀγωγός) *guide an old man*, S.*OC*348: c.acc., Πηλέα γ. Id.*Fr*.487, parodied by *Com.Adesp*.11, cf. Ar.*Eq*.1099. **-άριον**, τό, = γερόντιον, *Gloss*. **-εία**, ἡ, *membership of a* γερουσία, *OGI* 534 (Ephesus). **-ειος**, α, ον, *belonging to an old man* or *old age*, Ar.*Fr*.715. **-εύω**, *to be a senator*, γεροντεύσας *IG*5(1).254 (Sparta, i B. C.), al.:—Med., Hsch. s. v. γηρωπίζεται. **-ία**, ἡ, Lacon., = γερουσία, X.*Lac*.10.1. **-ίας**, ου, ὁ, *father's father* (Lacon.), Sch.Il.14. 118, Eust.971.23. **-ιάω**, *grow old* or *childish*, D.L.3.18. **-ικός**, ή, όν, *of* or *for old men*, λουτρά Pl.*Lg*.761c; κρᾶσις Ath.Med.ap.Orib. *inc*.23.6: **-κόν**, τό, *senate-house*, Str.14.1.43; cf. sq. Adv. **-κῶς** *like an old man*, v.l. in Ar.*V*.1132, cf. Plu.2.639d: Comp. **-κώτερον** Cic. *Att*.12.1.2. **-ιον**, τό, Dim. of γέρων, *little old man*, Hp.*Ep*.13, Ar.*Ach*.993, X.*An*.6.3.22, Theoc.4.58, Luc.*Bacch*.3. II. the Carthaginian *Senate*, Plb.6.51.2 (v.l. γεροντικόν).

γεροντο-γρᾴδιο [ᾰ], τό, (γραῦς) *old man-woman*, barbarism in Ar. *Th*.1199 (sed divisim leg.). **-διδάσκᾰλος**, ὁ, ἡ, *old man's master*, Pl.*Euthd*.272c. **-ειδής**, ές, *like an old man*, Eust.1923.63. **-κομεῖον**, τό, (κομέω) *hospital for the old*, *Cod.Just*.1.3.45.1:—also Subst. **-κόμος**, ὁ, *warden of such a hospital*, Just.*Nov*.7.1: **-κομικά**, τά, Sch. Pl.*Phdr*.240c. **-μᾰνία**, ἡ, *craze* or *dotage of old men*, name of a play by Anaxandrides, Arist.*Rh*.1413b26.

γερουσί-α, ἡ, *Council of Elders, senate*, E.*Rh*.401: esp. at Sparta, D.20.107, Arist.*Pol*.1270b24, *IG*5(2).345.10 (Orchom. Arc., ii/i B. C.); cf. γερωΐα and γεροντία; also of the Carthaginian *Senate*,

Arist.*Pol.*1272^{b}37; and the Roman, Plu.2.789e, Jul.*Or.*2.97b; of the Jewish *Sanhedrin*, *Act.Ap.*5.21, cf. Lxx *Ex.*3.16. 2. *sacred college*, ἱερὰ γ. *IG*3.702 (Eleusis), cf. 7.2808 (Hyettus, iii B.C.), etc. II. = πρεσβεία, E.*Rh.*936. **-ακός**, ά, όν, *of* or *belonging to the senate*, χρήματα *CIG*3080 (Teos). **-άρχης**, ου, ὁ, *president of Jewish elders*, ib.9902 (Rome). **-ας**, ου, ὁ, *member of the* γερουσία at Sparta, *IG*5(1).31, al.: pl., ib.62.19; also, *official* of a guild, ib.206, 209. **-αστής**, οῦ, ὁ, *member of a* γερουσία, Plb.7.9.1, *IG*7.2808.17 (Hyettus, iii B.C.). **-ος**, α, ον, *for* or *befitting the* γέροντες, γ. οἶνος wine *drunk only by the chiefs*, Il.4.259, Od.13.8; γ. ὅρκος an oath *taken by them*, Il.22.119; γερούσιον, τό, *perquisite of chiefs*, Hsch.

γερράδια, τά, *mats of plaited work*, Hsch.

γέρρον, τό, *anything made of wicker-work*: I. *oblong shield*, covered with ox-hide, Hdt.7.61, X.*Cyr.*7.1.33, etc.; Θρᾴκια γ. Plu. *Aem.*32. II. γέρρα, τά, *wattled screens* or *booths*, used in the Athen. market-place, τὰ γ. ἐνεπίμπρασαν D.18.169; τὰ γ. ἀναιρεῖν Id.59.90: generally, *wattles*, Str.4.4.3, Jul.*Or.*1.29d: metaph. of the eyelashes, Gal.*UP*10.6. III. *wicker body of a cart*, Str.7.2.3. IV. = γερροχελώνη, Plb.8.3.3 (pl.), D.H.6.92, Arr.*An.*1.21.5. V. *stake*, Eup.405; *dart*, dub. in Alcm.133. 2. = αἰδοῖον (Sicel) (or prob., = ὄλισβος, cf. Orion 43.24), Epich.235.

γερρο-φόροι, οἱ, *troops that used wicker shields*, X.*An.*1.8.9, Pl.*La.*191c, Str.7.3.17. **-φύλαξ** [ῠ], ακος, ὁ, *defender of wicker-work barrier*, *Sammelb.*1918, prob. in *OGI*111 (nisi leg. δροφύλαξ). **-χελώνη**, ἡ, *penthouse, mantlet*, used in siege-works, Ph.*Bel.*98.19.

γέρρω· ἀπόλωλα, Hsch. (i.e. ϝέρρω).

γέρσυμον, τό, *end of a fishing-rod*, Hsch.

γέρῡνος, ὁ, = γύρινος, Nic.*Th.*620, *Al.*563.

γερωΐα (i.e. γερωΐα), ἡ, Lacon. form of γερουσία, Ar.*Lys.*980 (γερωχία codd.); cf. **γερωνία**, Hsch.

γέρων, οντος, ὁ, *old man*, Il.1.33, etc.: pleon., παλαιοὶ γέροντες Ar. *Ach.*676; ἄνους τε καὶ γ. S.*Ant.*281, cf. Ar.*Eq.*1349; ἀεὶ γὰρ ἡβᾷ τοῖς γέρουσιν εὖ μαθεῖν A.*Ag.*584; καλὸν δὲ καὶ γέροντα μανθάνειν σοφά Id.*Fr.*396. 2. γέροντες, οἱ, *Elders, Chiefs*, κίκλησκεν δὲ γέροντας ἀριστῆας Παναχαιῶν Il.2.404 sq., cf. 9.574, Od.2.14; later, *Senators*, esp. at Sparta, Hdt.1.65, 6.57, Pl.*Lg.*692a, *IG*2^{2}.687, Arist.*Pol.*1265^{b}38 (sg. γέροντι *IG*5(1).1346, but usu. γερουσίας, q.v.); in other states, as at Elis, Arist.*Pol.*1306^{a}17, cf. 1272^{a}7, *OGI*479.11 (Dorylaeum). II. as Adj., *old*, γέρον σάκος Od.22.184; γ. γράμμα A.*Fr.*331; more freq. in masc., γ. πατήρ Il.1.358, Od.18.53; ἀνὴρ γ. Thgn.1351; γ. χαλκός Simon.144; γ. λόγος A.*Ag.*750 (lyr.); ἵππος S.*El.*25; πόνος Id.*OC*1258 (codd. but πίνος Scaliger, edd.); οἶνος Alex.167.5, cf. Eub.124; πέπλος, λέμβος, Theoc.7.17, 21.12: rarely in Prose, οἱ γέροντες τῶν ἰχθύων Arist.*HA*607^{b}28; of stags, ib.611^{b}3; Ἀντίγονος ὁ γ. Antigonus *the Elder*, Plu.*Pel.*2: neut. pl., γέροντα βουλεύεις (for ἀρχαῖα) S.*Fr.*794. III. *part of the spinning-wheel*, Pherecr.114. (Skt. *járant-* 'old', *járati* 'render infirm'; cf. γέρας.)

γερωνία and **γερωχία**, v. γερωΐα. **γερώνοιον**· κοῖλον, κενόν, Hsch. **γέσμα**· γεῦμα, Id. **γέστα**· γογγυλίς, Id.:—also **γεστία**· ἔνδυσις, and **γέστρα**· στολή, Id. **γέτορ**· ἔτος, and **γέτος**· ἐνιαυτός, Id. (γ = ϝ). **γεῦ**· γυνὸν τι ἄρα, Id.

γευθμός, ὁ, = γεῦσις, Nic.*Al.*399.

γεύλοφα, = γεώλοφα, Hsch.

γεῦμα, ατος, τό, (γεύω) *taste, smack* of a thing, E.*Cyc.*150; τρία γ. Ar.*Ach.*187; γεύματος χάριν Arist.*HA*491^{a}8. II. *food*, σιτηρὰ γ. Hp.*Acut.*10: metaph., ἄγευστοι τοῦ παντρόφου γ. σοφίας Ph.1.544.

γευματικός, ή, όν, dub. sens., χιτών *Schwyzer* 462 *B* 29 (Tanagra, iii B.C.).

γευνῶν· γονάτων, Hsch. (leg. γεύνων, cf. γόνυ).

γεῦος, τό, in pl. γεύη, perh. *ass*, *POxy.*1675.12 (iii A.D.).

γεῦσ-ις, εως, ἡ, *sense of taste*, Democr.11, Arist.*EN*1118^{a}26, *de An.*422^{a}29, etc. II. *a tasting*, Lxx *Da.*5.2. III. *food*, Lxx *Wi.*16.2, al. IV. *taste, flavour*, Dsc.1.12, *Gp.*5.7.3. V. *back of the tongue*, Poll.2.104. **-τέον**, *one must make to taste*, τινὰ αἵματος Pl.*R.*537a. **-τήριον**, τό, *cup for tasting with*, Ar.*Fr.*299, Pherecr.143.3. **-της**, ου, ὁ, *taster*, *CIG*2214.8 (Chios). **-τικός**, ή, όν, *of* or *for taste*, γ. αἰσθητήριον the seat of the sense *of taste*, Arist. *de An.*422^{b}5; αἴσθησις D.H.*Comp.*12; δύναμις Alex.Aphr.*Pr.*2.60; τὸ γ. Plu.2.990a. Adv. -κῶς Sch.Ven.Il.5.661. **-τός**, ή, όν, *that may be tasted*, τὸ γ. Arist.*Rh.*1370^{a}23, *de An.*422^{a}8, Plu.2.38a, Porph.*Abst.*1.33.

Γευστός, ὁ, name of a month at Lamia, *IG*9(2).66, al.

γευστρίνην· γαυλόν, Hsch.

γεύστριον, γευστρίδιον, and **γευστρίς**, = γευστήριον, *Gloss.*

γεύω, fut. γεύσω Anaxipp.1.27: aor. ἔγευσα Hdt.7.46, E.*Cyc.*149:—Med., fut. γεύσομαι Od.17.413, etc.: aor. ἐγευσάμην 20.181, etc.; γεύσεται, -σόμεθα, Ep. for -ηται, -ώμεθα, Il.21.61, 20.258; 3 pl. opt. γευσαίατο E.*IA*423: pf. γέγευμαι A. v. infr., etc. (γεύμεθα Theoc.14.51): plpf. ἐγέγευντο Th.2.70:—*give a taste* of, γλυκὺν γεύσας τὸν αἰῶνα Hdt.7.46; τινά τι E.*Cyc.*149, Theopomp.Com.65, Polyaen.1.1.1; τινά τινος Anaxipp. l.c., Alex.179, Pl.*Lg.*634a: metaph., τινὰ ἀγαθῶν λόγων dub. in Men.*Georg.*45; σ' ἔγευσ' ἂν τῶν ἐμῶν χειρῶν Herod.6.11: but, II. Med., γεύομαι, with pf. and plpf. Pass., *taste*, c. gen., προικὸς γεύσεσθαι Ἀχαιῶν Od.17.413; ἀλλήλων ἐγέγευντο *they had tasted, eaten of*.., Th.2.70; μέλιτος Pl.*R.*559d, etc. 2. *take food*, Hp.*Epid.*3.1.β', *Act.Ap.*10.10; *dine*, *PLond. ined.*2487 (iv A.D.). 3. metaph., *taste, make proof of, feel*, δουρὸς ἀκωκῆς ἡμετέροιο γεύσεται Il.21.60; ὀϊστοῦ Od.21.98; χειρῶν 20.181; ἀλλ' ἄγε.. γευσόμεθ' ἀλλήλων ἐγχείῃσιν *let us try* one another with the spear, Il.20.258; *taste the sweets of*, ἀρχῆς, ἐλευθερίης, Hdt.4.147, 6.5; ὕμνων Pi.*I.*5(4).20; ἀλκᾶς, στεφάνων, Id.*P.*9.35, *I.*1.21; εἰ δὲ γεύεται ἀνδρὸς ἀνήρ τι Id.*N.*7.86; of a married woman, ἀνδρὸς γεγευμένη A.*Fr.*243; γ. πόνων *to have experience of* them, Pi.*N.*6.24; μόχθων S.*Tr.*1101; πένθους E.*Alc.*1069; νόμων Pl.*Lg.*752c; ἀμφοτέρων Id.*R.*358e; γ. ἐμπύρων *make trial of* them, S.*Ant.*1005: rarely c. acc., ἔρσης ἰκμάδα γευόμενος *AP*6.120 (Leon.); κάππαριν Plu.2.687d: abs., S.*Aj.*844. (Cf. Skt. *juṣáte* 'enjoy', Lat. *gusto*.)

γέφῡρα (Boeot. **βέφυρα** Stratt.47.5), Lacon. **δίφουρα** Hsch., Cret. **δέφυρα** *GDI*5000 ii *b* 6 (Gortyn), ἡ (used by Hom. only in Il., always in pl.):—*dyke, dam*, ποταμῷ πλήθοντι ἐοικὼς χειμάρρῳ, ὅς τ' ὦκα ῥέων ἐκέδασσε γεφύρας· τὸν δ' οὔτ' ἄρ τε γέφυραι ἐεργμέναι ἰσχανόωσι Il.5.88; cf. γεφυρόω: metaph., πολέμοιο γέφυραι, expld. by Sch.Il. as αἱ δίοδοι τῶν φαλάγγων, i.e. the *open space* between hostile armies, but more prob. *limits* of the battlefield, Il.4.371, 11.160, etc.; πόντου γ. of the Isthmus of Corinth, *causeway* through the sea, Pi.*N.*6.39, cf. *I.*4(3).20; so, of the *causeway* between Athens and Eleusis, *Carm. Pop.*9; at the Euripus, Str.9.2.2. II. after Hom., in sg., *bridge*, γέφυραν ζευγνύναι Hdt.4.97, cf. 1.75 (pl.); γ. γαῖν δυοῖν ζευκτηρίαν A.*Pers.*736; γ. λῦσαι X.*An.*2.4.17; πόρον ὑπὲρ γεφυρῶν ἄγοντες Lib.*Or.*11.243; also, of *a tunnel*, ὑποστείχει γ. Philostr.*VA*1.25.

γεφῡρ-εργάτης [ᾰ], ου, ὁ, = γεφυροποιός, Tz.*H.*2.82. **-ίζω**, *abuse from the causeway*, in the procession from Athens to Eleusis, Hsch., Suid.: hence, *abuse freely*, Plu.*Sull.*6, 13. **-ιον**, τό, Dim. of γέφῡρα, Ael.*VH*8.14. **-ισμός**, ὁ, *gross abuse*, Str.9.1.24 (pl.). **-ιστής**, οῦ, ὁ, *abuser, reviler*, οἱ Ἀθήνῃσι γ. Plu.*Sull.*2.

γεφῡρο-ποιέω, *make a bridge*, Plb.3.64.1. **-ποιός**, ὁ, *bridge-maker*, = Lat. *pontifex*, Plu.*Num.*9.

γεφῡρ-ουργία, ἡ, *bridge-making*, Tz.*H.*1.931. **-όω**, (γέφυρα) *dam up* (cf. γέφυραι), γεφύρωσεν δέ μιν (sc. τὸν ποταμὸν ἡ πτελέη) Il.21.245; but in Prose, γ. τὸν ποταμόν *throw a bridge over* it, Hdt.4.118; Βόσπορον ib.88; τοὺς τῆς θαλάττης τροχούς Pl.*Criti.*115c; ἐγεφυρώθη ὁ πόρος Hdt.7.36; πλοίοις τὴν διάβασιν γ. Plb.3.66.6; also, *dam*, ποταμοὺς νεκροῖς Luc.*DMort.*12.2; τὰ δύσπορα Id.*Demon.*1, cf. Nonn.*D.*27.185. 2. *make into a causeway* or *embankment*, γεφύρωσεν δὲ κέλευθον Il.15.357. 3. metaph., νόστον Ἀτρείδαις γ. Pi.*I.*8(7)51. **-ωμα**, ατος, τό, *bridge*, J.*BJ*3.7.28 (pl.). **-ωσις**, εως, ἡ, *furnishing with a causeway* or *bridge*, Str.1.3.18 (pl.); γ. ἡ διὰ τῶν νεῶν Arr.*An.*5.7.3; in concrete sense, διέβη τὰς γ. Ctes.*Fr.*29.17. **-ωτής**, οῦ, ὁ, *bridge-builder*, Plu.*Luc.*26 (pl.).

γεωγρᾰφ-έω, *describe the earth's surface*, Str.1.1.16, Arist.*Mu.*393^{b}20:—Pass., τὰ γεωγραφούμενα *geographic description*, title of Strabo's work, Ath.14.657f. **-ία**, ἡ, *geography*, Phld.*Po.*5.1425.2, Str. l.c. II. *geographical work*, Democr.14^{c}, Plu.*Thes.*1 (pl.), Porph.*Antr.*4. 2. *map*, στρογγύλας γράφοντες τὰς γ. Gem.16.4. **-ικός**, ή, όν, *geographical*, γ. ἐμπειρία, γ. πίναξ, Str.1.1.2, 11. Adv. -κῶς Id.2.1.41, etc.: τὰ -κά *geographical treatise*, ib.1; of Strabo's work, Ath.3.121a. **-ος**, ον, *earth-describing*: Subst., *geographer*, Str.1.1.16, al.; ὁ γ., i.e. Strabo, Eust.ad D.P.11, al.

γεω-δαισία, ἡ, (δαίω) *land-dividing*: *mensuration*, opp. the science of geometry, Arist.*Metaph.*997^{b}26, Jul.*Gal.*178b, Procl. *in Euc.* p.25 F. **-δαίστης**, ου, ὁ, *land-surveyor*, Hero *Def.*138.3:—also **-δαίτης**, Call.*Oxy.ined.* (= *Fr.*158), Iamb.*Comm.Math.*26. **-δαιτέομαι**, *divide, parcel out land*, Eust.1619.2.

γεώδης, ες, *earth-like, earthy*, Pl.*Phd.*81c, Hierocl. *in CA Praef.* p.417 M.; γ. καὶ ἄλιθον *with deep soil*, X.*An.*6.4.5, al.; τὸ γ. Arist. *GA*753^{a}25, 782^{b}22; τὸ -έστερον ib.751^{b}3; γ. φῦλον Aristid.*Or.*43(1).14; ἄνθρακες -έστατοι Thphr.*HP*5.9.1. II. epith. of certain ζῴδια, Vett.Val.10.11.

γεω-λοφία, ἡ, *hill of earth*, Str.5.4.3, *AP*6.98 (Zon.). **-λοφος**, ον, *crested with earth*, ὄρη Str.16.2.16; χωρία Id.12.7.1. II. Subst. γεώλοφος, ὁ, *hill, hillock*, X.*Cyr.*3.3.28 codd., Plb.1.75.4, Ph.1.191; γεώλοφον, τό, Theoc.1.13, Numen.ap.Ath.7.305a. 2. γεώλοφος, ὁ, *boor, clod-hopper*, Ael.Dion.*Fr.*107.

γεωμαντ-εία, ἡ, *geomancy*, Varr.ap.Isid.8.9.13: Subst. **-ις**, εως, ὁ, Id.ap.Serv.Virg.*A.*3.359.

γεωμετρ-έω, prop., *measure, survey land*, *BGU*12.27 (ii A.D.):—but usu., *practise* or *profess geometry*, Pl.*Tht.*162e, *Men.*85e, Arist.*Rh.*1406^{b}30. II. generally, *measure*, c. acc., τὸν ἀέρα Ar.*Av.*995; τὰ ἐπίπεδα Pl.*Tht.*173e, cf. X.*Smp.*6.8, *BGU*12.27 (ii A.D.), Luc.*Icar.*21 (Pass.). **-ης**, ου, ὁ, *land-measurer*, ib.28 (ii A.D.):—but usu., *geometer*, Pl.*Tht.*143b, al., cf. Men.495, *CIG*3544 (Perg.). **-ητος**, ον, *geometrical*, λόγοι Procl. *in Euc.*p.201 F.; τὰ -τα ib.p.185 F. **-ία**, Ion. **-ίη**, ἡ, *geometry*, Hdt.2.109, Ar.*Nu.*202: pl., τὰ ἐν ταῖς γ. Pl.*Men.*76a, cf. Man.4.129. II. *land-survey*, τῶν ἀμπελώνων καὶ παραδείσων *PTeb.*24.42 (ii B.C.), cf. *POxy.*499.27 (ii A.D.). III. *land-tax*, *PLips.*67.2 (ii A.D.), *PFay.*55.11 (ii A.D.), etc. 2. *tax for surveying*, *PTeb.*93.2, al. (ii B.C.). **-ικός**, ή, όν, *of* or *for geometry, geometrical*, ἀριθμός Pl.*R.*546c, etc.; ἰσότης Id.*Grg.*508a; ἀναλογία Arist.*EN*1131^{b}13; μεσότης Theo Sm.p.106 H., etc. (cf. γαμετρικός); ἁρμονία Nicom.*Ar.*2.26; θεωρήματα Plu.2.720a (Sup.); γεωμετρική (sc. τέχνη), *geometry*, Pl.*Grg.*450d, Nicom.Com.1.18; τὰ -κά title of work on *geometry*, Democr.11^{n}, cf. Arist.*APo.*79^{a}9. Adv. -κῶς *by a rigidly deductive proof*, Procl. *in Prm.*p.897 S., Id. *in Ti.*1.345 D.: γ. *refellere*, prove wrong *to demonstration*, Cic.*Att.*12.5.3. II. *skilled in geometry*, Pl.*R.*511d, Plu.2.579b, Arist.*Pol.*1282^{a}9; γ. Βριάρεως, of Archimedes, Id.*Marc.*17: Comp. -ώτερος Ph.1.621. Adv. -κῶς Arist.*Top.*161^{a}35, Str.2.1.41, Plu.2.643c.

γεωμῐγής, ές, *mixed with earth*, Str.12.7.3, *Placit.*3.2.6.

γεωμορ-έω, *till* or *farm the land*, Alex.ap.Eus.*PE*9.22. **-ία**, ἡ, *portion of land*, Nic.*Al.*10: pl., *farms, cultivated lands*, Opp.*C.*4.434. II. = γεωργία, Alciphr.1.4, *AP*7.532 (Isid.). III. *harvest*, λιπαρὰ γ. *AP*6.258 (Addaeus). IV. *division of land*, Nicom.*Ar.* 1.3. **-ικός**, ή, όν, *concerning* γεωμορία, γ. νόμος an *agrarian* law, D.H.10.39. **-ος**, v. **γημόρος**. II. = γεωργός, Hsch.

γεώνιον, τό, *price of earth*, *SIG*[2].587.57.

γεω-νόμος, ον, (νέμω) *one who distributes land*, *IG*1[2].45 (pl.). 2. *receiving a portion of distributed lands, colonist*, D.C.38.1:—also **-νόμης**, ου, ὁ, Phryn.*PS*p.57 B.

γεώπεδον, τό, *portion* or *plot of ground, garden*, esp. within a town, Hdt.7.28 (v.l. γεοπέδων, γεωπεδίων); cf. γήπεδον.

γεωπείνης, ου, ὁ, *poor in land*, Hdt.2.6, 8.111, Aristid.1.191 J.

γεωπον-έω, *till the ground*, Ph.1.212; **γᾱπ-** E.*Rh.*75; **γεη-** Heph. Astr.2.28. **-ία**, Ion. **-ίη**, ἡ, *tillage*, Orph.*Fr.*280, *Epigr.Gr.*446 (Arabia), Max.Tyr.27.5:—also **γεη-** Ps.-Phoc.161, **γη-** Them.*Or.* 30.350a, Hld.10.6. **-ικός**, ή, όν, *of* or *for agriculture*, Gal.16. 311; τὰ γ. title of treatise on the subject compiled by Cassianus Bassus. **-ος**, ὁ, *husbandman*, *AP*7.175 (Antiphil.), 281 (Heraclid.); *labourer*, opp. γεωργός, Ph.1.211:—also **γεηπόνος** Democr. ap.Gal.13.40, Agath.2.17 (pl.), Babr.108.14: **γᾱπ-** E.*Supp.*420: **γηπ-** Them.*Or.*30.350c, Hld.5.23.

γεωργ-έω, *to be a husbandman, farmer*, Pl.*Lg.*805e, X.*Oec.*14.2, etc.; γ. ἐν τῇ γῇ And.1.92; ἐν τῇ Νάξῳ Pl.*Euthphr.*4c, etc.; γεωργεῖς ἐκ τούτων you *have become a landed proprietor* by these means (i.e. the fruits of treason), D.19.314: c. acc. cogn., γεωργίαν ζῶσαν γ. of pastoral nomads, Arist.*Pol.*1256[a]35:—Med., οἱ γεωργούμενοι Aristeas 112. II. c. acc., *till, plough, cultivate*, πολλήν (sc. γῆν) Ar.*Ec.*592; τὰς ἄλλας [νήσους] Th.3.88; γεωργῶν τὰ ἐκείνων D.18. 41:—Pass., of land, *IG*9(1).61 (Daulis); χώρας γεγεωργημένης καὶ γεωργηθησομένης *SIG*685.80 (Crete); τὰ γεωργούμενα φυτά Arist. *Pr.*896[a]10. 2. generally, *cultivate*, ἐλαίαν *Gp.*9.2.6: hence, γ. ἔλαιον, οἶνον, *produce* it, D.C.49.36, cf. *IG*2[2].1100; τοῦ γεωργουμένου οἴνου *Gp.*6.7.2. 3. metaph., *work at* a thing, *practise* or *exploit* it, D.25.82; φιλίαν Plu.2.776b; τέχνην Hld.6.6; τὸν ἱππόδρομον Lib.*Or.*35.13; *cultivate*, ψυχὰς δόγμασι Ph.2.348. 4. of a river, *fertilize*, Philostr.*Im.*1.11, *Ep.*59, Hld.2.28. **-ημα**, ατος, τό, in pl., *operations of husbandry*, Pl.*Lg.*674c. **-ήσιμος**, ον, *tilled* or *fit for tillage*, Arist.*Pr.*924[a]22, Str.16.4.18, Plb.1.56.4. **-ητέον**, *one must till the soil*, Them.*Or.*30 tit. **-ία**, ἡ, *tillage*, τῆς Χερσονήσου Th.1.11, etc.; *agriculture, farming*, Pl.*Smp.*187a, etc.; γ. ψιλή *tillage* of arable land and pasture, opp. πεφυτευμένη, of vineyards and orchards, Arist.*Pol.*1258[b]17. 2. in pl., *farms, tilled land*, τοῖς μὲν γεωργίας ἐπὶ μισθώσεσι παραδιδόντες Isoc.7.32, cf. Pl. *Lg.*806d, Luc.*Prom.*14, etc.; rarely in sg., D.30.30. II. metaph., *source of income*, Lib.*Or.*39.12. **-ικός**, ή, όν, *agricultural*, σκεύη Ar.*Pax* 552; κόποι γ. *CIG*4659 (Palestine, iii A.D.); ὑπηρεσία *BGU* 197.17 (i A.D.); βιβλίον γ. a book *on rural economy*, Plu.*CatoMa.*25; ἡ γ. (sc. τέχνη) *agriculture, farming*, Pl.*Lg.*889d, etc.; τὰ γ. *lands*, Chrysipp.*Stoic.*3.180; also, *treatise on agriculture*, Democr.26[b], Ath. 14.649d; esp. that of Nicander, Id.3.92c. II. *occupied* or *skilled in farming*, Arist.*Pol.*1317[a]25; δῆμος ib.1318[b]9; λεώς Ar.*Pax*920:— as Subst., *a good farmer*, Pl.*Ap.*20b, etc.; *fond of rural pursuits*, Plu.2.268c. Adv. **-κῶς** Poll.7.141. **-ιον**, τό, *field*, Ph.*Bel.*96.49 (pl.), Theagen.17 (pl.), *BGU*1092.10 (iv A.D.); *orchard*, Str.14.5.6: metaph., Θεοῦ γ. 1 *Ep.Cor.*3.9. II. *husbandry*, Lxx *Si.*27.6. III. *crop*, ib.*Pr.*24.5. IV. in pl., *tax* on land, dub. in *SIG*311.9 (Lagina, iv B.C.). **-ισσα**, ης, ἡ, fem. of γεωργός, Just.*Nov.*156 *Praef.* (pl.). **-ίτης**, ὁ, = γεωργός, Proll.Hermog.in*Rh.*7.45 W. **-ός**, όν, (γῆ, ἔργον) *tilling the ground*, βοΐδιον Ar.*Ach.*1036; *fertilizing*, Νεῖλος Lib.*Or.*13.39:—as Subst., γεωργός, ὁ, *husbandman*, Hdt.4. 18, Ar.*Pax* 296, Pl.*Phdr.*276b, etc.; οἱ γ., opp. οἱ μισθαρνοῦντες, Arist.*Pol.*1296[b]28; but γ., opp. ὁ δεσπότης τοῦ χωρίου, *IG*2[2].1100; so of vine-dressers, gardeners, etc., Pl.*Tht.*178d, Ael.*NA*7.28; γ. ὄχλος *the peasantry*, D.H.10.53; γ. βίος prob. in Ar.*Pax*589; δένδρων ὧν γ. αἵδε αἱ χεῖρες Philostr.*VA*2.26. **-ώδης**, ες, *agricultural*, Plu.2.8b.

γεῶρες· γεωφύλακες, Suid. (Cf. γειώρας.)

γεωρῠχ-έω, *dig in the earth, dig a mine*, Hdt.4.200, Ael.*NA*16. 15. **-ία**, *excavation*, *IG*2.1055.27, Ael.*NA*6.43. **-ος**, ον, (γῆ, ὀρύσσω) *burrowing*, λαγιδεῖς Str.3.2.6, cf. Hsch. s.v. σκάλοψ:—fem. **γεωρῠχίς**, ἡ, *mole*, prob. cj. in *Gloss.* (pl.).

γεωτομ-ία, ἡ, *turning up the earth, ploughing*, *Eleg.Alex.Adesp.*1.1, Max.499. **-ος**, ον, *cutting the ground*, ὅπλον *AP*10.101 (Bian.).

γεωτρᾰγία, ἡ, *an eating of earthy substances*, Hp.*Morb.*4.55.

γεωφᾰν-ής, ές, *looking like earth*, ἐπικλίνων ἐπὶ τὸ -έστερον Archig. ap.Orib.8.2.4: esp. in pl., γ. *a spot where a kind of ochre was dug*, at Samos, Thphr.*Lap.*61:—so **-ιον** or **-ειον**, τό, περὶ τοῦ γ. title of speech by Din., D.H.*Din.*10, cf. Sch.Nic.*Al.*149, Poll.7.99, *EM* 229.21.

γεωφύλαξ, v. γεῶρες.

γεωχᾰρής, ές, *fond of the earth*, of *creeping* plants, Jul.*Or.*5.175d.

γῆ, ἡ, occasionally in Hom., freq. in Hes., and the only form in Att. Prose for γαῖα: dual γαῖν A.*Pers.*736: pl. rare, γαῖ Arist.*Pr.* 934[b]9, γέαι *SIG*279.40 (Zelea), etc., *AP*9.430 (Crin.): gen. γεῶν Hdt.4.198, *GDI*5755.14 (Mylasa); γῶν *BGU*993 iii 10 (ii B.C.): acc. γέας [Democr.]299, *SIG*46.3 (Halic.), γᾶς *PTeb.*6.31 (ii B.C.), Str. 2.5.26; Cypr. ζᾶς *Inscr.Cypr.*135.30 H.: dat. pl. γέαις prob. in *CIG* 2693 f9 (Mylasa), *LW*415.9 (ibid.):—*earth* (including land and sea, Sapph.*Supp.*5.2) opp. *heaven*, or *land* opp. *sea*, Γῆ τε καὶ Ἠέλιος καὶ Ἐρινύες Il.19.259, cf. 3.104; τίς γῆ; Od.13.233; γῆς περίοδοι Hdt.4. 36, Arist.*Mete.*362[b]12, title of work by Hecat.: personified, Il. l.c., A.*Th.*69, *Pers.*629, etc.; κατὰ γῆν on *land*, by *land*, opp. ναυσί, Th. 1.18; opp. ἐκ θαλάσσης, Id.2.81; κατὰ γῆν στέλλεσθαι X.*An.*5.6.5, etc.; ἐπὶ γῆς on *earth*, opp. νέρθε, S.*OT*416; κατὰ γῆς below *the earth*, A.*Ch.*377, 475, etc.; κάτω γῆς S.*OT*968; ὑπὸ γῆς Id.*Fr.*572; γᾶς ὑπένερθε Pi.*Fr.*292: gen. with local Adverbs, ἵνα γῆς E.*Andr.* 168; ποῦ, ποῖ, ὅποι γ., S.*OT*108, *Ph.*1211, *El.*922; ὅπου γ. Ar.*Av.* 9. 2. *earth*, as an element, Xenoph.27, Anaxag.4, Pl.*Prt.*320d, *Lg.*889b, Arist.*Metaph.*989[a]5, *Cael.*306[a]18, etc. b. γῆν καὶ ὕδωρ αἰτεῖν, as tokens of submission, Hdt.5.18, Lycurg.71; γῆν καὶ ὕδωρ διδόναι Hdt.5.18, al. II. *land, country*, καὶ γῆν καὶ πόλιν A.*Eu.* 993; γῆν πρὸ γῆς ἐλαύνεσθαι, διώκειν, from *land to land*, Id.*Pr.*682, Ar.*Ach.*235; ἡ ἁγία γῆ Lxx *Wi.*12.3; one's *native land*, Thgn.1213, Tyrt.12.33, A.*Supp.*890 (lyr.), S.*OC*44, E.*Ph.*1090; freq. omitted with art., ἐκ τῆς ἐμαυτοῦ (sc. γῆς) δραπέτας Id.*Heracl.*140, etc. 2. freq. in Trag., *city*, αὐτός τε καὶ γῇ δορὶ πεσοῦσ' Ἑλληνικῷ Id.*Tr.* 868. III. *the earth* or *ground* as tilled, ἄροτον γῆς S.*OT*270; γᾶ φθίνουσα ib.665, etc.; τὴν γῆν ἐργάζεσθαι, θεραπεύειν, till *the ground*, Pl.*R.*420e, X.*Oec.*5.12; τὰ ἐκ τῆς γῆς φυόμενα Id.*Mem.*4.3.10. 2. *estate, farm*, γῆν πρίασθαι Lys.32.23; ἐπὶ γῇ δανείζειν lend on mortgage, D.36.6. IV. of particular *kinds of earth* or *minerals*, e.g. *fuller's earth*, Thphr.*Char.*10.14, cf. Gal.12.168; Κιμωλία γ. Ar.*Ra.* 712, cf. Hp.*Mul.*2.189.

γηγεν-έτης, ου, ὁ, = sq., ἄργυρος Tim.*Fr.*26; γίγας E.*Ph.*128 (lyr.). **-ής**, ές, Dor. **γᾱγενής** Hdn.Gr.2.419:—*earthborn*, βολβός Xenarch.1.5; of a potter's vessel, Antiph.182.3; *indigenous*, βούβαλις S.*Fr.*792. 2. *earthborn*, of primeval men, Ἐρεχθεύς Hdt.8.55; Παλαίχθων A.*Supp.*250; τοὺς ἔμπροσθεν φύεσθαι γηγενεῖς καὶ μὴ ἐξ ἀλλήλων γεννᾶσθαι Pl.*Plt.*269b, cf. Arist.*GA*762[b]29; of the Thebans, *Trag.Adesp.*84; γ. πρωτοπλάστης Lxx *Wi.*7.1; of body, opp. soul, Pl.*Lg.*727e. 3. οἱ γ. *the dead, the shades*, ib.*Pr.* 2.18, 9.18. II. *born of Gaia*, of Titans and Giants, Batr.7, A.*Pr.* 353, E.*Ba.*996 (lyr.); ὁ γ. στρατὸς Γιγάντων S.*Tr.*1058; τὴν ἐπὶ τῶν γηγενῶν (sc. ἀναστροφήν), opp. civilized life, Phld.*Sto.Herc.*339.19: in Com. with an insinuation of impiety, Ar.*Nu.*853; (but also *boorish*, βῶλος, ἄροτρον, γ. ἄνθρωπος Alex.108.5); of things, *Titanic*, i.e. *portentous*, γηγενεῖ φυσήματι Ar.*Ra.*825: Sup. **-έστατος** *most earthy*, i.e. limited in intelligence, Procl.*in Prm.*p.763 S.

γηγῆλιξ, ὁ, *field-mouse*, Hsch.:—also **γήλιγρος**, ὁ, Id. **γηγυρίδαι**· οἰκτροί, Id.

γήδιον, τό, Dim. of γῆ, *little farm, piece of land*, Ar.*Pax*570, *Fr.* 387.2, Arist.*Pol.*1320[a]39, Ph.2.541, *POxy.*1559.11 (pl., iv A.D.); μικρὸν γ. X.*Cyr.*8.3.38.

γηθᾰλάσσιος, ον, *amphibious*, ζῷον *Cat.Cod.Astr.*7.208.14.

γηθᾰλέος, α, ον, (γηθέω) *joyous*, Androm.ap.Gal.14.36.

γῆθεν, Adv. *out of* or *from the earth*, A.*Th.*247, *Eu.*904, S.*OC*1591; *from beneath*, Id.*El.*453: in late Prose, τὰ γ. J.*AJ*4.3.2; γ. ἥκεις Luc.*Icar.*4.

γηθέω, 3 sg. γηθεῖ (contr.) Il.14.140, Dor. γᾱθεῖ Theoc.1.54 (but pf. is always used for pres. in Trag., unless γηθούσῃ φρενί be read in A.*Ch.*772, and impf. ἐπ-εγήθει (v. infr.) in Id.*Pr.*157 (lyr.)): impf. ἐγήθεον Il.7.127, 214: fut. γηθήσω 8.378, etc.: aor. ἐγήθησα, Ep. γήθησα Hes.*Sc.*116, Dor. γάθησα Pi.*P.*4.122, cf. Limen.7: pf. γέγηθα (in pres. sense, v. supr.), Dor. γέγᾱθα with 3 sg. γεγάθει Epich. 109 (imper. γέγᾱθι *Hymn.Curet.*6), Il.8.559, etc.: plpf. ἐγεγήθειν restored by Elmsl. in A.*Pr.*157, Ep. γεγήθειν Il.11.683, 13.494, Boeot. 3 sg. γεγάθι Corinn.*Supp.*1.27. A collat. form **γήθω**, Dor. **γάθω**, mentioned by Hsch., is found in *CIG*3632 (Ilium), Orph.*H.*16.10, al.:—**Med.**, γήθομαι Q.S.14.92, *AP*6.261 (Crin.), S.E.*M.*11.107: (v. γαίω):—*rejoice*, c. acc. rei, τίς ἂν τάδε γηθήσειεν Il.9.77; γ. κατὰ θυμόν 13.416; νῶι γηθήσει προφανέντε *will rejoice* at our appearing, 8.378: freq. c. part., *rejoice in doing ..*, γέγηθας ζῶν S.*Ph.*1021; πίνων E.*Cyc.*168: γεγήθει φρένα Il.11.683 (but Ἀχιλλῆος κῆρ γηθεῖ 14.140); θυμῷ γηθήσας Hes.*Sc.*116; ἂν περὶ ψυχὰν γάθησεν Pi.*P.*4. 122; παλαιαῖσιν ἐν ἀρεταῖς γ. Id.*N.*3.33; γεγηθέναι ἐπί τινι S.*El.*1231, Hierocl.*in CA*5 p.427 M.: c. dat., ἄλλος ἄλλῳ γέγαθε Axiop.1.23; τοῖς μεγάλοις ἀεὶ κακοῖς γέγηθ' ὁ κόσμος Sotad.15.4: part. γεγηθώς, like χαίρων, Lat. *impune*, ἦ καὶ γ. ταῦτ' ἀεὶ λέξειν δοκεῖς; S.*OT*368; but simply, *cheerful*, φαιδρὸς καὶ γ. D.18.323.

γηθία· ἤθη, Hsch. (For ἤθεα.)

γῆθος, εος, τό, = sq., Epicur.*Fr.*423, Plu.*Ages.*29, Luc.*Am.*9, etc.

γηθο-σύνη, ἡ, *joy, delight*, Il.13.29, 21.390, Ph.1.354; = Φιλία (q.v.), Emp.17.24: in pl., *h.Cer.*437, A.R.2.878. **-συνος**, η, ον, also ος, ον Orph.*H.*27.14, *AP*6.235 (Thall.):—*joyful, glad*, Il.7.122; χάρμῃ 13.82. Adv. **-νως** Hp.*Ep.*17, Suid.

γηθυλλίς, Dor. **γᾱθ-** Epich.134, ίδος, ἡ, Dim. of γήθυον:—*spring onion* (acc. to Moer.115, the Att. equivalent for ἀμπελόπρασον), Epich. l.c., Eub.89.3, Nic.*Al.*431, Epaenet.ap.Ath.9.371e, *IG*5(1). 1511 (Sparta, prob.).

γήθυον, τό, = γήτειον, Ar.*Fr.*5, Phryn.Com.12, Thphr.7.1.2, etc.

γή-ινος, η, ον, *of earth*, τὴν δὲ .. πλάσαντες γηίνην Semon.7.21; πλίνθοι X.*An.*7.8.14; τείχη Pl.*Lg.*778e; σῶμα Id.*Phdr.*246c, cf. Hierocl.*in CA*4 p.425 M.; οὐδὲ τὸ ξύλον γῆ, ἀλλὰ γήινον Arist.*Metaph.* 1049[a]20; νόος *App.Anth.*3.146 (Theon.): Sup. **-ώτατος**, ἀριθμός Lyd.*Ost.*45. **-ΐτης** [ῑ], ου, ὁ, *husbandman*, S.*Tr.*32 (in contr. form γήτης). **-λεχής**, ές, *sleeping on the earth*, Call.*Del.*286.

γηλιᾶσθαι· κατέχεσθαι, Hsch. **γηλουμένους·** συνειλημμένους, Id.

γήλοφος, ὁ, = γεώλοφος, *hill*, X.*An*.1.5.8, Pl.*Criti*.113d; γ. χειροποίητος artificial *mound*, Jul.*Or*.2.63b; γήλοφον, τό, J.*BJ*1.21.10: as Adj., *Gp*.3.1.9; (in Dor. form) γαλόφῳ πρῶνι Limen.12.

γῆμα· ἱμάτιον, Hsch. (γ = ϝ).

γη-μόριον, τό, *burial plot*, *IG*7.2183 (Thespiae). **-μόρος,** ὁ, Dor. and Trag. **γᾱμόρος,** *Trag.Adesp*.208 (s. v. l.), A.*Supp*.613, *PLond.ined*.2134 (ii A. D.); cf. τῆσδε γαμόρῳ χθονός (Dobree for τῇ δέ γ' ἀμοίρου) A.*Eu*.890; Att. **γεωμόρος** (γῆ, μείρομαι):—*one who has a share of land, landowner*: οἱ γαμόροι, in Sicily, *the wealthy landowners*, Hdt.7.155: at Argos, A.*Supp*. l. c.; at Athens, γεωμόροι *landowners*, large or small, opp. εὐπατρίδαι, δημιουργοί, Arist.*Ath.Fr*.2, Pl.*Lg*.737e, etc. **2.** γεωμόροι, οἱ, = Lat. *tresviri agris dividundis*, D.H.9.52. **3.** metaph. of Ἅιδης, *Trag.Adesp*. l. c. **II.** as Adj., *dividing earth*, i. e. *ploughing*, βοῦς A.R.1.1214; γεωμόρος τέχνα *IG*9(1).880 (Corc.).

γήνεια· ὅσα ἐκ τῆς γῆς ὠφέλιμα, Hsch. (Fort. γήινα.) **γήνεσθαι·** κατέχεσθαι, Id. (Cf. ϝηλέω, = εἰλέω).

γη-οῦχος, ον, (ἔχω) *land-holding*, Eust.1392.23; cf. γαιήοχος. **-οχέω,** *hold land*, Hdt.7.190. **-πάτταλος,** ὁ, *oblong radish*, com. word in Luc.*Lex*.2. **-πεδον,** τό, = γεώπεδον, *plot of ground*, Pl.*Lg*.741c, Arist.*Pol*.1263ᵃ3. **II.** Trag. used Dor. form γάπεδον acc. to St. Byz.: hence γ. for δάπεδον (metri gr.), A.*Pr*.829 (Pors.). **-πετής,** ές, (πίπτω) *falling* or *fallen to earth*, E.*Ph*.668 (lyr.). **-πονέω, -πονία, -πονικός, -πόνος,** = γεωπ–, qq. v. **-ποτος,** ον, v. γάποτος.

γηράεις, εσσα, εν, = sq., Alc.*Oxy*.1233.16.

γηρ-αιός, ά, όν (also ός, όν Antipho 4.1.2): (γῆρας):—longer form of γεραιός, *aged, old*, γηραιὸς δὲ θάνοις Hes.*Op*.378, cf. Hdt.3.64, Pi.*P*.4.157, A.*Pers*.854 (lyr.), *Supp*.606, Th.6.54; γ. τελευτᾶν X.*Ages*.11.15, Pl.*Smp*.179e; τὸν μὲν ἄρ' αἰὼν γ. κατέπεφνε Maiist. 12. **-αλέος,** α, ον (also **γηράλιος,** Hsch., **γηράλεῖος,** *IG*12(7).113 (Amorg.)), = foreg., Xenoph.1.18, Pi.*P*.4.121, A.*Pers*.171, Cratin.126, J.*BJ*1.2.2; γ. ὀδόντες, ῥυτίδες, Anacr.43.2, *AP*5.128 (Autom.); σανίς ib.9.242 (Antiphil.); ἀπὸ κροτάφων πελόμεσθα πάντες γηραλέοι Theoc.14.69. **-ᾶμα,** ατος, τό, = γήρειον, Sch.Arat. 921. **-άμων·** γράζα, Hsch. **-άναι,** v. γηράσκω. **-άνιον·** γήραν, Hsch. **-ανσις,** εως, ἡ, *a growing old*, Arist.*Metaph*.1065ᵇ20, *Ph*.201ᵃ19. **-άός,** όν, = γηραιός, *IG*14.1721.

γηράς, v. γηράσκω.

γῆρας, τό, gen. γήραος Il.22.60, al., Archil.116, Mimn.2.6, Pi.*O*.8.71, etc.; γήρως Thgn.174, Att. (v. infr.): dat. γήραϊ Pi.*N*.7.99, Hdt.6.24, contr. γήρᾳ S.*Aj*.507, etc., γήρατι v. l. in Adam.*Phgn*.1.14 (cf. γῆρος):—*old age*, γ. λυγρόν Od.24.250; στυγερόν Il.19.336; ἐπὶ γήραος οὐδῷ (v. οὐδός) 22.60; opp. γ. λιπαρόν, Od.19.368, Pi. l. c.; γ. πολιόν Thgn.174; γῆρας ἐκδῦναι, ἀποσείσασθαι, Ar.*Pax*336, Lys.670 (with play on signf. II); ἐπὶ γήρως *in old age*, Id.*Eq*.524; ἐν τῷ γήρᾳ Pl.*R*.329c, Lys.2.73; σὺν γήρᾳ, ἐν γ. βαρύς, S.*OT*17, *Aj*.1017; διανοίας γ. Arist.*Pol*.1271ᵃ1: metaph., οὐκ ἔστι γῆρας τοῦδε τοῦ μιάσματος, i. e. it never wears out, A.*Th*.682. **II.** *cast skin, slough of a serpent*, γῆρας ἐκδύνειν Arist.*HA*549ᵇ26, Nic.*Th*.31, Antig.*Mir*.20, Antyll.ap.Orib.10.35.4; of crabs, Arist.*HA*600ᵇ20, Thphr.*Fr*.177.

γηράσιμος, η, ον, = γηραιός, *JHS*34.12 (Teos).

γηράσκω, fut. γηράσομαι [ᾰ] Critias 1.5 (and in compds., ἐγ-, κατα-, συγ-, Th.6.18, Ar.*Eq*.1308, E.*Fr*.1058); γηράσω Pl.*R*.393e: poet. inf. γηρᾱσέμεν Simon.85.9: aor. ἐγήρᾱσα (κατ-) Hdt.2.146, Pl.*Tht*.202d (also causal, cf. infr. II): acc. fem. part. γηράσασαν (v. l. γηρᾶσαν) Hdt.7.114: pf. γεγήρᾱκα S.*OC*727, etc.:—also **γηράω** X.*Cyr*.4.1.15, Arist.*EN*1135ᵇ2, Men.481.14, Plu.2.911b, part. γηρῶν Epict.*Fr*.3: aor. 2 (as if from γήρημι or γήρᾱμι) ἐγήρα Il.7.148, 17.197, Od.14.67, (κατ-) Hdt.6.72; inf. γηρᾶναι [ᾰ] A.*Ch*.908 (cum Sch.), S.*OC*870 (so *EM*230.53, but γηρᾶναι Moer.115), part. γηράς Il.17.197, dat. pl. γηράντεσσι Hes.*Op*.188, gen. pl. (ὑπερ-) γηράντων dub. in Ael.*NA*7.17; also γηρείς, έντος, Xenoph.9:—**Med.**, γηράσκομαι Hes.*Fr*.171:—**Pass.**, (ὑπερ-) γηραθείς Ps.-Callisth.1.25:—*grow old*, and in aor. and pf., *to be so*, κηρύσσων γήρασκε *grew old* in his office of herald, Il.17.325, cf. 2.663, etc.; of things, ὄγχνη ἐπ' ὄγχνῃ γ. Od.7.120; χρόνος γηράσκων A.*Pr*.981; πάλιν γὰρ αὖθις παῖς ὁ γ. ἀνήρ S.*Fr*.487; μετὰ τὴν δόσιν γ. χάρις Men.*Mon*.347; τὸ τῆσδε χώρας οὐ γεγήρακε σθένος S.*OC*727: c. acc. cogn., βίον τοιοῦτον γηράναι ib.870:—so in Med., Hes.*Fr*.171. **II.** causal in aor. I ἐγήρᾱσα, *bring to old age*, ἐγήρασάν με τροφῇ A.*Supp*.894; γηράσας πόδα (but perh. acc. cogn.) *AP*6.94 (Phil.). (Akin to γέρων, γῆρας.)

γήρειον, τό, *thistledown*, Arat.921, Nic.*Al*.126, *Th*.329.

γηροβοσκ-έω, *to feed* or *cherish in old age*, esp. one's parents, E.*Med*.1033, *Alc*.663; also τέκνα Demoph.*Sent*.43:—Pass., *to be cherished when old*, Ar.*Ach*.678 (γηρωβοσκήσει is read in Lib.*Decl*.49.22; γηρωβοσκήσαντα is v. l. in Stob.3.1.38; cf. γηρο-κομεῖον, -κομέω, -κομία, -κόμος: such forms might be due to contr. of γηραο–, but are more prob. misspellings). **-ία,** ἡ, *care of the aged*, Alex.312, Plu.2.111e; esp. of parents, *POxy*.1210.5 (i A. D.). **-ός,** όν, (βόσκω) *nourishing* or *taking care of in old age*, esp. one's parents, S.*Aj*.570, Hyp.*Fr*.233; γηροβοσκὸν οὐκ ἔχω . . παῖδα E.*Supp*.923 (lyr.); γ. ἀποδιδόναι χάριτας D.H.8.47; γ. ἐλπίδες hopes *of such nurture*, ib.51: Subst., X.*Oec*.7.12.

γηροκομ-εῖον, τό, *alms-house for the aged*, Suid. (γηρωκ- Hdn.*Epim*.205), Zonar. **-έω,** = γηροβοσκέω, abs., *Trag.Adesp*.25: c. acc., Call.*Ep*.51, J.*AJ*4.8.24, Ael.*NA*10.16, Luc.*Tox*.22, Max.Tyr.5.7:—**Pass.,** ἐν θυγατράσιν γ. Agath.2.14 (γηρωκ- J. l. c., Luc. l. c., Max.Tyr. l. c.). **-ία,** = γηροβοσκία, J.*AJ*5.9.4 (γηρωκ-), Plu.*Cat.Ma*.5 (pl., γηρωκ-), 2.583c. **-ικός,** ή, όν, *belonging to* γηροκομία, Gal.6.330. **-ος,** ον, (κομέω) *tending old age*, χήτει γηροκόμοιο for want *of one to tend one's age*, Hes.*Th*.605; ἃς δαίμων ἀντ' ἐμέθεν ὤπασε γηροκόμους, i. e. daughters, *Epigr.Gr*.536 (Tomi); χείρ γ. *IG*3.1335; φροντίδες γ. Opp.*H*.5.85: in later Prose (written γηρωκόμος), J.*AJ*1.13.3, Alciphr.3.16, Lib.*Decl*.49.25.

γῆρος, τό, = γῆρας, not found in nom., gen. γήρους Hp.*Int*.6, *Rev.Arch*.1913.247 (Selymbria), dat. γήρει Lxx *Ge*.15.15, al., *Ev.Luc*.1.36; γήρεϊ v. l. ap.Sch.Il.3.150. (These forms are also found as vv. ll. for γήραος, γήραϊ.)

γηροτροφ-έω, = γηροβοσκέω, Is.1.39, Pl.*Mx*.248d:—Pass., γηροτροφούμενοι Isoc.14.48: fut. Med. in pass. sense, γηροτροφήσονται D.60.32; ὑπὸ τῶν . . παίδων γηροτροφηθέντες Lys.13.45, cf. Lycurg.144. **-ία,** ἡ, = γηροβοσκία, Antipho Soph.66, *PFlor*.382.39 (iii A. D.); τὰς γ. ἀποτίνειν Plu.2.579e. **-ιον** or **-εῖον,** τό, *alms-house for the aged*, Suid. s. v. γηροκομεῖον. **-ος,** ον, (τρέφω) = γηροβοσκός, E.*Alc*.668; γ. ἐλπίς Pi.*Fr*.214, cf. *CIG*2240 (Chios); χάριν οὐ δυνάμην γ. τελέσαι *Supp.Epigr*.1.567.10 (Karanis).

γηροφορέω, *carry an old person*, Plu.2.983b.

γηρόω, v. γυρόω.

γηρυγόνος, η, ον, *born of sound*, κούρας γηρυγόνας, i. e. echoes, Theoc.*Syrinx*6.

γήρῡμα, ατος, τό, (γηρύω) *sound*, of a trumpet, A.*Eu*.569 (lyr.): pl., ἀδίδακτα γ. Plu.2.973a.

Γηρῠόνης, ου, ὁ, (γηρύω) the three-bodied Giant *Geryon*, Pi.*I*.1.13, etc.: **Γηρῠονεύς,** έως, Ep. ῆος, Hes.*Th*.287: **Γηρῠών,** όνος, A.*Ag*.870:—hence **Γηρῠονίς** or **-ηΐς,** ίδος, ἡ, *a poem on Geryon* by Stesichorus, Ath.11.499e, Paus.8.3.2.

γῆρυς, Dor. **γᾶρυς,** B.5.15, S.*Ichn*.65, υος, ἡ, *voice, speech*, Il.4.437; στονόεσσα γ. S.*OT*186 (lyr.); Ὀρφεία γ., i. e. Orpheus, E.*Alc*.969; Κολχίδα γῆρυν ἱεῖσα A.R.4.731: in later Prose, Plu.2.397c: metaph. of the *voice* of passion, Ph.1.373. (Cf. OIr. *gāir, gairm* 'shout', Welsh *gawr, garm*.)

γηρύω, Dor. and Aeol. **γᾱρύω,** Sapph.*Supp*.25.20, etc.; inf. γαρύεν, -έμεν Pi.*O*.1.3, *N*.3.32: fut. -ύσω: aor. ἐγήρυσα Ar.*Pax*805; Dor. ἐγάρυσα S.*Ichn*.244:—**Med.,** fut. -ύσομαι Pi.*I*.1.34, E.*Hipp*.213: aor. ἐγηρυσάμην Id.*El*.1327 (lyr.); Dor. opt. γαρύσαιντο Theoc.1.136, etc.; also ἐγηρύθην (v. infr.):—*sing* or *say, speak, cry*, Sapph. l. c., dub. in Simon.31: c. acc., *utter*, ἄκραντα Pi.*O*.2.96; φρονέοντι συνετὰ γ. B.3.85; γ. εὖχος Pi.*N*.6.58; ὅπα Ar.*Pax*805; θέσπιν αὐδάν S. l. c. **2.** trans., *sing of, celebrate*, τινά Pi.*N*.7.83; τι Id.*O*.13.50, etc. **II.** Med., abs., *sing*, *h.Merc*.426; τοὶ σκῶπες ἀηδόσι γαρύσαιντο let the owls *sing against* the nightingales, Theoc.1.136 (perh. f. l. for δηρίσαιντο): c. acc. cogn., γηρύετ' ἀνθρώπων νόον Hes.*Op*.260; γαρύσομαι αἶσαν Pi.*I*.1.34, cf. *P*.5.72; οὐ μὴ τάδε γηρύσῃ E.*Hipp*.213 (lyr.), cf. 1074; αὐδὴν τήνδε γηρυθεῖσ' ἔσει A.*Supp*.460. (ῠ in pres. Hes., Pi., etc.; ῡ A.*Pr*.78, Theoc.9.7, Orph.*A*.432, *AP*7.201 (Pamph.): ῡ always in fut. and aor.)

γηρωβοσκέω, γηρωκομέω, etc., v. γηρο–. **γηρωπίζεται·** γεροντεύεται, Hsch. **γήρως,** v. γῆρας.

γήτειον, τό, = γήθυον, *horn onion, Allium Cepa*, var., Ar.*Eq*.677, al., Anaxandr.41.57, Alex.127.7, Call.*Aet*.1.1.25: pl., Ph.1.665.

γήτης, ὁ, contr. for γηΐτης (q. v.).

γητικά, τά, a kind of *cup*, Epist.Alex.ap.Hsch.

γη-τομέω, *cleave the ground*, A.R.2.1005, Lyc.268. **-φᾰγέω,** *eat earth*, Arist.ap.*EM*222.9. **-φάγος** [ᾰ], ον, = γαιηφάγος, *herb-eating*, i. e. *poor*, Call.*Fr*.58. **-φοριών,** ῶνος, ὁ (sc. μήν), name of month at Iasus, *GDI*3750.

γήχῠτον, τό, (χέω) *the soft mould* or *soil* on the earth's surface, Gal.19.91.

γία· ἄνθη (i. e. ϝία), Hsch. **γίαι·** ὀδύναι, Id. **γίαρ[ες]·** ἔαρ, Id. **γιγαλία·** ἡ γῆ, Id.

Γῐγάντ-ειος, α, ον, *gigantic*, *AP*9.708 (Phil.), Luc.*Philops*.23:—also **Γῐγανταῖος,** α, ον, Aesop.53, Hsch. s. v. Ἀβραμιαῖος: **Γῐγαντιαῖος,** σώματα Pall. *in Hp*.2.143 D.: **Γῐγαντικός,** ή, όν, *of* or *for the Giants*, τὰ -κά Plu.2.360f; *monstrous*, θρασύτης Simp. *in Ph*.1145.4, cf. Procl. *in Prm*.p.659 S. **-ία,** ἡ, = Γιγαντομαχία, Philostr.*VS*1.21.5. **-ιάς,** άδος, ἡ, title of Epic by Dionysius, St.Byz. s. v. Δωδώνη. **-ιος,** ὁ (sc. μήν), name of month at Amphissa, *GDI*2091; at Triteia, ib.1813. **-ολέτης,** ου, *giantkiller*, name of Dionysus and Apollo, *AP*9.524,525, Ps.-Luc.*Philopatr*.4; of Zeus, prob. in Pancrat.*Oxy*.1085.25; **-ολέτωρ,** ορος, ὁ, Luc.*Tim*.4:—fem. **-ολέτειρα** and **-ολέτις,** ιδος, Suid., Ps.-Luc.*Philopatr*.8.

Γῐγαντο-μᾰχία, ἡ, *battle of the gods and giants*, Pl.*R*.378c (pl.), *Sph*.246a, Plu.*Ant*.60, etc. **-ραιστος,** ὁ, *giant-quelling*, Lyc.63. **-φθόρος,** ον, = sq., Sch.Lyc.63. **-φόνος,** ον, *giant-killing*, E.*HF*1193, Nonn.*D*.1.516. **-φόντις,** ιδος, ἡ, fem. of foreg., Corn.*ND*20.

Γῐγαντώδης, ες, *gigantic*, Ph.2.117, Eun.*Hist*.p.218 D.

γιγαρτίς· σταφίς, Hsch.

γίγαρτ-ον [ῐ], *grape-stone*, Simon.88, Ar.*Pax*634, Thphr.*HP*1.11.6, Lxx *Nu*.6.4, Apollon.*Mir*.15, etc.; *olive-stone*, *PSI*4.430.1 (iii B. C.), Phlp. *in Ph*.629.16. **-ώδης,** ες, *like grape-stones*, Thphr.*HP*3.17.6, Thd.*Is*.1.25. **-ώνιον,** τό, expld. by *unripe grapes*, *PLond.ined*.1821.

Γίγας [ῐ], αντος, ὁ, mostly in pl., *Giants*, ὑπέρθυμοι Od.7.59; Κύκλωπές τε καὶ ἄγρια φῦλα Γιγάντων ib.206; οὐκ ἄνδρεσσιν ἐοικότες ἀλλὰ Γίγασιν 10.120; γ. γηγενέται Hes.*Th.*185, cf. E.*Ph.*128 (lyr.); of Capaneus, A.*Th.*424. II. as Adj., *mighty* (γίγαντος· μεγάλου, ἰσχυροῦ, ὑπερφυοῦς, Hsch.), Ζεφύρου γίγαντος αὔρᾳ Id.*Ag.*692 (lyr.), cf. Eurytus (*PLG*3.639).

γιγγίδιον, τό, *a plant, Daucus Gingidium*, Dsc.2.137, 3.52: **γιγγικίδιον**, Sch.Nic.*Al.*432. II. = λεπίδιον, Dsc.2.174.

γιγγίς, ίδος, ἡ, kind of *turnip, French carrot*, Alex.Trall.1.15.

γίγγλᾰρος, ὁ, a kind of *flute* or *fife*, Poll.4.82 :—Dim. **γιγγλάριον**, τό, *AB*88; cf. γίγγρας.

γιγγλίαν· κάλυμμα κεφαλῆς ἐρεοῦν, Hsch.

γιγγλισμός, ὁ, *tickling*, Suid. II. = γίγγλυμος 5, Paus.Gr.*Fr.* 108.

γίγγλος· νᾶνος, Hsch.

γιγγλύμιον [ῠ], τό, Dim. of γίγγλυμος, Anthem.p.155 W. (γιγλ- codd.).

γιγγλῠμο-ειδής, ές, *like a hinge*, τοῦ βραχίονος τὸ γ. Hp.*Fract.*2, Gal.2.735. Adv. -δῶς Gal.18(1).513. **-ομαι**, *to be hinge-jointed*, γεγιγγλύμωνται πρὸς ἀλλήλους οἱ σφόνδυλοι Hp.*Art.*45.

γίγγλῠμος (**γιγγλυμός**, Hsch.), ὁ, *hinge*, οἷον εἰ γ. Hp.*Loc.Hom.*6, cf. Apollod.*Poliorc.*190.1: hence a species of *joint*, Arist. *de An.*433[b] 22, Gal.2.735. 2. metal *pivot* or *gudgeon* on which a door turns, = στρόφιγξ, *IG*4.1484.74 (Epid.), 11(2).165.15 (Delos, iii B.C.) :— written **γλυμός**, ib.142.49 (an engraver's error). 3. *joint in a coat of mail*, X.*Eq.*12.6. 4. *clasp, buckle*, J.*AJ*3.6.3,4. 5. *mode of kissing*, Hsch.

γιγγλῠμ-ώδης, ες, = γιγγλυμοειδής, Arist.*HA*529[a]32. **-ωτός**, όν, *hinged*, σανίδες Ph.*Bel.*91.29, Apollod.*Poliorc.*189.9. II. γ. φίλημα, = γίγγλυμος 5, Telecl.13.

γιγγρ-αΐνος, ον, *like the* γίγγρας, αὐλοί Ath.4.174f. **-αντός**, ή, όν, *composed for the* γίγγρας, μέλη γ. of 'scrannel pipes', Ath.4. 175b. **-ας**, ου, ὁ, *small Phoenician flute* or *fife*, of a high pitch and plaintive tone, Amphis 14 (from Γίγγρης, Phoenician name for Adonis, Ath.4.174f) :—also **γίγγρος** αὐλός Antiph.108, Men.259: **γίγγρον**, Hsch. 2. *its music*, Trypho *Fr.*109 V.; *dance to its tune*, Poll.4.102. **-ασμός**, ὁ, *the tone of the* γίγγρας, Hsch.

γιγγρί, an abusive interjection, Hsch. **γιγγρίας**, = γίγγρας, Id.

γίγνομαι, Ion. and after Arist. **γίνομαι** [ῑ], (Att. Inscrr. have γιγν- in fifth and fourth cent., cf. *IG*2.11.9, 1055.25, etc.); Thess. **γίνυμαι** *IG*9(2).517.22; Boeot. **γίνιουμαι** ib.7.3303: fut. γενήσομαι: aor. ἐγενόμην (ἐγενάμην Lxx *Je.*14.1, al. (προ-) Decr.Byz.ap.D.18.90), Ion. 2 sg. γένευ Il.5.897, 3 sg. γενέσκετο Od.11.208, ἔγεντο Hes.*Th.*705, Sapph.16, Pi.*P.*3.87, Parm.8.20, *IG*4.492 (Mycenae), prob. in *Scol.* 19; Ep. γέντο Hes.*Th.*199, Emp.98.5, Call.*Jov.*1.50, Theoc.14.27, etc. (γέ-το): pf. γέγονα Il.19.122, etc.: 3 pl. γέγοναν *Apoc.*21.6: plpf. ἐγεγόνει Lys.31.17, etc.; Ion. ἐγεγόνεε Hdt.2.2; Ep. forms (as if from pf. γέγᾰα), 2 pl. γεγάᾰτε Batr.143; γεγάᾱσι Il.4.325, freq. in Od.: 3 pl. γεγάκᾰσιν cj. in Emp.23.10: 3 dual plpf. ἐκ-γεγάτην [ᾰ] Od.10.138; inf. γεγάμεν [ᾰ] Pi.*O.*9.110, (ἐκ) Il.5.248, etc.; part. γεγᾰώς -ᾰυῖα, pl. -ᾰῶτες, -ᾰυῖαι Hom., etc., contr. γεγώς, -ῶσα S.*Aj.*472, E.*Med.*406; inf. γεγᾰκειν Pi.*O.*6.49: Med. forms ἐκ-γεγάασθε Epigr.Hom.16, ἐκ-γεγάονται (in fut. sense) *h.Ven.*197 (s.v.l.) :—**Pass.** forms, fut. γενηθήσομαι (only in Pl.*Prm.*141e, οὔτε γενήσεται, οὔτε γενηθήσεται, cf. Procl. *in Prm.*p.963 S.): aor. ἐγενήθην Epich.209, Archyt.1, Hp.*Epid.*6.8.32, 7.3, later Att., Philem. 95.2 and 167, *IG*2.630*b*10 (i B.C.) and Hellenistic Gk., Plb.2.67.8, D.S.13.51: pf. γεγένημαι Simon.69, freq. in Att. Poets and Prose, in Att. inscr. first in cent. iv, *IG*2.555: 3 pl. γεγενέανται Philet. ap.Eust.1885.51: plpf. ἐγεγένητο Th.7.18, al.; cf. γείνομαι :—*come into a new state of being*: hence, I. abs., *come into being* opp. εἶναι, Emp.17.11, Pl.*Phd.*102e, cf. *Ti.*29a; and so, 1. of persons, *to be born*, νέον γεγαώς new *born*, Od.19.400; ὑπὸ Τμώλῳ γεγαῶτας *born* (and so *living*) under Tmolus, Il.2.866; ἢ πρόσθε θανεῖν ἢ ἔπειτα γ. Hes.*Op.*175; γιγνομέναισι λάχη τάδ'.. ἐκράνθη *at our birth*, A.*Eu.*347; γ. ἔκ τινος Il.5.548, Hdt.7.11; πατρὸς ἐκ ταὐτοῦ E.*IA* 406, cf. Isoc.5.136; σέθεν.. ἐξ αἵματος A.*Th.* 142; less freq. ἀπό τινος Hdt.8.22, etc.; ἐσθλῶν E.*Hec.*380, etc.; γεγονέναι κακῶς, καλῶς, Ar.*Eq.*218, Isoc.7.37, etc.; κάλλιον, εὖ, Hdt. 1.146, 3.69; τὸ μὴ γενέσθαι not *to have been born*, A.*Fr.*401: freq. with Numerals, ἔτεα τρία καὶ δέκα γεγονώς Hdt.1.119; ἀμφὶ τὰ πέντε ἢ ἑκκαίδεκα ἔτη γενόμενος X.*Cyr.*1.4.16; γεγονὼς ἔτη περὶ πεντήκοντα D. 21.154; οἱ ὑπὲρ τὰ στρατεύσιμα ἔτη γεγονότες *those of an age* beyond .., X.*Cyr.*1.2.4: c. gen., γεγονὼς πλειόνων ἐτῶν ἢ πεντήκοντα Pl.*Lg.* 951c, etc.: rarely with ordinals, ὀγδοηκοστὸν ἔτος γεγονώς Luc.*Macr.* 22, cf. Plu.*Phil.*18. 2. of things, *to be produced*, ὅσα φύλλα καὶ ἄνθεα γίγνεται ὥρῃ Od.9.51; opp. ὄλλυσθαι, Parm.8.13,40; opp. ἀπόλλυσθαι, Anaxag.17, cf. Pl.*R.*527b, etc.; opp. ἀπολείπειν, Diog. Apoll.7; opp. ἀπολήγειν, Emp.17.30; τὰ γιγνόμενα καὶ ἐξ ὧν γίγνεται Pl.*Phlb.*27a; ἁπλῇ διηγήσει ἢ διὰ μιμήσεως γ. Id.*R.*392d; ὁ ἐκ τῆς χώρας γιγνόμενος σῖτος X.*Mem.*3.6.13; τὰ ἐν ἀγρῷ γιγνόμενα ib.2.9.4; of profits, καρποὶ οἱ ἐξ ἀγελῶν γ. Id.*Cyr.*1.1.2, etc.; τὰ ἆθλα ἀπὸ τεττάρων ταλάντων ἐγένοντο *were the produce of*, i.e. *were worth*, 4 talents, Id.*HG*4.2.7; τὸ ἀπὸ τῶν αἰχμαλώτων γενόμενον ἀργύριον *produced by* [the ransom of].., Id.*An.*5.3.4; of sums, ὁ γεγονὼς ἀριθμὸς τῶν ψήφων the *total* of the votes, Pl.*Ap.*36a; ἕκατον εἴκοσι στατήρων γίγνονται τρισχίλιαι τριακόσιαι ἑξήκοντα [δραχμαί] 120 staters *amount to* 3,360 drachmae, D.34.24; so in Math., of *products*, ὁ ἐξ αὐτῶν γενόμενος ἀριθμός Euc.7.24; ἀριθμὸς γενόμενος ἑκατοντάκις *multiplied* by 100, Papp.10.13; of times of day, ὡς ἡ ἡμέρα ἐγένετο Th.7.81, etc.; ἕως ἂν φῶς γένηται Pl.*Prt.*311a; ἅμα ἕῳ γιγνομένῃ Th.4.32; of Time in general, *elapse*, διέτης χρόνος ἐγεγόνεε ταῦτα πρήσσουσι Hdt.2.2; χρόνου γενομένου D.S.20.109. b. *fall due*, οἱ γιγνόμενοι δασμοί X.*An.*1.1. 8; τοὺς τόκους τοὺς γ. Isoc.17.37; τὸ τίμημα τὸ γ., τὸ γ. ἀργύριον, D.24. 82, Syngr.ap.eund.35.11; τὸ γ. μέρος X.*HG*7.4.33; τὸ γ. τοῖ πλήθι τᾶς ζαμίαν *IG*5(2).6 *A* 20 (Tegea, iv B.C.); c. dat., τὸ γ. τινὶ ἔλαιον *UPZ* 19.32 (ii B.C.); τοῖς γείτοσι τὸ γ. Thphr.*Fr.*97; τὰ γ. *dues*, *PHib.*1.92 and 111 (iii B.C.): hence γιγνόμενος *regular, normal*, τίμημα, χάρις, D. 38.25; ἐν ταῖς γ. ἡμέραις in the *usual number* of days, X.*Cyr.*5.4.51; freq. in later Gk., as Luc.*Tox.*18, etc. 3. of events, *take place, come to pass*, and in past tenses *to be*, καί σφιν ἄχος κατὰ θυμὸν ἐγίγνετο Il.13. 86, etc.; μάχη ἐγεγόνει Pl.*Chrm.*153b, etc.; ἐκεχειρία γίγνεταί τισι πρὸς ἀλλήλους Th.4.58; ἡ νόσος ἤρξατο γίγνεσθαι Id.2.47; πνεῦμα εἰώθει γ. ib.84; τὰ Ὀλύμπια γίγνεται, τραγῳδοὶ γίγνονται, *are held*, X.*HG*7. 4.28, Aeschin.3.41, etc.; ψήφισμα γ. *is passed*, X.*Cyr.*2.2.21; πιστὰ γ., ὅρκοι γ., pledges *are given*, oaths *taken*, ib.7.4.3, D.19.158; γίγνεταί τι ὑπό τινος (masc.), X.*An.*7.1.30, (neut.) Pl.*Tht.*200e; τὰ γιγνόμενα ὑπὸ τῶν Ἀθηναίων Th.6.88; τὰ γενόμενα ἐξ ἀνθρώπων Hdt.*Praef.*; ὕβρισμα ἐκ τῶν Σαμίων γενόμενον Id.3.48; ἀπό τινος γ. X.*An.*5.6.30; παρά τινος Pl.*R.*614a; ὃ μὴ γένοιτο which *God forbid*, D.10.27, 28. 21; but γένοιτο, = *Amen*, Lxx *Is.*25.1; γένοιτο γένοιτο ib.*Ps.*71(72). 19: Math., γεγονέτω *suppose it done*, Euc.6.23, etc.; γέγονε *it is done*, *Apoc.*16.17: c. dat. et part., γίγνεταί τί μοι βουλομένῳ, ἀσμένῳ (v. βούλομαι, ἄσμενος); οὐκ ἂν ἐμοί γε ἐλπομένῳ τὰ γένοιτο, i.e. I could not hope to see these things *take place*, Od.3.228; ἡδομένοισι ἡμῖν οἱ λόγοι γεγόνασι Hdt.9.46, etc.; of sacrifices, omens, etc., οὐ γάρ σφι ἐγίνετο τὰ σφάγια χρηστά ib.61, cf. 62; τὰ ἱερὰ καλὰ ἐγένετο X.*An.*6.4.9: abs., τὰ διαβατήρια ἐγ. *were favourable*, Th.5.55; θυομένῳ οὐκ ἐγίγνετο τὰ ἱερά X.*HG*3.1.17: in neut. part., τὸ γενόμενον *the event, the fact*, Th.6.54; τὰ γενόμενα *the facts*, X.*Cyr.*3.1.9, etc.; τὸ γιγνόμενον Pl.*Tht.*161b, etc.; τὰ γεγενημένα *the past*, X.*An.*6.2. 14; τὸ γενησόμενον *the future*, Th.1.138; τὰ γεγονότα, opp. ὄντα, μέλλοντα, Pl.*R.*392d, cf. *Lg.*896a: of Time, ὡς τρίτη ἡμέρη τῷ παιδίῳ ἐκκειμένῳ ἐγένετο Hdt.1.113; ἕως ἄν τινες χρόνοι γένωνται Pl.*Phd.* 108c; but in pf. and plpf., *to have passed*, ὡς διετὴς χρόνος ἐγεγόνεε Hdt.2.2; πρὶν ἓξ μῆνας γεγονέναι Pl.*Prt.*320a: impers., ἐγένετο or γέγονεν ὥστε.. *it happened, came to pass* that.., X.*HG*5.3.10, Isoc. 6.40, etc.; ἐγένετο, ὡς ἤκουσεν.. καὶ ἐθυμώθη *it came to pass*, when he heard.. that.., Lxx *Ge.*39.19; ἐγένετο ἐν τῷ πορεύεσθαι.. καὶ διήρχετο *Ev.Luc.*17.11: c. inf., γίνεται εὑρεῖν *it is possible* to find, Thgn.639; ἐγένετο, c. acc. et inf., *it came to pass* that, *Act.Ap.*9.3, al., *PAmh.*2. 135.10 (ii A.D.): c. dat. et inf., ἐάν σοι γένηται στραφῆναι Epict.*Ench.* 23. II. folld. by a Predicate, *come into a certain state, become*, and (in past tenses), *to be*, 1. folld. by Nouns and Adjs., δηΐοισι δὲ χάρμα γ. Il.6.82, cf. 8.282; σωτὴρ γενοῦ μοι A.*Ch.*2; κωλυτὴς γ. τινός Th.3.23; [οὖροι] νηῶν πομπῆες γ. Od.4.362, etc.; πάντα δὲ γιγνόμενος πειρήσεται *turning* every way, ib.417; παντοῖος γ., folld. by μή, c. inf., Hdt.3.124; παντοῖος γ. δεόμενος Id.7.10.γ´; ἐκ πλουσίου πένης γ. X.*An.*7.7.28; δημοτικὸς ἐξ ὀλιγαρχικοῦ γ. Pl.*R.*572d: rarely c. part., μὴ προδοὺς ἡμᾶς γένῃ, i.e. προδότης ἡμῶν, S.*Aj.*588, cf. *Ph.* 773; μὴ ἀπαρνηθεὶς γένῃ Pl.*Sph.*217c; ἀποτετραμμένοι ἐγένοντο Th. 3.68, etc.: with Pron., τί γένωμαι; *what am I to become*, i.e. what is to become of me? A.*Th.*297, cf. Theoc.15.51; οὐκ ἔχοντες ὅτι γένωνται Th.2.52; less freq. with masc., οὐδ' ἔχω τίς ἂν γενοίμαν A.*Pr.*905; γίγνονται πάνθ' ὅτι βούλονται Ar.*Nu.*348. b. in past tenses, *having ceased to be*, ὁ γενόμενος στρατηγός the *ex*-strategus, *POxy.*38.11 (i A.D.); ἡ γ. γυνή τινος the *former* wife, *PFlor.*99.4 (i/ii A.D.). 2. with Advbs., κακῶς χρῆν Κανδαύλῃ γενέσθαι Hdt.1.8; εὖ, καλῶς, ἡδέως γ., *it goes* well, etc., X.*An.*1.7.5, Arr.*Epict.*3.24.97, Lxx *To.* 7.9; with personal construction, οἱ παρὰ Πλάτωνι δειπνήσαντες ἐς αὔριον ἡδέως γίγνονται Plu.2.127b; δίχα γ. τοῦ σώματος *to be parted from*.., X.*Cyr.*8.7.20; τριχῇ γ. *to be* in three divisions, Id.*An.*6.2. 16; γ. ἐμποδών, ἐκποδών, E.*Hec.*372, X.*HG*6.5.38, etc. 3. folld. by oblique cases of Nouns, a. c. gen., γ. τῶν δικαστέων, τῶν γεραιτέρων, *become one of*.., Hdt.5.25, X.*Cyr.*1.2.15, cf. Ar.*Nu.*107, etc.; βουλῆς γεγονώς D.C.36.28 (cf. supr. I. b); *fall to, belong to*, ἡ νίκη Ἀγησιλάου ἐγεγένητο X.*HG*4.3.20; *to be under control of*, ὁ νοῦς ὅταν αὐτοῦ γένηται S.*OC*660, cf. Pl.*Phdr.*250a (s.v.l.); ὑμῶν αὐτῶν γενέσθαι D.4.7 (also ἐντὸς ἑωυτοῦ γ. Hdt.1.119; ἐν ἑαυτῷ γ. X.*An.*1. 5.17; ἐν σαυτοῦ γενοῦ S.*Ph.*950); τὴν πόλιν ἐλπίδος μεγάλης γινομένην Plu.*Phoc.*23: of things, *to be at*, i.e. *cost*, so much, αἱ τριχίδες εἰ γενοίαθ' ἑκατὸν τοὐβολοῦ Ar.*Eq.*662, cf. X.*Oec.*20.23. b. c. dat., *fall to*, i.e. as wife, Lxx *Nu.*36.11. c. with Preps., γ. ἀπὸ δείπνου, ἐκ θυσίας, *have done*.., Hdt.2.78, 1.50; πολὺν χρόνον γ. ἀπό τινος *to be separated* from.., X.*Mem.*1.2.25; γ. εἴς τι *turn* into, τὸ κακὸν γ. εἰς ἀγαθόν Thgn.162; freq. in Lxx, ἐγενήθη μοι εἰς γυναῖκα *Ge.*20.12; εἰς βρῶσιν ib.*La.*4.10; εἰς οὐδέν, εἰς κενόν, *Act.Ap.*5.36, 1 *Ep.Thess.* 3.5; ἐς Λακεδαίμονα Hdt.5.38 (in Hom. even without Prep., ἐμὲ χρεὼ γ. Od.4.634); γ. τι εἴς τινα *comes* to him, of a dowry, Is.3. 36; of a ward, And.1.117; γ. ἐξ ὀφθαλμῶν τινι *to be* out of sight, Hdt.5.24; ἐξ ἀνθρώπων γ. *disappear* from.., Paus.4.26.6; γ. ἐν Χίῳ Hdt.5.33, etc.; γ. ἐν.., *to be engaged* in.., οἱ ἐν ποιήσει γινόμενοι in poetry, Id.2.82; ἐν [πολέμῳ] Th.1.78; ἐν πείρᾳ γ. τινος X.*An.*1.9.1; ἐν ὀργῇ, ἐν αἰτίᾳ πρός τινα γ., Plu.*Flam.*16, *Rom.*7; of things, ἐν καιρῷ γ. *to be* in season, X.*HG*4.3.2; ἐν τύχῃ γ. τινί τι Th.4.73; γ. διὰ γηλόφων, of a road, X.*An.*3.4.24; but δι' ἔχθρας γ. τινί *to be* at enmity with, Ar.*Ra.*1412; γ. ἐπὶ ποταμῷ *arrive* or *be* at.., Hdt.1. 189, etc.; γ. ἐπί τινι *fall into* or *be in* one's power, X.*An.*3.1.13, etc.; ἐπὶ συμφοραῖς γ. D.21.58 codd. (-ᾶς Schaefer); γ. ἐπί τινι, also, *to be set* over.., X.*Cyr.*3.3.53; γ. ἐφ' ἡμῶν αὐτῶν *to be* alone, Aeschin.2.

36; γ. ἐπὶ τῆς διοικήσεως D.C.43.48; γ. ἐπ' ἐλπίδος *to be* in hope, Plu.*Sol.*14: Math., γ. ἐπὶ ἀριθμόν *to be multiplied* into a number, *Theol.Ar.*3; γ. κατά τινα or τι *to be* near.. or *opposite to*.., in battle, X.*Cyr.*7.1.14, *HG*4.2.18; but κατὰ ξυστάσεις γ. *to be formed* into groups, Th.2.21; καθ' ἓν γ. Id.3.10; καθ' αὑτοὺς γ. *to be* alone, D.10.52; γ. μετὰ τοῦ θείου *to be* with God, X.*Cyr.*8.7.27, etc.; ἡ νίκη γ. σύν τινι Id.*Ages.*2.13; γ. παρ' ἀμφοτέροις τοῖς πράγμασι *to be present* on both sides, Th.5.26; γ. παρά τι *to depend* upon.., D.18.232; γ. περὶ τὸ συμβουλεύειν *to be engaged* in.., Isoc.3.12; γενοῦ πρός τινα *go* to So-and-so, *PFay.*128, etc.; γ. πρὸς τῇ καρδίᾳ *to be at* or *near*.., Pl.*Phd.*118, etc.; γ. πρός τινι *to be engaged* in.., Isoc.12.270, D.18.176; αὐτὸς πρὸς αὑτῷ *meditate*, Plu.2.151c; so γ. πρὸς τὸ ἰᾶσθαι Pl.*R.*604d; πρὸς παρασκευήν Plb.1.22.2: impers., ἐπεὶ πρὸς ἡμέραν ἐγίγνετο X.*HG*2.4.6; γενέσθαι πρός τινων *to be* inclined towards them, Hdt.7.22; γ. πρὸ ὁδοῦ *to be* forward on the way, Il.4.382; γ. ὑπό τινι *to be* subject to.., Hdt.7.11, Th.7.64; γ. ὑπὸ ταῖς μηχαναῖς *to be* under the protection of.., X.*Cyr.*7.1.34. **4.** γίγνεται folld. by pl. nouns, ἵνα γίγνηται.. ἀρχαί τε καὶ γάμοι Pl.*R.*363a, cf. *Smp.*188b; ἐγένετο.. ἡμέραι ὀκτώ *Ev.Luc.*9.28. (Cf. *jánati* 'procreate', *jánas* (= γένος), Lat. *gigno*, *gnatus*.)

γιγνώσκω, Dor. (Epich.9, Pi.*O.*6.97), Aeol., Ion., and after Arist. **γινώσκω**, but γιγνώσκω in early Att. Inscrr., as $IG1^2$.127.19 (κατα–), etc.: fut. γνώσομαι Il.23.497, etc., Dor. 3 sg. γνωσεῖται Call.*Lav. Pall.*123 (γνώσω is f.l. in Hp.*Steril.*215); Cret. form ἀνα-γνώοντι dub. in *GDI*5075 (for aor. 1, v. ἀναγιγνώσκω): pf. ἔγνωκα Pi.*P.*4.287, etc.: aor. 2 ἔγνων Il.13.72, etc., Ep. dual γνώτην Od.21.36, Dor. 3 pl. ἔγνον Pi.*P.*4.120; imper. γνῶθι Epich.[264], etc.; subj. γνῶ, γνῷς, γνῷ Il.1.411, etc., Ep. also γνώω, γνώομεν Od.16.304, γνώωσι Il.23.610; opt. γνοίην Il.18.125, etc.; pl. γνοῖμεν Pl.*Alc.*1.129a; inf. γνῶναι Od.13.312, etc., Ep. γνώμεναι Il.21.266; part. γνούς S.*El.*731, etc.:—**Med.**, aor. 1 γνώσασθαι Man.2.342b:—**Pass.**, fut. γνωσθήσομαι Ar.*Nu.*918, Th.1.124, etc.: aor. ἐγνώσθην A.*Supp.* 7 (lyr.), E.*El.*852, Th.2.65: pf. ἔγνωσμαι E.*HF*1287, Th.3.38:—*come to know*, *perceive*, and in past tenses, *know*, c. acc., Il.12.272, etc.; as dist. fr. οἶδα *know by reflection*, γιγνώσκω, = *know by observation*, γνόντες δὲ εἰδότας περιορᾶν Th.1.69; ἐγὼ δ' οἶδ' ὅτι γιγνώσκετε τοῦτον ἅπαντες D.18.276; χαλεπόν ἐστι τὸ γνῶναι εἰ οἶδεν ἢ μή it is hard to *perceive* whether one knows or not, Arist.*APo.*76^{a}26; *discern*, *distinguish*, *recognize*, ὄφρ' εὖ γιγνώσκῃς ἠμὲν θεὸν ἠδὲ καὶ ἄνδρα Il.5.128; ἀσπίδι γιγνώσκων by his shield, ib.182; ironically, εὖ νύ τις αὐτὸν γνώσεται he will *learn* him to his cost, 18.270; νῦν ἔγνων τὸν Ἔρωτα Theoc.3.15: sts. c. gen., γνώτην ἀλλήλων *were aware of*.., Od.21.36, cf. 23.109. **2.** folld. by relat. clauses, γιγνώσκω δ' ὡς.. I *perceive* that.., 21.209; ἔγνως ὡς θεός εἰμι Il.22.10; ἔγνωκας ὡς οὐδὲν λέγεις Ar.*Nu.*1095; γ. ὅτι.. Heraclit.108, A.*Pr.*104,379, etc.; ἵν' εἰδῆτε ὑμεῖς καὶ γνῶτε ὅτι.. D.21.143; γνώμεναι εἴ μιν.. φοβέουσι Il.21.266; γ. τί πέπονθε πάθος Pl.*Phlb.*60d: c. acc. and relat. clause, Τυδείδην δ' οὐκ ἂν γνοίης, ποτέροισι μετείη Il.5.85; γ. θεοὺς οἵτινές εἰσι Heraclit.5; Σωκράτην γ. οἷος ἦν X.*Mem.*4.8.11; τοὺς Πέρσας γ. ὅτι.. Id.*Cyr.*2.1.11; also ἀλλοτρίας γῆς γ. ὅτι δύναται φέρειν Id.*Oec.*16.3: c. part., ἔγνων μιν.. οἰωνὸν ἐόντα *perceived* that he was.., Od.15.532; γνόντες οὐδεμίαν σφίσι τιμωρίαν οὖσαν Th.1.25; ἔγνωκα.. ἠπατημένη S.*Aj.*807; ἔγνων ἡττημένος I *felt that* I *was* beaten, Ar.*Eq.*658; χρυσῷ πάττων μ' οὐ γιγνώσκεις Id.*Nu.*912, cf. Antipho 5.33, X.*Cyr.*7.2.17: c. gen., ὡς γνῷ χωομένοιο when *he was aware of*.., Il.4.357, cf. Pl.*Ap.*27a: c. inf., ἵνα γνῷ τρέφειν τὴν γλῶσσαν ἡσυχεστέραν S.*Ant.*1089: c. acc. et inf., *recognize* that.., Th.1.43, etc.; *take* a thing *to mean* that.., Hdt.1.78: c. dupl. acc., *perceive* or *know* another to be.., οἵους γνώσεσθε τοὺς ἀνθρώπους X.*An.*1.7.4: abs., ὁ γιγνώσκων *the perceiver*, opp. τὰ γιγνωσκόμενα *the objects perceived*, Pl.*R.*508e; also ὁ γ. *one who knows*, *a prudent person*, ib.347d:—Pass., εἰ γνωσθεῖεν ᾧ.. if *it were known of them* in what.., Id.*Prt.*342b. **II.** *form a judgement*, *think*, ταὐτὰ Hdt.9.2; τἀναντία τούτοις γ. X.*HG*2.3.38; οὕτω γ. Id.*An.*6.1.19; τὰ δίκαια γ. Lys.22.2; ἃ γιγνώσκω λέγειν (= τὴν γνώμην λ.) D.4.1; περὶ τῆς βοηθείας ταῦτα γιγνώσκω Id.1.19; τοῦτο γιγνώσκων, ὅτι.. Men.572, cf. 648; ὡς ἐμοῦ ἀγωνιουμένου οὕτω γίγνωσκε X.*Cyr.*2.3.15: abs., αὐτὸς γνῶθι *see* thou to that, Pl.*Grg.*505c; esp. in dialogue, ἔγνων *I understand*, S.*Aj.*36; ἔγνως *you are right*, Id.*Tr.*1221, E.*Andr.*883; ἔγνωκας; Lat. *tenes?* Nausicr.1.5; *judge*, *determine*, *decree that*.., c. acc. et inf., Hdt.1.74, 6.85, Isoc.17.16: c. inf., *determine* to.., And.1.107:—Pass., *to be pronounced*, of a sentence or judgement, Th.3.36; παρανόμως γνωσθεῖσα δίαιτα D.33.33, cf. 59.47; κρίσις ἐγνωσμένη ὑπό τινος Isoc.6.30. **2.** Pass., of persons, *to be judged guilty*, A.*Supp.*7; γνωσθέντα ζημιοῦσιν οἱ νόμοι Arist.*Rh.Al.*1431^{b}30; τεθνάτω ἐὰν γνωσθῇ, ἐὰν δὲ φυγῇ γνωσθῇ, φευγέτω $IG1^2$.10.29. **3.** pf. Pass. with act. sense, ὡμολόγηκεν ὑμᾶς ὑπάρχειν ἐγνωσμένους are *determined*, D.18.228 (sed leg. ἡμᾶς). **III.** *know carnally*, Men.558.5, Heraclid.*Pol.*64, Lxx*Ge.*4.1, al., *Ev.Matt.*1.25, Plu.*Galb.*9, etc. **IV.** γ. χάριν, = εἰδέναι χάριν, D.C.39.9.

B. causal, *make known*, *celebrate*, γνώσομαι τὰν ὀλβίαν Κόρινθον Pi.*O.*13.3 acc. to Sch. ad loc., v. dub. (Root γνω–, cf. Skt. *jānāmi*, *jñātas*, Lat. *gnosco*, *gnotus*, etc.)

γιζί, ἡ, a kind of *cassia*, Gal.14.67; **γίζιρ** (v.l. ζίγιρ) Dsc.1.13; **γίζειρ** *Peripl.M.Rubr.*12; **γιζηρά**, Orib.*Syn.*2.56.17.

γιλός· ἑτερόφθαλμος, Hsch. **γιμάσαι**· σιαγόνες, Id. **γιμβάναι**· ζεύγανα, Id. **γίν**· σοί (leg. τίν), Id. **γινιπτήριον**, τό, perh. f.l. for γινιστ–, = Lat. *genista*, *broom*, *PLeid.X.*19.

γίννος or **γιννός**, ὁ, alleged offspring of mare by mule, Arist.*HA* 577^{b}25, cf. *GA*748^{b}34; *small mule*, Str.4.6.2; *hinny*, Hsch.; **γῖνος** *IG*12(1).677.23 (Ialysus).

γίνομαι, γινώσκω, v. γιγν–.

γίξαι· χωρῆσαι, Hsch. **γίο**· αὐτοῦ, Id. **γῖπον**· εἶπον, Id. **γίς**· ἱμὰς καὶ γῆ καὶ ἰσχύς (i.e. Ϝίς), Id. **γισάμεναι**· εἰδέναι, Id. **γίσας**· φθείρας, Id.: inf., γίσαι *deflower*, *App.Anth.* 4.73 (perh. Strat.). **γίσγον**· ἴσον, Hsch. (ϜίσϜον). **γίσιον**· μικρὸν τεῖχος, Id. (leg. γείσ–). **γιστία**· ἐσχάρα (ἐσχάτη cod.), Id. **γιστίαι**· ἱστουργοί, Id. **γιστιῶ**· παύσομαι, Id. **γισχύν**· ἰσχύν, Id. **γιτέα**· ἰτέα (ἐτέα cod.), Id. (In the above words, γ freq. = Ϝ.)

γῖτον, τό, dub. sens. in *UPZ*89.14 (pl., ii B.C.). **γίτονας**, v. γείτων.

γλᾰγ-άω, *to be milky*, *juicy*, γλαγόωντι σπέρματι *AP*9.384.23. **–έας**· γεγαλακτωμένας, Hsch. **–ερός**, ά, όν, *full of milk*, *AP*6.154 (Leon. or Gaet.). **2.** *soft*, *plump*, Opp.*C.*1.200,332.

γλᾰγό-εις, εσσα, εν, = foreg., μαζοί *AP*5.55 (Diosc.). **2.** *milky*, *milk-white*, Nic.*Th.*923, Opp.*H.*4.113. **–πήξ**, ῆγος, ὁ, ἡ, *curdling milk*, γαυλοὶ γ. bowls *for the purpose*, *AP*6.35 (Leon.).

γλάγος [ᾰ], εος, τό, poet. for γάλα (q.v.), *milk*, Il.2.471, Pi.*Fr.*106, Nic.*Al.*385.

γλᾰγότροφος, ον, *milk-fed*, Lyc.1260.

γλάζω, = κλάζω, *sing aloud*, μέλος Pi.*Fr.*97. **γλᾶθις**, ιος, ἡ, name of a *sacrifice* or *festival*, dub. sens. in *Riv.Fil.*53.208 (Crete, pl.).

γλαινοί or **γλαῖνοι**, οἱ, *star-shaped ornaments*, Hsch., *EM*232.40. **γλαισμοί**· λόφοι, Hsch. **γλακάω**, = γλαγάω, Id. **γλακκόν**· γαλαθηνόν, Id.

γλακτο-πᾰγής, ές, *full of milk*, μαστός *Jahrb.*19.*Anz.*186 (Smyrna). **–φάγος** [ᾰ], ον, shortd. for γαλακτ–, *living on milk*, Il.13.6: Γλακτοφάγοι, οἱ, Scythian people, Hes.*Fr.*54. **–φόρος**, ον, *milk-producing*, prob. in Marc.Sid.100.

γλάματα· ἀστράγαλοι, Hsch.

γλᾰμάω, = λημάω, Poll.4.185, Moer.111.

γλᾰμός· μύξα, Hsch. **γλάμπτειν**· πίνειν, Id.

γλᾰμυξιάω, = γλαμάω, and **γλᾰμυξος** [ᾰ], ον, = sq., *EM*232.42.

γλᾰμῠρός, ά, όν, *blear-eyed*, ὀφθαλμοί Hp.*Mul.*2.116,119; prov., ἐν τυφλῶν πόλει γ. βασιλεύει 'dans le royaume des aveugles le borgne est roi', Sch.Il.24.192. **II.** of birds, perh. = λαμυρός, S.*Fr.*396 (but ἐνυγροβίους *EM*232.44). (With γλαμάω, γλάμυξος (<γλαμο-μ.), γλαμυρός, γλαμώδης, cf. Lett. *glums* 'mucus', *glumt* 'become viscous', Engl. *clammy*.)

γλαμψοί· χαλινοὶ στόματος, Hsch.

γλᾰμώδης, ες, = γλαμυρός, *EM*232.44.

γλάμων [ᾰ], ον, = γλᾰμυρός, Ar.*Ra.*588, *Ec.*254, Eup.9, Lys.14.25.

γλάνις [ᾰ], ὁ (ἡ Paus.4.34.2), or **γλᾰνίς** (Hsch., also expld. as, = ἀργός), gen. ιδος Ephipp.12.1, Mnesim.4.32; γλάνιος (v.l. γλάνεως) Arist.*HA*568^{b}22, al.: acc. γλάνιν *AB*88: pl. γλάνεις, οἱ, Arist.*HA* 602^{b}24; γλάνιδες Archipp.26; γλάνιες Matro *Conv.*80:—*sheat-fish*, *Silurus*, esp. *Parasilurus Aristotelis*, Arist.*HA*568^{a}25, etc.:—also **γλάνιος**, ὁ, Hdn.Gr.1.94, *Gloss.*

γλανοί· ἀχρεῖοι, Hsch.

γλάνος, ὁ, *hyena*, Arist.*HA*594^{a}31.

γλάξ, v. γλαύξ III. **γλάπτω**, = γλάφω, *EM*233.7.

γλᾰρίς, ίδος, ἡ, *chisel*, whether for wood or stone work, S.*Fr.*529, *IG*11(2).161*A*87 (Delos, iii B.C.), Call.*Fr.*159 (pl.), Poll.7.118, 10.147. **II.** = ὅρος, Hsch.

γλάσσα, v. γλῶσσα:—hence **γλάσσων**· μωρός, Zonar.

γλαυκειοῦς, οῦν, = γλαύκινος, *IG*2.759 ii 11 (iv B.C.).

γλαυκηπόρος, ον, *blue-rolling*, κλύδων [Emp.]*Sphaer.*143.

γλαυκ-ία ἢ **γλαυκόν**· βοτάνη τις (cf. γλαύκιον), Hsch. **–ιάω**, Hom. only in Ep. part. γλαυκιόων, *glaring fiercely*, of a lion, Il.20.172; γ. ὄσσοις δεινόν Hes.*Sc.*430; of a sparkling stone, D.P.1121; γλαυκιόωσα σελήνη Man.5.250: 3 pl. γλαυκιόωσι Opp.*C.*3.70; late Prose, γλαυκιῶν τὸ βλέμμα Hld.7.10. **2.** *have a* γλαύκωμα, *glare blindly*, ὀφθαλμοί.. δυσαλθέα γλαυκιόωντες Q.S.12.408. **–ίδανον**, τό, name of an *eyesalve*, Gal.12.746. **–ίδιον**, τό, Dim. of γλαῦκος, Antiph.222.1. **2.** Dim. of γλαύξ, *IG*2.735.33. **–ίζω**, *to be bluish-grey*, of marble, Str.5.2.5; χρῶμα –ίζον Sch.Arat.367, cf. *PLeid.X.*100, al. **II.** = ἀμβλυωπέω, Hsch. **–ῑνίδιον** [νῐ], τό, = γλαυκίδιον, Amphis 35. **–ῖνος**, η, ον, *bluish-grey*, ἱμάτιον Plu.2.821e, cf. 565c. **II.** γ. ἔλαιον oil *flavoured with* γλαύκιον, *Edict. Diocl.*32.67. **–ιον**, τό, *juice of the horned poppy*, *Glaucium corniculatum*, Dsc.3.86, cf. 1.64, Gal.11.857. **II.** kind of *duck*, perh. *white-eyed duck*, *Anas leucophthalmus*, Ath.9.395c. **–ίσκος**, ὁ, a fish so called from its colour, Philem.79.21, Damox.2.18, *PEdgar* 15.4 (iii B.C.), *AP*5.184 (Asclep.). **II.** a *plant*, Hegesand.35. **–ισμός**, ὁ, *dyeing blue-grey*, *PHolm.*21.42.

γλαυκοειδής, ές, *grey*, Sch.Il.16.34.

γλαυκόμματος, ον, *grey-eyed*, Pl.*Phdr.*253e.

γλαυκός, ή, όν, orig. without any notion of colour, *gleaming* (cf. γλαύσσω, γλαυσός), once in Hom., γλαυκὴ δέ σε τίκτε θάλασσα Il.16.34 (hence γλαυκὴ δυσπέμφελος, = the sea, Hes.*Th.*440): so in Trag. (not A.), γ. λίμνα S.*Fr.*371,476; ἅλς E.*Cyc.*16; οἶδμα Id.*Hel.*1501 (lyr.); later γ. σελάνα Mesom.*h.Sol.*21; πλήθοντα πυρὸς γλαυκοῖο σελήνη Tryph.514; ἀστέρες Him.*Ecl.*13.37; γ. ἠώς Theoc.16.5; also γ. δράκων Pi.*O.*8.37 (expld. by Sch. as, = γλαύκωψ, γλαυκῶπις). **II.** later, of colour (κυανοῦς λευκῷ κεραννύμενος Pl.*Ti.*68c; cf. γλαυκότερον κυάνοιο φαείνεται Hegesianax 1), *bluish green* or *grey*, of the olive, S.*OC*701, E.*IT*1101, *Tr.*802 (all lyr.), etc.; of the elder,

Emp.93; ὀπώρα, of grapes, S.*Tr.*703; of vine leaves, *AP*9.87 (Marc. Arg.); of the beryl and topaz, D.P.1119 sq.; μάραγδος Nonn.*D.*5.178. 2. freq. of the eye, *light blue, grey*, opp. μέλας, χαροπός, Arist.*GA*779b13, *HA*492a3, cf. Paus.1.14.6; ἔθνος γ. ἰσχυρῶς καὶ πυρρόν Hdt.4.108, cf. Hp.*Aër.*14, Arist.*Pr.*892a3, etc.; γ. Ἀθάνα E.*Heracl.*754 (lyr.), Theoc.28.1, cf. Plot.4.4.19; cf. γλαυκῶπις:—this colour was not admired, Luc.*DMeretr.*2.1, Philostr. *VA*7.42.

γλαῦκος, ὁ, an eatable *fish of grey colour*, Epich.49,50, Cratin.161, Antiph.7.6, Arist.*HA*607b27, Numen.ap.Ath.7.295c, etc. II. as pr. n., esp. of a Chian inventor: hence prov., οὐχ ἡ Γλαύκου τέχνη, c. inf., 'it does not need a genius to..', Pl.*Phd.*108d, etc.

γλαυκότης, ητος, ἡ, *greyness*, of the eyes, Arist.*GA*778a18; ὀμμάτων γ. δεινῶς πικρά Plu.*Sull.*2; also γ. ἀέρος Corn.*ND*35.

γλαυκόφθαλμος, ον, = γλαυκόμματος, Dsc.1.125, Gal.12.740.

γλαυκοφόρβιδας· ἵππους εὐγενεστάτας, Hsch.

γλαυκο-χαίτης, ου, ὁ, *with greyish hair* or *mane*, Choerob.in *Cod. Barocc.*50f.200. **-χροος**, ὁ, ἡ, acc. γλαυκόχροα, *grey-coloured*, of the olive, Pi.*O.*3.13.

γλαυκόω, *dye blue-grey*, ἔρια *PHolm.*19.28, 26.30, cf. *EM*233.24. II. Pass., *to be affected with* γλαύκωμα, Hp.*Prorrh.*2.20, *Epid.*4.30; τὰς ὄψεις γλαυκωθῆναι J.*AJ*12.2.14.

Γλαυκώ, οῦς, name for the *moon*, Sch.Pi.*O.*6.76.

γλαυκ-ώδης, ες, *of the owl kind*, Arist.*HA*504a26. **-ώλενος**, ον, of Tethys, *with sea-grey arms*, *Hymn.Is.*148. **-ωμα**, ατος, τό, *opacity of the crystalline lens, cataract*, Arist.*GA*780a17; esp. of the supposedly incurable forms of this affection, opp. ὑπόχυμα, Ruf.ap. Orib.*Syn.*8.49, cf. Paul.Aeg.3.22, Gal.19.435. **-ώπιον**, τό, *temple of Athena Glaucopis*, prob. in Alc.32. **-ῶπις**, ἡ, gen. ιδος: acc. ιδα, also ιν Od.1.156:—in Hom., epith. of Athena, prob., *with gleaming eyes*, Il.1.206, al., cf. *IG*1².418, Sch.Ven.ad 5.458, Hsch. II. = γλαυκός, of the olive, Euph.150; of the moon, Emp.42.3, E.*Fr.* 1009. **-ωπός**, όν, = foreg., Corn.*ND*20, Ael.*NA*17.23, Eust.86. 46:—also -ώπης, ὁ, Eust.1389.2. **-ωσις**, εως, ἡ, *blindness from* γλαύκωμα, Hp.*Aph.*3.31 (pl.), Gal.*UP*10.6, etc. **-ώψ**, ῶπος, ὁ, ἡ, = γλαυκῶπις, δράκοντες Pi.*O.*6.45; ὄφις Id.*P.*4.249; Προνοίη Euph.2.

γλαυνός, ὁ, a kind of *tunic*, Poll.7.48.

γλαύξ, Att. **γλαῦξ**, γλαυκός, ἡ, Euphronius ap.Sch.Ar.*V.*1081, cf. Hdn.Gr.2.947:—*the little owl, Athene noctua*, so called from its *glaring eyes*, Epich.166, Arist.*HA*488a26, al.; freq. as emblem of Athena, Ar.*Av.*516, *Eq.*1093, etc.: prov., γλαῦκ' Ἀθήναζε, γλαῦκ' εἰς Ἀθήνας, 'carry coals to Newcastle', Ar.*Av.*301, Antiph.175.2; γλαῦξ ἐν πόλει 'Jack's as good as his master', Hsch., etc.; γλαῦκες Λαυρειωτικαί, of Athenian coins, from the type, Ar.*Av.*1106; so of figures of owls, *IG*2.678*B*76. 2. γ. θαλαττία, an unknown *bird*, Thphr. *Sign.*52. II. a kind of *dance*, Ath.14.629f. III. *wart cress, Coronopus procumbens*, Dsc.4.138, Gal.11.857:—also **γλάξ**, Hdn. Gr.1.395, al.

γλαυρόν· σεμνόν, Hsch. **γλαυσόν**· λαμπρόν, θρασύ, ἰταμόν, Id.

γλαύσσω, *shine, glitter*, Hsch.: aor. imper. γλαῦξον *EM*234.15. (Denom. fr. γλαυκός, cf. δια-γλαύσσω.)

γλᾰφίς, = γλυφίς, *EM*235.10.

γλάφυ [ᾰ], τό, (γλάφω) *hollow, cavern*, Hes.*Op.*533.

γλᾰφῠρ-ία, ἡ, *elegance*, Plu.*Pyrrh.*8 (pl.); of mathematical demonstrations, *neatness*, Iamb. *in Nic.*p.38P., al.: metaph., *smoothness* of manner, γ. καὶ πιθανότης Plu.2.1065d. **-ός**, ά, όν, (γλάφω) *hollow, hollowed*, νῆες Il.2.454, al.; γ. πέτρη, σπέος 2.88, 18.402; ἄντρον Agath.1.10 (Sup.); τὰ γ. τῆς γῆς Id.2.15; γ. φόρμιγξ Od. 17.262; γ. ἅρματα Pi.*N.*9.12; γ. λιμήν *a deep* harbour or cove, Od. 12.305.—In this sense Ep. and Lyr. (not in Trag.); twice in Com., Hermipp.63.11 (mock-Epic); [ποτήρια] ταπεινὰ καὶ γ. Epigen.4.3; later πόδες *arched*, Arist.*HA*538b11 (Comp.). II. *polished*: hence, 1. *hairless, smooth*, of spiders, Arist.*HA*555b11. 2. *neat, delicate*, ῥύγχος Id.*PA*662b8; κηρίον Id.*HA.*554b28 (Comp.); of dishes, *dainty*, δειπνάριον Diph.64.1; ἐμβαμμάτια Anaxipp.1.35. III. metaph., *subtle, exact*, of persons and things, ὦ σοφώτατ', ὦ γλαφυρώτατε Ar.*Av.*1272; γ. ἀστεῖός θ' ἅμα Macho ap.Ath.13.579b; γλαφυρώτερος τῶν νῦν νομοθετῶν Arist.*Pol.*1274b8; γλαφυρωτέραν ἔχειν τὴν διάνοιαν Id.*PA*650b19; εἴ τι κομψὸν ἢ σοφὸν ἢ γ. οἶσθα Dionys.Com. 3.1, cf. Plot.4.8.6; τὸ γ. *subtlety*, ποικίλλοντες τῷ γ. γεωμετρίαν Plu. *Marc.*14, cf. Iamb. *in Nic.*p.20P.; γ. τέχναι, θεωρία, Ph.1.270,566: Sup., Id.2.262. Adv., Comp. -οτέρως *more subtly*, Arist. *de An.*405a 8. 2. *skilful, neat*, χείρ Theoc.*Ep.*8.5; [ἀράχνιον] σοφώτατον καὶ -ώτατον Arist.*HA*623a8. Adv. -ρῶς, ἧττον γ. ἔχειν with less *finish*, Id.*Pol.*1271b21, cf. Alex.110.20. 3. *refined*, γλαφυρόν τι καὶ προσαγωγὸν ἐμειδίασεν Luc.*DDeor.*20.11; γ. διατριβαί Plu.*Cim.*13. Adv. -ρῶς, γ. καὶ περιττῶς διάγειν Id.2.989c; γ. βιώσας *CIG*2004 (Maced.). 4. of literary style, *polished, elegant*, γ. ἁρμονία D.H.*Dem.* 36; ῥυθμός Id.*Comp.*13; σύνθεσις, opp. αὐστηρά, ib.21. Adv. -ρῶς, λέγειν Id.*Isoc.*2; of music, ἐμελῴδει πάνυ γλαφυρὸν καὶ ἐναρμόνιον Luc. *DDeor.*7.4.

γλᾰφῠρότης, ητος, ἡ, *subtlety*, θεωρίας Ph.1.521, cf. 530 (pl.); *elegance*, ἔργων J.*AJ*12.2.9; παραβολῶν Luc.*Dem.Enc.*6, cf. Phld. *Rh.*1.165S.

γλάφω [ᾰ], *scrape up, dig up, hollow*, ποσσὶ γλάφει, of a lion, Hes. *Sc.*431. II. *engrave*, *CR*12.282 (ii A.D.).

γλάχων [ᾱ], Dor. for γλήχων, v. βλήχων.

γλέβα· ἀξίωμα συγκλήτου, Hsch. **γλεῖνος**, ὁ, v. γλῖνος.

γλευκ-ᾰγωγός, όν, *for carrying new wine*, βύρσα Pherecr.16. **-άω**, in aor. part. -ήσας, of *oversweetened* wine, Hsch. **-η**, ης, ἡ, = γλυκύτης, Sch.Nic.*Al.*171. **-ινος**, η, ον, *made with* γλεῦκος *as a vehicle*, μύρον, a special kind of confection or oil, Dsc.1.57, Androm. ap.Gal.13.1039, Aët.12.55; also γ. ἔλαιον Colum.12.53, Plin.*HN*23. 46. 2. *partly fermented*, οἶνος Gal.*UP*4.3. **-ίτης** [ῑ] (sc. οἶνος), ου, ὁ, = γλεῦκος I.1, Olymp. *in Mete.*311.13.

γλευκοπότης, ου, ὁ, *drinker of new wine*, Σάτυροι *AP*6.44 (Leon. (?)); Πάν *APl.*4.235 (Apollonid.).

γλεῦκος, εος (Dor. gen. γλεύκιος *GDI*4993 (Gortyn)), τό, *sweet new wine*, Arist.*Mete.*380b32, Nic.*Al.*184,299, *PPetr.*3p.149 (iii B.C.), *Act.Ap.*2.13, Dsc.5.6; οἴνου γλεύκους *PGrenf.*2.24.12 (ii B.C.), *PFlor.*65.8 (vi A.D.). 2. *grape-juice*, Gal.6.575. II. *sweetness*, Arist.*Pr.*931a18.

γλεῦξις, v. γλύξις. **γλέφαρον**, τό, Aeol. for βλέφαρον, Pi.*O.* 3.12, etc.

γλημώδης, ες, = γλαμυρός, Gal.19.91.

γλήν, ἡ, = sq., Hermesian.1.

γλήνη, ἡ, *eyeball*, Il.14.494, Od.9.390; τὸ εἴδωλον τὸ ἐν τῇ ὄψει, Ruf. *Onom.*24, cf. Poll.2.70; poet. *eye*, S.*OT*1277; Φαέθων μονάδι γλήνᾳ παραυγεῖ Cerc.4.18. II. ἔρρε, κακὴ γ. Il.8.164, perh. *doll, plaything* (since figures are reflected small in the pupil, cf. κόρη). III. *socket of a joint*, distd. from κοτύλη as being not so deep, Gal.2. 736. IV. *honeycomb*, *AB*233, Hsch. V. = γλίνη (q.v.), Hdn. Gr.1.330.

γληνίς (or γλῆνις), ἡ, perh. a measure of capacity, ἐλαίω κοτύλα γληνὶς *IG*5(1).1447 (Messene, iii/ii B.C.).

γληνοειδής, ές, *like a* γλήνη III, opp. κοτυλοειδής, Hp.*Art.*79; κοιλότης Gal.*UP*2.11: ἀποφύσεις Id.2.760.

γλῆνος, εος, τό, in pl., *gaudy things, playthings, trinkets*, Il.24.192, A.R.4.428 (expld. from **γληνόν**, = ποικίλον by Hsch.). II. = γλήνη I, Nic.*Th.*228. III. = φάος, Hsch., prob. in A.*Fr.*300.4: in pl., *stars*, Arat.318. IV. pl., = χρήματα (Elean), Sch.Il. l.c.

γληνῶσαι· διαφθεῖραι, Cyr., and **γληνωτά** (γλήνωσα cod.)· πονηρά, Hsch. **γληχυλίς**· πονηρά, Cyr. (**γληχυρίς**, Zonar.).

γλήχων, Dor. **γλάχων**, ἡ, v. βλήχων. II. γ. ἀγρία, = καλαμίνθη II, Ps.-Dsc.3.35; = δίκταμνον, ib.32.

γληχωνίτης οἶνος, ὁ, wine *prepared with* γλήχων, Dsc.5.52, *Gp.* 8.7.

γληχωνοειδές, τό, = δίκταμνον, Hsch.

γλία, ἡ, *glue*, *EM*234.24, Suid.; cf. γλοιός.

γλιᾶται· παίζει, Hsch.:—but **γλιῶσαι**· τὸ παίζειν, *EM*234.24.

γλίνη, ἡ, = γλοιός, Suid.: **γλίνα** *EM*234.26: **γλήνη** Hdn.Gr.1. 330:—Adj. **γλινώδης**, ες, = γλοιώδης, Arist.*Fr.*311 codd. Ath., Sch. Nic.*Al.*471, Dsc.4.82:—written **γληνώδης**, *Gp.*2.6.35,41.

γλῖνος or **γλεῖνος**, ὁ, *Cretan maple, Acer creticum*, Thphr.*HP*3.3. 1, 3.11.2.

γλίον, = εὔτονον or ἰσχυρόν, Hsch., *EM*234.24, Eust.1560.32.

γλισχρ-αίνομαι, Pass., *to be sticky, lubricated*, Hp.*Art.*55; *become tenacious*, of sputum, Gal.7.918. **-αντιλογεξεπίτριπτος**, ον, Com. word in Ar.*Nu.*1004, *hair-splitting-pettifogging-barefaced-knavish.* **-ασμα**, ατος, τό, *gluten*, Hp.*Acut.*10; *thick mucilage*, Aret.*CA*1.9; ἕως γλισχράσματος ἕψειν Dsc.*Eup.*1.1. **-εύομαι**, *to be close, stingy*, M.Ant.5.5. **-ία**, ἡ, = γλισχρότης, *stinginess*, Sch.Ar.*Pax*193 (but expld. by ἀτυχία).

γλισχρο-λογέομαι, *squabble about trifles*, Ph.1.526. **-λογία**, ἡ, *straw-splitting*, ib.698, D.L.2.30.

γλίσχρος, α, ον, *sticky*, Hp.*VC*14; γῆ Thphr.6.5.4; joined with λιπαρός, Pl.*Ti.*82d, 84a; γ. τὸ σίαλον Pherecr.69.3; of oil, Arist.*Mete.* 383b34; opp. ψαθυρός (q.v.), ib.385a17; *tough*, ξύλον Thphr.3.17. 5. II. metaph., 1. *sticking close, importunate*, γ. προσαιτῶν λιπαρῶν τε Ar.*Ach.*452: metaph., *clinging*, γ. ἡ ὁλκὴ τῆς ὁμοιότητος Pl.*Cra.*435c. Adv. -ρως, ἐπιθυμεῖν Id.*Cri.*53e; εἰκάζειν make a *close* comparison, Id.*R.*488a, cf. *Cra.*414c: Sup. -ότατα, σαρκάζοντες Ar. *Pax*482. 2. *penurious, niggardly*, Arist.*EN*1121b22; γλίσχρον βλέπειν Euphro10.16. Adv. -ρως καὶ κατὰ σμικρὸν φειδόμενος Pl.*R.*553c, cf. X.*Cyr.*8.3.37; φαύλως καὶ γ. παρείχοντο χρήματα *Hell.Oxy.*14.2; γ. ζῆν, opp. τρυφᾶν, Arist.*Pol.*1266b26; γ. λαμβάνειν, opp. ἀφθόνως διδόναι, ib.1314b3: hence, *with difficulty, hardly*, γ. καὶ μόλις λαμβάνειν D.37.38, cf. App.*Mith.*72; ἢ τὸ παράπαν οὐδέν.., ἢ γ. Arist.*Pol.*1275a 38; also τρόπον τινὰ γλίσχρον but *scantily*, Id.*PA*660b14. 3. of things, *mean, shabby*, of buildings, D.23.208; γ. δεῖπνον Plu.*Lyc.*17; of land, *poor*, Id.*Flam.*4; γ. τέχναι Luc.*Fug.*13; Χρύσιππος πολλαχοῦ γ. ἐστίν Plu.2.31e. 4. Adv. -ρως, of painting, *carefully, with elaborate detail*, Philostr.*Im.*2.12 and 28. (Cf. γλοιός.)

γλισχρότης, ητος, ἡ, *stickiness*, Arist.*HA*517b28, Thphr.*CP*1.6.4, etc.; *slipperiness*, Plb.26.1.14, Luc.*Anach.*29. II. metaph., *parsimony, stinginess*, opp. τρυφή, Arist.*Pol.*1326b38; *meanness*, Plu. *Them.*5, 2.125e. 2. γ. ὀνομάτων the 'birdlime' of verbiage (as *clogging* the intelligence), Ph.1.146.

γλισχρόχολος, ον, *viscous from bile*, Hp.*Epid.*4.26 (-χροος f.l. ap. Erot.).

γλισχρώδης, ες, *glutinous*, f.l. for βλιχ-, Hp.*VC*19.

γλίσχρων, ονος, ὁ, *niggard*, Ar.*Pax*193.

γλίττον, τό, = γλοιός, Hsch.; = ἀπόλυμα, Eust.1560.32.

γλίχομαι, only pres. and impf., exc. aor. 1 ἐγλιξάμην Pl.Com. 241:—*cling to, strive after, long for*, τινός Hdt.3.72; Αἰγύπτου Id. 4.152 (but γ. περὶ ἐλευθερίης Id.1.102 (s.v.l.)); ταῦτ' ἦν ὧν μάλιστ' ἐγλίχετο D.5.22; γ. τοῦ ζῆν Pl.*Phd.*117a, Charond.ap.Stob.4.2.24; κράτους Thphr.*Char.*26.1: c. acc., Hp.*Ep.*17 (dub.), Pl.*Hipparch.*

226e : folld. by a relat. clause, γλιχόμεθα τὴν μᾶζαν ἵνα λευκὴ παρῇ Alex.141.7 ; ὡς στρατηγήσεις γλίχεαι how thou shalt become general, Hdt.7.161 : c. inf., ὧν ἐγλίχοντο μὴ ἅψασθαι Th.8.15 ; εἰδέναι Pl.*Grg.* 489d ; λέγειν D.6.11 ; ἀποστερῆσαι Id.18.207 ; ζῆν Antiph.86.3 ; θιγεῖν Phld.*D.*3.1.—Not in Ep. or Trag. (γλῐ- : γλίχων [ῑ] is f.l. for γλήχων in Hdn.Gr.1.37.)

γλιχός, = γλίσχρος 2, Hsch. ; also, = περίεργος, Id. :—fem. **γλιχώ**, similarly expld. by *EM*234.26 ; = φειδωλία, Zonar.

γλιχύτης· ἀτυχὴς ἢ ἐπίπονος ἢ ἐρωτική, Hsch., cf. *EM*234.25.

γλοηρὸν χαλκοῦν, dub. sens. in *IG*2.716^{b}6.

γλοία or **γλοιά**, ἡ, = γλία, *glue*, Hsch.

γλοιάζω, *wink, twinkle with the eyes*, Hp.ap.Gal.19.91, *EM*234.45.

γλοιάς, άδος, ἡ, *vicious*, of mares, S.*Fr.*1037 :—masc. **γλοίης**, ητος, of horses, Hdn.Gr.2.680 ; also of persons, *slippery, shifty*, *EM* 234.44.

γλοιό-ομαι, *become sticky*, Dsc.5.79. **-ποιέομαι**, = foreg., Id. *Eup.*1.2. **-πότις**, ιδος, ἡ, *sucking up grease*, χλαμύς *AP*6.282 (Theodor.).

γλοιός, ὁ, *any glutinous substance, gum*, Hdt.3.112 ; ὁ γλισχρότατος γ. Arist.*Mir.*844^{a}14, cf. Sor.2.11, *Gp.*20.13, *POxy.*1220.16 (iii A.D. ; γλυοῦ Pap.) ; esp. *oil and dirt* scraped off the wrestler's skin with the στλεγγίς, Sch.Ar.*Nu.*449 : generally, *oily sediment* in baths, Semon.8, Telesp.41 H. ; γ. παιδικός substitute for butter in ointments, *Hippiatr.*69. II. as Adj. **γλοιός**, ά, όν, *slippery, knavish*, Ar.*Nu.* l.c. 2. = νωθρός, ἀσθενής, Hsch. Adv. **-ῶς**, = νυστακτικῶς, Id. 3. *thick*, παλλίολον *CPR*27.9 (ii A.D.). (For γλοι-ϝός, cf. γλία, γλίνη, etc., Lat. *glūs, glūten.*)

γλοιώδης, ες, *glutinous*, Pl.*Cra.*427b, Arist.*Fr.*311 (γλιν- codd. Ath.) ; τὸ γ. Thphr.*HP*5.4.1. Adv. **-δῶς** Sor.2.13, Gal.19.91. 2. *full of oily sediment*, ὕδωρ M.Ant.8.24.

γλουρός, οῦ, ὁ, *gold*, *AP*15.25.7 (Besant.), Hsch. :—hence **γλούρεα**· χρύσεα (Phryg.), Id.

γλούτια, τά, *medullary tubercles near the pineal gland of the brain*, Gal.*UP*8.14. II. *the great trochanter*, Id.2.773.

γλουτός, ὁ, *buttock*, γ. δεξιός Il.5.66, cf. Hp.*Fract.*13, Arist.*HA* 493^{a}23 : pl., Il.8.340, Hdt.4.9 : dual, τὼ γλουτώ X.*Eq.*7.2 : heterocl. pl., γλουτά, τά, Sch.Theoc.6.30. II. = σφαίρωμα τῆς κοτύλης, Hsch. (Cf. Skt. *glaús* 'round lump', Engl. *clot.*)

γλῠκ-άδιον, τό, *sweetmeat*, Hsch. 2. *vinegar*, Orus ap.*EM*626. 58, Choerob.*Rh.*p.251 S. **-άζω**, *sweeten*, τὴν κατάποσιν Epict. *Gnom.*22 ; *affect with a sensation of sweetness*, τοὺς ὑγιαίνοντας S.E. *P.*1.211 :—Pass., *receive a taste of sweetness*, Hierocl.p.29 A., S.E. *P.*1.20 ; but, *taste sweet*, *Gp.*2.39.4, and so intr. in Act. of wine, Ath. 1.26c ; μέλι γλυκάζον Lxx *Ez.*3.3, cf. Plot.4.3.26. **-αίνω**, fut. -ᾰνῶ Lxx *Si.*12.16 : aor. ἐγλύκᾰνα D.L.8.70 :—*sweeten*, Lxx *Si.*27. 23 ; opp. πικραίνω, D.L. l.c. ; *affect with a sensation of sweetness*, τὴν ἀκοήν D.H.*Comp.*15 : abs., *produce an effect of sweetness*, in Music, Aristox.*Harm.*p.23 M. :—more freq. in Pass., fut. γλυκανθήσομαι Lxx *Si.*49.1 : aor. ἐγλυκάνθην Hp.*Morb.*3.17, Mosch.3.110 : pf. γεγλύκασμαι Ath.9.384d, but ἀπ-εγλ. Diph.Siph.ib.2.55f :—*to be sweetened, turn sweet*, Hp.*Aër.*8, Arist.*Ph.*244^{b}23 ; *to be affected with a sensation of sweetness*, D.H.*Comp.*12, Ph.1.121. **-άνισον**, τό, = ἄνισον (= ἄνηθον), Sch.Theoc.7.63. **-ανσις**, εως, ἡ, *sweetening*, Thphr.*CP* 4.4.5. **-αντικός**, ή, όν, *of* or *for sweetening*, Ocell.1.9. Adv. **-κῶς** S.E.*M.*7.344 ; γ. διατίθεσθαι ib.367. **-ασμα**, ατος, τό, *sweetness*, Lxx *Pr.*16.24, al. ; *sweet wine*, ib.*Ne.*8.10, al. **-ασμός**, ὁ, *sweetness*, Dsc.*Alex.*7, Lxx *Ca.*5.16 (pl.) ; *sweet wine*, ib.*Am.*9.13. **-είδιον**, τό, Dim. of γλυκύς II, *BGU*417.18 (ii/iii A.D.). **-ειος**, α, ον, = γλυκύς, τῆς . . οὔτι γλυκειότερον *IG*14.1935. **-έλαιον**, τό, *sweet oil*, Xenocr.55, *Sammelb.*5747.8 (γλυκυέλ-), Gal.14.793. **-ερός**, ά, όν, = γλυκύς, Od.14.194, 17.41, Pi.*P.*4.32, E.*Med.*1099 (anap.), Arist. *PA*677^{a}23 ; opp. ὠφέλιμος, Crates Theb.10.5 : Comp. **-ώτερος** Od.9. 28, Them.*Or.*21.262c.

γλῠκερο-στάφῦλος [ᾰ], ον, *with sweet grapes*, Opp.*C.*1.465. **-χρως**, ωτος, ὁ, ἡ, *with sweet skin*, *AP*7.207 (Mel.).

γλυκή· βοτάνη τις ἐδώδιμος, Hsch. (Perh., = sq.)

γλῠκήρατον, τό, = γλυκύρριζα, Ps.-Dsc.3.5.

γλῠκ-ίζω, *treat with sweetmeats*, τοὺς πολίτας *IG*7.190.17 (Pagae). II. intr., *have a sweet flavour*, ὄξος -ίζον *Gp.*6.15.1, cf. 5. 26.10 :—also in Pass., *become sweet, form lead acetate*, Zos.Alch. p.248 B. **-ίνας**, ου, ὁ, in Crete, *cake made with sweet wine*, Seleuc. ap.Ath.14.645d, Hsch. **-ιος**, α, ον, *sugary, sickly*, Arist.*EE*1238^a 28 ; v.l. for Λύκιον in S.*Ph.*1461. **-ισμός**, ὁ, *distribution of sweetmeats* or *sweet wine*, Callix.2, *Inscr.Prien.*108.257 (ii B.C.), *IG*7.2712. 68 (Acraeph.).

γλύκκα, = γλυκύτης, and **γλυκκός**· γλυκύς, Hsch.

γλῠκόεις, εσσα, εν, = γλυκύς, ποτόν Nic.*Al.*444.

γλῠκύ-δακρυς, υ, *shedding sweet tears*, Ἔρως *AP*7.419 (Mel.), 12. 167 (Id.). **-δερκής**, ές, *with a sweet glance*, Hsch., Cyr. **-διον**, τό, = γλυκείδιον, *PLond.*2.239.13 (iv A.D. : -οίδιον Pap.). **-δρόμος**, ον, *faring pleasantly*, Νειλῶται *Lyr.Alex.Adesp.*32.3. **-δωρος**, ον, *with sweet gifts*, Κλειώ B.3.3 ; Νίκα Id.10.1 ; Ἔρως *AP*5.21 (Rufin.). II. γ. ἄγαλμα *sweet gift* brought in thy honour, B. 5.4. **-ηχής**, Dor. **-ᾱχής**, ές, *sweet-voiced*, *AP*9.26 (Antip. Thess.). **-θῡμέω**, *to be pleasant*, Hierocl. *in CA*26 p.479 M. **-θῡμία**, ἡ, *sweetness of mind*, γ. πρὸς τὰς ἡδονάς *readiness to indulge . .*, opp. τὸ καρτερεῖν, Pl.*Lg.*635c, cf. Plu.2.476d. II. *kindly disposition*, Id.*Them.*10, Id.2.970b ; πρός τινα *Sammelb.*4630.8 (ii A.D.). III. *pleasantness*, Iamb.*Myst.*5.11. **-θῡμος**, ον, *sweet of mood*, Il.20.467 ; of the Epicureans, Luc.*Herm.*16. II. Act., *charming the mind, delightful*, ἔρως, ὕπνος, Ar.*Lys.*551, *Nu.*705. **-κάλᾰμον** [κᾰ], τό, *scented lotus*, Zonar. **-καρπέω**, *bear sweet fruit*, Thphr.*CP*2.3.7. **-καρπος**, ον, *bearing sweet fruit*, ἄμπελος Theoc. 11.46, cf. Corn.*ND*14. **-κρεος**, ον, *of sweet flesh*, κογχύλιον Sophr. 24. **-λᾰλος**, ον, = sq., *Cat.Cod.Astr.*2.209. **-λογος**, ον, *sweet-speaking*, Sch.E.*Hec.*134. **-μαρίδες**, αἱ, a kind of *cockle*, Xenocr. 60,61, prob. in Gal.13.174. **-μήχᾰνος**, Dor. **-μάχᾰνος**, ον, *having pleasant devices*, Pi.*Pae.*2.80. **-μείλῐχος**, ον, *sweetly winning*, *h.Hom.*5.19.

γλυκυμή, = γλυκύρριζα, Hp.ap.Gal.19.91.

γλῠκύ-μηλον [κῠ], Aeol. and Dor. **γλῠκύ-μᾱλον**, τό, = μελίμηλον, *sweet-apple*, Sapph.93, Call.*Cer.*29, Dsc.1.115, Orib.5.31.3 ; as a term of endearment, Theoc.11.39. **-μῡθέω**, *speak sweetly*, *AP* 12.122 (Mel.). **-μῡθος**, ον, *sweetly-spoken*, ἔπος ib.5.194 (Id.). **-νους**, ουν, gen. ου, = γλυκύθυμος, Polem.*Phgn.*22. **-παις**, παιδος, ὁ, ἡ, *full of sweet boys*, Ῥόδος *AP*12.52 (Mel.). **-πάρθενος**, ἡ, *sweet maid*, in pl., Ὧραι ib.9.16 (Id.). **-πῐκρος**, ον, *sweetly bitter*, Ἔρος . . γ. ὄρπετον Sapph.40, cf. *AP*5.133 (Posid.), 12.109 (Mel.), Plu.2.681b ; of news, 'a gilded pill', Cic.*Att.*5.21.4 ; ἡδονή Ph.1.678 : later in literal sense, Gal.11.586. **-πότης**, ου, ὁ (γλυκο- codd.), *drinker of sweet wine*, Philagr.ap.Orib.5.19.6. **-πράτιον** [ᾱ], τό, *shop where sweetmeats are sold*, *Gloss.* :—also **γλυκεοπράτης** (sic), ου, ὁ, *dealer in sweetmeats*, ib. **-πῡρος**, ὁ, a kind of *wheat*, *BGU*1067.16 (ii A.D.). **-ρριζα**, ἡ, *sweet-root*, i.e. *liquorice*, *Glycyrrhiza glabra*, Dsc.3.5, Antyll.ap.Orib.10.24.4 :—also **-ρριζον**, τό, *Gp.*7.24.4, and **-ρριζος**, ἡ, Hsch.

γλῠκύς, εῖα (-ῆα Herod.4.2), ύ (-ύν *IG*14.1890), *sweet to the taste* or *smell*, νέκταρ Il.1.598 ; οἶνος Epich.124, etc. ; γλυκὺ ὄζειν Cratin.Jun. 1, prob. in Crates Com.2 ; opp. ὀξύς, Hp.*Vict.*2.55 ; opp. δριμύς, Plu. 2.708e : mostly metaph., even in Hom., *pleasant, delightful*, ἵμερος, ὕπνος, Il.3.139, Od.2.395 ; γ. αἰών 5.152, Hdt.7.46 ; πόλεμος γλυκίων γένετ' ἠὲ νέεσθαι Il.2.453 ; οὐδὲν γλύκιον ἧς πατρίδος οὐδὲ τοκήων Od.9. 34, cf. Pi.*N.*5.2, E.*Med.*1036, etc. ; γλυκὺ [ἐστι], c. inf., A.*Pr.*698, Alex. 210 ; θανεῖν γλύκιστον B.3.47 ; ὅτῳ . . μηδὲν ἦν ἰδεῖν γλυκύ S.*OT*1335 (lyr.), cf. 1390. b. of water, *sweet, fresh*, Xenoph.1.8, etc. ; opp. πικρός, Hdt.4.52 ; opp. ἁλμυρός, Arist.*Mete.*355^{a}33, etc. 2. after Hom. (but v. supr.), of persons, *sweet, dear*, γλυκεῖα (v.l. -ῆα) μᾶτερ Sapph. 90 ; γλυκεῖαι παῖδες ἀρχαίου Σκότου S.*OC*106 : c. inf., γ. φρὴν συμπόταισιν ὁμιλεῖν Pi.*P.*6.52 ; freq. in epitaphs, *IG*14.1472 (Sup.), etc. ; also ὑπὲρ τῆς γλυκυτάτης πατρίδος τελευτῆσαι *POxy.*33ii3 (ii A.D.) ; ὦ γλυκύτατε *my dear fellow*, Ar.*Ach.*462, cf. *Ec.*124 ; sts. in bad sense, *simple, silly*, ὡς γ. εἶ ! Pl.*Hp.Ma.*288b ; also applied κατ' ἀντίφρασιν to a swine, Gal.18(2).611 ; γλυκὺ πνεῖον, of mustard, Matro *Conv.*90. II. as Subst., ὁ γ. (sc. οἶνος) *grape-syrup*, Alex. 59, 172.14, Arist.*Pr.*875^{b}2, Herod.6.77, *POxy.*1088.51 ; also τὸ γ. Nic.*Al.*386, *POxy.*234ii6 (ii/iii A.D.). b. of the eye of Polyphemus, Theoc.6.22. 2. ἡ γ., = γλυκύρριζα, Thphr.*HP*9.13. 2. 3. ἡ γ., = χολή, Sch.Nic.*Th.*594. III. Comp. and Sup. γλυκίων Od.9.34 ; γλύκιστος B.3.47, Ael.*NA*12.46, etc. ; also γλυκύτερος, -τατος Pi.*O.*1.109, 19, etc. ; γλύσσων Xenoph.38.2. IV. Adv. -κέως Poll.4.24. (Perh. fr. *δλυκύς, cf. Lat. *dulcis.*)

γλῠκῠσίδη [ῑ], ἡ, *peony* (γ. ἄρρην, = *Paeonia officinalis*, γ. θήλεια, = *P. corallina*, Dsc.3.140), Hp.*Superf.*33, *Mul.*2.136, Pl.Com.61, Thphr.*HP*9.8.6.

γλύκυσμα, ατος, τό, *sweetness*, Lib.*Descr.*30.15. II. *sweetmeat*, Sch.Ar.*Pl.*660.

γλῠκύστρυφνος, ον, *sweet with an astringent taste*, Thphr.*HP*9. 20.5.

γλῠκύτης, ητος, ἡ, *sweetness of taste*, Hdt.4.177, Thphr.*CP*6.9.4 ; ὑδάτων D.S.4.84, cf. Arr.*Peripl.M.Eux.*49. 2. *sweetness, pleasantness*, γ. φυσική, of life, Arist.*Pol.*1278^{b}30 ; τῆς λέξεως D.H.*Comp.*11 ; μέλος καὶ γ. Phld.*Mus.*p.49 K. ; of persons, Plu.2.67b : in pl., *delights*, ἐπιθυμίαι πονηραὶ καὶ γλυκύτητες Phld.*Lib.*p.61 O.

γλῠκῠ-φᾰγία, ἡ, *the use of sweet food*, Alex.Trall.1.15. **-φαιον**, = ἐρυθρόδανον (Cret.), Hsch. **-φθογγος**, ον, *sweet-toned*, Sch. Pi.*O.*6.162. **-φρουροι**, οἱ, *those who love staying at home*, Hsch. **-φυλλον**, τό, dub. in Gal.19.730. **-φῠτον**, τό, = γλυκύρριζα, Ps.-Dsc.3.5. **-φωνέω**, *speak sweetly*, Theoc.15.146 (sed leg. γλυκὺ φωνεῖ). **-φωνία**, ἡ, *sweet voice* or *speech*, D.S.3.69, Heraclit.*Incred.*14. **-φωνος**, ον, *sweet-voiced, sweet-sounding*, Sch.Pi.*O.*4.4 ; rejected by Poll.2.113. **-χῡλος**, ον, *with sweet juices*, Hp.*Ep.*16, Xenoc.24,30. **-χῡμος**, ον, = foreg., Gal.11. 494 ; δίαιτα Paul.Aeg.2.15 :—Subst. **-χῡμία**, ἡ, Gal.14.749.

γλύκων, ωνος, ὁ, *sweet one* : ὦ γλύκων *you dear silly creature* ! Ar. *Ec.*985.

Γλῠκώνειος, α, ον, *Glyconic*, a kind of verse, so called from its inventor Glycon, Heph.10.2, Sch.Metr.Pi.*O.*1, etc.

γλύμμα, ατος, τό, (γλύφω) *engraved figure, signet*, Eup.4c6, Str. 14.1.16, *BGU*86.45 (ii A.D.) ; *inscription*, *AP*11.38 (Polemo Rex), Gal.12.773.

γλυμός, ὁ, prob. misspelt for γιγγλυμός, *IG*11(2).142.49 (Delos, iv B.C.).

γλύξις, εως, ἡ, *sweet insipid wine*, Phryn.Com.65, Polyzel.12 (pl.), cf. Ath.1.31e :—also written **γλεῦξις** in Hsch.

γλυπτ-ήρ, ῆρος, ὁ, (γλύφω) *graving tool, chisel*, *AP*6.68 (Jul.). **-ης**, Dor. **-ας**, ου, ὁ, *carver, sculptor*, *APl.*4.142,145. **-ικός**, ή, όν, *of engraving*, γλυπτικὴ σφραγίδων (sc. τέχνη) Poll.7.209.

γλυπτός, ή, όν, *fit for carving*, of wood or stone, Thphr.*Lap.*5. 2.

carved, λύγδου γ. *AP*5.193 (Posidipp. or Ascl.); γ. ὁμοίωμα Lxx *De.* 4.25; πρόσοψις Iamb.*Protr.*21.κγ'; γλυπτόν, τό, *carved image*, Lxx *Is.*44.10, al.: but γλυπτά, τά, *quarries*, ib.*Jd.*3.19.

γλύφ-ᾰνος [ῠ], ὁ, (γλύφω) *tool for carving, knife, chisel*, *h.Merc.*41, Theoc.1.28; γ. καλάμου pen-*knife*, *AP*6.63 (Damoch.). **-εῖον**, τό, = γλύφανος, Luc.*Somn.*13. **-εύς**, έως, ὁ, *carver*, J.*AJ*8.5.2, *IG*5(1).209 (Sparta); σφραγίδων Man.6.344 (pl.). **-ευτής**, οῦ, ὁ, *stone-mason* or *sculptor*, *PMasp.*147.8 (vi A.D.). **-ή**, ἡ, *carving*: *carved work*, D.S.5.44, *CPHerm.*127 (iii A.D.); γ. τῇ σφραγῖδι ποιεῖν its *emblem, device*, Plu.2.985b, cf. Iamb.*Protr.*21.κγ'; Δημητρίου γ. *the work* of D., under a carving, *IG*5(1).540 (Mistrá), cf. *CIG*4558 (Acre). II. *hole cut* in a beam, Anon.ap.Suid. v. καινοπρεπές. **-ικός**, ή, όν, *of* or *for carving*: γλυφική (sc. τέχνη) *Epigr.Gr.* 841 (Thrace). **-ίς**, ίδος, ἡ, in early writers always pl. γλυφίδες (but sg., opp. ἀκίς, of the constellation Sagitta, Hipparch.2.5.12), *notched end* of the arrow, ἕλκε δ' ὁμοῦ γλυφίδας τε λαβὼν καὶ νεῦρα Il. 4.122; ἕλκεν νευρὴν γλυφίδας τε Od.21.419; γλυφίδες μέσσῃ ἐγκάτθετο νευρῇ A.R.3.282; but perh. of *notches* or *grooves* for the fingers, παρὰ τὰς γλυφίδας περιειλίξαντες καὶ πτερώσαντες τὸ βυβλίον Hdt.8. 128, cf. Aen.Tact.31.26; τόξων πτερωταὶ γλυφίδες, poet. for *the arrow itself*, E.*Or.*274, cf. *AP*5.57 (Arch., sg.): also in pl., *notches in the arrow-head*, Paul.Aeg.6.88. II. *pen-knife*, *AP*6.62 (Phil.), 64 (Paul. Sil., pl.). 2. *chisel*, J.*BJ*5.5.2. III. in Architecture, *capitals* of columns, θριγκὸς.. λαΐνεος χαλκέῃσιν ἐπὶ γλυφίδεσσιν ἀρήρει A.R.3.218, cf. Sch. ad loc., *EM*235.13. IV. in pl., = θαλάμαι, Hsch.

γλύφω [ῠ], fut. γλύψω Lxx *Ex.*28.9: aor. ἔγλυψα Str.9.2.25:—**Med.**, aor. ἐγλυψάμην Theoc.*Epigr.*8, Plu.2.806d:—**Pass.**, aor. 1 part. γλυφθέν *AP*6.229 (Crin.), but aor. 2 γλυφέν [ῠ] *App.Anth.*3. 79 (Posidipp.), Ps.-Callisth.3.22, (δια-) Ael.*VH*14.7: pf. γέγλυμμαι *AP*9.752 (Ascl. or Antip. Thess.), Pl.*Smp.*216d, (ἐγ-) Hdt.2.106, but ἐξ-έγλ- Eup.331, Pl.*R.*616d:—*carve, cut out with a knife*, ναῦς τ' ἔγλυφεν Ar.*Nu.*879; γ. σφρηγῖδας *engrave* them, Hdt.7.69, cf. Pl. *Hp.Mi.*368c; of sculptors, opp. γράφω, Hdt.2.46, Str. l.c.; ἔγλυψέν με σίδηρος, written under a statue, *IG*14.973:—Med., *cause to be engraved*, Theoc. l.c., Plu. l.c. II. *note down* or *write* [on waxen tablets], τόκους *AP*11.289 (Pall.). III. Pass., *to be hatched*, ἕως γλυφῆναι τὰ ᾠά Antig.*Mir.*97. (Cf. Lat. *glūbo* 'peel', *glūma* 'husk', OHG. *klioban* 'cleave'.)

γλώνη· οὐδενὸς ἄξιον, Hsch.

γλώξ, ἡ, only pl. γλῶχες, *beard of corn*, Hes.*Sc.*398. (Cf. γλωχίν.)

γλωρεῖν· χρονίζειν, Hsch. **γλωρόν**· νομόν, Id.

γλῶσσα, Ion. γλάσσα, Herod.3.84, al., *SIG*1002.7 (Milet.), *Schwyzer*692 (Chios), Att. **γλῶττα**, ης, ἡ, *tongue*, Od.3.332, etc. b. γ. λάρυγγος, = γλωττίς, *larynx*, Gal.*UP*7.13. 2. *tongue*, as the organ of speech, γλώσσης χάριν through love *of talking*, Hes.*Op.*709, A.*Ch.* 266; γλώσσῃ ματαίᾳ Id.*Pr.*331, cf. *Eu.*830; γλώσσης ἀκρατὴς Id.*Pr.*884 (lyr.); μεγάλης γ. κόμποι S.*Ant.*128; γλώσσῃ δεινός, θρασύς, Id.*OC*806, *Aj.*1142; ἡ γ. ὀμώμοχ', ἡ δὲ φρὴν ἀνώμοτος E.*Hipp.*612: with Preps., ἀπὸ γλώσσης by *frankness of speech*, Thgn.63; φθέγγεσθαι Pi.*O.*6.13 (but ἀπὸ γ. ληίσσεται, opp. χερσὶ βίῃ, of fraud opp. violence, Hes. *Op.*322); also, by *word of mouth*, Hdt.1.123, Th.7.10, Arr.*An.*2. 14.1; τῷ νῷ θ' ὁμοίως κἀπὸ τῆς γ. λέγω S.*OC*936; τὰ γλώσσης ἄπο, i.e. *our words*, E.*Ba.*1049; ἀπὸ γ. φράσω by *heart*, opp. γράμμασιν, Cratin.122; οὐκ ἀπὸ γλώσσης not from *mere word of mouth*, but after full argument, A.*Ag.*813; μὴ διὰ γλώσσης without using *the tongue*, E.*Supp.*112; ἐν ὄμμασιν.. δεδορκὼς κοὐ κατὰ γλῶσσαν κλύων S.*Tr.* 747:—phrases: πᾶσαν γλῶτταν βασάνιζε try every *art of tongue*, Ar. *V.*547; πᾶσαν ἱέναι γλῶσσαν let loose one's whole *tongue*, speak without restraint, S.*El.*596; πολλὴν γ. ἐγχέας μάτην Id.*Fr.*929; κακὰ γ. slander, Pi.*P.*4.283: pl., ἐν κερτομίοις γλώσσαις, i.e. with blasphemies, S.*Ant.*962 (lyr.), cf. *Aj.*199 (lyr.): βοῦς, κλῄς ἐπὶ γλώσσῃ, v. βοῦς, κλείς. 3. of persons, *one who is all tongue, speaker*, of Pericles, μεγίστη γ. τῶν Ἑλληνίδων Cratin.293, cf. Ar.*Fr.*629 (s.v.l.). 4. ἡ γ. τοῦ ταμιείου the *advocacy* of the fiscus, Philostr.*VS*2.29. II. *language*, ἄλλη δ' ἄλλων γ. μεμιγμένη Od.19.175, cf. Il.2.804; γλῶσσαν ἱέναι speak a *language* or *dialect*, Hdt.1.57; γ. Ἑλληνίδα, Δωρίδα ἱέναι, Id.9.16, Th.3.112, cf. A.*Pers.*406, *Ch.*564; γλῶσσαν νομίζειν Hdt.1.142, 4.183; γλώσσῃ χρῆσθαι Id.4.109; κατὰ τὴν ἀρχαίαν γ. Arist.*Rh.*1357^{b}10; *dialect*, ἡ Ἀττικὴ γ. Demetr.*Eloc.*177; but also Δωρὶς διάλεκτος μία ὑφ' ἣν εἰσι γ. πολλαί Tryph.ap.Sch.D.T.p.320 H. 2. *obsolete* or *foreign word*, which needs explanation, Arist. *Rh.*1410^{b}12, *Po.*1457^{b}4, Plu.2.406f: hence Γλῶσσαι, title of works by Philemon and others. 3. *people speaking a distinct language*, Lxx *Ju.*3.8 (pl.), interpol. in Scyl.15. III. *anything shaped like the tongue* (cf. γλῶσσαι ὡσεὶ πυρός *Act.Ap.*2.3). 1. in Music, *reed* or *tongue of a pipe*, Aeschin.3.229, Arist.*HA*565^{a}24, Thphr.*HP*4.11. 4, etc. 2. *tongue* or *thong of leather, shoe-latchet*, Pl.Com.51, Aeschin.Socr.57. 3. *tongue of land*, App.*Pun.*121, cf. 95. 4. *ingot*, γ. χρυσῆ Lxx *Jo.*7.21. 5. *marking* on the liver, in divination, Hsch. (γλῶσσα from γλωχ-yᾰ, cf. γλώξ, γλωχίς; γλάσσα from *γλᾰχ-yᾰ, weak grade of same root.)

γλωσσ-αλγέω or (by dissimilation) **-αργέω**, *talk till one's tongue aches*, Poll.4.185. **-αλγία**, ἡ, *endless talking, wordiness*, E.*Med.* 525, *Andr.*689, Ph.2.165; but **γλωτταργία**, *idleness of the tongue*, σιωπὴν καὶ γ. ἡμῖν ἐπιβάλλει Luc.*Lex.*19. **-αλγος**, ον, (ἄλγος) *talking till one's tongue aches, garrulous*, Poll.6.119, Demoph.*Sent.* 7 (Sup.); *itching to speak*, Plu.2.510a:—also **-αργος**, [τέχνα] Pi. *Parth.Fr.*13^{b}67; ἡδονή J.*AJ*18.6.7; ἀηδών D.Chr.47.16: Sup., Ph. 2.571. **-άομαι**, pf. part. γεγλωσσαμένος, *tuneful*, στόμα κακκαβίδων prob. in Alcm.25. **-άριον**, τό, Dim. of γλῶσσα, Dsc.3.144, Gal.12.149. II. kind of *spoon* or *spatula*, *BGU*162.2 (ii/iii A.D.). **-ασπις**, ιδος, ὁ, *one who uses his tongue as his shield and defence*, *EM*235.39. **-ημα**, ατος, τό, = γλῶσσα II.2, Quint.*Inst.*1.8. 15, M.Ant.4.33. II. *tongue* or *point of a dart*, A.*Fr.*152. **-ηματικός**, ή, όν, (γλῶσσα II.2) *interlarded with* γλῶσσαι, λέξις, φράσις, D.H.*Amm.*2.2, *Th.*50, etc. Adv. **-κῶς** Tim.*Lex.Praef.* **-ίδιον**, Att. **γλωττ-**, τό, Dim. of γλῶσσα, Zen.5.65 (pl.). II. Dim. of γλωττίς II, Porph.*in Harm.*p.273. **-ίς**, ἡ, *inflammation of the tongue*, in horses, *Hippiatr.*130.

γλωσσο-γάστωρ, ορος, ὁ, ἡ, *living by one's tongue*, Com.ap.Poll. 2.108. **-γράφος** [ᾰ], ον, *writer on* γλῶσσαι, Str.13.1.19, Ath. 3.114b, 15.699e, Gal.19.106. **-ειδής**, ές, v. γλωττ-. **-κάτοχον**, τό, *tongue-depressor*, Heliod.ap.Orib.44.14.13. **-κηλόκομπος**, ον, *soothing with boastful tongue*, *Com.Adesp.*86. **-κομεῖον**, τό, (κομέω) *case to keep the reeds* or *tongues of musical instruments*, Lysipp.5: generally, *casket*, *BGU*824.9 (i A.D.), *PLond.*2.191.14 (ii A.D.): more freq. in form **-κομον**, τό, *case, casket*, *Test.Epict.*8.25, Apollod.Caryst.7, *PTeb.*414.21 (ii A.D.), *PMag.Lond.*122.55, etc.; = κιβωτός, *chest* (*Ark*), Lxx 2*Ki.*6.11 (v.l.); *money-box*, *Ev.Jo.*12.6, Plu. *Galb.*16; *compartment* in a water-organ, Hero *Spir.*1.42, cf. *Aut.*12. 1; *cage*, Longin.44.5; *coffin*, prob. in *AP*11.3; rejected by Phryn. 79:—also masc. **-κομος**, ὁ, *sarcophagus*, *BSA*17.235 (Pamphylia). II. *surgical instrument*, used for reducing fractures and dislocations, Heliod.ap.Orib.49.20. b. *box-splint*, Gal.10.442, *UP*7.14. III. *pudenda muliebria*, Eub.142. **-ποιΐα**, ἡ, *making of mouth-pieces* (γλῶσσα III.1), and **-ποιός**, όν, *making them*, Poll.2. 108, 7.153. **-πωγώνιον**, τό, *half a head with the tongue*, *POxy.* 108.14 (ii/iii A.D.).

γλωσσός, ή, όν, *talking, chattering*, Hdn.Gr.1.208.

γλωσσο-στροφεῖν· περιλαλεῖν καὶ στωμύλλεσθαι, Hsch. **-τέχνης**, ου, ὁ, *tongue-artificer*, opp. χειροτέχνης, D.Chr.7.124 (pl.). **-τμητος**, ον, *with the tongue cut out*, Lxx *Le.*22.22. **-τομέω**, *cut out the tongue*, ib.2*Ma.*7.4:—Pass., Plu.2.849b. **-χᾰρῐτέω**, = χαριτογλωσσέω, *flatter*, Lxx *Pr.*28.23.

γλωσσώδης, ες, = γλωσσοειδής: *talkative, babbling*, Lxx *Ps.*139 (140).11, Sext.*Sent.*13 M.

γλῶττα, ἡ, Att. for γλῶσσα.

γλωττήν, dub. in Pl.Com.239: perh. f.l. for γλωττ⟨οδέψ⟩ην.

γλωττ-ίζω, *kiss lasciviously, bill*, *AP*5.128 (Autom.). **-ικός**, ή, όν, *of the tongue*, τὸ γ. (sc. ὄργανον) Arist.*PA*683^{a}21. **-ίς**, ίδος, ἡ, *glottis, mouth of the windpipe*, Gal.*UP*7.13, al. II. *mouthpiece of a pipe, in which the reed was inserted*, Luc.*Harm.*1, Theo Sm.p.61 H.; of a trumpet, Hero *Spir.*1.16. III. *shoe-string*, Phryn.208; *latchet*, Lyd.*Mag.*2.13. IV. a bird, perh. *landrail*, Arist.*HA*597^b 16. **-ισμός**, ὁ, *lascivious kiss*, *AP*5.131 (Philod., pl.).

γλωττο-δεψέω, = Lat. *fellare*, *Com.Adesp.*32 D. **-ειδής**, ές, *tongue-shaped*, Arist.*HA*528^{b}30; γλωσσ-, v.l. in Dsc.4.88. **-ποιέω**, = γλωττοδεψέω, Ar.*V.*1283. **-στροφέω**, *ply the tongue*, Ar.*Nu.* 792.

γλωχίν [ῑ] or **γλωχίς** (cf. Hdn.Gr.2.431, 437), ἡ, gen. ῖνος:—*projecting point*: hence, 1. *end of the yoke-strap*, Il.24.274. 2. *barb* of an arrow, S.*Tr.*681, cf. Sch. ad loc., Gal.5.548; *point* of a penknife, *AP*6.63 (Damoch.); τριαίνης Nonn.*D.*36.111; κεραίας ib. 1.193; of the moon's horns, ib.40.314. 3. Pythagorean name for *an angle*, Hero *Deff.*15. 4. *extremity*, πυμάτη γ. D.P.184; *inlet*, θαλάττης γ. Agath.5.22. 5. *stigma* of saffron, *Gp.*11.261.

γλωχῑνωτός, ή, όν, *barbed*, βέλη Paul.Aeg.6.88.

γναθ-μός, ὁ, *jaw*, poet. form of sq., Il.17.617, al.: also in pl., Od. 18.29; γναθμοῖς ἀδήλοις φαρμάκων E.*Med.*1201; for ἀλλοτρίοις γναθμοῖσι γελᾶν, v. ἀλλότριος; also γναθμόν· τομώτατον καὶ αἱρετικώτατον, Hsch. **-ος** [ᾰ], ἡ, *jaw*, Prose form of γναθμός, also freq. in Poets, γ. ἱππείη Hom.*Epigr.*14.13; ἡ ἄνω, ἡ κάτω γ., Hp.*Art.*30, cf. Hdt. 2.68; καὶ γ. καὶ τὸ ἄνω τῆς γ. (where γνάθος, = *lower jaw*) Id.9.83; ἔπαγε γνάθον take your *teeth* to it! Ar.*V.*370; γνάθου δοῦλος a greedy fellow, E.*Fr.*282.5; also ὄνου γ. Eup.434: freq. in pl., Pl.*Phdr.* 254e, Arist.*PA*664^{a}11. 2. *cheek*, in pl., Hp.*VM*19, Gal.2.424, etc.; τὰς γ. φυσῶν D.19.314, cf. Ruf.*Onom.*47, Gal.18(1).423. 3. metaph., ποταμοὶ πυρὸς δάπτοντες ἀγρίαις γνάθοις A.*Pr.*370, cf. *Ch.* 280; also τραχεῖα πόντου Σαλμυδησσία γ., of jagged rocks, Id.*Pr.* 726. II. *point* of a wedge, ib.64. **-όω**, *hit on the cheek*, Phryn.Com.28. **-ων**, ωνος, ὁ, *full-mouth*, pr. n. of a parasite, Plu.2.707e, Longus 4.16:—also **Γναθωνάριον**, ibid.: **Γναθωνίδης** Luc.*Tim.*45. **-ώνειος**, ον, *like a* Γνάθων, Plu.2.707e.

γναμπ-τήρ, ῆρος, ὁ, *jaw*, λοβόλων Androm.ap.Gal.14.36. **-τός**, ή, όν, *curved, bent*, ἰχθυάασκον γναμπτοῖς ἀγκίστροισιν Od.4.369; μετὰ γναμπτῇσι γένυσσιν Il.11.416; πόρπας τε γναμπτάς θ' ἕλικας 18.401; ὄνυχες γ. Hes.*Op.*204; γ. δρόμοι, of the diaulos, Pi.*I.*1.57; γ. χαλινούς, Hsch. 2. *supple, pliant*, of the limbs of living men (opp. to the stark and stiff ones of the dead), ἐνὶ γναμπτοῖσι μέλεσσι Il.11. 669, 24.359, Od.11.394, etc. 3. metaph., *pliable*, οὔτε νόημα γναμπτὸν ἐνὶ στήθεσσι (of Achilles), Il.24.41. **-τω** (in codd. freq. κνάμπτω), fut. -ψω A.*Pr.*995, *Paean Oxy.*660.8, Lyc.1247: aor. ἔγναμψα, Ep. γνάμψα A.R.2.965:—poet. form of κάμπτω used by Hom. only in compds. in tmesi, ἐν δὲ γόνυ γνάμψεν Il.23.731; γ. τινά *bend* his will, A. l.c.; νόον Orph.*L.*195; in literal sense, δόρυ γ. Lyc. l.c.; ἄκρην *round* a headland, A.R. l.c., al.:—Pass., Nic.*Th.*423, Plu.*Arat.*13.

γναμφαί, = γνάθοι, Hsch. **γνάμψις**, εως, ἡ, *bending*, *EM*235.55. **γνα(π)ταὶ** ἀκταί, *curving* beach, Hsch.; γναπτὰς ἕλικας· τὰ καμφθέντα ψελλία, Id.; cf. γναμπτός. **γνάπτω**, = γνάμπτω, Id.

γνάπτωρ, ορος, ὁ, = γναφεύς, Man.4.422.

γνά-φαλον or **-φαλλον, -φεῖον, -φεύς, -φευτικός, -φεύω, -φικός, -φισσα, -φος, -φω**, v. κν-.

γνᾰφάδιον, τό, = sq., Hsch.

γνᾰφάλλιον, τό, *cotton-weed*, *Diotis maritima*, Dsc.3.117, Plin. *HN*27.88:—also **γνᾰφαλλίς**, ίδος, ἡ, Ps.-Dsc.3.117.

γνάφαλλον [ᾰ], τό, *flock of wool*, *Jahresh.*14 *Beibl.*52, *PMagd.*8.7 (iii B.C.):—hence Subst. **γναφαλλολόγος**, ὁ, *flock-picker*, *Ostr.*1081; more freq. by haplology **γναφαλλόγος**, ib.1082, 1086, *PPetr.*2 *Intr.* p.44 (iii B.C.).

γνάφαλος, ὁ, an unknown *bird*, Arist.*HA*616b16.

γνάψις, εως, ἡ, *dressing* of cloth, Pl.*Plt.*282e, Sch.Ar.*Pl.*166.

γνήσι-ος, α, ον, (γένος) *belonging to the race*, i.e. *lawfully begotten, born in wedlock*, νόθον καὶ γνήσιον Il.11.102, cf. Od.14.202, Hdt.3.2, *Leg.Gort.*10.41, Ar.*Av.*1665, And.1.127, D.44.49, etc.; παίδων ἐπ' ἀρότῳ γνησίων Men.*Pk.*435; ἀδελφός Ar.*Av.*1659; νόθος.. γνησίοις ἴσως σθένει S.*Fr.*87; φρονοῦντα γνήσια E.*Hipp.*309; γ. φρόνημα S.*Fr.* 307. 2. generally, *genuine, legitimate*, φίλος Phoc.2 A; γ. γυναῖκες *lawful* wives, opp. παλλακίδες, X.*Cyr.*4.3.1; πολῖται Arist.*Pol.*1278a30, cf. 1319b9; γ. τῆς Ἑλλάδος *true* Greeks, D.9.30; ἀκουστής D.H. *Isoc.*18 (Sup.); μήτηρ τῶν ἐρωτικῶν λόγων, of Aphrodite, Luc.*Am.*19; γ. ἀρεταί *real, unfeigned* virtues, Pi.*O.*2.11; γ. ὕμνοι *inspired* song, B.8.83; of fevers, γ. τριταῖος a *genuine* tertian, Hp.*Progn.*24; γ. ὄξος *genuine* vinegar, Eub.65; of writings, *genuine*, Gal.15.748, Harp.s.v. Ἀλκιβιάδης. Adv. -ίως *genuinely, truly*, E.*Alc.*678, Lys.2.76, D.*Ep.* 3.32, etc.; γ. φέρειν bear *nobly*, Antiph.281, Men.205; *lawfully*, τοῖς γ. συμβιώσασιν Phld.*Piet.*93. II. γνήσια, τά, *charges on land*, γ. δημόσια *PAmh.*86.15 (i A.D.), cf. *PLond.*3.1157.4 (ii A.D.). **-ότης**, ητος, ἡ, *legitimate birth*, ἀπ' ἀμφοῖν Arist.*Rh.*1360b35, cf. Phld.*Hom.* p.50 O. II. *genuineness, sincerity*, μετὰ πάσης γ. *POxy.*140.16 (vi A.D.).

γνίς· γέρανος (Tyrrhen.), Hsch.

Γνίφων, ωνος, ὁ, *niggard*, as pr. n., Luc.*Vit.Auct.*23; prob. in Alciphr.3.34.

γνοιῶσαι· γνοῦαι, Hsch. **γνοτέρα**, = βαλλωτή, Ps.-Dsc.3. 103. **γνόφεον**· μέλαν, Id.; cf. sq.

γνοφ-ίας, ου, ὁ, name of a wind, Lyd.*Mens.*4.119. **-ος**, later form for δνόφος, *darkness*, *Chron.Lind.*D.28, *Ep.Hebr.*12.18, D.Chr. 34.37 (pl.), Luc.*Per.*43: pl., *storm-clouds*, Arist.*Mu.*391b12. **-όω**, *darken*, Lxx *La.*2.1. **-ώδης**, ες, *dark, gloomy*, ib.*Pr.*7.9, Ph.2. 109, Plu.2.949a.

γνύθος [ῠ], εος, τό, *pit*, Lyc.485: but γνύθος, ὁ, *hollow*, Hsch.

γνύξ, Adv., (γόνυ) *with bent knee*, Il., always in phrase γνὺξ ἐριπών falling *on the knee*, 5.309, 357, al.; later γ. ἥμενος Arat.921; σφῆλεν γ. ἐπιόντα A.R.3.1310; γ. ἑδριόωσαι Orac.ap.Zos.2.6: in later Prose, Gal.*UP*3.15.

γνυπεσόν· ἀργόν, οἱ δὲ ἔκλυτον, Hsch.

γνύπετος, ον, (γόνυ, πίπτω) *falling on the knee*:—hence **γνυπτέω** (leg. γνυπετέω), *to be weak*, Hsch. **γνύποντι** (leg. -οῦντι)· ἀσθενοῦντι, Id., and **γνύπων**, ωνος, *depressed* or *weak*, Id.

γνυφαί· νάπαι, Hsch. **γνύων**· νωθραίνων, Id.

γνῶμα, ατος, τό, (γνῶναι) *mark, token*, Hdt.7.52; *test*, S.*Tr.*593; of an ass's teeth, Arist.*HA*577b3. II. *opinion, judgement*, A. *Ag.*1352, E.*Heracl.*407. III. = Lat. *groma*, Suid.

γνωμανάδοχος, ὁ, *surety for performance of a service*, *PMonac.*14. 63 (vi A.D.).

γνωμᾰτ-ευτής, οῦ, ὁ, *a dealer in maxims*, Sch.Il.10.31. **-εύω**, *discriminate, discern*, σκιὰς γ. Pl.*R.*516e (v. γνωμονεύω), cf. Philostr. *VA*2.30, Plot.5.8.11, v.l. in S.E.*M.*7.332; τὰ βουλεύματα τῶν πολεμίων Agath.1.14; γ. πήχει καὶ μέτρῳ τὴν ἀρετήν Them.*Or.*2.36b: abs., *exercise discrimination*, Plot.5.8.11; *decide*, c. acc. et inf., Men. Prot.p.47 D.

γνωμεισηγητής, οῦ, ὁ, *proposer of a motion*, *BGU*362 xv 8 (iii A.D.).

γνώμ-η, ἡ, *means of knowing*: hence, *mark, token*, Thgn.60 (pl.); of the teeth (cf. γνώμων III), Arist.*HA*576b15. II. *organ by which one perceives* or *knows, intelligence*, 1. *thought, judgement* (τῆς ψυχῆς ἡ γ. Pl.*Lg.*672b), ἐκμαθεῖν ψυχήν τε καὶ φρόνημα καὶ γ. S. *Ant.*176: acc. abs., γνώμην ἱκανός *intelligent*, Hdt.3.4; γ. ἀγαθός, κακός, S.*OT*687, *Ph.*910; τοιάδε τὴν γ. Id.*El.*1021; κατὰ γ. ἴδρις Id. *OT*1087 (lyr.); γνώμᾳ διπλόαν θέτο βουλάν Pi.*N.*10.89; γνώμῃ μαθεῖν τι S.*OC*403; γνώμῃ κυρήσας Id.*OT*398; γνώμῃ φρενῶν, opp. ὀργῇ, ib. 524; γνώμης ξύνεσις Th.1.75; γνώμης μᾶλλον ἐφόδῳ ἢ ἰσχύος Id.3.11; ταῖς γ. καὶ τοῖς σώμασι σφάλλεσθαι X.*Cyr.*1.3.10, cf. Th.1.70; γνώμῃ, opp. τύχῃ, σωφρονοῦντες Isoc.3.47; γνώμης ἅπτεσθαι affect *the head*, of wine or fever, Hp.*Acut.*63, *Fract.*11; γνώμην ἔχειν *understand*, S. *El.*214 (lyr.), Ar.*Ach.*396; πάντων γ. ἴσχειν S.*Ph.*837 (lyr.); προσέχειν γνώμην give *heed*, attend, δεῦρο τὴν γ. προσίσχετε Eup.37; πρὸς ἑτέρῳ ἔχειν γνώμην Aeschin.3.192; to be on one's *guard*, Th.1.95; δηλοῦν τὴν γ. ἔν τινι to show one's *wit* in.., Id.3.37; ἐν γνώμῃ τι παραστῆσαι D.4.17; ἀπὸ γνώμης φέρειν ψῆφον δικαίαν with a good *conscience*, A.*Eu.*674; but οὐκ ἀπὸ γ. λέγεις not without *judgement*, with good *sense*, S.*Tr.*389; ἄτερ γνώμης A.*Pr.*456; ἄνευ γ. S.*OC*594; γνώμῃ κολάζειν *with good reason*, X.*An.*2.6.10; γνώμῃ τῇ ἀρίστῃ (sc. κρίνειν or δικάζειν) *to the best of one's judgement*, in the dicasts' oath, Arist.*Rh.* 1375a29; ἡ καλουμένη γ. τοῦ ἐπιεικοῦς κρίσις ὀρθή Id.*EN*1143a19; so περὶ ὧν ἂν νόμοι μὴ ὦσι, γνώμῃ τῇ δικαιοτάτῃ κρινεῖν D.20.118; γ. τῇ δ. δικάσειν ὀμωμόκασιν Id.23.96, cf. 39.40; τῇ δ. γ. Arist.*Pol.*1287a 26; ὅστις γνώμῃ μὴ καθαρεύει has not a clear *conscience*, Ar.*Ra.* 355. 2. *will, disposition, inclination*, εὐσεβεῖ γνώμᾳ Pi.*O.*3.41; γ. Διός A.*Pr.*1003; ἐν γνώμῃ γεγονέναι τινί to stand *high in his favour*, Hdt.6.37; πάσῃ τῇ γ. with all *one's zeal*, Th.6.45; τίνα αὐτοὺς οἴεσθε γ. ἕξειν περὶ σφῶν αὐτῶν And.1.104; γ. ἕ. περί τινα Lys.10.21; πρὸς τοὺς Ἀθηναίους τὴν γ. ἔχειν *to be inclined* towards.., Th.5.44; ἐμπιμπλάναι τὴν γ. τινός satisfy his *wishes*, X.*An.*1.7.8, cf. *HG*6.1. 15 (pl.); ἀφ' ἑαυτοῦ γνώμης on his own *initiative*, Th.4.68; ἐκ μιᾶς γ. of one *accord*, with one *consent*, D.10.59; μιᾷ γνώμῃ Th.1.122, 6.17; διὰ μιᾶς γ. γίγνεσθαι Isoc.4.139; κατὰ γνώμην according to one's *mind* or *wishes*, ὅταν τακεῖ θῶ κατὰ γνώμην ἐμήν E.*Andr.*737; ἄν τι μὴ κατὰ γ. ἐκβῇ D.1.16: in pl., φίλιαι γνῶμαι friendly *sentiments*, Hdt. 9.4. III. *judgement, opinion*, βροτῶν γ. Parm.8.61; ταύτῃ.. τῇ γνώμῃ πλεῖστός εἰμι I incline mostly *to this view*, Hdt.7.220 (s. v. l.); also ταύτῃ πλεῖστος τὴν γνώμην εἰμί Id.1.120; ἡ πλείστη γ. ἐστί τινι Id.5.126; πλέον φέρει ἡ γ. τινί Id.8.100; τὸ πλεῖστον τῆς γ. εἶχεν.. προσμεῖξαι Th.3.31; γνώμην τίθεσθαι Hdt.3.80; οὕτως τὴν γ. ἔχειν to be of this *opinion*, Th.7.15, cf. X.*Cyr.*6.2.8, Ar.*Nu.*157; εἴ τινι γ. τοιαύτη παρειστήκει περὶ ἐμοῦ And.1.54; τὴν αὐτὴν γ. ἔχειν Th.2.55; τῆς αὐτῆς γ. εἶναι, ἔχεσθαι, Id.1.113, 140; ὁ αὐτὸς εἰμὶ τῇ γ. Id.3.38; κατὰ γ. τὴν ἐμήν in my *judgement* or *opinion*, Hdt.2.26, 5.3; ellipt., κατά γε τὴν ἐμήν Ar.*Ec.*153, cf. Plb.18.1.18, D.H.*Isoc.*3: abs., γνώμην ἐμήν Ar.*V.*983, *Pax* 232; παρὰ γνώμην τοῖς Ἕλλησιν ἐγένετο contrary to *general opinion*, Th.4.40; but παρὰ γ. κινδυνευταί *reckless* venturers, Id.1.70, cf. 4.19; εἰπὲ μὴ παρὰ γ. ἐμοί either contrary to *my wish*, or contrary to *your true opinion*, A.*Ag.*931, cf. *Supp.*454: freq. of *opinions* delivered publicly, ἑστάναι πρὸς τὴν γ. τινός Th.4. 56; Θεμιστοκλέους γνώμῃ *by the advice* of Th., Id.1.90, 93; γνώμην ἀποφαίνειν deliver *an opinion*, Hdt.1.40; ἀποδείκνυσθαι ib.207; ἐκφαίνειν Id.5.36; τίθεσθαι S.*Ph.*1448 (anap.), Ar.*Ec.*658; ἀποφαίνεσθαι E.*Supp.*336; ποιεῖσθαι περί τινων Th.3.36; γνώμας κατέθεντο have made up their *minds*, Parm.8.53. b. *verdict*, ἡ τοῦ δικαστοῦ γ. *IG*4.364 (Corinth, iv A.D.), cf. 685.32 (pl., Cret., ii B.C.). 2. *proposition, motion*, γνώμην εἰσφέρειν Hdt.3.80, 81; εἰπεῖν Th.8.68, etc.; (but γνώμας προτιθέναι hold a debate, Th.3.36); γνῶμαι τρεῖς προεκέατο Hdt.3.83: freq. in Inscrr., *resolution*, *IG*1².118.28, etc.; γ. στρατηγῶν ib.2².27; Κλεισόφου καὶ συμπρυτάνεων ib.1; ἡ ἐκφερομένη γ. ib.1051c26; γνώμην νικᾶν carry *a motion*, Ar.*V.*594, *Nu.*432; κρατεῖν τῇ γ. Plu.*Cor.*17. 3. γνῶμαι, αἱ, *practical maxims*, Heraclit. 78, S.*Aj.*1091, X.*Mem.*4.2.9, Arist.*Rh.*1395a11 (sg., 1394a22). 4. in pl., *fancies, illusions*, S.*Aj.*52. 5. *intention, purpose, resolve*, ἀπὸ τοιᾶσδε γνώμης with some such *purpose* as this, Th.3.92; γνώμην ποιεῖσθαι, c. inf., *propose* to do, Id.1.128; κατὰ γνώμην of *set purpose*, D.H. 6.81 (so also γνώμης Lib.*Or.*33.13, 50.12); τίνα ἔχουσα γνώμην; with what *purpose*? Hdt.3.119; οἶδα δ' οὐ γνώμῃ τίνι; with what *intent*? S.*OT*527, cf. *Aj.*448; ἡ ξύμπασα γ. τῶν λεχθέντων the general *purport*.., Th.1.22; ἦν τοῦ τείχους ἡ γνώμη.., ἵνα.. *the purpose* of it was.., that.., Id.8.90. **-ηδόν**, Adv. (γνώμη III. 2) *vote by vote*, πυνθάνεσθαι D.H.8.43. **-ηστός**, ὁ, *knowledge*, ἀφ' οὗ γ. as far as my *memory* goes, Hsch. s. h. v. **-ίδιον**, τό, Dim. of γνώμη, Ar. *Eq.*100, *Nu.*321, Luc.*Par.*42. **-ικός**, ή, όν, *normative* (nisi leg. γνωμονικά), γ. ἃ φύσις ἁ τοῦ ἀριθμοῦ Philol.11. 2. (γνώμη III. 3), *dealing in* or *suited to maxims, didactic*, περίοδος Hermog.*Inv.*4.3; τὰ γ. S.E.*M.*1.278; τὸ γ. D.Chr.52.17; σχῆμα γ. Sch.Od.15.74. Adv. -κῶς Phld.*Hom.*p.15 O., Ath.5.191e.

γνωμο-δοτέω, *give advice*, *IG*12(7).p.1 (Amorgos). **-λογέω**, *speak in maxims*, Arist.*Rh.*1394a21, *Rh.Al.*1439a3, Plu.2.481b, D.L. 8.78, Procop.Gaz.*Ep.*21. **-λογητέον**, *one must speak in maxims*, Arist.*Rh.Al.*1439a3. **-λογία**, ἡ, *sententious style*, Pl.*Phdr.*267c; *theory of maxims*, Arist.*Rh.*1394a19. 2. *collection of maxims*, Plu. *Cat.Ma.*2 (pl.), Suid. Θέογνις: pl., Plb.12.28.10, D.H.*Dem.*46, Plu. *Fab.*1, etc. **-λογικός**, ή, όν, *sententious*, τὰς τελευτὰς γ. ποιεῖσθαι Arist.*Rh.Al.*1439a5, Demetr.*Eloc.*9. Adv. -κῶς Theon *Prog.*5.

γνωμον-εύω, *measure as on a sun-dial, test*, v.l. in Pl.*R.*516e (ap. Tim.*Lex.*). **-ικός**, ή, όν, (γνώμων I) *judging by rule*, X.*Mem.*4. 2.10; *fit to judge of, skilled in* a thing, τινός Pl.*R.*467c, Iamb.*Myst.* 3.27. II. (γνώμων II. 2. a) *of* or *concerning sun-dials*, θεωρήματα Hipparch.1.9.8, cf. Str.1.1.20: -κός, ὁ, *expert in sun-dials*, *AP*14.139, Gal.5.652, Procl.*Hyp.*5.54: ἡ -κή (sc. τέχνη), *the art of making them*, Vitr.1.3. Adv. -κῶς Str.2.1.35. 2. *forming a* γνώμων (II. 2. c), τρίγωνα Iamb. *in Nic.*p.71 P. Adv. -κῶς ib.p.77 P. **-ιον**, τό, Dim. of γνώμων II. 2. a, *pointer* or *dial-hand*, Hero *Dioptr.*5, Procl.*Hyp.*3.26 (pl.).

γνωμο-σύνη, ἡ, *prudence, judgement*, Sol.16. **-τῠπέω**, *coin maxims*, Ar.*Th.*55. **-τῠπία**, ἡ, *coining of maxims*, Hsch. **-τῠπικός**, ή, όν, *clever at coining maxims*, Ar.*Eq.*1379. **-τύπος** [ῠ], ον, (τύπτω) *maxim-coining, sententious*, Id.*Ra.*877, *Nu.*952 (lyr.); γ. μάλιστα οἱ ἀγροῖκοι Arist.*Rh.*1395a7. **-φλυᾱκέω**, *babble of 'saws and instances'*, dub. cj. in Cerc.9.5.

γνώμων, ονος, ὁ, (γι-γνώ-σκω) *one that knows* or *examines, an interpreter, discerner*, θεσφάτων A.*Ag.*1130; τῶν παραχρῆμα Th.1.138; γλῶττα γ. (sc. γλυκέων καὶ δριμέων) X.*Mem.*1.4.5: γνώμονες, οἱ, *inspectors* of the sacred olives at Athens, Lys.7.25. 2. *expert witness* or *valuer*, *SIG*169.52 (Iasus, iv B.C.). 3. as Adj., *discerning*, νόος *Hymn.Is.*141. II. *carpenter's square*, Polyaen.4.3.21; [ὁ δημιουργὸς τῇ δεκάδι] ὥσπερ γνώμονι καὶ εὐθυντηρίῳ ἐχρήσατο *Theol. Ar.*59. 2. *pointer* of the sun-dial, Hdt.2.109, Phld.*Sign.*30, Plu. *Per.*6 (pl.), D.L.2.1. b. Geom., *gnomon*, Euc.2 *Def.*2, etc. c.

Arith., number added to a figurate number to obtain the next number of the same figure, Iamb.*inNic.*p.58 P.; esp. of the odd integers, Arist.*Ph.*203^{a}14, Theo Sm.p.32 H.; also of the original figurate number, *Theol.Ar.*9 (dub. l.). 3. = κλεψύδρα, Thphr.*Fr.* 159. 4. *point* of a drill, Apollod.*Poliorc.*149.4. 5. generally, *index*, τινός Plu.2.968f, Ael.*NA*6.34, al., Vett.Val.305.10; simply, *mark*, *POxy.*1409.18 (iii A.D.). 6. in pl., *teeth that mark* a horse's age, X.*Eq.*3.1. 7. metaph., *rule* of life, Thgn.543, cf. Luc.*Herm.* 76. 8. sens. obsc., ὁ γ. ἀνίσταται Diog.*Ep.*35. V. *tariff*, *OGI* 674.5 (Coptos), *BGU*1118.45 (i B.C.), *AB*233. 2. *code of regulations*, *PGnom.*1, *OGI*669.44 (i A.D.).

γνωρ-ίζω, fut. Att. -ιῶ: pf. ἐγνώρικα Pl.*Phdr.*262b:—*make known, point out*, A.*Pr.*487, Lxx 1*Ki.*10.8, al., *Ep.Rom.*9.22:—in this sense mostly Pass., *become known*, Pl.*R.*428a, Arist.*APr.*64^{b}35; τὰ γνωριζόμενα μέρη τῆς οἰκουμένης Plb.2.37.4. 2. c. acc. pers., *make known*, τινά τινι Plu.*Fab.*21; *commend*, τινὰ τῇ βουλῇ ἰσχυρῶς App. *Mac.*9.6. 3. *certify* a person's *identity*, *BGU*581.13 (ii A.D.), *POxy.* 1024.18 (ii A.D.). II. *gain knowledge of, become acquainted with, discover*, c. part., τοὔργον ὡς οὐ γνωριοῖμί σου τόδε δόλῳ προσέρπον S. *OT*538; τὰ καλὰ γ. οἱ εὐφυέες πρὸς αὐτά Democr.56, cf. E.*Alc.*564, Th.7.44, Arist.*Ph.*184^{a}12:—Pass., Th.5.103, Men.72; γ. περί τι or περί τινος Arist.*Metaph.*1005^{b}8, 1037^{a}16. 2. *become acquainted with*, τινά Pl.*La.*181c, D.35.6; τινὰς ὁποῖοί τινές εἰσι Isoc.2.28:—Pass., ἐγνωρισμένοι αὐτῷ *being made acquainted with* him, ibid.; πρός τινος Luc.*Tim.*5. **-ῐμος**, ον, rarely η, ον, Pl.*R.*614e, Luc. *Somn.*9:—*well-known*, γνώριμα λέγεις Pl.*R.*558c; φίλα τε καὶ συνήθη καὶ γ. Id.*Lg.*798e; λόγος γ. τινι D.3.23; ὀνόματα γ. *familiar*, Arist.*Po.*1451^{b}20, *Top.*149^{a}18 (Sup.); opp. ἄγνωστον, ibid.; γ. ἡμῖν, opp. ἁπλῶς, Id.*EN*1095^{b}3: more freq. in Comp. -ώτερον, ἁπλῶς, opp. γ. ἡμῖν, Id.*APo.*72^{a}3, al.; -ώτερα τεκμήρια Iamb.*Myst.*5.13. 2. of persons, γνωριμώτερον ποιεῖν τινά τινι X.*Cyr.*5.5.28. 3. Subst., *acquaintance*, ἑταῖρος ἢ καὶ γ. ἄλλος Od.16.9; less than φίλος, D.18. 284; τοῖς οἰκείοις καὶ τοῖς γ. Pl.*R.*343e, cf. X.*Mem.*2.3.1, D.21.73, etc. b. *pupil*, Ἰσοκράτους καὶ τῶν ἐκείνου γ. D.H.*Comp.*19, cf. Philostr.*VS*1.24.2, al., Plu.2.448e, *IG*3.774. c. *kinsman*, Lxx *Ru.*3.2. II. *notable, distinguished*, οἱ γνώριμοι *the notables* or *wealthy class*, X.*HG*2.2.6; opp. δῆμος, Arist.*Pol.*1291^{b}18, Plu. *Nic.*2, etc.: Sup. οἱ ἐν ταῖς πόλεσι -ώτατοι D.19.259; less freq. of things, *remarkable*, Luc.*Herm.*21. III. Adv. -μως *intelligibly*, γ. αἰνίζομαι E.*El.*946; γ. μοι πάνυ φράσεις Antiph.52.6; ἁπλῶς καὶ πᾶσι γ. γεγράφθαι D.24.68; γ. μᾶλλον λέγειν, opp. οὐ σαφῶς, Arist.*GA*747^{a}27. 2. *familiarly*, γ. ἔχειν τινί to be on *friendly terms* with one, D.53.4.—Rare in poetry. **-ῐμότης**, ητος, ἡ, *acquaintance*, Stob.2.7.5^{1}. **-ισις**, εως, ἡ, *making known*, Pl.*Plt.*257a. 2. οἰκειότης καὶ γ. ἀλλήλων Id.*Lg.*771d, etc. 3. *getting to know*, γνωρίσεως ἕνεκα τῶν τόπων ib.763b; *cognition*, Id.*Sph.*219c. **-ισμα**, τό, *that by which a thing is made known, mark, token*, X.*Cyr.*2.1.27 (pl.), Arist.*Phgn.*806^{a}15, etc.; ἴχνη καὶ γ. Plu.2.855b: in pl., *tokens by which* a lost child *is recognized*, Men.*Epit.*86, Plu.*Thes.*4, etc.: also in sg., Parth.1. 5. 2. in criminal trials, *corpus delicti*, *PMasp.*143.16, al. (vi A.D.). **-ισμός**, ὁ, *making known*, Arist.*APo.*90^{b}16. 2. *identification*, *PTeb.*288.15 (iii A.D.). II. *recognition*, *EM*735.25, Suid. **-ιστέον**, *one must know*, Arist.*EN*1180^{b}22; *one may recognize*, Alex.Trall.1.15. **-ιστής**, οῦ, ὁ, *one that takes cognizance of*, δίκης Antipho 5.94. II. *diviner*, Lxx 4*Ki.*23.24. **-ιστικός**, ή, όν, *capable of apprehending, cognitive*, Pl.*Def.*414c; κινητικὸν ἐδόκει ἡ ψυχὴ εἶναι καὶ γ. Arist.*de An.*404^{b}28; τοῦ εἴδους Id.*Ph.*194^{b}4; ἡ διαλεκτικὴ πειραστικὴ περὶ ὧν ἡ φιλοσοφία γ. Id.*Metaph.*1004^{b}26; ἡ τῆς γ. γραμμῆς τομή title of work ascribed to Archytas, Iamb.*Comm. Math.*2; *capable of knowing*, Plu.2.79d, Arr.*Epict.*2.20.21; γ. τοῦ μέλλοντος Max.Tyr.1.5. Adv. -κῶς, ζῆν Porph.*Gaur.*16.3. II. *corresponding with knowledge*, ἰδιότητες τοῦ ὄντος Porph.*Sent.*38.

γνωσῐ-γρᾰφία, ἡ, *picturing of the effect* of a verdict, as a Rhetorical device, Aps.p.304 H. **-δίκα** [ῐ], ἡ, *judicial decision*, *IG*5(2).262. 15 (Mantinea, v B.C.). **-μᾰχέω**, *fight with one's own opinion* (τῇ προτέρᾳ γνώμῃ μάχεσθαι Phryn.*PS*p.59 B.), or *recognize one's own fighting power* (as compared with the enemy): hence, *give way, submit*, Hdt.3.25, 7.130, E.*Heracl.*706 (anap.), Ar.*Av.*555, D.H.3.57; γ. μὴ εἶναι ὁμοῖοι *give way and confess* that.., Hdt.8.29. b. *admit one's error*, Isoc.5.7, *POxy.*1119.20 (iii A.D.), 71 ii 14 (iv A.D.). II. in later Prose, *contend obstinately*, in argument, Ph.1.526, al.; γνωσιμαχήσαντες πρὸς ἀλλήλους D.H.9.1 (s. v. l.): abs., *to be at variance*, Hp.*Ep.*27. **-μᾰχία**, ἡ, *obstinate contention*, Ph.1.693 (pl.).

γνῶσις, εως, ἡ, *seeking to know, inquiry, investigation*, esp. judicial, τὰς τῶν δικαστηρίων γ. D.18.224; τὴν κατὰ τοῦ διαιτητοῦ γ. Id.21.92, cf. 7.9, Lycurg.141; γ. περὶ τῆς δίκης *PHib.*1.92.13 (iii B.C.). 2. *result of investigation, decision*, *PPetr.*3p.118 (iii B.C.). II. *knowing, knowledge*, Heraclit.56; opp. ἀγνωσίη, Hp.*Vict.*1.23 (dub.); opp. ἄγνοια, Pl.*R.*478c; ἡ αἴσθησις γ. τις Arist.*GA*731^{a}33: pl., Θεὸς γνώσεων κύριος Lxx 1*Ki.*2.3. b. *higher, esoteric knowledge*, 1*Ep. Cor.*8.7, 10, *Ep.Eph.*3.19, etc.; χαρισάμενος ἡμῖν νοῦν, λόγον, γνῶσιν *PMag.Par.*2.290. 2. *acquaintance with* a person, πρός τινα Test. ap.Aeschin.1.50; τῶν Σεβαστῶν *IPE*1.47.6 (Olbia). 3. *recognizing*, Th.7.44. 4. *means of knowing*, [αἱ αἰσθήσεις] κυριώταται τῶν καθ' ἕκαστα γ. Arist.*Metaph.*981^{b}11. III. *being known*, γνῶσιν ἔχει τι, = γνωστόν ἐστι, Pl.*Tht.*206b. 2. *fame, credit*, Hdn.7.5.5, Luc.*Herod.*3. IV. *means of knowing*: hence, *statement in writing*, *PLond.*5.1708, etc. (vi A.D.). V. = γνῶμα, Hsch. s. h. v.

γνῶσμα, ατος, τό, *knowable object*, Dam.*Pr.*81.

γνωστ-εία, ἡ, *certification of identity*, *PFay.*65.5 (ii A.D.). **-έον**, *one must know*, Pl.*R.*396a. Adj. γνωστέα, τά, *things that must be known*, Gal.17(2).1. **-εύω**, *to be witness to identity* for a person, *BGU*895 (ii A.D.):—Pass., *to be certified*, ὑπό τινος *PFlor.*382.80 (iii A.D.). **-ήρ**, ῆρος, ὁ, *one that knows*: *surety*, X.*Cyr.*6.2.39, *BGU* 1032.11: *witness to identity*, *POxy.*496.16 (ii A.D.). 2. *inspector*, *PAmh.*2.139.23 (iv A.D.), *PLond.*3.1249.3 (iv A.D.). **-ης**, ου, ὁ, *one that knows*, τῶν ἐθῶν *Act.Ap.*26.3; τοῦ εὐαγγελίου *Sammelb.*421. 1 (iii A.D.): esp. *one who knows the future, diviner*, Lxx 1*Ki.*28.3. II. = γνωστήρ, *surety*, γ. τῆς πίστεως Plu.*Flam.*4; *expert witness* or *valuer*, *PLips.*106.10 (i A.D.). **-ικός**, ή, όν, *of* or *for knowing, cognitive*: ἡ -κή (sc. ἐπιστήμη), *theoretical* science (opp. πρακτική), Pl.*Plt.*258e, etc.; τὸ γ. ib.261b; ἕξεις γ. Arist.*APo.*100^{a}11 (Comp.); γ. εἰκόνες Hierocl.*in CA*25 p.475 M.: c. gen., *able to discern*, Ocell. 2.7. Adv. -κῶς Procl.*Inst.*39, Dam.*Pr.*79, Phlp.*in Ph.*241.22.

γνωστοποιός, όν, *creating the knowable*, Dam.*Pr.*80.

γνωστός, ή, όν, collat. form of γνωτός (q. v.), *known*, A.*Ch.*702, S. *OT*361, *Fr.*203, Pl.*Tht.*205d, X.*HG*2.3.44, etc.; γνωστόν, τό, *common knowledge*, τινός *PAmh.*145.9 (iv/v A.D.). Adv. -τῶς *clearly*, Lxx *Pr.*27.23, Eust.1540.1. 2. *knowable*, Arist.*Metaph.*1016^{b}20, *APo.*64^{b}37, etc.; γνωστὰ σαρκός bodily *symptoms* (of anger), Phld. *Ir.*p.24 W. II. pl., as Subst., = γνώριμοι, *notables*, Sm.*Pr.*31. 23; *acquaintance, friend*, *Ev.Luc.*2.44, al. III. Act., *knowing*, dub. in Lxx *Ge.*2.9 (γνωστικός ap.Ph.1.37).

γνωτέρα, = βαλλωτή, Ps.-Dsc.3.103 (γνοτέρα Wellm.).

γνωτός (A), ή, όν (ός, όν S.*OT*396), older and more correct form of γνωστός (Eust.400.26, 1450.62):—of things, *perceived, understood, known*, Il.7.401, Od.24.182; γνωτὰ κοὐκ ἄγνωτά μοι S.*OT*58; [μαντείαν] ἐκ θεῶν του γνωτόν ib.396. 2. of persons, *well-known*, ἐκ κάρτα βαιῶν γ. ἂν γένοιτ' ἀνήρ Id.*Fr.*282.

γνωτός (B), ἡ, *kinsman, kinswoman*, γνωτοί τε γνωταί τε *brothers* and *sisters*, Il.15.350; θάλαμον γνωτούς τε λιποῦσα 3.174, cf. 22.234; γνωτὸν μητρυιῆς 13.697; *brother*, A.R.1.53; *sister*, αὐτὴ .. γνωτή Nicaenet.1.9, cf. Nonn.*D.*3.313, al.; also, = ἐρωμένη, Hsch. (Cf. Lett. *znuots* 'son-in-law, brother-in-law', Skt. *jñātis* 'relative'.)

γνωτο-φόνος, ον, *murderer of another's brother*, Nonn.*D.*26.82:—fem. **-φόντις**, ιδος, ἡ, *murderess of a brother*, Lyc.1318.

γοάω, γοάει Mosch.3.88, -όουσι A.R.3.995, γοόωσι Q.S.2.648: Dor. 3pl. -άοντι Mosch.3.24; opt. γοάοιμεν Il.24.664; γοόωεν Od. 24.190; Ep. inf. γοήμεναι Il.14.502; part. γοόων, -όωσα 6.373, etc.: Ep. impf. γόων Od.10.567 (γόον Il.6.500 may be aor.), Ion. γοάασκεν Od.8.92: Ep. fut. γοήσομαι Il.21.124, later γοήσω *AP*7. 638 (Crin.), Nonn.*D.*2.137: aor. 1 ἐγόησα *IG*12(7).445 (Amorgos), *AP*7.599 (Jul.), 611 (Eutolm.):—**Med.**, Trag. (v. infr.) and once in Prose, X.*Cyr.*4.6.9:—**Pass.**, v. infr.:—*groan, weep*, Od.8.92, etc.: c. acc., *bewail*, Il.16.857, etc.; ὑπέρ τινος Mosch.4.83:—Med. (never in Hom. exc. in fut.), γοᾶσθε A.*Pers.*1072, cf. *Ch.*632; ὀδύρματα τὴν Ἡράκλειον ἔξοδον γοωμένην S.*Tr.*51; ἀμφί νιν γοώμενος ib.937:—Pass., γοᾶται A.*Ch.*632; μακρὰ γοηθεὶς *AP*7.371 (Crin.).

γοβρίαι· φανοί, λαμπτῆρες, Hsch.; cf. γράβιον.

γογγρίον, τό, Dim. of γόγγρος, Sch.Opp.*H.*1.113.

γογγρο-ειδής, ές, *like a conger*, Arist.*HA*505^{b}9 (Comp.). **-κτόνος**, ον, *conger-killing*, Plu.2.966a.

γόγγρος, ὁ, *conger-eel*, Antiph.26.12, Alex.15.15, Arist.*HA*571^{a} 28, etc. II. *tubercular disease in olive-trees*, Thphr.*HP*1.8.6.

γογγρύζω, *grunt*, Hsch., *EM*237.40.

γογγρώδης, ες, *like an excrescence*, ἔκφυσις Hsch. s. v. γόγγρος.

γογγρώνη, ἡ, *excrescence on the neck*, Hp.*Epid.*6.3.6, Gal.17(2).38. (Cf. γόγγρος II.)

γογγύζω, Ion. (Phryn.336) and later Gr. for Att. τονθορύζω, *mutter, murmur, grumble*, ἐπί τινι Lxx *Nu.*14.29, cf. 17.5; κατά τινος *Ev.Matt.*20.11; περί τινος *Ev.Jo.*6.41, etc.: abs., *PPetr.*3p.130 (iii B.C.), Lxx *Nu.*11.1, *POxy.*33 iii 14 (ii A.D.), Arr.*Epict.*1.29.55. 2. of doves, *coo*, Poll.5.89. (Cf. Skt. *gañgūyati* 'utter cries of joy'.)

γογγῠλάτης [ᾱ], ου, ὁ, of Zeus, *hurling balls of fire*, Lyc.435.

γογγύλη [ῠ], ἡ, = γογγυλίς, Poll.6.54; rejected by the Atticists, Phryn.81, but used in the jargon of a Scythian in Ar.*Th.*1185, also by Diocl.*Fr.*125, 141, Dsc.2.110, Gal.11.861, Str.5.4.10, *POxy.*1212. 6 (ii A.D.). II. γ. ἀγρία, *Eastern cress, Erucaria aleppica*, Dsc.l.c.

γογγῠλίδιον, τό, = καταπότιον, Hp.ap.Erot. (γογγυλίδα codd.), Gal.19.91.

γογγῠλίζω, v. γογγύλλω.

γογγῠλίς, ίδος, ἡ, *turnip, Brassica Rapa*, Ar.*Fr.*569.6, Eub.4 (pl., Id.74), Speus.ap.Ath.9.369b, Thphr.*HP*7.4.3, *PPetr.*3p.152 (iii B.C.), Dsc.5.20, *POxy.*736.5 (i A.D.).

γογγύλλω, *round* (μεταστρέφει Suid.), Ar.*Th.*56 (Pors. for γογγυλίζει); cf. γογγυλεῖν· συστρεφεῖν (perh. συστρέψειν), Hsch.

γογγῠλοειδής, ές, *roundish*, Sch.Nic.*Th.*855. Adv. -δῶς Dsc.5.18.

γογγῠλό-ρυγχος, ον, *with round nozzle*, *PMag.Par.*1.2183. **-σπάρᾰγον** [πᾰ], τό, *turnip-tops*, *Gp.*12.1.8.

γογγύλος [ῠ], η, ον, = στρογγύλος, *round*, A.*Fr.*199.7, S.*Ichn.*297, Pl.*Cra.*427c; [μᾶζα] Ar.*Pax* 28; λίθος ἄθετος *IG*1^{2}.372.22; ἐλαῖαι Plb. 12.2.4: Comp. -ώτερος Ath.4.139a. 2. = σκληρός, Hsch. II. Subst. γόγγῠλος, ὁ, (proparox. acc. to Hdn.Gr.1.164) = κόνδυλος, Sch.Lyc.435. 2. = ὄλυνθος, Nic.*Th.*855. (Redupl. form from root of γαυλός, γύλιος, etc.)

γογγυλόσκηνος, ον, *having a round body* (cf. σκῆνος), Hsch., *EM* 238.44; *having a round house*, Hsch. (Perh. epith. of a mollusc.)

γογγῠλ-ώδης, ες, *roundish*, Sch.Ar.*Pax* 788. **-ώματα**· στρογγυλεύματα, Hsch. **-ωπός**, όν, *round-faced, stout-looking*, Id. **-ωτόν**· *rapatum*, *Gloss.*

γόγγ-ῠσις, εως, ἡ, = sq., Lxx *Nu.* 14.27. **-υσμός**, ὁ, *murmuring, muttering, grumbling*, Anaxandr. 31, M.Ant. 9.37, Lxx *Ex.* 16.7–9, *Act.Ap.* 6.1, *Cat.Cod.Astr.* 7.139. **-ῠσος**, ὁ, = γογγυστής, Thd. *Pr.* 16.28, Hdn.Gr. 1.213. **-υστής**, οῦ, ὁ, *murmurer, mutterer, grumbler*, *Ep.Jud.* 16, Thd.*Pr.* 26.20. **-υστικός**, ή, όν, *inclined to murmur*, in Adv. -κῶς Erot. s. v. τρύζειν, *EM* 771.11.

γόγγων· μωρός, Hsch. **γόδα**, τά, = ἔντερα (Maced.), Id. **γοδᾶν**· κλαίειν (Cypr.), Id. **γόδατος**· θήρα, Id. **γοδόν**· γόητα, Id. **γοδοῦλος**, v. γοιδοῦλος.

γο-εδνός, ή, όν, = sq. 1, A.*Pers.* 1057 (lyr.), *Supp.* 73 (lyr.), 194. II. = sq. II, Id.*Pers.* 1039 (lyr.). **-ερός**, ά, όν, (γόος) of things, *mournful, distressful*, θρῆνοι Erinna 6.8 codd.; πάθη A.*Ag.* 1176 (lyr.); δάκρυα E.*Ph.* 1567 (lyr.); τὸ γ. καὶ ἡσύχιον μέλος Arist.*Pr.* 922ᵇ19. II. of persons, *wailing, lamenting*, ἥξει τι μέλος γοερὸν γοεραῖς E.*Hec.* 84; of the nightingale, Call.*Lav.Pall.* 94. Adv. -ρῶς D.T. 629.21, Eust. 1147.9. **-εροστ....ηνολαλήμων**, ονος, *uttering plaintive... notes*, ἀηδών Lyr. in *Philol.* 80.336. **-ήμεναι**, v. γοάω. **-ήμων**, ον, gen. ονος, = γοερός 1, φωνή *APl.* 4.101, Nonn.*D.* 11.196. II. = γ. II, ib. 20.162; κύνες ib. 5.454. **-ηρός**, ά, όν, poet. for γοερός, Lyc. 1057, *Epigr.Gr.* 790.7 (Dyme).

γόης, ητος, ὁ, *sorcerer, wizard*, Phoronis 2, Hdt. 2.33, 4.105, Pl.*R.* 380d, Phld.*Ir.* p. 29 W.; γ. ἐπῳδὸς Λυδίας ἀπὸ χθονός E.*Ba.* 234, cf. *Hipp.* 1038; prob. f.l. for βοῇσι Hdt. 7.191. 2. *juggler, cheat*, δεινὸς γ. καὶ φαρμακεὺς καὶ σοφιστής Pl.*Smp.* 203d; δεινὸν καὶ γ. καὶ σοφιστὴν.. ὀνομάζων D. 18.276; ἄπιστος γ. πονηρός Id. 19.109; μάγος καὶ γ. Aeschin. 3.137: Comp. γοητότερος Ach.Tat. 6.7 (s. v. l.). (Cf. Lith. *žavėti* 'incantare'.)

γοησίοδος· ᾠδός (leg. γοησιῳδός), ἀπατεών, Hsch.

γοητ-εία, ἡ, *witchcraft, jugglery*, γ. καὶ μαγεία Gorg.*Hel.* 10, cf. Pl. *Smp.* 203a: metaph., οὐδὲν ὑγιές, ἀλλὰ γ. τις Id.*R.* 584a, Andronic. Rhod. p. 573 M., etc.; ἀπάτη καὶ γ. Plb. 4.20.5, cf. Luc.*Nigr.* 15; γ. τῆς ὑποκρίσεως D.S. 1.76; ἡδονῆς δι' ὀμμάτων Plu. 2.961d; in a milder sense, '*finesse*', Cic.*Att.* 9.13.4; ἡ τῆς φύσεως γ. the *magic* of Nature, Plot. 4.4.44. **-ευμα**, ατος, τό, *spell, charm*, Pl.*Phlb.* 44c, Alciphr. 3.17, Ael. *NA* 3.17, Agath.*Praef.*; τὸ γ. τῆς φύσεως Porph.*Abst.* 1.43. **-ευσις**, εως, ἡ, *sorcery*, Plot. 4.4.43. **-ευτικός**, ή, όν, = γοητικός, Porph.*VP* 39, Poll. 4.48. Adv. -κῶς ib. 51. **-εύτρια**, ἡ, *sorceress*, Eust. 881.62. **-εύω**, *bewitch, beguile*, Pl.*Grg.* 483e, etc.:—Pass., Id.*R.* 412e, 413b, D. 19.102, etc.; *fascinate*, as a snake, Plot. 4.4.40. 2. abs., *play the wizard*, D.L. 8.59. **-ής**, οῦ, ὁ, *wailer*, γοητῶν νόμον A.*Ch.* 822 codd. (γοατάν Herm.), cf. Tim.*Pers.* 112. **-ικός**, ή, όν, (γόης) *skilled in witchcraft, juggling*, ἡ γ. μαγεία Arist.*Fr.* 36. Adv. -κῶς Poll. 4.51:—pecul. fem. **γοῆτις** μορφή *bewitching*, *AP* 12.192 (Strat.). **γοητός** (sic) is prob. f.l. for foreg. in *PHib.* 52.18 (iii B. C.).

γοῖ, γοῖ, to imitate the sound of pigs *grunting*, *AP* 11.327 (Antip. Thess.). II. γοῖ (i. e. ϝοῖ)· αὐτῷ, Hsch.

γοῖδα (i. e. ϝοῖδα)· οἶδα, Hsch. (prob. l.). **γοίδημι**· ἐπίσταμαι, Id. **γοιδοῦλος**· λαλιός, οἱ δὲ **γοδοῦλος**, Id. **γοιδύες**· ῥυτῆρες, Id. **γοίνακες**· βλαστοί, Id. **γοινά(ρ)υτις** (ϝοῖνος, ἀρύτω)· οἰνοχόη, Id. **γοινέες**· κόρακες, Id. **γοῖνος**· οἶνος, Id. **γοῖσος**· μέλαν, πλατύ, Id., cf. *EM* 238.45: **γοισοῦται**· πλατύνεται κτλ., *EM* 237.51. **γοῖτα**· οἶς (leg. ὗς), Hsch.; cf. γοῖ. **γοιταί**· κριθαί, γράστις, Id. **γοῖτος**· ῥύπος, πάθος, Id., cf. *EM* 51.17. **Γοιτόσυρος**, = Οἰτόσυρος (q. v.), Hsch. **γόλαμος**· διωγμός, Id. **γόλανα**· ἀγκύλη, ἀντιλαβεύς, Id. **γόλησις**· κακοδαιμονία, Id. **γόλλακα**· λάκκον, Id. **γόλμις**, = ψάρος, Id. **γολμοί**· στολμοί, Id. **γολοινά**· χλωρά, ἡ **γολονά**, Id. **γολομένη**, name of a *plant*, Id. **γολύριον**· κέλυφος (Tarent.), Id.

γομάριον, τό, Dim. of γόμος 2, *PFlor.* 274.5 (iii A. D.).

γόμνη· ὀρίγανον, Hsch.

γόμος, ὁ, (γέμω) *ship's freight, cargo*, A.*Supp.* 444 (dub.), D. 32.4; πεντακισχιλίων ταλάντων γόμον ἔχειν to be of 5,000 talents *burden*, Hdt. 1.194. 2. *beast's load*, Babr. 7.11, Lxx *Ex.* 23.5, al., *PAmh.* 2.138.11 (pl., iv A. D.); γ. καμηλικός *OGI* 629.87, al. (Palmyra, ii A. D.); γ. καρρικός ib. 16. 3. *guild of transport-agents* in Nubia, *CIG* 4980, al. II. γόμος· ζωμός, Hsch.

γομοφόρος, ον, *bearing loads*, *Gloss.*

γομόω, *load*, γομώσων τὸν ὄνον Babr. 111.9, cf. *PFlor.* 129.5 (iii A. D.), etc.:—Pass., ἅμαξα ξύλων γεγομωμένη *Edict.Diocl.* 14.8.

γομφ-αλγία, ἡ, *toothache*, Dsc. 4.164 (pl.). **-άριον**, τό, = κεστρεύς, Tz.ad Lyc. 664, Sch.Opp.*H.* 1.112, 3.339.

γομφι-άζω, *have pain in the back teeth* or *gnash* them, γ. τοὺς ὀδόντας Lxx *Si.* 30.10. 2. of the teeth, *suffer pain*, ib.*Ez.* 18.2. **-ᾰσις**, εως, ἡ, *toothache* or *gnashing of teeth*, Dsc. 2.59 (pl.). **-ασμός**, ὁ, Lxx *Am.* 4.6.

γομφιόδουπος, ον, *rattling in the teeth*, χαλινός *AP* 6.233 (Maec.).

γομφ-ίος (sc. ὀδούς), ὁ, more Att. than μύλος, Moer. 111: (γόμφος): —*grinder-tooth, molar*, chiefly in pl., Hp.*Epid.* 5.100, Hdt. 9.83, Ar. *Pax* 34, etc.; ψοφεῖ δ' ὁ γ. Epich. 21; γομφίους συγκρούων with his *teeth* chattering, Babr. 92.8; opp. προσθίος, X.*Mem.* 1.4.6, Arist.*PA* 661ᵇ8. II. *tooth of a key*, Ar.*Th.* 423. **-ίτης** [ῑ], ου, ὁ (fort. sc. νάρδος), a kind of στύραξ, Aet. 1.131, Steph. in *Hp.* 2.460 D.

γομφό-δετος, ον, *nail-bound*, δόρει A.*Supp.* 846 (lyr.). **-πᾰγής**, ές, *fastened with bolts*: metaph., *creaky*, ῥήματα γομφοπαγῆ, of the long compound words of Aeschylus, Ar.*Ra.* 824.

γόμφος, ὁ, *bolt*, for ship-building, Od. 5.248; for other uses, Hes. *Op.* 431, A.*Th.* 542; *dowel*, *SIG* 246 ii 40 (Delph., iv B. C.); γόμφοις καὶ περόνησιν ἀρηρότε Parm. 1.20; γόμφῳ ἢ κόλλῃ ἢ ἁφῇ Arist.*Ph.* 227ᵃ17, cf. *Metaph.* 1052ᵃ24: generally, *bond, fastening*, as of the *cross-ribs* of Egyptian canoes, Hdt. 2.96; of the ankle-joint, Arist.*PA* 654ᵇ21; of the invisible *bonds* uniting the particles of the body, Pl.*Ti.* 43a: metaph., γ. κατάστοργοι, of love, Emp. 87; τῶνδ' ἐφήλωται.. γόμφος διαμπάξ these things are *determined*, A.*Supp.* 945:—acc. to *EM* 238.4, γ. were prop. of wood; but cf. γ. χαλκοῖ *IG* 9(1).691 (Corc.), γ. σιδηροῖ Plb. 13.7.9. 2. *instrument for cautery*, *Hippiatr.* 97. 3. = γόμφιος, Hsch. II. *sea-fish*, = γομφάριον, *Gloss.* (Cf. Skt. *jámbhas* 'tooth', Lith. *žam̃bas* 'edge of a beam', etc.)

γομφ-όω, *fasten with bolts* or *nails*, esp. of ships, ἴκρια γομφώσαντες Nonn.*D.* 40.447:—mostly in Pass., γεγόμφωται σκάφος the ship's hull *is ready built*, A.*Supp.* 440, cf. Ar.*Eq.* 463, *AP* 11.248 (Bianor). II. metaph., *curdle*, γάλα λευκὸν ἐγόμφωσεν Emp. 33. **-ωμα**, ατος, τό, *that which is fastened by bolts, frame-work*, Plu.*Marc.* 15. 2. = γόμφος, Id. 2.321d, Longus 2.26. 3. metaph., κλειδῶν ἀχαλκεύτων γ. Vett.Val. 334.11 (pl.). **-ωσις**, εως, ἡ, *bolting together*, Sch. Theoc. 7.105. II. a mode of *articulation*, Gal. 2.738. 2. *framework* of the body, Eun.*VS* p. 474 B. **-ωτήρ**, ῆρος, ὁ, *a ship-builder*, *AP* 9.31 (Zelot.). II. *surgical instrument for excising bone*, Antyll.ap.Orib. 44.23.15. **-ωτήριον**, τό, *tenon*, *IG* 11(2).163 *A* 14 (Delos, iii B. C.), Hero *Aut.* 27.1; gloss on τέρετρα, Sch.Od. 5.246. **-ωτικός**, ή, όν, *of* or *fastening with nails*: ἡ -κή (sc. τέχνη), *the joiner's art, carpentry*, Pl.*Plt.* 280d. **-ωτός**, ή, όν, *fastened with bolts*: πλοῖα γ. ships *slightly put together*, so that they could be taken to pieces, Str. 16.1.11, cf. Aristeas 71.

γόμωσις, εως, ἡ, *loading*, ξύλων *PFlor.* 203.4 (iii A. D.).

γονάρ· μήτρα (Lacon.), Hsch.: **γονάδες**· μῆτραι, Id.

γονᾰτ-ίζω, *thrust with the knee*, Cratin. 399. II. *bend the knee*, Aq.*Ge.* 24.11, 41.43. III. σφυγμὸς γονατίζων, term coined by Archig.ap.Gal. 8.665. **-ιον**, τό, Dim. of γόνυ, Heliod.ap.Orib. 48.66.3, Ruf.ap.eund. 49.34.1, *POxy.* 52.17 (iv A. D.). 2. *hip-joint, groin*, Luc.*Asin.* 10, cf. Ph. 2.479, Sch.Nic.*Th.* 541, Ptol.*Alm.* 8.1, etc. II. = γύης 1, Procl.ad Hes.*Op.* 425, *Et.Gud.* III. *knot* or *joint* of a reed, Tz.*H.* 7.741.

γονᾰτόδεσμος, ὁ, *knee-band*, *Gloss.*

γονᾰτ-όομαι, Pass., *become* or *be jointed*, of grasses, reeds, etc., Thphr.*HP* 8.2.4, Dsc. 3.51. **-ώδης**, ες, *with joints*, Thphr.*HP* 1.5.3, Dsc. 1.1, 4.29.

γονάω, = γεννάω, Hsch.

γον-εά, Cret. = γενεά, *GDI* 5112 (Phaestus). **-εία**, ἡ, *generation*, Hdn.*Epim.* 16. **-εύς**, έως, ὁ, *begetter, father*, mostly in pl., *parents*, *h.Cer.* 240, Hes.*Op.* 235, Pi.*P.* 6.27, Pl.*Smp.* 178b, etc.: in sg., of a serpent, Hdt. 3.109; of a man, Pl.*R.* 457d; φράζε τίνος γονέως *IG* 12(5).310: generally, *progenitor, ancestor*, πέμπτος γ. *ancestor* in the fifth generation, Hdt. 1.91, cf. Is. 8.32; οἱ ἄνωθεν γ. Arist.*GA* 722ᵃ8. (Nom. pl. γονεῖες *Histria* 7.27: acc. pl. γονέας Antiph. 261: dat. pl. γονεῖσι *SIG* 1267.24 (Ios, iii A. D.).) **-εύω**, *produce, engender*, καρπούς Thphr. *CP* 1.14.1; ἀὴρ [σκώληκας] γονεύων Id.*HP* 8.10.5; of animals, Plu. 2.980d:—Pass., ib. 981d.

γονή, ἡ, (γενέσθαι) *offspring*, οἱ οὔ τι παίδων γ. γένετο κρειόντων Il. 24.539; γ. Ἀρκεισιάδαο Od. 4.755; τέκνων δίπτυχος γ. two *children*, E.*Med.* 1136: pl., εἰσὶ χἀτέροις γοναὶ κακαί S.*OC* 1192; γ. κατηκόους φύσαντες Id.*Ant.* 641; of animals, ταύρων γοναί A.*Fr.* 194; ἐν.. τετρασκελεῖ γ., i. e. among quadrupeds, S.*Fr.* 941.10; *fruits* of the earth, Pl.*Ax.* 371c. 2. *race, stock, family*, A.*Ag.* 1565 (lyr.); ὦ γονῇ γενναῖε S.*OT* 1469, cf. *El.* 156 (lyr.); ἁ Δαρδάνου γ. E.*Tr.* 1290: pl., μηδὲν ὢν γοναῖσι S.*Aj.* 1094; *parentage*, ἐξευρεῖν γονάς E.*Ion* 328. 3. *generation*, τριταίσιν ἐν γ. Pi.*P.* 4.143; τρίτος.. πρὸς δέκ' ἄλλαισιν γ. A.*Pr.* 774; τριτοσπόρῳ γονῇ Id.*Pers.* 818. II. *that which engenders, seed*, Hes.*Op.* 733, Hdt. 3.101, 109, Hp.*Genit.* 3, Arist.*GA* 726ᵃ18, etc.: pl., Pi.*N.* 7.84, S.*Ant.* 950 (lyr.). 2. *organs of generation*, generally, Hp.*Art.* 45, *Mochl.* 1 (also restricted to the *womb*, Ruf.*Onom.* 193, Gal. 2.889); πρὶν.. μητρὸς ἐκ γονῆς μολεῖν E.*Ph.* 1597. III. *act of generation*, Pi.*I.* 7(6).7; κατὰ φύσιν γονὰς ποιεῖσθαι Aeschin. 3.111. 2. of the mother, *child-birth*, E.*Ph.* 355, Theoc. 17.44. 3. of the child, *birth*, ἐκ γονῆς Hp.*Epid.* 4.31; γονῇ φῦναι γεραιτέρα S. *OC* 1294; γοναὶ ζῴων Arist.*Mu.* 399ᵃ28. 4. cure for sterility, Paul. Aeg. 3.74. IV. Pythag. name for *unity*, *Theol.Ar.* 6.

γόνημα, ατος, τό, = γένημα, *PLond.* 1.125.17.

γονής· νάρκισσος, Hsch.

γόνθος, = κόγχος, Hdn.Gr. 1.144.

γονιαῖος, *molaris*, *Gloss.* (leg. γομφ-).

γονίας χειμών, in A.*Ch.* 1067 (anap.), acc. to Hsch. εὐχερής, a *fair wind*; but, acc. to the Sch., ὅταν ἐξ εὐδίας κινηθῇ χαλεπὸν πνεῦμα.

γονικόθεν, Adv. *by inheritance from parents*, *PMasp.* 151.182 (vi A. D.).

γονικός, ή, όν, (γονή II. 1) *of the seed*, γ. ἔκκρισις Arist.*Pr.* 879ᵇ28. 2. *ancestral*, νόμοι Tim.*Lex.* s. v. πατρονομούμενοι.

γόνιμος, ον, also η, ον Hp.*Vict.* 1.25, Isyll. 53:—*productive, fertile, fruitful*, σπέρμα γ., opp. ἄγονον, Arist.*HA* 523ᵃ25; κύημα γ. Id.*GA* 736ᵃ35; ᾠὰ γ., opp. ὑπηνέμια, ib. 730ᵃ6; of women, Id.*Pr.* 876ᵇ12; of the male, Id.*HA* 546ᵃ2, al.; ἐν τῇσι ἡλικίῃσι τῇσι γονίμῃσι εἶναι Hp.l.c.; γ. μέλεα a *parent's* limbs, E.*El.* 1209 (lyr.); γ. φλέψ *AP* 6.218 (Alc.); γ. μέρεα *generative* organs, Aret.*SD* 2.5: hence (metaph.), ἀπο τίκτειν γ. τε καὶ ἀληθές Pl.*Tht.* 150c; γ. ἢ ἀνεμιαῖον ib. 151e; Νεῖλος γ., opp. πέλαγος, *Lyr.Alex.Adesp.* 32.6, cf. *Sammelb.* 2074 (Sup.). Adv. -μως, σπέρμα ἐν τῇ μήτρᾳ γ. κρατηθῆναι Porph.*Gaur.* 2.2. 2. c. gen. rei, νέφος γ. ὕδατος Arist.*Mu*.394^{a}27, cf. Thphr.*Ign*.44, Ael.*NA*7.5: metaph., πηγαὶ τῆς ὑψηγορίας γονιμώταται Longin.8.1. 3. metaph. of persons, ποιητὴς γ. poet *of true genius*, Ar.*Ra*.96; γονιμωτέρα γενέσθω ἡ γλῶσσα Luc.*Rh.Pr*.23. b. *born in lawful wedlock*, Man.6.56: metaph., ἀγαθὰ γ. τῇ αὐτῶν φύσει Pl.*R*.367d; γ. ὕδωρ ποταμῶν, opp. νόθον, *AP*9.277 (Antiph.). 4. = βιώσιμος, *viable*, παιδίον Hp. *Superf*.4; ἔμβρυον Arist.*HA*583^{b}31; βρέφη Ph.1.45. 5. *favourable to generation*, of uneven days, Pythagorean term, Plu.2.288c; of days in illness (because critical for life or death, Erot.s.v.), Hp. *Epid*.2.6.8, 2.5.12; γ. μήν, ἔτος, ib.6.10.

γονιμότης, ητος, ἡ, *vitality*, of the embryo, *Theol.Ar*.47, Simp.*in Ph*.503.31. 2. *generative power*, Dam.*Pr*.108.

γονιμώδης, ες, *fruitful*, Orph.*H*.55.19.

γονο-ειδής, ές, *like seed*, Hp.*Epid*.2.3.11, Aret.*SA*2.12, *SD*2.11. **-εις**, εσσα, εν, *fruitful*, Nic.*Al*.101, *Hymn.Is*.1. **-κτονέω**, *murder one's child*, Ps.-Plu.*Fluv*.22.1. **-κτονία**, ἡ, *murder of parents*, *Gloss*. **-ποιέω**, *impregnate*, Aët.16.17; *make fruitful*, Al.*Le*.26.9, *Gp*.19.4, Sch.Lyc.899. **-ποιΐα**, *production of offspring*, Alex.Aphr.*Pr*.2.68. **-πώτης**, ου, ὁ, *qui semen bibit*, Man.4.311 (pl.). **-ρροια**, ἡ, (ῥέω) *spermatorrhoea*, Antyll.ap.Orib.6.1.5, Aret. *SD*2.5, Sor.ap.Cael.Aur.*CP*3.18. II. in women, *blennorrhagia*, Aret.*SD*2.11. **-ρροϊκός**, ή, όν, *suffering from* or *subject to*, Antyll.ap.Orib.6.22.3, J.*BJ*6.9.3 (v.l. -οιοις); πάθος Ruf.*Sat.Gon*.15. **-ρρυέω**, *to be subject to spermatorrhoea*, Lxx *Le* 22.4 (v.l.), Sch. Nic.*Th*.721. **-ρρυής**, ές, = γονορροϊκός, Lxx *Le*.15.4, al., Ph.1.88.

γόνον· μίτον, Hsch. (leg. τόνον).

γόνος, ὁ, and (in signf. 1) ἡ, E.*IA*793: late Ion. **γοῦνος** Aret.*CD*2.5: —*that which is begotten, child*, Il.5.635, 6.191; *offspring*, 20.409, Hes. *Th*.919, etc.; ἄπαις ἔρσενος γόνου Hdt.1.109; πρεσβύτατος παντὸς τοῦ γ. Id.7.2; αὐτὸν καὶ γόνον *Schwyzer*415 (Elis); ὁ Πηλέως γ. his *son*, S.*Ph*.333, cf. 366, 416, etc.; of animals, γ. ὀρταλίχων Id.*Fr*.793; of fish, *roe*, Hegem.1, Archestr.*Fr*.9; of bees, Arist.*HA*554^{a}18. 2. *product*, of plants, γ. ἀμπέλου *Anacreont*.54.7; γ. πλουτόχθων, of the silver mines at Laureion, A.*Eu*.946 (lyr.); τοῦ φόρου τὸν γ. Ar.*V*.1116 codd. 3. ἐς ἔρσενα γόνον to any of the male *sex*, Hdt.6.135. II. *race, stock, descent*, οὔ πώ τις ἑὸν γ. αὐτὸς ἀνέγνω Od.1.216, cf. 11.234. III. *begetting, procreation*, A.*Supp*.172 (lyr.); γόνῳ πατήρ, opp. ποιητός, Lys.13.91; γόνῳ γεγονώς D.44.49; γ. υἱός Men.*Sam*.131, D.C.40.51, cf. *IG*3.1445, al. 2. of plants, *bearing*, Thphr.*CP*3.15.3. IV. *seed*, Hp.*Genit*.7, Arist.*GA*748^{a}22, Lxx *Le*.15.3; σπέρμα καὶ γ. Ti.Locr.100b, cf. Gal.19.450. 2. *genitals*, Hp.*Liqu*.2. V. γ. Ἑρμοῦ, = βούφθαλμος, Ps.-Dsc.3.139.

γονοτύλη [ῠ], ἡ, *callus on the knee*, Hsch.

γόνυ, τό, gen. γόνατος, Ep. and Ion. γούνατος (for γόνϝατος) Il.21.591, Hdt.2.80: pl. nom. γούνατα Il.5.176, Hes.*Op*.587, Hdt.1.199, *Schwyzer*694.7 (Chios, iv B.C.), gen. γουνάτων Hdt.9.76, dat. γούνασι Il.9.455, Hdt.4.152 (also Pi.*I*.2.26), γονάτεσσι Theoc.16.11, *Epigr.Gr*.782 (Halic.); also Ep. gen. γουνός (expl. as for γόνυος by Hdn.Gr.2.768, A.D.*Synt*.342.9) Il.11.547: pl. γοῦνα 6.511; γούνων 1.407, al.: dat. γούνεσσι 9.488, al. (v.l. γούνασσι):—Aeol. acc. pl. γόνα Alc.39.7 (prob.), but γόννα acc. to St.Byz. s.v. Γόννοι, Eust.335.39: gen. pl. γόνων Alc.*Supp*.10: E. has γουνάτων *Hec*.752, 839, γούνασι *Supp*.285 (lyr.), *Andr*.529 (lyr.), but not γουνός (γοῦν' acc. pl. was read by Sch. in *Ph*.852): gen. pl. γεύνων, Hsch.:—*knee*, γόνυ γουνὸς ἀμείβων Il.11.547, etc.: freq. of *clasping the knees* in earnest supplication, ἥψατο γούνων 1.512; ἑλεῖν, λαβεῖν γούνων 21.71, 1.407, etc.; τῶν γουνάτων λαβέσθαι Hdt.9.76; ποτὶ (v.l. περὶ) or ἀμφὶ γούνασί τινος χεῖρας βαλεῖν Od.6.310, 7.142; περὶ γόνυ χέρας ἱκεσίους ἔβαλον E.*Or*.1414, cf. *Ph*.1622, etc.; τὰ σὰ γούναθ' ἱκάνομαι Il.18.457, cf. Od.7.147, etc.; κιχανόμενοι τὰ σὰ γοῦνα ἱκόμεθ' 9.266; ἀντίος ἤλυθε γούνων Il.20.463; γόνυ σὸν ἀμπίσχειν χερί E.*Supp*.165; σοῖς προστίθημι γόνασιν ὠλένας Id.*Andr*.895; ἐς γούνατά τινι or τινος πεσεῖν Hdt.5.86, S.*OC*1607; ἀμφὶ γόνυ τινὸς πίπτειν E.*Hec*.787; γόνυ τινός or πρὸς γόνυ προσπίπτειν ib.339, *HF*79; γόνασί τινος προσπίπτειν Id.*Or*.1332 (but προσπίτνω σε γόνασιν *on my knees*, S.*Ph*.485); πίπτειν πρὸς τὰ γ. τινος, τινι, Lys.1.19, D.19.198; also γούνων λίσσεσθαι Il.9.451; ἐλλιτανεύειν Od.10.481; γουνάζεσθαι Il.22.345; ἄντεσθαι πρὸς τῶν γονάτων E.*Med*.710; ἱκετεῦσαι πρὸς τ. γ. D.58.70. 2. of a sitting posture, φημί μιν ἀσπασίως γ. κάμψειν will be glad to bend *the knee* so as to sit down and rest, Il.7.118, cf. 19.72; but also, bow *the knee* in submission, ἐμοὶ κάμψει (intr.) πᾶν γ. Lxx *Is*.45.23; γ. ὀκλάζειν τινί ib.3*Ki*.19.18, v. sub κάμπτω: ἐπὶ γούνασι *on* one's *knees*, ἐπὶ γούνασι πατρὸς Il.22.500; ποτὶ γ. 5.408; γούνασιν ἐφέσσεσθαι φίλον υἱόν 9.455; σ' ἐπ' ἐμοῖσι.. γούνεσσι καθίσσας 9.488; τόν ῥά οἱ.. ἐπὶ γούνασι θῆκεν Od.19.401; ἐν τοῖς γόνασί τινος στρέφεσθαι Pl.*R*.617b; πέπλον.. θεῖναι Ἀθηναίης ἐπὶ γούνασιν to lay it on her *lap* (as an offering), Il.6.92, cf. *Schwyzer* l.c.: hence metaph., θεῶν ἐν γούνασι κεῖται it rests *in the lap of* .., Il.17.514, Od.1.267, etc.; but ἐν γούνασιν πίτνοντα Νίκας victorious, Pi.*I*.2.26. 3. of the knees as the seat of strength, ἐν δὲ βίην ὤμοισι καὶ ἐν γούνεσσιν ἔθηκε Il.17.569; of swiftness, λαιψηρὰ γ. 22.204, etc.; γούνατά τινος λύειν disable, kill him, 5.176, etc.; ὑπὸ γούνατ' ἔλυσεν 11.579; βλάπτειν γ. τινι, κάματος δ' ὑπὸ γ. ἐδάμνα, 7.271, 21.52:—Pass., αὐτοῦ λύτο γούνατα 21.114, etc. 4. metaph., ἐς γόνυ βάλλειν bring down upon *the knee*, i.e. humble, conquer, Hdt.6.27; ἐς γ. ῥίπτειν, κλίνειν, App.*BC*3.20, 30; ἐς γ. ἐλθεῖν Procop.*Arc*.14, *Pers*.1.17; Ἀσία δὲ χθὼν.. ἐπὶ γόνυ κέκλιται A.*Pers*.931 (lyr.). 5. prov., ἀπωτέρω ἢ γόνυ κνάμα 'blood is thicker than water', 'charity begins at home', Theoc.16.18; γ. κνήμης ἔγγιον Arist.*EN*1168^{b}8, Ath.9.383b. II. *joint* of grasses or plants, Hdt.3.98, X.*An*.4.5.26, Thphr.*HP*8.2.4, Porph.*Antr*.19. (Cf. Skt. *jā́nu*, Lat. *genu*, etc.)

γονῠ-αλγής, ές, *suffering pain in the knee*, Hp.*Epid*.6.4.11. **-καμψεπίκυρτος**, ον, *twisting the knee awry*, of the gout, Luc.*Trag*.203. **-κανσαγρύπνα**, ἡ, *keeping awake by inflammation of the knee*, ib.201. **-κλῐνέω**, *bend the knee*, Eust.669.32. **-κλῐνής**, ές, *on bended knee*, γ. ἐχόμενός τινος *POxy*.1089.31 (iii A.D.). **-κλῐτέω**, = γονυκλινέω, Simp.*in Epict*.p.107 D. **-κροτος**, ον, *knocking the knees together*, of the gait of women, Arist.*HA*538^{b}10 (Comp.); of effeminate men, Anacr.144, Arist.*Phgn*.808^{a}13, 810^{a}34. **-πετέω**, *fall on the knee*, Plb.15.29.9, etc. 2. *fall down before* one, τινά *Ev.Matt*.17.14, cf. *Ev.Marc*.1.40: abs., Corn.*ND*12. **-πετής**, ές, (πεσεῖν) *falling on the knee*, Tim.*Pers*.189; ἕδραι γ. a *kneeling* posture, E.*Ph*.293. **-πλήξ**, *ruscus*, *Gloss*.

γονώδης, ες, = γονοειδής, Hp.*Coac*.446.

γονώνη· ὀρίγανος, Hsch. **γόον**, v. γοάω.

γόος, ὁ, *weeping, wailing*, σχέθε δ' ὄσσε γόοιο Od.4.758; also of *louder signs of grief*, ib.103; ἐρικλάγκταν γόον Pi.*P*.12.21; ἀρίδακρυς γ., πολύδακρυς γ., A.*Pers*.949 (lyr.), *Ch*.449 (lyr.); γόους δακρύειν S.*Aj*.579; οἰκτρᾶς γ. ὄρνιθος, of the nightingale, ib.629 (lyr.); γ. τινός *grief for* one, Q.S.3.644; so γόους πρὸς αὐτὴν [τούτων] θησόμεσθ', ἃ πάσχομεν *for* our sufferings, E.*Or*.1121: in late Prose, Lxx 3*Ma*.1.18 (pl.), al.

γοράπιες· ῥάφανοι, Hsch. **γοράτου**· ἠφινόν, οἱ δὲ ῥανῶ, Id.

Γοργάς, άδος, ἡ, = Γοργώ, Phot. s.v. πλόκιον Γοργάδος: pl., E. *Hyps.Fr*.41(64).77. 2. ἡ παλίμφρων Γ., of Hera, Lyc.1349. II. in pl., *sea-nymphs*, S.*Fr*.163:—also **Γοργίδες**, Hsch.

Γόργειος, α, ον, *of* or *belonging to the Gorgon*, Γοργείη κεφαλή Il.5.741, Od.11.634; Γόργειον, τό, *a Tragic mask*, *EM*238.46, Poll.10.167, etc.

γοργεύω, *move rapidly, hasten*, Sm.*Ec*.10.10, Hsch. 2. *busy oneself*, τινί or μετά τινος *PPar*.18.6.12 (ii A.D.).

γοργία, *agilitas*, *Gloss*.

Γοργῐ-άζω, *speak like Gorgias*, Philostr.*VS*1.16.2. **-ειος**, ον, *of Gorgias, Gorgias-like*, ῥήματα X.*Smp*.2.26; σχήματα D.H.*Dem*.5; of vases, *called after one Gorgias*, *IG*11(2).128.31, al. (Delos, iii B.C.).

Γοργολόφας, ου, ὁ, *he of the Gorgon-crest*, Ar.*Ach*.567:—fem. **Γοργολόφα**, ης, ἡ, Id.*Eq*.1181.

Γοργονεία (sc. λίθος), ἡ, *coral*, Plin.*HN*37.164: **Γοργονιὰς** βοτάνη, *Gorgon-like plant*, Dam.*Isid*.68.

Γοργόνειος, ον, = Γόργειος, πεδία A.*Pr*.793; τὸ Γ. *a Gorgon-mask*, *IG*2.654, al., cf. Plu.*Them*.10; *the Gorgon's head*, a group of stars in Perseus, Gem.3.11, Ptol.*Alm*.7.5, etc., Plu.*Them*.10; but also, the constellation *Medusa*, Hipparch.2.3.27, al.; *bogey*, Ruf.ap.Orib.*inc*.20.27; Orphic name for the *moon*, because of the face in it, Orph.*Fr*.33. II. Γ., τό, = λιθόσπερμον, Ps.-Dsc.3.141.

Γοργόνη, ἡ, = Γοργώ, Hdn.*Epim*.17, Suid.

Γοργόνιον, τό, = ἠρύγγη, Ps.-Dsc.3.21.

Γοργονώδης, ες, *Gorgon-like*, Sch.E.*Ph*.146.

Γοργόνωτος ἀσπίδος κύκλος, ἡ, a shield *with the Gorgon on it*, Ar.*Ach*.1124.

γοργόομαι, Pass., *to be spirited*, of a horse, X.*Eq*.10.4.

γοργός, ή, όν, *grim, fierce, terrible*, γ. ὄμμ' ἔχων, of Parthenopaeus, A.*Th*.537; ὄμμασι γοργός E.*Ph*.146 (lyr.); τοῖς κερτομοῦσι γοργὸν ὡς ἀναβλέπει looks *fiercely* at.., dub. l. in Id.*Supp*.322; γοργότεροι ἰδεῖν, δρᾶσθαι, *terrible* to behold, X.*Cyr*.4.4.3, *Smp*.1.10; γοργὸν βλέπειν look *terrible*, Ael.*VH*2.44; of horses, γ. ἰδεῖν X.*Eq*.10.17; ἵππου γ. βλέμμα Poll.1.192; in Ephebic Inscrr., φίλοι, γοργοί, γνήσιοι, *IG*3.1079. 2. *spirited, vigorous*, of persons, Luc.*DDeor*.7.3, *Asin*.8; of animals, *PRyl*.238.9 (iii A.D.); *quick*, c. inf., γ. ἐπινοεῖν Procop. *Arc*.16. Adv. -γῶς, τρέχειν Choerob.Rh.p.247 S. 3. of literary style, *vehement, vigorous*, v.l. in D.H.*Comp*.19 (Comp.), Hermog. *Id*.1.11, 2.1 (Comp.). Adv. -γῶς Syrian.*in Metaph*.130.6, Eust.1082.5, etc.

γοργότης, ητος, ἡ, *rapidity*, Sm.*Ec*.2.21, *Gloss*. II. of style, *vehemence, vigour*, Hermog.*Id*.2.1, Procl.*in Prm*.p.509 S., Sch.Od.1.110, etc.

Γοργοτομία, ἡ, (τέμνω) *cutting off the Gorgon's head*, Str.8.6.2.

γοργόφθαλμος, ον, = γοργωπός, Suid. s.v. γοργῶπις.

Γοργοφόνος, ον, *Gorgon-killing*, E.*Fr*.985: fem. **Γοργοφόνα**, as a name of Athena, Id.*Ion*1478 (lyr.).

γόργῡρα (Dor. γέργ-), ἡ, *underground drain* or *sewer*, Alcm.132, cf. *AB*233, Hsch.: used as *a dungeon*, Hdt.3.145, cf. Harp., etc.

Γοργώ, ἡ, *the Gorgon*, i.e. *the Grim One* (cf. γοργός), Hes.*Sc*.224, 230: acc. pl., Γοργοὺς Id.*Th*.276.—Sg. Γοργώ Il.11.36: gen. Γοργοῦς 8.349, Hes.*Sc*.224, E.*Or*.1521, *Ion*1003, etc.; also Γοργών Id.*Rh*.306: gen. Γοργόνος Id.*Fr*.360.46, *Ph*.456 (s.v.l.): acc. Γοργόνα Id. *Or*.1520: pl. Γοργόνες, acc. -ας, are the regul. forms (but v. supr.), Hes.*Sc*.230, A.*Pr*.799, al.: gen. Γοργόνων Pi.*P*.12.7, E.*Ba*.990 (lyr.).

γοργ-ωπός, όν, *fierce-eyed, grim-eyed*, σέλας A.*Pr*.358; κόραι E.*HF*868; ἴτυς Id.*Ion*210 (lyr.); γοργωπὰ λεύσσων Id.*Hyps.Fr*.16(18); ἀλέκτωρ *AP*7.428 (Mel.); τὸ γ. Corn.*ND*20. **-ώψ**, ῶπος, ὁ, ἡ, = foreg., E.*El*.1257, *Or*.261:—fem. **-ῶπις**, ιδος, of Athena, S.*Aj*.450, *Fr*.844.

γοργώψατο· πικρὸν ἔβλεψε, Hsch. **γορδελίζειν**· ἀδολεσχεῖν, Id.

Γόριλλαι, αἱ, name of a tribe of hairy women (but prob. *gorilla*), Hanno *Peripl*.18.

γορός· κυρτός, Hsch., Cyr., Zonar. (Perh. f. l. for γυρός.)

Γορπιαῖος, ὁ (sc. μήν), name of a Macedonian month, J.*BJ*2.17.8, Plu.*Thes.*20, etc.; at Nysa, *SIG*781.4 (i B.C.).

γόρτυξ· ὄρτυξ, Hsch. **γόρυνος**· μῦς, βάτραχος, Id.; ὁ μικρὸς βάτραχος, Zonar. (Cf. γύρινος.)

γορυνίας, Boeotian name for μυρσίνη ἀγρία, Ps.-Dsc.2.110.

γορφία, τά, *stocks from which olive-trees are struck* (Aram. g^e*rōphīth*), *Gp.*9.5.12.

γοτάν· ὗν (Maced.), Hsch.

γουβενάριον, τό, dub. in *POxy.*921 *Intr.* (iii A.D.).

γουβικός, f. l. for κυβικός, Hero *Stereom.*1.48.

γοῦν or **γ' οὖν**, Ion. and Dor. **γῶν** (γε οὖν); restrictive Particle with an inferential force, *at least then*, freq. scarcely distinguishable from simple γε: twice in Hom. (with a second γε added), εἴ γ' οὖν ἕτερός γε φύγῃσιν Il.5.258; μὴ ἐμέ γ' οὖν οὗτός γε 16.30 (so ἔοικα γοῦν τούτου γε.. σοφώτερος εἶναι Pl.*Ap.*21d); freq. later, δοκέων πάγχυ δευτερεῖα γῶν οἴσεσθαι Hdt.1.31; γνώσει.. ὀψὲ γοῦν τὸ σωφρονεῖν A.*Ag.*1425, cf. 432 (lyr.), etc.; freq. in adducing an instance, or a fact giving rise to a presumption, Heraclit.58, Th.1.2, X.*Cyr.*1.5.8; τὸν γοῦν ἄλλον χρόνον in past time *at all events*, D.20.16; emphasizing a personal or possessive pronoun, τὸ γ. ἐμόν S.*OT*626, cf. *Ant.*45; introducing an apodosis, Pl.*Alc.*1.112b; simply emphatic, *why yes*, E.*Ph.*618, Pl.*Sph.*219d, etc.; each Particle has its full force in τὰς γοῦν Ἀθήνας οἶδα *well* (οὖν), I know *Athens* (γε), S.*OC*24:—freq. separated by a word, πάνυ γ' ἂν οὖν Ar.*Ec.*806, cf. Th.1.76, etc.:—rarely γε οὖν in full, D.H.2.56 codd. (The negat. form is οὔκουν.. γε.)

γοῦνα, γούνων, poet. pl. of γόνυ (q. v.).

γουνάζομαι, fut. -σομαι: aor. 1 γουνασάμεσθα Orph.*A.*618, subj. γουνάσσηαι A.R.4.747, cf. Orph.*A.*943: (γόνυ):—Ep. Verb, *clasp* another's *knees* (v. sub γόνυ 1.2): hence, *implore, entreat*, abs., Il. 11.130: c. inf., τῶν ὕπερ.. γουνάζομαι οὐ παρεόντων ἑστάμεναι κρατερῶς in whose name.. I *implore* you to stand your ground, 15.665; νῦν δέ σε πρὸς πατρὸς γουνάζομαι Od.13.324; νῦν δέ σε τῶν ὄπιθεν γ., ..πρός τ' ἀλόχου καὶ πατρὸς 11.66; μή με.. γούνων γουνάζεο *entreat* me not by [clasping] my knees, Il.22.345.

γούν-ασμα, ατος, τό, *supplication*, Lyc.1243:—also **-ασμός**, ὁ, Eust.627.9.

γούνατα, γούνασι, Ep. **γούνεσσι**, etc., v. γόνυ.

γουνιαῖος τόπος, sine expl., Hsch. **γουννοννία**· σάμψυχος, Id.

γουνόομαι (also -έομαι, Hsch.), contr. -οῦμαι, = γουνάζομαι, only pres. and impf., γουνοῦμαι Il.21.74, Od.6.149, Archil.75, Anacr.1.1, etc.; γουνούμην Od.11.29; γουνοῦσθαι 10.521; γουνούμενος 4.433, etc.

γουνο-πᾰχής, ές, *thick-kneed*, v. l. **γουνο-πᾰγής**, *cramping the knees*, Ἀχλύς Hes.*Sc.*266.

γουνός, ὁ, *high ground*, φυτὸν ὣς γουνῷ ἀλωῆς Il.18.57; ἀνὰ γουνὸν ἀλωῆς οἰνοπέδοιο Od.1.193, etc.; ἐκ Κρήτης ἐς γουνὸν Ἀθηνάων 11.323; τῆς Ἀττικῆς.. τὸν γ. τὸν Σουνιακόν Hdt.4.99: pl., γουνοῖσιν Ἐλευθῆρος μεδέουσα Hes.*Th.*54; γουνοῖσιν κατένασσε Νεμείης ib.329; ἐν γουνοῖς Ἀθανᾶν Pi.*I.*4(3).25. (Expld. as τόπος γονιμώτατος by Sch.Il. l. c., but better as ὑψηλὸς τόπος (cf. γόνυ) Orion 38, *EM*239.5.)

γούντη, ἡ (Lydian word), *tomb*, Keil-Premerstein *Zweiter Bericht* 255 (iii A.D.):—also **γουτάριον**, τό, Ramsay *Cities and Bishoprics* No. 566.

γοῦρος, ὁ, a kind of *cake*, Sol.38.3.

γουττᾶτον, τό, a kind of *cake*, Chrysipp.Tyan.ap.Ath.14.647c.

γοώδης, ες, *mournful*, ἁρμονίαι Pl.*Lg.*800d (Sup.); φωνή Arist. *HA*615^{b}5.

γρᾶ, v. γράω.

γράα, ἡ, a kind of *serpent*, *Peripl.M.Rubr.*38.

γραβάν· σκάφιον, βόθρον, Hsch. **γράβατος**, v. κράβατος.

γράβδην, Adv., (γράφω) *grazing, scraping*, Eust.852.8, *EM*781. 27.

γραβδίς, ἡ, = sq., *EM*239.28 (acc. **γράβδις**, Sch.D.T.p.197 H.).

γράβιον, τό, *torch*, Strattis 50, Amerias ap.Ath.15.699e, prob. in S.*Fr.*177 (pl.).

γράζα, v. γηράμων. **γράθμα**, v. γράμμα.

γραῖα, late Poet. nom. **γραίη**, Dor. **γραία** (only gen. sg. in Hom.), ἡ, *old woman*, Od.1.438, S.*Tr.*870, E.*Tr.*465, al.: as Adj., γραῖαι δαίμονες, of the Eumenides, A.*Eu.*150 (lyr.), cf. 69. 2. as Adj., of things, *old*, γραίας ἐρείκης Id.*Ag.*295; γραίας ἀκάνθης S.*Fr.*868; γραῖαν ὠλένην E.*Ion* 1213; γραίᾳ χερί Id.*Hec.*877; γραιᾶν πηρᾶν Theoc.15.19; σταφυλὴ γραίη *raisins*, *AP*6.231 (Phil.). 3. Γραῖαι, αἱ, *the Graiae*, with hair grey from their birth, Hes.*Th.*270, prob. in A.*Fr.*262. II. = γραῦς II, *scum* or *skin which forms over boiled milk*, etc., Arist.*Pr.*893^{b}32. III. *folds of skin below the navel*, Ruf. *Onom.*99, Poll.2.170. IV. = γραῦς III, *sea-crab*, Epich.61. V. = κάρδοπος, Hsch.

γραιβία or **γραιτία** (i. e. γραιϝία)· πανηγυρίς (Tarent.), Hsch.

γρᾱΐδιον, τό, Dim. of γραῖς, *old hag*, Ar.*Pl.*536:—elsewh. contr. **γρᾴδιον**, ib.674, Philyll.5, X.*An.*6.3.22, D.18.260, Men.*Georg.*54, etc.: barbarous form γράδιο Ar.*Th.*1194.

γραΐζω (γραῦς II), *skim milk*, etc., Ar.*Fr.*446.

Γραικός, ὁ, *Greek*, "Ἕλληνες ὠνομάσθησαν τὸ πρότερον Γραικοὶ καλούμενοι *Marm.Par.*11 (iv B.C.), cf. Arist.*Mete.*352^{b}2, Apollod.1.7.3, Call.*Fr.*104, Lyc.532, etc.; Γραῖκες Alcm.134, S.*Fr.*518 is of doubtful meaning, cf. also Ῥαικός:—hence **Γραικ-ίτης**, ου, ὁ, Lyc.605: **-ίζω**, *speak Greek*, Hdn.*Epim.*12: **-ιστί**, *in Greek*, *EM*239.19. (Local name for a tribe in West Greece, applied by the Italians to Greeks in general.)

γραίνω, = γράω, *gnaw*, Hsch. **γραιολέας**· πονηρὰς ἢ ὀλεθρίας γραίας, Id.

γραιόομαι, Pass., *become aged, withered*, of a vine, *AP*9.261 (Epigon.).

γρᾱΐς, ΐδος, ἡ, = γραῦς, γραῖα, Chariton 6.1, *PMag.Lond.*125.21 (v A.D.), Palch. in *Cat.Cod.Astr.*1.95.

γραιωπίας, ου, ὁ, *man like an old woman*, Hsch. **γραμαιτιτά**, γραμματευτά, Hsch.

γράμμα, ατος, τό, Dor. **γράθμα**, prob. in *IG*4.506 (Heraeum, vi/v B.C.), cf. *An.Ox.*1.102, but **γράσσμα**, *IG*4.554 (Argos, v B.C.): late Aeol. pl. **γρόππατα**, *Epigr.Gr.*990.11 (Balbilla): (γράφω):—*that which is drawn*: pl., *lines of a drawing, picture*, etc., E.*Ion* 1146 (of tapestry), Theoc.15.81; *picture*, Ἀπέλλεω γ. Herod.4.73, cf. *AP* 6.352 (Erinna): sg., *drawing, picture*, Pl.*R.*472d, *Cra.*430e, cf. 431c: pl., *figures* in a picture, Procop.Gaz.*Ecphr.*p.157 B. II. *written character, letter*, Hdt.1.139, 148, etc.: in pl., *letters, characters*, γραμμάτων τε συνθέσεις A.*Pr.*460; πηλίκοις γ. *Ep.Gal.*6.11; *the letters, the alphabet*, Hdt.5.58; τὰ γ. καὶ τὰς συλλαβάς Pl.*Cra.*390e; γ. Φοινίκια S.*Fr.*514; Ἀσσύρια, Ἑλληνικά, Hdt.4.87; γράμματα ἐπίστασθαι Pl.*Lg.*689d; μαθεῖν to have learnt *to read*, Id.*Prt* 325e; γ. μὴ εἰδέναι *SIG*^{2}844.6; ἐδίδασκες γράμματα, ἐγὼ δ' ἐφοίτων you *kept school*—I went there, D.18.265; ἤτοι τέθνηκεν ἢ διδάσκει γ. *Com. Adesp.*20; παιδεύειν γράμματα Arist.*Pol.*1337^{b}24; τέχνη ἡμῶν γ. our profession is that of the *scribe*, *PTeb.*316.16 (i A.D.). b. *articulate sound, letter*, Pl.*Phlb.*18c; τὰ γ. πάθη ἐστὶ τῆς φωνῆς Arist.*Pr.*895^a 12; γράμματα φθέγγεσθαι ib.8, cf. *PA*660^{a}5. c. παρὰ γράμμα λέγοντα.. σκοπεῖν *etymologically*, Id.*MM*1185^{b}39; τὰ παρὰ γ. σκώμματα puns, Id.*Rh.*1412^{a}28; but ἀρετὴν παρὰ γ. διώκοντες, with ref. to Νικαρέτη, the mistress of Stilpo, Crates Theb.1. d. *inscription*, τὸ Δελφικὸν γ. Pl.*Phdr.*229e, cf. *Chrm.*164d, X.*Mem.*4.2.24, etc., *IG* 2.2876, al.: prov., εἰς πέλαγος.. γράμματα γράψαι *Epigr.Gr.*1038.8 (Attalia). 2. in pl., *notes* in music, *AP*11.78 (Lucill.). 3. mathematical *diagram*, Epigr.ap.D.L.8.12. 4. *letter* inscribed on the lots which the δικασταί drew, Ar.*Pl.*277, al., Arist.*Ath.*64.4; practically, = *division* of dicasts, ἐν ὁποίῳ γ. δειπνεῖ Ar.*Ec.*683; ἁ κατὰ γράμμα φυλακά the *roster* of guards, *SIG*569.21 (Cos, iii B.C.). b. *quarters* of a town, *PRein.*49.2; *accent*, *EM*240.42, Zonar. 5. a small weight, $\frac{1}{24}$ *ounce, scruple*, Androm.ap.Gal.13.114, *Gp.*7.13.2, *PLips.*62 ii 27 (iv A.D.). III. in pl., *set of written characters, piece of writing*, Hdt.1.124: hence, *letter*, Id.5.14, *IG*2^2.103.8, etc.; γραμμάτων πτυχαί S.*Fr.*144, cf. E.*IT*594, al., Pl.*Ep.*347c; *inscription, epitaph*, etc., ἐκόλαψε ἐς τὸν τάφον γράμματα λέγοντα τάδε Hdt. 1.187, cf. 4.91, And.3.12, Theoc.18.47, *IG*3.751. 2. *papers, documents*, Antipho 1.30, D.36.21, etc. (sg., D.Chr.65.14); τούτων τὰ γ. the *documents to prove* this, Lys.32.14; τὰ γ. τῆς δίκης Ar.*Nu.*772; τὰ δημόσια γ. the public *records*, Decr.ap.D.18.55; *title-deeds*, D.C.65. 14; *account* of loans, D.49.59; ἐπικαρπίαν ἐν γράμμασιν ἀποφέρειν Pl. *Lg.*955d; *contract* or *estimate*, *BCH*46.323 (Teos); *catalogue*, X.*Cyr.*7. 4.12: in sg., *bond*, *Ev.Luc.*16.7; *note of hand*, J.*AJ*18.6.3. 3. a man's *writings*, i. e. *book, treatise*, τὰ τοῦ Ζήνωνος γ. Pl.*Prm.*127c (but sg., ib.128a): pl., *books*, X.*Mem.*4.2.1; Πλάτωνος τὸ περὶ ψυχῆς γ. Call.*Ep.*25, cf. *AP*9.63 (Asclep.), Gal.18(2).928; τὰ ἱερὰ γ. the Holy *Scriptures*, *OGI*56.36 (iii B.C.), Ph.2.574, 2*Ep.Ti.*3.15, J.*Ap.*1.10; ἱερὰ γ., = Imperial *rescripts*, *IG*12(5).132 (Paros, iii A.D.); = *hieroglyphics*, *OGI*90.54 (Rosetta, ii B.C.): in sg., the *Law* of Moses, *Ep. Rom.*2.27, al.; opp. πνεῦμα, ib.29: sg., *article* of a treaty, Th. 5.29. 4. *laws* or *rules*, Pl.*R.*425b, *Plt.*292a, al., Ar.*Ec.*1050; κατὰ γράμματα ἄρχειν, opp. ἄνευ γραμμάτων, Pl.*Plt.*293a; ἡ κατὰ γ. καὶ νόμους πολιτεία Arist.*Pol.*1286^{a}15, cf. 1272^{a}38: οἱ κατὰ γ. νόμοι, opp. οἱ κατὰ τὰ ἔθη, ib.1287^{b}5, cf. Pl.*Plt.*299d; κατὰ γράμματα ἰατρεύεσθαι Arist.*Pol.*1287^{a}34; ἡ ἐκ τῶν γ. θεραπεία ib.40. IV. in pl., also, *letters, learning*, ἀπείρους γραμμάτων Pl.*Ap.*26d, etc.

γραμμαθέπτα· δραπέτα, Hsch. (leg. γράμμαθ' ἑπτά).

γραμμάριον, τό, *weight of two obols*, Aët.7.117.

γραμμᾰτ-εία, ἡ, *office of* γραμματεύς, *PTeb.*30.18 (ii B.C.), Plu. *Comp.Sert.Eum.*1, *BGU*587.11 (ii A.D.); the *term* of such office, *JRS*2.243 (Phrygia). II. *learning*, Lxx *Si.*44.4. **-είδιον**, τό, Dim. of γραμματεῖον, *small tablet*, Antipho 5.53, D.54.37, Thphr. *Char.*6.8, Plu.*Brut.*5, etc.; γ. δίθυρον Men.327; *menu*, Ath.2.49d; *memorandum*, Jul. *ad Ath.*277b. (γραμματίδιον which is freq. found in codd., cf. *PLips.*111.5 (iv A.D.), is expl. as Dim. of γράμματα by Gramm., cf. Hdn.Gr.2.488.) **-ειδιοποιός**, ὁ, *a maker of tablets*, title of plays by Apollodorus of Carystus (Ath.7.280d) and Apollodorus of Gela (Poll.4.19). **-εῖον**, τό, *that on which one writes, tablets*, Ar.*Fr.*157, Antipho 1.10, Pl.*Prt.*326d, prob. in Gorg.*Pal.*6; *tablet* on which names, etc., are recorded, λελευκωμένα γ. Arist.*Ath.* 47.2, cf. D.46.11, *IG*1^2.91.11, etc. 2. *bond, document, contract*, Lys. 32.7; κατὰ γραμματεῖον ἠταιρηκέναι Aeschin.1.165, cf. *POxy.*1012 *Fr.* 9 ii 15; *account-book, ledger*, Ar.*Nu.*19, D.45.33: freq. written γραμμάτιον. 3. τὸ ληξιαρχικὸν γ. *list in which* Athenian citizens *were enrolled*, *IG*1^2.79, Is.7.27, D.57.26. 4. *will, testament*, Is.6.29. 5. *pass* (?), *PPetr.*3 p.130. 6. *memorandum*, D.22.23, Jul. *ad Ath.* 283b; *petition*, Luc.*Peregr.*16. II. *place where* γράμματα *were taught, a school*, Anon.ap.Suid. III. *office of* γραμματεύς, Plb.4.87. 8, Poll.9.41. IV. *public dining-hall* in Syria, Posidon.18. **-εύς**, έως, ὁ, *secretary, registrar*, title of officials at Athens and elsewhere,

*IG*1².15, etc.; ὁ γ. ὁ τῆς πόλεως Th.7.10; γ. τοῦ δήμου *OGI*493.10 (Ephesus, ii A.D.), *Act.Ap.*19.35; γ. ἀνδραπόδων *PHib.*29.7; γ. τῶν μαχίμων *UPZ*110.145 (ii B.C.); γ. τοῦ θεοῦ *IG*9(2).1109.21 (Magn. Thess.); also of subordinate officials, *clerk*, sts. a term of contempt, ὄλεθρος γ. D.18.127; θεοῖς ἐχθρὸς καὶ γ. Id.19.95; ἡ γ., in joke, Ar. *Th.*432. 2. metaph., *recorder*, of memory, Pl.*Phlb.*39a. 3. *scholar*, γ. σαφής A.*Fr.*358 (s.v.l.). 4. *one who traces* or *marks out*, of Egyptian embalmers, D.S.1.91. **-ευτά,** v. γραμαιτιτά. **-εύω,** *to be secretary, hold his office*, *IG*1².392, Th.4.118, etc.: c. dat., *IG*1².352, etc.; later, c. gen., γ. τοῦ συνεδρίου *IG*3.752. **-ηφόρος,** ὁ, *letter-carrier*, D.H.20.4, Plu.*Galb.*8, al., *PFlor.*39.6 (iv A.D.), etc. **-ίας** (sc. λίθος), ου, ὁ, precious stone like an emerald, v.l. in Plin.*HN*37.118:—Hsch. has γραμματίας· περιεσπασμένους. **-ίδιον,** v. γραμματείδιον. **-ίζω,** *teach the spelling of a word*, Herod.3.24:—Pass., pf. *to be skilled in* γράμματα, Hsch.; γραμματισμένος (sic) *man of education*, *Cat.Cod.Astr.*6.65.8. II. *to be a secretary*, συνέδροις *IG*5(1).1432.19 (Messene); Boeot. γραμματίδδοντος *IG*7.1739 (Thespiae), al. **-ικεύομαι,** Dep., *to be a grammarian*, *AP*9.169 (Pall.).

γραμματικομάστιξ, ῖγος, ὁ, *scourge of critics*, title of Aus.*Idyll.*14.

γραμμᾰτ-ικός, ή, όν, *knowing one's letters, a good scholar*, X.*Mem.*4.2.20, Pl.*Tht.*207b, Arist.*EN*1105ᵃ21: Comp., Pl.*Plt.*285d, Ph.1.621; opp. ἀγράμματος, Arr.*Epict.*3.19.6; ἀνὴρ γ. Plu.2.582a. Adv. **-κῶς** Pl.*Tht.* l.c., etc. 2. γ. ἔκπωμα a cup *engraved with the alphabet* or *an inscription*, Eub.69, cf. Ath.11.466d, Luc.*Lex.*7. 3. γ. ἀνάγκαι f.l. for γραμμικαί, Alex.Aphr.*Pr.*2.46. II. Subst., γραμματικός, ὁ, *teacher of the rudiments*, Hp.*Epid.*4.37, Plu.2.59f:—fem. -κή, *Sammelb.*5753. 2. *one who occupies himself with literary texts, grammarian, critic*, Plb.32.2.5, D.L.3.61, D.Chr.53.1, *IG*14.1183, etc.; first used of Apollodorus of Cyrene, acc. to Clem.Al. *Strom.*1.16.79:—fem. -κή, ἡ, Ath.1.14d. 3. *concerned with textual criticism*, ἐξήγησις D.H.*Th.*51; γραμματικά, title of work by Eratosthenes, Clem.Al. l.c. III. ἡ -κή (with or without τέχνη) *grammar*, Pl.*Cra.*431e, *Sph.*253a, etc.; ἡ γ. ἐπιστήμη Arist.*Top.*142ᵇ31. b. *faculty of scholarship*, γ. ἐστιν ἕξις παντελὴς ἐν γράμμασι Eratosth.ap.Sch.D.T.p.160H., cf. Ph.1.502, *AP*7.588 (Paul. Sil.). 2. *alphabet, script*, Str.3.1.6, Plu.*Arist.*1, etc.; ἡ ἱερὰ γ. hieroglyphic *writing*, *OGI*56.64 (iii B.C.). IV. γραμματικόν, τό, *fee paid to scribes* in Egypt, *PHib.*1.110 (iii B.C.), *PTeb.*61ᵇ.89 (ii B.C.), etc. **-ιον,** τό, Dim. of γράμμα, Luc.*Merc.Cond.*36. II. = γραμματεῖον, *bond, contract*, *POxy.*71.5 (iv A.D.). **-ισμός·** *limpidus* (sic), *Gloss.* (Perh. *plinthium.*) **-ιστής,** οῦ, ὁ, = γραμματεύς, *clerk, registrar*, Hdt.2.28, 3.123, *IG*7.1745 (Thespiae), *SIG*529.4 (Dyme, iii B.C.), etc.: metaph., *recorder*, of memory (cf. γραμματεύς 2), Pl.*Phlb.*39b. II. *one who teaches* γράμματα, *elementary schoolmaster*, X.*Smp.*4.27, Pl.*Prt.*312b, al., D.19.281, D.H.11.28, Diog.Oen.11, etc. **-ιστική,** ἡ, *elementary teaching*, Phld.*Rh.*1.70S., S.E.*M.*1.44, Them.*Or.*23.297d (also -κά, τά, Id.*Or.*21.251a): but distd. fr. γραμματική as more elementary, Ph.1.540.

γραμμᾰτο-δῐδασκᾰλεῖον, τό, = γραμματεῖον II, Plu.2.712a, al. **-δῐδάσκᾰλος,** ὁ, *schoolmaster*, *SIG*578.8 (Teos), Teles p.50H., Phld. *Acad.Ind.*p.24M., Plu.*Alc.*7, Porph.*Plot.*3, *BGU*1214.4; cf. γραμμοδιδασκαλίδης. **-ειδής,** ές, *line-like*, διαφύσεις Sch.Il.21.169. **-εις,** εσσα, εν, *inscribed*, στήλη *Rev.Phil.*46.127 (Miscamus). **-εισαγωγεύς,** ὁ, *schoolmaster*: *governor*, Lxx *De.*1.15, al. **-κύφων** [ῠ], ωνος, nickname of a γραμματεύς, *porer over records*, D.18.209, Ph.2.536: pl., ib.520. **-λικρῖφίς,** ίδος, ὁ, *puzzle-headed grammarian*, *AP*11.140 (Lucill.). **-πίναξ** [ῐ], ακος, ὁ, *map-maker*, Sch.D.P.5. **-φορέω,** *carry* or *deliver letters*, Str.5.4.13. **-φόρος,** ὁ, *letter-carrier*, Plb.2.61.4, al., Plu.*Pel.*10. **-φῠλᾰκεῖον,** τό, = sq. I, J.*BJ*2.17.6, Plu.2.520c, S.E.*M.*2.27. **-φῠλάκιον** [ᾰκ], τό, *a place for keeping records*, Plu.*Arist.*21, *OGI*669.23 (i A.D.), *IG*5(2).516 (Lycosura, i A.D.), 5(1).20 (Sparta, ii A.D.): in pl., τὰ τῆς πόλεως γ. *BGU*913.4 (iii A.D.). II. *deed-box*, *EM*412.38. **-φύλαξ** [ῠ], ἄκος, ὁ, *recorder, registrar*, *IG*5(1).32*B*17 (Sparta), *OGI*229.51 (Smyrna), *Test.Epict.*8.27.

γραμμή, ἡ, (γράφω) *stroke* or *line* of a pen, *line*, as in mathematical figures, γραμμῆς λόγος ὁ τῶν δύο Pythagorei ap.Arist.*Metaph.*1036ᵇ12, cf. Pl.*Men.*82c, *R.*509d, etc.; περὶ ἀλόγων γ. title of work by Democritus, περὶ ἀτόμων γ., title of work ascribed to Arist.: hence γραμμαί, αἱ, *astronomy*, *AP*9.344 (Leon.); also in forming letters, *line* traced by teacher, Pl.*Prt.*326d; *outline*, opp. σκιά, Metop.ap.Stob.3.1.116, cf. Plb.2.14.8; ἡ ἐκτὸς γ. Hero *Aut.*27.2. II. = βαλβίς, *line across the course, starting-* or *winning-point*, Pi.*P.*9.118, cf. Ar.*Ach.*483; εὐθὺς ἀπὸ γ. Lib.*Or.*59.13: metaph. of life, πέλας γραμμῆς ἱκέσθαι E.*El.*956; ἐπ' ἄκραν ἥκομεν γ. κακῶν Id.*Fr.*169; ἡ ἐσχάτη τοῦ βίου γ. D.S.17.118: hence, *boundary-line, edge*, dub. l. in Hp.*Art.*80; *cutting edge* of a knife, Gal.2.673. III. *line* or *square on a chequer-board*: hence prov., τὸν ἀπὸ γραμμᾶς κινεῖν λίθον to move a piece from this line, i.e. try one's last chance, Theoc.6.18 (usu. called ἡ ἱερά (sc. γραμμή), cf. ἱερός); αἱ γ. *the board* itself, Poll.9.99. 2. διὰ γραμμῆς παίζειν to play at *tug-of-war* (διελκυστίνδα), Pl.Com.153.1, Pl.*Tht.*181a. IV. ἡ μακρά (sc. γραμμή), v. τιμάω III.1. V. Medic., *linea alba*, Gal.2.514. 2. = ζέα, *Hippiatr.*1.

γραμμ-ιαῖος, α, ον, *linear*, σχῆμα Dam.*Pr.*262. **-ίζω,** prob. f.l. for δια-, of a game (cf. γραμμή III.1), Eust.633.63. **-ικός,** ή, όν, *linear, geometrical*, θεωρία Gal.*UP*10.12; ἀπόδειξις Plu.*Marc.*14, *Theol.Ar.*26; ἀνάγκαι Olymp.*in Grg.*p.260J. Adv. **-κῶς** *by means of lines, geometrically*, ἀποδείκνυσθαι S.E.*M.*3.92, cf. Ptol.*Alm.*2.12, Procl.*in R.*2.27K. 2. γ. ἀριθμός *linear* number, Nicom.*Ar.*2.7, cf. Speus. ap.*Theol.Ar.*61. II. = γραμματικός, Plu.2.606c (s.v.l.). **-ιστήρ,** ῆρος, ὁ, *a surgical instrument*, *Hermes* 38.281. **-ιστός,** ή, όν, *chequered*, Eust.852.11.

γραμμο-δῐδασκᾰλίδης, = γραμματοδιδάσκαλος, in contempt, Timo 51. **-ειδής,** ές, *slender as a line*, φῶς Paul.Al.*G.*4. Adv. **-δῶς** *in wavy lines*, Arist.*Mu.*395ᵃ27. **-ποίκῐλος,** ον, *striped*, Arist.*Fr.*295.

γραμμός, ὁ, *act of writing*, Hdn.Gr.1.168.

γραμμοτόκος, ον, *mother of lines*, μέλασμα, of the leaden plummet, *AP*6.63 (Damoch.).

γραμμώδης, ες, = γραμμοειδής, *wiry*, Thphr.*HP*4.12.2; *with linear markings*, ib.7.3.2.

γρανθέωνα· γέροντα, Hsch.

γρᾶολογία, ἡ, *old wife's talk, gossip*, γραμματικὴ γ. S.E.*M.*1.141: pl., Porph.*Chr.*34.

γρᾶο-σόβης, ου, ὁ, *lover of old women*, Ar.*Pax* 812; cf. Sch.ad loc., and v. σοβάς. **-συλλέκτρια,** ἡ, *gossip-monger*, Suid. s.v. Τίμαιος. **-τρεφής,** ές, *reared by an old woman, coddled*, Eust.971.41. **-φῐλος,** ὁ, *lover of old women*, Sch.Ar.*Pax* 812.

γραπίνης· οἶνος τραχύς, Hsch., *EM*239.32.

γράπις, ιδος, ἡ, *cast slough* of serpents, etc., Hsch. 2. *wrinkled*, S.*Ichn.*177, *EM*239.31. 3. kind of *bird*, Hsch.

γραπτ-έον, *one must write* or *describe*, ὅπως.. X.*Eq.*2.1; *one must write, spell*, Str.9.4.5, Gal.15.720. 2. γραπτέος, α, ον, *to be written, described*, Pl.*Ep.*341d, Luc.*Im.*17. **-εύς,** έως, ὁ, = γραφεύς, Sch. Ar.*Th.*1103. **-ήρ,** ῆρος, ὁ, *writer*, *AP*6.66 (Paul. Sil.), Man.1.132 (pl.). **-ης,** ου, ὁ, *wrinkled*, Eust.633.56. **-ός,** ή, όν, *painted*, ζῷα Emp.128.5; τύποι E.*Fr.*764; κύρβις Achae.19; εἰκών *SIG* 1068.21 (Patmos): γραπτά, τά, *paintings*, opp. γλυπτά, D.H.*Comp.*25. 2. *marked as with letters*, ἁ γραπτὰ ὑάκινθος Theoc.10.28; γ. λίθος *IG*14.1089. II. *written*, νόμοι γ. Gorg.*Pal.*30, cf. Pl.*Lg.*773e, etc.; ἀσφάλεια *PAmh.*78.17 (ii A.D.): γραπτά, τά, *rescripts, proclamations*, Lxx 2*Ma.*11.15; *legal documents, bonds*, Man.3.214. **-ρα,** τά, *fee for writing* or *copying*, *PLond.ined.*2110 (ii A.D.), *BGU*1062.20 (iii A.D.), *POxy.*895.12 (iv A.D.). **-ύς,** ύος, ἡ, *scratching, tearing*, Od.24.229 (pl.). II. in pl., *writings*, A.R.4.279.

γράσθι, v. γράω.

γράσος, ὁ, prop., *smell of a goat*: hence, of men, A. or Ar.ap. Phot. s.v. ψό, Eup.242, Arist.*Pr.*879ᵃ23, Plu.2.180c, M.Ant.9.36.

γράσσμα, ατος, τό, Argive, = γράμμα, *IG*4.554 (pl.).

γραστ-ίζω, *feed at grass*, ἵππους *Gp.*16.1.11 (Pass.), *Hippiatr.*98. **-ισμός,** ὁ, *feeding at grass*, ib.10. **-ις,** εως, ἡ, (γράω) *grass, green fodder*, *PPetr.*2p.113 (corr. in 3p.333) (iii B.C.), etc.; γ. πυρίνη, κριθίνη, *Hippiatr.*68, 98, cf. Eust.633.47, Hsch.:—also **γράσσις,** *PHamb.*39 ii (ii A.D.); cf. κράστις.

γράσων, ωνος, ὁ, ἡ, (γράσος) *smelling like a goat*, M.Ant.11.15, Ath.13.585e; a term of abuse, Hsch. II. = γράσος, M.Ant.8.37 (s.v.l.).

γρασωνία, ἡ, = γράσος, Archig.ap.Aët.8.7 (pl.).

γραῦις, ιδος, ἡ, Dor. for γρηῦς, γραῦς, Call.*Fr.*326.

γραύκαλας· ὄρνις τεφρός, Hsch.

γραῦς, gen. γρᾱός, ἡ: Ion. **γρηῦς,** γρηός, voc. γρηῦ: poet. also **γρηΰς,** voc. γρηΰ: barbarous voc. γρᾶο in Ar.*Th.*1222: nom. pl. γρᾶες Ar.*Fr.*350, Timocl.25: acc. γραῦς E.*Andr.*612, etc.:—*old woman*, Hom., esp. in Od., 1.191, al., A.*Eu.*38, etc.; γ. παλαιή Od. 19.346: prov., γραῶν ὕθλος *old wives'* fables, Pl.*Tht.*176b: with Subst., γ. γυνή E.*Tr.*490, Ar.*Th.*345, D.19.283: Com., ὁ γραῦς of *an old man*, Ar.*Th.*1214 cod. R. II. *scum* of boiled milk, Id.*Pl.*1206, Arist.*GA*743ᵇ7. III. *sea-crab*, Arist.*HA*601ᵃ18 (as v.l.), Artem.2.14. IV. kind of *locust*, γ. σέριφος Zen.2.94.

γρᾰφ-είδιον (or -ίδιον), τό, Dim. of sq., Isoc.ap.Theon.*Prog.*5, *EM*240.16, Suid. **-εῖον,** τό, *pencil*, Hp.*Superf.*8 (f.l.), Arist.*Ph.*248ᵇ8, Macho ap.Ath.13.582c. 2. *paint-brush*, Plu.2.859e, S.E. *P.*1.28; *graving tool, chisel*, *Epigr.Gr.*980.4 (Philae). II. *registry, record-office*, *Michel* 595.12 (Halic.), *PRyl.*65.4 (i B.C.), *PAmh.*110.21 (i A.D.), etc.:—written **γράφιον,** *PPetr.*3p.155. III. *tax on writing-materials*, *BGU*277 ii 11: but in pl., *fees for copying*, ib.1214.12. **-εύς,** έως, ὁ, *painter*, Emp.23.1, E.*Hec.*807 (s.v.l.), And.4.17, Pl.*Phd.*110b, etc. II. = γραμματεύς, X.*HG*4.1.39, Plu.*Ages.*13; *private secretary*, τοῦ Δημοκρίτου Epicur.*Fr.*172. III. *writer*, D.S.21.17; *scribe, scrivener*, X.*Ages.*1.26; *copyist*, Arist.*Rh.*1409ᵃ20, Plb.12.4ᵃ.4, Str.13.1.54 (pl.); τὰ τῶν γραφέων παίσματα Porph.*Plot.*19; cf. γραφής, γροφεύς. **-ή,** ἡ, *representation by means of lines*: hence, I. *drawing, delineation*, Hdt.4.36; κατὰ γραφήν *in outline*, cj. in Pl.*Smp.*193a; also of *painting*, γραφῇ κοσμέειν Hdt.3.24; εἰκὼν γραφῇ εἰκασμένη Id.2.182; *the art of drawing* or *painting*, Pl.*Plt.*277c, *Ti.*19b. 2. *that which is drawn* or *painted, drawing, picture*, ὅσον γραφῇ only *in a picture*, Hdt.2.73; πρέπουσά θ' ὡς ἐν γραφαῖς A.*Ag.*242 (lyr.); σπόγγος ὤλεσεν γραφήν ib.1329; μήτε ἄγαλμα μήτε γ. Arist.*Pol.*1336ᵇ15; also of embroidery, A.*Ch.*232; γραφαὶ ἀπὸ κερκίδος Philostr.*Im.*2.5. 3. γ. παρειῶν *painting, rouging* the cheeks, Id.*Ep.*22. II. *writing* or *the art of writing*, Pl.*Phdr.*274b, etc.: pl., αἱ γ. τῶν δικῶν *the registration* of.., Arist.*Pol.*1321ᵇ36; γραφαὶ περὶ συμμαχίας, of treaties, ib.1280ᵃ40. 2. *that which is written, writing*, S.*Tr.*683, Agatho 4: hence, of various written documents, *letter*, Th.1.129: also in pl., E.*IT*735; ψευδεῖς γ. spurious *documents*, ap.D.18.55 (but in E.*Hipp.*1311 false *statements*); of published *writings*, τῶν φιλοσόφων Phld.Ir.p.73 W., cf. D.H.Orat.Vett.4; ἐν τῇ πρώτῃ γ. in the first book, Epicur.Nat.Herc.1431.16; written law, Pl.Lg.934c; contract, PAmh.2.43.13 (ii B.C.): pl., copies of judgements delivered in court, IG12(2).526d8 (Eresos). b. catalogue, list, return, ἱερῶν PTeb.88.2 (ii B.C.); τοῦ κατ' ἄνδρα OGI179.21 (Egypt, i B.C.); τὰς κατ' ἄνδρα γραφάς PTeb.27.7 (ii B.C.), etc.; price-list, D.S.1.91. c. inscription, Th.1.134, IG12(5).679 (Syros), Epigr.Gr.347 (Cios), D.C.37.21. d. MS. reading, Str.1.2.25, Gal.15.430, Alex.Aphr.in Sens.9.29, Herm.in Phdr.p.154A., etc. 3. the Holy Scripture, Aristeas155, 2Ep.Pet.1.20: pl., Ph.1.18, J.Ap.2.4, Ev.Matt.21.42, al.: also in sg., of a particular passage, Act.Ap.8.32, al. 4. γ. φαρμάκου medical prescription, Gal.12.293, 13.638, 15.918. 5. record-office, archive, IG11(2).203B101 (Delos, iii B.C.). III. (γράφομαι) as law-term, 1. bill of indictment in a public prosecution, λέγε, τὴν γ. αὐτὴν λαβών D.18.53. 2. criminal prosecution in the interest of the state (cf. Poll.8.41), γραφὴν ὕβρεως καὶ δίκην κακηγορίας ἰδίαν φεύξεται Id.21.32, cf. Lys.1.44, Is.11.28, etc.; γραφὴν γράφεσθαι Pl.Lg.929e, etc.; γρ. γ. τινά Id.Euthphr.2b, etc.; γ. ἀπενεγκεῖν Aeschin.3.217; γραφήν τινος διώκειν τινά D.19.293; πολλὰς γ. διώξας οὐδεμίαν εἷλεν Antipho 2.1.5; γραφὴν ἁλῶναι Id.2.2.9; γ. κατασκευάζειν κατά τινος, ἐπί τινα, D.21.103, 22.2; γ. εἰσέρχεσθαι, εἰσιέναι, appear before the court in a public prosecution, either as prosecutor or prosecuted, Id.18.105. 3. generally, an ordinary public action, opp. to special forms (such as εἰσαγγελία, εὔθυναι, etc.), γραφάς, εὐθύνας, εἰσαγγελίας, πάντα ταῦτ' ἐπαγόντων μοι D.18.249, cf. X.Ath.3.2, Lys.16.12. -ημα, ατος, τό, = γράμμα, AB787. -ής, ὁ, = γραφεύς II, IG5(2).8 (Tegea, iv B.C.), al. -ία, ἡ, = γραφή, Gloss. -ικός, ή, όν, capable of drawing or painting, Pl.Tht.144e, Ael.VH14.37: Comp., a better judge of painting, ib.2.3: -κή (sc. τέχνη), ἡ, the art of painting, Pl.Grg.450c, etc. 2. of things, as if painted, Ἔρωτες Plu.Ant.26 (so Adv. -κῶς ibid., 2.747c, Luc.Im.15); picturesque, πρόσοψις D.S.2.53. II. of or for writing, suited for writing: -κή, ἡ, the art of writing, Hp.VM20; γ. λέξις, opp. ἀγωνιστική, Arist.Rh.1413b8; δύναμις Alcid.Soph.29; γ. ῥέεθρον, i.e. ink, AP6.63 (Damoch.); κάλαμος Gp.10.75.8, PGrenf.2.38.7 (i A.D.); μέλαν Gal.6.565; in writing, γ. ἁμάρτημα a clerical error, Plb.34.3.11. 2. skilled in writing, Arr.Epict.2.18.2; shorthand writer, IG14.1528. 3. able to describe, Plu.2.874b, Luc.Alex.3; of style, graphic, lively, D.H.Amm.1.4; ὑπόθεσις γ. a subject for description, Plu.Alex.17.

γρᾰφιο-ειδής, ές, like a stylus, γ. ἔκφυσις styloid process of the temporal bone, Gal.UP7.19, 11.4. -θήκη, ἡ, case for γραφεῖα, Gloss.

γρᾰφίς, ίδος, ἡ, = γραφεῖον I, AP6.63 (Damoch.), 65 (Paul. Sil.), 67 (Jul.): esp. stilus for writing on waxen tablets, Pl.Prt.326d; paint-brush, APl.4.178 (Antip.); graving tool, Lxx Ex.32.4; σύμβολα.. γραφίδεσσι κατέξυσα Hymn.Is.11, cf. AP4.3b.72 (Agath.); needle for embroidering, APl.4.324. II. embroidery, AP5.275 (Agath.): but in pl., = paintings, Nonn.D.25.433.

γρᾰφίσκος, ὁ, surgical instrument for extracting arrows, etc., Cels.7.5.3.

γρᾰφοειδής, ές, ἀπόφυσις, of the styloid process of the ulna, Gal.2.252,271.

γράφος [ᾰ], εος, τό, = γράμμα, τὰ γράφεα SIG9 (Olympia, vi B.C.), IG5(2).343 (Orchom. Arc., iv B.C.).

γράφω [ᾰ], fut. -ψω Hdt.1.95, etc.: aor. ἔγραψα, Ep. γράψε Il.17.599: pf. γέγραφα Cratin.124, Th.5.26, etc.; later γεγράφηκα PHib.1.78.2 (iii B.C.):—Med., fut. γράψομαι Ar.Pax107, etc. (but in pass. sense, Gal.Protr.13): aor. ἐγραψάμην Ar.V.894, etc.:—Pass., fut. γρᾰφήσομαι Hp.Acut.26, Nicom.Com.1.39, (μετεγ-) Ar.Eq.1370; more freq. γεγράψομαι S.OT411, Theoc.18.47, etc.: aor. ἐγράφην [ᾰ], Hdt.4.91, Pl.Prm.128c, etc.; ἐγράφθην SIG57.5 (Milet., v B.C.), Archim.Fluit.2.4: pf. γέγραμμαι (also in med. sense, v. fin.), 3 sg. ἔγραπται Opp.C.3.274; part. ἐγραμμένος or ἠγρ- SIG9 (Elis, dub.), Leg.Gort.1.45, al.; later γεγράφημαι Ph.2.637: 3 pl. γεγράφαται IG 1^2.57.10, Dor. γεγράβανται Schwyzer90.12 (Argos): plpf. ἐγέγραπτο X.Mem.1.2.64: 3 pl. ἐγεγράφατο D.C.56.32. Used by Hom. only in aor. Act.:—scratch, graze, αἰχμὴ γράψεν οἱ ὀστέον ἄχρις Il.17.599; γράψας ἐν πίνακι πτυκτῷ θυμοφθόρα πολλά having marked or drawn signs thereon, 6.169: hence, later, represent by lines, draw, paint, Hdt.2.41, A.Eu.50, Pl.R.377e; γῆς περιόδους γ. draw maps, Hdt.4.36; γ. Ἔρωθ' ὑπόπτερον Eub.41.1; προσπεπατταλευμένον γ. τὸν Προμηθέα Men.535.2; ἀνδριάντα γ. Pl.R.420c; ζῷα γ., = ζωγραφεῖν (q.v.), Id.Grg.453c: metaph., ὁπόσα τοὺς λειμῶνας αἱ ὧραι γράφουσι Philostr.Im.Praef.:—Med., ζῷα γράφεσθαι Hdt.4.88:—Pass., εἰκὼν γεγραμμένη Ar.Ra.537; πίνακες γεγραμμένοι τὰ Ἀλεξάνδρου ἔργα Philostr.VA2.20. 2. Math., describe a figure, Euc.Post.3, al., Archim.Sph.Cyl.1.23, al., Gal.1.47. b. of a point or line in motion, generate a figure, Arist.Mech.848b10, al.; τὸ σαμεῖον ἕλικα γράψει Archim.Sph.Cyl.Def.1, cf. Apollon.Perg.Con.1.2, Hero Aut.8.1. 3. brand, mark, Opp.C.1.326:—Pass. in form γεγράφαται, ib.322. II. express by written characters, write, τι Hdt.1.125, etc.; γ. διαθήκην Pl.Lg.923c, cf. X.Cyr.4.5.34 (Pass.); γ. τινὶ ὅτι.. Th.7.14; γ. τινί, c. inf., SIG552.13 (Abae, iii B.C.); γ. τι εἰς διφθέρας Hdt.5.58: prov., ὅρκους.. γυναικὸς εἰς ὕδωρ γράφω S.Fr.811, cf. Xenarch.6; εἰς τέφραν γ. Philonid.7; εἰς ὕδωρ, ἐν ὕδατι, Men.Mon.25, Pl.Phdr.276c; ἐν χρυσῷ πίνακι Id.Criti.120c; ἐν φλοιῷ Theoc.18.47; καθ' ὕδατος Luc.Cat.21; εἰς πέλαγος γράμματα γράψαι Epigr.Gr.1038.8 (Attalia):—Pass., πόθι φρενὸς γέγραπται in what leaf of memory it is written, Pi.O.10(11).3. 2. inscribe, γ. εἰς σκῦλα, εἰς στήλην, E.Ph.574, D.9.41:—Pass., γράφεσθαί τι to be inscribed with a thing, S.Tr.157; ὧδε γέγραμμαι have my name inscribed, IG12(7).3* (dub.); ἐν τῷ προσώπῳ γραφεὶς τὴν συμφοράν having it branded on his forehead, Pl.Lg.854d; γεγραμμένα κωκύουσαν, of the hyacinth, Euph.40. 3. write down, γ. τινὰ αἴτιον set him down as the cause, Hdt.7.214; γ. τι ἱερόν τινι register as.., Pi.O.3.30; in magic, invoke a curse upon, Tab.Defix.Aud.14A1; γ. τινὰ κληρονόμον, ἐπίτροπον, institute by a written document, Pl.Lg.923c, 924a; register, enrol, ἐμὲ γράφε τῶν ἱππεύειν ὑπερεπιθυμούντων X.Cyr.4.3.21; οὐ Κρέοντος προστάτου γεγράψομαι, as a dependent of Cr., S.OT411. 4. γ. τινί write a letter to one, γ. σοὶ ἵνα εἰδῇς PGrenf.1.11ii21 (ii B.C.), etc.; εἴς τινα Luc.Syr.D.23. 5. γ. περί τίνος write on a subject, X.Cyn.13.2, etc.; ὑπέρ τινος Plb.1.1.4, etc.; εἴς τινα against.., Longin.4.3; πρός τινα address a work to.., Id.1.3; describe, οἱ ὑφ' ἡμῶν γραφόμενοι καιροί Plb.2.56.4; esp. of Prose, opp. ποιεῖν, Isoc.2.48: c. dupl. acc., τί.. γράψειειν ἄν σε μουσοποιὸς ἐν τάφῳ; E.Tr.1189. 6. write down a law to be proposed: hence, propose, move, γνώμην, νόμον, ψήφισμα, etc., X.HG1.7.34, Ar.Nu.1429, etc.: abs. (sc. νόμον), D.18.179; γ. καὶ νομοθετεῖν περί τινος Id.24.48; γ. πόλεμον, εἰρήνην, Id.10.55, 19.55: c. inf., σὺ γράφεις ταῦτ' εἶναι στρατιωτικά Id.1.19; ἔγραψα.. ἀποπλεῖν.. τοὺς πρέσβεις Id.18.25; enact, νόμοι οὓς τὸ πλῆθος συνελθὸν ἔγραψε X.Mem.1.2.42:—Pass., παρὰ τὰ γραφέντα δρᾶν Pl.Plt.295d; τὸ γεγραμμένον ὑπὸ σοῦ ψήφισμα Din.1.70. 7. prescribe, ordain, πότμος ἔγραψε Pi.N.6.7. 8. ὁ γράφων τὸν Ὀξυρυγχίτην (sc. νομόν) the secretary for the nome of Oxyrhynchus, POxy.239.1 (i A.D.); τῷ ἰδίῳ λόγῳ γράφοντι τὸν νομόν PFlor.358.5 (ii A.D.).

B. Med., write for oneself or for one's own use, note down, Hdt.2.82, IG 1^2.57.39, etc.; γ. τι ἐν φρεσίν A.Ch.450 (lyr.); φρενῶν ἔσω S.Ph.1325; ἐγραψάμην ὑπομνήματα I wrote me down some memoranda, Pl.Tht.143a; cause to be written, συγγραφήν D.56.6, etc.; γ. πρόσοδον πρὸς τὴν βουλήν petition for a hearing before the Council, Id.24.48. 2. enrol oneself, γράψασθαι φυλῆς καὶ δήμου καὶ φρατρίας IG 1^2.374.16, ib.2.115b21: abs., of colonists, Pl.Lg.850b; but also (cf. A.II.3), ἕνα τῶν μαθητῶν ἐμὲ γράφου enrol me as one of your disciples, Id.Cra.428b. 3. as law-term, γ. τινά to indict one, τινός for some public offence, e.g. τῆς αἰσχροκερδείας, Pl.Lg.754e; γ. [τινὰ] παρανόμων D.18.13; in full, γραφὴν γράψασθαί τινα Ar.Nu.1482 (but in Pass., εἴ σοι γράφοιτο δίκη ib.758); γράψασθαι δίκας SIG344.38 (Teos): c. acc. et inf., γ. τινὰ ἀδικεῖν Ar.V.894, cf. Pax107: abs., οἱ γραψάμενοι the prosecutors, Id.V.881; ἑτέροις οὐκ ἦν γράψασθαι And.1.75; also γράφεσθαί τι indict an act, i.e. the doer of it, as criminal, ἐγράψατο τὴν Χαβρίου δωρειάν he brought a γραφὴ παρανόμων against the person who proposed the grant to Chabrias, D.20.146, cf. 95; τὸ χάριν τούτων ἀποδοῦναι παρανόμων γράφει (2 sg.) Id.18.119. b. Pass., to be indicted, γραφεὶς ἀπέφυγον D.18.103; τοῦτο τὸ ψήφισμα ἐγράφη παρανόμων was indicted as illegal, Aeschin.3.62; ψηφίσματα ὑπὸ τούτου οὐδὲ γραφέντα not even indicted, D.18.222 (but in 18.28, εἰ μὴ τοῦτ' ἐγράφη if this decree had not been proposed, as Pass. of A.II.6); τὰ γεγραμμένα the articles of the indictment, Id.18.56; τὸ γεγραμμένον the penalty named in the indictment, Id.24.83:—but γέγραμμαι usu. takes the sense of the Med., indict, Id.18.59,119, cf. Pl.Euthphr.2b, Tht.210d.

γραψαῖος, ὁ, crab, Diph.Siph.ap.Ath.3.106d.

γραψείω, Desiderat. of γράφω, Gloss.

γράω, gnaw, eat, Call.Fr.200: hence γρά· φάγε (Cypr.), Hsch.; γράσθι (imper.), Inscr.Cypr.144 H. (Golgoi). (Cf. γράστις, Skt. grásati 'devour'?)

γρᾱώδης, ες, = γραϊκός, ἀδολεσχία Chrysipp.Stoic.2.255; μυθολογία Str.1.2.3; μυθάριον Cleom.2.1, cf. Iamb.VP23,105, 1Ep.Ti.4.7: Comp. -έστερος Gal.5.315.

γρεῦς, ἡ, collat. form of γραῦς, Hdn.Gr.1.401.

γρηγορ-έω, late pres., formed from pf. ἐγρήγορα (q.v.), to be or become fully awake, watch, Lxx Ne.7.3, Ev.Matt.24.43, al., Ach.Tat.4.17; ἐπί τισι Lxx Ba.2.9; ἐπὶ τὰς πόλεις ib.Je.5.6:—Pass., ἐγρηγορήθη ἐπὶ τὰ ἀσεβήματά μου ib.La.1.14; opp. καθεύδω, of life opp. death, 1Ep.Thess.5.10. -ησις, εως, ἡ, wakefulness, Lxx Da.5.11. -ία, ἡ, = foreg., Gloss. -ικός, ή, όν, wakeful, watchful, Id. -σις, εως, ἡ, = γρηγόρησις, Ph.1.510.

γρήϊος, ον, Ion. for γραῖος, Call.Fr.511.

γρήνη· ἄνθη σύμμικτα, EM241.14, Hsch.

γρῆνος or **γρῆνυς**, = ἀγρηνόν, Eratosth.Fr.33.

γρηῢς, **γρηΰς**, Ion. and Ep. for γραῦς.

γρῖνος, ὁ and ἡ, Aeol. for ῥινός (i.e. Ϝρῖνος), acc. to Eust.1926.56; cf. γρίνος· δέρμα, Hsch., EM241.47.

γρίντης, ου, ὁ, tanner, Hdn.Gr.2.429 (γρηντίς cod., Hsch.). 2. = ὑβριστής, Cyr., Zonar. 3. = οὐρανός Cyr. (γρίντις EM241.48).

γρῑπάομαι, to be contracted or convulsed, Hsch.

γρῑπ-εύς, έως, ὁ, fisher, Sapph.120, Theoc.1.39, Mosch.Fr.1.9, AP7.305 (Addaeus), Procop.Pers.1.4. 2. maker of fishing-nets, Hsch. -εύω, fish, Zonar. -έω, catch: metaph., gain, οὐδὲν ἐγρίπισαν LW2261 (Syria): pf. part. γεγριφώς, Hsch. -ηΐς τέχνη, ἡ, art of fishing, AP6.223 (Antip.). -ίζω, = γριπεύω, Hsch.: metaph., of netting a profit, Lib. et Bas.Epp.14.1, cf. Et.Gud.d s.v. γρυμεία. -ισμα, ατος, τό, that which is caught, gain, EM241.22, Zonar.

γρῖπος, ὁ, = γρῖφος, AP6.23, Artem.2.14. II. haul or take of fish, D.L.1.32.

γρίπων [ῐ], ὁ, (γρῖπος) *fisherman*, γρίπωνος γριπεὺς.. ἔχωσε τάφον *AP*7.504.12 (Leon). (Prob. a pr. n.)

γρίσων, ωνος, ὁ, *pig*, Hdn.Gr.2.429.

γριτή, ἡ, dub. sens. in Lib.et Bas.*Epp*.15.1, 16.2 (perh. f.l. for γρύτη).

γρῐφᾶσθαι, Lacon. = γράφειν, Hsch.; also, *scratch*, Id.: ἀλγήματα γριφόμενα (prob. -ώμενα) *lancinating* pains, Hp.*Prorrh*.1.100, cf. Gal.ad loc.

γρῑφεύω, *ask riddles*, Ath.10.451b (cf. Diph.50), Eust.884.10.

γρῑφο-ειδής, ές, *enigmatical*, Hsch. **-πλόκος,** ον, *weaving riddles*, Tz.ad Hes.*Op*.588.

γρῖφ-ος, ὁ, = γρῖπος, *fishing-basket, creel*, Plu.2.471d, Opp.*H*.3.80, *PTeb*.486 (ii/iii A.D.). 2. metaph., *anything intricate, dark saying, riddle*, Ar.*V*.20, Demetr.*Eloc*.153, Ath.10.448b sqq.; γ. προβάλλειν Antiph.74.5; λέγειν γρίφους παρὰ πότον Id.124.2; distd. fr. αἴνιγμα, Poll.6.19. b. *forfeit paid* for failing to guess a riddle, Hsch. **-ότης,** ητος, ἡ, *obscurity*, Hdn.*Epim*.6. **-ώδης,** ες, *like a riddle*, Luc.*JTr*.28, Ath.10.456c.

γρομφάζω, *grunt*, *Gloss.*:—from **γρόμφαινα,** ἡ, *old sow*, Id.:—also **γρομφάς,** άδος, ἡ, Hsch., and **γρόμφις,** ιος, ἡ, acc. γρόμφιν, Hippon.69.

γρονθάριον, τό, Dim. of γρόνθος II, marginal gloss on χελώνιον, Apollod.*Poliorc*.178.4 codd.

γρονθοκοπῶ, *beat with fists*, *Gloss.*

γρονθονεύεται· θυμοῦται, βρενθύεται, Hsch.

γρόνθος, ὁ, = πυγμή, *fist*, Gloss.*Oxy*.1099.18, Hsch., etc.; κατέκτειναν γρόνθοις καὶ λακτίσμασι *PAmh*.2.141.10 (iv A.D.); γρόνθῳ παίσας Sch.Il.2.220; γ. παλαστιαῖος, = σπιθαμή, Aq.*Jd*.3.16, al., cf. Hero *Geom*.4.11. II. *spoke* on a machine, Ps.-Apollod.*Poliorc*. p.46 Thévenot.

γρόνθων, ωνος, ὁ, *first lessons on the flute*, Poll.4.83, Hsch.

γρόππα, v. γράμμα.

γρόπτος, Aeol. for γραπτός, *Epigr.Gr*.991.14 (Balbilla).

γρόσυνον· τάραξον, Hsch. (cf. ὀροθύνω).

γροσφομάχος, ον, *fighting with the* γρόσφος, οἱ γ., = Lat. *velites*, Plb.1.33.9, 6.21.7.

γρόσφος, ὁ, a kind of *javelin*, Plb.6.22.4, Str.4.4.3, Plu.*Sull*.18.

γροσφοφόρος, ον, = γροσφομάχος, Plb.6.21.9.

γροῦμος· στρόβιλος, Hsch.

γρουνός, ὁ, = γρυνός, Call.*Fr.anon*.84.

γρούσσεται· μηρύεται, ἐκτείνεται, Hsch.

γροφά, Dor. for γραφή, *painting*, *IG*4.1484.271 (Epid.).

γροφ-εύς, έως, ὁ, Dor. and Arc. for γραμματεύς, *IG*4.498 (Mycenae); γ. βωλᾶς ib.12(3).1259.16 (Cimolus), 5(2).357.20 (Stymphalus). 2. = ζωγράφος, Hsch. **-εύω,** Dor. = γραμματεύω, *IG* 4.609.8 (Argos).

γροφίς, Dor. = γραφίς, *IG*4.1484.292 (Epid.).

γρόφω, Dor. = γράφω, *IG*12(3).1075 (Melos), *Schwyzer* 209 (Melian, from Olympia).

γρῦ, used with negs., ἀποκρινομένῳ.. οὐδὲ γρῦ not *a syllable*, Ar.*Pl*. 17, cf. D.19.39; μηδὲ γ. λέγε Men.521; ὄψου μηδὲν.. μηδὲ γ. not *a morsel*, not *a bit*, Antiph.190.13; διαφέρει Χαιρεφῶντος οὐδὲ γ. Men. 364, cf. *Sam*.310, Aristaenet.1.17, Jul.*ad Ath*.273b. (Expld. of the noise of swine, not even *a grunt*, by Sch.Ar. l.c.; also, *a small coin*, Suid.; but prop., = *dirt under the nail*, Hsch., who also explains it as = γρύτη, cf. γρύξ.)

γρυβός, ὁ, = γρύψ, Hsch., *EM*242.2.

γρύζω, fut. γρύξω, Ar.*Eq*.294 codd., Lxx *Ex*.11.7, γρύξομαι Alc. Com.22: aor. ἔγρυξα (v. infr.):—*say* γρῦ (v. sub voc.), *grumble, mutter*, γρύζειν δὲ καὶ τολμᾶτον..; Ar.*Pl*.454; παιδὸς φωνὴν γρύξαντος Id.*Nu*.963; εἴ τι γρύξει Id.*Eq*.294; μὴ φλαῦρον μηδὲν γρύζειν Id. *Pax* 97 (anap.); γρύζοντας οὐδὲ τουτὶ Id.*Ra*.913; οὐκ ἐτόλμα γρύξαι τὸ παράπαν prob. in Is.8.27: c. dupl. acc., ἐγὼ μὲν οὔτε χρηστὸν οὔτε σε γρύζω ἀπηνὲς οὐδέν Call.*Iamb*.1.257; later, *growl*, of a dog, Lxx l.c.; *grunt*, of a pig, Alciphr.3.73; *grumble, murmur*, πρός τινα Porph. *Abst*.1.27. II. fut. γρύσει, = τήξει *will liquefy*, Arist.*Pr*.876ᵇ18.

γρυήλιον· ῥωσμὴν δρυός, Hsch.

γρυκτός, ή, όν, (γρύζω) ἆρα γρυκτόν ἐστιν ὑμῖν; will ye *dare to grumble?* Ar.*Lys*.656.

γρῡλ-ίζω (γρυλλίζω is incorrect acc. to Phryn.*PS*p.58 B.), Dor. fut. γρυλιξεῖτε Ar.*Ach*.746:—*grunt*, of swine, Ar.l.c., *Pl*.307, D. Chr.7.74; of a person, Procop.*Arc*.17. **-ισμός,** ὁ, *grunting*, Arist.*HA*535ᵇ17 (written γρυλλ- in Poll.). **-ίων·** χοῖρος, Hsch.

γρύλλη· ὑῶν φωνή, Hsch.

γρυλλισμός, ὁ, *Egyptian dance*, Phryn.*PS*p.58 B.

γρυλλογρᾰφέω (γρύλλος 2), *draw caricatures*, opp. καλοὺς δημιουργεῖν πίνακας, Phld.*Rh*.2.297 S.

γρύλλος, ὁ, = γρυλλισμός, Phryn.*PS*p.58 B.; *performer in such a dance*, ibid. 2. *comic figure, caricature*, in painting, Plin.*HN*35. 114.

γρῦλος, later **γρύλλος,** Hsch., ὁ, *pig, porker*, Plu.2.986b, Zonar. 2. = γόγγρος, Diph.Siph.ap.Ath.8.356a, Nic.*Fr*.122.

γρῡμέα (in codd. freq. written γρυμαία), ἡ, *bag* or *chest* for old clothes, etc., Diph.127, Poll.10.160, Phryn.*PS*p.60 B.:—also **γρυμεῖα** or **-εία,** ibid., *Et.Gud.d.* II. = γρύτη I (Hsch.), *trash, trumpery*, Sotad.Com.1.3; of persons, *riff-raff*, ῥήτορας καὶ ποιητὰς καὶ πᾶσαν τὴν τοιαύτην γ. Phld.*Ir*.p.65 W., cf. Them.*Or*.21.257a; γ. παντοδαπῶν βιβλίων Dam.*Isid*.293:—hence **γρῡμεοπώλης,** ου, ὁ, Luc. *Lex*.3.

γρυμπάνειν, = γρύπτειν, Hsch.

γρύνη· λιβανωτός, Theognost.*Can*.108.

γρυνόν, = σίκυς ἄγριος, Ps.-Dsc.4.150.

γρῡνός, ὁ, *fagot, firebrand*, Hom.*Fr*.18, Lyc.86, 294.

γρῦνος, ὁ, = γρύψ, Hsch.

γρύξ· ὁ τόπος (leg. ῥύπος) τοῦ ὄνυχος, Hsch.

γρῡπάετος [ᾰ], ὁ, *a kind of griffin* or *wyvern*, Ar.*Ra*.929.

γρῡπαίνω, = γρυπόομαι, Dionys.ap.Harp., Hsch.

γρῡπᾰλώπηξ, ἡ, *griffin-fox*, nickname in Hp.*Epid*.6.8.29.

γρῡπᾰνίζω, *become wrinkled*, of the earth in earthquake, Antipho Soph.31.

γρῡπ-άνιος, ον, *wrinkled*, of the earth, Antipho Soph.30:—also **-άνιον** or **-άλιον,** τό, *old woman*, Hsch.

γρυπή, ἡ, in pl., *vulture's nests*, Hsch.

γρῡπ-νόν· στυγνόν, κατηφές, Hsch.; cf. γνύπων. **-όομαι,** Pass., *to become hooked*, of the nails, Hp.*Prog*.17, Alex.Aphr.*Pr*.2. 18, Gal.8.47. **-ός,** ή, όν, *hook-nosed, aquiline*, opp. σιμός, X.*Cyr*. 8.4.21, Pl.*R*.474d, etc.: generally, *hooked*, ὄνυχες Aret.*SA*2.1, *SD* 1.8; *curved*, γρυπὴ γαστήρ a *round* paunch, X. l.c.; γ. στέφανος Eub.105 (Sup.); τὸ γρυπόν, = γρυπότης, Arist.*Pol*.1309ᵇ24. **-ότης,** ητος, ἡ, *hookedness*, of the nose, opp. σιμότης, X.*Cyr*.8.4.21, Arist. *Rh*.1360ᵃ27; of a beak, Plu.2.994f; of talons, ib.641d. **-τω,** *become bent* or *wrinkled*, Hsch.: aor. 2 ἔγρυπον, *become wrinkled*: metaph. of the earth in an earthquake, Melanth.Hist.1: in pf. part. Pass., γᾶν ἐγρυμμέναν *Annuario* 3.195 (Gortyn). **-ωσις,** εως, ἡ, *crooking, hooking*, of the nails, Cael.Aur.*CP*2.32, Steph.*in Hp*.1. 187 D.

γρυσμός, ὁ, (γρύζω) *a grunting*, Agathocl.2.

γρῡτάριον, τό, Dim. of γρύτη, Zen.5.54, *CPHerm*.9.5 (pl., iii A.D.).

γρυτεύεται· παρασκευάζεται, Hsch.

γρύτη [ῡ], ἡ (also **γρῦτα,** ἡ, *Gloss.*), *woman's dressing-case* or *vanity-bag*, Sapph.156; σκευῶν γ. prob. a workman's *tool-bag*, *PPetr*.3 p.78. 2. *frippery*, Phryn.209, *PS*p.60 B.; cf. γριτή: pl., = σκεύη, Hsch. 3. of fish, λεπτὴ γ. small *fry*, *Gp*.20.12.2.

γρῡτο-δόκη, ἡ, = γρυμέα I, *AP*6.254 (Myrin.). **-πωλεῖον,** τό, *small-ware shop*, *Gloss.* **-πώλης,** ου, ὁ, *seller of small wares*, Sch.Ar.*Pl*.17: written κρυτ-, *BGU*9112 (iii A.D.).

γρύψ, gen. γρῡπός, ὁ, *griffin*, Aristeas ap.Hdt.3.116, cf. 4.13, A. *Pr*.804, *IG*1².280.80; τράπεζα ἔχουσα πόδας ἀναγλύπτους γρῦπας *SIG* 996.10 (Smyrna). II. a bird, prob. the *Lämmergeier*, Lxx *Le*. 11.13, *De*.14.13. III. pl., part of a ship's *tackle*, or *anchor*, Hsch.

γρωθύλοι· γωλιοί, σπήλαια, Hsch. **γρωθώνη·** σαπρὰ γραῦς, οἱ δὲ τὴν παλαιὰν ὄνησιν, Id. **γρώνα** (s. v. l.), ἡ, *sow* (Lacon.), and pl. **γρωνάδες,** Id.

γρῶνος, η, ον, (γράω) *eaten out, cavernous*, Lyc.631, 1280; *hollow*, πελλίδες Nic.*Al*.77. 2. in pl., *those who listen and do not speak*, Hsch. II. as Subst. **γρώνη** (sc. πέτρα), ἡ, *hole*, γ. μυοδόχοι Nic.*Th*.794 (pl.). 2. *hollow vessel, kneading-trough*, *AP*7.736 (Leon.).

γύαια, τά, (γύης II) = πρυμνήσια, *AP*10.1 (Leon.), Hsch.

γῠάλας [ᾰ], ὁ, *a* Megarian *cup*, Philet.ap.Ath.11.467c, Parth.ibid.

γῠᾰλοθώραξ, ᾶκος, ὁ, *cuirass composed of front- and back-piece*, Paus.10.26.2.

γύᾰλον [ῠ], τό, *hollow*, in Il. always of the *breast-* or *back-piece* of the cuirass, [θώρηκα] γυάλοισιν ἀρηρότα Il.15.530: sg., usu. of the *front-piece*, 5.99, al. 2. *hollow* of a vessel, κρατήρων γ. E.*IA*1052 (lyr.); *hollow vessel*, χρυσοῦ γέμοντα γύαλα θησαυροὺς βροτῶν Id. *Andr*.1093 (v. infr. 4). 3. κοίλας πέτρας γ. *hollow* of a rock, S.*Ph*. 1081 (lyr.); *cavern*, πέτρινα [μύχατα] γύαλα E.*Hel*.189 (lyr.). 4. pl., of *hollow ground, vales, dells*, γυάλοις ὕπο Παρνησοῖο Hes.*Th*. 499, cf. *h.Ap*.396; Νύσης *h.Hom*.26.5; γ. Θεράπνας Pi.*N*.10.56 (but γ. Πυθῶνος, Φοίβου Id.*P*.8.63, E.*Ph*.237 (lyr.), cf. *Ion* 245, S.*Fr*.460, may perh. refer to the rock-chambers of Delphi, cf. γύαλα· θησαυροί, ταμιεῖα, Hsch., and so perh. in E.*Andr*.1093 (v. supr.)); Λυδίᾳ τ' ἀγ γύαλα throughout *the vales* of Lydia, A.*Supp*.550 (lyr.); γύαλα χώρας Ar.*Th*.110 (lyr.); αἰθέρια γύαλα *the vault* of heaven, Opp.*C*. 1.281, cf. Orph.*H*.19.16.

γύᾰλος [ῠ], ὁ, *cubical stone*, *EM*243.12; also oxyt. as Adj., γυαλὸν λίθον ἀγκάσσασθαι Call.*Fr.anon*.331.

γυβᾷ· κολυμβᾷ, Hsch.

γῠβερνήτης, ὁ, = κυβ-, *PGrenf*.1.49.21 (iii A.D.).

γυγαί· πάπποι, Hsch. **γυγαίη** νύξ· ἡ σκοτεινή, Id.

γύγης, ου, ὁ, *a bird*, Dionys.*Av*.2.16.

γυέλιον· κόλπον, Hsch.

γύης [ῠ], ου, ὁ, *the curved piece of wood* in a plough, to which the share was fitted, *the tree*, Hes.*Op*.427, 436. II. *a measure of land*, rarely in sg., E.*Heracl*.839, v.l. in S.*Fr*.601; *field*, *PTeb*.105. 15 (ii B.C.); γ. ἄνυδρος *POxy*.918 ii 10 (ii A.D.): more freq. in pl., *lands*, Σικελίας λευροὺς γύας A.*Pr*.371; ἀνηρότους γύας ib.708; αὐτόσποροι γ. Id.*Fr*.196.5; οἱ πλησίοι γ. S.*OC*58, cf. *Tab.Heracl*.2.13. 2. metaph. of a wife, ἀρώσιμοι γ. S.*Ant*.569. 3. = ἀστραγάλων, σύνθεσις, Hsch. 4. γύαι· ὁδοί, Id. (Fem. (cf. γύη· μέτρον πλέθρου, Hsch.), E.*Hel*.89, *Ba*.13 codd.: but τούς, τούσδε Elmsl.)

γυήτης· χωλός, Hsch.; cf. ἀμφιγυήεις.

γυθίσσων (prob. γνυθ-)· διορύσσων, Hsch.

γυι-αλθής, ές, *nourishing the limbs*, Nic.*Th*.529. **-αλκής,** ές, *strong of limb*, σώματα B.8.38, cf. 11.8; ἥβη Opp.*H*.5.465; παλαισμοσύνη ib.2.277. **-αρκής,** ές, *strengthening the limbs*, νωδυνία Pi.*P*.3.6.

γυΐζω, *take in the hand*, coined by *EM*309.31, cf. Eust.250.36.

γυιο-βᾰρής, ές, *weighing down the limbs*, παλαίσματα, κάματος, A. *Ag.*63 (lyr.), *AP*10.12. **-βόρος**, ον, *gnawing the limbs, eating*, μελεδῶναι (v.l. γυιοκόρος, dub. sens.) Hes.*Op.*66; πῦρ *AP*9.443 (Paul. Sil.). **-δᾰμος**, η, ον, *taming limbs, conquering*, ἐν γυιοδάμαις.. χερσίν Pi.*I.*5(4).59: unless from Subst. -δάμας, ὁ, *athlete*. **-δόνητος**, ον, *with bruised limbs*, Phryn.Trag.2. **-κολλος**, ον, *binding the limbs*, Lyc.1202.

γυῖον, τό, *limb*, Hom., always pl., in phrases such as γυῖα λέλυντο Il.13.85; ὑπὸ τρόμος ἔλλαβε γυῖα 14.506; ὁππότε κέν μιν γυῖα λάβῃ κάματος 4.230, etc., cf. A.*Pers.*913 (lyr.), Id.*Eleg.*3; γυῖα ποδῶν *the feet*, Il.13.512; μητρὸς γυῖα *womb*, *h.Merc.*20; γυῖα *hands*, Theoc. 22.81; γυῖον, sg., *the hand*, ib.121 (so prob. as device on signet, *Tab. Heracl.*1.183); but γυῖον *the whole body*, Pi.*N.*7.73, Hp.*Epid.*6.4. 26.—Not in Att. Prose: later, opp. στέρνα καὶ κεφαλή, Plu.*Arist.*14.

γυιο-πᾰγής, ές, *stiffening the limbs*, νιφάς *AP*6.219 (Antip.); κάματοι *IG*3.779.6. **-πέδη**, ἡ, *fetter*: in pl., Pi.*P.*2.41, A.*Pr.*169 (lyr.).

γυιός, ή, όν, *lame*, Call.*Dian.*177, Lyc.144, Aret.*SD*2.12; γ. πόδας *AP*6.203 (Lacon. or Phil.).

γυιοτᾰκής, ές, *melting* or *wasting the limbs*, πενίη *AP*6.30 (Maced.). II. Pass., *with pining limbs*, ib.71 (Paul. Sil.).

γυιοῦχος, ον, *fettering the limbs*, Lyc.1076.

γυιόχαλκος, ον, *of brasen limb*, Dosiad.*Ara*6.

γυιόω, (γυιός) *lame*, γυιώσω.. ὑφ' ἅρμασιν ὠκέας ἵππους Il.8.402, cf. 416; *wound*, Nic.*Th.*731; γυιωθεὶς *lame*, Hes.*Th.*858, cf. Hp. *Art.*52; *weaken, reduce*, Id.*Acut.*59; γ. βίης *deprive* of strength, Orph.*Fr.*135.

γυλάριον, τό, = μυξῖνος, Sch.Opp.*H.*1.111.

γῠλιαύχην, ενος, ὁ, ἡ, *long-necked, scraggy-necked*, Ar.*Pax*789.

γυλιός (*AB*228, *EM*244.21; also **γύλιος, γύλλιον**, Hsch.), ὁ, *long-shaped wallet*, Ar.*Ach.*1097, *Pax*527 (ubi v. Sch.), Critias 34 D., Philem.35, *IG*4.951.80 (Epid.), Lib.*Decl.*33.41. II. *hedgehog*, Sophr.73.

γυλίσκος, ὁ, a *fish* (cf. γυλάριον), Hsch. **γύλλινα**· ἐρείσματα, γεῖσοι, Id.

γυλλάς, ἡ, kind of *cup* (Maced.), Hsch.; cf. γυάλας.

γυλλός, ὁ, *block of stone*, *Schwyzer* 725 (Milet., vi B.C.), *SIG*57.25 (Milet., v B.C.); also γυλλοί· στολμοί, Hsch.

γυμν-άδδομαι, Dor. for γυμνάζομαι, Ar.*Lys.*82. **-άζω**, fut. -άσω: aor. ἐγύμνασα A.*Ag.*540: pf. γεγύμνακα Id.*Pr.*586 (lyr.):—**Med.**, (v. infr.):—**Pass.**, aor. ἐγυμνάσθην [D.]61.43: pf. γεγύμνασμαι (v. infr.): (γυμνός):—*train naked, train in gymnastic exercise*: generally, *train, exercise*, τὸ σῶμα, τὴν ψυχήν, Isoc.2.11; ἑαυτὸν καὶ τοὺς ἵππους X.*An.*1.2.7; ἑαυτὸν πρός τι Arr.*Epict.*2.18.27: c. inf., γ. τοὺς παῖδάς τι ποιεῖν *train* or *accustom* them *to* do a thing, X.*Cyr.*1.6.32; γ. τινά τινι *accustom* him *to* it, ib.1.2.10; τινὰ περί τι Isoc.10.5; *teach rhetoric*, Phld.*Rh.*2.50 S.:—Med., *exercise for oneself, practise*, γυμνάσασθαι τέχνην Pl.*Grg.*514e; τὰ περὶ τὰς διαίτας Str.14.2.19; γυμνάσιον τὸ εἰωθὸς Ael.*VH*5.6; *practise gymnastic exercises*, Thgn. 1335, Hdt.7.208, Th.1.6, etc.; δρόμῳ *IG*4.955.8 (ii A.D.), etc.; generally, *practise*, ναῦς -ομένας X.*HG*1.1.16; of a disputer, Arist.*Top.* 108^{a}13, etc.:—Pass., ὁ γεγυμνασμένος *the trained* or *practised* orator, opp. ὁ εὐφυής, Id.*Rh.*1410^{b}8; γεγυμνάσθαι πρός τι, ἔν τινι, *be trained* or *practised for* or *in* a thing, Pl.*Lg.*626b, 635c; περὶ τὰ ὅπλα γυμνάζεσθαι X.*HG*6.5.23: c. acc., τὰ πρὸς τὰς πολεμικὰς πράξεις γεγυμνασμένοι τὰς ἕξεις.. Arist.*Pol.*1319^{a}22; θήραν Philostr.*VA*3.9: c. gen., γεγ. θαλάττης, πολέμων, σοφίας, Id.*Her.*2.15, 3.1, 10.1; καρδία γεγ. πλεονεξίας 2*Ep.Pet.*2.14; also ὕδωρ ὑπὸ συνεχῶν πληγῶν γεγ. καὶ κεκαθαρμένον J.*AJ*3.1.2. 2. *prepare*, βιβλίδιον *PFlor.*338.4 (iii A.D.). II. metaph., *wear out, harass*, ἅδην με.. πλάναι γεγυμνάκασι A.*Pr.*586; ἔρως πατρῴας τῆσδε γῆς σ' ἐγύμνασε Id.*Ag.*540; κρυμὸς.. πλευρὰ γυμνάζει χολῆς, of pleurisy, E.*Fr.*682:—Pass., τοὺς ὑπερμήκεις δρόμους.. γυμνάζεται A.*Pr.*592. 2. *investigate*, *Sammelb.*5941.12 (Pass., vi A.D.). III. = γυμνόω, *PSI*1.70 (Pass., vi A.D.). **-άς**, άδος, prop. fem. of γυμνός, *naked*, E.*Tr.*448: also with masc. Subst., γ. στόλος ἀνδρῶν Id.*Fr.*105. II. *trained, exercised*, ποδὶ γυμνάδος ἵππου (restored for γυμνάδας ἵππους) E.*Hipp.* 1134 (lyr.): masc., *trained, practised*, ἀμφ' ἀρετὴν *IG*3.1322. III. Subst., = γυμνασία or γυμνάσιον, γυμνάδος ἐν τεμένει *IG*12(7).447 (Amorg.), cf. 12(3).202 (Astypalaea); γυμνάδος.. πόνον ἐκτελέσαντα *Inscr.Cos* 419.5: pl., Orph.*H.*28.5. **-ᾰσία**, ἡ, *right to use* γυμνάσιον, Arist.*Pol.*1297^{a}17 (s.v.l.); *exercise*, σωματικὴ γ. 1*Ep.Ti.*4.8: pl., *IG*2^{2}.1006.65, *SIG*1073.19 (Olympia, ii A.D.); of *military exercises*, ἡ ἐν τοῖς ὅπλοις γ. Plb.4.7.6; generally, *struggle*, Str.3.2.7; αἱ καθ' ἡμέραν γ. *lessons*, D.H.*Comp.*20: metaph. of *mental exercise*, Iamb.*Comm.Math.*24; freq. of disputation, Pl.*Tht.*169c, Arist. *Top.*101^{a}27, al.; *training*, γ. πρὸς τὰς πολιτικὰς πράξεις Plb.1.1. 2. 2. Rhet., *practice*: hence, *arrangement, disposition*, τοῦ διηγήματος Theo *Prog.*4, cf. Aphth.*Prog.*6.

γυμνᾰσιαρχ-έω, *to be gymnasiarch*, at Athens and elsewhere, *IG* 3.1104, al., 5(1).481, al. (Sparta), 7.1669 (Plataea), *BGU*184.3 (i A.D.), etc.; εἰς Προμήθεια Lys.21.3, Is.7.36; γ. λαμπάδι (cf. λαμπαδηφορία) Id.6.60:—Med., γυμνασιαρχεῖσθαι ἐν ταῖς λαμπάσι X.*Vect.* 4.52. II. trans., *provide for, supply as gymnasiarch*, πάντα τὰ γυμνάσια Keil-Premerstein *Zweiter Bericht* No.69:—Pass., *to be supplied with gymnasiarchs*, γυμνασιαρχοῦσιν οἱ πλούσιοι.., ὁ δὲ δῆμος γυμνασιαρχεῖται X.*Ath.*1.13. **-ης**, ου, ὁ, = -αρχος, *IG*3.1104, Lex ap.Aeschin.1.39. 2. name of a throw at dice, Hsch. **-ία**, ἡ, *office of gymnasiarch*, X.*Ath.*1.13 (pl.), Arist.*Pol.*1323^{a}1, Pl.*Ax.* 367a, *IG*12(2).82 (Mytilene), 5(1).531 (Sparta), *PAmh.*70.3 (ii A.D.), etc. **-ικός**, ή, όν, *of* or *for a gymnasiarch*, ῥάβδοι Plu.*Ant.*33; πολιτεία Iamb.*VP*27.130; νόμος *IG*12(7).515.82 (Amorg.); ἔκλογος *CPHerm.*53.7 (iii A.D.). **-ίς**, ίδος, ἡ, fem. of -άρχης, *CIG*5132 (Cyren.), *PAmh.*64.6 (ii A.D.). **-ος**, ὁ, *gymnasiarch, superintendent of athletic training* at Athens and elsewhere, And.1.132, D. 35.48, *IG*2^{2}.1227.4, 5(1).20*A*5 (Sparta), *PAmh.*2.130.1 (i A.D.), etc.: fem. ἡ -αρχος, *IGRom.*3.802 (Pamphyl.). 2. *director of a* γυμνάσιον, Pl.*Erx.*399a, Phld.*Herc.*1040.

γυμνᾰσ-ίδιον, τό, Dim. of sq., Arr.*Epict.*2.16.29. **-ιον** [ᾰ], τό, I. in pl., *bodily exercises*, Pi.*Fr.*129.4, Hdt.9.33, Hp.*Art.*58, Pl.*R.*539d, etc. 2. metaph., γυμνάσιον γράφειν write *an exercise* or *essay*, Gal.19.17. II. *gymnastic school*, E.*Ph.*368, Antipho 3.2.3, Pl.*Criti.*117c (pl.), etc.; ἐκ θἠμετέρου γυμνασίου from our *school*, Ar.*V.* 526: pl., γ. τὰ ἱππόκροτα the *hippodrome*, E.*Hipp.*229 (anap.). b. οἱ ἀπὸ γ. in Egypt, *those who have received training as* ἔφηβοι, i.e. the Hellenized inhabitants of the μητροπόλεις, *PFlor.*179.24 (i A.D.), etc. 2. generally, *school*, ἐν γυμνασίοις Ἀκαδημίας Epicr.11.11; ἐν Ὁμηρείῳ γ. *Epigr.Gr.*860 (Chios); γ. ἀρετῆς Luc.*Nigr.*19; of a philosophic *school*, ἐκ τοῦ αὐτοῦ γ. Pl.*Grg.*493d, cf. ὁ ἀπὸ τοῦ αὐτοῦ γ. Dam.*Pr.*399: metaph., γῆ γ. ζωῆς Secund.*Sent.*15. 3. in collective sense, *the youths who attend the school*, *IPE*2.299.8 (Panticapaeum). **-ις**, εως, ἡ, *exercise*, Poll.3.153. **-ιώδης**, ες, *fit for a* γυμνάσιον, *ornamenta* Cic.*Att.*1.6.2. **-μα**, ατος, τό, *an exercise*, γ. καὶ ἀσκήματα τῆς ῥητορικῆς D.H.*Rh.*2.1, cf. J.*Ap.*1.10, Plu.2.1119d; γ. τῆς ψυχῆς Ph.1.590: in pl., rhetorical *text-books*, Theo *Prog.* 1. 2. physical *exercises*, Ruf.ap.Orib.*inc.*2.15, Luc.*Anach.*8, Ath. 10.413c. **-τέον**, *one must train*, τὸ σῶμα X.*Mem.*2.1.28; of disputation, Arist.*Top.*164^{b}9. II. Adj. -τέος, α, ον, Philostr.*Gym.*29, al. **-τήριον**, τό, = γυμνάσιον, Gal.6.186: metaph., δικῶν Aristaenet. 2.3. **-τής**, οῦ, ὁ, *trainer of professional athletes*, X.*Mem.*2.1.20, Pl.*Lg.*720e, etc.; ἰατρὸς καὶ γ. Arist.*EN*1180^{b}14. **-τικός**, ή, όν, *fond of athletic exercises, skilled in them*, Hp.*Aph.*1.3; γ. ἢ ἰατρός Pl. *Prt.*313d: Comp., Philostr.*Gym.*35: Sup., ib.11; *of the gymnastic master* (opp. παιδοτρίβης, q.v.), Arist.*Pol.*1288^{b}18; γ. [θεραπεία] Pl. *Grg.*464b: ἡ -κή (with or without τέχνη), *gymnastics*, Id.*Smp.*187a, etc. Adv. -κῶς Ar.*V.*1212. II. γ. λῆμμα (opp. ῥητορικόν) *suited for dialectical discussion*, *Stoic.*2.76. Adv. -κῶς *by means of testing*, Simp.*in Ph.*139.3.

γυμν-ηλός, ή, όν, *poor, needy*, Hsch., *EM*243.14. **-ής**, ῆτος, ὁ, = γυμνός, βίος D.S.3.8. II. Subst., *light-armed foot-soldier*, Tyrt.11.35, Hdt.9.63, E.*Ph.*1147, X.*An.*4.1.28, *Hell.Oxy.*6.5. 2. in pl., γυμνῆτες, οἱ, *Argive serfs*, Poll.3.83, *Et.Gud.*; also γυμνήσιοι, οἱ, St.Byz. s.v. Χίος, Eust. ad D.P.533. 3. = Γυμνοσοφισταί, Str.15. 1.70. **-ήσιαι** νῆσοι, αἱ, (γυμνής) the Balearic islands, from the skill of the inhabitants *as light-armed troops*, esp. slingers, Arist. *Mir.*837^{a}30, Str.3.5.1, D.S.5.17, etc.

γυμνήσιοι, v. γυμνής.

γυμνητ-εία (v.l. -ητία), ἡ, *light-armed troops*, Th.7.37. II. *nakedness*, Corn.*ND*15; *going unclothed*, as a symptom of insanity, Ptol.*Tetr.*170. **-εύω**, *to be naked*, 1*Ep.Cor.*4.11, Demoph.*Sent.* 8. 2. *to be lightly clad*, D.Chr.25.3. 3. *to be light-armed*, Plu. *Aem.*16. **-ης**, ου, ὁ, = f.l. for γυμνής II. 1, X.*An.*4.1.6. II. Adj., *naked*, Lyc.388, Luc.*Bacch.*3. **-ικός**, ή, όν, *of* or *for a* γυμνής, ὅπλα X.*Cyr.*1.2.4, Plu.*Flam.*4; τὸ γ., = γυμνητεία, Str.7.3.17. **-ις**, ιδος, ἡ, fem. of γυμνήτης, in signf. of γυμνής II. 3, σοφία, Plu.2.332b.

γυμνικός, ή, όν, *of* or *for gymnastic exercises*, γ. ἀγών a *gymnastic* contest, Hdt.2.91, etc., opp. ἱππικός, Id.1.167; opp. μουσικός, Th. 3.104, Pl.*Lg.*658a; τὰ γ. ἐπιδείκνυσθαι *POxy.*42.5 (iv A.D.): Sup., Luc.*Ner.*2.

γυμνο-δερκέομαι, Pass., *show oneself naked*, Luc.*Cyn.*1. **-καρπος**, ον, *huskless*, of fruits, Thphr.*CP*1.17.8. **-κοχλίας**, *snail*, *Gloss.* **-παιδίαι**, αἱ, *festival* at Sparta, *at which naked boys danced and went through gymnastic exercises*, Hdt.6.67, Th.5.82, etc.: later in sg., Plu.2.208d; ἡ τῶν Λυκαίων γ., = *Lupercalia*, D.C. 44.11. **-παιδική** (sc. ὄρχησις), ἡ, *dance of naked boys*, Ath.14. 630d: pl., Phld.*Mus.*p.15 K. **-περίβολος**, ον, *bare of coverings*, epith. of Γυμνοσοφισταί, Ps.-Callisth.3.5. **-ποδέω**, *go barefoot*, Socr.*Ep.*13. **-πόδης**, ου, ὁ, = γυμνόπους, Suid. **-πόδιον**, τό, *kind of sandal* or *slipper*, Poll.7.94. **-πους**, ὁ, ἡ, gen. ποδος, *barefooted*, Str.7.2.3, J.*BJ*2.15.1. **-ρρύπᾰρος** [ῠ], ον, *naked and dirty*, of Zeno, D.L.7.16.

γυμνός, ή, όν, *naked, unclad*, γ. περ ἐών Od.6.136, etc.; τὰ γ. Thphr.*Char.*4.4: Comp., Ἶρου γυμνότερος Procop.Gaz.*Ep.*122; γυμνὸν στάδιον, opp. ὁπλιτοδρόμος, Pi.*P.*11.49. 2. *unarmed*, οὐδ' ὑπέμεινε Πάτροκλον, γυμνόν περ ἐόντ' ἐν δηϊοτῆτι Il.16.815, etc.; γυμνὰ τὰ νῶτα παρέχειν Plu.*Fab.*11; τὰ γυμνά *parts not covered by armour, exposed parts*, Th.3.23, X.*HG*4.4.12; esp. *right side* (the left being covered by the shields), Th.5.10.71. 3. of things *bare*, γ. τόξον an *uncovered* bow, i.e. taken out of the case, Od.11.607; γ. ὀϊστός 21.417; γ. μάχαιραι Theoc.22.146; ξίφος A.R.1.1254; γ. τῇ κεφαλῇ Pl.*Phdr.*243b. 4. c. gen., *stripped of* a thing, κολεοῦ γ. φάσγανον Pi. *N.*1.52, cf. X.*Ages.*2.14; κᾶπος [δένδρων] γ. Pi.*O.*3.24; γ. ὀστράκων A.*Fr.*337; γ. προπομπῶν Id.*Pers.*1036 (lyr.); (but also γ. τῶν ἀριστείων ἄτερ S.*Aj.*464): in Prose, γ. ὅπλων Hdt.2.141 (v.l.); ἡ ψυχὴ γ. τοῦ σώματος Pl.*Cra.*403b, cf. *R.*577b, *Grg.*523d: Comp. ἀνδριάντων -ότερος D.Chr.34.3. 5. *lightly clad*, i.e. *in the undergarment only*, Hes.*Op.*391, Ar.*Nu.*498, Pl.*R.*474a, Luc.*Herm.*23;

μικροῦ γ. ἐν τῷ χιτωνίσκῳ D.21.216; of horses, *without harness*, Arr. *Cyn.*24.3. **6.** of facts, *naked, bald*, γυμνῶν τῶν πραγμάτων θεωρουμένων D.S.1.76; γ. τὸ ἔργον διηγήσασθαι Luc.*Tox.*42; γυμνοτέροις χρῆσασθαι τοῖς ὀνόμασιν Ph.1.5; γ. χρῆσθαι τῇ μιμήσει Demetr.*Eloc.* 112. Adv. -ῶς *baldly*, Sch.A.*Pers.*740. **7.** *destitute*, *PSI*6.605. 4 (iii B.C.), etc. **8.** *bare, mere*, κόκκος 1*Ep.Cor.*15.37. **9.** *beardless*, A.R.2.707. **10.** *scalped*, Archil.161. **11.** γυμνή· ἄνηβος, Hsch. **12.** prov. of impossibilities, γυμνῷ φυλακὴν ἐπιτάττεις Pherecr.144, Philem.12. (Akin to Skt. *nagnás*, Lat. *nūdus*, etc.; cf. λυγνός.)

γυμνο-σάνδᾰλος, ον, *without sandals, barefooted*, *PMag.Par.*1. 2481. **-σοφισταί**, ῶν, οἱ, *naked philosophers* of India, Arist.*Fr.*35, Str.16.2.39, Ph.2.27, Plu.*Alex.*64, Luc.*Fug.*7, Porph.*Abst.*4.17:—hence **-σοφιστεία**, ἡ, *their philosophy*, Suid. s. v. Ἀδάμ. **-σπέρματος** and **-σπερμος**, ον, *having the seed with no apparent pericarp*, Thphr.*HP*1.11.2 and 3.

γυμνότης, ητος, ἡ, *nakedness*, Lxx *De.*28.48, *Ep.Rom.*8.35, M.Ant. 10.27; γ. ψυχική Ph.1.77. **2.** *bare statement*, τῶν προτάσεων D.H. *Rh.*10.6.

γυμνο-φᾰνής, ές, *appearing naked*, πόρναι Lyd.*Mag.*3.65. **-χρους**, ὁ, ἡ, *having the body naked*, Nonn.*D.*7.124.

γυμν-όω, *strip naked*, τὰ ὀστέα τῶν κρεῶν γ. *strip* the bones of their flesh, Hdt.4.61; σῶμα γυμνώσαντες εὖ S.*Ant.*410:—Hom. only Med. and Pass., *strip oneself* or *be stripped naked*, αἰδέομαι γὰρ γυμνοῦσθαι Od.6.222; mostly of warriors, *to be exposed*, ὅτεῳ στρεφθέντι μετάφρενα γυμνωθείη Il.12.428; οὖτα Θόαντα στέρνον γυμνωθέντα παρ' ἀσπίδα 16.312, cf. Od.10.341, Call.*Iamb.*1.219; τεῖχος ἐγυμνώθη the wall *was left bare*, i. e. *defenceless*, Il.12.399: c. gen., γυμνώθη ῥακέων he *stripped himself* of his rags, Od.22.1; later γυμνωθὲν ξίφος, δόρυ, Hdt.3.64, A.*Th.*624: metaph., *to be stripped* or *deprived of* a thing, Pl.*R.*601b; ἀφορμῆς Antipho Soph.14. **2.** metaph., *lay bare*, φύσιν τῷ λόγῳ Ph.1.118:—Pass., Dam.*Pr.*400. **3.** *lay aside*, σάκκον Lxx *Ju.*9.1. **-ωσις**, εως, ἡ, *stripping*, παρθένων Plu. *Lyc.*14, cf. *Cat.Ma.*20, Dsc.2.173. **II.** *exposure*, Lxx *Ge.*9.22; ἐξαλλάσσειν τὴν ἑαυτοῦ γ. his *defenceless side* (cf. γυμνός 2), Th.5. 71. **-ωτέος**, α, ον, *to be stripped of*, τινός Pl.*R.*361c. **II.** γυμνωτέον, *one must strip*, Gal.10.448: pl., -τέα Them.*Or.*23.294c.

γῠναικ-άδελφος [ᾰ], ὁ, *wife's brother*, *PMasp.*95.14 (vi A.D.), Sch. S.*OT*70, Sch.E.*Hec.*833. **-άνηρ** [ᾰ], ανδρος, ὁ, *woman-man*: dat. pl., γυναικάνδρεσσι Epich.218, cf. Eust.1132.32. **-άνθη**, ἡ, = ἄμπελος μέλαινα, Plin.*HN*23.27. **-άριον**, τό, Dim. of γυνή, Diocl. Com.11, Epict.*Ench.*7, 2*Ep.Ti.*3.6, M.Ant.5.11. **-εῖος**, α, ον A. *Ch.*630 (lyr.), also ος, ον ib.878, E.*IA*233 (lyr.): Ion. **-ήιος**, η, ον: (γυνή):—*of* or *belonging to women, feminine*, γυναικεῖαι βουλαί *a woman's* designs, Od.11.437; λουτρόν Hes.*Op.*753; ἔργα Hdt.4.114; κόσμος Pl.*R.*373c; σκεῦος (i. e. *woman*) 1*Ep.Pet.*3.7; γ. αἰδοῖον, τόποι, χῶροι, Gal.*UP*15.3, Aret.*SA*2.11, *CA*2.10; κόλπος (= αἰδοῖον) Sor.1. 16; ῥοῦς *leucorrhoea*, Id.2.43; γονόρροια Aret.*SD*2.11; ἰατρός Sor.2.3; γ. ἀγορά Thphr.*Char.*2.9; ἡ γ. θεός, = Lat. *bona dea*, Plu.*Caes.*9, *Cic.* 19; γ. πόλεμος war *with women*, *AP*7.352 (Mel.(?)). **2.** in bad sense, *womanish, effeminate*, πένθος Archil.9.10; δράματα Ar.*Th.* 151; μαθήματα Pl.*Alc.*1.127a; γ. καὶ σμικρὰ διάνοια Id.*R.*469d. Adv. -είως, πικραίνεσθαι Id.*Lg.*731d; ἐμπικραίνεσθαι Eus.Mynd.54; διακεῖσθαι D.C.38.18. **II.** as Subst., **1.** ἡ γυναικεία, Ion. -ηΐη, = γυναικών, *part of the house reserved for the women*, Hdt.5.20, Lxx *To.*2.11. **b.** ἡ γ. (sc. ἀγορά), Thphr.*Char.*22.10. **2.** τὰ γυναικεῖα *partes muliebres*, Hp.*Epid.*1.26.ε', Aret.*SA*2.11. **b.** = τὰ καταμήνια, Hp.*Aph.*5.28, Arist.*PA*648^{a}31, al., Lxx *Ge.*18.11. **c.** *lochia*, Gal.17(2).817. **d.** *female disorders*, title of works by Hp. and Sor., cf. Thphr.*HP*4.8.6, Aret.*CA*1.3. **e.** (sc. φάρμακα) *remedies for female complaints*, Hp.*Mul.*1.64. **f.** *women's garments*, *PSI* 4.341.7 (iii B.C.). **3.** γυναικεῖον, τό, = στίβι, Dsc.5.84. **-εραστέω**, *to be a lover of women*, and **-εραστής**, οῦ, ὁ, *woman-lover*, Poll. 3.68,70. **-ήιος**, η, ον, Ion. for γυναικεῖος (q. v.). **-ηρός**, ά, όν, = γυναικεῖος, Diocl.Com.4; γ. τρόπος Phryn.*PS*p.55 B. **-ίας**, ου, ὁ, = γύννις, *weakling*, Eup.124 (dub.), Luc.*Pisc.*31, Lib.*Or.*64. 64. **-ίζω**, *to be womanish, play the woman*, Hp.*Aër.*22, Ar.*Th.* 268:—Med., Plb.32.15.7, J.*BJ*4.9.10. **II.** *muliebria pati*, Luc. *Gall.*19: = ἀφροδισιάζεσθαι, Hsch. **-ικός**, ή, όν, *womanish*, Arist. *Pr.*895^{a}32, *GA*766^{b}32 (Comp.); γυναικικώτεροι γίνονται οἱ μαστοί *more like those of women*, Id.*HA*582^{a}13. Adv. -κῶς Suid. **-ιον**, τό, Dim. of γυνή, Longus 3.6.15 (v.l. γύναιον). **-ισις**, εως, ἡ, *womanish behaviour*, Ar.*Th.*863, Lib.*Or.*64.74. **-ίσκιον**, τό, *young girl*, Hsch. **-ισμός**, ὁ, *womanish weakness*, Plb.30.18.5, cf. Phld.*Mus.*p.16 K., D.S.31.15, Plu.*Caes.*63. **-ιστί**, Adv. *like a woman*, Ath.12.528f.

γῠναικό-βουλος, ον, *devised by a woman*, μήτιδες A.*Ch.*626 (lyr.). **-γήρῡτος**, ον, *proclaimed by a woman*, κλέος Id.*Ag.*487 (lyr.). **-δίδακτος** [ῐ], ον, *taught by a woman*, Olymp. *in Alc.* p.136 C. **-ειδής**, ές, = γυναικώδης, Sch.Ar.*Nu.*289. **-ήθης**, ες, *of womanish disposition*, Hsch. s. v. μαλακός. **-θοίνας**, ὁ, *feasted by the women* or *feaster of women*, epith. of Ares at Tegea, Paus.8.48.4. **-θῡμος**, ον, *of womanish mind*, Ptol.*Tetr.*162. Adv. -μως Plb.2.8.12; χειρίζειν τι, of a man, Id.32.15.9. **-ϊέραξ**, ακος, ὁ, *woman-hunter*, Anon.ap.Suid. **-κλωψ**, ωπος, ὁ, *stealer of women*, Lyc.771. **-κοσμοι**, οἱ, = γυναικονόμοι, Poll.8. 112. **-κρᾱσία**, ἡ, (κρᾶσις) *womanish temper*, Str.3.4.18, Plu. *Cleom.*33 (s. v. l.), 2.20a. **-κρᾰτέομαι**, Pass., *to be ruled by women*, Arist.*Pol.*1269^{b}24, D.S.2.45, Plu.2.755c. **-κράτητος** [ᾰ], ον, *ruled by women*, Sch.E.*Or.*742. **-κρᾰτία** (-κράτεια Procop.*Arc.*5), ἡ, *dominion of women*, Arist.*Pol.*1313^{b}33, Plu.*Cat. Ma.*8: title of plays by Amphis and Alexis. **-κτόνος**, ον, *murdering women*, Ph.2.581, *Cat.Cod.Astr.*8(4).128. **-μᾰνέω**, *to be mad for women*, Ar.*Th.*576, J.*BJ*1.22.3. **-μᾰνής**, ές, *mad for women*, Chrysipp.*Stoic.*3.167, Ph.2.312, Gal.5.396, *AP*12.86 (Mel.), Luc.*Alex.*11. **-μᾰνία**, ἡ, *madness for women*, Chrysipp.*Stoic.*3. 167. **-μασθος** or **-μαστος**, ον, *having breasts like a woman*: -μασθον, τό, abnormal development of the mamma, Gal.19.444, cf. Paul.Aeg.6.46. **-μῑμος**, ον, *aping women*, γυναικομίμοις ὑπτιάσμασιν χερῶν A.*Pr.*1005; ἐσθήματα S.*Fr.*769; μόρφωμα E.*Antiop.* ii *A* 7 A.; στολά Id.*Ba.*980 (lyr.). **-μορφος**, ον, *in woman's shape*, ib.855, Ph.2.280. **-νομέω**, *to be a* γυναικονόμος, *BCH*47. 376 (Notium), Artem.2.31. **-νομία**, ἡ, *office of* γυναικονόμος, Arist.*Pol.*1322^{b}39. **-νόμος**, ὁ, *supervisor of women*, title of magistrate at Athens and elsewhere, Timocl.32.3, Men.272, Arist.*Pol.* 1299^{a}22, Philoch.103, *IG*5(1).170 (Sparta, iii A.D.), 1390.26 (Andania, i B.C.), *SIG*1219.17 (Gambreion).

γῠναικο-πᾰθέω, *to be effeminate*, Ath.12.523c. **-πίπης** [ῐ], ου, ὁ, (ὀπιπτεύω) *one who ogles women*, Eust.851.54. **-πληθής**, ές, *composed of women*, ὅμιλος A.*Pers.*122 (lyr.); ξύλλογοι E.*Alc.*952. **-ποινος**, ον, *woman-avenging*, πόλεμοι A.*Ag.*225 (lyr.). **-πρεπής**, ές, *befitting women, womanish*, Plu.2.102e: Comp., Procl.*Par.Ptol.*203. **-πρεπώδης**, ες, = foreg., Ptol.*Tetr.*144 (Comp.). **-πρόσωπος**, ον, *with woman's face*, *Mim.Oxy.*465.203, Sch.Il.1.131. **-τροφος**, ον, *reared by a woman*, Suid. s. v. τηθαλλαδοῦς. **-ϋφή**, ἡ, *women's weaving*, τεχνῖται τῆς κατὰ τὴν ἐρέαν πᾶσαν γυναικυνφη (sic), *PSI*4. 341.2 (iii B.C.). **-φίλης** [ῐ], ου, Dor. **-ας**, α, ὁ, *woman-loving*, Polyzel.10, Theoc.8.[60]: voc. -φίλα *AP*6.78 (Eratosth.). **-φόνος**, ον, *slaying women*, ἰχώρ Orph.*L.*488 (s. v. l.). **-φρων**, ον, gen. ονος, *of woman's mind*, E.*Fr.*362.34. **-φυής**, ές, *female by nature*, Emp.61.4. **-φωνος**, ον, '*speaking small like a woman*', Ar.*Th.*192. **-ψῡχος**, ον, *of womanish soul*, Procl.*Par.Ptol.* 228.

γῠναικόω, *make effeminate*, Ph.2.21:—Pass., Hp.*Epid.*6.8.32; παρθένος οὐδέποτε γυναικουμένη Ph.1.683.

γῠναικ-ώδης, ες, *woman-like, womanish*, τὸ ἀγεννὲς καὶ γ. Plb.2. 56.9, cf. D.S.2.24, Ph.1.366; ἄνανδρα καὶ γ. πάθη Plu.*Sol.*21: -ῶδες φθέγγεσθαι Luc.*Nigr.*11. Adv. -δῶς Sch.Ar.*Th.*575. **-ών**, ῶνος, ὁ, = sq., X.*Cyr.*5.5.2. **-ωνῖτις**, ιδος, ἡ, *women's apartments* in a house, opp. ἀνδρών (cf. γυναικών), Lys.1.9, Men.519, Ph.1.107, etc.; *harem* of an eastern prince, i. e. *the women*, Plu.*Cat.Mi.*30, 2. 819d; at Jerusalem, the *women's court* in the Temple, J.*BJ*5.5. 2. **2.** as Adj., ἡ γ. αὐλή the court *of the women's apartments*, D.S.17.50; ἑστία Ph.1.312.

γῠναι-μᾰνής, ές, = γυναικομανής, *mad for women*, Il.3.39, *h.Bacch.* 17, Ael.*NA*15.14, Q.S.1.726:—in late Ep. **-μανέων**, as if a part., ib. 735, Nonn.*D.*2.125, al. **II.** *making women mad*, Hsch.

γύναιος [ῠ], α, ον, = γυναικεῖος, γ. δῶρα presents *made to a woman*, Od.11.521, 15.247; φυὴ γυναίη Mosch.2.45. **II.** Subst. **γύναιον**, τό, *little woman*, term of endearment for a wife, Ar.*V.*610, *Th.*792: more freq. in a contemptuous sense, *weak woman*, And.1.130, etc.; γυναίου πρᾶγμ' ἐποίει D.25.57, cf. Arist.*EN*1171^{b}10: but simply, = γυνή, Aen.Tact.2.6, D.S.17.24, J.*AJ*1.12.4, al., Ph.1.99, al., Plu. *Pel.*9.

γύνανδρος [ῠ], ον, *of doubtful sex, womanish*, S.*Fr.*963, Ael.*Fr.*10, 290. **2.** of a woman, *virago*, Ph.1.183, 2.379.

γυνή, Dor. **γυνά**, Boeot. **βανά** (v. sub voce), ἡ, gen. γυναικός, acc. γυναῖκα, voc. γύναι (γυνή Alc.Com.32): dual γυναῖκε S.*Ant.*61: pl. γυναῖκες, γυναικῶν, etc. (as if from γύναιξ wh. is only found in Gramm., cf. Hdn.Gr.2.643): gen. γυναικείων Phoc.3 (s. v. l.): Aeol. dat. pl. γυναίκεσσι Sapph.*Supp.*7.6: Com. acc. γυνήν Pherecr.91: pl. nom. γυναί Philippid.2, Men.484, acc. γυνάς *Com.Adesp.*1336, cf. *EM*243.24, *AB*86:—*woman*, opp. *man*, Il.15.683, etc.: with a second Subst., γ. ταμίη housekeeper, 6.390; δέσποινα Od.7.347; γρηῦς (q. v.), ἀλετρίς (q. v.), δμῳαὶ γυναῖκες Il.9.477, al.; Περσίδες γ. Hdt.3.3: voc., as a term of respect or affection, *mistress, lady*, E.*Med.*290, Theoc.15.12, etc.; φαντὶ γυναῖκες *the lasses* say, Id.20.30; πρὸς γυναικὸς *like a woman*, A.*Ag.*592: prov., γ. μονωθεῖσ' οὐδέν Id.*Supp.* 749; ὅρκους γυναικὸς εἰς ὕδωρ γράφω (cf. γράφω II) S.*Fr.*811; γυναιξὶ κόσμον ἡ σιγὴ φέρει Id.*Aj.*293. **II.** *wife, spouse*, Il.6.160, Od.8. 523, Hdt.1.34, etc.; γ. καὶ παρθένοι X.*An.*3.2.25; opp. ἑταίρα, Is.3. 13; γ. γνησία, *PEleph.*1.3 (iv B.C.); also, *concubine*, Il.24.497. **III.** *mortal woman*, opp. *goddess*, 14.315, Od.10.228, etc. **IV.** *female*, *mate* of animals, Arist.*Pol.*1262^{a}22 (dub. sens.), Xenarch.14, etc.—Not to be taken as Adj. in γυναῖκα θήσατο μαζόν Il.24.58. (Cf. Ved. *gnā-* (freq. disyll.), Skt. *janis.*)

γύννις, ιδος, ὁ, *a womanish man*, ποδαπὸς ὁ γ.; of Bacchus, A.*Fr.* 61, cf. Theoc.22.69 (s. v. l.), Ael.*VH*12.12, Lib.*Or.*64.49. **2.** = ἵππουρις, Ps.-Dsc.4.46,47.

γύον, τό, = γύης, Sch.Od.18.374.

γύος, ὁ, = γύης II, *PLips.*106.16 (i A.D.), *PTeb.*373.7 (ii A.D.), etc.

γῡπ-αιεύς, έως, ὁ, title of Apollo, Conon 35.5. **-ἀλέκτωρ**, ορος, ὁ, *vulture-cock*, fabulous bird, *PMag.Berol.*2.18. **-άριον**, τό, Dim. of sq., *nest, cranny*, Ar.*Eq.*793.

γύπη [ῡ], ἡ, *vulture's nest*, Hsch.; κοίλωμα γῆς, θαλάμη, γωνία, Id.

γῡπιαῖος, α, ον, = γύπινος, Tz.*H.*12 No.439 tit.

γῡπ-ιάς, άδος, ἡ, *vulture-haunted*, πέτρα A.*Supp.*796 (lyr.). **-ινος**, η, ον, *of a vulture*, πτέρυξ Luc.*Icar.*11.

γῡπο-γίγας [ῐ], αντος, ὁ, in pl., 'men of prey', Marin.*Procl.* 15. **-ειδής**, ές, *vulture-like*: τὸ γ. Porph.ap.Eus.*PE*3.12.

γυπόν· μακρόν, Hsch.

γῡπώδης, ες, = γυποειδής, *hooknosed*, Arist.*Phgn.*808^{b}7.

γύπωνες, οἱ, dancers at Sparta, Poll.4.104.

γῡράλεος [ᾰ], α, ον, = γυρός, *rounded, curved*, Opp.*C.*1.57.

γυργᾰθίον, τό, Dim. of sq., in Alchemy, *net* for suspending substances in fluids, *PHolm.*18.17.

γυργᾰθός (on the accent v. Hdn.Gr.1.145, but γύργαθος in Mss.), ὁ, *wicker-basket, creel*, Ar.*Fr.*217, Aen.Tact.18.6, Timo38, Luc.*DMeretr.*14.2; of the *net* woven by phalangia, Arist.*HA*555^{b}10; *cage* for insane patients, Paul.Aeg.3.14: prov., γυργαθὸν φυσᾶν, of labour in vain, Aristaen.2.20:—also **γυργαθόν**, τό, *BGU*1092.29 (iv A.D.); cf. γεργαθός.

γῡρεύω, *run round in a circle*, Str.6.1.8: c. acc. cogn., καμπτῆρας Babr.29.4.

γῡρητόμος, ον, *tracing a circle*, αὖλαξ *AP*9.274 (Phil.).

γῡρίνη, ἡ, a kind of *cake*, Luc.*Trag.*158.

γῡρῖνος (so Hdn.Gr.1.183) or **γύρῑνος**, ὁ, *tadpole*, [βάτραχος] γ. Pl.*Tht.*161d, cf. Arat.947; χείρους γυρίνων οἱ ῥήτορες Lib.*Decl.*26.36.

γῡρῑνώδης, ες, *like a tadpole*, Arist.*HA*568^{a}1.

γύριος [ῡ], α, ον, (γυρός) *circular, round*, λίμνη Anon.ap.Suid.

γῦρις, εως, ἡ, *the finest meal*, Dsc.2.85, Sor.1.118, Ath.3.115d, *POxy.*520.12 (ii A.D.):—also **γύριος**, prob. in *PSI*4.428.44 (iii B.C.), cf. *girius*, = *farina, pollen*, *Gloss.*

γῡρ-ιστήριον κόσκινον, *sieve for* γῦρις, *Gloss.* **-ιστός**, ή, όν, *rounded, curved*, Sch.Philostr.p.579B. **-ίτης** [ῑ] (sc. ἄρτος), ου, ὁ, *bread of the finest meal*, *Gp.*20.41, Hsch.

γῡρο-δρόμος, ον, *running round in a circle*, πέτρος a millstone, *AP*9.20. **-ειδής**, ές, *like a circle, round.* Adv. -δῶς Dsc.2.173.

γῡρόθεν, Adv. *in a circle*, [Lib.]*Descr.*30.14.

γῡρόμαντις, εως, ὁ, (γῦρις) = ἀλευρόμαντις, dub. l. in Artem.2.69.

γῡρός, ά, όν, *rounded, curved, crooked*, γυρὸς ἐν ὤμοισι *round-shouldered*, Od.19.246, cf. D.H.14.10, *Hymn.Is.*29; κέρας, ἄγκιστρα, *AP*6.255 (Eryc.), 28 (Jul.); κόνις, of a tomb, ib.7.180 (Apollonid.); γ. πάλη, i.e. wrestling, Philostr.*Gym.*11: Comp. -ότερος Ael.*NA*4.34.

γῦρ-ος, ὁ, *ring, circle*, Plb.29.11.5; γ. οὐρανοῦ, γῆς, Lxx *Jb.*22.14, *Is.*40.22; perh. an *ornament, bangle*, Men.334. 2. *trench* made round a tree, Thphr.*CP*3.4.1, Orph.*Fr.*280.4; γύρους περισκάψας Alciphr.3.13. **-όω**, *make round*, οὐρανόν Lxx *Si.*43.12; *bend*, Opp.*H.*2.333; *wind*, τρίχα ἵππου *PHolm.*3.42 (γηρ- Pap.); *bind up*, Opp.*H.*4.419; ἐπ' αὐχένι δεσμὰ βραχίοσι γ. of a bride, ib. 159:—Pass., *to be bent*: hence of the aged, *to be weak* in body, *Com. Adesp.*969. II. *plant in a* γῦρος, Arat.9, Ph.2.294; *make a* γῦρος *round* a tree, ib.402, *Gp.*4.3.1:—Med., *dig, trench*, βώλακα γαίης Nic.*Al.*514. III. intr., *coil oneself up*, of the ichneumon, Opp.*C.*3.440.

γυρτεύς· ἀνακρωτόφονος, Hsch. **γυρτόν**· σκύφον, Id.

γύρ-ωσις [ῡ], εως, ἡ, *making of a* γῦρος, *POxy.*1631.11 (iii A.D.), *Gp.*2.46.4. **-ωτέον**, *one must surround with a* γῦρος, τοὺς ὀφθαλμούς ib.5.21.2.

γῦς, written for γύος, *PLond.*1.131^{r}.82, al. (i A.D.).

γύψ, γῡπός, ὁ (ἡ only as v.l. in Porph.ap.Eus.*PE*3.12), Ep. dat. γύπεσσι Il.11.162:—*vulture*, prob. including several species, 22.42, E.*Tr.*599, Arist.*HA*563^{a}5, etc.

γυψ-εμπλαστής, οῦ, ὁ, = γυψωτής, Zonar. **-εμπλαστικός**, ή, όν, *belonging to plasterers*, Phlp.*in APo.*382.16. **-ίζω**, *plaster with gypsum*, *PMag.Lond.*46.360. **-ική**, ἡ, *tax on plasterers*, *BGU*471.15, *PFay.*23a. **-ινος**, η, ον, *made of gypsum*, ἀγαλμάτιον *EM*530.15. II. γ., τό, *room plastered with gypsum*, *BGU* 1028.88 (ii A.D.). **-ίον**, τό, = γύψος, *Stud.Pal.*10.259 (vi A.D.). **-ισμός**, ὁ, *plastering with gypsum*, *BGU*952.8 (pl., ii/iii A.D.).

γυψοειδής, ές, = γυψώδης, Paul.Aeg.6.21.

γύψος, ἡ, *chalk*, Hdt.7.69, Pl.*Phd.*110c. II. *gypsum*, Thphr.*Lap.*64, *BGU*952.8 (ii/iii A.D.). III. *cement*, Thphr.*Lap.*65, Ph.*Bel.*79.5; ἐν γύψῳ κείμενος embedded in *cement*, D.S.2.10, Arr.*An.*2.21.4.

γυψ-όω, *rub with chalk, chalk over*, Hdt.3.24, 8.27, Polyaen.6.18.1. 2. *plaster with gypsum*, *Gp.*4.15.13. **-ώδης**, ες, *chalky*, γάλα Sor.1.91, cf. Eust.1304.27. **-ωσις**, εως, ἡ, *plastering*, *Gp.* 6 *Arg.*18. **-ωτής**, οῦ, ὁ, *plasterer*, *EM*811.36. **-ωτός**, ή, όν, *plastered*, Hsch. s.v. τιτανωτή.

γῶ, coined by Gramm., as etym. of χωρῶ, γαστήρ, γυνή, γωρυτός, etc., *Et.Gud.* s.v. γεγῶσα, cf. *EM*244.6, Philox.ap.Orion39.

γωγγάμη, = γαγγάμη, Hsch. **γωγώνη**· φάρυγξ, Id.

γωλεός, ὁ, *a hole*, Arist.*HA*603^{a}6 (v.l. φωλεός); **γωλιός**, Hsch.: heterocl. pl., φωλειοῦ ὑπὸ γωλεά Nic.*Th.*125; γωλειά Lyc.376. (Cf. Lith. *guõlis* 'lair'.)

γῶν, Ion. for γοῦν.

γωνία, ἡ, *corner, angle*, Hdt.1.51, Pl.*Men.*84d, etc.; γ. ἐπίπεδος, στερεά, *plane, solid angle*, Euc.1 *Def.*8, 11 *Def.*11; αἱ πρὸς τῇ βάσει γ. *the angles* at the base, Id.1.5; ἡ ὑπὸ ΒΑΓ or ὑπὸ τῶν ΒΑΓ γ. *the angle* ΒΑΓ, Id.1.9, al. 2. metaph., *corner, secluded spot*, ἐν γωνίᾳ ψιθυρίζειν Pl.*Grg.*485d; ἐν γ. πεπραγμένον *Act.Ap.*26.26. 3. of the four *quarters* of the compass, Ptol.*Tetr.*29. 4. *joint*, Arist.*PA* 690^{a}13. II. *joiner's square*, Pl.*Phlb.*51c, Plu.*Marc.*19. III. *cutwater* of a bridge, D.S.2.8. IV. of persons, *leader, chief*, Lxx 1*Ki.*14.38. (Akin to γόνυ.)

γωνι-άζω, *place at an angle*, Porph.*in Cat.*132.31. **-αῖος**, α, ον, *on* or *at the angle*, λίθος Lxx *Jb.*38.6, cf. *IG*1^{2}.372.19; στυλίς D.H.3.22; μέρος τείχους J.*BJ*5.3.5; also γωνιήϊος *BCH*26.64 (Delph.). II. *angular*, γ. ῥῆμα, i.e. hard to pronounce, Pl.Com.67. **-ακός**, ή, όν, *angular, of, in* or *at angles*, συμβολαί Procl. *in Euc.*p.129F.; κόσμοι Id. *in Ti.*1.454D.; ὀδούς Sch.Ar.*Pl.*1059. Adv. -κῶς, γ. καὶ ἐπιπέδως Procl. *in Ti.*2.217D. **-ασμός**, ὁ, *squaring off corners*, Lys.*Fr.*61; name of a *proposition in geometry*, Hsch.: metaph., ἐπῶν γωνιασμοί *finishing* of verses *by square and rule*, Ar.*Ra.*956.

γωνίδιον, τό, Dim. of γωνία, Luc.*Nec.*17, M.Ant.3.10.

γωνιο-βόμβυξ, ῦκος, ὁ, *one that buzzes in a corner*, nickname of Grammarians, Herodic.ap.Ath.5.222a. **-ειδής**, ές, *angular*, Arist.*GC*319^{b}14, Thphr.*HP*1.10.1, al. (γωνο- codd.), *PHib.*1.16.42 (Thphr.(?)). **-ομαι**, Pass., *become angular*, Dsc.3.7; γεγωνιωμένα σχήματα Procl. *in Euc.*p.163F. **-ποιέομαι**, *form into an angle*:—Pass., Erot. s.v. ἐγγώνιος πῆχυς. **-πους**, ὁ, ἡ, **-πουν**, τό, gen. ποδος, *crook-footed*, D.L.9.116.

γώνιος, = γωνιακός, εἴδη *Theol.Ar.*3 (s.v.l.); *angular*, σφυρίδια *PKlein.Form.*321.4 (vi A.D.).

γωνιόφυλλος, ον, *with pointed leaves*, Thphr.*HP*1.10.5.

γωνι-ώδης, ες, *angular*, Th.8.104; *at a sharp angle*, διαστροφή Hp.*Art.*47. **-ωμα**, ατος, τό, = γωνία, Eust.1082.28. **-ωσις**, εως, ἡ, name for a pulse, coined by Archig.ap.Gal.9.324. **-ωτός**, ή, όν, *angular*, Paul.Aeg.6.88.

γωνοειδής, ές, = γωνιο-, Democr.ap.Thphr.*Sens.*65, freq. written in codd. of Thphr.

γῶνορ, = γωνία (Lacon.), Hsch. **γωνορίσματα**· γνωρίσματα, τοποθεσίαι, Id. **γῶνος**· γουνός, ἕδος, καὶ παιδιά τις παλαιστρική, οἱ δὲ κώπη, Id. **γώνυμος**· φερώνυμος, Id. **γῶος**· μνημεῖον, Id. **γωροῦται**· σαρκοῖ (Lacon.), Id.

γωρῡτός, ὁ (ἡ *AP*6.34 (Rhian.)), *quiver*, ἀπὸ πασσάλου αἴνυτο τόξον αὐτῷ γωρυτῷ Od.21.54, cf. Lyc.458, *AP*6.34 (Rhian.), J.*BJ*3.5.5, Luc.*Herc.*1, Q.S.3.35; γ. πλήρεις οἰστῶν Anon.ap.Suid., cf. *EM*244.7; wrongly expld. as *bow-case*, Apollon.*Lex.*, Eust.1898.21.

γώψ· κολοιός (Maced.), Hsch.

Δ

Δ δ, **δέλτα** (q.v.), fourth letter of the Gr. alphabet: as numeral, δ' = τέσσαρες and τέταρτος, but ,δ = 4,000.

δα-, intens. Prefix, = ζα-, as in δάσκιος, δαφοινός.

δᾶ, expld. by the Sch.A.*Ag.*1072, *EM*60.8 as Dor. for γᾶ, γῆ, in Trag. (lyr.) φεῦ δᾶ, E.*Ph.*1296, Ar.*Lys.*198; οἰοῖ δᾶ φεῦ A.*Eu.*874; ἄλευ' ἃ δᾶ Id.*Pr.*567; ὀτοτοτοτοῖ ποποῖ δᾶ Id.*Ag.*1072; οὐ δᾶν no *by earth*, Theoc.4.17 (v.l. γᾶν):—prob. an exclamation of horror.

δαάναι· δύεσθαι, ὅσον εἰς τὴν χρείαν τοῦ στήμονος μεριζόμενον καθάπτεσθαι, Hsch. **δαβελός** [i.e. δαϝ], = δαλός (Lacon.), Id. **δαβῆ**· καυθῇ (Lacon.), Id.

δαγκάνω, = δάκνω, cf. Heraclid.ap.Eust.28.42, Hdn.Gr.1.451, etc.

δάγκολον, τό, = δρέπανον, Hsch.; cf. ζάγκλη.

δάγμα, ατος, τό, v. δάχμα.

δάγμνος (sic)· οἰκτρός, πένης, ἐλεεινός, Hsch.

δαγμός, ὁ, = δηγμός, Ruf.*Fr.*64.20.

δαγνόν· πυκνόν, Hsch. (leg. ἀδινόν). **δαγόμενον**· ἐρρωμένον, Id.

δᾱγύς, ῦδος, ἡ, *wax doll*, used in magic rites, *puppet*, Theoc.2.110.

δαδαίνω, = δανδαίνω, Hsch.

Δᾳδᾱφόριος, ὁ (sc. μήν), name of a month at Delphi, *SIG*729.1, etc.: **-φόρια**, τά, *torchlight festival held in this month*, *Michel*995*D*4.

δᾳδηφόρος, ον, *torch-bearing*, epith. of κόρη, *App.Anth.*1.266c (Eleusis).

δᾴδ-ινος, η, ον, (δᾴς) *of pine wood*, Gal.19.738, Aët.3.141. **-ίον**, τό, Dim. of δαΐς, δᾴς, *splinter of pine wood*, Dsc.1.69, 2.73; *little torch*, Iamb.*Protr.*21.ις', Procop.*Goth.*2.20, Poll.10.111; used of *firewood*, Ar.*Eq.*921. 2. *dilator* (cf. δαΐς 4), Hp.*Mul.*1.13, 2.133. **-ίς**, ίδος, ἡ, *a torch-feast*, Luc.*Alex.*39.

δᾳδοκοπέω πεύκην, *cut out the resin-glut* from it, Thphr.*CP*5.16.2 (Pass.).

δᾳδόομαι, Pass., (δᾴς) *become afflicted with resin-glut*, Thphr.*CP*5.11.3.

δᾳδουργ-έω, = δᾳδοκοπέω, Thphr.*CP*5.16.2:—Pass., Id.*HP*4.16.1. **-ός**, ὁ, *one who cuts pines for torches*, ib.3.9.3.

δᾳδουχ-έω, *carry a torch*, esp. in pageants, E.*Tr.*343, Luc.*Cat.*22. 2. *hold the office of* δᾳδοῦχος I.1, *IG*2.1413, 1414. II. c. acc., *celebrate*, τὰ μυστήρια Them.*Or.*5.71a:—Med., γόον οὐχ ὑμέναιον ἐδᾳδουχήσατο *Epigr.Gr.*413:—Pass., *to be illuminated*, Socr.Rhod.1. **-ία**, ἡ, *torch-bearing*, Lxx 2*Ma.*4.22, Plu.2.621c, Luc.*Alex.*38. **-ιον**, τό, *office of the* δᾳδοῦχος, *IG*1^{2}.6.99 (prob.). **-ος**, ὁ, (ἔχω) *torch-bearer*, App.*BC*2.17: but usu. of the holder of a hereditary office at the mysteries of the Eleusinian Demeter, X.*HG*6.3.3, Arist.*Rh.*1405^{a}20, *IG*1^{2}.76.25, *SIG*^{2}587.305; δ. Κόρης *IG*3.172.9. 2. metaph., δᾳδοῦχοι τῆς σοφίας Plu.2.10e. 3. of the Sun, Cleanth.*Stoic.*1.123. II. *torch-stand, candelabrum*, *CIG*4647 (Bostra): also in Lacon. form **δᾳδῶχορ**, Hsch.

δᾳδο-φορέω, *carry torches*, Luc.*Peregr.*36. II. *produce* δαΐς, Thphr.*HP*9.2.8. **-φόρος,** ον, *torch-bearing*, Ἑκάτα B.*Fr.*23.1.

δαδύσσομαι, *to be distracted*, ἐν ὅσσῳ δέει δαδύσσεσθε Sophr.117.

δᾳδ-ώδης, ες, *resinous*, Thphr.*HP*3.9.7, 9.2.5 (Comp.), Plu.2.648d. **-ωσις,** εως, ἡ, *the disease of resin-glut*, Thphr.*CP*5.11.3.

δαεγώ· οἶδα, ἐπίσταμαι, Hsch. **δαεινόν·** κλαύσιμον, Id. (leg. καυσ-).

Δάειρα [ᾰ], ἡ, *Knowing one*, epith. of Persephone at Athens, Pherecyd.45 J., Lyc.710, *IG*2.741 *A b* 2: **Δαῖρα,** A.*Fr.*277, *IG*2².1358.12: —**Δαειρίτης,** ου, ὁ, *her priest*, Poll.1.35.

δαείω, δαήμεναι, v. *δάω.

δαελός, Syracusan form of δαλός, Sophr.116; but, = δῆλος, Hsch.

δᾱερός, (δαίω A) *hot*, cj. in Emp.90; also, *black*, or *burnt*, Hsch.

δαηθμόν· ἐμπρησμόν, Hsch. **δαήμεναι·** ἔμπειροι γυναῖκες, Id.

δαημ-οσύνη, ἡ, *skill, knowledge*, A.R.2.175 (pl.), 4.1273, Orph.*A.* 728 (pl.), Them.*Or.*33.366a. **-ων,** ον, gen. ονος, (δαῆναι) *knowing, experienced in* a thing, τέκτονος ἐν παλάμῃσι δαήμονος Il.15.411; ἐν πάντεσσ' ἔργοισι δαήμονα 23.671: c. gen. rei, δαήμονι φωτὶ ἐΐσκω ἄθλων Od.8.159, cf. Democr.197: c. inf., κοσμῆσαι δ. *knowing best how to*.., Arr.*An.*7.28.2; χρήματα φυλάττειν δ. Them.*Or.*2.25c: Comp. -έστερος Eun.*VS*p.499 B., Procop.*Arc.Praef.*: Sup. -έστατος X.*Cyr.*1.2.12, Agath.5.6. Adv. Sup. -έστατα Id.3.25.

δαῆναι, v. *δάω.

δαήρ, έρος, ὁ, voc. δᾶερ, Il.3.180, 6.344, Men.135: dat. written τῷ δαιρι (sic) *JHS*37.105, cf. *BCH*8.382, Buresch *Aus Lydien* 116:—*husband's brother, brother-in-law*: gen. pl. as disyll., δαέρων ἢ γαλόων Il.24.769. (Cf. Skt. *devár-*, Lith. gen. sg. *dieveȓs*, Slav. *děverĭ*, Lat. *lēvir*.)

δαηρόν· θερμόν, λαμπρόν, καυματηρόν, *EM*244.42, cf. Hsch.; perh. to be read in Emp.90, cf. δαερός. **δάης·** μάχης μεγάλης, Hsch. **δάησις** [ᾰ], εως, ἡ, *learning, understanding*, δ. καὶ ἐμπειρία *EM*250.53.

δάθεα· ἅρπη, φρεάτια (Tarent.), Hsch.

δαί, colloquial form of δή, used after interrogatives, to express wonder or curiosity, τίς δ. ὅμιλος ὅδ' ἔπλετο; Od.1.225; ποῦ δ. νηῦς ἕστηκε; 24.299, cf. A.D.*Synt.*78.2 (but wrongly read by Aristarch. for δ' αἱ Il.10.408): freq. in Com., τί δ. σύ..πεποίηκας; Ar.*Eq.*351; mostly in a separate clause, τί δ.; *what? how?* Pherecr.93, Ar.*Eq.* 171, al.; τί δ. σύ; Id.*Av.*136; πῶς δ.; Id.*V.*1212; dub. l. in A.*Pr.* 933, *Ch.*900, S.*Ant.*318, but prob. to be read E.*Med.*1012, *Ion* 275, al.: freq. in codd. of Pl., but prob. f.l. for δέ, as in Ar.*Ach.*912.

δαΐ [ῐ], Ep. dat. of δαΐς.

δαϊγμός, ὁ, *division, partition*, *EM*613.45.

δαιδᾰλέοδμος, ον, *with artificial fragrance*, μύρα Emp.128.5.

δαιδάλ-εος [ᾰ] (not -έος, Hdn.Gr.1.114), α, ον: (δαιδάλλω):—*cunningly* or *curiously wrought*, in Hom. always of metal or wood, ζωστήρ, θώρηξ, σάκος, θρόνος, Il.4.135, 8.195, 19.380, Od.1.131; λάρναξ Simon.37.1, B.5.140; also of embroidery, Hes.*Th.*575, E.*Hec.* 470 (lyr.), Theopomp.Com.33. 2. of natural objects, *dappled, spotted*, etc., of fish, Alex.17; of deer, Nonn.*D.*5.391; *shot with light, sheeny*, Opp.*C.*1.218. II. *cunning*, χείρ Pl.*Epigr.*22: Ἥφαιστος *AP*9.755. **-εύομαι,** = δαιδάλλω, Ph.1.666. **-εύτρια,** ἡ, *skilful workwoman*, Lyc.578.

δαιδάλλω, Act. only in pres. and impf.:—*work cunningly, embellish*, σάκος..πάντοσε δαιδάλλων Il.18.479; λέχος ἔξεον..δαιδάλλων χρυσῷ τε καὶ ἀργύρῳ ἠδ' ἐλέφαντι Od.23.200; of a *painter* or *sculptor*, Opp.*C.*1.335, *IG*14.967:—Pass., to be *spotted, marked*, σφραγῖσι Opp.*C.*1.324. 2. metaph., δ. πόλιν εὐανορίαισι Pi.*O.*5.21; δ. ἔπεσιν Id.*Parth.*2.32:—Pass., δεδαιδαλμένοι ψεύδεσι μῦθοι Id.*O.*1.29; πλοῦτος ἀρεταῖς δεδ. ib.2.53; [μέλη] δαιδαλθέντ' ἀοιδαῖς Id.*N.*11.18.

δαίδαλ-μα, ατος, τό, *work of art*, θεῶν Theoc.1.32, cf. Luc.*Am.*13; τὰ τῆς οἰκοδομίας δ. Agath.2.15. **-όεις,** εσσα, εν, = δαιδάλεος, τεύχεα Q.S.1.141; βρέτας χρυσῷ δ. *AP*9.332 (Nossis). **-ος,** ον, *cunningly* or *curiously wrought*, μάχαιρα Pi.*N.*4.59 (Did., Δαιδάλου codd.); πέπλος A.*Eu.*635: in Hom. only neut. as Subst., ὃς χερσὶν ἐπίστατο δαίδαλα πάντα τεύχειν..to frame all *cunning works*, Il.5.60, al.; τεκτόνων δ. Pi.*P.*5.36, cf. Opp.*C.*1.355: also in sg., Od.19.227. 2. *spotted, speckled*, or perh. rather, *sheeny, shot with light*, of fish, Opp.*C.*1.58. II. as pr. n., Δαίδαλος, ὁ, *Daedalus*, i.e. *the Cunning Worker, the Artist*, traditional name for the first sculptor, Il.18.592, Pl.*Men.*97d: hence δαίδαλα, τά, = *statues*, Paus.9.3.2: also Δαίδαλα, τά, festival of Hera at Argos, ib., Plu.*Daed.*tit.

δαιδαλούργ-ημα, ατος, τό, = δαίδαλμα, δ. χάλκειον Vett.Val.275.4. **-ία,** ἡ, *cunning workmanship*, *Corp.Herm.*3.3.1. **-ός,** όν, *cunningly wrought*, ἀνδριάντες Zen.3.7.

δαιδᾰλόχειρ, ὁ, ἡ, gen. χειρος, *cunning of hand*, *AP*6.204 (Leon.).

δαιδαλόω, = δαιδάλλω, poet. inf. fut. -ωσέμεν Pi.*O.*1.105.

δαιδήσσουσι· βασανίζουσι, Hsch. **δαιδύσσεσθαι·** ἕλκεσθαι, Id.; cf. δαδύσσομαι. **δαιέλιξι·** τοῖς πεπυρακτωμένοις ξύλοις μετὰ προσβολῆς πυρσῶν (Arg.), Id. **δαιημός,** ὁ, *division*, Id. (leg. δαιθμός). **δαιῆσαι·** διδάξαι, Id.; cf. *δάω.

δαΐζω, aor. ἐδάϊξα (v. infr.):—Med. fut. δαΐσονται Man.4.615:—Pass. (v. infr., cf. δαίω B):—poet. (Trag. in lyr.), *cleave asunder*, πάντα διεμοιρᾶτο δαΐζων Od.14.434; χιτῶνα περὶ στήθεσσι δαΐξαι Il.2.416, cf. 7.247; δαΐζων ὀξεῖ χαλκῷ 24.393; κάρανα δαΐξας A.*Ch.*396. 2. *slay*, δαΐζων ἵππους τε καὶ ἀνέρας Il.11.497; τέκνον δαΐξω A.*Ag.*208: freq. in Pass., χαλκῷ δεδαϊγμένος Il.22.72, etc.; δεδαϊγμένος ἦτορ *pierced through* the heart, 17.535; δεδαϊγμένον ἦτορ a heart *torn* by misery, Od.13.320; ἐκ βελέων δαϊχθεὶς Pi.*P.*6.33; ἐξ ἐμᾶν χερῶν E.*IT*872. 3. *rend*, χερσὶ κόμην ᾔσχυνε δαΐζων Il.18.27 (so in Med. fut., Man. l.c.); δαΐζειν πόλιν *destroy* it *utterly*, A.*Supp.*680, cf. *Ch.* 396. 4. *divide*, ἐδαΐζετο θυμὸς ἐνὶ στήθεσσιν Ἀχαιῶν their soul *was divided* within them, Il.9.8; δαϊζόμενος κατὰ θυμὸν διχθάδια *divided* or *doubting* between two opinions, 14.20; δαΐζειν ἐννέα μοίρας *to divide into*.., Orph.*L.*712. 5. = δαινύναι (q.v.), θυσίας ἃς δαΐζοι ἁ πόλις *IG*7.207 (Aegosthena). [δᾰ-; but δᾱ- Il.11.497, A.*Ch.*396.] (Prob. δαϝίζω from *δα-ϝο-ς '*cut*'; cf. δᾰ-τέομαι.)

δαιθμός, ὁ, (δαίω B) *allotment* of land, *IG*14.352 ii 23 (Halaesa). II. *rule of distribution*, *IG*12(5).50 (Naxos).

δαϊκτάμενος, η, ον, *slain in battle*, Il.21.146, 301.

δαϊκτ-ήρ, ῆρος, ὁ, *slayer, murderer*, of Ares, Alc.28. 2. as Adj., *heart-rending*, γόος A.*Th.*916 (lyr.). **-ής,** οῦ, ὁ, = foreg. 2, φθόνος *Anacreont.*40.10 (prob.). **-ός,** ή, όν, *to be slain*, Orph.*A.* 976. **-ωρ,** ορος, ὁ, = δαϊκτήρ 2, γάμος A.*Supp.*798 (lyr.).

δαῖμα· σπιθαμήν, καὶ τὸ ἔγκωλον τοῦ σχοινίου, στήμονα δὲ (i.e. δίασμα) Ταραντῖνοι, Hsch. **δαιμοδία·** ἡ τῶν ἀρίστων ἐπιβολή, Id. **δαιμοί·** οἱ καταδικασθέντες τὰς οὐσίας εἰς βασιλέως, Id.

δαιμονάω, *to be under the power of a* δαίμων, *to suffer by a divine visitation*, δαιμονᾷ δόμος κακοῖς A.*Ch.*566; δαιμονῶντες ἐν ἄτᾳ Id.*Th.* 1008 (lyr.): abs., *to be possessed, to be mad*, E.*Ph.*888, X.*Mem.*1.1.9, Plu.*Marc.*20, etc.; δαιμονᾷς Men.140.

δαιμονητιᾷ· δαιμονίζεται (Cret.), Hsch.

δαιμονι-άζομαι, = δαιμονίζομαι III, *PMag.Par.*1.3007. **-ακός,** = δαιμονικός, *PMag.Osl.*1.143 (-ων-). **-άω,** *to be possessed of a God*, Phld.*D.*1.18. **-άρχης,** ου, ὁ, *ruler of demons*, Lact.*Inst.*2.14.6.

δαιμον-ίζομαι, Med., = δαιμονάω, ἄλλος κατ' ἄλλην δαιμονίζεται τύχην each one hath his own *fate appointed*, Philem.191. II. as Pass., *to be deified*, S.*Fr.*173 (so expld. by *AB*90; Act. in Hsch.). III. *to be possessed by a demon* or *evil spirit*, *Ev.Matt.*4.24, al., Plu.2.706d. **-ικός,** ή, όν, of persons or animals, *possessed by a demon*, ζῷον Plu.2.362f: of things, *sent by a demon*, οὐ θεῖον, ἀλλὰ δ. ib.996c, cf. 458c; δ. δύναμις ib.363a.

δαιμόνιον, τό, *divine Power, Divinity*, Hdt.5.87, E.*Ba.*894 (lyr.), Isoc.1.13, Pl.*R.*382e, etc.; τὸ δαιμόνιον ἄρ' ἢ θεὸς ἢ θεοῦ ἔργον Arist.*Rh.*1398ᵃ15, cf. 1419ᵃ9; οἱ θεοὶ εἴσονται καὶ τὸ δ. D.19.239; φοβεῖσθαι μή τι δ. πρᾶγμ' ἐλαύνῃ some *fatality*, Id.9.54; τὰ τοῦ δ. the favours of *fortune*, Pl.*Epin.*992d. II. *inferior divine being*, μεταξὺ θεοῦ τε καὶ θνητοῦ Id.*Smp.*202e; καινὰ δ. εἰσφέρειν X.*Mem.*1.1.2, Pl.*Ap.*24c, cf. Vett.Val.67.5, etc.; applied to the '*genius*' of Socrates, X.*Mem.*1.1.2, Pl.*Ap.*40a, *Tht.*151a, *Euthphr.*3b. 2. *evil spirit*, δ. φαῦλα Chrysipp.*Stoic.*2.338, cf. Lxx *De.*32.17, *To.*3.8, *Ev.Matt.*7.22, al., *PMag.Lond.*1.46.120 (iv A.D.).

δαιμονιό-πληκτος, ον, = δαιμονιόληπτος, *PMag.Leid.V.*9.1, Ptol.*Tetr.*169: Subst. **-πληξία,** ἡ, ib.170, Petas.ap.Olymp.Alch.p.95 B.

δαιμόνιος, α, ον: also ος, ον A.*Th.*892, Lys.6.32, *OGI*383.175 (Commagene):—*of* or *belonging to a* δαίμων: properly *miraculous, marvellous*, but: I. in Hom. only in voc., δαιμόνιε, -ίη, *good sir*, or *lady*, addressed to chiefs or commoners, Il.2.190, 200, al., Hes.*Th.*655: pl., Od.4.774: esp. in addressing strangers, 23.166, 174; used by husbands and wives, Il.6.407, 486 (Hector and Andromache), 24.194 (Priam to Hecuba): later c. gen., δαιμόνιε ἀνδρῶν Hdt.4.126, 7.48, 8.84: freq. in Com., in an iron. sense, ὦ δαιμόνι' ἀνδρῶν Ar.*Ec.*564, 784, etc.; ὦ δαιμόνι' Id.*Ra.*44, 175; ὦ δαιμόνι' ἀνθρώπων Id.*Av.*1638, cf. Pl.*R.*344d, 522b, *Grg.*489d, etc. II. from Hdt. and Pi. downwds. (Trag. in lyr.), *heaven-sent, miraculous, marvellous*, βῶλαξ Pi.*P.*4.37; τέρας B.15.35, S.*Ant.*376; ὁρμή Hdt.7.18; ἀραί, ἄχη, A.*Th.*892, *Pers.*581; ἡ φύσις δ. ἀλλ' οὐ θεία Arist.*Div.Somn.*463ᵇ14; εὐεργεσία D.2.1; εἰ μή τι δ. εἴη were it not *a divine intervention*, X.*Mem.*1.3.5, cf. S.*El.*1270; τὰ δαιμόνια *visitations of heaven, ways of God*, Th.2.64, X.*Mem.*1.1.12; πολλαὶ μορφαὶ τῶν δ. E.*Alc.*1159, al.; δ. ἀνάγκη Lys. l.c.; δ. τύχη of *ill* fortune, Pl.*Hp.Ma.*304b; Ἄπολλον, ἔφη, δαιμονίας ὑπερβολῆς! Id.*R.*509c. 2. of persons, τῷ δ. ὡς ἀληθῶς καὶ θαυμαστῷ Id.*Smp.*219b; ὁ περὶ τοιαῦτα σοφὸς δ. ἀνήρ ib.203a; δαιμόνιος τὴν σοφίαν Luc.*Philops.*32: Comp. -ώτερος D.C.53.8. III. Adv. -ίως *by Divine power*, opp. ἀνθρωπίνως, Aeschin.3.133, cf. Pl.*Ti.*25e; *marvellously*, Ar.*Nu.*76; δ. περί τι ἐσπουδακώς Aeschin.1.41; δ. ποιεῖ, of remedies, Aët.15.14, al.; [οἶνος] δ. καὶ μεγαλοπρεπῶς prob. in Epicur.*Fr.*183 (cf. δαΐος): neut. pl. as Adv., δαιμόνια Ar.*Pax*585; δαιμονιώτατα ἀποθνῄσκει *most clearly by the hand of the gods*, X.*HG*7.4.3: also in fem. dat., δαιμονίᾳ, formed like κοινῇ, θεσπεσίῃ, etc., Pi.*O.*9.110.

δαιμονιοῦχος αἰτία, *spiritual* cause, Procl.*in Prm.*p.513 S.

δαιμον-ίς, ίδος, ἡ, fem. of δαίμων, Procl.*in Ti.*1.47 D., *in Prm.*p.643 S., Herm.*in Phdr.*p.87 A.:—also **-ισσα,** ἡ, *PMag.Leid.W.*16.48. **-ισμός,** ὁ, *demoniac possession*, Vett.Val.2.18.

δαιμονιώδης, ες, *like a demon*, Sch.Ar.*Ra.*293; *demoniacal, devilish*, *Ep.Jac.*3.15; *like a* δαίμων, Procl.*in Ti.*1.113 D.

δαιμονο-βλάβεια [ᾰ], ἡ, *heaven-sent visitation*, Plb.28.9.4. **-μαχέω,** *fight against heaven*, Eust.1097.6. **-πλήξ,** ῆγος, *smitten of heaven*, cj. in S.*Fr.*221.13. **-πληξία,** ἡ, = δαιμονιοπλ-, Petas.ap.Olymp.Alch.p.97 B. **-τάκτης,** ου, ὁ, *ruler of demons*, *PMag.Par.*1.1374 (pl., written δαιμονατ.).

δαίμων, ονος, voc. δαίμων S.*OC*1480 (lyr.), δαῖμον Theoc.2.11, ὁ, ἡ, *god, goddess*, of individual gods or goddesses, Il.1.222, 3.420, etc.; δαίμονι ἶσος 5.438; ἐμίσγετο δαίμονι δαίμων, of Φιλίη and Νεῖκος, Emp.59.1:—but more freq. of *the Divine power* (while θεός denotes a God in person), *the Deity*, cf. Od.3.27; πρὸς δαίμονα against *the Divine power*, Il.17.98; σὺν δαίμονι by its grace, 11.792; κατὰ δαίμονα, almost, = τύχῃ, by *chance*, Hdt.1.111; τύχᾳ δαίμονος Pi.*O.*8.67; ἄμαχος δ., i.e. Destiny, B.15.23: in pl., ὅτι δαίμονες θέλωσιν, what *the Gods* ordain, Id.16.117; ταῦτα δ' ἐν τῷ δ. S.*OC*1443; ἡ τύχη καὶ ὁ δ. Lys. 13.63, cf. Aeschin.3.111; κατὰ δαίμονα καὶ συντυχίαν Ar.*Av*.544. 2. *the power controlling the destiny of individuals*: hence, one's *lot* or *fortune*, στυγερὸς δέ οἱ ἔχραε δ. Od.5.396, cf. 10.64; δαίμονος αἶσα κακή 11.61; δαίμονα δώσω I will deal thee *fate*, i.e. kill thee, Il.8.166; freq. in Trag. of *good* or *ill fortune*, ὅταν ὁ δ. εὐροῇ A.*Pers*.601; δ. ἀσινής Id.*Ag*.1342 (lyr.); κοινός Id.*Th*.812; γενναῖος πλὴν τοῦ δαίμονος S.*OC*76; δαίμονος σκληρότης Antipho 3.3.4; τὸν οἴακα στρέφει δ. ἑκάστῳ Anaxandr.4.6; personified as *the good* or *evil genius* of a family or person, δ. τῷ Πλεισθενιδῶν A.*Ag*.1569, cf. S.*OT*1194 (lyr.); ὁ ἑκάστου δ. Pl.*Phd*.107d, cf. *PMag.Lond*.121.505, Iamb.*Myst*.9.1; ὁ δ. ὁ τὴν ἡμετέραν μοῖραν λελογχώς Lys.2.78; ἅπαντι δ. ἀνδρὶ συμπαρίσταται εὐθὺς γενομένῳ μυσταγωγὸς τοῦ βίου Men.16.2 D.; δ. ἀλάστορες Id. 8 D.; ὁ μέγας [τοῦ Καίσαρος] δ. Plu.*Caes*.69; ὁ σὸς δ. κακός ibid.; ὁ βασιλέως δ. Id.*Art*.15; ἦθος ἀνθρώπῳ δ. Heraclit.119; Ξενοκράτης φησὶ τὴν ψυχὴν ἑκάστου εἶναι δ. Arist.*Top*.112ᵃ37. II. δαίμονες, *οἱ*, *souls of men of the golden age*, acting as tutelary deities, Hes.*Op*. 122, Thgn.1348, Phoc.15, Emp.115.5, etc.; θεῶν, δ., ἡρώων, τῶν ἐν Ἅιδου Pl.*R*.392a: less freq. in sg., δαίμονι δ' οἷος ἔησθα τὸ ἐργάζεσθαι ἄμεινον Hes.*Op*.314; τὸν τε δ. Δαρεῖον ἀγκαλεῖσθε, of the deified Darius, A.*Pers*.620; νῦν δ' ἐστὶ μάκαιρα δ., of Alcestis, E.*Alc*.1003 (lyr.), cf. *IG*12(5).305.5 (Paros): later, of *departed souls*, Luc.*Luct*.24; δαίμοσιν εὐσεβέσιν, = *Dis Manibus*, *IG*14.1683; so θεοὶ δ., ib.938, al.: also, *ghost*, Paus.6.6.8. 2. generally, *spiritual* or *semi-divine being* inferior to the Gods, Plu.2.415a, al., Sallust.12, Dam.*Pr*.183, etc.; esp. *evil spirit*, *demon*, *Ev.Matt*.8.31, J.*AJ*8.2.5; φαῦλοι δ. Alex.Aphr.*Pr*.2.46; δαίμονος ἔσοδος εἰς τὸν ἄνθρωπον, Aret.*SD*1. 4; πρᾶξις ἐκβάλλουσα δαίμονας *PMag.Par*.1227. 3. ἀγαθὸς δ. *the Good Genius* to whom a toast was drunk after dinner, Ar.*V*.525, Nicostr.Com.20, D.S.4.3, Plu.2.655e, Philonid.ap.Ath.15.675b, Paus.9.39.5, *IG*12(3).436 (Thera), etc.; of Nero, ἀ. δ. τῆς οἰκουμένης *OGI*666.3; of the Nile, ἀ. δ. ποταμός ib.672.7 (i A.D.); of the tutelary genius of individuals (supr. 1), ἀ. δ. Ποσειδωνίου *SIG*1044.9 (Halic.): pl., δαίμονες ἀ., = Lat. *Di Manes*, *SIG*1246 (Mylasa): Astrol., ἀγαθός, κακὸς δ., names of celestial κλῆροι, Paul.Al.*N*.4, *O*.1, etc. (Less correctly written Ἀγαθοδαίμων, q.v.).

B. = δαήμων, *knowing*, δ. μάχης *skilled in* fight, Archil.3.4. (Pl. *Cra*.398b, suggests this as the orig. sense; while others would write δαήμονες in Archil., and get rid of this sense altogether; cf. however αἴμων. More probably the Root of δαίμων (*deity*) is δαίω *to distribute destinies*; cf. Alcm.48.)

δαίνῡμι, imper. δαίνῡ Il.9.70, part. -ύντα Od.4.3: Ep. impf. δαίνῡ Il.23.29; δαίνυεν (from δαινύω) Call.*Cer*.84: fut. δαίσω Il.19.299, A.*Eu*.305: aor. ἔδαισα Pi.*N*.9.24, Hdt.1.162, E.*Or*.15:—Med., δαίνῠται Il.15.99: 2 sg. subj. δαινύῃ Od.19.328; Ep. 3 sg. opt. δαινῦτο Il.24.665; 3 pl. opt. δαινύατο Od.18.248; part. -ύμενος Cratin. 142; 2 sg. impf. δαίνυ' (i.e. -υο) Il.24.63: fut. δαίσομαι Lyc.668, Herod.4.93, etc., (μετα-) Od.18.48: aor. ἐδαισάμην Archil.99, Pi.*P*.10.31, etc.; δαισάμενοι Od.18.408; [δαινῦῃ Od.19.328; but δαινῦῃ 8.243 (for wh. δαινύεαι shd. be read)]. (V. δαίω B.):—poet. Verb (used by Hdt.), *give a banquet* or *feast*, δαίνυ δαῖτα γέρουσι Il.9. 70; ἔφασκες .. δαίσειν γάμον didst promise *to give* me a marriage-*feast*, 19.299, cf. Od.4.3, *h.Ven*.141, Pi.*N*.1.72; ὁ τοῖσι τάφον μενοεικέα δαίνυ Il.23.29, cf. Od.3.309; δ. ὑμεναίους, γάμους, E.*IA*123 (lyr.), 707. 2. c. acc. pers., *feast* one *on* a thing, τὸν..Ἀστυάγης ἀνόμῳ τραπέζῃ ἔδαισε Hdt.1.162, cf. E.*Or*.15; ζῶν με δαίσεις *thou shalt be* my living *feast*, A.*Eu*.305. II. Med., *have a feast given one*, *feast*, in Hom. more freq. than Act., Il.15.99, al., cf. Pi.*I*.6(5).36, Hdt.1. 211; δαίσασθαι γάμον Archil. l.c. 2. c. acc., *feast on*, *eat*, δαῖτα, ἑκατόμβας, κρέα, Od.3.66, Il.9.535, Od.12.30; κρέα δαίνυσθαι Hdt.3. 18, Ant.Lib.18.2 (but c. gen., Id.11.7); ἐδαίσατο παῖδα S.*Fr*.771.5, cf. *El*.543; μίαν δ. τράπεζαν *eat* at a common table, Theoc.13.38: of fire, *consume*, Pi.*N*.9.24, S.*Tr*.765; of poison, ib.1088.

δαΐξανδρος, ον, *man-destroying*, χεῖρες *Hymn.Is*.45, cf. *Sammelb*. 5829.

δάϊος, contr. **δᾷος**, α, ον, Dor. for Ep. **δήϊος** (contr. **δῇος** Thgn. 552b), η, ον: also **δάϊος**, ον, E.*Tr*.1301 (lyr.), *HF*915 (lyr.) (Trag. always use the Dor. form): (δαίω A):—*hostile*, *destructive*, Hom. only in Il., δηΐου ἐκ πολέμου 7.119; δ. ἄνδρα 6.481: esp. as epith. of πῦρ, *burning*, *consuming*, 8.181, al.; δάϊοι *enemies*, Pi.*N*.8.28, A.*Ag*.559; λάφυρα δᾴων Id.*Th*.278 (dub. l.); φόβημα δαΐων S.*OC*699 (lyr.): in sg., *fighting man*, Ar.*Ra*.1022; also δᾴου μάχας S.*Ichn*.239; δαΐον ὁρμάν *hostile*, Ar.*Nu*.335 (= [Philox.]18 (anap.)); ἔπιτε δαΐαν ὁδὸν Ar.*Ra*. 897 (lyr.). 2. *unhappy*, *wretched*, A.*Pers*.282 (lyr.), etc., S.*Aj*.784, E.*Andr*.838 (lyr.). II. (δαῆναι) *knowing*, *cunning*, τεχνίτης *APl*. 4.119 (Posid.). Adv. δαΐως Epicur.*Fr*.183 codd. Plu. (δαιμονίως Usener). [δάϊος: but disyll. in Hom. where the last syll. is long; Trag., when disyll., written δᾷος, A.*Pers*.282; δηΐων at the end of a pentam., *AP*6.123 (Anyte).]

δαϊόφρων, ονος, ὁ, ἡ, (φρήν) *unhappy in mind*, *miserable*, A.*Th*.918 (lyr.).

δαϊόω, v. δηιόω.

δαΐς, δαΐδος, Att. contr. **δᾴς**, δᾳδός, ἡ: (δαίω A):—*fire-brand*, *pine-torch*, δαΐδων ὕπο λαμπομενάων Il.18.492; δαΐδας μετὰ χερσὶν ἔχοντες Od.7.101; δᾷδες, = λαμπάδες, Philyll.29; ἀραμένη δαΐδας *IG*12(5).229. 8; ἔλαχεν μυστιπόλους δ., of a δᾳδοῦχος, ib.3.172: in sg., Ar.*Nu*. 1494, Antiph.199,272: collective in sg., metaph., ἐπὶ τὴν δᾷδα προελθεῖν to come to the *funeral-torch*, i.e. end of life, Plu.2.789a. 2. as collective noun, *pine-wood*, such as torches were made of, *SIG* 57.32 (Milet., v B.C.), Ar.*Nu*.612, Th.7.53, X.*Cyr*.7.5.23, Arist.*Col*. 791ᵇ24, *Supp.Epigr*.1.329.24. 3. *a disease in pines*, *resin-glut*, Thphr.*HP*3.9.5. 4. = δᾳδίον 2, Hp.*Mul*.2.133.

δαΐς (δαίω A), *war*, *battle*, mostly in apoc. dat. δαΐ, as always in Hom., Il.13.286, al., cf. Hes.*Th*.650, A.*Th*.925: acc. δάϊν Call.*Fr*. 243.

δαίς, δαιτός, ἡ, (δαίω B) *meal*, *banquet*, δαὶς ἐΐση, *duly shared*, Il.15.95, etc.; δαὶς πίειρα sumptuous *banquet*, 19.179; *sacrificial feast*, βωμὸς ἐδεύετο δαιτὸς ἐΐσης 24.69; δαῖτα θάλειαν Hom.*Fr.inc*. 4 Kinkel (cf. Od.17.382); Θυέστου δαῖτα παιδείων κρεῶν *the feast* of Th. on.., A.*Ag*.1242, cf. 1593: pl., Od.20.182, A.*Ch*.483: of beasts of prey, Il.24.43; [τούτοις] παρέξω δαῖθ' ὑφ' ὧν ἐφερβόμην S.*Ph*. 957. 2. *meat*, *food*, E.*Cyc*.245, cf. Od.18.279. 3. personified, S.*Fr*.605. Rare in Prose (exc. in Homeric allusions, Pl.*Phdr*.247a, etc.) as Hdt.1.133,211.

δαισάνη· πτισάνη, *EM*251.47.

δαίσιμος or **δαίσιος**, *eatable*, Hsch., *EM*352.29.

Δαίσιος, ὁ, a Macedonian month, *SIG*700.39 (ii B.C.), Plu.*Alex*.16, *Cam*.19, *Arat*.53, etc.

δαῖσις, εως, ἡ, *division of property*, *Leg.Gort*.4.25, 5.47.

δαΐσφαλτος, ον, *in which one is overthrown*, πάλη Lyc.170.

δαιτᾰλ-άομαι, *feast*, Lyc.654. **-εύς**, έως, ὁ, *banqueter*, ἄκλητος δ., of the eagle eating Prometheus' liver, A.*Pr*.1024: pl., *Com. Adesp*.30 D; Δαιταλῆς, play by Aristophanes. **-ουργία**, ἡ, *cookery*, Lyc.199.

δαίτη, ἡ, poet. for δαίς, *feast*, *banquet*, Il.10.217 (pl.), Od.3.44, A.R.2.761, Call.*Aet*.1.1.5; of beasts, Opp.*H*.2.251, Nic.*Al*.380.

δαίτηθεν, Adv. *from a feast*, Od.10.216, Theoc.17.28.

δαιτήριον, τό, *place of distribution*, *EM*251.52, Zonar.

δαίτης, ου, ὁ, *priest who divided the victims*, E.*Fr*.472.12.

δαῖτις, v. δέτις. II. epith. of Aphrodite at Ephesus, *Jahresh*. 17.146.

δαιτρ-εία, ἡ, *place where meat is cut up*, Hdn.*Epim*.19. **-ευτῶς**, Adv. *by dividing* or *distributing*, Zonar. **-εύω**, *divide*, esp. *cut up* meat, δαιτρεῦσαί τε καὶ ὀπτῆσαι *to cut up* and roast it, Od.15. 323; ἂν δὲ..ἵστατο δαιτρεύσων *to carve*, 14.433; τὰ δ' ἄλλ' ἐς δῆμον ἔδωκε δαιτρεύειν *to cut up for distribution* among the people, Il.11.705, cf. 688; ἵππους δαίτρευον, of the Amazons, A.R.2.1176; τὰ πιότερα τῶν προβάτων Them.*Or*.13.171c; of animals, *devour* prey, Opp.*H*.2. 294:—Med., ib.606, Nonn.*D*.5.363, al.:—Pass., Lyc.160, etc. **-όν**, τό, *one's portion*, δαιτρὸν πίνειν Il.4.262.

δαιτροπόνος, = σιτοπόνος, σιτοποιός, Hsch., *EM*252.4.

δαιτρός, ὁ, (δαίω) *one that carves and portions out*, esp. meat at table, Od.1.141, 17.331, Lyc.35, Nic.*Al*.258, Ath.1.12d. II. hereditary priest who officiated at the Dipolia, Porph.*Abst*.2.30.

δαιτροσύνη, ἡ, *art of carving meat into portions*, Od.16.253 (pl.).

δαιτῠμ-ονεύς, Ep. gen. ῆος, ὁ, = sq., Nonn.*D*.2.666. **-ών**, όνος, ὁ, (δαίς) *one that is entertained*, *guest*, (but in Od.4.621 of *those who bring each his portion*) Hom. only in pl., Od.7.102,148, al, cf. Hdt. 1.73, etc.: in sg., Pl.*R*.345c, Arist.*Pol*.1282ᵃ22.

δαιτύς, ύος, ἡ, Ep. for δαίς, *a meal*, Il.22.496.

δαΐφρων, ον, gen. ονος, 1. (δάϊς) *warlike*, *fiery*, Il.2.23, al. (not in Od.); Λατοῦς θυγάτηρ B.5.122, cf. 137, Q.S.1.47; δ. ἀλκή Id.1. 218. 2. (δαῆναι) *wise*, *prudent*, Ὀδυσῆα δ. ποικιλομήτην Il.11.482, cf. Od.1.48, al.; of a charioteer, Il.24.325; *craftsman*, Od.8.373; of a woman, 15.356: hence δ. Περσεφόνεια *h.Cer*.359, cf. Pi.*P*.9.84. (δα(σ)ι-, cf. Skt. *dasrás* 'working miracles'.)

δαίω (A), Act. only pres. and impf. (but ἔδευσε may be for ἔδαυσε aor. 1, cf. infr. II, *Berl.Sitzb*.1902.1098):—Pass., pres. and impf., Hom.: aor. 2 subj. δάηται Il.20.316: also intr. in pf. 2 Act. δέδηα, plpf. δεδήειν (v. infr.); Ep. part. fem. δεδᾰυῖα Nonn.*D*.6.305: aor. part. δαισθείς E.*Heracl*.914 (if not from δαίνυμι): also aor. 2 subj. δαβῇ, ἐκδαβῇ, Hsch.: pf. Pass. δέδαυμαι (v. infr. II). (*δαϝ-yω, cf. δε-δαυ-μένος, δαβελός, Skt. *dunóti* 'burn'):—poet. Verb, *light up*, *kindle*, δαῖέ οἱ ἐκ κόρυθός τε καὶ ἀσπίδος ἀκάματον πῦρ *she made* fire *burn* from.., Il.5.4, cf. 7; ἐκ δ' αὐτοῦ δαῖε φλόγα 18.206, cf. 227; so πῦρ καὶ φῶς δ. A.*Ch*.864 (lyr.); φλόγα Id.*Ag*.496: metaph., δαῖε δ' ἐν ὀφθαλμοῖς.. πόθον A.R.4.1147:—Pass., *blaze*, *burn fiercely*, ἐν πεδίῳ πῦρ δαίετο καῖε δὲ νεκρούς Il.21.343; πυρὶ ὄσσε δεδήει *blazed* with fire, 12.466; ἐν δέ οἱ ὄσσε δαίεται *blaze like fire*, Od.6.132; σεμνῶν ὀργίων ἐδαίετο φλόξ S.*Tr*.765: mostly metaph. sense, μάχη πόλεμός τε δέδηεν Il.20.18, al., cf. 12.35, 17.253; Ὄσσα δεδήει Rumour *spread like wild-fire*, 2.93; φιλοφροσύνη δεδήει *glowed*, Emp.130.2. II. *burn up*, μηρ' ἐπὶ βωμῶν *Epigr.Gr*.1035. 20 (Pergam.); σάρκας ἔδευσε (sic) πυρί *Berl.Sitzb*. l.c.; τὰν χώραν δ. Decr.Byz.ap.D.18.90; *use cautery*, Hp.*Haem*.2 (very rare in Prose):—Pass., φλογὶ σῶμα δαισθείς E. l.c.; μηρίων δεδαυμένων Semon.30; ἐν ἔρωτι δεδ., prob. in Call.*Epigr*.50 (cf. δάκνω III).

δαίω (B), *divide*:—Act. is not found in this sense (for aor. ἔδαισα v. δαίνυμι), δαΐζω being used:—Pass., δαίεται ἦτορ my heart *is torn*, *distracted*, Od.1.48: Ep. 3 pl. pf., Αἰθίοπας, τοὶ διχθὰ δεδαίαται ib.23:—more freq. in Med., *distribute*, κρέα δαίετο 15.140; κρέα πολλὰ δαιόμενος 17.332; πήματα..δαίονται βροτοῖς ἀθάνατοι Pi.*P*.3.81; cf. δατέομαι. II. aor. ἔδαισα, *feast*, from Hdt. downwards, though formed from δαίω, belongs in sense to δαίνυμι (q.v.):—Med., *feast on*, [ἀμβροσίην] δαίονται Matro *Conv*.72. (δαι- also in δαίς, δαίνυμι, etc.: prob. akin to δα- in δατέομαι.)

δάκαρ, v.l. for δάρκα, Dsc.1.13.

δακέθῡμος, ον, *heart-eating, heart-vexing,* ἱδρώς Simon.58.5; ἄτη S.*Ph.*705 (lyr.).

δακετόν or **δάκετον**, τό, = δάκος 1, Ar.*Av.*1069, Thphr.*HP*9.19.3, Ph.1.399, etc.: as Adj., δ. θηρία D.S.1.87, 20.42, Vett.Val.126.29.

δάκια· τὰ ἄγρια ὀρνιθάρια, Hsch.; but, = τὰ μικρὰ θηρία, *EM*245.33.

δακκύλιος, v. δάκτυλος.

δακν-άζω, = δάκνω, *AP*7.504 (Leon.). II. metaph. in Pass., *to be afflicted, mournful,* imper. δακνάζου A.*Pers.*571. **-ηρός**, ά, όν, *biting,* ἔπη Phld.*Ir.*p.31 W.; δακνηρόν, τό, ib.p.75 W., Herm.ap. Stob.1.49.44. **-ίς**, ἡ, a *bird,* Hsch. **-ιστήρ**, ῆρος, ὁ, *biter, stinger,* v. μακιστήρ. **-ω**, Hippon.49.6 (cj.), A.*Th.*399, etc.: fut. δήξομαι Hp.*Nat.Mul.*16, *Mul.*1.18 (v.l. δάξεται): pf. δέδηχα Babr. 77: aor. 1 ἔδηξα late, Luc.*Asin.*9: aor. 2 (the only tense in Hom.) ἔδᾰκον Batr.181, Tyrt.10.32, etc., Ep. δάκε Il.5.493, redupl. δέδακε *AP*12.15 (Strat.): Ep. inf. δακέειν Il.17.572:—**Pass.**, δάκνομαι Thgn.910: fut. δηχθήσομαι E.*Alc.*1100: aor. ἐδήχθην S.*Tr.*254, Ar. *Ach.*18, etc.; later ἐδάκην Aret.*SD*2.2: pf. δέδηγμαι Ar.*Ach.*1, etc.; Dor. δεδαγμένος Pi.*P.*8.87, Call.*Ep.*50 codd.:—*bite,* of dogs, δακέειν μὲν ἀπετρωπῶντο λεόντων Il.18.585; of a gnat, ἰσχανάᾳ δακέειν 17. 572; στόμιον δ. *champ* the bit, A.*Pr.*1009; χεῖλος ὀδοῦσι δακών, as a mark of stern determination, Tyrt.l.c.: abs., δακὼν ἀνάσχου Men. *Sam.*141; δ. στόμα *bite* one's tongue, so as to refrain from speaking, πρὸ τῶν τοιούτων χρὴ λόγων δ. στόμα A.*Fr.*397, cf. S.*Tr.*976; δ. ἑαυτόν *to bite* one's lips for fear of laughing, Ar.*Ra.*43; so (by a joke παρὰ προσδοκίαν) δ. θυμόν Id.*Nu.*1369; δ. χόλον A.R.3.1170. II. metaph. of pungent smoke and dust, *sting,* Ar.*Ach.*18, *Lys.*298, *Pl.* 822; δ. ὄμματα, of dry winds, Hp.*Aph.*3.17. III. of the mind, *bite, sting,* δάκε δὲ φρένας Ἕκτορι μῦθος Il.5.493, cf. Hes.*Th.*567; ἔδακε λύπη Hdt.7.16.α'; συμφορὰ δ. A.*Pers.*846; λόφοι δὲ κώδων τ' οὐ δάκνουσ' ἄνευ δορός *have* no *sting,* Id.*Th.*399; σαίνουσα δάκνεις S.*Fr.* 885; τὸ δάκνον τῆς συμβουλῆς Jul.*Or.*7.207d; of love, πάντες οἱ ἐν ὥρᾳ τὸν φιλόπαιδα δάκνουσι Pl.*R.*474d:—freq. in Pass., δηχθεῖσα κέντροις .. ἠράσθη E.*Hipp.*1303; ἔρωτι δεδαγμένος Call.l.c.; of vexation, δάκνομαι ψυχήν Thgn.910; συμφορᾷ δεδαγμένοι Pi.l.c.; δέδηγμαι καρδίαν Ar.*Ach.*1; ὑπὸ τῆς δαπάνης Id.*Nu.*12; πρός τι, ἐπί τινι, at a thing, S.*Ph.*378, X.*Cyr.*4.3.3; ὑπὸ τῶν ἐν φιλοσοφίᾳ λόγων Pl.*Smp.*218a: c.part., ἐδήχθη ἀκούσας X.*Cyr.*1.4.13. (Cf. Skt. *dáśati* 'bite', Goth. *tahjan* 'tear'.) **-ώδης**, ες, *biting, pungent,* Hp. *Aph.*5.20, Gal.6.237; *painful,* Mich.*in EN*499.3.

δάκος [ᾰ], εος, τό, (δάκνω) *animal of which the bite is dangerous, noxious beast,* A.*Pr.*583 (lyr.), *Th.*558; Ἀργεῖον δ., of the Trojan horse, Id.*Ag.*824; δάκη θηρῶν *ravenous* beasts, E.*Hipp.*646; θήρειον δ. Id.*Cyc.*325; generally, β. δάκος, of a whale, Opp.*H.*5.333. II. *bite, sting,* δ. κακαγοριᾶν Pi.*P.*2.53, cf. Opp.*H.*2.454, 5.30.

δακόσσαι· πορθῆσαι, Hsch.

δάκρυ, τό, used by Poets metri gr. for δάκρυον in sg. δάκρυ and dat. pl. δάκρυσι Il.9.570, etc.: dat. pl. sts. in Prose, Th.7.75, D.30. 32, *Ev.Luc.*7.38: pl., δάκρη *An.Ox.*1.121 (cj. Bgk. in Pi.*Fr.*122.3, cf. δάκρυον 2):—*tear,* Il.2.266, Od.4.114, A.*Pr.*638, etc.; τοῦ δ' γε δ. χέων Od.2.24. II. generally, *drop,* λιβάνου Pi.l.c.; δ. πεύκινον E.*Med.*1200. (Cf. Lat. *lacruma*, Goth. *tagr*, OE. *tear.*)

δακρ-ύδιον, τό, Dim. of δάκρυ, = σκαμμωνία, Ps.-Dsc.4.170, cf. Alex. Trall.*Febr.*5. **-ῡμα**, ατος, τό, *that which is wept for, a subject for tears,* Orac.ap.Hdt.7.169. II. *tear,* A.*Pers.*134 (lyr.), E.*Andr.* 92 (pl.).

δακρυο-γόνος, ον, *author of tears,* Ἄρης A.*Supp.*682 (lyr.). **-εις**, εσσα, εν, neut. -όειν A.R.4.1291: 1. of persons, *tearful,* Il.21. 506, etc.; γόος Od.24.323; δακρυόεν γελάσασα smiling *through tears,* Il.6.484. 2. of things, *causing tears,* πόλεμος, ἄλγεα, θάνατος, 5. 737, Hes.*Th.*227, etc.

δάκρυον, τό, used in sg. δάκρυον, pl. δάκρυα, -ύων, -υοις, Ep. gen. pl. δακρυόφι (-φιν) Il.17.696, Od.5.152, etc.: (v. δάκρυ):—*tear,* δ. θερμὰ χέων Il.16.3; δ. λείβειν, εἴβειν, 13.88, Od.4.153; βλεφάρων ἄπο δ. ἧκεν 23.33; ἐς δάκρυα πεσεῖν Hdt.6.21; ἴσχειν πηγὰς δακρύων S.*Ant.*803 (lyr.), etc.; μετὰ πολλῶν δ. ἱκετεύειν Pl.*Ap.*34c. 2. *that which drops like tears, gum, sap,* τῆς ἀκάνθης Hdt.2.96; κρομμύου Hp.*Mul.*2.201; τῶν δένδρων Arist.*HA*553^{b}28; ἀμπέλου *AP*11.298; τὸ ἤλεκτρον καὶ ὅσα λέγεται ὡς δάκρυα Arist.*Mete.*388^{b}19; δ. κάμωνος, = σκαμμωνία, Nic.*Al.*484; of the bulbils of κρίνον (q.v.), Thphr. *HP*2.2.1, al. II. = δάκρυμα 1, *AP*7.527 (Theodorid.).

δακρῠο-πετής, ές, *making tears fall,* πάθεα A.*Supp.*113 (lyr.). **-ποιός**, όν, *inducing tears,* Dsc.1.1. **-τῑμος**, ον, *honoured with tears,* Orph.*H.*56.6.

δακρυ-πλώω, (πλέω) *swim with tears,* of drunken men, Od.19. 122. **-ρροέω**, *melt into tears, shed tears,* S.*Tr.*326, Ph.2.179; χαρᾷ S.*El.*1313; ἐπὶ παισί E.*HF*1181; of the eyes, *run with tears,* Hp.*Epid.*4.25; ὄμμα δακρυρροοῦν E.*Alc.*826, cf. *Ph.*370 codd., Alex. 313. 2. of vines, '*weep*', Thphr.*CP*3.13.2, *Gp.*5.38. **-ρροια**, ἡ, *shedding of tears,* Ps.-Callisth.3.3, Sch.E.*Or.*788. **-ρροος**, ον, *flowing with tears,* E.*Supp.*773; τέκνων πηγαί Id.*HF*98.

δακρῠσίστακτος, ον, *in floods of tears,* neut. pl. as Adv., A.*Pr.* 400 (lyr.).

δακρῡτός, όν (ή, όν J.*AJ*4.8.48), *wept over, tearful,* ἐλπίς A.*Ch.* 236; μόρος *AP*7.495 (Alc.); ἀπαλλαγή J.l.c.: irreg. Sup. δακρυώτατος, Hsch.

δακρῠ-χάρής, ές, *delighting in tears,* Πλούτων *IG*14.769 (Naples); Λάθας κευθμὼν *Mon.Ant.*11.477 (Cret.); κνίσματα prob. l. in *AP*5.165 (Mel.). **-χέων**, ουσα, wrongly written for δάκρυ χέων in Hom., etc.: hence Nonn. formed δακρυχέειν in trans. sense, *bewail,* *D.*5. 532.

δακρύω, first in A.*Ch.*81: fut. -ύσω E.*El.*658, later -ύσομαι Tryph. 404: aor. ἐδάκρῡσα Hdt.1.112, etc., Ep. δάκρῡσα Od.11.55: pf. δεδάκρῡκα Alciphr.2.3.14:—**Med.**, δακρύεσθαι A.*Th.*815: aor. δακρύσατο Tryph.431:—**Pass.**, pres., E.*Hel.*1226: pf. δεδάκρῡμαι Il.16.7, etc.: [ῡ long in all tenses, except in late Poets, as *AP*9.148]: (for the Root, v. δάκρυ). I. intr., *weep, shed tears,* Od.l.c., etc.: c. acc. cogn., δ. γόους to lament *with tears,* S.*Aj.*580: c. gen. causae, δ. συμφορᾶς E.*HF*528 (dub. l.); δ. βλέφαρα *to flood* them *with tears,* Id.*Hel.*948; δ. χαρᾷ X.*HG*7.2.9; ἐπὶ ταῖς συμφοραῖς Isoc.4.168:—Pass., pf. δεδάκρυμαι *to be in tears,* τίπτε δεδάκρυσαι, Πατρόκλεες; Il. 16.7; δεδάκρυνται δὲ παρειαί 22.491; δεδακρυμένος *in tears,* Pl.*Ax.* 364b, Plu.*Publ.*6, etc. 2. of the eyes, *run,* Arist.*HA*620^{a}5. 3. of trees, *exude gum,* Thphr.*Fr.*121; ἤλεκτρον δακρύειν Luc.*Salt.* 55. II. c. acc., *weep for,* τινά A.*Ag.*1490 (lyr.), S.*OT*1486, Ar. *Ach.*1027, etc.:—Pass., *to be wept for,* συμφορὰ δακρύεται E.*Hel.*1226 (prob. Med. in A.*Th.*815).

δακρυώδης, ες, *exuding a watery fluid,* ἕλκος δ. καὶ ἀνεκπύητον Hp. *Fract.*25; *running* at the eyes, *Hippiatr.*1, al. 2. *tear-like,* συρροή, of the bulbils of κρίνον (cf. δάκρυον 1.2), Thphr.*HP*6.6.8. II. *tearful, lamentable,* Luc.*Vit.Auct.*14.

δακτῠλ-ήθρα, ἡ, (δάκτυλος) *finger-sheath,* X.*Cyr.*8.8.17, Clearch. 21; *thumb-screw,* Lxx 4*Ma.*8.13. **-ηθρον**, τό, *ring,* Them.*Or.* 21.253a. **-ιαῖος**, α, ον, *of a finger's length, breadth* or *thickness,* ῥάβδοι Hp.*Fract.*30; κάραβοι Arist.*HA*549^{b}10; τομοὶ δ. τῷ τε μήκει καὶ πάχει Democr.ap.Gal.13.1000: Astron., *a digit in extent,* Cleom. 2.3. II. *possessing* δάκτυλοι, δ. μέρη τοῦ σώματος, i.e. hands and feet, D.S.1.77. **-ίδιον** [λῐ], τό, Dim. of δακτύλιος, *ring, IG*11(2). 161*B*119 (Delos, iii B.C.), *BGU*1104.13 (8 B.C.), *PAmh.*126.55 (ii A.D.), Poll.2.155, 5.100, *BGU*843.8, etc., but rejected by Atticists, cf. *AB*88. II. **δακτυλίδιον** [λῐ], τό, Dim. of δάκτυλος, *toe,* Ar. *Lys.*417. **-ίδρυον**, τό, late spelling of δακτυλίδιον 1, *BGU*1036. 14 (ii A.D.):—also **δακτυριτριω(ν)** (sic, gen. pl.), *PLond.*2.193^{v}4 (ii A.D.), cf. ib.44. **-ίζω**, = δακτυλοδεικτέω (in bad sense), Hsch. s. vv. ἐδακτύλιζον, σκινδαρεύεσθαι. II. Pass. in metre, *to be made a dactyl,* Eust.874.8. **-ικός**, ή, όν, *of* or *for the finger*: αὐλὸς δ. a flute *played with the fingers,* Ath.4.176f; δ. ψῆφος a stone *for calculating, AP*11.290 (Pall.). 2. *for the anus,* ἔμπλαστρος Orib.*Fr.*83, Cass.Fel.74. II. *dactylic,* ῥυθμός Longin.39.4, Heph.4. Adv. -κῶς, ποδίζεσθαι Eust.11.25. III. = δακτυλιαῖος, διάστημα Theo Sm.p.125 H.

δακτῠλιο-γλῠφία, ἡ, *art of cutting gems,* Pl.*Alc.*1.128c. **-γλύφος**, ὁ, *engraver of gems,* Critias 66 D., Phld.*Po.Herc.*1676.5, D.L. 1.57, Gal.12.205. **-θήκη**, ἡ, *collection of gems,* Plin.*HN*37.11. II. *ring-case,* Mart.11.59.

δακτύλιον, τό, = sq. 1, *BGU*781 ii 15: = sq. II. 2, Aët.2.185 (s. v. l.); also v.l. for δακρύδιον Ps.-Dsc.4.170.

δακτύλιος [ῠ], Boeot. **δακκύλιος** (v. δάκτυλος), ὁ, *ring, signet,* Sapph.35, Hdt.2.38, Ar.*Pl.*884, Pl.*R.*359e; ὁ ἐπὶ τοῦ δ. keeper of the *signet,* Lxx *To.*1.22; ὁ τῆς πόλεως δ. *OGI*229.88 (Smyrna, iii B.C.); δ. φαρμακίτης Eup.87, cf. Antiph.177. II. *anything ring-shaped,* as, 1. *felloe* of a wheel, Poll.1.145. 2. *anus,* Dsc.1.70, Luc.*Demon.*17, *PRyl.*28.68 (iv A.D.). 3. pl., *movable rings* on a bit, X.*Eq.*10.9. 4. *stone* to which mooring-cables were attached, Hsch. 5. *door-handle,* Id. 6. *end of the steering-paddle,* Id.

δακτῠλιουργός, ὁ, *ring-maker,* Philyll.15, Pherecr.207.

δακτῠλ-ίς, ίδος, ἡ, name of a kind of *grape,* Plin.*HN*14.40. II. = δάκτυλος, Steph.*in Hp.Aph.*2.294 D. **-ίσκος**, ὁ, Dim. of δάκτυλος II, *IG*7.3073.115 (Lebad.). **-ιστής**, οῦ, ὁ, (δάκτυλος II) *measurer, surveyor, PFay.*112.11 (i A.D.), *PAmh.*126.32 (ii A.D.).

δακτῠλῖτις, ἡ, = ἀριστολοχεία μακρά, Dsc.3.4, Isid.*Etym.*17.9.52.

δακτῠλο-δεικτέω, *point with the finger,* D.25.68: c. acc., D.C.61. 17:—Pass., D.H.*Rh.*7.4, Ph.2.539. **-δεικτος**, ον, *pointed at with the finger,* μέλαθρα A.*Ag.*1332 (lyr.), cf. *PLond.ined.*1821. **-δικτος**, ον, (δικεῖν) *thrown from the fingers,* δ. μέλος, of the humming of a top, A.*Fr.*57 codd. Str. (-δεικτον edd.). **-δόχμη**, ἡ, *four fingers' breadth,* = παλαιστή, Poll.2.157. **-ειδής**, ές, *like a finger,* Philem. Gloss.ap.Ath.11.468f, Ruf.*Oss.*22. **-καμψόδῠνος**, ον, *wearying the fingers by keeping them bent, APl.*1.18. **-κοιλογλύφος** [λῠ], ὁ, = δακτυλιογλύφος, *IGRom.*4.1648 (Philadelphia). **-ποιητικός**, ή, όν, *finger-making,* δύναμις Phlp.*in GA*193.11. **-πους**, ὁ, gen. ποδος, *first phalanx,* δ. ἢ ῥιζοδάκτυλος *Cat.Cod.Astr.*7.238.25.

δάκτῠλος, ὁ, poet. pl. δάκτυλα Theoc.19.3, *AP*9.365 (Jul. Imp.), also Arist.*Phgn.*810^{a}22:—*finger,* ἐπὶ δακτύλων συμβάλλεσθαι τοὺς μῆνας to reckon on *the fingers,* Hdt.6.63; ὁ μέγας δ. *the thumb,* Id. 3.8, Diog.Apoll.6; ὁ μέσος Arist.*PA*687^{b}18; οἱ λιχανοί Hp.*Art.*37; ὁ ἔσχατος Id.*PA*687^{b}17: prov., ἄκρῳ δ. γεύεσθαι Procop.Gaz.*Ep.* 31; οὐκ ἄξια ψόφου δακτύλων Clearch.5. 2. οἱ δ. τῶν ποδῶν *the toes,* X.*An.*4.5.12; and, without ποδός, Batr.45, Ar.*Eq.*874, Arist. *HA*494^{a}12; τὸ τῶν δ. μέγεθος ἐναντίως ἔχει ἐπί τε τῶν ποδῶν καὶ τῶν χειρῶν Id.*PA*690^{a}30; ὁ μέσος δ. of a monkey, Id.*HA*502^{b}3; ὁ μείζων δ. the great *toe,* Plu.*Pyrrh.*3. b. of *the toes* of beasts, Arist.*HA*498^{a}34; of birds, Id.*PA*695^{a}22. II. a measure of length, *finger's breadth,* = about $\frac{7}{10}$ of an inch, Hdt.1.60, al.; πώνωμεν, δάκτυλος ἀμέρα Alc.41; δάκτυλος ἀώς *AP*12.50 (Asclep.): Astron., *digit,* i.e. twelfth part of the sun's or moon's apparent diameter, Cleom.2.3. III. metrical foot, *dactyl,* — ◡ ◡, Pl.*R.*400b; ῥυθμὸς κατὰ δάκτυλον Ar.*Nu.*651; δ. κατ' ἴαμβον, *diiambus,* Aristid.

Quint.1.17. 2. δάκτυλοι, οἱ, a *dance*, Ath.14.629d. IV. *date*, fruit of the φοῖνιξ, Arist.*Mete*.342^{a}10, Artem.5.89. 2. kind of *grape*, Plin.*HN*14.15, Colum.3.2.1. 3. = ἄγρωστις, Plin.*HN*24.182. V. Δάκτυλοι Ἰδαῖοι mythical *wizards* and *craftsmen* in Crete (or Phrygia, D.S.17.7), attached to the cult of Rhea Cybele, Hes.*Fr*.176, Pherecyd.47 J., S.*Fr*.364, Str.8.3.30, D.S.5.64, *IG*12(9).259.22 (Eretria). 2. δ. Ἰδαῖοι, = γλυκυσίδη, Dsc.3.140. b. fossil found in Crete, Plin.*HN*37.170. VI. δ. θεοῦ the *hand* of God, Lxx *Ex*.8.19, cf. *Ev.Luc*.11.20. (Orig. *δάτκυλος, cf. Boeot. δακκύλιος *Schwyzer* 462 *B* 51; δατ- = *dnt*, cf. Skt. *a-datkas* 'toothless'.)

δακτῠλότριπτος, ον, *worn by the fingers*, ἄτρακτος *AP*6.247.3 (Phil.).

δακτῠλωτός, ή, όν, *with finger-like handles*, ἔκπωμα Ion Trag.1, Didym.ap.Ath.11.468e.

δάλα· ἄμπελος, Hsch. **δάλαν**· λύμην, Id. (Cf. δηλέομαι.) **δαλάγχαν**· θάλασσαν (Maced.), Id. **δάλεμον**· κηδεμόνα, Id.

δᾰλέομαι, Dor. for δηλέομαι.

δᾰλερός, ά, όν, *burning, hot*, dub. l. in Emp.90.2.

δάλιδας· τὰς μεμνηστευμένας, Hsch. (leg. τάλιδας).

δᾰλίον, τό, Dim. of δαλός, Ar.*Pax*959.

Δάλιος, Dor. for Δήλιος (q. v.).

δαλιοχεῖν, = παιδὶ συνεῖναι (Ambrac.); also, = μοιχεύειν, Hsch.: **δαλιοχός**· μοιχός, Id. **δαλίς**· μωρός, Id. **δάλκιον**· πινάκιον, Id. **δάλλει**· κακουργεῖ, Id. (Cf. δηλέομαι.) **δαλλώ** or **δαλώ**, *old woman* (cf. δαλός II), Id. **δαλμᾶναι**· εἰκάσαι, Id.

Δαλμᾰτεῖς, οἱ, *Dalmatians*, Plb.12.5.2, Str.7.5.5:—also **Δαλμάται**, App.*Ill*.11: **Δαλματία**, ἡ, Str.7.5.3:—Adj. **-τικός**, ή, όν, Id. 7.5.5:—hence **Δαλμᾰτική**, ἡ, *a robe*, *CPR*21.16 (iii A. D.):—more freq. **Δελμ-**, *Edict.Diocl*.19.9, al., *BGU*93.7 (ii/iii A. D.):—Dim. **Δελματίκιον**, τό, *Sammelb*.1988, *POxy*.1026.10 (V A. D.):—also **δερματική**, *PTeb*.405.10 (iii A. D.):—Dim. **δερματίκιν**, *PTeb*.413.8 (ii/iii A. D.).

δαλμᾰτικομᾰφόρτης, ου, ὁ, *Dalmatian cloak with a hood*, *POxy*.1273.14 (iii A. D.) (δελμ-):—Dim. **δερμᾰτικομᾰφόρτιν**, ib.114.5 (ii/iii A. D.).

Δᾰλογενής, ές, Dor. for Δηλογενής.

δᾱλός, ὁ, (δαίω) *fire-brand*, Il.15.421, Od.5.488, E.*Cyc*.471,472, A.*Ch*.608 (lyr.), Arist.*Mete*.344^{a}26; *beacon-light*, *AP*9.675; of the thunderbolt, Il.13.320, cf. Luc.*Tim*.2. 2. a kind of *meteor*, Arist. *Mete*.341^{b}28. II. *burnt-out torch*: metaph. of an old man, *AP*12.41 (Mel.). (Contr. fr. δᾰϝελός, cf. δαβελός.)

δαλός· μελάνουρος ἰχθύς, Hsch. **δαλοῦν**· σύντομον, Id.

δάλτος, Cypr. = δέλτος, *Inscr.Cypr*.135.26 H. (Idalium).

δαμάζω A.*Ch*.324 (lyr.), etc.: fut. δαμάσω *AP*6.329 (Leon.); Ep. δαμάσσω Il.22.176, also δαμᾷ, δαμάᾳ, 1.61, 22.271; 3 pl. δαμόωσι 6.368 (v. δαμάω): aor. 1 ἐδάμᾰσα Pi.*N*.7.90 (part. δαμάσσαις *O*.9.92), Ep. ἐδάμασσα, δάμασσα, Il.5.191, Od.14.367: pf. δεδάμακα Stob. *Flor.Monac*.82:—Med., fut. Ep. δαμάσσομαι Il.21.226: aor. ἐδαμάσσατο, δαμάσαντο, δαμασσάμενος, Od.9.516, Il.10.210, Od.9.454; aor. 1 opt. δαμάσαιτο *Leg.Gort*.2.11: aor. 2 opt. δάμοιτο *CIG*4000.18 (Iconium):—Pass., fut. 3 δεδμήσομαι *h.Ap*.543; irreg. δαμοῦμαι *PMag.Par*.1.2906: aor. ἐδαμάσθην Od.8.231, Pi.*O*.2.20, A.*Pers*.279 (lyr.), E.*Ph*.563; Ep. δαμάσθην Il.19.9, cf. 16.816; ἐδμήθην, imper. δμηθήτω 9.158, δμηθείς 4.99, Hes.*Th*.1000, Dor. δμᾱθείς A. *Pers*.907 (lyr.), E. (lyr., v. infr.), Cerc.7.1: ἐδάμην [ᾰ] Il.13.812, Parm.7.1, etc.; Ep. δάμην Od.3.90; 3 pl. δάμεν Il.8.344; Ep. subj. δαμείω Od.18.54, 2 and 3 sg. δαμήῃς -ήῃ Il.3.436, 22.246, 2 pl. δαμήετε 7.72; opt. δαμείην Il.3.301, E.*Med*.648; inf. δαμῆναι Il.15.522, A.*Ch*.368 (lyr.), S.*Ph*.200, Ep. inf. δᾰμήμεναι Il.20.312; part. δαμείς 22.40, Sapph.90, etc. (only form of aor. used by S., and preferred by A. and E.): pf. δέδμημαι Il.5.878, etc., -ημένος 14.482, etc.; later δεδαμασμένος Nic.*Al*.29, *Epigr.Gr*.550.9: plpf. δέδμητο Od.3.305; 3 pl. -ήατο Il.3.183.—Poet. Verb, used by X. in pres. part. δαμάζων *Mem*.4.3.10: aor. Pass. δαμασθεῖεν ib.4.1.3; also inf. δαμασθῆναι is f. l. in Isoc.7.4:—*overpower*: I. of animals, *tame, break in*, twice in Hom., in Med., ἡμίονον. . ἥ τ' ἀλγίστη δαμάσασθαι Il.23.655; τῶν κέν τιν'. . δαμασαίμην Od.4.637:—later in Act., X.*Mem*.4.3.10:—Pass., ib.4.1.3. 2. of metals, *work*, σίδαρον E.*Alc*.980 (lyr.); of land, *clear*, *PSI*4.316 (iv(?) A. D.). II. of maidens, *make subject* to a husband, ἀνδρὶ δάμασσεν Il.18.432:—Med., *force, seduce*, *Leg.Gort*. l. c.:—Pass., Il.3.301, Od.3.269. III. *subdue, conquer*, Od.9.59, al.; βίῃ καὶ χερσὶ δ. Hes.*Th*.490:—Pass., *to be subject to* another, σοί τ' ἐπιπείθονται καὶ δεδμήμεσθα ἕκαστος Il.5.878; δέδμητο δὲ λαὸς ὑπ' αὐτῷ Od.3.305. b. of the gods, *bring low*, Il.9.118, 16.845, al. c. *subdue, gain the mastery over*, ἐπιθυμίαν Stob. l. c. 2. *lay low, kill*, esp. in fight, εἴ χ' ὑπ' ἐμοί γε θεὸς δαμάσῃ μνηστῆρας Od.21.213:—Pass., ὑπ' ἐμοὶ δμηθέντα Il.5.646; ὑπὸ δουρὶ δαμέντα ib.653. 3. of the powers of nature, etc., *overcome, overpower*, ἔρος. . θυμὸν ἐνὶ στήθεσσιν. . ἐδάμασσεν 14.316:—Med., δαμασσάμενος φρένας οἴνῳ Od.9.454, cf. 516:—Pass., *to be overcome*, αἴθρῳ καὶ καμάτῳ δεδμημένον 14.318; μαλακῷ δεδμημένοι ὕπνῳ Il.10.2; ὕπνῳ καὶ φιλότητι δαμείς 14.353; ἀλὶ δέδμητο φίλον κῆρ Od.5.454, cf. 8.231; δμαθέντες *dead*, E.*Alc*.127 (lyr.). IV. ἀγῶνα δαμάσσαι ἔργῳ *win* it, Pi.*P*.8.80. V. οὐ μήποτε τοῦτο δαμῇ, εἶναι μὴ ἐόντα it shall never be *proved* that. ., Parm.7.1. (δᾰμᾰ- : δμη- underlies δάμνημι, ἐδάμα(σ)σα, δέδμημαι; δαμάζω is a post-Homeric form of pres.; cf. Skt. *dámyati* 'to be tamed', *damitar-* 'tamer', etc.)

Δᾰμαῖος, ὁ, (δαμάζω) *Horse-Tamer*, epith. of Poseidon, Pi.*O*.13.69.

δᾰμάλη [μᾰ], ἡ, = δάμαλις, E.*Ba*.739, Theoc.4.12, *POxy*.1734.2, etc.

δᾰμᾰλήβοτος, ον, *browsed by heifers*, *APl*.4.230 (Leon.).

δᾰμάλης [μᾰ], ου, ὁ, (δαμάζω) *subduer*, Ἔρως Anacr.2.1. II. *young steer*, Arist.*HA*632^{a}15, *AP*6.96 (Eryc.).

δᾰμᾰληφάγος [φᾰ], ον, *beef-eating*, Ἀλκείδης *AP*9.237 (Eryc.).

δᾰμᾰλ-ίζω, poet. = δαμάζω, *to subdue*, Pi.*P*.5.121 codd.:—Med., πώλους δαμαλιζομένα E.*Hipp*.231 (lyr.). **-ιον**, τό, Dim. of δάμαλις, *PFlor*.150.2 (iii A. D.). **-ις**, εως, ἡ (ὁ D.H.1.39), (δαμάζω) *young cow, heifer*, A.*Supp*.351 (lyr.), Aen.Tact.27.1, D.H.1.35; of Io, B.18.24, Nic.*Al*.344; also masc., Hellanic.111 J. 2. δ. σῦς *IG*5(1).1390.34,69 (Andania, i B. C.). II. *girl*, Epicr.9, *AP*5.291 (Agath.).

δαμάλλοντες· δαρδάπτοντες, Hsch.

δᾰμᾰλοπόδια, ων, τά, *calves' feet*, Alex.Trall.7.8.

δάμᾰλος, ὁ, perh. *calf*, Hdn.Gr.1.159.

δᾰμαντήρ, ῆρος, ὁ, *tamer*, v. l. in Alcm.9.

δάμᾰρ [ᾰ], αρτος, ἡ, (δαμάζω II) *wife, spouse*, Il.3.122, Pi.*N*.4.57, A.*Pr*.834, etc.

δαμαρίππεως, ω, a kind of *fig*, Eup.407.

δαμαρούσιος· ὀχετὸς δημόσιος, Hsch.

δᾰμᾰσ-άνδρα, ἡ, *subduer of men*, of the moon, *Hymn.Mag*.5.43. **-ήνωρ**, ορος, *man-slaying*, λέων Pancrat.*Oxy*.1085.3.

δᾰμᾰσι-κόνδυλος, ον, *conquering with the knuckles*, Eup.408. **-μβροτος**, ον, *taming mortals, man-slaying*, Σπάρτη Simon.218; αἰχμή Pi.*O*.9.79; χαλκός B.12.50.

δᾰμάσιππος [μᾰ], ον, *horse-taming*, of Athena, Lamprocl.1.4 (perh. Stes., cf. Sch.Aristid.3.537 D.), cf. Corn.*ND*20; Λυδία B.3.23.

δᾰμᾰσις [δᾰ], εως, ἡ, *taming, subduing*, Sch.Pi.*O*.13.98.

δᾰμᾰσί-φρων, ον, gen. ονος, *heart-subduing* χρυσός Pi.*O*.13.78. **-φως**, ωτος, ὁ, ἡ, = δαμασίμβροτος, ὕπνος Simon.232; of Ares, prob. in Tim.*Pers*.22.

δᾰμᾰσίχθων, ονος, ὁ, *earth-subduer*, epith. of Poseidon, B.15.19.

Δαμασκηνόν, τό, *Damascus-plum, damson*, Ath.2.49d, Gal.6.353.

δᾰμᾰσ-τέον, *one must break in*, τριετῆ πῶλον *Gp*.16.1.11. II. Adj. -τέος, α, ον, Hsch. s. v. δματέα. **-τής**, οῦ, ὁ, *subduer*, *Gloss*., prob. epith. of Ἔρως, [Epich.]301. **-τικός**, ή, όν, gloss on Δαμαῖος, Sch.Pi.*O*.13.98.

δαμασώνιον, τό, = ἄλισμα, Dsc.3.152; = ἄλιμος, Ps.-Dsc.1.91. II. a diuretic, Pall.*inHp*.2.18 D.

δᾰμάτειρα [μᾰ], ἡ, fem. of δαμαντήρ, *AP*11.403 (Luc.).

Δαμάτηρ, v. Δημήτηρ.

δᾱμᾱτρίζειν (Δημήτηρ) *gather in the fruits of the earth* (Cypr.), Hsch.

δαμάτριον· ἄνθος ὅμοιον ναρκίσσῳ, Hsch.

Δᾱμάτριος, ὁ, Boeotian month, *IG*7.296, al., Plu.2.378e.

δᾰμάω, a form assumed as the 1st pers. of δαμᾷ, δαμάᾳ, δαμόωσι, which in Hom. are fut. of δαμάζω or δάμνημι: but δαμόωσι, δαμόωνται, are pres. in late Ep., Q.S.5.247,249.

Δάμεια, τά, festival at Tarentum, Hsch.

δᾰμείω, δᾰμήμεναι, v. δαμάζω.

δᾱμέτας, α, ὁ, = δημότης, *IG*12(1).1032.13 (Carpathus).

δᾱμία, Cret. for ζημία. **Δαμία**, ἡ, fertility-Goddess at Aegina, Hdt.5.82, Paus.2.30.4: also **Δαμοία**, *IG*5(1).363 (Sparta), 1314 (Thalamae).

δᾱμεύω, = δημοσιόω, *IG*4.554 (Argos), cf. Hsch.

δᾱμι-εργός, -οεργός, -οργός, Dor. for δημιουργός: **δᾱμιόργιον**, τό, *office of* δαμιοργοί, *LW*1572^b (Cnidus): **δάμιος**, Dor. for δήμιος: **δαμιόω**, Boeot. and Cret. for ζημιόω.

δαμναμένη, = κατανάγκη, Ps.-Dsc.4.131; = κῆμος, ib.133.

δαμνάω, = δαμάζω, Hom. only in 3 sg. pres. δαμνᾷ Od.11.221: impf. ἐδάμνα Il.21.52, Sapph.*Supp*.1.12; δάμνα Il.16.103, al.; Ion. δάμνασκε *h.Ven*.251: 2 sg. pres. δαμνᾷς Thgn.1388 (s.v.l.); imper. δάμνα Sapph.1.3. (These forms may belong orig. to δάμνᾱμι, Aeol. for sq.; Hsch. also gives pres. δάμνει and fut. δαμνήσει.)

δάμνημι (v. also foreg.), = δαμάζω, τὴν μὲν. . δάμνημ' ἐπέεσσι Il.5.893; δάμνησι στίχας ἀνδρῶν ib.746, etc.; ἄνδρ' ἀγαθὸν πενίη δάμνησι Thgn.173; πενία. . δ. λαόν Alc.92:—Med., ἵμερον, ᾧ τε σὺ πάντας δαμνᾷ ἀθανάτους Il.14.199; ἀλλά με χεῖμα δάμναται Od.14.488; Ἔρος δ. νόον Hes.*Th*.122, cf. Archil.85, A.*Pr*.165, Q.S.11.25:—Pass., πυκνὰ καρήαθ' ὑφ' Ἕκτορι δάμνατο Il.11.309; μηδ' οὕτω Τρώεσσιν ἔα δάμνασθαι Ἀχαιούς 8.244; Ἀχαιοὺς Τρωσὶν δαμναμένους 13.16; δάμναμαι A.*Supp*.904 (lyr.); imper. μηκέτι δάμναο θυμόν Maiist.51: pf. part. δεδαμναμένα *forced, seduced*, *Leg.Gort*.2.13.

δαμνῆτις, ιδος, ἡ, *she that subdues*, Hsch. **δάμνια**· θύματα, σφάγια, Id.

δάμνιππος, ον, *horse-taming*, Orph.*A*.740.

δαμνογόνη, δαμνοδάμεια, δαμνώ, *she that subdues*, epiths. of the Moon, *Hymn.Mag*.5.43.

δαμνόν· δεινόν, Hsch. **δάμνος**· ἵππος (Tyrrhen.), Id.

δᾱμογέρων, δαμόθεν, δαμόομαι, δᾱμόσιος, δᾶμος, δαμότης, Dor. for δημ-.

δᾱμοθοινία, Dor. = δημο-, *public feast*, *SIG*671 *A* 2, al. (Delph., ii B. C.).

Δαμοία, v. Δαμία.

δᾱμοσιομάστας, ὁ, official title, prob. = μαστρός (q. v.), *IG*5(1).47 (Sparta, ii A. D.); -μαστης, ib.554.

δᾱμοσιοργία, ἡ, = δημιουργία, *GDI*3052.10.

δᾱμοσιοφύλᾰκες [ῠ], οἱ, title of board of magistrates at Dyme, *GDI*1615, *SIG*529.4 (iii B. C.).

δαμοσόνιος, a plant, Hsch.; cf. δαμασώνιον. **δαμοῦαι**· οἱ ἐπὶ

Μελαντίας πεμπόμενοι (Lacon.), Id. **δαμοῦχοι,** οἱ, Dor. for δημ–, title of a board of magistrates, Id. **δαμοφανής,** = ἱμάτιον (Lacon.), Id. **δαμπόν,** = πυρίεφθον (Cret.), Id.

δᾱμώματα, τά, = τὰ δημοσίᾳ ᾀδόμενα, Ar.*Pax*797, from Stes.(*Fr.* 37): expld. by κοινώματα, δημοσιώματα, Hsch. **δαμώμενος·** ἀγαλλόμενος, οἱ δὲ παίζων, Id. **δαμώσεις·** δημόται, ἢ οἱ ἐντελεῖς (Lacon.), Id. **δαμώσικτον·** δεδοκιμασμένον (Lacon.), Id. **δᾶν,** v. δᾶ.

Δάν, = Ζεύς, *BpW*31.1578 (Delph.), Hdn.Gr.1.394.

δάν, δαναιός, Dor. for δήν, δηναιός.

Δανάη, ἡ, = δάφνη, Ps.-Dsc.4.145.

δάναε· δαιδοῦλαι (Tarent.), Hsch.

Δαναΐς, ἡ, = κόνυζα πλατύφυλλος, Ps.-Dsc.3.121.

δᾰνάκη [νᾰ], ἡ, *Persian coin*, worth rather more than an obol: hence, *the coin buried with a corpse* as Charon's fee, Call.*Fr.*110, Poll. 9.82, Hsch., *EM*247.41: Dim. **δανάκιον,** τό, prob. in Suid. (Pers. *dānak*.)

Δᾰναοί, οἱ, *the Danaäns*, subjects of Δάναος, king of Argos, but in Il.1.42, al., for *the Greeks* generally (but expl. as = νεκροί (cf. δάνος (B)), *EM*247.49): Com. Sup. Δαναώτατος Ar.*Fr.*259:—**Δαναΐδαι,** ῶν, οἱ, *the sons* or *descendants of Danaus*, E.*Ph.*466:—**Δαναΐδες,** αἱ, *his daughters*, name of a play of A.

δάνας· μερίδας (Caryst.), Hsch. **δανδαίνειν·** ἀτενίζειν, φροντίζειν, μεριμνᾶν, Id.

δανδαλίς, ίδος, ἡ, = δενδαλίς, Poll.6.77, Hsch.

δάνδαλος, ὁ, = ἐριθακός, Hsch. **δανδαρίκαι·** οἱ βολευταί, Id.

δᾰν-ειακός, ή, όν, *concerning loans*, *Cod.Just.*1.3.45, Just.*Nov.* 134.8. **-είζω,** fut. -είσω D.35.52: aor. ἐδάνεισα X.*Cyr.*3.1.34, etc.: pf. δεδάνεικα D.35.52:—Med., ibid.: fut. δανείσομαι Id.32.15: aor. ἐδανεισάμην Lys.12.59, etc.: pf. δεδάνεισμαι in med. sense, X. *HG*6.5.19, D.37.53:—Pass., aor. ἐδανείσθην X.*HG*2.4.28, D.33. 12: pf. δεδάνεισμαι Id.36.5, 49.53: (δάνος):—*put out money at usury, lend*, *IG*1².302.56, Ar.*Th.*842, al.; more fully, δ. ἐπὶ τόκῳ Pl.*Lg.* 742c; ἐπὶ ὀκτὼ ὀβολοῖς τὴν μνᾶν δ. τοῦ μηνὸς ἑκάστου D.53. 13, cf. Aeschin.1.107; δ. ἐπὶ τούτοις τοῖς ἀνδραπόδοις on the security of..., D.27.27; ἐπὶ τοῖς σώμασι Arist.*Ath.*9.1; εἰς τὰ ἡμέτερα D.27.28; δανεῖσαι χρήματα εἰς τὸν Πόντον καὶ πάλιν Ἀθήναζε Id.35.3. 2. Med., *have lent to one, borrow*, Ar.*Nu.*1306, etc.; ἀπό τινος Lys.17.2; ἐπὶ τοῖς μεγάλοις [τόκοις] D.1.15; δ. ἐγγείων τόκων 34.23:—Act. and Med. opposed, ἀποδώσουσι οἱ δανεισάμενοι τοῖς δανείσασι τὸ γιγνόμενον ἀργύριον ap.D.35.11:—Pass., of the money, *to be lent out*, Ar.*Nu.*756, X.*HG*2.4.28, D.33.12. 3. metaph. in Med., μόρια ἀπὸ τοῦ κόσμου Pl.*Ti.*42e; ἀποδώσετέ μοι ἃ ἐδανείσασθε ἐν τῷ λόγῳ Pl.*R.*612c.

δᾰνειοκόπος, ὁ, *usurer*, prob. in Mitteis *Chr.*80.27 (i A.D.).

δάν-ειον [ᾰ], τό, *loan*, δ. ἀπαιτεῖν D.34.12; ἀποδοτέον Arist.*EN* 1164ᵇ32: pl., Men.*Mon.*97; σπέρματα δάνεια *POxy.*1262.16 (ii A.D.): —written **δάνιον,** Lxx *De.*15.8, al. **-εισμα,** ατος, τό, = δάνειον, δ. ποιεῖσθαι, = δανείζεσθαι, Th.1.121; τῶν μαρτύρων τῶν παραγιγνομένων τῷ δ. D.35.9: metaph., οἷον δάνεισμα καὶ μόρια τοῦ μεγάλου κόσμου Gal.19.159. **-εισμός,** ὁ, *money-lending*, *IG*2².1172, Pl.*Lg.*842d (pl.), Arist.*EN*1131ᵃ3, etc. II. *borrowing*, Pl.*R.*573e (pl.), *POxy.*799 (i A.D.), Plu.2.706b: metaph., αἷμα δ' αἵματος πικρὸς δ. ἦλθε E.*El.* 858. **-ειστέον,** *one must lend money*, Plu.2.408c. **-ειστής,** οῦ, ὁ, *money-lender* or *creditor*, *IPE*1².32*B*84 (Olbia), Lxx 4*Ki.*4.1, *Ev. Luc.*7.41, Ph.2.284, al., Hierocl.p.57 A., *POxy.*68.25 (ii A.D.). II. *borrower*, *IG*12(7).67.41, 68.4 (Amorg.), Plu.*Sol.*13. **-ειστικός,** ή, όν, *concerning loans*, *BGU*1149.23 (i B.C.), Plu.*Agis*13, etc.; ὁ δ., = δανειστής, Luc.*Smp.*5.

δανές· ἀληθὲς ἢ δῶρον ἢ μερίδα ἢ ἰσχύν, γέρας ἢ δάνειον, Hsch. **δανήλοφα,** = μακροτράχηλα or ὑψηλοτράχηλα, Id. (i.e. ταν–).

δανίζω, Hellenistic form for δανείζω, Lxx *Pr.*19.14: fut. Act. δανιῶ and Med. δανιοῦμαι ib.*De.*28.12: aor. part. δανίσας *AP*11.309 (Lucill.), *Lyr.Alex.Adesp.*37.27.

δανός, ή, όν, *burnt, dry, parched*, ξύλα δ. Od.15.322: Sup. ξύλα δανότατα Ar.*Pax*1134. (Prob. from *δᾰϝεσ-νός, cf. δαίω.)

δάνος (A), [ᾰ], εος, τό, *gift, present*, Euph.42. II. *loan, debt*, Call. *Ep.*48, *PMasp.*126.11 (vi A.D.): metaph., ὁ χρόνος ἐστὶ δ. *Lyr.Alex. Adesp.*37.27; πνεῦμα λαβὼν δ. οὐρανόθεν..αὐτ' ἀπέδωκα *IG*14.2000.

δάνος (B), [ᾰ], ὁ, Maced. for θάνατος, Plu.2.22c.

δᾰνοτής, ῆτος, ἡ, perh. f.l. for δαϊοτῆτος (cf. δηι–), ἀμερίων μόχθων καὶ δανοτῆτος S.*Fr.*369.

δάντα· ζυγά, Hsch. **δανῶν·** κακοποιῶν, κτείνων (Maced.), Id.

δάξ, Adv. = ὀδάξ, Opp.*H.*4.60.

δάξα· θάλασσα (Epir.), Hsch.

δαξασμός, ὁ, = ὀδαγμός, ὀδαξησμός, Ti.Locr.103a.

δαόν· πολυχρόνιον, Hsch.

δάος [ᾰ], εος, τό, (δαίω) = δαΐς, δαλός, *firebrand, torch*, Il.24.647, Od.4.300, Q.S.9.454:—also **δάος,** ὁ, *JHS*32.163 (iii A.D.). II. Phryg., = λύκος, Hsch.

Δᾶος, ὁ, as the name of a slave, Lat. *Davus* (Δᾶϝος), Men.*Georg.* 32; from the name of a barbarous people, cf. Hdt.1.125.

δάοχος· μοιχός, Hsch.; cf. δαλιοχός.

δάπακες (cod. δαρπ–)· θυμάλωπες, Hsch.; cf. δαύακες.

δᾰπᾰν-άω:—Pass., pres. part. δαπανούμενα (as if from δαπανέω) *IG*5(1).1390.55 (Andania, i B.C.): fut. δαπανηθήσομαι Satyr.20, Plu.2.218d: aor. ἐδαπανήθην X.*Cyr.*2.4.11: pf. δεδαπάνημαι Hdt.2. 125, Lys.21.5, etc.: plpf. δεδαπάνητο (κατα–) Hdt.5.34:—Pass., also Med. δαπανάομαι Id.2.37, Ar.*Pl.*588, Pl., etc.; impf., Ar.*Fr.* 569.10, Lys.25.13: aor., Isoc.15.225, Is.5.43 (but -ήσας ib.45) (aor. Med. ἐδαπανησάμην Eun.*Hist.*p.271 D.): pf., Isoc.18.63:—*spend*, Th.7.29, etc.; ὑπὲρ τὴν οὐσίαν δ. Diph.32.7; δ. τὰ προσταττόμενα And.4.42; δ. εἴς τι *to spend* upon a thing, Th.8.45, X.*Mem.* 1.3.11, prob. in Arist.*Pol.*1307ᵇ34; δ. ἐκ τῶν αὑτοῦ Is.7.38; τἀναλώματα πάντα ἐκ τῶν ἰδίων ἐδαπανῶμεν *defrayed* all expenses, interpol. in D.21.154:—Pass., Hdt.2.125; τὰ λαμβανόμενα καὶ δαπανώμενα Arist.*Pol.*1314ᵇ5: also Med. (v. supr.), *spend*, Hdt.2.37; δ. μεγάλα And.4.32, cf. Lys.33.5: c. acc. cogn., τοσαύτας δαπάνας δαπανώμενος Id.21.3; ὅσα δεδαπάνησθε εἰς τὸν πόλεμον D.1.27, cf. Isoc.18.63; δαπανηθεὶς οὐδέν dub. l. in Is.5.43. 2. *consume, use up*, ἡ φύσις δ. τὸν θορόν Arist.*GA*757ᵃ25; χρόνον εἴς τι Onos.1.5:—Pass., Arist.*GA* 745ᵃ13; of time, App.*Pun.*130; *destroy, consume*, φλὸξ δ. πάντα Ph. 2.208; ἄνεμος [πόλιν] ἐδαπάνησεν App.*BC*1.94; of persons, *to be destroyed*, ὑπὸ θηρίων Ph.2.43; καθάπερ ὑπὸ πυρὸς ib.433; πρὸς θηρίων App. *BC*5.79; ἐν ταρτάροις καὶ βαράθροις δαπανωμένους D.H.4.81; ὑπὸ νόσου or νόσῳ δαπανᾶσθαι Plu.*Galb.*17, Lib.*Or.*55.27:—Med., πυρὶ καὶ φόνῳ καὶ σιδήρῳ πάντα δαπανήσασθαι Eun.l.c. II. causal, τὴν πόλιν δαπανᾶν *to put* it *to expense, exhaust* it, Th.4.3, cf. Ph.2.642. **-η,** ἡ, *cost, expenditure*, Hes.*Op.*723, al.; δ. χρυσοῦ καὶ ἀργύρου, χρημάτων, Th.1. 129, 3.13; δ. κοῦφα *the cost* is little, c. inf., E.*Ba.*893 (lyr.); εἰς κενὸν ἡ δ. *IG*14.1746.10: also in pl., Th.6.15; δαπάναι ἐλπίδων Pi.*I.*4 (5).57. II. *money spent*, ἵππων *on* horses, ib.3(4).47; δαπάνην παρέχειν *money for spending*, Hdt.1.41; ξυμφέρειν Th.1.99; ὅπως μὴ ἡ εἰς τὸν ἐνιαυτὸν κειμένη δ. εἰς τὸν μῆνα δαπανᾶται X.*Oec.*7. 36. III. *extravagance*, ἡ ἐν τῇ φύσει δ. Aeschin.3.218. **-ημα,** ατος, τό, *cost, expense*, mostly in pl., X.*Cyr.*8.1.9, Philem.96.6, *IG*7. 2712.32 (Acraeph.); τοῖς ἰδίοις δ. *BGU*1130.21 (i B.C.), etc.; δαπανημάτων ἔνδεια *want of necessaries*, Plb.9.42.4: sg. in Arist.*EN*1122ᵃ 24, *CIG*3600 (Ilium), etc. **-ηρία,** ἡ, *extravagance*, Arist.*EE* 1221ᵃ11. **-ηρός,** ά, όν, of men, *lavish, extravagant*, Pl.*R.*564b, X.*Mem.*2.6.2; εἰς ἑαυτόν, εἰς ἀκολασίαν, Arist.*EN*1123ᵃ4, 1119ᵇ 31. II. of things, *expensive*, πόλεμος D.5.5; λειτουργία Arist. *Pol.*1309ᵃ18, cf. *EN*1122ᵃ21: Comp. -ότερα, λειτουργήματα Jul. *Or.*1.21d. Adv. -ρῶς X.*HG*6.5.4. III. *consuming*, πῦρ Ph.2. 91. **-ησις,** εως, ἡ, *consuming, devouring*, Aristeas 146. **-ητής,** οῦ, ὁ, *spendthrift*, *EM*40.44. **-ητικός,** ή, όν, *consuming*, δύναμις Philagr.ap.Aët.12.67, cf. Iamb.*Myst.*2.5. Adv. -κῶς *extravagantly*, βιοῦν S.E.*P.*1.230.

δᾰπᾰνοθήκη, ἡ, *penuarium*, *Gloss.*

δᾰπᾰν-ος [δᾰ], ον, = δαπανηρός, ἐλπίς Th.5.103; ῥᾳθυμία cj. in Longin.44.11: c. gen., Plu.2.624d. **-όω,** = δαπανάω, *expend*, *IG* 5(1).1390.55 (Pass., Andania, i B.C.). **-υλλα,** ἡ, Dim. of δαπάνη, Cerc.4.18

δάπεδον [δᾰ], τό, *level surface*, ἐν τυκτῷ δαπέδῳ Od.4.627; *floor of a chamber*, 10.227, al., X.*Cyr.*8.8.16, *IG*4.952.44 (Epid.); *ground, soil*, γῆς ἀρότροις ῥήξας δ. Ar.*Pl.*515; πόλιος δ. Hdt.4.200; Συρίης δ. *AP*12.131 (Posidipp.): abs., *ground*, κείμενον ἐν δαπέδῳ Od.11.577: in pl., a ship's *decks* (fore and aft), *h.Ap.*416; but, *plain*, Pi.*N.*7.34, E.*Hipp.*230 (anap.); Βοιωτῶν δ. *AP*7.245 (Gaet.).—Mostly poet.; in later Prose, Luc.*Sacr.*8 alludes to Il.4.2. (From *dm-pedo- [dem-, dom-, dm̥-, = house; expld. by οἶκος, ἐρείπιον, Hsch.]; cf. ζάπεδον.)

δάπης, = δάπις, Hsch.

δᾰπίδιον, τό, Dim. of δάπις, Hipparch.Com.1.3.

δᾰπῐδῠφάντης, ου, ὁ, *carpet-weaver*, prob. in *Ostr.*1395.

δάπις [ᾰ], ιδος, ἡ, = τάπης, *carpet, rug*, Ar.*Pl.*528, Pherecr.185, v.l. in X.*Cyr.*8.8.16, in pl.; Καρχηδὼν δάπιδας καὶ ποικίλα προσκεφάλαια Hermipp.63.23, cf. Ar.*V.*676.

δάπτης, ου, ὁ, *eater, bloodsucker*, δάπταις αἱμοπώταισιν, of gnats, Lyc.1403.

δάπτω, fut. δάψω Il.13.831: aor. ἔδαψα, poet. δάψα Pi.*N.*8.23, Opp. *H.*3.333:—*devour*, as wild beasts, Il.16.159, etc.; ἀλλήλους δάπτοντες Emp.136; of fire, δώσω Πριαμίδην πυρὶ δαπτέμεν Il.23.183; of a spear, *rend*, χρόα λειριόεντα δάψει 13.831, cf. A.*Pr.*370; of moths and worms, [χρυσὸν] οὐ σὴς οὐδὲ κὶς δ. Pi.*Fr.*222; δ. τὰν παρειάν *tear* with the nails, A.*Supp.*70 (lyr.); *corrode*, ὑγρὸν δάπτον Aret.*SD*1.9: metaph., *consume*, δ. πόλιν, of a tyrant, Alc.*Supp.*23.7; of envy, Pi.*N.* 8.23; δάπτει τὸ μὴ 'νδικον S.*OT*682 (lyr.); οἰκτρὰ συμφορὰ δ. φρένας *Trag.Adesp.Oxy.*213(*a*).10:—Pass., συννοίᾳ δάπτομαι κέαρ A.*Pr.*437.

δάρατος, ὁ, a Thessalian kind of *bread*, Maced. δράμις, Seleuc.ap. Ath.3.114b: neut. **δάρατον,** τό, prob. in *IG*9(2).1202 (Coropa, vi/v B.C.). II. *unleavened bread*, Nic.*Fr.*184:—also fem. pl. **δαράται,** αἱ, *cakes* offered at marriage and registration ceremonies by a φρατρία, *Michel*995*A*5, al. (Delph., v/iv B.C.).

δάρδα, = μέλισσα, Hsch. **δαρδαίνει·** μολύνει, Id.

Δάρδᾰνος, ὁ, *Dardanus*, son of Zeus, founder of Dardania or Troy, Il.20.215: Adj. Δάρδανος ἀνήρ *Trojan*, 2.701, 16.807: mostly pl., Τρῶες καὶ Δάρδανοι 3.456, al.:—Adj. **Δαρδάνιος,** α, ον, *Trojan*, 2.819; **Δαρδάνειος,** E.*Tr.*840 (lyr.):—fem. **Δαρδανίς,** ίδος, ἡ, *Trojan woman*, Il.18.122; also, = κώνειον, Ps.-Dsc.4.78: **Δαρδανία** (sc. γῆ), ἡ, *Troy*, Il.20.216:—**Δαρδανίδης,** ου, ὁ, *son* or *descendant of Dardanus*, 3.303, al.: **Δαρδανίωνες,** οἱ, *sons of Dardanus*, 7.414.

δαρδάπτω, aor. subj. δαρδάψῃ Opp.*H.*4.628; inf. δαρδάψαι, Hsch.: pf. δεδάρδαφα, Id.:—*devour*, of wild beasts, Il.11.479, Hp.*Ep.*17, etc.; κτήματα, χρήματα δαρδάπτουσιν, *they devour* one's patrimony, Od.14.92, 16.315, cf. Ar.*Nu.*711; δ. με πόθος Εὐριπίδου Id.*Ra.*66: in late Prose, Luc.*Nec.*14. (Perh. dissim. from *δαρ-δϝπτω, cf. δρέπω.)

Δᾱρεικός, ὁ, a Persian gold coin (but Δ. ἀργύρειοι Plu.*Cim.*10), prop. Adj. agreeing with στατήρ (in full, Th.8.28, Hdt.7.28), Ar.*Ec.* 602, X.*An.*1.1.9, Herod.7.122, etc.; so χρυσὸς χαρακτῆρα Δαρεικὸν ἔχων D.S.17.66; χρυσὸς Δαρεικός Alciphr.1.5:—written **Δαρικός** and **Δαριχός**, *IG*5(1).1 (Sparta). (From Δαρεῖος, cf. Poll.3.87, acc. to some not D. Nothus, Harp.; the connection with Bab. *dariku* (dub. sens.) is v. doubtful.)

Δᾱρειογενής, ές, *born from Darius*, A.*Pers.*6,145 (anap.).

Δᾱρεῖος, ὁ, *Darius* (OPers. *Dārayavauš* '*upholder of the Good*'), name of several kings of Persia; acc. to Hdt.6.98, = Gr. ἐρξίης (q.v.):—also **Δαρειαῖος**, X.*HG*2.1.8 and 9, Ctes.*Fr.*29.49: **Δαρῖάν** A.*Pers.*651 (lyr.): **Δαριήκης** Str.16.4.27. II. a throw of the dice, Hsch.

δάρειρ, = σπιθαμή, Hsch.: **δάριν**· σπιθαμήν (Arc.), Id.

δαρθάνω, *sleep*, Hierocl.*in CA*19 p.461 M.: aor. 2 ἔδρᾰθον, ἔδραθ' ἐνὶ προδόμῳ Od.20.143. (Prob. akin to Lat. *dormio*, Slav. *drěmati*, Skt. *drāti* 'sleep'.)

Δαρικός, v. Δαρεικός.

δάρκα, a kind of κασσία, Dsc.1.13 (v.l. δάκαρ).

δάρκανος, = ἐρυθρόδανον, Ps.-Dsc.3.143.

δάρκες· δέσμαι, Hsch.

δαρκνά (for δαρχνά), Cret., = δραχμή, *GDI*4985, *Leg.Gort.*1.32, al.:—also **δαρκμά**, *GDI*5071 (Cnossus), al.: **δαρχμά** ib.1154 (Elis), *IG* 5(2).3 (Tegea).

δάρμα, ατος, τό, Delph., = δέρμα, *Michel* 995 *D* 35 (ca. 400 B.C.).

δᾱρός, δᾱρό-βιος, Dor. for δηρός, δηρό-βιος: δαρόν also expld. by ἑορτή, and ἄρτος ἄζυμος (cf. δάρατος), Hsch.

δάρυσος, = βουτύπιον, Hsch. **δάρπη**· σαργάνη, κόφινος, Id.

δάρσις, εως, ἡ, (δέρω) *separation of parts united by cellular tissue by tearing*, Herophil.ap.Gal.2.349, cf. Gal.2.483, etc.

δάρτης, ου, ὁ, *one who flogs*, *Gloss.* **δάρτινον**· πέπλον λινοῦν, Hsch.

δαρτός, ή, όν, (δέρω) *flayed*, ἵππων δ. πρόσωπα the skin *flayed from* horses' heads, Choeril.4.5; δ. χιτών, of skin *stripped off*, Paul.Aeg. 6.61. II. τὰ δ. *fish which must be skinned before dressing*, Mnesith. ap.Ath.8.357c; of animals, ἔν τι τῶν δ. ὀνομαζομένων Gal.2.644, cf. *IG*1².190, *SIG*57.31 (Milet., v. B.C.).

δάρυλλος, ἡ, Maced., = δρῦς, Hsch. **δαρχμά**, v. δαρκνά.

δάς· ἐπὶ τοῦ πολλοῦ καὶ μεγάλου, Hsch. **δᾴς**, v. δαΐς (A). **δάσασθαι, δασάσκετο, δασαίμεθα**, v. δατέομαι.

δασκάζει· ὑποφεύγει, Hsch.

δάσκιλλος, ὁ, name of *a fish*, Arist.*HA*591^{a}14.

δάσκῐος, ον, (δα-, σκιά) *thick-shaded*, *bushy*, ὕλη Od.5.470, B.10. 93, etc.; ὄρη E.*Ba.*218; γενειάς A.*Pers.*316, S.*Tr.*13.

δασκόν· δασύ, Hsch.

δάσμα, ατος, τό, (δάσασθαι) *share*, *portion*, Hsch.

δάσμευσις, εως, ἡ, *dividing*, *distributing*, X.*An.*7.1.37.

δασμο-λογέω, fut. -ήσω Isoc.*Ep.*7.4:—*collect as tribute*, ἀργύριον παρὰ τῶν ἐραστῶν D.59.31. 2. c. acc. pers., *subject* one *to tribute*, τοὺς νησιώτας δ. Isoc.4.132; δ. τοὺς ἐκλογεῖς Hyp.*Eux.*36:—Pass., Isoc.4.123. **-λογία**, ἡ, *collection of tribute*, Plu.*Ant.*23. **-λόγος**, ὁ, *exactor of tribute*, βίαιος καὶ δ. Str.10.4.8.

δασμός, ὁ, (δάσασθαι) *division of spoil*, ἤν ποτε δ. ἵκηται Il.1.166; διάτριχα δ. ἐτύχθη *h.Cer.*86. II. *tribute*, Isoc.10.27; σκληρᾶς ἀοιδοῦ δ. *tribute paid* to her, S.*OT*36; δ. τίνειν Id.*OC*635; δ. φέρειν X.*An.* 5.5.10; ἀποφέρειν, ἀποδιδόναι, Id.*Cyr.*4.6.9, 2.4.14: pl., Id.*An.*1.1.8.

δασμο-φορέω, *to be subject to tribute*, A.*Pers.*586 (lyr.):—Pass., δασμοφορεῖταί τινι *tribute is paid* one, X.*Cyr.*8.6.4. **-φορία**, ἡ, *payment of tribute*, Agath.5.2. **-φόρος**, ον, *tributary*, Hdt.3.97, etc.; δ. εἶναί τινι Id.7.51, X.*Cyr.*7.5.79.

δάσομαι, v. δατέομαι.

δάσος [ᾰ], εος, τό, (δασύς) *thicket*, *copse*, Men.*Epit.*25, Str.9.3.13, 17.2.2 (pl.), Ael.*NA*7.2, etc. II. *shagginess*, τοῦ σώματος Alciphr. 3.28; *roughness*, *PLeid.X.*74.

δάσοφρυς [ᾰ], υ, *with shaggy brows*, Adam.2.26.

δασπέτᾰλον· πολύφυλλον, Hsch.

δασπλῆτις, ἡ (voc. -πλῆτα *AP*5.240 (Paul. Sil.)), *horrid*, *frightful*, θεὰ δ. Ἐρινύς Od.15.234; of Hecate, Theoc.2.14:—also **δασπλής**, ῆτος, ὁ, ἡ, sc. δασπλῆτα Χάρυβδιν Simon.38; δασπλῆτες Εὐμενίδες Euph.94; δασπλῆτε δράκοντε Nic.*Th.*609; freq. in Nonn., γυναῖκες 46.210; μάχαιρα 22.219, al.:—nom. **δασπλῆτα**, Call.*Fr.*534: **δασπλήτης** *An.Ox.*1.149: **δάσπλη** (sic), Hsch.

δάσσα· λάχανα, Hsch. **δάσσασθαι**, v. δατέομαι.

δάσσω, = δατέομαι, *divide*, ἀνώμαλα δ. Call.*Fr.anon.*145.

δαστός, δαστῶ, etym. of δατέομαι, coined by *EM*249.37.

δᾰσῠ-γένειος, ον, *with thick beard*, v.l. for βαθυ-, Tz.ad Lyc. 307. **-γρᾰφέω**, *write with the rough breathing*, Hdn.*Epim.* 25. **-θριξ**, ὁ, ἡ, gen. τρῐχος, *hairy*, αἴξ *AP*6.113 (Simm.), Nonn. *D.*48.673; μῆλα *AP*9.136 (Cyr.); of a person, ib.11.345, cf. Polem. *Phgn.*5. **-κερκος**, ον, *bushy-tailed*, ἀλώπηξ Theoc.5.112. **-κλωνον**, τό, = πτερίς, Ps.-Dsc.4.184. **-κνήμις**, ῖδος, = sq., Nonn.*D.* 14.81. **-κνημος**, Dor. **-κναμος**, ον, *shaggy-legged*, Πάν *AP*6.32 (Agath.); γέρων Nonn.*D.*13.45. **-κνήμων**, Dor. **-κνάμων**, ον, gen. ονος, = foreg., *APl.*4.233 (Theaet.).

Δᾰσύλλιος, ον, epith. of Bacchus, Paus.1.43.5 (παρὰ τὸ δασύνειν τὰς ἀμπέλους, acc. to *EM*248.54).

δάσυλλις, ῖδος, ἡ, *bear*, *EM*248.55.

δάσῡμα [ᾰ], ατος, τό, = τράχωμα, Sever.ap.Aët.7.45.

δᾰσύ-μαλλος, ον, *thick-fleeced*, *woolly*, ὄϊες, αἰγίς, Od.9.425, E. *Cyc.*360. **-μέτωπος**, ον, *with hairy forehead*, κριός *Gp.*18.1.3.

δᾰσυν-τέον, *one must aspirate*, Ath.3.107f, Sch.Il.*Oxy.*221 xiv 2. **-τής**, οῦ, ὁ, *fond of the aspirate*, Ἀττικοί Moer.179,245. **-ω**, pf. Pass., δεδάσυμμαι or -υσμαι Hp.*Coac.*172: inf. -ύνθαι Adam. *Phgn.*2.26:—*make rough* or *hairy*, δ. τὰς ἀλωπεκίας *bring back the hair on* them, Dsc.1.125, *Gp.*12.22.12:—Pass., *become* or *be hairy*, Ar.*Ec.*66, Hp.*Epid.*6.8.32; opp. φαλακρόομαι, Arist.*HA*518^{b}27; *become bushy*, Thphr.*HP*2.6.12. II. *make thick and cloudy*, *overcast*, οὐρανόν Id.*Vent.*51, *Sign.*36. III. *aspirate*, Trypho *Fr.* 5, D.H.*Comp.*14, A.D.*Pron.*12.21, Seleuc.ap.Ath.9.398a. IV. Pass., of urine, *become cloudy*, Hp.*Prorrh.*1.95. 2. of breathing, *become rapid*, Agathin.ap.Orib.10.7.22. 3. of the voice, *become hoarse*, Dsc.3.80.

δᾰσῠ-πόδειος, α, ον, *of a hare*: τὸ δ. *the species hare*, Arist.*HA*574^b 13. **-πόδιον**, = ἴον πορφυροῦν, Ps.-Dsc.4.121. **-πους**, ποδος, ὁ, *rough-foot*, i.e. *hare*, *Lepus timidus*, Cratin.400, Alc.Com.17, Antiph.133.6, Arist.*HA*511^{a}31, Lxx *Le.*11.5, etc.; λαγωὸς δ. Babr. 69.1: prov., χελώνη παραδραμεῖται δασύποδα, Suid. II. in Plin., prob. *rabbit*, *Lepus cuniculus*, *HN*8.219, 10.173. **-πρωκτος**, ον, *rough-bottomed*, Pl.Com.3. **-πῡγος**, ον, = foreg., Sch.Theoc.5. 112. **-πώγων**, ωνος, ὁ, ἡ, *shaggy-bearded*, Ar.*Th.*33.

δᾰσύς, εῖα, ύ, Ion. fem. δασέα Hdt.3.32; opp. ψιλός in all senses: I. *with a shaggy surface*, 1. *hairy*, *shaggy*, δέρμα.. μέγα καὶ δ. Od.14.51; ὁ δ. γενέσθαι, of the bald, *recover their hair*, Hp. *Aph.*6.34; of young hares, *downy*, Hdt.3.108; γέρρα δ. βοῶν, βοῶν δασειῶν ὠμοβόεινα shields of skin *with the hair on*, X.*An.*5.4.12, 4.7. 22; ὀσφὺν δασέαν *SIG*1037.6 (Milet., iv/iii B.C.); of birds, Thphr. *Fr.*180; τὰ σώματα δασεῖς Arr.*Ind.*24: Sup., Arist.*Phgn.*812^{b}17. Adv. δασέως, ἔχειν περὶ τὴν κοιλίαν ib.15. 2. *thick with leaves*, Od.14.49; θρίδαξ δασέα, opp. παρατετιλμένη, Hdt.3.32; of places, *thickly wooded*, *bushy*, abs., Id.4.191, cf. Hp.*Aër.*1; διὰ.. τῶν δασέων through *the thickets*, Ar.*Nu.*325: c. dat. modi, δ. ὕλῃ παντοίῃ Hdt.4. 21; ἴδῃσι παντοίῃσι ib.109; ἐλαίαις Lys.7.7: rarely c. gen., δ. παντοίων δένδρων X.*An.*2.4.14; τὸ δ. *bushy country*, ib.4.7.7; δ. γῆ *Schwyzer* 734 (Zelea). 3. generally, *rough*, *thick*, μαλακαὶ καὶ δ. νεφέλαι D.S. 3.45. 4. δ. οὖρα *cloudy*, Hp.*Epid.*7.112. II. *hoarse*, ἀναπνοή Gal.18(1).574. 2. *aspirated*, Arist.*Aud.*804^{b}8, Ph.1.29, D.T.631. 22, etc.; ἡ δασεῖα (sc. προσῳδία) Seleuc.ap.Ath.9.398a, A.D.*Synt.*319. 20; δ. τὸ θ καὶ τὸ φ καὶ τὸ χ D.H.*Comp.*14. Adv. -έως, ἀναγνῶναι, ἐκφέρειν, A.D.*Pron.*78.16, S.E.*M.*1.59. III. δ. παράγωγος, Hsch. (Perh. for δη-σύς, cf. Lat. *densus*.)

δᾰσυσμός, ὁ, *making rough*, δ. φωνῆς *hoarseness*, Dsc.1.64 (pl.).

δᾰσύ-στερνος, ον, *shaggy-breasted*, Hes.*Op.*514; of Nessus, S. *Tr.*557; ὑμέναιοι, of a Satyr, Nonn.*D.*28.90. **-στηθος**, ον, = foreg., Procl.*Par.Ptol.*202. **-στομος**, ον, *with hoarse voice*, Gal. 16.509.

δᾰσύτης, ητος, ἡ, *roughness*, *hairiness*, opp. ψιλότης, Arist.*HA* 499^{a}11; γῆς Corn.*ND*27: in pl., D.S.3.35. II. in pronunciation, *aspiration*, opp. ψιλότης, Arist.*Po.*1456^{b}32, Plb.10.47.10, Phld.*Po. Herc.*994.33, D.H.*Comp.*14.

δασύ-τρωγλος, ον, = δασύπρωκτος, *AP*12.41 (Mel.). **-φλοιος**, ον, *with rough rind*, v.l. for λαχυ-, Nic.*Al.*269. **-χαίτης**, ου, ὁ, *shaggy-haired*, τράγος *AP*6.32 (Agath.).

δατέν· ζητεῖν, Hsch.

δᾰτ-έομαι Il.18.264, etc., irreg. inf. δατέασθαι (v.l. -έεσθαι) Hes. *Op.*767: fut. δάσομαι (κατα-) Il.22.354 (tm.): aor. ἐδασάμην, δασσάμην Od.14.208, Il.1.368, etc.; Ion. δασάσκετο 9.333 (δια-, tm.): pf. δέδασμαι Diog.Apoll.3, Q.S.2.57 in pass. sense (v. infr. II): aor. inf. δασθῆναι, Hsch.:—*divide among themselves*, ὅτε κεν δατεώμεθα ληΐδ' Ἀχαιοί Il.9.138; τὰ μὲν εὖ δάσσαντο μετὰ σφίσιν υἷες Ἀχαιῶν 1.368; ἄνδιχα πάντα δάσασθαι 18.511, cf. Od.2.335, etc.; χθόνα δατέοντο Ζεύς τε καὶ ἀθάνατοι Pi.*O.*7.55; μένος Ἄρηος δατεῦνται *they share*, i.e. *are alike filled with*, the fury of Ares, Il.18.264: freq. of banqueters, κρέα πολλὰ δατεῦντο Od.1.112; μοίρας δασσάμενοι δαίνυντ' 3.66; ὑπέστην Ἕκτορα .. δώσειν κυσὶν ὠμὰ δάσασθαι *tear* in pieces, Il.23.21, cf. Od.18.87, E.*Tr.*450. 2. [ἡμίονοι] χθόνα ποσσὶ δατεῦντο *measured* the ground with their feet, Il.23. 121. 3. *cut in two*, τὸν μὲν .. ἵπποι ἐπισσώτροις δατέοντο 20. 394. II. in act. sense, simply, *divide*, τρεῖς μοίρας δασάμενοι τὸν πεζόν *having divided into* .., Hdt.7.121; *divide* or *give* to others, τῶν θεῶν τῷ ταχίστῳ.. τῶν θνητῶν τὸ τάχιστον δατέονται Id.1.216; τοῖς παισὶ τὰ χρήματα Democr.279; μεῖον, πλέον δ. X.*Cyr.*4.2.43, *Oec.* 7.24; τὸ ἐπιβάλλον Corn.*ND*27: pf. in pass. sense, *to be divided*, *distributed*, Il.1.125, 15.189, Hdt.2.84, Diog.Apoll. l.c., E.*HF*1329.—Ep. and Ion., also Cret., *Leg.Gort.*4.28, al., and Arc., *IG*5(2).262 (Mantinea, v B.C.); rare in Trag., never in correct Att. Prose, exc. Lys.*Fr.*7 S. (Cf. δαίω (B).) **-ήριος**, α, ον, *dividing*, *distributing*, χρημάτων A.*Th.*711. **-ησις**, εως, ἡ, *division*, condemned by Poll. 8.136. **-ητής**, οῦ, ὁ, *distributer*, πικρὸς χρημάτων δ. Ἄρης A.*Th.* 943 (lyr.). II. in Att. law, *liquidator* of estates or partnerships, Arist.*Ath.*56.6, etc.

Δᾱτισμός, ὁ, *a speaking like Datis* (the Median commander at Marathon), i.e. *speaking broken Greek*, Hdn.*Philet.*p.443, Suid. s.v. Δᾶτις.

δατύς, = κουράλλιον; also νύμφη λευκόκηρος, Hsch.

δᾰτύσσω, *devour*, Hsch.; *swallow*, dub. l. in Aret.*SD*2.13.

δαυάκες· θυμάλωπες, Hsch. **δαυάς**· μέλαινα, καὶ πονηρά, Id. **δαῦγος**· δασύς, Id.

δαυκίτης οἶνος, wine flavoured with δαῦκος Κρητικός, Dsc.5.60.

δαῦκος, ὁ, an umbelliferous plant growing in Crete, *Athamanta*

Cretensis, Hp.*Acut.*23, Dsc.3.72 (who applies the name to two other species, *Peucedanum Cervaria* and *Psychotis Amnis*), *POxy.*1088.65, Gal.6.654; also, = σταφυλῖνος, *wild carrot, Daucus Carota*, Id.11.862, which is called **δαῦκον**, τό, by Thphr.*HP*9.15.5 (but, = *Malabaila aurea*, ib.9.15.8, 9.20.2): **δαύκειον**, τό, Nic.*Th.*858,939: **δαυκίν** (i.e. δαυκίον), *Gp.*12.1.2:—also **δαυχμός**, Nic.*Th.*94 (cf. Sch. ad loc.), *Al.*199.

δαῦκος· ὁ θρασύς, Hsch.

Δαυλιάς, ἡ, *woman of Daulis*, epith. of Procne, who was changed into *the nightingale*, Th.2.29 (Δαυλία κορώνη, Suid.); so her sister Philomela, changed into *the swallow*, was **Δαυλίς**, Plu.2.727d.

Δαυλίς, ίδος, ἡ, *Daulis*, a city of Phocis, Il.2.520, etc.; also name of a festival at Argos, Hsch. (Δαῦλις cod.), etc.: **Δαύλιος**, ὁ, *a Daulian*, Hdt.8.35, or **Δαυλιεύς**, έως, A.*Ch.*674: **Δαυλία** (sc. χώρα), ἡ, *the country of Daulis, Phocis*, S.*OT*734.

δαῦλον· ἡμίφλεκτον ξύλον, Hsch.; cf. δαελός.

δαυλός (Hdn.Gr.1.156, but δαῦλος Paus.Gr.*Fr.*117), όν, *thick, shaggy*, ὑπήνη A.*Fr.*27; γένεια Nonn.*D.*6.160: metaph., δαυλοὶ πραπίδων δάσκιοί τε πόροι *dark* devices, A.*Supp.*93 (lyr.).

δαυμάσαι (leg. δαῦσαι)· ἐκκαῦσαι, Hsch. **δαυνίς**, dub. sens. in Hdn.Gr.1.96. **δαύξ**, dub. sens. in *An.Ox.*3.243. **δαῦτα**· λάχανα, Hsch. **δαυχμός**, v. δαῦκος. II. **δαυχμόν**· εὔκαυστον ξύλον δάφνης, Hsch., cf. *EM*250.20.

δαύχνα, Thess., = δάφνη, found only in compds. (cf. ἀρχιδαυχναφορέω):—hence **δαυχνοφόρος**, = δαφνηφόρος, cj. in Alcm.17: **Δαυχναφόριος**, ὁ, prob. epith. of Apollo in Cyprus, *Ber.Sächs.Ges.*1908.3; cf. **Δαυχναῖος**, patron. fr. Δαύχνας, *IG*9(2).1228.26. (Perh. akin not to δάφνη, but to δαῦκος.)

δαύω, = ἰαύω, *sleep*, Sapph.83: aor. ἔδαυσεν, Hsch. (Cf. δαίω (A).)

δαφν-αία, ἡ, a precious stone, Plin.*HN*37.157. **-αῖος**, α, ον, = δαφνικός, *of bay*, πέταλα Nonn.*D.*19.73. II. epith. of Apollo, *AP*9.477, Nonn.*D.*13.82. **-έλαιον**, τό, *oil of bay*, Dsc.1.40 tit. (v.l.), Sch.Nic.*Al.*198. **-εών**, = δαφνών, *Gloss.*

δάφνη, ἡ, *sweet bay, Laurus nobilis*, Od.9.183, Hes.*Th.*30, prob. in Men.*Georg.*36; τὸ τῆς δ. (sc. τρύπανον) ἄριστον Thphr.*HP*5.9.7; δάφναν μὴ δρέπε *Supp.Epigr.*2.185 (Boeot., v B.C.); [Ἀπόλλων] χρείων ἐκ δάφνης γυάλων ὕπο Παρνησοῖο *h.Ap.*396; ἐξ ὧν εἶπέ μοι ὁ Φοῖβος..Πυθικὴν σείσας δάφνην Ar.*Pl.*213; ἐρέω τι τορώτερον ἢ ἀπὸ δάφνης Call.*Del.*94; στεφανῶσαι δάφνης στεφάνῳ *GDI*2507 (Delph.), cf. *Epigr.Gr.*786 (Halic.), *CIG*3641*b* 20 (add., Lampsacus). II. δ. Ἀλεξανδρεία, *Ruscus Hypoglossum*, Thphr.*HP*1.10.8, 3.17.4, Dsc.4.145. 2. = χαμαιδάφνη, Ps.-Dsc.4.147. III. *white mangrove, Avicennia officinalis*, Thphr.*HP*4.7.2. IV. a kind of *coral*, ibid. (ᾰ Theoc.11.45.)

δαφνή-εις, εσσα, εν, *abounding in bay*, Nonn.*D.*13.76. **-φᾰγία**, *eating of bay*, Tz.*Proll.Hes.*p.14. **-φάγος** [ᾰ], ον, *bay-eating*: hence, *inspired*, Lyc.6. **-φορεῖον**, τό, *temple of Apollo* δαφνηφόρος, Thphr.*Fr.*119. **-φορέω**, *bear boughs* or *crowns of bay*, Paus.9.10.4, Plu.*Aem.*34, *IG*14.1293*B*, Hdn.2.2.10; of the Roman *fasces laureati*, Id.7.6.2; to be read for δαφνοφορέω in D.C.37.21. **-φορία**, ἡ, *bay-bearing*, Boeotian festival in honour of Apollo, Procl.ap.Phot.*Bibl.*p.321 B. **-φορικός**, ή, όν, *of* or *for Apollo* δαφνηφόρος: τὰ -κά *songs in his honour*, Poll.4.53, Suid. s.v. Πίνδαρος, Procl.ap.Phot.*Bibl.*p.321 B. **-φόριος**, = δαφνηφόρος II, title of Apollo, *IG*7.3407 (Chaeronea). **-φόρος**, ον, *bay-bearing*, δ. τιμαῖς A.*Supp.*706; δ. κλῶνες branches *of bay borne in worship of* Apollo, E.*Ion*422; δ. ἄλση groves *of bay-trees*, Hdn.1.12.2. 2. Subst., *bearer of bays*, at Eleusis, *IG*2².1092*B*25. II. epith. of Apollo at Thebes, Paus.9.10.4; at Eretria, *IG*12(9).210.

δαφν-ιακός, ή, όν, *belonging to a bay*: δ. βίβλοι, = δαφνιακά, a poem by Agathias, *AP*6.80. **-ῐνος**, η, ον, *made of bay*, ἔλαιον Thphr.*Od.*28, Dsc.1.40; *of bay-wood*, ὅρπηξ Call.*h.Ap.*1. II. δάφνινον (sc. χρῶμα) *PLond.*3.928.13 (ii A.D.). **-ιος**, α, ον, f.l. for foreg., Hp.*Morb.*2.13; epith. of Artemis, Str.8.3.12. **-ίς**, ίδος, ἡ, *bay-berry*, Hp.*Morb.*2.13, *Nat.Mul.*33, Thphr.*HP*1.11.3. 2. *bay-tree*, *PEdgar* 21.3 (iii B.C.). **-ίτης** [ῑ], ου, ὁ, *laureate*, epith. of Apollo at Syracuse, Hsch. II. *of bay*, οἶνος *Gp.*8.8.

δαφνῖτις, ιδος, ἡ, = ἄχυ, Dsc.1.13, Gal.14.72. II. = χαμαιδάφνη, Ps.-Dsc.4.147. III. = δαφνοειδές, ib.146.

δαφνο-γηθής, ές, *delighting in the bay*, of Apollo, *AP*9.525.5. **-ειδής**, ές, *like bay*, δαῦκον Thphr.*HP*9.15.5 (s.v.l.); of certain corals, ib.4.7.1. II. τὸ δ. *spurge-laurel, Daphne Laureola*, Hp.*Nat.Mul.*33, Dsc.4.146. 2. = κληματίς, Dsc.4.7. **-κοκκον**, τό, = δαφνίς, Alex.Trall.8.2. **-κόμης**, ου, ὁ, = sq., Opp.*C.*1.365. **-κομος**, ον, *bay-crowned*, τρίποδες *AP*9.505.11. **-πώλης**, ου, ὁ, *bay-seller*, Com. epith. of Apollo, Ar.*Fr.*764.

δάφνος Σαμοθρᾳκική, = δάφνη Ἀλεξανδρεία, Ps.-Dsc.4.145.

δαφνόσκιος, ον, *bay-shaded*, ἄλσος Diog.Trag.1.

δαφν-ώδης, ες, *bay-wooded*, γύαλα E.*Ion*76. II. *like bay*, Thphr.*HP*9.10.1. **-ών**, ῶνος, ὁ, *laurel grove*, Str.16.4.14 (pl.), Petron.126, Gell.2.20.9 (pl.), *Peripl.M.Rubr.*11. **-ωτός**, ή, όν, *laurelized*, κινάραι, prob. in *Gp.*12.39.6 (δαφνάτους codd.).

δᾰφοινεός, όν, = δαφοινός, εἷμα δαφοινεὸν αἵματι *dark* with blood, Il.18.538, cf. Hes.*Sc.*159.

δᾰφοινήεις, εσσα, εν, later form of sq., Nonn.*D.*1.425.

δᾰφοινός, όν (ή, όν Opp.*C.*3.440; δαφοινή as etym. of δάφνη in Corn.*ND*32), epith. of savage animals, *tawny* (as expld. by most Gramm., though some also give *blood-reeking*), δαφοινὸν δέρμα λέοντος Il.10.23; δράκων ἐπὶ νῶτα δαφοινός 2.308; θῶες δ. 11.474; λαῖφος δ' ἐπὶ νῶτα δαφοινὸν λυγκὸς ἔχει *h.Pan.*23; πῆμα δ., of the dragon Python, *h.Ap.*304; δ. ἀετός A.*Pr.*1022; λεόντων ἃ δ. ἴλα E.*Alc.*581 (lyr.); δ. ἄγρα *tawny*, Pi.*N.*3.81. 2. metaph., δ. Κῆρες Hes.*Sc.*250; δαλός A.*Ch.*607 (lyr.).

δάχανος, ὁ, = νότος, *Peripl.M.Rubr.*50.

δαψίλ-εια [ῐ], ἡ, *abundance, plenty*, τροφῆς Arist.*HA*572ᵃ3; τοῦ ὑγροῦ Id.*GA*782ᵇ18; εὐωνία καὶ δ. Plb.2.15.4; μετάλλου D.S.5.13, cf. Agatharch.95; χρημάτων Onos.35.2: metaph., δ. τύφου Metrod.31. **-εύομαι**, *abound*, ἀγέλαις ἐλεφάντων Ph.Byz.*Mir.*3.2. 2. *to be anxious, careworn*, διά τινα Lxx 1 *Ki.*10.2. 3. Pass., *spend lavishly*, *SIG*708.34 (Istropolis), Andronic.Rhod.p.577 M.; *bestow lavishly*, τοῖς αἰτοῦσι τὸ ἔλεος Ph.*Fr.*104 H., cf. Eustr.*in EN*91.20. **-ής**, ές, *abundant, plentiful*, ὕδωρ Hp.*Acut.*65; ποτόν Hdt.2.121.δ′; δωρεή Id.3.130; τροφή Arist.*GA*774ᵇ26; τῷ ἁλὶ -εστέρῳ χρῆσθαι *in too great quantity*, Id.*HA*585ᵃ27; ἔπαινοι Phld.*Lib.*p.32 O.; ἔργα Herod.7.84; πλῆθος σωμάτων Plb.4.38.4 (Sup.); πηγαί Plu.*Num.*15; χώρα ib.16 (Comp.); ἐβένου τάλαντον δ. a *full* talent, *BCH* 35.286 (Delos, ii B.C.). Adv. -έως *in abundance*, Theoc.7.145; δαψιλῶς τοὺς φαγόντας βρέχειν Antiph.286; παρέχεσθαι πάντα D.S.5.14, cf. 19.3: neut. as Adv. δαψιλὲς ἠπείλησεν Call.*Del.*125: Comp. -έστερον J.*BJ*4.11.4; -εστέρως ib.8.3, Ptol.*Tetr.*56. 2. of space, *ample, wide*, ἐρημία Lyc.957. II. of persons, *liberal, profuse*, Arist.*VV*1280ᵇ25, Axiop.4.4; δ. χορηγός Plu.*Per.*16; so κακία δ. τοῖς πάθεσιν Id.2.500e. Adv. -ῶς, ζῆν X.*Mem.*2.7.6: Sup. -έστατα, χρῆσθαι Id.*Cyr.*1.6.17, cf. Ph.*Bel.*101.4. **-ός**, ή, όν, = foreg. I. 2, αἰθήρ Emp.39.1.

***δάω** [ᾰ], *learn* (also causal, *teach*, v. infr. II and cf. διδάσκω): I. intr., aor. ἐδάην Il.3.208, Trag. (in lyr.), A.*Ag.*123, S.*El.*169; subj. δαῶμεν Il.2.299, Ep. δαείω 16.423, Od.9.280; opt. δαείην A.R.2.415; inf. δαῆναι Od.4.493, *IG*4.760 (Troezen), Ep. δαήμεναι Il.21.487; part. δαείς Sol.13.50, A.*Ch.*603, Pi.*O.*7.91 (for aor. δέδαον, ἔδαον, v. infr. II): fut. δαήσομαι Od.3.187: pf. δεδάηκα 8.134,146, part. δεδαώς 17.519; also δεδάημαι *h.Merc.*483, Theoc.8.4, etc.:—*learn*, and in pf., *know*, ll. cc.: c. gen. pers., ἐμεῦ δαήσεαι *wilt learn* from me, Od.19.325: c. gen. rei, πολέμοιο δαήμεναι Il.21.487; Ἄρεος εὖ δεδαῶτες D.P.1004; σοφίης δεδαημένο Epic.*Oxy.*1015.20: c. acc. rei, φάρμακα Theoc.28.19; ἄξια Μοισᾶν *IG*3.771; ἀλεξητήρια νούσων ib.9(1).881 (Corc.); ἄκεσμα νόσου ib.14.1750; ἔργα Ἀθηναίης ib.12(5).30 (Sicinus); *perceive*, ἐδά ψυχάς B.5.64; δάεν ῥιπὰν μελιαδέος οἴνου *felt* the impulse of ..., Pi.*Fr.*166: abs., δαέντι *to one who knows*, Id.*O.*7.53.—Hom. has also inf. δεδάασθαι (perh. for δεδαέσθαι) *search out*, c. acc., Od.16.316.—The pres. in this sense is supplied by διδάσκομαι. II. causal, *teach*, Hom. only in redupl. aor. 2 δέδαε *he taught*, c. dupl. acc., ὃν Ἥφαιστος δέδαεν..παντοίην τέχνην Od.6.233, cf. 8.448, 23.160; ἔργα δ' Ἀθηναίη δέδαε κλυτὰ ἐργάζεσθαι 20.72, cf. Theoc.24.129 (v.l. ἔδαεν); 3 pl. δέδαον Hsch.; also δάε, ἔδαε, A.R.1.724, 4.989.—The pres. in this sense is supplied by διδάσκω.

δέ, *but*: adversative and copulative Particle, I. answering to μέν (q.v.), τὴν νῦν μὲν Βοιωτίαν, πρότερον δὲ Καδμηίδα γῆν καλουμένην Th.1.12, etc. II. without preceding μέν, 1. adversative, expressing dist. opposition, αἰεί τοι τὰ κάκ' ἐστὶ φίλα..μαντεύεσθαι, ἐσθλὸν δ' οὔτε τί πω εἶπας Il.1.108; ὀρθῶς ἔλεξας, οὐ φίλως δέ μοι λέγεις E.*Or.*100, cf. S.*Ant.*85, etc.; τέθνηκεν ἀνδρὸς οὐδενός, θεοῦ δ' ὕπο Id.*Ph.*334; so in Prose, οὐκ ἐπὶ κακῷ, ἐλευθερώσει δέ.. Th.4.86; οἱ αἰχμάλωτοι..ᾤχοντο εἰς Δεκέλειαν, οἱ δ' εἰς Μέγαρα X.*HG*1.2.14, cf. *Cyr.*4.5.46; ἡ δ' ἑτέρα *IG*2.652*A*45. 2. copulative, a. in explanatory clauses, ξυνέβησαν..τὰ μακρὰ τείχη ἑλεῖν (ἦν δὲ σταδίων μάλιστα ὀκτώ) Th.4.66, cf. Il.7.48: when a Subst. is folld. by words in apposition, Ἀρισταγόρῃ τῷ Μιλησίῳ, δούλῳ δὲ ἡμετέρῳ Hdt.7.8.β′; μήτηρ βασιλέως βασίλεια δ' ἐμή A.*Pers.*152; so in answers, διπλᾶ λέγειν.—Answ. διπλᾶ δ' ὁρᾶν Id.*Th.*974. b. in enumerations or transitions, Il.1.43–49, 345–351, X.*Cyr.*1.2.1, etc.; with repetition of a word in different relations, ὡς Ἀχιλεὺς θάμβησεν.., θάμβησαν δὲ καὶ ἄλλοι Il.24.483; σάκος εἷλε.., εἵλετο δ' ἔγχος 14.9 sq.; Ζεύς ἐστιν αἰθήρ, Ζεὺς δὲ γῆ, Ζεὺς δ' οὐρανός A.*Fr.*70; κινεῖ κραδίαν, κινεῖ δὲ χόλον E.*Med.*99; ὄζει ἴων, ὄζει δὲ ῥόδων, ὄζει δ' ὑακίνθου Hermipp.82.8; in rhetorical outbursts, οὐκ ἂν εὐθέως εἴποιεν· τὸν δὲ βάσκανον, τὸν δὲ ὄλεθρον, τοῦτον δὲ ὑβρίζειν,—ἀναπνεῖν δέ! D.21.209; in a climax, πᾶν γύναιον καὶ παιδίον καὶ θηρίον δέ *nay* even beast, Pl.*Tht.*171e, cf. X.*HG*5.2.37; in the combination καὶ δέ Il.23.80, al., καὶ ... δέ A.*Pr.*973, E.*El.*1117, etc., each particle retains its force. c. answering to τε (q.v.), ἃ τῶν τε ἀποβαινόντων ἕνεκα ἄξια κεκτῆσθαι, πολὺ δὲ μᾶλλον αὐτὰ αὑτῶν Pl.*R.*367c. 3. implying causal connexion, less direct than γάρ, Il.6.160, Od.1.433. 4. in questions, with implied opposition, ἑόρακας δ', ἔφη, τὴν γυναῖκα; X.*Cyr.*5.1.4; καὶ ὁ Σωκράτης, εἰπέ μοι, ἔφη, κύνας δὲ τρέφεις; Id.*Mem.*2.9.2, cf. 2.1.26, S.*Ant.*1172: in Trag. (not in Com. or Oratt.), when the speaker turns from one person to another, the voc. stands first, then the pers. Pron. folld. by δέ, as Μενέλαε, σοὶ δὲ τάδε λέγω.. E.*Or.*622, etc.; also in Hdt., ὦ δέσποτα, ἐγὼ δὲ ταῦτα ἐποίησα 1.115. b. τί δέ; what *then*? to mark a transition in dialogue; v. τίς. III. in apodosi: 1. after hypothetical clauses, εἰ δέ κε μὴ δώωσιν, ἐγὼ δέ κεν αὐτὸς ἕλωμαι if they will not give it, *then* I.., Il.1.137, cf. Od.12.54; εἰ μηδὲ τοῦτο βούλει ἀποκρίνασθαι, σὺ δὲ τοὐντεῦθεν λέγε X.*Cyr.*5.5.21, cf. Pi.*O.*3.43 (v.l.), A.*Ag.*1060, Hdt.5.1, etc. b. after temporal or relative clauses, with ἐπεί, ἕως, etc., Il.24.255, Hdt.9.70, etc.; μέχρι .. εἶχον τὰ βέλη, οἱ δὲ ἀντεῖχον Th.3.98; with demonstr. Pronouns or Advbs. answering to a preceding relative, οἵηπερ φύλλων γενεή, τοίη δὲ καὶ ἀνδρῶν Il.6.146, etc.; ἆθλα οἷς κεῖται ἀρετῆς μέγιστα, τοῖς δὲ καὶ ἄνδρες ἄριστοι πολιτεύουσιν Th.2.46; τοὺς δ' ἔλαβε τυράννους.. τούτους δὲ.. ἐξεδίδου Hdt.5.37, cf. Isoc.4.98, Pl.*La.*194d; οἷα μὲν ἕκαστα ἐμοὶ φαίνεται τοιαῦτα μὲν ἔστιν ἐμοί, οἷα δὲ σοί, τοιαῦτα δὲ αὖ σοί Id.*Tht.*152a: sts. after a participle, οἰόμενοι.. τιμῆς τεύξεσθαι, ἀντὶ δὲ τούτων οὐδ' ὅμοιοι.. ἐσόμεθα X.*An.*6.6.16, cf. Isoc.15.71 (v.l.). 2. to resume after an interruption or parenthesis, χρόνου δὲ ἐπιγινομένου καὶ κατεστραμμένων σχεδὸν πάντων..,—κατεστραμμένων δὲ τούτων.. Hdt.1.28,29; νῦν δ' αὖ πάλιν ὑπό τε πλούτου διαθρυπτόμενος.. καὶ ὑπ' ἀνθρώπων.. ὑπὸ τοιούτων δέ.. X.*Cyr.*7.2.23; with an anacoluthon, ἡ δὲ ψυχὴ ἄρα,—οἷ ἂν θεὸς θέλῃ...τῇ ἐμῇ ψυχῇ ἰτέον, αὕτη δὲ δή.. Pl.*Phd.*80d: for δ' οὖν, v. οὖν. 3. to begin a story, ἦμος δ' ἠέλιος.. *well*, when the sun.., Od.4.400. 4. to introduce a proof, τεκμήριον δέ, σημεῖον δέ, v. sub vocc.

B. Position of δέ. It usu. stands second: hence freq. between Art. and Subst. or Prep. and case; but also after Subst., or words forming a connected notion, hence it may stand third, γυναῖκα πιστὴν δ' ἐν δόμοις εὕροι A.*Ag.*606, cf. *Th.*411, *Eu.*531, S.*Ph.*959, etc.; fourth, Id.*OT*485, E.*Hel.*688, A.*Pr.*323,383, etc.; fifth, ib.401 codd.; even sixth, Epigen.7 (codd. Poll.); so in Prose after a neg., οὐχ ὑπ' ἐραστοῦ δέ, to avoid confusion between οὐ δέ and οὐδέ, Pl.*Phdr.*227c.

-δε, an enclitic post-position: joined, I. to names of Places in the acc., to denote *motion towards* that place, οἶκόνδε (Att. οἴκαδε) home-*wards*, ἅλαδε sea-*wards*, Οὔλυμπόνδε *to* Olympus, Αἴγυπτόνδε to the Nile, θύραζε (for θύρασδε) *to* the door (v. sub vocc.); repeated with the possess. Pron., ὅνδε δόμονδε Il.16.445; sts. after εἰς, εἰς ἅλαδε Od.10.351; after the gen. Ἄϊδόσδε. b. to names of persons, Πηλεΐωνάδε Il.24.338; to Prons., ἡμέτερόνδε, ὑμ–, Od.8.39, Il. 23.86; ὅνδε, v. supr. In Att. mostly joined to the names of places, Ἐλευσῖνάδε, etc.; also Ἀθήναζε, Θήβαζε (for Ἀθήνασδε, Θήβασδε); rarely, in Att., with appellatives, as οἴκαδε. c. to time-words, βουλυτόνδε (v. βουλυτός). 2. to denote *purpose* only, μήτι φόβονδ' ἀγόρευε Il.5.252. II. to the demonstr. Pron., to give it greater force, ὅδε, τοιόσδε, τοσόσδε, etc., such a man *as this* (v. sub vocc.).

δεά, = θεά (Tyrrhen.), Hsch.

δέατο, *seemed*, ἀεικέλιος δέατ' εἶναι *methought* he was a pitiful fellow, Od.6.242; εἰκ ἂν δέατοι, = ἢν δοκῇ, ὅσα ἂν δ., = ὅσῃ ἂν δοκῇ, *IG*5(2).6.10,18 (Tegea); ὀπόθ' ἂν δεάσητοι ἀμφοτέροις ib.343.24 (Orchom. Arc.); cf. δέαται· δοκεῖ, δεάμην· ἐδοκίμαζον, ἐδόξαζον, δέασθεν (prob.)· ἐδόκουν, Hsch. (Root δεyᾰ, cf. δῆλος, δοάσσατο, Skt. *dideti* 'appear'.)

δέατος, v. δέος.

δέγμενος, v. δέχομαι. **δέγμον**· ὁδόν, Hsch. **δεγμών**· χρόνος, Id. **δεδάασθαι, δέδαε, δεδάηκα, δεδαημένος**, v. *δάω. **δεδαίαται**, v. δαίω (B). **δεδάλας**· δέσμας, Id. **δέδαλοι**· προμαχῶνες, Id. **δέδασται**, v. δατέομαι. **δεδαώς**, v. *δάω. **δεδέαται**· δέδενται, Id. **δέδεια**· φοβοῦ, and **δεδειαί**· δειλίαι, Id. **δεδείκελος**, *timorous*, Id. **δεδειπνάναι**, v. δειπνέω. **δεδεῖσαι**· φοβῆσαι, Id. **δεδεῖσθαι**· εὐλαβεῖσθαι, φοβεῖσθαι, Id. **δεδέχαται**, v. δέχομαι. **δέδηε, δεδήει**, v. δαίω (A).

δεδημευμένως, *in a popular manner*, Procl.*in Prm.*p.880 S.

δεδηνῶσθαι· ἐνεχυράσασθαι, ἐνδήσασθαι ἐνεχύροις, Hsch.

δέδια, poet. **δείδια**, v. δείδω.

δεδιότως, Adv. of part. pf. δεδιώς, *in fear*, D.C.42.17, Vett.Val. 238.32, prob. in D.H.11.47.

δεδίσκηται· ἔρριπται, Hsch. (fort. –ευται).

δεδίσκομαι, v. δειδίσκομαι. II. v. δειδίσσομαι.

δεδιττέον, *one must fear*, ὑπέρ τινος Themist.*Ep.*8.

δεδίττομαι, v. δειδίσσομαι. **δεδμάων**· κριὸς ἡγεμών, Hsch.

δέδμημαι, pf. Pass. of δαμάζω and δέμω.

δεδοικότως, Adv. part. pf. of δείδω, = δεδιότως, Ruf.*Interrog.*2, Philostr.*VA*4.20.

δεδοίκω, Dor. pres., = δείδω, δέδια, Theoc.15.58: fut. δεδοικήσω Macr.*Diff.*p.610 K. (Syrac.).

δεδοκημένος, irreg. part. pf. of δέχομαι (Ion. δέκομαι), in act. sense, *waiting, watching*, Il.15.730, Hes.*Sc.*214, A.R.4.900; δ. ἥντινα ῥέξει μῆτιν *waiting to see*.., ib.1660: c. acc., *observing*, φάσιας Nic.*Th.* 122; *watching*, Nonn.*D.*30.88, al.: c. gen., ἤματος Arat.559.

δέδορκα, v. δέρκομαι. **δεδρίομεν**· ῥέξομεν, Hsch. **δεδροικώς**· δοικώς, Id. (leg. δεδϝοικώς· δεδοικώς).

δεείλη, = δείλη, Phryn.Trag.ap.Sch.Il.*Oxy.*221 iii 6.

δέελος, η, ον, resolved form of δῆλος, Il.10.466. II. = δεσμός, ἅμμα, Hsch. **δεήλαδες**· φύλακες, Id.

δέ-ημα, ατος, τό, (δέομαι) *entreaty*, δέημα δεῖσθαι Ar.*Ach.*1059. **–ησίδιον**, τό, Dim. of sq. I. 2, *Gloss.* **–ημος**· νόμος ἢ δεσμός, Hsch. **–ησις**, εως, ἡ, *entreaty*, Lys.2.15 (pl.), Isoc.8.138 (pl.), Pl.*Ep.*329d (pl.), etc.; δέομαι δ' ὑμῶν.. δικαίαν δέησιν D.29.4; δεήσεις ποιεῖσθαι *Ev.Luc.*5.33, cf. Wilcken *Chr.*41 ii 12 (iii A.D.). 2. written *petition*, *CPHerm.*6.10, J.*BJ*7.5.2, Ph.2.586, *PGen.*16.10 (iii A.D.). II. *want, need*, Antipho Soph.11; ἐν ἐπιθυμίαις τε καὶ δεήσεσιν Pl.*Erx.*405e; κατὰ τὰς δεήσεις according to their *needs*, Arist.*Pol.*1257ᵃ23; δεήσεις εἰσὶν αἱ ὀρέξεις Id.*Rh.*1385ᵃ22. **–ητέον**, *one must entreat*, Aristid.Quint.3.9. **–ητικός**, ή, όν, *disposed to ask*, Arist.*EN*1125ᵃ10; *suppliant*, φωνή D.S.17.44; λόγος Plu.*Cor.* 18; ἐπιστολαί Ph.2.590 (Sup.); εὐχαί Id.2.296 (Sup.).

δεῖ: subj. δέῃ, sts. contr. δῇ (in codd. of Com., as Ar.*Ra.*265); ὁπόσου κα δῇ *IG*4.1484.65 (Epid.), cf. *SIG*245 *G* 47 (Delph.); opt. δέοι Th.4.4; inf. δεῖν; part. δέον (v. infr. IV): impf. ἔδει, Ion. ἔδεε: fut. δεήσει E.*Hipp.*941, etc.: aor. 1 ἐδέησε Th.2.77, etc.—Impers. from δέω (A), *there is need* (the sense of moral obligation, prop. belonging to χρή, is later, S.*Ph.*583, etc.): I. c. acc. pers. et inf., *it is needful for* one to do, *one must*, once in Hom., τί δὲ δεῖ πολεμιζέμεναι..Ἀργείους why *need* the Argives fight? Il.9.337; δ. (μ') ἐλθεῖν Pi.*O.*6.28, etc.: with nom. of the Pron., ἡγούμην.. δεῖν.. μεγαλοψυχότερος φαίνεσθαι D.19.235: rarely δεῖ σ' ὅπως δείξεις, = δεῖ σε δεῖξαι, S.*Aj.*556, cf. *Ph.*54; δεῖ σ' ὅπως μηδὲν διοίσεις Cratin.108; (the full constr. in S.*Ph.*77 τοῦτο δεῖ σοφισθῆναι.. ὅπως γενήσῃ): rarely c. dat. pers., *there is need of*.. for.., θεοῖσι προσβαλεῖν χθονὶ ἄλλην δεήσει γαῖαν E.*Hipp.*941, cf. X.*An.*3.4.35, *Oec.*7.20: the acc. pers. is often omitted, ἐκ τῶν μανθάνειν δεῖ (sc. ἡμᾶς) Hdt.1.8, cf. A.*Ag.* 567, *Eu.*826, etc. 2. c. acc. rei et inf., δεῖ τι γενέσθαι Th.5.26; παραδείγματα, καθ' ἃ δέοι ἀποκρίνεσθαι Pl.*Men.*79a, etc.; also ἐπεί δέ οἱ ἔδεε κακῶς γενέσθαι since *it was fated* for him.., since he *was doomed*.., Hdt.2.161, cf. 8.53, 9.109, S.*OT*825; for οἴομαι δεῖν, v. οἴομαι. 3. abs. with inf. understood, μὴ πεῖθ' ἃ μὴ δεῖ (sc. πείθειν) S.*OC*1442, cf. *OT*1273; εἴ τι δέοι, ἣν τι δέῃ (sc. γενέσθαι), X. *Mem.*1.2.59, Th.1.44; κἂν δέῃ (sc. τροχάζειν), τροχάζω Philetaer. 3. II. c. gen. rei, *there is need of*, freq. with neg., οὐδὲν ἂν δέοι πολλοῦ ἀργυρίου Pl.*Cri.*45a, etc.; τί δεῖ τῆς ἀρετῆς; Arist.*Pol.*1309ᵇ 10; sts. with inf. added, μακροῦ λόγου δεῖ ταῦτ' ἐπεξελθεῖν A.*Pr.*870, cf. 875, *Supp.*407. b. freq. in phrases, πολλοῦ δεῖ *there wants much, far from it*, ὀλίγου δεῖ *there wants little, all but*; in full c. inf., πολλοῦ δεῖ οὕτως ἔχειν Pl.*Ap.*35d; τοὺς Πλαταιέας ἐλαχίστου ἐδέησε διαφθεῖραι [τὸ πῦρ] Th.2.77; πολλοῦ γε δεῖ, πολλοῦ γε καὶ δεῖ Ar.*Ach.* 543, D.18.300, 21.71; τοῦ πλεῦνος αἰεὶ ἔδεε *there was* always further *to travel*, Hdt.4.43; τοῦ παντὸς δεῖ Luc.*Merc.Cond.*13: also ὀλίγου δεῖν abs., in same sense, Pl.*Ap.*22a, etc.; μικροῦ δεῖν D.27.29. 2. with dat. pers. added, δεῖ μοί τινος A.*Ag.*848, E.*Med.*565, Th.1.71, etc. 3. with acc. pers. added, αὐτὸν γάρ σε δεῖ προμηθέως A.*Pr.* 86, cf. E.*Rh.*837, *Hipp.*23. 4. rarely with Subj. in nom., δεῖ μοί τι something *is needful* to me, ἓν δεῖ μόνον μοι E.*Supp.*594; εἴ τι δέοι τῷ χορῷ Antipho 6.12; πρῶτον μὲν τοῦτο δεῖ, ὑπειληφέναι.. D.10. 15. III. Med., δεῖται *there is need*, c. gen., δεῖταί σοι τῆς αὐτῆς ἐρωτήσεως Pl.*Men.*79c; ὅσων δέοιτο Aen.Tact.13.1; ἑτέρου δεῖσθαι στρατηγοῦ νομίζων Plu.*Pel.*26: c. inf., ὥστε βραχέ' ἐμοὶ δεῖσθαι φράσαι S.*OC*570 (codd.); δεήσεται.. ἀναγράφεσθαι Aen.Tact.31.9; τήν μευ γλῶσσαν ἐκταμεῖν δεῖται Herod.6.41. IV. neut. part. **δέον** (**δεῖν** is dub. in Ar.*Fr.*220, Lys.14.7, cf. A.D.*Adv.*132.30, Hdn.Gr.2. 328, al., Hsch.): abs., *it being needful* or *fitting*, Pl.*Prt.*355d, etc.; οὐκ ἀπήντα, δέον, he did not appear in court, *though he ought to have done so*, D.21.90: c. inf., Ar.*Nu.*988; οὐδὲν δέον *there being* no *need*, Hdt.3.65, etc.: fut. ὡς αὐτίκα δεῆσον διώκειν X.*Cyr.*3.2.8: aor. δεῆσαν Plu.*Fab.*9, etc.: also δέον ἂν εἴη, = δέοι ἄν, Plb.2.37.5, etc.: less freq. gen. abs. δέοντος, c. acc. inf., Corn.*ND*17. 2. Subst. **δέον**, τό (v. sub voc.).

Δεῖα, τά, = Δῖα, *games in honour of Zeus*, *JHS*37.89 (Philadelphia, iii A.D.).

δεία· ἔνδεια, Hsch.

δεῖγμα, ατος, τό, (δείκνυμι) *sample, pattern*, καρπῶν Isoc.15.54, cf. *POxy.*113.5 (ii A.D.); τοῦ βίου Ar.*Ach.*988; λαβὼν δ' Ἄδραστον δεῖγμα τῶν ἐμῶν λόγων taking him *as evidence* of.., E.*Supp.*354; μὴ ..αὐτοὶ καθ' ὑμῶν αὐτῶν δ. τοιοῦτον ἐξενέγκητε D.21.183; τοῦτο τὸ δ. ἐξενηνοχὼς περὶ αὑτοῦ Id.19.12, cf. Pl.*Lg.*788c; δείγματος εἵνεκα by way *of sample*, D.23.65; δείγματος χάριν S.E.*M.*11.40; δ. προφέρειν, ἐκτίθεσθαι, παρασχεῖν, Pl.*Lg.*718b, Plb.4.24.9, D.H.*Rh.*6.5; δ. μικροψυχίας Men.*Georg.Fr.*3; δ. ψυχῆς *sign* of life, Luc.*Prom.Es* 2 (s.v.l.); δ. φιλοσοφίας Ἀττικῆς Id.*Scyth.*7; [ἀνδριάντα] δ. ἀρετᾶς θεμένα *Epigr. Gr.*860.6, cf. *IG*14.967, etc. b. *plan, sketch*, *PGiss.*15.3. c. *sense-evidence*, τὰ ἐπὶ τοῦ ὀργάνου δείγματα Epicur.*Nat.*11.7. 2. *mart, bazaar*, in the Piraeus, X.*HG*5.1.21, Lys.*Fr.*75.6; περιεπάτουν ἐν τῷ δ. τῷ ἡμετέρῳ D.35.29; elsewh., *IPE*1.16ᴮ49 (Olbia), Aen. Tact.30.2, Plb.5.88.8, D.S.19.45. b. metaph., δ. δικῶν Ar.*Eq.* 979.

δειγμᾰτ-ίζω, *make a show of*, *Ep.Col.*2.15; *make an example of*, *Ev.Matt.*1.19; *furnish a sample*, in Pass., *PTeb.*576 (i B.C./i A.D.); δειγματισθήσεται ... ἀπολέσθαι *will be proved to*.., *PRyl.*1.28.32 (iv A.D.). 2. *make trial of, test*, *PHolm.*18.20, 22.29. II. intr., *appear*, Ar.Byz.*Epit.*41.19, Hp.*Ep.*19 (in *Hermes* 53.67). **–ισμός**, οῦ, ὁ, *public inspection, verification*, *PSI*4.358.8 (iii B.C.), *OGI*90.30 (Rosetta), *BGU*246.6 (ii/iii A.D.), al. III. *putting to shame, exposure*, in pl., Vett.Val.43.26, Heph.Astr.2.32,34, *PRyl.*1.28.70 (iv A.D.).

δειγμᾰτο-άρτης, ου, ὁ, *inspector of the market*, *POxy.*63.8 (ii/iii A.D.), *PLond.*3.1159.39 (ii A.D.). **–κατᾰγωγία**, ἡ, *conveyance of samples*, *POxy.*1254.5 (iii A.D.). **–κατᾰγωγός**, ὁ, *official who delivered samples* of corn, *PStrassb.*31.6 (iii A.D.).

δείδεκτο, δειδέχαται, δειδέχατο, v. δειδίσκομαι; **δειδέχθαι**, v. δέχομαι.

δειδήμων, ονος, (δείδω) *fearful, cowardly*, Il.3.56, Nonn.*D.*15. 199, al.

δείδια, δείδιμεν and **δειδέμεν**, v. δείδω.

δειδίσκομαι, (cf. δέχομαι) *greet, welcome*, δεξιτερῇ δειδίσκετο χειρί Od.20.197; δέπαϊ χρυσέῳ δειδίσκετο 18.121; δειδισκόμενος 15.150:—to the same verb the following forms probably belong, πλησάμενος δ' οἴνοιο δέπας δείδεκτ' Ἀχιλῆα *pledged* him, Il.9.224; τοὺς μὲν ἄρα χρυσέοισι κυπέλλοις .. δειδέχατο ib.671, cf. 4.4; δειδέχαται μύθοισι Od.7.72; δεικνύμενος *welcoming*, 4.59, Il.9.196; *pledging*, *h.Ap.* 11; so, δεδεγμένος Panyas.12. II. (δείκνυμι) *show*, A.R.1.558.

δειδίσσομαι, later **δεδίσσομαι**, Att. **-ττομαι**: impf. ἐδεδίσκετο Ar.*Lys.*564: fut. -ίξομαι Il.20.201: aor. 1 inf. δειδίξασθαι (v. infr.), δεδίξασθαι Hsch.; part. δεδιξάμενος D.19.291:—causal of δείδω, *frighten, alarm*, μὴ.. δειδίσσεο λαὸν Ἀχαιῶν Il.4.184, cf. 13.810, Pl. *Phdr.*245b, Luc.*Bis Acc.*7, etc.; μὴ δή μ' ἐπέεσσι.. ἔλπεο δειδίξεσθαι Il.20.201, cf. Hes.*Sc.*111; Ἕκτορα.. ἀπὸ νεκροῦ δειδίξασθαι *to scare* him *away* from the corpse, Il.18.164 (in 2.190 οὔ σε ἔοικε, κακὸν ὥς, δειδίσσεσθαι it may be taken in either sense, cf. 15.196): c. inf., φευγέμεν ἂψ ὀπίσω δειδίσσετο Theoc.25.74, D.19.291, *Prooem.*43, D.H.1.71, al.; cf. δεδίσκομαι II. II. intr., *fear*, ἣν ἡ γυνὴ.. δειδίσσηται (v.l. διδ-) Hp.*Mul.*1.25; μὴ.. λίην δειδίσσεο θυμῷ A.R. 2.1219, cf. Plu.*Dio* 57: c. acc., *to be afraid of*, Orph.*A.*56, etc.: aor. δειδισάμενος App.*BC*5.79; τὴν αὐγήν Aret.*CA*1.1; τὸν ἄνδρα Luc. *Sol.*5.

δείδω, (for δε-δϝοy-α) 1st sg. pf. in pres. sense, Il.14.44, Od.5.300 (δείδιτε should prob. be restored for δείδετε in *AP*9.147 (Antag.)): fut. δείσομαι Il.15.299, etc.; later δείσω Q.S.4.36, etc.: aor. ἔδεισα, in Hom. ἔδδεισα (i.e. ἔδϝεισα, cf. ὑποδδείσας, = ὑποδϝείσας): aor. 2 δίον Il.22.251 (v. infr. 7), 3 sg. δίε 5.566; pf. δέδοικα, ας, ε, (in pres. sense), freq. in sg., Thgn.39, A.*Pers.*751, Ar.*Eq.*38, etc.; rare in pl., δεδοίκαμεν Men.534.11, Luc.*Charid.*24, -κατε Ar.*Ec.*181; Ep. δείδοικα (i.e. δε-δϝ-) Il.1.555, al.; subj. δεδοίκωσι Hp.*Art.*37; inf. δεδοικέναι E.*Supp.*548, Ar.*V.*1091, Pl.*Ax.*372, etc.; part. -κώς Anacr.43, Ar.*Pax* 607, Hdt.1.107, etc.: plpf. in impf. sense, Ar. *Pl.*684, Pl.*R.*472a, etc.; 3 pl. -οίκεσαν Th.4.27, X.*An.*3.5.18:—also δέδια A.*Pr.*184 (lyr.), S.*OC*1469 (lyr.), commonly used in Prose, D.14.4, Luc.*Prom.Es*5, etc.; δέδιε Amphis 33.6, Men.223. 13; pl. δέδιμεν, δέδιτε, Th.3.53,56, 4.126, etc.; δεδίασι Ar.*Eq.*224, Pl.*Ap.*29a, etc. (once in Hom., Il.24.663); Ep. δείδια ib.13.49, al., 3 sg. δείδιε Od.16.306; pl. δείδιμεν Il.9.230, etc.; δείδιτε *AP* l.c. (v. supr.); imper. δέδιθι Ar.*Eq.*230, *V.*273, Ep. δείδιθι Il.5.827, etc.; later δείδῑθι Nic.*Al.*443 (δείδιχθι cod. opt.), δέδῑθι Babr.75.2 codd.; subj. δεδίῃ X.*Ath.*1.11; δεδίωσι Isoc.4.156, etc.; inf. δεδιέναι Th. 1.136, Pl.*Phd.*88b, etc., Ep. δειδίμεν (to be distd. from 1 pl. indic. δείδιμεν) Od.9.274, 10.381; part. δεδιώς Ar.*Ec.*643, *Pl.*448, Th.6.24, etc., fem. δεδιυῖα prob. in Pl.*Phdr.*254e, Ep. acc. δειδιότα, pl. -ιότες, -ιότων, -ιότας, Il.6.137, etc.: plpf. ἐδεδίειν, εις, ει, Hyp.*Lyc.*6, D.34. 27, etc.; Ep. 3 sg. δείδιε Il.18.34; 3 pl. ἐδεδίεσαν Th.4.55 codd., X. *An.*5.7.36, ἐδέδισαν Pl.*Lg.*685c; Ep. 1 pl. ἐδείδιμεν Il.6.99, 3 pl. ἐδείδισαν 5.790, al., δείδισαν 15.652 (hence in late Ep., impf. ἐδείδιον, -ιες, -ιε, Q.S.10.450, Nonn.*D.*2.608, 35.30):—in Prose the shorter forms are generally preferred:—*fear*, distd. from φοβέομαι (v. δέος): Construct.: 1. abs., Hom., etc. 2. folld. by a Prep., δ. περί τινι *to be alarmed, anxious* about.., Il.17.242, 5.566, etc.; ἀμφί τινι A.*Pr.* 184 (lyr.); τῆς τυραννίδος πέρι E.*Supp.*446; ὑπέρ τινος Th.1.74; δ. ἐκ τῶν ὕπνων Plb.5.52.13; θορύβῳ Plu.*Dem.*9. 3. folld. by a relat. clause, mostly with μή.., and folld. by subj., Il.1.555, etc.; rarely by indic., δείδω μὴ.. νημερτέα εἶπεν Od.5.300; ὃν δέδοικ' ἐγὼ μή μοι βεβήκῃ S.*Ph.*493, cf. *OT*767, Th.6.88; δέδοιχ' ὅπως μὴ.. ἀναρρήξει κακά, = δέδοικα μή.., S.*OT*1074, cf. D.8.53, 9.75, Ar.*Eq.*112; μὴ δείσῃς ποθ' ὡς.. ὄψεται S.*El.*1309; δ. μὴ οὐ, folld. by subj., δέδιμεν μὴ οὐ βέβαιοι ἦτε Th.3.57, cf. Hdt.7.163, X.*Mem.*2.3.10, E.*Andr.*626, etc.; also δ. ὅπως λάθω E.*IT*995; μὴ δείσητε ὡς οὐχ ἡδέως καθευδήσετε X. *Cyr.*6.2.30. 4. c. inf., *fear to do*, δεῖσαν δ' ὑποδέχθαι Il.7.93, Th.1. 136: c. acc. et inf., δ. νέμεσιν ἔσεσθαι Od.22.40; θανεῖν σε δείσας E. *Ion* 1564: c. inf. Pass., οὐκ ἐδεδίεσαν βασανισθῆναι Lys.13.27. 5. c. acc., *fear, dread*, Δία Od.14.389; σημάντορας ib.4.431, etc.; τὸ σὸν πρόσωπον S.*OT*448; τοὺς γονέας Pl.*R.*562e; coupled with φοβοῦμαι, τοὺς Ἀθηναίους ἡγούμενοι ἅπερ ἐδεδίεσαν φοβεῖσθαι Th.4.117; οὐδὲ δέδοικα οὐδὲ φοβοῦμαι τὸν μέλλοντα ἀγῶνα D.21.200, cf. Isoc.12.48, Pl.*Euthphr.*12b,c. 6. part. pf., τὸ δεδιός *one's fearing*, much like δέος, Th.1.36. 7. *flee from*, c. acc. (by assimilation to φοβήσομαι), Il.22.251.

δειελιάω, (δείελος) *take an afternoon meal*, σὺ δ' ἔρχεο δειελιήσας Od.17.599, cf. Ath.5.193a.

δειελίη, ἡ, (δείελος) f.l. for δείελον, Call.*Fr.*190.

δειελινός, ή, όν, = δείελος, *at evening*, Theoc.13.33; δειελινὴν τὴν δ' εἷλε κακὸς χλόος Call.*Aet.*3.1.12.

δείελος, ον, *of* or *belonging to* δείλη (q.v.), δ. ἦμαρ *the evening part of* day, *eventide*, Od.17.606, Theoc.25.86; δ. ὥρη A.R.3.417. II. Subst. (sc. ἡμέρα), *late evening*, εἰσόκεν ἔλθῃ δ. ὀψὲ δύων Il.21.232, cf. Call.*Hec.*1.4.1; ποτὶ or ὑπὸ δείελον at *even*, *AP*9.650 (Leont.), A.R. 1.1160. 2. δείελον, τό, *afternoon meal*, Call.*Fr.*190 (perh. = *Oxy.* 1362 ii *Fr.*4). (δειελός Hdn.Gr.1.161.)

δείεμα· βρῶμα, Hsch.

δεικᾰνάω, (δείκνυμι) *point out, show*, in Ion. and Ep. impf. δεικανάασκεν Theoc.24.57; Ep. 3 pl. pres. δεικανόωσι Arat.209: but II. Med., (cf. δειδίσκομαι) *salute, pledge*, δεικανόωντο δέπασσιν Il.15.86; δεικανόωντ' ἐπέεσσιν Od.18.111; cf. δεκανᾶται.

δείκᾰνον, τό, = δείκηλον, of *embroidered figures* in tapestry, *EM* 260.43 (pl.).

δείκελον, τό, = δείκηλον II.1, Democr.123, Hegesianax 2. 2. = δείκηλον II.2, Nonn.*D.*48.697, *AP*9.153 (Agath.).

δεικές· λαμπρόν, κτλ., Hsch.

δεικηλίκτας, α, ὁ, Dor. for δεικηλίστης, *one who represents*; esp. Lacon., = ὑποκριτής, *actor who played burlesque parts*, Plu.*Ages.*21, 2.212f, Ath.14.621e (δικ- codd.).

δείκηλον, τό, *representation, exhibition*, παθέων Hdt.2.171. II. *reflection, image*, A.R.1.746; *phantom*, Id.4.1672 (pl.). 2. *sculptured figure*, *IG*14.1301, Lyc.1179 (pl.), J.*BJ*2.10.4, Porph.ap.Eus. *PE*3.9.

δείκνυμι (also **δεικνύω** Hes.*Op.*451, Men.562; Ion. **δέκνυμι** *GDI* 5653*b*14 (ἀπο-, Chios), 5493*b*25 (ἀπο-, Milet.), freq. in Hdt.; Cret. **δίκνυμι** (προ-) *GDI*5112); 3 sg. δείκνυ Hes.*Op.*526; imper. δείκνυε ib.502, Pl.*Phdr.*228e, 3 sg. δεικνύτω S.*OC*1532: impf. 3 pl. ἐδείκνυσαν X.*An.*4.5.33, D.18.213, also -νον Hdt.4.150, Antipho 5.76, etc.; 3 sg. δείκνυεν Pi.*P.*4.220: fut. δείξω Od.12.25, etc., Ion. δέξω Hdt.4. 179, al.: aor. 1 ἔδειξα, Ep. δεῖξα Od.3.174, etc., Ion. ἔδεξα Hdt.2.30, al.: pf. δέδειχα Alex.268, (ἐπι-) D.26.16, (ἀνα-) Plb.4.48.3:—Med., with pf. Pass., for Ep. forms δεικνύμενος, δείδεκτο, δειδέχαται, δειδέχατο, v. δειδίσκομαι:—Pass., fut. δειχθήσομαι Isoc.5.1, 12.4; δεδείξομαι Plu.2.416d, A.D.*Synt.*23.26, al.: aor. ἐδείχθην E.*Supp.*1209, etc., Ion. ἐδέχθην (ἀπ-) Hdt.1 *Prooem.*: pf. δέδειγμαι S.*Fr.*432, Ion. δέδεκται Hp. *de Arte* 10:—*bring to light, show forth*, [θεὸς] ἡμῖν δεῖξε [τέρας] Od.3.178; δεικνὺς σῆμα βροτοῖσιν Il.13.244; ἄγος δ. S.*OT* 1427; τὸν κτανόντα ib.278; ἵν' ἐλαίας.. ἔδειξε κλάδον Ἀθάνα E.*Tr.* 802; of artists, *portray, represent*, Luc.*Im.*5; *cause*, δυσθέατα πήματα ἐδείξατ' A.*Th.*982 codd.; *render* so and so, τυφλοὺς τοὺς ἐμβλέποντας δεικνύει Men.83; τινὰ ὑπὸ τῶν τραυμάτων δείξας νεκρόν D.S.34.2. 21:—Med., δείκνυμαι *set before one*, ἄεθλα Il.23.701. 2. *show, point out*, δ. Ἀλέξανδρον Μενελάῳ Il.3.452; δέσμιον.. ἔδειξ' Ἀχαιοῖς (sc. αὐτόν) S.*Ph.*609, cf. 492,630; αὐτὸ δ. experiment *will show*, Cratin.177, cf. Pl.*Tht.*200e, *Hp.Ma.*288b; δείξει δὴ τάχα alone, *time will show*, Ar.*Ra.*1261; δ. εἴς τινα *point* towards, Hdt.4. 150:—Med., δείξατο δ' εἰς Κρονίωνα *h.Merc.*367. 3. *show, make known*, esp. by words, *explain*, ὁδόν Od.12.25, etc.; ἀντολὰς ἐγὼ ἄστρων ἔδειξα A.*Pr.*458, cf. 482. 4. *show, prove*, with part., ποῦ γὰρ ὢν δείξω φίλος; E.*Or.*802; ἔδειξαν ἕτοιμοι ὄντες Th.4.73, cf. 5.72; δεικνύω ἐσπουδακώς Men.562; δείξω αὐτὸν πολλῶν θανάτων ὄντ' ἄξιον D.21.21; εἰ.. δειχθήσεται τοῦτο πεποιηκώς ib.160; ἱκανώτατα δέδεικται ψυχὴ τῶν πάντων πρεσβυτάτη Pl.*Lg.*896b: folld. by a relat. clause with ὡς.., ὅτι.., εἰ.., etc., A.*Th.*176, Th.1.76,143, etc.; πᾶσα ἀπόδειξίς τι κατά τινος δείκνυσι Arist.*APo.*90ᵇ34: ὅπερ ἔδει δεῖξαι, = Q.E.D., Euc.1.4, al.: abs., δέδεικται *it is clear* or *proven*, Pl.*Phd.*66d, etc.; δεδείξεται A.D. l.c. 5. of accusers, *inform against*, τινά Ar.*Eq.*278 (Dobree ex Sch. ἐγὼ ἐνδείκνυμι). 6. *display, exhibit*, ἀγλαΐαν Pi.*P.*6.46; ἀρετήν, προθυμίαν, Th.1.37,6. 11. 7. *offer, proffer*, καὶ τὰ πίστ' ἐδειξάτην A.*Ag.*651. (Cf. Lat. *dīco*, Goth. *gateihan* 'announce', OHG. *zeigōn* 'show'.)

δεικ-τέον, *one must show, prove*, X.*Mem.*3.5.8; περί τινος Thphr. *CP*3.7.5; τοὺς νόμους δεικτέον μοι *it is* my *duty to point out..*, D.18. 58, cf. Porph.*Abst.*3.7. **-τηριάς**, άδος, ἡ, = Lat. *mima*, Plb.14. 11.4. **-τήριον**, τό, *place for showing*; at Samos, *place where* Athena *showed* Perseus *a representation of the Gorgon*, *EM*261.9. II. = δεῖγμα, *PPetr.*3 p.333. **-της**, ου, ὁ, *exhibitor*, Orph.*H.*8.16; τῶν ἱερῶν ἀγώνων prob. in *CIG*2932 (Tralles); ὁ λόγος δ. ἐστὶ πάντων τῶν ἀγαθῶν Zos.Alch.p.191 B. **-τικός**, ή, όν, *able to show*: in Logic, of syllogisms, *those which can be directly reduced*, Arist.*APr.*45ᵃ24; δ. ἐνθύμημα, opp. ἐλεγκτικόν, Id.*Rh.*1396ᵇ24. Adv. -κῶς Id.*APr.*29ᵃ 31. 2. *categorical*, πρότασις *Stoic.*2.85. II. Gramm., *demonstrative*, τὸ "τοῦτο" δεικτικόν Chrysipp.*Stoic.*2.65; δ. ὄνομα D.T. 636.12; ἄρθρα Apollod.Ath. and D.T.ap.A.D.*Pron.*5.19; ἀντωνυμία ib.9.17: -άτεραι γιγνόμεναι (sc. ἀντωνυμίαι) προσλαμβάνουσι τὸ ῑ ib. 59.16: -κόν, τό, Demetr.*Eloc.*289. Adv. -κῶς Chrysipp.*Stoic.*2.245, Plu.2.747d, S.E.*M.*7.267. **-τός**, ή, όν, *capable of proof*, Arist. *APo.*76ᵇ27. 2. *perceptible*, Phlp.*in Cat.*88.21.

δειλαινομένως, Adv. *with trepidation*, Gloss.

δειλαίνω, *to be a coward* or *cowardly*, Arist.*EN*1107ᵃ18, 1137ᵃ22, Plot.1.4.15:—Med., Luc.*Ocyp.*153, *PTeb.*58.27:—Pass., aor. δειλανθείς· κλεφθείς, ἀπατηθείς, Hsch.; δειλάσαι· δειλιάσαι, Id.

δείλαιος, α, ον (ος, ον *IG*14.1722.7), lengthd. form of δειλός (q.v.): —*wretched, sorry, paltry*, not in Hom., freq. in Trag., esp. of persons, A.*Pr.*580 (lyr.), etc.; δείλαιε τοῦ νοῦ S.*OT*1347 (lyr.); δ. χάρις a *sorry* kindness, A.*Ch.*517; δ. σποδός *paltry* dust, S.*El.*758; δ. ἄχεα, ἀλγηδών, δύα, Emp.145, S.*OC*513 (lyr.), *Ant.*1311 (lyr.); γῆρας E. *Hec.*156 (lyr.): sts. found in Com. (v. infr.) and Prose, Lys.24.23 (Sup.), Aeschin.1.172: in later Prose, Jul.*Or.*1.29b. (The penult. is short in S.*Ant.*1311, *El.*849 (lyr.), E.*Supp.*279 (lyr.), Ar.*Eq.*139, *V.*165, etc.)

δειλαιότης, ητος, ἡ, *misery*, Sch.Ar.*Eq.*1148.

δειλ-ακρίνας, = sq., *EM*261.38. **-ακρίων**, ωνος, ὁ, *pitiable creature*; in Com., *poor fellow!* Ar.*Pax*193, *Av.*143. **-ακρος**, α, ον, *pitiable*, Ar.*Pl.*973, *Carm.Pop.*27. **-ανδρέω**, *to be cowardly*, Lxx 2*Ma.*8.13, 4*Ma.*10.14. **-ανδρος**, ον, *cowardly*, Hdn.Gr.1. 204.

δεῖλαρ, ατος, τό, = δέλεαρ, Call.*Fr.*458 (pl.).

δείλη, ἡ, *afternoon* (δ. ἡμέρας τελευτή Pl.*Def.*411b), ἔσσεται ἢ ἠὼς ἢ δείλη ἢ μέσον ἦμαρ Il.21.111: divided into *early* and *late* (πρωΐα and ὀψία), περὶ δείλην πρωΐην γενομένην Hdt.8.6 (opp. δ. ὀψίην, ib.9); δείλης ὀψίης Id.7.167, cf. D.57.9; περὶ δείλην ἤδη ὀψίαν Th.8.26; later περὶ δ. ἑσπέραν Ph.2.533, Hdn.3.12.7. II. δ. alone, 1. *early afternoon*, δείλη δὲ τέμνεται ὀπώρα S.*Fr.*255; ἤδη ἦν μέσον ἡμέρας.., ἡνίκα δὲ δείλη ἐγένετο X.*An.*1.8.8; ἀμφὶ δείλην ib.2.2.14 (opp. ὀψέ, ib.16); περὶ δείλην Hdt.9.101, Th.4.69,103; ἀπὸ δείλης from *the hour of afternoon*, Arist.*HA*564ᵃ19; τῆς δείλης *in the course of the afternoon*, X.*An.*7.3.10; but also, b. *late afternoon*, τῆς ἡμέρας ὅλης διῆλθον.. ἀλλὰ δείλης ἀφίκοντο ib.3.3.11; ἡνίκα ἦν δ., opp. τῆς νυκτός, ib.3.4.34, cf. 4.2.1, 7.2.16; μέχρι δείλης ἐξ ἑωθινοῦ Id.*HG*1.1.5, cf. 4.1.22; ἀπ' ἠοῦς μέχρι δείλης Pl.*Def.*411a; ἕωθεν καὶ δείλης early in the morning and *late in the evening*, Arist.*Fr.*531; πρὸς τὴν δείλην Id.*HA* 596ᵃ23; δείλαν alone, Theoc.10.5. 2. in late Prose, *any time of day*, περὶ μεσημβρίαν δ. about mid-*day*, Ach.Tat.3.2. b. apparently, *day*, opp. *night*, δείλ(η)s ἐργ(άταις) *PLond.*1.131ʳ44 (ii A.D.), cf. 244.

δείληθι· φοβοῦ, Hsch. (leg. δείδιθι). **δειλήμων,** = δειδήμων (εἰδήμονες cod.), Id.

δειλία, ἡ, *timidity, cowardice*, Hdt.1.37, S.*OT*536, etc.; δειλίην ὀφλεῖν to be charged with *cowardice*, Hdt.8.26; δειλίας ὀφλεῖν (sc. δίκην) And.1.74; ἔνοχος δειλίας (sc. δίκῃ) Lys.1.45; opp. ἀνδρεία, θρασύτης, Pl.*Lg.*648b, *Ti.*87a. II. *misery*, Procop.*Goth.*4.32.

δειλι-αίνω, *make afraid*, Lxx *De.*20.8. **–ᾱσις,** εως, ἡ, *fright, faintheartedness*, Plu.*Fab.*17.

δειλίασμα, δειλινισμός, and **δείλισμα,** = Lat. *merenda, Gloss.*

δειλιάω, *to be afraid*, Lxx *De.*1.28, al., D.S.20.78, Paul.Aeg.3.76. (Later Gr. for ἀποδειλ–.)

δειλινός, ή, όν, (δείλη) = δειελινός, *in the afternoon*, δ. ἤρξατο *Com.Adesp.*609, cf. Luc.*Dem.Enc.*31, Secund.*Sent.*4, *BGU*513.3 (ii A.D.); τὸ δ., as Adv., *at even*, Lxx *Ge.*3.8, Luc.*Lex.*2; δ. ὁλοκαύτωμα Lxx 1*Es.*5.50; ὧραι Str.17.3.8; ἑσπέρα Ph.1.505 (s.v.l.); διατριβή Plu.2.70e. 2. *western*, κλίμα Str.9.2.41. II. τὸ δ. (sc. δεῖπνον) *evening meal*, f.l. in Ath.10.418b (quoting Plb.20.6.6), cf. Ath.1.11e.

δειλοκατα-φρονητής, οῦ, or **-φρόνητος,** ον, *cowardly and insolent*, Ptol.*Tetr.*66.

δειλοκοπέω, *cheat* or *terrify*, Hermipp.88.

δείλομαι (A), (δείλη) *verge towards afternoon*, δείλετό τ' ἠέλιος the sun *was westering*, Od.7.289 (Aristarch. and others for δύσετο).

δείλομαι (B), Delph. and Locr., = βούλομαι.

δειλόομαι, Pass., *to be afraid*, read by Nicanor in S.*Ichn.*150, cf. Lxx 1*Ma.*16.6, D.S.20.78.

δειλοποιός, όν, *making cowardly*, Sch.S.*Tr.*1028.

δειλός, ή, όν, (δέος): I. of persons, *cowardly*, opp. ἄλκιμος, Il.13.278; opp. ἀνδρεῖος, Pl.*Phdr.*239a, etc.: hence, *vile, worthless*, Il.1.293; δειλαί τοι δειλῶν γε καὶ ἐγγύαι Od.8.351; opp. ἐσθλός, *lowborn, mean*, Hes.*Fr.*164; πλοῦτος καὶ δειλοῖσιν ἀνθρώπων ὁμιλεῖ B.1.50; ἀγαθοὶ δειλῶν ἐπὶ δαῖτας ἴασιν Eup.289; of animals, Hdt.3.108: c. gen., δειλὸς μυάγρης *afraid of..*, *AP*9.410 (Tull. Sab.): c. inf., ib.6.232 (Crin.). Adv. **–λῶς** Theoc.*Adon.*15, Plu.2.26b. 2. more commonly, *miserable, wretched*, with a compassionate sense, δειλοὶ βροτοί *poor* mortals! Il.22.31, al.; ἆ δειλέ *poor wretch!* ἆ δειλοί *poor wretches!* 17.201, Od.20.351; ἆ δειλὲ ξείνων 14.361; Πατροκλῆος δειλοῖο Il.17.670. II. of things, *miserable, wretched*, γῆρας Hes.*Op.*113; δ. δ' ἐνὶ πυθμένι φειδώ ib.369; τὰ δ. κέρδη S.*Ant.*326; ἔργα, λόγος, etc., Thgn.307, E.*Andr.*757, etc.: Comp., Longin.2.1: Sup., Ar.*Pl.*123: neut. pl. as Adv., ὀχλεῖ μοι δειλὰ ὁ Τρωΐλος *PLand.*11.4 (iii A.D.).—Trag. use δειλός chiefly in former sense, δείλαιος in latter.

δειλότης, ητος, ἡ, = δειλία, *cowardice*, Hsch. s.v. δειλίην.

δειλόψῡχος, ον, *fainthearted*, Lxx 4*Ma.*8.16.

δεῖμα, ατος, τό, (δέος) *fear*, δεῖμα φέρων Δαναοῖσι Il.5.682; φρένα δείματι πάλλων S.*OT*153 (lyr.); ἔλαβέ τινα Hdt.6.74; ἐς δ. πεσεῖν, ἐν δείματι κατεστάναι, Id.8.118,36; opp. θάρσος, Aen.Tact.16.3: pl., S.*El.*636; φόβοι καὶ δ. Th.7.80, Phld.*D.*1.22, etc. II. *object of fear, terror*, ὦ πῦρ σὺ καὶ πᾶν δ. S.*Ph.*927; ἐκ δ. του νυκτέρου Id.*El.*410; ἀντιπάλοις δ. *a terror* to them, *Epigr.Gr.*343 (Germa): esp. in pl., A.*Pr.*691 (lyr.), *Ch.*524, A.R.4.735; δειμάτων ἄχη *fearful* plagues or monsters, A.*Ch.*586 (lyr.); δ. θηρῶν E.*HF*700 (lyr.).

δειμ-αίνω, only pres. and impf. (Ep. δειμαίνεσκε Q.S.2.439):—*to be afraid*, *h.Ap.*404, Hdt.3.51, etc., S.*OC*492, Pl.*R.*330c, etc.; δ. περὶ ἑωυτῷ, ὑπέρ τινος, Hdt.3.35, 8.140.β'; ἀμφί τινι S.*OC*492; ἐπί τινι Jul.*Or.*2.82a:—Pass., *to be frightened*, Q.S.2.499. 2. folld. by a relat. clause with μή.., Thgn.541, Hdt.1.165, S.*Tr.*481. 3. c. inf., Mosch.3.56, Opp.*H.*5.320. 4. c. acc., *fear*, τὴν Περσέων δύναμιν Hdt.1.159; πάντα δ. A.*Pers.*600, cf. *Pr.*41: c. acc. cogn., δεῖμ' ὃ δειμαίνεις E.*Andr.*868. **–ᾰλέος,** α, ον, *timid*, Arist.*Phgn.*810ᵃ23, Mosch.2.20, Opp.*C.*1.165. II. *horrible, fearful*, Batr.287, cj. in Thgn.1128.

δειμαλέτα· τὰ λεπτὰ τῶν βοσκημάτων, οἱ δὲ Λάκωνες νεκρά, Hsch.

δειμᾰτ-ηρός, ά, όν, *fearful, timid*, A.D.*Synt.*189.25. **–ίας,** ου, ὁ, epith. of Zeus, *the Scarer*, D.H.6.90. **–όεις,** εσσα, εν, *frightened, scared*, *AP*9.244 (Apollonid.).

δειμᾰτο-ποιός, όν, *terrifying*, Sch.E.*Hec.*70. **–στᾰγής,** ές, (στάζω) *reeking with horror*, A.*Ch.*842 (leg. αἱματοσταγές).

δειμᾰτ-όω, *frighten*, Hdt.6.3, Ar.*Ra.*144, Ph.2.204:—Pass., A.*Ch.*845, S.*Ichn.*142, E.*Andr.*42, Pl.*Ax.*370a, etc. **–ώδης,** ες, *terrible, frightful*, Aret.*SD*1.5, al., Hsch. **–ωσις,** εως, ἡ, *scaring*, Sch.Lyc.1182.

δειμός, ὁ, (δέος) *fear, terror*, δειμόν τινα ἀναπλάσσειν J.*Ap.*2.34. II. Δεῖμος, ὁ, personified as accompanying Φόβος, Ἔρις, Γοργώ, etc., Il.4.440, cf. 11.37, 15.119, Hes.*Th.*934.

δειμώδης, = φοβερός, Erot. (dub. l.).

δεῖν, v. δεῖ.

δεῖνα, ὁ, ἡ, τό, gen. δεῖνος, dat. δεῖνι, acc. δεῖνα: sts. indecl. (v. infr.): nom. δεῖν, δ. Sophr.58: gen. and dat. τοῦ δείνατος, τῷ δείνατι, A.D.*Pron.*60.12, *EM*614.51:—*such an one, so-and-so*, always with Art., ὁ δεῖνα Ar.*Ra.*918, etc.; τὸν δεῖνα τὸν τοῦ δεῖνα Id.*Th.*622; ὁ δεῖνα τοῦ δεῖνος τὸν δεῖν' εἰσήγγειλεν D.13.5; ἃ ἂν ὁ δ. ἢ ὁ δ. εἴπῃ Id.2.31; ὁ δ. καὶ ὁ δ. Arist.*Rh.*1416ᵃ23; ἡ δεῖνα Ant.Lib.22; τὸ δ., euphem. for τὸ πέος, Ar.*Ach.*1149, cf. Sch.Luc.*BisAcc.*23; τὸ δ. δ' ἐσθίεις; do you eat *such a fish?* Antiph.129.6: in gen., ἐμὸς ἢ τοῦ δεῖνος mine or *some other's*, Arist.*Pol.*1262ᵃ3: dat., τῷ δεῖνι μεμφόμενος D.20.104, cf. 37.56: pl., οἱ δεῖνες Id.24.180; τῶν δείνων Id.20.106. II. τὸ δ. in Com. as an interjection to express an idea which suddenly strikes one, *by the way, mark you*, Ar.*V.*524, *Pax* 268, etc.: in later Prose, Luc.*Vit.Auct.*19.

δεινάζω, *to be in straits*, Lxx 2*Ma.*4.35.

δειναυξῆσαι, *exaggerate, Gloss.*

δεινιάς (sc. ἐμβάς), άδος, ἡ, *shoe called after Dinias* (D.20.146), Cleanth.*Stoic.*1.133.

δεινο-βίης [ῐ], ου, ὁ, (βία) *terribly strong*, Orph.*A.*65. **–επής,** gloss on ἀπτοεπές, Sch.Il.8.209, *EM*133.45. **–θέτης,** Dor. **–ας,** ου, ὁ, (τίθημι) *knave*, Mosch.*Fr.*3.7. **–κάθεκτος,** ον, *hard to be repressed*, Orph.*H.*10.6. **–λεχής,** ές, *dreadfully married*, Id.*A.*906.

δεινόλινος· ὁ δεινῇ εἱμαρμένῃ ἐφθαρμένος, *EM*264.28.

δεινο-λογέομαι, *complain loudly*, ὅτι.. Hdt.1.44; εἰ.. Plu.*Sert.*6: abs., Hdt.4.68, Eus.Mynd.59. **–λογία,** ἡ, *exaggerated complaint*, Plb.33.11.3. **–πάθεια** [πᾰ], ἡ, *exaggerated complaint*, condemned by Poll.6.201, cf. Suid. s.v. τραγῳδία. **–πᾰθέω,** *complain loudly of sufferings*, D.40.53, Teles p.58 H., Plb.12.16.9, Luc.*Syr.D.*24; ἐπί τινι D.S.19.75, Plu.2.781a. **–πενθής,** ές, gloss on στονόεσσα, Sch.Il.24.721. **–ποιέω,** in Rhet., *amplify*, D.H.*Th.*23, Nicol.*Prog.*p.42 F.; *use terrifying expressions*, Porph.*Chr.*30. **–πους,** ὁ, ἡ, –πουν, τό, gen. ποδος, *with terrible foot*, Ἀρά (as if she were a hound upon the track), S.*OT*418. **–προσωπέω,** *to be stern of countenance*, περὶ τῆς τυραννίδος Arg.E.*Ph.*

δεινός, ή, όν, (δέος, cf. Pl.*La.*198b) *fearful, terrible*; in Hom., of persons and things, Χάρυβδις Od.12.260; κλαγγή Il.1.49; ὅπλα 10.254: freq. in neut., δεινὸν ἄϋσαι 11.10; βροντᾶν 20.56; δεινὸν δέρκεσθαι 3.342; παπταίνειν Od.11.608; δεινὰ δ' ὑπόδρα ἰδών Il.15.13; δ. ἰδέσθαι *fearful* to behold, Od.22.405; δ. μὲν ὁρᾶν, δ. δὲ κλύειν S.*OC*141; εἰ καὶ δεινόν τῳ ἀκοῦσαι Th.1.122; δεινὴ παρὰ τοῖς εἰδόσιν ἡ βάσανος And.1.30; in milder sense, *awful*, δεινή τε καὶ αἰδοίη θεός Il.18.394, cf. 3.172, Od.8.22, etc.; τὸ δεινόν *danger, suffering, horror*, A.*Ch.*634, etc.; *awe, terror*, Id.*Eu.*517; ὅπου τὸ δ. ἐλπὶς οὐδὲν ὠφελεῖ S.*Fr.*196; πρὸς τὸ δ. ἔρχεσθαι ib.351: in pl., ἐκτὸς ὄντα πημάτων τὰ δείν' ὁρᾶν Id.*Ph.*504; εἰ δείν' ἔδρασας, δεινὰ καὶ παθεῖν σε δεῖ Id.*Fr.*962, etc.; δεινὸν γίγνεται μή.. there is *danger* that.., Hdt.7.157; οὐδὲν δεινοὶ ἔσονται μὴ ἀποστέωσιν no *fear* of their revolting, Id.1.155, etc.; δεινότατον μή.. the *greatest danger* lest.., And.3.1; δεινόν ἐστι, c. inf., it is *dangerous* to do, Lys.12.87; δεινὸν ποιεῖσθαι *take ill, complain of, be indignant at* a thing: abs., Th.1.102, etc.: c. inf., ὑπὸ Μήδων ἄρχεσθαι Hdt.1.127, etc.; also δεινὰ ποιεῖν *make complaints*, Id.3.14, 5.41; ἐν δεινῷ τίθεσθαι J.*AJ*18.9.8; δεινόν τι ἔσχε αὐτὸν ἀτιμάζεσθαι Hdt.1.61; δεινὸν or δεινὰ παθεῖν suffer *illegal, arbitrary* treatment, Ar.*Ra.*252, cf. Pl.*Prt.*317b, etc.; δεινότερα π. Th.3.13; τὸ δ. τὸ πείσομαι Hdt.7.11: in Oratt., δεινὸν ἂν εἴη εἰ... And.1.30, Lys.12.88, etc. Adv. **–νῶς,** φέρειν Hdt.2.121.γ'; δ. καὶ ἀπόρως ἔχει μοι I am in *dire* straits, Antipho 1.1; δ. ἔχειν τῇ ἐνδείᾳ X.*An.*6.4.23; δ. διατεθῆναι τυπτόμενος Lys.3.27. II. *marvellously strong, powerful*: δ. σάκος the *mighty* shield, Il.7.245; simply, *wondrous, marvellous, strange*, τὸ συγγενές τοι δεινὸν ἥ θ' ὁμιλία kin and social ties *have strange power*, A.*Pr.*39; δ. τὸ κοινὸν σπλάγχνον Id.*Th.*1036; δ. τὸ τίκτειν S.*El.*770; πολλὰ τὰ δ. κοὐδὲν ἀνθρώπου –ότερον πέλει Id.*Ant.*333; δ. ἵμερος, ἔρως, Hdt.9.3, Pl.*Tht.*169c; οἶκτος S.*Tr.*298, etc.; δ. λέγεις πρᾶγμα Pl.*Euthd.*298c; δ. γ' εἶπας, εἰ καὶ ζῇς θανών S.*Aj.*1127; freq. δεινὸν ἂν εἴη εἰ... it were *strange* that.., as E.*Hec.*592. Adv. **–νῶς** *marvellously, exceedingly*, δ. μέλαινα, ἄνυδρος, Hdt.2.76,149; δ. ἐν φυλακῇσι εἶναι Id.3.152; δ. πῶς εἰμ' ἐπιλήσμων Metag.2, etc.: Comp. –οτέρως Sch.Min.Il.7.97. III. *clever, skilful*, first in Hdt.5.23 ἀνὴρ δ. τε καὶ σοφός; of Odysseus, γλώσσῃ.. δεινοῦ καὶ σοφοῦ S.*Ph.*440, cf. *OC*806, Antipho 2.2.3, Lys.7.12; σοφὸς καὶ δ. Pl.*Prt.*341a; opp. σοφός, of *practical ability*, Id.*Phdr.*245c, *Tht.*164d; opp. ἰδιώτης, D.4.35: c. inf., δεινὸς εὑρεῖν A.*Pr.*59; δεινοὶ πλέκειν τοι μηχανὰς Αἰγύπτιοι Id.*Fr.*373; δ. λέγειν *clever* at speaking, S.*OT*545, etc.; δ. εἰπεῖν is rare, D.20.150; νόσος δ. φαγεῖν Ar.*Nu.*243; δ. πράγμασι χρῆσθαι D.1.3; αἱ εὐπραξίαι δ. συγκρύψαι τὰ ὀνείδη are *wonderfully liable* to.., Id.2.20: c. acc., δ. τὴν τέχνην Ar.*Ec.*364; δ. περὶ τοὺς λόγους τοὺς εἰς τὰ δικαστήρια Pl.*Euthd.*304d; ἐς τὰ πάντα Ar.*Ra.*968; δ. περὶ τὸ ἀδικεῖν, περὶ Ὁμήρου, Pl.*R.*405c, *Ion* 531a; δ. ἀμφί τι Arr.*Tact.*9.5; δ. κατὰ χειρουργίαν Ael.*VH*3.1; ἐν λόγοισι δ. Ὑπερείδης Timocl.4.7 (but also of the *forcible, vehement*, style in oratory, Demetr.*Eloc.*240, al.); in bad sense, *over-clever*, Pl.*Euthphr.*3c; δ. ὑπὸ πανουργίας Id.*Tht.*176d, cf. Arist.*EN*1144ᵃ27. (For δϝεινός, cf. Δϝενία, gen. of pr.n. Δεινίας, *IG*4.858.)

δεῖνος (A), gen. of δεῖνα (q.v.).

δεῖνος (B), ὁ, = δῖνος, a name for *different round vessels*, Stratt.34, Dionys.Com.5, etc.: Cyren., = ποδανιπτήρ, Philet.ap.Ath.11.467d. II. a *dance*, Apolloph.1. III. *threshing-floor*, Telesilla 7. IV. *instrument for making* or *gilding pills*, Schwyzer 182a.3 (Gortyn, v/iv B.C.).

δείνοσμος (i.e. *evil-smelling*), = κόνυζα πλατύφυλλος, Ps.-Dsc.3.121.

δεινότης, ητος, ἡ, *terribleness*, Th.3.59, 4.10; *harshness, severity*, νόμων Id.3.46. II. *cleverness, shrewdness*, D.18.144, Arist.

*EN*1144a23; opp. ἀλήθεια, Antipho 5.5; esp. in an orator, Th.3.37, D.18.242,277; ἡ ἐν τοῖς λόγοις δ. Isoc.1.4; δεινότητα λόγου ἐπιδείκνυσθαι Plu.*Pomp.*77. III. Rhet., *intensity, forcefulness*, D.H. *Comp.*18, *Th.*53, al., Longin.34.4, Hermog.*Id.*2.9, al.: pl., Demetr. *Eloc.*243.

δειν-όω, *make terrible*: *exaggerate*, ἐπὶ τὸ μεῖζον πάντα δεινώσας Th. 8.74; δεινῶσαι τὰς συμφοράς Plu.*Per.*28. **-ωμα**, ατος, τό, *exaggerated view*, τὸ δ. τῶν κριτῶν Phld.*Rh.*1.286 S. **-ωπός**, όν, = δεινώψ, Hes.*Sc.*250. **-ωσις**, εως, ἡ, *exaggeration* or *exacerbation*, Pl.*Phdr.*272a, Quint.*Inst.*6.2.24, Longin.11.2, 12.5 (pl.), Demetr. *Eloc.*130; αὔξησις καὶ δ. D.H.*Vett.Cens.*2.5, cf. *Lys.*19 (pl.). II. *indignation*, Arist.*Rh.*1417a13, 1419b26. 2. *frowning*, ὀφρύες δεινώσιος μετέχουσαι Hp.*Acut.*42. **-ωτικός**, ή, όν, Rhet., *pertaining to* δείνωσις I, ὗλαι Corn.*Rh.*p.394 H. **-ώψ**, ῶπος, ὁ, ἡ, *fierce-eyed*, of the Erinyes, S.*OC*84.

δειομένη· δεισομένη, Hsch.

δεῖξις, εως, ἡ, (δείκνυμι) *mode of proof*, ἐκ τῶν σημείων Arist.*Rh.* 1408a26, cf. *APr.*34a4. 2. *proof, specimen*, δ. ἀνδρείας παρέχεσθαι, δ. εὐνοίας, Hdn.1.15.2, 2.3.5. II. *display, exhibition*, Macho ap.Ath.6.245e; δεῖξιν λόγων ποιεῖσθαι Ath.3.98c; anatomical *demonstration*, Gal.14.627. 2. *calling up*, θεῶν Alciphr.2.4.15, cf. *PMag. Leid.W.*6.42. 3. Gramm., *demonstrative force* or *reference*, Chrysipp.*Stoic.*2.65, al., A.D.*Pron.*9.8, al.

δείους, Ep. gen. of δέος (q.v.).

Δειπάτυρος· θεὸς παρὰ Στυμφαίοις, Hsch.

δειπν-άριον, τό, Dim. of δεῖπνον, Diph.64.1, *AP*11.10 (Lucill.). **-εύς**, έως, ὁ, divinity worshipped by cooks in Achaia, Ath.2. 39d. **-εύω**, = δειπνίζω, prob. in *CIG*2719 (Stratonicea). **-έω**, fut. -ήσω Ar.*Pax* 1084, X.*Cyr.*5.3.35, -ήσομαι D.S.11.9, Gal.11.6: aor. ἐδείπνησα, Ep. δείπνησα Od.14.111, etc.: pf. δεδείπνηκα Ar.*Ec.* 1133, etc.; Att. 1 pl. δεδείπναμεν Alex.109, Eub.91; inf. δεδειπνάναι Ar.*Fr.*464,249, Pl.Com.144: plpf. ἐδεδειπνήκεσαν Antipho 1.18; Ep. δεδειπνήκειν Od.17.359:—*make a meal*, Hom. (v. δεῖπνον): in Att. always, *take the chief meal, dine*, once in Trag., δειπνεῖν E.*Fr.*894 (dub. l.); δ. τὸ ἄριστον *make* breakfast *serve as dinner*, X.*Cyr.*1. 2.11; δ. παρά τινι *with* one, Antipho 1.18; [ἐν πρυτανείῳ] And.1. 45. 2. c. acc., δ. ἄρτον *make a meal on* bread, Hes.*Op.*442; δ. μοσχίον Ephipp.15.13; κοτύλην μίαν Alex.221.17; ξίφη Mnesim.7; δ. τἀλλότρια, of parasites, freq. in Com., Theopomp.34, Eub.72, etc.; also δ. ἀπό τινος Ar.*Pl.*890. II. Act., *entertain*, τινάς *Milet.*7.68, *Inscr.Cos* 131. **-ήεντα**· δειπνοφόρα, οὐ δυνάμενα φέρειν ἡμᾶς, Hsch. **-ηστος**, ὁ, *meal-time*, Od.17.170; δ. ἀκρόνυχος Nic.*Th.* 761 (v.l. -ητός). (Acc. to some Gramm., δειπνηστός (sc. καιρός) = *meal-time*, δείπνηστος = *meal*, Eust.1814.36.) **-ηστύς**, ύος, ἡ, *meal-time*, Hsch. **-ητήριον**, τό, *dining-room*, Plu.*Luc.*41, Inscr. ap.*PFay.*p.33, J.*BJ*2.8.5. **-ητής**, οῦ, ὁ, *diner, guest*, Plb.3.57. 7. **-ητικός**, ή, όν, *fond of dinner*, Anaxipp.1.36; ἐπιστολαὶ δ. letters *on cookery*, Ath.4.128a. Adv. -κῶς *like a cook, artistically*, Ar.*Ach.*1016. **-ίζω**, Att. fut. -ιῶ Diph.62: aor. ἐδείπνισα X. *Cyr.*4.5.5 (v. Od. infr. cit.):—*entertain at dinner*, κατέπεφνεν δειπνίσσας Od.4.535; δειπνίζοντες Ξέρξεα Hdt.7.118; δ. τὴν πόλιν ὅλην *IG*5(1).1346: also c. acc. cogn., δ. τινὰ δεῖπνον *give* one a dinner, Matro *Conv.*2:—Pass., βοὰς δεδειπνισμένων θεάτρων the applause of spectators *bribed by dinners*, Plu.2.92e. **-ίον**, ου, τό, Dim. of δεῖπνον, Ar.*Fr.*483. **-ιστήριον**, τό, = δειπνητήριον, *IG*5(2).268. 36 (Mantinea, i B.C.), 12(9).906.10 (Chalcis, iii A.D.), *Mon.Ant.*23. 124 (Side). **-ιστός**, ὁ, = δείπνηστος, Orus ap.*EM*262.45. **-ῖτις**, ιδος, ἡ, = fem. of δειπνητικός, στολή D.C.69.18.

δειπνο-θήρας, ου, ὁ, = δειπνολόχος, Ph.1.665. **-κλήτωρ**, ορος, ὁ, *one who invites to dinner*, v.l. in *Ev.Matt.*20.27. II = ἐδέατρος, Artem.ap.Ath.4.171b:—hence **-κλητόριον**, τό, Eust.766.58. **-κρίτης** [ῐ], ου, ὁ, *judge of the feasts*, of a religious official, Epigr. in *CRAcad.Inscr.*1907.141 (Janiculum). **-λογία**, ἡ, *poem on dining* by Archestratus, Ath.1.4e:—hence **-λόγος**, ὁ, *dinner-bard*, of Archestratus, ib.29a. **-λόχος**, η, ον, *laying traps, fishing for invitations to dinner, parasitic*, Hes.*Op.*704. **-μᾰνής**, ές, *mad after eating*, Timo 16.1.

δεῖπνον, τό, *meal*: in Hom. sts. *noonday meal*, Il.11.86; sts. = ἄριστον, *morning meal*, 2.381, 10.578, 19.171 sq., Od.15.94 sq., 500; sts. = δόρπον, *evening meal*, 17.176, 20.390 sq.; later, *the midday meal*, σῖτον εἰδέναι διώρισα, ἄριστα, δεῖπνα, δόρπα θ' αἱρεῖσθαι τρίτα A.*Fr.*182; later, *the afternoon meal, dinner* or *supper*, σοὶ δὲ μελήσει, ὅταν ᾖ δεκάπουν τὸ στοιχεῖον, λιπαρῷ χωρεῖν ἐπὶ δ. Ar.*Ec.*652: freq. in pl., S.*OT* 779, *El.*203 (lyr.); δ. Θυέστου E.*Or.*1008 (lyr.); ἀπὸ δείπνου straightway after *the meal*, ἀπὸ δ. αὐτοῦ θωρήσσοντο Il.8.54, cf. Antipho 1.17; καλεῖν ἐπὶ δεῖπνον, κεκλῆσθαι ἐπὶ δ., Eub.72,119.2; δ. παρασκευάζειν Pherecr.45,172; παραθεῖναι Id.184; ποιεῖν Dionys.Com.2.4; of animals, etc., Hom.*Epigr.*11, Ael.*VH*1.12, 12.27. 2. generally, *food, provender*, ἵπποισιν δεῖπνον δότε Il.2.383; ὄρνισι δεῖπνον A. *Supp.*801; κοράκεσσιν Epigr.ap.Philostr.*Her.*19.17.

δειπνο-πίθηκος [ῐ], ὁ, Com. name for a *parasite*, *Com.Adesp.*321. **-ποιέω**, *prepare a dinner*, X.*Cyr.*5.2.6 (v.l. -οῦντο), Alciphr.2.1:—Med., *dine*, Th.4.103, Plu.2.225d. **-ποιΐα**, ἡ, *preparing* or *taking dinner*, D.S.17.37. **-ποιός**, ὁ, *dinner-preparer, caterer*, Arist.*MM* 1206a27.

δεῖπνος, ὁ, late form of δεῖπνον, v.l. in D.S.4.3, Sch.Ar.*Pax* 564.

δειπνοσοφιστής, οῦ, ὁ, *one learned in the mysteries of the kitchen*: in pl., title of work by Athenaeus.

δειπνοσύνη, ἡ, Com. for δεῖπνον, Matro *Conv.*10 (pl.).

δειπνο-φορία, ἡ, *solemn procession with meat-offerings* to Herse, Pandrosos, and Aglauros, Is.*Fr.*151. **-φόρος**, ον, *carrying meals*, of birds, Arist.*HA*616b34, 619b24. II. *carrying meat-offerings*, Lys.*Fr.*311 S., Hyp.*Fr.*88, Plu.*Thes.*23, *IG*3.371.

δεῖρα· δείμοιρα (leg. διμοιρία, cf. δεισιάδα), τράχηλος, διαίρεσις, Hsch.

δειράδιον, τό, Dim. of δειρή I.2, Poll.2.235.

δειράζειν· κλέπτειν, Hsch.

δειραῖος, α, ον, *hilly, craggy*, Lyc.994.

δειράρ· κορυφή, Hsch. (Lacon. = sq.)

δειράς (Cret. **δηράς** *GDI*5024.19), άδος, ἡ, *ridge of a chain of hills*, *h.Ap.*281, S.*Aj.*697 (lyr.), Limen.22; of the isthmus of Corinth, Pi. *O.*8.52, *I.*1.10; of Trachis, S.*Ph.*491: in pl., E.*Ph.*206 (lyr.): metaph., τέγγει δ' ὑπ' ὀφρύσι δειράδας, of the petrified form of Niobe on Mt. Sipylus, which poured tears under the brow of the hill over its *ridges*, S.*Ant.*832 (lyr.). (δερσ-, cf. Skt. *dṛṣad-* 'rock'.)

δειρ-αχθής, ές, *heavy on the neck*, ἅμμα *AP*6.179 (Arch.): **-αγχής** (cf. Hsch.), cj. Brunck, which is dub. l. in *AP*7.473 (Aristodic.).

δειρή, ἡ, Att. **δέρη** A.*Ag.*329,875, etc.; Aeol. **δέρα** Sapph.*Supp.* 23.16 (v. infr.):—*neck, throat*, Il.11.26, etc.; τὰ ἀπὸ τῆς δ. *ornaments*, Hdt.1.51. 2. *collar*, Poll.2.235. II. in pl., *gully, glen*, Pi.*O.* 3.27, 9.59: but in sg., = δειράς, prob. in Hermesian.7.54. (The original form is preserved in Arc. **δερϝά** *BCH*39.55 (Orchom.): Aeol. **δέρρη** is coined by *EM*262.57 as etym. of δέρρις: Hsch. has δέρα· ὑπερβολὴ ὄρους, οἱ δὲ τὰ σιμὰ τῶν ὀρῶν by confusion with δειράς. Κοίλα δέρα, place-name in *Inscr.Olymp.*46.30. Prob. from root of ζέρεθρον, βιβρώσκω.)

δειρητής, ὁ, Elean, = στρουθός, Nic.*Fr.*123.

δειριᾶν· λοιδορεῖσθαι (Lacon.), Hsch.: also **δειρεῖοι**· λοίδοροι (Lacon.), Id., cf. δερίαι.

δειρο-κύπελλον [ῠ], τό, *long-necked cup*, Luc.*Lex.*7. **-παις**, αιδος, ὁ, ἡ, *producing young by the neck*, as weasels were supposed to do, Lyc.843.

δεῖρος, εος, τό, = δειρή, Euph.38 (pl.). II. = δειράς, Hsch.

δειροτομέω, fut. -ήσω, *cut the throat* of a person, σὺ δ' ἄμφω δειροτομήσεις Il.21.89, cf. 555, Od.22.349.

δείρω, v. δέρω.

δείς, δενός, *no one* or *thing*, Alc.76. II. *something*, μὴ μᾶλλον τὸ δὲν ἢ τὸ μηδὲν εἶναι (expld. as = σῶμα, opp. κενόν), Democr.156. (Abstracted from οὐδείς.)

δεῖσα, ἡ, *slime, filth*, *PTeb.*105.27,60, 106.26 (ii B.C.), *BGU*1119. 31 (i B.C.), Suid. II. = ἡ τῶν βοτανῶν συλλογή, *EM*651.48.

δεισαλία, ἡ, = foreg., Thd.*Is.*28.13.

δεισήνωρ, ορος, ὁ, ἡ, *fearing man*, A.*Ag.*154 (lyr.).

δεισία, ἡ, *distribution*, κρεῶν *IG*2^2.1356: cf. **δεισιάδα**· τὴν μοῖραν, οἱ δὲ διμοιρίαν, Hsch.

δεισῐδαιμ-ονέω, *have superstitious fears*, Plb.9.19.1, D.S.12.59, Polystr.9, etc.: rare in good sense, *to be religious*, Zaleuc.ap.Stob. 4.2.19. **-ονία**, ἡ, *fear of the gods, religious feeling*, Plb.6.56.7, Phld.*Herc.*1251.10, *CIG*2737b11 (Aphrodisias), D.S.1.70, etc.; ἡ τῶν θεῶν δ. Id.11.89. 2. in bad sense, *superstition*, Thphr.*Char.* 16, Plb.12.24.5; ἡ πρὸς τὰ ζῷα δ. D.S.1.83; περὶ Δεισιδαιμονίας, title of work by Plu. **-ων**, ον, gen. ονος, (δείδω) *fearing the gods*, 1. in good sense, *pious, religious*, X.*Cyr.*3.3.58, *Ages.*11.8; δ. εἶναι καὶ φροντίζειν τῶν θεῶν Arist.*Pol.*1315a1; φίλος θνητοῖς εἴς τ' ἀθανάτους δ. *IG*14.1683: Comp. -έστερος *Act.Ap.*17.22. 2. in bad sense, *superstitious*, Thphr.*Char.*16, Phld.*Piet.*105; δ. διάθεσις, = δεισιδαιμονία, D.S.1.62: Comp. -έστερος D.L.2.132: Sup. -έστατος Luc. *Pr.Im.*27. Adv. -όνως Aristeas 129, Ph.1.195, Corn.*ND*27.

δεισίθεος, ον, = foreg., Poll.1.21.

δεισιλός· δειλός, Hsch.

δείσοζος, ον, (δεῖσα) *smelling of filth*, *AP*6.305 (Leon.).

δέκᾰ, οἱ, αἱ, τά, indecl., *ten*, Il.2.372, Od.9.160, etc.; οἱ δ. *the Ten*, Isoc.18.6; ἡ τῶν δ. τυραννίς Arist.*Ath.*41.2; also οἱ δ. the *Attic Orators*, Philostr.*VS*2.1.14; τὰ δέκα [ἔτη] ἀφ' ἥβης those who are *ten* years past 20 (the age of military service), X.*HG*3.4.23; δ. ἄνδρες, = Lat. *decemviri*, App.*Hann.*56: compds. (not in early writers, but usu. in Hellenistic Gr.) **δεκᾰ-είς**, *Tab.Heracl.*2.34, Plu. *Num.*3: **-δύο**, *PSI*5.509.10 (iii B.C.), *IG*2^2.1013.31 (ii/i B.C.), Plu. *Cat.Mi.*44, *Act.Ap.*19.7: **-τρεῖς**, D.47.77,81, *BGU*644.5 (i A.D.): **-τέσσᾰρες**, α, Plb.1.36.11, etc.; Delph. **-τέτορες** *SIG*241 *A* 2 (iv B.C.): **-πέντε**, *PRev.Laws* 12.17 (iii B.C., prob.), D.S.2.13 codd.; Thess. **-πέμπε** *IG*9(2).553.13 (Larisa, i B.C.): **-έξ**, *Tab.Heracl.*2.40, *PSI*4. 379.6 (iii B.C.), Lxx *Ge.*46.18, Str.2.5.42: **-επτά**, *PSI*5.509.13 (iii B.C.), v.l. in D.S.12.36, J.*BJ*5.11.4, S.E.*M.*1.114, etc.: **-οκτώ**, *IG* 2.1054.47, Cleonid.*Harm.*2, *Ev.Luc.*13.11: **-εννέα**, *PSI*4.396.12 (iii B.C.), D.S.12.71, Plu.2.932b:—hence **-έννατος**, *nineteenth*, ἡμέρα Lyd.*Ost.*18.

δεκά-βαθμος [κᾰ], ον, *with ten steps*, κρηπίς Ph.Byz.*Mir.*6.2. **-βάμων** [βᾱ], ονος, ὁ, ἡ, *with ten steps* or *intervals*, ἐνδεκάχορδε λύρα, δεκαβάμονα τάξιν ἔχουσα Ion Lyr.3.1. **-βοιος**, ον, (βοῦς) *worth ten oxen*, τὸ δ. a coin attributed to Theseus, Plu.*Thes.*25; δεκάβοιον ἀποτίνειν, from a law of Draco, Poll.2.61. **-γονία**, ἡ, *the tenth generation*, Luc. *Herm.*77. **-γράμμᾰτος**, f.l. for ἑνδεκα-, Ath.10.455b. **-γώνιον**, τό, and **-γωνον**, τό, *decagon*, Hero *Geom.*21.21, *Stereom.*2.63, Ptol. *Alm.*1.10. 2. Adj. δεκάγωνος, ον, ἀριθμοί Theo Sm.p.40 H. **-δακτῠλιαῖος**, ον, = sq., Heliod.ap.Orib.49.7.4. **-δάκτῠλος**, ον, *ten fingers long* or *broad*, βάλανος Hp.*Morb.*3.14, cf. Ath.Mech.16.6. 2. *ten-fingered*, χεῖρες D.C.47.40.

δεκᾰδαρχ-έω, *to be a* δεκάδαρχος, Hsch. s. h. v. **-ης**, ου, ὁ, later form for δεκάδαρχος, = Lat. *decurio*, J.*BJ*2.20.7, Arr.*An*.7. 23.3, *IGRom*.4.1221 (Thyatira), *BGU*81.2 (ii A. D.), *PHamb*.10.1 (ii A. D.). II. -άρχαι, οἱ, with or without θεοί, name of an order of divine beings, Herm. *in Phdr*.p.134 A., Dam.*Pr*.351. **-ία**, ἡ, *government of ten*, v.l. in Isoc.4.110, cf. D.6.22; = Lat. *decemviratus*, D.H.11.27. II. *decuria of cavalry*, Arr.*Tact*.42.1. **-ος**, ὁ, = δεκάρχης, *commander of ten men*, X.*Cyr*.8.1.14, Plb.6.25.2, Arr.*Tact*. 42.1, Lxx*Ex*.18.21,25, *De*.1.15, 1*Ma*.3.55. II. = Lat. *decemvir*, D.H.10.60. III. = τελώνης, Hsch. (Cf. δεκατ-.)

δεκᾰδ-εύς, έως, ὁ, *one of a decury*, X.*Cyr*.2.2.30. II. *chairman of a board of ten*, in acc. sg. δεκαδῆ, *IG*4.748.21 (Troezen). **-ικός**, ή, όν, *of the* δεκάς, Herm. *in Phdr*.p.137 A. Adv. -κῶς Syrian. *in Metaph*.106.15. **-ιστής**, οῦ, ὁ, *one who celebrates the tenth day of the month*, cj. in Thphr.*Char*.27.11, cf. *IG*11(4).1227 (Delos), 2. 1139*b*:—fem. -ίστρια, ibid. **-οῦχος**, ὁ, *one of the ten*, Harp.

δεκά-δραχμος [κᾰ], ον, *at the price of ten drachmae*, Arist.*Oec*.1352^{b} 15, *BGU*1134.7 (i B. C.). II. Subst. δ., ὁ, *taxpayer assessed at ten* δραχμαί, ib.1181i9 (ii A. D.). **-δρομοι**, οἱ, *adults* (i.e. *those who have taken part in ten contests*) (Cret.), Hsch. **-δωρος**, ον, (δῶρον II) *ten palms long* or *broad*, Hes.*Op*.426. **-έτηρος**, ον, (ἔτος) *ten-yearly*: χρόνος δ. a space *of ten years*. Pl.*Lg*.772b codd.:— fem. **-ετηρὶς** πανήγυρις D.C.57.24: more freq. as Subst., *period of ten years*, prob. in Pl. l. c., Vett.Val.252.9, *OGI*722 (Egypt, iv A. D.):— also **-ετηρία**, ἡ, title of Orphic work, Suid. **-ετής**, ές, or **-έτης**, ες, *ten years old*, Hdt.1.114, Hp.*Epid*.1.10. II. *of* or *lasting ten years*, πόλεμος Th.5.25,26 codd., Jul.*Or*.2.74b. (Cf. δεκέτης.)— The statements of Gramm. as to the accentuation of this and similar words are confused, cf. Poll.1.54, *EM*765.21, Choerob. *in Thd*.1.167, 2.385: they were prob. parox. in Attic, oxyt. in the κοινή. **-ετία**, ἡ, *space of ten years*, δεκαετίαν (-έτειαν Pap.) ἄρχειν Arist.*Ath*.3.1, cf. D.H.1.71, Str.15.1.43, Ph.1.531, Plu.*Num*.10.

δεκάζω, *bribe, corrupt*, esp. judges, Isoc.8.50, Aeschin.1.87, Arist. *Ath*.27.5:—Pass., *to be bribed*, Lys.29.12, Plu.*Cat.Mi*.44. II. metaph. in Pass., *to be subject to allurements*, δεδεκασμέναι ἀκοαί Ph. 1.523, cf. Plot.6.8.13; ὑπὸ τῶν ἡδονῶν Porph.*Abst*.4.1. III. δεκάζων· ὁ εἰς δέκατον ἀριθμὸν ἥκων, Hsch.

δεκάκις, Adv. *ten-times*, Il.9.379, etc. 2. *tenfold*, *AP*5.117 (Marc. Arg.); in hyperbole, Men.*Sam*.131.

δεκά-κλῑνος, ον, (κλίνη) *holding ten dinner-couches*, στέγη X.*Oec*. 8.13. II. *ten* κλίναι *long*, κρήνη Arist.*Mir*.834^{b}8. **-κότῠλος**, ον, *holding ten* κοτύλαι, Str.3.2.7. **-κῡμία**, ἡ, (κῦμα) *tenth* (i.e. *overwhelming*) *wave*, Luc.*Merc.Cond*.2. **-λιτρος**, ον, *weighing* or *worth ten* λίτραι, στατήρ Epich.10, Arist.*Fr*.510: as Subst., δεκάλιτρον, τό, *coin worth ten* λίτραι, ὁ μισθὸς δ. Sophr.37, cf. Poll.9. 81. **-λογος**, ου, ἡ, *Decalogue*, Jul.*Gal*.152b. **-μαζος**, ον, *with ten breasts*, of Ephesian Artemis, *Epigr.Gr*.406.10. **-μετρος**, *of ten metrical units*: Subst. -μετρον (sc. κῶλον), τό, *decameter*, Sch.Ar.*Eq*.496, etc. **-μηναῖος**, α, ον, *in the tenth month*, Tz.*H*. 2.192. **-μηνιαῖος**, α, ον, = sq., χρόνος Plu.*Num*.12; βρέφη Alex. Aphr.*Pr*.1.40. **-μηνος**, ον, *ten months old*, σκύλαξ X.*Cyn*.7.6, cf. Theoc.24.1. 2. *in the tenth month*, ἡ αἵρεσις ἐγένετο ἔς τι δ. Hdt. 9.3; τὰ δ. (sc. παιδία) Hp.*Septim*.7; γυνὴ κυεῖ δ. prob. l. in Men. 413; τόκος δ. Arist.*GA*777^{b}14: neut. pl. as Adv., ib.772^{b}9. 3. *consisting of ten months*, ἡ δ. (sc. περίοδος) *Placit*.5.18.1: Subst. δεκάμηνον, τό, *Schwyzer* 195.12 (Delos, ii B. C.), *PRyl*.88.17 (ii A. D.). **-μναῖος** or **-μναιαῖος**, α, ον, = sq., Plb.13.2.3; πετροβόλος throwing a projectile *weighing ten minae*, Ph.*Bel*.51.49. **-μνους**, μνουν, (μνᾶ) *weighing* or *worth ten minae*, Ar.*Pax* 1224,1235; δεκάμνουν, τό, *weight of ten minae*, *IG*2^{2}.1013.55; written δεκάμνων in ib. 11.203*B*99 (Delos, iii B. C.). **-μοιρία**, ἡ, *space of ten degrees* of the zodiac, J.*AJ*3.7.7, Ptol.*Alm*.2.7, Anon.ap.Lyd.*Ost*.p.174 W.:— hence Adj. **-μοιριαῖος**, Heph.Astr.1.1. **-μοιρον**, τό, name of an *ointment*, Orib.ap.Aët.12.62: perh. f.l. for **δεκά-μῠρον**, τό, a similar remedy, Alex.Trall.7.8. **-μυξος**, ον, *with ten wicks*, λύχνος Roussel *Cultes Égyptiens* 235 (Delos, ii B. C.).

δεκάμφορος, ον, *holding ten* ἀμφορεῖς, κρατήρ E.*Cyc*.388; πίθος Sosith.2.8.

δεκᾰναΐα, ἡ, (ναῦς) *squadron of ten ships*, Plb.22.7.4, D.S.14.103, prob. in Str.7.7.6.

δεκανᾶται· ἀσπάζεται, Hsch.; cf. δεικανάω II.

δέκανδρος, ὁ, = Lat. *decemvir*, *OGI*482 (Acmonia):—hence **δεκανδρικός**, ή, όν, = Lat. *decemviralis*, ἀρχή Lyd.*Mag*.1.34.

δεκᾰνία, ἡ, = Lat. *decuria*, Arr.*Tact*.6.1. 2. *measure* or *division* of land, ἀμπέλων δ., δ. Κολπηνή, *IGRom*.4.1675 (Lydia), cf. *PFay*. 156 (ii A. D.), *POxy*.1512 (iv A. D.); also δ. πυροῦ *BGU*894.11. 3. *guard-house of a decuria*, *IGRom*.3.1286 (Arabia), *Princeton Exp. Inscr*.636.

δεκᾰνικός, ή, όν, *of* or *for a* δεκανός I, *PHib*.1.30.13 (iii B. C.), 96.21; δεκανικόν, τό, *tax for maintenance of* δεκανοί, δ. πλοίων *BGU*1.1 (ii/iii A. D.); δ. ἰχθυοθηρευτικῶν *PRyl*.196.6 (ii A. D.). II. *of a* δεκανός II, Paul.Al.*C*.2.

δεκᾰνός, ὁ, = Lat. *decurio*, *IGRom*.1.1046 (Alexandria); *police officer* in Egypt, *PTeb*.27.31 (ii B. C.), *POxy*.387 (i A. D.), etc. II. Astrol., δεκανοί, οἱ, *decans*, thirty-six divinities each of whom presided over ten degrees of the zodiac, Nech.ap.Firm.4.22.2, Herm.ap. Stob.1.21.9, Heph.Astr.1.1, Gal.11.797, *PMag.Par*.1.1203, Leont. *in Arat*.p.569 M., Ps.-Callisth.1.4, etc.

δεκᾰ-ολυμπῑονίκης [νῑ], ου, ὁ, *winner of ten victories at Olympia*, *Sammelb*.5225 (iii A. D.). **-πᾰλαι** [κᾰ], Adv. *a very long time ago*, Com. form of πάλαι (cf. δωδεκάπαλαι), Ar.*Eq*.1154, Philonid.8, Henioch.2.1. **-πεδον**, τό, *distance of ten feet*, *Klio* 16.170 (Delph., ii B. C.). **-πηχῠαῖος**, α, ον, = sq., *Gp*.9.9.10, 15.2.22. **-πηχυς**, υ, *ten cubits long*, Hdt.9.81, Plb.18.16.2, *IG*11.161*D*122 (Delos, iii B. C.), Luc.*Tim*.4. **-πλᾰσιάζω**, *multiply by ten*, Lxx*Ba*.4.28, Ph.1. 462. **-πλάσιος** [πλᾰ], ον, *tenfold*, Hp.*VM*16; δ. τὸ ἔκτεισμα τοῦ ἀδικήματος ἐκτίνειν Pl.*R*.615b: c. gen., *ten times greater than*, Plb.21. 22.15; τὴν δεκαπλασίαν (sc. τιμήν) καταδικάζειν mulct in *ten times the amount*, Lex ap.D.24.105 (dub.); δ. ὑφῃρῆσθαι rob the state of *a tenfold penalty*, D.24.82. Adv. -ως Hp.*VM*6. **-πλᾰσίων**, ον, gen. ονος, = foreg., Sch.Il.2.488, Thd.*Da*.1.20. **-πλεθρος**, ον, *enclosing ten* πλέθρα, προτείχισμα Th.6.102. **-πλευρος**, ον, *ten-sided*, Procl. *in Euc*.p.422 F. **-πληγος**, ἡ, *the ten plagues* of Egypt, *PMag. Par*.1.3037. **-πλοκος**, ον, *folded ten times*, Paul.Aeg.6.65. **-πλόος**, ον, contr. **-πλοῦς**, οῦν, = δεκαπλάσιος, D.24.83; τὸ γνωσθὲν ἀποτίνεται δ. Arist.*Ath*.54.2, cf. Hyp.*Dem.Fr*.7: also in fem. ἀποτεισάτω δεκαπλόαν *IG*5(1).1421.13 (Cyparissia, iv/iii B. C.). **-πολις**, εως, ἡ, *district with ten cities*, *Decapolis*, *Ev.Matt*.4.25, J.*BJ*3.9.7, *IGRom*.3. 1057 (ii A. D.). **-πους**, ὁ, ἡ, -πουν, τό, *ten feet long*, Ar.*Ec*.652; ἄκαινα Call.*Aet.Fr*.7.6 P. **-πρωτεία**, ἡ, *office of* δεκάπρωτοι, *IGRom*. 3.802 (Syllaeum), *POxy*.1204.4 (iii A. D.), etc. **-πρωτεύω**, *serve as member of* δεκάπρωτοι, *JHS*37.108 (Thyatira), *CIG*2929 (Tralles), etc. **-πρωτοι**, οἱ, = Lat. *decemprimi*, the chief municipal authorities of a city, γνώμη στρατηγῶν καὶ δεκαπρώτων *IG*12(7).395.4 (Amorgos), etc.: sg., ib.239.12, *Rev.Phil*.37.311 (Thyatira), *POxy*. 1204.4 (iii A. D.): fem. -πρώτη, ἡ, *PFlor*.76.11 (iii A. D.). II. = Lat. *decemviri*, Lyd.*Mag*.1.34 tit. **-πτῠχος**, ον, *with ten folds*: metaph., *comprised in ten tablets*, Orph.*Fr*.247.21.

δεκ-άρουρος [ᾰ], ον, *of ten arurae*, *PTeb*.5.44 (ii B. C.), *PLond*.3.604 *B*244 (i A. D.). **-άρτᾰβος**, ον, *of ten* ἀρτάβαι, *PRyl*.119.22 (i A. D.).

δεκάρχ-ης, ου, ὁ, = δεκαδάρχης, *decurion*, Hdt.7.81; = Lat. *decurio* (in form **δέκαρχος**), Arr.*Alan*.22, D.C.71.27. II. = Lat. *decemvir*, f.l. in D.H.2.14. **-ία**, ἡ, = δεκαδαρχία, X.*HG*3.4.2, Isoc.4. 110, al.

δεκάς, άδος, ἡ, *company of ten*, Il.2.126, Hdt.3.25; of ships, A. *Pers*.340, etc.: generally, *company*, ἧς καὶ σὺ φαίνει δεκάδος E.*Supp*. 219; *number, tale*, τῶν ἐτέων ἡ δ. οὐκ ὀλίγη Call.*Fr*.489; ἡ Ἀττικὴ δ., the *ten* Attic *Orators*, Luc.*Scyth*.10. 2. Λύκου δ. *the company* of Lycus, a name given to bribed dicasts at Athens, because the bribers were to be found near the statue of Lycus in the law-courts, Eratosth.ap.Harp. s. v. II. the number *ten*, περὶ τῆς δ., title of work by Archytas, cf. Philol.11, Arist.*Metaph*.1084^{a}12; τέλειον ἡ δ., Pythag., ib.986^{a}8, cf. *Fr*.203. III. = δεκάτη I, Hsch. s. v. δεκατευταί.

δεκά-σημος [κᾰ], ον, *of ten time-units* in Music, Aristid.Quint.1. 14. **-σκαλμος** ναῦς *with ten banks of oars*, Suid.

δεκασμός, ὁ, (δεκάζω) *bribery*, D.H.7.64, Plu.*Cat.Mi*.44: in pl., Id.*Cic*.29.

δεκά-σπορος χρόνος, ὁ, lapse *of ten seed-times*, i.e. *ten years*, E.*Tr*. 20, cf. *El*.1154. **-στᾰδιαῖος**, α, ον, *ten stadia high*, Theo Sm. p.125 H., al. **-στάδιον** [στᾰ], τό, *race-course of ten stadia*, *IG*4.951. 79 (Epid.), Herzog *Koische Forschungen* p.55. **-στάτηρος** [στᾰ], ον, *in receipt of ten staters*, Arr.*An*.7.23.3: Subst. -στάτηρον, τό, *sum of ten staters*, *Leg.Gort*.9.49, *Schwyzer* 179*a*5 (Crete); *weight of ten staters*, *IG*1^{2}.918. **-στεγος**, ον, *ten stories high*, πύργος Str.15. 3.7, Ath.Mech.11.8. **-στῐχος**, ον, *containing ten lines*, βίβλος Sch.Il.4.101. **-στῠλος**, ον, *with ten columns in front*, Vitr.3.2. 8. **-σχημος**, ον, *with ten forms*, of certain verses, Ps.-Plu.*Metr*. p.471 B.

δεκᾰταῖος, α, ον, *for ten days*, δ. τῶν νεκρῶν διεφθαρμένων Pl.*R*. 614b. II. *ten days old*, δεκαταίου δ' ἤδη ὄντος τοῦ ᾠοῦ Arist.*HA* 561^{a}26; βρέφος Luc.*Halc*.5.

δεκᾰτάλαντ-ία, ἡ, *sum of ten talents*, Poll.9.52. **-ος**, ον, *weighing* or *worth ten talents*, λίθος Ar.*Fr*.276; δίκη δ. an action *in which the damages were laid at ten talents*, Aeschin.2.99.

δεκᾰτάρχ-ης, ου, ὁ, = δεκάταρχος, Lat. *decurio*, in the Roman fleet, *IG*5(1).818.5 (Sparta, iii A. D.), *Supp.Epigr*.1.345 (Paros, i A. D.). **-ία**, ἡ (for δεκαδαρχία), *group of ten*, e.g. cultivators, Wilcken *Chr*.304 (iii B. C.). **-ος**, ὁ, *head of a* δεκαταρχία, *PSI* 4.337.4 (iii B. C.); τῶν λατόμων *PPetr*.2 p.6; v.l. for δεκαδάρχης, Lxx 1*Ma*.3.55.

δεκᾰτεία, ἡ, = δεκάτευσις, Plu.*Ant*.39.

δεκᾰτέσσᾰρες, α, v. δέκα.

δεκάτ-ευμα [κᾰ], ατος, τό, *tenth, tithe*, Call.*Ep*.40 (pl.). **-ευσις**, εως, ἡ, *decimation*, D.H.1.24. **-ευτήριον**, τό, *office for collection of* δεκάτη, *custom-house*, X.*HG*1.1.22. **-ευτής**, οῦ, ὁ, *tithe-farmer*, Harp. **-εύω**, *exact tithe from*, τινά D.22.77; τὰς πόλεις Jusj.ap. Lycurg.81; τούτους δεκατεῦσαι τῷ ἐν Δελφοῖσι θεῷ *make* them *pay a tithe* to Apollo, Hdt.7.132; of things, δ. τὰ ἐξ ἀγροῦ ὡραῖα *tithe* them (as an offering).., X.*An*.5.3.9; δ. τοὺς Θηβαίους τοῖς θεοῖς Plb.9.39. 5:—Pass., ἀναγκαίως ἔχει [τὰ χρήματα] δεκατευθῆναι τῷ Διί Hdt.1. 89; ἐλπὶς ἦν δεκατευθῆναι τὰς Θήβας, i.e. *that it would be taken and tithed*, X.*HG*6.3.20, 5.35. 2. abs., *to be a* δεκατευτής, Ar.*Fr*. 455. II. in war, *take out the tenth man for execution, decimate*, D.C.48.42, etc. 2. *divide into ten sections*, τινάς App.*BC*1.49. III. = ἀρκτεύω, Lys.*Fr*.250 S., D.ap.Harp. IV. metaph. in Astrol., *to be superior to*, Man.6.279.

δεκάτη, ἡ, v. δέκατος.

δεκᾰτη-λογία, ἡ, *collection of tithe*, Poll.1.169. **-λόγιον**, τό, =

δεκατευτήριον, Id.9.28. **-λόγος**, ὁ, (λέγω) = δεκατευτής, D.23.177. **-μοιρία**, ἡ, *tenth part*, Just.*Edict*.7.5. **-μόριον**, τό, (μέρος) *tenth part*, Pl.*Lg*.924a. **-φόρος**, ον, *tithe-paying*, ἀπαρχαί Call.*Del*.278. II. *receiving tithe*, epith. of Apollo at Megara, Paus. 1.42.5: Dor. **δεκατᾱφόρος** *GDI*5045 (Crete), etc.

δεκᾰτ-ισμός, ὁ, *formation of decuriae*, Them.*Or*.5.65d. **-ισταί**, οἱ, perh. = δεκαδισταί, *BCH*24.367 (Bithyn.).

δεκᾰτοκύριοι [ῡ], οἱ, prob. = δεκάταρχοι, *PPetr*.2 p.33.

δέκᾰτος (Arc. **δέκοτος** *IG*5(2).282 (Mantinea, v B.C.), also Aeol. in *Epigr.Gr*.988.5 (Balbilla)), η, ον: (δέκα):—*tenth*, Ἠώς Il.6.175, etc.; as a round number, Od.16.18, etc. II. **δεκάτη** (sc. μερίς), ἡ, *tenth part, tithe*, τᾶς δεκάτας δεκάταν Simon.141.4, cf. Hdt.2.135, etc.; τῇ θεῷ τὰς δ. ἐξαιρεθῆναι Lys.20.24; τὰ ἐκ τῆς δ. the produce *of the tenth*, *IG*1².91, cf. *Tab.Defix*.99.14: esp. as a customs-duty, D.20.60; δεκάτη μόσχων *PTeb*.307.8 (iii A.D.). 2. δεκάτη (sc. ἡμέρα), ἡ, *the tenth day*, Od.9.83, al. b. δ. προτέρα· ἡ πρὸ εἰκάδος, ὡς ὑστέρα· ἡ μετ' εἰκάδα, Hsch. 3. *festival on the tenth day after birth*, when the child has a name given it, τὴν δ. θύειν *to give a naming-day* feast, Ar.*Av*.922, cf. 494; δ. ὑπέρ τινος ἑστιᾶσαι D.40.28, cf. 39.22. 4. δεκάτα· τάξις, ἄθροισμα, καὶ ἡ τῶν εἴκοσιν ἁρμάτων τάξις, Hsch. 5. δέκατον, τό, *tenth part*, Lxx *Le*.23.13,17 (pl.).

δεκᾰτόσπορος, ον, *in the tenth generation*, Epigr.ap.Str.10.3.2.

δεκᾰτόω, *take tithe of* a person, τινά *Ep.Hebr*.7.6:—Pass., *pay tithe*, ib.9.

δεκα-τρεῖς, **-τρια**, v. sub δέκα.

δεκᾰτ-ώνης, ου, ὁ, *tithe-farmer*, Anaxil.8. **-ώνιον**, τό, *office of the* δεκατῶναι, Antiph.27.

δεκά-φυιος [κᾰ], ον, (φυή) *tenfold*, Call.*Fr*.162. **-φῡλος**, ον, *consisting of ten tribes*, Hdt.5.66. **-χαλκον**, τό, *coin worth ten* χαλκοῖ, = Lat. *denarius* (*worth ten asses*), Plu.*Cam*.13. **-χειλε**· πρὸς ἀποδοχὴν ἐπιτήδειον, Hsch. **-χειλοι**· δεκα(κι)σχίλιοι, Id.; cf. δεκάχιλοι.

δεκᾰχῆ, Adv. *in ten parts*, D.C.55.24, prob. in Hdt.5.69: Att. **δεκᾰχᾷ** *IG*2².1.34.

δεκά-χῑλοι [κᾰ], αι, α, *ten thousand*, Il.5.860, 14.148; cf. ἐννεάχιλοι. (Aristarch. read the true Ion. form -χειλοι (from *g̑hezl-*) which he mistranslated "ἐννέα χείλη ἔχοντες", Sch.T.Il.14.148.) **-χοια**· δεκαπλαῖ, Hsch. **-χορδος**, ον, *ten-stringed*, λύρα Ion Lyr.3 (fort. ἐνδεκάχορδος), Lxx *Ps*.32(33).2, al.

δεκάω, dub. l. et sens., *Ath.Mitt*.18.225 (Attica, viii B.C.(?)).

Δεκέλεια, Ion. -έη, ἡ, a place in Attica, Hdt., etc.:—**Δεκελεύς**, έως, ὁ, *a Decelean*, Hdt.9.73; but **Δεκελειεύς** Inscrr. Att., as *IG*2.660, al.; **-εεύς** ib.2.1247, al.: Adj. **Δεκελεικός**, ή, όν, *Decelean*, ὁ Δ. πόλεμος, name given to the latter part of the Pelop. war, Isoc.8.37, etc. Advbs. **Δεκελεῆθεν** *from D.*, Hdt. l. c.; **-ειόθεν** Lys.23.2: **Δεκελειᾶσιν** *at D.*, Isoc.8.84: **-είαζε** *to D.*, St.Byz.

δεκ-έμβολος, ον, *with ten beaks*, ναῦς A.*Fr*.133. **-ετηρικός** (sc. λόγος), *for the Decennalia* of an Emperor, Them.*Or*.11 tit. **-ετηρίς**, ίδος, ἡ, *space of ten years*, D.C.53.16 (pl.); = Lat. *Decennalia*, *BGU*362 iii 24 (iii A.D.). **-έτηρος**, ον, = sq., *AP*9.474. **-έτης**, ου, ὁ, *lasting ten years*, χρόνος S.*Ph*.715 (lyr.), Pl.*Lg*.682d; δεκέτεις ἀλάλημτο *for a space of ten years*, E.*Andr*.306 (lyr.): fem. δεκέτις, ιδος, παιδοποιΐα Pl.*Lg*.784b; προστασία D.C.56.28. II. *ten years old*, fem. δεκέτις Ar.*Lys*.644.

δεκήρης, ες, *with ten banks of oars*, ναῦς Plb.16.3.3, Plu.*Ant*.64.

δέκομαι, v. δέχομαι. **δέκοτος**, v. δέκατος.

δεκ-τέος, α, ον, (δέχομαι) *to be received*, Luc.*Herm*.74. II. **δεκτέον**, *one must take* or *understand*, Str.10.2.22, Sch.Th.*Oxy*.853 vii 9. **-τή**· χλαῖνα, χλανίς, Hsch. **-τήρ**, ῆρος, ὁ, title of an official *receiver*, *IG*5(2).274 (Mantinea, ii/i B.C.), cf. Hsch., Suid. **-της**, ου, ὁ, (δέχομαι) *receiver, beggar*, Od.4.248. **-τικός**, ή, όν, *fit for receiving*, τὸ τῆς τροφῆς δ. *the part that receives* the food (sc. ἡ κοιλία), Arist.*Pol*.1290ᵇ27, cf. *HA*489ᵃ3; αἰσθητήριον δ. τῶν αἰσθητῶν Id.*PA*647ᵃ7; [τοῦ εἴδους] Id.*Metaph*.1023ᵃ12: Comp., Id.*Pr*.966ᵃ12. 2. *capable of*, ἐπιστήμης Pl.*Def*.415a; ἐναντιώσεως Arist.*GC*320ᵃ4; τῆς ἕξεως Id.*Cat*.12ᵃ30; διατάξεως Porph.*Abst*.1.7; παθημάτων Hierocl.*in CA*24 p.470M.; θυμοῦ Phld.*Ir*.p.87W.; πόνων Demetr.Lac.*Herc*.1012.45F., cf. Phld.*D*.1.2. 3. abs., *capable of receiving, recipient*, Arist. *de An*.414ᵃ10, *Ph*.249ᵃ2. **-το**, v. δέχομαι. **-τός**, ή, όν, *to be received* or *accepted, acceptable*, Lxx *Is*.61.2, al., *Ev.Luc*.4.24; δεκτόν [ἐστι] it is *an accepted principle*, c. inf., Erot.*Praef*. 2. *to be grasped*, χείρ Iamb.*Protr*.21.ιθ'. II. *to be taken, understood*, Phld.*Rh*.2.269S. **-τρια**, ἡ, fem. of δεκτήρ, Archil.19, *AP*11.400 (Luc.). **-τωρ**, ορος, ὁ, *one who takes upon himself* or *on his own head*, αἵματος δ. νέου A.*Eu*.204.

δεκῠρεύω, *to be a decurio*, *IG*14.575 (Centuripa).

δεκώβολον, τό, *sum of ten obols*, *IG*2.837.23.

δέκων· ὁ δεκαζόμενος, Hsch.

δεκώρῠγος, ον, (ὀργυιά) *ten fathoms long*, X.*Cyn*.2.5.

δελαστρεύς, έως, ὁ, *using bait*, ἰχθυβολῆες Nic.*Th*.793.

δελε-άζω, (δέλεαρ) *entice* or *catch by a bait*, τὴν γραῦν δ. λεπαστῇ Antiph.45, cf. Hdn.2.15.3; δ. τινὰς ἐπὶ πλεονεξίαν Onos.6.10:—Pass., γαστρὶ δελεάζεσθαι X.*Mem*.2.1.4, cf. Isoc.8.34, Epicur.*Sent. Vat*.16, Phld.*Lib* p.14O.; ῥᾳστώνῃ καὶ σχολῇ D.18.45; ὑπὸ χρημάτων, ὑπὸ τῆς ἡδονῆς, Luc.*Apol*.9, Jul.*Or*.6.185a. II. c. acc. cogn., νῶτον ὑὸς περὶ ἄγκιστρον δ. *put* it on the hook *as a bait*, Hdt.2.70; but δ. ἄγκιστρον ἰσχάδι *bait* it with a fig, Luc.*Pisc*.47; δ. ἄγκιστρον ἐπ' ἄλλους to catch others, ib.48. **-ᾱμα**, ατος, τό, = sq., Anon.ap.Suid. s.v. ἔγκειται (fort. δελέασμα). **-αρ**, ατος, τό, Ep. **δεῖλαρ** (q.v.); Ep. gen. δελείατος Numen.ap.Ath.7.305a; dat. pl. δελέασσιν Opp.*H*.3.437: contr. in dat. δέλητι Hsch.; neut. pl. δέλητα cj. in Theoc.21.10:—*bait*, X.*Mem*.2.1.4, Plb.15.21.6 (pl.): metaph., δ. τινος *bait* for a person, E.*Andr*.264, cf. *Fr*.981.5, Luc.*Rh.Pr*.25 (pl.), etc.; τιμαὶ γάρ, ἆθλα, δ. ἃ ὁ θεὸς ἔδωκεν ἀνθρώποις Antipho Soph.49: c. gen. rei, *an incitement to* .., ἡδονὴ κακοῦ δέλεαρ Pl.*Ti*.69d, cf. J.*Ap*.2.39; δ. σοφίης *Epigr.Gr*.880.6 (Cyzicus). **-άρπαξ**, αγος, ὁ, ἡ, *snapping at the bait*, πέρκη *AP*7.504.3 (Leon.). **-ασμα**, ατος, τό, = δελέαμα, δέλεαρ, Ar.*Eq*.789. **-ασμάτιον**, τό, Dim. of foreg., Philox.2.5. **-ασμός**, ὁ, *catching with a bait*, Arist.*HA*535ᵃ7 (pl.); *enticement, allurement*, τινός A.D.*Pron*.41.1. **-άστρα**, ἡ, *baited trap* or *noose*, Cratin.216. **-αστρον**, τό, = foreg., Nicopho4. **-τρον**, τό, = δέλεαρ, Numen.ap.Ath.7.287c, 306c, Opp.*H*.2.431, 3.185. 2. *torch*, Timach.ap.Ath.15.699e, Hsch.

δελήτιον, τό, Dim. of δέλεαρ, Sophr.118 (= [S.]*Fr*.1124).

δελία· δάφνη, Hsch. **δέλιχρα**· τὰ ἡμίχοιρα, Id.

δελκανός, ὁ, a kind of *fish*, Euthyd.ap.Ath.3.118b.

δέλλει· καλεῖ, Hsch. (leg. βάλλει).

δελλίθιον [λῐ], τό, *the nest of the* δέλλις, Hsch.

δέλλῑς (A), ῑθος, ἡ, kind of *wasp*, Hdn.Gr.1.89, Hsch.

δέλλις (B), acc. δέλλιν, = δέλφαξ, *Annuario* 3.144 (Pisidia).

Δελματία, Δελματ-ική, -ίκιον, -ιον, v. Δαλμ-.

δέλος, εος, τό, = δέλεαρ, Eust.235.7: gen. pl. δελέων *PMag.Par*. 1.939.

δέλτα, τό, indecl., *the letter* δέλτα: gen. δέλτατος Democr.20. (Hebr. *dāleth* 'door'.) II. *anything shaped like a* Δ, esp. *island formed by the mouths of a large river*, as the Nile, Hdt.2.13, etc.; of the Indus, Str.15.1.33, Arr.*An*.5.4.1, etc. 2. adverbially, δ. παρατετιλμέναι Ar.*Lys*.151. III. = δελτωτόν, Ptol.*Tetr*.27.

δελτάριον, τό, Dim. of δέλτος, Plb.29.27.2, Plu.*Cat.Mi*.24. II. a surgical instrument, *Hermes* 38.284.

δελτίον, τό, Dim. of δέλτος, Hdt.7.239, *PLond*.5.1674 (vi A.D.).

δελτο-γράφημα [γρᾰ], ατος, τό, *official rescript*, τοῦ ἀνθυπάτου *OGI* 458.62 (i B.C./i A.D.). **-γράφος** [ᾰ], ον, *writing on a tablet, recording*, δελτογράφῳ δὲ πάντ' ἐπωπᾷ φρενί A.*Eu*.275. **-ειδής**, ές, *delta-shaped, triangular*, Hsch. s.v. καρχήσιον; of the *deltoid* muscle, Gal.2.354. Adv. -δῶς Ruf.*Oss*.10. **-ομαι**, Med., *note down on tablets for oneself*, τἄμ' ἔπη δελτουμένας A.*Supp*.179. **-ποιός**, *tabellarius*, Gloss.

δέλτος (A)· ἀγαθός, Phot.

δέλτος (B) (Cypr. **δάλτος** *Inscr.Cypr*.135.26H.), ἡ, *writing-tablet*, Batr.3 (pl.), Hdt.8.135, etc.; ἐν .. δέλτου πτυχαῖς γράψας E.*IA*98; χαλκῆς .. δύσνιπτον ἐκ δέλτου γραφήν S.*Tr*.683; δέλτον ἐγγεγραμμένην ξυνθήματα inscribed with .., ib.157; δέλτον ἀναθεῖναι *IG*12(2).58*b*17 (Mytilene): esp. pl., E.*IA*116,798 (both lyr.); πινάκων ξεστῶν δέλτοι Ar.*Th*.778: metaph., ἣν ἐγγράφου σὺ μνήμοσιν δέλτοις φρενῶν on *the tablets* of the heart, A.*Pr*.789; θὲς (cj. for σὲ δ') ἐν φρενὸς δέλτοισι τοὺς ἐμοὺς λόγους S.*Fr*.597. II. any *writing*: *letter*, Pl.*Ep*.312d; *will*, Luc.*Tim*.22, etc.; δέλτον χαλκῆν ἐκσφραγισθεῖσαν *BGU*265.21 (ii A.D.), cf. 780.15, 1032.3; Ὁμήρου δέλτον *the books* of Homer, *IG*9(1).880.10 (Corc.), cf. *AP*12.2 (Strato); αἱ δώδεκα δ. the Twelve *Tables*, D.H.2.27.

δελτωτός, ή, όν, *in the shape of the letter* Δ: τὸ δ. *the constellation Triangle*, Arat.235, Eratosth.*Cat*.20 tit.

δελφάκ-ειος [ᾰ], ον, *of a* δέλφαξ, πλευρὰ δ. ribs *of pork*, Pherecr.108.16, cf. Alex.124.2; ζωμός Dieuch.ap.Orib.4.6.1. **-ίνη** [ῑ], ἡ, = δέλφαξ, Epich.124.2. **-ιον**, τό, Dim. of δέλφαξ, *sucking-pig*, Ar.*Th*.237, *Lys*.1061, Aeschin.Socr.4, *BGU*949.8 (iii/iv A.D.), etc. II. *pudenda muliebria*, Hsch. **-ίς**, ίδος, ἡ, = foreg. 1, *Ostr*.1031 (i A.D.), *PGiss*.49.17 (iii A.D.). **-όομαι**, Pass., *grow up to pighood*, Ar.*Ach*.786.

δέλφαξ, ᾰκος, ἡ (cf. Ath.9.375a, ὁ, Epich.100.4, Sopat.5, Pl.Com.110), Hippon.70 B, Hdt.2.70, Ar.*Fr*.506.4, Eup.281, Theopomp.Com.48, Arist.*HA*573ᵇ13:—*pig*, ll. cc., etc.; full-grown, opp. χοῖρος, Ar. Byz ap.Ath. l. c.; sacrificed to Persephone, *IG*3.77.7.

Δελφίδιος, Dor., = Δελφίνιος, *SIG*712.13 (Cnossus).

δελφίν, ῖνος, ὁ, later form of δελφίς (q. v.).

δελφῑν-άριον, τό, *small dolphin*, Hero *Aut*.27.2. **-ιάς**, άδος, ἡ, = δελφίνιον II, Ps.-Dsc.3.73. **-ίζω**, *duck like a dolphin*, τὸ κάρα Luc.*Lex*.5. **-ιον** [φῖ], τό, *temple of Apollo Delphinios*, esp. at Athens, τὸ ἐπὶ Δελφινίῳ δικαστήριον the law-court *there*, Decr.ap.And.1.78, Arist.*Ath*.57.3, Plu.*Thes*.12.18, etc.: also at Chalcis, etc., Id.*Flam*.16, etc. II. *larkspur, Delphinium Ajacis*, Ps.-Dsc.3.73, *Gp*.20.2.2. b. *dolphin-flower, Delphinium Consolida*, Ps.-Dsc. l. c.

Δελφίνιος [φῖ], ὁ, epith. of Apollo, *h.Ap*.495, *SIG*57.11 (Milet., v B.C.), *IG*12(3).537 (Thera), Plu.2.984a, etc. II. (sc. μήν), name of month at Thera, Aegina, etc., *Test.Epict*.2.31, Sch.Pi.*N*.5.81, etc. 2. = δελφίνιον II, Hsch. III. Δελφίνια, τά, *festival of Apollo D.*, Sch.Pi.*O*.13.155, etc.

δελφῑνίς, ίδος, ἡ, τράπεζα, prob. *with dolphins for a base*, Luc.*Lex*.7.

δελφῑνίσκος, ὁ, Dim. of δελφίς, Arist.*HA*631ᵃ17.

δελφῑνο-ειδής, ές, *like a dolphin*, φυλλάρια Ps.-Dsc.3.73. **-σημος**, ον, *bearing a dolphin as a device*, Lyc.658. **-φόρος**, ον, *bearing dolphins*, A.*Fr*.150. II. *carrying* δελφῖνες II, κεραῖαι Th.7.41, cf. Pherecr.12.

δέλφιξ, ῖκος, ὁ, *tripod*, δέλφικας ἀργυροῦς Plu.*TG*2 (prob. for δελφῖνας); δέλφικα· τὸν τρίποδα *EM*255.10.

δελφίς (later **δελφίν**, Mosch.3.37 (dub.l.), Man.5.157), ῖνος, ὁ:—

dolphin, Il.21.22, Od.12.96, Archil.74.7, Pi.*P*.2.51, Hdt.1.24, Arist.*HA*489^{b}2, Opp.*H*.1.648, etc.; as an ornament, *IG*2.678^{B}37; cf. βελφίν. II. *mass of lead shaped like a dolphin*, hung at the yard-arm, and let down on the decks of the enemy's ships, τοὺς δ. μετεωρίζου Ar.*Eq*.762, cf. Sch. ad loc.; δ. κεροῦχος Pherecr.12. 2. = κερκέτης, Paus.Gr.*Fr*.118, Opp.*H*.3.290. 3. *stops* in a machine, Orib.48.4.44. III. *the constellation Dolphin*, Democr.14, Arist.*Mete*.345^{b}22, Arat.316, Eratosth.*Cat*.31 tit., etc.

Δελφοί, ῶν, οἱ, *Delphi*, Δελφῶν ἐς πίονα δῆμον *h.Hom*.27.14, cf. S.*OT*734; Δελφοῖς *at Delphi*, Th.1.143: also **Δαλφοί** *Schwyzer* 324.13, **Δερφοί** *Delph*.3(2).238, **Δολφοί** *GDI*3607.5; Aeol. **Βέλφοι** *EM* 200.27; Boeot. **Βελφός, Βελφίς**, etc., *IG*7.2385,619, etc. II. *the Delphians*, Hdt.1.54, etc.: sg., Δελφός, pr.n. of king of Delphi, A.*Eu*.16; Δ. ἀνήρ E.*Andr*.1151, etc.: fem. **Δελφίς** S.*OT*464 (lyr.), etc.; Δελφίς, ίδος, ἡ, *territory of Delphi*, *SIG*534.16 (Delph., iii B.C.); Δελφίδες (sc. δραχμαί) *Schwyzer* 322 (Delph., v/iv B.C.):—Adj. **Δελφικός**, ή, όν, *Delphic, Delphian*, S.*OC*413, Pl.*Lg*.686a, etc.; **Δέλφιος** is dub. in Call.*Aet*.3.1.20.

δέλφος, ους, τό, *pig*, dub. in *SIG*1039.15.

δελφύς, ύος, ἡ, *womb*, Hp.*Steril*.222, Arist.*HA*510^{b}13, Ath.9.375a:—Dor. **δελφύα**, ἡ, acc. to Greg.Cor.p.344S.

δέμα, ατος, τό, (δέω A) *band*, Plb.6.33.11; = σχοινίον, Hsch. II. Archit., *clamp, dowel*, *IG*7.3073.70 (Lebad.). III. *tow-rope*, Ph.*Bel*.73.24.

δέμας, τό, (δέμω) *bodily frame*, usu. of man, Hom. (v. infr.); rarely of other animals, Od.10.240, Pi.*O*.1.20; prop. *the living body*, but also of a corpse, νεκρὸν δ. Batr.106, cf. S.*Ant*.205, E.*Or*.40,1066, Sch.Ven.Il.1.115.—Hom. uses it only in acc. sg., usu. abs., μικρὸς δ. small *in stature*, Il.5.801; ἄριστος εἶδός τε δ. τε Od.8.116; δέμας εἴκυῖα θεῇσιν Il.8.305; δέμας ἀθανάτοισιν ὁμοῖος Od.8.14; οὐ..ἐστι χερείων οὐ δέμας οὐδὲ φυήν Il.1.115, cf. Od.5.212; δέμας καὶ εἶδος ἀγητός Il.24.376, cf. Od.18.251; χαρίεσσα δέμας Hes.*Th*.260; Κλύμενον ..ἀμώμητον δ. B.5.147: nom. in later poets, as S.*OC*110,501, etc.: dat. δέμαϊ Pi.*Pae*.6.80. 2. in Lyr. and Trag. as a periphrasis, Ἀστερίας δ., the island of Delos, ib.5.42; κτανεῖν μητρῷον δ. A.*Eu*.84; οἰκετῶν δ. S.*Tr*.908; Ἡράκλειον δ. E.*HF*1037 (lyr.); οἰνάνθης δ., i.e. the vine-*shoot*, S.*Fr*.255.4; ἀστερωπὸν οὐρανοῦ δ. v.l. in Critias 25.33 D.; Δάματρος ἀκτᾶς..δ., i.e. bread, E.*Hipp*.138: in later Ep., ὕλης δ. Orph.*L*.238. 3. Com., = πόσθη, Pl.Com.173.10. II. as Adv., δέμας πυρὸς αἰθομένοιο *in form* or *fashion like* burning fire, Il.11.596, cf. 17.366.

δεμάτιον, τό, Dim. of δέμα, *Hippiatr*.22, Sch.Theoc.4.18.

Δέματρος, ὁ (sc. μήν), month at Halos, *IG*9(2).109^{B}47.

δέμει· ὁδός, Hsch.

δεμελέας, τάς, acc. pl., *leeches*, *IG*4.951.98 (Epid.); cf. **δεμβλεῖς**· βδέλλαι, Hsch. (Nom. sg. unknown.)

δέμνιον, τό, (δέμω) mostly in pl. δέμνια, *bedstead, mattress*, Il.24.644, Od.4.297, etc. 2. generally, *bed*, freq. in pl., Od.6.20, 8.282, S.*Tr*.901,915: also in sg., Pi.*N*.1.3, E.*Or*.229, *Alc*.183 (δεμνίων 186), Call.*Del*.248.

δεμνιοτήρης, ες, *keeping one to one's bed*: μοῖρα δ. *a lingering* fate, A.*Ag*.1449 (lyr.); δ. πόνος ὀρταλίχων ib.53 (anap.).

δέμω, rare in pres. and impf., Ep. impf. δέμον Od.23.192, part. δέμων *h.Merc*.87: aor. ἔδειμα Il.21.446, Hdt.2.124, Ep. δεῖμα A.R.3.37, subj. δείμομεν for δείμωμεν Il.7.337:—**Med.**, aor. (v. infr.):—**Pass.**, pf. δέδμημαι 6.249, etc., Dor. 3 pl. δέδμανθ' Theoc.15.120: plpf. ἐδέδμητο Hdt.7.59,176:—*build*, τεῖχος ἔδειμαν Il.7.436, etc.; τείχη παλαιὰ δείμας E.*Rh*.232:—Med., ἐδείματο οἴκους he *built him* houses, Od.6.9; ἄστη Pl.*Ax*.370b. 2. generally, *construct, prepare*, δ. ἀλωήν *h.Merc*.87; δ. ὁδόν, Lat. *munire viam*, Hdt.2.124:—Pass., ἁμαξιτὸς δέδμηται Id.7.200: metaph. of persons, δέδμηνται πάσῃ κόσμος Ἰαονίῃ Haussoullier *Milet* p.141.

δεμώ· χρόνος, Hsch. **δέν**, v. δείς.

δενδαλίς, ίδος, ὁ, a kind of *barley-cake*, Nicopho 15, Eratosth.10; cf. δανδαλίς.

δενδίλλω, *turn the eyes* or *glance quickly*, πόλλ' ἐπέτελλε..δενδίλλων ἐς ἕκαστον Il.9.180; ὀξέα δενδίλλων A.R.3.281.—Ep. word, also S.*Fr*.1039.

δενδρ-αῖος, α, ον, *produced by trees*, ἐέρση *tree*-honey, Nonn.*D*.26.198. **-άς**, άδος, ἡ, *wooded*, λόχμη ib.13.399; χαίτη ib.11.514. **-ειος**, α, ον, = δενδρικός, prob. in Str.15.1.60, cf. Nonn.*D*.12.57.

δενδρεόθρεπτος, ον, *nourishing trees*, ῥεύματα Emp.111.8.

δένδρεον, δένδρον, and **δένδος**, τό (late δένδρος, ὁ, Ath.Med.ap. Orib.*inc*.7.4), δένδρεον always in Ep. (δενδρέῳ, δενδρέων, disyll., Il.3.152, Od.19.520), also Ion., Hdt.4.22, and Dor., *IG*4.951.90 (Epid., iii B.C.); Aeol. **δένδριον** Theoc.29.12; later Ep. **δένδρειον**, τό, Arat.1008, Nic.*Th*.832: δένδρος, τό, nom., *IG*14.1934i3; acc., Hdt.6.79; gen. δένδρεος *IG*4.951.91, δένδρους Meno *Iatr*.32.53; dat. δένδρει, Ion. -εϊ Hp.*Nat.Puer*.26, Meno *Iatr*.33.4, Arr.*Ind*.7.11: nom. pl. δένδρη E.*Fr*.484.5, Pherecr.130.9, *IG*4.951.121, *PHal*.1.99 (iii B.C.), Ant.Lib.31.5; dat. pl. δένδρεσι Hdt.2.138, Hp.*Nat.Puer*.26 (and so usu. in Att. Prose, as Th.2.75, Pl.*Lg*.625b, cf. Moer.131, and later, as *BCH*12.27 (Mylasa), Str.2.1.14), late δενδράσι v.l. in J.*BJ*6.1.1: indeterminate forms, nom. pl. δένδρεα Hecat.292(a) J., Hdt.1.17, al., E.*Ba*.563 (lyr.); gen. δενδρέων Hdt.1.202, al., *Tab.Heracl*.1.129, al.: δένδρον, τό, first in Hdt.1.193, 3.107, regul. in Att., Lys.7.28, etc., and later Gr. (exc. in dat. pl., v. supr.), cf. Ael.Dion.*Fr*.119:—*tree*: δένδρον ἐλάας an olive-*tree*, Ar.*Av*.617; δ. ἄρκτου, = ἀκτῆ, Ps.-Dsc.4.173; δένδρα *fruit-* or *mast-bearing trees*, opp. ὕλη, timber, Th.4.69; δ. ἥμερα καὶ ἄγρια Hdt.8.115; δένδρα *tall plants*, Id.1.193 (so of rattan, Thphr.*HP*5.4.7; mustard, *Ev.Matt*.13.32); αὖον δ. *stick*, Call.*Fr*.49.

δενδρ-ήεις, εσσα, εν, *wooded*, νῆσος, ἄλσος, Od.1.51, 9.200; ἀλωαί Theoc.25.30; νῆσος Jul.*Mis*.352a. 2. *with tree-like markings*, ἀχάτης Orph.*L*.236. II. = δενδρικός, *of* or *for a tree*, πόθος Opp.*H*.4.270. **-ιακός**, ή, όν, = δενδρικός, *AP*6.22 (Zon.). **-ίζω**, *to be like a tree*, δενδρίζον κουράλιον Dsc.5.122. **-ικός**, ή, όν, *of a tree*, σπέρματα Thphr.*CP*5.18.1; καρπός Heph.Astr.1.22. II. *wooded*, ἄρουρα *BGU*328 i 17 (ii A.D.); ἐδάφη *Stud.Pal*.20.65.13 (ii A.D.). **-ινος**, η, ον, = foreg., *Gloss*. **-ίον**, τό, Dim. of δένδρον, Agathocl.6. II. Aeol. form of δένδρεον, prob. in Alc.44, Theoc.29.12. **-ίτης** [ῑ], ου, ὁ, *of a tree*, καρπός Thphr.*Vent*.13; ὑάκινθος, a gem, Mart.Cap.1.75; name of Dionysus, Plu.2.675f; Δενδρῖται, οἱ, a fabulous people, Luc.*VH*1.22:—fem. **δενδρῖτις** γῆ soil *suited for planting*, D.H.1.37; opp. ψιλή, *Inscr.Prien*.12.23 (iii B.C.); ἄμπελος δ., = ἀναδενδράς, Str.5.3.5; νύμφη δ. *wood*-nymph, *AP*9.665 (Agath.): epith. of Helen at Rhodes, Paus.3.19.10. II. δενδρίτης· κροκόδειλος, f.l. in Hsch.

δενδρο-βατέω, *climb trees*, *AP*11.348 (Antiphan.). **-γάληνος** οἶνος, a Bithynian wine made from the μερσίτης ἄμπελος, *Gp*.5.2.10. **-έθειρα**, ἡ, *wooded*, πτυχαί Tim.*Pers*.116. **-ειδής**, ές, *tree-like*, Dsc.4.164.9, *Gloss*. **-κολάπτης**, ου, ὁ, *woodpecker*, *Gloss*. **-κόμης**, ου, ὁ, = δενδρόκομος I, *AP*5.18 (Rufin.). **-κομικός**, ή, όν, *of* or *like a woodman*, Ael.*NA*13.18. **-κομος**, ον, *grown with wood*, ἐναύλεια E.*Hel*.1107 (lyr.); ὀρέων κορυφαί Ar.*Nu*.280 (lyr.). II. δενδροκόμος, ον, *tree-tending*, Nonn.*D*.47.182, 199. **-κοπέω**, *cut down trees*, esp. *vines and fruit-trees*, X.*Mem*.2.1.13; δ. χώραν *to waste* a country *by cutting down the trees*, Decr. Byz.ap.D.18.90:—Pass., Corn.*ND*30. **-κόπιον**, τό, *tree-cutting*, name of a festival, Herzog *Koische Forschungen* p.133. **-κόπος**, ὁ, *woodcutter*, *Gloss*. **-λάχανα** [λᾰ], τά, *tall-growing potherbs*, etc., Thphr.*HP*1.3.4. **-λίβανον** [ῐ], τό, *rosemary, Rosmarinus officinalis*, Gal.12.67, Aët.1.130, *Gp*.11.15 tit. **-μαλάχη** [λᾰ], ἡ, *tree-mallow, Lavatera arborea*, ib.15.5.6, etc.

δένδρον, v. δένδρεον.

δενδροπήμων, ον, gen. ονος, *blasting trees*, βλάβα A.*Eu*.938 (lyr.).

δένδρος, εος, τό, v. δένδρεον.

δενδρότης, ητος, ἡ, *growth of trees*, Suid.

δενδρο-τομέω, *cut down trees*, πρὸς καῦσιν Str.14.6.5, cf. S.E.*M*.5.69: but usu., 2. *lay waste* a country, Th.1.108: metaph., δ. τὸ νῶτον Ar.*Pax* 747. **-τομία**, ἡ, *laying waste*, Ph.2.401,548 (pl.). **-τόμος**, ον, *cutting down trees*, Sch.rec.S.*El*.98. **-τρόφος**, ον, *rearing trees*, ὄρη Max.Tyr.31.7. **-φορέω**, *to bear trees* in procession, Artem.2.37. **-φορία**, ἡ, *carrying of trees*, as a religious ceremony, Str.10.3.10 (pl.). II. *bearing, production of trees*, *Gp*.2.9.3. **-φόρος**, ον, *bearing trees*, φάραγξ Theodor.ap.Ath.14.621b; ἄρουρα *BGU*328 i 17 (ii A.D.): Sup. -ώτατος Plu.*Sull*.12; ἡ δ. (sc. γῆ) Ph.2.583. II. in pl., *tree-bearers*, a guild in the cult of Cybele, μήτηρ δενδροφόρων *IGRom*.1.614 (Tomi, iii A.D.); freq. in Lat. Inscrr., cf. Lyd.*Mens*.4.59. **-φυέω**, *produce trees*, Porph.*Abst*.2.5. **-φυής**, ές, *tree-like*, *Lyr.Adesp*.84.7. **-φυτος**, ον, *planted with trees*, χώρα Plu.*Cam*.16, cf. *PRyl*.427. II. πέτρα δ. a kind of *agate, with tree-like marks*, Orph.*L*.232.

δενδρόω, *turn into a tree*, γυῖα Nonn.*D*.43.234:—Med., ἑὴν δενδρώσατο μορφήν ib.12.190. II. Pass., *grow into a tree*, Thphr.*HP*1.9.4. 2. *to be turned into a tree*, Plot.3.4.1.

δενδρ-υάζω, *lurk, hide in the wood*, Paus.Gr.*Fr*.119, Hsch. II. *dive and remain under water*, *EM*256.4. **-ύφιον**, τό, Dim. of δένδρον, M.Ant.4.20, Dsc.1.108; *toy tree*, Hero *Spir*.1.41, al.; of corals, Thphr.*HP*4.7.2. **-ύω**, = δενδρυάζω II, *IG*4.952.20 (Epid.); cf. δρυάσαι, δρύεται. **-ώδης**, ες, = δενδροειδής, *tree-like*, Arist.*Long*.467^{b}1, Dsc.4.164,173, Heraclit.*Incred*.23. 2. δ. Νύμφαι *wood-nymphs*, *AP*7.196 (Mel.). 3. *wooded*, ὄρη Hp.*Aër*.13. **-ωμα**, ατος, τό, = sq., Aq.1*Ki*.22.6. **-ών**, ῶνος, ὁ, *thicket*, Id.*Ge*.21.33, 1*Ki*.31.13. **-ωσις**, εως, ἡ, *growth into a tree*, Thphr.*CP*2.15.5. **-ῶτις**, ιδος, ἡ, *wooded*, πέτρα E.*HF*790; ὥρα f.l. in A.*Fr*.44.6.

δενέμω· κροκόδειλος, prob. in Hsch. **Δένθις**· οἶνος (Lacon.), Id. (Pr. n., cf. Alcm.117.)

δενν-άζω, (δέννος) *abuse, revile*, τινά Thgn.1211; τέχνην E.*Rh*.925; ἐπὶ ψόγοισι δεννάσεις ἐμέ S.*Ant*.759: c. acc. cogn., κακὰ ῥήματα δ. *to utter* words *of* foul *reproach*, Id.*Aj*.243 (lyr.). **-αστός**, ή, όν, *reviled*, Hsch.

δέννος, ὁ, *reproach*, prob. in Archil.65 (pl.), Hdt.9.107, Lyc.777 (pl.), Herod.7.104. II. δεννόν· κακολόγον, Hsch.

δέννω, = δέω (A), *PMag.Osl*.5.2, *POxy*.2061.

δεντή· δέλεαρ, Hsch.

δεξαμενή, ἡ, (aor. 1 part. of δέχομαι, with different accent) *receptacle* for water, *tank, cistern*, Hdt.3.9, 6.119, *PSI*1.66 (v A.D.); of the *veins*, Democr.135; *vehicle*, as matter of form, Pl.*Ti*.53a, Aen.Gaz. *Thphr*.p.66 B.: generally, *receptacle*, Ph.1.647, D.C.76.1.

δεξιά, Ion. -ιή (fem. of δεξιός), ἡ, *right hand*, opp. ἀριστερά (*left*), δεξιῇ ἠσπάζοντο Il.10.542; ἐκ δεξιᾶς on *the right*, Ar.*Eq*.639; δεξιᾶς abs., *IG*2.733*A*, 835; ἐν δεξιῇ ἔχειν τὰ οὔρεα keep them on *the right* (as you go), Hdt.7.217, cf. Th.2.19,98, etc.; ἐν δ. λαβεῖν τὴν Σικελίαν Id.7.1; so Ἐπίδαμνός ἐστι πόλις ἐν δ. ἐσπλέοντι.. on *your right* as you sail in.., Id.1.24; πορεύεσθαι τὴν εἰς δ. (sc. ὁδόν) Pl.*R*.614c; ἐπὶ δεξιᾷ τοῦ βήματος Plu.2.192f. 2. in welcoming or saluting (as we shake *hands*), δεξιὰν διδόναι Ar.*Nu*.81; προτείνειν, ἐμβάλλειν, etc. (v. sub vocc.); esp. as a sign of *assurance, pledge* or *treaty*, σπονδαὶ.. καὶ δεξιαὶ ἧς ἐπέπιθμεν Il.2.341; δεξιὰς δόντες καὶ λαβόντες having exchanged *assurances*, X.*An*.7.3.1, cf. 1.1.6; δεξιὰς παρὰ βασιλέως φέρειν μὴ μνησικακήσειν bring *pledges* that he would not.., ib.2.4.1; δεξιᾶς πίστις μεγίστη E.*Med*.21; φυλάσσειν, τηρεῖν τὴν δ., *PFay*.124.13, *POxy*.533.18:—χείρ is never expressed in Hom., but is used later, χεῖρα δ. S.*Ph*.912,1254, etc.; φεῦ δ. χείρ E.*Med*.496; χειρὸς δ. ib.899, etc.; τὴν χεῖρα δὸς τὴν δ. Ar.*Nu*.81.

δεξῐ-άζω, in Pass., = δεξιόομαι Lxx 2*Ma*.4.34. II. Med., *approve*, γάμον *PLips*.41.5 (iv A.D.). **-δωρος**, ον, (δέχομαι) = δωροδόκος, Suid. **-μηλος**, ον, *receiving sheep*, i.e. *rich in sacrifices*, δόμος, ἐσχάρα, ἀγάλματα, E.*Andr*.129 (lyr.), 1138, *Ph*.632.

δέξιμος, η, ον, *acceptable, satisfactory* in quality, πυρός *PFlor*.368.9 (i A.D.).

δεξιο-βόλος, v. δεξιολάβος. **-γυιος**, ον, (δεξιός IV) *ready of limb*, Pi.*O*.9.111. **-λάβος** [ᾰ], ὁ, *spearman*: in pl., *guards*, *Act.Ap*.23.23 (v.l. δεξιοβόλους).

δεξιόομαι, impf. ἐδεξιούμην X.*Cyr*.7.3.38, Ep. 3 pl. δεξιόωντο *h.Hom*.6.16, A.R.2.756: fut. -ώσομαι A.*Ag*.852, S.*El*.976: aor. ἐδεξιωσάμην Lys.2.37, X.*Cyr*.7.5.53, etc.:—Pass., aor. ἐδεξιώθην Pl.*R*.468b: (δεξιά, δεξιός):—*greet with the right hand, welcome*, c. acc. pers., Ar.*Pl*.753, Lys.2.37, X.*Cyr*.7.5.53; *canvass*, τὸν δῆμον Plu.*Cat.Mi*.49: but also c. dat. pers., δεξιοῦσθαι θεοῖς *to raise one's right hand* to the gods, *pay greeting* or *honour to* them, A.*Ag*.852: also c. dat. modi, δ. χερσί *h.Hom*. l.c.; ἐπαίνοις S.*El*.976; δώροις Arist.*Mu*.391b8; λόγοις χρηστοῖς καὶ ἔργοις Paus.2.16.2; στόματι Luc.*Alex*.41; ὀφθαλμοῖς Lib.*Decl*.4.18: c. acc. rei, πυκνὴν ἄμυστιν δεξιούμενοι *pledging one in* many a bumper, E.*Rh*.419:—Pass., Pl. l.c.; ζῷα δεξιούμενα *with right hands joined*, *IG*2.754.33. II. δεξιώσασθαι· ἐγγίσασθαι γυναικί, Hsch.

δεξιόπηρος, ον, *blind of the right eye*, Hierocl.*Facet*.63.

δεξιός, ά, όν, *on the right hand* or *side*, opp. ἀριστερός, δ. μαζός, γλουτός, ὦμος, Il.4.481, 5.66, Od.17.462; τὸ δ. (sc. κέρας) *the right* of an army, X.*Ages*.2.9, etc.: freq. in adverb. usages, ἐπὶ δεξιά on or to *the right*, νωμῆσαι βῶν Il.7.238, cf. Hdt.1.51; ἐν τῷ ἐπὶ δ. τοῦ ὀπισθοδόμου *IG*1².92.55; ἐπὶ δεξιόφιν (Ep. gen.) towards *the right*, Il.13.308; χειρὸς εἰς τὰ δ. S.*Fr*.598, cf. Arist.*Pr*.943b29; ἀπὸ τῶν δ. Id.*Cael*.284b28; ἐν τοῖς δ. *Ev.Marc*.16.5; ἐκ δεξιῶν Hero *Aut*.26.4, *Ev.Matt*.20.21, al.; ἐπὶ δ. χειρός Theoc.25.18; κατὰ δ. χειρός Arat.707; πρὸς δ. Hdt.7.69; εἰς δεξιά Pl.*Ti*.43b; δεξιά as Adv., Plb.3.82.9 (s.v.l.). II. *fortunate*, esp. of the flight of birds and other omens, δ. ὄρνις Il.13.821, cf. Od.2.154, A.*Pr*.489, *Michel* 727 (Ephesus); ἀοιδὰν.. δεξιωτάταν ὀπαδόν Pi.*N*.3.8; βροντή X.*Cyr*.7.1.3. Adv. -ῶς Hdn.3.9.12. III. Astron., *northerly*, Cleom.1.1. IV. metaph., *dexterous, ready, skilful, clever*, Pi.*I*.5(4).61, Ar.*Nu*.428, 834, al., Th.3.82, etc.; δεξιὸν ποιεῖν *a clever thing*, Antipho 1.19; Εὐριπίδου δρᾶμα δεξιώτατον Stratt.1; δ. περὶ τὰς δίκας Pl.*Hipparch*.225c. Adv. -ιῶς Antiph.229.2; δ. ἔχειν πρός τι Plu.2.660a; δ. φέρειν *in the right spirit*, Phld.*Lib*.pp.18,41 O.: Sup. δεξιώτατα Ar.*Nu*.148. V. *courteous, kindly*, Luc.*Nec*.13, *Alex*.57; τὸ δ. καὶ ἐπιεικές Gal.14.296. Adv. -ιῶς ib.211. (Cf. Skt. *dákṣiṇas*, Lat. *dexter*, etc.)

δεξιό-σειρος ἵππος, ὁ, *right-hand trace-*horse in team of four, which did the hardest work: hence, generally, *vigorous, impetuous*, S.*Ant*.140 (lyr.). **-στάτης** [ᾰ], ου, ὁ, *one who stands in the right file of* the Chorus, Poll.2.161, 4.106.

δεξιότης, ητος, ἡ, *dexterity*, esp. of mind, *sharpness, cleverness*, σοφίη καὶ δ. Hdt.8.124, cf. Ar.*Eq*.719, al.; opp. ἀμαθία, Th.3.37. II. = δεξίωσις, δ. καὶ φιλία Paus.7.7.5. III. *courtesy, kindliness* (cf. δεξιός V), Ph.2.30. IV. *fortune, felicity*, καιροῦ Lyd.*Mag*.1.3.

δεξιό-τοιχος, ον, *on the starboard side of a ship*, *AB*91, Hsch. **-φᾰνής**, ές, *not reversed* (of images in a mirror), Plu.2.930b; *not producing a reversed image*, κάτοπτρα Phlp. *in Mete*.28.17. **-φιν**, v. δεξιός. **-φύλαξ** [ῠ], ακος, ὁ, *right rear flank man*, Hsch. s.v. οὐραγός.

δεξίπῡρος [ῐ], ον, *receiving fire*, θυμέλαι E.*Supp*.64 (lyr.).

δέξις, εως, ἡ, *reception*, E.*IA*1182. II. δεξίς, *part of the liver* observed in divination, Hsch.

δεξίστρᾰτος, ον, *receiving the host*, ἀγορά B.14.43.

δεξῐτερός, ά, όν, (δεξιός) *right-hand of two*, δ. κατὰ μαζόν Il.5.393; δ. χειρί Od.20.197; ποδί Pi.*P*.4.96; δεξιτερά (sc. χείρ), ἡ, *the right hand*, Il.1.501; Ep. dat. δεξιτερῆφι 24.284; rare in Com., Antiph.174.6.

δεξί-ωμα, ατος, τό, *acceptable thing*, ὦ χρυσέ, δ. κάλλιστον βροτοῖς E.*Fr*.324.1. II. *pledge* or *mark of friendship*, S.*OC*619 (pl.), D.C.58.5 (pl.). **-ώνυμος**, ον, prop. *right* or *lucky in name*; but simply, = δεξιός, χερσὶ δεξιωνύμοις A.*Supp*.607. **-ωσις**, εως, ἡ, *offer of the right hand, greeting*, Ph.1.478, 2.124 (pl.), Plu.*Alex*.9 (pl.), *Pomp*.79; *canvassing*, φιλονεικίαι καὶ δ. ib.67 (pl.): metaph., *greeting*, τῶν διαστάντων Dam.*Pr*.83. **-ωτικός**, ή, όν, *welcoming, hospitable*, φιλοφροσύνη Eust.782.56.

δέξο, v. δέχομαι.

Δεξώ, οῦς, ὁ, *Receiver*, Com. name of a corrupt person, Cratin.401.

δεόμενος· νόμος, δεσμός, Hsch.

δέον (written δεῖον *PSI*4.361.4 (iii B.C.), etc.), οντος, τό, neut. Subst., prop. part. of impers. δεῖ (q.v.):—*that which is binding, needful, right*, μᾶλλον τοῦ δ. X.*Mem*.4.3.8; τὰ δ. Th.1.22, etc.; οὐδὲν τῶν δ. πράττοντες Isoc.3.25; πρὸ τοῦ δ. before *it be needful*, S.*Ph*.891; ἐν δέοντι (sc. καιρῷ) in *good time*, E.*Med*.1277, Plu.*Cim*.17; ἐν τῷ δ. Hdt.2.159; ἐς δέον ἐγεγόνεε Id.1.119, cf. 186; ἐς δ. πάρεστι S.*OT* 1416, cf. *Ant*.386; εἰς δ. λέγειν D.4.14; εἰς τὸ δ. for *needful purposes*, or *in case of need*, ἐς τὸ δ. χρῆσθαι Hdt.2.173: hence of *secret service*, εἰς τὸ δ. ἀπώλεσα Ar.*Nu*.859 (parody of Pericles' εἰς τὸ δ. ἀνήλωσα Sch. ad loc.); εἰς οὐδὲν δ. ἀναλίσκειν D.3.28: so in pl., εἰς δέοντα ἀναλωθῆναι Andronic.Rhod.p.577 M.

δεόντως, Adv. of δέον, *as it ought*, Pl.*Clit*.409c, Epicur.*Ep*.2 p.36 U., *SIG*615.6 (Delph., ii B.C.), Plb.1.12.7, al., Phld.*Sign*.17,18, Hero *Aut*.11.6, *BGU*613.29 (ii A.D.), etc.; δ. ἔχειν Plb.9.7.3; *suitably*, χρῆσθαι Orib.*Eup*.2.1, al.

Δεονῦς, Ion., = Διονύσιος, gen. Δεονῦος *IG*12(8).270 (Thasos), also Δεονῦδος *GDI*5644 (Abdera), 5694 (Erythrae).

δεός, = θεός, Hsch.

δέος, gen. δέους (also δέᾱτος S.*Fr*.328, Cerc.*Fr*.18 ii 4; δείους (written for δϝέεος) Il.10.376, 15.4), τό: pl., v. infr. II:—*fear, alarm*, χλωρὸν δέος pale *fear*, ib.7.479, etc.: distd. by Ammon. from φόβος, as being more lasting (δέος.. κακοῦ ὑπόνοια, φόβος δὲ ἡ παραυτίκα πτόησις), cf. Prodic.ap.Pl.*Prt*.358d; φόβος τε καὶ δ. Hdt.4.115; τὸ δ. καὶ ὁ φ. Lys.20.8; δέει καὶ φόβῳ D.21.124, cf. 23.103; also δέος.. αἰσχύνη θ' ὁμοῦ S.*Aj*.1079; ἵνα γὰρ δ., ἔνθα καὶ αἰδώς Poet.ap.Pl.*Euthphr*.12b; δ. τινός *fear of* a person or thing, Ar.*Ach*.581; δέει τῶν Κερκυραίων μή.. Th.1.26; τεθνᾶσι τῷ δέει τοὺς τοιούτους ἀποστόλους (τεθνᾶσι τῷ δέει = δεδίασι) D.4.45; τρέμειν τῷ δέει τί πείσεται Alex.110.6: c. inf., σοὶ δ' οὐ δ. ἔστ' ἀπολέσθαι Il.12.246: folld. by μή with subj., οὐχὶ δ. μή σε φιλήσῃ Ar.*Ec*.650; μέγα τὸ δ. ἐγένετο μή.. Th.3.33; δέος ἴσχετε μηδέν, ὅσ' αὐδῶ S.*OC*223; ἀδεὲς δ. δεδιέναι *to fear* where no fear is, Pl.*Smp*.198a; πρὸς δέους λαβεῖν τι Plu.*Flam*.7; of *reverence*, A.*Pers*.703. II. *reason for fear*, Il.1.515; *means of inspiring fear*, δ. δεινότερον Th.3.45: rarely in pl., δέη ἐπιπέμπει πολλὰ ὁ θεός Lys.6.20; δέα ποικίλα Ael.*NA*8.10; also δέατα Hecat.364 J. (δϝεy-os, cf. δεινός, Skt. *dveṣṭi* 'hate'.)

δεπάζω, etym. of δέπαστρον, *EM*443.56.

δέπας, αος, τό, dat. δέπα Od.10.316: pl. nom. δέπᾰ 15.466, etc.; δέπατα dub. in *IG*12(3).450a1 (Thera): Ep. dat. δεπάεσσι Il.1.471, δέπασσι 15.86:—*beaker, goblet*, Od.10.316, etc.; δ. ἀμφικύπελλον Il.1.584, al.; δ. χρυσείοις ἥλοισι πεπαρμένον 11.632; δ. σκύπφειον Stes.7; δ. ἐκ κεραμοίο *APl*.4.333 (Antiphil.); of the golden *bowl* in which the sun floated back from West to East during the night, Stes.8.1, Pherecyd.18(a) J.; δ. Ἡφαιστοτυκές A.*Fr*.69 (lyr.).

δεπαστραῖος, α, ον, *in* or *of a cup*, Lyc.489.

δέπαστρον, τό, = δέπας, Antim.21, cf. 15 (pl.), *Carm.Pop*.41.8.

δέρα, v. δειρή.

δερ-άγχη, ἡ, (δέρη) *collar*, *AP*6.109.3 (Antip.). **-αγχής**, ές, *throttling*, πάγαι ib.107 (Phil.).

δέραιον, τό, *necklace*, E.*Ion*1431 (pl.), Men.*Epit*.86 (pl.), Satyr.*Vit.Eur.Fr*.39 vii 14 (pl.); *collar*, X.*Cyn*.6:—the form **δεραιοί** is given by Hsch.

δεραιοπέδη, ἡ, *collar*, *AP*6.14 (Antip. Sid.), 9.76 (Antip.).

Δεραμῖτις, ἡ, epith. of Athena, *Schwyzer* 196 (Crete).

δέρας, ατος, τό, = δέρος (q.v.).

δερβιστήρ, = δέρος, *EM*257.52 (δερϝ-, cf. δειρή).

δέργ-μα, ατος, τό, (δέρκομαι) *look, glance*, κυανοῦν λεύσσων δέργμα δράκοντος looking the *look* of.., A.*Pers*.82, cf. E.*Med*.187, etc. II. *thing seen, sight*, Orph.*L*.339. **-μός**, ὁ, = foreg., Hsch.

δέρεθρον· λίμνη ἀποχώρησιν ἔχουσα, Hsch.; cf. βάραθρον, ζέρεθρον.

δέρϝα, δέρη, v. δειρή.

δερίαι· λοιδορίαι, Hsch. **δερίπιον**· φλοιόν, Id.

δέρις, ιος, ἡ, = δέρη, Alciphr.1.28, Hsch. II. = δέρρις, Poll.2.235.

δεριστήρ, ῆρος, ὁ, *horse-collar*, Hsch.: **δεριστής**· κυνάγχης περιαυχένιος, Id. (δερρ- cod.)

δερκευνής, ές, *sleeping with the eyes open*, Nic.*Al*.67.

δερκιάομαι, poet. for δέρκομαι, Hes.*Th*.911.

δέρκομαι (Act. only in Hsch.), Il.11.37, etc.: impf. ἐδερκόμην, Ep. δερκέσκετο Od.5.158: fut. δέρξομαι Androm.ap.Gal.6.37: pf. in pres. sense δέδορκα Il.22.95, Pi.*O*.1.94, A.*Th*.103 (lyr.), etc.; also later Prose, Arist.*Phgn*.808a4, Luc.*Herm*.20, *Icar*.6,14: aor. ἔδρᾰκον Od.10.197, A.*Eu*.34, E.*HF*951 (never in S.): aor. part. Pass. δρακείς Pi.*P*.2.20, *N*.7.3; ἐδέρχθην A.*Pr*.547 (lyr.); δέρχθη S.*Aj*.425 (lyr.), imper. δέρχθητε A.*Pr*.93 (lyr.), part. δερχθείς S.*Fr*.837; later in med. forms δέρξατο *APl*.4.166 (Even.), ἐδρακόμην *AP*7.224:—*see clearly, see*, Il.17.675; part. δεδορκώς *having sight*, opp. τυφλός, S.*OT*454, cf. *El*.66: hence, *alive, living*, ζῶντος καὶ ἐπὶ χθονὶ δερκομένοιο Il.1.88, cf. Od.16.439; δρακεῖσ' ἀσφαλές *since she lives* in safety, Pi.*P*.2.20; ἀλαοῖσι καὶ δεδορκόσι A.*Eu*.322 (lyr.); δεδορκότ' S.*El*.66: freq. with neut. Adj., δεινόν, σμερδαλέον δ., *look* terrible, Il.3.342, 22.95, etc.; δεινὰ.. ὀφθαλμοῖν δρακεῖν A.*Eu*.34; φόνια δ. Ar.*Ra*.1337 (lyr.): c. acc. cogn., πῦρ ὀφθαλμοῖσι δεδορκώς *flashing* fire from his eyes, Od.19.446; Ἄρη δεδορκότων A.*Th*.53; but σκότον δεδ. *blind*, E.*Ph*.377. 2. c. acc. objecti, *look on* or *at*, Il.13.86, etc.; τί.. ἥδιον δρ.; A.*Ag*.602; ἐδέρχθης ὀλιγοδρανίαν Id.*Pr*.547; so δ. εἰς τινα Hes.*Sc*.169, E.*HF*951; κατά τι A.*Pr*.679; *descry, perceive*, Od.10.197, E.*Andr*.545; κτύπον δέδορκα A.*Th*.103 (lyr.). b. *look with favour on*, of Destiny, Pi.*P*.3.85. II. of light, *flash, gleam*, like the eye, δέδορκεν φάος, φέγγος, Id.*N*.3.84, 9.41; δεδορκὸς βλέπειν to be *keen-eyed*, Chrysipp.*Stoic*.3.198; τὸ σφοδρὸν καὶ δεδορκός Plu.2.15b. (Cf. Skt. *dadárśa* 'have seen', *dṛṣṭás* 'seen'; prop. not merely of *sight*, but of *sharp sight*, cf. A.*Supp*.409, S.*Aj*.85.—Poet. and later Prose.)

δερκύλλειν· αἱμοποτεῖν, ἄλλοι **δερμύλλειν**, Hsch.

δέρμα, ατος, τό, (δέρω) *skin, hide*, συός Il.9.548, al.; κριοῦ Pi.*P*.4.

161; δ. αἴγειον *PEdgar*11.8 (iii B.C.), etc.; λέοντος a lion's *skin* for a cloak, Il.10.23; κελαινόν, of a shield, 6.117; of *skins prepared for bags, bottles*, etc., Od.2.291; of *a man's skin*, Il.16.341, Od.13.431, Pl.*Phd*.98d, etc.; of *a man's skin* stripped off, Hdt.4.64, 5.25; παλαιὸν δ. A.*Fr*.275.4; περὶ τῷ δ. δέδοικα Ar.*Eq*.27, cf. *Pax* 746; ἀνὴρ κατὰ δέρμα θαυμαστὸς οἷος Aristid.*Or*.51(27).38; of *the shell* of a tortoise, Ar.*V*.429, 1292. 2. *skin* of fruits, Thphr.*HP*4.14.10; περικαρπίων δέρματα *outer coverings* of seed-vessels, ib.1.2.6. *wallet, scrip*, Hsch.

δερμᾰτ-ηρά, ἡ, *tax on hides*, *PPetr*.3 p.66 (iii B.C.). **-ίκιον**, τό, prob. written for δελμ-, *PTeb*.413 (ii/iii A.D.), etc. **-ικός**, ή, όν, *of skin, like skin*, ὑμήν Arist.*HA*495^{a}8; of the wings of insects, Id.*PA*682^{b}19; σκέπη Id.*GA*719^{b}5. II. δερματικόν (sc. ἀργύριον), τό, the *money received for the sale of the hides* of sacrificial animals, *IG*2.741, Lycurg.*Fr*.1. III. v. δαλματικόν. **-ινος**, η, ον, *of skin, leathern*, ἠρτύναντο δ' ἐρετμὰ τροποῖς ἐν δ. Od.4.782; ἀσπίς Hdt. 7.79; ὑμήν Arist.*Fr*.335; πλοῖα Str.16.4.19; ζώνη *Ev.Marc*.1.6; ὑποδήματα *IG*5(1).1390.23 (Andania, i B.C.); τεύχη *Inscr.Prien*.114.11, 30 (i B.C.); ὄγκος Ph.1.100; χιτών (of the human skin), Porph. *Abst*.2.46. **-ιον**, τό, Dim. of δέρμα, Pl.*Erx*.400a, Arist.*Phgn*. 807^{b}18.

δερμᾰτο-μᾰλάκτης, ου, ὁ, *currier*, Sch.Pl.*Grg*.517e. **-πτερος**, ον, *with wings of skin*, of the bat, Ar.Byz.*Epit*.120.7.

δερμᾰτουργικός, ή, όν, *of* or *for tanning*, Pl.*Plt*.280c.

δερμᾰτο-φᾰγέω, *eat skin and all*, Str.16.4.17. **-φορέω**, *wear a skin* or *hide*, Sch.A.R.1.324. **-φόρος**, ον, *clothed in skins*, Str.16. 4.17. **-χίτων** [ῐ], ωνος, ὁ, *wearing a leathern jerkin*, Sch.Lyc.634.

δερμᾰτόω, in Pass., *to be turned into hide*, Hsch. s.v. ἰσχαλωμέναι.

δερμᾰτώδης, ες, *like skin*, κάλυμμα, φλέψ, Arist.*HA*505^{a}7, 513^{b}8; opp. σαρκώδης, Thphr.*HP*4.3.4 (Comp.); ἐπιφύσεις Gal.2.615, cf. Aët.16.1; *leathery*, Xenocr.29.

δέρμη· ὁδός, Hsch.

δερμηστής (-ιστής Hsch.), οῦ, ὁ, (δέρμα, ἔδω) *worm which eats skin* or *leather*, S.*Fr*.449, Lys.*Fr*.104S., Aristid.Mil.29; = ὄφις, Aristarch. ap.Harp.

δέρμητες· οἱ ἐξ ἐφήβων (ἐφ' ἡμῶν cod.) περισσοί, Hsch.

δερμό-πτερος, ον, *with membranous wings*, as a bat, τὰ δ. Arist. *HA*487^{b}22, 490^{a}7, Ael.*NA*11.37. **-τῡλον**, τό (-τοιλον Pap.), *leather cushion*, *PLond*.5.1790 (v/vi A.D.).

δερμύλλω, = φλάω, Sch.Ar.*Nu*.734; cf. δερκύλλειν.

δέρξις, εως, ἡ, *sense of sight*, Orac.ap.Plu.2.432b, Hsch.

δεροεργής, ές, *tanning*, Man.4.320.

δέρον, v. δέρω.

δέρος and **δέρας**, τό, poet. and Ion. (δέρας *GDI*iv p.875 (Chios)) for δέρμα, only nom. and acc. (exc. gen. δέρατος or δέρους in D.S.4.56): δέρος S.*Fr*.11, E.*Med*.5 cod. L, *Ph*.1120, *Ion*995, A.R.1.245, al., Epic. in *Arch.Pap*.7.3; δέρας E.*Med*.480 codd. plures, *Ba*.835.

δέρρη, v. δειρή.

δερρῐδόγομφος, ον, *with screens fastened upon them*, πύλαι *Com. Adesp*.858.

δέρριον· τρίχινον σακίον, Hsch.

δέρρις, εως, ἡ, (Att. form of *δέρσις, cf. δέρω) *skin*, δ. τριχίνη Lxx *Za*.13.4, cf. *AP*12.33 (Mel.). II. *leathern covering*, of a jerkin, Eup.328; of a curtain, Pl.Com.240, Myrtil.1. III. in pl. (sg., Ph.*Bel*.95.34), *screens of skin* or *hide*, hung before fortifications to deaden the enemy's missiles, Th.2.75, Cic.*Att*.4.19.1, D.S.20.9, Apollod.*Poliorc*.142.2, Polyaen.3.11.13: generally, *curtain*, Lxx *Ex*. 26.7, al., *IG*5(1).1390.35 (Andania, i B.C.).

δερρίσκος, ὁ, Dim. of foreg., *IG*2.678*B*73.

δερτόν, τό, *flayed sheep*, *SIG*1024.25 (Myconos); cf. δαρτός.

δέρτρον, τό, (δέρω) = ἐπίπλους, *caul* or *membrane which contains the bowels*, χολάδας δέρτροισι καλύψεις Antim.45, cf. Hp.*Epid*.5.26; γῦπε . . δέρτρον ἔσω δύνοντες even to *the bowels*, Od.11.579. II. in Od. l.c., δέρτρον is expld. by Gramm., as *EM*257.31, etc., of the vulture's *beak*: hence, of *a sharp point*, Lyc.880. III. pl., = τύμπανα, Hsch.

δέρω Ar.*V*.485, Pl.*Euthd*.285c, etc.:—also **δείρω** Hdt.2.39, Ar. *Nu*.442, *Av*.365, Cratin.361: impf. ἔδερον Il.23.167, Ep. δέρον Od. 8.61: fut. δερῶ Ar.*Eq*.370: aor. ἔδειρα Il.2.422, (ἀπ-) Hdt.5.25, (ἐκ-) Pl.*R*.616a:—Pass., fut. δαρήσομαι *Ev.Marc*.13. 9, *POxy*.653*b* (ii A.D.): aor. ἐδάρην [ᾰ] Men.*Mon*.422, (ἀπ-) X.*An*. 3.5.9, (ἐκ-) Hdt.7.26; part. δαρθείς Nicoch.8: pf. δέδαρμαι (v. infr.):—*skin, flay*, of animals, δ. βοῦς Il.23.167: prov., κύνα δ. δεδαρμένην 'flog a dead horse', Pherecr.179; ἀσκὸς δεδάρθαι *to have one's skin flayed off*, Sol.33.7; δερῶ σε θύλακον κλοπῆς I *will make* a thief's purse *of* your *skin*, Ar.*Eq*.370: prov., πρὶν ἐσφάχθαι δέρεις 'first catch your hare, then cook it', Eust.1792.45; ἀέρα δέρειν 'plough the sands', Id. 1215.50, Suid. 2. Anat., *separate by avulsion*, Herophil.ap.Gal. 2.349. II. colloquially, *cudgel, thrash*, δέδοκταί μοι δέρεσθαι καὶ δέρειν δι' ἡμέρας Ar.*V*.485, cf. *Nu*.442, *POxy*. l.c. (ii A.D., Pass.): prov., ὁ μὴ δαρεὶς ἄνθρωπος οὐ παιδεύεται 'spare the rod and spoil the child', Men. l.c., cf. *SIG*1109.91 (ii A.D.): metaph., εἰς πρόσωπόν τινα δ. 2*Ep.Cor*.11.20. (Cf. Lith. *derù* 'flay', Skt. *dṛṇāti* 'split'.)

δεσαύχενες· οἱ ἀσκοί, Hsch., *EM*258.28.

δέσις, εως, ἡ, (δέω A) *binding together*, Pl.*Cra*.418e; *setting* of stones, Lxx *Si*.45.11; *tying in bundles*, Hdn.8.4.5; ποδῶν δ., = ὑπόδημα, Ezek.*Exag*.97. II. *complication of a dramatic plot*, opp. λύσις, Arist.*Po*.1455^{b}26. III. = δέσμη (prob. of a belt-purse), *UPZ*121.9 (cf. δεσμός II). IV. Botan., *joint*, Sch.Orib.2 p.743D.

δέσκαλος, ἡ, dub. sens., ἀσπάζεται ἡμᾶς . . Ἀθηναῒς ἡ δέσκαλος *BGU* 332.9 (ii/iii A.D.).

δέσμα, ατος, τό, (δέω A) poet. for δεσμός, *bond, fetter*, σιδήρεα δέσματ' Od.1.204, cf. 8.278. II. *head-band*, ἀπὸ κρατὸς βάλε δέσματα Il. 22.468.

δεσμ-άτιον, τό, Dim. of δέσμα, Sch.Theoc.4.18. **-ευτήριον**, τό, = δεσμωτήριον, *PTeb*.567 (i A.D.). **-ευτής**, οῦ, ὁ, *one who binds*, Sch.Opp.*H*.3.373. **-ευτικός**, ή, όν, *of* or *for fetters*, Pl.*Lg*.847d. **-εύω**, *fetter, put in chains*, *h.Bacch*.17, E.*Ba*.616, Pl.*Lg*.808e; *tie together*, as corn in the sheaf, Hes.*Op*.481; δ. ἀγκάλας *PLond*.1.131^{r}426 (ii A.D.); χόρτον *PFlor*.322.31 (iii A.D.); δ. ἔκ τινος *bind fast to* . ., Plb.3.93.4, Apollod.2.1.3. II. *lay snares for*, Lxx 1*Ki*.24.12. **-έω**, = δεσμεύω (un-Attic, Moer.122), *Ev. Luc*.8.29, Hld.8.9:—Pass., Diog.Oen.39, Luc.*JTr*.20, Alex.Aphr. *Pr*.1.75, 106; of joints, *undergo ankylosis*, Gal.15.410. **-η**, ἡ, *package, bundle*, Test.ap.D.35.34, Alex.117, Arist.*Fr*.140, D.H.3. 61. 2. a *measure* in Egypt, φοινίκων *PFay*.119.4, al.; ἀσπαράγου *POxy*.1212.4 (ii A.D.). b. in Medicine, *handful*, Androm.ap. Gal.13.1033; ὑσσώπου κόμης Ezek.*Exag*.185. **-ή**· ὁδός, Hsch.; cf. δέρμη. **-ημα**, ατος, τό, = δεσμίς, Tz.ad Hes.*Op*.479. **-ίας**, ου, ὁ, *worthy of bonds*, Hsch. (-ίης cod.). **-ίδιον**, τό, Dim. of δεσμίς (= δέσμη 2b), Dsc.*Eup*.2.65, Aët.3.79, *POxy*.1288.9 (iv A.D.), 1130. 29 (v A.D.). 2. *small bandage*, Antyll.ap.Orib.44.23.74. **-ιον**, τό, = δεσμός, *AP*9.479 (pl.). **-ιος**, ον, *binding*: metaph., *binding as with a spell, enchaining*, c. gen., ὕμνος ἐξ Ἐρινύων δ. φρενῶν A.*Eu*. 332 (lyr.), cf. 306. II. Pass., *bound, captive*, S.*Aj*.299, *Ph*.608, E.*Ba*.226, *POxy*.580 (ii A.D.), etc.; *on leash*, [κύων] prob. in Aen. Tact.31.32; δ. φυγών, = ἐκ δεσμῶν, E.*Ba*.792. **-ίς**, ίδος, ἡ, = δέσμη, Hp.*Mul*.1.78, Thphr.*HP*9.16.2.

δεσμόβροχος, ὁ, *noose*, Man.5.133.

δεσμός, ὁ, pl. δεσμά *h.Merc*.157, al., Thgn.459, Hdt.6.91, and so mostly in Trag., A.*Pr*.513, etc., and Pl.*Euthphr*.9a; but δεσμοί A.*Pr*. 525, E.*Ba*.518, 634, usu. in Pl., as *Lg*.793b, al.: both forms in Att. Inscrr., δεσμοί *IG*2.678*B*48, δεσμά ib.791.31, the latter preferred by Thom.Mag.p.79R. (sg. δεσμόν *SIG*246 ii 36 (Delph.), Att. acc. to Hsch.): (δέω A):—*band, bond, anything for tying and fastening*, as *halter*, Il.6.507; *mooring-cable*, Od.13.100, etc.; *door-latch*, 21. 241; *yoke-strap*, X.*An*.3.5.10: metaph., any *bond of union* or *connexion*, Pl.*Ti*.31c, etc.; of the vowels, Id.*Sph*.253a; δεσμοὶ πολιτείας, of the laws, Id.*Lg*.793b; εἰς τὰ δεσμοῦ for *binding material*, *PTeb*.120.70 (i B.C.). 2. in pl. (never δεσμά in this sense), *bonds, chains*, ἐκ δεσμῶν λυθῆναι A.*Pr*.509, 770; πρὶν ἂν ἐξ ἀγρίων δ. χαλάσῃ ib.177; ἐν δεσμοῖσι S.*Fr*.63; εἰς δεσμοὺς ἄγειν E.*Ba*.518; δεσμοῖς Th.7.82; ὁ ἐπὶ τῶν δ., = δεσμοφύλαξ, Luc.*Tox*.29: in sg., collectively, *bonds, imprisonment*, δ. ἀχλυόεις Epigr.ap.Hdt.5.77 (= *IG*1^{2}.394); οὐδὲν ἄξιον δεσμοῦ Hdt.3.145; ἐν. δ. S.*Ant*.958; ἐν δημοσίῳ δ. δεθείς Pl.*Lg*.864e; ἔδησεν ἑαυτὸν τιμησάμενος δεσμοῦ Lys.6.21: metaph. of moral *bondage*, Porph.*Abst*.1.38, al. 3. *ligature*, Arist.*HA* 495^{b}13, al. 4. δ. ἄρθρου in Hp.*Fract*.37 is expld. by Gal. ad loc. as *ankylosis*. 5. *spell, charm*, Iamb.*Myst*.3.27. II. = δέσμη, Pap. in *Philol*.80.341, Poll.2.135, Eust.862.27; ἀσπαράγου δ. *BGU*1120. 14 (i B.C.); δ. ἀργυρίου Lxx *Ge*.42.27; cf. δέσις III.

δεσμό-τρῐχον, τό, gloss on κεκρύφαλος, Hsch. **-φῠλᾰκεία**, ἡ, *tax for maintenance of prisons*, *PFay*.53.6; *service as warder*, *PFlor*. 253 (iii A.D.), al. **-φῠλάκειον** [ᾰ], τό, *prison*, ib.2.100 (iii A.D.). **-φύλαξ** [ῠ], ακος, ὁ, *gaoler*, *BGU*1138.12 (i B.C.), *Act.Ap*. 16.23, Luc.*Tox*.30, Artem.2.60.

δεσμ-ωμα, ατος, τό, *bond, fetter*, A.*Pers*.745, S.*Fr*.29 (both pl.). **-ωτήριον**, τό, *prison*, Th.6.60, Pl.*Grg*.486a, D.9.60, etc.; δ. ἀνδρῶν Hdt.3.23: pl., = Lat. *ergastula*, Plu.*TG*8. **-ώτης**, ου, ὁ, *prisoner, captive*, Hdt.3.143, Th.5.35, etc.:—fem. **-ῶτις**, Hld.8.8: metaph. of the soul, Ph.1.289. II. as Adj., *in chains, fettered*, A.*Pr*.119 (the play is called Προμηθεὺς δ.): fem. δεσμῶτις ποίμνη S.*Aj*.234 (lyr.); Μελανίππη δ., name of a play by E. III. *gaoler*, Cratin.189.

δεσπόζω, mostly pres. and impf.: fut. -όσω A.*Pr*.210, al., Ep. -όσσω *h.Cer*.365: aor. inf. δεσπόσαι E.*Alc*.486: 1. abs., *to be lord* or *master, gain the mastery*, πρὸς βίαν δ. A.*Pr*.210; ἄρχειν καὶ δ. Pl.*Phd*.80a, al.: as law-term, *to be the legal proprietor*, opp. κρατεῖν, *PTheb.Bank*1.15, cf. *BGU*1187.9 (i B.C.), *PLond*.3.977.32 (iv A.D.). b. Astrol., of planets, *to be dominant* in a nativity, Vett. Val.72.5. 2. c. gen., *to be lord* or *master of*, *h.Cer*.365, Hdt.3. 142, etc.; Ζηνὸς (or Διὸς) δεσπόσαι A.*Pr*.930; δεσπόζοντ' ἐμοῦ E. *Supp*.518; δ. τινός, opp. δουλεύειν ἄλλῳ, Pl.*R*.576a; δεσπόζειν φόβης *own* it, A.*Ch*.188; *make oneself master of*, λέκτροις ὧν ἐδέσποζον E.*Andr*.928: metaph., τοῦδε δ. λόγου A.*Ag*.543. 3. c. acc., *lord it over*, δ. πόλιν E.*HF*28:—Pass., δεσπόζονται Hp.*Aër*.16; δεσποζόμεναι πόλεις Pl.*Lg*.712e; δ. ὑπό τινος D.S.18.60; πρός τινος Ph.1.337.

δέσποινα, ἡ, fem. of δεσπότης, *mistress, lady of the house*, of Penelope, Od.14.127; ἄλοχος δ., of the wife of Nestor, 3.403; γυνὴ δ., of Arete, 7.347; *mistress* of a slave, *POxy*.49.4 (i/ii A.D.), *BGU*55 ii 5 (ii A.D.). 2. *princess, queen*, δ. Κόλχων Pi.*P*.4.11; Κύπρου Id. *Fr*.122.14; δέσποιν' ἁπασῶν, πότνι' Ἀθηναίων πόλι *Com.Adesp*.340. 1. 3. coupled with the names of goddesses, δ. Ἑκάτη A.*Fr*.388; Ἄρτεμις S.*El*.626, cf. B.10.117, etc.; δ. νύμφη A.*Fr*.342; esp. as a name of Persephone, Pl.*Lg*.796b; in Arcadia, *IG*5(2).514 (Lycosura), Paus.8.37.1–10; of Κύπρις, Xenarch.4.21. 4. in Thessaly, simply, = γυνή, Hsch. 5. at Rome, *Empress*, *PSI*1.76.1 (vi A.D.), etc.

δεσποινικός, ή, όν, *belonging to the Imperial household*, *PMasp*.88. 10 (vi A.D.).

Δεσποσιοναῦται, ῶν, οἱ, Helots at Sparta *who were freed on condition of serving at sea*, Myro 2.

δεσπ-όσιος, ον, = δεσπόσυνος, ὕβρις A.*Supp*.845 (lyr.). II. Subst., = *verna*, Eust.846.13. **-οσμα**, ατος, τό, *act of authority*: pl., δ. Μοιρῶν *decrees* of fate, Man.4.38. **-οστός**, ή, όν, *suited to despotic rule*, of persons, cj. in Arist.*Pol*.1287ᵇ38 (v.l. δεσποτικόν), 1324ᵇ39. **-οσύνη**, ἡ, *absolute rule, despotism*, Hdt.7.102. **-όσυνος**, ον, also η, ον Pi.*P*.4.267:—*of* or *belonging to the master* or *lord*, λέχος *h.Cer*.144; δόμοι δ. A.*Ch*.942 (lyr.); μέλαθρα Ar.*Th*.42 (anap.); τὰ δ. χρήματα *the master's* property, X.*Oec*.9.16 (δεσπόσυνα, τά, ib.14.2, Phld.*Oec*.p.24 J.); δ. ἀνάγκαι *arbitrary rule*, A.*Pers*.587 (lyr.); also, = τῆς δεσποίνης, γόνατα Tim.*Pers*.136. II. Subst., = δεσπότης, Tyrt.6.2 (cf. Plu.*Lyc*.28), Anaxandr.41.33 (anap.), *GDI*4334 (Megiste). 2. = *verna*, Eust.846.13.

δεσποτ-εία, ἡ, *the power of a master* over slaves, or *the relation of master* to slaves, Pl.*Prm*.133e, Arist.*Pol*.1253ᵇ18, 1278ᵇ32; *of husband* over wife, Ph.1.40, cf.151. 2. *absolute rule, despotism*, Pl.*Lg*. 698a, Luc.*Luct*.6; δ. βαρβαρική Isoc.5.154. II. *ownership*, *BGU* 1187.32 (i B.C.), *POxy*.67.10 (iv A.D.), Just.*Nov*.2.2*Pr*. **-ειος**, α, ον, = δεσπόσυνος, Lyc.1183. **-ειρα**, ἡ, fem. of δεσπότης, *mistress*, S. *Fr*.1040. **-εύω**, = δεσπόζω, Lxx 3*Ma*.5.28, *CIG*3702 (Lopadium), D.C.60.28: c. gen., *enjoy ownership of*.., *PGen*.60.1 (iv A.D.). **-έω**, = δεσπόζω, c. gen., Pl.*Ti*.44d:—Pass., *to be despotically ruled*, πρὸς ἄλλης χερός A.*Ch*.104; σῇ χερί E.*Heracl*.884; δεσποτούμενος βίος, opp. ἀνάρχετος, A.*Eu*.527 (lyr.), cf. 696.

δεσπότ-ης, ου, ὁ; voc. δέσποτᾰ: Ion. acc. δεσπότεα Hdt.1.91, al., Luc.*Syr.D*.25:—*master, lord*, prop. *the master of the house*, δόμων A.*Eu*.60, etc.; ὄμμα γὰρ δόμων νομίζω δεσπότου παρουσίαν Id. *Pers*.169: pl., of a family, Id.*Ag*.32, *Ch*.53, 82 (lyr.); in respect of slaves, Pl.*Prm*.133d; δοῦλοι καὶ δ. οὐκ ἄν ποτε γένοιντο φίλοι Id.*Lg*. 757a, etc.; δ. καὶ δοῦλος Arist.*Pol*.1253ᵇ6, cf. 1278ᵇ35; ὦ δέσποτ' ἄναξ Ar.*Pax*90 (anap.); ὦναξ δέσποτα ib.389, *Fr*.598; δέσποτ' ἄναξ Men. 312.5. 2. *despot, absolute ruler*, Hdt.3.89, Th.6.77; τύραννος καὶ δ. Pl.*Lg*.859a; of the Roman *Emperors*, Ph.2.568, D.C.55.12, Hdn.1.6.4; γᾶς καὶ θαλάσσας δ. *IG*12(2).216 (Mytilene). 3. of the gods, S.*Fr*.535, E.*Hipp*.88, Ar.*V*.875, X.*An*.3.2.13. 4. *dominant planet*, Vett.Val.5.16. II. generally, *master, lord, owner*, κώμου, ναῶν, Pi.*O*.6.18, *P*.4.207; μαντευμάτων A.*Th*.27; τῶν Ἡρακλείων ὅπλων S.*Ph*.262; ἑπτὰ δεσποτῶν, of the seven *Chiefs* against Thebes, E.*Supp*.636; τοῦ ὄρτυγος Poll.9.108.—Not in Hom. (for metrical reasons), though he uses δέσποινα in Od. (Prob. for δεμσ-ποτ- 'lord of the house', cf. δόμος.) **-ίδιον**, τό, Dim. of δεσπότης, Aristaenet.1.24. **-ικός**, ή, όν, *of* or *for a master*, συμφοραί misfortunes *that befall one's master*, X.*Cyr*.7.5.64; δίκαιον a *master's* right, Arist.*EN*1134ᵇ8; ὑπομένειν τὴν δ. ἀρχήν Id.*Pol*.1285ᵃ22; ἡ δ., = δεσποτεία, ib.1259ᵃ37; τὸ δ. Pl.*Lg*.697c. 2. *Imperial*, νομισμάτια *PFlor*.95.10; κτήσεις *PLond*.2.234.1 (iv A.D.); νοτάριος ib.416.3 (iv A.D.). II. *fitted to rule*, ἀδικία -ώτερον δικαιοσύνης Pl.*R*.344c, etc.; *inclined to tyranny, despotic*, ὀλιγαρχία δ. Arist.*Pol*.1306ᵇ3; δῆμος ib.1292ᵃ16; of persons, *tyrannical*, Phld.*Ir*.p.59 W. Adv. -κῶς, βουλεύεσθαι Isoc.4.104; ἄρχειν Arist.*Pol*.1295ᵃ16: Comp. -ωτέρως Id.*Ath*.24.2. 2. c. gen., *exercising despotic power over*, τινός X. *Oec*.13.5; ἔστι δὲ τυραννὶς μοναρχία δ. τῆς πολιτικῆς κοινωνίας Arist. *Pol*.1279ᵇ16; δ. τῶν βελτιόνων ib.1292ᵃ19. **-ις**, ἡ, = δέσποινα, voc. δεσπότι Limen.39; acc. δεσπότιν S.*Tr*.407, *El*.597, E.*Med*.17, Pl.*Ti*.34c, Epicur.*Ep*.3 p.65 U.; gen. δεσπότιδος *POxy*.48.7 (i A.D.); dat. δεσπότιδι *AP*6.160.8 (Antip. Sid.). **-ίσκος**, ὁ, Dim. of δεσπότης, E.*Cyc*.267. **-ρια**, ἡ, = δέσποινα, Sch.E.*Hec*.397.

δέστρον, τό, part of an axle, Poll.1.145.

δετέον, *one must bind*, *Gp*.4.12.16.

δέτις, ιδος, ἡ, *torch*, Hp.ap.Erot. (dub.l.), Gal.19.92. 2. *head of garlic* (from being *bound up* like a faggot), Id. l.c. 3. = παλάθη (-άνθη cod.), Hsch.

δετός, ή, όν, *that may be bound*, παλάμαι Opp.*C*.4.289. II. δετή, ἡ, *faggot*, καιόμεναι δεταί Il.11.554; *torch*, Ar.*V*.1361; also, *fetter*, and *sheaf*, Hsch.

δέτρον, τό, = δέρτρον, Hsch., *Et.Gud*. **δετρός**· μάγειρος, Hsch. (leg. δαιτρός). **δεύασθαι**· γεύσασθαι, Id.

δευκής, ές, = γλυκύς, dub. in Nic.*Al*.328; cf. δευκές· λαμπρόν, ὅμοιον, Hsch.

δεῦκος, εος, τό, = γλεῦκος, Sch.A.R.1.1037; Aetol. acc. to Sch.Nic. *Th*.625.

δεύκω· βλέπω, *EM*260.54; cf. δεύκει· φροντίζει, Hsch. **δευλόν**· πονηρόν, ἀχρεῖον, Id.

δεῦμα, ατος, τό, (δεύω A) *that which is steeped, seethed*, δεύματα κρεῶν *boiled* flesh, dub. in Pi.*O*.1.50; cf. δεύτατος.

δεῦμαι, δεύμενον, v. δέομαι.

Δευνῦσος, ὁ, Ion. for Διόνυσος, Anacr.2.11:—from **δεῦνος**, Indian for βασιλεύς, acc. to *EM*259.32: v. Δεονῦς.

δεύομαι, Ep. for δέομαι; cf. δεύω (B).

δεῦρο (Aeol. **δεῦρυ** Hdn.Gr.2.933, who read δεύρω in Il.3.240), strengthd. in Att. **δευρί** Ar.*Nu*.323, And.2.10: sts. written δευρε in Att. Inscrr., as *IG*1².900: late **δευρεί** *Stud.Pal*.10.7.6 (iv/v A.D.). Adv.: I. of Place, *hither*, with all Verbs of motion, Il.1.153, etc.: strengthd., δ. τόδ' ἵκω Od.17.444, cf. Il.14.309; in pregn. sense with Verbs of rest, *to* [*have come hither and*] *be here*, δ. παρέστης 3. 405; πάρεστι δ. . . ὅδε S.*OC*1253; τὰ τῇδε καὶ τὰ δεῦρο πάντ' ἀνασκόπει Ar.*Th*.666: with Art., μακρὸν τὸ δ. πέλαγος S.*OC*663; τῆς δ. ὁδοῦ ib.1165; τὸ τῇδε καὶ τὸ κεῖσε καὶ τὸ δ. Ar.*Av*.426, cf. E.*Ph*. 266, [315]; δ. ἐλθών Pl.*Tht*.143a. b. later, *here*, τὰ δ., = *sensible objects*, Arist.*Metaph*.991ᵇ30; τὰ σώματα τὰ δ. Id.*Cael*.269ᵇ15; τὰ δ. κακά Max.Tyr.14.7. 2. used as Interjection, *come on!* in Hom. with 2 sg. imper. (δεῦτε (q.v.) being used with pl.), ἄγε δ. Il.11.314; δ. ἄγε Od.8.145; δ. ἴθι Il.3.130; δ. ἴτω 7.75; δ. ὅρσο Od.22.395: later with 2 pl. imper., δ. ἴτε A.*Eu*.1041 (lyr.); δ. ἕπεσθε E.*HF* 724. b. with 1 pl. subj., δεῦρο, φίλη, λέκτρονδε τραπείομεν *come* let us.., Od.8.292, cf. Il.17.120, al.; later in this sense with imper., καί μοι δ. εἰπέ *here now*, tell me, Pl.*Ap*.24c; δεῦρό σου στέψω κάρα *come* let me.., E.*Ba*.341. c. without a Verb, δ. δηὖτε Μοῖσαι Sapph.84; δεῦρο, σύ *here*, you! Ar.*Pax* 881; δ. παρὰ Σωκράτη (sc. καθίζου) Pl.*Tht*.144d; δ. δὴ πάλιν (sc. βλέπε) Id.*R*.477d. d. later, *go away!* Lxx 4*Ki*.3.13. 3. in arguments, μέχρι δ. τοῦ λόγου up *to this point* of the argument, Pl.*Smp*.217e; τὸ μέχρι δ. ἡμῖν εἰρήσθω Id.*Lg*.814d; δεῦρ' ἀεὶ προεληλύθαμεν Id.*Plt*.292c; ἄχρι δ. Gal.15.453. II. of Time, *until now, hitherto*, Trag. (v. infr.) and Prose, Pl.*Ti*.21d; μέχρι τοῦ δ. Th.3.64, Onos.*Praef*.7, *PLond*. 2.358.16 (ii A.D.); μέχρι δεύρου (sic) *PGen*.47.8 (iv A.D.); εἰς τὴν δ. Hld.1.19; ἐξ ἕω μέχρι δ. Pl.*Lg*.811c; δεῦρ' ἀεί E.*Med*.670, *Ion* 56, etc.; paratrag. in Ar.*Lys*.1135; δεῦρό γ' ἀεί A.*Eu*.596.

δευρόλας· ὁ ἐξ ἐφήβων Ἀθηναίων, Hsch.

Δεύς, Boeot. for Ζεύς, Corinn.*Supp*.2, Ar.*Ach*.911, Hdn.Gr.1.400, al.; also Lacon., *GDI*4417, *An.Ox*.4.325, Hsch.; on a Rhodian vase, *Schwyzer* 276a. (Expld. ἀπὸ τοῦ δεύειν τὴν γῆν Corn.*ND*2.)

δεύσιμος, η, ον, *fit for watering*, τόπος Sch.Il.12.21.

δευσοποι-έω, *dye, stain*, τὰς παρειάς Alciphr.3.11: metaph., Dam. *Pr*.427. **-ία**, ἡ, *dyeing*, Poll.1.49. **-ός**, όν, (δεύω A) *deeply dyed, fast*, of colours, δ. γίγνεται τὸ βαφὲν Pl.*R*.429e, cf. Alex.141.9, D.Chr. 77.4; δ. σπάργανα Diph.72.2; δ. φάρμακα Luc.*Im*.16; δ. καὶ δυσέκνιπτος Ael.*NA*16.1: metaph., δόξα δ. Pl.*R*.430a; πονηρία Din.2.4; δέος Plu.*Alex*.74. Adv. -ῶς Simp.*in Cat*.253.28. 2. title of play by Apollod.Gel., Suid. 3. = βαφεύς, Hsch.

δευσοπορούσιος, α, ον, (δεύω A, βοῦς) *dyed red*, prob. in *PMasp*.6 ii 81 (vi A.D.).

δευτάτιος [ᾰ], α, ον, poet. for δεύτατος, Max.350.

δεύτατος, η, ον, Sup. of δεύτερος, = ὕστατος, *the last*, Il.19.51, Mosch.4.65, *Schwyzer* 90.3, 92.2 (Argos, iii B.C.), etc.:—prob. f.l. in Pi.*O*.1.50.

δεῦτε, Adv., as pl. of δεῦρο, *come hither!* in Hom. with pl. imper. (exc. δεῦτ' ἄγε Φαιήκων ἡγήτορες Od.8.11), either expressed, δεῦτ' ἄγετ' Il.7.350, al.; or understood, δεῦτε, φίλοι 13.481; δεῦθ', ἵνα.. ἴδησθε Od.8.30: rarely in Lyr., Sapph.60, 65, and Trag., δεῦτε, λείπετε στέγος E.*Med*.894: in later Prose, δ. οἰκοδομήσωμεν Lxx *Ge*. 11.4; δ. ἴδετε *Ev.Matt*.28.6; δ. καὶ ἀκούσατε Arr.*Epict*.3.23.6; δ. πρός τινα Plu.*Cor*.33.

δευτερᾰγωνιστ-έω, *play second-class parts*, Poll.4.124. **-ής**, οῦ, ὁ, *actor who takes second-class parts*, Hsch. 2. metaph., *seconder, supporter*, D.19.10, Luc.*Peregr*.36.

δευτερ-αῖος, α, ον, *on the second day*, usu. agreeing with the subject of the Verb, δ. ἐκ τοῦ Ἀθηναίων ἄστεος ἦν ἐν Σπάρτῃ Hdt.6.106, cf. X.*Cyr*.5.2.2, etc.; also τῇ δ. (sc. ἡμέρᾳ) Hdt.4.113. **-εῖος**, α, ον, *of second quality*, Dsc.1.49; ἄρτοι *Gp*.2.32.3; βίρρος *Edict.Diocl*. 7.43. II. neut. pl. **δευτερεῖα** (sc. ἆθλα), τά, *second prize* in a contest, hence *second place* or *rank*, δ. νέμειν τινί Hdt.1.32; δευτερείοισι ὑπερβάλλειν *votes for second place*, Id.8.123, cf. Pl.*Phlb*.22c, etc.:—later in sg., *CIG*2360.29 (Delos), 2759 (Aphrodisias), D.L.2. 133. 2. *secondary action*, Arist.*Pr*.921ᵇ36. **-έσχᾰτος**, ον, *last but one*, Heliod.ap.Orib.46.11.23. **-εύω**, *to be second*, οὐδενὸς Plb. 18.55.5; δ. μετὰ τὸν βασιλέα D.S.1.73, cf. Str.8.6.18; δ. τινός *to be next best to* it, Dsc.3.39, cf. Herod.Med.ap.Orib.10.11.3; δ. τινί *to play second to*.., Plu.*Eum*.13, cf. Lxx*Es*.4.8. **-έω**, = foreg., v.l. in ib.*Je*.52.24, cf. Hld.10.6. **-ιάζω**, *play the second part*, Ar.*Ec*. 634. **-ίας** (sc. οἶνος), ὁ, *seconds*, a poor wine made from στέμφυλα, Dsc.5.6, Poll.1.248, 6.17, Hsch.; prob. l. in Nicopho 20. **-ίναρ**, = foreg., Hsch. **-ιος**, α, ον, *of inferior quality*, οἶνος Nicoph.20 codd.; cf. δευτερίας. 2. τὸ δ. or τὰ δ. *afterbirth*, Aq.*De*.28.57, prob. in Paul.Aeg.6.75. 3. = χόριον, Steph.*in Hp*.2.463 D.

δευτερο-βόλος, ον, *shedding the teeth a second time*, ἵππος Hierocl. *Facet*.4, cf. *Hippiatr*.20, *POxy*.1708.10 (iv A.D.); of camels, *BGU* 1088.4 (ii A.D.), etc. **-γενής**, ές, *produced later*, τρίχες Antig.*Mir*. 109. **-γονος**, ον, *second-born*, Aq.*Ge*.30.42.

δευτερ-οδέομαι (better -ῳδέομαι), Pass., *to be secondary, produced by repetition*, of numbers, *Theol.Ar*.22; μονάδες Nicom.*Ar*.1.19, cf. Syrian.*in Metaph*.149.23:—hence Subst. **-οδία** (better -ῳδία), ἡ, *secondary series*, *Theol.Ar*.34.

δευτερο-κοιτέω, *to have a bedfellow*, Ath.13.584b. **-λεπτον**, τό, Astron., *second of a minute of degree*, Rhetor. in *Cat.Cod.Astr*.7. 194.22. **-λογέω**, *speak a second time*, Lxx 2*Ma*.13.22. **-λογία**, *second speech*, Hermog.*Meth*.27, *Stat*.3 (pl.), Aphth.*Prog*.7, etc. **-λόγος**, ὁ, *second speaker*, Teles p.5 H. **-νόμιον**, τό, *second* or *repeated Law*, the fifth book of the Pentateuch, Lxx, cf. *De*.17.18, *Jo*.9.5(8.32). **-πάθεια** [πᾰ], ἡ, *secondary affection*, Gal. 8.31:—**πᾰθέω**, *have a secondary affection*, ibid. **-ποτμος**, ον, = ὑστερόποτμος, Hsch. **-πρωτον** σάββατον, τό, prob. corrupt in *Ev.Luc*.6.1 (no expl. is satisfactory).

δεύτερος, α, ον, *second*, (perh. from δύο with Comp. termination): I. *next* in Order (with a notion of Time), in Il. (not in Od.) of one who *comes in second* in a race, 23.265; δ. ἐλθεῖν 22. 207; δ. αὖτ'.. προΐει.. ἔγχος *next*, 20.273, etc.; οὔ μ' ἔτι δ. ὧδε ἵξετ' ἄχος no *second* grief, i.e. none *hereafter* like this, 23.46; as Comp., c. gen., ἐμεῖο δεύτεροι *after* my *time*, ib.248; σοὶ δ' οὐκέτι δ. ἔσται no *second choice* will be allowed thee, Hes.*Op*.34; in Att. and Trag. with Art., ὁ δ. S.*OC*1315, etc.; αἱ δ. πως φροντίδες σοφώτεραι *second* thoughts are wisest, E.*Hipp*.436: prov., δ. πλοῦς the *next best* way, Pl.*Phd*.99d, etc.; ὁ δ. πλοῦς ἐστι δήπου λεγόμενος, ἂν ἀποτύχῃ τις οὐρίου, κώπαισι πλεῖν Men.241. 2. of Time, *next, later*, δ. χρόνῳ in *after* time, Pi.*O*.1.43; δ. ἡμέρῃ on the *next* day, Hdt.1.82; δ. ἔτεϊ τούτων in the year *after* this, Id.6.46: neut. as Adv., δεύτερον αὖ, αὖτε, αὖτις, *a second time*, Il.3.332,191, Od.9.354; ἐν τᾷ δ. ἐκκλησίᾳ *SIG*644.20: with the Art., τὸ δ. Sapph.*Supp*.4.11, Hdt.1.79, A.*Ag*.1082, X.*Cyr*.2.2.1: also pl., Hdt.3.53, 9.3; τὰ δ. κινδυνεύσοντας about to run the *next* dangers, Th.6.78; later, ἐκ δευτέρου for *the second time*, *Ev.Marc*.14.72, Dsc.5.87.10; ἐκ δευτέρης Babr. 114.5, cf. *PStrassb*.100.22 (ii B.C.): regul. Adv. δευτέρως Pl.*Lg*. 955e, Sallust.18, etc. b. ὁ δ. the *younger*, *BGU*592.10 (ii A.D.). II. in Order or Rank (without any notion of Time), *second*, δ. μετ' ἐκεῖνον Hdt.1.31, cf. S.*Ph*.1442, etc.; πολὺ δ. Id.*OC*1228 (lyr.); πολὺ δ. μετά τι very much *behind*, Th.2.97; μετὰ τὸ πλουτεῖν δ. Antiph.144.9: c. gen., δ. οὐδενός *second* to none, Hdt.1.23, Plb.31. 27.16; δ. παιδὸς σῆς E.*Tr*.618; πάντα τἄλλα δεύτερ' ἦν τῶν προσδοκιῶν D.19.24; πρὸς τὰ χρήματα θνητοῖσι τἄλλα δεύτερ' S.*Fr*.354.5; τὰ ἄλλα πάντα δ. τε καὶ ὕστερα λεκτέον Pl.*Phlb*.59c; logically or metaphysically *posterior*, πᾶν πλῆθος δ. ἐστι τοῦ ἑνός Procl.*Inst*.5, cf. 36, Dam.*Pr*.126, al.; δεύτερ' ἡγεῖσθαι think *quite secondary*, S.*OC* 351; δεύτερον ἄγειν, δεύτερα ποιεῖσθαι, Luc.*Symp*.9, Plu.2.162e; ἐν δευτέρῳ τίθεσθαι Id.*Fab*.24, cf. Jul.*Or*.8.242b; ἱερὸν δ. *of the second class*, *OGI*56.59 (iii B.C.), etc. 2. *the second of two*, δ. αὐτή herself *with another*, Hdt.4.113, cf. *AB*89; ἑπτὰ δ. σοφοί a *second* seven sages, Euphro 1.12; εἷς καὶ δ. *unus et alter*, Hdn.Gr.2.934; εἷς ἢ δ. Jul.*Or*.6.190d; ἕν τι .. ἢ δεύτερον D.Chr.33.7; δ. καὶ τρίτος *two* or three, Plb.26.1.1; neut. as Adv., ἅπαξ καὶ δεύτερον once or *twice*, Jul. *ad Ath*.278c. 3. δ. ἀριθμός number *whose prime factors are odd*, Nicom.*Ar*.1.12. III. as Subst., τὰ δ., = δευτερεῖα, *the second prize* or *place*, Il.23.538; τὰ δ. φέρεσθαι Hdt.8.104. 2. *after-birth*, Dsc.1.48,50. 3. δευτέρα σαββάτου (sc. ἡμέρα) *second day of the week*, Lxx *Ps*.47(48) tit.

δευτερο-στάτης [ᾰ], ου, ὁ, *one who stands in the rear file of the Chorus*, Them.*Or*.13.175b. 2. in pl., *soldiers in the rear rank*, Arr.*Alan*.17. **-στολιστής**, οῦ, ὁ, στολιστής (q.v.) *of the second class*, *PTeb*.313.5 (iii A.D.).

δευτεροστρᾰτηλᾰτιανοί, οἱ, = Lat. *Comitatenses*, Lyd.*Mag*.2.7.

δευτερο-τᾰγής, ές, *in the second series*, Nicom.*Ar*.1.13. **-τόκος**, ον, *bearing a second time*, Arist.*HA*546^{a}12.

δευτερ-ουργής, ές, *vamped up, second-hand*, χλαῖνα Poll.7. 77. **-ουργός**, όν, *working in the second place, secondary*, opp. πρωτουργός, κινήσεις Pl.*Lg*.897a, cf. Iamb.*Myst*.3.1: but, II. Subst. δευτερουργός, ὁ, *one who vamps up old clothes*, Poll.7.77. **-οῦχος**, ον, = τὰ δευτερεῖα ἔχων, Lyc.204.

δευτερό-φωνος, ον, *speaking after one*, of Echo, Nonn.*D*.2.119. **-χύται** [ῠ], αἱ, *wine from the second pressing*, *PFlor*.178.2 (iii A.D.).

δευτερ-όω, *do the second time*: *repeat*, λόγον Lxx *Si*.7.14, al. 2. *change*, ὁδόν ib.*Je*.2.36. II. δ. τινί *to give* one *a second blow*, ib. 1*Ki*.26.8: c. acc., τινά *slay*, ib.3*Ki*.21(20).20. III. intr., *occur twice*, ib.*Ge*.41.32. **-ῳδέομαι, -ῳδία**, v. δευτεροδέομαι, -οδία. **-ωμα**, ατος, τό, *repetition*, Eust.80.10. **-ωσις**, εως, ἡ, *second rank* or *course*, Lxx 4*Ki*.23.4. II. *Jewish traditions*, Just.*Nov*.146.1.2.

δευτήρ, ῆρος, ὁ, *kettle, cauldron*, Demiopr.ap.Poll.10.105; cf. δεῦμα.

δεύω (A), impf. ἔδευον, Ep. δεῦον, Ion. δεύεσκον, Od.8.522, Il.13. 655, Od.7.260: fut. δεύσω Eub.90.4: aor. ἔδευσα Eup.332, Pl.Com. 173.9, S.*Aj*.376 (lyr.):—Med., Od.5.53:—Pass., ib.6.44, etc.: fut. δεύσομαι (ἀνα-) Gal.10.867: aor. ἐδεύθην Hp.*Ulc*.11, Thphr.*HP*9.9. 1: pf. δέδευμαι E.*Fr*.467.5, Pl.*Lg*.782c, X.*Cyr*.6.2.28:—*wet, drench*, δεῦε δὲ γαῖαν (sc. αἷμα) Il.13.655, cf. 23.220; γλάγος ἄγγεα δεύει 2. 471; δάκρυ δ' ἔδευε .. παρειάς Od.8.522; σπογγιὰν δεύων Hp.*Loc. Hom*.12: c. dat. modi, εἵματα δ' αἰεὶ δάκρυσι δεύεσκον Od.7.260:—Pass., δεύοντο δὲ δάκρυσι κόλποι Il.9.570; αἵματι δὲ χθὼν δεύετο 17. 361; χρίμασι δευόμενοι Xenoph.3.6; μέλιτι καρποὶ δεδευμένοι Pl.*Lg*. l. c.; *to be flooded* with light, ἀργέτι δεύεται αὐγῇ Emp.21.4; ῥίζα ὄξει δευθεῖσα *steeped* in .., Thphr. l. c.:—Med., πυκινὰ πτερὰ δεύεται ἅλμῃ *wets his* wings in the brine, Od.5.53, cf. E.*Alc*.184: rarely c. gen. modi, αἵματος ἔδευσε γαῖαν Id.*Ph*.674 (lyr.). 2. *mix* a dry mass *with liquid*, so as to make it fit to knead, Ar.*Fr*.271; δεῦσαι καὶ μάξαι X.*Oec*.10.11; ἄρτον ὕδατι δεδευμένον Id.*Cyr*.6.2.28; ἀλφίτοις δ. *knead up* with meal, D.H.7.72. 3. *smear*, δᾶδας πίττῃ δεδευμένας Hdn.8. 4.11:—Med., ἀμφὶ μελαίνῃ δευόμεναι σποδιῇ πλόκαμον *AP*7.10. II. causal, *make to flow, shed*, ἐρεμνὸν αἷμ' ἔδευσα S.*Aj*.376 (lyr.).

δεύω (B), Aeol. and Ep. form of δέω (B), *miss, want*, Act. used by Hom. only in aor., ἐδεύησεν δ' οἰήϊον ἄκρον ἱκέσθαι *he missed, failed* in reaching it, Od.9.483,540: δεύει, = δεῖ, *IG*12(2).526*A* 19 (Eresus); δεύοντος Alc.*Oxy*.1788.15 ii 3. II. Dep. **δεύομαι**, fut. δευήσομαι Od.6.192, = Att. δέομαι, *feel the want* or loss *of, be without*, θυμοῦ δευόμενος *reft of* life, Il.3.294, 20.472; *stand in need of*, βάκτρου E.*Tr*. 276; ἐν καίροις ἐπιμελήτας δευομένοις *IG*12(2).243 (Mytilene); αἴ κέ τινος δεύωνται ib.15.26; ἐδεύετο ἤματος ὥρη .. νέεσθαι the time of day *required* her to return, A.R.3.1138. 2. *to be wanting, deficient in*, δ. πολέμοιο Il.13.310; μάχης ἔρα πολλὸν ἐδεύεο 17.142: abs., δευόμενος *in need*, 22.492; τετράκις εἰς ἑκατὸν δεύοιτό κεν *it would fall short* .., A.R.2.974. 3. c. gen. pers., *to be inferior to*, ἄλλα τε πάντα δεύεαι Ἀργείων Il.23.484; οὔ τευ δευόμενον Od.4.264.

δεφιδασταί, οἱ, guild of fullers, *IG*4.608 (Argos).

δέφῡρα, ἡ, Cret., = γέφυρα, *GDI*5000 (Gortyn).

δέφω, *soften* by working with the hand: δ. ἑαυτόν, sens. obsc., = Lat. *masturbari*, Eub.120.5:—Med., Ar.*Eq*.24, *Pax*290.

δεχάμμᾰτος, ον, (δέκα, ἅμμα) *with ten meshes*, X.*Cyn*.10.2.

δεχάς, άδος, ἡ, *receptacle*, coined by Pythag. to expl. δεκάς, Ph.2. 184, *Theol.Ar*.59, Ascl.*in Metaph*.38.31, etc.

δέχαται, v. δέχομαι.

δεχεπτά, *seventeen*, J.*BJ*5.11.4.

δεχήμερος, ον, *for ten days, lasting ten days*, θυσία Pl.*Ep*.349d; ἐκεχειρία δ. truce *terminable at ten days' notice* (or, *renewable every ten days*), Th.5.26; ἀνοχαί Plb.20.9.5; σπονδαί Th.6.7,10; written δεκ- *BGU*812 ii 11 (ii/iii A.D.). II. δεχήμερον, τό, *a space of ten days*, Poll.1.63.

δέχνῡμαι, poet. for δέχομαι, Orph.*A*.564, Parth.*Fr*.4, *AP*9.553, Epic.in *Arch.Pap*.7.5, *IG*3.1347, Coluth.159, Q.S.12.585: in late Prose, Hld.3.2.

δεχοκτώ, *eighteen*, *IG*14.1648.

δέχομαι, Ion., Aeol., Cret. **δέκομαι**, Hdt.9.91, Sapph.1.22, Pi.*O*.2. 69, impf. ἐδεκόμην Hdt.3.135: fut. δέξομαι, Ep. also δεδέξομαι Il.5. 238, also in *AP*5.8 (Rufin.), Aristid.*Or*.28(49).24; δεξοῦμαι *SIG* 360.29 (Chersonesus); δεχθήσομαι (in pass. sense) Lxx *Le*.22.25: aor. ἐδεξάμην Il.18.238, etc., δεξάμην Pi.*P*.4.70; also ἐδέχθην (ὑπ-) E.*Heracl*.757 (lyr., δεχθείς in pass. sense), J.*AJ*18.6.4, (εἰσ-) D.40.14 (Pass.): pf. δέδεγμαι Il.4.107, Pi.*P*.1.100, etc.; imper. δέδεξο Il.5. 228, pl. δέδεχθε *h.Ap*.538; Ion. 3 pl. ἀπο-δεδέχαται Hdt.2.43, al.:—Hom. also has Ep. impf. ἐδέγμην Od.9.513, 3 sg. δέκτο Il.15.88, al., later ἔδεκτο Pi.*O*.2.54, Simon.184; imper. δέξο Il.19.10, pl. δέχθε A.R.4.1554; inf. δέχθαι E.*Rh*.525; part. δέγμενος Il.18.524 (also δέχμενος Hsch.); also a 3 pl. pres. δέχαται Il.12.147; cf. προτίδεγμαι, and v. δεδοκημένος:— I. of things as the object, *take, accept, receive*, etc., ἄποινα 1.20, etc.; μισθὸν τῆς φυλακῆς Pl.*R*.416e; φόρον Th.1.96; δ. τι χείρεσσι Od.19.355; τὸ διδόμενον παρά τινος Pl.*Grg*.499c; τι ἐν παρακαταθήκῃ παρά τινος Plb.33.6.2, etc.; δ. τί τινι *receive* something *at the hand of* another, δέξατό οἱ σκῆπτρον πατρώϊον Il.2.186, cf. *IG*12(3).1075 (Melos, vi B.C.), etc.; *accept* as legal tender, ὀδελός *GDI*5011 (Gortyn); τι παρά τινος Il.24.429; τι ἔκ τινος S. *OT*1107 (lyr.); τί τινος Il.1.596, 24.305, S.*OT*1163; also δ. τί τινος *receive in exchange for* .., χρυσὸν φίλου ἀνδρὸς ἐδέξατο Od.11.327; *choose*, τι δ. πρό τινος Pl.*Lg*.729d; μᾶλλον δ. τι ἀντί τινος Id.*Grg*. 475d: c. inf., *prefer*, δεξαίμην ἂν πάσας τὰς ἀσπίδας ἐρριφέναι ἢ .. Lys. 10.21, cf. Pl.*Phlb*.63b; δ. μᾶλλον .. X.*HG*5.1.14, *Smp*.4.12; οὐδεὶς ἂν δέξαιτο φεύγειν Th.1.143; Ὀρφεῖ συγγενέσθαι ἐπὶ πόσῳ ἄν τις δέξαιτ' ἂν ὑμῶν; Pl.*Ap*.41a; οὐκ ἂν δεξαίμην τι ἔχειν And.1.5. b. *catch*, as in a vessel, ὀπὸν .. κάδοις δ. S.*Fr*.534.3. 2. of mental reception, *take, accept* without complaint, χαλεπόν περ ἐόντα δεχώμεθα μῦθον Od.20.271; κῆρα δ' ἐγὼ τότε δέξομαι Il.18.115. b. *accept* graciously, τοῦτο δ' ἐγὼ πρόφρων δ. 23.647; of the gods, ἀλλ' ὅ γε δέκτο μὲν ἱρά 2.420; προσφιλῶς γέρα δ., of one dead, S.*El*.443; τὰ σφάγια δ. Ar.*Lys*.204, cf. Pi.*P*.5.86; τὸ χρησθέν, τὸν οἰωνὸν δ., *accept, hail* the oracle, the omen, Hdt.1.63, 9.91; δέχου τὸν ἄνδρα καὶ τὸν ὄρνιν Ar.*Pl*.63; δ. τὰ ἀγαθά *IG*2^2.410, al.; ἐδεξάμην τὸ ῥηθέν S.*El*.668: abs., δεχομένοις λέγεις θανεῖν σε A.*Ag*.1653, cf. X.*An*.1.8.17; *accept, approve*, τὸν λόγον, ξυμμαχίαν, Hdt.9.5, Th.1.37; τοὺς λόγους ib.95; διδόναι καὶ δέχεσθαι τὰ δίκαια ib.37, cf. *h.Merc*.312; δέχεσθαι ὅρκον, v. ὅρκος; *accept* a confession, and so *forgive*, ἀδικίαν Lxx *Ge*.50.17. c. simply, *give ear to, hear*, ὠσὶν ἠχήν E.*Ba*.1086; δ. ὀμφάν Id.*Med*.175 (lyr.); τὰ παραγγελλόμενα ὀξέως δ. Th.2.11, 89. d. *take* or *regard* as so and so, μηδὲ συμφορὰν δέχου τὸν ἄνδρα S.*Aj*.68; *understand* in a certain sense, ὅπῃ βούλει δέξασθαι ταύτῃ δέχου Pl.*Ep*.315c: c. inf., κῶλά με δέξαι νυνὶ λέγειν D.H.*Comp*.22, cf. Str.1.3.13, etc. e. *cap* verses, σκόλια δ. Ar.*V*.1222. 3. *take upon oneself*, τὴν δαπάνην Plb.31.28.5: c. inf., *undertake*, *SIG*245.34. II. of persons as the object, *welcome*, κόλπῳ Il.6.483; ἀγαθῷ νόῳ Hdt.1.60; ἐν μεγάροισι, ἐν δόμοισιν, Il.18.331, Od.17.110; δόμοις δ. τινά S.*OT*818; στέγαις, πυρὶ δ. τινά, E.*Or*.47; δ. χώρᾳ Id.*Med*.713; τῇ πόλει δ. *to admit* into the city, Th.4.103; ἀγορᾷ, ἄστει δ., Id.6.44; ἔσω ibid.; εἰς τὸ τεῖχος X.*An*.5.5.6; δ. τινὰ ξύμμαχον *accept* or *admit* as an ally, Th.1.43, etc.; *accept as security*, *PGrenf*.1.33.4, etc.: metaph. of places, τόποι τοὺς κατοικιζομένους ἵλεῳ δεχόμενοι Pl.*Lg*.747e; *entertain*, δείπνοις Anaxandr.41.2 (anap.); δωρήμασιν S.*OC*4. 2. *receive as an enemy, await the attack of*, ἐπιόντα δ. δουρί Il.5.238, cf. 15.745; of a hunter *waiting for* game, 4.107; of a wild boar *waiting for* the hunters, 12.147; of troops, εἰς χεῖρας δ. X.*An*.4.3.31; τοὺς Λακεδαιμονίους δ. Hdt.3.54, cf. 8.28, Th.4.43; ἐπιόντας δ. Id.7.77; δ. τὴν πρώτην ἔφοδον Id.4.126; ἐδέξατο πόλις πόνον E.*Supp*.393. 3. *expect, wait*, c. acc. et fut. inf., ἀλλ' αἰεί τινα φῶτα .. ἐδέγμην ἐνθάδ' ἐλεύσεσθαι Od.9.513, cf. 12.230; also δέγμενος Αἰακίδην, ὁπότε λήξειεν Il.9.191; δεδεγμένος εἰσόκεν ἔλθῃς 10.62.—In these two last senses, Hom. always uses fut. δεδέξομαι, pf. δέδεγμαι, and δεδεγμένος, cf. δεδεγμένος ὁππόθ' ἵκοιτο Theoc.25. 228; δέγμενος is used in sense 3 only, exc. in *h.Cer*.29, *Merc*.477: inf. δειδέχθαι as imper., *expect*, c. gen., βορέω Arat.795, cf. 907, 928. III. rarely with a thing as the subject, *occupy, engage* one, τίς ἀρχὰ δέξατο ναυτιλίας [αὐτούς]; Pi.*P*.4.70. 2. *receive, hold*, τὴν τροφήν Arist.*HA*531^{a}23, al.; οἰκίαι ἱκαναὶ δέξασθαι ὑμᾶς *SIG*344. 10. 3. *admit of*, ψεῦδος οὐδὲν δ. ἁ τῶ ἀριθμῶ φύσις Philol.11; τὸ μᾶλλον Arist.*Top*.146^{a}3, cf. D.H.*Isoc*.2. 4. Geom., *contain, circum-*

scribe, γωνίας ἴσας Euc.3 *Def.*11; πεντάγωνον Papp.422.34. IV. intr., *succeed, come next*, ὥς μοι δέχεται κακὸν ἐκ κακοῦ αἰεί Il.19.290; ἄλλος γ' ἐξ ἄλλου δέχεται χαλεπώτερος ἆθλος Hes.*Th.*800; ἄλλος ἐξ ἄλλου δ. Emp.115.12; of places, ἐκ τοῦ στεινοῦ τὸ Ἀρτεμίσιον δέκεται Hdt.7.176. (δέκομαι is prob. the original form, cf. Slav. *desiti*, *dositi* 'find'.)

δέψα, ἡ, *skin, hide*, Suid.

δέψω, aor. ἐδέψησα, *work* or *knead* a thing *till it is soft*, κηρὸν δεψήσας μελιηδέα Od.12.48; δέψει χερσὶ [τὸ δέρμα] Hdt.4.64.

δέω (A), imper. 3 pl. δεόντων Od.12.54 codd. (v. δίδημι): fut. δήσω: aor. ἔδησα, Ep. δῆσα Il.21.30: pf. δέδεκα D.24.207, v.l. δεδηκότας in Aeschin.2.134: plpf. ἐδεδήκει And.4.17 (prob.):—**Med.**, Ep. impf. δέοντο Il.18.553: aor. ἐδησάμην 24.340, al.; Ep. 3 sg. δησάσκετο ib.15:—**Pass.**, fut. δεθήσομαι D.24.126,131, etc., δεδήσομαι Pl.*R.*361e, X.*Cyr.*4.3.18; δεδέσομαι f.l. in Aristid.*Or.*41(4).7: aor. ἐδέθην D.24.132, etc.: pf. δέδεμαι (v. infr.): plpf. ἐδεδέμην And.1.48; Ep. δέδετο Il.5.387; Ion. 3 pl. ἐδεδέατο Hdt.1.66, etc.—In this Verb, though a disyll., εο and εω are occas. contr. τὸ δοῦν, τῷ δοῦντι, Pl.*Cra.*419b, 421c; δοῦσα Din.*Fr.*89.15:—*bind, tie, fetter*, δεσμῷ τινα δῆσαι Il.10.443, etc.; ἐνὶ δεσμῷ 5.386, etc.; ἐν πέδαις (v.l. ἐς πέδας) Hdt.5.77; δῆσε δ' ὀπίσσω χεῖρας.. ἱμᾶσιν Il.21.30; δ. τινὰ χεῖράς τε πόδας τε Od.12.50; δ. ἔκ τινος *to bind* from (i.e. to) a thing, ἐξ ἐπιδιφριάδος ἱμᾶσι δέδεντο Il.10.475, cf. Hdt.4.72; δῆσαί τινα ξύλῳ or ἐν ξύλῳ (cf. ξύλον II.2); ἐν κλίμακι Ar.*Ra.*619; δ. κύνα κλοιῷ *tie* a clog to a dog, Lex Solonis ap. Plu.*Sol.*24, cf. E.*Cyc.*234; δ. τινὰ πρὸς φάραγγι A.*Pr.*15; πρὸς κίονα, κίονι, S.*Aj.*108,240 (lyr.); δεδεμένοι πρὸς ἀλλήλους Th.4.47; δεδέσθαι ἐν τῇ ποδοκάκκῃ Lex Solonis ap.D.24.105. 2. alone, *bind, keep in bonds*, πῶς ἂν ἐγώ σε δέοιμι; says Hephaistos, pointing to the nets in which he had caught Ares, Od.8.352; αὐτὸς δ' ἔδησε πατέρα A.*Eu.*641; δήσαντες ἔχειν τινάς Th.1.30; δησάντων αὐτὸν οἱ ἕνδεκα Lex ap.D.24.105, etc. 3. metaph., *bind, enchain*, γλῶσσα δέ οἱ δέδεται Thgn.178; κέρδει καὶ σοφία δέδεται Pi.*P.*3.54; ψυχὰ δ. λύπῃ E.*Hipp.*160 (lyr.); later, *bind by spells*, τὸ στόμα *AP*11.138 (Lucill.), cf. *Tab. Defix.*96,108. 4. c. gen., *hinder from* a thing, ἔδησε κελεύθου Od.4.380,469. 5. Medic., *harden, brace up*, Hp.*Off.*17, etc. II. Med., *bind, tie, put on oneself*, ποσσὶ δ' ὑπὸ λιπαροῖσιν ἐδήσατο καλὰ πέδιλα *tied* them on *his* feet, Il.2.44, etc.:—Pass., περὶ δὲ κνήμῃσι βοείας κνημῖδας.. δέδετο he *had* greaves *bound* round his legs, Od.24.228. (Cf. Skt. *ditás* 'bound', *dā́ma* 'bond'.)

δέω (B), A.*Pr.*1006, etc.: fut. δεήσω Pl.*R.*395e: aor. ἐδέησα Lys.30.8, Ep. δῆσα only Il.18.100: pf. δεδέηκα Pl.*Plt.*277d:—**Med.**, fut. δεήσομαι Th.1.32, etc., Dor. δεοῦμαι Epich.120; later -θήσομαι Lxx *Jb.*5.8, Plu.2.213c, etc.: aor. ἐδεήθην Hdt.4.84, Ar.*Pl.*986, etc.: pf. δεδέημαι X.*An.*7.7.14, Is.8.22 (the forms δεήσω, etc., compared with the Ep. ἐδεύησα, δεύομαι, point to √δεϝ):—*lack, miss, stand in need of*, c. gen., ἐμεῖο δὲ δῆσε.. ἀλκτῆρα γενέσθαι Il. l.c. (elsewh. Hom. uses δεύω, q.v.); παραδείγματος τὸ παράδειγμα αὐτὸ δεδέηκεν Pl.*Plt.*277d, cf. X.*Mem.*4.2.10. 2. freq. in Att., πολλοῦ δέω I *want* much, i.e. *am* far *from*, mostly c. inf. pres., πολλοῦ δ. ἀπολογεῖσθαι I *am* far *from* defending myself, Pl.*Ap.*30d; πολλοῦ δεῖς εἰπεῖν Id.*Men.*79b; π. δ. ἀγνοεῖν Id.*Ly.*204e; π. γε δέουσι μαίνεσθαι Id.*Men.*92a; also μικροῦ ἔδεον ἐν χερσὶν εἶναι X.*HG*4.6.11, cf. Men.*Georg.*25; τοσούτου δέω ἱκανὸς εἶναι λέγειν ὥστε.. Lys.17.1; τοσούτου δέουσι μιμεῖσθαι Isoc.14.17 (also τοσοῦτον δέω εἰδέναι Pl.*Men.*71a); παρὰ μικρὸν ἐδέησα ἀποθανεῖν v.l. in Isoc.17.42; simply ἐδέησα κινδύνῳ περιπεσεῖν Alciphr.3.5: abs., πολλοῦ γε δέω I *am* far *from* it, Pl.*Phdr.*228a; τοῦ παντὸς δέω A.*Pr.*1006; παντὸς δεῖ τοιοῦτος εἶναι Pl.*Sph.*221d (impers. πολλοῦ δεῖ, etc., v. δεῖ II.1.b): in part., παλαστῆς δεόντων τεττάρων ποδῶν *IG*1².373.8; μικροῦ δέοντα τέτταρα τάλαντα D.27.35; the part. is freq. used to express numerals compounded with 8 or 9, ἀνδράσιν ἑνὸς δέουσι τριάκοντα *IG*1².374.413; δυοῖν δέοντα τεσσεράκοντα forty *lacking* two, thirty-eight, Hdt.1.14; πεντήκοντα δυοῖν δέοντα ἔτη Th.2.2; ἑνὸς δέον εἰκοστὸν ἔτος the 20th year *save* one, the 19th, Id.8.6; δυοῖν δεούσαις εἴκοσι ναυσίν X.*HG*1.1.5: later, the inf. stands abs., περὶ τὰ ἑνὸς δεῖν πεντήκοντα fifty *save* one, Arist.*Rh.*1390ᵇ11: part. in gen., τροφαλίδες μιᾶς δεούσης εἴκοσιν Id.*HA*522ᵃ31; πόλεων δυοῖν δεούσαιν ἑξήκοντα D.L.5.27; ἑξήκοντα ἑνὸς δέοντος ἔτη Plu.*Pomp.*79. 3. part. δέων, δέουσα, as Adj., *fit, proper*, ὁ καιρὸς οὐκ ἔστι χρόνος δέων Arist.*APr.*48ᵇ36; τοῖς δέουσι χρόνοις *IG*12(3).247.11 (Anaphe); ἡ δέουσα ἑκάστων χρῆσις Hierocl.p.61 A., etc.: esp. freq. in neut., v. δέον. 4. δεῖ impers., v. h. v. II. Dep. **δέομαι**: contr. δῆσθε Sophr.46, part. δεύμενος Id.36: fut. δεήσομαι Pl.*Phlb.*53b: aor. ἐδεήθην: always personal, and used by Hom. only in form δεύομαι (v. δεύω B): 1. abs., *to be in want* or *need, require*, mostly in part., κάρτα δεόμενος Hdt.8.59; οἱ δεόμενοι the *needy*, opp. οἱ κεκτημένοι τὰς οὐσίας, Isoc.6.67. b. *stand in need of, want*, c. gen., Hdt.1.36, etc.; τὰ σὰ δεῖται κολαστοῦ.. ἔπη S.*OT*1148; ῥώμης τινὸς δ. ib.1293; οὐδὲν δεῖσθαι τροφῆς *have* no *need of*..., Th.8.43; ἤν τι δέωνται βασιλέως if *they have* any *need* of him, ib.37: c. inf., τοῦτο ἔτι δέομαι μαθεῖν Pl.*R.*392d, cf. *Euthd.*275d, etc.; τὰ πράττεσθαι δεόμενα *things needing* to be done, X.*Cyr.*2.3.3; τὰ δεόμενα *necessaries*, *IG*2.573.4; ἐπισκευάσαι τὰ δεόμενα parts *needing* repair, ib.2².1176.15; τὸ δεόμενον *the point threatened*, Plb.15.15.7; δεῖται impers., v. δεῖ. 2. *beg* a thing *from* a person, c. dupl. gen. rei et pers., τῶν ἐδέετο σφέων Hdt.3.157, cf. Th.1.32, etc.; μή μου δεηθῇς. ΘΗ. πράγματος ποίου; S.*OC*1170: freq. with neut. Pron. in acc., τοῦτο ὑμῶν δέομαι Pl.*Ap.*17c, cf. *Smp.*173e, etc.: c. acc. cogn., δέημα, or oftener δέησιν, δεῖσθαί τινος, Ar.*Ach.*1059, Aeschin.2.43, etc.: also c. acc. rei only, ξυμφορὰ δ. Th.1.32; δυνατά τινος Pl.*Prt.*335e; δίκαια καὶ μέτρια ὑμῶν D.38.2; διαπράξωμαι ἃ δέομαι X.*An.*2.3.29: with gen. pers. only, δεηθεὶς ὑμῶν *having begged a favour* of you, D.21.108: c. gen. pers. et inf., ἐδέετο τοῦ δήμου φυλακῆς πρὸς αὐτοῦ κυρῆσαι Hdt.1.59, cf. Pl.*Prt.*336a, etc.; δ. τινὸς ὥστε.. Th.1.119; ὅπως.. Plu.*Ant.*84: rarely c. acc. pers., ἐδέοντο Βοιωτοὺς ὅπως παραδώσουσι Th.5.36: parenthetic, δέομαι *I pray*, Lxx *Ge.*44.18.

δέω (C), = δήω (A), Alc.102.

δή, prop. a temporal Particle (cf. ἤδη), *at this* or *that point*: hence, *now, then, already*, or *at length*: I. in Ep. (rarely Lyr.) sts. at the beginning of a sentence or clause, Τεῦκρε πέπον, δὴ νῶϊν ἀπέκτατο πιστὸς ἑταῖρος Il.15.437; δὴ πάμπαν ἀποίχεαι ἀνδρὸς ἑῆος 19.342; δὴ γὰρ μέγα νεῖκος ὄρωρεν 13.122; δὴ τότε, δή ῥα τότε, 1.476, 13.719, al., cf. Pi.*O.*3.25, A.*Th.*214 (lyr.): but usu. second (or nearly so), freq. with Numerals and temporal Particles, ὀκτὼ δὴ προέηκα.. ὀϊστούς Il.8.297; ἐννέα δὴ βεβάασι.. ἐνιαυτοί *full* nine years, 2.134; ἕκτον δὲ δὴ τόδ' ἦμαρ this is *just* the sixth day, E.*Or.*39, cf. Il.24.107, etc.: also after Advbs. of Time, πολλάκι δή many a time *and oft*, often *ere now*, 19.85; ὀψὲ δὲ δή 7.94; τρὶς δή Pi.*P.*9.91; πάλαι δή, Lat. *jamdudum*, S.*Ph.*806; νῦν δή *just* now, Ar.*Av.*923 (freq. written νυνδή, Pl.*Tht.*145b, etc.); νῦν τε καὶ ἄλλοτε δή ib.187d; now *at length*, Id.*R.*353a, etc.; τότε δή at that *very* time, Th.1.49, etc.; αὐτίκα δὴ μάλα this *very* instant, Pl.*R.*338b, etc.; ὕστερον δή *yet* later, Th.2.17: freq. with temporal Conjunctions, ἐπεὶ δή (written ἐπειδή, q.v.), etc. II. without temporal significance, as a Particle of emphasis, *in fact, of course, certainly*, ναὶ δή, ἢ δή, Il.1.286,518, etc.; οὐ δή *surely* not, S.*Ph.*246, cf. E.*Or.*1069, etc.; δῆλα δή, v. δῆλος; with Verbs, δὴ γὰρ ἴδον ὀφθαλμοῖσι Il.15.488; νῦν δὲ δὴ ὁρᾶτε δή X.*Cyr.*3.2.12; καὶ ἴστε δὴ οἷος.. Pl.*Ap.*21a: less freq. with Substs., σοφιστὴν δή τοι ὀνομάζουσι τὸν ἄνδρα εἶναι they call the man a sophist *as you know*, Id.*Prt.*311e: with Conjunctions, ἵνα δή, ὡς δή, Il.23.207, 5.24, etc.; ὅπως δή Th.5.85; γὰρ δή for *manifestly*, A.*Ch.*874,891, Pl.*Tht.*156c; οὐ γὰρ δή S.*OC*265: hence with a part. representing Conjunction and Verb, ἅτε δὴ ἐόντες since they *evidently* are, Hdt.8.90; but ὡς φόνον νίζουσα δή *as though* she were.., E.*IT*1338, cf. Hdt.1.66, X.*Cyr.*5.4.4, etc.; and so, ironically, ὡς δή Il.1.110, Ar.*V.*1315, *Eq.*693, Pl.*Prt.*342c, al.; freq. with σύ, ὡς δὴ σύ μοι τύραννος Ἀργείων ἔσῃ A.*Ag.*1633, cf. S.*OC*809, E.*Andr.*235, etc.; also ἵνα δὴ.. Pl.*R.*420e, *Men.*86d; ὅτι δή.. Id.*Phdr.*268d; also εἰσήγαγε τὰς ἑταιρίδας δή the *pretended* courtesans, X.*HG*5.4.6, cf. E.*Ion*1181, Th.4.67, 6.80. 2. freq. placed immediately after Pronouns, ἐμὲ δή me *of all persons*, Hdt.3.155; σὺ δή you *of all persons*, Id.1.115, S.*Aj.*1226; οὗτος δή this *and no other*, Hdt.1.43; ὑμεῖς δὲ κεῖνοι δή οἵ.. S.*Tr.*1091; οὗτος δὴ ὁ Σωκράτης, ironically, Pl.*Tht.*166a; τὸ λεγόμενον δὴ τοῦτο as the *well-known* saying goes, Id.*Grg.*514e, cf. E.*Hipp.*962; δή τις some one *you know of*, Pl.*Phd.*108c, al.: with possess. Pronouns, τὸ σὸν δὴ τοῦτο Pl.*Smp.*221b, cf. *Grg.*508d, etc.: with relatives, ὃς δὴ νῦν κρατέει Il.21.315; τὰ δὴ καὶ ἐγένετο Hdt.1.22; οἷος δὴ σύ *just* such as thou, Il.24.376, cf. Od.1.32, S.*Aj.*995, etc.; ὅσα δή Ar.*Ach.*1, etc.: with Adjs., οἴη δή, μοῦνος δή, Od.12.69, Hdt.1.25; ἐν πολλῇ δὴ ἀπορίᾳ ἦσαν X.*An.*3.1.2: freq. with Superlatives, μάχη ἐγένετο πλεῖστον δὴ χρόνου μεγίστη δὴ τῶν Ἑλληνικῶν Th.5.74; ἁπάντων δὴ ἄλγιστον S.*Aj.*992, etc. III. to mark a transition, with or without inference, *so, then*, νίκη μὲν δὴ φαίνετ'.. Il.3.457; τὴν μὲν δὴ τυραννίδα οὕτω ἔσχον Hdt.1.14; τοῦτο δὴ τὸ ἄγος οἱ Λακεδαιμόνιοι ἐκέλευον ἐλαύνειν Th.1.127. IV. with Indef. Particles, v. δήποθεν, δήποτε, δήπω, δήπουθεν: with interrogatives, τοῦ δὴ ἕνεκα; Pl.*Grg.*457e; τί δὲ δή..; Id.*Phd.*58c (simply τί δή; what *then?* *R.*357d); πότερα δή; S.*Ph.*1235 (and with Advbs., ποῖ δὴ καὶ πόθεν; Pl.*Phdr.*init.; ποῦ δή; πῇ δή; ib.228e, Il.2.339, etc.): with Indef. Pronouns, δή strengthens the indef. notion, ἄλλοισιν δὴ ταῦτ' ἐπιτέλλεο others *be they who they may*, Il.1.295; μηδεὶς δή no one *at all*, Pl.*Tht.*170e; δή τις some one *or other*, Id.*R.*498a (pl.), etc. (rarely τις δή E.*IT*946); the neut. δή τι is common, ἦ ἄρα δή τι εἴσκομεν ἄξιον εἶναι; in any way, *whatever it be*, Il.13.446; τὸ ἱππικόν, τῷ δή τι καὶ ἐπεῖχε ἐλλάμψεσθαι Hdt.1.80; οὕτω δή τι Id.3.108, etc.; θεῶν ὅτεῳ δή *whosoever it be*, Id.1.86; ἐπὶ μισθῷ ὅσῳ δή, Lat. *quantocumque*, ib.160, etc.; οἷα δή γε.. E.*Heracl.*632, cf. *Supp.*162; but θαυμαστὰ δὴ ὅσα Pl.*Smp.*220b; ὡς δή Il.5.24, etc.; so almost, = ἤδη, ἀναπέτομαι δὴ πρὸς Ὄλυμπον Anacr.24; καὶ δὴ φίλον τις ἔκταν' ἀγνοίας ὕπο A.*Supp.*499; ἤκουσα δή S.*Ant.*823; πάθη μὲν οὖν δὴ πόλλ' ἔγωγ' ἐκλαυσάμην Id.*Tr.*153; οἶσθα μὲν δή ib.627; so καὶ δή *already, in fact*, freq. not at the beginning of the sentence, κεῖται καὶ δὴ πάνθ' ἅπερ εἶπας Ar.*Ec.*514, cf. *Nu.*906, Theoc.5.83; but καὶ δή σφε λείπω A.*Supp.*507. 2. to continue a narrative, freq. after μέν, *then, so*, τότε μὲν δὴ.. ἡσυχίην εἶχε Hdt.1.11; Σόλων μὲν δὴ ἔνεμε ib.32; τὸν μὲν δὴ πέμπει ib.116; alone, εἷς δὴ τούτων.. so one of these.., ib.114, etc.: freq. in summing up, τοιαῦτα μὲν δὴ ταῦτα, Lat. *haec hactenus*, A.*Pr.*500, cf. Hdt.1.14, Th.2.4; τούτων δὴ ἕνεκα X.*Cyr.*3.2.28, etc.; in summing up numbers, γίγνονται δὴ οὗτοι χίλιοι these *then* amount to 1,000, ib.1.5.5; in resuming after a parenthesis, Ἀνδρομάχη, θυγάτηρ μεγαλήτορος Ἠετίωνος.., τοῦ περ δὴ θυγάτηρ Il.6.395; οὗτος δή.., ὁ μὲν δή Hdt.1.43. b. with imper. and subj., μὴ δὴ.. ἐπιέλπεο Il.1.545, cf. 5.684, etc.; χωρῶμεν δὴ πάντες S.*Ph.*1469; ἐννοεῖτε γὰρ δή for do *but* consider, X.*Cyr.*4.3.5; ἄγε δή, φέρε δή, ἴθι δή, σκόπει δή, λέγε δή, Pl.*Sph.*235a, *Phd.*63b, *Sph.*224c, *Phd.*80a, *Prt.*312c. 3. to express what follows *a fortiori*, καὶ μετὰ ὅπλων γε δή *above all* with arms, Th.4.78; μή τί γε δή not to mention, D.2.23; εἰ δὲ δὴ πόλεμος ἥξει Id.

1.27. 4. καὶ δή and *what is more*, adding an emphatic statement, Il.1.161, 15.251, Hdt.5.67, Lys.13.4; in Prose, freq. καὶ δὴ καί.., ἐς Αἴγυπτον ἀπίκετο.., καὶ δὴ καὶ ἐς Σάρδις Hdt.1.30, etc.; καὶ δὴ καὶ νῦν τί φῄς; and *now* what do you say? Pl.*Tht.*187c; καὶ δὴ μὲν οὖν παρόντα yes, and *actually* here present, S.*OC*31; esp. in a series, ὑγίεια καὶ ἰσχὺς καὶ κάλλος καὶ πλοῦτος δή and *of course* riches, Pl.*Men.*87e, cf. *Tht.*159c, *R.*367d; εἴτ'.. εἴτ'.. εἴτε δή ib.493d. b. καὶ δή is also used in answers, ἦ καὶ παρέστη κἀπὶ τέρμ' ἀφίκετο; Answ. καὶ δὴ 'πὶ δισσαῖς ἦν.. πύλαις *yes*, he was *even* so far as.., S.*Aj.*49; βλέψον κάτω. Answ. καὶ δὴ βλέπω *well*, I am looking, Ar. *Av.*175, cf. *Pax*327, *Pl.*227 sq., S.*El.*317 sq., 1436, etc.; πρόσθιγέ νύν μου. Answ. ψαύω καὶ δή S.*OC*173; without καί, ἀποκρίνου περὶ ὧν ἂν ἐρωτῶ. Answ. ἐρώτα δή Pl.*Tht.*157d; ἐρώτα. Answ. ἐρωτῶ δή Id. *Grg.*448b. c. in assumptions or suppositions, καὶ δὴ δέδεγμαι and *now suppose* I have accepted, A.*Eu.*894, cf. *Ch.*565, E.*Med.*386, *Hel.* 1059, not found in S., once in Ar.*V.*1224. 5. δή in apodosi, after εἰ or ἐάν, Il.5.898, Hdt.1.108, Pl.*R.*524e, etc.; after ὅτε, ἡνίκα, *even then*, S.*Ant.*170 sq., *El.*954; after ἐπεί, ἐπειδάν, X.*Cyr.*1.6.14, Pl. *Cra.*435e, etc.; after ὡς, X.*Cyr.*7.2.4; ἐν ᾧ δὲ ταῦτα ἐβουλεύοντο, καὶ δὴ ὁ βασιλεύς.. *already*, Id.*An.*1.10.10.

δῆ· γῆ, καὶ σιωπᾷ, Hsch. **δηαί**, = κριθαί (Cret.), *EM*264.13; cf. δητταί. **δήᾰλωτος**, ον, contr. for δηϊάλωτος (q.v.). **δηατάχα**· καὶ φθορὰ δένδρων, Hsch. **δηβοιλοί**· κιθαρῳδοί, Id. **δηγῆρες**, = στρουθοί, Id., Suid., *Et.Gud.*

δῆγμα, ατος, τό, *bite, sting*, X.*Mem.*1.3.12, Arist.*HA*604^{b}21, etc.: metaph., δ. λύπης A.*Ag.*791 (lyr.); ἔρωτος S.*Fr.*841; ψυχῆς cj. in Luc.*Prom.Es* 2. II. = σπάραγμα ὀδόντων, Hsch.

δηγμός, ὁ, *bite, sting*, μυίας Chrysipp.*Stoic.*3.51. 2. *gnawing pain*, Hp.*Coac.*626, Thphr.*HP*4.4.5; of mental *suffering*, *Stoic.*3. 107, Phld.*Mort.*25,35, *Lib.*p.48 O., Ph.1.212 (pl.); of a speech, δ. προσάγειν Plu.2.69a, cf. *Alc.*4: in pl., *painful operations*, Id.*Per.*15.

δηγοί· πληροί, Hsch.

δηθά, Ep. Adv. = δήν, *for a long time*, δηθά τε καὶ δολιχόν Il.10.52; δ. μάλα ib.5.587; οὐ μετὰ δ. not *long* after, A.R.2.651.

δηθαγόρος, ον, *prolix*, Hsch. **δηθαίων**, ωνος, ὁ, ἡ, *long-lived*, Id.

δηθάκι and **δηθάκις**, Adv. *often*, Nic.*Al.*215, Man.3.22, Opp.*C.* 1.27, etc.

δῆθεν (δῆθε E.*El.*268, cj. in Eup.7.1 D.), Adv., a strengthd. form of δή, ὡς Ζεὺς ἀνάσσοι δ. A.*Pr.*204; ὡς παῖδα δ. μὴ τέκοις E.*El.*268, cf. *Ion*831; τί δὴ ἀνδρωθέντες δ. ποιήσουσι; Hdt.6.138; ἄρτι δ. *I suppose*, Pl.*Plt.*297c. 2. more freq. ironically, *forsooth*, οἵ μιν ἠθέλησαν ἀπολέσαι δ... *as he pretended*, Hdt.1.59; δ. οὐδὲν ἱστορῶν S. *Tr.*382; οὐκ ἐπὶ κωλύμῃ ἀλλὰ γνώμης παραινέσει δ. Th.1.92, cf. 127, 3.111: freq. after ὡς, mostly with a word interposed, φέροντες ὡς ἄγρην δ. Hdt.1.73; ὡς κατασκόπους δ. ἐόντας Id.3.136, cf. 6.39, 8.5; also κέντρον δ. ὡς ἔχων χερί E.*HF*949; εἴσιμεν.. δ. ὡς θανούμενοι Id. *Or.*1119; θεατὴν δ., ὡς οὐκ ὄντ' ἐμόν Id.*Ion*656. II. *from that time, thenceforth*, *Anacreont.*1.16, Hsch.

δηθύνω, pres. and impf. only, Ep. subj. δηθύνησθα Od.12.121: (δηθά):—*tarry, delay*, Il.6.503, *AP*5.222.6 (Maced.); of disease, *to be prolonged*, Aret.*SD*1.2; δ. οὔασι *to be slow* of hearing, Orph.*L.* 467.

δηθυρεῖν· σχολάζειν, διατρίβειν, Hsch.

δηϊάλωτος [ᾰ], ον, (δήϊος, ἁλῶναι) *taken by the enemy, captive*, E. *Andr.*105 (lyr.); contr. **δηάλωτος**, A.*Th.*72.

Δηϊάνειρα [ᾱν], ἡ, *destroying her spouse*, the wife of Heracles—her name expressing the legend of his death, S., etc.

δήϊος, η, ον, Ep. for δάϊος (q.v.).

δηϊοτής, ῆτος, ἡ, *battle-strife, the battle*, Il.3.20, etc.; *mortal struggle, death*, Od.12.257; cf. δανοτής.

δηϊοῦσα, = κώνειον, Ps.-Dsc.4.78.

δηϊόω, Ep. opt. δηϊόῳεν Od.4.226, part. δηϊόων Il.17.566; Att. pres. δηῶ, δηοῦμεν, -οῦτε, X.*Cyr.*3.3.18, Ar.*Lys.*1146, part. δηῶν Il.17.65: impf. ἐδῄουν Th.1.65, X.*Cyr.*5.4.23, ἐδηΐουν Hdt.8.33,50 (ἐδῄευν v.l. in 5.89); Ep. δῄουν Il.11.71, al., δηϊάασκον (as if from δηϊάω) A.R. 2.142: fut. δηώσω Il.9.243, etc.: aor. ἐδῄωσα Th.1.114, subj. δηώσῃ, -ωσιν, Il.16.650, 4.416, part. δῃώσας 8.534, al., Ion. δηϊώσας Hdt.6. 135: pf. δεδῄωκα Rh.8.193 W. (Sopat.):—**Med.**, fut. δηώσεσθαι (in pass. sense) A.R.2.117: aor.1 δηώσασθαι v.l. in J.*BJ*2.13.2, cf. Q.S.5. 567, Opp.*H.*5.350:—**Pass.**, aor. ἐδηϊώθην Hdt.7.133, δηωθείς Il.4.417: pf., Hsch., part. δεδῃωμένος Luc.*DMort.*10.11.—Hom. has δη-, when ι is folld. by a long syll.: A.R. forms impf. ἐδήϊον (as if from δηΐω) 3. 1374, said by Sch. to be taken from Eumel. (*Fr.*9), cf. δήειν· πολεμεῖν, φονεύειν, Hsch. (δηεῖν cod.), Cyr., δηΐων· διακόπτων, Hsch., Cyr.: this is perh. a difft. Verb, and δήϊον, δήϊων might be read in Hom.:—*cut down, slay*, χαλκῷ δηϊόων Il.17.566, etc.; ἔγχεϊ δηϊόων περὶ Πατρόκλοιο θανόντος *slaying* [men].., 18.195: abs., δῄουν *were slaying*, 16. 771; δηϊόωντο *were being slain*, 13.675; Ἕκτορα δηώσαντε 22.218; Κικόνων ὕπο δηωθέντες Od.9.66. 2. *rend, tear, cleave*, δῄουν.. βοείας ἀσπίδας *were cleaving* shields, Il.5.452, etc.; of a spear, *cut asunder*, 14.518; of savage beasts, ἔγκατα πάντα λαφύσσει δηῶν 17. 65, cf. 16.158; τὸν πώγωνα δεδῃωμένος *having had* his beard *cut off*, Luc.*DMort.*10.11. II. after Hom., *waste, ravage* a country, Sol.13. 21, Hdt.5.89, 7.133, etc.; δ. χώραν Ar.*Lys.*1146, Th.1.81, etc.; ἄστυ δῃώσειν πυρί S.*OC*1319.

δηϊφόβος [ῐ], Dor. **δαϊφ-**, ον, *scaring the foe*, dub. in Alc.28:—in Hom. only pr. n.

δηΐω, v. δηϊόω.

δηκτ-ήριος, ον, *biting, torturing*, καρδίας E.*Hec.*235. **-ης**, ου, ὁ, *biter*, E.*Fr.*555: metaph. as Adj., δ. λόγος Plu.2.55b: with neut. Subst., δήκτα στόματι *APl.*4.266.7. **-ικός**, ή, όν, *biting, stinging*, φαλάγγια Arist.*HA*622^{b}28; τῶν ἰχθύων οἱ δ. Id.*PA*662^{a}31; *pungent*, Diph.Siph.ap.Ath.3.121a (Comp.), Diocl.*Fr.*138, Ruf.*Fr.*68.3, Dsc. 1.105; φάρμακον Luc.*Nigr.*37, etc.: metaph., of anger, Phld.*Ir.* p.77 W.; -κόν, τό, Ph.1.684; ἀστεῖον καὶ δ. Luc.*Demon.*50. Adv. -κῶς Sch.Ar.*V.*937.

δήκω, = δάκνω, cj. in Hippon.49.6.

δηλᾰδή (cf. δῆλος II.4), Adv. *clearly, manifestly*, Epich.149, S.*OT* 1501, E.*IA*1366, Timocl.3 D., etc.: ironically, προφάσιος τῆσδε δηλαδή on this pretext *forsooth*, Hdt.4.135: freq. in answers, οὐ πόλλ' ἔνεστι δεινὰ τῷ γήρᾳ κακά;—δηλαδή *yes plainly, of course*, Ar. *V.*441: but better written divisim in such phrases as ἦ δῆλα δὴ ὅτι..; Pl.*Prt.*309a, etc.; cf. δῆλα δὴ καὶ ταῦτα Id.*Cri.*48b.

δηλαίνουσι· παίζουσι, Hsch.

δηλαϊστός, v.l. for δείλαιος, Lxx*Ez.*5.15, cf. Hsch.

δηλαυγῶς· ἄγαν φανερῶς, Hsch.

δηλ-έομαι (A), Dor. **δᾱλ-** Theoc.15.48: fut. -ήσομαι: aor. ἐδηλησάμην: pf. δεδήλημαι, prob. in act. sense, E.*Hipp.*175 (in pass. sense, Hdt.4.198, 8.100): I. mostly of persons, *hurt, do a mischief to*, μήπως [ἵππους] δηλήσεαι, by accident, Il.23.428; also on purpose, Ἀχαιοὺς ὑπὲρ ὅρκια δηλήσασθαι 4.67; ἦέ σε.. ἄνδρες ἐδηλήσαντο *did* thee *a mischief*, i.e. *slew* thee, Od.11.401; μή με.. δηλήσεται ὀξέϊ χαλκῷ (Ep. subj.) 22.368; of the sword, ῥινὸν δηλήσατο χαλκός ib. 278; ἄλλον δηλήσομαι, ἄλλον ὀνήσω *h.Merc.*541; δ. τινὰ ἔργμασι λυγροῖς Mimn.7, = Thgn.795: in Ion. Prose, ἵνα μὴ ἔχοιέν σφεας δηλέεσθαι Hdt.6.36, cf. 7.51; πλεῖστόν σφεας ἐδηλέετο ἡ ἐσθής Id.9.63; τούς.. ποτῷ δαλήσατο Κίρκα Theoc.9.36. II. of things, *damage, spoil*, καρπὸν ἐδηλήσαντ' Il.1.156; so in Hdt., γῆν δ. πολλά 4.115; ἅλμην ἐπανθέουσαν, ὥστε καὶ τὰς πυραμίδας δηλέεσθαι Id.2.12: freq. in Hom. in the phrase, ὅρκια δηλήσασθαι *violate* a truce, Il.3.107, al.; of thieves, μή τις.. δηλήσεται (Ep. subj.) *should steal them*, Od.8. 444, cf. 13.124. 2. abs., *to do mischief, be hurtful*, ἔνθα κε σὴ βουλὴ δηλήσεται Il.14.102: c. acc. cogn., ἤδ' ὅσα.. ἄνδρες ἐδηλήσαντο all *the mischief* they *did*, Od.10.459. (Ep., Ion., and rarely Dor., Theoc. ll. cc.; cf. δάλλει, πανδάλητος, and perh. ἀδαλές.)

δηλέομαι (B), only in fut. Pass., δηληθήσονται· θεωρηθήσονται, Hsch.

δηληγατεύω, *assign* as tax to be paid, μέτρον ἐλαίου *PLips.*64.3 (iv A. D.). **δηληγατίων**, ωνος, ἡ, *delegatio, annual declaration by the state of the amount of taxes to be paid*, *BGU*836.3 (vi A. D.), 974.7 (iv A. D.), cf. Suid.

δηλ-ήεις, εσσα, εν, = δηλήμων, Orph.*A.*923: neut. sg. δηλῆειν prob. in Nic.*Al.*42. **-ημα**, ατος, τό, *mischief, bane*, ἄνεμοι χαλεποί, δηλήματα νηῶν Od.12.286; ὁδοιπόρων A.*Fr.*123; βροτοῖσιν *h.Ap.*364, cf. S.*OT*1495; τύχης δηλήμασι *IPE*2.197 (Panticapaeum). **-ήμων**, ον, gen. ονος, *baneful, noxious*, βροτῶν δηλήμονα πάντων Od.18.85, al.; ὄφιες ἀνθρώπων οὐδαμῶς δηλήμονες *doing* men no *hurt*, Hdt.2.74, cf. 3.109: abs., of the gods, σχέτλιοί ἐστε, θεοί, δηλήμονες Il.24.33 (in Od.5.118 nearly all codd. give ζηλήμονες): in late Prose, Jul.*Or.*2.87a. **-ησις**, εως, ἡ, *mischief*, μὴ κλῶπες ἐπὶ δηλήσι φανέωσι Hdt.1.41, cf. 4.112; ἀλεξητήριον τῆς δ. Thphr.*HP*7. 13.4; *injury of health*, ἐπὶ δηλήσι Hp.*Jusj.* **-ητήρ**, ῆρος, ὁ, *a destroyer*, Hom.*Epigr.*14.8. **-ητήριος**, ον, *noxious*, φάρμακα *SIG* 37 (Teos, v B. C.), cf. J.*BJ*1.13.10, Gal.*Nat.Fac.*3.7, Hdn.3.5.5. 2. δηλητήριον (sc. φάρμακον), τό, *poison*, Hp.*Ep.*19 (*Hermes* 53.69), Plu. 2.662c, Hdn.1.17.10, Lib.*Or.*64.33; τὰ ὑγιεινὰ καὶ τὰ νοσερὰ καὶ τὰ δ. Porph.*Abst.*3.8. **-ητηριώδης**, ες, *noxious*, Dav.*Proll.*32. 26.

δήλιοι· οἱ ἀδελφὰς γεγαμηκότες, Hsch.; cf. ἀέλιοι.

Δήλιος, Dor. **Δάλιος**, α, ον, also ος, ον E.*Tr.*89:—*Delian*, A.*Eu.* 9, etc.: ὁ Δ., name of Apollo, S.*Aj.*704, Th.1.13; τοῖς Δηλίοις καὶ ταῖσι Δηλίαισι, the gods and goddesses *worshipped at Delos*, Ar.*Th.* 334:—**Δήλιος**, ὁ, *a Delian*, Hdt.4.33, etc.:—also **Δηλιεύς**, *IG*12(7). 50 (Amorgos):—fem. **Δηλιάς**, άδος, ἡ, *Delian woman*, κοῦραι Δ. *h. Ap.*157, cf. E.*HF*687: with neut. Subst., Δηλιάσιν γυάλοις cj. in Id. *IT*1235:—Adj. **Δηλιακός**, ή, όν, χορός Th.3.104; πλοῖον Plu.2. 786f. II. **Δηλιάς** θεωρία mission *sent to Delos* every fourth year, Philoch.158:—hence **Δηλιασταί**, οἱ, *members of this* θεωρία, Lycurg. *Fr.*80, Herodicus ap.Ath.6.234e, Harp., Hsch. III. Δήλιον, τό, *precinct of Apollo* Δ., Herodicus l.c., *Schwyzer*688 *A* 7 (Chios, v B. C.), etc. IV. Δήλια (sc. ἱερά), τά, *festival of Apollo at Delos*, Th.3. 104, X.*Mem.*4.8.2; also at Tanagra, etc., *SIG*319.16, etc.

Δηλογενής, Dor. **Δᾱλ-**, ές, *Delos-born*, Simon.26 B, B.3.58, 10.15.

δήλομαι, Dor. for βούλομαι, Theoc.5.27, Ti.Locr.94d, Archyt.ap. Stob.3.1.105, Plu.2.219d, *Tab.Heracl.*1.146, *Chron.Lind.D.*66, *GDI* 3585.18 (Calymna): also Elean **δηλόμηρ**, = βουλόμενος, *Michel* 1334.5.

δηλονότι, i.e. δῆλόν [ἐστιν] ὅτι (cf. δῆλος II.3), used adverbially, *clearly, manifestly*, Pl.*Cri.*53a, *Grg.*487d, etc.; once in *NT*, 1*Ep. Cor.*15.27. II. freq. epexegetically, *that is to say, namely*, Pl. *Smp.*199a, X.*Cyr.*5.4.6, etc.: in Gramm. the common form for introducing an explanation, Sch.Ar.*Ach.*11, etc.

Δηλόπτης, ου, ὁ, a Thracian divinity associated with Bendis, *IG* 2^2.1324 (Piraeus), *Ath.Mitt.*25.172 (Samos).

Δῆλος, Dor. **Δᾶλος**, ἡ, *Delos*, Od.6.162, Pi.*Fr.*87, etc.: prov., ᾄδεις ὥσπερ εἰς Δ. πλέων, from the careless joviality of the Δηλιασταί (q.v.), Zen.2.37. (Expld. from δῆλος, because of the legend that it became *visible* on a sudden, Arist.*Fr.*488, *EM*264.22; but cf. sq.)

δῆλος (also Dor., Archyt.1, Theoc.11.79, etc., and Aeol., cf. πρόδηλος), η, ον, also ος, ον E.*Med.*1197: Ep. **δέελος**: I. prop. *visible, conspicuous,* δέελον δ' ἐπὶ σῆμά τ' ἔθηκε Il.10.466, but: II. commonly, *clear* to the mind, *manifest,* νῦν δ' ἤδη τόδε δ. Od.20.333, etc. 2. δ. εἰμι is freq. used c. part., δ. ἐστιν ἀλγεινῶς φέρων i.e. *it is clear* that he takes it ill, S.*Ph.*1011, cf. *OT*673,1008, etc.; οἱ ἂν δ. ὦσι μὴ ἐπιτρέψοντες who are *clearly* not going to permit, Th.1.71; with ὡς, δ. ἐστιν ὥς τι δρασείων κακόν S.*Aj.*326; δ. ἔσεσθε ὡς ὀργιζόμενοι Lys.12.90, cf. X.*An.*1.5.9; δ. δρᾶσθαι..ὢν being as was *plainly* to be seen, E.*Or.*350: with ὅτι and a Verb, δ. ἐστιν ὅτι.. ἀκήκοεν Ar.*Pl.*333; δ. ἡ οἰκοδομία ὅτι κατὰ σπουδὴν ἐγένετο Th.1.93; δ. ἔσται ὅτι.. Lys.12.50: sts. the part. or relat. clause must be supplied, καταγελᾷς μου, δ. εἶ (sc. καταγελῶν) Ar.*Av.*1407, cf. Id.*Lys.* 919; δῆλοι δέ (sc. οὐ μένοντες) Th.5.10. 3. δῆλον ποιεῖν *show plainly,* τινὶ ὅτι.. Id.6.34, etc.: c. part., δῆλον ἐποιήσατε..μηδίσαντες Id.3.64. 4. δῆλον (sc. ἐστί) *it is manifest,* αὐτὸς πρὸς αὑτοῦ· δῆλον S.*Aj.*906; ἀλγεινά, Πρόκνη, δῆλον Id.*Fr.*585; ἐκ πίθω ἀντλεῖς, δῆλον Theoc.10.13; δῆλον δέ, to introduce a proof, folld. by γάρ, Th.1.11, Arist.*Col.*799^{a}5, etc.; δῆλον γάρ S.*Fr.*63; δῆλον ὅτι Th.3.38, etc.; τὰ Κύρου δῆλον ὅτι οὕτως ἔχει X.*An.*1.3.9, cf. *Cyr.*2.4.24, etc., v. δηλονότι: in pl., δῆλα δή, δ. δ. καὶ ταῦτα Pl.*Cri.*48b; ἢ δ. δ. ὅτι..; Id. *Prt.*309a, etc.: hence as Adv., usu. written δηλαδή (q.v.). 5. Adv. δήλως is rejected by Att., Poll.6.207. III. δῆλοι, οἱ, *Urim,* Lxx 1*Ki.*28.6, al. (Cf. δέατο.)

δηλοφανής, ές, *manifest,* f.l. in Polus ap.Stob.3.9.51 (Comp.).

δηλ-όω:—Pass., fut. δηλωθήσομαι Th.1.144; δηλώσομαι in pass. sense, S.*OC*581; δεδηλώσομαι Hp.*Art.*45, Diog.Apoll.4:—*make visible* or *manifest, show, exhibit,* τὸν ἄνδρ' Ἀχαιοῖς δ. S.*Ph.*616; ποῖον ὄμμα πατρὶ δηλώσω; Id.*Aj.*462: with inf. added, ὡς γένος ἄτλητον ἀνθρώποισι δηλώσοιμ' ὁρᾶν Id.*OT*792, etc.:—Pass., *to be* or *become manifest,* Id.*OC*581, etc. 2. *make known, disclose, reveal,* A.*Pers.*519, S.*OT*77, etc.; *prove,* Id.*OC*146, Th.1.3; δηλοῖ ὁ λόγος ὅτι.. Democr.7; αὐτὸ δηλώσει D.19.157; *explain, set forth,* Th.2.62; *signify,* ἐδήλουν οὐδὲν ὅτι ἴσασιν *gave* no *sign* of knowing, Id.4.68: *indicate,* τὰς μεγίστας καὶ ἐλαχίστας Id.1.10, etc. Construct.: mostly δ. τινί τι Antipho 1.30; δ. τι πρός or εἴς τινα, S.*Tr.*369, Th.1.90; δ. περί τινος Lys.10.7; τινὶ περί τι Isoc.11.9: c. acc. et inf., *SIG*888.52 (Scaptopara, iii A.D.): folld. by a relat. clause, δ. ὅτι S.*El.*1106, Hdt.2.149, cf. 1.57, etc.; οἷα φρονῶ S.*El.*334; δ. περί τινος, ὡς.. Th.1.72,73: c. acc. et part., σκευή τε γάρ σε καὶ τὸ δύστηνον κάρα δηλοῦτον.. ὅνθ' ὃς εἶ S.*OC*555; ὥς σε δηλώσω κακὸν [ὄντα] ib.783, cf. *Ant.*471: c. part. nom., referring to the subject, δηλώσω πατρὶ μὴ ἄσπλαγχνος γεγώς *I will show* my father that I am no dastard, Id.*Aj.*472; δηλοῖς.. τι καλχαίνουσ' ἔπος thou *showest* that thou art pondering.., Id.*Ant.*20; δηλοῖς ὥς τι σημανῶν ib.242; δηλώσω οὐ παραγενόμενος I *will show* that I was not present, Antipho 2.4.8; δηλώσει μείζων γεγενημένος Th.1.21; also Λιβύη δηλοῖ ἑωυτὴν ἐοῦσα περίρρυτος Hdt.4.42; ἑαυτὸν ἐδήλωσεν ὅστις ἦν D.H.3.48. II. intr., *to be clear* or *plain,* δηλοῖ ὅτι οὐκ Ὁμήρου τὰ Κύπρια ἔπεά ἐστι Hdt.2.117; δηλοῖ δὲ ταῦτα.. ὅτι οὕτως ἔχει Pl.*Grg.*483d; δηλώσει ἡ ἔχθρα ὅταν πρῶτον.. And.4.12; *to be significant, possess a meaning,* c. dat., Pl.*Cra.*434c. 2. impers. δηλοῖ, = δῆλόν ἐστι, δηλοῖ μοι ὅτι.., Hdt.9.68, cf. Arist.*Pol.*1296^{a}20; δηλώσει Lys.10.20, Pl.*R.*497c; ἐδήλωσε X.*Mem.*1.2.32, cf. *Cyr.*7.1.30. **-ωμα**, ατος, τό, *a means of making known,* τινός Pl.*Lg.*792a, Plu.2.78e, etc.: pl., ib. 62d. **-ωσις**, εως, ἡ, *pointing out, explanation,* Th.1.73; αἰσθήσει ἢ δηλώσει Pl.*Min.*314a; ἡ τῶν ὄντων λόγῳ δ. Id.*Plt.*287a; δ. ποιεῖσθαι, = δηλοῦν, Th.4.40. 2. *direction, order,* ἡ τῶν ἀρχόντων δ. Pl.*Lg.* 942c. 3. *Urim,* Lxx *Le.*8.8. 4. *interpretation,* ib.*Da.*2.27. **-ωτέον**, *one must set forth,* Pl.*Ti.*48e, Ph.1.15. **-ωτικός**, ή, όν, *indicative,* τινός Hp.*Acut.*42, Arist.*Phgn.*808^{b}30, D.H.*Comp.*16: abs., *notificatory, PMonac.*2.15 (vi A.D.). Adv. -κῶς Aen.Tact.14.2. 2. *expressive,* of dancing, Poll.4.96. 3. *visible, PMag.Berol.*1.259. **-ωτός**, ή, όν, *able to be shown,* Arist.*Xen.* 979^{a}13.

δῆμα, ατος, τό, = δέμα, Sch.A.R.2.535.

δημᾰγωγ-έω, *to be a leader of the people,* καλῶς δ. Isoc.2.16; τῇ μὲν ἐξουσίᾳ τυραννῶν, ταῖς δ' εὐεργεσίαις δημαγωγῶν Id.10.37; cf. δημαγωγεῖ· στρατηγεῖ, Hsch.: usu. in bad sense, Ar.*Ra.*423, etc. 2. c. acc. pers., δ. ἄνδρας *curry favour with,* X.*An.*7.6.4, cf. Arist.*Pol.* 1305^{b}26, al.:—Pass., *to be won over, conciliated by popular arts,* J.*AJ* 16.2.5. b. = ψυχαγωγέω, τὸν πόθον, of a work of art, Him.*Ecl.*31.6; τὸ θέατρον, of Homer, Id.*Or.*20.3. 3. c. acc. rei, *introduce* measures *so as to win popularity,* τὰ πρὸς ἡδονὴν τῷ πλήθει D.H.*Dem.* 17; βουλὰς δ. Lxx 1*Es.*5.70(73). II. in causal sense, δ. τινά *make* him *popular,* App.*BC*5.53, *Pun.*133. **-ία**, ἡ, *control* or *leadership of the people,* Ar.*Eq.*191, Th.8.65, Arist.*Pol.*1305^{b}23, *Ath.*28.4, Luc.*Dem.Enc.*19; *demagogic method,* Plb.2.21.8. **-ικός**, ή, όν, *fit for* or *like a demagogue,* τὰ -κά *arts of a demagogue,* Ar.*Eq.*217, cf. Plb.15.21.1: generally, *popular,* of a dancer, Poll.4.96. Adv. -κῶς ib.4.26. **-ός**, ὁ, *popular leader,* as Cleon or Pericles, Th. 4.21, Isoc.8.126; δ. ἀγαθοί Lys.27.10; ὁ δίκαιος δ. Hyp.*Dem.Fr.* 5. 2. more freq. in bad sense, *leader of the mob, demagogue,* X. *HG*2.3.27; ὀχλοκόπος καὶ δ. Plb.3.80.3; λόγοι δημαγωγοῦ, opp. ἔργα τυράννου, And.4.27; ἔστι γὰρ ὁ δ. τοῦ δήμου κόλαξ Arist.*Pol.*1313^b 40, cf. 1292^{a}20, etc.

δημᾰκίδιον [κῐ], τό, Com. Dim. of *δῆμαξ, 'magnificative' of δῆμος, Ar.*Eq.*823; cf. δημίδιον.

δημάρᾱτος [μᾰ], ον, (ἀράομαι) *prayed for by the people*: hence as pr. n. of a king of Sparta, Hdt.5.75 (in Ion. form -άρητος), etc., cf. Eust.1093.57.

δημαρχ-έω, *to be* δήμαρχος at Athens, Is.12.11, D.57.26; at Chios, *Schwyzer* 687 A3; or *tribune* at Rome, App.*BC*1.2: pf. δεδημάρχηκα Arr.*Epict.*3.14.12. **-ία**, ἡ, *the office* or *rank of* δήμαρχος, D.57.63; at Rome, *tribunate,* Plu.*Fab.*9, etc. II. *office* in general, Ph.*Fr.* 33 H. (pl.). 2. = δημοκρατία, Hsch. **-ικός**, ή, όν, *tribunician,* δέλτοι Plu.*Cat.Mi.*40; δ. ἐξουσία, = Lat. *tribunicia potestas,* D.H.6. 89, *Mon.Anc.Gr.*5.18, D.C.54.28: freq. in Inscrr. and Pap., *IG*3. 40, *BGU*74.3, etc. **-ος**, ὁ, at Athens, *chief official of a* δῆμος, Ar. *Nu.*37, Lys.*Fr.*184 S., D.50.6, Lex ap.eund.43.58, Arist.*Ath.*21.5; also at Cos, *Inscr.Cos* 344, al.; at Chios, *Schwyzer* 687 C1. b. at Naples, one of the *chief magistrates* of the city, Str.5.4.7; at Eretria, *IG*12(9).189.24 (iv B.C.). 2. at Rome, = Lat. *tribunus plebis,* Plb. 6.12.2, D.H.6.89, Plu.*Cor.*7, etc.

δηματρεύεσθαι· ἐπὶ πολὺ ὑπερτίθεσθαι, Hsch. **δημεῖαι**· αἱ τῶν δήμων συστάσεις, Id. **δημελέητος**, ον, *object of general pity,* Id., Suid.

δημεραστ-έω, *to be a friend of the people,* Olymp.*in Grg.*p.385 J. **-ής**, οῦ, ὁ, *friend of the people,* Pl.*Alc.*1.132a, D.C.47.38:—hence Subst. **-ία**, ἡ, Poll.3.65, and Adj. **-ικός**, ή, όν, *friendly to the people,* Procl.*in Alc.*p.146 C.

δήμ-ευσις, εως, ἡ, *confiscation of property,* θάνατον ἢ φυγὴν ἢ δ. χρημάτων *IG*1^2.101.7, cf. Pl.*Prt.*325c (pl.), D.17.15; δ. alone, Arist. *Pol.*1298^{a}6; δημεύσει τῶν ὑπαρχόντων ζημιοῦν D.21.43; τῆς οὐσίης *SIG*167.26 (Mylasa, iv B.C.). **-εύω**, (δῆμος) *seize as public property,* esp. of a citizen's goods, *confiscate,* Th.5.60, And.1.51; πολλὰ δ. διὰ τῶν δικαστηρίων Arist.*Pol.*1320^{a}5: abs., D.8.69,71:—Pass., τὰ δημευόμενα Arist.*Ath.*43.4; τῶν ἐκ προνοίας δεδήμευται τὰ ὄντα D.23.45; later of persons, ἐδημεύθη τὴν οὐσίαν Philostr.*VS*2.1.2; δημευθήσεσθαι Hdn.2.14.3. II. generally, *make public,* δεδήμευται κράτος the power *is in the hands of the people,* E.*Cyc.*119:—Pass., also, *to be published,* Pl.*Phlb.*14d,e. III. δεδημευμένα ὀνόματα *vulgarized, hackneyed* words, Ammon.*in Int.*66.3. IV. = ἐνδημέω, and also, = δημαγωγέω, Hsch.

δημεχθηλός, όν, = sq., Hsch.

δημεχθής, ές, (ἔχθος) *hated by the people,* Call.*Fr.*472.

δημηγερσία, ἡ, *sedition, agitation, PFlor.*295.5 (vi A.D.); cf. δημοεγερτής.

δημηγορ-έω, *practise speaking in the assembly,* Ar.*Eq.*956, etc.; πρὸ τοῦ πολιτεύεσθαι καὶ δ. ἐμέ D.18.60; δ. περί τινος Lys.14.45; δ. πρός τινας Pl.*Lg.*817c; ἐν τοῖς ὄχλοις Arist.*Fr.*83: c. acc. cogn., δ. καὶ συνηγορεῖν λόγους D.19.15; δ. λόγον παρά τισι Id.23.110:—Pass., τὰ δεδημηγορημένα *public speeches,* Id.19.9. II. esp. *make popular speeches, use clap-trap,* ταῦτα δημηγορεῖς Pl.*Grg.*482c: abs., ib.503b, *Tht.*162d, *R.*350e; τῶν δημηγοριῶν ὧν δ. D.21.202; δ. πρὸς χάριν, πρὸς ἡδονήν, Id.3.3,4.38, cf. Hermog.*Meth.*1. **-ία**, ἡ, *deliberative speaking,* opp. forensic (δικανική), Arist.*Rh.*1354^{b}28. 2. *speech in the public assembly,* Aeschin.2.243, Jul.*Or.*2.75b (pl.). 3. *position of a public speaker,* Pl.*Ap.*36b (pl.). II. esp. *popular oratory, claptrap,* Id.*Tht.*162d. **-ικός**, ή, όν, *suited to public speaking,* opp. δικανικός, X.*Mem.*1.2.48; προοίμια, title of work by Critias, Hermog. *Id.*2.11; *popular,* Pl.*Grg.*482e; δ. καὶ δικανικὴ σοφία Id.*R.*365d, etc.; λέξις Arist.*Rh.*1413^{b}4: Comp. or Sup., ib.1418^{a}1:—ἡ -κή (sc. τέχνη), = δημηγορία, Pl.*Sph.*222c; τὰ -κά Arist.*Rh.*1354^{b}28. Adv. -κῶς Poll.4.26. **-ος**, ὁ, (ἀγορεύω) *popular orator,* mostly in a bad sense, Pl.*Grg.*520b, *Lg.*908d, etc.; ὅρκος ἑταίρας ταὐτὸ καὶ δημηγόρου Diph.101; but δ. ἀγαθοί, opp. ῥήτορες φαῦλοι, X.*Mem.*2.6.15: as Adj., δημηγόρος, ον, τιμαὶ δ. *a speaker's* honours, E.*Hec.*254; στροφαὶ δημηγόροι *rhetorical* tricks, A.*Supp.*623.

δημ-ηλᾰσία, ἡ, *banishment decreed by the people, exile,* A.*Supp.* 6 (anap.). **-ήλᾰτος** φυγή, = foreg., ib.614.

Δημήτηρ, τερος and τρος, ἡ: Dor., Arc., Boeot. **Δαμάτηρ**; also **Δημήτρα** Buresch *Aus Lydien* 69: acc. Δημήτραν Epigr.ap.Paus.1. 37.2: gen. Δαμάτρας *IG*7.2793 (Copae); Aeol. **Δωμάτηρ** Hoffmann *Griechische Dialekte* 2.153 (Aegae); Thess. dat. Δαμμάτερι *IG*9(2). 1235:—*Demeter,* Il.2.696, al., once in Od., 5.125, *h.Cer.*, etc. 2. appell., as a name for *bread,* Opp.*H.*3.463; cf. ἀκτή, καρπός. (Variously expld. by Gramm. as, = Γημήτηρ, δημομήτηρ, or from δηαί, = κριθαί, cf. *EM*265.54.)

Δημήτρειοι, οἱ, the *dead,* Plu.2.943b.

Δημητριακός, ή, όν, *of* or *belonging to Demeter,* καρποί D.S.2.36, cf. Corn.*ND*28, Alex.Aphr.*Pr.*2.68; σπέρματα Orib.3.2.5. II. Δημητριακόν (sc. βιβλίον), τό, work by Demetrius Lacon, Phld. *Sign.*28.

Δημητριάς, άδος, ἡ, fem. Adj.: I. (sc. φυλή) tribe *named in honour of Demetrius Poliorcetes,* Plu.*Demetr.*10. II. city founded by him, Plb.3.6.4, etc.:—hence **Δημητριεῖς**, οἱ, its citizens, Id.5.99. 3. III. as Subst., *six-rowed barley,* Hsch. 2. = περιστερεὼν ὕπτιος, Ps.-Dsc.4.60.

Δημητριασταί, οἱ, guild of *worshippers of Demeter* at Ephesus, *BMus.Inscr.*3.595, Ἀρχ.Δελτ.7.200.

Δημήτριος, ον (also Δημήτρειος, v. Δημήτρειοι), *of* or *belonging to Demeter,* βίος A.*Fr.*44.5; καρπὸς Δ. corn, Thphr.*CP*2.4.5; also Δ. σπέρματα, of leguminous plants, Gal.15.454: Δημήτριος (sc. μήν), ὁ, month in Bithynia, *Hemerolog.Flor.*: Boeot. **Δαμάτριος**, *IG*7.296, al., Plu.2.378e. II. τὸ Δημήτριον *the temple of D.,* Str.9.5. 14. III. τὰ Δημήτρια *her festival,* Poll.1.37, etc.; but later, *in honour of Demetrius,* Plu.*Demetr.*12:—also **Δημητριεία**, τά, *Supp. Epigr.*1.362.8 (Samos, iv B.C.).

Δημητριών, ῶνος, ὁ, name of a month at Cassandrea, *SIG*380; at Athens, new name given to the month Μουνυχιών, in honour of *Demetrius*, Plu.*Demetr.*12.

δημίδιον [μῐ], τό, Com. Dim. of δῆμος, Ar.*Eq.*726,1199; cf. δημακίδιον.

δημίζω, *pose as 'friend of the people'*, Ar.*V.*699.

δημιο-εργείη, ἡ, = δημιουργία, Procl.*H.*7.20. **-εργός**, όν, poet. for δημιουργός (q. v.). **-πληθής**, ές, *abounding for public use*, κτήνη δ. cattle *of which the people have large store*, A.*Ag.*129 (lyr.). **-πρᾶτα**, τά, *goods seized by public authority, and put up for sale*, Ar.*V.*659, Poll.10.96, Ath.11.476e, Phalar.*Ep.*95; περὶ τῶν δ. πρὸς Εὐθίαν, title of speech by Lys.

δήμιος, Dor. **δάμ-**, ον (α, ον A.*Ch.*57 (lyr.), δημίην· πόρνην (Cypr.), Hsch.): (δῆμος):—*belonging to the people*, οἶκος Od.20.264; αἰσυμνῆται δ. judges *elected by the people*, 8.259; πρῆξις δ' ἥδ' ἰδίη, οὐ δήμιος not *public*, 3.82; δήμιον ἢ ἴδιον; 4.314, cf. 2.32: epith. of Hestia at Paros, *IG*12(5).238 (v B.C.): neut. pl. as Adv., δήμια πίνειν *at the public cost*, Il.17.250; τὸ δ. *the sovereign people*, A.*Supp.*370,699 (lyr.). **II.** ὁ δ. (sc. δοῦλος) *public executioner*, Ar.*Ec.*81, Pl.*R.* 439e, Lys.13.56, Aeschin.2.126, etc. (δάμιος μαστίκτωρ in A.*Eu.* 160 (lyr.)); ὁ κοινὸς δ. Pl.*Lg.*872b. **2.** *public physician*, πτωχὸς ἦν καὶ δ. Phoenicid.4.13. **III.** δημίαι πύλαι, perh. a mistake for Διομῆσι, Hsch.

δημιουργ-εῖον, τό, *work-place*, App.*Pun.*93. **-έω** (cf. II. infr.), *practise a handicraft*, Pl.*Plt.*288d, etc.; τινί *for* one, Id.*Lg.*846e, *R.* 342e: metaph., ἡ δημιουργήσασα φύσις Arist.*PA*645^{a}9. **2.** c. acc. rei, *work at, fabricate*, Pl.*Plt.*288e; ἡ φύσις οὐδὲν δ. μάτην Arist.*IA*711^{a}18, cf. *PA*647^{b}5; δ. τὸν υἱὸν εἰς ἀρετήν *to train* him to.., Plu.*Cat.Ma.*20:—Pass., *to be wrought* or *fabricated*, Pl.*R.*414d, al.; τὰ δημιουργούμενα *products of arts and crafts*, Arist.*EN*1094^b 14. **3.** of divine power, *create*, τὸν ὁρατὸν κόσμον Ph.1.4; ὁ δημιουργῶν θεός Numen.ap.Eus.*PE*11.18.6, cf. Dam.*Pr.*304, etc.:—Pass., Procl.*Inst.*207. **II.** *hold office of* δημιουργός, *CIG*4415*b* (Iotapata), etc.; of a woman, *Supp.Epigr.*1.393 (Samos, i B.C.); δαμιοργέοντος Μίκκωνος *IG*9(1).330(Locr.); *to be a civil official*, opp. στρατηγέω, Artem.2.22. **b.** c. acc., *administer*, δαμιουργεόντων τὰ ἱερὰ *IG*9(1).32.44 (Stiris). **-ημα**, ατος, τό, *a work of art, piece of workmanship*, Longin.13.4 (pl.), Ath.11.497c, Herm.*in Phdr.* p.202 A.; δ. χειρῶν D.H.*Comp.*1; τὰ δ. Φειδίου Jul.*Or.*2.54b; οὐ τύχης οὐδ' ἀνθρώπων δ., of the universe, Zaleuc.ap.Stob.4.2.19, cf. Dam.*Pr.*175; θεοειδὲς δ. ᾧ λογιζόμεθα Ph.1.208; *creature*, πρὸς ἀπότεξιν εὐτρεπὲς δ. Hierocl.p.7A.; also of actions, Iamb.*Myst.*1.5, 2.7. **-ία**, ἡ, *workmanship, handicraft*, Pl.*R.*401a; τέχναι καὶ δ. ib.495d; *piece of mechanism*, Arist.*Mu.*400^{a}1. **2.** *making, creating*, ζῴων Pl.*Ti.*41c, etc.; δ. ἔκ τινος Id.*Plt.*280c; *creative activity*, μεριστὴ δ. Jul.*Or.*5.179b, al.; *the creation*, ἡ φανερὰ δ. ib.4.144b; ὁ κόσμος ὅδε καὶ ἁπλῶς ἡ δ. Dam.*Pr.*283. **3.** *physical function*, Arist.*HA*489^{a}13. **4.** δ. τῶν τεχνῶν *handling* or *practising* them, Pl.*Smp.*197a. **II.** *the office of* δημιουργός, *OGI*578.12 (pl., Tarsus), etc.: generally, *magistracy, office*, Arist.*Pol.*1310^{b}22 (pl.). **-ικός**, ή, όν, *of a craftsman*, βίος Pl.*Phdr.*248e; ἀρετή Id. *Prt.*322d; τεχνήματα *craftsmen's* works, Id.*Lg.*846d; τιμαί, of cooks, Clidem.2. Adv. -κῶς *in a workmanlike manner*, Ar.*Pax* 429. **2.** *creative*, θεός Numen.ap.Eus.*PE*11.18; τετρακτύς Hierocl.*in CA*20 p.466 M.; αἴτια, δυνάμεις, Iamb.*Myst.*5.26, 10.6; νοῦς Phlp.*in Mete.* 12.25; -κόν, τό, opp. πατρικόν (as οὐσιοποιόν to εἰδοποιόν), Procl.*Inst.* 157, cf. Dam.*Pr.*184. Adv. -κῶς Syrian.*in Metaph.*82.31. **II.** *of* or *for the magistrates*, τὸ δ. *the official class*, Arist.*Pol.*1291^a 34. **-ιον**, Dor. **δαμιόργιον** or **-ούργιον**, τό, *office of the* δημιουργοί, *GDI*3502 (Cnidus, also -εῖον, τό, ib.3501). **II.** *meeting of the* δ., ἐν ἐννόμῳ δαμιουργίῳ *SIG*830.3 (Delph., ii A.D.). **-ίς**, ίδος, ἡ, *office of* δημιουργός II, *IGRom.*3.800 (Pamphyl.), *Jahresh.*18*Beibl.*55 (Anazarba). **-ός**, Ep. **δημιοεργός** (also Hdt.7.31 codd.), ὁ, *one who works for the people, skilled workman, handicraftsman* (opp. ἰδιώτης, Pl. *Plt.*298c, *Prt.*327c, *Ion* 531c), Od.17.383, 19.135; ἐχάλκευσε ξίφος.. Αἰδης δ. ἄγριος S.*Aj.*1035; of medical *practitioners*, Hp.*VM*1, Pl.*Smp.* 186d; but opp. scientific physicians (ἀρχιτεκτονικοί), Arist.*Pol.*1282^a 3; of sculptors, Pl.*R.*529e; of confectioners and cooks, Hdt.7.31, Men.518.12 (fem.), Antiph.225, Alexandr.Com.3; μέλιτος δ., of the bee, Jul.*Or.*8.241a; οἱ δ. *the artisan class* at Athens, Arist.*Ath.*13. 2, Plu.*Thes.*25; opp. πολιτικοί, Pl.*Ap.*23e; δαμιουργοί, = πόρναι, Hsch. **2.** metaph., *maker*, ἡ μαντικὴ φιλίας θεῶν καὶ ἀνθρώπων δ. Pl.*Smp.*188d; νόμων, πολιτείας, Arist.*Pol.*1273^{b}32; λόγων Aeschin. 3.215; δ. κακῶν *author* of ill, E.*Fr.*1059.7; πειθοῦς δ. ἡ ῥητορική Pl. *Grg.*453a; ἀρετῆς Id.*R.*500d, Arist.*Pol.*1329^{a}21; ἐναργείας Demetr. *Eloc.*215; ὄρθρος δημιοεργός morn *that calls man to work*, *h.Merc.* 98. **3.** *creator, producer*, νυκτός τε καὶ ἡμέρας Pl.*Ti.*40c; οὐρανοῦ Id. *R.*530a; esp. in later philosophy, *the Creator* of the visible world, *Demiurge*, [Philol.]21, Hp.*Ep.*23, Ph.1.632, etc.; ὁ νοῦς ἀπεκύησε ἕτερον νοῦν δ. *Corp.Herm.*1.9; also name for μονάς, *Theol.Ar.*5.24: as Adj., δ. λόγος *creative* reason, Syrian.*in Metaph.*7.27. **II.** in many Greek states, title of *a magistrate*, Th.5.47 (Mantinea), Epist. Philipp.ap.D.18.157 (Peloponnesus), Plb.23.5.16 (Achaean League), etc.:—Dor. **δαμιωργός**, *IG*12(3).174 (Astypalaea); **δαμιουργός**, ib. 4.679 (Hermione); **δαμιοργός**, ib.5(1).1390.116 (Andania, i B.C.); **δαμιεργός**, ib.12(3).168 (Astypalaea):—Ion. **δημιοργός**, ib.12(7). 241 (Amorgos), *Michel* 368.1 (Samos).—In Arist.*Pol.*1275^{b}29 there is a play upon the double meaning. **III.** as a priestly title, δ. θεᾶς Ῥώμης *BGU*937.9 (iii A.D.).

δημιώδης, ες, = δημώδης, Phld.*Mus.*p.27 K. (s. v. l.).

δημιῶν· τὸν δῆμον διοικῶν, Hsch.

δημοαλῆ· περιβόητον, Hsch. (leg. -λαλῆ, cf. δημολάλητος).

δημο-βόητος, gloss on δημολάλητος, *notorious*, Hsch. **-βορέω**, *devour the people*, Eust.1143.46. **-βόρος**, ον, *devourer of the common stock*, δ. βασιλεύς Il.1.231; of Caligula, Ph.2.561. **-γέρων**, οντος, ὁ, *elder of the people*, Il.11.372: in pl., *nobles, chiefs*, 3.149, E. *Andr.*300 (lyr.), Plot.6.4.15; of the Jewish *elders*, δ. τοῦ ἔθνους Ph.2.94; δ. θεός, = Lat. *deus minorum gentium*, dub. l. in *AP*9. 334 (Pers.). **-δίωκτος** [ῐ], gloss on δημόσσοος, Hsch. **-εγερτής**, οῦ, ὁ, *sedition-monger, agitator*, Suid. **-ειδής**, ές, *vulgar*, κιβδηλίη Hp.*Art.*78. **-θεές**· θεωρόν, Hsch., and **-θέεση** (sic)· ἐθεώρει, Id.

δημόθεν, Adv. *at the public cost*, δημόθεν ἄλφιτα δῶκα Od.19. 197. **2.** *from among the people*, A.R.1.7. **II.** δ. Εὐπυρίδης an Eupyrian *by deme*, *IG*3.121.

δημοθοιν-έω, *give a public feast*, *IG*12(7).389 (Amorgos), *Ath.Mitt.* 36.159. **-ία**, ἡ, *public feast*, Arist.*Mu.*400^{b}21 (pl.), Luc.*Dem. Enc.*16, *CIG*2880 (Branchidae), Ph.2.55, *OGI*533.9 (Ancyra):—Delph. **δᾱμο-**, *SIG*672.53.

δημό-θροος, οον, contr. **-θρους**, ουν, *uttered by the people*, φήμη, ἀρὰ δ., A.*Ag.*938,1409; δ. ἀναρχία lawlessness *of popular clamour*, ib. 883. **-καλλίας** (-κας cod., but cf. καλλίας, = πίθηκος)· τοὺς περὶ τὰ δημόσια ἀναστρέφοντας, Hsch. **-κηδής**, ὁ, *caring for, friendly to the people* or *to democracy*, Str.14.2.5; = Lat. *Publicola*, D.H.5.19, Plu.*Publ.*10. **-κλίναρχος** [ῐ], ὁ, *president of a municipal religious association*, *Arch.Pap.*1.417 (Talmis). **-κοινος** (sc. δοῦλος), ὁ, = δήμιος II, *executioner*, S.*Fr.*780, Antipho 1.20, Isoc.17.15. **2.** = πόρνος, Hsch. **II.** as Adj., δημόκοινος, ον, *vile, common*, of coarse food, Lyc.Trag.2.4. **-κόλαξ**, ακος, ὁ, *mob-flatterer*, D.H.6.60, Luc.*Dem.Enc.*31.

δημοκοπ-έω, *court the mob*, Plu.*CG*9, Charito 1.5; opp. δημαγωγέω, Plu.2.802d; δ. ἔς τινας App.*Syr.*16; δ. τὸ πλῆθος ἐπί τισι Id.*BC* 4.94:—Med., Phld.*Rh.*1.380 S. **-ημα**, ατος, τό, *attempt to gain mob-favour*, App.*BC*1.24. **-ία**, ἡ, *courting the mob*, D.H.6.60, *IG*4.1153 (Epid.); *bribery*, Plu.*Dio* 47: pl., Str.14.5.14, Ph.*Fr.*33 H., App.*BC*1.34. **-ικός**, ή, όν, *of* or *suited to a* δημοκόπος, βίος δ. Pl.*Phdr.*248e; τὸ περὶ ἀνθρώπους δ. M.Ant.1.16: Sup., App.*Hisp.* 4. **-ος**, ὁ, *demagogue*, D.H.5.65, D.S.18.10, Ph.2.47, etc.

δημόκραντος, ον, *ratified by the people*, ἀρὰ δ. A.*Ag.*457 (lyr.).

δημοκρᾰτ-έομαι, Pass. with fut. Med. -κρατήσομαι Th.8.48, Lys. 34.4, D.24.99, but -κρατηθήσομαι v.l. in Th.8.75: pf. δεδημοκράτημαι D.C.52.13:—*have a democratic constitution*, Hdt.6.43, Ar.*Ach.*642, Lys.12.4, etc.; πόλις δημοκρατουμένη Lex ap.And.1.88, cf. Th.5. 29. **2.** impers., δημοκρατεῖται *democratic principles prevail*, Arist. *Pol.*1265^{b}38. **-ία** (Dor. **δᾱμο-** *SIG*360.14 (Chersonesus)), ἡ, *democracy, popular government*, Hdt.6.43, Antipho 6.45, etc.; ἐν δ. D.18.132; δ. καταλυθείσης And.1.95, cf. Th.6.89, Arist.*Pol.*1279^{b}18, al. **II.** personified, Paus.1.3.2; θυσία τῇ Δ. *IG*2.741.67; ἄγαλμα τῆς Δ. *SIG*694.31 (Elaea). **-ίζω**, *to be on the democratic side*, App. *Pun.*70. **-ικός**, ή, όν, *of* or *for a democracy*, νόμοι Pl.*R.*338e; δημοκρατικόν τι δρᾶν to do a *popular* act, Ar.*Ra.*952; τὸ δίκαιον τὸ δ. Arist.*Pol.*1280^{a}9. Adv. -κῶς D.S.2.32, Str.6.3.4. **II.** of persons (δημοτικός is more usu. in this sense), *favouring democracy* or *suited to democracy*, Lys.25.8, Pl.*R.*571a, Arist.*EN*1131^{a}27.

Δημοκρίτειοι, οἱ, *followers of Democritus* of Abdera, Ael.*VH*12. 25, Plu.2.1108e; ἡ Δ. φιλοσοφία S.E.*P.*1.213.

δημο-κώκῡτος (-τυτος cod.)· ἀθρήνητος, ἀνελεήμων, Hsch. **-λάλητος** [ᾰ], ον, *notorious*, Id., *EM*265.19. **-λευστος**, ον, *publicly stoned*, δ. φόνος death *by public stoning*, S.*Ant.*36; of a person, Lyc.331. **-λογέω**, = δημόομαι, μείλιχα δ. *AP*7.440 (Leon.). **-λογικός**, ή, όν, *suited to public speaking*: *popular, superficial*, Pl.*Sph.*268b:—hence **Δημολογοκλέων**, ὁ, a nickname given by the Chorus to Bdelycleon in Ar.*V.*342.

δημόομαι, Dor. **δαμ-**, *sing a popular song* (cf. δάμωμα), γλυκύ τι δαμωσόμεθα Pi.*I.*8(7).9; δημούμενον λέγειν talk *ad captandum*, Pl. *Tht.*161e; also δ. ἱερὰς ἐσθῆτας *display*, Jul.*Ep.*89b (s. v. l.). **II.** Pass., *to be made public*, D.C.53.19, *Fr.*57.80.

δημο-πίθηκος [ῐ], ὁ, *mob-jackanapes, charlatan*, Ar.*Ra.*1085. **-ποίητος**, ον, *made a citizen*, but not one by birth, Plu.*Sol.*24, Luc. *Scyth.*8, Aristid.1.103 J. **-πρακτος**, ον, *resolved by the people*, ψῆφος A.*Supp.*942. **-πράτης** [ᾱ], ου, ὁ, *auctioneer of public goods*, Poll.9.10. **-ρρῐφής**, ές, *hurled by the people*, ἀραί A.*Ag.*1616.

δῆμος, Dor. **δᾶμος** (cf. infr. IV), ὁ, *district, country, land*, Βοιωτοὶ μάλα πίονα δ. ἔχοντες Il.5.710; Λυκίης ἐν πίονι δ. 16.437, cf. Od.13. 322, etc.; Ἰθάκης ἐνὶ δ. 1.103; δήμῳ ἔνι Τρώων 13.266; λαοὶ ἀνὰ δῆμον 16.95: metaph., δῆμος ὀνείρων *the land* of dreams, 24.12. **2.** the *people, inhabitants* of such a district, πόληΐ τε παντί τε δήμῳ Il.3.50, cf. *h.Cer.*271; Βακτρίων ἔρρει πανώλης δ. A.*Pers.*732. **II.** hence (since the common people lived in the country, the chiefs in the city), *the commons, common people*, δήμου ἀνήρ, opp. βασιλεύς, ἔξοχος ἀνήρ, etc., Il.2.198,188, cf. 11.328, Hes.*Op.*261, Hdt.5.66, *Act.Ap.*12.22, etc. (rarely of a single person, δῆμον ἐόντα being *a commoner*, Il.12.213); opp. οἱ εὐδαίμονες, Hdt.1.196; opp. οἱ παχέες, Id.5.30; opp. οἱ δυνατοί, Th.5.4; οἱ.. ἐπαναστάντες τοῖς δυνατοῖς καὶ ὄντες δῆμος Id.8.73; = Lat. *plebs*, D.H.6.88, etc.; τοῦ πολλοῦ δ. εἷς *unus de plebe*, Luc. *Sat.*2; τοῦ δ. ὤν Id.*Gall.*22; in an army, *rank and file*, opp. officers, ὁ δ. τῶν στρατιωτῶν X.*Cyr.*6.1.14. **2.** metaph., δ. ἰχθύων Antiph. 206.7; τυράννων Philostr.*VS*1.15.1; πιθήκων Id.*VA*3.4; ὀρνέων

Alciphr.3.30. III. in a political sense, *the sovereign people, the free citizens*, A.*Th.*199,1011, etc.; ὁ δ. ὁ Ἀθηναίων *IG*1^2.10.37, etc.; προστάτης τοῦ δήμου Th.6.35, etc.; personified, Ar.*Eq.*42, al.; ἱερεὺς τοῦ Δ. καὶ τῶν Χαρίτων *IG*2^2.1028. 2. *popular government, democracy*, opp. ὀλιγαρχίη, Hdt.3.82; opp. οἱ τύραννοι, And.1.106; πολίτευμα εἶναι ἐν Χίῳ δ. *SIG*283.4 (iv B.C.); δήμου κατάλυσις X.*HG*2.3.28, Arist. *Ath.*8.4; ταῦτα καταλύει δῆμον, οὐ κωμῳδία Philippid.25.7; δ. καταστῆσαι, καταπαύειν, X.*HG*7.3.3, Th.1.107: in pl., *democracies*, Id. 3.82, D.20.15; δ. ὁ ἔσχατος Arist.*Pol.*1277^{b}3. 3. *the popular assembly*, λέγειν ἐν τῷ δ. Pl.*R.*565b; ἡ βουλὴ καὶ ὁ δ., formula in Inscrr., as *IG*1^2.39, etc.; of the *assembly* of Oxyrhynchus, *POxy.*41.19 (iii/iv A.D.), 1407.19 (iii A.D.). IV. *township, commune* (= Dor. κώμη acc. to Arist.*Po.*1448^{a}37; but διελόμενοι τὴν μὲν πόλιν κατὰ κώμας, τὴν δὲ χώραν κατὰ δήμους Isoc.7.46, cf. Pl.*Lg.*746d, and v. infr.), in Attica, Hdt.5.69, Arist.*Ath.*21.5, Str.9.1.16, *IG*1^2.76.9, al.; elsewh., ib.12(5).594 (Ceos), *PHib.*1.28.13 (iii A.D.), *OGI*49.14 (Ptolemais), etc.:—Dor. **δᾶμος**, *Michel*418.34 (Calymna), *IG*12(1).58.23 (Lindos): in indications of origin, Σωφάνης ἐκ δ. Δεκελεῆθεν Hdt.9.73; δήμου Ἁλαιεὺς Antiph.211; τῶν δήμων Πιτθεὺς Pl.*Euthphr.*2b; τῶν δ. Θορίκιος D.39.30, cf. Arist.*Ath.*21.4; ἐπιγράψαι τοὺς βουλευτὰς πατρόθεν καὶ τοῦ δ. *IG*2^2.223*B*4: metaph., οἱ τῆς θαλάσσης δ. Philostr.*Gym.* 44. V. name for a prostitute, Archil.184. VI. *faction* in the circus, *Tab.Defix.Aud.*15.8 (Syria, iii A.D.). VII. = κατανάγκη, Ps.-Dsc.4.131. (Perh. cognate with Skt. *dā́ti* 'reap', δαίομαι, δατέομαι.)

δημός, ὁ, *fat*, βοῦν..πίονα δημῷ Il.23.750, cf. Hes.*Th.*538, Ar.*V.* 40, etc.; δίπλακι δημῷ (of sacrificial meat) *with fat* above *and fat* below, Il.23.243; of men, κορέει κύνας ἠδ' οἰωνοὺς δημῷ 8.380.

Δημοσθέν-ειος, α, ον, *Demosthenic*, Longin.34.2:—also **-ικός**, ή, όν, D.H.*Rh.*11.10, Luc.*Dem.Enc.*15. Adv. -κῶς Aristid.*Rh.*1 p.510 S. **-ίζω**, *imitate Demosthenes*, Plu.*Cic.*24.

δημοσίᾳ, Adv., v. δημόσιος.

δημοσιεύω, Dor. **δᾱμ-**, *make public* or *common, confiscate*, τὰ χρήματα X.*HG*1.7.10. 2. *publish* a book, J.*Vit.*65, Gal.14.62; κοινοῦν καὶ δ. τὴν χρείαν [λόγου] Plu.2.34c:—Pass., τὰ δεδημοσιευμένα *sayings that have become public property*, Arist.*Rh.*1395^{a}19. 3. δ. τὴν τοῦ σώματος ὥραν *prostitute* it, D.H.1.84. 4. Pass., *to be manifested, displayed*, -εύεται ἡ θερμότης τινός Steph.*in Hp.*1.186 D. 5. Pass., *to be produced as evidence*, *PLond.*1.77.5 (vi A.D.), etc. II. intr., *to be in the public service*, esp. of physicians *in receipt of a salary from the state*, Ar.*Ach.*1030, Pl.*Grg.*514d, *POxy.*40.9 (ii/iii A.D.); οἱ ἰατροὶ οἱ δαμοσιεύοντες ἐν τᾷ πόλει *SIG*943.7 (Cos); δ. δωρεὰν *IG*2^2. 483.17: generally, *to be a public man*, opp. ἰδιωτεύω, Pl.*Grg.*515b, *Ap.*32a; φροντίσι δ. *devote oneself* in every thought *to the common good*, Plu.2.823c; but ἐπὶ μισθῷ δ. *to be a* paid *official*, Id.*Comp. Arist.Cat.*6; also of things, ἐν βαλανείῳ δημοσιεύοντι Id.*Phoc.*4.

δημοσιο-μάστης, v. δαμοσιομάστας. **-πρακτος**, ον, *engaged in public business*, *Cat.Cod.Astr.*1.150.

δημόσιος, Dor. **δᾱμ-**, α, ον (ος, ον Hp. (v. infr.)), *belonging to the people* or *state*, κτέανα Xenoph.2.8; τὰ δ. Hdt.5.29, Ar.*V.*554; δ. χρήματα Cratin.171; πλοῦτος Th.1.80; χώρα, opp. ἱερά, ἰδία, Arist.*Pol.* 1267^{b}34; ἡ δ. τράπεζα *IG*2^2.1013; τὰ ἱερὰ τὰ δ., opp. ἰδιωτικά, *SIG* 1015.9 (Halic.); ἀγῶνες, δίκαι, Aeschin.1.2, Arist.*Pol.*1320^{a}12; δ. λόγος, = Lat. *fiscus*, *BGU*193.27, *OGI*669.21; δημόσιον εἶναι, γίγνεσθαι, to be, become *state-property*, be *confiscated*, Th.2.13, *IG*2^2.1100.40 (Hadr.), Pl.*Lg.*742b, etc.; γῆν δ. ποιεῖν Lys.18.14. b. *used by the public*, βαλανεῖα, λουτρόν, Plb.26.1.12, Hdn.1.12.4. 2. *common*, δημοσιώτατος τρόπος, τόπος, Arist.*Top.*162^{a}35, *SE*165^{a}5; δημόσιος κακίη *epidemic*, Hp.*Ep.*19 (*Hermes* 53.67). II. as Subst.: a. δημόσιος (sc. δοῦλος), ὁ, *any public slave* or *servant*, as, *the public crier*, Hdt.6.121; *policeman*, Ar.*Lys.*436; *public notary*, = γραμματεύς, D. 19.129, etc.; *public executioner*, D.S.13.102: generally, *public official*, τὸν ἀρχέφοδον καὶ τοὺς ἄλλους δημοσίους *POxy.*69.13 (ii A.D.). b. *public victim*, = φάρμακος, Ar.*Eq.*1136, cf. Sch. ad loc. c. *harlot, prostitute*, Procop.*Arc.*9 (cf. Sapph.148). III. neut., δημόσιον, τό, *the state*, Hdt.1.14, Aeschin.3.58; οἱ ἐκ δ. *public officials*, X. *Lac.*3.3. b. *public building, hall*, Hdt.6.52. c. *treasury*, = τὸ κοινόν, ἀργύριον ὀφείλοντες τῷ δ. And.1.73, cf. D.21.182, Din.2.2; ὁ ἐκ δ. μισθὸς Th.6.31; ἡ ἐκ τοῦ δ. τροφὴ Pl.*R.*465d; τελεῖν εἰς τὸ δ. *BGU*1188.12 (Aug.), 1158.18 (i B.C.). d. *the public prison*, Th.5. 18. 2. τὰ δ. *public archives*, *OGI*229.108 (Smyrna). b. *public dues, taxes*, in pl., *PLond.*3.938.11 (iii A.D.), *BGU*1018.21 (iii A.D.). IV. fem., δαμοσία (sc. σκηνή), ἡ, *tent of the Spartan kings*: hence οἱ περὶ δαμοσίαν the *king's council*, X.*HG*4.5.8, *Lac.*13.7. V. as Adv.: 1. dat. δημοσίᾳ, Ion. -ίῃ, *at the public expense*, Hdt.1. 30, Ar.*Av.*396, etc.; *by public consent*, D.21.50; *on public service*, δ. ἀποδημεῖν Id.45.3; δ. κρίνειν try *in the public courts*, And.1.105; δ. τεθνάναι to die *by the hands of the public executioner*, D.45.81. 2. *as a community*, opp. ἰδίᾳ, Pl.*Ap.*30b. 3. *commonly, popularly*, τὰ δ. νομιζόμενα ἀγαθά Luc.*Nigr.*4. 4. regul. Adv. -ίως A.D. *Adv.*151.12; *on public business*, καταπλεῦσαι *SIG*520.7 (Naxos, iii B.C.).

δημοσιουργία, Dor. **δᾱμοσιοργία**, ἡ, *eligibility for public office*, *SIG*1009.10 (Chalcedon).

δημοσιοφύλαξ [ῠ], Dor. **δᾱμοσιο-**, ακος, ὁ, *treasury official*, *SIG* 529.4, 531.26 (Dyme, iii B.C.).

δημοσι-όω, *confiscate*, Th.3.68, Procop.*Arc.*11:—Pass., of the Ager Publicus at Rome, *to be converted to public use*, D.H.8.74; also δεδημοσιωμέναι γυναῖκες *prostitutes*, Plu.2.519e. II. *publish*, D.L.8.55:—usu. Pass., Pl.*Sph.*232d, Plu.2.507f. 2. *register* a deed, παρὰ τῷ ἀρχιδικαστῇ *Sammelb.*4651.6 (iii A.D.):—usu. Pass., *BGU*50.5 (ii A.D.), etc. **-ωμα**, gloss on δάμωμα, Hsch. **-ώνης**, ου, ὁ, *farmer of the revenue*, Str.12.3.40, D.S.34.38, al., *OGI*629.25 (Palmyra), *IG*7.413 (Oropus), *POxy.*44.8 (i A.D.), etc. **-ωνία**, ἡ, *leasing of the revenues*, Memn.38.2, *OGI*440.9 (Ilium). **-ώνιον**, τό, *office of revenue-leases*, Plu.2.820c. **-ωσις**, εως, ἡ, *registration* of a deed in the record office, *POxy.*906.9 (ii/iii A.D.), 1200.7 (iii A.D.), etc.

δημοσσόος, ον, (σῴζω) *saving the people*: but, II. δημόσσοος, (σεύω) *driven away by the people*:—both in Hsch.

δημο-στροφέω, *go about amongst the people*, Hsch. **-σώστης**, ου, ὁ, *saviour of the people*, *IGRom.*3.67 (Prusias): fem. **-σῶστις**, βουλή prob. l. in *Bayr.Sitzb.*1863.220. **-τελής**, ές, (τέλος) *at the public cost*, θυσίη Hdt.6.57, cf. Pl.*Lg.*935b, Plb.6.53.6, *CIG*3493.7 (Thyatira); ἑορτή Th.2.15, cf. *OGI*56.41 (iii B.C.); πανάγυριν δαμοτέλην (sic) *IG*12(2).645.44 (Nesus); δ. ἱερὰ τελεῖν Orac.ap.D.21.53. 2. *with public authority, sovereign*, ἐκκλησία *AJA*18.324 (Sardis). Adv. -λῶς Suid. II. epith. of Demeter, *IG*12(7).4.5 (Amorgos).

δημότερος, α, ον, poet. for δημοτικός II, A.R.3.606. II. = δημόσιος I. 1, χρήματα *AP*9.693. III. = δημόσιος I. 2, *common, vulgar*, Κύπρις ib.415.2 (Antiphil.).

δημοτερπής, ές, *popular, attractive*, Pl.*Min.*321a (Sup.), D.H.*Rh.* 1.8 (Comp.), Max.Tyr.10.6.

δημοτεύομαι, Pass., *to be a* δημότης, ἠρόμην ὁπόθεν δημοτεύοιτο Lys.23.2, cf. Antipho *Fr.*65, D.57.49.

δημότης, ου, ὁ, Dor. **δᾱμότας**, also **δᾱμέτας** (q.v.), *one of the people, commoner*, opp. a man of rank, Tyrt.4.5, Hdt.2.172, 5.11, X. *Cyr.*2.3.7; ἄνδρα δ. S.*Aj.*1071; δ. ὅμιλος Ar.*Pax*921; δ. τε καὶ ξένος E.*Supp.*895; δημόται καὶ πένητες X.*Mem.*1.2.58:—fem. **δημότις**, ιδος, opp. βασίλισσα, Plb.22.20.2: pl., opp. εὐγενέσταται, D.C.62. 15. 2. = ἰδιώτης, γνωστὰ λέγειν δημότῃσι speak *popularly*, Hp.*VM* 2, cf. *Acut.*8; ἀμαθὴ τῶν δ. Id.*Art.*67. II. *one of the same people, fellow-citizen*, Pi.*N.*7.65, E.*Alc.*1057. III. at Athens and elsewhere, *member of a deme* or *of the same deme*, S.*OC*78, Susario 1, Pl.*Ap.*33e, D.18.261, *IG*2^2.1172, etc.; φράτερας καὶ δ. Cratin.Jun. 9:—so fem. **δημότις**, ιδος, Ar.*Lys.*333, Theoc.28.22. **-ικός**, ή, όν, *of* or *for the people, in common use*, δ. γράμματα in Egypt, opp. ἱερά, Hdt.2.36; οἶνος Plu.*Mar.*44; of opinions and the like, ὑπόληψις *popular*, Arist.*Metaph.*989^{a}11; *common, ordinary*, ὀνόματα Luc. *Hist.Conscr.*22; ὕλη Max.Tyr.10.7; πράγματα μικρὰ καὶ δ. Plu.2. 408c. 2. = δημόσιος, τὰ -κά *public affairs*, Alciphr.1.4; δ. λειτουργία *PSI*1.86 (iv A.D.). II. *of the populace, one of them*, D.21. 209. Adv. -κῶς, ἐσταλμένος Luc.*Scyth.*5. 2. *on the popular* or *democratic side*, τὸ σόφισμα δ. Ar.*Nu.*205; ὄρνεα δ. Id.*Av.*1584; τὴν οὐ δ. παρανομίαν Th.6.28; opp. ὀλιγαρχικός, Isoc.16.37; λέγεις πόσα δεῖ προσεῖναι τῷ δ. D.18.122; οὐδὲν δ. πράττειν to do nothing *for the people*, X.*HG*2.3.39; δ. συκοφάνται Isoc.8.133: generally, *popular*, δ. καὶ φιλάνθρωπος X.*Mem.*1.2.60; τῶν μετρίων τινὰ καὶ δ. D.21.183; δημοτικὸν τοῦτο δρᾷ Antiph.190.19: hence, *generous, kindly, affable*, X.*Mem.*1.2.60; δ. τι καὶ πρᾶον Pl.*Euthd.*303d; πρᾶός τις καὶ δ. Plb. 10.26.1; δ. καὶ φιλάνθρωπα Plu.*Oth.*1. Adv. -κῶς *affably, kindly*, καλῶς καὶ δ. D.24.59; φιλανθρώπως καὶ δ. ib.24: Comp. -ώτερον Plu. *Demetr.*42. 3. of governments, *popular, democratic*, πολιτεία Arist.*Pol.*1292^{b}13: Comp. -ώτερα Id.*Ath.*22.1. 4. δ. δικαστήριον *trying suits between citizens*, *SIG*286.17 (Milet., iv B.C.). 5. Adv. χρῆσθαι ἀλλήλοις δ. *in a spirit of equality*, Arist.*Pol.*1308^{a}11; δ. πεπαιδευμένοι ib.1310^{a}17; δ. ἐρίζειν *like a free and independent citizen*, Luc.*Ner.*9. III. *of* or *belonging to a deme*, opp. δημόσιος, Lex ap. D.43.71; ἱερά Hsch. s. v. δημοτελῆ.

δημοῦχος, Dor. **δᾱμ-**, ον, (ἔχω) *protectors* or *possessors of the land*, epith. of guardian deities, S.*OC*458; δαμοῦχοι γᾶς ib.1087 (lyr.); ἄνδρες δ. χθονός ib.1348; title of the Heraclidae at Thespiae, D.S. 4.29.

δημο-φάγος [ᾰ], ον, = δημοβόρος, τύραννος Thgn.1181. **-φᾰνής**, ές, (φαίνω) *public, solemn*, ἑορτή Ph.2.169. II. *notorious*, πρᾶγμα Phryn.*PS*p.64 B. **-φαντος**, ον, = foreg., Hsch. **-φθόρος**, ον, *ruining the people*, f.l. for θυμο-, Callistr.*Stat.*14. **-φῐλής**, ές, = φιλόδημος, Sch.Ar.*Pl.*550.

Δημοφῶν, = θλάσπι, prob. l. in Ps.-Dsc.2.156 (Wellm.).

δημο-χᾰρής, ές, *pleasing the people, popular*, Paul.Al.*N.*2. **-χᾰριστής**, οῦ, ὁ, *mob-courtier*, E.*Hec.*132 (anap.). **-χᾰριστικῶς**, *like a* δημοχαριστής, Sch.Il.2.350.

δημ-όω, v. δημόομαι. **-ώδης**, ες, *popular*: μουσική, σωφροσύνη, *in the popular sense*, Pl.*Phd.*61a, *Lg.*710a; ἀρεταὶ καὶ κακίαι Phld.*Rh.* 1.217 S.; *hackneyed*, κοινὰ καὶ δ. ὀνόματα Longin.40.2; στιχίδια Plu. *Per.*30, cf. Ael.*VH*3.3; λόγος ib.3.45; τὸ δ. πλῆθος, of civilians, opp. στρατιωτικοί, Hdn.1.4.8, cf. 1.15.7; of a prostitute, *common*, *AP*7.345. Adv. -δῶς Apollon.Cit.1. **-ώλης**, ες, *having lost membership of a* δῆμος, *IG*1^2.913. **-ωμα**, v. δάμωμα. **-ωφελής**, ές, *of public use*, λόγοι Pl.*Phdr.*227d; πολιτεύματα Plu.2.784d; δ. τι πραχθὲν D.C.72.7, cf. Luc.*Bis Acc.*11; τὸ δ. *the common good*, Hdn. 2.3.8: Sup. τὸ -έστατον Ph.2.177. 2. of persons, Democr.282, Phld.*Rh.*2.92 S.; ἡγεμών Plu.*Sull.*30. 3. Adv. -λῶς *CIG*4415*b* (Iotapata), *IPE*1^2.39.36 (Olbia), *IGRom.*4.860 (Laodicea ad Lycum): Sup. -έστατα D.C.56.37. **-ωφελῶν**· δῆμον ὠφελῶν, Hsch.

Δήν, Δηνός, Cret., = Ζεύς, *SIG*527.18 (iii B.C.).

δήν, Dor. **δάν** (or **δοάν** Alcm.135, cf. A.D.*Adv.*160.18), Adv. *for a long while*, Il.5.412; οὐδὲ γὰρ..δ. ἦν nor was he *long-lived*, 6.131, cf. 16.736; δ. δη..φίλοι ὦμεν Thgn.1243; ἐπὶ δ. μετέπειτα A.R.1.516, cf. Euph.9.8; once in Trag., A.Pers.584 (lyr.). 2. long ago, δ. οἴχεσθαι Od.18.313. (δοάν, = δϝάν, cf. Lat. dudum: hence οὐδὲ δ(ϝ)ήν Il.16.736.)

δηναιός, ή, όν, Dor. **δᾱναιός**, ά, όν, long-lived, Il.5.407; δ. κλέος Theoc.16.54; long-continued, ὁδοιπορίη IG14.1780; χρόνος A.R.4.1547; βίος AP6.39.7 (Arch.): neut. as Adv., Man.3.143. 2. aged, κόραι A.Pr.794; ancient, θρόνοι ib.912 (and in Eu.846 (lyr.), δαναιᾶν should be restored with Dindorf for δαμαίων, cf. Call.Fr.105); ἀοιδοί Id.Jov.60; worn out, δένδρα Hsch. II. after a long time, δ. εἰσαφίκοντο A.R.4.645; late come, long absent, ἀδελφεός Opp.H.4.154: neut. δηναιόν, as Adv., A.R.3.590: so pl., δηναιά Maiist.8. III. personified, Θόωσα and Δηναιή, Overspeed and Loitering, Emp.122.3.

δηναιότης, ητος, ἡ, long life, Democr.201.

Δηναιών, ῶνος, ὁ (sc. μήν), name of month at Erythrae, SIG1014.24 (iii B.C.).

δηνάριον, τό, = Lat. denarius (usu. represented by δραχμή (q.v.)), Arr.Epict.1.4.16, Placit.4.11.5, etc.; = one tetradrachm, PLond.2.248.20 (iv A.D.), POxy.1431.3 (iv A.D.).

δήνεα, τά, only in pl., counsels, plans, arts, whether good or bad, δ. θεῶν Od.23.82; ἤπια δ. οἶδε Il.4.361, Hes.Th.236; ὀλοφώϊα Od.10.289; δ. πάντα καὶ τρόπους ἐπίσταται Semon.7.78; δ. Κίρκης A.R.4.559; δ. τέχνης Opp.H.1.7.—Sg. nom. **δῆνος**, εος, τό, Hsch.: **δήνεον** (sic), Suid.

δήξ, gen. δηκός, ὁ or ἡ, worm in wood, Tz. ad Hes.Op.418.

δηξίθῡμος [ῐ], ον, = δακέθυμος, ἔρωτος ἄνθος A.Ag.743 (lyr.); comically, δ. ὀξάλμη Sopat.21.

δῆξις, εως, ἡ, (δάκνω) bite, biting, Arist.HA623^{a}1; δήξιες σπλάγχνων gnawings, Hp.VM19: metaph., of mental anguish, pangs, Zeno Stoic.1.51 (pl.), Chrysipp.ib.3.119, Phld.D.3Fr.22; also, biting jokes, Plu.Lycurg.14.

δῆος· βωβός (Cret.), Hsch.

δηόω, contr. for δηϊόω.

δήποθεν, indef. Adv. (better written **δή ποθεν**) from any quarter, Pl.Ep.331e; dub. l. in A.Ch.632 (lyr.); perh. = δήπου, as in Orac. ap. Phleg.Olymp.Fr.1, Iamb.Myst.5.20.

δήποτε, indef. Adv. (better written **δή ποτε**), Ion. **δήκοτε**, Dor. **δήποκα**, at some time, once upon a time, Od.6.162, E.Supp.1131 (lyr.); αἰεὶ δ. Th.8.73; at length, A.Ag.577. 2. εἰ δή ποτε if ever, Il.1.40. 3. with interrog., τί δή ποτε; what in the world? what or why now? καίτοι τί δή ποτε; D.4.35; πόσοι δή ποτ' εἰσὶν οἱ..; how many do you suppose? Id.20.21. 4. esp. freq. with relatives, ὅτι δή κοτε πρήξαντα Hdt.6.134; ὅστις δ. ὤν Pl.Phdr.273c; ὅτι δή ποτε whatever it may be, 'so-and-so', D.21.32; ὁπόθεν δ. Id.35.6: strengthd. by οὖν, ὅντινα δή ποτ' οὖν τρόπον Id.40.8; οἷος δή ποτ' οὖν v.l. in Dsc.5.10; also δή ποτ' οὖν without relat., κατὰ πρεσβείαν ἢ κατ' ἄλλην δ. χρείαν Arch.Pap.6.9 (Delos).

δήπου, indef. Adv. (better written **δή που**) perhaps, it may be, ᾧ δή που ἀδελφεὸν ἔκτανε Il.24.736: in Trag. and Att. usu. doubtless, I presume, οὐ δήπου τλητόν A.Pr.1064; τῶν Λαΐου δ. τις ὠνομάζετο S.OT 1042, cf. Ar.Pl.491,582, Th.1.121, etc.; ἴστε γὰρ δή που, μέμνησθε γὰρ δή που, D.2.25, 19.113, cf. 18.249; σχεδὸν ἴσμεν ἅπαντες δή που Id.3.9; οὐδεὶς ἀγνοεῖ δή που Id.21.156. II. as interrog. implying an affirm. answer, τὴν αἰχμάλωτον κάτοισθα δή που; i.e. I presume you know, S.Tr.418; ἀνόμοιον δή που Pl.Tht.159b; οὐ δή που; surely it is not so? implying a neg. answer, as Ar.Ra.526, Pl.Men.73c.

δήπουθεν (-θε before a consonant, Bato 7.3), indef. Adv. = δήπου, chiefly used before a vowel (before a consonant, Pl.Ion 534a, etc.), freq. in Com., Ar.V.296, Pl.140, etc.; in answer to a rhetorical question, οὐ δ., ἀλλά.. Lys.6.36, cf. D.27.59, Pl.Phlb.62e, etc.

δηράς, ἡ, Cret., = δειράς (q.v.). **δηρή**, = δειρή, Hsch.: but **δήρη**· μάχη, Id.

[**δηρ**]**ιάζομαι**, = sq., περί τινος Pi.Pae.6.119 (prob.).

δηρῐάομαι, (δῆρις) contend, περὶ νεκροῦ δηριάασθαι (v.l. δηρίσασθαι) Il.17.734; ὥστ' ἀμφ' οὔροισι δύ' ἀνέρε δηριάασθον wrangle about boundaries, 12.421: abs., ὅ τ' ἄριστοι.. δηριόωντο Od.8.78; οἱ δ' αὐτοὶ δηριαάσθων Il.21.467; δ. τινί contend with one, A.R.4.1729.—Later Act. **δηρῐάω**, contest a prize, Pi.N.11.26; δίφροι δηριόωντες A.R.1.752, cf. Opp.C.1.230.—From **δηρίομαι** (used by Pi.O.13.44) Hom. has aor. 1 Med. δηρίσαντο Od.8.76: 3 dual aor. 1 Pass. δηρινθήτην (as if from δηρίνομαι) Il.16.756 (later δηρινθῆναι A.R.2.16, -θέντες Euph.98.3): fut. δηρίσομαι Theoc.22.70: also in aor. Act., δηρισάντοιν Thgn.995; οὐκ ἄν τοί τις ἐδήρισεν περὶ τιμῆς Theoc.25.82, cf. Lyc.1306. [ῐ in pres.: ῑ in fut. and aor.]

δῆρις, ἡ, battle, contest, Il.17.158, al. (only in acc.): nom. in A.Supp.412 (lyr.), Emp.122.2 (personified), Epigr.Gr.343 (Germa); gen. δήριος A.Ag.942, δήρεως Suid.

δηρίττειν· ἐρίζειν, Hsch.

δηρίφᾰτος [ῐ], ον, = ἀρείφατος, prob. in AP7.722 (Theodorid.).

δηρόβῐος, Dor. **δᾱρ-**, ον, long-lived, θεοί A.Th.524 (lyr.).

δηρός, Dor. **δᾱρός**, ά, όν, (cf. δήν) long, too long, δηρὸν χρόνον Il.14.206, h.Cer.282: more freq. δηρόν (sc. χρόνον) as Adv., all too long, Il.2.298, etc.; also ἐπὶ δηρὸν δέ μοι αἰὼν ἔσσεται 9.415, cf. Musae.291: freq. with neg., οὐδέ σέ φημι δ...ἀλύξειν Il.10.371, cf. 2.435, etc.: Trag. use only Dor. form, πολὺν δαρόν τε χρόνον S.Aj.414 (lyr.), cf. A.Supp.516, E.IT1339; δαρόν alone, A.Pr.648,940, S., etc.; also δαρὸν χρόνου πόδα time's lingering foot, E.Ba.889 (lyr.).

δηρότη(ς)· κακουργία, Hsch. (leg. δηϊότης).

δησάσκετο, v. δέω (A). **δῆσε**, aor. of δέω (A): also for ἐδέησε, aor. of δέω (B).

δῆτα, Adv., lengthd. and more emphatic form of δή, first as v.l. in Hdt.4.69, mostly used by Trag. and Pl. (v. infr.).—Never placed at the beginning of a sentence or verse, exc. in S.Aj.986. 1. in answers, mostly added to a word which echoes a statement or question, as ἴσασιν ὅστις ἦρξε.. Answ. ἴσασι δ. aye they know, E.Med.1373; γιγνώσκεθ' ὑμεῖς..; Answ. γιγνώσκομεν δ. yes we know her, Ar.Th.606, cf. Eq.6, al.; ἰωὰ δὴ κατ' ἄστυ. Answ. ἰωὰ δ. A.Pers.1071, cf. S.OC536 (lyr.), Pl.R.333a, Phd.90d, al. (with a word repeated in the same speech, ὥς μ' ἀπώλεσας· ἀπώλεσας δ. how hast thou destroyed me!—aye, destroyed indeed, S.El.1164; ἰὼ δύστηνε σύ, δύστηνε δῆτα Id.Ph.760); also to correct the previous speaker, οἴκτιρέ θ' ἡμᾶς.. Answ. οἴκτιρε δ... ἐκγόνους nay rather pity.., E.El.673, cf. 676; without repeating the word, αὐτὸς δ' ἀναλοῖ δ. yes truly.., A.Th.814; ἐκεῖνος αὐτὸς δ. Ar.Ra.552: freq. with a neg., not so, οὐ δῆτα μὰ τὸν Ἀπόλλω Id.Eq.870; οὐ δῆτ' ἔγωγε faith not I, Id.Av.1391, E.Med.1048; οὐ δ. Lacon.ap.Arist.Rh.1419^{a}34, cf. Pol.1313^{a}33. 2. in questions, to mark an inference or consequence (cf. δή), τί δ.; what then? A.Pr.627; τί δ. ἐρεῖς, ἦν..; Ar.Nu.1087; τί δ. ἐπειδὰν..; Id.Ach.1011; πῶς δ.; A.Ag.1211, Ar.Nu.79; ἆρ' οἶσθα δ.; S.OT1014; ἀλλὰ δ...; as the last of several questions, Id.Aj.466, etc.; ποῦ δῆθ' ὁ τῖμος; A.Ch.916; ποῖ δ. κρανεῖ; ib.1075, etc.; sts. expressing indignation, καὶ δῆτ' ἐτόλμας; and so thou hast dared? S.Ant.449; ταῦτα δῆτ' ἀνασχετά; Id.Ph.987; ἦ ταῦτα δῆτ' ἀνεκτά; Id.OT429; ἔγνωκας οὖν δῆτ'..; Ar.Eq.871; ironical, τῷ σῷ δικαίῳ δ. ἐπισπέσθαι με δεῖ; your principle of justice forsooth, S.El.1037, cf. OT364; in implied questions, esp. after ἀλλά, ἀλλ' ἢ τέκνων δῆτ' ὄψις ἦν ἐφίμερος ib.1375, cf. Ar.Av.375, Pl.Hp.Ma.283c; τὴν Εὐρυτείαν οἶσθα δ. παρθένον; of course you know.., S.Tr.1219. 3. in prayers or wishes, ἀπόλοιο δ. now a murrain take thee! Ar.Nu.6; λαβοῦ, λαβοῦ δ. take, oh take hold, E.Or.219, cf. 1231, etc.; σκόπει δ. just think, Pl.Grg.452c: with μή, it strengthens the deprecatory force, μὴ δ. τοῦτό γ' S.Ph.762, cf. 1367; μὴ δ. μὴ δ. ἴδοιμι Id.OT830, cf. 1153. 4. in resuming after a parenthesis, ἑσπέρας γε..—ἑσπέρας δ. Pl.Prt.310c. 5. καὶ δ., = καὶ δή, ibid., Ar.Av.511, Th.6.38. II. rarely, like δή I, to emphasize single words, ἅπασι δ. Ar.Ec.1144.

δητός (A), οῦ, ὁ, (δέω A) bundle, σχοινίων Sammelb.1.5 (pl., iii A.D.).

δητός (B)· ὕστερος, Hsch.

δητταί· αἱ ἐπτισμέναι κριθαί, Hsch.; cf. δηαί.

δηῦτε, contr. for δὴ αὖτε, freq. in Lyr.; v. αὖτε.

δήω (A), find, meet with, always in pres. (exc. impf. ἔδηεν Hsch.) with fut. sense, δήεις Il.13.260, Od.7.49, AP7.370 (Diod.); δήομεν Od.4.544; δήετε Il.9.418; δήουσι A.R.4.591; δήωμεν, δήοιμεν, ib.1336,1460. (Poet. exc. as etym. of Δηώ in Corn.ND28.)

δήω (B), burn, EM265.7.

Δηώ, όος, contr. οῦς, ἡ, = Δημήτηρ, Demeter, first in h.Cer.47, al.; Ἐλευσινίας Δηοῦς ἐν κόλποις S.Ant.1121 (lyr.); Δηοῦς ἐσχάραι, καρπός, E.Supp.290, Ar.Pl.515; dat. Δηοῖ Call.Ap.110, IG3.900.3:—Adj. **Δηῷος**, α, ον, sacred to Demeter, ib.14.1389 ii 5:—**Δηωΐνη**, ἡ, daughter of Demeter, Persephone, Call.Fr.48.

δήω, v. δηϊόω.

δήωσις, εως, ἡ, ravaging, Ph.2.548 (pl.), Polyaen.1.36.2.

Δί, Δία, v. Ζεύς.

διά, poet. **διαί** (Aeol. **ζά**, q.v.), Prep. governing gen. and acc.—Rad. sense, through; never anastroph. [Prop. δῐᾰ: but Hom. uses ῑ at the beginning of a line, Il.3.357, 4.135, al.: also ᾱ, metri gr., freq. in Hom., for which A. uses **διαί** in lyr., Ag.448, al.]

A. With Gen. I. of Place or Space: 1. of motion in a line, from one end to the other, right through, in Hom. freq. of the effect of weapons, διὰ μὲν ἀσπίδος ἦλθε.. ἔγχος καὶ διὰ θώρηκος.. Il.3.357; δουρὶ βάλεν Δάμασον κυνέης διά 12.183; δι' ὤμου.. ἔγχος ἦλθεν 4.481; in Prose, τιτρώσκειν διὰ τοῦ θώρακος X.An.1.8.26; διὰ τοῦ ὀρόφου ἐφαίνετο πῦρ ib.7.4.16: also of persons, διὰ Σκαιῶν πεδίονδ' ἔχον ὠκέας ἵππους out through the Scaean gate, Il.3.263; δι' ἠέρος αἰθέρ' ἵκανεν quite through the lower air even to the ether, Il.14.288, cf. 2.458; διὰ Τρώων πέτετο straight through them, 13.755; δι' ὄμματος.. λείβων δάκρυον S.OC1250, etc.: also in Compos. with πρό and ἐκ, v. διαπρό, διέκ: in adverbial phrases, διὰ πασῶν (sc. χορδῶν), v. διαπασῶν: διὰ πάσης throughout, Th.1.14; διὰ κενῆς idly, Id.4.126, etc. (cf. III.1.c). 2. of motion through a space, but not in a line, throughout, over, ἑπόμεσθα διὰ πεδίοιο Il.11.754; δι' ὄρεσφι 10.185, al.; ὀδύνη διὰ χροὸς ἦλθε through all his frame, 11.398; τεῦχε βοὴν διὰ ἄστεος Od.10.118; δι' ὁμίλου Il.6.226, etc.; θορύβου διὰ τῶν τάξεων ἰόντος X.An.1.8.16, cf. 2.4.26, etc.; later, in quoting an authority, ἱστορεῖ δ. τῆς δευτέρας in the course of.., Ath.10.438b. 3. in the midst of, Il.9.468; κεῖτο τανυσσάμενος δ. μήλων Od.9.298; between, δ. τῶν πλευρέων ταμόντα Hp.Morb.2.61: hence, of pre-eminence, ἔπρεπε καὶ δ. πάντων Il.12.104; τετίμακε δι' ἀνθρώπων Pi.I.4(3).37; εὐδοκιμέοντι δ. πάντων Hdt.6.63, cf. 1.25, etc. 4. in Prose, sts. of extension, along, παρήκει δ. τῆσδε τῆς θαλάσσης ἡ ἀκτή Id.4.39 (but πέταται δ. θαλάσσας across the sea, Pi.N.6.48); λόφος, δι' οὗ τὸ σταύρωμα περιεβέβλητο X.HG7.4.22. 5. in Prose, of Intervals of Space, δ. τριήκοντα δόμων at intervals of thirty layers, i.e. after every thirtieth layer, Hdt.1.179; δ. δέκα ἐπάλξεων at every tenth battlement, Th.3.21; cf. infr. II.3: of a single interval, δ. πέντε σταδίων at a distance of five stades, Hdt.7.30, cf. 198; δ. τοσούτου μᾶλλον ἢ δ. πολλῶν ἡμερῶν ὁδοῦ at so short a distance, etc., Th.2.29; δ. πολλοῦ at a great *distance apart*, Id.3.94; δ. πλείστου Id.2.97; δι' ἐλάσσονος Id.3.51; ὕδατα δ. μακροῦ ἀγόμενα Hp.*Aër*.9, etc. II. of Time, 1. of *duration* from one end of a period to the other, *throughout*, δ. παντὸς [τοῦ χρόνου] Hdt.9.13; δι' ὅλου τοῦ αἰῶνος Th.1.70; δι' αἰῶνος S.*El*.1024; δι' ἡμέρας ὅλης Ar.*Pax* 27; δι' ὅλης τῆς νυκτὸς X.*An*.4.2.4, etc.: without an Adj., δι' ἡμέρης *all* day *long*, Hdt.1.97; δ. νυκτός Th.2.4, X.*An*.4.6.22 (but δ. νυκτός *in the course of* the night, *by* night, *Act.Ap*.5.19, *PRyl*.138.15 (i A.D.), etc.); δ. νυκτὸς καὶ ἡμέρας Pl.*R*.343b; δι' ἐνιαυτοῦ, δι' ἔτους, Ar.*Fr*.569.8, *V*.1058; δ. βίου Pl.*Smp*.183e, etc.; δ. τέλους *from beginning to end*, A.*Pr*.275, Pl.*R*.519c, etc.: with Adjs. alone, δ. παντός *continually*, A.*Ch*.862 (lyr.), etc.; δι' ὀλίγου *for* a short time, Th.1.77; δ. μακροῦ E.*Hec*.320; ὁ δ. μέσου χρόνος Hdt. 8.27. 2. of the interval which has passed *between* two points of Time, δ. χρόνου πολλοῦ or δ. πολλοῦ χρ. *after* a long time, Id.3.27, Ar.*Pl*.1045; δ. μακρῶν χρόνων Pl.*Ti*.22d: without an Adj., δ. χρόνου *after* a time, S.*Ph*.758, X.*Cyr*.1.4.28, etc.; δι' ἡμερῶν *after* several days, *Ev.Marc*.2.1; and with Adjs. alone, δι' ὀλίγου Th.5.14; οὐ δ. μακροῦ Id.6.15,91; δ. πολλοῦ Luc.*Nigr*.2, etc.: with Numerals, δι' ἐτέων εἴκοσι Hdt.6.118, cf. *OGI*56.38 (iii B.C.), etc.: but δ. τῆς ἑβδόμης *till* the seventh day, Luc.*Hist.Conscr*.21: also distributively, χρόνος δ. χρόνου προὔβαινε time *after* time, S.*Ph*.285; ἄλλος δι' ἄλλου E.*Andr*.1248. 3. of successive Intervals, δ. τρίτης ἡμέρης every other day, Hdt.2.37; δ. τρίτου ἔτεος ib.4, etc.; δ. πεντετηρίδος every four years (with inclusive reckoning), Id.3.97; δι' ἔτους πέμπτου, of the Olympic games, Ar.*Pl*.584 (but δι' ἐνδεκάτου ἔτεος *in the course of* the eleventh year, Hdt.1.62). III. causal, *through, by*, a. of the Agent, δι' ἀγγέλων or -ου ἐπικηρυκεύεσθαι, ποιεῖσθαι, *by the mouth of*.., Id.1.69,6.4, cf. 1.113; δι' ἑρμηνέως λέγειν X.*An*.2.3.17, etc.; τὸ ῥηθὲν ὑπὸ Κυρίου δ. τοῦ προφήτου *Ev.Matt*.1.22; δι' ἑκόντων ἀλλ' οὐ δ. βίας ποιεῖσθαι Pl.*Phlb*.58b; πεσόντ' ἀλλοτρίας διαὶ γυναικός *by* her *doing*, A.*Ag*.448 (lyr.); ἐκ θεῶν γεγονὼς δ. βασιλέων πεφυκώς X.*Cyr*.7.2.24; δι' ἑαυτοῦ ποιεῖν τι *of oneself, not by another's agency*, ib.1.1.4, etc.; but also, *by oneself alone, unassisted*, D.15.14, cf. 22.38. b. of the Instrument or Means, δ. χειρῶν *by* hand (prop. *by holding between* the hands), δι' ὁσίων χ. θιγών S.*OC*470; also δ. χερῶν λαβεῖν, δ. χειρὸς ἔχειν *in* the hand, Id.*Ant*.916,1258 (but τὰ τῶν ξυμμάχων δ. χειρὸς ἔχειν to keep a *firm* hand on, Th.2.13); δ. στέρνων ἔχειν S.*Ant*.639; ἡ ἀκούουσα πηγὴ δι' ὤτων Id.*OT*1387; δ. στόματος ἔχειν X.*Cyr*.1.4.25; δ. μνήμης ἔχειν Luc.*Cat*.9; αἱ δ. τοῦ σώματος ἡδοναί X.*Mem*.1.5.6; δ. λόγων συγγίγνεσθαι to hold intercourse *by* word, Pl.*Plt*.272b; δ. λόγου ἀπαγγέλλειν *Act.Ap*.15.27; δι' ἐπιστολῶν 2*Ep.Cor*.10.9, *POxy*.1070.15 (iii A.D.). c. of Manner (where διά with its Noun freq. serves as an Adv.), δ. μέθης ποιήσασθαι τὴν συνουσίαν Pl.*Smp*.176e; παίω δι' ὀργῆς *through* passion, *in* passion, S.*OT*807; δ. τάχους, = ταχέως, Id.*Aj*.822, Th.1.63 (but δ. ταχέων ib.80, al.); δ. σπουδῆς *in* haste, hastily, E.*Ba*.212; δι' αἰδοῦς *with* reverence, respectfully, ib.441; δ. ψευδῶν ἔπη lying words, Id.*Hel*.309; αἱ δ. καρτερίας ἐπιμέλειαι *long-continued* exertions, X.*Mem*.2.1.20; δι' ἀκριβείας, δ. πάσης ἀκρ., Pl.*Ti*.23d, *Lg*.876c; δ. σιγῆς Id.*Grg*.450c; δ. ξυμφορῶν ἡ ξύμβασις ἐγένετο Th.6.10; οὐ δι' αἰνιγμάτων, ἀλλ' ἐναργῶς γέγραπται Aeschin.3.121; δι' αἵματος, οὐ δ. μέλανος τοὺς νόμους ὁ Δράκων ἔγραψεν Plu.*Sol*.17: also with Adjs., δ. βραχέων, δ. μακρῶν τοὺς λόγους ποιεῖσθαι, Isoc.14.3, Pl.*Grg*.449b; ἀποκρίνεσθαι δ. βραχυτάτων ibid. d; cf. infr. IV. 2. in later Prose, of Material *out of* which a thing is made, κατασκευάζειν εἴδωλα δι' ἐλέφαντος καὶ χρυσοῦ D.S.17.115; θυσίαι δι' ἀλφίτου καὶ σπονδῆς πεποιημέναι Plu.*Num*.8; βρώματα δ. μέλιτος καὶ γάλακτος γιγνόμενα Ath.14.646e; οἶνος δ. βουνίου Dsc.5.46. IV. διά τινος ἔχειν, εἶναι, γίγνεσθαι, to express conditions or states, ἀγὼν διὰ πάσης ἀγωνίης ἔχων extending *through* every kind of contest, Hdt.2.91; δι' ἡσυχίης εἶναι Id.1.206; δι' ὄχλου εἶναι to be trouble*some*, Ar.*Ec*.888; δ. φόβου εἶναι Th.6.59; δι' ἀπεχθείας γίγνεσθαι X.*Hier*.9.2; ἡ ἐπιμέλεια δ. χάριτος γίγνεται ibid.; δ. μιᾶς γνώμης γίγνεσθαι Isoc.4.138. b. with Verbs of motion, δ. μάχης ἐλεύσονται will engage *in* battle, Hdt.6.9; ἐλθεῖν Th.4.92; δ. παντὸς πολέμου, δ. φιλίας ἰέναι τινί, X.*An*.3.2.8; δ. δίκης ἰέναι τινί go *to* law with.., S.*Ant*.742, cf. Th.6.60; δ. τύχης ἰέναι S.*OT*773; δι' ὀργῆς ἥκειν Id.*OC*905; ἐμαυτῷ δ. λόγων ἀφικόμην I held converse with myself, E.*Med*.872; δ. λόγων, δ. γλώσσης ἰέναι come *to* open speech, Id.*Tr*.916, *Supp*.112; δ. φιλημάτων ἰέναι come *to* kissing, Id.*Andr*.416; δ. δικαιοσύνης ἰέναι καὶ σωφροσύνης Pl.*Prt*.323a, etc.; δ. πυρὸς ἰέναι (v. πῦρ): in pass. sense, δι' ἀπεχθείας ἐλθεῖν τινι to be *hated* by.., A.*Pr*.121 (anap.). c. with trans. Verbs, δι' αἰτίας ἔχειν or ἄγειν τινά hold *in* fault, Th.2.60, Ael.*VH*9.32; δι' ὀργῆς ἔχειν τινά Th.2.37, etc.; δ. φυλακῆς ἔχειν τι Id.7.8; δι' οἴκτου ἔχειν τινά, δι' αἰσχύνης ἔχειν τι, E.*Hec*.851, *IT*683; δ. πένθους τὸ γῆρας διάγειν X.*Cyr*.4.6.6; δι' οὐδενὸς ποιεῖσθαί τι S.*OC*584.

B. WITH ACC. I. of Place, only Poet., in same sense as διά c. gen.: 1. *through*, ἐξ δὲ δ. πτύχας ἦλθε.. χαλκός Il.7.247; ἤϊξε δ. δρυμὰ.. καὶ ὕλην 11.118, cf. 23.122, etc.; δ. τάφρον ἐλαύνειν *across* it, 12.62; δ. δώματα ποιπνύοντα 1.600; ἐπὶ χθόνα καὶ δ. πόντον βέβακεν Pi.*I*.4(3).41; φεύγειν δ. κῦμ' ἅλιον A.*Supp*.14 (anap.). 2. *through, among, in*, οἴκεον δι' ἄκριας Od.9.400; ἄραβος δὲ δ. στόμα γίγνετ' ὀδόντων Il.10.375 (but μῦθον, ὃν.. δ. στόμα.. ἄγοιτο *through* his mouth, 14.91; so δ. στόμα ὄσσαν ἱεῖσαι Hes.*Th*.65; ἀεὶ γὰρ ἡ γυνή σ' ἔχει δ. στόμα Ar.*Lys*.855); δ. κρατερὰς ὑσμίνας Hes.*Th*.631; νόμοι δι' αἰθέρα τεκνωθέντες S.*OT*867 (lyr.). II. of Time, also Poet., δ. νύκτα Il.2.57, etc.; δ. γλυκὺν ὕπνον *during* sweet sleep, Mosch.4.91. III. causal: 1. of persons, *thanks to, by aid of*, νικῆσαι δ.. Ἀθήνην Od.8.520, cf. 13.121; δ. δμῳὰς.. εἷλον 19.154; δ. σε *by* thy *fault* or *service*, S.*OC*1129, Ar.*Pl*.145, cf. 160,170: in Prose, *by reason of, on account of*, δι' ἡμᾶς Th.1.41, cf. X.*An*.7.6.33, D.18.249; οὐ δι' ἐμαυτόν And.1.144; so εἰ μὴ διά τινα if it had not been *for*.., εἰ μὴ δι' ἄνδρας ἀγαθοὺς Lys.12.60; Μιλτιάδην εἰς τὸ βάραθρον ἐμβαλεῖν ἐψηφίσαντο, καὶ εἰ μὴ δ. τὸν πρύτανιν ἐνέπεσεν ἄν Pl.*Grg*.516e, cf. D.19.74; εἰ μὴ δ. τὴν ἐκείνου μέλλησιν Th.2.18, cf. Ar.*V*.558; πλέον' ἔλπομαι λόγον Ὀδυσσέος ἢ πάθαν γενέσθαι δι' Ὅμηρον Pi.*N*.7.21. 2. of things, to express the Cause, Occasion, or Purpose, δι' ἐμὴν ἰότητα *because of* my will, Il.15.41; Διὸς μεγάλου δ. βουλάς Od.8.82; δι' ἀφραδίας *for, through* want of thought, 19.523; δι' ἀτασθαλίας 23.67; δι' ἔνδειαν *by reason of* poverty, X.*An*.7.8.6; δ. καῦμα, δ. χειμῶνα, ib.1.7.6; δι' ἄγνοιαν καὶ ἀμαθίαν Pl.*Prt*.360b, etc.: freq. also with neut. Adjs., δ. τί; *wherefore?*; δ. τοῦτο, δ. ταῦτα *on this account*; δι' ὅ, δι' ἅ *on* which *account*; δ. πολλά *for* many reasons, etc. 3. = ἕνεκα, to express Purpose, δι' ἀχθηδόνα *for the sake of* vexing, Th.4.40, cf. 5.53; δ. τὴν τούτου σαφήνειαν *with a view to* clearing this up, Pl.*R*.524c, cf. Arist.*EN* 1172b21; αὐτὴ δι' αὑτήν *for* its own *sake*, Pl.*R*.367b, etc.

C. WITHOUT CASE as Adv. *throughout*, δ. πρό (v. supr. A. I. 1); δ. δ' ἀμπερές Il.11.377.

D. IN COMPOS.: I. *through, right through*, of Space, διαβαίνω, διέχω, διιππεύω. II. *in different directions*, as in διαπέμπω, διαφορέω; of separation, *asunder*, διαιρέω, διαλύω; of difference or disagreement, *at variance*, διαφωνέω, διαφέρω; or simply mutual relation, *one with another*, διαγωνίζομαι, διᾴδω, διαθέω, διαπίνω, διαφιλοτιμέομαι. III. pre-eminence, διαπρέπω, διαφέρω. IV. completion, *to the end, utterly*, διεργάζομαι, διαμάχομαι, διαπράττω, διαφθείρω: of Time, διαβιόω. V. to add strength, *thoroughly, out and out*, διαγαληνίζω, etc.; cf. ζά. VI. of mixture, *between, partly*, esp. in Adj., as διάλευκος, διάχρυσος, διάχλωρος, etc. VII. of leaving an *interval* or *breach*, διαλείπω, διαναπαύω. (Cogn. with δύο, δίς.)

δῖα, ἡ, fem. of δῖος. **Δία**, acc. of Ζεύς.

Δῖα (sc. ἱερά), τά, = Δίασια, *SIG*38.34 (Teos, v B.C.); cf. Δεῖα.

διαβᾰδίζω, fut. -ιοῦμαι, later -ιῶ Luc.*Dem.Enc*.1, -βαδίσω D.C. 37.53:—*go across*, Th.6.101, Gal.6.185. 2. *walk to and fro*, App.*BC*1.25, Luc. l.c.: in pres. Med., Them.*Or*.21.253a.

δια-βάθρα, ἡ, *ladder*, Aristeas 106, Str.16.2.40, D.H.5.41, etc.: esp. *ship's gangway*, *PPetr*.2p.38 (iii B.C.). II. *drawbridge*, Apollod.*Poliorc*.170.1, al.: generally, *bridge*, *PSI*5.543 (iii B.C.). **-βαθρον**, τό, a kind of *slipper*, Alex.98.8, Herod.7.61, Alciphr.3.46; cf. Lat. *diabathrarii*, Plaut.*Aul*.513.

διαβαίνω, fut. -βήσομαι: aor. -έβην, Aeol. part. ζάβαις Alc.*Supp*.7.3: I. intr., *stride, walk* or *stand with legs apart*, εὖ διαβάς, of a man *planting himself firmly* for fighting, Il.12.458, Tyrt.11.21; ᾠδὶ διαβάς Ar.*V*.688; τοσόνδε βῆμα διαβεβηκότος Id.*Eq*.77; opp. συμβεβηκώς, X.*Eq*.1.14; πόδας μὴ -βεβῶτας Hp.*Art*.43, cf. D.S.4.76; κολοσσοὶ -βεβηκότες Plu.2.779f; simply, *spacious*, δόμοι Corn.*ND* 15: metaph., μεγάλα δ. ἐπί τινα *to go with* huge *strides* against.., Luc.*Anach*.32; ὀνόματα -βεβηκότα εἰς πλάτος *great straddling* words, D.H.*Comp*.22; [πούς] -βεβηκὼς *with a mighty stride*, ib.17: c. acc. cogn., αἱ ἁρμονίαι διαβεβήκασι εὐμεγέθεις διαβάσεις ib.20; also ἐξερείσματα χρόνων πρὸς ἑδραῖον -βεβηκότα μέγεθος Longin.40.4. II. c. acc., *step across, pass over*, τάφρον Il.12.50; πόρον Ὠκεανοῖο Hes.*Th*.292, cf. A.*Pers*.865 (lyr.); Ἀχέροντα Alc. l.c.; ποταμόν Hdt.1.75, etc., cf. 7.35; also διὰ ποταμοῦ X.*An*.4.8.2. 2. abs. (θάλασσαν or ποταμόν being omitted), *cross over*, Ἤλιδ' ἐς εὐρύχορον διαβήμεναι Od.4.635; ⟨ἐς⟩ τήνδε τὴν ἤπειρον Hdt.4.118; πλοίῳ Id.1.186, cf. Th.1.114, Pl.*Phdr*.229c, etc.: metaph., τῷ λόγῳ διέβαινε ἐς Εὐρυβιάδεα *he went over* to him, Hdt.8.62; δ. ἐπὶ τὰ μείζω Arr.*Epict*.1.18.18. b. πόθεν.. διαβέβηκε τὸ ἀργύριον from what sources the money *has mounted up*, Plu.2.829e. 3. *bestride*, *AP*5.54 (Diosc.). 4. *decide*, δίκας *SIG*426.7 (Teos, iii B.C.). 5. *come home to, affect*, εἴς τινα Diog. Oen.2, Steph. *in Rh*.281.5.

διαβάλλω, fut. -βᾰλῶ: pf. -βέβληκα:—*throw* or *carry over* or *across*, νέας Hdt.5.33,34; in wrestling, Ar.*Eq*.262 codd. 2. more freq. intr., *pass over, cross*, ἐκ.. ἐς.. Hdt.9.114; φυγῇ πρὸς Ἄργος E.*Supp*.931; πρὸς τὴν ἤπειρον Th.2.83: c. acc. spatii, δ. πόρον A.*Fr*.69 (dub.); γεφύρας E.*Rh*.117; τὸν Ἰόνιον Th.6.30; τὸ πέλαγος εἰς Μεσσαπίους Demetr.Com.Vet.1. 3. *put through*, τῆς θύρας δάκτυλον D.L.1.118; τύλος διαβεβλημένος διὰ τοῦ ῥυμοῦ Arr.*An*.2.3.7 (= Aristobul.*Fr*.4); κρίκων δι' ἀλλήλων διαβεβλημένων D.Chr.30.20; διαβληθέντων τῶν ἀγκώνων διὰ μέσων τῶν τόνων Hero*Bel*.101.12, cf. 108.6. II. in Ar.*Pax* 643 ἅττα διαβάλοι τις αὐτῷ, ταῦτ' ἂν ἥδιστ' ἤσθιεν, for παραβάλοι, whatever scraps *they threw to* him, with a play on signf. v. III. *set at variance*, ἐμὲ καὶ Ἀγάθωνα Pl.*Smp*.222c,d, cf. *R*.498c; δ. τινὰς ἀλλήλοις Arist.*Pol*.1313b16; *set against*, τινὰς πρὸς τὰ πάθη, πρὸς τὴν βρῶσιν, Plu.2.727d,73cf; *bring into discredit*, μή με διαβάλῃς στρατῷ S.*Ph*.582; δ. [τινὰ] τῇ πόλει Pl.*R*.566b:—Pass., *to be at variance with*, τινί Id.*Phd*.67e; *to be filled with suspicion and resentment against* another, Hdt.5.35, 6.64, Th.8.81,83; οὐδὲν ὑπολείπεται ὅτῳ ἄν μοι δικαίως διαβεβλῆσθε And.2.24; πρός τινα Hdt. 8.22, Arist.*Rh*.1404b21, Plb.30.19.2; τοὺς -βεβλημένους πρὸς τὴν φιλοσοφίαν Isoc.15.175; *to be brought into discredit*, ἐς τοὺς ξυμμάχους Th.4.22; διαβεβλημένος *discredited*, Lys.7.27,8.7. IV. *put off with evasions*, δ. τινὰ μίαν (sc. ἡμέραν) ἐκ μιᾶς *Sammelb*.5343.41 (ii A.D.), cf. *PFlor*.36.23 (iv A.D.). V. *attack* a man's character, *calumniate*, δ. τοὺς Ἀθηναίους πρὸς τὸν Ἀρταφρένεα Hdt.5.96; Πελοποννησίους ἐς τοὺς Ἕλληνας Th.3.109; διέβαλλον τοὺς Ἴωνας ὡς δι' ἐκείνους ἀπολοίατο αἱ νέες Hdt.8.90; διαβαλὼν αὐτοὺς ὡς οὐδὲν ἀληθὲς ἐν νῷ ἔχουσι Th.5.45; *accuse, complain of*, without implied malice or falsehood, *PTeb.*23.4 (ii B.C.): c. dat. rei, *reproach* a man *with*.., τῇ ἀτυχίᾳ Antipho 2.4.4; δ. τινὰ εἴς or πρός τι, Luc.*Demon.* 50, *Macr.*14:—Pass., διεβλήθη ὡς *Ev.Luc.*16.1; ἐπὶ βίῳ μὴ σώφρονι διαβεβλημένος Hdn.2.6.6. 2. c. acc. rei, *misrepresent*, D.18.225, 28.1, etc.: *speak* or *state slanderously*, ὡς οὗτος διέβαλλεν Id.18.20, cf. ib.14; τοῦτό μου διαβάλλει ib.28: generally, *give hostile information*, without any insinuation of falsehood, Th.3.4. 3. δ. τι εἴς τινα *lay the blame for* a thing on.., Procop.*Arc.*22.19. 4. *disprove* a scientific or philosophical doctrine, Gal.5.289:—Pass., Id.5.480, Plu.2.930b. 5. δ. ἔπος *declare* it *spurious*, Id.*Thes.* 34. VI. *deceive by false accounts, impose upon, mislead*, τινά Hdt.3.1, 5.50, 8.110, E.*Fr.*435:—Med., Hdt.9.116, Ar.*Av.*1648 (ubi v. Sch.), *Th.*1214:—Pass., Hp.*Nat.Puer.*30, Pl.*Phdr.*255a, Plu.2.563d. VII. *divert* from a course of action, πρὸς τὴν κακίαν τινάς ib.809f:—Pass., ψυχὴ -βέβληται πρὸς μάχην Arr.*Epict.*2.26.3. VIII. Med., *contract an obligation* (?), *Leg.Gort.*9.26. IX. διαβάλλεσθαι ἀστραγάλοις πρός τινα *throw* against him, Plu.2.148d, 272f.

διαβαπτίζομαι, *dive for a match*, πρός τινα Polyaen.4.2.6. 2. metaph., *contend in foul language with*, τινί D.25.41.

διάβαρος λίθος, a volcanic stone, dub. in Thphr.*Lap.*20 (leg. διάβορος, *porous*).

διαβᾰσᾰνίζω, *test thoroughly*, Pl.*Lg.*736c, J.*AJ*5.7.10, Arr.*Epict.* 3.26.13.

διαβᾰσείω, Desiderat. of διαβαίνω, D.C.40.32.

διαβᾰσῐλίζομαι, *to be a pretender to a kingdom*, *Com.Adesp.*322.

διάβᾰσις, εως, ἡ, *crossing over, passage*, δ. ποιεῖσθαι Hdt.1.186, etc.; *act of crossing*, αἱ δ. τῶν ὀχετῶν διασπῶσι τὰς φάλαγγας Arist.*Pol.*1303ᵇ12. 2. *means* or *place of crossing*, Hdt.1.205; δ. ποταμῶν *fords*, Th.7.74, cf. X.*An.*1.5.12, etc.; *bridge*, ib.2.3.10; *passage along a ship's deck, gangway*, Hp.*Ep.*14, Plu.*Cim.*12; *ferry-boat*, Lxx *2Ki.*19.18. II. the Jewish *Passover*, Ph.1.117. III. ἡ τῶν ὡρῶν δ. *transition* of the seasons, Ael.*NA*9.46. IV. in Gramm., *transitive force* of Verbs, τὰ ἐν δ. τοῦ προσώπου ῥήματα A.D.*Synt.*202.7, al. V. in Rhet. of *intervals* or *pauses* in pronunciation caused by long syllables and the like, ῥυθμοὶ πλείστην ἔχοντες δ. D.H.*Comp.*20; cf. διαβαίνω I.

διαβάσκω, = διαβαίνω, *strut*, διαβάσκει Ar.*Av.*486; cf. διαβιβάσκω.

διαβαστ-αγμός· *cunctatio*, *Gloss.* **-άζω**, *carry over*, Aq.*Is.*51.18, Sm.*Ex.*15.13:—Pass., Vett.Val.162.28. II. *weigh in the hand, estimate*, Plu.*Dem.*25, Luc.*Ep.Sat.*33. 2. *contain*, Vett. Val.222.1.

διαβᾰτ-έος, α, ον, *that must be crossed* or *passed through*, ποταμός X.*An.*2.4.6; νάπος ib.6.5.12. II. διαβατέον *one must cross*, Plb.5.51.5, Plu.*Luc.*31, etc. **-ήρια** (sc. ἱερά), τά, *offerings before crossing the border*, τὰ δ. προὐχώρει, τὰ δ. ἐγένετο, they were favourable, Th.5.54, 55, cf. X.*HG*4.7.2; also, *for crossing a river*, ἔθυσε τῷ Εὐφράτῃ ταῦρον δ. Plu.*Luc.*24; τὰ δ. δυσχερέστατα ἐγένετο D.C.40.18: also masc., Ζεὺς διαβατήριος Ctes.*Fr.*29.17. II. Jewish *Passover*, Ph.2.292, al. **-ης**, ου, ὁ, *one who ferries over* or *crosses*, Ar.*Fr.*765. II. = διαβήτης, Hsch. **-ικός**, ή, όν, of Verbs, *transitive*, A.D.*Synt.*43.18. II. *slipping through* the fingers, Sch.Ar.*Nu.*448. **-ός**, ή, όν, *to be crossed* or *passed, fordable*, Hdt.1.75, Th.2.5, etc.; νῆσον δ. ἐξ ἠπείρου *easily got at* from the main land, Hdt.4.195:—Aeol. **ζάβατος**, Sapph.158. II. **διάβατον**, τό, *passage for water*, *PLand.*52.14 (i A.D.).

διαβεβαι-όω, *confirm*, ὑπόληψιν D.L.8.70:—usu. Med. **-όομαι**, *maintain strongly, affirm, confirm*, D.17.30; οἱ πρεσβύτεροι δ. οὐδέν Arist.*Rh.*1389ᵇ16; δ. γεγονέναι τι D.S.13.90, cf. Aristeas 99, D.H.2.39, *BGU*1911 7 (ii A.D.), *POxy.*67.10 (iv A.D.); *to be positive*, περί τινος Plb.12.12.6, S.E.*P.*1.191:—Pass., Phld.*Rh.*1.226 S., *Sign.* 17. **-ωσις**, εως, ἡ, *assurance*, δοῦναι, ἐργάζεσθαι, ib.24, 35; *asseveration*, Hdn.*Fig.*p.96 S. **-ωτικός**, ή, όν, *affirmative*, δ. σύνδεσμος A.D.*Conj.*235.26, al., *EM*415.42; θεωρία Ptol.*Tetr.*7. Adv. -κῶς A.D.*Synt.*318.28, S.E.*P.*1.233.

διαβέτης, εος, ὁ, (perh. for δια-ϝέτης, cf. ἔτης) title of *official* at Sparta, *IG*5(1).32 *A* 2, al.

διά-βημα, ατος, τό, *a step across, a step*, Lxx *Jb.*31.4: metaph. in pl., *successive moments*, ἡ διακόσμησις τρισὶ διώρισται δ. Dam.*Pr.* 423. **-βημᾰτίζω**, *step out, pace out*, Aq.*2Ki.*6.13. **-βησείω**, later form, = -βᾰσείω, Agath.2.4. **-βήτης**, ου, ὁ, (διαβαίνω) *compass*, so called from its outstretched legs, Ar.*Nu.*178, *Av.*1003. 2. *carpenter's* or *stonemason's rule*, ξύσας ὀρθὸν πρὸς διαβήτην *IG*12(2).11.20 (Lesbos), cf. ib.2.1054.10, Pl.*Phlb.*56b, Plu.2.802f, Sch.Il.2.765. II. *siphon*, Colum.3.10, Hero *Spir.*1.29. III. Medic., the disease *diabetes*, Aret.*SD*2.2, Philagr.ap.Orib.5.19.9, Gal.8.394. **-βητίζομαι**, Med., *make straight by rule*, *IG*7.3073.186 (Lebad.). **-βήτινος**, η, ον, *made by rule*, ἐκτομάς *Stud.Pal.*20.211.9 (v/vi A.D.).

διαβῐάζομαι, strengthd. for βιάζομαι, E.*IT*1365, Lxx *Nu.*14.44; δ. τὴν ἀσθένειαν τῇ συνηθείᾳ τῇ πρὸ τοῦ Plb.23.12.2; of plants, *penetrate* the soil in germination, Thphr.*CP*2.17.7.

διαβῐβ-άζω, causal of διαβαίνω, *carry over* or *across, transport, lead over*, δ. τὸν στρατὸν κατὰ γεφύρας Hdt.1.75; ἐς τὴν νῆσον ὁπλίτας Th.4.8: also c. acc. loci, ποταμὸν δ. [τινά] *take* one *across* a river, Pl.*Lg.*900c, Plu.*Pel.*24: metaph., δ. ἐπὶ τὰ ὁμοειδῆ τὸ χρήσιμον Chrysipp.*Stoic.*2.31, cf. Apollon.Cit.1 (Pass.), Aristid.*Or.*28(49).29; *lead* to a conclusion, τινὰ εἰς πέρας τῷ λόγῳ Hld.2.24: in Music, *cause* the melody *to pass*, ἐπὶ τὴν παρυπάτην Plu.2.1134f. 2. δ. κλήρους *pass through* the heats or rounds of an athletic contest, *JRS*3.282 (Antioch in Pisidia). 3. Pass., of Verbs, *have a transitive force*, A.D.*Synt.*277.10, al. 4. later, *pass time*, Sch.Ar.*Pl.*847. **-άσκω**, = foreg., Hp.*Fract.*4, cf. Erot. (διέβασκον codd.). **-ασμός**, ὁ, Gramm., *transitive force*, A.D.*Pron.*113.21. **-αστικός**, ή, όν, of Verbs, *transitive*, Id.*Synt.*298.15.

διαβιβρώσκω Gal.13.553: fut. Pass. -βρωθήσομαι ib.466: mostly in pf. Pass. -βέβρωμαι:—*eat up, consume, corrode*, Hp.*Morb.*2.24, Pl.*Ti.*83a, etc., Luc.*Ind.*1: metaph., διαβιβρώσκονται ὑπὸ [λόγων] Plu.2.508d; ψυχὴ -βεβρωμένη Max.Tyr.6.7.

διαβῐ-όω, fut. -ώσομαι: aor. 2 -εβίων, inf. -βιῶναι (also -βιῶσαι· ζῆσαι, Hsch.): pf. -βεβίωκα Isoc.9.70:—*live through, pass*, χρόνον Pl.*Lg.*730c; τὸν βίον Id.*Men.*81b; τὸν ἐνθάδε χρόνον Isoc.l.c.: abs., *spend one's whole life*, δ. δικαίως Pl.*Grg.*526a: c. part., μελετῶν διαβεβιωκέναι X.*Ap.*3, *Mem.*4.8.4. 2. *survive*, Procop.*Pers.*2.5, al. 3. δ. ἀπὸ χρημάτων *live* on, Plu.*Publ.*3. **-ώσκω**, = foreg. 2, Agath.*Praef.* **-ωτέον**, *one must spend one's life*, δ. παίζοντα Pl.*Lg.*803e.

διαβλαστ-άνω, *sprout*, Thphr.*CP*4.8.1, Plu.*Crass.*22. **-ησις**, εως, ἡ, *germination*, Thphr.*CP*2.17.10.

διαβλέπω, *stare with eyes wide open*, Pl.*Phd.*86d, Arist.*Insomn.* 462ᵃ13; δ. εἴς τινα, πρός τινα, Plu.*Alex.*14, 2.548b. 2. *see clearly*, Dionys.Com.2.13; ἐν τοῖς σκοτεινοῖς Phld.*Rh.*1.252 S., cf. Luc.*Merc. Cond.*22: c. inf., διαβλέψεις ἐκβαλεῖν τὸ κάρφος *Ev.Matt.*7.5.

διά-βλημα, ατος, τό, *strap passing through* a shoe-buckle, Lyd.*Mag.*2.13. **-βλητικός**, ή, όν, = διαβολικός, Poll.5.118: -κή, ἡ, *art of calumny*, Phld.*Vit.*p.42 J. Adv. -κῶς Poll. l.c. **-βλήτωρ**, ορος, ὁ, *slanderer*, Man.4.236.

διαβλύζω, *gush forth*, κολώνης Nonn.*D.*22.21.

διαβο-άω, late fut. -βοήσω Hdn.2.2.2:—*proclaim, publish*, aor. subj. -βοάσω A.*Pers.*638 (lyr.): c. acc. et inf., ἐκεῖσε χωρεῖν τινὰς διεβόησαν Corn.*ND*35:—Pass., *to be the common talk*, ταῦτα δὴ διαβεβόηται Pl.*Ep.*312b; *to be celebrated*, of persons or things, Plu.*Sol.*11, *Them.*3; πρός τινα Id.*Per.*9; ἐπί τινι Luc.*Nec.*6, Ant.Lib.12.4. II. *cry aloud*, δ. ὡς.. Th.8.53, 78: abs., Luc.*Am.*17. III. Med., *contend in shouting*, D.26.19. **-ησις**, εως, ἡ, *crying out* or *aloud*, Plu.2.455b. **-ητος**, ον, *noised abroad, famous*, Plu.*Lyc.*5, Hdn.4.4.8; ἐφ' ὥρᾳ καὶ λαμπρίᾳ Plu.*Luc.*6, cf. X.Eph.1.2, D.Chr.3.72, Luc.*Alex.*4.

διαβολ-ή, ἡ, (διαβάλλω V) *false accusation, slander*, Epich.148; ἐπὶ διαβολῇ εἰπεῖν Hdt.3.66, 73; δ. λόγου Th.8.91; διαβολὰς ἐνδέχεσθαι, προσίεσθαι, to give ear to *them*, Hdt.3.80, 6.123; διαβολὰς ἔχειν ὡς.. to have *it slanderously said* that.., Isoc.8.125; ὀνείδους καὶ δ. τυγχάνειν Lys.25.6; ἐν δ. καθεστηκέναι ibid.; διαλύσειν τὴν δ. Th.1.131: of *charges* not necessarily false or malicious, δ. ταῖς ἐμαῖς *the accusations* which I bring, E.*Andr.*1005, cf. Isoc.1.17; τὰ πρὸς διαβολὴν κυροῦντα tending to *discredit*, Plb.12.15.9, cf. 2.11.4; ἐμὴ δ. *prejudice against* me, Pl.*Ap.*19b; δ. εἰς ἐμέ And.1.30; δ. καθ' αὑτοῦ παρέσχεν Plu.*Them.*4, cf. Phryn.Com.58; opp. δόξα, *ill-repute*, Men.723; δ. λῦσαι καὶ ποιῆσαι remove, create *prejudice* against an antagonist, Arist.*Rh.*1415ᵃ27; δ. ἀπολύεσθαι D.H.6.59. II. (διαβάλλω III) *quarrel, enmity*, κατὰ τὰς ἰδίας δ. Th.2.65; ἡ πρὸς τὸ συγγενὲς δ. Plu.2.479b; ἡ πρὸς θάνατον δ. *fear, aversion* from it, ib.110a: c. gen., δ. τοῦ πάθους ib.456b; εἰς διαβολήν τινος to *withstand* them, Lxx *Nu.*22.32. III. (διαβάλλω VIII) *legal obligation* (?), *Leg.Gort.*9.35. IV. *fraud*, Sch.Ar.*Pl.* 373. **-ία**, Ion. -ίη, ἡ, = διαβολή, Thgn.324; δεινόν ἐστιν ἡ δ. Hippias *Fr.*17 D.: in pl., Pi.*P.*2.76. (Perh. to be written διαιμετρι gr. in poetry.) **-ικός**, ή, όν, *slanderous*, κακοτεχνία Ph.*Fr.*98 H. II. *devilish*, δ. καὶ σατανικὴ ἐνέργεια *PLond.*5.1731.11 (vi A.D.). **-ος**, ον, *slanderous, backbiting*, γραῦς Men.878, cf. Phld.*Lib.*p.24 O.: Sup. -ώτατος Ar.*Eq.*45; διάβολόν τι, *aliquid invidiae*, And.2.24; τὸ δ. Plu.2.61d. II. Subst., *slanderer*, Pi.*Fr.*297, Arist.*Top.*126ᵃ31, Ath.11.508d; *enemy*, Lxx *Es.*7.4, 8.1: hence, = *Sâtân*, ib.*1Chr.*21.1; *the Devil*, *Ev.Matt.*4.1, etc. III. Adv. -λως *injuriously, invidiously*, Th.6.15; χρῆσθαί τινι Procop.*Arc.*2.

διαβορβορύζω, strengthd. for βορβορύζω, Hp.*Aph.*4.73.

διαβόρειος, ον, *stretching northwards*, Str.2.1.33 (s. v. l.).

διαβόρος, ον, (βιβρώσκω) *devouring*, νόσος S.*Tr.*1084, *Ph.*7. II. διάβορος, ον, Pass., *eaten up, consumed*, Id.*Tr.*676; cf. διάβαρος.

διαβόσκω, fut. -ήσω Socr.*Ep.*19:—*feed*, ὄροβοι καὶ τὰ ἐς βρῶσιν ἀναγκαῖα διέβοσκεν αὐτούς Philostr.*VA*1.15; τὴν γαστέρα ἐπί τινι Alciphr.3.7; *pasture*, *PMasp.*112.15 (vi A.D.).

διαβοστρῠχόομαι, Pass., *to be curled*, διαβεβοστρυχωμένος Archil. 162.

διαβουκολέω, *cheat with false hopes*, Luc.*DMort.*5.2:—Med., διαβουκολεῖσθαί τινι *beguile oneself with*.., Them.*Or.*21.255d.

διαβουλ-ευείρ· ὁ ἐν τοῖς ἱστοῖς πρόβολος (Lacon.), Hsch. **-εύω**, of a Council, *complete its term*, Arist.*Ath.*32.1. II. mostly in Med. (Dor. διαβωλ- *IG*5(2).343), *deliberate, discuss thoroughly*, And.2.19, Th.2.5, 7.50; δ. εἴτε.. εἴτε Pl.*Plt.*304e, cf. Luc.*Hist.Conscr.* 31; *decide*, c. inf., Id.*Pisc.*24. **-ία**, ἡ, = sq., Lxx *Ps.*5.10, *Ho.* 11.6. **-ιον**, τό, *debate, deliberation*, ib.*Wi.*1.9 (pl.), al.; δ. ἄγειν Plb.3.20.1, etc. II. *resolution, decree*, Id.4.24.2, etc. III. *meeting for debate*, Id.29.10.2, *IG*5(1).1390.172 (Andania, i B.C.). **-οι**· διπλοῖ, δίβουλοι, Hsch.

διαβουνίν, *sweetmeat eaten at dessert*, Hsch.

διαβρᾰβεύω, *bestow*, Aesop.24 (v.l.).

διάβραγχος, ὁ, *windpipe* (?), *Hippiatr.*20.

διά-βρεγμα, ατος, τό, *extract prepared by maceration*, Dieuch.ap. Orib.4.7.11 (pl.). **-βρεκτέον**, *one must macerate*, τυρὸν ὠμῇ λύσει *Gp.*18.19.9. **-βρεξις**, εως, ἡ, *soaking*, Erot. s.v. τέγξις. **-βρεχής**, ές, *wet through, soaked*, Luc.*Trag.*304. **-βρέχω**, *soak*, ταρτύματα A.*Fr.*306: abs., Arist.*Pr.*866ᵃ10 :—Pass., ἄλφιτα ζωμῷ διαβραχέντα Ael.*NA*1.23, cf. *Gp.*17.17.2; διαβεβρεγμένος, of a person, *soaked in liquor*, Hld.5.31; πρὶν διαβραχῆναι πικροτάτους εἶναι Zeno *Stoic.*1.65; ἐν οἴνῳ καὶ μέθῃ διαβραχείς Porph.*Chr.*30.

διαβρίθει· βαρύνει, Hsch., and **διαβρῑθής·** ἰσχυρός, Id.

διαβρῑμάομαι, strengthd. for βριμάομαι, Them.*Or.*21.261c.

διαβροχή, ἡ, *maceration*, v.l. in Dsc.2.107, cf. Antyll.ap.Orib.4. 11.2; *soaking, wetting*, σωμάτων ib.9.23.1.

διαβροχισμός, ὁ, *catching in a noose*, Antyll.ap.Orib.45.24.5, Gal. 18(2).679.

διάβροχος, ον, (διαβρέχω) *very wet, moist*, ὄμμα E.*El.*503; ἄγκος ὕδασι δ. Id.*Ba.*1051, cf. Call.*Del.*48; γῆ Hp.*Aër.*10, Arist.*SE*167ᵇ 7. 2. *soaked, sodden*, ναῦς δ. *leaky*, Th.7.12; σάρξ Arist.*Pr.*870ᵃ 11: metaph., ἔρωτι, μέθῃ δ., Luc.*Tox.*15, *Bis Acc.*17. 3. *tearful*, δ. δάκρυσι Hld.1.26.

διά-βρωμα, ατος, τό, (διαβιβρώσκω) *that which is eaten through*; *worm-eaten wood, parchment*, etc., Str.13.1.54. **-βρωσις**, εως, ἡ, *eating through*, τινός Plu.2.967f (pl.); *chewing*, Dsc.5.74. II. Medic., *erosion* of the coats of a vessel, Aret.*SA*2.2, *SD*2.9 (pl.), J.*BJ*7.11.4, Gal.8.262; of the tissues generally, ib.81; also βλεφάρων Dsc.1.105 (pl.). **-βρωτικός**, ή, όν, *corrosive*, Alex.Aphr.*Pr.* 1.99, Gal.1.280 (Sup.).

δια-βυνέω, -βύνω, v. διαβύω.

διαβύσσει· διακαμύσσει, Hsch.

διαβύω, *thrust through*, ἐς τὸ στόμα Hp.*Superf.*5:—Med. (from -βυνέω), διαβυνέονται ὀϊστοὺς διὰ τῆς ἀριστερῆς they *pass* arrows *through their* left hand, Hdt.4.71:—Pass. (from -βύνω), πηδάλιον διὰ τῆς τρόπιος διαβύνεται is *passed through* the keel, Id.2.96.

διαγᾰληνίζω, *make quite calm*, τὰ πρόσωπα Ar.*Eq.*646.

διαγᾰνακτ-έω, *to be full of indignation*, Lys.*Oxy.*1606.84, D.27. 63, Plu.2.74b, D.S.14.1; πρός τι J.*BJ*4.4.4. II. Medic., *to be severely affected*, Antyll.ap.Orib.44.8.1; *to be irritated*, Sor.1.81, 118. **-ησις**, εως, ἡ, *great indignation*, Ph.2.178, Plu.*Mar.*16 (pl.).

διαγᾰπάω, strengthd. for ἀγαπάω, *love*, τὸν αὐτῆς ἄνδρα *PMasp.* 112.15 (vi A.D.).

διαγαυριάω, *plume oneself, strut about*, *EM*270.38. **διάγγαρον·** δικέφαλον, Hsch.

διαγγ-ελία, ἡ, *notification*, J.*BJ*3.8.5. **-έλλω**, fut. -ελῶ: aor. διήγγειλα X.*An.*1.6.2:—*give notice by a messenger*, c. dat., Th.7.73, X. l. c., etc.; δ. εἰς.. Id.*Mem.*3.11.3; πρός τινα Philipp.ap.D.12.16: generally, *noise abroad, proclaim*, δ. ὅτι.. Pi.*N.*5.3; τι E.*Hel.*436, Pl.*Prt.*317a: c. inf., *order* to do, E.*IA*353:—Med., *pass* the word of command *from man to man*, X.*An.*3.4.36. **-ελμα**, ατος, τό, *a message, notice*, Lxx 3*Ki.*4.20(7). **-ελος**, ὁ, *messenger, negotiator*, esp. *secret informant, go-between*, Th.7.73. 2. military term, *adjutant*, Plu.2.678d; but, = Lat. *speculator*, Plu.*Galb.*24. **-ελτέον**, *one must notify*, τὰς παραινέσεις πᾶσι Ph.2.259.

διαγ[ειτ]ονία, ἡ, *local group*, prob. in *IG*12(1).922.4 (Lindus).

διαγελάω, *laugh at, mock*, τινά E.*Ba.*272,322, X.*An.*2.6.26, J.*AJ* 16.7.6, Phld.*Piet.*110, Plu.2.1118c; τῶν ἰαμάτων τινὰ δ. ὡς ἀπίθανα ἐόντα *IG*4.951.35 (Epid.): abs., Luc.*Pseudol.*16. 2. intr., *look bright*, of the weather, Thphr.*HP*8.2.4, *CP*1.2.8; δ. ἡ ἡμέρα Procop.*Aed.*1.1; of water, Plu.2.950b, cf. *Caes.*4.

διαγέλως, ωτος, ὁ, *derision*, prob. in Phld.*Herc.*1251.17.

διαγενής· εὐγενής, Hsch. (fort. διογενής).

διά-γευσις, εως, ἡ, *tasting*, *Gp.*7.7 tit. **-γεύω**, *give a taste of*, τινὰ τῆς φωνῆς καὶ τοῦ μέλους Eun.*Hist.*p.247 D. II. Med., *taste*, Plu.2.469c, *Gp.*7.7.1.

διαγιγγράζω, lit. *tune up*: metaph. of a cook, Athenio 1.31 (cj. Dobr.).

διαγίγνομαι, Ion. and later Att. **-γίνομαι** [γῑ], fut. -γενήσομαι: aor. διεγενόμην, also διεγενήθην Phld.*Piet.*37:—*go through, pass*, τοσάδε ἔτη Pl.*Ap.*32e; τὴν νύκτα X.*An.*1.10.19; δ. ἀπραγμόνως τὴν ἡμέραν Nicom.Com.1.42: abs., *go through life, live*, Ar.*Av.*45, Th.5.16; *survive*, v.l. in Hp.*Epid.*1.2; ἐὰν ἄρα διαγιγνώμεθα if we *live long enough*, Aeschin.1.51; ἂν διαγένωμαι Diog.Oen.66; δ. ἀπὸ τῆς τέχνης *to subsist* by it, Arist.*Pol.*1268ᵃ31; γενναίως δ. ἔν τινι *behave* nobly in.., Plu.2.119d: freq. c. part., διαγενέσθαι ἄρχων *continue in* the government, X.*Cyr.*1.1.1; οὐδὲν ἄλλο ποιῶν διαγεγένηται ἢ διασκοπῶν he *was never anything* but a theorist, Id.*Mem.*4.8.4; δ. κολακεύων D.23. 179. II. *intervene, elapse*, χρόνου μεταξὺ διαγενομένου Lys.1.15; χρόνων διαγενομένων Is.11.9, cf. Plu.*Rom.*22, etc.; οἴδαμεν..ἤδη τῇ κρίσει ἐκείνῃ διαγεγονότα ἔτη ὀκτώ Test.ap.D.21.82, cf. Plu.2.162c, Phld.*Piet.*37, *POxy.*68.18 (ii A.D.).

διαγιγνώσκω, Ion. and later Att. **-γῑνώσκω**, fut. -γνώσομαι D.50. 1:—*know one from the other, distinguish, discern*, εὖ διαγιγνώσκοντες Il.23.240; ἔνθα διαγνῶναι χαλεπῶς ἦν ἄνδρα ἕκαστον 7.424, cf. Ar.*Pl.* 91; δ. εἰ ὅμοιοί εἰσι *to distinguish* whether they are equals or no, Hdt.1.134; οὐδ' ἄν..διαγνοίη, λίνου ἢ καννάβιός ἐστι Id.4.74; δ. τὴν βοὴν ὁποτέρα μείζων Th.1.87; δ. διότι.. Arist.*Pol.*1266ᵇ16; δ. πότερον.., ἤ.. Id.*Mete.*389ᵃ5; δ. τὸν καλόν τε καὶ αἰσχρὸν ἔρωτα Pl. *Smp.*186c; δ. τὸ ὀρθὸν καὶ μή Aeschin.3.199; δ. τὴν θήλειαν καὶ τὸν ἄρρενα Arist.*HA*613ᵃ16; δ. τοὺς νεωτέρους καὶ πρεσβυτέρους ἐκ τῶν ὀδόντων ib.501ᵇ11; δ. ὑμᾶς ὄντας.., i.e. δ. ὑμῶν οἵτινές εἰσιν.., Ar.*Eq.*518:—Pass., τὸν χαλκὸν μὴ διαγινώσκεσθαι τῇ χροᾷ πρὸς τὸν χρυσόν Arist.*Mir.*834ᵃ2, cf. Thphr.*HP*5.3.2; *to be distinguished, celebrated*, ἀρεταῖς Pi.*Pae.*4.21. 2. *discern exactly, perceive, descry*, τι S.*El.*1186; δ. ὅτι.. Isoc.3.47. 3. Medic., *form a diagnosis*, Erasistr.ap.Gal.8.14. II. *determine* by vote or otherwise, c. inf., Hdt.6.138, Luc.*Am.*9, Hdn.4.4.2:—Pass., impers. διέγνωστο αὐτοῖς λελύσθαι τὰς σπονδάς Th.1.118. 2. law-term, *determine* or *decide* a suit, δίκην A.*Eu.*709, cf. *IG*5(2).159 (Tegea, v B.C.), Antipho 6.3; τὰ ἀμφισβητήσιμα Id.2.1.1; *give judgement*, περί τινος Th.4. 46, Lys.7.22, D.28.10; *take cognizance of* an action, *PPetr.*3p.118 (iii B.C.), etc.:—Pass., διεγνωσμένη κρίσις Th.3.53; μενέτωσαν ἐν τοῖς διαγνωσθεῖσι Lexap.D.21.94. III. = διαναγιγνώσκω (which shd. perh. be read), *read through*, Plb.3.32.2, Ph.2.555, al.

διαγκῠλόομαι, Dep., (ἀγκύλη) *hold a javelin by the thong*:—only pf. part. Pass. διηγκυλωμένος *ready to throw* or *shoot*, X.*An.*4.3.28 (v.l. -ισμένος), 5.2.12: later in form -ημένος (as if from -άομαι), τόξον, κεραυνόν, δ. *ready to shoot with*.., Hdn.1.14.9, Luc.*Jup.Conf.*15.

διάγκῠλος, ον, *with two loops*, βρόχος Heraclas ap.Orib.48.16.1: Subst. διάγκυλον, τό, *double loop*, Sor.*Fasc.*7.

διαγκων-ίζομαι, *lean on one's elbow*, Dam.*Isid.*134. II. διηγκωνισμένος σφυγμός, term coined by Archig., Gal.8.651. **-ισμός**, ὁ, *jostling with the elbow*, Plu.2.644a.

διαγλαίνειν· διαλυμαίνεσθαι, Hsch.

διαγλαύσσω, *shine brightly*, ἀταρποί A.R.1.1281.

διαγλάφω [ᾰ], *scoop out*, εὐνὰς ἐν ψαμάθοισι διαγλάψασ' (v.l. -γνάψ-) Od.4.438.

διά-γλυμμα, ατος, τό, in pl., *scrapings*, Sch.Ar.*Ra.*835, Hsch. s.v. σμιλεύματα. **-γλυπτος**, ον, *divided*, of a quill-pen, *AP*6.227 (Crin.). **-γλῠφή**, ἡ, *scooping out*, Orib.49.4.28. **-γλῠφος**, ον, *hollowed out, coffered*, of ceilings, *EM*789.18, Suid. **-γλύφω** [ῡ], *scoop out*, pf. Pass. διέγλυπται Androsth.ap.Ath.3.93b; *carve, engrave*, ἄγαλμα Ael.*VH*2.33; δακτυλίους ib.12.30:—Pass., διαγλυφέντες καὶ διατορευθέντες, metaph. of athletes, ib.14.7; ὀροφὴ φάτναις διαγεγλυμμένη D.S.1.66. 2. Medic., *shape, trim*, Gal.12.348, etc.

διάγματα· διασκευάσματα, Hsch.

διαγνοέω, *to be ignorant of*:—Pass., dub. in Philostr.*Her.Prooem.*

διάγνοια, ἡ, *deliberation*, dub. in J.*AJ*17.9.5.

δια-γνώμη, ἡ, *decree, resolution*, Th.1.87; διαγνώμας ποιεῖσθαι Id. 3.67; δ. προθεῖναι περί τινος ib.42. **-γνωμονέω**, *consider, reflect, deliberate*, Eust.1237.21. **-γνώμων**, ον, gen. ονος, *distinguishing*, and so *rewarding*, ὁσίων Antipho 3.3.3.

διαγνωρ-ίζω, *make known*, τί τινι *Ev.Luc.*2.15 (v.l.); *speak publicly*, περί τινος ib.17. **-ισμός**, ὁ, = διάγνωσις, Gal.17(1).141.

διά-γνωσις, εως, ἡ, *distinguishing*, τὴν δ. ποιεῖσθαι ὁποῖοι ἐκράτουν ἢ ἐκρατοῦντο Th.1.50; *means of distinguishing* or *discerning*, E.*Hipp.* 926; καλῶν ἢ μὴ τοιούτων τίς δ.; D.18.128; δ. φωνῆς καὶ σιγῆς Arist. *Cael.*290ᵇ27; of medical *diagnosis*, δ. ποιεῖσθαι Hp.*VC*10, Gal.8.766, etc. 2. *power of discernment*, E.*Hipp.*696. II. *resolving, deciding*, δ. ποιεῖσθαι Antipho 6.18; περί τινος D.18.7; ταχίστην ἔχει δ. Isoc.1.34; τοῦ δ πρακτέον ἐστίν Metrod.*Fr.*27; δ. τῆς ἀξίας ποιεῖσθαι to *determine* the value, Pl.*Lg.*865c; = Lat. *cognitio*, *Act.Ap.*25. 21, *BGU*19 i 20 (ii A.D.), 891ʳ24 (ii A.D.); ἐπὶ διαγνώσεων τοῦ Σεβαστοῦ, = Lat. *a cognitionibus Augusti*, *IG*14.1072, cf. *Ephes.*3 No.51 (iii A.D.). **-γνωστέον**, *one must distinguish*, Luc.*Herm.* 16. **-γνώστης**, ου, ὁ, *examining magistrate*, = Lat. *cognitor*, *Gloss.* **-γνωστικός**, ή, όν, *able to distinguish*, ἀληθῶν καὶ ψευδῶν λόγων S.E.*P.*2.229, cf. Luc.*Salt.*74; δ. καὶ διακριτικός Id.*Herm.*69, cf. Gal.*UP*5.10; δ. θεωρία Id.1.271; δ. σημεῖα, opp. προγνωστικά, ib. 313. II. *belonging to a* διάγνωσις II, ὑπομνήματα *PLips.*34.15 (iv A.D.). **-γνωστός**, ή, όν, *to be distinguished*, Gal.8.940.

διαγογγύζω, *mutter* or *murmur among themselves*, κατά τινος Lxx *Ex.*16.7; ἐπί τινι ib.*Nu.*14.2: abs., *Ev.Luc.*15.2, 19.7, Hld.7.27.

διαγόρ-ευσις, εως, ἡ, *declaration*, Porph.ap.Stob.2.8.42. **-εύω**, *declare, state explicitly*, συγγραφῆς -ούσης *PMagd.*3.4 (iii B.C.); ὡς ὁ νόμος δ. Lxx *Su.*61, cf. D.H.1.78 (v.l.), Jul.*Or.*1.3d; *give orders, command*, Ph.1.437; τι Id.2.291: c. inf., Id.2.324, al.; τινί, c. inf., Plu.*CG*16; so μή.. *forbid*, App.*BC*1.54:—Pass., *to be declared* or *established*, Pl.*Lg.*757a; τὰ διηγορευμένα *PTeb.*105.30 (ii B.C.), *PStrassb.*115.6 (ii B.C.). II. *relate in detail*, D.H.11.19. III. *speak of*, κακῶς δ. τινά Luc.*Pisc.*26 (v.l.). IV. = τὰ διάφορα καὶ οὐ τὰ αὐτὰ λέγειν, Is.*Fr.*18.

διάγραμμα, ατος, τό, *figure marked out by lines, plan*, Pl.*R.*529e: esp. *geometrical figure*, X.*Mem.*4.7.3, Pl.*Phd.*73b, Arist.*Cael.*280ᵃ 1, etc. b. *geometrical proposition*, Id.*EN*1112ᵇ21, *APr.*41ᵇ14, Ascl. *in Metaph.*174.9. 2. in Music, *scale*, Phan.Hist.17; but ἀφ' ἑνὸς δ. ὑποκρέκειν on one *note*, Plu.2.55d, cf. *Dem.*13. 3. *horoscope, nativity*, Id.*Mar.*42. 4. *map*, Jul.*Ep.*10. II. *list, register*, D. 14.21; *inventory*, σκευῶν Id.47.36; *register* of taxable property, *PRev. Laws* 39.17, al. (iii B.C.), Harp., Suid. III. *ordinance, regulation*, *GDI*5040.64 (Cret.), *PEleph.*14.27 (iii B.C.), D.S.18.57; τὸ δ. τῶ Ἀντιγόνω *OGI*7 (Cyme); = Lat. *edictum*, Plb.22.10.6, Plu.*Marc.*24.

διαγραμμ-ίζω, *divide by lines*: hence, *play at chequers*, Philem. 209. **-ισμός**, ὁ, *game of chequers*, Poll.9.99, Eust.633.65.

διαγραπ-τέον, (διαγράφω IV) *one must strike out, erase*, Phryn. 368. **-τος**, ον, *struck out of the list*, δίκη Hsch.

διαγρᾰφ-άριος· ὁ ἀπαιτῶν δημόσια, Hsch. **-εύς**, έως, ὁ, *one who makes a* διάγραμμα: at Athens, *one who drew up a register* of taxable properties, Harp. s.v. διάγραμμα. 2. *describer*, ἠθῶν δ. Marcellin.*Vit.Thuc.*51. —ή, ἡ, *delineation*, Pl.*R.*501a; *diagram*, Plu.*Phil.*4; ἡ δ. τῶν φύλλων *outline*, Thphr.*HP*3.13.1; *delimitation* of land, *PAmh.*2.40.11 (ii B.C.): in pl., *plans, specifications* of a building, *OGI*46.3 (Halic.). II. *outline, scheme*, τὰς δ. ποιεῖσθαι Arist.*Top.*105b13; *table, syllabus*, Id.*EN*1107a33, cf. *EE*1228a28 (cf. ὑπογραφή); *description* of goods sold, *PTheb.Bank*2.6; *register*, ἁπάντων τῶν γενῶν Diph.43.7, cf. *CIG*3060 (Teos), etc.; *list* of articles, *Sammelb.*3924.21. III. *decree, ordinance*, esp. of Alexander, *IG*12(2).526.35, al.; αἱ περὶ τῶν ἱερῶν δ. D.H.3.36. IV. *crossing out, cancelling*, of a debt: hence, *payment*, ποιεῖν τὴν δ. τινὶ τῶν εἴκοσι πέντε ταλάντων Plb.31.27.7, cf. *PTeb.*121.3 (i B.C.), al.; *payment by draft*, *SIG*742.52 (Ephesus, pl.); *certificate that such payment has been made*, *BGU*281.15 (ii A.D.). V. *contract*, *PTeb.*88.9 (ii B.C.). VI. *levy, tax*, Just.*Nov.*131.5, al. —ον, τό, dub. in *POxy.*127.2 (vi A.D.). —ω, *mark out by lines, delineate*, τὴν πόλιν Pl.*R.*500e; δ. λόγῳ *map out*, Id.*Lg.*778a; δ. τινά *describe* a person, Philostr.*VS*2.2.7, *Her.*2.1: abs., Plu.*Nic.*23, etc. b. δ. γραμμὴν *draw* a line *between*, Pl.Com.153.2. 2. *draft* a law, etc., D.H.6.88:—Pass., συνθηκῶν διαγραφεισῶν Plb.1.62.7. II. *draw out a list of*, προτάσεις Arist.*APr.*46a8 (Pass.), *Rh.*1378a28, cf. *PRev.Laws* 13.2. III. *enroll, levy*, στρατιώτας Plb.6.12.6. b. of things, *fix by written ordinance*, τὸ πλῆθος τὸ διαγραφὲν ἀποτινέτω *PRev.Laws*43.7 (iii B.C.). IV. *draw a line through, cross out, erase*, Pl.*R.*387b; δ. τινά *strike off* a person's name, E.*El.*1073; δ. δίκην, of the magistrates, *strike* a cause *out of the list*, Ar.*Nu.*774 (Pass.), cf. Lys.17.5 codd., D.48.26 (but in *SIG*2.511.28,47 (Pass.), prob. *to be entered in the list*):—Med., διαγράψασθαι δίκην, of the plaintiff, *give up* a cause, *withdraw* it, Lys.*Fr.*195 S., D.20.145. 2. *cancel, rescind*, δόγμα Plu.*Mar.*4; *rule out, exclude*, τὰ ἄλογα τῶν ζῴων Porph.*Abst.*3.1. 3. *reduce, degrade*, θεοὺς εἰς ὀνόματα στρατηγῶν Plu.2.360a, cf. 377d, 757b. V. *write an order for*, ὀψωνισμοὺς τοῖς στρατιώταις D.H.5.28, cf. *SIG*410.16 (Pass.); *pay by banker's draft*, *UPZ*114, *IG*11(2).287*A*135 (Delos, iii B.C.), etc.; simply, *pay*, στατῆρας ἑκατὸν *Milet.*3.147.12, cf. *SIG*577.9, *PRev. Laws*32.11 (iii B.C.), *PTeb.*100.3 (ii B.C.), Lxx 2*Ma.*4.9. VI. *distribute*, χώρας Plu.*Pomp.*31; σατραπείας D.S.18.50.

διαγρηγορέω, *start into full wakefulness*, *Ev.Luc.*9.32; *keep awake*, πάσης τῆς νυκτὸς ἐν φροντίσιν καὶ δέει δ. Hdn.3.4.4.

διαγριαίνω, strengthd. for ἀγριαίνω, Plu.*Ant.*86, *Brut.*20 (Pass.).

διαγρυπν-έω, *lie awake*, ἐν μακρῷ χρόνῳ νυκτὸς δ. Ar.*Ra.*931, cf. Luc.*Nec.*6, Porph.*Abst.*1.27; τὴν νύκτα D.S.14.105. —ητής, οῦ, ὁ, *one who lies awake*, Sch.Ar.*Eq.*277.

διάγυιος παιών, *the foot* – ‿ –, Aristid.Quint.1.16. (Perh. *two-limbed.*)

διαγυμν-άζω, *keep in hard exercise*, Polyaen.6.1.7; *continue exercise*, Gal.6.163:—Med., *take hard exercise*, Id.*Parv.Pil.*4. —όω, *strip naked, lay bare*, τὴν ἀλήθειαν δ. Eun.*Hist.*p.250 D.

διάγχω, strengthd. for ἄγχω, Luc.*Anach.*31.

διάγω [ᾰ], *carry over* or *across*, πορθμῆες δ' ἄρα τούς γε διήγαγον Od.20.187, cf. Th.4.78; δ. ἐπὶ σχεδίας ἄρτους X.*Cyr.*2.4.28. b. intr., *cross over*, Id.*An.*7.2.12. 2. *draw through*, τὴν προβοσκίδα Plu.2.968d. 3. Geom., *draw through* or *across, produce* a line, Euc.1.21, al. 4. *draw apart*, τὰ ὄμματα *IG*4.951.121 (Epid.). II. of Time, *pass, spend*, αἰῶνα *h.Hom.*20.7; βίοτον, βίον, A.*Pers.*711, S.*OC*1619, Ar.*Nu.*464; δ. τὸν βίον μαχόμενος Pl. *R.*579d; ἡσύχιον βίον δ. ἐν εὐσεβείᾳ 1*Ep.Tim.*2.2; γῆρας, νύκτα, X. *Cyr.*4.6.6, *An.*6.5.1; χρόνον Plu.*Tim.*10 (but χρόνος διῆγέ με, = χρόνον διῆγον, S.*El.*782); δ. ἑορτὴν *celebrate* it, Ath.8.363f: hence, 2. intr., without βίον, *pass life, live*, Democr.191, D.18.254, 25.82; = διαιτῶμαι, διατρίβω, Thom.Mag.pp.90,98 R.; δ. ἐν φιλοσοφίᾳ Pl.*Tht.* 174b; *tarry*, ἐν τῷ δικαστηρίῳ Id.*Euthphr.*3e; ἐν προαστείῳ Hdn.1.12.5:—Med., διαγόμενος Pl.*R.*344e, etc.; τὰ πρὸς τοὺς θεοὺς εὐσεβῶς δ. *Michel*352.15 (Iasus). b. *delay*, Th.1.90, D.C.57.3: c. acc., *spin out, protract*, τοὺς λόγους Philostr.*VA*1.17. c. c. acc. pers., *divert, fob off*, ἐλπίδας λέγων διῆγε [τοὺς στρατιώτας] X.*An.*1.2.11, cf. D.*Prooem.* 53, Luc.*Phal.*1.3. d. *continue*, δ. σιωπῇ X.*Cyr.*1.4.14: freq. c. part., *continue doing* so and so, δ. λιπαρέοντας Hdt.1.94; δ. μανθάνων, ἐπιμελόμενος, X.*Cyr.*1.2.6, 7.5.85. e. with Advbs., ἐν τοῖς χαλεπώτατα δ. Th.7.71; ἄριστα X.*Mem.*4.4.15; εὖ Arist.*HA*625b23; ἀκινδύνως Id.*Pol.*1295b33; also εὐσεβῆ δ. τρόπον περί τινα *conduct oneself piously*, Ar.*Ra.*457. III. *cause to continue, keep* in a certain state, πόλιν ὀρθοδίκαιον δ. A.*Eu.*995 (lyr.); πόλεις ἐν ὁμονοίᾳ Isoc.3.41; ἐν πᾶσι τοῖς κατὰ βίον .. διῆγεν ὑμᾶς D.18.89; τὸ ὑπήκοον ἐν ἡσυχίᾳ δ. D.C.40.30. IV. *entertain, feed*, τραγήμασι καὶ λαχάνοις τὸν στρατόν Philostr.*Her.*10.4:—Pass., [λέων] μελιτούτταις διήγετο Id.*VA* 5.42. V. *manage*, κάλλιστα πάντα δ. Pl.*Plt.*273c; πανηγυρικώτερον δ. τὰ κατὰ τὴν ἀρχήν Plb.5.34.3. VI. *separate, force apart*, τὰ σκέλεα Hp.*Ster.*230, Lxx *Ez.*16.25; τοὺς ὀδόντας Aret.*SA*1.6. 2. *divert*, τινα ἀπό τινος Philostr.*Her.Prooem.*3; simply, *divert*, τὰς βασιλείους φροντίδας Id.*VS*1.8.2.

διάγωγ-εύς, έως, ὁ, *conductor*, ψυχῶν, of Hermes, *EM*268.24. —ή, ἡ, *carrying across*, τριήρων Polyaen.5.2.6. 2. lit. *carrying through*: hence metaph., ἡ διὰ πάντων αὐτῶν δ. *taking a person through* a subject by instruction, Pl.*Ep.*343e; so, *course of instruction, lectures*, ἐν τῇ ἐνεστώσῃ δ. prob. in Phld.*Piet.*25. II. *passing of life, way* or *course of life*, δ. βίου Pl.*R.*344e: abs., Id.*Tht.*177a, etc. 2. *way of passing time, amusement*, δ. μετὰ παιδιᾶς Arist.*EN*1127b34, cf. 1177a27; δ. ἐλευθέριος Id.*Pol.*1339b5; διαγωγαὶ τοῦ συζῆν public *pastimes*, ib.1280b37, cf. Plu.126b (pl.). 3. *delay*, D.C. 57.3. III. *management*, τῶν πραγμάτων δ. *dispatch* of business, Id.48.5. IV. *station* for ships, f.l. in Hdn.4.2.8. V. διαγωγάν· διαίρεσιν, διανομήν, διέλευσιν, Hsch. —ικός, ή, όν, *of* or *for a passage*: τέλος δ., = sq., Str.4.3.2. —ιον, τό, *transit-duty, toll*, Plb.4.52.5.

διᾰγων-ία, ἡ, *struggle*, Max.Tyr.1.1. (Fort. διαφωνία.) —ιάω, pf. διηγωνίακα *IPE*12.32*B*22 (Olbia):—strengthd. for ἀγωνιάω, Aristeas 124, Lxx 2*Ma.*3.21; δ. μὴ σφαλῶσιν Plb.3.105.5: c. acc., *stand in dread of*, ib.102.10. —ίζομαι, *contend, struggle against*, τινί, πρός τινα, X.*Mem.*3.9.2, *Cyr.*1.6.26; ταῦτα δ. πρὸς ἀλλήλους ib. 1.2.12; τῷ Διὶ ὑπὲρ εὐδαιμονίας Epicur.*Fr.*602; ὑπὲρ τῆς ἀρχῆς D.H. 3.17; περί τινος Luc.*VH*2.8: abs., μάχῃ δ. Th.5.10; λόγῳ δ. Pl. *Grg.*456b, cf. 464e, D.7.8; *finish a contest*, of the Chorus, X.*HG*6. 4.16; but, *decide a contest*, περί τινος Aeschin.3.132:—Pass., διηγώνισται Plu.2.556e; πράξεις διαγωνισθεῖσαι Socr.*Ep.*30.9, etc.

διαγώνιος, ον, *from angle to angle, diagonal*, Str.2.1.36, Vitr.9.1.5, Aristid.Quint.3.3, Antyll.ap.Orib.6.23.3, Procl.*Hyp.*3.16; δ. πάσσαλος Nicom.*Harm.*6. Adv. –ίως Id.*Ar.*2.12.

διᾰγων-ισμός, ὁ, *a great straining*, τῆς κοιλίας Aët.9.30. —ιστέον, *one must make a great effort*, Ph.2.471.

διᾰγωνοθετέω, *set at variance*, Plb.25.4.7.

διαδάκνω, fut. –δήξομαι, *bite hard*, Max.Tyr.6.2: metaph. of calumny, δ. τινά Plb.4.87.5; of sarcasm, Iamb.*Protr.*21.λα':—Med., *have a biting-match with*, τῷ Κερβέρῳ Plu.2.1105a; *bite each other*, κυνίδια διαδακνόμενα M.Ant.5.33.

διαδακρύω [ῡ], *weep*, D.H.10.17 (s.v.l.).

διαδάπτω, *tear asunder, rend*, διὰ δὲ χρόα καλὸν ἔδαψεν Il.5.858, cf. 21.398.

διαδᾰτέομαι, aor. διεδασάμην Pi. (v. infr.): 1. in reciprocal sense, *divide among themselves*, διὰ κτῆσιν δατέοντο Il.5.158, Hes.*Th.* 606, cf. Pi.*O.*1.51; δ. τὴν ληΐην Hdt.8.121. 2. in act. sense, *divide, distribute*, διὰ παῦρα δασάσκετο (Ion. iterative form) Il.9.333; ἐς φυλὰς διεδάσαντο *distributed* them among the tribes, Hdt.4.145:—Pass., *to be divided*, γῆς διαδατουμένης App.*BC*1.1.

διαδείκνῡμι, fut. –δείξω, Ion. –δέξω, strengthd. for δείκνυμι, *show plainly*, Hdt.2.162, al.; φρόνημα καὶ μέγεθος ἀρετῆς Plu.2.968d: folld. by a relat. clause with ὅτι, Hdt.7.172, 9.58: also c. part., διαδεξάτω τις βασιλέος κηδόμενος Id.8.118; δ. τὴν Ἑλλήνων ἀλκὴν ἀπρόσμαχον οὖσαν Plu.*Arat.*9:—Med., *display*, ἐπιμέλειαν *BGU*778.6 (ii A.D.):—Pass., διαδεικνύσθω ἐὼν πολέμιος *let him be declared* the king's enemy, Hdt.3.72; ἀγαθοὶ διεδείχθησαν Lib.*Or.*11.105, cf. Hermog.*Inv.*3.4, Aen.Gaz.*Thphr.*p.56 B. II. sts. intr. in forms διέδεξε and ὡς διέδεξε, *it was clear, manifest*, Hdt.2.134, 3.82.

διαδεκ-τήρ, ῆρος, ὁ, (διαδέχομαι) *transmitter*, σημείων Aen.Tact. 6.4, 7.2. —τωρ, ορος, ὁ, *inheritor*, καμάτου Man.4.223. II. Pass. as Adj., πλοῦτος δ. *inherited* wealth, E.*Ion*478.

διαδέλλειν· διασπᾶν, Hsch.; cf. διαδηλέομαι.

διαδέξιος, ον, *of right good omen*, Hdt.7.180.

διάδεξις, εως, ἡ, *passage*, ὑποχονδρίων Hp.*Epid.*6.2.14; δ. ἐκ πατέρων hereditary *transmission*, Aret.*CD*2.12; δ. γένεος *procreation*, ib. 2.5. II. *transition* from one disease to another, ib.1.1.

διαδέρκομαι, aor. –έδρᾰκον, *see* one thing *through* another, οὐδ' ἂν νῶϊ διαδράκοι *would* not *see* us *through* [the cloud], Il.14.344. 2. *look about*, πάντῃ δὲ διέδρακεν ὀφθαλμοῖσι Theoc.25.233. II. *see over*, νῆσον Cypr.11.3.

διαδέρω, *strip off*, δέρμα Paul.Aeg.6.50:—Pass., ib.68.

διά-δεσις, εως, ἡ, (διαδέω) *bandaging*, Antyll.ap.Orib.7.9.7, Heliod.ib.10.18.3 (pl.). —δεσμα, ατος, τό, *tree-mallow, Lavatera arborea*, Zoroaster ap.Ps.-Dsc.2.118. —δεσμεύω, = sq., Sor.1.50. —δεσμέω, *bind*, τὴν κεφαλὴν δ. ταινίᾳ Lyd.*Mens.*1.20. —δεσμος, ὁ, *connecting band*, Hp.*Nat.Puer.*14; *bandage*, Aret.*CA*1.9; *ligature*, διαδέσμοις σφίγγων τὰ ἄκρα Philum.ap.Aët.9.12. —δετέον, *one must bind round*, Archig.ap.Orib.47.13.5, Gal.17(1).434. —δετος, ον, *bound fast*, χαλινοὶ διάδετοι γενύων ἱππίων bits *firm bound through* the horse's mouth, A.*Th.*122 (lyr.); δακτύλιος ἠλέκτρῳ δ. τὸν κύκλον *adorned with* a strip of amber *set in* . ., Hld.5.13; δ. ταινίαις τὰς κόμας Lib.*Decl.*12.27.

διαδέχομαι, fut. –ξομαι, *receive one from another*, δ. τὸν λόγον *take up* the word, i.e. *speak next*, Pl.*R.*576b; λόγον παρά τινος D.H. *Rh.*8.14: abs., διαδεξάμενοι ἔλεγον Hdt.8.142; ἀποκρινόμενοι διαδέχεσθε Pl.*Lg.*900c; δ. νόμους παρὰ τῶν θεῶν, τέχνην, Antipho 1.3, Lys.24.6; τὴν διατριβήν, leadership of a school of philosophy, Phld. *Acad.Ind.*p.58 M. 2. δ. βασιλείαν *succeed to* the kingdom, Plb.2.4.7; ἀρχὴν παρά τινος Id.9.28.8; τὴν ναῦν δ. τινί, of a trierarch (cf. διαδοχή I), D.50.38; πλοῦτον παρά τινος Luc.*DMort.*11.3. II. διαδέχεσθαί τινι *succeed* one, *take his place, relieve* him on guard, etc., Pl. *Lg.*758b, X.*Cyr.*8.6.18: later, δ. τινά Arist.*Pol.*1299b4, Plb.28.3.6; δ. τὰ κατὰ τὴν στρατηγίαν *act for* the στρατηγός, *BGU*18.3 (ii A.D.), etc.; τοὺς προφήτας στολισταὶ δ. *represent*, *PGnom.*193. b. *appoint a successor to*, τινά Eun.*Hist.*p.231 D.:—Pass., διεδέχθη τῆς στρατηγίας *was relieved of* his command, Id.p.243 D. 2. abs., *relieve one another*, τοῖς ἵπποις *with fresh* horses, X.*An.*1.5.2 (wrongly expld. as *closing in from both sides* by Demetr.*Eloc.*93); *succeed*, οἱ διαδεχόμενοι στρατηγοί Lys.13.62, cf. Arist.*Pol.*1293a29; οἱ διαδεξάμενοι *the successors* (of Alexander), Plb.9.34.11; οἱ τὰ Πύρρου δ. App.*Ill.*7: pf. part. Pass., νὺξ εἰσάγει καὶ νὺξ ἀπωθεῖ διαδεδεγμένη *in turns, by turns*, S.*Tr.*30; διαδεξάμενοι *Act.Ap.*7.45; οἱ διαδεχόμενοι καιροί Herod.Med.ap.Orib.7.8.3. III. *supersede*, τὸν ὕπατον D.S.24.1.

διαδέω, *bind on either side,* δ. τὸ πλοῖον ἀμφοτέρωθεν Hdt.2.29, cf. 4.154; δ. τὰ χαλκεῖα ταινίᾳ Arist.*Aud.*802^{a}40; *bandage,* Herod.Med. ap.Orib.10.18.2; *put in chains,* δοῦλον *POxy.*1423.9 (iv A.D.); ψυχὴ διαδεδεμένη ἐν τῷ σώματι *fast-bound,* Pl.*Phd.*82e:—Med., δ. ἱμάτια ταῖς λαιαῖς *bind, wrap them* round *their* left arms, App.*Mith.*86: abs., διαδεῖσθαι καυσίαις *bind one's head* (with a diadem), Plu.*Demetr.*41; ὁ διαδούμενος *the boy binding his hair,* a famous statue by Polyclitus, Plin.*HN*34.55; διαδησάμενος Plu.2.489f:—Pass., διαδέδεσθαι τὴν κεφαλὴν διαδήματι, μίτρᾳ, *have one's* head *bound* with.., D.S.4.4, Luc.*DMort.*12.3.

διαδηλέομαι, *do great harm to, rend in pieces,* ὀλίγου σε κύνες διεδηλήσαντο Od.14.37, cf. Theoc.24.85, A.R.2.284, Agath.5.7.

διάδηλ-ος, ον, also η, ον Arist.*HA*613^{b}1:—*distinguishable among others,* Th.4.68, Pl.*R.*474b, Plb.6.22.3; δ. παρὰ τοὺς ἄλλους D.H.1.72; of a person, *distinguished, OGI*504.9 (Aezani): c. part., δ. εἶναι εὐτακτῶν X.*Mem.*4.4.1: c. dat., δ. τῇσι μελεδώνῃσι Aret.*SD*2.4. **-όω,** *make manifest, indicate clearly, PRev.Laws* 16.17 (iii B.C.), J.*BJ*6.9.3, Plu.*Caes.*6, D.L.4.46, S.E.*M.*7.87, D.C.40.17.

διάδημα, ατος, τό, (διαδέω) *band* or *fillet*: esp. *band round the* τιάρα worn by the Persian king, X.*Cyr.*8.3.13, Plu.2.488d; by Alexander, Arr.*An.*7.22.2; by his successors, *OGI*248.17 (Pergam., Antiochus IV), Hdn.1.3.3; by kings generally, Plu.2.753d, D.S.20.54; δ. τῆς Ἀσίας Lxx 1*Ma.*13.32. II. Ὀσίριδος δ., = ἄλιμος, Ps.-Dsc.1.91.

διαδημᾰτίζομαι, *wear the* διάδημα, Aq.*Ps.*21(22).13.

διαδημᾰτοφόρος, ον, *bearing a diadem,* καυσία Plu.*Ant.*54.

διαδιδράσκω, Ion. **διαδιδρήσκω,** aor. 2 part. -δράντας Hdt.8.75: pf. -δέδρᾱκα Ar.*Ach.*601:—*run away, escape,* Hdt. l.c., Th.7.85, *PPetr.*2 p.101 (iii B.C.), etc.; διαδεδρακότες *shirkers,* Ar. l.c. 2. c. acc., *escape from,* τινά Hdt.3.135, etc.; τὸ πάθος, τὸν ὄλεθρον, Aret.*SA*1.10,2.8:—Pass., Hsch. 3. *fly in all directions,* Lxx 2*Ma.*8.13.

διαδίδωμι, fut. -δώσω Pl.*R.*328a:—*pass on, hand over,* ἐμοὶ τοῦτον διέδωκαν (sc. Μοῖσαι) ἀθάνατον πόνον Pi.*Pae.*9 *Fr.*16.16; λαμπάδια ἔχοντες διαδώσουσιν ἀλλήλοις Pl. l.c.; *propound* for consideration, Pall. *in Hp.Fract.*12.277 C.; *spread abroad,* λόγον Plu.*Them.*19:—Pass., λόγος διεδόθη v.l. in X.*Cyr.*4.2.10, cf. Plu.*Sol.*8; διαδοθέντος τοῦ λόγου Isoc.5.7, cf. 9.74; παρὰ τῶν ἀρχαίων δ. *to be handed down* by tradition, Arist.*Cael.*270^{b}17; ἐν παροιμίᾳ διαδοθῆναι Str.6.2.4. 2. *distribute,* τινί τι X.*An.*1.10.18, Th.4.38, D.49.14:—Pass., τῇ σάλπιγγι σιωπῆς εἰς ἅπαντας διαδοθείσης Plu.*Flam.*10; τὸ διαδιδόμενον εἰς τὰς φλέβας, of food, Arist.*PA*678^{a}18; of the bowels, *secrete,* τῆς κοιλίης ὑδατόχολα πολλὰ διαδιδούσης Hp.*Coac.*67. 3. δ. κόρας *cast* one's eyes *around,* E.*Ph.*1371, cj. in *Or.*1267. 4. διαδοῦναι δίκας *give* satisfaction to injured party, Hsch. II. intr., *spread about,* Arist.*HA*495^{b}8. 2. *remit,* Hp.*Acut.*(*Sp.*)5.

διαδῐκ-άζω, *give judgement,* And.1.28, Pl.*R.*614c, *Lg.*916b (Pass.); χορηγοῖς, ἀρχὰς δ., X.*Ath.*3.4; διεδίκαξαν δίκας *IG*7.21 (Megara); τὰς ἀμφισβητήσεις τισί Arist.*Ath.*57.2: c. gen., δ. ἀστρατείας X.*Ath.*3.5 (prob. l.). 2. *hold inquiry,* esp. at Athens, of naval matters, δ. εἴ τις τὴν ναῦν μὴ ἐπισκευάζει X.*Ath.*3.4; ἀριθμὸς τριήρων καὶ σκευῶν τῶν -δεδικασμένων *IG*2.795*f*60. 3. Med., *go to law, dispute,* διαδικασόμενος τῇ βουλῇ περὶ ἀληθείας Din.2.1; ταῦτα διαδικασόμεθα περὶ τῆς σοφίας Pl.*Smp.*175e, etc.; διαδικάσασθαι ἐν φίλοις τὰ πρὸς ἐμέ *to settle* by friendly arbitration, D.30.2; Διαδικαζόμενοι, title of play by Dioxippus, Suid., cf. *IG*2.975 iii 21, *BGU*1914 (ii A.D.). b. *submit oneself to trial,* Pl.*Phd.*107d, 113d, X.*HG*5.3.10: later, aor. Pass. διαδικασθῆναι, = διαδικάσασθαι, D.L.1.74, D.C.48.12. II. = διὰ ὅλου τοῦ ἔτους δικάζω, Critias *Fr.*71 D. **-αιόω,** *justify* an action, Th.4.106; *defend as matter of right,* ὑπέρ τινος, D.C.39.60; *defend* a person's *right,* τὰ τοῦ Καίσαρος Id.40.62. **-ᾰσία,** ἡ, *suit to decide between claimants,* e.g. to an estate, δ. κλήρου D.44.7; to a wardship, δ. ἐπιτροπῆς Arist.*Ath.*56.6; to exemption from a λειτουργία, D.28.17, cf. Lys.17.1, D.24.13, etc.; τὴν δ. ποιεῖσθαι *IG*12(5).722.48 (Andros); esp. of *judicial inquiries* relating to naval matters, D.47.26, Arist.*Ath.*61.1. 2. *judicial decision* or *settlement,* X.*Cyr.*8.1.18, *OGI* 437.78. 3. metaph., δ. τῷ βήματι πρὸς τὸ στρατήγιον *dispute* between the orators and the board of generals, Aeschin.3.146: generally, τὴν τῶν ἀριστείων δ. *the competition for* public honours, Pl.*Lg.*952d, cf. Polem.*Call.*53. 4. διαδικασίαν προθεῖναι ταῖς γνώμαις put *the question* to the vote, D.H.11.21. **-ασμα,** ατος, τό, *object of litigation in a* διαδικασία, Lys.17.10. **-ασμός,** ὁ, *lawsuit*: *contention,* Aq.*Ez.*48.28.

δια-δῐκέω (A), *contend at law,* πρός τινα *PRein.*19.16 (ii B.C.); οἱ διαδικοῦντες *the contending parties,* Plu.2.196c, *POxy.*1101.8 (iv A.D.). 2. *decide a suit,* οἱ διαδικοῦντες *the jurors,* D.C.40.55 (s. v.l.).

δι-ᾰδῐκέω (B), *do wrong, injure,* D.C.58.16.

διάδῐκος· τὸ εἰς δίκην καλεῖν (Att.), Hsch.

διαδιφρεύω, *drive* horses *as in a chariot-race,* E.*Or.*990 (lyr.).

διαδοιδῠκίζω, (δοίδυξ) *make a closed fist like a pestle, Com.Adesp.*973. II. = ὀρχεῖσθαι ἀσχημόνως, ibid.

διαδοκέω, plpf. Pass. διεδέδοκτο *it had been determined,* v.l. in J.*Vit.*11.

διαδοκῑμάζω, *distinguish by testing,* τὰ καλὰ καὶ κίβδηλα ἀργύρια X.*Oec.*19.16.

διαδοκίς, ίδος, ἡ, (δοκός) *cross-beam,* Hsch.

διάδομα, ατος, τό, (διαδίδωμι) *distribution of money, IG*7.2715.64 (Acraeph.), Ἀρχ.Δελτ.2.148 (pl.), *UPZ*2.8 (ii B.C.).

διαδοξάζω, *form a definite opinion,* Pl.*Phlb.*38b, Iamb.*Myst.*4.6:—Med., ib.8.5.

διαδορᾰτ-ίζομαι, *fight with spears,* and generally, *contend in battle,* Plb.5.84.2, J.*BJ*5.3.3, M.Ant.4.3: metaph., '*break a lance*', *contend,* Longin.13.4 (and so perh. in M.Ant. l.c.). **-ισμός,** ὁ, *fighting with the spear,* M.Ant.7.3 (pl.).

διά-δοσις, εως, ἡ, *distribution,* D.44.37; χώρας Plb.2.23.1; ἀννώνης *POxy.*1115.9 (iii A.D.): pl., *IGRom.*3.739. II. Medic., δ. οὔρων an *evacuation,* Hp.*Epid.*3.4; ἡ τῆς τροφῆς δ. its *distribution* through the body, Arist.*IA*705^{a}32. III. *exchange,* μειδιαμάτων Plu.*Sull.*35 (pl.). IV. *communication,* κινήσεως Epicur.*Ep.*2 p.48 U.; δ. ἐκ θεῶν εἰς ἀνθρώπους Arr.*Epict.*1.12.6; ταῖς ἀρίσταις διαδόσεσι κινεῖσθαι (of just men) Phld.*Piet.*68, cf. M.Ant.1.17.6 (pl.); ἐκ -δόσεως τῆς ἀφῆς γινώσκειν τι Heliod.ap.Orib.44.23.59: Astrol., of celestial influence, Ptol.*Tetr.*5 (pl.), 105. **-δοτέος,** έα, έον, *to be published,* Isoc.12.233. II. διαδοτέον *one must distribute,* Pl.*Ti.*19a. **-δότης,** ου, ὁ, an official, *distributor* of provisions to the soldiers, οἴνου *PRein.*56.9 (iv A.D.), *PLond.*3.1245.3 (iv A.D.), *BGU* 1025 xvi 15 (iv/v A.D.).

διαδοχ-ή, ἡ, (διαδέχομαι) *taking over from* another, νεώς, of a trierarch, D.50.1. 2. *succession,* ἄλλος παρ' ἄλλου διαδοχαῖς πληρούμενοι by *successions* or *reliefs,* A.*Ag.*313; διαδοχῇ τῶν ἐπιγιγνομένων Th.2.36; ἡ τῶν τέκνων δ. Arist.*Pol.*1334^{b}39: freq. in dat. pl., ἀνάσσειν διαδοχαῖσιν ἐν μέρει ἐνιαυσίαισιν E.*Supp.*406; διαδοχαῖς Ἐρινύων (apparently) *by successive attacks* of the Furies, Id.*IT*79; γένους μακραῖς δ. by long *pedigrees,* Hdn.1.2.2: with Preps., ἐκ διαδοχῆς ἀλλήλοις in *turns,* D.4.21, cf. Antiph.8 (but, in *succession,* Arist.*Ph.*228^{a}28); κατὰ διαδοχὴν χρόνου or κατὰ δ., Th.7.27,28; κατὰ διαδοχάς Arist.*Mu.*398^{a}33; τὰ κατὰ διαδοχὴν κληρονομηθέντα *POxy.*1201.7 (iii A.D.), cf. *BGU*907.13 (iii A.D.). II. concrete in military sense, *relief, relay,* ἡ δ. τῇ πρόσθεν φυλακῇ ἔρχεται X.*Cyr.*1.4.17, cf. D.21.164: metaph., σελήνη ἡλίου δ. Secund.*Sent.*6. 2. *the succession* (i.e. *successors*), Luc.*Nigr.*38; ἡ περὶ τὸν Πλάτωνα δ. the *school* of Plato, S.E.*M.*7.190; Στωϊκὴ δ. Plu.2.605b; ἡ Ἐπικούρου δ. *IG*2^{2}.1099 (Epist. Plotinae); αἱ Διαδοχαί, title of work by Sotion on *the Successions* or *successive heads* of the Philosophic Schools, Ath.4.162e, cf. D.L.*Prooem.*1, 2.12. **-ικός,** ή, όν, *belonging to a philosophic school,* τὰ δ. *endowments,* Olymp. *in Alc.*p.141 C., Suid. s.v. Πλάτων. **-ος,** ον, *succeeding* a person *in* a thing: 1. c. dat. pers. et gen. rei, δ. Μεγαβάζῳ τῆς στρατηγίης his *successor in* the command, Hdt.5.26, cf. 1.162, etc.; θνητοῖς.. διάδοχοι μοχθημάτων *succeeding* them *in,* i.e. *relieving* them *from,* toils, A.*Pr.*464, cf. 1027; σοι τῶνδε διάδοχος δόμων E.*Alc.*655. 2. c. gen. rei only, δ. τῆς Ἀστυόχου ναυαρχίας *succeeding to* his command, Th.8.85; δ. τῆς κληρονομίας Isoc.19.43; τῆς φιλοσοφίας Epicur.*Fr.*217. 3. c. gen. pers. only, φέγγος ὕπνου δ. sleep's *successor* light, S.*Ph.*867. 4. c. dat. pers. only, δ. Κλεάνδρῳ X.*An.*7.2.5: c. dat. rei, ἔργοισι δ' ἔργα διάδοχα E.*Andr.*743; κακὸν κακῷ δ. ib.803; quasi-act., λύπη.. δ. κακῶν κακοῖς *bringing a succession* of evils *after* evils, *Hec.*588; ἀγὼν.. γόων γόοις (γόων bis codd.) δ. *Supp.*72 (lyr.). 5. abs., διάδοχοι ἐφοίτων they went to work *in relays* or *gangs,* Hdt.7.22, cf. Th.1.110: neut. pl. as Adv., *in turn,* E.*Andr.*1200 (lyr.). 6. as Subst., οἱ Δ. the *Successors* of Alexander, D.S.18.42. b. the lowest grade of court officials at Alexandria, *OGI*100.4, *PAmh.*2.36.5, *PRyl.*67.2 (both ii B.C.). c. *substitute, deputy, BGU*852.4 (ii A.D.), *POxy.*54.7 (iii A.D.). d. *head of a school of philosophers,* τῆς σχολῆς Phld.*Ind.Sto.*53; δ. Στωικὸς *IG*3.661, cf. 2^{2}.1009 (Epist. Plotinae). e. a kind of *gem,* Plin.*HN*37.157.

διαδρᾱμᾰτίζω, *finish acting a play,* M.Ant.3.8, D.L.3.56.

διαδρᾱσῐπολῖται, οἱ, *citizens who shirk all state burdens,* Ar.*Ra.*1014.

διάδρᾱσις, εως, ἡ, (διαδιδράσκω) *an escape from,* ἀναγκῶν, πυρός, J.*AJ*17.4.2 and 10.2.

διαδράσσομαι, *seize hold of,* ἀλλήλων Plb.1.58.8, Ph.2.328.

διαδρηστεύω or **διαδρηπετεύω,** *run off, go over to,* suggested emendations for διεπρήστευσε in Hdt.4.79.

διαδρομ-ή, ἡ, (διαδραμεῖν) *running to and fro through* a city, A.*Th.*351 (pl.), cf. Hp.*Epid.*7.122, Plb.15.30.2; αἱ δ. τῶν ἀστέρων *shooting,* Arist.*Mete.*341^{a}33, al.; διαδρομὰς ὀξείας ἔχειν *spread* rapidly, of disease, Plu.2.825d. 2. *running across,* Antipho 3.4.4; *passage through,* σπιλάδος Plu.2.476a. 3. *race* (perh. *team-race*) or *parade, OGI* 339.36 (Sestos), 764.24 (Pergam.), *SIG*694.56 (Elaea, ii B.C.). 4. a *cavalry manœuvre,* Anon.ap.Suid. 5. Medic., δ. πνευμάτων, = βορβορυγμός, Dsc.5.45; *sensation,* δ. νυγματώδης, φρικώδης, Sor.2.17, Philum.*Ven.*17.1. 6. *course,* ἡμέρα δωδεκάωρος δ. Secund.*Sent.*4. II. *place for running through, passage,* X.*Cyn.*10.8; of fish-ponds, δ. ἰχθυοτρόφοι Plu.*Luc.*39. **-ος,** ον, *running through* or *about, wandering,* φυγαί A.*Th.*191; λέχος δ. *stray, lawless* love, E.*El.*1156 (lyr.); ἔμβολα κίοσι δ. the architrave *reeling, ready to fall,* Id.*Ba.*592 (lyr.). II. Subst. διάδρομος, ὁ, = διαδρομή II, Luc.*Hipp.*6.

διαδῠναστεύω, *prevail,* f.l. for δυναστεύω, Arist.*Mu.*395^{a}2.

δια-δύνω Hp.*Flat.*13, Arist. *de An.*404^{a}7: **διαδύω** Hdt.2.66 codd.; more freq. Dep. **διαδύομαι,** fut. -δύσομαι: aor. 2 διέδυν:—*slip through* a hole or gap, διαδύντες διὰ τοῦ τείχους Th.4.110; διὰ τούτων ἡ φιλία διαδυομένη X.*Mem.*2.6.22: abs., *slip through, slip away,* Hdt. l.c.; διαδὺς Ar.*V.*212; μῶν ὁ γέρων πῃ διαδύεται; ib.396. 2. c. acc., *evade, shirk,* τοῖς διαδυομένοις τὰς λειτουργίας Lys.21.12, cf. D.42.23; ὅπῃ... διαδύσεται τὸν λόγον Pl.*Sph.*231c, etc.; τὸ δίκην δοῦναι διαδὺς D.18.133. **-δῠσις,** εως, ἡ, *passing through, passage,* ἐς τὼς πόρως Ti.Locr.100e, cf. Thphr.*Od.*50: metaph. in pl., *evasions,* τῶν ἀδικημάτων, i.e. *escape from* the consequences of crimes, D.24.139, cf. 94, Plu.*Dem*.6: abs., Lib.*Or*.18.32. II. in pl., *passages, galleries*, in mines, etc., D.S.5.36: sg., prob. l. in Aen.Tact.24.5; *subterranean channel*, Demetr.Sceps.ap.Str.13.1.43. **-δῦτικός**, ή, όν, *penetrating*, ἀήρ Thphr.*CP*5.14.1 (Comp.).

διάδωμα, ατος, τό, prob. = διάζωμα, *IGRom*.4.914 (fort. διάδομα).

διαδωρέομαι, *distribute in presents*, X.*Cyr*.3.3.6, Posidon.24. 2. generally, *distribute, assign*, τινὰς εἰς τὰς ἐπαρχίας J.*BJ*6.9.2.

διαειδής, ές, *transparent*, ὕδωρ Theoc.16.62.

δια-είδω (i.e. διαϝείδω) (A), fut. -είσομαι, *discern, distinguish*, αὔριον ἣν ἀρετὴν διαείσεται *will test* his manhood, Il.8.535:—Pass., ἔνθα μάλιστ' ἀρετὴ διαείδεται *is discerned*, 13.277, cf. Aret.*SD*1.1; simply, *appear between*, A.R.2.579 (tm.).

δι-ᾱείδω (B), fut. -ᾱείσομαι: Att. **δι-ᾴδω**, -ᾴσομαι:—Med., aor. διᾴσασθαι Phryn.*PS*p.65 B.:—*contend in singing*, τινί *with* one, Theoc.5.22: abs., *contend in song, sing for the prize*, Arist.*Po*.1462^{a}7, Phryn. l. c. II. *to be dissonant*, opp. συνᾴδω, Heraclit.10.

διαειμένος, pf. part. Pass. of διΐημι. **διαειπέμεν, διαϝειπάμενος**, v. διεῖπον.

διαείρω, = διαιρέω, *divide*, τριχῆ θυσίας Orac.ap.Eus.*PE*4.9.2.

διᾱέριος, v. sub διηέριος.

διαζάω, Ion. **-ζώω**, inf. διαζῆν, *live through, pass*, ὀρθῶς τὸν βίον E.*IA*923; τὸ καθ' ἡμέραν Pl.*R*.561c, etc.: abs., καλῶς δ. X.*HG*7.1.8. 2. c. part., *live* by doing so and so, ποιηφαγέοντες διέζων *they supported life* by.., Hdt.3.25; δ. ἀπό τινος *live* off or by a thing, S.*Ph*.535, Ar.*Av*.1434, etc.; ἔκ τινος *Stoic*.3.187; πῶς οὖν διέζης ἢ πόθεν μηδὲν ποιῶν; Ar.*Pl*.906; δ. νομῇ of pastoral *life*, Pl.*Lg*.679a.

διά-ζευγμα, ατος, τό, dub. sens., perh. *bridge* over or *branch* of a canal, *PLond*.1.131.205 (I A.D.). **-ζευγμός**, ὁ, = διάζευξις, Plb.10.7.1. **-ζεύγνῡμι**, *part, separate*, διὰ γὰρ ζευγνῦσ' ἡμᾶς πατρίων μελάθρων μητρὸς κατάραι E.*El*.1323 (anap.), cf. Charito8.16; λίθους ἀλλήλων Lib.*Or*.30.38; *open* sluices, *PPetr*.3p.121 (iii B.C.); *take to pieces*, σκάφη Polyaen.3.11.3; *dissolve*, θάνατος δ. γάμον Ph.2.311; *disjoin, distinguish*, τί τινος ib.298, al.:—but more freq. Pass., *to be disjoined, parted*, τινός *from* one, Aeschin.2.179; ἀπό τινος X.*An*.4.2.10: abs., ὅπως αἱ πρότερον συνήθειαι διαζευχθῶσιν Arist.*Pol*.1319^{b}26; *to be divorced*, Pl.*Lg*.784b; διεζευγμένον (sc. ἀξίωμα) *disjunctive proposition*, Chrysipp.*Stoic*.2.5,71, etc. (with ἀξίωμα in full, Gell.16.8.12); λῆμμα Gal.*Nat.Fac*.2.7. 2. τὸ διεζ. σύστημα the *disjunct* scale, in which two tetrachords were so combined that the first note of one was a tone lower than the last note of the other, opp. συνημμένον, Cleonid.*Harm*.10; νήτη διεζευγμένων Euc.*Sect.Can*.15; [τετράχορδον] διεζευγμένων Plu.2.1029b. 3. Math., διεζευγμένη μεσότης, ἀναλογία, *discrete* mean, proportion, Nicom.*Ar*.2.21. 4. Medic., *reckon* periods *exclusively*, opp. συνάπτεσθαι, Gal.9.901. **-ζευκτικός**, ή, όν, *disjunctive*, σύνδεσμος Chrysipp.*Stoic*.2.68, A.D.*Conj*.216.10; συλλογισμός Chrysipp.*Stoic*.2.88; πρὸς τοὺς Ἀμεινίου -κούς (sc. λόγους), title of work by Chrysipp., *Stoic*.2.7. Adv. -κῶς A.D.*Synt*.9.27. **-ζευξις**, εως, ἡ, *disjoining, parting*, τοῦ σώματος Pl.*Phd*.88b; δ. τε καὶ σύζευξιν ποιεῖσθαι Id.*Lg*.930b; ἡ δ. τῶν γυναικῶν, in Crete, Arist.*Pol*.1272^{a}23. 2. Musical term, *disjunction* of two tetrachords, Plu.2.491a, Cleonid.*Harm*.10, etc. 3. Gramm., *disjunction*, κατὰ διάζευξιν παραλαμβάνεσθαι A.D.*Synt*.125.12: in Logic, συμπλοκαὶ καὶ διαζεύξεις Plu.2.1011a. 4. Medic., κατὰ διάζευξιν by *exclusive reckoning*, Gal.18(2).232, al.

διαζέω, *boil through*, Suid., cf. Hsch. s. v. διασμύχων.

διαζηλεύομαι, *to be lost in admiration*, Hp.*Praec*.13.

διαζηλοτῡπέομαι, *engage in rivalry*, τινί Ath.13.588e; πρός τινα Plb.36.8.2.

διάζησις, εως, ἡ, *way of living*, Hierocl.p.15 A., Porph.ap.Stob.2.8.40.

διαζητ-έω, *search through, examine*, Ar.*Eq*.1292, Pl.*Plt*.258b, etc. II. *seek out, invent*, λόγους εὖ διεζητημένους Ar.*Th*.439. **-ησις**, εως, ἡ, *inquiry, inquisition*, *Gloss*.

διάζομαι, *set the warp in the loom*, i.e. *begin the web*, Nicopho5; opp. προφορεῖσθαι τὸν στήμονα, Sch.Ar.*Av*.4; cf. δίασμα: διέζετο (post διαείδεται)· διεσχίζετο, Hsch.

διαζῠγή, ἡ, *division*, *Corp.Herm*.13.12 (pl.).

διαζῠγία, ἡ, = διάζευξις, *AP*5.8 (Rufin.).

διαζύγιον [ῠ], τό, *divorce*, Eust.893.51, 1667.33: pl. **διαζύγια**, τά, *differences, quarrels* between man and wife, Just.*Nov*.140.1 *Intr*.

διαζωγρᾰφ-έω, *paint in divers colours*, Pl.*Ti*.55c, Plu.2.1003d, Ael.*VH*12.41, Dam.*Isid*.70:—Subst. **-ησις**, εως, ἡ, Sch.D.T.p.490 H.

διάζωμα, ατος, τό, *that which is put round as a girdle*: hence, 1. *a girdle, drawers*, δ. ἔχειν περὶ τὰ αἰδοῖα Th.1.6. b. *bandage*, Hp.*Fist*.9. 2. φρενῶν δ., = διάφραγμα II, Arist.*PA*672^{b}10; τὸ δ. τὸ τοῦ θώρακος Id.*HA*497^{a}23: of the *pelvis*, ib.493^{a}22; *partition*, Id.*PA*681^{a}3. 3. *cornice* or *frieze* in Architecture, Thphr.*Lap*.7. 4. *gangway*, giving access to the seats in a theatre, *CIG*(add.)2755 (Aphrodisias), Vitr.5.6.7. 5. *vein, layer, marking*, in stone, Dsc.5.126. 6. *isthmus*, Plu.*Phoc*.13. 7. *layer, stratum* of atmosphere, Herm.ap.Stob.1.49.69; *vein*, of copper ore, Dsc.5.74 (pl.).

διαζωμάτιον, τό, Dim. of foreg. 1, *Gloss*.

διαζωμεύω, (ζωμός) *make into soup*, τὰ κρέα v.l. in Hp.*Int*.9.

δια-ζώνη, ἡ, *girdle*, Aq.*Ex*.29.9. **-ζώννῡμι** or **-ύω**, fut. -ζώσω: pf. Pass. διέζωμαι *IG*2.736*B*19, ib.11(2).161.35 (Delos, iii B.C.):—*gird round, encircle, embrace*, Gal.14.715: metaph., τὸν ὅλον ἄνθρωπον διέζωσεν [ἡ ψυχή] Diog.Oen.39:—Med., *undergird one's* ship, App.*BC*5.91; but usu. *gird oneself with*, διαζωσάμενοι τὸ τριβώνιον Luc.*Hist.Conscr*.3:—Pass., διαζώννυσθαι ἐσθῆτα, ἀκινάκην, Id.*Somn*.6, *Anach*.6: abs., διεζωσμένοι *wearing the* διάζωμα 1, Th.1.6 codd. (-ζωμένοι Phot., Suid.): metaph., ἀρχὴν διεζωσμένος *invested with* office, J.*AJ*14.9.3. II. metaph., *engirdle, encompass*, of fire, Plu.*Brut*.31; τὸν αὐχένα (i.e. the Chersonese) δ. ἐρύμασι Id.*Per*.19; νήσους Id.*Them*.12:—Pass., [ἡ Ἀττικὴ] μέση διέζωσται ὄρεσιν X.*Mem*.3.5.25; ῥάχει διεζῶσθαι Plb.5.69.1; also *pass like a girdle*, διὰ τῶν τροπικῶν Arist.*Mu*.392^{a}12. **-ζωσις**, εως, ἡ, *cincture*, ἡ τοῦ ζῳδιακοῦ δ. Eudem.ap.Theon.Sm.p.198 H., cf. Hero *Deff*.138.11. **-ζωσμα**, ατος, τό, = διάζωμα 1, Hp.*Haem*.2, Plu.2.132a. II. = διάζωμα 3, Callix.1. **-ζωστήρ**, ῆρος, ὁ, *twelfth vertebra in the spine*, Poll.2.179. **-ζώστρα**, ἡ, = διάζωμα 1, Pers.*Stoic*.1.100; condemned by Hermog.*Meth*.3.

διαζωτικός, ή, όν, *vital*, ἰδίωμα Procl.*in Prm*.p.576 S.

διαζώω, v. διαζάω.

διάημι [ᾰ], impf. διάην, Ep. Verb, *blow through*, c. acc., τοὺς [θάμνους]..οὔτ' ἀνέμων διάη μένος Od.5.478; πώεα..οὐ διάησι ἲς ἀνέμου Hes.*Op*.517: c. gen., τῶν [οὐρῶν] ψυχρὸς ἐὼν διάησι [Βορέας] ib.514.

διαθᾰλασσεύω, in Pass., *to be parted by the sea*, Alciphr.2.3.

διαθάλπω, *warm through*, Plu.2.799b.

διαθαρρέω, *take heart*, Ael.*NA*4.14.

διαθε-άομαι, *look through, look into, examine*, τι Pl.*Prt*.316a, *Cra*.424d; δ. ὅσην χώραν ἔχοιεν X.*An*.3.1.19. **-ᾱτέον**, *one must examine*, λογισμῷ Pl.*R*.611c.

διαθειόω, *fumigate thoroughly*, εὖ διεθείωσεν μέγαρον Od.22.494.

διαθέλγω, *soothe thoroughly*, Anon.ap.Suid. s. v. κατεπᾴδουσα.

διάθεμα, ατος, τό, *disposition* of the stars at one's nativity, Thrasyll.in *Cat.Cod.Astr*.8(3).101, S.E.*M*.5.53, Vett.Val.78.25, etc.

διαθερίζω, *pass the summer*, Lyd.*Mag*.1.46. II. *cut asunder*, Hsch. s. v. διαμῆσαι.

διαθερμ-αίνω, *warm through*, Pl.*Ti*.65e, Arist.*Pr*.880^{b}11, etc.:—Pass., *to be heated*, Thphr.*CP*6.9.3; *to be overheated*, Hp.*Art*.50; by drinking, D.19.197, Plu.2.622c. **-ᾰσία**, ἡ, *warming effect*, Epicur.*Fr*.58. **-ος**, ον, *thoroughly warm* or *hot*, Hp.*VM*16, Antig.*Mir*.82. II. *of a hot temperament*, Arist.*Rh*.1389^{a}19; δ. καὶ θαρραλέοι Id.*Pr*.947^{b}24.

διαθέρομαι, *to be heated*, Agath.5.7.

διάθεσις, εως, ἡ, (διατίθημι) *placing in order, arrangement* (ἡ τοῦ ἔχοντος μέρη τάξις Arist.*Metaph*.1022^{b}1), Antipho Soph.24a; πολιτείας Pl.*Lg*.710b; τῶν ξενίων Id.*Ti*.27a. 2. *disposition* or *composition* in a work of art (opp. εὕρεσις), Id.*Phdr*.236a; opp. ἱστορία, μῦθος, Plb.34.4.1, Plu.*Arat*.32, etc.; δ. ᾠδῆς Eup.303; τῶν ἐπῶν Phryn.Com.55; *plan* of a building, Plu.*Per*.13; *subject* of a picture, etc., Polem.ap.Ath.5.210b; δ. μυθολογίας Plu.2.16b; *representation* in a play, Hero *Aut*.20.2: in pl., *word-painting*, Plu.2.17b; of geographical *description*, Str.1.1.16; *rhetorical art*, μετ' αὐξήσεως καὶ διαθέσεως Plb.2.61.1. b. in oratory, *delivery*, Plu.*Dem*.7; δ. σώματός τε καὶ τόνου φωνῆς Longin.*Rh*.p.194 H. 3. *disposition* of property, *will, testament*, = διαθήκη, Lys.*Fr*.44, Pl.*Lg*.922b. 4. *disposing of, sale*, τῶν περιόντων Isoc.11.14, cf. *PTeb*.38.10 (ii B.C.), Str.11.2.12, Plu.*Sol*.24; οἷς δ. εὔπορος, perh. *means of disposing of* it, *of making away with* it, Arist.*Rh*.1372^{a}33 (possibly, *inventive disposition*). 5. δ. ἔγγραφος written *report*, *POxy*.52.13 (iv A.D.). 6. = διάθεμα, Procl.*in Cra*.p.10 P. (pl.). II. (from Pass.) *bodily state, condition*, Hp.*VM*7, Arist.*GA*778^{b}34; δ. τοῦ σώματος Philem.95.4; δ. ὑγιεινή, νοσώδης, Gal.5.826, 17(2).238; ἕξις defined as δ. μόνιμος Id.5.826; νευρικὴ δ. *OGI*331.11 (Pergam.); of the mind, Antipho Soph.24a; ἕξις ψυχῆς καὶ δ. Pl.*Phlb*.11d; distd. from ἕξις, Arist.*Cat*.8^{b}28, *de An*.417^{b}15, Zeno and Chrysipp.*Stoic*.1.50, 3.111; δ. ἁμαρτωλός Phld.*Lib*.p.56 O., al.; δ. σωματική, ψυχική, A.D.*Synt*.278.10: pl., Diotog.ap.Stob.4.7.62. b. *disposition* towards persons, Pl.*R*.489a; *propensity*, Cic.*Att*.14.3.2; πρός τινα Sch.E.*Hec*.8. 2. generally, *state, condition*, τὴν βασιλείαν εἰς τὴν ἀρχαίαν δ. κατέστησεν *OGI* 219.11 (Sigeum, iv/iii B.C.). 3. Gramm., *force, function*, τοῦ ὀνόματος δ. εἰσὶ δύο, ἐνέργεια καὶ πάθος (e.g. κριτής, κριτός) D.T.637.29; esp. of the *voices* of the verb, δ. εἰσὶ τρεῖς, ἐνέργεια, πάθος, μεσότης Id.638.8; δ. παθητική, μέση, A.D.*Synt*.210.19, 226.10; also of tense, χρονικὴ δ. ib.251.1 (s.v.l.); διαβατικὴ δ. transitive *force*, ib.43.18.

διαθεσμοθετ-έω, *prescribe severally, ordain*, πάντα αὐτοῖς ταῦτα Pl.*Ti*.42d, cf. Iamb.*VP*16.68, Hierocl.*in CA*19p.460 M., Procl.*in Cra*.p.49 P. **-ησις**, εως, ἡ, in pl., *ordinances*, Herm.*in Phdr*.p.149 A.

διαθετ-ήρ, ῆρος, ὁ, = sq., Pl.*Lg*.765a, Them.*Or*.26.321d. **-ης**, ου, ὁ, (διατίθημι) *one who arranges, sets in order*, χρησμῶν τῶν Μουσαίου Hdt.7.6; οἴκου Dam.*Isid*.24; συνουσίας Procl.*in Prm*.p.479 S. **-ικός**, ή, όν, *affecting*, πάθος δ. ψυχῆς Anon.Lond.2.14.

διαθέω, aor. 1 part. διαθεύσας Vett.Val.345.35:—*run about, run to and fro*, Th.8.92, Jul.*Mis*.338c, etc.; of reports, *spread*, X.*Oec*.20.3; of a panic, Id.*Cyr*.6.2.13; ἀστέρες διαθέοντες *shooting* stars, Arist.*Mete*.342^{b}21. II. *run a race*, Pl.*Tht*.148c; τινί *with* or *against*.., Id.*Prt*.335e; πρός τινα Plu.2.58f: c. acc. cogn., δ. τὴν λαμπάδα *run* the torch-*race*, Id.*Sol*.1.

διαθεωρέω, *examine closely*, ὅθεν ἂν τὸ πλεῖον αὔξοιτο Phld.*Oec*.p.55 J., cf. S.E.*M*.7.438.

διαθηγή, v. διαθιγή.

διαθήκη, ἡ, (διατίθημι) *disposition* of property by will, *testament*, Ar.*V*.584, 589, D.27.13, etc.; κατὰ διαθήκην by *will*, *OGI*753.8 (Cilicia), *Test.Epict*.4.8, *BGU*1113.5 (i B.C.), etc.: in pl., διαθήκας διαθέσθαι Lys.19.39; θέσθαι *CIG*2690 (Iasus). II. αἱ ἀπόρρητοι δ. mystic *deposits* on which the common weal depended, prob. oracles (cf. διαθέτης), Din.1.9 codd. 2. name of an eyesalve, because the recipe was *deposited* in a temple, Aët.7.118. III. *compact, covenant*, ἣν μὴ διαθῶνται διαθήκην ἐμοί Ar.*Av.*440; freq. in Lxx, *Ge.* 6.18, al.; καινή, παλαιὰ δ., *Ev.Luc.*22.20, 2*Ep.Cor.*3.14; *disposition* (with allusion to I), *Ep.Gal.*3.15, cf. *Ep.Hebr.*9.15. IV. = διάθεσις II, σώματος δ. Democr.9.

δια-θηκημιαῖος, α, *testamentary*, *Sammelb.*5294 (iii A.D.):—also **-θηκιμαῖος**, *PMasp.*15.1.9, al. (vi A.D.).

διαθηκογράφος [γρᾰ], ον, *notary who drafts wills, Gloss.*

διαθηλύνω, strengthd. for θηλύνω, Thphr.*CP*1.16.6.

διάθημα, ατος, τό, = διάθεμα, Ptol.ap.Heph.Astr.2.11.

διαθηράω, *hunt*, θηρίον Philostr.*Im.*1.6: metaph., ὥραν μειρακίου ib.28.

διαθηριόω, strengthd. for θηριόω, Plu.2.330b.

διαθῐγή, ἡ, (διαθιγγάνω) *mutual contact*, Leucipp. and Democr.ap. Arist.*Metaph.*985^{b}15, al.; v.l. **διαθηγή**, perh. = διάθεσις (cf. θήγη· θήκη, θέσις, τάξις, Hsch.).

διαθλάω, *break in pieces*, Ael.*NA*4.21, Nonn.*D.*17.167:—Pass., Antyll.ap.Orib.45.10.5.

διαθλ-εύω, = sq. II, δ. πολλοὺς ἀγῶνας Vett.Val.359.29, cf. 248. 27. **-έω**, *struggle desperately*, πρός τινα Ael.*VH*5.6; ὑπὲρ τοῦ γάμου Conon 10. II. *struggle through*, βίον Hld.7.5; ἀγῶνας Hierocl.*in CA*14 p.450 M. **-ητέον**, verb. Adj., *one must fight it out*, Ph.2.471.

διαθλίβω [λῑ], *break in pieces*, Call.*Fr.*67.

διαθολόω, *darken*, ἡ σκιὰ τῆς γῆς δ. τὸ φέγγος Plu.*Daed.*4:—Pass., τῆς θαλάσσης διαθολωθείσης Id.2.978b.

διάθονται, sine expl., Hsch.

διαθορῠβέω, *render uneasy, disquiet*, τινά Th.5.29, Luc.*Alex.*31, Eun.*Hist.*p.222 D.: abs., *make a great noise*, Plu.*Galb.*18.

διά-θραυστος, ον, *easily broken*, Thphr.*Lap.*11. **-θραύω**, *break in small pieces*, in Pass., Pl.*Ti.*57b, Arist.*HA*616^{a}27; τῇ μασήσει Thphr.*CP*6.9.3.

διαθρ-έω, *look closely into, examine closely*, Ar.*Eq.*543, *Th.*658, Ael. *VH*3.28, Luc.*Am.*13; *peruse*, βύβλους Epicur.*Ep.*1 p.3 U.: abs., Ar. *Nu.*700. **-ησις**, εως, ἡ, *perspicacity*, ψυχῆς Eun.*VS* p.476 B.

διαθρῐαμβεύω, strengthd. for θριαμβεύω, θρίαμβον App.*Pun.*135.

διαθρίζω, shortd. from διαθερίζω, Q.S.8.322.

διαθροέω, *spread a report, give out*, ὡς Th.6.46; δ. ἐν ταῖς πόλεσιν ὅτι.., X.*HG*1.6.4:—Pass., D.C.53.19, 61.8.

διαθροίζω, *collect*, Gal.12.185.

διαθρῠλέω, *spread abroad*, mostly in pf. and plpf. Pass., *to be commonly reported*, διετεθρύλητο ὡς.. X.*Mem.*1.1.2; *to be hackneyed*, of a quotation, Plu.*Cim.*15. II. Pass., *to be talked deaf*, διαθρυλουμένους ὑπό σου X.*Mem.*1.2.37; διατεθρύλημαι ἀκούων Pl.*Ly.*205b; διατεθρυλημένος τὰ ὦτα Id.*R.*358c.

διαθρυμμᾰτίς, ίδος, ἡ, = θρυμματίς, Antiph.90.

διαθρύπτω:—Pass., aor. διετρύφην [ῠ] Il.3.363, διεθρύφθην D.L. 7.153, διεθρύβην [ῠ] Lxx *Na.*1.6:—*break in pieces*, τὸ κρανίον Luc. *DMort.*20.2; φλὸξ δ. τὴν τῶν λίθων ἰσχύν Procop.*Pers.*2.17:—Pass., once in Hom., τριχθά τε καὶ τετραχθὰ διατρυφέν [τὸ ξίφος] Il. l. c.; of a drug, *to be crushed*, Hp.*Mul.*1.74; ἀσπίδες διατεθρυμμέναι X.*Ages.* 2.14, cf. D.H.9.21. II. metaph., *break down* by profligate living and indulgence, *enervate, pamper*, τινά Pl.*Ly.*210e; σώματα X.*Lac.* 2.1:—Pass., *to be enervated*, πλούτῳ A.*Pr.*891 (lyr.); διὰ τὸν πλοῦτον X.*Mem.*4.2.35; ὑπὸ πολλῶν ἀνθρώπων ib.1.2.24; διατεθρύφθαι τὸν βίον Ael.*VH*13.8; τῷ βίῳ Plu.*Pomp.*18; διατεθρυμμένος τὰ ὦτα κολακείαις Id.*Dio* 8. Adv. διατεθρυμμένως, ἔχειν Pl.*Lg.*922c. 2. Med., *give oneself airs*; of a prudish girl, *to be coy*, Theoc.6.15; of a singer, διαθρύπτεται ἤδη *is beginning her airs and graces*, Id.15.99; of a doctor, *have an affected 'bedside manner'*, Gal.17(2).148.

διαθρώσκω, *shoot forth, flash through*, φῶς ἔξω διαθρῷσκον Emp. 84.5, cf. Dam.*Pr.*81, Epic. in *Arch.Pap.*7.3; of eggs, *slip through*, Opp.*H.*1.549: c. gen., κόλπου Nonn.*D.*8.397.

διάθῠρα, ων, τά, *lattice across the doorway* of a Greek house, Vitr. 6.7.5.

διαθωκέω, pf. Pass. διατεθώκηται:—*separate*, Hsch.

διαί, διαιβολία, v. διά, διαβολία.

διαῖγδην, Adv., (διαΐσσω) *bursting through*, Opp.*H.*3.119.

διαίθομαι, Pass., *to be kept warm*, ἐρίοισι Aret.*SD*1.11.

διαιθριάζω, *become clear and fine*, ἐδόκει διαιθριάζειν it seemed likely *to be fine*, X.*An.*4.4.10 (or, it seemed best *to bivouac*).

δίαιθρος, ον, *clear and fine*, Plu.*Sull.*7; also, = δίυγρος, Hsch.

διαιθύσσω, *move rapidly in different directions*, διαιθύσσοισιν αὖραι *change rapidly*, Pi.*O.*7.95. II. c. acc., ἐλπὶς διαιθύσσει φρένας *causes* the heart *to flutter*, B.*Fr.*16.4; *shake out*, Nonn.*D.*11.498, 20.190.

δίαιμος, ον, *bloody*, Hp.*Dent.*17; ὄνυξ E.*Hec.*656 (lyr.); δίαιμον ἀναπτύειν spit *blood*, Plu.*Arat.*52, cf. Plb.8.12.5; δίαιμα ἐκκρινόμενα Antyll.ap.Aët.9.40.

διαινέω, (αἶνος III) *decree, resolve*, τὸ διαινεθὲν ἄκυρον ἔστω *GDI* 2642.23 (Delph., ii B.C.).

δῐαίνω, aor. ἐδίηνα, *wet, moisten*, ὑπερῴην δ' οὐκ ἐδίηνε Il.22.495; ὄμμα διῆναι Heliod.Med(?).ap.Stob.4.36.8 (hex.); διαίνετο.. ἄξων Il. 13.30; οἴνῳ διαίνων ἔντερ' Axionic.8.3:—Med., διαίνεσθαι ὄσσε *wet one's* eyes, A.*Pers.*1064 (lyr.): and abs., *weep*, ib.258 (lyr.); δίαινε πῆμα. Ans. διαίνομαι *weep for* the woe—I *weep*, ib.1038 (lyr.), cf. Sch. ad loc., S.*Fr.*210.35.—Rare in Prose, Arist.*Mete.*387^{a}28.

διαιολάω, *cajole, deceive*, Hsch.

διαιρ-έσιμος, ον, *divisible, Gloss.* **-εσις**, εως, ἡ, *divisibility*, Arist.*Metaph.*1016^{b}4, al. 2. Medic., *dissection*, ζῴων Gal.4. 664. b. *venesection*, Antyll.ap.Orib.7.9.2. c. *surgical operation*, Phld.*Lib.*p.56 O. d. pl., *wounds*, Diod.Rh.p.53 H. II. *dividing, distribution*, of money, Hdt.7.144; of spoil, X.*Cyr.*4.5.55; ἐν διαιρέσει [ψήφων] *in the reckoning* of the votes *on either side*, A. *Eu.*749; ἀντίγραφον διαιρέσεως *BGU*1013.1 (i A.D.). III. *distinction*, ἀγνωσίας τε καὶ γνώσεως Pl.*Sph.*267b; [τῆς δημοκρατίας καὶ τῆς ὀλιγαρχίας] Arist.*Pol.*1294^{a}34. IV. in Logic, *division* of genus into species, τῶν γενῶν κατ' εἴδη δ. Pl.*Sph.*267d; ἡ διὰ τῶν γενῶν δ. Arist.*APr.*46^{a}31; opp. συναγωγαί, Pl.*Phdr.*266b. b. *separation* of subject and predicate, περὶ σύνθεσιν καὶ δ. ἐστι τὸ ψεῦδος καὶ τὸ ἀληθές Arist.*Int.*16^{a}12. 2. ὁ παρὰ τὴν δ. [λόγος] the fallacy of *division* (cf. σύνθεσις), Id.*SE*177^{a}33. V. Rhet., *division* or *distribution* into heads, Hermog.*Prog.*7, *Stat.*1, Onos.2 tit., etc. VI. Gramm., *resolution* of a diphthong into two syllables, A.D.*Pron.*87.2, al.; of one word into two, κατὰ διαίρεσιν ἀναγνωστέον Ath.11.492a, cf. Trypho *Trop.*1.8. VII. in Metric, *division of a line at the close of a foot, diaeresis*, Aristid.Quint.1. 24. VIII. Math., δ. λόγου *transformation* of a ratio *dividendo*, Euc. 5 *Def.*15; κατὰ διαίρεσιν Archim.*Sph.Cyl.*2.6. IX. *division* of troops, of the Roman *cohors*, J.*AJ*7.14.9. **-ετέον**, *one must divide* or *distinguish*, Pl.*R.*412b, *Lg.*874e, Porph.*Abst.*2.38; δίχα δ. Pl.*Sph.*265a; τινὰς ἀπ' ἀλλήλων Id.*Plt.*287b; διαιρετέον πόσαι διαφοραί Arist.*Pol.*1289^{b}12. 2. *one must open* a vein, Antyll.ap.Orib. 7.2 tit., Aët.16.90. **-ετήρ**, ῆρος, ὁ, = δατητής, *EM*249.46. **-έτης**, ου, ὁ, *divider, distributor*, Dam.*Pr.*273 (pl.). **-ετικός**, ή, όν, *logically distinguishable*, Pl.*Sph.*226c. 2. *able to divide, separative*, Arist.*Pr.*884^{b}35; δ. δύναμις Plu.2.1026d, cf. 952b. 3. *given to resolving diphthongs*, -κώτατοι οἱ Ἴωνες A.D.*Pron.*95.4. 4. *suited for breaking up*, λίθων Gal.19.694. II. in Logic, *by means of division*, ὅροι Arist.*APo.*91^{b}39; διαιρετική, ἡ, as a branch of Dialectic, Ammon.*in APr.*7.31, cf. Iamb.*Comm.Math.*20; δ. μέθοδος Gal.10. 115; δ. συλλογισμός *disjunctive* syllogism, with contradictory alternatives, *Stoic.*2.87. Adv. -κῶς Plu.2.802f. III. Rhet., *concerned with distribution under heads*, τέχνη Hermog.*Inv.*3.4, cf. *Stat.*6, Lib. *Decl.*49 *Intr.*2. **-ετός**, ή, όν (ός, όν S.*Tr.*163), *divided, separated*, opp. σύνθετος, X.*Cyr.*4.3.20; δ. τυραννίδες, of extreme oligarchies and pure democracies, Arist.*Pol.*1312^{b}37. b. *having divisions*, ἀμφορεῖς Id.*Ath.*68.3. 2. *divisible*, Parm.8.22; πᾶν συνεχὲς δ. εἰς ἀεὶ διαιρετά Arist.*Ph.*231^{b}16, cf. *EN*1106^{a}26; opp. ἀδιαίρετος, Id.*APo.* 92^{a}23; δ. ψυχή Id.*deAn.*411^{b}27; δ. πλοῖα *which can be taken to pieces*, D.S.2.16. Adv. -τῶς Dam.*Pr.*174. II. *divided, distributed*, μοῖραν γῆς διαιρετὸν νέμειν S. l. c. III. *distinguishable*, τύχας οὐ λόγῳ δ. not *to be determined* by argument, Th.1.84. **-έω**, *take apart, cleave in twain, divide*, διὰ δ' ἀμφοτέρους ἕλε κύκλους ἀσπίδος Il. 20.280; παῖδα κατὰ μέλεα διελών Hdt.1.119; δ. λαγόν *cut* it *open*, ib.123; δ. πυλίδα *break* it *open*, Th.4.110, 6.51; δ. τὴν ὀροφήν *tear away, pull down*, Id.4.48; τοὺς σταυρούς X.*An.*5.2.21; δ. τοῦ τείχους *take down* part of the wall, *make a breach* in it, Th.2.75; τὸ διῃρημένον *the breach*, ib.76, 5.3; διῃρημένοι τὸ ὑπόζωμα, of insects, Arist. *HA*556^{a}18; διαιρουμένος τὴν καρδίαν Phld.*Sign.*1. II. *divide*, δύο μοίρας Λυδῶν *divide* the Lydians *into* two parts, Hdt.1.94, cf. 4.148; δύο μερίδας D.48.12; δ. τριχῇ ψυχήν Pl.*Phdr.*253c; δ. εἰς τὸ ἐλάχιστον Arist.*Sens.*440^{b}5; εἰς ὁμοιομερῆ Id.*HA*486^{a}5 (Pass.):—Med., *divide for themselves*, κατ' ὀλίγας ναῦς διελόμενοι *distributing* their ships in small divisions, Th.4.11; τοῖς δικάζουσι δ. τὰ ὦτα *lending* an ear *to both* parties, Lib.*Or.*52.4; *divide among themselves*, τιμάς Hes.*Th.*112; τὴν λῃτην Hdt.9.85; κατὰ πόλεις τὸ ἔργον Th.7.19; τἀδικήματα D.45.38: abs., δ. κατὰ πόλεις Th.5.114:—Pass., διῃρημένοι κατ' ἀναπαύλας *divided* into relays, Id.2.75; διαιρήσομαι as fut. Pass., Pl.*Plt.*261c; διῄρητο τὰ τῶν Ἑλλήνων εἰς δύο D.10.51. 2. *break up*, opp. συντιθέναι, Pl.*Phd.*78c, etc. 3. *dispense*, φάρμακον Plu.2.73b. III. *distinguish*, τυραννίδος εἴδη δύο διείλομεν Arist. *Pol.*1295^{a}8, etc.; δ. πότερα.. X.*Oec.*7.26: abs., Ar.*Nu.*742:—Med., Pl.*Tht.*182c; δ. τοὺς ἀμείνους καὶ τοὺς χείρονας Id.*Lg.*950c; δ. περί τινος Id.*Chrm.*163d. 2. *determine, decide*, διαφορὰς διαιρέοντες Hdt.4.23; δίκας A.*Eu.*472; τοῦτο πρᾶγμα ib.488; ψήφῳ δ. τοῦδε πράγματος πέρι ib.630; τὰ ἀμφίλογα X.*Vect.*3.3, cf. Pl.*R.*571a, *Prt.* 314b, al.; κλήρῳ δ. τὸν νικῶντα Id.*Lg.*946b; δ. περί τινος Arist.*Ph.* 239^{b}13, etc.; διαιρείσθω πόσα εἴδη, etc., Id.*Pol.*1300^{b}18, etc.: abs., Ar. *Ra.*1100; also δ. εἴτε E.*Ba.*206 codd. 3. *define expressly*, Hdt.7. 16.γ' and 103:—Med., c. acc. et inf., Id.7.47. 4. Med., *interpret*, τέρας, σημεῖον, D.H.4.60, 9.6. IV. in Logic, *divide*, δ. κατ' εἴδη τὰ ὄντα Pl.*Phdr.*273e; *divide* a genus into its species, Arist.*APo.* 96^{b}15, al.:—Med., Id.*PA*642^{b}5. V. Math., *divide*, Pl.*Lg.*895e (Pass.); διελόντι, *dividendo*, Archim.*Sph.Cyl.*1.6, al. VI. *divide words, punctuate* in reading, Isoc.12.17, Arist.*Rh.*1401^{a}24 (Pass.); Gramm., *resolve* a diphthong or contracted form, διῃρῆσθαι Ἰακῶς A.D.*Pron.*38.17, cf. Corn.*ND*5, Hdn.*Philet.*p.456 P. (Pass.). VII. *allocate* revenues, *OGI*573.24 (Cilicia). **-ημα**, ατος, τό, *part divided, division*, Dam.*Pr.*201. 2. *logical division*, Simp.*in Cat.* 425.1. 3. in pl., gloss on φακῶν ἐρέγματα, Erot.

διαίρω, aor. διῆρα D.H.1.35:—*raise up, lift up*, δ. ἄνω τὸν αὐχένα X.*Eq.*10.3: metaph., *exaggerate*, τὰ πράγματα Ph.2.575:—Med., *rise, become prominent*, of the breasts, Hp.*Gland.*16; *lift up oneself*, πρὸς τὴν τῶν ὅλων θέαν Arist.*Mu.*391^{a}3: c. acc., *lift up what is one's own*, δ. τὴν βακτηρίαν Plu.*Lys.*15; τοὺς ἄκοντας Luc.*Tox.*40; τόσον δ. *take* so much *on oneself*, dub. l. in Pl.*Ax.*370b:—Pass., δ. πρός, εἰς ὕψος, Ph.2.510, 619: metaph., πρὸς ἀλαζονείαν Plu.2.

116e. II. *separate, remove,* τὸν πόλεμον ἀπό.. Plu.*Ages.*15:—Med., διαράμενος (sc. τοὺς πόδας) *with long strides,* Thphr.*Char.*3. 6. 2. δ. τὸ στόμα *open* one's mouth, D.19.112,207: hence Rhet., διηρμένος *lofty, sublime,* D.H.*Rh.*6.6, *Vett.Cens.*5.3, Longin.2.2, Hermog.*Id.*2.9; λέξις ib.1.1; ποιητική Luc.*Hist.Conscr.*45. III. intr. (sc. ἑαυτόν, etc.), *lift oneself over, cross,* τὸ πέλαγος, of swans, Arist.*Fr.*344; τὸν πόρον Plb.1.37.1; εἰς Σαρδόνα ib.24.5, etc.; τὴν ἀκτήν D.H. l.c.

διαισθ-άνομαι, *perceive distinctly, distinguish,* τι Pl.*Sph.*253d; τὰς διαφοράς Arist.*GA*780^{b}17, al.; διάστημα Aristox.*Harm.*p.14 M.: abs., Pl.*Phdr.*250b. **-ησις,** εως, ἡ, *clear perception,* Apolloph. *Stoic.*1.90, Numen.ap.Eus.*PE*14.9.

διαίσιον, τό, = Lat. *repudium, notice of divorce,* Just.*Nov.*22.6, al., *Cod.Just.*1.3.52.15.

διαΐσσω, Att. **-ᾴσσω** or **-ᾴττω** (wrongly written διάττω in codd., Arist.*Mete.*341^{b}35, etc.), aor. 1 διῇξα (v. infr.):—*rush* or *dart through* or *across,* πυρὸς λαμπρὸν διαΐσσει μένος B.3.54; λαγὸς ἐς τὸ μέσον διήϊξε Hdt.4.134: also c. acc., Λύκι' ὄρεα διᾴσσει S.*OT*208 (lyr.); of sound, ἀχὼ .. διῇξεν ἄντρων μυχόν A.*Pr.*133 (lyr.) (but φήμη διῇξε *spread abroad,* E.*IA*426); of pain, σπασμὸς διῇξε πλευρῶν S.*Tr.* 1083, cf. Hp.*Morb.*1.22; φρῖκαι διὰ τοῦ σώματος δ. Id.*Mul.*1.35; διᾴττοντες [ἀστέρες] *shooting* stars, Anaxag.ap.D.L.2.9, Arist.*Cael.* 395^{a}32, Gem.17.47.

διαϊστόω, *make an end of,* Πέργαμον Pi.*Pae.*6.96 (dub.); αὐτήν S.*Tr.*881.

διαισχύνομαι, strengthd. for αἰσχύνομαι, Luc.*Electr.*3.

δίαιτα [ῐ], ἡ, *way of living, mode of life,* τὰ τῆς οἴκοι δ. S.*OC*352; πτωχῷ δ. ib.751; σκληρὰς δ. ἐκπονεῖν E.*Fr.*525.5; δ. εὐτελέστεραι X. *Cyr.*1.3.2; δ. ἔχειν A.*Pr.*490; δίαιταν ἔχειν ἐν Κροίσου, παρὰ τῇσι γυναιξί, Hdt.1.36,136; ξυνήθη τὴν δ. μεθ' ὅπλων ποιεῖσθαι Th.1.6; δ. ποιεῖσθαι ἐν ὕδατι pass *one's life,* Hdt.2.68 (but δ. ἐποιήσατο τῶν παίδων he made them *live,* Id.2.2); δ. τῆς ζόης μεταβάλλειν Id.1.157, cf. Th.2.16; παρὰ τὴν δ. at *table,* Ath.12.519b. 2. δίαιτα τοῦ οὐρανοῦ· τὸ φαγεῖν, τὸ πιεῖν, Hsch. II. *dwelling, abode,* Arist.*EN* 1096^{a}27; κοινὴ θεῶν ἁπάντων δ. *OGI*383.27 (i B.C.); δ. πολιτικαί public *buildings,* J.*AJ*15.9.6; *room* (or, more often, *suite* of rooms), Ar.*Ra.*114, *CIG*3268 (prob. Smyrna), Plu.*Publ.*15; τὰς τῶν θεραπόντων δ. Id.2.515f; sailors' *quarters* in a ship, Moschion ap.Ath. 5.207c; of fishes, Arist.*Mu.*398^{b}32. 2. Medic., *prescribed manner of life, regimen,* Hp.*Vict.*1.1, Pl.*R.*404a, etc.; esp. of *diet,* Hp. *Fract.*36, Gal.*Thras.*35, etc. b. *state, condition,* ἕλκεος Aret.*SD* 2.4. III. at Athens and elsewhere, *arbitration,* S.*El.*1073 (lyr.), Lex ap.And.1.87; opp. δίκη, Arist.*Rh.*1374^{b}20; ἐμμένειν τῇ δ. Ar. *V.*524; δίαιταν ἐπιτρέψαι τινί Lys.32.2, Isoc.18.13, Is.5.31 (prob. l.); ὀφλεῖν τὴν δ. to have *judgement* against one, D.29.58. 2. *the office of arbiter,* δ. λαβεῖν Hyp.*Eux.*31. IV. *discussion, investigation,* ταῦτα μακροτέρας ἐστὶ δ. Str.1.1.7; δ. ποιήσασθαι περί τινος 15. 1.10. (Cf. διαιτάω.)

δῐαιτ-άριος, ὁ, (δίαιτα II. 1) Lat. *diaetarius, house-steward,* *Dig.*33. 7.12.42, *Gloss.*; title of a subordinate official, Lyd.*Mag.*3.21. **-άρχης,** ου, ὁ, = foreg., *Dig.* l.c., *Gloss.* 2. *ship's steward,* *Dig.*4.9.1. 3. **-άω,** impf. διῄτων D.H.2.75, also ἐδιαίτων *AB*91, in compos. κατ-εδιῄτα D.49.19: fut. διαιτήσω Id.29.58: aor. 1 διῄτησα Is.2. 31, Plu.*Pomp.*12, etc.; ἀπ-εδιῄτησα Is.12.12, D.40.17; κατεδ- Id. 21.84,96; μετεδ- Luc.*DMort.*12.3; Dor. διαίτᾱσα Pi.*P.*9.68: pf. δεδιῄτηκα D.33.31: plpf. κατ-εδεδιῃτήκει Id.21.85:—Med. and Pass., impf. διῃτώμην Pl.Com.168, Lys.32.8, etc., but 2 sg. ἐδιητῶ Lib.*Or.*64.93; Ion. διαιτώμην, -ᾶτο, Hdt.3.65, 4.95, part. διαιτεύμενος Hp.*Ep.*19 (*Hermes* 53.64): fut. διαιτήσομαι Lys.16.4:—pass. forms, aor. διῃτήθην Th.7.87, Is.6.15; διαιτήθην Hdt.2.112 (aor. Med. only κατα-): pf. δεδιῄτημαι Th.7.77, later διῄτημαι Hdn.6.9.5, Gal.6.249: plpf. ἐξεδεδιῄτητο Th.1.132.—The double augm. and redupl. is the rule in compds., but in the simple Verb occurs only in pf. (but δεδιαιτ- in Arist.*Ath.*53.4 Pap.) and plpf.:—*treat,* τινά πως Hp.*Aph.*1.7; δ. τοὺς νοσοῦντας οἴκοι Plu.*Cat.Ma.*23; κατὰ ποτόν δ. Hp.*Epid.*3.9:—Pass., διαιτᾶται σκέλος Id.*Art.*58, cf. Porph. *Abst.*1.2. 2. Med. and Pass., *lead one's life, live,* ἐπ' ἀγροῦ Hdt. 1.120, cf. 123, Th.1.6; παρά τινι Hdt.2.112, S.*OC*928; τοὺν δόμοισιν ἦν διαιτᾶσθαι γλυκύ ib.769; ἄνω, κάτω, *live* up or down-stairs, Lys.1.9; ἐν Πειραιεῖ Id.32.8; ἐν πύργῳ Aen.Tact.11.3; πολλὰ ἐς θεοὺς νόμιμα δ. *live in the observance of..,* Th.7.77; ἐν ὅπλοις ἀεὶ καὶ πολεμικοῖς ἔργοις διῃτημένος Hdn. l.c.; δ. ἀκριβῶς And.4.32; ἀνειμένως Th.2.39, cf. 1.6, etc.; δίαιταν δ. μοχθηράν Pl.*Ep.*330c. II. *to be arbiter* or *umpire,* Is.2.29: c. inf., διῄτησαν ἡμᾶς ἀποστῆναι ib. 31; οὗτος διαιτῶν ἡμῖν D.21.84: c. acc. cogn., δ. δίαιταν Arist.*Ath.* 53.5; also οἱ τὴν Οἰνηΐδα διαιτῶντες *the panel of arbitrators for* the tribe Oeneis, D.47.12. 2. c. acc. rei, *arbitrate on,* παισὶ φιλήματα Theoc.12.34; νείκη D.H.7.52. b. *decide, prove* a thing, Pi.*P.* 9.68. c. *investigate, discuss,* τι Str.2.2.1, al.; περί τινος ib.3.8; *criticize,* τινάς Id.1.2.1. 3. generally, *regulate, govern,* πόλιν Pi. *O.*9.66: abs., αὐτοτελῶς Phld.*D.*1.22, cf. 24. 4. *reconcile,* τινά τινι App.*BC*5.93. 5. *moderate, regulate,* Hld.3.10, al.; *administer,* τὰ ἐκ τῶν διαθηκῶν Luc.*Tox.*23. (Perh. formed from δια-ιτάω from διά and *ἰτάω (εἶμι 'ibo'); for sense II cf. διαβαίνω II. 4: δίαιτα is a post-verbal creation.)

διαιτέω, *turn by entreaty,* Lxx *Ju.*8.16 (Pass.).

δῐαίτ-ημα, ατος, τό, mostly in pl., *food, diet,* Hp.*VM*13; *sustenance, provisions,* X.*Mem.*1.6.5: in sg., δ. τὸ καθ' ἡμέραν Arist.*Pr.* 866^{b}3. 2. pl., *rules of life, regimen,* esp. in regard of *diet,* Hp. *VM*3: generally, *institutions, customs,* Th.1.6, X.*Ath.*1.8. 3. *abode,* Hld.2.26; ὁ νοῦς ἐμόν ἐστιν δ. (v.l. ἐνδ-) Ph.1.160. **-ημάτώδης,** ες, *to be treated by dieting,* of disease, Hp.*Ep.*19 (*Hermes* 53. 64).

δῐαιτ-ήσιμος, ον, *belonging to a* διαιτητής, Is.*Fr.*153. **-ησις,** εως, ἡ, *way of life,* *PLips.*64.58 (iv A.D.). **-ητέον,** *one must treat,* v.l. in Hp.*Vict.*1.27, cf. Agath.4.4. 2. c. acc., δ. τὴν τροφόν Sor.1. 93. **-ητήριον,** τό, (δίαιτα II. 1) in pl., *dwelling-rooms,* X.*Oec.*9.4: sg., *dwelling-place,* Procop.*Aed.*1.9. **-ητής,** οῦ, ὁ, *arbitrator, umpire,* Hdt.5.95, Pl.*Lg.*956c, etc.; τῆς γὰρ δίκης .. γίγνεταί μοι δ. Στράτων D.21.83; δ. ὁ μέσος Arist.*Pol.*1297^{a}6; esp. at Athens, Id. *Ath.*53, etc. II. in later Law, = *judex pedaneus,* *Cod.Just.*4.20. 15, etc. **-ητικός,** ή, όν, *of* or *for diet*: ἡ δ. (sc. τέχνη) *dietetics,* Hp.*Acut.*(*Sp.*)54; τὸ δ. μέρος τῆς ἰατρικῆς Plb.12.25^d.3, Gal.*Thras.* 33; also of persons, δ. ἰατρός ib.24. II. (δίαιτα IV) λόγος δ. *critical* discussion, Str.10.2.24. III. **-κόν,** τό, *decision of an arbitrator,* *PLips.*43.5 (iv A.D.). **-ητός·** ὁ μὴ κατὰ κλῆρον δικαστής, Hsch.

διαιτός· κριτής, Hsch.

διαιτοχορηγία, ἡ, *maintenance,* *PMasp.*151.185 (vi A.D.).

δίαιτρον· δίοπτρον διαφανές, Hsch.

διαίτωμα, ατος, τό, = δίαιτα III, *BCH*25.350 (Delph., ii B.C.).

διαιων-ίζω, *perpetuate,* τὸ γένος Ph.2.318:—Pass., Id.*Fr.*64 H.; but usu. intr., *to be eternal,* Id.2.190, al. **-ιος,** α, ον (also ος, ον Phld.*Piet.*80, Ph.2.569), *everlasting,* φύσις Pl.*Ti.*39e; εὐδαιμονία Phld. l.c., cf. Ph. l.c., Jul.*Or.*4.144c; ζῷα Phld.*Piet.*111. Adv. -ίως Procl.*Theol.Plat.*5.37, Syrian.*in Metaph.*103.28, Jul.*Or.*4.145a.

διαιωρέομαι, Pass., *float about, move to and fro,* Pl.*Ti.*78e.

διακαής, ές, (διακαίω) *burnt through, very hot,* cj. in Thphr.*Vent.* 21, cf. Gal.11.21, etc.; ἀήρ Luc.*Anach.*16; πυρετοί Simp.*in Cael.* 602.9: metaph., τῷ ζήλῳ δ. Luc.*Dom.*31. Adv. -ῶς Alciphr.1.27, Alex.Trall.*Febr.*2.

διακᾰθ-αίρω, aor. part. -άρας *IG*11(2).287 *A* 79:—*purge thoroughly,* Ar.*Ec.*847, Pl.*R.*399e, Apollod.3.6.7; κρουνούς *IG* l.c.; ἅλωνα *Ev. Luc.*3.17: metaph., [φιλοσοφία] τέχνας δ. Iamb.*Comm.Math.*16; τινὰ τοῦ αἰσχροῦ ὀνόματος Procop.*Goth.*1.4:—Med., of *one's own* stock, Pl.*Lg.*735c. II. *prune,* Thphr.*HP*2.7.2 (Pass.); δένδρα Ph.2. 207. **-ᾰρίζω,** = foreg., *Ev.Matt.*3.12 (s.v.l.). **-αρσις,** εως, ἡ, *thorough cleansing* or *purging,* Pl.*Lg.*735d; ὤτων Erot. s.v. διαπτερώσιες. II. *pruning,* Thphr.*HP*2.7.2, *CP*3.7.5, dub. l. in Corn.*ND* 27. **-αρτέον,** *one must purge, purify, clear* from incongruous associations, Dam.*Pr.*39.

διακαθ-έζομαι, Med., *take up position,* of an army, ἐπὶ τῶν ὀρῶν J.*BJ*1.15.6; *take each his own seat,* Plu.2.412f. **-ημαι,** = foreg., of an army, *take up position,* J.*AJ*14.16.1, Arr.*Epict.*3.4.4; of birds, *perch,* Plu.*Cic.*47. **-ιζάνω,** *sit down apart,* i.e. *alvum solvere,* Lxx *De.*23.13(14): metaph., *hold aloof,* δ. ὁ νοῦς Ph.1.72. **-ίζω,** *cause to sit apart,* X.*Oec.*6.6. II. intr., = foreg., Lxx 2*Ki.*11.1.

διακαινίζομαι, Med., *surrender, hand over,* τὰ ἱερὰ τοῖς βαρβάροις *PMasp.*4.9 (vi A.D.).

διακαίνω· *interneco,* *Gloss.*

διακαίω, *burn through, heat to excess,* Hdt.2.26: freq. in pf. part. Pass., γῆ διάθερμος καὶ διακεκαυμένη Arist.*Pr.*906^{b}13, cf. *Mete.*345^a 17; ἀὴρ δ. Thphr.*Vent.*21; δ. εἰς τὸ μελάντατον Luc.*Herc.*1; ἡ δ. ζώνη the *torrid* zone, Str.2.1.13, al.; κύκλος *Placit.*2.30.1; ὥρα ἔτους Ar.Did.*Epit.*26; δ. ὑπ. ὀργῆς πρόσωπον *flushed* with anger, J.*AJ*11. 6.9. 2. *inflame,* ἄνεμοι δ. τὰς κόρας *Gp.*2.26.2: metaph., *inflame, excite,* τινά Plu.*Thes.*6, al.: c. acc. cogn., δ. φιλοτιμίαν Theopomp. Hist.300:—Pass., Luc.*Cal.*14. 3. in Surgery, *brand, apply cautery across* or *throughout,* ἐς τὸ πέρην Hp.*Art.*11; πέρην ib.40 (Pass.); καυτῆρι τὸ πρόσωπον *Gp.*17.20.4.

διακᾰλᾰμάσαρκες, epith. of ἔριφοι, Lex Rhod.ap.Hsch. (expld. as feeding on καλάμη σπερμάτων).

διακᾰλέομαι, *urge on from all quarters,* κυνορτικὸν σύριγμα δ. by means of.., S.*Ichn.*167.

διακᾰλ-ίνδω, aor. διεκάλῑσα, *transport by means of rollers,* ξύλα prob. in *SIG*²587.158. **-ῖσις,** εως, ἡ, *transportation by means of rollers,* *IG*4.742.12 (Hermione).

διακαλλωπίζω, *adorn,* Hsch. s.v. πρῷρα (Pass.).

διακᾰλοκᾰγᾰθίζομαι, (καλοκἀγαθία) *vie with another in virtue,* τινί Diog.ap.Stob.3.4.111.

διακᾰλύπτω :—Pass., fut. -καλυφθήσομαι D.11.13:—*reveal,* βουλεύματα D.H.5.54, cf. J.*BJ*6.3.4, Plu.2.764b:—Med., διακαλύψασθαι τὸ ἱμάτιον *throw aside* one's cloak, Ael.*VH*5.19:—Pass., D. l.c.

διακάμπτω, *bend* or *turn about,* Lxx 4*Ki.*4.34, dub. in Gal.16. 137.

διακαμπῠλόω, *bend,* Suid. s.v. διεκιρνῶντο.

διάκαμψις, εως, ἡ, *bending,* of the body, in exercise, Archig.ap. Aët.12.1.

διακᾰνάσσω, only aor. 1, μῶν τὸν λάρυγγα διεκάναξέ σου; has aught *run gurgling through* thy throat? E.*Cyc.*157.

διακᾰπηλεύω, *sell by retail,* ὅτι τύχοιεν ἕκαστος D.Chr.8.9.

διακᾰρᾰδοκέω, *expect anxiously,* νύκτα Diph.35; πόλεμον Plu.*Ant.* 56.

διακάρδιος, ον, *heart-piercing,* ὀδύνη J.*AJ*19.8.2.

διακαρτερ-έω, *endure to the end,* Hdt.3.52; ἐς τὸ ἔσχατον Id.7.107; εἰς τὴν πατρίδα δ. *stand by* one's country, Lycurg.85; ἐν τῇ συμμαχίᾳ X.*HG*7.2.1: c. part., δ. πολεμῶν ib.4.8, cf. Plu.*Sert.*7: c. inf., δ. μὴ λέγειν τἀληθῆ *to be obstinate* in refusing to speak the truth, Arist.*Rh.*

1377ᵃ4. 2. c. acc., *bear patiently*, δ. τηλικαύτην ἡμέραν Alex.233; κακοπάθειαν δ. Plb.36.16.4. **-ησις**, εως, ἡ, *endurance, perseverance*, Marin.*Procl.*26 (pl.).

διακατελέγχομαι, Med., *confute thoroughly*, τισί *Act.Ap.*18.28.

διακατέχω, *hold fast*, Apollon.Cit.1, Ruf.*Anat.*4; *hold* in the mouth, Heraclid.Tarent.ap.Gal.12.958; of splinters of bone, Aët. 15.14; *keep in check*, ἐπιβολάς Plb.2.51.2, etc. II. *hold in possession*, ib.70.3; *inhabit*, ib.17.5; *occupy, hold*, Lxx *Ju.*4.7(6), Onos. 18; ξενικοῖς ὅπλοις τὴν πόλιν D.S.14.32; δ. ἐπαρχείαν, = Lat. *obtinere provinciam*, *OGI*441.108; ἱερωσύνην Decr.ap.J.*AJ*14.10.4: of the head of a school, [σχολὴν] δυ' ἔτη Phld.*Acad.Ind.*p.100 M., cf. p.108 M. III. *keep on foot*, τὸν πόλεμον D.S.15.82.

διακάτιοι, αι, α, = διακόσιοι, *IG*5(2).159 (Tegea), 2².1126.29 (Lex Amphictyonum), etc.

διακατ-οχή, ἡ, *holding in possession*, *SIG*742.54 (Ephesus, pl.); = Lat. *bonorum possessio*, *POxy.*1201.15 (iii A.D.), etc. **-οχος**, ον, *holding, possessing*, *Gloss.*, = Lat. *bonorum possessor*, *PSI*3.183 (v A.D.), etc.

διακαυλέω, *run to stalk*, Thphr.*CP*2.12.4.

διάκαυμα, ατος, τό, *burning heat*, f.l. in *AP*6.291.

διακαυνιάζω, (καῦνος) *determine by lot*, Ar.*Pax*1081 (hex.).

διάκαυσις, εως, ἡ, (διακαίω) *the use of cautery*, ἡ πέρην δ. Hp.*Art.* 40, cf. Antyll.ap.Aët.12.1. II. *burnt-up remains*, ἀστέρος *Placit.* 3.1.2.

διακαυτέον, *one must burn through*, *Gp.*17.25.

διακεάζω, *cleave asunder*, διὰ ξύλα δανὰ κεάσσαι Od.15.322, cf. A.R.4.392.

διακεδάννυμι, *scatter abroad*, δούρατα A.R.2.1126 (tm.); *shed abroad*, κῶμα Nic.*Al.*458 (tm.).

διάκειμαι, 3sg. subj. διάκηται Sapph.*Supp.*2.9; inf. -κεῖσθαι: fut. -κείσομαι: first in Hes.*Sc.*20:—serving as Pass. to διατίθημι, δ. ὑπό τινος X.*HG*4.1.33, cf. 6.5.1; *to be served at table*, Philostr.*VA*2.28; of troops, *to be stationed*, *POxy.*1204.7 (iii A.D.), etc.: but mostly, II. *to be in* a certain *state* of mind, body, or circumstances, *to be disposed* or *affected* in a certain manner, Hdt.2.83, etc.: freq. with Adv., ὡς διάκειμαι what *a state* I *am in!* E.*Tr.*113 (lyr.); δρᾶτε ὡς δ. ὑπὸ τῆς νόσου Th.7.77, etc.; σχεδόν τι οὕτω διεκείμεθα, τοτὲ μὲν γελῶντες κτλ. Pl.*Phd.*59a; μοχθηρῶς, φαυλότατα δ., *to be in a* sorry *plight*, Id.*Grg.*504e, *Erx.*405d; οὕτω δ. τὴν γνώμην ὡς.. Isoc.2.13; εὖ δ. τινί, *to be* well *disposed* towards him, Is.4.18; πρός τινα κακῶς δ. Lys.16.2; πρὸς τοὺς ἄρχοντας Isoc.3.10; φιλικῶς τινί, οἰκείως πρός τινα, X.*An.*2.5.27, 7.5.16: abs., *to be well-disposed*, πρός τινα Philostr.*VA*1.7 (cf. ἀπὸ τοῦ διακειμένου ἀκροασάμενος Id.*VS*2.10.1); ἐπιφθόνως δ. τινί *to be* envied *by* him, Th.1.75; ὑπόπτως τῷ πλήθει δ. *to be* suspected *by* the people, Id.8.68; ἐρωτικῶς δ. τῶν καλῶν *to be* in love *with*.., Pl.*Smp.*216d; ἀπλήστως δ. πρὸς ἡδονὴν X.*Cyr.*4.1.14; λύπῃ δ., = λυμαίνεσθαι, Hdt.2.162; τὸ διακείμενον, of the *intransitive* Verb, opp. τὸ ποιοῦν, Arist.*SE*166ᵇ14. 2. of things, *to be settled, fixed*, or *ordered*, τῶς οἱ διέκειτο Hes. l.c.; τὰ διακείμενα *conditions, terms*, ἐπὶ διακειμένοισι μουνομαχῆσαι Hdt.9.26; of a gift, ἄμεινον διακείσεται *it will be* better *disposed of*, X.*An.*7.3.17. 3. of property, etc., *to be situated*, *PGiss.*119.3 (v A.D.), etc.

διακείρω, Ep. aor. διέκερσα (v. infr.), prop. *cut through*, τένοντας A.R.1.430; νεῦρα D.H.14.10: metaph., μή τις..πειράτω διακέρσαι ἐμὸν ἔπος *make* it *null, frustrate* it, Il.8.8:—Pass., σκευάρια διακεκαρμένος *shorn of* his trappings, Ar.*V.*1313.

διακεκρῐμένως, Adv., (διακρίνω) *differently*, Arist.*HA*600ᵃ18. II. *specially*, δ. ἀρίστη Paus.10.33.7. III. *separately, distinctly*, Procl. *Inst.*176, Jul.*Or.*5.164d.

διακέλ-ευμα (better than -ευσμα), ατος, τό, *an exhortation, command*, Pl.*Lg.*805c. **-εύομαι**, *exhort, give orders, direct*, δ. τινὶ εἶναι, ποιεῖν, etc., Hdt.1.36, Lys.25.28, etc.; οὐ τοῦτό σοι διεκελευόμην, c. inf., Pl.*Euthphr.*6d; so δ. ὅπως.. Id.*R.*549e; also δ. τινί τι (sc. ποιεῖν) Id.*Sph.*218a, etc.: abs., Id.*Tht.*148e, etc. 2. *encourage one another*, Hdt.1.1, 3.77; freq. with ἀλλήλοις added, *cheer* one another *on*, X.*An.*4.8.3; δ. ἑαυτῷ Id.*Cyr.*1.4.13; δ. τοῖς θέουσι Pl. *Phd.*61a. 3. *admonish, inform*, τινὶ περί τινος Isoc.9.78.—The Act. only in Suid. **-ευσμός**, ὁ, *exhortation, cheering on*, Th.7. 71, J.*AJ*3.2.4. **-ευστέον**, *one must direct*, προστάξεις τισί Pl.*Lg.* 631d.

δια-κενῆς or better **διὰ κενῆς** (sc. πράξεως), Adv. *in vain, idly, to no purpose*, Hp.*Epid.*7.5, E.*Tr.*758, Th.4.126; δ. ἄλλως Ar.*V.*929; μάτην δ. Pl.Com.174.21. **-κενος**, ον, *empty, hollow*, σφαῖρα Sor. 1.93; τὸ δ. *gap, breach*, Th.4.135, 5.71; τὸ δ. τοῦ ὀδόντος Antyll.ap. Orib.10.36.3; *interval*, Aristox.*Harm.*p.26 M.; τὰ δ. *hollows*, Pl.*Ti.* 58b, 60e; διάκενον δεδορκότα with *a vacant* stare, of skeletons, Luc. *Nec.*15. II. *empty* or *vain*, Pl.*Lg.*820e; δ. ἐλκυσμός, of *idle* fancies, Chrysipp.*Stoic.*2.22. Adv. -νως, ἕλκειν τὴν διάνοιαν Iamb. *Myst.*2.10; κοπιᾶν Macar.1.99. III. *thin, lank*, Plu.*Lyc.*17; δ. καὶ λαγαροί Id.*Publ.*15; δ. τοὺς βουβῶνας Philostr.*Gym.*37. IV. *porous*, Gal.8.672; δ. ἄρτοι *light* bread, Lxx *Nu.*21.5. V. Adv. διακένως, ζώνη δ. ὑφασμένη of a *gauzy* texture, J.*AJ*3.7.2. **-κενόω**, *empty outright*, Hp.*Nat.Puer.*30 (Pass.).

διακεντ-έω, *pierce through, make a puncture*, Hp.*Acut.*(*Sp.*)61:—Pass., *to be adorned with openwork*, Corn.*ND*24. **-ησις**, εως, ἡ, *piercing through*, of the teeth, Hp.*Dent.*11. **-ητέον**, *one must pierce, puncture*, Herod.Med. in *Rh.Mus.*58.85, *Gp.*17.19.2.

διακέν-ωμα, ατος, τό, *space, interval*, Pall. in Hp.*Fract.*12.282 C. **-ωσις**, εως, ἡ, *emptying out*, Hsch. s.v. διελάφυξας.

διᾰκέομαι, *repair*, *IG*11.154*A*10, 199*A*69, 103 (Delos, iii B.C.).

διακεράννῠμαι, Pass., *to be mixed up with*, τοῦ λόγου Philostr.*VS* 2.12.2.

διακερμᾰτίζομαι, *get changed into small coin*, δραχμήν Ar.*V.*789.

διακερτομέω, strengthd. for κερτομέω, *to mock at*, D.C.43.20.

διακεφᾰλαιῶσαι, gloss on διαπηνηκίσαι, Hsch. **διακεχλῐδέναι**· θρύπτεσθαι, and -κεχλιδώς (-οιδῶς cod.)· διαρρέων ὑπὸ τρυφῆς, Id.; cf. χλιδή.

διακεχῠμένως, Adv., (διαχέω) *immoderately*, δ. γελᾶν Suid. s.v. ἀπασκαρίζειν.

διακεχωρισμένως, Adv., (διαχωρίζω) *distinctly*, Suid. s.v. διακεκριμένως, Sch.Opp.*H.*1.498.

διακηρῡκεύομαι, *negotiate by herald*, πρός τινας Th.4.38.

διακήρῡξις, εως, ἡ, *sale by auction*, and Adj. **διακηρυκτικός**, ή, όν, *pertaining to such a sale*, *Gloss.*

διακηρύσσω, *proclaim by herald*, ἐν διακεκηρυγμένοις in *declared war*, Plu.*Arat.*10: metaph., ἀσεβὲς εἶναι.. Phld.*Herc.*862.12. 2. Med., = διακηρυκεύομαι, D.S.18.7. 3. *sell by auction*, τὴν οἰκίαν Philostr.*VS*2.21.1 (Pass.); τὴν οὐσίαν Plu.*Cic.*33. 4. *celebrate*, ἡ παροιμία δ. τινά Iamb.*VP*6.30.

διακιβδηλεύω, *corrupt*, Suid. s.v. Ἀδάμ.

διακιγκλίζω, strengthd. for κιγκλίζω, Hp.*Art.*79, Ar.*Fr.*29.

διακινδῡν-ευτέον, *one must risk*, τὸ φάναι Pl.*Ti.*72d: abs. in pl., ἐδόκει -ευτέα εἶναι Arr.*An.*1.1.8. **-εύω**, *run all risks, make a desperate attempt*, abs., ἀλόγως δ. Th.8.27; δ. τῷ σώματι Antipho 5.63; ἐς τὰς Ἐπιπολάς Th.7.47; πρὸς ὀλίγας [ναῦς] Id.1.142: c. inf., Id.7. 1; δ. ὑπὲρ τῆς Ἑλλάδος Lys.2.20; πρὸ βασιλέως X.*Cyr.*8.8.4; περὶ τῶν ὅλων D.*Ep.*3.12 (simply, *run the risk*, c. acc. et inf., δ. ἢ χρηστὸν [τὸ σῶμα] γενέσθαι ἢ πονηρόν Pl.*Prt.*313a):—Pass., διακεκινδυνευμένα φάρμακα *desperate* remedies, Isoc.11.22.

διακῑν-έω, *move slightly*, ἄρθρον Hp.*Art.*9:—Pass., *to be put in motion, move*, Hdt.3.108, Hp.*Art.*30; of *mincing* gait, Ar.*V.*688, Luc.*Merc.Cond.*16. 2. *throw into disorder, confound*, τὰ πεπραγμένα Th.5.25; *agitate*, τὰ συμμαχικά Plu.*CG*10; τὴν γνώμην Philostr. *VA*2.36. II. *sift thoroughly, scrutinize*, τὸν νοῦν Ar.*Nu.*477; τινὰ περί τινος Sosip.1.22. **-ημα**, ατος, τό, *displacement of a bone, partial dislocation*, Hp.*Fract.*37 (pl.), Gal.19.461, Id.ap.Orib. 47.5.1. **-ησις**, εως, ἡ, *slight movement*, Gal.18(1).742.

διάκινον· δυσκίνητον (Cret.), Hsch.; cf. διακόνιν.

διακιρνάω, *mix well*, τί τινι or ἔν τινι, Hp.*Vict.*2.56, *Int.*45.

διακίχρημι, *lend to various persons*:—Pass., διακεχρημένον τάλαντον D.27.11.

διά-κλᾰσις, εως, ἡ, *breaking-up* of light-rays, Procl.*Hyp.*7.14. **-κλάω**, *break in twain*, τόξα..χερσὶ διακλάσσας (Ep. for -κλάσας) Il. 5.216. II. Pass., = διαθρύπτομαι, διακλᾶσθαι Ἰωνικῶς *practise soft* Ionian airs, cj. in Ar.*Th.*163; διακεκλασμένος *enervated*, Luc.*Demon.* 18; δ. ὄμμα prob. in Zeno *Stoic.*1.58; διακλώμενοι ῥυθμοί, opp. ἀνδρώδεις, D.H.*Dem.*43, cf. *Comp.*17.

διά-κλεισις, εως, ἡ, *closing*, εἰσόδων τῶν πρός τινα J.*AJ*18.6.4. **-κλείω**, *shut out* or *off*, χορηγίας τινί Plb.1.82.13; τινὰ ἀπὸ τῆς χώρας ib.73.6; τινὰ τῆς εἰσόδου D.H.11.14: c. inf., διεκλείσθη συμμετασχεῖν J.*BJ*1.19.1. II. *close*, τὸ στόμα τοῦ Πόντου App.*Mith.*12.

διακλέπτω, *steal at different times*, ὅσα δὲ διακέκλεπται D.27.12; τὸ δὲ διακλαπὲν πολὺ *the number stolen* [by the soldiers] *and dispersed* was great, Th.7.85, cf. Plu.*Nic.*27:—Med., *steal away*, Lxx 2 *Ki.*19. 3(4). II. *keep alive* or *save by stealth*, τινά Hdt.1.38; ἑαυτήν Plu. *Sull.*22. III. *evade*, τῇ ἀπολογίᾳ δ. τὴν κατηγορίαν Lys.26.3; δ. τοῖς ἑαυτοῦ λόγοις τὴν ἀλήθειαν D.29.5; *disguise*, τῇ χάριτι τῆς συνθέσεως τὴν ἀνάγκην D.H.*Comp.*18; *pass in evasion of duty*, τὸν λοιπὸν χρόνον τῆς ὑπατείας Id.10.54.

διακληρονομέω, *disperse*, Longin.12.4 (Pass.).

διακληρ-όω, Dor. -κλᾱρόω, *assign by lot, allot*, ἐφ' ἑκάστῃ..φερνήν A.*Supp.*978 (anap.), cf. Arist.*Ath.*30.3, 50.2; ἐπὶ τὰς φυλάς *SIG*531. 29 (Dyme, iii B.C.):—Med., *have allotted to one*, τῦφον ἐκ νόμων Diog. *Ep.*28.1, cf. Procop.*Goth.*4.20, al.:—Pass., Pl.*Lg.*760c. 2. *choose by lot*, X.*Cyr.*6.3.36; τὸ δέκατον δ. θανεῖν, of *decimating* soldiers, App. *BC*2.47:—Med. c. acc., ib.18, Iamb.*Myst.*1.5, al.: but usu. abs., *cast lots*, Th.8.30, X.*Cyr.*6.3.34; πρὸς σφᾶς αὐτούς D.59.103. **-ωσις**, εως, ἡ, *allotment, apportionment*, App.*BC*1.14, Iamb.*Myst.*2.3. 2. perh. f.l. for ἀποκλήρωσις, Porph.*Abst.*1.41.

διακλῑμᾰκίζω, strengthd. for κλιμακίζω, Pl.Com.124.

δια-κλίνω [ῑ], *turn away, retreat from*, τῆς ἀγορᾶς Plb.11.9.8; ἀπό τινος Id.6.41.11. 2. c. acc., *evade, shun*, Id.35.4.6; φίλημα Plu. *Alex.*54. 3. *bend*, πῆχυν Philostr.*Im.*2.18. **-κλῐσις**, εως, ἡ, *avoidance of battle, retreat*, Plu.*Pyrrh.*21.

διακλονέω, *shake violently*, Hsch.

δια-κλύζω, *wash, wash out*, ἄντρ' ἃ πόντος νοτίδι δ. E.*IT*107; οἴνῳ τι Ath.9.381b:—Med., *wash out one's mouth*, Hp.*Epid.*7.2, Arist. *Pr.*948ᵃ2; *use a clyster*, Hp.*Aff.*27:—Pass., *to be washed out*, θερμῷ with hot water, Arist.*GA*739ᵇ12. **-κλυσμα**, ατος, τό, *lotion for washing out the mouth*, Gal.11.839; ὀδονταλγίας δ. to prevent toothache, Dsc.1.43, cf. 96, Apollonius ap.Gal.12.864, cf. Id.11.879. **-κλυσμός**, ὁ, *clyster*, Dsc.2.156. **-κλυστήριον**, τό, = ψυκτήρ, Suid. s.v. κύλιξ ῥοπαλωτή.

διακναίω, *scrape* or *grate away*, ὄψιν δ. *gouge out* his eye, E.*Cyc.* 487 (lyr.):—Pass., *to be lacerated*, Hp.*Mul.*2.120; διακναιομένης κάμακος the spear *being shivered*, A.*Ag.*65 (anap.). 2. *wear out, wear away*, ἡ ἀσιτίη δ. Hp.*Morb.*1.13; πόθος μ' ἔχει διακναίσας Ar.*Ec.*957, cf. E.*IA*27 (lyr.), *Heracl.*296 (lyr.); δ. Ὀρέστην *murder* Orestes (i.e.

the character, by bad acting), Stratt.1:—Pass., *to be worn quite away, destroyed*, αἰκίαις, μόχθοις, A.*Pr.*94,541 (lyr.), cf. E.*Med.*164 (lyr.), *Alc.*109 (lyr.); πόλις διακναισθήσεται Ar.*Pax* 251; τὸ χρῶμα διακεκναισμένος *with all one's* colour *scraped off*, Id.*Nu.*120.

διακνημόομαι, = διακναίω, in aor. 1 διεκνημώσατο, Hsch.

διακνίζω, *pull to pieces*, ἄνθεα *AP*4.1.32 (Mel.), cf. Dsc.1.44, al.; *make incisions in*, Orib.9.40.2:—Pass., Arist.*HA*570^{a}18, 583^{b}16. 2. metaph., *pick to pieces* (by attacking), δ. καὶ συκοφαντεῖ D.H.*Dem.* 35, cf. Phld.*Ir.*p.4 W. (dub.).

διακοιλαίνω, *hollow out*, Sch.Od.4.438.

διάκοιλος, ον, *quite hollow*, D.S.17.115.

διακοινοποιέω, *use interchangeably*, ὀνόματα Sch.Pi.*P.*4.25.

διακοιρᾰνέοντα· βασιλικῶς ἐπερχόμενον, ἢ ὡς κοίρανον διαπορευόμενον, διέποντα, Hsch.

διακολᾰκεύομαι, *vie with each other in flattery*, Isoc.12.159:—Act. only as v.l. in Sch.E.*Or.*714.

διακολάπτω, *dress stone with a chisel*, Agath.2.19:—also **διακολαπτηρίζω**, *IG*7.3073.185 (Lebad.).

διᾰκολλ-άω, *glue together*, Luc.*Ind.*16:—Pass., λίθῳ διακεκολλημένος *formed* of stones *morticed together*, Id.*Hipp.*6. **-ημα**, ατος, τό, *stuffing*, Eup.409. **-ησις**, εως, ἡ, *joining together*, σωλήνων *PLond.*3.1177.305 (ii A.D.). **-ητικός**, prob. f.l. for διακωλυτικός, ἔργα Poll.7.209.

διᾰκολουθέω, strengthd. for ἀκολουθέω, v.l. in S.E.*M.*7.275.

διακολυμβάω, *dive and swim across*, ἀπὸ τῶν πειρατῶν *IG*12(5).653.29 (Syros); πρός τινα Plb.5.46.8, cf. Lxx 1*Ma.*9.48, Palaeph.27; τὸν Τίβεριν D.S.14.116.

διακομ-ῐδή, Dor. -ῐδά, ἡ, *carrying over*, τῶν ἀνδρῶν ἐς τὴν νῆσον Th.3.76. II. (from Pass.) *passage, voyage*, ἐκ Κρήτας εἰς Ῥόδον *SIG*581.23 (Crete, ii B.C.). **-ίζω**, *carry over* or *across*, ἐς τὴν νῆσον Th.3.75; πέντε σταδίους δ. τινά Hdt.1.31; simply, *convey*, Luc.*Merc.Cond.*27, *PLips.*34.5 (iv A.D.):—Med., *carry over what is one's own*, δ. παῖδας Th.1.89:—Pass., *to be carried over*, ib.136, Pl.*Lg.* 905b; *pass over, cross*, Th.3.23, And.3.30. II. *recover, revive*, τινὰ σιτίοισι Hp.*Morb.*2.51.

διάκομμα, ατος, τό, *cut, gash*, Hp.*Prorrh.*2.15, Gal.12.816. II. *breach* in an embankment, *PPetr.*3p.80, al.

διακομπάζω, *boast one against the other*, πολλὰ δὴ διεκόμπασας σὺ κἀγώ Ar.*V.*1248 (Burges for -κομίσας).

διακομπέω, strengthd. for κομπέω, Pi.*Fr.*157, Posidon.41.

διᾱκον-έω, Ion. **διηκ-**, impf. ἐδιακόνουν E.*Cyc.*406 (dub.), Alc. Com.13, Nicostr.Com.36; later διηκόνουν *Ev.Matt.*4.11: fut. -ήσω Hdt.4.154, Pl.*Grg.*521a: aor. διηκόνησα Aristid.2.198 J.; inf. -ῆσαι Antipho 1.16: pf. δεδιακόνηκα Arched.3.8:—Med., impf. διηκονούμην Luc.*Philops.*35: fut. -ήσομαι Id.*DDeor.*4.4: aor. διηκονησάμην Id. *Tyr.*22:—Pass., fut. δεδιακονήσομαι J.*AJ*18.8.7: aor. ἐδιακονήθην D.50.2: pf. δεδιακόνημαι, v. infr. II: (διάκονος):—*minister, do service*, abs., E.*Ion* 396, Ar.*Av.*1323, *POxy.*275.10 (i A.D.): c. dat. pers., *serve*, D.19.69, etc.; δ. διακονικὰ ἔργα Arist.*Pol.*1333^{a}8; δ. ὑποθήκαις τινός Antipho 1.17; δ. παρὰ τῷ δεσπότῃ Posidipp.2; δ. πρὸς ὠνήν τε καὶ πρᾶσιν Pl.*R.*371d:—Med., *minister to one's own needs, serve oneself*, S.*Ph.*287; αὐτῷ διακονεῖται Ar.*Ach.*1017; διακονοῦντες καὶ διακονούμενοι ἑαυτοῖς *acting as servants* and *serving themselves*, Pl.*Lg.*763a: also simply like Act., οἶνον ἡμῖν χρυσίῳ διακονούμενοι Luc.*Asin.*53, cf. Lib.*Or.*53.9:—Pass., *to be served*, οὐκ ἦλθε διακονηθῆναι ἀλλὰ διακονῆσαι *Ev.Matt.*20.28. 2. *to be a deacon*, 1*Ep.Ti.*3.10,13. II. c. acc. rei, *render a service*, τινὶ ὅ τι ἂν δεηθῇ Hdt.4.154, cf. Pl.*Plt.*290a; δ. γάμους Posidipp.26.19:—Pass., *to be supplied*, τῇ πόλει ἐδιακονήθησαν [αἱ πράξεις] D.50.2; τῶν καλῶς δεδιακονημένων Id.51.7: c. dat. instr., ἐκπώμασι διακονείσθωσαν *OGI*383.159 (i B.C.). **-ημα**, ατος, τό, *servants' business, service*, δουλικὰ δ. Pl.*Tht.*175e; δ. ἐγκύκλια Arist.*Pol.*1255^{b}25, cf. *CIG*2811 *b* 24 (Aphrodisias, prob.). 2. *service* rendered to a god, Jul.*Or.*2.68c. II. pl., *instruments* or *utensils of service*, Ath.6.274b, Diog.*Ep.*37.3. **-ησις**, εως, ἡ, *serving, doing service*, Pl.*Lg.*633c. **-ητικός**, ή, όν, *pertaining to service*, Alex. Aphr.*de An.*59.14. **-ία**, ἡ, *service*, Th.1.133 (pl.), Pl.*R.*371c, etc.; οὐκ ἔστι ταῦτ' ἀρχή, ἀλλ' ἐπιμέλειά τις καὶ δ. Aeschin.3.13. 2. *attendance on a duty, ministration*, D.18.206; ἡ δ. ἡ καθημερινή, of *ministering* to external wants, *Act.Ap.*6.1; but also ἡ δ. τοῦ λόγου ib.4, cf. 1.17, etc. II. *body of servants* or *attendants*, Plb.15.25.21. III. *instruments of service*, = διακόνημα II, Moschio ap.Ath. 5.208b. **-ικός**, ή, όν, *serviceable*, Ar.*Pl.*1170, etc.; -κή (sc. τέχνη), ἡ, Pl.*Plt.*299d; δ. φύσις Id.ap.Plu.2.416f: Comp. -ώτερος Id. *Grg.*517b; αἱ δ. πράξεις, τὰ δ. ἔργα *servants'* business, *menial* work, Arist.*Pol.*1277^{a}36, 1333^{a}7; δ. ἀρεταί ib.1259^{b}23. Adv. -κῶς *in the course of service*, Men.113; *serviceably*, Sor.1.80.

διακόνιν· δυσκίνητον (Cret.), Hsch.; cf. διάκινον.

διᾱκονίομαι [νῑ], Pass., *roll in the dust*, Hp.*Ep.*27 (Oratio Thessali): hence, *prepare for combat*, Plu.2.970f.

διακόνιον, τό, a sort of *cake*, Pherecr.156.

διακονίς, ίδος, ἡ, a kind of coarsely woven *tunic*, Hsch.; also ἄνθρωπος ὁ μὴ πυκνὸς δ., Id.

διᾱκόνισσα, ἡ, *deaconess*, *IG*3.3527.

διάκονος [ᾱ], Ion. **διήκονος**, ὁ, later **διάκων** (q.v.):—*servant*, Hdt. 4.71,72, *PFlor.*121.3 (iii A.D.), etc.; *messenger*, A.*Pr.*942, S.*Ph.* 497; ὄρνιθα καὶ κήρυκα καὶ δ. Id.*Fr.*133:—as fem., Ar.*Ec.*1116, D. 24.197. 2. *attendant* or *official* in a temple or religious guild, *Inscr.Magn.*109,217, *IG*9(1).486 (Acarnania, ii/i B.C.), 4.774.12 (Troezen, iii B.C.): fem., *CIG*3037 (Metropolis in Lydia):—esp. in the Christian church, *deacon*, 1*Ep.Ti.*3.8, etc., *POxy.*1162.3 (iv A.D.): fem., *deaconess*, *Ep.Rom.*16.1. II. as Adj., *servile, menial*, ἐπιστήμη Pl.*Plt.*290c: irreg. Comp. διᾱκονέστερος Epich.159 Ahr. (Cf. ἐγ-κονέω, ἀ-κονιτί.)

διᾱκοντ-ίζομαι, Att. fut. -ιοῦμαι, *contend with others at throwing the javelin*, X.*Cyr.*1.4.4; τινί Thphr.*Char.*27.13; simply, *hurl darts*, J.*BJ*4.3.12, 5.7.3. **-ισμός**, ὁ, *competition in javelin-throwing*, *OGI*339.68.

διακόντωσις, εως, ἡ, = κόντωσις, Ael.*NA*12.43.

διακοπή, ἡ, *gash, cleft*, as in the skull, Hp.*VC*7, Gal.7.38; *deep-seated wound*, Id.18(1).27; διακοπαὶ σωμάτων Plu.*Mar.*19; *severance* of a musical string, Theo Sm.p.71 H. b. *rupture* of a blood-vessel, Gal.19.457. II. *cutting* or *canal* through an isthmus or mountain, Str.1.3.18 (pl.); through a wall or dam, *BGU*1188.8 (i B.C.); *narrow channel* or *passage*, Lxx *Jb.*28.4, al., cf. J.*AJ*7.4.2. III. *divorce*, Sm.*De.*24.3(1). IV. metaph., *breach, rupture, quarrel*, Lxx *Jd.*21.15: pl., δ. φίλων Vett.Val.3.2. V. *refutation*, λόγων Phld.*Rh.*1.11 S., al. VI. *intermission*, Herod.Med.ap.Orib. 6.20.19. VII. Gramm., *tmesis*, Charis.p.275 K.

διάκοπος, ὁ, *breach* in a dyke, *POxy.*1409.16 (iii A.D.), Ulp.ap. *Dig.*47.11.10. II. *chopping up* of firewood, *PGoodsp.Cair.*30.4, al. (ii A.D.). III. (sc. λόγος) *formula* or *spell for producing breach* or *separation*, esp. between husband and wife, *PMag.Leid.V.*11.15.

διάκοπρος, ον, *well-manured*, Thphr.*CP*4.12.3.

δια-κοπτέον, *one must cut short*, πρεσβείας ἀκαίρους Plu.2.819a. **-κόπτω**, *cut in two, cut through*, διὰ δέρην ἔκοψε μέσσην Anacr.80, cf. Th.2.4, X.*An.*7.1.17, etc.; χῶμα Wilcken *Chr.*11 *B* 6 (ii B.C.); ἰσθμόν Str.1.3.18; *gash*, σκέλος Men.*Georg.*48:—Pass., *receive a gash*, Hp.*Aph.*6.18, al., Plb.2.30.7; so διακέκοπται of base coin which *had a hole drilled* in it, Suid. 2. *break through* the enemy's line, δ. τάξιν X.*An.*1.8.10; τὴν φάλαγγα Plu.*Pyrrh.*7; τεῖχος Aen. Tact.32.7: abs., *break through* the enemy's line, X.*HG*7.5.23, etc.; διακεκοφότας πρὸς τὰς εἰσόδους Id.*Cyr.*3.3.66; so, of a weapon, δ. ἄχρι τοῦ διελθεῖν Luc.*Nigr.*37: metaph. of a remedy, *have decisive effect*, *SIG*1170.16 (Epid.). 3. *break off, interrupt*, τὴν περίοδον Arist.*Rh.*1409^{b}9 (Pass.); δ. τὰς διαλύσεις Plb.1.69.5; συνθήκας Id. 18.42.3; ἑορτήν, ῥῆσιν, Luc.*Lex.*11, *Dom.*14; ὕπνον Ael.*NA*3.37:—Pass., of the pulse, Gal.8.459; also, *to be checked*, τὰ πρὸς ἑταίρας δ. σωφρονισμοῖς Plu.2.712c; διακέκομμαι τὸ στόμα *I am struck dumb*, Men.*Sam.*334. 4. *refute*, in Pass., Phld.*Sign.*11.

διακόρ-ευσις, εως, ἡ, = διακόρησις, Sor.1.25, al. **-εύω**, (κόρη I) *deflower*, Ar.*Th.*480, Ephor.164, Sor.1.8, Luc.*DMeretr.*11.2, Artem. 2.65. **-έω**, = foreg., Luc.*Tox.*25:—Pass., Ael.*NA*11.16. **-ής**, ές, = διάκορος, τινός Pl.*Lg.*629b, Max.Tyr.7.6, D.C.61.13, Jul.*Or.*2.65d: abs., Plu.*Lyc.*15. **-ησις**, εως, ἡ, *deflowering*, prob. l. in J. *AJ*7.8.1, Sor.1.33, Sch.Il.18.493. **-ίζω**, = διακορέω, Hsch. s.v. δια(κε)κόρισται. II. Med., (κόρη III) *gaze intently*, Id.

διακορκορῠγέω, *rumble through*, τὴν γαστέρα Ar.*Nu.*387.

διάκορος, ον, *satiated*, c. gen., ἀλλήλων X.*Lac.*1.5: abs., σῶμα δ. Plu.2.996a; *saturated* with rain, Hdt.3.117; δ. ἤδη τοῦτο this is *quite enough*, Gal.7.498. Adv. -ρως *immoderately*, πίνειν D.C.68.7.

διᾱκοσι-άκις, Adv. *two hundred times*, Herod.Med.ap.Orib.6.20.11. **-άπρωτοι**, οἱ, *highest class of tax-payers* at Aphrodisias, *Rev. Ét.Gr.*19.242. **-οι**, Ion. **διηκ-**, αι, α, *two hundred*, Hdt.1.193, etc.: sg. with Noun of multitude, δ. ἵππος *two hundred* horse, Th.1.62; v. διακάτιοι. **-οντάχους**, ουν, *two-hundred-fold*, Str.15.3.11. **-οντάκις**, *two hundred times*, Suid.

διᾱκοσιο-και-τεσσᾰρᾰκοντά-χους, ουν, *two-hundred-and-forty-fold*, Str.17.3.11.

διᾱκοσιοστός, ή, όν, *two-hundredth*, D.H.8.83; -στή, ἡ, *tax of* ½% in Ptolemaic Egypt, *PHib.*1.66.1. (Written διακοσσιαστοῦ (gen.) in *Princeton Exp.Inscr.*797[2] (iv A.D.).)

διακοσκῑν(εύ)ω, *riddle, sift thoroughly*, Gal.10.355 (Pass.).

διακοσμ-έω, *divide and marshal, muster, array*, ὡς τοὺς ἡγεμόνες διεκόσμεον Il.2.476; πομπήν Th.1.20:—Pass., εἴ περ.. ἐς δεκάδας διακοσμηθεῖμεν Ἀχαιοί Il.2.126; διὰ τρίχα κοσμηθέντες ib.655. 2. *order, regulate*, Anaxag.12, Hdt.1.100, Th.2.100, Pl.*Lg.*864a, al., etc.:—Med., πᾶν μέγαρον διεκοσμήσαντο *got* it all *set in order*, Od.22.457; δ. τὸ σῶμα Hp.*Vict.*1.9. 3. Stoic t. t., *re-establish the world-order* after ἐκπύρωσις, εἶτ' αὖθις πάλιν -εῖσθαι [τὸν κόσμον] Zeno *Stoic.* 1.27. II. *adorn variously*, τινί τι Crobyl.10:—Pass., στιγμαῖς Philum.*Ven.*21.1. **-ησις** (hyperdor. **-āσις** Ocell.1.8), εως, ἡ, *setting in order, regulation*, ἡ περί τι δ. Pl.*Smp.*209a; τῶν νόμων Id. *Lg.*853a; θριάμβου Plb.2.31.6, cf. Phld.*Oec.*p.35 J., Corn.*ND*17, al.; τοῦ πόλου *OGI*56.46 (iii B.C.). 2. *the orderly arrangement* of the Universe, esp. in the Pythagorean system, Arist.*Metaph.*986^{a}6, Plu.*Per.*4, D.S.12.20, S.E.*M.*9.27, Porph.*Antr.*6, etc. 3. Stoic t. t., of the *new order* after ἐκπύρωσις, Zeno *Stoic.*1.28, etc. 4. *order, class* of beings, Procl.*Inst.*144, Dam.*Pr.*301, al. **-ητικός**, ή, όν, *regulative*, δύναμις Iamb.*Myst.*10.6. **-ος**, ὁ, = διακόσμησις, Parm.8.60; ὁ τοῦ βίου δ. Arist.*Mu.*399^{b}16; δ. οὐρανοῦ καὶ γῆς ib.400^{b}32; ὁ λογικὸς δ. εἰκὼν ὅλου τοῦ δημιουργοῦ Hierocl. *in CA* 1p.419 M., cf. Orph.*H.*34.18; θεῶν, νοεροὶ δ., Procl.*Inst.*145, Dam.*Pr.*81; μέγας, μικρὸς Διάκοσμος, titles of works by Leucippus and Democritus, D.L. 9.13; δ' Ἀναξαγόρειος δ. Satyr.*Vit.Eur.Fr.*37 iii 18. 2. *battle-order*, Th.4.93. II. *the Catalogue of ships in* Il.2, Str.12.3.5, Sch.Il. *Oxy.*221 vi 22.

διακουράζομαι· τὸ ἀτενὲς βλέπειν, *EM*267.27, Suid.

διακουστής, οῦ, ὁ, *hearer*, θεῶν καὶ ἀνθρώπων *PMag.Leid.V.*7.8.

διακουφίζω, intr., *become lighter for an interval, remit*, σμικρὰ δ. Hp.*Epid.*1.7. 2. trans., *relieve*, σπλῆνα Ruf.ap.Orib.45.30.69.

διᾰκούω, fut. -ακούσομαι *Act.Ap.*23.35 :—*hear out* or *to the end*, τι X.*Oec.*11.1 ; πάντα Men.*Epit.*471 : abs., of a court, *try out* a case, *OGI*335.71 (Pergam.) ; *hear* or *learn* from another, τινὸς ἅττα Pl.*Ep.* 338d ; παρά τινος Theopomp.Hist.244 ; δ. τὰ δόξαντα τοῖς ἄρχουσιν Arist.*Pol.*1273ᵃ10 : c. gen. rei, [λόγων] Pl.*Prm.*126c ; τῶν λεγομένων Plb.6.58.8 ; περί τινος Id.3.15.4 : c. gen. pers., of parties to a dispute, *SIG*599.20 (Priene), 685.29 (Crete), *PGrenf.*1.11 8 (ii B.C.), *Act.Ap.* l. c., etc. ; δ. μου πρὸς αὐτούς *BGU*168.28 (ii A.D.), cf. *PLond.* 3.924.16 (ii A.D.) ; also, *to be a hearer* or *disciple of*, Phld.*Rh.*1.96 S., Plu.*Cic.*4 ; τὰ γεωμετρικά τινος D.L.8.86 : abs., Phld.*Herc.*862.3.

διάκοψις, εως, ἡ, = διακοπή, Thphr.*CP*5.9.11 (pl.).

διακρᾰδαίνω, *shake violently*, σῶμα Tim.*Pers.*25, cf. Ar.Did.*Epit.* 13.

διακράζω, pf. διακέκρᾱγα, *have a screaming-match*, Ar.*Av.*306 ; δ. τινί *pit oneself against* another *at screaming*, Id.*Eq.*1403.

διακρᾰτ-έω, *hold fast, control*, τὰ ὅπλα Phylarch.24 ; τὸν ὅλον κόσμον Herm.ap.Stob.1.15.16, cf. Iamb.*Myst.*4.12 ; ὀργάδα D.H.1. 79 ; *hold*, ἐν τῷ στόματι Dsc.2.152 (Pass.), cf. *Gp.*12.30.3 (Pass.), etc. 2. *hold in possession*, *BGU*1047 ii 6 (ii A.D., Pass.). 3. *maintain, establish*, λόγον Stob.1.1.9 ; *retain, preserve*, in argument, Dam.*Pr.*439. 4. *hold up, support*, ἱστόν Erot. s. v. ὅπλα ; δέπας Ath.11.492b (Pass.) : metaph., *support, keep alive*, αὐτόν D.L.9.43. 5. *hold back, detain*, in Pass., πρὸς τῶν χρηστῶν App.*BC*2.8. **-ημα**, ατος, τό, *remedy to be held in the mouth*, Gal.12.268. II. *that which is held together*, Secund.*Sent.*1. **-ησις**, εως, ἡ, *holding fast, retention*, σπέρματος Sor.1.36, cf. Dsc.*Ther.Praef.*; *control*, Iamb. *Myst.*1.9 ; *possession*, Sch.Th.1.139, Suid. v. ἀόριστος : dub. in Eun. *Hist.*p.252 D. **-ητέον**, *one must hold fast*, Archig.ap.Gal.13. 176. **-ητικός**, ή, όν, *able to hold fast*, τινός S.E.*M.*9. 72. **-υντικός**, ή, όν, *making firm*, τῶν ὀδόντων Dsc.1.30.

Διακρεῖς, Att. **-κρῆς**, οἱ, *inhabitants of* Διακρία in Euboea, *IG*1². 211.25, al., Hsch., *EM*268.3 ; cf. Διάκριοι.

διακρέκω, *strike the strings* of the lyre, χέλυν *APl.*4.307 (Leon.).

διακρημνίζω, v.l. for κατακρημνίζω, J.*BJ*1.2.4.

διακρηνόω, Dor. **-κρᾱνόω**, *make to flow*, πῶμα Theoc.7.154 (v.l.).

διακρῑβ-εία, ἡ, *minute observance* of the law, Lxx 3 *Ki.*11.33 (pl.). **-ολογέομαι**, *inquire minutely*, Pl.*Sph.*245e ; ὑπέρ τινος Heraclit.*All.*49. **-όω**, *portray exactly*, Ἔρωτα *APl.*4.204 (Praxiteles). 2. *examine* or *discuss minutely* or *with precision*, τὰς τάξεις X.*Cyr.*2.1.27 ; τὸν ὅρον Arist.*SE*169ᵇ15, cf. *EN*1178ᵃ23 :—Med., Pl. *Tht.*184d ; περί τινος Isoc.4.18 :—Pass., διηκρίβωται *the subject has been examined minutely*, Arist.*Rh.*1366ᵃ21, cf. Phld.*Herc.*862.13 ; *to be brought to exactness* or *perfection*, Arist.*EN*1112ᵇ6, etc.; διηκριβωμένοι *accomplished* persons, Pl.*Lg.*965a ; διηκρ. ἑρμηνεία Aristox. *Harm.*p.16 M. ; διηκρ. τέχναι Ath.12.511d. **-ωσις**, εως, ἡ, *accurate investigation*, Ptol.*Geog.*8.1. **-ωτέον**, *one must examine minutely*, Plu.*Lys.*12.

δια-κρῐδά, Adv. = sq., Opp.*C.*2.496. **-κρῐδόν**, Adv., (διακρίνω) *eminently*, δ. εἶναι ἄριστοι Il.12.103, cf. 15.108, Hdt.4.53 ; δ. ἠσκημένη κόμη Luc.*Am.*3. 2. *precisely*, of measurement, Nic.*Th.*955 ; *in detail*, A.R.4.721 ; *distinctly*, *Hymn.Is.*14. 3. *separately*, A.R. 1.567, al. ; ἔνθα καὶ ἔνθα δ. Nonn.*D.*34.349, cf. Opp.*C.*2.130, Agath. 5.7 ; οὐ δ. without *distinction*, περὶ τῶν ὁσίων ἢ δικαίων App.*BC*5.9.

διάκρῐμα, ατος, τό, *discrete condition*, opp. σύγκριμα, συναίρεμα, ἕνωμα, Dam.*Pr.*53,56.

διακρίνω [ῑ], fut. -κρῐνῶ, Ep. and Delph. -κρῐνέω Il.2.387, *SIG*614. 8 (ii B.C.) :—*separate one from another*, ὥς τ' αἰπόλια.. αἰπόλοι ἄνδρες ῥεῖα διακρίνωσιν Il.2.475, cf. Hdt.8.114 ; *part* combatants, εἰς ὅ κε δαίμων ἄμμε διακρίνῃ Il.7.292, etc. ; εἰ μὴ νὺξ.. διακρινέει μένος ἀνδρῶν 2.387 ; δ. φιλέοντε Od.4.179 ; κρόκην καὶ στήμονας συγκεχυμένους δ. Pl. *Cra.*388b :—Pass., *to be parted*, of hair, Plu.*Rom.*15 : more freq. of combatants, διακρινθήμεναι (Ep. inf. aor. 1 Pass.) ἤδη Ἀργείους καὶ Τρῶας Il.3.98, cf. 102, 7.306, etc. : also in fut. Med., διακρινέεσθαι Od. 18.149, 20.180 ; διακριθέντες ἐκ τῆς ναυμαχίης Hdt.8.18 ; διακριθῆναι ἀπ' ἀλλήλων Th.1.105, cf. 3.9 ; διακρίνεσθαι πρός.. *part and join different* parties, Id.1.18. b. Pass., *to be divorced*, *Leg.Gort.*2.46. 2. in Philosophy, *separate, decompose into elemental parts*, opp. συγκρίνω, chiefly in Pass., Anaxag.12, cf. Arist.*Metaph.*985ᵃ28, [Epich.]245, Pl.*Phd.*71b, *Prm.*157a, etc. 3. ἄστρων διακρίνει φάη σελάνα prob. *sets apart, removes*, i.e. *outshines*, B.8.28. II. *distinguish*, καί κ' ἀλαὸς διακρίνειε τὸ σῆμα Od.8.195 ; οὐδένα δ. without *distinction* of persons, Hdt.3.39 ; οὐχὶ δ. τὴν πενιχρὰν ἢ πλουσίαν Diod.Com.2.8 : pf. Pass. in med. sense, διακεκρίμεθα τάς τε καθαρὰς ἡδονὰς καὶ.. Pl.*Phlb.* 52c : plpf. in pass. sense, διεκέκριτο οὐδέν no *distinction was made*, Th.1.49 ; διακεκριμέναι *distinct, varied*, B.*Fr.*24. III. *decide*, of judges, ὀρθᾷ δ. φρενί Pi.*O.*8.24 ; δ. δίκας Hdt.1.100 ; διὰ δὲ κρίνουσι θέμιστας Theoc.25.46 ; also, *determine* a fever, *mark* its *crisis*, Hp. *Coac.*137 ; ἡ νοῦσος μάλιστα διακρίνει ἐν οὐδενί *has* usually no *crisis* in any patient, Id.*Morb.*2.71 ; δ. αἵρεσιν Hdt.1.11 ; δ. εἰ.. Id.7.54 ; δ. περί τινος Ar.*Av.*719 :—Med., νεῖκος δ. *get* it *decided*, Hes.*Op.*35 ; τὸ ζητούμενον Pl.*Phlb.*46b ; *decide among yourselves*, ταῦτα.. ὅπως ποτ' ἔχει δ. D.32.28 :—Pass., *bring an issue to decision*, ἐπέεσσί γε νηπυτίοισι ὧδε διακρινθέντε Il.20.212 ; αἴ τινι τᾶν πολίων ᾖ ἀμφίλλογα, διακριθῆμεν Foed.Dor.ap.Th.5.79 ; διακριθεῖμεν περί τινος Pl.*Euthphr.* 7c ; of combatants, μάχῃ διακριθῆναι πρός τινα Hdt.9.58 ; πρός τινα ὑπέρ τινος Lxx *Jl.*3(4).2 ; ὅπλοις ἢ λόγοις διακρίνεσθαι Philipp.ap.D. 12.7 ; διακρίνεσθαι περὶ τῶν ὅλων Plb.3.111.2 ; τινί *with* one, *Ep. Jud.*9 : abs., *PMagd.*1.15 (iii B.C.), etc. ; also πόλεμος διακριθήσεται Hdt.7.206 ; of a person, *to be judged*, Polem.*Call.*18. IV. *set* [a place] *apart for holy purposes*, Pi.*O.*10(11).46. V. *interpret* a dream, etc., Ph.2.54, Junc.ap.Stob.4.50.95. VI. *question*, τοὺς ἰατρούς Arr.*Epict.*4.1.148. VII. *doubt, hesitate, waver*, *Act.Ap.* 11.12 (s.v.l.) : usu. in Med. and Pass., μηδὲν διακρινόμενος ib.10.20 ; μὴ διακριθῆτε *Ev.Matt.*21.21, cf. *Ep.Rom.*4.20.

Διάκριοι, οἱ, = Διακρεῖς, *IG*1².63.93 : esp. at Athens, *the Mountaineers*, one of the three political parties at Athens, after Solon's time, Ar.*V.*1223, Arist.*Ath.*13.4, Plu.*Sol.*13 ; cf. ὑπεράκριοι.

διά-κρῐσις, εως, ἡ, *separation, dissolution*, opp. σύγκρισις, Emp. 58, Anaxag.10, Pl.*Sph.*243b, al. ; *segregation*, τῶν ἡμαρτηκότων J.*BJ* 2.14.8 ; *discrimination*, καλοῦ τε καὶ κακοῦ *Ep.Hebr.*5.14 ; πνευμάτων 1*Ep.Cor.*12.10 ; *differentiation*, Dam.*Pr.*1. 2. in concrete sense, *resolved form*, ἡ ἀτμὶς ὕδατος δ. ἐστιν Arist.*Mete.*340ᵇ3, 341ᵇ15. II. *decision, determination*, Pl.*Lg.*765a, X.*Cyr.*8.2.27, A.R.4.1169 ; *judicial decision*, *PLond.*2.476.9 (i A.D.) : metaph., *Ep.Rom.*14.1 (pl.) ; *interpretation* of dreams or omens, Ph.2.55, Paus.1.34.5 ; δ. σημειώσεως medical *diagnosis*, Sor.2.23 : but in pl., αἱ ἐκ νούσων δ. *determinations, crises*, Hp.*Genit.*3. 2. *examination* or *revision of accounts*, δ. πρακτόρων Wilcken *Chr.*41 iii 6 (iii A.D.). III. *decision by battle*, τάξεων πρὸς ἀλλήλους Plb.18.28.3 ; *quarrel, dispute*, Epicur. *Ep.*1 p.29 U., Arat.109, *Milet.*3.149.39. IV. in X.*Cyn.*4.1, *space between the eyes* in dogs. V. *separation* of tumour from blood-vessels, Antyll.ap.Orib.45.2.9. 2. *secretion*, οὔρων Aret.*SA*1. 9, cf. Gal.6.382. VI. *a bandage*, Id.18(1).777. **-κρῐτέον**, *one must decide*, D.L.9.92 : pl. -έα Th.1.86. 2. *one must distinguish*, Dsc.5.106, Porph.*Abst.*2.50, Iamb.*Myst.*2.2 : Adj. -κριτέος, α, ον, *to be distinguished*, Philostr.*Gym.*33. 3. *one must separate*, Sor.2.89. **-κρῐτής**, οῦ, ὁ, *official in charge of revision of arrears of taxation*, δ. ἐχθέσεων ὅλου νομοῦ *PGiss.*58 ii 11 (ii A.D.) : pl., *BGU*734 ii 6 (iii A.D.). **-κρῐτικός**, ή, όν, *piercing, penetrating*, opp. *compressing* (συγκριτικός), Pl.*Ti.*67e ; χρῶμα Arist.*Metaph.* 1057ᵇ8. 2. *separative*, ἡ -κή, opp. ἡ συγκριτική (q. v.), Pl.*Plt.* 282b sqq. Adv. -κῶς Democr.164. II. *able to distinguish*, τῆς οὐσίας Pl.*Cra.*388c ; ὄψις ἕξις δ. σωμάτων Id.*Def.*411c : abs., Luc. *Herm.*69. **-κρῐτικότης**, ητος, ἡ, *power of discrimination*, Procl. *in Prm.*p.793 S. **-κρῐτος**, ον, *separated* : hence, *choice, excellent*, Theoc.22.163.

διακροβολ-ίζομαι, *skirmish*, J.*BJ*4.7.1, Onos.14.3. **-ισμός**, ὁ, *skirmishing, mock-fight*, Str.3.3.7.

διάκροκος, ον, *containing saffron*, κολλύρια Gal.12.608.

διακροτέω, *pierce through*, sens. obsc., E.*Cyc.*180. II. *resolve into components*, as words into their elements, opp. συγκροτέω, Pl. *Cra.*421c. III. *knock off*, κρίκους Plu.2.304b.

διακρότως, Adv. = ἀποκρότως, Hsch.

διά-κρουσις, εως, ἡ, *putting off*, ἐπὶ διακρούσει, *to gain time*, D.54. 27 ; *delay, evasion*, Plu.*Cor.*19 : pl., δ. καὶ ὑπερθέσεις Id.*Cic.*7 ; *escape from*, βασάνων Lib.*Or.*14.19. **-κρουστικός**, ή, όν, *expressive of deception*, ῥήματα A.D.*Synt.*284.20. **-κρούω**, *knock* or *drive through*, ὅταν οἱ σφῆνες διακρουσθῶσιν Thphr.*CP*2.15.4 ; *knock off*, δεσμά Paus.4.17.1. 2. *prove by knocking* or *ringing*, as one does an earthen vessel, δ. εἴτε ὑγιὲς εἴτε σαθρὸν φθέγγεται Pl.*Tht.*179d, cf. Luc.*Par.*4 :—perh. in a similar sense in *IG*7.3073.164 (Lebad.). II. Med., *drive from oneself, get rid of*, τοὺς Ἕλληνας Hdt.7.168 ; πρόσοδον [πρέσβεων] D.H.3.3 ; μακρὰς στρατηγίας Plu.*Nic.*6 ; *evade*, διακρούεσθαι τὸ δίκην δοῦναι D.21.128 ; διακρούεται τὰ χρήματα ἐκτῖσαι *POxy.*71 i 13 (iv A.D.) ; δ. τινά *evade* his creditor *by delays*, of a debtor, D.34.13 ; δ. τοὺς λοιδοροῦντας Plu.2.70d ; δ. τοὺς κυρίους μὴ καταθεῖναι D.38.12 ; so δ. τὸν παρόντα χρόνον Id.19.33 ; *evade, slur over* a difficult question, ψιλῇ παρατηρήσει A.D.*Pron.*41.8 ; *evade* an argument, Sor.1.58 : abs., *practise evasions and delays*, D.21.186, 201, *POxy.*237 viii 10 (ii A.D.) :—Pass., διακρουσθῆναι τῆς τιμωρίας *escape from* punishment, D.24.132. III. *hinder, entangle*, ἑαυτὸν διακρούειν ἐν τοῖς πράγμασι Plu.2.80d. IV. intr., *break away, escape*, Numen.ap.Eus.*PE*11.18. V. Med., *put aside for oneself, conceal, embezzle*, χόρτον *PSI*4.354.7 (iii B.C.).

διακρύπτω, strengthd. for κρύπτω, D.L.4.16 :—Med., Poll.6.209.

διακτενίζω, *comb well*, διεκτενισμένα μειράκια Philostr.*VA*8.7.

διακτέον, (διάγω) *one must treat* a patient, Hp.*Vict.*1.27.

διακτορία, *office of a* διάκτορος, *service*, Musae.6, *AP*6.68 (Jul.).

διάκτορος, ὁ, epith. of Hermes in Hom., δ. Ἀργεϊφόντης Il.2. 103, Od.5.43, etc. ; δ. alone, ib.12.390, 15.319 ; Ζηνὸς δ. *AP*13.2 (Phaedim.) : variously expld. by ancient writers, cf. Nessas 2, Corn. *ND*16, *EM*268.10, Eust.182.8, etc. : apptly. taken as *minister*, = διάκονος, by A.*Pr.*941 ; as *messenger* (διάγων ἀγγελίας), by later poets, ὄρνι Διὸς δ., of the eagle, *AP*7.161 (Antip. Sid.) ; applied to Iris by Nonn.*D.*31.107 ; to Athena, ib.30.250 (so perh. of Athena's owl, Call. *Fr.*164 ; πολέμων δ., of a poet, Luc.*Alex.*33) ; cf. συνδιάκτορος : used as neut. Adj., διάκτορα δηϊοτῆτος ἔγχεα Nonn.*D.*39.82 : cf. διάκτωρ.

διακτος, ον, *carried through pipes*, of oils or unguents used at the bath, *CIG*2820 (Aphrodisias), 3871 *b* (add., Sebaste) ; τὰ κατ' ἄνδρα δ. *IGRom.*4.860 (Laodicea ad Lycum).

διάκτωρ, ορος, ὁ, = διάκτορος, βούταν δ. *AP*10.101 (Bianor) ; διάκτορσι· ἡγεμόσι, βασιλεῦσιν, Hsch.

διακῠβερνάω, *steer through, pilot*, τὸ θνητὸν ζῷον, τἀνθρώπινα, Pl. *Ti.*42e, *Lg.*709b ; τὸν κόσμον Plu.2.1026f ; τὸν πότον ib.712b ; ἐμαυτήν τε καὶ τὸ παιδίον σοῦ *PLond.*1.42.16 (ii B.C.) ; of a physician, Arist.*Pr.*859ᵃ18 :—Pass., Iamb.*Myst.*8.3.

διακῠβεύω, *play at dice* with another, πρός τινα Plu.*Rom*.5 : abs., Id.2.128a ; περί τινος ib.70d.

διακῠβιστάω, *throw head over heels*, Suid.

διακυδόμεναι· διαχεόμεναι, Hsch.

διακῠκάω, *mix one with another, jumble*, ἄνω καὶ κάτω δ. D.18.111, cf. Agath.5.5 :—Pass., Id.4.17.

διακῠλινδέω, *to roll about*, Arist.*HA*613^{b}26.

διακῡμαίνω, *raise into waves*, τὸ πέλαγος Luc.*DMar*.15.4, cf. *Icar*. 26.

διακῡνοφθαλμίζομαι, Med., *to look askance one at another*, Com. *Adesp*.975, cf. Ael.Dion.*Fr*.124.

διακύπτω, *stoop and creep through* a narrow place, Hdt.3.145, Ar. *Ec*.930. **2.** *stoop so as to peep in*, Id.*Pax* 78 ; διὰ τῆς κεραμίδος Diph.84, cf. Men.*Epit*.463. **3.** *look out*, διὰ τῆς θυρίδος Lxx4*Ki*. 9.30, cf. *PMagd*.24.4 (iii B.C.), Luc.*Asin*.45.

διακῡρίττεσθαι, *fight*, prop. of rams, Hsch.

διακῡρόω, *confirm, ratify*, Phryn.*PS*p.62 B.

διακωδωνίζω, strengthd. for κωδωνίζω, Lys.*Fr*.313 S. (Pass.), D. 19.167, Porph.*Abst*.4.17 (Pass.), Harp. **II.** *bruit abroad*, Str. 2.3.4. **III.** *dismiss by the sound of a bell*, Philostr.*VS*2.27.5.

διακώλ-ῡμα, ατος, τό, *hindrance, obstacle*, ἔργων Pl.*Lg*.807d. **–ῡσις**, εως, ἡ, *hindering, preventing*, αἱ τῶν ἀναιρέσεων δ. Id.*R*.469e ; ἀπὸ προαιρέσεων Arist.*Rh.Al*.1421^{b}22. **–ῡτέον**, *one must prevent*, Pl.*R*.401b, Agath.2.6. **–ῡτής**, οῦ, ὁ, *a hinderer*, Hdt.6.56, Pl. *Phdr*.240a. **–ῡτικός**, ή, όν, *preventive*, Id.*Plt*.280d, prob. l. in Poll.7.209. **–ύω** [ῡ], *hinder, prevent*, τινὰ μὴ ποιεῖν Hdt.8.144, cf. Lys.20.36 ; δ. σε ὀρφανὸν εἶναι E.*Hec*.148 ; δ. τὰ ἱερὰ μὴ γίγνεσθαι Antipho 5.82 ; δ. ἄδικα γίγνεσθαι Pl.*Ap*.31e ; δ. τινά Th.8.92, *Ev. Matt*.3.14 ; δ. τινά τι (sc. ποιεῖν) Pl.*Ep*.315d ; δ. τινά τινος D.S.20. 79 ; δ. φόνον S.*OC*1771 (lyr.) ; δ. τὸ πρᾶγμα Alc.Com.3, cf. Arist. *EN*1159^{b}6 :—Pass., Th.1.101 ; διακωλυθεὶς τοῦ σκοποῦ τυχεῖν Antipho 3.2.7 : ἃ διεκωλύθη (sc. ποιεῖν) D.18.60.

διακωμῳδέω, *satirize*, Pl.*Grg*.462e, Arist.*Po*.1458^{b}6, Jul.*Or*.6.203a: abs., D.H.*Dem*.57.

διάκων, = διάκονος, *BGU*597.4 (i A.D.) ; pr. n., ib.1046.24 (ii A.D.).

διακωνέω, *daub with pitch*, Hsch.

διακωπηλᾰτέω, gloss on διερέττοντα, Suid. **διακωχή**, v. διοκωχή.

διαλᾰβή, ἡ, *seizing by the middle*, δόρατα ἐκ διαλαβῆς κρατούμενα D.H.20.11.

διαλαγχάνω, *divide* or *part by lot*, Hdt.4.68, A.*Th*.789 (lyr.), 816 (tm.), X.*Cyr*.7.3.1, etc. ; θηκτῷ σιδήρῳ δῶμα δ. E.*Ph*.68 : metaph., *tear in pieces*, Id.*Ba*.1291. **II.** *obtain a share by inheritance*, *Leg. Gort*.8.4,24 ; *obtain by lot*, D.H.3.48. **III.** *share with*, τινὶ λείας Procop.*Goth*.4.18.

διαλαιμοτομέομαι, Pass., *have one's throat cut*, Mnesim.4.16.

διαλᾰκέω, *crack asunder, burst*, Ar.*Nu*.410, *Hippiatr*.130.121.

διαλακτίζω, *kick away, spurn*, Theoc.24.25, Plu.2.648b.

διαλᾰλ-έω, *talk with*, τινὶ περί τινος Plb.1.85.2, cf. *POxy*.1417.24 (iv A.D.) ; ἐν ἑαυτοῖς ὑπέρ τινος Plb.9.32.1 ; κατὰ συμμορίας D.H.6. 57 ; πρὸς ἀλλήλους τί ἂν ποιήσειαν *Ev.Luc*.6.11 ; αὐτὴν ἐν αὑτῇ δ. Plu.2.141d. **II.** δ. τινί τι *talk over* a thing *with* another, E.*Cyc*. 175 :—Pass., *to be much talked of*, *Ev.Luc*.1.65. **–ησις**, εως, ἡ, *talking, discourse*, Sch.Pi.*O*.7.17 (pl.). **–ία**, ἡ, *verbal order*, Lyd. *Mag*.3.67. **II.** = Lat. *interlocutio*, Just.*Nov*.126.1, *Cod.Just*.4.20. 16, *PLond*.5.1674.45 (vi A.D.). **III.** *language*, Αἰγυπτιακὴ δ. ib. 1.77.69 (vi A.D.), *POxy*.1836 (vi A.D.).

διαλαμβάνω, fut. –λήψομαι : aor. διέλᾰβον : pf. διείληφα : pf. Pass. διείλημμαι, also διαλέλημμαι Ar.*Ec*.1090, Ion. –λέλαμμαι Hdt.4.68 :—*take* or *receive severally*, i.e. *each his own share*, ἵνα διαλαμβάνοιεν ἕκαστοι τὰ ἄξια X.*Cyr*.7.3.1, cf. *An*.5.3.4 ; δ. οἰκίας Lys.12.8. **II.** *grasp* or *lay hold of separately*, διαλαβόντες..τὰς χεῖρας καὶ τοὺς πόδας Hdt.4.94 : hence, *seize, arrest*, τινά Id.1.114, Pl.*R*.615e ; διαλελαμμένος ἄγεται Hdt.4.68, cf. Ar.*Ec*.1090 (v. Sch. ad loc.). **2.** in wrestling, *grasp round the waist, seize by the middle*, διαλαβὼν ἀγκυρίσας cj. Casaub. in Ar.*Eq*.262 ; διαλαμβάνων τοὺς νεανίσκους ἐτραχήλιζεν Plu.*Ant*.33 ; in full, μέσον δ. τινά Ach.Tat.3.13 ; also, *tie up*, σπάρτῳ *PHolm*.12.13 : metaph. of the soul, διειλημμένη ὑπὸ τοῦ σωματοειδοῦς Pl.*Phd*.81c. **3.** *treat, handle*, ταύτῃ τοὺς νόμους Lys. 14.4 ; τὸν ἡγεμόνα ὡς ἀνδράποδον Philostr.*VA*5.36. **4.** metaph., *embrace*, ὡς ἐπὶ τὸ πᾶν δ. *comprehend* in a general statement, Thphr. *HP*8.1.6. **III.** *divide*, τὸν ποταμὸν ἐς τριηκοσίας διώρυχας δ. Hdt.1.190, cf. 202, 5.52 ; τριχῇ δώδεκα μέρη δ. *divide* 12 parts into 3 (i.e. of 4 each), Pl.*Lg*.763c ; ἵνα χωρὶς ἡμᾶς διαλάβῃ, of a person taking his seat between two others, Id.*Smp*.222e ; δ. εἰς δύο πάντας *divide* them into two parties, Arist.*Pol*.1296^{a}11 ; δ. τὸν δῆμον, τοὺς ἀπόρους, ib.1272^{b}11, 1320^{b}8 ; τὴν σύμπασαν ἀρχὴν κατὰ ἔθνη Id. *Mu*.398^{a}29 :—Pass., ποταμὸς διαλελαμμένος πενταχοῦ *divided* into five channels, Hdt.3.117 ; of troops, Aen.Tact.10.25 ; θώρακες διειλημμένοι τὸ βάρος ὑπὸ τῶν ὤμων, στήθους κτλ. coat-armour *having* its weight *distributed* so as to be borne by.., X.*Mem*.3.10.13. **2.** *mark at intervals*, στήλαις δ. τοὺς ὅρους Decr.ap.D.18.154 ; τὰ τείχη δ. φυλακτηρίοις καὶ πύργοις *provide* them *at intervals with*.., Arist.*Pol*. 1331^{a}20 (Pass.), cf. *OGI*701.13 (Egypt) : of Time, τὰ τῶν ὡρῶν ἐνιαυτοῖς διειλημμένα Pl.*Lg*.886a. **b.** *make a pause*, δ. λέγοντα Id.*Prt*.346e : abs., διαλαβών *at intervals*, Hp.*Mul*.1.68. **c.** *give relief, make a break*, Arist.*Pr*.880^{b}22. **3.** *cut off, intercept*, τὰ στενόπορα Th.7. 73 codd. ; ὁ πορθμὸς ὁ δ. τὴν Σικελίαν Arist.*Mir*.840^{a}2 ; δ. τάφρῳ Plb. 5.99.9 ; δ. φυλακαῖς διαστήματα Id.1.18.4, etc. **4.** *mark off, distinguish*, αἱ πολιτεῖαι .. τοὺς πλείστους διειλήφασιν Isoc.4.16. **5.** *diversify, intersperse*, ἐπεισοδίοις δ. τὴν ποίησιν Arist.*Po*.1459^{a}36 ; λόγον περιόδοις D.H.*Comp*.2 ; παραπληρώμασι ib.16 ; ποιήσεις μέτροις ib.26 :—Pass., γῆ χρώμασι διειλημμένη *marked with various* colours, Pl.*Phd*.110b ; λειμῶνες παντοδαποῖς φυτοῖς διειλ. Luc.*Patr.Enc*. 10. **b.** in pf. part. Pass., διειλημμένος *distinct*, Phld.*D*.1.24 ; κατ' οὐ δ. δόξας ibid. ; cf. διειλημμένως. **6.** *divide* or *distinguish* in thought, ταῦτα δ. τοῖς διανοήμασι Pl.*Lg*.777a ; δ. δίχα [αὐτοὺς] τῷ παίζειν καὶ μή ib.935d, cf. E.*El*.373 ; διὰ τῶν ἔργων δ. τὴν πίστιν *draw distinctive* arguments from facts, dub. l. in Arist.*Pol*.1323^{a}40 ; περί τινος Id.*PA*665^{a}31, *PAmh*.2.35.44 (ii B.C.) : ὑπέρ τινος Plb. 2.42.7 ; δ. τί δεῖ ποιεῖν Id.4.25.1, cf. *PRyl*.68.23 (i B.C.) : hence, *determine, define*, τὸν καιρόν Plb.15.5.2 : c. inf., Id.30.9.2 ; *grasp, apprehend*, Epicur.*Ep*.1 p.5 U., al. ; *perceive*, ὅτι .. Phld.*Sign*.29 ; *give a judicial decision*, *BGU*195.36 (ii A.D.), 15 i 16 (ii A.D.) : in later Prose, simply, *think, believe*, J.*AJ*2.16.5, Anon.Lond.24.32, etc. **7.** *state distinctly*, Philipp.ap.D.12.23 ; περί τινος A.D.*Synt*. 22.8, etc. :—Med., ib.162.27. **8.** *to be pre-eminent throughout*, ἀρεταῖς πᾶσαν τὴν ὑφ' ἡλίῳ *OGI*520.5 (Iasus).

δια-λαμπής, ές, *white-hot*, *EM*109.33. **–λαμπρος**, ον, *clean, white*, ἐσθῆτες Demoph.*Sim*.25. **–λαμπρύνω**, *make splendid, illustrate*, λόγον παλαιόν Plu.2.734f ; *illuminate*, Dsc.*Ther.Praef*.p.50 S. (v.l.). **–λάμπω**, *shine through*, Arist.*HA*503^{b}20, 536^{a}17, Plu. 2.390b ; φῶς ἀληθείᾳ –λάμπον Porph.*Marc*.13 : metaph., δ. τὸ καλόν (sc. ἐν ταῖς ἀτυχίαις) Arist.*EN*1100^{b}30 ; ὥσπερ ἀστραπὴ –λάμψασα τῆς ψυχῆς Plu.2.382d. **2.** *dawn*, διέλαμψεν ἡμέρα Ar.*Pl*.744: abs., διαλάμποντος (sc. τοῦ ἡλίου) Plu.*Pyrrh*.32. **3.** metaph., *shine* or *be conspicuous* in a composition, δ. ἰδέαι Isoc.12.2 ; of men, *to be conspicuous*, πίνακες τῶν ἐν πάσῃ παιδείᾳ διαλαμψάντων, title of work by Callimachus, Suid. **II.** of a singer, *to be conspicuous* above a chorus, Arist.*Pr*.922^{a}36. **III.** Act., *cause to shine forth*, τὸ ἀνείδεον ἐν εἴδεσι Iamb.*Myst*.1.5, cf. Plu.2.393e. **–λαμψις**, εως, ἡ, *shining through*, Arist.*Mete*.369^{b}15, Paul.Al.*T*.1. **II.** Aeol. and Dor. form of Hellenistic διάλημψις, = –ληψις, *repute*, ἔχειν τινὰ ἐν τᾷ καλλίστᾳ διαλάμψει *Schwyzer* 647.28 (Cyme) ; *appreciation*, *SIG* 721.25 (Crete, found at Delos).

διαλανθάνω, fut. –λήσω Isoc.3.16, and as v.l. in Hp.*Acut*.(*Sp*.). 21 –λήσομαι : aor. διέλαθον : pf. διαλέληθα Pl.*Euthd*.278a :—*escape notice*, with part., διαλήσει χρηστὸς ὤν Isoc. l.c. ; but also διαλαθὼν ἐσέρχεται Th.3.25 : c. acc. pers., *escape the notice of*, θεοὺς X.*Mem*.1. 4.19 ; σὲ τοῦτο διαλέληθε Pl. l.c., Isoc.1.44 ; ὁ διαλεληθὼς (sc. λόγος), *a fallacy*, Chrysipp.*Stoic*.2.8. **II.** *abscond*, *BGU*1187.23 (i B.C.), *PSI*4.285.11 (iv A.D.).

διάλαυρος (sc. οἰκία), ἡ, *block of houses surrounded by streets*, Hsch.

διαλᾰφύσσω, aor. 1 διελάφυξα, *waste, squander*, Hsch.

διαλᾰχαίνω, *cut asunder as with a plough*, διὰ κῦμα λ. Opp.*H*.5. 264.

διαλγ-έω, strengthd. for ἀλγέω, Plb.4.4.2 ; ἐπί τινι Id.16.34. 10. **–ής**, ές, *grievous*, ἄτα A.*Ch*.68 (lyr.). **II.** *suffering great pain*, Plu.*Alex*.75. Adv. –γῶς, ἔχει *is pained*, Phld.*D*.3 *Fr*.77.

διαλεαίνω, *triturate*, Archig.ap.Gal.13.169 (Pass.) ; *grind small*, Gal.13.169. **II.** *plane, smooth* : hence metaph. in Med. aor. Boeot. διαλιάνασθη, = διαλεάνασθαι, *cancel* a debt, *IG*7.3172.158 (Orchom. Boeot.).

διαλεγδόν· διαφερόντως, Hsch.

διαλέγω, *pick out*, Hdt.8.107,113, X.*Oec*.8.9, etc. ; πτῶμα *glean* fallen olives, *PFay*.102.20 ; cf. διαλέγειν· ἀνακαθαίρειν, Hsch. ; *select, separate*, Pl.*Lg*.735b ; *examine, check* documents, *PFay*.11. 26 (ii B.C.), etc. **II.** διαλέγων τὴν ὀπὴν *picking open* the hole, to escape, Ar.*Lys*.720 ; cf. διαλέξαι· διορύξαι, Hsch.

B. as Dep., διαλέγομαι : fut. διαλέξομαι Isoc.12.5 and 112 ; also –λεχθήσομαι Id.9.34, D.18.252 ; –λεγήσομαι *Inscr.Perg*.5 (iii B.C.) ; aor. διελεξάμην Hom., Ar.*Fr*.343 ; Aeol. imper. ζάλεξαι Sapph.*Supp*. 16.3 ; also διελέχθην Hdt.3.51, and always in Att. Inscrr., *IG*2^2.657, etc. : less freq. aor. 2 διελέγην Arist.*Top*.154^{a}34, 159^{a}5, Scymn.7, *IG*5(1).5.5 (Lacon.), *GDI*5163^{a}2 (Crete), *PPetr*.3 p.130 (iii B.C.), *IG* 2^2.1236 ; 3 pl. διέλεγεν *CIG*3656.7 (Cyzic.) : pf. διείλεγμαι Pl.*Tht*. 158c, Isoc.5.81 : plpf. διείλεκτο D.21.119, but in pass. sense, Lys.9. 5 :—*hold converse with*, c. dat. pers., μοι ταῦτα φίλος διελέξατο θυμός Il.11.407, cf. Archil.80, Hdt.3.50,51, Ar.*Nu*.425, etc. ; πρὸς ἀλλήλους Pl.*Plt*.272c, etc. ; δ. τί τινι or πρός τινα, *discuss* a question with another, X.*Mem*.2.10.1, 1.6.1 ; δ. ὅρους *talk in* definitions, Arist.*APo*. 92^{b}32 ; δ. περί τινος Isoc.3.8, D.18.252 ; ἀνὴρ ἀνδρὶ δ. Th.8.93 ; δ. τινὶ μὴ ποιεῖν *argue with* one against doing, Id.5.59 ; εἰ τουτὶ τὸ ῥῆμα, ἀλλὰ μὴ τουτὶ διελέχθην ἐγώ D.18.232 ; οἱ νόμοι οὐδὲν τούτῳ δ. *have* nothing *to say* to him, *concern* him not, Id.43.59 ; ὁ νομοθέτης οὔπω τινὶ δ. Aeschin.1.17 ; δ. πρός τι *to argue on*.., Arist.*Top*.159^a 7 ; or *against*.., Id.*Ph*.185^{a}6 : abs., *to discourse, reason*, X.*Mem*.4. 5.12 ; δ. περί τινος Isoc.5.109, etc., freq. in Pl., *Ap*.33a, al. ; γλῶσσα εὔτροχος ἐν τῷ δ. Plu.*Per*.7 ; *reason, calculate*, = διαλογίζομαι, Id. *Marc*.18 :—the Act. in med. sense, Hermipp.40 ; οἱ διαλεγόμενοι, of logicians, Polystr.p.6 W., al. **2.** in Philosophy, *practise dialectic, elicit conclusions by discussion*, οὐκ ἐρίζειν ἀλλὰ δ. Pl.*R*.454a, cf. 511c, *Tht*.167e, etc. **3.** later, *discourse, lecture*, Philostr.*VS*2. 21.3. **4.** *use a dialect* or *language*, κατὰ ταὐτά τισι δ. Hdt.1.142 ; Φοινικιστί Plb.1.80.6 ; *write in prose*, opp. ποιεῖν, D.H.*Comp*.20. **b.** *speak articulately*, Arist.*HA*535^{b}2. **5.** in Att., euphem. for συνουσιάζω, *have intercourse*, Ar.*Ec*.890, *Pl*.1082, Hyp.*Fr*.171, Plu.*Sol*. 20, Hierocl.p.64 A. **6.** *have dealings with*, *OGI*484.23 (Pergam.).

διάλειμμα, ατος, τό, (διαλείπω) *interstice, gap*, Pl.*Ti*.59b, Arist.*PA* 680^{b}34, *BGU*12.31 (ii A.D.); in Music, *interval*, Arist.*Pr*.921^{b}10; of Time, Plb.1.66.2; *pause*, τὰ δ. τῆς ἐνεργείας D.H.*Comp*.20; ἐκ διαλειμμάτων at *intervals*, Epicur.*Ep*.3 p.64 U., Plu.*Per*.7; esp. of *intervals* between attacks of fever, Gal.7.414, cf. 427.

διᾰλειπτόν, τό, (διαλείφω) *liniment*, Hp.*Mul*.1.97.

διαλείπω, aor. διέλῐπον Ar.*Nu*.496: pf. -λέλοιπα Isoc.12.5:—*leave an interval between*, τὸ ὀλίγιστον Arist.*Ph*.226^{b}28:—Pass., διελέλειπτο *a gap had been left*, Hdt.7.40,41; διαλέλειπται μικρὰ χώρα Arist.*HA*503^{a}34. 2. *intermit*, τὴν ὀχείαν Id.*GA*757^{b}4: esp. of Time, διαλιπὼν ἡμέρας τὰς συγκειμένας, ἐνιαυτόν, *having left an interval of*.., Hdt.3.157, D.20.8; ἀκαρῆ διαλιπὼν *having waited* an instant, Ar.*Nu*.496; χρόνον ὀλίγον Isoc.5.8; πολὺν χρόνον Arist.*Pol*.1299^{a}37; later in gen., μιᾶς ἡμέρας δ. Hdn.7.8.9; so οὐ πολὺ διαλιπὼν *after* a short *time*, Th.5.10: abs., opp. εὐθύς, Men.*Sam*.198, cf. Hyp. *Eux*.32. II. intr., *stand at intervals*, δ. δύο πλέθρα ἀπ' ἀλλήλων Th.7.38; πίτυες διαλείπουσαι μεγάλαι X.*An*.4.7.6; τὸ δέρμα ταύτῃ δ. *is discontinuous* at this point, opp. συνεχές ἐστι, Arist.*HA*518^{a}3; τὸ -λεῖπον *an interval* or *gap*, X.*An*.4.8.13: impers., διαλείπει *there are intervals*, of the heavens, opp. πλήρη ἀστέρων εἶναι, Arist.*Mete*.346^{a}36. 2. c. part., mostly with neg., οὐ πώποτε διέλειπον ζητῶν X. *Ap*.16, etc.; οὐδένα διαλέλοιπα χρόνον διαβαλλόμενος I *have* never *ceased* to be slandered. Isoc.12.5; οὐ διέλιπον.. παραινῶν πείθεσθαι.. *BGU*747 i 7 (ii A.D.), cf. *POxy*.281.16 (i A.D.): without a neg., Luc. *Vit.Auct*.13, *DMeretr*.11.1. 3. of Time, διαλιπόντων ἐτῶν τριῶν, διαλιπούσης ἡμέρας, *after an interval* of.., Th.1.112, 3.74; τὸ διαλεῖπον *the interval of time*, Arist.*Ph*.228^{b}4. 4. in part., *intermittent*, διαλείποντες πνέουσιν οἱ ἄνεμοι Id.*Mete*.362^{a}28, cf. *GA*748^{a}19; δ. πυρετός Hp.*Aph*.4.43, *Coac*.139. 5. *die*, *GDI*1920.9, 2082.5 (Delph.).

διᾰλείφω, *anoint*, Hp.*Mul*.1.64. II. *plaster*, *SIG*^{2}587.107. III. *erase, strike out*, Plu.*Arat*.13; δίκην Chamael.ap.Ath.9.407c.

διαλείχω, *lick clean*, Ar.*Eq*.1034, *V*.904.

διάλειψις, εως, ἡ, *an interval, interstice*, v.l. in Hp.*Art*.35, cf. Arist. *Aud*.803^{b}37; δ. τῶν πλινθίδων *IG*2.1054.93; δ. φυλλική, *internode*, Thphr.*HP*3.18.11; *intermission*, Erot. s.v. τριταιοφυεῖς.

διαλεκτ-έον, (διαλέγομαι) *one must discourse*, Isoc.12.134, Pl.*Ly*. 211c: esp. philosophically, Arist.*APo*.77^{b}13, *Metaph*.1012^{b}7. **-ικεύομαι**, '*chop logic*', M.Ant.8.13, Gal.13.573. **-ικός**, ή, όν, *conversational*, χορός Demetr.*Eloc*.167. 2. δ. ὄργανα organs *of articulate speech*, opp. φωνητικά, Gal.16.204. II. *skilled in dialectic*, ὁ ἐρωτᾶν καὶ ἀποκρίνεσθαι ἐπιστάμενος Pl.*Cra*.390c; ἦ καὶ δ. καλεῖς τὸν λόγον ἑκάστου λαμβάνοντα τῆς οὐσίας; Id.*R*.534b; *dialectical*, Arist. *Metaph*.995^{b}23; δ. συλλογισμός Id.*Top*.100^{a}22; πρὸς τοὺς δ., title of work by Metrodorus, D.L.10.24, cf. Phld.*Rh*.1.279 S., al. III. ἡ διαλεκτική (sc. τέχνη) *dialectic, discussion by question and answer*, invented by Zeno of Elea, Arist.*Fr*.65; *philosophical method*, ὥσπερ θριγκὸς τοῖς μαθήμασιν ἡ δ. ἐπάνω κεῖται Pl.*R*.534e: τὸ -κόν Id.*Sph*. 253e; περὶ -κῆς, title of work by Cleanthes, D.L.7.174. 2. *the logic of probabilities*, ἡ δ. πειραστικὴ περὶ ὧν ἡ φιλοσοφία γνωριστική Arist.*Metaph*.1004^{b}25, cf. *Rh*.1354^{a}1. IV. Adv. **-κῶς** *dialectically*, Pl.*Phlb*.17a, etc.; *for the sake of argument*, opp. κατ' ἀλήθειαν, Arist. *Top*.105^{b}31, cf. *de An*.403^{a}2; *by argument on general principles*, opp. scientifically, Phld.*Rh*.2.134 S., *Mus*.p.89 K.: Comp. -ώτερον Pl.*Men*. 75d; *more logically*, Dam.*Pr*.97. **-ος**, ἡ, *discourse, conversation*, Hp.*Art*.30; θεοῖς πρὸς ἀνθρώπους Pl.*Smp*.203a; *discussion, debate, argument*, Id.*Tht*.146b; opp. ἔρις, Id.*R*.454a. 2. *common language, talk*, δ. ἡ πρὸς ἀλλήλους Arist.*Po*.1449^{a}26; ἡ εἰωθυῖα δ. Id.*Rh*. 1404^{b}24. II. *speech, language*, Ar.*Fr*.685; καινὴν δ. λαλῶν Antiph. 171; δ. ἀμνίου, opp. τὰ ἔνδον δράκοντος, Hermipp.3; *articulate speech, language*, opp. φωνή, Arist.*HA*535^{a}28; τοῦ ἀνθρώπου μία φωνή, ἀλλὰ διάλεκτοι πολλαί Id.*Pr*.895^{a}6; but also, *spoken*, opp. written *language*, D.H.*Comp*.11. 2. *the language of a country*, Plb.1.80.6, D.S.5.6, etc.: esp. *dialect*, as Ionic, Attic, etc., Diog.Bab.*Stoic*.3.213, D.H.*Comp*.3, S.E.*M*.1.59, Hdn.Gr.2.932; also, *local word* or *expression*, Plu.*Alex*.31. III. *way of speaking, accent*, D.37.55. 2. pl., *modes of expression*, Epicur.*Ep*.1 p.24 U. IV. *style*, πανηγυρική, ποιητικὴ δ., D.H.*Comp*.23,21: esp. *poetical diction*, Phld.*Po*. 2 *Fr*.33, al. V. of musical instruments, *quality*, '*idiom*', Arist. *de An*.420^{b}8.

διαλελυμένως, Adv., (διαλύω) *laxly*, Arist.*Pr*.900^{a}24. II. *not in composition*, Ath.15.676f; e.g. πόδας ὠκύς, as compared with ποδώκης, Eust.64.22. b. *in an uncontracted form*, e.g. χαλκέα, opp. χαλκῆ, Moer.414. c. *without conjunctions, in asyndeton*, Ph. 1.500. III. *in conversational style*, opp. ἐμμέτρως, Sch.Heph. p.115 C., cf. Sch.Ar.*Eq*.937.

διάλεξις, εως, ἡ, *discourse, argument*, Ar.*Nu*.317, Jul.*ad Them*. 255b (pl.), f.l. in Pl.*Ep*.350d, Philostr.*VA*4.40; *conversation, interview*, Wilcken *Chr*.155.17 (iii A.D.). II. = διάλεκτος II. 2, D.C. 60.17. III. *passage* in a book, *specimen of style*, D.H.*Dem*. 21; *phrase*, Ἀττικαὶ δ., title of work by Aristophanes of Byzantium. IV. *popular discourse, lecture*, Philostr.*VS*1.24.1, al., Diog.Oen.18, etc.; of the *discourses* of Epictetus, Gell.19.1.14.

διαλεπίζω, *strip of bark*, δένδρον *Gloss*.

διαλεπτολογέομαι, *discourse subtly*, '*chop logic*', τινί *with* one, Ar. *Nu*.1496.

διάλεπτ-ος, ον, *very small* or *narrow*, ὑμήν Eust.1157.18. **-ύνω**, *make thin, pare away, fine down*, Hp.*Fract*.11; *grind small*, Sch.E. *Ph*.1159:—Pass., *become thin, watery*, of a fluid, Ruf.*Sat.Gon*.15:—hence Subst. **-υνσις**, εως, ἡ, Aët.16.55.

διαλεσχαίνω, *prate, chatter*, Phryn.*PS* p.36 B.

διαλευκαίνω, *whiten*, Philostr.Jun.*Im*.12. 2. *illustrate, elucidate*, v.l. in Dsc.*Ther.Praef*.

διάλευκος, ον, *quite white*, Arist.*Pr*.894^{a}39, Lxx *Ge*.30.32, Str.17. 1.31, Plu.*Alex*.51, Aret.*SD*2.13; αἱ λίμναι -ότεραι τῆς θαλάττης Arist. *Pr*.932^{a}29.

διαληκάομαι, *laugh at*, Ael.Dion.*Fr*.125:—hence **διαληκίνδα**, a game, Theognost. in *AB*1353^{a}.

διάλημμα, ατος, τό, *windings* of a chain, Ath.Mech.24.6. II. *gap*, *PPetr*.3 p.290 (iii B.C.).

διάληξις, εως, ἡ, (διαλαγχάνω) *division* of an inheritance, Antipho *Fr*.64, Hsch., Suid.

διαληπτ-έον, *one must divide*, τὰς ἐπιστήμας Pl.*Plt*.258b; δ. ὡς.. *we must distinguish and say* that.., Arist.*Pol*.1290^{b}9. II. *one must hold an opinion, form a judgement*, τὸ παραπλήσιον δ. περί τινος Plb.6.44.1, 11.25.3. III. *one must discuss, treat*, Porph.*Abst*. 1.57. **-ικός**, ή, όν, *forming a judgement*, ἐπίστασις M.Ant.10.8, cf. Epicur.*Nat*.50 G. **-ός**, ή, όν, *distinguishable*, Id.*Ep*.1 p.16 U.

διαληρέω, *speak foolishly*, Eun.*Hist*.p.265 D.

διάληψις, later **διάλημψις**, in Doricized form **διάλᾱμψις** (q.v.), εως, ἡ, (διαλαμβάνω) *grasping with both hands*: ἐκ διαλήψεως, opp. ἐκ καταφορᾶς, as *thrusting* to cutting, Plb.2.33.6. 2. ἡ δ. τῆς χώρας *power of holding, capacity*, D.S.3.37. 3. *containing, storage*, *PPetr*. 3 p.141 (iii B.C.). II. *separating* or *distinguishing* in thought, Epicur.*Ep*.1 p.13 U., Phld.*D*.3.8; κατὰ διάληψιν *separately*, Id.*Ir*. p.76 W., *Rh*.1.91 S. III. *judgement, opinion*, Epicur.*Nat*.28.7; ἡ περὶ θεῶν δ. Plb.6.56.6; αἱ ὑπὲρ τῶν ἐν Ἅιδου δ. ib.12, cf. Lxx 2 *Ma*. 3.32; ἐγέννησε τὴν περὶ αὐτοῦ δ. ὡς.. D.S.18.54: esp. in good sense, τῆς προαιρέσεως ἐπ' ἀγαθῷ τὴν δ. ἐχούσης *Inscr.Prien*.117.60 (i B.C.); ἀρετῇ καὶ δ. *BCH*37.125 (Abdera, ii B.C.). 2. *sentence, punishment*, ἐνέχεσθαι ἱεροσυλίᾳ καὶ πίπτειν ὑπὸ πικροτέραν δ. *Annales du Service* 19.40, cf. 42 (Egypt, i B.C.). IV. *division*, Porph.*Sent*.36 (pl.); *distinction* of parts, Arist.*IA*705^{a}25: pl., *points of division* or *ramification*, Id.*PA*647^{b}2; of the *divisions* of the vertebrae, ib. 652^{a}17. 2. *interval*, = διάλειμμα, v.l. in Aret.*SD*1.12. V. *digression* in a narrative, Iamb.*Bab*.17.

διάλῐθος, ον, *set with precious stones*, *IG*2.652*B*13, Men.503, *Epit*.169, *OGI*56.59 (iii B.C.), Lxx *To*.10.7, Aristeas 62; ὅρμος ῥόδων δ. *IG*1^{2}.289; κόσμος Str.15.1.54; στέφανος D.C.44.6.

διαλιμπάνω, = διαλείπω, *intermit*, Gal.17(1).220, Mich. *in EN*560. 1, v.l. in *Act.Ap*.8.24.

διαλῑνάω, *slip through a net*, Phryn.*PS* p.64 B.:—Med., Eust.574. 31.

Διάλιος ἱερεύς, ὁ, = Lat. *flamen Dialis*, D.C.44.6.

διαλιχμάομαι, = διαλείχω, Iamb.*Bab*.3, Agath.2.3.

διαλλ-ᾰγή, ἡ, (διαλλάσσω) *interchange*, ὡς διαλλαγὰς ἔχοιμεν ἀλλήλοισιν ὧν πένοιτο γῆ E.*Supp*.209. II. *change*, δυναστειῶν, ἀρχόντων, D.C.47.5, 48.53; ἀριθμοῦ A.D.*Synt*.259.25: but esp. 2. *change* from enmity *to friendship, reconciliation*, Hdt.1.22, Is.7. 44; Δ. personified, Ar.*Ach*.989: in pl., E.*Ph*.375, Ar.*V*.472, etc.; διαλλαγαὶ πρός τινα Isoc.4.94, cf. D.2.1. III. *difference*, D.H.*Isoc*.11. **-αγμα**, ατος, τό, *substitute, changeling*, E.*Hel*. 586. II. *difference*, D.H.7.64. III. *renewal*, *PLips*.97 xxvi 13 (iv A.D.). **-ακτήρ**, ῆρος, ὁ, *mediator*, A.*Th*.908 (lyr.), *OGI* 43.2 (iii B.C.), D.H.2.76, App.*Mac*.4, Poll.1.153. **-ακτήριος**, ον, *mediating, conciliating*, λόγοι D.H.5.31. **-ακτής**, οῦ, ὁ, = διαλλακτήρ, E.*Ph*.468, Th.4.60, *IG*12(7).3.31 (Amorgos), Arist. *Ath*.38.4, etc. **-ακτικός**, ή, όν, *inclined to mediate*, D.H.7. 34. **-αξις**, εως, ἡ, *separation*, μιγέντων Emp.8.3, cf. Hp.*Vict*.1. 10. 2. pl., *attempts at reconciliation*, Pl.*Ep*.350d. **-άσσω**, Att. -ττω, fut. -ξω: pf. διήλλαχα Dionys.Com. (v. infr.), A.D.*Synt*.70. 11. I. Med., *interchange*, τὰς τάξεις Hdt.9.47, cf. Pi.*O*.11(10).21: abs., *make an exchange*, X.*Cyr*.8.3.32, *Test.Epict*.2.14. II. *exchange*, i.e., 1. *give in exchange*, τί τινι E.*Alc*.14; τί τινι ἀντὶ ἀργυρίου Pl. *R*.371d; τινὰ ὑπέρ τινος one for another, D.H.10.24; τὴν σκευὴν πρὸς τὸν δεσπότην D.C.47.10; or, 2. *take in exchange*, δ. ἀετοῦ βίον *take* an eagle's life *for* one's own, Pl.*R*.620b; ἐσθῆτα τῇ συμφορᾷ πρέπουσαν Plu.*Cic*.19; δ. Μακεδονίαν *change* one land *for* another, i.e. *pass through* a land, X.*HG*4.3.3 (also abs., ἐξ ἄλλης εἰς ἄλλην πόλιν δ. Pl. *Sph*.223d):—Med., τι ἀντί τινος D.H.2.3. 3. simply, *change, alter*, κελεύθους Emp.35.15; τοὺς ναυάρχους X.*HG*1.6.4; τοὺς λόγους Arist. *Rh.Al*.1434^{a}38. 4. abs., *change, alter*, Emp.17.12; δ. ἀπ' ἀλλήλων *to be discordant*, Hp.*Vict*.1.6; διαλλάττοντας *different*, opp. ὁμοίους, Phld.*Sign*.3, al. b. *depart this life, die*, Lycurg.*Fr*.33, Corn.*ND* 35. 5. *change money*, δ. τὸ δηνάριον *OGI*484.10 (ii A.D.). III. esp. *change enmity for friendship, reconcile* one to another, τινά τινι Th.2.95, 6.47, etc.; πόλεις πρὸς ἀλλήλας Isoc.5.111: most freq. c. acc. pl. only, E.*Ph*.436, Antipho 6.39, Test.ap.D.59.47, D.24.91: rarely c. acc. sg., *make it up with* one, διαλλάξεις με φιλάσας Theoc.23. 42:—Pass. with fut. διαλλαχθήσομαι Ar.*V*.1395, etc.; διαλλαγήσομαι Pl.*R*.471a: pf. διήλλαγμαι A.*Th*.885 (lyr.): aor. -ηλλάχθην Ar.*Lys*. 900, -ηλλάγην ib.1161:—*to be reconciled, to be made friends*, A.l.c., Pl. *Prt*.346b, etc.; τοῖς ἀποστᾶσι Isoc.9.63; πρός τινα περί τινος Id.3.33; τῆς πρόσθεν ἔχθρας ἐς φίλους E.*Med*.896, cf. And.2.26. IV. intr., c. dat. pers. et acc. rei, *differ from* one *in* a thing, εἶδος δ. οὐδὲν τοῖσι ἑτέροισι Hdt.7.70; δ. ταῖς ἡλικίαις Arist.*EN*1161^{a}5; κλήσει, οὐ φύσει D.H.1.29; πρός τινα Aristid.*Or*.36(48).16: also c. gen. pers., δ. τινός τινι Plb.2.37.11; ἔν τινι Luc.*Pisc*.23: abs., πολὺ διήλλαχεν Dionys.Com.2.10; τὸ διαλλάσσον τῆς γνώμης Th.3.10: pf. part.

διηλλαχῶς *differing*, τῇ ἐγκλίσει A.D. l. c. 2. *excel*, πολὺ δ. τῇ ἀρετῇ Arist.*EN*1165^{b}24; τινῶν τῷ μεγέθει D.S.1.35, D.H.*Th*.51:—so, V. Pass., *to be different*, τοῖς εἴδεσι διηλλαγμένα Th.3.82; πρὸς τὸν καιρόν Luc.*Salt*.19. **-ηλος**, ον, *reciprocating*, λόγος *Stoic*.2.90; *interchangeable*, of the order of words, A.D.*Adv*.126.2; *confused*, of argument, Id.*Pron*.50.20; δ. τρόπος argument *in a circle*, S.E.*P*.1.117, 2.68; δ. δεῖξις Dam.*Pr*.290. II. *interrelated, interdependent*, Plot.6.8.14. **-οιόω**, strengthd. for ἀλλοιόω, Thphr. *CP*5.6.12 (Pass.), *Od*.59.

διάλλομαι, *leap across*, τάφρον X.*Eq*.8.8, Plu.*Rom*.10.

διάλλῠδις, Adv. = ἄλλυδις (q.v.) ἄλλῃ, Epic. in *Arch.Pap*.7.4.

διαλλύος· ὁ ἀντὶ ἄλλου διακονῶν, Hsch. (Perh. f.l. for διάμοιος.)

δίαλμα, ατος, τό, as gymnastic term, = ἅλμα, Sch.Pi.*O*.13.39.

διᾰλοάω, strengthd. for ἀλοάω, Ael.*NA*1.9.

διαλογ-ή, ἡ, (διαλέγω) *estimate, enumeration*, τῶν ψήφων Arist.*Pol*.1268^{b}17; ἡ δ. τῶν ἕξεων καθ' ἕκαστα τὰ πάθη Id.*EE*1222^{b}5. 2. = διάλογος or διάλεξις, Ps.-Hdt.*Vit.Hom*.36. 3. *account*, *BGU*584.4, 578.4 (ii A.D.). 4. οἱ ἐπὶ τῆς δ. or πρὸς τῇ δ., officials in charge of *checking and transmission of documents* to the archives, *POxy*.34^{v}ii 3 (ii A.D.), *PLips*.10 ii 33 (iii A.D.). **-ίζομαι**, pf. -λελόγισμαι Amphis 33.9:—*balance accounts*, πρός τινα D.52.3; τινί *PSI*5.510.10 (iii B.C.):—Pass., *SIG*241 *C*127 (Delph., iv B.C.). 2. *calculate exactly*, ὁπόσον.. Diph.43.15, cf. Amphis l. c.; *consider*, ἀεί τι δ. καλόν Democr.112, cf. Isoc.6.90, Men.*Epit*.36; κενὰ δ. ib.347; πρὸς ὑμᾶς αὐτούς Is.7.45; *stop to consider*, D.18.98; *distinguish between*, τὰ καλὰ καὶ τὰ μή Aeschin.1.18. II. *debate, argue*, περί τινος X.*Mem*.3.5.1. III. *impute*, τί τινι Lxx 2*Ki*.19.19(20). IV. c. acc. loci, *hold a circuit court* (Lat. *conventus*) *for* a district, *PRyl*.74.8 (ii A.D.), *POxy*.484.24 (ii A.D.); ἐν Ἰουλιοπόλει *BGU*903.18 (ii A.D.). **-ικός**, ή, όν, *belonging to dialogue*, or *in dialogue form*, περίοδος Demetr.*Eloc*.19, 21; εἶδος συγγραφῆς Porph.*Plot*.9, 17; συγγράμματα Phlp.*in Cat*.3.15, cf. Dex.*in Cat*.4.2. Adv. -κῶς, ἀπαγγέλλειν Theon *Prog*.4. **-ισμα**, ατος, τό, = sq. II, in pl., Epicur.*Ep*.1 p.22, 2 p.35 U. **-ισμός**, ὁ, *balancing of accounts*, D.36.23, *PRev.Laws* 17.17 (pl.), *IG*5(1).1432.6 (Messene), etc.: hence, II. *calculation, consideration*, Pl.*Ax*.367a; δ. λαβεῖν περὶ σφῶν αὐτῶν Str.5.3.7; ὁ δ. οὗτος this *consideration*, Phld.*D*.1.15. III. *debate, argument, discussion*, Epicur.*Fr*.138 (pl.), Metrod.37, Plu.2.180c. IV. *circuit court*, τοῦ νομοῦ δ. ποιῆσαι *PLond*.2.358.19, cf. *BGU*19 i 13 (ii A.D.). V. *judicial inquiry*, *PTeb*.27.35 (ii B.C.), *PFay*.66.2 (ii A.D.). **-ιστέον**, *one must calculate*, Sor.1.96. **-ιστικός**, ή, όν, *of* or *for discourse*: ἡ -κή *the reasoning faculty*, Plu.2.1004d. **-ος**, ὁ, (διαλέγομαι) *conversation, dialogue*, Pl.*Prt*.335d, Demetr.*Eloc*.223; δ. τῆς ψυχῆς πρὸς αὐτήν Pl.*Sph*.263e; οἱ Σωκρατικοὶ δ. Arist.*Fr*.72; τὰ ἐν τοῖς δ. *debating arguments*, Id.*APo*.78^{a}12: generally, *talk, chat*, Cic.*Att*.5.5.2. II. perh. *speech* or *series of speeches, debate* (cf. διάλεξις), *IG*3.1128, al. III. = διαλογισμός I, *PHib*.1.122 (iii B.C.), *PTeb*.58.31 (ii B.C.).

διαλοιδορ-έομαι, *rail furiously at*, τινί Hdt.2.121.δ'; ἀπειλήσας καὶ διαλοιδορηθείς D.21.86.—Act. only in late authors, v.l. in Lib.*Decl*.40.11. **-ησις**, εως, ἡ, *railing, abuse*, Lxx *Si*.27.15.

δίαλον· φανερόν, and **διάλας**· τὰς δήλας καὶ φανεράς, Hsch.

διαλοξ-εύω, *turn aside* or *askance*, ὄμμα Lib.*Descr*.30.16. **-ος**, ον, *sidelong*, στροφαί ib.12.

διαλουφῶν· διατίλλων, Hsch.

δίαλσις, εως, ἡ, perh. *nourishing*, *GDI*5125 (Crete).

διαλῠγ-ίζω, *twist about*, and **-ισμα**, ατος, τό, *bend*, both in Hsch.

διαλῡμαίνομαι, aor. 1 διελυμηνάμην E.*Or*.1515:—*maltreat shamefully*, τινά Hdt.9.112; Ἑλλάδα δ. E. l. c.; ἵμερός με δ. Ar.*Ra*.59, etc. 2. *cheat grossly*, δ. τινὰ ταῖς κοτύλαις Id.*Pl*.436. 3. *falsify, corrupt*, τὸ νόμισμα Id.*Th*.348; of poetry, Id.*Ra*.1062. 4. *ruin, spoil*, τὰ πολλὰ Plu.*Ant*.24: c. dat., Jul.*Or*.2.54b. II. Pass., Orib.7.20.5: pf. part. διαλελυμασμένος in Hdt.9.112: aor. διελυμάνθην E.*Hipp*.1349 (lyr.).

διαλῡπέω, *grieve sorely*, Plu.2.578c (Pass.).

διά-λῠσις, εως, ἡ, (διαλύω) *separating, parting*, δ. τῆς ψυχῆς καὶ τοῦ σώματος Pl.*Grg*.524b; δ. τοῦ σώματος its *dissolution*, Id.*Phd*.88b, cf. Democr.297; τὴν τῶν γεφυρῶν οὐ δ. the failure to *break* the bridges, Th.1.137; *disbanding* of troops, X.*Cyr*.6.1.3; *breaking up* of an assembly, opp. συλλογή, Pl.*Lg*.758d; δ. ἀγορῆς *the time of* its *breaking up*, Hdt.3.104; τὴν δ. ἐποιήσαντο *broke off* the action, Th.1.51; χρεῶν δ. *liquidation* of debts, Pl.*Lg*.684d, cf. *POxy*.104.20 (i A.D.), etc.; δ. γάμου *divorce*, Plu.*Sull*.35, etc.; ἡ φθορὰ δ. οὐσίας Arist.*Top*.153^{b}31: hence abs., *dissolution*, opp. σύνθεσις, Id.*Cael*.304^{b}29, cf. Thphr.*Ign*.37; διάκρισις καὶ δ. Pl.*Phlb*.32a; opp. γένεσις, Phld.*D*.3.6; *resolution* into elements, e.g. of words into letters, D.H.*Comp*.14; *dissolution* of friendship, Arist.*EN*1164^{a}9, 1165^{b}36; of partnerships, κοινωνίαι καὶ -σεις Pl.*Lg*.632b; συμμαχία καὶ δ. Arist.*Pol*.1298^{a}5. 2. *ending, cessation*, κακῶν E.*Ph*.435; πολέμου Th.4.19, v.l. in Isoc.6.51: abs., *cessation of hostilities*, *Com.Adesp*.21.23 D.; *settlement, compromise*, *IG*12(2).6.20 (Mytilene, iv B.C.), *PAmh*.2.63.9 (iii A.D.), etc.: in pl., *settlement* of a dispute, ἠξίου δὲ καὶ πρὸς ἔμ' αὐτῷ..γίγνεσθαι τὰς διαλύσεις D.21.119, cf. Phoenicid.1. 3. *solution* of a problem, A.D.*Synt*.243.11; χρησμῶν Luc.*Alex*.49. 4. *refutation* of an argument, S.E.*P*.2.238. 5. *resolution of a diphthong*: ἐν διαλύσει, = διαλελυμένως, A.D.*Pron*.29.13. 6. Rhet., *asyndeton*, Alex.*Fig*.2.12, etc. 7. *discharge*, χορηγιῶν *PRyl*.181.10 (iii A.D.); τῶν χρεωστουμένων *POxy*.71.13 (iv A.D.). 8. *deed of separation* or *divorce*, *PLips*.39.10 (iv A.D.); ἔγγραφος δ. *PMasp*.153.16 (vi A.D.). 9. *division* of inheritance, *Sammelb*.6000.22 (vi A.D.), etc. **-λῡσίφῐλος** [σῐ], ον, *love-dissolving*, *AP*5.20 (Rufin.). **-λῡσος**, ὁ, *releaser*, coined as expl. of Διόνυσος, Corn.*ND*30. **-λῠτέον**, *one must dissolve*, φιλίαν Arist.*EN*1165^{b}17. **-λύτης** [ῠ], ου, ὁ, *dissolver, breaker-up*, τῆς ἑταιρίας Th.3.82; εἰρήνης Procop.*Pers*.1.14. **-λῠτικός**, ή, όν, *able to sever*, τινός (sc. τέχνη) Pl.*Plt*.281a; *destructive*, Id.*Ti*.60b; opp. γεννητικός, Phld.*D*.3.9. Adv. -κῶς Arist.*Top*.153^{b}32. II. Medic., *relaxing*, νότοι Hp.*Aph*.3.5. III. *embodying a settlement* or *compromise*, ὁμολογία *PMasp*.154.1 (vi A.D.). **-λῠτος**, ον, *relaxed*, Plu.2.136b; ἁρμογαί Luc.*Trag*.222. II. διαλῠτός, ή, όν, *capable of dissolution*, Pl.*Phd*.80b, v.l. in *Ti*.57b, Ph.1.495; = φθαρτός, Phld.*D*.3.9.

διαλύτρωσις, εως, ἡ, *ransom*, ἀνδρῶν, αἰχμαλώτων, Plb.6.58.11, 27.14.1.

διαλύω, fut. -λύσω, etc., *loose one from another, part asunder*, διαπλέκων καὶ διαλύων twining and *untwining*, Hdt.4.67; νὺξ δ. τοὺς ἀγωνιζομένους Id.8.11; δ. τὸν σύλλογον, τὴν συνουσίαν, τὴν πανήγυριν, etc., *break* it *up*, *dismiss* it, Id.7.10.δ', Pl.*Ly*.223b, X.*Cyr*.6.1.10, etc.; τὴν σκηνὴν εἰς κοίτην δ. *break up* the party and go to bed, ib.2.3.1; δ. τὴν στρατιάν ib.6.1.6; τὸ ναυτικόν *disband* it, Th.2.93:—Med., συνουσίας Pl.*Grg*.457d:—Pass., of an army, assembly, etc., *disperse*, Hdt.1.128, etc.; ἐκ τοῦ συλλόγου Id.3.73, cf. 8.56: in fut. Med., *part* from one's escort, Th.2.12; of a man, *die*, X.*Cyr*.8.7.20. 2. *dissolve* into its elements, *break up, destroy*, δ. καὶ ἀπολλύναι Pl.*R*.609a sq.; ἐξ ἑνὸς εἰς πολλὰ δ. Id.*Ti*.68d; *disperse, break up* a herd of sheep, *BGU*1012.12 (ii B.C.); *break up* a ship, παλαιὰν τριήρη δ. *IG*2.804, cf. *PSI*4.382 (iii B.C.); τρίπους, ὅρμος διαλελυμένος, *SIG*²588.169, 198 (Delos, ii B.C.); τὰς οἰκήσεις Plb.4.65.4; *dissolve*, κοινόν *Test.Epict*.8.6; σῴζεσθαι καὶ διαλυθεῖσαν οἴχεσθαι πολιτείαν Pl.*Lg*.945c; of the sun, *thaw* frozen things, X.*Cyn*.5.2:—Pass., ἐξ ὧν σύγκειται καὶ εἰς ἃ διαλύεται Arist.*GC*325^{b}19, cf. *Ph*.204^{b}33, etc. 3. *break off, put an end to* friendship, ὁμολογίας Isoc.4.175; φιλίαν Arist.*EN*1157^{b}10:—Pass., of married persons, *separate, be divorced*, *SIG*364.59 (Ephesus):—Med., διαλύσασθαι ξεινίην Hdt.4.154: abs., *dissolve friendship*, Arist.*EN*1162^{b}25:—Pass., αἱ σπονδαὶ διελέλυντο Th.5.1. 4. *put an end to* enmity, ἔχθραν, πόλεμον, Id.8.46:—Med., δ. ἔχθρας Is.7.11; διαφοράς Isoc.12.160; πολέμους Id.4.172, cf. D.4.15: in plpf. Pass. (with Med. signf.), διελέλυσθε τὸν πόλεμον Isoc.14.27 (v.l. διελύεσθε):—Pass., τὰς ἔχθρας διαλύεσθαι Th.4.19: hence, b. c. acc. pers., *reconcile*, πρὸς ἔμ' αὐτὸν διαλύειν ἠξίου D.21.122, cf. 41.14; δ. τινὰς ἐκ διαφορᾶς Plb.1.87.4; οὐ γὰρ ἦν ὁ διαλύσων οὔτε λόγος οὔτε ὅρκος Th.3.83; esp. in legal proceedings, *PHamb*.25.5 (iii B.C.), etc.:—Pass. and Med., c. gen. rei, διαλύεσθαι νείκους *to be parted from* quarrel, i.e. be reconciled, E.*Or*.1679 (v.l. νείκας); so διαλυθείσης τῆς διαφορᾶς prob. in D.S.14.110: also abs., *to be reconciled, make up a quarrel*, X.*HG*7.4.25, cf. Test.ap.Aeschin.1.66, Thphr.*Char*.12.14; πρός τινας D.38.24; περί τινος Lys.4.1: in fut. Med., ὅπως..μὴ διαλύσει D.21.216. 5. generally, *put an end to, do away with*, χρήμασι τὴν διαβολήν Th.1.131; πάσας αὐτοῦ διαλύσω τὰς ἀπολογίας D.27.58; τὸν ἐχόμενον φόβον δ. τῶν Ἑλλήνων Pl.*Mx*.241b:—so in Med., ἐγκλήματα δ. Th.1.140; δ. περὶ τῶν ἐγκλημάτων ib.145; διαβολάς Isoc.11.37, 15.16; τι τῶν κατηγορημένων Id.12.218; δ. ἃ ἐψηφίσασθε *cancel* your vote, Lys.18.15; διαλύσασθαι τὰ πρὸς ἀλλήλους *settle* mutual claims, Isoc.4.40. 6. *solve* a difficulty, Pl.*Sph*.252d; τὴν ἀπορίαν Arist.*Metaph*.1062^{b}31:—Med., διαλύσεσθαι σόφισμα S.E.*P*.2.238. 7. δ. τὰς τιμάς *pay the full* value, D.29.7; *pay, discharge*, τὴν δαπάνην Hdt.5.30; χρήματα D.20.12; τὰ συμβόλαια Arist.*Pol*.1276^{a}11; χρέος τινί Plb.31.27.4; πάντα διελέλυτο D.28.2: also c. acc. pers., δ. τὸν ναύκληρον *satisfy* him, i.e. *pay* him *off*, D.49.29, cf. 34.40, 36.50:—Med., *order* debts *to be paid*, διαλέλυμαι ταῦτα Arr.*An*.7.10.3; but also, *to have* them *paid to oneself*, D.Chr.46.6. II. *relax, weaken*, τὸ σῶμα Hp.*Aph*.3.17; esp. of the result of hunger, διαλύεσθαι τῷ λιμῷ *UPZ*11.27 (ii B.C.), cf. 42.9 (also in Act. intr., ὑπὸ τῆς λιμοῦ δ. ib.122.23 (ii B.C.)); *make supple and pliant*, Ar.*Pax*85:—Pass., δ. καὶ ἀδυνατεῖν Arist.*HA*585^{a}33; ἀνάπλους διαλελυμένος a sailing out *in loose order*, Plb.16.2.6; διαλελυμένη λέξις a *lax* style, D.H.*Lys*.9. 2. abs., *slacken one's hold, undo*, Theoc.24.32.

διαλφῐτόω, *to fill full of barley meal*, Ar.*Nu*.669.

διαλωβάομαι, Dep. strengthd. for λωβάομαι, Plb.11.7.2: pf. part. Pass., in pass. sense, Plu.*Caes*.68: metaph., δόξαι διαλελωβημέναι Id.2.986e.—Act. -λωβάω only late, Mich. *in EN*503.21.

διαμᾰγεύω, *charm with magic arts*, Luc.*Am*.41 (Pass.).

διᾰμᾰθύνω, *grind to powder, utterly destroy*, πόλιν διημάθυνεν A.*Ag*.824; κύνες διημάθυνον ἄνδρα δεσπότην (sc. Actaeon) Id.*Fr*.244.

διαμάλαξις [μᾰ], εως, ἡ, *softening*, Gal.11.714.

διαμᾰλάττω, strengthd. for μαλάττω, Sor.1.118, Luc.*Prom*.13:—Med., Hp.*Steril*.221.

διαμανθάνω, *learn by inquiry*, Philostr.*VA*1.16.

διαμαντ-εία, ἡ, *oracular response*, prob. in *SIG*987.39 (Chios, pl.). **-εύομαι**, *determine by an oracle*, τι Pl.*Lg*.696a; *make divinations*, Id.*Sis*.387e; ὄρνισι or ἐπ' ὄρνισι, Plu.*TG*17, *Cam*.32. II. *consult an oracle*, περί τινος D.H.3.69, Plu.2.302d.

διάμαξος [ᾰμ], ον, *for a chariot*, ὁδὸς δ. *carriage*-road, *GDI*5075.56 (Crete).

διαμάρανσις [μᾰ], εως, ἡ, *wasting away*, Alex.Aphr.*in Mete*.121.28.

διᾰμαρτ-άνω, fut. -αμαρτήσομαι D.19.151:—strengthd. for ἁμαρτάνω, *miss entirely, go quite astray from*, τῆς ὁδοῦ Th.1.106; τοῦ πράγματος D.21.192, 51.2; τοῦ ἑταίρου Pl.*Phdr*.257d; τῆς ὀρθοτάτης πολιτείας Arist.*Pol.*1293^{b}25. 2. *fail utterly of, fail of obtaining,* τινός Th.2.78; τῶν ἐλπίδων Isoc.4.93; τοῦ ἀγῶνος Is.6.52; τῆς εἰρήνης D.18.30; δυοῖν χρησίμοιν οὐ δ. not *to miss both of* two good things, Id.19.151. 3. abs., *fail utterly,* opp. τυγχάνω, Pl.*Tht.*178a; *to be quite wrong,* Macho 2.6; γνώμῃ in judgement, D.24.48,110; δ. τοῖς ὅλοις Arist.*EN*1098^{b}28; ἐν τῇ ἀρχῇ ib.1163^{a}3; περί τι Id.*Oec.* 1345^{b}10:—Pass., τὰ πολλὰ.. διημαρτημένα *utter failures,* Pl.*Lg.*639e; διημαρτημένας δόξας Diogenian.Epicur.2.32; διημαρτημένος *faulty,* of style, Phld.*Rh.*1.8 S., Longin.33.1, Demetr.*Eloc.*114 (also in act. sense, πολλαχῇ διημαρτημένου τοῦ Πλάτωνος Longin.32.8, cf. Plu.2.44e). Adv. διημαρτημένως Poll.6.205. **-ημα,** ατος, τό, *mistake,* *POxy.*1235.64 (Arg. Men.). **-ητέον,** οὐ δ. *one must* not *miss,* Agath.1.5. **-ία,** ἡ, *total mistake,* τοῦ Ἀννίβου Plu.*Fab.*6; τοῦ τόπου ibid.; δ. τῶν ἡμερῶν *wrong reckoning* of the days, Th.4.89; δ. τῆς γλώττης, *lapsus linguae,* Luc.*Laps.*1. 2. *gross fault,* ἄγνοιαι καὶ δ. Ph.1.345, cf. Plu.2.153b; δ. ἐρωτικὴ *guilty passion,* Philostr. *VA*1.13: pl., *faults,* δ. καὶ.. ἐλαττώσεις Phld.*Lib.*p.19O. II. *failure in obtaining, disappointment in,* τινός Luc.*Sacr.*1, cf. D.C. 49.28.

διαμαρτῠρ-έω, as Att. law-term, *use a* διαμαρτυρία (q.v.), πρός τινα D.44.27. 2. c. inf., *affirm by a* διαμαρτυρία *that..,* δ. μὴ ἐπίδικον.. τὸν κλῆρον εἶναι Is.3.3, cf. D.44.48:—Pass., aor. διεμαρτυρήθην, *to be affirmed in a* διαμαρτυρία to be so and so, διεμαρτυρήθη μὴ Πλαταιεὺς εἶναι Lys.23.13, cf. Is.3.5; τὰ διαμαρτυρηθέντα Isoc.18.15. 3. Med., *testify against,* τὰ πραττόμενα J.*AJ*9.8.3. 4. *attest,* -ουμένην τὴν παρὰ τῶν θεῶν εὐμένειαν *Inscr.Prien.*108.20, 110.15 (ii B.C.). **-ία,** ἡ, as Att. law-term, *obstructive plea,* put forward at the preliminary investigation to prevent a case from coming to trial, D.44.58, Is.3.5, Harp.; καθάπερ διαμαρτυρίαν θέμενος Satyr.*Vit.Eur.Fr.*39 xvii 21. 2. generally, *affidavit,* *CPR*232.6 (ii/iii A.D.), etc. II. generally, *testifying, solemn protest,* τοῦ ἔθνους Lxx 4*Ma.*16.16.

διαμαρτύρομαι [ῡ], aor. 1 -μαρτῠράμην: pf. -μεμαρτύρημαι [ῡ], Dep.:—abs., *call gods and men to witness, protest solemnly,* esp. in case of falsehood or wrong, βοᾶν καὶ δ. D.18.23,143; δ. μή.., c. inf., Id.33.20; δ. ὅπως μή.., c. fut., Id.42.28; δ. τινὶ μὴ ποιεῖν *protest against* his doing, Aeschin.2.89: c. inf., Plb.1.33.5, al.; *call to witness,* ὑμῖν τὸν οὐρανὸν Lxx*Ju.*7.28. 2. generally, *protest, asseverate,* Pl.*Phd.*101a, etc., *PSI*4.422 (iii B.C.): c. acc., *bear witness to,* τὸ εὐαγγέλιον *Act.Ap.*20.24; *testify,* Lxx*De.*32.46, al.; τῇ Ἱερουσαλὴμ τὰς ἀνομίας αὐτῆς ib.*Ez.*16.2. 3. abs., *beg earnestly of* one, *conjure* him, X.*Cyr.*7.1.9; δ. καὶ παρακαλεῖν *Act.Ap.*2.40; δ. τινὰ ἵνα .. 1*Ep.Ti.*5.21.

διαμᾰσ-άομαι, *chew up,* Arist.*HA*612^{a}1, Thphr.*CP*6.9.1, Apolloph.5, Lxx*Si.*34(31).16, Luc.*Alex.*12; δ. τὴν γλῶτταν, for ἐνδακεῖν, Alciphr.3.57:—Pass., *to be chewed,* Arist.*Pr.*890^{a}25, *Gp.*12.33. II. metaph., *carp at,* τι Philostr.*VSPraef.* **-ημα,** ατος, τό, *that which is chewed,* Hp.*Aff.*4, Dsc.1.96. **-ησις,** εως, ἡ, *chewing up,* Dsc.1.18. **-ητέον,** *one must chew,* Apollon.ap.Gal.12.999. **-ητός,** ή, όν, *fit for chewing,* Hp.*Aff.*4.

διαμάσσω, Att. -ττω, *bake to a turn,* μαζίσκας -μεμαγμένας Ar.*Eq.* 1105: metaph., λόγον δ. Id.*Av.*463.

διαμαστῑγ-όω, *scourge severely,* Phld.*Rh.*2.298 S.:—Pass., *bear marks of scourging,* Pl.*Grg.*524c. **-ωσις,** εως, ἡ, *severe scourging,* esp. of the Spartan boys, Plu.2.239d.

διάμαστος· θεός, Hsch. (Perh. of Artemis Ephesia.)

διαμαστροπεύω, *pander*: metaph. in Pass., -ομένης τῆς ἡγεμονίας γάμοις *bargained away* by a marriage, Plu.*Caes.*14.

διαμασχᾰλίζω, *stick under one's arm,* τι Ar.*Fr.*253.

διαμᾰχ-ετέον, *one must strive earnestly,* Pl.*Sph.*241d (v.l. διαμαχητέον), *R.*380b; *one must contend,* πρός τι D.Chr.8.35 (-ητέον). **-έω,** = διαμάχομαι, πρὸς τὴν ἀνάγκην J.*BJ*6.9.4. **-η,** ἡ, *a fight, struggle,* πρὸς φόβους καὶ λύπας Pl.*Lg.*633d, cf. J.*BJ*6.2.8 (pl.), Ph.1.7, al., Plu.2.74c, etc. **-ησις,** εως, ἡ, *struggle,* Gal.9.921 (ap.Aët.5.24). **-ομαι,** fut. -μαχέσομαι (v.l. for -μαχεσώμεθα aor. subj.) Hdt.9.48:—*fight, contend,* σιδήρῳ E.*Supp.*678; εἷς πρὸς ἕνα Pl.*Lg.* 833e; opp. λανθάνειν, Id.*R.*345a; πρός τι v.l. in D.17.18; περὶ τῆς χώρης τοῖς ἐπιοῦσιν Hdt.4.11; περὶ τοῦ πρότερος εἰπεῖν Ar.*Eq.*339, cf. Pl.*Men.*86c; περὶ τούτου ὡς οὐκ.. Lys.4.1; ὑπέρ τινος Pl.*Smp.*207b; δ. μὴ μεταγνῶναι ὑμᾶς I *resist to the uttermost* your change of opinion, Th.3.40; δ. τὸ μὴ θανεῖν E.*Alc.*694. 2. *exert oneself, strive earnestly,* περὶ τούτου ὅπως.. Pl.*Prt.*325d; ὅπως μή.. Id.*Grg.*502b. 3. in argument, *contend* or *maintain* that.., c. acc. et inf., Id.*Tht.*158d: with a neg., δ. τι μὴ εἶναι Th.3.42; δ. ὅτι οὐκ ἀπόλλυται Pl.*Phd.* 106c; ὡς οὐ.. Id.*Prm.*127e, etc.; also δ. τι *carry* a point, Id.*Sph.* 261a.

διαμαψαμένη· διασμηξαμένη, διαψησαμένη, Hsch.

διᾰμάω, fut. -ήσω, *to cut through,* χιτῶνα Il.3.359; λευκὴν παρηΐδα E.*El.*1023; διὰ λαιμὸν ἀμῆσαι A.R.4.374 (tm.). II. *scrape* or *clear away,* δακτύλοις δ. χθόνα E.*Ba.*709:—also in Med., διαμᾶσθαι τὸν κάχληκα Th.4.26; τὴν χιόνα Plb.3.55.6; τὴν ψάμμον J.*AJ*3.1.3.

διαμβλώττω, *procure abortion,* Et.Gud.

διαμεθίημι, *leave off,* μόχθον E.*Ba.*627; *give up,* τι Id.*El.*978.

διᾰμείβω, *exchange,* τι πρός τι one thing *with* another, Pl.*Plt.*289e; τὰς οἰκίας J.*BJ*1.6.1:—Med., τισὶ τῆς ἀρετῆς τὸν πλοῦτον Sol.15.2; τινί τι ἀντί τινος Pl.*Lg.*915e; τὰ ἱμάτια πρός τινα Plu.*Cim.*10; διαμεῖψαι Ἀσίαν Εὐρώπης *change* Asia *for* Europe, i.e. *pass into* Asia, E.*IT*397 (lyr.); δ. μεταβολὴν Dam.*Pr.*392; δ. τὴν φύσιν πρός τι ib. 396. 2. δ. ὁδὸν *finish* a journey, A.*Th.*334 (lyr.):—Med., δολιχῆς τέρμα κελεύθου διαμειψάμενος Id.*Pr.*287 (anap.); but in Med. also, *pass through,* πολλὰ φῦλα Id.*Supp.*543 (lyr.); πόντου πεδίον Id.*Fr.*150 (lyr.). b. *cross, traverse,* ὄρη Procop.*Goth.*3.40. 3. *change,* χρόα Parm.8.41 (tm.):—abs. in Med., *alter,* Hdt.9.108. 4. Med., ἀγορὰς διαποντίους δ. *trade in* foreign markets, D.H.5.66. 5. Med., *requite,* D.C.56.6.

διαμειδιάω, *smile,* Pl.*Ti.*21c, Plu.2.152c, D.C.71.32.

διάμειπτος [ᾰ], ον, *communicable,* Sapph.14.

διαμειρᾰκιεύομαι, *strive hotly with,* τινί Plu.*Comp.Dem.Cic.*2.

διάμειψις [ᾰ], εως, ἡ, *exchange* of prisoners, Plu.*Fab.*7; of arms, Id.*Pyrrh.*17. II. *change,* τῆς μορφῆς Iamb.*Myst.*7.3.

διαμελαίνω, *make quite dark,* τὸν ἀέρα Plu.*Flam.*4. II. intr., *to be* or *become so,* Id.2.921f.

διαμελεοί· οἰκέται, Hsch.

διαμελετάω, *practise diligently,* Pl.*Prm.*126c:—Med., Max.Tyr. 7.7:—Pass., Pl.*Lg.*830b, cf. Sm.*Ps.*76(77).13: c. inf., δ. τοῦ θανάτου καταφρονεῖν Iamb.*Protr.*20.

διαμελ-ίζομαι, *rival in singing,* Plu.2.973b. **-ίζω,** *dismember,* D.S.3.65:—Pass., Lxx*Da.*3.29(96), Plu.2.993b. **-ισμός,** ὁ, *dismemberment,* ib.996c: pl., ib.355b.

διαμέλλ-ησις, εως, ἡ, *postponement, procrastination,* πολλὴν δ. φυλακῆς long *postponement* of precautionary measures, Th.5.99, cf. D.C.*Fr.*40.21. **-ησμός,** ὁ, = foreg., *Gloss.* **-ω,** fut. -μελλήσω, *to be always going* to do, *to make a show* of doing: hence, *delay, put off,* Th.1.71,142, Ph.1.353, Luc.*Nigr.*10, al.:—Pass., Th.8.54.

διαμεμερισμένως, (διαμερίζω) *separately,* γράφειν Sch.D.T.p.191 H.

διαμέμφομαι, *blame greatly,* τι Th.8.89; τοὺς φιλοσοφοῦντας Isoc. 3.1; τινὰ ἐπί τινι D.C.46.51; τινὰ ὅτι.. Arist.*PA*663^{a}35.

διαμένω, fut. -μενῶ Epich.[265] (prob.), Men.*Epit.*513: aor. -έμεινα D.4.15: pf. -μεμένηκα Plb.3.55.1:—*continue, persist,* of disease, τοῖσι παιδίοισι Hp.*Aph.*3.28; διαμένει ἔτι καὶ νῦν τοῖς βασιλεῦσιν ἡ πολυδωρία X.*Cyr.*8.2.7: abs., *keep,* of seeds, Thphr.*HP*7.5.5; *persevere,* ἐν τῇ ἕξει Pl.*Prt.*344b; ἐπὶ τῇ διατριβῇ X.*Ap.*30; δ. ἐν ἑαυτῷ *maintain* his *purpose,* Plb.10.40.6: c. dat., τῇ φιλίᾳ D.S.14.48 codd.: abs., *hold out,* D.21.216; δ. ἕως.. Id.4.15; παρθένος δ. D.S.4.16; *to last, remain, live on,* Epich. l.c.; *endure, be strong,* Isoc.8.51; of form, colour, and the like, ταὐτὸν δ. *continue* the same, *be permanent,* Alex.34; χρῶμα διαμένον Nicol.1.28, cf. Antiph.232.2: c. part., δ. λέγων D.8.71; δ. ὅμοιοι ὄντες Arist.*EN*1159^{b}8: c. inf., *continue to..,* D.H.1.23.

διαμερ-ίζω, *divide,* Pl.*Phlb.*15e; *distribute,* τὸ ἐπιβάλλον Corn. *ND*27; τοὺς πόνους εἰς ἅπαν τὸ σῶμα Arist.*Pr.*885^{a}18:—Pass., *to be cut up,* Pl.*Lg.*849d. II. *part, separate,* Men.883:—Med., *divide* or *part among themselves,* *Ev.Matt.*27.35; πρὸς ἑαυτοὺς *PAmh.*2.152.18 (v/vi A.D.):—Pass., *to be set at variance,* *Ev.Luc.*12.52,53. **-ῐσις,** εως, ἡ, = sq., *Gloss.* **-ισμός,** ὁ, *division,* Pl.*Lg.*771d, *POxy.*12 vi 17, D.S.11.47, Lxx*Ez.*48.29 (pl.), J.*AJ*10.11.7. II. *dissension,* *Ev.Luc.*12.51. **-ιστής,** οῦ, ὁ, *a divider,* *Gloss.*

διάμεσος, ον, *midway between*: οἱ δ. *the middle class,* Hsch.

διαμέσταν· ἀλαζόνα, ἐξαλλάκτην, Hsch.; cf. διαμευστής.

διάμεστ-ος, ον, *brim-full,* Antiph.246; δ. εἰς τὸ ἥμισυ *exactly* half *full,* Arist.*Pr.*922^{b}36. **-όω,** *fill full,* ib.939^{a}4.

διαμετρ-έω, *measure through, measure out* or *off,* χῶρον δ. *measure* lists for combat, Il.3.315; *survey,* χώραν *OGI*502.12 (Aezani): abs., μετρῶν καὶ δ. καὶ λογιζόμενος D.Chr.40.7:—Med., Plb.6.41.3, Max. Tyr.6.3:—Pass., ἡμέρα διαμεμετρημένη *measured by the clepsydra,* D.19.120, Arist.*Ath.*67.3. 2. *measure out in portions, distribute,* μεδίμνους δ. τισὶ τῆς καθεστηκυίας τιμῆς D.34.39; οὐδὲν δ. τοῖς στρατιώταις *give out* no *rations,* X.*An.*7.1.40, cf. 41, etc.:—Med., *divide amongst themselves,* Orac.ap.Hdt.1.66, X.*Cyr.*7.5.9; *receive as one's share,* D.34.37:—Med. in act. sense, Call.*Ap.*55, *Dian.* 36. 3. Med., δ. τὸν βίον *die,* Procop.*Aed.*3.1. 4. *measure with the eye, scan,* Nonn.*D.*5.306, al. 5. *pass over, traverse,* Ὑδάσπην ib.23.149, cf. 22.42. II. Astron., δ. φάεσιν φάος ἀντικέλευθον *to be in opposition,* Man.4.74, cf. 296, Gal.19.557: c. acc., *to be diametrically opposite to,* τὸν ἥλιον Cleom.1.11: abs., ibid., Simp.*in Cael.*480.6; ὁκόταν ὁ χειμὼν διαμετρέῃ τῷ κατὰ λόγον Hp. *Ep.*19 (*Hermes* 53.70). **-ησις,** εως, ἡ, *measuring out,* Lxx 2*Ch.*3.3, J.*AJ*3.6.4, Plu.2.785d; *distribution* of corn, *SIG*976.55 (Samos, ii B.C.). II. Astron., *diametrical opposition,* Ptol.*Tetr.* 195, etc. **-ητός,** ή, όν, *measured out* or *off,* δ. ἐνὶ χώρῳ Il.3.344. II. *diametrical,* τὴν δ. (sc. ὁδὸν) διεξεληλυθέναι Dam.*Pr.* 87. **-ικός,** ή, όν, *diagonal*: [ἀριθμοί] *the numerators of the successive convergents to* $\sqrt{2}$ *expressed as a continued fraction,* *Theol.Ar.*3,59; cf. πλευρικός. **-ον,** τό, *measured allowance, soldiers' rations,* Plu. *Demetr.*40. **-ος,** ον, *diametrical*: Astrol., *diametrically opposed,* Ptol.*Tetr.*115, Man.1.89. II. Subst. δ. (sc. γραμμή), ἡ, *diagonal* of a parallelogram, Pl.*Men.*85b, al.; κατὰ δ. συντίθεσθαι, of triangles, *by the hypotenuses,* Id.*Ti.*54d; *diameter* of a circle, Arist.*Cael.*271^{a}12, etc.; *axis* of a sphere, Id.*MA*699^{a}29; *diameter* of other curves, Apollon.Perg.*Con.*1 *Def.*1; *axis* of a conic, Archim.*Aequil.*2.10; ἡ κατὰ διάμετρον σύζευξις, of circles, Arist.*EN*1133^{a}6; τὰ κατὰ δ. Id. *Cael.*277^{a}24; κεῖσθαι κατὰ δ. Id.*Mete.*363^{a}34, al.; κατὰ δ. κινεῖσθαι, of quadrupeds, which move the legs *cross-corner-wise,* as horses when *trotting* (opp. κατὰ πλευρὰν κινεῖσθαι ambling, in which the legs on either side move together), Id.*HA*490^{b}4, *IA*712^{a}25, cf. Plu. 2.43a; ἐκ διαμέτρου ἀντικείμενος, of planets, *in opposition,* *PMag. Par.*1.2221; ἐκ διαμέτρου ἡμῖν οἱ βίοι Luc.*Cat.*14. 2. prob. *mitre-square,* Ar.*Ra.*801.

διαμευστής, οῦ, ὁ, = ἀλαζών, Hsch.: also **διαμευτής** (-μέττης cod.), οῦ, ὁ, *cheat,* Id.

διαμήδομαι, = μήδομαι, Hom.*Epigr.*4.12.

διαμηκίζω, (μῆκος) *to be in direct opposition*, Ptol.*Tetr.*125,151.

διάμηκος, ον, *broad*, dub. in *Hippiatr.*14.

διαμηκύνω, *last out, live through*, ἡμέρας τέσσαρας *PMag.Leid.V.*11.29.

διαμηνύω, *point out clearly*, Str.11.14.4.

διαμηρ-ίζω, *femora diducere, inire*, Ar.*Av.*669, Zeno *Stoic.*1.59. **-ισμός**, ὁ, *femorum diductio*, ibid. (pl.).

διαμηρύω [ῡ], *arrange in kinks* (cf. μήρυμα), Hero *Aut.*10.3.

διαμηχᾰν-άομαι, *bring about, contrive*, δ. ὅπως.. Ar.*Eq.*917; δ. ζῶν εἰσιέναι ἐς Ἅιδου Pl.*Smp.*179d. **-ητέον**, *one must contrive*, Plu.2.131e.

διαμίγνῡμι or -ύω (Plu.2.1131e), fut. -μίξω, *to mix up*, l.c.:—Pass., διαμεμιγμένοι Pl.Com.174.9 codd. Ath.; cf. διαμίσγω.

διαμῑκρολογέομαι, *deal grudgingly*, πρός τινα Plu.*Sol.*30.

διάμιλλ-α [ᾰμ], ἡ, *fight*, of animals, Hierocl.pp.11,17 A. (pl.). **-άομαι**, fut. -ήσομαι Str.17.1.11:—*contend hotly, strive earnestly*, δέκα πρὸς δέκα ἀλλήλοις Pl.*Lg.*833e; τινί *with* one, Id.*R.*516e; πρός τινα Plb.16.21.6; δ. περί τινος about a thing, Pl.*R.*517d; τινὶ ἐν λόγοις καὶ ἐν ἔργοις ib.563a: c. gen. rei, δ. λειοτέρας ὁδοῦ Id.*Lg.*833b; τινὶ περὶ δεῖπνα Plu.*Them.*5: pf. διημίλληται in pass. sense, Luc.*Par.*58. **-ητέον**, *one must contend*, Plu.2.817d.

διαμιμνήσκομαι, only pf. Pass. διαμέμνημαι, *keep in memory*, X.*Mem.*1.4.13, D.H.4.9. II. *make mention of*, Ph.1.509, Lyd.*Mag.*1.7.

διαμῑνύρομαι [ῡ], *warble a plaintive ditty*, Ar.*Th.*100.

διαμίσγω, = διαμίγνυμι, Hp.*Mul.*1.64, Ph.*Bel.*88.13.

διαμῑσέω, *hate bitterly*, Arist.*Pol.*1274ᵃ34, Ph.1.396, J.*BJ*4.5.4, Plu.*Tim.*35 (Pass.), Ant.Lib.12.2 (Pass.).

διαμισθ-όω, *farm out*, *PAmh.*2.95.7, al., *OGI*669.14 (i A.D.), etc.:—Med., App.*BC*2.10. **-ωσις**, εως, ἡ, *farming out* of state land, *PTeb.*72.450 (ii B.C.), 376.15 (ii A.D.). **-ωτικόν**, τό, *rent* of state land, *BGU*475.1.

διαμιστύλλω, aor. 1 -εμίστῠλα, *cut up piecemeal*, Hdt.1.132.

διάμιτρος, ον, *veiled with a* μίτρα, Poll.4.151,154.

διαμμᾰτίζω, *knot* (a cord): pf. Pass., διημματισμένος κάλος Orib.49.22.8.

διαμμοιρηδά, Adv. *dividing in twain*, μέσσην νύκτα δ. φυλάξας A.R.3.1029.

δίαμμος, ον, *very sandy*, Plb.34.10.3, Str.1.3.7.

διαμνημον-ευτέον, *one must remember*, Aen.Tact.31.35. **-εύω**, *remember distinctly*, abs., Hdt.3.3, Lys.23.16, Antipho 5.54; c. gen. pers., Pl.*Smp.*180c; τι X.*Mem.*1.3.1, Phld.*Mort.*30, Plu.*Sol.*3, etc.:—Pass., διὰ τούτων διαμνημονεύονται D.S.12.13. 2. *mention, record*, Th.1.22; διαμνημονεύεται ἔχων he *is mentioned* as having, X.*Cyr.*1.1.2. 3. *call to mind*, τι Pl.*Epin.*976c.

διαμνημον-ικός, ή, όν, *having a good memory*, Suid. s. v. ἀνελέγετο:—also in form **-ητικός**, Id. s. v. Ἀπολλώνιος Τυανεύς.

διάμοιος· ὁ ἀντ' ἄλλου διακονῶν, Hsch. (fort. διαμοιβός).

διαμοιρ-άζω, *divide into equal portions, cut up*, κόστον Aët.1.138. **-ᾰσία**, ἡ, *division into equal portions*, βοός Tz. ad Hes.*Op.*56. **-άω**, *divide, rend asunder*, E.*Hipp.*1376 (lyr.):—Med., E.*Hec.*717, Orph.*Fr.*210:—Pass., Ath.1.12e. 2. Med., also, *portion out, distribute*, ἕπταχα πάντα διεμοιρᾶτο [ε̆] Od.14.434.

διαμολύνω [ῡ], *befoul with writing*, παλίμψηστα Plu.2.504d.

διαμονή, ἡ, (διαμένω) *continuance, permanence*, Arist.*Spir.*481ᵃ1, Epicur.*Ep.*2 p.38 U., Phld.*D.*3.8, *IG*12(5).659.5 (Syros), Ocell.1.9, Ph.1.2, al., Procl.*Inst.*129, *BGU*362 iv 11 (iii A.D.), etc.; of seeds or corn, *keeping*, Thphr.*HP*7.5.5, J.*BJ*7.8.4.

διαμόνῐμος, ον, *steadfast*, πιστὸν καὶ δ. Porph.*Abst.*1.52. Adv. -μως *permanently*, Phld.*Mus.*p.67 K.

διαμονομᾰχέω, *fight a single combat*, πρὸς ἀδελφούς Plu.2.482c, cf. Hld.7.16.

διάμονος, ον, *permanent*, ζωή *Sammelb.*4678.9 (vi A.D.).

διάμορφος, ον, *endued with various forms*, Emp.21.7. II. διάμορφον, = μανδραγόρας, prob. in Ps.-Dsc.4.75.

διαμορφοσκοπέομαι, *vie in beauty with*, τινί Ath.5.188d.

διαμορφ-όω, *give form to, shape*, ψυχὴν πρὸς εἶδος Ph.2.368; δρῦν ὥσπερ τρόπαιον Plu.*Rom.*16:—Pass., διαμεμορφωμένος *articulate*, Id.2.722c, cf. Ath.Med.ap.Orib.22.9.4. **-ωσις**, εως, ἡ, *forming, shaping*, τῆς ὕλης Plu.2.1023c; ἐμβρύων Ath.Med.ap.Orib.22.9.1. II. *gesture*, '*business*', in acting, Demetr.*Eloc.*195. **-ωτικός**, ή, όν, *formative*, φύσις Ptol.*Tetr.*142.

διάμοτ-ον, τό, *tent*, Paul.Aeg.4.54. **-όω**, (μότος) *put lint into* a wound, so as to keep it open, δ. ἕλκος Hp.*VC*14, Gal.13.752: hence **-ωσις**, εως, ἡ, Heliod.ap.Orib.44.14.14, Leonidas ap.Aët.6.1.

διαμ-πάξ (for δι-ανα-πάξ), Adv. *right through, through and through*, c. gen., στέρνων δ. A.*Pr.*65, cf. *Supp.*945, E.*Ba.*994 (lyr.); δι' αἴας Φρυγίας δ. A.*Supp.*548 (lyr.); ἐτέτρωτο τὸν μηρὸν δ. X.*HG*7.4.23; δ. ἄχρις Luc.*DMort.*27.4; πόδες δ. προσεληλαμένοι πρὸς τοὔδαφος Plu.*Crass.*25. **-πείρω**, poet. for διαναπ-, Q.S.1.614, Hsch. **-περές**, Adv., I. of Place, *through and through, right through*, c. gen., δ. ἀσπίδος Il.12.429, cf. 20.362; δ. στέρνων S.*Ph.*791: c. acc., βέβληαι κενεῶνα δ. Il.5.284; δ. οὖς prob. in A.*Ch.*380 (lyr.); δ. διὰ μέσου τοῦ [σφονδύλου] Pl.*R.*616e. 2. abs., *without break, continuously*, ἐκ κεφαλῆς..δ. ἐς πόδας ἄκρους Il.16.640; πέτρη ἠλίβατος ..δ. ἀμφοτέρωθεν Od.10.88; σταυροὺς..ἔλασσε δ. ἔνθα καὶ ἔνθα 14.11; ἡ δ' [the wall] ἕσπετο πᾶσα δ. all *in a piece*, Il.12.398. II. of Time, *throughout, for ever*, Od.8.245, Hes.*Th.*402, Emp.17.6; pleon., ἤματα πάντα δ. Il.16.499, cf. *Supp.Epigr.*1.409 (Eretria); αἰὲν διαμπερές *for ever and aye*, Il.15.70. (Found in tmesi διὰ δ' ἀμπερές 11.377, 17.309; cf. ἀμπερέως: poet. for δι-ανα-περές (πείρω).) **-περέως**, = foreg., *through and through*, of piercing pains, Hp.*Int.*8; also, διείσομαι πάντα δ. Nic.*Th.*495. **-περής**, ές, *piercing*, ὀδύνη Hp.*Mul.*2.125. **-περονάω** and **-πραθέειν**, perh. ff.ll. for διαπ-, Hsch.

διαμῠδαίνω, *putrefy*, A.*Fr.*54 A, cf. *AB*238, *EM*269.1.

διαμῡδᾰλέος, α, ον, *drenching*, δάκρυα A.*Pers.*539 (lyr.). (ῡ for ῠ metri gr.)

διαμῠδάω, *become fungoid*, of diseased bone, membrane, etc., Hp.*VC*21.

διαμύδησις [ῠ], εως, ἡ, *decay, mortification*, Sor.1.73.

διαμύθησις [ῡ], εως, ἡ, *deception, cajolery*, Hsch.

διαμῡθολογέω, *communicate by word of mouth, express in speech*, γλώσσῃ A.*Pr.*889 (lyr.); τι Pl.*Lg.*632e; δ. πρὸς ἀλλήλους *converse*, Id.*Ap.*39e; περί τινος Id.*Phd.*70b; *tell a story*, Max.Tyr.16.1.

διαμυκτηρίζω, strengthd. for μυκτηρίζω, D.L.9.113.

διαμυλλαίνω, *make mouths* (in scorn), Ar.*V.*1315.

διᾰμύσσω, *stimulate*, Paul.Aeg.3.9.

διαμφάδην [ᾰ], Adv., strengthd. for ἀμφάδην, Poll.2.129.

διαμφιβάλλω, *doubt*, ὅτι οὐ.. but that.., Simp.*in Cat.*417.5.

διαμφίδιος [φῐ], ον, *utterly different*, A.*Pr.*555 (lyr.; Hsch. also has -άδιον).

διαμφίς, Adv. *separately*, D.P.903.

διαμφισβητ-έω, *dispute, disagree*, πρὸς ἀλλήλους περί τινος Decr. ap.D.18.185, cf. Arist.*MM*1211ᵃ14; τινὶ περὶ μουσικῆς Ath.8.351a; ἀρετῆς κτλ. Plu.2.787d; δ. περί τινος *lay claim to*, Arist.*Pol.*1283ᵇ14; πρός τι ib.1287ᵇ35; δ. ποῖα θερμὰ τῶν ζῴων Id.*PA*648ᵃ24: abs., Id.*Pol.*1283ᵃ30, *CPR*1.20 (i A.D.), etc.:—Pass., διαμφισβητεῖται περὶ φιλίας οὐκ ὀλίγα not a few *questions are debateable*, Arist.*EN*1155ᵃ32; τὰ διαμφισβητούμενα the *points at issue*, D.44.57. **-ησις**, εως, ἡ, *disputing*, δ. ἔχει πότερον.. it admits of *dispute* whether.., Arist.*Pol.*1256ᵃ14; διαμφισβητήσεις ἔχειν contain *ambiguous points*, of Solon's laws, Id.*Ath.*35.2; χώρα ὑπὸ τὴν δ. ἠγμένη *disputed* territory, *SIG*685.55 (Crete); δ. παρέξειν πότερον.. Plu.*Tim.Praef.*: pl., Iamb.*Myst.*4.1.

διαμφοδ-έω, *miss the right* ἄμφοδος, Eust.789.54: metaph., *miss the right way* (in a question), S.E.*M.*9.31, cf. Hsch. s.v. ἀμφαλλάξαι. **-ησις**, εως, ἡ, *missing of the right* ἄμφοδος, Eust.789.51.

διαμωκ-άομαι, *mock* or *laugh at*, Phld.*Rh.*2.59 S., D.C.59.25, Iamb.*VP*33.234: abs., Aristaenet.1.27. **-ησις**, εως, ἡ, *mocking, raillery*, τινός Ath.5.200b.

διαμωλύω, *soften, mollify*, *BGU*1200.21 (i B.C.).

διανα-βάλλω, *delay, procrastinate*, *PTeb.*50.27 (ii B.C.):—Med., Hsch. s. v. διακρούεσθαι. **-βολή**, ἡ, *postponement, delay*, *EM*80.23 (pl.). **-γιγνώσκω**, *read through*, Isoc.12.201, Plb.31.21.9; Δημόκριτον πάντα δ. Damox.2.13:—Pass., D.C.58.10.

διᾰναγκ-άζω, *drill, train*, Pl.*Lg.*836a (Pass.); *reduce* dislocation, Hp.*Mochl.*38; δ. πόρους *force open* the pores, Id.*Vict.*2.64:—Pass., *to be dilated*, Id.*Fist.*4. **-ᾰσις**, εως, ἡ, *reduction* of dislocations, Id.*Mochl.*38. **-ασμός**, ὁ, = foreg.; *machine for this purpose*, Id.*Art.*47.

διανάγω, *bring back into its place*, Gal.18(1).421.

διανα-κᾰθίζω, = ἀνακαθίζω, Hp.*Mul.*2.201. **-κλάομαι**, Pass., *to be reflected*, Arist.*Pr.*934ᵃ22. **-κόπτω**, *pound up*, Sor.1.82. **-κύπτω**, *raise the head*, Aristeas 18; *look carefully into*, Ph.1.383.

διανᾰλίσκω, *consume*, dub. in D.C.*Fr.*55.1.

διανά-παυμα, ατος, τό, *intermission*, *AB*1167. **-παυσις**, εως, ἡ, *resting at intervals*, Arist.*Spir.*485ᵃ20, Diocl.*Fr.*142. **-παύω**, *allow to rest awhile*, Hp.*Aph.*2.48, Arist.*Pol.*1339ᵇ30, Plu.*Flam.*4; *interrupt*, τὸ συνεχές Luc.*Am.*7; δ. τὴν ταυτότητα *relieve* the monotony, D.H.*Comp.*12:—Med., *rest awhile*, Pl.*Lg.*625b, Ph.2.197, Porph.*Marc.*4:—also intr. in Act., Aristid.*Or.*51(27).17. **-πηδάω**, f.l. for ἀνα-, X.*Cyr.*1.4.4. **-πνοή**, ἡ, *breathing through*, Gal.18(2).899.

διαναρκάω, *grow stiff* or *numb*, Corn.*ND*35. 2. *remain torpid through* the winter, *hibernate*, f.l. in Thphr.*Fr.*171.7; cf. διαρκέω.

διαναρμοστέω, *to be out of time*, Poll.4.63.

διαναρτάομαι, f.l. in Iamb.*Protr.*13 (leg. δὴ ἀναρτᾶσθαι).

διανάσσω, *stop chinks*: *caulk ships*, Str.4.4.1:—Pass., pf. part. διανεναγμένος σφυγμός, name coined by Archig.ap.Gal.8.662.

διανά-στᾰσις, εως, ἡ, *rising up*, Hp.*Epid.*7.11 (of going to stool), Plb.5.70.8: pl., X.*Cyn.*10.18. **-στᾰτέον**, *one must make to get up*, τινά Sor.1.69. **-στρέφομαι**, *to be distorted, roll*, of the eyes, Herod.Med. in *Rh.Mus.*58.78.

διαναυμᾰχέω, *maintain a sea-fight*, Hdt.8.63, Th.8.27; πρός τινα Isoc.4.97.

διαναψύχω· *perfrigesco*, *Gloss.*

διανάω, *flow through, percolate*, Plu.*Aem.*14; cf. **διαναῦσαι**· διαπλεῦσαι, Hsch.

διανδής· πολυχρόνιος (Cret.), Hsch.

διάνδῐχα, Adv. = ἄνδιχα, *two ways*, δ. μερμηρίζειν halt *between two opinions*, Il.1.189; σοὶ δὲ δ. δῶκε endowed thee *by halves*, 9.37; in tmesi, διὰ δ' ἄνδιχα θυμὸν ἔχουσιν Hes.*Op.*13; διὰ δ' ἄνδιχα ἔαξα broke it *in twain*, Theoc.25.256, cf. A.R.2.1109; once in Trag., δ. κλῆθρα κλίνεται E.*HF*1029 (lyr.); also δ. νηὸς ἰούσης, perh. *with sails and oars*, A.R.1.934.

διανδρᾰγᾰθέω, *continue to behave honourably*, Wilcken *Chr.*10.3 (ii B.C.), *BGU*1204.6 (i B.C.).

διᾱνεκής, ές, v. διηνεκής.

διανέμ-ησις, εως, ἡ, *distribution*, Arist.*Mu*.401b13, J.*AJ*4.8.22, Corn.*ND*13, Plu.*Ant*.54. **-ητέον**, *one must distribute*, X.*Oec*.7.36, Iamb.*in Nic*.p.64P. **-ητής**, οῦ, ὁ, *distributor*, gloss on δατητής, *EM*249.43. **-ητικός**, ή, όν, *distributive*, τινὸς εἰς ἴσα μέρη Pl.*Ti*.55a, cf. Andronic.Rhod.p.576M.; τὸ δ. δίκαιον Arist.*EN*1131b27; of persons, ib.1134a3. **II.** Pass., *divisible*, εἰς ἴσα δ. Plu.2.1003c.

διᾰνεμόομαι, (ἄνεμος) Pass., *flutter in the wind*, Luc.*Im*.7, *AP*9.777 (Phil.); *to be blown away by the wind*, Eun.*Hist*.p.269D.

διανέμω, late fut. -νεμήσω App.*BC*5.3: aor. διένειμα X.*Cyr*.4.5.45, etc.; aor. regul. -ένειμα, but inf. διανεμῆσαι Did.*in D*.9.21: pf. -νενέμηκα X.*Cyr*.4.5.45:—*distribute, apportion*, τοῖς μὲν τιμάς, τοῖς δὲ ἀτιμίας Pl.*Lg*.830e, etc.; ἐπὶ τὰ αὐτῶν ἕκαστα ἐκμαγεῖα Id.*Tht*.194d; δ. μέρη *divide into* portions, Id.*Lg*.756c, cf. *Ti*.35b; ἡ χώρα κατὰ δώδεκα μέρη διανενέμηται Id.*Lg*.758e; δ. ἑαυτόν *distribute* oneself among friends, Arist.*EN*1171a3; δ. ἴσον αὐτόν [ὁ Πλοῦτος] Ar.*Pl*.510; ὁ διανέμων *the distributor*, Arist.*EN*1136b26; *assign*, Pl.*Cra*.430b, Arist.*Cael*.306b31:—Med., *divide among themselves*, τὰ κοινά And.1.135; τὴν ἀρχήν Pl.*Grg*.523a; δ. τὰ τῶν πλουσίων Arist.*Pol*.1281a15; also διανειμάμενοι δίχ' ἑαυτούς Pl.Com.153.2:—Pass., δ. εἰς τὸν λαόν *to be spread abroad*, *Act.Ap*.4.17. **II.** *set in order, govern*, ἄστυ Pi.*P*.4.261, cf. 8.62.

διανενοημένως, Adv., (διανοέω) *circumspectly*, Sch.A.R.1.1336.

διανεύω, *nod, beckon*, ταῖς κεφαλαῖς D.S.3.18; τινί to a person, Alex.261.12, *Ev.Luc*.1.22, Luc.*VH*2.25. **II.** *bend away from, avoid*, τὰς τῶν ὀργάνων ἐπιβολάς τι Plb.1.23.8; ὀργάς Plu.*Fr*.27.

διανέω, *swim across*, ἐς Σαλαμῖνα Hdt.8.89; τὸν Τίγρητα Luc.*Hist. Conscr*.19. **II.** c. acc., *swim through*, i.e. *get safe through*, δ. πέλαγος λόγων Pl.*Prm*.137a, cf. *R*.441c; ποταμόν Ael.*NA*3.6. **III.** metaph. in Med., *filter through*, c. gen., Marc.Sid.76.

διανήθω, in pf. part. Pass. -νενησμένος, *spin out*, Lxx *Ex*.35.6.

διάνημα, ατος, τό, *that which is spun, a thread*, Pl.*Plt*.309b.

διάνηξις, εως, ἡ, *swimming through*, Herm.ap.Stob.1.49.44.

διανηστ-εύω, *remain fasting*, Hp.*Aff*.27, J.*AJ*3.10.3. **-ισμός**, ὁ, *breakfast*, Philem.Gloss.ap.Ath.1.11d.

διανήχομαι, = διανέω, Hellanic.111J., J.*AJ*13.1.3, Plu.*Luc*.10, Ael.*NA*6.15, Palaeph.30, Porph.*Abst*.2.5; of sound, *penetrate*, Erinna 3: metaph., δ. τὸν βίον Vett.Val.68.12.

διάνηψις, εως, ἡ, *clearing off*, τῶν χυμῶν Aret.*CD*2.2 (perh. f.l. for -νιψις).

διανθ-έω, *flower again*, Plu. *in Arat*.7. **-ής**, ές, *double-flowering*, i.e. *twofold*, with outer (corolla) and inner (stamens and pistil) flower, Thphr.*HP*1.13.2. **II.** *flowering in succession*, ἀσφόδελος Nic.*Th*.534. **-ίζω**, *adorn with flowers*, δ. τὴν κεφαλὴν στεφάνοις Luc.*Bis Acc*.16 (Pass.); also with jewels, J.*AJ*8.5.2:—Pass., *to be picked out, decorated*, χλαμύδες διηνθισμέναι Plu.*Phil*.9; κέδρου ζῴδια χρυσῷ διηνθισμένα Paus.6.19.12; ξόανον χρυσῷ δ. Id.7.26.4, cf. Hdn.5.3.6; μηκέτι διηνθισμένος ποικιλίᾳ χρωμάτων, ὅλον δὲ λευκωθείς, of a leper, Ph.1.346.

διᾱνιάομαι, Pass., *grieve sorely*, Ael.*VH*1.24.

διανίζω, *wash out* or *thoroughly*, κύλικα, σκεῦος, λοπάδας, Crates Com.14.7, Eub.31, Damox.2.44; τὴν κοιλίαν Diocl.*Fr*.139:—Med., διανιψάσθω τὸ αἰδοῖον Hp.*Mul*.2.112.

διανίημι, *dissolve*, οἴνῳ *Hippiatr*.22.

διάνιον· κονία, Hsch.

διανίσσομαι, *go through*, τινός Pi.*P*.12.25, Opp.*H*.1.550: Ep. Subj. -νίσσεται Orph.*Fr*.285.56.

διανίστημι, fut. -στήσω, *awaken, rouse*, D.H.4.2, J.*AJ*6.13.9; *raise up*, opp. καταβάλλω, Ph.1.669:—Med., fut. -στήσομαι, *restore*, D.H.3.20. **II.** Pass., with aor. 2 and pf. Act., *stand up, rise*, νύκτωρ Arist.*Oec*.1345a16; *spring up* from ambush, Plb.3.74.1, cf. *PPetr*.2p.59 (iii B.C.), D.S.10.1, Plu.2.596a, etc. **2.** *stand aloof from, depart from*, τινός Th.4.128. **3.** *form factions*, περὶ σπουδὰς ὀρχηστῶν Plu.2.487f.

διάνιψις, εως, ἡ, (διανίζω) *ablution*, Hp.*Hum*.1; cf. διάνηψις.

διανο-έω, *have in mind*, Philostr.*Im*.2.1:—but in early writers always **-έομαι**, fut. -νοήσομαι: aor. διενοήθην, part. διανοηθείς in pass. sense, Pl.*Lg*.654c: aor. Med. -ησάμην D.S.20.3: pf. διανενόημαι Pl.*Alc*.1.106a: (νοέω):—*to be minded, intend, purpose*, c. inf. pres., fut., or aor., Hdt.2.121.δ' and 126, Ar.*Lys*.724, Pl.*R*.504e, etc.; μηδὲ δ. περὶ παραθήκης ἄλλο γε ἢ ἀποδιδόναι Hdt.6.86.δ'; διανενοημένοι βοηθεῖν Th.4.72, cf. 7.56; δ. τὴν ἀπόβασιν Id.4.29; διανοήθητε ἢ ὑπακούειν ἢ μὴ εἴξοντες Id.1.141; ὑπουργεῖν ἃ διανοούμεθα (sc. ὑπουργεῖν) Antipho 4.3.4. **II.** *have in mind*, τι Hp.*VM*7; τί διανοούμενος εἶπε what he really *meant* by his words, Pl.*Tht*.184a; περί τινος δ. οὑτωσί, ὀρθῶς περί τι, Id.*Lg*.644d, 686d: c. acc. et inf., *think* or *suppose* that.., Id.*Prt*.324b, etc.: c. gen. abs., διανοεῖσθαί τινων ὡς διαλλαγησομένων Id.*R*.470e: abs., *think*, λέγω νοῦν ᾧ δ.. ἡ ψυχή Arist.*de An*.429a23; τὸ διανοεῖσθαι *the process of thought*, Pl.*Tht*.189e; opp. νοεῖν, Arist.*de An*.408b25. **2.** *bethink oneself*, Lxx *Ge*.6.6. **III.** with Advbs., *to be minded* or *disposed* so and so, ἄλλως πως πρός τινας, Pl.*R*.343b; κακῶς δ. περὶ τῶν οἰκείων Isoc.1.35: with ὡς and part., ὅταν ὡς πετόμενοι διανοῶνται when they *are affected* as if flying, Pl.*Tht*.158b. **-ημα**, ατος, τό, *thought, notion*, X.*HG*7.5.19, Isoc.3.9, Pl.*Smp*.210d; διανοήματος εὐτέλεια Plu.2.40c; *thought*, opp. words, Pl.*Prt*.348d, Phld.*Po*.2.30,40: pl., *meanings* of words, Id.*Rh*.2.190S.; esp. *whim, sick fancy*, Hp.*Epid*.1.23; *intention*, *PLond*.5.1724.15, etc. **-ησις**, εως, ἡ, *process of thinking, thought*, Pl.*Plt*.306e; opp. βούλευσις, Plot.5.8.6: in pl., Pl.*Ti*.87c, Phld.*Herc*.1003, *Vit.Philonid*.p.4C., Plu.2.961d; διανοήσεως ἐκπίπτοντα πάσης, i.e. absurd, Phld.*Rh*.1.223S.; *cunning, skill*, Lxx 2*Ch*.2.14(13). **II.** *way of thinking*, Pl.*Lg*.888c. **-ητέον**, *one must think*, ib.626d, Plu.2.434b, etc. **-ητής**, οῦ, ὁ, *one who thinks*, gloss on φρόνιμος, Hsch. **-ητικός**, ή, όν, *of* or *for thinking, intellectual*, ἡ δ. κίνησις Pl.*Ti*.89a; ἀρετὴ δ., opp. ἠθική, Arist.*EN*1103a14, etc.; ἐπιστήμη δ. Id.*Metaph*.1025b6; δ. μέρη, of a play, parts *which display thought*, Id.*Po*.1460b4; δ. σύγκρισις Epicur.*Nat*.14.20; δ. φαντασίαι *mental* images, Cic.*Fam*.15.16.1; *discursive*, opp. νοερός, Dam.*Pr*.415: Comp. -ώτερος ib.219. Adv. -κῶς Arr.*Epict*.1.14.7. **-ητός**, ή, όν, *that which is* or *can be thought about*, τὸ δ. καὶ νοητόν Arist.*Metaph*.1012a2, cf. 1021a30; οὐδὲ δ. not even *thinkable*, Plu.2.1081a, cf. Procl.*Inst*.123.

διάνοιᾰ, ἡ, Aeol. **διανοΐα** Alc.*Supp*.1a.1 (nisi leg. δι' ἀνοΐα[ν]), poet. also **διανοίᾱ** acc. to Eust.1679.29:—*thought*, i.e. *intention, purpose*, Hdt.1.46,90, And.4.35, etc.; τῇ διανοίᾳ in the *spirit* of his action, D.21.219; ὤλοντ' ἀσεβεῖ διανοίᾳ A.*Th*.831 (lyr.); μαινόλις δ. Id.*Supp*.109 (lyr.); εὔφρονος ἐκ δ. Id.*Ag*.797 (lyr.), cf. *Eu*.1013 (anap.); τοῦ ὑπαπιέναι τὴν διάνοιαν ἔχειν Th.5.9; ἐπί τινι Isoc.5.14; πρός τινι Anaxipp.1.37; ἐπ' ἄλλο τι..τρέψαι τινὸς τὴν δ. Pl.*Euthd*.275b; ἐξ ὅλης τῆς δ. with all one's *heart*, Arr.*Epict*.2.2.13; ἐχθροὺς τῇ δ. *Ep.Col*.1.21. **2.** *thought, notion*, Hdt.2.169, Pl.*Phd*.63d, Arist.*Metaph*.986b10; ἀπὸ τῆς αὐτῆς δ. D.18.210. **II.** *process of thinking, thought*, ὁ ἐντὸς τῆς ψυχῆς πρὸς αὑτὴν διάλογος.. ἐπωνομάσθη δ. Pl.*Sph*.263d; πᾶσα δ. ἢ πρακτικὴ ἢ ποιητικὴ ἢ θεωρητική Arist.*Metaph*.1025b25; ταχίστη ἡ διανοίας κίνησις Id.*LI*968a25; esp. *discursive thought*, opp. νόησις, Procl.*Inst*.123. **III.** *thinking faculty, intelligence, understanding*, ὡς μεταξύ τι δόξης τε καὶ νοῦ τὴν δ. οὖσαν Pl.*R*.511d, al.; opp. σῶμα, Id.*Lg*.916a, cf. *R*.395b; ἔστιν ὥσπερ τοῦ σώματος καὶ τῆς δ. γῆρας Arist.*Pol*.1270b40; ἐπιτάττοντος τοῦ νοῦ καὶ λεγούσης τῆς δ. φεύγειν τι ἢ διώκειν Id.*de An*.433a2; ἔκστασις διανοίας Lxx *De*.28.28. **IV.** *thought expressed, meaning of* a word or passage, Pl.*Ly*.205b, *Phdr*.228d; τὰς τῶν ὀνομάτων δ. Id.*Cra*.418a; τὴν αὐτὴν ἔχει δ. Arist.*de An*.404a17; ἡ φυσικὴ δ. τοῦ νόμου Aristeas 171; so δ., opp. ῥητόν, *spirit*, opp. letter, Hermog.*Stat*.2. **V.** *intellectual capacity* revealed in speech or action by the characters in drama, Arist.*Po*.1450a6, b11, 1456a34, *Rh*.1404a19, al. (Rare in Poetry.)

διαν-οίγω, *lay open*, τοὺς ὀφθαλμούς Pl.*Ly*.210a; μήτραν *Ev.Luc*.2.23:—Pass., Lxx *Ge*.3.5, al., Sor.1.86; of a dead body, Arist.*HA*507a21. **II.** *open so as to connect*, τὸν Ἰνδικὸν καὶ Περσικὸν κόλπον Id.*Mu*.393b3. **III.** *reveal, explain*, τὰς γραφάς *Ev.Luc*.24.32, cf. *Act.Ap*.17.3; τὰ τῶν παλαιῶν ἀπόρρητα Aen.Gaz.*Thphr*.p.5B. **-οικίζω**, *build up, restore*, Philostr.*VS*2.9.2 codd. (Pass.). **-οιξις**, εως, ἡ, *opening*, Ruf.*Anat*.23, Thd.*Is*.61.1.

διανομ-εύς, έως, ὁ, *distributor*, Ph.*Fr*.15H., Plu.*Cim*.9, Polyaen.1.34.2. **-ή**, ἡ, *distribution*, Pl.*R*.535a, Arist.*Pol*.1329b41, etc.; παλαιὰς δ. καταφθίσας A.*Eu*.727; μισθῶν διανομαί Plu.*Per*.9; esp. of *doles* or *largess*, *IG*12(5).663.22 (Syros), 951.13 (Tenos), M.Ant.1.16, Luc.*Pisc*.41, App.*BC*1.27. **2.** *division* or *factorization* of numbers, Pl.*Lg*.747a, 771c, al. **II.** *regulation*, τῇ δ. τῶν πραγμάτων ἕπεσθαι Plu.2.102e; τὴν τοῦ νοῦ δ. ἐπονομάζοντας νόμον Pl.*Lg*.714a.

διανομοθετέω, *get* a motion *carried and made law*, νόμους Pl.*Lg*.628a, cf. D.C.36.40: abs., Id.37.50. **II.** *regulate by law*, τι Id.38.7:—Med., διενομοθετήσαντο τί τίνος ἔργον Pl.*Lg*.833e.

διάνομος, ὁ, = ὑπόνομος, *IG*1².325.19, *BCH*33.461 (Argos).

διανοσέω, in aor. διενόσησα *fall ill*, Hp.*Epid*.3.6, Gal.*Thras*.7.

διανοσφίζω, *separate, part asunder*, D.P.19 (tm.):—Med., *put aside for oneself, peculate*, D.S.19.71.

δίανσις [δῐ], εως, ἡ, *moistening*, Gal.11.740.

δίαντα, Adv. *right through*, τετρήατο prob. in Emp.84.9.

διανταῖος, α, ον (ος, ον E.*Ion* 766 (lyr.)), *extending throughout*, of ligaments *running the whole length of* the spine, Hp.*Art*.45; *right through*, διανταίαν πλαγὰν πεπλαγμένος A.*Th*.895 (lyr.); διανταίαν οὐτᾶν Id.*Ch*.640 (lyr.); δ. βέλει ib.184; ὀδύνα E.*Ion* 766 (lyr.); μοῖρα δ. *relentless* destiny, A.*Eu*.334 (lyr.). Adv. -αίως, παθεῖν Antyll.ap. Orib.44.23.14.

διανταίρω, *make war against*, πρός τινα prob. in Phld.*Acad.Ind*.p.57M.

δῐαντικός, ή, όν, (διαίνω) *able to wet*, ἔκκρισις Arist.*Mete*.387a26.

διαντλ-έω, *drain, exhaust*: only metaph., *drink to the dregs, endure to the end*, νοῦσον Pi.*P*.4.293; πόνους E.*Andr*.1217 (lyr.); οἰκουρίας Id.*HF*1373; βίου χρόνον Ph.1.161; ὕθλους καὶ λήρους Luc.*Pseudol*.25: abs., Heraclit.*Incred*.21:—Pass., πόλεμος διηντλήθη Pl.*Mx*.241e, cf. Lib.*Or*.59.94. **-ίζομαι**, Pass., *exhaust oneself, to be worried* or *troubled*, περὶ μισθαρίων Hp.*Praec*.7.

δῐαντός, ή, όν, *capable of being wetted*, Arist.*Mete*.385b10.

διανυκτερεύω, *pass the night*, νύκτα X.*HG*5.4.3, cf. *PTeb*.268.73 (iii A.D.): abs., Ph.2.488, Plu.*Aem*.16, al.; ἐν τῇ προσευχῇ *Ev.Luc*.6.12, cf. Hdn.1.16.5.

διάνῠσ-ις [ᾰ], εως, ἡ, *distance traversed*, δ. ἡμερήσιαι day's *journeys*, Ptol.*Geog*.1.8.1, cf. 1.9.5. **II.** *accomplishment*, ἔργων Iamb.*Myst*.4.3. **-μα**, ατος, τό, = foreg. 1, δ. ἡμερήσιον Plb.9.14.8: pl., ib.15.3.

Διάνυσος, ὁ, (διαίνω) coined as etym. of Διόνυσος, Corn.*ND*30.

διᾰνυστ-έον, *one must accomplish*, Agath.2.2. **-ικῶς**, Adv. *discursively*, γιγνώσκειν Ammon.*in APr*.25.24.

διανύττω, strengthd. for νύττω, Aristaenet.1.19, Paul.Aeg.3.70.

διανύχιος [ῠ], ον, *nocturnal*, read by Theon in S.*Ichn.*66 (lyr.).

διᾰνύω (also **διᾰνύτω** S.*Ichn.*64, X.*Mem.*2.4.7) [ῡ], pf. -ήνυκα Plb.4.11.7:—*bring quite to an end, accomplish, finish*, κέλευθα δ. *finish* a journey, *h.Cer.*380, cf. *h.Ap.*108; δίαυλον E.*El.*825; τὸ ἑξῆς τῆς ὁδοῦ X. l. c.; τὸν πλοῦν ἀπὸ Τύρου *Act.Ap.*21.7; πόνους Vett.Val. 330.9; τὰ προσήκοντα *POxy.*1469.4 (iii A.D.): c. acc. loci, πολὺν διὰ πόντον ἀνύσσας *having finished one's course over* the sea, Hes.*Op.*635; πλεῖον δ. *traverse*, of a point moving along a line, Arist.*LI*968^{a}25, cf. Archim.*Sph.Cyl.Praef.*, al.; τόπους Plb.4.11.7: abs., δ. εἰς τὰς ὑπερβολάς *arrive* at a place, Id.3.53.9:—Pass., ὁδὸς διηνυσμένη ib.63.7: aor. inf. διανυσθῆναι Hsch.: c. part., *finish doing* a thing, οὔ πω κακότητα διήνυσεν ἣν ἀγορεύων Od.17.517; but πόνοις σε διδοῦσα διήνυσεν *continued* giving.., E.*Or.*1663: abs., *live*, Vett.Val.58.17.

διαομῑλῶ, gloss on διαθρυλλῶ, Hsch.

διαξαίνω, aor. -έξᾱνα *Gp.*2.6.42, but inf. -ξῆναι Ar.*Lys.*578: pf. part. Pass. -εξαμμένος Gal.8.415, -εξασμένος Dsc.5.106, Simp.*in Cael.*571.6, Paul.Aeg.3.61:—*card, shred*, Ar.*Lys.*578; ἐσθῆτας Str. 11.14.8; ἔριον Paul.Aeg. l. c.; νεῦρον εἰς ἶνας Alex.Aphr.*Pr.*2.52, cf. Gal. l.c.; ἔντερον Ruf.ap.Orib.7.26.170; of flesh, Paul.Aeg.6. 77,88:—Pass., of alum, Dsc. l. c., *to be dispersed, broken up*, Simp. l. c. 2. metaph., κόμην, of the wind, Hld.3.3; δ. θάλασσαν πτερύγεσσι Opp.*H.*5.306; as a punishment, δ. τινά Ael.*Fr.*131:—Pass., ὑπὸ Ῥωμαίων ἐκτριβέντες διεξάνθησαν ib.130.

διαξέω, *smooth, polish off*, *IG*7.3073.138 (Lebad.), Poll.1.13. II. *erode*, Aët.5.41 (Pass.).

διαξηραίνω, *dry quite up*, D.S.1.10.

διάξηρος, ον, *quite dry*, *Gp.*6.2.4, v.l. in Arist.*Mete.*352^{b}19, cf. Olymp. ad loc.

διάξιμος, ον, *to be transferred*, *Cod.Just.*1.15.2.

διαξῐφ-ίζομαι, *fight to the death*, τινὶ περί τινος Ar.*Eq.*781. **-ισμός**, ὁ, *fighting with swords*, Plu.2.597f.

διαξόος, ὁ, *stone-dresser*, *SIG*247 *K*^1^ ii 55 (Delph.).

διάξῠλον, τό, *cross-piece*, Apollod.*Poliorc.*177.12. II. = ἀσπάλαθος 1, Dsc.1.20.

διαξῠράομαι, Med., *shave oneself*, Arr.*Epict.*1.2.29.

διά-ξυσμα, ατος, τό, *filings*: metaph., ἰσοτιμίας δ., of εὐγένεια, Chrysipp.*Stoic.*3.85. II. *flute* of a column, D.S.13.82. **-ξύω**, *cut into wrinkles*, τὰ περὶ τὸ πρόσωπον διεξυσμένα Arist.*Phgn.*808^{a}18 and 35: generally, *cut up*, Ael.*Fr.*85.

διαπαγκρᾰτιάζω, *contend in the* παγκράτιον, Plu.2.811d.

διαπαιγμός, ὁ, *jesting*, *Gloss.*

διαπαιδᾰγωγέω, *attend children*: generally, *guide*, Pl.*Ti.*89d; *entertain, amuse*, ἡδοναῖς τὴν πόλιν Plu.*Per.*11; δ. τὸν καιρόν *while away* the time, Id.*Sert.*16.

διαπαιδεύομαι, Pass., *take a course of education*, X.*Cyr.*1.2.15.

διαπαίζω, late fut. -ξω Gal.8.569: pf. -πέπαιχα Plu. (v. infr.):—*jest*, Gal. l. c.; διαπαίζων *in jest*, J.*Ap.*2.37 (dub.), D.L.8.6:—Pass., παιδιὰ καλῶς διαπεπαισμένη a sport well *kept up*, Pl.*Lg.*769a. II. *laugh, jest at*, c. acc., J.*BJ*5.7.4, Arr.*Epict.*2.18.22, Demetr.*Eloc.*147, D.L.4.53: abs., Phld.*Lib.*p.57 O. III. perh. *imitate playfully*, [ὁ Σοφοκλῆς] διαπεπαιχὼς τὸν Αἰσχύλου ὄγκον Plu.2.79b.

διαπαίκτης, ου, ὁ, *jester, deceiver*, *Gloss.*

διαπᾰλαίω, *continue wrestling*, Ar.*Eq.*573, Ph.2.544, J.*AJ*1.20.2; πρός τινα Ach.Tat.4.19: c. dat., νοσήματι *struggle with*, Gal.17(1). 569.

διαπάλη [πᾰ], ἡ, *hard struggle*, διαπάλαι πολέμου Plu.*Cor.*2, cf. 2.50f.

διαπάλλω, fut. -παλῶ A.*Fr.*304.4:—*brandish*, A. l. c.:—but in Pass., *to be driven to and fro*, of a hunted deer, Opp.*H.*2.620. II. *distribute by lot*, χθόνα ναίειν διαπήλας A.*Th.*731 (lyr.).

διαπᾰλύνω [ῡ], *grind to powder*, E.*Ph.*1159.

διαπαννυχ-ίζω, *pass the whole night*, Plu.2.775d. **-ισμός**, ὁ, *complete vigil*, D.H.2.19.

διαπαντάω, *meet*, Porph.*Abst.*3.10.

διαπαντός, Adv., later spelling of διὰ παντός, v. διά A. II. 1.

διαπαπταίνω, *look timidly round*, Plu.*Fab.*11.

διαπαρα-δίδωμι, *hand over* to a successor, *IG*9(2).1109.64,91 (Magn. Thess.). **-τηρέομαι**, *lie in wait for continually*, τινά Lxx 2*Ki.*3.30. **-τρῐβή**, ἡ, *constant wrangling*, 1*Ep.Ti.*6.5.

διαπαρθέν-ευσις, εως, ἡ, *deflowering of a maiden*, Hdn.*Epim.* 20. **-ευτής**, οῦ, ὁ, *one who deflowers*, *Gloss.* **-εύω**, *deflower a maiden*, Hdt.4.168 (Pass.), Diocl.Com.16, Antiph.75, Alex.314. **-ια** δῶρα, τά, presents *made to the bride on the morning after the wedding*, Amphis 49.

διαπαρίστημι, *set up statue of*, τινά *JHS*10.71 (Lydae).

διάπαρ-μα, ατος, τό, *transfixion*, *Gloss.* **-σις**, εως, ἡ, = foreg., Aret.*SA*1.7 (pl.).

διάπασμα, ατος, τό, (διαπάσσω) *scented powder to sprinkle over the person*, Dsc.1.7, Antyll.ap.Orib.10.31.1: freq. in pl., Thphr.*Od.*8, Plu.2.990c, Plin.*HN*13.19, Luc.*Am.*39.

διαπασσᾰλεύω, Att. **διαπαττ-**, *stretch out by nailing the extremities*, πρὸς σανίδα Hdt.7.33; of a hide *pegged out for tanning*, Ar.*Eq.* 371, cf. Plu.*Art.*17.

δια-πάσσω, Att. **-ττω**, *sprinkle*, -πάσας τοῦ ψήγματος ἐς τὰς τρίχας Hdt.6.125; σμύρνῃ δ. τὴν ὁδόν Eub.128; δασύποδας ἁλσὶ δ. Alc.Com. 17; μέλανι διαπεπασμένον χρῶμα Arist.*HA*526^{a}12; πυρρὰ διαπεπασμένα *with* red *spots*, ib.527^{b}30. **-παστέον**, *one must powder*, prob. in Philum.ap.Aët.5.128.

διαπάσχω, *endure, sustain*, χλεύην *POxy.*904.2 (v A.D.).

διαπᾱσῶν, ἡ, i. e. ἡ διὰ πασῶν χορδῶν συμφωνία, *concord of the first and last notes, octave*; more correctly divisim, τέταται διὰ πασῶν (sc. χορδῶν) Pl.*R.*432a; τὸ δὶς διὰ πασῶν Plu.2.1019b.

διαπᾰτάω, *deceive utterly*, Pl.*Lg.*738e, Ph.2.92:—Pass., Arist. *HA*496^{b}5.

διαπᾰτέω, *tread through*, τὴν χιόνα Plb.3.55.2; dub. in Ph.1.354 codd.

διάπαυ-μα, ατος, τό, *cessation, rest*, πόνων Pl.*Lg.*824a. 2. *gap*, *IG*14.352 ii 48 (Halaesa). **-σις**, εως, ἡ, *pause*, Arist.*Pr.* 894^{a}26. **-ω**, *bring to an end, conclude*, τὸν βίον, i. e. *die*, prob. in *SIG*494.4 (Delph., iii B.C.):—Med., *rest between times, pause*, Pl. *Smp.*191c, *R.*336b:—Pass., αἱ στρατιαὶ διεπέπαυντο *had ceased for the time being*, X.*HG*4.4.14.

διαπαφλάζω, *boil up, effervesce*, of anger, Nonn.*D.*31.24.

διάπεζος, ον, of women's robes, either *reaching to the feet* or *having a border* (πέζα), Callix.2.

διαπείθω, *convince*, ὁ διαπείθων λόγος dub. in Phld.*Ir.*p.80 W.:—Pass., *BGU*1062.19 (iii A.D.).

διᾰπειλέω, *threaten violently*, Hdt.7.15; δ. ὡς μηνύσει Id.2.121.γ': c. inf. fut., Plu.*Oth.*16:—Med., διαπειλεῖσθαί τινι Aeschin.1.43, Alex. 306, *PPetr.*2 p.1: c. inf., *forbid with threats*, μηθένα φέρειν ὅπλον Plb. 1.78.15; ἄλλα τε δ. καὶ ὡς.. Conon 50.3.

διαπεινάω, inf. -πεινῆν, *hunger one against the other, have a starving-match*, διαπεινᾶμες (Dor.), with a play on διαπίνομεν, Ar.*Ach.* 751.

διά-πειρα, ἡ, *crucial experiment, trial, proof*, ἐς διάπειράν τινος ἀπικέσθαι Hdt.2.28,77; ἀποπέμπειν ἐς τὴν δ. τινός Id.1.47; δ. βροτῶν ἔλεγχος Pi.*O.*4.18. **-πειράζω**, *tempt, make trial of*, τινά Lxx 3*Ma.* 5.40. II. *attempt, try*, c. inf., J.*AJ*15.4.2.

διαπειραίνω, *pierce through*, Man.2.106 (Pass.).

διαπειράομαι, aor. -επειράθην Antipho 5.34: pf. -πεπείραμαι Th. 6.91:—*make trial or proof of*, τῶν Περσέων Hdt.5.109, cf. 3.14, Cratin. Jun.7.2; *try to impose on* a man, Pl.*Lg.*921b: c. gen. rei, *have experience* of a thing, Th.6.91: abs., ὥσπερ αἴνιγμα συντιθέντι διαπειρωμένῳ Pl.*Ap.*27a, cf. *Lg.* l. c. 2. *attempt obstinately*, τὰ ψευδῆ λέγειν Antipho l.c. II. late in Act., διαπειρῶν δωροδοκίαις Plu. *Pomp.*51.

διαπείρω, *drive through*, σφυρῶν κέντρα E.*Ph.*26, cf. Il.16.405 (tm.); δ. ὀβελούς Iamb.*Myst.*3.4. 2. *pierce, transfix*, ἥλῳ τὰ στελέχη *Gp.* 5.36.3; βελόναις τὴν γλῶτταν Plu.*Art.*14; λίνῳ Dsc.2.61:—Pass., διαπεπαρμένος ἥλοις Plu.2.567f; τὴν χεῖρα διαπαρείς J.*AJ*10.1.2; *to be interpenetrated*, of muscle and flesh, Gal.8.74.

διάπεισμα (freq. misspelt **-πισμα**), ατος, τό, (διαπείθω) *present*, '*douceur*', *PTeb.*311.29 (ii A.D.), *POxy.*133.14 (vi A.D.), etc.; 'King's shilling' given to recruits, ib.1103.8 (iv A.D.).

διαπελάζω, *approach*, etym. of δασπλῆτις, Sch.Theoc.2.14.

διάπεμπτος, ἡ, *period of five days*, Gal.19.551, *Cat.Cod.Astr.*1. 119.9, 121.19; cf. διάτριτος.

διαπέμπω, *send off in different directions*, Hdt.1.48,84, etc.; ἄλλους ἄλλῃ δ. Th.8.64; φρουρὰς κατὰ χώραν Id.4.55; δ. τὴν ἰκμάδα (through the body), Arist.*PA*681^{a}30; τὸ πνεῦμα Id.*HA*496^{a}32; τὴν φωνὴν εἰς τὸ πρόσω Id.*PA*662^{b}22:—Med., *send out expeditions*, *OGI*199.35 (Adule). II. *send over* or *across*, τινὰ πρός τινα Ar.*Pl.*398; τινά τινι Th.4.123; *transmit*, *BGU*5 ii 19 (ii A.D.), etc.; ἐπιστολήν Th.1. 129:—Med., Id.3.75 (possibly Pass.), *SIG*741.33 (Nysa, i B.C.); ἐσθῆτά τινι Ph.2.43. III. Med., *send messages*, περὶ βοηθείας πρός τινα Plb.5.72.1; πρὸς τοὺς φίλους Plu.*Arat.*8. **-πεμψις**, εως, ἡ, *distribution* of nourishment in the body, Hp.*Vict.*1.9. 2. *transmission* of a letter, Themist.*Ep.*16.

διαπενθέω, *mourn throughout*, ἐνιαυτόν Plu.*Publ.*23.

διαπενταθλέω, *contend in the* πένταθλον, Tz. ad Lyc.860.

διαπεπονημένως, Adv., (διαπονέω) *elaborately*, Isoc.*Ep.*6.6.

διαπεραίνω, *bring to a conclusion*, λόγους E.*Andr.*333; *describe thoroughly*, τι Pl.*Phlb.*47b, etc.; διαπέραινέ μοι *tell me all*, E.*Andr.* 1056; δ. ὁδόν Pl.*Lg.*625b:—Med., μορφῆς διαπεράνασθαι κρίσιν *to get* the trial of beauty *decided*, E.*Hel.*26; διαπεράνασθαι λόγον Pl.*Phdr.* 263e, etc.:—Pass., Iamb.*Myst.*7.4. II. *traverse, pass through*, λοβόν Aret.*SA*2.8 (cf. διαπεράω).

διαπεραι-όω, *take across, ferry over*, Plu.*Sull.*27:—Pass., *to be carried over, cross*, ἐνθεῦτεν διαπεραιωθείς Hdt.5.23; δ. τὸν ποταμόν Id.2.124; ἐπεὶ πάντες διεπεπεραίωντο Th.3.23: in aor. Med., Pl. *Ax.*370b. 2. κολεῶν διεπεραιώθη ξίφη swords *were unsheathed*, S.*Aj.*730. **-ωσις**, εως, ἡ, *carrying over*, Sch.Th.3.76. II. *crossing over*, Marcian.*Peripl.*1.44 (pl.).

διαπέρᾱμα, ατος, τό, (διαπεράω) *strait of the sea, ferry*, Str.6.1.5, *Peripl.M.Rubr.*32, Ptol.*Geog.*1.13.8.

διαπεραντέον, *one must carry to its conclusion*, λόγον Pl.*Lg.*715e.

διαπεράσιμος [ρᾱ], ον, *penetrating*, Sch.Il.12.439, Eust.709.48.

διαπεράω, *go over* or *across*, ῥοάς E.*Tr.*1151; πελάγη Isoc.1.19; δ. ἐπ' οἶδμα E.*IT*395 (lyr.); δ. πόλιν *pass through* it, Ar.*Av.*1264; δ. Ἑλλάδα E.*Supp.*117; δ. εἰς Ἰταλίαν Arist.*Fr.*485; of Time, δ. τὸν βίον *pass through* life, X.*Oec.*11.7. b. διαπερᾶν Μολοσσίαν *reign through all* Molossia, E.*Andr.*1248 codd. 2. *pass through, pierce*, κνήμην διεπέρασεν Ἀργεῖον δόρυ Id.*Ph.*1394; *traverse*, ἧπαρ, of a vein, Aret. *SA*2.8 (cf. διαπεραίνω). 3. οἶσθα διαπερῶν *by traversing*, i. e. *by experience*, A.*Th.*994 (lyr.), cf. Sch. II. *reach, arrive at* a place, *PFlor.*247.9 (iii A.D.). III. trans., *carry over*, ὕδωρ ποταμοῦ σῶμα δ. Eub.151, cf. Luc.*DMort.*20.1.

διαπερδῐκίζω, *slip through like a partridge*, Com.*Adesp*.87.

διαπέρθω, aor. 1 -έπερσα Pi.*Pae*.6.104: aor. 2 -έπρᾰθον Il.1.367, Ep. inf. -πραθέειν 7.32: aor. Med. -επράθετο in pass. sense, Od.15.384:—*destroy utterly, sack, waste*, always of cities, ll.cc.

διαπεριπᾰτέω, *keep walking about*, Ath.4.157e, 12.539c.

διαπερονάω, *pin* or *pierce through*, σφυρὰ σιδήρῳ D.S.4.64; τινὰ διαμπάξ Agath.1.9:—Pass., Id.2.9, al., Luc.*Gall*.24; σαυνίῳ διὰ τοῦ θυρεοῦ διαπερονηθείς D.H.9.64.

διαπέρχομαι, *slip away one by one*, of soldiers deserting, D.49.14, 50.

διαπετάννῡμι, pf. -πεπέτακα D.S.17.115, Pass. -πεπέτασμαι ib. 10:—*open and spread out*, Ar.*Lys*.732,733; τὰς πλεκτάνας, of the polypus, Arist.*HA*541^{b}5; ἀετοὺς διαπεπετακότας τοὺς πτέρυγας D.S. 17.115:—Pass., pf. διαπέπ[τ]α[νται] πύλαι prob. in Pi.*Dith.Oxy*.2.4.

διαπέτεια, ἡ, *opening*, πόρων Eust.1842.48.

διαπετής, ές, *spread out, unfolded, open*, Hp.*Cord*.10.

διαπέτομαι (**διΐπταμαι** Hdn.,v.infr.), aor.-επτάμην (v.infr.): aor. Act. -έπτην Luc.*DMeretr*.9.4: pres. διαπέταται S.*OT*1310 (lyr.) is f.l. for διαπωτᾶται:—*fly through*, διὰ δ' ἔπτατο πικρὸς ὀϊστός Il.5.99; δρᾷς τὸν ἁβρὸν οὐ βέλος διέπτατο E.*Supp*.860; δ. διὰ τῆς πόλεως Ar.*Av*. 1217: c. acc., E.*Med*.1, Ar.*V*.1086. II. *fly away, vanish*, διαπτομένη οἴχεσθαι Pl.*Phd*.70a, 84b, etc.; of Time, E.*HF*507. III. of a report, *fly in all directions*, διϊπταμένη ἡ φήμη Hdn.2.8.7.

διαπεττεύω, *gamble*, δ. τὴν ἐλπίδα *try* one's luck *at play*, Luc.*Am*. 16.

διαπέττω, *digest*, τροφήν Arist.*GA*766^{b}13.

διαπεύθομαι, poet. for διαπυνθάνομαι, A.*Ag*.807 (anap.).

διαπέφλοιδεν· διακέχυται, and **διαπέφρυδεν**· χαίρει, διακέχυται, Hsch. **διαπεφρυκέναι**· διεσκέφθαι, καὶ καθεωρακέναι, Id.

διά-πηγα, τά, *panels*, Lxx 3*Ki*.7.31,32. **-πήγιον**, τό, = sq., *BGU*781 iii 8 (i A.D.). **-πηγμα**, ατος, τό, (διαπήγνυμι) *cross-bar*, Ph. *Bel*.54.19, Hero *Bel*.83.8, *Dioptr*.34, Heliod.ap.Orib.49.7.1; *partition*, Hero *Aut*.11.9. **-πηγμάτιον**, τό, Dim. of foreg., *small cross-bar*, Ph.*Bel*.64.7. **-πήγνῡμι**, *fix* or *thrust through*, ἀκόντιον διὰ πλευρῶν Antipho 3.3.5; *transfix*, διέπᾶξε σιδάρῳ Epigr. in *PTeb*.3.29 (i B.C.). II. *freeze hard*, Thphr.*Vent*.54: pf. -πέπηγα, intr., *to be frozen*, Arist.*Mir*.835^{a}30. III. Med., δ. σχεδίας *get* them *put together*, Luc.*DMort*.12.5.

διαπηδ-άω, fut. -πηδήσομαι, *leap across*, τάφρον Ar.*Ach*.1178, cf. X.*Eq*.3.7: metaph., *pass over lightly*, Philostr.*Her*.2.10: abs., *take a leap*, of a horse, X.*Cyr*.1.4.8. 2. Medic., *ooze through*, perh. f.l. for -πιδύω, Hp.*Hum*.11. 3. *leap apart, form a chasm*, of the earth, Lyd.*Ost*.53. **-ησις**, εως, ἡ, *leaping* or *starting through*: metaph. in Medic., of blood, etc., *transudation through the tissues*, Sor.1.23, v.l. in Hp.*Nat.Puer*.21.

διαπηνηκίζω λόγον *trick out deceitfully*, Cratin.282 (prob. l., cf. πήνη).

διάπηξ, ηγος, ὁ, = διάπηγμα, Apollod.*Poliorc*.172.7: as Adj., διάπηγες μοχλοί Ph.Byz.*Mir*.4.2.

διάπηξις, εως, ἡ, *fastening together, structure*, δ. σωματική bodily *frame*, Herm.ap.Stob.1.49.69.

διαπῑαίνω, *make very fat*, in Pass., Thphr.*CP*6.11.7, Theoc.16.91.

διαπῑδάω ὕδωρ *let* water *ooze through*, Arist.*Mete*.350^{a}8.

διαπῑδ-ύω, *ooze through*, διὰ τῶν πόρων Arist.*GA*743^{a}9, cf. Hp.*Nat. Puer*.21. **-υσις**, εως, ἡ, *transudation*, ibid.

διαπῑέζω, *press together*, Luc.*Lex*.11.

διαπῐθανεύομαι, *oppose by probable argument*, ἄλλου ἄλλως εἰκάζοντος καὶ διαπιθανευομένου S.E.*M*.8.324.

διαπῐθηκίζω, strengthd. for πιθηκίζω, *EM*269.38, Suid.

διαπικραίνομαι, Pass., *to be greatly embittered*, πρός τινα Plu.2. 457a.

διάπικρος, ον, *very bitter*, ὕδωρ D.S.2.48, 19.98.

διαπίμελος [ῐ], ον, *obese, adipose*, Ruf.*Onom*.175.

διαπίμπλημι, aor. inf. -πλῆσαι, *fill full*, οἰκίας Philostr.*Im*.2.27; λόγων τὴν οἰκουμένην Eun.*VS*p.493 D., cf. Nonn.*D*.5.194; in early writers in Pass., *to be filled with*, τινός Th.7.85; *to be satiated* or *tired*, διαπεπλησμένος τινός *of* one, And.1.125.

διαπίμπρημι, *burn*, ναῦς Plb.21.44.30; μοχλὸν διαπρήσας Aen. Tact.4.2 (nisi leg. -πρίσας):—Pass., *swell up* (cf. πρήθω), Nic.*Al*. 341; οἱ μυκτῆρες διαπέπρηνται *Hippiatr*.27.

διαπίνω [ῑ], *drink one against another*, Hdt.5.18, 9.16, Pl.*R*.420e; = προπίνειν, Epig.8:—Med., δ. ἀνδράσι Hedyl.ap.Ath.11.486c. II. *drink at intervals*, Anaxandr.57:—but Pass., *to be swallowed at a draught*, διαπινόμενοι Arist.*Pr*.872^{b}27.

διαπιπράσκω, *sell off*, *PTeb*.5.192 (ii B.C.), etc.; οὐσίαν Plu.*Comp. Lys.Sull*.3.

διαπίπτω, *fall through*, Arist.*Cael*.313^{b}1. II. *fall away, slip away, escape*, ἐν τῇ μάχῃ X.*HG*3.2.4; πρός τινα ib.4.3.18; εἰς τὴν Ἀσπίδα Plb.1.34.11, etc. 2. of reports and rumours, *spread abroad*, εἰς τὰ στρατεύματα Plu.*Galb*.22. 3. of Time, *elapse*, Arist.*Ath*.35. 4. III. *fall asunder, crumble in pieces*, διαπέσοιμι πανταχῇ Ar. *Eq*.695, cf. Pl.*Phd*.80c, Arist.*Mete*.365^{b}12; *burst*, of bubbles, Id.*Pr*. 936^{b}5; *rot*, Lxx *Nu*.5.21; *perish*, διέπεσε πᾶσα γενεὰ ἀνδρῶν ib.*De*. 2.14; *to be missing, lost*, of moneys, etc., *PEleph*.21.19 (iii B.C.), etc.; of books, *to be imperfect*, J.*AJ*12.2.4. b. of an *intermittent* pulse, Gal.19.636. 2. of things, *turn out ill, be useless*, τὸ συκοφάντημα διέπιπτεν αὐτῷ Aeschin.2.39, cf. Plb.5.26.16, *PAmh*.2.33.26 (ii B.C.), etc. 3. of persons, *make mistakes*, ἐν τοῖς σημαινομένοις Chrysipp.*Stoic*.3.33, cf. Phld.*Ir*.p.73 W.: c. gen., *fail of, miss*, Epicur.*Ep*.2 p.43 U., Phld.*Rh*.1.49 S.; δ. περὶ τῆς δόξης Socr.*Ep*.22; περὶ τῶν μεγίστων Arr.*Epict*.2.22.36: abs., *err*, Phld.*Ir*.p.91 W.; οὐ διαπεσούμεθα Iamb.*in Nic*.p.63 P.; *to be cheated*, ἐν χρήσει νομίσματος Arr.*Epict*.1.7.6. IV. ἡ διαπίπτουσα or ὁ τόπος ὁ διαπίπτων, *Tophet*, Lxx *Je*.19.12,13.

διαπιστεύω, *entrust to* one *in confidence*, τινὶ τὴν πόλιν, τὴν δυναστείαν, Aeschin.3.8, Plb.5.40.7; τῷ θεῷ τὰν ὠνάν Rüsch *Grammatik der delph.Inschr*.p.326 (ii B.C.); also δ. τινὶ περί τινος Aeschin.1. 188. II. *believe thoroughly*, τι Arist.*PA*673^{a}17, cf. Max.Tyr.10. 7. 2. c. dat., *have confidence in, believe*, *PHib*.1.147 (iii B.C.):—Pass., *to be trusted* or *believed*, D.10.51, Aen.Gaz.*Thphr*.p.18 B.

διᾰπιστέω, *distrust utterly*, τινί D.19.324, Arist.*Pol*.1314^{a}17: abs., *disbelieve*, *PSI*4.377.9 (iii B.C.), Aps.*Rh*.p.287 H.:—Med., *mistrust oneself*, Plb.18.46.7.

διαπλᾰνάω, *lead quite astray*, Plu.2.917e, Arr.*Epict*.1.20.10; *deceive, cheat*, *BGU*36.7 (ii A.D.):—Pass., *go astray, wander*, D.S.17. 116, Plu.*Fr.inc*.11 (v.l.).

διά-πλᾰσις, εως, ἡ, *putting into shape*: *setting of a dislocated limb*, Gal.18(2).332. II. *formation, modelling*, νεύρου Alex.Aphr.*Pr*.2.72; *conformation*, Gal.7.26; σώματος Hierocl.*in CA*10 p.437 M. III. *deformation* by mirrors, Phlp.*in Mete*.28.19. **-πλασμα**, ατος, τό, *model, shape*, or perh. *modelled jug*, Sch.Ar.*V*.614. **-πλασμός**, ὁ, v.l. for διάπλασις, *Placit*.1.3.18. 2. *massage* of infants, Sor.1. 101. **-πλάσσω**, Att. -ττω, *form, mould*, ζῷα Ph.1.15; ὕλην, ἄρτον, σῶμα, Plu.2.427b, 401f, Him.*Or*.14.13; διανοήματα ῥυθμοῖς Jul.*Or*.2.78d: metaph., ἐπίνοια J.*BJ*7.8.1; δ. τῷ λόγῳ Ael.*VH*3.1:—Pass., τέτταρσι διαπλασθέντα προσώποις μῦθον *AP*9.542 (Crin.); δ. τὰ μόρια [τοῦ ἐμβρύου] Arist.*GA*740^{a}36, cf. Epicur.*Ep*.2 p.38 U.: metaph., *to be concocted, invented*, *PMonac*.6.47 (vi A.D.). II. *plaster*, πηλῷ Thphr.*HP*4.15.2. III. Medic., *reshape* a broken nose, Heliod.ap.Orib.48.33.5, Gal.18(1).479. **-πλαστικός**, ή, όν, *formative*, δύναμις Alex.Aphr.*Pr*.1.47, Gal.*Nat.Fac*.1.6.

διαπλᾰτύνω, *dilate*, X.*Lac*.2.5; *flatten out*, Chrysipp.Tyan.ap. Ath.14.648a.

διάπλεγμα, ατος, τό, *woof* or *web*, Eust.1571.56.

διαπλέκω, *weave, plait*, σάνδαλα *h.Merc*.80; opp. διαλύω, Hdt.4. 67; τὰ τὸν ὄσχεον διαπλέκοντα σώματα Paul.Aeg.6.62: metaph., θρῆνον δ. Pi.*P*.12.8; ἀγὰν πάγχυ δ. *to try* every *twist, wind* all ways, ib.2.82:—Med., διαπλέξασθαι κόμας *plait one's* hair, Aristaenet.1.25:—Pass., ψυχὴ διαπλακεῖσα *interwoven* [with matter].., Pl.*Ti*.36e, cf. Plot.1.1.3. II. metaph., διαπλέξαντος τὸν βίον εὖ *finish the web of* one's life, Hdt.5.92.ζ'; δ. βίοτον λιπαρῷ γήραϊ Pi.*N*.7.99; ἁμέραν prob. in Alcm.23.38; ἀσκητικόν τινα βίον Pl.*Lg*.806a, cf. *Com.Adesp*.231: without βίον, δ. ζῶν ἡδέως Ar.*Av*.754.

διαπλευρισμός, ὁ, *cross-dyke*, *PLille* 1 16 (iii B.C.).

διαπλέω, Ion. -πλώω (q.v.), *sail through* a strait or gap, Th.4.24, Plb.14.10.12; sail *across*, Μέγαράδε Lys.12.17; εἰς Αἴγιναν Ar.*V*. 122, etc.: c. acc., δ. τὸ πέλαγος Plu.2.206d, *IG*14.1976: metaph., δ. βίον *sail through* life, *make* life's *voyage*, Pl.*Phd*.85d. 2. *flow through, pass*, τὰ ψαμμία σὺν τοῖσι οὔροισι δ. Aret.*SD*2.3.

διάπλεως, ων, *brim-full*, τινός Cratin.280, Plu.2.551a: pl., διάπλεα Thphr.*CP*2.1.4: fem. διάπλεαι Plu.*Tim*.11.

διαπληκτ-ίζομαι, *spar*, Lxx *Ex*.2.13; τινί Luc.*Anach*.11: generally, *skirmish with*, ἱππεῦσι Plu.*Luc*.31: metaph., *wrangle*, δ. τοῖς γυναίοις Id.*Tim*.14; πρὸς γύναιον Id.2.760a, cf. Agath.2.29: c. dat. modi, δ. τοῖς σκώμμασι Plu.*Sull*.2:—late in Act., Horap.1.70. **-ισις**, εως, ἡ, = sq., Sch.Il.1.138. **-ισμός**, ὁ, *sparring, disputing, wrangling*, πρὸς Σωκράτην περί τινος Plu.2.710c (pl.); δ. τε καὶ ὀργαί Porph. *Marc*.2.

διαπληρόω, strengthd. for πληρόω:—Pass., -πεπληρωμένοι λαφύρων Aen.Tact.16.8.

διαπλήσσω, *break in pieces, split, cleave*, δρῦς Il.23.120 (v.l. διαπλίσσοντες): aor. inf. -πλῆξαι read by Aristarch. in Od.8.507.

διαπλίσσομαι, *stand* or *walk with the legs apart*, διαπεπλιγμένος *long-shanked, straddling*, Archil.58: so in pf. part. Act., στόμα διαπεπλιχός *wide open*, Hp.*Mul*.2.167, cf. Hsch., and v. foreg.

δια-πλοκή, ἡ, *intermixture*, Hp.*Alim*.11. II. in pl., *crooked ways*, Aq.*Ps*.124(125).5. **-πλόκινος**, ον, = sq., σκάφιον Str.17.1. 50. **-πλοκος**, ον, *interwoven, plaited*, Hld.2.3.

διάπλοος, ον, contr. -πλους, ουν, I. Adj., *sailing across* or *sailing continually*, δ. καθίστασαν λεών they kept them *at the oar*, A. *Pers*.382. II. as Subst., **διάπλους**, ὁ, *a voyage across, passage*, πρὸς τὸ Κήναιον Th.3.93; ἀπὸ τῆς οἰκείας Id.6.31. 2. *room for sailing through, passage*, δυοῖν νεοῖν for two ships abreast, Id.4.8. 3. *cross-channel*, Pl.*Criti*.118e.

διάπλουτος, = ζάπλουτος (q.v.), *EM*407.8.

διαπλόω, *unfold*, Heb.*Ge*.38.29; διαπλοῦσθαι v.l. for διαπνεῖσθαι, X.*Smp*.2.25 as quoted by Ath.11.504d.

διαπλύνω, strengthd. for πλύνω, Ar.*Fr*.686.

διαπλώω, Ion. = -πλέω, A.R.2.629, Nic.*Al*.559, *AP*7.23 (Antip. Sid.).

δια-πνείω, poet. for διαπνέω, Nonn.*D*.29.201. **-πνευμα**, ατος, τό, *breeze*, dub.l. in Hp.*Aër*.19 (pl.). **-πνευσις**, εως, ἡ, = διαπνοή, *exhaling*, *Gp*.5.28.1. **-πνεύστας**· παραλογιστικός, prob. in Hsch. **-πνευστία**, ἡ, = διαπνοή, Gal.19.514. **-πνευστικός**, ή, όν, *promoting exhalation*, Aret.*CA*1.1. **-πνευστός**, όν, *easily dissipated, volatile*, ἀήρ Alex.Aphr.*in Sens*.36.4. **-πνέω**, Ep. -πνείω, fut. -πνεύσομαι, *blow through*, of air, δ. τὸ σῶμα Arist.*Pr*.967^{a}3, cf. *Mete*.370^{b}6, etc.:—Pass., αὔραις διαπνεῖσθαι X.*Smp*.2.25, cf. Arist.*HA*518^{a}16,

D.S.5.82. 2. intr., *admit air*, ἀπόφραξον ἅπαντα ὡς μὴ διαπνέειν Hero *Spir.*2.21. II. *breathe between times, get breath*, Plb.27.9.10, Plu.*Cim.*12, Ph.1.90, al.; ἐκ δυσχερείας Plb.31.4.1. III. intr., *disperse in vapour, evaporate*, Arist.*Resp.*479a17, *PA*671a20, cf. Ph. 2.42: so, IV. Pass., διαπίπτειν καὶ διαπνεῖσθαι Pl.*Phd.*80c; δ. καὶ σήπεται τὸ σῶμα Arist.*de An.*411b9. 2. Medic., *dissipate by exhalation*, Aret.*SA*1.7:—Pass., Gal.15.377 (also intr. in pass. sense, διέπνευσε τὸ ἄλγος Aret.*CA*1.10). 3. Pass., of plants, *exhale*, διαπνεῖται καὶ ἐξατμίζεται Thphr.*CP*1.1.3, cf. M.Ant.6.16; of human beings, *perspire*, Id.3.1, Gal.15.377:—so Med., Hp.*Alim.*28.

δια-πνοή, ἡ, *outlet, vent for the wind*, Arist.*Mete.*368b9: pl., *gap, interstice*, Erot. s. v. διαρόγχας; *pores*, Aret.*CA*2.7; *organs of respiration*, Id.*SA*1.5. II. *exhalation*, Thphr.*CP*6.16.6. III. *transpiration*, Hp.*Alim.*28, Alex.Aphr.*Pr.*2.60, Gal.15.180, Aret. *SA*1.10; of *vapours* or *humours*, Id.*CA*1.1, *CD*2.13. IV. *expulsion of flatus*, Id.*SD*2.8. **-πνοια**, ἡ, = foreg. 1, Poll.2.219, *Gp.*7.6.10, Simp.*in Cael.*524.10. II. *opening, gap*, Pall.*in Hp.Fract.*12.283C.

διαποδ-ίζω, *measure with the foot*, Hsch., *EM*269.25. **-ισμός**, ὁ, *jumping about*: a kind of *dance*, Poll.4.99.

διαπο-ζεύγνῡμαι, Pass., *to be utterly separated, depart*, Ph.1.255. **-θνήσκω**, *keep dying*, διαμάχεσθαι καὶ δ. Plb.16.31.8.

διαποιέω, *complete a transaction*, *BGU*1261.13 (i B.C.), *PTheb. Bank* 126.4.

διαποικίλλω, *variegate, adorn with variety*, mostly metaph., τοῖς διαιτήμασι Hp.*Vict.*3.68; ποίησιν Isoc.9.9; literally, δ. τι ἀργύρῳ καὶ χρυσῷ Plu.*Sert.*14:—Pass., μέλανι δ. *to be dappled*, Arist.*HA*503b5: metaph., δ. ἐκ.. *to be blended of various* sorts, Pl.*Lg.*693d, cf. 863a; ἀπάταις τὰ πολλὰ δ. τοῦ πολέμου Plu.*Lys.*7, cf. Iamb.*Myst.*7.3.

διαποίκῐλος, ον, *variegated*, Hp.*Coac.*603; ἄκανθα δ. τὴν χρόαν Arist.*Fr.*269; δ. ῥάβδοις *striated*, Id.*HA*525a12; δ. ψῆφοι Str.5.2.6. 2. metaph., ἀοιδά *Lyr.Alex.Adesp.*20.6. II. of persons, *clad in embroidered robes*, Luc.*Nec.*12.

διαποιμαίνω, *feed*: metaph. of educators, βίον Man.4.419.

διαπολεμ-έω, *carry a war through*, Hdt.7.158; δ. τὸν πόλεμον Pl. *Criti.*108e; δ. τινί *fight it out with* one, X.*An.*3.3.3, Plb.3.2.3, Plu. *Fab.*19; πρός τινα D.S.14.99:—Pass., διαπεπολεμήσεται [ὁ πόλεμος] the war *will be at an end*, Th.7.14, cf. 25, Jul.*Or.*2.55c. II. *carry on the war*, Th.6.37. **-ησις**, εως, ἡ, *finishing of a war*, Id.7.42.

διαπολῐορκέω, *carry a siege to its conclusion*, Th.3.17.

διαπολῑτ-εία, ἡ, *party-strife*, Plu.2.510c (pl.); αἱ πρός τινας δ. Cic. *Att.*9.4.2. **-εύομαι**, *to be a political rival*, Aeschin.3.194, Harp. s. v. διαγορεύων; δ. Περικλεῖ, of Thucydides son of Melesias, Marcellin.*Vit.Thuc.*28. **-ευτής**, οῦ, ὁ, *political opponent*, prob. in App. *Hisp.*8 (-πολῖται codd.).

διαπόλλῡμι, *destroy utterly*, Thphr.*HP*8.10.3.

διαπομπ-εύω, *carry the procession to an end*, Luc.*Nec.*16; Ῥάριον ὀργειῶνα νόμῳ -πομπεύουσα prob. in Hermesian.7.19. II. *carry all round*, ὕδωρ Critias 1.7 D. **-ή**, ἡ, *interchange of messages, negotiation*, πρὸς τὰς πόλεις Th.6.41 (pl.); φίλων, ἐραστῶν, App.*BC*5.71, *POxy.*471.61 (pl.): sg., App.*Hisp.*91. **-ησις**, εως, ἡ, = ἀποδιοπόμπησις, Sch.Ar.*Pl.*651. **-ιμος**, ον, *exported*, D.S.2.49, Opp. *C.*3.47.

διαπονδαρίζει (leg. -πυδ-)· διαναβάλλεται, διαναρρίπτεται, Hsch.

διαπον-έω, *work out with labour, elaborate*, Isoc.5.85; *cultivate, practise*, δ. γράμματα Pl.*Lg.*810b, cf. *R.*535c; τὰ πρὸς ἀγῶνας συντείνοντα Arist.*Pol.*1341a11; *exercise*, σώματα X.*Cyn.*4.10; σώματα δρόμοις καὶ πάλαις Plu.*Lyc.*14; αὐτὸν Id.*Dem.*5; στρατόν App.*Syr.*43; τοὺς νέους Luc.*Anach.*18:—Med., διαπονεῖσθαι ἐπιτηδεύματα, τέχνας, Pl.*Lg.*846d, cf. *Phdr.*273e, X.*Mem.*2.1.33:—Pass., Pl.*Criti.*118c, *Ep.*326d, etc.; οἴκου.. οὐχ ὡς τὰ πρόσθ' ἄριστα διαπονουμένου *managed, governed*, A.*Ag.*19; διαπονηθῆναι τὴν μουσικήν *to be taught* it *thoroughly*, Plu.*Per.*4; διαπεπονημένοι *veterans*, D.S.11.7; ὄψων.. περιττῶς διαπεπονημένων Plu.*Luc.*40. 2. *till* or *cultivate completely*, χώραν Plb.4.45.7:—Pass., *Hell.Oxy.*12.5. 3. Pass., *to be worn out, troubled*, *Act.Ap.*4.2, 16.18, *POxy.*743.22 (i B.C.). II. intr., *to work hard*, δ. τῇ διανοίᾳ καὶ τῷ σώματι Arist.*Pol.*1339a8, cf. Aristeas 92; περὶ τὸ σῶμα Arist.*EN*1178a26; περὶ τὰ δημιουργικὰ τεχνήματα Pl.*Lg.*846d: c. inf., δ. πᾶν ἰσόρροπον ποιεῖν X.*Smp.*2.17:—Med., δ. τὸ πᾶσαν πίστιν λαβεῖν Pl.*Lg.*966c; δ. περὶ τὸν γόνον Arist. *GA*759b1; οἱ διαπονούμενοι *the hard-working, hardy*, opp. ἄπονοι, X. *Lac.*5.8; *to be hard-worked*, of hounds, Arr.*Cyn.*32.1, al. **-ημα**, ατος, τό, *hard labour, exercise*, τὰ περὶ τὸν πόλεμον δ. Pl.*Lg.*813d. II. concrete, *work*, τὰ τῶν τεκτόνων δ. Id.*Criti.*114e; *achievement, work done*, βασιλέως Procop.*Aed.*2.7; *thing achieved, reward of toil*, Id. *Goth.*4.19.

διαπονηρεύομαι, *deal unfairly*, πρός τινα D.H.*Is.*3.

διαπόν-ησις, εως, ἡ, *working at, preparing*, πυροῦ Plu.2.693d. **-ητέον**, *one must work hard at*, Ph.2.235. **-ητότατα**, Adv. Sup., *most elaborately*, dub. l. in Id.2.20. **-ος**, ον, of persons, *exercised, hardy*, δ. τὰ σώματα Plu.*Mar.*26, al., cf. Onos.1.1. 2. *worn out*, σῶμα δ. πρός τι Plu.2.135f. II. Adv. -νως *with labour* or *toil*, Id. *Fab.*1.

διαπόντιος, ον, *beyond sea*, γᾶ A.*Ch.*352 (lyr.); στράτευμα Hermipp.58; πόλεμοι Th.1.141; λήμματα *revenues*, Antiph.196.8; πρεσβεία *IGRom.*4.881 (Tacina). II. *across the sea*, δ. πέτεσθαι Alex. 210; ναύτης δ. μονόμαχος Secund.*Sent.*18.

[διαπο]ντοπλᾰνής, ές, *wandering over the sea*, dub. in *Lyr.Alex. Adesp.*20.13.

διαπορ-εία, ἡ, *procession* of heavenly bodies, Pl.*Epin.*982c. II. *journey*, metaph., ἡ τοῦ λόγου δ. Id.*Criti.*106a. III. *mediation*, Id.*Epin.*984e. **-εύσιμος**, gloss on διαπρύσιος, Sch.Il.8.227, Hsch. **-ευσις**, εως, ἡ, gloss on διαπορεία, Suid. **-ευτός**, όν, *which may be traversed*, Apollon.*Lex.* s. v. ἀμαξιτός, Sch.X.*An.*1.2.21. **-εύω**, *carry over, conduct through*, X.*An.*2.5.18. II. mostly Med., with aor. Pass. διεπορεύθην:—*pass across*, ἐς Εὔβοιαν Hdt.4.33: c. acc., *go through*, Πελοπόννησον Th.5.52; χώραν X. *An.*3.3.3; δ. τὰς ὁδούς Pl.*Lg.*845a; στόμα δι' οὗ μέλη τε καὶ ἔπη δ. Satyr.*Vit.Eur.Fr.*39 xx 14; δ. γραμμήν *travel along* a line, Arist.*EN* 1174b1, cf. Archim.*Spir.*12: abs., Th.1.107, Pl.*Phd.*85d, Arist.*PA* 640b15; οἱ διαπορευόμενοι *the passers-by*, Aen.Tact.32.10. 2. *go through, detail*, εὐεργεσίας Plb.16.26.2; *perform*, τὰς κρούσεις Id.30.22.5. 3. of Time, *elapse*, *BGU*1116.11, al. (i B.C.).

διᾰπορ-έω, *to be quite at a loss, to be in doubt* or *difficulty*, τί χρὴ δρᾶν Pl.*Lg.*777c; ἐπὶ τοῖς συμβαίνουσι Plb.4.71.5: in aor. Pass., διηπορήθη Aeschin.2.34: pf. Pass., διηπορημένος Plu.*Alex.*25:—Med., δ. ὑπ' αἰσχύνης Pl.*Phdr.*237a. 2. *to be in want*, Arist.*Oec.*1353a26. II. *go through all the* ἀπορίαι, Id.*Pol.*1276b36, al.: but, 2. commonly only a stronger form of ἀπορέω, *raise an* ἀπορία, *start a difficulty*, Id.*EN*1096a11; ἔστι δὲ τοῖς εὐπορῆσαι βουλομένοις προὔργου τὸ διαπορῆσαι καλῶς Id.*Metaph.*995a28; περί τινος Plb.4.20.2, Phld. *Sign.*21; εἰ.. Epicur.*Fr.*21:—Med., διαπορεῖσθαί τι περί τινος Pl. *Sph.*217a:—Pass., *to be matter of doubt* or *discussion*, Pl.*Sph.*250e, Arist.*Metaph.*1086a19, al.; τὸ διαπορούμενον Pl.*Lg.*799e; τὸ διαπορεῖσθαι Arist.*EN*1101a35; τὸ διαπορηθέν Id.*Pol.*1282b8: impers., διαπορεῖται περί τινος *a question arises* about.., Id.*HA*631b2. **-ημα**, ατος, τό, *vexed question*, Id.*APo.*93b20 (pl.), al. II. *restlessness*, Hp.*Acut.*42. **-ησις**, εως, ἡ, *doubting, perplexity*, ὑπέρ τινος Plb. 28.3.6; εἰ δεῖ.. Id.35.5.1. **-ητέον**, *one must raise questions*, Id. 36.17.12, Ph.1.288, Longin.2.1. **-ητικός**, ή, όν, *at a loss, hesitating*, Plu.2.395a. II. Adv. -κῶς *in the form of a question*, περιοδεῦσαι Hermog.*Inv.*4.3.

διαπορθέω, = διαπέρθω, Il.2.691, Th.6.102, D.H.8.50, etc.:—Pass., *to be utterly ruined*, A.*Pers.*714, S.*Aj.*896 (lyr.), E.*Hel.*111, Paus.7. 17.1, D.C.47.45.

διαπορθμ-εύω, *carry over* or *across* a river or strait, Hdt.4.141, Acus.29 J., etc.; *carry a message from one to another*, Hdt.9.4:—Pass., *to be ferried across*, *BGU*1188.10 (i B.C.). 2. metaph., *transmit*, θεοῖς τὰ παρ' ἀνθρώπων καὶ ἀνθρώποις τὰ παρὰ θεῶν Pl.*Smp.*202e, cf. Procl.*Inst.*148, Iamb.*Myst.*1.5; κλῆρον εἰς τοὺς ἐκγόνους Jul. *Or.*2.81c. II. δ. ποταμόν, of ferry-boats, *ply across* a river, Hdt. 1.205, 5.52: abs., *cross over*, Iamb.*VP*2.11. **-ιος**, ον, *transmitting, mediating*, of certain spiritual beings, Orac.ap.Dam.*Pr.*339; τὸ ὄνομα τῶν ἰύγγων Procl.*in Cra.*33 P., cf. eund. *in Alc.*p.69 C.

διαπορίαι, αἱ, *Questions, Problems*, title of work by Epicurus, D.L.10.27; διαπορίας τοῖς ἰατροῖς παρέχειν Gal.5.721.

διαπορίζω, *furnish, render*, *POxy.*977 (iii A.D.).

διαπορπᾱκίζω, aor. inf. -κίξαι, *put the hand through the* πόρπαξ, Hsch.

διαπόρφῠρος, ον, *shot with purple*, ἄνθη Dsc.1.11; ἐσθάς Melissa *Ep.*1.

διαπο-στέλλω, *dispatch*, χρήματα εἰς Χίον D.35.54, cf. Plb.5.17.9, D.S.19.30; κήρυκας *Supp.Epigr.*2.261.6 (Delph., iii B.C.):—Pass., τοῦ παρ' ἡμῶν -ομένου παιδαρίου *UPZ*39.18 (ii B.C.); of a letter, Plb. 5.42.7; of scouts, Id.18.22.2:—Med. in act. sense, *IG*12(7).32.15 (Amorgos), *SIG*692.56 (Delph., ii B.C.); *send as a representative*, *POxy.*286.26 (i A.D.), etc. **-στολή**, ἡ, *sending of messages*, Plb. 5.37.3 (pl.), *OGI*248.58 (ii B.C.); πρεσβειῶν D.H.7.12.

διαποσῴζω, *carry safe through*, Arr.*Ind.*37.5.

διαπραγμᾰτεύομαι, *discuss* or *examine thoroughly*, τοῦτον τὸν λόγον Pl.*Phd.*77d; τὴν αἰτίαν ib.95e. II. *gain by trading*, *Ev.Luc.* 19.15. III. *accomplish*, τι πρὸς τοὺς θεούς Iamb.*Myst.*5.16.

διαπρακτ-έος, α, ον, *practicable*, Isoc.*Ep.*6.8. **-ικός**, ή, όν, *effective, operative*, Dam.*Pr.*34.

διάπραξις, εως, ἡ, *accomplishment of ends*, δ. πολιτικαί Pl.*Smp.* 184b, cf. Ph.1.429; *action, agency*, J.*AJ*17.1.1, Iamb.*Myst.*4.3.

διάπρᾱσις, εως, ἡ, *sale to various purchasers*, D.H.7.29, Plu.*Sull.* 33, *POxy.*83.8 (iv A.D.). II. *farming out*, προσόδων, τῶν τελωνικῶν, *PTeb.*8.15 (iii B.C.), *POxy.*44.4 (i A.D.).

διαπράσσω, Att. -ττω, Ion. -πρήσσω, *pass over*, c. gen., διέπρησσον πεδίοιο they *made their way over* the plain, Il.2.785, 3.14; also οἵ κε.. διαπρήσσωσι κέλευθον *may finish* their journey, Od.2.213, cf. 429: of Time, c. part., ἤματα.. διέπρησσον πολεμίζων I *went through* days in fighting, Il.9.326; κεν.. εἰς ἐνιαυτὸν ἅπαντα οὔ τι διαπρήξαιμι λέγων I *should* not *finish* speaking.., Od.14.197:—Med., διαπραξάμενος βίον Alex.262.2 (dub.). II. *bring about, accomplish*, Hdt.9.94; δ. τινί τι *get* a thing *done* for a man, Id.3.61, cf. A.*Eu.*953 (lyr.): c. inf., X.*Smp.*5.9: abs., Ar.*Eq.*93:—Pass., ἐπ' ἔργοις διαπεπραγμένοις καλῶς A.*Ch.*739:—freq. in Med., Hdt.1.2, 2.2, Ar.*Lys.*518, etc.; δι' ἑρμηνέων Hdt.4.24; οὐδὲν καινὸν διαπράττονται D.35.1: pf. Pass. in med. sense, τὸ αὐτὸ διαπεπραγμένοι εἰσὶν ὥσπερ ἂν εἰ.. Pl.*Grg.*479a; πολλοῖς πολλὰ παρὰ τοῦ πάππου ἀγαθὰ διεπέπρακτο X.*Cyr.*4.2.10, cf. *An.*2.3.25; ὃ οὗτοι διαπεπραγμένοι εἰσί D.35.26, cf. Din.1.97, Isoc. 4.137; τοὺς ἀνήκεστα δ. Theodect.ap.Arist.*Rh.*1399b4, cf. Men. *Per.Fr.*1: also strictly in sense of Med., *effect for oneself, gain one's point*, Hdt.9.41; τὸ ἴδιον Antipho 5.61; φιλίαν δ. πρός τινα X.*An.*7. 3.16; πλοῖα παρά τινος ib.6.2.17: c. inf., δ. τῶν ἀγγέλων γενέσθαι Pl.*R.*360a; δ. ὥστε folld. by inf., Lys.16.15, Pl.*Grg.*478e, by ind.,

X.*An*.4.2.23; δ. μὴ καίειν ib.3.5.5. 2. Med., *get for oneself, obtain*, πλοῖα ib.6.2.17, cf. 3.2.29. III. *make an end of, destroy*, in Pass., A.*Pers*.260 (lyr.), al., S.*Tr*.784, E.*Hel*.858; διαπέπρακται τὰ Καρχηδονίων Plu.*Fab*.5. IV. Med., *intrigue successfully*, Aeschin. 3.232 (so in Act., διαπρήσσει· ἀπατᾷ, ψεύδεται, Hsch.).

διαπραΰνω, *soothe*, Philostr.*VA*6.14, *VS*1.21.5.

διαπρέπ-εια, ἡ, *magnificence*, Aq.*Ps*.28(29).2, al. **-ής**, ές, *distinguished*, νᾶσος Pi.*I*.5(4).44; ἀρετῇ Th.2.34; ἐσθῆτι καὶ κόσμῳ δ. Democr.195, cf. E.*Supp*.841, *IA*1588; γυναικομίμῳ μορφώματι Id. *Antiop*.iiA7A.; τὸ δ. *magnificence*, Th.6.16. Adv. -πῶς *magnificently*, σκηνὴ δ. κεκοσμημένη Plu.*Alc*.12; δ. ἀγωνίσασθαι Id.*Mar*.28, J.*BJ*7.1.2 (Comp.): Sup. -πέστατα D.50.7. **-όντως**, *remarkably*, Sch.E.*Or*.1483. **-ω**, *appear prominent* or *conspicuous, strike the eye*, *h.Merc*.351, Pi.*O*.1.2; διαπρέπον κακόν A.*Pers*.1007 (lyr.). 2. *to be eminent*, ἔν τινι *AP*9.513 (Crin.); ἐπί τινι Luc.*Salt*.9, cf. D.C. 68.6; κάλλει, ὥρας ἀκμῇ, Plu.2.771e, D.C.42.34: c. gen., δ. πάντων ἀψυχίᾳ E.*Alc*.642. 3. *to be suitable*, κτητικὴ λεχθεῖσα ἂν διαπρέψειεν Pl.*Sph*.219c. II. c. acc. rei, *adorn*, E.*Fr*.185.

διαπρεσβ-εία, ἡ, *reciprocal embassy*, Plb.5.67.11. **-εύομαι**, *send embassies*, εἰς τὰς πόλεις X.*HG*3.2.24, cf. *SIG*633.121 (Milet., ii B.C.), Plb.1.11.11, D.S.11.68, Plu.*Sert*.23; τισί D.C.45.43:— later in Act., *serve as envoy*, *PPetr*.3 p.150. **-ευσις**, εως, ἡ, = διαπρεσβεία, App.*Gall*.18 (pl.); ἐς ἀλλήλους Id.*Syr*.2.

διαπρηστεύω, v. διαδρηστεύω.

δια-πρίζω, = -πρίω, Paul.Aeg.6.18:—Pass., Sor.1.80; cf. διαπρίζει· διαπερᾷ, Hsch. **-πριστος**, ον, *sawn through*, θύρα Demioprat. ap.Poll.10.24. **-πρίω** [ρῑ], *saw through, saw asunder*, Ar.*Eq*.768, cj. in Aen.Tact.4.2 (cf. διαπίμπρημι); *split*, κύμινον Jul.*Caes*.312a:— Pass., Hp.*VC*21; -πεπρισμένα [ξύλα] *SIG*^{2}587.304; διαπεπρισμένα ἡμίσε'.. ὡσπερεὶ τὰ σύμβολα Eub.70: metaph., διεπρίοντο ταῖς καρδίαις *Act.Ap*.7.54, cf. 5.33; also εἰς πλείω δ. τὴν Παλαιστίνην Lib.*Ep*. 334. II. δ. τοὺς ὀδόντας *gnash* the teeth, Luc.*Cal*.24. III. διαπρίεται· διαγοράζει, μαίνεται, Hsch.

διαπρί-ωσις [ρῑ], εως, ἡ, *sawing up* into planks, *SIG*248*N*8 (Delph., iv B.C.). **-ωτός**, ή, όν, = διάπριστος, Hp.*VC*21.

διαπρό, v. διά. **διάπροθι**, Adv. = foreg., Nic.*Al*.3.

διαπροστᾰτεύω, *continue to propose*, τι Plb.4.13.7.

διαπρύσιος [ῠ], α, ον, *going through, piercing*, in Hom. only as Adv., πρὼν πεδίοιο διαπρύσιον τετυχηκώς a hill *piercing into, running out into*, the plain, Il.17.748. 2. of sound, *piercing, thrilling*, ἤϋσεν δὲ διαπρύσιον he gave a *piercing* cry, 8.227; δ. κιθαρίζων *h.Ven*. 80: in late Prose, τορόν τι βοῶν καὶ δ. Agath.4.11. II. later as Adj., Ἀπείρῳ διαπρυσίᾳ *far-stretching*, Pi.*N*.4.51. 2. freq. of sound, *piercing*, ὀλολυγαί *h.Ven*.19; ὄτοβος S.*OC*1479 (lyr.); κέλαδος E.*Hel*. 1308 (lyr.): in late Prose, οἰμωγαί J.*BJ*2.1.2. 3. δ. κεραϊστής a *downright* thief, *h.Merc*.336; δ. πόλεμος *open* war, D.L.2.143. 4. Adv. -ίως *loudly*, ἱστορίας μαρτυρία κηρύττουσα δ. D.S.11.38: metaph., *intensely*, μισεῖσθαι ὑπό τινος Sch.Ar.*Pax* 481.

διαπταίω, *stutter much*, Luc.*Somn*.8.

διαπτερ-όω, *clean with* or *as with a feather*, Hp.*Acut*.58, Aret.*CD* 1.8. **-ύσσομαι**, *flutter about*, Ps.-Plu.*Fluv*.6.4. **-ωσις**, εως, ἡ, *cleaning with a feather*, v.l. in Hp.*Acut*.58, cf. Erot.

διαπτίσσω, aor. inf. -πτίσαι, *winnow, sift*, *EM*125.43.

διαπτο-έω, fut. -ήσω: Ep. aor. διεπτοίησα:—*scare away, startle and scatter*, ἐπέεσσι διεπτοίησε γυναῖκας Od.18.340; *strike with panic*, στρατὸν... φόβος διεπτόησε E.*Ba*.304; with personal subject, Plu. *Cleom*.5; τοὺς ἀντιπάλους Them.*Or*.21.257b:—Pass., *to be panic-stricken*, δείσαντες διεπτοήθημεν Pl.*R*.336b, cf. Plu.*Caes*.10, etc.; of horses, Plb.3.51.5. II. in Pass., = πτοέω II, διεπτόηντο ταῖς ὁρμαῖς πρὸς τὸν Τίτον Plu.*Flam*.5. **-ησις**, εως, ἡ, *violent excitement*, Pl.*Lg*.783c.

διά-πτυξις, εως, ἡ, *spreading out fanwise*, τῶν ἐπιπέδων Procl.*Hyp*. 5.110; *explication*, Gal.1.305. **-πτύσσω**, Att. -ττω, *open and spread out, unfold, disclose*: metaph., διαπτυχθέντες ὤφθησαν κενοί S.*Ant*.709, cf. E.*Hipp*.985, Pl.*Lg*.858e (Pass.); σύμβολα Iamb.*Protr*. 21; λόγῳ δ. Moschio Trag.6. 2. *split open*, κράνος D.S.17.20; *open up*, τὸ ἐπιγάστριον Gal.2.520. II. *fold one with another, intertwine*, Arist.*GA*720^{b}17. **-πτῠχή**, ἡ, *fold, folding leaf*, δέλτου διαπτυχαί, γραμμάτων δ., E.*IT*727, 793.

διαπτύω, *spit upon*, τινός Ael.*NA*4.22: abs., Gal.13.46: metaph., c. acc., ὁ σεμνὸς ἀνὴρ καὶ διαπτύων τοὺς ἄλλους D.18.258, cf. Lib.*Or*. 57.53, al.; of food, Plu.2.101c; δ. τὸν χαλινόν, Lat. *frenum respuere*, Philostr.*Im*.2.5:—Pass., D.Chr.38.38.

διά-πτωμα, ατος, τό, *stumble, slip*, Philem.60; *error*, Chrysipp. *Stoic*.2.215, Phld.*Herc*.1251.5; *failure*, opp. ἐπίτευγμα, Id.*Po*.5.21; μεγάλοις δ. περιπίπτειν fall in with great *losses*, *IPE*1^2.32.55 (Olbia), cf. *SIG*364.62 (Ephesus); *loss, deficiency* in accounts, *PHib*.1.52.9 (iii B.C.), etc. **-πτωσις**, εως, ἡ, *fall*, Gal.18(1).506: chiefly metaph., *failure*, Epicur.*Fr*.556; ἀγωνία φόβος διαπτώσεως *Stoic*. 3.98, cf. Phld.*Lib*.p.28 O., *Herc*.1251.7, S.E.*M*.7.423, Plu.2.800a, etc.

διαπῡδαρίζω, v. πυδαρίζω.

διαπῡ-έω, *suppurate*, Hp.*Aph*.4.82, etc. **-ημα**, ατος, τό, *collection of pus*, Id.*Prog*.7 (pl.). **-ησις**, εως, ἡ, *suppuration*, ibid., Sor.1. 76. **-ητικός**, ή, όν, *promoting suppuration*, Gal.11.118. **-ΐσκομαι**, Pass., *suppurate throughout*, Hp.*VC*2, M.Ant.4.39:—later in Act., Aret.*SD*1.9.

διάπυκνος, ον, v.l. for διάκοιλος in Dsc.4.114.

διαπυκτεύω, *spar, fight with*, τινί X.*Cyr*.7.5.53, Arr.*Epict*.2.21.11, etc.: abs., of cocks, Luc.*Anach*.37: metaph., Id.*Gall*.22.

διαπύλιον [ῠ], τό, (πύλη) *gate-toll*, Arist.*Oec*.1348^{a}26, *PTeb*.8.19 (iii/ii B.C.).

διαπυνθάνομαι (poet. διαπεύθομαι (q.v.)), *search out by questioning, find out*, τήν τινων συνουσίαν.. περὶ τῶν λόγων τίνες ἦσαν Pl.*Smp*.172a, etc.; τί τινος something *from* one, Plu.*Cat.Mi*.16; δ. τοῦ θεοῦ, πῶς χρή.. Pl.*R*.469a: abs., Id.*Hp.Mi*.369d.

διά-πῡος, ον, (πῦον) *suppurating*, Hp.*Aph*.7.45. **-πῡόω**, intr., *suppurate*, *Hippiatr*.16, 20.

διαπῠρ-ιάομαι, Pass., *to be thoroughly heated*, Hp.*Steril*.234. **-ίζω**, *heat thoroughly*:—Pass., metaph., *glow with anger*, Hsch. **-ινα**, τά, *cautery irons*, Gal.18(1).376. **-όομαι**, *set on fire*, E.*Cyc*.694: Pass., metaph., τῷ θυμῷ διεπυροῦτο Plu.*Phoc*.6; *to be consumed with thirst*, Lxx 4*Ma*.3.15. **-ος**, ον, *red-hot*, Anaxag.A.1, al., Hp.*Aër*. 17, E.*Cyc*.631, Arist.*Pr*.954^{a}18; σίδηρος Epicur.*Fr*.346b; διάπυρα, τά, *embers*, Pl.*Ti*.58c; *extremely hot*, πέτραι δ. ὑπὸ τοῦ ἡλίου Porph. *Abst*.1.13. 2. *inflamed*, Hp.*VM*18. 3. metaph., *ardent, fiery*, Pl.*R*.615e, *Lg*.783a (Sup.); δ. πρὸς ὀργήν, πρὸς δόξαν, Plu.2. 577a, *Luc*.4; ἐραστής Procop.*Pers*.2.12; δ. μῖσος Plu.*Arat*.3. Adv. -ρως *ardently*, προσέχειν σχολῇ εὐσεβείας Jul.*Ep*.89a; ἐρασθῆναί τινος Ael.*VH*2.4. 4. *using fire*, χρεία Max.Tyr.10.8.

διαπυρπᾰλᾰμάω, aor. -ησα, *juggle*, *h.Merc*.357.

διάπυρρος, ον, *bright red*, Xenocr.15.

διαπυρσεύω, *communicate by beacon*, τινί App.*Mith*.79: metaph., *blazon abroad as by beacon-fires*, τὰς πράξεις τῇ δόξῃ εἰς ἅπαντας τοὺς ἀνθρώπους Plu.*Demetr*.8: c. gen., Philostr.*VA*2.22 (v.l. -πυρσαίνω): —Med., *make signals by beacons*, Plb.1.19.7.

διαπύρσιος· μέγας, διαβόητος, Hsch.:—also **διαπύρσιον**· μέγα, διαπορεύσιμον, ἐξάκουστον (i.e. διαπρύσιον), κτλ., Cyr.

διαπύρωσις [ῠ], εως, ἡ, *severe inflammation*, Sor.1.82. II. *thorough heating*, *PHolm*.2.7.

διάπυστος, ον, *heard of, well-known*, δ. γίγνεσθαι Hdn.2.12.2.

διαπῠτίζω, Att. fut. -ιῶ, *spit* or *spirt out*, Arched.3.12.

διαπωλέω, *sell publicly*, X.*HG*4.6.6, Plu.*Oth*.4; *sell entirely*, πάντα τά τινος *PLips*.35.17 (iv A.D.):—Pass., *SIG*695.62 (Magn. Mae.).

διαπωρόομαι, Pass., *form a callus thoroughly*, of a broken bone, Hp.*Art*.21.

διᾰράομαι, *curse*, Aristeas 311.

διαρᾰπισμός, ὁ, *scourging*, prob. in *POxy*.1873 (v A.D.).

διᾰράσσω, *strike through*, διὰ σαρκὸς ἄραξα Hes.*Sc*.364; *smash in pieces*, τινὰ τῷ ῥοπάλῳ ὥσπερ πίθον παλαιόν D.Chr.8.31.

διάργεμος, ον, *flecked with white*, Babr.85.15.

διάρδω, *water, irrigate*, J.*BJ*3.10.8 (Pass.).

διάρημα, ατος, τό, = λέμβος, Procop.*Aed*.6.1 (pl.).

διαρθρ-έω, = ἐξαρθρέω, dub. in Gal.18(1).626. **-όω**, *divide by joints, articulate*, τὰ στήθη διήρθρου Pl.*Smp*.191a:—Pass., διηρθρωμένος *well-jointed, well-knit*, Hp.*Aër*.24, Pl.*Phdr*.253d (metaph., πρὸς σωφροσύνην πεπηγὸς καὶ δ. Eun.*Hist*.p.246 D.); πόδες, δάκτυλοι, Arist.*Phgn*.810^{a}16, *HA*504^{a}7; *to be differentiated*, of the embryo, ib.489^{b}9, cf. Hp.*Nat.Puer*.17; *to be movable-jointed*, Id.*Art*. 30; esp. *to be jointed by* διάρθρωσις (q.v.), Gal.2.656, 18(1).433; also διηρθρωμένον γράμμα a *distinct* birth-mark (opp. συγκεχυμένον), Arist.*GA*721^{b}34. 2. *endue with articulate speech*, τὴν γλῶτταν Luc.*Enc.Dem*.14, cf. Plu.*Dem*.11:—Med., φωνὴν καὶ ὀνόματα διηρθρώσατο τῇ τέχνῃ *invented articulate* speech and names, Pl.*Prt*. 322a. 3. *describe distinctly*, Id.*Lg*.963b, 645c (Pass.), Porph. *Plot*.18, Iamb.*VP*23.103, etc.; *perceive clearly, distinguish*, Phld.*D*. 1.22, *Mus*.p.39 K., *Vit.Philonid*.p.9 C.; διηρθρωμένη διάληψις Porph. *Abst*.2.43; opp. συγκεχυμένος, Id.*Marc*.10. 4. *complete in detail, fill up so as to form an organic whole*, lit., πρὶν διηρθρῶσθαι τὸ σῶμα Arist.*HA*521^{a}10 (Act. δ. σάρκα τῇ γλώττῃ of a bear *licking* its cub *into shape*, Ael.*NA*6.3): metaph., Arist.*EN*1098^{a}22:—Pass., Id. *Metaph*.986^{b}6; ἂν διαρθροῖτο ὁ συλλογισμός Id.*Top*.156^{a}20. 5. *distinguish*, τὸ γένος A.D.*Synt*.138.24. **-ωσις**, εως, ἡ, *articulation*, τῶν μελέων Hp.*Nat.Puer*.18; *differentiation*, δ. λαμβάνειν, of the embryo, Arist.*HA*583^{b}23, cf. *GA*744^{b}11; of the Universe, Epicur.*Ep*.2 p.38 U. (pl.). b. esp. *movable articulation, diarthrosis* (opp. συνάρθρωσις), Gal.2.735, 18(1).433. 2. of the voice, *articulate utterance*, Arist.*HA*535^{a}31; ἡ τῶν γραμμάτων δ. Id.*PA*660^{a}22. 3. *distinct statement*, ἠθικῶν ἐννοιῶν, title of work by Chrysipp., *Stoic*.2. 8, cf. Iamb.*Myst*.5.13; *distinctness*, λόγου Longin.ap.Porph.*Plot*.20, cf. Alex.Aphr. *in Metaph*.3.14. **-ωτέον**, *one must define precisely*, Arist.*EE*1248^{a}10, Porph.*Abst*.1.31, Simp. *in Epict*.p.2 D. **-ωτικός**, ή, όν, *explanatory*, Epict.*Ench*.52; δ. τέχνη S.E.*M*.1.300; *giving shape* or *form*, Sch.Hes.*Th*.139.

διᾰριθμ-έω, *reckon up one by one, enumerate*, ψήφους E.*IT*966, cf. Ar.*Av*.1622; τἀργύριον Phld.*Ir*.p.37 W.; ὑπολείποι ἂν ὁ αἰὼν διαριθμοῦντα Arist.*Rh*.1374^{a}33:—more freq. in Med., as Pl.*Cra*.437d, *Phdr*.273e, al.; *count and classify*, Id.*Grg*.501a; διαριθμήσασθαι περί τινος Id.*Lg*.633a:—Pass., Aeschin.3.207, Arist.*Ph*.322^{b}30. 2. *count out, pay*, δωρεάν τισι App.*BC*4.101. **-ησις**, εως, ἡ, *reckoning up*, χρημάτων Plu.2.27c; χρόνου Theo Sm.p.148 H. **-ητικός**, v.l. for διαρθρωτικός, Epict.*Ench*.52.

διάρῑνον, τό, *mustard*, Hsch., prob. in Polyaen.4.3.32.

διάριον, τό, = Lat. *diarium, day-wage*, *POxy*.1729 (iv A.D.), etc.

διαρίπτω, poet. for διαρρίπτω, dub. l. in Ar.*Th*.665 (lyr.).

διᾱριστάομαι, *eat at breakfast for a wager*, βοῦν αὐτῷ δ. *eat* an ox *against* another, Ath.9.412f.

διᾰριστεύομαι, *strive for the pre-eminence*, πρός τινα Longin.13.4.

διάρκ-εια, ἡ, *sufficiency*, τῆς τροφῆς Thphr.*CP*1.11.6. **-έω**, *suffice*, τρία ἔπεα διαρκέσει Pi.*N*.7.48, cf. X.*Cyr*.6.2.26, Phld.*Herc*. 1251.19, etc.; πρός τι Thphr.*CP*1.16.4; *endure, hold out*, Isoc.2.19; δ. πρός τινα *hold out* against..., Luc.*Luct*.24, etc. 2. in point of Time, *endure, last*, A.*Th*.842 (lyr.); οὐ διήρκεσε δεῦρο ὁ λόγος Pl.*Ti*. 21d: c. part., δ. πολιορκούμενος X.*HG*5.3.21; δ. ἐπὶ πολὺν χρόνον Arist. *Mete*.352^{b}4; οὐ διήρκεσε τῷ βίῳ πρὸς τὸ τοῦ πολέμου τέλος Plu.*Fab*.27; ἀπόσιτος [ὢν] ἐς ἑβδόμην δ. Luc.*Hist.Conscr*.21. II. *supply nourishment*, τινί Plu.*Sol*.22; *sustain*, τινάς Aeschin.*Ep*.5.3. **-ής**, ές, *sufficient*, χώρα Th.1.15; τροφή Arist.*HA*626^{a}2, Thphr.*CP*1.11.6; δυνάμεις D.H.4.23, etc. 2. *lasting*, ὠφέλεια D.3.33; ἐπὶ πολὺ D.H.6.54: Comp., Luc.*Anach*.24: Sup., *with staying power*, of an athlete, Paus.6.13.3; ἵπποι Them.*Or*.11.146a. Adv. -κῶς S.E.*P*. 3.115, Eun.*Hist*.p.209D., Demoph.*Sent*.10, etc.; δ. ἔχειν τι to be *amply* provided with, Procop.*Pers*.1.21, al.: Sup. διαρκέστατα ζῆν *in complete competence*, X.*Mem*.2.8.6. **-ούντως**, Adv. *sufficiently*, dub. l. in J.*AJ*14.13.9.

διάρμα, ατος, τό, (διαίρω) *passage by sea*, Plb.10.8.2, Agathem.3.13; *crossing of a channel*, Str.4.5.2. II. *elevation* of style, ὄγκος καὶ δ. Plu.2.853c, Longin.12.1; δ. ψυχῆς λαβεῖν D.L.9.7. III. = κούφισμα, Hsch.

διαρμόζω or **-ττω**, fut. -σω, *distribute in various places*, E.*Or*.1451 (lyr.): hence, 2. Med., *arrange, dispose*, ταῦτα πρὸς τὸ μέλλον Plb.8.25.5:—Pass., τὸν τρόπον τοῦτον διηρμοσμένοι ib.7.1; *regulate*, τὸν βίον Plu.2.88a.

διαρνέομαι, *deny*, Petr.Patr.p.434D., Just.*Nov*.18.10.

διαρόγχαι, αἱ, *gaps left in applying a bandage*, Hp.ap.Erot. (-ροχαί codd.); cf. διαρωχμίας.

διάρουρον, τό, *plot of two* ἄρουραι, *PBas*.17.3 (i A.D.).

διᾰρόω, *plough*, A.R.3.1053 (tm.).

διαρπ-ᾰγή, ἡ, *plundering*, Hdt.9.42, Plb.10.16.6, *PMasp*.4.13 (vi A.D.). **-άζω**, fut. -άσομαι Pl.*R*.336b, later -άσω App.*Pun*.55:—*tear in pieces*, [λύκοι] αἶψα διαρπάζουσι [ἄρνας] Il.16.355; of the wind, *carry away, efface*, τὰ ἴχνη X.*Cyn*.6.2; τείχη διηρπασμένα *dismantled*, Jul.*ad Ath*.279a. II. *spoil, plunder*, πόλιν Hdt.1.88, etc.:—Med., Συρίαν J.*AJ*1.9.1. 2. *seize as plunder*, χρήματα Hdt. l. c., cf. Lys. 7.6, 19.40, *Hell.Oxy*.13.3, Arist.*Pol*.1281^{a}25, etc.:—Pass., Pl.*Plt*. 274b; τὰν τῇ Βοιωτίᾳ διαρπασθησόμεν' ὑπὸ τοῦ πολέμου D.18.213, cf. Lys.19.41, Th.8.36. 3. *snatch from*, θηρείων παῖδα γενείων Nonn. *D*.48.290. **-ᾰσις**, εως, ἡ, = διαρπαγή, *AB*438.4.

διαρρᾰγή, ἡ, *tearing apart*, ὀστέων Hp.*Coac*.184.

διαρραίνω, pf. διέρραγκα Lxx *Pr*.7.17:—*sprinkle*, κόνιν Philostr. *Gym*.56; *shed*, ἀκτῖνας Lyd.*Ost*.10^{a}; *besprinkle*, Lxx l. c.; *purify by lustration*, οἰκίην *IG*12(5).593^{A}17 (Ceos, Pass.):—Pass., ἀφρῷ ἡ γῆ διέρρανται Philostr.*Im*.7.27:—also intr. in Act., Lyd.*Ost*.9^{b}. II. Pass., *to be diffused, dissipated*, S.*Tr*.14, Arist.*Mete*.341^{a}30.

διαρραίω, *dash in pieces, destroy*, διαρραῖσαι μεμαῶτες Il.2.473, etc.; οἶκον Od.2.49:—Pass., c. fut. Med., *to be destroyed, perish*, τάχα δ' ἄμμε διαρραίσεσθαι ὀΐω Il.24.355; διαρραισθέντας εἰς Ἅιδου μολεῖν A. *Pr*.238. II. ῥωχμαὶ σάρκα διαρραίουσι dub. in Marc.Sid.80.

διάρραμμα, ατος, τό, (διαρράπτω) *seam*, Plu.2.978a.

διαρρᾰπίζω, *cuff soundly*, Hld.7.7, 8.9 (Pass.).

διαρραπτέον, *one must insert a suture*, Archig.ap.Orib.47.13.5.

διαρράπτω, *sew through* or *together*, Str.15.1.67, Plu.2.978a; *insert a suture*, Gal.18(2).746.

διαρρᾰφή, ἡ, *sewing up*, Sor.2.40.

διαρρᾰχίζω, *carve*, Eub.15.4 (Pass.).

διαρρέμβομαι, *dawdle*, Anon.ap.Suid. s. v. ῥεμβώδης.

διαρρέπω, *oscillate*: *halt in one's gait*, Hp.*Art*.55.

διαρρέω, *flow through*, διὰ μέσου Hdt.7.108; δ. μέσου αὐτοῦ Ael. *VH*3.1: c. acc., τὴν χώραν Isoc.11.14; δ. εἰς τὴν θάλατταν, of rivers, Arist.*HA*569^{a}20:—Pass., Epicur.*Ep*.2p.47U.; *to be drenched*, ἱδρῶτι Hld.10.13; of a country, ποταμοῖς διαρρεῖσθαι Plu.2.951f: also intr. in Act., τὸ ἔδαφος διαρρέον καὶ τὴν ἰκμάδα παρέχον Thphr.*Ign*. 41. 2. *slip through*, τῶν χειρῶν Luc.*Anach*.28; διὰ τῶν δακτύλων Id.*DMort*.17.1. 3. of a vessel, *leak*, ib.10.1. 4. of a report, *fade away, die away*, Plu.*Aem*.24. 5. χείλη διερρυηκότα *gaping* lips, Ar.*Nu*.873. II. *fall away like water, die* or *waste away*, χάρις διαρρεῖ S.*Aj*.1267; of the moon, *wane*, πάλιν διαρρεῖ κἀπὶ μηδὲν ἔρχεται Id.*Fr*.871.8; to be 'boiled to rags', Ar.*V*.1156; of money, μὴ λαθεῖν διαρρυὲν τἀργύριον D.37.54; of soldiers, δ. ἐκ τῆς στρατοπεδείας Plb.1.74.10; δ. κατὰ πόλεις Plu.*Sull*.27, etc.; also δ. ὑπὸ πλούτου καὶ μαλακίας, Lat. *diffluere luxuria*, Id.2.32f, cf. *Ages*.14, Luc.*DMort*.11.4, etc.; δ. τῷ βίῳ *lead a loose* life, Ael.*VH*9.24.

διάρρηγμα, ατος, τό, *fragment*, prob. in Hsch. s. v. κεάσματα.

διαρρήγνῡμι, *break through*, Hom. only in Med., διά τε ῥήξασθαι ἐπάλξεις Il.12.308; διαρρήξασα χαλινόν *having broken* the bridle *asunder*, Thgn.259; μόγις ἂν.. διαρρήξειας [τὴν κεφαλήν] Hdt.3.12; πλευρὰν διαρρήξαντα.. φασγάνῳ *having cloven* it, S.*Aj*.834; δ. τὰς χορδάς Pl.*Phd*.86a:—Pass., *burst*, as with eating, X.*Cyr*.8.2.21, Anaxil.25, Phoenicid.3, etc.; δ. μυρίων ἀγαθῶν Men.10D.; with passion, διαρραγήσομαι Ar.*Eq*.340; ὑπὸ φθόνου Luc.*Tim*.40; οὐδ' ἂν σὺ διαρραγῇς ψευδόμενος D.18.21, cf. 87; διαρραγείης, as a curse, '*split you!*' Ar.*Av*.2, etc.: pf. διέρρωγα *to be broken* or *torn*, διερρωγυιῶν τῶν χορδῶν Pl.*Phd*. l. c.; ἀκεσαμένη τὸ διερρωγός Arist.*HA*623^{a}18; ὑπόδημα δ. Plu.2.82b: later pf. part. Pass. διερρηγμένος Jul.*Or*.2.64c.

διαρρήδην, Adv., (διαρρηθῆναι) *expressly, explicitly*, *h.Merc*.313, Plb.3.26.5; esp. of legal enactments or treaties, δ. γέγραπται Foed. ap.And.2.14; δ. εἴρηται μή.. Lys.1.20; ὁ νόμος δ. λέγει Is.3.68; δ. ψηφίσασθαι D.19.6; δ. πέμπειν Pl.*Lg*.698c; νομοθετεῖν ib.876c.

διαρρήκτης, ου, ὁ, *plotter*, Hsch.

διάρρηξις, εως, ἡ, = διαρραγή, Epicur.*Ep*.2p.49U., J.*AJ*18.9.1, Herod.Med. in *Rh.Mus*.49.552.

διάρρησις, εως, ἡ, *explicit enactment*, Pl.*Lg*.932e, dub. in *Leg. Gort*.9.36.

διαρρήσσω, = διαρρήγνυμι, Babr.38.7, *Ev.Luc*.8.29, Artem.4 *Praef*.:—Pass., Ps.-Callisth.1.46.

διαρρικνόομαι, *draw up and twist the body*, of an unseemly kind of dance, Cratin.219.

διάρριμμα, ατος, τό, *casting about, questing*, of a hound, X.*Cyn*.4. 4 (pl.).

διαρρῑν-άω, *file through* or *perforate*, Hero *Aut*.25.5, Sor.2.63: pf. part. Pass. διερρινημένος *perforated*, ἐπίθημα Arist.*Ath*.68.3, cf. Dsc. 4.114: metaph., *fine, critical*, ἀνὴρ λεπτὸς καὶ δ. τὴν γαστέρα Max. Tyr.36.4. **-ησις**, εως, ἡ, *filing through, perforation*, Heliod.ap. Orib.47.17.4.

διαρρῑπίζω, *blow away, disperse*, Hld.3.7: metaph. in Pass., Id. 9.14. II. *expose to draughts*, Hp.*Ep*.16 (Pass.).

διαρρίπτω, poet. **διαρίπτω**, also pres. **διαρριπτέω** Ar.*V*.59, X. *Cyn*.5.8, Aeschin.1.59, etc.:—*shoot through*, διαρρίπτασκεν ὀϊστόν Od.19.575. 2. *cast* or *throw about*, διάριψον ὄμμα πανταχῇ *fling* glances *round*, dub. in Ar.*Th*.665; τὰς ὄψιας πυκνὰ δ. Hp.*Coac*.214; δ. σκέλεα Id.*Prog*.3 (Pass.); δ. τὴν οὐράν, of a dog, *wag* the tail, X. *Cyn*.6.23. 3. *throw about*, as nuts, etc., among a crowd, Ar.*V*. 59; χρήματά τισι Plb.16.21.8: metaph., *toss about*, Pl.*Ep*.343d; *squander*, τὸν βίον Lib.*Or*.12.33: pf. part. Pass., *indiscriminate*, Pl. *Lg*.860c; *scattered, dispersed*, δ. κατὰ πόλεις Plu.*Phil*.8; διερριμμένην μνήμην ποιήσασθαι mention *here and there*, Plb.3.57.5. 4. *throw down*, τὸν περίβολον Id.16.1.6. II. intr., *plunge*, ἐν τῇ θαλάττῃ X.*Cyn*.5.8.

διαρρῑφή, Dor. **-φά**, ἡ, *casting about*, ποδός Pratin.Lyr.1.16.

διάρριψις, εως, ἡ, *scattering*, X.*An*.5.8.7, Thphr.*HP*6.3.4.

διάρροδος, ον, *compounded of roses*, κολλούριον Gal.12.765.

διαρροή, ἡ, *channel, pipe*, πνεύματος διαρροαί the *wind-pipe*, E.*Hec*. 567; of a stream, αἱ δ. τοῦ Ῥειτοῦ *SIG*86.15 (Eleusis, v B.C.). II. *flowing through*, ἡ ἄνω τε καὶ κάτω τοῦ ὠκεανοῦ διαρροή, ebb and flow, D.C.39.41.

διαρροθέω, *to roar* or *rustle through*, διαρροθῆσαι κάκην τινί *to inspire* fear *by clamour*, A.*Th*.192. II. διαροθεῦντα· διασοβοῦντα, Hsch.

διάρροια, ἡ, *flowing through, diarrhoea*, Hp.*Aph*.3.21 (pl.), Ar. *Fr*.150, Th.2.49, Pl.*Ti*.85e (pl.), Arist.*HA*605^{a}27; δ. κοιλίας Plu. *Mar*.30; δ. εἰς οὖρα *diabetes*, Gal.7.81.

διαρροιζέω, *to whizz through*, διερροίζησε στέρνων [ὁ ἰός] S.*Tr*. 568.

διαρροΐζομαι, *suffer from diarrhoea*, Dsc.4.88, Arr.*Epict*.4.10.11, Alex.Aphr.*Pr*.1.98.

διαρροϊκός, ή, όν, *suffering from diarrhoea*, Ruf.ap.Orib.7.26.6.

διαρρομβέομαι, *assume the figure of a rhombus*, Hero *Metr*.1.16.

διάρρομβος, ον, *rhomboid*, of a bandage, *Hippiatr*.74.

διάρρους, ου, ὁ, *passage, channel*, D.S.13.47, Str.4.1.2, Sch.Il. *Oxy*.221 i 17.

διαρρύδαν [ῠ], Dor. for -ρύδην, Adv. *flowing away, vanishing*, φόνος πέπηγεν οὐ δ. A.*Ch*.67 (lyr.).

διαρρυθμίζω, *adjust*, κανόνα *IG*1^{2}.373.70; *arrange in order*, Lxx 2*Ma*.7.22.

διαρρυμβονάω, *scatter, dissipate*, in aor. 1, Hsch.

διαρρύομαι, *deliver*, τινὰ ἐκ τοῦ δεσμωτηρίου Ph.1.95.

διαρρυπτικός, ή, όν, *cleansing*, φάρμακα Gal.11.744.

διαρρύπτω, *cleanse thoroughly*, τοὺς πόρους Gal.6.261; κηλῖδα Lib.*Decl*.33.31.

διάρρῠσις, εως, ἡ, = διάρρους, Hero *Spir*.1.1, al.

διάρρῠτος, ον, *intersected by streams*, Str.5.1.7, Epic. in *Arch.Pap*. 7.7; διαρρύτους· διηντλημένους, Hsch.

διαρρωγή, ἡ, *gap, interstice*, left in applying a bandage, Hp.*Art*. 35.

διαρρώξ, ῶγος, ὁ, ἡ, (διαρρήγνυμι) *rent asunder*, δ. κυμάτων σάλῳ ἀγμός a broken cliff *rent asunder* by the waves, E.*IT*262; πέτραι Opp.*H*.3.212. II. as Subst., *rent*, of the Straits of Messina, ib. 5.216.

δίαρσις, εως, ἡ, *raising up*, ἱστίων D.S.3.40; ἡ ἐκ διάρσεως μάχη fight *with broadswords*, Plb.2.33.5. II. = διάρμα II, Longin.8.1.

διαρτᾰβ-ία, ἡ, *tax of two* ἀρτάβαι, *PTeb*.2p.178. **-ος**, ον, *paying two* ἀρτάβαι *of rent*, *POxy*.1031.12 (iii A.D.).

διαρτάζω, *speak fitly*, dub. l. in A.*Fr*.318 (fort. διάρτισον).

διαρτᾰμέω, strengthd. for ἀρταμέω, *cut limb-meal*, A.*Pr*.1023, Anaxandr.6; διαρταμῶντες (as if from -αρταμάω) [σώματα] κατὰ μέλη is cj. in Ph.2.564.

διαρτ-άω, *suspend*, Hsch., dub. l. for διαττᾶσθαι, Plb.34.9.10. 2. *keep in suspense, keep engaged*, τινί in or *by*.., D.H.1.46; *mislead, deceive*, Men.1006. II. *to separate*, διδύμους Ph.2.303, al., cf. Heliod. ap.Orib.44.10.5; τὴν δύναμιν ἀπὸ Συρακουσῶν Plu.*Tim*.25; διηρτημένα ἀπ' ἀλλήλων Str.5.3.7: c. gen., σῶμα τοῦ ὅλου διαρτηθέν Ph.2. 509; *dismember*, Plot.6.9.5; *interrupt*, τὰς ἀκολουθίας D.H.*Dem*. 40; διηρτημένων τῶν λέξεων *forced apart*, Id.*Comp*.20; διηρτημένων .. φωνῶν Demetr.Lac.1014.48 F.; διηρτῆσθαι, of argument, *to lack connexion, be incoherent*, διηρτημένα τινὰ καὶ ψευδῆ ib.46 F., cf. S.E. *P*.2.153. III. = καταρτίζω, Hsch. (Pass.). **-ησις**, εως, ἡ, *incoherence, irrelevance*, κατὰ διάρτησιν λόγος *a non-sequitur*, *Stoic*.2.79

(perh. Chrysipp.). **-ίζω**, *mould, form*, Lxx *Jb.*33.6; *speak fitly*, Hsch. **-ισις**, εως, ἡ, *moulding, shaping*, *EM*361.8, Suid.; *composition*, prob. l. for διάρτησις, Gal.15.102. **-ισμός**, ὁ, = foreg., Sm.*Ez.*4.12.

διαρτύω, *dress, prepare*: metaph., πλάσις εἰς τὴν τῶν πολεμίων ἀπάτην διηρτυμένη Eun.*Hist.*p.248 D.

διαρύτω, strengthd. for ἀρύτω, Hsch., *EM*270.3.

Δίαρχοι, οἱ, *the Hellenodicae*, Hsch.

διάρχω, *hold office to the end*, Lys.*Fr.*177 S., D.C.40.66: c. acc. cogn., στρατηγίαν τὴν οἴκοι Id.36.41.

διαρωχμίας· διαστάσεις, Hsch.; cf. διαρόγχαι.

διασαικωνίζω, v. διασαλακωνίζω.

διασαίνω, strengthd. for σαίνω, ταῖς οὐραῖς X.*Cyn.*4.3.

διασαίρω, pf. part. -σεσηρώς, *grin, sneer*, Plu.*Mar.*12.

διασᾰλᾰκωνίζω, strengthd. for σαλακωνίζω, Ar.*V.*1169; but perh. better διασαικωνίζω, cf. Id.*Fr.*849.

διασάλ-ευσις [σᾰ], εως, ἡ, *agitated motion*, Marcellin.*Puls.*500. **-εύω**, *shake violently*, Plb.1.48.2, Luc.*VH*2.5; of missiles, Plb.16.30.4; κλεῖθρα Corn.*ND*30. 2. *confuse*, τὰς ἁρμονίας, τοὺς ἤχους, D.H. *Comp.*22,23; *cause excitement in*, πόλιν Luc.*Alex.*31; διασεσαλευμένος τὸ βάδισμα *negligent, easy* in gait, Id.*Rh.Pr.*11; δ. τὸ βλέμμα, of an ogler, Id.*Merc.Cond.*35. II. intr., = σαλεύω II. 3, Arist. *Phgn.*809b32. 2. = σαλεύω II. 2, ἐπ' ἀγκυρῶν App.*BC*5.89.

διασαρδᾰνόω, = διαγελάω, *EM*273.46.

διασαρκων-ίζω, = foreg., Hsch. (also **-σαρωνίζω**); but **-ισμα**· ἀσελγές τι σχῆμα, Id.

διασάτηρ· διαπαίζειν (Lacon.), Hsch.

διασάττω, *stuff with* a thing, αἵματι καὶ σαρξίν Gal.1.32: pf. part. Pass. διασεσαγμένος Archig.ap.eund.8.931; δ. ὑπό, c. gen., *gorged with*.., Macho ap.Ath.6.244c: c. gen., *Gp.*19.9.5: c. dat., σκυβάλοις Ruf.ap.Orib.8.24.13.

διασαυλόομαι, strengthd. for σαυλόομαι, Ar.*Fr.*624.

διασᾰφ-έω, *make quite clear, show plainly*, ἐλπίδας οὔσας κενὰς E. *Ph.*398; τι Pl.*Lg.*916e, Phld.*Lib.*p.13 O., etc.; δ. εἴτε.. εἴτε μή Pl. *Prt.*348b, cf. Phld.*Po.*5.13; also δ. περί τινος *make a clear statement* about.., Arist.*de An.*404b1; δ. εἰς Καρχηδόνα περί τινος *send clear information*.., Plb.3.87.4; δ. ὑπέρ τινος Id.2.19.13; *instruct plainly*, ἵνα.. Id.4.26.3, Lxx 2*Ma.*1.18; ὅπως *PEleph.*18.3 (iii B.C.):—Med., dub. in *PPar.*70 p.413:—Pass., Arist.*EN*1094b12, etc. **-ηνίζω**, *make clear*, X.*Mem.*3.1.11, *Ap.*1; τινὶ τὰ πεπραγμένα D.H.11.33, cf. Aët.13.15:—Pass., Hero *Bel.*98.6: **-ηνέω**, = foreg., dub. in Hp. *Ep.*12. **-ησις**, εως, ἡ, *explanation, interpretation*, Lxx *Ge.*40.8. **-ητέον**, *one must make quite clear*, Arist.*de An.*416b30; ὑπέρ τινος Thphr.*CP*6.14.5. **-ητικός**, ή, όν, *affirmative*, σύνδεσμος A.D.*Conj.*221.23; *explanatory*, Sch.Ar.*Av.*825, *An.Ox.*1.188; *declaratory*, *EM*415.27. **-ίζω**, = διασαφέω, Lxx 2*Ma.*1.21.

διά-σεισις, εως, ἡ, *succussion*, of the spine, Gal.18(1).520. II. = διασεισμός, *PTeb.*41.30 (ii B.C.). **-σεισμα**, ατος, τό, *extortion*, *BGU*1138.11 (i B.C.). **-σεισμός**, ὁ, *abuse of power, extortion*, συκοφαντία καὶ δ. *PTaur.*1v1 (ii B.C.), cf. *PTeb.*43.36 (ii B.C.), *POxy.* 1252r33 (iii A.D.). **-σειστος**, ον, *shaken about*, ἀστράγαλοι Aeschin.1.59, cf. Men.423; κύβοι Poll.7.203. **-σείω**, *shake violently*, Hp.*Morb.*1.6, dub. in Arist.*Ath.*64.2; τι εἰς ἀταξίαν Pl.*Ti.* 85e, cf. 88a; τὴν κεφαλὴν Plu.2.435c: c. dat., δ. τοῖν χεροῖν Aeschin. Socr.50; δ. τῇ οὐρᾷ *to keep wagging* the tail, X.*Cyn.*6.15:—Med., *shake* people *off, shake oneself free*, D.H.1.56. 2. *confound, throw into confusion*, τὰ τῶν Ἀθηναίων φρονήματα Hdt.6.109; τοὺς ἀκούοντας Plb.18.45.2; *intimidate, oppress*, Id.10.26.4, cf. *OGI*519.14 (Pass.); *browbeat*, *PTaur.*1v iii 13 (ii B.C.); *extort money by intimidation from* a person, *PPar.*15.37 (ii B.C.), *Ev.Luc.*3.14, etc.: c. gen., *PTeb.*41.10 (ii B.C.):—Pass., *POxy.*284.5 (i A.D.). 3. of political affairs, *throw into confusion*, Plu.*Cic.*10. 4. *stir up*, in Pass., Dam.*Pr.*29. 5. *sound, take the measure of*, Plu.2.580d,704d.

διασεύομαι, *dart through*, used by Hom. only in 3 sg. Ep. aor. Pass. διέσσῠτο, c. gen., τάφροιο δ. Il.10.194; αἰχμὴ δὲ στέρνοιο δ. 15. 542; ἐκ μεγάροιο δ. Od.4.37: less freq. c. acc., δ. λαὸν Ἀχαιῶν Il. 2.450: abs., αἰχμὴ δὲ δ. [μηροῦ or μηρόν] 5.661: later in part. διεσσύμενος Q.S.3.641: pf. διέσσυται Opp.*H.*2.259.

διασήθω, aor. -έσησα, *sift*, Hp.*VM*3, Dsc.5.75; prob. for διασείσας, Diocl.ap.Orib.8.41.3:—Pass., Aret.*CA*2.3.

διασηκόω, *weigh*, Suid. s.v. βαστάσας.

διασημ-αίνω, *mark out, point out clearly*, τι Hdt.5.86, X.*An.*2.1. 23; τινί τι Id.*Oec.*12.11. 2. *indicate by a signal*, σάλπιγγι τὸν καιρὸν τῆς προσβολῆς Plb.10.12.4. II. Med., *note the bearings of*, τόπους Arist.*HA*549b17. 2. *approve*, D.S.19.15. 3. *signify*, Str.17.1.6, Plu.*Dem.*19. III. intr., *show its symptoms, appear*, Hp.*Aph.*6.41. **-ᾰσία**, ἡ, *method of marking*, Ptol.*Alm.*7.4, 8. 3 (pl.). **-ειόομαι**, *cause to be placed on record*, *Inscr.Magn.*117.3 (ii A.D.). **-ος**, ον, (σῆμα) *clear, distinct*: neut. pl. as Adv., διάσημα θροεῖ S.*Ph.*209 (lyr.). II. *conspicuous, eminent*, Hippias Soph.4 (Sup.), Plu.*Dio* 54; δ. κράνος Id.*TG*17; γένει καὶ ἀξίᾳ *BMus.Inscr.* 481*.15 (ii A.D.): esp. in Sup., διασημοτάτη πόλις *Epigr.Gr.*904 (Erythrae); διασημότατος, = Lat. *clarissimus*, *IG*3.635; = *perfectissimus*, δ. ἡγεμών *BGU*198.5 (ii A.D.), al., *Epigr.Gr.*1078.10 (Adana); ἐπίτροπος *Sammelb.*4421.5 (iii A.D.).

διασήπω, *cause to putrefy*, χρῶτα Str.15.1.37, cf. Dsc.2.173, Gal. 18(2).455; τοῦ κακοῦ -σήψαντος τὰ οὖλα Ael.*NA*9.62:—freq. in Pass., with pf. διασέσηπα, *putrefy*, Thphr.*HP*5.7.5, Luc.*Luct.*18; διασαπεὶς τὸν πόδα Id.*Alex.*59.

διασθενέω, *to be exhausted*, of soil, *POxy.*1502v6 (iii A.D.).

Δῑάσια, τά, *the festival of Zeus* μειλίχιος, at Athens, Ar.*Nu.*408, Th.1.126, etc. [ᾰσ Ar. l.c., cf. Sch. ad v. 862.]

διασίζω, *hiss or whistle violently*, Aeschin.Socr.50.

διασιλλ-αίνω, *mock, jeer at*, c. acc., Luc.*Lex.*24; πράγματα καὶ δόγματα Iamb.*Protr.*21.λα'; τινὰ ἐπί τινι Alciphr.3.62. **-όω**, = foreg., *Com.Adesp.*978, D.C.59.25, 77.11.

διασῑωπάω, fut. -ήσομαι, *remain silent*, E.*Hel.*1551, X.*Mem.*3.6. 4. 2. *pause* in reading, Gal.16.742, al. II. trans., *pass over in silence*, E.*Ion* 1566; also in Dor. fut., διασωπάσομαί οἱ μόρον Pi.*O.* 13.91.

διασκαίρω, *bound through, dart along*, A.R.1.574.

διασκᾰλεύω, = sq., Plu.2.980e, Hsch. s.v. διαγλάψασ'.

διασκάλλω, *pick over*, τὸν ὄνθον Arist.*Fr.*354.

διασκάλων, v. διασκελίδα.

διασκανδῐκίζω, prop. *feed on chervil* (σκάνδιξ), Telecl.38: hence Com. for διευριπιδίζω, *to come Euripides over one* (his mother was said to be a λαχανόπωλις), Ar.*Eq.*19.

διασκάπτω, Dor. 3 pl. fut. -σκάψοντι *Tab.Heracl.*1.131:—*dig through*, ἰσθμόν Paus.2.1.5; δ. τὰ τείχη *make a breach in* them, Lys. 13.14; ῥόας τῷ ὕδατι *make a breach* for water in the canals, *Tab. Heracl.* l.c., cf. Ph.*Bel.*98.27: also c. gen., τοῦ τείχους Plu.*Pyrrh.* 33; *excavate*, τάφον Charito 8.7.

διασκᾰρῑφάομαι, *sketch in outline*: hence, *slur over*, τὰς εὐτυχίας ..διεσκαριφησάμεθα καὶ διελύσαμεν Isoc.7.12. II. Act., *scratch the ground*, of birds, Hsch.

διασκᾰτόομαι, Pass., *to be befouled* or *filthy*, ἄνανδρος καὶ διεσκατωμένη τρυφή, of the Epicureans, Diog.Sinop.1.

διασκεδ-άζω, = sq., Lxx *Ps.*32(33).10; *disperse* a tumour, Aët. 15.15. **-άννῡμι**, Att. fut. -σκεδῶ S.*Ant.*287, Ar.*V.*229, etc.:—*scatter abroad, scatter to the winds*, δούρατα Od.5.370; τῷ κέ τοι ἀγλαΐας γε διασκεδάσειεν 17.244; γῆν ἐκείνων καὶ νόμους διασκεδῶν S. l.c.; τὰ νῦν ξύμφωνα δεξιώματα δόρει διασκεδῶσιν Id.*OC*620; διασκεδᾶτε τὸ προσὸν νῦν νέφος Anaxandr.58; of the wind, διεσκέδασεν αὐτὰ (sc. ναυάγια καὶ νεκροὺς) πανταχῇ Th.1.54: metaph., *BGU*1253. 12 (ii B.C.):—Pass., Eus.Mynd.63. 2. in Hdt., τὸν στρατὸν διεσκέδασε *disbanded* it, 1.77, cf. 79:—Pass., 1.63, 5.15, Th.3.98, D.C. 47.38; δ. κατ' ἑωυτοὺς ἕκαστοι Hdt.8.57 (but also of an enemy, *scatter*, 8.68.β'). 3. *disperse* the soul, when it leaves the body, Pl.*Phd.*77e, cf. 70a, 78b. 4. in Pass., of reports, *to be spread abroad*, Hdn.7.6.9. 5. *reject*, βουλήν Lxx 3*Ki.*12.24. **-ᾰσις**, εως, ἡ, *scattering*, Thd.*Is.*24.19. **-ασμός**, ὁ, *scattering*, Hsch. s.v. Φαραί. **-αστής**, οῦ, ὁ, *scatterer*, as Adj., *extravagant, reckless*, τρόπος Ph.1.89. **-αστικός**, ή, όν, *fitted for dispersing* or *digesting*, ἀρχομένης ὑποχύσεως Dsc.3.80, cf. 5.115.

διασκελίδα· σπυρίδα ἥν ἔνιοι **διασκάλων**, Hsch.

διασκελίζομαι, in pf. part. Pass., *having the legs parted*, σῶμα διεσκελισμένον *PMag.Par.*1.2309; δ. καθῆσθαι Eust.1038.10, cf. *EM* 502.39.

διάσκεμμα, ατος, τό, *observation*, Gal.1.293 (pl.).

διασκεπάζω, *screen, hide*, αὐγήν D.C.60.26.

διασκεπ-τέον, *one must consider*, Pl.*Lg.*859b, Arist.*Pol.*1324a3, etc. **-τικός**, ή, όν, *cautious, considerate*, Poll.1.178. **-τομαι**, = διασκοπέω, Luc.*Vit.Auct.*27, *VH*2.18.

διασκευ-άζω, *get ready, set in order*, τι Plb.15.27.9:—Pass., *PTeb.* 24.32 (ii B.C.). II. *equip*, τινὰ βασιλικῶς Luc.*Nec.*16:—Pass., εἰς Σατύρους διεσκευασμένοι *dressed* as.., Plu.*Ant.*24; ὅπλοις Aen. Tact.26.1:—Med., *prepare for oneself, provide*, τἆλλα ὡς ἐς πλοῦν Th.4.38; *arm, equip* or *prepare oneself*, ὡς εἰς μάχην X.*HG*4.2.19; διεσκευάσθαι πρὸς τὸν δῆμον Din.1.70; διασκευάσασθαι πρὸς τοὺς δικαστάς *prepare all one's tricks* for a trial, X.*Ath.*3.7. III. Med., διασκευασάμενος τὴν οὐσίαν *having disposed of one's* property, D.29. 3. IV. *revise* or *edit* a work *for publication*, Aristeas 311, D.S. 1.5. 2. *compile*, ἐκ πολλῶν [βιβλίων] Gal.15.10. 3. *elaborate* with rhetorical devices, αἰτία μὲν κατασκευάζει, τρόπος δὲ δ. Hermog. *Inv.*2.7. **-ασμα**, gloss on διάγματα, Hsch. **-αστής**, οῦ, ὁ, *reviser, editor* of a poem, Sch.Il.6.441. **-αστικός**, ή, όν, *descriptive of dress*, σχῆμα Eust.169.31. **-ή**, ἡ, *construction*, Aristeas 64, al. II. *equipment*, δ. νομαδική Plb.8.29.7; δ. πολεμική D.S.4. 38; *furniture* or *vessels*, τῆς σκηνῆς Lxx *Ex.*31.7, cf. Plb.30.26.3, Agatharch.8 (pl.). III. *rhetorical elaboration* of a topic, Hermog. *Inv.*3.15; ποιεῖσθαι τὰς δ. τῶν μύθων Jul.*Or.*7.205b. 2. διασκευαί *set phrases*, Plb.15.34.1. IV. *new edition* or *recension* of a work, Aristeas 310, Ath.3.110b (pl.). V. = ἀνασκευή, δ. καὶ χλευασμὸς τοῦ διδασκαλείου Porph.*VP*53. VI. *theatrical performance*, κωμῳδίαι καὶ δ. D.Chr.32.94. **-ωρέω**, *revise, rehandle*, τι Pl.*Ep.* 316a:—Med., *set in order*, τὴν πόλιν Id.*R.*540e.

διάσκεψις, εως, ἡ, *inspection, examination*, περί τινος Pl.*Lg.*697c, Luc.*Anach.*21, Posidon.ap.Gal.5.469, cf. Lyd.*Mag.*1.45: in pl., *questions for decision*, Plu.*Tim.*38.

διασκέω, *deck out*, in Pass., διησκημένοι τὰς κόμας χρυσῷ Phylarch. 62. II. *train*, τινά Luc.*Vit.Auct.*9:—Pass., Id.*Peregr.*17. III. *practise*, ῥητορικά D.L.4.49.

διασκην-έω, *separate and retire each to his billet* (σκηναί), *take up one's quarters*, διασκηνῆσαι κατὰ τὰς κώμας X.*An.*4.4.8: abs., *go into billets*, ib.4.5.29, *Lac.*5.3. II. *leave* another's *tent*, διασκηνούντων μετὰ δεῖπνον Id.*Cyr.*3.1.38, dub. in Id.*HG*4.8.18. III. Act., *shade*, Lyd.*Mag.*3.70. **-ητέον**, *one must take up one's quarters*, εἰς στέγας X.*An.*4.4.14.

διασκηνίπτω, *crush, destroy*, ᾠεα Nic.*Th.*193.

διασκηνόω, *pitch like tents at intervals*, καπηλεῖα Ael.*VH*3.14 (Pass.). II. intr., = διασκηνέω I, X.*An.*4.4.10.

διασκηρίπτω, *prop on each side, prop up*, *AP*6.203 (Laco or Phil.).

διασκίδνημι, poet. for -σκεδάννυμι, Il.5.526, Hes.*Th.*875, Emp. 84.4, Hdt.2.25 :—Pass., Luc.*DDeor.*20.5, *Sacr.*13.

διασκιρτάω, *leap about*, Lxx *Wi.*19.9, Plu.*Eum.*11, Philostr.Jun. *Im.*10.

διασκοπέω (cf. διασκέπτομαι), fut. διασκέψομαι: aor. διεσκεψάμην: pf. διέσκεμμαι Ar.*Ra.*836, but διεσκέφθαι in pass. sense, Id.*Th.*687 :—*look at in different ways, examine* or *consider well*, Hdt.3.38, E.*Cyc.* 557, etc.; ἑξῆς δ. τὸν λόγον Pl.*R.*350e, cf. *Tht.*168e; also δ. πρὸς ἑαυτόν Id.*Chrm.*160e; περὶ σφᾶς αὐτούς, περί τινος, Th.7.71, Pl.*Phd.* 61e; δ. περί τινος εἰ.. Arist.*Pol.*1272^{a}26: c. gen., τῆς ἑαυτῶν ἀσφαλείας D.C.58.7 :—Med., πρὸς τὰ ἔξω διασκοπεῖσθαι Th.6.59: impf., Pl.*Plt.*259c. II. abs., *look round one, keep watching*, μὴ δρῶνται X.*Cyn.*9.3.

διασκοπιάομαι, *watch as from a* σκοπιά: hence, *spy out*, σε.. προέηκε διασκοπιᾶσθαι ἕκαστα, of Dolon, Il.10.388; *discern, distinguish*, ἀργαλέον.. διασκοπιᾶσθαι ἕκαστον 17.252.

διασκορπ-ίζω, *scatter abroad*, Lxx *Ge.*49.7 (v.l.), al. :—Pass., *Ev. Jo.*11.52, Plb.1.47.5, *BGU*1049.7 (iv A.D.); *squander*, οὐσίαν *Ev. Luc.*15.13; *confound*, ib.1.51; *winnow*, συνάγων ὅθεν οὐ διεσκόρπισας *Ev.Matt.*25.24. **-ῐσις**, εως, ἡ, *scattering abroad*, Zos.Alch.p.178 B. **-ισμός**, ὁ, *scattering, dispersal*, Lxx *Ez.*6.8, al.; *confusion*, τῆς φορολογίας *PTeb.*24.55 (ii B.C.). **-ιστικός**, ή, όν, *dissipative*, of waste-products, Antyll.ap.Orib.6.21.30.

διασκώπτω, *jest upon*, τινά dub. l. in Plu.2.82b; δεῖπνα Ath.2. 55d :—Med., *jest one with another, bandy jests*, X.*Cyr.*8.4.23.

δίασμα, ατος, τό, (διάζομαι) *warp*, διάσματα, φάρεος ἀρχήν Call.*Fr.* 244, cf. Lxx *Jd.*16.13, *Ostr.*1155, Nonn.*D.*6.151.

διασμάω, *wipe* or *rinse out*, ποτήρια Hdt.2.37.

διασμήχω, *rub well*, ψυχὴ πρὸς ὀξυωπίαν ἑαυτὴν διασμήξασα Hierocl. *in CA*21 p.467 M. :—Pass., ἁλσὶν διασμηχθεὶς ὄναιτ' ἂν οὑτοσί Ar.*Nu.* 1237: pf. διέσμηκται Plu.2.693d. 2. *rub off*, λύματα τρυφαλείης Nonn.*D.*30.92.

διασμῑλεύω, *polish off with the chisel*: metaph., δ. βίβλους *AP*15. 38 (Cometas); διεσμιλευμέναι φροντίδες *refined, subtle* theories, Alex. 221.8. Adv. διεσμιλευμένως Poll.6.150, Hsch.

διάσμυρνον, τό, name for various *eyesalves*, Gal.12.257,806; for a *plaster*, Asclep.ap.eund.13.967.

διασμύχομαι [ῡ], *smoulder*, πῦρ διασμυχόμενον Ph.2.143.

διασοβ-έω, *scare away*, Plu.2.133a; διασεσόβηται ὁ γάμος Hld.7. 26. II. *agitate, excite*, Alciphr.*Fr.*5, Agath.3.11 :—Pass., *to be excited, puffed up*, Plu.2.32d. **-ησις**, εως, ἡ, *trepidation*, M.Ant. 11.22.

διασοφίζομαι, *quibble like a sophist*, Ar.*Av.*1619.

διάσοφος, ον, *very wise*, dub. l. in *Lyr.Adesp.*135.

διασπᾰθ-άω, *squander away*, Plu.*Cic.*27. II. Med., *plunder, rob*, *POxy.*71 ii 12 (iv A.D.). **-ίζω**, = foreg. I, Lyd.*Mag.*2.19 :—Pass., ib.1.36.

διασπᾰρ-ακτός, ή, όν, *torn to pieces*, E.*Ba.*1220, Ael.*NA*12. 7. **-άσσω**, Att. -ττω, *rend in pieces*, A.*Pers.*195 :—Pass., Eub. 15.3. 2. metaph., δ. τινὰ τῷ λόγῳ Luc.*Icar.*21. II. *dilate forcibly*, Sor.2.59.

διά-σπᾰσις, εως, ἡ, *tearing asunder, forcible separation*, Arist.*Cael.* 313^{b}20, *Mete.*372^{b}19, Thphr.*Lass.*18, cj. in Epicur.*Ep.*2 p.44 U. II. *gap*, Plu.2.721a. **-σπασμα**, ατος, τό, = foreg. II, Id.*Aem.*20, Polyaen.4.3.17. **-σπασμός**, ὁ, *tearing in pieces*, Lxx *Je.*15.3, Phld.*Piet.*96. II. *interruption, interval*, in pl., Plu.2.129b, etc.; παντελὴς δ. complete *severance*, Dam.*Pr.*74: metaph., *distraction*, τῆς ψυχῆς Phld.*Ir.*p.29 W. **-σπαστέον**, *one must break up*, Arist. *PA*642^{b}17. **-σπαστος**, ον, *incoherent, disconnected*, ἐπιστολαί Alciphr.2.2. **-σπάω**, fut. -σπάσομαι [ᾰ] Ar.*Ra.*477, *Ec.*1076, also -σπάσω Hdt.7.236: aor. -έσπᾰσα, Med. -εσπασάμην E.*Hec.*1126, *Ba.*339, Plu.*Caes.*68: pf. -έσπᾰκα Sch.Th.*Oxy.*853 i 15 :—Pass., aor. -εσπάσθην: pf. -έσπασμαι (v. infr.) :—*tear asunder*, τοὺς ἄνδρας κρεοργηδὸν δ. Hdt.3.13, cf. E. and Ar. ll.cc., etc.; ἐμὲ καὶ τὸν ἄνδρα δ. X.*Cyr.*6.1.45; δ. τὸ σταύρωμα *to break through* or *tear down* the palisade, Id.*HG*4.4.10; δ. τὴν γέφυραν, τὸ ἔδαφος, Plb.6.55.1, Plu. *Cam.*5; *break up*, *SIG*364.10 (Ephesus, iii B.C.): metaph., διασπᾶν τὴν σύμπνοιαν τοῦ παντός Iamb.*Protr.*21.λ' :—Pass., διέσπασται μελέων φύσις Emp.63; τὸ Ἀττικὸν [ἔθνος].. διεσπασμένον ὑπὸ Πεισιστράτου Hdt.1.59; μόνον οὐ διεσπάσθην D.5.5; δ. ἀπὸ τῶν φίλων *to be torn away* from.., Arist.*Rh.*1386^{a}10. 2. in military sense, *separate* part of an army from the rest, X.*Cyr.*5.4.19; of army and fleet, Hdt.7.236; δ. τὰς φάλαγγας *break* them *up*, Arist.*Pol.*1303^{b}13: —Pass., στράτευμα διεσπασμένον an army *scattered and in disorder*, Th.6.98, cf. 7.44; of a fleet, Id.8.104; τῷ διεσπάσθαι τὰς δυνάμεις *to be widely scattered*, X.*An.*1.5.9. 3. metaph., *pull different ways*, πόλεις *distract* states, Pl.*Lg.*875a; τὰς πολιτείας D.4.48; τοὺς νόμους X.*Cyr.*8.5.25; διέσπακε τὴν ἱστορίαν *has broken the continuity of* the narrative, Sch.Th. l.c. :—Pass., διασπώμενος *distracted*, πρὸς τοσαύτας ὑπηρεσίας Luc.*DDeor.*24.1; ὑπὸ τῶν λόγων Id.*Icar.*23.

διασπείρω, aor. 2 Pass. -εσπάρην [ᾰ] S.*El.*748, etc. :—*scatter* or *spread about*, [τὰς μνέας].. αὐτοχειρίῃ διέσπειρε τῇ στρατιῇ Hdt.3. 13; διέσπειρε ἡμέας ἄλλην ἄλλῃ τάξας *dispersed* us, ib.68; δ. λόγον X.*HG*5.1.25; τοὔνομα εἰς τὴν Ἀσίαν Isoc.5.104; *squander*, S.*El.* 1291 :—Pass., *to be scattered*, κρατὸς διασπαρέντος αἵματός θ' ὁμοῦ Id. *Tr.*782; πῶλοι διεσπάρησαν ἐς μέσον δρόμον Id.*El.*748; of troops, διεσπαρμένοι Th.1.11, X.*HG*5.3.1, etc.; φύσεις ὁμοίως διεσπαρμέναι equally *distributed*, Pl.*R.*455d, cf. *Sph.*260b, etc.; ἡ ψυχὴ διασπείρεται *is dissipated*, Epicur.*Ep.*1 p.21 U.; τὸ διεσπαρμένον δόγμα the *current* opinion, Id.*Nat.*14.7; τῶν χρωμάτων διεσπαρμένων Ael.*NA* 11.21.

διασπεύδω, *work zealously*, Plb.4.33.9 :—Med., Is.*Fr.*56 S.; of political factions, D.C.*Fr.*83.5, cf. 52.7. II. *incite*, c. acc. et inf., Plb.*Fr.*126.

διάσπῑλος, ον, *all rocky*, *Peripl.M.Rubr.*43.

διασπλεκόω, strengthd. for σπλεκόω, Ar.*Pl.*1082.

διασποδέω, sens. obsc., = Lat. *subigitare*, Ar.*Ec.*939, cf. Hsch. s.v. διεσποδημένη; διεσποδήσατο· διέσεισε, διετίναξε, Id.

διασπορ-ά, ἡ, (διασπείρω) *scattering, dispersion*, Plu.2.1105a, Lxx *Je.*15.7; δ. ψυχική Ph.2.426. 2. collectively, = οἱ διεσπαρμένοι, Lxx *De.*28.25, *Ev.Jo.*7.35: pl., Lxx *Ps.*146(147).2. **-εύς**, έως, ὁ, *disperser*, Poll.3.129.

διασπουδάζω, *do zealously* :—and Pass., *to be anxiously done* or *looked to*, τί μάλιστα ἐν ἅπασι διεσπούδασται τοῖς νόμοις; D.20.157, cf. 23.78: c. inf., δ. μὴ λαβεῖν ὑμᾶς ib.182; διεσπούδαστο ἐλθεῖν J.*AJ* 15.8.1; διεσπουδάζετο abs., Arr.*An.*7.23.8. 2. *to be zealous*, περί τι D.H.*Lys.*14. II. *employ electoral corruption*, D.C.36.38: in fut. Med., Id.52.20.

διασσάω, v. διαττάω.

διᾴσσω, Att. **διᾴττω**, v. sub διαΐσσω.

διαστᾰδόν, Adv. *standing apart*, A.R.2.67; δ. ἀλλήλῃσι *apart from*.., Id.4.942, cf. Opp.*H.*1.502.

διαστάζω, *leak*, *Gp.*7.8.4; *pour off*, ἱδρὼς δ. μετώπων Nonn.*D.*37. 463. 2. trans., *pour*, ποτὸν κυπέλλῳ ib.44.136.

διασταθμ-άομαι, *separate*, αἰνῶ δ' ὃς βίοτον ἐκ πεφυρμένου θεῶν διεσταθμήσατο E.*Supp.*202 :—Act. -σταθμῆσαι· διελεῖν, Hsch. **-ησις**, εως, ἡ, *standard*, κατὰ τὴν δ. Phld.*D.*3 *Fr.*89. **-ίζω**, = διασταθμάομαι, Sm.*Is.*33.18.

διαστᾰλάσσω, *shed*, δάκρυον Lib.*Descr.*30.16.

διάσταλ-μά, ατος, τό, *ordinance, regulation*, *BGU*913.9 (iii A.D.). **-μός**, ὁ, *assessment for taxation*, *PLond.*5.1686.17 (vi A.D.). **-σις**, εως, ἡ, *arrangement, compact*, Lxx *2Ma.*13.25. II. = διαστολή, perh. to be read in Gal.8.736 for διάστασις. **-τέον**, *one must distinguish*, Plot.1.3.1, Nicom.*Ar.*2.18, Sch.Il.2.3. **-τικός**, ή, όν, *serving to distinguish*, προσώπων A.D.*Adv.*185.10, cf. D.L.4.33, Eust. 1610.3; *antithetic*, A.D.*Pron.*24.12. Adv. -κῶς ib.49.24, Eust.73. 31. II. of Music, *exciting, exalting*, Aristid.Quint.1.12, Cleonid. *Harm.*13.

διαστᾰσιάζω, *form into separate factions*, πάντας Arist.*Pol.*1303^b 26; τοὺς ἐποίκους.. πρὸς τοὺς εὐπόρους ib.1306^{a}3; τὸ πλῆθος, τὴν πόλιν, J.*BJ*1.11.5, Plu.*Cam.*36; *set at variance*, σῶμα καὶ ψυχήν J. *BJ*3.8.5. II. *to be at variance*, πρὸς σφᾶς, πρὸς ἀλλήλους, Plb. 1.82.4, etc.; τινί D.C.54.17; τοῖς ἀληθέσι Iamb.*Myst.*9.4: abs., ib. 4.9.

διά-στᾰσις, εως, ἡ, (διΐστημι) *parting, separation* (opp. ἕνωσις, Dam.*Pr.*273), ὀρέων Hdt.7.129; ὀστέων Hp.*Art.*20, cf. Gal.19.461; φάραγγες καὶ δ. τῆς γῆς *fissures*, Arist.*Mete.*350^{b}36; *breach* in a barrier, Ph.*Bel.*98.31; *opening*, τῆς γένυος Aret.*CD*1.3. b. κεφαλῆς δ. *splitting headache*, ibid. (pl.), v.l. in Pl.*R.*407c. c. *distension*, Arist.*PA*681^{b}24; φλεβῶν Aret.*SA*2.2. d. δ. κενεὴ *retching*, ib. 2.7. e. = διαστολή, of the pulse, Zeno ap.Gal.8.736. f. *expansion* of air, opp. πίλησις, Ph.*Bel.*77.23. 2. *setting at variance*, τοῖς νέοις ἐς τοὺς πρεσβυτέρους Th.6.18, cf. Plu.*Cor.*16; *cause of breach*, Arist.*Pol.*1303^{b}15. b. *contrasting*, Pl.*R.*360e. 3. *difference, contrast*, Arist.*Cael.*312^{a}13. 4. *disagreement*, δ. ἢ στάσις Pl. *Lg.*744d, cf. Arist.*Pol.*1296^{a}8, 1300^{b}37. 5. *divorce*, Plu.*Aem.*5, etc. II. Gramm., of vowels, διαίρεσις κατὰ διάστασιν (as in πάϊς) A.D.*Pron.*87.4. b. τὰ κατὰ δ. forms *written as two words*, e.g. ἐμέθεν αὐτῆς ib.114.11. III. *interval*, Pl.*Ti.*36a, etc.; in Music, Aristox.*Harm.*p.4 M., al.; of space, *extension*, Arist.*Top.*142^{b}5, al.; *dimension*, τὰς αὐτὰς διαστάσεις εἰς βάθος εἰληφός Epicur.*Nat.*2.7, cf. Gal.11.503, S.E.*M.*3.19; ἡ δ. ἡ τριχῇ *tridimensionality*, Plot.1.2.6, cf. 6.6.17, Porph.*Sent.*35, Dam.*Pr.*375. IV. = διακόσμησις, Antipho Soph.23. (Freq. confused with διάτασις, wh. shd. perh. be read in I.1.b,c,d.) **-στάτης**, gloss on δίορος, Hsch. **-στᾰτικός**, ή, όν, *disintegrating*, Ti.Locr.100e, Plu.2.952b; τινός Corn.*ND* 21. 2. *causing discord*, λόγοι Plu.*Pomp.*53, cf. Ph.*Fr.*101 H. 3. Adv. -κῶς *separately*, of vowels, -ώτερόν φαμεν τὸ γρηΰς A.D.*Adv.* 150.7; *in extension*, v.l. for διαστατῶς, Porph.*Sent.*2. **-στᾰτός**, όν, also ή, όν Lyd.*Mens.*4.76 :—*torn by faction*, πόλις Men.515. II. *having extension* or *dimension*, σῶμα δ. τριχῇ Apollodor.*Stoic.*3.259, cf. Ph.1.8, etc.; opp. ἀμερής, Procl.*Inst.*176; τὸ πάντῃ δ. Plu.2. 1023b; δ. πράγματα Dam.*Pr.*375. Adv. -τῶς *dimensionally* or *in extension*, Porph.*Sent.*33, Syrian. *in Metaph.*85.14; opp. νοερῶς, Procl. *in Cra.*p.55 P.

διασταυρόω, *cut off and fortify with a palisade*, D.C.41.50 :—Med., διασταυρώσασθαι τὸν ἰσθμόν *to have it fortified*, Th.6.97.

διαστείβω, *go through, across*, ἐπ' οἶδμα ναῒ θοᾷ Pi.*Fr.*221.4. II. *trample on*, τινά Nonn.*D.*36.239.

διαστείχω, aor. -έστῐχον (v. infr.), *go through* or *across*, πόλιν, γύαλα, E.*Andr.*1090,1092. 2. c. gen., δ. πλούτου *walk in ways* of wealth, Pi.*I.*3.17. 3. *go one's way*, ἀνεγρομένη γε διέστιχε Theoc. 27.69; *walk*, *AP*12.85 (Mel.), Coluth.215.

διαστέλλω, *put asunder, expand, separate*, συνεσταλμένα δ. Hp.

*Off.*11 ; τὸν ἀέρα ταῖς πτέρυξιν Arist.*IA*713^{a}12 ; τινὰς ξίφει J.*BJ*5.2. 2 ; δ. τι ταῖς ὄνυξι *to tear* it *open*, Plu.*Thes.*36 :—Pass., *to be dilated*, of the lungs or heart, Arist.*Aud.*800^{b}2, Gal.2.657, al. ; διασταλέντα τὰ ὑγρά *being dispersed*, Arist.*Pr.*891^{a}2 ; διασταλήτω πᾶσα σκοτία *let* all darkness *be dispelled*, *PMag.Par.*1.2472. 2. *divide*, δίχα Pl.*Plt.* 265e ; *distinguish*, τοὺς Τρῶας τῶν Δαρδάνων Sch.Il.*Oxy.*1086.115 ; τῷ τόνῳ *POxy.*1012*Fr.*16.5 (Pass.). b. *define precisely*, τὰ λεγόμενα Pl.*Euthd.*295d, cf. Arist.*Top.*134^{b}22, Phld.*Rh.*1.50S.; intr., ὅρασις διαστέλλουσα *distinct* vision, Lxx 1*Ki.*3.1 ; also, *to be distinctive*, opp. ἀπόλυτον εἶναι, A.D.*Pron.*39.1 :—Med., δ. περί τινος Arist. *Pol.*1268^{b}32, Phld.*D.*3*Fr.*8 : c. acc., Pl.*R.*535b :—Pass., διεσταλμένος *definite, determinate*, A.D.*Synt.*37.7, al. 3. *command expressly, give express orders*, ῥητῶς ὑπέρ τινος Plb.3.23.5 ; ἐπιτακτικῶς δ. περί τινων D.S.28.15 :—Med., Lxx*Jd.*1.19, al., *PHal.*7.6 (iii B.C.), *Ev.Marc.*5.43, etc. 4. *pronounce*, χείλεσι Lxx*Le.*5.4. 5. *give orders in writing*, *UPZ*111.6 (ii B.C.) :—more freq. in Med., ib.11.23 (ii B.C.), al. 6. *pay, render*, esp. in kind, *POxy.*88.5 (ii A.D.), al. ; *make an order for payment*, *Ostr.*1164 (ii/iii A.D.) ; *discharge* a vow, Lxx*Le.*22.21. 7. *set apart*, τινὰ ἑαυτῷ ib.3*Ki.*8.53; τὴν ἱερὰν γῆν *PRev.Laws*36.7 (iii B.C.), cf. *PTeb.*74.2 (ii B.C.). II. intr., *differ*, πρός τινα Plb.18.47.11.

διάστεμα, = διάστημα, *PRyl.*207^{a}27 (ii A.D.).

διάστενος, ον, *very narrow*, Gal.19.444.

διάστερος, ον, *starred, jewelled*, δ. λίθοις Luc.*Am.*41.

διάστημα, ατος, τό, (διαστῆναι) *interval*, freq. in Music, Archyt.2, Pl.*R.*531a, Aristox.*Harm.*p.4 M., al., Arist.*Pr.*922^{b}6, Damox.2.57 ; of Time, δ. τετραετές Plb.9.1.1 : generally, ἐκ μεγάλων δ. κινεῖσθαι Democr.191 ; δ. μεταξὺ κόσμων Epicur.*Ep.*2 p.37 U. ; *distance*, Phld. *D.*3.8,9. b. Geom., *radius*, κέντρῳ τῷ Α, διαστήματι τῷ ΑΒ, γεγράφθω κύκλος Euc.1.1, cf. Ph.*Bel.*52.14 ; of a sphere, Autol. 6. c. *aperture*, ἀγγεῖον ἔχον δ. μέγα Arist.*GA*787^{b}4 ; ἐκ πολλοῦ δ. Id.*Aud.*800^{a}36 ; τὰ δ. τῆς χειρὸς τῶν δακτύλων the *spaces* between the fingers, Aen.Tact.31.35. 2. Medic., *diastasis*, of bones, Hp.*Off.*23 (pl.), cf. Gal.18(2).887. 3. *difference*, τῶν ἡδονῶν μεγάλα τὰ δ. Nicom.Com.1.22. 4. *ratio*, Archyt.2, Arist.*Ph.*202^{a} 18. 5. in Aristotle's symbolism, *conjunction of two terms*, *APr.* 42^{b}10, *APo.*82^{b}7, al. 6. *extension, dimension*, χρόνος κινήσεως δ. Zeno *Stoic.*1.26, cf. Chrysipp.ib.2.164, Dam.*Pr.*389 ; of Space, Arist.*Ph.*209^{a}4, Plot.6.4.2 ; ὧν πρότερον διάστημα ἐνειστήκει whose *extension* (i.e. *surface*) it (the εἴδωλον) formerly occupied, Epicur. *Nat.*2.3. II. *distinction* of style, Longin.40.2.

διαστηματικός, ή, όν, *proceeding by intervals*, of musical progressions, δ. κίνησις Archyt.1, Aristox.*Harm.*p.9 M., etc. ; of Time, *measured by intervals*, Porph.*Sent.*44. II. *indicating distance*, of the pronoun ἐκεῖνος, A.D.*Pron.*57.10. III. *dimensional*, opp. ἀδιάστατος, φύσις Ph.2.184, cf. Dam.*Pr.*110 ; δ. φαντασία *spatial* representation, Procl.*in R.*2.249 K. IV. Adv. -κῶς, = διαστατικῶς, Simp.*in Epict.*p.5 D., Procl.*in Prm.*p.663 S., Syrian.*in Metaph.*24. 22 ; τοπικῶς καὶ δ. Procl.*in Ti.*2.104 D.

διαστήρ, ῆρος, ὁ, dub. sens. in *PLond.*3.1164.9 (iii A.D.).

διαστηρίζω, *make firm, strengthen*, *AP*6.203 (Laco or Phil.) :—Pass., *prop oneself up, secure one's footing*, Hp.*Ep.*17. II. *fix firmly*, Nonn.*D.*2.659, 36.369.

διάστησις, εως, ἡ, = διάστασις, τοῖν ποδοῖν Hld.3.13.

Διαστί, *in the language of Zeus*, prob. in D.Chr.11.23.

δια-στιγμή, ἡ, *punctuation*, *Gloss.* **-στίζω**, *distinguish by a mark, punctuate*, [οὐ] ῥᾴδιον διαστίξαι τὰ Ἡρακλείτου Arist.*Rh.*1407^{b} 13 : generally, *distinguish*, Stob.2.7.3^{c}. 2. *spot, mottle*, Nonn.*D.* 28.130. 3. *brand*, Just.*Nov.*115.4. **-στικτέον**, *one must punctuate*, Sch.S.*El.*878. **-στίκτης**, ου, ὁ, *one who punctuates*, *Gloss.*

διαστίλβω, *gleam*, Ar.*Pax*567, Nonn.*D.*42.420 ; *gleam through*, Ar.*Fr.*8, *AP*5.47 (Rufin.), Plu.2.497e.

διάστιξις, εως, ἡ, *branding*, Just.*Nov.*115.4.

διαστοιβάζω, *stuff in between*, Hdt.1.179.

διαστοιχίζομαι, Med., *arrange for oneself regularly, regulate exactly*, ἀρχὴν A.*Pr.*232.

διαστολ-εύς, έως, ὁ, *instrument for examining cavities, dilator*, Gal.19.110, Paul.Aeg.6.78 ; for opening a horse's mouth, *Hippiatr.* 2. II. *cashier*, title of official, *BGU*1064.19 (iii A.D.), *Cod.Just.*10. 71.4. **-ή**, ἡ, (διαστέλλω) *drawing asunder, dilatation*, of the lungs, Arist.*Aud.*800^{a}35 ; of the heart, Gal.2.597 ; of the pulse, Id.8.736, al. ; δ. χειλέων *parting* of the lips, i.e. *utterance*, Lxx*Nu.*30.7. b. *separation*, Thphr.*CP*3.16.3 ; *notch* or *nick*, Plu.*Cic.*1 ; *boundary, fence*, *Tab.Heracl.*2.46 ; *fencing off*, τῆς γῆς *PAmh.*2.40.25 (ii B.C.). 2. *distinction*, Chrysipp.*Stoic.*2.158, Lxx*Ex.*8.23, Epicur.*Nat.*28.7, Phld.*Piet.*123, *Ep.Rom.*3.22 ; ἁγίων καὶ βεβήλων Ph.2.159 ; μετὰ διαστολῆς προενεχθέντα with *discrimination*, Demetr.Lac.1014.48 F. ; *detailed statement* or *explanation*, Plb.1.15.6 ; ἀξίους μνήμης καὶ δ. Id. 16.14.2, cf. *SIG*284.11 (Chios), Apollon.Cit.3 ; *specification* of items in an account, *PRyl.*65.17 (i B.C.) ; *article* in a contract, etc., *PTheb. Bank*6.8, 7.7. 3. *command, injunction, order*, Lxx*Nu.*19.2, al., *PTeb.*24.45 (ii B.C.), etc. 4. *payment*, *BGU*485.26, *PTeb.*363. 1 (ii A.D.). II. Gramm., *comma* (as in ὅ, τι), D.T.629. b. *distinction*, γενῶν A.D.*Pron.*11.28, al. c. *opposition*, πρός τι ib.41. 24. 2. in Music, *distinctness*, of notes, 1*Ep.Cor.*14.7. **-ικόν**, τό, *official notification of payment due, writ*, *POxy.*68.33 (ii A.D.), al. ; in full, δ. ὑπόμνημα *BGU*613.18. **-ιον**, τό, = διαστολεύς 1, *Hippiatr.*16. **-ον**, τό, in pl., *dispositions* of a deed, *PLond.*1727. 58 (vi A.D.).

διαστομᾰλίζομαι· λοιδορέω, in impf., Hsch.

διαστόμ-ωσις, εως, ἡ, *expansion*, Alex.Aphr.*Pr.*1.93. **-ωτρίς** (with or without μήλη), εως, ἡ, = διαστολεύς 1, Hp.ap.Gal.19.122,92.

διαστοχάζομαι, *guess*, Hsch. s. v. διατεκμαίρομαι.

διάστρα, ἡ, (διάζω) *warp set up in a loom*, *Gloss.*

διαστράπτω, *glance like lightning*, Lxx*Wi.*16.22.

διαστρᾰτεύομαι, Med., *serve through one's campaigns* : διαστρατευσάμενος *a veteran*, D.C.58.18.

διαστρᾰτηγέω, *assume the position of general*, Plu.*Phoc.*25, *Aem.* 13, al. II. trans., *to out-general*, τοὺς Ῥωμαίους Plb.21.39.9 ; τοὺς βαρβάρους Dion.Byz.53. 2. δ. τι *practise stratagems*, Plb.16.37. 1. 3. δ. πόλεμον *conduct* a war *to its close*, Plu.*Sull.*23 ; δ. τὰν ἀρχάν Polus ap.Stob.3.9.51. 4. at Rome, *come to the end of one's praetorship*, D.C.54.33.

διαστρεβλόω, strengthd. for στρεβλόω, Aeschin.3.224.

διάστρεμμα, ατος, τό, *wrench, dislocation*, Hp.*Off.*23.

διαστρέφω, *turn different ways, twist about*, τὰ σώματα, as in the dance, X.*Smp.*7.3 ; δ. τὸ πρόσωπον *to distort* it, Plu.2.535a :—mostly Pass., *to be distorted* or *twisted*, of the eyes, limbs, etc., Hp.*Aph.*4. 49 ; ἡ ῥὶς δ. Id.*Art.*38 ; μέλη διεστραμμένα Pl.*Grg.*524c ; *to be warped*, τὰ διεστραμμένα τῶν ξύλων Arist.*EN*1109^{b}6 : also of persons, *to have one's eyes distorted*, or *to have one's neck twisted* (Scholl. give both interprr.), εὐδαιμονίζω δ' εἰ διαστραφήσομαι ; Ar.*Eq.*175 ; so ἀπολαύσομαί τί γ' εἰ δ. Id.*Av.*177 ; of the eyes, διεστράφην ἰδών Id.*Ach.*15 ; τὰ ὄμματα διαστρέφεσθαι Arist.*Pr.*960^{a}13 ; without ὄμματα, ib.9, cf. 957^{b}7 ; ὁ διεστραμμένος, opp. ὁ τυφλός, Eup.276.3 ; διεστρ. τοὺς πόδας *with* the feet *twisted*, Paus.5.18.1, cf. Arist.*Pr.*896^{b}5 : of torture, τῇ κλίμακι διαστρέφονται *Com.Adesp.*422 ; διεστράφησαν τὸν στόμαχον *had* their stomachs *turned*, Jul.*Or.*6.190d. 2. metaph., *distort, pervert*, [τρόπον χρηστόν] E.*Fr.*597 ; τοὺς νόμους Is.11.4 ; τὸν δικαστήν Arist.*Rh.*1354^{a}24 ; ὑπόληψιν Id.*EN*1140^{b}14 ; τῶν διαστρεφόντων (sc. παθῶν) Phld.*Lib.*p.32 O. ; διαστρέψαντες τἀληθῆ *having misrepresented* it, D.*Prooem.*46.2 :—Pass., διαστραφῆναι τὴν διάνοιαν Luc.*Vit. Auct.*24 ; γενεὰ διεστραμμένη *perverse*, Lxx*De.*32.5. II. *turn aside, divert*, ἴχνος τὸ πρόσθεν φρενῶν A.*Supp.*1017. III. sens. obsc., = βινεῖν, Eup.7 D.

διαστροβέω, *stir up*, πέλαγος *Trag.Adesp.*391. 2. = διασοβέω, Alciphr.3.9.

διαστροφ-εύς, gloss on παραχαράκτης, Hsch., etc. **-ή**, ἡ, *twisting*, of a fractured limb, Hp.*Fract.*16 ; *distortion*, Id.*Art.*46 ; τῶν ὀμμάτων Arist.*Pr.*958^{a}6, cf. 960^{a}20 : abs., of limbs, Sor.1.111. 2. metaph., *perversion*, Arist.*EE*1227^{a}21 ; τοῦ δήμου ἐπὶ τὸ χεῖρον Plb. 2.21.8, Porph.*Abst.*1.13, etc. ; γενῶν Plu.2.520c ; δ. κακή Lxx*Pr.*2. 14. 3. *distraction*, Metrod.*Herc.*831.7 ; *madness*, D.L.2.89. 4. *tergiversation*, Just.*Nov.*17.8.1 (pl.). **-ος**, ον, *twisted, distorted*, δ. καὶ ἔμπηρα καὶ ἀπόπληκτα Hdt.1.167 ; μορφὴ καὶ φρένες δ. A.*Pr.* 673, cf. S.*Aj.*447 ; ὀφθαλμός Id.*Tr.*794 ; δ. κόρας ἑλίσσουσ' E.*Ba.* 1122, cf. 1166 (lyr.) ; of a person, δ. τοὺς ὀφθαλμούς, τὸ σῶμα, Ath. 8.339f, Luc.*Ind.*7. Adv. -φως *incorrectly*, λέγειν S.E.*M.*1.152.

διάστρωμα, ατος, τό, *abstract of title-deeds* in land registry, *POxy.* 237 viii 39 (ii A.D.), etc. II. = *digestum*, *Gloss.*

διαστρώννῡμι, *spread* a couch, etc., κλισίαν Luc.*DDeor.*24.1 : abs., *spread*, Lxx 1*Ki.*9.25 :—Pass., Phylarch.43. II. Pass., of titles to property, *to be registered*, *POxy.*1725.17 (iii A.D.), etc.

διαστρωφάομαι, = διαστρέφομαι, Sm.*Ps.*54(55).5.

διαστυγνάζω, *make stern*, τὰ πρόσωπα Eun.*VS*p.503 D.

διαστύλ-ιον [ῠ], τό, in Architecture, *space between the columns*, Lat. *intercolumnium*, Bito 54.3. 2. ἀνέστησε δ. δύο perh. *a monument with three pillars*, Keil-Premerstein *Dritter Bericht* No.107. **-ος**, ον, *diastyle*, i.e. *having a space of three diameters between the columns*, Vitr.3.3.1. II. διάστυλον, τό, = foreg. 1, *IG*4.1484.63 (Epid.), *Ephes.*2.76, al. **-όω**, *support by pillars set at intervals*, Plb.5.100. 4 :—Pass., ib.4.8 ; διεστύλωτο δοκοῖς D.S.20.23.

διαστύρακοι, οἱ, *those with dark pupil and light iris*, Hsch.

διαστύφομαι [ῠ], aor. -εστύφθην, *become constipated*, *Hippiatr.*35.

διασυγ-χέω, *confuse utterly*, Plu.2.1078a. **-χύνω**, = foreg., A.D.*Adv.*202.15.

διασυκάξαι· διασκεδάσαι (Tarent.), Hsch.

διασυν-ιστάνω, = sq., τὸ μέλλον ἀγαθὸν δ. τῇ ψυχῇ Ph.1.603. **-ίστημι**, *set forth, signify clearly*, ib.237, al., D.L.3.79. II. *introduce, bring forward*, τινὰ λέγοντα Ph.1.368, al. :—Pass., *to be presented to the mind*, M.Ant.3.2. 2. *designate a successor to*, ἱερητείαν *SIG* 1014.155 (Erythrae, iii B.C.). **-τρέχω**, *revolve with*, τοῖς ἄλλοις, of heavenly bodies, Anon.*in Ptol.Tetr.*119.

διασῡριγμός, ὁ, f. l. for διασυρμός, D.S.14.109.

διασῡρίζω, *whistle*, of the wind, Lxx*Da.*3.50; f. l. in Theopomp. Hist.76 :—also **-σῡρίττω**, c. acc. metaph., τὸ τῆς φήμης πτερὸν τὴν ὕβριν ἀπανταχῇ δ. Lib.*Decl.*40.59 ; also, *whistle away, waste idly*, τὴν μέχρι τῆς αὐλῆς (sc. ὁδόν) Lyd.*Mag.*2.26.

διασυρ-μός, ὁ, *disparagement, ridicule*, Phld.*Vit.*p.37 J., D.S.14. 109, Longin.38.6, Ph.2.571 (pl.), Artem.3.25. **-σις**, εως, ἡ, *drawing through* a surgical dressing, Paul.Aeg.6.62. II. metaph., = foreg., Ptol.*Tetr.*160. **-τέον**, *one must ridicule*, Arist.*Rh.Al.* 1443^{a}9. **-της**, ου, ὁ, *detractor*, Ptol.*Tetr.*164. **-τικός**, ή, όν, *disparaging*, Phld.*Lib.*p.18 O., Ptol.*Tetr.*160 ; λόγος Trypho *Trop.* p.206 S. Adv. -κῶς Sch.E.*Hec.*925. **-τος**, ον, *drawn through*, λημνίσκος Paul.Aeg.6.34. **-ω** [ῡ], pf. -σέσυρκα Diph.75 :—Pass., pf. -σεσύρθαι Arist.*Rh.Al.*1433^{b}6 :—*tear in pieces*, κρέα prob. in Theopomp.Hist.76 : metaph., *pull to pieces*, i.e. *to disparage, ridi-*

cule, Alex.141.11,237; διεσύρε τὰ παρόντα D.13.12, al.; λοιδορούμενος καὶ διασύρων Id.18.180, cf. Plb.4.3.13, Phld.*Ir*.p.59 W., etc. II. *break up, disperse*, σύνοδον Plb.10.42.4. III. *draw through*, Paul. Aeg.6.25:—Pass., *to be drawn to one side, Hippiatr*.26.

διασύστᾰσις, εως, ἡ, *commending*, τοῦ ζητουμένου Ph.2.454; *introduction*, Id.1.26. II. *designation of a successor*, δ. ἱερητειῶν *SIG*1014.13 (pl., Erythrae, iii B.C.).

διασφᾰγ-ή, ἡ, *gap*, Lxx *Ne*.4.7(1); v. διασφάξ. 2. *sluice-gate*, Wilcken *Chr*.11 *B*6 (ii B.C.). **-μα**, ατος, τό, = διασφάξ II. 2, Hippon.68 A.

διασφαιρ-ίζω, *throw about like a ball*, σάρκα E.*Ba*.1136. **-όομαι**, *to be rolled up into a ball*, plpf. διεσφαίρωτο Nonn.*D*.3.137.

διασφακτήρ, ῆρος, ὁ, *murderous*, σίδηρος *AP*7.493 (Antip. Thess.).

διασφᾰλίζομαι, *secure firmly*, Plb.5.69.2, Ph.Byz.*Mir*.4.2, Herod. Med.ap.Orib.8.7.3:—Pass., σιδήρῳ διησφαλισμένα J.*AJ*15.11.3.

διασφάλλω, *overturn utterly*, τὴν τέχνην Luc.*Abd*.17:—Pass., *to fail of, be disappointed of*, τινός Aeschin.2.35, 3.91, D.S.20.10; τῇ προνοίᾳ, ἐν πράξεσι, Plb.5.81.7, 4.14.3, cf. Arist.*Ath*.19.3; πάντα δ. Vett.Val.116.34.

διασφάξ, ᾶγος, ἡ, (διασφάζω) *any opening made by violence, rent*, esp. *gorge*, through which a river runs, Hdt.2.158 (pl.), 3.117, etc.; *cleft* in the earth, Lyc.317. 2. Medic., of *divisions* of blood-vessels, Hp.*Loc.Hom*.3; *fissure* in the liver, Herophil.ap.Gal.2.570. 3. *sluice, POxy*.1188.24 (i A.D.). II. *gill-cavity*, in fishes, Opp.*H*. 1.744. 2. = τὸ θῆλυ μόριον, Eust.897.60.

διάσφαξις, εως, ἡ, = διασφάξ, Hp.*Epid*.2.1.8 (dub. l.).

διασφάττω, *slaughter*, f.l. in Lib.*Loc*.1.8.

διασφενδονάω, *scatter as by a sling*, D.S.17.83:—Pass., *to be hurled from slings*, Agath.3.25, 5.3; *to be scattered in all directions*, X.*An*. 4.2.3, Plu.*Marc*.15, D.C.56.14. II. *dismember*, Plu.*Alex*.43.

διασφετερίζομαι, f.l. for σφετερίζομαι, Ph.2.130.

διασφηκόομαι, Pass., *to be made like a wasp, be pinched in at the waist*, μέσος διεσφηκωμένος Ar.*V*.1072. II. later in Act., *bind tight*, Nonn.*D*.25.189, al.

διασφην-όω, *dilate as with a wedge*, Meges ap.Orib.44.24.2:—Pass., Antyll.ib.10.23.7; in literal sense, Apollod.*Poliorc*.180. 14. **-ωσις**, εως, ἡ, *plugging*, μοτῶν Sor.2.40 (pl.).

δια-σφίγγω, *bind tight*, ζώναις τὴν κοιλίαν Erasistr.ap.Gell.16.3.8, cf. Antyll.ap.Orib.7.9.3, Aret.*SA*1.5:—Pass., [σώματα] κατὰ τὸ μέσον διεσφιγμένα *narrow-waisted*, Eun.*Hist*.p.234 D.; also σφραγῖσι χρυσοδέτοις δ. ib.p.255 D.; dub. l. ib.p.261 D. **-σφιγκτέον**, *one must bind tightly*, Paul.Aeg.3.44. **-σφιγξις**, εως, ἡ, *binding tight, ligature*, Sor.2.41, Heliod.ap.Orib.10.18, Antyll.ib.7.9.3, Aret. *CA*2.2.

διασφρᾱγ-ίζομαι, *seal up*, Lxx *Je*.39(32).10.

διασφῡδόω, *cause to swell up*, Hsch.; cf. σφυδόω.

διάσφυξις, εως, ἡ, (σφύζω) *pulsation*, φλεβῶν Hp.*Alim*.48; ἀρτηρίης Aret.*SA*2.2; *throbbing*, ἐγκεφάλου Id.*CD*1.3.

διασχάζω, *open a vein*, Aret.*CA*2.10.

διάσχεσις, εως, ἡ, prob. = διάσχισμα II, Hsch., *EM*340.6.

διασχημᾰτ-ίζω, *shape, form variously*, Str.17.1.4, Plu.2.499e:—Med., of God, *mould as Creator*, Pl.*Ti*.53b:—Pass., ib.50c. 2. simply, *shape, model*, Luc.*Icar*.6, v.l. in *Prom*.11 (Pass.). 3. *shape oneself, prepare*, ἐπὶ πρᾶγμα Eun.*Hist*.p.269 D. **-ισις**, εως, ἡ, *formation*, i.e. *dimensions*, of a groove, Procl.*Hyp*.3.19: generally, Id. *in Ti*.3.261 D.

δια-σχῐδής, ές, *cloven, split, parted*, Ath.11.488e. **-σχίζω**, *cleave asunder, sever*, ἱστία δέ σφιν.. διέσχισεν ἲς ἀνέμοιο Od.9.71; ἐάν τις ἓν δ. Pl.*Phd*.97a, etc.:—Pass., *to be cloven asunder*, νεῦρα διεσχίσθη Il.16.316; opp. συγκρίνεσθαι, Pl.*Lg*.893e; θοἰμάτιον δ. Id.*Grg*. 469d; of soldiers, *to be separated, parted*, X.*Cyr*.4.5.13; *to be set at variance*, διέσχιστο ἡ πόλις Charito 6.1: impers., τούτοις διέσχισται they *have a cleft*, Arist.*Resp*.475^{a}2. **-σχίς**, ίδος, ἡ, *division*, φλεβός Hp.*Fract*.44, cf. Gal.14.706. **-σχῐσις**, εως, ἡ, *division, cleft*, Ath.11.488e; of roads, Them.*Or*.20.236b (pl.). **-σχισμα**, ατος, τό, *interval*, Sch.D.T.p.191 H. (Dind. for διάσχημα). II. in Music, *interval of half the* δίεσις, Philol.6. **-σχισμός**, ὁ, = διάσχισις, Sch.A.*Supp*.131. II. metaph., *dissension, BGU*923. 21 (i/ii A.D.).

διασχοινίζω, *scatter*, in pf. part. Pass., Hsch. (-σχην- cod.).

διασχολέω, strengthd. for ἀσχολέω, περί τι Hdn.7.6.7 (Med.).

διασῴζω, *preserve through* a danger, of persons, Ἀπόλλωνα δ. κατακρύψασα Hdt.2.156; δ. πόλιν E.*Ph*.783; δ. τινὰ ἐκ κινδύνων Isoc. 1.23:—Med., *save for oneself*, τὰ πλείστου ἄξια X.*Cyr*.4.2.28:—Pass., Pl.*Ti*.22d; *come safe through*, τοὺς διασωθέντας Id.*R*.540a, cf. 1*Ep. Pet*.3.20, etc.; διασῴζεσθαι ἐς.. or πρός.. *to come safe* to a place, Th.4.113, X.*An*.5.4.5, etc.; *recover* from illness, Id.*Mem*.2.10. 2. II. of things, *preserve, maintain*, ἀνδρὶ τἀμὰ δ. λέχη.. E.*Hel*. 65; *keep in memory*, X.*Mem*.3.5.22; δ. πίστιν τινί Id.*HG*7.2.17; δ. τὸν πρῶτον λόγον Pl.*R*.395b, cf. Arist.*Ph*.189^{b}1; τὰ παλαιά Isoc.10. 63:—Med., *preserve for oneself, retain*, εὐδαιμονίαν, εὐτυχίαν, Th.3.39, 5.16; δόξαν Lys.2.69; τὴν τῶν Μήδων μαλακίαν X.*Cyr*.8.8.15.

διασωμᾰτίζω, *dismember*, gloss on διασκηνίψαι, Hsch.

διασωπάσομαι, v. διασιωπάω.

διασωσ-τέον, *one must maintain*, Pl.*Ep*.360b, *Com.Adesp*.25.41 D. **-τής**, οῦ, ὁ, *policeman*, Just.*Nov*.130.1. **-τικός**, ή, όν, *preservative*, Max.Tyr.20.5, al.; δύναμις Gal.*Nat.Fac*.1.14; θεὸς δ. καὶ τῶν φύσεων τηρητικός *Theol.Ar*.5.

διασώχω, *rub to pieces*, Nic.*Th*.696 (tm.).

διατᾱγεύω, *arrange*, v.l. for διατάξαι in X.*Cyr*.8.3.33.

δια-τᾰγή, ἡ, *command, ordinance*, Lxx 2*Es*.4.11, *Ep.Rom*.13.2; ἐκ διαταγῆς *CIG*3465, *POxy*.92.3 (iv A.D.); *testamentary disposition, IGRom*.4.840.3, etc.; δ. τῆς τρύγης ποιήσασθαι make *arrangements* for.., *PFay*.133.4 (iv A.D.); πόλεως Ps.-Callisth.1.33; εἰς διαταγὰς ἀγγέλων *Act.Ap*.7.53; *medical regimen*, Ruf.ap.Orib.6.38. 13; = τάξις, *Placit*.1.15.8. **-ταγμα**, ατος, τό, *ordinance, edict*, Phld.*Rh*.2.289 S., D.S.18.64, Ph.1.180, *Ep.Hebr*.11.23, Plu.*Pomp*.6, *IG*2^{2}.1077.34; κατὰ τὸ δ. (sc. τῆς συγκλήτου) ib.12(3).173.10; = Lat. *edictum, OGI*458.81 (i B.C.), *BGU*1074.3 (iii A.D.), etc.; = Lat. *formula, IG*14.951.24,25 (Rome); *testamentary disposition, POxy*.1282. 27 (i A.D.). **-ταγματικός**, ή, όν, *edictalis, Gloss*. **-ταγμός**, ὁ, = διάταξις II, ib. **-τακτα**, τά, *miscellaneous treatises*, Anon.*Vit. Arist*. p.14.3 W. **-τακτέον**, *one must assign*, τὰ πρόσφορα χαρακτῆρι ἑκάστῳ Demetr.*Eloc*.59. **-τακτέω**, *issue a decree, Gloss*. **-τάκτης**, ου, ὁ, *assigner of posts*, Herm.ap.Stob.1.49.69. **-τακτικός**, ή, όν, *capable of ordering, arranging*, Phld.*Oec*.p.52 J., Ptol.*Tetr*.82. Adv. -κῶς *Gloss*. **-τάκτωρ**, ορος, ὁ, = -τάκτης, Orph.*Fr*.54, Sch.Il.1.16.

διατᾰλαντόομαι, Pass., *swing to and fro*, of a ship, Ach.Tat.3.1.

διατᾰμιεύω, *manage, dispense*, Pl.*Lg*.805e:—Med., *store, husband*, Id.*Criti*.111d.

διατάμνω, Ion. and Dor. for διατέμνω, Hdt.2.139, *Tab.Heracl*.1.12.

διατᾰνύω, = διατείνω, διὰ πτερὰ.. τανύσσας A.R.4.601.

διαταξίαρχος, ὁ, *assigner of offices, official of guild of* βουκόλοι, *IG Rom*.4.386 (Pergam.).

διάτᾰξις, εως, ἡ, (διατάσσω) *disposition, arrangement*, of troops, Hdt.9.26; ἡ δ. τῶν φυλάκων D.18.248; *disposition* of the elements, Pl.*Ti*.53b; ταύτην ὁ κόσμος ἔχει τὴν δ. Arist.*Cael*.300^{b}25; of a treatise, Ph.*Bel*.49.4; Rhet., *arrangement of topics*, Luc.*Hist.Conscr*. 24. II. *command*, Lxx *Ps*.118(119).91, Plb.4.19.10, Phld.*Herc*. 1251.20, *Po*.2.48 (pl.); *testamentary disposition*, Plb.4.87.5; *compact*, Id.8.16.12. 2. *imperial constitution*, θεῖαι δ. Wilcken *Chr*.41 iii 20 (iii A.D.); κατὰ διάταξιν τοῦ Ἁδριανοῦ *BGU*1022.9 (ii A.D.); νεαραὶ δ., title of Justinian's Novels; of the *decree* of the *praefectus Aegypti*, Wilcken *Chr*.27.10 (ii A.D.).

διατᾰράσσω, Att. -ττω, *throw into confusion*, X.*Mem*.4.2.40, Pl. *Lg*.693c, Plb.11.1.9, Phld.*Piet*.108:—Pass., δ. ἐν ταῖς τοῦ βίου μεταβολαῖς Isoc.2.39, cf. Epicur.*Ep*.3 p.66 U., D.S.18.7, Jul.*Or*.3.116d.

διατᾰρᾰχή, ἡ, *disturbance*, Plu.2.317b (pl.).

διάτᾰσις, εως, ἡ, *tension, dilatation*, ἔχειν δ. to have the *power of dilatation*, Arist.*PA*664^{a}33 (v.l.); κεφαλῆς διατάσεις καὶ ἰλίγγους Pl. *R*.407c (prob.). 2. *extension*, of a fractured or dislocated limb, Hp.*Off*.15, cf. Heliod.ap.Orib.49.8.33; σπαρτῶν Alciphr.2.4. 3. *stretching across*: hence Medic., δ. φρενῶν *diaphragm*, Hp.*VM*22; δ. alone, Id.*Coac*.394; also of vaginal *obstruction*, Paul.Aeg.6.72. II. *tension, exertion*, πνεύματος Thphr.*Sud*.32; of athletes and the like, Arist.*Pr*.885^{b}23, *IA*705^{a}18; διατάσεις καὶ κλαυθμοί, of infants, Id. *Pol*.1336^{a}34: metaph., ἡ εὔνοια.. οὐκ ἔχει δ. Id.*EN*1166^{b}33; ἐν δ. γενομένης τῆς ψυχῆς Plu.*Cor*.21; ἡ πρὸς τὸν ἥλιον δ., of plants, Iamb. *Protr*.21.λη'. 2. *contention, quarrel*, εἰς μεγάλην ἐλθεῖν δ. πρός τινα D.S.38/9.2 (s.v.l.).

διατάσσω, Att. -ττω, pf. διατέτᾰχα *BGU*1151.6 (i B.C.), prob. in *OGI*326.27 (Teos):—*appoint* or *ordain severally, dispose*, εὖ δὲ ἕκαστα ἀθανάτοις διέταξε Hes.*Th*.74; ἀνθρώποισι νόμον δ. Id.*Op*.276; *appoint to separate offices*, δ. τοὺς μὲν οἰκίας οἰκοδομέειν, τοὺς δὲ δορυφόρους εἶναι Hdt.1.114; δ. τι εἶναι Pl.*Ti*.45b; τίνας εἶναι χρεὼν τῶν ἐπιστημῶν.. ἡ πολιτικὴ δ. Arist.*EN*1094^{b}1: abs., *make arrangements*, πρὸς τὸ συμπῖπτον ἀεὶ δ. X.*Cyr*.8.5.16:—Med., *arrange for oneself, classify*, Pl.*Phdr*.271b; τινὶ περί τινος Plb.5.21.1; *undertake, pledge oneself*, πρός τινα c. fut. inf., ib.14.11; also in act. sense, περὶ θυσιῶν *OGI*331.53 (Pergam.):—Pass., *to be appointed, constituted*, Pl.*Lg*.932a; παρὰ τὰ -τεταγμένα contrary to *orders, BGU*1022.17 (ii A.D.): c. inf., v.l. in Hdt.1.110: c. acc., δ. γῆν *to be appointed to cultivate, POxy*.899.22 (200 A.D.). 2. esp. *draw up* an army, *set in array*, Hdt.6.107, Th.4.103; διέταξε χωρὶς ἑκάστους εἶναι Hdt.1. 103:—Med., διαταξάμενοι *posting themselves in battle-order*, Ar.*V*. 360, Th.8.104, X.*HG*7.1.20:—pf. Pass., διατετάχθαι *to be in battle-order*, Hdt.7.178, Th.4.31; διετέτακτο Hdt.6.112 (but in med. sense, J.*AJ*12.5.4). II. Med., *make testamentary dispositions*, περί τινος Plu.2.1129a; *order by will*, c. inf., *AP*11.133 (Lucill.); *bequeath, BGU*1151.6 (i B.C.):—Pass., *to be bequeathed, PFay*.97.13 (i A.D.).

διατᾰτικός, ή, όν, *on the stretch, urgent*, Plb.*Fr*.29 (Comp.). Adv. Comp. -ώτερον *by an extension of meaning*, S.E.*M*.1.45 codd.

διαταφρεύω, *cut off* or *fortify by a ditch*, Plb.3.105.11, Plu.*Pomp*. 62:—Pass., J.*BJ*5.4.2.

διατεθρυμμένως, Adv., (διαθρύπτω) *weakly*, Pl.*Lg*.922c.

διατείνω, *stretch to the uttermost*, δ. τὸ τόξον Hdt.3.35; *keep stretched out*, τὴν χεῖρα Hp.*Fract*.8; δ. τὰς χεῖρας ἐπί τι X.*Cyr*.1.3.4; ἀράχνιον δ. πρὸς τὰ πέρατα Arist.*HA*623^{a}9; τινὰ ὑπὲρ λεχέων *AP*5.54 (Diosc.):—Pass., *extend*, μία ἰδέα πάντῃ διατεταμένη Pl.*Sph*. 253d. II. intr., *extend*, Diog.Apoll.6; διὰ παντὸς τοῦ βίου Arist.*EN* 1172^{a}23; καθ' ἅπαν τὸ σῶμα Id.*HA*503^{b}21; κατὰ τὸ συνεχὲς ἕως εἰς.. Plb.3.37.9; *to continue*, γένος διέτεινε λαμπρόν Plu.*Marc*.30. 2. δ. εἰς, ποτί τι, *extend* or *relate to, concern, SIG*569.11,38 (Halasarna, iii B.C.), cf. Plb.8.29.6; πρὸς τὰ ὅλα Id.9.5.4. 3. *reach, arrive at, extend as far as*, πρός.. Epicur.*Ep*.1 p.13 U., Plb.5.86.4, D.S.12.70, etc.; *live until the time of*, εἴς τινα Plu.*Cat.Ma*.15.

B. Med. and Pass., *exert oneself*, τί οὖν.. διετεινάμην οὑτωσὶ σφοδρῶς; D.18.142; διατεινάμενος φεύγειν *at full speed*, X.*Mem*.4.2.23;

θεῖν διατεταμένους Pl.*R*.474a; ἰέναι ib.501c; πὺξ διατεινάμενος Theoc. 22.67; *strain, exert the voice*, Arist.*Pol*.1336a39; διατείνεσθαι πρός τι *exert oneself* for a purpose, X.*Mem*.3.7.9; διετείναντο αὐτὸν μὴ εἰσελθεῖν *prevented* him from going in, Antipho 5.46; δ. τὰ κάλλιστα πράττειν Arist.*EN*1169a9. 2. *maintain earnestly, contend*, δ. ὡς.. *maintain stoutly* that.., Pl.*Sph*.247c, Thphr.*HP*3.18.7, *CP*4.6.1, etc. b. *oppose*, opp. συναποφήνασθαι, Gal.4.759; πρός τινα ib. 773. II. in strict sense of Med., *stretch oneself*, Anaxandr.41. 67. 2. *to stretch out for oneself* or *what is one's own*, δ. τὸ τόξον Hdt.4.9; τὰ βέλεα ὡς ἀπήσοντες *to have their* lances *poised* as if they were about to throw, Id.9.18; διατεινάμενοι οἱ μὲν τὰ παλτὰ οἱ δὲ τὰ τόξα X.*Cyr*.1.4.23; διατεταμένοι τὰς μάστιγας Plb.15.28.2.

διατειχ-ίζω, *cut off and fortify by a wall*, Ar.*Eq*.818; τὸν Ἰσθμόν Lys.2.44; τὴν πόλιν ἀπὸ τῆς ἄκρας Plb.8.32.2. 2. *divide as by a wall*, ἡ ῥὶς διατετείχικε τὰ ὄμματα X.*Smp*.5.6: metaph., *keep apart*, φῶς καὶ σκότος Ph.1.632, al.; διατετείχισται ἡ ἱστορία πρὸς τὸ ἐγκώμιον *is separated* from it, Luc.*Hist.Conscr*.7. **–ιον**, τό, = sq., D.S.16. 12 (s.v.l.). **–ισμα**, ατος, τό, *place walled off and fortified*, Th.3. 34; *cross-wall*, Id.7.60. 2. *wall between two places*, *SIG*421.46 (Thermon, iii B.C.), Plb.8.34.9: metaph., *wall of partition*, Luc. *DMeretr*.11.4. **–ισμός**, ὁ, *fortifying*, τᾶς πόλιος *IG*4.757 *B* 25 (Troezen).

διατεκμαίρομαι, only aor. I –τεκμηράμην, *mark out, assign*, ἔργα ἀνθρώποισι Hes.*Op*.398, cf. D.P.1172; *mark, trace out*, A.R.4.284; *determine*, γενέθλην Μοῖραι δ. Man.6.750.

διατελευτάω, *bring to fulfilment*, θεὸς διὰ πάντα τ. Il.19.90.

διατελ-έω, fut. –τελέσω, Att. –τελῶ: pf. διατετέλεκα X.*Cyr*.1.5.4, *IG*2².223 *A* 5:—*bring quite to an end, accomplish*, ἐπεί περ ἠρξάμην, διατελέσαι βούλομαι X.*HG*7.3.4; δ. χάριν E.*Heracl*.434; so of Time, διατετελεκὼς τὰ ἐν τοῖς ἐφήβοις δέκα ἔτη X.*Cyr*. l. c. II. abs., 1. mostly c. part., *continue being* or *doing* so and so, τὸ λοιπὸν τῆς ζόης δ. ἐόντα τυφλόν Hdt.6.117; δ. ἐόντες ἐλεύθεροι Id. 7.111, cf. 1.32, etc.; δ. τὸν λοιπὸν βίον δουλεύοντες And.1.38; δ. καθεύδοντες Pl.*Ap*.31a; μινυρίζων δ. τὸν βίον ὅλον Id.*R*.411a; διετέλεσας πειρώμενος you *have been* trying *all along*, Id.*Tht*.206a: with Adjs., δ. πρόθυμος *continue* zealous, Th.6.89, cf. 1.34; δ. ἀχίτων X. *Mem*.1.6.2; ἡδὺς δ. Alex.45.9. 2. with no part. or Adj., *continue, live*, δ. μετ' ἀλλήλων διὰ βίου Pl.*Smp*.192c; δ. χαριέντως Id.*R*. 426a; ἐν ἀγρῷ Men.*Georg*.4. b. generally, *continue, persevere*, διατέλει ὥσπερ ἤρξω Pl.*Grg*.494c; δ. ἐν ὕπνῳ Arist.*GA*779a24; ἐν τῇ θαλάττῃ Id.*Pr*.933a14; of things, *continue*, ἐὰν αἱ μιμήσεις ἐκ νέων πόρρω δ. Pl.*R*.395d. **–ής**, ές, *continuous, incessant*, βρονταί S.*OC* 1514; *ever-flowing*, ὕδατα Ael.*VH*13.1; *permanent*, τυραννίδες Pl.*R*. 618a; *perpetual*, ἀρετή *IG*7.2509 (Thebes). (διὰ τέλους serves as the Adv.)

διατέμνω, Ion. and Dor. –τάμνω (q.v.), fut. –τεμῶ, *cut through, cut in twain, dissever*, διὰ δὲ γλῶσσαν τάμε μέσσην Il.17.618, cf. 522 (tm.), Hdt.2.139; διὰ κάρα τεμών S.*Fr*.799.6; διὰ κῦμα τεμών *cleaving* the wave, ib.271.5 (anap.); διχῇ γαῖαν δ. *part* it asunder, A.*Supp*.545 (lyr.); δίχα δ. Pl.*Smp*.190d; τι ἀπό τινος Id.*Plt*.280b: metaph., *disunite*, διατετμηκότα τὴν πολιτείαν Aeschin.3.207. 2. *cut up*, Hdt.2.41.

διατενής, ές, *tending*, πρὸς τὴν τελείωσιν Thphr.*CP*2.15.2.

διατέρπομαι, *take one's pleasure with*, γυναικί App.*Mith*.27.

διατερσαίνω, strengthd. for τερσαίνω, Prisc.p.301 D., Hsch.

διατετᾰμένως, Adv., (διατείνω) *with might and main, earnestly*, δ. φεύγειν Arist.*EN*1166b28; ἐνεργεῖν ib.1175a8, cf. Plu.*Cat.Mi*.26, Iamb.*Protr*.19, Hierocl.*in CA*20p.464M.

διατετηρημένως, *carefully*, prob. in Sch.D.P.1.

διατετραίνω, fut. (Ion.) –τετρανέω Hdt. (v. infr.), or –τρήσω Apollod.*Poliorc*.148.3: aor. –έτρησα Plu.2.370b, App.*Mith*.26:—Med., –τρήσαιο Gal.4.708:—Pass., aor. part. –τρηθείς *BGU*321.13: pf. part. –τετρημένος Apollod.*Poliorc*.152.2:—*bore through*, κεφαλάς Hdt. 3.12; ᾠόν Plu. l. c.:—Med., aor., ὦτα διετετρήνατο Ar.*Th*.18:—**διατιτραίνω** Thphr.*CP*1.17.9 (Pass.); also (as if from διατίτρημι) part. διατιτράντες D.C.69.12, impf. διετίτρη App.*Pun*.122:—late pres. **διατιτράω** Suid.: impf. διετίτρων App.*Hisp*.77; διετίτρα Gal.14.18.

διατήκω, *melt, soften by heat*, κηρόν Ar.*Nu*.149; *relax* the bowels, Hp.*Aër*.7. 2. *soak*, ἐν ἐλαίῳ Thphr.*Od*.29, Aët.15.13:—Pass., aor. –ετήχθην Ph.*Bel*.89.20. II. Pass., with pf. –τέτηκα, *melt away, thaw*, X.*An*.4.5.6; *waste away*, Arist.*Mete*.385a28, Agath.2.14.

διάτηξις· *tabes*, Gloss.

διατηρ-έω, Boeot. –τᾱρέω *Supp.Epigr*.1.132.8 (ii B.C.), but Dor. –τηρέω *SIG*541 *A* 4:—*watch closely, observe*, Pl.*Lg*.836d (v.l.), Arist. *HA*612b28; δ. μή τι πάθωσι D.9.20. 2. *maintain*, τὴν ἐλευθερίαν Decr.ap.D.18.184; τὴν τάξιν Decr.ib.37; τὸ πρέπον Arist.*EN*1178a 13; τὰ τοῦ βίου δίκαια Men.637; τὴν πόλιν καὶ τὴν ἑαυτῶν πίστιν Plb.1.7.7; τὴν εὔνοιαν *IG*12(7).506; τὴν ἀφθαρσίαν Phld.*D*.3*Fr*.19, etc.:—Med., –εῖται τὸν καιρόν *observes*, ib.*Fr*.77:—Pass., ὅταν διατηρηθῶσιν οἱ νόμοι τῇ πόλει Aeschin.3.6; ἀλειτούργητος –τηρείσθω ἡ θεία φύσις Epicur.*Ep*.2p.42U. 3. with predicates, βοῦς ἐννέα ἔτη δ. ἀνοχεύτους Arist.*HA*595b18; ἀβλαβεῖς δ. Plb.7.8.7; ἀφλυκταίνωτα δ. τὰ μέρη Dsc.5.156; δ. τὸν πόλεμον Plu.*Dio*33. 4. δ. ἑαυτὸν ἔκ τινος *keep* oneself from.., *Act.Ap*.15.29. **–ησις**, εως, ἡ, *preservation*, Lxx *Ex*.16.33, al.; ἑαυτῶν D.S.2.50; τῶν ἁγίων Ph. 1.203; γένους J.*AJ*1.3.2, etc. **–ητέον**, *one must preserve*, *Gp*. 9.11.10; *one must keep*, ἐν ἀγρυπνίᾳ Aët.13.12. **–ητικός**, ή, όν, *disposed for keeping*, φίλων M.Ant.1.16; ὑγιείας Porph.*Abst*.1.53, cf. Asp.*in EN*14.2.

διατίθημι, 3 pl. impf. διετίθουν Antipho Trag.1:—*arrange* each *in their several places, distribute*, τὰ κρέα, in sacrificing, Hdt.1.132; τὸ μὲν ἐπὶ δεξιά, τὸ δ' ἐπ' ἀριστερά Id.7.39; ᾗπερ οἱ θεοὶ διέθεσαν τὰ ὄντα X.*Mem*.2.1.27; δ. οἶνον εἰς ὀστράκια Arist.*HA*594a11. II. *manage* well or ill, usu. with Adv., κράτιστα δ. τὰ τοῦ πολέμου Th.6.15; καλὸν πρᾶγμα κακῶς δ. D.19.88; of persons, δ. ἑωυτὸν ἀνηκέστως *treat* himself barbarously, Hdt.3.155:—Pass., οὐ ῥᾳδίως διετέθη he *was* not very gently *handled*, Th.6.57; ἀπόρως διατεθέντας *reduced to* helplessness, Lys.18.23; ἀθλίως διατιθέμενος Pl.*Criti*.121b; σῶμα διατεθειμένῳ κακῶς Men.591. 2. c. acc. pers., with Advbs., *dispose* one so or so, ὅταν οὕτω διαθῇς τοὺς Ἕλληνας Isoc.5.80; οὕτω διαθεὶς.. τὰς πόλεις πρὸς ἀλλήλας D.18.168; δ. τινὰς ἀπίστως πρὸς ἡμᾶς αὐτούς Id.20.22; τὸν ἀκροατὴν δ. πως Arist.*Rh*.1356a3:—Pass., *to be disposed* in a certain manner, πρός τινα Pl.*Tht*.151c, Isoc.8.14; οἰκειότερον διατεθῆναί τινι Id.12.160; τὸν εἰρημένον τρόπον Arist.*Pol*.1302a35; ἐρωτικῶς δ., of animals, Pl.*Smp*.207c, cf. Longus1.15 (διάκειμαι is more usu. as Pass. in this sense). III. *set forth*, of speakers, minstrels, etc., *recite*, κακῶς ποιήματα Pl.*Chrm*.162d, cf. *Lg*.658d; cf. B.6. 2. *describe*, Str.1.1.16, etc.

B. Med., *arrange as one likes, dispose of*, τὴν θυγατέρα X.*Cyr*. 5.2.7; τὰ σώματα ἐπονειδίστως δ. Isoc.12.140; οὐθ' ὅσ' ἂν πορίσωσι.. ταῦτ' ἔχοντες διαθέσθαι D.2.16; εἰς καλὸν δ. τὰ πεπραγμένα Luc.*Hist. Conscr*.51, cf. *Merc.Cond*.25; *spend*, δ. τὰς οὐσίας εἴς τι Plb.20.6.5: metaph., τὸ πλεῖον τῆς ὀργῆς εἴς τινα Id.16.1.2. 2. *dispose of one's* property, *devise it by will*, Is.3.68; τὴν οὐσίαν ἑτέρῳ Id.7.1; δ. διαθήκας, διαθήκην, *make* a will, Lys.19.39, Pl.*Lg*.922c: abs., ibid., Lys. 6.41; κἂν ἀποθάνῃ μὴ διαθέμενος *intestate*, Arist.*Pol*.1270a28; ὁ δ. *the testator*, *Ep.Hebr*.9.16. 3. *dispose of* merchandise, φόρτον Hdt. 1.1,194, cf. X.*An*.7.3.10, *Ath*.2.11; τισί Pl.*Lg*.849d; ἔλαιον καὶ κίκι *PRev.Laws*48.4 (iii B.C.); δ. τὴν ὥραν καὶ τὴν σοφίαν X.*Mem*.1.6.13; δ. τι τριπλασίας τιμῆς ἢ πρότερον D.42.31. 4. *arrange* or *settle mutually*, δ. διαθήκην τινί *make a covenant with* one, Ar.*Av*.439; δ. διαθήκην πρός τινα *Act.Ap*.3.25; ἔριν δ. ἀλλήλοις *settle* a quarrel, X. *Mem*.2.6.23; ὡμολόγησαν καὶ διέθεντο ὀφείλειν *IG*12(7).67.58 (Amorgos). 5. *compose, make*, νόμους Pl.*Lg*.834a. 6. *set forth, recite*, λόγους, δημηγορίαν, etc., Plb.3.108.2, D.H.11.7, cf. D.S.12.17; πολλοὺς ἐπαίνους τινῶν D.H.3.17; δ. ῥῆσιν ἐφ' ἑαυτοῦ Luc.*Herm*. 1. b. Gramm., διατιθέναι and –τίθεσθαι *to act* and *be acted upon*, A.D.*Synt*.12.15; τὸ διατιθέν and τὸ διατιθέμενον *subject* and *object*, ib.127.22.

διατῑλάω, *pass excrements*, *Hippiatr*.31, al.

διατίλλω, lit., *pluck*, κουραῖς.. διατετιλμένη φόβην *having had its* mane *clipped*, S.*Fr*.659.7.

διάτιλμα, ατος, τό, *portion plucked off*, φύλλων *AP*6.71 (Paul. Sil.).

διατῑμ-άω, *finish honouring, honour no longer*, τὰ τοῦδε διατετίμηται θεοῖς A.*Th*.1052 Sch. (τοῦδ' οὐ codd.). 2. Med., *get* a thing *estimated* or *valued*, τὴν οὐσίαν D.S.4.21; τὸ ἀδίκημα ταλάντων πεντακοσίων Id.16.29; τὴν χώραν J.*AJ*13.9.2, cf. *CIG*2266.8 (Delos), *SIG*679.60 (ii B.C.):—also in Act., *PRev.Laws*26.10, Sm. *Le*.27.14. **–ησις**, εως, ἡ, *valuation*, δ. ποιεῖσθαι Ath.6.274e, cf. D.S.29.10, *POxy*.267.18 (i A.D.); *assessed value*, *PRev.Laws*55. 24. **–ητής**, οῦ, ὁ, *appraiser, valuer*, Just.*Nov*.64.1: pl., Id.*Edict*. 9.4. **–ητικός**, gloss on δοκιμαστικός, Suid.

διατῑνάσσω, *shake asunder, shake to pieces*, ἐπὴν σχεδίην.. διὰ κῦμα τινάξῃ Od.5.363; τὰ δώματα E.*Ba*.606: fut. Med. in pass. sense, ib.587 (lyr.). II. *shake violently*, κάρα δ. ἄνω κάτω Id.*IT*282; *shake out*, στρώματα Hierocl.p.63A.

διατινθᾰλέος, α, ον, = τινθαλέος, Ar.*V*.329.

διατιτραίνω, διατιτράω, διατίτρημι, v. διατετραίνω.

διατιτρώσκω, *pierce through, transfix*, δέρμα Hp.*Fract*.11; ταύρους D.C.63.3:—Pass., J.*BJ*6.3.1.

διατλῆναι, part. διατλάς, *endure, suffer*, Hsch.

διατμεύω, (ἀτμός) *evaporate*, Hp.*Morb*.4.45.

δια-τμήγω, aor. I διέτμηξα: aor. 2 διέτμᾰγον:—Pass., aor. 2 –τμάγην [μᾰ] (v. infr.):—Ep. for διατέμνω, *cut in twain*, ἔνθα διατμήξας.. then *having cut* [the Trojan host] *in twain*.., Il.21.3; νηχόμενος.. λαῖτμα διέτμαγον Od.7.276, cf. 5.409; ὦλκα δ., of ploughing, Mosch.2. 81 (Med., ἀρούρας διατμήξασθαι A.R.1.628); Ἀπόλλωνα ἠελίοιο χῶρι δ. *distinguish* him from the Sun, Call.*Fr*.48:—Pass., διέτμαγεν (3 pl. aor. 2 for –τμάγησαν) ἐν φιλότητι they *parted* friends, Il.7.302: abs., they *parted*, 1.531, Od.13.439; also, they *were scattered abroad*, Il. 16.354. **–τμημα**, ατος, τό, *space partitioned off*, Lyd.*Mag*.3. 37. **–τμητέον**· *decidendum*, Gloss.

διατμίζω, *evaporate*, Arist.*Mete*.344b23, 353b8, Sor.1.106, Corn. *ND*32, etc.: c. acc. cogn., ἱδρῶτα δ. Plu.2.695c:—Pass., in same sense, Arist.*Cael*.305b14; of perspiration, τὸ σύμπαν σκῆνος διητμίσθη Aret.*CA*1.1.

διατοιχέω, = ἀνατοιχέω (q.v.), Eub.51, Aristid.1.462J.

διάτοιχος, ον, *extending through the width of the wall*, ὑπερτόναια ξύλινα δ. *IG*2².463.57. II. Subst. διάτοιχος (sc. λίθος), ὁ, *bonding course* or *stone*, ib.11(2).144 *A* 57,97 (Delos, iv B.C.), 199 *C* 32 (iii B.C.), *Milet*.7.56,57 (pl.), cf. Hsch.

διατομή, ἡ, *cutting through, severance*, A.*Th*.934 (lyr., pl., dub.), Ael.*NA*13.20. II. *sharp edge*, ὀδόντων ib.1.31. III. *hole, perforation*, in a pipe, D.S.2.10.

διάτομος, ον, = διχότομος, Mart.Cap.8.864.

διατόναιον, τό, *joist*, *PPetr*.2 p.14 (iii B.C.); *curtain-rod*, Callix. 1:—so **–τόνιον**, *curtain-hook* or *-ring*, Lxx *Ex*.35.11.

διατονθορύζω, strengthd. for τονθορύζω, φοβερόν τι D.C.73.8.

διατονικός, ή, όν, = διάτονος ΙΙ, εἶδος, γένος, Ph.1.321, Aristid. Quint.2.19; διάστημα Cleonid.*Harm*.5. Adv. **-κῶς** Nicom.*Harm*. 11.2.

διατονόομαι, *to be in a state of tension*, Pall.*Febr*.12.

διάτονος, ον, (διατείνω) *on the stretch, vehement*, αὖραι Thphr.*CP* 2.3.1. 2. *extending from front to back*, of *bonding courses* in a wall, Vitr.2.8.7. II. in Music, διάτονον (sc. γένος), τό, *the diatonic scale*, opp. χρωματικόν, ἐναρμόνιον, Aristox.*Harm*.p.19 M., etc.; δ. μέλος Alciphr.1.18; δ. μελῳδία D.H.*Comp*.19.

διατοξ-εία, ἡ, *contest in archery*, *OGI*339.82 (Sestos). **-εύσιμος**, ον, *that can be shot across*, χώρα a place *within bowshot*, Plu.*Luc*. 28. **-εύω**, *shoot through*: metaph., δ. λόγον τινί *shoot* it *across* to him, Hld.5.32. II. Med., *contend with others in archery*, X. *Cyr*.1.4.4; τινί Parth.4.4.

διατόρ-ευμα, ατος, τό, *graven work*, Lxx 3*Ki*.7.17(30). **-εύω**, *engrave, chase*, S.*Fr*.315; δ. χρυσᾶς φιάλας στεφάνοις ἀμπέλου Aristeas 79; ὁ θεὸς ἐπίσταται τὰ ἑαυτοῦ δημιουργήματα δ. Ph.1.105; δ. ἐν σησάμῳ γράμμασιν ἔπη Plu.2.1083e:—Pass., Ael.*VH*14.7, Hierocl. p.37 A. **-έω**, *strike through, pierce*, Anon.ap.Suid. **-ία**, ἡ, *shrill, high-pitched music*, prob. in Thphr.*HP*4.11.4. **-νεύω**, *round off*, Lib.*Descr*.30.6. **-ος**, ον, (τείρω) *piercing*, πέδαι A.*Pr*. 76; δ. φόβος *thrilling* fear, ib.181 (lyr.); of sound, δ. Τυρσηνικὴ σάλπιγξ Id.*Eu*.567: neut. as Adv., διάτορον φθέγγεσθαι Plu.2.303e; ἀναβοᾶν Luc.*Gall*.1. II. Pass., *pierced, bored through*, ποδοῖν ἀκμαί S.*OT*1034.

διατρᾰγεῖν, v. διατρώγω.

διατρᾰγῳδέω, = τραγῳδέω, interpol. in D.18.22; also gloss on διακωμῳδέω, Hsch. (corrupt).

διάτρᾰμις, εως, ὁ, ἡ, = λισπόπυγος, Stratt.74.

διατρᾱνόω, *articulate clearly*, χρωματικὸν γένος Nicom.*Harm*.7; βρέφος διατετρανωμένον *Theol.Ar*.47: metaph., Iamb. *in Nic*.p.72 P.

διατρᾱνῶς, Adv. *clearly*, δ. [δρῶσι] Phld.*Lib*.p.58 O.

διατρᾰχηλίζομαι, *put one's neck under the yoke*, Telesp.10 H. II. *fall head over heels*, Plu.2.501e.

διατρᾱχύνω, *make quite rough*, Plu.2.979b (Pass.).

διατρεμέω, *to be very still*, Arr.*Peripl.M.Eux*.6.

διατρεπτικός, ή, όν, *dissuasive*, λόγος Plu.2.788f.

διατρέπω, fut. -τρέψω Plb.2.47.8:—*turn away, deter from* a thing, δ. τινὰ τοῦ μή.. Id.5.4.10; τινά τινος Plu.2.87f; τινὰ πρὸς τὸ μὴ ἀπολιπεῖν Arr.*Epict*.1.6.10:—Pass., fut. διατρᾰπήσομαι Epicur. (v. infr.), etc.: aor. διετράπην [ᾰ] D.25.95, etc.:—*turn aside from one's purpose*, Epicur.p.xxviii U.; *to be confounded* or *perplexed*, Hp.*Epid*.5.81, D. l. c., Plb.3.86.6, al.; ὑπὸ παντὸς δ. καὶ διαρρεῖν D.Chr.66.19: c. acc., *to be overawed by*, ὄχλον.., Epict.*Gnom*.65; *avoid, refuse to face*, τινάς Plu.2.532e, etc. II. *pervert*, Critias *Fr*.22 D. 2. *overthrow, do away with*, ὅρους S.E.*P*.2.212:—Pass., ib.194, al.

διατρέφω, fut. -θρέψω D.C.63.27:—*breed up, support*, dub. l. in Arar.16; τὸ τέκνιον ἡμᾶς -θρέψει D.C. l. c.; τινὰ ἀπό τινος X.*Mem*. 2.7.6; δ. σπουδαίως *keep* patient well *nourished*, Aët.16.36:—Pass., *to be sustained continually*, Th.4.39; *to be maintained*, *BGU*1024 vii 14 (iv A. D.), etc.

διατρέχω, aor. -έδρᾰμον Od.3.177, etc., also -έθρεξα Call.*Lav. Pall*.23, *AP*5.225 (Paul. Sil.):—*run across* or *over*, ἰχθυόεντα κέλευθα διέδραμον Od. l. c.; τίς δ' ἂν ἑκὼν τοσσόνδε διαδράμοι ἁλμυρὸν ὕδωρ; 5.100; ἀτρεμίζων καὶ μὴ διατρέχων Antipho 3.2.5; *pass through*, διὰ τῆς πόλεως *Sammelb*.3924.26 (i A. D.). 2. metaph., *run through*, τὸν βίον Pl.*Lg*.802a; τὰ ἡδέα X.*Mem*.2.1.31; δ. τὸν λόγον *get to the end of* it, Pl.*Phdr*.237a. II. abs., *run about*, δ. εἰς ἀγρὸν Ar.*Pax* 536, cf. Men.*Epit*.245; διατρέχοντες ἀστέρες Ar.*Pax*838; νεφέλαι διέδραμον Theoc.22.20: metaph., *run through, spread*, ἐν τῷ σώματι διέδραμε γαργαλισμός Hegesipp.Com.1.16; δ. σάλος ἁπάντων καὶ νεωτερισμός Plu.*Alex*.68; θροῦς δ. τῆς ἐκκλησίας Id.*Pyrrh*.13. 2. of Time, *pass away*, Hdn.2.6.3. 3. δ. εἰς... *come quite* to.., Hp.*Int*. 39; δ. μέχρι *penetrate* to.., Plu.*Pyrrh*.24; πρὸς τὴν οἰκονομίαν *PGiss*. 79 ii 4 (ii A. D.).

διατρέω, *run trembling about, flee all ways*, διέτρεσαν ἄλλυδις ἄλλος Il.11.486, cf. 17.729, Plu.*Marc*.29, *Bru*.18.

διά-τρημα, ατος, τό, *foramen* for spinal nerves, Gal.2.848. II. *dug-out, canoe*, Procop.*Aed*.6.1. **-τρησις**, εως, ἡ, *perforation*: *pore*, Hp.*Loc.Hom*.10, Gal.*UP*8.6. 2. *hole* in bone, ib.9. 5. **-τρητάριος**, ὁ, *maker of diatreta*, *Cod.Just*.10.66.1. **-τρητος**, ον, *bored through, pierced*, Gal.2.668. II. Lat. *diatreta, glass vessels with open-work decoration*, Mart.12.70.9.

διατρῐβή, ἡ, *wearing away*, esp. of Time, *way* or *manner of spending*, χρόνου τε διατριβὰς.. ἐφηῦρε.. πεσσοὺς κύβους τε *pastimes*, S. *Fr*.479.2: hence, abs., 1. *pastime, amusement*, Ar.*Pl*.923, Alex. 219.4, etc.; ἐν συνουσίᾳ τινὶ καὶ δ. D.21.71; γέλωτα καὶ δ. παρέχειν τινί Aeschin.1.175, cf. Plu.*Tim*.11; τοῦ συμποσίου δ. Alex.185; παρέσχε τοῖς κωμικοῖς δ. *materiem jocandi*, Plu.*Per*.4, cf. Jul.*Or*.2.52b; *place of amusement*, Men.481.10, Bato 2.4. 2. *serious occupation, study*, etc., τοὺς ἐν φιλοσοφίᾳ καὶ τῇ τοιᾷδε δ. τεθραμμένους Pl.*Tht*. 172c; διατριβὰς ποιεῖσθαι περί τι Lys.16.11, cf. Is.11.37; πρός τι Aeschin.2.38; ἐπί τινι Ar.*Ra*.1498; ἡ δ. τὰ πολλὰ ἐν λόγοις Pl.*Ly*. 204a. b. *discourse*, τὰς ἐμὰς δ. καὶ τοὺς λόγους Id.*Ap*.37d, cf. *Grg*. 484e, Isoc.12.19, etc.; αἱ πολιτικαὶ δ. D.H.10.15. c. *short ethical treatise* or *lecture*, δ. βραχέος διανοήματος ἠθικοῦ ἔκτασις Hermog. *Meth*.5, cf. Suid.: title of works by Zeno, Cleanthes, etc. d. *school* of philosophy, Ath.5.211d, al., Luc.*Alex*.5; Μωυσοῦ καὶ Χριστοῦ Gal. 8.579; Ἐπικούρου δ. Numen.ap.Eus.*PE*14.5; also, *a place of teaching, school*, ἡ ἐν τῷ κήπῳ δ. Epicur.*Fr*.217, cf. Phld.*Acad.Ind*.p.39 M., Luc.*Nigr*.25, Ath.8.350b. 3. *way of life, passing of time*, δ. ἐν ἀγορᾷ Ar.*Nu*.1055; δ. νέων ἐν δικαστηρίοις And.4.32; ἡ ἐν Σικελίᾳ δ. *stay* there, Pl.*Ep*.337e; ποιεῖσθαι ἐν τῷ ὑγρῷ τὴν δ., ἐν τῇ γῇ, Arist. *HA*487^{a}20, *Resp*.474^{b}26; διατριβὰς μετ' ἀλλήλων διατρίβειν Aeschin. 1.147. 4. *place of resort, haunt*, τὰς ἐν Λυκείῳ δ. Pl.*Euthphr*.2a; ᾗα ἐπὶ τὰς συνήθεις δ. Id.*Chrm*.153a. II. in bad sense, *waste of time, loss of time, delay*, with or without χρόνου, E.*Ph*.751, etc.; δ. ποιεῖσθαι Isoc.4.164: pl., δ. καὶ μελλήσεις Th.5.82; χρόνου δ. ἐμποιεῖν, παρέχειν, Id.3.38, X.*Oec*.8.13, etc.; ἐμβαλεῖν Plu.*Nic*.20; διατριβὴν ποτῷ ποιεῖν *prolong* a carouse, Alex.226.4. III. Rhet., *occasion for dwelling on a subject*, Arist.*Rh*.1418^{a}27 (pl.). IV. *continuance, permanence*, Id.*Mete*.374^{a}12. V. sens. obsc., = συνουσία, Procop. *Arc*.2.

διατρῐβικός, ή, όν, *scholastic, pedantic*, of persons, Plb.12.26^{d}.6; λόγοι ib.25^{k}.2; ῥητορική Phld.*Rh*.2.65 S.; οἱ δ. ib.1.32 S.

διατρίβω [ρῑ], pf. -τέτρῐφα Plb.4.57.3:—**Pass.**, aor. 2 διετρίβην [ῐ] (v. infr.):—*rub hard*, χερσὶ διατρίψας Il.11.847: more freq., *wear away, consume*, πάντα διατρίβουσιν Ἀχαιοί Od.2.265; χρήματα Thgn. 921; τὰ τῶν Πελοποννησίων Th.8.87; εἰς αἰτίας ἀλόγους δ. τὸ θεῖον *to fritter away* Providence into unreasoning causes, Plu.*Nic*.23:—Pass., κάκιστα διατριβῆναι *perish* utterly, Hdt.7.120 (v. l. ἐκ-), cf. Th. 8.78. II. *spend*, of Time, θερείην Hdt.1.189; freq. χρόνον δ. Lys. 3.11; παρά τινι Hdt.1.24, etc.; δ. τινὰς ἡμέρας X.*HG*6.5.49; ἔξ ἔτη Isoc.4.141 (later c. gen., ἐτῶν οὐκ ὀλίγων ἐν Ῥώμῃ δ. Hdn.3.10.2):—Pass., ἐνιαυτὸς διετρίβη Th.1.125. 2. abs. (without χρόνον), *waste time*, οὐ μὴ διατρίψεις..; *make* no more *delay*, Ar.*Ra*.462; δ. ἐν γυμνασίοις *pass all one's time* there, Id.*Nu*.1002; ἐν ἄστει Antipho 1.14; ἐν ἀγρῷ Philem.71.6; αὐτοῦ, ἔνδον, Pl.*Prt*.311a; δ. μετ' ἀλλήλων *go on talking*, Id.*Phd*.59d, etc.: hence, *busy, employ oneself*, ἐν ζητήσει Id. *Ap*.29c; ἐν φιλοσοφίᾳ Id.*Tht*.173c; ἐπί τινι Id.*Euthd*.305a, Isoc.3.19, D.2.16; ἀμφί τι X.*Eq*.2.1; περί τι Pl.*Phd*.90c, Isoc.1.4; πρὸς ἱππικῇ Pl.*Prm*.126c; πρὸς τοῖς ἔργοις Arist.*Pol*.1309^{a}8; πρὸς φιλοσοφίᾳ (prob. l. for -ίαν) Pl.*R*.540b: c. part., δ. μελετῶσαι X.*Cyr*.1.2.12. b. abs., *lose time, delay*, Il.19.150, Hp.*VC*19, Ar.*Eq*.515, etc.; λέγε καὶ μὴ διάτριβε Pl.*R*.472b; διατέτριφα I *have let the time slip by*.., Id. *Tht*.143a: c. part., καθ' ἕκαστα λέγων δ. *to waste time* in speaking, Isoc.3.35, cf. D.1.9. 3. *reside*, *PHal*.1.182 (iii B. C.), *PStrassb*. 22.6 (ii A. D.), etc. III. *put off by delay, thwart, hinder*, μή τι διατρίβειν ἐμὸν χόλον Il.4.42; οὔ τι διατρίβω μητρὸς γάμον Od.20.341; τἄριστον Ar.*Fr*.503: c. dupl. acc. pers. et rei, ὄφρα κεν ἥ γε διατρίβησιν Ἀχαιοὺς ὃν γάμον *put* them *off* in the matter of her wedding, Od. 2.204: c. gen. rei, μὴ δηθὰ διατρίβωμεν ὁδοῖο *let us* not *lose time* on the way, ib.404:—Med., μή τι διατριβώμεθα πείρης A.R.2.883.

διατρίζω, pf. -τέτρῑγα, *squeak, creak*, Agath.5.7: c. acc. cogn., φωνάς prob. in Plu.2.994e.

διάτριμμα, ατος, τό, *a sore from the skin being rubbed off* in riding, *Gloss*.

διατριπ-τέον, *one must spend time*, Arist.*Rh*.1417^{a}10, Men.*Rh*. p.359 S. II. *one must rub*, Hippiatr.1. **-τικός**, ή, όν, *fit for bruising*, μύρον Ar.*Lys*.943.

διατρῑταῖος, α, ον, = διάτριτος, in Lat. form, Cael.Aur.*CP*1.3.

διατρῑτάριος ἰατρός physician *who prescribes three days' fast*, Gal. 10.582.

διάτρῑτος, ον, *tertian*, opp. ἀμφημερινός, περίοδοι Ph.1.427: but more freq., II. δ. (sc. περίοδος), ἡ, *period of three days*, τὴν ἀπὸ ταύτης φυλακτέον δ. Herod.Med.ap.Orib.5.27.23; ἡ πρώτη δ. Thessal.ap.Gal.10.264; πρὸ τῆς πρώτης δ. S.E.*P*.2.237.

διάτριψις, εως, ἡ, *grinding*, Dsc.4.45; *trituration*, Sor.1.93.

διάτρῐχα, Adv. = τρίχα, *in three divisions, three ways*, usu. written divisim in Hom., as Il.2.655; as one word, *h.Cer*.86, A.R.2.997.

δια-τροπή, ἡ, *confusion, agitation*, *PTeb*.27.104 (ii B. C.), Plb.1.16. 4, al., Onos.42.2 (pl.); *fiasco, débâcle*, Cic.*Att*.9.13.7. 2. *disgust*, Metrod.*Herc*.831.7,19, cf. Phld.*Rh*.1.219 S.; δ. καὶ φόβος D.S.17. 41. 3. *pity, sympathy*, Anon.ap.Suid. 4. δ. τοῖς ἀδικοῦσι γίνεσθαι *divert* them *from* wrongdoing, J.*BJ*2.16.4. **-τρόπιος**, ον, dub. sens., χροία Paul.Aeg.5.19. **-τροπος**, ον, *various in dispositions*, τρόποις E.*IA*559 codd.

διατροφή, ἡ, *sustenance and support*, X.*Vect*.4.49, Men.14, *Epit*. 88, D.S.1.74, *BGU*321.7 (iii A. D.); τῷ τέρατι [the Minotaur] πρὸς διατροφὴν κατασκευάσαι λαβύρινθον D.S.4.77: pl., *means of subsistence*, 1*Ep.Ti*.6.8.

διατροχάδες, αἱ, title of a poetical form, Praxiph.ap.Hsch.

διατροχάζω, of a horse, *trot*, X.*Eq*.7.11; of a person, *ride to and fro*, App.*BC*4.125; also, *hasten*, ἐπί, ἐς.., ib.1.69, 5.105: abs., *bustle about*, Eun.*VS*p.463 B.

διατρύγιος [ῠ], ον, (τρύγη), διατρύγιος δὲ ἕκαστος [ὄρχος] ἤην each row *bore grapes in succession*, Od.24.342, cf. Eust. ad loc.

διατρῡπάω, *bore through, pierce*, Arist.*HA*528^{b}33:—Pass., Luc. *Sat*.24.

διατρῠφάω, strengthd. for τρυφάω, Pl.*Lg*.695c.

διατρῠφέν, v. sub διαθρύπτω.

διατρώγω, fut. -τρώξομαι Ar.*V*.164: aor. -έτρᾰγον ib.367:—*gnaw through*, τὸ δίκτυον ll.cc., cf. *Com.Adesp*.757; τὰς νευράς Arist. *Rh*.1401^{b}16; *keep munching*, Pl.Com.173.10:—Pass., Hp.*Mul*.1. 107. 2. c. gen. rei, *eat of*, Ael.*VH*1.10.

διαττ-άω, *sift, riddle*, Hp.*Ulc*.21, Pl.*Sph*.226b, al., *SIG*^{2}587.60, Ruf.ap.Orib.7.26.97:—Pass., Pl.*Cra*.402c, *IG*2^{2}.463.83, Thphr.

*HP*3.18.5. (The form διασσάω is given as etym. in *EM*271.37; διασσηθέντος dub. cj. in Emp.5.3; prop. δια-ττάω, cf. ἀλευρό-ττησις, ἐττημένα: hence pf. part. Pass. διεττημένης *IG*2².463.83 (but διηττ- codd. Thphr. l. c.).) **-ησις**, εως, ἡ, *sifting*, prob. in Plu.2.693e. **-ος**, ὁ, *sieve*, Hsch.

διάττω, v. διαΐσσω.

διατυγχάνω, *go wrong*, *make a mistake*, *PMasp.*76.15 (vi A. D.).

διατῠλίσσω, Att. **-ττω**, *unroll*, S.E.*M.*1.281.

διάτῠλος, ον, *callous*, of a fistula, Megesap.Orib.44.24.8.

διατῠπόω, *form*, χαρακτῆρας D.S.3.67; δ. νόμους *give* them *a lasting form*, Luc.*Jud.Voc.*5:—Pass., Lxx *Wi.*19.6, D.S.4.11, al., Sor.1.59; of seals, *to be engraved*, Arist.*Aud.*801^{b}5. 2. metaph., *imagine*, *conceive*, Act., Luc.*Alex.*4; δ. τῇ φαντασίᾳ Chor.p.213B., cf. Hdn.4.3.8; *represent*, *portray*, Plu.2.83a; χρώμασί τι Lib.*Eth.* 27.2. 3. *make dispositions*, of a testator, Just.*Nov.*1.2.2; of a legislator, ib.3*Praef.*:—Pass., ib.6.1.1; *to be arranged*, *regulated by agreement*, μεταξὺ τῶν Ἑλληνίδων πόλεων.. ὁπόσα χρὴ ἑκάστην.. λύειν *IG*7.24.4.

διατύπτομαι, = πληκτίζομαι, Sch.Ar.*Ec.*958.

διατύπ-ωσις [ῠ], εως, ἡ, *full and perfect shape*, Arist.*HA*551^{b}2; *configuration*, δ. ἀνδρείκελος Plu.*Alex.*72. 2. *system*, μηχανικῶν Hero *Mens.*23. 3. *vivid description*, Longin.20.1, Alex.*Fig.*3.25, etc. II. *regulation*, *apportionment*, *IG*12(9).907.9 (Chalcis, iv A. D.), 14.455 (Catana, v A. D.), *Ostr.Fay.*23 (iii A. D.), *PLips.*63.6 (iv A. D.); *disposition* made by a legislator, Just.*Nov.*117.13; by a testator, ib.1.1.2. **-ωτέον**, *one must represent*, λόγῳ ὁποῖος ἂν ὁ βίος γένοιτο D.H.*Rh.*2.6. **-ωτικός**, ή, όν, *descriptive*, *vivid*, Sch.A.R. 1.834. II. *formative*, *Theol.Ar.*34.

διατύφω [ῡ], pf. part. Pass. διατεθυμμένη *dazed*, Lib.*Or.*1.95 (nisi leg. -τεθρυμμένη).

διατωθάζω, *tease*, Alciphr.2.4.

διαυγ-άζω, *glance*, *shine through*, τῷ σχισμῷ *Placit.*3.3.3; ἕως οὗ ἡμέρα διαυγάσῃ 2*Ep.Pet.*1.19: impers., ἅμα τῷ διαυγάζειν (sc. τὴν ἡμέραν) Plb.3.104.5; *to be transparent*, Mnesith.ap.Orib.*inc.*15.11. II. = φωτίζω, Hsch.: and so metaph., διαυγασθεὶς *being enlightened, perceiving the truth*, J.*AJ*5.10.4. III. Astrol., *influence by its rays* (= ἐπιθεωρέω), *PLond.*1.130.70 (i A. D.). IV. Pass., *to be glazed*, of pottery, prob. in *BGU*1143.15 (i B. C.). **-ασμα**, ατος, τό, = sq., Aq.*Hb.*3.4. **-ασμός**, ὁ, *splendour bursting forth*, of lightning, *Placit.*3.3.1. **-εια**, ἡ, = foreg., Philostr.*Im.*2.1, Them. *Or.*13.175a, etc. 2. *translucency*, Plu.2.914b, Hierocl.*CA*26 p.480M.: metaph. of sayings, *clarity*, Plu.2.408e. II. *hole to admit light*, D.S.17.82; *peephole*, Procl.*Hyp.*3.25. **-έω**, *dawn*, ἡμέρας -ούσης Plu.*Arat.*22, D.H.5.49. II. ἧττον δ. *to be less obvious*, of a tumour, Antyll.ap.Orib.46.27.4. III. Pass., *to be transparent*, Gal.7.88, Hsch. **-ής**, ές, *translucent*, of water, Arist. *Mir.*840^{b}34, *AP*9.227 (Bianor), 277 (Antiphil.): Sup., v.l. in Arist. *Mu.*397^{a}16; τὰ ὑγρὰ τῶν ὀφθαλμῶν -έστατα Alex.Aphr.*Pr.*1.68, cf. Ecphant.ap.Stob.4.7.64; *radiant*, of metal, Call.*Lav.Pall.*21; of stars, A.R.2.1104; of gems, ἀμέθυστος *AP*5.204; ὀφθαλμοί Aristaenet.1.1. **-ίζω**, = -άζω, Aq.*Jb.*25.5. **-ιον**, τό, *vent*, Hero*Spir.*1.18, al.; *peephole*, Procl.*Hyp.*3.16.

διαυθεντέω, *to be certainly informed*, S.E.*M.*7.425.

διαυλ-έω, *accompany with a* διαύλιον, μάθησιν *BGU*1125.20 (i B. C.). **-ία**, ἡ, *duet on the flute*, Hsch., *EM*269.30. **-ίζω**· βαθύνω ἢ μηκύνω, Suid.:—Pass., διηυλίσθη· διεφθάρη, Hsch. **-ικός**, ή, όν, *of the* δίαυλος, τρόπος Iamb.*inNic.*p.89P. **-ιον**, τό, (αὐλός) *an air on the flute in the interval of the choral song*, Sch.Ar.*Ra.*1282, Hsch.: -ειον, Suid.

δῐαυλοδρομ-έω, *to run the* δίαυλος, Sch.Ar.*Av.*293; *return to the starting-point*, Arist.*GA*741^{b}21; of the moon, Ph.1.24; of evils, *recur*, Id.2.350. **-ης**, ου, ὁ, *runner in the* δίαυλος, Pi.*P.*10.9. **-ία**, ἡ, *running forwards and backwards*, Lyd.*Mens.*1.12. **-ος**, *running the* δίαυλος, *IG*7.1772 (Thespiae), *Liv.Ann.*3.146 (Thessaly): written -αδρόμος *CIG*2758 (Aphrodisias): metaph. of the cock, διὰ γὰρ τῆς αὐλῆς τρέχει interpol. in Artem.4.22.

δίαυλος [ῐ], ὁ, *double pipe* or *channel*: usu. in the race, *double course*, Pi.*O.*13.37, E.*El.*825, *IG*2².957, al.; compared with *recurrent* nerves, Gal.*UP*7.14. b. δ. ἵππιος, Hp.*Vict.*2.63. 2. metaph., κάμψαι διαύλου θάτερον κῶλον πάλιν to run the *homeward course*, retrace one's steps, A.*Ag.*344; δίαυλοι κυμάτων *ebb and flow*, *rise and fall* of the waves, E.*Hec.*29; εἰς αὐγὰς πάλιν ἁλίου δισσοὺς ἂν ἔβαν διαύλους they would twice *return*, Id.*HF*662 (lyr.), cf. 1102; τὸν ὕστατον τρέχων δ. τοῦ βίου Alex.235; ἐκπεριτρέχειν διαύλους to run *to and fro*, Aristaenet.1.27; of a wife's *return* to her husband, Anaxandr.56.4. II. *strait*, E.*Tr.*435. 2. in pl., of *air-passages*, Opp.*C.* 2.181.

διαυλων-ία, ἡ, (αὐλών) *narrow passage*, Eust.1917.32. **-ίζω**, *pass through a narrow channel*, Arist.*Resp.*478^{b}12, *Mete.*366^{a}27. 2. *admit a thorough draught*, Ath.5.189c. **-ισμός**, οῦ, ὁ, *passage of wind through a narrow opening*, Eust.1107.63.

διαυξάνω, *spread out*, Aët.7.1.

δίαυρος· δαλὸς διάπυρος, Hsch.

διαυχενίζομαι, *hold the neck erect*, Eun.*Hist.*pp.263,272 D.

διαυχένιος, ον, *running through the neck*, μυελός Pl.*Ti.*74a.

διαύχην· εὐεξίαν, Hsch.

διαύω, f. l. for ἰαύω, E.*HF*1049 (lyr.).

διαφᾰγεῖν, aor. 2 inf. of διεσθίω, *eat through*, Hdt.3.109, Hp.*Mul.* 1.2.

διαφάδην, Dor. **-άδαν** [φᾰ], Adv. *openly*, ὀνειδίσαι Sol.ap.Arist. *Ath.*12.5, cf. Alcm.23.56.

διαφαίκωσι· διαφαίνειν, Hsch.

διαφαίνω, *show through*, *let* a thing *be seen through*, τὴν λευκότητα δ. Arist.*GA*735^{b}20; Ἀὼς καλὸν διέφαινε πρόσωπον Theoc.18.26; δ. τὰς ἑαυτῶν φύσεις Plb.12.24.1. 2. *allow light to pass*, Hero*Aut.* 27.1. 3. *convey* (to the reader), κατασκευήν Phld.*Po.*2.35. II. Pass., *show through*, νεκύων δ. χῶρος *showed clear* of dead bodies, Il. 8.491; *to be seen through* a transparent substance, Hdt.3.24; μέλαν τὸ μὴ διαφαινόμενον *impervious to light*, Arist.*GA*780^{a}34, cf. *Pr.*936^{a}8; λίθος διαφαινόμενος *transparent* stone, Agatharch.82. 2. *to glow*, *to be red-hot*, μοχλὸς διεφαίνετο αἰνῶς Od.9.379. 3. metaph., *to be proved*, *show itself*, ἐν πείρᾳ τέλος -εται Pi.*N.*3.71, cf. Th.2.51; *to be conspicuous*, δυνάμει ταῦτα μέγιστα διεφάνη Id.1.18; *stand out*, *excel*, πάνθ' ἁπλῶς ἃ διαφαίνεται prob. in Phld.*Po.*5.4. III. intr., *show light through*, *to be transparent*, ἱμάτια -οντα Philem.81; *dawn*, ἡμέρης -ούσης Hdt.7.219, cf. 8.83: metaph., *shine through*, τὸ μεγαλοπρεπὲς διὰ τοῦ προσώπου διαφαίνει X.*Mem.*3.10.5. 2. πυρὰ διέφᾱνε (Dor. aor. 1) the pyre *parted its flames*, so as to allow a passage, Pi.*P.*3.44 (v. l. -φαινε).

διαφαιρέω, *take quite away*: aor. Med. διαφειλόμην v. l. in Paul. Aeg.6.35, prob. l. in Lxx 1*Ki.*17.39.

διαφάν-εια [φᾰ], ἡ, *transparency*, Pl.*Phd.*110d. **-ής**, ές, (φαίνω) *translucent*, *transparent*, [ὕαλος] Ar.*Nu.*767; οὖρα Hp.*Aph.* 4.72, *Epid.*1.26.β'; ὦτα Id.*Coac.*188; ὑδάτια Pl.*Phdr.*229b; χιτώνια Ar.*Lys.*48; χιτωνάριον Men.727, cf. *IG*5(1).1390.16,21; τὸ δ. Arist. *deAn.*418^{b}4, al. 2. *red-hot*, Hdt.2.9, 4.73,75, Hp.*Art.*11. II. metaph., *manifest*, τάδ' ἤδη διαφανῆ S.*OT*754; *distinct*, *distinctly seen*, φλέβες Hp.*Epid.*6.3.17; εἶδος δ. Pl.*R.*544c, 548c (Sup.). Adv. -νῶς Th.2.65, X.*An.*6.1.24: Sup. -έστατα D.C.37.46. 2. *conspicuous*, ἐν τοῖς ἄλλοις Pl.*R.*600b; εἰς ἅπαντας ἀνθρώπους ἀρετῇ Id. *Ti.*25b. III. Subst. δ., τό, *talc*, Gal.13.663, Orib.*Fr.*99.

διαφαρμᾰκεύω, *give medicine to*, τινάς v. l. in Plu.2.157c.

διάφαρος χιτών *made in two pieces*, *EM*175.39.

διάφᾰσις, εως, ἡ, (διαφαίνω) *view through*, opp. ἔμφασις, Thphr. *Lap.*30: metaph., ἐκφάσεις καὶ δ. τῆς ἀληθείας Plu.2.354b, cf. Cic. *Att.*2.3.2.

διᾰφάσσειν· διασιλλαίνειν, Hsch.

διαφαυλίζω, *hold cheap*, *depreciate*, Pl.*Lg.*804b, Hierocl.p.59A., Lib.*Decl.*50.48.

διά-φαυμα, ατος, τό, *daybreak*, *PLond.*5.1684.4 (vi A. D.). **-φαυσις**, εως, ἡ, *shining through*, Plu.2.929b.

διαφαύσκω, Ion. (and later Prose, D.H.9.63) **-φώσκω**, aor. -έφαυσα Lxx *Ge.*44.3, al.:—*show light through*, *dawn*, ἅμ' ἡμέρῃ διαφωσκούσῃ as soon as day *began to dawn*, Hdt.3.86, 9.45; ἄρτι διαφαύσκοντος (abs.) Plb.31.14.13.

διαφεγγής, ές, *pellucid*: Adv. Comp., ὑέλου -έστερον ἀπαστράπτειν Luc.*Am.*26.

διαφερόντως, Adv. pres. part. Act. of διαφέρω, *differently from*, δ. ἢ.., Lys.31.20, Pl.*R.*538b, *Phd.*85b. 2. c. gen., δ. τῶν ἄλλων *above* all others, Id.*Cri.*52b; πάντων δ. προθυμότατος Th.8.68. II. abs., *differently*, *in different ways* or *degrees*, Arist.*EN*1098^{a}29, *Pol.* 1260^{a}11, Hierocl.*inCA*7p.430M. 2. *especially*, *pre-eminently*, Th.1.38, etc.; δ. ἧττον πολὺ Pl.*Lg.*862d.

διαφέρω, fut. διοίσω S.*OT*321, διοίσομαι *h.Merc.*255, etc.: aor. 1 διήνεγκα, Ion. διήνεικα: aor. 2 διήνεγκον:—*carry over* or *across*, δ. ναῦς τὸν Ἰσθμόν Th.8.8; *carry from one to another*, διαφέρεις κηρύγματα E.*Supp.*382; [τὸ ἤλεκτρον] διαφέρεται εἰς τοὺς Ἕλληνας Arist. *Mir.*836^{b}6: metaph., γλῶσσαν διοίσει *will put* the tongue *in motion*, will speak, S.*Tr.*323 codd. 2. of Time, δ. τὸν αἰῶνα, τὸν βίον, *go through* life, Hdt.3.40, E.*Hel.*[10]; νύκτα Id.*Rh.*600: abs., ἅπαις διοίσει ib.982:—Med., *live*, *continue*, ὑγιηροὶ τἆλλα διαφέρονται Hp. *Art.*56; σοῦ διοίσεται μόνος *will pass his life* apart from thee, S.*Aj.* 511; σκοπούμενος διοίσει X.*Mem.*2.1.24 (cj. Dind. for διέσῃ). 3. *bear through*, *bear to the end*, σκῆπτρα E.*IA*1195; γαστρὸς ὄγκον δ., of a woman, Id.*Ion*15, cf. X.*Mem.*2.2.5: hence, 4. *bear to the end*, *go through with*, πόλεμον Hdt.1.25, Th.1.11; but also, *bear the burden of* war, Id.6.54; *endure*, *support*, with an Adv., ῥᾷστα γὰρ τὸ σόν τε σὺ κἀγὼ διοίσω τοὐμόν S.*OT*321; δ. πότμον δάκρυσι E.*Hipp.*1143 (lyr.): abs., of patients in disease, δ. ἕως τῶν εἰκοσιτεσσάρων ἡμερέων Hp.*Int.*40; δ. φθειρόμενος ib.12 (also ἡ νοῦσος δ. ἐννέα ἔτεα ibid.). II. *carry different ways*, Ar.*Lys.*570, etc.; δ. ἕκαστα εἰς τὰς χώρας τὰς προσηκούσας X.*Oec.*9.8; *toss about*, ὅπλισμα.. διαφέρων ἐσφενδόνα E.*Supp.*715; δ. τὰς κόρας *to turn* the eyes *about*, Id.*Ba.*1087, *Or.* 1261 (lyr.):—Pass., *to be drawn apart*, *disrupted*, opp. συμφέρεσθαι, Heraclit.10, Pl.*Sph.*242e, Epicur.*Nat.*908.2; *to be tossed about*, dub. in Str.3.2.5; δ. ἐν τῷ Ἀδρίᾳ *Act.Ap.*27.27, cf. Plu.*Galb.*26. 2. δ. τινὰ *spread* his *fame abroad*, Pi.*P.*11.60; εἰς ἅπαντας τὴν ἐκείνου μνήμην δ. D.61.46:—Pass., φήμη διηνέχθη Plu.2.163c. 3. *tear asunder*, E.*Ba.*754; *disjoin*, Arist.*Po.*1451^{a}34 (Pass.): metaph., *distract*, τὰς ψυχὰς φροντίσιν Plu.2.133d, cf. 97f (Pass.), D.Chr.32.46 (Pass.). 4. δ. τὴν ψῆφον *give* one's vote *a different way*, i. e. against another, Hdt.4.138, etc.; but also, *give each man* his vote, E.*Or.*49, Th.4.74, X.*Smp.*5.8. 5. ἐράνους δ., = διαλύεσθαι, *pay* them *up*, *discharge* them, Lycurg.22. 6. *defer*, *reserve* for judgement, τὸν αἴτιον A.*Ch.*68 (lyr., διασπαράσσει Sch.). 7. *plunder*, Herod.7.90:—Pass., τῶν ἀπὸ [τῆς οἰκίας] φορτίων διενηνεγμένων *PLond.*1.45.9 (ii B. C.). 8. *excel*, ἀρετῇ τοὺς ἄλλους D.S.11.67, cf. 2.5; καλλιτεκνίᾳ πάσας γυναῖκας *Stud.Pont.*3.123 (Amasia). III.

intr., *differ*, φυᾷ δ. Pi.*N*.7.54 ; ἆρ' οἱ τεκόντες διαφέρουσιν ἢ τροφαί; is it one's parents or nurture *that make the difference?* E.*Hec*.599: c. gen., *to be different from*, Id.*Or*.251, Th.5.86, etc.; οὐδὲν διοίσεις Χαιρεφῶντος τὴν φύσιν Ar.*Nu*.503, cf. Pl.*Prt*.329d ; τὸ δ'..ἀφανίζειν ἱερὰ ἔσθ' ὅτι τοῦ κόπτειν διαφέρει; D.21.147 ; δ. τὰς μορφὰς Arist.*HA* 497ᵇ15 ; δ. εἴς τι, ἔν τινι, X.*Hier*.1.2,7 ; παρὰ τὴν Βεβρυκίαν App.*Mith*. 1 ; καθ' ὑπεροχὴν καὶ ἔλλειψιν Arist.*HA*486ᵃ22 ; κατὰ τὴν θέσιν Id. *Mete*.341ᵇ24 ; πρός τι Id.*HA*505ᵃ21 ; τίνι δ. τὰ ἄρρενα τῶν θηλειῶν.. θεωρείσθω Id.*PA*684ᵇ3 : c. inf., μόνῃ τῇ μορφῇ μὴ οὐχὶ πρόβατα εἶναι δ. Luc.*Alex*.15: with Art., τρεῖς μόναι ψῆφοι διήνεγκαν τὸ μὴ θανάτου τιμῆσαι three votes *made the difference* (i.e. majority) against capital punishment, D.23.167 ; also διαφέρει τὸ ἥμισυ τοῦ ἔργου *makes a difference* equal to half the effort expended, X.*Oec*.20.17. 2. impers., διαφέρει *it makes a difference*, πλεῖστον δ. Hp.*Aph*.5.22 ; βραχὺ δ. τοῖς θανοῦσιν εἰ.. E.*Tr*.1248, etc.; οὐδὲν δ. *it makes* no *odds*, Pl.*Phd*.89c, cf. Men.*Epit*.193 ; σμικρὸν οἴει διαφέρειν; Pl.*R*. 467c: c. dat. pers., δ. μοι *it makes a difference* to me, Antipho 5.13, Pl.*Prt*.316b, etc.; ἰδίᾳ τι αὐτῷ δ. he *has* some private *interest at stake*, Th.3.42 ; εἰ ὑμῖν μή τι δ. if you *see* no *objection*, Pl.*La*.187d ; τί δέ σοι τοῦτο δ. εἴτε.. εἴτε μή; Id.*R*.349a, cf. *Grg*.497b, etc.: c. inf., οὐδέ τί οἱ διέφερεν ἀποθανεῖν Hdt.1.85 : with personal constr., πράγματά τινι διαφέροντα Plu.*Caes*.65 ; *to be of importance*, πρός or εἴς τι, Gal.15.420,428 ; τῷ ζῴῳ Id.*UP*9.5. 3. τὸ δ. *the difference, the odds*, Pl.*Phlb*.45d ;=τὸ συμφέρον Antiph.31 ; περὶ μεγίστων δὴ τῶν -όντων βουλεύεσθαι Th.6.92, cf. Lys.31.5, Is.4.12 ; τὰ ἀναγκαιότερα τῷ ταμιείῳ δ. vital *interests*, *PThead*.15.17 (iii A.D.) ; τὸ δ. μέρος τῶν ἀποφάσεων the *essential* part, *POxy*.1204.11 (iii A.D.) ; τὰ δ. *vital* matters, *Ep.Rom*.2.18 ; ἐπιστάμενος τὰ δ. παραβαίνειν τολμᾷ And. 3.19 (but τὰ δ. also simply, *points of difference*, in character and the like, Th.1.70, etc.). 4. *to be different from* a person: generally, *in point of excess, surpass, excel* him (cf. supr. II.8), τινός v.l. for -όντως in Th.3.39 ; τινί *in* a thing, Id.2.39, Alex.36.6 ; ἔν τινι Isoc.3. 39 ; εἴς τι Pl.*Ap*.35b ; κατὰ μέγεθος X.*Lac*.1.10 ; πρός τι Aeschin.1. 181 : c. inf., δ. τινὸς μεταβιβάζειν τινά Pl.*Grg*.517b : sts. folld. by ἤ, πολὺ διέφερεν ἀλέξασθαι ἤ.. *it was* far *better*..than.., X.*An*.3.4.33, cf. *Mem*.3.11.14, *Vect*.4.25 (where it means *to differ in point of diminution*) ; also δ. μέγα τι παρὰ τὰς ἄλλας πόλεις Plb.10.27.5 : abs., *excel*, ἐπί τινι Isoc.10.12 ; τάχει Jul.*Or*.2.53c ; οἱ τόποι διαφέρουσι Thphr.*CP*5.14.9 ; διαφέρον τι πεπραχέναι *a remarkable achievement*, Plb.6.39.2. 5. *prevail*, ἐπὶ πολὺ διήνεγκε Th.3.83. 6. *quarrel, struggle*, Telecl.20 ; οἱ διαφέροντες *the parties, litigants*, *PPar*.69ᴮ 10 (iii A.D.). 7. *come between, intervene*, ὁ διαφέρων χρόνος Antipho 5.94. 8. *belong to*, τινί, as property, Ph.1.207, *PLond*. 3.940.23 (iii A.D.) ; of persons, *belong to* a household, *PStrassb*.26.5 (iv A.D.) ; οἱ -φέροντες *kinsfolk*, *Annuario* 4/5.476 (Bargylia); *appertain to*, τῇ ὠνῇ *BGU*1062.21 (iii A.D.) ; τὰ εἰς τοῦτο -φέροντα πράγματα Mitteis *Chr*.372 v 3 (ii A.D.). IV. Med. and Pass., *be at variance, quarrel*, τινί Heraclit.72, cf. Amphis 32, etc.; περί τινος Hdt.1.173, Pl.*Euthphr*.7b ; δ. ἀλλήλοις *differ with*, ibid., cf. Antipho 5.42 ; τινὶ περί τινος Th.5.31, cf. X.*Oec*.17.4 ; πρὸς ἀλλήλους Lys.18. 17, cf. Hyp.*Oxy*.1607*Fr*.1 iii 60, etc.; τὰ πρὸς ἀλλήλους *Supp.Epigr*. 1.363.5 (Samos, iii B.C.) ; ἀμφί τινος X.*An*.4.5.17 ; διενεχθέντας γνώμῃ Hdt.7.220 ; δ. ὡς.. *maintain on the contrary* that.., D.56.46 ; οὐ διαφέρομαι, = οὔ μοι διαφέρει, Id.9.8 ; μηδὲν διὰ τοῦτο διαφέρου *let there be* no *dispute* on this ground, Lys.10.17 ; οἱ -φερόμενοι *the litigants*, *SIG*685.29 (Crete, ii B.C.).—Not in Ep.

διάφεσις, εως, ἡ, *IG*2².1036.4 (dub. sens.).

δια-φεύγω, fut. -φεύξομαι Pl.*Prm*.135d :—*get away from, escape*, τινά or τι, Hdt.1.204, 3.19, Antipho 5.90, etc.; θάνατον Pl.*Ap*.39a ; κίνδυνον Isoc.2.6 ; *survive*, [νόσημα] Arist.*HA*603ᵇ11 ; γάμον Men. *Georg*.21 : abs., Democr.239, Hdt.1.10, etc.; μὴ.. ἀθῷος διαφύγῃ *PTeb*.44.28 (ii B.C.) ; ἐκ τῆς Μήλου Th.8.39 ; δ. ἐκ πόνων εἰς ἀγαθά Pl.*Lg*.815e ; διαφεύγει δ' οὐδὲ νῦν but *it is* not even now *too late*, D.10. 31 :—Pass., διεφεύχθη ὁ κίνδυνος J.*AJ*18.8.9. 2. *escape one's notice* or *memory*, Pl.*Phd*.95e, *Men*.96e ; σὲ διαφεύξεται ἡ ἀλήθεια Id.*Prm*. 135d ; δ. τὰ πολλὰ τῶν νοσημάτων αὐτούς Jul.*Or*.7.228a ; πολλά με διαπέφευγε Isoc.4.187. -**φευκτέον**, *one must avoid*, Gal.13. 27. -**φευκτικός**, ή, όν, *able to escape*, Luc.*Tim*.29. -**φευξις**, εως, ἡ, *escaping, means of escape*, Th.3.23, J.*AJ*17.10.7, Plu.*TG*5 (v.l. -φυξις), D.C.40.32 ; *avoidance*, Phld.*Rh*.1.192 S.

διαφημέω, *bring discredit on*, τὴν εὐγένειαν dub. in Plu.*Nob*.19.

διαφημίζω, *make known, spread abroad*, D.H.11.46, *Ev.Marc*.1. 45 ; ὡς.. Palaeph.13 :—Pass., c. inf., διεφημίσθη θνήσκειν ὁ βασιλεύς J.*BJ*1.33.3 : abs., *to be celebrated*, ἐπὶ ταῖς καλοκἀγαθίαις Vett.Val. 250.5 :—Med., aor. 1 διεφημίξαντο D.P.26. II. *call, name*, Arat. 221 :—Med., Id.442 (v.l.), D.P.50.

διαφθαρτικός, ή, όν, *destructive, fatal*, Arist.*Pr*.865ᵃ8, Poll.5.132.

διαφθέγγομαι, *utter, speak*, Porph.*Chr*.63, al.

διαφθείρω, fut. -φθερῶ S.*OT*438, etc., Ep. -φθέρσω Il.13.625 : pf. διέφθαρκα E.*Med*.226, Pl.*Ap*.30d, etc.; also διέφθορα (v. infr. III) :—**Pass.**, fut. διαφθᾰρήσομαι Th.4.37 ; Ion. διαφθερέομαι Hdt.8.108, 9.42 : 3 pl. plpf. διεφθάρατο Id.8.90 :—*destroy utterly*, πόλιν Il.13.625 ; ἔργα διαφθείρεσκε Hdt.1.36 ; *make away with, kill*, τινά Id.9.88, etc.; *destroy, ruin*, ἥδ' ἡμέρα φύσει σε καὶ διαφθερεῖ S. l. c. ; τὴν τύχην Id. *Ph*.1069 ; δ. χεῖρα *weaken, slacken* one's hand, E.*Med*.1055 ; *spoil, break*, ὑγιῆ λίθον *IG*7.3073.33 (Lebad., ii B.C.) ; τὰ θυρώματα διεφθάρθαι *IG*2².1046.11 ; δ. τὴν συνουσίαν *break up* the party, Pl.*Prt*. 338d. 2. in moral sense, *corrupt, ruin*, γνώμην A.*Ag*.932 ; δ. τοὺς νέους, τοὺς νεωτέρους, Pl.*Ap*.30b, 25a ; νεανίσκον συνὼν δ. Eup. 337 ; esp. *corrupt by bribes*, Hdt.5.51 ; ἀργυρίῳ δ. τινά Lys.28.9 ; διαφθειρομένων ἐπὶ χρήμασι D.18.45 ; δ. γυναῖκα *seduce* a woman, Lys.1.16, etc., cf. E.*Ba*.318 (Pass.) ; δ. τοὺς νόμους *falsify, counterfeit* them, Isoc.18.11 ; γραμματεῖον Id.17.33 (Pass., ib.24) ; τὰ ϝεϝαδηκότα *IG*9(1).334.37 (Locr., v B.C.). 3. οὐδὲν διαφθείρας τοῦ χρώματος *having changed* nothing of his colour, Pl.*Phd*.117b. 4. of a woman, *to lose by miscarriage* or *premature birth*, ἔμβρυα, βρέφος, Hp.*Aph*.5.53, Plu.2.242c : abs., *miscarry*, Hp.*Epid*.7.73, Is.8. 36 :—Pass., τῶν διαφθαρεισῶν τὰ ἔμβρυα Hp.*Mul*.1.72. 5. *lose, forget*, E.*Hipp*.389. 6. = διάγω, dub. in Id.*Fr*.280. II. Pass., *to be destroyed*, δ. ἐπὶ τοῖς ἱματίοις *to be murdered* for the clothes he wore, Antipho 2.2.5 ; of animals, freq. in Pap., *POxy*.74.14 (ii A.D.), etc.; esp. *to be crippled, disabled*, Hdt.1.34 ; of ships, ib.166, And.1. 142 ; *to be spoilt*, γάλα *BGU*1109.11 (i B.C.), cf. Th.7.84 ; *to be corrupted*, αἷμα Gal.15.297, al. ; τὴν ἀκοὴν διεφθαρμένος *deaf*, Hdt.1.38 ; τὰ σκέλεα διεφθάρησαν *had their* legs *broken*, Id.8.28 ; διέφθαρμαι δέμας τὸ πᾶν S.*Tr*.1056 ; τὰ ὄμματα δ. *blinded*, Pl.*R*.517a ; σὰς φρένας E.*Hel*.1192 ; τὸ φρενῶν διαφθαρέν, = φρενοβλάβεια, Id.*Or*.297, cf. X.*Cyr*.4.1.8 : abs., *decomposed*, of a corpse, Pl.*R*. 614b. III. pf. διέφθορα intr., *to have lost one's wits*, διέφθορας Il. 15.128 ; also in Hp., διεφθορὸς αἷμα *corrupted* blood, *Mul*.2.134 ; freq. in later Prose, γάλα δ. ἤδη J.*AJ*5.5.4 ; τὰ δ. σώματα Plu.2.87c, cf. 128e, Luc.*Sol*.3, etc. ; but, 2. in Trag. and Com. always trans. (cf. Ammon.42, Moer.127), τὰς.. ἐλπίδας διέφθορεν S.*El*.306 ; τὰς φρένας διέφθορε.. μοναρχία E.*Hipp*.1014 ; τὸν λόγον δ. Cratin. 292, cf. Eup. l. c., Pherecr.145.15, Ar.*Fr*.490, Men.3. IV. aor. διέφθειρα intr., *became corrupt*, Lxx *Jd*.2.19.

διαφθίνω, pf. part. διεφθῑνηκώς *wasted away*, Sch.Theoc.10.18.

διαφθονέω, *envy*, τινί Lxx *Es*.6.3 (v.l.) :—Pass., *to be grudged, deprived of* one's good fortune, J.*AJ*2.6.7 ; *to be envied*, Agath.1. 16.

διαφθορ-ά, Ion. -ρή, ἡ, (διαφθείρω) *destruction, ruin*, ἐπὶ -φθορᾷ τῆς πόλεως Th.8.86 ; ἀπέστειλε ἐπὶ διαφθορῇ Hdt.4.164 ; μέχρι διαφθορᾶς Pl.*Mx*.242d : pl., S.*OT*573, etc. 2. *destruction, blight*, of things, ὀμμάτων διαφθοραί Id.*OC*552 ; διαφθορὰ μορφῆς A.*Pr*.643. 3. in moral sense, *corruption, seduction*, νέων X.*Ap*.19 ; κριτῶν Arist. *Rh*.1372ᵃ34 (pl.). 4. *miscarriage, abortion*, Hp.*Mul*.1.3, *Coac*. 505, *Mélanges Holleaux* 265 (ii/i B.C.). 5. stomachic *disorder*, Aret.*CA*1.5. II. concrete, ἰχθύσιν δ. *a prey* for fishes, of a corpse, S.*Aj*.1297 ; πολεμίοις ὕβρισμα καὶ δ. E.*HF*459. -**εύς**, έως, ὁ, *corrupter*, νόμων, ἀνθρώπων, Pl.*Cri*.53c ; τῶν νέων Them.*Or*.23.296b : as fem., E.*Hipp*.682. -**έω**, = διαφθείρω, dub. in Procop.*Aed*.6.5.

διαφίημι, aor. διαφῆκα X. and Plb. (v. infr.) : inf. διαφεῖναι D.23. 171 : fut. διαφήσουσι is f.l. in Th.7.32 :—*dismiss, disband*, τὸ στράτευμα ἐκ τῆς χώρας X.*HG*3.2.24 ; τὴν δύναμιν D. l. c. ; an assembly, Plb.3.63.14, al.

διαφῐλο-νῑκέω, *dispute earnestly*, Arist.*SE*165ᵇ13, Plu.*Alex*.29, D.L.3.34. -**τεκνέω**, *persist in philoprogenitiveness*, Phld.*Sto*.339. 9. -**τῑμέομαι**, *strive emulously* or *earnestly*, Thphr.*HP*4.4.1 ; τινὶ ὑπέρ τινος Plu.*Arist*.16.

διαφλέγω, *burn up*, Lxx *Ps*.82(83).15 :—Pass., Plu.*Alc*.39 : metaph., *inflame*, τὰς ψυχάς Id.*Mar*.16 ; οἱ διαφλέξαντες Ἀχιλλέα θυμοί Heraclit.*All*.20.

διάφλοισβοι· τεταραγμένοι, Hsch.

διαφλύω, in Pass., *to be permeated*, ὑπὸ θερμοῦ Hp.*Mul*.1.77.

δια-φλύζω and -**φλύω**, *to be in exuberant health* :—also Subst. -**φλυξις**, εως, ἡ, = ὑπέρβλυσις, Gal.19.92.

διάφοβος, ον, *timorous*, Tz. ad Lyc.1242.

διαφοιβάζω, *drive mad*, διαπεφοιβάσθαι κακοῖς S.*Aj*.332.

διαφοιγοιμόρ· ἐπὶ πάσῃ ἡμέρᾳ τῆς τῶν φιδιτίων σιτήσεως (Lacon.), Hsch.

διαφοινίσσομαι, *become quite red*, Hp.*Coac*.458.

διαφοιτάω, Aeol. part. ζαφοίταισ' Sapph.*Supp*.25.15 :—*wander, roam*, l.c., Hdt.1.60 ; *go backwards and forwards*, ib.186 ; of hounds on the scent, X.*Cyn*.3.3 ; δ. διὰ τῆς χώρας Ar.*Av*.557 ; ἀν' ἐρῆμον δρίος prob. in *Lyr.Alex.Adesp*.7.2 ; δ. τῆς Ἰταλίας Plu.*Caes*.33 : c. acc., διαφοιτῶντες [τὸ ζεῦγμα] Philostr.*Im*.2.17 ; οἰμωγὴ δ. τὸν στρατόν Id.*Her*.19.12 ; of a report, *spread*, εἰς Ῥώμην Plu.*Fab*.8, cf. Luc.*Alex*.7, Hdn.1.4.8, etc. II. *permeate*, ψυχὴ διαπεφοιτηκυῖα (sc. σώματος) Plot.1.1.4, cf. M.Ant.8.54 ; [δημιουργὸς] τῆς ὅλης [τῆς ὕλης] διαπεφοιτηκώς Gal.4.561.

διαφορ-ά, ἡ, (διαφέρω) *moving hither and thither*, πεσσῶν διαφοραί *moves*, E.*Fr*.360.9. 2. *dislocation*, τοῦ ὤμου Heliod.ap.Orib.49. 8.4, 49.9 tit. II. *difference*, Th.3.10 (pl.), etc.; περί τι D.H. *Comp*.15 ; θεοῦ πρὸς ἄνθρωπον Plu.2.1075c ; διαφορὰν ἔχειν to *differ*, Men.426. 2. in Logic, *the differentia* of a species, ἐκ τοῦ γένους καὶ τῶν διαφορῶν τὰ εἴδη Arist.*Metaph*.1057ᵇ7, cf. *Top*.139ᵃ29 : hence in pl. of *species* or *kinds*, Id.*Pol*.1285ᵃ1, 1289ᵃ20, Thphr. *HP*6.4.5 ; εἴδη καὶ δ. Plu.2.719e ; also κατὰ διαφορὰν ποιός *Stoic*.2. 128, al. III. *variance, disagreement*, Hdt.1.1 ; δ. ἔχειν τινί E. *Med*.75 : pl., τὰς διαφορὰς διαιρέειν, καταλαμβάνειν, settle *the differences*, Hdt.4.23, 7.9.β' ; δ. θέσθαι καλῶς And.1.140 ; διαφοραὶ πρός τινας Pl.*Phdr*.231b ; δ. πρὸς ἀλλήλους περί τινος Lys.25.10 ; ἐν δ. καταστῆναί τινι Antipho 1.1 ; δ. φιλοσοφίᾳ καὶ ποιητικῇ Pl.*R*. 607b. IV. *distinction, excellence*, Id.*Ti*.23a ; ναυπηγίας Plb.1.51. 4. V. *advantage, profit*, Antipho 2.3.3 ; πᾶν τὸ πῖπτον εἰς διαφορᾶς λόγον, *valuables*, Agatharch.102. VI. *vote, division*, in an assembly, δ. ποιήσασθαι *IG*12(2).526ᵃ18 (Eresus). VII. *delay*, *PMagd*.11.10 (iii B.C.). VIII. δ. διανοίας *being beside oneself*, Dsc.

*Ther.*7. **-έω**, = διαφέρω, *spread abroad, disperse*, κλέος εὐρὺ διὰ ξεῖνοι φορέουσι Od.19.333; σωρὸν . . διαφορῆσαι ῥᾴδιον Diph.100; τὴν ὑγρότητα Plu.2.366c, etc.; πολλὰ τῆς οὐσίας ib.484a; δ. κραιπάλη τὴν κραιπάλην ib.127f:—Pass., διαπεφορῆσθαι Critias *Fr.*62 D.; τὰ διαπεφορημένα τῶν εἰδώλων Arist.*Div.Somn.*464^{b}13. 2. *carry away*, τοὺς σταυρούς Th.6.100; esp. as plunder, χρήματα τὰ σὰ διαφορέει Hdt.1.88; ὧν κοινῇ διαπεφορημένων D.27.29. 3. *plunder*, ἐπαρχίας Plu.*Brut.*6, etc.:—Med., *PSI*5.522.5 (iii B.C.):—most freq. in Pass., οἶκον διαφορηθέντα Hdt.3.53; διαφορουμένης τῆς χώρας ὑπὸ λῃστῶν D.19.315; διαφορεῖσθαι τὴν γνώμην *to be robbed* of one's wits, Pl.*Lg.*672b. 4. *tear in pieces*, ἄλλαι δὲ δαμάλας διεφόρουν E.*Ba.*739; τινὰς τοξεύμασι Id.*HF*571; ὑπὸ κυνῶν τε καὶ ὀρνίθων διαφορεύμενος Hdt. 7.10.θ', cf. Ar.*Av.*338. 5. Pass., of ice, *break up*, *Gp.*19.6.4. II. = διαφέρω I. 1, *carry across from one place to another*, ἀπὸ τῶν ξυμμάχων προσόδου διαφορουμένης Th.6.91. III. Medic. (cf. διαφόρησις, -ητικός): 1. *dissipate* by evaporation, perspiration, etc., in Pass., Aret.*SD*2.1, Alex.Aphr.*Pr.*1.68, Gal.10.657, al. 2. '*discuss*', *disperse* by drugs or treatment, φύματα Dsc.5.156, cf. Gal.10. 392: abs., Dsc.1.30. 3. *exhaust by dissipating, weaken*, καρδιακόν με διαφορεῖ πάθος Diog.Oen.66: metaph., ὁ μερισμὸς δ. καὶ ἐκλύει τὴν ἑκάστου δύναμιν Procl.*Inst.*86:—Pass., Gal.14.735. IV. Pass., *dispute, debate*, S.E.*M.*1.205. V. διαφορούμενον ἀξίωμα, v. διφορέω. **-ημα**, ατος, τό, *thing thrown to and fro*; *the game of ball*, Hsch., Suid. II. *thing torn to pieces, prey*, Lxx *Je.*37.16. **-ησις**, εως, ἡ, *plundering, stealing*, προβάτων *PTeb.*72.239 (ii B.C.): pl., Plu. *Cor.*9, *Cic.*14. II. *evaporation, dissipation*, Sor.1.22, Olymp.*in Mete.*145.14; *perspiration*, Cic.*Fam.*16.18.1; δ. τῶν ἱδρώτων Plu.*Fr. inc.*149. 2. *dispersion, discussion*, Gal.10.919. 3. *exhaustion*, Cael.Aur.*CP*1.15, al. III. *dubitation, perplexity*, Plu.2. 389a. **-ητικός**, ή, όν, *promoting perspiration*, etc., Antyll.ap. Orib.6.21.30: Comp., Dsc.1.30. 2. *capable of dispersing, discutient*, δύναμις δ. οἰδημάτων Id.4.112, cf. Gal.13.925. 3. *perspiring*, Cael.Aur.*CP*2.36. **-ητος**, ον, *torn in pieces*, σάρξ prob. in E. *Cyc.*344. **-ία**, ἡ, = διαφορά I, f.l. in D.H.*Rh.*11.10. **-ος**, ον, *different, unlike*, Hdt.2.83, 4.81, Pl.*Lg.*964a, etc.; παρά τι Iamb. *Myst.*3.30: c. gen., *differing from*, Pl.*Phlb.*61d, etc. b. *several, various*, κατὰ τὰς δ. ὕλας Phld.*Sign.*24; δ. πρόσωπα *POxy.*1033. 88 (iv A.D.), cf. *Ep.Hebr.*9.13. c. *ambiguous*, Hsch. 2. *differing* or *disagreeing with* another, πολλοῖς δ. εἰμι E.*Med.*579; esp. in hostile sense, *at variance with*, Κλεομένεϊ Hdt.5.75; τοῖς οἰκείοις Lys.14.44; ἀλλήλοις, ἑαυτοῖς, Pl.*Prt.*337b, *Lg.*679b; ἀνώμαλος καὶ δ. πρὸς ἑαυτόν Plu.*Sull.*6: c. gen., δ. τινος one's *adversary*, D.29.15, cf. Antiph.209.1, Philem.162. 3. *excellent, distinguished, remarkable*, Antiph.175.3; δ. γλυκύτητι D.S.2.57; πρὸς ἀρετήν Plu.*Cleom.*16: Comp., ὄνομα *Ep.Hebr.*1.4. 4. *making a difference to one*, a. in good sense, *advantageous, profitable, important*, δ. ἑτέρου μᾶλλον Th.4.3; πρὸς σωτηρίαν Pl.*Lg.*779b. b. rarely in bad sense, *disagreeable*, γείτονα γείτονι μηδὲν ποιεῖν δ. ib. 843c. II. as Subst., διάφορον, τό, 1. *difference*, σμικρόν τι τὸ δ. εὕροι τις ἄν Hdt.2.7; διάφορα πολλὰ θεῶν βροτοῖσιν εἰσορῶ I see many *differences* between gods and men, E.*Supp.*612 (lyr.); μέγα τὸ δ. ἐστι (v.l. διαφέρον) Hp.*Art.*14; ἆρα μικρὰ τὰ δ. ἑκατέροις τῆς οὐσίας; Is.11.47; ἡλίκα γ' ἐστὶν τὰ διάφορ' ἐνθάδ' ἢ ἐκεῖ πολεμεῖν D.1.27. 2. *what concerns one*, τῶν ἡμῖν ἐς τὰ μέγιστα διαφόρων *matters of* the greatest *concern* to us, Th.4.87; τηλικούτων ὄντων αὐτῷ τῶν δ. D.19. 68, cf. Arist.*Oec.*1352^{b}2. 3. *difference, disagreement*, ἕνεκα τῶν αὐτοῖς ἰδίᾳ δ. on account of their private *differences*, Th.1.68, cf. 2.37; τὸ Ἀθηναίων δ. *difference with* the A., Id.2.27. 4. in reference to money-matters, *difference, balance*, Hyp.*Eux.*17, cf. Epict.*Ench.*25. 4; *expenditure*, Arist.*VV*1251^{b}10; ἡ μικρολογία ἐστὶ φειδωλία τοῦ δ. Thphr.*Char.*10.1: in pl., *expenses*, D.32.18, *IG*5(1).1390.45 (Andania, i B.C.); *losses*, *OGI*90.30 (ii B.C.), Wilcken *Chr.*11 *B* 8 (ii B.C.). b. *ready money, cash*, χρείας γενομένης ἀναγκαίας τῷ δήμῳ διαφόρου *IG*12(7).388.7 (Amorgos); *sum of money*, *PSI*4.330.8 (iii B.C.), *UPZ*3.7 (ii B.C.), Plb.4.18.8, *IG*12(5).653.56 (Syros, i B.C.), etc.: pl., Plb.31.27.13, *CIG*2695 (Iasus); *interest*, ἐπὶ διαφόρῳ ἡμιολίας *POxy.*1040.8 (ii A.D.); *price*, Luc.*Herm.*81, D.L.6.9. 5. *expenses of carriage*, *PAmh.*2.69.12 (ii A.D.), *PFay.*86*a*11 (ii A.D.). III. Adv. -ρως *with a difference*, τοῖς παροῦσιν ἤθεσι δ. πολιτεύειν Th.6.18, cf. Pl.*Ion* 531b: c. gen., δ. τῶν λοιπῶν δένδρων *Gp.*10.37.1; *in a variety of ways*, Phld.*D.*3.9: Comp. -ώτερον Id.*Mus.*p.109 K. 2. δ. ἔχειν *differ*, Pl.*Phlb.*25e, etc.; δ. ἔχειν τινί *to differ with*.., D.33. 18. 3. *pre-eminently*, πρᾶος καὶ φιλάνθρωπος τῶν ἄλλων δ. ὤν Id. 24.196, cf. J.*BJ*2.8.9 (Sup.); δ. συναρέσκει Men.*Epit.*333, cf. *Pk.*72; *excellently, with distinction*, ἀγωνίσασθαι Sosyl.p.30 B.; δ. ἀπειργασμένος Plb.13.7.2: Comp. -ώτερον Hsch.

διαφορότης, ητος, ἡ, *difference*, Pl.*R.*587e, Ph.2.370, J.*AJ*18.1.5, Ael.*NA*1.12, Iamb.*Comm.Math.*14.

διαφουλλαί· διακοπαί, διαλογαί, Hsch. **διαφράγιον**· ἀλλοῖον καὶ διάφορον, Id.

διάφραγμα, ατος, τό, *partition* or *barrier*, Th.1.133, Hero *Spir.*1.8; στοᾶς *Inscr.Prien.*99.19; *lock* in a canal, *PPetr.*3 p.343 (iii B.C.), D.S.1.33. II. *muscle which divides the thorax from the abdomen, midriff, diaphragm*, Pl.*Ti.*70a, 84d, Gal.*UP*4.14, etc. b. δ. [τοῦ μυκτῆρος] *cartilage which divides* the nostrils, Arist.*HA*492^{b}16, cf. Ruf.*Onom.*34, Gal.17(1).824. c. the *velum palati*, Hp.*Epid.*2.2. 24. d. *septum lucidum* of the brain, Gal.2.719.

διαφραγμάτιον, τό, Dim. of foreg., *small partition*, *IG*11(2).199*A* 15, 45 (Delos, iii B.C.).

διαφράγνῡμι, *barricade*, Plu.*Cam.*34 (Med.):—Pass., *to be barricaded*, ἐρύμασι καὶ προτειχίσμασι Id.*Aem.*13.

διαφρᾰδής, ές, *distinct*, of sound: in Adv. -έως Hp.*Loc.Hom.*2.

διαφράζω, only in pf. διαπέφρᾰδε, *show plainly*, ὡς .. μοι μήτηρ διεπέφραδε Il.18.9; διεπέφραδε κούρη Od.6.47, cf. 17.590, A.R.1.848, Opp.*C.*4.378, Q.S.3.80.

διαφρακτέον, *one must partition off*, Ph.*Bel.*95.34.

διάφραξις, εως, ἡ, *midriff*, Hp.*Virg.*1.

διαφράσσω, Att. -ττω, = διαφράγνυμι, διαφάρξαντι τὰ μετακιόνια *IG*1^2.373.251; δ. μεταστύλιον ib.2.1054.63, cf. D.S.17.96, Them. *Or.*20.235d:—Pass., *to be divided off*, δ. ὑμέσι Dsc.2.24; μήνιγξι Erasistr.ap.Gal.5.603, cf. Hdn.3.1.4; διαφρᾰγείς *obstructed*, Ruf. *Anat.*30; but ἔλλοβα διαπεφραγμένα *with divisions*, Thphr.*HP*8.5.2.

διαφρέω, *let through, let pass*, διὰ τῆς πόλεως . . τὴν κνῖσαν οὐ διαφρήσετε Ar.*Av.*193; ὅπως μὴ διαφρήσωσι τοὺς πολεμίους Th.7.32.

διαφρίσσω, strengthd. for φρίσσω, Poll.1.107.

διαφρονέω, *meditate*, Hsch. (-φορέων cod.). II. *quarrel*, Id., *Lyr.Alex.Adesp.*37.2 (s.v.l.).

διαφροντίζω, *meditate on, consider*, τι Hp.*Aër.*1; δ. δρᾶμα *compose*, Ael.*VH*2.21: abs., *meditate*, Epicr.11.22. 2. c. gen., *take care of, pay regard to*, Arist.*Pol.*1262^{b}20.

δίαφρος, ον, *foamy*, Gal.19.93.

διαφρουρέω, *to keep one's post*: metaph., διαπεφρούρηται βίος A.*Fr.* 265.

δια-φρύγω [ῡ], *bake*, *Hippiatr.*103, Lyd.*Ost.*27. **-φρυκτος**, ον, *parched*, of beans used in voting, Hsch.:—hence **-φρυκτόω**, *vote* or *cast lots*, Id., *EM*271.50, Suid.

διαφῠάς, άδος, ἡ, = διαφυή, D.S.1.47.

διαφυγγάνω, = διαφεύγω, Heraclit.86, Th.7.44, Aeschin.3.10, J. *AJ*19.1.15.

διαφῠγετεῖν· παρ' ἐλπίδα σωθῆναι, Hsch.

διαφῠγή, ἡ, *refuge, means of escape*, Th.8.11; τινός from a thing, Pl.*Prt.*321a (pl.), al.; ἔκ τινος Plu.*Alc.*25.

διαφῠή, ἡ, (διαφύω) *natural break, joint, suture*, τὰ ὀστᾶ . . διαφυὰς ἔχει χωρὶς ἀπ' ἀλλήλων Pl.*Phd.*98c, cf. Philostr.*VA*4.28; *distinction*, Pl.*Plt.*259d; *dissepiment*, as in chestnuts, X.*An.*5.4.29, cf. Plu.*Cic.*1; *joint* in reeds or grasses, Longus 1.10; *divisions* between the teeth, Plu.*Pyrrh.*3; *cleft* in rocks, D.S.5.22. II. *stratum* or *vein* of earth, stone, metal, Thphr.*Lap.*63; δ. καὶ φλέβες D.S.3.12. III. *string-basket*, *PRyl.*97.7 (ii B.C.).

διαφῠλακ-τέος, α, ον, *to be watched, preserved*, v.l. for φυλακτέα, X.*Cyr.*5.3.43. 2. διαφυλακτέον *one must preserve*, Arist.*Rh.Al.* 1423^{a}31. **-τικός**, ή, όν, *fit for preserving*, ἕξις Pl.*Def.*412a, cf. Plu.2.276a; τριχῶν Crito ap.Gal.12.438.

διαφῠλάσσω, Att. -ττω, Cret. -δδω (written -δω), *GDI*5169.11, al.:—*watch closely, guard carefully*, τὰ τείχεα, τὴν πόλιν, Hdt.6.101, 133; τὴν πάροδον Lys.2.30; τὰ ἀγαθά Isoc.2.6, cf. *SIG*577.15 (Milet., iii/ii B.C.); esp. of providential care, Lxx *Ps.*90(91).11, al., cf. *PGiss.* 17.7 (Hadr.), etc.:—Med., *guard for oneself*, πόλιν E.*IA*369. 2. *observe closely*, τὰ μέτρα Hdt.2.121.α'. 3. *observe, maintain*, τοὺς νόμους Pl.*Lg.*951b, cf. *SIG*1044.10 (Halic., iv/iii B.C.), *PTeb.*25.3 (ii B.C., Pass.); εἰρήνην Philipp.ap.D.18.78; τὴν πρός τινα πίστιν Plb. 1.78.8; εὔνοιαν *IG*12(7).241.22 (Amorgos, iii B.C.); δ. τὸ μὴ σπουδάζειν *guard against* being too particular.., Pl.*Plt.*261e; πλῆθος δ. ὅτι μάλιστα ταὐτὸν αὐτῶν εἶναι *take care* that.., Id.*Criti.*112d. 4. *remember, retain*, Luc.*Tim.*1, *Cont.*7.

διάφυξις, εως, ἡ, v.l. for -φευξις (q.v.).

διαφύομαι, Pass., fut. -φύσομαι Philostr.Jun.*Im.*13: with aor. 2 Act. διέφῡν: pf. διαπέφῡκα:—*germinate*, of seeds, Thphr.*CP*2.17. 7. II. *to be disjoined*, διαφύντος ἑνός Emp.17.10. III. *grow between*, Arist.*Fr.*335, Thphr.*CP*3.7.9; *intervene*, χρόνος διέφυ καὶ πάντα ἐξήρτυτο Hdt.1.61; βαθὺς δ. αὐλών Eratosth.8. IV. *to be different from*, ἀπ' ἀλλήλων Philostr.*Im.*2.32. V. *to be inseparably connected with*, τινός Philostr.Jun. l. c.; *to identify oneself with*, τυραννίδος Plu.*Dio* 12; *to be intimately acquainted with*, τῶν Ἑλληνικῶν D.C.72.6, cf. 77.13; δι' ὅλης τῆς Ἰταλίας *to pervade, leaven* all Italy (of Sulla's veterans), Plu.*Cic.*14. [ῡ only metri gr., Eratosth. l. c.]

διαφῡσ-άω, *blow in different directions, disperse*, μή . . ὁ ἄνεμος αὐτὴν (sc. τὴν ψυχὴν) διαφυσᾷ Pl.*Phd.*77d:—Pass., ib.80d, 84b. II. *blow* or *breathe through*, Luc.*Herm.*68; ἐκ τοῦ στόματος Plu.2.950c (Pass.). III. *inflate, fill with air*, μήτραν Hp.*Steril.*228, cf. Gal. 1.605. **-ησις**, εως, ἡ, *exhalation* from the body, Arist.*Pr.*908^{a}17 (pl.). II. *distension by* πνεῦμα, αἰδοίου Gal.7.266.

διαφῠσικεύομαι, *study natural philosophy*, Julian.ap.Gal.18(1). 256.

διάφῠσις, εως, ἡ, (διαφύω) *germination*, Thphr.*HP*8.1.6. II. *division*, Arist.*HA*495^{b}9 (pl.), Hp.*Mochl.*1 (pl.); *partition*, Arist.*HA* 562^{a}26, Hp. *de Arte* 10; *crack, crevice* in rocks, Ph.*Bel.*102.21 (pl.); *gorge*, Ph.2.117 (pl.); *point* or *line of separation between* the stalk and branch, Hp.*Oct.*12. III. *spinous process of the tibia*, Id.*Fract.* 12, Gal.18(2).475.

διάφυσον· φασκίς, Hsch.

διαφύσσω, aor. -ήφυσα, *draw continually*, οἶνον διαφυσσόμενον Od. 16.110. II. *draw away, tear away*, πολλὸν δὲ διήφυσε σαρκὸς ὀδόντι 19.450; διὰ δ' ἔντερα χαλκὸς ἤφυσ' Il.13.508. III. *draw out*, χίμετλα Nic.*Th.*682.

διαφῠτεύω, *transplant*, Thphr.*HP*4.4.3 (Pass.); *plant*, πλάτανον Ar.*Fr.*111; νῆσον δένδρεσι Philostr.*VA*7.25.

διαφων-έω, *to be a discord*, in Music, Aristox.*Harm.*p.45 M.; *to be* *out of tune*, Pl.*Grg*.482b. 2. generally, *disagree*, Id.*Lg*.860a, etc.; δ. περί τινος Arist.*Metaph*.$1085^{b}36$; διαφωνεῖ τι τῶν χρημάτων there *is a discrepancy* in the accounts, Plb.21.43.23; τῷ ῥηθέντι Pl.*Plt*.292b, etc.; ἀλλήλοις συμφωνεῖν ἢ δ. Id.*Phd*.101d; τῷ ψευδεῖ δ. τἀληθές Arist. *EN*$1098^{b}12$, al.; πρὸς τὴν ἀλήθειαν Iamb.*Myst*.9.3:—Pass., διαπεφώνηται *it has been disputed*, D.H.1.45. 3. *fail to answer roll-calls, desert*, Lxx*Ex*.24.11, al.; δ. ἐν μηδενὶ τῶν ἀγαθῶν *fail*, Ph.*Fr*.59 H.: metaph. of promises, *fail, be found wanting*, Lxx 3*Ki*.8.56. b. *to be lost, perish*, *SIG*521.25 (Amorgos, iii B.C.), 611.10 (Delph., ii B.C.), Agatharch.84, S.E.*M*.1.267; of plants or animals, *BGU*530.31 (i B.C.), *Hippiatr*.2; διαπεφωνήκαμεν we *are lost*, Lxx*Ez*.37.11; *to be lost*, of things, *PSI*5.527.15 (iii B.C.); of books, D.S.16.3:—in pf. Pass., *PRein*.17.14 (ii B.C.). **-ία**, ἡ, *discord, disagreement*, Pl.*Lg*.689a, 691a, Str.2.1.7, Plu.2.861a, etc.; δ. πρὸς ἑαυτόν *inconsistency*, Phld. *Po*.994.4; esp. in Music, *discord*, Bacch.*Harm*.59, prob. in Cleonid. *Harm*.5. **-ος**, ον, *discordant, inconsistent*, ἱστορίαι D.S.4.55, cf. Plu.2.1039d, etc.; τινί *with* one, Luc.*Cyn*.16; esp. in Music, διάφωνον ἕλκειν strike a *false note*, Damox.2.61, cf. Hp.*Vict*.1.18 (metaph. of tastes), etc.; opp. σύμφωνος, Euc.*Sect.Can.Praef*., Theo Sm.p.49 H. Adv. -νως Plu.2.1137c: c. dat., S.E.*M*.7.170: metaph., δ. ἵστασθαι πρός τινα Phld.*Rh*.1.90 S.

διαφώσκω, Ion. for διαφαύσκω.

διαφωτ-ίζω, *enlighten*, τὴν ψυχήν Plu.2.76b; βίᾳ διαφωτίσαι τόπον *clear* a place by force, Id.*Cat.Ma*.20; *throw light upon*, νυκτερινὰς διατριβάς Luc.*Icar*.21: abs., *dawn*, Lxx*Ne*.8.3. **-ισις**, εως, ἡ, *clearing up, explanation*, *PGiss*.67.14 (ii A.D.).

διαχάζομαι, *withdraw*, X.*Cyr*.7.1.31; cf. διχάζω II.

διαχάλ-ᾰσις [χᾰ], εως, ἡ, *disjoining* in the sutures of the skull, Hp. *VC*12. **-ασμα**, ατος, τό, *loosening*, τῶν ἁρμονιῶν D.H.*Comp*. 22. **-αστέον**, *one must relax*, Sor.1.56. **-άω**, *loosen, relax*, τὸ πῦρ δ. τὸ πεπηγός Arist.*Pr*.$886^{b}2$; τὰς ἁρμονίας τοῦ σώματος Epicr. 3.19; δ. μέλαθρα *unbar*, E.*IA*1340. II. *make supple by exercise*, X.*Eq*.7.11. III. intr., *to be disjointed, gape*, ὀστέον Hp.*VC*12 (v. l. διαχαλασθῇ).

διαχᾰρακτηρίζω· *persono*, *Gloss*.

διαχάραξις [χᾰ], εως, ἡ, *cleaving*, αὔλαξ.. δ. τοῦ ἀρότρου *EM*170.33.

διαχᾰράσσω, Att. -ττω, *sever, divide*, D.H.*Dem*.43 (Pass.); *strip off*, ἐκ τοῦ αὐχένος τὸ δέρμα Agath.4.23; *carve, give shape to*, Plu. 2.636c (Pass.), cf. Ph.1.649 (Pass.); *sharpen*, τὸν ὀφθαλμόν Plu.2. 974b:—Med., *scrape*, S.*Ichn*.255:—Pass., πέτραις -κεχαραγμένοι τὰ σκέλη Agath.4.20.

διαχᾰρίζομαι, *distribute as presents*, D.S.19.20.

διαχάσκω, aor. 2 -έχᾰνον: pf. -κέχηνα:—*gape, yawn*, Ar.*Eq*.533, Thphr.*HP*3.9.1, Plu.2.976b, 980b; ἀμφί, πρός τι, Agath.2.32, 5.3.

διαχεθῇ· διαχεσθῇ, Hsch.

διαχειμάζω, *pass the winter*, Th.7.42, X.*An*.7.6.31.

διαχειρ-έω, = -ίζω, χρήματα *IG*2.574e24. **-ησις**, v. διαχείρισις. **-ίζω**, *have in hand, conduct, manage*, χρήματα, πράγματα, And.1.147, 2.17, cf. Lys.9.12, Pl.*Grg*.526b, etc.; αἱ ἀρχαὶ δ. πολλὰ τῶν κοινῶν Arist.*Pol*.$1322^{b}8$; χρήματα *OGI*218.74 (Ilium, iii B.C.), etc.:—so in Med., fut. part. -ιούμενος Hp.*Mul*.2.111, etc.:—Pass., X.*An*.1.9.17. II. Med., *lay hands on, slay*, Plb.8.21.8, *Act.Ap*.5.30, Plu.2.220b, D.C.72.14. **-ισις**, εως, ἡ, *management, administration*, πραγμάτων Th.1.97, cf. Lib.*Ep*.245. 2. in Rhet., *treatment*, prob. for διαχείρησις, Aristid.*Rh*.1 p.501 S. **-ισμός**, ὁ, *manipulation*, φαρμάκων Hp.*Epid*.2.3.2. **-ιστικόν**, τό, *commission paid for handling* grain, *PLond.ined*.2093 (iii B.C.).

διαχειροτον-έω, *choose between two* persons or proposals *by show of hands*, εἴτε.. ἤ, εἴτε.. εἴτε, *IG*1^{2}.57,98, cf. D.47.43, etc.:—Pass., X.*HG*1.7.34; *to be selected*, Pl.*Lg*.755d. 2. *vote on* a person's case, δ. τινὰ πότερον ἐπιτήδειός ἐστιν ἢ οὔ Arist.*Ath*.49.2. **-ία**, ἡ, *choice between two* persons or things, *election*, δ. ποιεῖν, = διαχειροτονεῖν, D. 24.25, *IG*12(7).237.19 (Amorgos, ii/i B.C.); δ. διδόναι to allow *a right of election*, Aeschin.3.39.

διαχείρως, Adv. *in the appropriate manner* (?), κατακαίειν Zos.Alch. p.108 B.

διαχέω, fut. -χεῶ, later -χύσω *Gp*.7.8.4: aor. -έχεα, Ep. -έχευα (the only tense used by Hom.):—*pour different ways, scatter*, τὸν χοῦν Hdt.2.150. b. in Hom., *cut up* a victim into joints, αἶψ' ἄρα μιν διέχευαν Od.3.456, cf. Il.7.316, al.; χαλκὸς ἔγκατα διέχευεν Theoc.22.203. 2. *disperse*, τὰ συγκεκριμένα Pl.*Phlb*.46e; ἡ θερμότης δ. τὸ ὑγρόν Arist.*Pr*.$869^{a}15$; *melt, fuse*, χαλκόν Paus.9.41.1; *liquefy*, opp. πηγνύναι, Pl.*Ti*.46d; νῆα.. διέχευαν ἄελλαι A.R.3.320; δ. ἀποστήματα *disperse* abscesses, Thphr.*Od*.59(61); δ. ἴχνη *to destroy* the scent, X.*Cyn*.5.3:—Pass., ib.8.1:—also Med., *dissolve*, Nic. *Al*.373. 3. metaph., *confound*, τὰ βεβουλευμένα Hdt.8.57. 4. *put in a good humour*, τινὰ ὁμιλίαις καὶ λόγοις Plu.2.74d, cf. Philostr. *VS*2.10.1, Hermog.*Id*.2.9. II. more freq. in Pass., *to be poured from one vessel into another*, Hdt.6.119. 2. *run through, spread*, Th.2.75,76, Arist.*Fr*.243. 3. *to be dissolved, liquefied*, X.*Cyn*. 8.1, Arist.*Pr*.$890^{b}17$, etc.; of a corpse, Hdt.3.16; *disperse*, of soldiers, X.*HG*7.4.34; of humours, Hp.*Epid*.4.45. 4. metaph., *to be* or *become diffused* or *relaxed*, εὐφραινόμενον -χεῖται, opp. λυπούμενον συσπειρᾶται, Pl.*Smp*.206d; ὑπὸ μέθης διακεχυμένος Id.*Lg*.775c, cf. Plb.8.27.4; [αἱ ἐπιθυμίαι] οὐ διαχέονται Epicur.*Sent*.30; μαλακὸν καὶ διακεχυμένον βλέπειν Arist.*Phgn*.$813^{a}26$; φαιδρὸν καὶ δ. πρόσωπον Plu.*Alex*.19; τῆς ψυχῆς τὸ παθητικὸν διακεχυμένον ὑπὸ τοῦ λόγου Zeno ap.eund.2.82f, cf. Tryph.*Trop*.p.205 S.

διαχλαινόω, strengthd. for χλαινόω, τινά τινι Nonn.*D*.2.166.

διαχλευάζω, strengthd. for χλευάζω, c. acc., D.50.49, Pl.*Ax*.364b: abs., Plb.30.22.12. 2. *deceive*, τοὺς ὠνουμένους *Gp*.7.7.5.

διαχλῐαίνω, v. l. for χλιαίνω, Hp.*Mul*.2.208.

***διαχλίδω**, = θρύπτομαι, only pf. part. διακεχλῑδώς Archipp.45 (-οιδώς Hsch.).

διάχλωρος, ον, *of translucent green*, λίθος Ph.Byz.*Mir*.2.3, dub. in Gal.18(1).495; of a garment, *CPR*24.6 (ii A.D.).

διάχολος, ον, *bilious*, Hp.*Hebd*. in *Hermes* 46.439.

διαχόω, *bank up*: διαχοῦν τὸ χῶμα *complete* the mound, Hdt.8. 97. 2. *block with a mole*, πορθμόν Str.9.1.13, cf. 7.4.7.

διαχράομαι, fut. -ήσομαι, Dor. 3sg. διαχρησεῖται Theoc.15.54. I. Dep., c. dat. rei, *use constantly* or *habitually*, chiefly in Hdt., τῇ αὐτῇ γλώσσῃ 1.58; τῷ αὐτῷ τρόπῳ 2.127; οὐκ οἴνῳ διαχρέωνται 1.71, cf. 2.77; ἐσθῆτι φοινικηΐῃ 4.43; τῇ ἀληθείῃ δ. speak the truth, 3.72; οἰμωγῇ ἀφθόνῳ 3.66, cf. 6.58; ἀρετῇ 7.102; ἀγνωμοσύνῃ 6.10; ἀναιδείῃ τε καὶ ἀβουλίῃ 7.210; νόμοις τοῖς προτέροισιν Ar.*Ec*.609; λιμῷ ὥσπερ ὄψῳ δ. *use* hunger as a sauce, X.*Cyr*.1.5.12. b. of passive states, *meet with, suffer under*, συμφορῇ μεγάλῃ, τοιούτῳ μόρῳ, Hdt. 3.117, 1.167; αὐχμῷ δ. Id.2.13. 2. *treat, handle*, ἀνομώτατα Str. 6.1.8: c. acc., *destroy, kill*, Hdt.1.24,110, Antipho 1.23, Th.3.36, etc. II. Pass., *to be lent out to different persons*, v. διακίχρημι. 2. *to be killed*, D.L.1.102. III. later in Act., διαχράω *reveal by oracle*, τελετήν Orac.ap.Phleg.*Olymp.Fr*.1.

διαχρέμπτομαι, strengthd. for χρέμπτομαι, Phryn.*PS*p.126 B.

διαχρέομαι, subj. **διαχρέωμαι**, Ion. for διαχράομαι (q. v.).

διάχρηστος, ον, dub. in Hsch. s. v. λαβροστομία.

διά-χρῑσις, εως, ἡ, *anointing*, Archig.ap.Aët.6.39; *smearing with pitch*, *Gp*.6.9.2. **-χρισμα**, ατος, τό, *unguent, salve*, Archig.ap. Aët.6.27. II. *preparation for smearing, pitching*, πίθων *Gp*.6.9 tit. **-χρισμός**, ὁ, v. l. for -χρῖσις, Paul.Aeg.1.46 tit. **-χριστέον**, *one must anoint*, Sor.2.16. **-χριστος**, ον, *anointed*: hence δ. ἐσχαρίτης, a *rich* cake, Lynceus ap.Ath.3.109e: -χριστα, τά, *salves, ointments*, Dsc.1.30, Antyll.ap.Orib.10.34 tit., Aret.*CA*1.1.

διαχρίω [ῑ], *smear all over*, Hp.*Fist*.3,9, *Gp*.6.9.1; τινί with a thing, Arist.*HA*$623^{b}30$.

διαχρόν· χλιαρόν, Hsch.

διάχρῡσος, ον, *interwoven with gold*, ἱμάτιον Test.ap.D.21.22; ἐσθῆτες Plb.6.53.7; σκηναί D.S.14.109; ὑποδήματα Plu.2.142c.

διάχῠλ-ος, ον, *juicy, succulent*, σάρξ Arist.*HA*$603^{b}20$. **-όομαι**, *to be made into a syrup*, σεμίδαλις -κεχυλωμένη ὕδατι *Hippiatr*.32.

διάχῠμα, ατος, τό, gloss on γέλασμα, Sch.A.*Pr*.90.

διάχῠσις, εως, ἡ, *diffusion*, Hp.*Vict*.2.60, Pl.*Cra*.419c; *extension*, Plu.2.771b; *spreading*, γῆς *Gp*.5.25.2; δ. λιμνώδη λαμβάνειν to *spread out* like a lake, Plu.*Mar*.37. 2. *waste, loss*, σπέρματος Thphr.*CP*4.4.7. 3. *softening*, ib.4.12.2. II. *dissolution, liquefaction*, opp. πῆξις, Arist.*Mete*.$382^{a}30$. III. *relaxation*, συστολαὶ καὶ δ. Epicur.*Fr*.410, cf. Chrysipp.*Stoic*.3.119; τὰς ἐπὶ σαρκὶ τῆς ψυχῆς δ. Epicur. l. c., cf. Aret.*SD*1.5; *cheerfulness*, ψυχῆς Sor.1. 97; *merriment*, Plu.*Cat.Mi*.46, Hierocl.p.54 A., Hdn.*Fig*.p.92 S.; *ridicule*, Phld.*Lib*.p.37 O.; *cheerful expression*, Plu.*Dem*.25. IV. δ. ὀμμάτων '*melting*' look, Id.2.335c. V. = δελφίνιον, Ps.-Dsc. 3.73.

διαχῠτικός, ή, όν, *able to dissolve*, Pl.*Ti*.60a, Thphr.*Sens*.84, Dsc. 1.71 (dub. l.).

διαχυτλάζω, *besprinkle*, Hsch.

διάχῠτον, τό, *wine made from partly dried grapes*, Plin.*HN*14.84.

διαχωλεύω, *limp*, Hsch.

διάχωμα, ατος, τό, *embankment*, *PSI*4.337.6 (iii B.C.), etc. II. *tax for maintenance of embankments*, *PHib*.1.104.4 (iii B.C.).

διαχωρ-έω, *pass through*, Pl.*Ti*.78a, *PFlor*.200.4 (iii A.D.). 2. *abscond*, *PSI*4.359.7 (iii B.C.). 3. of food, *to be excreted*, Hp.*Vict*. 2.45 (also Pass., ibid.): impers., κάτω διεχώρει αὐτοῖς they suffered from *diarrhoea*, X.*An*.4.8.20, cf. Pl.*Phdr*.268b; of a person, Anon. Lond.*Fr*.1.1; δ. ἄπεπτα *pass* food, Arist.*PA*$675^{a}20$, cf. Hp.*Morb*.4. 44. 4. of coins, *to be current*, Luc.*Luct*.10. 5. metaph., *pass muster, obtain credence*, Plb.18.43.3. II. *part asunder, divide*, Arr. *An*.1.1.8; δ. εἰς πλάτος or εἰς βάθος, of a mountain-range, *part* so as to leave a plain *between*, ib.2.8.2,7. 2. *depart*, *PSI*4.359.7 (iii B.C.), Gal.18(2).40. **-ημα**, ατος, τό, *excrement*, Hp.*Aph*.2.14, Str. 14.5.14, Aret.*SA*2.5, etc. **-ησις**, εως, ἡ, *excretion*, Hp.*Aph*.2.18, Arist.*PA*$675^{a}22$, Phld.*D*.3.14 (pl.), Porph.*Abst*.1.45; δ. αἵματος Hp.*Aph*.5.64. **-ητικός**, ή, όν, *laxative*, Id.*Aër*.7, prob. in Aristox. *Fr.Hist*.7: Comp., Hp.*Acut*.50, Arist.*Pr*.$928^{a}18$: Sup., Hp.*Int*.13, etc. **-ίζω**, *separate*, X.*Oec*.9.7; τι ἀπό τινος Pl.*Plt*.262b; τι καί τι Epicr.11.14:—Med., Ar.*Th*.14:—Pass., Pl.*Ti*.59c, *Phlb*.17a; γυνὴ -χωρισθεῖσα *divorced*, J.*AJ*15.7.10. **-ισις**, εως, ἡ, *separation*, Arist.*GA*$723^{b}15$. **-ισμα**, ατος, τό, *cleft, division*, Luc.*VH*2. 43. **-ισμός**, ὁ, = διαχώρισις, J.*AJ*6.11.10, Gal.1.249. **-ιστέον**, gloss on διοριστέον, Hsch. **-ιστής**, οῦ, ὁ, *separator*, *Gloss*. **-οι**, οἱ, *intervals* in order of battle, Suid.

διάχωσις, εως, ἡ, *the making of a mound*, D.S.13.47.

διαψᾰθάλλω, *feel with the fingers, scratch*, Hsch.

διαψαίρω, *brush away, blow away*, θυμιαμάτων αὖραι διαψαίρουσι πλεκτάνην καπνοῦ Ar.*Av*.1717; διαψαίρουσα πέπλους (sc. αὔρα) Hermipp.6; *cleanse*, γλώσσῃ διαψαίρουσα μυκτήρων πόρους E.*Fr*.926; *scratch through*, of birds, Opp.*H*.2.115. II. intr., *flutter* in the wind, Nic.*Al*.127.

διαψᾰλάττομαι, = διαψαθάλλω, Hsch.

διαψᾰλίζω, *clip with scissors*, Paul.Aeg.4.48:—Pass., Gal.11.130.

διαψάλλω, strengthd. for ψάλλω, abs., Eup.77: c. acc., πρὶν διαψήλῃ τὴν λύραν Him.*Or.*17.2.

διάψαλμα, ατος, τό, *musical interlude*, used by the Lxx, in the Psalms, for the Hebr. *Selah*.

διαψαμμόω, *polish with sand*, *IG*12(2).11 (Lesbos).

διαψαύω, strengthd. for ψαύω, in Med., Hp.*Art.*57.

διαψάω, *cleanse* nostrils or ears, Dsc.*Eup.*1.7, Archig.ap.Gal.12.621. II. *massage*, Max.Tyr.12.2. III. *scratch through*, ἄμμον Anon.ap.Suid. (s. v. l.).

διαψέγω, strengthd. for ψέγω, Pl.*Lg.*639a, Ael.*VH*2.2.

δια-ψεύδω, *deceive*, D.*Ep.*3.34:—Med., abs., And.1.42: c. acc., Plu.*Fab.*7. 2. Med., *deny, disclaim*, A.D.*Synt.*115.24, *Pron.*81.17. II. *cheat*, [πατρίδα ἐλπίδων] Plb.3.109.12:—usu. Pass.: pf. διέψευσμαι: aor. διεψεύσθην:—*to be deceived, mistaken*, Isoc.5.1, D.1.22; τινός *to be cheated of, deceived in* a person or thing, X.*Mem.*4.2.27, D.23.19; τῆς ψυχῆς τινῶν πέρι Pl.*Ep.*351d; περί τι Arist.*EN* 1144ᵃ35; τι *in* a thing, Id.*Pol.*1323ᵃ33; ὑπολήψει καὶ δόξῃ Id.*EN* 1139ᵇ17; λογισμοῖς Plb.3.16.5: abs., μηδὲν διεψεῦσθαι *BGU*21 i 13 (iv A.D.). **-ψευσις**, εως, ἡ, *deceit*, Stob.2.7.11[l]. **-ψευσμα**, ατος, τό, *falsehood*, Aq.*Ps.*61(62).5. **-ψευστῶς**, Adv. *with fraudulent purpose*, Stob.2.7.11[m].

διαψηλᾰφ-άω, *handle* a thing, Herod.Med.ap.Orib.6.20.10, Sor.1.100, Aq.*Ge.*31.34, Sm.*Is.*59.10. **-ητέον**, *one must handle*, Paul.Aeg.2.43.

διαψηφ-ίζω, Dor. aor. inf. διαψᾶφίξαι, *put to the vote*, τὰν γνώμαν *IG*12(3).249.38 (Anaphe); δ. τοὺς φόρους *keep account of* tribute, of the *rationales*, Lyd.*Mag.*3.46. II. more freq. Dep. διαψηφίζομαι, Att. fut. -ιοῦμαι, *vote by ballot*, Antipho 5.8, Hyp.*Eux.*40, etc.; δ. περὶ δίκης Pl.*Lg.*937a; δ. κρύβδην, κρύφα, And.4.3, Th.4.88. 2. *decide by vote*, τι Lys.26.1; ταύτῃ διαψηφίσασθε v.l. in D.28.23. III. Pass., διαψηφισθεὶς εἰ γνήσιός ἐστι Lib.*Decl.*16.29. **-ισις**, εως, ἡ, *voting by ballot*, Pl.*Lg.*855d; esp. of a *vote* on claims to registration of citizens, Aeschin.1.77, D.57.26 (pl.); προτιθέναι τὴν δ. X.*HG*1.7.14; ῥᾳδίαν τὴν δ. ποιεῖν, of a criminal confessing his guilt, Lys.12.34. **-ισμός**, ὁ, = foreg., Arist.*Ath.*13.5, Ath.5.218a. II. *reckoning, assessment*, τᾶς ὀκτωβόλου εἰσφορᾶς *IG*5(1).1432 (Messene, i B.C.). **-ιστής**, οῦ, ὁ, = Lat. *rationalis*, Lyd.*Mag.*3.7, cf. *PLips.*34.4. **-ιστός**, ή, όν, *elected*, ἀρχαὶ κρυπτῇ ψήφῳ δ. Arist.*Rh.Al.*1424ᵇ2.

διαψηφοφορέομαι, of candidates for office, *to be submitted to a ballot*, *Ath.Mitt.*32.294 (Pergam.).

διαψήχω, *wear down, fritter away*, δύναμιν Plu.*Lys.*23.

διαψῐθῠρίζω, *whisper*, πρὸς τὸ οὖς προσπίπτων δ. Thphr.*Char.*2.10. II. *whisper among themselves*, Lxx *Si.*12.18, Plb.15.26.8, Luc.*Gall.*25.

διάψῑλος, ον, *uncultivated*, γῆ *POxy.*707.23 (ii A.D.), *CPR*34.6 (ii A.D.).

διαψοφέω, = παραψοφέω, Hsch.

διά-ψυγμα, ατος, τό, *dry*, i.e. *unfruitful land*, *BGU*277 ii 5 (ii A.D.). **-ψυκτικός**, ή, όν, *cooling, refreshing*, Hp.*Vict.*2.65. **-ψυξις**, εως, ἡ, *cooling*, Plu.2.967f (pl.), Aët.5.44. **-ψύχω**, *cool*, σῶμα Hp.*VM*16:—Pass., *to be chilly*, τὰ ἄκρα Id.*Acut.*30. 2. *air, dry and clean*, ναῦς Th.7.12, cf. Luc.*Cont.*23, etc.: metaph. of misers bringing out their hoards, X.*Cyr.*8.2.21. 3. Pass., *become dry*, i.e. *unfruitful*, ἵνα μὴ ἡ γῆ διαψυγῇ *PSI*6.603.11 (iii B.C.). 4. f. l. for διαψήχω in Plu.*Lys.*23.

διάω, v. διάημι.

διβάλανα· κάρυα Ποντικά, Hsch. (διαβ- cod.). **δίβαλον**· μέλι καὶ μελίκρατον, Id. (διαβ- cod.).

δίβᾰμος, ον, (βῆμα) *on two legs*, E.*Rh.*215.

δίβαν· ὄφιν (Cret.), Hsch.

διβᾰφ-ής, ές, = sq., Sm., Thd.*Ex.*25.4. **-ος**, ον, *double-dyed*, of purple cloth, Sm.*Ex.*28.5, *Edict.Diocl.*24.6; ἡ δ. (sc. ἐσθής) Cic.*Att.*2.9.2.

δῐβολ-έω, *harrow*, *PSI*4.422 (iii B.C.), *PFay.*112.5 (i A.D.). **-ητός**, ὁ, *harrowing*, *PAmh.*2.91.11 (ii A.D.), *PTeb.*378.19 (iii A.D.). **-ητρος**, ὁ, = foreg., *PFay.*112.4 (i A.D.). **-ία**, ἡ, = δίβολος χλαῖνα, Plu.2.754f. II. *double-pointed lance, halbert*, Ar.*Fr.*476, Men.*Kol.*30, Hdn.2.13.4; of a German weapon, Plu.*Mar.*25. **-ος**, ον, (βάλλω) *twice-thrown*, δ. χλαῖνα a garment *doubled and thrown over* the shoulders, Poll.7.47, Hsch. II. *two-pointed*, ἄκων E.*Rh.*374 (lyr.); περόνα *AP*6.282 (Theod.); *in two pieces*, ξύλον *SIG*²587.307: generally, *redoubled*, v. διόβολος. III. δίβολον· φᾶρος διπλοῦν, Hsch.

δίβος [ῐ], ὁ, name of a *square on the draught-board*, *AP*9.482 (Agath.).

δίβουλος, ον, *of two minds*, Hsch. s. v. διάβουλοι.

δίβρᾰχυς, εια, υ, *of two short syllables*, Arc.92.7, Ter.Maur.1365, etc.

δίβροχος, ον, (βρέχω) *prepared with a double infusion*, Dsc.1.55.

δίγαμμα, τό, indecl., Priscian.*Inst.*1.12, Donat.ad Ter.*Andr.*173:—also **δίγαμμος** *littera*, Ter.Maur.163, cf. 645, and **δίγαμμον** (sc. στοιχεῖον) Quint.*Inst.*1.4.7, Prob.ad Verg.*G.*1.70:—*digamma*, Trypho *Pass.*11; δ. Αἰολικόν A.D.*Pron.*76.32, al.; described, though not named, by D.H.1.20: ὥσπερ γάμμα διτταῖς ἐπὶ μίαν ὀρθὴν ἐπιζευγνύμενον ταῖς πλαγίοις, ὡς Ϝελένη καὶ Ϝάναξ καὶ Ϝοῖκος καὶ Ϝαήρ.

δί-γᾰμος [ῐ], ον, *married to two people, adulterous*, Stes.26, Man.5.291. **-γενής**, ές, *of doubtful sex*, Eust.150.27.

δίγηρες· στρουθοί, Hsch.

δί-γληνος, ον, *with two eye-balls*, Theoc.*Ep.*6. **-γλωσσος**, Att. -ττος, ον, *speaking two languages*, Th.8.85, 4.109, Gal.8.585:—as Subst., δίγλωσσος, ὁ, *interpreter, dragoman*, Plu.*Them.*6. II. *double-tongued, deceitful*, Lxx *Si.*5.9, al. **-γνωμος**, ον, *of two minds, vacillating*, Simp. *in Epict.*p.134 D., Diogenian.4.32. **-γνώμων**, ὁ, ἡ, gen. ονος, = foreg., Sch.E.*Or.*633. **-γομία**, ἡ, *double burden, load*, Lxx *Jd.*5.16. **-γόνᾰτος**, ον, *with two joints*, κλωνία Dsc.4.189. **-γονέω**, = διδυμογονέω, Phlp. *in GA*17.24. **-γονία**, ἡ, *double parturition*, Arist.*GA*719ᵃ24. **-γονος**, ον, *twice-born*, Βάκχος E.*Hipp.*560 (lyr.), cf. *AP*9.524.5. 2. *twin*: *double*, μάσθλης δ. S.*Fr.*129 (nisi leg. δίτονον); δ. σώματα *two* bodies, E.*El.*1178 (lyr.); but, II. parox., διγόνος, ον, *bearing twice*, Emp.69; *bearing twins*, Man.5.291. III. δίγονος· περιστερά, Hsch. **-γυιος**, ον, (γυῖον) *of two members*, Mart.Cap.9.989,990. II. as expl. of διάγυιος, Aristid.Quint.1.16. **-γωνία**, ἡ, *angle half-way between cardinal points*, Adam.ap.Aët.3.163.

δίδαγμα [ῐ], ατος, τό, *lesson, instruction*, Hp.*Fract.*1, Ar.*Nu.*668, X.*Eq.*9.10, Pl.*Clit.*409b, Mosch.*Fr.*2.7, etc.; χρόνος δ. ποικιλώτατον E.*Fr.*291; *evidence, proof*, τινός Plu.*Galb.*17.

δῐδαγμοσύνη, ἡ, = διδασκαλία, Doroth.ap.Heph.Astr.2.19.

δῐδακ-τέον, *one must teach*, Pl.*R.*451e, D.S.1.89, Jul.*Ep.*89b. **-τήρ**, ῆρος, ὁ, *ox-goad*, Aq.*Jd.*3.31. **-τήριος**, ον, = sq.: τὸ δ. *proof*, Hp.*Acut.*39. **-τικός**, ή, όν, *apt at teaching*, Ph.2.412, 1 *Ep.Ti.*3.2, 2 *Ep.Ti.*2.24. **-τός**, ή, όν, also ός, όν Pl.*Erx.*398d: I. of things, *taught, learnt*, ἅπαντα γάρ σοι τἀμὰ νουθετήματα κείνης διδακτά *of* her *teaching*, S.*El.*344; δ. ἀνθρωπίνης σοφίας λόγοι 1 *Ep.Cor.*2.13; ὅσοις δ. μηδέν, ἀλλ' ἐν τῇ φύσει τὸ σωφρονεῖν εἴληχεν E.*Hipp.*79. 2. *that can be taught* or *learnt*, τὰ δ. *things which may be taught by study and experience*, Pi.*N.*3.41; opp. ἄρρητα, S.*OT*300; δίδαξον . . . εἰ διδακτά μοι if I *may learn* them, Id.*Tr.*64, cf. 671; τὰ μὲν δ. μανθάνω, τὰ δ' εὑρετὰ ζητῶ Id.*Fr.*843; κἄστ' οὐ διδακτόν (sc. τὸ τῆς τύχης) E.*Alc.*786, cf. *Supp.*914; καθ' ὅσον δ. Isoc.13.20; ἀρετὴν . . εἴτε δ. εἴτε μὴ δ. Pl.*Men.*71a, cf. *Prt.*328c, *Euthd.*274e; ἐπιστήμη Arist.*EN*1139ᵇ25. II. of persons, *taught, instructed*, πολέμου Lxx 1 *Ma.*4.7; also δ. θεοῦ *taught* by God, ib.*Is.*54.13 (= *Ev.Jo.*6.45). **-τρα**, τά, *teacher's fee*, Theoc.8.86, Poll.6.186.

δῐδακτῠλ-ιαῖος, α, ον, *two fingers long* or *broad*, διάστημα S.E.*M.*10.156, cf. Heliod.ap.Orib.48.23.2, etc.:—so **-ος**, ον, Hp.*Art.*7, Thphr.*HP*9.5.3, *IG*2².463.78.

δίδαξις [δῐ], εως, ἡ, *teaching, instruction*, E.*Hec.*601, Arist.*Ph.*202ᵃ32, Phld.*Rh.*2.249 S. (pl., dub.), *PRyl.*62.21 (iii A.D.).

δῐδασκᾰλ-εῖον, τό, *teaching-place, school*, [S.]*Fr.*1120.3, Antipho 6.11, Th.7.29, prob. in Pl.*Lg.*764c; εἰς τὸ δ. ἰέναι Aeschin.1.9; τὰ παιδία τὰ ἐκ τῶν διδασκαλείων Hyp.*Eux.*22; τὰ δ. τῶν ῥητορικῶν Epicur.*Fr.*50; τὸ Σωκρατικὸν δ. D.H.*Dem.*2. II. in pl., = δίδακτρα, Ps.-Hdt.*Vit.Hom.*26. **-ία**, ἡ, *teaching, instruction*, Pi.*P.*4.102, Even.1, Hp.*Lex* 2, X.*Cyr.*8.7.24, Pl.*R.*493b, etc.; δ. ποιεῖσθαι, c. acc. et inf., Th.2.42; δ. παρέχειν serve as a *lesson*, ib.87; ἐκ δ., opp. ἐξ ἔθους, Arist.*EN*1103ᵃ15. 2. *elucidation*, Id.*Po.*1456ᵇ5. 3. *official instructions*, *PLips.*64.24 (iv A.D.); πρὸς διδασκαλίαν for *information*, *POxy.*1101.4 (iv A.D.). II. *training, rehearsing* of a chorus, etc., δ. τῶν χορῶν Pl.*Grg.*501e, cf. Simon.147.5, Plu.2.1096a, etc.; also, *the dramas produced*, Id.2.839d, *Cim.*8, *Per.*5, *AP*7.37 (Diosc.). 2. διδασκαλίαι, αἱ, *Catalogues of the Dramas*, their writers, dates, and success, title of compilation by Arist. and others, D.L.5.26, cf. Sch.Ar.*Ra.*1155, etc. **-ικός**, ή, όν, *of* or *for teaching*, τινός Philol.11; ὄργανον Pl.*Cra.*388b; λόγοι X.*Mem.*1.2.21; πειθὼ δ. περί τι Pl.*Grg.*453e, cf. 455a: ἡ -κή (sc. τέχνη) *the faculty of giving instruction*, Id.*Sph.*231b; τὸ -κόν Id.*Lg.*813b; so, in disparagement, τὸ πρεσβυτικὸν καὶ δ. *the didactic manner* of old age, of Isocrates, Hermog.*Id.*2.11: Comp. -ώτερος Arist.*Metaph.*982ᵃ13. Adv. -κῶς Pl.*Cra.*388c, Plb.6.3.5: Comp. -ώτερον Dioph.1 p.474 T., Hermog.*Inv.*1.1. 2. -κή (sc. ὁμολογία), ἡ, *contract of apprenticeship*, *POxy.*275.34 (i A.D.). 3. Gramm., τόπος δ., *locus classicus*, Sch.Il.5.857. **-ιον**, τό, *thing taught, science* or *art* (= αὐτὸ τὸ μάθημα, Suid.), Hdt.5.58; *lesson*, X.*Eq.*11.5. II. in pl., = δίδακτρα, Plu.*Lyc.*14, *Alex.*7, al. **-ος**, ὁ (but fem., *h.Merc.*556, A.*Pr.*110, cf. ξυμφορὴ γίνεται δ. Democr.76; πενία ἐπινοιῶν δ. Secund.*Sent.*10), *teacher, master*, μαντείης *h.Merc.* l. c.; δ. τέχνης πάσης βροτοῖς A.*Pr.* l. c.; δεινῶν ἔργων Lys.12.78; πόλεμος βίαιος δ. Th.3.82; διδάσκαλον λαβεῖν get *a master*, [S.]*Fr.*1120.8; εἰς διδασκάλου (sc. οἶκον) φοιτᾶν go to *school*, Pl.*Alc.*1.109d, etc.; διδασκάλων or ἐκ διδασκάλων ἀπαλλαγῆναι leave *school*, Id.*Grg.*514c, *Prt.*326c; ἐν διδασκάλων at *school*, Id.*Alc.*1.110b. II. *trainer* of a dithyrambic or dramatic chorus, *producer* of a play, etc., ἴτω δὲ καὶ τραγῳδίας ὁ Κλεομάχου δ. Cratin.256, cf. Ar.*Av.*912, *Ach.*628, Antipho 6.13, etc.; δ. τοῦ μεγάλου χοροῦ *SIG*698.8 (Delph., ii B.C.).

δῐδάσκω, Ep. inf. -έμεναι and -έμεν, Il.9.442, 23.308: fut. διδάξω A.*Supp.*519, etc.: aor. ἐδίδαξα Il.23.307, etc.; poet. ἐδιδάσκησα *h.Cer.*144 (prob.), Hes.*Op.*64, Pi.*P.*4.217: pf. δεδίδαχα X.*Cyr.*1.3.18, Pl.*Men.*85e:—Med., fut. διδάξομαι: aor. ἐδιδαξάμην:—Pass., fut. διδαχθήσομαι D.H.3.70, etc.: aor. ἐδιδάχθην Sol.13.51, Hdt.3.81, Ar.*Nu.*637, etc.: pf. δεδίδαγμαι Il.11.831, Pl.*Phdr.*269c, etc. Redupl. form of δάω (q. v.) in causal sense:—*instruct* a person, or *teach* a thing, Il.11.832, 9.442: c. dupl. acc., σε . . ἱπποσύνας ἐδίδαξαν they *taught* thee riding, 23.307, cf. Od.8.481; πολλὰ διδάσκει μ' ὁ πολὺς βίοτος E.*Hipp.*252 (lyr.), etc.; also δ. τινὰ περί τινος Ar.*Nu.*382; δ. τῶν γενομένων τισὶ τὴν ἀλήθειαν Pl.*Tht.*201b: c. acc. pers. et inf., σε διδάσκουσιν θεοὶ αὐτοὶ ὑψαγόρην ἔμεναι *teach* thee to be . ., Od.1.384: c. inf. only, δίδαξε γὰρ Ἄρτεμις αὐτὴ βάλλειν ἄγρια πάντα she *taught how* to shoot, Il.5.51, etc.: without inf., πολλοὶ τοὺς υἱοὺς ῥήτορας διδάσκουσιν Aristonym.ap.Stob.3.4.105; δ. πολλοὺς αὐλητάς Charon

9; τούτους ἱππέας ἐδίδαξεν οὐδενὸς χείρους Pl.*Men.*94b; also δ. τινὰ σοφόν E.*Heracl.*575: with an abstract subject, πολυμαθίη νόον οὐ διδάσκει Heraclit.40; ξενιτείη αὐτάρκειαν δ. Democr.246:—Med., *teach oneself, learn*, φθέγμα καὶ ἀστυνόμους ὀργὰς ἐδιδάξατο S.*Ant.* 356 (lyr.); but usu., *have* one *taught* or *educated*, esp. of a father, τὰ ἄλλα .. διδάσκεσθαι τοὺς ὑεῖς Pl.*Prt.*325b; δ. τοὺς ὑεῖς τὰς κούφας ἐργασίας Arist.*Pol.*1321^{a}24: c. inf., δ. τινὰ ἱππεύειν Pl.*R.*467e; δ. τινα ἱππέα Id.*Men.*93d, cf. X.*Mem.*4.4.5 (this distn. between Act. and Med. was neglected by some Poets and late Prose writers, Med. being used like Act. in Pi.*O.*8.59, Luc.*Somn.*10, etc.; but in Ar.*Nu.*783 Elmsl. restored διδάξαιμ' ἄν σ' ἔτι for διδαξαίμην σ' ἔτι, and in Pl.*R.*421e Cobet cj. διδάξει for -εται: Med. is used of gods, [θεοί] .. ὅπλων χρῆσιν διδαξάμενοι Id.*Mx.*238b):—Pass., *to be taught, learn*, c. gen., διδασκόμενος πολέμοιο *trained, skilled* in war, Il. 16.811: c. acc., τά σε προτί φασιν Ἀχιλλῆος δεδιδάχθαι which [medicines] they say thou *wert taught* by Achilles, 11.831, cf. Arat.529; ὃς οὔτ' ἐδιδάχθη οὔτε εἶδε καλὸν οὐδέν Hdt.3.81; διδάξω καὶ διδάξομαι λόγους E.*Andr.*739: freq. c. inf., δεδιδαγμένον εἶναι χειροήθεα Hdt.2.69; βρέφος διδάσκεται λέγειν ἀκούειν θ' E.*Supp.*914; διδάσκεσθαι ὡς.. X. *HG*2.3.45. 2. c. gen., *indicate, give sign of*, χειμῶνος συναγειρομένοιο Arat.793, cf. 734. II. abs., *explain*, πῶς δή; δίδαξον A.*Eu.* 431; σαφῶς δ. Th.2.60, etc.; *show by argument, prove*, λέγων διδασκέτω X.*An.*5.7.11, etc.; δ. περί τινος ὡς... Th.3.71; ἡλίκον ἐστὶ τὸ ἀλαζόνευμα..πειράσομαι..διδάξαι Aeschin.3.238; ποιητὴς δ. ὅτι..Jul. *Or.*2.50b. III. of dithyrambic and dramatic Poets (cf. διδάσκαλος II), δ. διθύραμβον, δρᾶμα, *produce* a piece, Hdt.1.23, 6.21; Πέρσας Ar.*Ra.*1026, cf. Pl.*Prt.*327d, *IG*1^2.770, al.:—Med., διδάξασθαι χορόν *train one's own* chorus, Simon.145.

δῐδᾰχή, ἡ, *teaching*, Democr.33, Th.1.120, Pl.*R.*536d; ἐκ διδαχῆς λέγειν Hdt.3.134; δ. ποιεῖσθαι Th.4.126.—Poet. only late, Ps.-Phoc. 89. 2. military *regulations* or *discipline*, τοὐναντίον αὐτῶν τῆς στρατιωτικῆς δ. πεποιηκότων *BGU*140.16 (ii A.D.). II. = διδασκαλία II. 2, *IG*14.2124.

δίδημι, Aeol. inf. δίδην and pres. ind. δίδει Hsch., part. διδείς, εἶσα, έν, *GDI*2156, al. (Delph.), fem. δ[ιδέ]ουσα *Delph.*3(2).131: redupl. form of δέω (A):—*bind, fetter*, ὥ ποτ' Ἀχιλλεὺς..δίδη μόσχοισι λύγοισιν (Ep. 3 impf. for ἐδίδη) Il.11.105; οἱ δέ σ'.. ἐν δεσμοῖσι διδέντων (Aristarch. for δεόντων) *let them bind* thee, Od.12.54: 3 pl. ind. διδέασι X.*An.*5.8.24 (v.l. δεσμεύουσι).

δίδραγμον, τό, *weight of two* δραγμαί, Hero *Mens.*60.4; cf. δίδραχμον.

διδράσκω, *run away*, Hsch.: pf., δέδρᾱκα τοῦ καπηλείου Eun.*Hist.* p.255 D.: aor. imper. δράντων prob. l. in *Tab.Defix.Aud.*26 (Crete, iii B.C.); part. δράσαντα *POxy.*1423.6 (iv A.D.); but mostly found in compds., esp. ἀπο-.

δῐδραχμ-ία, ἡ, *tax of two* δραχμαί in Roman Egypt, δ. τοῦ Σούχου θεοῦ *BGU*741 iii 3 (i A.D.). **-ιαῖος**, α, ον, = sq. I, Critias 58 D. **-ος**, ον, *priced at two drachms*, Arist.*Oec.*1353^{a}17; δ. ὁπλῖται soldiers *with pay of two drachms a day*, Th.3.[17]. II. *weighing two drachms*, ὁλκή Eudem.ap.Gal.14.185. III. δ. τόκος interest *at two drachms* per mina per month (24 %), *IG*5(1).1146.38 (Gythium, i B.C.), *BGU* 1126.17 (i B.C.). IV. δίδραχμον, τό, *coin of two drachms*, *IG*1^2.79, Arist.*Ath.*10.7, etc.: esp. *half-shekel*, paid to the temple-treasury at Jerusalem, Lxx*Nu.*3.47, al. (freq. with v.l. δίδραγμον, q.v.), *Ev. Matt.*17.24.

δῐδῠμᾰγενεῖς, οἱ, *twins*, *BGU*447.10 (ii A.D.), *POxy.*1119.26 (iii A.D.).

δῐδῠμαῖον, τό, = ὄρχις, Hp.*Int.*30 (διδύμη, Gal.19.93).

Δῐδῠμαῖος, ὁ, a name of Zeus as worshipped at Didyma in Miletus jointly with Apollo, Nic.*Fr.*1; of Apollo, *SIG*906 *A* (so **Δῐδῠμεύς**, ὁ, of Apollo, Orph.*H.*34.7); τὸ Διδυμαῖον, *their temple* at Miletus, Plu.*Pomp.*24:—**Δῐδύμεια**, τά, *their festival* there, *CIG*2881, al. (Branchidae), *IG*3.129.8.

δῐδῠμάνωρ [ᾱ], ορος, ὁ, ἡ, τό, *touching both the men*, κακά A.*Th.* 849 (lyr.).

δῐδῠμ-άων [ᾱ], ονος, ὁ, ἡ, poet. for δίδυμος, used by Hom. only in dual nom. and pl. dat., *twins*, Il.5.548: later of things, μαζοί Nonn. *D.*3.390; simply, *two*, δούρατα ib.23.33: sg., *double*, κεραίη ib.15.30; βουλή ib.4.179. **-εύω**, *bear twins*, Lxx*Ca.*4.2.

διδύμη, v. διδυμαῖον.

δῐδῠμη-τοκέω, *bear twins*, Scymn.379. **-τόκος**, Dor. **διδυμᾱτόκος**, ον, = διδυμοτόκος, Theoc.1.25, Call.*Ap.*54, *AP*6.99 (Phil.), etc. 2. *twin-born*, Man.4.455.

δῐδύμια [ῠ], τά, *small convexities near the pineal gland of the brain*, Gal.*UP*8.14, al. II. Dim. of δίδυμος III. 2, Paul.Aeg.6.68. III. διδυμίου ῥίζα, = ὄρχις, Hsch.

δῐδύμιος [ῠ], = δίδυμος, *Sammelb.*1068.

δῐδυμνος [ῐ], poet. for δίδυμος (cf. νώνυμνος for νώνυμος), to be read metri gr. in Pi.*O.*3.35.

δῐδῠμο-γενής, ές, *twin-born*, E.*Hel.*206 (lyr.); cf. διδυμαγενεῖς. **-γονος**, ον, = foreg., Ptol.*Tetr.*110, Vett.Val.299.9. **-ζῠγος**, ον, *with a pair of horses*; *twofold*, ὕδωρ Nonn.*D.*15.21; μόρος ib.34. 240. **-ζυξ**, ὑγος, ὁ, ἡ, = foreg., δίφρος ib.21.212; αὐλός ib.23. 211. **-θροος**, ον, *double-voiced*, αὐλός ib.10.234, al. **-κτῠπος**, ον, *double-sounding*, ib.20.307; ἠχώ ib.36.12.

δίδῠμος [ῐ], η, ον, also ος, ον v.l. in Pi.*P.*4.209, E.*HF*656 (lyr.), Pl.*Criti.*113e:—redupl. from δύο, *double, twofold*, Od.19.227, etc.; διδύμαιν χειροῖν S.*El.*206 (lyr.): also in sg., χερὶ διδύμᾳ with *both* hands, Pi.*P.*2.9; δ. ἅλς, i.e. the Pontus and Bosporus, S.*Ant.*967 (lyr.); δ. γένος *AP*7.72 (Men.); δ. ξύλον *forked*, Lxx*Jo.*8.29; τὸ γλυκύ μοι δ., of a wife, *IG*14.1974. II. *twin*, δ. κασίγνητος Pi.*N.*1. 36; δ. τέκνων ἄριστα S.*OC*1693 (lyr.); δ. τέκεα E.*Hel.*220 (lyr.). III. Subst., δίδυμοι *twins*, Il.23.641, Hdt.5.41: of *the Twins* in the zodiac, Eudox.ap.Hipparch.1.2.8, Arat.147, *IG*14.1307; also δίδυμα, τά, Hdt. 6.52; δύο διδύμω E.*Or.*1401 (lyr.). 2. *the testicles*, Lxx*De.*25.11, *AP*5.125 (Phld.): sg., Herophil.ap.Gal.*UP*14.11. 3. *ovaries*, Herophil. l. c., Sor.1.12.

δῐδῠμόστροφος, ον, *turning this way and that*, Man.4.590.

δῐδῠμότης, ητος, ἡ, *duality*, Pl.*Phlb.*57d, Aristid.Quint.2.26, Gal. *UP*8.10.

δῐδῠμο-τοκέω, *to bear twins*, Arist.*HA*573^{b}30. **-τοκία**, ἡ, *a bearing of twins*, Id.*GA*772^{b}14. **-τόκος**, ον, *producing twins*, Id. *HA*573^{b}32. **-χροος**, ον, *two-coloured*, Musae.59: heterocl. dat. sg. διδυμόχροϊ Nonn.*D.*11.378, acc. pl. -χροας ib.21.216.

Δῐδῠμών, ῶνος, ὁ (sc. μήν), name of month at Alexandria, Ptol. *Alm.*9.7.

δίδυξ (leg. δοῖδυξ)· τὸ τριβήδιν (leg. τριβίδιον) τοῦ ὅλμ[ί]ου, Hsch.

δίδωμι, Il.23.620, etc. (late **δίδω** *POxy.*121 (iii A.D.)); late forms, 1 pl. διδόαμεν v.l. in J.*BJ*3.8.5, etc., 3 pl. δίδωσι (παρα-) Id.*AJ*10.4.1, etc.; but thematic forms are freq. used, esp. in Ep. and Ion., διδοῖς, διδοῖσθα, Il.9.164, 19.270, διδοῖ Od.17.350, Mimn.2.16, Hdt.2.48, Hp.*Aër.*12 (ἀνα-), A.*Supp.*1010, etc., διδοῦσι Il.19.265 (always in Hom.), dub. in Att., Antiph.156; imper. δίδου Thgn.1303, Hdt.3. 140, E.*Or.*642, δίδοι Pi.*O.*1.85, Epigr. in *Class.Phil.*4.78, Ep. δίδωθι Od.3.380; inf. διδόναι, also διδοῦν Thgn.1329, Ep. διδοῦναι Il.24.425, Aeol. δίδων Theoc.29.9; part. διδούς, Aeol. δίδοις Alc.*Supp.*23.13: impf. ἐδίδουν -ους -ου, Ar.*Eq.*678, Od.19.367, 11.289 (Ep. δίδου Il. 5.165), etc.; 3 pl. ἐδίδοσαν Hdt.8.9, etc., ἐδίδουν (v.l. ἐδίδων) Hes. *Op.*139, D.H.5.6 codd. (ἀπ-), also ἔδιδον prob. in *h.Cer.*437, δίδον ib.328; Ep. iter. δόσκον Il.14.382: fut. δώσω 14.268, etc., Ep. διδώσω Od.13.358, 24.314; inf. δωσέμεναι Il.13.369: aor. 1 ἔδωκα, used only in ind., Od.9.361, etc., Ep. δῶκα Il.4.43: aor. 2 ἔδων, used in pl. ind. ἔδομεν ἔδοτε ἔδοσαν (Lacon. ἔδον *IG*5(1).1 *B*1), and in moods, δός, δῶ, δοίην, δοῦναι, δούς; Ep. forms of aor., subj. 3 sg. δώῃ, δώῃσι, δῷσι, Il.16.725, 1.324, Od.2.144; 3 sg. δώῃ, Boeot. δώει *SIG*^{2}858.17 (Delph.), *IG*7.3054 (Lebad.), δοῖ *PPetr.*2 p.24; 1 pl. δώομεν Il.7.299, Od.16.184, 3 pl. δώωσι Il.1.137; 3 sg. opt. is written δόη *UPZ*1.4, δοῖ *IG*14.1488, etc.; inf. δόμεναι Il.1.116, δόμεν 4.379 (also Dor., Ar.*Lys.*1163 (ἀπο-), δόμειν *SIG*942 (Dodona)); Cypr. inf. δοϝέναι *Inscr.Cypr.*135.5 H. (also opt. δυϝάνοι ib. 6); Arc. part. ἀπυ-δόας *IG*5(2).6.13 (Tegea); inf. δῶναι *Schwyzer* 666.2 (Orchom., iii B.C.), also in later Greek, *BGU*38.13 (ii A.D.): pf. δέδωκα Pi.*N.*2.8, etc.; Boeot. 3 pl. ἀπο-δεδόανθι *IG*7.3171.35 (Orchom.): plpf. ἐδεδώκει X.*Cyr.*1.4.26:—Med. only in compds.:—Pass., fut. δοθήσομαι E.*Ph.*1650, Is.3.39, etc.: aor. ἐδόθην Od.2.78, etc.: pf. δέδομαι Il.5.428, A.*Supp.*1041, Th.1.26, etc.; 3 pl. δέδονται E.*Supp.*757: plpf. ἐδέδοτο Th.3.109:—*give freely*, τινί τι Od.24.274, etc.: in pres. and impf., *to be ready to give, offer*, Il.9.519, Hdt.5.94, 9.109, Ar.*Fr.*100, X.*An.*6.3.9, etc.; τὰ διδόμενα *things offered*, D.18. 119. 2. of the gods, *grant, assign*, κῦδος, νίκην, etc., Il.19.204, 11.397, etc.; of evils, δ. ἄλγεα, ἄτας, κήδεα, etc., 1.96, 19.270, Od.9. 15, etc.; twice in Hom. in Pass., οὔ τοι δέδοται πολεμήϊα ἔργα not to thee *have* deeds of war *been granted*, Il.5.428, cf. Od.2.78; later εὖ διδόναι τινί *give* good fortune, *provide* well *for*.., S.*OT*1081, *OC*642, E.*Andr.*750: abs., of the laws, *grant permission*, δόντων αὐτῷ τῶν νόμων Is.7.2, cf. Pl.*Lg.*813c. 3. *offer* to the gods, ἑκατόμβας, ἱρὰ θεοῖσιν, Il.12.6, Od.1.67, etc. 4. with inf. added, ξεῖνος γάρ οἱ ἔδωκεν ... ἐς πόλεμον φορέειν *gave* it him to wear in war, Il.15.532, cf. 23.183; δῶκε [τεύχεα] θεράποντι φορῆναι 7.149: later freq. of *giving* to eat or drink, ἐκ χειρὸς διδοῖ πιεῖν Hdt.4.172, cf. Cratin.124, Pherecr.69, etc.; ἐδίδου ῥοφεῖν Ar.*Fr.*203; δίδου μασᾶσθαι Eup. 253; δὸς καταφαγεῖν Hegem.1; τὴν κύλικα δὸς ἐμπιεῖν Pherecr.41; δὸς τὴν μεγάλην σπάσαι Diph.17.7; with inf. omitted, φιάλην ἔδωκε κεράσας Ephipp.10; εὐζωρότερον δός Diph.58; also of *giving* water to wash with, δίδου κατὰ χειρός (sc. νίψασθαι) Arched.2.3, cf. Alex.261. 2. 5. Prose phrases, δ. ὅρκον, opp. λαμβάνειν, *tender* an oath, δοκεῖ κἂν ὀμόσαι εἴ τις αὐτῷ ὅρκον διδοίη Is.9.24, cf. D.39.3, Arist. *Rh.*1377^{a}8; δ. ψῆφον, γνώμην, *put* a proposal to the vote, *propose* a resolution, D.21.87, 24.13: δ. χάριν, = χαρίζεσθαι, S.*Aj.*1354, Cratin. 317; ὀργῇ χάριν δούς *having indulged* .., S.*OC*855; λόγον τινὶ δ. *give* one leave to speak, X.*HG*5.2.20; δ. λόγον σφίσι *deliberate*, Hdt. 1.97; οὐκ, εἰ διδοίης..σαυτῷ λόγον S.*OT*583; δοῦναι, λαβεῖν λόγον, Arist.*SE*165^{a}27 (but δ. λόγον, εὐθύνας, *render* accounts, *IG*1^2.91, al.): δ. δίκην or δίκας, v. δίκη: ἀκοὴν δ. λόγοις *lend* an ear to.., S. *El.*30, etc.; δ. ἐργασίαν *give* diligence, = Lat. *dare operam*, *OGI*441. 109 (Lagina, i B.C.), *POxy.*742.11: c. inf., *Ev.Luc.*12.58: abs., sc. πληγήν, λίθῳ δ. τινί *PLips.*13 iii 3; ἐμβολὰς διδόναι, *ram*, of ships, D.S.13.10. II. c. acc. pers., *hand over, deliver up*, ἀχέεσσί με δώσεις Od.19.167; μιν..ὀδύνῃσιν ἔδωκεν Il.5.397; Ἕκτορα κυσὶν 23. 21; πυρί τινα Od.24.65; πληγαῖς τινά Pl.*R.*574c; ἔδωκε θῆρας φόβῳ Pi.*P.*5.60. 2. of parents, *give* their daughter *to wife*, θυγατέρα ἀνδρί Il.6.192, Od.4.7; also of Telemachus, ἀνέρι μητέρα δώσω 2. 223; τήν..Σάμηνδε ἔδοσαν *gave* her *in marriage* to go to Samé, 15. 367, cf. 17.442; with inf. added, δώσω σοι Χαρίτων μίαν ὀπυιέμεναι Il. 14.268: in Prose and Trag., θυγατέρα δ. τινὶ γυναῖκα Hdt.1.107, cf. Th.6.59, X.*HG*4.1.4, etc.: abs., ἐδίδοσαν καὶ ἤγοντο ἐξ ἀλλήλων Hdt. 5.92.β', cf. E.*Med.*288; also δ. κόρᾳ ἄνδρα Pi.*P.*9.117. 3. διδόναι τινά τινι *grant* another to one's entreaties, *pardon* him at one's request, X.*An*.6.6.31; διδόναι τινί τι *forgive* one a thing, *condone* it, E.*Cyc*.296 (s.v.l.). 4. δ. ἑαυτόν τινι *give* oneself *up*, δ. σφέας αὐτοὺς τοῖσι Ἀθηναίοισι Hdt.6.108, cf. S.*Ph*.84, Th.2.68; τινὶ εἰς χεῖρας S.*El*.1348; δ. ἑαυτὸν τοῖς δεινοῖς D.18.97; εἰς τοὺς κινδύνους Plb.3.17.8; εἰς ἔντευξιν Id.3.15.4; εἰς τρυφήν, εἰς λῃστείας, D.S.17.108, 18.47: c. inf., δίδωσ' ἑκὼν κτείνειν ἑαυτόν S.*Ph*.1341. 5. *appoint, establish*, of a priest, Lxx *Ex*.31.6; δῶμεν ἀρχηγόν ib.*Nu*.14.4; δ. τινὰ εἰς ἔθνος μέγα ib.*Ge*.17.20; *place*, τινὰ ὑπεράνω πάντα τὰ ἔθνη ib.*De*.28.1:—Pass., οἱ δεδομένοι, = *Nethinim, ministers* of the Temple, ib.*Ne*.5.3; ἐδόθη αὐτοῖς ἵνα.. *orders were given* them that.., *Apoc*.9.5. III. in vows and prayers, c. acc. pers. et inf., *grant, allow, bring about that*..., esp. in prayers, δὸς ἀποφθίμενον δῦναι δόμον Ἄϊδος εἴσω *grant that* he may go.., Il.3.322; τὸν κασίγνητον δότε τυίδ' ἴκεσθαι Sapph.*Supp*.1.2; δός με τείσασθαι *give* me *to*..., A.*Ch*.18, cf. *Eu*.31; also c. dat. pers., τούτῳ.. εὐτυχεῖν δοῖεν θεοί Id.*Th*.422; θεοὶ δοῖέν ποτ' αὐτοῖς..παθεῖν S.*Ph*.316, cf. *OC*1101, 1287, Pl.*Lg*.737b. 2. *grant, concede* in argument, δ. καὶ συγχωρεῖν Id.*Phd*.100b, cf. Arist.*Metaph*.990ᵃ12, al.: c. inf., Id.*Ph*.239ᵇ29; δ. εἶναι θεούς Iamb.*Myst*.1.3; ἑνὸς ἀτόπου δοθέντος τἆλλα συμβαίνει Arist.*Ph*.186ᵃ9; δεδομένα, τά, *data*, title of work by Euclid; ἡ δοθεῖσα γραμμή, γωνία, etc., Pl.*Men*.87a, Euc.1.9, etc.; δεδόσθω κύκλος Archim.*Sph.Cyl*.1.6, al.; also in Alchemy, δός *take* certain substances, *PLeid.X*.69. IV. Gramm., *describe, record*, Sch.Pi.*P*.5.93, Sch.Il.16.207. V. seemingly intr., *give oneself up, devote oneself*, c. dat., esp. ἡδονῇ E.*Ph*.21, Plu.*Publ*.13; ἡδοναῖς Philostr.*VS*1.12; ἐλπίδι J.*AJ*17.12.2; εἰς δημοκοπίαν D.S.25.8; δρόμῳ δοὺς φέρεσθαι *at full speed*, Alciphr.3.47.

δῖε, v. δῖος. II. δίε, v. δίω. III. διέ, Thess., = διά, *IG*9(2).517.16 (Larisa).

διεγγελάω, gloss on γλοιάζω, Hsch.

διεγγύ-α, ἡ, (ἐγγύη) *surety, bail*, Sch.Th.3.70. **-άω**, I. *give bail to produce*, σώματα D.H.7.12:—Med., *to take bail for*, κατεγγυῶντος (v.l. δι-) Μενεξένου τὸν παῖδα, Πασίων αὐτὸν ἑπτὰ ταλάντων διεγγυήσατο Isoc.17.14, cf. Plu.*Caes*.11:—Pass., *to be bailed* by any one, ὀκτακοσίων ταλάντων τοῖς προξένοις διηγγυημένοι *bailed* by their Proxeni for eight hundred talents, Th.3.70. 2. *give security*, *SIG*976.49 (Samos, ii B.C.). II. *take pledges, distrain*, ib.629.20 (ii B.C.). III. abs., *mortgage* one's property, Lxx *Ne*.5.3. **-ημα**, ατος, τό, *pledge, security*, *PTeb*.5.12 (ii B.C.), *BGU*112.12 (i A.D.), etc. **-ησις**, εως, ἡ, *giving bail* or *security*, D.24.73, *IG*11(2).287*A*136 (Delos, iii B.C.), D.Chr.11.18 (pl.). II. *giving bail for production*, τοῦ σώματος D.H.11.32.

διεγ-είρω, *wake up*, Anaxipp.1.47, J.*AJ*8.13.7, Hdn.2.1.5; *stir up, arouse*, Lxx *2Ma*.7.21; *excite, promote*, αὔξησιν φυτοῦ *Gp*.9.3.7:—Pass., Hp.*Ep*.15, Arist.*Pr*.876ᵃ22, Lxx *Es*.11.11, Ph.2.485, Longus 2.35; *to be raised up* from a sick-bed, *AP*11.171 (Lucill.); Ep. aor. διέγρετο ib.5.274 (Paul. Sil.). II. *raise*, τὸν αὐχένα Hld.4.4; χώματα J.*BJ*6.1.1, 6.2.7:—Pass., πύλας διεγειρομένας εἰς ὕψος πηχῶν ἑβδομήκοντα Lxx *Ju*.1.4; τοῖς πηδήμασι πρὸς οὐρανὸν διεγείρεσθε μέσον Procop.Gaz.ἠθοπ.ποιμένος p.137 B. **-ερσις**, εως, ἡ, *arousing*, σώματος *Hippiatr*.128. **-ερτέον**, *one must arouse*, Ath.Med.ap.Orib.*inc*.23.19, Archig.ap.Gal.13.176. **-ερτικός**, ή, όν, *exciting, stimulant*, S.E.*M*.6.19; ἀφροδισίων Diph.Siph.ap.Ath.2.64b, cf. Philum.ap.Orib.*Syn*.8.6.4.

διεγκόπτω, strengthd. for ἐγκόπτω, Stob.1.36.2.

διέδεξε, v. διαδείκνυμι.

διέδην, Adv., (διΐημι) *throughout, to the end*, Hsch.

διεδρεία, ἡ, *sitting apart*, of birds whose position was ominous of strife, opp. συνεδρία, Arist.*HA*608ᵇ27 (pl.), Id.*EE*1236ᵇ10 (pl.).

διέδριον, τό, (ἕδρα) *seat for two persons*, Anon.ap.Suid.

δίεδρος, ον, (ἕδρα) *sitting apart*, opp. σύνεδρος, Arist.*HA*608ᵇ28. 2. = διαφανής, Hsch. II. δίεδρον, τό, *tripod-stand*, Callix.2. 2. *chaise-longue*, Antyll.ap.Orib.10.37.5, Erot. (pl.), Suid. s.v. ζεῦγος ἡμιονικόν.

διεζευγμένως, Adv., (διαζεύγνυμι) *discretely*, of ratios, Nicom.*Ar*.2.24.

διεθίζω, *become chronic*, Aret.*CD*1.2. II. of persons, *become habituated*, ἐμέτῳ Archig.ap.Orib.8.23.1.

διειδής, ές, (διεῖδον) *transparent, clear*, Thphr.*CP*6.19.2, Ael.*NA*4.30, Philostr.*Ep*.33; ποταμοί Max.Tyr.36.1: Sup., Luc.*Bacch*.6.

διεῖδον, inf. διϊδεῖν, aor. 2 with no pres. in use (διοράω being used), *see thoroughly, discern* (on the Homeric usage v. δια-είδω), τι Ar.*Nu*.168, Pl.*Phdr*.264c; λόγος οὐ ῥᾴδιος διϊδεῖν Id.*Phd*.62b. 2. *see through*:—Pass., διειδομένη ἐν ὕδατι νῆσος Call.*Del*.191; ἀτραπὸς .. διειδομένη πεδίοιο *seen through* or *across* the plain, A.R.1.546. II. pf. δίοιδα, inf. διειδέναι, Ep. διΐδμεναι Id.4.1360, *distinguish, discern*, ἀνδρῶν..τὸν κακὸν διειδέναι E.*Med*.518, cf. Ar.*Ra*.975, Pl.*Phdr*.262a: fut., διείσεται ἡ χείρ Orib.8.36.6; *decide*, S.*OC*295.

διεικάζομαι, Pass., pf. inf. διεικάσθαι *to be like*, c. dat., Philostr.*Im*.1.19.

διειλέω, *unroll* a book, Plu.2.1039e, dub. in Phld.*Rh*.1.340 S.

διειλημμένως, Adv., (διαλαμβάνω) *distinctly, precisely*, X.*Oec*.11.25, Ptol.*Tetr*.11; opp. ἀδιαλήπτως, Phld.*Ir*.p.83 W., *Rh*.1.158 S.

διειλοκομπάσας· σκιᾷ καὶ κόμπῳ ἐξαπατήσας, Hsch.

διειλύομαι, Pass., *slip out of*, διειλυσθεῖσα δόμοιο A.R.4.35.

δίειμι, serving as fut. to διέρχομαι, impf. διῄειν: fut. διείσομαι Nic.*Th*.494, 837, cf. Hsch.:—*go to and fro, roam about*, Ar.*Ach*.845; of a report, *spread*, λόγος διῄει Plu.*Ant*.56. 2. *pass through*, δι' αὐτῶν μέσων Th.3.21; *get through, escape*, διὰ τῶν πόρων Arist.*Cael*.307ᵇ13; ἔξω Thphr.*CP*5.9.12: abs., Arist.*Ph*.204ᵃ4. 3. *pass*, ἡμέρα χειμέριος δίεισιν Thphr.*Sign*.46; *proceed*, of a play, Ar.*Ra*.920. II. c. acc., *go through, traverse*, Id.*Av*.1392: c. acc. cogn., δ. τὸν θεῖον δρόμον Pl.*Ax*.370e. b. *go through a subject* in speaking or writing, *narrate, describe, discuss*, Id.*Cri*.47c; δ. τῷ λόγῳ Id.*Grg*.505e, cf. Nic. ll. cc., Luc.*Icar*.3.

δίειξις· διάστασις, Hsch. **Διειπετής**, v. Διϊπετής.

διεῖπον, in Hom. also διαεῖπον (v. infr.), serving as aor. 2 to διαγορεύω:—*tell fully* or *distinctly*, μεμιγμένοι .. ἦ ἀπάνευθε; δίειπέ μοι, ὄφρα δαείω Il.10.425; τρόπον πόνων S.*Tr*.22; *declare*, of an oracle, Id.*OT*854; *interpret* a riddle, ib.394, cf. Pl.*Plt*.275a. 2. *speak one with another, converse*, διαειπέμεν ἀλλήλοισιν Od.4.215. II. Med., *fix upon, agree*, διειπάμενος ἐν ᾧ [χρόνῳ] ἀποδώσει Arist.*Oec*.1351ᵇ5: abs., Id.*EE*1243ᵃ31, *Leg.Gort*.9.27.

διειργασμένως, Adv. *elaborately*, Men.Rh.p.387 S.

διείργω, Ep. and Ion. **διέργω**, Ep. also **διεέργω**:—*keep asunder, separate*, τοὺς διέεργον ἐπάλξιες Il.12.424, cf. Hdt.1.180, Pi.*N*.6.2, Th.3.107, E.*Fr*.382.6, *PTeb*.50.6 (ii B.C.); δ. τινὰ τοῦ μὴ συγκεχύσθαι Arist.*HA*562ᵃ25; ποταμοὶ δ. [τινὰς] τῆς οἴκαδε ὁδοῦ X.*An*.3.1.2:—Pass., πόρῳ διείργεται τῆς Ἀττικῆς ἡ νῆσος Plu.*Them*.13; χώρα ἰσθμῷ δ. μὴ νῆσον εἶναι Polyaen.2.2.4: c. inf., *to be prevented from* .., Porph.*Abst*.2.47. 2. *ward off*, Pl.*Criti*.115e; *exclude*, τινὰς παντὸς λόγου Philostr.*VA*3.31.

διείρηκα, v. διερῶ. **διείρομαι**, v. διέρομαι.

δίειρον, τό, dub. sens. in *PFay*.117.21 (ii A.D.).

διειρύω, Ep. and Ion. for διερύω, *draw across*, τὰς νέας τὸν ἰσθμόν Hdt.7.24; *draw through*, νειοῖο ἄροτρον A.R.1.687.

διείρω, aor. inf. διέρσαι Hp.*Art*.11, al., but διεῖραι Id.*Morb*.2.5; imper. δίειρον Aen.Tact.31.18; part. διείρας Luc.*Alex*.26, Ael.*VH*4.28: pf. διεῖρκα X.*Cyr*.8.3.10: pf. part. Pass. διηρμένη Hp.*Art*.70, but διειρμένα *PHolm*.3.14:—*pass* or *draw through*, ὑπάλειπτρον διὰ καυμάτων Hp.*Art*.11; χεῖρας διὰ τῶν κανδύων X. l.c.; τὸν δάκτυλον διὰ τῆς ὀπῆς Ael. l.c.; βελόνας Aeschin.3.166; *insert*, παττάλους Thphr.*CP*2.14.4; λίνον Aen.Tact. l.c.; βελόνην διὰ τῶν ὀφθαλμῶν *PMag.Par*.1.2949: intr., δάκτυλοι οἷον διείροντες Philostr.*VA*4.28. 2. *string* upon, κάνθαρον χρυσῷ *PMag.Lond*.46.229:—Pass., *PHolm*. l.c. II. *string together in order, weave* a story, Philostr.*VA*8.12:—Pass., λόγος διειρόμενος, = εἰρόμενος, f.l. in D.H.*Comp*.26.

διειρωνόξενος, ον, (εἴρων) *dissembling with one's guests, treacherous under the mask of hospitality*, Ar.*Pax* 623.

διείς, v. διΐημι.

διεισ-δύνω or **-δύω**, *go into and through*, [τὴν γῆν] Alex.Aphr.*Pr*.1.127; εἰς τοὺς πόρους ib.2.76, cf. Phlp.*in Mete*.93.37, al. **-δῠσις**, εως, ἡ, *passing through*, Id.*in Cat*.5.33.

διεισέρχομαι, Medic., *effect an entrance through* pores or membranes, Steph.*in Hp*.1.165 D., al.; also **διεισκρίνομαι**, ibid.

διέκ, before a vowel **διέξ** (but διὲξ σωλῆνος Archil.5), *out through*, δ. προθύρου, μεγάροιο, Il.15.124, Od.10.388, etc.; cf. παρέκ.

διεκ-βαίνω, *go through and out of*, τὰ ὄρη Str.12.2.4. **-βάλλω**, *pass* a needle, string, etc., *through, thread*, Hero *Bel*.98.10, Heliod.ap.Orib.44.10.4, Gal.10.417. 2. *subtract from* ζῴδια *in succession*, Vett.Val.175.35. 3. *pay through a bank*, *BGU*1200.23 (Pass., i B.C.). II. intr. (sc. στρατόν), *march through*, Στυμφαλίαν Plb.4.68.5, prob. in Plu.*Pel*.17. 2. of rivers, boundaries, etc., δ. τὰ ὅρια εἰς.. Lxx *Jo*.15.8; ὁ Εὐφράτης δ. διὰ τοῦ Ταύρου Str.16.1.13; δ. εἰς νότον καὶ βορρᾶ(ν) *PLond*.2.154.9 (i A.D.). **-βλητέον**, *one must pass a needle through*, Antyll.ap.Orib.45.24.9. **-βολή**, ἡ, *mountain-pass*, in pl., Plb.1.75.4, 3.40.1: sg., D.S.17.68. II. *estuary*, Str.9.5.22. III. *way out* of a city, J.*AJ*15.7.10 (pl.). IV. *traversing*, Onos.7.1; *passing through*, of needle, Heliod.ap.Orib.44.14.14. V. *acknowledgement of payment received* by a bank, *PTeb*.389.3 (ii A.D.), *BGU*445.8 (ii A.D.). **-βόλιον**, τό, *medicine to eject a dead foetus*, Hp.*Mul*.1.91. **-δίδωμι**, = διαδίδωμι, ibid. **-δικέω**, strengthd. for ἐκδικέω, ἑαυτήν Zos.Alch.p.112 B., cf. *PMasp*.299.14 (vi A.D.), Arg. 3 Hes.*Sc*., Sch.E.*Hec*.1027. II. *claim*, = Lat. *vindicare*, *Cod.Just*.10.16.1 (Pass.). **-δικητής**, οῦ, ὁ, = Lat. *defensor*, ib.10.11.8.7a (pl.). **-δρομή**, ἡ, *darting forth*, ἀστέρων Ptol.*Tetr*.102; *passing through*, Ezek.*Exag*.199 (pl.). **-δύομαι**, aor. διεξέδυν (but διεκδῦσαι· ἀποδρᾶσαι, Hsch.), *slip out through*, Hp.*Morb.Sacr*.7; δ. τὸν ὄχλον Plu.*Tim*.10: abs., prob. in Id.*Pel*.17. **-δῠσις**, εως, ἡ, *means of escape*, δ. μυῶν *mouse-holes*, Ath.3.98d, cf. Plu.*Sert*.13. **-θέστερον**· ἀκριβέστερον, Hsch.; cf. διεκτελέστερον. **-θέω**, *run through, extend*, ἄχρι τῆς γῆς Arist.*Mu*.395ᵃ22; διά τινος Plu.2.666b: c. gen., ib.589d: abs., Id.*Dio* 30; ἐς ἔμετον, of bile, Aret.*SA*2.5. **-θρώσκω**, aor. inf. -θορέειν, *leap through*, Opp.*H*.4.674.

διεκί, Thess., = διότι, *IG*9(2).517.11 (Larisa), 1229.36 (Phalanna).

διεκ-κύπτω, *peep out*, Lxx *2Ma*.3.19, Eust.1754.44. **-λαμβάνω**, *rent, hire*, *PSI*6.584.12 (iii B.C.). **-λάμπω**, *shine out through*, Hld.2.31. **-λανθάνομαι**, Med., *forget utterly*, Q.S.13.380 (tm.). **-λύω**, *dissolve, relax*, Gal.19.70; *remove* hindrances, Vett.Val.183.2:—Pass., Alex.Aphr.*Pr*.1.135. **-μηρύομαι**, *unwind*, Ph.*Bel*.57.44. **-μυζάω**, *suck out*, *Gp*.7.15.2. **-νέομαι**, *depart from among*, A.R.4.409 (tm.); διὲξ ἁλὸς οἶδμα νέοντο they *crossed* the sea, ib.659. **-παίω**, *break* or *burst through*, τῆς ἵππου J.*BJ*5.2.2, cf. Philostr.*Her*.19.4, *Im*.2.23; διά τινος Paus.7.16.5: c. acc., στοάν Diox.3, cf. App.*BC*5.34, etc.: abs., Luc.*Tox*.61:—Med., δ. τὰς πύλας D.H.11.37; τοὺς πολεμίους Plu.*Sert*.21: abs., J.*BJ*7.6.4, Polyaen.4.2.14; δ. ἔξω Iamb.*VP*35.249. **-παυσις**, εως, ἡ, *intermission*, τοῦ κακοῦ Vett.Val.209.25. **-περαίνω**, *go through with*, τὰ τούτων ἐχόμενα δ. X.*Oec.*6.1:—Pass., πρὶν.. βίος διεκπερανθῇ S.*Fr.*646. **-περαιόομαι,** Pass., *pass out through,* Str.12.2.3. **-περάω,** *pass out through,* c. acc., τὰς Ἡρακλέας στήλας Hdt.4.152; δ. τὴν ἄνυδρον *pass quite through* it, Id.3.4; τὸν ποταμόν Id.5.52; βίον E.*Supp.*954; *traverse,* ἀταρπόν Orac.ap.Jul.*Ep.*89b. 2. abs., δ. ἐς χθόνα A.*Pers.*485; of food, like διαχωρέω, Pl.*Ti.*73a. II. *pass by, overlook,* Ar.*Pl.*283, v. Sch. **-περδῑκίζω,** = διαπερδικίζω, Suid. **-πηδάω,** *jump, run about,* Antyll.ap.Orib.6.26.6; *bound violently,* καρδία Aristaenet.2.13. **-πίπτω,** *issue, escape through,* φωτὸς -πίπτοντος διὰ τῶν νεφῶν Epicur.*Ep.*2 p.45 U., cf. Ph.*Bel.*57.3: abs., *escape,* Arist.*Pr.*910ᵃ17; *exude,* τῶν πόρων Plu.2.51a, Gal.10.948; τι Onos. 21.1, Hld.10.28; διὰ τῆς πόλεως Arr.*An.*1.8.7. 2. *escape,* εἰς Θήβας D.S.4.54, cf. 12.56. II. *spread abroad,* of a proverbial saying, Eust.ad D.P.809. **-πλέκω,** dub. sens. in Alex.*Fig.*2.20. **-πλέω,** Ion. **-πλώω,** aor. -έπλωσα:—*sail out through,* τὸν Ἑλλήσποντον Hdt.7.147; τὰς Κυανέας Id.4.89; τὴν διώρυχα Id.7.122; σχοίνους δυώδεκα Id.2.29; Ἡρακλέων στηλέων Id.4.42: abs., *sail out,* ib.43. II. in naval tactics, *break the enemy's line by sailing through it,* so as to be able to charge their ships in flank or rear, Hdt.6.15, Th.1.50, 7.36, Sosyl.p.31 B., Plb.1.51.9. **-πλοος,** contr. **διέκπλους,** ὁ, *passage,* τῶν βραχέων *through* the shallows, Hdt.4.179; δ. ὑπόφαυσιν καταλιπεῖν Id.7.36, cf. Pl.*Criti.*115e. II. *breaking the enemy's line* in a sea-fight, δ. ποιεύμενος Hdt.6.12, cf. Th.1.49, 7.36. **-πλώω,** v. διεκπλέω. **-πνέω,** *blow from start to finish,* of winds, Arist.*Mu.*394ᵇ35. **-πνοή,** ἡ, *exhalation,* Thphr.*CP*4.12.12; πυρός *Placit.*2.24.2. II. *ventilation-hole,* Ph.*Bel.*87.4 (pl.). **-πονέω,** *work out, calculate,* Gal.19.529; prob. for -ποιέω, ib.531. **-πορεύομαι,** *go out through,* D.H.9.26; *pass through, traverse,* διὰ τῆς τῶν ὅλων οὐσίας M.Ant.7.19. **-πτύω,** *spit all about,* Philostr.*Im.*2.23. **-πτωσις,** εως, ἡ, *issue,* of nerves from the spine, Gal.8.57. II. *passage through* a sieve, of powders, Id.11.134. **-ρέω,** *flow out,* ὅκως ἀθρόως δ. τὸ αἷμα Aret.*CA*2.5. **-ροος,** ὁ, *passage for the stream to escape,* Hdt.7.129. **-σεύω,** *drive through,* νῆα διὲκ πέλαγος σεῦεν A.R.2.620. **-τείνω,** *stretch out, extend,* v.l. in Hp.*Mochl.*38 for δεῖ ἐκτ-, cf. Hero *Bel.*99.1:—Pass., fut. -ταθήσομαι Iamb.*in Nic.*p.71 P. **-τελέστερον·** ἀκριβέστερον, Hsch. **-τελέω,** *accomplish,* τὴν οἰκονομίαν *PMag.Par.*1.2107. **-τέλλω,** *arise, grow from,* Nic.*Fr.*74.30. **-τέμνω,** *divide through the midst,* v.l. in J.*BJ*3.10.7. **-τετραίνω,** gloss on διεκπαίω, Hsch.; -τετρημένος v.l. for διατετρ-, Heliod.ap.Orib.49.23.15. **-τρέχω,** aor. -έδρᾰμον, *traverse,* Ph.*Bel.*77.36; ὁππότ' ἂν.. ἠέλιος Κριὸν.. διεκτρέχῃ Orph.*Fr.*285.5: abs., *sally, rush out,* J.*AJ*5.2.11; κυνὸς διεκδραμόντος Plu.2.490d. **-τρησις,** εως, ἡ, *hole bored quite through,* Gal.*UP*10.5 (pl.). **-τρῡπάω,** gloss on διεκπαίω, Suid. **-τῡλόω,** *remove a callus,* Sor.1.46. **-τύλωσις,** εως, ἡ, *removal of a callus,* ibid. **-φαίνω,** strengthd. for ἐκφαίνω, Eust.1538.17:—Pass., Philostr.*Im.*1.14. **-φέρω,** strengthd. for ἐκφέρω, Hsch. s.v. διεξαγάγῃ, A.R.3.73 (tm.). **-φεύγω,** strengthd. for ἐκφεύγω, Plu.*Cam.*27 (v.l.); κακίαν *Corp.Herm.*12.7; διὲκ πέτρας φ. A.R.2.616. **-φύω,** *spring from,* of veins and muscles, Gal.2.786, 18(1).446. **-χέω,** strengthd. for ἐκχέω, Aret.*CA*2.5.

διέλᾰσις, εως, ἡ, *driving through,* of a nail, Plu.2.659d. II. *charge* or *exercise of cavalry,* ἡ εἰς τάχος δ. X.*Eq.Mag.*3.4.

διελαύνω, Att. fut. διελῶ: aor. 1 διήλᾰσα:—*drive through* or *across,* τάφροιο διήλασε μώνυχας ἵππους Il.12.120, cf. 12.120, E.*Supp.*676. b. ἥδε σ' ἡμέρα διήλασε *has brought* you *to the end* (sc. of servitude), Id.*Heracl.*788. 2. *thrust through,* λαπάρης δὲ διήλασε χάλκεον ἔγχος Il.16.318, cf. 13.161; νεκροῦ παρὰ τὴν ἄκανθαν ξύλον.. δ. Hdt.4.72. 3. δ. τινὰ λόγχῃ *thrust* one *through* with a lance, Plu.*Marc.*29, cf. Luc.*DMort.*27.4 (Pass.). II. intr., *ride through,* X.*An.*1.5.12, etc.; *charge through,* ib.1.10.7, al.: c. acc. cogn., δ. ὁδόν Id.*Cyr.*4.4.4. III. Pass., *to be driven through,* $IG1^2$.81.12. 2. *dart through,* of a shooting pain, Aret.*SA*2.7. 3. *to be distributed,* of the branches of an artery, ib.2.1. IV. Med., διηλάσω· διηγήσω, διῆλθες, Hsch.

διελεγκτέον, *one must refute,* Plu.2.450b.

διελέγχω, *refute,* Pl.*Grg.*457e, Arist.*Fr.*94, Plb.7.3.3, Luc.*Prom.*6, etc. II. *convict, expose,* Ph.1.265, al., Plu.2.437b, *PLips.*40iii23 (iv A.D.):—Pass., Philostr.Jun.*Im.*1, *BGU*321.14 (iii A.D.). III. *prove, try,* Philostr.*Gym.*17; *investigate,* Jul.*Or.*3.118b:—Pass., πάντα δ. φωτί Ph.2.345. IV. Med. or Pass., *dispute,* Lxx *Is.*1.18, *Mi.*6.2. 2. Pass., *to be distinguished,* Phlp. *in Mete.*128.30.

διελευθερόω, *liberate,* εἱργμῶν τὸν νοῦν Porph.*VP*46.

διέλευσις, εως, ἡ, *transit,* Ptol.*Tetr.*135.

διέλθυρις· διάμφοδος, Hsch.

διελινήσατο· ἐξέφυγε, Hsch.

διελῑνύω, *to cease entirely from labour or exercise,* Hp.*Acut.*45.

διελίσσω, Att. **-ττω,** *unfold*: *deploy,* of military evolutions, D.C.74.5: metaph., *expose,* Plu.2.411b:—Med., *roll over,* Q.S.6.565.

διελίτην· δόλιον, κακοῦργον καὶ πανταχοῦ διερχόμενον (i.e. διηλύτην), Hsch.; cf. διηλίτης.

διελκ-υσμός, ὁ, *pushing about,* D.H.*Comp.*20. 2. *delay,* *PTeb.*25.2 (ii B.C.). 3. *brawl,* Arg.1 Ar.*Ach.* **-υστίνδα** παίζειν, *tug-of-war,* Poll.9.112. **-ω,** fut. διελκύσω: aor. -είλκῠσα Ar.*Pl.*1036, Pl.*R.*440a:—*tear asunder, open wide,* τοὺς ὀφθαλμοὺς Pl.l.c.; τὸ στόμα D.L.7.20. 2. metaph. in Pass., *diverge, vary,* of Ms. readings, τὸ.. "παντὸς" διέλκεται κατὰ τὰ ἀντίγραφα Demetr.Lac.1012.23 F. II. *pull through,* διὰ δακτυλίου Ar.l.c.; βρόχῳ Hp.*Aff.*5. 2. *haul* ships *across* an isthmus, D.S.4.56. III. of Time, in Pass., *to be protracted,* Plb.31.18.4:—Act., δ. βίον *drag on* life, Plu.2.1033d; δ. τὸν φόρον *postpone payment of* a tax, *BGU*1116.21 (i B.C.), cf. 1120.35 (i B.C.):—Med., *procrastinate,* 2 dual aor. διηλκύσασθον Hsch. IV. *continue drinking,* Ar.*Pax*1131 (where others supply τὸν βίον), cf. *Fr.*109 (dub.).

δίεμαι, Pass., *speed,* ἵπποι πεδίοιο δίενται *speed* over the plain, Il.23.475; οὐ.. μέμονε.. δίεσθαι he is not minded *to hasten away,* 12.304. II. *fear,* c. inf., A.*Pers.*701 (lyr., δείομαι cod. Med.). (Cf. δίω.)

διεμβάλλω, *put in through,* Lxx *Nu.*4.6, al., Gal.2.574, Aët.15.12.

διέμενος, v. δΐημι.

διεμ-μένω, *keep in place,* Gal.18(1).828. **-πῖλος,** ον, *well-capped, well-hatted,* κεφαλή Luc.*Lex.*13. **-πίμπλημι,** *fill completely,* Lxx 2*Ma.*4.40, Hsch. **-πίπτω,** *fall quite into,* εἴς τι Plb.38.9.4. **-πολάω,** *sell to different buyers* or *sell in lots,* E.*Ba.*512; ἐμπορικὰ χρήματα δ. Ar.*Ach.*973. 2. metaph., τί με.. διεμπολᾷ λόγοισι πρός σε; what *bargain* is he *driving*? S.*Ph.*579; of a mercenary marriage, ὠθούμεθ' ἔξω καὶ διεμπολώμεθα Id.*Fr.*583.7. **-φαίνω,** *show through,* ὀφθαλμοὶ.. γοργὸν δ. Luc.*Alex.*3 (dub. l.). **-φᾰνίζω,** *let* a thing *be seen,* Aristaenet.2.16.

διεμφύομαι, *breed in,* τερηδόνων, ἃ διεμφύεται τοῖς δένδρεσι Procl. ad Hes.*Op.*412.

διενέγκαι, Ion. **-ενεῖκαι,** v. διαφέρω.

διεν-ειλέω, *involve,* λόγος διενειλημένος Ps.-Luc.*Philopatr.*1. **-είργω,** *shut quite up,* Gal.17(1).453 (Pass.).

διενεκτέον, (διαφέρω) *one must excel,* Luc.*Astr.*1.

διεν-εργέω, strengthd. for ἐνεργέω, Crito ap.Stob.3.3.64. **-εργητικός,** ή, όν, strengthd. for ἐνεργητικός, δύναμις Herod.Med. in *Rh. Mus.*58.76. **-θῡμέομαι,** *consider, reflect,* περί τινος *Act.Ap.*10.19.

διενῐαυτίζω, *live out the year,* Hdt.4.7. II. *spend a whole year,* *POxy.*899.11 (ii/iii A.D.).

διενίημι, *insert,* Orib.10.24.3, Ruf.ap.eund.8.24.29.

δίενος [ῐ], ον, *two years old,* Thphr.*HP*7.5.5, 8.11.5.

διενοχλέω, *annoy,* τινί Ph.2.590, J.*AJ*9.3.1 (v.l.), Aristaenet.1.5: abs., Luc.*Symp.*14:—Pass., ὑπὸ τῶν πρακτόρων *BGU*830.8 (i A.D.).

διεντέρευμα, ατος, τό, (ἔντερον) *looking through entrails,* Com. word for *sharp-sightedness,* coined by Ar.*Nu.*166.

διέξ, v. διέκ.

διεξ-αγνέω, = sq., *IG*5(1).26.9 (Sparta, ii B.C.). **-άγω** [ᾰ], Aeol. aor. 1 Pass. διεξάχθην *Milet.*3 No.152.25 (ii B.C.):—*lead through,* δύναμιν διὰ τειχῶν D.S.14.20. b. τροφὴ διεξάγουσα *laxative* diet, Aret.*CA*2.5. 2. *bring to an end, settle,* λόγῳ ἀμφισβήτησιν Plb.5.1.5, etc.; *try* a cause, *GDI*5040.69 (Crete):—Pass., *PTeb.*5.219 (ii B.C.), al., *PSI*2.173.15 (ii B.C.); τὸ δίκαιον διεξάγεται Plb.4.73.8. 3. *arrange, manage,* Chrysipp.*Stoic.*3.185; *administer, conduct,* ἀσφαλῶς τὰ κατὰ τὴν ἀρχὴν Plb.1.9.6, cf. *PLond.*3.1221.2 (ii A.D.); ταμιείαν $IG2^2$.1326.38:—Pass., ὁ τῆς φύσεως νόμος καθ' ὃν διεξάγεται τὰ γιγνόμενα Plu.2.568d. 4. *treat,* τινὰς ἐν τῇ πάσῃ φιλανθρωπίᾳ Plb.3.77.4. II. δ. τοὺς βίους ἀπό τινος *support* life, Id.1.71.1: abs., Plu.1090b. **-ᾰγωγή,** ἡ, *settlement* of a dispute, Plb.5.102.3. II. *inquiry, inquest,* *PTeb.*14.6 (ii B.C.), *PRyl.*65.10 (i B.C.). 2. *trial,* δ. ποιήσασθαι *GDI*5040.59 (Crete). III. δ. τοῦ βίου *a way of living,* D.S.4.30, cf. Hierocl.p.53 A., S.E.*M.*7.158, al.: abs., Phld.*Sto.*339.19, Arr.*Epict.*1.6.21, Ecphant.ap.Stob.4.7.64; τὰς δ. ποιεῖσθαι S.E.*M.*1.178. **-ᾰγωγός,** ὁ, *steward, manager,* Sch.Pi.*O.*14.13. **-αιρέω,** strengthd. for ἐξαιρέω, Demetr.*Eloc.*299. **-ᾱΐσσω,** Att. **-ᾴττω,** *rush forth,* Theoc.13.23, Arist.*Mu.*394ᵇ15, 397ᵃ31. **-ᾰμείβομαι,** Pass., *to be passed,* ἐτῶν διεξάμειπτο διπλόα δεκάς *IG*12(8).441.11 (Thasos). **-άνθημα,** ατος, τό, *pustule,* Aret.*SA*1.9. **-ανθίζω,** *variegate with flowers,* cj. Pors. in Eub.99. **-ανίσταμαι,** *rise up, prepare to deal with,* ἐπὶ τὰ λειπόμενα τῶν πραγμάτων Eun.*Hist.*p.263 D. **-ᾰνύω,** *complete,* πλοῦν Iamb.*VP*3.16. **-αρκέω,** *suffice,* πρὸς τὸ παρόν Ph.1.607; εἰς ἑκάστην ἡμέραν Id.2.297, cf. Anon.Lond.37.47. **-αρτάομαι,** *depend on,* τῆς λογικῆς φύσεως Ph.1.446. **-ατμίζω,** strengthd. for ἐξατμίζω, Hp.*Morb.*4.47. **-ᾴττω,** v. διεξαΐσσω. **-ειμι,** (εἶμι *ibo*) *go out through,* διεξίμεναι πεδίονδε Il.6.393; ἐξ αὐλῆς ἐς.. Hdt.2.148. 2. *go through, pass through* a country, δ. τῆς Λιβύης τὰ ἄνω ib.25; τὴν Μιλησίην Id.5.29; διὰ πάσης Εὐρώπης Id.2.36; διὰ παντὸς τοῦ σώματος Th.2.49, cf. 3.45; χώραν, τόπον, Plb.4.25.4, Plu.2.149a. 3. *traverse the whole length of* a line, Arist.*EN*1174ᵃ34. II. in counting or recounting, *go through in detail, relate circumstantially,* Hdt.1.116, 7.77, etc.; περί τινος Isoc.5.4, Pl.*Prt.*361e, etc.; *go through,* by way of examining, E.*Hipp.*1024; *expound,* Epicur.*Nat.*2.11; *deliver,* ἐγκώμιον Plu.*Ant.*14. **-έλᾰσις,** εως, ἡ, = διέλασις, Id.*Sull.*18, Hld.9.18. **-ελαύνω,** Att. fut. -ελῶ: intr., *drive, ride, march through,* abs., Hdt.1.187: c. acc. loci, δ. τὴν ἄνυδρον Id.3.11; τὰς πύλας Id.5.52, etc.; also κατὰ τὸ προάστειον Id.3.86; δ. ἐπὶ ἅρματος Id.7.100; δ. ἵππῳ τὸν πόρον Plu.*Publ.*19: c. gen. loci, δ. τῆς Ῥώμης Id.*Cam.*7. **-ελέγχω,** *refute utterly,* Luc.*Alex.*61, Plu.2.922e, Gal.4.518:—Pass., ὅταν ἀμαθέστεροι διεξελέγχωνται when they *are convicted of* ignorance, Them.*Or.*21.259b. **-έλευσις,** εως, ἡ, = διέξοδος, Sch.A.R.4.1573. **-ελίσσω,** Ion. **-ειλίσσω,** *unroll, untie,* Hdt.4.67. **-εργάζομαι,** *work out, effect,* κακά Pl.*Lg.*798d. II. *make away with,* v.l. in Hdt.5.92.γ' and D.H.6.35. **-ερέομαι,** *question closely,* c. dupl. acc., ἐμὲ ταῦτα Il.10.432, cf. A.R.1.327. **-ερευνάω,** *examine* or *survey closely,* Pi.*N.*3.24 (tm.):—Med., χώραν Pl.*Lg.*763a, cf. *Phlb.*58d. **-έρπω,** *run his course,* of the sun, Arist.*Mu.*399ᵃ24: fut. διεξερπύσει ib.398ᵇ33. **-ερύγησις** [ῠ], εως, ἡ, *power of belching forth,* Orac.ap.Porph.

ap.Eus.*PE*6.3. **–έρχομαι,** fut. –ελεύσομαι, = διέξειμι:—*go through, pass through,* τὸ χωρίον Hdt.2.29, cf. 5.29; πεδίον *Hell.Oxy.*7.3, etc. 2. *go completely through,* νόμον τὸν ὄρθιον Hdt.1.24; πάντας φίλους E.*Alc.*15; τὴν ὁδόν Pl.*Lg.*822a; τὴν δίκην ib.856a; δ. πόνους S.*Ph.*1419: c. part., δ. πωλέων *be done* selling, Hdt.1.196. 3. folld. by διά, *go through in succession,* διὰ πάντων δ. τῶν παίδων, i.e. killing them one after another, Id.3.11; διὰ τῶν δέκα Id.5.92.γ'; διὰ τῶν πόλεων Pl.*Prt.*315a. 4. *go through in detail, relate circumstantially,* Hdt.3.75, 7.18, D.18.21; λόγον Pl.*Lg.*893a; ἡ ψυχὴ δ. λόγον πρὸς αὐτήν Id.*Tht.*189e; τῷ λόγῳ Polystr.p.30 W.; περὶ νόμων Pl.*Lg.*857e. II. intr., *to be past, gone by,* of time, Hdt.2.52; ἡμέρα διεξῆλθεν ἀργή Plu.*Arist.*16. 2. *to be gone through,* of legal formalities, πάντα δ' ἤδη διεξεληλύθει D.21.84, cf. Pl.*Lg.*805b. **–ετάζω,** strengthd. for ἐξετάζω, Iamb.*in Nic.*p.88 P., Asp.*in EN*114.22; διεξητασμένος, of a surgeon, Eun.*VS*p.499 B. **–ηγέομαι,** strengthd. for ἐξηγέομαι, v.l. in X.*Mem.*4.2.12. **–ίημι,** strengthd. for ἐξίημι, *let pass through,* διεξῆκαν αὐτοὺς διὰ τῆς πόλεως Hdt.4.203. II. intr., of a river, *empty itself,* ἐς θάλασσαν Th.2.102 (s.v.l.). **–ικνέομαι,** *arrive at,* εἰς.. Plb.10.29.3. **–ιππάζομαι,** *ride out through,* dub. for διεξεπαίσατο (cf. διεκπαίω), Polyaen.5.16.5. **–ῑτέον,** *one must narrate, describe,* Pl.*Ti.*44d, Arist.*Rh.Al.*1425^{b}2, Agath. *Praef.* **–ιχνεύω,** *search through,* δικαιώματα *PMasp.*167.35 (vi A.D.). **–οδευτικός,** ή, όν, *giving issue,* ποταμῶν δ. ἀφέσεις εἰς θάλατταν *EM*692.52. **–οδεύω,** *have a way out, escape,* Hp.*Epid.*2.3.8; *march out,* J.*BJ*7.5.4. II. c. acc., *go through,* λόγον S.E.*M.*2.9, al. III. Pass., *to be regularized,* διεξωδευμένη φαντασία ib.7.166, al. **–οδικός,** ή, όν, *of* or *for going through*: τὸ δ. *fundament,* Arist. *HA*493^{a}23. 2. Math., *produced by traversing,* of loci (e.g. line by point or surface by line), Papp.662.2. II. *detailed,* λόγος Plb.12.25^{b}4; ἱστορία Plu.*Fab.*16. Adv. –κῶς *in detail,* δ. ἀποκρίνεσθαι, of an answer *involving a statement* (opp. 'yes' or 'no'), *Stoic.* 2.62, etc.: Comp., J.*BJ Prooem.*6, Phlp.*in GA*101.36; *verbatim,* ἀναγραφῆναι *SIG*694.38 (Pergam., ii B.C.); also, *by discursive reasoning,* Ammon.*in APr.*25.2; opp. συμβολικῶς, Porph.*VP*36. **–οδος,** ἡ, *outlet, passage,* Hp.*Aph.*7.51, Arist.*PA*684^{b}26, etc.; ἀποκεκλῃμένου τοῦ ὕδατος τῆς δ. Hdt.3.117, cf. 4.140; διέξοδοι ὁδῶν *passage*-ways, Id.1.199; ἀνέμων διέξοδοι (through the body), S.*Fr.*477; ὅταν πλεύμων μὴ καθαρὰς παρέχῃ τὰς δ. Pl.*Ti.*84d, cf. 91c; *way out from,* Th. 3.98; αἱ δ. τῶν ὁδῶν *Ev.Matt.*22.9; of the main *roads out of* a town, Aristeas 105; δ. ὑδάτων, of a spring, Lxx 4*Ki.*2.21; of tears, ib.*Ps.* 118(119).136. 2. *pathway, orbit,* of the sun, Hdt.2.24; τρεῖς ἡλίου διέξοδοι three *days,* E.*Andr.*1086; of planets, Arist.*Mu.*399^{a}3: metaph., πολλὰς φροντίδων δ. Henioch.4.5; δ. τῶν βουλευμάτων the *paths* of his counsels, Hdt.3.156; δ. τῆς φύσεως, τῆς οὐσίας, Ocell. 1.5, 12; [ὁ νοῦς] ἔχων τὴν αὐτὴν διὰ τῶν οὐκ αὐτῶν δ. Plot.6.7.13. 3. *issue, event,* δ. λαβεῖν Plb.2.1.3, etc. 4. *means of escape,* πάσας δ. διεξελθών Pl.*R.*405c; δ. πραγμάτων *way out of* difficulties, Chrysipp. *Stoic.*3.66. 5. Medic., *evacuation,* Hp.*Prog.*11, Gal.17(1).132 (pl.). II. *detailed narrative* or *description,* ἡ τοῦ λόγου δ. *the course* of the narrative or argument, Pl.*Criti.*109a, cf. *Prt.*361d, Chrysipp.*Stoic.*2.250, Ph.1.407; *exposition,* Phld.*Sign.*38, *Mus.* p.110 K., al.; ἡ διὰ στοιχείου δ. *description* by resolving into elements, Pl.*Tht.*207c; κατὰ διέξοδον in *detail,* Aristid.*Rh.*1 p.505 S.; δ. καὶ ἔπαινοι *narratives, tales,* Pl.*Prt.*326a, etc. III. *military evolution,* δ. τακτικαί Id.*Lg.*813e, cf. D.C.74.5. 2. *excursion,* Pl.*Phdr.* 247a. 3. *repeated experiment,* Gal.10.169. **–οίγνῡμι,** *lay quite open,* πλευρὰ διεξῴξεν Q.S.13.41. **–οιδάω** or **–έω,** pf. part. διεξῳδηκώς, *to swell out,* Philostr.*Im.*1.13. **–ουρέω,** strengthd. for ἐξουρέω, Hp.*Int.*14, Gal.19.652.

διεξωδέστερον, Adv. = διεξοδικώτερον, *more fully, in greater detail,* incorrect formation in Wilcken *Chr.*238.4 (ii A.D.).

διεορτάζω, *keep the feast throughout,* τὰ Ἴσθμια Th.8.9, cf. Plu. *Pyrrh.*20: plpf. διεωρτάκει D.C.47.20:—Pass., ταῦτα διεωρτάσθη these *festivities were kept,* Id.51.21.

διεπαχήσατο· διεπράξατο, Hsch. **διεπέμφρακτο·** διέφθαρτο, Id.

διεπέφρᾰδε, v. διαφράζω.

διεπι-βαίνω, *overlap,* Gal.2.564. **–στέλλω,** *dispatch, PLips.* 10 ii 32. **–φώσκω,** strengthd. for ἐπιφώσκω, D.H.9.63 (prob. f.l. for διέφωσκε).

διέπρᾰθ-ον, –όμην, v. διαπέρθω. **διέπτατο,** v. διαπέτομαι.

διέπω, *manage, conduct,* τὸ πλεῖον πολέμοιο Il.1.166; στρατόν 2.207; ἕκαστα 11.706; σκηπανίῳ δίεπ' ἀνέρας *drove* them *away,* 24.247; δ. πόλιν, ἄλσος, Pi.*O.*6.93, *B.*3.21; μάχας Xenoph.1.21; δ. τὰ πρήγματα, τὸν ἀγῶνα, Hdt.3.53, 5.22: rare in Trag. (lyr.), A.*Pers.*105, *Eu.*931: abs., ἀνὰ στρατιὴν διέπουσαν Sulla ap.App.*BC*1.97: in Prose, Arist.*Mu.*399^{a}18, Ecphant.ap.Stob.4.7.64; δ. ἀρχήν Plu.*Lyc.* 3; ἐπάρχειον *IPE*1^2.174.8 (Olbia, ii A.D.); τὴν τῶν στεμμάτων διοίκησιν *PRyl.*77.30 (ii A.D.); esp. as deputy or substitute, δ. τὰ κατὰ τὴν στρατηγίαν, τὴν ἀρχιδικαστείαν, *PTeb.*522 (ii A.D.), *PLond.*3. 908.19 (ii A.D.). b. Astrol., τὸν πολεύοντα καὶ διέποντα [ἀστέρα] Serapio in *Cat.Cod.Astr.*1.99, cf. Paul.Al.*C.*2. 2. *traverse,* ἅλα *AP*10.24 (Crin.). II. Med., *to be ever engaged in,* γόοις E.*El.* 146 (lyr.).

διέρ-ᾱμα, ατος, τό, *funnel, strainer,* Plu.2.1088e. II. *hopper for lading corn in bulk, PThead.*26, 27 (pl., iii A.D.): hence, **–ᾱμᾰτίτης,** ου, ὁ, *contractor for use* of διέραμα II, *POxy.*1197.4 (iii A.D.).

διέρᾱμαι, *love passionately,* c. gen., f.l. in Pl.*Ax.*370b (cf. διαίρω).

διέρᾱσις, εως, ἡ, *lading of corn in bulk* (cf. διέραμα), *PTeb.*328 (ii A.D.), *POxy.*1197.11 (iii A.D.).

διεραυνάω, later form of διερευνάω, *PMasp.*166.22 (vi A.D.).

διεράω, *strain through,* Plu.2.692c (Pass.).

διεργάζομαι, *work thoroughly, cultivate,* but pf. part. with pass. sense, γῆ διειργασμένη Thphr.*CP*5.13.10, al.; διεργασθέν *dressed,* of wool, Arist.*Pr.*931^{a}14. 2. *work out,* Isoc.10.69; πολλὰ καὶ κακὰ δ. Plb.3.73.7. II. *make an end of, kill, destroy,* ἑωυτόν Hdt.1.213; τινά E.*Hec.*369, cf. Pl.*Lg.*865c (Pass.), Ant.Lib.21.3; μὴ..πόλιν διεργάσῃ S.*OC*1417: plpf. in pass. sense, διέργαστο ἂν τὰ πρήγματα Hdt.7.10.γ'; also aor. διεργασθεῖτ' ἂν E.*Heracl.*174.

διεργάτινος [ᾰ], η, ον, *busy, laborious,* παλάμαι *IG*12(2).129.7 (Mytilene).

διέργω, v. διείργω.

διερεθ-ίζω, *provoke greatly,* Plb.9.18.9, Phld.*Ir.*p.48 W., al., Ph.1. 602, Aesop.250:—Pass., δ. πρὸς ἀλλήλους Arist.*Mir.*837^{b}17; ἔκ τινος Plu.*Oth.*4. 2. *stimulate,* τὰς ἐκκρίσεις Herod.Med.ap.Orib.8.4. 1. **–ισις,** εως, ἡ, *excitation,* Phlp.*in GA*196.33. **–ισμα,** ατος, τό, *provocation,* App.*BC*5.53. **–ισμός,** ὁ, *provocation,* Phld.*Ir.*p.26 W.: pl., ib.p.29 W.; *irritation,* Paul.Aeg.3.66. **–ιστέον,** *one must provoke, stimulate,* Herod.Med.ap.Orib.5.30.27. **–ιστικός,** ή, όν, *provocative,* τῶν συμπτωμάτων ib.23; δ. σημεῖον Phlp.*in GA*197.18.

διερείδω, *prop up,* Plu.2.529c, Luc.*VH*2.1. 2. *hold apart,* as the collar-bones do the shoulders, Sor.2.63: so metaph., of vowels, *thrust apart,* D.H.*Comp.*22. II. Med., *lean upon,* τινί E.*Hec.*66: c. acc., σχῆμα βακτηρίᾳ δ. *lean one's* body *on..,* Ar.*Ec.*150. 2. δ. πρός τι *set oneself firmly, struggle* against.., Plb.21.24.14, Plu.*Phil.* 17, prob. in Phld.*D.*3*Fr.*32; περί τινος for a thing, Plb.5.84.3.

διερείκω, aor. –ήρῐκον (also aor. 1 part. –ερείξας Hsch.), *cleave,* πλευρὰ καὶ θώρηκα Euph.41, Alex.Aet.3.21 (tm.).

διέρ-εισμα, ατος, τό, *supporting beam, IG*2.1054.68, 11(2).287*A* 84 (Delos, iii B.C.); also δ. χαλκᾶ ib.2.652*A*25. **–εισμός,** ὁ, *thrusting apart, separation,* D.H.*Comp.*22. **–ειστέον,** *one must prop up,* Sor.1.114.

διερέσσω, aor. –ήρεσα, poet. –ήρεσσα Od.14.351:—*row about,* χερσὶ δ. *to swim,* 12.444, 14.351. 2. c. acc., δ. χέρας *wave* them *about,* E.*Tr.*1258 (lyr.).

διερευν-άω, *track down,* Pl.*Sph.*241b; *search, examine, CPHerm.* 8 ii 5 (ii A.D.), Jul.*Or.*7.222c, etc.:—freq. in Med., Pl.*Phd.*78a, *Mx.* 240b, Onos.6.7, Plu.*Them.*10, etc.; δ. τί ἐστιν ἑκάτερον Pl.*R.*368c:—Pass., Plb.14.2.1. **–ησις,** εως, ἡ, *investigation,* Str.16.4.5, Iamb. *Comm.Math.*22, dub. in Epicur.*Nat.*135 G. **–ητέον,** *one must track down,* Pl.*Sph.*260e, *Lg.*654e. **–ητής,** οῦ, ὁ, *scout* or *vedette,* X. *Cyr.*5.4.4, 6.3.2. II. *spy,* D.H.4.43. **–ητικός,** ή, όν, Ptol. *Tetr.*57. Adv. –κῶς ib.7.

διερέω, (διερός) *wet, moisten,* prob. l. in Arist.*Pr.*939^{a}28.

διερίζω, *strive with one another,* interpol. in Epigr. in Gell.3.11; περί τι Iamb.*Bab.*4:—Med., *contend with,* τινί Plu.*Cat.Ma.*15.

διερμήν-ευσις, εως, ἡ, *parleying,* Pl.*Ti.*19c; *interpretation,* Iamb. *Myst.*5.5. **–ευτέον,** *one must interpret,* Ph.1.481. **–ευτής,** οῦ, ὁ, *interpreter,* v.l. in 1*Ep.Cor.*14.28. **–ευτικός,** ή, όν, *interpretative,* τοῖς τῆδε τῶν ἀπὸ τῶν θεῶν Olymp.*in Alc.*p.17 C. **–εύω,** *interpret, expound,* Plb.3.22.3, Epicur.*Nat.*1431.17, Phld.*Rh.*1.84 S., 1*Ep.Cor.* 14.27; *translate,* Aristeas 15:—Pass., Lxx 2*Ma.*1.36, *PTaur.*1^{v}4, Ph.1.226.

διέρομαι, Ep. **διείρομαι,** *ask* or *question closely,* τί με ταῦτα διείρεαι; Od.4.492; μὴ ταῦτα διείρεο Il.1.550, etc.: aor. inf., διερέσθαι τινὰ ἐρώτησιν Pl.*Phlb.*42e; διήρετο D.C.38.4.

διερός, ά, όν, *active, alive,* twice in Hom., οὐκ ἔσθ' οὗτος ἀνὴρ διερὸς βροτός Od.6.201, cf. Aristarch. ad loc. (but perh. for δϝι-ερός, 'to be feared'); διερῷ ποδί with *nimble* foot, 9.43; διερῇ φλογί *AP*7. 123 (Diog. Laert.). II. after Hom., *wet, liquid,* ὕδατι διερόν cj. in Pi.*Fr.*107.14; αἷμα τὸ δ. A.*Eu.*263; τὸ δ., opp. ξηρόν, Anaxag. 4, 12; of the air, opp. λαμπρός, v.l. in Hp.*Aër.*15; of birds, which *float* through the air, Ar.*Nu.*337; δ. μέλεα, of the nightingale's notes, dub. l. in Id.*Av.*213; δ. καὶ βαρεῖα γῆ Thphr.*CP*3.23.2; δ. φῦκος Ph. *Bel.*99.24; τοῦ δ. παγέντος Alciphr.1.23; δ. κέλευθος, of the sea, A.R.1.184; πώγων δ. [ὀστρέου] *AP*9.86 (Antiphil.); διερὰς χαίτας εὐώδεας Orph.*Fr.*142; δ. μόρος death *by drowning,* Opp.*H.*5.345; δ. πῦρ the *watery* star, i.e. the constellation Eridanus, Nonn.*D.*23.301. (Prop., acc. to Arist.*GC*330^{a}16 διερὸν μέν ἐστι τὸ ἔχον ἀλλοτρίαν ὑγρότητα ἐπιπολῆς, opp. βεβρεγμένον (*soaked through*), but cf. σπόγγος ὄξει διερός Dsc.*Eup.*1.141; διερά, = σεσηπότα, Hsch.) (In signf. I, perh. cogn. with δίεμαι (but not with βίος): in signf. II, prob. connected with διαίνω.)

διερπύζω, = sq., c. acc., Opp.*H.*2.261, Hld.6.1: c. gen., Nonn.*D.* 13.565, al.

διέρπω, *creep* or *pass through,* πῦρ δ., of the ordeal of fire, S.*Ant.* 265; διά τινος Plu.2.517a: metaph., τὸ διέρπον τῶν μηχανημάτων Eun.*Hist.*p.254 D.: abs., of disease, *spread,* Ph.2.349.

διερριμμένως, Adv. *in a disjointed way,* Plb.3.58.3.

διέρρωγα, v. διαρρήγνυμι.

διέρσις, εως, ἡ, (διείρω) *drawing through,* dub. cj. in Arist.*Pr.*915^a 9 for διαιρέσει: δ. λίνου Aen.Tact.31.18, cf. Gal.19.134.

διέρυθρος, ον, *shot with red,* Dsc.3.9.

διερύκω [ῡ], *keep off,* Arat.299 (tm.); *hinder,* ἀψιμαχίαν Plu. *Lyc.*2.

διερύω, v. διειρύω.

διέρχομαι, fut. διελεύσομαι (but δίειμι is used in Att. as fut., and διῄειν as impf.): aor. διῆλθον:—*go through, pass through,* abs., ἀντικρὺ δὲ διῆλθε βέλος Il.23.876, etc.: c. gen., φάτο... ἔγχος ῥέα διελεύσεσθαι.. Αἰνείαο 20.263, cf. 100; σφαγῶν διελθὼν ἰός S.*Tr.*717; δ. διὰ τῆς νήσου Hdt.6.31; διέρχεται ἅπαντα διὰ τούτου Ar.*Av.*181; δ. διὰ πάντων *Act.Ap.*9.32; εἰ σῶμα οὖσα ἡ ψυχὴ... διῆλθε διὰ παντός Plot. 4.7.8: c. acc., δ. πῶυ, ἄστυ, Il.3.198, 6.392; θύρας (pl.) Lys.12.16; τὴν πολεμίαν Th.5.64; τρεῖς σταθμούς X.*An.*3.3.8. 2. *pass through, complete*, τὸ πέμπτον μέρος τῆς ὁδοῦ Hdt.3.25; τὸν βίον Pl. *R.*365b, etc.; παιδείαν X.*Cyr.*1.5.1. 3. of reports, βάξις διῆλθ' Ἀχαιούς S.*Aj.*999: abs., διῆλθεν ὁ λόγος *went abroad, spread*, Th.6.46, cf. X.*An.*1.4.7; κληδὼν γῆς διῆλθε S.*Ph.*256. 4. of pain, *shoot through* one, ib.743; of passion, ἵμερος δ. Ἡρακλῆ Id.*Tr.*477; ἐμὲ διῆλθέ τι a thought *shot through* me, E.*Supp.*288. 5. *pass through and reach, arrive at*, βίου τέλος Pi.*I.*4(3).5. 6. *go through in detail, recount*, λόγον Id.*N.*4.72; χρησμόν A.*Pr.*874; ἃ διῆλθον the *details I have gone through*, Th.1.21; ὀλίγα διελθών a little *further on*, Pl.*Prt.*344b; δ. περί τινος Isoc.4.66, 9.12, Pl.*Prt.*347a; ὑπέρ τινος Plb.1.13.10; πάντα μετὰ φρεσί *h.Ven.*276; πρὸς αὐτόν Isoc.11.47; δ. τίς πολιτεία... συμφέρει Arist.*Pol.*1296b14. II. intr. of Time, *pass, elapse*, χρόνου οὐ πολλοῦ διελθόντος Hdt.1.8, cf. 3.152, D.23. 153, Plb.20.10.17; τοῦ διεληλυθότος ἔτους the *past* year, *BGU*410.7 (ii A.D.), etc.; διελθουσῶν τῶν σπονδῶν Th.4.115; διελθὼν ἐς βραχὺν χρόνον *having waited*, E.*HF*957 codd. (fort. ὡς).

διερῶ serving as fut., **διείρηκα** as pf., of διαγορεύω (διεῖπον (q.v.), being aor.):—*say fully, distinctly, expressly*, Pl.*Lg.*809e, etc.; διείρηκεν ὁ νόμος D.20.28, cf. 23.72:—Pass., aor. διερρήθην Pl.*Lg.*932e: pf. διείρημαι ib.813a, etc.; διειρημένον *it having been expressly stated*, D.17.28.

διερωτ-άω, *cross-question*, τινά Pl.*Ap.*22b, *Grg.*458a, etc.; δ. τινά τι Id.*Prt.*315c. II. *ask constantly* or *continually*, οἱ διερωτῶντες ὑμᾶς.. τί βούλεσθε; D.3.22. **–ητέον**, *one must cross-question*, Gal.18(2).638.

διεσθίω, fut. –έδομαι Plu.2.170a: aor. διέφᾰγον Hp.*Mul.*1.2:—*eat through*, δ. τὴν μητέρα (v.l. μήτραν), of young vipers, Hdt.3.109, cf. Arist.*HA*558a30. II. *consume, corrode*, Hp. l.c., Plu. l.c.: metaph., D.L.5.76:—Med., τὴν ψυχήν Ph.2.541.

διεσιαῖος, α, ον, (δίεσις III) *consisting of quarter-tones*, διαστήματα Aristid.Quint.3.11; τόπος Cleonid.*Harm.*6; λεῖμμα Theo Sm. p.91 H.

δίεσις, εως, ἡ, (διΐημι) *sending through, discharge*, of a liquid, f.l. for δέξις, Hp.*Superf.*29; *putting through*, τῆς πλεκτάνης διὰ τοῦ αὐλοῦ Arist.*GA*720b33; *letting through*, opp. σύλληψις, Plu.*Art.*3. 2. *release, discharge*, *Sammelb.*4638.21 (ii B.C.). 3. *dismissal* of a wife, *divorce*, *PMasp.*153.17 (vi A.D.), etc. II. *moistening, wetting*, Hp.*Ulc.*14, Dsc.1.26. III. in Music, the *smallest interval* in the scale, [ἡ ἀρχὴ] ἐν μέλει δ. Arist.*APo.*84b39, cf. *Metaph.*1053a 12, D.H.*Comp.*11, etc.; *semi-tone* in the diatonic scale, Philol.6, Arist.*Pr.*917b36; in enharmonic, *quarter-tone*, Aristox.*Harm.*p.21 M., etc., cf. Theo Sm.p.55 H.

διεσκεμμένως, Adv. *prudently*, X.*Oec.*7.18.

διεσκευασμένως (–σκεδ– cod.)· διατετυπωμένως, Hsch.

διεσμιλευμένως, Adv. *in polished style*, Poll.6.150, Hsch.

διεσπαρμένως, Adv., (διασπείρω) *in a disjointed manner*, Aristid. Quint.1.2, v.l. for sq. in Gal.*UP*16.1.

διεσπασμένως, Adv. *intermittently*, δ. πνεῖν (al. διεσπαρμένως) Hp. *Epid.*1.1, 3.2; *in a disjointed manner*, Gal.*UP*16.1.

διεσπουδασμένως, Adv. *diligently*, D.H.1.6 codd.

διέσσῠτο, v. sub διασεύομαι.

διεστραμμένως, Adv., (διαστρέφω) *perversely*, Lxx *Si.*4.17; *distortedly*, τῶν ὄψεων δ. ἔχειν Hld.2.19.

διεσφαλμένως, Adv. *wrongly*, Arr.*Epict.*3.23.3.

διετᾰρίστρια, ἡ, = τριβάς, Hsch.

δι-ετηρίς, ίδος, ἡ, (διετής) *space of two years*, Lxx *2Ki.*13.23, *IG Rom.*4.850 (Laodicea ad Lycum). **–ετήρων**, ον, gen. ονος, = sq., μόσχος *Epigr.Gr.*1035.21 (Pergam.). **–ετής**, ές, or **διέτης**, ες, *of* or *lasting two years*, χρόνος Hdt.2.2, etc.; κύησις Arist.*GA*777b15, etc.; ἀρξάμενος ἀπὸ διετοῦς Id.*HA*500a11; ἐπὶ διετὲς ἡβᾶν to be *two years* past puberty, Is.10.12, Aeschin.3.122, Lexap.D.46.20. II. *two years old*, Arist.*HA*545b11. III. = sq., Hsch. **–ετήσιος**, ον, *lasting through the year*, θυσίαι Th.2.38, cf. *Inscr.Prien.*112.69 (i B.C.). Adv. –ίως Ar.*Fr.*766. **–ετία**, ἡ, = διετηρίς, Ph.2.536, *Act. Ap.*24.27, 28.30; διετίᾳ Cleom.1.3, *CIG*5033 (Nubia), *Inscr.Magn.* 164.12, *POxy.*707.24 (ii A.D.), Theo Sm.p.136 H.; ἐκ διετίας βήσσοντα *SIG*1171.4 (Lebena). **–ετίζω**, (ἔτος) *live the year through*, i.e. *live more than a year*, of wasps, Arist.*HA*627b29; of plants, *to be biennial*, Thphr.*HP*1.2.2.

διέτμᾰγεν, διέτμᾰγον, v. διατμήγω.

διευεργετέω, *to be a firm friend to*, τινά Sch.A.*Pers.*854 (prob.).

διευθετ-έω, *set in order*, Cic.*Att.*6.5.2 (prob.), Sch.A.*Pers.*854. **–ησις**, εως, ἡ, *good order*, Eust.26.27.

διευθηνέω, *continue in prosperity*, οὐκ ἐπὶ πολὺ δ. Ptol.*Tetr.*194.

διευθυδρομέω, *persevere with*, τὰς πράξεις *Cat.Cod.Astr.*7.218.23.

διευθ-υντήρ, ῆρος, ὁ, *pilot, governor*, Man.4.106. II. δ. ψήφων *accountant, auditor*, *Cat.Cod.Astr.*2.172 (pl.). **–ύνω**, *make* or *keep straight*, δρόμον Ph.1.327. II. *set right, amend*, Luc.*Prom.* 19, Man.4.90. III. *settle* an account, *PLond.*3.924.8.

διευκρῑν-έω, pf. διευκρίνηκα Phld.*Rh.*2.47 S.:—*arrange carefully*, διηυκρινημένοι ὁπλῖται X.*Oec.*8.6. II. *examine thoroughly, elucidate*, ὑπέρ τινος Plb.2.56.4; περί τινος ποτέροις.. Id.3.28.5; τὰ ἀπορούμενα D.H.*Comp.*20, cf. Phld. l.c., Porph.*Abst.*2.4, etc.:—Pass., ὁ περί τινος λόγος –εῖται Plb.6.5.1, cf. Iamb.*Myst.*8.4, al.:—Att., only in Med., as Pl.*Prm.*135b, D.27.15. 2. *judge rightly*, τὰ διαφέροντα Plb.31.8.1, al. **–ημένως**, *distinctly*, Vett.Val.309.12; *in careful order*, Simp. *in Cat.*301.20. **–ής**, ές, *clear, distinct*, Suid. **–ησις**, εως, ἡ, *analysis, discussion, elucidation*, Ptol.*Alm.*12.3, Simp.*in Cael.*194.2.

διευλᾰβ-έομαι, aor. –ηυλαβήθην Pl.*Lg.*843e:—*take good heed to, beware of, be on one's guard against*, c. acc., Id.*Phd.*81e, *Lg.*797a, Lxx *De.*28.60, Plb.14.2.7, etc.: c. gen., Pl.*Lg.*843e; δ. μὴ... ib.789e; but δ. μὴ παθεῖν Id.*Ep.*351c. 2. *reverence*, τινά Id.*Lg.*879c. **–ητέον**, *one must take heed to*, τὰ τοιαῦτα Id.*R.*536a.

διευλῠτ-έω, *pay off, liquidate* debts, etc., *BGU*1151.42 (i B.C.), J. *AJ*16.9.3:—Pass., *POxy.*268.15 (i A.D.). **–ησις**, εως, ἡ, *discharge* of a debt, *PLips.*120.12 (i A.D.). **–όω**, = διευλυτέω, *pay off* a debt, *PTeb.*381.18 (ii A.D.). II. αἰτιῶν ἑαυτοὺς δ. *clear* themselves from charges, Just.*Nov.*123.22. **–ωσις**, εως, ἡ, *discharge* of a debt, *Gloss.*, prob. in Petersen-Luschan *Reisen in Lykien* p.12 No.19.

διευημερέω, *enjoy good success throughout*, Paul.Al.*N.*4.

διευνάω, *lay asleep*, τὸν βίοτον E.*Hipp.*1377 (lyr.).

διευπρᾱγέω, *continue fortunate*, J.*AJ*6.10.2.

διευρῑπῑδίζω, *play the part of Euripides*, Sch.Ar.*Eq.*19.

διευρῑπίζω, *to be constantly changing like the tide of the Euripus*, Arist.*Pr.*940a3 (διαρριπίζω cj. Dind.).

διευρύνω, *dilate*, in Pass., Hp.*Morb.*4.52, Aen.Tact.31.12, Arist. *de An.*422a3.

διευστοχέω, strengthd. for εὐστοχέω, D.H.*Comp.*11.

διευσχημονέω, *preserve decorum*, Plu.*Ages.*29, *PSI*6.571.12.

διευτακτέω, *pay interest regularly*, *BSA*22.205 (Mylasa, i B.C.). II. Pass., *to be regularly arranged in sequence*, Iamb. *in Nic.*p.46 P., al.

διευτελίζω, *hold very cheap*, Ael.*VH*14.49.

διευτονέω, *make one's way through, win through*, Thphr.*Sens.*7; πρὸς χώραν Plb.4.43.8. II. *acquire strength*, Sor.1.95.

διευτρεπίζω, *prepare*, Suid. s.v. Σεμίραμις.

διευτῠχέω, *continue prosperous*, τῇ οὐσίᾳ D.42.4; λήξεως Ael.*NA* 17.27; περί τι Theopomp.Hist.111: abs., Men.531.3, etc.; διευτύχει *fare thee well*, *CIG*4076 (Ancyra), cf. *PMag.Berol.*1.194, *BGU* 1197.23 (i B.C.).

διεφθάρᾰτο, v. διαφθείρω.

διέφθος, ον, *well-boiled*, opp. ὀπτός, Hp.*Aff.*40 (Comp.), Antig.*Mir.* 82, prob.l. in Dsc.2.120, etc.; ἀκροκώλια Pherecr.108.14, Telecl.48.

διεφικνέομαι, pf. διέφιγμαι dub. sens. in Eun.*Hist.*p.361 D. (leg. διέσφιγκται).

διέχ-εια, ἡ, *breach of continuity*, Aristid.Quint.3.10, Sch.Ar.*Pax* 938; κατὰ διέχειαν ἀριθμεῖσθαι to be reckoned *exclusively*, Steph. *in Hp.*1.198 D. **–ής**, ές, *discontinuous*, opp. συνεχής, Plu.2.115f, Aristid.Quint.3.10; σπεῖρα Procl.*in Euc.*p.119 F.

διεχθρ-αίνω, strengthd. for ἐχθραίνω, τινί S.E.*M.*1.49. **–εύω**, strengthd. for ἐχθρεύω, τινί D.H.4.70, Arr.*Cyn.*12.5; τὸ –εῦον *enmity*, Alciphr.2.3.

διέχω: I. trans., *keep apart* or *separate*, ὁ ποταμὸς δ. τὰ ῥέεθρα Hdt.9.51; δ. τὴν φάλαγγα *leave gaps in* it, Arr.*An.*1.1.10 (so abs., διασχεῖν *make way for* a person, Plu.*TG*18); δ. τοὺς μαχομένους Id. *Caes.*20; δ. τὰς χεῖρας *spread* them *out*, esp. for the purpose *of parting* combatants, Plb.4.52.1; τὰς χεῖρας ἐν μέσῳ δ. Plu.*Cim.*19; διασχοῦσα τὰς χεῖρας Id.*Ant.*20: c. gen., τῆς ἐσθῆτος διασχών Id.*Aem.* 31. 2. *hold fast*, κόντους Paus.10.25.2. II. intr., *go through, hold its way*, ἀντικρὺ δὲ διέσχε [ὀϊστός] Il.5.100, 11.253; δι' ὤμου δ' ὄβριμον ἔγχος ἔσχεν 13.520; διά τινος δ. Arist.*HA*496b31; *extend, reach*, ἐς τὸν Ἀράβιον κόλπον Hdt.4.42, cf. 7.122; ἀπὸ τῶν νεύρων πρὸς τὰς φλέβας Arist.*HA*515b28. 2. *stand apart, be separated, distant*, ἑκὰς δ. Thgn.970; ὅταν διάσχῃ τὰ κέρατα X.*An.*3.4.20, cf. Th. 8.95 (v.l.); δ. πολὺ ἀπ' ἀλλήλων Id.2.81; δ. ἀλλήλων ὡς τεσσαράκοντα στάδια X.*An.*1.10.4; διέχοντες πολὺ ᾖσαν they marched *with* broad *intervals*, Th.3.22; ὁ Ἑλλήσποντος ταύτῃ σταδίους ὡς πεντήκοντα διεῖχε *was* about fifty stades *wide* at this point, X.*HG*2.1. 21. 3. of Time, παιδὸς δὲ βλάστας οὐ διέσχον ἡμέραι τρεῖς not three days *parted* the birth (sc. from what followed), S.*OT*717. 4. of the earth, *open*, σεισμῷ Philostr.*Her.*1.2; of a river, *broaden out*, Arr.*An.*6.5.3. 5. *differ*, γέννη τε κρήσει τε Emp.22.6, cf. Arist. *Rh.*1412a12; οὐθὲν ἂν διέχοι φαγεῖν ἢ μὴ φαγεῖν Id.*Metaph.*1063a 31. b. *excel*, τόλμῃ καὶ προθυμίᾳ App.*Pun.*132.

διεψευσμένως, Adv. *falsely* or *mistakenly*, Str.1.3.1 codd., M.Ant. 2.17.

διέψω, *scorch thoroughly*, δ. ἀνθρώπους, of the effect of the westering sun, in Hp.*Aër.*6.

δίζα· αἴξ (Lacon.), Hsch.

δίζημαι, Hdt.7.103, Anacr.4, Theoc.16.68: 2 sg. δίζηαι Od.11. 100: 3 pl. δίζηνται B.1.67, once in Trag., A.*Supp.*821 (lyr.); part. διζήμενος Od.16.391, al., Hdt.7.142, al.: impf. ἐδίζητο Id.3.41, Phoen.1.4: fut. διζήσομαι Od.16.239, Lyc.682; 2 sg. διζήσεαι Parm. 8.6: aor. ἐδιζησάμην Heraclit.101. (Ep., Ion., Lyr., = Att. ζητέω (which occurs only once in Hom.); cf. δίζω II):—*seek out, look for* among many, Πάνδαρον... διζημένη εἴ που ἐφεύροι Il.4.88, cf. 5.168, Anacr.4; ἐδιζησάμην ἐμεωυτόν Heraclit. l.c. II. *seek for*, ἢ καὶ διζησόμεθ' ἄλλους Od.16.239; νόστον δίζηαι; 11.100; νόστον ἑταίροισιν διζήμενος ἠδ' ἐμοὶ αὐτῷ *devising means for* a return, 23.253; μνάσθω ἐέδνοισιν διζήμενος *seeking to win her* by gifts, 16.391; γύην... κατ' ὄρος δ. ἢ κατ' ἄρουραν Hes.*Op.*428; δ. τὸ μαντήϊον *to seek out, seek the meaning of*, Hdt.7.142; ἀγγέλους δ. εἰ... *to inquire of* them whether.., Id.4.151; δ. ἐπ' ᾧ ἄν.. Id.3.41; ὅτινι.. Theoc.16.68:

abs., Democr.108. III. c. inf., *seek, desire* to do, πλέον δ. ἔχειν Hdt.2.147, cf. A. l. c., B. l. c., and later Ep., Tryph.525, etc.: c. acc. et inf., *demand, require that*.., σὲ δ. εἴκοσι εἶναι ἀντάξιον Hdt.7.103. (Perh. redupl. fr. root of ζητέω.)

δίζησις, εως, ἡ, *inquiry*, Parm.1.33, 4.2, Orph.*Fr.*333 (pl.).

δι-ζῡγής, ές, = δίζυξ, πῆχυς *containing two bones*, Heliod.ap. Orib.44.23.26. **-ζῠγία**, ἡ, *double yoke of draught-cattle*, *Gp.* 2.23.14. **-ζῠγος**, ον, = δίζυξ, μέλος, οὐρή, Nonn.*D.*15.55, 39. 330. **-ζυξ**, ζυγος, *double-yoked*, ἵπποι Il.5.195, 10.473; *double*, δίζυγος ἠπείροιο *AP*4.3b.40 (Agath.); δ. χαλκός *castanets*, ib.9.139 (Claudian): neut. pl., δίζυγα ξύλα *IG*12(9).907.30 (Chalcis); δίζυγι πυρί Nonn.*D.*22.352; δ. κῶλα *having two bones* (cf. διζυγής), Paul. Aeg.6.107.

δίζῠφον, τό, = ζίζυφον, *POxy.*920.1 (pl., ii/iii A. D.).

δίζω, Ep. impf. δίζον Il.16.713:—*to be in doubt, at a loss*, δίζε γὰρ ἠὲ μάχοιτο.., ἦ λαοὺς ὁμοκλήσειε l. c.; δίζω ἤ σε θεὸν μαντεύσομαι ἢ ἄνθρωπον Orac.ap.Hdt.1.65:—Med., δ. ὅτι.., μή.., Eus.Mynd.58, Tryph.240. II. Med., = δίζημαι II, ἄτεκνον ἔριθον δίζεσθαι Hes.*Op.* 603 codd.; δίζεαι Theoc.25.37; δίζετο Bion *Fr.*14.2, Coluth.81, Epic. in *Arch.Pap.*7.9, etc.; διζόμεσθα Herod.8.12; δίζοντο Q.S.4.16; opt. δίζοιτο Ecphant.ap.Stob.4.7.64; part. διζόμενος *APl.*4.146, *Epigr. Gr.*226.10. (Perh. fr. δίς, cf. διστάζω.)

δίζῳδος, ον, (ζῴδιον) *bearing two figures*, of coins, *PLips.*13.10 (iv A. D.), *BGU*316.16 (iv A. D.).

δίζωος, ον, (ζωή) *with two lives*, φὼρ δίζωος, i. e. Sisyphus, who returned from Hades, Dosiad.*Ara*17.

δίζως, ων, *of double form*, of Pan, Theoc.*Syrinx*5.

διηγανές· λαμπρόν, Hsch.

διηγ-έομαι, *set out in detail, describe*, [ἔργα] Heraclit.1; πρᾶγμα Ar. *Av.*198; τὴν ἀλήθειαν περί τινος Antipho1.13, cf. Th.6.54, Pl.*Prt.* 310a, al.; περὶ ταύτης εἰπεῖν καὶ διηγήσασθαι D.21.77: c. acc. pers., οἷον.. σὺ τοῦτον διηγῇ such as you *describe* him, Pl.*Tht.*144c. **-ημα**, ατος, τό, *tale*, λέγειν Phoenicid.4.15; δ. ἀνωφελές Plb.1.14.6, cf. Lxx *De.*28.37, Polem.*Call.*42, Porph.*Antr.*4, etc. **-ηματικός**, ή, όν, *descriptive, narrative*, δ. ποίησις, μίμησις, Arist.*Po.*1459^{a}17, ^{b}36; παρεκβάσεις Plb.38.6.1; διάλογοι Plu.2.711c; ποιητής Sch.Il.*Oxy.*1086. 59. Adv. -κῶς Corn.*Rh.*p.371 H., D.L.9.103. II. *fond of narrating*, τινός Plu.2.631a, cf. 513d. **-ημάτιον**, τό, Dim. of διήγημα, Str.14.2.3. **-ησις**, εως, ἡ, *narration, narrative*, Pl.*R.*392d, *Phdr.* 246a, Aristeas 1, *Ev.Luc.*1.1, etc.; in a speech, *statement of the case*, Arist.*Rh.*1416^{b}29, Zeno*Stoic.*1.23. **-ητέον**, *one must narrate*, Aps.*Rh.*p.250 H., Trypho *Trop.*4, etc. **-ητής**, οῦ, ὁ, *narrator*, Ach.Tat.4.15. **-ητικός**, ή, όν, = διηγηματικός I, Arist.*Po.*1459^b 33. II. = δ. II, Id.*EN*1117^{b}34.

διηέριος, α, ον, also ος, ον, *through the air*, δ. ποτέονται A.R.2.227, etc.:—in Prose, **διαέριος**, ον, Luc.*Salt.*42, etc.; διαέρια λέγειν, = μετέωρα λ., Id.*Icar.*1.

διηθ-έω, *strain through, filter*, Hp.*Acut.*7, Pl.*Sph.*226b, *Ti.*45c; οἶνον δ. πυρέττοντι Plu.2.101c, cf. *Mim.Oxy.*413.161:—Pass., Arist. *Mete.*368^{a}22, Plb.34.9.10; of air in the lungs, Gal.2.705; καθαρὸν καὶ διηθημένον [γένος], opp. μικτόν, Ph.2.3. 2. *wash out, cleanse*, τὴν κοιλίην οἴνῳ, θυμιήμασι, Hdt.2.86. II. intr., of liquid, *filter through, percolate*, Id.2.93. **-ημα**, ατος, τό, *product of sifting*: δ. γῆς *riddled* earth, Sor.2.88; δ. αἵματος, of urine, Steph.*Urin.* 1. **-ησις**, εως, ἡ, *straining, percolation*, Epicur.*Ep.*2 p.45 U., Thphr.*CP*6.1.1, Plu.*Ant.*3: pl., D.Chr.33.6; *filtering* of urine in kidneys, Aret.*SD*2.3; *haemorrhage*, κατὰ δ. Aët.15.10. **-ητέον**, *one must strain*, Dsc.2.76.6. **-μεύω**, = διηθέω, Hsch. s. v. διυλίζοντες.

διηκονέω, διήκονος, διηκόσιοι, Ion. for διακ-.

διηκρῑβωμένως, Adv., (διακριβόω) *exactly, carefully*, Arist.*Rh.Al.* 1420^{a}10, Ph.1.92, cj. in Pl.*Lg.*965a.

διήκω, fut. -ξω Gal.*Anim.Pass.*1:—*extend* or *reach* from one place to another, ἐκ... εἰς or ἐπί..., Hdt.2.106, 6.31; μέχρι.. Id.4.185; ἄχρις... Ti.Locr.101a; δ. ἔς τε τὸ ἔσω.. καὶ ἐς τὸ ἔξω, i. e. *right through*, Th.3.21; ἀπό... πρός... Luc.*VH*1.19; διὰ πάντων Corn.*ND* 11; κατά, περί τι, Iamb.*Comm.Math.*4, 15. II. c. acc., *pervade*, πόλιν διήκει.. βάξις A.*Ag.*476 (lyr.), cf. *Th.*900 (lyr.); τὸ σὸν ὄνομα δ. πάντας, *volitat per ora*, S.*OC*306 (but in an inverted constr. σῶφρον γὰρ ὄμμα τοὐμὸν Ἑλλήνων λόγος πολὺς διήκει E.*Hyps.Fr.*34(60).45); διὰ πάντων διήκουσα δύναμις Arist.*Mu.*396^{b}29; κατὰ στενὸν δ. ib.393^b 5; αἱ κοιναὶ καὶ διήκουσαι κακίαι *pervading* faults, Phld.*Sign.*28: c. gen., φρόνημα δ. λόγου Philostr.*VS*1.17.3; ἡδονὴ δ. [ποιημάτων] Id.*Her.*18.1. 2. *pass over*, ἡλίου κύκλος μέσον πόρον διῆκε A.*Pers.* 505. 3. *discuss in detail*, Gal. l. c.

διήλᾰσε, v. διελαύνω. **διηλᾰσίην**· δίοδον, Hsch.

διηλιόω, *expose to the sun's heat*, Thphr.*CP*4.12.12 (Pass.).

διηλίτης· κακοῦργος, ἀπατεών, Hsch.; cf. διελίτην.

διηλῐφής, ές, (ἀλείφω) *sleek with unguents*, γένειον S.*Fr.*564.

διηλλαγμένως, Adv. *differently*, Str.13.1.3, D.S.2.31.

διηλόω, *drive a nail through, nail fast*, Lxx *Jd.*5.26:—Pass., τεῖχος πασσάλοις δ. Jul.*Or.*2.76a.

διήλῠσις, εως, ἡ, *passage through*, πόντοιο A.R.4.1573.

διημαρτημένως, Adv. *erroneously*, Hipparch.1.1.4, al., Alex.Aphr. *in Metaph.*172.5.

διημερεύω, *pass the day*, μετά τινος Pl.*Phd.*59d, X.*Cyr.*7.5.53; ἔν τινι in a thing, ib.86, Isoc.7.48, D.S.16.46: c. dat., Thphr.*Char.*8. 14 codd.; ψυχαὶ ἐν τῷ τοῦ παντὸς θεάτρῳ δ. Ph.1.266: c. part., *pass the whole day* in doing, Arist.*HA*540^{a}16; δ. ἀνάριστον καὶ ἄδειπνον Plu.2.157d. 2. of things, *continue all day*, Arist.*Pr.*947^{a}25.

διήμερον, τό, *period of twenty-four hours* (?), Lyd.*Ost.*66.

διημερόω, *cultivate thoroughly*, γῆς -ωθείσης Thphr.*CP*3.20.6.

διηνεκής, Dor. **διᾱνεκής** (v. infr.) *Supp.Epigr.*1.327.10 (Callatis, i A. D.), ές:—*continuous, unbroken*, ἀτραπιτοί τε διηνεκέες Od.13.195; νώτοισι.. διηνεκέεσσι with slices *cut the whole length* of the chine, Il.7.321; ῥίζαι, ῥάβδοι, 12.134, 297; εἰ ὦλκα διηνεκέα προταμοίμην Od. 18.375; so δ. σώματα Pl.*Hp.Ma.*301b, cf. Anaxandr.6, *BGU*646.22 (ii A. D.); ὅρος δ. Str.3.1.3; κανών *IG*7.3073.108 (Lebad., ii B. C.); τὸ δ. *regularity*, Gal.2.355; of Time, *perpetual*, δ. νυκτί Luc.*VH*1.19; δικτάτωρ εἰς τὸ δ. App.*BC*1.4. Adv. διηνεκέως in phrase δ. ἀγορεύειν to tell *from beginning to end*, Od.7.241, 12.56 (*distinctly, positively*, 4.836); ἅπαντα δ. κατέλεξε Hes.*Th.*627; cf. τὰ ἕκαστα διηνεκὲς ἐξενέποντα A.R.2.391; Boeot. and Dor. διανεκῶς *without ceasing*, εὕδειν Corinn.9 (dub.), cf. *SIG*793.3 (Cos, i A. D.); διηνεκῶς once in Trag., A.*Ag.*319, *Com.Adesp.*382, M.Ant.2.17, *OGI*194.12 (Egypt, i B. C.), D.Chr.49.8, etc.; so διηνεκές *h.Ap.*255, Call.*Fr.*158; also εἰς τὸ διηνεκές in *perpetuity*, *Ep.Hebr.*7.3, *PRyl.*2.427 (ii A. D.), *JHS*33.338 (Macedonia, ii A. D.); -κῶς *invariably*, opp. πλεονάκις, Gal.18(2). 315.—The Aeol. and Dor. form διᾱνεκής is used also in Att., as Pl.*Hp.Ma.*301b, e (cf. Diogenian.ap.Sch.ad loc.), Anaxandr. l. c., *IG*2.1054.81; but νόμος διηνεκής a *perpetual* law is read in Pl.*Lg.* 839a.

διήνεμος, ον, *blown through, wind-swept*, πάτρα S.*Tr.*327.

διηπειρόω, *make dry land of*, θάλασσαν *AP*9.708 (Phil.).

διήρεσα, v. διερέσσω.

διηρεφής, ές, (ἐρέφω) *all covered*, Q.S.6.325.

διῃρημένως, Adv., (διαιρέω) *separately*, M.Ant.11.6, Alex.Aphr. *in Metaph.*296.4, Hld.10.23.

διηρθρωμένως, Adv. *articulately, distinctly*, Gal.17(2).160, Alex. Aphr. *in Metaph.*61.3, *Theol.Ar.*49.

δίήρης, ες, (ἀραρίσκω) *double*, διῆρες ὑπερῷον *upper* story, *upper chamber*, Pl.Com.112; μελάθρων διῆρες ἔσχατον (sc. ὑπερῷον) E.*Ph.* 90, cf. Plu.2.77e. II. ἡ δ. (sc. ναῦς) *bireme, ship with two banks of oars*, Poll.1.82.

διητανές· λιτόν, διατεταμένον, Hsch.

διηυκρῑνημένως, Adv., (διευκρινέω) *carefully, exactly*, v.l. in D.S. 1.93.

διηχ-έω, *ring with*, τὸ μέγεθος τοῦ κατορθώματος Plu.*Tim.*21: abs., *resound*, *Placit.*4.16.2:—Pass., pf. part. διηχημένος *commonly spoken of*, ποιότητες Archig.ap.Gal.8.578. **-ής**, ές, *conducting sound*, Ar.Did.*Epit.*17, Plu.2.721e, Phlp.*in de An.*353.12, al. II. *loud*, βρονταί Lyd.*Ost.*22 (Sup.). **-ήτας**· ἄρτου εἶδος, Hsch. **-ητικός**, ή, όν, *sonorous*, Prisc.Lyd.16.6.

δῐ-θάλασσος, Att. -ττος [θᾰ], ον, *divided into two seas*, of the Euxine, Str.2.5.22, cf. D.P.156; of the Atlantic, Str.1.1.8. II. *between two seas, where two seas meet*, as is often the case off a headland, *Act.Ap.*27.41; βραχέα καὶ διθάλαττα shallows and *meetings of currents*, in the Syrtes, D.Chr.5.9. **-θαλλος**, ον, *feeding on two kinds of food*, Arist.*HA*616^{b}27 (dub.). **-θηκτος**, ον, *two-edged*, ξίφος A.*Pr.*863. **-θρονος**, ον, *two-throned*, Ἀχαιῶν δ. κράτος the *two-throned* might of the Achaeans, i. e. the brother-kings, Id.*Ag.* 109 (lyr.), cf. 43 (anap.). **-θροος**, ον, of sound, *redoubled*, Nonn. *D.*47.26. **-θῡμία**, ἡ, *dissension*, Hsch., *EM*275.5, Eust.936. 36. **-θῡμος**, ον, *at variance*, Lxx *Pr.*26.20.

δῑθῠραμβ-έω, *sing a dithyramb*, Philoch.21. **-ικός**, ή, όν, *dithyrambic*, D.H.*Th.*29; τὰ δ. *dithyrambic poems*, Arist.*Po.*1447^b 26. Adv. -κῶς Demetr.*Eloc.*91. **-ιος**, ὁ (sc. μήν), name of a month at Gonni, Ἀρχ.Ἐφ.1911.130, al.

Δῑθῠραμβο-γενής, v. διθύραμβος II.

δῑθῠραμβο-γράφος [γρᾰ], ὁ, *writer of dithyrambs*, Tz.*H.*10.839. **-δῐδάσκᾰλος**, ὁ, *dithyrambic poet who trained his own chorus*, Ar. *Pax*829. **-ποιητική** (sc. ποίησις), ἡ, *writing of dithyrambic poetry*, Arist.*Po.*1447^{a}14. **-ποιός**, ὁ, *dithyrambic poet*, Id.*Rh.* 1406^{b}21, D.S.15.6, Plu.2.952f.

δῑθύραμβος [ῠ], ὁ, metapl. acc. sg. διθύραμβα Pi.*Fr.*86:—*dithyramb*, Archil.77, Epich.132, Hdt.1.23, Pi.*O.*13.19, Pherecr.145.11, Pl.*Lg.*700b, Arist.*Pol.*1342^{b}7, *Pr.*918^{b}18, etc.; μιξοβόας δ. A.*Fr.* 355: metaph. of *bombastic language*, τοσουτονὶ δ. ᾄσας Pl.*Hp.Ma.* 292c; οὐκέτι πόρρω διθυράμβων φθέγγομαι Id.*Phdr.*238d. II. a name of Dionysus, E.*Ba.*526 (lyr.), Philod.Scarph.1:—hence **Δῑθυραμβογενής**, *AP*9.524. (Pi. is said to have written it λυθίραμβος (*Fr.*85)—as if from λῦθι ῥάμμα, the cry of Bacchus when sewn up in his father's thigh.)

δῑθῠραμβοχώνα, ἡ, *funnel of dithyrambs*, Μοῦσα prob. in *AP*13. 21 (Theodorid.) (-χανα cod.).

δῑθῠραμβώδης, ες, *fitted for the dithyramb*, ὄνομα Pl.*Cra.*409c, cf. D.H.*Dem.*29, Demetr.*Eloc.*116.

δί-θῠρος [ῐ], ον, *with two doors* or *entrances*, νεώς, ἄντρον, Plu.*Num.* 20, Porph.*Antr.*3; *bivalve*, of shell-fish, Arist.*HA*528^{a}12; of the mouth, Corn.*ND*30, etc.; *of two leaves*, δ. γραμματείδιον *a diptych*, Men.327, cf. Lib.*Or.*51.11, *Ep.*1021.1; of seeds, *which split in germinating*, Arist.*Juv.*468^{b}19, Thphr.*HP*8.2.2; δίθυρον, τό, *door with two leaves*, *Annales du Service* 19.63, 64 (ii B. C.), *BGU*1028.9 (ii A. D.). II. τὰ δ. *seat of honour*, = Lat. *tribunal*, Plb.27.1.6. **-θυρσον**, τό, *a double thyrsus*, *AP*6.172 (Agath.(?)). **-ίαμβος**, ὁ, *syzygy of two iambic feet*, Heph.3.3, D.T.p.120 U., Aristid.Quint.1.22.

διιδεῖν, v. διεῖδον.

δίϊδρ-ος, ον, (ἱδρώς) *perspiring*, Gal.19.93. **-όω**, *transude*, Hp. *Loc.Hom.*27, Gal.8.644 (Pass.), Hsch. s. v. κηκίειν.

διΐημι (3 sg. fut. διαήσει Hsch.), *drive, thrust* or *pass through*, διὰ δ' ἧκε σιδήρου (sc. τὸν ὀϊστόν) Od.21.328; δ. ξίφος λαιμῶν E.*Ph.*1092; δίες στυπτηρίαν ὄξους *PHolm.*12.45: c. dupl. acc., στέρνα δ. λόγχην E.*Ph.*1398. 2. *let* people *go through* a country, *give* them *a passage through*, εἰ μήτε οἱ ποταμοὶ διήσουσιν.. X.*An.*3.2.23, etc.; διέντες αὐτοὺς ἐφ' ὑμᾶς D.18.213, cf. ib.146: c. gen., ξυμφορὰς τοῦ σοῦ διῆκας στόματος *didst let* them *pass through* thy mouth, *gavest utterance to* them, S.*OC*963, cf. διαφέρω I. 1:—Pass., *pass through*, Arist.*Mir.*835ᵇ20: Ep. pf. part. διαειμένος A.R.2.372. II. *dismiss, disband*, στράτευμα X.*HG*2.4.39, etc.; τοὺς ὀδόντας δ. *unclose* them, D.S.10.17. 2. *soak*, Hp.*Acut.*21; ἐλαδίῳ διείς Sotad.Com. 1.27, cf. Arist.*HA*583ᵃ24:—Med., διέμενος ὄξει *having diluted* it with vinegar, Ar.*Pl.*720:—Pass., Alex.188.3. 3. *release* prisoners, *PGoodsp.Cair.*5.2 (ii B.C.), J.*AJ*15.10.3; διειμένος *set free*, Plu. *Demetr.*39.

διΐθ-υντήρ, ῆρος, ὁ, = διευθυντήρ, Man.4.40:—also **-υντής**, οῦ, ὁ, Hsch. **-ύνω**, *direct by steering*, εὔπλοΐην *AP*9.107 (Leon.(?)); τὸν πλοῦν Them.*Or.*4.50b, cf. Numen.ap.Eus.*PE*11.18.

διϊκαδία· ἐπὶ ὁμοίων καὶ ἀπαραλλάκτων, Hsch.

διϊκμάζω, *moisten*, Thphr.*CP*3.4.3 (Pass.).

διϊκμάω, *winnow thoroughly*, Thphr.*CP*4.12.9 (Pass.).

διϊκνέομαι, fut. -ίξομαι: aor. -ικόμην:—*go through, penetrate*, ποτὶ τὰν ψυχὰν δι' ὤτων Ti.Locr.101a; ἐφ' ὅσον -εῖται τὸ ὕδωρ Thphr. *CP*3.20.4; διῖκτο ἡ δόξα μέχρι βασιλέως Plu.*Dem.*20, cf. D.Chr.12.35; *reach*, with missiles, Th.7.79; βραδέως τοῦ παραγγέλματος διικνουμένου Plu.*Nic.*27. 2. in speaking, *go through, tell of*, πάντα δ. Il.9.61, 19.186, A.R.2.411. 3. of Time, *intervene*, διετοῦς χρόνου διικνουμένου Longus 1.4.

Διίκτυννα, coined (ἀπὸ τοῦ διικνεῖσθαι) as etym. of Δίκτυννα by Corn.*ND*34.

δίϊξις, εως, ἡ, *interpenetration*, δι' ἀλλήλων Procl. *in Ti.*2.88 D., cf. Olymp. *in Alc.*p.215 C.; *penetration* of sensations to consciousness, Prisc.Lyd.14.22.

Δίϊος, ον, *of Zeus*, v.l. in Pl.*Phdr.*252e, cf. Plu.2.421e, Them.*Or.* 13.165c.

Διϊπετής (better **Διειπετής**, cf. Zenodor.ap.Sch.Od.4.477), ές, (πίπτω) *fallen from Zeus*, i.e. *from heaven*, Ep. epith. of streams, *fed* or *swollen by rain*, Il.16.174, Od.4.477, Hes.*Fr.*217; νάματ' οὐ δ., of stagnant water, E.*Hyps.Fr.*5(3).31; δ. ὕδατα, of rain, Plu.*Mar.* 21. 2. generally, *divine, bright*, χαλκός Emp.100.9; αἰθὴρ διϊπετὴς *divine, holy*, E.*Ba.*1267; δ. πυρσοῖς *gleaming* with fires, Id.*Rh.*43 (lyr.). 3. *in continual flow*, Hp.*Mul.*1.24 (expld. as = διαυγής, καθαρός, Erot.). 4. διϊπετέες οἰωνοί, prob. *hovering in the sky*, *h.Ven.*4.

Διιπόλεια, Διιπόλια, Διιπολιώδης, v. sub Διπολ-.

διϊππ-ασία, ἡ, *riding through*, Suid., *EM*274.55. **-ευσις**, εως, ἡ, *charging through* the enemy's ranks, Ascl.*Tact.*7.3, al. **-εύω**, *ride through*, D.S.19.30; διὰ τῆς θαλάσσης D.C.59.17; *traverse*, τὴν ὠκεάνιον ζώνην ἐν κύκλῳ Porph.*Chr.*69: metaph. of Time, *elapse*, ib.60.

διίπταμαι, late pres., = διαπέτομαι, Arist.*Mir.*839ᵃ23, Hdn.2.8.7, Luc.*Am.*6, Max.Tyr.22.6; impf. διιπτάμην J.*BJ*3.7.20.

διϊσθμίζω, (ἰσθμός) *draw ships across the Isthmus*, Plb.4.19.7.

διϊστάνω, = διΐστημι, Phld.*Mort.*27; τὴν φιλίαν D.S.19.46; τὸ πλῆθος App.*Hisp.*36:—also **διϊστάω**, D.T.642.31, Lyd.*Mag.*3.54.

διϊστέον, (δίοιδα) *one must learn*, v.l. for διοιστέον, E.*Hipp.*491.

διΐστημι, fut. διαστήσω, *set apart, separate*, τοὺς λόχους Th.4.74; κατ' εἴδη Pl.*Phlb.*23d; διέστησεν [αὐτοὺς] εἰς μέρη πολλά D.18.61; ζῶντας ἡμᾶς οὐθὲν ἀλλήλων διέστησε Plu.*Ant.*84:—Pass., κίονες διεστάθησαν Callix.2. 2. *set* one *at variance with* another, τινά τινος Ar. *V.*41, Th.6.77; δ. τὴν Ἑλλάδα *divide* it *into factions*, Hdt.9.2; δ. τοὺς πένητας ἀπὸ τῶν εὐπόρων D.H.9.17. 3. μέσας διαστήσας ἡμέρας δύο *having left an interval of* two days, *Epigr.Gr.*996.7, cf. *BKT*3.20. 4. *distinguish*, τί τινος Ath.7.305d, cf. Aret.*SA*2.2. 5. *inflate*, κενοὺς ἀσκούς Demoph.*Sim.*57. II. more freq. in Pass., with aor. 2, pf., and plpf. Act.:—*stand apart, be divided*, Il., mostly in aor. 2, 24. 718, al.: once in impf. Med., θάλασσα διΐστατο the sea *made way, opened*, 13.29; διαστὰν γῆς βάθρον *yawning wide*, S.*OC*1662; τὰ διεστεῶτα ὑπὸ σεισμοῦ Hdt.7.129; διεστῶτα, opp. ἡνωμένα, Chrysipp. *Stoic.*2.124, al.; ἔτους διεστῶτος *after an interval of* a year, *SIG*344.119 (Teos). b. *stand with legs apart*, Luc.*Ner.*7. 2. of persons, *stand apart, be at variance*, διαστήτην ἐρίσαντε Il.1.6; εἴ τινές που διασταῖεν Th.1.18; διέστη ἐς ξυμμαχίαν ἑκατέρων *sided* with one or the other party, ib.15; κατὰ πόλεις διέσταμεν Id.4.61; διεστηκότες εἰς δύο D.10.4, cf. 18.18; ἐρίζειν καὶ διεστάναι Id.2.29; simply, *differ, be different*, πλούτου ἀρετὴ διέστηκεν Pl.*R.*550e; πρὸς ἄλληλα Arist.*Pol.*1256ᵃ29, cf. *Po.*1448ᵃ17; ἡ ἀριστοκρατία διέστηκεν ἀπὸ ταύτης πολὺ τῆς πολιτείας Id.*Pol.*1289ᵇ3; οὖρα διεστηκότα *not homogeneous*, Hp.*Aph.*7.33. 3. *part* after fighting, Hdt.1.76, 8.16, 18: hence, *to be reconciled*, Isoc.5.38. b. of an army, *retire*, Plb.10.3.6. 4. *stand at certain distances* or *intervals*, Hdt.2.66; of guards in a row, Id.3.72; of post-stations, Id.8.98; of soldiers, δ. κατὰ διακοσίους Th.4.32; διάστηθι *mark distances!* a word of command, Ael. *Tact.*12.11: Geom., ἴσα ἀπ' ἀλλάλων διέστακεν *are equidistant* from one another, Archim.*Aequil.*1.6. III. Med., sts. trans., *separate*, γεώδη γένη διϊστάμενοι Pl.*Ti.*63c: chiefly in aor. 1, δ. τόν τε δικαιότατον καὶ τὸν ἀδικώτατον *contrast*, Id.*R.*360e; ἀράχνια, of spiders, *spread*, Theoc.16.97.

διϊστορέω, *relate*, Phld.*Rh.*2.150 S.

διϊσχάνω, poet. for διέχω, *cleave*, νύκτ' ὀλοὴν οὐκ ἄστρα διίσχανεν οὐκ ἀμαρυγαὶ μήνης A.R.4.1696.

διϊσχναίνω, *make very lean*, f.l. in Hp.*Loc.Hom.*38.

διϊσχῡρ-ιείω, *wish* or *mean to affirm*, Hp.*Art.*1. **-ίζομαι**, *lean upon, rely on*, τῷ λόγῳ Antipho 5.33, cf. Aeschin.1.1. II. *affirm confidently*, τι Pl.*Phd.*63c, etc.; δ. ταῦτα οὕτως ἔχειν ib.114d; δ. ὡς.. Id.*Tht.*154a; δ. περί τινος And.2.4, Lys.13.85; τι ὑπέρ τινος Pl.*Men.* 86b; περὶ σοῦ ὡς.. Id.*Ep.*317c: abs., ὁμοίως ἐφ' ἑκατέροις δ. Id.*Tht.* 158d, etc. **-ιστέον**, *one must affirm*, Str.6.3.8.

διϊσχύω, strengthd. for ἰσχύω, Ph.2.627.

Διϊσωτήρια, τά, *festival of Zeus Soter* at Athens, *IG*2².1008.21, al.

διϊτέον [ῐτ], (δίειμι) *one must go through*, Pl.*R.*545a.

διϊτικός [ῐτ], ή, όν, (δίειμι) *penetrable*, in Comp., Arist.*Pr.*905ᵇ13.

διΐφῐλος [ῐφ], ον, *dear to Zeus*, usu. written divisim, Il.1.74, etc., but cf. *EM*275.6, etc.

διϊχνεύω, *track out*, Plb.4.68.3, Opp.*H.*3.37.

δῐκᾰδία, ἡ, *vessel containing two* κάδοι, *IG*2.856.

δῐκάζω, fut. δικάσω Il.23.579, Ar.*Eq.*1089, *V.*689, 801, Pl.*Criti.* 120a, etc.; Ion. δικῶ Hdt.1.97; inf. δικᾶν *GDI* iv p.880 (Chios), *SIG* 134*b*23 (Milet.): aor. ἐδίκασα, Ep. δίκασα, δίκασσα, Od.11.547, Il.23. 574: pf. δεδίκακα Heraclid.Cum.1:—**Med.** (v. infr. II), fut. -άσομαι Hdt.1.96, D.37.37: aor. ἐδικασάμην Lys.12.4, D.38.17, etc.: plpf. ἐδεδίκαστο (v. infr. II):—**Pass.**, fut. δικασθήσομαι D.H.5.61, δεδικάσομαι Luc.*Bis Acc.*14: aor. ἐδικάσθην Th.1.28, Pl.*Cri.*50b: pf. δεδίκασμαι Lys.21.18: plpf. ἐδεδίκαστο D.33.27: (δίκη):—*judge, sit in judgement*, Il.23.579, Hdt.1.14, Antipho 5.90, etc.; *sit as a juror*, D.21.75; δ. καὶ ἐκκλησιάζειν Lys.26.2, cf. Arist.*Pol.*1293ᵃ9, etc. 2. c. acc. rei, *give judgement on, decide, determine*, Il.1.542; δ. δίκην Hes.*Op.*39, etc.; ἀλιτρά Pi.*O.*2.65; πρᾶγμα A.*Eu.* 471, cf. 601; τἀμπλακήματα Id.*Supp.*230; δ. δίκην ἄδικον *give* an unjust *judgement*, Hdt.5.25; δ. ἐμπορικὰς δίκας D.35.46; less freq., γραφάς δ. Lycurg.7; εὐθύνας D.19.132; ἀγῶνα Din.1.46: c. acc. cogn., δίκας δ. *adjudge* a penalty, Hdt.6.139; δ. φυγήν τινι *decree* it as his *punishment*, A.*Ag.*1412; δ. φόνον ματέρος *ordain* her slaughter, E.*Or.*164 (lyr.): c. gen., δικάζειν τοὺς βασιλέας αἰτιῶν φόνου Lex Draconis ap.*IG*1².115.11; δ. τοῦ ἐγκλήματος (sc. δίκην) X.*Cyr.*1.2.7:—Pass., δίκαι δικασθεῖσαι Pl.*Cri.*50b, cf. Lys.17.3; ὁποτέρων ἂν δικασθῇ εἶναι τὴν ἀποικίαν *it may be decided..*, Th.1.28. b. *pass judgement on, condemn*, γάμον ἄγαμον S.*OT*1214 (lyr.). 3. φόνον δ. *plead in a case of* murder, E.*Or.*580: abs., *plead*, D.C.69.18. 4. c. dat. pers., *decide between* persons, *judge* their *cause*, Τρωσί τε καὶ Δαναοῖσι δικαζέτω ὡς ἐπιεικές Il.8.431; ἐς μέσον ἀμφοτέροισι δικάσσατε 23.574, cf. Hdt.1.97; τοῖσι Πέρσῃσι δίκας δ. Id.3.31; ἑκάστῳ κατὰ τὸ μέγαθος τοῦ ἀδικήματος *passed judgement* on each, Id.2.137. 5. c. inf., δικαξάτω λαγάσαι *Leg.Gort.*1.5; ἐδίκασαν δέκα ἀνταπόλλυσθαι Hdt.3.14; δ. ὡς.. Id.1.84. 6. Pass., αἰσχρὰς δίκας δ. *to have actions brought against one*, Lys.21.18. II. Med., of the party, *plead one's cause, go to law*, Od.11.545, 12.440, Hdt.1.96, Th.1.77; πρὸς τοὺς ἀστυνόμους Pl.*Lg.*845e; δίκην δικάζεσθαί τινι *go to law* with one, Lys.12.4, D.55.31; simply, δ. τινί Pl.*Euthphr.*4e; πρός τινας Th. 3.44; prop. of a private suit, opp. a public prosecution, D.21.26: with gen. added, δ. τινὶ κακηγορίας Lys.10.12; κλοπῆς D.22.27, etc.; ἐδεδίκαστο ἄν μοι τῆς ἐγγύης Id.33.27; δ. τινὶ περί τινος ib.26. 2. τὸ δ. *forensic speaking*, Arist.*Rh.*1354ᵇ26, cf. Antipho 2.2.12.

δῐκαία, Ion. -αίη, ἡ, poet. for δίκη, like Σεληναίη for Σελήνη, Cerc.18.5, cf. *EM*24.48.

δῐκαιάδῐκος [ᾰ], ὁ, *one neither just nor unjust*, Ph.2.346.

δῐκαιαρχία· ἀρχὴ δικαία, Hsch.

δῐκαϊκός, ή, όν, *inclined to justice*, διάθεσις M.Ant.5.34.

δῐκαιο-δοσία, ἡ, *jurisdiction*, Plb.20.6.2, etc.; *trial*, ἑλκομένης δ. Id. 22.4.2: pl., εἰς δ. προκαλεῖσθαί τινα Id.4.16.4; ἡ πρὸς ἀλλήλους δ. *Milet.* 3 No.154.5 (ii B.C.), cf. *IG*12(9).903 (Chalcis, ii B.C.); *administration of justice*, Str.13.1.55, al., D.S.37.8, al., *BGU*226.11 (i A.D.). II. *international compact for trying suits in the forum rei*, Plb.23.1.2, 32. 17.4. **-δοτέω**, *administer justice*, Str.11.3.6, Plu.2.779b, Epist.ap. J.*AJ*16.6.7, *POxy.*484.25 (ii A.D.): c. acc., *administer as juridicus*, ἐπαρχίαν *IGRom.*4.401 (Pergam., i B.C.). **-δότης**, ου, ὁ, = Lat. *juridicus*, at Alexandria, Str.17.1.12, *POxy.*237 vii 39 (ii A.D.), etc.: generally, δ. τοῦ ἔθνους *governor* of the province, J.*AJ*18.1.1; = Lat. *legatus juridicus*, δ. Σπανίας Dessau *Inscr.Lat.Sel.*8842. **-θέτης**, ου, ὁ, = foreg., Baillet *Inscr. des tombeaux des rois* 1836 (s.v.l.). **-κρῐσία**, ἡ, *righteous judgement*, *Ep.Rom.*2.5, Heph.Astr.3.34, *POxy.*71 i 4 (iv A.D.). **-κρίτης** [ῑ], ου, ὁ, *righteous judge*, Lxx 2 *Ma.*12.41, *PRyl.*113.35 (ii A.D.). **-λογέομαι**, fut. -ήσομαι Plb.4.3.12: aor. ἐδικαιολογησάμην Luc.*Prom.*4, or Pass. ἐδικαιολογήθην Plb.31.12.8:—*plead one's cause before the judge, come to issue with* a person, abs., Aeschin.2.21; περί τινος Lys.*Fr.*34; πρός τινα Hyp.*Eux.*20, Plb.4.3.12, D.Chr.48.10: metaph., Iamb.*Myst.*3.19. 2. *remonstrate*, Luc. *Alex.*55. II. later in Act., δ. ὑπὲρ τῆς πόλεως *Inscr.Prien.*111.126 (i B.C.), cf. 108.105; οἱ δικαιολογοῦντες *advocates*, Luc.*Tim.*11, cf. *Apol.*12. **-λόγητον**, *allegandum*, Gloss. **-λογία**, ἡ, *plea in justification*, Demad.7, Arist.*Rh.Al.*1438ᵃ25, Lxx 2 *Ma.*4.44, *PFlor.*6. 13 (iii A.D.): generally, *pleading*, Plb.3.21.3, al. II. pl., *forensic speeches*, Arist.*Rh.Al.*1421ᵇ13, 1432ᵇ33. **-λογίζομαι**, = -λογέομαι, Sch.Ar.*Ach.*361. **-λογικός**, ή, όν, *of* or *for pleading, judicial*, Sch.S.*OC*237. Adv. -κῶς, Comp. -κώτερον ibid. **-λόγος**, ὁ, *advocate*, Arc.89.19, Sch.Ar.*Av.*1702. **-μετρον** (sc. ἀγγεῖον), τό, *vessel which pours out an equal volume of liquid each time*, Hero *Spir.* 2.1. **-νομέω**, = δικαιοδοτέω, Ph.1.126. **-νομία**, ἡ, = δικαιοδοσία, Id.2.365, *IG*7.21.21 (Megara). **-νόμος**, ον, = *juridicus*,

D.C.78.22. **-ποιέω**, *act honestly*, Simp.*in Epict.*p.129 D. **-πολις**, εως, ὁ, ἡ, *strict in public faith*, Pi.*P.*8.22.

δῐκαιοπρᾱγ-έω, *act honestly*, Arist.*EN*1135^{a}16, *PTeb.*183 (ii B. C.), Ceb.41, Plu.*Sol.*5, Sallust.19, etc.; τὰ μεγάλα Jason ap.Plu.2.135f; πρός τινα Arist.*Rh.*1373^{b}22. **-ημα**, ατος, τό, *just* or *righteous act*, Id.*EN*1135^{a}12, Chrysipp.*Stoic.*3.73. **-ής**, ές, *acting justly*, *PSI*1. 76.5 (vi A. D.), Sch.Ar.*Av.*1354, Suid. s. v. ἀντιπελαργεῖν. **-ητέον**, *one must deal justly*, Iamb.*Protr.*21.ιθ'. **-ία**, ἡ, *just* or *righteous dealing*, Arist.*EN*1133^{b}30, Phld.*Rh.*1.266S., Porph.*Marc.*11, Jul. *Ep.*89; περὶ δ., title of work by Epicurus. **-μοσύνη**, ἡ, = foreg., Heraclit.*Ep.*2 (v. l.).

δίκαιος [ῐ], α, ον, also ος, ον E.*Heracl.*901 (lyr.), *IT*1202, D.S.5.72: (δίκη): A. in Hom. and all writers, of persons, *observant of custom* or *rule*, Od.3.52; esp. *of social rule, well-ordered, civilized*, ὑβρισταί τε καὶ ἄγριοι οὐδὲ δ. 9.175, cf. 8.575; [Γαλακτοφάγοι] δικαιότατοι Il.13.6; [Χείρων] δικαιότατος Κενταύρων 11.832, cf. Thgn.314, 794; δ. πολίτης a *good* citizen, D.3.21, etc.: metaph. of the sea, Sol.12.2 (Sup.); δικαίη ζόη a *civilized* way of living, Hdt.2.177. Adv. δικαίως, μνᾶσθαι woo *in due form, decently*, Od.14.90; ὑπὸ ζυγῷ λόφον δ. εἶχον *loyally*, S.*Ant.*292. 2. *observant of duty* to gods and men, *righteous*, Od.13.209, etc.; δ. πρὸς πᾶσαν ὁμιλίην Hp.*Medic.* 2; ἰθὺς καὶ δ. Hdt.1.96; opp. δυσσεβής, A.*Th.*598, cf. 610; δ. καὶ ὅσιος Pl.*Grg.*507b; δικαίων ἀδίκους φρένας παρασπᾷς S.*Ant.*791 (lyr.); also of actions, etc., *righteous*, ἐπὶ ῥηθέντι δικαίῳ a thing *rightly* said, Od.18.414, etc. 3. ὁ δίκαιος, euphem. of a sacred snake, *GDI* 5056 (Crete).

B. later: I. *equal, even, well-balanced*, ἅρμα δίκαιον *even-going* chariot, X.*Cyr.*2.2.26: so metaph., νωμᾷ δικαίῳ πηδαλίῳ στρατόν Pi.*P.*1.86; δικαιόταται ἀντιρροπαί Hp.*Art.*7; δικαιότατα μοχλεύειν ibid.: hence, *fair, impartial*, βάσανος Antipho 1.8; συγγραφεύς Luc.*Hist.Conscr.*39. b. *legally exact, precise*, τῷ δικαιοτάτῳ τῶν λόγων to speak *quite exactly*, Hdt.7.108, cf. Th.3.44; of Numbers, αἱ ἑκατὸν ὀργυιαὶ δίκαιαι Hdt.2.149. Adv. -αίως, πάντα δ. ὑμῖν τετήρηται D.21.3; δ. ἐξετάζειν ib.154. 2. *lawful, just*, esp. τὸ δ. *right*, opp. τὸ ἄδικον, Hdt.1.96, A.*Pr.*189 (lyr.), etc.; τὸ δ. τὸ νόμιμον καὶ τὸ ἴσον Arist.*EN*1129^{a}34; δ. διορθωτικόν, διανεμητικόν, ib.1131^{b}25, 27; τὸ πολιτικὸν δ. ib.1134^{b}18; ἔστι ἐπιεικὲς τὸ παρὰ τὸν γεγραμμένον νόμον δ. Id.*Rh.*1374^{a}27, cf. *EN*1137^{b}12; καὶ δίκαια κἄδικα Ar. *Nu.*99; τὰ ἴσα καὶ τὰ δ. D.21.67; τοὐμὸν δ. my own *right*, E.*IA*810; ἐλθεῖν ἐπὶ τοῦτο τὸ δ. bring the case to this *issue*, Antipho 6.24; οὐδὲν τῶν δ. ποιεῖν τινί not to do *what is just and right* by a man, X.*HG*5.3. 10; τὰ δ. ἔχειν, λαμβάνειν, receive *one's due*, Id.*An.*7.7.14,17; τὰ δ. πράττεσθαι πόλιν give a city its *deserts*, A.*Ag.*812; ἐκ τοῦ δικαίου, = δικαίως, Ar.*Av.*1435, cf. Th.2.89; so ἀπὸ τοῦ δικαίου, τῶν δικαίων, *Inscr.Prien.*50.8 (ii B. C.), 123.8 (i B. C.); μετὰ τοῦ δ. Lys.2.12, D.21. 177; τὸ δίκαιον *lawful claim*, ἃ ἔχομεν δίκαια πρός.. Th.3.54, cf. D. 21.179, Plu.*Luc.*3, etc.; τὰ πρὸς ἀλλήλους δ. mutual *obligations* or *contracts*, Plb.3.21.10; ἐπὶ συγκειμένοις τισὶ δικαίοις on certain agreed *terms*, D.H.3.51. Adv. -αίως *rightly, justly*, Hdt.6.137; μεῖζον ἢ δ. A.*Ag.*376 (lyr.); καὶ δ. καὶ ἀδίκως And.1.135. II. of persons and things, *meet and right, fitting*, δ. τοὖδε τοῦ φόνου ῥαφεὺς A.*Ag.*1604; κόσμος οὐ φέρειν δ. Id.*Eu.*55; ἵππον δ. ποιεῖσθαί τινι make a horse *fit for* another's *use*, X.*Mem.*4.4.5, cf. *Cyn.*7.4 (ἵππος δ. τὴν σιαγόνα having a *good* mouth, Poll.1.196). b. *normal*, σχήματα Hp.*Art.*69; φύσις Id.*Fract.*1 (Sup.). 2. *real, genuine*, γόνος S.*Fr.*[1119]; ποιῶν τὰ ἐν τῇ τέχνῃ δ. *Supp.Epigr.*2.184.7 (Tanagra, ii B. C.). Adv., εἴπερ δικαίως ἔστ' ἐμὸς *really and truly* mine, S.*Aj.*547, cf. Pl.*Cra.*418e. 3. ὁ δ. λόγος the plea *of equity*, Th.1.76. Adv. -αίως *with reason*, Id.6. 34, cf. S.*OT*675: Comp. -ότερον Ar.*V.*1149, etc.; also -οτέρως Isoc. 15.170: Sup. -ότατα Ar.*Av.*1222; Aeol. δικαίτατα *IG*12(2).526c17 (Eresus). III. ψυχὴ ἐς τὸ δ. ἔβη 'the land of the leal', *IG*7. 2543.3 (Thebes).

C. in Prose, δίκαιός εἰμι, c. inf., δίκαιοί ἐστε ἰέναι you *are bound* to come, Hdt.9.60, cf. 8.137; δ. εἰμεν ἔχειν Id.9.27; δ. εἰμι κολάζειν I *have a right* to punish, Ar.*Nu.*1434, cf. S.*Ant.*400; δ. ἐστι περιπεσεῖν κακοῖς Antipho 3.3.7; δ. εἰσι ἀπιστότατοι εἶναι they *have most reason* to distrust, Th.4.17; δ. βλάπτεσθαι Lys.20.12; δ. ἐστιν ἀπολωλέναι *dignus est qui pereat*, D.6.37; ὁ σπουδαῖος ἄρχειν δ. *has a right* to.., Arist.*Pol.*1287^{b}12; with a non-personal subject, ἔλεος δ. ἀντιδίδοσθαι Th.3.40: less freq. in Comp. and Sup., δικαιότεροι χαρίσασθαι Lys.20.34; δικαιότατος εἶ ἀπαγγέλλειν Pl.*Smp.*172b; but δίκαιόν ἐστι is also found, Hdt.1.39, A.*Pr.*611, etc.: pl., δίκαια γὰρ τόνδ' εὐτυχεῖν S.*Aj.*1126, cf. *Tr.*495,1116; δικαίως ἄν, c. opt., Pl. *Phdr.*276a. [δικαίων with penult. short in Orph.*Fr.*247.2; cf. οὐ δίκαον· οὐ δίκαιον, Hsch.]

δῐκαι-οσύνη, ἡ, *righteousness, justice*, Thgn.147, Hdt.1.96, al., Pl. *R.*433a, Lxx *Ge.*15.6, etc.; δ. δικαστική *legal justice*, Arist.*Pol.*1291^{a} 27; opp. ἐπιείκεια, Id.*EN*1137^{a}32. 2. *fulfilment of the Law*, Lxx *Is.*26.2, al., *Ev.Matt.*3.15, al. II. *justice, the business of a judge*, Pl.*Grg.*464b,c (v. l. δικαστική), *Clit.*408b. III. Δ., personified, *AP*9.164; Ἶσις Δ. *SIG*1131 (Delos), *IG*3.203. IV. Pythag. name for *four*, *Theol.Ar.*23. V. δικαιοσύνη· ἡ χοῖνιξ, μυστικῶς, Hsch. **-όσυνος**, ὁ, *Guardian of justice*, of Zeus, *AJA*1905.302 (Sinope), *Com.Adesp.*752, Eust.918.47: generally, *just*, Simp.*in Cat.*264.24. **-ότης**, ητος, ἡ, = δικαιοσύνη, X.*An.*2.6.26, Pl.*Prt.* 331b, Ph.2.641, Plot.4.7.8. **-οφᾰνής**, ές, *having an appearance of justice*, Sch.Th.6.80. **-όω**, Ion. impf. ἐδικαίευν Hdt.1.100: fut. -ώσω Orac.ap.eund.5.92.β', Th.5.26; -ώσομαι Id.3.40: aor. ἐδικαίωσα Id.2.71:—Pass., fut. -ωθήσομαι Lxx *Si.*18.2: aor. ἐδικαιώθην A.*Ag.* 393 (lyr.): pf. δεδικαίωμαι Lxx *Ez.*21.13(18). I. *set right*, νόμος.. δικαιῶν τὸ βιαιότατον Pi.*Fr.*169.3; δικαιωθείς *proved, tested*, A. l.c. II. *hold* or *deem right, claim* or *demand as a right*, c. inf., Hdt.1.89,133, Hp.*Fract.*31; δεινά με δικαιοῖ δρᾶν S.*OT*640, cf. 575; δικαιοῦντες μὴ ἀφαιρεθῆναι αὐτήν Th.2.41: with inf. omitted, οὕτω δ. (sc. γενέσθαι) Hdt.9.42; δίκας δ. (sc. γενέσθαι) ib.93; ὅποι ποτὲ θεὸς δικαιοῖ S.*Ph.*781; οὐκ ὀρθῶς δ. Th.5.26; *pronounce judgement*, Id. 2.71: c. inf., ἐδικαίωσεν ἀποδοῦναι ἡμᾶς τὸ κεφάλαιον *PRyl.*119.14 (i A. D.); *consent*, δουλεύειν Hdt.2.172, cf. 6.86; οὐκ ἐδικαίου οὐδένα οἱ ἐσαγγεῖλαι he *would* not *allow*.., Id.3.118:—Pass., τὸ δικαιωθὲν ὑπό τινος *that which is ordained*, D.H.10.1. III. *do a man right* or *justice*: hence, 1. *chastise, punish*, Hdt.1.100:—Pass., Id.3. 29, Pl.*Lg.*934b, D.C.*Fr.*57.47; *pass sentence on*, ὑμᾶς αὐτοὺς δικαιώσεσθε Th.3.40. 2. Pass., also, *have right done one*, opp. ἀδικεῖσθαι, Arist.*EN*1136^{a}18. 3. *pronounce and treat as righteous, justify, vindicate*, Lxx *Ex.*23.7, *Je.*3.11; ἑαυτούς *Ev.Luc.*16.15, etc.:—freq. in Pass., ib.7.35, etc.

δίκαιρον, τό, an Indian *bird*, Ctes.*Fr.*57.17, Ael.*NA*4.41. (The properties of opium are ascribed to its dung, ll. cc.).

δῐκαί-ωμα, ατος, τό, *act of right*, opp. ἀδίκημα, Arist.*Rh.*1359^{a}25; *duty*, τὰ πρὸς ἀνθρώπους δ. Ph.2.199; prop. *amendment of a wrong*, opp. δικαιοπράγημα, Arist.*EN*1135^{a}13: hence, a. *judgement, penalty*, Pl.*Lg.*864e. b. *justification, plea of right*, Th.1.41, Isoc. 6.25, Arist.*Cael.*279^{b}9, Lxx 2*Ki.*19.28(29), *PLond.*2.360.8 (ii A. D.), etc.; δικαιώματα Ἑλληνίδων πόλεων, compiled by Arist. for Philip, Harp. s. v. Δρύμος. c. pl., *pleadings, documents* in a suit, *OGI*13. 13 (Samos), *PLille* 29.25 (iii B. C.), etc.; also, *credentials*, *BGU*113.10 (ii A. D.), al. d. *act of* δικαίωσις I. 3, *Ep.Rom.*5.16. II. *ordinance, decree*, Lxx *Ge.*26.5, *Ex.*15.26 (pl.), al., *Ep.Rom.*1.32, 2.26 (pl.), al. **-ωσις**, εως, ἡ, *setting right, doing justice to*: hence, 1. *condemnation, punishment*, Th.8.66, D.C.40.43 (pl.), cj. in Plu.2.421d. 2. *plea of legal right, justification*, Lys.9.8, cf. Harp. 3. *making* or *accounting righteous, justification*, *Ep.Rom.*4.25, etc. II. *demand of right* or *as of right, just claim*, Th.1.141, Plu.*Demetr.*18. III. *judgement of what is right*, ἀντήλλαξαν τῇ δικαιώσει altered *at their will and pleasure*, Th.3.82. **-ωτήριον**, τό, *place of punishment*, Pl. *Phdr.*249a (pl.); *place of judgement*, Junc.ap.Stob.4.53.35 (pl.). II. = κριτήριον, Hsch. **-ωτής**, οῦ, ὁ, *judge*, αἰσχρῶν καὶ καλῶν Plu. *Art.*23, cf. 2.549d.

δῐκαμπ-ής, ές, *with a double twist*, ψέλια *BGU*1065.8 (i A. D.). **-ίας** οἶνος wine *which has undergone two* τροπαί, *Com.Adesp.*983.

δίκανα· ποικίλα ἱμάτια, Hsch.

δῐκᾰνικός, ή, όν, I. of persons, *skilled in pleading*, Pl.*Grg.*512b, *Tht.*201a, X.*Mem.*1.2.48, etc.: in bad sense, *lawyer-like, pettifogging*, σμικρὸς τὴν ψυχὴν καὶ δ. Pl.*Tht.*175d. II. *belonging to trials, judicial*, λόγοι Isoc.13.20; ῥημάτιον δ. *law-term*, Ar.*Pax*534; ἡ -κή (sc. τέχνη) *forensic oratory*, Pl.*R.*405a, Arist.*Rh.*1371^{a}7; μετὰ δικανικήν after *serving as advocate*, *Epigr.Gr.*919; τὸ δ. S.E.*M.*2.89; τὰ δικανικά Arist.*Rh.*1354^{b}23. 2. in bad sense, *savouring of the law-courts*, φορτικὰ μὲν καὶ δ. Pl.*Ap.*32a; ὡς μακρὸν τὸ ἐνύπνιον καὶ δ. Luc.*Somn.*17. Adv. -κῶς Charito 5.4.

δῐκανούς· τοὺς περὶ τὰς δίκας διατρίβοντας, Hsch.

δῐ-κάρδιος, ον, *with two hearts*, Ar.Byz.*Epit.*28.16, Ael.*NA*11.40; τὸ δ. a kind of *lettuce*, *Gp.*12.1.2. **-κάρηνος**, Dor. **-ᾱνος** [κᾰ], ον, *two-headed*, Batr.298, *AP*6.306 (Aristo). **-καρπέω**, *bear two crops*, Thphr.*CP*1.13.9. **-καρπος**, ον, *bearing two crops*, γῆ Str. 17.3.11.

δῐκᾰσ-ία, ἡ, *lawsuit*, Aq.*De.*1.12, al., Sm., Thd.*Pr.*25.9. **-ιμος**, ον, *judicial*, δ. ἡμέρα *when the courts are open*, Men.969; τῇ ἑξῆς δ. (sc. ἡμέρα) *PLips.*32.13 (iii A. D.); δ. μῆνες Pl.*Lg.*958b. **-ις**, εως, ἡ, *exercise of the function of a* δικαστής, Sch.Ar.*Pl.*277.

δῐκασκόποι, οἱ, title of *judges* at Mytilene, *IG*12(2).6.12 (iv B. C.); at Cyme, *BCH*37.157 (iii B. C.).

δῐκασμός, ὁ, *giving judgement*, Ph.1.133.

δῐκασ-πολέω, *judge*, Diotog.ap.Stob.4.7.61. **-πολία**, ἡ, *judgement*, *Hymn.Is.*36, Man.2.261, Coluth.12, *AP*11.376 (Agath.): pl., *IG*14.1363, *Inscr.Magn.*202.2. II. *office of a judge*, Orph.*A.* 381, Q.S.5.172. **-πόλος**, ὁ, (q^{u}el, cf. τελέω) *one who gives law, judge*, Il.1.238, Phoen.1.7; fem., Orph.*H.*69.11: as Adj., δ. ἄνδρα Od.11.186; σκῆπτρον δ. A.R.4.1178; δ. χρόνος Maiist.52.

δῐκαστ-ᾰγωγός, ὁ, *official who escorted foreign* δικασταί *to their homes*, *Milet.*3.152.94 (ii B. C.); δ. ἀπὸ Ἀσίας ἐπὶ Ἀγητορίδα *IG*5(1). 39 (Sparta, ii A. D.). **-εία**, ἡ, *function of a* δικαστής, ib.12(9).4.8 (Carystus), *CIG*3184 (Smyrna), Ἀρχ.Ἐφ.1911.134 (Gonni). **-έον**, *one must sue at law*, Ph.1.90. **-ήρ**, ῆρος, ὁ, = δικαστής, *Foed.Delph. Pell.*1 A 7, *IG*9(1).334.33 (Locr., v B. C.), Rhet.*Oxy.*410.11, Babr. 118.3. **-ηριακός**, ή, όν, *connected with law-courts*, Phld.*Rh.*1. 212S. **-ηρίδιον** [ρῐ], τό, Dim. of sq., Ar.*V.*803. **-ήριον**, τό, *court of justice*, δ. συνάγειν Hdt.6.85; συγκλῄειν Ar.*Eq.*1317; ὑπὸ δ. ὑπαχθείς Hdt.6.72, cf. 104; εἰς δ. ἄγεσθαι Pl.*Phdr.*273b; ἀναβὰς ἐς τὸ δ. Antipho 6.21; παραδιδόναι τῷ δ. And.1.17; ἐπὶ δ. ἐλθεῖν Is.1.1; ἐπὶ τοῦ δ. Id.5.29; πρὸ τῶν δικαστηρίων κληροῦσθαι Isoc.7. 54; in Egypt, *office of the governor*, *PLips.*64.24 (iv A. D.). 2. *the court*, i. e. *the judges*, Ar.*V.*624, Pl.*Lg.*880d, etc.; ἐπειδὰν ἀναστῇ τὸ δ. D.21.221. **-ής**, οῦ, ὁ, *a judge*, Hdt.1.96, 3.14,31, A.*Ch.*120, *Eu.*81, etc. 2. of stars, δ. τῶν ὅλων D.S.2.31. 3. at Athens and elsewh., *juror*, S.*Aj.*1136, etc.; opp. νομοθέτης, Lys.14.4, cf. Antipho 1.23, X.*Smp.*5.10. II. δ. αἵματος *avenger*, E.*HF* 1150. **-ικός**, ή, όν, *of* or *for law* or *trials, practised in them*, X.

*Mem.*2.6.38; *νόμος* δ. Plu.*CG*5; *μισθός* Sch.Ar.*V.*299; ἡ -κή (sc. *τέχνη*) *business of a judge* or *juryman*, Pl.*Plt.*303e, etc.; τὸ δ. *juror's fee*, Arist.*Pol.*1320^{a}26 (but τὸ δ. the *judicial element* in the state, 1300^{b}13). Adv. -κῶς Luc.*Herm.*47.

δῐκαστοφῠλᾰκέω, *to be a member of the bodyguard of a jury*, *Inscr. Magn.*93a.23.

δῐκάστρια, ἡ, fem. of *δικαστής*, Luc.*Pisc.*9.

δῐκαστύς, ύος, ἡ, *judgement*, Μίνως.. δικαστύας ἔξοχα κρίνων Epigr. in *Abh.Berl.Akad.*1909.62.

δῐκατάληκτος, ον, *having two καταλήξεις*, Heph.15.23 and 24: hence **δῐκαταληξία,** ἡ, Mar.Vict.p.62 K.

δικάτωρ· *ὁ διπλασίαν τὴν ἀρχὴν ἔχων*, Hsch.

δῐκαυλέω, *have two stems*, Thphr.*HP*6.6.8.

δῐκεῖν, inf. of *ἔδῐκον*, an aor. used by Pi. and Trag. (the pres. *δίκει* Aristaenet.2.1 is prob. f.l. for *δίεπει*):—*throw, cast*, τι Pi.*P.*9.123, A.*Ch.*99; *πεδόσε σώματα* E.*Ba.*600; *χεῖρ' ἐς οὐρανόν* Id.*HF* 498. 2. *strike*, δ. *πέτρῳ* Pi.*O.*10(11).72; *κρᾶτα φόνιον.. ὠλένας δικὼν βολαῖς* E.*Ph.*664.

δί-κελλα [ῐ], ης, ἡ, (*κέλλω*) *two-pronged fork*, Ps.-Phoc.158, A.*Fr.*196, S.*Ant.*250, E.*Ph.*1155, *IG*11.159*A*57 (Delos, iii B.C.), etc.; *ἀπαλλαγεὶς δικέλλης καὶ κακῶν* Men.*Georg.*65. **-κελλίτης** [λῑ], ου, ὁ, *a digger*, Luc.*Tim.*8. **-κελλον·** *δικράδεστος· ξένος δύο κλάδους ἔχων*, Hsch. **-κέντητον,** τό, name of an *eyesalve*, Dem. Ophth.ap.Aët.7.117. **-κεντρος,** ου, *with two stings*, Ael.*NA*6.20, 16.42. **-κέντρων,** a *throw at dice*, Hsch. **-κέραιος,** ον, *two-horned, two-pointed*, *στόρθυγξ* *AP*6.111 (Antip.(?)). **-κερας,** ατος, τό, *double horn*, Callix.2. **-κέρᾰτος,** ον, *two-horned*, *PMag. Lond.*121.757, Antig.*Mir.*53. **-κερκος,** ον, *with two tails*, Ael. *NA*12.3. **-κερως,** ωτος, ὁ, ἡ, *two-horned*, *h.Hom.*19.2, *AP*6.32 (Agath.), etc.: also *δίκερως*, ων, Orph.*Fr.*274, Arist.*HA*499^{b}18. **-κέφᾰλος,** ον, *two-headed*, ib.540^{b}3, *GA*770^{a}24, Paul.Aeg.3.76; *δράκων* D.C.50.8.

δῐκέω, *mulct*, prob. an error in *IG*2^{2}.1092*B*17 (Pass.).

δίκη [ῐ], ἡ, *custom, usage*, *αὕτη* δ. *ἐστὶ βροτῶν* this is the *way* of mortals, Od.11.218; *ἡ γὰρ* δ. *ἐστὶ γερόντων* 24.255, etc.; *ἥ τ' ἐστὶ* δ. *θείων βασιλήων* 4.691; *ἡ γὰρ δμώων* δ. *ἐστίν* 14.59, etc.; *ἡ γὰρ* δ., *ὁππότε..* this is always *the way*, when.., 19.168 (so in late Prose, *ἧπερ ἱππομαχίας* δ. Arr.*An.*3.15.2); *δίκαν ἐφέπειν τινός* to imitate him, Pi.*P.*1.50; δ. *ἐπέχειν τινός* to be *like*.., Anon.Lond.6.18; *normal course of nature*, *ἐκ τουτέων ὁ θάνατος οὐ γίνεται κατά γε δίκην, οὐδ' ἢν γένηται* Hp.*VC*3: hence, 2. adverb. in acc. *δίκην*, *in the way of, after the manner of*, c. gen., *λύκοιο* Pi.*P.*2.84; *πώλου* S.*Fr.*659; *τοξότου* Pl.*Lg.*705e; in later Prose, Arist.*Mu.*395^{b}22, Luc.*Dem.Enc.*31, Alciphr.1.6, etc.: mostly of living creatures or persons, but also of things, as *δίκην ὕδατος, ἀγγείου*, A.*Th.*85 (lyr.), Pl.*Phdr.*235d. II. *order, right*, *μή τι δίκης ἐπιδευές* nothing short of *what is fit*, Il.19.180; opp. *βία*, might, 16.388; opp. *σχέτλια ἔργα*, Od.14.84; personified, Hes.*Th.*902, A.*Th.*662, etc.; *Δίκης βωμός* Id.*Ag.*383 (lyr.), *Eu.*539 (lyr.); *Truth*, Pi.*P.*8.71. 2. *δίκη ἐστί*, = *δίκαιόν ἐστι*, A.*Ag.*259, cf. 811, *Eu.*277. 3. Adverb. usages, *δίκῃ* *duly, rightly*, Il.23.542, Pl.*Criti.*112e; *ἐν δίκᾳ* Pi.*O.*6.12, cf. S.*Tr.*1069, etc.; *σὺν δίκῃ* Thgn.197, Pi.*P.*9.96, A.*Th.*444, etc.; *κατὰ δίκην* Hdt.7.35, E.*Tr.*888, etc.; *μετὰ δίκης* Pl.*Lg.*643e; *πρὸς δίκης* S.*OT*1014, *El.*1211 (but *πρὸς δίκας* on the score *of justice*, Id.*OC*546 (lyr.)); *διαὶ δίκας* A.*Ch.*641; *ἐκ δίκης* Herod.4.77: opp. *παρὰ δίκαν* Pi.*O.*2.18, etc.; *ἄνευ δίκης* A.*Eu.*554; *πέρα δίκης* Id.*Pr.*30; *βίᾳ δίκης* Id.*Supp.*430 (lyr.); *δίχα δίκης* without *trial*, Plu.*Ages.*32; *πρὸ δίκης* in preference to *legal proceedings*, Th.1.141. III. *judgement*, *δίκην ἰθύντατα εἰπεῖν* give *judgement* most righteously (cf. *ἰθύς*), Il.18.508: esp. in pl., *Λυκίην εἴρυτο δίκῃσί τε καὶ σθένεϊ ᾧ* 16.542; *περὶ οἶδε δίκας* Od.3.244, etc.; *δίκαι σκολιαί* Hes.*Op.*219,250; *κρῖνε εὐθεῖαν δίκην* A.*Eu.*433. IV. after Hom., of *proceedings instituted to determine legal rights*, hence, 1. *lawsuit*, Pl.*Euthphr.*2a, D.18.210, etc.; prop. *private suit* or *action*, opp. *γραφή* (q.v.), Lys.1.44, etc.; *ἐκαλοῦντο αἱ γραφαὶ δίκαι, οὐ μέντοι αἱ δίκαι καὶ γραφαί* Poll.8.41; *οἱ δίκην ἔχοντες* the parties to *a suit*, *IG*7.21.8 (Megara), cf. Plu.*Cic.*17. 2. *trial* of the case, *πρὸ δίκης* Is.5.10, etc.; *μέχρι τοῦ δίκην γενέσθαι* Th.2.53; *court* by which it was tried, *ἐν ὑμῖν ἐστι καὶ τῇ δίκῃ* Antipho 6.6. b. *δίκην εἰπεῖν* to plead a *cause*, X.*Mem.*4.8.1; δ. *μακρὰν λέγειν* Ar.*V.*776, cf. Men.*Epit.*12. 3. *the object* or *consequence of the action, atonement, satisfaction, penalty*, *δίκην ἐκτίνειν, τίνειν*, Hdt.9.94, S.*Aj.*113: adverbially in acc., *τοῦ δίκην πάσχεις τάδε;* A.*Pr.*614; freq. *δίκην* or *δίκας διδόναι* suffer *punishment*, i.e. make *amends* (but *δίκας* δ., in A.*Supp.*703 (lyr.), to grant *arbitration*); *δίκας διδόναι τινί τινος* Hdt.1.2, cf. 5.106; *ἔμελλε τῶνδέ μοι δώσειν δίκην* S.*El.*538, etc.; also *ἀντί* or *ὑπέρ τινος*, Ar.*Pl.*433, Lys.3.42; also *δίκην διδόναι ὑπὸ θεῶν to be punished* by.., Pl.*Grg.*525b; but *δίκας ἤθελον δοῦναι* they consented to submit to *trial*, Th.1.28; *δίκας λαμβάνειν* sts. = δ. *διδόναι*, Hdt.1.115; *δίκην ἀξίαν ἐλάμβανες* E.*Ba.*1312, *Heracl.*852; more freq. its correlative, inflict *punishment*, take *vengeance*, Lys.1.29, etc.; *λαβεῖν δίκην παρά τινος* D.21.92, cf. 9.2, etc.; so *δίκην ἔχειν* to have *one's punishment*, Antipho 3.4.9, Pl.*R.*529c (but *ἔχω τὴν* δ. have *satisfaction*, Id.*Ep.*319e; *παρά τινος* Hdt.1.45); *δίκας* or *δίκην ὑπέχειν* stand *trial*, Id.2.118, cf. S.*OT*552; *δίκην παρασχεῖν* E.*Hipp.*50; *θανάτου δίκην ὀφλεῖν ὑπό τινος* to incur the death *penalty*, Pl.*Ap.*39b; *δίκας λαγχάνειν τινί* D.21.78; *δίκης τυχεῖν παρά τινος* ib.142; *δίκην ὀφείλειν, ὀφλεῖν*, Id.21.77, 47.63; *ἐρήμην ὀφλεῖν τὴν* δ. Antipho 5.13; *δίκην φεύγειν* try to escape *it*, be the defendant in *the trial* (opp. *διώκειν* prosecute), D.38.2; *δίκας αἰτέειν* demand *satisfaction*, *τινός for* a thing, Hdt.8.114; δ. *ἐπιτιθέναι τινί* Id.1.120; *τινός for* a thing, Antipho 4.1.5; *δίκαι ἐπιφερόμεναι* Arist.*Pol.*1302^{b}24; *δίκας ἀφιέναι τινί* D.21.79; *δίκας ἑλεῖν*, v. *ἔρημος* II; *δίκην τείσασθαι*, v. *τίνω* II; *δὸς δὲ δίκην καὶ δέξο παρὰ Ζηνί* *h.Merc.*312; *δίκας διδόναι καὶ λαμβάνειν παρ' ἀλλήλων*, of communities, submit *causes* to trial, Hdt.5.83; *δίκην δοῦναι καὶ λαβεῖν ἐν τῷ δήμῳ* X.*Ath.*1.18, etc.; *δίκας δοῦναι καὶ δέξασθαι* submit differences to a peaceful settlement, Th.5.59. V. Pythag. name for *three*, Plu.2.381f, *Theol.Ar.*12; for *five*, ib.31. (Cf. Skt. *diś-, diśā* 'direction', 'quarter of the heavens'.)

δῐκήγορος, ὁ, *advocate*, Lyd.*Mag.*3.66, Agath.5.7, Suid. s.v. *Ἀλέξανδρος Αἰγαῖος*, Eust.131.2.

δίκηλον, written for *δείκηλον*, Hsch.

δίκηλος [ῐ], ον, (*κήλη*) *with double hernia*, Heliod.ap.Orib.50.42.3. II. *with double hydrocele*, Paul.Aeg.6.62.

δίκησις [ῐ], εως, ἡ, *vengeance*, = *ἐκδίκησις*, LXX *Si.*47.25 (v.l.).

δῐκη-τροπεῖ· *φυγαδεύει*, Suid. **-φόρος,** ον, *bringing justice, avenging*, *Ζεύς* A.*Ag.*525; *ἡμέρα* δ. the day of *vengeance*, ib.1577; ὁ δ. *avenger*, opp. *δικαστής*, Id.*Ch.*120.

δῐκίδιον [ῐδ], τό, Dim. of *δίκη*, *little trial*, Ar.*Eq.*347, *V.*511.

δίκληρος, Dor. **δίκλᾱρος,** ον, *occupying the space of two κλῆροι*, *ἐλαιοκόμιον* *IG*14.352 i 69 (Halaesa).

δικλίς, ίδος, ἡ, (*κλίνω*) *double-folding*, epith. of doors or gates, mostly in pl. with *σανίδες, θύραι, πύλαι*, Od.2.345, 17.268, Il.12.455; later *δικλίδες* alone, *folding-doors*, *AP*7.182 (Mel.), 5.144 (Asclep.), 255 (Paul. Sil.), etc.: rarely in sg., Theoc.14.42, *AP*5.241 (Eratosth.); δ. *θύρη* Arat.193:—written **δίκλεις,** ειδος, as if from *κλείς*, *double-fastened*, Hp.*Art.*7 (cf. Gal. ad loc.).

δῐκο-γρᾰφία, ἡ, *composition of forensic speeches*, Isoc.15.2. **-γρᾰφικῶς,** Adv. *like a writer of forensic speeches*, Id.ap.Poll.8.24. **-γράφος** [ᾰ], ὁ, (*γράφω*) *composer of forensic speeches*, Hyp.*Fr.*234, D.L.6.15. **-δίφης** [δῑφ], ου, ὁ, *one who grubs for lawsuits*, Luc.*Lex.*9.

δίκοκκος [ῐ], ον, *with two grains*, *ζέα*, of rice-wheat, Dsc.2.89. 2. *δίκοκκον*, τό, = *χόνδρος*, Ps.-Dsc.2.96.

δῐκολέκτης, ου, ὁ, = *δικολόγος*, *AP*10.48 (Pall.), *APl.*4.313.

δῐκόλλῠβος, *sum of two κόλλυβοι*, Ar.*Fr.*3.

δῐκο-λογέω, *plead causes*, Arist.*Rh.*1355^{a}20. **-λογία,** ἡ, *pleading*, ib.1354^{b}29. **-λόγος,** ὁ, *pleader, advocate*, Plu.*Luc.*1, Ptol.*Tetr.*180, *Edict.Diocl.*7.72, *PFlor.*71.692 (iv A.D.), Artem.2.29 (pl.).

δῐ-κόλουρος, ον, *doubly truncated*, *πυραμίδες* Nicom.*Ar.*2.14. **-κολπος,** ον, *with two sinuses*, Gal.2.890.

δῐκο-λύμης [ῡ], ου, ὁ, *one who destroys by lawsuits*, *Com.Adesp.*859. **-μᾰχέω,** *carry on a lawsuit*, Alciphr.3.29 (vulg. *ἀδικ-*). **-μήτρα,** ἡ, *mother of lawsuits*, *Com.Adesp.*984.

δῐ-κόνδῠλος, ον, *double-knuckled*, *δάκτυλοι* Arist.*HA*493^{b}30. 2. *provided with two knobs* (?), *Sammelb.*1958. **-κορίασις,** εως, ἡ, (*κόρη*) *possession of double pupil*, Dem.Ophth.ap.Simon.Januens. **-κορμος,** ον, *with two trunks*, *δένδρον* v.l. in Artem.5.74. **-κορος,** ον, *having a double pupil*, Ptol.Chenn.p.192 W., Suid., Eust.295.44.

δῐκο-ρράπτης, ου, ὁ, = *δικορράφος*, Phryn.*PS* p.62 B. **-ρρᾰφέω,** *stitch*, i.e. *get up, a lawsuit*, Ar.*Nu.*1483, Apollod.Com.13.12. **-ρρᾰφία,** ἡ, *getting up a lawsuit*, Man.2.296, Sch.Ar.*Nu.*1015. **-ρράφος** [ᾰ], ὁ, (*ῥάπτω*) *pettifogger*, D.Chr.7.123, Aristaenet.2.3, Phryn.*PS* p.62 B.

δί-κορσος [ῐ], ον, *two-headed*, *Lex.Rh.*ap.Eust.947.28, Hsch. **-κόρυμβος,** ον, *twin-peaked*, *ἕδρανα*, of Parnassus, *Pae.Delph.*4, cf. Luc.*Cont.*5.

δῐ-κόρῠφος, ον, *two-peaked*, δ. *πλάξ*, of Parnassus, E.*Ba.*307; *λάμπουσα πέτρα..* δ. *σέλας* Id.*Ph.*227 (lyr.); *κλειτύς* Limen.2. 2. *with two crowns*, of the hair on the head, Arist.*HA*491^{b}7, Poll.2.43. 3. *with two tops*, *ἐνθέματα* *Gp.*10.75.7.

δῐκοτέχνης, ου, ὁ, *professional advocate*, D.Chr.7.124.

δικοτροπεῖ· *φυγαδεύει*, Hsch.

δῐ-κοτύλιον [ῠ], τό, *measure of two κοτύλαι*, Orib.*Fr.*83. **-κότῠλος,** ον, *with two rows of tentacula*, like the poulp, Arist.*HA*525^{a}19, *PA*685^{b}12. II. *holding two κοτύλαι*, Hp.*Int.*12, Sotad.Com.1.33, Polyaen.8.16.2. 2. Subst. *δικότυλον*, τό, *measure of two κοτύλαι*, *POxy.*937.27 (iii A.D.). **-κραιόομαι,** *branch, fork*, prob. in Hp.*Epid.*2.4.1 (but cf. *Oss.*10); cf. Erot. **-κραιος,** ον, *forked, cleft*, Hp.*Loc.Hom.*6, al. **-κραιότης,** ητος, ἡ, *division*, ibid. **-κραιρος,** ον, *two-horned*, *AP*6.32 (Agath.). II. *forked*, *δίκραιρα..κήτεος ὁλκαίη* A.R.4.1613. **-κρᾱνίζω,** *fork up earth*, *PFay.*110.17 (Pass.). **-κρᾱνος,** ον, *two-headed*, Parm.6.5. II. Subst. **δίκρᾱνον,** τό, *pitchfork*, *δικράνοις ἐξωθεῖν* Luc.*Tim.*12. III. *δικράνους· τὰς τριόδους*, Hsch. **-κρᾱνοφόρος,** *furcifer*, *Gloss.* **-κρᾰτής,** ές, *holding joint authority*, *δικρατεῖς Ἀτρεῖδαι* S.*Aj.*252 (lyr.); *δικρατεῖς λόγχας στήσαντε* *double-slaying* spears, of Eteocles and Polynices, Id.*Ant.*145 (lyr.). **-κρατον** *νόμισμα ἢ* **δίκρανον,** Hsch. **-κρεας,** τό, *double portion of meat*, *νώτου* *SIG*1025.53 (Cos); also **δίκρεως** *μερίς* ib.1013.5 (Chios); *δύο μοίρας δίκρεως* *BCH*37.195 (Chios, iv B.C.).

δικράδεστος, v. *δίκελλον*.

δί-κροος, α, ον, contr. **δίκρους,** α, ουν; or **δικρόος,** contr. **δικροῦς,** ᾶ, οῦν; also written **δίκρος,** α, ον:—*forked, cloven*, *γλώσσημα* A.*Fr.*152, cf. X.*Cyn.*10.7; *ξύλον* Timocl.9.6; *χηλή* Arist.*HA*590^{b}25, etc.; of a serpent's tongue, Id.*PA*660^{b}6, al.; of the womb, in selachians, Id.*HA*511^{a}6; of muscles and tendons, Gal.2.369; *δίκρα ῥίζα* Thphr.*HP*9.11.3; *δικροῖς ἐώθουν τὴν θεὸν—κεκράγμασιν* (*παρὰ προσδοκίαν* for *ξύλοις*) Ar.*Pax* 637; *δίκρουν* or *δικροῦν*, τό, *bifurcation*, Hp.*Coac.*

225, cf. Pl.*Ti.*78b; also δικρόα, ἡ, X.*Cyn.*9.19, Thphr.*HP*2.6.9. **-κρόσσιον,** τό, *double-fringed cloth, Peripl.M.Rubr.*6. **-κροσσος,** ον, *double-bordered* or *fringed*, Poll.7.72, *EM*430.30. **-κροτίζω,** *beat double*, of the pulse, Gal.19.640. **-κροτος,** ον, *double-beating*, ῥόθια κώπας E.*IT*408 (lyr.); of the pulse, Archig.ap.Gal.8.537, al., Ruf.*Syn.Puls.*8.5. 2. of ships, *with only two banks of oars manned*, X.*HG*2.1.28; later, = διήρης, Arr.*An.*6.5.2, Luc.*Am.*6: Subst. δίκροτον, τό, Plb.5.62.3, App.*Mith.*17; δίκροτος, ἡ, *AP*7.640 (Antip.). II. δ. ἁμαξιτός a road *for two carriages*, E.*El.*775. **-κρουνος,** ον, *with two springs*, ῥυτὸν δ. a vase *from which two kinds of wine could be poured*, Damox.1.3; δ., τό, Haussoullier *Milet* p.199.

Δικταῖος, ὁ, epith. of Zeus, from the Cretan mountain *Dicte*, Str.10.4.12.

δικταμνίτης [νῖ] οἶνος wine *flavoured with dittany*, Dsc.5.47.

δικταμνοειδές, name of a *plant*, prob. = ψευδοδίκταμνον, Hsch.

δίκταμνον, τό, Arist.*HA*612^{a}4, Thphr.*HP*9.16.1: **δίκταμον,** Arist.*Mir.*830^{b}21:—*dittany of Crete, Origanum Dictamnus.* 2. *bastard dittany, Ballota acetabulosa*, Dsc.3.32.

δικτάτωρ [ᾰ], ορος or ωρος, ὁ, Lat. *dictator*, Plb.3.87.7, etc.: hence **δικτᾱτωρ-εία,** ἡ, *the dictatorship*, D.H.6.22 (-ία, Plu.*Fab.*3): **-εύω,** *to be dictator*, D.C.43.1.

δίκτον, τό, = δίκταμνον, Arat.33 (Zenod.ap.Sch., but prob. pr.n.).

δίκτυ, = δίκτυον, *EM*275.27.

δικτῠ-ἀγωγός, ὁ, *drawer of nets*, Poll.5.17. **-αρχέω,** *hold office in the cult of Isis*, or (less prob.) *in a fishery guild*, *IGRom.*1.817 (Callipolis). **-βολέω,** *cast the net*, dub. l. in *AP*6.186 (Diocles). **-βόλος,** ον, *a fisherman*, ib.105 (Apollonid.), Opp.*H.*4.578. **-διον,** τό, Dim. of δίκτυον, Poll.7.179. **-εία** or **-ῖα,** ἡ, *net-fishing*, Ael.*NA*12.43. **-εύς,** έως, ὁ, *one who fishes with nets*, Str.8.7.2, Ael.*NA*1.12.

Δίκτυννα, ἡ, (δίκτυον) epith. of Artemis as *goddess of the chase*, Hdt.3.59, E.*Hipp.*145 (lyr.), etc.:—hence **Δικτυνναῖος,** ὁ (sc. μήν), name of month in Crete, *GDI*5173.

δικτῠο-βόλος, ον, = δικτυβόλος, Poll.7.137. **-ειδής,** ές, *net-like*, δ. πλέγμα *rete mirabile Galeni*, Herophil.ap.Gal.5.155, Gal.*UP*9.4. **-θήρας,** ου, ὁ, *net-fisher*, Sch.Theoc.1.40. **-θηρευτική** (sc. τέχνη), ἡ, *net-fishing*, Poll.7.139. **-κλωστος,** ον, (κλώθω) *woven in meshes*, σπεῖραι δ. *the net's meshy* coils, S.*Ant.*347 (lyr.).

δίκτυον, τό, (δικεῖν) *net*: 1. *fishing-net*, δικτύῳ ἐξέρυσαν πολυωπῷ (sc. ἰχθύας) Od.22.386; φελλοὶ δ' ὣς ἄγουσι δ. A.*Ch.*506; μολυβδὶς ὥστε δ. κατέσπασεν S.*Fr.*840; δ. καθιέναι, ἀναιρεῖσθαι, Arist.*HA*533^{b}19, 602^{b}8. 2. *hunting-net*, Hdt.1.123, Ar.*Av.*1083, etc.; larger than ἄρκυς, X.*Cyn.*2.5, cf. Poll.5.26, 27. 3. metaph., δ. ἄτης, Ἅιδου, A.*Pr.*1078 (anap.), *Ag.*1115 (lyr.), cf. S.*Fr.*932. 4. *lattice-work*, *IG*11(2).165.4, 13 (Delos, iii B.C.). 5. *bottom of a sieve*, Hsch.

δικτῠόομαι, Pass., *to be wrought in net-work*, Lxx 3*Ki.*7.18(6). II. *to be caught in a net*, Babr.107.11.

δικτῠοπλόκος, ον, *weaving nets*, Poll.7.139.

δικτῠουλκός, όν, *drawing nets*, Poll.7.137. II. Subst., *fisher*, Iamb.*VP*8.36: Δικτυουλκοί, οἱ, title of play by A.

δικτῠοῦχος, ὁ, = *retiarius*, *Gloss.*; also **δικτυοφόρος,** ὁ, Id.

δίκτῠπος, ον, *double-sounding*, ἠχώ Nonn.*D.*10.225.

δίκτυς, υος, ὁ, an unknown Libyan animal, Hdt.4.192. II. = ἰκτῖνος (Lacon.), Hsch.

δικτῠ-ώδης, ες, = δικτυοειδής, Sch.Ar.*V.*99, Poll.4.116. II. Subst. -ῶδες, τό, = δ. πλέγμα, Hp.*Ep.*19 (*Hermes* 53.69). **-ωτός,** ἡ, όν, *made in net-fashion*, θύσανος D.S.18.26; *latticed, trellised*, θύραι Plb.15.30.8; θυρὶς δ. *lattice*-window, Lxx *Ez.*41.16: Subst. δικτυωτόν, τό, = θυρὶς δ., ib.4*Ki.*1.2.

δί-κυκλος [ῐ], ον, *two-wheeled*, ὄχημα Lib.*Or.*1.33; δ. [ἅρμα] *two-wheeled* car, D.C.76.7. **-κῡμος,** ον, *bearing twins*, πρόβατα Suid. **-κύπελλος** [ῠ], ον, gloss on ἀμφικύπελλος, Eust.159.4. **-κυρτος,** ον, *two-humped*, of the Bactrian camel, *An.Ox.*4.264, *Gp.*16.22.4.

***δίκω,** v. δικεῖν.

δῐ-κωλία, ἡ, *period of two members*, Mar.Vict.p.182 K. **-κωλος,** ον, *with two limbs* or *legs*, Lyc.636; ἀκρίδια Dsc.2.94; of a crane, μηχανή *Milet.*7.60; *in two sections*, σύριγγες Nicom.*Harm.*10. II. in Rhet., *with two members*, περίοδος Demetr.*Eloc.*34, Hermog.*Inv.*4.3, Hdn.*Fig.*p.98 S.:—also in metre, Sch.Ar.*Ach.*1212, etc. **-κωπέω,** *ply a pair of sculls*, sens. obsc., ἀμφοτέρας δ. Ar.*Ec.*1091. **-κωπία,** ἡ, *pair of sculls*, Luc.*Cont.*1, Sch.Th.4.67. **-κωπος,** ον, *two-oared*, σκάφος E.*Alc.*252 (lyr.), cf. 444 (lyr.), Plb.34.3.2.

δίλαξ· ἀρία (Lacon.), Hsch.

δίλασσον, τό, a kind of *garment*, dub. sens. in *BGU*814.25, 816.17 (ii A.D.); cf. τετράλασσον.

δῑλέκῐθος, ον, *with two yolks*, ᾠόν Sch.E.*Or.*463.

διλέσβιος, ον, dub. sens., διλέσβια λευκά (sc. κεράμια?) *PSI*5.535.28.

δῐ-λήκῠθον, τό, *double* λήκυθος, Hippoloch.ap.Ath.4.129c. **-λημμα,** ατος, τό, *ambiguous proposition*, Roman.2, Suid. **-λήμμᾰτος,** ον, *involving two propositions*, συλλογισμός Gal.*Inst.Log.*6.5: -τον, τό, *dilemma*, Hermog.*Inv.*4.6. Adv. -τως Ulp.ad D.3.13. II. *ambiguous*, λέξεις Sch.Ar.*Nu.*480. III. *two-handled*, gloss on περιδέξιος, *EM*699.41. **-λήμνιον,** τό, *double lemniscus*, *IG*12(1).155.56 (Rhodes), *BCH*11.308 (Caria, written διλεμνίωι). **-ληπτος,** ον, *ambiguous*, Sch.Il.2.642. **-λιτραῖος,** ον, *weighing two pounds*, μῆλα Tz.*H.*9.342:—also **-λιτρόμηλα,** ib.347. **-λιτρον,** τό, *weight of two pounds*, *Gloss.* **-λογέω,** *repeat*, X.*Eq.*8.2; περὶ τῶν αὐτῶν D.S.16.46:—Pass., διλογηθὲν ὄνομα Demetr.*Eloc.*267: **-ητέον,** *one must repeat*, ib.197. **-λογία,** ἡ, *repetition*, X.*Eq.*8.2: as a rhetorical figure, Demetr.*Eloc.*211. **-λογος,** ον, *double-tongued, doubtful*, 1*Ep.Ti.*3.8. **-λογχος,** ον, *double-pointed, twofold*, ἄτη A.*Ag.*643; epith. of Βενδῖς (i.e. Artemis) from her *twofold* attributes, Cratin.80. **-λοφος,** ον, *double-crested*, πέτρα, of Parnassus, S.*Ant.*1126 (lyr.); ἀλέκτωρ *PMag.Leid.V.*9.21. **-λοχία,** ἡ, *double company*, Aen.Tact.15.3, Plb.10.23.4; *body of thirty-two men*, Ascl.*Tact.*2.8, Arr.*Tact.*10.1. **-λοχίτης** [χῑ], ου, ὁ, *commander of a* διλοχία, Ascl. and Arr. ll. cc. **-λωρος,** ον, dub. sens., *BGU*620.9 (iii A.D.). **-μαλλος,** ον, *with double fleece*, *Gloss.* **-μάχαιρος** [μᾰ], ον, *with two swords*, of gladiators, Artem.2.32. **-μάχης** [ᾰ], ου, ὁ, *mounted infantryman*, D.S.5.33 (with vv.ll.), Poll.1.132. **-μέδιμνον,** τό, *measure holding two* μέδιμνοι, Hsch. **-μελος** (?), *two-membered*, *Gloss.* **-μερής,** ές, *bipartite*, of the human body, the brain, etc., Arist.*PA*667^{b}32, al.; δ. ψυχή Ph.1.523; δ. κλισία J.*AJ*12.2.12; φιλοσοφία Jul.*Or.*6.190a. Adv. -ρῶς *in two instalments*, *Jahresh.*18 *Beibl.*23 (Seleucia in Cilicia, ii A.D.). **-μέτρητος,** ον, *holding two* μετρηταί, κώδων Callix.2, cf. *CIG*3071 (Teos). **-μετρος,** ον, of a verse, *having two metres*, Heph.5.3, etc. II. δίμετρον, τό, *double measure*, Lxx 4*Ki.*7.1, al. **-μέτωπος,** ον, *with two fronts*, App.*BC*5.33. **-μηνία,** ἡ, *period of two months*, prob. in *SIG*344.107 (Teos). **-μηνιαῖος,** α, ον, *two months old*, Hp.*Nat.Mul.*19, *Mul.*1.47; *of two months*, χρόνος Cleom.1.7, Gem.6.14, *Gp.*17.3.3 (v.l. -μηναῖος). **-μηνος,** ον, *of* or *for two months*, δ. πυρὸς *maturing in two months*, Thphr.*HP*8.4.4; ἀνοχαί Plb.18.10.4; δίμηνα ἐκτιτρώσκειν Hp.*Aph.*5.45; δίμηνος, ἡ, *space of two months*, Arist.*HA*573^{a}12; εἰς δ. Id.*Oec.*1353^{a}22; ἐντὸς διμήνου *POxy.*1032.22 (ii A.D.); τὴν δ. ἄρχειν Plb.6.34.3. **-μηρον,** *bicoxum*, *Gloss.* **-μήτωρ,** Dor. **-μάτωρ,** ορος, ὁ, ἡ, *twice-born*, of Bacchus, Alex.283, Orph.*H.*52.9, D.S.3.62:—also **-μήτριος,** *Et.Gud.*, Hdn.*Epim.*265. **-μῐτος,** ον, *of double thread*, καυσία Eust.393.4. **-μιτρος,** ον, *with double mitre*, Plu.*Demetr.*41. **-μναιαῖος,** α, ον, *paid at the rate of two minae*, ὁμιληταί Them.*Or.*23.290c. **-μναῖος,** α, ον, Ion. **-μνεως,** (μνᾶ) *worth* or *costing two minae*, δίμνεως (v.l. διμναίας) ἀποτιμήσασθαι to value *at two minae*, Hdt.5.77; δ. τιμήσασθαί τι Arist.*Oec.*1347^{a}23; μισθώματα διμναῖα Luc.*DMeretr.*14.4:—also **-μνους,** ουν, Ph.*Bel.*69.13: Subst. δίμνουν, τό, *weight of two minae*, *IG*2^2.1013.55. **-μνωος** χόρτος, dub. sens. in *PRyl.*183.17, etc.

δῐμοιρ-αῖος, gloss on διμοιρίτης, Hsch. II. δ. τόκος interest *at two-thirds of the legal maximum*, Just.*Nov.*136.4, *PMasp.*126.23 (vi A.D.). **-ία,** ἡ, *double share*, X.*An.*7.2.36, *Lac.*15.4; δ. βασιλέως Antiph.81.5; *double pay*, X.*HG*6.1.6 (pl.). 2. *two-thirds*, D.H.8.77, *BGU*136.8 (pl., ii A.D.). II. = ἡμιλόχιον, Ascl.*Tact.*2.2, Ael.*Tact.*5.2, Arr.*Tact.*6.2. **-ιαῖος,** α, ον, *of two-thirds*, μῆκος Apollod.*Poliorc.*162.7. **-ίτης** [ρῖ], ου, ὁ, *one who receives double pay*, *PLille* 27.3 (iii B.C.), Men.*Kol.*28 (v. Sch.), Arr.*An.*7.23.3. 2. = Lat. *duplarius*, Id.*Tact.*42.1. II. *leader of a* διμοιρία, Ascl.*Tact.*2.2, Luc.*DMeretr.*9.5; *mate* of a ship, Id.*JTr.*48. **-ος,** ον, *two-thirds*, esp. in neut., δίμοιρον, τό, A.*Supp.*1070 (lyr.), Euc.1.3, *BGU*661.22 (i A.D.), Nicom.*Harm.*10, etc.; διμοίρου ὀρθῆς ἐστιν ἡ γωνία the angle measures *two-thirds* of a right angle, Papp.178.23; δ. σπιθαμῆς Hero *Mens.*60.14, cf. *Gp.*8.36.3. 2. *half a drachma*, Pl.*Ax.*366c: at Rome, *half a libra*, Plu.*CG*17. II. in A.*Th.*850 (lyr.), Herm. restored δίμορα τέλεα (for δίμοιρα τέλεια) metri gr.

δί-μορφος [ῐ], ον, *two-formed*, Lyc.111, 892; *of twin form*, Vett.Val.13.3; *androgynous*, D.S.32.12. **-μόρφωτος,** ον, *of twin form*, ζῴδια, i.e. Gemini and Pisces, Man.4.452. **-μυξος,** ον, *with two wicks*, Philyll.26, Philonid.4, Pl.Com.84, Metagen.12, *CIG*3071.9 (Teos).

δῑνάζω, = δινέω, Artem.ap.Ath.8.333f: aor. Med. δινάσσατο in Pi.*Fr.*101.3 is corrupt.

δῑνάκω, *change, amend*, dub. in *Schwyzer*412.4 (Elis).

δίν-ευμα [ῑ], τό, *whirling round*, esp. in dancing, prob. in Ar.*Th.*122; *wheeling*, of a horse, X.*Eq.*3.11; *rotation*, ῥόμβου Orph.*H.*8.7 (pl.). **-εύω,** mostly in pres. and impf. (iter. δινεύεσκον Il.24.12), but aor. part. δινεύσας A.R.3.310:—also **δῑνέω,** A.*Th.*462: impf. ἐδίνεον, Ep. δίνεον Il.18.494, Od.9.384: aor. ἐδίνησα Il.23.840, A.*Th.*490: Aeol. **δίννημι** Sapph.1.11:—Med. (v. περιδ-):—**Pass.,** δινεύομαι Arat.455, Opp.*H.*1.376: aor. ἐδινήθην Od.22.85 (as v.l.), E.*Rh.*353 (lyr.): pf. δεδίνημαι (ἀμφι-) Il.23.562: also impf. or plpf. δίνηντο from δίνημι, B.16.107.—Poet. Verbs, also in X. and Pl. and later Prose (v. infr.): (δίνη):—*whirl, spin round*, ἧκε δὲ δινήσας [τὸν σόλον] *after whirling* it, Il.23.840; ζεύγεα δινεύοντες *driving* them *round a circle*, 18.543; μοχλὸν ἑλόντες δινέομεν *twirled* the stake *round* in the Cyclops' eye, Od.9.388; δ. πτέρα Sapph.1.11; ἵππους, [ἀσπίδα], A.*Th.*462, 490; ὄμμα E.*Or.*1459 (lyr.):—Pass., *whirl, roll about*, ὄσσε .. πάντοσε δινείσθην Il.17.680; κάππεσε δινηθεὶς v.l. for ἰδνωθείς, Od.22.85; of a river, *eddy*, E.*Rh.*353 (lyr.); *whirl round* in the dance, X.*An.*6.1.9, prob. for δον- in Id.*Smp.*2.8; of tumblers, ἐπὶ τροχοῦ δινεῖσθαι Pl.*Euthd.*294e; *writhe*, ἐκ τῶν ἀλγηδόνων J.*BJ*6.2.10. 2. Pass., *roam about*, ἐδινεόμεσθα κατ' αὐτήν [νῆσον] Od.9.153; βροτῶν ἐπὶ ἄστεα δινηθῆναι 16.63; κατ' ἀμευσίπορον τρίοδον ἐδινήθην Pi.*P.*11.38. 3. ἀμφὶ χαίταις δίνηντο ταινίαι were *twined*, B.16.107. II. intr. in Act., *whirl about*, ὀρχηστῆρες ἐδίνεον Il.18.494; of tumblers, ἐδίνευον κατὰ μέσσους ib.606; of a warrior, ὅστις ...δινεύοι κατὰ μέσσον 4.541; δινεύουσαν ὑπὸ πτέρυγος βάλε *as it was circling in its flight*, of a pigeon, 23.875: generally, δ. ἐν ἅρμασιν A.R.3.310; *roam about*, δινεύεσκ' ἀλύων παρὰ θῖν' ἁλὸς Il.24.12; δινεύων κατὰ οἶκον Od.19.67; ἀνὰ νῆσον ἐδίνεον A.R.2.695; δινεύων βλεφάροις look wildly about, E.*Or.*837 (dub.). **-η**, ἡ, *whirlpool, eddy*, Il.21.213, A.*Eu.*559, E.*Tr.*210, Pl.*Cra.*439c, etc.: pl., Il. 21.353, Hes.*Th.*791, Hdt.2.28, etc.; ἐπὶ Κυανέας δ. *CIG*3797 (Chalcedon): generally, of the sea, Τυρσηνὶς δ. *AP*9.308 (Bianor). 2. of the *rotating heaven*, Emp.35.4; αἰθέρος δῖναι Id.115.11, cf. Pl.*Phd.* 99b, Arist.*Cael.*295ᵃ13, *Ph.*196ᵃ26. 3. *whirlwind*, Ar.*Av.*697; δῖναι νεφέλας E.*Alc.*244 (lyr.). 4. generally, *circular motion, rotation*, Ar.*Av.*1198; ἀτράκτου Pl.*R.*620e, cf. Epicur.*Ep.*2 p.40 U., al. 5. metaph., ἀνάγκης στερραῖς δ. A.*Pr.*1052 (anap.); τελεσφόροις δίναις κυκλούμενον κέαρ Id.*Ag.*997 (lyr.). **-ήεις**, Dor. **-άεις**, Aeol. **διννάεις** Alc.*Supp.*7.2, εσσα, εν, gen. contr. δινᾶντος B.12.78:— *whirling, eddying*, Ξάνθῳ ἐπὶ δινήεντι Il.5.479, cf. Od.6.89, Simon.53. 2, E.*Cyc.*46, etc. II. *rounded*, ταλάροιο Mosch.2.55. **-ημα**, ατος, τό, *rotation*, κόσμου Man.4.553. **-ησις**, εως, ἡ, *whirling motion, rotation*, Arist.*Cael.*295ᵃ10, *Ph.*243ᵃ17, Epicur.*Ep.*2 p.38 U. (pl.); *vertigo*, Aret.*SD*1.4. **-ητός**, ή, όν, *whirled round*, *AP*7.394 (Phil.).

δίνομον [ῐ], τό, *coin worth two* νοῦμμοι, *SIG*²588.215 (Delos, ii B.C.), *BCH*35.260 (ibid.).

δῖνος, ὁ, like δίνη, *whirling, rotation*, such as Anaxagoras held to be the effect of νοῦς as the regulator of the Universe, Clem.Al.*Str.*2. 14 (pl.); personified, Δῖνος βασιλεύει τὸν Δί' ἐξεληλακώς Ar.*Nu.*828: generally, ὁ τοῦ κοσκίνου δ. Democr.164; σφενδόνης δ. Onos.17. 2. *eddy, whirlpool*, Epicur.*Ep.*2 pp.38,47 U., Arist.*Pr.*932ᵃ5, Plu.2.404f; δ. ἀπὸ τοῦ παντὸς ἀποκριθῆναι παντοίων εἰδέων Democr.167: metaph., δῖνοι ἡδυλόγου σοφίης cj. in Timo67.4. 3. a *dance*, Hdn.Gr.2.492, Eust.1166.10. II. *vertigo*, Hp.*VC*11. III. *round threshing-floor*, Telesill.7, cj. in X.*Oec.*18.5. IV. *round goblet*, Ar.*V.*618, *IG*11(2).110 (Delos, iii B.C.), al. (cf. δεῖνος, which is freq. v.l. and is found in puns with δεινός, Apolloph.1, Arched.1.4).

δίνουμμον [ῐ], τό, *coin of the value of two* νοῦμμοι (q.v.), *Gloss.*

δινόω, *turn with a lathe*, Eust.412.31, etc.

Δίνυσος, v. Διόνυσος.

δίν-ω [ῑ], used only in pres., *thresh out on the* δῖνος III, ἱερὸν ἀκτὴν δινέμεν Hes.*Op.*598:—Pass., δινομένην ὑπὸ (v.l. περὶ) βουσὶν... ἅλωα *trodden by the circling* oxen, Call.*Fr.*51:—Aeol. **δίννω** Hdn.Gr.2.492: Dor. 3 pl. ἀπο-δίνωντι *Tab.Heracl.*1.102. **-ώδης**, ες, *eddying*, D.C. 68.13; τὰ δινώδη *eddies*, Plu.*Cat.Ma.*20.

Δινών, ῶνος, ὁ (sc. μήν), name of month in Locris, *GDI*1908.

δῑνωτός, ή, όν, *turned, rounded*, λέχη, κλισίη, Il.3.391, Od.19.56; ῥινοῖσι βοῶν καὶ νώροπι χαλκῷ δινωτήν (sc. ἀσπίδα) *covered with... circular plates* (or *adorned with spirals*), Il.13.407; θρόνος A.R.3. 44. II. *whirling*, κύκλοι Parm.1.7; πτέρυγες *Epic.Alex.Adesp.* 4.14 Pap.

διξᾶται, *pandat*, *Gloss.*

δίξεστον, τό, *measure of two* ξέσται, Sch.Ar.*Th.*354.

δίξοος, ον, (ξέω) *cleft, forked*, Thphr.*HP*5.1.9,10.

διξός, ή, όν, Ion., = δισσός, Anacr.88, Hdt.2.44, etc.

δίξυλος, ον, *with two blocks*, τροχιλίαι Heliod.ap.Orib.49.8.9.

Διο- (in Ep. **Δῑο-** metri gr.), in compds., both *sprung from Zeus* or *the gods*, and *godlike*.

διό, Conj., for δι' ὅ, *wherefore, on which account*, Pl.*R.*358d, etc.; διὸ δή Th.2.21, Pl.*Cra.*412a, al.; διὸ καί, διὸ δὴ καί, Id.*Phdr.*258e, *Smp.* 203c; διόπερ Th.1.71,120, 8.92, etc.

διοβελία, ἡ, = διωβελία, *IG*2².1103.

Διο-βλής, ῆτος, ὁ, ἡ, *hurled by Zeus*, Sch.Pi.*P.*8.23. **-βλητος**, ον, = foreg., Democr.152, Nonn.*D.*2.511. 2. *smitten by Zeus*, ib.21. 223, Ael.*NA*6.62, *Fr.*250, Anon.*Incred.*17. **-βολος**, ον, = foreg. I, of the thunderbolt, κτύπος S.*OC*1464 (lyr.), E.*Alc.*128 (lyr.).

Διογένειον, τό, *the school of Diogenes*, *IG*3.1133.170. II. Διογένεια, τά, festival at Athens *in honour of Diogenes* the Macedonian, *IG*2².1028.24.

Διο-γενέτωρ, ορος, ὁ, *giving birth to Zeus*, Διογενέτορες ἔναυλοι *natal* cave *of Zeus*, E.*Ba.*122 (lyr.). **-γενής**, ές, *sprung from Zeus*, in Hom. epith. of kings, *ordained and upheld by Zeus*, Il.1.337, al.; δ. Ὀδυσεύς Od.2.352; later, Δ. θεοί A.*Th.*301 (lyr.), *Supp.*631 (lyr.), Ar.*Av.*1263; Διογενὲς κράτος, of Pallas, A.*Th.*127 (lyr.); δ. τέκνον S.*Aj.*91; Ἀμφίων A.*Th.*528; αἷμα τὸ δ., of Achilles, E.*Andr.* 1195 (lyr.): generally, *divine*, φάος Id.*Med.*1258 (lyr.). II. parox., Διογένης, ους, ὁ, pr. n. [Δῐ- in Ep., ῐ in Trag.]

Διογενισμός, ὁ, *life after the manner of Diogenes*, Jul.*Or.*6. 186c.

διογκ-όω, *distend, blow out*, πυρόν Plu.2.676b; λέξις δ. τὸ στόμα Hermog.*Id.*1.6; τὸ ω̄ καὶ τὸ ᾱ δ. τὸν λόγον ibid., cf. Alex.Aphr.*Pr.* 1.59:—Pass., *swell* or *be distended*, Hp.*Acut.*10,28, Plu.*Ages.*27, Sor.2.37: metaph., *to be lifted up, raised to a higher position*, Artem. 1.14; *to be puffed up*, Eun.*VS* p.478 B.; λέξεις διωγκωμέναι (cf. supra) Hermog. l.c.; of a lake, *rise, overflow*, Plu.*Cam.*3. **-ύλλομαι**, *to be puffed up with pride*, Eun.*VS* p.502 B. **-ωσις**, εως, ἡ, *swelling*, Sor.1.55, Plu.2.771b; *tumour*, Gal.1.185. II. *diastole*, Marcellin. *Puls.*478.

Διόγνητος, ον, contr. for Διογένητος, = Διογενής, Hes.*Sc.*340.

Διόγονος, ον, f.l. for δίγονος, Βάκχος E.*Hipp.*560 (lyr.).

διοδ-εία, ἡ, *passage through*, τῶν στρατευμάτων *BSA*23.73 (Macedonia, ii A.D.), cf. Suid. **-ευσις**, εως, ἡ, = foreg., Hp.*Flat.*9. **-εύω**, *travel through*, τὴν χώραν Plb.2.15.5; *march through*, Plu.*Ages.*17; πανδοκεῖον Arr.*Epict.*2.23,26; διὰ τῶν νομῶν *OGI*665.22 (Oasis Magna): c. gen., διοδεύσει πάντων ἡ τύχη J.*BJ*3.8.7: abs., X.Eph.4.1; *pass away*, of the cause of disease, Gal.8.20:—Pass., Sor.2.59, *AP* 9.708 (Phil.). **-ία**, *bivium*, *Gloss.* **-ιον**, τό, *passage through*, τὸ δ. τῆς λιθοτομίας *IG*2².1035.49 (i B.C.).

διοδοιπορέω, = διοδεύω, τὰς δύο μοίρας [τῆς ὁδοῦ] Hdt.8.129, cf. J. *Ap.*2.16.

διοδοποιέω, = foreg., dub. l. in Thphr.*Ign.*59.

δίοδος, ἡ, *way through, passage, pass*, of Thermopylae, Hdt.7. 201, cf. 9.99, Ar.*Th.*658, *IG*2².463.122, etc.; δ. ὕδατος Th.2.102; ἄστρων δίοδοι their *pathways, orbits*, A.*Pr.*1050 (lyr.); δ. ἔχειν to command *the road*, Th.7.32; αἱ δ. τῶν πτερῶν Pl.*Phdr.*255d; δ. αἰτεῖσθαι, αἰτεῖν, ask *leave to pass*, demand *a safe-conduct*, Ar.*Av.*189, Aeschin.3.151. II. *passing* through the bowels, μελάνων Hp. *Prorrh.*1.127.

Διόδοτος, ον, v. Διόσδοτος.

δἴόδους, *bidens*, *Gloss.*

διοζόομαι, Pass., *branch out*, Hp.*Nat.Puer.*19.

δίοζος [ῐ], ον, *with two knots* or *eyes*, Thphr.*HP*1.8.3.

Διόθεν, Adv. *sent from Zeus, according to his will*, Δ. βλαφθέντα βέλεμνα Il.15.489; Δ. ἄγγελος ἦλθε 24.194, cf. A.*Ag.*43 (anap.); ἐκ Δ. Hes.*Op.*765.

διοίγνῡμι, *open*, τὰς γνάθους διοίγνυτε Ar.*Ec.*852: metaph., τὸ τῆς ψυχῆς ὄμμα Ph.1.442:—Pass., Id.2.414:—also **διοίγω**, S.*Aj.*346, *OT*1287,1295 (Pass.), Pl.*Smp.*222a (Pass.), etc.; ᾗ δ' ἂν διοίξῃς σφάγια (sc. τῇ μαχαίρᾳ) E.*Supp.*1205.

δίοιδα, v. διεῖδον.

διοιδ-αίνω, = sq., Aët.3.34: metaph., διοίδαινον τῶν ὄχλων αἱ ψυχαί Hdn.7.3.6; also οἱ στρατιῶται δ. τὰς ψυχάς Id.8.8.1. **-έω**, pf. and plpf., διῴδηκα, -ειν, Luc.*Gall.*10, *Nec.*18:—strengthd. for οἰδέω, Hp. *Art.*79 (prob.), J.*BJ*5.12.3, Luc. ll. cc.; of the sea, Str.3.5.8: metaph. of a person, *swell with anger*, Ph.2.583; of a city, *to be in a ferment*, D.H.9.48:—Med., metaph., διοιδουμένη καὶ οὐκ ἄνευ ζηλοτυπίας Hld. 7.7. **-ής**, ές, *swollen, turgid*, μαζός Nic.*Al.*90. **-ησις**, εως, ἡ, *swelling*, Heliod.ap.Orib.50.52.1. II. *ebullition* of temper, Phld.*Ir.*p.26 W. **-ίσκομαι**, = διοιδέω, Gal.5.523.

διοικ-εία, ἡ, = διοίκησις, dub. in Eustr.*in EN*179.8. **-εσις**, εως, ἡ, = διοίκησις, *IG*12(2).15.34 (Mytilene). **-έω**, impf. διῴκουν Th.8. 21, etc.: fut. -ήσω Pl.*Men.*73b: aor. διῴκησα Isoc.1.35, etc.: pf. διῴκηκα Pl.*Ti.*19e, D.24.202:—**Med.**, fut. -ήσομαι Id.8.13 (also in pass. sense, Hdn.8.7.6): aor. διῳκησάμην D.18.247: pf. (in med. sense) διῴκημαι (v. infr.):—Pass., aor. διῳκήθην Luc.*Nec.*19: pf. διῴκημαι Arist.*Ath.*25.2, dub. l. in Antiph.191.18, D.22.74: plpf. διῴκητο (προ-) Id.23.14; but with both augm. and redupl., pf. δεδιῴκημαι Antiph.155, Machoap.Ath.8.341c, Phld.*Rh.*2.266 S.:—*keep house*: hence, generally, *control, manage, administer*, τὴν πόλιν Th.8.21, etc.; τὰ τῆς πόλεως Ar.*Ec.*305; τάς τε οἰκίας καὶ τὰς πόλεις Pl.*Men.* 91a; τὸν κόσμον Id.*Phdr.*246c; τὸν οὐρανόν Id.*Lg.*896e; τὰ ἀνθρώπινα ib.713c; τὸν ἑαυτοῦ βίον Isoc.1.10; τὴν οὐσίαν D.27.50, etc.; τὰ κοινά Id.1.22; τὴν ἀρχήν Arist.*Pol.*1313ᵃ35; τὰ μέγιστα ὁ λογισμὸς διῴκηκε Epicur.*Sent.*16; δ. πάντα ἀκριβῶς, of a housekeeper, Lys. 1.7; πολέμους Din.1.69; of a financier, δ. τὰ πρὸς τὴν πόλιν, ἐπὶ τῇ τραπέζῃ, D.27.60, 45.33; πεντεκαίδεκα τάλαντα, ἃ Καλλισθένης διῴκησεν Id.20.33; *administer as deputy*, τὴν λογιστείαν *Stud.Pal.*8.1010.1 (iii/iv A.D.):—Pass., *to be ordered, managed*, etc., τύχῃ δ. Hp.*VM*1, Aeschin.1.4; ἅπας ὁ βίος φύσει καὶ νόμοις δ. D.25.15:—Med., *manage after one's own will and pleasure*, τὰ πράγματα διοικήσασθαι Id.4.12: pf. Pass. (in med. sense), ἵν' ἃ βουλόμεθα ὦμεν διῳκημένοι Id.18.178; διοικούμενος οὕτως ἀδίκους πλεονεξίας *managing to make* such iniquitous profits, Id.44.38, cf. 40; διοικεῖσθαι πρὸς ἀλλήλους *act collusively* with.., Id.58.20, cf. 19. b. abs., *exercise authority, govern*, τυραννικώτερον Arist.*Pol.*1313ᵃ2, cf. 1298ᵇ12. 2. *provide, furnish*, ἀπορῶ τἄλλα ὁπόθεν διοικῶ D.27.66, cf. Decr.ap.eund.24.27 (Pass.); δ. τὴν ἀδελφήν *provide for, settle* her, D.24.202:—Pass., *to be nourished* or *supported*, ὑπό τινος Str.14.2.24; γάλακτι Ath.2.46e (dub. l.). 3. *rent, farm*, νομῶν τῶν πρὸς χαλκὸν διοικουμένων *PTeb.*79.8 (ii B.C.), al. 4. *digest* food, D.L.6.34. 5. Rhet., Med., *distribute, arrange in a discourse*, D.H.*Rh.*9.4. II. *inhabit distinct places*, Pl.*Ti.*19e:—Med., *live apart*, κατὰ κώμας X.*HG*5.2.5 (s.v.l.; διοικ(ι)οῖντο Cobet). **-ημα**, ατος, τό, *sum of money administered*, Hsch., Suid.s.v. ἀλογίου δίκη. **-ησις**, εως, ἡ, prop. *housekeeping*: hence, generally, *internal administration*, τῆς πόλεως Pl.*Prt.*319d, cf. Arist. *Pol.*1287ᵃ6, Lys.30.22, etc.; ἐγκύκλιος δ. Arist.*Ath.*43.1; κοινὴ δ. Aeschin.2.149; esp. of *financial administration*, δ. ἱερὰ καὶ ὅσια D. 24.96, cf. X.*HG*6.1.2; *department of finance* in Egypt, *PTeb.*7.4 (ii B.C.), al.; ὅπως ... ἡ δ. γένηται ἱκανή Decr.ap.D.24.27; ὁ ἐπὶ τῇ δ. *treasurer*, *IG*2.251, al., Poll.8.113; ὁ ἐπὶ τῆς διοικήσεως *IG*2².677, Decr.ap.D.18.38 (in Egypt, = διοικητής, *PRev.Laws* 19.7); τὰ περιόντα χρήματα τῆς δ. D.59.4. 2. *farming, renting*, [χωρῶν] *PTeb.*61(*a*).206 (ii B.C.), etc. II. = Lat. *conventus, assize-district*, Str.13.4.12, Cic.*Fam.*13.53.2, 67.1, *OGI*458.65 (Eumenia); later, *group of provinces*, *CIL*3.352 (iv A.D.), etc. **-ητής**, οῦ, ὁ, *administrator, governor*, στρατοπέδων Men.*Pk.*90, cf. *Kol.*6, Plb.27.13. 2; esp. *treasurer*, Lxx 2*Es.*8.36, al., *IG*9(1).694.144 (Corc.), Plu.2. 179f; *chief financial official* in Egypt, *OGI*53.7 (iii B.C.), *PTeb.*5. 27 (ii B.C.), etc.; = Lat. *procurator*, Str.17.3.25, Plu.*Ant.*67, etc.: Astrol., *controller*, of the Seven Planets, *Corp.Herm.*1.9. **-ητικός**, ή, όν, *controlling*, δύναμις Chrysipp.*Stoic.*2.264, cf. Ptol.*Tetr.*160: c. gen., πολέμων Corn.*ND*20. II. *digestive*, Orib.45.29.17. III. *pertaining to the chief financial officer*, χρηματισμοί *PTeb.*24.61 (ii B.C.), al.; ὑπηρέτης *PFlor.*312.7 (i A.D.). **-ήτρια**, ἡ, *housekeeper*, Sch.Ar. *Ec.*212. **-ήτωρ**, τορος, ὁ, = διοικητής, of the planets, *Corp.Herm.*

1.14. **-ίζω**, Att. fut. -ιῶ D.5.10:—*cause to live apart, disperse*, opp. συνοικίζω, δ. τὰς πόλεις *break* them *up* into villages (κῶμαι), Isoc. 5.43, cf. Arist.*Pol.*1311ᵃ14; τὴν Θηβαίων πόλιν διοικιεῖν D. l. c.; δ. Μαντινεῖς ἐκ μιᾶς πόλεως εἰς πλείους Plb.4.27.6:—Pass., διῳκίσθη ἡ Μαντίνεια τετραχῇ X.*HG*5.2.7; διῳκισμένοι κατὰ κώμας D.19.81: generally, *to be scattered abroad*, Pl.*Smp.*193a; *remove, migrate*, ἐκ Κολλυτοῦ εἰς.. Lys.32.14; διῳκισμένοι τινός *separated from..*, Luc. *Charid.*19: metaph. of rich and poor, διῳκίσμεθα καὶ δύο πόλεις ἔχομεν D.H.6.36. **-ισις**, εως, ἡ, *removal, change of abode*, Lys. 32.14. **-ισμός**, ὁ, = foreg., Ph.1.459, Plu.*Cam.*9; *living apart* (cf. διοικίζω fin.), D.H.6.81.

διοικο-δομέω, *build across, wall off*, Th.4.69, 8.90. 2. *to set a partition-wall between*: metaph., ἰσθμὸν καὶ ὅρον δ. τῆς τε κεφαλῆς καὶ τοῦ στήθους Pl.*Ti.*69e; δ. τοῦ θώρακος .. τὸ κύτος ibid. II. *barricade*, ὁδούς D.S.13.56. **-δομή**, ἡ, *construction*, Aristeas 87. **-δόμησις**, εως, ἡ, *fortification*, *IG*4.757 *A* 42, *B* 33 (Troezen, ii B.C.). **-νομέω**, strengthd. for οἰκονομέω, Phld.*Oec.*p.9 J. (dub.), Anon.Lond.22.49, Poll.5.156:—Pass., Arist.*Mu.*400ᵇ32.

διοινόομαι, Pass., *to be quite full of wine*, pf. part. διῳνωμένος Pl. *Lg.*775c.

διοινοχοέω, *mix wine for drinking*, Posidon.1 J. (Pass.).

δίοιξις, εως, ἡ, (διοίγνυμι) *opening*, ἀνθῶν Thphr.*CP*2.19.3.

διοιστέον, (διαφέρω) *one must move round*, ὄμμα πανταχῇ E.*Ph.* 265.

διοϊστεύω, *shoot an arrow between*, ὅς κε.. διοϊστεύσῃ πελέκεων Od. 19.578, al. II. abs., καί κεν διοϊστεύσειας thou mightest *reach it with an arrow*, i.e. thou art but a bow-shot from it, 12.102.

διοιστρέω, strengthd. for οἰστρέω, D.S.4.12, Philostr.*VA*1.33 (Pass.).

διοίσω, διοίσομαι, v. διαφέρω.

διοιχνέω, *go through*, ἀσινὴς δ' αἰῶνα διοιχνεῖ A.*Eu.*315 (anap.), cf. Lyc.10. II. abs., *wander about*, ἐν πέτρῃσιν *h.Hom.*19.10.

διοίχομαι, fut. -οιχήσομαι: pf. -οίχημαι Hdt.4.136:—*to be quite gone by*, ἡμέραι διοίχηνται Id. l. c.; of persons and things, *to be clean gone, to have perished*, τἀμὰ γὰρ διοίχεται A.*Fr.*138, cf. S.*Aj.*973, E. *Or.*181 (lyr.), Ar.*Th.*609, etc.; rare in Prose, Hdt. l.c., Pl.*Phd.* 87e. II. *to be gone through, ended*, ὁ λόγος διοίχεται S.*OC*574 (codd. recc. for διέρχεται); χὴ δίκη δ. E.*Supp.*530.

διοκνέω, *to be much afraid*, Antig.Car.ap.Ath.13.607e.

διοκωχή, ἡ, = διοχή, *cessation*, Th.3.87; esp. *armistice*, D.C.39. 47, etc.

διολισθάνω (in Pl.*Ly.*216d codd. -αίνω, cf. Luc.*Cont.*1, al., Lib. *Or.*11.225), Ion. aor. -ωλίσθησα Hp.*Art.*63: aor. 2 inf. διολισθεῖν Ar.*Nu.*434:—*slip through*, ὑπὸ τοὺς δακτύλους Hp.*Art.*40; of a bone put out, ib.63; δ. τοὺς χρήστας *to give* them *the slip*, Ar. l. c.; δ. καὶ διαδύεται ἡμᾶς Pl. l. c.; ἐπ' ἄκρων δ. κυμάτων, of a ship, Luc.*Dom.* 12: abs., *slip away*, Id.*Anach.*28, 29; δ. τὴν γλῶσσαν *slipping* with his tongue, of one drunken, Id.*Vit.Auct.*12.

διολκή, ἡ, (διέλκω) *drawing away*, διολκὴν εἰς τἀναντία γίνεσθαι Phld.*Mus.*p.35 K.; *extraction* of the foetus, Sor.2.62 (pl.). II. *diversity of opinion*, S.E.*M.*8.322, Numen.ap.Eus.*PE*14.5.

δίολκος, ὁ, *slipway* for passage of ships across the Isthmus of Corinth, Str.7.2.1.

διόλλυμι or -ύω (Them.*Or.*32.356a), fut. -ολέσω, Att. -ολῶ S.*Tr.* (v. infr.):—*destroy utterly, bring to naught*, Emp.139, S.*OT*442, *Tr.* 1028 (lyr.), Pl.*Cri.*47c, etc.; δ. γυναῖκα *ruin* a woman, E.*El.*921:—Pass., with fut. -ολοῦμαι, pf. -όλωλα, *perish utterly, come to naught*, Th.3.40, etc.; διώλετο ἔκ τινος by some one's hand, S.*OT*225. II. *blot out of one's mind, forget*, εἰδὼς διώλεσα ib.318.

διόλου, Adv. for δι' ὅλου (cf. καθόλου), *altogether*, Phoc.2 A, Arist.*Po.*1459ᵇ16, etc.; of Time, *always*, Lxx 1 *Ma.*6.18, *AP*5.157 (Asclep.), *Lyr.Alex.Adesp.*37.5, *Ev.Jo.*19.23, etc.

διολούφειν· διατίλλειν ἢ διασιλλαίνειν, Hsch.

διολοφύρομαι [ῠ], strengthd. for ὀλοφύρομαι, πρὸς αὐτόν Plb.21. 26.11.

δίομαι, v. δίω.

διομᾰλ-ίζω, pf. διωμάλικα Phld.*Po.Herc.*1425.34:—*maintain a standard*, ἀρετὴ διομαλίζουσα Id.*Rh.*1.264 S., cf. Longin.33.4, Plu. *Cat.Ma.*4, S.E.*M.*11.207; *to be consistent*, of observations, ib.5. 103. **-ισμός**, ὁ, *consistency, steadiness*, τῶν πράξεων S.E.*P.*3.244, cf. *M.*11.206: pl., *uniform periods*, in illness, Herod.Med.ap.Orib. 7.8.5. **-ύνω**, *distribute evenly*, Plu.2.130d.

Διομᾰνής, ές, *driven mad by Zeus* or *raging against Zeus*, Hsch.

διομβρ-έω, *soak through*, τὰ χώματα *PPetr.*2 p.17. **-ος**, ον, *wet through*, Arist.*Pr.*870ᵇ25; *rainy*, χώρα Ath.Med.ap.Orib.9.12. 13.

Δῐομειᾰλαζών, όνος, ὁ, *a braggart of the deme Diomea*, Ar.*Ach.*605.

Διομήδεια ἀνάγκη *absolute, dire* necessity; -εία Pl.*R.*493d codd.; -ειος Hsch., Ar.*Ec.*1029, Zen.3.8; proverbial expression variously expld.

Διομήδης, εος, ὁ, *Jove-counselled*; only as a pr. n. *Diomedes*.

Διομηνία, Ep. -ίη, ἡ, *wrath of Zeus*, Orph.*Fr.*285.21 (dub.).

Δῐομήτωρ, ορος, ὁ, Pythag. name for δυάς, *Theol.Ar.*12.

διόμνῡμι or -ύω (*BGU*647.22 (ii A.D.)), *swear solemnly, declare on oath*, esp. in courts of justice, c. fut. inf., ὅρκον αὐτῷ προσβαλὼν διώμοσεν, ἦ μὴν .. δουλώσειν S.*Tr.*255; δ. κτείνειν (κτενεῖν Cobet) Lycurg.127:—more freq. in Med., διόμνῠμαι, fut. -ομοῦμαι: aor. -ωμοσάμην, *vow, asseverate*, S.*Aj.*1233, *Tr.*378: c. inf., Ῥωμύλον ἰδεῖν Plu.*Num.*2; ζημιώσειν Id.*Cam.*39: esp. of the διωμοσία (q.v.), δ. ὅρκον Antipho 5.12; ταῦτα διωμόσω ἐν τῇ ἀντιγραφῇ *you swore to* this *in the oath* you took in support of the indictment, Pl.*Ap.*27c, cf. Lys.3.4; δ. ὑπέρ τινος Antipho 1.28; ἠρνεῖσθε διομνύμενοι *on oath*, D.18.286; διομόσασθαι τὸν υἱόν *swear by* his head, Id.47.73; τοὺς θεούς Din.1.47.

διομολογ-έω, *make an agreement*, ἀποστήσεσθαι X.*Ages.*3.5; *agree, concede*, c. acc. et inf., Luc.*Nigr.*26:—Pass., *to be agreed on*, mostly in pf., διωμολογημένον ἐμοί τε καὶ σοί Pl.*Euthd.*282c, cf. *BGU*350.17 (ii A.D.), etc.; ἡ Ἀσία διωμολόγηται παρ' ἡμῶν βασιλέως εἶναι Isoc.4.137; also τὰ διομολογούμενα Plb.31.19.1: aor., δεῖ διομολογηθῆναι ὅτι .. Pl.*R.*456c. II. more freq. in Med., aor. -ωμολογησάμην, *agree mutually, agree upon* certain points, *take* them *as granted, concede, grant*, δ. τὴν δικαιοσύνην ἀρετὴν εἶναι ib.350d; τι ib.507a, al.; δ. τοὺς τόκους *agree on* the interest to be paid, D.56.5; δ. περί τινος Pl.*Tht* 169e, Is.3.39; ἅπαντα διωμολογημένος πρὸς τὸν πατέρα *having agreed* with my father to do everything, D.28.14: c. inf. pres., Is.3.28, fut., ibid., aor., 8.23; folld. by a relat. Conj., δ. πότερον.. Pl.*R.*394d; δ. εἰ.. Id.*Grg.*500e; τί ποτ' ἔστιν Id.*Sph.*260a. **-ησις**, εως, ἡ, *convention*, πρός τινα Plb.3.27.9 (pl.), D.S.9.10 (pl.). **-ητέον**, *one must agree on* or *concede*, Pl.*R.*527b, al. II. -έος, α, ον, *to be conceded*, Id.*Prm.*142b. **-ία**, ἡ, *agreement, contract*, δ. ποιεῖν περί τινος Is.11.21, 23; γίνεται δ. τῆς ὑπουργίας Arist.*EN*1164ᵃ34.

δῖον, v. δῖος. **δίον**, v. δείδω.

διονομάζω, *distinguish by a name*, Pl.*Plt.*263d:—Pass., διωνόμασται *have received a name*, Arist.*HA*494ᵇ20, cf. *Mete.*350ᵇ12. II. Pass., *to be widely known*, Isoc.20.19, Str.2.5.17, D.H.*Th.*4; ἐπ' ἀνδρείᾳ Id.5.25.

Δῐονῦ, as voc. of Διόνυσος in Phryn.Com.10 (Meineke); cf. διονῦς· ὁ γυναικίας καὶ παράθηλυς, Hsch.; διοννύς· ἡ γυναικεία καὶ θῆλυς ἐσθής, Eust.629.42.

δῐόνυξ, -ῠχος, ὁ, *double nail*, as a superficial measure, Hero *Stereom.*1.95.

Δῐόνυξος, coined as etym. of Διόνυσος, Corn.*ND*30, *EM*277.35 (νύττω, from the legend of his birth).

Δῐονῦσ-ἀλέξανδρος, ὁ, *Dionysus masquerading as Paris*, title of play by Cratinus, *POxy.*663, etc. **-ια** (sc. ἱερά), τά, *festival of Dionysus*, *IG*1².57, Foed.ap.Th.5.23, etc.; τὰ ἐν ἄστει *IG*2².1299.31; τὰ ἀστικά Th.5.20; τὰ μεγάλα *IG*2².654.41; τὰ κατ' ἀγρούς Ar.*Ach.*202, Aeschin.1.157; τὰ ἐπὶ Ληναίῳ *IG*2.741.10; elsewh., *SIG*285.14 (Erythrae), *IG*12(1).6.3 (Rhodes, from Erythrae), etc.; Δ. παίδων ib.11 (2).105 (Delos, iii B.C.), al. **-ιάζω**, *keep the Dionysia*: Διονυσιάζουσαι, αἱ, title of play by Timocles, Ath.6.223b: hence, *live festively* or *extravagantly*, Luc.*Dem.Enc.*35, Philomnest.2. **-ιακός**, ή, όν, *belonging to the Dionysia* or *to Dionysus*, Δ. θέατρον Th.8.93; ἀγών Arist.*Rh.*1416ᵃ32, cf. *Pol.*1323ᵃ2: Διονυσιακά, τά, *poems on the legend of Bacchus*, e.g. by Nonnus: -κόν, τό, prob., = Διονύσιος III, Gal.12. 423. **-ιάς**, άδος, ἡ, pecul. fem. of Διονυσιακός, θυμέλα Pratin.1.2; λοιβά E.*HF*894 (lyr.); Πηγή Paus.4.36.5. 2. as Subst., *Bacchante*, Id.3.13.7. 3. a plaster, Orib.*Fr.*96, Philum.ap.Aët.16.38. 4. name of Naxos, Call.*Aet.*3.1.41. II. = ἀνδρόσαιμον, Dsc.3.156; = καταναγκη, Ps.-Dsc.4.131. **-ιασταί**, οἱ, guild of *worshippers of D.*, *IG*2².1325.20, 12(1).155.43, 12(3).104.17 (Nisyros), etc. **-ιον** (sc. ἱερόν), τό, *the temple of Dionysus*, Th.8.93, Ar.*Fr.*131, Paus.1.43. 5, etc. **-ιος**, α, ον, *of Dionysus*, δῶρα B.*Scol.Oxy.Fr.*1.9. II. Δ., ὁ (sc. μήν), name of month in Aetolia, *IG*9(1).374, cf. *SIG*524.14 (Crete), 1009.20 (Chalcedon), etc. III. Διονύσιον, τό, fruit of κισσός, Dsc.2.179. **-ίσκος**, ὁ, Dim. of Διόνυσος, *person who has bony excrescences on the temples*, Heliod.ap.Orib.46.28.2, Gal.19.443.

Δῐονῦσο-δότης, ου, ὁ, *bestower of Dionysus*, Olymp.*in Phd.*p.111 N. **-κόλᾰκες**, οἱ, nickname of the τεχνῖται Διονυσιακοί, Theopomp. Hist.267, Arist.*Rh.*1405ᵃ23, Chares ap.Ath.12.538f, Alciphr.3.48: hence, II. *flatterers of Dionysius* the Tyrant, and the school of Plato, Epicur.*Fr.*238, Thphr.ap.Ath.8.249f, 10.435e. **-κουροπυρώνων**, Comic compd., corrupt in Cratin.208. **-μᾰνέω**, *to be full of Bacchic frenzy*, Philostr.*VA*5.32. **-νυμφάς**, άδος, ἡ, *burnet, Poterium Sanguisorba*, Plin.*HN*24.165. **-πλάτων** [ᾰ], ωνος, ὁ, *double herm of Dionysus and Plato* as a signet, *POxy.*105. 20. **-φόροι**· ἀρχή τις ἐν Συρακούσαις, Hsch.

Δῐόνῡσος, ὁ, Od.11.325, S.*Ant.*957, etc.:—Ep. also **Διώνῡσος**, Il. 6.132, 14.325, Od.24.74, Hes.*Th.*947, Archil.77, Thgn.976:—Boeot. **Διώνουσος**, *IG*7.2468a, al., and **Δεύννσος** (q.v.):—also **Δίνυσος**, Ἀρχ.Ἐφ.1913.221 (Mytilene): **Διένυσος**, *IG*12(7).78 (Amorgos):—*Dionysus*, Διονύσου γοναί, name of comedies by Polyzelus and Anaxandrides, *IG*14.1098.

δῐόνῠχος, ον, *with cloven hoof*, ζῷα *EM*811.16.

διοξειῶν, v. ὀξύς.

Δῐό-παις, παιδος, ὁ, *son of Zeus*, *AP*9.525. **-πᾶν**, πᾶνος, ὁ, *Zeus-Pan*, *Epigr.Gr.*827b (Caesarea Panias). **-πεμπτος**, ον, *sent from Zeus*, ὄνειροι Eust.48.29.

διόπερ or δι' ὅπερ, v. διό.

Διοπετής, ές, *that fell from Zeus*, ἄγαλμα E.*IT*977; Παλλάδιον D.H.2.66; πέλτη Plu.*Num.*13, cf. D.H.2.71; ὄρνις Alciphr.3.59; Μένιππος Luc.*Icar.*2; οἰκίαι, i.e. 'taboo', Aristopho 3; διοπετές (sc. ἄγαλμα), τό, *Act.Ap.*19.35.

διοπεύω, *to be captain of* a ship, δ. τὴν ναῦν (Harp., διοπτεύων codd.) Test.ap.D.35.20, 34.

διόπη, ἡ, (διά, ὀπή) kind of *ear-ring*, Ar.*Fr.*320.10, *IG*1².291, 2.652 *B* 26. 2. kind of *shoe*, Hsch.

διοπλήκταν (prob. l.)· ἰσχυροπλήκτην, Hsch.

δῑοπομπ-έομαι, = ἀποδιοπ. (q.v.), Hsch., Suid., *EM*125.33. **-ή**, = πέμψις, *Et.Gud.*147.54.

δίοπος (A) [ῐ], ὁ, (διέπω) *ruler, commander*, A.*Pers.*44 (anap.), E.*Rh.*741 (anap.); θεὸς δ. πάντων Ph.2.369, cf. 1.145. II. *captain of a ship*, Hp.*Epid.*7.36, 5.74, *EM*18.28.

δίοπος (B) [ῐ], ον, (ὀπή) *with two holes*, φῶτες *IG*4.1488.46 (Epid.); αὐλοί Ath.4.176f.

διοπτάω, *roast thoroughly*, Zos.Alch.p.247 B.

διοπτ-εία, ἡ, *seeing through*, τὴν δ. ἀκώλυτον παρέχειν Procl.*Hyp.* 3.17. II. *use of the* διόπτρα, Hero *Deff.*135.8. **-ευσις**, εως, ἡ, *examination with the* διόπτρα, Ptol.*Alm.*5.1, al. **-ευτήριον**, τό, dub. sens. in Petos.*Fr.*24 R. **-εύω**, *watch accurately, spy about*, ἠὲ διοπτεύσων Il.10.451; *look into*, στέγος S.*Aj.*307, cf. Antipho Soph.6, Critias *Fr.*53 D.; δ. τί... X.*Cyr.*8.2.10: c. acc., D.C. 52.37:—Pass., *to be overlooked* by a neighbour, Agath.5.6. II. *take a sight*, διὰ τοῦ μήκους τῆς σύριγγος Hero *Bel.*86.7; esp. *through the* διόπτρα, Id.*Dioptr.*4. **-ήρ**, ῆρος, ὁ, *spy, scout*, στρατοῦ Il.10. 562: in late Prose, Agath.2.2. II. διάγγελοι καὶ διοπτῆρες, the *optiones* and *tesserarii* of the Romans, Plu.*Galb.*24. III. = διόπτρα III, Aët.16.105. **-ης**, ου, ὁ, *looker through*, ὦ Ζεῦ διόπτα! says Dicaeopolis in Ar.*Ach.*435, holding up a ragged garment to the light. II. = foreg. I, E.*Rh.*234 (lyr.). III. = διόπτρα I, Hsch. **-ιον**, τό, *sighting instrument for the* ἑλέπολις, Bito 53. I. **-ος**, ον, *transparent*, Alex.Aphr.*in Sens.*46.17; τὰ δ. ib.45.12.

διόπτρ-α, ἡ, *optical instrument* for measuring angles, altitudes, etc., Euc.*Phaen.*p.10 M., Plb.10.46.1, Attal.ap.Hipparch.1.10.24, Gem. 1.4, Ptol.*Alm.*5.14, etc.; ἡ τῶν δ. θεωρία Gem.5.11. 2. *aperture-sight* in a torsion-engine, Ph.*Bel.*64.9, 76.48. II. *plate of talc* for glazing windows, Str.12.2.10. III. = διαστολεύς, Aët.16.89, Paul.Aeg.6.73. IV. σημεῖον ἐν θυτικῇ, Hsch. **-ίζω**, *use the speculum*, Paul.Aeg.3.75. **-ικός**, ή, όν, *of, belonging to the use of the* διόπτρα I, ὄργανον δ., = διόπτρα, Str.2.1.35; τὰ δ. *the science of dioptrics*, Plu.2.1093e: also -κή, ἡ, Procl.*in Euc.*p.42 F. **-ιον**, τό, *small speculum*, Leonid.ap.Paul.Aeg.6.78. **-ισμός**, ὁ, *use of the speculum*, Sor.2.40, Paul.Aeg.6.73. **-ίτης** [ῑ] λίθος *talc*, *PHolm.* 3.39. **-ον**, τό, *means for seeing through*, οἶνος γὰρ ἀνθρώπῳ δ. Alc. 53. II. = διόπτρα I, Hsch. s.v. ἀστραβιστήρ.

διοπωπ-έας· τοὺς βασιλεῖς, *EM*278.12. **-εύω**, = διέπω, *AB* 237.

διορ-ᾱτικός, ή, όν, *clear-sighted*, Ph.1.478: c. gen., Luc.*Salt.*4 (Comp.); τῶν ὄντων Max.Tyr.16.3, cf. Asp.*in EN*79.28. **-άω**, *see through, see clearly*, X.*An.*5.2.30; δ. τὸ ἀληθές Pl.*Prm.*136c, etc. II. *distinguish*, τοὺς.. κολακεύοντας καὶ τοὺς.. θεραπεύοντας Isoc.2.28; τὰς φύσεις τῶν ἀνθρώπων Id.3.16; πότε ὑπάρχει καὶ πότε οὔ οὐ ῥᾴδιον διιδεῖν Arist.*Mete.*390a20; δόξας διορᾶν Epicur.*Nat.*15. 24, cf. 11.8.

διοργᾰν-ίζω, *dispose suitably*, in Pass., Zos.Alch.p.251 B., Syn. Alch.p.62 B. **-όομαι**, *to be provided with organs*, Iamb.*VP*15.66; of the foetus, Agath.4.25. **-ωσις**, εως, ἡ, *formation, fashioning*, Iamb.*VP*15.67; *structural differentiation*, Procl. *in Prm.*p.616 S., Simp.*in Cael.*389.19.

διοργίζομαι, *to be very angry*, Plb.2.8.13; τινί Lxx 3*Ma.*3.1 (v.l.), Plu.*Ages.*6; διωργισμένος Phld.*Ir.*p.9 W.; διοργισθείς D.S.14.14.

διοργυι-όομαι, *stretch out the arms*: διωργυιωμένος *with arms akimbo*, Hipparch.1.7.22: metaph., Ἀνάγκην -ωμένην ἐν παντὶ τῷ κόσμῳ Dam.*Pr.*123 bis. **-ος**, ον, *two fathoms deep, high*, etc., Hdt. 4.195, X.*Cyn.*2.5.

διορθ-εύω, = sq., only in E.*Supp.*417 μὴ διορθεύων λόγους not *judging rightly of* words. **-όω**, *make straight*, Hp.*Art.*38. 2. δ. λόγον *tell* my tale *aright*, Pi.*O.*7.21. II. *set right, restore to order*, Isoc.9.47; δ. λόγοις ἔριν *make up* a quarrel, E.*Hel.*1159 (lyr.); δ. ἀδικήματα *amend* them, Plb.4.24.4; δ. τὴν Ἰλιάδα *correct* or *revise* it, Plu.*Alex.*8, cf. *Alc.*7 (Pass.), Porph.*Plot.*7, al.:—Med., *amend for oneself*, διορθοῦσθαι τὰ μέλλοντα Isoc.4.181; τἀγνοούμενα D.*Ep.*1.3; σφᾶς αὐτούς Plb.24.10.12; δ. πίστιν *make good, redeem* it, Id.1.7.12; τὰ προσοφειλόμενα *pay off*, Id.12.28.5 (cf. III); *maintain in argument*, Aeschin.2.112:—but freq. like Act., ἐξέστω διορθώσασθαι τὰς συνθήκας *SIG*581.85 (Crete, ii B.C.); δ. τὴν Ἰλλυριῶν ἄγνοιαν Plb.3.16.4, etc.; also διορθοῦσθαι ὑπέρ τινος *take full security* for.., D.33. 11. III. *pay*, τὸ λοιπόν *PHib.*1.63.13 (iii B.C.); τόκον *POxy.*483. 16 (ii A.D.):—Med., *PRev.Laws* 18.14, al. (iii B.C.); φόρους *PEleph.* 14.1 (iii B.C.), cf. *PSI*5.509.13 (iii B.C.), etc.; ἀργύριον *BCH*46.420 (Caria, i B.C.). IV. *reconcile*, τινά τινι Philostr.*VS*1.17.2.

διορθρίζω, *rise early*, v.l. in Lxx 1*Ki.*29.10.

διόρθ-ωμα, ατος, τό, *making straight, setting right*, Hp.*Art.*33 (pl.); *instrument* or *means of setting right*, δ. τι ἐντιθέναι εἰς.. ib.37; *means of correction*, Arist.*Pol.*1284b20. II. *amendment*, Plu.*Num.*17; *revision*, νόμου *PRev.Laws* 57.1 (iii B.C.). **-ωσις**, εως, ἡ, *making straight*, as in the setting of a limb, Hp.*Off.*16, cf. *Mochl.*38; *setting straight, restoration*, οἰκοδομημάτων καὶ ὁδῶν Arist.*Pol.*1321b21. 2. *correction, chastisement*, ἐπὶ διορθώσει Plb.2.56.14; διορθώσεως σφίσι δεῖν D.H.6.20. II. generally, *amendment, correction*, of men, Plb.7.11.2: pl., Arist.*Pol.*1317a35, Plb.3.118.12; τῶν νόμων *IG*9(1). 694.137 (Corc.); *correction*, ἐρωτημάτων Arist.*SE*176b34, cf. *Pol.* 1275a20; εἰς δ. ἄγειν Plb.3.58.4; δ., opp. βλάβη, Id.5.88.2; ὑδάτων Orib.5.4 tit. 2. *right treatment*, τινός Pl.*Lg.*642a. III. *recension, revised edition* of a work, Sch.Il.10.397: in pl., *emendations*, D.L.3.66. IV. *payment*, ὀψωνίων Plb.5.50.7, cf. *PTeb.*61 (*a*). 33 (ii B.C.). **-ωτέος**, α, ον, *to be set*, of joints, Hp.*Mochl.*38. II. -τέον, *one must correct*, Ath.Med.ap.Orib.*inc.*5.1; δόγματα Simp.*in Epict.*p.28 D. **-ωτήρ**, ῆρος, ὁ, = sq., *IG*9(1).694.138 (pl.). **-ωτής**, οῦ, ὁ, *a corrector*, τῶν σοφῶν Lxx *Wi.*7.15; τῆς πολιτείας Plu.*Sol.*16; = Lat. *corrector civitatium*, Arr.*Epict.*3.7.1. 2. esp. *of books, editor, reviser*, D.S.15.6, Gal.8.758. **-ωτικός**, ή, όν, *corrective*, Arist.*EN*1131a1; τὰ -κά, title of works on textual criticism by Seleucus and Crates, Sch.Il.*Oxy.*221 xv 25, xvii 31. Adv. -κῶς Eust. 936.43.

διορία, v. διωρία.

διορ-ίζω, Ion. **διουρίζω**, Att. fut. -ιῶ Pl.*Lg.*860e: fut. Med. in pass. sense (v. infr. I. 3):—*draw a boundary through, delimit, separate*, Hdt.4.42; τὴν Εὐρώπην ἀπὸ τῆς Ἀσίης D.S.1.55; δίχα δ. Pl.*Sph.* 267a: metaph., οὐ στενῷ τῷ ἰσθμῷ διώρισται ἡ ἱστορία πρὸς τὸ ἐγκώμιον Luc.*Hist.Conscr.*7. 2. *distinguish, determine, define*, τὰ οὐνόματα Hdt.4.45; θεοῖσι..γέρα τίς ἄλλος ἢ 'γὼ.. διώρισεν; A.*Pr.* 440; πτῆσιν οἰωνῶν.. διώρισα, of auguries, ib.489; σῖτον δ' εἰδέναι δ. so as to know it, Id.*Fr.*182; γλυκὺν οἶνον καὶ οἰνώδεα Hp.*Acut.*50; δ. ἀκούσιά τε καὶ ἑκούσια Pl.*Lg.*860e, cf. *Cra.*391d; δ. περὶ ἐνεργείας τί ἐστιν Arist.*Metaph.*1048a26; *define* logically, δ. κατὰ τὰς διαφορὰς Id.*Top.*146b20, cf. *EN*1103a3 (Pass.), etc.:—Med., διορίζεσθαι τῷ στόματι τὰ γράμματα *pronounce clearly*, Alex.301. 3. *determine, declare*, τοιαῦτα φῆμαι μαντικαὶ διώρισαν S.*OT*723: c. inf., *determine* one *to be* so and so, καθαρὸν διώρισεν εἶναι D.20.158: with inf. omitted, οἱ συγγενεῖς μηνές με μικρὸν καὶ μέγαν διώρισαν S.*OT*1083:—Med., δηλοῖ καὶ δ. ὅτι.. D.18.40; διορισαμένων ὅπως.. Id.56.11; διορίσασθαι τίς αἱρετώτατος βίος Arist.*Pol.*1323a15: pf. Pass. in med. sense, ἃ χρὴ ποιεῖν διωρίσμεθα D.24.192:—Pass., διώρισται ὁπότερον .. And.4.8; διωρισμένον *it being prescribed*, Lys.30.4; τὸν νόμον ὡς ἐτέθη καὶ πρὸς οὓς διωρίσθη D.59.93; ἐν τῷ διωρισμένῳ χρόνῳ *PTeb.* 105.33 (ii B.C.), etc.: impers., διοριεῖται περί τινος we *will give precepts* about.., Hp.*Art.*9; ἐν οἷς [λόγοις] διώρισται περὶ τῶν ἠθικῶν Arist.*Pol.*1282b20, cf. *EN*1136a10. 4. *draw distinctions, lay down definitions*, οὐδ' ὁτιοῦν διορίζων D.21.104; τοῦτό μοι.. διόρισον Pl. *Grg.*488d:—mostly in Med., δ. περί τινος And.3.12, Isoc.3.5, Arist. *Ph.*200b15; πρὸς ἀλλήλους Pl.*Grg.*457c; δίκην διωρίσω *didst settle the conditions of* the trial, Ar.*Ach.*364. II. *remove across the frontier, banish*, ἔξω τῶν ὅρων Pl.*Lg.*873e; τὸν ἐνθένδε πόλεμον εἰς τὴν ἤπειρον Isoc.4.174; τινὰ ὑπὲρ θυμέλας E.*Ion* 46: generally, *carry abroad*, στράτευμα Τροίαν ἔπι Id.*Hel.*394; δ. πόδα to depart, ib.828. III. *send out a branch*, of the Bosporus, Plb.4.43.7. IV. Pass., *to be discontinuous*, opp. συνάπτω, Arist.*Cat.*4b28; διωρισμένος, opp. συνεχής, ib.20. **-ῐσις**, εως, ἡ, *distinction*, Pl.*Lg.*777b; *separation*, Arist. *Ph.*213b26. **-ισμα**, ατος, τό, *ordinance*, Porph.*Abst.*1.7. **-ισμός**, ὁ, *division, distinction*, Pl.*Ti.*38c, Arist.*EN*1134b33, Porph.*Abst.*3. 20. II. *logical distinction*, Pl.*Plt.*282c; *definition*, Arist.*SE*168a 23, al. III. Math., *particular enunciation* of a problem, Procl.*in Euc.*p.203 F. 2. *statement of limits of possibility* of a problem, Apollon.Perg.*Con.Praef.*, Archim.*Sph.Cyl.*2.4, Phld.*Acad.Ind.*p.17 M. **-ιστέον**, *one must distinguish*, Pl.*Lg.*874d, Arist.*Ph.*204a 2, Longin.11.3, etc. **-ιστικός**, ή, όν, *capable of distinguishing*, S.E.*M.*10.128: -ιστική (sc. τέχνη), ἡ, Syrian.*in Metaph.*56.3. 2. *limiting*, Iamb.*in Nic.*pp.88, 89 P.

διορκ-ίζω, *adjure*, *Sammelb.*4324.13:—Pass., of an oath, *to be sworn*, dub. in Wilcken *Chr.*110 *A* 27 (ii B.C.). **-ισμός**, ὁ, *assurance on oath*, Plb.16.26.6.

διορμάομαι, *to be impelled*, c. inf., θεῖν Max.Tyr.41.5.

διορμίζω, strengthd. for ὁρμίζω, τὰς ναῦς Longus 2.25:—Pass., D.S.20.88: metaph., διορμίζεται ὁ βίος Hierocl.p.56 A.

διόρνῡμαι, *hurry through*, A.*Supp.*552 (lyr.).

δίορος, = διαστάτης, Hsch.; *stone used in the game* ἐφεδρισμός, Poll.9.119.

διορόω, *turn into serum*, Hp.*Morb.*1.30, Gal.19.93:—Pass., *become serous*, of the blood, Hp.*Steril.*213, Arist.*HA*521a13; of milk, ib.521b34.

διορρωδέω, f.l. in D.Chr.3.69.

διορ-ῠγή, ἡ, = διωρυχή, Lxx *Je.*38(31).9. **-υγμα**, ατος, τό, *cut, canal*, as that across the isthmus of Mount Athos, Th.4.109. II. *digging through, house-breaking*, Lxx *Ex.*22.2(1), *Je.*2.34. III. *hole made in wall by* χελώνη, Aen.Tact.32.12. IV. *siege-mine*, D.S.20.94. **-υκτρὶς** χελώνη *battering*-ram, Apollod.*Poliorc.*138. 19. **-υξις**, εως, ἡ, *digging through*, Sch.Theoc.1.67. **-ύσσω**, Att. -ττω, *dig through*, διὰ τάφρον ὀρύξας *having dug* a trench *across* or *along*, Od.21.120; τοῖχον δ., = τοιχωρυχέω, Hdt.9.37, cf. Ar.*Pl.* 565, Th.2.3, D.54.37; δεσμωτήριον Id.25.56; οἰκίαν X.*Smp.*4.30, *PPetr.*3 p.60: c. acc. loci, τὸν Ἄθω Lys.2.29, cf. Pl.*Lg.*699a, D.6.30:—Pass., *Ev.Matt.*24.43. 2. metaph., *undermine, ruin*, D.45.30; φιλίαν Lib.*Or.*1.123; δημοκρατίαν Id.*Decl.*1.41:—Pass., διορωρυγμένα δωροδοκίαις Plu.*Phoc.*12, cf. Him.*Ecl.*5.6 (but *to be entrenched* in our *several* cities, D.9.28). II. *worm out*, ἀπόρρητα Bato 6; τὰ βουλευόμενα Plu.2.87c. III. Pass., *to be shut up in a funeral vault*, D.S.4.43. **-ῠχή**, ἡ, = διωρυχή, Χερσονήσου D.7.40; φρεάτων Ph.1.626; τοίχων Lib.*Decl.*8.19: metaph., *undermining*, νόμων, δικαστηρίων, Id.*Or.*63.21.

διορχέομαι, *dance across* or *along*, Opp.*H.*5.440. II. *dance a match*, Ar.*V.*1481.

διόρωσις, εως, ἡ, *becoming* or *making serous*, Hp.*Morb.*1.30.

δῖος, δῖα (Hom., v. infr.), δῖον, fem. δία in E.*Rh.*226 (lyr.), *IT*404 (lyr.) (δίη Hes.*Th.*260 codd.); fem. δῖος E.*Ba.*599 (anap.):—in Ep., *heavenly*, δ. γένος Il.9.538, etc., used by Hom., 1. of goddesses, δῖα θεά 10.290; more freq. δῖα θεάων, with superl. force, 18.388, 19.6, etc.; δαίμονα δῖον Hes. *Th.*991. 2. of illustrious men or women, *noble*, Il.2.221, etc.; δῖα γυναικῶν *noblest* of women, Od.4.305; *excellent*, δ. ὑφορβός 16.20, al. 3. of nations, etc., δῖοι Ἀχαιοί Il. 5.451; δ. Πελασγοί Od.19.177; δ. ἑταῖροι Il.5.692; of cities, as Elis, 2.615; Lacedaemon, Od.3.326. 4. of a *noble* horse, Il.8.185, 23.346. 5. of things, esp. of the powers of nature, *divine, awful, marvellous*, αἰθέρος ἐκ δίης, εἰς ἅλα δῖαν, χθὼν δῖα, Il.16.365, 1.141, 14.347, cf. Emp.109.2; δῖον πῦρ E.*Alc.*5, etc.; δῖα Χάρυβδις Od.12.104. II. first in Trag. as Adj. of Ζεύς, Δ. βούλευμα A.*Pr.*619; Δ. ὄμμα, στόμα, ib.654, 1033, etc. (For *dī̆v-ĭyos*, cf. Skt. *div-yá-* 'heavenly' (freq. trisyll.), but fem. δῖα for *div-ya*.)

Δῖος, ὁ (sc. μήν), the first month of the Maced. year, *PEleph.*1.2 (iv B.C.), J.*BJ*2.19.9, etc.; in Aetolia, *SIG*²845.1; in Thessaly, *IG* 9(1).689.8 (found in Corc.).

Διός [ῐ], gen. of Ζεύς.

διοσ-, the first element in various compound names of plants: **διόσ-ανθος**, ὁ, *carnation, Dianthus inodorus*, Thphr.*HP*6.1.1, al., Nic.*Fr.*74.59. **-βάλᾰνος** [βᾰ], *sweet chestnut, Castanea vesca*, Thphr.*HP*4.5.1, al., Dsc.1.106. **-ηλᾰκάτη** [κᾰ], ἡ, = πολύκνημον, Ps.-Dsc.3.94; = περιστερεὼν ὕπτιος, Id.4.60. **-κύᾰμος** [ῠ], ὁ, = ὑοσκ., ib.68. **-πῦρον**, τό, *fruit of nettle-tree, Celtis australis*, Thphr. *HP*3.13.3:—but **-πυρος**, ὁ, = λιθόσπερμον, Dsc.3.141. **-πώγων**, ωνος, ὁ, = χρυσοκόμη, Ps.-Dsc.4.55.

Δῐοσ-ᾰτᾱβῡρῐασταί, οἱ, *worshippers of Zeus Atabyrios*, *IG*12(1).161 (Rhodes):—also **Διοσ-ξενιασταί** or **-ξενιασταί**, *worshippers of Zeus Xenios*, ibid.: **Διοσσωτηριασταί**, οἱ, *worshippers of Zeus Soter*, ib.162: **Διοσμειλῐχιασταί**, οἱ, *worshippers of Zeus Meilichios*, *IG*12(3).104 (Nisyros).

Δῐόσδοτος, ον, (δίδωμι) *given by Zeus, heaven-sent*, αἴγλα Pi.*P.*8.96; σκῆπτρα A.*Eu.*626; γάνος Id.*Ag.*1391 (Porson): in Id.*Th.*946 the metre requires Διοδότων.

Διοσηλακάτη, v. διοσ-.

Δῐοσημ-ᾰσία, ἡ, = Διοσημία, Lyd.*Ost.*47. **-ειακός**, ή, όν, *portent-bearing*, ἀστέρες ib.15. **-ία**, ἡ, *a sign from Zeus, an omen from the sky*, esp. of thunder, lightning, rain, διοσημία 'στί Ar.*Ach.*171: pl., *Stoic.*2.203, D.S.2.19, Plu.2.419e, Philostr.*VA*2.33, Jul. *Or.*7.212b. (Freq. written -εία in codd.)

Διοσθεών, ὁ, name of a month at Stratonicea, *BCH*44.71.

Διόσθυος, ὁ, name of a month in Rhodes, *IG*12(1).155.1; Thera, *Test.Epict.*4.1, cf. Call.ap.*EM*278.28.

διοσκέω, *look earnestly at*, Anacr.3; also expld. by διαφορεῖσθαι τῷ σώματι καὶ τῇ ψυχῇ, διαπολέσαι, διαφθεῖραι, Hsch.

Δῐοσ-κόρειον, τό, *temple of the Dioscuri*, Th.4.110 (-κουρ- codd.), D.19.158, etc.:—also **Διοσκούριον**, *PPetr.*3p.295 (iii B.C.), *IG*11(2).154*A* 37 (Delos, iii B.C.): **Διοσκούρειον**, Plu.*Sull.*33, etc. II. **Διοσκούρεια**, τά, *festival of the Dioscuri*, *IG*5(1).559 (Sparta): -κορήϊα *SIG*²438.175 (Delph.): -κούρια *SIG*1067.15 (Rhodes). **-κόριος**, ὁ, name of a month in Syria, cj. in Lxx 2*Ma.*11.21; in Crete, *Hemerolog.Flor.* **-κοροι** (the Att. form, Phryn.212), Ion. and later **Διόσ-κουροι**, οἱ, *the sons of Zeus*, i.e. *the twins of Leda*, Castor and Polydeuces, *h.Hom.*33.1, etc.: dual Διοσκόρω, τώ, Ar.*Pax*285, *Ec.*1069, E.*Or.*465, Amphis9, Men.846, Them.*Or.*21.253d: sg. dub. in Hippon.120, cf. Varro *LL*5.66: Διόσκοροι is required by metre in E.*Hel.*1643, *El.*1239: -κούρων Pl.*Euthd.*293a; -κόρων Id.*Lg.*796b, cod. Laur. in Th.3.75: both forms in codd. of Hdt.2.43, 6.127. II. constellation named from them *the Twins*, Eratosth.*Cat.*10. III. = παρωτίδες, Gal.19.440, Eust.410.17. **-κουριασταί**, οἱ, *guild of worshippers of Dioscuri*, *Arch.Pap.*5.158 (iii B.C.).

Διοσκύαμος, v. διοσ-.

δίοσμος, ον, (ὄζω) *transmitting smells*, ἀήρ *EM*136.23, cf. Alex. Aphr.*in Sens.*89.2, Them.*in de An.*62.32.

Διόσ-πυρος and **-πώγων**, v. διοσ-.

δῐόστεος, ον, *double-boned*, Arist.*HA*494ᵃ5.

διοσφραίνω, *give a smell to, perfume*, Sch.Ar.*Ra.*1107.

διοτήρ· κατάσκοπος, Hsch. (leg. διοπτήρ).

διότι, Conj. for διὰ τοῦτο ὅτι.. (cf. A.D.*Conj.*242.1), *because, for the reason that, since*, Hdt.1.44, 3.55, Th.1.52, Thphr.*Char.*17.4; οὐδὲ δι' ἓν ἄλλο ἢ διότι.. Pl.*Phd.*100c; answering to διὰ τί; Id.*Plt.*310d, Amphis14.6, Timocl.2.4D., etc. 2. indirect, *wherefore, for what reason*, φράσω διότι.. Hdt.2.24; σκοπεῖν διότι.. Th.1.77; ἐρωτᾶν διότι.. Henioch.4.7. II. = ὅτι, *that*, Hdt.2.43, 50, Isoc.4.48, D.12.18, Is.3.50, Arist.*Metaph.*1062ᵃ6, al., Phld.*Ir.*p.84 W.; τὸ δ. Arist. *APr.*53ᵇ9: folld. by inf., Plb.31.12.4, v.l. in D.S.4.76.

διοτιδήποτε, *for whatever reason*, Simp.*in Ph.*50.20.

διότιπερ, strengthd. for διότι, *because*, Iamb.*in Nic.*p.83 P.

Διο-τρεφής, ές, *fostered, cherished by Zeus*, βασιλῆες Il.2.196, Hes. *Th.*82, etc.; αἰζηοί Il.2.660; also of the Scamander, *fed by rain*, 21.223. (Cf. Διειτρεφής.)

Διοτρόφος, ον, *nurse of Zeus*, Κρήτα E.*Hyps.Fr.*3 iii 23 (lyr.).

διού, Boeot., = δύο, *IG*7.3193.

δῐούγκιον, τό, *weight of two ounces*, *IGRom.*1.668 (Tomi): written διούγγιον, Orib.*Fr.*88.

διουργέω, *cultivate* (metaph.), *Klio* 18.302 (Delph.).

διουρ-έω, *pass in urine*, τι Dsc.*Eup.*2.65:—Pass., Hp.*Aër.*7: hence, *to have diuretic properties*, Id.*Aff.*48. II. intr., *pass urine*, Id.*Aer.*9. **-ητικός**, ή, όν, *diuretic*, Id.*Acut.*50, Diocl.*Fr.*112, Aret.*CA*1.1, etc. **-ίζω**, Ion. for διορίζω, Hdt. II. *percolate*, Orib.*Fr.*97.

διοφανής, dub. l. (for δια-), Them.*Or.*4.60d.

διοχετ-εία, ἡ, in pl., *irrigation-works*, Str.10.2.19. **-εύω**, *furnish with channels*, σῶμα Pl.*Ti.*77c. 2. *distribute by conduits*, Luc.*VH*1.33:—Pass., διωχετευμένων ὑδάτων D.S.20.8: metaph. of the spinal cord, δ. διὰ τῶν σφονδύλων Ruf.*Anat.*7. II. in Pass., of a country, *to be irrigated*, Str.5.1.5.

διοχεύομαι, *to be impregnated*, διὰ φωτός Plu.*in Hes.*84 (prob. for διοιχηθείσῃ).

διοχή, ἡ, (διέχω) *distance, interval*, Ph.*Bel.*75.6.

διοχλ-έω, *annoy exceedingly*, πόλεις Lys.6.6; *weary, bore*, D.19.329: pf. διώχληκα Jul.*Or.*2.78b; *press for payment*, *POxy.*286.13 (i A.D.); later, τινί Aeschin.*Ep.*2.2, Plu.*Cim.*18, Longus 3.20: abs., Ph.1.356:—Pass., Luc.*Am.*50, *IG*3.48 (iii A.D.); ὑπὸ ῥυθμῶν D.H. *Comp.*11. **-ησις**, εως, ἡ, *annoyance*, *IG*3.48 (iii A.D.). **-ίζω**, *move asunder, open*, Nic.*Al.*226 (tm.).

διοχῠρόω, strengthd. for ὀχυρόω, Plb.5.46.3 (Pass.).

δίοψ· οἰκονόμος (cf. δίοπος A), Hsch.

δίοψις, εως, ἡ, *a view through*, Plu.2.915a; *transparency*, ib.408e: metaph., ἤθους Id.*Comp.Dem.Cic.*1. II. metaph., *consideration*, Pl.*Ti.*40d codd. (δι' ὄψεως Procl.).

διόψομαι, v. διοράω.

δίπαις [ῐ], παιδος, ὁ, ἡ, *with two children*, A.*Supp.*319: Cypr. **δίπας**, *Inscr.Cypr.*93 H. 2. δ. θρῆνος a dirge *chanted by one's two children*, A.*Ch.*334 (lyr.).

δῐ-πάλαιστος [πᾰ], ον, *two palms broad* or *long*, X.*Cyn.*2.4, Plb.27.11.2:—also **δῐπᾰλαιστιαῖος**, α, ον, Heliod.ap.Orib.49.8.6, *Gp.*9.10.2. **-παλτος**, ον, *brandished with both hands*, ξίφη E.*IT*323; δ. πῦρ lightning *hurled* by Zeus *with both hands*, i.e. *with all his might*, Id.*Tr.*1103 (lyr.); πᾶς.. στρατὸς δίπαλτος ἄν με χειρὶ φονεύοι all the host would kill me *with sword brandished in both hands*, i.e. *with all their might*, S.*Aj.*408 (lyr.).

διπάνας· τοὺς διδύμους γεγενημένους, Hsch.

δί-πελμος [ῐ], ον, *with double soles*, *Edict.Diocl.*9.12a, 15. **-πενθημῐμερής**, ές, *consisting of two members of 2½ feet* (sc. μέτρον), Heph.15.10; κῶλα Sch.Ar.*Pax*775:—also **-μερικός**, ή, όν, Sacerd.p.512 K. **-πηχῠαῖος**, α, ον, = sq., Dsc.1.28, S.E.*M.*8.459. **-πηχυς**, υ, *two cubits long, broad*, etc., Hdt.2.78, Hp.*Art.*7, etc.

διπλάδιος [ᾰ], ον, *double*, poet. for διπλάσιος, *AP*11.158 (Antip. (?)). II. Subst. δ., τό, *a measure* of wine, *Sammelb.*4425 ii 9, al.

διπλάζω, = διπλασιάζω, *double*, φόρον And.4.11 (s.v.l.), Alex.122:—Pass., *to be doubled*, στρατηλάταις δορὸς διπλάζεται τιμά E.*Supp.*781 (lyr.), cf. Men.319.10. II. intr., *to be twofold* or *double*, τό τοι διπλάζον μεῖζον κακόν S.*Aj.*268.

δίπλαξ, ᾰκος, ὁ, ἡ, *in double folds* or *layers*, δημός Il.23.243: generally, *twofold, double*, θεσμός Orph.*Fr.*247.37. II. as Subst., δίπλαξ, ἡ, *double-folded mantle*, Il.3.126, Od.19.241, Lyd.*Mag.*1.17: dat. pl. διπλάκεσσιν dub. l. in A.*Pers.*277 (lyr.).

διπλᾰσι-άζω, *double*, Pl.*Lg.*920a, Hierocl.*in CA*20p.465 M., etc.:—Pass., Prodic.7, X.*Ages.*5.1, Ph.2.534; δ. λέγεται διχῶς· ἢ γὰρ τόπον.. μένοντος τοῦ πλήθους τῶν ἀνδρῶν, ἢ τὸν ἀριθμόν Ascl.*Tact.*10.17; so δ. τὸ βάθος Plb.18.24.8. 2. Gramm., *reduplicate*, A.D. *Pron.*62.23, al.:—Pass., Id.*Synt.*237.23. b. *double* a consonant, Hdn.Gr.2.932, etc. 3. *repeat* a metrical phrase, in Pass., Aristid. Quint.1.24. II. intr., *to be twice the size of*, τινός D.S.4.84; *to be doubled in value*, Lys.32.25. **-ᾰσις**, εως, ἡ, = sq., τῶν ἀνδρῶν Ascl. *Tact.*10.17; τῆς χώρας Nicom.*Ar.*1.13. **-ασμός**, ὁ, *doubling*, Antipho Soph.75; τοῦ κύβου Pl.*Sis.*388e; τοῦ στερεοῦ Plu.2.718f. II. Gramm., *the Ionic doubling of consonants*, as in τόσσος, *EM*68.47, Eust.73.3, etc. b. *reduplication*, A.D.*Synt.*323.6. III. in Tactics, *doubling of front*, Ascl.*Tact.*10.18, etc.; of Numbers, ib.17, etc. IV. in Anatomy, *cross-action* of muscles, Gal.18(2).974. V. = δίπλωσις II, *PHolm.*1.39. **-αστικός**, ή, όν, *of* or *for doubling*, Alex.Aphr.*in Metaph.*756.24. **-επιδίμοιρος** [δῐμ], ον, Gaud.*Harm.*10, and **-επιδῐμερής**, ές, Nicom.*Ar.*1.23, 2⅔ *times as great*: **-επιδῐτρῐτος**, ον, ibid., Domnin. in *Rev.Phil.*7.90, 2⅔ *times as great*: **-επίεκτος**, ον, Nicom.*Ar.*1.22, 2⅙ *times as great*: **-επίπεμπτος**, ον, ibid., 2⅕ *times as great*: **-επιτέταρτος**, ον, ibid., 2¼ *times as great*: **-επιτετραμερής**, ές, ib.23, and **-επιτετράπεμπτος**, ον, ibid., 2⅘ *times as great*: **-επιτρῐμερής**, ές, ibid., 2¾ *times as great*: **-επιτρῐτέταρτος**, 2¾ *times as great*, ibid.: **-επίτρῐτος**, ον, ib.22, Theo Sm.p.110 H., 2⅓ *times as great*: **-εφήμῐσυς**, υ, Nicom.*Ar.*1.22, 2½ *times as great*. **-ημιόλιος**, ον, ἀναλογία *ratio of* $\frac{5}{2}$, Theo Sm.p.110 H.

διπλᾰσιο-λογία, ἡ, *repetition of words*, Pl.*Phdr.*267c. **-ομαι**, Pass., *to be doubled*, Th.1.69, *PLeid.X.*87. **-πλευρος**, ον, *with two sides twice as long as the other two*, κλίνη Arist.*Mech.*856ᵃ39.

διπλ-άσιος [ᾰ], α, ον, Ion. **-ήσιος**, η, ον, *twofold, double*, Hdt.4.68, etc.: never in Trag. (δίκρουν is prob. in A.*Fr.*152): freq. as Comp. folld. by ἤ... Hdt.6.57, Th.1.10, etc.; also διπλήσιον ἢ ὅσον.. Hdt.7.23: or c. gen., *twice the size of*, Id.6.133; δ. ἐγίνετο αὐτὸς ἑωυτοῦ Id.8.137; διπλάσια τῶν ἄλλων D.18.238; δ. τῆς ἀληθείας Philem.160; διπλασίοις ἔλαττω (sc. τὰ χρήματα) D.27.52. 2. Subst. διπλήσιον, τό, *as much again*, Hdt.7.103: as Adv., διπλάσιον σπεύδουσι Thgn.229. 3. διπλασίαν (sc. ζημίαν), πράττεσθαι Pl.*Lg.*762b; τὴν δ. καταδικάζειν Lex ap.D.24.105. 4. Adv. -ως Th.8.1, Men.645; δ. ἄμεινον Aeschin.2.122, *AP*7.611 (Eutolm.). **-ᾰσίων**, ον, gen. ονος, later form for διπλάσιος, Arist.*Pr.*923ᵃ3, *Mu.*399ᵃ9, Arr.*Tact.*16.11, *PLips.*64.31 (iv A.D.), etc.; δ. λόγος *duplicate* ratio, Ph.1.22, Plu.2.1138e. **-ασμός**, ὁ, = διπλασιασμός, Eust.1396.52, prob. l. in Plot.6.1.9.

διπλεθρ-ία, ἡ, *a measure of two* πλέθρα, *IG*9(1).693.20 (Corc.).

-**ος**, *ον*, *two* πλέθρα *long* or *broad*, Theopomp.Hist.350, Luc.*VH*1. 16. 2. Subst. δίπλεθρον, τό, *space of two* πλέθρα, Plb.34.12.4.

διπλεία or **-ηΐα**, ἡ, *double*, τὰν διπλείαν τᾶς τιμᾶς *Leg.Gort.*6.42, cf. *GDI*4982. **δίπλειον**, τό, *PPetr.*2 p.42.

δίπλευρος, ον, *with two fronts*, Ael.*Tact.*36.4, Arr.*Tact.*28.4.

διπλῆ, ἡ, (διπλοῦς) a marg. mark used by Gramm. (⋗ >, ⋖ ⩤), to indicate vv.ll., rejected verses, etc., and, in dramatic poetry, a new speaker, Cic.*Att.*8.2.4, Heph.*Poëm.*p.74C., Sch.Il.*Oxy.*1086 ii 55, etc. II. *a dance*, Poll.4.105, Hsch. III. διπλαῖ, αἱ, = δίπλωμα, *IG*14.1054*b*: also sg., *PSI*5.446 (ii A.D.). IV. = διπλοΐς, Ap.Ty. *Ep.*3.

διπλῇ (Dor. **διπλεῖ** *Tab.Heracl.*1.109, *Leg.Gort.*2.7), Adv. *twice*, E.*Ion* 760, cj. in S.*Ant.*725. II. *twice as much*, opp. ἁπλῇ, *IG*1^2.6.47; folld. by ἤ, Pl.*R.*330c.

διπληγίς, ίδος, ὁ, = διπλοΐς, Poll.7.47.

διπλήθης, ες, *double in quantity*, Nic.*Al.*153 (v.l. διπλήρης).

διπλήσιος, η, ον, Ion. for διπλάσιος.

δίπλινθος, ον, *of two bricks in height*, θυρίδας διπλίνθους *IG*2^2.463.55.

διπλοείματος, ον, *with double cloak*, Cerc.1.3.

διπλόη, ἡ, *fold, doubling*, Gal.2.710: but usu., II. *porous substance between the double plates in the bones in the skull*, Hp.*VC*1,17, Heliod.ap.Orib.46.9.4, Ruf.*Onom.*135: generally, *spongy core* of bone, Paul.Aeg.6.77; also, *tissue between layers* of intestine, Aret. *SD*2.9: hence, 2. *weak spot, flaw* in metal, Pl.*Sph.*267e, Ph. *Bel.*71.28, Plu.2.802b: metaph., αἱ δ. τῆς ψυχῆς ib.715f, cf. 441d; 'patchiness', Plot.5.2.1; also, *concealed sense*, in oracles, Plu.2. 407c. III. *hollow sting* of the scorpion, Ael.*NA*9.4.

διπλόθριξ, ὁ, ἡ, gen. τριχος, *with geminate leaves*, of the stone-pine, Dionys.*Av.*1.27.

διπλοΐδιον, τό, Dim. of διπλοΐς I, Poll.7.49.

διπλοΐζω, = διπλασιάζω, A.*Ag.*835; cf. ἐπιδιπλοΐζω.

διπλοΐς, ΐδος, ἡ, *double cloak*, Lxx 1*Ki.*2.19, J.*AJ*6.14.2, etc.; worn by Cynics, *AP*7.65 (Antip. (?)). II. = διπλόη I, Hp.*Morb.* 2.23. 2. *abscess* in horse's ear, *Hippiatr.*17.

διπλο-ϊσότης, ητος, ἡ, *double equation*, Dioph.p.96T. **-κάριος**, ὁ, = Lat. *duplicarius, receiving double pay*, *PGrenf.*2.51.5 (ii A.D., -κάρις Pap.). **-κεράμιον** [ᾰ], τό, *measure of wine in Egypt*, *Ostr.* 1166, al., *POxy.*1751.3 (iv A.D., -μον Pap.).

διπλόος, η, ον, contr. **διπλοῦς**, ῆ, οῦν, Ion. fem. διπλέη Hdt.3.42 codd., but διπλῆν or -ῆν Id.5.90, διπλάς or -ᾶς Id.3.28: contr. always in Trag., exc. διπλόοι A.*Fr.*39: (cf. ἁπλόος):—*twofold, double*, prop. of cloaks and articles of dress, χλαῖνα διπλῆ, = δίπλαξ or διπλοΐς, Il.10. 134, Od.19.226; ὅθι.. διπλόος ἤντετο θώρηξ where the cuirass met [the buckle] *so as to be double*, Il.4.133; τὴν ἐπωμίδα πτύξας διπλῆν having folded it *double*, Apollod.Car.4: generally, καλύβη διπλῇ διαφράγματι Th.1.133; διπλόος θάνατος Hdt.6.104; παῖσον διπλῆν (sc. πληγήν) S.*El.*1415; δ. οἰκίδιον *of two stories*, Lys.1.9; διπλῇ ἄκανθα spine *bent double* by age, E.*El.*492; διπλῇ ⟨ῥάχις⟩ X.*Eq.*1.11; σύμβολον δ. *executed in duplicate*, *PHib.*1.29 (iii B.C.). 2. διπλῇ χερὶ θανεῖν by *mutual* slaughter, S.*Ant.*14. 3. δ. ὀνόματα *compound* words, Arist.*Po.*1459^{a}9, *Rh.*1404^{b}29, etc. 4. of fevers in which two paroxysms took place in a given time, δ. ἀμφημερινός, τριταῖος, Gal.7.472, 9.677. 5. δ. ἰσότης, = διπλοϊσότης (q.v.), Dioph.p.98T., etc. 6. δ. ἄνδρας· τὰ δισύλλαβα ἀνδρῶν ὀνόματα, Hsch. II. as Comp., *twice as much, large*, etc., βίος Pl.*Ti.*75b; δίκη Id.*Lg.*865c; δ. ἤ ... *twice as much as*.. (v. διπλῇ): c. gen., Id.*Ti.*35b; διπλοῦν ὀφείλειν ὅσον.. Lex ap.D.23.28; διπλῷ, = διπλῇ, Pl.*Lg.*722b. III. pl., in Trag., = δύο, A.*Pr.*950, *Ch.*761, S.*Aj.*960, *OT*20, *Ant.*51. IV. *double, doubtful*, οὐ γνώμᾳ διπλόαν θέτο βουλάν Pi.*N.*10.89; διπλᾶς καὶ ἀμφιβόλους λέξεις Ph.1.302. 2. *double-minded, treacherous*, E.*Rh.*395, etc.; οὐδὲν δ. X.*HG*4.1.32; δ. καὶ ποικίλος D.H.*Rh.*11. 5; also, *playing two parts*, Pl.*R.*397e; *at variance with oneself*, ib. 554d. V. διπλοῦν, τό, = δίπλωμα III, Androm.ap.Gal.13.29, al.

διπλόρους, ουν, *spelt with* ρρ, Tz.*H.*12.636.

διπλός, ή, όν, poet. for διπλόος (cf. ἁπλός), Opp.*C.*2.449, *AP*10. 101 (Bianor): Comp. διπλότερος, = διπλάσιος, App.*Praef.*10, *Ev. Matt.*23.15.

διπλο-σήμαντος, ον, *with double meaning*, Sch.Ar.*Nu.*225:—also **-σημος**, ον, Eust.1356.60.

διπλ-όω, *repeat* a process, Arist.*APo.*91^{a}21; *double*, τρίβωνα, of philosophers, D.L.6.22; *multiply by two*, Vett.Val.159.27:—Pass., ἐδεδίπλωτο ἡ φάλαγξ X.*HG*6.5.19; of swords, *to be bent double*, Plu. *Cam.*41; of a bow-string, Ach.Tat.3.8; of fevers (cf. διπλοῦς), Gal. 7.472; δεδιπλωμένον ἔμβρυον, of position of foetus at birth, Aspasia ap.Aët.16.22, cf. Sor.2.55. II. *repay twofold*, δ. διπλᾶ κατὰ τὰ ἔργα αὐτῆς *Apoc.*18.6. **-ῳδέομαι**, *recur*, τῶν διατόνων καθ' ἕκαστον τετραχορδον διπλῳδουμένων Theo Sm.p.93 H. **-ωμα**, ατος, τό, *anything double*: hence of the parallel streams of the 'milky way', Arist.*Mete.* 346^{a}24; of 'doubled' position of foetus at birth, Sor.2.60, Philum. ap.Aët.16.23. II. *folded paper*: hence, *letter of recommendation*, esp. *passport*, Cic.*Att.*10.17.4, *Fam.*6.12.3; later, *order enabling a traveller to use the public post*, Plu.*Galb.*8, *OGI*665.25 (Egypt, i A.D.), etc.; *receipt* for payment of licences or taxes, *PAmh.*2.92 (ii A.D.), etc. 2. *duplicate, counterpart*, *CIG*3276 (Smyrna). 3. δ. ὄνων, tax in Egypt, *BGU*213 (ii A.D.); δ. ἵππων *PAmh.*2.92.21 (ii A.D.). III. *double pot* for boiling unguents, etc., Dsc.2.77, Crito ap.Gal.13.37. **-ωσις**, εως, ἡ, *compounding of words*, Arist.*Rh.* 1406^{a}6. II. *doubling*, μήνιγγος Gal.*UP*9.6 (pl.); esp. in Alch., δ. ἀργύρου Zos.Alch.p.183 B., cf. *PHolm.*2.18, al. III. *folding*, Eust.633.20, Hsch. s. v. πτύξις.

δί-πνοος, ον, *with two breathing apertures*, Gal.19.93 (δίπνος codd.); cf. **δίπνοια** τρώματα· εἰς κενὰ τραύματα, Hsch. **-πόδης** [ῐ], gen. -πόδου, *two feet long, broad*, etc., X.*Oec.*19.3. **-ποδία**, ἡ, *two-footedness*, Arist.*PA*643^{a}3, Plot.6.3.5. II. *a Lacedaemonian dance*, Cratin.162. III. in Metric, *combination of two feet*, Anon.*Oxy.* 220 viii 1, Heph.4.3, Aristid.Quint.1.24, etc. **-ποδιάζω**, fut. -άξω, *dance the* διποδία, Ar.*Lys.*1243. **-ποδισμός**, ὁ, = διποδία II, Hsch.

δῐπολητ́ς, ΐδος, ἡ, *of* or *through two cities*, φήμη Man.4.376.

Δῑπολίεια, τά, contr. from Διιπ-, an ancient *festival of Zeus Polieus* at Athens, *IG*1^2.188,843; Διιπόλεια codd. in Ar.*Pax* 420, Antipho 2.4.8, cf. Sch.Ar. l. c.; Διιπόλεια Hdn.Gr.2.493.

δῐ-πολις, εως, ὁ, ἡ, *of* or *divided into two cities*, Str.3.4.8, 14.2. 15. **-πολίτης** [λῑ], ου, ὁ, *citizen of two cities*, Man.5.291.

Δῑπολιώδης, ες, *like the feast of Dipolia, old-world*, Ar.*Nu.*984.

δί-πολος [ῐ], ον, (πολέω) *twice-ploughed*, Procl. ad Hes.*Op.*460. II. = διπλόος, A.*Fr.*209 (dub.). **-πορος**, ον, *with two roads* or *openings*, δ. κορυφὰν Ἰσθμίου E.*Tr.*1097 (lyr.). **-πος**, = δίπους, Pythag.ap.Iamb. *VP*25.144. **-πότᾰμος**, ον, *between two rivers*, πόλις E.*Supp.*621 (lyr.). **-πους**, ποδος (acc. δίπουν *IG*2.1054.24, etc.), ὁ, ἡ, neut. πουν, *two-footed*, A.*Ag.*1258, *Supp.*895 (lyr.), Pl.*Plt.*276c, etc.: δίποδα, τά, *two-footed animals*, Plu.2.636e. 2. δίπους, ὁ, *jerboa*, which springs *from its two hind feet*, Hdt.4.192. II. *two feet long*, γραμμή Pl.*Men.*83d; διάμετρος δυνάμει δ. Id.*Plt.*266b. **-πρόσωπος**, ον, *two-faced*, ἄγαλμα Hdn.1.16.2; ποτήριον, σκάφιον, *IG*11(4).1308, 1309 (Delos, ii B.C.). 2. *ambiguous*, Luc.*JTr.*43. 3. Gramm., *denoting two persons*, A.D.*Pron.*17.1, 110.24. 4. διπρόσωπος, ἡ, name of a *plaster*, Gal.11.127. **-πρυμνος**, ον, v. sq. **-πρῳρος**, ον, ναῦς δ. καὶ δίπρυμνος a ship *double-prowed* and *double-sterned*, i.e. a *twin* ship, Callix.1, Promathidas ap.Ath.11.489b (here perh., = ἀμφίπρῳρος). **-πτερος**, ον, *two-winged*, of insects, opp. τετράπτερος, Arist.*HA*490^{a}16, al. II. ὁ δ. (sc. ναός) temple *with double peristyle*, Vitr.3.2.7. **-πτέρῠγος**, ον, = foreg. I, *AP*5.150 (Mel.), cf. 9.570 (Phld.). II. δ., τό, *mantle with two* πτερά (cf. πτέρον III. 10), *IG*2.754.38, *Jahresh.*16 *Beibl.*53. **-πτυον**, τό, a Cyprian *measure* (perh., = ½ μέδιμνος), Hsch. **-πτῠχής**, ές, = δίπτυχος, Arist.*HA*515^{b}8. **-πτῠχίζω**, Dor. aor. imper. -ιξον, *fold, double*, Hsch. (-διξον cod.). **-πτῠχος**, ον, (πτύσσω) *double-folded, doubled*, δίπτυχον ἀμφ' ὤμοισιν ἔχων.. λώπην Od.13.224 (so δίπτυχα λώπην, metaplast. acc. as if from δίπτυξ, A.R.2.32); δ. δελτίον *a pair of* tablets, Hdt.7.239; δ. κάτοπτρον *folding* mirror, *BGU*717.12; κωδίκιλλοι δ. ib.326 ii 15 (ii A.D.):—in the Homeric phrase δίπτυχα ποιήσαντες [τὴν κνίσην], δίπτυχα is interpr. by Sch.BT as an Adv., *having doubled* the fat, i.e. putting one layer of fat under the thighs (μηροί) and another over them, but may be acc., = *fold*, Il.1.461, al. II. *twofold*, δ. δῶρον E.*Ion* 1010; γλῶσσα Id.*Tr.*286: in pl., = δισσοί, *two*, δ. ὀδύναι S.*Fr.*152; νεανίαι E.*IT*242, cf. *Or.*633, *Andr.*578, Ar.*Fr.*558. III. δίπτυχα, τά, = Lat. *tabulae*, *SIG*827 i 9 (Delph., ii A.D.). **-πτωτος**, ον, *having one form for two cases*, A.D.*Pron.* 91.7. **-πῠλος**, ον, *double-gated, with two entrances*, S.*Ph.*952. II. δίπυλον, τό, a name for the Θριάσιαι πύλαι at Athens, Plb.16.25.7, Plu.*Per.*30; at Rome for the temple of Janus, Id.2.322a. 2. = ὑπερῷον, Hsch. **-πυργία** οἰκία house *with two wings*, *POxy.*247. 23 (i A.D.), *PLond.*2.348 (iii A.D.), etc.:—also **-πυργιαία**, *POxy.* 1703.12 (iii A.D.). **-πύρηνος**, ον, (πυρήν) *with two knobs*: Subst. -πύρηνον, τό, *probe*, Herophil.ap.Sor.2.85, Cael.Aur.*CP*3.3, Gal.2. 574, al. **-πῡρίτης** [ρῑ] (sc. ἄρτος), ὁ, *twice-baked bread, biscuit*, Hp. *Int.*25. **-πῡρος** (sc. ἄρτος), ον, *twice fired*, i.e. *baked*, = foreg., Eub.18, Alex.172.10: pl., Alc.Com.5; δ. σῖτος *JHS*32.154. II. διπύρους ἀνέχουσα λαμπάδας... Ἑκάτα Hecate holding up *two flaming* torches, Ar.*Ra.*1361. **-πωλος**, ον, *with two horses*, ἅρμα (Ἄρης cod.) Hsch. s. v. συνωρίδα.

δίρηγες· στρουθοί, Hsch.; cf. δίγηρες.

διρκαία, ἡ, = κιρκαία, Dsc.3.119: **δίρκαιον**, τό, = δαῦκος, Ps.-Dsc. 3.72; = στρύχνον ὑπνωτικόν, Id.4.72. **δίρκος**, ὁ, = φθείρ III, Paus. Gr.*Fr.*131.

δί-ρραβδος, ον, *with two stripes*, Arist.*Fr.*294. **-ρρυθμος**, ον, = δίμετρος, in paeonic metre, Sch.Ar.*Eq.*613, etc. **-ρρῡμία**, ἡ, *double pole*, A.*Fr.*324. **-ρρῡμος**, ον, *with two poles*, i.e. three horses, Id.*Pers.*47 (anap.).

δίς [ῐ], Adv. *twice, doubly*, with Nouns, δ. τόσσον *twice* as much, Od. 9.491, cf. Th.6.57, etc.; ἀληθὴς ὁ λόγος ὡς δ. παῖς γέρων Cratin.24; δ. παῖδες οἱ γέροντες Theopomp.Com.69: more freq. with Verbs, τοῦτο δ. ἤδη ἐγένετο Hdt.8.104; δ. φράσαι A.*Pers.*173, cf. *Ag.*1384; δ. αἰάζειν καὶ τρίς S.*Aj.*432; δ. καὶ τρίς φασι καλὸν εἶναι τὰ καλὰ λέγειν Pl.*Grg.*498e, cf. *Phlb.*60a, Emp.25; δ. βιῶναι *twice over*, Men.223.4; δειπνεῖν... δ. τῆς ἡμέρας Pl.Com.207; ἐς δ. App.*Mith.*78: ὁ δ. **Νέωνος**, = *son and grandson* of N., *GDI*3092.18 (Aegosthena); Αὐρήλιος Αὐξάνων δ. *BCH*17.249 (Apamea); Αὐρ. Δοῦ⟨ρ⟩λος δ. *JHS*19.301 (Selmea [Lycaonia]).—In compds. δι-, but δισ- in δισμύριοι, δισχίλιοι, δισθανής, δίσαβος, δισάρπαγος, δίσευνος, etc. (Cf. Skt. *dvis* 'twice', Lat. *bis.*)

-δις, inseparable Suffix, signifying motion to a place, like -δε, but only used in a few words, as ἄλλυδις, οἴκαδις, χαμάδις.

Δίς, ὁ, = Ζεύς, Rhinth.14; otherwise only in oblique cases, Διός, Διΐ, Δία (pl. Δίες, Δίας, Plu.2.425e): the contr. dat. Δί *SIG*35, Pi.*N.* 1.72, etc.: apocop. acc. Δί in νηδί, v. Ζεύς.

δίσᾱβος [ῐ], ον, hyperdor. for δίσηβος, *twice young*, *AP*15.26 (Dosiad.).

δῐσάκκ-ιον, τό, *saddle-bag, panniers*, *PFay.*347 (ii A. D.), *PStrassb.* 37.17 (iii A. D.):—Dim. **-ίδιον**, τό, *POxy.*741.2 (ii A. D.).

δίσαλα· ἀκαθαρσία, and **δισαλέος**· ῥυπαρός, Hsch. (cf. δεῖσα, etc.).

δῐσ-άρπᾰγος, ον, *twice ravished*, Lyc.513. **-εβδομηκοντάπηχυς**, υ, 140 *cubits long*, Tz.*H.*3.942. **-έβδομος**, ον, *fourteenth*, ib.9.781. **-έκγονοι**, οἱ, *second cousins*, Asp. *in EN*184.26. **-έκτωρ**, dub. sens. in *Stud.Pal.*20.75 i 22 (iii/iv A. D.). **-εξάδελφος** [ᾰ], ον, ὁ, *great-nephew*, Sch.A.R.3.359. **-ευνος**, ον, *with two wives*, *AP* 15.26 (Dosiad.).

δί-σημος [ῐ], ον, *of two times*, πούς Aristid.Quint.1.14 (but in Music, *of four times*, acc. to Elias *in Cat.*189.9). II. *of doubtful quantity*, Sch.D.T.p.38 H. III. in Rhythm, *of two time-units*, χρόνος, μέγεθος, Aristox.*Rhyth.*2.10,31, cf. Aristid.Quint.1.14. IV. of a garment, *with double border*, *PTeb.*406.17 (iii A. D.), *POxy.*1051.5 (iii A. D.).

δισθᾰνής, ές, *twice dead*, Od.12.22.

δῐσῑτέομαι, *eat two meals a day*, Herod.Med.ap.Aët.9.13.

δισκ-άζομαι, = διαφέρομαι, Hsch. **-άριον**, τό, Dim. of δίσκος, Orib.*Syn.*7.44.1. **-ελλα**· σπυρίς, Hsch. **-εύς**, έως, ὁ, a kind of *comet*, Lyd.*Ost.*10^{a}, 15^{a}. **-ευτής**, οῦ, ὁ, *one who pitches quoits*, Mich. *in EN*487.31. **-εύω**, = δισκέω, Sosith.3, Philostr.*Ep.*7; δ. αὐτόν D.L.1.118, Porph.*Chr.*48:—Pass., *to be pitched* or *thrown*, *AP*9.14 (Antiphil.), v.l. in E.*Ion* 1268; cf. sq. **-έω**, *pitch the quoit*, δίσκον.. στιβαρώτερον οὐκ ὀλίγον περ ἢ οἵῳ.. ἐδίσκεον ἀλλήλοισιν Od. 8.188; μακρὰ δισκήσαις *having made a long throw*, Pi.*I.*2.35; αἴ τις δισκίοι *IG*5(1).828 (Sparta):—Pass., *to be hurled*, of a person, E.*Ion* 1268 (v.l. -ευθήσεται); of a squid, *AP*9.227 (Bianor). **-ημα**, ατος, τό, *a thing thrown*, δ. πικρόν, of Astyanax, E.*Tr.*1121. II. *quoit-throw*, S.*Fr.*380.

δί-σκηπτρος, ον, *two-sceptred*, τιμή, of the Atridae, A.*Ag.*43 (anap.).

δισκο-βολέω, *pitch the quoit*, Gal.*Thras.*33, Hsch. s. v. δισκεύει: *throw down like a quoit*, *Epigr.Gr.*336 (Alexandria Troas). **-βολία**, ἡ, *quoit-throwing*, Gal.6.325. **-βόλος**, ὁ, *quoit-thrower*, subject of statues, by Myron, Luc.*Philops.*18; by Naucydes, Plin.*HN*34.80. **-ειδής**, ές, *quoit-shaped*, Agatharch.105, Dsc.2.156, *Placit.*2.27.3, Ruf.*Anat.*16. **-ομαι**, Pass., *to be made in the form of a disk*, Lyd.*Ost.*6.

δισκόραξ, ακος, ὁ, *double-dyed Korax* (with play on κόραξ), Luc. *Pseudol.*30.

δίσκος, ὁ, (δικεῖν) *quoit*, Il.2.774, Od.8.186, E.*IA*200, al., Arist. *Fr.*533, etc.; δίσκου οὖρα *quoit's cast*, Il.23.431; λιθίνοις ἐν δ. Pi.*I.* 1.25. II. *anything quoit-shaped*: 1. *dish, trencher*, *AP*11.371 (Pall.), Lib.*Decl.*30.24; *salver*, *BGU*388 ii 22 (ii/iii A. D.). 2. *round mirror*, *AP*6.18 (Jul.). 3. the sun's *disk*, Alex.Aphr.*Pr.* 2.46, *Placit.*2.24.1, al. 4. *gong*, S.E.*M.*5.28, al. 5. *reliquary*, Procop.*Aed.*1.7. III. *marigold, Calendula arvensis*, Alex.Trall. 12. (Cf. δικεῖν.)

δίσκ-ουρα, τά, (οὖρος) *quoit's cast*, as a measure of distance, ἐς δίσκουρα λέλειπτο Il.23.523:—also **-ούρια**, Hsch.

δισκοφόρος, ον, *bringing the discus*, Luc.*Philops.*18.

δισ-μῡρίανδρος πόλις a city *of twenty thousand inhabitants*, Str.12.7.3. **-μύριοι** [ῠ], αι, α, *twenty thousand*, Hdt.1.32, Pl.*Ion* 535d: sg., δισμύριος, α, ον, with collective Nouns, ἵππος δισμυρία Luc.*Zeux.*8.

δισπερίοδος, ὁ, *twice a* περιοδονίκης (q. v.), κῆρυξ *IG*3.129 (iii A. D.).

δι-σπῐθᾰμαῖος, α, ον, = sq., Dsc.2.144. **-σπῐθᾰμος**, ον, *of two spans' length*, ib.156. **-σπόνδειος**, ὁ, *double spondee*, Heph.3.3, Aristid.Quint.1.22, Hermog.*Id.*1.6. **-σπορέω**, (σπόρος) *sow twice*, *PEdgar* 27.2 (iii B. C.), Str.16.4.2 (Pass.).

δισσ-άκις [ᾰ], poet. **-ι**, Adv. *twice over*, Arat.968, Q.S.2.56, *AP* 6.223 (Antip.). **-άρχης**, ου, ὁ, *joint-ruling*, δισσάρχαι βασιλεῖς S.*Aj.*390 (lyr.). **-ᾰχῆ**, Adv. *at two points*, Arist. *de An.*406^{b}32. **-ᾰχοῦ**, Att. **διττ-**, Adv. = foreg., Thphr.*Lap.*25.

δισσο-γονέω, Att. **διττ-**, *bear doubly*, i. e. to be both viviparous and oviparous, Arist.*GA*719^{a}14. **-γρᾰφία**, ἡ, *dittography, repetition of words* by copyist, Simp. *in Cat.*88.24. **-λογέω**, Att. **διττ-**, *say twice, repeat*, as in phrases like ἄπιστ' ἄπιστα, καινὰ καινά, Sch.E. *Hec.*688; *go over again*, Vett.Val.249.20. II. *call in question, leave doubtful*, Simp. *in Cael.*194.17. **-λογία**, ἡ, *repetition of words*, Sch.Od.1.406. **-λόγος**, ον, *speaking two languages*, Man.5.291. **-ποιός**, όν, *making doubtful, perplexing*, Sch.S.*El.* 645.

δισσός, Att. **διττός**, Ion. **διξός** (q. v.), ή, όν, (δίς) *twofold, double*, Hdt.2.44, 7.70, Pl.*Tht.*198d, etc. Adv. διττῶς, opp. ἁπλῶς, *doubly, in two ways*, δ. [γνώριμα] Arist.*EN*1095^{b}2; δ. λέγεσθαι ib.1096^{b}13, al. 2. *executed in duplicate*, ἀποχή *POxy.*1024.39 (ii A. D.), etc. II. pl., *two*, Pi.*N.*1.44, Hdt.5.40,52, A.*Pr.*957, S.*Aj.*57, etc.: with a dual, δισσοὶ προάγοντε μάλιστα Iamb.*Comm.Math.* 25. III. metaph., *divided, disagreeing* in mind, λήμασι δισσούς (λήμασιν ἴσους Dind.) A.*Ag.*122 (lyr.). 2. *doubtful, ambiguous*, ὄνειροι S.*El.*645; τὸ δ. *ambiguity*, Arist.*Pol.*1261^{b}29. Adv. διττῶς Id.*SE*180^{a}15.

δισσο-τόκος, ον, *bearing twice*, Nonn.*D.*5.199. II. proparox., δισσότοκος, ον, *twice-born*, of Bacchus, ib.1.4. **-φῠής**, ές, *of double nature*, ib.14.97, etc.

δίστ-αγμα, ατος, τό, *doubt, uncertainty*, Phld.*Rh.*1.111 S.:—also **-αγμός**, ὁ, Agatharch.21, Plu.2.214f, Steph. *in Hp.*1.59 D.

δι-στάδιος [ᾰ], ον, *two stadia long*, διάστημα App.*Hann.*37.

διστ-άζω, fut. -άσω Phld.*Sign.*1, al.: (δίς):—*doubt, hesitate*, abs., Pl.*Tht.*190a, *Ion* 534e, etc.; δ. εἰ.. Id.*Lg.*897b, *BGU*388 i 17 (ii/iii A. D.); μή.. Pl.*Sph.*235a; μή ποτε, c. ind., Phld.*Sign.*13,21; πῶς.. Arist.*EN*1112^{b}2; πότερον.. Id.*Metaph.*1091^{a}14; περί τι Id.*EN*1112^{b}8; περί τινος Plu.2.62a:—Pass., *to be in doubt*, D.S.17.9; τὰ -όμενα *OGI*315.66 (Pessinus), Phld.*Lib.*p.23 O. **-ακτικός**, ή, όν, *expressive of doubt*, ἔγκλισις, of the subjunctive, Sch.D.T.p.245 H., cf. A.D. *Synt.*264.18. Adv. -κῶς Sch.E.*Or.*632, Sch.Il.1.100.

διστάσιος [ᾰ], ον, *of twice the value*, Pl.*Hipparch.*231d, Aglaïas 19.

διστασμός, ὁ, = δισταγμός, Thphr.*Metaph.*31, Sch.Od.2.276.

δι-στεγής, ές, = δίστεγος, *EM*274.27. **-στεγία**, ἡ, *second story*, Poll.4.130. **-στεγος**, ον, *of two stories*, οἰκία, πύργος, *Sammelb.* 5246 (i B. C.), *POxy.*243.15 (i A. D.), cf. Str.15.3.8, J.*BJ*5.4.3, Sor. 1.70, etc. 2. *of two chambers* on the same floor, J.*BJ*5.5.4. 3. δίστεγον, τό, *room on the upper floor*, *Gp.*8.25.1. **-στεφής**, ές, *twice-crowned*, Call.*Sos.*7.2. **-στῐχής**, ές, = δίστιχος, ὀδόντες Ar. Byz.*Epit.*120.9. **-στῐχία**, ἡ, *double row* or *line*, of fruit, J.*AJ*8.3.4; of ships, Sch.Il.14.31. 2. *couplet, distich*, Heph.*Poëm.*1, Sch. Ar.*Nu.*1348. II. Medic., *growth of a second row* of eyelashes, Gal. 14.767. **-στῐχίασις**, εως, ἡ, = διστιχία II, Sever.ap.Aët.7.68, Paul. Aeg.6.8. **-στῐχος**, ον, *with two rows*, κριθαί *Placit.*5.10.2. 2. *of two verses*, ἐπίγραμμα *AP*9.369 (Cyrill.); δίστιχον, τό, *distich*, *AP* 6.329 (Leon.); '*a couple of lines*', of a brief letter, *PGiss.*20.23 (ii A. D.). 3. *doubly woven*, μαφόρια *PMasp.*6 ii 80 (vi A. D.). **-στοιχία**, ἡ, *double row*, Thphr.*HP*4.8.6, Ael.*NA*9.40. **-στοιχος**, ον, *in two rows*, ὀδόντες Arist.*HA*501^{a}24; [βράγχια] ib.505^{a}16; κριθὴ δ. *two-rowed* barley, Thphr.*HP*8.4.2; *in two courses*, ὑπερτόναια *SIG* 969.32. **-στολος**, ον, *in pairs, two together*, or simply, *two*, ἀδελφαί S.*OC*1055 (lyr.). **-στομος**, ον, (στόμα) *double-mouthed, with two entrances*, πέτρα S.*Ph.*16; δ. ὁδοί *double-branching* roads, Id.*OC* 900; so of rivers *with two mouths*, Plb.34.10.5; *with two harbours*, Hsch. II. of a weapon, *two-edged*, ξίφος E.*Hel.*983; πελέκεως γέννυς Id.*Fr.*530.5.

διστραλίον, τό, *single-bladed axe*, Sch.Il.23.851 (Lat. *dextrale*).

δίστροπον, τό, *vessel for libations*, *BGU*590 (ii A. D.).

δίστροφος, ον, *doubly twisted*, of cords, Meges ap.Orib.44.24.12. II. *of two turns*, ἕλιξ Papp.1110.15.

δῐσυλλᾰβ-έω, *to be of two syllables*, Hdn.Gr.2.908, A.D.*Pron.*78.24. **-ία**, ἡ, *pair of syllables*, καταληκτικὸν εἰς δ. Sch.Ar.*Av.*904, etc. **-ος**, ον, *of two syllables*, Demetr.Poliorc.ap.Phylarch.12 J. (of slave-names), D.H.*Comp.*11, A.D.*Pron.*49.14, Luc.*Gall.*29; δισυλλάβῳ περιττεύειν Heph.4.4. Adv. -βως A.D.*Pron.*35.25, Ath.10. 446e, Sch.Th.*Oxy.*853 v 12.

δῐσύν-απτος, ον, *double-plaited*, στέφανος Philox.1. **-εγγυάω**, *become joint surety twice*, *Sammelb.*4369 ii 6 (iii B. C.).

δῐσύπᾰτος [ῠ], ὁ, *twice consul*, Plu.2.777b, Arr.*Epict.*4.1.6, Philostr. *VS*2.1.1 (pl.).

δισχέλιοι, οἱ, Aeol. for δισχίλιοι.

δισχῐδ-ής, ές, (σχίζω) *cloven-hoofed*, opp. ἀσχιδής, πολυσχιδής, Arist.*HA*499^{b}9. 2. *cloven*, ποδότης Id.*PA*642^{b}29. 3. *divided, parted*, κόμη Callistr.*Stat.*7; ὁδός *Trag.Adesp.*338. Adv. -δῶς Dosith.p.412 K. 4. *branching*, of arteries, etc., Gal.*UP*16.10, etc. **-όν**, Adv. of foreg., *in double columns*, of writing, Sch. D.T.p.191 H., al. (wrongly expld. as = στιχηδόν).

δισχῑλιάς, άδος, ἡ, *number of twenty thousand*, Lxx 1 *Ma.*9.4.

δισχίλιοι [χῑ], αι, α, Aeol. **δισχέλιοι** Alc.*Supp.*22.2:—*two thousand*, Hdt.2.44, Ar.*V.*660, Pl.*Criti.*118a, etc.: poet. dat. pl., δισχίλοις ἀνδραπόδοισιν *IG*1^{2}.1085: sg., δισχίλιος, α, ον, with collective Nouns, e. g. ἵππος Hdt.7.158.

δί-σχοινος, ον, *measuring two* σχοῖνοι (i. e. 60 *stades*), χώρα δ. κύκλῳ Str.12.3.34. **-σώματος**, ον, *double-bodied*, D.S.4.12, Orph. *H.*71.5, *Fr.*57, Ph.2.481; *with two chambers*, εἰσώστης *CIG*2842 (Aphrodisias). **-σωμος**, ον, applied to certain constellations, Serapio in *Cat.Cod.Astr.*1.100, S.E.*M.*5.6, Vett.Val.7.25, etc.

δισώνῠμος, ον, *with two names*, Sch.Od.12.22.

Δῐσωτήριον, τό, contr. for Διοσ-, *the temple of* Ζεὺς Σωτήρ on the Acropolis at Athens, *AB*91; cf. Δισωτήρια.

δῐ-τάλαντος [τᾰ], ον, *weighing two talents*, σταθμός Hdt.1.50, 2.96; *worth two talents*, δ. εἶχες ἔρανον D.18.312; οἶκοι δ. Id.27.64: neut. as Subst., δ. ἀργυρίου Lxx 4 *Ki.*5.23. **-τοιχος**· ἀναίσθητος, Hsch. **-τοκέω**, *bear two at a birth*, Arist.*HA*558^{b}23, *GA*772^{a}35:—also **δῐτοκεύω**, Nic.*Fr.*73.1. **-τόκος**, ον, *having borne two at a birth*, Anacr.145: opp. μονοτόκος, Arist.*GA*774^{b}9; but perh. *having borne two children*, *AJA*17.162 (Cyrene). **-τομία**, *second cutting* of reeds, *POxy.*1631.14 (iii A. D.). **-τονέω**, *have a double accent*, A.D.*Synt.*307.15; or *two accents*, Id.*Pron.*60.16. **-τονιαῖος**, α, ον, = δίτονος, Aristox.*Harm.*p.66 M. **-τονίζω**, *accent in two ways*, Sch.rec.S.*Aj.*733. **-τονος**, ον, *of two tones*, διάστημα Gaud.*Harm.*3; δίτονον, τό, the *major third*, Aristox.*Harm.*p.65 M., Cleonid.*Harm.*5, Plu.2.430a; also, = περισπώμενον, prob. in *Gramm. Lat.*4.527 K. **-τορμία**, ἡ, *double socket* or *tenon*, Ph.*Bel.*63.24, Hero *Bel.*92.9, *Spir.*1.42. **-τρῐχιάω**, *have double eyelashes*, Gal.14.771. **-τροπος**, ον, expl. of δίχολος, Diogenian.4.32. **-τρόχαιος**, ὁ, *double trochee*, Heph.3.3, Aristid.Quint.1.22. **-τροχία**, ἡ, *windlass with two wheels*, Bito 63.10. **-τροχος**, ον, *two-wheeled*, ἅμαξα *Edict.Diocl.*15.40; καθέδρα Men.Prot.p.51 D.

διττάμενον· ἀρνούμενον (Cret.), Hsch.

διτταχῶς· διχῶς, Hsch. **διττός**, etc., v. δισσ-.

δίτῠλος, ον, *with two humps*, κάμηλοι D.S.2.54.

διυγιαίνω, *to be healthy throughout*, Plu.2.135c, Iamb.*VP*22.102.

διυγραίνω, *soak thoroughly*, Thphr.*CP*2.9.3:—Pass., Hp.*Aph*.7.51.

δίυγρος, ον, *washed out, pale*, δ. τὴν εἰδέην Hp.*Int*.43 (A.*Th*.990 is corrupt). 2. of a *melting* glance, νεῦμα δ. *AP*12.68.7 (Mel.). II. *liquid, moist*, Arist.*Pr*.887^{b}25; ἀναθυμίασις Porph. *Sent*.29; στοιχεῖον δ., of the sea, Id.ap.Eus.*PE*3.11; τὸ δ. τῆς ὕλης Jul.*Or*.5.165d; πνεῦμα Iamb.*Myst*.4.13; *watery*, αἷμα Steph.*in Hp*.1.132D.

διῠδᾰτίζω, *give water to drink*, Sch.Il.6.307.

δίυδρος, ον, (ὕδωρ) *full of water*, γαστήρ Hp.*Int*.26.

διῡλ-ίζω, *strain, filter thoroughly*, οἶνον Mim.*Oxy*.413.154, Dsc.5.72, Artem.4.48:—Pass., διυλισμένος οἶνος Lxx *Am*.6.6: metaph., διυλισμένα ἀρετὰ ἀπὸ παντὸς τῶ θνατῶ πάθεος Archyt.ap.Stob.3.1.108, cf. Pl.*Ti*.69a. II. *strain off*, κώνωπα *Ev.Matt*.23.24. **-ῐσις**, εως, ἡ, *filtering, refining, purifying*, Suid. **-ισμα**, ατος, τό, *filtered* or *clarified liquor*, Gal.12.836. **-ιστήρ**, ῆρος, ὁ, *filter, strainer*, Sch. Ar.*Pax* 534. **-ιστήριον**, τό, gloss on ἠθμάριον, Hsch. **-ιστός**, ή, όν, *filtered, strained*, ἔλαιον *PRyl*.97.3, cf. Gal.19.688.

διυπερτίθημι, *postpone*, *POxy*.1479.6 (i B.C.).

διυπηρετέομαι, *serve*, Sch.E.*Ph*.1435.

διυπνίζω, (ὕπνος) *awake from sleep*, trans., Ael.*NA*7.46: intr., Luc.*Ocyp*.108:—Pass., Diocl.*Fr*.141, J.*AJ*5.10.4 (v.l.), Zos.Alch. p.117B., *AP*9.378 (Pall.): but, II. *fall asleep*, Simp. *in Ph*. 1258.25.

διυπο-βάλλω, in Pass., of wrestlers in a *clinch*, Theo Sm.p.122 H. **-βλέπω**, gloss on διακυνοφθαλμίζομαι, Hsch.

διυποπτεύω, *dissimulate* (?), Zos.Alch.p.208 B.

δι-ϋφαίνω, *fill up by weaving*, τὰς διαστάσεις Gal.2.904, cf. Luc. *VH*1.15:—Pass. ἀράχνιον μήπω διυφασμένον Gal.2.569. 2. *interweave*, in Pass., Ael.*NA*9.17; ζώνη διυφασμένη καλλίστοις χρώμασιν Aristeas 97, cf. Lxx *Ex*.36.31 (39.23). **-ύφαντος** [ῠ], ον, *doubly woven*, *PMasp*.6 ii 98 (vi A.D.). **-ῠφή**, ἡ, *woven fabric*, Aristeas 86.

διυφίημι, *let fall, drop*, of offspring, in Pass., Ph.2.319 (s.v.l.).

διφαδεύει· ἐξελεῖται, Hsch. **δίφακος**, a *plant*, Id.

δῐφᾰλαγγ-άρχης, ου, ὁ, *leader of a* διφαλαγγαρχία, Suid. **-αρχία**, ἡ, *corps of two* φαλαγγαρχίαι or 8,192 men (half a phalanx), Ael.*Tact*.9.9, Arr.*Tact*.10.7. **-ία**, ἡ, *phalanx marching in two divisions*, Plb.2.66.9, 12.20.7, Ael.*Tact*.36.3, Arr. *Tact*.28.6. 2. = διφαλαγγαρχία, Ascl.*Tact*.2.10, Ael.*Tact*.33.5.

δῐφᾰλέος, α, ον, (διφάω) *searching, sagacious*, *Hymn.Is*.10.

διφάνινος λύχνος, dub. sens. in *PLond*.2.193.29 (ii A.D.).

δίφας, ἡ, a kind of *serpent*, Artem.2.13; cf. δίβαν, δίφατον.

δῐφᾰσία, ἡ, (δίφατος) = διλογία, Hsch.

δῐφάσιος [ᾰ], α, ον, Ion. Adj., *of two kinds*, γράμματα Hdt.2.36; αἰτίαι Id.3.122, cf. *Schwyzer* 725 (Milet.), Eus.Mynd.63. II. in pl., = δύο, Hdt.1.18, 2.17, al.

δίφατον· ὄφιν (Cret.), Hsch.

δῐφᾰτος [ῐ], ον, *ambiguous*, Hsch.

δῑφ-άω, only pres., *search after*, πόντῳ ἐν ἰχθυόεντι.. τήθεα διφῶν Il.16.747; τεὴν διφῶσα καλιήν Hes.*Op*.374; ἐν οὔρεσι πάντα λαγωὸν διφᾷ Call.*Epigr*.33, cf. *Fr*.165; διφᾶν τὰ καλύμματα (or καλλύσματα, q.v.) *search* them *well*, Thphr.*Char*.10.6: abs., Herod.6.73; εἴ ποθι διφώωσα.. ἀθρήσειεν Nonn.*D*.48.592:—Ion. **διφέω**, *AP*9.559 (Crin.). **-ήτωρ**, ορος, ὁ, *a searcher*, βυθῶν διφήτορες Opp.*H*.2.435.

διφθέρα, ἡ, *prepared hide, piece of leather*, Hdt.1.194; ἐκ διφθερέων πεποιημέναι κυνέαι Id.7.77; διφθέραι, opp. δέρρεις (hides), Th.2.75; of a *drum*, Hero *Aut*.20.4; esp. as writing-material, τὰς βύβλους διφθέρας καλέουσι ἀπὸ τοῦ παλαιοῦ οἱ Ἴωνες Hdt.5.58; δ. μελαγγραφεῖς E.*Fr*.627; δ. βασιλικαί, of Persian records, Ctes.ap.D.S.2.32; δ. ἱεραί, at Carthage, Plu.2.942c; χαλκαῖ δ., ib.297a, cf. Sch.Il.1.175: prov., ἀρχαιότερα τῆς διφθέρας λέγεις Diogenian.3.2; used for bindings, διφθέρας περιβάλλειν (sc. βιβλίοις) Luc.*Ind*.16. II. *anything made of leather, leathern jerkin*, Ar.*Nu*.72, Pl.*Cri*.53d, *SIG* 1259.6 (iv B.C.), Men.*Epit*.12, Luc.*Tim*.6,38, Arr.*An*.7.9.2, etc.; properly, *of goatskin*, opp. μηλωτή, Ammon.*Diff*.p.44V. 2. *wallet, bag*, X.*An*.5.2.12, Lib.*Or*.58.5. 3. pl., *skins used as tents*, X.*An*.1.5.10, Phylarch.41 J.

διφθερ-άλοιφος [ᾰ], ὁ, Cypr. for *a schoolmaster*, *JHS*12.330, Hsch. **-άριος**, ὁ, *parchment-maker*, *Edict.Diocl.Asin*.7.38. **-ίας**, ου, ὁ, *clad in a leathern jerkin*; the dress of old men in Tragedy, of boors in Comedy, Posidipp.ap.Ath.10.414e, Luc.*Tim*.8, Poll.4.137. **-ινος**, η, ον, *of tanned leather*, σχεδίαι X.*An*.2.4.28; πλοῖα Str.3.3.7. **-ιον**, τό, Dim. of διφθέρα, Theognost.*Can*.125.25. **-ίς**, ίδος, ἡ, = διφθέρα, *AP*9.546 (Antiphil.). **-ῖτις**, ιδος, fem. of διφθερίας, Poll.4.138. **-όομαι**, Pass., *to be clad in leather*, Str.17.3.11.

διφθεροπώλης, ου, ὁ, *leather-seller*, Nicoph.19.

διφθέρωμα, ατος, τό, = διφθέρα, Thd.*Is*.8.1.

διφθογγ-ίζω, *write with a diphthong*, Eust.1571.29. **-ιστέον**, *one must write with a diphthong*, Tz.*H*.5.690.

διφθογγογρᾰφέω, = διφθογγίζω, Sch.rec.S.*Aj*.715, etc.

διφθογγόομαι, *to be written with a diphthong*, Hdn.*Epim*.276.

δίφθογγος, ον, *with two sounds*, γραφή Tz.*H*.5.694: δίφθογγος, ἡ, *diphthong*, D.T.639.15, A.D.*Adv*.128.8, al.: later δίφθογγον, τό, Hdn.*Epim*.245.

δῐφορ-έω, *to bear double*, esp. of fruit, Thphr.*CP*1.14.1. II. Pass., *to be spelt* or *pronounced in two ways*, Hdn.Gr.2.543, *EM*197.51, al. III. διφορούμενος συλλογισμός syllogism with an identical proposition as premise, *Stoic*.2.87, al. **-ησις**, εως, ἡ, *double mode of writing*, Eust.74.1. **-ος**, ον, *bearing fruit twice in the year*, Ar. *Ec*.708, Pherecr.97, Antiph.198, Thphr.*HP*1.14.1. 2. *bearing two kinds of fruit*, Ph.2.369. II. metaph., *paying twice over*, of Ephorus, Hsch.

διφοῦρα, = γέφυρα (Lacon.), Hsch. **διφράγες**, name of a corps of Parthian soldiers, Id.

δίφρ-ακον, ου, τό, = δίφρος, *seat*, *Michel* 832.46 (Samos, iv B.C.). **-αξ**, ἄκος, ἡ, poet. for δίφρος, *seat, chair*, Theoc.14.41:—also **-άς**, άδος, ἡ, Hom.*Epigr*.15.8 (v.l. δίφρακα). **-εία**, ἡ, *chariot-driving*, X.*Cyr*.6.1.27, Procl.*H*.1.11 (pl.), Lib.*Decl*.12.14; δ. ἁρμάτων, ἵππων, Arr.*Tact*.19.4. **-ελάτειρα** [ᾰ], ἡ, pecul. fem. of διφρηλάτης, *APl*.4.359. **-ευτής**, οῦ, ὁ, *charioteer*, S.*Aj*.857. **-ευτικός**, ή, όν, *concerned with chariot-driving*, ἐπιστήμη Ephor.97 J. **-εύω**, *drive a chariot*, E.*Andr*.108 (eleg.), Heraclit.*Incred*.22. 2. c.acc., *drive over*, δ. ἅλιον πέλαγος E.*Andr*.1010 (lyr.); νὺξ.. νῶτα διφρεύουσ' αἰθέρος Id.*Fr*.114. 3. c. acc. cogn., αἴγλαν ἐδίφρευ' Ἅλιος.. κατ' αἰθέρα Id.*Supp*.991 (lyr.); ὅταν Φαέθων πυμάτην ἀψῖδα διφρεύῃ Archestr.*Fr*.33. 4. = διακαθίζω, Hsch. **-ηλᾰσία**, ἡ, *chariot-driving*, Pi.*O*.3.38. **-ηλᾰτέω**, *drive a chariot*, τὸν οὐρανὸν δ., of the Sun, S.*Aj*.845; δ. ἵππους E.*Rh*.781: in late Prose, Phlp. *in Mete*.101.27. **-ηλάτης** [ᾰ], ου, ὁ, *charioteer*, Pi.*P*.9.81, A.*Eu*.156 (lyr.), S.*El*.753, E.*IA*216 (lyr.), etc.—Poet. and later Prose, Luc.*DDeor*.25.1. **-ήλᾰτος**, ον, *car-borne*, E.*Fr*.1108. **-ίδιον**, τό, Dim. of δίφρος, *EM*718.45 (pl.). **-ίον**, τό, Dim. of δίφρος, Tim.*Lex*. s.v. σκολύθρια. **-ιος**, α, ον, *of a chariot*: neut. pl. as Adv., δίφρια συρόμενος dragged *at the chariot wheels*, *AP*7.152. **-ις**, ὁ, *sedentary person*, Hsch. (fort. διφρίας). **-ίσκος**, ὁ, Dim. of δίφρος, Ar.*Nu*.31.

δί-φροντις, ιδος, ὁ, ἡ, *divided in mind, doubting*, A.*Ch*.196.

διφροπηγία, ἡ, *cart-building*, Thphr.*HP*5.7.6.

δίφρος, ὁ, heterocl. pl. δίφρα, τά, Call.*Dian*.135, Nonn.*D*.27.238: (perh. for διφόρος):—*chariot-board*, on which *two* could stand, the driver (ἡνίοχος) and the combatant (παραιβάτης), Il.5.160, 11.748, Hes.*Sc*.61: metaph., ἕστηκεν ἐν τῷ δ. τῆς πόλεως Pl.*R*.566d. 2. *chariot*, Il.10.305, al., Pi.*P*.2.10, al., Arr.*Tact*.19.3, etc.; ἐϋπλέκτῳ ἐνὶ δίφρῳ Il.23.335; μεταμείβοντος δίφρον ἐκ δίφρου Jul.*Or*.3.122b; of the Sun's *chariot*, E.*Ph*.2, Call.*Dian*.111; Μοισᾶν δ. Pi.*O*.9.81; *travelling-car*, Od.3.324; *litter*, δ. κατάστεγος D.C.60.2. II. *seat, couch, stool*, Il.3.424, 6.354, Od.19.97, Ar.*Eq*.1164, Pl.*R*.328c, etc.; δ. Θετταλικός Eup.58; = Lat. *sella curulis*, Plb.6.53.9, etc.; judge's *seat of office*, Lxx 1*Ki*.1.9, al.; royal *throne*, *OGI*199.38 (i A.D.); *night-stool*, Aristid.*Or*.49(25).19.

διφρ-ουλκέω, (ἕλκω) *draw a chariot*, *AP*9.285 (Phil.). **-ουργία**, ἡ, (ἔργον) *making chairs*, Thphr.*HP*3.10.1. **-οῦχος**, ον, (ἔχω) *with a seat*, ἅρμα Melanipp.1.

διφρο-φορέω, *carry in a chair* or *litter*, D.C.47.10:—Pass., *travel in one*, οἱ διφροφορούμενοι, of the Persian princes, Hdt.3.146, cf. D.C.60.2, Lib.*Or*.25.32. II. *carry a camp-stool* (cf. sq.), Ar.*Av*.1552. **-φόρος**, ον, *carrying a camp-stool*; esp. of the female μέτοικοι, who had to carry seats for the use of the κανηφόροι, Id.*Ec*.734, Hermipp.26, Nicoph.16, Strattis 8; also ὁ βασιλέως δ. Dinon 18.

δι-φρῠγής, ές, (φρύγω) *twice roasted*: διφρυγές, τό, *baked clay* or *pyrites from copper-mines*, Dsc.5.103,125, Gal.12.214. **-φῠής**, ές: neut. pl. διφυῆ, also διφυᾶ Arist.*PA*669^{b}18 (s.v.l.):—*of double nature* or *form*, ἔχιδνα μειξοπάρθενος δ. Hdt.4.9; of Centaurs, S.*Tr*.1095, Pherecyd.50 J.; of Pan, Pl.*Cra*.408d; Κέκροψ, i.e. man and serpent, but expld. as *of double sex* (Suid.), or *of double race* (Egyptian and Greek), D.S.1.28; δ. Ἔρως *sexual intercourse*, Orph.*A*.14. 2. generally, *twofold, double*, κόραι Ion Lyr.16; ὀφρύες Arist. *HA*491^{b}14; στῆθος διφυὲς μαστοῖς ib.493^{a}12; ἡ τῶν μυκτήρων δύναμις Id.*PA*657^{a}4; μῦς, of the biceps, Gal.*UP*13.13; αὐλός Aret.*SD*2.13. **-φῠΐα**, ἡ, *bipartition*, τῶν κώλων Arist.*PA*668^{b}22. **-φυιος** [ῐ], ον, = διφυής, Antag.1.7. II. = δύο, A.*Ag*.1469 (lyr.). III. = διπλοῦς, *Schwyzer* 411.5, 419.8 (Elis): **ζίφ-** prob. in ib.410.1 (ibid.). **-φωνος**, ον, *speaking two languages*, Philist.62, D.S.17.110.

δίχᾰ [ῐ], (δίς), I. Adv. *in two, asunder*, δ. πάντας.. ἠρίθμεον Od.10.203; δ. πάντα δέδασται 15.412; πλευροκοπῶν δ. ἀνερρήγνυ S. *Aj*.236; δ. πρίσαντες Th.4.100; τέμνειν δ. Pl.*Sph*.265e; δ. διαλαβεῖν Id.*Tht*.147e; δ. τὸ στράτευμα ποιεῖν X.*An*.6.4.11; δ. τὴν δύναμιν λαβεῖν catch the force *divided*, Th.6.10; ὅτι δ. πέφυκε (sc. ἡ Σικελία) is *divided against itself*, Id.4.61: generally, *apart, aloof*, διαστῆναι Hdt.4.180; κεῖσθαι Pi.*P*.5.93; οἰκεῖν S.*OC*602. 2. metaph., *at two, two ways*, whether with others or oneself, *at variance* or *in doubt*, δ. δέ σφισι ἥνδανε βουλή Il.18.510; δίχα θυμὸν ἔχοντες 20.32; δ. δέ σφιν ἐνὶ φρεσὶ θυμὸς ἄητο 21.386; δ. θυμὸς ἐνὶ φρεσὶ μερμηρίζει Od.16.73; δ. θυμὸς ὀρώρεται ἔνθα καὶ ἔνθα 19.524; δίχα βάζομεν 3.127; δ. μοι τὰ νοήμματα prob. in Sapph.36; μιῇ γλώσσῃ δ. ἔχειν νόον Thgn.91, etc.; ἐγίνοντο δ. αἱ γνῶμαι Hdt.6.109; δόξα δ' ἐχώρει δίχα E.*Hec*.117; μαθήσεται ὅσον τό τ' ἄρχειν καὶ τὸ δουλεύειν δίχα *differ*, A.*Pr*.927; τὸ γὰρ τοπάζειν τοῦ σάφ' εἰδέναι δ. Id.*Ag*.1369; δ. ψηφίζεσθαι *on different sides*, X.*Mem*.4.4.8; ἐὰν δ. γένηται τὸ δικαστήριον Arist.*Pol*.1318^{a}40. II. Prep., c. gen., *apart from*, Emp.21.19; *without*, πυρός, ἄρσενος, A.*Th*.25, *Ag*.861; ἀνθρώπων δ. S.*Ph*.31; οἷος Ἀτρειδῶν δ. Id.*Aj*.750; μόνη.. φασγάνου δ. Id.*Tr*.1063; δ. τέλους *Supp.Epigr*.1.329.25 (Istros, i A.D.); δ. γνώμης ἐμῆς καὶ συγκαταθέσεως *PFlor*.58.8 (iii A.D.); δ. πραγμάτων Jul.*Or*.7.212a, etc. 2. *differently from, unlike*, δ. ἄλλων A.*Ag*.757; σῆς δ. γνώμης λέγω S.*El*.

547. 3. πόλεως δ. *against the will of*, Id.*OC*48, cf. *Aj.*768. 4. *except*, δ. γε Διός A.*Pr.*163; τῶν λελεγμένων δ. Id.*Ch.*778. 5. *besides*, dub. in D.H.7.19.—As a Prep. it commonly follows its case in Trag., but precedes it in A.*Pr.* l. c., S.*Ph.*195, al., E.*IT*185.

δῐχάδε, Adv. = δίχα, διοιχθέντες Pl.*Smp.*215b.

δῐχάδεια, = δίχα (?), Theognost.*Can.*164.26.

δῐχάζω, fut. -άσω Plot.5.3.10:—*divide in two*, Pl.*Plt.*264d (of logical dichotomy):—Pass., Nonn.*D.*3.33, al.; αἴγειρος.. δισσοῖσι κλάδοις δεδιχασμένη ἑνὸς ἐκ στελέχους Lyr.in*Philol.*80.334; δεδιχασμένον διχασμῷ Aq.*De.*14.6. b. *divide by two*, Nicom.*Ar.*1.7, al. (Pass.). 2. δ. τινὰ κατά τινος *divide* one against another, *Ev.Matt.*10.35. II. intr., *to be divided*, interpol. in X.*An.*4.8.18; διχαζούσης ἡμέρας at *mid*-day, Anon.ap.Suid.

δῐ́χαιος, coined to expl. δίκαιος, Arist.*EN*1132^{a}32.

δῐχαίτης, *disulcis*, *Gloss.*

δῐχαίω, = διχάζω, in Pass., Arat.495,807.

δῐ-χάλα, ἡ, Dor. for διχήλη, the *fork* of the legs, Medici ap.Gal. 14.707. **-χαλκον**, τό, *double chalcus*, a copper coin, = $\frac{1}{4}$ of an obol, *AP*11.165 (Lucill.), Poll.9.65; as a weight (variously expld.), Dsc.4.150, etc. **-χᾱλος**, Dor. for δίχηλος (q. v.). II. δίχαλον· ζυγόν· τὸν ἑκατέρωθεν κεκοιλασμένον, Hsch.

δῐχάμετρος, ον, to explain διάμετρος, Arist.*Pr.*910^{b}20.

δῐ́χανον· κεχωρισμένον, Hsch.

δῐχάρακτος [χᾰ], ον, [νόμισμα] *doubly stamped*, i. e. in mint condition, *IGRom.*4.595 (Phrygia).

δῐχ-άς, άδος, ἡ, *the half, middle*, Arat.807. **-ᾰσις**, εως, ἡ, *division, halving*, Id.737. **-ασμός**, ὁ, *division into two parts*, Aq.*De.*14. 6. 2. *division by two*, Nicom.*Ar.*1.10. II. *payment in two instalments*, dub. in Ἀρχ.Ἐφ.1917.133 (Perrhaebia). **-αστής**, οῦ, ὁ, *divider*, to explain δικαστής, Arist.*EN*1132^{a}32. **-αστῆρες** ὀδόντες, οἱ, *the incisors*, Poll.2.91. **-αστός**, ή, όν, *divisible by two*, *Theol.Ar.*35. **-άω**, poet. for διχάζω, Ep. part. διχόωντι, -όωσα, Arat.512,605:—Med., διχόωνται Id.856:—Pass., διχόωντο A.R.4. 1616.

δίχειλον, *bilabrum*, *Gloss.*

δῐχή, ἡ, *bisection*, Ascl.*in Metaph.*34.19.

δῐχῇ, Adv. = δίχα, *in two, asunder*, A.*Supp.*544 (lyr.), Pl.*Ti.*62c, etc. 2. *in two ways*, δ. ἐπονομασθῆναι Id.*R.*445d; δεῖ δ. τὴν βοήθειαν εἶναι D.1.18.

δῐχηλ-έω, ὁπλὴν δ. *divide* the hoof, Arist.*PA*695^{a}18 (v.l.), Aristeas150, Lxx *Le.*11.3, al., Ph.2.353 (**διχηλεύω** is v.l. in Lxx *De.*14. 6). **-ησις**, εως, ἡ, *dividing of the hoofs*, Ph.1.321: -ία, ἡ, = foreg., Aristeas161. **-ος**, ον, *cloven-hoofed*, Hdt.2.71; δ. ἔμβασις E.*Ba.*740:—freq. in Dor. form **δῐ́χᾱλος**, Arist.*PA*663^{a}31, al. II. *with two pincers, prongs*, or *claws*, πυραγρέτης *AP*6.92 (Phil.); πάγουρος ib.196 (Stat. Flacc.), cf. Hero*Bel.*76.10; δίχιλα (sic) ξύλα *BGU* 37.4 (i A. D.); εἰς δίχηλον διεσχισμένος Hero*Spir.*1.28. III. Subst., δίχηλα ὕεια pigs' *trotters*, Luc.*Lex.*6; cf. διχάλα.

δῐχήρης, ες, *dividing in twain*, κύκλος... μηνὸς διχήρης, of the moon, E.*Ion*1156.

διχθά, Adv., Ep. for δίχα, δ. δεδαίαται they are parted *in twain*, Od.1.23; δ. δέ μοι κραδίη μέμονε my heart is *divided*, Il.16.435.

διχθάδιος [ᾰ], α, ον, *twofold, double*, κῆρες Il.9.411, 14.21; δ. κατὰ κῶλον *in either* leg, *APl.*1.15; simply, *two*, *AP*6.4 (Leon.), al.

διχθάς, άδος, ἡ, fem. of foreg., Musae.298.

δῐχίτων [χῐ], ωνος, ὁ, ἡ, *with two coats*, ἀρτηρίαι Gal.4.728:—also **δῐχίτωνος**, ον, Id.19.366.

δῐχό-βουλος, ον, *of different counsel, adverse*, Νέμεσις Pi.*O.*8. 86. **-γνωμέω**, = sq., Poll.2.229. **-γνωμονέω**, *to differ in opinion*, X.*Mem.*2.6.21, D.C.44.25; δ. πρὸς ἑαυτόν Iamb.ap.Stob.2. 33.15. 2. *doubt*, Lib.*Decl.*43.43. **-γνωμος**, ον, *ambiguous*, Sch.E.*Or.*890. **-γνωμοσύνη**, ἡ, *discord*, Poll.8.153. **-γνώμων**, ὁ, ἡ, gen. ονος, *divided between two opinions*, Plu.2.11c. Adv. -γνωμόνως Poll.8.154. **-γρᾰφέω**, *write in two ways*, St.Byz. s.v. Δώτιον (Pass.). **-ζωνος**, ον, = διχόμηνος, Doroth. in *Cat.Cod.Astr.* 2.82. **-θεν**, Adv. *from both sides, both ways*, A.*Pers.*76 (lyr.), Ar. *Pax*477, Th.2.44, etc.; δ. μισθοφορεῖν D.24.123; *from two sources*, τὸ δίκαιον δ. συνίσταται Aps.*Rh.*p.294H. **-θῡμος**, ον, *wavering*, cj. in Pittac.1 Bgk.

δῐχοινῑκ-ία, ἡ, *tax of two* χοίνικες *per* ἄρουρα, *PLond.*372.25 (ap. *PTeb.*ii p.339) (ii A. D.), etc. **-ιος**, ον, = sq., *PSI*1.33.18 (iii A. D.). **-ος**, ον, *holding two* χοίνικες, Ar.*Nu.*640. II. Subst. διχοίνικον, τό, *measure of two* χ., *SIG*945.4 (pl., Assos, iv B. C.).

δῐ́-χολος [ῐ], ον, *with double gall*, Ael.*NA*11.29. II. *at variance*, πόλις cj. in Alc.37 A; δ. γνῶμαι, = διάφοροι, Achae.39. **-χόλωτος**, ον, *doubly furious*, v.l. for τριχόλωτος, ἀνάγκη *AP*9.168 (Pall.).

δῐχό-μην, ηνος, ὁ, ἡ, = διχόμηνος, σελήνη Arat.78, cf. 737. **-μηνία**, ἡ, *full moon*, *IG*1^{2}.6.62, *PRev.Laws*56.18 (iii B. C.), Lxx*Si.*39.12, Gem.8.1, etc.; δ. μηνὸς Μεταγειτνιῶνος *Inscr.Prien.*4.45 (iv B. C.); ἡ σελήνη δ. ἦγεν Plu.*Dio*23. 2. *mid-menstrual period*, Hp. *Oct.*13. **-μηνιαία** (sc. ἡμέρα), ἡ, *day of full moon*, Gal.9.908; also, = Lat. *Idus*, Suid. **-μηνιάς**, άδος, ἡ, = διχόμηνις, Max. 454. **-μηνις**, ιδος, ὁ, ἡ, = sq., Μήνα Pi.*O.*3.19, cf. A.R.4.167; δ. ἑσπέραι evenings *at the full of the moon*, Pi.*I.*8(7).47; νύξ B.8. 29. II. ἡμέρα, = Lat. *Idus*, D.H.1.38, etc. **-μηνος**, ον, (μήν) *dividing the month*, i. e. *at* or *of the full moon*, ἑσπερίη *h.Hom.*32.11; δ. σελήνη *Gp.*10.48.2, cf. Plu.*Flam.*4; διχόμηνος, ἡ, Arat.808, Ph.2. 293; διχομήνη, ἡ, *Gp.*2.14.7, *Cat.Cod.Astr.*1.173. **-μῡθος**, ον, *double-speaking*, νόημα Pittac.1 Bgk.; γλῶσσα Sol.42.4; *double-dealing, deceptive*, Ant.Lib.23; λέγειν διχόμυθα speak *ambiguously*, E.*Or.*890.

διχόνδις· ἀπύγων, Hsch.

δῐχο-νοέω, = διχογνωμονέω, condemned by Poll.2.228. **-νοητικός**, ή, όν, *indicating doubt*, Eust.166.28. Adv. -κῶς *discordantly*, *Gloss.* **-νοια**, ἡ, *discord, disagreement*, Pl.*Alc.*1.126c, Plu.2. 70c; δ. περὶ τοῦ ἀρίστου Ph.2.181: c. gen., *disagreement with*, τῆς Ἀντωνίου γνώμης App.*BC*5.33. **-νοος**, ον, contr. **-νους**, ουν, *double-minded*, Ph.2.269, cf. 663. **-ποιός**, όν, *productive of division*, opp. ἑνοποιός, Alex.Aphr.*in Metaph.*58.11.

δῐ́-χορδος [ῐ], ον, *two-stringed*, πηκτίς Sopat.11:—Subst. **-χορδον**, τό, Euphro1.34. **-χόρειος** (sc. πούς), ὁ, *ditrochaeus*, Longin. 41.1. **-χορία**, ἡ, *division of a chorus into two parts*, Poll.4.107, Arg.Ar.*Lys.*1. **-χοριάζω**, *sing in two halves*, of a chorus, Hsch.

δῐχο-ρρᾰγής, ές, (ῥήγνυμι) *broken in twain*, E.*HF*1008 (lyr.). **-ρροπος**, ον, *oscillating*, γνώμη *Trag.Adesp.*341. Adv. -πως *waveringly, doubtfully*, used only by A., and always with a neg., οὐ or μὴ δ. *Ag.*349,815,1272, *Supp.*605,982. **-στᾰσία**, ἡ, *dissension*, B. 10.67 (pl.), Hdt.5.75, Eus.Mynd.45, Plu.2.20c; *sedition*, Sol.4.38, Thgn.78, Lxx1*Ma.*3.29. **-στᾰτέω**, (στῆναι) *stand apart, disagree*, ὄξος τ' ἄλειφά τ'... διχοστατοῦντ' ἂν οὐ φίλως προσεννέποις A.*Ag.* 323; δ. λάχη Id.*Eu.*386 (lyr.); λόγος S.*Fr.*867; δ. πρός τινα E.*Med.* 15, Pl.*R.*465b. II. *feel doubts*, Alex.Aphr.*Pr.Praef.* **-στομος**, ον, = δίστομος II, δορὸς πλᾶκτρον S.*Fr.*152. **-τομέω**, *cut in twain*: *bisect* a line, Plb.6.28.2:—Pass., Arist.*Pr.*913^{b}31; σώματος -ηθέντος Plu.*Pyrrh.*24: metaph. of the medial raphe of the perineum, Paul.Aeg.6.62, etc. 2. *punish with the last severity*, *Ev.Matt.*24. 51. 3. *divide into two* (logically), Pl.*Plt.*302e, Arist.*PA*642^{b}22, 644^{b}19. 4. intr., of the moon, dub. in Plu.2.929f. **-τόμημα**, ατος, τό, *half of a thing cut in two*: hence, generally, *any portion of a thing cut up*, Lxx *Ex.*29.17, *Le.*1.8, Ph.1.503 (pl.). **-τόμησις**, εως, ἡ, = sq., κύκλου S.E.*M.*9.284. **-τομία**, ἡ, *dividing in two*, of the moon's quarters, Arist.*GA*777^{b}22, Gem.9.3, Simp.*in Ph.*455.22; *bisection*, Theo Sm.p.184H. 2. *point of bisection*, Archim.*Aequil.* 1.6, al. b. *point of division* between wings of army, Ascl.*Tact.*2. 6. II. *division into two parts* (logically), *dichotomy*, Arist.*PA* 644^{a}9, Iamb.*Comm.Math.*1. **-τομιαῖος**, α, ον, = sq., Paul.Al.*G.* 4. **-τόμος**, ον, *cutting in two*, Ammon.p.44V.: but, II. proparox., διχότομος, ον, *cut in half, divided equally*, μυκτήρ Arist. *HA*492^{b}17; δ. σελήνη the *half*-moon, Id.*Pr.*911^{b}36, Aristarch.Sam. *Hyp.*3, Gem.9.8, prob. in Plu.2.929f; σελήνης σύμβολον τὸ δ. Porph. ap.Eus.*PE*3.11; μέχρι διχοτόμου till *the second quarter*, Antyll.ap. Orib.9.3.2; κατ' ἀμφοτέρας τὰς διχοτόμους (sc. φάσεις) at *the first and third quarters*, Ptol.*Alm.*5.1.

δῐχοῦ, Adv. = δίχα, δ. σφέας διελόντες Hdt.4.120, Choer.*in Theod.* 1.388.

δῐ́-χους [ῐ], ουν, neut. pl. δίχοα, *holding two* χόες, Posidon.25 J., Arist.*Ath.*67.2; δίχουν, τό, Dsc.5.57.

δῐχο-φορέω, = sq., Plu.2.447d. **-φρονέω**, *to hold different opinions*, ib.763e. **-φροσύνη**, ἡ, *discord, faction*, ib.824d (pl.), Ocell.4.6, D.Chr.44.10, Anon.ap.Iamb.*VP*7.34. **-φρων**, ον, gen. ονος, (φρήν) *at variance*, πότμος δ. a destiny *full of discord*, A.*Th.*899 (lyr.). **-φυής**, ές, *forked*, Gal.14.707. **-φυΐα**, ἡ, *a disease of the hair, when it splits*, Id.19.430. **-φωνέω**, *disagree*, Pythagorei ap.Iamb.*in Nic.*p.73P. **-φωνία**, ἡ, (φωνή) *discord*, Id.*VP*7.34.

διχόω, f.l. for δικραιόω in Hp.*Oss.*10.

δῐ́-χροια, ἡ, *double colour*, Arist.*GA*751^{a}32. **-χρονία**, ἡ, in Metric, *two short syllables*, Sch.Heph.p.110C. II. Pythag. name for *six*, *Theol.Ar.*37. **-χρονος**, ον, in Metre, *of two quantities, common*, D.H.*Comp.*14, Plu.2.737e, S.E.*M.*1.100; περὶ διχρόνων, title of treatise by Hdn.Gr. II. *consisting of two short syllables*, [πούς] Heph.3.1, cf. Arc.139.20: metaph. of the pulse, Ruf.*Syn. Puls.*4.4. III. *equivalent to two time-units*, Longin.*Proll.Heph.* p.87C. **-χροος**, ον, contr. **-χρους**, ουν, *two-coloured*, ᾠά Arist.*HA* 489^{b}14, *GA*749^{a}18. **-χρωμος**, ον, = foreg., Luc.*Prom.Es*4, Gal.13. 460. II. Subst. δίχρωμος, ἡ, name of a *plaster*, Aët.15.13. 2. δίχρωμον, τό, = περιστερεὼν ὕπτιος, Ps.-Dsc.4.60. **-χρως**, ων, = foreg., Arist.*HA*564^{b}24. **-χρωτος**, ον, = foreg., *Gloss.*

δίχωρον, τό, *a measure of wine* in Egypt, = eight χόες, *BGU*531 ii 5 (i A. D.), etc.

δῐχῶς, Adv. *doubly, in two ways*, A.*Ch.*915 (dub.), Arist.*Mu.*393^{a} 24, Ascl.*Tact.*10.10; *in two senses*, Arist.*Po.*1457^{a}28.

δῐ́ψα, ης, ἡ, *thirst*, δ. τε καὶ λιμός Il.19.166; πεῖνα καὶ δ. Pl.*R.*585a; δίψῃ ξυνέχεσθαι Th.2.49, etc.; of trees, Antiph.231.6, *PFlor.*176.12 (iii A.D.): pl., Arist.*EN*1154^{b}3. 2. c. gen., *thirst for*, ποτοῦ Pl. *R.*437d: metaph., ἀοιδᾶν δ. Pi.*P.*9.104.—The form **δίψη** occurs in Opp.*C.*4.339, and in codd. of A.*Ch.*756; cf. δίψος.

δῐ́ψαι· βλάψαι, Hsch.; cf. δίψιος I. fin.

διψ-ᾰκερός, ά, όν, *thirsty*, *EM*801.48; expld. by ταλαίπωρον, Hsch. **-ᾰκος**, ὁ, prob. a kind of *diabetes, attended with violent thirst*, Gal.8.394, Alex.Trall.11.6. II. *teasel*, *Dipsacus fullonum*, Dsc.3.11, Gal.11.864. **-ᾰλέος**, α, ον, *thirsty*, μῦς Batr.9; ἀνήρ Call. *Jov.*27, cf. *AP*9.128; ἐπιθυμία Ph.1.116; δ. θρυαλλίδιον *wanting oil*, Luc.*Tim.*14; ὀδύνη δ. the pain *of thirst*, Id.*Dips.*6; ὄργανα δ. *subject to thirst*, Aret.*SA*2.4. 2. *dry, parched*, ἀήρ A.R.4.678, Nonn.*D.* 22.260, al. II. *thirst-provoking*, χοῖρος *AP*9.487 (Pall.). **-άρα**· δέλτος, οἱ δὲ διφθέρα, Hsch. **-άς**, άδος, used as fem. of δίψιος, βοτάναι Euph.141; χῶραι J.*BJ*3.3.4, cf. Opp.*C.*4.322, etc. II. Subst., *venomous serpent, whose bite caused intense thirst*, Nic.*Th.*334, Ael.

*NA*6.51; δ. ἔχιδνα *AP*7.172 (Antip. Sid.), *IG*4.620.4 (Argos). 2. δ. ἄκανθα a desert *thorn*, *Acacia tortilis*, Thphr.*HP*4.7.1. **-άω**, late Ep. -ώω Tryph.548, *AP*11.57 (Agath.): Ion. -έω Archil.68; part. διψεῦσα *AP*6.21; contr. 3 sg. διψῇ Pi.*N*.3.6, Pl.*Phlb*.35b; inf. διψῆν Hdt.2.24, S.*Fr*.735, Ar.*Nu*.441, etc.: impf. 3 sg. ἐδίψη Hp. *Epid*.3.1.β′, γ′ (διψᾶς, -ᾷ, -ᾶν only in later writers, *APl*.4.137 (Phil.), Pl.*Ax*.366a, Lxx *Is*.29.8, Gal.5.837): fut. -ήσω X.*Mem*.2.1.17: aor. ἐδίψησα Pl.*R*.562c: pf. δεδίψηκα Hp.*Cord*.2, Plu.*Pomp*.73:—Med. (v. infr.):—*thirst*, στεῦτο δὲ διψάων [ᾱ] Od.11.584, etc.; of the ground, *to be thirsty, parched*, Hdt.2.24; δ. ὑπὸ καύματος Alc.39.2; of trees, Thphr.*CP*3.22.5:—Med., διψώμεθα Hermipp.25. 2. metaph., δ. τινός *thirst after* a thing, Pi.*N*.3.6; ἐλευθερίας Pl.*R*.562c: later c. acc., δ. Χῖον Teles p.8 H.; φόνον *APl*.4.137 (Phil.); δικαιοσύνην *Ev.Matt*. 5.6; αἷμα J.*BJ*1.32.2; also δ. πρὸς τὸν θεόν Lxx *Ps*.41(42).2: c. dat., ὕδατι ib.*Ex*.17.3: c. inf., διψῶ χαρίζεσθαι ὑμῖν X.*Cyr*.5.1.1; ἀκρατῶς ἐδίψη οἶνον πίνειν Ael.*VH*2.41, etc. **-ηρός**, ά, όν, = δίψιος, Hp.*Aër*.7; [οἶνος] Posidipp.34 (s. v. l.):—also **-ήρης**, ες, Nic.*Th*. 371. **-ησις**, εως, ἡ, *a thirst, longing*, Ath.1.10b; cf. δίψα. **-ητικός**, ή, όν, *thirsty*, Arist.*PA*671ᵃ2. 2. *provoking thirst*, ὁ φόβος -κόν Id.*Pr*.947ᵇ39: Comp., Dsc.1.128. **-ιος**, α, ον, also ος, ον A.*Ch*. 185, Nic.*Th*.147: (δίψα):—*thirsty*, and of things, *dry, parched*, δ. κόνις A.*Ag*.495, S.*Ant*.246; χθών E.*Alc*.560; πῦρ θεοῦ Id.*Rh*.417; ἐξ ὀμμάτων δὲ δίψιοι πίπτουσι σταγόνες, perh. tears *checked in their flow*, A.*Ch*.185; δίψιον, expld. by βεβλαμμένον, S.*Fr*.296, by βλαπτικόν, Hsch.; cf. δῖψαι. II. *causing thirst*, ὕδατα Hermipp.ap.J.*Ap*.1. 22; δ. σήψ Nic.*Th*.147; cf. διψάς II.

διψοποιός, όν, *provoking thirst*, Dsc.5.6, Sch.Theoc.7.66.

δίψος, εος, τό, = δίψα, Th.7.87 codd., X.*Cyr*.8.1.36, Pl.*Phd*.94b, Nic.*Th*.774, Luc.*Hist.Conscr*.28, etc., v. l. for δίψα in Ar.*Eq*.534, Th. 4.35. (Sch.Il.19.166 calls δίψος Attic, δίψα Ionic; both forms in Lxx, cf. *Wi*.11.4,8; δίψος 2*Ep.Cor*.11.27.)

διψοσύνη [ῠ], ἡ, = δίψα, Orac.ap.Porph.ap.Eus.*PE*6.2.

διψυχ-ία· ἀπορία, Hsch. **-ος**, ον, *double-minded*, Ph.2.663, *Ep.Jac*.1.8.

διψώδης, ες, *thirsty*, Hp.*Aph*.4.54, Plu.2.129b, Aret.*SA*2.4; τοῦ πάθους τὸ μανικὸν καὶ δ. Plu.2.555c. II. *exciting thirst*, Hp.*Acut*. 50, Diph.Siph.ap.Ath.2.71e.

δίω [ῐ], Ep. Verb (used also by A. in lyr. passages, v. sub fin.), only pres. and impf. Med. (of which Hom. has subj. δίωμαι, δίηται, δίωνται, opt. δίοιτο Od.17.317, but mostly inf. δίεσθαι; for δίον v. δείδω):—*put to flight*, δηΐους προτὶ ἄστυ δίεσθαι Il.12.276; [μητέρα] ἀπὸ μεγάροιο δίεσθαι Od.20.343; μή σε .. ἀγρόνδε δίωμαι βάλλων χερμαδίοισι 21.370; ὡς δ᾽ ὅτε νεβρὸν .. κύων .. δίηται Il.22.189; ἐπεί κ᾽ ἀπὸ ναῦφι μάχην .. δίηται 16.246; rarely, *drive*, ὅς τ᾽ .. ἵππους .. προτὶ ἄστυ δίηται 15.681; also in A., ἀτίετα διόμεναι λάχη *pursuing* a dishonoured office, *Eu*.385 (lyr.); and intr. folld. by Prep., *give chase, hunt*, ἐπὶ τὸν ὦ διόμεναι ib.357 codd. (ὧδ᾽ ἱέμεναι Ahrens); μετά με δρόμοισι διόμενοι Id.*Supp*.819; f. l. for δίεμαι, Id.*Pers*.700.

δῐ-ωβελία, ἡ, (ὀβολός) at Athens, *a daily allowance of two obols* to needy citizens, *IG*1².304, al., prob. for Δεκελείας in X.*HG*1.7.2, cf. Arist.*Pol*.1267ᵇ2 (-βολία codd.). **-ωβολιαῖος**, α, ον, *weighing two obols*, Archig.ap.Gal.13.264, etc. **-ώβολον**, τό, *double obol*, Ar.*Fr*.3, Alex.186, Theopomp.Com.55, Arist.*Ath*.41.3.

δίωγ-μα, ατος, τό, *pursuit, chase*, A.*Eu*.139 (pl.), Plb.1.34.9, Onos. 10.6 (pl.); δ. πώλων, = τοὺς διώκοντας πώλους, E.*Or*.988; ὑπ᾽ αἰετοῦ δ. φεύγων Id.*Hel*.20; δ. ξιφοκτόνον, i. e. the sword, ib.354; τὰ πλούτου δ. *eager pursuit* of wealth, Pl.*Plt*.310b. II. *that which is chased*, X. *Cyn*.3.9. III. a secret rite in the Thesmophoria, *from which men were driven away*, Hsch. **-μείτης**, ου, ὁ, *mounted policeman*, *CIG*3831a8 (Aezani). **-μητικά**, τά, *fees*, = Lat. *persecutiones*, *Cod.Just*.10.30.4.4. **-μός**, ὁ, *the chase*, X.*Cyr*.1.4.21, etc. 2. *pursuit*, D.S.4.13, al., Ael.*Tact*.34.4, Iamb.*VP*31.191. II. *persecution, harassing*, in pl., A.*Supp*.148,1046, E.*Or*.412; also in later Prose, Plu.2.483a: sg., *Ev.Matt*.13.21, *Act.Ap*.8.1.

διώδῠνος, ον, (ὀδύνη) *with thrilling anguish*, σπαραγμός S.*Tr*. 777.

διωθ-έω, aor. διῶσα Hom. (v. infr.), διέωσα X.*HG*2.1.8, ἐδίωσα codd. in Hero *Aut*.24.3:—*push asunder, tear away*, [πτελέη] ἐκ ῥιζέων ἐριποῦσα κρημνὸν .. διῶσε the elm as it fell uprooted *tore* the bank *away*, Il.21.244; διώσας καὶ κατακτείνας ἐχθρούς E.*Heracl*.995; *drive apart*, τῶν ὀφθαλμῶν τὰς διεξόδους Pl.*Ti*.67e. 2. *thrust through*, τι διά τινος X.*HG*2.1.8, Plb.21.28.14. II. more freq. in Med. (fut. διώσομαι Democr.191), *force one's way through, break through*, τὰ γέρρα Hdt.9.102; τὸν ὄχλον X.*Cyr*.7.5.39; τὰς τάξεις Plb.11.1. 12; δ. τὴν ὕλην, of roots, Thphr.*HP*8.11.8; τὴν θάλατταν, of a river, Plb.4.41.4. 2. *push from oneself, push away*, τοῖς κόντοις διεωθοῦντο, of sailors, Th.2.84; ἡ γαστὴρ δ. τὸ περιττὸν εἰς τὴν νῆστιν Gal. 5.567; *repulse*, στρατὸν ἰθυμαχίῃ Hdt.4.102; οἷς [πέτροις] .. διώσει στρατόν A.*Fr*.199.9 (Dobr.); κῆρας Democr. l. c.; τὰς τύχας E.*HF* 315; ψευδῆ λόγον καὶ συκοφαντίαν *repel* it, D.21.124; τὴν ἐπιβουλὴν Id.58.65: abs., *get rid of danger*, Hdt.9.88. 3. *reject*, τὴν εὔνοιαν Id.7.104; ὃ μὴ προσίενται Th.4.108; τὴν ἐπικουρίαν Arist.*EN*1163ᵇ 25; of bribes, D.19.139: abs., *refuse*, Hdt.6.86.β′, Plu.*Brut*.52: so pf. Pass. διῶσμαι cj. for δίωμαι in this sense, Thgn.1311. **-ησις**, εως, ἡ, *thrusting*, Hero *Spir*.1.11. **-ίζομαι**, *scuffle, jostle*, App.*BC* 2.117. **-ισμός**, ὁ, *pushing about, scuffle*, Plu.*Cam*.29 (pl.).

διωκ-άθω [ᾰ], pres. assumed by Gramm. as lengthd. form of διώκω and read in Pl.*Euthphr*.15d, E.*Fr*.362.25 codd. Stob.: the remaining forms may be referred to an aor. **διωκαθεῖν**: Subj. διωκάθω Ar. *Nu*.1482: 2 sg. ἐδιώκαθες Pl.*Grg*.483a, etc. **-τέος**, α, ον, verb. Adj. of διώκω, *to be pursued*, Hdt.9.58, Ar.*Ach*.221. 2. of objects, *to be pursued*, Pl.*Tht*.167d, etc. II. διωκτέον *one must pursue*, Id.*Grg*.507d, al.: pl., διωκτέα ἐφαίνετο Arr.*An*.3.21.6. **-τήρ**, ῆρος, ὁ, *pursuer*, Babr.128.14. **-της**, ου, ὁ, = foreg., 1*Ep.Ti*.1. 13. **-τικός**, ή, όν, *apt to pursue, follow* a course [χρυσὸς] δ. τῆς ἐπὶ τὸ μέσον φορᾶς Iamb.*Protr*.21.λε′; *swift in pursuit*, *EM*468. 23. **-τός**, ή, όν, *driven into exile, banished*, S.*Fr*.1041. 2. of objects, *to be pursued*, Chrysipp.ap.Ath.1.8d, Arist.*EN*1097ᵃ31. **-τρια**, ἡ, fem. of διωκτήρ, Sch.A.*Eu*.206. **-τύς**, ύος, ἡ, Ion. for δίωξις, *persecution*, Call.*Dian*.194. **-τωρ**, ορος, ὁ, = διωκτήρ, cj. for διάκτορα, *AP*10.101 (Bianor).

διώκω, Ep. inf. διωκέμεναι, -έμεν (v. infr.): fut. -ξω Sapph.1.21, Pi.*O*.3.45, X.*Cyr*.6.3.13 (s. v. l.), *An*.1.4.8, D.38.16 codd.; but διώξομαι Ar.*Eq*.368 (and Elmsl. restored διώξει for -εις in *Eq*.969, *Nu*.1296, *Th*.1224), Pl.*Tht*.168a: aor. ἐδίωξα: aor. 2 ἐδιώκαθον (v. διωκάθω): pf. δεδίωχα Hyp.*Lyc*.16:—Med. (v. infr.):—Pass., fut. διωχθήσομαι D.S.19.95, Polyaen.2.13; but διώξομαι in pass. sense, Lxx *Am*.2.16, D.H.3.20: aor. ἐδιώχθην Hdt.5.73, Antipho 2.1.3,6, (ἐπ-, κατ-) Th.3.69, 3.4: pf. δεδίωγμαι *Ev.Matt*.5.10: (cf. ϝιώκω *GDI*3153 (Corinthian vase); v. δίω):—*cause to run, set in quick motion*, opp. φεύγω: 1. *pursue, chase*, in war or hunting, φεύγοντα διώκειν Il.22.199, etc.: abs., πεδίοιο διωκέμεν ἠδὲ φέβεσθαι 5.223, cf. Hdt.9.11:—Med., διώκεσθαί τινα πεδίοιο, δόμοιο, *chase* one over or across .., Il.21.602, Od.18.8. b. c. acc. pers., of a lover, Sapph. l. c.; *follow*, X.*HG*1.1.13; τοὺς εὐγνώμονας Id.*Mem*.2.8.6; δ. καὶ φιλεῖν τινα Pl.*Tht*.168a, cf. *Ev.Luc*.17.23. 2. *pursue* an object, *seek after*, ἀκίχητα διώκειν Il.17.75; σὸν μόρον δ. S.*Aj*.997; τιμὰς δ. Th.2.63; ἡδονήν, τὸ ἀγαθὸν καὶ καλόν, Pl.*Phdr*.251a, *Grg*.482c; ἀλήθειαν ib.482e; δικαιοσύνην *Ep.Rom*.9.30; λαθραίαν Κύπριν Eub. 67.9: prov., τὰ πετόμενα δ. Arist.*Metaph*.1009ᵇ38; κατὰ σκοπὸν δ. *Ep.Phil*.3.14; of plants, δ. τοὺς ξηροὺς τόπους *seek* them, Thphr. *HP*1.4.2; δ. τὰ συμβάντα or τὸ συμβαῖνον *follow* or *wait for* the event, D.4.39, 10.21:—Med., διώκεσθαι τὸ πλέον ἔχειν D.H.1.87 (s. v. l.); μοῖρα διωξαμένη [αὐτούς] *IG*5(1).1355 (Messenia). 3. *pursue* an argument, τὴν ἐναντίωσιν Pl.*R*.454a; also, *describe*, ὕμνῳ ἀρετάς Pi.*I*.4(3).21; τὴν Ἡρακλέους παίδευσιν X.*Mem*.2.1.34; *recite*, λόγον *PMag.Par*.1.958, cf. 335 (Pass.). II. *drive* or *chase away*, διώκω οὔτιν᾽ ἔγωγε I don't *force* any one *away*, Od.18.409; ἐκ γῆς Hdt.9.77; *banish*, Id.5.92.ε′: metaph., διώκεις μ᾽ ᾗ μάλιστ᾽ ἐγὼ ᾽σφάλην you *push* or *press* me .., E.*Supp*.156. III. of the wind, *drive* a ship, Od.5.332; of rowers, *impel, speed on her way*, ῥίμφα διώκοντες (sc. τὴν νῆα) 12.182; νηῦς ῥίμφα διωκομένη 13.162; Συρηγενὲς ἅρμα διώκων *driving* it, Orac.ap.Hdt.7.140, cf. A.*Pers*.84; ἄτρυτον δ. πόδα Id.*Eu*.403, cf. *Th*.371. 2. seemingly intr., *drive, drive on*, Il.23.344,424; *gallop, run*, etc., dub. in A.*Th*.91 (lyr.); ἀναπηδήσαντες ἐδίωκον X.*An*.7.2.20; ἅμα διώκοντος *on the march*, Plu. *Caes*.17: c. acc. spatii, διώξας περὶ ὀκτακοσίους σταδίους Chares 17. 3. *urge, impel*, βέλος χερί Pi.*I*.8(7).35; φόρμιγγα πλάκτρῳ Id.*N*.5.24; esp. of music, δ. μοῦσαν Pratin.Lyr.5; δ. μέλος Simon. 29:—Pass., ὑφ᾽ ἡδονῆς διώκομαι .. σὺν τάχει μολεῖν S.*El*.871. 4. of work, *urge on, carry forward*, σκαφήτρους *PFay*.112.2 (i A. D.). 5. pf. part. Pass. δεδιωγμένος *hurried, rapid*, σφυγμοί Aret.*SA*2. 8. IV. as law-term, *prosecute*, ὁ διώκων *the prosecutor*, opp. ὁ φεύγων, the defendant, Hdt.6.82 (pl.), A.*Eu*.583, etc.; ὁ διώκων τοῦ ψηφίσματος τὸ λέγειν .., *he who impeaches* the clause in the decree ..., D.18.59; γραφὰς δ. Antipho 2.1.5; γραφήν δ. τινά *indict*, D. 59.69; δ. εἰσαγγελίαν Hyp.*Eux*.9; δ. τινὰ περὶ θανάτου X.*HG*7.3.6: c. gen. criminis, *accuse of* .., *prosecute for* .., δ. τινὰ τυραννίδος Hdt. 6.104; δειλίας Ar.*Eq*.368; παρανόμων And.1.22, cf. διωκάθειν; ψευδομαρτυρίων D.29.13, etc.; δ. ἀπάτης εἵνεκεν Hdt.6.136; φόνον τινὸς δ. *avenge* another's murder, E.*Or*.1534 (anap.), cf. Arist.*Pol*.1269ᵃ2; δίκην δ. *pursue* one's rights at law, D.54.41; δίκας μὴ οὔσας δ. Lys. 32.2: c. acc. et inf., *accuse* one of doing, App.*BC*4.50:—Pass., ὁ διωκόμενος Antipho 2.1.5; θανάτου ὑπό τινος -εσθαι X.*Ap*.21; with play on I. 1, Ar.*Ach*.698 sq. V. *persecute*, *Ev.Jo*.5.16, al.; δεδιωγμένοι ἕνεκα δικαιοσύνης *Ev.Matt*.5.10.

διωλένιος, ον, *AP*7.711 (Antip.(?)); also η, ον Arat.202:—*with stretched-out arms*, Id. l. c.; δ. φλόγα πεύκας, of torches, *upheld in both arms*, *AP* l. c.

διωλύγιος [ῠ], ον, *immense, enormous*, μήκη δ. Pl.*Lg*.890e; μακρὰ .. καὶ δ. φλυαρία Id.*Tht*.162a (Sch. expl. both by περιβόητος and σκοτεινός); πράγματα Is.*Fr*.123; μακρὸς ὁ λόγος καὶ δ. Jul.*Or*.2.101d; κῦμα δ. Call.*Fr*.111; ἤπειρος A.R.4.1258; σκότος Dam.*Isid*.303; τιμαί Them.*Or*.11.146b; πνεῦμα δ., of a water-clock striking, perh. *far-sounding*, *AP*7.641 (Antiphil.); *loud, piercing*, φθέγμα θρηνῶδες καὶ δ. Agath.1.12: neut. as Adv., δ. ἀνῴμωζον J.*BJ*7.6.4; δ. ἀνεβόησεν Charito 3.3, Lib.*Decl*.26.47. (Etym. unknown: expld. by ἠχοῦν ἐπὶ πολύ, μέγα καὶ σφοδρόν, διατεταμένον, Hsch.; by μέγα καὶ ἐπὶ πολὺ διῆκον, Suid.)

διωμοσία, ἡ, *an oath taken by both parties at the* ἀνάκρισις *before the trial came on*, Antipho 5.88 (pl.), D.23.69; τὰς δ. ποιεῖσθαι Lys.10.11.

διώμοτος, ον, *bound by oath*, c. inf., S.*Ph*.593: abs., Aristid.*Or*. 34(50).42. Adv. -τως, ὁμαιχμίαν ποιεῖσθαι Procop.*Goth*.4.25.

διωνέομαι, *buy up*, *PPar*.21.38.

Δῐώνη, ἡ, *Dione*, mother of Aphrodite by Zeus, Il.5.370, Hes.*Th*. 17, Str.7.7.12. II. later, as a Metronymic, *daughter of Dione*, i. e. *Aphrodite*, Theoc.7.116, dub. l. in Bion 1.93:—Adj. **Διωναῖος**, α, ον, Κύπρι Δ. Theoc.15.106; Διωναίη alone, D.P.853.

δῐωνῠμ-έω, *use two names*, Eust.288.20. **-ία**, ἡ, *pair of names* or *double name*, Vett.Val.187.25, Man.4.376, Hdn.*Fig*.p.103 S. **-ος**, ον, (δίς, ὄνυμα, ὄνομα) *with two names*, D.T.636.11 (s. v. l.); or, of two persons, *named together*, θεαί E.*Ph*.683 (lyr.). II. (διά) *far-famed*, εὐτυχία Plu.*Tim*.30; στρατηγός App.*BC*4.54; χῶρος J.*BJ* 5.1.3.

Διώνῡσος, etc., Ep. for Διον-.

διωξῐκέλευθος, ον, *urging on the way*, κέντρα *AP*6.246 (Phld. or Marc. Arg.).

δῐώξιππος, ον, *horse-driving*, Κυράνα Pi.*P*.9.4; Ἄρης B.8.44, *AP* 9.322.9 (Leon.); μύωψ ib.6.233 (Maec.).

δίωξις [ῐ], εως, ἡ, (διώκω) *chase, pursuit*, esp. of soldiers or ships, Th.3.33, etc.; δ. ποιεῖσθαι Id.8.102. 2. *pursuit* of an object, τοῦ ὅλου Pl.*Smp*.192e; opp. φυγή, Arist.*EN*1139ᵃ22, Epicur.*Sent*.25; δ. τῶν καλῶν Plu.2.550e. II. as law-term, *prosecution*, δίωξιν εἶναι κατὰ τῶν ἐλεγχθέντων *IG*1².10.10; δ. ποιεῖσθαι Antipho6.7, cf. D.45.50; δ. τῶν ἀδικούντων Plu.*Per*.10.

διωργισμένως, Adv. *angrily*, Phld.*Rh*.1.200 S.

διωρία, ἡ, either (ὅρος) *fixed space* or *interval*, or (ὥρα) *appointed time*, J.*BJ*5.9.1.

διωρισμένως, Adv. pf. part. Pass. of διορίζω, *distinctly, separately*, Arist.*HA*521ᵃ15, Iamb.*Protr*.4; *definitely*, Plu.2.415b.

δίωρος [ῐ], ον, (ὅρος) *having two boundary stones*, λόφος *Schwyzer* 664.20 (Orchom. Arc., iv B.C.). II. δίωρον· ἀσύμφωνον, οἱ δὲ ἀνόμοιον, διάφωνον, Hsch.

δῐώροφος, ον, (ὄροφος) *with two roofs* or *stories*, Lxx *Ge*.6.16, App. *Pun*.95:—written **διώρυφος**, *PPetr*.3p.39.

διωρῠγή, ἡ, v.l. for διωρυχή.

διωρύγιον [ῠ], τό, Dim. of διῶρυξ, *PLond*.1.131ʳ633 (i A.D.).

δῐώργυος, ον, = διόργυιος, X.*Cyn*.2.5.

διῶρυξ, ῠχος (sts. in Pap., *BGU*543.7 (i B.C.), etc.; later Gr. more freq. ῠγος *PPetr*.3p.60 (iii B.C.), *Tab.Heracl*.1.59, *PTeb*.72.72 (ii B.C.), J.*Vit*.31, etc.), ἡ (ὁ, *PRyl*.154.18):—*trench, conduit, canal*, Hdt.1.75, Hp.*Aër*.15, Th.1.109, etc.; κρυπτὴ δ. an underground *passage*, Hdt.3.146; = *fossa*, Plu.*Fab*.1 (pl.).

διωρῠχή, ἡ, *digging* or *cutting through*, Χερρονήσου v.l. for διορυχή in D.7.40, cf. Polyaen.4.18.1, Aristid.*Or*.17(15).14. (διορυγή is f.l. in Plu.*Fab*.1 (cf. foreg.), Them.*Or*.2.36d.)

δίωσ-ις, εως, ἡ, *pushing asunder, forcing open*, Arist.*Pr*.964ᵃ22, *Ph*. 243ᵇ4. II. *putting off 'sine die'*, δίκης Id.*Rh*.1372ᵃ33. **-μός**, ὁ, = foreg. 1, χειρῶν, in gymnastics, Aret.*CD*1.3. 2. in surgery, *pushing through* of embedded weapons, Paul.Aeg.6.88. **-τήρ**, ῆρος, ὁ, *instrument for pushing out* embedded weapons, ibid. II. *pole running through rings*, for carrying the ark, Lxx *Ex*.38.10 (37.13). **-τρα**, ἡ, *projector* or *barrel* of a torsion-engine, Ph.*Bel*.74.22, Hero *Bel*.77.9, al.

δίωτος [ῐ], ον, (οὖς, ὠτός) *two-eared*; of vessels, *two-handled*, Pl. *Hp.Ma*.288d; καδίσκος Anticlid.13; ψυκτήρ *OGI*214.57 (Branchidae, iii B.C.); πίναξ *IG*2².120.44.

διώττας· ἐργοδιώκτας, Hsch. **διωφέλλειν**· διορύσσειν, Id.

διωχής, ές, (ἔχω) *that will hold two*, δίφρος Pherecr.3, Paus.Gr.*Fr*. 132.

δίωχμος, ὁ, Aeol. for διωγμός, *EM*371.21.

δμηθείς, δμηθήτω, v. δαμάζω.

δμῆσις, εως, ἡ, (δαμάζω) *taming, breaking*, ἵππων Il.17.476.

δμητέος, Dor. **δματέος**, = δαμαστέος, Hsch.

δμητήρ, ῆρος, ὁ, *tamer*, ἵππων *h.Hom*.22.5, cf. Alcm.9: fem., νὺξ δμήτειρα θεῶν Il.14.259.

δμητός, ή, όν, *tamed*, Hsch., *EM*389.46.

δμῳ-ή (Choerob. *in Theod*.1.405) or **δμω-ή** (both spellings freq. in codd.), ἡ, (δαμάω) prop. *female slave taken in war*, δμῳαὶ δ' ἃς Ἀχιλεὺς ληΐσσατο (cf. δμώς) Il.18.28, cf. 9.658, 24.643: generally, *female slave, serving-woman*, only in pl. in Hom., mostly joined with γυναῖκες: δμῳαί A.*Ag*.908, S.*Ant*.1189; δ. γυναῖκες A.*Ch*.84; rare in Prose, X.*Cyr*.5.1.6, Philostr.*VA*1.5: later in sg., Q.S.5.561; of things, δμωὴν.. Αἶδος.. μάκελλαν *IG*14.1389ii25. **-ιάς**, άδος, ἡ, = foreg., Q.S.3.684, 9.341: also as disyll., **δμῳάς** Man.2.276. **-ιος**, ον, *in servile condition*, βρέφος *AP*9.407 (Antip. Sid. (but prob. Thess.)). **-ίς**, ίδος, ἡ, = δμωή, A.*Th*.363 (lyr.), *Supp*.335, E.*Ba*. 514, Lyc.1123, A.R.1.285.

δμῶος, ὁ, = sq., Hes.*Op*.430, Leucon ap.Sch.Il.*Oxy*.1087.55, Call. *Hec*.1.4.15 (pl.).

δμώς, ωός, ὁ, (δαμάω) *slave taken in war*, δμώων οὓς.. ληΐσσατο δῖος Ὀδυσσεύς (cf. δμωή) Od.1.398: generally, *slave*, τεῦ δμὼς εἰς ἀνδρῶν; 24.257: mostly in pl., κτῆσιν ἐμὴν δμῶάς τε Il.19.333: dat. pl. δμώεσσι Od.6.71, etc.—Once in S.*Ant*.578; freq. in E., *Med*.188 (lyr.), al., but not found in Prose.

δνοπᾰλ-ίζω, *shake violently, fling down*, ἀνὴρ ἄνδρ' ἐδνοπάλιζεν Il. 4.472; τὰ σὰ ῥάκεα δνοπαλίξεις *'wrap* thy old cloak *about thee'*, Od. 14.512:—Pass., γυῖα δνοπαλίζεται, of the polypus, its arms *wave about*, Opp.*H*.2.295. **-ιξις**, εως, ἡ, *shaking, fluttering*, Sch.Opp. *H*.2.295.

δνοφ-έος, α, ον, = sq., κάλυμμα B.15.32, cf. Hsch. **-ερός**, ά, όν, *dark, murky*, νύξ Od.13.269; ὕδωρ Il.9.15, cf. Thgn.243; ἀχλύς A. *Eu*.379 (lyr.); κατὰ δ. γᾶς E.*IT*1266 (lyr.), etc.: metaph., δ. κᾶδος Pi.*P*.4.112; πένθος A.*Pers*.536 (lyr.).—Poet. word; but τὸ δνοφερόν *gloom*, Hp.*Morb.Sacr*.16. **-ερώδης**, ες, v.l. for δνοφώδης, Id. l.c. **-όεις**, εσσα, εν, = δνοφερός, ὄμβρος Emp.21.5. **-ος**, ὁ, *darkness, dusk, gloom*, Simon.37.8: pl., A.*Ch*.52 (lyr.).—Poet. word, though its collat. form γνόφος (q. v.) occurs in later Prose. **-ώδης**, ες, = δνοφερός, E.*Tr*.79 (as Dind. for γνοφώδη), Hp.*Morb.Sacr*.16; later γνοφ- (q. v.).

δνόψ· χιτῶνος εἶδος, βάθος, Hsch.

δοάν, Dor. for δήν (q. v.), Alcm.135.

δοάσσατο, Homeric aor. form, mostly impers., = Att. ἔδοξε, *it seemed*, in phrase ὧδε δέ (or ὡς ἄρα) οἱ φρονέοντι δοάσσατο κέρδιον εἶναι so *it seemed* to him to be best, Il.13.458, Od.5.474, al.; also ὡς ἂν τοι πλήμνη γε δοάσσεται (Ep. for δοάσσηται) ἄκρον ἱκέσθαι till the nave *appear* even to graze, Il.23.339. II. for δοάσσαι, δοάσσατο, as used by A.R., v. δοιάζω. (For δο-άσσατο: δέ-ατο cf. τροχ-άζω: τρέχω.)

δόγμα, ατος, τό, (δοκέω) *that which seems to one, opinion* or *belief*, Pl.*R*.538c; δ. πόλεως κοινόν Id.*Lg*.644d, etc.; esp. of philosophical *doctrines*, Epicur.*Nat*.14.7, 15.28, Str.15.1.59, Ph.1.204, etc.; *notion*, Pl.*Tht*.158d, al. 2. *decision, judgement*, Id.*Lg*.926d (pl.); *public decree, ordinance*, And.4.6; τὰ τῶν Ἀμφικτυόνων δ. D.5.19, cf. 18. 154; δόγμα ποιήσασθαι, c. inf., X.*An*.3.3.5; esp. of Roman *Senatus-consulta*, δ. συγκλήτου Plb.6.13.2, *IG*12(3).173.22; δ. τῆς βουλῆς D.H.8.87.

δογμᾰτ-ίας, ου, ὁ, *sententious person*, Philostr.*VS*1.16.4. **-ίζω**, *lay down as an opinion*, ἀϊδίους εἶναι Phld.*Piet*.19; τὰ αἰσχρά Arr.*Epict*. 3.7.18: abs., S.E.*P*.1.13, al.; οἱ -οντες, = οἱ δογματικοί, Gal.18(1). 270:—Pass., τὰ -όμενα S.E.*P*.1.18. 2. *decree by ordinance*, c. inf., D.S.4.83, Lxx 1 *Es*.6.34; of the Roman Senate, J.*AJ*14.10.22; δ. τινὰ καλὴν *declare* her beautiful, *AP*9.576 (Nicarch.):—Pass., τὰ δογματισθέντα *IG*12(3).173.53 (Astypalaea), cf. ib.14.759.13 (Naples). 3. in Pass., of persons, *submit to ordinances*, *Ep.Col*.2.20. **-ικός**, ή, όν, *of* or *for doctrines, didactic*, [διάλογοι] Quint.*Inst*.2.15.26. II. of persons, δ. ἰατροί physicians *who go by general principles*, opp. ἐμπειρικοί and μεθοδικοί, Dsc.*Ther.Praef*., Gal.1.65; in Philosophy, S.E.*M*.7.1, D.L.9.70, etc.; δ. ὑπολήψεις Id.9.83; δ. φιλοσοφία S.E. *P*.1.4. Adv. -κῶς D.L.9.74, S.E.*P*.1.197: Comp. -κώτερον Id.*M*. 6.4.

δογμᾰτο-γρᾰφέω, *draft decrees*, *Ephes*.2.20 (ii A.D.). **-γράφος** [γρᾰ], ὁ, *drafter of decrees*, *IG*5(1).26 (Amyclae), *IGRom*.4.259 (Assos), 661 (Acmonia), etc. **-λογία**, ἡ, *expounding of a doctrine*, S.E.*M*.8.367 (pl.). **-ποιέω**, *make a decree*, c. inf., Plb.1.81.4:—also Med., *IG*5(1).1390.57 (Andania). **-ποιΐα**, ἡ, *maintenance of* δόγματα, Aristob.ap.Eus.*PE*13.12.

δοειδές· διαφανές, Hsch.

δοθῑήν, ῆνος, ὁ, *small abscess, boil*, Hp.*Hum*.20, Hermipp.30, Ar. *V*.1172, Telecl.43, Dsc.1.128.6, etc.

δοθῑηνικόν, τό, *remedy for boils*, Paul.Aeg.4.23.

δοθῑών, όνος, ὁ, = δοθιήν, Anon.Lond.19.31, Hdn.Gr.2.923.

δοιάζω or **δοάζω**, *consider in two ways, be in two minds*: hence, *have a mind to*, aor., δοίαξε φάσγανον ἐν στέρνοισι πᾶξαι B.10.87; also βουλὰς δοιάζεσκε *was hesitating between*.., A.R.3.819; ὁππότε δοῦπον ..δοάσσαι (poet. aor. opt.) when she *imagined* a noise, ib.955:—Med., δοάσσατο she *doubted*, ib.770; δοιάζοντο λεύσσειν *imagined* they saw, Id.4.576. (The forms in δοα- and some meanings are due to confusion with δοάσσατο.)

δοιάς, άδος, ἡ, *duality*, Gloss.

δοιδῠκο-ποιός, ὁ, *pestle-maker*, Plu.*Phoc*.4. **-φόβα**, ἡ, *pestle-fearing*, Luc.*Trag*.201.

δοίδυξ, ῠκος, ὁ, *pestle*, Ar.*Eq*.984, Gal.12.189, etc.

δοιέτης, ου, *two years old*, *TAM*2.369 (Xanthus).

δοιή, ἡ, *doubt, perplexity*, ἐν δοιῇ Il.9.230, Call.*Jov*.5, Antag.1.1. (Cf. Skt. dat. sg. *dvayyái* (*dvayī* 'duality').)

δοιοί, αί, ά, Ep. for δύο, *two, both*, Il.5.206, Hes.*Op*.432, etc.: neut. pl. δοιά as Adv., *in two ways, in two points*, Od.2.46. 2. sg., δοιός, ή, όν, *twofold, double*, Emp.17.3, Call.*Ep*.1.3, *AP*9.46 (Antip. Thess.), etc.—Ep. word, also Dor., *IG*12(3).378 (Thera), and Aret. *SD*2.9, 11.

δοιοτόκος, ον, *bearing twins*, prob. in *AP*7.742 (Apollonid.).

δοῖτρον· πύελον, σκάφην, Hsch. (Perh. for δροῖτρον, cf. δροίτη.)

δοιώ, = δοιοί (of which it is properly the dual), = δύο, indecl., Hom.; commonly masc., Il.3.236, al.; but neut. in 24.648.

δοκάζω, *wait for*, πλόον Sophr.52, cf. S.*Fr*.221.23.

δόκᾰνα, τά, (δοκός) at Sparta, *two upright parallel bars* joined towards each end (as symbols of the Dioscuri), Plu.2.478a.

δοκάνη [ᾰ], ἡ, (δοκή, δέχομαι) = στάλιξ, *forked pole* on which hunting-nets are fixed, Hsch.

δοκεύς, έως, ὁ, = δοκός II, Heph.Astr.1.24.

δοκεύω, *keep an eye upon, watch narrowly*, ἑλισσόμενόν τε δοκεύει [the hound] *watches* [the boar] turning to bay, Il.8.340; Θόωνα μεταστρεφθέντα δοκεύσας *having watched for* his turning round, 13.545; Ἀμφικλον ἐφορμηθέντα δοκεύσας 16.313; τὸν πρὸ ἔχοντα δοκεύει *watches* him that is before [in the race], 23.325; of the Great Bear, ἥ τ'.. Ὠρίωνα δοκεύει *watches* the hunter Orion, 18.488; λόχμαισι δ. *lie in wait for* [them] in.., Pi.*O*.10(11).30, cf. *AP*6.45, Theoc.9.26; νιν.. ὄψεται δοκεύοντα will see him *playing the spy*, E.*Ba*.984 (lyr.); ἃ μὴ θέμις οὐκ ἐδόκευσα *sought* not *for*, *IG*14.2068. 2. *expect*, c. acc., Arat.987, al.: c. gen., ἀνέμοιο γαληναίης τε δ. Id.813. 3. in later Poets, *observe, see*, Nonn.*D*.1.530, al., *AP*5.252 (Iren.), Man.6.142; also, *think*, Orph.*A*.891, 1083.

δοκέω Il.7.192, Att. impf. ἐδόκουν, Ep. δοκέεσκον *AP*5.298 (Agath.):—**Med.**, δοκέοντο Opp.*C*.4.296: part. δοκεύμενος ib.109: the fut. and other tenses are twofold: 1. fut. δόξω and aor. 1 ἔδοξα

Pi.*N.*4.37, *h.Merc.*208, etc.: pf. δέδοχα inferred from plpf. ἐδεδόχεσαν D.C.44.26:—Pass., aor. ἐδόχθην Plb.21.10.8, etc., (κατ–) Antipho 2.2.2: pf. δέδογμαι Hdt.8.100, etc.: plpf. ἐδέδοκτο Id.9.74. 2. regul. forms (chiefly Trag., Com., and late Prose), fut. δοκήσω A.*Pr.*388, Ar.*Nu.*562, etc. (once in Hdt., 4.74); Dor. δοκησῶ or –ᾱσῶ Theoc.1.150: aor. ἐδόκησα, Ep. δόκ– Od.10.415, Pi.*O.*13.56, A.*Th.*1041, Ar.*Ra.*1485, etc.: pf. δεδόκηκα A.*Eu.*309 (lyr.):—Pass., aor. ἐδοκήθην E.*Med.*1417 (anap.): pf. δεδόκημαι Pi.*N.*5.19, E.*Med.*763 (anap.), Ar.*V.*726, also in Hdt.7.16.γ′; but δεδοκημένος (q.v.) belongs to δέχομαι.

I. *expect* (Iterat. of δέκομαι, cf. δέχομαι II. 3): hence, *think, suppose, imagine,* (opp. φρονέω, S.*Aj.*942 (lyr.), Pherecr.146.4): 1. c. acc. et inf., δοκέω νικησέμεν Ἕκτορα Il.7.192; οὔ σε δοκέω πείθεσθαι Hdt.1.8, cf. 11,27, al., Antipho 2.4.5, etc.: rarely with inf. omitted, δοκῶ.. οὐδὲν ῥῆμα.. κακὸν [εἶναι] S.*El.*61; τούτους τι δοκεῖτε [εἶναι] X.*An.*5.7.26; freq. in relating a dream or vision, τεκεῖν δράκοντ' ἔδοξεν she *thought* a serpent produced young, A.*Ch.*527; ἐδόκουν αἰετὸν.. φέρειν *methought* an eagle was carrying, Ar.*V.*15; ὁρᾷς γὰρ οὐδὲν ὢν δοκεῖς σάφ' εἰδέναι E.*Or.*259: with inf. only, ἔδοξ' ἰδεῖν *methought* I saw, ib.408; ἔδοξ' ἀκοῦσαι Pl.*Prt.*315e; ἔδοξ' ἐν ὕπνῳ.. οἰκεῖν ἐν Ἄργει E.*IT*44 (sts. also, as in signf. II, ἐδοξάτην μοι δύο γυναῖκε.. μολεῖν A.*Pers.*181; ἐν τῷ σταδίῳ.. μέ τις ἐδόκει στεφανοῦν Alex.272.4). b. *think* to do, *purpose,* ὅταν δ' ἀείδειν.. δοκῶ A.*Ag.*16. 2. abs., *have* or *form an opinion,* περί τινος Hdt.9.65; mostly in parenthetic phrases, ὡς δοκῶ Pl.*Phdr.*264e; δοκῶ alone, Hdt.9.65, Ar.*Pax*47, Pl.*Prm.*126b; πῶς δοκεῖς; to call attention to something remarked, τοῦτον, πῶς δοκεῖς; καθύβρισεν E.*Hipp.*446, cf. *Hec.*1160, Diph.96, etc.; πόσον δοκεῖς; Ar.*Ec.*399. 3. δοκῶ μοι I *seem to myself, methinks,* c. inf., ἐγώ μοι δοκέω κατανοέειν τοῦτο Hdt.2.93, etc.; ἡδέως ἄν μοι δοκῶ κοινωνῆσαί τινος X.*Cyr.*8.7.25, cf. *Oec.*6.11; οὔ μοι δοκῶ I *think* not.., Pl.*Tht.*158e; δοκῶ μοι parenthetic, Id.*Thg.*121d. b. δοκῶ μοι I *am determined, resolved,* c. inf. pres., Ar.*V.*177, etc.: c. inf. fut., Aeschin.3.53, etc.: c. inf. aor., dub. in Ar.*Av.*671, etc.: rarely without μοι, *think fit,* σὺ δ' αὐτὸς ἤδη γνῶθι τίνα πέμπειν δοκεῖς A.*Th.*650. 4. *seem, pretend,* c. inf. (with or without neg.), ὁρέων μὲν οὐδέν, δοκέων δὲ [ὁρᾶν] dub. l. in Alcm.87; οὔτε ἔδοξε μαθέειν Hdt.1.10; οὐδὲ γιγνώσκειν δοκῶν Pherecr.163; τὰ μὲν ποιεῖν, τὰ δὲ δοκεῖν Arist.*Pol.*1314ᵃ39; ἤκουσά του λέγοντος, οὐ δοκῶν κλύειν E.*Med.*67; πόσους δοκεῖς.. ὁρῶντας.. μὴ δοκεῖν ὁρᾶν; Id.*Hipp.*462, cf. Ar.*Eq.*1146, X.*HG*4.5.6. 5. Pass., *to be considered,* δοκεῖσθαι οὕτω Pl.*R.*612d; τὰ νῦν δοκούμενα περί τινος *the current opinions,* ib.490a. 6. Med., Opp.*C.*4.296; δοκεύμενος.. ἀλύξειν ib.109.

II. of an Object, *seem,* c. dat. pers. et inf. pres., δοκέεις δέ μοι οὐκ ἀπινύσσειν Od.5.342; δόκησε δ' ἄρα σφίσι θυμὸς ὣς ἔμεν ὡς εἰ.. their heart *seemed* just as if.., *felt* as though.., 10.415: c. inf. fut., *seem likely,* δοκέει δέ μοι ὧδε λώϊον ἔσσεσθαι Il.6.338: c. inf. aor. (never in Hom.), τί δ' ἂν δοκεῖ σοι Πρίαμος (sc. ποιῆσαι); A.*Ag.*935; *seem* or *be thought* to have done, esp. of suspected persons, Th.2.21; *to be convicted,* ἂν ἁλῷ καὶ δοκῇ τοὔργον εἰργάσθαι D.23.71. 2. abs., *seem,* as opp. to reality, τὸ δοκεῖν καὶ τὰν ἀλάθειαν βιᾶται Simon.76; οὐ δοκεῖν ἄριστος ἀλλ' εἶναι θέλει A.*Th.*592, cf. Pl.*Grg.*527b; in full, τὸ δοκεῖν εἶναι A.*Ag.*788 (anap.). 3. *seem good, be resolved on,* εἰ δοκεῖ σοι ταῦτα ib.944; τοιαῦτ' ἔδοξε τῷδε Καδμείων τέλει Id.*Th.*1030. 4. freq. impers., δοκεῖ μοι *it seems* to me, *methinks,* ὥς μοι δοκεῖ εἶναι ἄριστα Il.12.215; ὡς ἐμοὶ δοκεῖ as I *think,* A.*Th.*369, etc.; τὸ σοὶ δοκοῦν your *opinion,* Pl.*R.*487d: freq. in inf. in parenth. clause, ὡς ἐμοὶ δοκέειν *to* my *thinking,* Hdt.9.113; δοκέειν ἐμοὶ Id.1.172; ἀλλ', ἐμοὶ δοκεῖν, τάχ' εἴσει A.*Pers.*246, etc.; without μοι, X.*An.*4.5.1. b. *it seems good* to me, *it is* my *pleasure,* δοκεῖ ἡμῖν χρῆσθαι Th.4.118, cf. A.*Ag.*1350: freq. of a public resolution, τοῖσι Ἕλλησι δόξαι.. ἀπαιτέειν Hdt.1.3, etc.; ἔδοξεν Ἀργείοισιν A.*Supp.*605, cf. *Th.*1010; esp. in decrees and the like, ἔδοξε τῇ βουλῇ, τῷ δήμῳ, Ar.*Th.*372, Th.4.118, cf. *IG*1.32, etc.; τὰ δόξαντα S.*El.*29, D.3.14; παρὰ τὸ δοκοῦν ἡμῖν Th.1.84, etc.:—Pass., δέδοκται Hdt.4.68; οὕτω δέδοκται; S.*Ph.*1277, etc.; εἰ ἐπαινῆσαι δεδόκηται Pi.*N.*5.19; δεδόχθω τὸ ἄτοπον τοῦτο Pl.*Lg.*799e, etc.; τοῦτ' ἔστ' ἐμοὶ δεδογμένον E.*Heracl.*1; δεδογμέν' [ἐστί].. τήνδε κατθανεῖν S.*Ant.*576, cf. *OC*1431; τὰ δεδογμένα Hdt.3.76; δεδόχθαι τῇ βουλῇ καὶ τῷ δήμῳ *IG*2².1.12, etc. c. acc. abs., δόξαν *when it was decreed* or *resolved,* δόξαν αὐτοῖς ὥστε διαναυμαχεῖν Th.8.79; δόξαν δέ σφι (sc. λιπέσθαι) Hdt.2.148; δόξαν ἡμῖν ταῦτα Pl.*Prt.*314c, cf. X.*An.*4.1.13; ἰδίᾳ δοκῆσάν σοι τόδ'..; E.*Supp.*129; also δεδογμένον αὐτοῖς Th.1.125, etc.; but also δόξαντος τούτου X.*HG*1.1.36; δόξαντα ταῦτα καὶ περανθέντα ib.3.2.19. 5. *to be reputed,* c. inf., Pi.*O.*13.56, *P.*6.40; ἄξιοι ὑμῖν δοκοῦντες Th.1.76; δοκοῦντες εἶναί τι *men who are held* to be something, *men of repute,* Pl.*Grg.*472a; τὸ δοκεῖν τινὲς εἶναι.. προσειληφότες D.21.213; τὸ φρονεῖν ἐδόκει τις εἶναι περιττός Plu.*Arist.*1; οἱ δοκοῦντες Heraclit.28 (dub.), E.*Hec.*295; τὰ δοκοῦντα, opp. τὰ μηδὲν ὄντα, Id.*Tr.*613; μετ' ἀρετῆς δοκούσης ἐς ἀλλήλους γίγνεσθαι Th.3.10; *to be an established, current opinion,* Arist.*APo.*76ᵇ24, al.; τὰ δοκοῦντα Id.*Metaph.*1088ᵃ16, al.:—Pass., οἱ δεδογμένοι ἀνδροφόνοι *those who have been found guilty* of homicide, D.23.28; also αἱ δοκούμεναι Πέρσαις τέχναι Polem.*Call.*60. (The two senses of δοκέω are sts. contrasted, τὰ ἀεὶ δοκοῦντα.. τῷ δοκοῦντι εἶναι ἀληθῆ that which *seems* true is true *to him who thinks* it, Pl.*Tht.*158e; τὸ δοκοῦν ἑκάστῳ τοῦτο καὶ εἶναι τῷ δοκοῦντι ib.162c.)

δοκή, ἡ, *vision, fancy,* Hdn.Gr.1.313. **II.** = δοχή, Hsch.

δόκημα, ατος, τό, *vision, fancy,* δ. ὀνείρων E.*HF*111 (lyr.); τὰ δοκήμασιν σοφά Id.*Tr.*411; δοκήματα *make-believes,* of adopted sons, Id.*Fr.*359. 2. *opinion, expectation,* δοκημάτων ἐκτός Id.*HF*771 (lyr.). **II.** = δόγμα, δ. τοῦ συνεδρίου *IG*12(3).1259.3 (Cimolus), *Schwyzer*91.27 (Argos, iii B.C.).

δοκησί-δέξιος, ον, *clever in one's own conceit,* Pherecr.154, Callias Com.27. **–νους**, ουν, = foreg., ibid.

δόκησις, εως, ἡ, (δοκέω) *opinion, fancy,* δ. δὲ δεῖ λέγειν Hdt.7.185, cf. Chrysipp.*Stoic.*2.22, etc.; δ. εἰπεῖν, opp. ἐξακριβῶσαι λόγον, S.*Tr.*426; δ. ἀγνὼς λόγων ἦλθε a vague *suspicion* was thrown out, Id.*OT*681 (lyr.); δ. τῆς ἀληθείας Th.2.35; δώρων δ. *suspicion* of bribery, Id.5.16; δ. παρέχειν ὡς.. Plu.*Pomp.*54. 2. *apparition, phantom,* κενὴν δ. E.*Hel.*36; σκοπεῖτε μὴ δόκησιν εἴχετ' ἐκ θεῶν ib.119; οὕτω δοκεῖτε τὴν δ. ἀσφαλῆ ib.121. 3. *appearance,* opp. reality, Ph.1.222; φάσμα καὶ δ. ἑαυτῆς παρέχειν Plu.2.392a; δ. ἰσχίου Aret.*SD* 2.12. **II.** *repute, credit,* Th.4.18, *Stoic.*3.38; ὁ στρατηγὸς τὴν δ. ἄρνυται E.*Andr.*696.

δοκησί-σοφία, ἡ, *conceit of wisdom,* Pl.(?) ap.Poll.4.9. **–σοφος**, ον, *wise in one's own conceit,* Ar.*Pax*44, Antipho Soph.105, Ph.1.122; δ. φρόνημα ib.605.

δοκίας, ου, ὁ, = δοκός II, Phlp. *in Mete.*92.24, Suid. s.v. κομῆται. **δοκίδιον**, τό, Dim. of δοκός, Harp.

δοκικῶ, com. barbarism for δοκέω, Hermipp.12.

δοκῐμάζω, (δόκιμος) *assay, test,* πορφύραν καὶ χρυσόν Isoc.12.39; τοὺς οἴνους Arist.*EN*1118ᵃ28; τὰ νομίσματα Id.*HA*491ᵃ21:—Med., *prove for oneself, choose,* χώραν X.*Oec.*8.10, cf. Men.532.11 (dub.):—Pass., ἐπειδὰν τὸ ἔργον.. δοκιμασθῇ *CIG*2266.15 (Delos). 2. of persons, δ. αὐτοὺς *put* them *to the test, make trial of* them, Isoc.2.50; δ. τοὺς μηνυτάς Th.6.53; φίλους X.*Mem.*2.6.1, cf. *PEleph.*1.8 (iv B.C.), etc.; also of Apis-bulls, Hdt.2.38. **II.** *approve, sanction,* μετὰ δεδοκιμασμένου [λόγου] μὴ ξυνέπεσθαι Th.3.38; ἐψηφίσασθε δοκιμάσαντες τοὺς νόμους, εἶτ' ἀναγράψαι τούτους οἳ ἂν δοκιμασθῶσι And.1.82; ἄρρενας ἔρωτας Plu.2.11e; ὅπῃ ταύτῃ ἀρετὴ δοκιμάζεται Pl.*R.*407c: c. inf., ἐκπονεῖν ἐδοκίμαζε he *approved of* their working, X.*Mem.*1.2.4; ἐπειδὴ.. ἐδοκιμάσθη ταῦτα καλῶς ἔχειν Th.2.35. 2. as a political term, a. *approve after scrutiny as fit* for an office, Lys.16.3, Pl.*Lg.*759d, Arist.*Ath.*45.3:—Pass., *to be approved as fit,* Lys.15.6, etc.; δοκιμασθεὶς ἀρχέτω Pl.*Lg.*765b; μου δοκιμαζομένου *when I was undergoing a scrutiny,* D.21.111; δεδοκιμασμένος [ἰατρός] *PFay.*106.24 (ii A.D.), cf. *PGnom.*201 (ii A.D.): metaph., ὃν δ' Ἥφαιστος ἐδοκίμασεν *OGI*90.3 (ii B.C.); ὑπὲρ τοῦ στεφανωθῆναι δοκιμάζομαι D.18.266. b. *pass as fit to serve,* ἱππεύειν δεδοκιμασμένος Lys.14.22, cf. X.*An.*3.3.20, *IG*2².1126.15, 1369. c. *examine and admit* boys *to the class of* ἔφηβοι or ἔφηβοι *to the rights of manhood,* Ar.*V.*578 (Pass.), Arist.*Ath.*42.2, etc.; ἕως ἐγὼ ἀνὴρ εἶναι δοκιμασθείην D.27.5; εἰς ἄνδρας δεδοκιμασμένοι Isoc.12.28. d. *test* an orator's *right to speak* (cf. δοκιμασία 4), *AB*310. 3. c. inf., *think fit* to do, Luc.*BisAcc.*31, J.*AJ*2.7.4, etc.: with neg., *refuse* to do, *Ep.Rom.*1.28: abs., *BGU*248.19 (i A.D.), etc.

δοκῐμαίνονται· δοκιμάζουσι, Hsch.

δοκῐμ-ᾰσία, ἡ, *examination, scrutiny*: 1. of magistrates after election, to see if they fulfil the legal requirements of legitimacy, full citizenship, etc., ἡ δ. τῶν στρατηγῶν Lys.15.2, cf. 16.9 (pl.); τῶν ἱερέων Pl.*Lg.*759d; δ. εἰσάγειν ταῖς ἀρχαῖς Arist.*Ath.*59.4 (pl.), cf. *IG* 2².856, 980. 2. δ. τῶν ἱππέων *passing muster,* X.*Eq.Mag.*3.9 (pl.). 3. δ. (sc. ἐφήβων), before admission to the rights of manhood, D.44.41, v.l. in 57.62. 4. δ. τῶν ῥητόρων a judicial *process to determine the right* of a man *to speak* in the ἐκκλησία or in the law-courts, Aeschin.1.2. 5. *examination of recruits,* *PLond.*3.982.6 (iv A.D.). 6. generally, *test,* δ. ἱκανήν [τινος] λαβεῖν make full *trial of,* Is.7.34 (but, receive *assurance* of.., Plb.3.31.8); ἡ κατὰ τὸν χρόνον δ. Arist.*EN*1162ᵃ14; κρίσιν καὶ δ. τινῶν ποιεῖν Plu.*Cleom.*10; λίθος δοκιμασίας LXX *Si.*6.21; δ. οἰκοδόμων *PSI*3.176 (v A.D.). **–αστέος**, α, ον, *to be approved after scrutiny,* Luc.*Eun.*8. **II.** impers., **δοκιμαστέον**, *one must approve after scrutiny,* Lys.21.25, Epicur.*Sent.Vat.*28, Plu.2.3d, Max.Tyr.7.9. **–αστήρ**, ῆρος, ὁ, = δοκιμαστής, τῶν κοινῶν Plb.24.7.5, cf. 6.8. **–αστήριον**, τό, *test, means of trial,* Men.*Mon.*537, Arr.*Epict.*3.6.10; μύρων, of the nose, Artem.4.27. **–αστής**, οῦ, ὁ, *examiner, scrutineer,* Lys.26.16, Pl.*Lg.*802b; πράγματος D.48.3; διαίτης Aeschin.2.146 (pl.); *money-changer,* Men.532.8. **II.** *approver, panegyrist,* D.21.127; δ. καὶ ἐπαινετής D.C.38.4. **–αστικός**, ή, όν, *of* or *for scrutiny,* δύναμις Arr.*Epict.*1.1.1, cf. S.E.*M.*1.64, *Theol.Ar.*52, v.l. in Diog.Bab.*Stoic.*3.219. Adv. –κῶς *approvingly,* διακεῖσθαι *Stoic.*3.160. **II.** –κόν, τό, *commission paid to an assayer,* *PHib.*29.24, al. **–αστός**, ή, όν, *approved,* Diog.Bab.*Stoic.*3.219, cf. 49, D.L.7.105. **–άω**, = –άζω, *PTeb.*24.78 (ii B.C.). **–εῖον**, τό, *test, means of testing,* Pl.*Ti.*65c (v.l. **δοκίμιον**, as in D.H.*Rh.*11.1, *Ep.Jac.*1.3, 1*Ep.Pet.*1.7, S.E.*M.*7.430, Lib.*Decl.*16.55), *IG*7.303.31 (Orop.); *proof,* εὐσεβείας *OGI*308.16 (Hierapolis), cf. Zos.3.13. **–εῖος** (freq. written **δοκίμιος**), α, ον, = δόκιμος, χρυσίον *BGU* 717.8, cf. *IG*2.684.5, etc. **–ή**, ἡ, *proof, test,* interpol. in Dsc.4.184. 2. *tried* or *approved character,* *Ep.Phil.*2.22, cf. 2*Ep.Cor.*2.9. **–ος**, ον (Dor. α, ον *Tab.Heracl.*1.103), (δέχομαι) *acceptable*: hence, 1. of persons, *trustworthy,* Heraclit.28 (Sup.), Democr.67; *approved, esteemed,* Hdt.1.65, al.; δ. παρά τινι Id.7.117; δοκιμώτατος Ἑλλάδι *most approved* by Hellas, her *noblest* son, E.*Supp.*277 (anap.): c. inf., *of approved ability* to do.., δόκιμος δ' οὔτις.. εἴργειν A.*Pers.*87 (lyr.). 2. of things, *excellent,* τὸ ἔαρ –ώτατον Hdt.7.162; *notable, considerable,* ποταμός Id.7.129; *approved,* κριθὰ καθαρὰ δ. *Tab.Heracl.* l.c.; δ. ἀργύριον *legal* tender, D.35.24, cf. *PLond.*3.938.6 (iii A.D.); ὕμνος *acceptable,* Pi.*N.*3.11. 3. Adv. –μως *really, genuinely,* A.*Pers.*547 (lyr.), X.*Cyr.*1.6.7. **–όω**, = δοκιμάζω,

Parm.1.32, Pherecyd.ap.D.L.1.122, Theoc.30.25, Hsch. **-ωμι,** Aeol. form of δοκιμόω, = δοκέω, Sapph.69, cf. 37 (dub.), *Epigr.Gr.* 991.7 (Balbilla).

δοκίον, τό, = δοκίς, Arist.*HA*532^{b}21, *IG*11.146*A*68 (Delos, iv B.C.), D.S.18.42.

δοκίς, ἴδος, ἡ, *plank,* Hp.*Fract.*13, X.*Cyn.*9.15, *IG*11.287*A* 24 (Delos, iii B.C.). 2. *screen* or *shield* used by sappers, = χελώνη ὀρυκτρίς, Ph.*Bel.*81.28, al. II. = δοκός II, Arist.*Mu.*392^{b}4, Ptol. *Tetr.*90; πυρίνη δ. D.S.15.50, cf. Nonn.*D.*2.199. III. *number of the form mn^2 ($m>n$),* Theo Sm.p.42 H., Nicom.*Ar.*2.17.

δοκίτης, ου, ὁ, = δοκός II, Suid.

δοκοθήκη, ἡ, *stone with hole for insertion of roof-beam, IG*11(2).161*A*55 (Delos, iii B.C.). **δοκόν,** τό, = δοκός, *PLond.*3.1259.13 (iv A.D.). **δοκοποιός,** *tignarius, Gloss.*

δοκός, ἡ, later also ὁ, Luc.*VH*2.1: (δέχομαι):—*bearing-beam, main beam,* esp. in the roof or floor of a house, Od.22.176, Ar.*Nu.* 1496; any *balk* or *beam,* Il.17.744, Th.4.112; *bar* of a gate or door, Ar.*V.*201: also, in pl., *firewood, PFlor.*127.5 (iii A.D.): prov., ὁ τὴν δοκὸν φέρων *one who has 'swallowed a poker',* Ar.*Rh.*1413^{b}28; ἐν δοκοῖσι is prob. f.l. for ἐνδόκοισι in Archil.66.3, cf. Hsch. s.v. ἔνδοκος. II. a kind of *meteor,* Plin.*HN*2.96, Lyd.*Ost.*10^b, Hsch.; cf. δοκεύς, δοκίας, δοκίς II.

δόκος, ὁ, = δόκησις, Xenoph.34.4, Call.*Fr.*100; περὶ τοῦ δ., title of work by Demetrius of Phalerum, D.L.5.81. II. = ἀγχονή, Ar. *Fr.*515.

δοκοτέκτων, ονος, ὁ, *carpenter, Gloss.*

δοκόω, *furnish with rafters,* in Pass., S.E.*P.*3.99; οἰκία δεδοκωμένη *Sammelb.*5105.3 (ii B.C.), *PGrenf.*2.35 (i B.C.).

δοκώ, όος, contr. οῦς, ἡ, = δόκησις, E.*El.*747.

δοκ-ώδης, ες, *beam-like, Gloss.* **-ωσις,** εως, ἡ, *furnishing with rafters, roofing,* Lxx*Ec.*10.18, Plu.2.1112e (pl.), S.E.*P.*3.99, *M.*9. 343, *POxy.*1648.60 (ii A.D.).

δολάν (leg. δοάν)· ἀντὶ τοῦ δήν, Hsch. **δολάνα·** μαστροπός, Id. (cf. δολομάν). **δολβαί·** θύματα, οἱ δὲ μικρὰ (μικτὰ cod.) πλακούντια, Id.; cf. δόλπαι.

δολερός, ά, όν, (δόλος) *deceitful, treacherous,* νόος Hdt.2.151; ἄνθρωποι, εἵματα, Id.3.22; φρήν S.*Ph.*1112 (lyr.), cf. X.*Cyr.*1.6.27, Ant.Lib.29.3; δολερὸν πέφυκεν ἄνθρωπος Arr.*An.*4.5.1; δ. ἔρως Pl. *Smp.*205d. Adv. -ρῶς Ph.2.314, J.*AJ*14.13.6, Poll.3.132.

δόλευμα, ατος, τό, *stratagem, ruse,* Aen.Tact.39 tit.

δολέων· δοθιήν, Hsch.

δολία, ἡ, = κώνειον, Ps.-Dsc.4.78.

δολῐεύομαι, *deal treacherously,* Aq., Sm.*Ge.*37.18. 2. λόγος δεδολιευμένος *a sophism,* S.E.*P.*2.229.

δολίζω, *adulterate,* Dsc.1.64, al.

δολῐό-βουλος, ον, gloss on δολόμητις, Suid. **-γνωμος,** ον, gloss on δολομῆτα, Hsch. **-μήτης,** voc. -μῆτα, ὁ, = sq., Id. **-μητις,** ιδος, ὁ, ἡ, *crafty-minded,* A.*Supp.*750 (lyr.). **-μῦθος,** ον, *crafty of speech,* prob. for δολό-, S.*Tr.*839 (lyr.). **-πους,** ὁ, ἡ, πουν, τό, *stealthy of foot,* Id.*El.*1392 (lyr.).

δόλιος, α, ον (ος, ον E.*Alc.*33, *Tr.*530), Lxx*Ps.*51(52).6, etc. (lyr.): —*crafty, deceitful, treacherous,* in Od. always of things, ἔπεα, τέχνη, 9.282, 4.455; ὁππότε... δόλιον περὶ κύκλον ἄγωσιν the *treacherous* circle, i.e. the net, 4.792; μῆνις A.*Ag.*155 (lyr.); of persons, Pi.*P.*2.82, etc.; δόλιον ὄμμ' ἔχων A.*Pr.*569; epith. of Aphrodite, B.16.116, E.*Hel.*238 (lyr.); of Hermes, S.*Ph.*133, Ar.*Pl.*1157; in later Prose, Plb.21.34.1; δ. χείλη Lxx*Pr.*26.23; ἀνελεύθερος καὶ δ. Phld.*Ir.* p.60 W. Adv. -ίως Batr.93, *Epigr.Gr.*387.7 (Apamea), Lxx*Je.*9.4 (3), D.L.9.35.

δολιότης, ητος, ἡ, *deceit, subtlety,* Lxx*Nu.*25.17, al.

δολιό-τροπος, ον, *crafty,* γνώμη Tz.*H.*3.443. **-φρων,** ὁ, ἡ, gen. ονος, *crafty of mind, wily,* ποινά A.*Ch.*947 (lyr.); Κύπρις E.*IA* 1300.

δολιόω, 3 pl. impf. ἐδολιοῦσαν, *deal treacherously with* one, Lxx *Ps.*5.10, al.: abs., *to be treacherous,* Sm.*Pr.*26.19.

δολίσκος, ὁ, Dim. of δόλων II, Hsch. **δολίφονον·** πέπαικται δὲ τοῦ δολοφονίου, Id.

δολῐχ-αίων, ὁ, ἡ, gen. ωνος, *long-lived, immortal,* θεοί Emp.21.12, 23.8. **-άορος** [ᾱ], ον, *with long sword,* Ἀθηναίη Philet.23. **-αυλος,** ον, *with a long tube,* δ. αἰγανέη a spear *with a long iron socket* for the shaft, Od.9.156. **-αύχην,** ενος, ὁ, ἡ, *long-necked,* πταναί E.*Hel.* 1487 (lyr.); κύκνος B.15.6, E.*IA*793 (lyr.). **-εγχής,** ές, *with tall spear,* Παίονες Il.21.155. **-εύω,** = δολιχοδρομέω, *AP*11.82 (Nicarch.): generally, δρόμον δ. *go through a long* course, Ph.1.331; δ. τὴν φύσιν *prolong* its existence, ib.9; δ. πολλοὺς πλοῦς Ael.*Fr.*71.

δολῐχήπους, ὁ, ἡ, gen. ποδος, *with long feet,* Numen.ap.Ath.7.305a.

δολῐχ-ήρετμος, ον, (ἐρετμός) *long-oared,* of a ship, Od.4.499, etc.; of the Phaeacians, *using long oars,* 8.191; δ. Αἴγινα Pi.*O.*8. 20. **-ήρης,** ες, = δολιχός, *long,* Nic.*Th.*183, Opp.*C.*1.408.

δολῐχο-γρᾰφία, ἡ, *prolix writing, AP*6.327 (Leon.). II. *long-continued writing,* ib.65 (Paul. Sil.). **-δειρος,** Ep. δουλ-, ον, *long-necked,* κύκνοι Il.2.460. **-δρομέω,** *run the* δόλιχος, Aeschin. 3.91. **-δρόμος,** ον, *running the* δόλιχος, Pl.*Prt.*335e, X.*Smp.*2. 17:—Aeol. and Dor. **δολιχαδρόμος,** *IG*12(2).388 (Mytilene), *CIG* 2758 (Aphrodisias), *IG*5(1).19 (Sparta). **-εις,** εσσα, εν, Ion. δουλ-, = δολιχός, *AP*6.4 (Leon.). **-κρότᾰφος,** ον, *long-headed, IG*2.1310.

δολῐχό-ουρος or **δολίχ-ουρος,** ον, *long-tailed*: metaph. of verses with a syll. redundant (as Od.5.231), Sch.Heph.p.290 C., Eust.12.33.

δολῐχό-πους, ὁ, ἡ, πουν, τό, = δολιχήπους.

δολῐχός, ή, όν, *long,* ἔγχεα, δόρυ, Il.4.533, al.; also of Time, νύξ, νοῦσος, Od.23.243, 11.172; δολιχόν, as Adv., Il.10.52; σχελίδες Archipp.11.3 (lyr.); ἐλάται A.R.1.914; πρυμνήσια *AP*10.4 (Marc. Arg.); some phrases, as δ. πλόος, δ. ὁδός, unite both senses, Od.3.169, 4. 393. (Cf. Skt. *dīrghas* 'long'.)

δόλιχος, ὁ, *the long course,* in racing, opp. στάδιον, *IG*2^2.956, etc.; τὸν δ. ἁμιλλᾶσθαι Pl.*Lg.*833b; θεῖν X.*An.*4.8.27; νικᾶν Luc.*Hist. Conscr.*30; δολίχῳ κρατεῖν Paus.3.21.1: metaph., δ. κατατείνουσι τοῦ λόγου Pl.*Prt.*329a; δόλιχον τοῖς ἔτεσι... τρέχειν Epicr.3.18; δόλιχον βιότου σταδιεύσας *Epigr.Gr.*311; γήρως δ. ib.231. 2. a *measure of length,* = 12 *stades,* Hero *Geom.*4.13. II. *calavance, Vigna sinensis,* Thphr.*HP*8.3.2, Diocl.*Fr.*117.

δολῐχ-όσκιος, ον, (σκιά) *casting a long shadow,* Homeric epith. of ἔγχος, Il.3.346, etc.: in later Ep. as a general epith., *long,* οὐρή Opp.*C.*1.411; αὐχήν Nonn.*D.*12.181; *far-reaching,* ἰός Id.2.612, etc. **-ούᾰτος,** ον, (οὖας) *long-eared,* Opp.*C.*3.186.

δολῐχόφρων, ὁ, ἡ, gen. ονος, *far-reaching,* μέριμναι Emp.11.1.

δολιχωπά· μακρά, Hsch.

δολό-εις, εσσα, εν, (δόλος) *subtle, wily,* Καλυψώ, Κίρκη, Od.7.245, 9.32. II. of things, *craftily contrived, artful,* δέσματα 8.281; θάνατος Hellanic.69(a) J.; Τροίας ἕδη E.*IA*1527 (lyr.). **-εργής,** ές, *working by fraud,* Man.4.394:—also **-εργός,** όν, ib.57, al. **-κτᾰσία,** ἡ, (κτείνω) *murder by treachery,* A.R.4.479 (pl.).

δολομάν· μαστροπόν (Lacon.), Hsch.

δολο-μήδης, ες, gen. εος, *wily, crafty,* f. l. in Simon.43. **-μήτης,** ου, ὁ, voc. δολομῆτα, = sq., Il.1.540. **-μητις,** ι, *crafty of counsel, wily,* of persons, Od.1.300; Ἀφροδίτα prob. in Simon.43; ἀπάτα A. *Pers.*93 (lyr.). **-μήχᾰνος,** ον, *contriving wiles,* Ἄρης Simon.43 (codd. of Sch.A.R.), Theoc.30.25. **-μῦθος,** ον, *subtle-speaking,* f.l. in S.*Tr.*839 (lyr.).

δολοπεύω, *plot,* Hsch. (cf. δόλοψ).

δολο-πλᾰνής, ές, *treacherous,* Nonn.*D.*8.126. **-πλοκία,** ἡ, *subtlety, craft,* in pl., Thgn.226, Hp.*Ep.*17. **-πλόκος,** ον (α, ον v.l. in *Lyr.Adesp.*129), *weaving wiles,* Ἀφροδίτα Sapph.1.2; μῦθος Tryph.264. **-ποιός,** όν, *treacherous, ensnaring,* ἀνάγκα S.*Tr.*832 (lyr.).

δολορρᾰφ-έω, *lay snares,* Ctes.*Fr.*29.4. **-ής,** ές, *treacherously wrought,* of nets, Opp.*H.*3.84. II. *weaving treacherously,* Nonn. *D.*20.182, al. **-ία,** ἡ, *artful contrivance, AP*5.285 (Paul. Sil.). **-ος,** ον, (ῥάπτω) *treacherous,* Tz.*H.*8.925.

δόλος (A), ὁ, prop. *bait* for fish, Od.12.252: hence, *any cunning contrivance for deceiving* or *catching,* as the net in which Hephaestus catches Ares, 8.276; the Trojan horse, ib.494; Ixion's bride, Pi. *P.*2.39; the robe of Penelope, Od.19.137 (pl.); ξύλινος δ. mouse-trap, Batr.116. b. generally, *any trick* or *stratagem,* πυκινὸν δ. ἄλλον ὕφαινε Il.6.187, etc.: in pl., *wiles,* δόλοι καὶ μήδεα 3.202; δόλοισι κεκασμένε 4.339, etc. 2. in the abstract, *craft, cunning, treachery,* δόλῳ ἠὲ βίηφι Od.9.406; ἔπεφνε δόλῳ, οὔ τι κράτεΐ γε Il.7. 142; οὐ κατ' ἰσχὺν... δόλῳ δέ... A.*Pr.*215, cf. *Ch.*556, etc.; δόλοις ib.888, S.*OT*960, etc.; ἐκ δόλου Id.*El.*279; ἐν δόλῳ Id.*Ph.*102; σὺν δόλῳ A.*Pers.*775; μετὰ δόλου καὶ τέχνης Isoc.9.36; δόλῳ πονηρῷ, = Lat. *dolo malo, Supp.Epigr.*1.161.53; μετὰ δόλου πονηροῦ *IG*12(2). 510.9 (Methymna); χωρὶς δ. π. *OGI*629.112 (Palmyra). 3. *spy,* Hsch.

δόλος (B)· πάσσαλος, Hsch.

δολοσχερής, ές, neut. pl. τὰ δολοσχερέα, of parts of a bier, *IG*12 (5).593 (Ceos); cf. foreg. (Perh. τὰ δ' ὁλοσχερέα.)

δολοφον-έω, *slay by treachery,* Str.5.3.2, al., Ph.1.412:—Pass., Plb. 32.5.11; but freq. simply, *murder* (with no implication of treachery), Ph.1.205, al., App.*Syr.*69:—Pass., D.19.194, Arist.*Mir.*836^{a}16, *POxy.*12^{r}v8, *BGU*388i23 (ii/iii A.D.), etc. **-ησις,** εως, ἡ, = sq., App.*Syr.*69. **-ία,** ἡ, *slaying by treachery,* Arist.*EN*1131^{a}7; *murder,* Plb.6.13.4 (pl.). **-ος,** ον, *slaying by treachery, privy to treacherous murder,* λέβης δ. A.*Ag.*1129 (lyr.).

δολο-φρᾰδής, ές, *wily-minded, h.Merc.*282, Pi.*N.*8.33. **-φράδμων,** ον, gen. ονος, = foreg., Ἀφροδίτη Nonn.*D.*4.68, 32.1. **-φρονέων,** ουσα, ον, *planning craft, wily-minded,* Il.3.405, Od.10.339, Archil. 93. **-φροσύνη,** ἡ, *craft, subtlety,* Il.19.97, 112. **-φρων,** ον, gen. ονος, = δολοφραδής, f. l. in A.*Supp.*750 (lyr.); Ἀπάτα *AP* 7.145 (Asclep.).

δόλοψ, οπος, ὁ, *lurker in ambush,* Hsch.

δολόω, *beguile, ensnare, take by craft,* A.*Ag.*273, 1636; φαρμάκῳ δ. Hdt.1.212; ὃς πλέγμασι δ. X.*Cyr.*1.6.28; δολοῦν τινὰ γάμοις *beguile* by the anticipation of..., E.*IA*898 (anap.):—Med., *Leg.Gort.*2.36, 44:—Pass., Hes.*Th.*494, S.*Ph.*1288. II. *disguise,* μορφήν ib. 129; *adulterate* incense, wine, etc., Dsc.1.81, Luc.*Herm.*59; *alloy,* Gal.14.48 (Pass.); *dye,* τὰ ἔρια Poll.7.169.

δόλπαι, αἱ, *small cakes* (Cos), Hsch.; cf. δολβαί. **Δολφοί,** v. Δελφοί. **δολφός,** ὁ, (cf. δελφύς) *womb,* Id.

δόλωμα, ατος, τό, *trick, deceit,* A.*Ch.*1003; *stratagem, ruse,* Aen. Tact.8.2 (pl.).

δόλων, ωνος, ὁ, *flying jib,* Plb.16.15.2, D.S.20.61. 2. *spar which carries such a sail,* Poll.1.91. II. *secret weapon, poniard, stiletto,* Plu.*TG*10. III. *fishing-rod* (?), Artem.2.14.

δολωνικός, ή, όν, *pertaining to a top-sail,* ξύλον εἰς τράπεζαν δολωνικὴν *PLond.ined.*2305 (iii B.C.).

δολ-ῶπις, ιδος, ἡ, *artful-looking, treacherous,* S.*Tr.*1050. **-ωσις,** εως, ἡ, *tricking,* X.*Cyr.*1.6.28 (pl.). 2. *alloying,* Gal.14.48.

δόμα (A), ατος, τό, (δίδωμι) *gift*, Pl.*Def.*415b, Lxx *Ge.*25.6 (pl.), Plu.2.182e. 2. *payment*, *PPetr.*2 p.11 (iii B.C.).

δόμα (B), ατος, τό, = δῶμα, Max.448, = τειχίον, Hsch.

δομαῖος, α, ον, (δομή) *for building*: δομαῖοι (sc. λίθοι) *foundation-stones*, A.R.1.737; δ. λᾶα *APl.*4.279.

δομᾰτίζω, *bestow presents on*, Sm.*Ez.*16.33:—Pass., Ps.-Callisth. 1.11 (cod. A).

δομ-άω, = δέμω:—Pass., λίθοι εὖ δεδομημένοι Aristid.1.821 J., cf. J.*BJ*5.4.2, al., Arr.*An.*7.22.2.

δόμεναι, δόμεν, v. sub δίδωμι.

δομ-έοντι· οἰκοδομοῦντι, Hsch. **–ή**, ἡ, (δέμω) *building*, dub. l. in J.*AJ*15.11.3, cf. Hsch. II. Alex. word for δέμας, A.R.3.1395, Nic.*Th.*153, Lyc.334,597,783.

δόμημα, ατος, τό, *building*, J.*BJ*5.5.1.

δόμ-ησις, εως, ἡ, = δομή 1, J.*BJ*1.21.6, al. **–ήτωρ**, ορος, ὁ, *builder*, Anon.*Prog.* in Rh.1.642 W.

δόμονδε, Adv. *homeward*, Hom.; ὅνδε δόμονδε *to* his own *house*, Od.1.83; also δόμον Archestr.*Fr.*26.

δόμορτις· γυνή, Hsch.

δόμος, ὁ, (δέμω, cf. Lat. *domus*): 1. *house*, Il.2.513, Sapph.1.7, etc.; also, *part of a house, room, chamber*, Od.8.57, 22.204: freq. in pl. for *a house*, Hes.*Op.*96, etc.; freq. in Trag., A.*Supp.*433, etc.: chiefly poet., οἶκος or οἰκία being used in Prose. 2. *house* of a god, *temple*, Διὸς δόμος Il.8.375; δ. Ἀρτέμιδος Ar.*Ra.*1273; Ἐρεχθῆος πυκινὸν δόμον *the building* of Erechtheus, i.e. *the temple* of Athena, Od.7.81; Ἄϊδος δ., of the nether world, Il.3.322, etc.; δ. δίκας A. *Eu.*516 (lyr.); μυστοδόκος δ., of the *temple* at Eleusis, Ar.*Nu.*303: so in pl., εἰν Ἀΐδαο δόμοισι Il.22.52; δόμων τῶν Λοξίου A.*Eu.*35, cf. E.*Ion* 249; *chamber* in a temple, χρύσεος δ. ἐν Διὸς οἴκῳ Theoc.17. 17. 3. *abode* of animals, e.g. sheep*fold*, Il.12.301; κοῖλος δ. wasps' or bees' *nest*, ib.169; serpent's *hole*, Ael.*NA*2.9. 4. ξύλινος δ. *pyre*, B.3.49. 5. κέδρινοι δόμοι *closet* or *chest* of cedar, E.*Alc.* 160. II. in Trag., *household, family*, A.*Ch.*263, S.*OC*370, E.*Or.* 70, *Med.*114 (anap.); *one's father's house*, ἔξω δόμων τε καὶ πάτρας ὠθεῖν ἐμέ A.*Pr.*665, etc. III. *course* of stone or bricks in a building, ὑποδείμας τὸν πρῶτον δ. λίθου Αἰθιοπικοῦ Hdt.2.127; διὰ τριήκοντα δόμων πλίνθου at every thirtieth *layer* of bricks, Id.1.179, cf. Lxx 1*Es.*6.24, D.S.1.64; καθ' ἕνα δόμον Plb.10.22.7. 2. *ply* or *strand* of gut in the τόνοι of a torsion-engine, Ph.*Bel.*65.42, Hero *Bel.*82.1.

δομο-σφᾰλής, ές, *shaking the house*, κτύπος A.*Ag.*1533 (lyr.). **–τέκτων**, ονος, ὁ, = *valvarius, Gloss.*; *carpenter*, *Ath.Mitt.*25.123 (Philadelphia).

δομόω, *provide with lodging*, *PMasp.*96.29 (Pass., vi A.D.).

δονᾰκ-εύομαι, *fowl with reed and birdlime*, *AP*9.264 (Apollonid. or Phil.). **–εύς**, ῆος or έως, ὁ, (δόναξ) *thicket of reeds*, Il.18.576: pl., Opp.*H.*4.507. II. *fowler*, Id.*C.*1.73. III. = δόναξ, *AP* 6.64 (Paul. Sil.). **–ηδόν**, Adv. *like a reed*, A.D.*Adv.*197. 19. **–ήματα**· ἀναλήμματα, Hsch. **–ινος**, η, ον, *made of reeds*, κερκίδες Hsch. s.h.v. **–ῖτις**, ιδος, ἡ, *of reed*, ψήκτρα *AP*6.307 (Phan.). II. Subst., = λευκὴ ἄκανθα, Ps.-Dsc.3.12.

δονᾰκο-γλύφος [ῠ], ον, *reed-cutting, pen-making*, σμίλα *AP*6.295 (Phan.). **–δίφης** [ῐ], poet. **δουν–**, ου, ὁ, *one who searches among reeds*, prob. in ib.10.22 (Bianor). **–εις**, εσσα, εν, *reedy*, δονακόεντος Εὐρώτα E.*Hel.*210 (lyr.); δόλος δ. a reed covered with birdlime, *AP* 9.273 (Bianor). **–τρόφος**, ον, *producing reeds*, Εὐρώτας Thgn.785, E.*IA*179 (lyr.); Λάδων Corinn.12. **–φοίτης**, v. δουν–. **–χλοος**, ον, contr. **–χλους**, ουν, *green with reeds*, E.*IT*400.

Δονάκτας, ου, ὁ, epith. of Apollo, prob. in Theopomp.Hist.281.

δονᾰκ-ώδης, ες, *reedy*, Νεῖλος B.*Fr.*22, cf. A.R.2.818; *reed-like*, μορφή Nonn.*D.*42.385; *made by a reed*, μέλος ib.1.440. **–ών**, ῶνος, ὁ, *a thicket of reeds*, Paus.9.31.7 (as pr. n.), Epic. in *Arch.Pap.*7.7.

δόναξ, ᾰκος, ὁ, poet. gen. δούνακος *AP* (v. infr.), dat. δώνακι Theoc. (v. infr.): (δονέω, 'a reed *shaken with the wind*'):—*pole-reed, Arundo Donax*, smaller than the κάλαμος (Eust.Il.1165.23), Il.10.467, Od. 14.474, Thphr.*HP*4.11.11, etc.; δόνακες καλάμοιο reed-*stalks*, *h.Merc.* 47. 2. *bed of reeds*, App.*BC*3.67, al. II. *anything made of reed*, 1. *shaft of an arrow*, Il.11.584. 2. *shepherd's pipe*, Pi. *P.*12.25 (pl.), A.*Pr.*574 (lyr.), Theoc.20.29. 3. *fishing-rod* or *limed reed*, *AP*7.702 (Apollonid.). 4. *bridge* of the lyre, Ar.*Ra.* 232. III. shell-fish, = σωλήν, Diph.Siph.ap.Ath.3.90d.

δον-έω, *shake*, of the effects of the wind, τὸ δέ τε πνοιαὶ δονέουσιν they *shake* the young tree, Il.17.55; ἄνεμος... νέφεα σκιόεντα δονήσας *having driven* them, 12.157; ἀνέμῳ δεδονημένον αὖον ἄχερδον Theoc. 24.90: generally, *shake*, δ. γάλα, in order to make butter, Hdt.4.2; δ. ἄκοντα Pi.*P.*1.44:—Pass., δονοῦνται τὸ νευρῶδες *have twitchings in* the tendons, Paul.Aeg.6.74. 2. *drive about*, τὰς.. οἶστρος... ἐδόνησεν (sc. τὰς βόας) Od.22.300; *disturb, terrify*, Tim.*Pers.*222: hence of love, *agitate, excite*, Sapph.40, Ar.*Ec.*954 (lyr.); ποθεινὰ Ἑλλὰς αὐτὰν δ. μάστιγι πειθοῦς Pi.*P.*4.219, cf. 6.36 (Pass.); θυμὸν δονέουσι μέριμναι B.1.69 (but δ. καρδίαν *to agitate* one's mind, *Fr.*8); ὀσμὴ.. μυκτῆρα δονεῖ Mnesim.4.60; ἡμᾶς ἐδόνησεν ἡ μουσική Alciphr.*Fr.*6. 12:—Pass., ἡ Ἀσίη ἐδονέετο Asia *was in commotion*, Hdt.7.1; τὰ ὑπερόρια πολέμοις ἐδονεῖτο App.*BC*4.52; πελέκεσσι δονεῖσθαι Corinn. 18; Ἔρωτι δονεύμενος Bion *Fr.*6.5; παῖδα ποθῶν δεδόνητο Theoc.13. 65: fut. Med. in pass. sense, ἅρματα καλὰ δονήσεται *h.Ap.*270. 3. Pass., *wheel*, of troops, Arist.*Mu.*399^{b}9. II. of sound, *murmur, buzz*, of bees, prob. in *h.Merc.*563; δ. θρόον ὕμνων *rouse* the voice of song, Pi.*N.*7.81:—also in Med. or Pass., λυρᾶν τε βοαὶ καναχαί τ' αὐλῶν δονέονται Id.*P.*10.39; of bees, Choeril.2; ῥοιζήμασιν αἰθὴρ δονεῖται Ar.*Av.*1183.—Poet. word, used in Ion., X.*Smp.*2.8, and late Prose; of medical *percussion*, Aret.*SD*2.1. **–ημα**, ατος, τό, *agitation, waving*, δένδρου Luc.*Salt.*19.

δόξᾰ, ἡ, (δοκέω, δέκομαι) *expectation*, οὐδ' ἀπὸ δόξης not otherwise than *one expects*, Il.10.324, Od.11.344; in Prose, παρὰ δόξαν ἢ ὡς κατεδόκεε Hdt.1.79, etc.; ἐν δόξᾳ θέμενος εὖχος *hoping for*.., Pi.*O.* 10(11).63; δόξαν παρέχειν τινὶ μὴ ποιήσεσθαι... to make one *expect* that..., X.*HG*7.5.21; δόξαν παρέχεσθαί τινι ὡς..., c. part., Pl.*Sph.* 216d; ἀπὸ τῆς δ. πεσέειν, = Lat. *spe excidere*, Hdt.7.203. II. after Hom., *notion, opinion, judgement*, whether well grounded or not, βροτῶν δόξαι Parm.1.30, cf. 8.51; ψυχῆς εὐτλήμονι δόξῃ A.*Pers.*28 (anap.); ἃ δόξῃ τοπάζω S.*Fr.*235; δόξῃ γοῦν ἐμῇ Id.*Tr.*718; κατά γε τὴν ἐμήν, with or without δόξαν, Pl.*Grg.*472e, *Phlb.*41b: opp. ἐπιστήμη, Id.*Tht.*187b sq., *R.*506c, Hp.*Lex* 4, Arist.*Metaph.*1074^{b}36; φάσεις καὶ δ. Id.*EN*1143^{b}13; opp. νόησις, Pl.*R.*534a; ἀληθεῖ δόξῃ δοξασταί capable of being subjects of true *opinion*, Id.*Tht.*202b; δ. ἀληθεῖς ἢ ψευδεῖς Id.*Phlb.*36c; δόξης ὀρθότης ἀλήθεια Arist.*EN*1142^b 11; δ. ἐμποιεῖν περί τινος Id.*Pol.*1314^{b}22; κύριαι δ. philosophical *maxims*, title of work by Epicurus, Phld.*Ir.*p.86 W., etc.; αἱ κοιναὶ δ. *axioms*, Arist.*Metaph.*996^{b}28. 2. *mere opinion, conjecture*, δόξῃ ἐπίστασθαι, ἡγεῖσθαι, *imagine, suppose* (wrongly), Hdt.8.132, Th.5.105; δόξης ἁμαρτία Id.1.32; δόξαι joined with φαντασίαι, Pl.*Tht.*161e, cf. Arist.*Ph.*254^{a}29 (but distd. fr. φαντασίαι, Id.*de An.*428^{a}20); κατὰ δόξαν, opp. κατ' οὐσίαν, Pl.*R.*534c; ὡς δόξῃ χρώμενοι speaking *by guess*, Isoc.8.8, cf. 13.8. 3. *fancy, vision*, δ. ἀκόνας λιγυρᾶς Pi.*O.*6.82; δ. βριζούσης φρενός A.*Ag.*275; οὐκ εἰσὶ δόξαι τῶνδε πημάτων Id.*Ch.* 1053, cf. 1051; of a dream, E.*Rh.*780; δ. ἐνυπνίου Philostr.*VA*1.23: pl., *hallucinations*, Alex.Trall.1.17. III. *the opinion which others have of one, estimation, repute*, first in Sol.13.4 ἀνθρώπων δόξαν ἔχειν ἀγαθήν, cf. 34; δ. ἐπ' ἀμφότερα φέρεσθαι Th.2.11. 2. mostly, *good repute, honour, glory*, Alc.*Supp.*25.11, A.*Eu.*373 (lyr., pl.), Pi.*O.*8.64, etc.; δόξαν φύσας Hdt.5.91; δόξαν σχεῖν τινός *for* a thing, E.*HF*157; ἐπὶ σοφίᾳ δ. εἰληφώς Isoc.13.2; ἐπὶ καλοκἀγαθίᾳ καὶ σωφροσύνῃ δ. ὁμολογουμένην πεποιημένος Plb.35.4.8; δόξαν ἀντὶ τοῦ ζῆν ᾑρημένος D.2.15; δόξαν εἶχον ἄμαχοι εἶναι Pl.*Mx.*241b; δ. ἔχειν ὥς εἰσι... D.2.17; δ. καταλιπεῖν Id.3.24: in pl., οἱ ἐν ταῖς μεγίσταις δόξαις ὄντες Isoc.4.51. 3. rarely of *ill repute*, [δ.] ἀντὶ καλῆς αἰσχρὰν τῇ πόλει περιάπτειν D.20.10; λαμβάνειν δ. φαύλην Id.*Ep.*3.5; κληρονομήσειν τὴν ἐπ' ἀσεβείᾳ δ. Plb. 15.22.3. 4. *popular repute* or *estimate*, εἰσφέρων οὐκ ἀφ' ὑπαρχούσης οὐσίας.. ἀλλ' ἀπὸ τῆς δόξης ὧν ὁ πατήρ μοι κατέλιπεν D.21.157. IV. of external appearance, *glory, splendour*, esp. of the *Shechinah*, Lxx *Ex.*16.10, al.; δ. τοῦ φωτός *Act.Ap.*22.11: generally, *magnificence*, πλοῦτον καὶ δ. Lxx *Ge.*31.16, cf. *Ev.Matt.*4.8, al.; esp. of *celestial beatitude*, 2*Ep.Cor.*4.17: pl., 1*Ep.Pet.*1.11; also of *illustrious persons, dignities*, δόξας οὐ τρέμουσιν 2*Ep.Pet.*2.10; δ. βλασφημεῖν *Ep.Jud.*8.

δοξ-άζω, *think, imagine*, c. acc. et inf., A.Ag.673, E.*Supp.*1043, etc.; c. dupl. acc., πῶς ταῦτ' ἀληθῆ.. δοξάσω; how *can I suppose* this to be true? A.*Ch.*844; δ. βελτίους ἑαυτούς Pl.*Phlb.*48e; τὰ εὔχρηστα τῶν ζῴων θεοὺς ἐδόξασαν D.L.1.11; also abs., μετ' ἀσφαλείας δ. Th.1. 120; δοξάζων μὲν οὔ not *expecting* it, S.*Ph.*545:—Pass., δ. εἶναι *to be supposed* to be, Pl.*Ti.*46d, al.; ὅση δοξάζεται (sc. εἶναι) Id.*Phd.* 108c; δ. κακοί Id.*Lg.*646e; δ. δίκαιος Id.*R.*588b; τὰ δοξαζόμενα Id. *Plt.*278b. 2. c. part., δοξάσει τις ἀκούων *will suppose that* he hears, A.*Supp.*60 (lyr.). 3. c. acc. cogn., δόξας δ. *entertain* opinions, Pl. *Cri.*46d; δ. ψευδῆ *hold* false *opinions*, Id.*Tht.*189c; ψευδῶς δοξαζόμενα Polystr.p.26 W. 4. abs., *form* or *hold an opinion*, Pl.*Tht.*187a, al.; περί τινος Id.*Grg.*461b; κακῶς δ. Id.*R.*327c; παρὰ τὰ ὄντα Id. *Phdr.*262b; opp. γιγνώσκω, Id.*R.*476d; opp. ἐπίσταμαι, Arist.*APo.* 89^{a}7; δ. ἄνευ ἐπιστήμης Pl.*Tht.*201c. 5. Pass., *to be matter of opinion*, ταῦτα δεδοξάσθαι Xenoph.35, cf. Epicur.*Sent.*22. II. *magnify, extol*, ἐπὶ πλέον τι αὐτὸν δ. Th.3.45, cf. Lxx *Ex.*15.2, al.; τὸν θεόν *Ep.Rom.*1.21, al.:—Pass., *to be distinguished, held in honour, magnified*, Dionys.Com.2.24; δεδοξασμένος ἐπ' ἀρετῇ Plb.6.53.10, cf. Lxx *Ex.*15.1, al., *Ev.Jo.*7.39, al.; ἱερὸν δεδοξασμένον ἐξ ἀρχαίων *OGI* 168.56 (ii B.C.). **–άριον**, τό, Dim. of δόξα, Arr.*Epict.*2.22.11, Luc.*Peregr.*8. **–ᾰσία**, ἡ, *opinion*, D.C.53.19. **–ασις**, εως, ἡ, *formation of opinion*, Simp. in *Ph.*268.16 (pl.). **–ασμα**, ατος, τό, *opinion, notion, conjecture*, Th.1.141, Pl.*Phdr.*274c, etc.; *fancy*, E.*El.* 383; *idea, presentation*, Pl.*Tht.*158e. II. *glory*, Lxx *Is.*46.13, *La.*2. 1. **–ασμός**, ὁ, *formation of opinions*, κατὰ δοξασμόν Chrysipp.*Stoic.* 2.107. II. *glorification*, Sm.*Is.*13.3, Al.2*Ki.*22.25. **–αστέον**, *one must opine*, τὰ παραπλήσια Ph.1.4; ὡς.. Epicur.*Ep.*1 p.23 U. **–αστής**, οῦ, ὁ, *one who forms opinions* or *conjectures*, opp. κριτής, Antipho 5.94, cf. S.E.*M.*7.157; opp. ἐπιστήμων, Pl.*Tht.* 208e. II. δοξασταί· δικασταί, Hsch. **–αστικός**, ή, όν, *forming opinions, conjecturing*, opp. ἐπιστήμων, Pl.*Tht.*207c; δ. ἐπιστήμη *conjectural* knowledge, Id.*Sph.*233c, cf. 268c; δ. ἔννοιαι *pertaining to judgement*, Epicur.*Sent.*24; τὰς δοξαστικὰς (sc. φαντασίας) *belonging to opinion*, Phld.*Herc.*1003; τὸ δ. [μέρος τῆς ψυχῆς], opp. τὸ ἐπιστημονικόν, Arist.*EN*1140^{b}26. 2. in good sense, *original, full of ideas*, ψυχὴ ἀνδρικὴ καὶ δ. Isoc.13.17: τὸ –κόν Antig.Nic.ap.Heph. Astr.2.18. II. Adv. –κῶς, opp. κατ' ἀλήθειαν, Arist.*APr.*43^{b}8, cf. Phld.*Oec.*p.14 J., S.E.*M.*11.156, Procl. in *Prm.*p.609 S. **–αστός**, ή, όν, *matter of opinion, conjectural*, opp. νοητός, Pl.*R.*534a, Plu.2. 1114c; opp. γνωστός, Pl.*R.*478b, etc.; opp. ἐπιστητός, Arist.*APo.* 88^{b}30; opp. ὁρατός, δ. θεός Plu.2.756d; συλλαβὰς.. ἀληθεῖ δόξῃ δοξαστάς Pl.*Tht.*202b; τροφὴ δοξαστὴ food *of opinion*, Id.*Phdr.*248b. Adv. –τῶς S.E.*M.*2.53. II. *glorified*, Lxx *De.*26.19; *held in honour*, prob. in Hp.*Decent.*18.

δόξις, εως, ἡ, = δόξα, Democr.7.

δοξο-καθαιρετικός, ή, όν, *clever at removing suspicion*, Paul.Aeg. 2.12. **-κᾰλία**, ἡ, *conceit of beauty*, Pl.*Phlb*.49d. **-κομπέω**, = sq., Simp.*in Epict*.p.86 D. (s. v. l.). **-κοπέω**, *court popularity*, Plb.12.25ᵉ.3, D.Chr.66.1, Plu.*Per*.5. 2. *strike, impress the imagination*, τῷ ὄχλῳ τοῦ ἀριθμοῦ Longin.23.2. **-κοπία**, ἡ, *thirst for fame* or *popularity*, Phld.*Lib*.p.57 O., Heraclit.*Ep*.2, Plu.*Per*.5, M.Ant.11.18, Luc.*Peregr*.2, App.*BC*2.44, *Hann*.9, etc.; δ. ἄκρατος Epicur.*Fr*.120. **-κοπικός**, ή, όν, *popularity-hunting*, Apollon.ap. Stob.*App*.p.14 Gaisf. **-κόπος**, ον, = *thirsting for notoriety*, Teles p.39 H., Ph.2.269, Muson.*Fr*.7 p.29 H., D.Chr.32.24. **-λογία**, ἡ, *laudation*, Iamb.*Myst*.2.10. **-μᾰνέω**, *to be mad after fame*, Ph. 1.550. **-μᾰνής**, ές, *mad after fame*, Chrysipp.*Stoic*.3.167, Ph. 1.564, Iamb.*VP*12.58. **-μᾰνία**, ἡ, *mad thirst for fame*, Plu.*Sull*. 7. **-μᾰταιόσοφος**, ον, *would-be philosopher*, Epigr.ap.Hegesand. 1. **-μῑμητής**, οῦ, ὁ, *one who imitates mere semblance* (and not reality), Pl.*Sph*.267e. **-μῑμητική** (sc. τέχνη), ἡ, *his art*, ibid. **-παιδευτικός**, ή, όν, *having the semblance of education*, τέχνη ib.223b. **-ποιέω**, *glorify, praise* a god, *PMag.Berol*.2. 176. II. Pass., *possess the power of judgement*, τὸ τῶν ἀνθρώπων γένος δεδοξοποιημένον Plb.18.15.16. **-σοφία**, ἡ, *conceit of wisdom*, Pl.*Sph*.231b, *Phlb*.49a,d, Plu.2.999f. **-σοφος**, ον, *wise in one's own conceit*, Pl.*Phdr*.275b; *pretending to wisdom*, Arist.*Rh*.1387ᵇ 32. **-φᾰγία**, ἡ, *hunger after fame*, Plb.6.9.7. **-φαυλος**, ον, *apparently bad*, γάλα Sor.1.92. **-φόρος**, ον, *winning fame*, Man. 4.514.

δοξόω, only Pass., **δοξόομαι**, *have the character* or *credit* of being, ἐδοξώθη εἶναι σοφώτατος Hdt.8.124; δεδόξωσθε εἶναι ἀγαθοί Id.7.135, cf. 9.48.

δορά (A), ἡ, (δέρω) *skin when taken off, hide*, of beasts, δ. αἰγῶν Thgn.55; θηρῶν E.*Cyc*.330, cf. Diog.Oen.10; of birds, Hdt.4.175; of men, Pl.*Euthd*.285c; σατύρου Id.*Smp*.221e; grape-*skin*, Ruf. *Anat*.12. 2. rarely, *skin* on the living body, Ph.2.100, Hld.9. 18. II. *flaying*, Gal.2.423.

δορά (B), = δοκός (Cret.), *EM*284.12; cf. δόρυ.

δοράζει· κολάζει, *EM*284.15; but λογχάζει, Hsch.

δόραντον, τό, *horn for glue*, Hsch.

δορᾰτ-ίζομαι, *fight with spears*, Hsch., *EM*284.15. **-ιον**, τό, Dim. of δόρυ, Hdt.1.34, Th.4.34, Aen.Tact.29.6, Onos.26.1. **-ισμός**, ὁ, *fighting with spears*, Plu.*Pyrrh*.7, *Tim*.28, cj. in Lib.*Descr*.1.6.

δορᾰτο-θήκη, ἡ, *spear-case*, *EM*736.29. **-μᾰχέω**, *to fight with spears*, *AB*357, Suid. s. v. αἰχμάσσουσι. **-ξόος**, ον, = δορυξόος, τέκτων Nic.*Th*.170. **-πᾰχής**, ές, *of a spear-shaft's thickness*, X. *Cyn*.10.3. **-φόρος**, ον, = δορυφόρος, *Lyr.Adesp*.108, Lxx 1 *Ch*.12. 24, Ascl.*Tact*.1.3, etc.

δορεύς, έως, ὁ, *flayer*, prob. in Herod.8.64; name of a *throw of the dice*, Eub.57.5.

δορήϊος, α, ον, (δόρυ) *wooden*, *AP*15.14 (Theophanes).

δορίαλλος, ὁ, *pudendum muliebre*, Ar.*Fr*.367.

δορῐ-ἁλωσία, ἡ, *a being taken by storm*, App.*BC*4.52. **-ἄλωτος** [ᾰ], ον, *captive of the spear, taken in war*, χώρα Hdt.8.74, 9.4; of persons, *captive*, E.*Tr*.518 (lyr.), Isoc.4.177; πόλεις Decr.ap.D.18. 181, cf. Plb.23.10.6; Ion. δουριάλωτον λέχος, of Tecmessa, S.*Aj*. 211 (lyr.):—δορυάλωτος is a freq. v.l., as in Hp.*Ep*.27, X.*Cyr*.7.5. 35, *HG*5.2.5, Ph.2.526, etc., cf. *IG*14.1293.57. **-γαμβρος**, ον, *bride of battles*, i.e. *causing war by marriage*, or *wooed by battle*, of Helen, A.*Ag*.686 (lyr.). **-δμητος**, ον, *subdued by the spear*, *Sammelb*. 5829.6. **-θήρᾱτος**, ον, *hunted and taken by the spear*, E.*Hec*.103 (anap.), *Tr*.574 (lyr.). **-θρᾰσής**, ές, v. δορυθαρσής. **-κᾰνής**, ές, *slain by the spear*, δ. μόρος A.*Supp*.987. **-κμής**, ῆτος, ὁ, ἡ, Ion. **δουρ-**, = foreg., λαός Id.*Ch*.365 (lyr.). **-κός**, ή, όν, *of skin* or *hide*, ἱμάτια Hp.*Nat.Puer*.24. **-κρᾶνος**, ον, *spear-headed*, λόγχη A.*Pers*. 148 (lyr., δορυκρ- cod. Med.). **-κτητος**, ον, *won by the spear*, γυνή E.*Andr*.155, cf. Lyc.933, etc.: in Hom., also the Ion. fem. δουρικτήτη Il.9.343, cf. A.R.1.806: **δορύκτητος** Tryph.553; fem. -τη Id.630, Plu.2.232a. **-κτῠπος**, ον, *spear-clashing*, Pi.*N*.3.60. **-ληπτος**, ον, *won by the spear*, S.*Aj*.146 (anap.), E.*Hec*.478 (lyr.), etc.; Ion. **δουρίλ-** S.*Aj*.894; = κατηγορούμενος, Hsch. **-λύμαντος** [ῠ], ον, *destroyed by the spear*, A.*Fr*.131.2 (anap.). **-μᾰνής**, ές, *raging with the spear*, E.*Supp*.485. **-μαργος**, ον, *raging with the spear*, A.*Th*.687 (lyr.). **-μᾰχος**, ον, *fighting with the spear*, ἀρετά Tim.*Fr*. 14; Ion. **δουρίμᾰχος** Orac.ap.Sch.Il.2.543. **-μήστωρ**, ορος, ὁ, *master of the spear*, E.*Andr*.1016 (lyr.). **-παλτος**, ον, (πάλλω) *wielding the spear*, ἐκ χερὸς δοριπάλτου on the *right* hand, A.*Ag*.117 (lyr., δορυ- cod. Med.). **-πετής**, ές, (πίπτω) *fallen by the spear*, πεσήματα, ἀγωνία δ., *death by the spear*, E.*Andr*.653, *Tr*.1003. **-πληκτος**, ον, *smitten by the spear*, Sch.E.*Andr*.653. **-πονος**, ον, *toiling with the spear, bearing the brunt of war*, πόλις A.*Th*.169 (lyr.); ἄνδρες E.*El*.479 (lyr.); δ. κακά A.*Th*.628 (lyr.); δ. ἀσπίδες E.*IA*771 (lyr.). **-πτοίητος**, ον, *scattered by the spear*, *AP*7.297 (Polystr.).

δορίς, ίδος, ἡ, *sacrificial knife*, Anaxipp.6.3, Call.*Aet*.3.1.11.

δορι-σθενής, ές, *mighty with the spear*, A.*Ch*.158 (δορυσθενής cod. Med., as in *h.Hom*.8.3); βασιλῆες *AP*9.475. **-στέφᾰνος**, ον, *crowned for bravery*, Σπάρτα ib.596. **-τίνακτος** [τῐ], ον, *shaken by battle*, αἰθήρ A.*Th*.155 (lyr.). **-τμητος**, ον, *pierced by the spear*, Id. *Ch*.347 (lyr.). **-τολμος**, ον, *bold in war*, *APl*.4.46.

δορκάδ-ειος [ᾰ], α, ον, (δορκάς) *of an antelope* or *gazelle*, ἀστράγαλοι Thphr.*Char*.5.9, Plb.26.1.8:—also written **δορκάδεοι**, ἀστράγαλοι *IG*2.766.23, cf. *PSI*4.331.2, 444.2 (iii B.C.). **-ίζω**, *bound like an antelope*, of the pulse, Herophil.ap.Gal.8.556, al. **-ιον**, τό, Dim. of δορκάς, Lxx *Is*.13.14, Hsch. s. v. βούβαλος; *silver ornament in that shape*, *IG*11(2).203 *A* 10 (Delos, iii B.C.). II. = δίκταμνον, Ps.-Dsc.3.32.

δορκάζω, = περιβλέπω, Hsch. **δόρκαι**· κονίδες, Id.

δορκᾰλίς, ίδος, ἡ, = δορκάς, Call.*Ep*.33.2, *AP*7.578 (Agath.), Opp. *C*.1.165; of a girl, *AP*5.291.12 (Agath.). II. **δορκαλῖδες**, ων, αἱ, = δορκάδειοι ἀστράγαλοι, Herod.3.19.

δόρκανα, Adv., (δέρκομαι) *quick-sightedly, accurately* (Crete), Hsch.

δορκάς, άδος [ᾰ], ἡ, (δέρκομαι, δέδορκα) *an animal of the deer kind* (so called from its large bright eyes), in Greece, *roe, Cervus capreolus*, E.*Ba*.699, X.*Cyr*.1.4.7; in Syria and Africa, *gazelle, Antilope dorcas*, Hdt.4.192 (in form ζορκάς), 7.69.—Other forms:—**δόρξ**, **δορκός**, ἡ, E.*HF*376 (prob.), Call.*Lav.Pall*.91, Luc.*Am*.16: **δόρκος**, ὁ, Dsc.2.75, Opp.*C*.2.315, 3.3: **δόρκων**, ωνος, ὁ, Palamed.ap.Ath.11. 397a, Lxx *Ca*.2.17, Ar.Byz.*Epit*.3.15: **ζορκάς** (v. supr.): **ζόρξ**, Call. *Dian*.97, *Fr*.239, Nic.*Th*.42: **ἴορκος**, Opp.*C*.2.296, 3.3. (δόρκος and ἴορκος are distd. fr. δορκάς.)

δόρκειος, α, ον, *of a deer*, Theognost.*Can*.185.29: **δόρκιος**, *Edict. Diocl*.8.21.

δόρκων, ωνος, v. δορκάς. II. a kind of *ship*, David *Proll*.22.2.

δοροεργής, ές, *tanning* or *currying hides*, Man.4.320.

δορός, ὁ, (δέρω) *leathern bag* or *wallet*, Od.2.354, 380.

δορόω, *coat, plaster*, πηλῷ ἠχυρωμένῳ *IG*2².463.68, cf. 2.1054.58, dub. in ib.11(2).287 *A* 121 (Delos, iii B.C.).

δορπέω, *take supper*, Il.23.11, Od.8.539.

δορπήϊον, τό, *food, a meal*, Nic.*Al*.166 (pl.).

δορπηστός, ὁ, *supper-time, evening*, Hp.*Epid*.5.22, Ar.*V*.103, X. *An*.1.10.17: acc. to Philem.ap.Ath.1.11d, some made it = ἄριστον.

Δορπία, ἡ, *the first day of the feast Apaturia*, celebrated by public suppers in each phratria, personified in Philyll.8.2: πρόπεμπτα τῆς Δ. *IG*2.841 *b* 62; but τῆς ὀρτῆς τῇ δορπίῃ on the *eve* of the feast, Hdt. 2.48.

δορπιάζω, *take an evening meal*, Hsch.

δόρπιος, ον, *belonging to the feast*, ἁρμονίη Nonn.*D*.12.148. II. Subst. **δόρπιον**, τό, *supper-time*, v. l. (Erot.*Fr*.18) in Hp.*Epid*.5. 22.

δόρπον, τό, in Hom., *evening meal*, Od.12.439; taken at sunset, Il.19.208, Od.4.429, Pi.*O*.10(11).47; ἄριστα, δεῖπνα, δόρπα θ' αἱρεῖσθαι τρίτα A.*Fr*.182.3, cf. Sch.Od.2.20.—In later Ep., generally, *meal, food*, *h.Ap*.511, A.R.2.304, Q.S.4.278, Opp.*H*.1.26 (pl.); δόρποιο ποτοῦ θ' ἅλις Orph.*A*.406.

δόρπος, ὁ, = foreg., Nic.*Al*.66, *AP*9.551 (Antiphil.), Q.S.9.431.

δορποφόρος, ον, *offering supper*, βωμός *IG*12(5).244 (Paros).

δόρυ, τό, Att. gen. δόρατος, rare in Poets, as Ar.*Ach*.1120, late Ep. dat. pl. δοράτεσσι Q.S.6.363: Ep. and Ion. decl., gen. δούρατος (also in Pi.*P*.4.38); dat. δούρατι (also in S.*Ph*.721 (lyr.)); pl. δούρατα, δούρασι (but codd. of Hdt. usu. have δόρατα, δόρασι): more commonly δουρός, δουρί (but δορί Archil.2.1); dual δοῦρε; pl. δοῦρα, δούρων, δούρεσσι; dat. pl. δούροις Opp.*H*.3.573: Trag., gen. δορός; dat. δορί or δόρει, the former required by metre in A.*Th*.347, 456, 958, *Ag*.111, E.*Hec*. 909, *Ph*.186, etc. (all lyr.), also in Id.*Hec*.5; δόρει is required in S.*OC*620, 1314, 1386; ξὺν δορὶ ξὺν ἀσπίδι Ar.*V*.1081, but σὺν δόρει σὺν ἀσπίδι Achae.29, cf. Choerob.*in Theod*.1.346; δορί occurs in Prose in the phrases δορὶ ἑλεῖν, λαβεῖν (v. infr. II. 2): nom. pl. δόρη E. *Rh*.274, Theopomp.Com.25; gen. δορῶν Hsch.: nom. δοῦρας *AP*6. 97 (Antiphil.). Exc. sg. δόρυ, Hom. uses only the Ion. forms: I. *stem, tree*, οὔπω τοῖον ἀνήλυθεν ἐκ δόρυ γαίης Od.6.167; but commonly, *plank* or *beam*, δοῦρ' ἐλάτης κέρσαντες Il.24.450; δούρατα μακρὰ ταμών Od.5.162, cf. Il.3.61; δούρατα πύργων 12.36; δούρατ' ἀμάξης Hes.*Op*.456; mostly of ships, δόρυ νήϊον ship's *plank*, Il.15.410, etc.; νήϊα δοῦρα Od.9.498; also, *mast*, E.*Tr*.1148: hence, 2. δ. εἰνάλιον, ἀμφῆρες, of a *ship*, Pi.*P*.4.27, E.*Cyc*.15; δ. ποντοπόρον S.*Ph*. 721 (lyr.); also δόρυ alone, A.*Pers*.411, *Ag*.1618, E.*Hel*.1611; ἐπ' Ἀργῴου δορός Id.*Andr*.793; also δούρων, of *oars*, *Hymn.Is*.152. 3. *pillory, stocks*, ἐν δουρὶ δεθεὶς αὐχένα Anacr.21.9. II. *shaft of a spear*, δόρυ μείλινον the ashen *shaft*, Il.5.666, al.: hence, generally, *spear itself*, δ. χάλκεον 13.247; ἀσπίδα καὶ δύο δοῦρε Od.1.256, etc.; *hunting-spear*, Il.12.303; δόρατα ναύμαχα boarding-*pikes*, Hdt.7.89: freq. in military phrases, v. πέλεκυς I; εἰς δόρατος πληγήν within *spear's* throw, X.*Eq*.8.10; εἰς δόρυ ἀφικόμενοι Id.*HG*4.3.17; ἐπὶ δόρυ to *the right hand*, in which the spear was held, opp. ἐπ' ἀσπίδα, Id. *An*.4.3.29 (cf. κλίνω IV. 3, κλίσις III); παρὰ δόρυ Id.*Lac*.11.10; εἰς δόρυ Id.*HG*6.5.18; τὴν ἐμβολὴν ἐκ δόρατος ποιεῖσθαι Plb.3.115.9:—ὑπὸ δόρυ πωλεῖσθαι, = Lat. *sub hasta venire*, D.H.4.24, cf. Str.4.6. 7. b. *pole* of a standard, X.*Cyr*.7.1.4. c. *sceptre*, E.*Hec*. 9. d. *stick* used as tourniquet, Hp.*Nat.Puer*.24. 2. metaph., δουρὶ κτεατίζειν win wealth *by the spear*, i.e. *in war*, Il.16.57; ὑπὸ δουρὶ πόλιν πέρθαι ib.708; in Prose, δορὶ ἑλεῖν, λαβεῖν, Th.1.128, App. *BC*4.8; *an armed force*, συμμάχῳ δ. A.*Eu*.773; δ. ἐπακτοῦ S.*OC* 1525; καὶ τὸ δ. καὶ τὸ κηρύκειον πέμπειν to offer *war* or peace, Plb. 4.52.4. (Cf. Skt. *dāru* 'piece of wood', δορά (B), δρῦς.)

δορύαλλος, = δορίαλλος, Hsch.

δορῠ-άλωτος, v. δοριάλωτος. **-βόλος**, ον, *hurling spears*, μηχάνημα J.*AJ*9.10.3; δορυβόλον alone, Ph.*Bel*.95.20.

δορύδιον, τό, Dim. of δόρυ, *shaft* of a hook or probe, Heliod.(?) ap. Orib.47.17.5.

δορυ-δρέπᾰνον, τό, a kind of *halbert*, Pl.*La*.183d; esp. a large kind *used for cutting off* halyards in sea-fights, Str.4.4.1; in sieges, *for pulling down* battlements, Plb.21.27.4. **-θαρσής**, ές, = δορίτολμος, *Epigr.Gr.*1035.18 (Pergam.), *APl.*4.170 (Hermodor.):—also **-θρᾰσής**, ές, Nonn.*D.*17.100, 21.164, al.

δορύκαι· δουροδόκαι, Hsch.

δορῠκέντειρα, ἡ, *piercing with the spear*, v.l. in Corn.*ND*20.

δορυκνίδιον, τό, Dim. of sq. 1, Gal.11.864.

δορύκνιον, τό, *Convolvulus oleaefolius*, Dsc.4.74, Plu.*Demetr.* 20. 2. = μελισσόφυλλον, Nic.*Al.*376 (cf. Sch.ad loc.). 3. = πύρεθρον, Ps.-Dsc.3.73. 4. = στρύχνον μανικόν, ib.4.72.

δορύκρᾱνος, δορύκτητος, δορύμᾰχος, v. δορι-.

δορύλλιον, τό, Dim. of δόρυ, Suid. s.v. ξυστόν. **δορυμήστωρ**, ορος, ὁ, *skilled with the spear*, Hsch. **δορυμόλπης**· ὁ προηγούμενος τοῦ θυομένου βοὸς τῷ Διί, Id. **δορυξε⟨ί⟩ον**, τό, *workshop where spear-shafts are made*, Id.

δορύ-ξενος, ὁ, ἡ, *spear-friend*, i.e. *war-friend, ally* (wrongly expld. as ἐκ δορυαλώτου δ. προσαγορευόμενος by Plu.2.295b), A.*Ag.*880; ξένος τε καὶ δ. δόμων Id.*Ch.*562, cf. S.*El.*46, etc.: as Adj., δόμοι δορύξενοι A.*Ch.*914; ἑστία S.*OC*632. **-ξόος**, ον, contr. **-ξοῦς**, ουν, (ξέω) *spear-polishing*: *maker of spears*, Plu.*Pel.*12:—also **-ξός**, ὁ, Ar.*Pax* 447, 1213; **-ξύς**, *PTeb.*278.4 (i A.D.). **-πᾱγής** [ῠ], ές, *compact of beams*, νῆας A.*Supp.*743 (lyr.):—Ion. **δουροπ-** Opp.*H.*1.358. **-πῦρος**, ον, *with fiery spears*, ἄστρων στρατὸς *Lyr.Adesp.*128.

δορυσθενής, v. δορι-.

δορυσ-σόητος, ον, = sq., μόχθων δορυσσοήτων of the toils *of battle*, S.*Aj.*1188. **-σόος**, ον, contr. **-σοῦς**, οῦν (v. infr.): (σεύω):—*brandishing the lance*, of persons, Hes.*Sc.*54, A.*Supp.*182, 985; πόνος δ. Thgn.987: contr. -σοῦς S.*OC*1313, A.*Th.*125, prob. in E.*Heracl.* 774 (lyr.).

δορυφία· καρποφορία ἀγαθή, Hsch.

δορῠφόνος, ον, *slaying with the spear*, Ar.*Fr.*196, Telecl.29 (s.v.l.).

δορῠφορ-έω, *attend as a body-guard*, τινά Hdt.2.168, 3.127, Th.1.130; τὸν ἔπαρχον *PAmh.*2.79.52 (ii A.D.): generally, *keep guard over*, τὴν ἑκάστου σωτηρίαν D.23.123:—Med., ψυχὴν λογισμῷ Them.*Or.*1.5b:—Pass., *to be guarded*, στρατοπέδοις D.17.12; δορυφορεῖσθαι τῇ τῶν πολιτῶν εὐνοίᾳ Isoc.10.37: metaph., ὑπὸ μανίας Pl.*R.*573a, cf. Ph.2.239, al. b. Astrol., of planets, *attend*, i.e. *flank*, the Sun, etc., Ptol.*Tetr.*114, al., S.E.*M.*5.38 (Pass.). 2. c. dat., *attend as guard*, ἡμῖν αὐτοῖς X.*Cyr.*7.5.84; πειθαρχοῦντας αὐτῷ καὶ -φοροῦντας Plb.32.8.6. 3. metaph. of numbers in a series, *flank*, Iamb.*in Nic.* p.77P.:—Pass., ib.p.40P. **-ημα**, ατος, τό, *body-guard*: used of the κωφὰ πρόσωπα or *mute characters* on the stage, Luc.*Hist.Conscr.*4, Jul.*Caes.*310c: hence of Aridaeus, who was put up as the successor of Alexander, ὁ δέ, ὥσπερ ἐπὶ σκηνῆς δ., κωφὸν ἦν ὄνομα βασιλείας Plu.2.791e, cf. Id.*Alex.*77. **-ησις**, εως, ἡ, *protection of body-guard*, M.Ant.1.17 (pl.). **-ία**, ἡ, *guard kept over*, τῆς ἐπιστολῆς X.*Cyr.*2.2.10: abs., Iamb.*Myst.*2.7; concrete, *body-guard*, Lxx 2*Ma.*3.28. II. Astron., κατὰ δορυφορίαν τῶν τροπικῶν κύκλων *Placit.*2.23.6. **-ικός**, ή, όν, *of* or *for the guard*, οἴκησις Pl.*Ti.*70b, *Criti.* 117c; δ. σημεῖα, = Lat. *signa praetoria*, standards *of the praetorian guard*, D.C.60.35; τὸ δ. *the guard*, Id.42.52. **-ος**, ον, *spear-bearing*, ὀπάονες A.*Ch.*769. II. Subst., *spearman*, X.*An.*5.2.4. 2. esp. *one of the body-guard* of kings and tyrants, Hdt.1.59, etc.; [ὁ Περίανδρος] πρῶτος -φόρους ἔσχε Arist.*Fr.*516. b. at Rome, of *the praetorians*, Plu.*Galb.*13, Hdn.5.4.8. 3. metaph., ἡδοναὶ δ. *mere satellite* pleasures, Pl.*R.*587c, cf. 573e; δ. τῶν ἐπιθυμιῶν τινος *pandering to* his lusts, Luc.*Tyr.*4. 4. in Drama, *mute character*, Hsch., *EM*284.21.

δορχελοί· ἀστράγαλοι, Hsch.

δορ-ώσιμος, η, ον, (δορόω) *for plastering*, *PPetr.*3 p.139 (iii B.C.). **-ωσις**, εως, ἡ, *plastering*, ibid.

δός, δόθι, v. δίδωμι.

δοσείδιον, τό, Dim. of δόσις II. 5, *IG*14.956*A*22.

δοσείω, Desiderat., *to be inclined to give*, Hsch.

δοσίδῐκος, ον, f.l. for δωσίδικος, Hdt.6.42, Plb.4.4.3.

δόσιμος, η, ον, of houses, *liable to be surrendered as billets*, *PTeb.*5.176 (ii B.C.).

δοσίπῡγος, v. δωσίπυγος.

δόσις, εως, ἡ, (δίδωμι) *giving*, φαρμάκου Antipho 1.18; χρημάτων Hdt.1.61; μισθοῦ Th.1.143; opp. αἴτησις, Pl.*Euthphr.*14d; δ. χρημάτων καὶ λῆψις Arist.*EN*1107^{b}8; λήψεις καὶ δόσεις Arr.*Epict.*2.9.12, cf. Lxx *Si.*41.19, *Ep.Phil.*4.15. b. *licence, permission*, *SIG* 987.33 (Chios, iv B.C.). 2. ἐμβολῶν δ. *ramming* in naval tactics, D.S.13.10. II. *gift*, καὶ οἱ δ. ἔσσεται ἐσθλή Il.10.213; δ. ὀλίγη τε φίλη τε Od.6.208, 14.58, cf. Hdt.1.90, 9.93, S.*OT*1518, etc.; δόσιν κακὰν κακῶν κακοῖς A.*Pers.*1041 (lyr.); θεῶν εἰς ἀνθρώπους Pl.*Phlb.* 16c. 2. *bequest, legacy*: κατὰ δόσιν by *will* (opp. κατὰ γένος, as heir-at-law), Is.4.7, Isoc.19.45, cf. Harp. 3. *largess*, = Lat. *congiarium*, Hdn.6.8.8 (pl.). 4. *contribution* towards the fulfilment of a purpose, Chrysipp.(?)*Stoic.*3.30. 5. *payment on account, instalment*, *IG*1^{2}.296, 7.303.35 (Orop.), etc.; *payment in kind*, *PMasp.*146.4 (vi A.D.), al. 6. *portion*, Lxx *Ge.*47.22, al., *BGU*1122.12 (i B.C.); διελὼν εἰς δόσεις Plu.*Arat.*13. 7. *dose of medicine*, Dsc.2.171; δ. τελεία full *dose*, Ruf.ap.Orib.8.57.5, etc., cf. Luc.*Abd.*4. 8. τῆς οἰκονομίας πολλὴν ποιεῖσθαι δ. lay great *stress* on an arrangement, D.H.*Dem.*51; οὐ τοσαύτην ποιούμενοι τῆς ἡδονῆς δ. ὅσην τῆς ἀληθείας ib.18. 9. *destiny, fate* of an individual, ἡ ἀνθρωπίνη δ. Iamb.*Myst.* 1.3; esp. of planetary *influence*, Plot.2.3.2, al.

δόσκον, Ep. iterative of δίδωμι (q.v.).

δοσοληψία, ἡ, *give-and-take, exchange, barter*, Orph.*Fr.*278 (pl.), Vett.Val. in *Cat.Cod.Astr.*2.163.

δότ-ειρα, ἡ, fem. of δοτήρ, Hes.*Op.*356, Nic.*Al.*612. **-έος**, α, ον, (δίδωμι) *to be given*, Hdt.8.111. II. δοτέον *one must give*, Pl.*R.*452e, Alex.250, etc.; *one must allow*, c. inf., Luc.*Abd.*9. **-ήρ**, ῆρος, ὁ, *giver, dispenser*, ταμίαι .. σίτοιο δοτῆρες Il.19.44; ὀϊστοὶ θανάτοιο δ. Hes.*Sc.*131; esp. of the gods, δ. εὐθηλέος ἥβης *h.Hom.*8.9; μαντευμάτων Pi.*Pae.*7.1; πυρὸς βροτοῖς δοτῆρα A.*Pr.*612.—Poet. form used by X.*Cyr.*8.1.9, and in later Prose, θεὸς δ. παντὸς ἀγαθοῦ D.H.2.62, cf. J.*AJ*1.18.6, Iamb.*Myst.*3.31. **-ης**, ου, ὁ, later form of δοτήρ, Lxx *Pr.*22.8, 2*Ep.Cor.*9.7. **-ικός**, ή, όν, *inclined to give, giving freely*, Arist.*EN*1121^{b}16. Adv. -κῶς Hsch. s.v. δοσείειν. II. ἡ -κή (sc. πτῶσις), *the dative case*, *Stoic.*2.59, Str.14.1.41, D.T.636.4, A.D.*Synt.*28.23, etc. **-ός**, ή, όν, (δίδωμι) *granted*, Lxx 1*Ki.*1.11, Ph.1.273; *that may* or *must be granted*, Max.Tyr.11.7.

δουκηνάριος, ὁ, = Lat. *ducenarius*, *official receiving salary of* 200,000 *sesterces*, *IG*14.1347, *POxy.*1711.4 (iii A.D.), etc. II. fem. **δουκηναρία**, ἡ, *assessment of* 200,000 *sesterces*, ib.1274.14 (iii A.D.).

δουκικός, ή, όν, = Lat. *ducianus*, Just.*Edict.*13.2.

δουλᾰγωγ-έω, *make a slave, treat as such*, dub. in D.S.12.24, cf. Arr.*Epict.*3.24.76. 2. metaph. of pleasure, etc., δ. τοὺς βίους Longin.44.6, cf. Charito 2.7; τὸ σῶμα *bring* it *into subjection*, 1*Ep.Cor.*9.27. **-ία**, ἡ, *enslavement*, *IG*9(1).39, 42 (Stiris), *POxy.*38.10 (i A.D.). **-ός**, όν, *enslaving*, δ. θηρίον ἡ ἡδονή Plu.*Volupt.Fr.*2.

δουλ-ᾰπᾰτία, ἡ, *enticement of slaves from their master*, Arist.*EN* 1131^{a}7. **-άριον**, τό, Dim. of δούλη, Ar.*Th.*537, Metag.19, etc.; not used of male slaves, acc. to Luc.*Lex.*25, but cf. Arr.*Epict.*2.21.11. **-εία**, ἡ, Ion. **-ηΐη** Anacr.114, Hdt.6.12: also **δουλία** Pi.*P.*1.75:—*slavery, bondage*, ll.cc., A.*Th.*253; δουλείας γάγγαμον, ζυγά, Id. *Ag.*360 (anap.), S.*Aj.*944 (lyr.); δ. καὶ ὑπηρεσία Ar.*V.*602; ἡ τῶν κρεισσόνων δ. *imposed by* them, Th.1.8; ἡ ὑπὸ τῶν βαρβάρων δ. Pl.*R.*469c; applied to the condition of the subject allies of Athens, Th.5.9. II. collectively, *slaves*, δουλεύοντα δουλείαις ἐμαῖς E.*Ba.*803; ἤν .. ἡ δ. ἐπανιστῆται if *the slave-class* rise in rebellion, Th.5.23; ἡ Ἡρακλεωτῶν δ. Pl.*Lg.*776d; τὰς .. Εἱλωτείας καὶ Πενεστείας καὶ δουλείας Arist. *Pol.*1264^{a}36. III. *service for hire*, μισθὸν δουλείας Lxx 3*Ki.*5.6. **-ειος**, α, ον, also ος, ον Pi.*Fr.*223, E.*Tr.*1330 (lyr.):—*slavish, servile*, εἶδος Od.24.252; κεφαλή Thgn.535; τύχα Pi.l.c.; δούλειον ἦμαρ E.*Hec.*56, *Andr.*99, cf. *Tr.*1330; ζυγόν Pl.*Lg.*770e; ἤθη ib. 790a. **-έκδουλος**, ὁ, *a born slave*, Seleuc.ap.Ath.6.267c, D.S.10 *Fr.*1. **-ελεύθερος**, ὁ, *freedman*, Vett.Val.7.8, al. **-εος**, α, ον, poet. for δούλειος, δ. δεσμὰ γυναικῶν A.R.*Fr.*12.13. **-ευμα**, ατος, τό, *a service*, E.*Or.*221. II. *a slave*, S.*Ant.*756, cf. E.*Ion* 748. **-ευσις**, εως, ἡ, *slavery*, prob. f.l. for δούλωσις, Porph.*Abst.*1.8. **-ευτέον**, *one must be a slave*, τινί E.*Ph.*395, *Ba.*366; οὐ μὴν δουλευτέον τοὺς νοῦν ἔχοντας τοῖς κακῶς φρονοῦσιν Isoc.9.7. **-ευτός**, ή, όν, *servile*, Al.*Le.*23.7. **-εύτρια**, ἡ, *female attendant*, Eust.1661.47. **-εύω**, (δοῦλος) *to be a slave*, Hdt.2.56, And.1.138, Pl.*Lg.* 777d, etc.; παρά τινι D.18.129: c. acc. cogn., δουλείαν δ. X.*Mem.*3.12.2, Pl.*Smp.*183a, al. 2. *serve, be subject*, τό τ' ἄρχειν καὶ τὸ δ. δίχα A.*Pr.*927, etc.; δ. ζεύγλαις ib.463; τοῖς ἄρχουσι καὶ τοῖς νόμοις Pl.*Lg.*698b; ἡδονῇ Id.*Phdr.*238e, etc.; δ. γαστρί, ὕπνῳ, λαγνείᾳ, X. *Mem.*1.6.8; κεναῖς δόξαις Polystr.p.29W.; τῇ γῇ δ. *make oneself a slave* to one's land, i.e. give up rights that one may keep it, Th.1.81; so δ. τῇ κτήσει αὐτοῦ Pl.*R.*494d; δουλεύομεν δόξαισιν Philem.93.8; δ. τῷ καιρῷ *accommodate oneself* to the occasion, *AP*9.441 (Pall.); θυμῷ Hdn.1.17.6. 3. *render a service*, τινά *PLond.*5.1727.11 (vi A.D.). **-ία**, v. δουλεία. **-ίδιον**, τό, Dim. of δουλίς, Hsch. s.v. θεράπνιον. **-ικός**, ή, όν, = sq. 1, ὅπλον X.*Cyr.*7.4.15 (Sup.); διακονήματα Pl.*Tht.*175e; ἔργον Araros 18; δ. καὶ ταπεινὰ πράγματα ποιεῖν D.57.45; -ώτεροι τὰ ἤθη Arist.*Pol.*1285^{a}20; δ. πόλεμος *slave-war*, Plu.*Crass.*10. Adv. -κῶς Phryn.Com.2D., X.*Oec.*10.10: Comp. -ώτερον Arr.*Epict.*4.1.25. 2. = sq. 2, παιδίον, σώματα, *BGU*1120.10 (i B.C.), 26.23 (i A.D.). **-ιος**, α, ον (ος, ον *AP*7.401 (Crin.)), *slavish, servile*, in Hom. only δούλιον ἦμαρ the day *of slavery*, Il.6.463, al., cf. *IG*1^{2}.763; ἐσθῆτι δουλίῃ (δουληΐῃ is f.l.) Hdt.3.14; δ. ζυγόν Id.7.8.γ', A.*Ag.*953, *Th.*471; δ. τροφή S.*Aj.*499. 2. *of a slave*, δ. φρήν a *slave's* mind, A.*Ag.*1084 (lyr.); ἔργον (prob.) *PGrenf.*2.78.11 (iv A.D.).—In a few places the Med. Ms. of A. gives δούλειος (*Th.*75, 471, 793), but the metre freq. requires δούλιος (*Pers.*50 (anap.), *Ag.* 953, 1041, al., so in S.*Aj.*499), never δούλειος: in E., however, δούλειος is certainly required (v. sub v.). The common form in Att. Prose is δουλικός, and δοῦλος is used as Adj. in same sense. **-ίς**, ίδος, ἡ, = δούλη, Hyp.*Fr.*235, *AP*5.17 (Rufin.), *IG*14.1839.8: condemned by Poll.3.74.

δουλῐχό-δειρος, ον, Ion. for δολιχόδ-. **-εις**, εσσα, εν, Ion. for δολιχόεις.

δουλό-βοτος, ον, *eaten up by slaves*, τὰ αὑτοῦ Philostr.*VS*1.21.4. **-γάμος** [ᾰ], ον, = δουλομίκτης, *Cat.Cod.Astr.*8(4).127. **-γνώμων**, ον, gen. ονος, *of slavish mind*, *AB*393, Suid. s.v. ἀνδραποδώδεις. **-δῐδάσκᾰλος**, ὁ, *teacher of slaves*, title of play by Pherecr., cf. Ath.6.262b; of Theodora, Procop.*Arc.*15. **-κοίτης**, ου, ὁ, *consorting with slaves*, Paul.Al.*O.*2. **-κρᾰτέομαι**, Pass., *to be ruled by slaves*, D.C.60.2; or, *like slaves*, Lib.*Decl.*43.35. **-κρᾰτία**, ἡ, *slave-government*, J.*AJ*19.4.4. **-μᾰχία**, ἡ, *servile war*, Lyd. *Ost.*34. **-μίκτης**, ου, ὁ, *one who consorts with slaves*, Tz.*H.*6.466. **-μιξία**, ἡ, *consorting with slaves*, ib.467. **-ποιέω**, *enslave*, Herm.ap.Stob.1.49.45. **-ποιός**, όν, *enslaving*, Sch.E.*Or.* 488. **-πόνηρος**, ον, *bad like a slave's*, κόλυθρον Telecl.3. **-πρέ-**

πεια, ἡ, *slavish spirit*, Pl.*Alc.*1.135c, Theopomp.Com.87. **-πρεπής**, ές, *befitting a slave, servile*, πόνος Hdt.1.126; opp. ἐλευθέριος, X.*Mem.* 2.8.4 (Comp.), cf. Pl.*Grg.*485b, 518a, etc.: Sup., Phld.*Herc.*1457.3. Adv. -πῶς, φθαρῆναι D.C.61.15, cf. Gal.17(2).146: Sup. -έστατα Cratin.403.

δοῦλος (A), Cret. **δῶλος** *Leg.Gort.*1.1, al., ὁ:—prop. *born bondman* or *slave*, opp. *one made a slave*, τὰ ἀνδράποδα πάντα καὶ δοῦλα καὶ ἐλεύθερα Th.8.28, cf. E.*IA*330: then, generally, *bondman, slave*, opp. δεσπότης (q.v.): not in Hom., who twice has fem. **δούλη**, ἡ, *bondwoman*, Il.3.409, Od.4.12, cf. A.*Ag.*1326, X.*Cyr.*5.1.4, Pl.*R.* 395e, etc.: freq. of Persians and other nations subject to a despot, Hdt., etc.; οὔ τινος δοῦλοι κέκληνται, of the Greeks, A.*Pers.*242: metaph., χρημάτων δ. *slaves to* money, E.*Hec.*865; so γνάθου δ. Id.*Fr.* 282.5; τῶν αἰεὶ ἀτόπων Th.3.38; λιχνειῶν, λαγνειῶν, X.*Oec.*1.22, cf. *Mem.*1.3.11. II. Adj. (not in A.), δοῦλος, η, ον, *slavish, servile, subject*, δ. πόλις S.*OC*917, X.*Mem.*4.2.29; γνώμαισι δούλαις S.*Tr.*53; δ. ἔχειν βίον ib.302; σῶμα δ., opp. νοῦς ἐλεύθερος, Id.*Fr.*940; τοὺς τρόπους δούλους παρασχεῖν E.*Supp.*877; δ. θάνατος, ζυγόν, πούς, Id.*Or.* 1170, *Tr.*678, 507; δ. καὶ τυραννουμένη πόλις Pl.*R.*577d; δ. ἡδοναί, = δουλοπρεπεῖς, ib.587c, etc.: Comp. δουλότερος *more enslaved*, Αἴγυπτον δ. ποιεῖν Hdt.7.7. 2. τὸ δ., = οἱ δοῦλοι, E.*Ion*983, etc.; also, *slavery, a slavish life*, ib.556 (troch.). 3. *ancillary*, δ. ἐπιστῆμαι Arist.*Metaph.*996^{b}11.

δοῦλος (B)· ἡ οἰκία ἢ τὴν ἐπὶ τὸ αὐτὸ συνέλευσιν τῶν γυναικῶν, Hsch.; cf. δωλοδομεῖς, δωλέννετος.

δουλό-σύνη, ἡ, poet. and Ion. for δουλεία, *slavery*, Od.22.423, Pi. *P.*12.15, A.*Th.*112, E.*Ph.*192 (anap.), Hdt.1.129, al. **-συνος**, ον, = δοῦλος (A) II, *enslaved*, τινί E.*Hec.*448 (lyr.). **-φᾰνής**, ές, *slave-like, slavish to look on*, σῶμα J.*BJ*2.7.2. **-ψῡχος**, ον, = foreg., Ptol.*Tetr.*66.

δουλ-όω, *enslave*, Hdt.1.27; δουλοῖς καὶ σὲ καὶ πᾶσαν πόλιν A.*Th.* 254, cf. S.*Tr.*467; δ. φρόνημα Th.2.61:—mostly in Pass., *to be enslaved*, ὑπὸ Πέρσῃσι, ὑπὸ Ἁρπάγου, Hdt.1.94, 174, cf. Th.1.98; αἱ ψυχαὶ δεδούλωνται Hp.*Aër.*23; δεδουλωμένοι τῇ γνώμῃ, τὴν γνώμην ἐδουλοῦντο, Th.4.34, 7.71; ἐλεύθερος πᾶς ἐνὶ δεδούλωται, νόμῳ Men.699, cf *Sam.*280:—Med. (with pf. δεδουλῶσθαι Th.6.82), *make subject to oneself, enslave*, Id.1.18, 5.29, 7.68, 75, Pl.*Mx.*239d; τὸν ἥσσονα δουλούμεθ' ἄνδρα E.*Supp.*493; ἐπιθυμίαν Pl.*Lg.*838d; τὸ ἑαυτοῦ θειότατον ὑπὸ τῷ ἀθεωτάτῳ . . δουλοῦται Id.*R.*589e. **-ωσις**, εως, ἡ, *enslavement*, Th.3.10, Plu.*Publ.*21, D.C.53.7. 2. *constraint*, opp. τρυφή, Pl. *Lg.*791d. **-ωτικός**, ή, όν, *pertaining to service*, πρᾶγμα Plu.*Nob.*2.

δοῦναξ, δουνακόεις, poet. for δον-.

δούξ, δουκός, ὁ, = Lat. *dux*, *PLond.*2.141.18 (iv A.D.), Just.*Edict.* 13.18 *Intr.*, etc.

δουπέω, fut. -ήσω *AP*9.427 (s.v.l., Barb.): Ep. aor. δούπησα Il.4.504, al.; also ἐγδούπησα (from γδουπέω) 11.45: pf. δέδουπα 23. 679, Nic.*Al.*15, A.R.1.1304, Euph.40; not freq. exc. in Ep.: (δοῦπος):—*sound heavy* or *dead*; in Hom., of *the heavy thud of a corpse*, opp. the clashing of the armour, δούπησεν δὲ πεσών, ἀράβησε δὲ τεύχε' ἐπ' αὐτῷ Il.4.504, al.; ἢ αὐτὸς δουπῆσαι ἀμύνων λοιγὸν Ἀχαιοῖς 13.426; δεδουπότος Οἰδιπόδαο 23.679, cf. A.R.1.1304, Euph.40; δουπεῖ χεὶρ γυναικῶν *falls with heavy sound* upon their breasts, E.*Alc.*104 (lyr.); of rowers, κώπῃ δουπεῖν dub. in *AP*9.427 (Barb.); of soldiers, *strike heavily*, ταῖς ἀσπίσι πρὸς τὰ δόρατα ἐδούπησαν X.*An.*1.8.18; τοῖς δόρασι δ. πρὸς τὰς ἀσπίδας Arr.*An.*1.6.4:—Pass., aor. δουπήθησαν *AP* 9.283 (Crin.).—Rare in Prose, cf. Luc.*Hist.Conscr.*22. (Said to be Cypr., *AB*1095.)

δουπήτωρ, ορος, ὁ, *clattering*, χαλκός *AP*4.3b.13 (Agath.).

δοῦπος, ὁ, *any dead, heavy sound, thud*, δ. ἀκόντων Il.11.364, 16. 361; δ. ὀρώρει πύργων βαλλομένων 9.573, cf. 12.289; of the distant *din* of battle, 16.635; of the *sound* of footsteps, 10.354, Od.16.10; of *the measured tread* of infantry, Il.23.234, Hes.*Th.*70; ὅμαδον καὶ δ., of a multitude, Od.10.556; of the *roar* of the sea dashing against rocks or of a distant torrent, 5.401, Il.4.455.—Rare in Trag., δ. μαράγνης A.*Ch.*376 (lyr.); χερόπλακτοι δ' ἐν στέρνοισι πεσοῦνται δοῦποι the *loud* beating of breasts, S.*Aj.*634, cf. E.*Ba.*513; ἀκούομεν πυλῶν δ. *the noise* of opening gates, Id.*Ion*516. Rare in Prose, Th. 3.22 (v.l. ψόφον); θόρυβος καὶ δ. X.*An.*2.2.19.

δοῦρας, τό, a nom. sg. formed from the Homeric pl. δούρατα (v. sub δόρυ), *AP*6.97 (Antiphil.).

δουράτεος [ᾰ], α, ον, *of planks* or *beams of wood*, ἵππος δ. the *wooden* horse, Od.8.493, 512; ὀβελοί *h.Merc.*121; πύργοι A.R.2.381.

δουρᾰτόγλῠφος, ον, *carved from wood*, Lyc.361.

δούρειος, α, ον, = δουράτεος, E.*Tr.*14, Pl.*Tht.*184d.

δουρεμηκές· δόρατος μῆκος, Hsch.

δουρηνεκής, ές, (ἐνεγκεῖν) *a spear's throw off* or *distant*, only neut. as Adv., Il.10.357.

δουρῐ-ᾰλής (-άλης cod.)· αἰχμάλωτος, Hsch. **-άλωτος**, ον, Ion. for δοριάλ-. **-βᾰρής** κάματος burden *of a heavy spear*, *Wien.Stud.* 25.3 (Crete). **-κλειτός**, ον, *famed for the spear*, Homeric epith. of heroes, Il.5.55, Od.15.52. **-κλῠτός**, ον, = foreg., Il.2.645, Od. 15.544, Archil.3: dat. pl. δουρικλύτοις (sic) A.*Pers.*85 (lyr.).

δουρι-κμής, -κτητος, -ληπτος, -μανής, -μαχος, Ion. for δορι-.

δούριος, α, ον, = δούρειος, Ar.*Av.*1128.

δουρί-πηκτος, ον, *fixed on spears*, λάφυρα δάων δουρίπηχθ' A.*Th.* 278. **-τῠπής**, ές, *wood-splitting*, σφῦρα *AP*6.103 (Phil.). II. *smitten with the spear*, *IPE*2.298.8 (Panticapaeum, ii A.D.). **-φᾰτος**, ον, *slain by the spear*, Opp.*H.*4.556.

δουρο-δόκη, ἡ, (δέχομαι) *case* or *stand for spears*, Od.1.128. **-δόκος**, ὁ, *one of the principal beams* of the roof, Harp. s.v. στρωτήρ, *EM* 731.10. **-μᾰνής**, ές, poet. for δοριμανής, πόλεμος *AP*9.553. **-πᾰγής**, ές, poet. for δορυπαγής, Opp.*H.*1.358, Nonn.*D.*4.230. **-τόμος**, poet. for δρυτόμος, Opp.*H.*5.198; πελέκεις *AP*7.445 (Pers.).

δοχ-αῖος, α, ον, *fit for holding*, σκαφίδες Nic.*Th.*618; κραδίην Id. *Al.*21 (s.v.l., Sch. δοχεῖον). **-εῖον**, Ion. -ήϊον, τό, *holder*, μέλανος δ. ink-*horn*, *AP*6.66 (Paul. Sil.), cf. 63 (Damoch.), Gal.14.719; τὸ θῆλυ ὥσπερ γονῆς τι δ. Luc.*Am.*19. **-εύς**, έως, ὁ, *recipient*, esp. of oracles or inspiration, Orac.ap.Porph.ap.Eus.*PE*5.9, Herm. *in Phdr.*pp.105, 111 A. **-ή**, ἡ, = δοχεῖον, *receptacle*, E.*El.*828, Pl. *Ti.*71c. II. *reception, entertainment*, Macho ap.Ath.8.348f, Lxx *Ge.*21.8, al., *PTeb.*112.89 (ii B.C.), *Ev.Luc.*5.29, etc.; = ἄριστον, Hsch. III. σημεῖον ἐν θυτικῇ, Id.

δοχικός, ή, όν, δ. μέτρον *receiving* measure (officially prescribed for use by revenue officials), opp. ἀνηλωτικόν, *PHib.*1.74 (iii B.C.), al., cf. *PTeb.*11.6, *PPar.*66.26, etc.

δοχμαϊκός, v. δόχμιος. **δοχμαλόν**· χαμαίζηλον, ταπεινόν, Hsch.

δοχμή or **δόχμη**, ἡ, (δέχομαι) *space contained in a hand's breadth*, Cratin.350, Ar.*Eq.*318, *Com.Adesp.*571, Scyl.112: expld. as, = παλαιστή, Sch.Ar. ad loc.; but also as, = σπιθαμή, Phot. s.h.v.; Hsch. and Suid. give both senses. (On the accent, v. Ael.Dion.*Fr.*136, Poll.2.157.)

δοχμιάζω, *use the dochmiac metre*, Sch.E.*Or.*140.

δόχμιος, α, ον, *across, aslant*, δόχμια . . ἦλθον Il.23.116, cf. E.*Or.* 1261 (lyr.); δ. κέλευθον ἐμβάνειν Id.*Alc.*1000 (lyr.), cf. 575 (lyr.); πέσε δ. A.R.1.1169. II. in Prosody, ποὺς δ. *the dochmiac measure*, Choerob. *in Heph.*p.219 C.; ῥυθμὸς δ. Aristid.Quint.1.17, Bacch. *Harm.*100:—hence Adj. forms, **δοχμιακός** Aristid.Quint. l.c.: **δοχμικός, -αϊκός**, Sch.A.*Th.*128, Sch.Ar.*Av.*937. (Perh. cf. Skt. *jihmá-* 'oblique'.)

δοχμό-κορσοι· πλαγιοχαῖται, Hsch. **-λοφος**, ον, *with slanting, nodding plume*, A.*Th.*114 (lyr.). **-ομαι**, *turn sideways*, δοχμωθείς, of a boar *turning himself* to whet his tusks or rip up his enemy, Hes. *Sc.*389; of Hermes *turning himself* to dart through the keyhole, *h.Merc.*146.—Later in aor. Act. δόχμωσε, Med. δοχμώσατο, Nonn.*D.* 42.193, 37.254.

δοχμός, όν (Delph. ά, όν, v. infr.), = δόχμιος I, δοχμὼ ἀΐσσοντε rushing on *slantwise*, Il.12.148; δοχμοὶ μῆτραι *lying obliquely*, Hp.*Mul.* 2.141; δ. ἀπὸ προβολῆς κλινθείς Theoc.22.120; δ. ἀνακρούων θηρὸς πάτον Nic.*Th.*479; ἁ ὁδὸς ἁ δοχμά the *cross*-road, *Klio*16.170 (Delph., ii B.C.). II. = δόχμιος II, συζυγία Sch.Ar.*Ach.*283.

δοχός, όν, (δέχομαι) *containing, able to hold*, θερμοῦ καὶ ὑγροῦ Thphr. *CP*2.4.11. II. Subst. δοχός, ὁ, *receptacle*, Hsch.; also, = λουτήρ, Id.

δράβη, ἡ, *Arabian mustard, Lepidium Draba*, Dsc.2.157.

δραγατεύω, *to be a watcher of a field* or *vineyard* (cf. Mod. Gr. δραγάτης), Ἀρχ.Ἐφ.1913.27 (Thess.).

δράγδην, Adv. *in the grasp, with the hand*, Plu.2.418e, Q.S.13.91.

δραγκάζειν· κρύπτειν, Hsch. **δραγκαλακτᾶν**· βριμοῦσθαι, Id.

δράγ-λη, ἡ, a kind of *javelin*, *PLond.*2.191.12 (ii A.D.). (Cf. Lat. *tragula*.) **-μα**, ατος, τό, (δράσσομαι) *handful*; esp. *as many stalks of corn as the reaper can grasp* in his left hand, *truss*, Il.11.69, 18.552; also, *sheaf*, = ἄμαλλα, X.*HG*7.2.8, Theoc.10.44, Ph.*Bel.*86.24, *BGU* 757.16 (i A.D.), Plu.*Publ.*8. II. later, *uncut corn*, *AP*11.365.10 (Agath.), Luc.*Hes.*7: metaph., πρώτης δράγματα φυταλιῆς *first-fruits*, *AP*6.44 (Leon. (?)), cf. Lxx *Le.*23.12. III. ἐποίησεν ἡ γῆ δράγματα brought forth *by handfuls*, i.e. *plenty*, ib.*Ge.*41.47.

δραγμᾶναι· αἱ ἐν ταῖς τοῦ ἐγκεφάλου κοιλότησι . . , Hsch.

δραγμᾰτ-εύω, = δραγμεύω, Eust.1162.17. **-ηγέω**, *convey sheaves*, *BGU*698.14 (ii A.D.). **-ηγία**, ἡ, *conveyance of sheaves*, ib.831.13, *PFlor.*2.185.17 (iii A.D.). **-ηγός**, ὁ, *labourer who conveys sheaves*, *BGU*698.24 (ii A.D.). **-ηφόρος**, ον, *carrying sheaves*, Babr.88.16.

δραγμᾰτο-κλεπτέω, *steal sheaves*, *PPetr.*3 p.60 (iii B.C.). **-λόγος**, ον, *gleaning*, Hsch.

δραγ-μεύω, *collect the corn into sheaves*, Il.18.555. **-μή**, ἡ, *handful*, *EM*285.52. II. = δραχμή (q.v.). **-μίς**, ίδος, ἡ, *small handful, pinch*, v.l. for δραχμίς, Hp.*Morb.*2.55. **-μός**, ὁ, *grasping*, E.*Cyc.*170, dub. l. in Q.S.1.350.

δραϝεός, ἡ, uncertain object dedicated to Athena, *GDI*1537 (Phocis, pl.).

δραθεῖν, v. δαρθάνω.

δραίνω, *to be ready to do*, Il.10.96. II. *have strength*, δ. μυΐ' ὅσον Herod.1.15, cf. 2.95.

δραιόν· μακρόν· πυλεόν (fort. l. μάκτραν, πύελον), Hsch. **δραιώμη**· ὠφέλεια, Id.

δράκαινα, ης, ἡ, fem. of δράκων, *she-dragon*, *h.Ap.*300; of the Erinyes, A.*Eu.*128; Ἅιδου δ., of the Erinys of Clytaemnestra, E.*IT* 286; compared with a courtesan, δ. ἄμεικτος Anaxil.22.3, cf. Secund. *Sent.*8. II. *scourge*, Ar.*Fr.*767.

δρᾰκαινίς, ίδος, ἡ, = δράκων III, Ephipp.12.6, Mnesim.4.42.

δράκαυλος [ᾰ], ον, prob. *living with a snake*, epith. of the daughters of Cecrops, S.*Fr.*643.

δρᾰκείς, δρακῆναι, δράκον, v. δέρκομαι:—but **δράκεν**· ἐνεργεῖ, πράσσει, is prob. f.l. for δέδρακεν, Hsch.

δρακ-ίζω, *play the buffoon*, Gloss. **-ις**, ὁ, dub. sens. in S.*Ichn.* 177. **-ιστής**, οῦ, ὁ, *buffoon*, Gloss.

δρᾰκονθόμῐλος, ον, *of dragon brood*, A.*Supp.*267.

δρᾰκόντειος, ον, *of a dragon*, κρημνοί E.*Ph.*1315; νῶτα *AP*12.257 (Mel.); δειραί *APl.*4.90; πούς Luc.*Philops.*4.

δρᾰκοντία μεγάλη, = δρακόντιον III, Ps.-Dsc.2.166; δ. μικρά, = ἄρον, ib.167.

δρᾰκοντίας πυρός, ὁ, a wheat *with coarse straw*, Thphr.*CP*3.21.2. 2. δ. πελειάς, ἡ, a kind of *pigeon*, Nic.*Fr.*73. 3. δ. σίκυς, = σ. ἄγριος, Euthyd.ap.Ath.3.74b. 4. *stone found in a serpent's head*, Plin.*HN*37.158.

δρακοντίασις, εως, ἡ, *guinea-worm disease*, Gal.14.790.

δρᾰκόντ-ιον, τό, Dim. of δράκων I, δ. ἀργυροῦν *IG*11(2).203*B*44 (Delos, iii B.C.). II. a kind of *fish* (v.l. for δράκων III), Hp.*Int.*21. III. *edder-wort, Dracunculus vulgaris*, ib.1, Thphr.*HP*7.12.2, Dsc.2.166 (where δρακοντία, ἡ, Ps.-Dsc.: -εία βοτάνη *Gp.*13.8.7). IV. *guinea-worm, Filaria medinensis*, Plu.2.733b, Sor.ap. Paul.Aeg.4.58, Gal.19.449. V. a kind of *fig*, Ath.3.78a. VI. a pigment, *dragon's-blood*, Alex.Aphr.*in Mete.*161.5 (but δρακόντιον αἷμα *cinnabar*, *PHolm.*10.32). -ίς, ίδος, ἡ, a kind of *bird*, Ant. Lib.9.3. II. in pl., certain *vessels* near the heart, Hp.ap.Ruf. *Onom.*202. -ίτης [ῑ] (sc. λίθος), ου, ὁ, *dragon-stone*, conferring sharp vision, Ptol.Chenn.p.192 W.

δρᾰκοντο-βόλος, ον, *dragon-hurling*(?), Nonn.*D.*36.177. -βότος, ον, *feeding dragons*, ib.4.356, al. -γενής, ές, *dragon-gendered*, of Thebans, Sch.S.*Ant.*126. -έθειρα, ἡ, *with snaky locks*, Γοργών Orph.*L.*542. -ειδής, ές, *snake-like*, ὄφεις δ. τὴν κεφαλήν *Peripl.M.Rubr.*55. Adv. -δῶς, ῥεῖν to have a *serpentine* course, Str. 9.3.16. -ζωνες, dub. in Poet.Magic.ap.Afric.*Cest.Oxy.*412 i 29. -κέφᾰλος, ον, *with a serpent's head*, *BGU*1065.9 (i A.D.), Suid. s. v. Ἑκάτην. -κομος, ον, *with snaky locks*, Nonn.*D.*1.18, 47.552. -κτονία, ἡ, *slaying of a serpent*, Arg.Pi.*P.*

δρᾰκοντ-ολέτης, ου, ὁ, *serpent-slayer*, of Apollo, *AP*9.525.

δρᾰκοντό-μαλλος, ον, *with snaky locks*, Γοργόνες A.*Pr.*799. -μῖμος, ον, *serpent-like*, τορεύματα Sopat.19. -μορφος, ον, *of serpent-form*, Lyc.1043, *POxy.*490.12 (ii A.D.). -πους, ὁ, ἡ, gen. ποδος, *snake-footed, with serpents for feet*, Tz. ad Lyc.63, *EM*371.46. -τρῐχέω, *have snaky hair*, Tz.*H.*5.720. -φόνος, ον, *serpent-slaying*, Orph.*L.*158, Nonn.*D.*25.453. -φόροι, οἱ, = Lat. *draconarii*, Lyd.*Mag.*1.46. II. Adj. -φόρος, ον, *snaky*, κόμαι Nonn.*D.*25.221 (s.v.l.). -φρουρος, ον, *watched by a dragon*, Lyc.1311.

δρᾰκοντώδης, ες, = δρακοντοειδής, κόραι, τύραννος, E.*Or.*256, Plu.2.551e; *vermiform*, κάθισμα, worm of a still, Zos.Alch.p.224 B.

δρᾰκος [ᾰ], εος, τό, (δέρκομαι) *eye*, Nic.*Al.*481. II. (δράσσομαι) = δράγμα, Lxx 3*Ma.*5.2.

δρακτόν, τό, *small vase* (cf. δράξ), *OGI*479.10 (Dorylaeum), *BCH* 11.385 (Panamara), etc.

δρᾰκών, δρᾰκόμενος, v. δέρκομαι.

δράκων [ᾰ], οντος, ὁ: (prob. from δέρκομαι, δρᾰκεῖν, cf. Porph.*Abst.*3.8):—*dragon, serpent*, Il.11.39, al.; interchangeable with ὄφις, 12.202, 208, cf. Hes.*Th.*322, 825, Pi.*N.*1.40, A.*Th.*292 (lyr.); ἀετὸς καὶ δ. πολέμια Arist.*HA*609ᵃ4; perh. a *water-snake*, ib.602ᵇ25. II. the constellation *Draco*, Arat.46, al., Man.2.69. III. a sea-fish, *the great weever*, Epich.60, Arist.*HA*598ᵃ11, Hp.*Vict.*2.48. IV. = κηρύκειον, prob. *a wand with a serpent coiled round it*, S.*Fr.*700 (cf. 701). 2. *serpent-shaped bracelet* or *necklace*, Luc.*Am.*41. 3. a *noose* or *crossed bandage* for the ankle, Heraclas ap.Orib.48.5.1. 4. *dragon-standard*, Lib.*Or.*1.144, Them.*Or.*18.219a, cf. *Or.*1.2a: hence, *corps of* 1,000 *men* in the Parthian army, Luc.*Hist. Conscr.*29.

δράλαινα· λαμυρά (Cos), Hsch.

δρᾶμα, ατος, τό, (δράω) *deed, act*, opp. πάθος, A.*Ag.*533; *office, business, duty*, Pl.*Tht.*150a, *R.*451c; τὸ δ. δρᾶν to go about one's *business*, Id.*Tht.*169b. II. *action* represented on the stage, *drama, play*, Ar.*Ra.*920, Arist.*Po.*1448ᵃ28, etc.; μὴ ἐν τῷ δ. not in *the action on the stage*, ib.1460ᵃ31; ἔξω τοῦ δ. ib.1453ᵇ32; δ. ποιεῖν Ar.*Ra.*1021; σατυρικὸν δ. Pl.*Smp.*222d (with play on I): metaph., *stage-effect* of any kind, τὰ ἐλεινὰ ταῦτα δ. εἰσάγειν Id.*Ap.*35b: also, *tragical event*, Plb.23.10.12, Him.*Ecl.*1.12, etc.

δρᾶμᾰτ-ικός, ή, όν, *dramatic*, μιμήσεις Arist.*Po.*1448ᵇ35; μῦθοι ib.1459ᵃ19; δ. ἀτοπία *such as is found in plays*, D.H.1.84. Adv. -κῶς Ammon.*in Cat.*14.15, Eust.6.11. -ιον, τό, Dim. of δρᾶμα, Plu.*Dem.*4; δ. σατυρικόν Ath.13.595e.

δρᾶμᾰτοποι-έω, *put into dramatic form*, τὸ γελοῖον Arist.*Po.*1448ᵇ37. -ΐα, ἡ, *dramatic composition*, Ph.2.597. -ός, οῦ, ὁ, *dramatic poet*, Heph.8.1, Ps.-Luc.*Philopatr.*13: metaph., *melodramatic*, δ. καὶ τερατευτής Phld.*Herc.*1457.12.

δρᾶμᾰτουργ-έω, = δραματοποιέω, τὸν διάλογον Ath.*Epit.*1.1f, cf. Max.Tyr.7.1; '*act a part*', πάντα δ. J.*BJ*1.24.1, Alciphr.2.3. II. = πανουργέω, Hsch. -ημα, ατος, τό, *dramatic composition*, Id. -ία, ἡ, = δραματοποιία, Luc.*Salt.*68: metaph. of life, Sopat. ap.Stob.4.5.52, Max.Tyr.7.10; the *action* of a play, Str.1.2.27. -ός, όν, *contriver*, μύσους J.*BJ*1.26.4.

δρᾰμεῖν, v. τρέχω.

δράμ-ημα [ᾰ], ατος, τό (cf. *EM*316.50), *running, course*, Hdt.8.98, A.*Pers.*247 (anap.), S.*OT*193 (lyr.), *Ichn.*74, Ion Trag.1, E.*Ba.*872 (lyr.), al.; κυμάτων δ. Id.*Tr.*693 (pl.): the later form δρόμημα is found in codd. of Id.*Med.*1180, al., cf. *APl.*5.385 (pl.), Ar.Byz.*Epit.*73.14. -ητέον, *one must run*, S.E.*M.*8.271.

δράμις, ἡ, a kind of *loaf*, Maced. word, Seleuc.ap.Ath.3.114b.

δρᾱμοσύνη, ἡ, *ceremony*, *IG*2².1358ii 34, 40 (iv B.C.).

δρᾰμοῦμαι, v. τρέχω.

δρανεῖς· δραστικοί, Hsch.

δρᾶνος, εος, τό, (δράω) *doing, deed, power*; also, = ὄργανον, ἄγαλμα, κατασκεύασμα, Hsch. (δρανός cod.).

δράξ, ἄκός, ἡ, *handful*, πηλοῦ Batr.237; ἀλφίτων Porph.*Abst.*2.17. II. *the hand*, τίς ἐμέτρησε τὴν γῆν δρακί; Lxx *Is.*40.12 (so δράξ· παλάμη, Hsch.); τὰς δράκας καρτερῶς σφίγξαι Herm.ap.Stob. 1.49.44; the *claw* of the constellation Leo, Ptol.*Alm.*7.5. III. a *measure*, Dsc.5.87, Hero *Mens.*61.9, Hsch. IV. βακχικαὶ δ., = θύρσοι, Sch.Il.6.134.

δραξών, a temple in Sicily, Hsch. II. *thief*, *EM*286.32. 2. = πορνοβοσκός, Hsch.

δράπᾰνον [δρᾰ], τό, = δρέπανον, Epigr. in *BKT*5(1)p.77.

δραπενίδες· εἶδος ὀρνέου, Hsch.

δρᾱπετ-ᾰγωγός, όν, *recovering a runaway slave*: Δ., ὁ, a comedy by Antiphanes, Ath.4.161d. -εία, ἡ, *running away*, Hsch. s. v. δράσκασις. -ευμα, ατος, τό, = foreg., Diocl.Com.12. -εύω, *run away*, X.*Mem.*2.1.16; τινά *from* one, Pl.*Smp.*216b; παρά τινος Luc.*Somn.*12; δραπετεύσουσι ὑπὸ ταῖς ἀσπίσιν *will skulk* behind.., X.*HG*2.4.16; δραπετεύοντα πολεμεῖν Id.*Ages.*1.23: metaph., *shirk public service*, D.42.25; [αἱ δόξαι] δ. ἐκ τῆς ψυχῆς Pl.*Men.*98a; ἐκ τοῦ βίου Luc.*Peregr.*21; ἐκ φιλοσοφίας Plu.2.46e; *slip away*, εἰς τὸ βάθος, of fluids, Paul.Aeg.6.3. -ης, ου, Ion. δρηπέτης, εω, ὁ, (διδράσκω, δρᾶναι) *runaway*, βασιλέος *from* the king, Hdt.3.137; esp. *runaway slave*, δούλοισι, καὶ τοῦτο δρηπέτῃσι Id.6.11, cf. Ar.*Ach.*1187, Herod. 3.13, etc.; δ. ἀνήρ S.*Fr.*63. 2. Adj., πούς δ. E.*Or.*1498 (lyr.), cf. Aeschin.3.152; βίος δ. *fugitive* life, *AP*10.87 (Pall.); οὐ δραπέτην τὸν κλῆρον..μεθείς no *skulker's* lot, i. e. not a lump of earth which would fall in pieces, of the lot of Cresphontes, S.*Aj.*1285. II. fem. **δρᾱπέτις**, ιδος, Luc.*Asin.*25: as Adj., στέγη a home *whose occupants are shifting*, S.*Fr.*174; ψυχή *AP*12.80 (Mel.); μέλισσαι Ael.*Ep.*5; Δραπέτιδες, title of play by Cratinus. -ίδης, ου, Dor. -δᾱς, ὁ, = foreg., δ. ἐμός ἐστιν Mosch.1.3. -ικός, ή, όν, *of* or *for a* δραπέτης, δ. θρίαμβος a triumph *over runaway slaves*, Plu.*Pomp.*31; δ. σώματα *CIG*2554.102 (Crete); δραπετικοί, οἱ, *IG*5(1).1390.83 (Andania); of a slave, *likely to run away*, *BGU*887.5 (ii A.D.). -ίνδα (Adv.) παίζειν, a game *where one chased the rest*, *EM*286.48; expld. by δραπετικῶς, Hsch. -ις, ιδος, ἡ, fem. of δραπέτης (q.v.). -ίσκος, ὁ, Dim. of δραπέτης, Luc.*Fug.*33.

δράπων, ὁ, = δραπέτης, Hdn.Gr.1.34, al.

δρᾱσείω, Desiderat. of δράω, *have a mind to do*, S.*Aj.*326, 585, E.*Ph.*1208, *Med.*93, Ar.*Pax*62.

δράσῑμος [ᾱ], ον, = δραστήριος: τὸ δ. *activity, vigour*, A.*Th.*554.

δρᾶσις, εως, ἡ, *strength, efficacy*, Luc.*Trag.*276. 2. *sacrifice*, Hsch. 3. Gramm., *active force* of a verb, A.D.*Pron.*44.1, *Synt.*283.23: generally, *action*, opp. *passivity*, Mich.*in EN*275.8. II. (δράω B) *vision*, *EM*287.8.

δρασκ-άζω, (διδράσκω) *attempt an escape*, Lex ap.Lys.10.17: prov., ἐν ἅλῳ δρασκάζεις, of those who 'bury their head in the sand', Zen. 3.74. -ᾰσις, εως, ἡ, *running away, escape*, Hsch.

δρασματικός, ή, όν, = δραστήριος, *Cat.Cod.Astr.*2.165.

δρασμάτων· πανουργημάτων, Hsch.

δρασμός, Ion. **δρησμός**, ὁ, (διδράσκω) *running away, flight*, δρησμὸν βουλεύειν Hdt.5.124; δρησμῷ ἐπιχειρέειν Id.6.70; δρασμῷ κρυφαίῳ A.*Pers.*360; δρασμὸν εὑρεῖν ib.370: in pl., E.*Or.*1374 (lyr.), etc.: not freq. in Prose, δρασμῷ χρῆσθαι Aeschin.3.21, cf. Plb.5.26.14, *BGU*987.23 (i A.D.), Jul.*Or.*2.57b.

δράσσομαι, Att. **δράττομαι**, Hdt.3.13; impf. ἐδραττόμην Ar.*Ra.*545: fut. δράξομαι *APl.*4.275.10 (Posidipp.), Lxx *Nu.*5.26: aor. ἐδραξάμην Pl.*Ly.*209e, etc.: pf. δέδραγμαι, 2 pers. δέδραξαι E.*Tr.*750, part. δεδραγμένος Il.13.393:—the Act., δράσσω only in Poll.3.155, *EM*285.43, prob. in *PLond.*3.1170ᵛ113 (iii A.D.), cf. δράξαι· κρατῆσαι, Hsch.: (cf. δράξ, δράγμα, δραχμή):—*grasp* with the hand, c. gen. rei, κόνιος δεδραγμένος αἱματοέσσης *clutching handfuls* of gory dust, Il. l. c.: metaph., ἐλπίδος δεδραγμένος S.*Ant.*235 (vv. ll. πεπρ-, πεφρ-), cf. Plb.36.15.7; δραξάμενοι τῶν ἁλῶν *taking a handful* of salt, Pl. l. c., etc. 2. *lay hold of*, τί μου δέδραξαι χερσί; E.*Tr.*750; δραξάμενος φάρυγος *having seized* [them] by the throat, Theoc.24.28, cf. 25.145, *POxy.*1298.10 (iv A.D.): metaph., δράξασθαι καιροῦ D.S.12.67; μείζονος οἴκου (i.e. by marriage), Call.*Epigr.*1.14; μεγάλης ἀπήνης *AP* 11.238 (Demod.); τᾶς κραδίας Theoc.30.9; [ὧν χρ]ὴ δράξασθαι τὸ στόμα sounds the mouth has to *grip*, i.e. *make*, dub. in Phld.*Po.*2.41. II. c. acc., *take by handfuls*, ταύτας [τὰς μνέας] δ. Hdt.3.13; also, *catch*, τοὺς σοφοὺς ἐν τῇ πανουργίᾳ αὐτῶν 1*Ep.Cor.*3.20.

δραστ-έος, α, ον, *to be done*, S.*Tr.*1204. II. δραστέον *one must do*, Id.*OT*1443, E.*IA*1024, D.Chr.12.16. -ην· κόφινον, Hsch. -ήρ, ῆρος, ὁ, *cook*, Id.; cf. δρηστήρ. -ηρά· δραστικά, Id. -ήριος, ον, *active, efficacious*, μηχανή A.*Th.*1046; φάρμακον E.*Ion*1185; ἀνὴρ δ. ἐς τὰ πάντα Th.4.81; τὸ δ. *activity, energy*, Id.2.63. Adv. -ίως Ph.1.104, Jul.*Ep.*10, Hierocl.*in CA*26p.479 M. 2. rarely in bad sense, τὰ δεινὰ καὶ δ. *audacious deeds*, E.*Or.*1554. 3. *active*, opp. *passive*, Plot.6.1.29: esp. in Gramm., of verbs, D.H.*Th.*24. Adv. -ίως Syrian.*in Metaph.*82.31. -ηριότης, ητος, ἡ, *activity, energy*, Eust.123.46. -ηριώδης, ες, = δραστήριος, Gal.12.123 (Comp.).

δράστης and **δράστας**, ὁ, Att. and Dor. for δρήστης.

δραστικός, ή, όν, = δραστήριος, σχήματα *representing attack*, in a war-dance, Pl.*Lg.*815a; *efficient* (cause), δ. αἴτιον ὀργῆς Phld.*Ir.* p.98 W., cf. *D.*1.14; δραστικοὺς τῶν κακῶν (τοὺς θεούς) ib.19, cf. Max. Tyr.18.2; παχυμεροῦς ὕλης δ., of river fish, Xenocr.9; of persons, Plu.*Cor.*21: Comp. διάνοια -ώτερον χειρός Ph.1.542: Sup., Onos.22.4. 2. *active*, opp. *passive*, δ. ποιότητες, ἀρχαί, *Stoic.*2.133,134;

–ώτατον τὸ θερμόν ib.135; –ώτατα στοιχεῖα Ph.2.142. 3. as Medic. term, *drastic*, Dsc.1.19.4 (Sup.); φάρμακον *Gp.*13.14.5, cf. Xenocr.ap.Orib.2.58.50. Adv. –κῶς Gal.10.368. 4. Gramm., δ. διάβασις, = δρᾶσις I. 3, A.D.*Pron.*115.6.

δράστις, = βύσσος, and **δραστιουργοί,** *flax-* or *linen-workers*, Hsch.

δραστοσύνη, v. δρηστοσύνη.

δρᾰτός, ή, όν, = δαρτός, (δέρω) *skinned, flayed*, δρατὰ σώματα Il.23.169 (v.l. δρετά).

δραύκιον, τό, *necklace, Gloss.*

δραχμ-αῖος, α, ον, = δραχμιαῖος, Nic.*Th.*519. **–ή,** ἡ, (δράσσομαι, prop. *as much as one can hold in the hand*, cf. Plu.*Lys.*17): I. a weight, *drachm*, [κρεῶν] prob. in *IG*1².10.4, Thphr.*Od.*17, etc. 2. a silver coin, *drachma*, worth six obols, Hdt.7.144, And.4.18, *IG*7.3171.52 (Orchom. Boeot.), 9(1).694.54 (Corc.), etc. [The penult. is long in Simon.157, and sts. in Com., Ar.*V.*691 (anap.), *Pax* 1201, *Pl.*1019, Pl.Com.174.17: **δαρχμή** is found in Hsch.; cf. δαρκνά.] **–ῆος,** α, ον, Ion. for δραχμαῖος, *weighing a drachm*, ἄχθος Nic.*Th.*604. **–ιαῖος,** α, ον, *worth* or *costing a drachma*, Ar.*Fr.*425; [ἐπίδειξις] Pl.*Cra.*384b; δ. συναλλάγματα Arist.*Pol.*1300ᵇ33; δ. τόκος interest *at the rate of 1 dr. per 100 denarii per month*, *IGRom.*4.788 (Apamea), cf. *BGU*1038.20 (ii A.D.). 2. *weighing one drachm*, Archig.ap.Gal.12.876, etc. **–ίον,** τό, Dim. of δραχμή, Aristeas 5. **–ός,** ὁ, = δραγμός, v.l. in Q.S.1.350.

δράω (A), Aeol. 3 pl. δραῖσι Alc.*Supp.*27.11, subj. δρῶ, δρᾷς, δρᾷ, opt. δρῴην, Ep. δρώοιμι Od.15.317; παρα-δρώωσι ib.324: impf. ἔδρων: fut. δράσω: aor. 1 ἔδρᾱσα, Ion. ἔδρησα Thgn.954: pf. δέδρᾱκα:—Pass., aor. 1 ἐδράσθην, δρασθείς, Th.3.38, 6.53: pf. δέδρᾱμαι (δεδρασμένων is f.l. in Id.3.54):—*do, accomplish*, esp. *do some great thing*, good or bad (acc. to some δ. was the equiv. Dor. Verb for Att. πράττειν, Arist.*Po.*1448ᵇ1), αἶψά κεν εὖ δρώοιμι μετὰ σφίσιν ἅσσ' ἐθέλοιεν Od.15.317 (where the Sch. interprets it διακονοίην, δουλεύοιμι I *would serve*.., cf. δρήστης); ἄνδρες δραῖσιν ἀτάσθαλοι Alc. l.c.; opp. πάσχω, freq. in Trag., εὖ δρῶσαν, εὖ πάσχουσαν A.*Eu.*868; ἄξια δράσας ἄξια πάσχων Id.*Ag.*1527; κακῶς δράσαντες οὐκ ἐλάσσονα πάσχουσι Id.*Pers.*813; of one in extreme perplexity, τί πάθω; τί δὲ δρῶ; Id.*Th.*1062, cf. *Ch.*899; δρῶν ἀντιπάσχω χρηστά S.*Ph.*584; prov., "δράσαντι παθεῖν" τριγέρων μῦθος τάδε φωνεῖ A.*Ch.*313; δράσαντι γάρ τοι καὶ παθεῖν ὀφείλεται Id.*Fr.*456, cf. S.*OT*1272; τά γ' ἔργα μου πεπονθότα.. μᾶλλον ἢ δεδρακότα acts of suffering rather than of *doing*, Id.*OC*267; ὁ δρῶν *the doer*, whoever he be, A.*Ag.*1359, etc.; ὁ δράσας the *culprit*, Pl.*Lg.*879a, cf. S.*Tr.*1108; ὁ δεδρακὼς Id. *OT*246, D.23.40; used to avoid repetition of a verb, Th.2.49, al.: c. dupl. acc., οἷ' ἔργ' ὁ παῖς μ' ἔδρασεν S.*Ph.*940, cf. *OC*854, etc.: with Adv., εὖ, κακῶς δρᾶν τινά, *do* one a good or ill turn, Thgn.108, S.*Aj.*1154; δρᾶν τι εἴς τινα Id.*OC*976; τί τινι Id.*OT*1402; πάντα δρᾶν *try* every way, cj. in E.*Hipp.*284; παντὸς εἶχε δρῶντος ἡδονήν was satisfied with *the doing*, S.*OC*1604; τὰ δρώμενα *what is doing* or *being done*, ib.1644, cf. D.C.37.57: sg., τὸ δρώμενον S.*El.*40, Th.5.102; τί δράσω; to express helplessness or despair, S.*Aj.*920, etc.; for οἶσθ' οὖν ὃ δρᾶσον; v. *εἴδω fin. 2. of things, τουτὶ τί δρᾷ τὸ ποτήριον; Ar.*Eq.*237; ὅπερ ἡ λίθος δρᾷ τὸν σίδηρον Luc.*Im.*1: so, generally, *to be active*, εἰς ἄλληλα πάσχειν καὶ δ. Chrysipp.*Stoic.*2.135, cf. Prisc.Lyd.4.10. II. *offer sacrifice* or *perform mystical rites*, δ. τὰ ἱερὰ *IG*1².4, cf. 188, Ath.14.660a, Paus.1.43.2, Iamb.*Myst.*1.21, etc.:—Pass., τὰ δρώμενα Gal.*UP*7.14, Sopat.in Rh.8.1 W., etc.; τὰ δημοσίᾳ δρώμενα Plu.*Num.*9.

δράω (B), = ὁράω, A.D.*Adv.*139.8, *EM*287.7.

δρέμμα· κλέμμα (fort. κλῆμα), οἱ δὲ κλάσμα, Hsch.

δρεπάνη [ᾰ], ἡ, (δρέπω) *sickle, reaping-hook*, ἤμων ὀξείας δρεπάνας ἐν χερσὶν ἔχοντες Il.18.551, cf. *AP*9.383.9; *pruning-hook*, ἐτρύγων... δρεπάνας ἐν χ. ἔχ. Hes.*Sc.*292: rare in Prose, Plu.*Cleom.*26, Alciphr.3.19.

δρεπᾰνηΐς, ΐδος, ἡ, poet. for foreg., Nic.*Fr.*21.

δρεπᾰνηφόρος, ον, *bearing a scythe* or *hook*, ἅρμα δ. *scythed* car, X.*An.*1.7.10, Plb.5.53.10, D.S.17.53, Ascl.*Tact.*8, Ph.2.107.

δρεπᾰνίον [ᾰ], τό, Dim. of δρέπανον, Seleuc.ap.Ath.4.155e.

δρεπᾰνίς, ίδος, ἡ (also **δραπενίς** Hsch.), a kind of *bird*, so called from the shape of its wings, prob. the *Alpine swift, Cypselus melba*, Arist.*HA*487ᵇ27; = κεγχρίς (κέγχρος cod.), Hsch.

δρεπᾰνο-ειδής, ές, *sickle-shaped*, Th.6.4, Str.8.2.3. **–μάχαιρα** [μᾰ], ἡ, *scimitar*, Sch.Ar.*Th.*1138. **–ποιός,** ὁ, *sickle-maker, Gloss.*

δρέπᾰνον, τό, also **δράπανον** (q.v.), (δρέπω) = δρεπάνη, δ. εὐκαμπές Od.18.368; χαλκέοις ἥμα δ. S.*Fr.*534; the usual form in Prose and Com., Hdt.1.125, etc.; δ. θεριστικόν *PMagd.*8.6 (iii B.C.). 2. *pruning-knife*, Pl.*R.*333d. 3. *scythe*, X.*Cyr.*6.1.30. 4. *curved sword, scimitar*, Hdt.5.112, 7.93, Ar.*Ra.*576.

δρεπᾰνουργός, ὁ, *sword-maker, armourer*, Pherecr.130.2, Ar.*Pax* 548.

δρεπᾰνοφόρος, ον, = δρεπανηφόρος, τέθριππα Anon.Hist.in *Rev. Ét.Gr.*5.323.

δρεπᾰνώδης, ες, = δρεπανοειδής, αἰχμαί Agath.5.22, cf. *EM*219.2.

δρεπ-τεύς, έως, ὁ, *vintager*, Hsch. (but **δρεπεῖς** *EM*287.30). **–τικῶς,** Adv. *carptim, Gloss.*, Dosith.p.412 K. **–τός,** ή, όν, *plucked*: δρεπτόν, a name for a kiss, Teleclid.13. **–τω,** poet. for sq., *pluck*, Ep. impf. δρέπτον Mosch.2.69:—more freq. in Med., Opp.*C.*2.38, *APl.*4.231 (Anyte), etc. **–ω,** Ep. impf. δρέπον *h.Cer.*425: aor. 1 ἔδρεψα Hdt.2.92, (ἀπο-) Pi.*P.*9.110: aor. 2 ἔδρᾰπον ib.4.130: Aeol. subj. δρόπωσιν Alc.*Oxy.*1788 *Fr.*15 ii 23:—**Med.,** Dor. fut. δρεψεῦμαι Theoc.18.40: aor. ἐδρεψάμην Od.12.357, etc.:—**Pass.,** aor. ἐδρέφθην Philostr.*VA*8.7.5:—*pluck*, ἄνθεα *h.Cer.*425, Hdt.2.92, cf. E.*El.*778, *Ion* 889 (lyr.); κασίην Hdt.3.110: metaph., *gain possession* or *enjoyment of*, δ. τιμάν, ἥβαν, Pi.*P.*1.49, 6.48, etc.; δραπὼν εὐζωᾶς ἄωτον ib.4.130; δ. κορυφὰς ἀρετᾶν ἄπο Id.*O.*1.13; σοφίας καρπὸν δ. Id.*Fr.*209; λειμῶνα Μουσῶν δ., of a poet, Ar.*Ra.*1300. II. Med., *pluck for oneself, cull*, φύλλα δρεψάμενοι.. δρυὸς Od.12.357; νάρκισσον... δρεπόμην *h.Cer.*429; 'Ισθμιάδων δρέπεσθαι ἄωτον Pi.*N.*2.9; ἀπὸ κρηνῶν μελιρρύτων δρεπόμενοι τὰ μέλη Pl.*Ion*534b; στεφάνως δρεψεύμεναι Theoc.18.40; κενεὰς ἐλπίδας ἐδρεπόμαν *AP*12.125 (Mel.); ἡδύσματα παρὰ τῆς ποιητικῆς Μούσης Jul.*Or.*7.207c; ψυχὴν θείαν Orph.*Fr.*228; αἷμα δρέψασθαι *cull the fruits of* murder, A.*Th.*718, cf. Bion 1.22: abs., E.*Hipp.*81: c. gen., κατὰ καιρὸν ἐρώτων δ. Pi.*Fr.*123.1.

δρέχμονες· νεφροί, Hsch.

δρῆγες· στρουθοί (Maced.), Id.; cf. δίγηρες, δρίξ. **δρηλοῖ·** φοβεῖται, Id. (Fort. δϝηλοῖ.)

Δρηνεία, ἡ, title of Artemis, 'Αρχ.'Εφ.1913.227 (Lesbos).

δρηπέτης, δρησμός, Ion. for δραπέτης, δρασμός.

δρησμοσύνη, ἡ, = δρηστοσύνη, δ. ἱερῶν *care* of the holy rites, *h.Cer.*476. II. = δρασμός, Max.351.

δρηστ-εύω, *perform rites*, θεοῖς 'Αρχ.'Εφ.1913.223 (Lesbos). **–ήρ,** ῆρος, ὁ, (δράω A) *labourer, working man*, Od.16.248: fem. δρήστειρα *workwoman*, 10.349, 19.345. II. (διδράσκω) *runaway*, λῃστής Babr.128.14. **–ης,** Att. **δράστης,** ου, Dor. **δράστας,** α, ὁ, *worker*, Archil.72; θεράπων, οὐ δράστας as an attendant, not *a slave*, Pi.*P.*4.287; *doer, actor*, αὐτουργὸς καὶ δράστης Plb.12.25ʰ.6. 2. as Adj., *energetic*, Man.5.85. II. = δραπέτης, Hsch. **–ις,** ιος, ἡ, (διδράσκω) = δραπέτις, Call.*Ep.*42. **–οσύνη,** ἡ, Ep. for δραστ–, *service*, Od.15.321; δμωὶς δρηστοσύνῃσι κεκασμένη *IG*3.1310.

δριάεντα· χλωρά, Hsch.; **δριάουσαν·** θάλλουσαν, Id. **δριαλεῖν·** ποιεῖν, Id. **δρικηαί,** in pl., a kind of *bird*, Id.: cf. δρίξ. **δρίλαξ,** ακος, *leech* (Elean), Id.

δρῖλος, ὁ, expld. by Lat. *verpus*, sens. obsc., *AP*11.197 (Lucill.); **δρεῖλος,** *Supp.Epigr.*2.353 (Amphissa).

δρίμαι· ψῦχος, Hsch.

δρῑμεύω, *itch*, Anon. *in EN*448.3.

δρῑμυγμός, ὁ, *pungency*, θύμου Tz.*H.*11.374.

δρῑμῠλέων, οντος, ὁ, epith. applied by Menodotus the Empiric to the dogmatic physicians, Gal.*Subf.Emp.*11 p.63 Bonnet.

δρῑμύλος [ῠ], ον, Dim., ὄμμα δ. *a piercing little* eye, Mosch.1.8.

δρῑμύμωρος [ῠ], ον, = ὀξύμωρος, used of the dogmatic physicians by Menodotus the Empiric, Gal.*Subf.Emp.*11 p.63 Bonnet.

δρίμυξις [ῐ], εως, ἡ, *smarting*, Orib.*Fr.*64, Sor.(?)ap.Aët.16.77.

δρῑμῠποιέω, *make pungent*, Herod.Med. in *Rh.Mus.*58.82.

δρῑμύς, εῖα, ύ, *piercing, sharp, keen*, βέλος Il.11.270: metaph., δριμεῖα μάχη 15.696, Hes.*Sc.*261; δ. χόλος Il.18.322; μένος Od.24.319; ἄχος Hes.*Sc.*457; θυμός A.*Ch.*391 (lyr.). II. of things which affect the eyes or taste, *keen, pungent, acrid*, of smoke, δριμύτατος καπνῶν Ar.*V.*146; of radish, etc., opp. γλυκύς, X.*Mem.*1.4.5, cf. Pl.Com.154 (Sup.); χυμὸς Arist.*de An.*422ᵇ13; ὀσμαί ib.421ᵃ30; δριμέσιν ἰητρεύειν *with pungent drugs*, Hp.*Fract.*27; δ. οἶνος Luc.*Merc.Cond.*18. Adv. –έως: Comp. δριμύτερον, ὄζειν Arist.*Pr.*907ᵃ13; ῥεύματος δριμυτέρου γενομένου Hp.*VM*18. III. metaph., of persons, *bitter, fierce*, ἀλάστωρ A.*Ag.*1501 (lyr.); ἄγροικος Ar.*Eq.*808, etc.; also, *keen, shrewd*, κρόταλον E.*Cyc.*104; ἔντονοι καὶ δ. Pl.*Tht.*173a; δ. καὶ δικανικός ib.175d; δ. ἐν τῷ ἀποκρίνεσθαι Arist.*Top.*156ᵇ37; λόγος δριμύτατος Id.*SE*182ᵇ37 (but λέξις and λόγος δ. of *striking* turns of phrase, Hermog.*Id.*1.2, 2.5): neut. as Adv., δριμὺ βλέπειν look *bitter*, Ar.*Ra.*562; but also to look *sharply, keenly*, Pl.*R.*519a, Luc.*Symp.*16; ἐνορᾶν Id.*Cat.*3, Ael.*VH*14.22, D.C.59.26:—regul. Adv. δριμέως, Anaxandr.15.3; ἐρασθῆναι Ael.*NA*7.15; δριμύτατα ἀλγεῖν Id.*VH* 12.1.

δρῑμύσσω, *cause to smart*, ὀφθαλμούς Alex.Trall.2:—Pass., οἱ δριμυττόμενοι τὰ βλέφαρα Aët.7.15. II. *treat severely*, Eust.201.23; δριμύξεται τὰ ἐναγώνια Lib.*Decl.*43 *Intr.*4.

δρῑμύτης, ητος, ἡ, *acridness* of humours, Hp.*VM*18 (pl.); *pungency* of taste, etc., Anaxipp.1.46, Alex.Aphr.*Pr.*2.70: pl., Arched.2.7, Thphr.*CP*1.16.9; *itches*, Agatharch.58; of smoke, Plb.21.28.16. II. metaph., *keenness, eagerness*, Pl.*Plt.*311a; δ. πρὸς τὰ μαθήματα Id.*R.*535b; *keenness* of wit or satire, Plu.2.48a, Luc.*Alex.*4; πανουργία καὶ δ. ib.483f; ποικιλία καὶ δ. Arr.*Epict.*2.23.40; *bitterness* in controversy, Phld.*Ir.*p.22 W. 2. esp. in Lit. Crit., *use of striking words and turns of phrase*, Id.*Piet.*15, Hermog.*Id.*2.5, *Inv.*3.13, Aristid.*Rh.*2 pp.513, 524 S. 3. *fierceness, grimness*, τοῦ προσώπου App.*BC*1.70.

δρῑμῠφάγ-έω, *live on acrid food*, Sor.1.64, Paul.Aeg.4.1. **–ία,** ἡ, *acrid diet*, Dsc.2.31 (pl.), Philum.ap.Orib.45.29.13, Aët.16.75.

δρίξ· στρουθός, Cyr.; cf. δρῆγες.

δρίος [ῐ], εος, τό, *copse, thicket*, δρίος ὕλης *copse*-wood, Od.14.353; δ. εὔδενδρον, ὑλῆεν, *AP*7.193 (Simm.), 203 (Id.); ἅπαν Opp.*H.*4.588; ἀν' ἐρῆμον δ. *Lyr.Alex.Adesp.*7.3: heterocl. pl. δρία, τά, Hes.*Op.*530, S.*Tr.*1012 (hex.), E.*Hel.*1326 (lyr.): also dat. pl. δρισί (as if from δρίες) dub. in *IG*14.217.43.

δρίς· δύναμις, Hsch. **δρίφακτος·** κράββατος, Id.

δρίφος, = δίφρος, Sophr.10.

δροιόν· καλόν (Cret.), Hsch. (Fort. κᾶλον.)

δροίτη, ἡ, *bathing-tub, bath*, A.*Ag.*1540 (lyr.), *Ch.*999 (985), *Eu.*633, Nic.*Al.*462, Lyc.1108. 2. *cradle*, Alex.Aet.16. 3. *bier*, Parth.*Fr.*44, cf. *EM*288.4. 4. a *dance*, Hsch. (The form δρύτη cited from Hermipp. in *EM* is due to a false derivation from δρῦς.)

δρομάασκε, v. δρομάω.

δρομ-ᾱγετέω, *act as clerk of the course, IG*12(2).134,258 (Mytil.). **-αδάριος** or **-εδάριος,** ὁ, = Lat. *dromedarius, POxy.*1652 *a* 6, *BGU* 827^v, etc. **-άδην** [ᾰ], Adv., (δρόμος) *in running,* Hsch. **-αῖος,** α, ον, also ος, ον E.*Alc.*245 (lyr.):—*running at full speed, swift,* κἀγὼ δρομαία βᾶσα S.*Tr.*927; οὐχ ὡς δ. πῶλος E.*Hel.*543; νεφέλας δρομαίου Id.*Alc.* l.c.; χωρεῖ δρομαίαν Id.*Fr.*495.4; δρομαίαν πτέρυγ' ἐκτείνων Ar.*Pax* 160: in Prose, λαγὼς δ. a hare *run by hounds,* opp. εὐναῖος, X.*Cyn.*5.9; ἴχνη δ., opp. εὐναῖα, the track *of a running hare,* ib.3.8: metaph., δ. τῆς ψυχῆς ὁρμή Alcid.ap.Arist.*Rh.*1406^{a}23. Adv. -ως Sch.E.*Or.*1416. **II.** epith. of Apollo, as patron of racing, Plu.2.724c, *IG*5(1).497, al. (Sparta). **-αξ,** ακος, ὁ, *good at running,* κάμηλος *Gp.*16.22.7. **-άς,** άδος, ὁ, ἡ, *running,* πρός σ' ἔβαν δρομὰς ἐξ οἴκων E.*Supp.*1000 (lyr.); ἄντυξ δ. the *whirling* wheel, S.*Ph.*678 (lyr.); ὁλκάδες Ar.*Fr.*420; δ. κάμηλος *dromedary,* D.S.19.37, Str.15.2.10, J.*AJ*6.14.6, Plu.*Alex.*31: also with a neut., δρομάσι κώλῳ E.*Hel.*1301 (lyr.); δρομάσι βλεφάροις Id.*Or.*837 (lyr.). **2.** *wildly roaming, frantic,* Ναΐς, παρθένος, Id.*Hipp.*549 (lyr.), *Tr.*42; Γαλλαὶ μητρὸς ὀρείης φιλόθυρσοι δρομάδες *Lyr.Adesp.*121. **II.** of certain fish, *migratory,* Arist.*HA*488^{a}6. **III.** *street-walker,* Phryn. Com.33. **-άσσειν·** τρέχειν, Hsch.

***δρομ-άω** (not found in pres.), = τρέχω: Ep. iter. δρομάασκε Hes.*Fr.*117 (v.l. φοίτασκε): aor. 1 part. δρομήσασα Vett.Val.345.33 (but inf. δρομῆσαι dub. in Hp.*Fract.*4): pf. ὑπα-δεδρόμακε Sapph.2.10. **-εδάριος,** v. δρομαδ-. **-εύς,** έως, ὁ, *runner,* E.*El.*824, Ar. *V.*1206, Pl.*Lg.*822b, Lxx *Jb.*9.25, *BGU*141 ii 11 (iii A.D.), etc.: pl., δρομῆς Eup.94, Pl.*R.*613b; later dat. δρομέσι Call.*Fr.*555. **2.** in Crete, = ἔφηβος, *Leg.Gort.*1.40; cf. δρόμος II.3. **3.** *race-horse* (?), *PMag.Lond.*121.390. **-ή,** ἡ, = δρόμος, Hdn.Gr.1.325. **-ήϊος,** ὁ (sc. μήν), name of month in Crete, *GDI*5040. **-ημα,** v. δράμημα.

δρομιάφιον ἦμαρ, = ἀμφιδρόμια, Hsch.

δρομ-ίας, ου, ὁ, a kind of *fish,* Eratosth.*Fr.*12. **II.** *horseman-crab,* Ael.*NA*7.24. **-ικός,** ή, όν, *good at running, swift,* Pl.*Tht.*148c, Arist.*EN*1101^{b}16: Comp., Philostr.*Her.*3.4: Sup., Polyaen.3.11.10. **2.** *belonging to the foot-race,* τὰ δ. τοῦ πεντάθλου X.*HG*7.4.29; τὰ δ. γυμνάζεσθαι D.61.24; τῷ δρομικῷ ἀγωνίσασθαι D.C.67.8. Adv. -κῶς, ἀποχωρεῖν Pl.*Lg.*706c. **II.** *set up in race-courses,* οἱ δ. τῶν Ἑρμῶν Philostr.*Her.*2.21. **-ικότης,** ητος, ἡ, *fleetness of foot,* Simp.*in Cat.*24.18. **-ιον,** τό, *race-course, Tab.Defix.Aud.*163.80 (Rome, iv/v A.D.).

Δρόμιος, ὁ, *god of the race-course,* epith. of Hermes in Crete, *GDI* 5115. **II.** in Metric, δρόμιος (sc. πούς), ὁ, the foot ⏑ ⏑ – ⏑, Choerob.*in Heph.*p.218 C.

δρομοκῆρυξ, ῦκος, ὁ, *runner, postman,* Aeschin.2.130, Aen.Tact. 22.3, Polyaen.5.26 (pl.), Philostr.*Gym.*4, D.C.78.35.

δρόμος, ὁ, (δραμεῖν) *course, race,* in Il. mostly of horses, ἵπποισι τάθη δρόμος 23.375; also of men, τέτατο δρόμος ib.758; οὐρίῳ δρόμῳ with prosperous *course,* S.*Aj.*889 (lyr.); ἅπαντι χρῆσθαι τῷ δρόμῳ at full *speed,* Luc.*Dom.*10: of *any quick movement,* e.g. *flight,* A.*Pers.*207: of Time, ἡμέρης δ. a day's *running,* i.e. the distance one can go in a day, Hdt.2.5; κατανύσαι τὸν προκείμενον δ. Id.8.98; ἵππου δ. ἡμέρας D.19.273: of Things, δ. νεφέλης, ἡλίου τε καὶ σελήνης, E.*Ph.*163, Pl.*Ax.*370b (pl.), etc.; οἱ δ. τῶν ἀστέρων Procl.*Par.Ptol.*136; δρόμῳ *at a run,* freq. with Verbs of motion, δρόμῳ διαβάντας τὸν Ἀσωπὸν Hdt.9.59; ἰέναι Id.3.77; χρῆσθαι Id.6.112; χωρεῖν Th.4.31; δ. ξυνῆψαν E.*Ph.*1101; βοηθῆσαι δ. Ar.*Fr.*551: in pl., δρόμοις A.*Pr.*838, *Supp.*819. **2.** *foot-race,* as a contest, *IG*2.594.11, al.: prov., περὶ τοῦ παντὸς δρόμου (-μου codd.) θεῖν to *run* for one's life, Hdt.8.74; τὸν περὶ ψυχῆς δρόμον δραμεῖν Ar.*V.*375; περὶ ψυχῆς ὁ δ. Pl.*Tht.*173a: generally, *contest,* πλαγᾶν δρόμος, i.e. a pugilistic *contest,* Pi.*I.*5(4).60. **3.** *lap* in a race, S.*El.*726 (interpol. ib.691); ἐν τῷ δευτέρῳ δ. Arist.*HA* 579^{a}8. **4.** in speaking, *rapid delivery,* Longin.*Rh.*p.312 S. **II.** *place for running,* δρόμοι εὐρέες *runs* for cattle, Od.4.605. **2.** *race-course,* Hdt.6.126, E.*Andr.*599. **3.** *public walk,* ἐν εὐσκίοις δ. Ἀκαδήμου Eup.32, cf. *IG*2^2.1126.36, etc.; *colonnade,* Pl.*Tht.*144c; κατάστεγος δ. *cloister,* Id.*Euthd.*273a; δ. ξυστός Aristias 5; in Crete, = γυμνάσιον, Suid., cf. *SIG*463.14 (Itanos, iii B.C.); δύ' ἢ τρεῖς δρόμους περιεληλυθότε having taken two or three *turns in the cloister,* Pl.*Euthd.* l.c.; in Egypt, *avenue* of Sphinxes at entrance of temples, *OGI*56.52 (Canopus, Ptol. III), Str.17.1.28, etc.; δ. τοῦ ἱεροῦ *BGU* 1130.10 (i B.C.). **4.** *orchestra* in the theatre (Tarent.), Hsch. **5.** metaph., ἔξω δρόμου or ἐκτὸς δρόμου φέρεσθαι get off the *course,* i.e. wander from the point, A.*Pr.*883 (anap.), Pl.*Cra.*414b; ἐκ δρόμου πεσεῖν A.*Ag.*1245; οὐδέν ἐστ' ἔξω δρόμου 'tis not foreign to the purpose, Id.*Ch.*514. **III.** δ. δημόσιος, = Lat. *cursus publicus,* Procop.*Vand.*1.16, *Arc.*30, Lyd.*Mag.*2.10; δ. ὀξύς, = Lat. *cursus velox,* ib.3.61, *POxy.*900.7 (iv A.D.), etc.

δρομόω, *hasten,* Aq.*Ps.*67(68).32.

δρόμων, ωνος, ὁ, *a light vessel,* Procop.*Vand.*1.11, Lyd.*Mag.*2.14, etc. **II.** = δρομίας II, Hsch.

δρόξιμα, τά, late form for τρώξιμα, *uncooked fruit, PLond.*5.1674 (v A.D.), *PMasp.*2 iii 10 (vi A.D.).

δροόν· ἰσχυρόν (Argive), Hsch.

δροπά, = δρεπτά, S.*Fr.*481. (Perh. due to wrong division of a compd., e.g. ἀρτίδροπος.)

δρόπις· τρυγητός, Hsch. **δροπίσκος,** ὁ, *flower-basket,* Id.

δρόσαλλις, ιδος, ἡ, a kind of *vine, Gp.*5.17.3 (Bithynian).

δροσ-ερός, ά, όν, (δρόσος) *dewy, watery,* αἰθήρ, πηγαί, E.*Ba.*865 (lyr.), *Hel.*1335; νεφέλαι Ar.*Nu.*338 (anap.); *dewy, fresh,* λάχανα Id. *Pl.*298. **2.** *tender, soft,* στόματα *AP*5.243 (Paul. Sil.). **-ία,** poet. -ίη, ἡ, *foam* of a horse's mouth, Orac.ap.Luc.*Alex.*53; *dew, Cat.Cod. Astr.*1.172. **-ίζω,** *bedew, besprinkle,* in Med., Ar.*Ra.*1312 (lyr.), prob. in E.*Hyps.Fr.*9.4:—later in Act., Posidon.20 J., Babr.12.16:—Pass., Hp.*Ulc.*12; δεδροσισμένον νέφος *dewy,* D.L.7.152: metaph., ἡνίκ' ἂν ὑπὸ τοῦ οἴνου δροσισθῇ ἡ ψυχή Epict.*Gnom.*26. **II.** intr., *form dew,* Arist.*Pr.*939^{b}38; δροσίζων ἱδρώς Herod.Med. in *Rh.Mus.* 58.99; *to be in a flaccid condition,* of the body, Philostr.*Gym.*48, cf. Archig.ap.Aët.6.3. **-ιμος,** ον, = sq., Plu.2.918a. **-ινός,** ή, όν, = δροσερός, *AP*9.570 (Phld.). **-ισμός,** ὁ, *exposure to dew,* Olymp.Alch.p.87 B.

δροσο-βολέω, *to shed dew,* ὁ ἀὴρ δροσοβολεῖ Plu.2.659b. **-βόλος,** ον, *dewy,* χῶραι Thphr.*CP*3.24.4; ἀήρ ib.6.18.3; πανσέληνοι Plu.2.917f. **-γόνος,** ον, *dew-producing,* of the sign Aquarius, *Cat.Cod. Astr.*7.209. **-ειδής,** ές, *dew-like,* Adv. -ειδῶς Gal.*Nat.Fac.*2.3, al., Paul.Aeg.4.17. **-είμων,** ον, gen. ονος, *dew-clad,* νεφέλαι Orph.*H.*21.6, 51.6. **-εις,** εσσα, εν, *dewy,* Sapph.*Supp.*24.12, etc.; πεδία A.R.1.1282, cf. Coluth.343; *shedding dew,* Σελήνη Nonn.*D.*40.376; *fresh,* λουτρά E.*Tr.*833; χείλεα *AP*5.269 (Paul. Sil.). **-λιθος,** ὁ, a *gem,* Isid.*Etym.*16.12.2. **-μελι,** ιτος, τό, = ἀερόμελι, Gal.6.739. **-ομαι,** Pass., *to be wet with dew, Anacreont.*53.31. **-πᾰγής,** ές, *dew-nourished,* Ph.Byz.*Mir.*1. **-πάχνη,** ἡ, *hoar-frost, rime,* Arist. *Mu.*394^{a}26.

δρόσος, ἡ, *dew,* Hdt.2.68, Pl.*Ti.*59e: pl., A.*Ag.*336, S.*Aj.*1208 (lyr.), etc. **2.** in Poets, *pure water,* ποντία δ. A.*Eu.*904; δρόσῳ ἐναλίᾳ, θαλασσίᾳ, E.*IT*255, 1192; ποταμίᾳ δ. Id.*Hipp.*127 (lyr.); ποταμίαισι δρόσοις ib.78; ἐπὶ κρηναίαισι δρόσοις Id.*IA*182 (lyr.); δρόσος alone, Ἀχελῴου δ. Id.*Andr.*167; καθαραῖς δρόσοις Id.*Ion* 96 (lyr.); ἐκ ποταμῶν δρόσον ἄρατε Ar.*Ra.*1339. **3.** of other liquids, δ. ἀμπέλου Pi.*O.*7.2; δ. φοινία A.*Ag.*1390, etc.; ἀπόπτυστος Ar.*Eq.*1285; of oil, *AP*5.3 (Phld.); of honey, Philostr.*Her.*19.19; δ. καλάμου *sugar,* Antyll.ap.Orib.10.27.18: metaph., δρόσος κώμων Pi.*P.*5.99. **4.** *down* on the cheek, δ. καὶ χνοῦς Ar.*Nu.*978, cf. Plu.2.79d. **II.** metaph., *the young of animals,* A.*Ag.*141 (lyr., pl.): in sg., δ. Ἡφαίστοιο Call.*Hec.*1.2.3.

δροσώδης, ες, *dewy, moist,* κύπειρος Pherecr.109; λιβάς Antiph. 52.13; κρεάδια Alex.124.12; ἱδρώς Plu.2.695c; δ. ὕδατος νοτίς a spring of *fresh* water, E.*Ba.*705.

Δρουίδης, = Δρυΐδης, prob. in D.S.5.31.

δροῦνα· ἡ ἀρχή (Tyrrhen.), Hsch.

δρυάζειν· φλυαρεῖν, Hsch.:—also **δρυάσαι·** κατακολυμβῆσαι, Id.; cf. δενδρυάζω II. **δρύακες,** = δρύοχοι, Id.

δρῠάριον, τό, Dim. of δρῦς, Eust.1715.52.

Δρυᾰς, άδος, ἡ, (δρῦς) *a Dryad,* nymph whose life was bound up with that of her tree, Plu.*Caes.*9. **II.** a *snake,* Androm.ap.Gal. 14.33.

δρυαταί· ἄδιψοι, ψεῦσται, Hsch.

δρῠᾰχαρνεύς, έως, ὁ, *tough Acharnian, Com.Adesp.*75.

δρύεται· κρύπτεται, Hsch.

δρῠηκόπος, ον, (κόπτω) *wood-cutting,* Lyc.1378.

Δρυΐδης, ου, ὁ, *Druid,* Arist.*Fr.*35, Str.4.4.4.

δρῠ-ΐνας, ου, ὁ, *serpent living in hollow oaks,* Nic.*Th.*411, Dsc. *Ther.*11. **-ῐνος,** η, ον, (δρῦς) *oaken,* Od.21.43, Hp.*Fract.*13, E.*Ba.*1103, etc.; δ. πῦρ a fire *of oak-wood,* Theoc.9.19; μέλι δ. honey *from the hollow of an oak, AP*9.72 (Antip.(?)); ὁ δ. στέφανος *Mon.Anc. Gr.*17.24. **-ῑνών,** ῶνος, ὁ, *oak-coppice, IG*1^2.328 (dub.). **-ΐτης** [ῑ], ου, ὁ, in Thphr.*CP*1.2.2, said to be a kind of *cypress.* **II.** δ. λίθος a *precious stone,* Plin.37.188. **-καρπον,** τό, *acorn* or *similar fruit,* Lyc.83, Eust.773.49 (in pl.). **-κολάπτης,** v. δρυοκολάπτης.

δρυμάζω or **-σσω,** = δρύπτω; fut. δρυμάξω *Com.Adesp.*986.

δρυμεῖτις (sc. γῆ), ιδος, ἡ, *woodland, Stud.Pal.*22.159 (ii A.D.).

δρύμιος, α, ον, *passing through a copse,* ῥόϝος *Inscr.Cypr.*135.19 H.

δρυμίους· τοὺς κατὰ τὴν χώραν κακοποιοῦντας, Hsch.

δρυμίς, ίδος, ἡ, = δρυάς, δ. Νύμφαι *An.Ox.*1.225.

δρυμόνιος, α, ον, *haunting the woods,* epith. of Artemis, Orph.*H.* 36.12.

δρῡμός, ὁ, *copse, thicket,* S.*OT*1399, *SIG*57.28 (Milet., v B.C.), E. *Hipp.*1127 (lyr.), *Tab.Heracl.*1.19, *PLille* 5.13 (iii B.C.), Lxx *Ec.*2.6, Plb.2.15.2, *AP*7.544, etc.: pl., A.*Fr.*304.10, Theoc.1.117, *AP*6.13 (Leon.), 9.4 (Cyllen.), 84 (Antiphan.), Plu.*Comp.Per.Fab.*1. **II.** Hom. has only pl., δρῡμά, τά, Il.11.118, Od.10.150, 197, 251, also in Simm.15 (prob.); δρῦμά in late Ep., D.P.492, Opp.*C.*1.64. **III.** δρυμός· φρούριον, Hsch., perh. in this sense in *PPetr.*2 p.140. (Cf. Skt. *drumá-* 'tree', Slav. *drŭmŭ* 'thicket': ῠ is original, ῡ borrowed from δρῦς.)

δρῡμο-φύλαξ, *saltuarius, Gloss.* **-χᾰρής,** ές, *delighting in the woods,* Orph.*H.*51.13.

δρῡμ-ώδης, ες, *woody,* τόποι D.S.3.26, cf. Str.8.3.25; λόφος *Inscr. Prien.*42.46 (ii/i B.C.). **-ών,** ῶνος, ὁ, = δρυμός, J.*AJ*8.6.5, al., Babr.45.11, Opp.*C.*2.78.

δρῠο-βάλᾰνος [βᾰ], ἡ, *acorn,* Str.15.3.18: sg. in collect. sense, Id.3.3.7. **-βᾰφής,** ές, *dyed with oak-bark,* ἱμάτια Hsch. **-γόνος,** ον, (γενέσθαι) *oak-grown,* ὄρη Ar.*Th.*114. **-εις,** εσσα, εν, *full of oaks, woody,* Il.2.783^a, Nonn.*D.*5.60. **II.** *made of oak-wood,* ib. 17.322, al. **-κοίτης,** ου, ὁ, *dweller on the oak,* τέττιξ *AP*7.190 (Anyte or Leon.). **-κολάπτης,** ου, ὁ, *woodpecker,* of which Arist. distinguishes four species, the *great black, Picus martius,* the *green, Picus viridis,* and the *spotted* (both *greater* and *less*), *Picus major* and *minor, HA*593^{a}5, cf. 614^{b}7, Str.5.4.2; = Lat. *picus,* D.H.1.14:—also

δρῠκολάπτης, Ar.*Av.*480,979; **δρῠοκόλαψ**, Hsch. s.v. ἵπτα (prob. l.); **δρῠοκόπος**, Arist.*PA*662ᵇ7. **-πᾰγὴς** στόλος, in S.*Fr.*702, expld. by Eust.1726.16 as ὁ δρύϊνος πάσσαλος, the *oak-fastening* instrument, an *oaken* bolt. (Cf. στόλος, = ἔμβολον, A.*Pers.*408.) **-πε-τής**, ές, = δρυπετής (v. δρυπεπής), Gal.6.608; δαφνίδες Dsc.1.40 (s.v.l.). **-πτερίς**, έως, ὁ, *black oak-fern, Asplenium onopteris*, Dsc. 4.187.

δρύος, ὁ, *woodland*, *POxy.*1044.8, al. (ii/iii A.D.).

δρῠο-τομία, ἡ, *felling of trees for timber*, Pl.*Lg.*678d. **-τομική** (sc. τέχνη), ἡ, = foreg., Id.*Plt.*288d. **-τόμος**, ὁ, = δρυτόμος, Aesop. 35, Gal.13.573, etc. [δρῡ- v.l. in Q.S.1.250.] **-φακτος**, coined as etym. of δρύφακτος, Sch.Ar.*Eq.*672.

δρύοχοι [ῠ], οἱ, (δρυ- 'wooden structure', 'ship' (cf. δόρυ), ἔχω) *props* or *shores* upon which is laid the frame of a new ship, Od.19.574, cf. Eust. et Sch. ad loc.; κατὰ δρυόχων ἐπάγη σανίς Epigr.ap.Moschion. ap.Ath.5.209c; ἐκ δρυόχων ναυπηγεῖσθαι to build a ship from *the keel*, Plb.1.38.5; δρυόχους ἐπεβάλλετο νηός A.R.1.723: metaph., δρυόχους τιθέναι δράματος ἀρχάς to lay *the keel* of a new play, Ar.*Th.*52: οἷον ἐκ δρυόχων Pl.*Ti.*81b, cf. Plu.2.321e: sg. only in Poll.1.85. II. = δρυμά, *woods*, *AP*6.16 (Arch.): heterocl. pl. δρύοχα E.*El.*1163 (lyr.).

δρύοψ [ῠ], οπος, ὁ, a kind of *woodpecker*, Ar.*Av.*304.

δρῠπεπής, ές, *ripened on the tree, quite ripe*, ἐλάα Chionid.7, Eup. 312; αἱ δρυπεπεῖς (sc. ἰσχάδες) Ar.*Lys.*564, Callias Com.21: by a com. metaph., μᾶζαι δ. Cratin.165, Telecl.38; δ. ἑταῖραι Ar.*Fr.* 141: heterocl. acc. sg., τὴν ἀλίπαστον δρύπεπα, as Subst., *AP*6.191 (Longus):—**δρυπετής** or **-πέτης** (πίπτω), *ready to fall, over-ripe*, is a constant v.l., cf. Sch.Orib.2 p.746 D., Hsch.

δρυπίς, ίδος, ἡ, (δρύπτω) *knot-wort, Drypis spinosa*, Thphr.*HP*1. 10.6.

δρυπολεῖ· ταλαιπωρεῖ, ὀρειβατεῖ, πυρὶ πολιορκεῖ, Hsch.

δρύππᾱ, ἡ, *olive*, *AP*6.299 (Phan.), Ath.2.56a.

δρύππιος, α, ον, perh. *planted with olives*, ἀγρός *IG*9(1).61.20 (Daulis).

δρυπτερίς, = δρυοπτερίς, Hsch.

δρύπτην· ἀλήτην, Hsch.; cf. δρώπτης.

δρύπτω, E.*El.*150: fut. δρύψω (κατα-) v.l. in *AP*5.42 (Rufin.): aor. ἔδρυψα, Ep. δρύψα Il.16.324:—**Med.**, Hes.*Sc.*243 (κατα-, tm.), E.*Hec.* 655 (lyr.): aor. δρυψάμενος Od.2.153:—**Pass.**, *AP*7.2 (Antip. Sid.): plpf. δέδρυπτο Q.S.14.391:—*tear, strip*, βραχίονα δουρὸς ἀκωκὴ δρύψ' ἀπὸ μυώνων Il. l.c.:—Med., δρυψαμένω δ' ὀνύχεσσι παρειὰς ἀμφί τε δειράς *tearing each other's* cheeks and necks all round, Od. l.c.: mostly in sign of mourning, δρύπτεν κάρα E.*El.*150 (lyr.); ἑκάτερθε παρειάς A.R.3.672; also δρύπτεσθαι παρειάν *to tear one's* cheek, E. *Hec.*655; without παρειάν, X.*Cyr.*3.1.13. 2. metaph., τὴν δὲ χοῖρον αὐονὴ δρύπτει Herod.8.2.—Poet., X. and later Prose, as Philostr. *VA*3.38.

δρῦς, ἡ (Pelop. ὁ, acc. to Sch.Ar.*Nu.*401, cf. *IG*9(1).485.5 (Thyrrheum), but fem. in Arc., *Schwyzer*664.23): gen. δρυός: acc. δρῦν (δρύα Q.S.3.280): nom. pl. δρύες Il.12.132, A.*Pr.*832, etc., δρῦς Thphr.*CP*2.9.2, Paus.8.12.1: acc. pl. δρῦς Ar.*Eq.*528, *Nu.*402, δρύας S.*Fr.*403, Call.*Del.*84, *AP*7.8 (Antip. Sid.): gen. δρυῶν Hdt.7.218: dual δρύε Hdn.Gr.1.420. [ῠ, exc. in δρῦς, δρῦν: gen. δρῡός at the beginning of a verse, Hes.*Op.*436]:—originally, *tree* (δρῦν ἐκάλουν οἱ παλαιοὶ.. πᾶν δένδρον Sch.Il.11.86, cf. Hsch.); including various trees, Thphr.*HP*3.8.2; esp. *Quercus Aegilops* (φηγός) and *Quercus Ilex* (πρῖνος), cf. ἡ φηγὸς καὶ ἡ πρῖνος εἴδη δρυός Dsc.1.106; opp. πεύκη, Il.11.494; opp. πίτυς, Od.9.186, cf. Il.13.389, 23.328, etc.; στέφανος δρυός crown *of oak leaves*, *SIG*[2]588.7 (Delos, ii B.C.); commonly, *the oak*, δ. ὑψικάρηνοι, ὑψίκομοι, Il.12.132, 14.398, cf. 13. 389, 23.328, etc.; sacred to Zeus, who gave his oracles from the oaks of Dodona, Od.14.328; αἱ προσήγοροι δρύες A.*Pr.*832; πολύγλωσσος δ. S.*Tr.*1168, cf. Pl.*Phdr.*275b: prov., οὐ γὰρ ἀπὸ δρυός ἐσσι.. οὐδ' ἀπὸ πέτρης thou art no foundling from *the woods* or rocks, i.e. thou hast parents and a country, Od.19.163, cf. Pl.*Ap.*34d, *R.* 544d, *AP*10.55 (Pall.); but οὐ μέν πως νῦν ἔστιν ἀπὸ δρυὸς οὐδ' ἀπὸ πέτρης.. ὀαρίζειν 'tis no time now to talk at ease from *tree* or rock, like lovers, Il.22.126; ἀλλὰ τί ἦ μοι ταῦτα περὶ δρῦν ἢ περὶ πέτρην; why all this about *trees* and rocks (i.e. things we have nothing to do with)? Hes.*Th.*35; also διὰ πέτρας καὶ διὰ δρυὸς ὁρᾶν 'to see through a brick wall', Plu.2.1083d. II. of other trees bearing acorns or mast (Paus.8.1.6), πίειρα δρῦς the resinous *wood* (of the pine), S.*Tr.*766; of the olive, E.*Cyc.*615 (lyr.); δ. θαλασσία, = ἁλίφλοιος, Ps.-Democr.*Symp.Ant.*p.5 G. III. δ. ποντία, *gulf-weed, Sargassum vulgare*, Thphr.*HP*4.6.9. IV. metaph., *worn-out old man*, *AP*6.254 (Myrin.), Artem.2.25. (Cogn. with δόρυ; cf. Skt. *dru-* 'wood', in compds.)

δρύσσομαι, aor. part. δρυξάμενος, perh. = δρυφάσσω, δ. τῆς γῆς ἀπὸ τῶν ὁρίων *PGrenf.*1.11.14 (ii B.C.).

δρῠτόμος, ον, *wood-cutter*, Il.11.86, Theoc.5.64, Philostr.*Im.*2.33, al.; cf. δρυοτόμος. [δρῡ- Q.S.9.163,453, 13.56.]

δρῠφάδες, αἱ, *nail-parings*, Hsch.; also, = λῦπαι, ὀδύναι, i.e. *lancinating pains* or *weals, bruises*, Id.

δρυφάζω, aor. inf. δρυφάξαι· δακεῖν, Hsch. **δρυφαίνηκα**· τὸν οὐ μέγαν (Elean), Id.

δρύφακτ-ος [ῠ], ὁ, later **τρύφακτος** *BCH*35.23 (Delos, iv B.C.), *OGI*598.3 (Jerusalem), Hdn.Gr.2.595:—*railing* or *latticed partition*, serving as *the bar* of the courts of law, the council-chamber, etc., Ar. *V.*380: mostly in pl., ὑπερεπήδων τοὺς δ. Id.*Eq.*675; ὑπὸ τοῖς δ. Id.*V.* 386; ἐπὶ τοῖς δ. ib.552, X.*HG*2.3.55: sg., δρυφάκτου τρόπῳ Apollod. *Poliorc.*172.1. 2. *hand-rail*, Plb.1.22.6, 10. 3. *balcony*, Arist. *Ath.*50.2:—written **δρύφρακτοι**, Lib.*Or.*11.217. (By dissim. for δρύ-φρακτος (φράσσω), cf. Lib. l.c., Hellad.ap.Sch.Orib.2 p.746 D., Sch.Ar.*Eq.* l.c.) **-όω**, *fence, fortify*, Plb.8.4.4. **-ωμα**, ατος, τό, *enclosure*, Str.13.4.14.

δρῠφάσσω, *fence round, guard by a fence*, Lyc.758 (Pass.).

δρύφειν· περαίνειν, and **δρυφόμενοι**· φθειρόμενοι, Hsch.

δρυφή [ῠ], ἡ, (δρύπτω) *tearing*, and **δρυφοί**, οἱ, *scrapings*, Hsch.: —also **δρύφη**, = κλάσματα, Id. s.v. πύρνα, cf. Suid.

δρῠφόροι, οἱ, religious guild at Thessalonica (cf. δενδροφόρος), *BCH*38.41 (δροι- lapis).

δρύψελον, τό, lit. *bark*: of a *leaf*, Parth.*Fr.*26: **δρύψαλα**, Hsch.

δρύψια, τά, = foreg., δ. τυρῶν *AP*6.299 (Phan.).

δρυψο-γέρων, οντος, ὁ, (δρύπτω) *worn-out old man*, and **-παις**, παιδος, ὁ, ἡ, *coquette*, Hsch.; also, = ἐλεεινός, Id.

δρῠώδης, ες, gloss on δρυόεις, Hsch.

δρωκτάζεις (δροκτ- cod.)· περιβλέπεις, Hsch.; cf. δρωπάζω, δρώπτω. **δρωμᾷ**· τρέχει, and **δρωμίσσουσα**· τρέχουσα, Id.

δρωπάζω (δράω B), *gaze at*, A.D.*Adv.*139.8, Hsch.

δρωπᾰκ-ίζω, *apply a depilatory*, δ. μέλιτι Orib.*Eup.*4.7:—Med., Arr.*Epict.*3.22.10, Hierocl.*Facet.*64:—Pass., Luc.*Demon.*50. **-ισμός**, ὁ, *the application of a pitch-plaster*, as a counter-irritant, Dsc. *Ther.*3. **-ιστέον**, *one must apply a pitch-plaster*, Orib.*Fr.* 75. **-ιστής**, οῦ, ὁ, = *depilator*, *Gloss.* **-ιστός**, ή, όν, *serving as a counter-irritant*, Gal.18(2).894. **-ίστρια**, ἡ, = παρατίλτρια, Phot.

δρῶπαξ, ἄκος, ὁ, (δρέπω) *pitch-plaster*, Hp.*Ep.*19 (*Hermes* 53.71), Gal.6.416, Dsc.*Eup.*1.233, Archig.ap.Aët.3.180:—also neut. pl. **δρώπακα** (sc. φάρμακα), Gal.18(2).894. [ᾰ in Lat. gen., Mart.3.74, 10.65.]

δρώπτης· πλανήτης, πτωχός, Hsch.

δρώπτω, = διακόπτω ἢ διασκοπῶ, A.*Fr.*278.

δρώψ· ἄνθρωπος, Hsch. **δύα**, Dor. for δύη. II. δύαν· κρήνην, Id.

δῠᾰδ-ίζω, *make into a dyad*, in Pass., ἡ δυαδιζομένη μονάς Dam.*Pr.* 147. **-ικός**, ή, όν, (δύο) *of* or *for the number two*, Plu.2.1025d; opp. μοναδικός, Dam.*Pr.*119; δ. πᾶσα πρόοδος ib.47. Adv. **-κῶς** Procl.*in Prm.*p.915 S., Herm.*in Phdr.*p.151 A. **-ισμός**, ὁ, *making into a dyad*, Dam.*Pr.*193.

δῠ-άζω, *express in the dual number*, Eust.47.28. 2. Pass., *to be impressed with the sense of a thing's being double, see double*, etc., S.E.*M.*7.193. II. *make into two*, Ascl.*in Metaph.*432.12 (Pass.): —Pass., *to be halved*, of the moon, *Theol.Ar.*12. 2. *double*, Theo Sm.p.29 H., Iamb.*in Nic.*p.60 P. III. δυάζει· φλυαρεῖ, Hsch., Cyr. (cf. δρυάζω); also δυαεῖ Hsch. **-άκις**, Adv. *twice*, Ar.*Fr.* 769. **-άνδρες**, οἱ, = Lat. *duumviri*, *Wien.Stud.*24.288 (Olbasa). **-ανδρικός**, ή, όν, = *duumviralis*, ib.289. **-ᾰνερικός**, ή, όν, = foreg., *CIG*3979 (Antioch. Pisid.). **-άς**, άδος, ἡ, *the number two*, Pl.*Phd.*101c, *Prm.*149c, Arist.*Ph.*220ᵃ27, etc. 2. *dyad*, ἡ ἀόριστος δ. Arist.*Metaph.*1081ᵃ14, Alex.Aphr.*in Metaph.*58.12. 3. *pair*, Philostr.*Im.*1.6, Lib.*Or.*61.7.

δῠάω, (δύη) *plunge in misery*, δυόωσιν.. ἀνθρώπους Od.20.195:— Pass., pf. part. δεδυημένη Hsch.

δυγός, Dor. for ζυγός, *Schwyzer*180 (Crete), 317 (Delph.), *EM* 316.57; Aeol., ib.466.36; Boeot., Choerob.*in Theod.*2.390.

δῠ-ειδής, ές, *of the class of the dyad*, μεσότης Dam.*Pr.*189. **-ενῐαυσίως**, Adv. *twice yearly*, *PAmh.*2.148.8 (v A.D.).

δῠερός, ά, όν, (δύη) *miserable*, δυεροῦ θανάτοιο τυχεῖν *IG*3.1337, cf. Max.65,182.

δυϝάνοι, v. δίδωμι.

δύη [ῠ], ἡ, Dor. (not in Trag.) **δύα**, poet. Noun, *misery, anguish*, Od.14.215, etc.; πῆμα δύης height *of woe*, ib.338; πέλαγος ἀτηρᾶς δύης A.*Pr.*746; γενναία δ. S.*Aj.*938 (lyr.): pl., πημοναῖς δύαις τε A. *Pr.*513, cf. 181 (lyr.), 525, etc.: also in late Prose, App.*BC*4.42; Pythag. name for *two* (by false etym.), *Theol.Ar.*12.

δῠη-πᾰθέω, *endure misery*, Nonn.*D.*26.113. **-πᾰθής**, ές, *much-suffering*, A.R.4.1165, Opp.*H.*2.436; *painful*, τοκετός Nonn.*D.*41. 411. **-πᾰθία**, poet. **-ίη**, ἡ, *misery*, A.R.4.1395, *APl.*4.113 (Jul.), Hsch.:—written **-πάθεια**, *EM*291.10. **-πᾰθος**, ον, = δυηπαθής, *h.Merc.*486.

δυθμή, = δυσμή (q.v.).

δῠϊκός, ή, όν, *dual*, D.T.635.30; τὸ δ. *the dual number*, A.D. *Pron.*10.28, S.E.*M.*1.142. Adv. **-κῶς** *in the dual number*, Phoeb. *Fig.*1.4, Anon.*in Tht.*73.4; = διττῶς, Suid.

δῠίος [ῠ], α, ον, = δυερός, A.*Supp.*829 (lyr.).

δῦμα, ατος, τό, = ἔνδυμα, *POxy.*929.8, 15 (ii/iii A.D.).

δύμεναι [ῡ], Ep. aor. 2 inf. Act. of δύω.

δύνᾰμαι [ῠ], 2 sg. δύνασαι Il.1.393, Od.4.374, S.*Aj.*1164 (anap.), Ar.*Nu.*811 (lyr.), *Pl.*574, X.*An.*7.7.8, etc.; δύνῃ *Carm.Aur.*19, also in codd. of S.*Ph.*798, E.*Hec.*253, *Andr.*239, and later Prose, Plb. 7.11.5, Ael.*VH*13.32; Aeol. and Dor. δύνᾳ Alc.*Oxy.*1788 *Fr.*15 ii 16, Theoc.10.2, also S.*Ph.*849 (lyr.), dub. in *OT*696 (lyr.); δύνῃ is subj., Ar.*Eq.*491, cf. Phryn.337; Ion. 3 pl. δυνέαται Hdt.2.142; subj. δύνωμαι, Ion. 2 sg. δύνηαι Il.6.229 (δυνεώμεθα -ωνται as vv.ll. in Hdt.4.97, 7.163); also δύνᾱμαι Sapph.*Supp.*3.3, *GDI*4952 *A* 42 (Crete): impf. 2 sg. ἐδύνω *h.Merc.*405, X.*An.*1.6.7; later ἐδύνασο Hp.*Ep.*16 (v.l. ἠδ.), Luc.*DMort.*9.1; Ion. 3 pl. ἐδυνέατο Hdt.4.110, al. (ἠδ- codd.): fut. δυνήσομαι Od.16.238, etc.; Dor. δυνᾱσοῦμαι Archyt.3; later δυνηθήσομαι D.C.52.37: aor. ἐδυνησάμην Il.14.33, Ep. δυν- 5.621; subj. δυνήσωνται Semon.1.17, never in good Att., f.l. in

D.19.323: Pass. forms, Ep., Ion., Lyr., ἐδυνάσθην or δυνάσθην Il.23.465, al., Hdt.2.19, al., Pi.*O.*1.56, Hp.*Art.*48 (v.l. δυνηθείη), also in X.*Mem.*1.2.24, *An.*7.6.20; Trag. and Att. Prose ἐδυνήθην S.*Aj.* 1067, *OT* 1212 (lyr.), E.*Ion* 867 (anap.), D.21.80,186: pf. δεδύνημαι D.4.30, Din.2.14, Phld.*Rh.*1.261 S.—The double augment ἠδυνάμην is Att. acc. to Moer.175, but Ion. acc. to *An.Ox.*2.374, and is found in codd. of Hdt.4.110, al., Hp.*Epid.*1.26.β', al.; ἠδύνω is required by metre in Philippid.16; but is not found in Att. Inscrr. before 300 B.C., *IG*2².678.12, al., cf. ἠδύνασθε ib.7.2711 (Acraeph., i A.D.); both forms occur in later writers: ἠδυνήθην occurs in A.*Pr.*208, and codd. of Th.4.33, Lys.3.42, etc.: δύνομαι is a late form freq. in Pap. as *UPZ* 9 (ii B.C.), al. [ῠ, exc. in δυναμένοιο Od.1.276, 11.414, Hom. *Epigr.*15.1, and pr. n. Δῡναμένη, metri gr.]

I. *to be able, strong enough* to do, c. inf. pres. et aor., Il.19.163, 1.562, etc.: fut. inf. is f.l. (πείσειν for πείθειν) in S.*Ph.*1394, (κωλύσειν for κωλῦσαι) Plb.21.11.13, etc.: freq. abs., with inf. supplied from the context, εἰ δύνασαί γε if at least thou *canst* (sc. περισχέσθαι), Il. 1.393: also c. acc. Pron. or Adj., ὅσσον δύναμαι χερσίν τε ποσίν τε 20.360; [Ζεὺς] δύναται ἅπαντα Od.4.237; μέγα δυνάμενος very *powerful, mighty*, 1.276, cf. 11.414; δ. μέγιστον ξείνων Hdt.9.9, etc.; μέγα δύναται, *multum valet*, A.*Eu.*950 (lyr.); δ. Διὸς ἄγχιστα Id.*Supp.*1035; οἱ δυνάμενοι *men of power, rank, and influence*, E.*Or.*889, Th.6.39, etc.; οἱ δυνάμενοι, opp. οἱ μὴ ἔχοντες, Democr.255; opp. οἱ πένητες, Archyt.3; δυνάμενος παρά τινι *having influence* with him, Hdt.7.5, And. 4.26, etc.; δύνασθαι ἐν τοῖς πρώτοις Th.4.105; δ. τοῖς χρήμασι, τῷ σώματι, Lys.6.48, 24.4; ὁ δυνάμενος *one that can maintain himself*, Id. 24.12; of things, [διαφέρει] οἷς δύνανται differ in their *potentialities*, Plot.6.3.17. 2. of moral possibility, *to be able, dare, bear* to do a thing, mostly with neg., οὔτε τελευτὴν ποιῆσαι δύναται Od.1.250; σε .. οὐ δύναμαι προλιπεῖν 13.331, cf. S.*Ant.*455; οὐκέτι ἐδύνατο ἐν τῷ καθεστῶτι τρόπῳ βιοτεύειν Th.1.130; οὐδὲ σθένειν τοσοῦτον ᾠόμην τὰ σὰ κηρύγμαθ' ὥστε .. θεῶν νόμιμα δύνασθαι .. ὑπερδραμεῖν S.*Ant.* 455. b. *enjoy a legal right*, δ. τῆς γεωργίας ἀπηλλάχθαι *POxy.*899.31 (ii/iii A.D.), etc. 3. with ὡς and Sup., ὡς ἐδύναντο ἀδηλότατα as secretly as they *could*, Th.7.50; ὡς δύναμαι μάλιστα κατατείνας as forcibly as I *possibly can*, Pl.*R.*367b; ὡς δύναιτο κάλλιστον Id.*Smp.*214c; ὡς ἂν δύνωμαι διὰ βραχυτάτων D.27.3, etc.; simply ὡς ἐδύνατο in the best way he *could*, X.*An.*2.6.2: with relat., ὅσους ἐδύνατο πλείστους ἀθροίσας Id.*HG*2.2.9; λαβεῖν .. οὓς ἂν σοφωτάτους δύνωμαι Alex. 213. II. *to be equivalent to*, λόγοι ἔργα δυνάμενοι words *that are as good as* deeds, Th.6.40: hence, 1. of money, *to be worth*, c. acc., ὁ σίγλος δύναται ἑπτὰ ὀβολούς X.*An.*1.5.6, cf. D.34.23: abs., *pass, be current*, Luc.*Luct.*10. 2. of Number, etc., *to be equal* or *equivalent to*, τριηκόσιαι γενεαὶ δυνέαται μύρια ἔτεα Hdt.2.142; δυνήσεται τὴν ὑποτείνουσαν *will be equivalent to* the hypotenuse, Arist.*IA* 709ᵃ19. 3. of words, *signify, mean*, Hdt.4.110, al.; τὸ πειρηθῆναι καὶ τὸ ποιεῖν ἴσον δύναται Id.6.86.γ'; δύναται ἴσον τῷ δρᾶν τὸ νοεῖν Ar. *Fr.*691; δύναται τὸ νεοδαμῶδες ἤδη ἐλεύθερον εἶναι Th.7.58: in later Greek, δύναται τὸ "μνασθέντι" ἀντὶ τοῦ "μνασθέντος" *is equivalent to*.., Sch.Pi.*O.*7.110. b. *avail to produce*, οὐδένα καιρὸν δύναται *brings* no advantage, E.*Med.*128 (anap.), cf. Pl.*Phlb.*23d. c. of things, *mean*, '*spell*', τὸ τριβώνιον τί δύναται; Ar.*Pl.*842; αἱ ἀγγελίαι τοῦτο δύνανται they *mean* this much, Th.6.36; τὴν αὐτὴν δ. δούλωσιν Id.1.141, cf. Arist.*Pol.*1313ᵇ25. 4. Math., δύνασθαί τι *to be equivalent when squared to* a number or area, τοῖς ἐπιπέδοις ἃ δύνανται in the areas of which they [the lines] *are the roots*, Pl.*Tht.*148b; ἡ ΒΓ τῆς Α μεῖζον δύναται τῇ ΔΖ *the square on* ΒΓ *is greater* than *the square on* Α by the *square on* ΔΖ, Euc.10.17; αἱ δυνάμεναι αὐτὰ [τὰ μεγέθη] the lines *representing* their *square roots*, ib.*Def.*4, cf. *Prop.* 22; αὐξήσεις δυνάμεναί τε καὶ δυναστευόμεναι increments both *in the roots* and *powers* of numbers, Pl.*R.*546b; τὴν ὑποτείνουσαν ταῖς περὶ τὴν ὀρθὴν ἴσον δυναμένην Plu.2.720a, cf. Iamb.*Comm.Math.*17; ἡ δυναμένη, Pythag. name for the *hypotenuse* of a right-angled triangle, Alex.Aphr. *in Metaph.*75.31. b. of numbers multiplied together, *come to*, Papp.1.24,27. III. impers., οὐ δύναται, c. aor. inf., *it cannot be, is not to be*, τοῖσι Σπαρτιήτῃσι καλλιερῆσαι οὐκ ἐδύνατο Hdt. 7.134, cf. 9.45; δύναται *it is possible*, Plu.2.440e (s. v.l.).

δῠνᾰμερός, ά, όν, *potent*, of drugs: hence as Subst., φυσικὰ δυναμερά, title of work by Ps.-Bolus, Suid. s. v. Βῶλος, cf. Archig.ap.Aët. 3.114.

δῠνᾰμικός, ή, όν, *powerful, efficacious*, ἐρωτήματα Chrysipp.*Stoic.* 2.90 (Comp.); τὸ τοῦ λόγου δ. Phld.*Rh.*1.378 S. (Sup.); λόγος, of a magician's spell, Ps.-Callisth.1.3; πρός τι Plb.22.21.4, Onos.12.2 (Comp.); κατὰ τὴν σωματικὴν ἕξιν Plb.36.16.3 (Sup.); of wine, *potent*, Ath.1.26b (Sup.). 2. *potential*, τὸ δ., opp. τὸ ὑποστατικόν, τὸ ἐνεργητικόν, Dam.*Pr.*61. b. Gramm., *expressing possibility*, δ. σύνδεσμος (of κα) Sch.Theoc.1.4.

δύνᾰμις [ῠ], ἡ, gen. εως, Ion. ιος, Ion. dat. δυνάμι: (δύναμαι):— *power, might*, in Hom., esp. of *bodily strength*, εἴ μοι δ. γε παρείη Od. 2.62, cf. Il.8.294; οἵη ἐμὴ δ. καὶ χεῖρες Od.20.237; ἡ δ. τῶν νέων Antipho 4.3.2, etc.: generally, *strength, power, ability* to do anything, πὰρ δύναμιν beyond one's *strength*, Il.13.787; in Prose, παρὰ δ. τολμηταί Th.1.70, etc.; ὑπὲρ δ. D.18.193; opp. κατὰ δ. as far as *lies in one*, Hdt.3.142, etc. (κὰδ δ. Hes.*Op.*336); εἰς δύναμιν Cratin.172, Pl.*R.* 458e, etc.; πρὸς τὴν δ. Id.*Phdr.*231a. 2. *outward power, influence, authority*, A.*Pers.*174 (anap.), *Ag.*779 (lyr.); καταπαύσαντα τὴν Κύρου δ. Hdt.1.90; δυνάμει προὔχοντες Th.7.21, etc.; ἐν δ. εἶναι, γενέσθαι, X.*HG*4.4.5, D.13.29. 3. *force for war, forces*, δ. ἀνδρῶν Hdt.5.100, cf. Pl.*Mx.*240d, Plb.1.41.2, Lxx *Ge.*21.22, *OGI* 139.8 (ii B.C.); μετὰ δυνάμεων ἱκανῶν Wilcken *Chr.*10 (ii B.C.), etc.; δ. καὶ πεζὴ καὶ ἱππικὴ καὶ ναυτική X.*An.*1.3.12; πέντε δυνάμεσι πεφρουρημένον, of the five projecting rows of sarissae in the phalanx, Ascl.*Tact.*5.2, al. 4. *a power, quantity*, χρημάτων δ. Hdt.7.9.α'. 5. *means*, κατὰ δύναμιν Arist.*EE* 1243ᵇ12; opp. παρὰ δ., 2*Ep.Cor.*8.3; κατὰ δ. τῶν ὑπαρχόντων *BGU* 1051.17 (Aug.). II. *power, faculty, capacity*, αἱ ἀμφὶ τὸ σῶμα δ. Hp.*VM* 14; αἱ τοῦ σώματος δυνάμεις Pl.*Tht.*185e; ἡ τῆς ὄψεως δ. Id.*R.* 532a; ἡ τῶν λεγόντων δ. D.22.11: c. gen. rei, *capacity for*, τῶν ἔργων Arist.*Pol.*1309ᵃ35; τοῦ λέγειν Id.*Rh.*1362ᵇ22; τοῦ λόγου, τῶν λόγων, Men.578, Alex.94; δ. στρατηγική Plb.1.84.6; δ. ἐν πραγματείᾳ Id.2. 56.5; δ. συνθετική D.H.*Comp.*2: abs., any *natural capacity* or *faculty*, that may be improved and may be used for good or ill, Arist.*Top.* 126ᵃ37, cf. *MM* 1183ᵇ28. 2. *elementary force*, such as heat, cold, etc., Hp.*VM* 16, Arist.*PA* 646ᵃ14; ἡ τοῦ θερμοῦ δ. ib.650ᵃ5; θερμαντικὴ δ. Epicur.*Fr.*60, cf. Polystr.p.23 W. b. *property, quality*, ἰδίην δύναμιν καὶ φύσιν ἔχειν Hp.*VM* 13, cf. *Nat.Hom.*5, *Vict.*1.10; esp. of the *natural properties* of plants, etc., αἱ δ. τῶν φυομένων, τῶν σπερμάτων, X.*Cyr.*8.8.14, Thphr.*HP* 8.11.1; *productive power*, τῆς γῆς Id. *Oec.*16.4; μετάλλων Id.*Vect.*4.1: generally, *function, faculty*, δύναμις φυσική, ζωική, ψυχική, Gal.10.635; περὶ φυσικῶν δ., title of work by Galen. c. in pl., *agencies*, ὑπάρχειν ἐν τῇ φύσει τὰς τοιαύτας δυνάμεις (sc. the gods) Polystr.p.10 W. d. *function, meaning*, of part in whole, Id.p.17 W. e. in Music, *function, value*, of a note in the scale, δ. ἐστι τάξις φθόγγου ἐν συστήματι Cleonid.*Harm.*14, cf. Aristox.*Harm.*p.69 M.; μέση κατὰ δύναμιν, opp. κατὰ θέσιν, Ptol. *Harm.*2.5. 3. *faculty, art*, or *craft*, Pl.*R.*532d, Arist.*Metaph.* 1018ᵃ30, *EN* 1094ᵃ10, Arr.*Epict.*1.1.1; δ. σκεπτική the *doctrine* of the Sceptics, S.E.*M.*7.1. 4. *a medicine*, Timostr.7, etc.; δ. ἁπλαῖ Hp.*Decent.*9, Aret.*CD* 1.4, etc.; δ. πολυφάρμακοι Plu.2.403c, Gal.13. 365: in pl., *collection of formulae* or *prescriptions*, Orib.10.33. b. *action* of medicines, περὶ τῆς ἁπλῶν φαρμάκων δ., title of work by Galen; also, *potency*, δυνάμει θερμά, ψυχρά, Id.1.672, al. 5. *magically potent substance* or *object*, *PMag.Leid.V.*8.12: in pl., *magical powers*, Hld.4.7. III. *force* or *meaning* of a word, Lys.10.7, Pl. *Cra.*394b, Diog.Oen.12, Phld.*Sign.*31, etc. b. phonetic *value* of sounds or letters, Plb.10.47.8, D.H.*Comp.*12, Luc.*Jud.Voc.*5, etc. 2. *worth* or *value* of money, Th.6.46, 2.97, Plu.*Lyc.*9, *Sol.* 15. IV. *capability of existing* or *acting, potentiality*, opp. *actuality* (ἐνέργεια), Arist.*Metaph.*1047ᵇ31, 1051ᵃ5, etc.: hence δυνάμει as Adv., *virtually*, ὕστερον ὂν τῇ τάξει, πρότερον τῇ δυνάμει .. ἐστί D.3. 15; opp. ἐνεργείᾳ, Arist.*APo.*86ᵃ28, al.; opp. ἐντελεχείᾳ, Id.*Ph.*193ᵇ 8, al. V. Math., *power*, κατὰ μεταφορὰν ἡ ἐν γεωμετρίᾳ λέγεται δ. Id.*Metaph.*1019ᵇ33; usu. *second power, square*, κατὰ δύναμιν in *square*, Pl.*Ti.*54b, cf. *Theol.Ar.*11, etc.: chiefly in dat., [εὐθεῖα] δυνάμει ἴση a line *the square* on which is equal to an area, ἡ ΒΑ ἐλάσσων ἐστὶν ἢ διπλασίων δυνάμει τῆς ΑΚ the *square* on ΒΑ is less than double of the *square* on ΑΚ, Archim.*Sph.Cyl.*2.9: εὐθεῖαι δ. σύμμετροι commensurable *in square*, Euc.10 *Def.*2; ἡ δυνάμει δεκάς the series $1^2 + 2^2 \ldots + 10^2$, *Theol.Ar.*64. b. *square number*, Pl.*Ti.*32a. c. *square* of an unknown quantity (x^2), Dioph.*Def.*2, al. 2. *square root* of a number which is not a perfect square, *surd*, opp. μῆκος, Pl. *Tht.*147d. 3. *product* of two numbers, ἡ ἀμφοῖν (sc. τριάδος καὶ δυάδος) δ. ἑξάς Ph.1.3, cf. Iamb. *in Nic.*p.108 P.; δυνάμει *in product*, Hero *Metr.*1.15, *Theol.Ar.*33. VI. concrete, *powers*, esp. of divine beings, αἱ δ. τῶν οὐρανῶν Lxx *Is.*34.4, cf. 1*Ep.Pet.*3.22, al., Ph.1.587, *Corp.Herm.*1.26, Porph.*Abst.*2.34: sg., *Act.Ap.*8.10, *PMag.Par.*1. 1275; πολυώνυμος δ., of God, Secund.*Sent.*3. VII. *manifestation of divine power, miracle*, *Ev.Matt.*11.21, al., Buresch *Aus Lydien* 113, etc.

δῠνᾰμο-δύνᾰμις, εως, ἡ, *square multiplied by square, fourth power*, Hero *Metr.*1.17; *fourth power of unknown quantity* (x^4), Dioph. *Def.*1 (pl.), al.:—hence **-δῠνᾰμοστόν**, τό, *the fraction* $1/x^4$, Id.*Def.*3, al. **-κῠβος**, ὁ, *square multiplied by cube, fifth power*, Hippol. *Haer.*1.2.10; *fifth power of unknown quantity* (x^5), Dioph.*Def.*1 (pl.), al.:—hence **-κῠβοστόν**, τό, *the fraction* $1/x^5$, Id.*Def.*3, al.

δῠνᾰμοστόν, τό, *the fraction* $1/x^2$, Dioph.*Def.*3, al.

δῠνᾰμ-όω, *strengthen*, Lxx *Ec.*10.10, Thd.*Da.*9.27, Polem.*Call.* 30, Porph.*Sent.*35, Sall.16, Procl.*Inst.*70, al.:—Pass., *Ep.Col.*1.11, etc. 2. in magic, *put power into*, σῶμα *PMag.Leid.W.*7.16; πρᾶγμα ib.*V.*8.19; τινά *PMag.Par.*1.197:—Pass., *PMag.Berol.*2. 121. **-ωσις**, εως, ἡ, *strengthening, fortifying, invigoration*, ψυχῆς Plot.4.6.3. **-ωτικός**, ή, όν, *strengthening*, ἡ δύναμις τῶν πάντων -ώτατον (sc. αἴτιον) Dam.*Pr.*61.

δύνᾰσις [ῠ], εως, ἡ, poet. for δύναμις, Pi.*P.*4.238, B.9.49, S.*Ant.* 604 (lyr.), 952 (lyr.), E.*Ion* 1012; ἐν (i.e. ἐς) δύνασιν *pro virili parte*, *IG*2².1126.5 (Amphict. Delph.).

δῠναστ-εία, ἡ, *power, lordship, domination*, S.*OT* 593, D.18.67; δ. ὀλίγων ἀνδρῶν Th.3.62; πολιτικαὶ δ. *the exercise of* political *power*, Pl. *Tht.*176c; οἱ τὰς δ. ἔχοντες Isoc.2.8, cf. 9.19, Plb.3.18.1. II. *close oligarchy*, opp. ἰσονομία, Th.4.78, cf. And.2.27, X.*HG*5.4.46, etc.; ὑπὸ τῶν ὀλίγων δ. Pl.*Plt.*291d; opp. πολιτεία, Arist.*Pol.*1272ᵇ10; distd. fr. ὀλιγαρχία, ib.1292ᵇ10, cf. 1293ᵃ31: in pl., of the Roman Senate, D.C. 52.1. III. in pl., *mighty deeds*, Lxx 4*Ki.*13.12, al. **-ειρα**, ἡ, fem. of δυνάστης, *Tab.Defix.Aud.*38.11 (Alexandria, iii A.D.). **-ευμα**, ατος, τό, in pl., *natural resources*, τὰ δ. τοῦ Λιβάνου Lxx 3*Ki.*2. 46c. **-ευτικός**, ή, όν, *arbitrary*, ὀλιγαρχία Arist.*Pol.*1298ᵃ32; *oligarchical*, αἵρεσις ib.1306ᵃ18; ἰατρεία (opp. πολιτική) ib.1272ᵇ3; πόλεις καὶ χῶραι Phld.*Rh.*2.145 S.; λόγος Plu.2.818a; *tyrannical*, δούλωσις Porph.*Abst.*1.8. **-εύω**, *hold power* or *lordship, be powerful* or *influential*, Hdt.9.2, Isoc.12.82, *OGI* 56.12, etc.; τὸ -εῦον, opp.

δῆμος, Th.6.89; ἡ πόλις τῶν λοιπέων ἐδυνάστευε μέγιστον Hdt.5.97: c. gen., *to be lord over*, Οἰχαλίας D.S.4.31: metaph., αἱ ἄλογοι ἡδοναὶ δ. ψυχῆς Ph.1.19: c. dat., Ath.14.624d: generally, *prevail, be prevalent*, of a wind, of climate, Hp.*Aph*.3.5, *Aër*.12; *to be influential, potent*, ἐν τῷ σώματι Id.*VM*16, cf. Herophil.ap.Gal.12.619:—Pass., *to be ruled*, πρὸς μυρίων Ph.2.503. II. Math., in Pass., *to be concerned with powers* of numbers, Pl.*R*.546b. **-ης**, ου, ὁ, *lord, master, ruler*, of Zeus, S.*Ant*.608 (lyr.); ἄνδρες δ. *the chief men* in a state, Hdt.2.32, cf. Pl.*R*.473d, etc.; *petty chief, princelet*, Th.7.33, etc.; ἡγεμόσι καὶ δ. καὶ βασιλεῦσιν Plb.9.23.5, cf. 10.34.2, Posidon.50 J., Str. 17.3.25; λαμπροὶ δυνάσται, of the stars, A.*Ag*.6. **-ικός**, ή, όν, *of* or *for a* δυνάστης, *arbitrary*, Arist.*Pol*.1320b31 (Sup.): Comp., *more potent*, Gal.6.396. **-ις**, ιδος, ἡ, fem. of δυνάστης, Demetr.*Eloc*. 292; τύχη ἡ πάντων δ. ἀνθρώπων dub. in Phld.*Mort*.24. **-ωρ**, ορος, ὁ, = δυνάστης, E.*IA*280 (lyr.).

δῠνᾰτ-έω, = δύναμαι, δυνατήσει τὸ συμβαῖνον ἴσχειν Phld.*Sign*. 11. 2. *to be mighty*, 2*Ep.Cor*.13.3. **-ης**, ου, ὁ, poet. for δυνάστης, ὦ δυνάτα A.*Pers*.674 (lyr., cod. Med.). **-ός**, ή, όν, also ός, όν Pi.*N*.2.14, Apollon.Cit.2:—*strong, mighty*, in body or mind, ὅ τι ἦν αὐτῶν δυνατώτατον *the ablest-bodied men*, Hdt.9.31; *sound in limb*, opp. ἀδύνατος, Lys.24.12; σῶμα δ. πρός τι X.*Oec*.7.23; χερσὶ καὶ ψυχᾷ δ. Pi.*N*.9.39; τοῖς σώμασι καὶ ταῖς ψυχαῖς X.*Mem*.2.1.19; εἴς τι Pl.*Hp.Mi*.366a; κατά τι ib.366d (Sup.): c. acc., ibid. (Sup.); of ships, *fit for service*, Th.7.60; of things, δυνατώτερον ἀδικία δικαιοσύνης Pl.*R*.351a; λόγος a *powerful* argument, Epicur.*Ep*.1 p.31 U.; δ. προτείχισμα Plb.10.31.8. 2. c. inf., *able* to do, Hdt.1.97, etc.; δ. λῦσαι *mighty* to loose, Pi.*O*.10(11).9; λέγειν τε καὶ πράσσειν -ώτατος Th.1.139, Pl.*Prt*.319a; -ώτατοι καὶ τοῖς σώμασιν καὶ τοῖς χρήμασιν λητουργεῖν Decr.ap.Arist.*Ath*.29.5; ἐὰν τοὺς δ. ἄρχειν X.*Ath*.1.3; ὅσονπερ δ. εἰμι, with inf. omitted, E.*Or*.523. 3. of outward power, *powerful, influential*, S.*El*.219; τῶν Ἑλλήνων δυνατώτατοι Hdt.1.53; οἱ δ. *the chief men of rank and influence*, Th.2.65; χρήμασι δ. Id.1.13, etc., cf. *OGI*669.13 (i A.D.). 4. *able to produce, productive*, χώρα -ωτέρα εἰς τὴν καρπῶν ἔκφυσιν *Gp*.2.21.5. 5. *potential*, Arist.*Metaph*.1048a27. II. Pass., of things, *possible*, οὐ δύνατον γένεσθαι Sapph.*Supp*.5.21, cf. Hdt.9.111, A.*Ag*.97 (lyr.), etc.; ὁδὸς δυνατὴ καὶ τοῖς ὑποζυγίοις πορεύεσθαι *practicable*, X.*An*.4.1.24; λόγου δ. κατανοῆσαι Pl.*Phd*.90c; βίον τοῖς πλείστοις κοινωνῆσαι δ. Arist.*Pol*.1295a30; κατὰ τὸ δυνατόν, *quantum fieri possit*, Pl.*Cra*.422d, D.3.6, etc.; ἐς τὸ δ. Hdt.3.24; εἰς ὅσον ἀνθρώπῳ δ. μάλιστα Pl.*Phdr*.277a; ἐκ τῶν δυνατῶν X.*An*.4.2.23; ἐπὶ τὸ δ. Id.*Cyn*. 5.8; ἐν δυνατῷ εἶναι *BCH*29.172 (Delos, ii B.C.); also ὅσον δυνατόν E.*IA*997; ὅσον καθ' ἡμᾶς δ. Id.*Ba*.183; esp. with Sup., ὡς δ. πλεῖστον Isoc.12.278; ὡς δ. κακίστους X.*Mem*.4.5.5; γνώμη ὡς δ. δικαιοτάτη D.24.13; τὰ δ. things *which are practicable*, Th.5.89, cf. Arist. *Rh*.1359b1. III. Adv. -τῶς *strongly, powerfully*, εἰπεῖν δ. Aeschin. 2.48: Sup. -ώτατα *most ably*, Pl.*R*.516d. 2. δ. ἔχει it is *possible*, Hdt.7.11.

δῠνᾰτοτερέω (sic), *to be more capable* of financial burdens, τινός *PFlor*.296.37 (vi A.D.).

δυνδεκάτη· ἡμέρᾳ δωδεκάτῃ, Hsch.

δῠνητικός, ή, όν, *potential*, of the particle ἄν, κεν, A.D.*Synt*.205.5, 265.15, cf. Sch.E.*Or*.379.

δύο [ῠ], also **δύω** in Ep., Eleg. and late, *SIG*1231 (Nicomedia, iii/iv A.D.), not in Ion. Inscrr. nor in Trag. (δύο ῥοπάς shd. be read in E.*Hel*.1090), nor in Att. Prose or Inscrr.: Lacon. acc. δύε *IG*5(1). 1; Thess. fem. δύας ib.9(2).517: gen. and dat. δυοῖν Hp.*Vict*.1.3, but f.l. in Hdt.1.11,91 [used as monos. in S.*OT*640, cf. δώδεκα for δυώδ-]; later Att. also δυεῖν (esp. in fem. gen.) found in codd. of E.*El*. 536, cited fr. Th. by Ael.Dion.(?)*Fr*.372, cf. 1.20 (cod. Laur.); Boeot. δουῖν Corinn.*Supp*.2.54; later δυσί, δυσὶν ἡμέραις Th.8.101 codd., δυσὶν ἡμέρῃσι v.l. in Hp.*Acut*.(*Sp*.)67; δυοῖν ὄμμασι καὶ δυσὶν ἀκοαῖς Arist.*Pol*.1287b27, cf. Men.699, *SIG*344.26 (Teos, iv B.C.), etc.: early Att. Inscrr. have δυοῖν *IG*1².3.10, al., later δυεῖν *SIG*²587.286, *IG*2². 463.78, al., from cent. iii on δυσί ib.1028.27, al.; Ion. gen. δυῶν *GDI*5653*d*9 (Chios), Hdt.1.94,130, etc., dat. δυοῖσι ib.32,7.104; δυῶν also Dor., *Leg.Gort*.1.40, *Tab.Heracl*.1.139; δυοῖς *Leg.Gort*.7.46.—Used indecl., like ἄμφω, by Hom. (who has no gen. or dat. δυοῖν), τῶν δύο μοιράων Il.10.253; δύω κανόνεσσι 13.407, etc.; so in Hdt. and Att., δύο νεῶν Hdt.8.82; δύο ζεύγεσι Id.3.130; δύο νεῶν Th.3. 89; δύο πλέθρων X.*An*.3.4.9; with dual, δύο μναῖν dub. l. Id.*Mem*. 2.5.2; but not in Trag. and rare in Com., ἔτεσιν δύο Alex.105; δύ' ἔτεσιν Damox.2.3: not in Att. Inscrr. before the Roman period, *IG*3.1443, al.:—*two*, Il.1.16, etc.; in Hom., δύο and δύω are sts. joined with plural Nouns, δύο δ' ἄνδρες 18.498, al.; also in Trag., δύο κριούς S.*Aj*.237 (lyr.); in Att. Prose, δύο τέχνας Pl.*Grg*.464b; but δυοῖν is rare with plural Nouns, ὀρθοστάταις δυοῖν *IG*2.1054.64; ἕνα καὶ δύο one or *two*, a few, Il.2.346; δύ' ἢ τρεῖς Ar.*Pax*829, cf. X.*HG* 3.5.20; εἰς δύο *two and two*, Id.*Cyr*.7.5.17; σὺν δύο *two* together, Il. 10.224, Hdt.4.66; δύο ποιεῖν τὴν πόλιν to split the state into *two*, divide it, Arist.*Pol*.1310a4.

δυογόν, coined as etym. of ζυγόν, Pl.*Cra*.418d.

δῠοδεκάς, -δεκᾰδικός, v. δυω-. **δῠοδεκαπλάσιος**, = δωδ-, Bito 59.8. **δῠοδεκᾰτημόριον**, τό, = δωδεκ-, Paul.Al.*K*.1. **δυόδεκο**, v. δυώδεκα.

δῠοειδής, ές, *of two forms, double, dual*, λόγος Porph.*VP*50; τὸ δ. τῆς ψυχῆς Herm.*in Phdr*.p.167 A. Adv. -δῶς Dam.*Pr*.55.

δῠοκαίδεκα, οἱ, αἱ, τά, *twelve*, Il.2.557, etc.

δῠοκαιδεκά-δελτος, ὁ, or **-δελτον**, τό, *the Laws of the Twelve Tables*, Lyd.*Mag*.1.26,42. **-ζῳδος** κύκλος *zodiac*, Vett.Val.172. 32. **-μηνος**, ον, = δωδεκάμηνος, χρόνοι S.*Tr*.648 (lyr.). **-τος**, ον, *twelfth*, Hp.*Morb*.3.16, *Epid*.7.5.

δῠοκαι-εβδομηκοστός, ή, όν, *seventy-second*, *SIG*1011.21 (Chalcedon, iii/ii B.C.). **-εικοσίπηχυς** [σῐ], υ, *of two and twenty cubits*, Eust.644.39. **-εικοστός**, ή, όν, *twenty-second*, *IG*1².212, Archim. *Aren*.4. **-πεντηκοστός**, ή, όν, Dor. **-πεντᾱ-**, *fifty-second*, ib.14.

δῠόμῐσυ, (δύο, ἥμισυ) *two and a half*, *Supp.Epigr*.2.705 (Perga).

δῠοποιός, όν, *making two*, Arist.*Metaph*.1083b36, Procl.*in Prm*. p.548 S.

δῠοστός, ή, όν, *second*, τὸ δ. (sc. μόριον) answering the question ποστημόριον, i.e. *half*, Sch.E.*Hec*.32.

δυοχοῖ, = πωματίζει, Democr.136; δυοχῶσαι· πωμάσαι, Hsch.

δύπτης, ου, ὁ, *diver*, Call.*Fr*.167, Opp.*H*.2.436: as Adj., κηρύλος Lyc.387; of persons, Id.73.

δύπτω (lengthd. from δύω), *duck, dive*, ἠΰτε τις καύηξ δύπτῃσιν ἐς ἁλμυρὸν ὕδωρ Antim.*Eleg*.6 (nisi leg. δύπτης); πρὸς κῦμα δυπτούσας Lyc.715: without a Prep., ἔδυψε Νηρέως τάφους Id.164; νειόθι δύψας A.R.1.1326: c. acc., δύπτοντες κεφαλάς ib.1008.

δύρομαι [ῡ], poet. for ὀδύρομαι (q.v.).

δυσ-, insepar. Prefix, opp. εὖ, *un-*, *mis-*, with notion of *hard, bad, unlucky*, etc., as δυσήλιος, δύσαγνος; *destroying the good sense* of a word, or *increasing its bad sense*: hence, joined even to words expressing negation, as δυσάμμορος, δυσανάσχετος; poet. in strong contrasts, as Πάρις Δύσπαρις, γάμος δύσγαμος. Before στ, σθ, σπ, σφ, σχ, the final σ was omitted, v. δυστ-. (Cf. Skt. *dus-*, *dur-*, e.g. *durmanās*, = δυσμενής; ONorse *tor-*, e.g. *torsóttligr* (δύσμαχος); OIr. *du-*, *do-*, e.g. *dochruth* 'misshapen'.)

δῠσ-άγγελος, ον, *messenger of ill*, Nonn.*D*.20.184. **-ᾰγέω**, *to be impious*, *IG*14.432 (Tauromenium). **-ᾰγής**, ές, (ἄγος) *impious*, opp. εὐαγής, Man.5.180, Poll.1.33. **-αγκόμιστος**, **-άγκρῐτος**, poet. for δυσανακ-. **-αγνος**, ον, *unchaste*, A.*Supp*.751 (lyr.), Orac.ap.Luc. *Alex*.54. **-αγρέω**, *have bad sport in fishing*, Plu.*Ant*.29. **-αγρής**, ές, *unluckily caught*, of fish, Opp.*H*.3.272. **-αγρία**, ἡ, *bad sport*, Poll.5.13. **-άγωγος** [ᾰ], ον, *hard to guide*, D.H.2.28, Luc.*Abd*. 3,17; ἐπὶ τὸ καλόν D.H.9.8; of horses, *Hippiatr.Praef*. **-άγων** [ᾰ], ωνος, ὁ, ἡ, *having seen hard service*, Plu.*Tim*.36. **-ᾰγώνιστος**, ον, *impregnable*, Poll.3.141, 5.79,105. **-άδελφος** [ᾰ], ον, *unhappy in one's brothers*, A.*Th*.871 (lyr., Sup.), Vett.Val.18.5. **-άεθλος** [ᾰ], ον, *laborious*, Eust.740.54. **-ᾱερία**, ἡ, *badness of air*, Str. 5.1.7, *Cat.Cod.Astr*.2.161: pl., *fogs*, Str.4.1.8. **-άερος** [ᾰ], ον, *having bad air*, δεσμωτήριον (sc. ὁ κόσμος) D.Chr.30.11; *unwholesome*, of the atmosphere, Procl.*Par.Ptol*.122, cf. Sabin.ap.Orib.9. 20.8. **-ᾱής**, ές, (ἄημι) *ill-blowing, stormy*, ἀνέμοιο δυσαέος Il.5. 865; Ζεφύροιο δ. 23.200, al.: poet. gen. pl. δυσαήων for δυσαέων, Od.13.99. 2. generally, *excessive*, δ. κρυμός Call.*Dian*.115; καῦμα Q.S.13.134; κῦμα *AP*7.739 (Phaedim.). II. *ill-smelling*, of a seal, Opp.*C*.3.114; φάρμακα Id.*H*.4.662. **-άθλιος**, ον, *most miserable*, τροφαί S.*OC*330, Lxx 3*Ma*.4.4. **-αίακτος**, ον, *most mournful, miserable*, ib.6.31. **-αιᾱνής**, ές, *most melancholy*, βοά A.*Pers*.281 (lyr.). **-αίθριος**, ον, *not clear, murky*, ὄρφνη E.*Heracl*. 857. **-αιμορράγητος** [ρᾰ], ον, *bleeding with difficulty*, Aët.8. 44. **-αίνητος**, ον, *of ill fame*, Orph.*A*.1340. **-αίνιγμα**, ατος, τό, *riddle of woe*, Sch.E.*Ph*.45. **-αίρετος**, ον, *hard to take, impregnable*, Poll.1.170. **-αισθησία**, ἡ, *low degree of sensibility*, Ti. Locr.102e, Gal.7.55 (pl.), prob. in Phld.*Piet*.67. **-αισθητέω**, *to be hardly sensible*, Alex.Trall.1.13. **-αίσθητος**, ον, *insensible*, σώματα Alex.Aphr.*Pr*.1.72, cf. Adam.1.7; τὸ δυσαίσθητον, = ἀναισθησία, Gal.4.784. II. Pass., *scarcely perceptible*, Alex.Aphr.*in Sens*.85. 24; *hard to trace*, Poll.5.12. **-αιτῐολόγητος**, ον, *hard to account for*, Ph.2.644, Gal.13.605. **-αίων**, ωνος, ὁ, ἡ, *most miserable*, Trag. only lyr., A.*Th*.926 (prob.), S.*OC*151; αἰὼν δ. a life *that is no life*, E.*Hel*.213; δ. ὁ βίος Id.*Supp*.960. **-άκεστος** [ᾰ], ον, *hard to heal*, ἐκτρίμματα Hp.*Fract*.29. **-ᾰκής**, ές, = foreg., Hsch. s.v. δυσηκῆ. **-άλγημα**, ατος, τό, *severe pain*, Herod.Med. in *Rh.Mus*. 58.82. **-ᾰλγής**, ές, *very painful*, A.*Ag*.1165, Plu.2.106d, Q.S. 14.68. **-άλγητος**, ον, *hard to be borne, most painful*, Eup. 410. II. *unfeeling, hard-hearted*, S.*OT*12; δειλὸς ἢ δ. φρένας Id. *Fr*.952. **-αλθής**, ές, = sq., Hp.*Art*.41, Cass.*Probl*.1 (Comp.); τὸ τῆς φύσεως δ. Pl.*Ax*.367b. Adv. -θῶς Philum.ap.Orib.45.29.36. 2. *deadly*, Nic.*Al*.12,157, Luc.*Dem.Enc*.13: neut. pl. as Adv., Q.S.12. 408. **-άλθητος**, ον, *hard to cure, inveterate*, Id.9.388 (-άλθετος Hsch.). **-άλιος** [ᾱ], ον, Dor. for δυσήλιος. **-αλλοίωτος**, ον, *hard to alter*, Gal.*Protr*.11; *hard to digest*, Hp.*Alim*.49; χυμός Alex.Aphr. *Pr*.1.83. **-άλυκτος** [ᾰ], ον, *hard to escape*, Nic.*Al*.251,537, Lxx *Wi*.17.17, Man.3.247. **-άλωτος** [ᾰ], ον, *hard to catch or take*, ἄγρα Pl.*Ly*.206a (Comp.); of birds and fish, Arist.*HA*615a17, 599b25; ἐρύματα Ph.2.133. 2. *hard to conquer*, ἀρχά A.*Pr*.167 (lyr.); πάθος Luc.*Abd*.18 (Sup.); *immune*, τοῖς ἔξωθεν αἰτίοις δ. σῶμα Gal.4.742; πρὸς νόσους Sor.1.32 (Comp.): c. gen., δ. κακῶν *beyond reach* of ills, S. *OC*1723 (lyr.). 3. *hard to comprehend*, Pl.*Ti*.51a (Sup.). **-ᾰμάρτητος**, ον, *making unfortunate mistakes*, Vett.Val.11.16. **-άμβᾰτος**, ον, poet. for δυσανάβατος, πέτραι Simon.58.2. **-ᾱμερία**, Dor. for δυσημ-. **-άμμορος**, ον, *most miserable*, Il.19.315, 22.428,485, A.R. 2.218. **-ανάβᾰτος**, ον, *hard to climb*, Corn.*ND*14. **-αναβλαστέω**, prob. f.l. for δυσαναβλυστέω, *well up with difficulty*, Plu.2. 688e. **-(ανά)γνωστος**, ον, *hard to read*, prob. for δύσγνωστος, Plb.3.32.1. **-ανάγωγος** [ᾰγ], ον, *hard to throw up*, ὑγρά Dsc.1.1, cf. Androm.ap.Gal.13.28.

δῠσανά-δοτος, ον, *hard to assimilate*, Diph.Siph.ap.Ath.3.91e, Gal. 19.364, *Hippiatr.*1. **-θῡμίᾱτος**, ον, *hard to evaporate*, Artem. 1.1. **-κάθαρτος** [κᾰ], ον, *hard to cleanse*, ἕλκωσις Gal.ap.Orib. *Syn.*9.3.8. **-κλητος**, ον, *hard to call back*, Plu.2.74e; J.*BJ*2.18.8 (but simply, *hard to summon, call together*, Plu.*Thes.*24), etc. 2. *hard to restore*, of hysterics, Sor.2.29 (Comp.), cf. Herod.Med. in *Rh.Mus.*58.74; or to good spirits, Max.Tyr.33.6. Adv. -τως, ἔχειν to be *hard to restore* to one's senses, Dsc.*Alex.*16. **-κόμιστος**, ον, *hard to carry upwards*, ψυχή Plu.*Rom.*28:—poet. **δυσαγκόμιστος**, *hard to recall*, αἷμα A.*Eu.*262 (lyr.). **-κρᾶτος**, ον, *hard to mix* or *temper*, κοινωνία Plu.2.1024d. **-κρῐτος**, ον, *hard to determine*: poet. **-άγκρῐτος**, πόνοι A.*Supp.*126 (lyr.). **-ληπτος**, ον, *hard to recover*, μνήμη Alcid.*Soph.*19. II. *hard to recover from*, ἀρρωστία Jul.*Or.*6.181a. Adv. -λήπτως, ἔχειν to be *in a bad way for recovery*, Ruf.ap.Orib.8.47.4. 2. of an athlete, *unable to return to ordinary habits*, Ath.Med.ap.Orib.*inc.*1.6. **-ληψία**, ἡ, *difficult convalescence*, Vett.Val.236.17. **-λῠτος**, ον, *hard to analyse*, Porph. *in Cat.*132.9. Adv. -τως Simp. *in Cat.*212.16.

δῠσανάλωτος [ᾱλ], ον, *hard to destroy, consume*, στοιχεῖον Ph.2. 505.

δῠσανά-παυστος, ον, *restless*, Eust.1296.58. **-πειστος**, ον, *hard to convince*, Pl.*Prm.*135a. **-πλους**, ουν, *hard to sail up*, ὁ Ῥοδανός Str.4.1.14. **-πλωτος**, ον, = foreg., Id.5.2.5. **-πνευστος**, ον, *offensive to inhalation*, Arist.*Sens.*443b12. 2. *transpiring with difficulty*, Gal.7.287. **-πόρευτος**, ον, *hard to pass*, Ph. 1.672, 2.118. **-σκεύαστος**, ον, *hard to restore*, Alex.Trall.*Febr.* 7. **-σφαλτος**, ον, *hardly recovering from an illness*, Hp.*Alim.* 28. **-σχετέω**, *bear ill*, Th.7.71; *to be greatly vexed*, ἐπί τινι, πρός τι, Plu.*Cam.*35, Plb.16.12.5; περί τινος Phalar.*Ep.*37; τοῖς γενομένοις J.*AJ*13.16.2: abs., Eus.Mynd.59, Aët.8.44. **-σχετος**, ον, *hard to bear, intolerable*, ὕβρεις Ph.2.92; κήδη Phleg.*Macr.*4, cf. Dsc. *Eup.*1.235, Porph.*Abst.*3.20: poet. **-άνσχετος** A.R.2.272. II. Act., *bearing hardly*, in Adv. -τως, ἔχειν A.D.*Synt.*218.9, cf. Poll.3. 130. **-τρεπτος**, ον, *hard to overthrow*, δύναμις Plu.*Caes.*4, cf. Gal. 18(1).604. **-φορικός**· δυσκόλως ἀναφερόμενος, Hsch.

δῠσ-ανδρία, ἡ, (ἀνήρ) *want of men*, App.*BC*1.7. **-άνεκτος**, ον, = δυσανάσχετος I, interpol. in X.*Mem.*2.2.8, cf. Gal.7.181. Adv. -τως Poll.3.130. **-άνεμος** [ᾰ], ον, Dor. for δυσήνεμος, S.*Ant.*591 (lyr.). **-ανθής**, ές, *shy of flowering*, Poll.1.231. **-άνῐος** [ᾰ], ον, (ἀνία) *soon vexed, ill to please*, Antipho Soph.89, Critias *Fr.*42 D., Men.803 (but better -ήνιον (q.v.)); opp. εὔθυμος, Arist.*Phgn.*805b6; *vexed, annoyed*, in Comp. -ιώτερος Phld.*Acad.Ind.*p.50 M. **-ανῐῶν**, ῶσα, ῶν, (ἀνιάω) *much vexing*, Plu.2.106d. **-άνοικτος**, ον, *hard to open*, πυξίδες Diog.*Ep.*50. **-άνολβος**, ον, strengthd. for ἄνολβος, Emp.124. **-άνσχετος**, ον, poet. for δυσανάσχετος. **-ανταγώνιστος**, ον, *hard to struggle against*, Paus.1.17.6, D.L.2.134, Jul.*Or.*1. 34b. **-άντης** or **-αντής**, ές, = sq. I, φῦλα Opp.*C.*3.262; μῆνις Nonn. *D.*42.380. II. = sq. II, κύματα ib.6.310, cf. Musae.324. III. *hard to climb*, ὁδός Ph.1.255; κολῶναι Opp.*C.*4.432. **-άντητος**, ον, *disagreeable to meet, boding of ill*, opp. εὐάντητος, Luc.*Tim.*5, etc. II. *hard to withstand*, πάθη Plu.2.118c; ὀδύναι Procl.*H.*3. 5; κακά Max.Tyr.5.3.

δῠσαντί-βλεπτος, ον, *hard to look in the face*, Plu.*Marc.*23; -βλεπτον στίλβειν ἀπὸ τῶν ὀμμάτων Corn.*ND*20; *hard to face*, ἀπορία χαλεπωτάτη καὶ δ. Syrian. *in Metaph.*178.30; *hard to vie with*, Philostr. Jun.*Im.Praef.*; ὠφέλεια Agathin.ap.Orib.10.7.6. **-λεκτος**, ον, *hard to gainsay*, D.H.5.18: metaph., ἐπιθυμία J.*AJ*18.9.5. **-ρρητος**, ον, = foreg., gloss on ἐχυρόν, Hsch., *EM*406.7. Adv. -τως Plb. 9.31.7.

δῠσ-αντοφθάλμητος, ον, *hard to resist*, Plb.22.8.13. **-άνωρ** [ᾱ] γάμος marriage *with a bad husband*, A.*Supp.*1064. **-αξίωτος**, ον, *inexorable*, Sch.S.*OT*334.

δῠσαπ-άλειπτος [ᾰλ], ον, *hard to wipe out*, Sch.S.*Tr.*682. **-αλλακτία**, ἡ, *the quality of being difficult to get rid of, persistency*, Pl. *Phlb.*46c. **-άλλακτος**, ον, *hard to get rid of*, νοῦσος Hp.*Nat.Mul.* 40; ὀδύναι S.*Tr.*959 (lyr.); πρόσταγμα Isoc.10.28; ἀρρώστημα Arist. *PA*671b9, cf. *Cat.*10a4: c. gen., -ότεραι τῶν ἐμβρύων *having difficulty in bringing forth*, Id.*HA*587b1; δ. ἀπὸ λόγου a person *hard to draw away* from.., Pl.*Tht.*195c. Adv. -τως, ἔχειν τινός Eust.1389.46, cf. Eustr. *in EN*140.18. **-άντητος**, ον, = δυσάντητος, Eust.1054.30, Suid.

δῠσάπιστος, ον, *very disobedient*, *AP*12.179 (Strato):—hence **-απιστέω**, *AB*1285.

δῠσαπο-βίβαστος [ῐ], v.l. for δυσυπο-, Gal.6.535. **-βλητος**, ον, *hard to get rid of*, πυρετός Alex.Aphr.*Febr.*19; *hard to cast away*, Olymp. *in Alc.*p.51C.; *hard to lose*, Id. *in Cat.*116.25, cf. Ammon. *in Cat.*82.8, Simp. *in Cat.*228.23. **-δεικτος**, ον, *hard to demonstrate*, Pl.*R.*488a. **-δίδακτος** [ῐ], ον, *hard to unlearn*, J.*AJ*16.2. 4. **-δίωκτος** [ῐ], ον, *hard to drive away*, Sch.Theoc.10.11. **-δοτος**, ον, *hard to render* or *define*, S.E.*M.*7.242, Bacch.*Harm.*95. **-θετος**, ον, *hard to put aside*, πάθος Olymp. *in Alc.*p.101C. **-κατάστᾰσις**, εως, ἡ, *difficulty of recovering, mortal sickness*, Erot. s.v. δυσθεσίην. **-κατάστᾰτος**, ον, *hard to restore*, M.Ant.11.8, Gal.14. 792. II. *hard to recover from*, ὀργαί Phld.*Ir.*p.63 W. **-κλίτως** [ῐ], Adv. *with difficulty in bending*, Herod.Med. in *Rh.Mus.*58. 90. **-κρῐτος**, ον, *hard to answer*, Luc.*Vit.Auct.*22. Adv. -τως, ἔχειν, of a letter, Mithr.*Ep.*1. II. Act., *hardly answering*, Paul. Aeg.3.9. **-ληπτος**, ον, *hard to catch*, Alex.Aphr. *in Sens.*26.18; *irreparable*, *Gloss.* **-λόγητος**, ον, *hard to defend* or *excuse*, Plb. 1.10.4, cf. Ph.1.562, J.*AJ*16.4.2; *hard to answer*, Aristeas 213; *hard to explain*, Str.4.1.7. Adv. -τως, ἔχειν Eust.147.23. **-λῠτος**, ον, *hard to get free of*, δ. πάθος τὸ φιλότιμον Olymp. *in Alc.*p.51C. Adv. -τως Erot. s.v. βλακεύειν, Gal.8.284. **-νιπτος**, ον, *hard to wash off* or *out*, Zen.1.47, Sch.E.*Ph.*63: Comp., *Theol.Ar.*22. **-πτωτος**, ον, *not apt to fall off*, καρπός Thphr.*CP*1.11.8. **-σπαστος**, ον, *hard to tear away*, Posidon.15 J., Secund.*Sent.*10, Dsc.3.14. Adv. δυσαποσπάστως, ἔχειν Pl.*Ax.*365b, Aristeas 123, D.S.20.51. II. *from which it is hard to tear oneself away*, Ph.2.11,14; κάλλος Charito 5.8. **-σχετος**, ον, *hard to abstain from*, S.E.*M.*9.152. **-τέλεστος**, ον, *hard to accomplish*, Eust.1956.18. **-τρεπτος**, ον, *hard to dissuade, refractory*, X.*Mem.*4.1.4, Aristaenet.1.28. **-τριπτος**, ον, *hard to rub off* and so *get rid of*, ὀνείδη Macar.8.47, cf. Ph.1.459,615 (Sup.), Thessal.ap.Gal.10.252; of persons, Plu.2.55e. **-τροπος**, ον, *difficult to avert*, ἄτη *IG*2.1660.22.

δῠσαποῦλωτος, ον, *hard to cicatrize*, Dsc.4.41, Aët.1.243, *Hippiatr.* 26: Comp., Phlp. *in APo.*182.13.

δυσαρεεῖ· δυσφροντίστῳ, Hsch.

δυσαρεσκόμενος, incorrect form for δυσαρεστούμενος, Hsch.

δῠσᾰρεστ-έω, *suffer annoyance*, Arist.*HA*560b24; *to be displeased*, τινί *at* a thing, Plb.4.22.9, D.S.5.9, J.*AJ*8.5.3, Aq., Sm., Thd.*Ps.*94 (95).10; δ. ὅτι D.H.*Comp.*11: Medic., *suffer malaise*, Gal.10.551, Aët.5.5:—also Med., τινί Plb.5.94.2; ἐπί τινι 11.28.11. II. c. dat. pers., *to be displeasing to*, Id.7.5.6, D.S.18.62; τῷ θεῷ Ph.2.6:—also Med. -ουμένη φιλία Plu.2.94d, cf. Iamb.*VP*35.255. **-ημα**, ατος, τό, Medic., *malaise, distress*, Antyll.ap.Stob.4.37.15, Sor.1.26. **-ησις**, εως, ἡ, *distress*, Pl.*Ax.*366d; *dissatisfaction*, τινί or ἐπί τινι, Plb.4.21. 7, 23.7.5. II. Medic., *malaise*, Cael.Aur.*TP*3.6, Sor.1.56. **-ία**, ἡ, *distress, malaise*, Herod.Med. in *Hermes* 40.584, prob. in Aët.16. 18 (for -ησίαι), Hierocl. *in CA*11 p.442 M. **-ικός**, ή, όν, *distressing*, σύμπτωμα Herod.Med.ap.Orib.6.20.21. **-ος**, ον, *hard to appease, implacable*, δαίμονες A.*Eu.*928; *ill-pleased*, τι *at* a thing, Luc.*Nav.*46; *ill to please, fastidious, peevish*, δυσάρεστον οἱ νοσοῦντες E.*Or.*232, cf. Isoc.1.31, 12.8, X.*Mem.*3.13.3 (Comp.), Diph.63, Nicostr.31 (Comp.), Plu.2.128d; ἀνοίας νόσημα δυσάρεστον Polystr.*Herc.*1520.1; τὸ δ. *displeasure*, Plu.*Sol.*25. Adv. -τως, ἔχειν πρός τι Id.2.476b.

δῠσ-ᾰρίθμητος, ον, *hard to count up*, App.*BC*2.73. **-ᾰριστοτόκεια**, ἡ, *unhappy mother of the noblest son*, as Thetis calls herself, Il.18.54. **-αρκτος**, ον, *hard to govern*, φρένες A.*Ch.*1024; στρατόπεδα J.*AJ*4.2.1; οὐδὲν ἀνθρώπου -ότερον Plu.*Luc.*2; ἔθνος -ότατον App.*BC*2.149. **-αρμοστία**, ἡ, *disharmony*, ἠθῶν Plu.*Aem.* 5. **-άρμοστος**, ον, *ill-united*, Id.*Eum.*13; *insecure*, πύργος App. *Mith.*34. **-αρχία**, ἡ, *ill discipline*, App.*BC*5.17. **-αυγής**, ές, *blinding*, Poet. *de herb.*65. **-αύλητος**· δυσεγκλήμων, Hsch. **-αυλία**, ἡ, *ill* or *hard lodging*, A.*Ag.*555 (pl.), Ph.1.195 (pl.). **-αυλις**, ἡ, dub. sens., St.Byz. s.v. αὐλή (expld. as compd. of Αὖλις). **-αύλιστος**, gloss on sq., Hsch. **-αυλος**, ον, (αὐλή) *bad for lodging, inhospitable*, of frost, S.*Ant.*356 (lyr.). **-αυλος** ἔρις *an unhappy contest with the flute* (αὐλός), *AP*9.266 (Antip.). **-αυξής**, ές, *hardly* or *slowly growing*, Arist.*Aud.*802a25, Thphr.*CP*1.8.4, J.*AJ*3.1.3:—also **-αύξητος**, ον, Thphr.*CP*1.8.2. **-αυρία**, ἡ, *stormy wind*, Ar. Byz.*Epit.*24.18 (s.v.l.). **-αυχής**, ές, *idly boasting, vain-glorious*, A.R.3.976. **-αφαίρετος**, ον, *hard to take away*, Arist.*EN*1095b 26; *hard to remove*, of an application, Gal.12.356. **-ᾰφής**, ές, *hard to the touch*, σάρξ Id.6.100. **-ᾱχής**, ές, Dor. for δυσηχής, πόλεμος Anacr.107. **-ᾰχής**, ές, (ἄχος) *most painful*, πάθος A.*Eu.*145 (lyr.). **-αχθής**, ές, *very grievous*, Tryph.42, Max. 308. **-βάρνακος**· δυσκατανόητος, βάρνακα γὰρ ἄγρια λάχανα δύσπλυτα *EM*291.45. **-βᾰσᾰνίστως**, gloss on ἀβασανίστως, Hsch. **-βάστακτος**, ον, *intolerable, grievous to be borne*, Lxx *Pr.* 27.3, *Ev.Matt.*23.4, Plu.2.915f, etc.; of persons, Antisth.ap.Ph.2. 449. **-βᾰτοποιέομαι**, *make impassable*, dub. l. in X.*Eq.Mag.*8.9 (prob. for δύσβατα ποιούμενον). **-βᾰτος**, ον, *hard to traverse, impassable*, ἀμαχανίαι Pi.*N.*7.97; τόπος Pl.*R.*432c; τὰ δ., = δυσχωρίαι, X.*Cyr.*2.4.27: metaph., δ. καὶ μακρὰ διερμήνευσις Iamb.*Myst.*5. 5. II. *trodden in sorrow*, Περσὶς αἶα A.*Pers.*1069 (lyr.). **-βήρης** or **-βηρής**, ές, = δύσβατος, Hsch., *EM*291.43. **-βῐος**, ον, = sq., *AB*323. **-βίοτος** [ῐ], ον, *making life wretched*, πενίη *AP*7.648 (Leon.). **-βλεπτέω**, *see badly*, Hsch. s.v. κικυμώττειν. **-βοήθητος**, ον, *hard to help* or *cure*, Hp.*Coac.*491, D.S.3.47, 11.15, Paul. Aeg.5.29: Comp., Dsc.*Eup.*2.159. Adv. -τως Gal.5.122. **-βολος**, ον, *throwing badly*, esp. with dice, Poll.9.94. **-βούλευτος**, ον, *ill-advised*, *EM*3.51. **-βουλία**, ἡ, *ill counsel*, A.*Th.*802, *Ag.*1609, S.*Ant.*95: pl., ib.1269 (lyr.). **-βράκᾰνος** [ρᾰ], ον, *hard to deal with*, Cratin.404; cf. βρακεῖν. **-βωλος**, ον, *of ill soil, unfruitful*, γῆ Hom.*Epigr.*7; χθών *AP*7.401 (Crin.).

δυσγᾰμ-έω, *to be unhappily married*, Heph.Astr.1.1. **-ία**, ἡ, *an ill marriage*, Man.1.19. **-ος**, ον, *ill-wedded*, γάμοι δ. E.*Ph.*1047 (lyr.); ῥυστάγματα Lyc.1089, cf. Paul.Al.*N.*2; δύσγαμον αἶσχος ἑλών, of Menelaus, E.*Tr.*1114; χελιδών Luc.*Trag.*49.

δυσ-γάργᾰλις, ι, *very ticklish, skittish*, ἵππος X.*Eq.*3.10, cf. Ar.*Fr.* 43, Ael.*NA*16.9:—also **-γαργάλιστος**, ον, prob. l. in *Gp.*16.2.1, cf. Tim.Gaz.148.3: **-γάργᾰλος**, ον, Lib.*Ep.*234.1 codd., Phryn.*PS* p.65 B. **-γένεια**, ἡ, *low birth*, S.*OT*1079, E.*IA*446, Pl.*R.*618d (pl.), Cerc.17.36, Plu.2.1b, etc. II. *meanness*, E.*HF*663 (lyr.), Plu.*Alex.* 62. **-γενής**, ές, *low-born*, E.*Ion*1477, Ar.*Ra.*1219, etc.: Comp., Men.533.10. II. *low-minded, mean*, E.*El.*363, etc.; δ. ἐν τῷ τρόπῳ Com.ap.Stob.4.30.6a. **-γεφύρωτος** [ῡ], ον, *hard to make a bridge over*, Str.4.3.3. **-γεώργητος**, ον, *hard to till* or *cultivate*, Id.17.3.

25. **-γνοια**, ἡ, *ignorance, doubt*, E.*HF*1107. **-γνώμων**, gloss on δυσέκτων (sic), Suid. **-γνώριστος**, ον, *hard to recognize*, Gal.7.804, al., Poll.5.150. Adv. -τως ib.160. **-γνωσία**, ἡ, *difficulty of knowing*, δυσγνωσίαν εἶχον προσώπου I did *not know* thy face, E.*El*.767. **-γνωστος**, ον, *hard to understand*, Pl.*Alc*.2.147c. 2. *hard to recognize*, τισί Plb.3.78.4: Sup., Aen.Tact.25.2. **-γοήτευτος**, ον, *hard to seduce by enchantments*, Pl.*R*.413e. **-γονος**, ον, *conceiving with difficulty*, Vett.Val.18.24, *Cat.Cod.Astr*.2.207. **-γράμμᾰτος**, ον, *hard to write*, Aristid.2.360 J. II. *unlearned*, Philostr.*VS*2.1.10. **-γρίπιστος** [ῐπ], ον, *very grasping*, Lib.Bas.*Ep*.13.

δύσγω· ἀποδύω, Hsch.

δυσδαιμ-ονέω, *to be wretched*, Longin.9.7. **-ονία**, ἡ, *misery*, E.*IT*1120(lyr.), And.2.7. **-ων**, ον, gen. ονος, *ill-starred, unhappy*, πότμος Emp.9.4, A.*Th*.827, S.*Ant*.274; μοῖρα Id.*OT*1302 (anap.); τύχη Pl.*Lg*.905c; νέρτεροι Ti.Locr.104d; of a person, *BGU*1024 vii 24 (iv A.D.): Comp. -έστερος And.2.9. Adv. -νως Eust.1064.44.

δυσ-δάκρῡτος, ον, *sorely wept*, A.*Ag*.442 (lyr.). II. Act., *sorely weeping*, *AP*12.80 (Mel.); δάκρυα δ. tears *of anguish*, ib.7.476 (Id.). **-δᾰμαρ**, αρτος, ὁ, ἡ, *ill-wedded*, A.*Ag*.1319. **-δάμαστος** [δᾰ], ον, *hard to subdue*: hence, *hard to work*, σίδηρος Sch.Hes.*Sc*.122. **-δεικτος**, ον, *hard to prove*, θεωρήματα Gal.15.139. **-δέρκετος**, ον, = sq., Opp.*C*.2.607. **-δερκής**, ές, *ill to look upon, grim, ugly*, ib.3.263, *H*.1.47. II. *hard to see, faint*, ἴχνη Id.*C*.1.102, cf. 451. **-δηλις**, ιδος, ὁ, ἡ, (δηλέομαι) *baneful*, Hsch. **-δηνίας**· δύσνους, κακὰ βουλευομένους, Id. **-δηρις**, ι, gen. ιος, *hard to fight with*, Nic.*Th*.738.

δυσδιά-βᾰτος, ον, *hard to get through*, ποταμός Aen.Tact.8.1, cf. X.*An*.6.5.19; τόποι Plb.1.39.13; ῥεῦμα D.S.17.93. **-γνω⟨σ⟩τικός**, ή, όν, τὸ δ. *the difficulty in diagnosis*, Alex.Trall.8.2. **-γνωστος**, ον, *hard to distinguish*, Cic.*Att*.5.4.1, D.H.2.71, Gal.9.433, etc.

δυσδιάγωγος [ᾰ], ον, *unpleasant to live in*, πόλις Str.16.2.23: Comp., Ptol.*Tetr*.168.

δυσδιάθετος, ον, *hard to dispose of* (in marriage), χαλεπόν γε θυγάτηρ κτῆμα καὶ δυσδιάθετον Men.18. 2. *hard to manage* or *settle*, Plu.*Caes*.11, D.C.73.15, Hierocl.*in CA*11p.438 M.

δυσδιαίρετος, ον, *hard to divide* or *split*, Arist.*Pr*.928ᵃ29, Thphr.*HP*7.11.3, Sor.1.118, *Theol.Ar*.5.

δυσδιαίτητος, ον, *hard to decide*, Plu.*Comp.Cim.Luc*.3; λόγος Porph.*Abst*.2.1.

δυσδιακόμιστος, ον, *hard to carry through*, Hsch.

δυσδιᾰκόντιστος, ον, *hard to pierce*, Ael.*NA*17.44.

δυσδιάκρῐτος, ον, *hard to distinguish*, Str.13.4.12, Clytus 1; ἀξίαι Plu.2.617d; δ. ἀπό.. Corn.*ND*31. II. of litigants, *whose case is hard to decide*, D.S.33.28a. III. *hard to digest*, Xenocr.9.

δυσδιάλλακτος, ον, *hard to reconcile*, Suid. Adv. -τως Ammon.63.

δυσδιά-λῠτος, ον, *hard to dissolve*, Arist.*Pr*.870ᵇ31 (Comp.): σχῆμα τῆς τάξεως Plb.1.26.16. 2. *hard to digest*, Philotim.ap.Ath.2.53f, Gal.16.760. II. *hard to reconcile*, Arist.*EN*1126ᵃ20. **-νόητος**, ον, *hard to understand*, Sch.E.*Ph*.30.

δυσδιάνοικτος, ον, *hard to open*, ὀφθαλμός *Hippiatr*.1.

δυσδιά-πνευστος, ον, *slow to evaporate*, Thphr.*CP*1.2.4, Dsc.5.6. II. *slow to perspire*, Herod.Med.ap.Orib.5.27.3. **-σπαστος**, ον, *hard to break*, τάξις Plb.15.15.7; *hard to pull up*, of a palisade, Ph.*Bel*.82.35. **-στᾰτέω**, *to be unstable*, dub. in Plu.2.993e. **-στᾰτος**, ον, *hard to separate*, Herod.Med. in *Rh.Mus*.58.90. **-τηκτος**, ον, *hard to soften*, prob.l., Thphr.*CP*2.15.2. **-φευκτος** or **-φυκτος**, ον, *hard to escape*, Suid., Hsch. (-διαφύ[λα]κτον cod.). **-φθαρτος**, ον, *hard to break up*, τὰ δ. βραδυπεψίας ἐργάζεται Gal.7.209. **-φορησία**, ἡ, *difficulty of dissipation*, Cass.*Pr*.66. **-φόρητος**, ον, *hard to disperse* or *dissipate*, Gal.11.119. II. *hardly evaporating*, Id.10.657; *not excreting readily*, Id.17(1).188; διάθεσις Alex.Trall.8.2; cf. δυσδιαχώρητος. **-φύλακτος**, v. δυσδιάφευκτος. **-χώρητος**, ον, *indigestible*, Arist.*Pr*.927ᵇ21 (Comp.); *hard to pass*, prob. for -φόρητος, Xenocr.34. II. Act., *costive*, Alex.Aphr.*Pr*.1.90, Sever. p.6 D.

δυσδίδακτος [ῐ], ον, *hard to instruct*, Hp.*Ep*.17.

δυσδι-έγερτος, ον, *hard to be roused from*, καταφορά Gal.19.413, cf. Herod.(?)Med. in *Rh.Mus*.58.77. **-έξακτος**, ον, *hard to pass*, βίος Porph.*Abst*.4.18. **-εξίτητος** [ῐτ], ον, *hard to get through*, v.l. in D.S.3.44. **-εξόδευτος**, ον, = sq. II, *Hippiatr*.69. **-έξοδος**, ον, *hard to get through, traverse*, D.S.5.34, D.C.60.20. II. *hard to pass*, Gal.6.535. **-ερεύνητος**, ον, *hard to search thoroughly*, Pl.*R*.432c, D.C.51.26, Them.*Or*.21.254d. **-ήγητος**, ον, *hard to narrate*, Lxx *Wi*.17.1. **-όδευτος**, ον, = -ήλῠτος, Hsch.; of a child's tissues, Sor.1.95. **-οδος**, ον, *hard to pass through*, Plb.3.61.3, etc. **-οίκητος**, ον, *hard to manage*, J.*BJ*2.16.4, Poll.5.105 (vulg. -ητικός). II. *hard to digest*, Xenocr.31, Sor.1.93. **-όρᾱτος**, ον, *hard to see one's way in*, τόπος διὰ τὸ σκοτεινόν Alcin.*Intr*.35. **-όρθωτος**, ον, *hard to set right*, Hsch. **-όριστος**, ον, *hard to delimit*, ἀπ' ἀλλήλων S.E.*M*.5.74; *hard to distinguish*, φαντασία ib.7.416.

δυσδίωκτος [ῐ], ον, gloss on δύσσοα, Sch.Theoc.4.45.

δυσδοκίμαστος [ῐ], ον, *hard to test*, τῇ γεύσει Dsc.3.82.

δύσδωρος, ον, = ἄδωρος, Opp.*H*.3.303.

δύσεα· τοῦ τοίχου τὰ πέριξ (Cypr.), Hsch.

δῠσέγερτος, ον, *hard to wake*, Gal.16.645, Paul.Aeg.3.9.

δῠσεγ-καρτέρητος, ον, *hard to sustain*, S.E.*M*.9.152. **-κλήμων**, v. δυσαύλητος. **-χείρητος**, ον, *hard to take in hand*, J.*AJ*15.11.2. **-χωστος**, ον, *hard to dam up*, prob. in Str.16.1.10.

δύσ-εδρος [ῠ], ον, *bringing evil in one's abode*, A.*Ag*.746 (lyr.). 2. *fitting ill, awry*, D.H.*Comp*.6. **-είδεια**, ἡ, *ugliness*, D.L.2.33. **-ειδής**, ές, *unshapely, ugly*, Hdt.6.61, S.*Fr*.88.9, Pl.*Sph*.228a, Agatharch.74; of sounds, ἧττον δ. τοῦ ε τὸ ο D.H.*Comp*.14. II. *difficult to discern*, τὸ δ. τῆς οὐσίας Procl.*Theol.Plat*.5.23. **-είκαστος**, ον, *hard to make out*, of Thucydides' style, D.H.*Lys*.4, cf. Luc.*Icar*.4. **-εικτος**, ον, *unyielding, stiff*, Paul.Aeg.2.11.21.

δῠσειμ-ᾰτέω, *to wear mean clothes*, Plu.2.299e. **-ᾰτος**, ον, *meanly clad*, E.*El*.1107. **-ονία**, ἡ, *mean clothing*, Sch.E.*Hec*.240. **-ων**, ον, gen. ονος, *ill-clad*, Ps.-Hes.ap.Ath.3.116a.

δῠσειρεσία, ἡ, *difficulty in rowing*, Suid.

δῠσείσ-βολος, ον, *hard to enter* or *invade*, of Laconia, E.*Fr*.1083, cf. Aen.Tact.16.17; of a river, Str.4.1.8: Sup. -ώτατος, ον, *least accessible*, of Locris, Th.3.101. **-οδος**, ον, *difficult to enter*, σπήλαιον *TAM*2(1).174 *C*13 (Sidyma). **-πλους**, ουν, gen. ου, *hard to sail into*, Str.4.1.8. **-πλωτος**, ον, = foreg., prob. l. for δυσεκ-, Sch.Th.3.2.

δῠσέκ-βᾰτος, ον, *hard to get out of*, D.C.56.19, Nonn.*D*.45.269 (but f.l. for δυσέμβ-, φλόξ 2.487). **-βίαστος** [ῐ], ον, *hard to overpower*, ἐπιθυμίαι Plu.2.127a, cf. *Cor*.2, Eun.*VS*p.500 B. **-δεκτος**, ον, *hard to endure, intolerable*, Gal.19.2. **-δρομος**, ον, *hard to escape*, Nic.*Al*.14. **-δῠτος**, ον, *hard to shake off*, Hsch. s. v. νήδυμον. **-θέρμαντος**, ον, *hard to warm*, Plu.2.625a, Gal.6.608, Antyll.ap.Orib.10.13.9. Adv. -τως Id.ib.10.29.3, Gal.10.674. **-θῠτος**, ον, *hard to avert by sacrifice*, σημεῖα Plu.*Crass*.18. **-κάθαρτος** [κᾰ], ον, *hard to wash away*, D.H.4.24. **-καρτέρητος**, ον, *hard to endure*, κακόν Phld.*D*.1.12. **-κένωτος**, ον, *hard to evacuate*, Gal.8.192. **-κόμιστος**, ον, *hard to carry out*, Hsch. and Suid. s. v. δυσέξοιστον. **-κρῐτος**, ον, *hard to digest and pass*, Diph.Siph.ap.Ath.2.69e, Xenocr.38. Adv. -τως, ἀθροίζεσθαι Gal.*UP*10.10. 2. Act., *excreting with difficulty*, γαστέρες Id.6.462. **-κρουστος**, ον, *hard to disturb, shake*, φυλακή S.E.*M*.7.23. **-λάλητος** [ᾰ], ον, *hard to express*, Cic.*Att*.5.10.3 (prob.), D.H.*Lys*.11. **-λειπτος**, ον, *hard to escape from*, Plu.2.829b. **-ληπτως**, Adv. dub. in Gal.*Anim.Pass*.1.5 (leg. δυσεξάλειπτον). **-λόγιστος**, ον, *hard to calculate*, Suid. **-λῠτος**, ον, *hard to undo*, τέχνημα A.*Fr*.375 (Dind. δυσέκδυτον *hard to escape from*); δόξα Ph.1.192, cf. Vett.Val.71.23, al. Adv. -τως *indissolubly*, A.*Pr*.60. **-μόχλευτος**, ον, *hard to dislodge*, of disease, Antyll.ap.Orib.10.29.3. **-μύζητος**, ον, *hard to suck out*, Sor.1.87. **-νευστος**, ον, *hard to swim out of*, Max.Tyr.17.10. **-νιπτος**, ον, *hard to wash out*, Pl.*R*.378d, *Trag.Adesp.* in *Gött.Nachr*.1922.26, Cerc.3, Ach.Tat.6.11, Porph.*Abst*.4.20; μῖσος Them.*Or*.21.249c. Adv. -τως Gal.8.36, al. 2. *hard to cleanse*, ὀδόντες Ael.*NA*1.48. **-πέρᾱτος**, ον, *hard to pass out from, hard to escape*, E.*Hipp*.678 (lyr.), 883 (lyr., v.l. δυσεκπέραντος). **-πληκτος**, ον, *hard to terrify*, ὑπὸ φόβων Arist.*VV*1250ᵃ7. **-πλήρωτος**, ον, *hardly realizable*, Phld.*D*.1.12. **-πλοκος**, ον, *tangled, inextricable*, Gloss. **-πλους**, ουν, *hard to sail out of*, Plb.34.2.5, Str.1.2.15. **-πλῠτος**, ον, *hard to wash out*, Ph.2.182,487, Plu.2.488b. II. *hard to cleanse*, ὀδόντες Ael.*NA*1.48: metaph., ψυχαί Ph.1.558. **-πνευστος**, ον, *hard to breathe out*, Sch.E.*Ph*.1438. **-πόνητος**, ον, τιμωρίας καὶ πόνους δυσ[εκπο]νήτους *hard to endure*, Phld.*Herc*.1251.12 (dub. rest.). **-πόρευτος**, ον, *hard to get out of*, πύλαι Ph.*Bel*.79.25; τέλμα J.*AJ*13.2.4. **-πτωτος**, ον, *not easily dislocated*, Paul.Aeg.6.114. **-πύητος** [ῠ], ον, *hard to bring to suppuration*, Gal.11.119, Paul.Aeg.4.18. **-ρίζωτος** [ῐ], ον, *hard to extirpate*, πλάνη Ph.*Fr*.105 H. **-ρίπτος**, ον, *not easily displaced*. Adv. -τως Orib.49.22.17. **-ρυπτος**, ον, *hard to wash out*, Xenocr.58. **-τηκτος**, ον, *hard to melt*, dub. in Hp.*Alim*.51. **-φευκτος**, ον, *hard to escape from*, Tim.*Pers*.130, Theodect.10, Plb.1.77.7, Man.4.477; *hardly escaping*, Tim.*Pers*.140. Adv. δυσεκφύκτως *APl*.4.198 (Maec.).

δῠσεκ-φόρητος, ον, = sq., D.H.*Comp*.22. **-φορος**, ον, *hard to pronounce* or *utter*, Phld.*Po*.994 *Fr*.22, 1676.8, D.H.*Comp*.12,16 (Sup.); λαλιά *Cat.Cod.Astr*.2.167. Adv. -ρως, δ. καὶ τραχέως λαλεῖν Str.14.2.28. **-φώνητος**, ον, *hard to pronounce*, Eust.76.33.

δῠσέλεγκτος, ον, *hard to refute*, of persons or arguments, Str.1.2.1 (Comp.), 11.6.4, Luc.*Pisc*.17.

Δῠσελένα, ἡ, *ill-starred Helen*, E.*Or*.1388 (lyr.); cf. Δύσπαρις.

δῠσ-έλικτος, ον, *hard to undo*, Eust.229.38; *hard to unroll* and read, βίβλοι Jul.*Or*.7.227b. **-ελκής**, ές, *unfavourable for the healing of sores*, of a constitution, opp. εὐελκής, Hp.*Acut*.46, cf. *Morb*.2.52, Gal.10.387. **-ελκία**, ἡ, *the constitution of a* δυσελκής, Hp.*Epid*.2.10 (pl.).

δῠσελπ-ίζω, incorrect spelling for δυσελπιστέω, Plb.16.33.1, 21.13.2. **-ις**, ι, gen. ιδος, *hardly hoping, despondent*, A.*Ch*.412 (lyr.), Hp.*Nat.Mul*.41 (prob.), X.*HG*5.4.31, Arist.*Rh*.1390ᵃ4; δ. τι ἐρεῖν Luc.*Herm*.69. II. Pass., *hardly hoped for*, νίκη Onos.38.2. **-ιστέω**, *to have scarce a hope*, τοῖς ὅλοις, ἐπὶ ταῖς βοηθείαις, Plb.2.10.8, 4.60.4:—Pass., *to be despaired of*, Epicur.*Sent.Vat*.17. **-ιστία**, ἡ, *despondency*, Arist.*VV*1251ᵇ25, Plb.1.39.14, Telesp.35 H., Ph.1.119, App.*BC*4.12. **-ιστος**, ον, = δύσελπις, *Lyr.Adesp*.138, Epicur.*Fr*.470, Plu.*Fab*.17. Adv. δυσελπίστως, ἔχειν Plb.1.87.1. II. *unhoped for*, ἐκ δυσελπίστων *unexpectedly*, X.*Cyr*.6.1.47, cf. Vett.Val.124.25.

δῠσέμ-βᾰτος, ον, *hard to walk on, rugged*, τοῦ χωρίου τὸ δ. Th.4.10;

inaccessible, οἰωνοῖσι D.P.1150. **-βλητος,** ον, *hard to set*, of dislocations, Hp.*Art.*71. **-βολος,** ον, = foreg., Id.*Fract.*38 (Comp.). II. *hard to enter*, δυσεμβολωτάτη ἡ Λακωνική X.*HG*6.5.24; δ. τοῖς πολεμίοις [χώρα] Arist.*Pol.*$1326^{b}41$; ὄρη Plb.3.49.7, cf. J.*AJ*17.2.1.

δῠσεμ-έω, *not to vomit easily*, Philum.ap.Aët.9.23. **-ής,** ές, *hard to make to vomit*, Gal.17(2).329, prob. l. in Dsc.4.153; cf. δυσημής.

δῠσέμπρηστος, ον, *hard to burn*, Ph.*Bel.*82.23.

δῠσέμπτωτος, ον, *not easily falling into* a thing, Nicom.*Harm.*11, Gal.5.433. Adv. -τως Nicom.*Harm.*4.

δῠσενέδρευτος, ον, *hard to way-lay*, App.*Hisp.*88.

δῠσενέργ-εια, ἡ, *lassitude*, Dsc.5.49. **-ητος,** ον, *sluggish*, Sch. Ar.*Pl.*313. II. of food, *badly digested*, Sor.1.34.

δῠσεντερ-ία, ἡ, *dysentery*, Hp.*Aph.*3.12 (pl.), al., Hdt.8.115, Pl. *Ti.*86a (pl.), Arist.*Pr.*$861^{b}16$, etc. **-ιάω,** *suffer from dysentery*, *Hippiatr.*39, Alex.Trall.9.3. **-ικός,** ή, όν, *afflicted with dysentery*, Hp.*Coac.*451, Arr.*Epict.*2.21.22, Mnesith.ap.Orib.4.4.4; *liable to it*, Plu.2.101c; δ. πάθη Epicur.*Fr.*138; τὰ δ. Dsc.1.51. **-ιον,** τό, late form of δυσεντερία, *Act.Ap.*28.8, Moeris 129. **-ιώδης,** ες, *ill with dysentery*, Hp.*Epid.*1.5, 3.8; *symptomatic of* or *belonging to it*, ib.3.17.θ'; τρόπος Aret.*SD*2.9. **-ος,** ον, *suffering from dysentery*, Nic.*Al.*382.

δῠσέν-τευκτος, ον, *unpleasant to meet, physically repulsive*, δ. καὶ ἀηδής Thphr.*Char.*19; but more usu. *unpleasant to deal with*, Plb. 5.34.4, Plu.2.27e; τὸ δ. Ph.2.520, J.*AJ*13.2.1. **-τευξία,** ἡ, *repulsive demeanour*, D.S.19.9, Cass.*Pr.*80 (pl.).

δῠσένωτος, ον, (ἑνόω) *hard to unite*, M.Ant.11.8.

δῠσεξ-άγωγος [ᾰ], ον, *difficult to carry off* or *get rid of*, Hp.*Insomn.* 89, Arist.*Pr.*$871^{a}19$ (Comp.). **-άκουστος** [ᾰ], ον, *difficult to hear*, τὰ διὰ φωνῆς (sc. παραγγέλματα) Ael.*Tact.*35.3. **-άλειπτος** [ᾰ], ον, *hard to wipe out*, εὔνοια Plb.39.3.1; συνήθεια D.S.3.6; μνήμη Longin.7.3; ψυχῆς διάθεσις Corn.*Rh.*p.353 H. **-άλυκτος** [ᾰ], ον, *hard to avoid*, Hsch. **-ανάλωτος** [ᾰλ], ον, = δυσανάλωτος, Hp. *Alim.*49. **-ἄπάτητος** [πᾱ], ον, *hard to deceive*, Pl.*R.*413c, X.*Ages.* 11.12. **-απτος,** ον, *hard to unbind*, ψυχὴ δ. *hard to loose from* the bonds of the body, Plu.*Rom.*28. II. *hard to kindle*, χυμός Gal. 7.341, cf. Steph.*in Hp.*1.284 D. **-ἄρίθμητος,** ον, *hard to count*, Plb.3.58.6, Plu.2.667e. **-άτμιστος,** ον, *hard to evaporate*, Gal. 14.776. **-ειλήτως,** v. -ίλλητος. **-έλεγκτος,** ον, *hard to refute*, Pl.*Phd.*85c (Sup.), Ptol.*Tetr.*164. II. *hard to discover*, φάρμακα D.H.3.5. **-έλευστος,** ον, *hard to get out of*, Tz.*H.*11.556. **-έλικτος,** ον, *hard to unfold, involved*, πλοκή D.H.*Thuc.*29, cf. *Amm.*2.2, Plu.*Brut.*13; δυσεξέλικτα κυματούμενος κλύδων Luc.*Trag.*25; *twisted, contorted*, ὀδόντες Ael.*NA*14.8. **-έργαστος,** ον, *hard to work out*, Eust.1394.7. **-ερεύνητος,** ον, *hard to explore*, Arist.*Pol.*$1330^{b}26$. **-εύρετος,** ον, *hard to find out*, Id.*HA*$611^{a}26$, Plu.2.407f. **-ήγητος,** ον, *hard to explain*, Darius ap. D.L.9.13, Gal.17(2).71. **-ημέρωτος,** ον, *hard to tame*, Plu.*Art.*25. **-ήνυστος,** ον, *indissoluble*, δεσμός E.*Hipp.*1237. **-ίλαστος** [ῐ], ον, *hard to appease*, πένθη Plu.2.609f. **-ίλλητος,** ον, *hard to unravel*, Cic. *Att.*5.10.3 (s.v.l.). Adv., in form δυσεξειλήτως, v.l. in Sch.Theoc. 14.51. **-ίτηλος** [ῑ], ον, *not easily perishing*, ἄνθος φαρμάκων Str. 11.8.7, cf. Plu.2.696d, Philum.*Ven.*4.3. **-ίτητος** [ῑ], ον, = sq., Hsch., *EM*238.42. **-ῖτος,** ον, *hard to get out of*, D.S.3.44 (v.l. δυσδιεξίτητος). **-όδευτος,** ον, = δυσδιέξοδος, Procl.*Par.Ptol.* 153. **-οδος,** ον, *hard to get out of*, Arist.*Pol.*$1330^{b}26$, Lyc.1099, Paus.2.31.1: metaph., ἐρώτησις Luc.*Fug.*10. 2. *hard to remedy*, Hp.*Epid* 4.30. **-οιστος,** ον, *hard to explain*: τὸ δ. Porph.*VP*48, cf. Hsch. II. = δυσεκκόμιστος, Id. **-οχος,** ον, *craggy, rugged*, Eust. ad D.P.389. **-ῠβωτός,** ον, *not easily displaced outwards*, Sor.1.102. **-ώθητος,** ον, *hard to dislodge*, Simp.*in Ph.*677.29.

δῠσέπ-ακτος, ον, *hard to draw back*, of overwound strands of gut, Ph.*Bel.*58.23. **-ανόρθωτος,** ον, *hard to correct* or *reform*, Vett. Val.77.6; πολιτεία Theo *Prog.*12. **-έκτᾰτος,** ον, *hard to extend* or *distend*, Gal.8.288, al. **-ήβολος,** ον, *hard to master*, Suid. s.v. Ἀγάπιος.

δῠσεπί-βᾰτος, ον, *hard to get at*, D.S.1.69. **-βλητος,** ον, *hard to attain to*, παράδειγμα *OGI*764.17 (Pergam.). **-βολος,** ον, *hard to assail*, χώρα Aen.Tact.8.1 codd.; *risky to undertake*, πλοῦς *Peripl. M.Rubr.*39; *unsuccessful*, Paul.Al.*N.*4. **-βούλευτος,** ον, *hard to attack secretly*, X.*Eq.Mag.*4.11 (Comp.), *Ages.*6.7 (Sup.). 2. *hard to damage*, Apollod.*Poliorc.*139.7. **-γνωστος,** ον, *hard to identify* or *find out*, *SIG*1023.9 (Cos, iii/ii B.C.), App.*BC*1.18. **-θετος,** ον, *hard to attack*, Aen.Tact.*Praef.*2. **-κούρητος,** ον, *hard to meet*, ἀπορία Alcid.*Soph.*21. **-κρῐτος,** ον, *hard to decide*, Ap.Ty. *Ep.*19, Gal.13.789. **-λόγιστος,** ον, *hard to conceive*, Diog.Oen. 38. **-μικτος,** ον, *disinclined for intercourse*, τινί Str.11.2.2: abs., *unsociable*, Id.3.3.8; τὸ ἄστοργον καὶ δ. Plu.2.917c, Porph.*Abst.*4. 6. **-νόητος,** ον, *hard to understand*, M.Ant.6.17; *hard to devise* or *plan out*, Jul.*Or.*1.12b. **-στροφος,** ον, *hard to turn* or *guide*, ἅρματα App.*Mith.*42. **-σχετος,** ον, *hard to check*, of bleeding, Gal.19.457, Aret.*CA*2.6. Adv. -τως Gal.7.725, Herod.Med. in *Rh. Mus.*58.99. **-τευκτος,** ον, *hard to accomplish*, στρατεία D.S.17. 93; *ineffective*, Vett.Val.43.12, al., *Cat.Cod.Astr.*1.164. Adv. -τως Vett.Val.194.27. 2. *hard to treat*, *Hippiatr.*26. **-τίμητος** [τῑ], ον, *hard to criticize*, Alex.Aphr.*in Top.*543.5. **-χείρητος,** ον, *hard to prove*, πρόβλημα Arist.*APr.*$42^{b}31$. 2. *hard to attack*, θέσις Id.*Top.*$159^{a}3$; πρόβλημα ib.$158^{b}16$: Sup. -ότατοι τῶν ὅρων ib. $158^{b}8$; of a person, J.*BJ*4.3.10, Plu.2.281a, App.*Pun.*118.

δῠσεπούλωτος, ον, *hard to cicatrize*, Gal.6.751, v.l. in Dsc.4.41.

δῠσέραστος, ον, *unhappy in love*, Max.Tyr.3.5 (Comp., wrongly spelt δυσερασίστερος). II. *unfavourable to love*, ὄρθρος *AP*5.171 (Mel.), 172 (Id.).

δῠσεργ-ᾰσία, ἡ, *difficulty of performing*, Artem.1.67. **-αστος,** ον, *difficult to construct*, χώματα J.*BJ*5.9.2. **-εια,** ἡ, *difficulty*, Sor.2.53, Orib.45.18.14; *functional defect*, Paul.Aeg.6.42, al. **-έω,** *to be sluggish*, καταμήνια -γοῦντα, of dysmenorrhoea, Hp.*Ep.* 21. **-ημα,** ατος, τό, *difficulty, hindrance*, Dsc.*Ther.Praef.* **-ής,** ές, *difficult*, App.*Hisp.*73, al.; τὸ δ. *OGI*502.6 (Aezani): Comp., of an operation, Antyll.(?) ap. Orib.44.23.23; *making it hard to work*, βαρύτητες Plu.2.1129d. **-ία,** ἡ, *difficulty in working* or *construction*, δυσεργίαν παρέχειν Ph.*Bel.*56.42, cf. Hero *Aut.*23.8 (in form -έργεια), Plu.*Aem.*16; *difficulty* in pronouncing, ἡ ἐν τῇ προφορᾷ δ. Phld.*Po.*2.42; *inability to exert oneself*, Hp.*VM*10 (v.l. δυσοργίη); *inability to act*, App.*Syr.*19. **-ος,** ον, *hard to work*, ὕλη Thphr.*HP* 5.1.1; λίθοι Paus.3.21.4; *unfit to be worked*, σίδηρος Plu.*Lyc.*9; *hard to manage*, ὁπλισμός Id.*Flam.*8; δ. χρῆσθαι Id.*Tim.*28; πόλις -οτέρα *harder to besiege*, Id.*Nic.*17. 2. *hard to effect, difficult*, Plb.28.8. 3, Ph.1.272 (Sup.); πόλεμος App.*Hisp.*63 (Sup.); τὸ παραφυλάττειν τὰς ἐξόδους -ότερον J.*BJ*5.12.1. Adv. -γως, κινηθῆναι Plu.*Demetr.* 43. II. Act., *incapable of work, useless*, πρός τι App.*Syr.*16; χεῖμα δ., *hiems ignava*, Bion *Fr.*15.5; *idle*, νωθρὸς καὶ δ. Plu.*Alex.*33.

δῠσ-ερεύνητος, ον, *hard to search*, χωρία J.*BJ*1.16.5. **-έρημος,** ον, *very lonely, desolate*, πάγος *AP*9.561 (Phil.). **-ερις,** ι, gen. ιδος, *quarrelsome, contentious*, Isoc.1.31, Arist.*Rh.*$1381^{a}32$, *EN*$1108^{a}30$, al.; δ. λόγος Pl.*Lg.*864a. II. Act., *producing unhappy strife*, φθόνος Plu.*Pel.*4; τὸ δανείζειν δ. App.*BC*1.54. **-εριστία,** ἡ, *contentious disposition*, Procl.*in Prm.*p.539 S.; *irreconcilability*, Iamb. *Myst.*1.2. **-έριστος,** ον, *pertaining to unholy strife*, αἷμα S.*El.* 1385 (lyr.); σπουδή Cleanth.*Stoic.*1.122. **-ερμήνευτος,** ον, *hard to interpret*, *Ep.Hebr.*5.11, Gal.11.454, *Cat.Cod.Astr.*1.114.26; *hard to describe*, χρόαι D.S.2.52; θέα Ph.1.649. **-ερμος,** ον, *not favoured by Hermes, unlucky*, Suid.:—hence **-ερμία,** ἡ, *ill luck*, Hsch., *EM*291. 49. **-ερνής,** ές, *hardly shooting* or *sprouting*, Poll.1.231. **-ερως,** ωτος, ὁ, ἡ, *madly* or *disastrously loving*, τινός E.*Hipp.*193; τῶν ἀπόντων Th.6.13; τῶν ἀφροδισίων X.*Oec.*11.13; *mali cupidus*, Max. Tyr.36.4; εἰς χρήματα Jul.*Or.*2.85c: abs., Lys.4.8 (s.v.l.), Call.*Ep.* 42.6, *AP*5.244 (Maced.), al.; of bees, *Lyr.Alex.Adesp.*7.16; δ. ἔρως Plu.*Per.*20. II. *laggard in love*, Theoc.1.85, 6.7. **-ερωτιάω,** *to be desperately in love*, Ach.Tat.5.1, Plu.*Fr.*21.2. **-ετηρία,** ἡ, (ἔτος) *bad season*, Poll.1.52. **-ετῠμολόγητος,** ον, *hard to derive*, ὄνομα Corn.*ND*20. **-ευνήτωρ,** Dor. -άτωρ, ορος, ὁ, *ill bedfellow*, A.*Th.*293 (lyr.):—expld. by **-εύνητος,** *ill-bedded*, in Sch. ad loc. **-ευπόριστος,** ον, *hard to procure*, Alex.Trall.1.15. **-εύρετος,** ον, *hard to find out*, A.*Pr.*816; λόγος Porph.ap.Eus.*PE*3.11; δ. τό τινων γένος Ph.1.234. 2. *hard to find* or *get*, X.*Mem.*3.14.7, Secund.*Sent.*11; σπάνιον καὶ δ. Plu.2.97b. 3. *hard to find one's way through, impenetrable*, ὕλη E.*Ba.*1221. **-έφικτος,** ον, *hard to come at*, Plb.31.25.3, Plu.2.65e, Phld.*Rh.*2.119 S.; ἀνθρώπῳ Ecphant.ap. Stob.4.7.64; *hard to understand*, Vett.Val.272.8, al. **-έφοδος,** ον, *hard to get at, inaccessible*, D.S.1.57 (Sup.); τὸ δ. Phld.*Rh.*1.325 S. (nisi leg. δυσέφικτον). **-εψᾰνος** [ᾰ], ον, *hard to digest*, Suid. s.vv. ἔψανον, τέραμνον. **-έψητος,** ον, = foreg., Phryn.*PS*p.33 B.; *hard to cook*, Gal.6.541 (Comp.). **-ζηλία,** ἡ, *jealousy*, Ath.13. 589a. **-ζηλος,** ον, *exceeding jealous*, Od.7.307; ἐπί τινι A.R.4. 1089; γυνή Plu.*Alex.*9; τὸ δ. Id.2.471a. Adv. -λως, ἔχειν πρός τινα Id.*Alex.*77. 2. *eager*, ὁρμή Emp.114.3. II. *rivalling in hardship*, αἰθύῃσι βίον δύσζηλον ἔχοντες Hom.*Epigr.*8. **-ζήτητος,** ον, *hard to seek* or *track*, X.*Cyn.*8.1, Poll.5.50. **-ζωΐα,** v.l. for δυσοδία, Ps.-Callisth.3.9. **-ζωος,** ον, *wretched*, βίοτος δ. *AP*9. 574. **-ήβολον·** δυσάν⟨τ⟩ητον, Hsch. **-ήκεστος,** ον, *hard to heal* or *cure*, Hp.*Fract.*29, *AP*3.19 (Cyzicus). **-ηκής,** ές, = foreg., Hsch.

δῠσηκο-έω, *to be hard of hearing*, Antyll.ap.Orib.10.13.5. **-ΐα,** ἡ, *hardness of hearing*, Dsc.5.17, Plu.2.1073d, Vett.Val.109.31; *disobedience*, Plu.2.794d. **-ος,** ον, *hard of hearing*, ὦτα Ph.2.35; δυσήκοος ὦ Στρατονίκη, epitaph in *Inscr.Mus.Alex.*299 (iii B.C.); *disobedient*, Plu.2.13f. II. *ill-sounding, terrible to hear*, prob. in S. *Fr.*220; *unpleasant to the ear*, Demetr.*Eloc.*48, Poll.2.117, Philostr. *VS*1.12; of an orator, Eun.*VS*p.456 B.

δῠσ-ηλάκᾰτος [λᾰ], ον, *spinner of ill*, Μοῖρα Nonn.*D.*1.367; Φιλομήλη ib.4.321. **-ήλᾰτος,** ον, *hard to drive through* or *over*, Poll. 1.186. **-ηλεγής,** ές, (ἄλγος, ἀλεγ-εινός) Homeric epith. of death and war, *bringing bitter grief, cruel, ruthless*, θάνατος, πόλεμος, Od.22. 325, Il.20.154; πηγάδες... δυσηλεγέες *cruel* frosts, Hes.*Op.*506; δυσηλεγέος ἀπὸ δεσμοῦ Id.*Th.*652; also of men, πολῖται Thgn.795; γείτονες Max.87. **-ήλιος,** Dor. -άλιος, ον, *ill-sunned, sunless*, κνέφας A.*Eu.*396 (lyr.), cf. E.*Rh.*247 (lyr.), Plu.*Mar.*11, etc. II. *too much sunned, parched*, θέρος *Trag.Adesp.*340.

δῠσημερ-έω, *have an unlucky day, be unlucky*, Pherecr.98; κατὰ τὰς μάχας D.H.1.57. **-ημα,** ατος, τό, *ill luck*, Sch.Il.6.336. **-ία,** Dor. **-ᾱμερία,** ἡ, *unlucky day*: *mishap, misery*, δυσαμεριᾶν πρύτανιν A.*Fr.*236; μοῖρα δυσαμερίας S.*Fr.*591, cf. Plu.*Eum.*9.

δῠσ-ήμερος, ον, (ἥμερος) *hard to tame, restive*, Str.3.3.8, Ptol.*Tetr.* 56. **-ήμετος,** ον, = sq., Hp.*Epid.*6.8.26. **-ημής,** ές, = δυσεμής, Id.*Aph.*4.7. **-ήνεμον·** δυστάραχον, τὸ κακοὺς ἀνέμους ἔχον, Hsch. **-ηνίαστος,** ον, *hard to bridle*, Tim.Gaz.124.11. **-ήνιος,** ον, (ἡνία) = foreg., *refractory*, Epict.*Gnom.*63; γυνὴ δυσήνιόν ἐστι

(v. l. -ἀνιόν) Men.803. B. (ἀνία) = δυσάνιος, *ill at ease, uneasy*, Hp.*Epid*.3.17.ιαʹ codd. **-ηνίοχητος**, ον, *hard to hold in, ungovernable*, Luc.*Abd*.17. **-ήνῠτος**, ον, (ἀνύω) *hard to accomplish*, J.*BJ*5.12.1; also **-ήνυκτος**, Hsch. **-ήρης**, ες, *difficult*, opp. εὐήρης, Suid. **-ηρις**, ιδος, ὁ, ἡ, = δύσερις 1, Pi.*O*.6.19, Axiop.1.4: Att. form of δύσερις acc. to Moer.126. **-ήριστος**, ον, = foreg., Hsch.; also, = ἀμφίβολος, Id. **-ήροτος**, ον, (ἀρόω) *hard to plough*, Call.*Del*.268, Poll.1.227. **-ήττητος**, ον, *hard to conquer*, ib. 157. **-ήτωρ**, ορος, ὁ, ἡ, *heavy at heart*, Hsch. **-ηχής**, Dor. **-ᾱχής**, ές, (ἠχέω) *ill-sounding*, Phld.*Po*.2.16, v.l. in D.H.*Comp*.14; *giving a dull sound*, of metals, Plu.2.721c; ἰσθμοῖο δ. Emp.100.19:— in Hom., epith. of πόλεμος, Il.2.686 (cf. Anacr.107), al.; and of θάνατος, Il.16.442, al. (where it should perh. be taken, = *bringer of great woe* (ἄχος), cf. Apollon.*Lex*.), of φόνος Emp.136.1; *of ill-repute*, δ. ἀνδράσιν *h.Ap*.64. **-ηχία**, ἡ, *unpleasantness of sound*, Phld.*Po*.2.24, *Po.Herc*.994.23. **-ηχος**, ον, *ill-sounding*, ῥυθμός Hermog.*Id*.1.7; συνθήκη ibid. **-θάλασσος** [θᾰ], ον, *subject to sea-sickness*, Sor.1.109. **-θαλής**, ές, *hardly growing*, Cratin.405, Alex.Mynd.ap.Ath.9.393a. **-θᾰλία**, ας, ἡ, *a misfortune*, Sophr. 83 (pl.). **-θαλπής**, ές, *hard to warm*: *chilly*, χειμών Il.17.549. II. *over-warm, burning hot*, Q.S.11.156 codd.

δυσθᾰνᾰτ-άω, strengthd. for θανατάω, *long for death*, J.*BJ*5.9.3, 6.6.2, Agath.3.22, cf. *EM*442.48; but freq. confused with sq., as in Ph.2.390. 2. δυσθανατῶσα γραῦς 'with one foot in the grave', Chrysipp.*Stoic*.3.50. **-έω**, *to be loath to die*, Hdt.9.72; *struggle against death, die hard*, Pl.*R*.406b, Thphr.*HP*3.11.3, Plu.*Ant*.77, etc.; also, *to be sick to death with desire*, περί τι Ph.2.167; *to be deadly obstinate*, περί τι ib.100: abs., *to be in deadly terror*, ib.173. **-ος**, ον, *bringing a hard death*, Hp.*Prorrh*.1.55; κρατῆρες E.*Ion* 1051 (lyr.).

δυσ-θᾰνής, ές, *unhappy in death*, *AP*9.81 (Crin.). **-θέᾱτος**, ον, *ill to look on*, A.*Pr*.69 (lyr.), S.*Aj*.1004. II. *hard to see*, ἀμαυρὸν αἴθυγμα καὶ δ. Plu.2.966b, cf. Ael.*NA*9.61. **-θενέω**, (σθένος) *to be weak and powerless*, Hp.*Morb*.2.54, al. **-θεος**, ον, *godless, ungodly*, A.*Ag*.1590, *Ch*.46 (lyr.); ὦ δ. μίσημα S.*El*.289. 2. *miserable, wretched*, μισθὸς εὐσεβίης *AJA*17.170 (Cyrene, written δύσθιον). **-θερᾰπευσία**, ἡ, *difficulty of treatment*, Cass.*Pr*. 1. **-θεράπευτος** [ᾰ], ον, *hard to cure*, Hp.*Medic*.10, S.*Aj*.609 (lyr.); εὐήθεια Ph.1.334. **-θερέας**· δυσαλθήτους, Hsch. **-θέρμαντος**, ον, *cold*, Sch.Il.17.549. **-θερος**, ον, *over-hot, parched*, Poll.5. 110. **-θεσία**, ἡ, *bad condition*: *fretfulness, peevishness*, Hp.*Fract*. 33 (v.l. δυσαισθησίη). **-θετέω**, *to be dissatisfied*, ταῖς συνθήκαις Plb.*Fr*.128; *to be in distress*, D.S.14.113. II. mostly in Med., abs., *to be vexed*, X.*Cyr*.2.2.5; τινί Plb.33.17.1; *to be in straits*, Id. 8.5.4. **-θετος**, ον, (τίθημι) *in bad case*, κακόν Ph.1.97; τὸ δ. *bad condition*, J.*AJ*15.9.6. II. *hard to set right*, Hp.*Fract*.38 (Comp.). **-θεώρητος**, ον, *hard to observe*, Arist.*HA*511^{b}13; *scarcely visible*, τρύπημα Hero*Spir*.1.31, cf. Philum.*Ven*.15.6. II. *hard to understand* or *reduce to theory*, τέχνη Ph.*Bel*.49.19, cf. Plb.3. 31.7, Phld.*Rh*.1.141 S., Ph.2.84. **-θήρᾱτος**, ον, *hard to catch*, Arist.*HA*615^{a}22, Plu.*Pomp*.38: metaph., τὸ δ. [τῆς φιλοσοφίας] Ph.1.234; δ. τἀληθές Plu.*Per*.13, cf. Ph.2.217, al. **-θήρευτος**, ον, = foreg., Pl.*Sph*.218d, 261a. **-θηρία**, ἡ, *bad hunting*, Poll.5.13. **-θηρος**, ον, *having bad sport*, Opp.*H*.3.431, Poll.5. 13. **-θησαύριστος**, ον, *hard to store*, καρπός Pl.*Criti*.115b, cf. Arist.*Mu*.401^{a}5. **-θιος**, v. δύσθεος. **-θλαστος**, ον, *hard to crush, tough*, Thphr.*HP*8.4.1 (Comp.), Gal.*UP*11.17. **-θνήσκω**, = δυσθανατέω, only in part., E.*El*.843, *Rh*.791. **-θνητέω**, = foreg., Nic.Dam.p.36 D. **-θραυστος**, ον, *hard to break*, Dsc.4.154, Gal. *UP*11.17. **-θρήνητος**, ον, *loud-wailing, most mournful*, ἔπος S. *Ant*.1211; θρῆνοι E.*IT*144 (anap.):—also **-θρηνος**, gloss on δυσηχής, Apollon.*Lex*. **-θροος**, ον, *ill-sounding*, φωνά Pi.*P*.4.63; βάγματα, αὐδά, γόοι, A.*Pers*.637 (lyr.), 942 (anap.), 1076 (lyr.). **-θρυπτος**, ον, *hard to break in pieces*, στερρότης Plu.ap.*EM*104.1 (dub. l.).

δυσθῡμ-αίνω, *to be dispirited, despond*, *h.Cer*.362. **-έω**, = foreg., Hdt.8.100, Onos.10.26; δ. ταῖς ἐλπίσιν Plu.*Tim*.34:—Med., *to be melancholy, angry*, Democr.286, E.*Med*.91. **-ία**, ἡ, *despondency, despair*, Hp.*VM*10, Pl.*Lg*.666b, etc.; πρὶν ἐλθεῖν ξυμμάχοις δυσθυμίαν E.*Supp*.696: pl., Id.*Med*.691, S.*Fr*.663, Arist.*Pr*.954^{b}35, Ph.2. 99. II. *ill-temper*, Them.*Or*.13.172c. **-ικός**, ή, όν, *melancholy*, Arist.*Phgn*.813^{a}33. **-ος**, ον, *desponding, melancholy*, S.*El*. 218 (lyr.), X.*Cyr*.5.2.34, Arist.*Pr*.955^{a}17 (Comp.), Phld.*Herc*.1251. 10; τοῖς πεπραγμένοις S.*El*.550; τὸ δ., = δυσθυμία, Plu.*Per*.15. Adv. **-μως**, ἔχειν Plb.1.87.1, Phld.*Mort*.27: Comp. -ότερον Pl.*Phd*.85b.

δυσ-ῐᾱτέω, *to be hard to heal*, Paul.Aeg.3.18. **-ίᾱτος**, Ion. **-ίητος** [ι], ον, *hard to heal*, κλητ̄ς Hp.*Art*.14 (Comp.), cf. Cass.*Pr*.1 (Comp.); κακὸν δ. an ill *that none can cure*, A.*Ag*.1103 (lyr.); ὀργή E.*Med*.520; νόσημα Pl.*Lg*.916a, cf. Ph.1.40, al.; of persons, *implacable*, Them.*Or*.15.192c. Adv. -τως, μόριον πεπονθὸς δ. Gal.18(2). 273. **-ίδρως**, ωτος, ὁ, ἡ, *hardly perspiring*, Thphr.*Sud*.18. **-ῐερέω**, *to have bad omens in a sacrifice*, Plu.*Caes*.63, 2.587c.

δῠσῐθάλασσος [θᾰ], Att. **-ττος**, ον, (δύω) *dipped in the sea*, *AP*6.38 (Phil.).

δύσικμος [ῠ], ον, (ἰκμάς) *with scanty secretions*, Hp.*Mul*.1.34; δ. πάθος Orib.*Fr*.78.

δῠσικός, ή, όν, = δυτικός, *PLond*.1.98.51.

δῠσ-ίμερος [ῐ], ον, κάματος, πῆμα, *of the torments of love*, A.R.3. 961, 4.4. II. *tormented by love*, Nonn.*D*.42.202, al. **-ίππαστος**, ον, = sq., τόπος Anon.Hist.in*Rev.Ét.Gr*.5.320, Sch.Pl.*Mx*. 240c, cf. Poll.1.186 (v.l.). **-ιππος**, ον, *hard to ride in*: τὰ δ. *parts unfit for cavalry-service*, X.*HG*3.4.12; δ. χώρα Plu.*Phil*.14.

δύσις [ῠ], εως, ἡ, (δύω) *setting of the sun* or *stars*, opp. ἀνατολή, Heraclit.120, A.*Pr*.458; ἀμφὶ Πλειάδων δύσιν (cf. Πλειάδες) Id.*Ag*. 826; περὶ δύσιν Πλειάδος Damox.2.19; δ. χειμερινή, θερινή, ἰσημερινή, Cleom.1.9; δ. τροπική Str.2.4.7; ἄχρι ἡλίου δύσεως *IG*4.597 (Argos); ἀλίου ἄχρι δ. ib.606 (ibid.); Κυνὸς ψυχρὰν δ. S.*Fr*.432.11; personified, *PMag.Berol*.2.94: pl., δύσιες, opp. ἀντολαί, A.R.1.85: metaph., δ. τοῦ λογισμοῦ Ph.1.511. 2. *quarter in which the sun sets, west*, πρὸς ἡλίου δύσιν Th.2.96; πρὸς δύσεις Arist.*Mu*.393^{a}18; ἀπὸ δύσεως *CIG*1755 (Opus); πρὸς δύσει Plb.1.42.5; πρὸς τὰς δύσεις βλέπειν Id. 5.104.7. II. *hiding-place*, Opp.*H*.1.330.

δῠσ-ίχνευτος, ον, *hard to track*, Sch.S.*Aj*.32. **-ίωτος** [ῑ], ον, *not easily rusted*, in Comp., Orib.49.3.5. **-κᾰής**, ές, *hard to burn, burning badly*, Plu.2.952c. **-καθαίρετος**, ον, *hard to overthrow*, Ph.1.61; στάσις J.*BJ*2.17.4. **-κάθαρτος** [κᾰ], ον, *hard to purify*, Ph.1.239, al.; *hard to purge*, πνεύματα Plu.2.991b, cf. Dsc.5.69. II. *hard to satisfy by purification* or *atonement*, δ. Ἅιδου λιμήν, of the house of the Labdacidae in which murders never ceased, S.*Ant*. 1284 (lyr.); δαίμων Ar.*Pax*1250. **-κάθεκτος**, ον, *hard to hold in*, ἵπποι X.*Mem*.4.1.3 (Sup.); πλήθη Plu.*Num*.4: metaph., Corn.*ND*30; πλοῦτος Luc.*Tim*.29 (s. v. l., al. δυσκάτοχος); *hard to keep in mind, retain*, Plu.2.408b. **-κάθοδος**, ον, *hard to go down into*, σπήλαιον Conon 35.1. **-καμπής**, ές, *hard to bend*, Plu.2.650d, Aret.*SD*2.3: Comp., Sabin.ap.Orib.9.19.2. **-καμπτος**, ον, = foreg., Cass. *Pr*.61, Sch.Ar.*Th*.74. Adv. -τως, ἔχειν Aët.16.8. **-καπνος**, ον, *noisome from smoke*, δώματα A.*Ag*.774 (lyr.). II. *producing an unpleasant smoke*, Thphr.*Ign*.72; φοῖνιξ Chaerem.39 (Sup.). **-καρτέρητος**, ον, *hard to endure*, Ph.2.73, Plu.*Phoc*.4, etc. Adv. -τως Porph.*Marc*.8, Herod.Med.ap.Aët.9.2. **-κατάγωγός**, όν, *making a landing difficult*, βράχη *Stad*.114. **-κατᾰγώνιστος**, ον, *hard to overcome*, Plb.15.15.8, D.H.3.7; *hard to refute*, Id.*Rh*.8.3; τὸ δ. *impregnability*, Corn.*ND*20. **-κατάθετος**, ον, *hard to bring*, πρὸς φιλίαν, f.l. for δυσσυγκάθετος, Iamb.*VP*31.194. **-κάτακτος**, ον, *hard to break*, Thphr.*HP*3.7.4, Dsc.3.22, Apollod.*Poliorc*.139. 8. **-κατάληπτος**, ον, *hard to comprehend*, D.S.1.3, Ph.2.216, M.Ant.5.10. **-κατάλλακτος**, ον, *hard to reconcile*, Plu.2.13d, Ath. 14.625b.

δυσκατά-λῠτος, ον, *hard to bring to an end*, πόλεμοι Str.14.1.28; *hard to overthrow*, δυναστεία J.*BJ*4.5.5. **-μάθητος** [μᾰ], ον, *hard to learn* or *understand*, Isoc.10.11, Pl.*Plt*.303d (Comp.), D.H.*Th*.9. Adv. -μαθήτως, ἔχειν Isoc.2.33. **-μάχητος** [μᾰ], ον, *hard to overcome*, D.S.3.35; νόσος (sc. πενία) Lib.*Decl*.34.4. **-νόητος**, ον, *hard to understand*, διάλεκτος D.S.5.14, cf. Plu.2.47c. **-παυστος**, ον, *hard to check*, ἄλγος A.*Ch*.470 (lyr.); βοή Lxx 3*Ma*.5.7; of persons, Plu.*Alex*.31; *restless*, ψυχή E.*Med*.109 (anap.); τὸ -ότερον Thphr. *Vent*.35. **-πεπτος**, ον, *hard to digest*, Id.*CP*1.14.4. **-πληκτος**, ον, *hard to keep in awe*, Plb.1.67.4. **-πολέμητος**, ον, *hard to conquer*, D.S.2.48. **-πόνητος**, ον, *hard to execute*, M.Ant.6.19, Arr.*Epict*.3. 12.8; *hard to digest*, Sor.2.32. **-ποσία**, ἡ, *difficulty of swallowing*, Herod.Med. in *Rh.Mus*.58.86, Philum.ap.Aët.8.48. **-ποτέω**, *have difficulty in swallowing*, Herod.Med.ap.Orib.5.30.12. **-ποτος**, ον, *hard to swallow*, Arist.*Sens*.443^{b}12, Archig.ap.Gal.12.976. **-πρακτος**, ον, *hard to effect*, X.*Cyr*.8.7.12 (Comp.).

δυσκατάρτιστος, ον, *hard to place rightly*, ἐν τῇ ἐπιβάσει, of stallions, *Hippiatr*.14.

δυσκατά-σβεστος, ον, *hard to extinguish*, D.S.4.54, Plu.2.417b. **-στᾰτος**, ον, *hard to restore* or *rally*, X.*Cyr*.5.3.43 (Comp.). **-φρόνητος**, ον, *not to be despised*, ib.8.1.42 (Comp.).

δυσκατ-εργᾰσία, ἡ, *indigestion*, Anon.Lond.6.10. **-έργαστος**, ον, *hard to work*, λίθος Str.17.1.33; καρποὶ -ότεροι *slower to mature*, Thphr.*CP*1.14.4; *hard of digestion*, Dsc.2.93, Ph.2.244. II. = δυσκατάπρακτος, X.*Mem*.4.2.7 (Comp.). III. *hard to tame*, γένος ταύρων Agatharch.76 (Sup.); *hard to overcome*, Luc.*Tyr*. 15. **-οπτος**· δυσθεώρητος, Hsch. **-όρθωτος**, ον, *hard to succeed in*, ἔργον Demetr.*Eloc*.127, Ph.2.83, Gal.*UP*15.7; τυραννίς Chio *Ep*.15 (Comp.). II. *hard to set right, remedy*, σπάνις τῶν ἀναγκαίων J.*AJ*2.5.6. **-ούλωτος**, ον, *hard to cicatrize*, Dsc.5.81; ἕλκη Apollon.*Mir*.42.

δυσκάτοχος, v. δυσκάθεκτος.

δύσκαυστος, ον, *hard to burn*, Apollod.*Poliorc*.139.8.

δύσκε, v. δύω.

δυσ-κέλᾰδος, ον, *ill-sounding, shrieking*, φόβος Il.16.357; ζῆλος δ. envy *with its tongue of malice*, Hes.*Op*.196; δ. ὕμνος Ἐρινύος A.*Th*. 867 (anap.), cf. *Fr*.451 I; μοῦσα E.*Ion*1098 (lyr.). **-κένωτος**, ον, *hard to excrete*, Gal.18(1).580 (Sup.). **-κέραστος**, ον, *hard to temper*, φύσις πρὸς τὸ πιθανὸν δ. Plu.*Dio*52; δύσμικτα καὶ δ. Id.2. 754c. **-κερδής**, ές, *with ill gains, ill-gotten*, Opp.*H*.2.417. **-κηδής**, ές, (κῆδος) *full of misery*, δυσκηδέα νύκτα φυλάσσω Od.5.466. II. (κήδομαι) δυσκηδέα· δυσφύλακτον, χαλεπόν, Hsch. **-κηλος**, ον, (κηλέω) *past remedy*, A.*Eu*.825 (cf. Sch.ad loc.): but perh. rather formed by analogy from εὔκηλος: hence, *spiteful*. **-κημον**· ἄφρονα, δυσοιώνιστον, Hsch.

δυσκῑν-ησία, Ion. -ίη, ἡ, *difficulty of moving*, Hp.*Aph*.3.17, Arist. *GA*780^{a}25, *PA*685^{a}8. **-ητέω**, *move with difficulty*, Herod.Med. in *Rh.Mus*.58.104. **-ητος**, ον, *hard to move*, Pl.*Ti*.56a, Ph.2.227 (Comp.), Thphr.*Vent*.35 (Sup.); πλοῖα Plb.1.22.3. Adv. -τως, ἔχειν πρὸς τοὺς ἀνέμους Arist.*Cael*.294^{b}17. II. in mental relations, δ. πρὸς τοὺς φόβους Pl.*R*.503d; δ. ὑπὸ ὀργῆς Arist.*VV*1250^{a}5; δ. ποιεῖν τὴν διάνοιαν Id.*PA*686ᵃ30; ἕξις -οτέρα διαθέσεως Id.*Cat.*9ᵃ10; τὸ -ον *obstinacy*, Phld.*Lib.*p.55 O.; of language, *clumsiness*, τὸ ἄσχημον καὶ δ. Id.*Po.*994.35. Adv. -τως καὶ δυσμαθῶς ἔχειν Pl.*R.*503d. 2. *firm, resolute*, Plu.*Thes.*36; *inexorable*, Ἅιδης *AP*7.221. 3. *impervious to motion*, of the soul, Plot.1.4.8.

δυσ-κλεής, ές, *inglorious*, Il.9.22 (poet. acc. δυσκλέᾶ for δυσκλεέα); *infamous, shameful*, of persons and things, δ. θέα A.*Pr.*243; δυσκλεεστάτῳ μόρῳ Id.*Pers.*444; πρῶτον μὲν οὐκ οὖσ' ἄδικός εἰμι δυσκλεὴς E.*Hel.*270, cf. X.*Cyr.*3.3.53, Lxx 3 *Ma.*3.23 (Sup.). Adv. -εῶς S.*El.*1006, E.*Hel.*993 codd., Plu.2.169a. **-κλεια**, ἡ, *ill-fame, infamy*, S.*Fr.*188, E.*Med.*218, Th.3.58, Pl.*Lg.*663a, etc.; ἐπὶ δυσκλείᾳ tending to *disgrace them*, S.*Aj.*143 (anap.). II. *ingloriousness*, D.60.24. **-κληδόνιστος**, ον, *of ill name, boding ill*, Luc.*Am.*39. **-κληρέω**, *to be unlucky in one's lot*, esp. in standing for an office, opp. λαγχάνω, Pl.*Lg.*690c. **-κλήρημα**, ατος, τό, *piece of ill luck*, Plb.30.20.9 (pl.); τῆς πατρίδος D.S.32.22 (pl.). **-κληρος**, ον, *unlucky*, Phryn.*PS* p.61 B. **-κλής**, poet. for δυσκλεής, Simm. *Secur.*6. **-κλητος**, ον, *in bad repute*, Heraclid.Tar.ap.Ath.3.120d. **-κλῐτος**, ον, *hard to inflect, irregular*, δ. ῥήματα, title of work by Eulogius, *EM*809.33. **-κλῠδώνιστον**· δυσέκβατον, Suid. **-κλῠτος**, ον, *ill-famed*, Hsch. **-κοίλιος**, ον, *bad for the bowels*, Dsc.1.105, Plu.2.137a. 2. *costive*, Paul.Aeg.1.44. **-κοινώνητος**, ον, *unsocial*, Pl.*R.*486b; ἀρχή Plu.*Demetr.*3. **-κοιτέω**, *to have bad nights*, Hp.*VM*10, *Acut.*30. **-κοιτος**, ον, *making bed unpleasant*, Aristaenet.2.7. **-κολαίνω**, impf. ἐδυσκόλαινον Pl.*Phlb.*26d: fut. -κολᾰνῶ Isoc.15.149:—*to be peevish*, Ar.*Nu.*36; of a baby, Lys.1.11, cf. X.*Mem.*2.2.8; τινί D.37.15; *feel a difficulty*, δ. ὡς.. Pl. l.c.; in argument, *to be captious*, Arist.*Top.*160ᵇ3, al. 2. *cause trouble* or *annoyance*, οὔρησις δυσκολαίνουσα Hp.*Prorrh.*1.109. **-κολία**, ἡ, *discontent, peevishness*, Ar.*V.*106, Pl.*R.*411c. II. of things, *difficulty*, δ. ἔχειν D.5.1, Arist.*Pol.*1281ᵃ14, etc.; πλείους παρέχειν δυσκολίας ib.1263ᵃ11; δ. ὀνομάτων J.*AJ*2.7.4. **-κόλλητος**, ον, *hard to glue together*, Gal.11.124,133; *ill-glued* or *fastened, loose*, Luc.*Hist.Conscr.*11.

δυσκολό-καμπτος, ον, *hard to bend*: δ. καμπή an *intricate* flourish in singing, Ar.*Nu.*971. **-κοιτος**, ον, *making bed uneasy*, μέριμνα ib.420.

δύσ-κολος, ον, (κόλον): I. of persons, prop. *hard to satisfy with food* (cf. Ath.6.262a): but, generally, *hard to please, discontented, fretful, peevish*, Ar.*V.*942; γῆρας E.*Ba.*1251; δ. ψυχὴ καὶ ἀγρία Pl.*Lg.*649e, cf. Arist.*EN*1108ᵃ30, etc.; τὸ δ. Pl.*Lg.*791c; of animals, *intractable*, Id.*Tht.*174d (Comp.): so in Adv. δυσκόλως ἔχειν, διακεῖσθαι πρός τινα, D.19.132, Isoc.3.33; δυσκολώτερον διακεῖσθαι Pl.*Phd.*84e. II. of things, *troublesome, harassing*, δ. ἡ ἡνιόχησις Id.*Phdr.*246b; πυρετοί Hp.*Coac.*38: generally, *unpleasant*, ἄν τι δ. συμβῇ D.18.189, cf. Men.89; εἴ τι δ. πέπρακται Θηβαίοις πρὸς ἡμᾶς D.18.176; καιροὶ δ. *difficult* times, *IG*2².682.33. Adv. -λως, ὑπακούειν Hp.*Epid.*3.8. 2. *difficult to explain*, Arist.*SE*180ᵇ5, *Metaph.*1001ᵇ1; δ. ἐστι it is *difficult*, *Ev.Marc.*10.24, cf. Onos.1.15 (Comp.); τὰ μὲν ῥάδια.. τὰ δὲ δ. Phld.*Po.*994.24. Adv. -λως *hardly, with difficulty*, *Ev.Marc.*10.23, al. **-κολπος**, ον, *with luckless womb*, γαστήρ, of a woman whose child was dead before birth, *AP*7.583 (Agath.). **-κόμιστος**, ον, *hard to bear, intolerable*, πότμος S.*Ant.*1346 (lyr.); τέκνα E.*HF*1422. **-κοπάνιστος** [ᾰ], ον, *hard to bake*, ἄρτος *EM*150.35. **-κοπος**, ον, (κόπτω) *hard to bruise*, Damocr.ap.Gal.13.636. **-κρᾱής**, ές, *intemperate*, Opp.*H.*2.517. **-κρανές**· αὐχμηρόν, Hsch.; cf. δυσχρανής. **-κρᾱσία**, ἡ, *bad temperament*, of the air, Str.6.4.1, Plu.*Alex.*58 (pl.); σώματος *Stoic.*3.216; τῶν ἐν ἡμῖν δυνάμεων Ph.1.29. (δυσκρᾰσίη Man.4.543.) **-κρᾰτής**, ές, = sq., δυσκρατέστατον πάντων ὁ λόγος Stob.3.33.10. **-κράτητος** [ᾰ], ον, *hard to control*, τὸ δ. τῆς ἐπιβολῆς D.S.3.3; *ungovernable, ill-disciplined*, J.*AJ*19.4.1; γηρῶντι ἤδη δ. εἶναι (sc. τὴν ἀρχήν) App.*Syr.*61. **-κρᾱτος**, ον, *of bad temperament*, ἀήρ Str.2.3.1, cf. Gal.9.912. Adv. -τως Id.10.518; διακεῖσθαι Ps.-Plu.*Vit.Hom.*202. **-κρῐνής**, ές, *hard to distinguish*, Plu.2.922a; = sq., Aët.5.10. **-κρίσιμος** [κρῐ], ον, = sq., Sch.Hp.2.272 D. **-κρῐτος**, ον, *hard to discern* or *interpret*, ἄστρων δύσεις A.*Pr.*458; κληδόνες ib.486; ὀνείρατα Id.*Ag.*981 (lyr.), cf. S.*Tr.*949 (lyr.); δ. νοῦσοι *hard to determine, doubtful*, Hp.*Aph.*3.8; but δύσκριτα ἐγένετο there was an *obscure crisis*, Id.*Epid.*3.12; δ. ἐστι πότερον.. ἤ.. *difficult of solution*, Id.*Aph.*1.12, Pl.*R.*433c. Adv. -τως *doubtfully, darkly*, A.*Pr.*662; δ. ἔχειν to be *in doubt*, Ar.*Ra.*1433. **-κροτος**, ον, *badly put together*: Adv. -τως, διακεῖσθαι to be in *bad* condition, Meno *Iatr.*13.20, cf. 9.16. **-κτητος**, ον, *hard to come by*, πραγματεία Plb.3.32.1; τἀγαθόν Phld.*Herc.*1251.4 (dub.). **-κῠβέω**, *to be unlucky at dice*, Ath.15.666d, Poll.9.94. **-κῠλίστως**, Adv. *rolling with difficulty*, δ. ἔχειν Philostr.Jun.*Im.*10. **-κύμαντος** [ῠ], ον, in A.*Ag.*653 δυσκύμαντα κακά evils *from the stormy sea*. **-κωφέω**, *to be hard of hearing*, Gal.12.653, *AP*7.731 (Leon.), Dsc.4.162. **-κωφία**, ἡ, *deafness*, Id.*Eup.*1.61. **-κωφος**, ον, *hard of hearing*, Hp.*Coac.*193, Arist.*Insomn.*459ᵇ21, Lxx *Ex.*4.11, Str.14.2.21; τὸ τοῦ γήρως δ. Plu.2.13e. **-λέαντος**, (λεαίνω) *hard to pound* or *bray*, Archig.ap.Aët.3.184. **-λείωτος**, ον, = foreg., opp. εὐλείωτος, Asclep.ap.Gal.13.677. **-λεκτος**, ον, *hard to tell*, A.*Pers.*702 (anap.). **-λεκτρος**, ον, *ill-wedded*, Sch.S.*El.*492. **-λεπής**, ές, *rough-husked*, κάρυον Nic.*Al.*271. **-λεχής**, gloss on δυσηλεγής, Hsch. **-ληπτος**, ον, *hard to take hold of*, Sor.1.88; *hard to catch*, μοχθηρία Ph.2.366, cf. Luc.*Anach.*27; *hard to comprehend*, Str.13.4.12, A.D.*Synt.*225.28, Plu.2.17d. **-λίμενος** [λῐ], ον, gloss on δύσορμος, Sch.rec.A.*Pers.*448. **-λόγιστος**, ον, *hard to compute*, Anaximen.ap.Stob.2.8.17, Plu.2.981e, Gal.18(2).631, D.C.73.15. II. Act., *ill-calculating, misguided*, χείρ S.*Aj.*40. **-λοφος**, ον, *hard for the neck, hard to bear*, ζεύγλη, ζυγόν, Thgn.848, 1024; χείρ B.12.46; δ. φρενί prob. l. in S.*Ichn.*4; δυσλοφωτέρους πόνους A.*Pr.*931. II. *impatient of the yoke*, ἡμίονοι Ael.*NA*16.9. Adv. -φως, φέρειν E.*Tr.*303. **-λῠτος**, ον, *indissoluble*, δυσλύτοις χαλκεύμασι A.*Pr.*19; ἄκος τῶν δ. πόνων E.*Andr.*121 (lyr.); ὦμοι *stiff*, Arist.*Phgn.*811ᵃ4. Adv. -τως, ἔχειν X.*Oec.*8.13. 2. *insoluble*, of a problem, Luc.*JTr.*12, Alex.Aphr. *in Metaph.*223.2; αἴνιγμα Plu.*Fr.*25.3; *hard to refute*, Alex.Aphr. *in Top.*558.25. **-λώσων**· δυσχερῶν, Hsch.

δυσμᾰθ-έω, *to be slow at recognizing*, A.*Ch.*225. **-ής**, ές, *hard to learn*, Id.*Ag.*1255; δ. ἰδεῖν *hard to know* at sight, E.*Med.*1196; τὸ δ. *difficulty of knowing*, Id.*IT*478. II. Act., *slow at learning, dull*, Pl.*R.*358a, etc.: Comp., Plu.2.992d: Sup., Ph.2.175, Jul.*Or.*7.225b. Adv. δυσμαθῶς, ἔχειν Pl.*R.*503d. **-ία**, ἡ, *slowness at learning*, ib.618d (pl.), *Lg.*812e, etc.:—written **-μάθεια**, Id.*Ep.*315c, Iamb.*VP*20.95.

Δύσμαιναι (perh. f. l. for Δύμ-), = βάκχαι, at Sparta, Hsch.; title of play by Pratinas, Ath.9.392f.

δυσ-μάλακτος [μᾰ], ον, *hard to soften*, Ruf.ap.Orib.8.24.22. **-μᾱνής**, ές, *thick*, ὕδατα Thphr.*HP*7.5.2. **-μάραντος** [μᾰ], ον, *unfading*, *Trag.Adesp.*339. **-μᾰρής**, ές, *difficult*, opp. εὐμαρής, ἀποτέλεσμα Phld.*Rh.*2.119S. **-μάσητος** [μᾰ], ον, *hard to chew*, Gal.16.760. **-μάτωρ**, Dor. for δυσμήτωρ.

δυσμᾰχ-έω, *fight in vain against* or *fight an unholy fight with*, θεοῖσι δυσμαχοῦντες S.*Tr.*492; πρὸς τὴν βελτίονα [δύναμιν] Plu.2.371a: abs., *fight desperately*, ib.661c. **-ητέον**, *one must fight a losing battle with*, ἀνάγκῃ δ' οὐχὶ δ. S.*Ant.*1106. **-ητος**, ον, *keenly contested*, δῶρα Μοισᾶν *Lyr.Adesp.*86 B (cf. B.*Fr.*32). **-ος**, ον, *hard to fight with, unconquerable*, X.*HG*4.2.10 (Comp.), E.*Hec.*1055 (Sup.); πάντων -ώτατον γυνή Id.*Fr.*544; of things, A.*Pr.*921, Pl.*Lg.*863b, D.1.4, etc. 2. generally, *difficult*, δ. κρῖναι A.*Ag.*1561 (lyr.).

δυσ-μεικτος or **-μικτος**, ον, *hard to mix*: *without affinity*, Pl.*Ti.*35a, etc. II. *unsocial*: Adv. -τως, ἔχειν Plu.2.640d. **-μείλικτος**, ον, *hard to appease*, Id.*Art.*19; πικρία Id.2.553a. **-μελῴδητος**, ον, *hard to employ in melody*, of enharmonic intervals, Theo Sm.p.56 H. (Sup.).

δυσμεν-αίνω, *bear ill-will*, τινί *against* another, E.*Med.*874; δ. τοῖς κοινοῖς ἀγαθοῖς D.18.217; δ. τῆς ποτὲ βίας App.*Pun.*60: abs., Ph.1.145. **-εια**, Ion. -ίη, ἡ, *ill-will, enmity*, ἡ ἐκ σοῦ δ. S.*El.*619; ἐν δ. εἶναι ib.1124; δ. ἄρασθαί τινι E.*Heracl.*991: in Prose, Democr.191, Antipho 4.1.3, etc.; φθόνος καὶ δ. Isoc.5.68, Pl.*R.*500c; φθόνοι καὶ ἄλλαι δ. Id.*Prt.*316d. **-έων**, participial form, only masc., *bearing ill-will, hostile*, Od.2.72; δυσμενέοντες ib.73, 20.314. **-ής**, ές, (μένος) *hostile*, ἄνδρες δ. Il.5.488; δυσμενέες *enemies*, 16.521, cf. *Schwyzer* 84.12; δυσμενέων ὄχλος A.*Th.*234 (lyr.), cf. 366 (lyr.), Hdt.3.82, S.*Aj.*662 (Sup.), etc.; οἱ ὑμέτεροι δ. X.*HG*5.2.33: c. dat., τῷ πατοῦντι δυσμενεῖς A.*Ag.*1193, cf. S.*Ph.*585; οὐδὲν τυράννου -έστερον πόλει E.*Supp.*429: less freq. c. gen., ἄνδρα δ. χθονός *an enemy of* the land, S.*Ant.*187, cf. Ph.2.136. Adv. -νῶς Pl.*Tht.*168b; δ. ἔχειν τινί Isoc.3.5; πρὸς τὴν πόλιν Id.14.6:—poet. **δυσμενέως**, Nonn.*D.*21.85 (v.l.). II. rarely of things, δ. χοαί S.*El.*440; δυσμενὲς ὁ τοῦ πλεονεκτεῖν ἔρως X.*Mem.*2.6.21, cf. E.*Alc.*617 (v.l.). **-ίδης**, ου, ὁ, = foreg., Ael.*VH*3.7. **-ικός**, ή, όν, *like an enemy, hostile*, Plb.6.7.8, etc. Adv. -κῶς Id.8.8.1.

δυσμέριστος, ον, *hard to chew up*, τραγήματα Philum.ap.Aët.9.23.

δυσμετα-βλησία, ἡ, *difficulty of alteration*, Sor.1.91. **-βλητος**, ον, *hard to alter*, Hp.*Alim.*51, Plu.2.952c. **-βολος**, ον, = foreg., Damocr.ap.Gal.13.1003. Adv. -λως ib.1004. **-δοτος**, ον, *not imparting freely*, Str.17.1.29: c. gen., *reluctant to part with*, τῶν ἀναγκαίων Phld.*Herc.*1251.20. **-θετος**, ον, *hard to alter*, of persons, *opinionated*, Plb.12.26ᵈ.5; προαίρεσις Plu.2.799b; *hard to remove*, Gal.11.215. **-κίνητος** [ῑ], ον, *hard to shift*, ψυχὴ δ. ἀπὸ τῶν χειρόνων J.*AJ*6.11.8; γυνή Plu.2.288d, Eust.1733.32. Adv. -τως, ἔχειν Alex.Trall.1.16. **-κλαστος**, ον, *hard to break* or *move*, Sch.S.*OT*12. **-κλητος**, ον, *hard to cure of a habit*, *Gp.*19.2.13. **-στρεπτος**, ον, *hard to divert*, Gal.19.489. Adv. -τως, gloss on ἀσκελέως, Apollon. *Lex.* **-τρεπτος**, ον, = foreg., Eust.1461.43. **-χείριστος**, ον, *hard to manage*, παῖς Pl.*Lg.*808d (Sup.), cf. Plu.*Mar.*37, al., Aen.Tact.39.7; ζῷα Ael.*NA*4.44; δίκτυα X.*Cyn.*2.6. 2. *hard to attack*, στρατός Hdt.7.236, J.*BJ*1.7.1; of the tortoise's shell, Hierocl. p.13 A.

δυσμέτρητος, ον, *hard to measure*, Antipho Soph.106. 2. *hard to traverse*, πέλαγος Philostr.*VA*4.15.

δυσμή, ἡ, (δύω) = δύσις, *setting*, mostly in pl., ἀελίου δ. S.*OC*1245, cf. A.*Fr.*69, Hp.*Epid.*7.5, Pl.*Phd.*61e; ἐπὶ δυσμῇσιν ἐών at the point of *setting*, Hdt.3.104; περὶ ἡλίου δυσμάς Lys.1.39; ἥλιος ἦν ἤδη περὶ δυσμάς *Hell.Oxy.*15.5: metaph., τὸ γῆρας δυσμαὶ βίου Arist.*Po.*1457ᵇ25, cf. D.H.4.79, Ph.1.678, S.E.*M.*9.90, Diog.Oen.2, etc. II. *the quarter of sunset, west*, ἀπὸ ἑσπέρης τε καὶ [ἡλίου] δυσμέων Hdt.2.31; πρὸς ἡλίου δυσμέων Id.7.115, cf. 2.33; πρὸς δυσμαῖς A.*Pers.*232; opp. ἀνατολαί, *BGU*1049.8 (iv A.D.):—also **δυθμή**, Call.*Cer.*10 (pl.), *Fr.*539 (sg.).

δύσ-μηνις, ι, *wrathful*, θεός Poll.1.39; χόλος *AP*9.69 (Parmenion). **-μήνῐτος**, ον, = foreg., δένδρεα *AP*7.141 (Antiphil.); ψυχαί Ptol.*Tetr.*159 (-ίτας). **-μήτηρ**, ερος, ἡ, in Od.23.97 μῆτερ ἐμὴ δύσμητερ my mother *yet no mother*, cf. Lyc.1174, Nonn.*D.*46.194. **-μητις**, ι, *contriving ill*, Suid., Hsch. (cod. -ήτης). **-μήτωρ**,

Dor. **-μάτωρ,** ορος, ὁ, ἡ, in A.*Supp.*67 (lyr.) δ. κότος *an ill mother's wrath.* **-μηχᾰνέω,** *to be at loss how* to do, c. inf., A.*Ag.* 1360. **-μήχᾰνος,** ον, *hard to effect,* Epimen.ap.D.L.1.113; *difficult,* Ἀρχύτεω δυσμήχανα ἔργα κυλίνδρων Eratosth.*Fr.*35.7; prob. f.l. for δύσμαχον, J.*BJ*4.1.2. II. Act., *at a loss,* πρός τι Them.*Or.* 10.137b. III. *devising ill,* Nonn.*D.*44.210; δόλος ib.35.273; also, *ill-devised, wicked,* ἔργον Opp.*H.*3.404.

δυσμικός, ή, όν, (δυσμή) = δυτικός, *western,* Str.2.5.11, Hld.8.15: Comp., Str.2.1.34, Ptol.*Alm.*2.13, Theo Sm.p.137 H.: Sup., Str. 2.1.32, Ptol.*Geog.*2.3.18.

δύσ-μικτος, v. δύσμεικτος. **-μίμητος** [ῑ], ον, *hard to imitate,* D.S.1.61, Luc.*Alex.*20, *CIG*3187 (Smyrna); τὸ δ. Plu.*Cat.Mi.*8: Sup., Anon.*Oxy.*1012 ii 34. **-μίσητος** [ῑ], ον, *much hated,* Lyc. 841. **-μνημόνευτος,** ον, *hard to remember,* Arist.*Rh.*1416^{b}22, Aen.Tact.24.2, Epicur.*Ep.*2 p.35 U., D.S.1.3. II. Act., *remembering ill, unmindful,* Pl.*Ti.*74e (Comp.). **-μοιρος,** ον, (μοῖρα) = δύσμορος, S.*OC*327. **-μορία,** ἡ, *a hard fate, AP*9.351 (Leon.). **-μορος,** ον, *ill-fated,* Il.22.60, etc.; δυσμόρου γε δύσμορα (sc. σκῆπτρα) S. *OC*1109, cf. Men.*Sam.*40, Lyc.897, Opp.*C.*3.217: in Prose, Antipho 3.2.11. Adv. -ρως *with ill fortune,* prob. in A.*Th.*837 (lyr., cod. M -φόρως). **-μορφία,** ἡ, *misshapenness, ugliness,* Hdt.6.61, Phld. *Mort.*29, etc. **-μορφος,** ον, *misshapen, ill-favoured,* ἐσθής E.*Hel.* 1204, Lyc.692, Plu.2.670a. **-μουσος,** ον, = ἄμουσος, *unmusical,* αὐλός *AP*9.216 (Honestus). **-μόχλευτος,** ον, *hard to dislodge,* Aët.3.34, Simp.*in Cat.*236.27. **-νίκητος** [ῑ], ον, *hard to conquer,* ἔρως J.*AJ*18.1.6, cf. Plu.*Comp.Pel.Marc.*2, D.C.43.28. **-νιπτος,** ον, *hard to wash out,* δ. ἐκ δέλτου γραφή S.*Tr.*683. **-νῐφος,** ον, (νίψ) *snowed upon,* Nonn.*D.*2.685. 2. *chilly, wintry,* ὕδωρ ib.3. 210; οἶδμα ib.13.533. **-νοέω,** *to be ill-affected,* τινί Lxx 3 *Ma.*3.24, Plu.*Cic.*38. **-νόητος,** ον, *hard to be understood,* Darius ap. D.L. 9.13, 2 *Ep.Pet.*3.16; χρησμοί Luc.*Alex.*54. II. Act., *slow of understanding,* Vett.Val.345.26. **-νοια,** ἡ, *disaffection, ill-will, malevolence,* S.*El.*654, E.*Hec.*973, Pl.*Tht.*151d, Plu.*Demetr.*3, Phld. *Lib.*p.29 O., etc. **-νομία,** Ep. and Ion. -ίη, ἡ, *lawlessness, bad constitution,* Sol.4.32: personified in Hes.*Th.*230. **-νομος,** ον, *lawless, unrighteous, AP*6.316 (Nicodem.). **-νοος,** ον, contr. **-νους,** ουν, *ill-affected, disaffected,* τινί S.*Ant.*212; τῇ πόλει Th.2.60; πρὸς τὰ πράγματα X.*HG*2.1.2: abs., E.*IT*350, Plu.2.176b. Adv. δυσνως Poll.2.230. **-νοστος** νόστος a return *that is no return,* E. *Tr.*75. II. *from which no traveller returns,* ῥόος *App.Anth.*4. 54. **-νουθέτητος,** ον, *hard to be corrected,* θηρίον (sc. πενία) Men. *Georg.*78. **-νύμφευτος,** ον, *ill-wedded, AP*7.401 (Crin.). **-νυμφος,** ον, *ill-wedded* or *ill-betrothed,* E.*IT*216 (lyr.), *Tr.*144 (lyr.). **-ξενος,** ον, *inhospitable,* Poll.9.22. **-ξήραντος,** ον, *hard to dry,* Thphr.*CP* 1.4.3, Plu.2.627d, etc. **-ξύμβλητος,** ον, *hard to understand,* Corn.*ND*28, D.C.56.29. **-ξύμβολος,** ον, *hard to deal with, driving a hard bargain,* Pl.*R.*486b, X.*Mem.*2.6.3, Plu.*Phoc.*5. II. = foreg., Poll.5.150. III. *ill to meet,* ζῷα Artem.4.56 (v.l. δυσσυμβούλευτα). **-ξύνετος,** ον, *hard to understand,* δυσξύνετον ξυνετὸς μέλος ἔγνω E.*Ph.*1506 (lyr.); διαγράμματα X.*Mem.*4.7.3; τὸ δ., τὰ δ., Plu.2.975f (δυσξύνθετον codd.), Iamb.*VP*35.252. **-ογκος,** ον, *overheavy, burdensome,* πλοῦτος Plu.*Aem.*12.

δυσόδ-ευτος, ον, *hardly passable,* App.*Syr.*21. **-έω,** *make bad way, get on slowly,* Plu.*Pyrrh.*32; of difficult breathing or childbirth, Ph.2.563, Sor.2.59: metaph., Arr.*Epict.*3.19.3. **-ία,** ἡ, *badness of roads,* App.*Syr.*21: pl., in concrete sense, Ptol.*Tetr.*197: metaph., *difficulty,* -ίαν παρέχειν τῷ λόγῳ Plu.2.448a, cf. Ph.2.67; δυσοδία ἐντροχάζειν δοκεῖ Demetr.Lac.1012.50 F.; δ. σκυβάλων Sor. 2.20.

δύσ-οδμία, δύσοδμος, v. sub δυσοσμ-. **-οδοπαίπᾰλος,** ον, *difficult and rugged,* prop. of a mountain road: metaph., A.*Eu.*387 (lyr.). **-οδος,** ον, *hard to pass, scarce passable,* Th.1.107, Poll.3. 96. **-οίζω** (aor. ἐδύσοιξα Hsch.), *to be distressed,* E.*Rh.*724 (lyr.); *fear, tremble at,* οὔτοι δυσοίζω θάμνον ὡς ὄρνις φόβῳ A.*Ag.*1316:— Med., *fear,* E.*Rh.*805. (Lacon. acc. to Hsch.) **-οίκητος,** ον, *bad to dwell in,* Hp.*Aër.*19, X.*Cyr.*8.6.21. **-οικονόμητος,** ον, *hard to digest,* Diph.Siph.ap.Ath.2.70a, Xenocr.73. II. *difficult to manage,* τὸ δ. Artem.2.58. **-οικος,** ον, gloss on ἄοικος, Sch.S. *Ph.*534. **-οικτος·** δυσθρήνητος, Hsch. **-οιμος,** ον, acc. to Sch. and Hsch., = δύσοδος, τύχα δ. A.*Ch.*945 (lyr.); or perh. (οἴμη), *a sad theme,* cf. δύσοιμος· ἐπὶ κακῷ ἤκουσα, Hsch. **-οινος,** ον, *yielding bad wine,* Poll.6.21. **-οιστος,** ον, (οἴσω) *hard to bear, insufferable,* ὀδμή Hp.*Mul.*2.181; πήματα, ἄλγη, πόνοι, A.*Pr.*690 (lyr.), *Ch.*745, S.*Ph.*508 (lyr.); βίου δύσοιστον ἕξομεν τροφάν Id.*OC* 1688 (lyr.); δ. ἀήρ Str.12.3.40; ὀργή Jul.*Gal.*161b.

δῠσοιων-έω, (οἰωνός) *augur ill of* a thing, Phryn.*PS*p.62 B. **-ισμός,** ὁ, *an ill omen,* Hsch. s.v. ἀπήχεια. **-ιστικός,** ή, όν, *ill-omened,* Suid. s.v. ἐς κόρακας. **-ιστος,** ον, = foreg., Ph.2.542, Hermog. *Stat.*3, Luc.*Eun.*6, D.C.41.49.

δύσ-οκνος [ῠ], ον, *very lazy*: Adv. -κνως, ἐξεγείρεσθαι M.Ant.5.1; *unwillingly,* καταλείπειν τέκνα Hdn.6.7.1. **-όλισθος,** ον, *not slipping easily,* Paul.Aeg.3.76.

δύσομαι, v. δύω.

δύσομβρος [ῠ], ον, *stormy*: metaph., βέλη S.*Ant.*358 (lyr.).

δυσομίλ-ητος [ῑ], ον, *hard to live with,* σκαιὸς καὶ δ. Hierocl.p.59 A.; δ. παροικοῦσα πόλις ἐχθρά D.Chr.40.27. **-ία,** ἡ, *unsociableness,* Satyr.*Vit.Eur.Fr.*39 x 5. **-ος,** ον, *hard to live with,* Plu. *Demetr.*42. II. *bringing evil in one's company,* Ἐρινύς A.*Ag.*746 (lyr.).

δῠσ-όμμᾰτος, ον, *scarce-seeing, purblind,* A.*Eu.*388 (lyr.). **-όμοιος,** ον, *unlike,* Stratt.75, Hsch. **-οναρ,** *infaustus, Gloss.* **-όνειρος,** ον, *full of ill dreams,* ὕπνος Plu.2.15b. II. *bringing ill dreams,* βρώματα ib.734f, cf. Dsc.2.105. **-οπαίοντα·** δυστυχοῦντα, Hsch. **-οπον·** δύσφωνον, Id. **-οπτος,** ον, (ὄψομαι) *hard to detect,* Gal.*Anim.Pass.*2.3; τὸ δ. τῆς ἡμέρας *gloominess,* Plb.18.21. 2. **-ορᾱσία,** ἡ, *dim sight,* Ruf.ap.Orib.7.26.15 (pl.). **-ὅρᾱτος,** ον, *hard to see,* X.*Cyr.*1.6.40, Ph.1.570; δι' ὑπερβολὰν λαμπρότατος δ. Ecphant.ap.Stob.4.7.64; τὰ δυσόρατα *dark corners,* X.*Eq.Mag.*4. 18. II. *ill to look on, horrible,* App.*Hisp.*97.

δῠσοργ-ησία, ἡ, = *passionateness,* Hp.*Hum.*9 (pl.). **-ητος,** ον, = δύσοργος, Arist.*Phgn.*811^{a}31, [Babr.]11.12; θεός Poll.1.39. Adv. -τως D.H.6.47. **-ία,** ἡ, = δυσοργησία, v.l. in Hp.*VM* 10. **-ος,** ον, *quick to anger,* S.*Aj.*1017, *Ph.*377, *Tr.*1118 (wrongly expld. by κακοεργός, Hsch.).

δῠσ-ορεξία, ἡ, *lack of appetite,* Gal.7.128. **-όριστος,** ον, *difficult to adapt to a limit,* Arist.*Mete.*378^{b}24, *GC*329^{b}32. II. *difficult to define,* χαρακτήρ D.H.*Din.*5. **-ορκέω,** (ὅρκος) *swear falsely,* Phryn.*PS*p.65 B. **-όρμιστος,** ον, (ὁρμίζω) = sq., Poll.1. 101. **-ορμος,** ον, *with bad anchorage,* νῆσος .. δ. ναυσί A.*Pers.* 448; also τὰ δ. *rough* ground, *where one can scarce get footing,* X.*Cyn.* 10.7. II. Act., πνοαὶ δ. *that detained* the fleet *in harbour* or *that kept* it *from reaching harbour, foul* winds, A.*Ag.*193 (lyr.). **-ορνις,** ῑθος, ὁ, ἡ, = δυσοιώνιστος, *boding ill,* Id.*Th.*838 (lyr.), E.*Hipp.*757 (lyr.); *with ill auspices,* Plu.*Marc.*4. **-όρφναιος,** α, ον, *dusky,* τρύχη E.*Ph.*325 (lyr.). **-οσμία,** ἡ, *an ill smell,* S.*Ph.*876, *Fr.*538, Luc.*Tox.*29; -ίη Man.4.270. **-οσμος,** Ion. **-οδμος,** ον, (ὀσμή) *ill-smelling,* ἐν δυσοδμοτάτῳ [τόπῳ] γινόμενον εὐωδέστατόν ἐστι Hdt. 3.112; ὀσμή Arist.*Pr.*908^{b}29 (Comp.). II. *bad for scent,* in hunting, οἱ ὄμβροι τὴν γῆν ποιοῦσι δύσοσμον X.*Cyn.*5.3. III. Act., *having a bad nose,* Arist.*Insomn.*459^{b}22. IV. δύσοσμον, τό, = σκόρδιον, Ps.-Dsc.3.111.

δῠσούλωτος, ον, *hard to scar over,* Alex.Trall.4.1, Poll.4.196.

δῠσουρ-έω, *to have difficulty in micturition,* Diocl.*Fr.*141, Ruf.ap. Orib.8.24.6, Dsc.1.6, *POxy.*468.1, Aret.*SD*2.4:—Med., Hp.*Vict.*2. 54. **-ητικός,** ή, όν, *suffering from* δυσουρία, *Gloss.* **-ία,** Ion. **-ίη,** ἡ, *difficult micturition,* Hp.*Aph.*3.31 (pl.), Arist.*Fr.*486; ἐν -ίᾳ γενέσθαι Plu.2.733c. **-ίασις,** εως, ἡ, = foreg., Ar.Byz.*Epit.*146. 5, Suid. s.v. τέτανος. **-ιάω,** = δυσουρέω, Dsc.1.33, *Hippiatr.* 31. **-ικός,** ή, όν: πάθος δ., = δυσουρία, f.l. in Cic.*Fam.*7.26.

δῠσ-ούριστος, ον, (οὐρίζω) *driven by a too favourable wind, fatally favourable,* S.*OT*1315 (lyr.). **-ουρον·** δυσφύλακτον, Hsch. **-όφθαλμος,** ον, *offensive to the sight,* αἶσχος Telest.1.3.

δυσπάθ-εια [πᾰ], or **-ία** (Hsch.), ἡ, *deep affliction,* Plu.2.112b. II. *firmness in resisting,* Plu.*Demetr.*21: in pl., *capabilities of endurance,* Id.2.666b; *insensitivity,* Alex.Aphr.*Pr.*1.39. **-έω,** *suffer a hard fate,* Mosch.4.84; of sickness, *suffer severely,* ῥινῷ δ. Nic.*Th.*381; *to be in a bad way,* Plb.29.7.4. II. *to be impatient,* ἐπί τινι, πρός τι, Plu.*Aem.*36, *Per.*33; ἔν τινι Id.2.77e. **-ής,** ές, (παθεῖν) *feeling to excess,* opp. ἀπαθής, ib.102d. II. *not easily affected,* τὸ ὅμοιον ὑπὸ τοῦ ὁμοίου -έστερον ib.651c: abs., *impassive,* ib.454c, Luc.*Anach.* 24, Plot.1.4.8.

δῠσ-παίπᾰλος, ον, *rough and steep,* βῆσσαι Archil.115; κύματα B. 5.26; Ὄθρυς Nic.*Th.*145; *rough,* λάχνη Opp.*H.*2.369, cf. *C.*2.381, al. **-παις,** *unhappy child,* Sch.rec.S.*OT*1243. **-πάλαιστος** [πᾰ], ον, *hard to wrestle with,* [Epich.]254; ἀρά A.*Ch.*692; πράγματα Id.*Supp.*468; γῆρας E.*Supp.*1108; δύναμις X.*HG*5.2.18; cf. δυσπέλαστος. 2. *unskilled at wrestling,* Philostr.*Gym.*40. **-πάλᾰμος** [πᾰ], ον, *hard to struggle with,* δόλοι θεῶν A.*Eu.*847 (lyr.); *hard to beat,* περὶ τὴν τέχνην Tz.ap.Suid. s.v. Λυκόφρων. II. *helpless*: Adv. δυσπαλάμως, ὀλέσθαι to perish *helplessly,* A.*Supp.*867 (lyr.). **-πᾰλής,** ές, *hard to wrestle with,* δίνα Id.*Eu.*559 (lyr.); *difficult,* c. inf., διακρίνειν .. δυσπαλές [ἐστι] Pi.*O.*8.25, cf. *P.*4.273, Cerc.*Fr.Oxy.*26. 2. *dangerous, noxious,* ῥίζαι A.R.4.52. 3. *stubborn,* Nicom.*Harm.* 3. **-πάμφαλος·** δυστάραχος, δυσκίνητος, Hsch.; cf. δυσπέμφελος.

δυσπαρά-βᾰτος, gloss on δυσοδοπαίπαλος, Sch.A.*Eu.*387. **-βλητος,** ον, *incomparable,* Plu.*Ant.*27. **-βοήθητος,** ον, *hard to assist,* Plb.5.22.7. **-βουλος,** ον, *hard to persuade,* A.*Supp.*108 (lyr.).

δυσπαράγγελτος, ον, *hardly to be reduced to rule* or *formulated,* Plb.12.25^{i}.7.

δυσπαράγρᾰφος, ον, *hard to define,* ποσότης Plb.16.12.10; *hard to state precisely,* Id.18.15.1; *hard to terminate,* of life, Phld.*Herc.* 1251.16.

δυσπαράγωγος [ᾰγ], ον, *hard to mislead,* Poll.8.10.

δυσπαρά-δεκτος, ον, *hard to admit* or *believe,* S.E.*M.*9.42, Alex. Aphr.*in Sens.*18.18. II. Act., *hardly admitting,* Sor.2.62. Adv., metaph., δυσπαραδέκτως ἔχειν *to be sceptical,* Plb.12.4.7. **-θελκτος,** ον, *hard to assuage,* A.*Supp.*386 (lyr.).

δυσπαραίτητος, ον, *hard to move by prayer, inexorable,* φρένες A. *Pr.*34; ὀργή Plb.30.31.13; of a person, Plu.*Cat.Mi.*1. 2. *difficult to refuse,* Id.2.531d, 602f.

δυσπαράκλητος, ον, *inexorable,* Sch.S.*OT*334; τὸ δ. τοῦ τρόπου J.*AJ*16.5.4 (v.l. δυσπαραιτ-).

δυσπαρᾰκολούθητος, ον, *hard to follow,* i.e. *hard to understand,* Men.490, D.H.*Pomp.*5, Corn.*ND*7, J.*AJ*11.3.10, Arr.*Epict.*2.12. 10. II. Act., *hard of understanding, dull,* M.Ant.5.5 (Comp.).

δυσπαρα-κόμιστος, ον, *hard to carry along,* Plu.*Demetr.*19; πλοῦς δ. a *difficult* voyage, Plb.3.61.2. **-μύθητος** [μῡ], ον, *hard to appease,* Pl.*Ti.*69d, Plu.*Mar.*45. II. *admitting no consolation,* συμφορά, πάθος, J.*AJ*2.9.2, Poll.3.101. **-πειστος**, ον, *hard to dissuade*, prob. in Arist.*Phgn.*809a35 (Comp.). **-πλευστος**, ον, *hard to sail along*, Str.16.4.18. **-πλους**, ουν, = foreg., D.S.3.44. **-ποίητος**, ον, *hard to alter* or *forge*, Gal.14.52, Ammon.*Diff.*74. **-τήρητος**, ον, *hard to observe*, Antig.*Mir.*126, Porph.*Abst.*3.4. **-τρεπτος**, ον, *hard to seduce* or *bribe*, Poll.8.10.

δυσπάρευνος, ον, *ill-mated*, λέκτρον S.*Tr.*791.

δυσπαρηγόρητος, ον, = sq., ἐπιθυμία J.*AJ*16.7.4. II. *inconsolable*, Plu.2.74e; *admitting no consolation*, συμφορά Phalar.*Ep.*144.1; *hard to soothe*, ἄλγημα Herod.Med.ap.Aët.9.2.

δυσπαρήγορος, ον, *hard to appease*, A.*Eu.*384 (lyr.).

δυσπάρθενος, ον, *a virgin to her cost*, Ἠχώ Nonn.*D.*16.324; Αὔρη ib.48.421.

Δύσπᾰρις, ιδος, ὁ, *unhappy Paris, Paris of ill omen*, Il.3.39, 13.769, Luc.*DMort.*19.1.

δυσπάρ-ῐτος, ον, *hard to pass*, X.*An.*4.1.25. **-οδος**, ον, *hard to enter*, Apollod.Hist.ap.Ath.15.682d. **-οξύνομαι**, Pass., *have a severe attack*, of fever, Alex.Trall.*Febr.*2.

δυσ-πάτητος [ᾰ], ον, *hard to the feet*, ὁδός Luc.*Trag.*227. **-παυστος**, ον, *hard to stop* or *appease*, Gal.1.334.

δυσπειθ-εια, ἡ, *indiscipline, disobedience*, App.*BC*1.48. **-έω**, *to be refractory*, *POxy.*44.6 (i A.D.). **-ής**, ές, *hard to persuade, not easily talked over*, Pl.*Phdr.*271d. 2. *self-willed, disobedient*, Id.*Lg.*880a, Hierocl.p.63A.; κύνες X.*Mem.*4.1.3 (Sup.). 3. *hard to believe*, Phld.*D.*3.12. 4. Adv. -θῶς, ἔχειν πρός τι Plu.*Galb.*25; δ. φέρειν Id.*Lys.*15; *with difficulty*, κάμπτεσθαι Hero *Bel.*75.9.

δυσ-πειρία, Ion. -ίη, ἡ, *difficulty of learning by experiment*, Hp.*Hum.*1. **-πειστέω**, *disbelieve*, Tz.*H.*7.34. **-πειστος**, ον, *hard to persuade, opinionated*, Arist.*EN*1151b6; ὄμματα ἀκοῆς D.Chr.12.71 (Comp.). Adv. -τως, ἔχειν to be *incredulous*, Isoc.4.18. II. *disobedient*, X.*Eq.Mag.*1.23. **-πέλαστος**, ον, *dangerous to come near*, δ. ἀμαθία κακόν (Nauck δυσπάλαιστον) S.*Fr.*924. **-πεμπτος**, ον, *hard to banish*, A.*Ag.*1190. **-πέμφελος**, ον, *rough and stormy*, εἰ καὶ δυσπέμφελος εἴη (sc. πόντος) Il.16.748: as a general epith. of the sea, οἳ γλαυκὴν δυσπέμφελον ἐργάζονται Hes.*Th.*440; ναυτιλίη δ. *stormy* passage, Id.*Op.*618; αὔρη Nonn.*D.*2.550: metaph., *rude, uncourteous*, Hes.*Op.*722; δ. εὐνή, of a wife, Max.88. **-πένθερος**, ον, *of an evil father-in-law*, θεσμά Nonn.*D.*3.309.

δυσπενθ-έω, *to be sore afflicted*, Plu.2.106a (v.l.). **-ής**, ές, *bringing sore affliction, direful*, κάματος Pi.*P.*12.10; δόλος ib.11.18; θαλάμοιο ..δυσπενθέα κόσμον *Epigr.Gr.*431 (Antioch); Ἀΐδας *IPE*2.286.5 (Panticapaeum). 2. *bitterly lamented*, of the dead, Opp.*H.*4.261.

δυσ-πέπαντος, ον, *hard to soften*, Sch.S.*Aj.*205. **-πεπτέω**, *digest with difficulty*, Dsc.5.6:—Pass., Id.4.82. **-πεπτος**, ον, *hard to digest*, Arist.*GA*776a12, al., Nicom.Com.1.31, Dsc.1.125; *refusing to be assimilated*, Pl.*Ti.*83a. 2. *unripe*, v.l. ap.Sch. in Nic.*Al.*297. **-περαίωτος**, ον, = sq., ποταμός Ps.-Callisth.3.10. **-πέρᾱτος**, ον, *hard to pass* or *cross*, ὑπερβολαὶ ὄρους Str.4.6.6, cf. 15.1.26 (Comp.): metaph., ἀμηχανίας δ. αἰών E.*Med.*646 (lyr.).

δυσπερι-άγωγος [ᾰγ], ον, *hard to wheel about*, Arr.*Tact.*16.8. **-αίρετος**, ον, *hard to strip off, peel*, φλοιός prob. in Thphr.*HP*5.1.1. **-γένητος**, ον, *hard to overcome*, Ph.1.621. **-γράφος**, ον, *hard to treat comprehensively*, πραγματεία Sor.1.78. **-κάθαρτος** [κᾰ], ον, *hard to peel, clean off*, φλοιός Thphr.*HP*5.1.1 codd. (leg. -αίρετος). **-κτητος**, ον, *not successful in acquiring property*, Paul.Al.*N.*3. **-ληπτος**, ον, *hard to encompass*, γαστήρ Posidon.6J.; πόλις τοῖς ἐναντίοις δ. Arist.*Pol.*1330b3; στελέχη δ. πέντε ἀνθρώποις Str.15.1.21. II. *hard to embrace in one view, treat synoptically*, D.S.1.3. III. *hard to get*, φιλήματα *AP*12.200 (Strat.). **-νόητος**, ον, *hard to conceive*, Ph.1.570. **-τρεπτος**, ον, *hard to overturn*, ἕδρα Gal.*UP*3.9. Adv. -τως Id.18(1).591. **-ψυκτος**, ον, *hard to chill*, Dsc.1.30, Sor.1.100.

δυσπετ-έω, *fall out ill*, Suid. **-ημα**, ατος, τό, *misfortune*, Lxx 2*Ma.*5.20. **-ής**, ές, *falling out ill, most difficult*, μαθεῖν δ. S.*Aj.*1046. Adv. -τῶς, Ion. -έως Hdt.3.107; δ. φέρειν Hp.*Prog.*15, A.*Pr.*752: Comp. -εστέρως Hp.*Morb.*1.22.

δυσ-πεψία, ἡ, *indigestion*, Macho ap.Ath.8.341b, Ph.2.352, Dsc.5.45, Gal.7.66. **-πήμαντος**, ον, *full of grievous evil, disastrous*, A.*Eu.*481 (as Scaliger for δυσπῆμαθ'; cf. δυσκύμαντος). **-πῐνής**, ές, *squalid*, στολαί S.*OC*1597, cf. Ar.*Ach.*426. **-πιστέω**, *mistrust*, τινί Plu.2.593a. **-πιστία**, ἡ, *disbelief*, Aët.7.118. **-πιστος**, ον, *hard of belief, distrustful*: Adv. -τως, ἔχειν πρός τι to be *incredulous* about a thing, Pl.*Erx.*405b. II. Pass., *hard to be believed*, Vett.Val.108.13, Palaeph.30: Comp., D.Chr.32.64. III. *superstitious*, Hsch. **-πλᾰνος**, ον, *wandering in misery*, A.*Pr.*608 (lyr.); δ. ἀλατεῖαι ib.900 (lyr.). **-πληκτος**, ον, *not easily terrified*, ὑπὸ φόβων Ph.2.665, cf. Andronic.Rhod.p.575M. II. *hard to hit*, Simp.*in Cat.*247.7. **-πλήρωτος**, ον, *hard to fill* or *fulfil*, Poll.9.21. **-πλῆτις**, f.l. for δασ-, Lyc.1452, Suid. **-πλοΐα**, Ion. -πλοΐη, ἡ, *difficulty of sailing*, *AP*7.630 (Antiphil.), Str.1.2.31: pl., Ph.1.601:—written -πλωΐα, *Cat.Cod.Astr.*2.178. **-πλοος**, ον, contr. -πλους, ουν, *dangerous for ships*, Κρήτα *AP*7.275 (Gaet.). **-πλῠτος**, ον, *hard to wash clean*, Hp.*Mul.*2.122. **-πλωτος**, ον, = δύσπλοος, *AP*7.699. **-πνευστος**, ον, gloss on δυσαής, Hsch. **-πνοέω**, Ion. **-πνοιέω**, *breathe with difficulty*, Aret.*SD*1.11, Gal.19.423. **-πνόητος**, ον, dub. in Hp.*Judic.*35. **-πνοια**, ἡ, *difficulty of breathing, shortness of breath*, Id.*Aph.*3.31, X.*Cyn.*9.20, Nymphis 16, Aret.*SA*1.9, etc. II. *contrary winds*, Sch.A.R.4.1. **-πνοϊκός**, ή, όν, *short of breath*, Dsc.4.134 (v.l.), Asclep.ap.Gal.13.108, *Hippiatr.*27. **-πνοος**, ον, contr. **-πνους**, ουν, *scant of breath*, Hp.*Prog.*17 (Comp.), S.*Ant.*224. II. *unfit to breathe*, ἀήρ Thphr.*Ign.*24. III. δ. πνοαί *contrary* winds, S.*Ant.*588 (lyr.).

δυσ-πολέμητος, ον, *hard to war with*, A.*Supp.*648 (lyr., s.v.l.), Isoc.4.138; εἰ δέ τις .. δ. οἴεται τὸν Φίλιππον εἶναι D.4.4; δ. ὅπλον, of friendship, Luc.*Tox.*36. **-πόλεμος**, ον, *unlucky in war*, A.*Pers.*1013 (lyr.). II. = foreg., Γαλάται *IG*11(4).1105 (Delos, iii B.C.), Lxx 2*Ma.*12.21. **-πολιόρκητος**, ον, *hard to take by siege*, X.*HG*4.8.5 (Comp.), Plb.5.3.4, J.*AJ*2.10.2; τὸ δ. Corn.*ND*20. **-πολίτευτος** [ῑ], ον, *unfit for public business*, τὸ δ. Plu.*Dio* 32.

δυσπον-ής, ές, *toilsome*, δυσπονέος καμάτοιο Od.5.493. Adv. -έως Max.194. **-ητος**, ον, *bringing toil and trouble*, δαίμων A.*Pers.*515; δυσπόνητον ἕξετ' ἀμφ' ἐμοὶ τροφὴν *laborious*, S.*OC*1614. **-ία**, ἡ, *toil and trouble*, Man.4.260. **-ος**, ον, *toilsome*, S.*Ant.*1276 (lyr.).

δυσπόρ-ευτος, ον, *hard to pass*, πηλὸς ταῖς ἁμάξαις δ. X.*An.*1.5.7; ἀνοδίαι Ph.2.14; ὁδοί D.C.53.22. **-έω**, *have a toilsome march*, J.*BJ* 3.6.2.

δυσπόρθητος, ον, *hard to sack*, Sch.rec.A.*Pr.*166.

δυσπορία, ἡ, *difficulty of passing*, τοῦ ποταμοῦ X.*An.*4.3.7.

δυσπόριστος, ον, *hard to come by* or *procure*, opp. εὐπ., Epicur.*Ep.*3p.63U., cf. Phld.*Herc.*1251.12, D.H.1.37, D.Chr.7.152, Muson.*Fr.*18Ap.94H., Plu.2.156f; σχήματα Alex.*Fig.*1.1; δ. ἡ ἀρετὴ τοῦ σωφρονεῖν J.*AJ*19.2.5; τὸ δ. *difficulty of getting*, τῶν ἀναγκαίων Ph.1.19, cf. Plu.*Sol.*23.

δύσπορος, ον, *scarcely passable*, Pl.*Cra.*420e, X.*An.*6.5.12. 2. *difficult to get*, τροφή Corn.*ND*28, Poll.5.105.

δυσποτμ-έω, *despair of oneself*, ἐν ἀρρωστίαις Plb.33.17.1. **-ία**, ἡ, *ill luck, ill success*, D.H.9.28, Them.*Or.*13.170a. **-ος**, ον, *unlucky, ill-starred*, of persons and things, δ. θεός, of Prometheus, A.*Pr.*119; δ. βοῦς, of Io, Id.*Supp.*306; δ. εὐχαί, i.e. *curses*, Id.*Th.*820; χλιδά S.*OT*888 (lyr.); θήρα E.*Ba.*1144, cf. Ar.*Ach.*419; τύχαι D.H.1.17: Comp. -ώτερος E.*Ph.*1348: Sup. -ότατος Plu.*Comp.Per.Fab.*1. Adv. -μως A.*Pers.*272 (lyr.): Sup. -ότατα Plu.*Fab.*18.

δύσποτος, ον, *unpalatable*, πῶμα A.*Eu.*266.

δύσπους, ποδος, ὁ, ἡ, *slow of foot*, Call.*Fr.*1.63P.

δυσπρᾱγ-έω, *to be unlucky*, A.*Ag.*790 (anap.), Plu.*Ant.*63, Al.*Jb.*5.24. **-ής**, ές, *faring ill*, Vett.Val.16.21. **-ία**, *ill luck, ill success*, Gorg.*Hel.*9 (pl.), Antipho 2.49, Ph.2.75, Jul. *ad Them.*257b.

δυσ-πραγμάτευτος [μᾰ], ον, *hard to manage*, λαός Plu.2.348f. **-πρακτος**, ον, *hard to do*, Poll.3.131, 5.105. **-πραξία**, ἡ, *ill success, ill luck*, A.*Pr.*966, S.*OC*1399, And.2.5, Men.707: pl., A.*Eu.*769, S.*Aj.*759, Isoc.6.102. **-πρᾱτος**, ον, *hard to sell*: name of a play by Antiphanes, Ath.6.262c. **-πράϋντος** [ᾱ], ον, *hard to tame*, Hsch. s.v. δυσγάργαλις. **-πρέπεια**, ἡ, *indecency*, J.*AJ*3.7.4. **-πρεπής**, ές, *base, undignified*, E.*Hel.*300. **-πριστος**, ον, *hard to saw through*, Thphr.*HP*5.6.3. **-πρόκοπος**, ον, *making progress with difficulty*, Vett.Val.76.24.

δυσπρόσ-βᾰτος, ον, *hard to approach*, Th.4.129, D.C.56.12. **-δεκτος**, ον, *hardly admitted, disagreeable*, Plu.2.39d. II. Act., *disinclined to entertain*, διαβολῆς M.Ant.1.5. **-ήγορος**, ον, *hard to speak with, repulsive*, D.C.*Fr.*11.6, Poll.1.42. Adv. -ρως Id.5.139. **-ῐτος**, ον, *difficult of access* or *attack*, πόλις D.H.4.54, cf. D.S.15.42, Onos.11.6; λιμὴν δ. ναυσί J.*BJ*4.10.5; τεῖχος D.C.40.34; of a man, E.*IA*345. **-μᾰχος**, ον, *hard to attack*, Plu.*Tim.*21. **-μεικτος**, ον, *hard to get into*, λιμήν Poll.1.101. **-οδος**, ον, *difficult of access*, χωρίον Th.5.65, cf. Aen.Tact.28.1 (Sup.); δ. τοῖς ἐναντίοις πόλις Arist.*Pol.*1330b3; *hard to assault*, τάξις, παρεμβολή, Plb.1.26.10, 2.65.12. 2. of men, *unsocial*, δ. αὑτὸν παρέχειν Th.1.130, cf. X.*Ages.*9.2, Luc.*Scyth.*6, Plu.*Demetr.*42, D.C.*Fr.*11.6. **-οιστος**, ον, *hard to approach*, στόμα S.*OC*1277. **-οπτος**, ον, *hard to look on, horrid to behold*, κάρα τὸ δ. ib.286; ὀνείρατα Id.*El.*460; ὄψις καὶ κίνησις Plu.*Aem.*12. Adv. -τως Agatharch.26. **-όρμιστος**, ον, *hard to land on, having few ports*, Plb.1.37.4; δ. ἀπόβασις a *difficult* landing, D.S.1.31. **-ορμος**, ον, = foreg., Scymn.726. **-πέλαστος**, ον, *hard to get at*, Plu.*Pomp.*28; gloss on δασπλῆτις, Sch.Od.15.234. **-πόριστος**, ον, *bad for foraging in*, χώρα Aen.Tact.8.1. **-πτωτος**, ον, *hard to apply*, of stiff ointment, Gal.11.134 (ap. Orib.44.15.21). **-ρητος**, ον, *hard to speak with*, condemned by Poll.5.138.

δυσ-πρόσωπος, ον, *of ill aspect, sour looks*, Artem.3.47, f.l. in Plu.*Mar.*15, cf. Men.Rh.p.416S. **-πρόφορος**, ον, *hard to pronounce*, Mart.Cap.5.514. **-ρᾰγής**, ές, *hard to break*, Luc.*Anach.*24 (Comp.). **-ρᾰχῖτις**, ιδος, ἡ, name of a *plaster*, Crito ap.Gal.13.797. **-ρευστος**, ον, *hardly flowing*, of thick water, S.E.*M.*5.75 (Comp.). **-ρηκτος**, ον, *hard to break through*, Gal.*UP*15.5, D.C.62.8. **-ρητος**, ον, *that should not be spoken*, Demetr.*Eloc.*302. II. *hard to give a name to*, Gal.12.501. **-ρῖγος**, ον, *impatient of cold, sensitive to cold*, ζῷα Hdt.5.10, cf. Arist.*HA*605a20 (Sup.), Men.1007, J.*AJ*7.14.3, Plu.2.916a; of plants, Thphr.*HP*6.7.3. Adv. -γως Ruf.ap.Orib.8.24.61, Agathin.ib.10.7.17: Comp. -οτέρως, διάγειν Arist.*Pr.*863a2.

δυσ-ροέω, *flow ill*, i.e. *to be unlucky*, Arr.*Epict.*1.28.30, al. **-ροητικός**, ή, όν, *leading to ill luck*, ib.4.1.58. **-ροια**, ἡ, *bad circulation*, Anon.Lond.4.17: metaph., *ill luck, misfortune*, Arr.*Epict.*2.17.18. **-ροος**, ον, contr. -ρους, -ρουν, *sluggish*, γαστήρ Orib.8.35.6, cf. Gal.8.358. **-σάρκωτος**, ον, *healing with difficulty*, of ulcers, Id.12.188, Aët.2.187.

δυσσέβ-εια, ἡ, *impiety, ungodliness*, πρὸς δυσσεβείας ἦν it verged on *impiety*, A.*Ch.*704; παντὸς ἔργου δ. S.*Ant.*301; *a charge of impiety*, τὴν δ. εὐσεβοῦσ' ἐκτησάμην ib.924.—In Lyrics also **-ία**, A.*Eu.*

533; -ίη Nonn.*D*.20.404. **-έω**, *to be ungodly*, S.*Tr*.1245; οἱ δυσσεβοῦντες A.*Eu*.910, E.*Med*.755. **-ημα**, ατος, τό, *impious act*, Lxx 2*Ma*.12.3, D.H.7.44, Scymn.684, etc. **-ής**, ές, *ungodly, impious, profane*, of persons, A.*Th*.598 (Comp. or Sup.), and their acts, δ. χάρις S.*Ant*.514; τὰ τῶν κακίστων δυσσεβέστατα Id.*OC*1190; δ. μέλαθρα E.*IT*694. Adv. -βῶς Id.*Fr*.825.—This family of words is chiefly found in Trag. (δυσσεβής occurs in Men.540, Diph.105, and later Prose as Jul.*Or*.5.174b (Sup.)); εὐσεβής, etc., are freq. also in Prose. **-ία**, ἡ, v. δυσσέβεια.

δύσ-σειστος, ον, *hard to shake*, Hsch. **-σηπτος**, ον, *not easily rotting*, κρέα Plu.2.725b; δένδρα Id.*in Hes*.7, cf. Gal.10.942, al. **-σοος**, ον, *hard to save, ruined*, Theoc.3.24; τὰ δ. *the rogues*, Id.4.45, cf. *Riv. Indogr*.8.266 (Camarina, v B.C.).

δυσσυγκάθετος, ον, *condescending with difficulty*, πρὸς τὰς ἐξωτερικὰς φιλίας prob. cj. in Iamb.*VP*31.194.

δυσσύλληπτος, ον, *hard to conceive*, σπέρματα Sor.1.41.

δυσσυλλόγιστος, ον, *hard to reason out*, Gal.8.882.

δυσσύμ-βᾰτος, ον, *ill-agreeing*, πρὸς τὸ ἀλλόφυλον Plu.2.661c. **-βλητος**, **-βολος**, v. δυσξυμβ-. **-βούλευτος**, v. δυσξύμβολος. **-πτωσία**, ἡ, *difficulty in coalescing*, Gal.19.401. **-πτωτος**, ον, *not coalescing easily*, Id.8.873. **-φῠτος**, ον, *hardly growing together*, Id.10.336; τραύματα Sor.1.38.

δυσσυν-αίσθητος, ον, *hard to grasp as a whole*, of an argument, Simp.*in Ph*.1272.13. **-ακτος**, ον, *hard to bring together*, πλῆθος J.*BJ*4.4.6. **-άλλακτος**, ον, *hard to deal with*, Vett.Val.115.9. **-είδητος**, ον, *with a bad conscience*, Id.37.29, al. **-εσία**, ἡ, *lack of understanding*, Simp.*in Ph*.1147.9. **-οπτος**, ον, *hard to get a view of*, Plb.3.84.2, etc.: metaph., Iamb.*VP*30.182.

δυσ-σώστως, Adv. *with small chance of survival*, ἔχειν Hippiatr. 71. **-τακτος**, ον, *ill-regulated, disordered*, Pl.*Lg*.781a. II. (for δύσ-στακτον) = κακοδάκρυτον, Hsch. **-τάλᾱς**, αινα, ἄν, *most miserable*, S.*Aj*.410, etc.: freq. in E. in fem., *Med*.1028, al., masc. twice in E., δ. σὺ τῆσδε συμφορᾶς *Hipp*.1407, cf. *Supp*.1034. **-ταλτος**, ον, (στέλλω) *hard to check*, Hippiatr.9. **-τᾰμίευτος** [ῐ], ον, *hard to manage*, πνεῦμα Arist.*Aud*.800^{b}31. **-τάρᾰχος** [τᾰ], ον, *very stormy*, Hsch. s. v. δυσήνεμον.

δυστᾰτέω, *to be unstable*, αἰσθήσεις Plu.2.1124b.

δυσ-τέκμαρτος, ον, *hard to make out from signs, hard to trace*, ἴχνος S.*OT*109; δ. τέχνη, of the art of interpreting auspices, A.*Pr*. 497; ποικίλον τι καὶ δ. E.*Hel*.712; τέλος D.H.4.29; γνώμη Plu.*Cat. Mi*.72; δ. πατὴρ τῶν ὅλων Ph.1.467; *hard to estimate*, Aret.*CA*1. 4. **-τεκνία**, ἡ, *ill luck in the matter of children*, Man.2.179. **-τεκνος**, ον, *unfortunate in one's children*, S.*OT*1248, Vett.Val.18.5, *Cat. Cod.Astr*.1.149. **-τέρματον**· δυσχερὲς τέλος ἔχον, ἢ μὴ ἔχον τέλος, Hsch. **-τερπής**, ές, *ill-pleasing*, A.*Ch*.277. **-τευκτος**, ον, *unsuccessful*, Doroth.in *Cat.Cod.Astr*.2.174. **-τευξία**, ἡ, *difficulty in securing*, πραγμάτων Heph.Astr.2.28. **-τηκτος**, ον, (τήκω) *hard to melt*, Hp.*Alim*.51, Plu.2.701b.

δυστηνία, ἡ, = μοχθηρία, Hsch.

δύστηνος, Dor. **δύστᾱνος**, ον, *wretched, unhappy, unfortunate, disastrous*, poet. Adj.: 1. mostly of persons, as always in Hom. and mostly Trag., A.*Pers*.909 (anap.), etc.; δυστήνων δέ τε παῖδες ἐμῷ μένει ἀντιόωσιν *unhappy are they* whose sons.., Il.6.127. 2. of sufferings and the like, μόχθος δ. Pi.*P*.4.268; θέρος A.*Ag*.1655; αἰκίαι S.*El*.511 (lyr.); ὄνειδος Id.*Aj*.1191 (lyr.); ὄνειρος Ar.*Ra*.1333 (lyr.); πάθος D.H.6.20. Adv., Sup. δυστανοτάτως γηράσκω E.*Supp*. 967 (lyr.). II. after Hom., in moral sense, *wretched*, S.*El*.121 (Sup., lyr.), *Ph*.1016; λόγοι E.*HF*1346.—Rare in Prose, though D. 19.255 has δ. λογάρια, in latter sense: Sup. (v. supr. 1); no Comp. is found. (Cf. ἄστηνος.)

δυστήρητος, ον, *hard to keep*, κάλλος Ps.-Phoc.217; θηρίον Plu. *Cleom*.36.

δυστίβευτος [ῐ], ον, *bad for scent*, Plu.2.917e, 918a.

δυσ-τῐθάσευτος [ᾰ], ον, *hard to tame*, Str.15.1.42, Plu.2.529b; τὸ δ. Artem.3.12. **-τλήμων**, ον, gen. ονος, *suffering hard things*, h.*Ap*. 532, Orph.*Fr*.49 vi 95. **-τλητος**, ον, *hard to bear*, Ἀνάγκη Emp. 116, A.*Ag*.1571 (anap.); δύστλητα τολυπεύειν *IG*14.2123.

δυστόκ-εια, ἡ, *one who has borne a child to misery*, dub. in Hsch. **-εύς**, έως, ὁ, ἡ, *suffering in child-birth*, δυστοκέες ἀλετρίδες Call.*Del*. 242; *unhappy parent*, δ. τοκέες *IG*14.2125. **-έω**, *suffer in child-birth*, Hp.*Aph*.5.35, Pl.*Tht*.149d, Arist.*HA*587^{a}4: metaph., ἡ πόλις δυστοκεῖ Ar.*Ra*.1423, cf. Aristid.*Or*.31(11).11. **-ία**, ἡ, *painful delivery*, Arist.*HA*587^{a}10 (pl.), Thphr.*HP*9.16.1 (pl.). II. = δυστεκνία, Man.1.46. **-ος**, ον, *born for mischief*, δάκος E.*Fr*.863.

δυστομέω, (στόμα) *speak evil of*, τινά τι S.*OC*986.

δυστομία, ἡ, (στόμα) *difficulty in pronunciation*, Phld.*Po*.2.24.

δύστομος (A), ον, (στόμα) *hard-mouthed*, of a horse, ἵππείη *APl*.4. 361, *Hippiatr.Praef*. II. *hard to pronounce*, συλλαβή Phld.*Po*.2.15.

δύστομος (B), ον, (τέμνω) *hard to cut*, Thphr.*HP*3.14.1.

δύστονος, ον, (στένω) *lamentable, grievous*, A.*Th*.989 (lyr., codd.), *Ch*.469 (lyr.).

δυστοπ-άζοντες· δυσχερῶς ὑπονοήσαντες, Hsch. **-αστος**, ον, *hard to guess*, ὅστις ποτ' εἶ σύ, δυστόπαστος εἰδέναι E.*Tr*.885; Φοίβου δυστόπαστ' αἰνίγματα Id.*Supp*.138, cf. Phld.*Mort*.37; αἰτία Plu.*Rom*. 21; κοσμοποιός Ph.1.570.

δύστος, = δύστηνος, Hdn.Gr.1.217.

δυστόχαστος, ον, *hard to hit upon*, καιρός Plu.*Ant*.28, cf. Dsc.*Ther. Praef*.

δυσ-τράπεζος [ᾰ], ον, *fed on horrid food*, E.*HF*385 (lyr.). **-τρᾰπελία** or **-εία**, ἡ, *difficulty of managing*, D.S.4.11, 5.15; ἐν τοῖς καταγείοις Id.17.82; *unhealthiness*, τόπου Iamb.*VP*19.92. **-τράπελος** [ᾰ], ον, *difficult to deal with*, φλέψ Hp.*Oss*.16; πρᾶγμα Henioch. 4.4, cf. Plu.2.419a; ὀφθαλμία Sor.2.15. 2. of persons, *intractable, stubborn*, S.*Aj*.914 (lyr.), Arist.*EE*1234^{a}5. Adv. -λως *awkwardly, clumsily*, X.*Oec*.8.16; *with difficulty*, Gal.14.114.

δυστρᾰτοπέδευτος, ον, *ill-suited for encamping*, Aen.Tact.8.1.

δυσ-τρᾰχηλέω, *to be stiff-necked, stubborn*, Tz.*H*.1.427. **-τρητος**, ον, *hard to pierce or bore*, of inferior pearls, Suid. **-τριπτος**, ον, *hard to bruise or grind*, Artem.1.70, *Hippiatr*.1. **-τροπία**, ἡ, *peevishness*, Poll.5.119, Jul.*Mis*.365b, Alex.Trall.7.9. **-τροπικός**, ή, όν, *peevish*, Sch.Ar.*Ra*.848. **-τροπος**, ον, (τρόπος) *ill-conditioned, surly, peevish*, δ. γυναικῶν ἁρμονία E.*Hipp*.161; δύσκολος καὶ δ. D.6. 30, Ph.1.621; δ. καὶ σκυθρωπαὶ φύσεις Plu.2.361b. Adv. -πως, λογιστεύειν Philostr.*VS*1.19.2.

Δύστρος μήν, ὁ, name of a Macedonian month, *OGI*55 (iii B.C.), *AP*11.243 (Nicarch.), etc.

δύσ-τροφος, ον, *hard to rear*, Thphr.*CP*1.8.4. **-τρύπητος** [ῠ], ον, *hard to bore through*, Id.*HP*5.6.3 (Comp.). **-τρωτος**, ον, *hard to injure*, σιδήρῳ καὶ λίθῳ Plu.2.983d, cf. Apollod.*Poliorc*.139.8: Comp., Gal.*UP*1.2. **-τύπωτος** [τῠ], ον, *not easily taking an impress*, Id.1.322.

δυστῠχ-έω, Ion. impf. ἐδυστύχεον Hdt.8.105: aor. ἐδυστύχησα Pl. *Mx*.243a: pf. δεδυστύχηκα Id.*La*.183c, Isoc.4.55, Lyc.Trag.5:—Pass., v. infr.:—*to be unlucky, unfortunate*, Hdt. l. c., etc.; ἐπεύχομαι τῷδε μὲν εὐτυχεῖν.. τοῖσι δὲ δ. A.*Th*.482 (lyr.), cf. S.*Ant*.1159; γάμοις E.*Ph*.424; παίδων πέρι Id.*Andr*.713; ἔν τινι Ar.*Ra*.1449; εἴς τι Pl.*La*. 183c; κατὰ γῆν καὶ κατὰ θάλατταν Id.*Alc*.2.148d; περί τι Plu.*Cam*. 11: c. acc., πάντα δυστυχῶ E.*Hec*.429; δυστυχεῖν ἄμορφον γυναῖκα *to be curst with*.., *AP*11.287 (Pall.); μανίαν Ach.Tat.4.17; τῆς ἀλλοδαπῆς βαρυτέραν τὴν πατρίδα δυστυχήσασα Hld.10.16:—Pass. in same sense, ὅταν τις δυστυχηθῇ *is made unfortunate*, Pl.*Lg*.877e; τὰ ὑφ' ἑτέρων δυστυχηθέντα Lys.2.70, cf. Plu.*Pyrrh*.4. **-ημα**, ατος, τό, *piece of ill luck, failure, misfortune*, And.2.9, Lys.24.3 (pl.), Pl.*Cra*.395d (pl.), Onos.36.4 (pl.); esp. of *defeat* in war, X.*HG*4.5.18, etc. **-ής**, ές, *unlucky, unfortunate*, of persons and things, Th.7.87, Pl.*Lg*.832a, etc.; freq. in Trag., δυστυχῆ πράσσειν A.*Th*.339 (lyr.); δ. βίος S. *El*.602; δ. εἴς τι E.*Ph*.1642; τά τ' ἔνδον τά τε θύραζε δ. Id.*Or*.604; τὸ δυστυχές A.*Ch*.913. Adv. -χῶς Id.*Ag*.1660, Pl.*Lg*.687e, etc. 2. of the Erinyes, δ. κόραι *ill-starred, harbingers of ill*, A.*Eu*.791 (lyr.). **-ία**, ἡ, *ill luck, ill fortune*, E.*Ba*.388 (lyr.), al.; τοῦ πάθους ἡ δ. Th.6.55, etc.

δύσ-υδρος [δῠ], ον, *scant of water*, J.*AJ*2.11.2, Ph.2.516. **-υπέρβᾰτος**, ον, *hard to pass over*, Ph.*Bel*.82.35.

δῠσυπν-έω, *sleep ill*, Pl.*Lg*.790d. **-ήτως**, Adv. ἔχειν suffer from *insomnia*, Agathin.ap.Orib.10.7.27. **-ος**, ον, *sleeping badly*, ib.10.

δῠσυποβίβαστος [ῐ], ον, *hard to carry off by purging*, etc., Diph. Siph.ap.Ath.3.74c, Gal.6.535.

δῠσύποιστος, ον, *hard to endure*, *AP*5.162 (Mel.), J.*AJ*15.7.1; *hard to carry*, βάρος Archig.ap.Aët.13.120.

δῠσυπο-μένητος, ον, = sq., S.E.*M*.9.154. **-μόνητος**, ον, *hard to abide*, Ph.2.287, 432, Sor.1.80. **-νόητος**, ον, *hard to detect the nature of*, of a person, Ph.2.268; μῖσος ib.201. **-στᾰτος**, ον, *hard to withstand*, βία D.S.17.11; of a person, Plu.*Cor*.8. **-χώρητος**, gloss on δυσύποιστος, Suid.

δυσ-φαής, ές, *scarce visible*, ἥλιος Plu.2.431f. **-φᾰνής**, ές, *dark, obscure*, νύξ Id.*Luc*.9: metaph., σώματος ψυχὴ -έστερόν τι χρῆμα Them.*Or*.1.2c.

δύσφαλτον· δύσμαχον, Hsch.

δυσ-φάνταστος, ον, *hard to imagine*, Plu.2.432c. **-φᾰτος**, ον, *hard to speak, unutterable*, A.*Ag*.1152 (lyr.). II. *hard to explain*, Lyc.10. **-φεγγής**, ές, *shining ill, gloomy*, Poll.5.109. **-φερής**, ές, *intolerable*, Hsch. **-φευκτος**, ον, *hard to be avoided*, κακόν Men. *Georg*.12, cf. Ph.2.268.

δυσφημ-έω, *use ill words*, esp. *words of ill omen*, A.*Ag*.1078, S.*El*. 905, Plu.*Cic*.22. II. trans., *speak ill of*, S.*El*.1183, E.*Heracl*.600, *Hec*.181 (lyr.), Phld.*Rh*.1.215 S., Them.*Or*.13.178a:—Pass., Phld. *Mort*.36. **-ημα**, ᾰτος, τό, *word of ill omen*, Plu.2.1065e. **-ία**, ἡ, *ill language*, esp. *words of ill omen*, κατεῖχε.. πᾶν στρατόπεδον δυσφημίαις S.*Ph*.10, dub. in J.*AJ*16.4.1: pl., *curses*, Plu.2.587f, cf. *Pel*.8; but, *unsavoury details*, Demetr.*Eloc*.302. II. *blasphemy, slander*, D.H.6.48, etc. III. *ill fame, obloquy*, S.*Fr*.178 (pl.), Them.*Or*.7.99c. **-ιστος**, ον, = sq., Suid. s. v. δυσκληδόνιστος. **-ος**, Dor. **-φᾱμος**, ον, *of ill omen, boding*, Hes.*Op*.735; opp. εὔφημος, E.*Andr*.1144, Pl.*Hp.Ma*.293a. Adv. -μως, ἱερουργεῖν Zen.4.95. II. *slanderous, shameful*, ἔπη Thgn.307; λόγος Men. 715; *abusive*, Plu.*Luc*.18. Adv. -μως Phryn.*PS* p.62 B. III. *of ill fame, evil*, κλέος Pi.*N*.8.37. **-οσύνη**, ἡ, *evil talk*, Phld.*Sto*. 339.20.

δύσ-φθαρτος, ον, *hard to destroy*, S.E.*M*.9.19; *not easily spoilt*, Diph.Siph.ap.Ath.3.121c, Hices.ib.87d, Xenocr.73 (Comp.), Dsc. 2.9. **-φθεγκτος**, ον, *unfit to be uttered*, Poll.3.129, 5.123. **-φθογγος**, ον, *hard-sounding*, Demetr.*Eloc*.246. **-φῐλής**, ές, *hateful*, δάκος A.*Ag*.1232; γαμήλευμα Id.*Ch*.624; γέρων S.*OC*1258, etc.

δυσφορ-έω, impf. ἐδυσφόρουν Hp.*Epid*.3.1.γ', X.*Cyr*.2.2.8:—*to be impatient, angry, vexed*, Hdt.5.19, A.*Supp*.513, S.*El*.255, Pherecr. 22 D., Ar.*Th*.73, Men.543.7, etc.; κακοῖς E.*Andr*.1234; ἐπί τινι A. *Th*.780 (lyr.), J.*AJ*1.10.4, Hdn.3.9.7; περὶ τὰς ἀναστάσιας *to feel* *ill* on getting up, Hp.l.c.; διά τι D.S.4.61 :—Med., X.*Cyr.*2.2.8, Procop.*Arc.*10,12 :—Pass., S.*Ichn.*329, v.l. in X.*Cyr.*2.2.5. **-ητος**, ον, *hard to be borne*, Hsch.; f.l. for διαφόρητος, E.*Cyc.*344. **-ία**, ἡ, *malaise, discomfort*, Hp.*Acut.*54, *Epid.*1.26.η', *Coac.*260; classed as εἶδος λύπης, *Stoic.*3.100. 2. *vexation, distress*, Epicur.*Fr.*445 (pl.), Simp. *in Epict.*p.117 D. **-ικός**, ή, όν, *indicative of vexation*, Eust. 1581.22.

δυσ-φόρμιγξ, ιγγος, ὁ, ἡ, *unlike the lyre, mournful*, E.*IT*225 (lyr.). **-φορος**, ον, *hard to bear, heavy*, θώρακες X.*Mem.*3.10.13. 2. mostly of sufferings, *hard to bear, grievous*, θάμβος, μέριμνα, Pi.*N.*1.55, *Fr.* 248; ἄτα, βίος, A.*Eu.*372 (lyr., codd.), *Ag.*859, etc.; δ. γνῶμαι *false, blinding* fancies, S.*Aj.*51; τὰ δ. our *troubles, sorrows*, Id.*OT*87, cf. *El.*144 (lyr.); δύσφορόν [ἐστι] X.*Cyr.*1.6.17. Adv. δυσφόρως, διάγειν τὴν νύκτα Hp.*Epid.*5.95; δ. φέρειν Id.*Aph.*1.18 (Sup.), Hdn.1.8.4; δ. ἔχειν S.*OT*770; *impatiently*, τοὔνειδος ἦγον ib.783. 3. of food, *oppressive*, X.*Cyr.*1.6.17. 4. *bearing bad crops*, χώρα Men.Rh. p.345 S. II. (from Pass.) *moving with difficulty, slow of motion*, σώματα Pl.*Ti.*74e; ἵππος X.*Eq.*1.12 (Comp.). **-φορτος**, ον, *hard to be borne* or *carried*, *CIG*3127 (Teos). **-φράδεια** [φρᾰ], ἡ, *difficulty of pronunciation*, Eust.852.58. **-φρακτος**, ον, *cohesive*, Steph. *in Hp.*1.298 D. **-φραστος**, ον, *hard to tell* or *explain, mysterious*, Pl.*Ti.*50c: generally, *difficult*, κέλευθα Opp.*H.*2.60. II. Act., *speaking with difficulty*, γλῶσσα Ezek.*Exag.*114. Adv. -τως Lyc.1466. **-φρόνη**, ἡ, = -φροσύνη, in pl., *anxieties, troubles*, δυσφρονέων ἐπιλήθεται Hes.*Th.*102; in Pi.*O.*2.52, παραλύει δυσφρονᾶν should be read (metri gr.) for δυσφροσύναν παραλύει, cf. ἀφρόνη, εὐφρόνη. **-φροντις**, = δυσκηδής, Eust.1546.41. **-φρόντιστος**, gloss on δυσαρεής, Hsch. **-φροσύνη**, ἡ, *anxiety, care*, Hes. *Th.*528, Simon.86 (both times in Ep. gen. pl. δυσφροσυνάων): pl., E.*Tr.*597 (lyr.), Ph.2.75. **-φρων**, ον, gen. ονος, *sad at heart, sorrowful*, τὸ δ. στύγος A.*Ag.*547; ἄτα S.*OC*202 (lyr.); λῦπαι E. *Andr.*1043 (lyr.). II. *ill-disposed, malignant*, δράκοντες A.*Supp.* 511; ἰός Id.*Ag.*834; οἱ δ. ib.608; λόγοι E.*Andr.*288 (lyr.). III. = ἄφρων, *senseless, insensate*, A.*Th.*875 (lyr.); φρενῶν δυσφρόνων ἁμαρτήματα S.*Ant.*1261 (lyr.). Adv. -όνως *foolishly, rashly*, A.*Pers.* 552 (lyr.). **-φυής**, ές, *germinating tardily*, Thphr.*HP*7.1.3: Sup., ibid. **-φῠΐα**, ἡ, *tardy germination*, opp. ταχυβλαστία, Id.*CP* 4.8.2. **-φῠλακτέω**, = δυσωρέομαι, Eust.797.28. **-φύλακτος** [ῠ], ον, *hard to guard*, δυσφύλακτον οὐδὲν ὡς γυνή Alex.339; of a city, Plb.2.55.2; πλοῦτος Str.9.3.8; ἀρχή D.C.56.33. II. *hard to keep off* or *prevent*, κακά E.*Ph.*924, cf. *Andr.*728; *hard to guard against* or *avoid*, τενάγη Str.11.4.2; τὸ οἰδεῖν -ότατον Longin.3. 3. **-φῠσις**· κακὴ φύσις, Hsch. **-φωνία**, ἡ, *roughness of sound*, Demetr.*Eloc.*48, Poll.2.112, *Cat.Cod.Astr.*2.167. **-φωνος**, ον, *ill-sounding, harsh*, Demetr.*Eloc.*69 (Comp.), 105; κολοιοί Babr.33. 4. **-φώρᾱτος**, ον, *hard to detect*, Plu.2.51d. **-χᾰλέες**· βλάσφημοι, χαλεποί, Hsch. **-χᾰλίνωτος** [ῐ], ον, *hard to rein, unbridled*, Gal.19.94 (s.v. δυσήνιος). **-χάριστος** [ᾰ], ον, *thankless*, τῶν πυκνῶν φιλημάτων A.*Fr.*135. **-χειμερινός**, ή, όν, = sq., τὰ δ. *wintry climates*, Thphr.*HP*8.8.1. **-χείμερος**, ον, *wintry* or *stormy*, Hom. (only in Il.) epith. of Dodona, 2.750, al.; χώρη Hdt.4.28, cf. Arist. *HA*606^{b}5; φάραγξ A.*Pr.*15: metaph., δ. πέλαγος δύης ib.746; δ. ἆται Id.*Ch.*271. II. *bearing winter ill*, Arist.*HA*596^{b}5, *Gp.*19.2. 8. **-χείμων**, ον, gen. ονος, = foreg. 1, A.R.4.635. **-χείρωμα**, ατος, τό, *a hard conquest*, incorrect formation in S.*Ant.*126. **-χείρωτος**, ον, *hard to subdue*, Hdt.7.9.β' (Sup.), D.61.37, Plu.*Alc.*4, D.C. 53.25 (Comp.): Sup. δυσχειρότατον is prob. f.l. in D.S.5.34.

δυσχερ-αινόντως, Adv. part. pres., *with disgust*, v.l. in Arist.*Rh.* 1408^{a}17. **-αίνω**, impf. ἐδυσχέραινον Pl.*Tht.*169d: aor. ἐδυσχέρᾶνα S.*OC*1282, Isoc.12.201: aor. Pass. ἐδυσχεράνθην Plu.2.820f: (δυσχερής):—*to be unable to endure* or *put up with, to be disgusted at*, c. acc., Isoc.14.46, Pl.*Tht.*195c, D.19.116, etc.; θεούς Pl.*Lg.*900a; δ. τὸ γενέσθαι τι X.*HG*7.4.2; τὸ ἀδικεῖν Pl.*R.*362b: c. acc. et part., *to be annoyed at* his doing, Aeschin.1.158. 2. mostly intr., *feel dislike, disgust* or *annoyance, to be displeased*, περί τινος And.3.35; τινί *at* a thing, D.55.11; ἐπί τινι Isoc.1.26; πρός τι D.H.*Th.*34, Plu. *Pyrrh.*21; κατά τινος Luc.*Nav.*10; also δ. ἑαυτῷ *to have misgivings*, Arist.*Metaph.*984^{a}29:—Pass., *to be hateful*, ὄνομα δυσχεραινόμενον Plu.*Publ.*1; δ. ὑπὸ πολλῶν Id.*Cic.*24. 3. c. inf., *scorn* to do a thing, Pl.*R.*388a: c. acc., δ. τι τῶν λεχθέντων *feel qualms about*, Id. *Plt.*294a; ταῦτ' οὐκ ἐδυσχέραινεν *felt* no *scruple about*, Aeschin.1. 54; *to be fastidious*, περὶ τὰ μαθήματα Pl.*R.*475b. II. causal, *cause annoyance*, ῥήματ' ἢ τέρψαντά τι ἢ δυσχεράναντ' S.*OC*1282; δ. τὴν ὁδόν *make* it *difficult*, App.*Ill.*18:—Pass., *to be disagreeable*, τοῖς ἀκούουσι Arist.*Rh.Al.*1432^{b}19: abs., ib.1437^{a}33. III. δ. ἐν τοῖς λόγοις *to make difficulties* in argument, *to be captious*, Pl.*Grg.* 450e. **-ανσις**, εως, ἡ, *disgust*, Andronic.Rhod.p.570 M., Plot. 1.9, Simp. *in Epict.*p.45 D. **-αντέον**, *one must boggle at*, θεόν Pl. *Lg.*828d, al. **-αντικός**, ή, όν, *peevish*, M.Ant.1.8, Hierocl. *in CA*11p.444 M. Adv. -κῶς, ζῆν Simp. *in Epict.*p.35 D. **-ασμα**, ατος, τό, in pl., *harsh judgements*, Pl.*Phlb.*44d; *inconveniences*, Dam.*Isid.*66:—condemned by Poll.3.133. **-εια**, ἡ, opp. εὐχέρεια, I. of things, *annoyance, disgust* caused by a thing, τοῦ φορήματος, τοῦ νοσήματος, S.*Ph.*473, 900, cf. Pl.*Plt.*286b; *unpleasantness*, of food, D.C.68.31: pl., Plu.2.654b. b. *odium, unpopularity*, Pl.*Lg.*967c (pl.). 2. *difficulty, troublesome question*, Id.*R.* 502d, Isoc.5.12 (pl.), etc.; δ. παρέχειν Plb.1.20.10; εἰς δ. ἐμπεσεῖν Id.8.7.1; κατὰ τὴν προφοράν, opp. εὐχέρεια, Phld.*Po.*994.8. 3. in argument, *difficulties*, δ. λογικαί Arist.*Metaph.*1005^{b}22, cf. 995^a 33. II. of persons, *harshness*, Pl.*Phlb.*44c; *offensiveness*, Thphr. *Char.*19. 2. *loathing, nausea*, Pl.*Prt.*334c. **-ής**, ές, (χείρ) *hard to take in hand* or *manage*, opp. εὐχερής: I. of things, *annoying, vexatious*, θεωρία A.*Pr.*802; πᾶσι θαῦμα δ. S.*Ant.*254; Ἁρπάλου ἄφιξις Din.2.5; of actions, *odious, unpopular*, Isoc.12.63 (Sup.); *disagreeable*, Pl.*Lg.*779e (Comp.); τὸ δ., = δυσχέρεια, E.*Ph.* 390; δυσχερὲς εἰπεῖν D.18.3; δυσχερὲς ποιεῖσθαι to raise *difficulties*, Th.4.85. 2. *difficult*, Pl.*Hp.Mi.*369b (Sup.), etc.; τύχη Lys.24.6 (Sup.); βίος D.60.24; τὰ δυσχερῆ *difficulties*, Id.10.58, al.; καιροὶ δ. *difficult* times, *Inscr.Prien.*37.132. 3. of arguments, *contradictory, captious*, Pl.*Prt.*333d, D.20.113; τὰ δυσχερῆ *difficulties* in an argument or discussion, Arist.*EN*1145^{b}6, *Metaph.*1067^{b}35. II. of persons, *ill-tempered, unfriendly*, τινί to one, S.*El.*929; πρός τινα E. *Ion* 398; ἄτοποι καὶ δ. D.19.308; δ. περὶ τὰ σιτία *fastidious*, Pl.*R.*475c, cf. Arist.*EE*1221^{b}3. 2. *unpleasant, offensive*, Thphr.*Char.*19.1; ὕδωρ D.C.68.31. III. Adv. δυσχερῶς, φέρειν, Lat. *aegre ferre*, Hp. *Aph.*1.25; ἀποδέχεσθαι Pl.*Euthphr.*6a; δ. ἔχειν to be *annoyed*, πρός τι Id.*Prt.*332a; ἐπί τινι Amphis 34.

δυσχιδώτερον· κακοτροπώτερον (Tarent.), Hsch.

δύσχῑμος, ον, *troublesome, dangerous, fearful*, δράκων A.*Th.*503; πλημμυρίς Id.*Ch.*186; κέλευθοι Id.*Pers.*567 (lyr.); ὄρη Id.*Fr.*342; χθών, πνεύματα, E.*Ba.*15, *Supp.*962 (lyr.). (It is doubtful whether -χῑμος (required by the metre in A.) is cognate with χεῖμα, *hiems*, cf. μελάγ-χῐμος: the form δύσχειμος is corrupt in A.*Fr.*342, E. ll. cc.)

δύσχιστος, ον, *hard to split*, Thphr.*CP*5.16.4.

δυσχλαινία, ἡ, *mean* or *shabby clothing*, E.*Hec.*240: in pl., τὰς ἐμὰς δυσχλαινίας Id.*Hel.*416.

δυσχορήγητος, ον, *difficult to stage*, Plu.2.712e.

δύσχορτος, ον, *with little grass* or *food*, δ. οἶκοι *inhospitable* dwellings, E.*IT*219 (lyr.).

δυσχραής· δυσχερής, and **δυσχρανής**· αὐχμηρός, Hsch.

δυσχρηστ-έω, *to be intractable*, Plb.27.7.10. II. *to be in difficulties* or *distress*, Id.4.60.8; ταῖς εἰρεσίαις Id.16.4.10; διά τι Id.1.51. 6; περὶ τὴν ἔξοδον ib.75.7:—also in Med., δ. ἐν τοῖς κινδύνοις ib.87.7; πράγμασι, λόγοις, Id.1.18.7, 3.11.4; of things, *to be useless*, Id.16.3.5:—Pass., *to be brought into distress*, ἐπὶ τοῖς ἀπαντωμένοις ὑπ' Ἀρχιμήδους Id.8.6.5; *to be annoyed*, D.S.18.39; ἐπί τινι Id.19.77. **-ημα**, ατος, τό, *inconvenience*, *Stoic.*3.23. **-ία**, ἡ, *difficult position, awkward circumstances*, εἰς δ. ἥκειν Plb.11.25.1, cf. 5.26.2, al.; *distress*, Phld.*Ir.*p.52 W., *Mort.*26 (pl.); of things, *inconvenience, disadvantage*, Plb.5.46.5: pl., Id.1.53.13; χρείας καὶ δ. Str.2.5.17; opp. πλεονέκτημα, Corn.*ND*18, cf. Plu.2.600a. II. (χράω) *difficulty in obtaining loans*, '*tightness*' *of money*, Cic.*Att.*16.7.6. **-ος**, ον, (χράομαι) *hard to use, inconvenient*, opp. εὔχρηστος, Hp.*Aph.*2.54, cf. Sch.Il.*Oxy.*221 vii 14; ἱππικὸν στράτευμα ἐν νυκτὶ.. δ. X.*Cyr.*3.3. 26; *intractable*, κύνες Id.*Cyn.*3.11; of troops, Plb.4.11.8 (Sup.); δ. ἐξουσία *hard to use well*, Isoc.8.103; δύσχρηστα *inconveniences*, Cic. *Att.*7.5.3, cf. D.S.4.8. Adv. -τως, διακεῖσθαι to be *in difficulties, unmanageable*, of ships, Plb.1.61.4; of troops, ἀπαλλάττειν Id.4.64.7; δ. ἔχειν Plu.*Aem.*19:—synon. for οὐ χρησίμως, Str.17.2.4.

δύσ-χροια, ἡ, *bad colour*, Dsc.*Ther.*6, Gal.17(2).215, Asp. *in EN* 44.6. **-χροος**, ον, contr. **-χρους**, ουν, = sq., Hp.*Aph.*5.42. **-χρως**, ωτος, ὁ, ἡ, *of a bad colour, discoloured*, Id.*Coac.*136.

δύσχῡλος, ον, *with bad juices, ill-savoured*, Xenocr.12.

δυσχῡμ-ία, ἡ, *an ill taste*, Thphr.*CP*6.12.12. **-ος**, ον, *ill-savoured*, Arist.*GA*776^{a}30, Thphr.*CP*6.12.4.

δυσχώρ-ητος, ον, *hard to traverse*: *inextricable*, ἀκρισία Plb.23.1. 13 (s.v.l.). II. *difficult to digest*, τροφή Aët.9.30. **-ία**, ἡ, *rough ground*, X.*Cyr.*1.6.35; τῶν Ἰταλῶν Jul.*Or.*1.38c: in pl., X. *Cyr.*1.4.7, Isoc.6.80, Onos.11.3, Gal.*UP*3.1, etc. II. *want of room*, Ph.2.563, Ath.4.129c. III. *difficulty*, Alex.Aphr.*Fat.*200. 23.

δυσχώριστος, ον, *hard to separate*, Gal.2.700 (Comp.); *hard to distinguish*, ἡ κολακεία τῆς φιλίας δ. Plu.2.51a.

δυσχῶται· δυσχωρῆ, διακωλύεται, Hsch.

δύσψυκτος, ον, *not easily affected by cold*, Gal.1.346.

δῠσωδέω, *to be ill-smelling*, Ph.2.563.

δῠσώδ-ης, ες, (ὄζω) *ill-smelling, stinking, foul*, χωλός, δ. S.*Ph.* 1032; δ. πῦον Hp.*Prog.*7; καρπός Hdt.2.94; πνεῦμα Th.2.49; ὀσμαί Arist.*HA*626^{a}27: Comp., κόπρος Plu.*Fr.inc.*149. **-ία**, ἡ, *foul smell*, Arist.*Pol.*1311^{b}34, *HA*626^{b}20, Ph.2.96, Plu.2.90b, Phld. *Herc.*19.27, etc.

δῠσώδῑνος, ον, *causing grievous pangs*, *AP*6.272 (Pers.).

δῠσώλεθρος, ον, *hard to kill, tenacious of life*, Thphr.*HP*3.12.5.

δῠσώμοτος, ον, *hardly*, i.e. *reluctantly, swearing*, Poll.1.39.

δῠσων-έω, impf. ἐδυσώνουν *AP*11.169 (Nicarch.):—*beat down the price, cheapen*, Pl.Com.224:—Med., Arist.*Fr.*558. **-ης**, ου, ὁ, *one who beats down the price, hard bargainer*, Lync.ap.Ath.6.228c; οὐδεὶς δ. χρηστὸν ὀψωνεῖ κρέας *Com.Adesp.*277. **-ος**, ον, *hard to buy*, Hdn. *Epim.*213.

δῠσωνῠμ-έω, *have a bad name*, Hdn.*Epim.*203. **-ος**, ον, *bearing an ill name, hateful*, υἷες Ἀχαιῶν Il.6.255; ἠώς Od.19.571; μοῖρα Il.12.116; λέκτρα S.*OC*528 (lyr.); φθόνος E.*Fr.*403; κήρ A.R.2.258; esp. *bearing a name of ill omen*, such as Αἴας, S.*Aj.*914 (lyr.): Comp., Ph.1.680:—in S.*Fr.*88.9 (lyr.) perh. δ. γλώσσῃ *whose tongue earned him an ill name* (of Thersites).

δῠσωπ-έω, aor. ἐδυσώπησα Luc.*Asin.*38: (ὤψ):—*put out of countenance, abash*, τινά Ph.1.291, Plu.2.418e, Luc.l.c., S.E.*P.*3.66, etc.; οὐδὲν αὐτὴν ἐδυσώπει X.Eph.4.5: c. acc. inf., *shame* a person with doing a thing, J.*BJ*1.6.5, al.: esp. of importunate persons, δ. τινὰ δεήσει ib.3.8.6; so, *entreat*, ἥκειν ὑμᾶς καὶ παρακαλῶ καὶ δ. Hld.10.2: abs., *to be importunate*, αἰσχυνόμενοι ἀντιλέγειν τοῖς ἀγνωμόνως δυσωποῦσιν ὕστερον δυσωποῦνται τοὺς δικαίως ἐγκαλοῦντας Plu.2.532d:—Pass., θεὸν εἶναι τὴν ἠχὼ δυσωποῦμαι *I am constrained to believe* that, Jul.*Ep.*189, cf. Marcellin.*Puls.*23; *to be susceptible to importunity*, τὴν ὑπὸ τῶν ἀναισχύντως λιπαρούντων ἧτταν, ἣν ἔνιοι δυσωπεῖσθαι καλοῦσιν Plu.*Brut.*6; δυσωπεῖν τὴν ὄψιν *to disgust*, Id.*Lyc.*9; *alarm*, πάθος δ. τινά Procop.*Arc.*2. II. in early writers only Pass., impf. ἐδυσωπούμην Pl.*Phdr.*242c:—*to be put out of countenance*, abs., Id.*Plt.*285b, etc.; πρὸς ἀλλήλους Id.*Lg.*933a; δ. μή.. Id.*Phdr.* l.c.; τινί Plb.20.12.6; ἐπί τινι Ph.1.639; εἰ.. Id.2.423; περί τινος Phld.*Rh.*1.297S.; of animals, *to be shy, timid*, X.*Mem.*2.1.4. 2. c. acc., *to be put to shame by*, τὴν ἀρετήν τινος Plu.*Cor.*15; τὴν χάριν Lib.*Decl.*37.19: but more freq. *fight shy of*, ὄνομα D.H.*Comp.*12 (so in Act., *look askance at*, δ. καὶ ὑποπτεύω μήποτ' οὐ Λυσίου ὁ λόγος Id.*Lys.*11), cf. Phryn.166; ὑφορᾶν καὶ δ.Them.*Or.*26.330b; διὰ τοὔνομα τὴν μοναρχίαν Plu.*Sol.*14; *regard with aversion*, ὄψα Ael.*Fr.*182; *disapprove of*, Phld.*Hom.*p.55O.: c. inf., *to be ashamed to do*, ..εἰπεῖν D.Chr.32.7, cf. 36.54; also τὴν ἀντίδοσιν δ. *feel ashamed to reply*, Jul.*Ep.*184. III. intr. in Act., *to see with difficulty*, Luc.*Lex.*4. **-ημα**, ατος, τό, *a means of making* one *ashamed*, and so, *a corrective*, τῶν ἡμαρτημένων J.*BJ*1.25.5, cf. D.Chr.*Fr.*8. **-ητέον**, *one must be shy of using*, τὴν ταυτολογίαν Eust.173.12. **-ητικός**, ή, όν, *importunate*, Id.105.15 (Comp.), etc. Adv. -κῶς Sch.Ar.*Pl.*21 (v.l. -ωπικῶς). **-ία**, ἡ, *confusion of face, shamefacedness*, Phld.*Lib.* p.24O., Ph.2.603 (pl.), Plu.2.95b; *false modesty*, ib.528e, al.; *cause for shame*, ib.707e, Cic.*Att.*13.33.2; δυσωπίαν *habere*, to have *an ugly look*, ib.16.15.2; τὰς δ. (v.l. δυστροπίας) τὰς ἐν τοῖς διαπορηθεῖσι dub. in Ph.1.330.

δῡσωρέομαι, (ὥρα) *keep painful watch*, ὡς δὲ κύνες περὶ μῆλα δυσωρήσονται ἐν αὐλῇ Il.10.183; but Apollon.*Lex.* read δυσωρήσωσιν, cf. Hsch., *EM*292.49.

δύσωρος, ον, (ὥρα) *unseasonable*, Poll.5.109.

δυσωχεῖν· δυσχεραίνειν, Hsch.

δύτη, Dor. **δύτα**, ἡ, *shrine* (?), *IG*4.823.42 (Troezen), 7.2477 (Cabireum).

δύτης [ῠ], ου, ὁ, (δύω) *diver*, Hdt.8.8; δ. βύθιος Poll.1.97.

δῠτικός, ή, όν, *able to dive*, ζῷον Arist.*Fr.*496; ἡ -κή (sc. τέχνη) Poll.7.139. II. (δύσις) later form for δυσμικός, *setting*, Euc.*Phaen.*p.10M. 2. *western*, στοά J.*AJ*20.8.11; opp. ἀνατολικός, Ptol.*Alm.*2.11: Comp. -ώτερος *farther west*, ib.2.13; δ. ὠκεανός Nonn.*D.*12.1; -κόν, τό, *closing at sunset*, = κλύμενον, Ps.-Dsc.4.13; = φοῖνιξ, ib.43.

δυτῖνος, ὁ, unknown *water-bird*, Dionys.*Av.*2.13, 3.24.

δύω, v. δύο.

δύω (v. infr.), δύνω: A. causal Tenses, *cause to sink, sink, plunge in*; pres. only in Thphr.*HP*5.4.8 οὐκ ἐν ἴσῳ βάθει πάντα δύοντες τῆς θαλάσσης: aor. 1 ἔδῡσα (ἐξ-) Od.14.341; cf. the compds. ἀπο-, ἐκ-, ἐν-, κατα-δύω.

B. non-causal, *get* or *go into*, c. acc.: pres. δύω (v. 1.4); more freq. δύνω Il.17.202, Hes.*Op.*616, S.*Ph.*1331, etc.; Ep. impf. δῦνον Il.11.268: aor. ἔδῡνα Batr.245, part. δύνας Plb.9.15.9, Paus.2.11.7, Ael.*VH*4.1, but ἔδῡσα *Ev.Marc.*1.32, etc.: more freq. Med. δύομαι Il.5.140, E.*Rh.*529 (lyr.), etc. (also in Att. Inscrr., as *IG*2².1241): impf. ἐδυόμην Pl.*Plt.*269a; Ep. δύοντο Il.15.345: fut. δύσομαι [ῡ] 7.298, E.*El.*1271: aor. ἐδῡσάμην A.R.4.865, (ἀπό) Nic.*Al.*302; Ep. 3 pl. δύσαντο Il.23.739, opt. δυσαίατο prob. in 18.376 (Prose and Com. in Compds.); Hom. mostly uses the Ep. forms ἐδύσετο, ἐδύσετο, imper. δύσεο 19.36, Hes.*Sc.*108, part. δυσόμενος (in pres. sense) Od.1.24, Hes.*Op.*384: more freq. aor. ἔδυν (as if from *δῦμι) Il.11.63, etc.; 3 dual ἐδύτην [ῡ] 10.254; 1 pl. ἔδῡμεν S.*Fr.*367; ἔδῡτε Od.24.106; ἔδῡσαν, Ep. ἔδυν Il.11.263; Ion. 3 sg. δύσκεν 8.271; imper. δῦθι, δῦτε, 16.64, 18.140; subj. δύω [ῡ] 6.340, 22.99, but δύῃ [ῡ] Hes.*Op.*728; Ep. opt. δύη [ῡ] (for δυίη) Od.18.348; inf. δῦναι Il.10.221, Att., Ep. δύμεναι [ῡ] 14.63, ἐκ-δῦμεν 16.99; part. δύς, δῦσα, Hdt.8.8: pf. δέδῡκα Il.5.811, Sapph.52, Pl.*Phd.*116e; Dor. inf. δεδυκεῖν [ῠ] Theoc.1.102:—Pass., fut. and aor. δῠθήσομαι, ἐδύθην [ῠ], and a pf. δέδῠμαι only in compds., v. ἀπο-, ἐκ-, ἐν-δύω. [ῠ in δύω in pres. and impf. Act. and Med., Hom.; but A.R. has δῡομαι, δῡετο 1.581, part. δῡόμενος ib.925, Call.*Ep.*22; δῡεται Nonn.*D.*7.286; ἐκ-δέδῡκας *AP*5.72 (Rufin.).] I. of Places or Countries, *enter, make one's way into*, in Hom. the most freq. use, εἰ..κε πύλας καὶ τείχεα δύω (aor. 2) Il.22.99; πόλιν δύσεσθαι Od.7.18; ἔδυ νέφεα *plunged into* the clouds, of a star, Il.11.63; δῦτε θαλάσσης εὐρέα κόλπον *plunge into* the lap of Ocean, 18.140; γαῖαν ἐδύτην *went beneath* the earth, i.e. died, 6.19, cf. 411, etc.; πόλεμον δύμεναι *plunge into*.., 14.63; θεῖον δύσονται ἀγῶνα 7.298; ἐδύσετο οὐλαμὸν ἀνδρῶν 20.379; δύσεο δὲ μνηστῆρας *go in to* them, Od.17.276; rarely in Trag., αἰθέρα δ. S.*Aj.*1192 (lyr.), cf. E.*El.*1271. 2. in Ep. less freq. with Preps., ἔδυν δόμον Ἄϊδος εἴσω Il.11.263; δύσομαι εἰς Ἀΐδαο Od.12.383; ἐς πόντον ἐδύσετο 5.352; δέρτρον ἔσω δύνοντες 11.579; δύσεθ' ἁλὸς κατὰ κῦμα Il.6.136; ὑπὸ κῦμα θαλάσσης αὐτίκ' ἔδυσαν 18.145; κατὰ σταθμοὺς δύεται *slinks* into the fold, 5.140; καθ' ὅμιλον ἔδυ Τρώων 3.36 (rarely c. gen., κατὰ σπείους κοίλοιο δέδυκεν Od.12.93); παῖς ὣς ὑπὸ μητέρα δύσκεν εἰς Αἴαντα *he got himself unto* Ajax, i.e. *got behind* his shield, Il.8.271; βέλος δ' εἰς ἐγκέφαλον δῦ ib.85; ἀκίδες δεδυκυῖαι διὰ φλεβῶν Plu.*Crass.*25; in Prose and Trag. mostly with a Prep. (but δυόμενοι abs., *diving*, Th.7.25), δῦναι ἐς θάλασσαν Hdt.8.8; ἐς ἄντρον A.*Fr.*261; ἁρμὸν..πρὸς αὐτὸ στόμιον S.*Ant.*1217; κατὰ βάθος Pl.*Lg.*905a; κατὰ τῆς γῆς Id.*Phd.*113c, etc. 3. abs., εἴσω ἔδυ ξίφος the sword *entered his body*, Il.16.340; δύνει ἀλοιφή *sinks in* (where however βοείην may be supplied), 17.392:—Med., δύου πάλιν Ar.*V.*148. 4. of Sun and Stars, *sink into* [the sea], *set*, ἠέλιος μὲν ἔδυ Il.18.241, cf. Od.3.329, etc.; ἔδυ φάος ἠελίοιο 13.35; δύσετό τ' ἠέλιος 2.388, cf. Il.7.465, etc.; ἀελίω δύντος Sapph.*Supp.*25.8; so Βοώτης ὀψὲ δύων *late-setting* Boötes, Od.5.272; δείελος ὀψὲ δύων Il.21.232; [σελαναία] δύεν Bion *Fr.*8.6; πρὸ δύντος ἡλίου Hdt.7.149; πρὸ ἡλίου δύντος D.15.22; δυσόμενος Ὑπερίων (to mark the West) Od.1.24; ἐδύετο εἰς τόπον [ὁ ἥλιος] Pl.*Plt.*269a; πρὸς δύνοντος ἡλίου towards the West, A.*Supp.*255: metaph., βίου δύντος αὐγαί Id.*Ag.*1123 (lyr.); ἔδυ πρόπας δόμος ib.1011 (lyr.); δεδυκὸς ζῆν live *in retirement*, Pl.*Lg.*781c. II. of clothes and armour, *get into*, Ἀρήϊα τεύχεα δ. Il.6.340, etc.; κυνέην δ. *put on* one's helmet, 5.845; δῦ δὲ χιτῶν' 18.416: metaph., εἰ μὴ σύ γε δύσεαι ἀλκήν if thou *wilt* not *put on* strength, 9.231; so ἀνάγκας ἔδυ λέπαδνον A.*Ag.*218 (lyr.): hence, 2. trans., *put on*, ἀμφ' ὤμοισιν ἐδύσετο τεύχεα Il.3.328, etc.; ὤμοιϊν..τεύχεα δῦθι 16.64; χιτῶνα περὶ χροΐ..δῦνεν Od.15.61; χρυσὸν.. ἔδυνε περὶ χροΐ Il.8.43. 3. rarely abs. with a Prep., ὅπλοισιν ἔνι δεινοῖσιν ἐδύτην 10.272, cf. A.R.1.638; ἐς τεύχεα δύντε Od.22.201. III. of sufferings, passions, and the like, *enter, come over* or *upon*, κάματος..γυῖα δέδυκεν Il.5.811; ὄφρ' ἔτι μᾶλλον δύῃ ἄχος κραδίην Od.18.348; ἦτορ δῦν' ἄχος Il.19.367; ὀδύναι δῦνον μένος 11.272; κρατερὴ δέ ἑ λύσσα δέδυκε madness *is come over* him, 9.239; δῦ μιν Ἄρης Ares, i.e. the spirit of war, *filled* him, 17.210; μιν ἔδυ χόλος 19.16.

δύωβολιαῖος, α, ον, *weighing two obols*, Gal.13.92, al.

δύώδεκα, Ion., Ep., Lyr.; Att. **δώδεκα**, *twelve*, in all genders, Il.2.637, Hdt.1.16, Pi.*N.*4.28, etc.; οἱ δώδεκα θεοί Aeschin.Socr.5, *Com.Adesp.*39.9D.:—also **δυόδεκο**, *IG*5(2).3 (Tegea, iv B.C.).

δῠωδεκάβοιος [ᾰ], ον, *worth twelve oxen*, Il.23.703.

δῠωδεκᾰδικός, ή, όν, *belonging to the* δυωδεκάς 1, Dam.*Pr.*276.

δῠωδεκά-δρομος, ον, *running the course twelve times*, τέθριππα Pi.*O.*2.50. **-εθλος**, v. δωδ-.

δῠωδεκᾰϝέτης, = δωδεκέτης, *Leg.Gort.*12.34.

δῠωδεκαΐς, ΐδος, Att.; Ion. **δωδεκηΐς**, ΐδος, and **-ηΐς**, -ῆδος, ἡ, *sacrifice of twelve victims*, *SIG*²438*D*37 (Delph.), *SIG*³604.9 (Delph., ii B.C.), Porph.*Abst.*1.22, etc.: as Adj., θυσίαι Eust.1386.48: hence name of a sacred mission to Delphi, *SIG*773.2 (i B.C.).

δῠωδεκά-μηνος, δῠωδεκαταῖος, δῠωδέκατος, v. δωδ-. **-μοιρος**, ον, *divided into twelve parts*, *AP*7.641 (Antiphil.). **-πηχυς**, υ, *of twelve cubits*, εὖρος Opp.*H.*2.143. **-πλους**, ουν, *twelvefold*, *IG*14.644 (Brutt.). **-πολις**, ιος, *formed of twelve united states*, Ἴωνες Hdt.7.95.

δῠωδεκάς, άδος, ἡ, *the number twelve*, Procl. *in Euc.*p.174F.; *group of twelve* divinities, Dam.*Pr.*348. II. *twelfth part*, of the signs of the zodiac, Arat.555 (pl.), 703; of an hour, *AP*9.779, 782 (Paul. Sil.).

δῠωδεκᾰτειχής, ές, *having twelve walled cities*, λαός Tim.*Pers.*247.

δῠωδεκᾰτεύς (sc. μήν), έος, ὁ, *twelfth month*, *IG*14.425iv, 427ii (Tauromenium).

δῠωκαιεικοσί-μετρος [σῐ], ον, *holding twenty-two measures*, τρίπους Il.23.264. **-πηχυς**, υ, *twenty-two cubits long*, 15.678.

δῶ, τό, shortd. Ep. form for δῶμα, *house, dwelling*, Hom. only in nom. as Od.1.392, and acc. as Il.1.426.—As pl. for δώματα, only in Hes.*Th.*933.

δωαί· δικαίως, ὁσίως, Hsch.

δώδεκα, v. δυώδεκα.

δωδεκᾰ-ακτῖονίκης [νῑ], ου, ὁ, *twelve times victorious in the Actian games*, *BGU*1074.23 (iii A.D.). **-βοιος**, ον, *of twelve oxen*, θυσία *IGRom.*4.555 (Ancyra). **-βωμος**, ον, *with twelve altars*, ναός Lyd.*Mens.*4.2. **-γναμπτος**, ον, *bent twelve times*, τέρμα the post (in the race-course) *that has been doubled twelve times*, Pi.*O.*3.33. **-γωνον**, τό, *dodecagon*, Plu.2.363a. **-δάκτῠλος**, ον, *twelve fingers long* or *broad*, Apollod.*Poliorc.*178.3; *of twelve digits*, of the apparent diameter of sun and moon, Cleom.2.3; δ. ἔκφυσις *the duodenum*, Herophil.ap.Gal.2.572, Ruf.*Anat.*42.

δωδεκάδαρχος [κᾰ], ὁ, *leader of twelve*, X.*Cyr.*3.3.11; codd. have -δεκάρχας, -δεκαδάρχας in ib.2.4.4.

δωδεκά-δραχμος, ον, *sold at twelve drachmae*, οἶνος D.42.20. II. *privileged to pay as poll-tax only twelve dr.*, *POxy.*258.8 (i A.D.), al. **-δωρος**, ον, *twelve palms long*, κέρα *AP*6.96 (Eryc.). **-εδρος**, ον, (ἕδρα) *with twelve surfaces*: δωδεκάεδρον, τό, *dodecahedron*, Euc.11 *Def.*28, 13.17, Arist.*Cael.*307ᵃ16.

δωδεκάεθλος [ᾰ], ον, *conqueror in twelve contests*, *Sammelb.*2134.4, *APl.*4.99 (also δύω- Nonn.*D.*35.335).

δωδεκᾰ-ετηρίς, ίδος, ἡ, *cycle of twelve years*, τοῦ Διός *Gp.*1.12 tit.: pl., title of Orphic work, Suid. **-ετής**, ές, or **-έτης**, ες, (ἔτος) *lasting twelve years*, χρόνος J.*AJ*15.9.6. II. *twelve years old*, Plu.*Comp.Lyc.Num.*4, 2.198c. **-ετία**, ἡ, *space of twelve years*, Ptol.*Tetr.*206; ὑπὲρ τῆς δ., title of a speech of Demades. II. *age of twelve years*, *BGU*592i3 (ii A.D.). **-ζῴδιος**, ον, *having twelve signs*, οὐρανός Lyd.*Mens.*4.67.

δωδεκᾰ-ήμερος, ον, *of twelve days*, Eust.128.13. **-θεος**, ον, *of twelve Gods*, *cena*, Suet.*Aug.*70. II. Subst. **-θεον**, τό, *temple of the twelve Gods*, *Inscr.Cos*43. 2. *medicine compounded of twelve ingredients*, Paul.Aeg.7.11. 3. *primrose, Primula acaulis*, Plin.*HN*25.28.

δωδεκάκις, Adv. *twelve times*, Ar.*Pl.*852, Arist.*Fr.*347, D.C.60.7, etc.

δωδεκά-κλῖνος, ον, *holding twelve* κλῖναι, Anaxandr.41.11. **-κρουνος**, ον, *with twelve springs*, Cratin.186, Philostr.*VS*1.22.4. **-κυκλος**, ον, dub. sens., *Sammelb.*1958. **-κωλος**, ον, *of twelve clauses*, Sch.Ar.*Eq.*821. **-λῖνος**, ον, *of twelve threads*, X.*Cyn.*2.5. **-μηνος**, ον, *of twelve months*, τέλος Pi.*N.*11.10 (but δυω- codd.): -μηνον, τό, *year*, Thd.*Da.*4.26, *POxy.*506.15 (ii A. D.):—poet. **δυωδεκάμ-**, *twelve months old*, Hes.*Op.*752. **-μήχᾰνος**, ον, (μηχανή) *knowing twelve arts* or *tricks*, ἄστρον E.*Fr.*755 (lyr.); of a courtesan, Ar.*Ra.* 1327 (et Sch.), cf. Pl.Com.134. **-μν(α)ιαῖος**, α, ον, *weighing twelve minae*, Hsch. s. v. πέλεκυς. **-μορφος**, ον, *of twelve forms*, Olymp. *in Phd.*p.199 N. **-μοχθος**, ον, *of twelve labours*, epith. of Heracles, Lyd.*Mens.*4.67. **-όργυιος**, ον, *of twelve fathoms*, Hero *Geom.*4. 12. **-παις**, παιδος, ὁ, ἡ, *with twelve children*, λοχείη *APl.*4.132 (Theodorid.). **-πᾰλαι**, Adv. *twelve times* πάλαι, *ever so long ago*, Ar.*Eq.*1154; cf. δεκάπαλαι, μυριόπαλαι. **-πηχυς**, υ, *twelve cubits high*, κολοσσοί Hdt.2.153 (δυω-); σιρός Anaxandr.41.28, cf. *BCH*35. 243 (Delos, ii B. C.), Philostr.*VA*4.16. **-πλᾰσιάζω**, *multiply by twelve*, Heph.Astr.2.2. **-πλᾰσιασμός**, ὁ, *multiplication by twelve*, *Cat.Cod.Astr.*4.44. **-πλάσιος**, ον, *twelvefold*, Plu.2.1028c; also **-πλᾰσίων**, ον, gen. ονος, Orib.*Fr.*102. **-πλευρον**, τό, *twelve-sided figure*, v.l. in Gal.*Anim.Pass.*2.3. **-πλους**, ουν, = δωδεκαπλάσιος, Papp.609. **-πους**, ὁ, ἡ, πουν, τό, gen. ποδος, *twelve feet long*, Men. 364, Gal.10.33.

δωδεκάρχης, ου, ὁ, v. δωδεκάδαρχος:—also **-αρχος**, Hsch. s. v. δεκαδάρχαι.

δωδεκάς, άδος, ἡ, *group of twelve*, Pl.*Lg.*756b. II. = δυωδεκαΐς, Hsch. (pl.).

δωδεκά-σεληνος [ᾰ], ον, *having twelve moons*, ἐνιαυτός Sch.E.*Tr.* 1075. **-σημος**, ον, *of twelve times*, in music, Aristid.Quint.1.14, Sch.Ar.*Nu.*456 cod. Ven. **-σκαλμος**, ον, *twelve-oared*, Plu.*Caes.* 38. **-σκῦτος**, ον, *of twelve strips of leather*, σφαῖρα Pl.*Phd.*110b, Plu.2.1003d. **-στάδιος** [στᾰ], ον, *twelve stades long*, etc., Posidon. 18 J., Str.13.1.36. **-στάσιος** [στᾰ], ον, (ἵστημι) *weighing twelve times as much*, Pl.*Hipparch.*231d. **-στεγος**, ον, *with twelve stories*, πύργος Ps.-Callisth.2.18. **-στῦλος** (sc. οἶκος), ὁ, *colonnade of twelve columns*, *Milet.*7.59 (Didyma). **-σύλλᾰβος**, ον, *of twelve syllables*, Ἀλκαϊκὸν δ. (sc. μέτρον) Heph.10.3, 14.4. **-σχοινος**, ἡ, name of a district in Egypt, *OGI*210.5, 670.5, Ptol.*Geog.*4.5.74.

δωδεκᾰταῖος, α, ον, *on the twelfth day, in twelve days*, δ. ἀνεβίω Pl. *R.*614b, cf. Thphr.*HP*7.1.3; δυωδεκαταῖος ἀφ' ὧτέ νιν οὐδὲ ποτεῖδον Theoc.2.157. II. *twelve days old*, Hes.*Op.*751 (in poet. form δυωδ-), Arist.*HA*567ᵃ5.

δωδεκᾰτημόριον, τό, *twelfth part*, [χώρας] Pl.*Lg.*848c, cf. *IG*12(7). 237.56 (Amorgos, ii/i B. C.), Ph.1.673; *sign of the zodiac*, Hipparch. 2.1.7, Ptol.*Tetr.*93, etc.

δωδεκᾰτημόριος, ον, = δυωδεκάμοιρος, Man.4.167:—also **-τήμορος**, ον, *PHib.*1.27.122 (iv/iii B. C.).

δωδέκᾰτος, η, ον, *twelfth*, Il.24.781, etc.; δ. τόκοι, $8\frac{1}{3}\%$, *SIG*364.74 (Ephesus, iii B. C.), etc.:—Ep. **δυωδ-**, Il.1.493, etc. II. δωδεκάτη, ἡ, = Χόες, Hsch.

δωδεκά-τροπος, ἡ, *fixed circle of twelve divisions* through which the zodiac is supposed to revolve, Vett.Val.179.33, *Cat.Cod.Astr.*5 (3).89, al. **-φόρος**, ον, *bearing twelve times a year*, Luc.*VH*2. 13. **-φυλλος**, ον, *with twelve petals*, ῥόδα δ. Thphr.*HP*6.6.4. II. *with twelve leaves*, κλάδος *PMag.Berol.*2.67. **-φῦλος**, ον, *of twelve tribes*, τὸ δ. *the twelve tribes* of Israel, *Act.Ap.*26.7. **-χορδος**, ον, *with twelve strings*, ὄργανον *EM*813.43.

δωδεκᾰχῶς, Adv. *in twelve ways*, *An.Ox.*2.3 (Theognost.).

δωδεκά-χους [ᾰ], χουν, *holding twelve* χόες, *PRev.Laws*40.11 (iii B. C.), al. **-ωρος**, ον, *of twelve hours*, Secund.*Sent.*4, S.E.*M.*10. 182. II. δωδεκάωρος, ἡ, *circle of twelve animal figures* typifying the *double hours* of the Chaldaean νυχθήμερον, Teucer in *Cat.Cod. Astr.*7.195, al.

δωδεκέμβριος, ὁ, = *Dodecember*, month invented by Licinus, D.C. 54.21.

δωδεκ-έτης, ου, or **-ετής**, οῦ, ὁ, *twelve years old*, Call.*Ep.*21 (δωδεκένη Meineke), Plu.*Aem.*35:—in form **δωδεχέτης**, *IG*4.51 (Aegina), *Annuario* 4/5.467 (Halic., iv B. C.):—fem. **-έτις**, ιδος, *AP*11.70 (Leon.). **-εύς**, έως, ὁ, = χοεύς *which held twelve cotylae*, Hsch. **-ήμερος**, ἡ, *period of twelve days*, *IG*1².374.89. **-ήρης**, ους, ἡ, *a ship with twelve banks of oars*, Callix.1.

δωδεκηΐς, ῆδος, ἡ, v. δυωδεκαΐς.

δωδεκόμφᾰλος, ον, *with twelve knobs*, πόπανον *IG*2².1367.

Δωδώνη, ἡ, *Dodona*, in Epirus, the seat of the most ancient oracle of Zeus, Il.16.234, Od.14.327, Hes.*Fr.*134, 212, A.*Pr.*830, etc.: heterocl. forms **Δωδῶνος**, **-ῶνι** (as if from Δωδών), S.*Fr.*460, *Tr.*172: Δωδώνᾱθεν Pi.*N.*4.53; Δωδώνηθε Call.*Del.*284: a nom. Δωδώ, Simm. ap.Str.8.5.3:—Adj. **Δωδωναῖος**, α, ον, Il.16.233, A.*Supp.*258, Cratin.5: prov., Δωδωναῖον χαλκεῖον *chatterbox*, Eust.335.45:—fem. **Δωδωνίς**, ίδος, S.*Fr.*456, Hdt.2.53, Pherecyd.90 J.

δωΐα· ὁμοία, Hsch.

δωλέννετος· ὑπόβλητος, Hsch.; cf. sq.

δωλοδομεῖς· οἰκογενεῖς, Hsch. (cf. δοῦλος and ἐβάθη· ἐγεννήθη, Id.: Lith. *gimti* 'to be born').

δῶλος, Dor., = δοῦλος, *Leg.Gort.*1.1, al.; voc. δῶλε Theoc.5.5: but δῶλα· ὦτα (Cret.), Hsch.

δῶμα, ατος, τό, (δέμω) *house*, πατρώϊον ἵκετο δ. Il.21.44, etc.; mainly poet., but once in Hdt., 2.62 (pl.), and in late Prose (v. infr.), but never in Att. Prose: also, *chief room, hall*, θάλαμον καὶ δ. καὶ αὐλήν Il.6.316, cf. Od.17.329, al.: hence, pl. for *a single house*, 2.259, freq. in Trag., A.*Ag.*607, S.*Tr.*332, E.*Or.*301, etc. 2. of the gods, ἀθάνατοι Ὀλύμπια δώματ' ἔχοντες Il.2.13, etc.; κλυτὰ δ. βένθεσι λίμνης, of Poseidon, 13.21; freq. of Pluto, δῶμ' Ἀΐδαο the nether world, Od.12.21; ὦ δῶμ' Ἀΐδου καὶ Περσεφόνης S.*El.*110; Πλούτωνος δ. E.*HF*808 (lyr.); of a temple, Pi.*P.*4.53, A.*Eu.*242, etc.: pl., Hdt.2.62, S.*OT*71. 3. δῶμα Καδμεῖον, i. e. Thebes, ib.29. 4. *housetop*, Lxx *De.*22.8, *Ev.Matt.*24.17, Babr.5.5, *POxy.*475.22 (ii A. D.), etc. II. *household, family*, A.*Ag.*1468 (lyr.), S.*OT*1226, etc.; cf. δῶ.

δωμάτ-ιον [ᾰ], τό, Dim. of δῶμα, Ar.*Ra.*100, *IG*12(8).442.8 (Thasos), Jul. *ad Them.*263a. II. *chamber, bedchamber*, Ar.*Lys.* 160, Lys.1.17, 24, Pl.*R.*390c, and so prob. in X.Eph.2.1, Procop. *Arc.*23. III. *housetop* (cf. foreg. 1.4), J.*BJ*2.21.5, Hdn.1.12. 8. **-ίτης** [ῑ], ου, ὁ, *of, belonging to the house*, Ποσειδῶν Paus.3.14. 7, *IG*5(1).497, al. (Sparta); Ἀπόλλων Sch.Pi.*N.*5.81: fem., δωματῖτις ἑστία A.*Ag.*968. **-όομαι**, Pass., *have a house built for one, to be housed*, δεδωμάτωμαι οὐ σμικρᾷ χερί Id.*Supp.*958.

δωμᾰτοφθορέω, *ruin the house*, cj. for σωματοφθ-, A.*Ag.*948.

δωμ-άω, *build*, A.R.2.531, *IG*14.1868, *AP*7.142:—more freq. in Med., ib.11.400 (Luc.), Coluth.287, Orph.*A.*570: metaph., *build up, restore to life*, τινά Lyc.48:—Pass., δ. ἐκ λίθων Antyll.ap.Orib.9. 13.6; of a statue, *to be set up*, *App.Anth.*2.534 (Halic.). **-ημα**, ατος, τό, *chamber*, δω[μ]ήματι τύμβου Benndorf-Niemann *Reisen in Lykien* p.80 No.59 (Sidyma). **-ησις**, εως, ἡ, and **-ητύς**, ύος, ἡ, *building*, Hsch. **-ήτωρ**, ορος, ὁ, *builder*, Man.6.415.

δωμός, Dor. for ζωμός, Epil.3 (prob. l.), *EM*316.56.

δώνακος, δώνακι, v. δόναξ.

δωός, v. ζωός.

δωράκινον (sc. μῆλον), τό, = Lat. *duracinum*, a kind of **peach**, *clingstone*, *Gp.*3.1.4, 10.13.1.

δώραξ· σπλήν (Maced.), Hsch.

δωρ-εά, Ion. **-εή**, ἡ: δωρειά in earlier Attic Inscrr., *IG*1².77, al., δωρεᾶ first in ib.2².1.68:—*gift, present*, esp. *bounty* (= δόσις ἀναπόδοτος Arist.*Top.*125ᵃ18), Hdt.2.140; δωρεὰν διδόναι Id.6.130, A.*Pr.*340; πορεῖν ib.616; δωρεῖσθαι Pl.*Plt.*290c; δ. δέχεσθαι, λαμβάνειν, Isoc.6. 31, 15.40; ironically, θάνατόν τινι δωρεὰν ἀποδοῦναι Antipho 5.34; δ. ἔχειν S.*Aj.*1032, D.18.312; ἐν χάριτος μέρει καὶ δωρειᾶς D.21.165; δωρειὰν καὶ χάριν ib.172, cf. Pl.*Lg.*844d; of a *legacy*, D.27.41, 65; δωρεαί *privileges* and *immunities*, opp. δῶρα, *gifts in cash* or *kind*, Philostr.*VS*2.10.4. 2. *estate granted* by a king, *fief*, Phoenicid. 4.7, *PSI*5.511.4, 518.2 (iii B. C.). II. acc. δωρεάν as Adv., *as a free gift, freely*, Hdt.5.23, prob. in And.1.4; μηδὲν δ. πράττειν Plb. 18.34.7, cf. Lxx *Jb.*1.9; δ. λειτουργεῖν *Test.Epict.*4.27, cf. *Inscr.Prien.* 4.17 (iv B. C.); so κατὰ δωρεάν *IG*7.2711.13, al. (Acraeph., i A. D.); ἐν δωρεᾷ προσνεῖμαι Plb.22.5.4; but γῆν (ἀμπελῶνα, etc.) ἐν δωρεᾷ ἔχειν to hold land by a royal *grant*, *PRev.Laws*36.15 (iii B. C.), cf. 43.11, 44.3. 2. *to no purpose, for naught*, *Ep.Gal.*2.21. **-εαῖος**, α, ον, *held by royal grant*, γῆ *Sammelb.*1178a, b, cf. 3937, 3938 (iii B. C.); v. foreg. II. **-εαστικός**, ή, όν, *concerning grants*, γράμμα *PMasp.* 13.26 (vi A. D.). **-ετικός**, ή, όν, = foreg., ὁμολογία *Sammelb.*4678. 13 (vi A. D.). **-έω**, fut. -ήσω Hom.*Fr.*17: aor. ἐδώρησα Hes.*Op.* 82, Pi.*O.*6.78:—*give, present*, δῶρον Hes. l. c.; *present* one *with*, θυσίαις Ἑρμᾶν Pi. l. c.:—Pass., aor. δωρηθῆναι *to be given* or *presented*, Hdt.1.87, Isoc.4.26: in pf. Pass., παρὰ θεῶν δῶρα ὑμῖν δεδώρηται Pl. *Plt.*274c; and of persons, *to be presented with* a thing, χώρῃ Hdt.8. 85, cf. S.*Aj.*1029. II. more freq. Med. **δωρέομαι**, ῥεῖα θεὸς ... ἵππους δωρήσαιτ' Il.10.557; δωρέεσθαί τί τινι *present* a thing *to* one, Hdt.2.126, 5.37, A.*Pr.*253, X.*An.*7.3.20, etc.; σπέρμα εἰς Πελοπόννησον δωρήσασθε Id.*HG*6.3.6; also δ. τινά τινι *present* one *with* a thing, Hdt.1.54, 3.130, A.*Pr.*778; δ. τινά *to make* him *presents*, Hdt. 1.55: pf., δεδώρηται Pl.*Ti.*46e, *Lg.*672b, X.*Cyr.*[5.2.8]. 2. in pres. and impf. also, *offer*, E.*Supp.*875. **-ημα**, ατος, τό, *gift, present*, Hdt.7.38, etc.: c. dat. pers., A.*Pers.*523, *Eu.*402, S.*Tr.*668: pl., E.*Or.*123, etc.—Rare in Prose, X.*Hier.*8.4, Arist.*EN*1099ᵇ11, and later, Ph.2.9, *Ep.Jac.*1.17. **-ημᾰτικός**, ή, όν, = δωρητικός, D.H.8.60, Vett.Val.41.3. **-ητήρ**, ῆρος, ὁ, *giver*, *AP*6.305 (Leon.). **-ητής**, οῦ, ὁ, *benefactor*, *IG*12(2).645ᵇ64 (Nesus, iv B. C.). **-ητικός**, ή, όν, *concerned with giving*, Pl.*Sph.*223c. II. *munificent*, Ph.1.254. **-ητός**, όν, of persons, *open to gifts* or *presents*, Il.9.526. II. of things, *freely given*, δ., οὐκ αἰτητόν S. *OT*384, cf. Plu.*Cor.*16.

Δωρι-άζω, *dress like a Dorian girl*, i. e. in a single garment open at the side, Anacr.59. II. = Δωρίζω, *Anacreont.*10.6, Philostr.*VS* 1.24.2. **-ᾰκός**, ή, όν, poet. for Δωρικός, πόλεμος Orac.ap.Th.2. 54. **-αρχέω**, *to be archon of the Dorians*, *SIG*668.12 (Delph., ii B. C.), 770ᴮ2 (Delph., i B. C.). **-εια**, τά, *festival at Cnidus*, *GDI* 4271 (Cedreae):—also **Δώρεια**, ib.3660 (Cos). **-εύς**, έως, ὁ, *Dorian, descendant of Dorus* son of Hellen, *IG*12(5).225 (Paros): pl., Δωριεῖς, Ion. -ιέες, Att. -ιῆς, οἱ, *the Dorians*, Od.19.177, etc. II. as Adj., = Δωρικός, Pi.*P.*8.20.

Δωρ-ίζω, Dor. -ίσδω, *imitate the Dorians in life, dialect*, etc., *speak Doric Greek*, Theoc.15.93, Str.8.1.2, Plu.2.421b:—Pass., *to be written in the Doric dialect*, δ. τὰ Ἀλκμᾶνος A.D.*Synt.*279.25. **-ικός**, ή, όν, *Doric*, Hdt.8.43, Th.3.95, etc.: Comp. -ώτερος A.D.*Adv.*159.27. Adv. -κῶς Id.*Pron.*48.27, S.E.*M.*1.78: Comp. -ώτερον A.D.*Synt.* 159.16. **-ιος**, α, ον, also ος, ον Pratin.Lyr.1.17, Arist.*Pol.*1276ᵇ9: —*Dorian*, Pi.*O.*3.5; ἁπλοῦν τε καὶ Δ. Plu.*Lys.*5, etc.; esp. of the *Dorian* mode in music, Arist.*Pol.* l. c., 1290ᵃ22. **-ίς**, ίδος, ἡ, fem. Adj. *Dorian*, ἐσθής Hdt.5.88; φωνή Th.6.5, etc.: hence, 1. Δ. νᾶσος the *Dorian* island, of Aegina and Peloponnesus, Pi.*N*.3.3, S.*OC*696 (lyr.), etc. 2. (with or without γῆ) *Doris*, in Northern Greece, Hdt.8.31, Plu.*Them*.9, etc. 3. Δ. κόρα a *Dorian* damsel, E.*Hec*.934 (lyr.). 4. (sc. κοπίς) *Dorian knife* used at sacrifices, Id. *El*.819. 5. Δωρίς, = ἔχιον, Dsc.4.27. b. = λεοντοπέταλον, Ps.-Dsc.3.96 (also δωριπτερίς ibid.). **-ίσδω**, Dor. for Δωρίζω. **-ισμός**, ὁ, *speaking in the Doric dialect*, Demetr.*Eloc*.177. **-ιστί** [ῐ], Adv. *in Dorian fashion*, Δ. ζῆν Pl.*Ep*.336c. 2. *in the Dorian dialect*, λαλοῦσι Δ. Call.*Iamb*.1.354. II. ἡ Δ. ἁρμονία the *Dorian* mode or measure in music, Arist.*Pol*.1340ᵇ4; so Δ. alone, Pl.*R*.399a; in Ar.*Eq*.989 (lyr.) with a play on δῶρον.

δωρίτης [ῑ] ἀγών, ὁ, game *in which the conqueror received a present*, Plu.2.820d.

δωρο-γραφία, ἡ, dub. sens. in *Ostr.Strassb*.277.11, al. (ii A.D.). **-δειπνος**, ον, *giving dinner*, παῖς δ., i.e. a waiter, Ath.15.701b. **-δέκτης**, ου, ὁ, *one that takes bribes*, Lxx *Jb*.15.34. **-δοκέω**, *accept as a present*, esp. *take as a bribe*, ἀργύριον πολλόν Hdt.6.72; χρυσόν Pl.*R*.590a; κατὰ πεντήκοντα τάλαντα Ar.*V*.669. 2. abs., *take bribes*, Hdt.6.82, D.18.45, etc.; ἐπί τινι Lys.21.22, D.18.49. II. c. acc. pers. (only in later Gr., for δωροδοκοῦσιν is f.l. in Ar.*V*.675 and δωροδοκοῦντας (abs.) is interpol. in D.9.45), *corrupt by bribes*, D.S.13.64, Arr.*Epict*.4.1.148, Luc.*Pisc*.9, etc. 2. simply, *bestow gifts*, *AP*9.335 (Leon.): c. acc., ib.12.204 (Strat.). III. Pass., of persons, *to have a bribe given one*, Cratin.128, cf. Plb.6.56.2, D.H.4.55 (as v.l.); also ταῦθ' ἁπλῶς δεδωροδόκηται this *has been accomplished by bribery*, D.19.329 (v.l. -ηνται); τὰ περὶ τὴν Εὔβοιαν δωροδοκηθέντα *the bribery* in the matter of Euboea, Aeschin.3.221; τὸ δεδωροδοκημένον χρυσίον Din.1.66. **-δόκημα**, ατος, τό, *acceptance of a bribe, corruption*, D.18.20,31. 2. *bribe*, καταλαβεῖν Pl.Com.119. **-δοκία**, ἡ, *taking of bribes*, freq. in Oratt., as And.4.30; δωροδοκίαν καταγνῶναί τινος Lys.21.21; -ίας κατηγορεῖν Aeschin.2.3: pl., ibid.; also, *giving of bribes, corruption*, in pl., D.C.39.55, 50.7. **-δοκιστί**, Adv. *in bribe-fashion*, Ar.*Eq*.996, with a play on Δωριστί. **-δόκος**, ον, *taking presents* or *bribes, corrupt*, Pl.*R*.390d, D.18.61; Com., δωροδόκοισιν ἐπ' ἄνθεσιν ἵζων Ar.*Eq*.403. II. Act., *bribing*, Sch.Pl.*Alc*.2.149a, cf. *AB*242. 2. *munificent*, Aret.*SD*2.12. **-δοτέω**, *give presents*, Aq.*Ez*.16.33. **-δότης**, ου, ὁ, *giver of presents*, λάθας δ. *AP*12.49 (Mel.). **-δοχεῖον**, τό, *receptacle for offerings, alms-box*, Zonar. s. v. Κορβωνᾶς. **-κοπέω**, *bribe*, Lxx *Si*.32(35).12:—Pass., ib.3 *Ma*.4.19. **-κοπία**, ἡ, *bribery*, Aq.*De*.10.17, Sm.*Ps*.25(26).10. **-κόπος**, *one who bribes*, *Gloss*. **-ληπτέω**, *take presents*, Eust.91.17. **-λήπτης**, ου, ὁ, *greedy of gain*, Lxx *Pr*.15.27. **-ληψία**, ἡ, *taking of presents*, *Com.Adesp*.987, D.C.39.55.

δῶρον, τό, (δίδωμι) *gift, present, gift of honour*, ἀγλαὰ δ. Il.1.213, etc.; *votive gift* or *offering* to a god, φέρε δῶρον Ἀθήνῃ 6.293, cf. Lxx *Ge*.4.4, *Ev.Marc*.7.11; βωμοὶ δώροισι φλέγονται A.*Ag*.91; ποῦ μοι τὰ ..δ. κἀκροθίνια; Id.*Fr*.184; δῶρά τινος *the gifts of*, i.e. *given by*, him, θεῶν ἐρικυδέα δ. Il.20.265, cf. Od.18.142; δῶρ' Ἀφροδίτης, i.e. personal charms, Il.3.54,64; δ. Κύπριδος E.*Hel*.363 (lyr.); δ. τῶν Μουσῶν καὶ Ἀπόλλωνος, of μουσική, Pl.*Lg*.796e: c. gen. rei, ὕπνου δ. *the blessing* of sleep, Il.7.482; δῶρα *presents* given as tribute, 17.225; δῶρον τοῦ ποταμοῦ, of the land of Egypt, Hdt.2.5. 2. δῶρα *presents*, as retaining fees or bribes, D.18.109, Jusj.ib.24.150, Arist.*Ath*.55.5, *SIG*953.7 (Calymna), etc. (the usual sense of the word in Att. Oratt.): hence in Att. law, δώρων γραφή an indictment *for being bribed*, Aeschin.3.232, etc., cf. Harp.; δώρων κριθῆναι to be tried *for taking bribes*, Lys.27.3; δώρων ἑλεῖν τινα to convict him *of taking bribes*, Ar.*Nu*.591; δ. ὀφλεῖν to be found guilty *of taking bribes*, And.1.74; δώρων δίωξις Plu.*Per*.32. 3. in pl., *good qualities, talents*, τὰ βασιλέως δ. Lib.*Ep*.19. II. *front part of palm*, Poll.2.144. 2. *hand's breadth, palm*, as a measure of length, Nic.*Th*.398, Vitr.2.3.3, *Milet*.7.57 (Didyma); cf. δεκάδωρος.

δωρο-ξενίας γραφή, ἡ, *indictment of a ξένος for bribing the judges to declare him an Athenian*, Lys.*Fr*.196 S., Hyp.*Fr*.20, Arist.*Ath*.59.3. **-τελέω**, *bring presents*, Orac.ap.D.43.66. **-φάγος** [ᾰ], ον, *devouring gifts, greedy of presents*, Hes.*Op*.221, 264, Plb.6.9.7. **-φορέω**, *bring presents*, τινί Pl.*Phdr*.266c, cf. *Euthphr*.14e, prob. in Epigr. ap.Ath.5.209e (Archimelos); *give as presents* or *bribes*, τί τινι Ar.*V*.675, cf. D.C.40.53. II. δ. τινά present him *with gifts*, Ael.*VH*1.32. **-φορία**, ἡ, *bringing of presents*, v.l. in *Ep.Rom*.15.31, Alciphr.1.6 (pl.), Poll.4.47. **-φορικός**, ή, όν, = sq., Pl.*Sph*.222d. II. *given as a present*, στολή Ael.*VH*1.22. **-φόρος**, ον, *bringing presents*, Pi.*P*.5.86, f.l. in Epigr.ap.Ath.5.209e (Archimelos); *tributary*, Euph.78.

δωρύττομαι, Dor. for δωρέομαι, Theoc.7.43.

δωρώνιον, = σίον, corrupt in Ps.-Dsc.2.127.

δώς, ἡ, = δόσις, only in nom., Hes.*Op*.356.

δωσί-άραις· κακὰ διδούσαις, Hsch. **-βιος**, ον, *life-giving*, *Mus. Belg*.16.70. **-δικία**, ἡ, *administration of justice*, *IGRom*.3.563 (Tlos). **-δικος**, ον, *referring disputes to a court*, Hdt.6.42. 2. *subject to jurisdiction*, δ. παρασχεῖν τοὺς ἠδικηκότας Plb.4.4.3, cf. *UPZ*121.14. **-πῡγος** or **δοσίπῡγος**, ον, = κίναιδος, Suid. s. v. ἀφέλεια.

δώσων, οντος, ὁ, fut. part. of δίδωμι, *always going to give, always promising*: hence Δώσων as a name of Antigonus II, Plu.*Cor*.11.

δώτειρα, ἡ, fem. of sq., Linus ap.Stob.3.1.70, Arat.113, Man.2.447, Nonn.*D*.19.45.

δωτήρ, ῆρος, ὁ, *giver*, δωτῆρες ἑάων *givers* of good, i.e. the gods, Od.8.325, Hes.*Th*.46, etc.: voc. δῶτερ ὑγείης *Rev.Arch*.1911.439 (Thrace).

δώτης, ου, ὁ, = foreg., Hes.*Op*.355.

δωτῑνάζω, *receive* or *collect presents*, Hdt.2.180.

δωτίνη [ῑ], ἡ, *gift, present*, Il.9.155, Od.9.268, Hdt.1.61; δωτίνην δοῦναι give *as a free gift*, ib.69, cf. Them.*Or*.21.260d. II. *rent in kind*, *IG*4.841.8,11 (Calauria, iii B.C.).

δῶττις· δώς, φέρνη, Hsch.

δωτύς, ύος, ἡ, Ion., = τροφή, Suid. (leg. ἐδητύς).

Δωτώ, οῦς, ἡ, *Giver*, name of a Nereid, Il.18.43, Hes.*Th*.248.

δώτωρ, ορος, ὁ, = δωτήρ, δῶτορ ἑάων *giver* of goods, addressed to Hermes, Od.8.335, *h.Hom*.18.12, cf. Luc.*Sat*.14; to Zeus, Call.*Jov*.91; θεοὶ τούτων δώτορες ἀμφοτέρων Thgn.134, cf. E.*Hyps.Fr*.7.5.

E

E ε, ἒ ψιλόν, fifth letter of the Gr. alphabet: as numeral ε′ = πέντε and πέμπτος, but ͵ε = 5,000:—its name was εἶ, q.v., later ἒ ψιλόν; cf. ψιλός.

ἒ ἔ, or repeated **ἒ ἒ ἒ ἔ**, an exclamation of pain or grief; *woe! woe!* A.*Ag*.1114, etc.; always doubled either once or twice and better written ἐέ (as in cod. Med. of A. and S.), or (where the metre requires an iambus) ἐή S.*OC*149; but ἠέ cod. Med. in A.*Th*.966.

ἕ, v. οὗ.

ἔᾱ, exclam. of surprise or displeasure, *ha! oho!* esp. before a question, ἔα, τί χρῆμα; A.*Pr*.300, E.*Or*.1573; ἔα, τίς οὗτος...; Id. *Hec*.501, cf. 733, al.; ἔα, τίς ἔσθ'; Ar.*Pl*.824; sts. extra versum, E. *Hec*.1116, *Med*.1005, al.; sts. doubled, ἔ. ἔα, ἄπεχε A.*Pr*.688 (lyr.); ἔα [ἔα], ἰδού S.*OC*1477 (lyr.).—Rare in Prose, ἔα, ἔφη, σοφισταί τινες Pl.*Prt*.314d; ἔα, τί ἡμῖν καὶ σοί; *Ev.Luc*.4.34.

ἔᾱ, Ep. and Ion. for ἦν, impf. of εἰμί. **ἔᾱγα, ἐάγην** [ᾰ], v. ἄγνυμι. **ἔακεν**· ἀλγεῖ, Hsch. **ἕαδα**, part. ἑαδώς, v. ἁνδάνω. **ἑάλη**, v. εἴλω. **ἐαλόν**· λυπηρόν, λυτήριον, Hsch. **ἑάλωκα, ἑαλώκειν**, v. ἁλίσκομαι.

ἐάν (so early Attic Inscrr., as *IG*1².3.20, εἰάν sts. after B.C. 400, ib.2².28.17, cf. *PEleph*.1.8,10 (iv B.C.)), also contr. ἤν and ἄν, v. ἤν, ἄν (B) [ᾱ], which by crasis with καί become κἄν:—*if haply, if*, regularly folld. by subj.: for its use and for examples, v. εἰ B. II, and ἄν (A) B. I. 1. II. In Hellenistic and late Greek, = ἄν after relative Pronouns and Conjunctions, as ὃς ἐάν whosoever, Lxx *Ge*.15.14, *PTeb*.107.8 (ii B.C.), *Ev.Matt*.5.19, al.; ὅσος ἐάν *PPetr*.3p.120 (iii B.C.), *Ev.Matt*.18.18; ὅστις ἐάν Ph.1.220, M.Ant.9.23; ὅπου ἐάν *Ev.Matt*.8.19, etc.; ὅθεν ἐάν *Gp*.1.3.3: folld. by ind., Lxx 1*Ki*.2.14. [The second syll. of ἐάν is long, S.*OC*1407, Ar.*V*.228, Sopat.6.9.]

ἑάνδανε, v. ἁνδάνω.

ἑανηφόρος, ον, (ἑανός, ὁ) *wearing a thin robe*, Ἠώς Antim.84.

ἑανός, ή, όν, Ep. Adj. (never in Od.):—*fine*, of fabrics and materials for wearing, ἑανῷ λιτί with *fine* linen, Il.18.352, 23.254; πέπλος ἑανός 5.734, 8.385; ἑανοῦ κασσιτέροιο tin *beaten out fine*, 18.613; ἱμάτιον Sapph.(?)122. II. as Subst., **ἑανός**, ὁ, *fine robe*, once in nom., ἀμφὶ δ' ἄρ' ἀμβρόσιος ἑανὸς τρέμε Il.21.507; νεκταρέου ἑανοῦ 3.385; ἑανῷ ἀργῆτι φαεινῷ ib.419; ἀμβρόσιον ἑανόν (acc.) 14.178; ἑανῶν πτύχας ἱμεροέντων *h.Cer*.176; λεπταλέῳ ἑανῷ A.R.4.169; ἑανοῖς χρυσειδέσι *Hymn.Is*.109; also with the first syll. long, εἱανοῦ ἁπτομένη Il.16.9; cf. ἵανον. 2. *sail*, λῦε ἑανοῦ πτέρυγας *Lyr.Alex.Adesp*.20.9. [Hom. always makes ᾱ in the Adj., ᾰ in the Subst.; but later poets use ᾱ or ᾰ, as suits the metre, as Orph.*A*.877, 1223.] (Cf. ἕννυμι (q.v.); the Subst. has the digamma, Il.14.178, 21.507, whereas the Adj. has not, 18.352, 613, 23.254.)

ἐάνπερ, v. εἰ B. II. **ἔαντο**· ἦσαν, Hsch.

ἔαξα, v. ἄγνυμι.

ἔᾰρ (A), τό, Hom. (only gen. ἔαρος), etc.; contr. ἦρ Alcm.76: gen., dat., ἦρος, ἦρι, Lyr. (Alc.45), Att., and prob. Ion., cf. Hdt.1.77, Hp. *Epid*.1.1 (but ἔαρος is found in codd. of Hdt.5.31, 7.162, al., Hp.l.c.): poet. gen., dat., εἴαρος, εἴαρι (metri gr.), Alcm.26, *h.Cer*.174 (nisi leg. ἤαρος), and later Poets (whence was formed late nom. εἶαρ Numen. ap.Ath.9.371e, Ter.Maur.653); cf. Hdn.Gr.1.408 (Hes. used ἔαρ as a monos., and ἔαρι as a trochee, *Op*.492, 462):—*spring*, ἔαρος δ' ἐπιγίγνεται ὥρη Il.6.148; ἔαρος νέον ἱσταμένοιο early *spring*, Od.19.519; ἔαρι πολεῖν Hes.*Op*.462; ἅμα τῷ ἔαρι at the beginning of *spring*, Hdt.5.31, cf. Th.4.117, 6.8; πρὸς ἔαρ Id.5.56, etc.; πρὸς τὸ ἔ. ib.17; περὶ τὸ ἔ. Id.3.116; ἐξ ἦρος εἰς Ἀρκτοῦρον S.*OT*1137: prov., μία χελιδὼν ἔαρ οὐ ποιεῖ Cratin.33; also of the *prime, flower* of anything, ἐφήβοι. .ἔ. τοῦ δήμου Demad.*Fr*.4 S., cf. Hdt.7.162, Arist.*Rh*.1411ᵃ3; ἔ. δρώωσα looking *fresh and bright*, Theoc.13.45; γενύων ἔ. *the first down* on a youth's face, *AP*6.242 (Crin.); ὕμνων ἔ. *the freshest, brightest* of their kind, ib.7.12; τὸ ἔ. τῶν πτερῶν, of a peacock, Luc. *Dom*.11. (Ϝεσϝ-, cf. γέαρ, γίαρ[ες], Lat. *vēr*, Skt. *vasantas*, Lith. *vasara* 'summer'.)

ἔᾱρ (B) or **εἶᾰρ** (Hsch. **ἦαρ, ἴαρα**), τό, in Alex. Poets, *blood*, λύθρῳ τε καὶ εἴαρι πεπλήθασι Call.*Fr.anon*.20; Αἰακίδαο εἴαρος Euph.39.3; τὸ δ' ἐκ μέλαν εἶαρ ἔλαπτεν Call.*Fr*.247, cf. Nic.*Al*.314, Opp.*H*.2.618; cf. εἰαροπότης, εἰαροπῶτις. 2. *juice*, εἶαρ ἐλαίης Nic.*Al*.87; ἐκ λύχνου πῖον ἔλειξαν ἔαρ Call.*Fr*.201. (Cypr. acc. to Hsch.; identified with ἔαρ *spring*, by *EM*307.44, Suid.; cf. Skt. *ásṛk*, gen. *asnás*, Lett. *asinis* 'blood'.)

ἐαρδάλη· ἐπλησίασεν, Hsch. **ἐαρίδας**· τὰς κανθαρίδας, Id.

ἐᾱρίδρεπτος (-δροπος Bgk.), ον, *plucked in spring*, Pi.*Fr.*75.6.

ἐᾱρίζω, *pass the spring*, X.*An.*3.5.15. II. *bloom as in spring*, Ph.2.99:—Med., λειμῶνες ἄνθεσιν ἐαριζόμενοι Pl.*Ax.*371c. III. *to be like spring*, μετοπώρου ἐαρίζοντος Ph.1.13, cf. 2.643.

ἐᾱρῐνός, ή, όν, Ep. **εἰαρινός** (also **ἠαρινός** *h.Cer.*401, *PPetr.*3 p.152 (iii B.C.)); in other Poets, **ἠρινός**:—*of spring*, εἰαρινὴ ὥρη *springtime*, Il.16.643, cf. Plb.3.34.6; εἰαρινὰ ἄνθεα Il.2.89; πλόος εἰαρινός Hes.*Op.*678; θάλπος ἐαρινόν the heat *of spring*, X.*Cyr.*8.6.22; ἄνεμος ἠρινός Sol.13.19; ἠρινὰ φύλλα Pi.*P.*9.46; λειμῶνος ἠρινοῦ στάχυν E.*Supp.*448; ἐ. πυλαία *IG*9(1).111 (Elatea); τροπαί Ph.2.163; μῆλα ἐ. *apricots*, *PCair.Zen.*33.13 (iii B.C.):—neut. as Adv., *in spring-time*, μέλισσα λειμῶν' ἠρινὸν διέρχεται E.*Hipp.*77 (s.v.l., ἐαρινή Sch.); γῆ ἠρινὸν θάλλουσα Id.*Fr.*316.3: ἠρινὰ κελαδεῖν, of the swallow, Ar.*Pax* 800 (lyr.). Adv. ἐαρινῶς Hsch. s.v. ἦρις ὡς.

ἐάριον· ῥόδον, Hsch.

ἔᾱρον, τό, *ewer*, *IG*12(3).450[a]1 (Thera, pl.); ἐαρόν, Hsch.

ἐᾰρο-τρεφής, ές, *flourishing in spring*, λειμῶνες Mosch.2.67. **-χροος**, ον, *spring-coloured, fresh green*, ἴασπις Orph.*L.*267.

ἐάρτερος, α, ον, poet. for ἐαρινός, Nic.*Th.*380.

ἔᾱσι, Ep. 3 pl. of εἰμί. **ἔασκον**, Ion. and Ep. impf. of ἐάω. **ἔασσα**, Dor. part. fem. of εἰμί.

ἐασφόρος· ἑωσφόρος, Hsch. **ἕᾰται, ἕατο**, Ion. 3 pl. pres. and impf. of ἧμαι.

ἐᾱτέος, α, ον, (ἐάω) *to be suffered*, E.*Ph.*1210: c. inf., ἐατέος ἐστὶ φεύγειν Hdt.8.108, cf. Pl.*R.*401b. 2. ἐατέον *one must suffer*, E.*HF* 173, etc. II. *to be let alone* or *given up*, ἐ. ὁ πλοῦτος Id.*Hel.*905, cf. Ph.1.564. 2. τὴν πόλιν ἐατέον τῆς κατοικίσεως we *must let* it *alone* as to foundation, Pl.*Lg.*969c; *one must dismiss* from one's mind, Id.*Grg.*512e; *one must omit*, Str.2.5.18.

ἑαυτάδελφος [ᾰ], ὁ, incorrect form for αὐτ-, *CPR*1.155.

ἑαυτότης, ητος, ἡ, *self-hood*, Procl.*Theol.Plat.*5.37.

ἑαυτοῦ, ῆς, οῦ, ἑαυτῷ, ῇ, ῷ, ἑαυτόν, ήν, ό, pl. ἑαυτῶν, ἑαυτοῖς, ἑαυτούς άς, ά: Ion. **ἑωυτοῦ** *SIG*57.44 (Milet., v B.C.), etc.; also ὡὐτῆς Herod. 6.84, ὡὐτέου Aret.*SA*1.7 (Ion. ἑων- by contraction of ἑο αὐ-, from which also Att. ἑᾱυ-, freq. written ἑατοῦ in Pap. and Inscrr., as *SIG* 774.2 (Delph., i B.C.): Att. contr. **αὑτοῦ**, etc., which is the usual form in Trag., though ἑαυτοῦ, etc., are used (though rarely) when the metre requires, A.*Pr.*188 (anap.), al.; in Att. Inscrr. αὑτοῦ prevails after B.C. 300; Cret. **ϝιαυτοῦ** Kohler-Ziebarth *Stadtrecht von Gortyn* p.34; Dor. **αὐταυτοῦ, αὑσαυτοῦ** (q.v.); Thess. **εὑτοῦ** (dat.), *IG*9(2). 517.16: gen. pl. **ηὑτῶν** *Schwyzer* 251 *A* 44 (Cos):—reflex. Pron. of 3rd pers., *of himself, herself, itself*, etc.; first in Alc.78, Hdt., and Att. (Hom. has ἑο αὐτοῦ, οἷ αὐτῷ, ἓ αὐτόν): αὐτὸ ἐφ' ἑαυτό (v.l. -τοῦ) itself by *itself, absolutely*, Pl.*Tht.*152b; αὐτὸ ἐφ' αὑτοῦ ib.160b; ὅταν τὸ ἐφ' ἑαυτὸν ἕκαστος σπεύδῃ Th.1.141; αὐτὸ καθ' αὑτό Pl.*Tht.*157a; αὐτὰ πρὸς αὑτά ib.154e; ἀφ' ἑαυτῶν, ἑαυτοῦ, of *themselves, himself*, Th. 5.60, X.*Mem.*2.10.3; ἐφ' ἑαυτοῦ, v. ἐπί; ἐν ἑαυτῷ γίγνεσθαι, ἐντὸς ἑαυτοῦ γ., v. ἐν, ἐντός; παρ' ἑαυτῷ at *his own* house, ib.3.13.3, etc.: esp. with Comp. and Sup., ἐγένοντο ἀμείνονες αὐτοὶ ἑωυτῶν they surpassed *themselves*, Hdt.8.86; πλουσιώτεροι ἑαυτῶν continually richer, Th.1.8; θαρραλεώτεροι αὐτοὶ ἑαυτῶν Pl.*Prt.*350a, cf. d; τῇ αὐτὸ ἑωυτοῦ ἐστι μακρότατον at its very greatest length, Hdt.2.8, cf. 149, 4.85, 198. II. in Att., Trag., and later, αὑτοῦ, etc., is used for the 1st or 2nd pers., as for ἐμαυτοῦ, αὐτὸς καθ' αὑτοῦ τἄρα μηχανορραφῶ A.*Ch.*221, cf. S.*OT*138, etc.; for σεαυτοῦ, μόρον τὸν αὑτῆς οἶσθα A.*Ag.*1297, cf. 1141, Pl.*Phd.*101c (v.l.), Ph.*Bel.*59.16, etc.: so in pl., τὰ αὑτῶν (= ἡμῶν αὐτῶν) ἐκποριζώμεθα Th.1.82; δώσομεν ἑαυτούς Epicur.*Sent.Vat.*47; ἐφ' ἑαυτοῖς by *ourselves*, Lxx 1 *Ki.*14.9, cf. *PPar.*47.26 (ii B.C.), 2 *Ep.Cor.*7.1, etc.; ἑαυτῶν, = ὑμῶν αὐτῶν, *PPar.* 63.128 (ii B.C.). III. pl., ἑαυτῶν, ἑαυτοῖς, etc., is sts. used for ἀλλήλων, ἀλλήλοις, *one another*, διάφοροι ἑωυτοῖσι Hdt.3.49; παρακελευόμενοι ἐν ἑαυτοῖς Th.4.25, etc.; καθ' αὑτοῖν *one* against *the other*, S.*Ant.*144 (anap.); πρὸς αὑτούς D.18.19; περιιόντες αὑτῶν πυνθάνονται Id.4.10, cf. Pl.*Ly.*215b.

ἑάφθη, found only in Il.13.543 ἐπὶ δ' ἀσπὶς ἑάφθη καὶ κόρυς and 14. 419 ἐπ' αὐτῷ ἀσπὶς ἑάφθη. (Acc. to Tyrannio ap.Sch.A, = ἥφθη, upon him *was fastened*, i.e. to him *clung*, his shield; acc. to Aristarch., connected with ἕπομαι, shield and helmet *followed after*: ἑ- Aristarch., ἐ- most Mss.; possibly connected with ἰάπτω (q.v.), *was hurled* over him; glossed by ἐκάμφθη, ἐβλάβη, Hsch.)

ἐάω, contr. ἐῶ Il.8.428, etc.; Ep. **εἰῶ** 4.55; Ep. 2 and 3 sg. ἐάᾳς, ἐάᾳ, Od.12.137, Il.8.414; inf. ἐᾶαν Od.8.509: impf. εἴων, ας, α, Il.18.448, Od.19.25, Th.1.28, etc.; Ion. and Ep. ἔων Hdt.9.2, ἔα Il.5.517, 16. 731; also ἔασκον or εἴασκον, 2.832, 5.802, etc.: fut. ἐάσω [ᾱ] 18.296, etc.: aor. εἴασα (εἴασεν is v.l. for εἴασ' in 10.299) 24.684, etc.; Ep. ἔασα 11.437: pf. εἴακα D.8.37, 43.78, Cerc.17.35:—**Pass.**, fut. ἐάσομαι in pass. sense, E.*IA*331, Th.1.142: aor. εἰάθην Isoc.4.97: pf. Pass. εἴᾱμαι D.45.22.—Hdt. never uses the augm. in this Verb. [ᾰ in pres. and impf., ᾱ in fut. and aor. even in Ion. (so prob. in Anacr.56, 57; forms with -ασσ- occur as vv.ll. in Hom. and Parm. 8.7). Synizesis occurs in 3 sg. ἐᾷ Il.5.256, in 1 subj. ἐῶμεν 10.344, and prob. in ἐάσουσιν Od.21.233; also in Trag., in imper. ἔα S.*OT* 1451, *Ant.*95, Ar.*Nu.*932; ind. ἐῶ Id.*Lys.*734: Hsch. has the form ἦσεν· εἴασεν, cf. ἦσαι· παῦσαι]:—*suffer, permit*, c. acc. pers. et inf., τούσδε δ' ἔα φθινύθειν *leave* them *alone* to perish, Il.2.346; αἴ κεν ἐᾷ με ... ζώειν Od.13.359, etc.; ἐᾶν οἰκεῖν Th.3.48, cf. *IG*1².1; ἐ. τοὺς Ἕλληνας αὐτονόμους ib.2.17.9; ἐᾶν ἄκλαυτον, ἄταφον S.*Ant.*29, cf. *Tr.* 1083; ἐᾶν τί τινι Plu.2.233d:—so in Pass., Κρέοντί γε θρόνους ἐᾶσθαι *should be given up*, S.*OC*368. b. *concede, allow* in argument, c. acc. et inf., Pl.*Prm.*135b. 2. with neg., οὐκ ἐᾶν not *to suffer*: hence, *forbid, prevent*, τρεῖν μ' οὐκ ἐᾷ Παλλὰς Ἀθήνη Il.5.256; εἴπερ γὰρ φθονέω τε καὶ οὐκ εἰῶ διαπέρσαι 4.55; esp. of the law, Aeschin.3.21; δμωὰς δ' οὐκ εἴας προβλωσκέμεν Od.19.25, etc.: used elliptically with ἀλλά following, οὐκ ἐῶν φεύγειν, ἀλλὰ [κελεύων] μένοντας ἐπικρατέειν Hdt.7.104, cf. Th.2.21; also, *persuade* or *advise* not to do.., Id.1.133: an inf. may freq. be supplied, οὐκ ἐάσει σε τοῦτο will not *allow* thee [to do] this, S.*Ant.*538; κἂν μηδεὶς ἐᾷ even if all men *forbid*, Id.*Aj.* 1184, cf. *Ph.*444:—so in Pass., οὐκ ἐᾶσθαι, c. inf., *to be hindered*, E.*IT*1344, Th.1.142, D.2.16. II. *let alone, let be*, c. acc., ἔα χόλον Il.9.260; μνηστήρων μὲν ἔα βουλήν *heed not* the suitors' plan, Od. 2.281; ἐπεί με πρῶτον ἐάσας as soon as thou *hast dismissed* me, Il. 24.557, cf. 569, 684; ἥ κέν μιν ἐρύσσεαι, ἦ κεν ἐάσῃς or *wilt leave* him *alone*, 20.311, cf. Hdt.6.108, etc.; ἐάσωμεν ἕκηλον αὐτόν S.*Ph.*825; [πρᾶγμα] ἀκάθαρτον ἐᾶν Id.*OT*256; τὰ παθήματα.. παρεῖσ' ἐάσω Id.*OC*363, cf. Th.2.36; ἐᾶν φιλοσοφίαν Pl.*Grg.*484c: c. inf., ἐπὶ Σκύθας ἰέναι.. ἔασον *let it alone*, Hdt.3.134; κλέψαι μὲν ἐάσομεν Ἕκτορα we *will have done with* stealing Hector, Il.24.71; ἐᾶν περί τινος Pl.*Prt.* 347c, etc.; ἐῶ γὰρ εἰ φίλον D.21.122: abs., ἀλλ' ἄγε δὴ καὶ ἔασον *have done, let be*, Il.21.221, cf. A.*Pr.*334; οὐ χρὴ μάχεσθαι πρὸς τὸ θεῖον, ἀλλ' ἐᾶν E.*Fr.*491.5; θεὸς τὸ μὲν δώσει, τὸ δ' ἐάσει he will give one thing, the other he will *let alone*, Od.14.444:—Pass., ἡ δ' οὖν ἐάσθω S.*Tr.*329, etc. 2. for ἐᾶν χαίρειν, v. χαίρω sub fin. (ἐϝάω, cf. ἔβασον· ἔασον, and εὖα· ἔα, Hsch. who also has ἥσον· ἔασον.)

ἑάων, v. ἐΰς.

ἐβαδίαστον· μελανόβροχον, Hsch. **ἐβάθη**· ἐγεννήθη, Id.; cf. Lith. *gim̃ti*. **ἐβάμωσεν**· ἡττήθη, Id.

ἑβδεμαῖος, Dor., = ἑβδομαῖος, *IG*4.952.26 (Epid.).

ἑβδεμήκοντα, Dor. for ἑβδομ-, *GDI*2562.18 (Delph.), *Tab.Heracl.* 1.23:—also **ἑβδέματος**, ον, = ἕβδομος, *Philol.*71.6 (Argos, iv B.C.).

ἑβδομᾰ-γενής, ές, *born on the seventh day* [of the month], epith. of Apollo, Plu.2.717e.

ἑβδομ-ᾱγέτης, ου, ὁ, (ἡγέομαι) epith. of Apollo, to whom the Spartans *offered sacrifices on the seventh of every month*, A.*Th.*800, cf. Hdt.6.57. **-ᾰδικός**, ή, όν, *weekly*, ἀριθμός Antyll.ap.Orib. 9.3.1; περίοδος Gal.9.914, *Theol.Ar.*45. Adv. -κῶς Steph.*in Hp.*1. 198 D. II. *septenary*, Procl.*in Ti.*3.108 D., Dam.*Pr.*264, 265. Adv. -κῶς ib.263. **-άζω**, *keep the Sabbath*, Lxx *Ez.*21.23(28), Tz.*H.*10.675. **-αῖος**, α, ον, *on the seventh day*, ἱδρώς Hp.*Aph.*4.36; ἑ. πυρετός a fever *recurring every seven days*, Id.*Epid.*1.24: ἑ. τραγῳδοί Luc.*Hist.Conscr.*1: with a Verb, διεφθείροντο ἑβδομαῖοι Th.2.49, cf. X.*HG*5.3.19, Plu.*Galb.*7; ἑ. ἡμέρα *PSI*6.690 (i/ii A.D.). 2. *seven days old*, τράγος Horap.1.48. II. **-αῖον**, τό, monthly festival of Apollo, *IG*2².1357 (iv B.C.), cf. ἑβδομαγέτης: pl., *Schwyzer* 687 *B*4 (Chios, vii/vi B.C.), 726.6 (Milet., v B.C.). **-άκις**, Adv. *seven times*, Call.*Del.*251. **-άς**, άδος, ἡ, *the number seven*, Ph.1.21, Dam.*Pr.*264, etc. II. *a number of seven*, *APl.*4.131 (Antip.(?)). 2. *period of seven days, week*, Hp.*Aph.*2.24, Lxx *Ex.*34.22, etc. b. *period of seven years*, Sol.27.7, Arist.*Pol.*1336[b]40, *Placit.*4.11.4; ἐτῶν ἑ. J.*AJ*3.12.3.

ἑβδομ-ᾰτικός, = -αδικός, Ph.2.206, J.*AJ*11.8.6. **-ᾰτος**, ον, = ἕβδομος, *seventh*, Il.7.248, al. **-ειος**, *worshipped on the seventh day*, epith. of Apollo, *IG*2.1653. **-εύομαι**, Pass., of children, *receive a name at seven days of age*, as was customary, Lys.*Fr.*95 S.

ἑβδομηκονθ-εβδόμᾰδος, ον, *of seventy weeks*, χρόνος Tz.*H.*8.54. **-εκτος**, ον, *seventy-sixth*, ἡμέρας -ον (sc. μέρος) Gem.8.59.

ἑβδομήκοντα, οἱ, αἱ, τά, indecl., *seventy*, Hdt.1.32, X.*An.*4.7.8, etc.

ἑβδομηκοντάβιβλος (sc. πραγματεία), ἡ, *work in seventy books*, Paul.Aeg.*Praef.*

ἑβδομηκοντακαιεκᾰτονταπλᾰσίων, ον, gen. ονος, *170 times as great*, Procl.*Hyp.*4.104.

ἑβδομηκοντάκις, Adv. *seventy times*, Lxx *Ge.*4.24, *Ev.Matt.*18.22.

ἑβδομηκοντάπηχυς, υ, *seventy cubits high*, Ph.Byz.*Mir.*4.3.

ἑβδομηκοντάρουρος [ᾰ], ον, *possessing seventy ἄρουραι*, *PCair.Zen.* 1.23 (iii B.C.), *PTeb.*62.30 (ii B.C.).

ἑβδομηκοντάς, άδος, ἡ, *group of seventy*, Tz.*H.*1.974.

ἑβδομηκονταστάδιος [στᾰ], ον, *seventy stades broad*, πορθμός Str. 9.5.13.

ἑβδομηκοντούτης, ου, ὁ, *seventy years old*, Luc.*Alex.*34: fem. -οῦτις Id.*Rh.Pr.*24, D.C.46.18.

ἑβδομηκοστό-δῠος, ον, *seventy-second*, μόριον Plu.2.932a. **-μονος**, ον, *seventy-first*: τὸ ἑ. *one seventy-first part*, Archim.*Circ.*3. **-πεμπτος**, η, ον, *seventy-fifth*, Tz.*H.*12.908. **-τρῖτος**, ον, *seventy-third*, ib.13.439.

ἑβδομηκοστός, ή, όν, *seventieth*, Hp.*Epid.*7.7, Lxx *Za.*1.12.

ἕβδομος, η, ον, (ἑπτά) *seventh*, Il.19.117, etc.; ἡ ἑβδόμη *the seventh day*, Hdt.6.57 (pl.), Arist.*HA*588[a]8; *sabbath*, Ph.1.675, *Ep. Hebr.*4.4. 2. = ἑπτά, ἑβδόμαις πύλαις A.*Th.*125 (lyr., s.v.l.), cf. Thom.Mag.p.133 R.; ἐν κύκλοισιν ἑβδόμοις *Milet.*6.46. 3. ἕβδομα, τά, *seven years' work*, Lxx *Ge.*29.27.

ἐβέβλις· θήκη ἀργυρίου, καὶ κίστη, Hsch.

ἐβένη, v. ἔβενος.

ἐβένινος, η, ον, *of ebony*, δίφρος *CIG*3071 (Teos), cf. Str.15.1.54, *Peripl.M.Rubr.*36, *PMag.Berol.*1.279.

ἐβενῖτις, ιδος, ἡ, = πόλιον τὸ ὀρεινόν, Ps.-Dsc.3.110.

ἔβενος, ἡ (ὁ in *BCH*35.286 (Delos, ii B.C.)), *ebony*, Hdt.3.97, Theoc. 15.123:—being the black heart-wood of various species of Diospyrus, ἐ. Αἰθιοπική, = *D. mespiliformis*, ἐ. Ἰνδική, = *D. Ebenum*, Dsc. 1.98, cf. Arist.*Mete*.384^{b}17, Thphr.*HP*1.5.4 (but ἐβένη, ἡ, ib.4.4.6). (Prob. an Egyptian word.)

ἐβενότρῐχον, = ἀδίαντον, Ps.-Dsc.4.134; = καλλίτριχον, ibid.

ἔβην, ἐβησάμην, ἐβήσετο, v. βαίνω.

ἐβῆνοι· ἀλωπεκίδες, Hsch.; cf. εἴβηνος.

ἐβίσκος, ἡ, = ἀλθαία, Gal.11.867, Aët.1.96.

ἔβλητο, v. βάλλω. **ἐβλόν**· ἀπόπληκτον, Hsch.

Ἑβραῖος, α, ον, *Hebrew*: and as Subst., *a Hebrew*, 2*Ep.Cor*.11.22, Paus.1.5.5, App.*BC*2.71; Ἑ. ἐξ Ἑβραίων *Ep.Phil*.3.5, etc.; opp. Ἑλληνιστής, a Jew who used the Hebrew (Aramaic) language, *Act. Ap*.6.1:—Adj. **Ἑβραϊκός**, ή, όν, *Hebrew*, γράμματα *Ev.Luc*.23.38 (s.v.l.):—fem. **Ἑβραΐς**, ίδος, διάλεκτος *Act.Ap*.21.40; γυναῖκες J. *AJ*2.9.5:—Verb **Ἑβραΐζω**, *speak Hebrew*, Id.*BJ*6.2.1:—Adv. **Ἑβραϊστί**, *in the Hebrew tongue*, Lxx*Si.prol.*, *Ev.Jo*.19.20, etc.

ἐβρατάγησεν· ἐψόφησεν, Hsch.; cf. βαθαγέω.

ἔβρᾰχε, v. βραχεῖν.

ἔβρος, ὁ, *he-goat*, Hsch.

ἐγ, for ἐν in compos. before γ κ χ ξ; also for ἐκ in Inscrr. and Pap. before δ λ μ.

ἔγαν· ἐγένετο, Hsch.

ἐγγᾱγὶς πέτρα, = γαγάτης, Nic.*Th*.37.

ἐγγᾱέω, = ἐνοικέω, ἐν τᾷ πόλι *IG*4.853.26 (Methana).

ἔγγαιος, α, ον, more commonly **ἔγγειος**, ον, (γαῖα, γῆ) *in* or *of the land, native*, ἥβα A.*Pers*.922 (anap.); τις... οἰωνοπόλων ἔγγαιος Id. *Supp*.59 (lyr.). 2. *within the land*, opp. ὑπερόριος, X.*Smp*.4.31. II. of property, *in land, consisting of land*, οὐσία Lys.*Fr*.91, D.36.5; κτήσεις ἔγγειοι καὶ οἰκίαι *IG*9(2).338.9 (Thess.), cf. *CIG* 2056 (Odessus), Plb.6.45.3; τὰ ἔγγεια *the fixtures* of a farm, D.30.30; συμβόλαιον ἔγγειον Id.33.3; στατῆρας δανεισάμενος ἐγγείων τόκων *on mortgage*, Id.34.23 (ἑκατὸν μνᾶς ἐγγείους (v.l. ἐγγύους) ἐπὶ τόκῳ δεδανεισμένας is read by codd. in Lys.32.15); ἔγγεια καὶ ναυτικά *PEleph*.1.13 (iv B.C.). III. *in* or *of the earth*, [φυτὰ] ἔγγεια *plants*, Pl.*R*.491d; φυτὸν οὐκ ἔγγειον, ἀλλὰ οὐράνιον Id.*Ti*.90a; λίθων τὰ ἔγγαια μέρη Plu.2.701c. IV. *in* or *below the earth*, = χθόνιος, Ἀϊδωνεύς *AP*7.480 (Leon.); χθόνιον καὶ ἔ. σκότος Plu.2.953a; opp. ἐναέριος, Them.*Or*.13.168b.

ἐγγᾰληνίζω τῷ βίῳ, *spend* life *calmly*, Epicur.*Ep*.1 p.4 U.

ἔγγᾰλος, ον, (γάλα) *giving milk, in milk*, of a ewe, Hsch.

ἐγγᾰμ-έω, *marry into a family*, Aesop.21c, Hsch. **-ίζω**, *give in marriage*, Eust.758.54, *Gloss.* **-ιος**, ον, *nuptial*, *PSI*2.220 (iii A.D.).

ἐγγανᾶται· διέφθαρται, Hsch.

ἐγγᾰρ-εύω, = ἀγγαρεύω, *PTeb*.5.182 (ii B.C.). **-έω**, dub. sens. in *Inscr.Olymp*.335.

ἐγγαστρί-μαντις [ρῐ], ὁ, ἡ, *one that prophesies from the belly*, Poll. 2.168, Suid. s. v. ἐγγαστρίμυθος. **-μάχαιρα** [μᾰ], ἡ, comic name of a glutton in Hippon.85, *one who makes havoc with his belly*. **-μῡθος**, ον, *ventriloquist*, mostly of women who delivered oracles by this means: hence, = ἐγγαστρίμαντις, Hp.*Epid*.5.63, Philoch.192, Lxx *Le*.19.31, Ph.1.654, Plu.2.414e, Luc.*Lex*.20; also, *the familiar spirit* of such a person, Lxx 1*Ki*.28.8.

ἐγγάστριος, ον, *in the womb*, Man.1.189.

ἐγγαστρίτης [ῑ], ου, ὁ, = ἐγγαστρίμυθος, in Sch.Ar.*V*.1014.

ἐγγαστρόχειρ, χειρος, ὁ, = ἐγχειρογάστωρ, Sch.Par.A.R.1.989.

ἔγγαυρον· νοτερόν, ὑγρόν; also ἄωρον, πρόσφατον, Hsch. **ἔγγαυσον**· ἔνσκαμβον, Id.; cf. γαυσός. **ἐγγέαβλος**· νεωκόρος, Id.

ἐγγέγαα, Ep. pf. of ἐγγίγνομαι. **ἐγγεγωνώς**· βοήσας, Hsch.

ἐγγείνωνται, 3 pl. aor. 1 subj. in causal sense (no pres. ἐγ-γείνομαι being found), μὴ μυῖαι εὐλὰς ἐγγείνωνται lest the flies *breed* maggots *in* [the wounds], Il.19.26.

ἔγγειος, v. ἔγγαιος.

ἐγγειό-τοκος or **ἐγγεό-**, ον, *growing in the earth*, of truffles, Thphr. *HP*1.6.9, cf. *Fr*.167. **-φυλλος**, ον, *having leaves close to the ground*, Id.*HP*6.6.7.

ἐγγείσωμα, ατος, τό, (γεῖσον) *fracture of the skull*, such that one piece slips under the bone *like a cornice*, Heliod.ap.Orib.46.15.1, Sor. *Fract*.5, Gal.14.782.

ἐγγελ-αστής, οῦ, ὁ, *mocker, scorner*, E.*Hipp*.1000. **-άω**, fut. -άσομαι [ᾰ], *laugh at, mock*, τοῖς ποιουμένοις S.*El*.277, cf. E.*Med*. 1355; in tmesi, γέλωτ' ἐν σοὶ γελῶ S.*Ant*.551 codd.; κατά τινος Id. *OC*1339: without dat. expressed, Id.*El*.807, E.*Med*.1362; εἴς τινα Herod.1.77:—Pass., Luc.*Ind*.15. II. *laugh in* or *among*, αὔρα ἐγγελῶσα κύμασιν Sosicr.2.

ἐγγεν-έτης, ου, ὁ, *inborn, native*, δαίμονες A.R.4.1549. **-ής**, ές, *native*, Αἰγύπτιοι Hdt.2.47; opp. μέτοικος, ἐ. Θηβαῖος S.*OT*452; θεοὺς τοὺς ἐ. gods *of the race* or *country*, A.*Th*.582, S.*Ant*.199, cf. *El*.428; νόμος J.*AJ*15.7.10. 2. *born of the same race, kindred*, S.*OT*1168,1506, *Inscr.Cos*124; ἐ. κηδεία connexion *with a kinsman*, E.*Supp*.134. Adv. -νῶς *like kinsmen*, S.*OT*1225. II. of qualities, *inborn, innate*, νοῦς Id.*El*.1328; σφίσιν ἐγγενὲς ἔμμεν ἀεθληταῖς ἀγαθοῖσιν *'tis in their race* to be good athletes, Pi.*N*.10.51; πόνος ἐ. *in the family*, A.*Ch*.466 (lyr.); τἀγγενῆ κακά S.*OT*1430. III. = Lat. *ingenuus*, *PGnom*.29. **-ικός**, ή, όν, *hereditary*, ἱερεύς *OGI*583.5 (Cyprus, i A.D.).

ἐγγενν-άω, *generate* or *produce in*, τινί Plu.2.132e: abs., Them.*Or*. 13.166d. **-ησις**, εως, ἡ, *place of generation*, νεοττῶν Pl.*Lg*.776a.

ἔγγεον· ἰοῦγον, Hsch.; cf. Lat. *jugum* 'taxable unit of land, etc.'

ἐγγεότοκος, ον, v. ἐγγειότοκος.

ἐγγεύομαι, Pass., *taste of*, αἵματος Plb.7.13.7.

ἐγγηΐσταί, οἱ, *residents in a country*, *Supp.Epigr*.1.325 (Thrace).

ἐγγήναλοι· ὑπογραμματοί, Hsch.

ἐγγήρ-ᾱμα, ατος, τό, *employment for old age*, Cic.*Att*.12.25.2, Plu. *Cat.Ma*.24. **-άσκω**, Lib.*Or*.61.9 (-άω Anon. *in EN*237.2), fut. -άσομαι [ᾰ] (v. infr.):—*grow old with* or *in*, μεγέθει σώματος Hp.*Aph*. 2.54; ταῖς βασιλείαις Plb.6.7.4, cf. D.S.11.23, Plu.*Tim*.15. 2. abs., *grow old in one, decay*, τὴν ἐπιστήμην ἐγγηράσεσθαι Th.6.18; πρὶν ἐγγηρᾶσαι τὴν ἀκμὴν τῆς ἐλπίδος Plu.*Nic*.14.

ἐγγηροτροφέω, = γηροτροφέω, Poll.2.13 (Pass.).

ἐγγῆρυς· ἡ γῆ, παρὰ Ἀττικοῖς, Hsch.

ἐγγιάω, *to be near akin*, Lxx*Ne*.13.4 (s.v.l.).

ἐγγίγνομαι, Ion. and later **ἐγγίνομαι** [ῐ], fut. ἐγγενήσομαι: 3 pl. Ep. pf. ἐγγεγάᾱσι (the only tense used by Hom.):—*to be born in*, τοὶ Ἰλίῳ ἐγγεγάασιν Il.6.493, cf. Od.13.233; of vermin, *to be bred in* the skin, Hdt.2.37; of stones, ἐν τῷ καρπῷ ἐ. ib.92. 2. of things, qualities, etc., *spring up, appear in* or *among*, ὅσα ἐν ἀνθρώπου φύσι ... ἐ. Id.8.83, cf. Pl.*R*.351d; αἴσθημά τι κἂν νηπίοις γε ... ἐ. E.*IA*1244: c. dat., ἃ παρθένοις ἐγγίγνεται νοσήμαθ' Id.*Ion*1524, cf. Th.2.49, X. *Mem*.1.2.21, etc.; of persons, Pl.*Grg*.526a. 3. of events and the like, *take place* or *happen in* or *among*, τισί Hdt.5.3, cf. 3.1; χεῖμα σφοδρὸν ἐ. Pl.*Ax*.371d. II. *come in, intervene*, λόγους ἐγγίνεσθαι Hdt.2.121.δ'; χρόνου ἐγγινομένου, ἐγγενομένου, Id.1.190, Th.1.113, etc.; ἵνα μοι χρόνος ἐγγένηται τῇ σκέψει Pl.*Prt*.339e, cf. *Smp*. 184a. III. ἐγγίγνεται, impers., *it is allowed* or *possible*, c. inf., Hdt.1.132, 6.38, And.1.141, Pl.*Phd*.66c; ὥστε μὴ ἐγγενέσθαι μοι ποιῆσαι Antipho 5.17; ἐγγενόμενον ἡμῖν *when it was in* our *power*, Is.5.19. IV. for aor. ἐγγείνασθαι, v. ἐγγείνωνται.

ἐγγιγνώσκω, Ion. **ἐγγῑν-**, *acknowledge*, ἔρωτα Aret.*SD*1.5.

ἐγγίζω, aor. ἤγγισα Arist. (v. infr.): pf. ἤγγικα Lxx*Ez*.7.4(7), *Ev. Matt*.3.2: (ἐγγύς):—*bring near, bring up to*, τῇ γῇ τὰς ναῦς Plb.8.4.7; τὰ φιλήματα τοῖς χείλεσι Ach.Tat.2.37; τινὰ πρός τινα Lxx*Ge*.48.10. II. mostly intr., *approach*, Arist.*Mir*.845^{a}20; τινί Plb.18.4.1: c. gen., τῆς Αἰτωλίας Id.4.62.5, etc.; πρὸς τὸν θεόν Lxx*Ex*.19.21; εἰς θάνατον ib.*Jb*.33.22; ἕως ib.*Si*.37.30(33); μέχρι θανάτου *Ep.Phil*.2.30; *to be imminent*, ἤγγικεν ἡ παρουσία τοῦ Κυρίου *Ep.Jac*.5.8: also, c. gen., *approximate to*, Phld.*Herc*.1457.4. 2. *to be next of kin*, Lxx*Le*. 21.3. III. c. inf., *to be on the point of* doing, ναοῦ -οντος συμπεσεῖν *IG*12(1).1270.8 (Syme).

ἐγγίων, ον, **ἔγγιστος**, η, ον, Comp. and Sup. Adj., formed from Adv. ἐγγύς:—*nearer, nearest*, οὐδὲν ἡμῖν ἐστιν ἔγγιον ἡμῶν αὐτῶν Procl. *in Alc*.p.6C.; ἔτη δέκα τὰ ἔγγιστα *IG*7.2225.24 (Thisbe): neut. ἔγγιον, ἔγγιστα, as Adv., Hp.*Vict*.1.35 (also -υτάτα ibid.), 2.44, etc.; ἐξ ἐγγίονος App.*BC*4.108; τοὺς ἔγγιστα τῆς Ἀττικῆς τόπους Decr.ap. D.18.165; οἱ ἔγγιστα the *next of kin*, Antipho 4.4.1; ἔγγιστα *approximately*, of numbers, Autol.1.6, Vett.Val.153.21, etc.; αἱ ἔγγιστα τᾶς τοῦ ἀμβλυγώνου κώνου τομᾶς *asymptotes* of the hyperbola, Archim. *Con.Sph.Praef.*; of Time, *next, forthcoming*, ἡ ἔγγιστα ἀρίθμησις *POxy*.1258.7 (i A.D.).

ἔγγλαυκ-ος, ον, *blueish*, D.S.1.12. **-ῶσαι**· ἐμβλέψαι, Hsch.

ἐγγλωψούμενα· ἔνωχρα, ἄχροα, Hsch.

ἐγγλῠκ-άζω, gloss on ἐγγλύσσει, Hsch. **-υς**, υ, *sweetish*, Dsc. 5.6.

ἔγγλυμμα, ατος, τό, in pl., *ornamental carvings*, *IG*4.1485.91,96 (Epid.). 2. *intaglio*, Them.*Or*.4.62b.

ἐγγλύσσω, *to have a sweet taste*, Hdt.2.92.

ἐγγλῠφ-ή, ἡ, *carving, engraving*, Phld.*Po*.1676.5. **-ος**, ον, *carved*, *TAM*2.210 (Sidyma), Prisc.p.311 D. **-ω**, *carve*, ζῷα ἐν λίθοισι Hdt.2.4; ζῷα ἐγγεγλυμμένα ib.124; αἱμασιὴ ἐγγεγλυμμένη τύποισι ib.138; λίθος εἰκόνα -γεγλυμμένος J.*AJ*19.2.3; *hollow out*, [γογγύλην] Dsc.2.110, al.:—Pass., ὀστοῦ -γλυφέντος *having a groove*, Gal.2.255.

ἐγγλωττογάστωρ, ορος, ὁ, ἡ, = γλωσσογάστωρ, Ar.*Av*.1695, cf. *EM* 309.51, etc.

ἔγγλωττος, gloss on κατεγλωττισμένος, Suid., cf. Sch.Ar.*Th*.138.

ἐγγλωττοτῠπέω, *talk loudly of*, Ar.*Eq*.782.

ἐγγνάμπτω, *bend in*, ἐν δὲ γόνυ γνάμψεν, i.e. caught the back of the knee with his foot so as to trip him up and throw him, Il.23.731.

ἐγγοητεύω, *bring on by charms*, ὕπνον ἐ. τινί Philostr.*VA*3.8.

ἔγγομος, ον, *laden*, κάμηλοι *OGI*629.166 (Palmyra, ii A.D.), *Gloss.*

ἐγγομφ-όω, *nail, fix in*, Gal.2.336:—Pass., of the teeth, ib.754 (ap.Orib.25.6.4). **-ωσις**, εως, ἡ, *fixing in of teeth*, Gal.12.851.

Ἐγγόνασιν (= ἐν γόνασιν), ὁ, indecl., *kneeling figure*, name of the constellation Hercules, Arat.66,669, Gal.9.936, etc.

ἐγγονεῖν, written for ἐγκονεῖν in Hsch.

ἔγγονος, ὁ, properly, *grandson*, D.H.6.37, etc.: **ἐγγόνη**, ἡ, *granddaughter*, *IGRom*.4.882 (Themisonium), Artem.4.69, Lyd.*Mag*.2.1; also ἔγγονος, ἡ, Plu.*Per*.3. 2. simply, = ἔκγονος, *descendant*, Pl.*R*.364e, D.19.48,54, etc.; ἔκγ- is v.l. in ll.cc., and may be right in Arist.*Pol*.1335^{a}13, cf. ib.^{b}30; τὰ ἔγγονα *issue*, *Inscr.Cos* 36^{a}4, *PFreib*.10.8, etc.; of animals, Ph.2.396, al.; Ἔρως πυρὸς ἔγγονε *APl*.4.212 (Alph.). 3. *productive*, κακίας, μνήμης, Callistr.*Stat*. 10. [ἐγγ- may represent ἐκγ- (q.v.), both forms are found in Att. Inscrr. up to ca. 300 B.C.; ἐγγ- is rare in Hellenistic Greek, *OGI*49.12 (iii B.C.), *PTeb*.124.25,33 (ii B.C.); but more freq. later; ἐνγ- is written in *SIG*333.25 (Samos, iv B.C.), dub. in *CIG*3185 (Smyrna).]

ἐγγοργῶν· φοβερῶς βλέψας, Hsch.:—also aor. Med. **ἐ⟨γ⟩γοργώψατο**, Id.; cf. γοργώψατο.

ἐγγράμμᾰτος, ον, *written*, λόγος φωνῇ ἐ. Pl.*Def*.414d, cf. Ph.1.321, Arr.*Epict*.1.20.4, S.E.*M*.1.100. II. *containing letters, descriptive of letters*, ῥῆσις Ath.10.454b. III. *literate*, *POxy*.1467.13 (iii A.D.).

ἔγγραπτος, ον, = ἔγγραφος, συνθῆκαι Plb.12.9.3, al.; νόμοι Str.6.1.8, D.S.1.94; πρᾶγμα ἔ. καὶ ἄγραφον *PAmh*.2.110 (i A.D.), etc.: ἔγγραπτον, τό, *written document*, *PMagd*.18.5 (iii B.C.).

ἐγγραυλίς, ίδος, ἡ, a fish, = ἐγκρασίχολος, Ael.*NA*8.18: pl., ἐγγραύλεις Opp.*H*.4.470.

ἐγγρᾰφ-εύς, έως, ὁ, *registrar*, *Gloss*. **-ή**, ἡ, Dor. **ἐγγροφά** *IG*4.1485.126 (Epid.), *registration*, πολιτῶν Arist.*Ath*.43.1, cf. Ph.2.51; of persons on the list of their deme, D.39.5 (pl.), *IG*2^2.1028.6 (pl.); of ἄτιμοι, D.25.28; of public debtors, Id.37.6; of those subject to penalties, Arist.*Pol*.1322^{a}1 (pl.). II. *engraving of an inscription*, Ἀρχ.Ἐφ.1911.141 (Gonni). 2. Geom., *inscribing* of a figure, Papp.150.8, al.; cf. ἐκγραφή. **-ής**, ές, = ἔγγραφος, Anon. *in EN*245.30. **-ος**, ον, Dor. **ἔγγροφος** *SIG*712.35 (Crete), *written*, Plb.3.21.4, Luc.*Herm*.24, etc.; ἔγγραφα, τά, *documents*, *OGI*335.137 (Pergam.). Adv. -φως *Inscr.Prien*.113.37 (i B.C.), J.*BJ*1.27.1, *SIG*880.68 (Pizus), Porph.*Chr*.27. II. *enrolled*, *IG*1^2.949. III. ἔγγραφοι πατέρες, = *patres conscripti*, D.H.2.12. **-ω**, *make incisions into*, τὸ στέλεχος Thphr.*HP*5.1.2. 2. *mark in* or *on*, *paint on*, ζῷα ἐς τὴν ἐσθῆτα ἐ. Hdt.1.203; opp. ἐξαλείφω, Pl.*R*.501b. 3. *engrave, inscribe*, ἐν τῇσι στήλῃσι Hdt.2.102, cf. 4.91; νόμους Lys.30.2 (of codifiers, opp. ἐξαλείφω):—Med., ἣν ἐγγράφου σὺ μνήμοσιν δέλτοις φρενῶν A.*Pr*.789:—Pass., *to be written in*, ἐνεγέγραπτο δὲ τάδε ἐν αὐτῇ (sc. τῇ ἐπιστολῇ) Th.1.128; αὑτὸν εὗρεν ἐγγεγραμμένον κτείνειν found his name *entered in the letter* for execution, ib.132; δέλτον ἐγγεγραμμένην συνθήμαθ' S.*Tr*.157. 4. metaph., εἰ μέλλουσι τοιαῦται διάνοιαι ἐγγραφήσεσθαι ἀνθρώποις X.*Cyr*.3.3.52. 5. Geom., *inscribe* a figure in another, εἰς.. Euc.4.4, al.; ἐν.. Archim.*Sph.Cyl*.1.13, al. (Pass.). 6. Medic., *include in a prescription*, οἶνος ἐγγεγράφθω Aret.*CD*1.2. II. *enter in the public register*, esp. of one's deme or phratria, ἐς τὰ κοινὰ γραμματεῖα Is.7.1; ἐγγράψαι τὸν υἱὸν εἰς ἄνδρας D.19.230; εἰς τοὺς φράτερας Id.39.4; ἐ. εἰς τοὺς ἀτίμους Plu.*Them*.6; also ἱερὰν ἐ. τὴν οὐσίαν Alex.276:—Pass., εἰς τοὺς δημότας ἐγγραφῆναι D.18.261; Μαντίθεος ἐνεγεγράμμην by the name of M., Id.39.4; τοὺς μήπω δι' ἡλικίαν ἐγγεγραμμένους Arist.*Pol*.1275^{a}15; πρὶν ἐγγραφῆναι καὶ λαβεῖν τὸ χλαμύδιον Antid.2; εἰς τοὺς ἐφήβους Pl.*Ax*.366e. (A.*Ch*.699 is corrupt.) 2. *indict*, Ar.*Pax*1180, D.37.24:—Pass., ἐγγράφεσθαι λιποταξίου *to be indicted* for desertion, Aeschin.2.148. 3. of state-debtors, *enter their names*, ἐγγραφόντων οἱ ἄρχοντες τοῖς πράκτορσιν Lex ap.D.43.71; ἐγγεγραμμένος [ἐν ἀκροπόλει] *registered* among the state-debtors, D.25.4, cf. Arist.*Ath*.48.1; also of ἄτιμοι, Pl.*Lg*.784d. (Perh. written ἐκγρ-, *SIG*742.29.)

ἐγγριμᾶσθαι· ἐναγίσαι, Hsch. **ἐγγρισμός**· παροξυσμός, Id.; cf. ἀγγρίζειν. **ἐγγυάζων**· ἀντιφωνῶν, Id.

ἐγγυᾰλίζω, Ep. and Lyr. Verb, (γύαλον) prop. *put into the palm of the hand, put into the hand*, ἔεδνα ὅσσα οἱ ἐγγυάλιξα Od.8.319; ἐγὼ δέ τοι ἐγγυαλίξω I *will put* him *into* your *hands*, 16.66; ὁ δ' αὐτ' ἐμοὶ ἐγγυάλιξεν (sc. τοὺς ἵππους) Il.23.278; freq. of the gods, καί τοι Ζεὺς ἐγγυάλιξε σκῆπτρόν τ' ἠδὲ θέμιστας 9.98; τιμήν.. ὄφελλεν Ὀλύμπιος ἐγγυαλίξαι 1.353; τότε οἱ κράτος ἐγγυαλίξω 11.192; ὀτέοισιν κῦδος.. ἐγγυαλίξῃ 15.491, cf. A.R.2.55, etc.; ἐ. ὄλβον Pi.*Pae*.6.133, cf. *I*.8(7).46, Hegem.ap.Ath.15.698d.

ἐγγύαλον, = κοῖλον, Orion 51.2.

ἐγγύαν· ὀψωνίαν (Lacon.), Hsch.

ἐγγῠάω, impf. ἠγγύων (παρ-) S.*OC*94, E.*Supp*.700, X.*An*.4.1.17, etc.: aor. ἠγγύησα E.*IA*703, D.29.47, etc.: pf. ἠγγύηκα D.C.38.9: plpf. ἠγγυήκει Is.3.58:—**Med.**, fut. -ήσομαι D.24.46: aor. ἠγγυησάμην And.1.44,73, D.22.53:—**Pass.**, aor. ἠγγυήθην (ἐξ-, κατ-) Lys.23.11, D.59.49: pf. ἠγγύημαι (δι-) Th.3.70:—also treated as a compd., ἐνεγυησάμεθα *PEleph*.27.9 (iii B.C.), and freq. in codd.: impf. ἐνεγύων Is.3.45, D.41.16; ἐνεγύησα Is.3.36,70: pf. ἐγγεγύηκα ib.40, D.59.53: impf. Pass. ἐνεγυᾶτο Is.3.70: pf. ἐγγεγύημαι D.33.24, *POxy*.259.7 (i A.D.): plpf. ἐνεγεγύητο Is.3.55: but these forms are incorrect: (ἐγγύη):—*give* or *hand over as a pledge*:—Med., *have a thing pledged* to one, *accept as a surety*, δειλαί τοι δειλῶν γε καὶ ἐγγύαι ἐγγυάασθαι Od.8.351 (nowhere else in Hom.). 2. esp. of a father, *plight, betroth*, θυγατέρα ἐγγυᾶν τινι Hdt.6.57 (v. infr.); Ζεὺς ἠγγύησε καὶ δίδωσ' E.*IA*703:—Med., *have* a woman *plighted* or *betrothed to one*, c. acc., D.57.41:—Act. and Med. opposed, Hdt.6.130:—Pass., of the man, *to be betrothed*, θυγατρί τινος Pl.*Lg*.923d. II. Med., *pledge oneself, give security*, ἐγγύας ἐγγυησάμενοι πρὸς τὸ δημόσιον And.1.73, cf. Pl.*Lg*.953e; ἐπί τισι Lys.23.9; ἐ. τινὶ ὅτι.. Pl.*Euthd*.274b. 2. c. acc. et inf. fut., *promise* or *engage that*.., Pi.*O*.11(10).16, Ar.*Pl*.1202, X.*An*.7.4.13, Pl.*Prt*.336d, etc.; ἐγγυᾶσθαι [τινα] καὶ ὁμολογεῖν παρέξειν Lys.13.23; ἐγγυωμένη δώσειν Babr.58.10. 3. c. acc. rei, *answer for*, ἐγγυᾶσθαι τὰ μέλλοντ' ἔσεσθαι D.18.191: c. acc. pers., Pl.*Lg*.855b; ἐγγυᾶσθαί τινά τινι *give surety for* him to another, D.33.28; ἐγγύην ἐγγυᾶσθαί τινα πρός τινα Pl.*Phd*.115d; ἐ. τὰ μετέωρα *give guarantees* without security, *SIG*364.46 (Ephesus, iii B.C.).

ἐγγῠβᾰθής, ές, = ἀγχιβαθής, Dion.Byz.1:—written **-βαθος** in Suid.

ἐγγύδιον· ἔγγιον, Hsch.

ἐγγῠεύω, = ἐγγυάομαι, *GDI*1804.3 (Delph.).

ἐγγύ-η (rarely **ἐγγύα**; but τὴν ἐγγύαν *IG*11(2).226*A*29 (Delph., iii B.C.), cf. Epich. (v. infr.), *PSI*4.346 (iii B.C.)), ἡ: (ἐν, γύαλον, cf. ἐγγυαλίζω):—*pledge put into one's hand*: generally, *surety, security*, whether received or given, Od.8.351; ἐ. τιθέναι τινί A.*Eu*.898; ἐγγύας ἀποτίνειν ὑπέρ τινος Antipho 2.2.12; ἐ. ἐγγυᾶσθαι (v. ἐγγυάω II); ἀποδιδόναι D.53.27; ἐ. ὁμολογεῖν, = Lat. *vadimonium facere*, D.H.11.32, *OGI*455.3 (Epist. M. Antonii); τῆς ἐ. τῆς ἐπὶ τὴν τράπεζαν D.33.10; ἐγγύας ἄτα 'στι θυγάτηρ, ἐγγύα δὲ ζαμίας Epich.268: prov., ἐγγύη, πάρα δ' ἄτη Pl.*Chrm*.165a, etc. 2. *betrothal*, Pl.*Lg*.774e; ἐ. ποιεῖσθαί τινος Is.3.28. 3. ἐ.· σημεῖον ἐν θυτικῇ, Hsch. [ῠ; ῡ only in *AP*9.366.] **-ημα**, ατος, τό, *security*, *PMasp*.169.14 (vi A.D.). **-ησις**, εως, ἡ, *security*, *CIG*2953*b*38 (Delos(?)), *BGU*981.36 (i A.D.), v.l. in D.24.73; *right of giving security*, *IG*2^2.10. II. *betrothal*, Is.3.53; κατ' ἐγγύησιν Alciphr.3.1. **-ητής**, οῦ, ὁ, *one who gives security, surety, guarantor*, ἐγγυητὴν καθιστάναι Hdt.1.196, Antipho 5.17, Lys.23.12, *IG*2^2.1172.22, etc.; ἄξιος ἐ. τινος Thphr.*Char*.18.6; παρέχειν Pl.*Lg*.871e; λαμβάνειν τινὰ ἐ. D.33.7; διδόναι Plb.12.16.3, etc.; ἐπ' ἐγγυητῶν ἐκμισθοῦν under *securities*, X.*Vect*.3.14; ἐ. τοῦ ἀργυρίου ἀξιόχρεως for the money, Pl.*Ap*.38c; οἱ ἐ. τῆς τραπέζης *those who had given security* for the bank (and were liable in case of its failure), D.33.10; ὁ νόμος ἐ. ἀλλήλοις τῶν δικαίων Arist.*Pol*.1280^{b}11; τὸ νόμισμα οἷον ἐ. ὑπὲρ τῆς ἀλλαγῆς Id.*EN*1133^{b}12; εἰ μή τις θεῶν ἐστιν ἐ., ὡς.. D.H.11.41. **-ητικός**, ή, όν, *connected with suretyship*, πράγματα, πρόσωπα, Heph.Astr.2.28,30. **-ητός**, ή, όν, always of a wife, *plighted, wedded*, ἐγγυητὴ γυνή, opp. to an ἑταίρα, Is.3.77, D.59.60. **-ήτρια**, ἡ, fem. of ἐγγυητής, *Stud.Pal*.20.139 (vi A.D.).

ἐγγύθεν [ῡ], Adv., (ἐγγύς) *from nigh at hand*, ἐ. ἐλθεῖν to *approach*, Il.5.72; ἐ. σκοπεῖν S.*Ph*.467, cf. Th.3.13, Pl.*Plt*.289d, etc. 2. with Verbs of rest, *hard by*, ἐ. ἱσταμένη Il.10.508; ἐ. εἰσίν Od.6.279. 3. c. dat., ἐ. τινί *hard by* him, Il.17.554, etc.; ἐπεὶ φόνος ἐ. αὐτῷ 18.133, cf. 19.409: c. gen., ἐ. Ἀρήνης 11.723; θνήσκοντος ἐ. παρών A.*Ch*.852. 4. of kinship, Od.7.205.

ἐγγῠθήκη, ἡ, *stand for vessels, tripods*, etc., Lys.*Fr*.34, Hegesand.45; cf. ἐγγυοθήκη.

ἐγγύθι [ῡ], Adv. *hard by, near*, in Ep. mostly c. gen., Il.6.317, Hes.*Op*.343; αὐτοῖιν Theoc.21.8: less freq. c. dat., Il.22.300: abs., 7.341, Hes.*Op*.288. II. of Time, *nigh at hand*, ἐγγύθι δ' ἠώς Il.10.251.

ἐγγυιόω, *stretch the limbs upon*, v.l. for συνέκαμψεν, Lxx 4*Ki*.4.35; cf. ἐγγυιώσεται· συμπλακήσεται, ἐναγκαλισθήσεται, Hsch.

ἐγγυμν-άζω, *exercise in*, τὴν ψυχὴν θεάμασιν ἐ. Luc.*Salt*.6; τὴν γνώμην ἐνθυμήμασιν Polyaen.3*Praef*.:—more freq. in Med., ἐν σοὶ ἐγγυμνασόμενος *to practise* upon you, Pl.*Phdr*.228e; *practise oneself in*.., πολέμοις Plu.*Caes*.28, cf. Ph.1.551, Luc.*Lex*.22, Jul.*Or*.1.37c; ἐν ταῖς πράξεσιν D.C.36.32, cf. *BKT*3 p.25:—Pass., Hp.*Vict*.2.63; ἐγγυμνασθέντες περί τι Vett.Val.353.5; λόγοις Luc.*Hipp*.2. **-αστέον**, *one must practise oneself in*, Them.*Or*.4.51b.

ἐγγῠοθήκη, ἡ, = ἐγγυθήκη, Luc.*Lex*.2.

ἔγγυος, ον, (ἐγγύη, cf. ἀμφίγυος) *secured, under good security*, μνᾶς.. ἐγγύους ἐπὶ τόκῳ δεδανεισμένας Lys.32.15 (but v. ἔγγαιος II). 2. *reliable*, in Comp., ὅπλα -ώτερα Them.*Or*.15.197c (nisi leg. ἐχεγγ-). II. Subst., = ἐγγυητής, ἔγγυον παρέχειν Thgn.286, cf. X.*Vect*.4.20, Arist.*Oec*.1350^{a}19, *SIG*364.41 (Ephesus), 976.13 (Samos), *PEleph*.8.19, *Ep.Hebr*.7.22, etc.; ἔ. τῆς προξενίας *giving security* for.., *IG*9(2).4 (Hypata), etc.: fem. in Aeschin.*Ep*.11.12, *BGU*1051.10 (i B.C./i A.D.).

ἐγγύς [ῠ], Adv., Comp. ἐγγυτέρω (-τέρῳ *Hell.Oxy*.6.3), also -ύτερον Pl.*Lg*.704e: Sup. ἐγγυτάτω or -ύτατα (first in Hp., and Att.); also ἔγγιον, ἔγγιστα (v. ἐγγίων). I. of Place, *near, nigh, at hand*: freq. in Hom., ἐ. γὰρ νυκτός τε καὶ ἤματός εἰσι κέλευθοι Od.10.86: c. gen., *hard by, near to*; so λύπας ἐγγυτέρω *nearer to* grief, S.*OC*1217: c. dat., Il.11.340, E.*Heracl*.37; ἐγγὺς ὁδῷ dub. in *IG*1^2.974: mostly with Verbs of rest, ἐ. ἑστάναι, παρεστάναι, A.*Pers*.686, *Eu*.65; but ἐ. χωρεῖν Id.*Th*.59: c. gen., οἱ ἐγγυτάτω τῆς ἀγορᾶς κατεσκευασμένοι Lys.24.20, etc. II. of Time, *nigh at hand*, Il.22.453; ἐ. ἡμῖν ὁ ἀγών X.*Cyr*.2.3.2. III. of Numbers, etc., *nearly*, ἔτεσι ἐ. εἴκοσι Th.6.5; μισθὸς ἐ. ἐνιαυτοῦ X.*HG*3.1.28: generally, *nearly, almost*, ἐ. ἔγνως S.*Ichn*.301; οὐδ' ἐ. τινος not *nearly*, i.e. not *by a great deal*, nothing *like* it, Pl.*Smp*.198b; ἔχει οὐχ οὕτω ταῦτα οὐδ' ἐ. not so.. nor yet *nearly so*, D.21.30; οὐκ ἐποίουν τοῦτο, οὐδ' ἐ. Id.18.96; *mostly*, Hp.*Mochl*.34. IV. of Qualities, *coming near*, ἐ. τι καὶ παραπλήσιον Pl.*Grg*.520a; ἐγγύτατα τοῦ νῦν τρόπου, τῆς ξυμπάσης γνώμης, Th.1.13,22; ὅτι ἐγγύτατα τούτων Id.7.86; κοινῇ δὲ πᾶσιν οὐδεὶς ἐγγυτέρω D.18.288; δοκεῖς δηλῶσαι ἐγγύτατα τὴν ῥητορικήν Pl.*Grg*.452e; ἐ. εἶναι, c. gen., Id.*Phd*.116b; ἐ. τυφλῶν Id.*R*.508c; ἐ. τι τείνειν τοῦ τεθνάναι *very near* death, Id.*Phd*.65a; κακῶς παθεῖν ἐγγύτατα D.21.123. V. of Relationship, *akin to*, οἱ Ζηνὸς ἐ. A.*Fr*.162; ἐγγυτέρω γένει or γένους, Pl.*Ap*.30a, Is.3.72; ἐγγύτατα γένους A.*Supp*.388, Lys.*Fr*.41, Pl.*Hp.Ma*.304d; ἐγγυτάτω γένους *IG*1^2.77, Ar.*Av*.1666.

ἐγγύτερος [ῠ], α, ον, Comp. Adj., (ἐγγύς) *nearer*, Procop.Gaz.*Ep*.62: Sup. **ἐγγύτατος**, η, ον, *nearest*, Aen.Tact.28.3 (s.v.l.), Lxx *Jb*.6.15; δι' ἐγγυτάτου, = ἐγγυτάτω, Th.8.96.

ἐγγύτης [ῠ], ητος, ἡ, *nearness*, Str.8.6.19, A.D.*Pron*.24.4, Alex.Aphr.*Pr*.2.35, Them.*Or*.14.182b, etc.

ἐγγώνιος, ον, (γωνία) *forming an angle*, esp. *right angle*, σχῆμα Hp.*Art*.22; λίθοι ἐντομῇ ἐγγώνιοι cut *square*, Th.1.93; πύργοι J.*BJ*7.8.3. Adv. -ίως Paul.Aeg.6.115. II. *cut into angles*, of ivy-leaves, Thphr.*HP*3.15.4 (Comp.).

ἐγγωνοειδής, ές, = foreg. II, Thphr.*HP*3.12.5.

ἔγγωνον, τό, *angular piece of land*, *Tab.Heracl*.2.107.

ἐγδ-, freq. for ἐκδ- in Inscrr. and Papyri:—also **ἐγδάκτυλος**, = ἐξαδ-, *IG*2.809^{b}195.

ἐγδούπησαν, v. γδουπέω.

ἐγειρόφρων, ον, gen. ονος, (φρήν) gloss on ἀερσίφρων, *EM*20.47.

ἐγείλασαν· συνήλωσαν, Hsch. (Perh. ἐϝ–, cf. γάλλοι.)

ἐγείρω, Aeol. inf. ἐγέρρην Alc.*Supp*.16.12, cf. *Et.Gud*.157.48: Ep. impf. ἔγειρον Il.15.594: fut. ἐγερῶ Pl.*Epigr*.28 (cf. ἐξ–, ἐπ–): aor. ἤγειρα, Ep. ἔγ– Od.15.44: pf. ἐγήγερκα Philostr.*Ep*.16: plpf. –κειν J.*AJ*17.7.4, D.C.42.48:—**Pass.**, Pl.*R*.330e, etc.: fut. ἐγερθήσομαι Babr.49.3 (also fut. Med. ἐγεροῦμαι dub. in Polyaen.1.30.5): aor. ἠγέρθην Hdt.4.9, etc.; Ep. 3 pl. ἔγερθεν v.l. for ἄγ. in Il.23.287: pf. ἐγήγερμαι v.l. in Th.7.51: plpf. ἐγήγερτο Luc.*Alex*.19: also, in pass. sense, poet. aor. ἠγρόμην (ἐξ–) Ar.*Ra*.51; 3 sg. ἔγρετο, imper. ἔγρεο, Il.2.41, Od.23.5; 2 sg. subj. ἔγρῃ Ar.*V*.774; opt. ἔγροιτο Od.6.113; inf. ἐγρέσθαι (freq. written ἔγρεσθαι, as if from a pres. ἔγρομαι, cf. ἔγρω) ib.13.124; part. ἐγρόμενος 10.50 (and late Prose, Iamb.*Myst*. 1.15): intr. pf. ἐγρήγορα (as pres.) Ar.*Lys*.306, Pl.*Prt*.310b, etc.: plpf. ἠγρηγόρη (as impf.) Ar.*Ec*.32; 3 pl. ἐγρηγόρεσαν Id.*Pl*.744; 3 sg. ἐγρηγόρει X.*Cyr*.1.4.20: Ep. pf. 3 pl. ἐγρηγόρθασι Il.10.419; imper. ἐγρήγορθε (v. infr. II); inf. ἐγρήγορθαι ib.67. I. Act., *awaken, rouse*, ἐ. τινὰ ἐξ ὕπνου 5.413, etc.; τοὺς δ'..ὑπνώοντας ἐγείρει 24.344; ἐ. τινὰ εὐνῆς E.*HF*1050 (lyr.); simply, ἐ. τινά A.*Eu*.140, etc.: metaph., τὰς τέχνας Theoc.21.1. 2. *rouse, stir up*, Il.5.208; ἐπεί μιν ἔγειρε Διὸς νόος 15.242; ἐγείρειν Ἄρηα *stir* the fight, 2.440, etc.; ἐ. μάχην, φύλοπιν, etc., 13.778, 5.496, etc.; Τρωσὶν θυμὸν ἐ. (v.l. ἀγεῖραι) ib.510; ἐ. τινὰ ἐπὶ ἔργον Hes.*Op*.20; ἔγειρε νῆα *h.Ap*.408; ἐκδοχὴν πομποῦ πυρὸς ἐ. *wake up* the bale-fire, A.*Ag*.299; λαμπάδας ἐ. Ar.*Ra*.340: freq. metaph., ἐ. ἀοιδάν, λύραν, μέλος, θρῆνον, Pi.*P*.9.104, *N*.10.21, Cratin.222, S.*OC*1778 (anap.); μῦθον Pl.*Plt*.272d; τὸ οὖς ἐ. '*prick up*' the ears, Plot.5.1.12. 3. *raise* from the dead, νεκροὺς *Ev.Matt*. 10.8, cf. 1*Ep.Cor*.15.42 (Pass.); or from a sick-bed, *Ep.Jac*.5.15. 4. *raise, erect* a building, Hyp.*Fr*.103, Call.*Ap*.64, *OGI*677.3 (ii A.D.); ναόν *Ev.Jo*.2.19, cf. Luc.*Alex*.10:—Pass., στῦλος ἐγηγερμένος Bito 66.5, cf. Plu.*Alex*.19, Jul.*Caes*.320c. II. Pass., with pf. Act. ἐγρήγορα, *wake*, ἐγειρομένων ἀνθρώπων Od.20.100, cf. Hdt.4.9, etc.; ἔγρετο δ' ἐξ ὕπνου Il.2.41: metaph., ἐγειρόμενος εἰς ἐμαυτὸν ἐκ τοῦ σώματος Plot.4.8.1: in pf., *to be awake*, ἐγρηγόρθασι Il.10.419; ἐγρήγορθε *stay awake!* 7.371, 18.299 (whereas ἔγρεο is *wake up!* Od.15.46); ἐγρήγορας ἢ καθεύδεις; Pl.*Prt*.310b; πόλις ζῶσα καὶ ἐγρηγορυῖα Id.*Lg*. 809d; καὶ ἐφρόνει καὶ ἐγρηγόρει X.*Cyr*.1.4.20, etc.; of things, ἐγειρομένου χειμῶνος *arising*, Hdt.7.49: so metaph., τὰ ἐκ τοῦ βαρβάρου ἐγειρόμενα ib.148; ἐγρηγορὸς φρούρημα A.*Eu*.706; ἐ. τὸ πῆμα Id.*Ag*. 346, etc. 2. *rouse* or *stir oneself, be excited* by passion, etc., Hes. *Sc*.176, D.19.305: c. inf., ἐγηγερμένοι ἦσαν μὴ ἀνιέναι τὰ τῶν Ἀθηναίων they *were encouraged* to prevent the departure of the Athenians, v.l. in Th.7.51. III. intr. in Act., *arouse oneself*, Aesop.16b. IV. in ἀμφὶ πυρὴν...ἔγρετο λαός Il.7.434, 24.789, ἔγρ. is for ἤγρ– (ἀγείρω); so in Maiist.52.

ἐγέλα· χαλινοί, Hsch. **ἐγέλωτοι**· ἀστέρες, Id. **ἔγεντο**, v. γίγνομαι. **ἐγεργεῖ**· γρηγορεῖ, Id.

ἐγερσι-βόης, ου, ὁ, *raising the cry, loud-voiced*, *IG*3.82. **–βροτος**, ον, *awakening men*, Procl.*H*.7.18. **–γελως**, ωτος, ὁ, ἡ, *laughter-stirring*, *AP*11.60 (Paul. Sil.); Ἀφροδίτη Orph.*Fr*.183. **–θέατρος**, ον, *exciting the theatre*, *APl*.4.361. **–μάχας** [μᾰ], ου, ὁ, *battle-stirring*, *AP*7.424 (Antip. Sid.):—fem. **–χη**, ib.6.122 (Nicias). **–μᾰχέω**, *arouse strife*, Tz.*H*.12.654. **–μοθος**, ον, = ἐγερσιμάχας, Opp.*C*.1. 207, Nonn.*D*.3.39.

ἐγέρσῐμος, ον, *from which one wakes*, ὕπνος, opp. the sleep of death, Theoc.24.7.

ἐγερσίνοος [ῐ], ον, *soul-stirring*, μέθη Nonn.*D*.12.376; φωνή ib. 37.673; βίβλοι Procl.*H*.3.4.

ἔγερσις, εως, ἡ, *awaking*, Hp.*Coac*.82; personified in Emp.123.1: pl., Phld.*Rh*.2.206S., Polyaen.2.2.6: metaph., ἡ τοῦ θυμοῦ ἔ. Pl.*Ti*. 70c, Arist.*EN*1116^{b}30. b. *awaking* from death, *Ev.Matt*.27.53; *recovery*, ἐκ τοῦ πάθεος Aret.*SA*2.11. 2. *raising, erection*, τειχίων Hdn.8.5.4 (pl.), cf. Men.Eph.ap.J.*AJ*8.5.3.

ἐγερσι-φάής, ές, *light-stirring*, ἐ. πέτρος the flint, *AP*6.5 (Phil.). **–χορος**, ον, *leading the dance*, Opp.*C*.4.236.

ἐγερ-τέον, *one must raise*, E.*Rh*.690. **–τήριον**, τό, *excitement*, Ael.*VH*2.44: pl., –τήρια δρόμου, of the ears of a hare, Id.*NA* 13.14. **–τί** [ῐ], Adv. *eagerly, busily*, κινεῖν τινα S.*Ant*.413; *wakefully*, Heraclit.63, E.*Rh*.524. **–τικός**, ή, όν, *waking, stirring*, νοήσεως Pl.*R*.523e, 524d. II. in Gramm., *enclitic*, because changing the grave accent of the preceding word into the acute, ἐ. ἐπίρρημα *AB*1147. **–τός**, ή, όν, = ἐγέρσιμος, ὕπνος Arist.*Somn.Vig*. 454^{b}14.

ἐγϝηληθίωντι, v. ἐξειλέω. **ἐγήγαρτος**· ἐπίχαρτος, ἐπιχαρής, Hsch. (leg. ἔγχαρτος). **ἐγήρα**, v. γηράσκω.

ἐγκαθαιρέω, aor. inf. ἐγκαθελεῖν· καταβαλεῖν, Hsch.

ἐγκαθ-αρμόζω, *fit in*, Ar.*Lys*.682. **–εδρος**, ὁ, *assessor*, *Gloss*. **–έζομαι**, fut. –εδοῦμαι, *sit* or *settle oneself in*, Ar.*Ec*.23; εἰς θᾶκον Id.*Ra*.1523; εἰς ἐνέδραν Arr.*Tact*.15.5; *encamp in* a place, Th.3.1, 4.2; τῶν δαιμονίων –καθεζομένων J.*AJ*6.11.2. **–είργω** and **–γνῡμι**, *shut up, enclose*, ib.5.1.2; φορβειᾷ τὸ ῥαγδαῖον Plu.2.456c:—Pass., ib.951b, Jul.*Or*.7.206b:—also **ἐγκατείργω**, Agath.1.11, al.:—Pass., Aret.*SA*1.5, Herm.ap.Stob.1.49.44. **–ειρκτος**, ον, *shut in, enclosed*, Aesop.40. **–ετος**, ον, (ἐγκαθίημι) *put in secretly, suborned*, προέδρους ἐ. ὑφέντες Pl.*Ax*.368e, cf. D.*Ep*.3.34, Plb.13.5.1, *Ev.Luc*.20.20, J.*BJ*6.5.2. Adv. –τως, δημηγορεῖν D.S.16.68. II. of a child, = εἰσποιητός, Hyp.*Fr*.56. **–εύδω**, fut. –ευδήσω, *sleep among*, Arist.*HA*610^{b}31; *sleep upon*, ποδήρη ὦτα ὡς ἐγκαθεύδειν Str. 15.1.57; στιβάδα ἐγκαθεύδειν τινὶ παρασκευάσαι Ael.*NA*6.42. 2. generally, *lie abed*, Ar.*Lys*.614. 3. *sleep in a temple* to effect a cure, *IG*4.951.25 (Epid.), 7.235 (Orop.), etc. **–έψω**, *boil in* anything, Hp.*Mul*.2.133. **–ηβάω**, *pass one's youth in*, E.*Hipp*. 1096. **–ηλόω**, *fix in*, Heliod.ap.Orib.49.4.25 (Pass.). **–ημα**, ατος, τό, *that which settles in* a place, of foreign bodies in the eye, Orib.*Eup*.4.31. **–ημαι**, *sit in* or *on*, X.*Eq*.1.11; *lie in ambush*, ἐν τοῖς τρίβωσιν Ar.*Ach*.343, cf. *Th*.600; ἐ. καὶ ἐνεδρεύειν Aeschin.3. 206; of garrisons, *lie in* a place, Plb.18.11.6, J.*BJ*5.1.2; *lie couched in*, as the men in the Trojan horse, Pl.*Tht*.184d: metaph., ἐ. μεταξύ.. Id.*Prm*.156d; ἐγκαθημένου ταῖς ψυχαῖς τοῦ φόβου Plb.2.23.7; ἐμπόδιον ἐγκαθήμενον Plot.6.9.7; *take one's stand upon*, τῷ ῥητῷ Mich.*in EN*68.31. **–ιδρύω** [ῡ], *erect* or *set up in*, ἄγαλμα ἐ. χθονί E.*IT*978, cf. Ath.11.473b, J.*BJ*2.13.7:—Pass., Philox.3.5 codd. Ath., Arist. *Mu*.397^{b}27, Hld.5.13. **–ίζω**, Ion. **–κατίζω**, *seat in* or *upon*, εἰς θρόνον Pl.*R*.553c; ἐ. στρατιὰν ἐν τοῖς τόποις *station* a force *in* a place, Plb.16.37.4: aor. 1 Med., ναὸν ἐγκαθείσατο (vulg. ἐγκαθίσατο, cf. ἐγκαθισάμενοι τὰ ὅπλα v.l. in J.*BJ*5.1.2) *founded* a temple *there*, E. *Hipp*.31. 2. *administer a sitz-bath to* one, Sor.1.64, Herod.Med. ap.Orib.6.20.18, etc.:—Pass., Hp.*Mul*.1.35; also, *to be used for such*, Dsc.5.13, 30. 3. *cause to subside upon*, τοῖς κοιλώμασι τὴν ὑπερκειμένην γῆν Lyd.*Ost*.53. II. intr., *sit in* or *upon*, [θρόνῳ] Pi. *P*.4.153:—Med., ἐγκατίζεσθαι εἰς θρόνον *take one's seat on*..., Hdt.5. 26. **–ίημι**, *let down*, ἐς τὴν χύτραν Ar.*Lys*.308. 2. *send in* as agents, Plu.*Pyrrh*.11:—Pass., of a catheter, *to be passed*, Ruf. *Ren.Ves*.7.11. II. *commit, entrust*, Ζεὺς ἐγκαθεῖ (for –ίησι) Λοξίᾳ θεσπίσματα A.*Fr*.86. **–ιννῠμαι**, = ἐγκαθίζω 2, Hp.*Mul*.2. 210. **–ισμα**, ατος, τό, *sitz-bath*, Dsc.3.113, *Gp*.12.23.5, Sor.1. 56, etc. II. *dwelling on a syllable in pronunciation*, D.H.*Comp*. 20, 22 fin. **–ισμός**, ὁ, = foreg. II, Id.*Dem*.43 (pl.). **–ιστέον**, *one must administer a sitz-bath*, Sor.2.11, Herod.Med. in *Rh.Mus*. 58.109. **–ίστημι**, *place* or *establish in*, as king or chief, σὲ.. Μυκήναις ἐγκαταστήσω πάλιν E.*IT*982; ἐ. τινὰς ἡγεμόνας Th.1.4; τινὰ τύραννον D.17.10; also, *place as a garrison in* a place, v.l. in Id. 9.15; φρουράν Plu.*Alc*.30; of institutions, ἐ. δημοκρατίας Arr.*An*.1. 18.2:—Med., *establish for oneself*, βασιλείην Hellanic.79(a) J. II. Pass., with aor. 2, pf. and plpf. Act., *to be established* as ruler *in* a place, Lys.2.59, Th.1.122; also αὐλητῶν νόμῳ ἐγκαθεστώτων Id. 5.70. **–οράω**, *look closely into*, τινὸς τῷ προσώπῳ Plu.*Demetr*.38; εἰς τὸ ὕδωρ *IG*4.951.66 (Epid.): abs., Pl.*Epin*.990e. II. *remark* something *in* a person or thing, Plu.*Brut*.16. **–ορμίζομαι**, Med., *run into harbour, come to anchor*, αὐτόσε Th.4.1, cf. D.C.48. 49: aor. Pass., Arr.*An*.2.20.8. **–όρμισις**, εως, ἡ, *putting into harbour*, ib.1.18.5. **–υβρίζω**, *riot* or *revel in*, τρυφαῖς E.*Tr*. 997. **–υφαίνω**, v.l. for καθ–, Lxx *Ex*.28.17.

ἐγκαίν-ια, τά, (καινός) *feast of renovation* or *consecration*, Thd.*Da*. 3.2, Lxx 2*Es*.6.16; esp. that established by Judas Maccabaeus *at the reconsecration* of the Temple, *Ev.Jo*.10.22. **–ίζω**, *restore*, τεῖχος Lxx *Is*.16.11; βασιλείαν 1*Ki*.11.14; *make afresh*, ὁδόν *Ep.Hebr*.10. 20; *consecrate, inaugurate*, οἶκον Κυρίου Lxx 3*Ki*.8.63:—Pass., *Ep. Hebr*.9.18, *IG*12(5).712.58 (Syros); χύτρα –ισμένα Archig.ap.Orib. 8.46.4. II. *innovate*, prob. in *PPar*.16.24 (ii B.C.). **–ίς**, ίδος, ἡ, dub. sens. in Agath.5.21. (Perh. ἐγκενίς, = ἐπηγκενίς.) **–ισις**, εως, ἡ, *consecration*, Lxx *Nu*.7.88 (v.l. –ωσις). **–ισμός**, ὁ, = foreg., ib.1*Ma*.4.56 (v.l. –ιασμός), *Nu*.7.10, al.

ἐγκαιρ-ία, ἡ, *seasonableness*, opp. ἀκαιρία, Pl.*Plt*.305d; τροφῆς Aret.*CA*1.1. **–ιος**, ον, = ἔγκαιρος, Pl.*Ti*.51d (Sup.), *PGrenf*.1. 64. **–ιότης**, ητος, ἡ, = ἐγκαιρία, Sch.E.*Ph*.471. **–ος**, ον, *timely, seasonable*, Pl.*Plt*.282e, *Lg*.928a, Them.*Or*.26.331a: Sup., Pl.*Lg*.717a. Adv. –ρως Aristaenet.1.15: Sup. –ότατα Them.*Or*.9. 120c.

ἐγκαίω, aor. 1 part. ἐγκέας *IG*1^2.374.96, but –καύσας *SIG*^{2}587. 186:—*burn* or *heat in*, ὀβελοὶ ἐγκεκαυμένοι πυρί E.*Cyc*.393. 2. *brand*, Luc.*Pisc*.46:—Pass., βοῦς ἐγκεκαυμένας ῥόπαλον Arr.*An*.5.3. 4. 3. *scorch*, of the sun, *Gp*.18.17.1. 4. *paint in encaustic*, i.e. *with colours mixed with wax*, *IG* l.c., 11(2).199*A* 80 (Delos, iii B.C.), Lxx 2*Ma*.2.29, Plin.35.122. 5. Medic. in Pass., *to be overheated*, Gal.2.870, Aret.*CD*1.5. II. *make* a fire *in*, πῦρ Plu.*Alex*. 24; οἶκοι ἐγκαιόμενοι *heated* chambers, Luc.*VH*2.11. III. metaph. of passion, Sm.*Ps*.38.4. IV. abs., *offer sacrifice*, Ἀπόλλωνι Paus. 1.42.6.

ἐγκᾰκέω, *behave remissly in* a thing, ἐνεκάκησαν τὸ πέμπειν they *culpably omitted* to send, Plb.4.19.10, cf. Thd.*Pr*.3.11, Sm.*Ge*.27.46: c. part., τὸ καλὸν ποιοῦντες μὴ ἐγκακῶμεν *Ep.Gal*.6.9: abs., *Ev.Luc*. 18.1, al., cf. *BGU*1043.3 (iii A.D.); cf. ἐκκακέω. II. ἐγκακοῦμεν· ὑψοῦμεν, Hsch.

ἐγκᾰλέω, *call in* a debt, Isoc.17.44, X.*An*.7.7.33, D.31.6, 36.14: generally, *demand* as one's due, ἀργύριον Lys.3.26. 2. *invoke*, τὴν τῶν θεῶν ἰατρείαν Str.14.1.44. II. *bring a charge* or *accusation against* a person:—Constr.: c. dat. pers. et acc. rei, *charge* something *against* one, φόνους ἐ. τινί S.*El*.778, cf. Pl.*Ap*.26c, etc.; ἐ. ἔγκλημά τινι Hyp.*Lyc*.18, cf. *Eux*.24; χόλον κατ' αὐτῶν ἐ. S. *Ph*.328: folld. by a relat. clause, ἐ. τινὶ ὅτι.. X.*An*.7.5.7: c. inf., ἐστὶν ἃ ἐνεκάλει τοῖς Ἀθηναίοις παραβαίνειν τὰς σπονδάς Th.4.123: c. part., ἐ. αὐτοῖς ἀμελοῦσιν Pl.*Prt*.346a: freq. c. dat. pers. only, *accuse*, Antipho 4.2.2, etc.; ἐ. περί τινων *Inscr.Prien*.28.8 (ii B.C.); ἐπὶ τοῖς διῳκημένοις ib.37.128 (ii B.C.): c. acc. rei only, *bring as a charge*, εἴ τι ἄλλο ἐνεκάλουν Th.5.46, cf. 6.53; τὸ νεῖκος ἐγκαλεῖν *throw the blame* of quarrel on another, S.*OT*702: abs., οἱ ἐγκαλέσαντες Arist.

*Rh.Al.*1437ᵃ17: rarely c. gen. rei, τῆς βραδύτητος αὐτοῖς ἐνεκάλει Plu. *Arist.*10 :—Pass., ἐγκαλεῖται τῇ τύχῃ *a charge is brought against*.., Arist.*EN*1120ᵇ17 ; ἐνίων ἐγκληθέντων ἐπὶ τῷ βίῳ Phld.*Piet.*p.93 G.; τὰ ἐγκεκλημένα *charges*, *OGI*90.14 (ii B.C.): also with person. constr., ἐγκαλεῖσθαι ὑπέρ τινος D.H.7.46 ; τινός D.C.58.4 :—Locr. part. ἐγκαλείμενος may be either Med. or Pass., *IG*9(1).334.41. 2. as law-term, *prosecute, take proceedings against*, οὔτ' ἐγκαλοῦντες οὔτ' ἐγκαλούμενοι D.34.1 ; ἐ. δίκην τινί Id.40.19 ; ἐ. τινὶ περί τινος Isoc.4.40 : abs., Ar.*Av.*1455. 3. *object*, c. acc. et inf., Phld.*Sign.*29.

ἐγκᾰλινδέομαι, *roll about in*, τῆσι ψάμμοισι Aret.*CD*1.2 : metaph., πολλῇσι συμφορῇσι Hp.*Ep.*17 ; ταραχαῖς καὶ κινδύνοις Agath.4.27 ; *wallow in*, ταῖς λιχνείαις Ath.6.262b, cf. Them.*Or.*29.346b.

ἐγκαλλωπ-ίζομαι, *take pride in*, τοῖς αἰσχροῖς Plu.*Ant.*36 ; βωμολοχίαις Agath.1.13, cf. Arr.*Epict.*3.22.59, Ael.*VH*9.35 ; *boast of*, ταῖς φίλαις τῇ ἀξιώσει J.*AJ*18.3.4 : abs., Ph.2.28. **-ισμα**, ατος, τό, *ornament, decoration*, Th.2.62, Plot.3.5.9, Them.*Or.*6.83c ; of a person, γένους Agath.*Praef.*p.135 D.

ἐγκᾰλοσκελής, οῦς, ὁ, *having his legs in the stocks*, *Com.Adesp.*988.

ἐγκᾰλ-υμμός, ὁ, *covering, wrapping up*, cj. in Ar.*Av.*1496. **-υπτέος**, α, ον, *fit to be veiled, hidden*, Ap.Ty.*Ep.*18. **-υπτήρια**, τά, *veiling-feast*, opp. ἀνακαλυπτήρια, Philostr.*VS*2.25.4. **-ύπτω**, *veil, wrap up*, Ar.*Ra.*911 :—Pass., *to be veiled* or *enwrapped*, Id.*Pl.*714, Pl.*Phdr.*243b ; *to be wrapped up* (as for sleep), X.*An.*4.5.19, Pl.*Prt.* 315d ; ἐγκεκαλυμμένος λόγος, a noted fallacy, *Stoic.*2.8,90, etc. II. Med., *hide oneself, hide one's face*, Ar.*Pl.*707, etc. ; ἐγκαλυπτόμενος καθεύδειν And.1.17 ; of persons at the point of death, X.*Cyr.*8.7.26, Pl.*Phd.*118a, etc.: metaph., *conceal one's feelings*, c. part., νεμεσῶν ἐνεκαλύπτετο App.*BC*2.69. 2. as a mark of shame, Pl.*Phd.*117c, D.*Ep.*3.42, Aeschin.2.107 : c. acc. pers., *feel shame before* a person, θεοὺς ἐγκαλυπτόμενος ὧν ἔμελλε δράσειν App.*BC*1.16 : c. inf., *to be ashamed to*.., *PMasp.*295.12 (V A.D.). 3. -καλυπτόμενος σφυγμός, term invented by Archig., Gal.8.662. **-υψις**, εως, ἡ, *concealment*, Str.10.2.12 (pl.) ; τῆς ψυχῆς ὑπὸ τοῦ σώματος Plu.2.266e ; ἐν ἐγκαλύψει εἶναι to be *wrapped in obscurity*, M.Ant.5.10.

ἐγκάμνω, *grow weary* or *slack in* or *at* a thing, τινί J.*AJ*2.15.5 ; *become slack*, ταῖς εὐτυχίαις Id.*BJ*3.10.2 ; ἐς ἔργον Aret.*SD*1.15.

ἐγκάμπτω, *bend in, bend*, X.*Eq.*1.8, Gal.18(2).353.

ἐγκᾰνάσσω, *pour in* wine, ἐγκάναξον E.*Cyc.*152, Ar.*Eq.*105 ; κύλικα Alciphr.3.36.

ἐγκᾰνᾰχάομαι, *make a sound on* a thing, ἐ. κόχλῳ *blow on* a conch, Theoc.9.27.

ἐγκάνθιος, α, ον, *in* or *of the inner angle of the eye*, Dsc.*Eup.*1.8, Gal.19.437.

ἐγκανθίς, ίδος, ἡ, *tumour in the inner angle of the eye*, Cels.7.7.5, Gal.*UP*10.11, etc.

ἐγκαπῆ· ἐπικαρπία, Hsch. **ἐγκάπνισμα**, ατος, τό, *fumigation*, *Gloss.*

ἐγκάπτω, pf. ἐγκέκᾰφα *AP*9.316.6 (Leon.) :—*gulp down greedily, snap up*, Ar.*Pax*7, *V.*791, Stratt.25, Hermipp.26, Alex.128.7 ; ἐ. αἰθέρα γνάθοις *hold* one's breath, E.*Cyc.*629. II. ἐγκάπτει· ἐκπνεῖ, Hsch.

ἔγκᾰρ, ἄρος, ὁ, = φθείρ, Eust.757.27.

ἐγκαρδι-αῖος, α, ον, = sq., φῶς Iamb.*Myst.*2.7. **-ος**, ον, *in the heart*, ἐγκάρδιόν ἐστί (or γίγνεταί) τί τινι it goes *to* his *heart*, Democr. 262, D.S.1.45 ; τἀγκ. τις ἐρεῖ *what is in* his *heart*, Phld.*Lib.*p.14 O. Adv., ὅταν γεννηθῇς ἐγκαρδίως *PMag.Par.*1.1785. 2. *in close proximity*, of planets, Antioch.Astr. in *Cat.Cod.Astr.*8(3).105. II. ἐγκάρδιον, τό (ἐγκάρδιος, ὁ, S.E.*M.*9.119), *heart-wood, core*, Thphr. *HP*3.8.5, 5.3.2 ; *pith*, Dsc.1.109.5, *Gp.*12.25.3. 2. generally, *core*, Roussel *Cultes Égyptiens* 236 (Delos, ii B.C.).

ἔγκᾰρος, ὁ, (κάρ, κάρα) *the brain*, *AP*9.519.3 (Alc.), Lyc.1104.

ἐγκαρπ-ασθέντας· ἐγκριθέντας, ἐντυχόντας, Hsch. **-ία**, ἡ, perh. f.l. for εὐκ-, *EM*797.27. **-ιος**, ον, of fruit, *containing seed*: hence, *ripe*, Hp.*Vict.*2.55. II. ἐγκάρπια, τά, *unreaped crops*, *SIG*633.87 (Milet., ii B.C.). **-ος**, ον, *containing fruit*, κάλυξιν ἐγκάρποις χθονὸς S.*OT*25 ; *fruitful*, σπέρματα Pl.*Phdr.*276b ; of soil, Thphr.*CP*2.4.2 ; γᾶν ἔγκαρπον φέρειν may the earth bear *produce*, *SIG*526.41 (Crete) ; δένδρα Plu.2.2e ; τέλη ἔγκαρπα tithe *of produce*, S.*Tr.*238 : metaph., χρήσιμον καὶ ἔ. *fruitful*, Plu.2.776b, cf. Luc.*Merc.Cond.*39 (Sup.). Adv. -πως, διακεῖσθαι Aen.Tact.7.1. II. ἔγκαρπα, τά, *festoons of fruit* on friezes or the capitals of columns, Lat. *encarpa*, Vitr.4.1. 7. 2. ἔγκαρπα or ἔγκαρτα, = τοὺς κεκουρευμένους πυρούς, Phryn. Trag.4 (ap.Hsch.). **-ωσις**, εως, ἡ, *being in seed*, Gal.13.570.

ἐγκάρσιος, α, ον (ος, ον Gal.*UP*5.12 codd.), *athwart, oblique*, Th. 2.76, 6.99, Ach.Tat.3.2, Hld.3.2 ; of the ecliptic, Arist.*Mu.*392ᵃ12 (v.l. -ίως).

ἐγκαρτερέω, *persevere* or *persist in* a thing, τινί v.l. in X.*Mem.*2.6. 22 ; ἐγκαρτερεῖν [τούτοις] ἃ ἔγνωτε Th.2.61 ; πρὸς δίψαν Plu.2.987e : c. inf., μὴ φιληθῆναι Id.*Ages.*11. 2. c. acc., *await stedfastly*, θάνατον E.*HF*1351, *Andr.*262. 3. abs., *hold out, remain firm under*, c. dat., ταῖς πληγαῖς Plu.*Pomp.*79 ; τοῖς δεινοῖς Luc.*Anach.*38 : abs., Plu.*Lyc.*18, *PAmh.*2.78 (ii A.D.).

ἐγκάς, Adv. *deep in*, prob. in Hp.*VC*5, cf. Gal.19.94.

ἔγκᾰτα, τά, *inwards, entrails*, Hom., always in acc., as Od.9.293, exc. dat. ἔγκασι in Il.11.438 ; ἐν ἔγκασιν ᾄδου *AP*15.40.42 (Comet.) : later, nom. sg. ἔγκατον Lxx 3*Ki.*17.22, Luc.*Lex.*3.

ἐγκατα-βαίνω, *go down into, put oneself in*, c. acc., κροκωτὸν σπάργανον ἐγκατέβα Pi.*N.*1.38 : c. dat., dub. l. in D.S.14.28 ; εἰς.. Gal. *UP*2.15 : abs., Id.8.686. **-βάλλω**, *throw down into*, μέσῃ δ' ἐνικάββαλε δίνῃ A.R.1.1239 (but written divisim, μέσῳ δ' ἐνὶ κ. ὁμίλῳ Il. 12.206) ; εἰς.. Alex.Aphr.*Pr.*2.67 (Pass.). **-βιόω**, *pass one's life in*, Plu.2.783d, Longin.44.11. **-βρέχω**, *wet* or *soak with*, *Gp.*13.1. 7. **-βυσσόομαι**, *penetrate deeply*, Democr.*A.*77 D. **-γηράσκω**, = ἐγγηράσκω, *grow old in*, τῇ ἀρχῇ Arist.*Ath.*17.1 ; ἐν πενίᾳ Plu.*Phoc.* 30 ; *become inveterate in*, Din.2.3 :—also **-γηράω**, ταῖς μοναρχίαις Them.*Or.*19.232c.

ἐγκατάγομαι [ᾰγ], *put up at* a place, Nic.Dam.p.138 D., Poll. 1.73.

ἐγκατα-γράφω [γρᾰ], *write down among*, Ael.*Fr.*67 ; *portray*, Aen. Gaz.*Ep.*12. **-δᾰμάζω**, *overpower* :—Pass., ὑπὸ κωνώπων ἐγκαταδαμασθεὶς dub. in Hp.*Epid.*7.79 (sed leg. ἐν καταδήγμασιν). **-δαρθάνω**, *sleep in*, Plu.2.647f. II. *go to sleep over* a thing, τῷ διψῆν ib. 688f. **-δέω**, *bind fast in*, τινί Pl.*Phd.*84a, Them.*Or.*23.297a (Pass.), Opp.*H.*3.201. **-δύνω** [ῡ], aor. -κατέδυν, of the sun, *set upon* a place, Hp.*Aër.*6 ; *sink beneath*, ὕδασιν *AP*7.532 (Isid.) ; μυχόν Opp. *H.*1.153 : abs., *sink, be absorbed in*, Archig.ap.Aët.3.167, Gal.7.217 : metaph., *to be immersed in*, c. dat., Dam.*Pr.*10 :—Med., τοῖς οἰκείοις ἐπιτηδεύμασι Procop.*Arc.*1. **-ζεύγνῡμι**, *associate with, adapt to*, νέας βουλὰς νέοισιν ἐγκαταζεύξας τρόποις S.*Aj.*736. **-θνήσκω**, Ep. aor. ἐνικάτθανε, *die in*, A.R.2.834. **-κειμαι**, *lie in*, c. dat., κλισμῷ Thgn.1191. 2. *lie in bed, sleep*, παρά τινι Ar.*Pl.*742. **-κενόω**, *empty out into*, *Hippiatr.*74. **-κλεισις**, εως, ἡ, *enclosing*, Herod. Med. in *Rh.Mus.*49.553. **-κλειστος**, ον, *shut up in* a place, E.*Fr.* 1132.39. **-κλείω**, *shut up in, enclose*, τινὰ τῷ νεῷ Alex.40.3, cf. Arist.*Pr.*937ᵃ29 ; τὸ θερμὸν Thphr.*CP*5.13.2 :—Pass., Hp.*Acut.*16, Arist.*Mete.*378ᵃ29. **-κλίνω** [ῑ], *put to bed in* a place, Ar.*Pl.* 621 :—Pass., *lie down in*, σισύραν ἐγκατακλῑνῆναι μαλθακήν Id.*Av.* 122 ; ἐγκατακλιθῆναι εἰς τὸ ἱερόν Hyp.*Eux.*14. **-κλώθω**, *interweave*, Hsch. **-κνᾰκομῑγής**, ές, *compounded of* ἔγκατα *and* κνάκων, Philox.3.11. **-κοιμάομαι**, = ἐγκοιμάομαι, Hdt.8.134, *IG*4.952.9 (Epid.). **-κρούω**, χορείαν τοῖς μύσταις *tread* a measure *among* them, Ar.*Ra.*330. **-κρύπτω**, *hide in*, τί τινι Lyc.1231, cf. Gal. 2.305, al. ; ὄνομα βυθοῖς in religious mysteries, *IG*3.900. **-λαμβάνω**, *catch in* a place, *hem in*, Th.4.116 ; ἐ. τινὰ ὅρκοις *trammel* by oaths, ib.19 ; ἐὰν λογισμὸς ἐγκαταλαμβάνῃ αὐτόν Aeschin.3.60 :—Pass., Th.3.33, Arist.*Pr.*926ᵇ31. II. *follow in immediate succession*, παννυχὶς ἐ. ἑορτήν Aristid.*Or.*47(23).6, cf. 26(14).84 ; *attack immediately after*, ἡ ἐπὶ τῷ ἐμέτῳ ἀσιτία [τινὰ] ἐ. Id.47(23).60. **-λέγω**, *build in*, πολλαὶ στῆλαι ἐγκατελέγησαν *were built into* the wall, Th. 1.93. 2. *count* or *reckon among*, Luc.*Par.*3 ; τινὰς εἰς τοὺς Εὐπατρίδας, = Lat. *adlegere inter patricios*, D.C.43.47 ; *enlist soldiers*, *AP* 11.265 (Lucill.). II. Pass., *lie in* or *on*, Ep. aor. ἐγκατέλεκτο A.R. 4.431. **-λειμμα**, ατος, τό, *remnant, residue, trace*, Arist.*Fr.*13, cf. Lxx *Je.*11.23, al. 2. *residual trace*, εἰδώλου Epicur.*Ep.*1 p.12 U. 3. *kneading trough*, Lxx *De.*28.5,17. 4. *sediment*: hence, *silting-up*, *PPetr.*2 p.14 (iii B.C.). **-λείπω**, *leave behind*, παῖδα Hes.*Op.*378 ; ἐ. φρουρὰν ἐν τῇ νήσῳ Th.3.51 ; πλεῖον ἐ. ἐξιόντες ἐκ τῆς ὠνῆς *PRev.Laws*53.12 ; ἐ. τὸ κέντρον, of a bee, Pl.*Phd.*91c : hence of Pericles, τὸ κέντρον ἐγκατέλιπε τοῖς ἀκροωμένοις Eup.94.7 ; ἐ. τὴν μάχαιραν ἐν τῇ σφαγῇ Antipho 5.69. 2. *leave in the lurch*, Pl.*Smp.* 179a, Lycurg.2, D.57.58, *Ev.Matt.*27.46, *Lyr.Alex.Adesp.*4.22, etc. ; *abandon*, νεκροὺς Th.4.44 ; ἀκρόπολιν X.*HG*5.4.13. 3. *leave out, omit*, Hdt.3.119. 4. *leave traces behind*, Epicur.*Nat.Herc.* 1420. II. Pass., *to be left behind* in a race, Hdt.8.59. 2. *leave residual symptoms* or *sequelae*, Hp.*Epid.*6.2.6, 6.7.7.

ἐγκατᾰλείφω, *mix in an ointment*, λίπος Hp.*Acut.*(*Sp.*)33.

ἐγκατά-λειψις, εως, ἡ, *residual symptom* (v. -ληψις). **-λεκτέος**, α, ον, *to be reckoned among*, [πόλεσιν] εὖ πραττούσαις Philostr.*VS*2. 24.1. **-ληπτικός**, ή, όν, *inclusive*, Gal.19.235. **-ληψις**, εως, ἡ, *catching* or *being caught in* a place, *being hemmed in*, Th.5.72 ; *suppression* of urine, Hp.*Epid.*6.2.7 (codd. sed leg. ἐγκατάλειψις). 2. *concept* (= κατάληψις), Gal.14.685, cf. 19.350. **-λιμπάνω**, = ἐγκαταλείπω, Hp.*Aph.*2.12 (Pass.), Arist.*Rh.*1368ᵇ19. **-λογίζομαι**, *reckon in*, Is.11.45. **-λοχίζω**, *divide into relays* or *courses*, Lxx 2*Ch.*31.18. **-μείγνῡμι** (-ύω Luc.*Lex.*25), *mix with*, τί τινι Timo 33, Luc.*Hist.Conscr.*13, etc. ; φάρμακον πότῳ Ach.Tat.4.15 ; τινὰς λόχοις D.H.6.2 ; ἑαυτοὺς τοῖς στρατιώταις Hdn.7.12.7 : metaph., κέντρον τωθασμοῖς Ph.2.570 ; θεὸν ἀνθρωπίναις χρείαις Plu.2.414f ; of a sculptor, μανίην λίθῳ *APl.*4.57 (Paul. Sil.), cf. *AP*9.593 :—Pass., *to be mixed in* or *with*, ἐγκαταμειγνύμενος ὕδατι Hp.*Aër.*6 ; ἐγκαταμιγμένα τοῖς λεγομένοις Isoc.15.10 ; ὀνόματα -μιγέντα τῇ λέξει D.H. *Comp.*25. **-μεμιγμένως**, Adv. *in a mixed manner*, Sch.rec.S.*OT* 95. **-μένω**, *remain in*, Thphr.*HP*1.3.4, Hld.1.33, etc. ; *continue the use of*, τισί Antyll.ap.Aët.9.42. **-μιξις**, εως, ἡ, *intermingling, infusion*, Alex.Aphr. in *Sens.*74.26, Olymp. in *Mete.*157.29. **-μίσγω**, = -μείγνυμι, τῇ διηγήσει τὰς θεατρικὰς γοητείας D.H.*Th.*7 :—Pass., Id.*Dem.*22, cf. *EM*770.52, *Et.Gud.*533.49. **-μυκτηρίζω**, gloss on ἐγκατιλλῶψαι, Hsch.

ἐγκατάνα· κατὰ γνώμην, κατὰ νοῦν, Hsch.

ἐγκατα-ναίω, aor. 1 -ένασσα, *make to dwell in*, οὐρανῷ τινά A.R.3. 116, Moero 1. **-νέμω**, *bestow upon*, τί τινι Jul.*Or.*5.179b.

ἐγκαταντλ-έω, *wash over with* a thing, *Hippiatr.*26. **-ησις**, εως, ἡ, *washing over*, Hp.*Decent.*8.

ἐγκατα-νωτίζομαι, *to be backed*, μέρεσι ἱππείοις Tz.*H.*6.965. **-ξηρος**, ον, *dry*, opp. κάθυγρος, γῆ *Gp.*2.13 tit. **-παίζω**, *mock at*, τινί Lxx *Jb.*40.14(19). **-πήγνῡμι**, *thrust firmly in*, ξίφος... κουλεῷ ἐγκατέπηξ' Od.11.98 ; ἐν δὲ σκόλοπας κατέπηξεν *planted* or *fixed* them *in*, Il.9.350 ; τὴν κεφαλὴν δόρατι ἐ. *having fixed* it *on*, Hdn.1.13.4. 2.

sheathe, ξίφος Plu.2.313e. **-πίμπρημι**, *burn in*, τινά τινι Phalar. *Ep.*122.4. **-πίνομαι** [ῐ], pf. -πέπομαι: aor. -επόθην, *to be swallowed up*, of a ship, Ph.1.670: metaph. of persons, Id.2.300, al.; *to be absorbed*, *immersed*, Dam.*Pr.*67. **-πίπτω**, poet. aor. ἐνικάππεσον, *fall* or *throw oneself upon*, λέκτροισιν A.R.3.655; ὅρμῳ *AP* 9.82 (Antip. Thess.). **-πλέκω**, *interweave*, *entwine*, ἀκάνθας δι' ἀλλήλων Plu.2.494a:—Pass., X.*Cyn.*9.12. **-πνίγω** [ῑ], *suffocate in*, Gal.7.673:—Pass., aor. inf. -πνῐγῆναι Diocl.*Fr.*55. **-ποσις**, εως, ἡ, *swallowing up*, Ph.1.116.

ἐγκατᾰριθμέω, *count*, *number*, *reckon in* or *among*, τὴν ἔκφρασιν τοῖς γυμνάσμασιν Hermog.*Prog.*10, cf. Alex.Aphr.*in Metaph.*46.9:—Pass., *to be counted in* or *among*, Arist.*SE*167^{b}24.

ἐγκατα-ρράπτω (poet. aor. -ἔραψα Orph.*H.*48.3), *sew in*, Aen. Tact.31.4:—Pass., X.*Cyn.*6.1. **-σβέννῡμι** or -ύω, *quench in* a thing, τὸ λογικὸν ἐγκατέσβεσται τῆς ψυχῆς Plu.2.975c, cf.987d. **-σήπομαι**, *grow rotten* or *corrupt in*, Hp.*Mul.*1.63, E.ap.Stob.3.41.6. **-σκάπτω**, *demolish*, Tz.*H.*1.787. **-σκευάζω**, *prepare in* a place, ἐν ταῖς πόλεσι προδότας D.S.16.54; but the Prep. ἐν freq. has little force, Id.2.24 (s.v.l.), 14.91. **-σκευος**, ον, *elaborate*, *ornate*, of style, opp. ἁπλοῦς, D.H.*Comp.*18, al., cf. Phld.*Rh.*1.164S., Demetr.*Eloc.*15. Adv. -ως S.E.*M.*2.56. **-σκήπτω**, *fall upon*, of lightning, εἴς τινα D.C.49.15; of epidemics, πολλαχόσε ἐ. Th.2.47, cf. Gal.10.880: metaph., Ph.2.471, Ael.*Fr.*348. II. trans., *hurl down among* or *upon*, of lightning, ἐγκατάσκηψον βέλος S.*Tr.*1087; κακῶν ἃ Πέρσαις ἐγκατέσκηψεν θεός A.*Pers.*514. **-σκηψις**, εως, ἡ, *sudden attack*, Philum.*Ven.*4.5. **-σκιρόομαι**, Pass., *to be engrained*, κηλῖδας ἐγκατεσκιρωμένας Hipparch.ap.Stob.4.44.81. **-σπείρω**, *scatter*, *sow*, *implant in* or *among*, ἐλπίδα τῷ γένει τῶν ἀνθρώπων Ph.2.673; τι τῇ ὕλῃ Plu.2.1001b; φήμην Hdn.2.1.3:—Pass., Plu. *Cic.*14, Aen.Gaz.*Thphr.*p.69B. **-στηρίζω**, *fix firmly in*, Corn. *ND*6 (Pass.). **-στοιχειόομαι**, *to be implanted as a principle in*, τινί Plu.*Lyc.*13, 2.353e. **-στρέφω**, *return* a ball in a game, Antiph.234.6. **-συφράζω**· ἐνυβρίζω, Hsch. **-σφάττω**, *slaughter in*, τὸν υἱὸν τῷ κόλπῳ Plu.*Dem.*31:—also **-σφάζω**, γονέων ἐν ὄμμασι καὶ κόλποις τέκνα D.S.35.12. **-σχάζω**, *scarify*, Dsc.*Ther.*19 (Pass.). **-τᾰράσσω**, *throw into confusion*, Plu.2.592a (Pass.). **-τάσσω**, Att. -ττω, *arrange* or *place in*, Longin.10.7, Marcellin.*Puls.*474:—Pass., Onos.10.3; ῥυθμοὶ -τεταγμένοι ἀδήλως rhythms *introduced* unobtrusively, D.H.*Comp.*25 (cf. ἐγκαταχωρίζω). **-τέμνω**, *cut up* the foetus *in* the womb, Hp.*Foet.Exsect.*1. II. *cut up among* a number, Pl.*R.*565d. **-τίθημι**, *lay* or *put in*, ⟨ἔν⟩ τινι τι Orph.*H.*25.9; Ἐριχθόνιον... νηῷ ἐγκατέθηκε *IG*14.1389ii31. II. Hom. only in Med., ἱμάντα τεῷ ἐγκάτθεο κόλπῳ *put* the band *upon* or *round* thy waist, Il.14.219, cf. 223; ἄτην ἐῷ ἐγκάτθετο θυμῷ *stored up*, *devised* mischief *in* his heart, Od.23.223; τελαμῶνα ἐῇ ἐγκάτθετο τέχνῃ *stored up* the belt in his art, *designed* it by his art, Od.11.614; σὺ ταῦτα τεῷ ἐνικάτθεο θυμῷ *store it* up *in* thy heart, Hes.*Op.*27; στέρνοις ἐγκατέθεντο Simon.85.5; ὅκα φρεσὶν ἐγκατάθοιτο βουλάν Theoc.17.14; γλυφίδας ..ἐνικάτθετο νευρῇ A.R.3.282. **-τίλλω**, *shred in* lint, Hp.*Mul.* 2.205. **-τομή**, ἡ, *cutting up* of the foetus *in* the womb, Id. *Foet.Exsect.*tit. **-φλέγω**, *burn in*, βόθροις *Gp.*9.6.3. **-φῡσάω**, *spray*, οἴνῳ καὶ ἐλαίῳ *Hippiatr.*26. **-φύω**, gloss on ἠγκυροβόληται, Gal.19.102. **-χέω**, *pour out besides*, φόνον Epigr.ap.Plu.*Marc.* 30. **-χρίω** [ῑ], *smear over*, Dsc.*Eup.*1.118. **-χώννῡμι**, *overwhelm*, τινὰ τῷ πλήθει τῶν βελῶν D.H.9.21; *bury*, τὸ δεύτερον τοῦ κλήματος μέρος *Gp.*4.3.3:—Pass., μνήμη -χώννυται τῷ αἰῶνι M.Ant. 7.10. **-χωρίζω**, *place in*:—Pass., ῥυθμοὶ -κεχωρισμένοι ἀδήλως D.H.*Dem.*50 (cf. ἐγκατατάσσω).

ἐγκατ-ειλέομαι, *to be cooped up in*, Arist.*Mu.*395^{b}33, dub. in Ph. 2.504. **-είργω**, v. ἐγκαθείργω. **-ερείδω**, *support heavily on*, τὸ ἰσχίον τῇ βάσει Philostr.*Gym.*31. **-εφάλλομαι**, Ep. aor. 2 ἐγκατέπαλτο, *leap down into*, Opp.*H.*4.661. **-έχω**, *contain within*, σῶμα κόρης...τύμβος ὅδ' ἐ. *IG*12(8).609.2; *retain*, Sor.1.46, Ruf.ap. Orib.8.24.8:—Pass., *to be contained*, Plu.2.691f; esp. *to be confined* in a temple, *UPZ*6.8 (ii B.C.). II. Pass., *to be owned* or *possessed*, *PFlor.*97.3 (ii A.D.). **-ίλλω**, f.l. for ἐγκατατίλλω (q.v.), Hp.*Mul.* 2.205. **-ιλλώπτω**, *scoff at*, ὑμῖν ἐγκατιλλώψας μέγα A.*Eu.*113, cf. *Fr.*226 (dub.).

ἐγκᾰτόεις, εσσα, εν, (ἔγκατα) *containing* or *enclosing intestines*, κεκρύφαλος Nic.*Th.*580.

ἐγκατοικ-έω, *dwell in*, Hdt.4.204; δόμοις E.*Fr.*188; *dwell among*, αὐτοῖς 2*Ep.Pet.*2.8. **-ίζω**, Att. fut. -ιῶ Lyc.1261:—*settle* or *place in* or *on*, Luc.*Asin.*25: metaph., τῇδε τῇ τάξει τὸ φρουρητικόν Dam. *Pr.*257; *implant*, Plu.2.779f (Pass.). **-οδομέω**, *to build in* a place, Th.3.18 (Pass.). II. *build in*, *immure*, εἰς ἔρημον οἰκίαν Aeschin. 1.182:—metaph. in Pass., ὁ [ἀὴρ] ἐν τοῖς ὠσὶν ἐγκατῳκοδόμηται Arist. *de An.*420^{a}9, cf. Porph.*Abst.*4.3. **-ος**, ον, *indwelling*, Sch.Il.2.125.

ἔγκατον, v. ἔγκατα.

ἐγκατ-οπτρίζομαι, Med., aor. -ίξασθαι *IG*4.951.64 (Epid.):—*look at oneself as in a mirror*, ἐς τὸ ὕδωρ l. c.; λεκάνῃ Artem.3.30. II. *contemplate as in a mirror*, τὸ τῆς τέχνης ἔργον Ph.Byz.*Mir.Praef.* 2. **-ορύσσω**, Att. -ττω, *bury in*:—Pass., ἐγκατωρύχθαι τὴν ψυχὴν ἐν τῷ σώματι D.H.*Rh.*6.5, cf. Jul.*Or.*6.189c. **-οχέω**, (κάτοχος) *to be a recluse* (cf. sq.), τῷ κυρίῳ Σαράπιδι *IGRom.*4.1403 (Smyrna, iii A.D.). **-οχος**, ὁ, *recluse*, ἱερῶν Ptol.*Tetr.*163; ἐν ἱεροῖς Vett.Val.63.29, cf. *Sammelb.*1066. II. Adj., *fixing*, τὸ ἐ. Olymp.Alch.p.74B.

ἐγκαττύω, *stitch into the shoe-sole*, Alex.98.8 (Pass.).

ἐγκᾰτώδης, ες, *like the entrails*, Sch.Ar.*Eq.*1176.

ἐγκαυλέω, *to be in stalk*, Arist.*Pr.*926^{a}26, Thphr.*HP*1.2.2.

ἔγ-καυμα, ατος, τό, (ἐγκαίω) *mark burnt in*, *sore from burning*, Luc.*DDeor.*13.2, al. II. *encaustic picture*, Pl.*Ti.*26c, *JHS*41.195 (Delos, ii B.C.), Dicaearch.1.8, Plu.2.759c. III. *ulcer in the eye*, Aët.7.27. **-καυσις**, εως, ἡ, *encaustic painting*, *IG*2.808^d.52, 4. 1484.266 (Epid., iv B.C.), *SIG*977^a.7 (Delos), *IG*7.3073.11 (Lebad.), etc. II. *heat-stroke*, Dsc.5.13 (pl.), Gal.12.504: pl., Plu.2. 127b. **-καυστήρια**, τά, *instruments used by encaustic painters*, *IG* 11(2).287 A44 (Delos, iii B.C.). **-καυστής**, οῦ, ὁ, *encaustic painter*, Plu.2.348f; ἀγαλματοποιὸς ἐ. *IG*14.1494:—also **-καυτής**, ib.1^2.374, *CIG*4958c. **-καυστικός**, ή, όν, *of* or *for burning in*: ἡ ἐ. (sc. τέχνη) *the art of encaustic painting*, Plin.*HN*35.122. 2. *inflammatory*, πυρετός Herod.Med.ap.Aët.5.129. **-καυστος**, ον, *burnt in*, *painted in encaustic*, Mart.4.47: *encausto pingere*, Plin.*HN*35.149; *encausta pictura*, ib.122.

ἐγκαυχάομαι, *pride oneself on*, ἔν τινι Lxx *Ps.*73(74).4; τινί Aesop. 230, Eustr. *in EN*272.14.

ἔγκᾰφος, (ἐγκάπτω) *mouthful*, *morsel*, Eup.330.

ἐγκαψικίδαλος, ον, (κίδαλον) *onion-eating*, Luc.*Lex.*10 (prob. f. l. for ἐγκαψιπήδαλος, cf. καψιπήδαλος).

ἔγκειμαι, fut. -κείσομαι: used as Pass. of ἐντίθημι: I. *lie in*, *be wrapped in*, ἐπεὶ οὐκ ἐγκείσεαι αὐτοῖς [τοῖς εἵμασι] Il.22.513; so, Hdt.2.73 (v.l. ἐσκειμένον); simply, *to be in*, ὀφθαλμὸς ἕεις ἐνέκειτο μετώπῳ Hes.*Th.*145: in mal. part., Herod.5.3. 2. ἐγκεῖσθαί τινι *to be involved in*, πόθῳ Archil.84; βλάβαις S.*Ph.*1318; μόχθοις E.*Ion* 181 (anap.); πολλαῖς ξυμφοραῖς Id.*Hel.*269; κακοπαθείαις Plb.14.9.5 codd.: c. acc., μελεδῶνας ἔγκειμαι I *have* cares *laid on me*, A.R.2.627. b. *to be implied*, *involved in*, ἐ. τὸ αἰσθητικὸν εἶναι ἐν τῷ εἴδει Plot.6.7. 3. 3. abs., *to be inserted*, Pl.*Cra.*402e, *R.*616d. II. *press hard*, esp. of troops *pressing upon* a defeated or retreating enemy, Th.1. 49,144, etc.; of opponents in politics or argument, ἐνέκειντο τῷ Περικλεῖ Id.2.59, cf. 5.43, etc.: freq. with Adj. or Adv., πολλὸς ἐνέκειτο λέγων *was* very *urgent*, Hdt.7.158, cf. Th.4.22; πολὺς τοῖς συμβεβηκόσι ἔγκειται he *insists* much upon..., D.18.199; ἄγαν ἐ. τινί to *be vehement against* one, Ar.*Ach.*309; ἰσχυρῶς ἐ. Th.1.69; βαρὺς ἐγκεῖσθαι D.H.6.62; ὅλος ἐγκεῖσθαί τινι *to be devoted to* one, Theoc. 3.33; ἐ. ἐπὶ τὰ πονηρά Lxx *Ge.*8.21. III. *to be upon*, ὁ δέ οἱ περὶ ποσσὶ... ἐνέκειτο, of a sandal, *IG*14.1389i27. IV. *to be a burden*, *annoyance*, Herod.4.47 (prob.).

ἐγκείρω, in pf. part. Pass., ἐγκεκαρμένῳ κάρᾳ with *shorn* head, E. *El.*108 (v.l. ἐν κεκ.).

ἐγκεκαροῦται· ἐγκαταβλέπει, Hsch.

ἐγκεκλῐμένως, Adv. *with the accent thrown back*, Sch.Il.1.277, 6. 289.

ἐγκέλᾰδος, ὁ, *a buzzing insect*, like βομβύλιος, Sch.Ar.*Nu.*158.

ἐγκέλ-ευμα or -ευσμα, ατος, τό, *encouragement*, X.*Cyn.*6.24, Cic. *Att.*6.1.8. **-ευσις**, εως, ἡ, = foreg., Str.13.1.35, *Sammelb.*4284.8 (iii A.D.), Them.*Or* 19.232b: pl., A.D.*Synt.*258.20; ἐξ ἐ. by *command*, *IG*14.926 (Portus, dub.), Zucker *Les temples immergés de la Nubie* p.3 (ii A.D.). **-ευσμᾰτικός**, ή, όν, = ἐγκελευστικός, ἐπίρρημα *EM*115.27. **-ευσμός**, ὁ, = -ευσις, ἐς ἀλλήλους Arr.*An.*2.21. 9. **-ευστικός**, ή, όν, *encouraging*, Max.Tyr.23.5; *hortatory*, ἐπίρρημα A.D.*Synt.*258.11. **-ευστος**, ον, *urged on*, ὑπό τινος X.*An.* 1.3.13. **-εύω**, *urge on*, *cheer on*, A.*Pr.*72; ἐ. κυσί X.*Cyn.*9.7:—Med., D.H.3.20, etc.; τὸ πολεμικὸν ἐγκελεύεσθαι *sound* a charge, Plu.*Arist.*21, cf. *Pomp.*70. 2. in Med. also, *command*, Arist. *Fr.*11; τοῖς στραταγοῖς *IPE*1^2.79.23 (Olbia), cf. Asp.*in EN*135.13: c. acc., *enjoin*, Ti.Locr.104a.

ἐγκέλλω, aor. 1 ἐνέκελσα, *fit into*, as a socket, Hp.*Fract.*30.

ἐγκεντ-έω, *puncture*, *Gloss.* II. = ἐγκεντρίζω, Eust.1308. 62. **-ρια**, τά, *spurs*, Hsch. II. ἐγκέντριον, τό, *graft*, Mich. *in PN*105.9. **-ρίζω**, *goad*, *spur on*, Lxx *Wi.*16.11 (Pass.). II. of plants, *graft*, Thphr.*HP*2.2.5, Porph.*Gaur.*10.1 (Pass.), etc.: metaph., *Ep.Rom.*11.17, Plot.2.9.7; of a Centaur, ὃν φύσις ἐνεκέντρισεν ἵππῳ *APl.*4.116 (Euodus). III. (κέντρον) *concentrate*, Dam.*Pr.*74:—Pass., ib.263. **-ρίς**, ίδος, ἡ, *sting*, Ar.*V.*427. 2. *goad*, X.*Cyn.*6.1, Pl.Com.40; also, *spur*, Pherecr.48. 3. *pointed stile* for writing, Poll.8.16, Aristaenet.1.20. 4. *spike worn on the leg* for climbing, περιθέμενον.. ἐγκεντρίδας ἀναδραμεῖν εἰς τοὺς τοίχους Arist.*Fr.*84. **-ρισις**, εως, ἡ, *inoculation* or *grafting of trees*, Colum. 3.9.6, Jul.*Ep.*180 (pl.). **-ρισμα**, ατος, τό, = foreg., *Gloss.* **-ρισμός**, ὁ, = foreg., *Gp.*4.12.2, *PSI*6.624.20. **-ριστής**, οῦ, ὁ, *agitator*, *instigator*, *Gloss.* **-ρος**, ον, *furnished with a sting*, [σφῆκες] Arist. *HA*627^{b}27. II. of stars, *occupying a cardinal point*, Vett.Val.57. 30, Sch.Ptol.*Tetr.*148. 2. ἐ. κύκλος, opp. ἔκκεντρος, Theo Sm. p.162 H., al. **-ρόω**, *thrust in a sting*: *fix firmly in*, Hsch. (Pass.): —Pass., *to be furnished with a sting*, Sch.Ar.*V.*1069.

ἐγκεράννῡμι or -ύω, *mix*, esp. wine, οἰνόν τ' ἐγκεράσασα πιεῖν Il.8. 189; τρεῖς μόνους κρατῆρας ἐγκεραννύω Eub.94.1 (cf. ἐγκίρνημι); ἐ. τι εἰς ὄνομα Pl.*Cra.*427c:—Med., *mix for oneself*: metaph., *concoct*, πρήγματα μεγάλα Hdt.5.124; ἐγκεράσασθαι παιδιάν *mix in* a little amusement, Pl.*Plt.*268d, cf. Luc.*Am.*19. II. Pass., *to be multiplied together*, of numbers, *Theol.Ar.*45.

ἐγκέραστος, ον, *mixed*, *blended*, Plu.2.660c.

ἐγκεραυλ-έω, *play* on the Phrygian flute, Hsch.:—hence **-ης**, ου, ὁ, Id.

ἐγκερτομέω, *abuse*, *mock at*, E.*IA*1006.

ἐγκέρχνω, *make hoarse*, Hp.*Acut.*58.

ἐγκεφᾰλ-αίωμα, ατος, τό, = κεφαλαίωμα, *PLond.*2.38. **-ιον**, τό,

Dim. of ἐγκέφαλος I, *BGU*348.33. **-ίς,** ίδος, ἡ, *cerebellum*, f.l. for παρεγκεφαλίς, Gal.*UP*8.6. **-ίτης** [ῑ], ου, ὁ, *of the brain*, μυελός ib. 4. **-ος,** ον, (κεφαλή) *within the head*: as Subst., ἐγκέφαλος (sc. μυελός), ὁ, **I.** *brain*, Il.3.300, Od.9.458, etc.; τὸν ἐ. σεσεῖσθαι Ar. *Nu.*1276; ὁ ἐ. ἐστιν ὁ τὰς αἰσθήσεις παρέχων τοῦ ἀκούειν κτλ. Pl.*Phd.* 96b, cf. Arist.*Sens.*438^{b}25 (but cf. *Metaph.*1013^{a}6). **II.** *the heart* or '*cabbage*' of the date-palm, X.*An.*2.3.16, Thphr.*HP*2.6.2. **III.** Διὸς ἐ., prov. of rare and costly food, 'morsel for a king', Ephipp. 13.7, Clearch.5.

ἐγκέχοδα, v. ἐγχέζω. **ἐγκεχρημένος,** v. ἐγχράω.

ἐγκηδεύω, *bury in* a place, Lxx 4*Ma.*17.9 (Pass.), J.*AJ*9.5.3, *JHS* 6.359.

ἐγκηρίς, ίδος, ἡ, *lump of wax*, Androm.ap.Gal.13.693, al.

ἔγκηροι (κήρ)· θνητοί, Hsch.

ἐγκηρόω, *wax over, rub with wax*, *Gp.*10.21.5.

ἐγκηρύσσω, *invite tenders* for a contract, *PPetr.*3 p.101 (iii B.C.).

ἐγκῐθᾰρίζω, *play the harp in the midst*, *h.Ap.*201; μέσῳ ἤματι *at midday*, *h.Merc.*17.

ἐγκίρνημι, = ἐγκεράννυμι, Dor. imper. ἐγκίκρα Sophr.48.

ἐγκῐλῐκ-εύομαι, = sq., Suid. s.v. Κιλίκιος τράγος. **-ίζω,** (Κίλιξ) *play the Cilician to* one, τινί, i.e. *cheat*, Pherecr.166. **-ίστρια·** περιαγνίστρια, Hsch.

ἐγκίλλαφον and **ἔγκιλλον,** = οὐρά, Hsch.

ἐγκινδῡνεύω, *take a risk*, *Cod.Just.*1.3.39.

ἐγκῑνέομαι, Med., *disturb, trouble*, τισί Ar.*Fr.*69.

ἐγκίνῡμαι [ῑ], *to be moved*, Q.S.13.245.

ἐγκίρνημι, poet. for ἐγκεράννυμι, *mix by pouring in*, [κρητῆρα] Pi.*N.* 9.50; ἐν δὲ κέρναις οἶνον (Aeol. for ἐγκιρνάς) Alc.34.4: metaph., ἤθεσι θεωρήματα Lysis ap.Iamb.*VP*17.77; τῇ μεταβολῇ τὸ ἀμετάβλητον Dam.*Pr.*412:—Pass., ἐν δ' ἐκίρνατο οἶνος *Com.Adesp.*1203.3, cf. Iamb. *in Nic.*p.81 P.

ἔγκιρρος, ον, *pale-yellow*, Dsc.1.13.

ἐγκισσάω, *have yearnings like one pregnant*, Lxx *Ge.*30.38.

ἐγκισσεύομαι, Pass., *twine like ivy*: metaph., *form a plexus*, φλεβίοις ἐς τὸν μυελὸν Hp.*Oss.*14.

ἐγκίσσησις, εως, ἡ, *impregnation*, Zonar. (vulg. ἐγκίσσωσις).

ἐγκλαστρίδια, ων, τά, *ear-rings*, Poll.5.97.

ἐγκλάω, Ep. **ἐνικλάω,** aor. ἐνέκλασα, *thwart, frustrate*, μοι ἔωθεν ἐνικλᾶν ὅττι κεν εἴπω Il.8.408; ἦε τίς ἄτη σωομένους ... ἐνέκλασεν; A.R. 3.307; later lit., *break in*, σιλφίον ἐ. Hp.*Mul.*2.133:—Pass., φωνὴ ἐγκεκλασμένη *weak* voice, Phld.*Mus.*p.80 K. **II.** Pass., *to be bent, inclined*, Apollod.*Poliorc.*187.16; of the eyes of swine, Plu.2.671a (s.v.l.); of a diadem, Heraclit.*Ep.*8.1.

ἐγ-κλεισμός, ὁ, *shutting up*, λόγου Eust.1391.63; ἐν ἐγκλεισμῷ under *lock and key*, *POxy.*1734.6. **-κλειστέον,** *one must shut up*, *Gp.*14.7.18. **-κλείω,** Ion. **-κληΐω,** Att. **-κλῄω,** Ep. **ἐνικλείω** A.R. 2.1029:—*shut in, close*, ὅκως τὰς πύλας ἐγκληΐσειε Hdt.4.78; θύρα ἐγκεκλῃμένη Pl.*Prt.*314d. **II.** *shut* or *confine within*, ἑρκέων ἐγκεκλῃμένος (for ἐντὸς ἑρκέων κεκλῃμένος) S.*Aj.*1274; δόμοις ἐγκεκλῃμένος Id.*Tr.*579: generally, *shut up, confine*, γλῶσσαν ἐγκλῄσας ἔχει Id.*Ant.*180; εἰ μὴ γλῶσσαν ἐγκλῄοι φόβος ib.505; στόμα ἐ. E.*Hec.* 1284. **III.** Med., *shut oneself up in*, X.*HG*6.5.9. **2.** *shut up with oneself*, Luc.*Alex.*41.

ἐγκλεπίς· ἐπιθυμία, and **ἐγκλεφές·** ἐπιθυμητικόν, Hsch. **ἐγκλέφωνος,** = ἐρεθιστής, διεφθαρμένος, Id.

ἔγ-κλημα, ατος, τό, (ἐγκαλέω) *accusation, charge*, ἔ. τινι ἔχειν S.*Ph.* 323, cf. *Tr.*361, Antipho 3.2.9, etc.; ἐγκλήματα ἔχειν τινός, = ἐγκαλεῖν τι, Th.1.26; ἔ. ποιεῖν τι make a thing *matter of complaint*, Id.3.53; ἐγκλήματα ποιεῖσθαι bring *accusations*, Id.1.126; τὰ ἐ. τὰ ἔς τινας *complaints* respecting..., ib.79; ἐν ἐγκλήματι γίγνεσθαι D.18.251; γίγνεται or ἐστὶ ἔγκλημά μοι πρός τινα I have *ground of complaint* respecting him, X.*Cyr.*1.2.6, Lys.10.23; λύειν ἔ. *clear away* a charge, Plb.2.52.4; λόγοις τὰ ἐ. διαλύεσθαι Th.1.140. **II.** in Law, *written complaint*: generally, of *complaints* which were to lead to private suits, ἔ. λαγχάνειν τινί file *a complaint* against.., D.34.16, al., cf. *PTeb.*616 (ii A.D.). **III.** concrete, *a standing reproach*, τῆς τύχης καὶ τῶν θεῶν Plu.*Dio* 58. **2.** *defect*, Gal.14.20. **-κλημᾰτίζω,** = ἐγκαλέω, *PFlor.*58.16 (iii A.D.), *Gloss.* **-κλημᾰτικός,** ή, όν, *liable to cause disputes*, Arist.*EN*1162^{b}16, *Pol.*1335^{a}4. Adv. **-κῶς** Vett.Val.293.35. **II.** ἐ. δίκη *criminal* suit, *Cod.Just.*4.20.16; αἰτία ἐ. *PMonac.*7.62 (vi A.D.). **-κλημάτιον,** τό, Dim. of ἔγκλημα, *PFlor.*332.26 (ii A.D.). **-κλημᾰτογρᾰφέω,** *draw up an indictment against*, ἐμέ *UPZ*124. **-κλημᾰτόομαι,** Pass., *shoot into twigs*; v. ἐκκλημ-. **-κλήμων,** ον, gen. ονος, *liable to a charge*, *AP*5.187 (Leon.).

ἐγκληρ-όομαι, Pass., *to be assigned* or *planted by lot*, Ael.*VH*8. 1. **-ος,** ον, *having a lot* or *share in*..., c. gen., οὔθ' ὑμεναίων ἔ. S. *Ant.*814 (lyr.); λαχεῖν ἔγκληρά τινι to have *an equal share with*..., ib.837 (lyr., dub.). **2.** *having a share of an inheritance, heir* or *heiress*, E.*IT* 682; ἔ. εὐνή a marriage *which brings wealth*, Id.*Hipp.* 1011; ἔ. πεδία land *possessed as an inheritance*, Id.*HF*468. **3.** Astrol., *occupying a* κλῆρος, Serapio in *Cat.Cod.Astr.*8(4).225.

ἐγκλησία, ἡ, *blame, adverse criticism*, Anon.*Vit.Arist.*p.14 W.

ἔγ-κλησις, εως, ἡ, *accusation*, *PRyl.*65.16 (i B.C.), Man.1.221 (pl.), etc. **-κλητέος,** α, ον, *to be blamed*, ἀμέλειαι Plu.2.1051c. **II.** ἐγκλητέον *one must blame*, τινί Plb.4.60.9; τῇ προνοίᾳ M.Ant.12. 24. **-κλητος,** ον, *liable to a charge*, *PTeb.*27.42 (ii B.C.), Plu.2. 1051b, *PMasp.*97 ii 50 (vi A.D.). **2.** written for ἔκκλ-, Hsch.

ἐγκλῄω, Att. for ἐγκλείω.

ἐγ-κλῐδόν, Adv. *leaning, bent down*, *h.Hom.*23.3; ἐ. ὄσσε βαλοῦσα *aslant* or *askance*, A.R.3.1008; ἐ. ὤμῳ κεφαλὴν ἐρεισαμένη *AP*5.249 (Paul. Sil.). **-κλιζε·** τὰ ἑτέρων ἑτέροις ἐδίδου, Hsch. **-κλῐμα,** ατος, τό, *slope*, Plb.5.59.9 (pl.). **2.** *inclination, tilt*, τοῦ κόσμου Hipparch.1.3.5, Gem.6.24; of an engine, Bito 55.10 (pl.). **3.** *latitude*, Vett.Val.316.32. **II.** *turning*, i.e. *rout*, of an army, Plb.1.19.11; cj. for ἔκκλημα in D.S.20.12. **III.** Gramm., *inflected form*, A.D. *Synt.*83.2. **2.** *form pronounced with grave accent*, Id.*Pron.*90.12.

ἐγκλῐμᾰτικός, = ἐγκλιτικός, *AB*1144.

ἐγκλίνω [ῑ], fut. -κλῐνῶ: pf. ἐγκέκλῐκα Plu.*Sull.*1: pf. Pass. ἐγκέκλῐμαι (v. infr.):—*bend in* or *inwards*, τὴν κνήμην Arist.*Mech.*857^b 36; *bend*, τινά A.R.1.62 (v.l. ἀγκλῖναι):—Pass., σκέλη ἐγκεκλιμένα μικρὸν X.*Cyn.*5.30; τὰ ἐγκλιθέντα v.l. for ἐκκλ- in Hp.*Art.*38. **2.** *cause to incline*, τι εἰς δεξιά Pl.*R.*436e; τὰ πράγματά τισι Arist.*Oec.* 1348^{b}3:—Med., ἐ. εἰς τὰ δεξιὰ *lean* to the right, Id.*Phgn.*813^{a}17. **3.** Pass., *lean on*, X.*Smp.*3.13: metaph., πόνος ὔμμι ἐγκέκλιται labour *lies upon* you, Il.6.78. **4.** ἐ. νῶτόν τινι *turn* one's back *towards* another, E.*Hec.*739. **5.** Pass., *give way*, ὑπείκει καὶ θέλων ἐγκλίνεται Id.*Fr.*431.5. **6.** Gramm., *pronounce as an enclitic*, A.D.*Synt.* 120.10; *pronounce with the grave accent*, Trypho ap.eund.*Conj.*255. 16:—Pass., A.D.*Pron.*35.26. **b.** ἐγκλινόμενα, τά, *inflected forms*, opp. ὀρθά, D.H.*Comp.*5, cf. A.D.*Synt.*30.11 (s.v.l.). **7.** ἐ. φωνὴν *lower* the voice, Luc.*Philops.*6. **II.** intr., *incline towards*, [ἡ καρδία] μικρὸν ἐ. εἰς τὸν ἀριστερὸν μαστόν Arist.*HA*496^{a}16, cf. *PPetr.*2 p.126 (iii B.C.); [ἡ πολιτεία] ἐγκλίνειν βούλεται πρὸς τὴν ὀλιγαρχίαν Arist. *Pol.*1266^{a}7, cf. 1307^{a}21. **2.** abs., *give way, flee*, X.*HG*7.2.14, *Cyr.* 3.3.65, Plb.1.57.8, Plu.*Fab.*12, etc.; also ἐ. τινί *give way* to him, D.H.5.54: c. acc., *give way to*, Plb.14.8.8. **3.** *decline, become worse*, Plu.*Sull.*1, etc. **4.** in Tactics, *wheel*, ἐπὶ δόρυ ἢ ἐπὶ ἀσπίδα Arr.*Tact.*21.3.

ἐγκλίς· ἡ καγκελλωτὴ θύρα, *EM*518.22.

ἔγ-κλῐσις, εως, ἡ, *inclination*, ἔ. λαβεῖν, of the earth, D.L.2.9, cf. Pl.*Amat.*132b; of the ecliptic (ὁ λοξὸς κύκλος), Arist.*GC*336^{b}4; of ground, ἔ. ἔχειν πρὸς ἕω Id.*Pol.*1330^{a}39; εἰς νότον Porph.*Antr.* 26; ἐγκλίσεις τῆς κεφαλῆς εἰς τὰ δεξιὰ Arist.*Phgn.*808^{a}13; ἐ. σχημάτων τριγώνων Onos.10.28 (pl.); ἐ. δορατίου, in signalling, Id.26.1. **2.** *the inclination* or *slope*, as of a wave, κατὰ τὴν ἔ. σκιασθῆναι Arist.*Col.* 792^{a}22. **3.** Medic., *displacement*, Hp.*Fract.*39 (pl.): generally, ὄγκων cj. in Epicur.*Ep.*1 p.14 U. **4.** *modulation* of a singer's voice, D.Chr.32.49. **5.** *failure, defeat*, *PMag.Par.*1.2445. **II.** in Gramm., **1.** *mood of a verb*, D.H.*Comp.*6, D.T.638.7, A.D. *Synt.*248.14, etc. **2.** *throwing back* of the accent, Id.*Pron.*8. 7, al.; *change of acute to grave accent*, Id.*Adv.*169.23. **3.** *inflexion*, Simp.*in Cat.*65.8, Dexipp.*in Cat.*33.8: generally, of *derivative forms*, Simp.*in Cat.*37.11. **-κλῐτέον,** *one must use as enclitic*, Sch.Il.12.204, Sch.Th.*Oxy.*853 vi 25. **-κλῐτικός,** ή, όν, of a word *which leans* (ἐγκλίνει) *its accent upon the one before* (cf. A.D.*Synt.*98. 2), *enclitic*, Trypho ap.eund.*Conj.*255.11, etc. Adv. **-κῶς,** ἀναγιγνώσκειν *EM*124.9, A.D.*Synt.*222.22, Hdn.Gr.2.70: Comp. **-ώτερον** A.D.*Synt.*140.28.

ἐγκλοιόω, *enclose in a collar*, Lxx *Pr.*6.21 (Med.).

ἐγκλονέομαι, Pass., *gurgle in*, Hp.*Mul.*1.2.

ἐγκλῠδ-άζομαι, Pass., *make a splash*, Hp.*Morb.*1.15. **-αξις,** εως, ἡ, *splashing*, Diocl.*Fr.*43. **-αστικός,** ή, όν, *gurgling*, '*splashy*', Hp.*Acut.*62.

ἐγ-κλύζω, fut. -ύσω, *rinse the inside of* a thing, οἴνῳ with wine, D.S. 1.91. **2.** *soak*, Dsc.5.75. **3.** *treat by clysters*, τινά Id.4.154:—Pass., *to be administered as a clyster* or *injection*, Id.1.73, *Eup.*1.197, etc. **-κλυσμα,** ατος, τό, *injection, clyster*, Id.4.3, al. **-κλυστέον,** *one must give a douche*, Paul.Aeg.3.66.

ἐγκλώθω, *spin* or *fasten to*, Sch.rec.S.*OT*1264.

ἐγκνήθω, *grate in*, in Med., Nic.*Th.*911 (ἐνικν-), *Al.*368.

ἔγκνισμα, ατος, τό, *a piece of meat*, Argive word in Plu.2.296f.

ἐγκνώσσω, *sleep in*, Mosch.2.6 (in poet. form ἐνικν-).

ἐγκοακίσαι· ἐγχέαι λάθρα, Hsch.

ἐγκοιλ-αίνω, *hollow, scoop out*, f.l. in Hdt.2.73:—Pass., Thphr. *HP*5.2.4. **-ιος,** ον, (κοιλία) *in the belly*:—as Subst., ἐγκοίλια, τά (sg. -ιον D.S.1.35). **1.** *intestines*, Id.1.91, *SIG*958.13 (Ceos), Lxx *Le.*1.9. **2.** *ribs of a ship, belly-timbers*, Thphr.*HP*4.2.8, Moschio ap.Ath.5.206f. **II.** *flat-bellied*, *Cat.Cod.Astr.*7.202. **-ος,** ον, *hollow, sunken*, ὀφθαλμοὶ Hp.*Prog.*2; ἔγκοιλόν τι a *sinking in* of the lip, Arist.*HA*604^{a}28; τὰ ἔ. τῆς γῆς Pl.*Phd.*111c: Comp. **-ότερος** *deeper*, Lxx *Le.*13.30. **II.** *concave*, Thphr.*HP*7.13.1.

ἐγκοιμ-άομαι, Pass. with fut. Med., *sleep in* a place, [ἐν σπηλαίῳ] Arist.*Mir.*839^{a}3; esp. *sleep in* a temple, to seek prophetic dreams or to obtain cure for a disease, Str.11.7.1, 16.2.35, Plu.2.109c; ὑπὲρ ἐνεργείας Arr.*Epict.*2.16.17. **2.** *sleep upon* or *after* a meal, Hp.*Acut.* 29. **-ησις,** εως, ἡ, *a sleeping in a temple* (v. foreg.), D.S.1. 53. **-ητήριος,** α, ον, *for sleeping on*, ψίαθοι Poll.6.11: **-τήριον,** τό, *grave*, *BSA*18.145 (Beroea, ii B.C.). **-ήτριον,** τό, = sq., in form -ητριν, *UPZ*85.8 (ii B.C.). **-ητρον,** τό, *counterpane*, *PCair.Zen.* 48.4 (iii B.C.), Ammon.p.140 V.; expld. by *dormitorium*, *Gloss.* (also -ηθρον, -ητρα, ib.). **-ήτωρ** χιτών *night*-gown, Poll.10.123. **-ίζω,** *lull to sleep in*..., *AP*7.260 (Carph.): metaph., Hero *Aut.*16.2:—Pass., *IG*4.951.90 (Epid.).

ἐγκοισῠρόομαι, Pass., *to be luxurious as Coesyra* (a female name in the Alcmaeonid family), ἐγκεκοισυρωμένη Ar.*Nu.*48.

ἐγκοιτ-άζομαι, = ἐγκοιμάομαι, *IG*4.951.95 (Epid.). **II.** *to be embedded*, μέχρι τοῦ ἡμίσους Apollod.*Poliorc.*161.4; *to be soaked*,

*PLeid.X.*98. **-άς**, άδος, ἡ, *serving for a bed*, ἀκρώρειαι *AP*7.626. **-έω**, *sleep in* or *on*, τῷ Καπιτωλίῳ D.C.65.8. **-ιος**, ον, *belonging to a bed*, στρώματα *EM*255.44: ἐγκοίτιον, τό, = ἐγκοίμητρον, Hsch. s. v. ἐνευναίου.

ἐγκοιωτός, ά, όν, (κοῖον) *given as security*, *Leg.Gort.*9.35.

ἐγκόλ-αμμα, ατος, τό, *anything engraven*, Lxx *Ex.*36.13(39.6); *engraved inscription*, *Inscr.Prien.*42.9(pl.). **-απτός**, όν, *engraven, sculptured*, ἱστορία Ath.11.781e, cf. *Inscr.Prien.*37.168 (ii B.C.), Lxx 3*Ki.*6.28(29). **-άπτω**, *cut* or *carve upon* stone, ἐ. γράμματα ἐς τὸν τάφον Hdt.1.187, cf. *IG*1^2.313.166; ἐν τᾷ στάλᾳ ib.12(1).694.9 (Camirus); τύποι ἐν πέτρῃσι ἐγκεκολαμμένοι, γράμματα ἐν λίθῳ ἐγκ., Hdt.2.106, 136, al., cf. Lxx 3*Ki.*6.33(35); ἐπὶ τρίποσι Hdt.5.59; ἐπὶ πίνακος Suid. s. v. βοῦς ἕβδομος; εἰς τὸ μέτωπον Plu.*Per.*21: metaph., [νόμους] ἡ φύσις κατὰ μέσης ἐνεκόλαψε τῆς ψυχῆς Lib.*Decl.*43.49. **-αψις**, εως, ἡ, *engraving, inscribing*, *IG*4.1484.265 (Epid.), 7.3073.11 (Lebad.).

ἐγκολεήσατο, *sheathed his sword*, Hsch., Suid.

ἐγκοληβάζω, in Ar.*Eq.*263, *gulp down, swallow up*, v. Sch. ad loc., Hsch.; also expld. by ἐπὶ κόλοις βαίνειν, Suid. s. v. ἐκολαβῆσαι.

ἐγκολλ-άω, *glue on* or *to*, *IG*1^2.373.208, Lxx *Za.*14.5 (Pass.), Hero *Aut.*24.2. **-ησις**, εως, Dor. **ἐγκόλλᾱσις**, ιος, ἡ, *fastening, soldering*, *IG*4.1485.167 (Epid.). **-ος**, ον, (κόλλα) *adhering, fitting*, Ph. 1.610, al.

ἐγκόλλουρα, *torunda*, a kind of *bread*, *Gloss.*

ἐγκολπ-ίας ἄνεμος, a local wind *blowing from a bay*, Arist.*Mu.*394^{b}15. **-ίζω**, *form a bay*, ἠϊὼν ἐγκολπίζουσα Str.5.4.5. 2. *go into* or *follow the bay*, Id.9.5.22. 3. *inject into the vagina*, Aët.1.126. II. Med., with pf. Pass., *take in one's bosom*, ὥσπερ ἑρπετὰ τοὺς ἀπορρήτους λόγους Plu.2.508d, cf. Plot.1.4.6; *embrace*, θεὸς ἐγκεκόλπισται τὰ ὅλα Ph.1.425; περίοδος πολλοὺς ἀγκῶνας ἐγκολπιζομένη a period *embracing* many turns of expression, D.H.*Dem.*4 (vulg. ἐγκαλλωπιζομένη); [ἰχθῦς] ἐ. τῇ σαγήνῃ *to catch* fish *in the belly* of the net, Alciphr.1.18. 2. *conceive*, Porph.*Gaur.*5.4. 3. *embrace in a bay*, ἄκρα πολὺν -ομένη λιμένα Dion.Byz.53. **-ιος**, ον, *in* or *on the bosom*, διδόναι τι ἐ. τῷ ἀέρι Heraclit.*All.*39. **-ισμός**, ὁ, *vaginal douche* or *clyster*, Aët.3.153. **-όω**, *make full and round, like the folds of a robe*, Orph.*A.*1183 (tm.):—Pass., ἐγκεκολπῶσθαι *to be curved into a bay* or *bays*, Arist.*Mu.*393^{a}23:—Med., *put in the fold of one's robe*: hence metaph., 'have in one's pocket', τὴν τοῦ Καίσαρος ἰσχὺν D.C.48.52:—Pass., *to have folded round one*, χιτῶνα ἐνεκεκόλπωτο Id.62.2: metaph., ἀρετήν Mich.*in EN*603.24.

ἐγκομβ-όομαι, Med., (κόμβος) *bind* a thing *on oneself*, *wear* it *constantly*, Apollod.Car.4, 1*Ep.Pet.*5.5. II. Pass., = δέομαι, ἐνειλοῦμαι (Hsch.), Epich.7. **-ωμα**, ατος, τό, a sort of *frock* or *apron*, worn esp. by slaves to keep the ἐξωμίς clean, Longus 2.33, Poll.4.119, Thd. *Is.*3.20, cf. Varro ap.Non.p.870 L.

ἔγκομμα, ατος, τό, *obstacle, hindrance*, *PSI*5.500 (iii B.C.), Al.*Ex.*34.12, Hsch.

ἐγκον-έω, *to be quick and active*, esp. *in service*, Hom., only part. pres., with another Verb, ἐπεὶ στόρεσαν λέχος ἐγκονέουσαι *in haste*, Od.7.340, Il.24.648, cf. Critias *Fr.*16 D.: later also in imper., ἐγκόνει *make haste!* S.*Aj.*988, Ar.*Ach.*1088; also ἐγκονῶμεν S.*Aj.*811; ἐγκονεῖτε Id.*Tr.*1255, E.*HF*521; οὐ θᾶττον ἐγκονήσεις; Ar.*Av.*1324: c. acc. cogn., κέλευθον ἥνπερ ἦλθες ἐγκόνει πάλιν *hasten* back the way by which thou camest, A.*Pr.*962: c. inf., Opp.*H.*4.103, Q.S.1.157.—Rare in Prose, Luc.*Anach.*4. 2. *urge on, incite*, κυσίν *AP*6.268 (Mnasalc., s. v. l.). **-ητί**, Adv. *actively, vigorously, by perseverance*, Pi.*N.*3.36. **-ῑμα**, ατος, τό, *room for sprinkling sand* (cf. sq.), *IG*9(2).31 (Hypata, prob.). **-ίομαι**, Med., (κονίω) *sprinkle sand over oneself* after anointing, and before wrestling, X.*Smp.*3.8:—Pass., Luc.*Am.*45; *to be in the dust*, prob. l. in Hp.*Vict.*3.76. **-ίς**, ίδος, ἡ, *maid-servant*, Suid. **-ιστής**, Boeot. **-άς**, οῦ, ὁ, *sprinkler*, χρούσιος ἐ. *IG*7.2420 (votive offering to Cabiri). **-ως**, Adv. *eagerly*, Hsch.

ἐγκοπ-εύς, έως, ὁ, *tool for cutting stone, chisel*, Luc.*Somn.*3. **-ή**, ἡ, *incision*, Gal.7.38; *fracture* of skull, Sor.*Fract.*3, cf. Heliod.ap. Orib.46.12.1. 2. *steps* cut in the wall of wells, etc., Ael.Dion.*Fr.*90. II. *hindrance*, οἴησις προκοπῆς ἐ. Heraclit.131, cf. Phld.*D.*3.6, 1*Ep.Cor.*9.12, Vett.Val.2.7 (pl.); material *obstacle*, D.S.1.32; *interruption, check*, τῆς ἁρμονίας D.H.*Comp.*22; τοῦ λόγου Aristid.*Rh.*2 p.514 S., cf. Iamb.*Protr.*21; κατ' ἐγκοπάς *disjointedly*, Longin.41.3.

ἐγ-κοπιάω, *labour without ceasing*, ἔργων ἐπιμελείαις καὶ κατασκευαῖς *IPE*1^2.40.21 (Olbia). **-κοπος**, ον, *wearied*, *AP*6.33 (Maec.), Lxx *Jb.*19.2, *Is.*43.23. II. *wearisome*, ib.*Ec.*1.8. III. *interrupted, checked*, πρᾶξις *Cat.Cod.Astr.*2.161. Adv. **-πως** Phld.*Rh.*1.23 S.

ἔγκοπρος, ον, *full of manure*, Hsch.

ἐγκοπτικός, ή, όν, *checking, hindering*, Ath.Med.ap.Orib.*inc.*21.8, Vett.Val.182.12, al., Eust.1216.52.

ἐγκόπτω, *knock in*, πάτταλον Thphr.*HP*2.7.6; χιλίας (i. e. πληγὰς) ἐς τὸ νῶτον ἐγκόψαι Herod.5.33. 2. *engrave*, τὸ ψήφισμα ἐς στήλην *SIG*279.33 (Zelea):—Med., *IG*12(3).536 (Thera). 3. *incise*, Dsc.*Eup.*1.141 (Pass.). II. *oppose*, Hp.*Praec.*13; λόγον λόγῳ Olymp.*in Mete.*125.9. III. *check, hold* the breath, Sor.1.69: generally, *hinder, thwart*, τισί *Sammelb.*4305; τῇ δικαιοδοσίᾳ f.l. in Plb.23.1.12; *delay*, *Act.Ap.*24.4:—Pass., ἐνεκοπτόμην τοῦ ἐλθεῖν *Ep. Rom.*15.22, cf. Porph.*Antr.*19. IV. intr., *come to a stop*, Vett. Val.260.24.

ἐγκορδυλέω, *wrap up in coverlets*, Ar.*Nu.*10.

ἐγκορύπτω, fut. ἐγκορύψομαι, *butt at*, ἐ. ἐπί τινι πληγήν Lyc.558.

ἐγκοσμέω, *arrange in*, ἐγκοσμεῖτε τὰ τεύχε᾽.. νηΐ Od.15.218:—Pass., εἰς ἑτέραν σύγκρισιν Simp.*in Ph.*28.21 (ἐκκ- codd.). II. Pass., *to be adorned*, v.l. in Aristid.*Or.*26(14).99; εὐσχημοσύνῃ Lxx 4*Ma.*6.2 (v. l. ἐκκ-).

ἐγκόσμιος, ον, *mundane*, δυνάμεις Porph.*Antr.*9, cf. Sall.6, Procl. *Inst.*165, Dam.*Pr.*24; αἴτια Iamb.*Myst.*5.3; θεοί Procl.*in Alc.*p.68 C.; νοῦ Id.*in Prm.*p.588 S.

ἐγκοσμογενεῖς· τοὺς ἅμα τῷ κόσμῳ ἐγκριθέντας, Hsch.

ἐγκοτ-έω, *to be indignant at*, τινί A.*Ch.*41 (lyr.), S.*Fr.*1042, Lxx *Ge.*27.41. **-ημα**, ατος, τό, = sq., ib.*Je.*31(48).39, Hsch. **-ησις**, εως, ἡ, *anger at one, hatred*, Aq.*Ho.*9.7. **-ητικός**, gloss on ζάκοτος, Apollon.*Lex.* **-ος**, ον, *bearing a grudge, spiteful, malignant*, στύγος A.*Ch.*392 (lyr.); of the Erinyes, ib.924, 1054; φθόνος *AP*7.40 (Diod.). Adv. **-τως**, ἔχειν Ph.2.520. II. Subst. ἔγκοτος, ὁ, *grudge*, ἔγκοτον ἔχειν τινί Hdt.3.59, 9.110; τινός *for* a thing, Id.8.29; διά τι Id.6.73, cf. 133; also ἔγκοτον, τό, D.H.9.7.

ἐγκοτύλη [ῠ], ἡ, *a game of pick-a-back*, in which a boy was carried about kneeling *on the hollow* of another's folded hands (κοτύλαι) (cf. Poll.9.122), Ath.11.479a, Paus.Gr.*Fr.*143.

ἐγκουράς, άδος, ἡ, *painting on the ceiling*, A.*Fr.*142; also pl., = τὰ ἐν τῷ προσώπῳ στίγματα, Hsch.

ἐγκραγγάνω, = ἐμβοάω, Hsch.

ἐγκράζω, aor. ἐνέκρᾰγον: pf. -κέκρᾱγα:—*to cry aloud at* one, esp. *in anger*, τινί v.l. in Ar.*Pl.*428; ἐπί τινα v. l. in Th.8.84; φωνεῖν ὀξὺ καὶ ἐγκεκραγός Arist.*Phgn.*813^{b}5.

ἐγκραιπᾰλ-άω, *to be drunk at* or *with*, τρυφῇ Hdn.2.10.6:—also **-ίζω**, dub. in Phld.*Rh.*1.173 S.

ἐγ-κράνῑον [ᾱ], τό, *cerebellum*, Gal.*UP*8.6:—also **-κρᾱνίς**, ίδος, ἡ, ib.11.

ἔγκρᾱσις, εως, ἡ, *blending* of sounds, Nicom.*Harm.*2: metaph., *multiplication* of numbers, κατ' ἔγκρασιν, opp. κατὰ σύνθεσιν (addition), *Theol.Ar.*9, 37.

ἐγκρᾱσίχολος [ῐ], a small fish, *anchovy*, Arist.*HA*569^{b}27, Call.*Fr.*38, Ael.*NA*8.18.

ἐγκράτ-εια [ρᾰ], ἡ, *mastery over*, ἐ. ἑαυτοῦ *self-control*, Pl.*R.*390b; ἐ. ἡδονῶν καὶ ἐπιθυμιῶν *control over* them, ib.430e, cf. X.*Mem.*2.1.1, Isoc.1.21; περί τι Arist.*EN*1149^{a}21, al. II. abs., *self-control*, X.*Mem.*1.5.1, Isoc.3.44, Arist.*EN*1145^{b}8, al., Lxx *Si.*18.30, *Act.Ap.*24.25, etc. **-ευμα**, ατος, τό, *instance of self-control*, Iamb.*VP*17.72 (pl.). **-εύομαι**, *exercise self-control*, Arist.*EE*1223^{b}12, Lxx *Ge.*43.31, 1*Ep.Cor.*7.9; *force oneself* to do a thing, Lxx 1*Ki.*13.12; *starve oneself*, Vett.Val.127.20 (cf. ἀποκαρτερεῖν). II. *to be a member of the Encratite sect*, *Anatolian Studies* 87 (Phrygia). **-ευτής**, οῦ, ὁ, *ascetic*, esp. *faster*, Eust.554.8. **-έω**, *to be master of, exercise control over*, τῷ ἀλόγῳ Metop.ap.Stob.3.1.115, cf. Lxx *Ex.*9.2. **-ής**, ές, (κράτος) *in possession of power*, S.*OT*941. II. *holding fast*, χεὶρ -εστάτη a hand *with the firmest hold*, X.*Eq.*7.8. 2. *stout, strong*, ἐ. σθένει A.*Pr.*55; τὸν -έστατον σίδηρον S.*Ant.*474; ἐ. σῶμα X.*HG*7.1.23. III. c. gen. rei, *having possession of*, χωρέων Hdt.8.49, cf. 9.106, S.*Ph.*75, *SIG*58.7 (Milet., v B.C.), etc.; ναὸς ἐγκρατῆ πόδα the sheet *that controls* the ship, S.*Ant.*715; ἐ. αὑτῶν *masters of* themselves, Pl.*Phdr.*256b, al.; ἐ. ἀφροδισίων καὶ γαστρός X.*Mem.*1.2.1, cf. 2.1.7, *Oec.*12.16. 2. abs., *master of oneself, self-controlled*, Pl.*Def.*415d; *self-disciplined*, Arist.*EN*1145^{b}13, al. IV. Adv. **-τῶς**, Ion. **-τέως** Hp.*Foet.Exsect.*4, etc.; *with a strong hand, by force*, ἄρχειν Th.1.76; ἐ. ἔχειν τὴν ἀρχήν Arist.*Pol.*1284^{a}40; -τέως *forcibly*, Theoc.25.266. 2. *with self-control, temperately*, ἐ. ἔχειν Pl.*Lg.*710a; φέρειν τι D.Chr.2.53; -τέως Archestr.*Fr.*23.20. **-ησις**, εως, ἡ, *holding in* the breath, D.L.6.77. **-ίτης**, ου, ὁ, *member of the Encratite sect*, *Cod.Theod.*16.5.9. **-ούντως**, Adv. = ἐγκρατῶς, Phld.*Rh.*2.62 S.

ἐγκραυγάζω, *shout at* a person, Phld.*Lib.*p.5 O. (Pass.).

ἐγκρέκων σφυγμός, term coined by Archig.ap.Gal.8.662.

ἐγκρεμάννῠμαι, Pass., *to be hung up in*, *Gp.*2.4.2, al.

ἐγκρέμᾰσις, εως, ἡ, *suspension*, Hp.*Art.*76 (v. l. ἐκκρ-).

ἐγκρί· κοίλῳ καὶ κενῷ, Hsch.

ἐγκρῑδοπώλης, ου, ὁ, *dealer in* ἐγκρίδες, Ar.*Fr.*256, Nicopho 19.

ἐγκρῑκάδεια, = ἐγκοτύλη, Hsch., Theognost.*Can.*164.27.

ἐγκρίκια· ξύλα κεκαμμένα, Hsch.

ἐγκρῑκόω, *enclose as in a ring, bind as in a hoop*, Hp.*Oss.*18.

ἐγκρίμνᾰμαι, *to be suspended*, Hp.*Art.*76 (v.l. ἐκκρ-).

ἐγκρίνω [ῑ], *reckon in* or *among*: *reckon as*, τίν' ἄνδρ' ἄριστον ἐγκρίνειεν ἄν; E.*HF*183. 2. of persons, *select, admit*, ἐ. συγκρ. 2*Ep.Cor.*10.12:—Pass., εἰς τὴν αἵρεσιν Pl.*Lg.*755d; εἰς τὴν γερουσίαν D.20.107; ⟨εἰς⟩ τὸ στάδιον X.*HG*4.1.40; of ἔφηβοι, *IG*7.29 (iii/ii B.C.); of athletes, Artem.1.59; ἐγκρινόμενος, ὁ, subject of statue by Alcamenes, Plin.*HN*34.72. 3. *admit, accept*, opp. ἀποκρίνω, Pl.*Lg.*936a; ἐν τοῖς φιλοσόφοις Id.*R.*486d, cf. *Lg.*952a, al.; τρία γένη σημείων Phld.*Sign.*32; παλιγγενεσίαν Sch.Pi.*O.*2.104; *regard as genuine*, νομίσματα Phld.*Rh.*1.256 S.; *admit, sanction*, e. g. an author as classical, Suid. s. v. Δείναρχος. 4. *approve*, Plb.9.2.4 (Pass.), Plu.2.11f; ἀριθμὸς ἐγκρίνεται *is adopted*, Ael.*Tact.*8.3.

ἐγκρίς, ίδος, ἡ, *a cake made with oil and honey*, Stesich.2, Pherecr.83, Antiph.275, Lxx *Ex.*16.31, Ph.1.214; also expld. as, = ἀμανίτης, Hsch.

ἔγ-κρῐσις, εως, ἡ, (ἐγκρίνω) *approval, judgement*, *IG*9(2).338.17 (Epist. Flaminini). 2. *examination* of athletes before admitting them to a contest, Luc.*Pr.Im.*11, Artem.1.59, Aristid.*Or.*29(40).18 (pl.). II. *junction, meeting*, ἡ ἐπὶ τοὺς μηροὺς ἔ. Alciphr.1.

39. **-κρῐτέον**, *one must admit*, εἰς ἀριθμόν τινα, opp. ἀποκρ-, Pl.*R.*537a, cf. 413d; διορισμὸν ἐ. ὡς πιθανώτατον Dam.*Pr.*436, cf. Jul.*Or.*7.219a; *one must approve, recommend,* αἰώρας Herod.Med. in *Rh.Mus.*58.86: also pl. ἐγκριτέα ib.112. **-κρῐτήριος**, α, ον, *of* or *for admission*: ἐ. οἶκοι rooms *where* the athletes *were examined before they were admitted* as candidates, *IG*4.203.12 (Corinth, ii A.D.). **-κρῐτος**, ον, *admitted, accepted,* Pl.*Lg.*966d, *IG*12(9).189.9 (Eretria, iv B.C.); ἔ. θεά Herod.Med. in *Rh.Mus.*58.106.

ἐγκροαίνω, *spread oneself in*, διηγήσεσιν Eust.1050.31.

ἐγκροστόω, = Lat. *incrustare, veneer* with marble, *Supp.Epigr.*2.698 (Attalia).

ἐγκρότᾰφος· ὁ ἀντικέφαλος, *Et.Gud.*

ἐγκροτέω, *strike on* the ground, ἐς ἓν μέλος ἐγκροτέοισαι ποσσίν *beating time* with the feet to one tune, Theoc.18.7:—Med., πυγμαὶ δ' ἦσαν ἐγκροτούμεναι the fists were *dashing one against the other*, E.*IT* 1368. II. Pass., *to be fastened by nails*, τοίχῳ Philostr.*VA*2.20.

ἐγκρούω, *knock* or *hammer in*, παττάλους εἰς τὸν τοῖχον Ar.*V.*130; ἥλους εἰς τὰ ὑποδήματα Thphr.*Char.*4.13; *strike*, ἐγκρούουσα ποσσὶ λάλους πτέρυγας, of the locust, *AP*7.195.4 (Mel.). II. *dance*, Ar.*Ra.*374.

ἐγ-κρύβω [ῠ], late form of ἐγκρύπτω, D.S.1.80 (Pass.), Apollod.3.13.6, Gal.6.620, *PHolm.*5.7. **-κρυμμα**, ατος, τό, *anything concealed, an ambuscade*, Eust.932.17. **-κρυπτέον**, *one must bury, cover up*, Herod.Med.ap.Orib.10.8.10. **-κρυπτος**, = ἐγκρυφίας, Hsch. **-κρύπτω**, *hide* or *conceal in*, δαλὸν σποδιῇ ἐνέκρυψε μελαίνῃ Od.5.488, cf. Sotad.Com.1.29; [ᾠὰ] ἐν δέρματι λαγωοῦ Arist.*HA* 619b15; τι εἴς τι *Ev.Matt.*13.33, Apollod.1.5.1 (Pass.), etc. 2. πῦρ ἐ. *bank* it *up*, Ar.*Av.*841. 3. Med., *hide oneself*, μελάθροις Nonn.*D.*32.285. **-κρῠφιάζω**, intr., *keep oneself hidden, act underhand*, Ar.*Eq.*822. 2. *hide, conceal*, πάθος Procop.*Arc.*1: abs., Id.*Vand.*1.25. **-κρῠφίας** ἄρτος loaf *baked in the ashes*, Hp.*Vict.*2.42, Nicostr.Com.14, Luc.*DMort.*20.4, Ath.3.110b. **-κρύφιος**, ον, = sq., πῦρ *AP*5.123 (Phld.). **-κρῠφος**, ον, *hidden*, ἥβη Nonn.*D.*28.295. **-κρύφω** [ῠ], = ἐγκρύπτω, impf. ἐνέκρῠφεν Q.S.14.556, Nonn.*D.*6.135. **-κρυψις**, εως, ἡ, *banking up* of a fire, Arist.*Juv.* 470a12.

ἐγκτάομαι, *acquire possessions in* a foreign country, πόλιν ἐν Θρηΐκῃ (v.l. for ἐγκτισ-) Hdt.5.23; οἱ ἐγκεκτημένοι citizens *who possess property in* a deme not their own, opp. δημόται, D.50.8, cf. X.*Vect.*2.4, *PGnom.*243.

ἐγκτερεΐζω, *bury in*, τύμβῳ A.R.1.1060, cf. Tryph.179.

ἔγ-κτημα, ατος, τό, *land held in a country* by a person not belonging to it, And.3.15, D.7.42, *IG*2^2.43.27, App.*Mith.*47. **-κτησις**, Dor. **-κτᾶσις**, εως, ἡ, *tenure of land in a country* or *district* by a person not belonging to it, X.*HG*5.2.19 (pl.); *the right of holding such property*, freq. granted as a privilege or reward to foreigners, ἔγκτασιν γᾶς καὶ οἰκιᾶν Decr.Byz.ap.D.18.91, cf. *IG*5(1).4.12 (Sparta), etc.; εἶναι δὲ αὐτῷ οἰκίας ἔγκτησιν ib.2^2.53. 2. *estate, property*, Lxx *Le.*25.13, etc.; βιβλιοθήκη ἐγκτήσεων register *of properties*, *BGU*76 (ii A.D.), etc. 3. *acquisition of territory*, Plb.28.20.8 (prob. l.). **-κτητικόν**, τό, *a land-tax paid for the right of holding* ἐγκτήματα, *IG*2^2.1214. **-κτητος**, η, ον, *possessed in* a foreign country, Lxx *Le.*14.34, al. **-κτήτωρ**, ορος, ὁ, *landowner*, Keil-Premerstein *Dritter Bericht* 86.

ἐγκτίζω, *found, build among*, πόλεις ἔθνεσιν Plu.2.328e:—Med., πόλιν ἐν Θρηΐκῃ v.l. in Hdt.5.23 (cf. ἐγκτάομαι).

ἔγκῠαρ, ᾶρος, ἡ, *pregnant*, ὄϊς *Schwyzer* 725.6 (Milet., vi B.C.).

ἐγκῠβιστάω, *plunge headlong into*, πράγμασιν Suid. s.v. κύβος.

ἔγκῠδον· ἔνδοξον, Hsch.

ἐγκῠ-έομαι, *to be borne in the womb*, Theon *Prog.*2. **-ησις**, εως, ἡ, *germination*, in plants, Thphr.*CP*1.6.3. **-ητήριον**, τό, *drug which promotes conception*, Hp.*Steril.*231.

ἐγκῠκάω, *mix up in*, Ar.*Ach.*939 (Med.):—Act., Dsc.*Ther.*2, Lyc.674.

ἐγκυκλ-έομαι, Pass., *roll* or *rotate in* the sockets, of the joints, Hp.*de Arte* 10. II. in com. sense, *to be cooped up*, οὐκ οἶδ' ὅπῃ ἐγκεκύκλησαι Ar.*V.*699. III. Med., *surround*, Plu.*TG*5; τοὺς ἀμφὶ πλουσίαν τράπεζαν -κυκλουμένους Id.2.50d. **-ηθρον**, τό, Eust.976.15, is prob. f.l. for ἐκκύκληθρον, = ἐκκύκλημα. **-ημα**, ατος, τό (v. ἐκκύκλημα); but, II. ἐγκυκλήματα, τά, *movable property*, Arist.*Oec.*1346a13. **-ίζω**, *revolve*, τὰ ὀπίσθια *Hippiatr.*30. **-ιος**, ον, also α, ον Orph.*A.*981: (κύκλος):—*circular, round*, χοροί E.*IT*429 (lyr.), Aeschin.1.10; τὸ ἐ. σῶμα Arist.*Cael.*286a11; ἐ. κίνησις, φορά, motion *in a circle*, ib.293a11, 296a35; δρόμημα θεῶν *Corp.Herm.*3.3. Adv. -ίως *in a circle*, φέρεσθαι Arist.*Mete.*339a12, cf. Euc.*Phaen.*p.2 M., Hero *Aut.*11.8, Plu.2.1004c; καθῆσθαι Asp.*in EN*10.31. II. *revolving in a cycle, recurrent*: hence, at Athens, λητουργίαι ἐ. public services *required regularly* every year, opp. to those required at uncertain times, D.20.21; ἐ. δίκαια rights *common to all citizens*, Id.25.74. III. *ordinary, everyday*, ἐν τοῖς ἐ. καὶ τοῖς καθ' ἡμέραν γιγνομένοις Isoc.3.22, cf. 8.87, Arist.*Pol.*1269b35; ἐ. διακονίαι *everyday* duties, ib.1263a21; τὰ ἐ. καὶ πολιτικά Epicur.*Sent.Vat.*58; ἡ ἐ. διοίκησις *IG*12(5).653.56 (Syros, i B.C.); ἐ. ἀναλώματα ib.1.329; ἐ. [τέλη] taxes *farmed out annually*, ib.11(2).161 *A* 36, 203 *A* 29 (Delos, iii B.C.); ταμίαι τῶν ἐ. *SIG*577.11 (Milet., iii/ii B.C.). b. μεγάλοις ἐ. συμπτώμασιν (sc. πάθος) *commonly liable to*, Phld.*Ir.*p.29 W. 2. Arist., τὰ ἐ. φιλοσοφήματα or τὰ ἐ., = τὰ ἐξωτερικά, *Cael.*279a30; ἐν τοῖς ἐ. εἴρηται *EN*1096a3. 3. ἐ. παιδεία *general* education, prior to professional studies, D.H.*Comp.*25, Plu.2.1135d; οἱ περὶ τὰ ἐ. παιδευταί Id.*Alex.*7; τὰ ἐ. παιδεύματα Id.2.7c, cf. Vitr.6 *Praef.*4, Quint.*Inst.*1.10.1, Ath.4.184b, Luc.*Am.*45; also ἐ. ἀγωγή instruction *in general knowledge*, Str.1.1.22; ἐ. τέχνη Olymp.Alch.p.91 B. IV. ἐγκύκλιον, τό, *tax on sales*, *PLond.*3.1200 (ii B.C.), *PAmh.*2.53 (ii B.C.), etc.

ἐγκυκλοπαιδεία, f.l. for ἐγκύκλιος παιδεία, Quint.*Inst.*1.10.1, cf. Plin.*HN Praef.*

ἔγκυκλ-ος, ον, *circular*, δίνη Epicur.*Ep.*2 p.52 U.; *round*, Matro *Conv.*116, Ezek.*Exag.*77. Adv. -ως Gal.18(2).439. II. ἔγκυκλον, τό, *woman's upper garment*, Ar.*Th.*261, *Lys.*113; ἐ. ποικίλον *IG*2.754.48. III. ἔγκυκλα· τὰ ἐγκυκλούμενα τῷ βίῳ καὶ συνήθη, Hsch. **-όω**, *move round in a circle*, ὀφθαλμόν E.*IT*76. II. *surround*, Str.2.5.24:—more freq. in Med. with pf. part. Pass., *encompass, encircle*, τοῦ χθόν' ἐγκυκλουμένου αἰθέρος E.*Ba.*292, cf. Ar.*V.*699; φωνή μέ τις ἐγκεκύκλωται a voice *has echoed around* me, ib.395; *surround, hem in*, Plu.*Marc.*6, etc.; of rivers or mountains, Str.2.1.36, D.C.49.37:—Pass., *to be surrounded*, Id.56.12 (s.v.l.). 2. in late Prose, *wander, roam about*, ἐγκυκλωθῆναι Σικελίαν D.S.4.23, etc. **-ωσις**, εως, ἡ, *surrounding, encompassing*, Str.2.1.36.

ἐγκῠλίδωτος (leg. ἐγκυλίωτος), ον, *rolled up*, ἔριον Hp.*Mul.*1.75.

ἐγκῠλίνδ-ησις, εως, ἡ, *rolling among*, ἐν πόρναις Plu.*Oth.*2. **-ω** (ἐγκυλίω Hp.*Mul.*1.75, Arist.*Pr.*914a22, Vett.Val.118.15, etc.), fut. -κυλίσω [ῑ]:—*roll* or *wrap up in*, πολλοῖς ἐμαυτὸν ἐγκυλῖσαι πράγμασιν Pherecr.146.2; τι ἐς ἔριον Hp. l.c. II. metaph. in Pass., *to be involved in*, εἰς ἔρωτας ἐγκυλισθείς X.*Mem.*1.2.22, cf. Vett.Val. l.c.; εἰς τὰς πολιτικὰς πράξεις D.H.11.36; ἐν κακοῖς Porph.*Chr.*26; πράγμασι *Cat.Cod.Astr.*7.208:—in aor. Med., ἐγκυλίσασθαι Luc.*Hipp.*6.

ἐγκύλ-ισμα [ῠ], ατος, τό, = ἁλινδήθρα, Sch.Ar.*Nu.*32. **-ισμός**, ὁ, = ἐγκυλίνδησις, in mal. part., Vett.Val.118.17 (pl.).

ἐγκύμᾰτος [ῡ], ον, *on the waves*, ὁδοιπορία Secund.*Sent.*17.

ἐγκῠμ-ονέω, *become pregnant*, *Gp.*14.26.2; τὸν Δία *conceive*, Apollod.1.1.5. **-ων**, ον, gen. ονος, (κῦμα B) *pregnant*, X.*Cyn.*7.2, Arist.*HA*546b10, etc.; ἐ. γενέσθαι ὑπό τινος Id.*Fr.*76; ἵππος ἐ. τευχέων *big with* arms, of the Trojan horse, E.*Tr.*11; ἐ. ἄμυλος Pl.Com.174.8; πόα ἐ. σπέρματος Dsc.3.7: metaph., of the mind, Pl.*Smp.*209b, Ph.1.651, etc.; καμάτων ἐγκύμονα βίβλον *AP*9.210.

ἐγκῠοποιέω, *impregnate*: metaph. of a chemical reaction, Zos. Alch.p.211 B.

ἔγκῠος, ον, (κύω) = ἐγκύμων, Hdt.1.5, 6.131, Hp.*Aph.*5.42, etc.; πῶλος ἡσυχίης ἔγκυος, of the Trojan horse, *AP*9.156 (Antiphil.); γαστρὸς ἀπωσαμέναν μόρον ἔγκυον, of one dying in child-birth, *Epigr.Gr.*238 (Smyrna), cf. *IG*12(7).301 (Amorgos). 2. of plants, Arist.*HA*595b27.

ἐγκύπτω, *stoop down and peep in*, ἐ. εἴς τι *look closely* into, Hdt.7.152; κατὰ [τὰς θυρίδας] Pl.*R.*359d: abs., ἐγκεκυφότες *stooping to the ground*, Ar.*Nu.*191, Th.4.4; δάκτυλοι ἐγκύπτοντες *retracted*, Hp.*Hebd.*51.

ἐγκῠρ-έω, v. ἐγκύρω. **-ησις**, εως, ἡ, *meeting with* or *happening*, Phld.*Rh.*1.71 S., S.E.*P.*1.37. 2. in Medicine, *definite phenomenon*, *BKT*3 p.30.

ἐγκυρσεύω, = ἐγκυρέω, Heraclit.17 (s.v.l.).

ἐγκύρτ-ια, τά, (κύρτος) *passages into the* κύρτος or *creel* or *fish-trap*, to which Pl. compares the throat, *Ti.*78b–d, cf. Gal. ad loc.p.20 D. **-ος**, ον, *curved* or *crooked*, Hp.*Mochl.*1, Arist.*Pr.*908b29. **-ωσις**, εως, ἡ, *curvature*, Cass.*Pr.*38.

ἐγκύρω [ῡ], impf. ἐνέκῡρον: fut. ἐγκύρσω: aor. ἐνέκυρσα:—**Pass.**, ἐγκύρομαι: **ἐγκῠρέω**, aor. 1 ἐνεκύρησα, less freq. in early writers, Heraclit.72, freq. in Phld. as *Sign.*21, al., cf. Plb. and D.H. (v. infr.), Ael.*Tact.*1.2:—*fall in with, light upon, meet with*, c. dat., ἐνέκυρσε φάλαγξι Il.13.145; ἐγκύρσας ἀάτῃσιν Hes.*Op.*216; ὁκοίοις ἐγκυρέωσιν ἔργμασι Archil.70; ἐγκύρσαις (Aeol. aor. 1 part.) ἑκατονταετεῖ βιοτᾷ Pi.*P.*4.282, cf. 1.100; δύᾳ B.*Fr.*21; τμητοῖς ὁλκοῖς ἐγκῦρσαι S.*El.*863 (lyr.); στρατῷ ἐνέκυρσε ἀμφοτέρῃσι τῇσι μοίρῃσι Hdt.4.125; ἐνεκύρησαν στρατῷ Id.7.218, cf. Plb.8.35.5, etc.; δυσχωρίαις ἐγκυρήσαντες D.H.3.59; τυράννοις Phld.*Ir.*p.30 W.: in Hdt.7.208, c. gen., ἀλογίης ἐνέκυρσε πολλῆς (here Valck. proposed ἐκύρησε, which has been received by edd.): c. acc., Ἅιδαν ἐγκύρσαντες ἀλάμπετον *Epigr.Gr.*241 (Smyrna).—Not in Att. Prose, once in Com., ἐγκυρῆσαι Cratin.35.

ἐγκῡσίκωλος [ῐ] or **ἐγκῡσόχωλος**, = ἄνωθεν ἀπὸ τοῦ κυσοῦ χωλός, *Com.Adesp.*6 D.

ἔγκῡτα, τά, Lacon., = ἔγκατα, Hsch.

ἐγκῡτί, Adv., (κύτος) *to the skin*, ἐγκυτὶ κεκαρμένος *close* shaven, Archil.37, cf. Call.*Fr.*311. [ῑ Archil., ῐ Call.]

ἐγκύφωσις [ῠ], εως, ἡ, *curvature*, Gal.8.246.

ἐγκώλεος, *trunculus*, *Gloss.*

ἐγκωλύω, aor. ἐνεκώλυσα, f.l. for ἐνεκόλλησα, Hero *Aut.*24.2.

ἐγκωμάζω, *take part in a* κῶμος, *revel*, *Gloss.*

ἐγκωμι-άζω, impf. ἐνεκωμίαζον Aeschin.3.86: fut. -άσω Pl.*Grg.*518e, 519a, Isoc.12.111, but -άσομαι Pl.*Smp.*198d, Aeschin.1.33: aor. ἐνεκωμίασα Pl.*La.*191b: pf. ἐγκεκωμίακα Id.*Lg.*629c, Isoc.7.71:—**Pass.**, aor. ἐγκωμιασθείς Hdt.5.5: pf. ἐγκεκωμίασμαι Pl.*Smp.*177c (the tenses being formed as if the Verb were a compound of ἐν and *κωμιάζω, and not derived directly from ἐγκώμιος):—*praise, laud, extol*, c. dupl. acc., ταῦτα τὴν δικαιοσύνην Id.*R.*363d; τινὰ ἐπὶ σοφίᾳ Id.*Euthphr.*9b; κατὰ τοῦτο Id.*La.*191b; περὶ τὴν μάχην Id.*Tht.*142b; τὴν τέχνην τινός Id.*Grg.*448e: abs., Phld.*Herc.*1457.8:—Pass., *to be praised*, Hdt.5.5, Pl.*Smp.*181a; *to be said in panegyric*, Phld.*Herc.*

1457 *Fr.*14, etc. **-αστέον,** *one must eulogize*, Id.*Rh.*1.219S., S.E. *M.*2.101; θεούς Hermog.*Prog.*7. **-αστής,** οῦ, ὁ, *praiser, panegyrist*, Str.15.1.68, Plu.2.605a. **-αστικός,** ή, όν, *panegyrical*, Arist.*Rh.Al.*1421^{b}9, Plb.8.11.2, Ph.2.31; -ικόν, τό, Plu.2.743d, Longin.8.3, Demetr.*Eloc.*120. Adv. -κῶς Poll.4.26. **-αστός,** ή, όν, *to be praised*, Ph.1.453.

ἐγκωμικός, ή, όν, = ἐγκωμιαστικός, λόγοι *IG*12(9).95^a (Tamynae).

ἐγκωμιο-γράφος [ᾰ], ὁ, *panegyric-writer*, Artem.1.56 (pl.); εἰς τὸν αὐτοκράτορα *IG*7.1773.11 (Thebes). **-λογικόν** (sc. μέτρον), τό, *metre used in* ἐγκώμια, Heph.15.10. **-λόγος,** ὁ, *one who delivers panegyrics*, *IG*12(9).94 (Tamynae, i B.C.).

ἐγκώμιον, τό, v. sq. II. 2.

ἐγκώμιος, ον, (κώμη) *in the village*: hence, *native, common*, v.l. for ἐγχώριος, Hes.*Op.*344. II. (κῶμος) *belonging to a* κῶμος, esp. that which escorted a victor in the games: hence, *belonging to the praise of a conqueror*, ἐ. μέλη, ὕμνοι, Pi.*O.*2.47, *P.*10.53; ἐ. ἀμφὶ τρόπον Id. *O.*10(11).77; στεφάνων ἐγκώμιος τεθμός the law *of praise* for prizes won, ib.13.29. 2. Subst. ἐγκώμιον, τό, *laudatory ode*, D.S.11.11, Ath.13.573f; generally, *eulogy, panegyric*, Ar.*Nu.*1205, D.18.207 (pl.), Thphr.*Char.*3.2, etc.; ἐγκώμια παλαιῶν ἀνδρῶν Pl.*Prt.*326a; ἐ. εἴς τινα, κατά τινος, Pl.*Min.*319c, D.6.9; ἐ. λογικόν in prose, *IG*7.2727 (Acraephia); ἐ. ἐπικόν ib.419 (Oropus); ὁ ἔπαινος τῆς ἀρετῆς, opp. τὰ ἐ. τῶν ἔργων, Arist.*EN*1101^{b}33, cf. *Rh.*1367^{b}28.

ἔγκων, coined as etym. of ἀγκών, Chrysipp.*Stoic.*2.47.

ἐγκώπαια· περιδέραια, Suid.

ἔγκωπον, τό, *part* of the ship *between the foremost and hindmost oars*, Callix.1.

ἔγμα· ὀχύρωμα, στῦλος, Hsch. **ἔγμεν·** ἔχειν, Id. **ἐγνωδώς·** σὺν θεῷ, Id.

ἐγξέω, *scratch, scrape*, E.*Fr.*298 (cj. Heath for ἐγξύσαι).

ἐγξηραίνω, *dry in*, Hp.*Mul.*1.104.

ἔγξῠλος, ον, *wooden*, δέλτος f.l. in Aen.Tact.31.14; πυραί Tz.*H.* 10.502.

ἐγξύρω [ῡ], *shave*, κεφαλήν Tz.*H.*3.512.

ἐγξύω [ῡ], = ἐγξέω, Hp.*Int.*42; *shred in*, ἐς μέλι Thphr.*HP*9.13.3.

ἐγρε-κύδοιμος [ῠ], ον, *rousing the din of war, strife-stirring*, epith. of Pallas, Hes.*Th.*925, Lamprocl.1. **-μάχης** [ᾰ], ου, ὁ, *exciting, rousing the fight*, S.*OC*1054 (lyr.): fem. ἐγρεμάχη, epith. of Pallas, *h.Cer.*424, *IG*1^2.573. **-μοθος,** ον, *stirring strife*, Nonn.*D.*20. 291, al.

ἔγρεο, ἔγρετο, v. ἐγείρω and ἔγρω.

ἐγρεσί-κωμος [ῐ], ον, *stirring up to revelry*, epith. of Dionysus, *AP* 9.524.6. **-οικος,** ον, *building houses*, prob. in Man.4.325.

ἐγρήγορα, ἐγρήγορθε, -θαι, -θασι, v. ἐγείρω.

ἐγρηγορ-έω, f.l. in X.*Cyn.*5.11, Arist.*Pr.*877^{a}9, etc. **-ικός,** ή, όν, *waking*, πράξεις, κινήσεις, Arist.*Somn.Vig.*456^{a}28, *Div.Somn.*463^a 9. **-ος,** ον, *wakeful*, Adam.*Phgn.*2.28, Poll.3.120. Adv. -ρως Mich.*in PN*70.2, al., Sch.Il.10.182. **-ότως,** Adv. part. of ἐγρήγορα, *waking*, Plu.2.32a, Luc.*Herm.*1 (v.l.), Porph.*Plot.*9. **-όων,** Ep. part., *watching, awake*, Od.20.6. **-σιος,** ον, *keeping awake*, Pherecr.208. **-σις,** εως, ἡ, *waking, wakefulness*, Hp.*Hum.*9, Arist.*HA*536^{b}24, Ph.1.71, al., Onos.10.11, D.Chr.3.85, Plot.6.8.16; περὶ ὕπνου καὶ ἐγρηγόρσεως, title of work by Arist. **-τέον,** *one must keep awake*, Antyll.ap.Orib.6.6.3. **-τί** [ῑ], Adv. *awake, watching*, Il.10.182.

ἔγρηνται· ᾕρηνται, Hsch. **ἐγρήσασα·** μαθοῦσα, Id.

ἐγρήσσω, (ἐγείρω) *watch, awake*, Il.11.551, Od.20.33,53, A.R.2. 308, Aret.*CA*1.1, etc.

ἐγρῆτα· παρακαταβολὴν ἢ δίκης ἢ κρίσεως, Hsch. **ἐγρυπνεῖ·** ἀγρυπνεῖ, Id. **ἔγρυσις,** v. ἔκρ-.

ἔγρω, later form of ἐγείρω, imper. ἐγρέτω cj. in Sopat.10; ἔγρει Call.*Hec.*1.4.13:—Pass., ἔγρεσθε E.*Rh.*532; ἔγρεται Opp.*H.*5.241: ἔγρονται E.*Fr.*773.29 (lyr.); ἔγρετο Opp.*C.*3.421.

ἐγχαδές (prob. ἐγχαλές, cf. χάλις)· νέον ἄκρατον, Hsch.

***ἐγχαίνω,** v. ἐγχάσκω.

ἐγχᾰλάω, *relax*, in Pass., Plu.2.690a, Antyll.ap.Orib.44.8.4.

ἐγχαλεῖν· καταχασμᾶσθαι (Lacon.), Hsch. **ἐγχαλίδες·** διαπεπαρμένοι ἧλοι, Id.

ἐγχᾰλῑνόω, *put a bit in the mouth of*, ἵππον Babr.76.14:—Pass., τὰ στόματα ἐγκεχαλινωμένους *having the bit in* their mouths, Hdt.3.14, cf. X.*An.*7.2.21. 2. metaph., Ph.1.117:—Pass., τὸν δῆμον ἐγκεχαλινωμένον τῇ ὀλιγαρχίᾳ *held in check* by the oligarchy, Plu.*Lys.*21; ὀργῇ -ωμένῃ τῷ λόγῳ Them.*Or.*17.214d. 3. metaph. of reins, *to be in the form of a bit*, Hp.*Oss.*19.

ἐγχαλκ-εύω, *to impress* or *design on brass*, Sch.B.Il.18.468. **-ος,** ον, *in* or *with brass*: *moneyed, rich*, *AP*11.425. II. *for sale*, Ath. 13.584e. III. *with a flavour of copper*, Dsc.5.103.

ἐγχανδής, v. εὐχανδής.

ἐγχᾰρ-ακτέον, *one must scarify*, Paul.Aeg.3.27. **-αξις,** εως, ἡ, *scarification*, Apollon.ap.Orib.7.19 tit., Aret.*CD*1.2. II. *furrow*, gloss on ὁλκός, Sch.A.R.3.413. **-άσσω,** Att. -ττω, *engrave*, τινί *upon* a thing, D.H.2.55; ἐς στάλλαν *IG*12(2).67 (Mytilene); εἰς τὸ ἱερόν *GDI*2322.16 (Delph.), cf. Plu.*Per.*21, etc.; κατά τινος Id.*Them.*9; *insert* in a document, *CPR*19.18 (iv A.D.): metaph., *imitate*, ἐ. τὸν Ἀντισθένειον τύπον Jul.*Or.*7.217a:—Pass., τὰ ἐγκεχαραγμένα ἀγαθά *OGI*666.17 (i A.D.); μεγάλως ἐγκεχαραγμένος *with a great record*, Charito 2.6; of coins, Luc.*Alex.*58; δραχμαὶ ἐγκεχαραγμέναι γράμμασιν Ἑλληνικοῖς ἐπίσημα *Peripl.M.Rubr.*47; of soldiers, *to be entered on a muster-roll*, Agath.5.15. II. *to make an incision into* a thing, *Gp.*5.38.2; *scarify*, Antyll.ap.Orib.7. 16.3.

ἐγχᾰρίζομαι, = χαρίζομαι, *AP*9.114 (Parmen., dub.).

ἐγχάσκω, fut. ἐγχανοῦμαι: aor. ἐγχανεῖν:—lit., *gape*, πρὸς τὴν σελήνην Luc.*Icar.*13; ἐ. τῷ πλακοῦντι *to gape for* it, Alciphr.1.22. II. *grin* or *scoff at* one, ἐγχάσκειν σοι Ar.*V.*721; προσέχειν διαλεγομένῳ καὶ ἐ. Phld.*Vit.*p.41 J., cf. Luc.*Merc.Cond.*14; τῇ 'μῇ μωρίᾳ S.*Ichn.* 343; ἐγχανεῖται ταῖς ἐμαῖς τύχαισι Ar.*Ach.*1197; ἐγχανεῖται τῇ πόλει Id.*Eq.*1313: c. part., μὴ γὰρ ἐγχάνῃ ποτὲ... ἐκφυγών *let* him not *taunt* [us] *with* his having escaped, Id.*Ach.*221.

ἐγχέζω, fut. -χέσω or -χεσοῦμαι: pf. ἐγκέχοδα, = Lat. *incacare*, Ar.*Ra.*479: c. acc., *to be in a horrid fright at* one, Id.*V.*627.

ἐγχει-βρόμος, ον, *thundering with the spear*, κόρα Pi.*O.*7.43. **-γάστωρ·** ὁ διὰ τοῦ δόρατος ζῶν, Zonar.

ἐγχεῖδαι· τηρηταὶ δανείων, Hsch.

ἐγχείη, ἡ, Ep. form of ἔγχος, *spear, lance*, Hom., esp. in Il.: gen. pl., ἐγχειάων 5.167; ἐγχείῃ ἐκέκαστο he excelled all *in the spear*, 2. 530.

ἐγχείῃ, Ep. 3 sg. pres. subj. of ἐγχέω, Od.9.10.

ἐγχεικέραυνος, ον, *hurling the thunderbolt*, Ζῆνα Pi.*P.*4.194, *O.*13. 77, Eust.839.10, etc.

ἐγχειμάζω, *pass the winter in*, Jul.*Ep.*185, Poll.1.62; πόλις ἐγχειμάσαι οἵα χειρίστη Dicaearch.1.21.

ἐγχεί-μαργος, ον, = ἐγχεσίμαργος, *EM*313.14. **-μορος,** ον, *dealing death with the spear*, ib.630.24.

ἐγχειρ-έω, Arc. ἰγχηρέω *IG*5(2).6.12 (Tegea, iv B.C.): (χείρ):—*take* a thing *in hand, undertake, attempt*, c. dat. rei, E.*Med.*377, X.*Vect.* 6.1, etc.: later, c. acc. rei, ἔργον *PPetr.*2 p.37 (iii B.C.): c. inf., Pl. *Prt.*310c, X.*Mem.*2.3.12, etc.; τὸν ἐγχειρήσαντα συκοφαντεῖν Hyp. *Eux.*34: abs., *to make an attempt* or *beginning*, S.*El.*1026, Th.4.4, etc. 2. *lay hands on, attack*, πόλεσι ib.122: abs., X.*HG*4.5.16; πρὸς τὰ κατὰ τοὺς πολεμίους Plb.2.22.11. 3. *put hand to* a case requiring medical treatment, τινί Hp.*de Arte* 3; τῇσι νούσοισιν ib. 13. 4. *try one's hand* in argument, εἰς ἑκάτερον Plu.*Cic.*21:—Pass., *to be discussed*, Id.2.687e codd. II. in late Poets, *take in hand*, c. acc., ἔργον *Epigr.Gr.*1038.36.—ἐπιχειρέω is more common in Att. **-ημα,** ατος, τό, *undertaking, attempt*, S.*OT*540, Pl. *Plt.*290d, Antiph.29, D.27.34, Aen.Tact.24.15, Plu.*Cleom.*25, etc.; *essay in argument*, Epicur.*Dial.*1413.7 (pl.). **-ησις,** εως, ἡ, *taking in hand, undertaking*, Th.6.83, Plu.*Caes.*66, etc. II. ἀνατομικαὶ ἐ., *Practical* Anatomy, title of work by Gal. **-ητέον,** *one must undertake*, X.*Ages.*1.1, Pl.*Plt.*304a, D.Chr.18.5: pl., -ητέα τῷ ἔργῳ Agath. *Praef.*p.133 D. **-ητής,** οῦ, ὁ, *one who undertakes*, καινῶν ἔργων Ar. *Av.*257; πράξεως Ph.2.27: abs., Adam.*Phgn.*2.39. **-ητικός,** ή, όν, *enterprising, adventurous*, X.*HG*4.8.22. Adv. -κῶς Archyt.ap.Stob.4. 50.2. **-ία,** ἡ, *manipulation*, v.l. for εὐχ-, Hp.*Art.*35, cf. Phld.*Hom.* p.45 O.: pl., Hsch. **-ίδιος,** ον, (χείρ) *in the hand*, ἱκετῶν κλάδοι A.*Supp.*21 (anap.). II. as Subst., -ίδιον, τό, *hand-knife, dagger*, Hdt.1.12,214, Th.3.70, etc.; ἐγχειριδίῳ πλήττειν Lys.4.6, etc. 2. *handle*, Thphr.*HP*4.3.4, Callix.1. 3. *manual, handbook*, title of works by Epict. and others, cf. Demetr.Lac.*Herc.*1013.12 F., Philostr. *VS*2.1.14, Longin.*Proll.Heph.*p.86 C. 4. *tool, implement*, Lxx *Ex.*20.25. [-ῑδιον Hermipp.46.] **-ίζω,** Att. fut. -ιῶ X.*Oec.*8. 10: pf. ἐγκεχείρικα Plu.*Phoc.*34:—*put into one's hands, entrust*, τί τινι or τινά τινι, Hdt.5.92.γʹ, Th.2.67, etc.; τὰς ἀρχὰς ἐ. τινί Hdt.5. 72, cf. Arist.*Pol.*1305^{a}16, prob. in Thphr.*Char.*30.15; ἐ. τινὶ τὴν φυλακήν Arist.*Pol.*1306^{a}22; ἐ. ἐμαυτὸν τῇ ἀτυχίᾳ Antipho 2.4.1, etc.:—Pass., *to be entrusted*, τινί to one, Plb.5.44.1; τὴν ἐγχειρισθεῖσαν ἑαυτῷ πίστιν *IG*2^2.1028.72; ἡ -ισθεῖσά τινι χρεία *PFlor.*2. 9 (iii A.D.); but ἐγχειρίζεσθαί τι *to be entrusted with* a thing, Luc. *Prom.*3, *Am.*39, Hdn.1.12.3, etc.: c. inf., διοικεῖν τὰ τῆς ἀρχῆς ἐγκεχειρίσμεθα we *have been entrusted with* the administration of the government, Id.8.7.5:—Med., *take in hand, encounter*, κινδύνους Th. 5.108, D.C.*Fr.*29.6, v.l. in S.E.*P.*1.91. II. *treat surgically*, *Hippiatr.*18.

ἐγχειρίθετος [ρῐ], ον, *put into one's hands*, ἐ. τινα παραδιδόναι Hdt. 5.106: Aeol. **ἐγχερρίθετος** prob. in Sapph.*Oxy.*1787 *Fr.*9.

ἐγχειριστέον, *one must undertake*, Aët.6.22.

ἐγχειρο-γάστωρ, ορος, ὁ, = γαστρόχειρ, Cleanth.ap.Clearch.16, Zonar. **-τονέω,** *elect*, Poll.2.150.

ἐγχείω, Ep. for ἐγχέω, Hom.

ἐγχέλ-ειον, τό, Dim. of ἔγχελυς, in sg., Ar.*Fr.*318.7, Antiph.222. 4: mostly in pl., Pherecr.108.12, Callias Com.3, Posidipp.14; ὀπτᾶτε τἀγχέλεια Ar.*Ach.*1043: but in ll.cc. prob. neut. pl. of ἐγχέλειος (sc. κρέα or τεμάχη); so τέμαχος ἐγχέλειον Pherecr.45, cf. Eust. 1231.36. **-εών** or **-ῠών,** ῶνος, ὁ, *eel-trap*, Arist.*HA*592^{a}4,16. **-ις,** = ἔγχελυς, Id.*Fr.*311. **-ύδιον** [ῠ], τό, Dim. of ἔγχελυς, Amphis 35, Ephipp.15.6.

ἐγχελῠοτρόφος, ον, *keeping eels*, Arist.*HA*592^{a}2, *Fr.*311.

ἔγχελυς Matro *Conv.*39, acc. -υν Archestr.*Fr.*8 (the accent ἐγχέλυς, etc., is sts. found as v.l.), ἡ (ὁ, is f.l. in Luc.*Anach.*1), Att. gen. εως, nom. pl. εις, cf. Ael.Dion.*Fr.*145; gen. pl. ἐγγέλεων acc. to Choerob.*in Theod.*1.331; but the Ion. forms -υος, -υες or -υς, -ύων, -υσι are freq. found as v.l. in Arist.*HA*; dat. sg. -υϊ Hp.*Mul.*2.115; acc. pl. ἐγχέλυας Archil.101:—*eel*, ἐγχέλυές τε καὶ ἰχθύες Il.21.203, cf. Epich.73, Arist.*HA*538^{a}3, al., etc.; ἐ. Κωπαΐδας Ar.*Ach.*880; ἐ. Βοιώτιαι Antiph.236: prov., ἐγχέλεις θηρᾶσθαι, i.e. to 'fish in troubled waters', Ar.*Eq.*864, cf. *Nu.*559, Arist.*HA*592^{a}6.

ἐγχελυών, v. ἐγχελεών.

ἐγχελῠωπός, όν, *eel-faced*, Luc.*VH*1.35.

ἔγχερα, τά, = ἐπίχειρα, *IG*2².1126.4 (Decr. Amphict.).

ἔγχερσος, = χερσός, ἄρουρα *POxy.*1912.138 (vi A.D.).

ἐγχεσί-μαργος [ῐ], ον, *raging with the spear*, *EM*313.7, Hsch. **-μωρος**, ον, *fighting with the spear*, Il.2.692, al., Od.3.188, Cerc.6.9: Comp., with play on μῶρος, *AP*11.16. (-μωρος is perh. cogn. with μάρναμαι.) **-παλοι**, οἱ, *wielders of the spear*, Hsch. **-χειρ**, χειρος, ὁ, *living by war*, Orph.*Fr.*285.18.

ἐγχέσ-πᾰλος, ον, (πάλλω) *wielding the spear*, Il.2.131, B.5.69, etc. **-φόρος**, ον, *spear-bearing*, Pi.*N.*3.61.

ἐγχέω, Ep. subj. ἐγχείῃ (v. infr.): fut. -χέω, late ἐγχύσω f.l. in Hero*Spir.*1.33: aor. ἐνέχεα, Ep. ἐνέχευα, but 3 pl. ἐνέχεαν in tmesi Od.8.436; imper. ἔγχεον E.*Cyc.*568: pf. Pass. ἐγκέχῠμαι:—*pour in*, ἐν δ' οἶνον ἔχευεν Od.3.40, 6.77; μέθυ.. ἐγχείῃ δεπάεσσι 9.10; ἔγχεε κέρναις ἕνα καὶ δύο Alc.41.4; οἶνον ἐς κύλικα Hdt.4.70; ὄξος τ' ἄλειφά τ' ἐγχέας ταὐτῷ κύτει A.*Ag.*322; φάρμακα X.*Cyr.*1.3.9; κἂν οἶνόν μοι μὴ 'γχῇς σὺ πιεῖν Ar.*V.*616; ἐγχεῖν alone, *fill the cup*, τοῖς νεανίσκοις ἐγχεῖν ἐκέλευε X.*An.*4.3.13, cf. Pl.*Smp.*214a: c. gen., *in honour of*, τινός Call.*Epigr.*31, *AP*5.135,136 (Mel.): also c. dat., ἔγχει καὶ Κήδωνι *Scol.*27; ἐγχεῖν σπονδήν *pour in* wine for a libation, Ar.*Pax* 1102, Antipho 1.19:—Med., ὕδωρ δ' ἐνεχεύατο πουλύ (with no med. sense) Od.19.387; but in strict sense of Med., *pour in wine for oneself, fill one's cup*, Ar.*V.*617; εἰς τὴν χεῖρα ἐγχέασθαι *pour* [wine] into *one's own* hand, X.*Cyr.*1.3.9; ποτὸν ἐγχεῖσθαι Id.*Smp.*2.26. 2. of dry things, *pour in, shoot in*, ἐν δέ μοι ἄλφιτα χεῦον... δοροῖσιν Od.2.354. b. ἐ. ἐς τὰς ῥῖνας πτερά *thrust* in, Ar.*Av.*1081. 3. metaph., *infuse, instil*, in Pass., πᾶσιν ἡμῖν θανάσιμον -κέχυται τὸ τῆς γενέσεως φάρμακον Metrod.53; τὸ δ' αὖ τῆς ἡδονῆς πολὺ πλέον ἐγκεχυμένον Pl.*Phlb.*47a. II. sts. with acc. of the cup, *fill by pouring in*, κρατῆρα S.*Fr.*563; φιάλην X.*Smp.*2.23; ἔγχεον.. Διός γε τήνδε σωτῆρος Alex.232; ἐγχέασα..ἀγαθοῦ δαίμονος (sc. κύλικα) Nicostr.20. III. ἐγχεῖν ὕδωρ τινί (v. κλεψύδρα) D.19.213, cf. 43.8:—Pass., ἐγχεῖται τὸ πρῶτον ὕδωρ Aeschin.3.197.

ἔγχηλος, ὁ, *bandage*, Hsch. **ἐγχημώμενοι**· ἐγχάσκοντες, Id. (leg. ἐγχασμ-). **ἐγχηρωτύλει**· ἐπιχαίρουσιν, Id.

ἐγχθόνιος, ον, *in the earth*, σποδιὴ κειμένη ἐ. *Epigr.Gr.*298, prob. in *AP*7.740 (Leon.). II. *of the country*, κύλιξ *APl.*4.235 (Apollonid.).

ἐγχίδιον· ἔγγιον, Hsch.

ἐγχίκτῠπος, ον, *making a noise with the spear*, *EM*630.26.

ἐγχλαινόομαι, Pass., *to be clothed in*, ἐσθῆτα Lyc.974, cf. 1347.

ἐγχλᾰμῠδόομαι, *to be wrapped in a cloak*, Hsch. s. v. ἐντεθετταλίσθαι.

ἐγχλῐαίνω, *warm*, in Pass., Dsc.*Eup.*1.228.

ἐγχλίαμα· μαῦρον ὄνομα, Hsch.

ἐγχλίω [ῐ], *to deal wantonly with, insult*, Ἕλλησιν A.*Supp.*914.

ἐγχλοάω, *to be of a greenish hue*, Nic.*Th.*154. II. ἐγχλοᾶσθαι· ἐμφῦναι, Hsch.

ἔγχλοος, ον, = ἔγχλωρος, Nic.*Th.*506, al.; metapl. acc. ἔγχλοα ib. 676.

ἐγχλωρίζω, = ἐγχλοάω, Sch.Nic.*Th.*154.

ἔγχλωρος, ον, *greenish*, Thphr.*HP*3.12.5 (Comp.), Dsc.3.37.

ἔγχνοος, ον, contr. -χνους, ουν, *downy*, Nic.*Th.*762, Dsc.3.146.

ἐγχόδια· ἀθρόα, Hsch.

ἐγχοιριλόω, pf. part. Pass. ἐγκεχοιριλωμένην, = λεπράν, Hsch.

ἐγχονδρ-ίζω, *form into grains*, Archig.ap.Gal.12.661. **-ος**, ον, *in grains*, of manna, Dsc.1.68.6.

ἔγχορδος, ον, (χορδή) *stringed*, Poll.4.58.

ἐγχορεύω, *dance in*, ἐν Ἰνδίᾳ Plu.2.332b: generally, *disport oneself, take pleasure in*, παιδεύμασι, etc., Ph.1.252, al.; of birds, *sport in* the air, c. acc., Vett.Val.344.22 (s. v. l.).

ἔγχορτος, ον, *grass-grown*, *POxy.*1911.103 (vi A.D.), 1912.134 (vi A.D.).

ἔγχος, εος, τό, *spear, lance*, Il.6.319, etc.; ἔ. λογχωτά B.*Fr.*3. II. *weapon* in general: *sword*, S.*Aj.*287, al., E.*El.*696, etc.: pl., *weapons*, ἄτερ ἐγχέων Pi.*P.*9.28; πτερωτὰ ἔγχη *arrows*, E.*HF*1098; πῦρ.. Ἑκάτης ἔγχος S.*Fr.*535 (anap.); of Nausicaa's *ball*, τὸ δ' ἔ. ἐν ποσὶν κυλίνδεται ib.782: metaph., φροντίδος ἔ. Id.*OT*170 (lyr.). III. meton., *armed force*, Ἠπύγων ἔγχος ἀπωσάμενοι Call.*Fr.*444.

ἐγχοῦν· τὸν στεάτινον (Lacon.), Hsch.

ἔγχουσα, ἡ, Att. for ἄγχουσα (q. v.), Ar.*Lys.*48, X.*Oec.*10.2.

ἐγχουσίζομαι, *rouge*, τὸ πρόσωπον, *EM*313.37; cf. ἀγχουσίζομαι.

ἐγχόω, = ἐγχώννυμι, impf. ἐνέχουν Str.7.4.7:—Pass., ἐγχούμενοι πόροι Id.9.2.18.

ἐγχράω and **ἐγχραύω**, Ep. **ἐνιχραύω** Nic.*Th.*277:—like ἐγχρίμπτω, *dash against*, ἐνέχραυεν ἐς τὸ πρόσωπον τὸ σκῆπτρον Hdt.6.75; κυνόδοντά τισι Nic. l. c. II. Pass., ἦσαν δὲ πρός τινας καὶ ἄλλους ἐγκεχρημένοι (sc. πόλεμοι) *there were* wars *undertaken*.., Hdt.7.145 (prob. f.l. for ἐγκεκρημένοι).

ἐγχρεμετίζω, fut. -ίσω, *to neigh in*, Poll.10.56.

ἔγχρεμμα, ατος, τό, *spitting*, in pl., Plu.2.82b (dub. l.).

ἐγχρέμπτομαι, *expectorate*, Luc.*Gall.*10.

ἐγχρῄζω, fut. -χρήσω Phld.*Rh.*1.147 S.:—*want, have need of*, c. gen., ib.1.3 S., *POxy.*1766.10 (iii A.D.). II. intr., *to be needful* or *useful*, εἰς ὕδωρ *Gp.*20.19 tit.; ἰατροῖς ἐγχρῄζει τὸ ψέγειν prob. in Phld.*Ir.*p.21 W., cf. *BGU*226.9 (i A.D.), Apollon.*Mir.*36; τὰ ἐγχρῄζοντα *necessaries*, condemned by Luc.*Hist.Conscr.*22.

ἐγχρημᾰτίζω, *execute* a deed, *PPetr.*2p.43.

ἐγχρίμπτω or -χρίπτω, Philostr.*VA*8.19 (also -χριπτᾶται· ἐγγίζει, Hsch.): aor. ἐνέχριμψα Il.23.334, Hdt.2.60 (v. l. -χρίψαντες):—**Med.**, fut. -χρίμψομαι A.R.4.939:—**Pass.**, aor. ἐνεχρίμφθην Il.23.338:—*bring near to*, with collat. notion of force, *strike* or *dash against*, τῷ [τέρματι] σὺ μάλ' ἐγχρίμψας ἐλάαν σχεδὸν ἅρμα drive the chariot close *so as almost to touch* the post, ib.334 (so ἐν νύσσῃ δέ τοι ἵππος.. ἐγχριμφθήτω *let* him *almost touch* the post, ib.338); ἐ. τὴν βᾶριν τῇ γῇ *to bring* the boat *close to* land, Hdt.2.60; ἐ. (sc. τὴν ναῦν) τῷ αἰγιαλῷ Id.9.98; ἐ. τὸν ἵππον τῇ θηλέῃ Id.3.85; ἐ. ἐς τὴν γῆν App.*BC* 5.81. II. intr., *approach*, τινί S.*El.*898:—more freq. in Pass. in this sense, ἐγχριμφθείς *having come near to assault* one, Il.13.146; ἐνιχριμφθέντα πύλῃσιν 17.405; αἰχμὴ ὀστέῳ ἐγχριμφθεῖσα the point *driven to* the very bone, 5.662; ἀσπίδ' (i.e. ἀσπίδι) ἐνιχριμφθείς *dashed against* his shield, 7.272; νωλεμὲς ἐγχρίμπτοντο they *pressed* unceasing *on*, 17.413; later, *keep close to*, ἐ. (sc. τῇ γῇ), of fish, Hdt. 2.93; ἐν οὐδενὶ Maiist.24; ἐ. γυναικί, = πλησιάζω, Hdt.4.113; κύνες ἐλάφοις ἐγχριμπτόμεναι *pursuing* them, E.*Hipp.*218 (anap.); of serpents, *attack*, τινί v. l. for -σκίμψῃ in Nic.*Th.*336, cf. A.R.4.1512, Philostr. l. c.; of elephants, Opp.*C.*2.535; of disease, *attack* a particular part, ἐς τοὺς βουβῶνας Hp.*Mul.*2.137; ἀρθρῖτις ἐ. ἐς ἄρθρα Aret.*SD*2.12.—Poet., Ion. and late Prose.

ἔγ-χρῐσις, εως, ἡ, (ἐγχρίω) *anointing, rubbing in*, Hp.*Decent.* 8. II. *slight wound, scratch*, Ael.*NA*3.22. **-χρισμα**, ατος, τό, *liniment, embrocation*, Hp.*Hum.*5. **-χριστέον**, *one must anoint*, Sor.2.16, *Gp.*16.6.1. **-χριστος**, ον, *rubbed in as an ointment*, Theoc.11.2; εἰς τοὺς ὀφθαλμούς Arist.*GA*747ᵃ9.

ἐγχρίω [ῑ], *anoint*, ἀλείμμασιν ἑαυτόν Duris 10 J., cf. *AP*11.117 (Strat.); τοὺς ὀφθαλμούς *Apoc.*3.18: metaph., ψευδηγόροις φήμαις ἐγχρίειν ἔπη Lyc.1455:—Med., *anoint oneself*, ἰξοῦ Str.15.1.29; ἐ. τὸ πρόσωπον Nic.Dam.p.2 D.: abs., Arr.*Epict.*2.21.20, etc.:—Pass., Ph. 1.526. II. *sting, prick*, τινί Pl.*Phdr.*251d:—Pass., ἰὸς ἐγχρισθείς poison *injected by a sting*, Ael.*NA*1.54. 2. *stick in*, τὸ κέντρον ib. 6.20.

ἐγχρον-ία, Ion. -ίη, ἡ, *chronic character*, νούσου dub. in Hp.*Praec.* 14. **-ίζω**, *to be long about* a thing, *delay*, Th.3.27; περὶ ὑποχόνδριον Hp.*Acut.*50; ἐγχρονίσας *after long delay*, *Epigr.Gr.*815.7; ἐ. πρὸς τὸν γάμον Arist.*Rh.*1411ᵃ19; εἰς καιρόν Phld.*Lib.*p.13 O.; τινί *in* a thing, Plb.15.36.6; ἐν τόπῳ D.C.44.46:—Pass., Pl.*Ep.*362a. II. *become chronic*, ἐγχρονίζει τὰ ἐμπυήματα Hp.*Prog.*17; ἐγχρονίζον ἔθος Ph.2.203; *continue in*, τῷ καταστήματι Procl.*Par.Ptol.*51:—Pass., ἐγχρονισθὲν τὸ νόσημα Pl.*Grg.*480b, cf. Arist.*HA*586ᵃ18. III. Act., c. acc. pers., *waste* a person's *time*, Vett.Val.150.10. **-ιος**, ον, *temporal*, φύσεις Procl.*in Prm.*p.638 S. **-ισμός**, ὁ, *prolonged use*, Sor.1.46, Antyll.ap.Orib.9.23.10. **-ος**, ον, *lasting a short time*, App.*Fr.*3 (expld. by Suid. as *recent*). 2. *in time, temporal*, opp. αἰώνιος, Ocell.1.2, Ascl.*in Metaph.*424.7, Procl.*Inst.*53, al., Dam. *Pr.*90, al., Simp.*in Ph.*461.12.

ἐγ-χρύσεος [ῡ], ον, = sq., *IG*14.268 (Selinus). **-χρῡσος**, ον, *golden*, ὅπλον *Schwyzer* 647.35 (Cyme, i A.D.); στολή Philostr.*Im.*1. 22; πρόσοψις D.S.3.39. **-χρῡσόω**, *gild*, Tz.*H.*3.975 (Pass.).

ἐγχρῴζομαι, Pass., *to be engrained*, ἐν ἅπασι τοῖς μέρεσιν ἐγκέχρωσται ἡ λευκότης Arist.*Xen.*978ᵃ11: metaph., *to be amalgamated with*, πάθος ἐγκεχρωσμένον τῷ βίῳ Id.*EN*1105ᵃ3; νόμον ἐν τοῖς ἤθεσι καὶ τοῖς ἐπιταδεύμασι τῶν πολιτᾶν ἐγχρῴζεσθαι δεῖ Archyt.ap.Stob. 4.1.138:—Act. only ἐγχρώσας· χρίσας, Hsch.

ἐγχρωκουρίας, ου, ὁ, = ἐν χρῷ κεκαρμένος, Orus ap.*Et.Gen.* s. v. ἐν χρῷ.

ἐγχρώμᾰτος, ον, *parti-coloured*, Sch.Ar.*Pl.*530.

ἐγχῡλ-ης, a kind of *fish*, Hsch. **-ίζω**, *convert into juice* (by pressing), Thphr.*CP*6.11.14. **-όομαι**, *to be converted into chyle*, τὰ ἐγκεχυλωμένα Gal.8.369. **-ος**, ον, *juicy, succulent*, Hp.*Aff.*59, Thphr.*CP*6.11.15 (Comp.); ἰχθύς Agatharch.40; *savoury*, Alex.124. 12; *soft-boiled*, of eggs, Gal.6.707. Adv. -λως dub. in Archig.ap. Gal.8.931. **-ωσις**, εως, ἡ, = ἔγχυμα II, Paul.Aeg.2.11, Aret.*CD* 2.13.

ἔγχῠμα, ατος, τό, *instillation*, Gal.12.649. II. *filling, content*, of a vessel, Hp.*Cord.*8, Gal.11.260, 7.524. III. = ἔγχυτος II, Hsch.

ἐγχῡμᾰτ-ίζω, *make an infusion* of, τι Dsc.1.45 (Pass.), *Gp.*4.7.3, Aesop.18. II. ἐ. τινά *treat by injections*, *Hippiatr.*129. III. *instil, inject*, Sor.1.64, Archig.ap.Gal.12.621, etc. **-ισμός**, ὁ, *injection, instillation*, Antyll.ap.Orib.10.26.1, Sor.1.56, *Hippiatr.* 68. **-ιστά**, τά, *injections*, Dsc.*Eup.*1.55. **-ιστέον**, *one must inject*, Sor.1.69, Orib.46.25.4. II. *one must make an infusion*, *Gp.*18.17.1.

ἔγχῡμος, ον, *moistened*, ἔγχυμα χυμῷ Hp.*Off.*11; *juicy, succulent*, σάρξ Pl.*Ti.*74d, cf. Thphr.*CP*5.4.3; *sapid*, Arist.*Sens.*442ᵇ29.

ἐγχύμωσις [ῡ], εως, ἡ, *stirring up, enlivening*, in pl., Hp.*Epid.* 2.4.4.

ἐγχύνω, late form of ἐγχέω, Luc.*Pr.Im.*29, etc.

ἔγχῠσις, εως, ἡ, (ἐγχέω) *pouring in*, Plu.2.38f, Hero*Spir.*1. 12. II. *pouring* of wine *into* casks, *PPetr.*2p.136 (iii B.C.).

ἐγχῠτέον, *one must pour in*, *Gp.*6.7.4, al.

ἐγχυτλόω, *pour libations*, τοῖς καμοῦσι Herod.5.84.

ἔγχῠτος, ον, *poured in, infused*, Aret.*CD*2.3; ἔγχυτον, τό, *injection*, Hp.*Mul.*1.34, Apollon.ap.Gal.12.582. II. ἔγχυτος (sc. πλακοῦς), ὁ, *cake cast into a shape*, Hippon.37, Men.518.9, Euang.1.7:—also **ἐγχῠτοῦς**, ὁ, *Gloss.* 2. ἔγχυτον, τό, = ἔγχυμα, *infusion*, Aret.*CA* 2.10.

ἐγχύτρ-ιαι· αἱ τὰς χόας τοῖς τετελευτηκόσιν ἐπιφέρουσαι, Sch.rec. Ar.*V.*289. **-ίζω**, *expose children in an earthenware vessel*, Hsch.: hence, *make away with*, Ar.*V.*289. **-ίστρια**, ἡ, *woman who* *gathered the bones from* a funeral pile *into an urn*, Pl.*Min*.315c (v.l. ἐγχυτίστρια), cf. *EM*313.41. **II.** *woman who exposed children*, acc. to Sch.Ar.*V*.289 (but cf. ἐγχύτριαι).

ἔγχωμα, ατος, τό, *bar of a river*, Plb.4.39.9.

ἐγχώννῡμι or -ύω, *fill up by depositing earth*, of rivers, Plb.4.40.4 (Pass.); ἐ. τάφρον App.*BC*5.36. **II.** *throw in earth*, εἰς τάφρον ἐνεχώννυον ib.2.75, cf. D.S.17.42.

ἐγχωρ-έω, *give room* to do a thing, *allow*, ὁ χρόνος οὐκ ἐγχωρεῖ, c. inf., Lys.26.6, X.*Eq*.12.13: abs., ὅσον ἐνεχώρεε ἡ δεκάτη so far as the money *allowed* her to go, Hdt.2.135; ἂν ἐγχωρῇ τὸ ὕδωρ (i.e. the water-clock), D.44.45. **b.** c. acc., *admit of*, κλίσιν Arr.*Tact*. 11.4. **2.** ἐγχωρεῖ, impers., *there is time, it is possible* or *allowable*, c. dat. pers. et inf., ἐ. αὐτῷ εἰδέναι Antipho 1.7, cf. 5.90, Pl. *Prt*.321d, X.*HG*2.3.16, etc.; οἷς ἐ. ὑβρισταῖς εἶναι Lys.24.15: also abs., ἔτι ἐ. *there is* yet *time*, Pl.*Phd*.116e; οὐκέτ' ἐγχωρεῖ D.4.41; = ἐνδέχεται, Arist.*APr*.25b10, al.; ἐφ' ὁπόσον ἂν ἐγχωρῇ D.H.*Comp*.6; ἐγχωροῦν ἐστί Paus.3.24.11; κατὰ τὸ ἐγχωροῦν as far as *possible*, Paul. Aeg.6.99. **II.** *pass*, εἰς ἑτέραν ὑποθήκην *BGU*907.15 (iii A.D.). **-ιος**, ον, also η or α, ον Hdt.6.35, Pi.*O*.5.11: (χώρα):—*in* or *of the country*, ἐσθὴς ἐγχωρίη Hdt. l. c.; ἐγχωρία λίμνα Pi. l. c.; βασιλῆες ib.9.56; ἐ. θεοί A.*Th*.14, S.*Tr*.183, *Sammelb*.5680 (iii B.C.); θεοὶ καὶ ἥρωες Th. 2.74; Ἑλληνικοῖς καὶ ἐ. γράμμασι *OGI*194.30 (i B.C.); κάρτα δ' ἔστ' ἐ. *a true-born* Theban, A.*Th*.413; ἐ. [πυροί], opp. ἐπείσακτοι, Arist.*Mir*. 836b22; of winds, *local*, Thphr.*CP*5.12.11. **2.** Subst., *dweller in* the land, ἐ. τῆσδε γῆς *inhabitants*, S.*OC*871, cf. E.*Ion*1167; οἱ ἐ. Arist.*PA*673a18, Wilcken *Chr*.1.2 (iii B.C.), etc. **3.** τὸ ἐ. as Adv., *according to the custom of the country*, Th.4.78. Adv. -ίως Sch.E. *Ph*.134. **II.** *of* or *for the country, rustic*, Hes.*Op*.344 (v.l. ἐγκώμιον). **III.** ἐγχώριον· τόκος, δάνειον, Hsch. **-ος**, ον, (χώρα) = foreg., S.*Ph*.692 (lyr.), *OC*125 (lyr.), Lyc.509, etc.; φάσματα S.*Ichn*. 322 (lyr.).

ἔγχωσις, εως, ἡ, *silting up* of a channel, Arist.*Mete*.352b34, Plb.4. 39.10, etc.: pl., Str.5.3.8. **II.** *bank, dyke*, αἱ ἐ. τῶν τάφρων Ph. *Bel*.100.24, cf. *Ostr.Strassb*.777.

ἐγχωστήριος, ον, *useful for filling up*, ὄργανα App.*BC*5.36.

ἐγώ, *I*: Pron. of the first person:—Ep. mostly **ἐγών** before vowels (so in Dor., before consonants, Epich.85, Sophr.81, Ar.*Ach*.748,754), rarely in Trag., A.*Pers*.932 (lyr.); Boeot. **ἰών** A.D.*Pron*.51.4:—strengthd. **ἔγωγε**, *I at least, for my part, indeed, for myself* (more freq. in Att. than in Hom.): Dor. **ἐγώνγα** Alcm.51, Ar.*Ach*.736, *Lys*.986, dat. ἐμίνγα *IG*2².1126.7 (Amphict. Delph.): Boeot. **ἰώνγα** Corinn.21; **ἰώνει** Ead.10; **ἰώγα** Ar.*Ach*.898: Lacon. and Tarent. **ἐγώνη**, Hsch., A.D.*Conj*.255.29. **II.** oblique cases from a difft. root, gen. ἐμοῦ, enclit. μου; Ion. and Ep. ἐμέο, ἐμεῦ, μευ, also ἐμέθεν Il.1.525, E.*Hel*. 177 (lyr.); Aeol. ἔμεθεν Sapph.*Supp*.23.7; ἐμεῖο *IG*3.1337; μεθέν Sophr.20; Dor. ἐμέος, ἐμεῦς, Epich.144; Boeot. ἐμοῦς Corinn.37; also ἐμῶς, ἐμίο, ἐμίω, ἐμίως A.D.*Pron*.74.17:—dat. ἐμοί, enclit. μοι (which may be compared with Skt. gen. *me* in κλῦθί μοι Il.5.115, al.); ὅ μοι πόσις *Schwyzer*683 (Cypr.); Dor. ἐμίν Epich.99, *AJA*29.461 (Rhodian, v B.C.), Ar.*Ach*.733, Theoc.4.30; Tarent. ἐμίνη Rhinth.13: acc. ἐμέ, enclit. με; Cypr. μι *Inscr.Cypr*.59,60 H. **III.** dual, nom. and acc., **νῶι**, *we two*, Il.5.34, etc.; acc. νῶιν Zenod.ad Il.8.377; Att. νώ Pl.*Phdr*.278b (also Il.5.219, Od.15.475); νῶε Antim.39, Corinn.5: gen., dat. νῶιν; νῷν S.*Ant*.3; νῶι dat., Orph.*L*.773; νῶιν, = ἡμῖν, Q.S.1.213, etc. **IV.** pl., nom. ἡμεῖς (ἡμέες f.l. in Hdt.2.6, al., rejected by A.D.*Pron*.93.1); Aeol. ἄμμες Od.9.303, Alc.18.3, Pi.*P*. 4.144; Dor. ἁμές Alcm.65, Epich.42, Ar.*Lys*.168:—gen. ἡμῶν (also ἥμων A.D.*Synt*.130.23); Ion. ἡμέων Hdt.1.112, etc.; ἡμείων Od.24. 170, Herod.1.46; Aeol. ἀμμέων Alc.88, *Milet*.3 No.152.29; ἄμμων ib.74, A.D.*Pron*.95.3; Dor. ἁμέων Alcm.66; ἁμῶν [Epich.]266, Ar. *Lys*.168, Theoc.2.158; Cret., Boeot. ἁμίων *SIG*528.5, A.D.*Pron*.95. 21:—dat. ἡμῖν, in S. also ἥμιν (ῐ) (or ἡμιν Aristarch.ad Il.1.214, A.D. *Pron*.95.3); also rarely in Com., Phryn.Com.37, Ar.*Av*.386 (dub.): Aeol. ἄμμιν, ἄμμι, Il.1.384, Alc.80, al., Pi.*P*.4.155, A.*Th*.156 (lyr.), *Milet*.3 No.152; ἄμμεσιν Alc.100; Dor. also ἁμίν or ἅμιν, Alcm.77,78, A.*Eu*.347 (lyr.), Ar.*Lys*.1081; with ῑ, Id.*Ach*.821, Theoc.7.145:—acc. ἡμᾶς (also ἥμας Od.16.372); Ion. ἡμέας Il.8.211, *SIG*273.25 (Milet., iv B.C.); ἥμεας Od.4.294 (cf. Hdn.Gr.2.140); Aeol. ἄμμε Il.1.59, Sapph.115, Theocr.8.25; Dor. ἁμέ *SIG*1 (Abu Simbel, vi B.C.), Epich.173, Ar.*Ach*.759 codd., *Lys*.95.—On these dialectic varieties, v. A.D.*Pron*.50 sqq. (Cf. Skt. *ahám* (ἐγών), acc. pl. *asmā́n*; for νώ cf. Skt. *nau*):—freq. in answers, as an affirmative, esp. in form ἔγωγε, S.*Tr*.1248, Pl.*Tht*.149b, etc.; οὗτος ἐ. here am *I*, Pi.*O*. 4.26; ὅδ' ἐκεῖνος ἐ. S.*OC*138 (lyr.); rarely with Art., τὸν ἐμὲ *myself*, Pl.*Tht*.166a, *Sph*.239b (but ὁ ἐ. *the Self, the Ego*, Dam.*Pr*.444); τίς ὢν οὗτος ὁ ἐγὼ τυγχάνω; Plu.2.1119a; τί ἐστι φίλος; ἄλλος ἐ. Pythag. ap.Herm.*in Phdr*.p.166 A.; τί τοῦτ' ἐμοί; ἡμῖν τί τοῦτ' ἔστ'; Lat. *quid mea hoc refert?* Ar.*Th*.498, etc.; ἐγώ; in a question, Ar.*Eq*. 1336, al.; ἡμεῖς *the self*, ἔνθα δὴ ἡμεῖς μάλιστα Plot.1.1.7.

ἐγώγυος or -ιος, = ὠγύγιος, Hsch., Suid.

ἐγᾦδα, ἐγᾦμαι, Att. crasis for ἐγὼ οἶδα, ἐγὼ οἶμαι. **ἐγών, ἐγώνγα, ἐγώνη**, dialectic forms of ἐγώ, ἔγωγε (q. v.). **ἐδααία**· ἐρημία, Hsch. **ἐδάην**, ης, η, aor. 2 of *δάω. **ἐδαλάχθη**· ἐδήχθη, Id. **ἐδάμην**, ης, η, Ep. aor. 2 Pass. of δαμάω. **ἐδάνη**· εἶδος ἀμπέλου, Id.

ἐδᾰνός, ή, όν, *eatable*: ἐδανόν, τό, *food*, A.*Ag*.1407.

ἑδᾰνός, ή, όν, as epith. of oil, Il.14.172, cj. in *h.Ven*.63; expld. by Gramm. as cogn. with ἡδύς, ἥδομαι, ἁνδάνω (q. v.), *sweet*, cf. Hdn.Gr. 2.89, Apollon.*Lex*. s. v.

ἔδαρ· βρῶμα, Hsch. (i.e. ἔδϝαρ, cf. εἶδαρ).

ἐδᾰφ-εινός, etym. of ταπεινός, *EM*745.54. **-αῖος**, α, ον, *belonging to a floor*, Tz.*H*.3.211; gloss on γονυπετής, Sch.E.*Ph*. 293. **-ίζω**, *beat level and firm like a floor* or *pavement*, Plb.6.33. 6, Thphr.*HP*9.3.1:—Pass., Id.*CP*4.8.2, Arist.*Pr*.934b10. **II.** *provide with a floor*, οἶκον *IG*11(2).158*A*66 (iii B.C.), cf. *BCH*29. 475. **III.** *dash to the ground*, Lxx*Ps*.136(137).9, *Ev.Luc*.19. 44. **-ικός**, ή, όν, *pertaining to land*, ἔργα *PLond*.2.163.19 (i A.D.); ἐλάσσωμα *BGU*20.8 (ii A.D.). **-ιον**, τό, Dim. of ἔδαφος 4, Alex. Aphr.*in Metaph*.738.17; τῶν κατηγοριῶν τὰ ἐ. Dexipp.*in Cat*.5.14, cf. Eust.1532.63, Tz.*H*.4.202, Sch.Pi.*O*.5.1. **-ιστήριον**, τό, = λίστρον, Hsch. s.h.v. **-ίτης** [ῑ], ου, ὁ, = ἐδαφιαῖος, Tz.*H*.1.906.

ἐδᾰφοποιέω, *raze to the ground*, J.*Vit*.19.

ἔδᾰφος, εος, τό, *bottom, foundation, base* of anything, τῆς κατασκευῆς τὰ ἐ. Th.1.10; ἔ. νηός *bottom* of a ship, Od.5.249; ἔ. πλοίου D.32.5, cf. Pherecr.12; ἔ. ποταμοῦ, τῆς θαλάττης, X.*Cyr*.7.5.18, Arist.*HA*534a11; [ποτηρίου] Pherecr.143.2. **2.** *ground-floor, pavement*, οἴκου Hdt.8.137; καθελεῖν ἐς ἔ. raze to the *ground*, Th. 3.68; τὸ ἔ. ὁμαλίσασι *IG*11(2).161*A*57 (Delos, iii B.C.); ἔπεσον εἰς τὸ ἔ. *Act.Ap*.22.7; ἀπὸ ἐδάφους μέχρι παντὸς ὕψους *CPR*95.17 (iii A.D.), etc. **3.** *ground, soil*, περὶ τοῦ τῆς πατρίδος ἐδάφους ἀγωνίζεσθαι for our country's *soil*, Aeschin.3.134, cf. D.26.11 (pl.); ἐχθρὸς τῷ τῆς πόλεως ἐδάφει, of a mortal foe, Id.8.39, 10.11; δακρύειν ἔ. *Eleg.Alex. Adesp*.1.7; *soil*, viewed in regard to its quality, Thphr.*CP*2.4.1 (pl.), 4.11.8: pl., ἐδάφη *lands and tenements* (incl. houses), Is.11.42, *IG* 2.780, *PTeb*.302.10 (i A.D.); also, *masses of earth*, Epicur.*Ep*.2 p.48 U. **4.** *text* of a manuscript, opp. margin (μέτωπον), Gal.16.837, 18(2).864. **b.** *manuscript*, Id.16.468 (s. v.l.). **5.** *background* of puppet-theatre, Hero *Aut*.30.1, al.

ἐδαφόω, pf. Pass. ἠδάφωται, *establish*, Hsch.

ἐδέατρος, ὁ, among the Persians, *one who tasted first, and named the order of dishes*, = θαλίαρχος, *seneschal*, Phylarch.*Fr*.44 J., cf. *EM* 315.37, Suid.; *steward*, *PCair.Zen*.31.18; cf. ἐλέατρος.

ἐδέγμην, v. δέχομαι. **ἐδεδέατο**, v. δέω *bind*. **ἐδεδμήατο**, v. δέμω. **ἐδέζετο**· ἐπολεμεῖτο, Hsch.

ἑδέθλιον, τό, = sq., Call.*Ap*.62, A.R.4.630, Nonn.*D*.3.258, al.

ἕδεθλον, τό, = ἔδαφος, Antim.28, Call.*Ap*.73, Lyc.987, A.R.4.331; τὰ χρυσόπαστα δ' ἕδεθλα should be read (with Auratus) in A.*Ag*.776 for ἐσθλά. **II.** *precinct, shrine*, *SIG*364.21 (Ephesus, iii B.C.); τόδε νάσω ἕ. *Epigr.Gr*.978.9 (Philae).

ἐδείδῐμεν, -δῐσαν, v. δείδω. **ἔδεκτο**, v. δέχομαι.

ἐδελώνη· ἄνθος, Hsch. **ἕδεος**· Θεσσαλικὸς θρόνος, Id.

ἔδεσμα, ατος, τό, (ἔδω) *meat, food*, Pl.*Ti*.73a, Antiph.26.10: pl., *eatables, meats*, Batr.31, X.*Hier*.1.23, Pl.*R*.559b, Antiph.82.1, Porph. *Abst*.1.55: metaph., οὐ γὰρ ἡδύσματι χρῆται ἀλλ' ὡς ἐδέσματι τοῖς ἐπιθέτοις Arist.*Rh*.1406a19:—Dim. **ἐδεσμάτιον**, τό, Procl.ad Hes.*Op*.41.

ἐδεσμᾰτοθήκη, ἡ, *food-hamper*, Sch.Od.6.76.

ἐδεσ-τέον, *one must eat*, Pl.*Cri*.47b, *Prt*.314a. **-τής**, οῦ, ὁ, *eater*, Hdt.3.99, Antiph.26.15. **-τός**, ή, όν, *eatable, good for food*, ζῷον Arist.*Pol*.1324b41; ἐδεστά *eatables, meats*, E.*Fr*.472.19, Pl.*Ti*. 72e: sg., Call.*Fr*.128. **II.** *eaten*, S.*Ant*.206; *consumed*, ἐξ αὐτοῦ Id.*Tr*.677.

ἐδήδοκα, ἐδήδεσμαι, ἐδήδοται, ἐδηδώς, v. ἔδω, ἐσθίω.

ἐδηδών, όνος, ἡ, = φαγέδαινα, Hsch.

ἐδητύς, ύος, ἡ, *meat, food*, in Hom. always in phrase, πόσιος καὶ ἐδητύος ἐξ ἔρον ἕντο Il.1.469, etc.; exc. Od.6.250 δηρὸν γὰρ ἐδητύος ἦεν ἄπαστος.

ἔδμεναι, v. ἔδω.

ἑδν-άς· ἡ ἀπὸ τῶν ἕδνων ἐδητύς, Hsch. **-εύειν**· ἐνεχυράζειν, Id. **-ιος**, α, ον, *bridal*, χιτών Id.

ἕδνον, τό, Pi.*O*.9.10, Call.*Fr*.193, Theoc.25.114, 27.33, Orph.*A*. 873, Nonn.*D*.42.28, al.; elsewh. only pl. **ἕδνα, ἔεδνα**:—*bride-price* or *wedding-gifts* (φερνή being the bride's *portion*), ὄπυιε πορὼν ἀπερείσια ἕ. Il.16.178; ἠγάγετο .. ἐπεὶ πόρε μυρία ἕ. ib.190, cf. 22.472; μνάσθω ἐέδνοισιν διζήμενος Od.16.391; εἰς ὅ κέ μοι.. πατὴρ ἀποδῷσιν ἔεδνα 8.318; rare in Trag., ἕδνοις ἄγαγες Ἡσιόναν πιθὼν δάμαρτα A. *Pr*.559 (lyr.): later Prose, Parth.20.1. **II.** *wedding-gifts* made to the bride *by those of her own household*, Od.1.277, 2.196, E.*Andr*. 2, Pi.*O*.9.10; but, **III.** in Id.*P*.3.94, Orph. l. c., D.C.79.12, *wedding-presents* to a wedded pair *by their guests*. **IV.** generally, *gift*, Theoc.25.114.

ἑδνοφορέω, *bring wedding-presents*, Eust.1414.49.

ἑδν-όω, Ep. ἐεδν-, (ἕδνον) *promise for wedding-presents, betroth*, ἡμῖν ἕδνωσε θύγατρας Theoc.22.147:—Med. in Hom., of a father, ὥς κ' αὐτὸς ἐεδνώσαιτο θύγατρα Od.2.53; ἐδνώσομαί τε θυγατέρ' (Herm. for ἐδώσομαι) E.*Hel*.933. **II.** Med., of a husband, *dower* a wife, Hes. *Fr*.94.47; simply, *marry*, γυναῖκα *AP*7.648 (Leon.); *woo*, Nonn.*D*. 6.3. **-ωτή**, ἡ, *bride betrothed for* ἕδνα, Hsch. **-ωτής**, Ep. ἐεδν-, οῦ, ὁ, *father who portions a bride*, οὗ τοι ἐεδνωταὶ κακοὶ εἰμεν Il.13.382.

ἔδομαι, fut. of ἐσθίω, ἔδω. **ἔδον**, Ep. and Dor. 3 pl. aor. 2 of δίδωμι. **II.** impf. of ἔδω.

ἐδοξοεῖ· ἀγαλματοποιεῖ, Hsch. **ἐδοργύπευσεν**· ἔσφαξεν ἢ ἐπέρανεν, Id.

ἕδος, εος, τό, Ep. dat. pl. ἑδέεσσιν *IG*14.1389 ii 19:—*sitting-place*: **1.** *seat, stool*, Il.1.534 (pl.), 581 (pl.), 9.194, etc.; ἕ. Θεσσαλικόν *straight-backed chair*, Hp.*Art*.7. **2.** *seat, abode, dwelling-place*, esp. of the gods, ἐς Ὄλυμπον ..ἵν' ἀθανάτων ἕ. ἐστί Il.5.360; ἵκοντο θεῶν ἕ. αἰπὺν Ὄλυμπον ib.367, cf. Theoc.7.116; periphr., ἕ. Οὐλύμποιο, = Ὄλυμπος, Il.24.144, cf. Pi.*O*.2.12; of the abodes of men,

Θήβης ἕ. Il.4.406; Ἰθάκης ἕ. Od.13.344; ἕ. Μάκαρος *the abode* of Macar, Il.24.544: periphr., Τροίας ἕ. B.8.46; ἔποικον ἕ., = ἐποικίαι, A.*Pr.*412. **3.** *seated statue* of a god, S.*OT*886 (lyr.), *El.*1374, *IG* 2.754, al., Isoc.15.2, X.*HG*1.4.12, Porph.*Abst.*2.18, Polem.Hist.90, Plu.*Per.*13, Paus.8.46.2; τὰ ἕ. τῶν θεῶν, i.e. the Lat. *Penates*, D.H. 1.47; also of a man worshipped as a hero, *IG*14.2133; τὰ τῶν θεῶν ἕδη καὶ τοὺς νεώς Isoc.4.155; τοὺς νεὼς καὶ τὰ ἕδη καὶ τὰ τεμένη Lycurg.143; θεῶν ἕδη (v.l. ἄλση) καὶ ἱερά Pl.*Phd.*111b, cf. Tim.*Lex.* ἕδος· τὸ ἄγαλμα, καὶ ὁ τόπος ἐν ᾧ ἵδρυται, but this latter use is doubtful in early Prose; later, *temple*, Ph.2.314; ἕ. ὑπαίθριον D.C.51. 1. **4.** *foundation, base,* Hes.*Th.*117, Epigr.ap.Vitr.8.3.23. **II.** *act of sitting,* οὐχ ἕδος ἐστί 'tis no *time to sit idle*, Il.11.648, 23.205; cf. ἕδρα II. (Cf. Skt. *sádas* 'seat'.)

ἕδρ-α, Ep. and Ion. **ἕδρη**, ἡ: (ἕδος): **I.** *sitting-place*: **1.** *seat, chair, stool, bench,* Il.19.77, Od.3.7; ἀγοραί τε καὶ ἕδραι 8.16, cf. 3.31; *seat of honour,* περὶ μέν σε τίον... ἕδρῃ τε κρέασίν τε Il.8.162, 12. 311; ἕδραις γεραίρειν τινά X.*Cyr.*8.1.39; τιμίαν ἕ. ἔχειν A.*Eu.*855; *throne,* ἐκβαλεῖν ἕδρας Κρόνου Id.*Pr.*203; θακεῖν παγκρατεῖς ἕ. to sit on an almighty *throne*, ib.391, cf. *Pers.*466. **2.** *seat, abode,* freq. in pl., Pi.*O.*7.76, *P.*11.63, etc.; esp. of the gods, *sanctuary, temple,* Id. *I.*7(6).44, A.*Ag.*596, etc.; also νέοικος ἕ. *station* for ships, Pi.*O.*5.8; ναύλοχοι ἕδραι S.*Aj.*460: periphr., ἕδραισι Θεράπνας Pi.*P.*11.63; Παρνησοῦ ἕδραι A.*Eu.*11, cf. E.*Tr.*557 (lyr.); βλεφάρων ἕ. the eye, Id.*Rh.* 8 (anap.); ὄμματος ἕ. ib.554 (lyr.). **3.** *seat* or *place* of anything, ἐξ ἕδρας out of its *right place*, Id.*Ba.*928, cf. Plu.*Fab.*3; καταναγκάσαι ἐς ἕδρην Hp.*Mochl.*38; ὁ ἥλιος ἐκλιπὼν τὴν ἕ. Hdt.7.37; τὴν τοῦ ἥπατος ἕ., σπλάγχνου, etc., Pl.*Ti.*67b, 72c, etc.; ἐκ τῆς ἕ. ὠθεῖν ib.79b; ἔχειν ἕδραν to keep its *place*, Arist.*Mete.*356ᵃ4; μεταθέσεις ἐξ ἕδρας ἀτόμων Epicur.*Fr.*61; ἕδραν στρέφειν to *wriggle*, Thphr.*Char.*27.14; στοὰν εἰς τὴν ἀρχαίαν ἕ. ἐπαναγαγεῖν D.C.57.21; *base*, Plu.*Demetr.*21: metaph. in Rhet., D.H.*Dem.*31, etc.; of a plant, *Gp.*5.9.9. **4.** ἡ ἕ. τοῦ ἵππου *the back* of the horse, *on which the rider sits*, X.*Eq.*5.5, 12.9, *Eq. Mag.*4.1. **5.** in pl., *quarters* of the sky in which omens appear, A.*Ag.*118 (lyr.), E.*HF*596. **6.** *seat* of a physiological process, ἕ. ἀναθρέψεως Gal.18(2).105. **II.** *sitting*, esp. of suppliants, ἕδραν ἔχειν προστρόπαιον A.*Eu.*41, cf. S.*OT*13, *OC*112. **2.** *sitting still,* Hp.*Aër.*20: hence, *inactivity, delay,* περιημέκτεε τῇ ἕδρῃ Hdt.9.41; ἀχθομένων τῇ ἕ. Th.5.7; οὐχ ἕδρας ἀκμή S.*Aj.*811; οὐχ ἕδρας ἀγών E.*Or.*1291; οὐχ ἕδρας ἔργον B.*Fr.*11; also οἰκίης ἕδρῃ *sitting* at home, Herod.4.92. **3.** *position,* γονυπετεῖς ἕδραι kneeling, E.*Ph.*293 (lyr.); βέλεος ἕδρη *place occupied by* a weapon which fixes itself in the skull, Hp.*VC*7. **4.** *sitting, session* of a council, etc., εὐθὺς ἐξ ἕδρας when he rose from *the sitting*, S.*Aj.*780 (but ἐξ ἕδρας ἀνίσταται ib.788, means from *quietude*); ἕδραν ποιεῖν to hold *a sitting*, And.1. 111, cf. *IG*1².110.41. **III.** *seat, breech, fundament,* Hdt.2.87, Hp. *Aph.*5.22, Ar.*Th.*133, etc.; of birds and animals, *rump*, Arist.*HA* 633ᵇ8, Simon *Eq.*9, etc. **IV.** Geom., *face* of a regular solid, *Theol. Ar.*37. **-άζω**, *cause to sit, place,* ἐπὶ πλευρᾶς D.H.*Comp.*6; ἄλλυδις *AP*15.24 (Simm.); *settle, establish,* Jul.*Or.*5.165a, Procl. *Inst.*64, Simp.*in Ph.*528.21, Sch.A.R.4.947:—Med. or Pass., *to be seated* or *fixed*, Callix.1, Haussoullier *Milet* p.163, Porph.*Marc.*19, Dam.*Pr.*138; ἡδρασμένος *secure*, θρόνος D.Chr.1.78, cf. Sor.2.22.

ἕδρᾰθον, ες, ε, poet. aor. 2 of δαρθάνω.

ἑδραῖος, α, ον, also ος, ον Pl.*R.*407b, Plu.2.288d:—*sitting, sedentary*, of persons or their occupations, ἔργον Hp.*Art.*53; οἱ πολλοὶ τῶν τὰς τέχνας ἐχόντων ἑδραῖοί εἰσι X.*Lac.*1.3; ἑ. ἀρχαί, opp. στρατεῖαι, Pl. *R.*407b; ἑ. βίος *AP*11.42 (Crin.). **2.** ἑδραία ῥάχις the horse's back *on which the rider sits*, E.*Rh.*783. **II.** *steady, steadfast,* κάθησ' ἑδραία Id.*Andr.*266; δεῖ τὴν γυναῖκα ὥσπερ κύβον ἑδραῖον εἶναι Plu.2.288d, cf. 952d; κύβος -ότατον σῶμα Ti.Locr.98c; ἑ. βάσεις Pl.*Ti.*59d; ἑδραιότατον στοιχεῖον εἶναι τὴν γῆν Heraclit.*All.*41; ὃν τὸ πάντων -ότατον Plot.6.2.8; ἑ. ὕπνος *sound* sleep, Hp.*Epid.*6.4.15; of a cup, Ath.11. 496a: metaph. in Rhet., *firmly based*, κατάληξις Demetr.*Eloc.*19, cf. Longin.40.4. Adv. -αίως *firmly*, Ath.Mech.36.10, Hdn.3.14.5; *steadily*, Procl.*Hyp.*3.21. **2.** *permanently appointed*, *PStrassb.*40. 11 (vi A.D.).

ἑδραι-ότης, ητος, ἡ, *stability*, Corn.*ND*14, Procl.*in Prm.*p.794 S., *in Ti.*2.49 D. **II.** *sedentary occupation*, D.Chr.7.110. **-όω**, *make stable*, Hdn.Gr.1.453:—Pass., *become* or *be stable*, Ps.-Luc. *Philopatr.*16. **-ωμα**, ατος, τό, *stay, support,* τῆς ἀληθείας 1*Ep.Ti.* 3.15. **-ωσις**, εως, ἡ, *establishing*, Tz.*Il.*120.11.

ἕδρᾰκον, aor. 2 of δέρκομαι.

ἕδρᾱμα, ατος, τό, = ἕδρα I, *IG*4.951.115 (Epid.).

ἕδρᾰμον, aor. 2 of τρέχω.

ἕδρᾰνον, τό, poet. form of ἕδρα, *seat, abode, dwelling*, Πελασγῶν Hes. *Fr.*212, cf. Orph.*H.*18.7; ἕ. κόσμου ib.26.4: mostly in pl., A.*Pers.*4, *Supp.*103, S.*OC*176, 233, *Pae.Delph.*5, Maiist.36; ἀλλ' ἄνα ἐξ ἑδράνων rise from thy *rest* or *idleness*, S.*Aj.*192; Trag. only in lyr. exc. Id. *Fr.*1128.7 γῆ ἑδράνων ἔρημος, which is Stoic. **2.** *chair*, Hsch. **II.** *stay, support*, said of an anchor, in sg., *AP*6.28 (Jul.).

ἑδρᾰνῶς, = στερεῶς, Eust.769.23, 29.

ἕδρ-ασμα, ατος, τό, = ἕδρα, E.*Fr.*305, Ph.1.336, *PMag.Par.*1.1153 (pl.). **II.** Pythag. name for *eight*, *Theol.Ar.*55. **-ασμός**, ὁ, *placing in position*, πίθων *Gp.*6.2 tit. **-αστέον**, (ἑδράζω) *one must place*, ib.6.2.2. **II.** (ἑδράζομαι) *one must sit*, Sch.Il.23. 205. **-αστικός**, ή, όν, *establishing, making stable,* δυνάμεις Procl. *in Ti.*3.138 D., cf. Dam.*Pr.*138; τοῦ δημιουργοῦ ἀγαθότης Simp.*in Ph.* 1355.6. **II.** = ἑδρικός, φάρμακα Orib.*Eup.*4.12.

ἑδρήεις, εσσα, εν, = ἑδραῖος, Hsch. **ἕδρησα**, Ion. aor. 1 of δράω.

ἑδρ-ίας, ου, *blowing steadily*, of wind, Hsch. **-ιάω**, *seat* or *set*:— Pass., *sit*, only in Ep. forms ἑδριόωνται Hes.*Th.*388; ἑδριόωντο Il.10. 198, Od.7.98; ἑδριάασθαι 3.35. **II.** intr. in Act., *sit*, Theoc.17.19, A.R.3.170. **-ικός**, ή, όν, *belonging to the anus*, Heliod.ap.Orib. 48.58.7, Crito ap.Gal.13.306, Aët.14.3, etc. **-ιον**, τό, Dim. of ἕδρα II. 4, Hsch. **2.** Dim. of ἕδρα I. 3, Id. s.v. ἑδώλια. **-ίς**· ἑδραῖος, Id. **-ισο**· καθῆσο, Id. **-ίτης** [ῑ], ου, ὁ, *suppliant sitting* on the hearth, Suid., *EM*316.53 (-ηστής Zonar.).

ἑδρο-διαστολεύς, έως, ὁ, *instrument for widening the passage of the anus*, Heliod.ap.Orib.44.23.66, Leonidas ap.Paul.Aeg.6.78, Gal.19. 110. **-στρόφος**, ὁ, *wrestler who throws his adversary*, Argive fashion, *by a cross-buttock*, Theoc.24.111.

ἐδύνη, = ὀδύνη, Greg.Cor.p.597 S.

ἔδω, old Ep. pres. (also Hp.*VM*4 (v.l.), Theoc.5.128), for which in Att. **ἐσθίω** is used, Ep. inf. ἔδμεναι, ἐέδμεναι Emp.128.10 (s.v.l.): impf. ἔδον, Ion. 3 sg. ἔδεσκε Il.22.501: fut. ἔδομαι 18.271, Od.9.369, Theoc.3.53: pf. part. ἐδηδώς Il.17.542, *h.Merc.*560:—Pass., pf. ἐδήδοται Od.22.56: aor. 1 subj. ἐδεσθῇ dub. l. in Hp.*Vict.*2.54:—for the Att. forms, v. sub ἐσθίω; cf. also ἔσθω:—*eat*, εἰωθότες ἔδμεναι ἄδην Il. 5.203; ὅσσα τοι ἐκπέποται καὶ ἐδήδοται Od.22.56; of worms, Il.22. 509, cf. Od.21.395; κύτισόν τε καὶ αἴγιλον αἶγες ἔδοντι Theoc.5. 128.—Rare in Com., Alc.Com.36, Eub.28; also E.*Cyc.*245. **II.** *eat up, devour,* esp. in phrases, βίοτον καὶ κτήματα, οἶκον, χρήματα ἔ., Od.2.123, 16.431, 389; ἡμέτερον κάματον νήποινον ἔδουσι 14.417. **III.** metaph., καμάτῳ τε καὶ ἄλγεσι θυμὸν ἔδοντες 9.75, cf. 10.379, Il.24. 129, Semon.1.24 (s.v.l.).

ἐδωγαθή· ἡ τροφή, Hsch.

ἐδωδή, ἡ, *food, meat, victuals*, Il.19.167, Od.3.70, Hp.*Acut.*47, X. *Hier.*1.19, etc.; ἐ. καὶ πόσις Pl.*Lg.*782e, cf. *R.*350a, al.: pl., τῶν.. περὶ ἐδωδὰς ἡδονῶν ib.389e, cf. 519b. **2.** *forage, fodder* for cattle, Il.8.504. **3.** *bait* for fish, Theoc.21.43. **II.** *act of eating*, ὀδόντας ἔχει... ἐδωδῆς χάριν Arist.*PA*683ᵃ4; τῇ ἐ. τοῦ βοὸς [χαίρει] ὁ λέων Id.*EN*1118ᵃ20; πουλύποδος Jul.*Or.*6.181a, al. **2.** *meal*, ἐπὶ μιᾶς ἐ. Arist.*HA*596ᵃ4. **3.** [ἀετὸς] ἀχθόμενος τῇ ἐ. wearied with *feeding* the young birds, ib.563ᵃ22.

ἐδώδιμος, ον, Thphr.*CP*6.11.10, 6.12.12; η, ον Hdt.2.92:—*eatable*, Hdt. l.c., 3.108, etc.; ἐδώδιμα *eatables, provisions,* Th.7.39, Arist.*Rh.*1373ᵃ30, Porph.*Abst.*1.12, etc. **II.** *prepared for eating, cooked*, Orib.15.1.8.

ἐδωδός, όν, *given to eating* (rather than drinking), Hp.*Aër.*7.

ἑδωλι-άζω, *furnish with seats*, *IG*11(2).287 *A*81 (Delos, iii B.C.), Lycurg.*Fr.*2, Poll.4.121; ἡδωλιασμένη θέα *IG*2².1176.12. **II.** *lay a floor*, Suid. **-ον**, τό, *seat*, mostly pl., *abodes*, πωλικά, νυμφικά, A.*Th.*455 (lyr.), *Ch.*71 (lyr.); ἀρχαιόπλουτα S.*El.*1393 (lyr.), cf. *Fr.* 566: Com. phrase, κριβάνων ἑ. Ar.*Fr.*155. **II.** ἑδώλια, τά, in a ship, a *raised quarter-deck* at the stern, Hdt.1.24, S.*Aj.*1277, E.*Cyc.* 238, *Hel.*1571, Lyc.296; expld. as *rowers' benches* by Hsch., Suid., Eust.153.35. **2.** sg., *step of the mast*, Arist.*Mech.*851ᵃ40. **III.** in a theatre, *semicircle of benches*, Poll.4.132 (on the breathing, cf. *EM*317.9; ἐδ- in codd. of A.*Th.* l.c., E. ll. cc.).

ἑδώλιος or **ἑδωλιός**, ὁ, a *bird* in Sch.Ar.*Av.*884, Hsch.

ἕδωλον, τό, = ἑδώλιον II, Lyc.1320.

ἐδωλός, name of a λόχος at Sparta, Hsch.

ἕε, poet. for ἕ, *him*, acc. of οὗ. **ἔεδνα, ἐεδνόω, ἐεδνωτής**, Ep. for ἐδν-. **ἐεικοσάβοιος, ἐείκοσι, -κόσορος, -κοστός**, Ep. for εἰκοσ-. **ἐεικώς**, v. εἴκω. **ἐείλεον**, v. εἴλω. **ἔειπα, ἔειπον**, Ep. for εἶπα, εἶπον.

ἔεις, Ep. for εἷς, Hes.*Th.*145, *IGRom.*1.1299.

ἐεισάμην, ἐείσαο, part. ἐεισάμενος, Ep. aor. of εἴδομαι, v. *εἴδω :— but **ἐείσατο, ἐεισάσθην**, v. εἶσομαι II.

ἐέλδομαι, ἐέλδωρ, Ep. for ἔλδ-. **ἐέλμεθα, ἐελμένος**, v. εἴλω. **ἐέλπομαι**, Ep. for ἔλπομαι. **ἐέλσαι**, v. εἴλω. **ἐεργάθω, ἔεργε, ἐεργμένος, ἐέργνυμι, ἐέργω**, Ep. for εἰργ-. **ἐερμένος, ἔερτο**, v. εἴρω. **ἐέρση, ἐερσήεις**, Ep. for ἐρσ-. **ἐέρχατο**, v. εἴργω. **ἐέσσατο** (A), Ep. 3 sg. aor. 1 Med. of ἵζω; v. sub ἐφίζω I. **ἐέσσατο** (B), Ep. 3 sg. aor. Med. of ἕννυμι. **ἔεστο**, Ep. 3 sg. plpf. Pass. of ἕννυμι.

ἐετῶς, *easily*, Hsch., Suid. **ἐεχμένη**· συνεχομένη, Hsch. **ἐϜέρην**, v. εἴρω. **ἔζελεν**· ἔβαλεν, Id. (cf. ζέλλω). **ἔζινεν**· ἐπεσβέννυεν, Id.

ἕζομαι, imper. ἕζευ Il.24.522: impf. and aor. 2 ἑζόμην: aor. 1 Pass. ἕσθην, only ᾗ 'σθῶ; S.*OC*195 (s.v.l.):—*seat oneself, sit*, in Hom. only pres. and impf., εἰνὶ θρόνῳ Il.15.150; ἐς θρόνους Od.4.51; ἐπὶ δίφρῳ Il.6.354; κατὰ κλισμούς Od.3.389; ποτὶ βωμόν 22.379; ἐπὶ βάθρου S.*OC*100, cf. Ar.*Ra.*682 (s.v.l.); ἕ. ἐς Κολοφῶνα Mimn.9; ἀμφὶ κλάδοις E.*Ph.*1516 (anap.): c. acc. only, τόδ' ἕζετο μαντεῖον A. *Eu.*3; εἰρεσίας ζυγὸν ἑζόμενον S.*Aj.*249 (lyr.); ἐπὶ χθονὶ ... ἑζέσθην they *sank* to the earth, of a pair of scales, Il.8.74; once in Hdt., ἐκ τοῦ μέσου ἡμῖν ἕζεσθε 8.22, and in late Prose, J.*AJ*18.6.6, Luc.*Syr. D.*31, *Astr.*10; in Att. Prose καθέζομαι was always used. **2.** *crouch*, in a posture of defence, Il.22.275, Od.14.31. **3.** *sink* to the ground, *collapse*, Il.13.653, 14.495. **II.** Act., ἕζω *set, place*, is not found: for εἷσα, εἰσάμην, εἵσομαι, εἷμαι, v. ἵζω. (Cf. ἕδος.)

ἑή, fem. of ἑός. **ἑή**, exclam., v. ἔ. **ἐήλακεν**· ἐλήφθη, Hsch. **ἔην**, Ep. 3 sg. impf. of εἰμί (*sum*), Hom.: 1st pers., only Il.11.762 vulg.; v. εἰμί. **ἐήνδᾰνε**, Ep. 3 sg. impf. Act. of ἁνδάνω. **ἑῆος**, gen. masc. of ἐΰς (q.v.); cf. ἑός. **ἕης**, Ep. gen. of ὅς, *who*, Il.16.208:—but **ἑῆς**, gen. fem. of ἑός, *his*. **ἔησθα**, Ep. 2 sg. impf. of εἰμί (*sum*). **ἔησι**, Ep. 3 sg. subj. pres. of εἰμί (*sum*). **ἐητύς**, ύος, ἡ, *goodness*, Hsch. **ἔθα**· πάλιν, Id.

ἐθάς, άδος, ὁ, ἡ, (ἔθος) *accustomed*, ἐ. γενέσθαι Hp.*Mul.*1.12; ἐ. γενέσθαι τινός Th.2.44; εἶναι Plu.*Oth.*5; of persons, *familiar*, Philostr. *VA*8.30: c. dat., τῇ νούσῳ Hp.*Morb.Sacr.*12, cf. Opp.*H.*5.499. II. of things, *customary, usual*, νοῦσοι ἐ. ἀπὸ νεότητος Hp.*Mul.*2.125; ἡδονή Ph.1.316. III. *tame*, Them.*Or.*22.273c.

ἐθεῖν· ἐξ ἔθους ἔρχεσθαι, Hsch.

ἔθειρα, ἡ, *hair*, poet. Noun, Hom. only in Il., and always in pl., either of *a horse's mane*, 8.42; or of the *horsehair crest* on helmets, 16.795, 19.382. II. later sg., *hair of the head*, Pi.*I.*5(4).9, A.*Pers.* 1062 (lyr.), E.*Hel.*1124 (lyr.), Theoc.5.91, etc.: also pl., *h.Ven.*228, A.*Ch.*175, E.*Hel.*632, Euph.23, *IG*3.1376, etc.; of a lion's *mane*, Theoc.25.244; porcupine's *quills*, Opp.*C.*3.395; a bird's *feathers*, ib. 123; κρόκου θυόεσσαν ἔθειραν, of the *filiform stigmas* of the saffron, Mosch.2.68.

ἐθειράζω, *have long hair*, Theoc.1.34.

ἐθειράς, άδος, ἡ, = ἔθειρα, an old reading in Od.16.176, for γενειάδες, cf. Sch.Theoc.1.34.

ἐθειρολόγος, ὁ, *tweezer*, *Hermes* 38.282 (s.v.l.).

ἐθείρω, *tend, till*, once in Hom., χαίρει δέ μιν (sc. ἀλωήν) ὅστις ἐθείρῃ Il.21.347:—but in Pass., χρυσέαις φολίδεσσιν ἐθείρεται he *is decked* with golden scales, Orph.*A.*929, cf. Hsch.

ἐθελ-ακρίβεια [ῐ], ἡ, *pretence of accuracy*, Sch.Luc.*Gall.*32. **-ακρῑβής,** ές, *making pretence of accuracy*, Sch.Luc.*Vit.Auct.*21. **-άστειος,** ον, *aiming at fashion, foppish*, Hld.7.10. **-εχθρέω,** *bear a grudge against*, ὁ ἐμφανισθεὶς ἂν ἐθελεχθρῇ τῷ μηνύσαντι Charond.ap.Stob. 4.2.24. **-εχθρος,** ον, *bearing one a grudge*, Cratin.407, Ph.2.269. Adv. -ρως, ἔχειν πρός τινα D.39.36, cf. Ph.2.120, Paus.4.4.4. **-ημός,** όν, *willing, voluntary*, Hes.*Op.*118, Call.*Dian.*31, A.R.2.656. Adv. -μῶς Hsch. **-ήμων,** ον, gen. ονος, = foreg., Pl.*Cra.*406a.

ἐθελο-δουλεία (-ία Suid.), ἡ, *voluntary subjection*, Pl.*Smp.*184c, D.C.*Fr.*17.2, Procl.*in Prm.*p.737S. **-δουλέω,** *be* or *become a slave willingly*, D.C.45.35. **-δουλος,** ον, *serving voluntarily*, Pl.*R.*562d, Ph.1.376, Aristaenet.2.2. Adv. -λως, ἔχειν Plu.*Arat.*25. **-θρησκεία,** ἡ, *will-worship, self-chosen service*, *Ep.Col.*2.23. **-κᾰκέω,** of soldiers who let themselves be beaten, *play the coward deliberately*, Hdt. 1.127, 5.78, 9.67, Plb.4.38.6, Luc.*Somn.*18, Paus.1.35.2, etc. II. *do wrong deliberately, act of malice prepense*, Ph.2.523, al., *PMasp.*151. 216 (vi A.D.); ἐ. ἐπὶ συμφοραῖς *exult wrongfully* over..., Ph.2.73, cf. 539. **-κάκησις** [ᾰ], εως, ἡ, *wilful neglect of duty*, Plb.3.68.10; εἰς ἐ. ἄγειν to refer a thing to *malice prepense*, Id.27.15.13. **-κᾰκία,** ἡ, = foreg., Suid. **-κᾰκος,** ον, = κακὰ θέλων, Hsch. II. *guilty of wilful cowardice*, of soldiers, τὸ τῶν στρατιωτῶν ἐ. D.H.9.7. Adv. -κως App.*Ital.*7 *Fr.* **-κᾰλος,** ον, *showing goodwill*, Phld.*Herc.* 1457.11. **-κίνδῡνος,** ον, *courting danger, foolhardy*, Poll.3.134. Adv. -νως App.*Pun.*120. **-κωφέω,** *affect deafness*, ἐπείγεσθαι S.E.*M.*11.202, Str.1.2.30, Procop.*Goth.*4.12. **-κωφία,** ἡ, *pretended deafness*, Phld.*Rh.*2.118S. **-κωφος,** ον, *pretending deafness, unwilling to hear*, Suid.

ἐθελοντ-ηδόν, Adv. *voluntarily, spontaneously*, Th.8.98, D.C.53.8; f.l. for sq., Plb.6.31.2. **-ήν,** Adv. *voluntarily*, Hdt.1.5, X.*Mem.* 2.1.3, Plb.1.49.5, al. **-ήρ,** ῆρος, ὁ, *volunteer*, Od.2.292. **-ής,** οῦ, ὁ, Prose form of foreg. (used by S.*Aj.*24), Hdt.5.104, 110, *IG*1[2].97. 15, Th.1.60, And.1.3: as Adj., ἐ. φίλος X.*An.*1.6.9 (dub.); τῶν ἐ. τριηράρχων D.18.99. II. = δεικηλιστής, Eust.884.27. **-ί,** Adv. = ἐθελοντηδόν, Th.8.2, Plb.2.22.5, D.S.18.53, etc. **-ως,** = foreg., Sch.Il.19.79.

ἐθελό-πονος, ον, *willing to work*, X.*Cyr.*2.1.22, Ael.*NA*4.43. **-πορνος,** ον, *voluntary catamite*, Anacr.21.7. **-πρόξενος,** ον, *one who voluntarily charges himself with the office of* πρόξενος (q.v.) to a foreigner or foreign state, Th.3.70. **-ρήτωρ,** ορος, ὁ, *would-be orator*, *AB*95.18. **-σέβεια,** ἡ, gloss on ἐθελοθρησκεία, Hsch. **-συχνος,** ον, *fond of repetition, a bore*, Crates Com.48 (s.v.l.).

ἐθελ-ουργέω, *work freely, indefatigably*, Ael.*NA*7.13. **-ουργός,** όν, *willing to work, indefatigable*, X.*Eq.*10.17, Ael.*NA*4.43; τὸ ἐ. Ph. 2.448. Adv. -γῶς Poll.3.121. **-ούσιος,** α, ον, *voluntary*, X.*Cyr.* 4.2.11; ἀνάγκη ἐ. Id.*Smp.*8.13; *of one's free will*, Pherecyd.(?)98J.; ἐθελούσιον ἱκετεύσαντα D.C.43.12; ἐθελουσία [τῇ προνοίᾳ] καὶ κατὰ γνώμην Jul.*Or.*5.166b. II. of things, *optional*, [τὸ ἐρᾶν] ἐθελούσιόν ἐστι love is *a matter of free choice*, X.*Cyr.*5.1.10; γνώμη Ph.2. 482; ἐθελουσίᾳ (sc. γνώμῃ) *voluntarily*, Hierocl.p.33A.: regul. Adv. -ίως X.*Hier.*11.12.

ἐθελοφῐλόσοφος, ον, *would-be philosopher*, *EM*722.17.

ἐθέλω or **θέλω** (v. infr.), Ep. subj. ἐθέλωμι Il.1.549, 9.397: impf. ἤθελον 14.120, etc.; Ep. and Lyr. ἔθελον 6.336, Thgn.606, B.10.73; Ion. ἐθέλεσκον Il.13.106, Hdt.6.12: fut. ἐθελήσω Il.18.262, etc.; θελήσω Antipho 5.99: aor. 1 ἠθέλησα Hdt.2.2, etc.; Ep. ἐθέλησα Il.18. 396; imper. θέλησον A.*Pr.*783; subj. θελήσῃ ib.1028, X.*Cyr.*2.4.19, etc.; opt. θελήσαιμι S.*OC*1133; part. θελήσας Id.*OT*649 (lyr.): pf. ἠθέληκα X.*Cyr.*5.2.9, Aeschin.2.139, D.47.5; τεθέληκα (Alexandrian acc. to Phryn.307) Lxx *Ps.*40(41).12, Phld.*Rh.*2.76S., S.E.*M.*2.37: plpf. ἠθελήκει X.*HG*6.5.21; ἐτεθελήκεσαν D.C.44.26 codd. (elsewh. ἠθελήκεσαν as 46.47):—θέλω is never found in Hom. or Hes. exc. Il.1.277 (dub.), ὅττι θέλοιεν Od.15.317 as v.l. (ἅσσ' ἐθέλοιεν Aristarch.), nor in Aeol.; rarely in early Ep. and Eleg., θέλοι *h.Ap.*46, θέλει Sol.27.12; but is found in Ion. Inscrr., *SIG*45.16 (Halic., v B.C.), 1037.7 (Milet., iv B.C.), and in Semon.7.13, Hippon.22B, Anacr.92:—both forms in codd. of Hdt. and Hp. and in Heraclit. and Democr., also in Pi. and B.: Trag. never use ἐθέλω exc. in augmented forms, ἤθελον, -ησα: Com. never use θέλω exc. in phrases such as ἢν θεὸς θέλῃ, εἰ θεὸς θέλοι, Ar.*Pl.*347, *Ra.*533, or parodies of Trag.: early Att. Inscrr. have ἐθέλω *IG*1[2].6.41, etc., till 250 B.C., when θέλω becomes common: Att. Prose writers rarely use θέλω exc. in phrases such as ἂν θεὸς θέλῃ Din.2.3 or after a long vowel, e.g. μὴ θελῆσαι Th.5.72, μὴ θελήσας Is. 8.11, μὴ θέλοντας And.1.22, τῷ θέλοντι Id.4.7, etc.; but θέλω Antipho 3.4.3, θελήσουσιν Id.5.99: in later Gr. θέλω is regular exc. in the augmented forms; ἐθέλω is not found in Lxx or NT:—*to be willing* (of consent rather than desire, v. βούλομαι I), but also generally, *wish*, Od.3.324:—Constr.: abs., esp. in part., ἐθέλων ἐθέλουσαν ἀνήγαγεν ib.272; εἰ σύ γε σῷ θυμῷ ἐθέλοις Il.23.894; ἀλλά μοι ἤθελε θυμός Od.11.566: freq. folld. by inf. pres. or aor., *wish to...*, Il.7.364, etc.: with inf. supplied, εἰ δ' ἐθέλεις πεζός (sc. ἰέναι) Od.3.324: c. acc. et inf., *wish that...*, Il.19.274, Hdt.1.3; rarely folld. by ὥστε, E.*Hipp.*1327: later c. ἵνα, *Ev.Matt.*7.12, etc.: not used c. acc. only, exc. when an inf. is easily supplied, εὔκηλος τὰ φράζεαι ἅσσ' ἐθέλησθα (sc. φράζεσθαι) Il.1.554, cf. 9.397, 7.182, Od.14.172; σιτέονται δὲ οὐκ ὅσα ἐθέλουσι (sc. σιτέεσθαι) Hdt.1.71, cf. Th.5.50; εἰ καὶ τῆς ἀξίας ἔλαττον ἐθελήσειέ τις (sc. φράσαι) Jul.*Or.*1.132a: also with neut. Pron. or Adj., τί δὴ θέλων; with what *intent?* A.*Pr.*118. 2. with neg., almost, = δύναμαι, as μίμνειν οὐκ ἐθέλεσκον ἐναντίον they *cared* not to make a stand, i.e. they *were* un*able*, Il.13.106; οὐδ'.. ἤθελε θυμὸς τειρομένοις ἑτάροισιν ἀμυνέμεν 17.702: metaph. of things, of a stream, οὐδ' ἔθελε προρέειν ἀλλ' ἴσχετο *would* not run on, but stopped, 21.366, cf. Od.8.223, 316, *h.Cer.*45; αὔλειοι δ' ἔτ' ἔχειν οὐκ ἐθέλουσι θύραι Sol.4.28; τὰ δένδρα οὐδέν μ' ἐθέλει διδάσκειν Pl.*Phdr.* 230d, cf. *R.*370b (said to be an Att. use, Greg.Cor.p.135S.). 3. part., ἐθέλων or θέλων *willingly, gladly*, Od.3.272, etc. (also πιθοῦ θελήσας S.*OT*649 (lyr.)); οὐκ ἐθέλων, = ἀέκων, Il.4.300; with Art. like ὁ βουλόμενος, *whoever will*, i.e. *any one*, S.*Ph.*619, *Aj.*1146, Pl. *Grg.*508c, etc. 4. θέλεις οὐ θέλεις *nolens volens*, Arr.*Epict.*3.9.16; θέλει οὐ θέλει ib.3.3, M.Ant.11.15. 5. μὴ ἔθελε, c. inf., *do* not, Il.1.277, 2.247, E.*Fr.*174. 6. εἰ θέλεις if you *please*, S.*OT*343. 7. folld. by subj., τί σοι θέλεις δῆτ' εἰκάθω; in what *wilt* thou that I give way to thee? ib.651 (lyr.); θέλεις μείνωμεν αὐτοῦ; Id.*El.*80. 8. *maintain, hold*, c. acc. et inf., Plu.2.883e, Paus.1.4.6. 9. *delight in, love*, ἔν τινι Lxx 1*Ki.*18.22; τινά ib.*Ps.*17(18).20; but οἱ κακῶς τινὰς θέλοντες their ill-*wishers*, *Cat.Cod.Astr.*7.234. 10. *ordain, decree*, ἠθέλησεν [ὁ ἡγεμὼν] τὸν κίνδυνον τῆς προβολῆς εἶναι πρός τινας *CPR* 20.17 (iii A.D.), etc. II. of inanimate things (cf. supr. I. 2), 1. to express a *future* event, like our *will* or *shall*, εἰ ἐθελήσει ἀναβῆναι ἡ τυραννίς Hdt.1.109; εἰ ἐθελήσει ἐκτρέψαι τὸ ῥέεθρον ὁ Νεῖλος Id.2.11; εἰ θέλει τοι μηδὲν ἀντίξοον καταστῆναι Id.7.49, cf. Pl.*R.*370b, etc.:—in this sense, very rarely of living things, οὐ δοῦναι θέλοι, = οὐκ ἂν δοίη, A.*Eu.*429; εἴπερ..οὗτός ⟨σ'⟩ ἐθέλει κρατῆσαι Ar.*V.*536, cf. Pi.*N.*7.90, Pl.*R.*375a. 2. *to be naturally disposed, to be wont* or *accustomed*, c. inf., συμβάσιες ἰσχυραὶ οὐκ ἐ. συμμένειν Hdt.1.74; μεγάλα πρήγματα μεγάλοισι κινδύνοισι ἐ. καταιρέεσθαι Id.7.50; αἱ πλευραὶ οὐκ ἐθέλουσιν ἐς τὸ εὐρὺ αὔξεσθαι Hp.*Art.*41; οὐκ ἐ. αἱ γνῶμαι ... ὁμοῖαι εἶναι Th.2.89; τοῦτ' ἐνδελεχὲς ἐ. γίγνεσθαι Arist.*Mete.*347^{a}5, cf. *Metaph.*1013^{b}27, al.; οὐ θέλει ζῆν, of premature births, Id.*HA*575^a 28. 3. in phrases expressive of meaning, τὸ θέλει σημαίνειν τὸ τέρας Hdt.1.78; τὸ θέλει τὸ ἔπος εἶπαι Id.6.37; τὸ θέλει τὰ δῶρα λέγειν Id.4.131; τὸ ἔπος τοῦτο ἐθέλει λέγειν ὡς.. Id.2.13. 4. τοῦ θέλοντος, = τοῦ θελήματος, S.*OC*1220 (lyr., s.v.l.).

ἕθεν (i.e. ϝέθεν, cf. A.D.*Pron.*77.4), Ep., Lyr., and Trag. gen. for ἕο, οὗ, masc. and fem., *his, her, of him, of her*, Hom., etc.; αὐτοῦ ἕθεν, = ἑαυτοῦ, *IG*4.952.106 (Epid.). II. = ἑκάς, Hsch.

ἐθημο-λογέω, *gather customarily*, *AP*9.551 (Antiphil.). **-σύνη,** ἡ, *custom*, Hsch., Suid.

ἐθήμων, ον, gen. ονος, *accustomed*, c. dat., ἐλπίδι Musae.312: c. gen., κυδοιμοῦ Nonn.*D.*36.464. 2. *customary*, ib.1.433, al.

ἔθην, aor. 1 Pass. of ἵημι: but **ἔθην,** aor. 2 Act. of τίθημι.

ἐθ-ίζω, poet. **εἰθ-** *Carm.Aur.*35: Att. fut. ἐθιῶ X.*Cyr.*3.3.53: aor. εἴθισα D.20.68: pf. εἴθικα Pl.*Men.*70b, X.*HG*6.1.15:—Pass., fut. ἐθισθήσομαι D.H.4.11: aor. εἰθίσθην Ar.*V.*512, Hp.*Art.*41, Pl.*Lg.*681b: pf. εἴθισμαι E.*Med.*122 (anap.), Th.1.77; 3 pl. ἐθίδαται Hp.*Acut.*36; late ἤθισμαι *IG*12(5).662.14 (Syros, ii A.D.): plpf. εἴθιστο X.*Ages.*11. 2: (ἔθος):—*accustom*, ἐ. αὐτὸν χαίρειν Pl.*Grg.*510d, cf. Isoc.3.57; τὸ προαιρεῖσθαι..πότερον ἂν ἐθίζοιμεν X.*Mem.*2.1.2: c. inf., ἐθίσας ἀεί τι λήξεσθαι App.*Hann.*44: c. acc. cogn., ἔθη ἐ. πονηρά Pl.*Lg.*706d; ἐ. τινὰ ταὐτά X.*HG*6.1.15; ἐ. τινὰ πρός τι Luc.*Anach.*20:—Pass., *to be* or *become accustomed* or *used to* do, c. inf., Hp.*Art.*41, Ar.*V.*512, Lys. 14.31, Th.1.77, etc.; εἰθισμένος ἀναισχυντεῖν And.2.4: c. acc. cogn., ἐθίζεσθαι ἔθη Pl.*Lg.*681b; ἐθίζεσθαι σὺν ἔθει τινί X.*Cyr.*1.6.33 (s.v.l.); ἐθίζεσθαι πρός τι Arist.*EN*1119^{a}25; τι ib.1121^{a}23; τινί Thphr.*CP*5.9. 11: abs., καθότι εἴθισται as *is the custom*, *PPetr.*3p.116 (iii B.C.); κατὰ τὰ εἰθισμένα *BGU*1073.12 (iii A.D.), etc.:—in Plu.*Lyc.*12, Bekk. restored εἰθίζοντο from Porph. for the intr. Act. εἴθιζον. II. intr. in Act., *become accustomed*, M.Ant.10.22: c. inf., Id.12.2: c. acc., ἔθιζε καὶ ὅσα ἀπογινώσκεις ib.6: with inf. supplied, ὅπως ἀναγραφῇ τὸ ψήφισμα οὗ καὶ τὰ ἄλλα ἐθίζουσιν (sc. ἀναγράψαι) *BCH*48.370 (Thaumaci, i B.C.). **-ικός,** ή, όν, *arising from habit*, ἀρεταί Plu.2.3a. **-ιμος,** ον, *accustomed, usual*, ἔθιμόν [ἐστί] μοι D.S.29.32; τὰν ἐ. τοῖς ἐφήβοις θυσίαν *Supp.Epigr.*1.327.3 (Callatis); ὁ ἐ. Ῥωμαίων ὅρκος *BGU*581.5 (ii A.D.), etc.; τὸ ἐ. *usage*, A.D.*Synt.*77.27; τὰ ἐ. *customs*, Ath.4. 151e; κατὰ τὰ ἐ. *IG*12(7).237.26 (Amorgos, i B.C.). Adv. -μως A.D. *Pron.*78.25. **-ισμα,** ατος, τό, (ἐθίζω) *custom, habit*, Pl.*Lg.* 793d. **-ισμός,** ὁ, *accustoming, habituation*, Arist.*EN*1098^{b}4, al.; τὰ κατ' ἐθισμόν τινος Lxx *Ge.*31.35; πρός τι Hierocl.*in CA* 26 p.479M.:

pl., *habits*, Arist.*Pol.*1331ᵇ6; *usages*, Posidipp.25, Plb.1.17.11; οἱ ἐξ ἀρχῆς ἐ. *PTeb.*40.20 (ii B.C.); οἱ νόμοι καὶ οἱ ἐ. Phld.*Piet.*102, cf. *IG*2².1043.30 (i B.C.); οἱ πολύτροποι ἐ. τῶν λέξεων *customary modes* of speech, Epicur.*Nat.*28.1, al. **-ιστέον**, *one must accustom*, τῇ γνώμῃ ὑπηρετεῖν ἐ. τὸ σῶμα X.*Mem.*2.1.28, cf. Pl.*R.*396a, etc. **-ιστός**, ή, όν, *to be acquired by habit*, ἀρετή, opp. μαθητόν, Arist.*EN*1099ᵃ9, al. 2. *acquired by habit*, τὸ ἐ. ἐν τοῖς ἡδέσιν Id.*Rh.*1369ᵇ16.

ἐθμή, ἡ, *vapour*, Hsch. **ἐθμοί**· πολλοί, δεσμοί, πλόκαμοι, Id.

ἐθν-άρχης, ου, ὁ, *ruler of a tribe* or *nation*, Ἄσανδρος ἀντὶ ἐθνάρχου βασιλεὺς ἀναγορευθεὶς Βοσπόρου Luc.*Macr.*17; *sheikh*, *OGI*616.2 (Arabia); of Abraham, Ph.1.513. 2. title of Jewish official, Lxx 1*Ma.*14.47, Str.17.1.13, Nic.Dam.p.143 D., 2*Ep.Cor.*11.32, J.*AJ* 13.6.7. II. Adj., *ruling over nations*, ἐ. θεοί Jul.*Gal.*115d, cf. 143a. **-αρχία**, ἡ, *office of ethnarch*, J.*AJ*17.13.1. **-ηδόν**, Adv. *by nations, as a whole nation*, Lxx 4*Ma.*2.19. **-ικός**, ή, όν, *national*, συστάσεις Plb.30.13.6; διαστάσεις Id.4.21.2; χρεῖαι D.S.18.13; ἰδιότητες Phld.*Rh.*1.154 S.; διαφοραί Str.2.3.1. II. *foreign, gentile*, *Ev.Matt.*5.47; ἐθνικῇ.. ἐν σοφίᾳ *Epigr.Gr.*430.6. Adv. -κῶς, opp. Ἰουδαϊκῶς, *Ep.Gal.*2.14. b. in the Roman Empire, *provincial*, *Cod. Just.*12.63.2.6. III. Gramm., *indicating nationality*, Str.14.2.28, D.T.636.11, A.D.*Synt.*190.20. Adv. -κῶς, παραχθέν ib.5, cf. Str.4. 1.1, D.L.7.56. 2. *dialectal*, ἔθος A.D.*Synt.*46.1. IV. ἐθνικός, ὁ, *tax-collector*, *POxy.*126.13 (vi A.D.). **-ίτης** [ῑ], ου, ὁ, *of the same nation*, Eust.901.9, Suid.; **ἐθνιστής**, Hsch.

ἔθνος, εος, τό: (Ϝέθνος, cf. Il.2.87, 7.115, al.):—*number of people living together, company, body of men*, ἑτάρων ἔ., ἔ. ἑταίρων, *band* of comrades, Il.3.32, 7.115, etc.; ἔθνος λαῶν *host* of men, 13.495; of particular tribes, Λυκίων μέγα ἔ. 12.330; Ἀχαιῶν ἔ. 17.552: pl., ἔθνεα πεζῶν 11.724, cf. 2.91; ἔ. νεκρῶν Od.10.526; of animals, ἔ. μελισσάων, ὀρνίθων, μυιάων, *swarms, flocks*, etc., Il.2.87,459,469; ἔθνη θηρῶν S.*Ph.*1147 (lyr.), *Ant.*344; ἔ. ἀνέρων, γυναικῶν, Pi.*O.*1. 66, *P.*4.252; ἔ. βρότεον, θνατόν, Id.*N.*3.74, 11.42; ἔ. τόδε, of the Erinyes, A.*Eu.*366 (lyr.). 2. after Hom., *nation, people*, τὸ Μηδικὸν ἔ. (γένος being a subdivision of ἔθνος) Hdt.1.101; ἔ. ἠπειρογενές, μαχαιροφόρον, A.*Pers.*43,56 (anap.), etc.; τῶν μηδισάντων ἐθνέων τῶν Ἑλληνικῶν Hdt.9.106. b. later, τὰ ἔ. *foreign, barbarous nations*, opp. Ἕλληνες, Arist.*Pol.*1324ᵇ10; ἔ. νομάδων, of Bedawin, *LW*2203 (Syria); at Athens, athletic *clubs of non-Athenians*, *IG*2. 444, al.; in Lxx, *non-Jews*, *Ps.*2.1, al., cf. *Act.Ap.*7.45; *Gentiles*, τῶν ἐθνῶν τε καὶ Ἰουδαίων ib.14.5, etc.; used of *Gentile Christians*, *Ep. Rom.*15.27. c. at Rome, = *provinciae*, App.*BC*2.13, Hdn.1.2.1, *PStrassb.*22.19 (iii A.D.), D.C.36.41, etc.: so in sg., *province*, ὁ τυραννήσας τοῦ ἔθνους D.Chr.43.11; ὁ ἡγούμενος τοῦ ἔθνους the governor of the *province*, *POxy.*1020.5 (iii A.D.). 3. *class* of men, *caste, tribe*, τὸ Θετταλῶν.. πενεστικὸν ἔ. Pl.*Lg.*776d; ἔθνος κηρυκικόν Id. *Plt.*290b; οἶσθά τι ἔ. ἠλιθιώτερον ῥαψῳδῶν; X.*Smp.*3.6; δημιουργικὸν ἔ. Pl.*Grg.*455b, cf. Arist.*Ath.Fr.*3; ἔ. Βραχμάνων D.S.17.102; τὰ ἱερὰ ἔ. the *orders* of priests, *OGI*90.17 (ii B.C.); *trade-associations* or *guilds*, ἔθνη καὶ ἐργαστήρια *PPetr.*3 p.67 (iii B.C.), al.; *class* in respect to rank or station, οὐ πρὸς τοῦτο βλέποντες.. ὅπως.. ἕν τι ἔ. ἔσται διαφερόντως εὔδαιμον Pl.*R.*420b, cf. 421c, D.21.131. 4. *sex*, θῆλυ, ἄρρεν ἔ., X.*Oec.*7.26. 5. *part, member*, Hp.*Loc.Hom.*1. II. of a single person, *a relation*, Pi.*N.*5.43.

ἐθνοφύλαξ, *gentilicius*, *Gloss.*

ἔθος, εος, τό, (ἔθω) *custom, habit*, ἔ. τὸ πρόσθε τοκήων (but prob. f.l. for ἦθος) A.*Ag.*728 (lyr.); τὸ σύνηθες ἔ. S.*Ph.*894; εἰ τὸ ἔ. συνθήκη Pl.*Cra.*435a; πάτρια ἔ. Id.*Plt.*295a: prov., "ἔ.", φασί, "δευτέρη φύσις" Jul.*Mis.*353a; ἐν ἔθει τῇ πόλει εἶναι to be *the habit*, Th.2.64; ἔ. ἐστίν τινι, c. inf., Cratin.Jun.7.1, Alex.253; ἔθος ἔχειν, c. inf., Plu. *Them.*4; ἔθει *by habit, habitually*, opp. φύσει, Arist.*EN*1179ᵇ21; ἐν ἔθει Id.*Fr.*122; δι' ἔθος, opp. ἐκ γενετῆς, Id.*EN*1154ᵃ33; ἐξ ἔθους ib. 1103ᵃ17; κατὰ τὰ Ῥωμαίων ἔ. *PSI*3.182 (iii A.D.), etc. (σϜέθ-, cf. Lat. *suesco*; v. βεσόν.)

ἐθρίς· τομίας (ταλμ- cod.) κριός, Hsch.; cf. ἴθρις.

ἔθρισεν, v. θερίζω.

ἔθω, *to be accustomed, to be wont*: pres. only in part., κακὰ πόλλ' ἔρδεσκεν ἔθων much ill he wrought *after his wont*, Il.9.540; οὓς παῖδες ἐριδμαίνωσιν ἔθοντες 16.260 (in these passages some Gramm. expld. ἔθων as, = βλάπτων, φθείρων (and it was so used by Call.*Fr.*108), and (in 16.260) ἐρεθίζων, cf. ἔθει· φθείρει, ἐρεθίζει, Hsch., ἐθρίς, ἴθρις): pf. εἴωθα Il.5.766, etc., Ep. and Ion. ἔωθα 8.408, etc., is used as pres.; plpf. εἰώθειν, Ion. ἐώθεα, as impf.; part. εἰωθώς, Ion. ἐωθώς, also in Archipp.48, Araros 19; Dor. 3 pl. pf. ἐθώκατι Hsch.: mostly c. inf., Il.5.766, Hdt.3.31, Th.1.99, etc.: impers., ὡς εἴωθε as *is the custom*, Ar.*Ec.*282; ὥσπερ εἰώθει Plu.*Sull.*9, etc.: freq. abs. in part., of persons, *accustomed, customary, usual*, ἡνιόχῳ εἰωθότι Il.5.231; ὑμῖν.. τοῖς εἰώθοσιν *who are used* [to hear me], S.*Ph.*939; οὐκ ἐωθὼς *praeter morem*, Hdt.1.111; of things, τὰ ἐωθότα νοήματα Id.3.80; ἐν τῷ εἰ. τρόπῳ Pl.*Ap.*27b, etc.: freq. in neut., παρὰ τὸ εἰ. contrary to *custom*, Th.4.17,55; τὰ εἰ. *ordinary things*, Ar.*Ra.*1, Th.2.51, etc.

εἶ, indecl., name of the letter ε, pronounced like the letter itself, Pl.*Cra.*393d, 437a, al., *Michel* 832.46 (Samos, iv B.C.), etc.; later pronounced ῑ, Hdn.Gr.2.390; written ῑ, *BGU*427.15.

εἶ, Dor., = *where*, *IG*9(1).682 (Corc.), 14.352 ii 13 (Halaesa); but **εἶ μήν**, later Greek, = ἦ μήν, Lxx *Ge.*22.17, al., *PTeb.*22.13 (ii B.C.), etc.; Dor. εἰ μάν *IG*5(1).1390.27 (Andania, i B.C.).

εἰ, Att.-Ion. and Arc. (for εἰκ, v. infr. II ad init.), = Dor. and Aeol. αἰ, αἰκ (q.v.), Cypr. ἤ *Inscr.Cypr.*135.10 H., both εἰ and αἰ in Ep.:— Particle used interjectionally with imper. and to express a wish, but usu. either in conditions, *if*, or in indirect questions, *whether*. In the former use its regular negative is μή; in the latter, οὐ.

A. INTERJECTIONALLY, in Hom., *come now!* c. imper., εἰ δὲ.. ἄκουσον Il.9.262; εἰ δὲ καὶ αὐτοὶ φευγόντων ib.46; most freq. with ἄγε (q.v.), 1.302, al. 2. in wishes, c. opt., ἀλλ' εἴ τις.. καλέσειεν 10.111, cf. 24.74; so later, εἴ μοι ξυνείη μοῖρα S.*OT*863 (lyr.); εἴ μοι γένοιτο φθόγγος ἐν βραχίοσιν E.*Hec.*836: more freq. folld. by γάρ, αἲ γὰρ δὴ οὕτως εἴη Il.4.189, al.; εἰ γὰρ γενοίμην ἀντὶ σοῦ νεκρός E.*Hipp.* 1410; εἰ γὰρ γένοιτο X.*Cyr.*6.1.38; εἰ γὰρ ἐν τούτῳ εἴη Pl.*Prt.*310d; of unattained wishes, in Hom. only c. opt., εἰ γὰρ ἐγών.. Διὸς πάϊς αἰγιόχοιο εἴην Il.13.825; Ζεῦ πάτερ, αἲ γὰρ ἐμὸς πόσις εἴη Alcm.29; later with past tenses of ind., εἰ γάρ μ' ὑπὸ γῆν.. ἧκεν A.*Pr.*152 (anap.); εἰ γὰρ τοσαύτην δύναμιν εἶχον ὥστε.. E.*Alc.*1072: twice in Od. c. inf. (cf. the use of inf. in commands), αἲ γὰρ τοῖος ἐών.. ἐμὸς γαμβρὸς καλέεσθαι 7.311, cf. 24.376. b. εἴθε, Ep. αἴθε, is freq. used in wishes in the above constructions, εἴθε οἱ αὐτῷ Ζεὺς ἀγαθὸν τελέσειεν 2.33; εἴθ' ὣς ἡβώοιμι Il.7.157; ἰὼ γᾶ, εἴθ' ἔμ' ἐδέξω A.*Ag.*1537 (lyr.); εἴθε σοι, ὦ Περίκλεις, τότε συνεγενόμην X.*Mem.*1.2.46: later c. inf., γαίης χθαμαλωτέρη εἴθε.. κεῖσθαι *AP*9.284 (Crin.). c. εἰ γάρ, εἴθε are also used with ὤφελον (Ep. ὤφελλον), of past unattained wishes, αἴθ' ὤφελλες στρατοῦ ἄλλου σημαίνειν Il.14.84; εἰ γὰρ ὤφελον [κατιδεῖν] Pl.*R.*432c. d. folld. by a clause expressing a consequence of the fulfilment of the wish, αἲ γὰρ τοῦτο.. ἔπος τετελεσμένον εἴη· τῷ κε τάχα γνοίης.. Od.15.536, cf. 17.496, al.; sts. hard to distinguish from εἰ in conditions (which may be derived from this use), εἴ μοί τι πίθοιο, τό κεν πολὺ κέρδιον εἴη Il.7.28.

B. IN CONDITIONS, *if*: I. with INDIC., 1. with all tenses (for fut., v. infr. 2), to state a condition, with nothing implied as to its fulfilment, εἰ δ' οὕτω τοῦτ' ἐστίν, ἐμοὶ μέλλει φίλον εἶναι but *if* this is so, it will be.., Il.1.564: any form of the Verb may stand in apodosi, εἰ θεοί τι δρῶσιν αἰσχρόν, οὐκ εἰσὶν θεοί E.*Fr.*292.7; εἰ δοκεῖ, πλέωμεν S.*Ph.* 526; εἰ Φαῖδρον ἀγνοῶ, καὶ ἐμαυτοῦ ἐπιλέλησμαι Pl.*Phdr.*228a; κάκιστ' ἀπολοίμην, Ξανθίαν εἰ μὴ φιλῶ Ar.*Ra.*579, cf. Od.17.475; εἰ θεοῦ ἦν, οὐκ ἦν αἰσχροκερδής· εἰ δ' αἰσχροκερδής, οὐκ ἦν θεοῦ Pl.*R.*408c; εἰ ταῦτα λέγων διαφθείρω τοὺς νέους, ταῦτ' ἂν εἴη βλαβερά Id.*Ap.*30b, cf. 25b; εἰ οὗτοι ὀρθῶς ἀπέστησαν, ὑμεῖς ἂν οὐ χρεὼν ἄρχοιτε *if* these were right in their revolt, (it would follow that) you rule when you have no right, Th.3.40. b. to express a general condition, *if ever, whenever*, sts. with pres., εἴ τις δύο ἢ καὶ πλείους τις ἡμέρας λογίζεται, μάταιός ἐστιν S.*Tr.*943: with impf., εἴ τίς τι ἠρώτα ἀπεκρίνοντο Th.7.10: rarely with aor., D.S.31.26.1, S.E.*P.*1.84; cf. III. 2. 2. with fut. (much less freq. than ἐάν c. subj.), either to express a future supposition emphatically, εἰ φθάσομεν τοὺς πολεμίους κατακαίνοντες οὐδεὶς ἡμῶν ἀποθανεῖται X.*Cyr.*7.1.19; εἰ μὴ βοηθήσετε οὐ περιέσται τἀκεῖ Th.6.91; εἰ αὕτη ἡ πόλις ληφθήσεται, ἔχεται ἡ πᾶσα Σικελία ibid.; in threats or warnings, εἰ μὴ καθέξεις γλῶσσαν ἔσται σοι κακά E.*Fr.*5; εἰ τιμωρήσεις Πατρόκλῳ, αὐτὸς ἀποθανῇ Pl.*Ap.*28c, cf. D.28.21: or, b. to express a present intention or expectation, αἶρε πλῆκτρον εἰ μαχεῖ *if* you mean to fight, Ar.*Av.*759; ἐγὼ μὲν οὐκ ἀνήρ.. εἰ ταῦτ' ἀνατεὶ τῇδε κείσεται κράτη S.*Ant.*485, cf. Il.1.61, E.*Hec.*863. 3. with historical tenses, implying that the condition is or was unfulfilled. a. with impf., referring to present time or to continued or repeated action in past time (in Hom. always the latter, Il.24.715, al.): ταῦτα οὐκ ἂν ἐδύναντο ποιεῖν, εἰ μὴ διαίτῃ μετρίᾳ ἐχρῶντο they would not be able to do this (as they do), *if* they did not live an abstemious life, X.*Cyr.*1.2.16, cf. Pl.*R.*489b; οὐκ ἂν νήσων ἐκράτει, εἰ μή τι καὶ ναυτικὸν εἶχεν he (Agamemnon) would not have been master of islands, *if* he had not had also some naval force, Th.1.9; αἰ δ' ἦχες ἔσλων ἵμερον ἢ κάλων.. αἶδώς κεν.. ἦχεν Sapph.28; εἰ ἦσαν ἄνδρες ἀγαθοί.. οὐκ ἄν ποτε ταῦτα ἔπασχον *if* they had been good men, they would never have suffered as they did, Pl.*Grg.*516e, cf. X.*Mem.*1.1.5; εἰ γὰρ ἐγὼ τάδε ᾔδε'.. οὐκ ἂν ὑπεξέφυγε *if* I had known this.., Il.8. 366. b. with aor. referring to past time, εἰ μὴ ἔφυσε θεὸς μέλι.. ἔφασκον γλύσσονα σῦκα πέλεσθαι Xenoph.38; εἰ μὴ ὑμεῖς ἤλθετε, ἐπορευόμεθα ἂν ἐπὶ βασιλέα had you not come, we should be on our way..., X.*An.*2.1.4; καὶ ἴσως ἂν ἀπέθανον, εἰ μὴ ἡ ἀρχὴ διὰ ταχέων κατελύθη Pl.*Ap.*32d, cf. Il.5.680, Od.4.364, D.4.5, 27.63: with plpf. in apodosi, εἰ τριάκοντα μόναι μετέπεσον τῶν ψήφων, ἀπεπεφεύγη ἂν Pl. *Ap.*36a. c. rarely with plpf. referring to action finished in past or present time, λοιπὸν δ' ἂν ἦν ἡμῖν ἔτι περὶ τῆς πόλεως διαλεχθῆναι, εἰ μὴ προτέρα τῶν ἄλλων τὴν εἰρήνην ἐπεποίητο *if* she had not (as she has done) made peace before the rest, Isoc.5.56, cf. Pl.*Ti.*21c. II. with SUBJ., εἰ is regularly joined with ἄν (Ep. κε, κεν), cf. ἐάν: Arc. εἰκαν in Tegean Inscrr. of iv B.C. (*IG*5(2).3.16,31,6.2, *SIG*306.34) should be understood as εἰκ ἄν (εἰ: εἰκ = οὐ: οὐκ), since εἰ δ' ἄν is also found in *IG*5(2).3.2,6.45, and εἰκ alone, ib.3.21; but ἄν (κε, κεν) are freq. absent in Hom. as Od.5.221, 14.373 (and cf. infr. 2), and Lyr., Pi. (who never uses εἰ with ἄν or κε(ν)) *P.*4.266, al.; in dialects, αἰ δείλητ' ἀγχωρεῖν *IG*9(1).334.6 (Locr., v B.C.), cf. Foed.Dor.ap.Th.5. 79; rarely in Hdt., εἰ μὴ ἀναβῇ 2.13; occasionally in Trag., A.*Eu.* 234, S.*OT*198 (lyr.), etc.; very rarely in Att. Prose, εἰ ξυστῶσιν αἱ πόλεις Th.6.21; εἴ τι που ἄλσος ἢ τέμενος ἀφειμένον ᾖ Pl.*Lg.*761c: in later Prose, εἴ τις θελήσῃ *Apoc.*11.5; εἰ φονεύῃ Plot.2.9.9, cf. Procl. *Inst.*26. 1. when the apodosis is fut., to express a future condition more distinctly and vividly than εἰ c. opt., but less so than εἰ c. fut. ind. (supr. I. 2a); εἰ δέ κεν ὣς ἔρξῃς καί τοι πείθωνται Ἀχαιοί, γνώσῃ ἔπειθ'.. *if* thou do thus.., thou shalt know, Il.2.364, cf. 1.128, 3.281, Od.17.549; ἂν δέ τις ἀνθιστῆται, σὺν ὑμῖν πειρασόμεθα χειροῦσθαι X. *An.*7.3.11; ἂν μὴ νῦν ἐθέλωμεν ἐκεῖ πολεμεῖν αὐτῷ, ἐνθάδ' ἴσως ἀναγκασθησόμεθα τοῦτο ποιεῖν *if* we be not now willing, D.4.50, cf. X.*Cyr.* 5.3.27: folld. by imper., ἢν εἰρήνης δοκῆτε δεῖσθαι, ἄνευ ὅπλων ἥκετε ib.3.2.13, cf. 5.4.30. 2. when the apodosis is present, denoting customary or repeated action, to express a general condition, *if ever*, ἤν ποτε δασμὸς ἵκηται, σοὶ τὸ γέρας πολὺ μεῖζον (sc. ἐστί) *whenever* a division comes, your prize is (always) greater, Il.1.166; ἢν ἐγγὺς ἔλθῃ θάνατος, οὐδεὶς βούλεται θνῄσκειν *if* death come near, E.*Alc.* 671; with ἄν omitted, εἴ περ γάρ τε χόλον.. καταπέψῃ ἀλλά.. ἔχει κότον Il.1.81. b. with Rhet. present in apodosis, ἐὰν μὴ οἱ φιλόσοφοι βασιλεύσωσιν, οὐκ ἔστι κακῶν παῦλα there is (i.e. can be, will be) no rest .., Pl.*R.*473d. III. with OPTATIVE (never with ἄν in early Gr., later ἐάν c. opt., Dam.*Pr.*114, al.), 1. to express a future condition less definitely than ἐάν c. subj., usu. with opt. with ἄν in apod., ἦ κεν γηθήσαι Πρίαμος Πριάμοιό τε παῖδες.. εἰ σφῶιν τάδε πάντα πυθοίατο μαρναμένοιιν surely they would exult, *if* they should hear.., Il.1.255, cf. 7.28, Od.3.223; εἴης φορητὸς οὐκ ἄν, εἰ πράσσοις καλῶς A.*Pr.*979; οὐδὲ γὰρ ἄν με ἐπαινοίη, εἰ ἐξελαύνοιμι τοὺς εὐεργέτας X.*An.*7.7.11; οἶκος δ' αὐτός, εἰ φθογγὴν λάβοι, σαφέστατ' ἂν λέξειεν A.*Ag.*37, etc.: fut. opt. is f.l. in Pl.*Tht.*164a: with pres. ind. in apod., Xenoph.34. 3, Democr.253: with fut. ind., Meliss.5. b. in Hom. sts. with pres. opt., to express an unfulfilled present condition, εἰ μὲν νῦν ἐπὶ ἄλλῳ ἀεθλεύοιμεν, ἦ τ' ἂν ἐγὼ τὰ πρῶτα φεροίμην *if* we were now contending, etc., Il.23.274: rarely in Trag., εἰ μὴ κνίζοι (= εἰ μὴ ἔκνιζε) E.*Med.*568; also εἰ ἀναγκαῖον εἴη ἀδικεῖν ἢ ἀδικεῖσθαι, ἑλοίμην ἂν μᾶλλον ἀδικεῖσθαι Pl.*Grg.*469c. 2. when the apodosis is past, denoting customary or repeated action, to express a general condition in past time (corresponding to use of subj. in present time, supr. II. 2); once in Hom., εἴ τίς με.. ἐνίπτοι, ἀλλὰ σὺ τόν γ'.. κατέρυκες Il.24.768; εἰ δέ τινας θορυβουμένους αἴσθοιτο.., κατασβεννύναι τὴν ταραχὴν ἐπειρᾶτο *if* he should see (*whenever* he saw) any troops in confusion, he (always) tried, X.*Cyr.*5.3.55, cf. *An.*4.5.13, *Mem.*4.2.40; εἴ τις ἀντείποι, εὐθὺς ἐτεθνήκει *if* any one made objection, he was a dead man at once, Th. 8.66; ἀλλ' εἴ τι μὴ φέροιμεν, ὤτρυνεν φέρειν E.*Alc.*755. For εἰ c. ind. in this sense v. supr. I. 1: ind. and opt. are found in same sentence, ἐμίσει, οὐκ εἴ τις κακῶς πάσχων ἠμύνετο, ἀλλ' εἴ τις εὐεργετούμενος ἀχάριστος φαίνοιτο X.*Ages.*11.3. 3. in oratio obliqua after past tenses, representing ἐάν c. subj. or εἰ with a primary (never an historical) tense of the ind. in oratio recta, ἐλογίζοντο ὡς, εἰ μὴ μάχοιντο, ἀποστήσοιντο αἱ πόλεις (representing ἐὰν μὴ μαχώμεθα, ἀποστήσονται) X.*HG*6.4.6, cf. D.21.104, X.*HG*5.2.2; ἔλεγεν ὅτι, εἰ βλαβερὰ πεπραχὼς εἴη, δίκαιος εἴη ζημιοῦσθαι (representing εἰ βλαβερὰ πέπραχε, δίκαιός ἐστι) ib.32, cf. *An.*6.6.25; εἰ δέ τινα φεύγοντα λήψοιτο, προηγόρευεν ὅτι ὡς πολεμίῳ χρήσοιτο (representing εἴ τινα λήψομαι, χρήσομαι) Id.*Cyr.*3.1.3; also, where oratio obliqua is implied in the leading clause, οὐκ ἦν τοῦ πολέμου πέρας Φιλίππῳ, εἰ μὴ Θηβαίους .. ἐχθροὺς ποιήσειε τῇ πόλει, i.e. Philip thought there would be no end to the war, *un*less he should make.. (his thought having been ἐὰν μὴ ποιήσω), D.18.145; ἐβούλοντο γὰρ σφίσιν, εἴ τινα λάβοιεν, ὑπάρχειν ἀντὶ τῶν ἔνδον, ἢν ἄρα τύχωσί τινες ἐζωγρημένοι Th.2.5. 4. c. opt. with ἄν, only when the clause serves as apodosis as well as protasis, cf. Pl.*Prt.*329b, D.4.18, X.*Mem.*1.5.3 (v. ἄν A. III. d). IV. c. INF., in oratio obliqua, only in Hdt., εἰ γὰρ δὴ δεῖν πάντως περιθεῖναι ἄλλῳ τέῳ τὴν βασιληΐην, [ἔφη] δικαιότερον εἶναι κτλ. 1.129; εἰ εἶναι τοῦτο μὴ φίλον 2.64, cf. 172, 3.105,108. V. after Verbs denoting *wonder, delight, indignation, disappointment, contentment*, and similar emotions, εἰ c. ind. is used instead of ὅτι, to express the object of the feeling in a hypothetical form, θαυμάζω εἰ μηδεὶς ὑμῶν μήτ' ἐνθυμεῖται μήτ' ὀργίζεται, ὁρῶν.. I wonder *that* no one of you is either concerned or angry when he sees.., D.4.43; οὐκ ἀγαπᾷ εἰ μὴ δίκην δέδωκεν, ἀλλ' εἰ μὴ καὶ χρυσῷ στεφάνῳ στεφανωθήσεται ἀγανακτεῖ Aeschin.3. 147: after past tenses, ἐθαύμασε δ' εἰ μὴ φανερόν ἐστιν X.*Mem.*1.1.13; δεινὸν εἰσῄει, εἰ μὴ.. δόξει D.19.33; ἐθαύμαζον εἴ τι ἕξει τις χρήσασθαι τῷ λόγῳ Pl.*Phd.*95a; οὐδὲ ᾐσχύνθη εἰ.. ἐπάγει D.21.105: in oratio obliqua (expressed or implied) c. opt., ἐπεῖπεν ὡς δεινὸν (sc. εἴη) εἰ.. μεγαλόψυχος γένοιτο Aeschin.2.157; ᾤκτιρον εἰ ἁλώσοιντο X.*An.*1.4.7; ἐθαύμαζε δ' εἴ τις ἀρετὴν ἐπαγγελλόμενος ἀργύριον πράττοιτο he wondered *that* any one should demand money, Id.*Mem.*1.2.7; ἔχαιρον ἀγαπῶν εἴ τις ἐάσοι I rejoiced, being content *if* any one should let it pass, Pl.*R.*450a:—in this use the neg. οὐ is also found, ἀγανακτῶ εἰ ὁ Φίλιππος ἁρπάζων οὐ λυπεῖ D.8.55; δεινὸν ἂν εἴη εἰ οἱ ἐκείνων ξύμμαχοι οὐκ ἀπεροῦσιν Th.1.121; τέρας λέγεις, εἰ οὐκ ἂν δύναιντο λαθεῖν Pl.*Men.*91d, etc. VI. in citing a fact as a ground of argument or appeal, *as surely as, since*, εἴ ποτ' ἔην γε *if* there was [as there was], i.e. *as sure as* there was such an one, Il.3.180, al.; εἰ τότε κοῦρος ἔα, νῦν αὖτέ με γῆρας ὀπάζει 4.321; πολλοὺς γὰρ οἶκε εἶναι εὐπετέστερον διαβάλλειν ἢ ἕνα, εἰ Κλεομένεα μὲν μοῦνον οὐκ οἷός τε ἐγένετο διαβαλεῖν, τρεῖς δὲ μυριάδας Ἀθηναίων ἐποίησε τοῦτο it seems easier to deceive many than one, *if* (as was the fact, i.e. *since*) he was not able.., Hdt.5.97, cf. 1.60, al. VII. ELLIPTICAL CONSTRUCTIONS: 1. with apodosis implied in the context, εἰ having the force of *in case, supposing that*, πρὸς τὴν πόλιν, εἰ ἐπιβοηθοῖεν, ἐχώρουν they marched towards the city [so as to meet the citizens], *in case* they should rush out, Th.6.100; ἱκέται πρὸς σὲ δεῦρ' ἀφίγμεθα, εἴ τινα πόλιν φράσειας ἡμῖν εὔερον we have come hither to you, *in case* you should tell us of some fleecy city (i.e. that we might hear of it), Ar.*Av.*120; παρέζεο καὶ λαβὲ γούνων, αἴ κέν πως ἐθέλῃσιν ἐπὶ Τρώεσσιν ἀρῆξαι sit by him and grasp his knees [so as to persuade him], *in case* he be willing to help the Trojans, Il.1.408, cf. 66, Od.1.94, 3.92; ἄκουσον καὶ ἐμοῦ, ἐάν σοι ἔτι ταὐτὰ δοκῇ hear me also [that you may assent], *in case* the same opinion please you, Pl.*R.*358b; ἰδὲ δή, ἐάν σοι ὅπερ ἐμοὶ συνδοκῇ look now, *in case* you approve what I do, ib. 434a. 2. with apodosis suppressed for rhetorical reasons, εἴ περ γάρ κ' ἐθέλῃσιν Ὀλύμπιος.. στυφελίξαι *if* he wish to thrust him away, [he will do so], Il.1.580; εἰ μὲν δώσουσι γέρας—· εἰ δέ κε μὴ δώωσιν, ἐγὼ δέ κεν αὐτὸς ἕλωμαι *if* they shall give me a prize, [well and good]; but *if* they give not, then I will take one for myself, 1.135, cf. 6.150, Ar.*Pl.*468; καὶ ἢν μὲν ξυμβῇ ἡ πεῖρα—· εἰ δὲ μή.. and *if* the attempt succeed, [well]; otherwise.., Th.3.3, cf. Pl.*Prt.*325d. 3. with the Verb of the protasis omitted, chiefly in the following expressions: a. εἰ μή *except*, οὐδὲν ἄλλο σιτέονται, εἰ μὴ ἰχθῦς μοῦνον Hdt. 1.200; μὰ τὼ θεώ, εἰ μὴ Κρίτυλλά γ' [εἰμί]—nay, *if* I'm not Critylla! i.e. I am, Ar.*Th.*898; εἰ μὴ ὅσον *except* only, ἐγὼ μέν μιν οὐκ εἶδον, εἰ μὴ ὅσον γραφῇ Hdt.2.73, cf. 1.45, 2.20; εἰ μὴ εἰ Th.1.17, Pl.*Grg.*480b, etc.; εἰ μή τι οὖν, ἀλλὰ σμικρόν γέ μοι τῆς ἀρχῆς χάλασον *if* nothing else, yet.., Id.*Men.*86e; ironical, εἰ μὴ ἄρα ἡ τῆς ἀρετῆς ἐπιμέλεια διαφθορά ἐστιν X.*Mem.*1.2.8; εἰ μή πέρ γε τὸν ὑοσκύαμον χρήματα εἶναι φήσομεν Id.*Oec.*1.13. b. εἰ δὲ μή but *if* not, i.e. *otherwise*, προηγόρευε τοῖς Λαμψακηνοῖσι μετιέναι Μιλτιάδεα, εἰ δὲ μή, σφέας πίτυος τρόπον ἀπείλεε ἐκτρίψειν Hdt.6.37, cf. 56; after μάλιστα μέν, Th.1.32,35, etc.:—after a preceding neg., μὴ τύπτ'· εἰ δὲ μή, σαυτόν ποτ' αἰτιάσει don't beat me; *otherwise*, you will have yourself to blame, Ar.*Nu.* 1433; ὦ Κῦρε, μὴ οὕτω λέγε· εἰ δὲ μή, οὐ θαρροῦντά με ἕξεις X.*Cyr.*3.1.35; οὔτ' ἐν τῷ ὕδατι τὰ ὅπλα ἦν ἔχειν· εἰ δὲ μή Id.*An.*4.3.6, cf. Th.1.28,131, Pl.*Phd.*91c. c. εἰ δέ sts. stands for εἰ δὲ μή, εἰ μὲν βούλεται, ἐψέτω· εἰ δ', ὅτι βούλεται, τοῦτο ποιείτω Pl.*Euthd.*285c, cf. *Smp.*212c; εἰ δ' οὖν S.*Ant.*722; εἰ δ' οὕτως Arist.*EN*1094ᵃ24; εἰ δὲ τοῦτο and *if* so, Str.2.1.29. d. εἰ γάρ for *if* so, Id.7.3.6. e. εἴ τις *if* any, i.e. *as much as* or *more than* any, τῶν γε νῦν αἵ τις ἐπιχθονίων, ὀρθῶς B.5.5; ὅτλον ἄλγιστον ἔσχον, εἴ τις Αἰτωλὶς γυνή S.*Tr.*8, cf. *OC*734; εἴ τις ἄλλος, *siquis alius*, E.*Andr.*6, etc.; εἴ τινες καὶ ἄλλοι Hdt.3.2, etc.; εἴπερ τις ἄλλος Pl.*R.*501d; also κατ' εἰ δέ τινα τρόπον in *any* way, *IG* 5(2).6.27 (Tegea). f. εἴ ποτε or εἴπερ ποτέ *now if* ever, ἡμῖν δὲ καλῶς, εἴπερ ποτέ, ἔχει.. ἡ ξυναλλαγή Th.4.20, cf. Ar.*Eq.*594; αἴ ποτα κἀτέρωτα Alc.*Supp.*7.11, cf. X.*An.*6.4.12, etc.; but in prayers, εἴ ποτέ τοι ἐπὶ νηὸν ἔρεψα.. τόδε μοι κρήηνον ἐέλδωρ Il.1.39. g. εἴ ποθεν (sc. δυνατόν ἐστι) *if* from any quarter, i.e. from some quarter or other, S.*Ph.* 1204 (lyr.); so εἴ ποθι somewhere, anywhere, Id.*Aj.*885 (lyr.); εἴ που Od.4.193. h. εἴ πως ib.388, X.*An.*2.3.11: in an elliptical sentence (cf. VII. 1), πρέσβεις πέμψαντες, εἴ πως πείσειαν Th.1.58. VIII. with other PARTICLES: 1. for the distinction between καὶ εἰ (or καὶ ἐάν, or κἄν) even *if*, and εἰ καί (or ἐὰν καί) even *though*, v. καί:—the opposite of καὶ εἰ is οὐδ' εἰ, not even *if*; that of εἰ καί is εἰ μηδέ, *if* (*although*) not even. 2. for ὡς εἰ, ὡς εἴ τε, ὥσπερ εἰ, etc., v. ὡς and ὥσπερ. 3. for εἰ ἄρα, v. ἄρα; for εἰ δή, εἴπερ, v. εἰ δή, εἴπερ; for εἴ γε, v. γέ. IX. in neg. oaths, = Hebr. *im*, LXX *Ps.*94(95).11, *Ev.Marc.*8.12, al.

C. IN INDIRECT QUESTIONS, *whether*, folld. by the ind., subj., or opt., according to the principles of oratio obliqua: 1. with IND. after primary tenses, representing the same tense in the direct question, σάφα δ' οὐκ οἶδ' εἰ θεός ἐστιν *whether* he is a god, Il.5.183; εἰ ξυμπονήσεις.. σκόπει S.*Ant.*41. 2. with SUBJ. after primary tenses, representing a dubitative subj. in the direct question, τὰ ἐκπώματα οὐκ οἶδ' εἰ Χρυσάντᾳ τουτῳῒ δῶ *whether* I should give them, X.*Cyr.*8.4.16: sts. elliptical, ἐς τὰ χρηστήρια ἔπεμπε, εἰ στρατεύηται ἐπὶ τοὺς Πέρσας Hdt.1.75. 3. OPT. after past tenses, representing either of the two previous constructions in the direct question, ἤρετο εἴ τις ἐμοῦ εἴη σοφώτερος he asked *whether* any one was wiser than I (direct ἔστι τις σοφώτερος;), Pl.*Ap.*21a; ἐπεκηρυκεύετο Πεισιστράτῳ, εἰ βούλοιτό οἱ τὴν θυγατέρα ἔχειν γυναῖκα Hdt.1.60: rarely aor. opt. for the aor. ind., ἠρώτων αὐτὸν εἰ ἀναπλεύσειεν I asked him *whether* he had set sail (direct ἀνέπλευσας;), D.50.55: but aor. opt. usually represents aor. subj., τὸν θεὸν ἐπήροντο εἰ παραδοῖεν Κορινθίοις τὴν πόλιν ..καὶ τιμωρίαν τινὰ πειρῷντ' ἀπ' αὐτῶν ποιεῖσθαι they asked *whether* they should deliver their city to the Corinthians, and should try.., Th.1.25:—in both constructions the ind. or subj. may be retained, ψῆφον ἐβούλοντο ἐπαγαγεῖν εἰ χρὴ πολεμεῖν ib.119; ἐβουλεύοντο εἴτε κατακαύσωσιν.. εἴτε τι ἄλλο χρήσωνται *whether* they should burn them or should dispose of them in some other way, Id.2.4; ἀνακοινοῦσθαι αὐτὸν αὐτῷ εἰ δῷ ἐπιψηφίσαι τοῖς προέδροις [he said that] he consulted him *whether* he should give.., Aeschin.2.68. 4. with OPT. and ἄν when this was the form of the direct question, ἠρώτων εἰ δοῖεν ἂν τούτων τὰ πιστά they asked *whether* they would give (direct δοίητε ἄν;), X.*An.*4.8.7. 5. the NEG. used with εἰ in indirect questions is οὐ, when οὐ would be used in the direct question, ἐνετέλλετο ..εἰρωτᾶν εἰ οὔ τι ἐπαισχύνεται *whether* he is not ashamed, Hdt.1.90, etc.; but if μή would be required in the direct form, it is retained in the indirect, οὐ τοῦτο ἐρωτῶ, ἀλλ' εἰ τοῦ μὲν δικαίου μὴ ἀξιοῖ πλέον ἔχειν μηδὲ βούλεται ὁ δίκαιος, τοῦ δὲ ἀδίκου (the direct question would be μὴ ἀξιοῖ μηδὲ βούλεται; he does not see fit nor wish, does he?) Pl.*R.* 349b:—in double indirect questions, εἴτε.. εἴτε..; εἰ.. εἴτε..; εἴτε.. ἤ.., either οὐ or μή can be used in the second clause, ὅπως ἴδῃς εἴτ' ἔνδον εἴτ' οὐκ ἔνδον S.*Aj.*7; σκοπῶμεν εἰ ἡμῖν πρέπει ἢ οὔ Pl.*R.*451d; εἰ ἀληθὲς ἢ μή, πειράσομαι μαθεῖν ib.339a; πολλὰ ἂν περιεσκέψω, εἴτε ἐπιτρεπτέον εἴτε οὔ.. οὐδένα λόγον οὐδὲ συμβουλὴν ποιῇ, εἴτε χρὴ ἐπιτρέπειν σαυτὸν αὐτῷ εἴτε μή Id.*Prt.*313a,b; ἀνάγκη τὴν ἐμὴν μητέρα, εἴτε θυγάτηρ ἦν Κίρωνος εἴτε μή, καὶ εἰ παρ' ἐκείνῳ διῃτᾶτο ἢ οὔ, καὶ γάμους εἰ διττοὺς ὑπὲρ ταύτης εἰστίασεν ἢ μή.. πάντα ταῦτα εἰδέναι τοὺς οἰκέτας Is.8.9; τοὺς νόμους καταμανθάνειν εἰ καλῶς κεῖνται ἢ μή.. τοὺς λόγους εἰ ὀρθῶς ὑμᾶς διδάσκουσιν ἢ οὔ Antipho 5.14.

εἶα, an exclamation used to cheer or urge on, *on! up! away!* used with the imper. sg. or pl., cf. E.*Med.*820, etc.; εἶα δή *come then!* A. *Ag.*1650, Ar.*Th.*659; εἶά νυν *well now!* Id.*Pax*467; ἄγ' εἶα Id.*Ra.* 396; ἀλλ' εἶα E.*HF*622, Ar.*Pl.*760; ὦ εἶα Id.*Pax*459; εἶα ὦ ib.468; ἀλλ' εἶα δή..σκεψώμεθα Pl.*Sph.*239b:—with interrog. οὐ, where the question is equivalent to a command, οὐκ εἶα.. δραμεῖσθε; E.*IT*1423, cf. *Hel.*1597. (εἶα S.*Ichn.*87, cf. Hdn.Gr.1.495.)

εἰάζω, *cry* εἶα, E.*Fr.*844; cf. **εἰαγχοῦν** (fort. ἴαχον)· βοῶσαν, Hsch.

εἰαί· τῶν ὀσπρίων τὰ ἀποκαθάρματα, Hsch.; cf. εἶοι. **εἰακέν**· ἀσθενεῖν, Id.

εἰαμενή or **εἰᾰμενή**, ἡ, *a river-side pasture, meadow*, ἐν εἰαμενῇ ἕλεος in a marshy *meadow*, Il.4.483; λειμῶνες ὑπόδροσοι εἰαμεναί τε Theoc. 25.16, cf. Call.*Dian.*193, A.R.3.1202, Euph.138; εἰαμενὴ δὲ καὶ οὐ βυθός ἐστι θαλάσσης, of a *shallow creek*, Dem.Bith.4.5 (prob. a participial form): cf. also **εἰαμένον**· νήνεμον, κοῖλον, βοτανώδη, Hsch.

εἰᾱνός, ή, όν, Ep. for ἑανός, Il.16.9.

εἶαρ, **εἰᾰρινός**, v. ἔαρ (A and B), ἐαρινός.

εἰᾰρό-εις, εσσα, εν, poet., = ἐαρινός, Man.4.275. **-μασθος**, ον, *with youthful breasts*, *AP*5.75 (Rufin.). **-πότης**, ου, ὁ, = αἱμοπότης, Hsch. **-πῶτις**, v.l. for ἠεροφοῖτις in Il.19.87; cf. ἔαρ (B). **-τερπής**, ές, *joying in spring*, Orph.*H.*51.15.

εἴασκον, Ion. and Ep. impf. of ἐάω.

εἴαται, **εἴατο**, Ep. 3 pl. pres. and impf. of ἧμαι. II. εἴατο, Med. form for ἦσαν (impf. of εἰμί *sum*), read by Aristarch. in Od.20. 106. 2. εἵατο, 3 pl. plpf. Med. of ἕννυμι.

εἰβάτας, Thess., = ἡβητής, *IG*9(2).234 (Pharsalus).

εἴβηνος, ὁ, name of a breed of horses: metaph., of a maiden, Alcm. 23.59; cf. ἐβῆνοι, ἴβηνος.

εἴβιμος, ον, *trickling*, Eust.1471.30: as pr. n., Id.1336.28.

εἰβιοβοσκός, v. ἰβιοβοσκός.

εἴβω, Ep. for λείβω, *drop, let fall in drops*, ὑπ' ὀφρύσι δάκρυον εἶβε Od.4.153:—Med., ἀπ' ὄσσων..δ' εἰβομένα ῥέος (prob. for λειβ-) A.*Pr.* 401; δάκρυ' εἰβομένη (Triclin. for δάκρυα λειβ-) S.*Ant.*527 (anap.):—Pass., *trickle down*, Hes.*Th.*910, A.R.2.664.

εἰ γάρ, v. εἰ A. **εἴγε**, v. γε. **εἰ δ' ἄγε**, v. εἰ A.

εἰδαίνομαι, aor. 1 εἰδήνατο, = εἴδομαι, *to be like*, τινί Nic.*Al.*76,600.

εἰδαλίζεται· ἐναλίζεται, Hsch.

εἰδάλιμος, η, ον, (εἶδος) *shapely, comely*, Od.24.279. II. *like, looking like*, c. gen., *AP*7.491 (Mnasalc.).

εἰδαλίς· ὄρνις ποιός, Hsch.

εἰδάλλομαι, = εἰδαίνομαι, ἰνδάλλομαι, Hsch.

εἶδαρ, ατος, τό, Ep. word, *food*, παρὰ δ' ἀμβρόσιον βάλεν εἶ., of the horses of the gods, Il.5.369, 13.35; εἴδατα πόλλ' ἐπιθεῖσα, on the table, Od.1.140, 4.56, etc.; ἄνθινον εἶ., of the Lotophagi, 9.84; μελίσσης ἄνθιμον εἶ., of honey-cakes, Orph.*L.*735, cf. Theoc.15.115. (ἔδϝαρ, cf. ἔδαρ, ἔδω.)

εἶδας· εἰς αὔριον, Hsch. (Fort. ἔνας (v. ἔνος); sed cf. ἓνς ἄς.)

εἰδέα, written for ἰδέα in codd., as Ar.*Th.*436 (lyr.), Lxx *Ge.*5.3, *Ev.Matt.*28.3.

εἰδετικός, = εἰδητικός, Olymp. *in Alc.*p.18 C.

εἰδέχθ-εια, ἡ, *odious, ugly look*, Lxx *Wi.*16.3, Ph.1.38. **-θής**, ές, *of hateful look, ugly*, εἰ. ἀπὸ τοῦ προσώπου Thphr.*Char.*28.4, cf. *Com.Adesp.*21 (Comp.), *Stoic.*2.307, Plb.36.15.1, D.S.3.29, Ph.2.56 (Sup.); εἰ. ὁρᾶν Porph.*Abst.*3.20. II. *putrid, fetid*, Hp.*Mul.*2. 115,125.

εἰ δή, *if indeed*, S.*Tr.*27; *if that is to say*, Pl.*Smp.*218e, Arist.*Rh.* 1370^{a}30; εἰ δή..γε Pl.*Tht.*166c, etc.

εἰδηθμός· συστροφή, φυγή, Hsch. (leg. εἰλ-). **εἰδηλήγε**· ἀναμάρτητον, Id.

εἴδ-ημα, ατος, τό, *knowledge*, Oenom.ap.Eus.*PE*5.21 (pl.). **-ημονικός**, ή, όν, *belonging to knowledge*, ἀρχά, opp. κοινανικά, Archyt.ap. Stob.2.31.120. Adv. -κῶς *with knowledge, skilfully*, Suid. **-ήμων**, ον, gen. ονος, *acquainted with* or *expert in* a thing, τινός D.L.6.14, *AP* 9.505.4, *IG*14.885 (Suessa), S.E.*M.*1.79. Adv. -νως Hermog.*Meth.* 13, Vett.Val.348.19, Hsch.

εἴδ-ησις, εως, ἡ, *knowledge*, τῶν πραγμάτων Nausiph.2; = γνῶσις, Arist.*de An.*402^{a}1; γραμμάτων S.E.*M.*1.44, cf. *SIG*685.24 (Magn. Mae., ii B.C.), Lxx *Si.*42.18, Ph.1.335, Porph.*Sent.*32, Plot.4.4.12, al., Iamb.*Protr.*3, etc.: in pl., *forms of knowledge*, μαρτυροῦσι δὲ καὶ αἱ αἰσθήσεις, εἰδήσεις εἶναι θέλουσαι Plot.6.7.29. **-ητικός**, ή, όν, *constituting an* εἶδος III. 2, ἀριθμός, opp. μαθηματικός, Arist.*Metaph.*1086^{a} 5, 1088^{b}34 (but later εἰ. ἀριθμός *capable of being represented by a geometrical pattern, figurate*, Iamb.*Comm.Math.*19); *formal*, αἰτία Alex. Aphr. *in Metaph.*124.9, Procl.*Inst.*178; αἴτια Olymp. *in Mete.*302.28; opp. εἰδητός (q.v.), Dam.*Pr.*81. 2. *concerned with* εἴδη, νόησις ib.5; ἀποδείξεις ibid.; *specific*, Alex.Aphr. *in Metaph.*113.6. II. Adv. -κῶς Dam.*Pr.*284,321, Procl. *in Prm.*pp.625,649 S. **-ητός**, ή, όν, *knowable*, εἶδος γάρ, ὅτι εἰδητὸν καὶ εἰδητικόν Dam.*Pr.*81, cf. ib. 303. **-ικός**, ή, όν, (εἶδος) *specific*, opp. γενικός, ὄνομα D.T.636.14, A.D.*Synt.*230.11 (Sup.), cf. Porph.*Intr.*4.16 (Sup.), al.; ἀντίρρησις S.E.*M.*1.39 (Comp.); ἀρεταί Phld.*D.*3 *Fr.*82, cf. Ph.1.140; τὰς γενικὰς καὶ τὰς εἰ. τῶν σημείων παραλλαγάς Phld.*Sign.Fr.*2; αἰσθήσεις *Placit.*4.10.1; εἰδικώτατον, τό, = Lat. *infima species*, *Stoic.*3.214, cf. Dam.*Pr.*87. Adv. -κῶς *specifically*, *Stoic.*2.77, Dsc.5.75. II. *special*, opp. *general*, Phlp. *in Mete.*4.27 (Comp.). Adv. -κῶς *specially*, *CIG* 2222.15 (Chios). III. *formal*, opp. *material*, διαφοραί Plot.5.7.1.

εἴδιον· νενοτισμένον, ὑγρόν, Hsch. (Perh. for ἴδιον, cf. ἰδίω.)

εἰδογράφος [ᾰ], ὁ, *classifier of literary forms*, of the critic Apollonius, *POxy.*1241 ii 10, Sch.Pi.*P.*2.1, *EM*295.51.

εἰδοί or **ἰδοί**, ῶν, αἱ, = Lat. *Idus*, D.H.6.89, Plu.*Rom.*23, *Tab.Defix. Aud.*242.49 (Carthage, i A.D.): gen. pl. εἰδυῶν *IG*7.2225 (Thisbe); cf. εἴδυιοί.

εἰδομᾰλίδας, ὁ, *fair-cheeked* (?), Alc.150 (cf. Alc.Com.37).

εἰδοποι-έω, *endue with form*, εἰ. ἕκαστα καὶ σχηματίζειν Chrysipp. *Stoic.*2.148; τὸν βίον Plu.*Alex.*1; αὐτοὺς εἰς ἀνθρώπους, of the gods, Hld.3.13; ἰδέαι εἰ. ἕκαστα τῶν ὄντων Ph.2.219; *characterize*, αἵρεσιν Gal.1.161:—Pass., Ph.2.261, Corn.*ND*6, Plot.1.8.5, al., Syrian. *in Metaph.*8.13, etc.: c. acc., ἀριθμὸς τὴν ἐπ' ἄπειρον προχώρησιν -ούμενος *fashioned into the pattern of* an infinite progression, *Theol.Ar.*34: c. dat., *to be characterized by*, Asp. *in EN*87.5. II. *portray, describe*, τινά Callistr.*Stat.*8. 2. *add specific detail to*, γραφήν Str.15.1.14 (prob.). **-ημα**, ατος, τό, *copy of an* εἶδος or *pattern*, τινός *Theol.Ar.*9 (pl.). **-ησις**, εως, ἡ, *construction of a typical form*, ἀριθμοῦ ib.36, cf. 34, Iamb. *in Nic.*p.15 P. **-ητικός**, ή, όν, = εἰδοποιός, Plot.1.8.3, Olymp. *in Mete.*297.28. **-ία**, ἡ, *formation, structure*, αἱ κατὰ μέρος εἰ., opp. οἰκοδομία, Ph.*Bel.*50.51: in sg., *specific form*, Str.1.1.18. 2. Rhet., *descriptive quality*, σχημάτων Longin.18.1. 3. Philos., *production of forms*, Iamb.*Comm.Math.*14, Procl.*Inst.*144,157, Syrian. *in Metaph.*86.1. **-ός**, όν, *constituting a species, specific*, διαφορά Arist.*Top.*143^{b}7, cf. *EN*1174^{b}5, Plot.6.3.18, Dam.*Pr.*308. II. *creating forms*, Procl.*Inst.*157, Dam.*Pr.*310: c. gen., *creating a form* or *pattern*, ἀριθμός..δικαιοσύνης εἰ. *Theol.Ar.*28, cf. 10.

εἶδος, εος, τό, (εἴδω A) *that which is seen*: *form, shape*, freq. in Hom., of the human *form* or *figure*, esp. abs. in acc. with Adjs., εἶδος ἄριστος, ἀγητός, κακός, Il.3.39, 5.787, 10.316; ἀλίγκιος ἀθανάτοισιν Od.8.174; opp. φρένες, 17.454; opp. βίη, Il.21.316; δευτέρα πεδ' Ἀγιδὼν τὸ εἶ. Alcm.23.58; τὸ εἶδος τῆς γυναικὸς ὑπερεπαινέων Hdt.1.8, etc.; *appearance*, of a dog, Od.17.308; ὄφιες ποικίλοι τὰ εἴδεα Hdt.3.107; εἴδεα [τῶν θεῶν] σημήναντες Id.2.53; γυνή τό γ' εἶδος Ar.*Th.*267: hence, periphr. for *person*, S.*El.*1177; τὸ ἐπ' εἴδει καλόν Pl.*Smp.*210b. b. esp. of *beauty of person, comeliness*, εἴδεος ἐπαμμένος Hdt.1.199; πλούτῳ καὶ εἴδει προφέρων Id.6.127. c. Medic., *physique, habit of body, constitution*, Hp.*Nat.Hom.*9, *Hum.*1: more freq. in pl., Id.*Aër.*3, al.; εἴδεα εὔχροά τε καὶ ἀνθηρά ib.5. 2. generally, *shape*, σχῆμα καὶ εἶδος Id.*Off.*3, cf. *Mochl.*6, etc.; *pattern*, of 'figurate' numbers, Arist. *Ph.*203^{a}15; ἡ μονὰς εἶδος εἰδῶν τυγχάνει *Theol.Ar.*4, cf. 17; *decorative pattern* or *figure*, Plu.*Them.*29 (pl.); of a musical scale, τοῦ διὰ τεσσάρων τρία εἴδη Aristox.*Harm.*p.74 M. (identified with σχῆμα, ibid.): in pl., *shapes*, i.e. *various kinds of atoms* (cf. ἰδέα), Democr.ap.Thphr. *Sens.*51. b. Geom., δύο εἴδη τῷ εἴδει δεδομένα two *figures* given *in species*, Euc.*Dat.*53, etc.; esp. in central conics, *rectangle formed by a transverse diameter and the corresponding parameter*, Apollon.Perg. *Con.*1.14,21, al.; also, *species* of numbers, of the terms in an algebraical expression involving different powers of the unknown quantity, Dioph.*Def.*11. II. *form, kind*, or *nature*, τῶν ἀλλέων παιγνιέων τὰ εἴδεα Hdt.1.94; τὸ εἶ. τῆς νόσου Th.2.50, etc.; ἐν ἁρμονίας εἴδει εἶναι, γενέσθαι, to be or become *like*.., Pl.*Phd.*91d, cf. *Cra.*394d; ὡς ἐν φαρμάκου εἴδει by *way* of medicine, Id.*R.*389b; νόμων ἔχει εἶδος is in *the province* of law, Arist.*Pol.*1286^{a}3; *situation, state* of things, σκέψασθε ἐν οἵῳ εἴδει..τοῦτο ἔπραξαν Th.3.62; *plan of action, policy*, ἐπὶ εἶδος τρέπεσθαι Id.6.77, 8.56; ἐπ' ἄλλ' εἶδος τρέπεσθαι take up another *line*, Ar.*Pl.*317; *specific notion, meaning, idea*, ἂν παρέχῃ τὸ ἓν εἶ. δύο ὀνόματα.., περὶ ἑνὸς εἴδεος δύο ὀνόματα οὐ τὰ αὐτά Aen.Tact.24. 1; *department*, Hp.*VM*12 (but also, *elementary nature* or *quality*, ib. 15); *type, sort*, πυρετῶν Id.*Epid.*3.12; αὐγῆς Id.*Off.*3, etc.: Rhet., *style* of writing, τὰ εἴδη τῶν λόγων Isoc.13.17, cf. Arist.*Rh.Al.* 1441^{b}9 (pl.); later, *definite literary form*, Men.Rh.init., Procl.*Chrest.* p.243 W., *EM*295.52; also, *example of a style*, ὅλοις εἴδεσι Isoc.15.74; later, *single poem*, applied to Pindar's odes by Sch.; also, *written statement*, ἀναγνωσθέντος εἴδους *PAmh.*2.65.11 (ii A.D.), cf. *PTeb.*287. 12 (ii A.D.). III. *class, kind*, πᾶν τὸ τῶν πίστεων εἶδος Isoc.15. 280, cf. D.24.192: freq. in Pl., περὶ παντὸς τοῦ εἴδους..ἐν ᾧ.. *Tht.* 178a; ἑνὶ εἴδει περιλαβεῖν ib.148d; εἰς ταὐτὸν ἐμπέπτωκεν εἶδος ib. 205d, etc.; *logical species*, *Sph.*235d; ἓν εἶδος ἀποχωρίζειν *Plt.*262e; τὰς διαφορὰς ὁπόσαιπερ ἐν εἴδεσι κεῖνται, ib.285b, al., cf. Arist.*Metaph.* 1057^{b}7, al., *Cat.*2^{b}7; as a subdivision of γένος, Id.*Rh.*1393^{a}27; ἐπὶ τοῦ αὐτοῦ γένους τεύχη, εἴδει διαφέρουσα, Dsc.1.69. 2. = ἰδέα II. 2, Pl.*Phd.*103e, *R.*596a, *Prm.*132a, al., Arist.*Metaph.*990^{b}9, al., etc. 3. *form*, opp. matter (ὕλη), Id.*Ph.*187^{a}18, al., *Metaph.*1029^{a}29: hence, *formal cause, essence*, ib.1032^{b}1, etc. IV. in later Gr., *wares* of different kinds, *goods*, *POxy.*109.1 (iii/iv A.D.), *PFay.*34.7 (ii A.D.): hence, *payments in kind*, opp. χρυσίον, Just.*Nov.*17.8, cf. *Cod.Just.*1. 4.18, al.; *spices*, Lyd.*Mag.*3.61; *groceries*, Anon.post Max.p.120 L.; εἰ. ἰατρικόν *drug*, Hsch. s.v. νίτρον, cf. *Hippiatr.*129.54 and v. ἐξάειδος, τετράειδος, τρίειδος; of a chemical *reagent*, Zos.Alch.p.205 B.

εἰδότης, ητος, ἡ, *the quality of an* εἶδος, *'formality'*, Dam.*Pr.*65.

εἰδότως, Adv. of εἰδώς, *knowingly*, Aeschin.1.111; *as one who knows, scientifically*, Arist.*Ph.*188^{a}5.

εἰ δ' οὖν, v. εἰ B. VII. 4 c.

εἰδοφορ-έω, *represent* or *express* (in dancing), D.H.7.72. **-ος**, ὁ, *part of a tomb which bore the figure* of the deceased (cf. ζωφόρος), *CIG*2840, al. (Aphrodisias).

εἴδυιοί, οἱ, = εἰδοί, *SIG*664.18 (Delos, ii B.C.).

εἰδύλλιον, τό, Dim. of εἶδος II: *short, highly wrought descriptive poem*, mostly *on pastoral subjects*, as those of Theoc., Bion, Mosch., *idyll*, Sch.Theoc.*Proll.*, cf. Plin.*Ep.*4.14.

εἰδύλλομαι, = εἰδάλλομαι, Pempel.ap.Stob.4.25.52 (nisi leg. εἰδυλλέτω).

εἰδύλος [ῠ], ον, = εἰδήμων, *EM*295.30, etc.:—fem. **εἰδυλίς**, ίδος, Call.*Fr.*451.

***εἴδω**, no Act. pres. in use, ὁράω being used:—**Med.**, v. infr. A. II: aor. 2 **εἶδον** always in sense of *see* (so in pres. and aor. 1 Med., *to be seen*, i.e. *seem*): but pf. **οἶδα**, in pres. sense, *know*. (With ἔ-ϝιδον, cf. (ϝ)είδομαι, (ϝ)εἶδος, Lat. *videre*; with (ϝ)οἶδα, cf. Skt. *véda*, Goth. *wait*, OE. *wát* 'know'.)

A. aor. 2 εἶδον (late εἶδα Orph.*A.*118), serving as aor. to ὁράω, Ep. ἴδον, iter. ἴδεσκε Il.3.217, late Aeol. εὔιδον *Epigr.Gr.*990.11 (Balbilla); imper. ἴδε (in Att. written as Adv. ἰδέ, *behold!* Hdn.Gr.2.23), ἴδετε; subj. ἴδω, Ep. ἴδωμι Il.18.63; opt. ἴδοιμι; inf. ἰδεῖν, Ep. ἰδέειν; part. ἰδών: hence, fut. ἰδησῶ Theoc.3.37:—**Med.**, aor. 2 εἰδόμην, Ep. ἰδόμην, in same sense, poet., Ion., and later Prose (c. gen., Arat.430) (so in compds., even in Att. Prose, v. ἐπ-, προ-, ὑπ-ειδόμην); imper. ἰδοῦ (freq. written as Adv. ἰδού, = ἰδέ); subj. ἴδωμαι; opt. ἰδοίμην; inf. ἰδέσθαι; part. ἰδόμενος Hdt.1.88, al.: **1.** *see, perceive, behold*, ὀφθαλμοῖσι or ἐν ὀφθαλμοῖσι ἰδέσθαι *see* before the eyes, Il.1.587, etc.; ἰδεῖν ἐν ὄμμασιν E.*Or.*1020; ἄγε, πειρήσομαι ἠδὲ ἴδωμαι well, I will try and *see*, Od.6.126, cf. 21.159; *mark, observe*, Il.4.476, Od.4.412, etc.: folld. by relat. clause, ἴδωμ' ὅτιν' ἔργα τέτυκται Il.22.450; ἀλλ' ἄγε θᾶσσον ἰδώμεθα ὅττι τάδ' ἐστίν Od.10.44: freq. in inf. after Subst. or Adj., θαῦμα ἰδέσθαι a marvel *to behold*, Il.5.725; οἰκτραῖσιν ἰδεῖν A.*Pr.*240; ἐλεινὸς ἰδεῖν Pl.*R.*620a. **b.** *see* a person, i.e. *meet* him, *speak with* him, Th.4.125, X.*An.*2.4.15, etc. **c.** *see*, i.e. *experience*, νόστιμον ἦμαρ ἰδέσθαι Od.3.233, etc.; δούλειον ἦμαρ ἰδεῖν E.*Hec.*56; ἀέλιον ἕτερον ἰδεῖν S.*Tr.*835; τὴν δίκην ἰδεῖν Id.*Ant.*1270 (lyr.); ἀλόχου κουριδίης.. οὔ τι χάριν ἴδε he *saw* (i.e. *enjoyed*) not the favour of his wedded wife, Il.11.243. **2.** *look*, ἰδεῖν ἐς.. *look* at or towards, 2.271, etc.; ἰδεῖν ἐπί.. 23.143; πρός.. Od.12.244; εἰς ὦπα ἰδέσθαι *look* him in the face, Il.9.373, etc.; κατ' ἐνῶπα ἰδών 15.320; ἄντα, ἐσάντα, or ἄντην ἰδεῖν, 13.184, 17.334, Od.5.78, etc.: qualified by Adv. or Adj., ὑπόδρα ἰδών *looking* askance, Il.1.148, al.; ἀχρεῖον ἰδών *looking* helpless, 2.269; κέρδος ἰδεῖν *look to* gain, A.*Eu.*541 (lyr.). **3.** *see mentally, perceive*, ἰδέσθαι ἐν φρεσίν '*to see* in his mind's eye', Il.21.61, cf. 4.249; ἰδεῖν τῇ διανοίᾳ Pl.*R.*511a. **b.** *examine, investigate*, Id.*Phd.*70e, *Tht.*192e; *consider*, ἴδωμεν τί λέγομεν Id.*Grg.*455a. **II.** Med., pres. **εἴδομαι**, Ep. ἐείδεται Theoc.25.58, part. ἐειδόμενος Pi.*N.*10.15: aor. εἰσάμην, Ep. part. ἐεισάμενος Il.2.22, al.:—only Ep. and Lyr., *to be seen, appear*, εἴδεται ἄστρα they *are visible, appear*, 8.559; εἰ. ἦμαρ ὑπὸ Τρώεσσι δαμῆναι 13.98; εἴσατο δέ σφι δεξιός 24.319; ὅπῃ τὸ Ταρτάρειον εἴδεται βάθρον *Epigr.Gr.*1034.19 (Callipolis), cf. Od.5.283; perh. also οὔ πῃ χροὸς εἴσατο none of the skin *was visible*, Il.13.191. **2.** c. inf., *appear* or *seem* to be, τὸ δέ τοι κὴρ εἴδεται εἶναι 1.228; τοῦτό τί μοι κάλλιστον ἐνὶ φρεσὶν εἴδεται εἶναι Od.9.11, etc.: with inf. omitted, οἵ τό γε κέρδιον εἴσατο θυμῷ 19.283, etc.; οὐ μέν μοι κακὸς εἴδεται Il.14.472, cf. Theoc.25.58; also, *look like* or *make a show of..*, εἴσατ' ἴμεν ἐς Λῆμνον he *made a show of* going to Lemnos, Od.8.283; εἴσατο δ' ὡς ὅτε ῥινόν it *had the look as of* a shield, 5.281. **3.** strictly middle, c. dat., εἴσατο φθογγὴν Πολίτῃ she *made herself like* Polites in voice, Il.2.791, cf. 20.81; αὐδὴν εἰσάμενός τινι Rhian.50: esp. in part., *like*, εἰδομένη κήρυκι Il.2.280, etc.; τῷ δ' ὄψιν ἐειδόμενος Pi.*N.*10.15; εἰδόμενος τοκεῦσιν A.*Ag.*771 (lyr.); φάσμα εἰδόμενόν τινι Hdt.6.69.

B. pf., οἶδα I *see with the mind's eye*, i.e. I *know*, used as pres.: plpf. ᾔδεα (v. infr.), I *knew*, used as impf.:—pf. οἶδα, Aeol. ὄϊδα Alc.145; 2 sg. οἶδας once in Hom., Od.1.337, cf. *h.Merc.*456, Thgn.491, Hippon.89, Hp.*Acut.*67, E.*Alc.*780, Philem.44.3 codd.; οἶσθα elsewh. in Hom., Att., etc.; in Com. also sts. οἶσθας Cratin.105, Alex.15.11, Men.348.5, cf. Herod.2.55; pl., ἴσμεν, Ep., Aeol., and Dor. ἴδμεν, also Ion., Hdt.1.6, al.; ἴστε, ἴσασι [ῐσ- Od.2.211, al., but ῑσ- ib.283, al.]; οἴδαμεν Hdt.2.17, οἴδατε *AP*12.81 (Mel.), οἴδᾱσι Hdt.2.43, X.*Oec.*20.14 codd.; dual, οἴδατον Socr.*Ep.*22.1: imper. ἴσθι, ἴστω, Boeot. ἴττω, late ἰδέτω Phalar.*Ep.*122 codd.: from 3 pl. ἴσασι (ἴσαντι Epich.53) were formed Dor. 1 sg. ἴσᾱμι Epich.254, Pi.*P.*4.248; 3 sg. ἴσατι *IG*14.644.4 (Bruttii); 1 pl. ἴσᾱμεν Pi.*N.*7.14, ἴσαμες prob. in *Dialex.*6.12; Cret. 3 pl. subj. ἴθθαντι *GDI*5024; inf. ϝισάμην Kohler-Ziebarth *Stadtrecht von Gortyn* 34 No.3.19; part. ἴσας A.D.*Adv.*175.19, dat. sg. ἴσαντι Pi.*P.*3.29, Cret. pl. ἴθθαντες *GDI*5024: subj. εἰδῶ (εἰδέω, ἰδέω, Il.14.235, Od.16.236), Ion. 3 pl. εἰδέωσι *SIG*45.21 (Halic., v B.C.); Ep. also εἴδω Od.1.174, al. (cf. Hdn.Gr.2.131), εἴδομεν Il.1.363, εἴδετε Od.9.17: opt. εἰδείην, 1 pl. εἰδεῖμεν Pl.*La.*190b, *R.*582a: inf. εἰδέναι, Ep. ἴδμεναι, ἴδμεν, also ἰδέμεν Pi.*N.*7.25: part. εἰδώς, εἰδυῖα, Ep. also ἰδυῖα, Elean ϝειζώς Schwyzer 409:—plpf. ᾔδεα Il.14.71, Hdt.2.150, contr. ᾔδη S.*Ant.*18, Ar.*Av.*511, Pl.*Smp.*119a, ᾔδησθα Od.19.93, Eup.416, etc. (but ᾔδεισθα freq. in codd., Ar.*Ec.*551, E.*Cyc.*108, Pl.*Men.*80d, al.), ᾔδεε(ν) Il.17.402, al., ᾔδη 1.70, al. (also later Att., acc. to Aristarch.ap.Choerob.*in Theod.*2.86), Att. contr. ᾔδει(ν) E.*Ion* 1187, Ar.*V.*558, etc.; Ep. 2 and 3 sg. ἠείδης, ἠείδη (v.l. -εις, -ει), Il.22.280, Od.9.206; Att. also 1 sg. ᾔδειν D.37.24, 2 sg. ᾔδεις Ar.*Th.*554, etc.; pl., ᾔδειμεν Aeschin.3.82, Arist.*APo.*87^{b}40, ᾔδεμεν Men.14D. (to be read in S.*OT*1232), ᾔδειτε D.55.9, etc. (ᾔδετε prob. in E.*Ba.*1345), Ion. ᾐδέατε Hdt.9.58 (συν-), ᾔδεισαν Lxx *Ge.*42.23, Str.15.3.23, ᾔδεσαν Hdt.7.175, Thgn.54, etc.; late Ep. ᾔδειν, ἠείδειν, A.R.2.65, 4.1700, also ᾖσμεν, ᾖστε, ᾖσαν, Ar.*Fr.*149.4 (prob.), S.*Fr.*340, E.*Cyc.*231, etc.; Ep. 3 pl. ἴσαν Il.18.405, Od.4.772:—fut., in this sense, εἴσομαι Il.1.548, Hp.*VM*20, Ar.*Ach.*332, etc.; also εἰδήσω Od.7.327, Hdt.7.234, Isoc.1.44, Aen.Tact.31.5, Arist.*Top.*108^{a}28, Herod.5.78, Apollon.Perg.*Con.*1 *Praef.*, etc.; inf. εἰδησέμεν Od.6.257.—The aor. and pf. are usu. supplied by γιγνώσκω; aor. 1 inf. εἰδῆσαι is found in Hp.*Acut.*(*Sp.*)22, *Epid.*6.8.25 (ἐξ-), Arist.*EN*1156^{b}27, Thphr.*Char.Prooem.*4; imper. εἴδησον *PCair.Zen.*36.2 (iii B.C.); 3 pl. subj. εἰδήσωσιν Herzog *Koische Forschungen* No.190 (ii/i B.C.):—*know, have knowledge of, be acquainted with*, Hom., etc.: c. acc. rei, ὃς ᾔδη τά τ' ἐόντα τά τ' ἐσσόμενα πρό τ' ἐόντα Il.1.70; νοήματα, μήδεα οἶδε, Od.2.122, Il.18.363, etc.: less freq. c. acc. pers., τούτους μὲν δὴ οἶδα Od.4.551, cf. Pl.*R.*365e, D.54.34, etc.; πρῶτος ὧν ἡμεῖς ἴδμεν the first we *know of*, Hdt.1.6, etc.; παλαίτατος ὧν ἀκοῇ ἴσμεν Th.1.4: strengthd. by εὖ or σάφα, εὖ τόδ' ἴσθι *know* well, *be assured* of this, E.*Med.*593; σάφ' οἶδ' ἐγώ A.*Supp.*740, etc.: freq. in Hom. with neut. Adj., to express character or disposition, ἄγρια οἶδε *has* fierceness *in his heart*, Il.24.41; ἀθεμίστια ᾔδη *had* lawlessness *in his heart*, Od.9.189; αἴσιμα, ἄρτια ᾔδη, 14.433, 19.248; εἴ μοι ἤπια εἰδείη if he *were* kindly *disposed* towards me, Il.16.73; φίλα εἰδότες ἀλλήλοισιν Od.3.277; κεχαρισμένα, πεπνυμένα εἰδώς, 8.584, 24.442: c. gen., ὃς σάφα θυμῷ εἰδείη τεράων Il.12.229; ὃς πάσης εἰδῇ σοφίης 15.412; τόξων εὖ εἰδὼς *cunning with* the bow, 2.718; αἰχμῆς εὖ εἰ. 15.525; οἰωνῶν σάφα εἰδὼς Od.1.202; εὖ εἰδὼς τεκτοσυνάων 5.250; μάχης εὖ εἰδότε πάσης Il.2.823; κύνε εἰδότε θήρης 10.360; παῖδ' ἔτ' ἐόντ' οὔ πω μάλα εἰδότε θούριδος ἀλκῆς 11.710; εἰδὼς πυγμαχίης 23.665; θεοπροπίων εὖ εἰδὼς 6.438; χάριν εἰδέναι τινί *acknowledge* a debt to another, *thank* him, 14.235, Hdt.3.21, etc.: imper., freq. in protestations, ἴστω νῦν Ζεὺς αὐτός *be* Zeus *my witness*, Il.10.329; ἴστω νῦν τόδε Γαῖα 15.36, etc.; Boeot. ἴττω Ἡρακλῆς, etc., Ar.*Ach.*860, etc.: part. εἰδώς, abs., *one who knows, one acquainted with the fact*, ἰδυίῃ πάντ' ἀγορεύω Il.1.365; μετ' εἰδόσιν ἀγορεύειν 10.250; μακρηγορεῖν ἐν εἰδόσιν Th.2.36, cf. 3.53; μαθεῖν παρὰ τοῦ εἰδότος Pl.*R.*337d, etc.; also ἰδυίῃσι πραπίδεσσι with *knowing* mind, Il.1.608, al. **2.** c. inf., *know how* to do, οἶδ' ἐπὶ δεξιά, οἶδ' ἐπ' ἀριστερὰ νωμῆσαι βῶν 7.238, cf. S.*Ph.*1010, Ar.*V.*376; also, *to be in a condition, be able, have the power*, E.*Med.*664, D.4.40; of drugs, ὅσα λεπτύνειν οἶδε Alex. Trall.*Febr.*6; of a festival, οἶδε ἐκπέμπουσα δάκνειν Chor.p.124B.; *learn*, ἵν' εἰδῇ μὴ 'πὶ τοῖς ἐμοῖς κακοῖς ὑψηλὸς εἶναι E.*Hipp.*729. **3.** c. part., *to know that* such and such *is* the fact, the part. being in nom. when it is a predicate of the Subject of the Verb, ἴσθι μοι δώσων *know that* thou wilt give, A.*Ag.*1670; ἴστω ὑπὸ τοῦ ἀδελφεοῦ ἀποθανών Hdt.4.76; οὐ γὰρ οἶδα δεσπότας κεκτημένος E.*Hec.*397: in acc. when it is predicate of the Object, τοὺς φιλτάτους γὰρ οἶδα νῷν ὄντας πικρούς A.*Ch.*234; τὸν Μῆδον ἴσμεν ἐκ περάτων γῆς ἐλθόντα Th.1.69: with part. omitted, γῆν αὐτὰ οἶδεν ἀμφότερα (sc. ὄντα) Jul.*Or.*7.226a. **4.** less freq. c. acc. et inf., πλήθους.. ἂν σάφ' ἴσθ' ἕκατι βάρβαρον ναυσὶν κρατῆσαι A.*Pers.*337, cf. S.*Ph.*1329; εὖ ἴσθι τοῦτον.. ἰσχυρῶς ἀνιᾶσθαι X.*Cyr.*8.3.44; also εὖ τόδ' ἴσθι, μηδάμ' ἡμέρᾳ μιᾷ πλῆθος τοσουτάριθμον ἀνθρώπων θανεῖν A.*Pers.*431; ἕν γ' ἀκούσασ' ἴσθι, μὴ ψευδῶς μ' ἐρεῖν E.*IA*1005. **5.** c. acc. folld. by ὡς, ὅτι, etc., οἶδα κἀμαυτὴν ὅτι ἀλγῶ S.*El.*332; ἐάν τινα εἰδῶσιν ὅτι ἄδικός ἐστι Pl.*Prt.*323b, etc. **6.** οὐκ οἶδ' εἰ.. I *know* not whether, to express disbelief or doubt, sts. with ἄν transposed, οὐκ οἶδ' ἂν εἰ πείσαιμί σε E.*Alc.*48, cf. D.45.7: with Verb omitted after εἰ, as οὐκ οἶδ' εἴ τις ἄλλος *perhaps* no other, Isoc.6.1, 12.10. **7.** in similar ellipses with other Conjunctions, οὐκ οἶδ' ὅπως I *know* not how, Pl.*R.*400b; οὐκ οἶδ' ὁπόθεν Id.*Cra.*396d. **8.** οἶδα, ἴσθι are freq. parenthetic, οἶδ' ἐγώ E.*Med.*948; σάφ' οἶδα ib.94, 963; also οἶδ' ὅτι, οἶσθ' ὅτι, ἴσθ' ὅτι, πάρειμι δ' ἄκων οὐχ ἑκοῦσιν, οἶδ' ὅτι (sc. πάρειμι) I *know it* well, S.*Ant.*276; οἶδ' ὅτι, freq. in D., as 9.1, al.; σάφ' ἴσθ' ὅτι Ar.*Pl.*889:—οἶσθ' ὅ, οἶσθ' ὡς, with imper., are common in Trag. and Com., οἶσθ' οὖν ὃ δρᾶσον; do—thou *know'st* what, i.e. make haste and do, Ar.*Eq.*1158, cf. *Pax* 1051, etc.; οἶσθ' ὡς πόησον; S.*OT*543; also οἶσθ'.. ὡς νῦν μὴ σφαλῇς; Id.*OC*75; οἶσθα νῦν ἅ μοι γενέσθω; E.*IT*1203: rarely with the fut., οἶσθ' οὖν ὃ δράσεις (nisi leg. δρᾶσον); Id.*Cyc.*131, cf. *Med.*600 codd.

εἰδώ· φρόνησιν, ὄψιν, Hsch.

εἰδωλ-εῖον or **-ιον**, τό, *idol's temple*, Lxx 1*Ma.*1.47, 1*Ep.Cor.*8.10. **-ικός**, ή, όν, *symbolical*, Sch.Pl.*Grg.*452d. Adv. **-κῶς** Porph. *Sent.*10, Sch.Pl.*Grg.*456a. **2.** *imaginary*, Syrian. *in Metaph.*7.32, Dam.*Pr.*453. **3.** *phantasmal*, ἔμφασις Iamb.*Myst.*3.13.

εἰδωλό-θυσία, ἡ, *sacrifice to idols*, *Gloss.* **-θυτος**, ον, *sacrificed to idols*: Subst. εἰδωλόθυτα, τά, *meats offered to idols*, *Act.Ap.*15.29, 1*Ep.Cor.*8.1, etc. **-λάτρης**, ου, ὁ, ἡ, *idol-worshipper, idolater*, ib.5.10, etc. **-λατρία**, ἡ, *idolatry*, *Ep.Gal.*5.20, 1*Ep.Cor.*10.14. **-μορφος**, ον, *formed after an image*, *Gp.*10.9.1. **2.** *like a phantom*, of comets, Sch.Ptol.*Tetr.*75.

εἴδωλον, τό, (εἶδος) *phantom*, Il.5.451, Od.4.796, Hdt.5.92.η', Pl.*Lg.*959b; βροτῶν εἴδωλα καμόντων, of ghosts, Od.11.476, etc.; ψυχῶν Procl.*Inst.*64. **2.** *any unsubstantial form*, εἴδωλον σκιᾶς A.*Ag.*839, S.*Fr.*659.6, Chaerem.14.15; οὐδὲν ἄλλο πλὴν εἴδωλα.. ἢ κούφην σκιάν S.*Aj.*126; εἰ. ἄλλως a mere *form*, Id.*Ph.*947; αἰῶνος εἰ. Pi.*Fr.*131.3. **3.** *image reflected* in a mirror or in water, Pl.*Sph.*266b, Arist.*Div.Somn.*464^{b}9. **4.** in the system of Epicurus, *film* given off by any object and conveying an impression to the eye, Epicur.*Ep.*1 p.10 U., *Nat.*2.1, al., Cic.*Fam.*15.16.1, etc. **II.** *image in the mind, idea*, X.*Smp.*4.21; *phantom of the mind, fancy*, Pl.*Phd.*66c; εἰ. καὶ ψεῦδος Id.*Tht.*150c. **III.** *image, likeness*, γυναικὸς εἰ. χρύσεον Hdt.1.51, cf. 6.58: metaph., λόγος εἰ. ψυχῆς Isoc.3.7. **IV.** later, *image of a god, idol*, Lxx 4*Ki.*17.12, 1*Ep.Cor.*12.2, *OGI*201.8 (Silco, vi A.D.), etc. **V.** εἰ. οὐράνια *constellations*, A.R.3.1004, cf. Max.56.

εἰδωλο-πλαστέω, *form, model*, Heraclit.*All.*66. **-πλαστος**, ον, *modelled*: hence, *ideal*, Lyc.173. **-ποιέω**, *form an image*, esp. in the mind, εἴδωλα εἰ. Pl.*R.*605c, cf. Arist.*de An.*427^{b}20; ὅσα εἰ. ὁ τῦφος Ph.1.671. **II.** *represent by an art-type*, Diogenian.

Epicur.2.61, Theo Sm.p.133 H.(Pass.); *portray in a bust*, D.S.31.25.2 (Pass.). b. *depict in words*, ὄψιν Longin.15.7. **–ποίησις**, εως, ἡ, *formation of mental images*, S.E.*P.*2.222 (pl.). **–ποιητής**, οῦ, ὁ, *seer of phantoms*, θεῶν ἢ νεκρῶν Vett.Val.112.34. **–ποιητικός**, ή, όν, *calling up phantasms*, τέχνη Iamb.*Myst.*3.28. **–ποιία**, ἡ, *formation of images*, as in a mirror, Pl.*Ti.*46a; or by painters, Id.*Criti.* 107b. 2. *image formed in the mind, imagination*, D.S.1.96: pl., Longin.15.1. 3. *putting of words into the mouth of one dead*, Hermog.*Prog.*9, Aphth.*Prog.*11. 4. *production of mental images*, Iamb.*Myst.*2.10. 5. *manufacture of idols*, ib.3.28. **–ποιικός**, ή, όν, *of* or *for image-making*, ἡ εἰ. (with or without τέχνη) Pl.*Sph.* 235b, 236c, al. II. *producing* εἴδωλα (in the Epicurean sense), σώματα Diog.Oen.7. **–ποιός**, ὁ, *image-maker*, Pl.*Sph.*239d, Iamb. *Myst.*3.28. II. Adj., *producing phantasmal appearances*, δύναμις ib.10.2, cf. 2.10.

εἰδωλουργικός, ή, όν, = εἰδωλοποιικός: –κή, ἡ, Pl.*Sph.*266d.

εἰδωλο-φᾰνής, ές, *like an image*, *Placit.*5.19.5. **–χᾰρής**, ές, *delighting in images*, Dam.*Pr.*453.

εἶελος· εἴλιγγος, Hsch.

εἶέν (for the aspiration, found in cod. Rav. of Ar., etc., cf. A.D. *Synt.*319.26, *An.Bachm.*1.208), Particle used in dialogue and oratory, in passing to the next point, *well, quite so, very good*, Ar.*Nu.* 1075, Pl.*Ap.*19a, etc.; "εἶέν" ἐρῶ καὶ κατανεύσομαι καὶ ἀνανεύσομαι Id.*R.*350e: folld. by a question, Ar.*Nu.*176, etc.; εἶέν· τί δῆτα..; S.*Ph.*1308; εἶέν· καὶ δὴ τεθνᾶσι E.*Med.*386: folld. by imper., S.*El.* 534; in argument, *so far so good*: εἶέν, ἐρεῖ δέ.. Antipho 4.2.3; εἶέν, τοῦτο μὲν ἡμῖν κείσθω· ἔφαμεν δέ.. Pl.*R.*350d; εἶέν, ἀλλὰ νὴ Δία.. D.20.75, cf. D.Chr.17.19, etc.; εἶὲν δή Pl.*Smp.*213e. [At the beginning of a trimeter, εἶέν, ἀκούω, A.*Ch.*657, Ar.*Pax* 663: extra versum in E. l.c.]

εἴεω, a battle-cry of young warriors, Hsch.

εἵην, aor. 2 opt. of ἵημι: but **εἴην**, pres. opt. of εἰμί (*sum*).

εἶθαρ, Adv. *at once, forthwith*, Il.5.337, Theoc.25.213, Antim.16.5, A.R.2.408, Nic.*Th.*547.

εἴθε, Ep. αἴθε, v. εἰ A. **εἰθεῖν**· μαθεῖν, Hsch.

εἰθίζω, poet. for ἐθίζω.

εἰθισμένως, Adv., (ἐθίζω) *in the accustomed manner*, Arcesil.ap. D.L.4.35.

εἰκ, v. εἰ. **εἶκα**, pf. of ἵημι.

εἰκᾰδάρχης, ου, ὁ, *commander of twenty*, Hsch.

εἰκάδιος [ᾰ], α, ον, *belonging to, celebrated on the* εἰκάς, *EM* 297.59, *Et.Gud.*164.22.

εἰκᾰδισταί, ῶν, οἱ, epith. of the Epicureans, because they commemorated their founder's death *on the twentieth* (εἰκάς) of Gamelion, Ath.7.298d.

εἰκάζω, Aeol. **εἰκάσδω** Sapph.104: impf. εἴκαζον Hdt.4.133, but Att. ᾔκαζον Ar.*Ec.*385: fut. -άσω A.*Eu.*49: aor. εἴκασα Hdt.2.104, Att. ᾔκασα Ar.*Nu.*350, etc.: pf. εἴκακα Sch.Ar.*V.*151:—Pass., fut. εἰκασθήσομαι Ar.*Ach.*783: aor. εἰκάσθην X.*HG*7.5.22: pf. εἴκασμαι Hdt.3.28, Att. ᾔκασμαι (ἐξ-) Ar.*Eq.*230 (but εἴκασται Pl.*Cra.*439a).— This is the only Verb that augments εἰ- by ᾐ-:—*represent by an image* or *likeness, portray*, γυναῖκα γραφῇ εἰκάσας X.*Oec.*10.1; εἰκὼν γραφῇ εἰκασμένη a figure *painted to the life*, Hdt.2.182; αἰετὸς εἰκασμένος *a figure like* an eagle, Id.3.28; χειρὶ τεκτόνων δέμας.. εἰκασθέν E.*Alc.*349; κενταύροις ᾔκασαν αὑτάς *made* themselves *like* Centaurs, Ar.*Nu.*350; τοῦ θεοῦ.. ᾧπερ εἰκάζεις σεαυτόν Id.*Ra.*594. II. *liken, compare*, ὄρπακι βραδίνῳ σε μάλιστ' ἐϊκάσδω Sapph. l.c., cf. A.*Ch.*633 (lyr.), *Eu.*49, etc.; *describe by a comparison*, εἰ. τι ὡς εἰ.. Hdt.7.162, cf. 4.31, Arist.*EN* 1106ᵇ30:—Pass., *to be like, resemble*, τινί E.*Ba.*942, 1253, etc.; πρός τινα Ar.*Ach.*783. III. *infer from comparison, form a conjecture*, Hdt.1.68, 7.49, S.*OC* 1504, 1677 (lyr.), Isoc.3.26; freq. in phrase ὡς εἰκάσαι so far as *one can guess*, ὡς εἰκάσαι, βασιλήϊην τε καὶ πολιτήϊην αἰτεομένους Hdt.9.34, cf. 1.34, etc.; rarely without ὡς, ἀλλ', εἰκάσαι μέν, ἡδύς S.*OT* 82: c. acc. et inf., Hdt.4.132, Antipho Soph.53, Th.5.9, etc.: omisso inf., 'Αμαζόνας.. ἂν ᾔκασ' ὑμᾶς (sc. εἶναι) A.*Supp.*288; τί τοῦτ' ἂν εἰκάσειας (sc. εἶναι); S.*Ant.*1244; εἰ. τι ἔκ τινος A.*Th.*356 (lyr.), Th.3.20; ἀπό τινος Id.1.10; εἰ. τι *make a guess* about it, A.*Ch.*518, Antipho 5.64; τινί Th.1.9, Plu.*Publ.*14; *estimate*, τὴν κριθήν, τὰ τετρυγημένα εἰς.., at a given quantity, *PSI* 5.522 (iii B.C.), *PGurob* 8.14 (iii B.C.): abs., εἰ. τεκμαιρόμενος Lys. 6.20; εἰ. καλῶς Men.852.

εἰκαθεῖν, inf. of aor. εἴκαθον, from εἴκω *yield*; subj. εἰκάθω S.*OT* 651 (lyr.), *Ph.*1352; inf. εἰκαθεῖν Id.*El.*396, *Ant.*1096; part. εἰκαθών Id. *Tr.*1177. Cf. παρ-, ὑπ-εικαθεῖν.

εἰκαιο-βουλία, ἡ, *rashness*, Hsch. **–λογέω**, *talk at random*, Dosith.p.431 K. **–λογία**, ἡ, *random talking*, Ph.1.674. **–λόγος**, ον, *talking at random*, Phld.*Rh.*1.191 S. (Comp.). **–μῡθέω**, = εἰκαιολογέω, Hsch., Suid. **–μῡθία**, ἡ, *random talking*, Id. **–ρρημοσύνη**, ἡ, = εἰκαιομυθέω, Id. **–ρρημοσύνη**, ἡ, = εἰκαιομυθία, Id.

εἰκαῖος, α, ον, (εἰκῇ) *without aim* or *purpose*, 1. of things, *random, purposeless*, τίκτει γὰρ οὐδὲν ἐσθλὸν εἰκαία σχολή S.*Fr.*308; ὡς εἰκαῖον ὄν as being *useless*, Luc.*JConf.*6; εἰ. διήγημα J.*BJ Prooem.* 1. Adv. -ως, δοξάζειν cj. in Epicur.*Ep.*1 p.30 U., cf. Diotog.ap. Stob.4.1.96, D.L.2.128, Procl.*in Cra.*p.26 P.: Comp. -ότερον S.E. *M.*1.276: neut. pl. as Adv., Lyc.748. 2. of persons, *rash, hasty*, Plb.7.7.5, etc.; οἱ πολλοὶ καὶ εἰ. Cebes 12; τὸ εἰ. *PRyl.*235.12 (ii A.D.). 3. *ordinary, casual*, J.*BJ*2.10.2, Luc.*Am.*33; *taken at random*, ξύλα Iamb.*Comm.Math.*4; *careless*, σφίξις Heliod.ap.Orib. 50.9.10.

εἰκαιοσύνη, ἡ, *thoughtlessness*, Timo 36.

εἰκαιότης, ητος, ἡ, = foreg., Phld.*Rh.*1.190 S., *Vit.*p.29 J., Ph.1. 193, D.L.7.48.

εἰκαιόψογοι ψόγοι *random censure*, Demetr.*Eloc.*291 (dub. l.).

εἰκάς, άδος, ἡ, Aeol. dat. pl. εἰκάδεσσι B.*Scol.Oxy.*1361 *Fr.*1.5: (εἴκοσι):—*twentieth day of the month* (sc. ἡμέρα), Hes.*Op.*792, 820, Plu.2.1089c, etc.: pl., B. l.c., Epicur.*Fr.*217; ἡ πρώτη, δευτέρα, etc., μετ' εἰκάδα, εἰκάδας, the 21st, 22nd, etc., Men.320.3, *IG*2². 890, etc.; τετάρτῃ ἐπὶ εἰκάδι *IG*9(1).694.2 (Corc.): hence εἰκάδες, αἱ, *the last ten days* of the month, And.1.121; σελήνην ἄγουσαν εἰκάδας Ar.*Nu.*17; τρίτῃ εἰκάδι, i.e. the 23rd, Pl.*Lg.*849b. II. name of the sixth day of the Eleusinian mysteries (= Boedromion 20), E.*Ion* 1076 (pl., lyr.), cf. Plu.*Phoc.*28. III. pl., divisions of a tribe, Hsch.

ἐϊκάσδω, v. εἰκάζω.

εἰκ-ᾰσία, ἡ, *likeness, representation*, X.*Mem.*3.10.1. II. *comparison*, Plu.*Them.*29; *estimate*, ἐξ εἰκασίας *PTeb.*61(*a*).186, al. (ii B.C.). III. *conjecture*, Hp.*Morb.*1.1, Pl.*Sis.*390c, Ph.2.91, Hierocl. p.37 A. (pl.), etc.; *doubt*, Phld.*Rh.*1.249 S. IV. *apprehension of* or *by means of images* or *shadows*, Pl.*R.*511e, 534a. **–άσιμος**, ον, *that can be estimated*, Gloss. **–ασμα**, ατος, τό, *likeness*, A.*Th.*523 (lyr.), Porph.*Plot.*1, Iamb.*Comm.Math.*8; θεὸς πολύμορφον εἰ. Secund. *Sent.*3. II. *probability*, Max.Tyr.9.3 (pl.). **–ασμός**, ὁ, *conjecturing, guessing*, D.H.6.71 (pl.); εἰκασμοῦ ἐπίρρημα *conjectural* adverb (ἴσως), D.T.642.8; ἐξ εἰκασμοῦ λέγειν Str.17.3.1, cf. Plu.*Mar.*11, Luc. *Herm.*16. **–αστέον**, *one must liken, compare*, τί τινι Plu.2.374a, Max.Tyr.33.6. **–αστής**, οῦ, ὁ, *one who conjectures, diviner*, τῶν μελλόντων Th.1.138, cf. J.*AJ*18.9.2. II. *one who portrays, represents*, ἀληθείας D.H.*Isoc.*11, cf. *Lys.*19. **–αστικός**, ή, όν, *able to represent*: ἡ –κὴ τέχνη the art of *copying* or *portraying*, Pl.*Sph.*235d, etc. II. *able* or *liable to conjecture*, ψευδῶν Ph.1.160; τὸ εἰ. *the faculty of conjecturing*, Luc.*Alex.*22. Adv. -κῶς *conjecturally*, Phld. *Rh.*2.91 S. (dub.), Procl.*in Alc.*p.23 C. 2. τὸ εἰ. *matter of conjecture*, Vett.Val.312.32. **–αστός**, ή, όν, *comparable, similar*, S.*Tr.* 699. 2. *apprehended through an image*, opp. αἰσθητός, Ascl.*in Metaph.*142.10, Iamb.*Comm.Math.*8, Sch.Pl.*R.*509d. 3. *conjectural*, Procl.*in Alc.*p.23 C.

εἴκᾰτι, εἰκατίδειος, v. εἴκοσι, εἰκοσιδύω. **εἴ κε, εἴ κεν**, v. εἰ B. II.

εἰκέλιος, α, ον, = εἴκελος, Man.3.237, 6.346.

εἰκελόνειρος, ον, *dream-like*, ἀνέρες Ar.*Av.*687 (anap.).

εἴκελος, η, ον, (εἰκός) *like*, τινί Il.22.134; χελιδόνι εἰ. αὐδήν Od.21. 411, cf. Hdt.8.8 (v.l. for ἴκελος), S.*Fr.*574.4, Plu.2.410e.

εἰκελόφωνος, ον, *of like voice*, χελιδόσιν *AP*6.247 (Phil.).

εἰκέναι, Att. for ἐοικέναι, inf. of ἔοικα.

εἰκῇ, *without plan* or *purpose, at random, at a venture*, Xenoph. 2.13, Heraclit.47, Hp.*Epid.*7.9, A.*Pr.*450, 885, Ar.*Eq.*431, D.28.5; εἰ. ζῆν S.*OT* 979; πράττειν Pl.*Prt.*326d; λέγεσθαι Id.*Ap.*17c, etc.; νήφων παρ' εἰ. λέγοντας Arist.*Metaph.*984ᵇ17, etc.; ἄρμενα εἰ. ἀποκλασθέντα Theoc.22.14. II. *in vain*, *PLips.*104.29 (i B.C.), 1*Ep. Cor.*15.2, al. III. *slightly, moderately*, ἀγγεῖα εἰ. πεπυρωμένα Agatharch.61. (Prob. for ἐϝεκῇ 'at will', cf. ἑκών.)

εἰκλεῖ· δειπνεῖ, and **εἶκλον**· δεῖπνον, Hsch.; cf. αἶκλον. **εἰκνεῖται**· ἄλλος αὐτὸν εἰσφέρει, Id.

εἰκο-βολέω, *talk at random*, γλῶσσ' εἰκοβολεῖ περὶ τῶν ἀφανῶν E. *Fr.*913.4, cf. Ar.*Fr.*689, Phld.*Rh.*1.247 S., *EM* 297.32. II. *discharge missiles at random*, Plb.*Fr.*35. **–βολία**, ἡ, *talking at random*, Phld.*Rh.*2.98 S. (pl.).

εἰκον-ίδιον, τό, Dim. of εἰκών I. 1, *POxy.*1449.8 (iii A.D.). **–ίζω**, *copy* from a pattern, *PPar.*65.12 (ii B.C.). 2. *draw up an official description*, *PFay.*36.23 (ii A.D.), etc. 3. *mould into form*, τὰς ἀμόρφους ὕλας *Placit.*1.10.1; εἰ. ἀλήθειαν *to give the semblance of* truth, Aphth.*Prog.*1:—Med., *picture to oneself*, θάνατον Vett.Val.226. 19. **–ικός**, ή, όν, *representing a figure, copied from it*, εἰ. ἄγαλμά τινος *a portrait* statue, Callix.1; πίνακες *IG*2².995.8, cf. Plu.*Lys.*1; ὅπλον εἰ. shield *with* embossed *portrait*, *IGRom.*4.144; of actor's masks, Poll.4.148. II. *counterfeited, pretended*, *AP*11.233 (Lucill.). III. *belonging to* or *employing images*, φαντασία Plot. 3.6.18; διάκοσμος Dam.*Pr.*284, cf. 423 (Comp.). Adv. -κῶς Procl. *Inst.*65, *in Euc.*p.16 F., Dam.*Pr.*330, Simp.*in Ph.*160.24. **–ιον**, τό, Dim. of εἰκών, Polem.Hist.18, Plu.2.753b, *BGU* 423.21 (ii A.D.). **–ισμα**, ατος, τό, *image*, λιθουργές S.*Fr.*573, cf. *AP* 13.6 (Phal.), Porph.*Sent.*43, Plot.1.4.10; *portrait*, Herod.4.38. **–ισμός**, ὁ, *delineation, description*, Plu.2.54b. II. *registered description* of individuals for purposes of census, *PRyl.*161.15 (i A.D.), *PLond.ined.* 2196 (i A.D.), etc.; term used by *publicani*, Sen.*Ep.*95 (pl.). **–ιστής**, οῦ, ὁ, *registrar*, *POxy.*1.34ᵛ i 12 (ii A.D.).

εἰκονο-γρᾰφέω, *depict*, Ph.2.588; *describe*, Longin.10.6, Heraclit. *Incred.*15. 2. *make an image*, dub. in *PPetr.*2 p.9. **–γρᾰφία**, ἡ, *sketch, description*, Str.15.1.69. **–γράφος** [ᾰ], ὁ, *portrait-painter*, Arist.*Po.*1454ᵇ9, Them.*Or.*24.309b; prob. in *IG*7.3064 (Lebad.). **–λογέω**, *speak figuratively*, prob. in Antig.*Mir.*127. **–λογία**, ἡ, *figurative speaking*, Pl.*Phdr.*267c, 269a (pl.). **–μορφος**, ὁ, *portrait-sculptor*, Man.4.343 (pl.). **–ποιία**, ἡ, *image-making*, Dam.*Pr.* 341. **–ποιός**, ὁ, *portrait-sculptor* or *-painter*, Arist.*Po.*1460ᵇ 9. **–στάσιον** [ᾰ], τό, *shrine*, Anon.*in Rh.*78.2.

εἰκονώδης, ες, *fantastic*, Gloss.

εἰκός, Ion. οἰκός, ότος, τό, neut. part. of ἔοικα, *like truth*, i.e. *likely, probable, reasonable*, εἰ. (with or without ἐστί), c. inf. pres., aor., or fut.,

S.*El.*1026, A.*Ag.*575, Is.4.18; οὐ γὰρ εἰ., c. inf., S.*Ph.*230; οἷς εἰ. (sc. δοῦναι) ib.973; ὥσπερ εἰ. ἦν Ar.*Fr.*621, etc.: also pl., ἐοικότα γάρ.. τυχεῖν Pi.*P.*1.34. 2. neut. Subst., εἰκός, τό, *likelihood, probability*, τὰ οἰκότα *likelihoods*, Hdt.1.155, etc.; τὸ οὐκ εἰ. Th.2.89; κατὰ τὸ εἰ. in all *likelihood*, Id.1.121; ἐκ τοῦ εἰκότος Id.4.17; τῷ εἰκότι Id.6.18; παντὶ τῷ οἰκότι Hdt.7.103; τοῦ εἰκότος πέρα S.*OT*74; τῷ εἰκότι χρῆσθαι, opp. ἀπόδειξιν λέγειν, Pl.*Tht.*162e: in Poets without Art., λέγεις μὲν εἰκότα S.*Ph.*1373; εἰκὸς πέπονθα E.*IA*501; ἦν γ' ἐρωτᾷς εἰκότ', εἰκότα κλύεις ib.1134. b. in Logic, *probable proposition*, opp. positive fact, Arist.*APr.*70ᵃ4, *Rh.*1357ᵃ34. II. *reasonable, fair, equitable*, Th.2.74, Isoc.3.53, etc.; τὰ εἰ. καὶ δίκαια Th.5.90; παρὰ τὸ εἰ. *unreasonably*, 2.62: Comp. εἰκότερον Antipho 2.2.3.

εἰκοσά-βοιος, poet. ἐεικ– [ᾰ], ον, *worth twenty oxen*, Od.1.431. **–γράμμᾰτος**, ον, *of twenty letters*, [ὄνομα] *PMag.Par.*1.2634. **–γωνος**, ον, *having twenty angles*: τὸ εἰ. Iamb.*VP*34.247.

εἰκοσά-εδρος [ᾰ], ον, *of twenty surfaces*: εἰκοσάεδρον, τό, *body with twenty surfaces*, Plu.2.719e, Gal.5.668. **–ετηρίς**, ίδος, ἡ, *period of twenty years*, Ptol.*Tetr.*205. **–ετής**, ές, or **–έτης**, ες, *of twenty years*, παῖς Hdt.1.136; χρόνος Plu.2.113d, Wilcken *Chr.*41 iii 21 (iii A.D.):—better **εἰκοσιετής**, fem. –ετίς, Pl.*R.*460e, D.C.55.9; ϝικατιϝέτιες *IG*7.3068 (Lebad.). **–ετία**, ἡ, *period of twenty years*, Ph.2.224, J.*AJ*8.5.3, *PTeb.*287.7.

εἰκοσάκις, *twenty times*, Il.9.379, Pl.*Lg.*771b, etc.

εἰκοσά-κλῖνος, ον, = εἰκοσίκλινος, D.S.1.49, Ath.12.548a. **–κωλος**, ον, *of twenty members*, εἴσθεσις Sch.Ar.*Nu.*1153. **–κωπος**, ον, *with twenty oars*, Hsch. s. v. ἐεικοσόροιο, etc. **–μηνος**, ον, *twenty months old*, *AP*7.662 (Leon.). **–μναῖος**, α, ον, *weighing twenty minae*, Ph.*Bel.*95.10. **–πηχυς**, υ, = εἰκοσιπ–, Chares ap.Ath.12.538d, Luc.*DMort.*27.4. **–πλάσιος** [πλᾰ], α, ον, = sq., Aristarch. Sam.7, Procl.*Hyp.*3.68. **–πλασίων**, ον, gen. ονος, *twentyfold*, Plu. 2.925c. **–πλοῦς**, οῦν, *twentyfold*, Sch.Il.22.349, Hsch. s. v. ἐεικοσαβοιέων. **–πρωτοι**, οἱ, *municipal council of twenty*, *OGI*629.10 (Palmyra), *Rev.Ét.Gr.*6.120 (Iasos):—hence **–πρωτεία**, ἡ, *office of* εἰ., *Dig.*50.4.18.26, and **–πρωτεύω**, *hold such office*, *JHS*15.118 (Lycia), *Jahresh.*5.199 (Arneae).

εἰκοσ-άριθμος [ᾰ], ον, gloss on εἰκοσινήριτος, *EM*297.44, Suid. **–άρουρος** [ᾰ], ὁ, *holder of twenty* ἄρουραι of land, *PTeb.*61(*a*).65 (ii B.C.), al.

εἰκοσάς, άδος, ἡ, *score*, Orac.ap.Luc.*Alex.*11, Vett.Val.339.1, S.E. *M.*4.32, Hierocl. *in CA* 20p.464M.

εἰκοσα-στάδιος [στᾰ], ον, *of twenty stadia*, Str.9.4.4. **–στεγος**, ον, *having twenty stories*, Ath.Mech.12.4.

εἰκοσ-ετηρίς, ίδος, ἡ, = Lat. *Vicennalia*, D.C.58.24. **–έτης**, ου, ὁ, = εἰκοσαετής, *BMus.Inscr.*2.390 (Cypr.):—fem. **–ετίς**, ίδος, ἡ, *AP* 7.166 (Diosc. or Nicarch.). **–ήρης**, ες, *with twenty banks of oars*, Ath.5.203d.

εἴκοσι (for εἴκοσιν v. infr.), Att., Ion., also Arc., *IG*5(2).3.1 (Tegea), and Aeol., ib.12(2).6.21 (Lesbos):—indecl., *twenty*, Il.2. 510,748, etc.; in Hom. more freq. in Ep. form **ἐείκοσι**, before a vowel ἐείκοσιν, 1.309, 6.217, al.; Dor. ϝίκατι *Leg.Gort.*4.13, etc.; ϝείκατι *Tab.Heracl.*2.71; Lacon. **βείκατι** Hsch.; **εἴκατι** *IG*9(1).693. 10 (Corc.), Theoc.4.10, 5.86. (Orig. ϝίκατι and *ἐϝίκοσι, whence ἐείκοσι in Hom.; ϝείκατι and εἴκατι are late spellings of (ϝ)ῑκατι; εἴκοσι is contr. from *ἐϝίκοσι. Cf. Lat. *vīginti*, Skt. *viṁśatis*. εἴκοσιν is the only form used by Ar., whether before vowels or consonants (εἴκοσ' ἀπολογίζεται is dub. in *Fr.*465); also (before consonants) Herod.3.91, Phld.*Piet.*3, etc., but not common in Inscrr. or Pap., e.g. (before consonants) *Schwyzer* 707*B*2 (Ephesus, vi B.C.), *IG*2.804.155 (iv B.C.), (before a vowel) *PGrenf.*2.75.7 (iv A.D.); εἴκοσι ἔτη, εἴκοσι ἡμερῶν, *IG*1².94,49.)

εἰκοσί-δύω or **–δύο**, *two and twenty*, *PSI*4.390 (iii B.C.), Eust. 726.13. **–εδρος**, ον, = εἰκοσάεδρος, Ti.Locr.98d. **–είς**, ενός, *twenty-one*, *UPZ*81 ii 14 (ii B.C.). **–εκταῖος**, α, ον, *on the twenty-sixth day*, Gal.7.501. **–εννέα**, *nine and twenty*, *BGU*339 (ii A.D.), Ath.13.608a: **–έξ**, *six and twenty*, *Vit.Eur.*: **–επτά**, *seven and twenty*, Hp.*Oss.*1. **–επτάετής**, ὁ, ἡ, *twenty-seven years old*, *Annales du Service* 22.16. **–ετής**, ές, v. εἰκοσαετής. **–καιτετραπλάσίων**, ον, gen. ονος, *twenty-four times as great*, Procl.*Hyp.*3.51. **–κλῖνος**, ον, *with twenty places at table*, Antig.Caryst.ap.Ath.12.548a, D.S.1. 49. **–μετρος**, ον, *holding twenty measures*, τρίπος Nonn.*D.*37.548, 610. **–μνως**, ων, *of twenty minae*, ἔρανος Lys.*Fr.*19.

εἰκοσινήρῐτος, ον, (εἴκοσιν, ἀρι– 'count', cf. ἀριθμός), δεκάκις τε καὶ εἰ. ἄποινα a ten-, yea *twentyfold* ransom, Il.22.349.

εἰκοσῐ-οκτώ, *twenty-eight*, D.S.14.102, *BGU*458 (iii A.D.), etc. **–πεδος**, ον, *twenty feet wide or long*, in Dor. form ϝικατίπεδος *Tab. Heracl.*1.62, al. **–πενταέτης**, *twenty-five years old*, *IG*3.1376 (fem.). **–πεντάρουρος** [ᾰ], *holding twenty-five* ἄρουραι, *PHib.*1.87 (iii B.C.). **–πέντε**, *twenty-five*, Syngr.ap.D.35.10. **–πηχυς**, υ, *of twenty cubits*, βάθος Hdt.3.60. **–στάδιος** [ᾰ], ον, *of twenty stadia*, μέτρον Th.6.1. **–τέσσᾰρες**, ρα, *twenty-four*, Hp.*Oss.*1, D.S. 14.92. **–τρεῖς**, neut. **–τρία**, *twenty-three*, Ath.13.585b. **–φυλλος**, ον, *with twenty petals*, ῥόδον Thphr.*HP*6.6.4.

εἰκόσορος, poet. ἐεικ–, ον, (εἴκοσι, ἐρέσσω) *with twenty oars*, Od. 9.322, Teles p.27H., *AP*5.203.10 (Mel.), 6.222 (Theodorid.): as Subst., εἰ. (sc. ναῦς), ἡ, D.35.18.

εἰκοσταῖος, α, ον, *on the twentieth day*, Hp.*Prog.*15, Antipho 1.20; εἰκοσταῖοί ἐσμεν ἀφ' οὗ ἐγδημοῦμεν *PLond.ined.*2090 (iii B.C.).

εἰκοστή, ἡ, v. εἰκοστός II.

εἰκοστόγδοον, τό, *one twenty-eighth*, Nicom.*Ar.*1.16.

εἰκοστο-έβδομος, ον, *twenty-seventh*, Plu.2.1027f. **–εκταῖος**, α, ον, *on the twenty-sixth day*, Gal.7.501. **–λόγος**, ὁ, ἡ, *one who collects the twentieth, tax-* or *toll-collector*, Ar.*Ra.*363. **–πεμπτος**, ον, *twenty-fifth*, *Gp.*8.23.2, Nicom.*Ar.*1.12. **–πρωτος**, ον, *twenty-first*, ibid.

εἰκοστός, ή, όν, *twentieth*, Od.5.34, etc.; Ep. also ἐεικοστός Il.24. 765. II. εἰκοστή, ἡ, *a tax of a twentieth*, εἰ. τῶν γιγνομένων, τῶν κατὰ θάλασσαν, Th.6.54, 7.28. 2. εἰ. ἐλευθερίας or –ιῶν, = Lat. *vicesima manumissionum*, *IG*3.1446, *BGU*96.8, etc.

εἰκοστο-τέταρτος, ον, *twenty-fourth*, Plu.2.935e:—also **–τεταρταῖος**, α, ον, Gal.7.501.

εἰκοστώνης, ου, ὁ, *farmer of the vicesima*, Arr.*Epict.*4.1.33.

εἰκοσώρῠγος, ον, (ὀργυιά) *of twenty fathoms*, δίκτυα X.*Cyn.*2.5.

εἰκοτο-λογέω, *infer from probabilities*, Str.13.3.2. **–λογία**, ἡ, *probability* or *inference therefrom*, Archyt.ap.Stob.1.41.5, Phld.*Rh.* 1.80S., Str.13.3.1, Iamb.*VP*18.86 (pl.), Herm. *in Phdr.*p.74A. (pl.), Simp. *in Ph.*18.30.

εἰκότως, Adv. of εἰκώς, Att. pf. part. of ἔοικα, *suitably*, c. dat., A. *Ag.*915; *fairly, reasonably*, Id.*Supp.*403 (lyr.), S.*OC*432,977, Isoc.12. 101, etc.; εἰ. ἔχει *'tis reasonable*, E.*IT*911, cf. *Or.*737 (troch.); εἰ. δοκεῖ And.1.140, cf. 142; οὐκ εἰ. *unreasonably*, Th.1.37: folld. by γάρ, ib.77: freq. at the end of sentences, D.1.10, al., Pl.*La.*183b.

εἰκτέον, (εἴκω) *one must yield*, Ph.2.68.

εἰκτικός, ή, όν, (εἴκω) *readily yielding*, φύσις, of the void, Phld. *Sign.*18, cf. Max.Tyr.13.3 (Comp.), Heliod.ap.Orib.44.10.2, Them. *in de An.*92.36: metaph., *weak, easily refuted*, λόγος Phld.*Sign.*13.

ἔϊκτον, ἐΐκτην, ἔϊκτο, v. ἔοικα.

εἰκτός, ή, όν, (εἴκω) *yielding*, Alex.Aphr.*Quaest.*62.4, *EM*297. 8. II. (ἔοικα) *like*, Theognost.*Can.*15.

***εἴκω**, *to be like, seem likely*, v. ἔοικα.

εἴκω, Il.12.48, etc.: impf. εἶκον 16.305 (ὑπό–), Hdt.8.3: fut. εἴξω Th.1.141, etc.: aor. 1 εἶξα Il.24.718, etc., poet. ἔειξα or ἔϝειξα Alcm. 31, Ion. εἴξασκε Od.5.332: pf. part. ἐεικώς *Chron.Lind.*D.96:—*give way, retire*, ὀπίσσω εἶκετε Il.5.606; ὅππῃ τ' ἰθύσῃ τῇ τ' εἴκουσι στίχες ἀνδρῶν 12.48: c. dat., *make way for*, οὐρεῦσι 24.716; *yield* to pressure, Gal.18(1).97. 2. c. dat. pers. et gen. loci, μηδ' εἴκετε χάρμης Ἀργείοις *shrink* not *from* the fight for them, 4.509; εἴκειν τινὶ τῆς ὁδοῦ Hdt.2.80; εἴξατέ μοι νίκης Coluth.171: c. gen. only, εἴκειν πολέμου καὶ δηϊοτῆτος *withdraw from* war and strife, Il.5.348; εἶκε, γέρον, προθύρου *retire from* the door, Od.18.10, cf. Jul.*Or.*2.67b. 3. *give way*, as a mark of honour, Il.24.100, Od.2.14; τῇ πατρίδι Jul.*Or.*8. 246a. 4. *give way to* any passion or impulse, ᾧ θυμῷ εἴξας Il.9. 598; ὄκνῳ καὶ ἀφραδίῃσι 10.122; ὕβρει Od.14.262; βίῃ καὶ κάρτεϊ εἴκειν *give full play to* one's might and strength, 13.143; ὀργῇ δ' εἶξα μᾶλλον ἤ μ' ἐχρῆν E.*Hel.*80; τῇ ἡλικίῃ εἴκειν Hdt.7.18; of circumstances, πενίῃ εἴκων Od.14.157; κακοῖς A.*Pr.*322; ἀνάγκῃ Id.*Ag.*1071; ξυμφοραῖς Th.1.84; ζημίαις *to the force of* punishment, X.*Cyr.*1.6.21:—in S.*Ant.*718 θυμοῦ shd. prob. be read for θυμῷ. 5. εἴκειν τινί τι *yield to* another *in* a thing, τὸ ὃν μένος οὐδενὶ εἴκων *inferior to* none *in*.., Il. 22.459, Od.11.515: c. acc. cogn., εἴκοντας ἃ δεῖ *yielding* in.., S.*OC* 172 (lyr.), cf. *Aj.*1243: also c. dupl. dat., ἕλεσκον ἀνδρῶν.. ὅ τέ μοι εἴξειε πόδεσσι whoever *was inferior* to me *in* swiftness of foot, Od. 14.221. 6. c. gen., *retire from*, ἱερατείας *Chron.Lind.* l. c. II. trans., *yield up, give up*, εἶξαί τέ οἱ ἡνία *give* [the horse] the rein, Il.23. 337; Εὖρος Ζεφύρῳ εἴξασκε διώκειν *gave up* [the ship] to Zephyrus to chase, Od.5.332. 2. *grant, allow*, ὁπηνίκ' ἂν θεὸς πλοῦν ἡμὶν εἴκῃ S.*Ph.*465. III. impers., *it is allowable* or *possible*, ὅπῃ εἴξειε μάλιστα Il.22.321: c. inf., ὅθι σφίσιν εἶκε λοχῆσαι 18.520; φώναισ' οὐδὲν ἔτ' εἴκει Sapph.2.8; φερόμενοι πρὸς τὸ εἶκον attacking on the *line of least resistance*, Plu.*Fab.*16.

εἰκών, ἡ, gen. όνος, acc. όνα, etc.: poet. and Ion. nom. **εἰκώ** is implied (though not found) in gen. εἰκοῦς E.*Hel.*77, acc. εἰκώ A.*Th.*559, E.*Med.*1162, Hdt.7.69 (but εἰκόνα 2.143, both εἰκόνα and εἰκώ in Pl.*Ti.* 37d), Maiist.15: acc. pl. εἰκούς E.*Tr.*1178, Ar.*Nu.*559: (*εἴκω, ἔοικα, ϝεικ– *Inscr.Cypr.*151H.):—*likeness, image*, whether picture or statue, Hdt.2.130,143, A.*Th.*559, etc.; εἰ. γεγραμμένη Plu.2.1117c; εἰ. γραπτά *IG*4.940.23, cf. 3.1330; of needlework, E.*IT*223 (anap.); *bust*, Luc.*Alex.*18; εἰ. βασιλικαί, = Lat. *imagines imperatorum*, Lib. *Or.*56.13: generally, εἰ. τοῦ νοητοῦ θεὸς αἰσθητός Pl.*Ti.*92c. 2. *image in a mirror*, E.*Med.*1162, Pl.*R.*402b. 3. *personal description*, *PTeb.*32.21 (ii B.C.), etc. 4. metaph., *living image, representation*, εἰ. ζῶσα τοῦ Διός *OGI*90.3 (Rosetta, ii B.C.); τοῦ θεοῦ 2*Ep.Cor.*4. 4. II. *semblance, phantom*, E.*HF*1002; οὐ γὰρ ἐκεῖνος τέθνηκεν, ἀλλ' ἐγὼ ἡ εἰ. αὐτοῦ Luc.*DMort.*16.1; *imaginary form*, Pl.*R.*588b; *image in the mind*, εἰκοὺς πατρός E.*Tr.*1178; δοξῶν καὶ λόγων Pl.*Phlb.* 39c, etc.; εἰκόνας σῆς ἀρετῆς thy virtue's *counterparts*, of children, *Epigr.Gr.*435.4; περίβολον ἔχειν δεσμωτηρίου εἰκόνα Pl.*Cra.*400c; ἐν εἰκόνι βασιλείας Hdn.7.9.10. III. *similitude, comparison*, Ar.*Nu.* 559, *Ra.*906, Pl.*Phd.*87b, *Men.*80c, Men.536.1; δι' εἰκόνος λέγεσθαι Pl.*R.*487e, cf. Arist.*Rh.*1407ᵃ11, Lib.*Ep.*8.1. IV. *pattern, archetype*, ποτὶ τὰν εἰκόνα [κόσμος] ἀπειργασμένος Ti.Locr.99d.

εἰκώς, v. ἔοικ–. **εἶλα·** ὀσπρίων καλάμη, Hsch.; cf. εἴλη II. 2.

εἰλαμίδες, αἱ, *membranes* of the brain or spinal cord, Poll.2.44.

εἰλαδόν or **ἰλαδόν**, Adv., (εἴλη) = ἰληδόν, Hdt.1.172, App.*BC*2. 63.

εἰλᾰπῐν-άζω, used by Hom. only in pres., *revel in a large company*, Od.2.57, so Pi.*P.*10.40: impf., Q.S.6.179: trans., *feast on*, Nonn. *D.*12.49, al.; δαῖτα Opp.*H.*3.219. **–αστής**, οῦ, ὁ, *feaster, guest, boon-companion*, Il.17.577, Orph.*Fr.*207. II. name of Zeus at

Cyprus, Hegesand.30. -η, ἡ, *solemn feast* or *banquet* (Ath.8.362e), γάμοι τ' ἔσαν εἰλαπίναι τε Il.18.491; εἰλαπίνη ἠὲ γάμος, both opp. ἔρανος, Od.1.226, cf. E.*Med.*193 (lyr.), *Hel.*1337 (lyr.), Pl.*Ax.* 371d (pl.), A.R.1.13, Plu.2.169d (pl.), Ant.Lib.4.4, *BGU*1080.10 (iii A.D.); cf. ἐλλαπίνα. -ουργός, ὁ, *maker of feasts*, Man.4.300.

εἶλαρ, τό, used only in nom. and acc. sg., *covering, shelter, defence*, εἶ. νηῶν τε καὶ αὐτῶν *shelter for* ship and crew, Il.7.338, etc.; κύματος εἶ. *fence against* the waves, Od.5.257. (ϝέλϝαρ, cf. ἔλαρ Hsch., εἴλω.)

εἰλαρχέω, εἰλάρχης, v. ἰλ-.

εἰλάτινος, Ep. for ἐλάτινος.

εἴλεα· ἄθλια, χαλινοί, δεσμοί, φιμοί, δέραια, Hsch.; v. εἶλος.

Εἰλείθυια, ἡ, (ἐλυθ- *she that comes* in need, a participial form) *Ilithyia*, the goddess of child-birth, pl. in Hom., Il.11.270, 19.119, sg. in Hes.*Th.*922, etc. II. *parturition*, in pl., Opp.*H.*1.477, al.; *offspring*, ib.4.505. 2. metaph., σταφυλὴ βότρυος εἰ. Nonn.*D.*16.203. (There are numerous varieties of spelling, e.g. **Ἐλείθυια** Pi. *P.*3.9, *N.*7.1, *SIG*602 (Delph.), *IG*3.1320, etc.: **Ἐλείθυα** ib.12(3).192 (Astypalaea): **Εἰλήθυια** (q.v.) *IG*12(5).197 (Paros, prob.), Call. *Del.*132, *AP*6.200 (Leon.), Paus.2.5.4, etc.: **Ἐλευθία**, Ion. **-ίη**, *GDI* 4584 (Hippola), *IG*12(5).187 (Paros): Lacon. Ἐλευσία ib.5(1).236: Cret. Ἐλεύθυια *GDI*5149, al.: Boeot. **Εἰλείθεια, -ια**, *IG*7.2228, 3410; cf. Εἰλιόνεια, Ἐλευθώ.) **Εἰλειθυιαῖον** or **-υαῖον**, τό, *temple of Ilithyia*, ib.11(2).161*B*114,118 (Delos, iii B.C.), *Inscr.Delos*338*A b*84:—also **Εἰλείθυιον**, τό, *Lex.Rhet.*ap.Eust.1053.61.

εἰλεός or **ἰλεός**, ὁ, (εἰλέω) *intestinal obstruction*, Hp.*Aph.*3.22, Aret.*SA*2.6, v.l. (-ειοῖο) in Nic.*Al.*597, etc.; distd. fr. χορδαψός, Diocl.*Fr.*73; of other diseases, as *nephritis*, Hp.*Int.*44; εἰ. ἰκτερώδης *jaundice*, ib.45; εἰ. αἱματίτης *scurvy*, ib.46, cf. Lyc.ap.Orib.8.28.1, etc.; *staggers*, Arist.*HA*604ᵃ30. II. *lurking-place, den, hole*, εἰλεόν, οὐκ οἴκησιν Theoc.15.9. III. = ἐλεός, *butcher's block*, Eust.749.7. IV. a kind of *vine*, Hippys 7.

εἰλετίας (sc. κάλαμος), ου, ὁ, a kind of *reed*, *Ammophila arundinacea*, Thphr.*HP*4.11.13; **εἰλεσίας**, Hsch.

εἰλέτις· βλάσφημος, Hsch.

εἰλέω, εἰλέω, v. εἴλω.

εἰλέω, Ion. **εἰλ-**, (εἴλη) *sun*, Eust.1573.45:—Pass., πρὸς τὸν ἥλιον εἰληθέντες Hp.*Int.*45.

εἰλεώδης, ες, *of the nature of* εἰλεός I, τὰ εἰ. the symptoms thereof, Hp.*Epid.*3.1.θ'; οἱ εἰ. *those who suffer therefrom*, Dsc.1.30; *causing this disease*, Aret.*SA*2.6 (dub.). Adv. -ωδῶς Sor.2.29, Herod.Med. in *Rh.Mus.*58.108.

εἴλη, = ἴλη (q.v.).

εἵλη, ἡ, *the sun's heat* or *warmth*, Ar.*V.*772 (dub.), *Fr.*627, Luc. *Lex.*2, Alciphr.1.2, 12; cf. γέλαν (i.e. ϝέλαν)· αὐγὴν ἡλίου, Hsch. II. *chaff*, Id. 2. τῶν ὀσπρίων ἡ καλάμη, Id.; cf. εἶλα.

εἰληδόν, εἰληδά, Adv., (εἴλη) = ἰληδόν, εἰληδὰ φέρονται Arat. 917. II. (εἰλέω) *by twisting* or *coiling round*, εἰληδὸν ἔδησε πόδας *AP*9.14.6 (Antiphil.).

εἰληθερ-έω, *bask in the sun*, Hp.*Morb.*2.68, 70, Xenarch.4.5, Philostr.*Gym.*58:—Med., Luc.*Rh.Pr.*17. -ής, ές, (εἵλη, θέρω) *warmed by the sun*: *warm*, Hp.*Morb.*2.30, Gal.11.389; cf. ἐλαθερής.

εἴληθι, v. ἱλάσκομαι.

εἰληθμός (εἰδ- cod.), ὁ, *coiling up*, Hsch.

Εἰλήθυια, v. Εἰλείθυια. II. name of a kind of *comet*, Heph. Astr.1.24.

εἰλήϊον· ἐν ἡλίῳ θερμανθέν, Hsch.

εἰλήλουθα, εἰληλούθειν, εἰλήλουθμεν, v. ἔρχομαι.

εἴλημα, ατος, τό, (εἰλέω) *veil, covering, wrapper*, [Hdt.] ap.Stob.3.28.18ᵃ. II. = εἰλεός I, Hp.*Flat.*9 (pl., dub.). 2. *a coil*, σχοινίου S.E.*M.*7.187; *roll* of a bandage, Gal.18(1).809. III. Archit., *arch* spanning intercolumniation, *Arch.Anz.*19.8 (Milet.), *CIG*2782.31 (Aphrodisias). IV. *vault, cellar*, prob. in *PLond.ined.*1821.387.

εἰλῆς εἶ· ἵλεως εἶ, Hsch.

εἴλησις, Att. **εἴλ-**, εως, ἡ, (εἰλέω) *eddy, vortex* of wind, fire, etc., Plot.1.8.14, *EM*20.3, Sch.A.R.1.438, Phryn.374; *revolution* of heavenly bodies, Poll.4.156.

εἴλησις, εως, ἡ, (εἰλέω) *sun-heat*, Pl.*R.*380e (pl.), 404b (pl.), Arist. *Ph.*197ᵃ23, Plu.2.688a (pl.).

εἰλ-ητάριον, τό, *wrapper, roll*, Aët.15.13. -ητικός, v.l. for ἰλυσπαστικός (q.v.) in Arist.*HA*487ᵇ21. -ητός, Att. **εἰλ-**, ή, όν, (εἰλέω) *wound*, Sch.Ar.*Ra.*342; *rolled*, ἐπίδεσμος Gal.18(1).813, cf. Heliod.ap.Orib.48.20.1.

εἰλιγγιάω, εἴλιγγος, v. ἰλ-.

εἰλίγδην, Adv. *wriggling*, ἕρπων Orac. in *App.Anth.*6.140.10.

εἴλιγμα, ατος, τό, Horap.1.59, *EM*723.35: -μός, ὁ, Mnesith.ap. Orib.8.38.9, Orph.*H.*38.12; poet. and Ion. for ἑλιγ-.

εἶλιγξ, v. εἶλιξ.

εἰλικο-ειδής, ές, = ἑλικ-, Suid., Zonar. -εις, εσσα, εν, = ἕλιξ, ἀσπίδες Nic.*Th.*201; κτίλοι *with crooked horns*, Opp.*C.*1.388; βότρυς Nonn.*D.*12.343; δράκων ib.9.130. -μορφος, ον, (ἕλιξ) *of twisted* or *spiral form*, Opp.*C.*2.98.

εἰλικρίν-εια [ρῐ], ἡ, *unmixedness, purity*, opp. μίξις, Arist.*Col.*793ᵃ10; ἀέρος S.E.*M.*9.73, cf. Alex.Aphr. *in Sens.*137.1: metaph., λογισμοῦ Iamb.*VP*16.68 (pl.); in bad sense, *unrelievedness*, κακοῦ Phld. *Ir.*p.25 W. II. *sincerity, uprightness*, 1*Ep.Cor.*5.8, al., *POxy.* 1252 vii 38 (iii A.D.). -έω, *purify*, Arist.*Mu.*397ᵃ35 (Pass.). II. *separate, distinguish*, Buther.ap.Stob.1 *Prooem.*5 (Pass.). -ής, ές, *unmixed, without alloy, pure*, ἐκ πυρὸς τοῦ -εστάτου καὶ ὕδατος Hp. *Vict.*1.35; θέρμη, ψῦξις, Id.*VM*19; διὰ τὸ εἰλικρινῆ ἕκαστα εἶναι (sc. τὰ φῦλα) *distinct and separate*, X.*Cyr.*8.5.14; εἴ τῳ γένοιτο αὐτὸ τὸ καλὸν ἰδεῖν εἰ., καθαρόν, ἄμεικτον Pl.*Smp.*211e; τὸ ἧττον εἰ., opp. τὸ καθαρώτερον, Arist.*Mete.*340ᵇ8; τῶν χρωμάτων οὐδὲν ὁρῶμεν εἰ. οἷόν ἐστιν, ἀλλὰ πάντα κεκραμένα Id.*Col.*793ᵇ13; τὸ λευκὸν [μέλι] οὐκ ἐκ θύμου εἰλικρινοῦς Id.*HA*627ᵃ3; εἰ. καὶ ἀμιγής Id.*de An.*426ᵇ4; ἐν μεγάλῳ εἰ. καὶ κενῷ Epicur.*Ep.*2 p.37 U. (fort. καὶ εἰ.); τὸ ἓν εἰ. καὶ καθαρόν Plu. 2.393c. 2. *pure, simple, absolute*, αὐτῇ καθ' αὑτὴν εἰλικρινεῖ τῇ διανοίᾳ χρώμενος the *pure and absolute* intellect, Pl.*Phd.*66a; ψυχὴν αὐτὴν καθ' αὑτὴν εἰ. ἀπαλλάξεσθαι ib.81c; γνωσόμεθα..πᾶν τὸ εἰ. *the pure and absolute*, ib.67b; τὸ καθαρόν τε καὶ εἰ. Id.*Phlb.*52d; τὰς τέρψεις εἰ. ἀποδιδόναι Isoc.1.46; ἡδονὴ εἰ. Arist.*EN*1176ᵇ20; εὐπορία -εστάτη Epicur.*Sent.*14; also of evil things, *sheer, absolute*, ἀδικία X.*Mem.*2.2.3. 3. *sincere*, ἀπόδεξις *OGI*227.12 (Didyma, iii B.C.); εὔνοια ib.763.41 (Milet., ii B.C.); of persons, *Ep.Phil.*1.10. Adv. -νῶς *OGI*441.5 (i B.C.). 4. *total*, ἐκλείψεις Cleom.2.5. II. Adv. -νῶς *without mixture, of itself, simply, absolutely*, διὰ τὸ εἰ. εἶναι Ἕλληνας καὶ ἀμιγεῖς βαρβάρων Pl.*Mx.*245d; τὸ εἰ. ὂν *absolute* being, Id.*R.*477a; εἰ. ὑπὸ τοῦ ἔρωτος ὡρμημένους Id.*Smp.*181c; εἰ. ὅλον λευκόν Arist.*Ph.*187ᵇ4; *without qualification*, -νῶς Ταραντῖνοι Arr.*Tact.* 4.6: Ion. -έως, κρίνεσθαι to have a *clear* crisis, Hp.*Epid.*4.7.—The word is confined to Prose.

εἰλικρῖνότης, ητος, ἡ, *sincerity*, *Gloss.*

εἰλικτήρ, ῆρος, ὁ, = ἑλ., *IG*2.660.52, 698 ii 23.

εἰλικτός, ή, όν, (εἱλίσσω) poet. and Ion. for ἑλικτός, f.l. E.*Ion*40; of flames, *enveloping*, Ps.-Democr.Alch.p.50B.

εἰλίνδησις, εως, ἡ, = ἀλινδ-, Aq.*Ps.*54(55).6:—so **εἰλινδούμενοι**, v.l. in Alciphr.1.26.

εἶλιξ, ικος, ἡ, poet. for ἕλιξ; cf. **εἶλιξ** (fort. εἶλιγξ)· σκότωσις (prob. for εἰλισκότ- cod.), στρόφος, Hsch.

Εἰλιόνεια, ἡ, = Εἰλείθυια, Plu.2.277b.

εἰλίονες, poet. pl., = *brothers-in-law*, whose wives are sisters, Pollux 3.32. (Prob. metri gr. for *ἐλίονες, cf. ἀέλιοι, OIcel. *svilar* (same meaning), Skt. *syālás* 'wife's brother'?)

εἰλῐπόδης, ου, ὁ, later form for sq., Nonn.*D.*1.60; Ἥφαιστος ib. 29.356; ὀρχηθμός ib.17.214: metaph. of the scazon, Aus.*Ep.*10.31.

εἰλίπους [ῐ], ὁ, ἡ, πουν, τό, gen. ποδος: (εἴλω, πούς):—*rolling in their gait*, in Hom. (only in dat. and acc. pl., Il.6.424, 9.466) as epith. of oxen, which *bring round their hind legs with a circling* or *rolling motion*, cf. Hp.*Art.*8; εἰλίποδες, abs., for *oxen* or *kine*, Theoc.25.131; also of women, *having a rolling gait*, Eup.161; also expld. sens. obsc., Anacr.164, cf. Paus.Gr.*Fr.*154; cf. ἀνελλίπους.

εἰλίσσω, v. ἑλίσσω.

εἰλῐτενής, ές, epith. of the plant ἄγρωστις, Theoc.13.42, prob. (from ἕλος, τείνω) *spreading through marshes*.

εἰλίχατο, v. ἑλίσσω. **εἰλκτής**· αἴτιος, Hsch. **εἴλλω, εἴλλω**, v. εἴλω.

εἰλόπεδον, τό, v.l. for θειλόπεδον in Od.7.123, cf. *EM*449.29, Eust. 43.38.

εἶλος, = δεσμός, Hsch.; cf. εἴλεα. **εἰλύ**· μέλαν, Id.

εἰλυθμός, ὁ, (εἰλύω) *lurking-place, den*, Nic.*Th.*285; glossed by ἕλκος, τρόμος, Hsch. **εἰλῦΐος**, ὁ, *wood-worm*, Id.

εἴλῡμα, ατος, τό, *wrapper*, εἴ. σπείρων Od.6.179, cf. Anacr.21.6, A.R.2.1129, Gal.19.367. (Cf. ἔλυμα.)

εἰλῠός or **ἰλ-** [ῐ], ὁ, = εἰλυθμός, X.*Cyn.*5.16, A.R.1.1144, Nic.*Th.* 143.

εἰλύς, ύος, ἡ, = ἰλύς, *mire, morass*, Hsch.

εἴλῡσις, εως, ἡ, *crawling* or *wriggling along*, Sch.S.*Ph.*291, Simp. *in Ph.*1229.22.

εἰλυσπ-άομαι, freq. v.l. for ἰλυσπάομαι. -όα, perh., = ἄγρωστις, Porph.*Abst.*2.7. -ωμα, ατος, τό, *worm-like motion*, Eust.1413.43.

εἰλύσσεται· εἰλεῖται, Hsch.

εἰλυστήριον, *place for rolling*, *Gloss.*

εἰλυτά (sc. μᾶζα), cake offered to Trophonius, *IG*7.3055 (Lebad.). (Cf. ἐλλ-.)

εἰλῡφάζω, = εἰλύω, only pres. and impf., *roll along*, ἄνεμος φλόγα Il.20.492. II. intr., *roll* or *whirl about*, of a blazing torch, Hes. *Sc.*275.

εἰλῡφάω, = foreg., Ep. part. -όων Il.11.156, Hes.*Th.*692; intr., Nonn.*D.*30.81. (Perh. wrongly expanded, for εἰλύφων.)

εἰλύω, Arat.432: fut. εἰλύσω [ῡ] Il.21.319:—**Med.**, part. εἰλῠόμενος, impf. εἰλῠόμην, S.*Ph.*702 (lyr.), 291:—**Pass.**, pf. εἴλῡμαι, Ep. 3 pl. εἰλύαται, plpf. εἴλῡτο, Il.5.186, Od.20.352, Il.16.640. [ῡ always in Hom. exc. in εἰλῠ́αται, also in S.; ῠ in Metag. (v. infr.), and late Ep., Arat.432, Nic.*Al.*18 (but εἰλῡμένα *Th.*754).]:—*enfold, enwrap*, Act. once in Hom., κὰδ δέ μιν αὐτὸν εἰλύσω ψαμάθοισι Il.21.319; ὀλίγη δέ μιν εἰλύει ἀχλὺς Arat. l.c.:—Pass., *to be wrapped, covered*, βοέῃς εἰλυμένω ὤμους Il.17.492; εἰλυμένοι αἴθοπι χαλκῷ 18.522; νεφέλῃ εἰλυμένος ὤμους 5.186; αἵματι καὶ κονίῃσιν εἴλυτο 16.640; εἴλυτο δὲ πάνθ' ἁλὸς ἄχνη Od.5.403; νυκτὶ μὲν ὑμέων εἰλύαται κεφαλαί 20.352, cf. Il.12.286. II. Pass., after Hom., = ἰλυσπάομαι, *crawl, wriggle along*, of a lame man, εἰλυόμην δύστηνον ἐξέλκων πόδα S.*Ph.*291; εἰλυόμενος, παῖς ἄτερ ὡς..τιθήνας ib.702; of a shoal of fish, Metag. 6.4. 2. in Theoc.25.246 εἰλυθεὶς is used like ἐλυσθείς in Hom., *rolled up, crouching*; but εἰλυμένος is part. of ἐλύω (q.v.) in A.R. 3.296.

εἴλω (also **εἰλέω, εἰλέω, εἴλλω, εἴλλω, ἴλλω**; εἰλῶνται is f.l. in Aret.*SD*1.2), a word whose meanings are traceable to various roots of similar form, v. infr. D.—From εἴλω (pres. in Hom. only Pass. part. εἰλόμενος (v. infr.)), we have Ep. aor. ἔλσα Il.11.413, inf. ἐέλσαι 21.295, Dor. part. ἔλσαις Pi.*O.*10(11).43:—**Med.**, aor. ἠλσάμην Semon.17:—**Pass.**, aor. 2 ἐάλην [ᾰ] Il.13.408; inf. ἀλῆναι, ἀλήμεναι, 16.714, 18.76; part. ἀλείς, εἶσα, έν 22.308: pf. ἔελμαι, part. -μένος 13.524:—for ἐόλει, ἐόλητο, v. ἐόλει.—From **εἰλέω** Il.2.294: impf. εἴλεον Od.22.460; contr. εἴλει Il.8.215, Od.12.210; ἐείλεον Il.18.447: fut. εἰλήσω Lxx *Jb.*40.21(26), *AP*12.208 (Strat.): aor. εἴλησα Lxx 4*Ki.*2.8, Dsc.5.87 (ἐν-):—**Med.**, impf. εἰλεῦντο Il.21.8; part. εἰλεύμενος Hdt.2.76:—**Pass.**, aor. εἰλήθην Hp.*Morb.*4.52: pf. εἴλημαι Lxx 1*Ki.*21.9(10) and *Is.*11.5 (s. v. l.), Lyc.1202: plpf. εἴληντο J.*AJ* 12.1.9.

A. *shut in* (less freq. *shut out*, εἰλέσθων τοῦ ἱαροῦ *let them be shut out* from the temple, *IG*2².1126.48 (iv B.C.)); [Ὀδυσῆα] ἔλσαν ἐν μέσσοισι μετὰ σφίσι, πῆμα δὲ ἔλσαν (Zenod., v.l. πῆμα τιθέντες) Il.11.413; ὅτε Κύκλωψ εἴλει ἐνὶ σπῆϊ Od.12.210, cf. 22.460; ἔνθα δυώδεκα μὲν μένον ἤματα δῖοι Ἀχαιοί· εἴλει γὰρ Βορέης ἄνεμος μέγας οὐδ' ἐπὶ γαίῃ εἴα ἵστασθαι Od.19.200; ὅν περ ἀελλαι χειμέριαι εἰλέωσιν Il.2.294; εἰλεῖσθαι ἐν τῷ τόπῳ, μὴ δυνάμενον ἐκπλεῦσαι Arist.*Mir.* 840ᵃ33, cf. *EM*298.29; εἰς ἄστυ ἅλεν (for ἀλησαν) Il.22.12; κατὰ ἄστυ ἐέλμεθα 24.662; ἐελμένοι ἔνδοθι πύργων 18.287; νηυσὶν ἔπι γλαφυρῇσιν ἐελμένοι 12.38; χειμέριον ἀλὲν ὕδωρ *ponded* water, *prevented* from flowing away, Il.23.420; ὅσοι πικροὶ ... χυμοὶ κατὰ τὸ σῶμα πλανηθέντες ἔξω μὲν μὴ λάβωσιν ἀναπνοήν, ἐντὸς δὲ εἰλλόμενοι (v.l. εἰλόμενοι) τὴν ἀφ' αὐτῶν ἀτμίδα τῇ τῆς ψυχῆς φορᾷ συμμείξαντες ἀνακερασθῶσι, Pl.*Ti.*86e. 2. *hinder, hold in check, prevent*, ἧστο Διὸς βουλῇσιν ἐελμένος Il.13.524, cf. A.*Fr.*25: ἔλλοψ (as though ἴλλοψ) is derived from ἴλλεσθαι = εἴργεσθαι and ὄψ = φωνή by Ath.7. 308c. 3. *enclose, cover, protect*, ὑπ' ἀσπίδος ἄλκιμον ἦτορ ἔλσας Callin.1.11; τῇ ὕπο (sc. τῇ ἀσπίδι) πᾶς ἐάλη he *was* entirely *covered*, Il.13.408.

B. *press*, as olives and grapes, Paus.Gr.*Fr.*155; ἀμφὶ βίην Διομήδεος . . εἰλόμενοι *huddling* around him, Il.5.782; ἵππων φειδόμενος, μή μοι δευοίατο φορβῆς ἀνδρῶν εἰλομένων, εἰωθότες ἔδμεναι ἄδην here where men *throng*, ib.203; πλῆθεν...ἵππων τε καὶ ἀνδρῶν εἰλομένων· εἴλει δὲ..Ἕκτωρ 8.215, cf. 1.409, 18.447, 21.295; πόλις δ' ἔμπλητο ἀλέντων ib.607; ἐς ποταμὸν εἰλεῦντο they *were forced* into the river, ib.8; εἰλουμένης τῆς τροφῆς the nourishment being *concentrated*, Thphr.*CP*6.11.8; θῆρας ὁμοῦ εἰλεῦντα Od.11.573; [λέων] ἰλλόμενός περ ὁμίλῳ hard-*pressed*, A.R.2.27; ἀπωθούμενον ὑπὸ τοῦ περιεστῶτος ἔξωθεν πνεύματος πάλιν ἐντὸς ὑπὸ τὸ δέρμα εἰλλόμενον κατερριζοῦτο Pl.*Ti.*76b:—Pass., of crowds, *swarm, jostle one another*, ἐν ὀλίγῳ εἰλουμένους Plu.*Crass.*25; of ants, Luc.*Icar.*19. 2. in aor. Pass., of a man or animal, *contract* his body, *draw himself together*, Αἰνείας δ' ἐάλη καὶ ἀπὸ ἕθεν ἀσπίδ' ἀνέσχεν Il.20.278; ἐνὶ δίφρῳ ἧστο ἀλείς (*huddled up*), ἐκ γὰρ πλήγη φρένας 16.403; of a lion when struck, ἐάλη τε χανών 20.168; of a warrior, Ἀχιλῆα ἀλεὶς μένεν 21.571; οἴμησεν δὲ ἀλεὶς ὥς τ' αἰετὸς ὑψιπετήεις 22.308, Od. 24.538. II. without the idea of pressure, *collect*, ἐν Πίσᾳ ἔλσαις στρατὸν λείαν τε πᾶσαν Pi.*O.*10(11).43:—Pass., Ἀργείους ἐκέλευσα ἀλήμεναι ἐνθάδε πάντας *to assemble*, Il.5.823.

C. (found only in the forms εἰλέω (εἰλ-), ἴλλω) *wind, turn round*, σκολιήν τε καὶ οὐ μίαν ἀτραπὸν ἴλλων Nic.*Th.*478; ἀπὸ δὲ τῶ[ν πετρῶν] ἴλλει ἡ στεφάνη ἐπὶ τὸν λόφον *GDI* iv p.847 (iv B.C.); νῆα δ' ἔπειτα πέριξ εἴλει ῥόος A.R.2.571; *roll*, γλῶσσαν dub. in Call.*Iamb.*1.144:—Pass., *revolve, move to and fro*, ἰλλομένων ἀρότρων S.*Ant.*340 (lyr.); οἱ ἀστέρες ἐν τῷ οὐρανῷ εἰλέονται Luc.*Astr.*29; περὶ τὴν γῆν ἀεὶ εἰλεῖν ἰών, as etym. of ἥλιος (ἀέλιος), Pl.*Cra.*409a; εἰλέονται ἐπὶ τὸ ὑγιὲς σκέλος they *pivot* or *swing round* on the sound leg, Hp.*Art.*52, cf. *Mochl.*20; of a flame, περὶ δ' αὐτὸν εἰλεῖτο φλόξ Mosch.4.104; κατ' αὐτὸν (sc. τὸν κισσὸν) ἕλιξ εἰλεῖται *is twined* round, Theoc.1.31; δαίμων ἐν μέσῳ τοῦ παντὸς εἰλουμένη Herm.ap.Stob.1.3.52; also of hair on the crown, *to be whorled*, Ruf.*Onom.*13. II. *roll up tight*, [κῶας] εἴλει ἀφασσόμενος A.R.4.181; τὴν μηλωτὴν εἰλήσας Lxx 4*Ki.* 2.8:—Pass., ἰλλομένη ἐπὶ λαίφεσι *furled*, A.R.1.329. 2. *bind fast*, δεσμοῖς ἰλλόμενος A.R.1.129, cf. 2.1249 (Pass.), cf. S.*Fr.* 158. III. metaph. in Pass., ἐν ποσὶ εἰλεῖσθαι to be familiar, Hdt. 2.76; οἱ περὶ τὰς δίκας εἰλούμενοι Max.Tyr.28.3, cf. Alciphr.3.60,64.

D. It seems impossible to derive all the above uses from an orig. sense *squeeze*, though most of those under A and B, as well as C. II, might be so explained; but A seems to imply a root meaning *bar*, cf. ἀποϝηλέω, ἐγϝηληθίωντι, ϝήλημα (βήλημα), εἶλαρ, and C is to be compared with εἰλύω, Lat. *volvo*: some passages are doubtful in meaning, μή νυν περὶ σαυτὸν εἶλλε τὴν γνώμην ἀεί do not *roll* or *wrap* your thought round you, or do not *confine* your thought within you, Ar.*Nu.*761; γῆν ... ἰλλομένην (v.l. εἰλλ-, εἱλλ-) τὴν περὶ τὸν διὰ παντὸς πόλον τεταμένον Pl.*Ti.*40b was taken to mean *revolving* by Arist.*Cael.*293ᵇ31 (cf. περὶ τὸ μέσον εἰλεῖσθαι *Mete.*356ᵃ5) but expld. (omitting τήν) as *packed tightly* about.. by Procl.*in Ti.*3.136 D.; ἐν δὲ τῇ ταραχῇ (in the churning) εὐρυχωρίης γινομένης, εἰλέεται (sc. τὸ ὑγρόν) ἀποκεκριμένον καὶ θερμαίνει τὸ σῶμα perh. *is squeezed out*, Hp. *Morb.*4.51; πρὶν δὲ ταραχθῆναι οὐκ ἔχει ἐκχωρέειν τὸ πλεῖον τοῦ ὑγροῦ, ἀλλ' ἄνω καὶ κάτω εἰλέεται μεμιγμένον τῷ ἄλλῳ ὑγρῷ *is driven up and down*, ibid.:—νῆα κεραυνῷ Ζεὺς ἔλσας (ἐλάσας Zenod.) ἐκέασσε prob. *striking* the ship.., Od.5.132, cf. 7.250 (only here in this sense).

Εἵλως, ωτος, Th.4.80, etc., and **Εἱλώτης**, ου, ὁ, Hdt.6.58, etc.; fem. **Εἱλωτίς**, ίδος, ἡ, Plu.*Ages.*3:—*Helot*, name of the Spartan *serfs*, derived by Hellanic.188 J., Theopomp.Hist.14, etc., from Ἕλος, a town of Laconia, whose inhabitants were enslaved: by others from Pass. of *ἕλω, = αἱρέω, cf. *EM*332.53.

Εἱλωτ-εία, ἡ, *the system of serfdom* at Sparta, Pl.*Lg.*776c. II. *the body of Helots*, Arist.*Pol.*1269ᵇ12, cf. 1264ᵃ35 (pl.). **-εύω**, *to be a Helot* or *serf*, Isoc.4.131. **-ίζομαι**, Pass., *to be Helotized*, cj. in Hermipp.71. **-ικός**, ή, όν, *of Helots*, τὸ Εἱ. *the Helots* collectively, Paus.4.23.1; Εἱ. πλῆθος Plu.*Sol.*22.

εἷμα, ατος, τό, Aeol. ἔμμα Alc.*Supp.*4.21 (pl.), *Lyr.Alex.Adesp.*9 (pl.); Cret. ϝῆμα *Leg.Gort.*3.38 (but gen. fem. ϝήμας 5.40): (ἕννυμι):—*garment*, freq. in Hom., in pl., φᾶρός τε χιτῶνά τε εἵματ' ἔθηκαν Od.6.214; χλαῖνάν τε χιτῶνά τε εἵματα ἕσσεν 10.542: in Hdt. mostly, *over-garment*, like ἱμάτιον, 1.155, 2.81, cf. A.*Ch.*81 (lyr.), S. *OT*1268; ἀγῶνα γυμνικὸν ἐν εἵμασι *Inscr.Prien.*112.91 (i B.C.). II. *rug, carpet*, A.*Ag.*921,963, S.*Aj.*1145.

εἱμάδες· ποιμένων οἰκίαι, Hsch.

εἷμαι, pf. Pass. of ἕννυμι. II. pf. Pass. of ἵημι.

εἱμάρσην, ενος, ἡ, *woman clad in man's dress*, Dosiad.*Ara* 1.

εἵμαρται, εἵμαρτο, εἱμαρμένος, Εἱμαρμένη, v. μείρομαι.

εἱμαρτός, ή, όν, *fixed by fate*, χρόνος Plu.*Alex.*30, cf. *Epigr.Gr.*339; τὸ ἐπὶ πάντων ἀνθρώπων εἱ. *IG*12(7).396.21 (Amorgos, ii A.D.).

εἱμᾰτᾰνωπερίβαλλος, ὁ, *one who wraps his cloak about him*, com. word in Hegesand.2.

εἱμάτ-ιον, v. ἱμάτιον. **-ισμός**, ὁ, *clothing*, *PEleph.*1.4 (iv B.C.), *IG*4.1390.15 (Andania), *SIG*999.5 (Lycosura).

εἱματο-πώλης, -φυλάκιον, -φύλαξ, v. ἱματ-.

εἱμένος, pf. part. Pass. of ἕννυμι and ἵημι.

εἰμί (*sum*), Aeol. ἔμμι Sapph.2.15, Theoc.20.32; Cret. ἠμί *GDI* 4959a; 2 sg. εἶ, Ep. and Ion. εἰς Od.17.388, al., Aeol. ἔσσι, Ep. and Dor. ἐσσί Il.1.176, Pi.*O.*6.90, Sophr.134; ἐσί *GDI*4959a; 3 sg. ἐστί, Dor. ἐντί *IG*12(1).677 (Rhodes), Theoc.1.17, etc.; 3 dual ἐστόν Th.3. 112; 1 pl. ἐσμέν, Ep. and Ion. εἰμέν (also in Pi.*P.*3.60), ἐμέν Call.*Fr.* 294, Dor. εἰμές Theoc.15.73, but ἠμέν *GDI*5178.34; 3 pl. εἰσί (-ίν), Ep. and Ion. ἔασι (-ιν) Il.7.73, Xenoph.8.1, Antim.29, Herod.4.84, Dor. ἐντί Pi.*N.*1.24, Theoc.11.45, *IG*9(1).32.22 (Phocis), etc.: imper. ἴσθι (ἔσθι Hecat.361 J.), Ep. and Lyr. also in Med. form ἔσσο Od.3. 200, Sapph.1.28, Maced.*Pae.*31, late Prose ἔσο Plu.2.241d, M.Ant.3. 5, Hld.5.12, Porph.*Marc.*34; 3 sg. ἔστω (ἤτω Lxx *Ps.*103.31, and late Inscrr., *CIG*2664, al.; but in Pl.*R.*361c leg. ἴτω), Dor. εἴτω, ἤτω, Heraclid.ap.Eust.1411.21, Elean ἤστω *Schwyzer*424; 3 pl. ἔστωσαν, but ἔστων Hom., Pl.*R.*502a, ὄντων Id.*Lg.*879b, and early Att. Inscrr., *IG*1².22, etc. (ἔστωσαν first in ii B.C., ib.2².1328), Dor. ἐόντων ib.1126: subj. ὦ, ᾖς, ᾖ, Ep. ἔω Od.9.18; 3 sg. ἔῃ Il.12.300, al. (also ἔῃσι 2.366, al., ᾖσι(ν) 19.202, Hes.*Op.*294), also Boeot. ἔνθω *IG*7.3172.165, μετείω Il.23.47 and perh. εἴῃ 9.245, etc.; Dor. 3 pl. ὦντι *SIG*940.3 (Crete), ἔωντι *GDI*5040.14 (Hierapytna), Boeot. ἴωνθι *IG*7.3171.46 (iii B.C.): opt. εἴην, -ης (εἴησθα Thgn.715), -η, also ἔοις, ἔοι, Il.9.284, 142, al., cf. Hdt.7.6; 3 pl. εἴοισαν Ἀρχ.Ἐφ.1911.133 (Gonni); 3 dual εἴτην Pl. *Prm.*149e, *Sph.*243e; 1 pl. εἶμεν E.*Alc.*921 (lyr.), Pl.; 2 pl. εἶτε Od. 21.195; 3 pl. εἶεν Il.2.372, etc., εἴησαν Hdt.1.2, etc.; Elean ἔα, = εἴη, *SIG*9 (vi B.C.), and σύν-εαν, = συνεῖεν, *GDI*1149 (vi B.C.): inf. εἶναι, Arc. ἦναι *SIG*306.9 (Tegea, iv B.C.); Ep. ἔμμεναι (also Aeol. ἔμμεν' Sapph.34), ἔμμεν (also Pi.*P.*6.42, S.*Ant.*623 (lyr.)), ἔμεναι, ἔμεν, also ἔμειν *SIG*1166 (Dodona); Dor. εἶμεν Foed.ap.Th.5.77,79, *IG*7.1.7 (Megara), ἦμεν *Test.Epict.*5.16, *Tab.Herad.*1.75, Cret. ἦμεν or ἤμην *Leg.Gort.*1.15, al., *GDI*4998 i 2, al., Megar. εἴμεναι Ar.*Ach.* 775, εἴμειν *IG*12(1).155.100 (Rhodes), 14.952 (Agrigentum); εἶν ib. 12(9).211.10 (Eretria), *SIG*135.4 (Olynthus), etc.: part. ὤν, Ep. ἐών, ἐοῦσα, ἐόν, Cypr. ἰών *Inscr.Cypr.*135.23 H.; Boeot. fem. ἰῶσα *IG* 7.3172.15 (Orchom.), Aeol. and Dor. fem. ἔσσα Sapph.75.4, *IG*4. 952.2 (Epid.), Theoc.28.16, ἔοισα Pi.*P.*4.265, ἔασσα *Lyr.Alex.Adesp.* 9, Diotog.ap.Stob.4.7.62, εὖσα Erinn.5.5 (also Ion., Herod.5.16, εὔντων 2.85), ἐᾶσα Ti.Locr.96d, *IG*5(1).1470.8 (Messene), ἴαττα *Leg. Gort.*8.47; acc. sg. εὖντα Theoc.2.3; nom. sg. εἷς in Heraclid.ap. Eust.1756.13, pl. ἔντες *Tab.Herad.*1.117; dat. pl. ἔντασσι ib.104; gen. pl. παρ-έντων Alcm.64: impf. ἦν Il.2.77, etc., Ep. ἔον (also Aeol., Alc.127, Sapph.*Oxy.*1787 *Fr.*3 ii 21), in Att. ἦ (dub. in Aeol., Alc. *Supp.*14.9), Ar.*Pl.*77, Pl.*Phd.*61b, etc., but usu. altered to ἦν in codd. (and ἦν is required by metre in E.*Ion* 280), contr. from Ep. and Ion. ἦα (Il.5.808, al., *IG*12(8).449.2 (Thasos), whence Hom. and later Ion. ἔα Il.4.321, al., ἔας Hdt.1.187, ἔατε Id.4.119); Ep. 3 sg. ἦεν, always with ν in Hom.; ἔην as 1 sg., only Il.11.762 (s. v.l., al. ἔον), freq. as 3 sg. (generally before a consonant, so that ἔεν is possible), sts. also ἤην; 2 sg. ἦσθα, later ἦς (wh. is v.l. in Pi.*I.*1.26), sts. in Lxx (*Jd.* 11.35, *Ru.*3.2, al.), cf. Pl.*Ax.*365e, Erinn.4.4, *Ev.Matt.*25.21, al., ἦσθας Men.*Epit.*156, Ep. ἔησθα; 3 sg. ἦν, Ep. ἔην, ἤην, ἦεν (v. supr.), Dor. and Aeol. ἦς Alc.*Supp.*30.1, Epich.102, Sophr.59, Theoc.2.90, *SIG*241.145 (Delph.); 3 dual ἤστην Il.5.10, E.*Hipp.*387, Ar.*Eq.*982, Pl.*Euthd.*272a, al.; Dor. 1 pl. ἦμες Plu.*Lyc.*21; 2 pl. ἦτε Pl.*Euthd.* 276c, ἦστε Ar.*Pax*821, *Ec.*1086; 3 pl. ἦσαν, Ion. and Poet. ἔσαν (in Hes.*Th.*321,825, ἦν is not pl. for ἦσαν, but is rather a peculiarity of syntax, v. infr. v, but is 3 pl. in Epich.46, al., *SIG*560.15 (Epidamnus, iii B.C.)); Aeol. ἔον *Schwyzer*644.12; later ἤμην *PSI*4.362.21 (iii B.C.), *SIG*527.46 (Crete, iii B.C.), *IGRom.*4.1740 (Cyme), always in Lxx as *Ba.*1.19, cf. *Ev.Matt.*23.30, Plu.2.174a, etc., and sts. in codd. of earlier writers, Lys.7.34, *Trag.Adesp.*124 (cited from E. *Hel.*931 by Choerob. and from Id.*Tr.*474 by Aps.), X.*Cyr.*6.1.9, Hyp.*Ath.*26, 2 sg. ἦσο *Epigr.Gr.*379 (Aezani), 3 sg. ἦστο *Supp.Epigr.* 1.455.7 (Phrygia), 1 pl. ἤμεθα *PPetr.*2 p.11 (iii B.C.), Lxx *Ba.*1.19, 1*Ki.*25.16, *Ep.Eph.*2.3; subj. ὦμαι *PBaden*48.12 (ii B.C.), ἦται *GDI*

1696, ἧνται prob. in *IG*5(1).1390.83 (Andania); Ion. and Ep. also ἔσκον, used by A.*Pers.*656 (lyr.): fut. ἔσομαι, ἔσται, Ep. and Aeol. also ἔσσομαι, ἔσεται, ἔσσεται; Aeol. 2 sg. ἔσσῃ prob. in Alc.67,87; Dor. 2 and 3 sg. ἐσσῇ, ἐσσεῖται, Il.2.393, 13.317, Theoc.10.5, 3 pl. ἐσσοῦνται Foed.ap.Th.5.77 codd. (but ἔσσονται *Tab.Heracl.*1.113), inf. ἐσσεῖσθαι Sophr.57.—All forms of the pres. ind. are enclitic (exc. 2 sg. εἶ and 3 pl. ἔασι); but 3 sg. is written ἔστι when it begins a sentence or verse, or when it immediately follows οὐκ, καί, εἰ, ὡς, ἀλλά, or τοῦτ', Hdn.Gr.1.553 (also μή acc. to *EM*301.3); later Gramm. wrote ἔστι as Subst. Verb, Phot., Eust.880.22. A. as the Subst. Verb, I. of persons, *exist*, οὐκ ἔσθ' οὗτος ἀνήρ, οὐδ' ἔσσεται Od.16.437; ἔτ' εἰσί they *are* still *in being*, 15.433, cf. S.*Ph.*445, etc.; τεθνηῶτος.. μηδ' ἔτ' ἐόντος Od.1.289; οὐκέτ' ἐστί he *is* no more, E.*Hipp.*1162; οὐδὲ δὴν ἦν he *was* not long-*lived*, Il.6.131; ὁ οὐκ ὤν, οἱ οὐκ ὄντες, of *those who are* no more, Th.2.45,44; οἱ ὄντες the *living*, Plb.9.29.2; ὁ ὤν the *Eternal*, Lxx *Ex.*3.14, al., Ph.1.289; θεοὶ αἰὲν ἐόντες Il.1.290; ἐσσόμενοι *posterity*, 2.119; κἀγὼ γὰρ ἦ ποτ', ἀλλὰ νῦν οὐκ εἴμ' ἔτι E.*Hec.*284; ὡς ἂν εἶεν ἄνθρωποι *might continue in being*, Pl.*Smp.*190c; ζώντων καὶ ὄντων Ἀθηναίων D.18.72, cf. Arist.*GC*318^{b}25; of things, εἰ ἔστι ἀληθέως [ἡ τράπεζα] Hdt.3.17, etc.; of cities, ὄλωλεν, οὐδ' ἔτ' ἐστὶ Τροία E.*Tr.*1292, cf. *Heracl.*491; δοκεῖ μοι Καρχηδόνα μὴ εἶναι *censeo Carthaginem esse delendam*, Plu.*Cat.Ma.*27; ἂν ᾖ τὸ στράτευμα *be in existence*, D.8.17; of money, *to be in hand*, τῶν ὄντων χρημάτων καὶ τῶν προσιόντων *IG*1^{2}.91.25; τὰ ὄντα *property*, Pl.*Grg.*511a, Plu.*Ant.*24, etc.; τὸ ἐσόμενον ἐκ.. *future revenue* from.., *BCH*46.420 (Olymos, i B.C.); of place, τὴν οὖσαν ἐκκλησίαν the *local* church, *Act.Ap.*13.1; of time, τοῦ ὄντος μηνός in the *current* month, *BGU*146.4, etc.; *in office*, ἱερέων τῶν ὄντων *PPar.*5.4 (ii B.C.); αἱ οὖσαι [ἐξουσίαι] the powers *that be*, *Ep.Rom.*13.1. II. of the *real* world, *be*, opp. become, γίγνεται πάντα ἃ δή φαμεν εἶναι Pl.*Tht.*152d, etc.; τὸ ὄν *Being*, Parm.8.35, Protag.2, Pl.*Ti.*27d, etc.; opp. τὸ μὴ ὄν, Gorg.*Fr.*3 D., etc.; οὐδὲν γίνεται ἐκ τοῦ μὴ ὄντος Epicur.*Ep.*1 p.5 U.; ἐξ οὐκ ὄντων ἐποίησεν αὐτὰ ὁ θεός Lxx 2*Ma.*7.28; τὰ ὄντα the *world of things*, Heraclit.7, Emp.129.5, etc.; ὄν indecl., τῶν ὂν εἰδῶν species *of Being*, Plot.6.2.10. 2. of circumstances, events, etc., *to happen*, τά τ' ἐόντα, τά τ' ἐσσόμενα, πρό τ' ἐόντα Il.1.70; ἡ ἐσβολὴ ἔμελλεν ἔσεσθαι Th.2.13, etc.; τῆς προδοσίας οὔσης since treachery *was there*, Id.4.103; ἕως ἂν ὁ πόλεμος ᾖ so long as it *last*, Id.1.58; αἱ σπονδαὶ ἐνιαυτὸν ἔσονται Id.4.118; τί ἐστιν; what *is* it? what's the matter? Ar.*Th.*193; τί οὖν ἦν τοῦτο; how *came* it *to pass*? Pl.*Phd.*58a: repeated with a relat. to avoid a positive assertion, ἔστι δ' ὅπῃ νῦν ἔ. things *are* as they *are*, i.e. are ill, A.*Ag.*67. III. *be the fact* or *the case*, διπλασίαν ἂν τὴν δύναμιν εἰκάζεσθαι ἢ ἔστιν twice as large as it *really is*, Th.1.10; αὐτὸ ὃ ἔστι καλόν beauty *in its essence*, Pl.*Smp.*211c, cf. *Phd.*74b; freq. in part., τὸν ἐόντα λόγον λέγειν or φαίνειν the *true* story, Hdt.1.95,116; τῷ ἐόντι χρήσασθαι tell the *truth*, ib. 30; τὰ ὄντα ἀπαγγέλλειν Th.7.8; σκῆψιν οὐκ οὖσαν, λόγον οὐκ ὄντα, S.*El.*584, Ar.*Ra.*1052; τῷ ὄντι *in reality, in fact*, Pl.*Prt.*328d, etc.; to apply a quotation to a case in point, τῷ ὄντι κλαυσίγελως *real* 'smiles through tears' (with allusion to Il.6.484), X.*HG*7.2.9, cf. Pl. *La.*196d; κατὰ τὸ ἐόν according to the *fact, right*ly, Hdt.1.97; πᾶν τὸ ἐόν the whole *truth*, Id.9.11; τοῦ ἐόντος ἀποτεύξεται Hp.*VM* 2. IV. folld. by the relat., οὐκ ἔστιν ὃς or ὅστις *no one*, οὐκ ἔσθ' ὃς.. ἀπαλάλκοι Il.22.348; οὐκ ἔ. οὐδεὶς ὃς E.*El.*903; οὐκ ἔ. ὅτῳ, = οὐδενί, A.*Pr.*293 (anap.), cf. 989: freq. in pl., εἰσὶν οἵ, = Lat. *sunt qui*, used exactly like ἔνιοι, Th.6.88, 7.44, Pl.*Men.*77d, *Grg.*503a, etc. (εἰσί τινες οἵ.. Th.3.24); ἔστιν ἃ χωρία, πολίσματα, Id.1.12,65; ἔστιν ἃ εἰπεῖν Id.2.67; ἦσαν οἵ X.*An.*5.2.14; the sg. Verb is used even with masc. and fem. pl., ἔστιν οἵ, αἵ, Hp.*Fract.*1, *VC*4, X.*Cyr.*2.3.16; more freq. in oblique cases, ποταμῶν ἐστὶ ὧν Hdt.7.187; ἔστιν ἀφ' ὧν Th.8.65; ἐστὶ παρ' οἷς, ἔστιν ἐν οἷς, Id.1.23, 5.25: in questions ὅστις is used, ἔστιν ἥντινα δόξαν... ἀπεκρίνατο; Pl.*Men.*85b: with relat. Particles, ἔστιν ἔνθα, = Lat. *est ubi*, X.*Cyr.*7.4.15, etc.; ἔ. ὅπῃ, ἔσθ' ὅπου, *some*how, *some*where, Pl.*Prt.*331d, A.*Eu.*517, S.*OT*448, etc.; in questions expecting a neg. answer, ἔ. ὁπόθεν, ὅπως; Pl.*Phlb.*35a, *R.*493e, etc.; οὐ γάρ ἐσθ' ὅπως Pi.*Fr.*61, cf. Hdt.7.102, A.*Ag.*620; οὐκ ἔ. ὅπως οὐ *in any case, necessarily*, Ar.*Pax* 188; οὐκ ἔ. ὡς Pl. *Men.*76e, etc.; ἔ. ὅτε, ἔσθ' ὅτε, *some*times, Pi.*Fr.*180.2, S.*Aj.*56, Th. 7.21, etc. V. ἦν is sts. used with pl. masc. and fem., usu. at the beginning of a sentence, *there was*, τῆς δ' ἦν τρεῖς κεφαλαί Hes.*Th.*321; (but in ἦν δ' ἐρῳδιοί τε πολλοί Epich.46, cf. 59, al., it may be taken as Dor. 3 pl.); ἦν δ' ἀμφίπλεκτοι κλίμακες S.*Tr.*520 (lyr.); ἦν ἄρα κἀκεῖνοι ταλακάρδιοι Epigr.ap.Aeschin.3.184; less freq. ἔστι, ἔστι δὲ μεταξὺ... ἑπτὰ στάδιοι Hdt.1.26, cf. 7.34; ἔστι... ἄρχοντές τε καὶ δῆμος Pl.*R.*463a; before dual Nouns, Ar.*V.*58, Pl.*Grg.*500d. VI. ἔστι impers., c. inf., *it is possible*, ἔστι γὰρ ἀμφοτέροισιν ὀνείδεα μυθήσασθαι Il.20.246; ἔστι μὲν εὕδειν, ἔστι δὲ τερπομένοισιν ἀκούειν Od.15.392; εἴ τί πού ἐστι (sc. πιθέσθαι) 4.193; τοιάδε.. ἐστὶν ἀκοῦσαι A.*Pr.*1055 (anap.); ἔστι τεκμήρια δρᾶν X.*An.*3.2.13, cf. Ar.*Ra.*1163, Aeschin.3.105, D.18.272, Arist.*Ath.*53.6, etc.; so in imper., opt., and subj., ἔστω ἀποφέρεσθαι τῷ βουλομένῳ *IG*1^{2}.10.7; μυρία ἂν εἴη λέγειν Pl.*Plt.*271e; ὅπως ἂν ᾖ δρᾶν *IG*2.1054.91: more freq. in neg. clauses, Il.6.267, etc.; folld. by ὥστε c. inf., S.*Ph.*656: c. acc. et inf., ἀδόντα δ' εἴη με τοῖς ἀγαθοῖς ὁμιλεῖν Pi.*P.*2.96; ἔστιν ἐκπεσεῖν ἀρχῆς Δία A.*Pr.*757: sts. not impers. in this sense, θάλασσα δ' οὐκέτ' ἦν ἰδεῖν Id.*Pers.*419. b. ἔστω in argument, *let it be granted*, ἔστω τοῦτο ἀληθὲς εἶναι D.H.*Comp.*25; ἔστω σοι τοῦθ' οὕτως Plu.2.987b; ἔστω εἶναί τινα τοιοῦτον D.Chr.74.24.

B. most freq., *to be*, the Copula connecting the predicate with the Subject, both being in the same case: hence, *signify, import*, τὸ γὰρ εἴρειν λέγειν ἐστίν Pl.*Cra.*398d; esp. in the phrase τοῦτ' ἔστι, *hoc est*; Σκαιόλαν, ὅπερ ἐστὶ Λαιόν Plu.*Publ.*17: with numerals, τὰ δὶς πέντε δέκα ἐστίν twice five *are* ten, X.*Mem.*4.4.7; εἶναί τις or τι, *to be* somebody, something, *be* of some consequence, v. τις; οὐδὲν εἶναι Pl.*R.*562d, etc. 2. periphr. with the Participle to represent the finite Verb: with pf. part. once in Hom., τετληότες εἰμέν, for τετλήκαμεν, Il.5.873; so in Trag. and Att., ἦν τεθνηκώς, for ἐτεθνήκει, A.*Ag.*869; ἔσται δεδορκώς ib.1179; εἰμὶ γεγώς S.*Aj.*1299; πεφυκός ἐστι Ar.*Av.*1473; δεδρακότες εἰσίν Th.3.68; κατακεκονότες ἔσεσθε X.*An.*7.6.36: with aor. part., once in Hom., βλήμενος ἦν Il.4.211; so προδείσας εἰμί, οὐ σιωπήσας ἔσει; S.*OT*90,1146, cf. A.*Supp.*460: with pres. part., ἦν προκείμενον Id.*Pers.*371; φεύγων Ὀρέστης ἐστίν Id.*Ch.*136; εἴην οὐκ ἂν εὖ φρονῶν S.*Aj.*1330; τί δ' ἐστί.. φέρον; Id. *OT*991, cf. 274,708; λέγων ἐστίν τις E.*Hec.*1179; ἦν τίς σ' ὑβρίζων Id. *HF*313; πόρρω ἤδη εἶ πορευόμενος Pl.*Ly.*204b; βαδίζων εἰμί Ar.*Ra.*36; freq. in Hdt., ἦσαν ἰέντες 1.57, al.; even εἰσὶ διάφοροι ἐόντες 3.49 (s.v.l.):—if the Art. is joined with the Part., the noun is made emphatic, Κᾶρές εἰσι οἱ καταδέξαντες the persons who showed her *were* Carians, Id.1.171; αὐτὸς ἦν ὁ μαρτυρῶν A.*Eu.*798; δόλος ἦν ὁ φράσας S.*El.*197 (anap.).

C. εἶναι is freq. modified in sense by the addition of Advbs., or the cases of Nouns without or with Preps.: I. εἶναι with Advbs., where the Adv. often merely represents a Noun and stands as the predicate, ἅλις δέ οἱ ἦσαν ἄρουραι Il.14.122, etc.; ἀκέων, ἀκήν εἶναι, *to be* silent, 4.22, Od.2.82; σῖγα πᾶς ἔστω λεώς E.*Hec.*532; διαγνῶναι χαλεπῶς ἦν ἄνδρα ἕκαστον Il.7.424; ἀσφαλέως ἡ κομιδὴ ἔσται *will go on* safely, Hdt.4.134; ἐγγύς, πόρρω εἶναι, Th.6.88, Pl.*Prt.*356e: freq. impers. with words implying good or ill fortune, Κουρήτεσσι κακῶς ἦν *it fared* ill with them, Il.9.551; εὖ γὰρ ἔσται E.*Med.*89, cf. Ar.*Pl.*1188, etc.; ἡδέως ἂν αὐτοῖς εἴη D.59.30. II. c. gen., to express descent or extraction, πατρὸς δ' εἴμ' ἀγαθοῖο Il.21.109; αἵματός εἰς ἀγαθοῖο Od.4.611, cf. Hdt.3.71, Th.2.71, etc.; πόλεως μεγίστης εἶ X.*An.*7.3.19. b. to express the material of which a thing is made, ἡ κρηπὶς ἐστι λίθων μεγάλων *consists of*.., Hdt.1.93; τῆς πόλιος ἐούσης δύο φαρσέων ib.186; τοιούτων ἔργων ἐστὶ ἡ τυραννὶς *is made up of*.., Id.5.92.η', etc. c. to express the class to which a person or thing belongs, εἶ γὰρ τῶν φίλων *you are one of* them, Ar.*Pl.*345; ἐτύγχανε βουλῆς ὤν Th.3.70; ὅσοι ἦσαν τῶν προτέρων στρατιωτῶν Id.7.44; Κριτίας τῶν τριάκοντα ὤν X.*Mem.*1.2.31; ἔστι τῶν αἰσχρῶν *it is in the class of* disgraceful things, i.e. *it is* disgraceful, D.2.2. d. to express that a thing belongs to another, Τροίαν Ἀχαιῶν οὖσαν A.*Ag.*269; τὸ πεδίον ἦν μέν κοτε Χορασμίων Hdt.3.117, etc.: hence, *to be of the party of*, ἦσαν.. τινὲς μὲν Φιλίππου, τινὲς δὲ τοῦ βελτίστου D.9.56, cf. 37.53; *to be dependent upon*, S.*Ant.*737, etc.; *to be at the mercy of*, ἔστι τοῦ λέγοντος, ἢν φόβους λέγῃ Id.*OT*917. e. to express one's duty, business, custom, nature, and the like, οὔτοι γυναικός ἐστι '*tis* not a woman's *part*, A.*Ag.*940; τὸ ἐπιτιμᾶν παντὸς εἶναι D.1.16; τὸ δὲ ναυτικὸν τέχνης ἐστίν *is matter of* art, *requires* art, Th.1.142, cf. 83. f. in Lxx, *to be occupied about*, ἦσαν τοῦ θύειν 2*Ch.*30.17; ἔσεσθαι, c. gen., *to be about to*, ἐσόμεθα τοῦ σῶσαί σε 2*Ki.*10.11. III. with the dat., ἐστί μοι I *have*, freq. in Hom., etc. 2. with two dats., σφίσι τε καὶ Ἀθηναίοισι εἶναι οὐδὲν πρῆγμα that they and the Athenians *have* nothing *to do* one with another, Hdt.5.84; μηδὲν εἶναι σοὶ καὶ Φιλίππῳ πρᾶγμα D.18.283; more shortly, σοί τε καὶ τούτοισι πρήγμασι τί ἐστι; Hdt.5.33; τί τῷ νόμῳ καὶ τῇ βασάνῳ; D.29.36; τί ἐμοὶ καὶ σοί; Lat. *quid tecum est mihi? Ev.Marc.*5.7, etc.; also ἐμοὶ οὐδὲν πρὸς τοὺς τοιούτους (sc. ἐστίν) Isoc.4.12; ἐν οἷς πρὸς τοὺς ἐναντίους ἐστὶ τῷ δήμῳ D.18.278; ἔσται αὐτῷ πρὸς τὸν θεόν, in tomb inscriptions, *JHS*18.113, etc. 3. with ἄσμενος, βουλόμενος, etc., added, ἐμοὶ δέ κεν ἀσμένῳ εἴη '*twould be* to my delight, Il.14.108; οὐκ ἂν σφίσι βουλομένοις εἶναι Th.7.35; προσδεχομένῳ Id.6.46; θέλοντι S.*OT*1356 (lyr.); ἡδομένοις Pl.*La.*187c. IV. with Preps., εἶναι ἀπό τινος, = εἶναί τινος (supr. II.a), X.*Mem.*1.6.9; εἰσὶν ἀπ' ἐναντίων αὗται πραγμάτων Pl.*Phlb.*12d; but εἶναι ἀπ' οἴκου *to be* away from.., Th.1.99. 2. εἶναι ἔκ τινος *to be sprung* from, εἴμ' ἐκ Παιονίης, Μυρμιδόνων ἐξ εἰμί, Il.21.154, 24.397, etc.; ἔστιν ἐξ ἀνάγκης *it is* of necessity, i.e. necessary, Pl.*Sph.*256d. 3. εἶναι ἐν... *to be* in a certain state, ἐν εὐπαθείῃσι Hdt.1.22; ἐν ἀθυμίᾳ, etc., Th.6.46, etc.; ἐν ταραχαῖς D.18.218; εἶναι ἐν ἀξιώματι *to be* in esteem, Th.1.130; οἱ ἐν τέλεϊ ἐόντες those in office, Hdt.3.18, etc.; but εἶναι ἐν τέχνῃ, ἐν φιλοσοφίᾳ, *to be engaged* in.., S.*OT*562, Pl.*Phd.*59a. b. ἐν σοί ἐστι *it depends* on thee, Hdt.6.109, S.*Ph.*963; ἐν σοὶ γάρ ἐσμεν Id.*OT*314; so also ἐπί τινι Id.*Ph.*1003, X.*Cyr.*1.6.2, etc. 4. εἶναι διά.., much like εἶναι ἐν..., εἶναι διὰ φόβου, = φοβεῖσθαι, Th.6.34; εἶναι δι' ὄχλου, = ὀχληρὸν εἶναι, Id.1.73; εἶναι διὰ μόχθων X.*Cyr.*1.6.25; εἶναι δι' αἰτίας, = αἰτιᾶσθαι, D.H.1.70; Geom., *pass* through, διὰ τᾶς ἑτέρας διαμέτρου ἐόντος τοῦ ἐπιπέδου Archim.*Con.Sph.*20. 5. εἶναι ἐφ' ἑαυτῆς *to be* by oneself, D.25.23; εἶναι ἐπὶ ὀνόματος *to bear* a name, Id.39.21; εἶναι ἐπὶ τοῖς πράγμασιν *to be engaged* in.., Id.2.12; εἶναι ἐπί τινα *to be* against him, Id.6.33; εἶναι ἐφ' ἑξήκοντα στάδια *to reach* sixty stadia, X.*An.*4.6.11; εἶναι ἐπὶ τὰς ἁφὰς *pass* through the points of contact, Apollon.Perg.*Con.*4.1; εἶναι ἐπί τινι, v. supr. 3b. 6. εἶναι πρός τινος *to be* in one's favour, Th.4.10,29, etc.; *to suit*, X.*An.*1.2.11, etc.; εἶναι πρός τινι *engaged* in, Pl.*Phd.*84c, Philostr.*VA*5.31; πρὸς τοῖς ἰδίοις *mind* one's own affairs, Arist.*Pol.*1309^{a}6, *Ath.*16.3; εἶναι πρὸς τὸ κωλύειν Plb.1.26.3; πρὸς τὸ πονεῖν Teles p.46 H.; εἶναι περί τι X.*An.*3.5.7, etc. 7. εἶναι παρά τινι or τινα, = παρεῖναι, Id. *Cyr.*6.2.15, Hdt.8.140.α' (s.v.l.). 8. εἶναι ὑπό τινα or τινι *to be* subject to.., X.*HG*5.2.17 (s.v.l.), 6.2.4. **9.** περὶ τούτων ἐστὶν that *is* the question, Men.*Epit.*30. **10.** εἶναι ἀπό.., in Geom., *to be constructed* upon, Archim.*Sph.Cyl.*2.9, *Con.Sph.*7.

D. ἐστί is very freq. omitted, mostly in the pres. ind. before certain predicates, as ἀνάγκη, ἄξιον, δυνατόν, εἰκός, ἕτοιμον, οἷόν τε, ῥᾴδιον, χρεών, etc., and after the neut. of Verbals in -τέος, and such forms as θαυμαστὸν ὅσον: less freq. with other persons and moods, εἰμί omitted, S.*OT*92, *Aj.*813; εἶ, Od.4.206; ἐσμέν, S.*Ant.*634; ἐστέ, Od.10.463; εἰσί, S.*OT*499 (lyr.), *IG*2.778*B*; subj. ᾖ, Il.14.376, E.*Hipp.*659, Antipho 5.32; opt. εἴη, *IG*2².1183.12; impf. ἦν, ib.2.778*B*; fut. ἔσονται, Od.14.394.

E. the Inf. freq. seems redundant, **1.** in phrases implying power or will to do a thing, ἑκὼν εἶναι (v. ἑκών); κατὰ δύναμιν εἶναι Is.2.32; εἰς δύναμιν εἶναι Pl.*Plt.*300c; τὸ ἐπ' ἐκείνοις εἶναι, *quantum in illis esset*, Th.8.48, X.*HG*3.5.9, cf. Lys.13.58; τὸ ἐπὶ σφᾶς εἶναι Th.4.28; τὸ κατὰ τοῦτον εἶναι X.*An.*1.6.9; κατὰ τοῦτο εἶναι Pl.*Prt.*317a; τὸ τήμερον, τὸ νῦν εἶναι, Id.*Cra.*396e, *La.*201c, Theopomp. Com.98, Decr.ap.Arist.*Ath.*31.2, etc. **2.** after Verbs of naming or choosing, σοφιστὴν ὀνομάζουσι τὸν ἄνδρα εἶναι Pl.*Prt.*311e; σύμμαχόν μιν εἵλοντο εἶναι Hdt.8.134; of giving, δῶκε ξεινήϊον εἶναι Il.11.20.

F. impf. ἦν is sts. used where other languages take the pres., **1.** after ἄρα, to express a fact which *is and has always been* the same, δέρμα δὲ ἀνθρώπου ... ἦν ἄρα σχεδὸν δερμάτων πάντων λαμπρότατον human skin then *it appears is*.., Hdt.4.64; Κύπρις οὐκ ἄρ' ἦν θεός E.*Hipp.*359; ὡς ἄρ' ἦσθ' ἐμὸς πατὴρ ὀρθῶς ib.1169; ἦ πολύμοχθον ἄρ' ἦν γένος.. ἁμερίων Id.*IA*1330; ἦ στωμύλος ἦσθα Theoc.5.79; so also when there is reference to a past thought, τουτὶ τί ἦν; what *is* this? Ar.*Ach.*157, cf. Pl.*Cra.*387c: so in the Aristotelian formula τὸ τί ἦν εἶναι (*APo.*82ᵇ38, al.), used to express *the essential nature* of a thing, where τί ἦν (for ἐστί) takes the place of the dat. in such phrases as τὸ ἀγαθῷ εἶναι, τὸ μεγέθει εἶναι, *APr.*67ᵇ12, *de An.*429ᵇ10.

G. ἐγώ εἰμι, in Lxx, pleonastic for ἐγώ, ἐγώ εἰμι οὐχ ἥμαρτον *Jd.*11.27, cf. 6.18; also ἔσται πᾶς ἀποκτενεῖ με *Ge.*4.14.

εἶμι (*ibo*), 2 sg. εἶ S.*Tr.*83, Ar.*Av.*990, Ep. and Ion. εἶς Hes.*Op.*208, εἶσθα Il.10.450, Od.19.69; 3 sg. εἶσι; pl. ἴμεν, ἴτε, ἴασι: imper. ἴθι (also εἶ in the compd. ἔξει Ar.*Nu.*633 acc. to Sch., but prob. indic.), 3 pl. ἴτωσαν E.*IT*1480, Pl.*Lg.*765a, also ἴτων A.*Eu.*32, ἰόντων Th.4.118, etc.: subj. ἴω (εἴω Sophr.48); Ep. 2 sg. ἴῃσθα Il.10.67; Ep. 3 sg. ἴῃσι 9.701; Ep. pl. ἴομεν (for -ωμεν) 2.440: opt. ἴοιμι, οις, οι, 14.21, etc.; ἰοίην Sapph.159, *IG*4.760 (Troezen), X.*Smp.*4.16, (διεξ-) Isoc.5.98; Ep. ἰείη Il.19.209, cf. περι-ιεῖεν *IG*2².1126.18 (Amphict. Delph.), εἴη Il.24.139, Od.14.496, εἴηι *GDI*4986.7 (Crete): inf. ἰέναι, Ep. ἴμεναι (ι in Il.20.365) or ἴμεν, also ἰέμεν Archyt.ap.Stob.3.1.106 (dub. l.), ἶναι [ῑ] Orac.ap.Str.9.2.23, (ἐξ-) Macho ap.Ath.13.580c, cf. *EM*467.18 (προσ-εῖναι dub. in Hes.*Op.*353): part. ἰών, ἰοῦσα, ἰόν: impf. ᾔειν, ᾔεις (δι-ῄεισθα Pl.*Ti.*26c, ἐπεξ-ῄεισθα *Euthphr.*4b), ᾔει or -ειν Id.*Ti.*38c, *Criti.*117e; Ep. and Ion. ἤϊα, 3 sg. ἤϊε (-εν), contr. ᾖε Od.18.257; dual ᾔτην Pl.*Euthd.*294d; 1 and 2 pl., ᾖμεν, ᾖτε; 3 pl., Ep. and Ion. ἤϊσαν, Ep. also ἴσαν, Att. ᾖσαν (μετ-) Ar.*Eq.*605, cf. *Fr.*161, (ἐπ-) Od.19.445, later ᾔεσαν (εἰσ-) Arist.*Ath.*32.1, etc.; also 3 sg. ἴε Il.2.872, al.; Ep. 1 pl. ἤομεν Od.10.251, al., 3 dual ἴτην Il.1.347; 3 pl. ἤϊον Od.23.370:—Med. pres. and impf. ἵεμαι, ἱέμην are mere mistakes for ἵεμαι, ἱέμην (from ἵημι), cf. S.*OT*1242, E.*Supp.*698:—for fut. εἴσομαι and aor. Med. εἰσάμην, in 3 sg. εἴσατο, ἐείσατο, 3 dual ἐεισάσθην, v. εἴσομαι II.—The ind. εἶμι usu. has pres. sense in Hom. (fut., Il.1.426, 18.280), but in Ion. Prose and Att. it serves as fut. to ἔρχομαι (q.v.), I *shall go, shall come*: the pres. sense is sts. found in Poetry, prov. αὐτόματοι δ' ἀγαθοὶ ἀγαθῶν ἐπὶ δαῖτας ἴασι (cf. Pl.*Smp.*174b), cf. Theoc.25.90, also in compds. (προσ-) A.*Eu.*242, (ἐπ-) Th.4.61, (συν-) Str.3.2.2. [ῐ- in all tenses, exc. in Ep. Subj. ῑομεν for ἴωμεν at the beginning of a verse]:—*come* or *go*, the special senses being given by the context, οἴκαδ' ἴμεν *go* home, Il.17.155; τάχ' εἶσθα θύραζε Od.19.69, etc.; *come*, οὐδέ μιν οἴω νῦν ἰέναι Il.17.710, etc.; *go, depart*, Od.2.367; ὑπὸ τεῖχος ἰόντας Il.12.264. **II.** c. acc., **1.** c. acc. loci, *go to* or *into*, Od.1.176, 18.194, S.*OT*637. **2.** c. acc. cogn., ὁδὸν ἰέναι *go* a road, Od.10.103; so τὴν ὀρεινήν (sc. ὁδόν) X.*Cyr.*2.4.22: metaph., ἄδικον ὁδὸν ἰέναι Th.3.64. **3.** *go through* or *over*, τὸ μέσον τοῦ οὐρανοῦ, of the sun, Hdt.2.25, cf. 26: in Hom., freq. c. gen., ἰὼν πεδίοιο *going across* the plain, Il.5.597. **III.** c. inf. aor., ἀλλά τις εἴη εἰπεῖν Ἀτρεΐδῃ Od.14.496.—On the Homeric βῆ δ' ἴμεν, etc., v. βαίνω. **2.** c. part. fut., Ἑλένην καλέουσ' ἴε *went* to call her, Il.3.383, cf. 14.200, Od.15.213; ἤϊα λέξων I *was going* to tell, Hdt.4.82; ἴτω θύσων Pl.*Lg.*909d; εἴ τις ἱστορίαν γράψων ἴῃ Luc.*Hist.Conscr.*39. **IV.** also of other motions besides walking or running, as of *going in a ship*, esp. ἐπὶ νηὸς ἰέναι Od.2.332, etc.; of the *flight* of bees, Il.2.87. **2.** of the *motion* of things, [πέλεκυς] εἶσιν διὰ δουρός the axe *goes* through the beam, 3.61; of clouds or vapour, 4.278; of the stars, 22.317; of time, ἔτος εἶσι the year *will pass*, Od.2.89; φάτις εἶσι the report *goes*, 23.362; χρόνος... ἰὼν πόρσω Pi.*O.*10(11).55; ἴτω κλαγγά, βοά, S.*Tr.*208 (lyr.), Ar.*Av.*857 (lyr.); ἡ μοῖρ' ὅποιπερ εἶσ' ἴτω S.*OT*1458, cf. Pl.*Ap.*19a. **V.** metaph. usages, ἰέναι ἐς λόγους τινί *to enter* on a conference with.., Th.3.80, etc.; ἰέναι ἐς τοὺς πολέμους, ἐς τὴν ξυμμαχίαν, Id.1.78, 5.30; ἰέναι ἐς χεῖρας *to come* to blows, Id.2.3, 81; ἰέναι ἐς τὰ παραγγελλόμενα *to obey* orders, Id.1.121; διὰ δίκης ἰὼν πατρί S.*Ant.*742; ἰέναι διὰ μάχης, διὰ φιλίας, etc., v. διά A.IV.b. **VI.** imper. ἴθι (with or without δή) *come now!* mostly folld. by 2 sg. imper., ἴ. ἐξήγεο Hdt.3.72; ἴθ' ἐγκόνει, ἴθ' ἐκκάλυψον, S.*Aj.*988, 1003; ἴ. πέραινε Ar.*Ra.*1170; in full, ἴ. καὶ πειρῶ *go and* try, Hdt.8.57: with 1 pl., ἴ. οὖν ἐπισκεψώμεθα X.*Mem.*1.6.4, cf. Pl.*Prt.*332d; ἴτε δὴ ἀκούσωμεν Id.*Lg.*797d: 2 dual, ἴθι δὴ παρίστασθον Ar.*Ra.*1378: also 2 pl., ἴτε νεύσατε S.*OC*248, cf. *OT*1413. **2.** ἴτω *let it pass, well then*, Id.*Ph.*120, E.*Med.*798. **VII.** part. added to Verbs, φρονείτω μεῖζον ἢ κατ' ἄνδρ' ἰών let him *go and* think.., S.*Ant.*768, cf. *OC*1393, *Aj.*304; βακχεύσεις ἰών E.*Ba.*343.—Cf. ἴσκω.

εἴμορος· πεπρωμένος, Hsch.

εἰν, Ep. and Lyr. (metri gr.) for ἐν, *in*, Il.2.783, al.; Trag. in lyr., A.*Supp.*871 (dub.), E.*Alc.*436; exc. εἰν Ἅιδου v.l. in S.*Ant.*1241; cf. εἰνί; also *Schwyzer*707 *A*3 (Ephesus, vi B.C.), and in compds., εἰνάλιος, εἰνόδιος.

εἵν, = οἱ, Corinn.36; cf. εἵν· ἀντωνυμία, ἐκεῖνος, Hsch.

εἶν, v. εἰμί.

εἰνα-ετής, ές, or **-έτης**, ες, *of nine years, nine years old*, Orph.*L.*348: neut. εἰνάετες, as Adv., *nine years long*, Od.14.240: fem. εἰναέτις, ιδος, *AP*7.643 (Crin.). **-ετίζομαι**, poet. for ἐνναετίζομαι, Call.*Dian.*179.

εἰνάκις, εἰνακισχίλιοι, εἰνακόσιοι, αι, α, v. ἐνάκις, etc.

εἰνᾰλίδῖνος [λῐ], η, ον, = ἐν ἁλὶ δινεύων, αἴθυιαι Arat.918.

εἰνάλιος, η, ον, poet. for ἐνάλιος.

εἰνᾰλίφοιτος [ῐ], ον, *roaming the sea*, of nets, *AP*6.16 (Arch.).

εἰνάνυχες [ᾰ], as Adv., *nine nights long*, Il.9.470; cf. εἰνάετες.

εἶναξ· κάλλος, Hsch.

εἰνάπηχυς, υ, poet. for ἐννεάπηχυς, Lyc.860.

εἰνάς, άδος, ἡ, poet. for ἐννεάς 11, Hes.*Op.*810.

εἰνάτερες [ᾰ], αἱ, *wives of brothers* or *of husbands' brothers, sisters-in-law*, Il.6.378, al. (never in Od.). (Sg. ἐνάτηρ Keil-Premerstein *Zweiter Bericht*138 (not εἰνάτηρ as stated by Hdn.Gr.1.48, al.); dat. ἐνατρί Buresch *Aus Lydien* 147; καίνετ[έ]ραν (acc. sg.) is dub. in *Jahresh.*18*Beibl.*33 (Cilicia)), voc. εἴνατερ Hdn.Gr.1.419, gen. εἰνάτερος Id.2.747, al.: εἰν- metri gr. in Ep., with ἐνάτηρ cf. Skt. *yā́tar-*, Lith. *jéntė*, gen. *jenters*, Lat. *janitrīces* 'sisters-in-law'.)

εἰνάτιον· λοξόν, Hsch. **εἴνᾰτος**, v. ἔνατος.

εἰνᾰφόωσσων, ον, gen. ωνος, *with nine sails*, στόλος Lyc.101.

εἵνεκα, εἵνεκεν, v. ἕνεκα.

εἰνεσίαι· ἐπιστολαί, Hsch.; cf. ἐννεσίη.

εἰνί, Ep. (metri gr.) for ἐνί, = ἐν (q.v.).

εἰνόδιος, ον, Ep. and Lyr. for ἐνόδ-, Il.16.260, E.*Ion* 1048, etc.

εἰνοσίγαιος, = ἐννοσίγαιος (q.v.).

εἴνοσις, = ἔνοσις, Hsch.

εἰνοσίφυλλος [ῐ], ον, (ἔνοσις) *with quivering foliage*, of wooded mountains, Il.2.632, Od.9.22, etc.

εἴνυμι or **-ύω**, v. καταέννυμι. **εἴξασι**, v. ἔοικα: **εἴξασκε**, v. εἴκω.

εἶξις, εως, ἡ, *giving way, yielding*, Sor.2.31, Plu.2.1122c, S.E.*M.*10.221, D.L.10.43: pl., Plu.2.447a.

εἶο, v. οὗ. **εἶοι**· ὀσπρίων τὰ καθάρσια, Hsch.; cf. εἰαί. **εἷος**, v. ἕως. **εἰπάδεον**· ἐπίπονον, Id. (Fort. εἰπαλέον, cf. εἶπος.)

εἴπερ or **εἴ περ**, strengthd. for εἰ, *if really, if indeed*, Il.3.25, etc.; esp. *even if, even though*, Il.7.117, Od.1.167, etc.; εἴ. καί 9.35; εἴ. τε Il.10.225; εἴ. γε A.*Ch.*198, Pl.*Prt.*312a, etc.; εἴ. γε δή Id.*Tht.*182c; with words between, εἴ. γάρ τε χόλον γε.. Il.1.81; εἴπερ ἔσται γε A.*Ag.*1249, cf. Pl.*Plt.*275e; καλῶς, εἴπερ ποτέ, ἔχει Th.4.20; εἴπερ ἄρα Jul.*Or.*7.216b. **II.** in Att. and Trag. to imply that the supposition agrees with the fact, *if as is the fact, since*, Th.6.14, etc.; but with impf. it implies that it is contrary to the fact, εἴπερ ἦν πέλας *if* I had been (but I was not), S.*El.*312, cf. 604; also εἴ. ἐκτελεῖς ἅπερ λέγεις *if only* you will keep your word, Id.*Ichn.*48. **III.** with an ellipse, *if you must*, Ar.*Nu.*227; ἀλλ' εἴ. but *if so*, Pl.*Prm.*150b, Arist.*EN*1101ᵃ12; cf. εἰ B.VII.

εἶπερ, Dor. Adv. *where*, *IG*2².1126.15.

εἶπον (pres. ἔπω is used by Nic.*Al.*429, 490, etc., but the pres. in use is φημί, λέγω, ἀγορεύω (v. infr. IV), the fut. ἐρέω, ἐρῶ, the pf. εἴρηκα), Ep. and Lyr. ἔειπον Il.1.552, al., Pi.*O.*4.25; subj. εἴπω (Ep. εἴπωμι Od.22.392, -ῃσθα 11.224, -ῃσι Il.7.87); opt. εἴποιμι; inf. εἰπεῖν, Ep. -έμεναι, -έμεν, 7.375, 9.688, Dor. εἴπην (v. infr.); part. εἰπών: also aor. 1 εἶπα (ἔειπα Emp.17.15, Theoc.22.153), ὅπερ εἶπα as I *said*, Satyr.*Vit.Eur.Fr.*39xvii 14, mostly in Ion. Prose, also Men.*Pk.*128, Herod.3.26, *UPZ*62.14 (ii B.C.), and the 2nd persons ind. and imper. of this form are preferred in Att., 2 sg. ind. εἶπας Il.1.106, 108, etc.; imper. εἶπον (on the accent v. Hdn.Gr.1.460) Simon.154, Pl.*Men.*71d, Men.891, Theoc.14.11, εἰπάτω (ἀν-ειπάτω *IG*2².1186.19 (iv B.C.), but ἀν-ειπέτω ib.1247.13 (iii B.C.)), -ατον, -ατε; 3 pl. εἶπαν *SIG*333.3 (Samos, iv B.C.), later εἴπασαν *IG*7.2225.51 (Thisbe); part. εἴπας Philem.42, Aeol. εἴπαις Pi.*O.*8.46, cf. Ael.Dion.*Fr.*156; in compds. Med. ἀπείπασθαι (q.v.), διείπασθαι (q.v.), but never in good Att.: (redupl. aor. 2 from ϝεπ- 'say'; ϝείπην only cj. in Alc.55, Sapph.28.2; ϝεῖπαι *Leg.Gort.*8.15; with ἔ-(ϝ)ειπον cf. Skt. *avocam*, redupl. aor. of *vac-* 'say'; cf. ἔπος):—*speak, say*, ὡς εἰπών Il.1.68, etc.; τινί 17.692, etc.; εἰς ἅπαντας E.*Hec.*303; εἰπεῖν ἔν τισιν or μετά τισιν *speak* among a number, Il.10.445, 3.85, etc.: c. acc. cogn., ἔπος, μῦθον, θεοπρόπιον, οὐνόματα, etc., 3.204, 1.552, 85, 17.260, etc.; τινί τι Od.1.169, al.; τι Alc., Sapph. ll. cc., etc.; τι ἐς or πρός τινα, S.*Tr.*487, *Aj.*292; εἰπεῖν περί τινος, ἀμφί τινι, Od.15.347, 14.364: c. gen., πατρός τε καὶ υἱέος *of* them, 11.174; εἰπεῖν ὅτι or ὡς *to say* that.., Il.17.655, Od.22.373, etc.: but also c. inf., Hdt.2.30, Th.7.35, Pl.*Grg.*473a, etc. **b.** *recite*, ἔπη Id.*Ion* 535b. **2.** in parenthesis, ὡς ἔπος εἰπεῖν so *to say*, limiting a general statement, A.*Pers.*714, etc.; *speaking loosely*, opp.

ὄντως, Pl.*Lg.*656e; opp. ἀκριβεῖ λόγῳ, Id.*R.*341b; ὡς εἰπεῖν Th.3.38, al., Pl.*Phdr.*258e, al.; ὡς ἀξίως εἰπεῖν Arist.*PA*651^{b}36: without ὡς, οὐ πολλῷ λόγῳ εἰπεῖν Hdt.1.61; ἐς τὸ ἀκριβὲς εἰπεῖν Th.6.82; σχεδὸν εἰπεῖν Pl.*Sph.*237c: καθόλου εἰπεῖν Arist.*Cat.*12^{a}27; ἡ ἁπλῶς εἰπεῖν ἀπόδειξις Id.*APo.*75^{b}23; τὸ ξύμπαν εἶπαι, εἰπεῖν, Hdt.7.143, Th.1.138. 3. εἴποι τις *as one might say*, dub. l. in Plb.15.35.1; ὥσπερ εἴποι τις Ar.*Av.*180 (s. v. l.); ὡς εἴποι τις D.Chr.64.5 (s. v. l.). II. c. acc. pers., *address, accost* one, Il.12.210, etc. 2. *name, mention*, ib.1.90, etc. 3. *call* one so and so, πολλοί τέ μιν ἐσθλὸν ἔειπον Od.19.334, cf. S.*OC*43, E.*Med.*465, etc. 4. c. dupl. acc. pers. et rei, *tell* or *proclaim* so *of* one, Il.6.479 (where ἀνιόντα depends on εἴποι); εἰπεῖν τινα ὅτι.. Pi.*O.*14.22; ἀτάσθαλόν τι εἰ. τινά Od.22.314; κακὰ εἰ. τινά Ar.*Ach.*649; μηδὲν φλαῦρον εἰ. τ. Id.*Nu.*834; εὖ εἰ. τινά Od.1.302; εἰ. τεθνεῶτ' Ὀρέστην *speak of* him *as* dead, A.*Ch.*682. 5. *celebrate*, of poets, Αἴαντος βίαν *AP*7.2.6 (Antip. Sid.). III. c. dat. pers. et inf., *order* or *command* one to.., Od.15.76, 22.262, etc.; also εἰπεῖν πρός τινα, c. inf., 16.151: c. acc. et inf., εἶπον τὰς παῖδας δεῦρ' ἄγειν τινά S.*OC*932, cf. Pl.*Phd.*59e, Herod. 6.26: folld. by ἵνα, freq. in *NT*, *Ev.Matt.*4.3, al. IV. *propose, move* a measure in the assembly, εἰπὼν τὰ βέλτιστα D.3.12; εἰπεῖν τὰ δέοντα ib.15; εἶπε ψήφισμα Id.24.11: freq. as a formal prefix to decrees and laws, Λάχης εἶπε Th.4.118, cf. *IG*1^{2}.24, al.; cf. ἀγορεύω. V. *plead*, δίκην Il.18.508; δικίδιον Ar.*Eq.*347. VI. *promise, offer*, χρυσὸν εἴφ' ὃς ἂν κτάνῃ E.*El.*33. VII. imper. εἰπέ sts. used in addressing several persons, Ar.*Ach.*328, *Av.*366, D.4.10.

εἶπος, ὁ, = ἶπος, Call.*Fr.*233.

εἴποτε or **εἴ ποτε**, *if ever*, Il.1.39; strengthd. εἴ ποτε δή ib.503: used in asking a favour of any one, to call something to his mind, for εἴποτ' ἔην γε, i. e. *as surely as* he was. II. indirect, *if* or *whether ever*, Il.2.97, etc.

εἴπου or **εἴ που**, *if anywhere, if at all*, Od.3.93, etc.; εἴ τί που ἔστι *if* it is *any way* possible, 4.193; πάσας ξυνήθροισεν εἴ πού τις ἦν X.*HG*2.1.10, etc. II. indirect, *whether anywhere*, πευσόμενος.. εἴ που ἔτ' εἴης Od.13.415, etc.

εἶρ· λαῖλαψ, Hsch.: εἴρ, Suid.

Εἰρᾰφιών, ῶνος, ὁ, name of month at Amorgos, *IG*12(7).62.28; cf. sq.

Εἰρᾰφιώτης, ου, ὁ (Aeol. **Ἐρραφεώτας** Alc.90), epith. of Bacchus, *h.Hom.*1.2, al., Call.*Fr.anon.*89, D.P.576, *IGRom.*4.360.27 (Pergam.); for various etymologies cf. Corn.*ND*30, Porph.*Abst.*3.17, *EM*302.53, 372.1. II. = ἔριφος (Lacon.), Hsch.

εἰργαθεῖν, v. ἐργαθεῖν.

εἰργμός, later **εἱργμός**, ὁ, (εἴργω) *cage, prison*, Pl.*R.*495d, *Phd.*82e. 2. *imprisonment*, J.*AJ*18.1.3, Plu.2.84f: pl., Mitteis *Chr.* 71.10 (iv A. D.); εἰργμοὶ καὶ δεσμοί, of a snake's *coils*, Ael.*NA*17.37; εἰργμοῦ γραφή action *for malicious imprisonment*, Poll.6.154.

εἰργμοφύλαξ [ῠ], ἄκος, ὁ, ἡ, *gaoler*, X.*HG*5.4.8.

εἰργνῡμι (-ύω And.4.27), Ep. impf. ἐέργνυ:—*shut in* or *up*, Od.10.238.

εἴργω or **εἵργω**, v. ἔργω. **εἰρέα**, ἡ, v. sub εἴρη (A). **εἰρέαται**, Ion. 3 pl. pf. Pass. of ἐρῶ. **εἰρέβαδε**, = εἰς ἔρεβος, Hsch. **εἰρεθύρη**· ὀρσοθύρα, ὁ στροφεύς, Id.

εἰρελάω, Eretrian for εἰσ-, *IG*12(9).90.11 (Tamynae, iv B. C.).

εἴρεμος (ἥρ- cod.), etym. of Ἑρμῆς, Hsch. s. v. Ἀργειφόντης.

εἴρερος, ὁ, *bondage, slavery*, εἴρερον εἰσανάγουσι Od.8.529.

εἰρεσία, Ion. -ίη, ἡ, (ἐρέσσω) *rowing, oarage*, πρῶτα μὲν εἰρεσίη, μετέπειτα δὲ κάλλιμος οὖρος Od.11.640; εἰρεσίῃ χρᾶσθαι Hdt.1.203, 4.110; εἰρεσίας ζυγόν S.*Aj.*249 (lyr.); εἰ. τῶν τριήρων Arist.*Mete.*369^{b}10: metaph., εἰ. πτερῶν Luc.*Tim.*40; παρὰ δ' εἰρεσίᾳ μαστῶν ἕπεται Ἀστυάναξ close to her *throbbing* breast, E.*Tr.*570 (anap.); εἰρεσίῃ γλώσσης Dionys.Eleg.4.3. 2. *oar*, Ph.1.352,385. II. in collective sense, *rowers, oarsmen*, E.*Hel.*1453 (lyr.), *AP*7.287 (Antip.(?)); ξυνέχειν τὴν εἰ. keep *the oars* together or make *the rowers* keep time, Th.7.14. 2. *boat-song, to which the rowers kept time*, αὐλεῖν εἰρεσίαν Plu.*Alc.*32, cf. Luc.*VH*1.40. III. pl., *rowers' benches*, Plb.1.21.2. (The Ep. form, due to metrical lengthening, is retained in Prose.)

εἰρεσιώνη, ἡ, (εἶρος) *branch* of olive or laurel *wound round with wool and hung with fruits*, dedicated to Apollo and borne about by singing boys at the Πυανόψια and Θαργήλια, while offerings were made to Helios and the Hours, and afterwards hung up at the house-door, Eup.119, Ar.*Eq.*729, *V.*399, *Pl.*1054, cf. Paus.Gr.*Fr.*157, Sch.Ar. ll. cc. 2. the song itself, Hom.*Epigr.*15, Plu.*Thes.*22. II. *crown* hung up in honour of the dead, *IG*3.1337, Alciphr. 3.37. 2. generally, *wreath*, J.*AJ*3.10.4; cf. εἰρυσιώνη.

εἰρέω, *say*, only in Ep. part. fem. εἰρεῦσαι Hes.*Th.*38; for εἰρήσομαι, εἴρημαι, v. ἐρῶ. II. εἰρεῦντα· ἐρωτῶντα, Hsch.

εἴρη (A), ἡ, (εἴρω 'speak') old Ion., = ἀγορά or ἐκκλησία, *a place of assembly*, εἰράων προπάροιθε καθήμενοι Il.18.531 (cf. Sch. ad loc. and *EM*483.3); ἐπιμίσγεται.. εἴρας ἐς ἀθανάτων Hes.*Th.*804 (Herm. for εἰρέας): expld. by Hsch. as = ἐρώτησις, φήμη, κληδών (also written ἱρά, ἰρά, by Gramm., cf. Apollon.*Lex.*, *EM*475.12, Suid.).

εἴρη (B), ἡ, v. εἶρις: also, = ἶρις, *rainbow*, Hsch.

εἰρήδεται· ἐρίζεται, Hsch.

εἰρήν, ενος, or **ἰρήν**, ένος, ὁ, *Lacedaemonian youth who had completed his twentieth year*, X.*Lac.*2.11, Plu.*Lyc.*17, *IG*5(1).279.

εἰρηνάζει· κρατεῖ, Hsch.

εἰρηναῖος, α, ον, *peaceful*, εἰρηναῖον εἶναί τινι to live *peaceably* with any one, Hdt.2.68; οὐδὲν εἰ. ἀπαγγέλλειν Th.1.29; τὰ εἰ. *matters of peace*, Hdt.6.57; εἰ. βίος Phld.*Oec.*p.20 J.; εἰ. καὶ βέβαιος πλοῦς Dion. Byz.24: Sup., Max.Tyr.30.5. Adv. -αίως Hdt.3.145, Phld.*Oec.* p.39 J. II. εἰρηναῖον, τό, = Lat. *Templum Pacis*, D.C.72.24.

εἰρηναρχ-εῖον, τό, *office of* εἰρηνάρχης, *POxy.*141.5 (vi A. D.). **-έω**, *hold office of* εἰρηνάρχης, *OGI*537.6 (Pessinus), *BSA*18.149 (Beroea, ii/iii A. D.), *IGRom.*4.1437 (Smyrna), 3.208 (Ancyra). **-ης**, ου, ὁ, *police magistrate*, ib.203 (Ancyra), *OGI*550 (Phrygia), *BGU*151.4, *Cod.Just.*10.77, etc.:—also **εἰρήναρχος**, ὁ, *Milet.*1(7) No.263, *IGRom.*4.1543 (Erythrae), *Cod.Just.*10.1.9. **-ικός**, ή, όν, *of* or *for such an officer*, τιμαί *BCH*9.347 (Caria), cf. Sch.Ar.*Ra.*1103.

εἰρήν-ευσις, εως, ἡ, *reconciliation*, ἐναντίων δυνάμεων Iamb.*VP*33.229. **-εύω**, *bring to peace, reconcile*, D.C.77.12, gloss on Babr. 39.4. II. intr., *keep peace, live peaceably*, Pl.*Tht.*180b; πρός τινα D.S.21.16; μετὰ πάντων *Ep.Rom.*12.18:—Med., πρὸς τοὺς κρείττους εἰρηνεύεσθαι Arist.*Rh.*1359^{b}39, cf. *OGI*199.1 (Adule); χώρα -ομένη ἐκ παλαιοῦ Plb.5.8.7. **-έω**, = εἰρηνεύω II, Arist.*HA*608^{b}29, D.L. 2.5, D.C.37.52.

εἰρήν-η (v. infr.), ἡ, *peace*, Od.24.486, etc.; ἐπ' εἰρήνης in *time of peace*, Il.2.797; ἔθηκε πᾶσιν εἰ. φίλοις A.*Pers.*769; εἰ. τἀκεῖθεν τέκνοις on that side they have *peace*, have naught to fear, E.*Med.*1004; εἰ. γίγνεται *peace* is made, Hdt.1.74: hence later, *a peace, treaty of peace*, ἡ βασιλέως εἰ. *IG*2^{2}.103.24, etc.; εἰ. ποιεῖν Ἀρμενίοις καὶ Χαλδαίοις make *peace* between.., X.*Cyr.*3.2.12; εἰ. ποιεῖσθαι And.3.8, Aeschin. 2.77; εἰ. κατεργάζεσθαι, πράττειν, And.3.8,17; διαπράξασθαι X.*HG* 6.3.4; εἰρήνης δεῖσθαι ib.2.2.13; εἰρήνην δέχεσθαι to accept *it*, ib.22; λαβεῖν And.3.7; εἰ. ἄγειν keep *peace*, be at *peace*, Ar.*Av.*386, etc.; πρὸς ἀλλήλους Pl.*R.*465b; εἰ. ἄγειν (v. l. ἔχειν) enjoy *peace*, X.*An.*2.6.6; λύειν break *it*, D.18.71; πολλὴ εἰ. τινὸς γίγνεται profound *peace*, Pl.*R.*329c; ἐν εἰρήνῃ λέγειν, τὸν βίον διάγειν, Id.*Smp.*189b, *R.*372d; πόλεμον εἰρήνης χάριν [αἱρεῖσθαι] Arist.*Pol.*1333^{a}35; εἰρήνης ἄρξας, = εἰρηναρχήσας, *IGRom.*3.784, cf. 452. II. *the goddess of peace*, daughter of Zeus and Themis, Hes.*Th.*902, cf. Pi.*O.*13.7, B.*Fr.*3.1, *IG*3.170, Plu.*Cim.*13, etc. III. Pythag. name for *three*, *Theol.Ar.* 16; for *six*, ib.37. IV. Hebraism in Lxx, ἐρωτῆσαί τινα εἰς εἰρήνην *greet* a person, inquire after their health, *Jd.*18.15, 1*Ki.*17.22; ἐρ. τινὰ τὰ εἰς εἰ. ib.10.4; so ἐπερωτᾶν εἰς εἰ. τοῦ πολέμου 2*Ki.*11.7; in salutations, εἰ. σοι; 4*Ki.*4.26, cf. *Ev.Luc.*24.36, al.; εἰ. ἡ εἴσοδός σου 3*Ki.*2.13. (Ϝειράνα *IG*5(1).1509 (Sparta, iv B. C., dub.); ἰράνα ib.4.917 (Epid.), 12(3).29.12 (Telos); cf. Boeot. πολέμω καἰράνας ib.7.2407, but Cret. πολέμω χ[ἰ]ρήνας *GDI*5018.5; εἰρήνα Pi. l. c., B. l. c., *SIG*241.80 (Delph., iv B. C.), later εἰράνα *IG*5(1).935.14 (ii B. C.).) **-ικός**, ή, όν, *of* or *for peace*, λόγων -ώτατος Isoc.5.3; χρεία Arist.*Pol.*1254^{b}32; θυσίαι *peace* offerings, Lxx 1*Ki.*11.15, al.; ἄγγελοι καὶ δαίμονες Herm.ap.Stob.1.49.45. 2. *of* or *in peace, peaceful*, βίος, πρᾶξις, etc., Pl.*Lg.*829a, *R.*399b, etc.; ἐπιστῆμαι X.*Oec.*1.17; Sup., Ph. 2.634. Adv. -κῶς *peaceably*, opp. πολεμικῶς, Isoc.5.46, Phld.*Hom.* p.45 O., etc.: Comp. -ώτερον Luc.*Fug.*5. 3. *peaceable*, of persons, Isoc.2.24.

εἰρηνο-δίκαι [ῐ], ῶν, οἱ, = Lat. *Fetiales*, D.H.2.72, al.: sg., ib.15.9, App.*Sam.*5. **-πάτριος**, ὁ, *Father of Peace*, title of Chosroes, Men. Prot.p.16 D. **-ποιέω**, *to make peace*, Lxx *Pr.*10.10, *Ep.Col.*1.20, *Cat.Cod.Astr.*2.203:—Med., *make peaceful*, [ψυχὴ] τὸν ἴδιον δρόμον -εῖται Herm.ap.Stob.1.49.45. **-ποιός**, ὁ, *peace-maker*, X.*HG* 6.3.4, *Ev.Matt.*5.9, Corn.*ND*23, Plu.*Nic.*11. II. pl., = Lat. *Fetiales*, Id.2.279b. **-φῠλᾰκέω**, *to be a guardian of peace*, Ph.2.209. **-φύλαξ** [ῠ], ἄκος, ὁ, ἡ, *guardian of peace*, X.*Vect.*5.1, Aeschin.3.159; of Caesar, Ph.2.567; title of police magistrate, Lib. *Or.*48.9 (pl.), *Sammelb.*4636.32,36 (Panopolis, iii A. D.). II. pl., = εἰρηνοδίκαι, Plu.*Num.*12.

εἰρητής· αἴτιος, Hsch. **εἰρίνεος, εἴριον**, v. ἐρίνεος, ἔριον.

εἶρις, ἡ, = ἶρις II. 3, *SIG*1171.15 (Crete, acc. sg. written εἴρην): **εἴρινος**, = ἴρινος, *Edict.Diocl.* in *BCH*22.403 (Delph.). II. v. Ἶρις.

εἰρκτέον, (εἴργω) *one must prevent*, S.*Aj.*1250.

εἱρκτή or **εἰρκ-**, Ion. **ἑρκτή**, ἡ, (εἵργω) *an inclosure, prison*, Hdt.4.146,148, Th.1.131, *PTeb.*5.260 (ii B. C.), etc.; of the body as *prison* of the soul, J.*BJ*2.8.11 (pl.): pl., E.*Ba.*497, X.*Cyr.*3.1.19. II. *inner part of the house, women's apartments*, Id.*Mem.*2.1.5.

εἱρκτικός, ή, όν, *preventive*, Gloss.

εἱρκτο-φῠλᾰκέω, *to be a gaoler*, Ph.1.290. **-φύλαξ** [ῠ], ἄκος, ὁ, *gaoler*, Ph.1.289, 2.53, J.*AJ*17.7.1.

εἱρμός, ὁ, (εἴρω A) *train, series, sequence*, Arist.*Pr.*916^{a}31, Ph.1.6, Plot.3.1.2, etc.; εἰ. αἰτιῶν *concatenation* of causes, *Placit.*1.28.4, cf. Iamb.ap.Stob.1.5.17; so εἱρμός alone, Chrysipp.*Stoic.*2.284, cf. Hierocl. *in CA*11 p.442 M. 2. *connexion*, εἰ. λόγου πρὸς βίον Ph. 1.569.

εἶρξις, εως, ἡ, *fencing in*, *IG*1^{2}.94.8. II. gloss on μεσόδμη, Gal. 19.122.

εἰροκόμος, ον, *working in wool*, Il.3.387: as Subst., *AP*6.160 (Antip. Sid.).

εἴρομαι, Ion. for ἔρομαι, *ask*; v. εἴρω (C).

εἰρομένως, Adv. *running on*: *in order*, *PSI*4.439 (iii B. C.); *in continuation*, Apollon.Cit.2.

εἰρο-πόκος, ον, *wool-fleeced, woolly*, εἰροπόκοις ὀΐεσσιν Il.5.137; εἰροπόκων ὀΐων Od.9.443, Theoc.8.9, cf. Hes.*Op.*234. **-πόνος**, ον, *working in wool*, Suid.

εἶρος, εος, τό, *wool*, Od.4.135, 9.426. II. = γναφάλλιον, Ps.-Dsc.3.117. III. a kind of *fever*, Hp.ap.Erot. (with other expll.).

εἰροχᾰρής, ές, *delighting in wool*, τάλαρος *AP*6.39 (Arch.).

εἴροψ, οπος, ὁ, Boeot., = μέροψ, Arist.*HA* 559ᵃ4.

εἰρτός, ή, όν, (εἴρω A) *that can be threaded* or *sewn*, *Gloss.*

εἰρύαται, εἰρύμεναι [ῠ], v. ἐρύω.

εἰρύσῐμον [ῠ], τό, Ep. for ἐρύσιμον, Nic.*Th.*894.

εἰρῠσῐώνη, ἡ, = εἰρεσιώνη II. 2, *wreath* dedicated to Apollo, Roussel *Cultes Égyptiens* 172 (Delos, i B.C.).

εἰρύω, εἰρύομαι, poet. for ἐρύω, ἐρύομαι (q.v.).

εἴρω (A), aor. εἶρα (v. infr.), also ἔρσα (v. διείρω) :—Pass., pf. part. ἐρμένος (ἐν-) Hdt.4.190; Ep. ἐερμένος (v. infr.):—mostly in compds., ἀν-, δι-, ἐν-, ἐξ-, συν-είρω :—*fasten together in rows, string*, used by Hom. only in Ep. pf. Pass., ἠλέκτροισιν ἐερμένος [a necklace] *strung* with pieces of amber, Od.18.296, and plpf. Pass., μετὰ δ' ἠλέκτροισιν ἔερτο 15.460; περὶ στήθεσσιν ἔερτο [μίτρη] A.R.3.868; τὸ εὖ εἰρόμενον *a connected system*, Plot.2.3.7. II. after Hom. in Act., στεφάνους εἴ. Pi.*N.*7.77; εἴ. τὰ θεῖα Plu.2.1029c; *insert*, εἰς βρόχον εἴρας τὸν τράχηλον Zaleuc.ap.Stob.4.2.19 ad fin., cf. *PMag.Par.*1.259; esp. in speech, *string together*, ὁ εἴρας καὶ συνυφάνας ἕκαστα [λόγος] Ph.1.499; θρῆνον J.*BJ*6.5.3; πολλὰ ὀνόματα Philostr.*VA* 1.20, cf. 6.17; οἱ μηδὲ δύο σχεδὸν ῥήματα δεξιῶς εἴρειν δυνάμενοι S.E.*M.*1.98:—Pass., εἰρομένη λέξις *continuous, running* style, i.e. not antithetic or with balanced periods, Arist.*Rh.*1409ᵃ29. 2. εἰρόμενον, τό, '*dossier*' of documents, Mitteis *Chr.*184.9 (iii A.D.); εἰ. τραπεζιτικόν *PLips.*9.22. (Etym. dub., cf. either Lat. *sero* or Lith. *vérti* 'thread'.)

εἴρω (B), *say, speak, tell*:—Act. is used by Hom. only in Od., and in 1 pers., μνηστῆρσιν δ' . . τάδε εἴρω 2.162, cf. 13.7; τὰ δέ τοι νημερτέα εἴρω 11.137:—Med. in same sense, καὶ εἴρετο δεύτερον αὖτις Il.1.513; εἴροντο δὲ κήδε' ἑκάστη Od.11.542, cf. Nic.*Th.*359:—Pass., 3 sg. εἴρεται *is said*, Arat.172,261: for other forms v. ἐρῶ. (ϝέρ-yω, fr. root of ἐρῶ, q.v.)

***εἴρω** (C), *ask*: for Act. forms (stem ἐρε(ϝ)-), v. ἐρέω (A): for Med. forms (stems ἐρε(ϝ)- and ἐρ(ϝ)-), v. ἔρομαι, ἐπείρομαι.

εἴρων, ωνος, ὁ, ἡ, *dissembler, one who says less than he thinks*, Ar.*Nu.*449, etc.; opp. ἀληθευτικός, Arist.*EN*1124ᵇ30, Thphr.*Char.*1.1; opp. ἀλαζών, Arist.*EN*1108ᵃ23; ἀλώπηξ εἴ. τῇ φύσει Philem.89.6; ὁ εἴ. ὡς ἐπὶ τὸ πλεῖστον ἀλαζόνος εἶδος Phld.*Vit.*p.38 J.; εἴ. ἐν τοῖς λόγοις Luc.*Anach.*18, cf. Cic.*Off.*1.30.108, J.*BJ*1.26.2.

εἰρων-εία, ἡ, *dissimulation*, i.e. *ignorance purposely affected* to provoke or confound an antagonist, a mode of argument used by Socrates against the Sophists, Pl.*R.*337a, cf. Arist.*EN*1124ᵇ30, Cic.*Acad.Pr.*2.5.15: generally, *mock-modesty*, opp. ἀλαζονεία, Arist.*EN*1108ᵃ22; *sarcasm*, Hermog.*Id.*2.8, al.; *understatement*, Phld.*Lib.*p.13 O. II. *pretence, assumption*, when a person at first appears willing, but then draws back, D.4.7; τὴν ἡμετέραν βραδυτῆτα καὶ εἰρωνείαν ib.37. III. generally, *dissembling*, Ph.1.345 (pl.), al. 2. *pretext*, *PSI*5.452.23 (iv A.D.). **-ευμα**, ατος, τό, in pl., *ironies*, Max. Tyr.24.5, 38.4. **-εύομαι**, *feign ignorance*, so as to perplex, Arist.*Rh.*1379ᵇ31; πρός τινα Pl.*Cra.*384a; πρὸς ὑμᾶς αὐτούς Din.2.11; *banter*, Arist.*Pol.*1275ᵇ27: generally, *dissemble, shuffle*, Ar.*Av.*1211, Pl.*Ap.*38a, D.60.18. 2. *employ understatement*, Polystr.p.15 W. II. trans., *treat with sarcasm*, τινά Him.*Ecl.*1.13. **-ευτής**, οῦ, ὁ, = εἴρων, Timo 25.3. **-ευτικός**, ή, όν, = foreg., Sch.A.R.1.486. **-ίζω**, = εἰρωνεύομαι, Philostr.*VS*1.7.1 (v.l. for εἰρωνικόν). **-ικός**, ή, όν, *dissembling*: hence, *hollow, insincere*, Pl.*Sph.*268a; τὸ εἰ. εἶδος Id.*Lg.*908e; εἰρωνικόν τι ὑπομειδιάσας Hld.10.14. Adv. **-κῶς** *mockingly*, Ar.*V.*174, Pl.*Smp.*218d, etc.

εἰρωτάω, Ep., and **εἰρωτέω**, Ion., for ἐρωτάω.

εἰς or **ἐς**, PREP. WITH ACC. ONLY:—both forms are found in Hom., Ion. poets, and early metrical Inscrr.; ἐς is best attested in Hdt. and Hp., and is found in nearly all early Ion. Inscrr. (exc. *IG*12(8).262.16 (Thasos, v B.C.), ib.7.235.1 (Oropus, iv B.C.)); εἰς in Att. Inscrr. from iv B.C., *IG*2.115, etc.; and usu. in Att. Prose (exc. Th.) and Com. (exc. in parody): Trag. apptly. prefer εἰς, but ἐς is used before vowels metri gr.; ἐς was retained in the phrases ἐς κόρακας (whence the Verb σκορακίζω), ἐς μακαρίαν. Aeol. poets have εἰς before vowels, ἐς before consonants, and this is given as the rule in Hom. by *An.Ox.*1.172, cf. Hellad.ap.Phot.*Bibl.*p.533 B. (Orig. ἐνς, as in *IG*4.554.7 (Argos), *GDI*4986.11 (Crete); cf. ἐν, ἰν. The diphthong is genuine in Aeol. εἰς, but spurious in Att.-Ion.) Radical sense *into*, and then more loosely, *to*: I. OF PLACE, the oldest and commonest usage, εἰς ἅλα *into* or *to* the sea, Il.1.141, al.; εἰς ἅλαδε Od.10.351; ἐς ῥ' ἀσαμίνθους 4.48; ἐς οἶνον βάλε φάρμακον ib.220; freq. of places, *to*, εἰς Εὔβοιαν 3.174; ἐς Αἴγυπτον, etc., Hdt.1.5, etc.; ἐς Μίλητον *into the territory of* Miletus, ib.14; εἰς Ἑλλήσποντον εἰσέπλει X.*HG*1.1.2; ἀφίκετο εἰς Μήδους πρὸς Κυαξάρην Id.*Cyr.*2.1.2; εἰς ἅρματα βαίνειν to step *into*.., Il.8.115; εἰς ἐλάτην ἀναβῆναι 14.287; opp. ἐκ, in such phrases as ἐς σφυρὸν ἐκ πτέρνης, ἐς πόδας ἐκ κεφαλῆς, from heel *to* ankle-joint, from head *to* foot, 22.397, 23.169; ἐκ πάτου ἐς σκοπιήν 20.137; ἐς μυχὸν ἐξ οὐδοῦ Od.7.87; κῆς ἔτος ἐξ ἔτεος from year *to* year, Theoc.18.15: with Verbs implying motion or direction, as of looking, ἰδεῖν εἰς οὐρανόν Il.3.364; εἰς ὦπα ἰδέσθαι to look *in* the face, 9.373, etc.; εἰς ὦπα ἔοικεν he is like *in* face (sc. ἰδόντι), 3.158, etc.; ἐς ὀφθαλμούς τινος ἐλθεῖν to come *before* another's eyes, 24.204; ἐς ὄψιν ἀπικνέεσθαί τινος Hdt.1.136; καλέσαι τινὰ ἐς ὄψιν Id.5.106, etc.; ἐς ταὐτὸν ἥκειν come *to* the same point, E.*Hipp.*273: less freq. after a Subst., ὁδὸς ἐς λαύρην Od.22.128; τὸ ἐς Παλλήνην τεῖχος *facing* Pallene, Th.1.56; ξύνοδος ἐς τὴν Δῆλον Id.3.104, cf. Pl.*Tht.*173d. b. Ep. and Ion., also c. acc. pers. (Att. ὡς, πρός, παρά), Il.7.312, 15.402, Od.14.127, Hdt.4.147; also in Att. with collective Nouns, ἐς τὸν δῆμον παρελθόντες Th.5.45, or plurals, εἰς ὑμᾶς εἰσῆλθον D.18.103; esp. of consulting an oracle, ἐς θεὸν ἐλθεῖν Pi.*O.*7.31; εἰς Ἄμμων' ἐλθόντες Ar.*Av.*619. 2. with Verbs expressing *rest in* a place, when a previous motion *into* or *to* it is implied, ἐς μέγαρον κατέθηκεν ἐπὶ θρόνου he put it *in* the house (i.e. he brought it *into* the house, and put it *there*), Od.20.96; ἐς θρόνους ἕζοντο they sat them down *upon* the seats, 4.51, cf. 1.130; ἐφάνη λὶς εἰς ὁδόν the lion appeared *in* the path, Il.15.276; ἀπόστολος ἐς τὴν Μίλητον ἦν Hdt.1.21 (s.v.l.); αὐτὸς ἐς Λακεδαίμονα ἀπόστολος ἐγίνετο Id.5.38; ἐς κώμην παραγίνονται Id.1.185; παρῆν ἐς Σάρδις Id.6.1; ἐς δόμους μένειν S.*Aj.*80 (cod. Laur.); ἐς τὴν νῆσον κατέκλησε Th.1.109, cf. Hdt.3.13; ἀπόβασιν ποιήσασθαι ἐς.. Th.2.33, etc.; later used like ἐν, τὴν γῆν εἰς ἣν ὑμεῖς κατοικεῖτε Lxx *Nu.*35.34; τὸ χρυσίον ὃ εἰλήφεσαν εἰς Ῥώμην D.S.14.117; οἰκεῖν εἰς τὰ Ὕπατα Luc.*Asin.*1; εἰς Ἐκβάτανα ἀποθανεῖν Ael.*VH*7.8; εἰς ἅπασαν τὴν γῆν Suid. s.v. Καλλίμαχος: generally, τοὔνομα εἰς τὴν Ἑλλάδα, φασίν, Ἱππομιγὴς δύναται Ael.*VH*9.16. 3. with Verbs of saying or speaking, εἰς relates to the persons *to* or *before* whom one speaks, εἰπεῖν ἐς πάντας, ἐς πάντας αὐδᾶ, Hdt.8.26, S.*OT*93; λέγειν εἰς τὸ μέσον τῶν ταξιάρχων X.*Cyr.*3.3.7; αἱ ἐς τὸ φανερὸν λεγόμεναι αἰτίαι Th.1.23: with other Verbs, εἰς τοὺς Ἕλληνας σαυτὸν σοφιστὴν παρέχων Pl.*Prt.*312a; καλὸν ἐς τοὺς Ἕλληνας τὸ ἀγώνισμα φανεῖσθαι Th.7.56; ἐπαχθὴς ἦν ἐς τοὺς πολλούς Id.6.54; στρατιὰν ἐπαγγέλλων ἐς τοὺς ξυμμάχους Id.7.17; διαβεβλῆσθαι εἴς τινα Pl.*R.*539c. 4. elliptical usages, a. after Verbs which have no sense of motion to or into a place, τὴν πόλιν ἐξέλιπον εἰς χωρίον ὀχυρόν they quitted the city *for* a strong position, i.e. to seek a strong position, X.*An.*1.2.24; γράμματα ἑάλωσαν εἰς Ἀθήνας letters were captured [and sent] *to* Athens, Id.*HG*1.1.23, cf. Pl.*R.*468a; ἀνίστασθαι ἐς Ἄργος E.*Heracl.*59, cf. Pl.*Phd.*116a. b. participles signifying motion are freq. omitted with εἰς, τοῖς στρατηγοῖς τοῖς εἰς Σικελίαν (sc. ἀποδειχθεῖσιν) And.1.11, etc. c. c. gen., mostly of proper names, as εἰς Ἀΐδαο, Att. εἰς Ἅιδου [δόμους], Il.21.48; ἐς Ἀθηναίης [ἱερόν] *to* the temple of Athena, 6.379; ἐς Πριάμοιο [οἶκον] 24.160, cf. 309; εἰς Αἰγύπτοιο [ῥόον] Od.4.581; ἐς τοῦ Κλεομένεος Hdt.5.51; εἰς Ἀσκληπιοῦ Ar.*Pl.*411; ἐπὶ δεῖπνον [ἰέναι] εἰς Ἀγάθωνος Pl.*Smp.*174a: with Appellatives, ἀνδρὸς ἐς ἀφνειοῦ *to* a rich man's house, Il.24.482; ἐς πατρός Od.2.195; πέμπειν εἰς διδασκάλων send *to* school, X.*Lac.*2.1; εἰς δ. φοιτᾶν Pl.*Prt.*326c; ἐς σεωυτοῦ, ἑωυτοῦ, Hdt.1.108, 9.108, etc. II. OF TIME, 1. to denote a certain point or limit of time, *up to, until*, ἐς ἠῶ Od.11.375; ἐς ἠέλιον καταδύντα *till* sunset, 9.161 (but also, *towards* or *near* sunset, 3.138); ἐκ νεότητος ἐς γῆρας Il.14.86; ἐκ παιδὸς ἐς γῆρας Aeschin.1.180; ἐς ἐμέ *up to* my time, Hdt.1.92, al.: with Advbs., ἐς ὅτε (cf. ἔς τε) *against* the time when .., Od.2.99; εἰς πότε; *until* when? how long? S.*Aj.*1185 (lyr., cf. εἰσόκε); εἰς ὁπότε Aeschin.3.99; ἐς τί; = εἰς πότε; Il.5.465; ἐς ὅ *until*, Hdt.1.93, etc.; ἐς οὗ Id.1.67, 3.31, etc.; ἐς τόδε Id.7.29, etc. 2. to determine a period, εἰς ἐνιαυτόν *for* a year, i.e. a whole year, Il.19.32, Od.4.526; *within* the year, ib.86 (cf. ἐς ἐνίαυτον Alc.*Supp.*8.12); εἰς ὥρας Od.9.135; ἐς θέρος ἢ ἐς ὀπώρην *for* the summer, i.e. *throughout* it, 14.384; ἡ εἰς ἐνιαυτὸν κειμένη δαπάνη εἰς τὸν μῆνα δαπανᾶται the expenditure *for* a year is expended *in* the month, X.*Oec.*7.36; μισθοδοτεῖν τινὰς εἰς ἓξ μῆνας D.S.19.15; χοίνικα κριθῶν εἰς τέσσαρας ἡμέρας διεμέτρει Posidon.36 J.; εἰς ἑσπέραν ἥκειν to come *at* even, Ar.*Pl.*998; εἰς τρίτην ἡμέραν or εἰς τρίτην alone, *on* the third day, *in* two days, Pl.*Hp.Ma.*286b, X.*Cyr.*5.3.27; ἥκειν ἐς τὴν ὑστεραίαν Id.*An.*2.3.25; ἥκειν εἰς τὸ ἔαρ *Hell.Oxy.*17.4; ἐς τέλος *at* last, Hdt.3.40; ἐς καιρόν *in* season, Id.4.139; οὐκ ἐς ἀναβολάς, ἀμβολάς, *with* no delay, Id.8.21, E.*Heracl.*270, etc.; ἐς τότε *at* this time, v.l. in Od.7.317 (but εἰς τότε *at* that time (in the fut.), D.14.24, Pl.*Lg.*830b); ἐς ὕστερον or τὸ ὕστερον, Od.12.126, Th.2.20: with Advbs., ἐς αὔριον Il.8.538, Pl.*Lg.*858b; ἐς περ ὀπίσσω Od.20.199; ἐς αὖθις Th.4.63 (v. εἰσαῦθις); ἐς αὐτίκα μάλ' Ar.*Pax* 367; εἰς ἔπειτα (v. εἰσέπειτα); ἐς τὸ ἔ., Th.2.64; ἐς ὀψέ Id.8.23; εἰς ἅπαξ, v. εἰσάπαξ; εἰς ἔτι, v. εἰσέτι. III. to express MEASURE OR LIMIT, without reference to Time, ἐς δίσκουρα λέλειπτο was left behind *as far as* a quoit's throw, Il.23.523; ἐς δραχμὴν διέδωκε paid them *as much as* a drachma, Th.8.29; ἱματισμὸν ζητῆσαι εἰς δύο τάλαντα Thphr.*Char.*23.8; so ἐς τὰ μάλιστα *to* the greatest degree, Hdt.1.20, etc.; ἐς τοσοῦτο τύχης ἀπίκεν Id.1.124; εἰς τοσοῦτο ἥκειν Lys.27.10; εἰς τοῦτο θράσους καὶ ἀναιδείας ἀφίκετο D.21.194; ἐς ὃ ἐμέμνηντο *so far as* they remembered, Th.5.66; ἐς τὸ ἔσχατον Hdt.7.229, etc.; εἰς ἅλις Theoc.25.17. 2. freq. with Numerals, ἐς τριακάδας δέκα ναῶν A.*Pers.*339; ναῦς ἐς τὰς τετρακοσίας, διακοσίας, *to the number of* 400, etc., Th.1.74, 100, etc.; εἰς ἕνα, εἰς δύο, εἰς τέσσαρας, one, two, four *deep*, X.*Cyr.*2.3.21; but εἰς τέσσαρας four *abreast*, Aen.Tact.40.6: with Advbs., ἐς τρίς or ἐστρίς *thrice*, Pi.*O.*2.68, Hdt.1.86; of round numbers, *about*, X.*An.*1.1.10. 3. distributive, εἰς φυλάς *by* tribes, Lxx 1 *Ki.*10.21, cf. 2 *Ki.*18.4. IV. to express RELATION, *towards, in regard to*, ἐξαμαρτεῖν εἰς θεούς A.*Pr.*945, etc.; ἁμάρτημα εἴς τινα, αἰτίαι ἐς ἀλλήλους, Isoc.8.96, Th.1.66; ὄνειδος ὀνειδίζειν εἴς τινα S.*Ph.*522; ἔχθρη ἔς τινα Hdt.6.65; φιλία ἐς ἀμφοτέρους Th.2.9; λέγειν ἐς.. Hdt.1.86; γνώμη ἀποδεχθεῖσα ἐς τὴν γέφυραν Id.4.98; ἡ ἐς γῆν καὶ θάλασσαν ἀρχή Th.8.46. b. of the subject of a work, esp. in titles, e.g. τὰ ἐς Ἀπολλώνιον Philostr. *VA*; of the object of a dedication, as in titles of hymns, ἐπινίκια, etc. 2. *in regard to*, πρῶτος εἰς εὐψυχίαν A.*Pers.*326; σκώπτειν ἐς τὰ ῥάκια Ar.*Pax* 740, cf. *Eq.*90; διαβάλλειν τινὰ ἔς τι Th.8.88; αἰτία ἐπιφερομένη ἐς μαλακίαν Id.5.75; μέμφεσθαι εἰς φιλίαν X.*An.*2.6.30; εἰς τὰ πολεμικὰ καταφρονεῖσθαι Id.*HG*7.4.30; πόλεως εὐδοκιμωτάτης εἰς σοφίαν Pl.*Ap.*29d; *in respect of*, εὐτυχεῖν ἐς τέκνα E.*Or.*542, cf. Pl.*Ap.*35b, etc.; εἰς χρήματα ζημιοῦσθαι Id.*Lg.*774b, cf. D.22.55;

ἐς τὰ ἄλλα Th.1.1; εἰς ἅπαντα S.*Tr*.489; ἐς τὰ πάνθ' ὁμῶς A.*Pr*.736; εἰς μὲν ταῦτα Pl.*Ly*.210a; τό γ' εἰς ἑαυτόν, τὸ εἰς ἐμέ, S.*OT*706, E. *IT*691, cf. S.*Ichn*.346; ἐς ὀλίγους μᾶλλον τὰς ἀρχὰς ποιεῖν Th.8.53; ἐς πλείονας οἰκεῖν Id.2.37; for τελεῖν ἐς Ἕλληνας, Βοιωτούς, ἄνδρας, etc., v. τελέω. 3. of Manner, ἐς τὸν νῦν τρόπον Id.1.6; τίθεμεν τἆλλα εἰς τὸν αὐτὸν λόγον; Pl.*R*.353d; ἐς ἓν μέλος Theoc.18.7: freq. periphr. for Advbs., ἐς κοινὸν φράζειν, λέγειν, A.*Pr*.844, *Eu*.408; ἐς τὸ πᾶν, = πάντως, Id.*Ag*.682 (lyr.); ἐς τάχος, = ταχέως, Ar.*Ach*.686; ἐς εὐτέλειαν, = εὐτελῶς, Id.*Av*.805; ἐς τἀρχαῖον Id.*Nu*.593; εἰς καλόν S. *OT*78, cf. Pl.*Phd*.76e; ἐς δέον γεγονέναι Hdt.1.119, cf. S.*OT*1416, and v. δέον. V. of an end or limit, ἔρχεσθαι, τελευτᾶν, λήγειν ἐς.., to end *in*.., Hdt.1.120, 3.125, 4.39, etc.; ἐς ἑβδομήκοντα ἔτεα οὖρον ἀνθρώπῳ προτίθημι Id.1.32; καταξαίνειν ἐς φοινικίδα to cut *into* red rags, Ar.*Ach*.320 (troch.); στρέφειν τι εἰς αἷμα *Apoc*.11.6; εἰς ἄνδρας ἐκ μειρακίων τελευτᾶν, εἰς ἄνδρα γενειᾶν, Pl.*Tht*.173b, Theoc.14.28; ἐκτρέφειν τὸ σπέρμα εἰς καρπόν X.*Oec*.17.10: so with εἶναι or γίγνομαι to form a predicate, ἔσται εἰς ἔθνη Lxx *Ge*.17.16; ἐγενήθη εἰς γυναῖκα ib.20.12; πιστὸς (sc. ἦν) εἰς προφήτην ib.1*Ki*.3.20; ἐγένετο εἰς δένδρον *Ev.Luc*.13.19, al. 2. of Purpose or Object, εἰπεῖν εἰς ἀγαθόν, πείσεται εἰς ἀγαθόν, *for* good, *for* his good, Il.9.102, 11.789; εἰς ἀγαθὰ μυθεῖσθαι 23.305; ἐς πόλεμον θωρήξομαι 8.376, cf. Hdt.7.29, etc.; ἐς φόβον *to cause* fear, Il.15.310; ἐς ὑποδήματα δεδόσθαι Hdt.2.98; κόσμος ὁ εἰς ἑορτάς X.*Oec*.9.6; ἐπιτηδεότατος, εὐπρεπής, ἔς τι Hdt.1.115, 2.116; εἰς κάλλος ζῆν to live *for* show, X.*Cyr*.8.1.33, cf. *Ages*. 9.1; ἐς δαίτην ἐκάλεσσε Call.*Aet*.1.1.5; εἰς κέρδος τι δρᾶν S.*Ph*.111; πάσας φωνὰς ἱέντων εἰς ἀπόφυξιν Ar.*V*.562; εἰς γράμματα παιδὶ δεκετεῖ ἐνιαυτοὶ τρεῖς Pl.*Lg*.809e; εἰς τὸ πρᾶγμα εἶναι to be *pertinent, to the purpose*, D.36.54; freq. of expenditure *on* an object, *IG*2².102.11, 116.41, al.; ἐς τὸ δέον Ar.*Nu*.859, etc.; ἐς δᾷδα ib.612.

B. Position: εἰς is sts. parted from its acc. by several words, εἰς ἀμφοτέρω Διομήδεος ἅρματα βήτην Il.8.115; εἰς δὲ μονάρχου δῆμος ἀϊδρίῃ δουλοσύνην ἔπεσεν Sol.9: seldom (only in Poets) put after its case, Il.15.59, Od.3.137, 15.541, S.*OC*126 (lyr.): after an Adv., αὔριον ἔς· τῆμος δὲ.. Od.7.318.

εἷς, μία, ἕν (μίη only in late Ion. Prose): gen. ἑνός, μιᾶς, ἑνός:—Ep. ἕεις Hes.*Th*.145, *AP*7.341 (Procl.), cj. in Il.5.603:—Dor. ἧς Rhinth. 12, *Tab.Heracl*.1.136:—Ep., Aeol., and Ion. fem. ἴα Il.13.354, prob. in Hp.*Morb*.4.37; acc. ἴαν Alc.33.6 (prob.), Sapph.69.1 (cf. μηδεΐα), Corinn.*Supp*.2.56, *IG*9(2).517.22 (Thess.); gen. ἰῆς Il.16.173, 24.496; dat. ἰῇ 9.319, 11.174, etc.: neut. dat. (ἰῷ κίον ἤματι) 6.422. (In Com. οὐδὲ (μηδὲ) εἷς, οὐδὲ (μηδὲ) ἕν, occur, mostly at the end of an iambic trimeter, without elision, Cratin.302, Ar.*Ra*.927, *Pl*.37, 138, al.) (Orig. ἕνς, assim. ἕν(δ) prob. in *Leg.Gort*.9.50, from *ἕμς, I.-Eur. *sem*- (cf. ὁμός); μία from *sm-ia*; ἴα is not related to μία, but prob. to pronom. stem *i*- (Lat. *is*), cf. ἰός.) 1. as a Numeral, εἷς κοίρανος ἔστω Il.2.204, etc.; strengthd., εἷς οἷος, μία οἴη, a single *one, one* alone, 4.397, Od.7.65; μία μούνη 23.227; εἷς μοῦνος Hdt.1.119, Ar.*Pl*.1053, etc.; εἷς καὶ μόνος D.H.1.74; εἷς ὢν S.*OT*247, E.*Ph*.894, etc.; opp. πολύς, μία τὰς πολλὰς ψυχὰς ὀλέσασα A.*Ag*.1456, cf. 1465, *Ch*.299, etc. b. emphatically with a Sup., εἷς οἰωνὸς ἄριστος Il.12.243, etc.: freq. in Trag., εἷς ἀνὴρ πλεῖστον.. πόνον παρασχὼν A.*Pers*.327; πλείστας ἀνὴρ εἷς.. ἔγημε S.*Tr*.460; κάλλιστ' ἀνὴρ εἷς Id.*OT*1380; ἕνα κριθέντ' ἄριστον Id. *Ph*.1344; also in Prose, ἐπὶ πλεῖστον δὴ χλιδῆς εἷς ἀνὴρ ἀπίκετο Hdt.6.127, cf. Th.8.68; Μυτιληναίους μάλιστα δὴ μίαν πόλιν Id.3.39; πάντων εἷς ἀνὴρ μεγίστων αἴτιος κακῶν D.18.143: without a Sup., Ἐτεοκλέης ἂν εἷς πολὺς κατὰ πτόλιν ὑμνοῖθ' A.*Th*.6. c. in oppos., made emphatic by the Art., ὁ εἷς, ἡ μία, Il.20.272, Od.20.110, Pl.*Cri*.48a; τοῦ ἑνὸς οἱ δύο ἀγαθοὶ βελτίους Arist.*Pol*.1287ᵇ13, cf. Theoc.6.22. d. with a neg., εἷς οὐδεὶς no *single man*, Hdt.1.32; ἓν οὐδὲν ἴαμα Th.2.51; οὐκ ἐν ἄλλῳ ἑνί γε χωρίῳ in no other *single* country, Id.1.80; οὐχ εἷς, i.e. more than *one*, A.*Th*.103, E.*Andr*.96; εἷς οὐ.., εἷς μή.., emphatic for οὐδείς, μηδείς, Ar.*Th*.549, X.*An*.5.6.12; more emphatic, οὐδὲ εἷς, μηδὲ εἷς, v. οὐδείς, μηδείς. e. εἷς ἕκαστος each *one*, each *by himself*, Hdt.1.123, Pl.*Prt*.332c, etc.; αἰσθήσεις μία ἑνός (sc. γένους) *one of each*, Arist.*Metaph*.1003ᵇ19: pl., ἑκάτεροι ἕνες *POxy*.276.8 (i A.D.). f. with κατά, καθ' ἓν ἕκαστον each *singly*, piece by piece, Hdt.1.9, etc.; καθ' ἓν *one* by *one*, Pl.*Sph*.217a, etc.; καθ' ἕν, τό, *list*, *PEleph*.20.7 (iii B.C.), etc.; καθ' ἕν' ἡμῶν ἕκαστον ἀποστερεῖν to deprive each of us *singly*, D.21.142, cf. Men.*Epit*.164, 186; εἷς κατὰ εἷς *one* by *one*, *Ev.Marc*.14.19; but καθ' ἓν γίγνεσθαι, εἶναι, to be *united*, Th.8.46, X. *HG*5.2.16. g. with other Preps., ἓν ἀνθ' ἑνός *above all*, Pl.*R*. 331b, *Phlb*.63c; but μίαν ἀντὶ μιᾶς *alternately*, *PStrassb*.25.13, etc.; ἐπὶ μίαν ἑκάστην ῥάβδον τιθέντες θεσπίζουσι *one by one, separately*, Hdt.4.67; ἐπὶ ἑνός Pl.*Tht*.157a; ἓν ἐφ' ἑνί Id.*Sph*.229b, *Lg*.758b: ἓν πρὸς ἕν, with or without συμβάλλειν, in comparisons, Hdt.4.50, Pl.*Lg*. 647b; πρὸς ἕν' εἷς D.21.131: παρ' ἕνα *alternately*, Luc.*Salt*.12; εἰς ἓν συναγαγεῖν E.*Or*.1640; ἰσχὺς τοσαύτη εἰς ἓν ξυστᾶσα Th.6.85; εἰς ἓν μοίρας συνέκυρσας E.*Andr*.1172; ἐς μίαν βουλεύειν Il.2.379; in full, ἐς μίαν βουλήν Th.5.111; εἰς μίαν νοεῖν Ael.*NA*5.9; ἓν ἐξ ἑνὸς ἐπισεσώρευκεν Arr.*Epict*.1.10.5, cf. Luc.*Asin*.54; ἀπὸ μιᾶς with *one accord*, *Ev.Luc*.14.18; ὑφ' ἓν *at once*, S.E.*M*.10.124; also ὑφ' ἓν θέσθαι τὸ ὂν τῷ μὴ ὄντι Plot.6.2.1; cf. ὑφέν. h. in compd. numerals, as an ordinal, τῷ ἑνὶ καὶ τριηκοστῷ [ἔτει] Hdt.5.89, cf. Th.8.109, etc.; so in Att. Inscrr., *IG*2.660.30, al.: later εἷς alone, = *first*, Lxx *Ge*.1.5; μιᾷ τοῦ μηνός ib.8.13. i. μίαν μίαν, = κατὰ μίαν, S.*Fr*.201; εἷς εἷς Lxx 1*Ch*.24.6. 2. *one*, i.e. *the same*, τώ μοι μία γείνατο μήτηρ Il. 3.238, etc.; εἷς καὶ ὁ αὐτὸς *one* and the same, ἓν καὶ ταὐτὸν ἀριθμῷ Arist.*Metaph*.1039ᵃ28, etc.; ὑπὸ μίαν καὶ τὰν αὐτὰν ἀρχάν Perict.ap. Stob.3.1.121; ταὐτὸν καὶ ἓν Arist.*Ph*.201ᵇ3; so ἓν καὶ ὅμοιον Pl.*Phdr*. 271a; εἷς καὶ κοινός Plu.2.699f: c. dat., ἐμοὶ μιᾶς ἐγένετ' ἐκ ματρός E. *Ph*.156; ἐκ μιᾶς οἰνοχόης Ἐπικούρῳ πεπωκότες Plu.2.1089a. b. *possessing unity*, ἧττον μία ἡ μίμησις ἡ τῶν ἐποποιῶν Arist.*Po*.1462ᵇ3; λίαν ἓν ποιεῖν τὴν πόλιν Id.*Pol*.1263ᵇ7; τὰ κυρίως ἕνα Dam.*Pr*. 437. 3. *one*, opp. *another*, ἓν μὲν.. ἓν δὲ.. Arist.*EN*1139ᵃ6, *Pol*. 1285ᵇ38, etc.; ὁ μὲν... εἷς δὲ... εἷς δ' αὖ... Od.3.421 sq., cf. Pl.*R*.369d; εἷς μὲν... ἕτερος δὲ... X.*HG*1.7.23. 4. indefinitely, εἷς τις some *one*, S.*OT*118, Pl.*Grg*.471e, etc.; ἐξ ἑνός γέ του τρόπου Th.6.34; rarely τις εἷς S.*Ant*.269, Pl.*Prm*.145d; εἷς γάρ τις ἦν ἕκαστος οὐξειργασμένος each *single* one was suspected, S.*Ant*.262; εἷς ὁστισοῦν Arist.*Pol*. 1325ᵇ28; εἷς ὁ πρῶτος, Germ. *der erste beste*, Is.8.33, D.1.9, cf. Luc. *Herm*.61: alone, like our indef. Art., *a, an*, Κάδμου θυγατέρων μιᾷ E.*Ba*.917; εἷς κάπηλος, στρατηγός, Ar.*Av*.1292, Th.4.50; εἷς Ἀθηναίων D.21.87, cf. Lxx *Ge*.21.15, *Ev.Matt*.21.19, etc.; εἷς ἀπό.. Lxx *Le*.6.3(22). 5. οὐχ εἷς *many*, A.*Th*.103, Call.*Dian*.33; οὐχ εἷς οὐδὲ δύο not *one* or two only, D.29.12; οὐ μίαν οὐδὲ δύο not *once* nor twice, Lxx 4*Ki*.6.10; ἓν ἢ καὶ δύο ληφθὲν μαρτύριον Plb.2.38.10; εἷς ἢ δεύτερος Jul.*Or*.6.190d: prov., εἷς ἀνὴρ οὐδεὶς ἀνήρ *one* man's no man, D.Chr.48.10. 6. Math., τὸ ἓν *unity*, opp. πλῆθος, Pythag.*Fr*.5, etc.: pl., ἕνα *units*, Arist.*Metaph*.1056ᵇ21; ὁ ἀριθμός ἐστιν ἕνα πλείω Id.*Ph*. 207ᵇ7; τῶν προτέρων ἑνῶν Dam.*Pr*.460. 7. Philos., ἕν, τό, *unity*, the *One*, ἐκ πάντων ἓν καὶ ἐξ ἑνὸς πάντα Heraclit.10, cf. Emp.17.1, etc.: later indecl., ἓν εἶναι τοῦ ἓν παρουσίᾳ Plot.6.6.14, cf. 5.5.5.

εἶσα, v. ἵζω I.

εἰσάγᾱν, Adv., strengthd. for ἄγαν, Tz.*H*.1.11, 210.

εἰσαγγελ-εύς, έως, ὁ, *one who announces, usher* at the Persian and Ptolemaic courts, Hdt.3.84, D.S.16.47, *Klio*12.365 (Alexandria, ii B.C.), *PTeb*.179 (ii B.C.), cf. Plu.*Alex*.46, Jul.*Mis*.365b, etc. 2. metaph. of the senses, Them.*in de An*.87.8. II. *accuser*, Suid. **-ία,** ἡ, *information, news*, Plb.9.9.7. 2. *public announcement*, *IG*12(3).325.16 (Thera, ii B.C.). 3. *application* to an authority, *PStrassb*.56.25 (iii A.D.). II. at Athens, *state prosecution, impeachment*, Σόλωνος θέντος νόμον εἰσαγγελίας Arist.*Ath*.8.4, cf. And.1.43, Lys.30.22, X.*HG*1.7.9, Isoc.8.130, etc.; εἰ. δέδωκας ὑπέρ τινος Hyp.*Lyc*.12; εἰ. ἐδόθη εἰς τὴν βουλὴν ὑπὲρ Ἀριστάρχου Test.ap.D.21.121; εἰ. εἰσαγγέλλειν Arist.*Ath*.59.2. 2. *a process* brought before the chief Archon, *to punish* κάκωσις (q.v.) or *maltreatment of parents by children, of* ἐπίκληροι *by their husbands*, or *of wards by their guardians*, Is.3.47. 3. *a procedure employed against unfair arbitrators*, Harp. **-λω,** *go in and announce* a person, Hdt. 3.118, Lys.1.20, etc.; πρός τινα X.*Cyr*.8.3.20. b. *submit* a person's name, *PCair.Preis*.18.7 (iv A.D.), etc. 2. *take a message in*, E.*Ba*.173: generally, *announce, report* a thing, τὰ ἐσαγγελλόμενα Th.6.41; of the senses, εἰ. πολλὰς διαφοράς Arist.*Sens*.437ᵃ2, cf. *Insomn*.461ᵇ3:—Pass., ἐσαγγελθέντων ὅτι... *information having been given that*..., Th.1.116, cf. 3.3, 6.52. 3. *lay information*, = μηνύω, X.*HG*3.3.5, *OGI*669.39 (Egypt, i A.D.). II. in the technical sense of εἰσαγγελία, *lay an impeachment*, περί τινος εἰς τὴν βουλήν Antipho 6.35, cf. And.1.37: abs., D.18.13; τινὰ περί τινος Id.20.79; τινὰ τῇ βουλῇ And.2.21; ἐν τῷ δήμῳ περί τινος Delat.ap.eund.1.14; τινὰ πρὸς τοὺς ἄρχοντας Pl.*Lg*.763e; τοῖς νομοφύλαξιν ib.910c; τινὰ εἰς τὸν δῆμον ἐπὶ τυραννίδος αἰτίᾳ D.H.8.77: c. inf., εἰ. τινὰ δημηγορεῖν Lys. 10.1:—Med., εἰσαγγειλαμένων τῶν στρατηγῶν *SIG*742.21 (Ephesus, i B.C.):—Pass., *to be impeached*, D.18.250, Hyp.*Eux*.3. **-σις,** εως, ἡ, *announcing*, Pl.*Def*.414c. **-τικός,** ή, όν, *of* or *for an impeachment*, νόμος Lex ap.D.24.63, Hyp.*Eux*.3; λόγος D.H.*Din*.10.

εἰσᾰγείρω, *collect into* a place, ἐς (ἐν Aristarch.) δ' ἐρέτας... ἀγείρομεν (sc. ἐς τὴν νῆα) Il.1.142, Od.16.349:—Med., νέον δ' ἐσαγείρετο (v.l. -ατο) θυμόν he *gathered* fresh courage, Il.15.240, cf. 21.417:—Pass., θοῶς δ' ἐσαγείρετο λαὸς [ἐς τὰς νῆας] Od.14.248.

εἰσάγω [ᾰ], Ion. impf. ἐσάγεσκον Hdt.1.196: pf. -αγήοχα Epist. Philipp.ap.D.18.39: pf. Pass. ἐσῆγμαι Hdt.2.49:—*lead in* or *into*, esp. *into one's dwelling, introduce*, c. dupl. acc., αὐτοὺς εἰσῆγον θεῖον δόμον Od.4.43; Κρήτην εἰσήγαγ' ἑταίρους *he led* his comrades *to* Crete, 3.191; ἐσ. τινὰ ἐς... Hdt.1.196, etc.: c. dat., τινὰ δόμοις E.*Alc*.1112 codd.; εἰ. ψυχᾷ χάριν Id.*Hipp*.526 (lyr.); ὅταν σε καιρὸς εἰσάγῃ, = ὅταν καιρὸς ᾖ σὲ εἰσιέναι, S.*El*.39; νὺξ εἰ. πόνον Id.*Tr*.29:—Med., *admit* forces into a city, Th.8.16, 108; *take in with one, introduce into* a league or conspiracy, Ὀτάνης ἐσάγεται Ἰνταφρένεα Hdt.3.70:—Pass., τὴν θερμότητα εἰσάγεσθαι εἰς τοὺς πόρους Thphr.*Ign*.38. 2. ἐσαγαγεῖν or ἐσαγαγέσθαι γυναῖκα *to lead* a wife *into one's house*, Hdt. 5.40, 6.63. 3. *bring in*, σῖτον Th.4.26; *import*, οἶνον Ἀθήναζε κατ' ἐμπορίαν D.35.35:—Med., εἰσάγεσθαι καὶ ἐξάγεσθαι X.*Ath*.2.3, cf. D. 18.145; εἰ. ὧν ἐνδεεῖς Arist.*Pol*.1257ᵃ32:—Pass., εἰσαγόμενα καὶ ἐξαγ. *imports* and exports, Id.*Rh*.1359ᵇ22, cf. Hdt.3.6, *SIG*37 (Teos, v B.C.). 4. εἰ. εἰς τοὺς φράτερας *introduce* a child to the members of one's φρατρία, Lys.30.2 (Pass.), Is.3.75, cf. D.57.54; εἰς Κήρυκας And.1.127; εἰ. τινὰς εἰς τὴν πολιτείαν Arist.*Pol*.1308ᵃ8; τινὰς ἐς σπονδάς *secure* their *adhesion*, Th.5.35; ἰατρὸν εἰσάγειν τινί *call in* a physician *for* another, X.*Mem*.2.4.3, cf. D.47.67:—Med., of the physician himself when ill, εἰσάγεσθαι ἄλλους ἰατρούς Arist.*Pol*.1287ᵃ41. 5. *introduce new* customs, Hdt.2.49 (Pass.); τελετὰς πονηρὰς E. *Ba*.260; σόφισμα Id.*Ph*.1408; δεινότατον ἔθος εἰς τὴν πολιτείαν D.19. 2; εἰ. τὰ εἴδη the doctrine of ideas, Arist.*EN*1096ᵃ13; αὐλὸν καὶ ῥυθμὸν εἰς τὸν πόλεμον ἀντὶ σάλπιγγος Plb.4.20.6. 6. δούλιον εἰσᾶγον αἶσαν, for δ. ἄγον εἰς αἶσαν, A.*Ch*.77 (lyr.). II. *bring in, bring forward*, esp. on the stage, χορόν Ar.*Ach*.11; Ἥραν ἠλλοιωμένην Pl.*R*. 381d; δράματα Id.*Ap*.35b, cf. Luc.*Hist.Conscr*.58; of an orator, εἰ. σεαυτὸν ποιόν τινα Arist.*Rh*.1417ᵇ7; *represent* in art, Corn.*ND*28, al.

(Pass.). 2. εἰ. τινὰ εἰς τὴν βουλὴν *bring* a culprit *before* the Council, X.*HG*7.3.5, etc. 3. as law-term, εἰ. δίκην or γραφήν *to bring* a cause *into court*, of *the prosecutor*, A.*Eu*.580,582, cf. D.24.10, *PHal*.1.125, etc.; ὑπόθεσιν *OGI*669.41 (Egypt, i A.D.); also of the εἰσαγωγεύς II, Antipho 6.42, *IG*12(7).3.40 (Arcesine), etc.; οἱ δὲ θεσμοθέται εἰσαγόντων εἰς τὴν Ἡλιαίαν Lex ap.D.21.47. b. εἰ. τινά *bring forward* the case of an officer at the εὔθυναι (q.v.), D.18.117: generally, *bring* a person *into court*, *prosecute*, Pl.*Ap*.25c, al.; in full, εἰ. εἰς δικαστήριον ib.29a, *Grg*.521c (Pass.), cf. *Lg*.910e, al. 4. *pay in*, τὴν τιμὴν ἐπὶ τὴν δημοσίαν τράπεζαν *IG*2².1013.28; ἀργύριον *PHib*.46.18 (iii B.C.), etc. 5. *enter*, *register*, *POxy*.1535.8 (Pass.), etc. III. *introduce to* a subject, *instruct*:—Pass., εἰσαγόμενοι, οἱ, *beginners*, Ph.1.175, Gal.*Libr.Propr.Prooem*., etc. IV. intr., *enter*, Sch.T.Il.6.252.

εἰσᾰγωγ-εύς, έως, ὁ, *introducer*, Schwyzer 784a7 (Tenos); δικαιοσύνης Arr.*Epict*.3.26.32; *director* of choruses, Pl.*Lg*.765a, cf. *IG*3.1193, *BCH*27.297 (Larymna). II. at Athens and elsewhere, *magistrate who brought cases into court*, *IG*1².63.7, Arist.*Ath*.52.2, D.37.33, *SIG* 364.5 (Ephesus), *IG*12(7).3 (Amorgos), *PHal*.1.40, *PTeb*.29.1 (ii B.C.), etc. III. in pl., at Samos, *importers* of corn on account of the state, *Ath.Mitt*.37.216 (ii/i B.C.). IV. *conduit*, Horap.1.21. **-έω**, *guide*, Zonar. **-ή**, ἡ, *bringing in*, ὑδάτων, ὕδατος, Str.5.3.8, *IGRom*. 3.804 (Aspendus); σίτου *PSI*5.500 (iii B.C.). 2. *introduction*, as of heirs by adoption, Is.10.9 (pl.); of children to a φρατρία, *IG*2². 1237.108. 3. *importation* of goods, etc., Pl.*Lg*.847d, Arist.*Rh*. 1360a14, *SIG*278.11 (Priene). 4. *raising* of taxes, *PAmh*.2.31.6 (ii B.C.), etc. II. as law-term, *bringing of causes into court*, Pl. *Lg*.855d (pl.); τῶν κλήρων Is.4.12 (pl.). III. *introduction* to a subject, *elementary teaching*, Ph.*Bel*.56.12, D.H.*Amm*.2.1 (pl.), Ph.1. 487, Arr.*Epict*.1.29.23, S.E.*M*.8.428 (pl.); *elementary treatise*, Εἰ. εἰς τὴν περὶ ἀγαθῶν καὶ κακῶν πραγματείαν, title of work by Chrysippus, cf. Plu.2.43f (pl.), Gal.*Libr.Propr.Prooem*. IV. *channel of entrance* to a harbour, Str.17.1.18, *Peripl.M.Rubr*.37. V. *office of* εἰσαγωγεύς II, Hsch. **-ικός**, ή, όν, *of* or *for importation*, τέλη *import* duties, opp. ἐξαγωγικά, Str.17.1.13. II. *introductory*, *elementary*, συλλογισμοί Chrysipp.*Stoic*.2.7, Ptol.*Tetr*.16, etc. Adv. -κῶς Papp. ad Apollon.Perg.*Con.Prooem*.5: Comp. -ώτερον Ph.*Fr*.8 H. **-ιμος**, ον, *that can* or *may be imported*, opp. ἐξαγώγιμος, Arist.*Oec*.1345a21; τὰ εἰ. *imports*, Id.*Pol*.1280a39; τέχνη εἰ. *requiring to be imported*, *foreign*, Pl.*Lg*.847d; εἰ. λαβεῖν E.*Fr*.984; εἰ. πόλεις, of colonies, opp. the αὐτόχθονες of Athens, ib.360.10. II. as law-term, of a plea, *maintainable*, μὴ εἰσαγώγιμον εἶναι τὴν δίκην D.33.3, 35.45, cf. Lys.23.5, Din.1.46, *PHal*.1.37; εἰ. χρήματα, with play on sense I, D.32.23. **-ιον**, τό, *entrance-fee*, *SIG*1106.51 (Cos). **-ός**, ὁ, = εἰσαγωγεύς I, *CIG*2932 (Tralles). II. epith. of Hermes, *watching over imports*, *Ath.Mitt*.37.216 (Samos, ii/i B.C.). III. *conduit*, *PTeb*.86.4 (ii B.C.), etc.

εἰσᾰεί, for εἰς ἀεί, *for ever*, A.*Pr*.732, S.*Aj*.570; ἐσαιεί A.*Eu*. 836.

εἰσᾰείρομαι, Med., *take to oneself*, Διωνύσου δῶρ' ἐσαειράμενος Thgn. 976 codd.

εἰσαθρέω, *look at*, *descry*, εἴ που ἐσαθρήσειεν Ἀλέξανδρον Il.3.450, cf. Theoc.25.215; εἰκόνα τήνδ' ἐσάθρει *Epigr.Gr*.906 (Gortyn); ἀστέρας ἐσαθρεῖς Pl.*Epigr*.14: metaph., ἱστορίην ἐσαθρήσας *IG*3.716.—Poet. Verb.

εἰσαίρω, *bring* or *carry in*, ἡ τράπεζ' εἰσήρετο Ar.*Ra*.518, cf. Anaxandr.2 (prob.).

εἰσᾴσσω, contr. -ᾄσσω, Att. -ᾴττω, fut. -ᾴξω: aor. -ῇξα:—*to dart in* or *into*, Ar.*Nu*.543, Aristid.*Or*.49(25).16, prob. in D.C.37. 32; cf. εἰσήκω.

εἴσαιτο, aor. opt. Med. of *εἴδω, Il.2.215.

εἰσᾰΐω, poet., = εἰσακούω, *catch the sound of*, *hear*, Sapph.*Supp*.1. 13, *Oxy*.1787 *Fr*.3; *listen*, *hearken to*, c. gen., Theoc.7.88, A.R.1. 764: c. acc., ὕμνον *AP*9.189, cf. Call.*Jov*.54, Nic.*Al*.220, Orac.ap. Luc.*Alex*.50: abs., Rhian.19. II. *perceive*, *feel the effect of*, Hp. *Morb*.4.37; contr. fut. and aor. forms ἐσᾴσει, ἐσᾴσειεν are prob. in ib.35,38, al.

εἰσᾰκοή, ἡ, *listening*, *hearkening*, Ph.1.593.

εἰσᾰκοντίζω, *throw* or *hurl javelins at*, τινά Hdt.1.43, 9.49; ἐς τὰ γυμνά Th.3.23: c. acc., τὴν χίμαιραν εἰσηκοντικώς Epin.2.10:—Pass., *dart*, εἰ. μυῖα καθάπερ βέλος Ph.2.101. 2. abs., *spout*, of blood, E.*Hel*.1588.

εἰσᾰκούω, *hearken* or *give ear to* one, ὣς ἔφατ', οὐδ' ἐσάκουσε.. Ὀδυσσεύς Il.8.97, cf. Hdt.4.133, al.: c. acc., φωνὴν ἐσάκουσαν *h.Cer*.284, cf. E.*Hec*.559, etc.: c. gen. pers., S.*Aj*.789; τῶν ἐμῶν λόγων E.*IA* 1368: c. dat. pers., Hdt.1.214, etc.; τινί τι Id.9.60; *give way*, *yield* to a request, Th.1.126, 3.4; of God, τινός or τῆς προσευχῆς Lxx *Ps*. 4.2, etc.:—so in Pass., of the prayer, *Ev.Luc*.1.13; of the person, *Ev.Matt*.6.7. 2. in Poets, simply, *hear*, τούτου λέγοντος εἰσήκουσ' ἐγώ, ὡς.. S.*Tr*.351; τίνος βροτῶν λόγον τόνδ' εἰ.; Id.*El*.884, cf. *Aj*. 318, Axiop.1.12; ζῶντ' εἰσακούσας παῖδα E.*El*.416. 3. *perceive*, *feel effect of*, τοῦ ἐγκεφάλου ἐσακούσαντος τοῦ τρώματος Hp.*Prorrh*.2. 14. II. Pass. in strict sense, ἔξωθεν εἰς τὰς οἰκίας εἰσακούεται μᾶλλον ἢ ἔσωθεν ἔξω Arist.*Pr*.903b13 (v.l. εἴσω ἀκ.).

εἰσακτέον, *one must bring into court* (cf. εἰσάγω II.3), ἀδίκημα Ar. *V*.840; τινάς X.*Eq.Mag*.1.10. II. *one must introduce*, in speaking, Hermog.*Id*.2.9; in argument, S.E.*M*.6.36.

εἰσάκτης, ου, ὁ, *introducer*, Gloss.

εἰσᾰλείφω, *smear* or *rub in*, ἐς τὸ στόμα τῶν ὑστερέων Hp.*Nat.Mul*. 9; *anoint*, Aristid.2.292 J.

εἰσάλλομαι, Ep. 3 sg. aor. 2 ἐσᾶλτο:—*spring* or *rush into*, ἐσήλατο τεῖχος Ἀχαιῶν Il.12.438; πύλας καὶ τεῖχος ἐσᾶλτο 13.679, cf. 12.466; πύργον -όμενοι Pi.*O*.8.38; later ἐσ. ἐς τὸ πῦρ *leap into it*, Hdt.2.66; εἰ. εἰς τὰ τείχη v.l. in X.*Cyr*.7.4.4; ἀνακειμένῳ εἰς τὸν αὐχέν' εἰσαλοίμην S.*Fr*.756; [εἰς ἀσκόν] upon a bladder, Eub.8; ἐπὶ κρατί μοι πότμος εἰσήλατο S.*Ant*.1345 (lyr.).

εἰσᾰμείβω, *go into*, *enter*, τεῖχος A.*Th*.558.

εἰσάμην, v. εἴσομαι II. II. Ep. aor. Med. of *εἴδω. III. εἰσάμην, aor. Med. of ἵζω, *SIG*1041.8.

εἶσαν· ὑπῆ⟨ρ⟩χον, συνῆκαν, ἢ εἴδησαν, ἢ ἐπεγίνωσκον, Hsch.

εἰσαναβαίνω, *go up to* or *into*, Ἴλιον εἰσανέβησαν Il.6.74; εἰσαναβᾶσ' ὑπερῶϊα Od.16.449, cf. 19.602; so λέχος, ἀκτὴν εἰσαναβαίνειν, Il. 8.291, v.l. in 24.97; ἀκροτάταν εἰσαναβᾶσ' S.*OT*876 codd. (lyr.).

εἰσᾰναγκάζω, *force* one thing *into* another, Hp.*Art*.47 (Pass.). 2. *constrain*, τινά A.*Pr*.292 (anap.): c. inf., Pl.*Ti*.49a.

εἰσαν-άγω [ᾰγ], *lead up into*, εἴρερον *into* slavery, Od.8.529; ψυχὴν οὐρανὸν εἰ. *APl*.4.201 (Marian.); ζωγρείᾳ πρός τινα εἰσαναχθῆναι Plb. 1.82.2. **-αίρω**, *carry off*, *plunder*, *PFay*.108.16 (ii A.D.). **-ᾱλίσκω**, *expend upon*, τι εἰς ἑαυτόν Antiph.204.10 (troch.), *PPetr*.2 p.6.

εἰσανδρόω, *fill with men*, Λῆμνον παισίν A.R.1.874.

εἰσαν-εῖδον, *look up to*, οὐρανὸν εἰσανιδὼν Il.16.232, 24.307. **-ειμι**, *go up into*, ἠέλιος.. οὐρανὸν εἰσανιών 7.423, Hes.*Th*.761; ἱερόν A.R.1. 1092. **-έχω**, intr., *rise above*, c. gen., ib.1360, cf. 4.291: c. acc., γαῖαν εἰσανέχει πέλαγος ib.1578. **-ορούω**, *rush up to*, οὐρανόν Q.S.2.658, 14.2.

εἰσάντᾰ, Adv. *right opposite*: ἐσάντα ἰδών looking *in the face*, Il.17. 334; ἰδεῖν Od.11.143; εἰ. ἰδέσθαι 5.217:—also **εἰσάνταν** B.5.110.

εἰσαντλέω, *pour in*, κεχηνότι τὴν τροφήν Clearch.12.

εἰσάπαν, shd. be read divisim εἰς ἅπαν as in Epict.*Ench*.33.5, Ph. 1.125, etc.

εἰσάπαξ [σᾰ], = εἰς ἅπαξ, *at once*, *once for all*, Hdt.6.125, A.*Pr*.750, Th.5.85, etc.

εἰσαπο-βαίνω, *pass out to*.., c. acc., A.R.4.650, etc. **-δίδωμι**, *repay*, *refund*, *BGU*190 ii 3. **-κλείω**, *shut up in*, v.l. for ἐν-, Sever. in Rh.1 p.546 W. **-στέλλω**, *send in* or *to*, *PPetr*.3 p.113 (dub.), Ant.Lib.41.2.

εἰσαπωξεία, ἡ, dub. sens. in *POxy*.2052.5 (vi A.D.).

εἰσᾰράσσω, Att. -ττω, *dash* or *force into*, τὴν ἵππον ἐσ. *drive* the enemy's horse *in upon* his foot, Hdt.4.128, cf. D.C.51.26; σφέας ἐς τὰς νέας Id.5.116.

εἰσαρπάζω, *seize and carry in*, Lys.1.27 (Pass.), 3.11.

εἰσαρτίζω, *join* or *fit into*, ἔς τι Hp.*Morb*.2.33 vulg.

εἰσᾰρύομαι, *drain*, *exhaust*, dub. in Hp.*Gland*.12.

εἰσάττω, Att. for εἰσαΐσσω (q.v.).

εἰσαυγάζω, *look at*, *view*, *AP*5.105 (Diotim.).

εἰσαῦθις, = αὖθις, Ar.*Ec*.983.

εἰσάφ-ασμα [ᾰφ], ατος, τό, *touch*, *grasp*, A.*Fr*.204 (pl.). **-άσσω**, *feel in*, ἐσαφάσσειν τὸν δάκτυλον *feel by putting in* the finger, Hp.*Nat. Mul*.11; but ἐ. τῷ δακτύλῳ ib.36, al.

εἰσαφέτης, ου, ὁ, *charioteer*, Gloss.

εἰσαφ-ίημι, *admit*, X.*Cyr*.4.5.14 codd., Str.15.1.42, J.*BJ*1.13.3:—Pass., Aen.Tact.32.9. **-ῐκάνω** [ᾱ], = sq., πατέρα Od.22.99; δόμον Hes.*Sc*.45; Βέβρυκας Theoc.22.29. **-ικνέομαι**, Ion. ἐσαπικνέομαι, 2 sg. aor. subj. εἰσαφίκηαι Hes.*Fr*.170:—*come into* or *to*, *arrive at*, c. acc., Ἴλιον εἰσαφικέσθαι Il.22.17; συβώτην εἰ. *go into* his house, Od.13.404; Σειρῆνας S.*Fr*.861; Ἑλλάδα E.*Andr*.13; ὅς τινα εἰ. Isoc.4.45: c. dat., τῇ τε ἄλλῃ (sc. χώρῃ) καὶ δὴ καὶ ἐς τὸ Ἄργος Hdt.1.1; φήμη ἐσ. τοῖσι Ἕλλησι Id.9.100: abs., *arrive*, ib.101; οἱ εἰσαφικνούμενοι *visitors* to a country, X.*Vect*.3.12, cf. Pl.*Men*.92b, *IG*2².1191.17: c. gen., σοφιστοῦ (nisi leg. ⟨ἐς⟩) D.Chr.19.3. **-ιξις**, εως, ἡ, *right of settlement*, ἐς Μίλητον *SIG*273.7 (Milet., iv B.C.); εἰς Κύζικον ib. 645.88 (Seleucia in Cilicia, ii B.C.).

εἰσᾰφύσσω, *draw into*, A.R.4.1692 (Med.).

εἰσβαίνω, *go on board* a ship, mostly abs., *embark*, Od.9.103, Th.7. 13, etc.; ἐς [πεντηκόντερον] Hdt.3.41: c. acc., σκάφος E.*Tr*.686. 2. generally, *enter*, πρὸς κόρης νυμφεῖον εἰ. S.*Ant*.1205; δόμους E.*Med*. 380; εἰ. κακά *come into* miseries, S.*OC*997; ἄτης ἄβυσσον πέλαγος A. *Supp*.470; reversely, ἐμοὶ γὰρ οἶκτος.. εἰσέβη S.*Tr*.298; κἀμὲ γὰρ τὸ δυσχερὲς τοῦτ' εἰσβέβηκεν E.*Hyps.Fr*.5(3).20. 3. *come in*, *be imported*, εἰσέβαινον ἰσχάδες Alex.117. 4. *project into*, *PTeb*.86.24 (ii B.C.), etc. II. causal in aor. 1, *make to go into*, *put into*, ἐς δ' ἑκατόμβην βῆσε θεῷ (sc. ἐς νῆα) Il.1.310, cf. E.*Alc*.1055 (lyr.), *Ba*. 466; ληΐδα A.R.2.167.

εἰσβάλλω, *throw into*, ἄνδρα εἰς ἕρκη S.*Aj*.60; εἰς πῆμα A.*Pr*.1075; φάρμακα ἐς φρέατα Th.2.48; ἐσ. στρατιὴν ἐς Μίλητον *throw* an army *into* the Milesian territory, Hdt.1.14; ἐσ. ὗς ἐς [τὴν ἄρουραν] Id.2.14, cf. E.*El*.79; πρόβατα *IG*12(1).677.31 (Rhodes, iii B.C.): c. dupl. acc., βοῦς πόντον εἰσεβάλλομεν *were driving* them *to* the sea, E.*IT*261:—Med., *put on board one's ship*, ἐς τὴν νέα Hdt.1.1, cf. 6.95: abs., Th. 8.31. II. ἐσ. τὴν στρατιὴν ἐς.., of an invasion, Hdt.1.18: but usually without στρατιάν, *throw oneself* into, *make an inroad* into, ἐς Μίλητον ib.15, cf. 16, Th.2.47, etc.; ἐσβάλλειν ἐς τοὺς ὁπλίτας *to fall upon* them, Id.6.70; πρὸς πόλιν ἐσβάλλειν *make an assault* upon it, Id. 4.25: abs., Ar.*Ach*.762; of disease, *come on*, Aret.*CD*1.1, al.: *enter* a country, εἰς τὸν τόπον Thphr.*HP*9.7.1: poet. c. acc., χῶρον εἰ. E. *Hipp*.1198; λέπας Id.*Ba*.1045; *come upon*, *fall in with*, Βρομίου πόλιν ἔοιγμεν εἰσβαλεῖν Id.*Cyc*.99: abs., ἤφριζον, εἰσέβαλλον ἱππικαὶ πνοαί the horse's breath was foaming, *was close upon them*, S.*El*.719. 2. of rivers, *empty themselves into*, *fall into*, ἐς τὰ ἀρχαῖα (sc. ῥέεθρα) Hdt.

1.75, cf. 4.48, al., Arist.*Mete.*351ᵃ10, Plb.4.41.1; ἐσ. ἐς τὸν Εὐφρήτην ποταμὸν τὸ ῥέεθρον Hdt.1.179. 3. of ships, *make entrance* (sc. εἰς Πόντον), Syngr.ap.D.35.13. 4. abs., *begin*, ἀπό τινος Sch.Pi.*N.* 7.1; εἰς λόγον Olymp.*in Mete.*102.12; κατὰ τὸ ἔαρ εἰσβάλλον Gal. 18(1).470.

εἴσ-βᾰσις, εως, ἡ, *an entrance*, εἰσβάσεις μηχανώμενοι devising *ways of entrance*, E.*IT*101; *embarkation*, Th.7.30, D.C.41.42; *introductory process*, *first stage* of a magical operation, *PMag.Par.*1. 397. **-βᾰτικόν**, τό, tax in Egypt, *PLond.*2.333. **-βᾰτός**, ή, όν, *accessible*, τῇ τόλμῃ Th.2.41.

εἰσβδάλλω, *suck in*, cj. in Gal.*UP*4.7.

εἰσβῐάζομαι, *force one's way into*, εἰς τὰ πρῶτα γένη Plu.*Num.*1; πρός τινα D.S.14.9; ἐς τὸν Βόσπορον D.C.42.47. 2. *force oneself in*, ὁ μὲν γὰρ ὢν οὐκ ἀστὸς ἐσβιάζεται Ar.*Av.*32; τῶν αὑτοὺς εἰσβιαζομένων.. ποιεῖσθαι *who force* [others] to adopt them into a family, D. 39.33, cf. *CIG*2685 (Iasos), *OGI*736.6 (Fayûm), *PPetr.*3 p.39 (iii B.C.), etc.

εἰσβῐβάζω, causal of εἰσβαίνω, *put on board ship*, τὸν στρατὸν [ἐς τὰς νέας] Hdt.6.95, cf. Th.7.60, etc.; τοὺς ξένους καὶ τοὺς δούλους ναύτας εἰ. *impress* them, Isoc.8.48. 2. generally, *make to go into*, ἐς τὸ περιοικοδομημένον Hdt.7.60; ἐς ἅρμα Id.1.60.

εἰσβλέπω, *look at*, *look upon*, mostly with εἰς, Hdt.7.147, 8.77, X. *Cyn.*10.12: c. acc., E.*Or.*105: abs., X.*Smp.*4.3, Lxx *Is.*37.17.

εἰσβλητέον, *one must throw in*, Dsc.2.76.

εἰσβολή, ἡ, (εἰσβάλλω II) *inroad*, *invasion*, Hdt.6.92, E.*Ion*722 (lyr.), etc.; ποταμῶν Plb.4.40.9; διὰ τὴν ἐς Σάρδις ἐσβολὴν Hdt.7.1; ἐ. ποιεῖσθαι τῇ πόλει Th.8.31 codd.; *irruption* of false opinions, Polystr.p.19 W.; of an illness, *attack*, Aret.*SD*2.12, *CA*1.1. 2. *entrance*, *pass*, ἐ. ἐξ ὀρέων στεινῶν ἐς πεδίον Hdt.2.75; ἡ ἐ. ἡ Ὀλυμπική *the pass* of Mount Olympus, Id.7.172, cf. Th.3.112; Συμπληγάδων ἐ. E.*Med.*1264 (lyr.): pl., of Thermopylae, Hdt.7.176, cf. 1. 185, 2.141, Jul.*Or.*2.98b. b. pl., *mouth of a river*, v.l. for ἐκβ. in Hdt.7.182. 3. *entering upon a thing*, *beginning*, καινὰς ἐσβολὰς ὁρῶ λόγων E.*Supp.*92; ἐ. στεναγμάτων Id.*Ion*677 (lyr.); σοφισμάτων Ar.*Ra.*1104; κανόνων ib.956; *proem*, *preface*, of a play, Antiph.191. 20, cf. D.H.*Lys.*17 (pl.), Longin.38.2.

εἰσγένεσις, εως, ἡ, *produce* of live-stock, *PStrassb.*24.43.

εἰσγίγνομαι, *arrive*, *PGiss.*69.17; dub. in Aeschin.*Ep.*11.8. II. τὰ εἰσγενόμενα *incomings*, *revenue*, *PBaden* 47 (ii B.C.).

εἰσγρᾰφή, ἡ, *enrolment*, εἰς τοὺς ἐφήβους D.C.59.2.

εἰσγράφω [ᾰ], *inscribe*, στηλῶν ἐς ἃς οἱ νόμοι ἐσεγράφοντο D.C.37.9; *enrol*, τινὰ εἰς τοὺς φίλους Id.36.53; τινὰς ἐς τὸν κατάλογον Id.*Fr.*109. 5; also of painting, πορφυραῖ σκιαὶ τοὺς ὀφθαλμοὺς εἰς κάλλος -ουσιν Ael.*NA*12.25:—Med., ἐς τὰς σπονδὰς ἐσγράψασθαι ἑαυτούς *to have* themselves *enrolled* in the league, Th.1.31:—Pass., D.C.61.21. 2. simply, *write down*, μαντεῖα S.*Tr.*1167; *send in a report*, *BCH*46. 400 (Mylasa).

εἰσδᾰνείζω, *lend at interest as well*, Pl.*R.*555c.

εἰσδεκτός, ή, όν, *acceptable*, Lxx *Le.*22.29 (s.v.l.).

εἰσδέρκομαι, with aor. Act. εἰσέδρᾰκον: pf. εἰσδέδορκα:—*look at* or *upon*, νῆσον ἐσέδρακον ὀφθαλμοῖσιν Od.9.146; ἐσέδρακον ἄντην Il.24. 223; τί μ' εἰσδέδορκεν; E.*El.*558, cf. *Andr.*615.

εἰσδέχομαι, Ion. ἐσδέκ-, *take into*, *admit*, ἐς τὸ ἱρόν Hdt.1.144, cf. 206: c. acc. pers., S.*OT*238; εἰ. φρουράν *IG*2².43.22: c. acc. loc., οὐκ εἰσεδέξατ' οἶκον E.*Supp.*876: c. dat., ἄντροις εἰ. τινά *receive* him in the cave, Id.*Cyc.*35: rarely c. gen., τόνδ' εἰσεδέξω τειχέων, = τειχέων εἴσω ἐδέξω (cf. Sch. ad loc.), E.*Ph.*451: c. acc. dupl., ἐσδέξασθαί τινα συνοικιστῆρα *admit* him as a fellow-colonist, Pi.*Fr.*186; εἰ. τινὰ ὑπόστεγον S.*Tr.*376: aor. 1 εἰσδεχθῆναι in pass. sense, Luc.*Tox.*30, *Merc.Cond.*10. 2. c. acc. rei, σκῆψιν ἄγων οὗτος οὐκ ἐσδέξεται Ar. *Ach.*392; εἰ. εὐνομίαν διὰ τῆς μουσικῆς Pl.*R.*425a. 3. of certain animals, *take in* their young after birth, Arist.*HA*566ᵇ17, *GA*754ᵃ 29.

εἰσδίδωμι, intr., of rivers, *flow into*, ἐς.. dub. l. in Hdt.4.49, 50. II. *hand in a report* or *memorandum*, εἰ. περί τινος Aristeas 28, prob. in J.*AJ*12.2.3:—Pass., τὸ εἰσδοθέν *PTeb.*72.462 (ii B.C.); also of a question, *to be brought up* for discussion, ἐν ἀγᾶρρει *IG*14. 759.12. 2. *send in* the name of a person liable to service or taxation, *BGU*619.8 (ii A.D.), 1198.16 (i A.D.), etc. b. *lay information against*, τινά *PSI*4.417 (ii B.C.), etc. 3. *pay in*, *PPetr.*2 p.31 (iii B.C.).

εἴσδοσις, εως, ἡ, *report*, *memorandum*, Aristeas 28, 33, *PLond.*1.23 iv 1 (ii B.C.), prob. in J.*AJ*12.2.3.

εἰσδοχή, ἡ, *reception*, Olymp.*in Mete.*5.6; τοῦ σπέρματος Alex. Aphr.*Pr.*2.64; εἰσδοχαὶ δόμων *a hospitable* house, E.*El.*396. 2. *receipt* of corn, etc., *PTeb.*123.4 (i B.C.).

εἰσδρομή, ἡ, *inroad*, *onslaught*, E.*Rh.*604; of one who throws himself into a besieged place, Th.2.25; into a house, J.*BJ*5.10.3.

εἰσδύνω, and Med. **εἰσδύομαι** (v. δύω): fut. -δύσομαι, with aor. 2 -έδῡν: pf. -δέδῡκα:—*get* or *crawl into*, ἐς τὸν θησαυρόν Hdt.2.121. β'; ψυχὴ ἐς ἄλλο ζῷον ἐσδύεται ib.123; εἰσεδύοντο εἰς τοὺς πόδας οἱ ἱμάντες the thongs *entered into* their feet, X.*An.*4.5.14; εἰς τὴν Ἀμφικτυονίαν εἰσδεδυκώς *having wormed his way into* the League, D.11.4. 2. c. acc., *go into*, *enter*, ἀκοντιστὺν ἐσδύσεαι Il.23.622; ὁ ψὴν τὴν βάλανον ἐσδύνων Hdt.1.193; ἄκακον.. τρόπον εἰσδύς *having put on*.., Anaxil.33.3. 3. folld. by relat., οὐκ εἶδεν οὗ γῆς εἰσέδυ saw not into what part of the earth she *entered*, E.*IA*1583. II. of feelings, δεινόν τι ἐσέδυνέ σφι great fear *came upon* them, Hdt. 6.138; εἰσέδυ με.. οἴστρημα καὶ μνήμη κακῶν S.*OT*1317; [ἡ ἀλήθεια] εἰς τὰς ψυχὰς εἰσδύεται Plb.13.5.5; λύπη εἰσδύνουσα Andronic.Rhod. p.571 M.

εἴσδῠσις, εως, ἡ, *entrance*, Arist.*HA*616ᵃ28, Agath.2.5; *room for* or *means of entrance*, εἴ. οὐδ' ἀθέρι prob. in *Lyr.Adesp.*2 B, cf. *Gp.*15.2.26.

εἰσεάω, *let in*, *Gp.*15.2.27.

εἰσεγγίζω, *approach*, dub. l. in Plb.12.19.6 (prob. ἐγγίζοντα).

εἰσεῖδον, Ep. εἰσίδον and in Med. form εἰσιδόμην, v. εἰσοράω.

εἴσειμι, inf. -ιέναι, serving as fut. to εἰσέρχομαι: impf. εἰσῄειν:— *enter*, *go into*, οὐδ' Ἀχιλῆος ὀφθαλμοὺς εἴσειμι I *will* not *come before* Achilles' eyes, Il.24.463: more freq. with Preps., οὐκ εἴσειμι μετ' ἀνέρας Od.18.184; παρὰ βασιλέα Hdt.1.99; mostly with εἰς, ἐς τὸ μέγαρον ib.65, etc.; πρός τινα S.*Ph.*953, X.*Cyr.*2.4.5; ἐσιέναι ἐς σπονδάς *enter* into a treaty, Th.5.30: abs., τὸν εἰσιόντα μῆνα the *ensuing* month, And.1.42; τὸν εἰσιόντα ἐνιαυτόν Arist.*Ath.*31.2, cf. *POxy.*1278.17 (iii A.D.), etc. II. of the Chorus or actors, *come upon* the stage, *enter*, Pl.*Lg.*664c; τὸ τοὺς τυράννους.. εἰσιέναι *take the part of* king, D.19.247, cf. Lib.*Or.*30.28. III. of public speakers, *come into the assembly*, εἰς ἀγοράν D.24.60; καθ' ὅτι ἂν ἐσίῃ ἡ πρεσβεία Th.4.118; of judges, *come into court*, εἰ. κρινοῦντες D.18. 210. 2. of the parties to a lawsuit, *come before the court*, εἰς ὑμᾶς Antipho 5.80, etc.; εἰ. περί τινος D.19.211; πρός τινα Id.54.32. 3. of the charges or actions, ἡ δίκη εἰσῄει Is.5.17; δίκας εἰσιέναι κατά τινος *enter upon* actions, D.28.17, cf. Is.8.44. 4. *enter on* an office, εἰς ἀρχήν D.59.72; ὁ ἐσιών the *new* king, Hdt.6.59. IV. metaph., *come into one's mind*, Ἀστυάγεα ἀνάγνωσις ἐσῄιε Id.1.116; καίτοι μ' ἐσῄει δεῖμα E.*Or.*1668; ἔλεος εἰσῄει με Pl.*Phd.*58e: c. dat., ἄλγος εἰσῄει φρενί E.*IA*1580, cf. Pl.*Phd.*59a; δέος τινὶ εἰσῄει περί τινος Id.*R.*330d. 2. impers., εἰσῄει αὐτοὺς ὅπως ἂν.. they *began to think* how they might.., X.*An.*5.9.17: c. inf., οὐδενὸς εἰσῄει μοι φθονεῖν D.23.188. V. rarely of things, τὰ εἰσιόντα *what enters into one*, *food*, X.*Cyr.*1.6.17.

εἰσέλ-ᾰσις, εως, ἡ, *charge*, of scythe-chariots, Plu.*Art.*7. **-αστικός**, ή, όν, *celebrated by a triumphal entry*, ἀγῶνες εἰ. *CIG*2932 (Tralles), 3426 (Philadelphia), *IGRom.*3.370 (Adada), cf. Plin.*Ep.*10.118; ἱεροὶ εἰ. [ἀγῶνες] *Ath.Mitt.*26.239 (Tralles). **-αύνω**, Ep. -ελάω: fut. -ελάσω [ᾰ], Att. -ελῶ:—*drive in*, ποιμὴν εἰσελάων [τὴν ποίμνην] Od. 10.83; ἵππους δ' εἰσελάσαντες Il.15.385; τὴν θήλειαν ὁ ἄρρην εἰ. πρὸς τὰ ᾠά Plu.2.962f; εἰσελαύνειν τινὰ εἰς τὸν τοῦ πράγματος δρόμον *to keep* him to the point, Aeschin.1.176, cf. 3.206. II. as if intr., ἔνθ' οἵ γ' εἰσέλασαν [τὴν νῆα] that way they *rowed in*, Od.13.113; ἐπεὶ εἰσήλασεν εἰς τὴν πόλιν [τὸν ἵππον] when he *marched into*.., X.*An.*1.2.26, etc.: c. acc. loci, εἰ. λιμένα A.R.2.672, cf. 1265; *enter in triumphal procession*, Plu.*Marc.*8; τεθρίππῳ Id.*Publ.*9; εἰς τὰς Ἀθήνας Ael.*VH*12.58: c. acc. cogn., εἰσελαύνειν θρίαμβον Plu.*Mar.*12, *Cat.Mi.*31.

εἰσελεύσιον, τό, worse form for εἰσηλύσιον, *Gloss.*

εἰσέλευσις, εως, ἡ, *entrance*, *arrival*, Vett.Val.226.22, Hsch. s.v. ἧξις (prob. l.), Thom.Mag.p.302 R.

εἰσέλκω, *draw*, *haul*, *in* or *into*, Xenarch.4.13: aor. -είλκῠσα Hdt. 2.175, Ar.*Ach.*379.

εἰσεμ-βαίνω, *go on board*, *AP*7.374 (Marc. Arg., nisi leg. εἰσανέβην). **-πλέκω**, aor. 2 Pass. εἰσενεπλάκη, gloss on ἐνεδιάσθη, Hsch. **-πορεύομαι**, Pass., *enter* a country *as a trader*, εἰς τὴν χώραν *IG*1².57.20: expld. by τὸ εἰς πολεμίους ἐμπορίας χάριν ἀπιέναι, Hsch.

εἰσεντίθημι, *place in*, εἰσενέθηκε *Epigr.Gr.*517.8 (Edessa).

εἰσέπειτα, Adv. *for hereafter*, τὰ.. πάρος τά τ' εἰ. S.*Aj.*35, etc.

εἰσεπιδημέω, *visit a foreign state*, Pl.*Lg.*952d.

εἰσέργνῡμι, *shut up in* (a mummy-case), τὸν νεκρόν Hdt.2.86.

εἰσέρπω, aor. εἰσείρπῠσα, *to go into*, ἐσέρπει ἐς ἄνθρωπον ψυχή Hp. *Vict.*1.7, cf. Plu.*Cleom.*8; ἐς τὸ ἱερὸν μὴ ἐσέρπεν (Dor. inf.) *IG*12(3). 183 (Astypalaea, iv/iii B.C.); διὰ τοῦ στομίου Luc.*DMort.*3.2: c. dat., φθόνος βραχέσιν εἰσερπύσας χωρίοις Ph.2.553.

εἰσέρρω, *go into*, *get in*: pf. εἰσήρρηκα Ar.*Th.*1075: aor. εἰσήρρησεν Id.*Eq.*4, Agath.*Praef.*p.139 D.

εἴσερσις, εως, ἡ, (εἴρω A) *binding in* or *to*, Sch.Th.1.6.

εἰσερύω, *draw into*, [νῆα] κοῖλον σπέος εἰσερύσαντες Od.12.317.

εἰσέρχομαι, fut. -ελεύσομαι: aor. -ήλῠθον, -ῆλθον: in Att., fut. is supplied by εἴσειμι, and impf. by εἰσῄειν:—*go in* or *into*, *enter*, in Hom. and Poets mostly c. acc., Φρυγίην εἰσήλυθον Il.3.184; ἀλλ' εἰσέρχεο τεῖχος 22.56; αὐλάν Pi.*N.*10.16; ἄλσος, δόμους, S.*Tr.*1167, E.*Alc.*563; οἴκαδε X.*HG*5.4.28; οἴκαδε εἰς ἐμαυτοῦ Pl.*Hp.Ma.*304d; εἰσῆλθ' ἑκατόμβας *invaded* the hecatombs, Il.2.321: but in Prose mostly with Preps., ἐς οἴκημα Th.1.134, etc.; ἐσ. ἐς τὰς σπονδάς *come into* the treaty, Id.5.36; εἰς τὸν πόλεμον v.l. in X.*An.*7.1.27; εἰ. εἰς τοὺς ἐφήβους *enter the ranks of* the Ephebi, Id.*Cyr.*1.5.1; also εἰ. πρός τινα *enter* his *house*, *visit* him, ib.3.3.13; of a doctor, *pay a visit*, Gal.18(2).36; εἰ. ἐπὶ τὸ δεῖπνον X.*An.*7.3.21: abs., of money, etc., *come in*, προσόδους εἰσελθούσας Id.*Vect.*5.12. II. of the Chorus, actors, etc., *come upon* the stage, *enter*, Pl.*R.*580b, X.*An.* 6.1.9, etc.; *enter the lists*, in a contest, S.*El.*700; πρός τινα in competition with.., D.18.319. III. as law-term, of the accuser, *come into court*, εἰς ὑμᾶς (sc. τοὺς δικαστάς) D.59.1; but also τοὺς ὑπὲρ τῶν κοινῶν -εληλυθότας δικαστάς Id.18.278. 2. of the parties, c. acc., εἰ. τὴν γραφήν *enter* the charge, Id.18.105; εἰ. δίκας Id.28.17 (so also εἰ. [τὴν καταχειροτονίαν] Id.21.6; εἰ. λόγον κατά τινος Arg. Isoc.11). 3. of the accused, *come before the court*, δεῦρο Pl.*Ap.*29c; εἰς δικαστήριον Id.*Grg.*522b; εἰς ὑμᾶς D.18.103, cf. 21.176; εἰσελθόντες δ' ὡς ὑμᾶς is prob. in Arist.*Rh.*1410ᵃ18. 4. of the cause, *to be brought in*, ποῖ οὖν δεῖ ταύτην εἰσελθεῖν τὴν δίκην; D.35.49. IV.

enter on an office, Antipho 6.44; ἐσ. ἐς τὴν ὑπατείαν D.C.41.39; ἐπὶ τὴν ἀρχήν Id.64.7. V. *consult* a table, εἰ. εἰς ὄργανον Vett.Val.20.12. VI. metaph., [μένος] ἄνδρας ἐσέρχεται courage *enters into* the men, Il.17.157; πείνη δ' οὔ ποτε δῆμον ἐσέρχεται famine never *enters* the land, Od.15.407; Κροῖσον γέλως ἐσῆλθε Hdt.6.125; ὥς με πόλλ' εἰσέρχεται.. ἄλγη A.*Pers*.845; πόθος μ' εἰσέρχεται E.*IA* 1410; νιν εἰσῆλθεν τάδε ib.57: c. dat., εἰσῆλθε τοῖν τρὶς ἀθλίοιν ἔρις S.*OC*372; [Κύπρις] εἰσέρχεται μὲν ἰχθύων.. γένει Id.*Fr*.941.9; δέος εἰ. τινὶ περί τινος Pl.*R*.330d; ὑποψία εἰ. μοι Id.*Ly*.218c. 2. *come into one's mind*, Κροίσῳ ἐσελθεῖν τὸ τοῦ Σόλωνος Hdt.1.86, cf. Pl.*Tht*.147c; ἐσελθεῖν τισὶ ἡδονήν, οἶκτον, Hdt.1.24, 3.14. b. impers., c. inf., τὸν δὲ ἐσῆλθε θεῖον εἶναι τὸ πρῆγμα *it came into* his *head* that.., Id.3.42; ἐσῆλθέ με κατοικτῖραι Id.7.46; εἰσῆλθε δή με.. φοβηθῆναι Pl.*Lg*.835d; τὸν δὲ ἐσῆλθε ὡς εἴη τέρας Hdt.8.137; εἰσελθέτω σε μήποθ' ὡς.. A.*Pr*.1002.

εἰσέτι, Adv. *still, yet*, Theoc.27.19, etc.

εἰσευπορέω, *procure in plenty*, τὸ πλεῖστον *Supp.Epigr*.1.366.40 (Samos, iii B.C.); χρήματα τῇ πόλει D.S.16.40; ποθόδους τοῖς ἐγχωρίοις *GDI*3069 (Selymbria): abs., *SIG*364.74 (Ephesus).

εἰσέχω, used intr. by Hdt., *stretch into*, κόλπος ἐκ τῆς βορηΐης θαλάσσης ἐσέχων ἐπὶ Αἰθιοπίης a bay *running in* from the north sea towards Ethiopia, Hdt.2.11; ἡ μεγίστη τῶν διωρύχων ἐσέχει ἐς ποταμόν Id.1.193; ἦν θάλαμος ἐσέχων ἐς τὸν ἀνδρεῶνα the chamber *opened into* the men's apartment, Id.3.78; ἐς τὸν οἶκον ἐσέχων ὁ ἥλιος the sun *shining* into the house, Id.8.137: abs., ἐκ τοῦ Νείλου διώρυχες ἐσέχουσι (sc. ἐς τὴν γῆν) Id.2.138. II. in pictures, τὸ ἐσέχον is *the retiring part, the shade*, opp. ἐξέχον (the high lights), Philostr.*VA* 2.20. b. στέρνα ἐσέχοντα *hollow* chests, Id.*Gym*.35.

εἰσέω· ἱκετεύω, Hsch.

εἰσηγ-έομαι, Dor. **εἰσᾱγ–**, fut. –ήσομαι, *lead in*, εἰσηγοῦ σὺ λαβὼν ἡμᾶς Ar.*Av*.647; *bring in, introduce*, ἀοιδάς Simon.174 (dub.); of religious rites, Hdt.2.49; δημαγωγίαν Plb.2.21.8; ἔθος D.H.11.50. 2. *introduce, propose*, τὴν πεῖραν Th.3.20; γῆς ἀναδασμούς Pl.*Lg*.684e; νόμον Diph.38, cf. D.18.148, etc.; δόγμα Ph.1.140, al.; εἰ. περί τινος *make a proposal* on a subject, Isoc.4.170: c. inf., *propose*, εἰ. τὴν αὐλητρίδα χαίρειν ἐᾶν to let her go, Pl.*Smp*.176e, cf. *Cri*.48a, cf. D.H. 6.51, Plu.*Publ*.16; τοῦτο τὸ μάθημα, ὅτι καλὸν εἴη Pl.*La*.179e; εἰ. ὅπως.. Plu.*Them*.20; εἰσηγουμένου τινός *at* his *proposal, on* his *motion*, Th.4.76, cf. *IG*5(1).1451.6 (Messene, ii A.D.), etc. 3. εἰσηγεῖσθαί τινι *represent* to a person, ἐσηγεῖται.. τοῖς ἐν τέλει οὖσιν ὡς οὐ χρεών.. Th.7.73: hence, *advise, instruct*, τοιαῦτα μέντοὐγὼ φρονεῖν τούτοισιν εἰσηγησάμην Ar.*Ra*.972; τοῖς νεωτέροις Isoc.1.4; εἰ. τοῖς πολεμίοις ἃ χρὴ καταλαβεῖν τῶν χωρίων Lys.14.35. 4. *relate, narrate, explain*, τινί τι Pl.*Smp*.189d; λόγον τινί Id.*Ti*.20d. –ημα, ατος, τό, *motion, proposal*, Aeschin.1.82: pl., Isoc.*Ep*.1.2. 2. *precept*, Nic.Dam.p.26 D. –ησις, εως, ἡ, *proposing, advising*, Th.5.30, Ph.2.211, Plu.2.11d; *introduction*, ἐθῶν καὶ νομίμων Ph.1.166 (pl.); δογμάτων ib.410. II. *a motion*, D.C.36.38. –ητέον, *one must move*, Th.6.90. –ητήρια, τά, = εἰσιτήρια (quod fort. leg.), Hsch. –ητής, οῦ, ὁ, *one who brings in, author*, τῶν κακῶν τῷ δήμῳ Th.8.48, cf. Hyp.*Epit*.3, Arist.*Ath*.27.4, Aeschin.1.172, Ph.1.103, al., Luc.*Anach*.14, etc. –ήτρια, ἡ, fem. of foreg., *she that introduces*, καινοῦ θεοῦ Corn.*Rh*.p.390 H. –ορία, ἡ, *reproach*, Suid., Zonar.

εἰσηθέω, *inject by a syringe*, Hdt.2.87.

εἰσήκω, *to have come in*, v.l. in Ar.*V*.606; of revenues, *BCH*6.18 (Delos, ii B.C.): fut., *to be about to come in*, ἔοικεν.. ἐσήξειν (nisi leg. ἐσάξειν) A.*Ag*.1181; εἰς τὴν οἰκίαν ἐσήξειν (nisi leg. –άξειν) D.C. 37.32.

εἰσηλεῖν· εἰσάγειν, εἰσελαύνειν, Hsch. (prob. = εἰσειλεῖν).

εἰσηλ-ῠσία, ἡ, *coming in, entrance*, *AP*9.625 (Maced.). –ύσιον, τό, *entrance-fee*, *IG*2².1368.37, *Ath.Mitt*.32.294 (Pergam., ii A.D.). –**ῠσις**, εως, ἡ, *entrance, right of entrance*, *CIG*3278 (Smyrna).

εἶσθα, Ep. 2 sg. of εἶμι (*ibo*), Il.10.450, Od.19.69.

εἶσθαι, pf. inf. Pass. of ἵημι (v. ἀφίημι).

εἴσθεσις, εως, ἡ, *putting in*, Ph.1.278; opp. ἀφαίρεσις, Dam.*Pr*. 102. II. *insetting* of short lines in lyric strophes, Sch.Ar.*Pl*.253, *Ach*.565.

εἰσθέω, *run into* or *in*, J.*BJ*6.4.6, Philostr.*VA*1.28, D.C.62.16, etc.; ἐσθεῖ πρὸς ἡμᾶς *runs up* to us, Ar.*Av*.1169.

εἰσθεωρέω, *investigate*, Heph.Astr.3.37.

εἴσθλᾰσις, **εἰσθλάω**, v. εἴσφλ–.

εἰσ-θλίβω [ῑ], prob. f.l. for ἐκθλ– in Plu.2.688b, Them.*Or*.14. 197a. –θλιψις, prob. f.l. for ἔκθλ. in Philagr.ap.Orib.5.17.10.

εἰσθρῴσκω, aor. –έθορον, *leap into* or *in*, ὁ δ' ἄρ' ἔσθορε φαίδιμος Ἕκτωρ Il.12.462, cf. 21.18; διά τινος Ael.*NA*14.24: c. acc., πρὶν ἐμὸν ἐσθορεῖν δόμον A.*Th*.454 (lyr.).

εἰσί, 3 pl. of εἰμί (*sum*). **εἶσι**, 3 sg. of εἶμι (*ibo*). **εἰσιδεῖν**, Ep. εἰσιδέειν, aor. inf. of εἰσεῖδον; v. εἰσοράω.

εἰσιδρύω, *build in*, ἐσίδρυται σφι Ἄρηος ἱρόν v.l. in Hdt.4.62.

εἰσίζομαι, *take one's station in*, ἐσίζεσθαι λόχον ἀνδρῶν Il.13.285.

εἰσίημι, fut. –ήσω: aor. –ῆκα:—*send into*, ἐς τὴν [λίμνην] εἰ. τὸ ὕδωρ, of rivers, Hdt.7.109; εἰ. τοὺς Πέρσας ἐς τὸ τεῖχος *let* them *in*, Id.3.158; τὴν [κεδρίην] (sc. ἐς τὴν κοιλίην) Id.2.87:—Med., τοὺς πολεμίους ἔφη εἰσέσθαι said he *had let* them *in*, X.*HG*1.3.19; χάριτας *Sammelb*. 4324.8:—Pass., *IG*1².115.18 (Lex Draconis). II. Med., αὖλιν ἐσιέμεναι *betaking themselves into their own* roost, Od.22.470.

εἰσίθμη, ἡ, (εἴσειμι) *entrance*, Od.6.264, Opp.*H*.1.738.

εἰσικνέομαι, *go into*, c. acc. loci, Hermesian.7.23. II. *penetrate*, Hdt.3.108; εἰσικνουμένου βέλει *piercing* her with a shaft, A.*Supp*. 556 (lyr.), s.v.l.

εἰσιππεύω, *ride into* or *in*, εἰς τὴν πόλιν D.S.17.12: abs., D.C.44.10.

εἰσίπτᾰμαι, = εἰσπέτομαι (q.v.).

εἰσῐτ-έον, *one must go in*, Iamb.*VP*23.105, al. –ημα, ατος, τό, *revenue*, *BCH*6.26 (Delos, ii B.C.): pl., Dor. –άματα *SIG*244*A* 20 (Delph.). –ήριος, ον, (εἴσειμι) *belonging to entrance*: εἰσιτήρια (sc. ἱερά), τά, *a sacrifice at the beginning* of a year or *entrance on* an office, D.19.190; εἰ. ὑπὲρ τῆς βουλῆς ἱεροποιῆσαι Id.21.114, cf. *SIG* 695.25 (Magn. Mae., ii B.C.), D.C.45.17; εἰσιτήριοι θυσίαι Hld.7.2: sg., εἰσιτήριον, τό, *entrance-deposit*, *PRyl*.77.37 (ii A.D., ἰσητ– Pap.):— Att. Inscrr. have **εἰσιτητήρια**, *IG*2².17, al. –ητέον, *one must go in*, Luc.*Herm*.73. –ητός, ή, όν, *accessible*, Alciphr.1.23; εἰσιτητὰ τῷ στόλῳ ποιεῖν Procop.*Vand*.1.20: also **εἰσιτός** J.*BJ*6.4.5, Zonar.

Εἰσῖτύχη [ῠ], ἡ, *Isis-Fortuna*, *CIL*4.4138, 14.2867.

εἰσκαθίημι, *dispatch to* a place, ἀργύριον ἐσκατιέναι (sic) Ἀθήναζε *IG*1².6.116.

εἰσκαθοράω, *look down upon*, πόλιν ἐσκατορᾷς (Ion. form), Bgk. for ἐγκ–, Anacr.1.6.

εἰσκαιεικοστός, όν, *twenty-first*, *IG*11(2).164*A* 45 (Delos, iii B.C.).

εἰσκᾰλᾰμάομαι, (κάλαμος I. 2) *haul in*, as an angler the fish which he has hooked, Ar.*V*.381.

εἰσκᾰλέω, *call in*, μάρτυρας Ar.*V*.936, D.28.5; τινὰ πρὸς αὑτόν X.*Cyr*.8.3.1, cf. Theoc.2.132, *PPetr*.2 p.31 (iii B.C.), etc.:—Med., *invite to one's house*, *Act.Ap*.10.23; also, *call* or *have called in*, Plb.21.22.2; [ἰητρόν] Hp.*Prog*.1; *summon*, *PPetr*.3 p.62 (iii A.D.).

εἰσκατα-βαίνω, *go down into*, c. acc., ὄρχατον Od.24.222; δόμον Orac.ap.Hdt.5.92.ε'. –δύνω, = foreg., Timo 34.1. –ρρήγνῡμι, *break inwards*:—Pass., ἐσκαταρραγῆναι ῥωγμῇσι Hp.*VC*17. –τίθημι, *put down into*:—Med., ἑὴν ἐσκάτθετο νηδύν Hes.*Th*.487, 890 (v.l. ἐγκάτθετο).

εἴσκειμαι, used as Pass. of εἰστίθημι, *to be put on board ship*, Th. 6.32.

εἰσκέλλω, intr., *put to land*, ποίαν δὲ χώραν εἰσεκέλσαμεν σκάφει; Ar.*Th*.877.

εἰσκηρύσσω, Att. –ττω, *proclaim by herald*, Ar.*Ach*.135 (Pass.), *Inscr.Prien*.5.9 (Pass., iv B.C.); *call into the lists for combat*, S.*El*. 690:—Pass., εἰ. εἰς τοὺς ἀγῶνας *SIG*286.11 (Milet., iv B.C.), cf. D.C. 61.20.

εἰσκλάω, in Pass., *grow in*, of eyelashes, Dsc.*Eup*.1.50.

εἰσκλείω, *place under lock and key*, ἐν θησαυρῷ *PThead*.28.8 (iv A.D.).

εἴσκλησις, εως, ἡ, *summons*, *Cat.Cod.Astr*.2.195.

εἰσκλύζω, f.l. for ἐκκλύζω (q.v.) in Str.5.1.7.

εἰσκλύω, poet. for εἰσακούω, τευ ἐσέκλυον αὐδήσαντος *IGRom*.1.1195 (Memnon), cf. Q.S.1.509.

εἰσκνάω, in Pass., ἐσκνᾶσθαι· ξυρῆσαι, Hsch.

εἰσκολάπτω, *carve upon*, in Pass., Lxx 3*Ki*.6.33(35) (s.v.l.).

εἰσκολυμβάω, *swim into*, Sch.Th.4.26.

εἰσκομ-ῐδή, ἡ, *importation* of supplies, ἡ ἐσκομιδὴ τῶν ἐπιτηδείων Th.7.4: pl., ib.24; *bringing in*, Orib.*Eup*.3.7.5. –ίζω, pf. –κεκόμικα Porph. (v. infr.):—*carry in*, χόρτον Hes.*Op*.606; *guide in*, A.*Ag*.951:—Med., *bring in for oneself*, τὰ ἐκ τῶν ἀγρῶν ἐσκομίζεσθαι Th.2.13, cf. 1.117:—Pass., ἐσκομίζεσθαι εἰς τὰ τείχη *take shelter in*.., Id.2.100; ἐπειδὰν εἰσκομισθῶσιν πόλει E.*HF*242; τὸν σῖτον ἐκ τῆς χώρας –κομισθῆναι *IG*2.331.36; τοῖς εἰς ταὐτὸ διὰ ταὐτοῦ –ομένοις Plu.2.699f. II. metaph., *import* into a discussion, *introduce*, δύο λύσεις Porph.*in Cat*.139.30. –ισμα, ατος, τό, *that which is brought in*, and –ιστέον, *one must bring in*, Gloss.

εἰσκρεμάννῡμι, fut. –κρεμάσω, *hang up in* a place, *PLond*.3.964.19 (ii/iii A.D.).

εἰσ-κρίνω [ρῑ], *enrol, admit*, εἰς τοὺς ἐφήβους *POxy*.477.10 (ii A.D.), etc. II. *cause to enter*, πνεῦμα Iamb.*Myst*.3.13, cf. *PMag.Lond*. 121.432; ὀνείρους μερόπεσσιν Orac. in *App.Anth*.6.197: but more freq., III. Pass., *enter into, penetrate*, D.L.1.7, Ph.2.604, *Gp*. 15.6.2, Iamb.*Myst*.1.8. 2. *to be adjudged*, σοφός *AP*9.578 (Leo Phil.). –κρίσις, εως, ἡ, *entering in, penetration*, τοῦ ψυχικοῦ θερμοῦ *Placit*.5.25.3, cf. Plot.4.3.9, Zos.Alch.p.205 B.: pl., κατακλίνονται ταῖς εἰ. ἀκολουθοῦντες *order of admission*, Ph.2.481. II. *enrolment, admission*, *PFlor*.79.9 (i A.D.), etc. –κρῐτικόν, τό, *due paid on enrolment* by ἔφηβοι, *Ostr*.136.

εἰσκρούω, *knock in*, πύνδακα Pherecr.105, Thphr.*Char*.30.11 (cj.).

εἰσκτάομαι, *acquire*, εὔκλειαν E.*Fr*.238.

εἰσκυκλ-έω, *wheel in*, esp. in a theatre, *turn* a thing *inwards by machinery*, and so, *withdraw it from the eyes of the spectators*, Ar.*Th*. 265, cf. Luc.*Lex*.8: generally, ὄψων παρασκευὴν εἰσκυκλουμένην Ath. 6.270e: metaph., πράγματα δαίμων τις ἐσκεκύκληκεν ἐς τὴν οἰκίαν some spirit *has wheeled* ill luck into the house, Ar.*V*.1475:—Pass., *plunge into*, τοῖς τῆς ἱστορίας διηγήμασι Lxx 2*Ma*.2.24:—Med., c. acc., [ἥρῳ ἔπη].. εἰσκυκλήσομαι Poet. in *BKT*5(1) p.84. II. εἰσκυκλήσας· περιελθών, Hsch. –ημα, ατος, τό, *the mechanism on which the* ἐκκύκλημα *turns*, Poll.4.128.

εἰσκῠλίνδω, fut. –κυλίσω [ῑ], *roll into*, [νήσους] ὤχλισσε καὶ εἰσεκύλισε θαλάσσῃ Call.*Del*.33: Com., εἰς οἷ' ἐμαυτὸν εἰσεκύλισα πράγματα what trouble I'*ve rolled* myself *into*, Ar.*Th*.651.

εἰσκύπτω, *pop in*, ὄμματα ἐκκύπτοντα.. κεἰσκύπτοντα, of a snail, Teucer ap.Ath.10.455e. 2. of a road, *overhang*, ἐπὶ Γαί Lxx 1*Ki*. 13.18.

εἰσκύρω [ῡ], *enter*, aor. εἰσέκυρσα Ezek.*Exag*.231.

εἴσκω, poet. Verb, only pres. and impf. (exc. fut. εἴξω, τίνι [σε] εἴξομεν; Jul.*Or.*2.52d):—*make like* (cf. ἴσκω), αὐτὸν... ἤϊσκεν δέκτῃ he *made* him *like* a beggar, Od.4.247, cf. 13.313:—Pass., δέμας ἶσον ἔϊσκετό τινι he *became like*, Nonn.*D*.4.72. **II.** *deem like, liken*, τάδε νυκτὶ ἐΐσκει Od.20.362, cf. Il.5.181; Ἀρτέμιδί σε... ἐΐσκω I *compare* thee to her, Od.6.152, cf. Il.3.197, Sapph.*Supp.*13.5, Ibyc.*Oxy.* 1790.45; οὔ σε δαήμονι φωτὶ ἐΐσκω I *do* not *deem* thee *like*, i.e. *take* thee *for*, a wise man, Od.8.159. **2.** c. acc. et inf., *deem, suppose*, οὔ τί σ' ἐΐσκομεν.. ἠπεροπῆα ἔμεν 11.363, cf. Il.13.446; ἄντα σέθεν γὰρ Ξάνθον... ἤϊσκομεν εἶναι 21.332, cf. Theoc.25.199. **3.** abs., ὡς σὺ ἐΐσκεις as thou *deemest*, Od.4.148. (*ϝε-ϝίκ-σκω, cf. (ϝ)έ-(ϝ)οικ-α, (ϝ)ε-(ϝ)ικ-υῖα.)

εἰσκωμάζω, (κῶμος) *burst in like a party of revellers*: generally, *burst in upon*, τινί Luc.*Lex.*9; εἰς τὴν πόλιν Aristid.*Or.*51(27).30: c. acc. loci, Lyc.1355: metaph., εἰσεκώμασεν ὁ ἄργυρος silver *came romping in*, Ath.6.231e.

εἰσλάμπω, *shine in*, Thphr.*CP*2.7.4, Plu.2.929c, Plot.5.1.2.

εἰσλεύσσω, *look upon*, οἰκεῖα πάθη S.*Aj.*260 (anap.), cf. Man.4.36.

εἰσμαίομαι, used by Hom. only in Ep. aor. 1, *touch to the quick, affect greatly*, μάλα γάρ με θανὼν ἐσεμάσσατο θυμὸν Il.17.564; ὃς ἐμόν γε μάλιστ' ἐσεμάσσατο θυμόν 20.425.—The pres. εἰσμαίομαι is not found, cf. ἐπιμαίομαι, εἰσματέομαι.

εἰσμαρτῠρέω, *introduce evidence*, Sch.E.*Or.*812.

εἰσμάσσομαι, Med., Dor. aor. 1 ἐσεμαξάμαν, *wipe upon*, κόλπον ἐς εὐώδη ... ἐσεμάξατο χεῖρας, metaph., of Aphrodite *imparting* her charms, Theoc.17.37.

εἰσμᾰτέομαι, *put in the hand to feel*, Hp.*Art.*32; ἐσμασάμενος ἐς τὴν κοιλίην ib.46; in full, τὴν χεῖρα ἔσω ἐσμάσασθαι Aret.*SD*2.9.—The spelling ἐσματευόμενον Hp.*Art.*38, *Mul.*1.70 (v.l.), is corrupt for ἐσματεύμενον, while ἐσματτευόμενον Bacch.ap.Erot. and ἐσμάττεσθαι Gal.18(1).453 are Atticizing forms.

εἰσμετρέω, *deliver corn*, *PEleph.*10.3 (iii B.C.), *PPetr.*2p.132 (Pass.), etc.

εἰσναίω, aor. Med. ἐσενασσάμην, *dwell in*, Hermesian.7.31.

εἰσνέομαι, *go into*, ἐς δὲ νέονται οὐρανὸν *AP*9.59 (Antip. [Thess.]).

εἰσνέω, fut. -νεύσομαι, *swim into*, Th.4.26, Ael.*NA*13.6.

εἰσνήχομαι, *swim into*, Ael.*NA*14.24.

εἰσνοέω, *perceive, remark*, Il.24.700, Od.11.572, A.R.1.1053, *AP* 5.266 (Agath.).

εἰσόβδην, v. ὄβδη.

εἰσοδ-εύω, = εἴσειμι, εἰ. καὶ ἐξοδεύειν *PRyl.*162.25 (ii A.D.), cf. *Sammelb.*6152.14. **-ιάζω**, *collect* money, Eust.1788.2, etc.:—Pass., *come in*, of revenue, Lxx 4*Ki.*12.4, Vett.Val.291.27; *to be paid*, ὅπως -οδιασθῇ τὰ ὀφειλόμενα *IG*5(1).1432.7 (Messene, i B.C./i A.D.). **-ιασμός**, ὁ, *ingathering of revenue*, Charis.p.577 K., *Gloss.*: generally, *receipts*, opp. ἐξοδιασμός, *Arch.Pap.*1.493. **-ιος**, ον (α, ον D.H.11.29), *going* or *coming in*, Suid., Zonar.: εἰσόδιοι, οἱ, *visitors*, Antip.ap.Stob.4.22.103 (s.v.l.), cf. D.H. l.c.: εἰσόδιον, τό, *income, revenue*, *PPetr.*2p.54 (iii B.C.): pl., *PHib.*1.116 (iii B.C., -εια Pap.), Thd.*Da.*11.13. **II.** εἰσόδιον, τό, *introduction* to a speech, Aristid. 2.321 J.

εἰσοδοιπορέω, *walk in*, ἐς τὸ τέμενος *IG*12(1).677.11 (Ialysus).

εἴσοδος or **ἔσοδος**, ἡ, *entrance*: **I.** *place of entrance, entry*, Od. 10.90, Hdt.1.9, etc.; ἐσόδους Φοίβου *the entrance* to his temple, E. *Ion* 104 (anap.); of a mountain-pass, ἡ διὰ Τρηχῖνος ἔ. ἐς τὴν Ἑλλάδα Hdt.7.176; in a theatre, *entrance* for the Chorus, Ar.*Nu.*326, *Av.* 296, v. Sch.; *entrance-door* of a court of justice, Arist.*Ath.*63.2, etc.: metaph., καλῶν ἔσοδοι *paths* to glory, Pi.*P.*5.116. **II.** *entering, entrance*, εἴ. παρασχεῖν X.*HG*4.4.7, etc.: pl., A.*Eu.*30. **2.** *entrance into the lists* to contend in the games, ἱππείαν ἔ. (cf. εἰσέρχομαι II) Pi.*P.*6.50; also ἡ εἴ. τῆς δίκης εἰς τὸ δικαστήριον *the introduction* of it, Pl.*Cri.*45e. **3.** *right* or *privilege of entrance*, ἔσοδον εἶναι παρὰ βασιλέα ἄνευ ἀγγέλου Hdt.3.118. **4.** *visit*, κακῶν γυναικῶν εἴσοδοι E.*Andr.*930, cf. 952, Lys.1.20; of a doctor, Gal.16.523. **5.** *study, investigation*, Vett.Val.259.7; ἀκροθιγεῖς τὰς εἰσόδους ποιήσασθαι ib. 222.11; also, *method*, ib.108.19. **III.** *that which comes in, revenue*, opp. ἔξοδος, Plb.6.13.1, cf. *IG*14.423 (Tauromenium), 5(1).1390.64 (Andania), *PPetr.*3p.151.

εἰσοιδαίνω, *cause to swell*, τὸ δέρμα Aret.*CD*1.2.

εἰσοικ-ειόω, *bring in as a friend*, τινὰ γάμοις Plu.*Alex.*10:—Pass., *become intimate with*, X.*HG*5.2.25. **-έω**, *settle in*, dub. in *AP*7.320 (Hegesipp., leg. ἐν-). **-ησις**, εως, ἡ, *place for dwelling in, home*, ἄοικος εἰ. S.*Ph.*534 (dub.). **-ίζω**, *bring in as a dweller* or *settler*, Plb.5.100.8:—Med. and Pass., *establish oneself* or *be established in*, ἐσοικισθέντων ἐς τοὺς Αἰθίοπας Hdt.2.30; ἐς τὴν Κρήτην Id.7.171; εἰς τὸ ἐργαστήριον Aeschin.1.124: c. acc., εἰσοικίσασθαι χώραν Plu.*Sol.* 7: abs., -σαμένου τοῦ ἐσμοῦ *Gp.*15.4.2; βίᾳ εἰσῳκισμένοι Aristid.*Or.* 26(14).29; οἱ ὑπὸ σοῦ εἰσοικισθησόμενοι τῷ οἴκῳ *POxy.*1641.4 (i A.D.): metaph., *make oneself at home*, ἡ παρανομία κατὰ σμικρὸν εἰσοικισαμένη Pl.*R.*424d; λιμὸς εἰσοικίζεται Men.841: c. acc., Κυδίππην κρυμὸς ἐσῳκίσατο Call.*Aet.*3.1.19: c. dat., ἐμὸς αἰὼν κύμασιν αἰθυίης μᾶλλον ἐσῳκίσατο Id.*Fr.*111; but, *take to oneself, give entrance to*, τὴν ψυχὴν Porph.*Gaur.*3.5; γυναῖκα *take* to wife, Just.*Nov.*18.11; ψυχῆς εἰσοικισθείσης Plot.5.1.2. **-ισμός**, ὁ, *bringing in as settler*, Hld.8.1.

εἰσοικοδομέω, *build into*, πλίνθους ἐς τεῖχος Th.2.75.

εἰσοιστέος, α, ον, *to be brought in*, νόμος D.24.25.

εἰσοιχνέω, poet. Verb, *go into, enter*, c. acc., χορὸν εἰσοιχνεῦσαν Od.6.157; οὐδέ μιν (sc. νῆσον) εἰσοιχνεῦσι κυνηγέται 9.120; ὁπόσοι τὴν Διὸς αὐλὴν εἰσοιχνεῦσιν A.*Pr.*122 (anap.).

εἰσόκα, Dor. for sq., Bion *Fr.*10.14.

εἰσόκε, before a vowel -κεν, (εἰς ὅ κε) *until*, mostly with subj., Il. 2.332, 10.62, al. (in 3.409 ποιήσεται is Ep. for ποιήσηται), Emp.26.7, al.; rarely with opt., Il.15.70; in later Ep. with past tenses of ind., A.R.1.820, etc. **II.** *so long as*, c. subj., Il.9.609.

εἰσολισθάνω, aor. -ώλισθον, *slip in*, Plu.2.972b.

εἴσομαι, fut. of οἶδα (*εἴδω). **II.** Ep. fut. of (ϝ)ει- 'rush', 'hasten', δεῦρ' εἴσεται Od.15.213: 3 sg. aor. εἴσατο Il.5.538, etc.; ἐείσατο 15.415; but sts. simply *go*, as εἴσῃ Od.16.313; πάλιν εἴσομαι Il.24.462, al.: c. inf. fut., ἐεισάσθην συλήσειν 15.544.

εἰσομῑλέω, *flatter, toady*, in impf., Hsch.

εἰσομόργνῡμι, *impress upon*, in Med., Chaerem.14.15 (codd. Ath., sed leg. ἐξ-).

εἶσον, imper. of εἶσα (ἵζω).

εἰσόπιν, (ὄπις) Adv. *back*: c. gen., εἰσόπιν χρόνου *hereafter*, A.*Supp.* 617.

εἰσοπίσω [ῐ], Adv. *in time to come, hereafter*, *h.Ven.*104, S.*Ph.*1104 (lyr.), Rhian.66. **II.** *backwards*, Opp.*C.*4.362, Q.S.1.243, al.

εἴσοπτος, ον, *visible*, βλεφάροις θνατῶν ἔσ. Simon.58.4, cf. Hdt.2. 138, Antipho Soph.6.

εἰσοπτρ-ίζω, *reflect like a glass*, Plu.2.696a:—Med., *look at oneself in a glass*, ib.141c, Iamb.*Protr.*21.κδ'; *see as in a glass*, ἀμυδρῶς τὴν πάλαι λαμπρότητα Lyd.*Mag.*3.1. **-ικός**, ή, όν, *seen in a mirror*, εἰκόνες Plu.2.920f. **-ίς**, ίδος, ἡ, = εἴσοπτρον, *AP*6.307 (Phanias). **-ισμα**, ατος, τό, = sq., Secund.*Sent.*4. **-ισμός**, ὁ, *reflection as in a mirror*, Plu.2.936e.

εἰσοπτροειδής (ἐσ-), ές, *like a mirror* or *reflection*, *Placit.*2.20.12.

εἴσοπτρον (so *CPR*21.20 (iii A.D.)), mostly in the form **ἔσοπτρον**, τό, (ὄψομαι) *looking-glass, mirror*, Pi.*N.*7.14, J.*AJ*12.2.9, Plu.2.85b, 139f, *Lyr.Alex.Adesp.*37.26, *Anacreont.*6.3.

εἰσοράω, Ep. part. εἰσορόων, inf. Med. εἰσοράασθαι: fut. εἰσόψομαι: aor. εἰσεῖδον, Ep. inf. -ιδέειν:—*look into, look upon, behold*, common in Poets, Od.4.142, al., Sapph.*Supp.*13.3, etc., but rare in Prose (as X.*Cyr.*5.1.16, Pl.*Grg.*526c); ἐσορᾶν καλός Pi.*O.*8.19; ἐλεινὸς εἰσορᾶν A.*Pr.*248; ἐσ. τὴν νέα Hdt.8.92:—Med. in same sense, freq. in Hom., εἰσοράασθε ἵππους Il.23.495: mostly in inf., οὗ.. ὀξύτατον... φάος εἰσοράασθαι whose eye is quickest *to discern*, 14.345; ὅς τε... ἀθάνατος ἰνδάλλεται εἰσοράασθαι he is like an immortal *to behold*, Od.3. 246; μείζονες εἰσοράασθαι 10.396, cf. 24.252: aor. εἰσειδόμην, imper. ἐσίδεσθ' A.*Pr.*141 (anap.); εἰσιδόμαν ib.427 (lyr.):—Pass., ὅσσον... ἠελίοιο μεσσηγὺς δυσιές τε καὶ ἀντολαὶ εἰσορόωνται A.R.1.85. **b.** c. part., εἰσορῶ τινὰ στείχοντα E.*Hipp.*51; πόλιν.. μοι ξυνοῦσαν εὔνουν S.*OC*772: parenthetic, ὡς ἕρποντος (εἰσορᾷς) ἐμοῦ since I (thou *seest*) am coming, Id.*Tr.*394 (s.v.l.). **2.** *look upon with admiration*, πάντες δὲ θεοὺς ὡς εἰσορόωσι Il.12.312; μιν.. θεὸν ὣς εἰσορόωντες Od. 7.71; simply, σε μᾶλλον Ἀχαιοὶ εἰσορόωσιν.. 20.166: hence, *pay regard to, respect*, πλοῦτον ἢ εὐγένειαν E.*El.*1097: with a Prep., ἐσορῶντες ἐς τὴν μαντικὴν Hdt.4.68: generally, *look at* or *gaze upon steadily*, A.*Pers.*111 (lyr.), E.*Med.*264. **3.** *look on with the mind's eye, perceive*, οὐκ εἰσορᾷς; S.*El.*997, cf. 611; εἰ. ὡς.. Id.*Ph.*501. **4.** of angry gods, *visit*, θεοὶ γὰρ εὖ μὲν ὀψὲ δ' εἰσορῶσι Id.*OC*1536, cf. 1370. **5.** folld. by μή, *take care lest...*, Id.*El.*584.

εἰσορμάω, *bring forcibly into*, ῥυθμὸν Μούσῃ *AP*7.707 (Diosc.):—Pass., *rush into*, c. acc., θάλαμον εἰσορμωμένην S.*Tr.*913:—intr. in Act., εἰσορμᾶν πρὸς Ἱππότας Plu.2.775a.

εἰσορμίζω, *bring into port*:—Pass., *run into port*, of seafaring men, εἰσορμισθέντας X.*Vect.*3.1: aor. Med., εἰς τὸν ποταμὸν εἰσωρμίσαντο Plu.*Cim.*12.

εἰσορούω, *rush in*, v.l. in Pi.*O.*8.40.

ἐΐσος, η, ον [ῑ], Ep. form of ἴσος, *alike, equal*, Hom., only fem. sg. and pl., always in set phrases (exc. [ἵππους].. σταφύλῃ ἐπὶ νῶτον ἐΐσας *equal in height*, Il.2.765): **1.** most freq. of a feast, *equal*, i.e. *equally shared, of which each partakes alike*, esp. of sacrificial feasts or of meals given to a stranger (for on other occasions the greatest men had the best portions), δαιτὸς ἐΐσης 1.468, al. **2.** of ships, *even* or *well-balanced*, νηὸς ἐΐσης 15.729; νῆες ἐΐσαι Od.5.175, al. **3.** of a shield, *evenly balanced*, ἀσπίδα πάντοσ' ἐΐσην Il.12.294, 13.157, 160, etc. **4.** of the mind, *even, well-balanced*, φρένας ἔνδον ἐΐσας Od. 11.337, 14.178.

εἰσότε, for εἰς ὅτε, *against the time when*, Od.2.99, al.

εἰσοφάγος or **εἰσωφάγος** [ᾰ], etym. of οἰσοφάγος, Gal.19.125, Pall. *in Hp.*2.192 D.

εἰσοχετεύω, *conduct into*, Hld.9.3.

εἰσοχή, ἡ, (εἰσέχω) *hollow, recess*, opp. ἐξοχή, Str.2.5.22 (pl.), cf. 12.2.4 (pl.); of intaglios, κατ' εἰσοχήν, opp. κατ' ἐξοχήν, *Stoic.*1.108.

εἴσοψις, εως, ἡ, *spectacle*, E.*El.*1085 codd.

εἰσόψομαι, fut. of εἰσοράω, Ep. ἐσ- Il.5.212, 24.206.

εἰσπαίω, aor. εἰσέπαισα, *burst* or *rush in*, S.*OT*1252, Xenarch.1.3, J.*BJ*4.1.9: c. acc. loci, κρυπτὸν λόχον εἰσπαίσας E.*Rh.*560 (lyr.).

⟨εἰσ⟩παραδέχομαι, *receive* (?), Hierocl.p.29 A.

εἰσπαραδύομαι, *slide gently into*, Ph.2.432.

εἰσπέμπω, *send in*, σύ μ' ἐσπέμπεις δόμους E.*HF*850, cf. Th.4.16; γράμματα πρὸς βασιλέα Id.1.137; *suborn* agents, S.*OT*705, And.2.4; ῥήτορας *send* them *into court, instruct* them, Pl.*Euthd.*305b; τῷ μὴ καλῷ θάρρει τὸν κάλλιστον φόβον *pit* against..., Id.*Lg.*671d.

εἰσπεράω, fut. -άσω [ᾱ], Ion. -ήσω, *pass over into*, Χαλκίδα τ' εἰσεπέρησα Hes.*Op.*655: abs., Orph.*A.*442.

εἰσπέτομαι, fut. -πτήσομαι: aor. εἰσεπτόμην Ar. (v. infr.), but 3 sg. -έπτατο Il.21.494; part. ἐσπτόμενοι D.C.45.17: also in Act.

form -έπτην Ath.9.395a, Plu.2.461e, etc.: aor. Pass. in med. sense, -πετασθῆναι Arist.*HA*624b6:—*fly into, fly in*, c. acc., κοίλην εἰσέπτατο πέτρην Il. l. c.; ἐς τὸν ἀέρα Ar.*Av.*1173; of weapons, ἐς τοὺς ὀφθαλμοὺς καὶ πρὸς τὰς χεῖρας D.C.40.22: metaph. of reports, Hdt.9.100, 101.

εἰσπηδάω, *leap in*, ἐς τὰς λίμνας Hdt.4.132; εἰς τὸν πηλόν X.*An.* 1.5.8. 2. *burst in*, εἰσπηδήσας πρός με νύκτωρ Μειδίας Test.ap.D. 21.22; εἰς τὴν οἰκίαν ib.78, cf. *PHal.*1.169 (iii B.C.); εἰς τὰ συνέδρια *Hell.Oxy.*10.2: abs., *rush in*, Men.*Sam.*219, *Act.Ap.*16.29.

εἰσπηδησιών, ῶνος, ὁ, *house-breaker, Gloss.*

εἰσπίπτω, fut. -πεσοῦμαι: aor. -έπεσον:—*fall into*, generally with a notion of violence, *rush* or *burst in*, ἐς τὰς πόλιας Hdt.5.15; ἐς τὰς νέας Id.8.56; ἐς οἴκημα Th.2.4, etc.; of the sea, Id.4.24: poet. c. dat., ἐσπίπτει δόμοις E.*Ion*1196. 2. simply, *fall into*, ἐς χωρίον Th.1.106; ἐς χαράδρας Id.3.98, etc.; ἐσ. ἐς εἱρκτήν *to be thrown* into prison, Id.1.131: in Poets, c. acc., ἐσπεσοῦσα δικτύων βρόχους E.*Or.* 1315; ὄχλον γὰρ ἐσπεσεῖν ᾐσχυνόμην *to go into* the crowd, Id.*Hel.* 415; ἐσ. πέπλους *seek shelter within* my robes, Id.*Tr.*1181; πτέρυγας ἐσπίτνων ἐμάς ib.751; κτύπου κέλευθον ἐσπεσόντος a noise *having come into* the street, Id.*Or.*1312. 3. *fall into a certain condition*, δούλειον ἦμαρ εἰ. Id.*Andr.*99; ξυμφοράν ib.983; γῆρας Id.*Ion*700: in Th.4.4 ἐνέπεσε shd. be read. II. *make an onset, attack*, Hdt. 1.63, S.*Aj.*55; εἰ. ἐς τὸν πεζόν Hdt.4.128; ἐς τοὺς ἀγρούς Th.2.22; ἐπὶ τὰς θύρας 'besiege the door', Plu.*Oth.*17. III. *come in*, of payments, Meyer *Ostr.*82.4 (iv A.D.).

εἰσπίτνω, poet. form of εἰσπίπτω, E.*Tr.*751.

εἰσπίφρημι, inf. -πιφράναι, = εἰσφρέω (q.v.), Arist.*HA*541b11: aor. εἰσέφρηκα; inf. -φρῆναι Hsch.

εἰσπλέω, fut. -πλεύσομαι, *sail into, enter*, ἐς τὰ στενά Th.2.86, cf. 89, etc.: poet. c. acc., E.*IT*1389: c. acc. et dat., ὑμέναιον δόμοις εἰσέπλευσας S.*OT*423. 2. abs., *sail in*, ἐπ' ἀριστερὰ ἐσπλέοντι *as one sails in*, Hdt.6.33; στόμα ναυσὶ ταῖς μεγίσταις ἱκανὸν εἰσπλεῖν Pl.*Criti.*115d; εἰσπλέοντάς ἐκπλέοντάς τε Pl.Com.183; Μεγαρεῦσι μηδὲν ἐσπλεῖν Th.3.51, cf. X.*HG*2.4.29; of corn, *to be imported*, D. 20.31.

εἰσπληρόω, *fill full*, in Med., Epicur.*Sent.*10 codd. (ἐκπλ- Diog. Oen.). II. *pay in full*, *PLond.*5.1841.26 (vi A.D.).

εἴσπλοια, ἡ, = sq., *EM*89.36.

εἴσπλοος, contr. -πλους, ὁ, *sailing in* of ships, βιάσασθαι τὸν ἔσ. Th.7.22, cf. 24 (pl.), X.*HG*2.2.9. 2. *right of entry*, εἶναι αὐτῷ εἴ. καὶ ἔκπλουν αὐτοῖς εἶναι καὶ ἐν πολέμῳ καὶ ἐν εἰρήνῃ *IG*12(7).8 (Amorgos), etc. II. *entrance of a harbour*, Th.4.8 (pl.); λιμὴν στενόν τινα ἔχων εἴ. Pl.*Ti.*25a.

εἴσ-πνευσις, εως, ἡ, *inhalation*, opp. ἔκπνευσις, Arist.*Ph.*243b 26. **-πνευστέον**, *one must inhale*, Gal.6.359.

εἰσπνέω, fut. -πνεύσομαι, *inhale*, opp. ἀναπνέω, ἐκπνέω, Arist.*Resp.* 472b3, *Pr.*887b17. 2. c. acc., *inhale*, ἀέρα Hld.2.35; εὐοσμίας Aristaenet.1.3. II. *breathe upon*, με αὔρα τις εἰσέπνευσε Ar.*Ra.* 314 (Pass., ἀνέμῳ ἐσπνεῖσθαι Philostr.*VA*2.8); τινί Ael.*VH*3.12 (a Lacedaemonian phrase for *inspire with love*); ἐς τὴν ἀναπνοὴν Aret. *SA*1.7.

εἰσπνήλας or **εἴσπνηλος**, ου, ὁ, *lover* (cf. foreg. II), Call.*Fr.*169, Theoc.12.13.

εἰσπνοή, ἡ, *inspiration, inhalation*, opp. ἐκπνοή, Arist.*Resp.*471a8, cf. Str.3.5.7; μιᾷ ἐσπνοῇ θνήσκουσι Aret.*SA*1.7.

εἴσπνοος, ον, *inhaling*, Hp.*Epid.*6.6.1.

εἰσποι-έω, *give in adoption*, υἱόν τινι Pl.*Lg.*878a; τὸν παῖδα εἰς τὸν οἶκόν τινος D.43.15; τοὺς σφετέρους παῖδας εἰς ἑτέρους οἴκους εἰσποιοῦσιν Is.10.17 (but the same phrase is used of a father who *begets*, Id.6.22); εἰ. τινὰ εἰς τὰ χρήματά τινος *make* him *heir* to the property, Id.10.12, cf. 16, 17, etc.; εἰ. σαυτὸν Ἄμμωνι, of Alexander, Plu.*Alex.* 50: metaph., [ἡ παντάρβη] πᾶν τὸ ἐγγὺς ἐσποιεῖ αὐτῇ *attracts*, Philostr. *VA*3.46:—Med., *adopt as one's son*, D.44.34, Ph.2.86, D.C.44.5:—Pass., εἰσποιηθῆναι πρός τινα *to be adopted* into his family, D.44.27; ἐπὶ τὸ ὄνομά τινος ib.36. 2. generally, εἰ. τινὰς εἰς λῃτουργίαν *bring new* persons *into* the public service, Id.20.19, 20; τῶν πραττομένων εἰσεποίει κοινωνὸν αὑτόν *forced* himself *in* as partaker, Din.1.32; εἰ. ἐγκώμιον εἰς τὴν ἱστορίαν *introduce* panegyric into history, Luc. *Hist.Conscr.*9; εἰ. ἑαυτὸν εἰς δύναμίν τινος *thrust* himself into another's authority, Plu.*Pomp.*16; εἰ. Ἡσιόδῳ Θεογονίαν *father* it on him, Paus.9.27.2. 3. τὸ τάχος [τὴν τίγριν] ἐσ. τοῖς ἀνέμοις *adopts into the family of* winds, i. e. *makes* it *as swift as* the winds, Philostr.*VA* 3.48. II. Med., *intervene, meddle* in an affair, *CPHerm.*6.10 (iii A.D.). **-ησις**, εως, ἡ, *adoption*, Is.10.14, Plu.*Oth.*16, etc. **-ητός**, ή, όν, *adopted*, Lys.*Fr.*55, D.44.34, 60.4.

εἰσπομπή, ἡ, *introduction*, Suid.

εἰσπορεύω, *lead in*, οἴκαδε E.*El.*1285:—Pass., *go into, enter*, X. *Cyr.*2.3.21, *UPZ*6.30 (iii B.C.); εἰς τὸ ἄδυτον *OGI*56.4 (iii B.C.); πρός τινα *Act.Ap.*28.30. Used for εἰσέρχομαι in later Gr., cf. *AB*91.

εἰσπορίζω, *supply*, v.l. in Isoc.5.121.

εἰσ-πράκτης, ου, ὁ, *exactor, taskmaster*, Aq.*Ex.*5.13. **-πρακτος**, ον, *chargeable*, *BGU*486.13 (ii A.D.). **-πράκτωρ**, ορος, ὁ, = εἰσπράκτης, Hsch. **-πραξις**, εως, ἡ, *getting in* or *collection* of taxes or dues, τοῦ θύματος Th.5.53; τῶν εἰσφορῶν D.24.8, cf. *SIG*364*A*50 (Ephesus), *IG*2².1273.24, etc.; βαρύνεσθαι.. ἀδίκοις εἰσπράξεσι *exactions*, *OGI*669.5, cf. Plu.*Demetr.*27. II. *levy* of recruits, Wilcken *Chr.* 469.4 (iv A.D.).

εἰσπράσσω, Att. -ττω, *get in* or *exact*, φόρον *IG*1².65.16, cf. 2².1172. 18, Pl.*Lg.*949d, Plb.13.7.3, Plu.2.1044a: c. acc. pers., τοὺς ὑπερημέρους D.21.11, cf. 24.13; οὐκ εἰσέπραξε τὸν δῆμον *did* not *charge* the people [with it], Decr.ap.D.18.115: c. dupl. acc., τοσοῦτον πλῆθος χρημάτων εἰ. τοὺς συμμάχους Isoc.5.146; προσήκει ὑμᾶς τοῦτον εἰσπρᾶξαί μοι τὰ ἀναλώματα Id.50.67:—Med., *exact for oneself, have paid one*, κακὸν δίκαιον εἰσεπράξατο E.*IT*559; Med. is freq. interchangeable with Act., D.21.155: so in pf. Pass., πικρῶς εἰσπράττειν με, ὥσπερ καὶ παρὰ τῶν ἄλλων εἰσπέπρακται Id.35.44; also εἰ. τιμωρίαν *exact* vengeance, Jul.*Or.*2.58a:—Pass., of the money, *to be exacted*, D.19.21, *IG*2.814*a* *A*24; of persons, *have* money *exacted from one, have to pay* it, D.33.24.

εἰσπτήματα, gloss on εἰσαφάσματα, Hsch.

εἰσπτύω, *spit upon*, τινί Arist.*HA*613a4.

εἰσράπτω, *sew on*, in Pass., Gal.18(2).578.

εἰσρέω, fut. -ρυήσομαι Isoc.8.140, Luc.*Alex.*42: aor. -ερρύην:—*stream in* or *into*, E.*IT*260; opp. ἐκρεῖν, Pl.*Phd.*112b: metaph., πλοῦτος εἰ. εἰς τὴν πόλιν Isoc. l. c.; εἰσερρύη νόμισμα εἰς τὴν Σπάρτην Plu.*Lyc.*30; τὸ πάθος εἰσερρύη *slipped in*, Pl.*Phdr.*262b; ἐπιστῆμαι εἰσρέουσι Id.*Phlb.*62c; ἁμάρτημα εἰσρεῖ D.H.*Rh.*10.17; πόθος εἰσερρύη πάντας εὐνομίας Plu.*Num.*20.

εἰσρήσσω, gloss on *irrumpo*, Dosith.p.434K.

εἰσ-ροή, ἡ, *influx*, Ael.*NA*1.53, Marcian.*Peripl.*1.1; τοῦ ἀέρος Porph.*Gaur.*3.3. **-ροια**, ἡ, = foreg., ὑδάτων *POxy.*1409.19 (iii A.D.). **-ροος**, contr. -ρους, = foreg., Arist.*Mu.*393a19. **-ρῦσις**, εως, ἡ, = foreg., *IG*11(2).199*A*55 (Delos, iii B.C.).

εἰσσπάομαι, *draw into oneself*, τινὰ εἰς τὸν οἶκον Lxx *Ge.*19.10.

εἴστε, Delph., = ἔστε, *SIG*241.69, 120.

εἰστείχω (for εἰσστ-), = εἰσέρχομαι, *Schwyzer* 633.1, al. (Lesbos).

εἰστελέω, *contribute*, *PFay.*20.2 (iii/iv A.D.). II. Pass., *to be received into* a class, εἰς γένος Pl.*Plt.*290e.

εἰστίθημι, *put into, place in*, τι ἔς τι Th.4.100, cf. Hdt.1.123; τινὰ ἐς τὰς χεῖράς τινι ib.208, etc.; νεκρὸν ἐς ἅμαξαν Id.9.25. 2. esp. *put on board* ship, πάντα ἐσθέντες (sc. ἐς τὰς πεντηκοντέρους) Id.1. 164:—Med., ἐσθέμενοι τέκνα καὶ γυναῖκας ibid., cf. 4.179, E.*Hel.*1566, X.*HG*1.6.20; *to take*, ἐς φορεῖον App.*BC*4.19. 3. Pass., *to be entered*, of a judgement in court, *PPetr.*3p.39 (iii B.C.).

εἰστιτρώσκω, aor. ἐσέτρωσα, *perforate, pierce*, τῷ ὀστέῳ μέσφα μήνιγγος Aret.*CD*1.2.

εἰστοξεύω, *shoot arrows at*, Hdt.9.49. II. ἐσ. βιβλία ἐς τὸ στρατόπεδον *shoot* papers *attached to arrows into*.., D.C.48.25. III. metaph., τὰ δρώμενα τὰ πάθη ταῖς ψυχαῖς εἰστοξεύονται Hld.3.7.

εἰστρέπομαι, *turn in*, [τὰ ἐκτὸς] ἐντὸς εἰ. *turn* outside *in*, Arist. *HA*621a8, cf. Heliod.ap.Orib.46.10.4:—Pass., fut. εἰστραπήσομαι Antyll.ap.Aët.7.74.

εἰστρέχω, aor. 1 subj. εἰσθρέξωσιν Lyc.1163: aor. 2 -έδραμον Th. 4.67, Theoc.13.24: pf. εἰσδεδράμηκα Men.*Sam.*146:—*run in*, Th. l. c.; εἰσέδραμε Φᾶσιν, of a ship, Theoc. l. c.; ἡ θεὸς (sc. ποδάγρα) διὰ ποδῶν εἰ. Luc.*Ocyp.Praef.*

εἰστρῡπάω, intr., *slip in through a hole*, Ael.Dion.*Fr.*161, Suid.; cf. ἐκτρυπάω II.

εἰσφαίνω, *inform*, f.l. in Philomnest.Hist.1.

εἰσφέρω, fut. εἰσοίσω E.*Ba.*367: aor. 1 εἰσήνεγκα Archil.78.2 (s.v.l.): pf. εἰσενήνοχα D.27.36: plpf. -όχειν Id.24.19:—*carry in*, εἴσω Od.7.6; ἐσ. ἀγγελίας Hdt.1.114; ἐς τὠυτὸ ἐσ. Id.9.70; τινὰ εἰς τὸ λογιστήριον *PAmh.*2.77.22 (ii A.D.). 2. *bring in, contribute*, τῖμον Archil. l. c.; χρήματα X.*Hier.*9.7, Plu.*Publ.*12; εἰ. τινὶ ἔρανον Pl.*Smp.*177c, cf. X.*Cyr.*7.1.12; at Athens, etc., *pay the property-tax* (v. εἰσφορά II), ἐσ. ἐσφοράν Th.3.19, etc.; εἰσφορὰς Antipho 2.2. 12, Lys.18.7: and abs., εἰ. εἰς τὴν πόλιν D.27.36; εἰ. ἀφ' ὑπαρχούσης οὐσίας Id.21.157. 3. *bring in* or *upon*, πένθος δόμοις E.*Ba.*367; νόσον καινὴν γυναιξί ib.353; πόλεμον Ἑλλήνων χθονί Id.*Hel.*38; δειλίαν ἐσφέρει τοῖς ἀλκίμοισι *brings* cowardice *into* the brave, Id.*Supp.* 540. 4. *introduce*, καινὰ δαιμόνια X.*Mem.*1.1.2; ψεῦδος Plb.2.58.12; esp. of political measures, *bring forward, propose*, γνώμην Hdt.3.80; γνώμην ἐς τὸν δῆμον Th.8.67; εἰ. νόμον, = Lat. *legem rogare*, D.23. 218, 24.19; ψηφίσματα *IG*2².1329.10; τιμάς ib.1343.29: abs., ἐσ. ἐς τὰς βουλὰς περί τινος Th.5.38; εἰς τοὺς νομοφύλακας Pl.*Lg.*772c; τὴν δὲ βουλὴν εἰσενεγκεῖν, ὅτῳ τρόπῳ.. X.*HG*1.7.7:—Pass., τὰ εἰσφερόμενα [ψηφίσματα] Arist.*Pol.*1298b33. b. of persons, *propose, nominate*, Pl.*Lg.*961b:—Pass., ibid.; τοὺς -ομένους ὑπὸ τῶν ὑπάτων πρεσβευτάς Plb.35.4.5. II. Med., fut. ἐσοίσομαι E.*Hel.*664 (lyr.): Ion. aor. 1 ἐσενείκασθαι Hdt. (v. infr.): pf. Pass. εἰσενήνεγμαι (v. infr.):—*carry with one, sweep along*, of a river, Il.11.495. 2. *bring in for oneself*, τὰ ἐκ τῶν ἀγρῶν ἐς τὸ τεῖχος Hdt.5.34, cf. Th.5.115:—so in Pass., σῖτον ἐσενηνεῖχθαι or -έχθαι Hdt.9.41. 3. *bring in with one, introduce*, τοὔνομα ἐς τὴν ποίησιν Id.2.23; πῶμ' ηὗρε κεἰσηνέγκατο θνητοῖς E.*Ba.*279; [λόγον] ἐσφέρεσθαι *to utter* it, Id.*Hel.*664 (lyr.); ν' μνᾶς εἰς τὸν οἶκον εἰσενηνεγμένη *having brought* 50 minae *as a dowry* into the family, D.27.4, cf. 41.4; προῖκα εἰσενεγκαμένη Thphr.*Char.*22.10. 4. *contribute*, εἰσενήνεκται.. οὐκ ἔλαττον μ' μνῶν Lys.19.43, cf. *Michel* 473. 9 (Mylasa, ii B.C.); *apply, employ*, πᾶσαν εἰ. σπουδὴν καὶ φιλοτιμίαν Plb.21.29.12, cf. Chrysipp.*Stoic.*2.293, *IG*2².1343.23, *Inscr.Prien.* 111.126 (i B.C.), D.S.1.84; ἀνδρείαν Onos.4.2; θάρσος J.*AJ*18.8.5; ἰσχύν ib.17.5.6; φιλονεικίαν Ael.*VH*12.64. 5. like προσφέρεσθαι, *eat*, Hp.*VM*3, Ant.Lib.11.1; *drink* water, Arist.*GA*767a32. 6. *draw breath*, Id.*Somn.Vig.*456a17. III. Pass., *to be brought in, introduced*, ἐσενειχθέντος σιδηρίου Hdt.9.37. 2. *rush in*, ἐς τὴν ὕλην Th.3.98.

εἰσφθείρομαι, aor. -εφθάρην [ᾰ], *make entry to one's undoing*, εἰς τὴν βασιλείαν J.*BJ*1.26.1, cf. Poll.9.158, Suid. s. v. εἰσέρρησεν; as an abusive term, οὐκ εἰσφθερεῖσθε θᾶττον.. ἐκποδών; Men.*Pk.*276; θᾶττον εἰσφθάρηθι σύ Id.*Sam.*229.

εἴσφλᾰσις, ιος, ἡ, Ion. for ἔσθλ–, *crushing inwards*, Hp.*VC*3.

εἰσφλάω, Ion. for ἐσθλ–, *crush in*, Hp.*VC*2 (Pass.).

εἰσφοιτ-άω, pf. –πεφοίτηκα, *go often into*, ἐς τοὐπτάνιον Ar.*Eq.*1033; πρὸς τὴν ἄλοχον E.*Andr.*945: abs., Lys.*Fr.*58: c. acc., κλισίας Q.S.3.433; *to be imported*, of goods, D.C.43.24, 60.11. **–ησις**, εως, ἡ, *inroad, invasion*, τῶν Περσῶν Agath.4.19 (pl.).

εἰσ-φορά, ἡ, (εἰσφέρω) *carrying* or *gathering in*, X.*Oec.*7.40. II. at Athens, etc., *property-tax* levied for purposes of war, εἰσφορὰς εἰσφέρειν Antipho 2.2.12, Lys.30.26, cf. Th.3.19, etc. b. in Egypt, *special tax*, *PTeb.*89.74, 124.35 (pl.), etc. 2. generally, *contribution*, χρημάτων Pl.*Lg.*955d; αἱ εἰ. τῶν τελῶν Arist.*Pol.*1313b 26. III. *introduction, proposal*, νόμων D.H.10.4, cf. D.C.37.51. **–φορέω**, = εἰσφέρω, Od.6.91, 19.32, Th.2.75, Diph.60.9, A.R.4.1145. 2. Med., = εἰσφέρω II. 5, Parth.9.5. **–φόριον**, τό, *tax-payment*, *PFlor.*151.6. **–φορος**, ὁ, *person liable to pay*, *POxy.*1117.15 (ii A.D.).

εἰσφράσσω, aor. 2 Pass., εἰσφρᾰγέντων τῶν τρυπημάτων v.l. in Nicom.*Harm.*10.

εἰσφρέω, impf. εἰσέφρουν D.20.53: fut. –φρήσω Ar.*V.*892, –φρήσομαι (in same sense) D.8.15: aor. 1 –έφρησα Plb.21.27.7, *PLips.*39.11 (iv A.D.): impf. Med. εἰσεφρούμην E.*Tr.*652; cf. εἰσπίφρημι:—*let in, admit*, Ar. l.c.; στράτευμα D.20.53:—Med., *bring in with one*, E. l.c.; also εἰσφρήσασθαι· καυχήσασθαι, μετὰ σπουδῆς εἰσενεγκεῖν, Hsch. 2. *swallow*, Arist.*Mir.*831b 11. II. intr., *let oneself in, enter*, Plb. l.c., Alciphr.3.53, Jul.*Caes.*315a.

εἰσφύρω [ῠ], *to mix in*, ἀναμὶξ πάντα ἐν τοῖς λόγοις Max.Tyr.28.6 (Pass.).

εἰσχειρίζω, *put into one's hands, entrust*, [ἀρχὴν] ἐμοὶ πόλις δωρητὸν οὐκ αἰτητὸν εἰσεχείρισεν S.*OT*384.

εἰσχέω, *pour in* or *into*, Hdt.4.2, E.*Cyc.*389 (s.v.l.):—Med., aor. εἰσεχεάμην Aristid.*Or.*39(18).4:—Pass. with Ep. aor. ἐσεχύμην [ῠ], *stream in*, ἐσσυμένως ἐσέχυντο ἐς πόλιν Il.21.610, cf. Hdt.9.70; ψυχὴν ἔξωθεν οἷον εἰσχυθεῖσαν Plot.5.1.2.

εἰσχράομαι, *use*, μέτροις *POxy.*717.2 (i B.C.).

εἴσχῠσις, εως, ἡ, *estuary*, Ptol.*Geog.*2.3.1, al.

εἰσχωρέω, *penetrate*, διὰ τοῦ στομίου Hero *Spir.*1.19.

εἴσω, ἔσω, used by Ep., Lyr., and Trag. Poets acc. as a spondee or iambus is required; ἔσω (as ἐς for εἰς) prevailed in Ion. and old Att. Prose; but in other Prose and in Com. εἴσω was the only form admitted, whereas ἔσωθεν with the Comp. and Sup. ἐσώτερος, ἐσώτατος, ἐσωτέρω, ἐσωτάτω, seem to have been the only forms in use:—Adv. of εἰς, ἐς, *to within, into*: abs., μή πού τις ἐπαγγείλῃσι καὶ εἴσω lest some one may carry the news *into the house*, Od.4.775, cf. Hdt.1.111, al.; so εἴπατε δ' εἴσω Od.3.427; also εἴσω δ' ἀσπίδ' ἔαξε he brake it through *to the inside*, Il.7.270; so ὀστέα δ' εἴσω ἔθλασεν Od.18.96; εἴσω ἐπιγράψαι τέρενα χρόα Il.13.553; ἐσσύμενοι εἴσω Pi.*P.*4.135; εἴσω κομίζου A.*Ag.*1035; πέπληγμαι.. ἔσω ib.1343; εἴσω.. δεῦρ' εἴσιθ' Ar.*Pl.*231; ἡγεῖσθαι εἴσω, φεύγειν εἴσω, X.*Cyr.*2.3.21, 7.5.26; παρακαλέσαι εἴσω Id.*An.*1.6.5. b. when a case follows, Hom. prefers the acc., δῦναι δόμον Ἄϊδος εἴσω Il.3.322; πέρησε δ' ἄρ' ὀστέον εἴσω αἰχμή 6.10, etc.; ἡγήσατο.. Ἴλιον εἴσω 1.71, etc.; more rarely with gen., κατελθόντ' Ἄϊδος εἴσω 6.284, cf. 22.425; ἐβήσετο δώματος εἴσω Od.7.135, cf. 8.290; so in Prose and Trag., Κύκλωπος ἔσω βλεφάρων ὤσας E.*Cyc.*485; it generally follows its case, but precedes in Il.21.125, 24.155, Od.8.290. 2. with Verbs of Rest, = ἔνδον, *inside, within*, εἴσω δόρπον ἐκόσμει 7.13; ἄντρον ἔσω ναίουσα *h.Merc.*6; ἔσω καθῆσθαι A.*Ch.*919; θακεῖν S.*Aj.*105; οὔτε πύργος οὔτε ναῦς ἔρημος ἀνδρῶν μὴ ξυνοικούντων ἔσω Id.*OT*57; τὸ ἔσω μέτωπον the *inner* front, Th.3.21; τὰ εἴσω νενοσηκότα σώματα Pl.*R.*407d; εἴσω τὴν χεῖρα ἔχειν ἀναβεβλημένον D.19.251. b. c. gen., μένειν εἴσω δόμων A.*Th.*232; γλῶσσαν εἴσω πυλῶν ῥέουσαν ib.557; εἴσω στέγης S.*Tr.*202; εἴσω ξίφους *within reach* of sword, E.*Or.*1531; εἴσω τῶν ὅπλων *within* the heavy-armed troops, i.e. *encircled by* them, X.*An.*3.3.7, 3.4.26; εἴσω τῶν ὀρέων *within*, i.e. *on this side of*, the mountains, ib.1.2.21; εἴσω τούτων *inside of* these people, i.e. *farther inland*, Th.2.100; εἴσω βέλους *within* bow-shot, Arr.*An.*1.6.8; τὰ δένδρα τῆς ὁδοῦ ποιεῖν εἴσω, i.e. *inside*, i.e. *by the side of*, the road, D.55.22; εἴσω τῆς εἰρωνείας ἀφικνεῖσθαι Id.*Prooem.*14; πάντα εἴσω τῆς συμφορᾶς Lib.*Or.*61.18. II. later of Time, *within*, εἴσω ἡμερῶν εἴκοσι *PGiss.*34.6 (iii A.D.), Hermog.*Stat.*8, Arg.2 Ar.*Eq.* III. for Comp. and Sup., v. ἔσω.

εἰσωθ-έω, *thrust into*, τι ἐς τὸ ἔσω μέρος Hp.*Art.*34; χεῖρα Aret.*SD* 2.1; ἔνδον τὰς στάλικας Lib.*Descr.*10.4:—Med., *force oneself into, press in*, X.*An.*5.2.18; εἰς τοὺς ὄχλους Porph.*Hist.Phil.Fr.*12. **–ίζομαι**, = foreg., App.*BC*4.78.

εἰσωπή, ἡ, *aspect*, Opp.*H.*4.358.

εἰσωπός, όν, *within*, i.e. *between* (perh. connected with ὀπή), εἰσωποὶ δ' ἐγένοντο νεῶν Il.15.653: abs., *in harbour*, A.R.2.751. 2. (ὤψ) *visible*, Arat.79, 122.

εἴσωσις, εως, ἡ, *inward thrust*, of spinal curvature, Gal.14.796.

εἰσώστη, ἡ, *tomb*, in pl., *CIG*2824 (Aphrodisias), *JHS*20.76 (Caria). (Prob. from ὠθέω, cf. ὑπώστη.)

εἶτα, Ion. εἶτεν (q.v., cf. ἔπειτα, –εν), Adv., used to denote the Sequence of one act or state upon another: I. of Sequence in time, without any notion of Cause, *then, next*, πρῶτα μέν.., εἶτα.. S.*El.*262, cf. Pl.*Phdr.*251a, etc.; *soon, presently*, S.*OT*452; εἶτα τί τοῦτο; *well*, what *then?* Ar.*Nu.*347, Pl.*Prt.*309a; εἶτα.. τότε *then.. after that*, Ar.*Eq.*1036 codd. (fort. τόδε): freq. repeated, sts. alternating with ἔπειτα, *then.., next.., then.., after* that.., etc., Men.154, etc.; with πάλιν, *SIG*1171; εἶτ' οὖν *also*, Sch.Pi.*O.*7.68. 2. freq. with finite Verb after a part., expressing surprise or incongruity, *and then, and yet*, μή μοι προτείνων κέρδος εἶτ' ἀποστέρει A.*Pr.*777; ἆρα κλύουσα, μῆτερ, εἶτ' ἔρξεις κακῶς; E.*El.*1058, cf. S.*El.*53, *Aj.*468, 1092, 1094, X.*An.*1.2.25, etc.; cf. ἔπειτα 1.3. II. to denote Consequence, *and so, therefore, accordingly*; esp. in questions or exclamations to express surprise, indignation, contempt, sarcasm, and the like, *and then..? and so..?* κᾆτ' οὐ δέχονται λιτάς; S.*Ant.*1019, cf. *OC*418; εἶτ' ἐγὼ μὲν οὐ φρονῶ; E.*Andr.*666; κᾆτα ποῦ 'στιν ἡ δίκη; Id.*Ph.*548; εἶτ' ἐσίγας, Πλοῦτος ὤν; Ar.*Pl.*79; εἶτ' ἄνδρα τῶν αὑτοῦ τι χρὴ προϊέναι; Id.*Nu.*1214; εἶτ' οὐκ αἰσχύνεσθε; D.1.24, cf. Pl.*Ap.*28b; οὐκ οἴεσθε δεῖν χρήματα εἰσφέρειν, εἶτα θαυμάζετε..; D.21.203; εἶτ' οὐκ ἐπῳδούς φασιν ἰσχύειν τινές; Antiph.217.15; εἶτ' οὐ περίεργόν ἐστιν ἄνθρωπος φυτόν; Alex.141.1, etc.

εἶται, 3 sg. pf. Pass. of ἕννυμι, Od.11.191.

εἰτακεῖν· ἐληλυθέναι, Hsch.

εἴτε, Dor. **αἴτε**, generally doubled, εἴτε.. εἴτε.., Lat. *sive...sive..*, *either..or.., whether..or..*, so that two cases are put as equally possible or equivalent; thrice repeated, S.*El.*606; εἴτ' οὖν.., εἴτε... Id.*OT*1049; εἴτ' οὖν.., εἴτε καί.. A.*Ag.*843; εἴτ' οὖν.., εἴτ' οὖν.. Id.*Ch.*683; εἴτε.., εἴτ' ἄρ' οὖν.. S.*Ph.*345; εἴτε.., εἴτ' αὖ... Pl.*Phlb.*34b; εἴτε καί.., εἴτε καί.. Id.*R.*471d: with Substantives, τὴν εἴθ' ἡδονὴν εἴτε ἀπονίαν ἢ εὐστάθειαν Plu.2.1089d: the first εἴτε is sts. omitted in Poets, ξεῖνος, αἴτ' ὦν ἀστός Pi.*P.*4.78; αἰνεῖν, εἴτε με ψέγειν θέλεις A.*Ag.*1403; μύραινά γ', εἴτ' ἔχιδν' ἔφυ Id.*Ch.*1002; λόγοισιν, εἴτ' ἔργοισιν S.*OT*517, cf. *Tr.*236; and even in Prose, πόλις, εἴτε ἰδιῶται Pl.*Lg.*864a, cf. 907d, *Sph.*224e: the first εἴτε is sts. replaced by εἰ, as εἰ... εἴτε.., Lat. *utrum..an...*, v.l. in Hdt.3.35; εἰ... εἴτε καί... A.*Ch.*768; εἰ.. εἴτε μή Id.*Eu.*468; εἰ μὲν.., εἴτε καὶ μή... X.*Cyr.*2.1.7; sts. ἤ (ἠὲ καί.. v.l. in Il.2.349) stands for the second εἴτε, E.*El.*896, Pl.*Phdr.*277d, *IG*1.40.5; or for the first, S.*Aj.*178 (lyr.), E.*Alc.*115 (lyr.); εἴτε... εἴτε.., c. subj. (cf. εἰ), v.l. in Archyt. ap.Stob.3.1.105. II. in indirect questions, Od.3.90, etc.; σκοπεῖτε εἴτ' ὀρθῶς λογίζομαι ταῦτ' εἴτε μή D.15.11.

εἶτε, = εἴητε, 2 pl. pres. opt. of εἰμί (*sum*), Od.21.195.

εἰτέα, v. ἰτέα.

εἶτεν, = εἶτα, *SIG*57.29 (Milet., v B.C.), Scymn.330, al., *Ev.Marc.*4.28, *IG*5(1).1390.31 (Andania), 7.3073.150 (Lebad.): condemned by Phryn.101; Ion. acc. to Ael.Dion.ap.Eust.1158.38.

εἰτισκαί· πηγή, παρὰ τῶς Κλειτῶς (prob. τοῖς Κλειτορίοις), Hsch.

εἴχεται· οἴχεται, Hsch. **εἰχόμενος**· κατεχόμενος, Id.

εἰωθάς, άδος, ἡ, = ἐθάς, of the domestic pigeon, Hdn.*Philet.*p.446 P.

εἰωθότως, Adv. of εἴωθα (v. ἔθω), *in customary wise*, S.*El.*1456, Aristid.*Or.*51(27).48, etc.; εἰ. ἔλεξεν in his *usual manner*, Pl.*Smp.*218d.

εἴως, Ep. for ἕως. **εἰῶσεν**· ἀπεώσατο, Hsch.

ἐκ, before a vowel **ἐξ**, also ἐξ τῷ ϝοίκῳ *Inscr.Cypr.*135.5 H., in Att. Inscrr. before σ ξ ζ ρ and less freq. λ; ἐγ– in Inscrr. before β γ δ λ μ ν; Cret. and Boeot. **ἐς** *Leg.Gort.*2.49, Corinn.*Supp.*2.67; ἐχ freq. in Att. Inscrr. before χ φ θ (and in early Inscrr. before σ, *IG*1^2.304.20); also ἐ Ναυπάκτω ib.9(1).334.8 (Locr.); (ἐτ is for ἐπὶ in ib.9(2).517.14 (Thess.)):—Prep. governing GEN. only (exc. in Cypr. and Arc., c. dat., *Inscr.Cypr.*135.5 H. (Idalium), (in form ἐς) *IG*5(2).6.49 (Tegea, iv B.C.)):—radical sense, *from out of*, freq. also simply, *from*. I. OF PLACE, the most freq. usage, variously modified: 1. of Motion, *out of, forth from*, ἐκ Πύλου ἐλθὼν τηλόθεν ἐξ ἀπίης γαίης Il.1.269, cf. Pl.*Prt.*321c, etc.; μάχης ἐκ Il.17.207; ἂψ ἐκ δυσμενέων ἀνδρῶν 24.288; ἐξ ὀχέων, ἐξ ἕδρης, 3.29, 19.77; φεύγειν ἐκ πολέμοιο 7.119; ἐκ τῶν πολεμίων ἐλθεῖν X.*Cyr.*6.2.9; ἐκ χειρῶν γέρας εἵλετο Il.9.344, cf. S.*Ph.*1287 (but ἐκ χειρὸς βάλλειν or παίειν to strike with a spear in the hand, opp. ἀντιτοξεύειν or ἀκοντίζειν, X.*An.*3.3.15, *Cyr.*4.3.16; ἐκ χειρὸς τὴν μάχην ποιεῖσθαι ib.6.2.16, cf. 6.3.24, etc.); ἐκ χρυσῶν φιαλῶν πίνειν ib.5.3.3; ἐξ ἀγορᾶς ὠνεῖσθαι Pl.Com.190. 2. ἐκ θυμοῦ φίλεον I loved her *from* my heart, *with all* my heart, Il.9.343; ἐκ τῆς ψυχῆς ἀσπάσασθαι X.*Oec.*10.4; μέγαν ἐκ θυμοῦ κλάζοντες Ἄρη A.*Ag.*48 (anap.); δακρυχέων ἐκ φρενός Id.*Th.*919 (anap.); οὐδὲν ἐκ σαυτῆς λέγεις S.*El.*344; ἐξ εὐμενῶν στέρνων δέχεσθαι receive *with* kindly heart, Id.*OC*486; ἐξ ὀμμάτων ὀρθῶν δὲ κἀξ ὀρθῆς φρενὸς Id.*OT*528; ὀρθὸς ἐξ ὀρθῶν δίφρων *with* chariot still upright, Id.*El.*742; ἐξ ἀκινήτου ποδός Id.*Tr.*875; ἐξ ἑνὸς ποδὸς Id.*Ph.*91. 3. to denote change or succession, freq. with an antithetic repetition of the same word, δέχεται κακὸν ἐκ κακοῦ one evil comes *from* (or *after*) another, Il.19.290; ἐκ φόβου φόβον τρέφω S.*Tr.*28; πόλιν ἐκ πόλεως ἀμείβειν, ἀλλάττειν, Pl.*Sph.*224b, *Plt.*289e; λόγον ἐκ λόγου λέγειν D.18.313; πόρους ἐκ πόρων ὑπισχνούμενοι Alciphr.1.8; ἀπαλλάττειν τινὰ ἐκ γόων S.*El.*291; ἐκ κακῶν πεφευγέναι Id.*Ant.*437: hence, *instead of*, τυφλὸς ἐκ δεδορκότος Id.*OT*454; λευκὴν.. ἐκ μελαίνης ἀμφιβάλλομαι τρίχα Id.*Ant.*1093; ἐλεύθερος ἐκ δούλου καὶ πλούσιος ἐκ πτωχοῦ γεγονὼς D.18.131, cf. X.*An.*7.7.28, etc. 4. to express separation or distinction *from* a number, ἐκ πολέων πίσυρες four *out of* many, Il.15.680; μοῦνος ἐξ ἁπάντων σωθῆναι Hdt.5.87; εἶναι ἐκ τῶν δυναμένων to be *one of* the wealthy, Pl.*Grg.*525e; ἐμοὶ ἐκ πασέων Ζεὺς ἄλγε' ἔδωκεν to me *out of* (i.e. *above*) all, Il.18.431, cf. 432; ἐκ πάντων μάλιστα 4.96, cf. S.*Ant.*1137 (lyr.), etc.; redundant, εἷς τῶν ἐκ τῶν φίλων σου LXX *Jd.*15.2. 5. of Position, *outside of, beyond*, chiefly in early writers, ἐκ βελέων *out of* shot, Il.14.130, etc.; ἐκ καπνοῦ *out of* the smoke, Od.19.7; ἐκ πατρίδος *banished from* one's country, 15.272; ἐκ μέσου κατῆστο sate down *apart from* the company, Hdt.3.83; ἐξ ἠθέων τὸν ἥλιον ἀνατεῖλαι *out of* its accustomed quarters, Id.2.142; ἐξ ὀφθαλμῶν *out of* sight, Id.5.24; ἐξ ὁδοῦ *out of* the road, S.*OC*113. **6.** with Verbs of Rest, where previous motion is implied, *on, in*, δαῖέ οἱ ἐκ κόρυθος..πῦρ lighted a fire *from* (i.e. *on*) his helmet, Il.5.4; ἐκ ποταμοῦ χρόα νίζετο washed his body *in* the river (*with water from* the river), Od.6.224: freq. with Verbs signifying hang or fasten, σειρήν..ἐξ οὐρανόθεν κρεμάσαντες having hung a chain *from* heaven, Il.8.19; ἐκ πασσαλόφι κρέμασεν φόρμιγγα he hung his lyre *from* (i.e. *on*) the peg, Od.8.67; ἀνάπτεσθαι ἔκ τινος fasten *from* (i.e. *upon*) a thing, 12.51; μαχαίρας εἶχον ἐξ ἀργυρέων τελαμώνων Il.18.598; πρισθεὶς ἐξ ἀντύγων gripped *to* the chariot-rail, S.*Aj.*1030, etc.; ἐκ τοῦ βραχίονος ἵππον ἐπέλκουσα leading it [by a rein] *upon* her arm, Hdt.5.12: with Verbs signifying hold, lead, ἐξ ἐκείνων ἔχειν τὰς ἐλπίδας to have their hopes *dependent upon* them, Th.1.84; ἐκ χειρὸς ἄγειν lead *by* the hand, Bion *Fr.*7.2; ἐκ ποδὸς ἕπεσθαι ib.6.2; ἐκ τῆς οὐρᾶς λαμβάνεσθαι Luc.*Asin.*23: with the Art. indicating the place of origin, οἱ ἐκ τῶν νήσων κακοῦργοι the robbers *of* the islands, Th.1.8, cf. 2.5,13; τοὺς ἐκ τῆς ναυμαχίας those *in* the sea-fight, Pl. *Ap.*32b; τοὺς ἐκ τῶν σκηνῶν those *in* the tents, D.18.169; ἁρπασόμενοι τὰ ἐκ τῶν οἰκιῶν X.*Cyr.*7.2.5; οἱ ἐκ τοῦ πεδίου ἔθεον Id.*An.* 4.6.25: even with Verbs of sitting or standing, εἰσεῖδε στάσ' ἐξ Οὐλύμποιο *from* Olympus where she stood, Il.14.154; καθῆσθαι ἐκ πάγων to sit *on* the heights and look *from* them, S.*Ant.*411; στὰς ἐξ ἐπάλξεων ἄκρων E.*Ph.*1009; ἐκ βυθοῦ *at* the bottom, Theoc.22.40: phrases, ἐκ δεξιᾶς, ἐξ ἀριστερᾶς, *on* the right, left, X.*Cyr.*8.3.10, etc.; οἱ ἐξ ἐναντίας, οἱ ἐκ πλαγίου, ib.7.1.20; ἐκ θαλάσσης, opp. ἐκ τῆς μεσογείας, D.18.301. **7.** νικᾶν ἔκ τινος win a victory *over*.., *Apoc.*15.2. **II.** OF TIME, elliptic with Pron. relat. and demonstr., ἐξ οὗ [χρόνου] *since*, Il.1.6, Od.2.27, etc.; in apod., ἐκ τοῦ *from* that time, Il.8.296; ἐκ τούτου X.*An.*5.8.15, etc. (but ἐκ τοῖο thereafter, Il.1.493, and ἐκ τούτων or ἐκ τῶνδε usu. *after* this, X.*Mem.*2.9.4, S.*OT*235); ἐξ ἐκείνου Th.2.15; ἐκ πολλοῦ (sc. χρόνου) *for* a long time, Id.1.68, etc.; ἐκ πλέονος χρόνου Id.8.45; ἐκ πλείστου ib.68; ἐξ ὀλίγου *at* short notice, Id.2.11 (but also a short time *since*, Plu.*Caes.*28); ἐκ παλαιοῦ X.*Mem.*3.5.8; ἐκ παλαιτάτου Th.1.18. **2.** of particular points of time, ἐκ νεότητος..ἐς γῆρας Il.14.86; ἐκ γενετῆς 24.535; ἐκ νέου, ἐκ παιδός, *from* boyhood, Pl.*Grg.*510d, *R.*374c, etc.; ἐκ μικροῦ παιδαρίου D.53.19; ἐξ ἀρχῆς A.*Eu.*284, etc.; καύματος ἐξ *after* hot weather, Il.5.865; νέφος ἔρχεται οὐρανὸν εἴσω αἰθέρος ἐκ δίης *after* clear weather, 16.365; ἐκ δὲ αἰθρίης καὶ νηνεμίης συνδραμεῖν ἐξαπίνης νέφεα Hdt.1.87; so (like ἀπό II) ἐκ τῆς θυσίης γενέσθαι to have *just finished* sacrifice, ib.50, etc.; ἐκ τοῦ ἀρίστου *after* breakfast, X.*An.*4.6.21; ἐξ εἰρήνης πολεμεῖν to go to war *after* peace, Th. 1.120; γελάσαι ἐκ τῶν ἔμπροσθεν δακρύων X.*Cyr.*1.4.28; κάλλιστον ἦμαρ εἰσιδεῖν ἐκ χείματος A.*Ag.*900; τὴν θάλασσαν ἐκ Διονυσίων πλόϊμον εἶναι Thphr.*Char.*3.3; ἐκ χειμῶνος *at the end of* winter, Plu. *Nic.*20. **3.** *at, in*, ἐκ νυκτῶν Od.12.286; ἐκ νυκτός X.*Cyr.*1.4.2, etc.; ἐξ ἡμέρας S.*El.*780; ἐκ μέσω ἄματος Theoc.10.5; ἐκ τοῦ λοιποῦ or ἐκ τῶν λοιπῶν *for* the future, X.*Smp.*4.56, Pl.*Lg.*709e. **III.** OF ORIGIN, **1.** of Material, *out of* or *of* which things are made, γίγνεταί τι ἔκ τινος Parm.8.12; ποιεῦνται ἐκ ξύλων τὰ πλοῖα Hdt.1. 194; πίνοντας ἐκ κριθῶν μέθυ A.*Supp.*953; εἶναι ἐξ ἀδάμαντος Pl.*R.* 616c; ἐκ λευκῶ ἐλέφαντος αἰετοί Theoc.15.123; στράτευμα ἀλκιμώτατον ἂν γένοιτο ἐκ παιδικῶν X.*Smp.*8.32; συνετάττετο ἐκ τῶν ἔτι προσιόντων formed line of battle *from* the troops as they marched up, Id.*An.*1.8.14. **2.** of Parentage, ἔκ τινος εἶναι, γενέσθαι, etc., Il. 20.106, 6.206, etc.; ἐκ γὰρ ἐμεῦ γένος ἐσσί (where γένος is acc. abs.) 5.896; σῆς ἐξ αἵματός εἰσι γενέθλης 19.111; ὦ παῖ πατρὸς ἐξ Ἀχιλλέως S.*Ph.*260; πίρωμις ἐκ πιρώμιος Hdt.2.143; ἀγαθοὶ καὶ ἐξ ἀγαθῶν Pl.*Phdr.*246a; τὸν ἐξ ἐμῆς μητρός S.*Ant.*466, etc. **3.** of Place of Origin or Birth, ἐκ Σιδῶνος..εὔχομαι εἶναι Od.15.425, cf. Th.1.25, etc.; ἐκ τῶν ἄνω εἰμί *Ev.Jo.*8.23; ἡ ἐξ Ἀρείου πάγου βουλή the Areopagus, Arist.*Ath.*4.4, etc.; οἱ ἐκ τῆς διατριβῆς ταύτης Aeschin.1.54; οἱ ἐκ τοῦ Περιπάτου the Peripatetics, Luc.*Pisc.*43; ὁ ἐξ Ἀκαδημείας the Academic, Ath.1.34b; οἱ ἐκ πίστεως *Ep.Gal.*3.7; οἱ ἐξ ἐριθείας *Ep.Rom.*2.8. **4.** of the Author or Occasion of a thing, ὄναρ, τιμὴ ἐκ Διός ἐστιν, Il.1.63, 2.197, cf. Od.1.33, A.*Pers.*707, etc.; θάνατος ἐκ μνηστήρων death *by the hand of* the suitors, Od.16.447; τὰ ἐξ Ἑλλήνων τείχεα walls *built by* them, Hdt.2.148; κίνημα ἐξ αὐτοῦ *spontaneous* motion, Plot.6.1.21; ὕμνος ἐξ Ἐρινύων A.*Eu.*331 (lyr.); ἡ ἐξ ἐμοῦ δυσβουλία S.*Ant.*95; ὁ ἐξ ἐμοῦ πόθος Id.*Tr.*631. **5.** with the agent after Pass. Verbs, *by*, Poet. and early Prose, ἐφίληθεν ἐκ Διός they were beloved *of* (i.e. *by*) Zeus, Il.2.669; κήδε' ἐφῆπται ἐκ Διός ib. 70; προδεδόσθαι ἐκ Πρηξάσπεος Hdt.3.62; τὰ λεχθέντα ἐξ Ἀλεξάνδρου Id.7.175, cf. S.*El.*124 (lyr.), *Ant.*93, Th.3.69, Pl.*Ti.*47b; ἐξ ἁπάντων ἀμφισβητήσεται Id.*Tht.*171b; ὁμολογουμένους ἐκ πάντων X.*An.*2.6.1; τὰς ἐκ θεῶν τύχας δοθείσας S.*Ph.*1316, cf. Pl.*Ly.*204c: with neut. Verbs, ἐκ...πατρὸς κακὰ πείσομαι Od.2.134, cf. A.*Pr.*759; τλῆναί τι ἔκ τινος Il.5.384; θνῄσκειν ἔκ τινος S.*El.*579, *OT*854, etc.; τὰ γενόμενα ἐξ ἀνθρώπων Hdt.1.1. **6.** of Cause, Instrument, or Means *by* which a thing is done, ἐκ πατέρων φιλότητος *in consequence* of our fathers' friendship, Od.15.197; μήνιος ἐξ ὀλοῆς 3.135; ἐξ ἔριδος Il. 7.111; τελευτῆσαι ἐκ τοῦ τρώματος Hdt.3.29; ἐκ τίνος λόγου; E. *Andr.*548; ἐκ τοῦ; *wherefore?* Id.*Hel.*93; λέξον ἐκ τίνος ἐπλήγης X. *An.*5.8.4; ποιεῖτε ὑμῖν φίλους ἐκ τοῦ Μαμωνᾶ τῆς ἀδικίας make yourselves friends *of* (i.e. *by means of*).., *Ev.Luc.*16.9; ζῆν ἔκ τινος X. *HG*3.2.11 codd.; ἐκ τῶν ἰδίων τρέφειν ἐμαυτόν Isoc.15.152; ἐκ τόξων ἀνύσαι γαστρὶ φορβάν S.*Ph.*710 (lyr.). **7.** *in accordance with*, ἐκ τῶν λογίων Hdt.1.64; ὁ ἐκ τῶν νόμων χρόνος D.24.28; ἐκ κελεύματος A. *Pers.*397, cf. Sophr.25; ἐκ τῶν ξυγκειμένων Th.5.25; ἐκ τῶν παρόντων ib.40, etc.; ἐκ τῶν ἔργων κρινόμενοι X.*Cyr.*2.2.21, cf. A.*Pr.*485. **8.** freq. as periphr. for Adv., ἐκ προνοίας *IG*1[2].115.11; ἐκ βίας *by* force, S.*Ph.*563; ἐκ δόλου Id.*El.*279; ἐκ παντὸς τρόπου ζητεῖν Pl.*R.*499a: esp. with neut. Adjs., ἐξ ἀγχιμόλοιο, = ἀγχίμολον, Il.24.352; ἐκ τοῦ ἐμφανέος Hdt.3.150; ἐκ τοῦ φανεροῦ, ἐκ τοῦ προφανοῦς, Th.4.106, 6.73; ἐκ προδήλου S.*El.*1429; ἐξ ἴσου, ἐκ τοῦ ἴσου, Id.*Tr.*485, Th.2. 3; ἐξ ἀέλπτου Hdt.1.111, etc.: with fem. Adj., ἐκ τῆς ἰθέης Id.3. 127; ἐκ νέης Id.5.116; ἐξ ὑστέρης Id.6.85; ἐκ τῆς ἀντίης Id.8.6; ἐκ καινῆς Th.3.92; ἐξ ἑκουσίας S.*Tr.*727; ἐκ ταχείας ib.395. **9.** of Number or Measurement, with numerals, ἐκ τρίτων *in* the third *place*, E.*Or.*1178, Pl.*Grg.*500a, *Smp.*213b; distributively, *apiece*, Ath.15.671b. **b.** of Price, ἐξ ὀκτὼ ὀβολῶν *SIG*[2]587.206; ἐκ τριῶν δραχμῶν ib.283; συμφωνήσας ἐκ δηναρίου *Ev.Matt.*20.2. **c.** of Weight, ἐπιπέμματα ἐξ ἡμιχοινικίου *Inscr.Prien.*362 (iv B.C.). **d.** of Space, θινώδης ὢν ὁ τόπος ἐξ εἴκοσι σταδίων *by the space of* twenty stades, Str.8.3.19.

B. ἐκ is freq. separated from its CASE, Il.11.109, etc.—It takes an accent in anastrophe, 14.472, Od.17.518.—Ep. use it with Advbs. in -θεν, ἐξ οὐρανόθεν, ἐξ ἁλόθεν, ἐξ Αἰσύμηθεν, Il.17.548, 21. 335, 8.304; ἐκ Διόθεν Hes.*Op.*765; ἐκ πρῴρηθεν Theoc.22.11.—It is combined with other Preps. to make the sense more definite, as διέκ, παρέκ, ὑπέκ.

C. IN COMPOS. the sense of *removal* prevails; *out, away, off.* **2.** to express *completion*, like our *utterly*, ἐκπέρθω, ἐξαλαπάζω, ἐκβαρβαρόω, ἐκδιδάσκω, ἐκδιψάω, ἐκδωριεύομαι, ἐξοπλίζω, ἐξομματόω, ἔκλευκος, ἔκπικρος.

D. AS ADVERB, *therefrom*, Il.18.480.

ἐκαβόλος, ον, Dor. for ἑκηβόλος.

Ἑκαδήμεια, ἡ, old form for Ἀκαδήμεια, from the name of a hero Hecademos, D.L.3.8.

Ἑκάεργος, ὁ, expld. by Gramm. (*EM*319.51, etc.) as, = ὁ ἕκαθεν εἴργων or ἐργαζόμενος, Ep. epith. of Apollo, either Subst., Il.1.147, etc., or Adj., 5.439, Od.8.323, Call.*Ap.*11, etc.: fem., ὦ ἑκάεργε, of Artemis, Ar.*Th.*972 (lyr.):—also **Ἑκαέργη**, a daughter of Boreas, Call.*Del.*292. **II.** Pythag. name for *nine*, ἀπὸ τοῦ εἴργειν τὴν ἑκὰς πρόβασιν τοῦ ἀριθμοῦ *Theol.Ar.*58. (This word and its cognates (e.g. ἑκατηβελέτης), although connected by Greek writers with ἑκάς, may have originally contained the stem ἑκητ- (cf. ἑκών) 'at will'; for the formation of ϝεκα(τ)-ϝεργός, cf. γυναι(κ)-μανής.)

ἕκαθεν, Adv., (ἑκάς) *from afar*, Il.2.456, Pi.*O.*10(11).7, A.*Supp.* 421 (lyr.), and late Prose, Corn.*ND*32, D.C.50.33: c. gen., ἕκαθεν πόλιος Il.13.107 (al. ἑκάς). **II.** = ἑκάς, *far off, far away*, Od.17. 25. **III.** = ἀνέκαθεν, *Schwyzer* 702 (Erythrae, iv B.C.).

Ἑκάλειος Ζεύς [ᾰ], from Ἑκάλη, a lady who entertained Theseus, and for this received at Athens the yearly honour of the **Ἑκαλήσια** [ἱερά]: hence the epith. was given to Zeus as worshipped on the same day, Plu.*Thes.*14.

ἑκαλία· πόρρωθεν, Hsch. **ἑκάλλιθμος**· ἱερός, ἀφειμένος, Id.

ἕκαλος, Dor. for ἕκηλος, Pi.*O.*9.58, *I.*7(6).41.

ἑκανόμος· ἀγελαῖος φιμός, Hsch.

ἑκάς, Adv. *afar, far off*, Il.20.422, etc.; οὐχ ἑκάς που S.*Ph.*41; rare in Prose, Th.1.69, 80 (and later, Nic.Dam.p.6 D.): c. gen., *far from, far away from*, ἑ. Ἄργεος Il.9.246, etc.: freq. following its case, 13.263, Od.14.496, al.; οὐ Χαρίτων ἑ. Pi.*P.*8.21, cf. E.*Ph.*907; ἑ. ἀπὸ τείχεος Il.18.256; ἀπὸ τῆς νήσου ἑ. Hdt.3.41. **2.** Comp. ἑκαστέρω *farther*, Od.7.321, *h.Bacch.*29, Alc.*Supp.*5.8 (ἐκ-), Hdt.6.108, E.*HF*1047 (lyr.), etc.: c. gen., Hdt.2.169, al.; also ἑκαστοτέρω dub. in Theoc.15.7: Sup. ἑκαστάτω *farthest*, Il.10.113, Hdt.4.33: c. gen., τοὺς ἑωυτῶν ἑ. οἰκημένους *farthest from*.., Id.1.134; τῆς Λιβύης ἑ. ἦλθε *to the farthest point* of Libya, Id.4.204, cf. 9.14. **II.** of Time, ἑ. ἐών *afar*, i.e. *long after*, Pi.*P.*2.54; οὐχ ἑ. χρόνου in no *long* time, Hdt.8.144; οὐχ ἑ. A.*Ag.*1650. [ᾰ; ᾱ only in Call.*Ap.*2, in arsi.] (Prob. from ἕ and -κάς as in ἀνδρακάς; lit. 'by himself'.)

ἑκάς, άδος, ἡ, a division of land (?), *Rev.Phil.*48.98 (Dura).

ἑκαστ-άκις, Adv., (ἕκαστος) *each* or *every time*, *IG*9(1).694.8 (Corc.); οἱ ἑκαστάκις ἐόντες ἄρχοντες, = οἱ ἀεὶ ἄ., ib.22: **-άκι** *GDI* 3051 (Chalcedon). **-άτω**, v. ἑκάς. **-άχη**, Adv. *everywhere*, Suid.; f.l. for ἕκαστα in X.*Cyr.*6.2.5. **-αχόθεν**, Adv. *from every side*, Th.7.20, 21, X.*HG*3.4.3. **-αχόθι**, Adv. = ἑκάστοθι, *on each side*, Plu.*Lys.*19, *PLips.*119[r]. **-αχοῖ**, Adv. *to each side, every way*, Plu.*Mar.*20, Hdn.Gr.1.502. **-αχόσε**, Adv. *to each side*, Th.4.55, 8.5, Pl.*Criti.*116a. **-άχου**, Adv. *everywhere*, Th.3.82, Pl.*Phdr.* 257e, al. **-έρω**, v. ἑκάς. **-οθεν**, Adv. = ἑκασταχόθεν, Cleobul. ap.D.L.1.93. **-οθι**, Adv. *for each* or *every one*, Od.3.8 (v.l. ἑκάστοθεν), Aen.Tact.11.11.

ἕκαστος, η, ον, *each*, opp. the whole body, Il.2.805, etc.: sg. with pl. Verb, ἔβαν οἰκόνδε ἕκαστος they went home *each* to his own house, 1.606; δεδμήμεσθα ἕκαστος 5.878, cf. Hdt.3.158; so in Att., Ar.*Pl.* 785, Pl.*Prt.*327e, etc.; ὅτι ἕκαστος ἐπίστασθε ἀγαθόν X.*Smp.*3.3: sg. in apposition with pl. Noun or Pron., which expresses the whole, Τρῶας δὲ τρόμος αἰνὸς ὑπήλυθε γυῖα ἕκαστον Il.7.215; ὔμμι..ἑκάστῳ 15.109; αἱ δὲ γυναῖκες..θαύμαζον..ἑκάστη 18.496, etc.; Περσίδες δ'.. ἑκάστα..λείπεται A.*Pers.*135 (lyr.); αἱ ἄλλαι πᾶσαι [τέχναι] τὸ αὑτῆς ἑκάστη ἔργον ἐργάζεται Pl.*R.*346d, cf. *Grg.*503e; ὅστις ἕκαστος *every one* which.. (nisi leg. ὥς τις), Hes.*Th.*459. **2.** the Art. is sts. added to the Subst. (so regularly in earlier Att. Inscrr., *IG*1[2].22.14, al., exc. ἑκάστου μηνός ib.6.125) with which ἕκαστος agrees, in which case ἕκαστος is commonly put first, καθ' ἑ. τὴν ἡμέραν *every single* day, Isoc.12.211, etc.; περὶ ἑ. τῆς τέχνης Pl.*Phdr.*274e: also following the Subst., κατὰ τὸν ὁπλίτην ἕκαστον Th.5.49; κατὰ τὴν ἡμέραν ἑκάστην Id.6.63, al. II. in pl., *all and each severally*, Il.1.550, al., A. *Supp.*932, etc.; οἷστισιν ἑκάστοις to whichsoever *severally*, Pl.*Lg.* 799a. 2. *each* of two or more groups or parties, Od.9.164, Hdt. 1.169, A.*Pr.*491, Th.6.77, etc. III. strengthd. by the addition of other Prons., εἷς ἑ. (v. εἷς); εἷς τις ἑ. S.*Ant.*262; ἕκαστός τις *each* one, Pi.*N.*4.92, Th.3.45, etc.; ταῦτα ἕκαστα Hdt.5.13, etc.; αὔθ' ἕκαστα *all in exact detail*, A.*Pr.*950. 2. with Preps., esp. κατά, καθ' ἕκαστον *singly, by itself*, Pl.*Tht.*188a, al.; καθ' ἑ. καὶ σύμπαντα Id. *Sph.*259b; τὸ καθ' ἑ., τὰ καθ' ἕκαστα, *particulars*, Arist.*Ph.*189^{a}6, *EN* 1143^{b}4, al.; παρ' ἕκαστον, παρ' ἕκαστα, in *every case*, Plb.4.82.5, 3.57.4, etc.; παρ' ἕκαστον καὶ ἔργον καὶ λόγον διδάσκοντες Pl.*Prt.*325d; παρ' ἕκαστον λέγων *constantly* interjecting, Men.*Epit.*48. 3. ὡς ἕκαστοι *each by himself*, Hdt.6.79, Th.1.15, etc.: in sg., τῶν δὲ ὡς ἑκάστῳ θύειν θέλει Hdt.1.132, cf. Pi.*P.*9.98; οὐχ ὡς ἕ. ἀλλὰ πάντες Arist.*Pol.* 1292^{a}12, cf. 1283^{b}34. IV. later, = ἑκάτερος, D.H.3.2 codd. (Ϝέκαστος *Leg.Gort.*1.9, al., *Schwyzer* 409.4 (Elis), *IG*9(1).334.9 (Locris). Apptly. connected with ἑκάς by Dam.*Pr.*423.)

ἑκάστοτε, Adv. *each time, on each occasion*, Parm.16.1, Hdt.1.90, Antipho 6.13, X.*An.*2.4.10, Pl.*R.*393b; ἀεὶ.. ἑ. Ar.*Nu.*1280; ἑ. πολλάκις Pl.*Phlb.*58a; ἵνα ἑ. wherever *on each occasion*, Hdt.8.115.

ἑκαστοτέρω, v. ἑκάς.

ἑκᾰτᾱβόλος, ον, Dor. for ἑκατηβ-, Terp.2, Tim.*Pers.*249.

Ἑκᾰταῖος, α, ον, *of Hecate*, μαγίδες S.*Fr.*734. II. Ἑκάταιον or Ἑκάτειον (cj. in Ar.*V.*804, cf. Suid.), τό, *statue* or *chapel of Hecate*, placed at the entrance of houses or where three roads meet (ἐν τριόδοις), Ar. l. c., *Ra.*366, cf. Hsch. 2. Ἑκαταῖα, τά, v. Ἑκάτη II.

ἑκᾰτερ-άκις, Adv., (ἑκάτερος) *at each time*, X.*Cyr.*4.6.4; *in both directions*, Gal.*UP*8.7. **-έω**, in dancing, *kick the rump with one heel after another*, Hsch. (but cf. ἑκατερίς). **-η**, Cret. Adv. *on either side*, *Schwyzer* 197.4 (iii B.C.); Ϝεκ- ib.186.18 (ii B.C.). **-θε**, before a vowel **-θεν**, poet. Adv. = ἑκατέρωθεν, *on each side, on either hand*, ἀμφίπολός οἱ.. ἑ. παρέστη Od.1.335; τρεῖς ἑ. Il.11.27, cf. A.R. 1.564: also in late Ion. Prose, Aret.*SD*2.3. 2. c. gen., ἑ. ὁμίλου Il.3.340, 23.813, cf. 329; ἑ. πόληος Od.6.263. **-ίς**, ίδος, ἡ, a dance with χειρῶν κίνησις, Poll.4.102 (but cf. ἑκατερέω). **-ος** (Dor. Ϝεκ- *Leg.Gort.*1.18, *Michel* 995 *A* 49 (Delph.)), α, ον, *each of two, each singly*, opp. ἀμφότεροι, Lys.2.33; εἷς ἑ. Syngr.ap.D.35.12; αὐτὸ τὸ ἑ. καὶ τὸ ἀμφότερον Pl.*Hp.Ma.*303a, cf. Pi.*I.*8(7).31, Th.1.20, etc.; when joined with a Subst., the Subst. almost always takes the Art. (so in Att. Inscrr. exc. *IG*1^2.372.137), as ἐφ' ἑ. τῷ κέρᾳ Th.5.67; ἐπὶ τῷ κέρᾳ ἑ. Id.4.93; ἑ. τῇ πόλει Id.5.16: sts. with Noun or Pron. in gen., ἑκάτερος ἡμῶν Id.6.17; ἑκατέρᾳ τῶν χειρῶν D.S.4.10: as nom. to pl. Verb, sts. in pl., esp. when one or both parties are in pl., ἐδικαίευν ἑκάτεροι Hdt.9.26, Pl.*R.*348b, etc.: in sg. with Verb in pl., ταῦτα εἰπόντες ἀπῆλθον ἑκάτερος ἐπὶ τὰ προσήκοντα X.*Cyr.*5.2.22, cf. 6. 1.19; repeated in ref. to each of two parties, ἐὰν ἑκάτεροι ἑκατέρων τέμνωσιν ἀγρούς Pl.*R.*470d: with Particles and Preps., ὡς ἑκάτεροι Th.3.74; ἐφ' ἑκάτερα *both* ways, Id.5.73; καθ' ἑκάτερα X.*An.*5.6.7; ἐξ ἑκατέρων Luc.*Am.*14. 2. = ἕκαστος, Id.*Alex.*49. **-ω**, Dor. Adv. *on either side*, τᾶς τραπέζας *Schwyzer* 251 *A* 10 (Cos). **-ωθεν**, Adv. *on each side, on either hand*, Hdt.3.102, Th.2.75: c. gen., ἑ. τῆς πόλεως Id.3.6; τὸ ἑ. μέρος Pl.*Phd.*112e; *at each end*, *Gp.*5.27.4. 2. *on both sides, by father and mother*, Poll.8.85. **-ωθι**, Adv. *on either side*, Pi.*O.*2.69, Hdt.2.19, 106, Arist.*Ath.*54.8, etc. **-ως**, Adv. *in either way*, Pl.*Lg.*895e, Ph.1.316; *in both languages*, i.e. Greek and Latin, *Inscr.Prien.*105.30 (i B.C.). **-ωσε**, Adv. *to either side, either way*, ἀποβλέπειν, φοιτᾶν, X.*An.*1.8.14, Pl.*Grg.* 523c. 2. *both ways*, καθιέναι Id.*Phd.*112e; τὰ ὑπερβάλλοντα ἑ. Id.*R.*619a.

Ἑκάτη [ᾰ], ἡ, (ἕκᾰτος) *Hecate*, lit. *she who works her will*, Hes.*Th.* 411, *h.Cer.*25, 52, E.*Fr.*955, etc.; Ἑ. φωσφόρος Ar.*Fr.*594a, E.*Fr.* 968. b. v. ἕκατος. II. Ἑκάτης δεῖπνον *Hecate's* dinner, a meal set out by rich persons at the foot of her statue ἐν τριόδοις on the 30th day of each month, when it became a sort of dole for beggars and paupers, Ar.*Pl.*594 et Sch. ad loc., cf. Plu.2.280c, 290d, *AB*247: hence, as it consisted of offal, Ἑκαταῖα κατεσθίειν, of a rapscallion, D.54.39, cf. Luc.*DMort.*1.1.

ἑκάτη, ἡ, *stake* to which criminals were bound for scourging, Hsch.

ἑκᾰτη-βελέτης, ου, ὁ, = sq., ἄναξ Il.1.75, Hes.*Sc.*100: Subst., *h.Ap.*157:—fem. **-βελέτις**, ιδος, ἡ, Pythag. name for *six*, *Theol.Ar.* 37.

ἑκᾰτηβόλος, ον, Dor. ἑκατᾱ- (q.v.), epith. of Apollo, Hom., Hes.: as Subst., Il.15.231; also of Artemis, *h.Hom.*9.6. (Expld. by the ancients as, = *far-darting*, Hsch., etc. (or, *shooting a hundred* βέλη, Id.); but perh. originally, *hitting the mark at will*, cf. ἑκάεργος.)

Ἑκᾰτήσιον, τό, = Ἑκάταιον, Plu.2.193f. II. Ἑκατήσια, τά, *festival of Hecate*, *SIG*1066.15 (Cos). III. Adj., Ἑκατήσιος, α, ον, *of Hecate*, Man.5.302, Poll.1.37.

ἕκᾰτι, Dor. and Trag. for ἕκητι (q.v.), Pi.*O.*4.10, E.*Or.*26, etc.

Ἑκᾰτικός, ή, όν, *of Hecate*, φάσματα Marin.*Procl.*28; λόγοι *Tab. Defix.Aud.*41 *A* 11 (written -ικίοις).

ἑκᾰτόγ-γυιος, ον, *with a hundred limbs* or *bodies*, κορᾶν ἀγέλα ἑκατόγγυιος a band of 100 maidens, Pi.*Fr.*122.15. **-κάρᾱνος** [κᾰ], ον, = sq., A.*Pr.*355. **-κεφάλας** [φᾰ], α, ὁ, *hundred-headed*, Pi. *O.*4.8, Ar.*Ra.*473, *Nu.*336. **-κέφᾰλος**, ον, = foreg., E.*HF*883 (anap.). **-κρᾱνος**, ον, = foreg., Pi.*P.*8.16. **-χειρ**, χειρος, ὁ, ἡ, = sq., Acus.8 J., Pi.*Pae.*8.31, Orph.*Fr.*57, al., Corn.*ND*17, etc. **-χειρος**, ον, *hundred-handed*, of Briareus, Il.1.402.

ἑκατόζῠγος, ον, *with* 100 *benches for rowers*, Il.20.247.

ἑκᾰτόμ-βαιος, α, ον, epith. of Apollo and Zeus, *to whom hecatombs were offered*, Hsch., *EM*321.7. 2. (sc. μήν) name of a month, *Hemerolog.Flor.* II. ἑκατόμβαια, τά, = ἑκατόμβοια, *CIG*1715 (Delph.). **-βαιών**, ῶνος, ὁ, *the month Hecatombaeon*, in which ἑκατόμβαι were offered at Athens and elsewhere, Antipho 6.44, Plu. *Thes.*12, *IG*11(2).203 *A* 31, al. (Delos, iii B.C.), etc.; μῆνα ἐμβάλλειν Ἑ. ib.1^2.76.53. **-βεύς**, έως, ὁ (sc. μήν), = foreg., at Sparta, Hsch. **-βη**, ἡ, (ἑκατόν, βοῦς) prop. *an offering of a hundred oxen*; but even in Hom., generally, *sacrifice*, Il.6.115 (apptly. of twelve oxen, cf. 93), Od.3.59; of bulls and goats, Il.1.315; of fifty rams, 23.146; of three victims, *Schwyzer* 726.19 (Milet.); Com., πουλυπόδων ἑ. Anaxandr.41. 29 (anap.); ᾠῶν ἑ. Ephipp.8.4: metaph., ὅστις στρατηγεῖ μὴ στρατιώτης γενόμενος οὗτος ἑ. ἐξάγει τοῖς πολεμίοις Men.640. II. name of an *eye-salve*, Alex.Trall.2. III. festival at Geronthrae, *IG*5(1). 1120. **-βιος**, ὁ, epith. of Apollo, *SIG*1024.30 (Myconos). II. (sc. μήν) name of month at Halos, *IG*9(2).109*b* 50. III. Ἑκατόμβιον, τό, *shrine of Apollo* Ἑκατόμβιος, ib.9(1).87.76 (Hyampolis). 2. Ἑκατόμβια, τά, = Ἑκατόμβοια, at Amorgos, *IG*12(7).388, al. **-βοΐδιον**· ἑκατὸν βοῶν τιμή, Hsch. **-βοιος**, ον, (βοῦς) *worth a hundred oxen*, Il.2.449, etc.: expld. as *worth* 100 *pieces of money*, the ancient coins being stamped with an ox, Eust.252.18, *EM*320.47. II. ἑκατόμβοια (sc. ἱερά), τά, *festival at which hecatombs were offered*, *SIG* 36.36 (Delph., v B.C.), 82.6 (Delph., v B.C.), *BCH*29.243 (Delos), *IG* 5(2).142 (Tegea), Str.8.4.11 codd.: dat. Ἑκατομβούοις (sic) *Schwyzer* 91.19 (Argos). **-πεδος**, ον, (πούς) *a hundred feet long*, πυρὴ ἑκατόμπεδος ἔνθα καὶ ἔνθα *a hundred feet* all ways, Il.23.164; νεώς Th. 3.68 (v.l. -ποδος), *IG*1^2.256, al., cf. Pi.*I.*6(5).22, *Tab.Heracl.*2.24, al.; ὁ ἑ. Παρθενών Plu.*Per.*13; ἡ ἑ. Id.*Dio*45; τὸ Ἑ. on the Acropolis of Athens, *IG*1^2.4.10, 18; at Dodona, Ptol.*Geog.*3.13.5. **-πηχυς**, υ, *of* 100 *cubits*, Hsch. and Apollon.*Lex.* s.v. ἑκατόγχειρον. **-πολις**, ι, *with a hundred cities*, Κρήτη Il.2.649; of Laconia, Str.8.4.11:—also **ἑκᾰτοντάπολις** [τᾰ], Κρήτη Id.10.4.15. **-πους**, ποδος, ὁ, ἡ, *hundred-footed*: in S.*OC*718 (lyr.), ἑκατόμποδες Νηρῇδες, some take it literally to mean *the* 50 *Nereids* (the number assigned to them by Hes.*Th.*264, Pi.*I.*6(5).6, A.*Fr.*174, E.*IT*427), others *the* 100 *Nereids* (Pl.*Criti.* 116e), others merely to express a notion of *multitude*. **-πτολίεθρος**, ον, = ἑκατόμπολις, E.*Fr.*472.3 (anap.). **-πῠλός**, ον, *hundred-gated*, Θῆβαι Il.9.383, D.P.249. **-φόνια** (sc. ἱερά), τά, *sacrifice for a hundred enemies slain*, Paus.4.19.3, Plu.2.159e, *Rom.*25, Polyaen.2. 31.2.

ἑκᾰτόν, Arc. ἑκοτόν *IG*5(2).3 (Tegea, iv B.C.), οἱ, αἱ, τά, indecl.:—*a hundred*, Il.2.510, etc.: in compds. freq. loosely for *very many*. (Dissim. from *sém k̂m̥tóm*, cf. εἷς and Lat. *centum*, Lith. *šimtas*, etc.)

ἑκᾰτον-δεκάρουρος [ᾰρ], ὁ, *holder of* 110 ἄρουραι, *PCair.Zen.*1.23 (iii B.C.). **-ζυγος**, = ἑκατόζυγος, Hsch. **-σεμνον**· πολύ, μέγα, Id.

ἑκᾰτονστάτηρον [στᾰ], τό, *sum of* 100 *staters*, *Leg.Gort.*9.47.

ἑκᾰτοντά-βιβλος [τᾰ], ον, *in a hundred books*, πραγματεῖαι Gal. 10.37. **-γράμμᾰτος**, ον, *having a hundred letters*, ὄνομα *PMag. Par.*1.1209, 1380. **-δόχος**, ον, *holding a hundred*, ἀνδρῶνες Jul. *Ep.*180. **-δραχμος**, ον, *weighing a hundred drachms*, Gal. 13.491. **-εβδομηκονταπλᾰσίων**, ον, gen. ονος, 170 *times as great*, Olymp.*in Mete.*118.21:—also **ἑκατοντᾰκαιεβδ-**, Ptol.*Alm.*5. 16. **-ετηρίς**, ίδος, ἡ, *period of* 100 *years*, Pl.*R.*615a. **-έτηρος**, ον, *of a hundred years*, Orph.*A.*1108. **-έτης**, ες, *of a hundred years*, βιοτά Pi.*P.*4.282; 100 *years old*, Lxx *Ge.*17.17. **-ετία**, ἡ, *period of* 100 *years*, Ph.1.101. **-θύσᾰνος** [ῠ], ον, *with a hundred tassels*, αἰγίς Jul.*Ep.*180. **-κάρηνος**, Dor. -ᾱνος [κᾰ], ον, *hundred-headed*, Pi. *P.*1.16. **-κέφᾰλος**, ον, = foreg., γίγας Jul.*Ep.*180. **-κικαιεικοσάκι**, 120 *times*, Ptol.*Alm.*5.19. **-κις**, Adv. *hundred times*, Hero *Bel.*113.7, Orib.*Fr.*113. **-κλῖνος**, ον, *with* 100 *couches, with room for* 100 *couches*, of a room, Chares ap.Ath.12.538c, D.S.17.16, J.*BJ*5. 4.4. **-κρήπις**, ιδος, ὁ, ἡ, *with a hundred steps*, βωμοί Jul.*Ep.*180.

ἑκᾰτον-τᾰλαντία, ἡ, *sum of* 100 *talents*, Poll.9.52. **-τάλαντος** [τᾰ], ον, *worth* 100 *talents*, γραφὴ ἑ. an action *for damages laid at that sum*, Ar.*Eq.*442.

ἑκᾰτοντά-μᾰχος [τᾰ], ον, *able to fight* 100 *men*, J.*AJ*13.12.5. **-μιγμα**, ατος, τό, *a compound remedy*, Gal.14.152.

ἑκᾰτόντ-ανδρος, ον, *consisting of* 100 *men*, λοχαγία Jul.*Ep.*180.

ἑκᾰτοντά-πεδος [τᾰ], ον, = ἑκατόμπεδος, νεώς Jul.*Ep.*180. **-πηχυς**, υ, *of* 100 *cubits*, J.*BJ*2.10.2. **-πλάσιος** [πλᾰ], ον, = sq., Simp.*in Ph.*1115.33. Adv. -ίως Lxx 1 *Ch.*21.3. **-πλᾰσίων**, ον, gen. ονος, *a hundred times as much* or *many*, c. gen., X.*Oec.*2.3: without gen., *a hundredfold*, Lxx 2 *Ki.*24.3; καρπός *Ev.Luc.*8.8. **-πλεθρος**, ον, *of* 100 *plethra*, ἄρουραι Jul.*Ep.*180. **-πολις**, v. ἑκατόμπολις. **-πῠλος**, ον, = ἑκατόμπυλος, Θήβη *AP*7.7, cf. Jul.*Ep.*180; Ῥώμη *IG*14.1389 ii 3 (-οπυλ- lapis).

ἑκᾰτοντ-άρουρος [ᾰρ], ον, *holder of* 100 ἄρουραι, *PHal.*20.4, 5 (iii B.C.), *PGiss.*2.10 (ii B.C.), etc. **-αρχέω**, *to be a centurion*, D.C.52. 25. **-άρχης**, ου, ὁ, *leader of a hundred*, Hdt.7.81, A.*Fr.*182; = ταξίαρχος (q.v.), Ascl.*Tact.*2.8, etc.; = Lat. *centurio*, D.H.2.13 (v.l. -χοι), *Act.Ap.*10.1, J.*AJ*9.7.2, Plu.*Pomp.*78, etc. **-αρχία**, ἡ, *post of a centurion*, Onos.34.2 (pl.), D.C.78.5. II. *centurion's command, century*, J.*BJ*3.6.2, Ph.2.33 (pl.). 2. *body of* 128 *light-armed troops*, Ascl.*Tact.*6.3, etc. **-άρχιον**, τό, name of an *eye-salve*,

Aët.7.11, al. **-αρχος,** ὁ, = ἑκατοντάρχης, X.*Cyr.*5.3.41, *Ev.Matt.* 8.5, Ph.2.131, Plu.*Luc.*35, Arr.*Tact.*10.3. **-άς,** άδος, ἡ, the number *a hundred*, Hdt.7.184: pl., Ph.2.423, Jul.*Ep.*180.

ἑκᾰτοντά-στῡλος, ον, *having* 100 *columns*, Aristeas 116, *BCH*11.100 (Thyatira). **-φυλλος,** ον, *with* 100 *petals*, ῥόδα Thphr.*HP* 6.6.4. **-χειρ,** χειρος, ὁ, ἡ, = ἑκατόγχειρ, Plu.2.478f (as v.l.), Jul. *Ep.*180: also **-χειρος,** ον, Hsch. s.v. Βριάρεῳ. **-χοος,** ον, contr. **-χους,** ουν, *of* 100 *measures*: *yielding fruit a hundredfold*, Thphr.*HP* 8.7.4; κριθή Str.15.3.11.

ἑκᾰτοντ-έρῐφον, τό, *sacrifice of* 100 *kids*, *IG*12(5).908 (Tenos). **-όργυιος,** ον, 100 *fathoms high*, ἀνδριάς Pi.*Fr.*282: in Ar.*Av.*1131 μῆκος ἑκατοντορόγυιον shd. be read. **-ορος,** ον, (ἐρέσσω) *hundred-oared*, Poll.1.82. **-ούτης,** ου, ὁ, contr. for ἑκατονταέτης, Luc.*Macr.* 14:—fem. **-οῦτις,** ιδος, Ath.15.697e.

ἕκᾰτος, ὁ, shortd. fr. ἑκατη-βόλος (q.v.), epith. of Apollo, Il.7.83, 20.295:—as Subst., **ἕκατος,** ὁ, 1.385, 20.71 (connected with ἑκατόν (sc. βέλη) by Simon.26A):—fem. **ἑκάτη,** epith. of Artemis, A.*Supp.* 676 (lyr.), Corn.*ND*32.

ἑκᾰτοστ-εύω, *bear a hundredfold*, Lxx *Ge.*26.12. **-ήριος,** α, ον, *subject to a tax of one per cent.*, οἰκίη *GDI*5661.13 (Chios):—Subst. **-ηρία,** Ion. **-ίη,** ἡ, *tax of one per cent.*, ib.48, *PCair.Zen.*12.76, al. **-ιαῖος,** α, ον, = ἑκατοστός: ἑκατοστιαῖοι τόκοι interest *of* $\frac{1}{100}$ *monthly*, i.e. twelve per cent. per ann., *IG*2^{2}.1104.4, *PGrenf.*2.89 (vi A.D.).

ἑκᾰτοστο-εικοστόγδοον, τό, *a* 128*th part*, Nicom.*Ar.*1.8. **-εικοστός,** ή, όν, 120*th*, Paul.Aeg.2.6.

ἑκᾰτόστομος, ον, *hundred-mouthed*, E.*Ba.*406 (lyr.).

ἑκᾰτοστός, ή, όν, *hundredth*, Hdt.1.47, etc.; ἐπ' ἑκατοστὰ ἐκφέρειν to bear *a hundredfold*, Id.4.198. II. ἑκατοστή, ἡ, *tax of one per cent.*, Ar.*V.*658, X.*Ath.*1.17, *PGnom.*85, etc.; ἐκ τῶν χρημάτων ἑ. *IG*2.721*A* i 12: also, = τόκοι ἑκατοστιαῖοι, Plu.*Luc.*20.

ἑκᾰτόστῡλος, ον, = ἑκατοντάστυλος, *having* 100 *columns* (sc. κρήνη), *Abh.Berl.Akad.*1904(2).13.

ἑκᾰτοστύς, ύος, ἡ, = ἑκατοντάς, X.*Cyr.*6.3.34, Plu.*Rom.*8. II. a division of a community, *a hundred*, Aen.Tact.11.10a, *IPE*1^{2}.79.30 (Olbia, i A.D.), *Milet.*3 No.153 (Byzantium), *SIG*645.61 (Seleucia Cilic., ii B.C.), *CIG*3641*b* (Lampsacus), etc.

ἑκᾰτόφυλλον, τό, *hundred-petalled rose*, *Gloss.*

ἑκᾰτῶρυξ, ῠγος, ὁ, dub. sens. in *IPE*4.80*B*6.

ἔκαχεν· ὑπήντησεν, Hsch. (leg. ἔκιχεν).

ἐκβᾰβάζω (or perh. **-βαβράζω**), glossed by ἐκσαλεύω, S.*Fr.*139 (ap.Hsch.).

ἐκβάζω, *speak out, declare*, A.*Ag.*498.

ἐκβαίνω, fut. -βήσομαι: aor. ἐξέβην: pf. ἐκβέβηκα:—*step out of* or *off from*, c. gen., πέτρης ἐκβαίνοντα Il.4.107; ἔκβαιν' ἀπήνης A.*Ag.* 906; ἐ. ἐκ τῆς νεώς Th.1.137 (so in tmesi, ἐκ δὲ Χρυσηῒς νηὸς βῆ Il.1.439): abs., *step out of* a ship or chariot, *disembark, dismount*, ἐκ δ' ἔβαν αὐτοί 3.113, cf. 1.437, Hdt.4.196, etc.; *step out of* the sea, Od. 5.415, 7.278; *debouch from* a defile, X.*An.*4.2.3; καταστρατοπεδεύσασθαι ἐπὶ λόφον ἐκβάντες ib.6.3.20: rarely exc. of persons, but βοὴ ..ἐξέβη νάπους S.*Aj.*892. 2. *go out of, depart from*, ψυχὴ ἐ. ἐκ τοῦ σώματος Pl.*Phd.*77d; ἐκ τοῦ πολέμου Plb.3.40.7: c. gen., ἐ. τύχης E.*IT*907; ἐ. τῆς ἑαυτοῦ ἰδέας Pl.*R.*380d; τῆς λεκτικῆς ἁρμονίας Arist.*Po.*1449^{a}27; τι τῆς εἰωθυίας διαίτης Pl.*R.*406b; ἔνθεν ἐ. Id. *Ti.*44e; *withdraw from*, ἐκ τῆς νομοθεσίας Id.*Lg.*744a; μισθώσεως, γεωργίας, *BGU*1120.52 (i B.C.), *PTeb.*309.14 (ii A.D.). 3. c. acc., *leave*, τὴν πλατεῖαν Herod.6.53, cf. Phld.*D.*3.11: but, b. usu. with the sense, *outstep, overstep*, γαίας ὅρια E.*HF*82; τὴν ἡλικίαν τοῦ γεννᾶν Pl.*R.*461b; τριάκοντα ἔτη ib.537d; τὸν ὅρκον v.l. in Id.*Smp.* 183b; τὸ μέσον Arist.*Pol.*1296^{a}26. 4. in Poets, the instrument of motion is added in acc., ἐκβὰς..ἁρμάτων πόδα E.*Heracl.*802. 5. *to be produced*, of crops, οἱ ἐκβησόμενοι καρποί *PLips.*23.20 (iv A.D.), etc. 6. *project*, of ground, *PTeb.*84.91 (ii B.C.). II. metaph., 1. *come out, turn out*, Hdt.7.209; τῇ περ ὤρων ἐκβησόμενα πρήγματα ταῦτα ibid.; τὰ μέλλοντά σφι ἐκβαίνειν ib.221, cf. Th.7.14, etc.; of a total obtained by measurement, *PAmh.*2.31 (ii B.C.). 2. *to be fulfilled*, of prophecies, etc., D.19.28; also τοιοῦτον ἐκβέβηκεν S.*Tr.*672; κάκιστος ἐ. *to prove* a villain, E.*Med.*229; κατὰ νοῦν ἐ. τινί Pl.*Mx.*247d; ἄν τι μὴ κατὰ γνώμην ἐκβῇ D.1.16; τὸ ἐκβάν, τὰ ἐκβαίνοντα, *the issue, event*, D.1.11, Plb.2.27.5. 3. *go out of due bounds*, ἐς τοῦτ' ἐκβέβηκ' ἀλγηδόνος E.*Med.*56; ποῖ ποτ' ἐξέβης λόγῳ; S.*Ph.*896; ἐξέβην γὰρ ἄλλοσε I *wandered* elsewhere in thought, E. *IT*781; in writing, *digress*, ἐπάνειμι ἔνθεν ἐξέβην X.*HG*6.5.1, cf. 7.4.1, D.18.211, Pl.*Lg.*864c. 4. *project, extend beyond* a limit, *POxy.* 918 xi 20 (ii A.D.): metaph., *transcend*, ἐ. ὑπὲρ τὸ μέγα ὂν καὶ ὑπὲρ τὸ μικρόν Porph.*Sent.*34. 5. *lapse*, πρὶν ἐκβῆναί τινι τὴν στρατηγίαν App.*Syr.*23. 6. ἐκβαίνοντος μηνός, = φθίνοντος μ., *IG*14.105 (Syracus.).

B. causal, in aor. 1 -έβησα:—*cause to go out*, esp. *put ashore, land from* a ship, ἐκ δ' ἑκατόμβην βῆσαν Il.1.438; οἵ δ' ἐκβήσαντές [σε] ἔβησαν (where ἔβησαν is aor. 2) Od.24.301; ἐς γαῖαν ἐξέβησέ [με] E. *Hel.*1616.

ἐκβάκχ-ευσις, εως, ἡ, *Bacchic enthusiasm*, Eun.*VS* p.470B. **-εύω,** *excite to Bacchic frenzy*, φρένας E.*Tr.*408, cf. Pl.*Phdr.*245a; τὰς σοφιστικὰς ὑποθέσεις Philostr.*VS*2.10.4; *cause to rage* with anger, Phld. *Ir.*p.63 W.:—Pass., *to be filled with Bacchic frenzy*, πᾶσα δ' ἐξεβακχεύθη πόλις E.*Ba.*1295, cf. Pl.*R.*561a, Hdn.5.8.1, etc.; ἔρωτι Aristaenet. 1.16; ὑπὸ τοῦ ἔρωτος Max.Tyr.24.9:—Med., E.*Supp.*1001 (lyr.):—intr. in Act., Alex.141.13; of anger, Phld.*Ir.*p.35 W.

ἐκβάλλω, Arc. **ἐσδέλλω** *IG*5(2).6.49 (Tegea, iv B.C.), fut. -βᾰλῶ: aor. -έβαλον: pf. -βέβληκα:—Pass., fut. -βεβλήσομαι E.*Ba.*1313:—*throw* or *cast out of*, c. gen., 'Οδίον μέγαν ἔκβαλε δίφρου Il.5.39, etc.: abs., *throw out*, ἐκ δ' εὐνὰς ἔβαλον 1.436, etc.; καὶ τὴν μὲν..ἰχθύσι κύρμα γενέσθαι ἔκβαλον *threw* her *overboard*, Od.15.481, cf. Hdt.1.24: then in various relations, ἐκπίπτω being freq. used as its Pass.: 1. *throw ashore*, τὸν δ' ἄρ'..νεὸς ἔκβαλε κῦμ' ἐπὶ χέρσου Od.19.278; ἄνεμος..τρηχέως περιέσπε..πολλὰς τῶν νεῶν ἐκβάλλων πρὸς τὸν Ἄθων Hdt.6.44; ἐ. ἐς τὴν γῆν Id.7.170 (but in 2.113 ἄνεμοι..ἐκβάλλουσι ἐς τὸ πέλαγος *carry out* to sea; ἐξέβαλεν ἄνεμος ἡμᾶς *drove* us *out of* our *course*, E.*Cyc.*20):—Med., *put ashore*, ἵππους ἐξεβάλλοντο Hdt. 6.101; *jettison*, Syngr.ap.D.35.11. 2. *cast out of* a place, Κιμμερίους ἐκβαλόντες ἐκ τῆς Εὐρώπης Hdt.1.103; ἐ. ἐκ τῆς χώρας, of an enemy, Lycurg.99, cf. D.60.8; esp. of banishment, ἐκ πόλεως ἐ. *drive out of* the country, Pl.*Grg.*468d, cf. Ar.*Pl.*430, etc.; of a corpse, ἔξω τῆς πόλεως, τῶν ὁρίων, Pl.*Lg.*873b, 909c: c. acc. only, *drive out, banish*, Heraclit.121, S.*OC*646, 770, etc.; *turn out*, νεοττούς Arist.*HA*618^{b}12; *cast out of* the synagogue, *Ev.Jo.*9.34; ἐκ τοῦ τάγματος J.*BJ*2.8.8; *exorcize, cast out* evil spirits, *Ev.Marc.*1.34, al.; also in weakened sense, *cause to depart*, ib.43. 3. *expose* on a desert island, S.*Ph.*257, 1034, 1390; *expose* a dead body, ταφῆς ἄτερ Id.*Aj.*1388; ἐ. τέκνα *expose* children, E.*Ion*964. 4. ἐ. γυναῖκα ἐκ τῆς οἰκίας *divorce* her, D. 59.83: with simple acc., And.1.125, D.59.63, D.S.12.18, etc.:—Pass., Lxx *Le.*21.7. 5. *cast out of* his seat, *depose* a king, ἐ. ἕδρας Κρόνον A.*Pr.*203; ἐκ τυραννίδος θρόνου τ' ib.910; ἐκ τῆς τιμῆς X.*Cyr.*1.3.9: without ἐκ, ἐ. τινὰ πλούτου S.*El.*649:—Pass., *to be ejected*, of an occupier, *PPetr.*2 p.143 (iii B.C.), *PMagd.*12.8 (iii B.C.), etc.; χάριτος ἐκβεβλημένη S.*Aj.*808; ἐκ τῆς φιλίας X.*An.*7.5.6; ἐκ τῆς ἀρχῆς ἐξεβλήθησαν Isoc.4.70. 6. *throw decisively* in wrestling, τίν' οὐ παλαίουσ' ἐς τρὶς ἐ.; S.*Fr.*941.13. 7. ἐ. φρέατα *dig* wells, Plu.*Pomp.*32. 8. of drugs, *get rid of*, τοξεύματα Dsc.3.32. 9. *expel* afterbirth, Hp. *Mul.*1.78. 10. *publish*, σύνταξιν Plb.30.4.11; *issue*, δόγμα ib.19.6; ἀπόκρισιν Id.29.19.5. II. *strike out of*, χειρῶν δ' ἔκβαλλε κύπελλα Od.2.396, cf. Theoc.22.210; ἐκβάλλεθ'..τευχέων πάλους *throw* them *out of* the urns, A.*Eu.*742: abs., δοῦρα ἐ. *fell* trees (prop., *cut* them *out of* the forest), Od.5.244. 2. *strike open, break in*, ἐ. θύρετρα, πύλας, θύρας, E.*Or.*1474, *Hec.*1044, Lys.3.23, D.47.53. III. *let fall, drop*, χειρὸς δ' ἔκβαλεν ἔγχος Il.14.419; σφῦραν B.17.28; ξίφος E. *Andr.*629, cf. Ar.*Lys.*156; οἰστούς X.*An.*2.1.6: metaph., ἦ ῥ' ἅλιον ἔπος ἔκβαλον *let fall* an idle word, Il.18.324; εἰ μὴ ὑπερφίαλον ἔπος ἔκβαλε Od.4.503, cf. Hdt.6.69, A.*Ag.*1662, etc.; ἐ. ῥῆμα Pl.*R.* 473e: abs., *utter, speak*, D.L.9.7; *shed*, δάκρυα δ' ἔκβαλε θερμά Od. 19.362; ἐ. ἕρκος ὀδόντων *cast, shed* one's teeth, Sol.27, cf. E.*Cyc.*644, etc.; *throw up* blood, S.*Ant.*1238; *spit out*, Thphr.*HP*4.8.4; ἐκβαλεῦσι τὰς κούρας their eyes *will drop out*, prov. of covetous persons, Herod.4.64. IV. *throw away, cast aside, reject*, εὐμένειαν, χάριν, S.*OC*631, 636, cf. Plb.1.14.4; προγόνων παλαιὰ θέσμια E.*Fr.*360.45; θεούς Ar.*Nu.*1477; *recall, repudiate*, ἐ. λόγους Pl.*Cri.*46b; *annul*, τοὔπος S.*OT*849; *remove* an official from his post, D.21.87; *drive* an actor from the stage, Id.19.337: metaph., of a politician, Pl.*Ax.*368d:—Pass., Ar.*Eq.*525; ἐκβάλλεσθαι ἄξια Antipho 4.3.1. V. *lose*, properly by one's own fault, φρένας, τἀγαθόν, S.*Ant.*649, *Aj.*965, cf. Ar.*Eq.*404, *Ec.*751. VI. *produce*, of women, Hp.*Epid.*4.25 (of premature birth), Plu.*Publ.*21; esp. in case of a miscarriage or abortion, Hp.*Mul.*1.60, Thphr.*HP*9.18.8; βρέφος ἐκ τῆς γαστρός Ant.Lib. 34; with play on 1.2, D.L.2.102, etc.; *hatch* chicks, Sch.Ar.*Av.* 251. b. of plants, ἐ. καρπόν *put forth* fruit, Hp.*Nat.Puer.*22; ἐ. στάχυν E.*Ba.*750:—Pass., τὰ ἐκβαλλόμενα *BGU*197.12 (i A.D.). VII. *put out* a bone or joint, Hp.*Fract.*31, *Art.*67; χεῖρα Arr.*Epict.*3.15.4. VIII. *upset, undo the effect of* a speech, Plb.11.10.6. IX. Math., *produce* a line, in Pass., Arist.*Cael.*271^{b}29, *Mech.*850^{a}11, Str. 2.1.29, etc.; ἐ. εἰς ἄπειρον *produce* to infinity, in metaph. sense, τὰ δεινά Phld.*D.*1.12, cf. 13. 2. *start counting*, in astronomical calculations, Procl.*Par.Ptol.*252. X. intr., *go out, depart*, ἵν' ἐκβάλω ποδὶ ἄλλην ἐπ' αἶαν E.*El.*96; of the sea, *break out of its bed*, Arist. *Mete.*367^{b}13; of a river, *branch off*, Pl.*Phd.*113a: metaph., ἐπειδὰν ἐς μειράκια ἐκβάλωσιν D.C.52.26.

ἐκβαρβᾰρ-όω, *make quite barbarous*, πόλιν Isoc.9.20:—Pass., *become so*, Pl.*Ep.*353a, Aristox.*Fr.Hist.*90, Plb.3.58.8. **-ωσις,** εως, ἡ, *barbarization*, Plu.*Tim.*17.

ἐκβᾰσᾰνίζω, *put to the question*, in Pass., J.*AJ*15.8.4; *test thoroughly*, *BGU*1141.47 (i B.C.), Philostr.*VA*2.31 (Pass.).

ἐκβᾰσῐλίζομαι, *to be raised to royal rank*, *POxy.*471.54 (ii A.D.):—prob. to be read for **ἐκβολίζεται·** εἰς βασιλέως ἔθη τρέπεται, Hsch.

ἐκβάσιος [ᾰ], ον, epith. of Apollo, = ἐκβατήριος, A.R.1.966.

ἔκβᾰσις, εως, ἡ, *way out of*, esp. *out of* the sea, Od.5.410; κατὰ τὴν ἔκβασιν τὴν εἰς τὰ..ὄρη X.*An.*4.3.20, cf. 4.1.20; περὶ τὰς ἐκβάσεις about the *landing-places*, Plb.3.14.6. 2. *going out of*, esp. *out of* a ship, *disembarkation*, ἔ. στρατοῦ A.*Supp.*771, cf. A.R.2.1049, Plb.4.64.5: metaph., ἄτης ἔ. *escape from..*, E.*Med.*279, cf. Plu. *Pyrrh.*23. 3. = μετάβασις, Arist.*Cael.*268^{b}3. 4. *end* of a person's life, Lxx *Wi.*2.17: generally, *termination, completion*, ἐλαιουργίας *PFay.*91.21 (i A.D.); *accomplishment*, τῶν ἔργων Ruf.*Anat.* 1. 5. *deviation, declension, departure*, παρὰ [τοῦ ἀγαθοῦ] Plot.1.8.7, cf. 3.7.6. II. *issue, event*, Men.696, Arr.*Epict.*2.7.9 (pl.); *fulfilment* of divination, Zeno *Stoic.*1.44, Chrysipp.ib.2.342. III. *emanation, procession*, Porph.*Sent.*35, Dam.*Pr.*283. IV. *produce*, ἐδαφῶν *PRyl.*122.5 (ii A.D.). V. *digression*, Serv. ad Virg. *G.*2.209.

ἐκβασμίδωσις [ῐδ], εως, ἡ, in pl., *steps for descending from* an altar,

*Epigr.Gr.*229 (Ephesus):—also **ἐκβάσμωσις**, *IGRom.*4.514 (Pergam.), *BCH*4.381 (Aeolis).

ἐκ-βᾰτήριος, α, ον, *of* or *for disembarkation*, μέλη Him.*Ecl.*13.38; ἐκβατήρια (sc. ἱερά) νόσου *a sacrifice offered for escape* from an illness, Philostr.*VS*2.1.12. II. Subst. ἐκβατηρία, ἡ, *landing-place*, *PPetr.*3 p.89 (iii B.C.), Lyc.516, *PTeb.*33.9 (ii B.C.). **-βάτης** [ᾰ], ου, ὁ, = ἡνίοχος ἐκβιβάζων, *IG*2.1316. **-βᾰτός**, ή, όν, *coming to pass*, Gal. 19.354.

ἐκβάω, Dor. for ἐκβαίνω, ἐκβῶντας Foed.Dor.ap.Th.5.77.

ἐκβεβαι-όομαι, *confirm*, *establish*, Plu.2.283a; νίκημα Id.*Pomp.*19, cf. *Ages.*19. **-ωσις**, εως, ἡ, *confirmation*, Id.2.85c.

ἐκβεβηλόω, *profane*, v.l. in Lxx*Le.*21.9 (Pass.).

ἐκβήσσω, *cough up*, Arist.*HA*495b19:—Pass., Hp.*Morb.*2.46.

ἐκβῐ-άζω, *to force out, dislodge, expel*, prob. f.l. for -βιβάζω in Plu. 2.243d, 662a; also χεῖρα κατά τινος *lay violent* hands on, Lib.*Decl.*40.1 (s.v.l.):—elsewh. in Med. (fut. -βιάσομαι Men.*Pk.*252), Thphr.*HP* 8.10.4, *PSI*4.340.16 (iii B.C.), Plb.18.23.4; δίψαν Plu.2.584e:—Pass., τόξον χειρῶν ἐκβεβιασμένον the bow *forced from* mine hands, S. *Ph.*1129 (lyr.); ἐκβιασθέντες *forced from their position*, Plb.1.28.6, cf. Plu.*Thes.*27, etc.: rare in pres., τοὺς ἐκβιαζομένους Id.*Alex.*60. 2. Med., *constrain*, Hdn.2.3.4: c. inf., ἐ. τινὰ ὑπακοῦσαι Id.2.2.5; ἐς τὸ γράφειν Eun.*Hist.*p.216 D.:—Pass., τούτους ἀνελεῖν -βιασθήσομαι Lib.*Decl.*40.14. II. Med., *project with force*, Arist.*Aud.*800b12: metaph., *exploit to the full*, τὴν τόλμαν Eun.*Hist.*p.258D. 2. *press upon*, ὅταν ἐκβιάσηται τὰ σπλάγχνα [ἡ ὑστέρη] Aret.*SA*2.11. III. Pass., *to be expressed in a forced, elaborate way*, of works of art, Plu. *Tim.*36. IV. in argument, *insist*, c. acc. et inf., Phld.*Rh.*1.74 S. **-άομαι**, = foreg., Hp.*de Arte*12:—Act., aor. ἐκβιᾶσαι Lxx*Jd.* 14.15. **-ασμα**, ατος, τό, prob. f.l. for ἔκβρασμα II, Vett.Val.161.18 (pl.). **-αστής**, οῦ, ὁ, *exactor*, *oppressor*, Aq., Thd.*Pr.*6.7. **-αστικός**, ή, όν, *oppressive*, *tyrannical*, Ptol.*Tetr.*155 (s.v.l.); cf. ἐκβιβ-.

ἐκβῐβ-άζω, Att. fut. -βιβῶ, causal of ἐκβαίνω, *make to go* or *come out*, ἐκβίβασον ἐκ τοῦ βουτόμου τοὐρνίθιον Ar.*Av.*662; ἐ. ποταμὸν ἐκ τοῦ αὐλῶνος *turn* a river *out of* its channel, Hdt.7.130; ἐ. τῶν ὁδῶν X.*Eq.Mag.*1.18; ἐ. τινὰ δικαίων λόγων *stop* one *from* discussing the question of justice, Th.5.98. b. in athletic contests, ἐ. κλήρους *eliminate*, i.e. *win* heats, *IGRom.*3.626 (Xanthus), al.; ἅρματι ἐγβιβάζων *SIG*728 *H* (Delph., i B.C.). c. *bring to a close*, μέτρον, κῶλον, Phld.*Po.Herc.*1676.12. 2. esp. *land* persons or goods *from* a ship, *disembark*, Th.7.39, Pl.*Grg.*512a, *PMeyer*21.8 (iii/iv A.D.):—Pass., Artem.Eph.ap.Porph.*Antr.*4. 3. = ἐμβιβάζω 3 (quod fort. leg.), εἰς τὸν πόλεμον Plb.27.7.8. II. *carry out* a measure, etc., εἵνεκεν τοῦ τὸ ἐπίταγμα ἐκβιβασθῆμεν *IG*5(1).1432.8 (Messene), cf. *POxy.*1195 (ii A.D.). III. *levy execution on*, τινά *Cod.Just.*3.2.4, 12.60.7.3 (Pass.). IV. *satisfy* a person's claim, *PTeb.*398.18 (ii A.D.). **-ασμός**, ὁ, *execution* of a sentence or judgement, Aq.1*Ki.*15.23, *Cod.Just.*12.60.7.1. **-αστής**, οῦ, ὁ, *one who executes* a sentence, Aq.*De.*16.18, Lyd.*Mag.*3.11,12, *Cod.Just.*3. 2.4.2. **-αστικός**, ή, όν, *extortionate*, *oppressive*, Procl.*Par.Ptol.* 219 (s.v.l.), cf. ἐκβιαστικός; *efficacious*, *Gloss.*

ἐκβιβρώσκω, *devour*, ἐκ μὲν ἐσχάτας βέβρωκε σάρκας S.*Tr.*1054:—Pass., *Gp.*2.35.7: metaph., Corn.*ND*18.

ἔκβῐος, ον, *deprived of life*, Artem.4.32.

ἐκβιούζει (i.e. ἐκϝιύζει)· θρηνεῖ μετὰ κραυγῆς, Hsch.

ἐκβῐόω, *live out, complete*, ἑξηκοστὸν ἔτος *IG*14.400 (Lipara).

ἐκβλαστ-άνω, aor. 1 ἐξεβλάστησα Hp.*Alim.*6, but inf. ἐκβλαστεῖν Thphr.*CP*3.23.1:—*shoot*, *sprout*, Id.*HP*7.2.3: metaph., τύραννος ἐκ προστατικῆς ῥίζης ἐ. Pl.*R.*565d, cf. Procl.*Inst.*36. 2. c. acc., *grow out of*, τὴν ἰδίην ἰδέην Hp. l. c. II. *cause to grow*, *produce*, ἔξοδον χλόης Lxx*Jb.*38.27; *cause to revive*, τὴν φυήν Aret.*CA*2.3. **-έω**, = foreg., Sm.*Ps.*103(104).14. **-ημα**, ατος, τό, *new shoot*, *sprout*, v.l. in Dsc.5.92, cf. Ph.1.48, Gal.12.349. **-ησις**, εως, ἡ, *shooting*, *budding*, φύλλων Dsc.1.81, cf. *Gp.*5.25.1. 2. esp. *later budding*, Thphr.*HP*3.5.3 (nisi leg. ἐπι-).

ἐκβλέπω, *look*, ἁπαλά (prob.) Philostr.Jun.*Im.*1, cf. Aristid.*Or.* 48(24).32 (dub.). II. *get the power of sight*, Ael.*NA*3.25.

ἐκ-βλήσιμος, ον, *to be rejected*, *PGiss.*40 ii 17 (iii A.D.). **-βλητέον**, (ἐκβάλλω) *one must reject*, μύθους Pl.*R.*377c; *one must get rid of*, Orib.*Fr.*130. 2. Medic., ἐ. διαιρέσεις *one must make* incisions, Antyll.ap.Aët.7.74. **-βλητικός**, ή, όν, *serviceable for expelling*, τοξευμάτων Arist.*HA*612a5; βελῶν Antig.*Mir.*30. **-βλητος**, ον, *cast overboard*, E.*Hec.*699. II. *to be thrown out*, νέκυες κοπρίων ἐκβλητότεροι Heraclit.96, cf. Ph.1.477 (Comp.).

ἐκβλίσαι· ἐκθλῖψαι, and **ἐκβλιστέος**· ἐκθλιπτέος, Hsch.

ἐκ-βλύζω, *gush out*, Orph.*L.*490; οἴνῳ Lxx*Pr.*3.10. II. trans., *cause to gush out*, ἄμπελος ἐκβλύσει τὸν οἶνον Orph.*Fr.*255; νεκρὸς ὑγρῶν πλῆθος ἐξέβλυσεν Plu.*TG*13. **-βλυσμα**, ατος, τό, *sluice*, *PIand.*52.14 (i A.D.). **-βλύω**, = ἐκβλύζω, A.R.4.1417 [where ἐκβλύοντα].

ἐκβλώσκω, *come forth*, only aor. imper. ἔκμολε Il.11.604.

ἐκβοάω, *call out*, *cry aloud*, X.*Cyn.*6.10, Pl.*R.*492b, A.R.3.631 (tm.), Ph.1.129, al., Polyaen.8.52: c. acc., *drive away* (nisi leg. ἐκσοβῆσαι), *Anacreont.*25.19:—Pass., κραυγαὶ ἐξεβοῶντο *POxy.*1242. 54 (ii A.D.); ἐκβεβοημένος *notorious*, Sch.Lib.*Or.*11.207.

ἐκβοήθ-εια, ἡ, *sally*, Th.3.18; *marching out*, Arist.*Pol.*1327a 6. **-έω**, *march out to aid*, πανδημεί Hdt.6.16; ἐς τὸν Ἰσθμόν Id.9. 26: abs., Polyaen.1.1.3, Plu.2.773f; *make a sally*, Th.1.105, Thphr. *Char.*25.3. **-ησις**, εως, ἡ, *protection*, ἐμπυρισμῶν against fire, Ath. Mech.12.6.

ἐκβόησις, εως, ἡ, *crying out* or *aloud*, Ph.2.159, al., Hld.10.17; ἡ ἐπὶ τῷ ἥδεσθαι ἐ. S.E.*M.*1.143: pl., *Anatolian Studies* 154 (Ephesus, v A.D.), *Cod.Just.*1.12.8.1.

ἐκβολάς, άδος, ἡ, *anything thrown out*; = σκωρία, *dross*, Str.9.1. 23. 2. ἐ. μήτρα, Lat. *vulva ejectitia*, a Roman dish, Hipparch.ap. Ath.3.101a, Sopat.8. II. an Egyptian *grape*, causing abortion, Plin.*HN*14.117.

ἐκβολβίζω, *peel*, as one does an onion of its outer coats, ἐ. τινὰ τῶν κῳδίων Ar.*Pax*1123. II. metaph., *uproot*, *destroy*, *Com.Adesp.*992.

ἐκβόλ-ειον σύαγρον, τό, prob. = ἐκβολὰς μήτρα, Dionys.Trag. 1. **-εύς**, έως, ὁ, *inspector of dykes*, *PLond.*5.1648 (vi A.D.), al. **-ή**, ἡ, (ἐκβάλλω) *throwing out*, ψήφων ἐ. *casting* the votes *out of* the urn, A. *Eu.*748. 2. *jettisoning* of cargo, Id.*Th.*769 (lyr.), Arist.*EN*1110a 9, *Act.Ap.*27.18 (but simply, *unloading*, *Sammelb.*1207): metaph., ἐ. τῆς δόξης *casting out* of it, *getting rid* of it, Pl.*Sph.*230b, *R.*412e; ἐ. ἐλέου Aphth.*Prog.*7, cf. Diog.Oen.4. II. *expulsion*, *banishment*, A.*Supp.*421 (lyr., pl.); μετὰ τὴν τῶν τυράννων ἐ. Arist.*Pol.*1275b36; ἐκβολαὶ ἐκ τῆς πόλεως Pl.*Lg.*847b; *dislodgement*, *ejection*, Plb.4.8. 4. 2. *divorce*, *repudiation*, γυναικός Lib.*Decl.*26.45. III. *letting fall* or *drop*, δακρύων ἐκβολαί E.*HF*742 (lyr.); ἐ. [ὀδόντων] *casting* or *shedding* of teeth, Arist.*GA*789a15. IV. *expulsion* of a foetus, Hp. *Mul.*1.78. 2. ἐ. σίτου *the time when* the corn *comes into ear*, Th.4. 1. 3. *shoot*, καυλοῦ Dsc.3.114. V. *putting out* of a joint, *dislocation*, ἐκβολαὶ τῶν ἄρθρων Plu.2.164f. VI. *putting forth*, *exposing*, μαστῶν Plb.2.56.7. VII. *debouchure*, *outlet*, ἐ. Πηνειοῦ Hdt.7. 128; *mouth* of a river, in pl., Th.2.102; in sg., Id.7.35, Pl.*Phd.* 113a: *pass leading out* of a chain of mountains, αἱ ἐκβολαὶ τοῦ Κιθαιρῶνος Hdt.9.38. 2. *by-way*, ἐ. ἐκ τῆς ὁδοῦ τῆς εὐθείας Paus.3.10.7: metaph., ἐ. λόγου *digression*, Th.1.97, Philostr.*Her.*19.14 (pl.), etc. 3. *close* of a verse, Eust.900.24. 4. *projection*, στόματος a snout, Philostr.Jun.*Im.*12. VIII. (from Pass.), *that which is cast out*, δικέλλης ἐ. *earth thrown up* by a mattock, *upcast*, S.*Ant.* 250; οὐρεία ἐ. *children cast* or *exposed* on the mountains, E.*Hec.*1079 (anap.). 2. *cargo thrown overboard*, *jetsam*, πλὴν ἐκβολῆς, ἣν ἂν.. ἐκβάλωνται Syngr.ap.D.35.11; so ἐκβολαὶ νεώς *wrecked* seamen, E.*IT*1424. IX. in Music, *interval of five* διέσεις, Plu.2.1141b, Bacch.*Harm.*42, Aristid.Quint.1.10. X. = ἐκβολάς I, Str.14.5. 28. **-ίζεται**, v. ἐκβασιλίζομαι. **-ῐμαῖος**, α, ον, = sq., Heph. Astr.1.1. **-ιμος**, ον, *thrown out*, *ejected*: ἐκβόλιμον *abortion*, Arist. *HA*575a28; τὰ ἐ. τῶν ἐμβρύων Id.*PA*665b1; τῶν ᾠῶν Id.*GA*752b4, cf. *POxy.*464.21. 2. metaph., *abortive*, *futile*, [δόξα] Phld.*Po.*5. 29, cf. Plu.2.44d; *to be rejected*, ἄκυρον καὶ ἐ. *PGrenf.*2.71 ii 11 (iii A.D.). **-ιον**, τό, *drug* or *other means for expelling the foetus* or *placenta*, Hp.*Mul.*1.78, Sor.1.60, Plu.2.134f. II. = δίκταμνον, Ps.-Dsc.3.32. **-ος**, ον, *thrown out* or *away*, *exposed*, ἔκβολον οἴκων βρέφος E.*Ph.*804 (lyr.); *rejected*, σφόνδυλοι *Supp.Epigr.*2.569.22 (Didyma); ἔ. βροτῶν βίου Luc.*Trag.*215. 2. *frustrated*, Lxx*Ju.* 11.11. 3. *cast out*, [ἔφοδος] ὡσανεὶ κόσκινον [ἀριθμοὺς] ὥσπερ ἐ. ἀποχωρίσει Iamb.*in Nic.*p.29 P.; τὰ διὰ κοσκίνου ἔ. ib.p.30 P. II. Subst. ἔκβολον, τό, *outcast*, ἔ. κόρης E.*Ion*555; νηδύος ἔ. Id.*Ba.*91 (lyr.). 2. ναὸς ἔκβολα seem to be *rags cast out from* the ship, Id. *Hel.*422; but, 3. in Id.*IT*1042 πόντου ἔκβολον *an outbreak*, a place where the sea *has broken in upon* the land.

ἐκβομβ-έω, *thunder forth*, Poll.1.118. **-ησις**, εως, ἡ, *shouting in token of approbation*, Them.*Or.*23.282d.

ἐκβόσκω, aor. ἐξεβόσκησα, *consume*, τὰ ὑγρά Alex.Aphr.*Pr.*2.29:—Med., ἐκβόσκομαι *feed on*, τι Nic.*Th.*803; *absorb*, ἰκμάδα Gal.1.517: metaph. of grief, ὀδύνη ἐ. με Aristaenet.2.5.

ἐκβοτᾰνίζω, *exherbo*, *Gloss.*

ἐκβραγμός, v.l. for ἐκβρασμός, Lxx*Na.*2.10(11).

ἐκ-βράζω or **-βράσσω**, fut. -βράσω: aor. -έβρασα:—*throw out*, *cast on shore*, ἐ. ποταμὸς περὶ τὰ χείλη χρυσίον Arist.*Mir.*833b16; of the sea, D.S.14.68, etc.; ἑαυτὸν ἐκβράσαι, of a dolphin, Ael.*NA*6.15:—Pass., τὰ ἐκ τῆς θαλάσσης -βρασσόμενα βρυώδη *Gp.*2.22.2; of ships, *to be cast ashore*, ἐς Κασθαναίην ἐξεβράσσοντο Hdt.7.188, cf. 190, Ath. 6.259b; of persons, Plu.2.294f. II. *throw off* humours, Hp.*Mul.* 2.113:—Pass., *gush out*, Id.*Gland.*4:—Med., Id.*Int.*1. III. *expel*, *drive out*, Lxx*Ne.*13.28, 2*Ma.*1.12: metaph., ὁ θυμὸς ἐ. τῆς ψυχῆς ἀκόλαστα ῥήματα Plu.2.456c. IV. intr. in Act., *boil over*, of water, Apollod.1.6.3; *pullulate*, of shoots, ἐκ μιᾶς ῥίζης *Gp.*2.6. 28. **-βρᾰσις**, εως, ἡ, *pullulation*, φθειρῶν Suid. 2. αἱ κοῖλαι ἐ. *breakers*, *EM*494.14. **-βρασμα**, ατος, τό, *thing cast up*, πόντου *Com.Adesp.*1218; *excretion*, Dsc.5.92, *Hippiatr.*85. II. *cutaneous eruption*, Ruf.ap.Orib.8.24.30 (pl.), cf. Crito ap.Gal.12.448; *scab*, Sm. *Le.*13.6. **-βρασμός**, ὁ, = foreg. II, Suid. and Phot. s.v. πομφόλυξ. II. *trembling*, *shaking*, Lxx*Na.*2.10(11); *confusion*, Hsch.

ἐκβράσσω, v. ἐκβράζω:—Ion. **ἐκβρήσσω**, Gal.19.95.

ἐκ-βρεκτέον, *one must soak*, Herod.Med.ap.Aët.4.47. **-βρέχω**, *cause to rot*, of water, in Pass., τὰ ἐκβεβρεγμένα ὑπὸ τοῦ ποταμοῦ *PPetr.*3 p.120.

ἐκβροντάω, *to strike out by lightning*, ἐξεβροντήθη σθένος he *had* strength *struck out of him by lightning*, A.*Pr.*364. II. intr., *thunder loud*, Poll.1.118.

ἐκβρῡχάομαι, *bellow forth* or *aloud*, E.*Hel.*1557; στεναγμὸν ἡδὺν ἐ. Id.*IT.*1390.

ἔκβρωμα, ατος, τό, *anything eaten out*, πρίονος ἔ. *saw-dust*, S.*Tr.* 700 (pl.); *piece eaten away*, Arist.*HA*625a9.

ἐκβῠθίζομαι, Pass., *come forth from the deep*, v.l. in Callistr.*Stat.*14.

ἐκβυρσεύω, *flay*, Al.*Le.*11.40.

ἐκβυρσ-όω, *cause to project from the skin*, Gal.18(2).721. **-ωμα**, ατος, τό, *projecting of the bones out of the skin*, ib.714. **-ωσις**, εως, ἡ, = foreg., Orib.*Fr.*88.

ἐκγᾰλακτόω, *turn into sap*, Thphr.*CP*3.23.1 :—Pass., *to be turned into sap*, of the seeds of plants, Id.*HP*8.6.1 ; also, *become like milk*, Sch.Hes.*Th.*353.

ἐκγᾰληνίζω, fut. -ιῶ, *soothe*, φρένας prob. in E.*Hyps.Fr.*3(1).3.

ἐκγᾰμ-έομαι, Pass., *to be given in marriage*, *AB*259, Suid. **-ιστής**, οῦ, ὁ, *matchmaker*, *Cat.Cod.Astr.*8(4).212.

ἐκγαυρόομαι, Pass., *to be proud of*, *admire greatly*, τι E.*IA*101.

ἐκγέγᾰα, ἐκγεγάονται, v. ἐκγίγνομαι.

ἐκγείνασθαι, aor. inf. Med., with no pres., *bring forth*, Luc.*Trag.*4.

ἐκγελάω, Ep. aor. ἐξεγέλασσα *h.Merc.*389, Theoc.4.37 :—*laugh out*, *laugh loud*, ἡδὺ δ' ἄρ' ἐκγελάσας μετεφώνεε Od.16.354, 18.35, cf. X.*Cyr.*1.3.9, etc. ; γέλωτι ὥσπερ κῦμα ἐ. Pl.*R.*473c ; ἐάν τις κνήσῃ, ἐ. Arist.*Pr.*965ᵃ24 : metaph. of a liquid that rushes out with a *gurgling* sound, ἐκγελᾷ φόνος E.*Tr.*1176.

ἐκγελιώσαιμι· ἐ(κ)χλευάσαιμι, Hsch.

ἔκγελως, ωτος, ὁ, *loud laughter*, Poll.6.199.

ἐκγενέτης, ου, ὁ, = ἔκγονος, δεσπόταις . . Λακεδαίμονος ἐκγενέταισι E.*Andr.*128 codd. (lyr.), cf. *Ba.*1155 (lyr.).

ἐκγενής, ές, v. ἐγγενής.

ἐκγενν-άω, *beget*, v.l. in Lxx*Ps.*109(110).3 ; also, *bring forth*, Eup. 99 : Boeot. 3 pl. fut. ἐσγεννάσονθ' Corinn.*Supp.*2.62. **-ημα**, Dor. -ᾱμα, ατος, τό, *offspring*, *issue*, *Supp.Epigr.*2.310.12 (Delph.).

ἐκγῐγαρτίζω, *take out the stone from*, τὴν σταφίδα Dsc.1.25, cf. Androm.ap.Gal.13.23, Archig.ib.12.585 ; μῆλα *Gp.*8.27.1.

ἐκγίγνομαι, later and Ion. **ἐκγίν-** [ῑ], fut. -γενήσομαι : Ep. pf. ἐκγέγαα, 3 dual ἐκγεγάτην ; part. ἐκγεγαώς, Aeol. ἐκγεγόνων Alc. *Supp.*25.10 :—*to be born of* a father, c. gen., οἳ Διὸς ἐξεγένοντο Il.5. 637, cf. 20.231, etc. ; ἐκγεγάτην . . Ἠελίοιο Od.10.138 ; Ἑλένη Διὸς ἐκγεγαυῖα Il.3.199,418 ; τοίων πατέρων ἐξ αἵματος ἐκγεγάατε Hom. *Epigr.*16.3 (ἐκγεγάασθε Suid.) ; οἱ πὰρ θεοῦ ἐκγεγάαντο *AP*15.40.20 (Comet.). 2. c. dat., *to be born to*, Πορθεῖ μὲν τρεῖς παῖδες . . ἐξεγένοντο Il.14.115, cf. Hdt.1.30, 4.155 : fut. perf., παῖδες παίδεσσι διαμπερὲς ἐκγεγάονται *h.Ven.*197. 3. simply, *come into being*, Emp. 59.3, *PMasp.*153.12 (vi A.D.), *PLond.*5.1708.207 (vi A.D.). II. aor., *to be gone away*, c. gen., ἐκγενέσθαι τοῦ ζῆν *to have departed* this life, X.*HG*6.4.23 (s.v.l.). III. impers., ἐκγίγνεται *it is allowed*, *it is granted*, c. dat. pers. et inf., mostly with neg., οὐκ ἐξεγένετό τινι ἀπαγγεῖλαι *it was* not *granted* him to . ., Hdt.1.78, cf. 5.51, Ar.*Eq.*851, Lys.7.37 ; δικαιοτάτῳ ἀνδρῶν βουλομένῳ γενέσθαι οὐκ ἐξεγένετο Hdt.3. 142 : without a neg., ἐκγενέσθαι μοι . . τείσασθαι [I pray] *that it may be allowed* me to . ., Id.5.105 ; εἰ . . τότ' ἐξεγένετο D.28.2 : abs. in part., ἐκγενόμενον Isoc.16.36 : rarely c. acc. et inf., εἰ γὰρ ἐκγένοιτ' ἰδεῖν ταύτην με τὴν ἡμέραν Ar.*Pax* 346.

ἐκγλευκίζομαι, *cease fermenting*, ἐκγεγλευκισμένος οἶνος *newly fermented* wine, Hp.*Epid.*7.64.

ἐκγλισχραίνω, *make very sticky*, Aret.*CD*2.3.

ἐκγλῠκαίνομαι, *grow sweet*, Olymp. *in Mete.*110.26.

ἐκγλῠφή, ἡ, *hatching*, Ael.*NA*4.12.

ἐκγλύφω [ῠ], *scoop out*, τὸν χόνδρον Meges ap.Orib.44.24.1 : pf. Pass. ἐξέγλυμμαι Pl.*R.*616d ; part. ἐκγεγλυμμένη Gal.18(2). 618. II. *hatch*, τὰ νεόττια Ael.*NA*2.33 :—Med., ᾠὰ ἐξεγλύψαντο Plu.*TG*17 :—also intr. in Act., τὰ ᾠὰ διὰ κα' (sc. ἡμερῶν) ἐκγλύφει *Gp.* 14.7.28.

ἐκγοητεύω, strengthd. for γοητεύω, Gorg.*Hel.*14, J.*BJ*1.11.3.

ἔκγονος, ον (η, ον E.*Hel.*1647 codd., *Milet.*7.71 (Didyma), *IGRom.* 4.912 (Cibyra)), Dor., Arc. etc. **ἔσγονος**, *Schwyzer* 191.32 (Crete), *SIG*306.53 (Tegea, iv B.C.), etc. :—*born of*, *sprung from*, esp. Subst., *child*, whether *son* or *daughter*, Il.5.813, Od.11.236, Hdt.1.35, etc. ; ὁ Διὸς ἔ. E.*HF*876 (anap.) : pl., ἔκγονοι *descendants*, Hdt.2.167, 4. 179, E.*Hipp.*450, etc. ; ἐκγόνων ἔκγονοι *children's children*, Pl.*Criti.* 112c : metaph., τῆς χώρας ἔκγονοι Id.*Mx.*239d ; ἀδικία ἔ. ὕβρεως Id. *Lg.*691c ; δειλίας ἔ. ἀργία ib.901e ; also of interest as *the child* of the principal, Id.*R.*555e, cf. 507a. b. *grandchild*, *Milet.* l. c., *SIG*900. 5, etc. 2. neut., ἔκγονά τινος one's *offspring*, A.*Pr.*137 (lyr.) ; ἔ. κλυτᾶς χθονός S.*OT*171 (lyr.) ; [ποιηταὶ] ἔ. ἑαυτῶν καταλείπουσιν Pl. *Smp.*209d ; τὰ [ζωγραφίας] ἔ. Id.*Phdr.*275d ; cf. ἔγγονος.

ἐκγρᾰφή, ἡ, *erasure* from a list, in pl., *SIG*742.31 (Ephesus, but perh. written for ἐγγραφή).

ἐκγράφω [ᾰ], *write out*, *copy*, *IG*9(1).687.12 (Corc.), cf. *CIG*2266 (Delos) :—Med., *copy for oneself*, [χρησμὸν] παρὰ τἀπόλλωνος ἐξεγραψάμην Ar.*Av.*982 ; Μορσίμου ῥῆσιν ἐξεγράψατο Id.*Ra.*151, cf. D.48.48, etc. II. *strike out*, *expunge from* a list, *IG*1².84.28, Decr.ap. And.1.77 (Pass.) ; τινὰ τῆς βουλῆς D.H.19.18. (Written ἐγγρ- *IG* 5(2).357.14 (Stymphalus, iii B.C.).)

ἐκγρῡτεύω, (γρύτη) *search out from old lumber*, aor. ἐξεγρύτευσα, Hsch.

ἐκγυμν-άζω, *exercise*, *train*, *Gloss.* **-όω**, *bare*, *expose*, Hsch. s.v. ἐξώργησα.

ἐκδαβῆ (i. e. ἐκδαϝῆ)· ἐκκαυθῇ (Lacon.), Hsch. ; cf. δαίω.

ἐκδᾳδόομαι, *become glutted with resin*, Thphr.*CP*6.11.9.

ἐκδακρύω, *burst into tears*, *weep aloud*, S.*Ph.*278, E.*Ph.*1344 ; of trees, *exude* drops of gum, J.*BJ*1.6.6, Plu.2.384b.

ἐκδάκτῠλος, ον, Att. for ἐξαδάκτυλος, *IG*2.1054*f*6.

ἐκδᾰν-είζω, *lend out at interest*, χρήματα Arist.*Oec.*1350ᵃ14 : fut. part. ἐκδανεισοῦντας *IG*9(1).694 (Corc., iii B.C.) ; 3 pl. -οῦντι ib.4. 841.16 (Calauria, iii B.C.) ; fut. also ἐκδανιῶ Lxx*De.*28.12 : pf. ἐκδεδάνεικα *AP*11.173 (Phil.) :—Med., *borrow*, *SIG*1068.15 (Patmos) : —Pass., *IG*12(7).237.23 (Amorgos). **-εισις**, εως, ἡ, *lending at interest*, ib.9(1).694 (Corc.). **-εισμός**, ὁ, *lending at interest*, ib. 12(7).515 (Amorgos), *BGU*362 xiv 21 (iii A.D.) ; εἶναι ἐν ἐ. *OGI*509. 16 (Aphrodisias). **-ειστής**, οῦ, ὁ, *one who lends at interest*, *Test. Epict.*6.30, *BMus.Inscr.*481*.131. **-ειστικός**, ή, όν, *relating to loans*, ἔγγραφα ib.311.

ἐκδᾰπᾰνάω, *exhaust*, χορηγίας Plb.21.10.9 ; προσόδους Id.24.7.4, cf. *PBaden* 19.19 (ii A.D.) ; τὸ αἷμα, τὸ ὑγρόν, Gal.10.192, 15.86 : metaph., τὰς προθυμίας εἰς τοὺς ἐχθρούς J.*AJ*15.5.1 ; τὸν θυμὸν εἴς τινας Lib.*Decl.*37.30 :—Pass., ἐκδεδαπανῆσθαι ὑπὲρ τῶν ψυχῶν ὑμῶν 2*Ep.Cor.*12.15.

ἔκδαρμα, ατος, τό, *excoriation*, Crito ap.Gal.12.449 (pl.) ; *hide*, *Et. Gud.* s. v. δορά.

ἐκδαρτικός, ή, όν, *suitable for flaying*, Tz. ad Hes.*Op.*502.

ἐκδᾰσύνομαι, Pass., pf. inf. -δεδασύνθαι, *become hairy*, Hsch.

ἐκδεῐητημένως, Adv. *luxuriously*, Poll.6.185.

ἐκδεής, ές, (δέω B) *wanting*, *imperfect*, Anon.ap.Suid.

ἔκδεια, ἡ, *falling short*, *being in arrear*, φόρων καὶ νεῶν in tribute and ships, Th.1.99 (pl.), cf. Hyp.*Fr.*136, *BGU*976.19 (ii A.D.), Lib. *Or.*36.10 (pl.), v. l. in D.32.30. 2. *deficit*, *PRev.Laws* 17.1, al. (iii B.C.). 3. *shortage*, *lack*, ὕδατος *PRyl.*81.13 (ii A.D.).

ἐκδείκνῡμι, *exhibit*, *display*, S.*El.*348, E.*Hipp.*1298 :—Med., ἔθος τόδ' εἰς Ἕλληνας ἐξεδειξάμην, prob. for -λεξάμην, Id.*Supp.*341. II. *point out*, S.*OC*1021.

ἐκδειμαίνω, strengthd. for δειμαίνω, Hld.9.8, Hierocl. *in CA*13 p.448 M.

ἐκδειμᾰτόω, strengthd. for δειματόω, Pl.*R.*381e, Porph.*Chr.*49, Aen.Gaz.*Thphr.*p.68 B. :—Pass., Lxx*Wi.*17.6, D.H.*Dem.*54.

ἐκδεινόω, strengthd. for δεινόω, J.*AJ*17.5.5.

ἐκδειπνέω, *finish a meal*, Poll.6.112.

ἐκδείρω, v. ἐκδέρω.

ἐκδεκᾰτεύω, *pay tithe of*, Ἡρακλεῖ τὴν οὐσίαν D.S.4.21.

ἐκδεκτέον, *one must admit*, *include*, Ath.5.189d, Dam.*Pr.*437.

ἐκδέκτωρ, ορος, ὁ, *one who takes from another*, πόνων *one who relieves another's* toil, A.*Fr.*194. 2. *successor*, τῆς βασιλείας Nic.Dam. p.45 D.

ἐκδέννῡμι, = ἐκδέω, Papp.1130.15, al.

ἐκδεξιάζομαι, *salute*, *PTeb.*43.11 (ii B.C.).

ἔκδεξις, εως, ἡ, *succession*, τῆς βασιληΐης Hdt.7.3.

ἐκδέρκομαι, *look out from*, Il.23.477 (sed leg. κεφαλῆς ἐκ δέρκεται) ; λεπτὸν ἐκδέδορκε Adam.1.5.

ἐκδερμᾰτ-ίζω, *flay*, *skin*, Hsch. s.v. ἔδειραν, Suid. s.v. ἀσκὸν δέρειν. **-όω**, = foreg., Sch.Ar.*Th.*765.

ἐκδέρω, Ion. -δείρω, fut. -δερῶ, *strip off the skin from* one, κριὸν Hdt.2.42, cf. 7.26 (Pass.) ; βῶν *Dialex.*2.11 ; also δῶκε δέ μ' ἐκδείρας ἀσκὸν βοὸς Od.10.19 ; βύρσαν ἐ. E.*El.*824. II. *cudgel soundly*, '*hide*', Ar.*V.*450, Pl.*R.*616a, Hyp.*Fr.*200, *PSI*4.403 (ii B.C.) :— Pass., Macho ap.Ath.13.580b (Pass.).

ἐκδεσμεύω, *make binding*, *secure*, τὴν ἑκατέρων πίστιν εἰς ἀλλήλους Plb.3.33.8.

ἔκδετος, ον, (ἐκδέω) *fastened to*, ἐξ ἵππων *AP*9.97 (Alph.).

ἐκδέχομαι, Ion. **ἐκδέκ-**, Ep. 3 pl. ἐκδέχαται Tryph.197 : fut. -δέξομαι :—Pass. (v. infr. I. 6). I. mostly of persons, 1. *take* or *receive from* another, οἵ οἱ σάκος ἐξεδέχοντο Il.13.710 ; Ὀρέστην ἐξεδεξάμην πατρί A.*Ch.*762 ; of a beacon-fire, τρίτον Ἄθῳον αἶπος . . ἐξεδέξατο Id. *Ag.*285 ; ἐ. τὴν αἰτίαν *take* it *on oneself*, D.19.37. 2. of a successor, ἐ. τὴν βασιληΐην Hdt.1.26, etc. : freq. with acc. omitted, ἐξεδέξατο Σαδυάττης (sc. τὴν βασιληΐην) S. *succeeded*, ib.16, cf. 103, al. ; παῖς παρὰ πατρὸς ἐκδεκόμενος τὴν ἀρχήν, [τὴν τέχνην], Id.1.7, 2.166 ; so ἐκδεξάμενοι (sc. τὴν μάχην) Id.7.211. 3. *take up the argument*, ὥσπερ σφαῖραν ἐ. τὸν λόγον Pl.*Euthd.*277b ; ἐκδεξάμενος (sc. τὸν λόγον) εἰπεῖν Id. *Smp.*189a ; ὁ μὲν πρῶτος εἰπών . . ὁ δ' ἐκδεξάμενος D.18.21. 4. *wait for*, *expect*, κεῖνον ἐνθάδ' ἐ. S.*Ph.*123 ; ἐλέφαντας Plb.3.45.6 ; ἀλλήλους 1*Ep.Cor.*11.33 ; ἐ. μεθ' ἡσυχίας ἕως . . D.H.6.67 ; πότε . . . Tryph. l. c. : abs., *wait*, ἕως . . *POxy.*1673.8 (ii A.D.). 5. *take* or *understand in a certain sense*, οὕτω δὴ τὴν ἀσωτίαν ἐκδεχόμεθα Arist.*EN*1120ᵃ3 ; τοὺς λόγους Plb.10.18.12 ; πρὸς τὸ συμφέρον D.S.14.56. 6. *entertain*, μεγαλοπρεπέστερον ἐγδεχθῆναι *PTeb.*33.7 (ii B.C.). 7. *to be surety for*, τινά *PSI*4.349 (iii B.C.), Lxx*Ge.*43.9. II. of events, *await*, τοὺς Σκύθας . . ἐξεδέξατο οὐκ ἐλάσσων πόνος Hdt.4.1 ; ἐ. [αὐτοὺς] περίοδος τῆς λίμνης μακρή Id.1.185. 2. of contiguous countries, *come next*, ἀπὸ ταύτης (sc. τῆς Περσικῆς) ἐ. Ἀσσυρίη Id.4.39, cf. 99, *Peripl.M. Rubr.*27. 3. in Archit., *support*, καμάραν D.S.18.26.

ἐκδέψηται· ἐκμαστιγώσηται, Hsch.

ἐκδέω, *bind so as to hang from*, *fasten to* or *on*, c. gen., πέτρης ἐκ πείσματα δήσας Od.10.96 ; [δρῦς] ἔκδεον ἡμιόνων they *bound* the oaks *to* the mules, i. e. they *yoked* the mules to them, Il.23.121 ; τοῦ τείχους Aen.Tact.11.6 : abs., σανίδας ἐκδῆσαι ὄπισθε *bind* planks behind, Od. 22.174 ; χέρας βρόχοισιν ἐκδήσαντες E.*Andr.*556 : metaph., *trace the dependence of* one thing *on* another, Plot.3.3.1 :—Med., *bind a thing to oneself*, *hang it round one*, ἐκδήσασθαι ἀγάλματα Hdt.4.76 ; also, *bind* or *fasten for oneself*, ἀκταῖσιν . . . πεισμάτων ἀρχὰς E.*Hipp.*761 (lyr.) ; τὸν νεκρὸν ἐκ τοῦ δίφρου *IG*14.1284 :—Pass., Luc.*Hist.Conscr.* 29, al.

ἐκδηθύνω, *to be protracted*, of disease, Aret.*CD*1.1.

ἐκδηῐόω, *destroy*, *ravage*, in aor. 1, Hsch. :—Med., Procop.*Arc.*19.

ἔκδηλος, ον, strengthd. for δῆλος, *conspicuous*, ἵν' ἔ. μετὰ πᾶσιν Ἀργείοισι γένοιτο Il.5.2 : hence, *considerable*, σίτου μοῖρα *CPHerm.*

6.4. II. *quite plain*, πάντ' ἐποίησεν ἔκδηλα D.2.21, cf. *OGI*665.13 (i A.D.), etc.: Sup., ἐκδηλοτάτη ἐνάργεια Phld.*Herc.*1251.13. III. Adv. -λως *openly, manifestly, plainly*, Id.*Vit.*p.40 J., Ph.1.111, Plu. *Oth.*17, etc.: Comp., Id.2.625d, Them.*Or.*15.192a: Sup., Philostr. *Her.*19.12, D.C.60.3.

ἐκδηλόω, *show plainly*, Thphr.*Vent.*35.

ἐκδημᾰγωγέω, *win by the arts of a demagogue*, τὸ πλῆθος D.H.7.4.

ἐκδημ-έω, *to be abroad, to be on one's travels*, Hdt.1.30, S.*OT*114, etc.; *to be in exile*, Pl.*Lg.*864e; εἰς πόλιν *PPetr.*3p.76. II. c. acc., *travel through*, δύσιν καὶ ἀνατολήν *IG*14.905. -ητικός, ή, όν, *on foreign service*, ἔξοδος στρατιωτῶν *Gloss.*, cf. *Cat.Cod.Astr.*8(3).99; (sc. λόγος) title of a satire, Varro *Sat. Men.*p.191 B. -ία, ἡ, *going* or *being abroad*, E.*Fr.*768: pl., Id.*Hyps.Fr.*5(3).15 (prob.); ἐ. πολιτικαί (opp. κατὰ πόλεμον καὶ στρατείας ἀποδημίαι) public *missions*, Pl.*Lg.*950e. 2. *exile*, ib.869e. 3. metaph., *departure from life*, *AP*3.5 (lemma).

ἐκδημοκοπέω, strengthd. for δημοκοπέω, τοὺς δουλωθέντας Chio *Ep.*15.2.

ἔκδημος, ον, *away from home, abroad*, X.*Cyr.*8.5.26: c. gen., ἔ. τῆσδε χθονός E.*Hipp.*281; ἔ. στρατεῖαι expeditions *abroad*, Th.1.15; ἔ. ἔξοδος, φυγή, Id.2.10, E.*Hipp.*37; ἔ. ἔρως ib.32.

ἐκδημοσιεύω, in Pass., *to be made known*, D.C.61.12, 52.31.

ἐκδιαβαίνω, *pass quite over*, τάφρον Il.10.198.

ἐκδῐαιτ-άω, *decide a case as* διαιτητής, Arist.*Ath.*53.5; also, = κακῶς διαιτάω, in aor. 1, Hsch. II. more freq. Med. or Pass., *regulate one's habits*, Hp.*Insomn.*89; *change one's mode of life*, εἴ τί που ἐξεδεδιῄτητο ἐκ τῶν καθεστώτων νομίμων Th.1.132, cf. D.H.5.74; εἰς τὰ ἀμείνω καὶ Ἑλληνικὰ ἐκδεδιῃτημένη Ath.13.556c: abs., ἐκδεδιῃτημένος *having gone astray*, Ph.2.48; βίος ἐκδεδιῃτημένος *undisciplined*, Men.Prot. p.2 D.: later c. acc., Ph.2.128; ἐκδεδιῃτημένος τὰς ὑπογαστρίους ἡδονάς Dam.*Isid.*266:—so in Act., ἐξεδιῄτησε τὴν πάτριον ἁγνείαν J.*BJ*7.8.1; causal, *make to change one's habits*, ἔθνος Lxx 4*Ma.*4.19. -ησις, εως, ἡ, *change of habits*, Ph.1.360, Plu.*Alex.*45: c. gen., τῶν πατρίων, τοῦ κατὰ φύσιν βίου, Ph.2.76, Plu.2.493c.

ἐκδιᾶν· σπᾶν, καὶ κέραμον συντετριμμένον, Hsch.

ἐκδιαπρίζω, *saw off*, App.*BC*4.20 (prob. f.l. for διαπρίζων).

ἐκδῐάστρα· κλῶσμα, ὁ στήμων, Hsch.; cf. δίασμα.

ἐκδιαφορ-έω, *draw out and dissipate*, τὸ θερμόν Phlp.*in GC*146.37, cf. Olymp.*in Mete.*278.18:—Pass., Pall.*in Hp.*2.121 D., Phlp.*in Ph.*625.25. -ησις, εως, ἡ, *dissipation*, ib.157.2.

ἐκδίδαγμα [ῐ], ατος, τό, *prentice-work*, κερκίδος E.*Ion* 1419.

ἐκδιδάσκω, poet. aor. -διδάσκησα Pi.*P.*4.217:—*teach thoroughly*, τινά Sapph.71, Th.6.80, Pl.*Prt.*328e, etc.; ἐ. πάνθ' ὁ γηράσκων χρόνος A.*Pr.*981; λέγ' ἐκδίδασκε ib.698, etc.; ἐ. τινά τι Pi. l. c., S.*OC*1539, Antipho 5.14, Theoc.6.40:—Med., *have another taught*, of the parents, Hdt.2.154, E.*Med.*295, Pl.*Ep.*360e:—Pass., c. inf., S.*Tr.*1110, etc.; αἰσχροῖς γὰρ αἰσχρὰ πράγματ' ἐκδιδάσκεται Id.*El.*621; ὀψ' ἐκδιδαχθεὶς τῶν κατ' οἶκον.. *having learnt* too late from those at home, Id.*Tr.*934. 2. c. acc. pers. et inf., *to teach* one *to be* so and so, εἶναι κακήν Id.*El.*395, cf. *Ant.*298; ἐπιθυμεῖν (sc. αὐτοὺς) ἐξεδίδαξα Ar.*Ra.*1026: with inf. omitted, γενναίους ἐ. ib.1019. 3. *explain, expound*, ἐ. ὡς.. Hdt.4.118, S.*OT*1370: abs., ἐ. σαφῶς *Com.Adesp.*14.9 D.

ἐκδιδράσκω, Ion. -διδρήσκω, fut. -δράσομαι [ᾱ]: aor. ἐξέδραν E.*Heracl.*14 (nowhere else in Trag.), D.C.37.47; part. ἐκδράς Hdt.4.148, Ar.*Ec.*55:—*run away, escape*, ἐξ Αἰγύπτου Hdt.3.4, cf. 9.88, etc.; διὰ τῶν ὑδρορροῶν Ar.*V.*126: abs., Id.*Ec.*55, Th.1.126.

ἐκδιδύσκω, = ἐκδύω, *strip, despoil*, νεκρούς Lxx 1*Ki.*31.8; *plunder*, πόλεις ὅλας J.*BJ*2.14.2.

ἐκδίδωμι, 3 sg. ἐκδιδοῖ Hdt.1.80, al.:—*give up*, esp. something seized and detained unlawfully, Ἑλένην καὶ κτήμαθ' ἅμ' αὐτῇ Il.3.459, cf. Hdt.1.3: generally, *surrender*, esp. of *giving up* refugees, ib.74, 158 sq.; τινὰ τοῖς ἐχθροῖς S.*Ph.*1386, cf. *OT*1040, etc.; ἐ. τινὰ τοῖς κατηγόροις D.21.30, cf. 29.38; ἐ. δοῦλον *give up* a slave to be examined by torture, Antipho 6.27, D.29.14; αὐτὸν ἐξέδωκεν μαστιγῶσαι Εὐριπίδῃ Arist.*Pol.*1311^{b}32; αὐτὸν ἐς τιμωρίαν τοῖς δικασταῖς Polyaen.6.7.1; *surrender* a city, Ἀμφίπολιν D.19.253, cf. 257:—Med., θυμὸν ἐκδόσθαι πρὸς ἥβαν *give up one's* heart to jollity, Pi.*P.*4.295. 2. *give out of one's house*, a. ἐ. θυγατέρα *give* one's daughter *in marriage*, τινί Hdt.1.196, E.*IA*132 (anap.), cf. Thphr.*Char.*22.4; θυγατέρας παρὰ σφῶν αὐτῶν ἐκδόντες *having provided for* their *marriage* at their own expense, D.27.69; Ἄλκηστιν ἐ. πρὸς γάμον D.S.4.53; freq. also without any acc., *give in marriage*, ἐ. εἰς οὓς ἂν ἐθέλωσι Pl.*R.*613d, cf. 362b, Th.8.21, etc.: metaph., of the elements, συνοικίζειν καὶ ἐ. Pl. *Sph.*242d:—less freq. in Med., ἐκδίδοσθαι θυγατέρα Hdt.2.47, Thphr. *Char.*30.19; ἐξέδου κόρην ὅτῳ σε θυμὸς ἦγεν E.*Med.*309:—Pass., Arc. ἐσδοθένσα (= ἐκδοθεῖσα) *given in marriage*, *SIG*306.7 (Tegea, iv B.C.). b. *give* one's son *for adoption*, τοὺς μὲν (sc. υἱοὺς) εἰς ἑτέρας οἰκίας Plb.31.28.2, cf. *POxy.*1206.6 (iv A.D.); also ἐ. τὸν παῖδα ἐπὶ τέχνην *put* him *out* as an apprentice, X.*Eq.*2.2, cf. *BGU*1021.6, etc. 3. *farm out, let for hire*, τὴν αὐλήν Hdt.1.68, cf. *SIG*1044.29 (Halic., iv/iii B.C.), etc.; ἐ. ἀνδράποδα *to let out* slaves for work, X.*Vect.*4.15; πῶλον Id.*Eq.*2.2 (also in Med., ἐξέδοτο [ἀμπελῶνα] γεωργοῖς *Ev.Marc.*12.1): c. inf., χαλινὸν χαλκεῖ ἐ. σκευάσαι Pl.*Prm.*127a; ἐ. [θύλακον] τῷ σκυτοδέψῃ ἐπιρράψαι Thphr.*Char.*16.6; ὅταν ἐκδῷ θοἰμάτιον ἐκπλῦναι ib.22.8; ἐκδόντος μοι Δημοσθένους.. στέφανον χρυσοῦν ὥστε κατασκευάσαι Test.ap.D.21.22; ὥσπερ ἀνδριάντ' ἐκδεδωκὼς κατὰ συγγραφήν like *one who has contracted for* the execution of a statue, D.18.122. 4. *give in charge* to another, πολλοὺς ἐξέδωκα Προδίκῳ (with play on signf. 2) Pl.*Tht.*151b; ἐκδιδοὺς νεικέων so as to be out of the way of quarrels, E.*Ba.*293 (s.v.l.): c. inf., Δὶ τοῦτ'.. ἐκδώσομεν πράσσειν Pi.*O.*13.106. 5. *bring out*, ἀλλ' ἐκδότω τις.. δᾷδας Ar.*Pl.*1194; ἐκδότω δέ τις.. δίφρω δύο Id.*Fr.*348. 6. *lend out money* on security, etc., Lex ap.D.35.51; ναυτικὰ ἐκδεδομένα Lys.32.6. b. simply, *pay out*, Arist.*Oec.*1349^{b}31, *PSI*3.204 (ii A.D.). 7. *put out, publish*, of books, etc., chiefly in Pass., λόγος ὁ πρότερον ἐκδοθείς Isoc.5.11, cf. Plb.2.37.6, Str.1.2.2; τοῖς ἐκδεδομένοις λόγοις Arist. *Po.*1454^{b}18:—in Act., Plu.*Rom.*8. 8. of a woman, *bring to the birth*, App.*BC*1.83. 9. of land, etc., *return, yield, produce*, μέταλλα.. μονολίθους ἐκδιδόντα πλάκας Str.5.2.5. 10. *hand over, deliver* a document, ἀποχήν *BGU*260.6 (i A.D.), etc.:—Med., *PFlor.*384.113 (v A.D.). 11. *betray*, Hsch. II. intr., of rivers, *empty themselves, disembogue*, ἐς θάλασσαν, ἐς τὴν Σύρτιν, ἐς τὸν Μαίανδρον, etc., Hdt.1.80, 2.150, 7.26, etc. 2. τῶν ἄλλων [ζῴων] τὰ μὲν εἰς ὀδόντας ἐκδίδωσι.. τὰ δὲ εἰς κέρατα.. *run to* teeth, etc., Arist.*Pr.*898^{a}22; *find an outlet*, εἰς κεφαλήν ib.29. 3. *emerge*, τὴν Ἀφροδίτην ἐκδοῦναι τῆς θαλάσσης Philostr.*Im.*2.1 (leg. -δῦναι).

ἐκδιέρχομαι, *pass through, endure*, βλάβη καὶ δαπανήματα *BGU* 1105.39 (i A.D.).

ἐκδιηγέομαι, *tell in detail*, Hp.*Prog.*1, Arist.*Rh.Al.*1434^{b}4, Ph.2.118, Lxx *Jb.*12.8, etc.

ἐκδιηθέω, *filter out*, Hp.*Morb.*4.37 (Pass.).

ἐκδιΐστᾰμαι, *to be distinct, separate*, Gal.18(2).994.

ἐκδῐκ-άζω, pf. ἐκδεδίκακα *OGI*7.3 (Cyme):—Med., fut. -δικῶμαι Lxx *Le.*19.18:—*decide*, μίαν (sc. δίκην) Ar.*Eq.*50, cf. Lys.17.5; δίκας καὶ γραφὰς καὶ εὐθύνας X.*Ath.*3.2:—Pass., of the suit, *to be settled*, Pl.*Lg.*958a:—Med., *prosecute one's right against another*, Is. *Fr.*77, *Delph.*3(2).205 (iii B.C.); περί τινος *CIG*4259, cf. *Tab.Heracl.*1.129:—also in Pass., *have right done to one*, *BGU*195.37 (ii A.D.). II. *avenge*, πατέρων.. ἐκδικάζοντες φόνον E.*Supp.*1215, cf. 154 (dub. l.). -αιόομαι, fut. -ώσομαι, = ἐκδικέω III, Keil-Premerstein *Dritter Bericht* 117 (Tire, i A.D.); *conduct legal proceedings*, *AJA*16.14 (Sardes). -ασία, ἡ, = ἐκδικία I, ib.17.29 (pl., Sardes, i B.C.). -ᾰσις, ιος, ἁ, Dor. for foreg., *SIG*563.14 (Aetol., found at Teos). -αστής, οῦ, ὁ, *avenger*, πατρός E.*Supp.*1152 (lyr.).

ἔκδικεν· ἐξέβαλεν, Hsch.

ἐκδῐκ-έω, *avenge, punish*, φόνον Ctes.*Fr.*37; παρακοήν 2*Ep.Cor.*10.6; τινάς *PGen.*47.17 (iv A.D.); *exact vengeance for*, τὰ αἵματα τῶν δούλων Lxx 2*Ki.*4.8; τὸ αἷμα τὸ ἀναίτιον *SIG*1181.12 (Jewish, circ. ii/i B.C.). 2. *decide* a case, δίκην, ἀγῶνα, Ph.2.432, *POxy.*1020.6 (ii A.D.). II. *avenge* or *vindicate* a person, by taking up his cause, Apollod.2.5.11, *PAmh.*2.134.10 (ii A.D.), Plu.*Comp.Ag.Gracch.*5; ἑαυτούς *Ep.Rom.*12.19, etc.; ἐ. τινὰ ἀπό τινος *avenge* one on another, *Ev.Luc.*18.3: c. dat., Sch.Ar.*Pl.*627:—Pass., Lxx *Ps.*36(37).28. 2. *act as* ἔκδικος II.3, *AJA*18.325 (Sardes, i B.C.), cf. *CIG*2824 (Aphrodisias), *BCH*23.182 (Pisidia). III. *claim*, *CIG*3488 (Thyatira), *Inscr.Perg.*245; σιτία καὶ ποτά Hierocl.*in CA*8 p.431 M. IV. ἐ. τισί *make retribution for* them, Aesop.279b. -ησία, ἡ, = sq., Lxx *Jd.*16.28 (dub.). -ησις, εως, ἡ, *avenging*, ἐ. ποιεῖσθαι to give *satisfaction*, Plb.3.8.10; ἐ. ποιεῖσθαί τινος obtain it from.., *CIG*2826 (Aphrodisias); *legal remedy*, *PLond.*5.1674.102 (vi A.D.); ἐ. ποιεῖν τινι *avenge* him, *Act.Ap.*7.24; τινός *Ev.Luc.*18.7, 8. -ητής, οῦ, ὁ, *avenger, vindicator*, Lxx *Ps.*8.3; τοῦ θεοῦ καὶ τοῦ νόμου J.*AJ* 17.9.6. -ητικός, ή, όν, *revengeful*, Tz. ad Lyc.406. -ία, ἡ, = ἐκδίκησις, J.*AJ*13.1.4; τοῦ πατρός Gal.14.239, Sch.Pi.*Pae.*6.119; ἡ ἀπὸ θεῶν ἐ. Herm.ap.Stob.1.49.44; ἐ. ποιεῖσθαι Onos.37.4; ἐ. γίγνοιτο *IG*2^2.1121.45 (iv A.D.). 2. *decision* of a case, D.C.38.7. II. *office of* ἔκδικος II.3, *CIG*2719 (pl.), 2771 (Aphrodisias), *POxy.*901.3 (iv A.D.); ἔχειν τὴν περί τινος ἐ. *BMus.Inscr.* 481*.219. -ος, ον, *lawless, unjust*, ἔκδικα πάσχω A.*Pr.*1093 (anap.); of persons, S.*OC*920, Ael.*NA*16.5 (Sup.). Adv. -κως A. *Pr.*976, etc. II. *maintaining the right, avenging*, ἔχει θεὸς ἔ. ὄμμα Batr.97; ἔ. χρόνος *AP*12.35 (Diocl.), cf. Lxx *Wi.*12.12. 2. Subst., *avenger*, Hdn.7.4.5; αἱ Ἰβύκου ἔ. Plu.2.509f. 3. *public advocate* or *prosecutor*, *IG*9(1).61, Cic.*Fam.*13.56.1, *Michel* 459 (Telmessus), *BMus.Inscr.*481*.315 (Ephesus, ii A.D.). 4. generally, *legal representative*, *POxy.*261.14 (i A.D.), Plin.*Ep.Traj.*110, etc.

ἐκδῐκόφως, *punishing mortals*, *PMag.Par.*1.1373.

ἐκδιοικ-έω, *collect* dues, etc., *PTeb.*27.57 (ii B.C., Pass.), al. -ήσιμος, ον, *alienable*, of property, *PTheb.Bank* 1.9 (ii B.C.). -ησις, εως, ἡ, *collection of dues*, *PTeb.*27.37.

ἐκδιορύσσω, *break open*, τάφον Tz.*H.*3.978.

ἐκδῑφάω, '*ferret out*', Herod.7.78: aor. 1, Hsch.

ἐκδιφρεύω, *throw from a chariot*, in Pass., Luc.*DDeor.*25.3, *Electr.*2.

ἐκδιψάω, *to be parched with drought*, of plants, Thphr.*CP*5.9.3; of a person, *to be very thirsty*, Plu.*Cleom.*29.

ἔκδιψος, ον, *very thirsty*, D.S.19.109.

ἐκδῐ-ωκτέον, *one must chase away*, Plu.2.13c. -ώκω, *chase away, banish*, Th.1.24; ἐκ τοῦ τόπου Arist.*HA*618^{b}12; τῆς οἰκίας Luc.*Tim.*10; *attack, persecute*, *PMasp.*2 iii 4 (vi A.D.), etc.:—Pass., Hyp.*Fr.*238. -ωξις, εως, ἡ, *pursuit*, Plu.2.293c. II. *repulse*, βαρβαρικῆς ἐπιδρομῆς *PLond.*5.1663 (vi A.D.).

ἐκδοκῐμάζω, *test thoroughly*, Aq., Sm.*Jb.*7.18.

ἐκδονέω, *shake utterly, confound*, in Pass., ἐκδεδόνηντο.. φρένες *AP* 11.64 (Agath.).

ἐκδορά, ἡ, *stripping off, removing*, λειχήνων Gal.12.844.

ἐκδόριος or -ειος, ον, *of* or *for flaying*: τὰ ἐ. (sc. φάρμακα) *medica-*

ments which take off the skin, Dsc.3.62, Aët.2.174; ἐπιθέματα Crito ap.Gal.12.448.

ἐκ-δόσιμος, ον, *contracted for, let out*, Poll.7.200, Ath.15.680d. 2. ἐκδόσιμον, τό, *certificate* of delivery of a document, service of summons, etc., *POxy*.34ᵛ ii 6 (ii A.D.), etc. **-δοσις**, εως, ἡ, Arc. **ἔσδοσις** *IG*5(2).6.16:—*giving up, surrendering*, ἱκετέων Hdt.1.159; δμηρειῶν ἐκδόσεις εἰς ἀλλήλους Pl.*Plt*.310e. 2. *giving in marriage, dowering*, ἐ. ποιεῖσθαι τῶν θυγατέρων Id.*Lg*.924d, cf. Arist.*Pol*.1335ᵃ 22; τὰς ἐ. τῶν γυναικῶν D.44.66. 3. *letting, hiring*, or *farming out*, *PPetr*.3 p.148 (iii B.C.); τὰς ἐ. ἀγοράζειν παρὰ τῶν τιμητῶν Plb. 6.17.4; τὰς ἐ. ποιεῖσθαι *IG*7.303.27 (Orop.); ἐ. ἱερῶν ἔργων Plu.*Cat. Ma*.19, cf. *IG*5(2).l.c. 4. *lending money on ships* or *exported goods, bottomry*, D.27.11, 29.35. 5. *publication* of a book, D.H. *Amm*.1.10, Ael.*Tact.Praef*.4: in concrete sense, *a 'publication', treatise*, A.D.*Synt*.3.4, 313.6, Iamb.*VP*23.104. b. *edition*, of an author's work, Ἀριστοφάνειος Heph.*Poëm*.p.74 C., cf. A.D.*Pron*.89. 22, etc. c. *translation*, J.*AJ*12.2.4 (dub.). II. *bursting forth*, πηγῶν Philostr.*Im*.2.17; *delivery*, ἐμβρύου Sor.1.71. 2. *motions* of the bowels, Archig.ap.Aët.6.27. **-δοτέον**, *one must give up*, τοὺς αἰτίους Plb.3.21.7; Καίσαρα τοῖς βαρβάροις Plu.*Caes*.22, cf. Ph.2.314. 2. *one must give in marriage*, Ar.*Av*.1635, Pl.*Ep*. 361d. **-δοτήρ**, Arc. **ἐσδοτήρ**, ῆρος, ὁ, = sq., *IG*5(2).6.6 (Tegea, iv B.C.); ἐγδ- *IG*4.1485.4 (Epid.). **-δότης**, ου, ὁ, *one who farms out contracts* or *taxes*, ib.12(5).653.63, etc. II. *one who gives his daughter in marriage*, *POxy*.497.15 (ii A.D.). III. *betrayer*, Hsch. **-δότις**, ιδος, ἡ, *bride's mother*, *POxy*.1273.26 (iii A.D.). **-δοτος**, ον, *given up, delivered*, esp. *betrayed*, ἔκδοτόν μιν ἐποίησε ἐς τοὺς Πέρσας Hdt.3.1, cf. Isoc.4.122; τὴν Βοιωτίαν Θηβαίοις Aeschin.3.142; ἱκέτην ἐ. διδόναι D.23.85, etc.; τοῖς πολεμίοις παραδιδόναι Lycurg.85; οὔτε σοὶ οὔτε ἄλλῃ οὐδεμιᾷ περιστάσει δώσομεν ἑαυτοὺς ἐ. Metrod.*Fr*.49; λαβών τινα ἐ. ὑπὸ τοῦ ὕπνου J.*AJ*6.13.9; ἔκδοτος ἄγεσθαι Hdt.6.85; γίγνεσθαι ibid., E.*Ion* 1251; ἐ. διὰ χειρὸς ἀνόμων *Act.Ap*.2.23: metaph., παρέχειν ἑαυτὴν ἐ. τινι to *give* herself *entirely up* to him, Luc.*DDeor*.20.13; ἐ. σεαυτὴν τῷ ποταμῷ ἐᾶσαι Porph. *Marc*.5; [χώρα] ἐ. τῷ κακῷ Id.*Chr*.49; πρὸς ὕβριν ἐ. Iamb.*Protr*. 2. II. *given in marriage*, *PMasp*.5.10 (vi A.D.).

ἔκδουλος, ὁ, *child of a slave*, Suid. s.v. Ἕρμιππος. **ἐκδούπησαν**· ἐβρόντησαν, Hsch. (ἐκ- for ἐγ-).

ἐκδοχ-εῖον, τό, *reservoir, tank*, J.*BJ*1.15.1, *Peripl.M.Rubr*.27. **-εύς**, έως, ὁ, *forwarding agent*, *PEdgar*5.11 (iii B.C.), *OGI*140.8 (Delos, ii B.C.), Ptol.*Tetr*.179, *POxy*.1669.2 (iii A.D.). **-ή**, ἡ, Arc. **ἐσδοκά** *IG*5(2).6.40:—*receiving from* or *at the hands of another, succession*, πομποῦ πυρός A.*Ag*.299; ἐκδοχαῖς ἐπιφέρει θεὸς κακόν E.*Hipp*. 866; ἐ. ποιεῖσθαι πολέμου to *continue* the war, Aeschin.2.30. 2. *receiving, containing*, ὄμβρων J.*BJ*5.4.3, cf. Paul.Aeg.6.106. II. *taking* or *understanding in a certain sense, interpretation*, ἐ. ποιεῖσθαι Plb.3.29.4, cf. *UPZ*110.86 (ii B.C.); ἐξ ὧν ἦν λαμβάνειν ἐκδοχὴν ὅτι.. Plb.22.7.6, cf. *SIG*557.18 (Magn. Mae., iii B.C.), Sch.Pi.*O*.13. 100. III. = προσδοκία, κρίσεως *Ep.Hebr*.10.27. IV. = ἀποδοχή, *recognition* for services rendered, *IG*12(5).722.8 (Andros). V. *giving of security*, προειδὼς ἀσφαλῆ τὴν ἐ. οὖσαν *PSI*4.349 (iii B.C.). VI. *contract*, *IG*5(2). l.c. **-ιον**, τό, = ἐκδοχεῖον, ὕδατος *Inscr.Prien*.208 (i B.C.); ἰχθύων θήρας ἐ. Dion.Byz.28: metaph., Μουσάων μυστικὸν ἐ. *AP*14.60. **-ιος**, ον, *receptive*, κόλπος τῆς θεότητος Procl. *in Ti*.3.175 D., cf. *Theol.Plat*.5.11.

ἐκδρᾰκοντόομαι, Pass., *become a very serpent*, A.*Ch*.549.

ἐκδρᾰμεῖν, v. ἐκτρέχω.

ἐκδρασκάζω, = ἐκδιδράσκω, Tz.*H*.5.889.

ἔκδραχμος, ον, *of six drachms*, Hsch.

ἐκδρέπομαι, *pluck off*, τούτων φύλλον Aristaenet.1.3 (Pass.).

ἐκδρομ-άς, άδος, ὁ, *one who has outrun the age of youth*, Eub.11, cf. Eust.1915.20. **-ή**, ἡ, *running out, sally, charge*, X.*HG*3.2.4, Arr. *An*.1.2.5, al.; τῶν ἐτησίων Aristid.*Or*.36(48).8. 2. abstr. for concrete, *party of skirmishers*, Th.4.127. II. *shooting, sprouting*, of trees, Thphr.*CP*2.1.3. 2. *issue*, ὕδατος Hp.*Morb*.4.57, cf. Herod. Med. in *Rh.Mus*.58.77. III. *digression in speaking*, Aristid.1.92 J. (pl.); ἡ ἐ. τοῦ λόγου Agath.1.3, cf. 4.29. IV. *lapse* of time, ἐτῶν τετρακοσίων Tz.*H*.8.56. **-ος**, ὁ, *one that runs out*: ἔκδρομοι *skirmishers*, Th.4.125, X.*HG*4.5.16.

ἐκδῠάζομαι, Pass., *to be conjoined*, ποικίλως σὺν ἀλλήλαις Phld. *Herc*.1003.

ἐκδῠάς, άδος, ἡ, fanciful etym. of ὀγδοάς, *Theol.Ar*.55.

ἔκδῠμα, f.l. in *AP*5.198 (Hedyl.; leg. ἐνδ-).

ἐκδῠνᾰμόω, gloss on ἐξανεμόω, Sch.Vind.Hp.*Mul*.1.34 (Pass.).

ἐκδῠναστεύω, *overpower, prevail over*, τινός Sm.*Je*.50(27).17.

ἐκδύνω, v. ἐκδύω. **ἐκδύον**· καλόν, κομψόν, Hsch.

ἐκδύσια [ῠ] (sc. ἱερά), τά, festival at Phaestus, in Crete, when Galatea *put off* her woman's *clothes*, Ant.Lib.17.6.

ἔκδῠσις, εως, ἡ, *getting out, escape*, opp. ἔσοδος, Hdt.2.121.γ'; τὴν ἐ. ποιεῖσθαι to make their *way out*, Id.3.109; οὐκ ἔστι Ἕλλησι οὐδεμία ἐ. μὴ οὐκ εἶναι δούλους Id.8.100, cf. Pl.*Cra*.426a; πόθεν ἔκδυσιν εὗρες λατρείης δοξῶν; Timo 48 (v.l. ἔκλυσιν). II. *stripping, deprivation*, Man.4.331 (pl.).

ἐκδῠσωπέω, *put to shame*, τινά Hld.8.3; τὴν πλεονεξίαν τινός J. *BJ*1.2.2; ἐ. τινὰ μὴ ἁμαρτάνειν Id.*AJ*15.4.1.

ἐκδῠτ-ήριον, τό, = ἀποδυτήριον, *Gloss*. **-ης**, ου, ὁ, *one who undresses*, Id.

ἐκδύω (**ἐκδύνω** Hdt.1.9, etc.): I. causal in pres. ἐκδύω: impf. ἐξέδυον· fut. ἐκδύσω: aor. 1 ἐξέδῡσα: late pf. ἐκδέδῠκα *AP*5.72 (Rufin.):—*take off, strip off*, c. dupl. acc. pers. et rei, ἐκ μέν με χλαῖναν ἔδυσαν they *stripped* me *of* my cloak, Od.14.341; ἐκδύων ἐμὲ.. ἐσθῆτα A.*Ag*.1269; ἐκδύσας αὐτὸν [τὸν χιτῶνα] X.*Cyr*.1.3.17: c. acc. only, *strip*, πάντας ἐ. D.24.204; ἐξέδυσαν [ἐκεῖνον] Id.54.8. 2. Pass., ἐκδύομαι, aor. 1 ἐξεδύθην [ῠ]: pf. ἐκδέδῠμαι:—*to be stripped of* a thing, τὸν χιτωνίσκον ἐκδεδύσθαι Lys.10.10; [Μαρσύας] τὸ δέρμα ἐκδύεται Palaeph.47: abs., *to be stripped*, ἐκδυθῆναι Antipho 2.2.5, cf. Plb.15. 27.9. 3. Med., ἐκδύομαι, Cret. ἐσδ- *GDI*5100, fut. -δύσομαι: aor. 1 ἐξεδυσάμην:—*strip oneself of* a thing, *put off*, τεύχεά τ' ἐξεδύοντο they *were putting off their* armour, Il.3.114; ἐκδύσασθαι (leg. -δύσεσθαι) τὸν κιθῶνα Hdt.5.106; ἐκδεδύσθαι θοἰμάτιον D.54.35; θηρία ἐκδύεται τὸ ἄγριον Plu.*Pomp*.28: abs., *put off one's clothes, strip*, θᾶττον ἐκδυώμεθα Ar.*Lys*.686, cf. X.*HG*2.4.19; technically, of ephebi, *SIG*527.99 (Dreros, iii B.C.), *GDI*5100: metaph. of death, 2*Ep.Cor*. 5.4. II. Act. in med. sense, *put off*, μαλακὸν δ' ἔκδυνε χιτῶνα Od. 1.437; ἐκδὺς χλαῖναν 14.460; τῶν ἱματίων κατὰ ἓν ἕκαστον ἐκδύνουσα Hdt.1.9: metaph., τὸ γῆρας ἐκδύς Ar.*Pax* 336, cf. Arist.*HA*600ᵇ15; τὸ κέλυφος ib.549ᵇ25:—Pass., of the clothes, *to be put off*, ἅμα κιθῶνι ἐκδυομένῳ Hdt.1.8. III. aor. 2 ἐξέδυν: pf. ἐκδέδῡκα:—*go* or *get out of*, c. gen., ἐκδὺς μεγάροιο Od.22.334; ἐκδὺς καὶ ἀνακύψας τῆς θαλάσσης *emerging from*.., Pl.*Phd*.109d: metaph., ἐξέδυ δίκης E.*Supp*.416; ἐκδῦναι κακῶν Id.*IT*602. 2. pf. and aor. 2 c. acc., *escape, shun*, νῶϊν δ' ἐκδῦμεν ὄλεθρον [grant] us *to escape*.., Il.16.99; ἐκδεδυκέναι τὰς λῃτουργίας D.20.1; τὸν φθόνον ἐκδύς Plu.*Pomp*.30; τὴν ἀληθινὴν οὐσίαν ἐκδεδυκέναι ταῦτα Plot.6.6.8. 3. abs., *escape*, Thgn.358; *escape one's memory*, Pl.*Alc*.2.147e.

ἐκδωριεύομαι, Pass., *become a thorough Dorian*, Hdt.8.73 (pf. ἐκδεδωρίευνται: ἐκδεδωρίωνται Valck., ἐκδεδωρίδαται Dind.).

ἐκεῖ (not in Hom.), Aeol. **κῆ** Sapph.51: Dor. **τηνεῖ** (q.v.):—Adv. *there, in that place*, opp. ἐνθάδε, Th.6.83; οἱ ἐ. S.*El*.685, etc.; τἀκεῖ *what is* or *happens there, events there*, E.*Fr*.578.5, Th.1.90; redundant, οὗ ἦν ἐ. Lxx 1*Ki*.9.10. 2. freq. as euphem. for ἐν Ἅιδου, *in another world*, κἀκεῖ δικάζει τἀμπλακήματα Ζεὺς ἄλλος A.*Supp*.230, cf. *Ch*.359 (lyr.), S.*Ant*.76; εὐδαιμονοίτην, ἀλλ' ἐ. E.*Med*.1073; εὔκολος μὲν ἐνθάδ', εὔκολος δ' ἐκεῖ Ar.*Ra*.82, cf. Pl.*Phd*.64a, al.; in full, ἐκεῖ δ' ἐν Ἅιδου E.*Hec*.418; οἱ ἐ. euphem. for *the dead*, A.*Ch*.355 (lyr.), S.*OT*776, Pl.*R*.427b, Isoc.14.61. 3. Philos., *in the intelligible world*, Plot.1.2.7, 2.4.5, etc. II. with Verbs of motion, for ἐκεῖσε, *thither*, ἐ. πλέομεν Hdt.7.147; ἐ. ἀπικέσθαι v.l. in Id.9.108; ὁδοῦ τῆς ἐ. S.*OC*1019; οἱ ἐ. καταπεφευγότες Th.3.71, cf. Plb.5.101.10; βλέψον δὲ κἀκεῖ Men.*Epit*.103. III. rarely, of Time, *then*, S.*Ph*.395 (lyr.), D.22.38.

ἔκελεν· ἐκέντησεν, Hsch.

ἐκεῖθεν, poet. **κεῖθεν** (the only form used by Hom., also in Trag. where metre requires): Aeol. **κήνοθεν** Alc.86: Dor. **τηνῶθεν** Ar.*Ach*. 754; **τηνῶθε** Theoc.3.10:—Adv. *from that place, thence*, opp. ἐκεῖσε, S.*Ph*.490, etc.; of a person, τἀκεῖθεν εἰ ποθούμεθα *on his part*, Id.*Tr*. 632; ὁ ἐ. ἄγγελος Pl.*R*.619b; τὸ σκῆπτρον ἐ. παραλαβόντες Jul.*Or*. 6.181b. 2. = ἐκεῖ, οἱ ἐ. Th.1.62: c. gen., τοὐκεῖθεν ἄλσους *on yon side of* the grove, S.*OC*505; ἕζοντο τὸ κεῖθεν ὅθενπερ ἥκει S.*OC*1227 codd. (lyr.). II. *thence, from that fact*, γνοίη δ' ἄν τις ἐ. Isoc.12.224, cf. D.45.48, etc. III. of Time, *thenceforward*, Il.15.234; ἐ. ἤδη D.C.54.25.

ἐκεῖθι and **κεῖθι** (the only form used by Hom. exc. Od.17.10, also by Trag. where metre requires), Aeol. **κῆθι** Sapph.*Supp*.25.18 (prob.): Dor. **τηνόθι** Theoc.8.44: poet. for ἐκεῖ, Il.3.402, Od.17.10: in late Prose, οἱ ἐκεῖθι Ael.*NA*6.15; κεῖθι Alciphr.3.53, Them.*Or*.4. 57a. II. = ἐκεῖσε, κεῖθι μολών Hes.*Fr*.134.10, cf. Musae.23, Opp. *H*.4.274, dub. in A.*Th*.809.

ἐκείνῃ, v. ἐκεῖνος III.

ἐκείνινος, η, ον, (ἐκεῖνος) *made of that material*, Arist.*Metaph*.1033ᵃ 7, 1049ᵃ21.

ἐκεῖνος, ἐκείνη, ἐκεῖνο, also **κεῖνος** (regular in Ep., Ion. (as *SIG*37. 3 (Teos, v B.C.), though Hdt. prefers ἐκεῖνος), and Lyr., in Trag. κεῖνος only where the metre requires, cf. A.*Pers*.230, 792, S.*Aj*.220 (anap.), etc.; but not in Att. Prose, and in Com. only in mock Trag. passages): Aeol. **κῆνος** Sapph.2.1: Dor. **τῆνος** Theoc.1.4, etc.: in Com., strengthd. **ἐκεινοσί** Eup.277 (prob.), Ar.*Eq*.1196, etc.; **ἐκεινοσίν** A.D.*Pron*.59.24: (ἐκεῖ):—demonstr. Pron. *the person there, that person* or *thing*, Hom., etc.: generally with reference to what has gone immediately before, Pl.*Phd*.106c, X.*Cyr*.1.6.9, etc.; but when οὗτος and ἐκεῖνος refer to two things before mentioned, ἐκεῖνος, prop. belongs to *the more remote*, in time, place, or thought, οὗτος to *the nearer*, Pl.*Euthd*.271b, etc.: but ἐκεῖνος sts. = *the latter*, X.*Mem*. 1.3.13, D.8.72, Arist.*Pol*.1325ᵃ7, etc.: ἐκεῖνος is freq. the predicate to οὗτος or ὅδε, οὗτος ἐκεῖνος τὸν σὺ ζητέεις Hdt.1.32; τοῦτ' ἔστ' ἐκεῖνο E.*Hel*.622; ἆρ' οὗτός ἐστ' ἐκεῖνος ὅν..; Ar.*Pax* 240, etc.: also joined as if one Pron., τοῦτ' ἐκεῖνο..δέρκομαι S.*El*.1115, etc.; κατ' ἐκεῖνο καιροῦ at *that point* of time, Plu.*Alex*.32, etc.; ἐς ἐ. τοῦ χρόνου D.C. 46.49; ἀλλ' ἐκεῖνο, *à propos*, Luc.*Nigr*.8. 2. to denote well-known persons, etc., κεῖνος μέγας θεός Il.24.90; ἐκεῖνος ἡνίκ' ἦν Θουκυδίδης Ar.*Ach*.708; καίτοι φασὶν Ἰφικράτην ποτ' ἐκεῖνον.. D.21. 62; ὦ παῖ 'κείνου τἀνδρός Pl.*Phlb*.36d. b. ἐκεῖνα *the ideal world*, Id.*Phdr*.250a. 3. for things, of which one cannot remember or must not mention the name, = ὁ δεῖνα, *so-and-so*, Ar.*Nu*.195. b. in formulae, τεθνάτω καὶ οἱ παῖδες οἱ ἐξ ἐκείνου *IG*1².10.33. 4. with simple demonstr. force, Ἶρος ἐκεῖνος ἧσται Irus sits *there*, Od.18.239; νῆες ἐκεῖναι ἐπιπλέουσιν *there* are ships sailing up, Th.1.51. 5.

in orat. obliq. where prop. the reflex. Pron. αὐτοῦ would stand, X. *HG*1.6.14, Is.8.22, etc. 6. after a Relat. in apodosi almost pleon., X.*Cyr.*1.4.19 (s.v.l.). 7. in Aeol. and Att. the Subst. with ἐκεῖνος prop. has the Art. (κῆνος ὤνηρ Alc.*Supp.*25.6), and ἐκεῖνος may precede or follow the Subst., ἐκείνῃ τῇ ἡμέρᾳ Th.1.20, Pl.*Phd.*57a; τὴν στρατείαν ἐ., τὸν ἄνδρ' ἐ., Th.1.10, Ar.*Pax*649: in Poets the Art. is freq. omitted, ἤματι κείνῳ Il.2.37, etc.; but when this is the case in Prose, ἐκεῖνος follows the Subst., ἡμέρας ἐκείνης Th.3.59, etc. II. Adv. ἐκείνως *in that case*, Id.1.77, 3.46; *in that way*, Hp.*Fract.*27; ζῆν Pl.*R.*516d, etc.: Ion. **κείνως** Hdt.1.120. III. dat. fem. ἐκείνῃ as Adv., 1. of Place, *at that place, in that neighbourhood*, Hdt.8.106, Th.4.77, etc.; κείνῃ (sc. ὁδῷ) Od.13.111. 2. of Manner, *in that manner*, Pl.*R.*556a, etc. IV. with Preps., ἐξ ἐκείνου from *that time*, X.*Ages.*1.17; ἀπ' ἐκείνου Luc.*DMar.*2.2; κατ' ἐκεῖνα *in that region*, X.*HG*3.5.17, etc.; μετ' ἐκεῖνα *afterwards*, Th.5.81; cf. ἐπέκεινα.

ἐκεῖσε, poet. **κεῖσε** (the only form in Hom., used by Trag. where the metre requires), Adv. *thither, to that place*, opp. ἐκεῖθεν or ἐνθένδε, Hdt.2.29, A.*Pers.*717, etc.; ἐκεῖσε κἀκεῖσε *hither and thither*, E.*Andr.*1131, *Hel.*533; δεῦρο καὶ αὖθις ἐ. ib.1141 (lyr.); κἀκεῖσε καὶ τὸ δεῦρο Id.*Ph.*266; τῇδε ἐ. Id.*Tr.*333 (anap.); τὸ κεῖσε δεῦρό τε S.*Tr.*929; τὸ τῇδε καὶ τὸ κεῖσε καὶ τὸ δεῦρο Ar.*Av.*425. 2. *to the other world*, E.*Alc.*363; ἐνθένδε ἐ. from this world *to the other*, Pl.*Phd.*117c. 3. c. gen., ἄνειμι δ' ἐ. τοῦ λόγου Hdt.7.239, cf. Pl.*Lg.*864c. II. = ἐκεῖ, Hp.*Vict.*2.38, Chrysipp.*Stoic.*2.244, Plb.5.51.3, Lxx *Jb.*39.29, J.*AJ* 3.2.1, Sch.Pi.*O.*9.108; τοὺς ἐ. ὄντας *Act.Ap.*22.5.

ἐκέκαστο, v. καίνυμαι. **ἐκεκήδει**· ὑπε(κε)χωρήκει, Hsch. **ἐκέκλετο**, v. κέλομαι.

ἐκεχειρία, ἡ, (ἔχω, χείρ) *cessation of hostilities, armistice, truce*, *IG* 1².96.22, etc.; ἐ. ποιεῖσθαι Th.4.117; ἄγειν, ἔχειν, Id.5.26, X.*HG*4.2.16; ἐ. γίγνεταί τισι πρὸς ἀλλήλους Th.4.58; ἀπειπεῖν τὴν ἐ. denounce the *truce*, Id.5.32; ἡ Ὀλυμπιακὴ ἐ. Arist.*Fr.*533; Dor. **ἐκεχηρία** *IG* 2².1126.49, cf. *SIG*559.32 (Megalop., found at Magn. Mae.). 2. generally, *rest from work, holiday*, J.*AJ*1.1.1, Luc.*Herm.*11, *Sammelb.*4224.17; ἐ. πόνων Jul.*Or.*4.153c; *leisure, opportunity*, τοῦ διαμαρτάνειν, εἰς τὸ ἁμαρτάνειν, Ph.1.430, 2.76: c. inf., ib.444. 3. in Ar.*Pax*908 ὑπέχοντα τὴν ἐκεχειρίαν is a pun—'alleging the *truce*', and 'presenting the *hand-for-holding*' (as a beggar does). 4. *licence, leave*, to do a thing, ἐ. διδόναι τινί Ph.2.542; coupled with ἄδεια, ib.447, al.; *time of licence*, ib.529. 5. *self-restraint, abstinence*, περὶ τὰς κλοπάς Str.15.1.53.

ἐκεχείριον, τό, *travelling allowance for* θεωροί *who announce a sacred truce*, *Inscr.Magn.*33.18.

ἐκέχειρον, τό, = foreg., *IG*12(5).1341.53 (Paros), 629.26 (Pergam., ii B.C.); cf. ἐκέχειρον· τὸ ἀργύριον, Hsch.

ἐκεχειροφόρος, ὁ, *herald of truce*, Poll.4.94: metaph., ἔδωκεν αὐτοῖς ὥσπερ ἐ. τὸν ἀέρα *mediator* between fire and water, Max.Tyr.15.3.

ἐκζᾰλόομαι, *to be surf-tossed, wave-beaten*, Gloss.

ἔκ-ζεμα, ατος, τό, *a cutaneous eruption, eczema*, Dsc.1.43 (pl.), Erot. s.v. ἐκθύματα (pl.), *Gp.*1.12.19 (pl.). **-ζεσις**, εως, ἡ, *boiling out* or *over, breaking out*, ἑλκῶν Arist.*Pr.*954ᵃ25 (pl.). II. = foreg., Erot. s.v. αἰθόλικες (pl.). **-ζεσμα**, ατος, τό, = ἔκζεμα, Archig.ap.Gal.12.468 (pl.), Crito ap.eund.12.485 (pl.). **-ζεστός**, όν, *boiled*, τευτλίον Diph.Siph.ap.Ath.9.371a; θρῖδαξ Did.ap.Aët.9.42; *hard-boiled*, ᾠά Alex.Trall.2. **-ζέω**, *boil out* or *over*: *break out*, in disease, Arist.*Pr.*861ᵇ10; ὅταν ἐκζέῃ τὸ αἷμα Ant.Lib.19.2: metaph., ἐξέζεσεν γὰρ Οἰδίπου κατεύγματα A.*Th.*709. 2. c. gen., ζῶσα εὐλέων ἐξέζεσε *bred* worms, Hdt.4.205: c. dat., ἐκζεῖν φθειρσί D.L.4.4: c. acc., σκώληκας Lxx *Ex.*16.20; of a country, ἐ. μύας ib.1*Ki.*6.1. 3. *ferment*, Dsc.5.7. II. Pass., *to be boiled to a decoction*, Aret.*CD*2.5.

ἐκζητ-έω, *seek out*, Aristid.1.488 J., *PMag.Osl.*1.354; τινάς *POxy.*1465.11 (i B.C.); περί τινος 1*Ep.Pet.*1.10. II. *demand an account of*, τὸ αἷμα Lxx 2*Ki.*4.11, al., cf. *Ev.Luc.*11.50 (Pass.). **-ησις**, εως, ἡ, *research*, 1*Ep.Ti.*1.4 (pl.). **-ητής**, οῦ, ὁ, *searcher out*, Lxx *Ba.*3.23.

ἐκζωόομαι, Pass., *become full of worms*, Thphr.*CP*4.8.4.

ἐκζωπῠρ-έω, *rekindle*, πόλεμον Ar.*Pax*310; ἄνθρακας Plu.*Mar.*44; παλαιὰν συγγένειαν Id.*Rom.*29. **-ησις**, εως, ἡ, *rekindling*, ἀνθράκων Id.2.156b.

ἔκηα, v. καίω.

ἐκηβελέτης, ου, ὁ, = ἑκηβόλος, Orph.*Fr.*297.11.

ἑκηβολ-έω, *to be an archer*, Max.Tyr.7.3. **-ία**, Ep. **-ίη**, ἡ, *skill in archery*, Il.5.54 (pl.): later in sg., Call.*Ap.*99, Str.8.3.33, *AP*6.26 (Jul.).

ἑκηβόλος, Dor. **ἑκᾱβόλος**, ον, (ἑκών, βάλλω) *attaining his aim*, epith. of Apollo, Il.1.14, al.; also Ἑκηβόλος alone, ib.96, *h.Ap.*45, Pi.*Pae.*9.38, al.; of Artemis, S.*Fr.*401; ἑκηβόλοι Διὸς χέρες E.*Ion* 213 (lyr.); τόξα A.*Pr.*711, *Eu.*628; σφενδόναι E.*Ph.*1142; ἔθνος ὀϊστῶν Opp.*H.*4.205; in later Prose, ἑ. βέλη Plb.13.3.4; μάχαι D.H.10.16; ἑ. ἄνδρες Plu.*Luc.*28; τὰ ἑ. Onos.20.1; τοξεύματα, ὅπλα, Ael.*Tact.*2.8, Arr.*Tact.*3.3; τοξόται καὶ ἑκηβόλοι Agath.3.17: Dor. Sup. ἑκαβολέστατος Archyt.ap.Iamb.*Protr.*4. Adv. **-λως**, τοξεύειν Ath.1.25d. (Understood by later writers as *far-shooting* (ἑκάς).)

ἐκηλία, ἡ, = εὐκηλία, *rest, peace*, Hsch.

ἕκηλος, Dor. **ἕκᾱλος**, ον, *at rest, at one's ease*, in Hom. esp. of persons feasting and enjoying themselves, οἱ δὲ ἕκηλοι τέρπονται Il.5.759; ἕκηλος πῖνε Od.21.309; ἕκηλοι νεκροὺς ἂμ πεδίον συλήσετε ye will plunder them *at your ease*, i.e. *without let* or *hindrance*, Il.6.70; ἕκηλος ἐρρέτω let him be off *in peace*, 9.376; of mere inaction, *quiet*, only twice in Hom., ἔσθι' ἕκηλος Od.17.478; ἕκηλοι κάτθετε 21.259, cf. Theoc.25.100; ἕκαλος ἔπειμι γῆρας Pi.*I.*7(6).41; ἕ. εὕδειν S.*Ph.*769; ἐὰν ἕκηλόν τινα ib.826: neut. as Adv., ἕκηλα ἡμερεύειν Id.*El.*786: metaph. of a field, *lying at rest* or *fallow*, *h.Cer.*451; of trees, *unmoved*, A.R.3.969.

ἕκητι, Dor. **ἕκᾱτι** (so always used by Trag., as E.*Or.*26, al.): prob. an old case-form, used adverbially, but always with a gen., which usually precedes, *by the will of, by means of, by virtue of*, Hom. only in Od. (in Il. he uses ἰότητι, but cf. ἀέκητι), and always of gods, Διὸς.. ἕκητι *by the grace* or *aid* of Zeus, Od.20.42; Ἑρμείαο ἕ. 15.319; Ἀπόλλωνός γε ἕ. 19.86; Διὸς ἕ. B.1.6; Παλλάδος καὶ Λοξίου ἕκατι A.*Eu.*759, cf. *Ch.*214; ἕ. μὲν δαιμόνων, ἕ. δ' ἁμᾶν χερῶν ib.436 (lyr.). II. in Lyr. and Trag. of things, 1. *on account of, for the sake of*, ἕκατι ποδῶν Pi.*N.*8.47; κεδνῶν ἕκατι πραγμάτων A.*Ch.*701; ἀρετῆς ἕ. S.*Ph.*669, cf. *Tr.*274, 353; γάμων ἕ. E.*Med.*1235: in Com., ὧν ἕ. τοῦτ' ἔδωκε Telecl.41.4. 2. *as to*, πλήθους ἕ. A.*Pers.*337; κελευμάτων δ' ἕ. E.*Cyc.*655; ἐμεῦ μὲν ἕκητι *so far as* I *am concerned*, *AP*11.361.7 (Autom.); ἕκητ' ἀλκῆς *as far as* strength *goes*, Herod.2.77: in later Prose, βιβλίων ἕ. Jul.*Or.*3.124a, cf. 119c. III. = χωρίς, Hsch. (Perh. cogn. with ἑκών.)

ἐκθᾰλαττόομαι, Pass., *become all sea*, Str.1.3.7.

ἐκθαλίς, = ἐρυσίβη, *EM*378.49 (s.v.l.).

ἐκθάλλω, *put forth blossoms*, Sm.*Ca.*2.13, Al.*Hb.*3.17. 2. metaph., *become active*, of heat in the ground, Adam.ap.Aët.3.163.

ἐκθάλπω, *warm thoroughly*, metaph. in Pass., ἔρωτι Phryn.*PS* p.71 B., cj. in S.*Fr.*474.

ἐκθαμβ-έω, *to be amazed*, Orph.*A.*1218 (tm.). II. trans., *amaze, astonish*, Lxx *Si.*30.9:—Pass., *Ev.Marc.*9.15, Gal.16.493. **-ησις**, εως, ἡ, *amazement*, Aq.*Is.*52.12. **-ητικός**, ή, όν, *astonishing*, Eust.1420.5. **-ος**, ον, *amazed, astounded*, Plb.20.10.9, *Act.Ap.*3.11, *Tab.Defix.*5.20, Orph.*Fr.*49 vi 88. II. *terrible*, Thd.*Da.*7.7.

ἐκθαμνίζω, *root out, extirpate*, A.*Th.*72, Tz.*H.*1.780 (Pass.).

ἐκθαμνόομαι, Pass., *grow bushy*, Thphr.*HP*1.3.3.

ἐκθάπτω, *disinter*, *CIG*2826.4, al. (Aphrodisias).

ἐκθαρρ-έω, strengthd. for θαρρέω, *have full confidence*, ἐκτεθαρρηκὼς τοῖς πράγμασι Plu.*Rom.*26; *to be encouraged*, ὑπό τινος Id.*Galb.*7. **-ησις**, εως, ἡ, *full confidence*, Porph.*Abst.*1.50.

ἐκθάρσημα, ατος, τό, *ground for confidence*, Plu.2.1103a.

ἐκθαυμάζω, strengthd. for θαυμάζω, Aristeas 312, D.H.*Th.*34, Longin.44.8; ἐπί τινος Lxx *Si.*27.23; ἐπί τινι *Ev.Marc.*12.17.

ἐκθεάομαι, *see out, see to the end*, S.*OT*1253. II. Pass., *to be made visible*, prob. for ἐκθειασθῇ in Ph.1.96.

ἐκθεᾱτρίζω, *bring out on the stage*, metaph. in Pass., Ath.11.506f; in bad sense, *make a public show of*, τὴν αὐτῶν ἀκρισίαν Plb.11.8.7; *expose to public shame*, τοὺς πολεμίους Id.3.91.10, etc.

ἐκθει-άζω, *make a god of, deify*, Luc.*Tox.*2, S.E.*M.*9.35 (Pass.), Hdn.4.2.1: metaph., τοὺς Αἰγυπτίους ὡς ἀρχαίους Herm.*in Phdr.* p.199 A.; *worship as a god*, τὰ θνητά Plu.*Rom.*28, cf. Ptol.*Tetr.*123, Jul.*Gal.*155d; τὴν φύσιν Vett.Val.251.28; τὴν Ὁμήρου σοφίαν ἐκτεθείακεν αἰὼν ὁ σύμπας Heraclit.*All.*79. II. of things, *treat* or *regard as supernatural*, Plu.*Sert.*11, Hdn.1.14.6 (Pass.). **-ασμός**, ὁ, *inspiration*, Sch.Ar.*V.*8. **-όω** (A), *make a god of, worship as such*, Pass., ἐκτεθειῶσθαι *to be deified*, D.H.2.75; ταῖς τιμαῖς Plu.2.856e. **-όω** (B), *desulphurate*, Zos.Alch.p.147 B.

ἔκθεμα, ατος, τό, *public notice, proclamation, edict*, *PRev.Laws*33.10 (iii B.C.), Plb.31.6(10).1 (pl.); ἀπ' ἐκθέματος, = Lat. *ex edicto*, *IG* 7.2712.26, 73 (Acraephia), cf. *SIG*1023.61 (Cos).

ἐκθεμᾰτίζω, *give public notice*, *PTeb.*27.108 (Pass., ii B.C.).

ἐκθέμεναι or **ἐκθέμεν**, v. ἐκτίθημι.

ἐκθεολογέω, *attribute to the Deity*, ἡ τοῦ παντὸς ἐκτεθεολόγηται γένεσις Heraclit.*All.*40.

ἐκθεόω, = ἐκθειόω (A), Ael.*NA*10.23, Porph.*Marc.*17:—Pass., *to be made* or *become divine*, Herm.*in Phdr.*p.135 A., Dam.*Pr.*100, Procl.*Inst.*129, al. II. of temples or places, *consecrate*, βωμόν App.*BC* 3.3. III. *drawn for magical purposes* (cf. ἀποθεόω), *PMag.Par.*1.2456.

ἐκθερᾰπεύω, strengthd. for θεραπεύω: 1. *cure perfectly*, Plb.3.88.1, Agath.1.15:—Med., *get oneself quite cured*, Hp.*Vict.*3.83. 2. *gain over*, Aeschin.1.169, D.S.14.19, Plu.*Sol.*31, *PSI*6.614.5 (iii B.C.), Agath.*Praef.*p.137 D.; τινὰς φιλανθρωπίαις D.H.5.76:—Pass., παρὰ τῶν κληρονόμων *Cod.Just.*1.3.45.6. 3. Pass., *to be complied with*, Agath.5.10.

ἐκθερίζω, *reap* or *mow completely*, of a crop, θέρος D.53.21, cf. *PEdgar*27.5 (iii B.C.), Lxx *Le.*19.9, Alciphr.3.16: metaph. of men, τοὺς γηγενεῖς ἐξεθερίσατε Sch.A.R.4.1031, cf. E.*Fr.*373:—Pass., Thphr.*CP*4.6.1. 2. *cut out*, τὴν γλῶσσαν ἐκθερίξω (aor. subj.) *Anacreont.*9.7.

ἐκθερμ-αίνω, strengthd. for θερμαίνω, *warm thoroughly*, Arist.*HA*580ᵃ9, *Pr.*878ᵃ38, Philostr.*Gym.*35; ποτῷ γυῖα Nic.*Al.*461:—Pass., *become hot*, Hp.*VM*16, Arist.*Pr.*863ᵇ27; with wine, Timae.114. II. *cause to evaporate by heat*, Arist.*Pr.*870ᵃ17 (Pass.): metaph., τὸν εὐρῶτα τῆς ψυχῆς οὐκ ἐκτεθέρμαγκε διὰ φιλοσοφίας Plu.2.48c. **-αντέον**, *one must heat*, Herod.Med. in *Rh.Mus.*58.101. **-ος**, ον, *very hot*, Vett.Val.162.23, Gal.4.490, Aspasia ap. Aët.16.22.

ἐκ-θεσία, Ep. **-ίη**, ἡ, *exposure*, βρεφέων Man.4.368: abs., ib.596. **-θέσιμος**, ον, *exposed*, Vett.Val.61.18, Gloss. **-θεσις**, εως, ἡ, *exposure*, of a child, Hdt.1.116, E.*Ion* 956; also of *the putting out* of Ulysses on the shore of Ithaca, Arist.*Po.*1460^{a}36. 2. *exhibition*, ἀργυρωμάτων D.S.34/5.2.35 (pl.). II. *setting forth, exposition*, τῶν ὅρων Arist.*APr.*48^{a}25, 49^{b}6. b. *exhibition* of a particular instance, ἀποδεῖξαι τῇ ἐκθέσει ib.28^{b}14; κατὰ τὴν ἔ. ἑκάστου Id. *Metaph.*1090^{a}17, cf. 992^{b}10, Epicur.*Nat.*15.23, Chrysipp.*Stoic.*2.7 (pl.). III. pl., *stakes*, at play, Alciphr.3.54. IV. *public notice*, ἔ. ποιεῖσθαι *SIG* 685.37 (Crete), cf. *PHib.*1.29.10 (iii B.C.). V. Medic., *prescription*, Alex.Trall.1.11. VI. Math., *setting out* of terms in a series, *Theol.Ar.*51 (pl.); *series*, Moderat.ap.Stob.1 *Prooem.*9, Nicom.*Ar.*1.7. b. Geom., *particular enunciation*, Procl.*in Euc.* p.203 F., al. VII. *salient angle*, Ph.*Bel.*82.3 (pl.); *projection* of bastions, *GDI* 5597 (Ephesus). 2. *writing* of lyric verses *to the left* of the previous line, opp. εἴσθεσις (q.v.), Sch.Ar.*Ra.*1548, al. VIII. *list, schedule*, *POxy.*291.3 (i A.D.), etc. IX. *table* of musical notes, Aristid.Quint.1.11. X. = ὀφειλὴ παλαιά, Hsch.

ἔκθεσμος, ον, *lawless, unlawful*, Ph.2.502, Phint.ap.Stob.4.23.61, *POxy.*129.4 (vi A.D.); *monstrous*, ὄναρ Plu.*Caes.*32; ὑποθέσεις Phld. *Sto.*339.18; εὑρήματα Ph.1.335 (Sup.).

ἐκ-θετέον, (ἐκτίθημι) *one must set forth*, Str.17.1.1; *one must arrange, tabulate*, ἐφ' ἑνὸς στίχου πάντας [ἀριθμούς] Plu.2.1027d, cf. Iamb.*in Nic.*p.44 P. **-θέτης**, ου, ὁ, *balcony*, Sm.3*Ki.*6.4. **-θετικός**, ή, όν, *expository*, λόγος ἔ. τινος Aphth.*Prog.*8, cf. Theo *Prog.*4. II. ἔ. τρόπος, = ἔκθεσις II.b, Alex.Aphr.*in APr.*34.7. Adv. **-κῶς** Simp. *in Ph.*948.25. III. *enunciatory*, *Stoic.*2.62. **-θετος**, ον, *sent out of the house, sent away*, E.*Andr.*70; *exposed*, of a child, *Act.Ap.* 7.19, Man.6.52; *cast away*, Hsch. II. *projecting, salient*, Sor.1. 68; opp. κρυπτός, Heliod.(?) ap.Orib.49.4.23. b. neut., ἔκθετον, τό, = ἐκθέτης, Al.*Ez.*42.3.

ἐκθέω, *run out*: *make a sally*, Ar.*Lys.*456; ἐκ τοῦ τείχους X.*HG* 3.1.7; of javelins, *fly out*, Plu.*Marc.*16: *rush, hurry out*, Arist.*EN* 1149^{a}28.

ἐκθέ-ωσις, εως, ἡ, *deification, consecration*, *OGI* 56.53 (Canopus, iii B.C.), Ph.2.594, al. **-ωτικός**, ή, όν, *divinizing*, Procl.*in Prm.* p.838 S., *in Ti.*3.205 D.

ἐκθηλάζω, *suck the breast*, Lxx *Is.*66.11:—Pass., Hp.*Mul.*1.73; *to be sucked out*, Arist.*HA* 587^{b}27.

ἐκθήλ-υνσις, εως, ἡ, *becoming soft, relaxation*, σαρκῶν Hp.*Aph.*5. 16, cf. *Art.*52:—also **-ῠσις** Nic.*Fr.*135. **-ύνω**, aor. -εθήλυνα D.H. 7.9:—*soften, weaken*, τὸ σκέλος ἐκτεθηλυσμένον γίνεται Hp.*Art.*52, cf. 56; *make effeminate*, στρατιὰν ταῖς ἡδοναῖς Str.5.4.13; τὴν νεότητα ταῖς ἀγωγαῖς D.H. l. c.; ψυχάς Corn.*ND* 20:—Pass., ἐκτεθηλυμμένος καὶ τῇ ψυχῇ καὶ τῷ σώματι Plb.36.15.2, cf. 28.21.3, D.C.50.27; of plants, *become enfeebled*, Thphr.*CP* 3.1.3. II. Gramm., *make a feminine of*, *EM* 473.35.

ἐκθηρ-άομαι, *hunt out, catch*, X.*Cyn.*5.25, Plu.*Pomp.*26; τῇ ἀκοῇ πότερον.. Max.Tyr.31.3. **-ατέον**, *one must hunt out*, Plu.*Comp. Nic.Crass.*4, Max.Tyr.34.4. **-εύω**, = ἐκθηράομαι, Hdt.6.31, Arist. *Mir.*832^{a}29, Plu.*Crass.*31.

ἐκθηριόω, *make savage*, τινάς Ph.*Fr.*98 H.; ἑαυτόν Longus 1.20:—Pass., *become quite wild* or *savage*, Ph.1.430, Iamb.*Protr.*5; also, *assume animal shape*, E.*Ba.*1331.

ἐκθησαυρίζω, *exhaust a treasure*, Phalar.*Ep.*12 (dub. l.).

ἔκθιβος and **ἔκθροιβος**· τὸ λῶμα τοῦ χιτῶνος, Hsch.; cf. ὄχθοιβος.

ἐκ-θλῐβή, ἡ, *oppression*, Lxx *Mi.*7.2. **-θλίβω** [ῑ], *squeeze out*, Arist.*HA* 578^{b}4, 626^{a}20, Epicur.*Ep.*2 p.50 U., Nic.*Al.*626:—Pass., Arist.*HA* 522^{a}20; *to be forced from* one's position, Plu.*Sull.*19. 2. Pass., *to be crowded, cramped*, of troops, X.*An.*3.4.19. 3. *squeeze, press*, σταφυλήν Lxx *Ge.*40.11:—Pass., aor. 2 part. ἐκθλῐβεὶς Dsc.1. 112. b. *squeeze out*, Arist.*Mete.*342^{a}9 (Pass.). 4. Gramm., *elide* a letter at the beginning or end of a word, οὐ γὰρ οἷόν τε εὑρέσθαι τὸ ῡ -όμενον A.D.*Conj.*228.17, cf. D.H.*Dem.*43. **-θλιμμα**, ατος, τό, *pressure, bruise*, Hp.ap.Gal.18(2).510, cf. 12.343. **-θλιπτέον**, *one must squeeze out*, *Gp.*18.17.1. II. Adj. -τέος, α, ον, gloss on ἐκβλιστέος, Hsch. **-θλιψις**, εως, ἡ, *squeezing out*, Hp.*Aph.*7.85, Arist.*Mete.*342^{a}15, Epicur.*Ep.*2 p.50 U.; τοῦ λοιποῦ (sc. οὔρου) Gal. *UP* 5.16. II. *affliction, distress*, Lxx *Ez.*12.18. III. Gramm., *ecthlipsis, ejection* of a letter, as σκῆπτρον, σκᾶπτον, A.D.*Conj.*230.10, etc.; also, *elision*, Eust.984.15 (pl.).

ἐκθνῄσκω, fut. -θᾰνοῦμαι: aor. ἐξέθᾰνον:—*die away, to be like to die*, γέλῳ (for γέλωτι) ἔκθανον *were like to die* with laughing, Od.18.100; ὁρῶντες ἐξέθνῃσκον ἐπὶ τῷ πράγματι Antiph.190.7; ὑπὸ γέλωτος ἐ. Plu. 2.54c; ὑπὸ τοῦ δέους Luc.*Icar.*23, etc. 2. *to be in a death-like swoon*, ἐξέθανε πεντάκις ὥστε τεθνάναι δοκέειν, Hp.*Epid.*5.42, cf. Philem.1. 6D.; ὁ ἐκτεθνεώς, opp. ὁ ὄντως τεθνηκώς, Pl.*Lg.*959a; opp. ἀποθνῄσκειν, Arist.*HA* 521^{a}11, cf. *Pr.*962^{b}4:—so in S.*Tr.*568 (though Nessus was really dying) ἐκθνῄσκων may retain its usual sense, *fainting away, at the point of death*. 3. *become mortified*, τὸ φλεγμαῖνον ἐκτέθνηκεν Hp.*VC* 19. 4. c. acc., *to be terrified of*, τὰς νόσους ἐκτεθνήκασι Phld.*Herc.*1251.18. II. later, = ἀποθνῄσκω, Luc.*Hist.Conscr.* 27, Aret.*SD* 2.13, D.C.48.37.

ἐκθοινάομαι, *feast on*, c. acc., A.*Pr.*1025.

ἐκθολόω, *make turbid*, Procl.*Par.Ptol.*183.

ἐκθόοντας· ἐξερχομένους, Hsch. (leg. -θέοντας). **ἐκθοράξει**· ἐκδιώξει, Id. (fort. ἐκθράξει, = ἐκταράξει).

ἐκθορέω, = ἐκθρῴσκω, aor. -εθόρησα, Plu.*Nob.*19.

ἐκθόρνῠμαι, later (unless read for ἐξέσσυται Democr.32 ap.Gal.17 (2).28) collat. form for ἐκθρῴσκω, τῇ ψυχῇ M.Ant.8.51; *start up* from sleep, Aret.*SA* 2.9.

ἐκθορῠβέω, *disturb, disquiet*, Poll.1.117:—Pass., ἐκ τῶν ὕπνων ἐκθορυβούμενοι Aret.*SD* 1.5.

ἔκθρεψις, εως, ἡ, *bringing up, rearing*, Ael.*NA* 3.8, Porph.ap.Eus. *PE* 3.11.

ἐκθρηνέω, *lament aloud for*, Luc.*Ocyp.*113.

ἐκθριαμβίζω, *make public, noise abroad*, *BGU* 1061.19 (Pass., i B.C.).

ἐκθροέω, *speak out loud*, Poll.6.207. II. Pass., *to be startled out of*, τῶν ὕπνων Gal.16.221. **ἔκθροιβος**, v. ἔκθιβος.

ἐκθρομβ-όω, *clear from clots*, σώματα Antyll.ap.Orib.45.2.10; ἕλκος Paul.Aeg.6.60. **-ωσις**, εως, ἡ, *coagulation*, αἵματος Dsc.1.128.7; *curdling* of milk, Gal.14.142.

ἐκθρῡλέω, *chatter out*, Poll.6.207:—Pass., ἐκτεθρυλημένος ib.206.

ἐκθρῴσκω, fut. -θοροῦμαι: aor. -έθορον:—*leap out of*, c. gen., ἔκθορε δίφρου Il.16.427; ἐκ δ' ἔθορε κλῆρος κυνέης 7.182, cf. 23.353; ἐ. ναῶν A.*Pers.*457; κραδίη δέ μοι ἔξω στηθέων ἐκθρῴσκει, of the violent *beating* of the heart, Il.10.95: abs., *leap forth*, Ἀπόλλων ἀντίος ἐξέθορε 21.539, cf. Corn.*ND* 19: rarely c. acc., δίκτυον ἐ. *AP* 9.371; *start up*, ἀπὸ τοῦ ὕπνου Luc.*DMar.*2.3; *come from the womb, to be born*, *h.Ap.* 119.

ἐκθυελλόω, *carry away as by a storm*, Moschio *Hyp.*1.

ἔκθῠμα, ατος, τό, (ἐκθύω II) *pustule*, Hp.*Epid.*3.7 (pl.), al. II. (ἐκθύω I) *expiatory sacrifice*, Arist.*Ath.*54.6 (pl.).

ἐκθῠμαίνω, strengthd. for θυμαίνω, aor. ἐξεθύμηνα (-θύμησαν codd.) Ant.Lib.7.4: fut. ἐκθυμᾰνῶ Phld.*Ir.*p.16 W.

ἐκθύμενος· ταχύς, Hsch.

ἐκθῠμία, ἡ, *ardour, eagerness*, Plb.3.115.6.

ἐκθῡμι-άω, *burn as incense*, E.*Ion* 1174. 2. *turn into vapour*, Str.15.1.22, Heraclit.*Ep.*6.4:—Pass., *to pass off in fumes*, Arist. *Mete.*388^{a}8, v.l. in Dsc.1.98, Ph.1.500, M.Ant.6.4. **-ασις**, εως, ἡ, *evaporation, expansion*, θερμοῦ Marcellin.*Puls.*59.

ἔκθῡμος, ον, *spirited, ardent*, φίλων ὑπηρεσίαι Plu.*Aem.*12, cf. App. *BC* 5.38 (Sup.). Adv. **-μως** *ardently*, Diog.Oen.15; ἐρίζειν Luc.*JTr.* 16; *vehemently, bravely*, ὥρμησε Plb.2.67.7, cf. 1.17.9 (Comp.); ἀγωνίζεσθαι D.H.2.54, etc.

ἐκθῡρίζω, *stray, play truant*, Eust.1020.13.

ἐκ-θῡσία, ἡ, = ἔκθυσις I, Vett.Val.183.26 (pl.), Zos.2.1.2 (pl.):—written **ἐχθυσία**, *IG* 11(2).142.59 (Delos, iv B.C.). **-θύσιμος** [ῠ], ον, *needing atonement*, Plu.2.518b. **-θῠσις**, εως, ἡ, (ἐκθύω I) *atonement, expiatory rites*, Id.*Marc.*28. 2. *averting by sacrifices*, τῶν εἱμαρμένων Iamb.*Myst.*9.3, cf. 1.13 (pl.) (leg. ἐκλ-). II. (ἐκθύω II) *breaking out, eruption*, Hp.*Coac.*168. **-θῠτέον**, *one must eradicate*, φιλαυτίαν τῆς διανοίας Ph.*Fr.*100 H. **-θῠτικός**, ή, όν, = ἐκθύσιμος, Hsch. s. v. ἐξιατρός. **-θύω** [ῡ], *sacrifice*, S.*El.*572, E.*Cyc.*371 (lyr.); *destroy utterly*, Id.*Or.*191 (lyr.):—Med., ἐχθυσεῦνται (Dor. fut.) τὰ ἱερά *SIG* 1106.65 (Cos). 2. Med., *atone for, expiate by offerings*, c. acc. rei, ἄγος Hdt.6.91; τὰ ἀναγκαῖα Iamb.*Myst.*9.3 (leg. ἐκλ-): c. acc. pers., *propitiate, appease*, τινὰ μακάρων E.*Fr.*912.12 (anap.): abs., *make atonement*, ὑπέρ τινος (thing or person) Thphr.*HP* 5.9.8, Plu.*Alex.*50, D.C.41.14; τοῖς θεοῖς Str.6.2.11. 3. Med., *avert by sacrifices*, τὰ εἱμαρμένα Iamb.*Myst.*9.3. II. *break out as heat* or *humours*, Hp. *Liqu.*6.

ἐκθωπεύω, gloss on sq., Hsch.

ἐκθώπτω, aor. -έθωψα, *gain by flattery, wheedle over*, S.*Fr.*857.

ἐκκαγχάζω, *burst out into loud laughter*, X.*Smp.*1.16; ἀθρόον ἐ. Arist.*EN* 1150^{b}11:—spelt **ἐκκακχάζω**, Phld.*Ir.*p.49 W.: **ἐκκαχάζω**, v. l. in Sch.Ar.*Nu.*1242.

ἐκ-κᾰθαίρω, Ion. aor. 1 -εκάθηρα Hdt.2.86, Att. -εκάθᾱρα Din.2.5:—*cleanse out*: 1. with acc. of the thing cleansed, *clear out*, οὐρούς τ' ἐξεκάθαιρον Il.2.153; τὴν κοιλίην Hdt. l. c.; μήτρας, ὀδόντας, Hp. *Mul.*1.88, Orib.*Syn.*5.25.3; χθόνα ἐκκαθαίρει κνωδάλων he clears this land of monsters, A.*Supp.*264; τὸν βίον (i. e. the world) Luc.*DDeor.* 13.1; ἐ. τινά, ὥσπερ ἀνδριάντα, εἰς τὴν κρίσιν *clear* him *of all roughness, polish* him *up*, metaph. from the finishing touches of a sculptor, Pl.*R.* 361d; ἐκκαθαίρειν ἀπό τινος 2*Ep.Ti.*2.21; ἐ. λογισμόν *clear off* an account, Plu.2.64f:—Pass., *to be cleansed, purified*, ἐκκεκαθαρμένοι τὰς ψυχάς X.*Smp.*1.4, cf. Pl.*R.*527d; *to be cleared up, explained*, Epicur.*Ep.*2 p.36 U. 2. with acc. of the thing removed, *clear away*, Pl.*Euthphr.* 3a, cf. Arist.*HA* 625^{b}34; τὸ τοιοῦτον ἐ. γένος Diph.32.17; τὴν δωροδοκίαν ἐκ τῆς πόλεως Din. l. c.; κόπρον *APl.*4.92.7. **-κᾰθᾱρίζω**, = foreg., Lxx *De.*32.43. **-κάθαρσις** [κᾰ], εως, ἡ, *complete cleansing, purification*, Muson.*Fr.*20 p.111 H. 2. *sweeping out*, Hierocl.*in CA* 14 p.451 M. 3. *polishing up*, θυρᾶν *IG* 4.1484.283 (Epid.).

ἐκκαθεύδω, *sleep out of one's quarters*, X.*HG* 2.4.24.

ἐκκαίδεκα, οἱ, αἱ, τά, indecl., *sixteen*, Hdt.2.13, etc.

ἐκκαιδεκά-γωνος [ᾰ], ον, *having sixteen angles*, Hero *Geep.*164, Simp.*in Ph.*55.3. **-δάκτῠλος**, ον, *sixteen fingers long, broad*, etc., Ath.Mech.35.1. **-δωρος**, ον, *sixteen palms long*, Il.4.109. **-εδρον**, τό, *solid with sixteen surfaces*, Ps.-Ptol.*Centil.*60. **-ετηρίς**, ίδος, ἡ, *period of sixteen years*, Gem.8.39. **-έτης**, ου, ὁ, *sixteen years old*, Plu.2.754e. II. *consisting of sixteen years*, χρόνος D.C.69. 8. **-κις**, *sixteen times*, Dioph.2.29. **-κωλος**, ον, *of sixteen members* (sc. περίοδος), Sch.Ar.*Pax* 382. **-λῐνος**, ον, *consisting of sixteen threads*, δίκτυον X.*Cyn.*2.5. **-πάλαιστος** [πᾰ], ον, *of sixteen palms*, Poll.2.157. **-πηχυς**, Dor. **-πᾶχυς**, υ, gen. εος, contr. ους, *sixteen cubits long* or *high*, Decr.Byz.ap.D.18.91, *IG* 11(2).161 *D* 120 (Delos, iii B.C.), Plb.5.89.6. **-πλάσιος** [πλᾰ], ον, *sixteen times as great*, Androm.ap.Gal.13.913. **-πους**, ποδος, ὁ, ἡ, *sixteen feet long*, Anon. *in Tht.*34.31.

ἐκκαιδεκάς, άδος, ἡ, *the number sixteen*, Dam.*Pr.*382.

ἐκκαιδεκά-σημος [ᾰ], ον, *of sixteen times*, χρόνος Aristid.Quint.1. 14. **-στάδιος** [στᾰ], ον, *sixteen stades long*, περίβολος Str.12.4. 7. **-σύλλᾰβος**, ον, *of sixteen syllables*, Σαπφικὸν -ον (sc. -μέτρον) Heph.10.6, Arg.Theoc.28.

ἐκκαιδεκᾰταῖος, α, ον, *sixteen days old*, [σελήνη] Sch.Ar.*Th*.86.

ἐκκαιδεκᾰτάλαντος [τᾰ], ον, *worth sixteen talents*, γύναιον ἑ. *with a dowry of sixteen talents*, cj. in Men.402.11.

ἑκκαιδέκᾰτος, η, ον, *sixteenth*, Hdt.2.143, etc.

ἑκκαιδεκ-έτις, ιδος, ἡ, *sixteen years old*, *AP*7.600 (Jul.). **-ήρης**, ους, ἡ, *ship of sixteen banks*, Plb.18.44.6.

ἑκκαιεβδομηκοντᾰετηρίς, ίδος, ἡ, *period of seventy-six years*, Gem. 8.59.

ἑκκαιεικοσάεδρον [ᾰ], τό, *solid with twenty-six surfaces*, Papp. in Archim.2 p.536 H.

ἐκκαινόω, *restore, repair*, *Ostr.Strassb*.736.

ἑκκαιπεντηκοντάγωνον [ᾰ], τό, *figure of fifty-six sides*, prob. in Plu. 2.363a (ὀκτωκαι- codd.).

ἔκκαιρος, ον, *out of date, antiquated*, *AP*11.417; *unseasonable*, *POxy*.729.18 (ii A.D.).

ἐκκαίω, Att. **ἐκκάω**, fut. -καύσω: aor. 1 ἐξέκαυσα Hdt.4.134, but part. ἐκκέαντες E.*Rh*.97:—*burn out*, τοὺς ὀφθαλμούς τινος Hdt.7.18; τὸ φῶς Κύκλωπος E.*Cyc*.633, cf. 657 (anap.):—Pass., ἐκκάεσθαι τοὺς ὀφθαλμούς *to have one's* eyes *burnt out*, Pl.*Grg*.473c. II. *light up, kindle*, τὰ πυρά Hdt.4.134, cf. E.*Rh*. l.c.; ἐκκέας τῶν ξύλων ἅττ' ἂν ᾖ δανότατα Ar.*Pax* 1133 (lyr.): metaph., ἐ. πόλεμον, ἐλπίδα, Plb.3.3. 3, 5.108.5; τοὺς θυμούς D.H.7.35; τὴν πρὸς αὐτὸν ὀργήν Plu.*Fab*.7; *provoke* to anger, ἔκ με κάεις Herod.4.49; *inflame* with curiosity, *excite*, τινά Luc.*Alex*.30; ἴσῃ φιλοτιμίᾳ πρός τε τὸν δῆμον ἑαυτοὺς καὶ τὸν δῆμον πρὸς ἑαυτοὺς ἐκκαύσαντες Plu.*Agis* 2:—Pass., *to be kindled, burn up*, τὸ πῦρ ἐκκάεται Eup.340; ἐ. τὸ κακόν Pl.*R*.556a; ὀργὴν ἐκκαῆναι Lxx 2*Ki*.24.1; ὁ δῆμος ἐξεκάετο Plu.*TG*13, cf. Luc.*Cal*.3, etc.; ἐ. εἰς ἔρωτα Alciphr.3.67, cf. Charito 1.1; ὑπὸ μέθης Parth.24. 2. 2. *stimulate*, τὴν βλάστησιν Thphr.*CP*2.1.3. III. *scorch*, ἐκκαίων ὁ ἥλιος Arist.*Pr*.867a20; of thirst, *parch*, Luc.*Dips*.4.

ἐκκᾰκέω, *to be faint-hearted, lose heart, grow weary*, v.l. for ἐγκ-, *Ev.Luc*.18.1, 2*Ep.Cor*.4.1,16, al., cf. Vett.Val.201.15, *Gloss*.

ἐκκακή· ὧδε, Hsch.

ἐκκᾰλᾰμάομαι, *pull out with a* καλάμη, *fish out*: hence metaph., *wheedle out*, Ar.*V*.609.

ἐκκαλάξαι· κλῖναι τὸ ἱστίον, Hsch. (i.e. ἐκχαλάσαι).

ἐκκᾰλέω, *call out* or *forth, summon forth*, Il.24.582, etc.; τινὰ δόμων E.*Ba*.170; ἔνδοθεν Lys.3.8; *crave speech of*, τινά S.*OT*597 codd. II. Med., *call out to oneself*, ψυχάς Od.24.1, cf. Hdt.8.79, S.*Ph*.1264. 2. *call forth, elicit*, χαρὰ δάκρυον ἐκκαλουμένη A.*Ag*.270; ὀργὴν Aeschin. 2.3; ἴσως ἂν ἐκκαλέσαιθ' ὑμᾶς D.4.42, cf. Pl.*Euthd*.288d; λιμὸν ἐ. Antiph.217.23; τοὺς ἱππεῖς *entice, provoke to battle*, Plb.1.19.2, cf. Ascl.*Tact*.7.1. 3. c. inf., *call on* one *to* do, S.*Tr*.1206; ἐ. [τινὰ] ποτὶ ἔργα Ti.Locr.104b: plpf. in med. sense, ἐξεκέκλητο πρὸς τὴν πρᾶξίν τινας Plb.4.57.4:—Pass., -κληθῆναι πρὸς τὰς ὠφελείας Id.3.51.11; *to be provoked*, εἴς, ἐπί τι, Phld.*Ir*.pp.52,95 W.; ἐς ὀργήν, δάκρυα, Philostr.*VS*2.8.4, 2.10.1. 4. *demand, require*, ὡς τὰ φαινόμενα -εῖται Epicur.*Ep*.2 p.36 U., cf. 53 U. III. Pass., = Lat. *evocari*, of foreign *numina*, Plu.2.278f. IV. Med., *appeal against*, κρίσιν ἐπί τινα ib.178f; *refer*, προβλήματα ἐπὶ τὴν τῶν ἀλόγων φύσιν ὥσπερ ἀλλοδαπὴν πόλιν ib.493b.

ἐκκαλλύνω, *sweep clean*, ἔδαφος πτεροῖς Arr.*Peripl.M.Eux*.21, cf. Hsch. s.v. ἐκκοροῦσι:—Pass., *EM*322.18.

ἐκκάλυμμα, ατος, τό, *means of discovery, token*, Plu.2.463a (pl.).

ἐκκαλυπτικός, ή, όν, *suited for discovery, indicative of*, c. gen., *Stoic*. 2.36,72. Adv. -κῶς S.E.*P*.2.141.

ἐκκᾰλύπτω, *uncover*, τὸ παιδίον Hdt.1.112; *disclose, reveal*, ὀργὴ νόον ἐξεκάλυψεν Even.5; πάντ' ἐκκάλυψον A.*Pr*.195, cf. S.*Aj*.1003; πάντ' ἐ. ὁ χρόνος Id.*Fr*.918; λέγ' ἐκκαλύψας κρᾶτα E.*Supp*.111; ἐ. μυστικοὺς λόγους Phld.*Ir*.p.46 W.: folld. by relat., ἐκκάλυπτε..ἡμῖν οὕστινας λέγεις λόγους E.*IA*872:—Med., *uncover one's head, unveil oneself*, Od.10.179 (tm.): pf. fut. ἐκκεκαλύψομαι Ar.*Av*.1503; opp. ἐγκαλύπτομαι, Pl.*Phd*.118a. 2. *unmask*, τινά Aeschin.3.55.

ἐκκάμνω, *grow quite weary of* a thing, τὰς ὀλοφύρσεις Th.2.51: c. part., πολεμοῦντες ἐξέκαμον Plu.*Sol*.8, cf. *Pomp*.32, D.C.40.24; ἐξέκαμεν ὑπὸ γήρως πρὸς τὰ δημόσια he *became unfit* through age for.., Plu.*Cat.Ma*.24; σίδηρος ἐξέκαμε πληγαῖς it *is worn out* (gnomic) with blows, Id.*Caes*.37; ἐ. ἡ ἀρετή τισι Max.Tyr.29.2.

ἐκκᾰνάσσω, *drink off*, τήνδ'..ἐκκανάξει (sc. κύλικα) Eup.272, cf. Ael.*Ep*.4.

ἐκκᾰπηλεύω, lit., *sell off*:—Pass., ἐκκαπηλεύεσθαι τῆς χώρας Philostr.*VA*1.15. II. *adulterate*, Hsch.

ἐκκαπνίζομαι, *evaporate in smoke*, Olymp.Alch.p.73 B.

ἐκκαρδιόω, *cut out the heart*, Alex.Trall.1.15.

ἐκκαρπ-εύομαι, = ἐκκαρπόομαι, *PPetr*.2 p.143 (iii B.C.). **-έω**, *grow to seed*, Hp.*Art*.8, Gal.6.537. **-ησις**, εως, ἡ, *growing to seed*, ib.665. **-ίζομαι**, Med., *yield as produce*, A.*Th*.601. II. *reap, enjoy*, τὰ ἐκ τῆς γῆς γενήματα *PTeb*.105.30 (ii B.C.). III. of land, *exhaust*, Thphr.*CP*4.8.3. **-όομαι**, Med., *gather* or *enjoy the fruit of*, ἄλλης γυναικὸς παῖδας ἐ. *to have* children *by* another wife, E. *Ion* 815; ἐ. φιλίαν D.C.37.56. II. *enjoy the fruit of* a thing, c. part., ἀμφοτέροις ἔνσπονδοι ὄντες ἐκκαρπώσασθαι Th.5.28; ἐ. τινάς *exhaust* them, *drain* them *dry*, D.24.2.

ἐκκᾰρῡκεύω, *make into* καρύκη (q.v.), in Pass., Hsch., Suid.

ἐκκατᾰράσσω, *damage completely*, Alex.Aphr.*Pr*.1.96 (Pass.).

ἐκκατεῖδον, aor. with no pres. ἐκκαθοράω in use, *look down from*, Περγάμου ἐκκατιδών Il.4.508, cf. Q.S.8.430.

ἐκκαυλ-έω, *run to stalk*, Arist.*Pr*.924b27, Dsc.2.136, cf. ἐκκαυλῆσαι· ἐπιδοῦναι, Hsch.; *develop a stem*, Thphr.*HP*1.2.2, *CP*4.3. 5. **-ημα**, ατος, τό, *stalk put forth*, Gal.19.153 (s. v. φύσιγγα). **-ησις**, εως, ἡ, *shooting into a stalk*, Thphr.*CP*4.3.5. **-ίζω**, *pull out the stalk*: metaph., καυλοὺς τῶν εὐθυνῶν ἐ. *pull off* the sprouts, i.e. the profits, Ar.*Eq*.825.

ἔκ-καυμα, ατος, τό, (ἐκκαίω) *wood for lighting fires*, in pl., S.*Fr*.225, D.S.2.49: sg., Thphr.*Ign*.73: metaph., ἔ. τόλμης E.*Fr*.1031; *source of heat*, Aret.*CA*2.11. **-καυσις**, εως, ἡ, *kindling, burning*, Arist. *Mete*.342a2, Anthem.p.154 W. 2. *heating* of the body, Aret. *SA*1.7 (pl.); of baths, *PFlor*.385.88 (v A.D.), *Cod.Just*.1.4.26 *Intr*. (pl.). II. *sunstroke*, Gal.2.884; ἡλίου Alex.Aphr.*Pr*.1.88. **-καυστικός**, ή, όν, *inflammatory*, Ael.*VH*11.12.

ἐκκαυχάομαι, strengthd. for καυχάομαι, E.*Ba*.31.

ἐκκαχλάζω, *break, plash*, of waves, Apollon.*Lex*. s.v. κωφόν.

ἐκκαχρύζω, '*pearl*' barley, Hsch.

ἐκκάω, Att. for ἐκκαίω.

ἐκκεδάννῡμι, *scatter*, ἦτορ ἀπὸ μελέων Q.S.10.124 (tm.).

ἔκκειμαι, serving as Pass. of ἐκτίθημι, *to be cast out* or *exposed*, ἐπορᾶν ἐκκείμενον (sc. τὸν παῖδα) Hdt.1.110, cf. 122, Longus 1.3; ἁπλοῦν τὸ ἦθος καὶ παντὶ ἰδεῖν ἐκκείμενον D.H.*Rh*.10.1. 2. of public notices, decrees, etc., *to be set up in public, posted up*, ἵν' ἐκκέοιτο πρὸ τῶν ἐπωνύμων D.21.103, cf. 58.9; *to be set forth*, ἡ ἐμὴ προθυμία ἐκκείσθω *POxy*.220 vi 5; ἐκκειμένων οὖν τῶν βίων Plu.*Comp.Ages.Pomp*.1. 3. *to be proposed*, ὁ σκοπὸς ἐ. καλῶς Arist.*Pol*.1331b31; μισθοὶ παρὰ βασιλέως ἔκκεινται Str.15.1.46; ἔλασσον τοῦ ἐκκειμένου *SIG*577.66 (Milet., iii/ii B.C.). 4. c. dat., *to be exposed to, be at the mercy of*, Str.5.2.6, Alciphr.3.29; τύχαις Plot.6.8.15; τῷ μέλλοντι Id.3.6.18; also πρὸς τὸ πάσχειν Procl.*Inst*.80. 5. *to be set forth, expounded*, Arist.*Rh*. 1419b23; in logical sense, Id.*Top*.103b29, cf. *APr*.48a8, Epicur.*Nat*. 28.1, Phld.*Sign*.19, etc. 6. Geom., *to be set out, 'taken'*, ἐκκείσθω κύκλος, ὁ ἐκκείμενος κῶνος, Archim.*Sph.Cyl*.1.5,28. II. c. gen., *fall from out, be left bare of*, μηροὶ..ἐξέκειντο πιμελῆς S.*Ant*.1011. 2. *project*, ἐκκειμένη εἰς θάλατταν ἄκρα Str.5.4.8; πύργοι ἔξω ἐκκείμενοι D.C.74.10; στέρνα προέχοντα καὶ ἐκκείμενα Philostr.*Gym*.35; φλέβες ἐκκ. Gal.17(2).97; in painting, *stand out*, Philostr.*Im*.2.1.

ἐκκειμένως, Adv. *openly*, ἐ. τοῦ ἤθους ἔχειν to be *open, frank*, Philostr.*VS*2.17.

ἐκκεινόω, v. ἐκκενόω.

ἐκκείρω, *shear completely*, Σκυθιστὶ ἐκκεκαρμένος *shorn* in Scythian fashion, S.*Fr*.473. II. *cut off*, ἐκ θέρος ἀνδρῶν κείρατε A.R.4.1033.

ἐκ⟨κε⟩κελλήρικεν· ἐκκέκληκεν, Hsch.

ἐκκεκλασμένως, Adv., gloss on σκεπαρνηδόν, Gal.19.138.

ἐκκέλευθος, ον, *out of the road*, λαθραῖα κἀκκέλευθα Lyc.1162 (but Dind. κἀκ κέλευθα, i.e. κατὰ κέλευθα).

ἐκκενόω, poet. **ἐκκεινόω**, *empty out, leave desolate*, ἄστυ Σούσων ἐξεκείνωσεν A.*Pers*.761, cf. Lxx *Ps*.136(137).7; *clear out*, οἴκημα Pl. *Prt*.315d; στωμυλίαν ἢ 'ξεκένωσε τὰς παλαίστρας Ar.*Ra*.1070; ἐ. θυμὸν ἐς σχεδίαν γέροντος *pour out* one's spirit into Charon's boat, i.e. *give up* the ghost, Theoc.16.40; χολῆς περισσὸν..ἐ. τῶν ἐγκάτων *App. Anth*.3.158; ἐ. ἰούς *to shoot all* one's arrows, *AP*6.326 (Leon.):—Pass., *to be left desolate*, στένει γαῖ' Ἀσὶς ἐκκενουμένα A.*Pers*.549 (lyr.), cf. *Th*.330 (lyr.); Ἀττικὴ τῆς τῶν ἀνθρώπων ἀγέλης ἐκκενωθεῖσα Philostr.*VS*1.16.1; Μοιράων..μίτος ἐξεκενώθη *was exhausted, spun out*, *IG*14.2002. 2. *unsheath*, μάχαιραν Lxx *Ez*.5.2. 3. *clear away*, πέτρας *Sammelb*.4368.

ἐκκεντέω, *prick out, put out*, ὄμματα Arist.*HA*508b6. II. *pierce, stab*, Plb.5.56.12, Lxx *Nu*.22.29, Polyaen.5.3.8. 2. *massacre*, Lxx *Jo*.16.10. III. intr., of hair, *stand out, project*, Luc. *Sat*.24.

ἐκκεντρεπίκυκλος, ον, *requiring both eccentric and epicycle*, ὑπόθεσις Procl.*Hyp*.2.3.

ἐκκεντρίζω, prob. written for ἐγκ-, *Cat.Cod.Astr*.7.185; f.l. for ἐκκεντέω, Alex.Trall.5.6.

ἔκκεντρος, ον, Astron., κύκλος *not having the earth as centre, eccentric*, Cleom.1.6, Gem.1.34, Ptol.*Alm*.3.3, etc. II. *not occupying a cardinal point*, opp. ἐγκ., Vett.Val.97.11.

ἐκκεντρότης, ητος, ἡ, *eccentricity*, Eudem.ap.Theon.Sm.p.201 H., Gem.1.39, Ptol.*Alm*.3.3, Iamb.*VP*6.31 (pl.), etc.

ἐκκενωτέον, *one must empty*, of venesection, Gal.10.313.

ἐκκερᾰΐζω, *plunder, pillage, sack*, Call.*Cer*.50; *cut down*, πίτυν *AP* 9.312 (Zon.).

ἐκκεράννῡμι, *pour out and mix*, Ath.2.38a codd. (εἰσ- Kaibel).

ἐκκερδαίνω, *make a profit*, Just.*Nov*.102 *Pr*.

ἐκκεχῠμένως, Adv. pf. part. Pass. of ἐκχέω, *profusely, extravagantly*, ἐ. ζῆν Isoc.15.207; ἐ. λέγειν *without reserve*, Pl.*Euthphr*.3d; ἀγαπᾶν Aristaenet.2.16; πράττειν τι Just.*Nov*.74.4.

ἐκκηλέω, *cast a spell upon*, in aor. ἐξεκήλησεν, Hsch.

ἐκκηραίνω, *enfeeble, exhaust*, A.*Eu*.128.

ἐκκηριόω, *amaze, confound*, Hsch., in pf. Pass.; cf. ἐξεκηρίωσας· ἐξέστησας, Id.

ἐκκηρ-υγμός, ὁ, *banishment by proclamation*, Sch.BT Il.21.575. **-υκτος**, ον, *banished, cast away*, Lxx *Je*.22.30, Hsch. **-ύσσω**, Att. **-ττω**, *proclaim by voice of herald*:—Pass., νέκυν ἀστοῖσί φασιν ἐκκεκηρῦχθαι τὸ μὴ τάφῳ καλύψαι S.*Ant*.27, cf. 203. II. *banish by proclamation*, Hdt.3.148, Plb.4.21.8, D.S.14.97; τῆς πόλεως, ἐκ τῆς πόλεως, Aeschin.3.258, Lys.12.3:—Pass., ἐκ τοῦ γένους ἐκκεκηρῦχθαι

Pl.*Lg*.929b; ἐξεκηρύχθην φυγάς S.*OC*430. **2.** *cashier, 'drum out'* of the army, prob. in Arist.*Ath*.61.2.

ἐκκῐναιδίζομαι, strengthd. for κιναιδίζομαι, D.C.50.27.

ἐκκῑνέω, *move out of* [his lair], *put up*, ἔλαφον S.*El*.567: metaph., ἐ. τὴν νόσον Id.*Tr*.979 (anap.); τόδε τὸ ῥῆμα Id.*OT*354; so σὺ γάρ μ' ἀπ' εὐνασθέντος ἐ. κακοῦ Id.*Tr*.1242:—Pass., σκώμμασι μᾶλλον ἢ λοιδορίαις ἐκκινούμεθα Plu.2.631c.

ἐκκιρρόω, pf. ἐκκεκίρρωκα, *become hardened*, *Hippiatr*.104.

ἐκκίω, *go out*, Od.24.492 (tm.).

ἐκκλάζω, *cry aloud*, ἐκ δ' ἔκλαγξ' ὄπα E.*Ion* 1204.

ἐκκλαστρίδιον, τό, *a woman's ornament*, *IG*11(2).219*B*23 (Delos, iii B.C.), etc.

ἐκκλάω, *break off*, Pl.*R*.611d (Pass.), Alciphr.2.4 (Pass.); δάκτυλον Paus.8.40.2. **II.** Pass., *grow weak*, *to be enfeebled*, Plu.2.671a (s. v. l.); τὸ θράσος ἐκκέκλασται ib.762f, cf. Max.Tyr.35.3.

ἐκκλείω, Ion. **ἐκκληΐω** or **-κλῄω**, old Att. **ἐκκλῄω**: Att. fut. -κλῄσω E.*Or*.1127: Dor. aor. 1 -κλᾳξα *Com.Adesp*.1203.7 (dub.): pf. ἐκκέκλεικα Men.*Sam*.201:—*shut out from*, c. gen., ἐ. ἄλλον ἄλλοσε στέγης E. l. c.:—Pass., *to be shut out*, Id.*HF*330. **2.** metaph., *shut out*, *exclude from*, πόλιν τῆς μετοχῆς Hdt.1.144; τῆς συμμαχίας, τῶν ὅρκων, Aeschin.2.85, 3.74: c. acc. et inf., ἐξέκλειον λόγου τυγχάνειν τοὺς ἄλλους D.19.26. **3.** *hinder*, *prevent*, τῷ καιρῷ τὴν κατηγορίαν Plb.18.8.2; τὴν θήραν D.S.3.16:—Pass., ἐκκληϊόμενοι τῇ ὥρῃ *being prevented* by [want of] time, Hdt.1.31; ἐκκλεισθεὶς ὑπὸ τῶν καιρῶν D.S.18.3: c. inf., ἐ. ποιεῖν τι Id.4.32, cf. Arist.*MM*1198^{b}16. **4.** *shut off*, *cut off*, ζωῆς ὁδούς Opp.*C*.2.342.

ἐκκλέπτω, aor. 2 Pass. -εκλάπην X.*HG*5.4.12:—*steal and carry off*, of persons, [Ἑρμῆς] ἐξέκλεψεν Ἄρηα he *stole away* Ares *from* his chains, Il.5.390, cf. Hdt.2.115 (s. v. l.), A.*Ag*.662, *Eu*.153, X.*Ap*. 23, Plu.*Pyrrh*.2; τοὺς ὁμήρους ἐ. ἐκ Λήμνου Th.1.115, cf. D.S.12.27; τοὺς ἀδικοῦντας οἱ κατήγοροι ἐκκλέπτουσιν Lys.20.7; ἐκ δόμων πόδα E. *Or*.1499: c. gen., τῆνδε.. ἐκκλέψαι χθονὸς Id.*Hel*.741; ἐ. φόνου Id. *El*.286; ἐ. μὴ θανεῖν ib.540; ἐ. τι τοῦ λόγου *to steal* it *from* the story, Pl.*R*.449c:—Pass., ὑπὸ τῆς ἀμήτορος παρθένου ἐκκλαπεῖσα Jul.*Mis*. 352b. **II.** ἐ. τινὰ λόγοις *to deceive* him, S.*Ph*.55, cf. 968; μὴ.. ἐκκλέψῃς λόγον *disguise* not the matter, *speak* not *falsely*, Id.*Tr*.437.

ἐκκληΐω, Ion. for ἐκκλείω.

ἔκκλημα, ατος, τό, *subject of appeal*, *Jahresh*.14.168 (Tolophon, iii B.C.), *Foed.Delph.Pell*.2*B*20 (pl., iii B.C.).

ἐκκλημᾰτόομαι, Pass., *put forth* κλήματα, *run to wood*, Thphr.*CP* 3.15.4, *Gp*.5.40.1.

ἐκκληπεῖ· ἐκπορεύεται, Hsch.

ἔκκληρος, ον, *without share* or *lot*, *Gloss*.

ἐκκλησί-α, ἡ, (ἔκκλητος) *assembly duly summoned*, less general than σύλλογος, Th.2.22, Pl.*Grg*.456b, etc.; applied to the Homeric Assemblies, Arist.*Pol*.1285^{a}11; to the Samian Assembly, Hdt.3. 142; to the Spartan, Th.1.87; to the meeting of the Amphictyons at Delphi, Aeschin.3.124; at Athens, ἐ. κύριαι, opp. σύγκλητοι, Arist.*Ath*.43.4; κυρία ἐ., at Amorgos, *IG*12(7).237.46; ἐ. συναγείρειν, συνάγειν, συλλέγειν, ἀθροίζειν, call *an assembly*, Hdt.3.142, Th.2.60, 8.97, X.*HG*1.6.8; ἐ. ποιεῖν Ar.*Eq*.746, Th.1.139, al.; ἐ. ποιεῖν τινί Ar.*Ach*.169; διδόναι τινί Plb.4.34.6; ἐ. γίγνεται *an assembly* is held, Th.6.8; καταστάσης ἐ. Id.1.31; ἦν ἐ. τοῖς στρατηγοῖς And.1.2; ἐ. διαλύειν, ἀναστῆσαι, dissolve *it*, Th.8.69 (Pass.), X.*HG*2.4.42; ἀφιέναι Plu.*TG*16; ἐ. ἀνεβλήθη was adjourned, Th.5.45; ἐ. περί τινος Ar. *Av*.1030, etc. **2.** = Lat. *Comitia*, ἐ. λοχῖτις, φρατρική, = *Comitia Centuriata*, *Curiata*, D.H.4.20. **3.** = ψήφισμα, ἀναγιγνωσκομένης ἐ. Philostr.*VS*2.1.11. **II.** in Lxx, *the Jewish congregation*, *De*. 31.30, al. **2.** in *NT*, *the Church*, as a body of Christians, *Ev.Matt*. 16.18, 1*Ep.Cor*.11.22; ἡ κατ' οἶκόν τινος ἐ. *Ep.Rom*.16.5; as a building, *Cod.Just*.1.1.5 *Intr*., etc. **-άζω**, fut. -άσω Ar.*Ec*.161, Isoc.8.2: impf. ἠκκλησίαζον D.18.265, 19.60; also ἐκκλησίαζον Lys.12.73 codd., but usu. with irreg. augm., as if the Verb were a compd. of ἐκ and *κλησιάζω, impf. ἐξεκλησίαζον Lys.13.73,76: aor. ἐξεκλησίασα Th.8. 93, D.21.193 (freq. with vv. ll. ἐξεκκλησίαζον, ἐξεκκλησίασα):—Med., ἐξεκκλησιάσατο, = ἀγορήσατο, Hsch. s. h. v.:—*hold an assembly*, *debate therein*, X.*Ath*.1.9, Ar.*Av*.1027, X.*An*.5.6.37; περί τινος Th.7.2, Isoc. 8.2; περί μου ἐπ' ὀλέθρῳ Ar.*Th*.84; ὑπὲρ τῆς πόλεως Isoc.8.13; τοιαῦτα ἐκκλησιάσαντες *having* thus *deliberated*, Th.8.77; ἐ. τὰς ἀναγκαίας ἐκκλησίας Arist.*Pol*.1292^{b}28. **2.** *to be a member of the Assembly*, ἐ. ἀπὸ τιμήματος οὐδενὸς ib.1294^{b}3. **II.** trans., *summon to an assembly*, *convene*, τοὺς αὐτοῦ στρατιώτας Aen.Tact.9.1; λαόν D.S.21.16; συναγωγήν Lxx *Le*.8.3, al.:—Pass., *to be called together*, ib.*Je*.33(26).9, al. **2.** metaph., τινὰ πρὸς ἑαυτὸν ἐ. *summon* considerations before one's mind, Eun.*Hist*.p.210 D. **-ασμός**, ὁ, *the holding an* ἐκκλησία, Plb.15.26.9. **-αστήριον**, τό, *the hall of the* ἐκκλησία, *IPE*1^2.24.9 (Olbia, iv B.C.), *BCH*35.76 (Delos), *CIG*2270.4 (Delos); = Lat. *Comitium*, D.H.4.38. **-αστής**, οῦ, ὁ, *member of the* ἐκκλησία, Pl.*Grg*. 452e, *Ap*.25a, Arist.*Pol*.1275^{a}26, *Rh*.1354^{b}7. **-αστικός**, ή, όν, *of* or *for the* ἐκκλησία, ἐ. πίναξ register *of voters*, D.44.35; αἱ ἐ. ψῆφοι Plu.*Cor*.14; τὸ ἐ. [ἀργύριον] *pay received for sitting in the* ἐκκλησία at Athens and elsewhere, Sch.Ar.*Eq*.51 (also μισθὸς ἐκκλησιαστικός Luc.*Dem.Enc*.25, etc.), cf. *Michel*466 (Iasos, iii B.C.); τὰ ἐ. *IG*2^2. 1272. **II.** *clerical*, *Cat.Cod.Astr*.7.216, *Cod.Just*.1.2.17.4. Adv. -κῶς Just.*Nov*.83.1. **-έκδικος**, ὁ, = Lat. *defensor ecclesiae*, *Cod. Just*.1.3.41.20, al.

ἔκ-κλησις, εως, ἡ, *appeal*, *IGRom*.4.1044 (Cos), Hsch. s. v. ἔφεσις. **2.** *challenging*, Plb.*Fr*.131 (pl.). **3.** = Lat. *evocatio numinum*, Plu.2.278f (pl.). **-κλητεύσιμος**, ον, gloss on ἐφέσι⟨μ⟩ον, Hsch. (ἐγκλ- cod.). **-κλητεύω**, *summon a witness under subpoena*, Aeschin.2.68:—Pass., Id.1.46, cf. Harp. s. v. κλητῆρες. **-κλητής**, οῦ, ὁ, *appellant*, *Gloss*. **-κλητικός**, ή, όν, *provocative*, *stimulative*, ὀρέξεως Dsc.2.151. Adv. -κῶς Suid. **-κλητος**, ον, (ἐκκαλέω) *selected to judge* or *arbitrate* on a point, ἐ. πόλις an *umpire* city, Aeschin.1.89, *IG*2^2.111.49, al., cf. Plu.2.215c; ἐν ἐκκλήτῳ δικάσασθαι *Michel*1335.30; δίκην ὠφληκὼς ἐν τῇ ἐ. *IG*12(7).67.63 (Amorgos); χρόνος ἔ. time-limit *for appeals*, *PRev.Laws*21.15 (iii B.C.). **2.** οἱ ἔκκλητοι, in Sparta and elsewhere, *a committee of citizens chosen to report* on certain questions, X.*HG*2.4.38; ἔ. Ἀργείων ὄχλος E.*Or*. 612, cf. 949. **3.** *subject to appeal*, δίκας *IG*2^2.111.74, D.C.52.22; κρίσις *PHal*.1.68 (iii B.C.); τὰς ἐκκλήτους [δίκας].. ἐφ' αὑτὸν ποιούμενος, prob. for ἐγκ–, Arist.*Oec*.1348^{b}14; ἔκκλητον δικάζειν exercise *appellate* jurisdiction, D.C.51.19.

ἐκκλῄω, old Att. for ἐκκλείω.

ἔκκλῐμα, ατος, τό, *movement to a flank*, D.S.20.12.

ἐκκλῑμᾰκίζω, *torture on the rack*, *EM*322.38; cf. κλῖμαξ.

ἐκ-κλῐνής, ές, *inclined outwards*, Arist.*Phgn*.809^{b}23; ὁ ἥλιος -έστερον ἡμῖν ποιεῖ τὸν κύκλον Id.*Pr*.912^{a}12. **-κλίνω** [ῑ], *bend out of the regular line*, *bend outwards* or *away*, opp. ἐγκλίνω, Hp.*Art*.38 (s. v. l.); *change the form of* a word, Pl.*Cra*.404d. **2.** *dislocate*, Hp.*Art*.7 (Pass.). **3.** *embezzle*, Dionys.Com.3.10. **4.** *pervert*, δικαιώματα Lxx 1*Ki*.8.3. **II.** intr., *turn away*, ἀπό τινος Th.5. 73, Lxx *Nu*.22.32(33); ἐκ τῆς ὁδοῦ ib.23; ἐκ νόμου θεοῦ ib.*Jb*.34. 27: abs., *give ground*, *retire*, X.*Cyr*.1.4.23; *give way*, *fall from its place*, Id.*Cyn*.6.10. **2.** c. acc., *avoid*, *shun*, ἐ. τι καὶ μὴ πράττειν Pl.*Lg*.746c; ἐπερχόμενον ἐ. νέφος Demad.15; τὴν τῶν θηρίων ἔφοδον Plb.1.34.4; στρατείαν Id.5.42.4, etc.:—Pass., Epict.*Ench*.2. **3.** with Prep., *turn away* or *aside towards*, κατά τι X.*Cyr*.7.1.30; ἐπὶ τὰς ἔξω οἰκίας *BGU*1215.9 (iii B.C.); ἐ. εἰς δῆμον, εἰς ὀλιγαρχίαν, *decline* into a democracy or oligarchy, Arist.*Pol*.1273^{a}5; πρός τινα *visit* a person on one's journey, Lxx *Ge*.19.3. **-κλῐσις**, εως, ἡ, *turning out of one's course*, *deflexion*, τῆς σελήνης Plu.2.929c (pl.). **2.** *tendency*, Arist.*Pr*.863^{b}24. **II.** *dislocation*, Hp.*Art*.62. **III.** *avoidance*, *refusal*, opp. αἵρεσις, Cleanth.*Stoic*.1.129 (pl.); opp. ἐκλογή, *Stoic*.3.190; opp. ὄρεξις, Epict.*Ench*.2; τῶν ὀχληρῶν S.E.*M*.1.51; τῆς βλάβης Gal.13.124, cf. Plot.1.4.6, etc. **IV.** *moral declension*, ib.8.15. **-κλῐτέον**, *one must avoid*, τὸν εὖ βάλλοντα τῶν πολεμίων Plu.2.584d; *one must shun*, τὰς ἀθρόας πόσεις Ath.3.120d, cf. Menemach.ap.Orib.7.22.3. **-κλίτης** [ῐ], ου, ὁ, *shirker*, dub. word in D.L.2.130. **-κλῐτικός**, ή, όν, *disposed to decline* or *shirk*, opp. ὀρεκτικός, δύναμις Arr.*Epict*.1.1.12. Adv. -κῶς, ἔχειν πόνου ib.3.12. 7. **-κλῐτός**, όν, *to be avoided*, opp. ὀρεκτός, Simp.*in Epict*.p.109 D., cf. Phot. s. v. παλιναίρετα.

ἐκ-κλύζω, fut. -ύσω M.Ant.8.51:—*wash out*, *wash away*, τὴν βαφήν Pl.*R*.430a; τὸν ῥύπον Luc.*Vit.Auct*.3:—in Pass., Hp.*Loc. Hom*.13; ἐ. τὰ λύματα εἰς τὸν Τίβεριν Str.5.3.8; restored in ib.1.7; *to be washed ashore*, εἰς τὸ ξηρόν Arist.*HA*525^{a}23. **2.** *wash thoroughly*, σῶμα Plu.*Sull*.36:—Med., Diocl.*Fr*.141. **II.** intr., *stream out*, Apollod.1.6.3 (nisi leg. -έβλυσεν). **-κλυσμα**, ατος, τό, *that which is washed away*, τὸ τῆς ἡδονῆς ἔ. Plu.2.1089b; *that which is washed up*, *produce of the sea*, of purple dye, Zos.Alch.p.164 B. **-κλυστέον**, *one must wash out*, Aët.16.89. **-κλυστος**, ον, *washed out*, prob. in Eup.147.

ἐκκναίω, *wear out*: metaph. of troublesome loquacity, Theoc.15. 88 (in Dor. 3 pl. fut. ἐκκναισεῦντι).

ἐκκνάω, aor. -έκνησα, *scrape off*, τὸν κηρὸν τοῦ δελτίου Hdt.7.239, cf. Aen.Tact.31.14 (prob.).

ἐκκνημόω, *destroy*, Call.*Iamb*.1.199:—Pass., Hsch.; cf. κνημόω.

ἐκκοβᾰλῑκεύομαι, *cheat by juggling tricks*, *cajole*, dub. in Ar.*Eq*. 270.

ἐκκοδοάζω, Dor. aor. 1 ἐξεκοδόαξα, *pour out*, Hsch.; cf. ἐγκοακίσαι.

ἐκκοδομεύω, *bake in an oven*, Id.

ἐκκοιλαίνω, *hollow out*, Plb.10.48.7.

ἐκκοιλίζω, (κοιλία) *disembowel*, Mithaec.ap.Ath.7.325f.

ἔκκοιλος, ον, *sunken*, ὀφθαλμός Hp.*Int*.43 (fort. ἔγκοιλος).

ἐκκοιμάομαι, *sleep off* the effects of a potion, Pl.*Lg*.648a.

ἐκκοιτ-έω, *keep night-watch*, *bivouac*, J.*BJ*6.2.6. **-ησις**, εως, ἡ, = sq., *Gloss*. **-ία**, ἡ, (κοίτη) *night-watch*, *bivouac*, in pl., Aen. Tact.13.3, Ph.*Bel*.93.5, D.S.30.10. **-ίζω**, gloss on ἐκκοχύζω, Hsch. **-ισμός**, ὁ, = ἐκκοιτία, *Gloss*.

ἐκκοκκίζω, Att. fut. -ιῶ Ar.*Lys*.364:—*take out kernels* or *seeds*, e.g. from pomegranates, Apollon.ap.Gal.12.649: hence metaph., οὐσίδιον.. ἐξεκόκκισα Nicom.Com.3; ἐ. σφυρόν *put out* one's ankle, Ar.*Ach*.1179; ἐ. τὰς τρίχας *pluck out* the hair, Id.*Lys*.448; ἐ. τὸ γῆρας *drive away* old age, ib.364; ἐ. τὰς πόλεις *sack*, *gut* the cities, Id.*Pax*63.

ἐκκοκκύζω, = μέγα κοκκύζω, Hyp.*Fr*.239.

ἐκκολ-άπτω, *erase*, *obliterate*, τὸ ἐλεγεῖον Th.1.132; τὸ ψήφισμα D.57.64; τῆς ἐπιγραφῆς any part of.., *CIG*(add.)4224*d* (Anticragus), cf. Aristid.1.425 J. **II.** *peck* the chick *out of* the egg, *hatch*, Arist. *HA*618^{a}13; ἐ. τοὺς ἀνθρώπους Luc.*VH*1.22; ἧπαρ Id.*Prom*.9:—Pass., Arist.*HA*562^{a}14; ᾠὸν ἐκκεκολαμμένον *empty* egg-shell, Thphr. *HP*3.16.4; of a seam of ore, Gal.12.239. **-αψις**, εως, ἡ, *breaking the shell*, of a chick, Arist.*HA*561^{b}29.

ἐκκολλαβήσαντα· ἐκλακέντα, ἐκφρονήσαντα, Hsch.

ἐκκολυμβάω, *plunge into the sea from*.., c. gen., ναὸς E.*Hel*.1609: abs., Ar.*Fr*.80, cf. D.S.20.86, *Act.Ap*.27.42; *swim ashore*, εἰς τὴν γῆν D.H.5.24, cf. App.*Syr*.6.

ἐκκομ-ῐδή, ἡ, *removal*, Hdt.8.44; σίτου *IG*2².655.12. b. *purgation*, τῶν περιττωμάτων Dsc.4.176, cf. 2.103. 2. of a corpse, *burial*, ἐ. πολυτελής D.H.4.8, cf. *AP*11.92 (Lucill.), *IG*12(7).395.27 (Amorgos), *IPE*1².34.5 (Olbia, i B.C.). **-ίζω**, *carry* or *bring out*, Hdt. 1.34, 3.24, E.*Tr*.294; esp. to a place of safety, Hdt.1.160, 3.122, Th. 2.6; ἐκκομίζειν τινὰ ἐκ τοῦ μέλλοντος γίνεσθαι πρήγματος *to keep* him *out* of trouble, Hdt.3.43:—Med., Id.8.20, Th.2.78; ἐσεκομίσαντο καὶ ἐξεκομίσαντο ἃ ἐβούλοντο, of those relieved from a state of siege, Id.1. 117: abs., *remove*, ἐς τοὺς Λοκρούς Hdt.8.32. 2. esp. *carry out* a corpse, *bury*, Plb.35.6.2 (Pass.), Plu.*Cic*.42 (Pass.), etc. 3. ἐ. σῖτον, of a horse, *throw* the provender *out of* the manger, X.*Eq*.4.2. 4. *carry home*, ἄνδρας Id.*An*.6.6.36. II. *endure to the end*, τὸ πεπρωμένον E.*Andr*.1269. III. Med., *receive* what is due, λόγους, ὀψώνια, *PLille* 3.79 (iii B.C.), *PSI*4.436 (iii B.C.). **-ισμός**, ὁ, *exportation*, Str.3.2.4. II. *funeral*, Phld.*D*.1.25. **-ιστής**, οῦ, ὁ, *one who brings out*, Gloss.

ἐκκομπ-άζω, *boast loudly*, κατά τι S.*El*.569. **-έω**, aor. 1 ἐξεκόμπησεν· ἐξέπληξεν, Hsch.

ἐκκομψεύομαι, Med., *set forth in fair terms*, E.*IA*333 (but prob. εὖ κεκόμψευσαι).

ἐκκονεῖ· ἐγχωρεῖ, Hsch.

ἐκκονίομαι [ῑ], Pass., *to be in the dust*, Hp.*Vict*.3.76 (nisi leg. ἐγκ–); cf. ἐκκεκονίσθαι· τὸ εἰς κονίαν ἀναλελύσθαι, Hsch.

ἐκκοπ-εύς, έως, ἡ, *a knife for excising*, Heliod.ap.Orib.44.11.6, Gal. 2.592, prob. in Paul.Aeg.6.88. **-ή**, ἡ, *cutting out*, ὀφθαλμῶν Phld. *Ir*.p.33 W.; *excision* of ribs, Heliod.ap.Orib.44.11 tit. 2. *mutilation*, ἐ. μελῶν Vett.Val.110.10 (pl.). 3. *chiselling out, erasure*, γραμμάτων *SIG*252.41 (Delph., iv B.C.); of an arrow-point from a bone, Plu.*Alex*.63. II. *cutting down, felling*, δένδρων Plb.2.65.6 (pl.), cf. *BGU*1121.27 (i B.C.), etc.; ἐκκοπαὶ λόφων *levelling* of hills, Str. 5.3.8; ἐ. πυλῶν Onos.42.17. III. *incision, notch, mortise*, Ph. *Bel*.65.20, Hero *Aut*.27.1, *Bel*.92.4, Ath.Mech.30.3, Sor.1.83. **-ος**, ον, *weary*, Thd.*Is*.43.24.

ἐκκοπρ-ίζω, *discharge excrement*, ἀθρόα πολλά Hp.*Epid*.3.17.δ', cf. *Hippiatr*.31. **-όω**, *empty of excrement*, τὴν κοιλίην Hp.*Acut*.(*Sp*.) 71, cf. Dieuch.ap.Orib.4.8.11:—Pass., Aret.*CA*1.4. **-ωσις**, εως, ἡ, *cleansing from excrement*: ἐ. τῆς κοιλίης *emptying* of the stomach *by purging*, Hp.*Prog*.15. **-ωτικός**, ή, όν, *promoting passage of faeces*, Herod.Med.ap.Aët.9.2, Suid. s. v. ἀλοή.

ἐκκοπτ-έον, *one must excise*, Antyll.ap.Aët.7.74; *one must remove*, τὴν αἰτίαν Gal.10.662, al. II. *one must cut to pieces*, i. e. *destroy*, Plu.*Luc*.24, *Comp.Nic.Crass*.4. **-ης**, ου, ὁ, *one who excises*, Gloss. **-ικός**, ή, όν, *suitable for eradicating* or *expelling*, τύλων, ὑγρῶν, Asclep.ap.Gal.13.850, Herod.Med. in *Rh.Mus*.49.553. **-ω**, *cut out, knock out*, τοὺς γομφίους Phryn.Com.68; τῶν ἑρπετῶν ἐξέκοψε τὸ φθέγμα Call.*Iamb*.1.163:—Pass., ἦν . . τωφθαλμὼ 'κκοπῇς *have* your eyes *knocked out*, Ar.*Av*.342; τὸν ὀφθαλμὸν ἐκκεκομμένος D.18.67; ἐξεκέκοπτο τὴν φωνήν *had lost* his voice, Luc.*JTr*.16. 2. *cut* [trees] *out of* a wood, *fell*, Hdt.6.37 (Pass.), 9.97, Th.6.99, etc.; δένδρα ἐκκεκόφασι X.*HG*6.5.37; παράδεισον *laid waste* the park, Id.*An*.1.4.10; χωρία D.H.8.87; νήσους καὶ πόλεις Plu.*Pomp*.24: hence, b. metaph., *cut off, make an end of*, τοὺς ἄνδρας Hdt.4.110; ἐ. φενακισμόν, ἱεροσυλίαν, Din.2.4, Is.8.39; *eradicate* abuses, *OGI*669.64 (Egypt, i A.D.); τὴν αἰσθητικὴν ἐνέργειαν Arist.*PA*656ᵃ5; *extirpate*, [λύπας] Diog.Oen.2:—Pass., ἡ θρασύτης ἐξεκέκοπτο Pl.*Chrm*.155c. c. ἐ. πλοῖα *scuttle* ships, *IG*12(7).386.9 (Amorgos). 3. as military term, *beat off, repulse*, τὰς ἀκροβολίσεις X.*Cyr*.6.2.15; τοὺς ἐπὶ τῷ λόφῳ Id. *HG*7.4.26. 4. *win*, in throwing the dice, Alex.44, Menecr.1 D.:—Pass., *to be ruined at play*, Hsch. 5. ἐ. θύρας *break open*, Lys.3.6; οἰκίαν ἐ. Plb.4.3.10. 6. *cut out* or *erase* an inscription, *SIG*38.38 (Teos, v B.C.), Arist.*Rh*.1400ᵃ33; οὐδενὶ ἐξέσται . . γράμμα ἐκκόψαι *CIG*3028 (Ephesus), al.; ἐ. τὴν χεῖρα *Ev.Matt*.5.30; *cut out*, as a surgeon does, Luc.*Cat*.24. 7. *coin, stamp* money, D.S.11.26. b. metaph., φαντασίαν ἐ. ὡς . . Phld.*Lib*.p.56 O.; γένη οὐκ ἐκκοπτόμενα ἰδίοις τέλεσι genders not *marked* by different terminations, A.D. *Synt*.104.23; ἐ. ἀναφθέγματα *coin* expressions, Phld.*D*.3.14. 8. *hinder, bring to a stop*, *PAlex*.4.1 (iii B.C.), Vett.Val.268.6. II. intr., *pause, come to a stop*, Id.260.24.

ἐκκορᾰκίζω, in Suid., Zonar., perh. f.l. for ἐσκορακίζω or σκορακίζω.

ἐκκορέω, *sweep clean*, τὰς κλίνας Thphr.*Char*.22.12 (nisi leg. ἐκκορίσας): metaph., μὴ 'κκόρει τὴν Ἑλλάδα Ar.*Pax* 59; and (with a play on κόρη) τίς ἐξεκόρησέ σε; who *has robbed* you *of your daughter?* Id.*Th*.760: generally, *sweep away*, τὸν τῦφον, τὴν κραιπάλην, Alciphr.1.37; ἐκκορηθείης σύ γε *clear out! pack off!* Men. *Georg*.53: prov., ἐκκόρει, κόρη, κορώνην maiden, *drive away* the crow—the opening of a wedding song—the crow being a prognostic of widowhood, *Carm.Pop*.25, cf. Horap.1.8.

ἐκκορίζω, (κόρις) *to clear of bugs*, *AP*9.113 (Parmen.), cf. foreg. II. (κόρη) sens. obsc., Eup.233.

ἐκκορῠφόω λόγον *tell* a tale *summarily, state the main points*, Hes. *Op*.106:—Pass., ἐκκεκορύφωται ὁ λόγος Hp.*Morb*.4.48.

ἐκκοσμ-έω, *deck out, adorn*, in Pass., Lxx 4 *Ma*.6.2, Aristid.1.148 J. **-ησις**, εως, ἡ, *decoration*, v.l. for κόσμησις, Dsc.5.94.

ἐκκοττίζω, in pf. part. Pass. -κεκοττισμένος *ruined at play*, Hsch. s. v. ἐκκεκομμένος.

ἐκκότῠλος, ον, *having a dislocated hip*, Gloss.

ἐκκουφίζω, *raise up, exalt*, Plu.*Mar*.9. II. *relieve* pain, etc., Id. *Crass*.33 (v.l.), Ruf.*Fr*.117. III. *weigh anchor*, Ael.*Fr*.71.

ἐκκοχύζω· ἐκκοιτίζω, Hsch.

ἐκκραγγάνω, *shout*, ἤκουσα τῶν ἐκκραγγανομένων Men.22 D.

ἐκκράζω, *cry out*, κυνηδὸν ἐξέκραξαν cj. in S.*Fr*.722; ἐ. μέγα Plu. *Mar*.44; ἐ. πολλὰ κυνηδόν D.C.66.15.

ἐκκραυγάζω, = ἐκκράζω, Epicur.*Fr*.605.

ἐκκρέμ-αμαι, Pass., *hang, be suspended*, v.l. in Hp.*Art*.76; τὴν γυναῖκα ἐκκρεμαμένην ἀποσεισάμενος Luc.*Tox*.61: c. gen., *hang from*, Pl.*Ion* 536a. II. *depend upon*, ἐξ ἐπιθυμιῶν Id.*Lg*.732e; τῆς τοῦ ζῆν ἐπιθυμίας Plu.*Mar*.12; ἐλπίδος *AP*9.411 (Maec.). **-άννῡμι**, fut. -κρεμάσω, *hang from* or *upon* a thing, Hp.*Art*.22 (dub.); τι ἔκ τινος Ar.*Eq*.1363; λίθον τοῦ ποδός *AP*11.100 (Lucill.); τινὰ ἐξ Ὀλύμπου Apollod.1.3.5. II. Pass., like ἐκκρέμαμαι, *hang on by, cling to*, c. gen., τῶν τε ξυσκήνων ἤδη ἀπιόντων ἐκκρεμαννύμενοι Th.7.75, cf. Luc.*Tox*.6. 2. metaph., *to be devoted to*, Ἄρεος E. *El*.950. **-ασις**, εως, ἡ, *hanging from* or *upon*, v.l. in Hp.*Art*. 76. **-ασμός**, ὁ, = foreg., Cass.*Pr*.6. **-ής**, ές, *suspended*, πήρα Hdn.1.9.3; τὸ -ές the *lobe* of the ear, Ruf.*Onom*.43: c. gen., *hanging from* or *upon*, χείλεος *AP*5.246 (Maced.); ἐπί τινι ib.240.8 (Paul. Sil.); ἀπὸ τοῦ ὤμου Agath.3.17; ἐπὶ γαστέρα ἐ. προβάλλειν Aret.*CA*1.5, cf. Porph.*Gaur*.3.3. II. Adv. -μῶς, Gramm., *in dependent construction*, opp. ἀπολύτως, Eust.1752.47.

ἐκκρήμναμαι or -κριμν-, = ἐκκρέμαμαι, v.l. in Hp.*Art*.76: c. gen., E.*HF*520; ῥόπτρων χέρας ἐκκρημνάμεσθα we *hang on to* the door-knocker by the hands, Id.*Ion* 1612:—later in Act. part. ἐκκρημνάς or -κριμνάς *hanging up*, Iamb.*VP*33.238.

ἐκκρῐδόν, Adv. *apart, alone*, prob. l. in Tryph.224.

ἐκκρῑθιάσας, in gloss on ἀγοστήσας, *AB*213.

ἔκ-κρῐμα, ατος, τό, *secretion*, Thphr.*Ign*.76. **-κρίνω** [ῑ], *single out*, Th.6.96:—Pass., ἀρετῇ πρῶτος ἐκκριθείς S.*Ph*.1425, cf. Th.6. 31. 2. *separate*, Arist.*HA*578ᵃ11, 572ᵇ22 (Pass.); ἐκ τοῦ μείγματος ἐκκρίνουσι τἆλλα *hold that* the rest *are separated out* from . . ., Id.*Ph*.187ᵃ23. 3. *exclude, expel*, X.*Cyr*.1.2.14 (Act. and Pass.), Luc.*Salt*.3 (Pass.); *reject, condemn*, Gal.18(2).693. 4. *secrete*, of the animal functions, Arist.*GA*765ᵇ10, al.; τραῦμα ἐ. ἰχῶρας Zen.6. 46:—freq. in Pass., Arist.*GA*738ᵃ1, al.; ἐκ πυρὸς -κρινόμενον καπνόν *given off* by . . ., Phld.*Sign*.36: metaph., ὅταν . . καθαρὸς ὁ νοῦς ἐκκριθῇ X. *Cyr*.8.7.20. 5. Pass., also of *excretions*, Hp.*Aph*.4.47, 76, etc. 6. of drugs, *remove*, λίθους Dsc.2.127. **-κρῐσις**, εως, ἡ, *separation*, Arist. *Mete*.342ᵃ15, Onos.9.1 (pl.). II. *secretion*, of the animal functions, Arist.*PA*689ᵃ16, *GA*727ᵃ2; τῶν ὑγρῶν Eun.*Hist*.p.263 D. III. = ἔκκριμα, of excrement, Hp.*Aph*.2.15; of the menses, Arist.*HA*583ᵃ 2, etc. **-κρῐτέον**, *one must pick out*, Pl.*Plt*.303b. **-κρῐτικός**, ή, όν, *secretive*, Arist.*Ph*.243ᵇ14; τῆς θερμότητος Thphr.*CP*6.1.3. 2. *tending to remove*, φυσῶν Dsc.2.152. **-κρῐτος**, ον, *picked out, select*, ἔ. δεκάς a *chosen* ten, A.*Pers*.340; πλῆθος ἔ. στρατοῦ ib.803, cf. *Th*. 57; ἔ. δικασταί Pl.*Lg*.926d; ἔ. δώρημα, = ἐξαίρετον, S.*Aj*.1302; ἔ. ἄλλων A.R.4.1185; ἔ. νομίζεσθαι Philostr.*Gym*.23: neut. ἔκκριτον, as Adv., *above all, eminently*, E.*Tr*.1241. 2. *evacuated*, Arist.*Pr*. 861ᵃ36.

ἐκκροτέω, *beat* or *knock out*, ὅπλα τῆς χειρός J.*AJ*6.2.2. II. *hammer out, form, educate*, Phryn.*PS*p.68 B.

ἐκκρουνίζω, *gush forth*, Sch.Il.20.470.

ἔκ-κρουσις, εως, ἡ, *beating out, driving away*, X.*Cyn*.10.12. II. *deduction*, *PTeb*.121.133 (i B.C.). **-κρουσμός**, ὁ, *waning* of the moon, ἐ. καὶ μείωσις Paul.Al.*G*.4. **-κρουστικός**, ή, όν, *fitted for expelling*, τοῦ ἐλέου Arist.*Rh*.1386ᵃ22; τοῦ λόγου Arr.*Epict*.2.18. 29. **-κρουστος**, ον, *beaten out, embossed*, A.*Th*.542. **-κρούω**, *knock out*, παττάλους Ar.*Fr*.402b; τι ἐκ τῶν χειρῶν X.*Cyn*.10.12; for Ar.*Fr*.270 (Med.), v. πύνδαξ:—Pass., *BGU*1007.16 (iii B.C.). b. metaph., ἡ μείζων κίνησις ἐ. τὴν ἐλάττω *expels*, Arist.*Sens*.447ᵃ15; [ἡ ἡδίων ἐνέργεια] ἐ. τὴν ἑτέραν Id.*EN*1175ᵇ8; ἐ. τὸν λογισμόν, τὴν λύπην, ib.1119ᵇ10, 1154ᵃ27. 2. *drive back, repulse*, Th.4.131, X.*HG* 7.4.16; ἀπὸ [λόφου] Th.4.128: metaph., ἐ. τινὰ ἐλπίδος *to frustrate, cheat* one *of* . ., Pl.*Phdr*.228e; τῆς προαιρέσεως Plu.*Sol*.14; ἵνα μὴ . . τοῦ παρόντος ἐμαυτὸν ἐκκρούσω D.18.313:—Pass., τὸν λογισμὸν ἐκκρουσθείς Plu.*Pyrrh*.30. 3. *hiss* an actor *off* the stage, ἐβόων, ἐξέκρουόν με D.19.23. 4. *put off, adjourn by evasions*, εἰς ὑστεραίαν τὴν . . γνώμην ib.144; [τὴν δίκην] Id.36.2, cf. 54.30; τοσαύτας τέχνας . . εὑρίσκων ἐκκρούει Id.21.81; ἐ. τοὺς λόγους *elude*, Pl.*Prt*.336c; ἐ. πρᾶγμα τῷ χρόνῳ 'talk out', Plu.*Caes*.13:—Pass., γραφῆς ἐκκρουομένης D.45. 4. 5. *discharge*, βέλη ἐκ μηχανῶν D.C.75.11. 6. Math., *subtract*, κοινὸν ἐκκεκρούσθω τὸ ἀπὸ ΒΖ *let* the square on ΒΖ *be subtracted* from both, Papp.946.16; *cast out* by division, Vett.Val.20.20, 174.2; *deduct*, in Pass., *PTeb*.189, 241 (i B.C.), etc. II. Med., *get rid of*, βῆχα Plu.2.515a. III. intr., *break forth*, κέρατα τῶν κροτάφων ἐκκρούει Philostr.*VA*1.19.

ἐκκτῠπέω, *burst forth with noise*, of thunder, Poll.1.118.

ἐκκῠβεύω, *play at dice*: metaph., ἐ. τοῖς ὅλοις, ὑπὲρ τῶν ὅλων, *to stake* one's all, Phylarch.58 J., Plb.1.87.8, cf. 3.94.4: c. acc., τὴν ἄδηλον τύχην Onos.32.3. II. Pass., *to be gambled out of, lose at play*, χιλίους ἐκκυβευθεῖσα δαρεικούς Plu.*Art*.17.

ἐκκῠβιστάω, *tumble headlong out of*, δίφρων ἐς κρᾶτα πρὸς γῆν ἐκκυβιστώντων βίᾳ E.*Supp*.692; ἐ. ὑπέρ τινος *to throw a somersault* over a thing, of dancers, X.*Smp*.2.11, cf. *An*.6.1.9.

ἐκκύεις· ἐρεθίζεις, ἐπισείεις, Hsch.

ἐκκῠέω, *bring forth, put forth as leaves*, *AP*7.385 (Phil.).

ἐκκυκλ-έω, *wheel out*, esp. by means of the ἐκκύκλημα (q. v.), ἀλλ' ἐκκυκλήθητι come, *wheel yourself out!* i. e. *show yourself*, Ar.*Ach*. 408; Answ., ἀλλ' ἐκκυκλήσομαι ib.409; ποῖός ἐστιν; Answ., οὗτος οὑκκυκλούμενος Id.*Th*.96; ἐφ' ὑψηλῆς μηχανῆς ἐ. τὴν φιλοσοφίαν Philostr.*VA*6.11. 2. metaph., *publish, divulge*, τι εἰς ἀγοράν Plu.2.80a: f.l. for ἐκκλίνω in D.H.*Rh*.10.9. —ημα, ατος, τό, *theatrical machine*, used to display an interior, Poll.4.128. —ηθρον, v. ἐγκ—.

ἐκκῠλ-ίνδω, *roll out*, ᾧ' ἐκκυλίνδων Ar.*Pax* 134: mostly in aor. 1, σε καταιγίδες ἐξεκύλισαν.. γυμνὸν ἐπ' ἠϊόνι *AP*7.501 (Pers.), cf. 582 (Jul.); *overthrow*, πίτυν.. γαίης ἐξεκύλισε ib.9.131; ἐξεκύλισε βίην ib. 543 (Phil.):—Pass., S.*OT*812: elsewh. aor. 1, ἐκ δίφροιο.. ἐξεκυλίσθη he *rolled headlong from* the chariot, Il.6.42, 23.394, cf. *AP*11.399 (Apollinar.); but ἐκκυλισθέντος τοῦ τροχοῦ Pherecyd.37(a)J.; *plunge headlong*, εἰς ἔρωτας love-intrigues, v.l. for ἐγκ—, X.*Mem*.1.2.22, cf. Opp.*H*.4.20; γένος εἰς κακίαν ἐσχάτην ἐκκεκυλισμένον Max.Tyr.30.3. 2. *extricate*, ὅστις δὴ τρόπος ἐξεκύλισέ νιν Pi.*Fr*.7, cf. *AP*7.176 (Antiphil.):—Pass., *to be extricated from*, ὅτῳ τρόπῳ τῆσδ' ἐκκυλισθήσει τύχης A.*Pr*.87; ἐκκυλισθῆναι ἐκ δικτύων X.*Cyn*.8.8, cf. Plu.*Galb*.27. 3. Pass., *to be published abroad*, εἰς ἀγοράν Id.2.507e. —ίομαι, *to be unrolled*, Arist.*Mech*.855ᵃ30, al., S.E.*M*.3.75, al. —ιστὸς στέφανος a garland *closely wreathed* or *rolled together*, Archipp.40, etc.

ἐκκῡμ-αίνω, *swerve, bulge from the straight line*, of a line of soldiers, X.*An*.1.8.18, cf. Demetr.*Eloc*.84. 2. *cause to burst from their sockets*, τὤμματα Herod.6.68. II. Pass., *to be cast up by the waves*, D.H.10.53; ὑπὸ τῆς θαλάσσης Plu.2.357a. —ανσις, εως, ἡ, *breaking of waves on a beach*, Eust.31.45.

ἐκκύματα· ἐξανθήματα, Hsch. (prob. ἐκθύματα, q.v.).

ἐκκῡμᾰτίζομαι, Pass., *to be cast up by the waves*, Str.6.3.9.

ἐκκῠνέω, (ἔκκυνος) of hounds, *keep questing about*, X.*Cyn*.3.10, Poll.5.65:—also **ἐκκῠνόω**, ibid.

ἐκκῡνηγέσσω, aor. 1 inf. -κυνηγέσαι, *track out*, S.*Ichn*.75.

ἐκκῡνηγετ-έω, *pursue in the chase, hunt down*, τινά E.*Ion* 1422, prob. in A.*Eu*.231. —ητέον, *one must chase*, ἀρχάς Dam.*Pr*.45.

ἔκκῠνος, ον, (κύων) of a hound, *questing about*, X.*Cyn*.7.10, Poll.5.65. II ἔκκυνοι· νόσημά τι κυνῶν, Hsch.

ἐκκύπτω, *peep out of*, αἰγείρου Babr.50.13; ἐκ τῶν οἴκων Ant.Lib. 39.6; ἐκκύψασαν ἁλῶναι to be caught *peeping out* (Reiske for ἐγκ—), Ar.*Th*.790: generally, *pop out*, Id.*Ec*.1052; of a snail's eyes, Teucer ap.Ath.10.455e: metaph., *proceed forth*, τοῦ νοητοῦ εἰς οὐρανόν Plot. 4.3.15; cf. ἐκκέκυφεν· ἀνωρθώθη (—ωσεν cod.), Hsch. II. trans., *put forth*, Ael.*NA*15.21.

ἐκκυρτόω, *make curved*, in Pass., Philostr.Jun.*Im*.12 (nisi leg. ἐγκ—).

ἐκκωδωνίζω, *proclaim by a bell, publish abroad*, Ath.5.219b.

ἐκκωμάζω, *rush wildly out*, εἰς ἄλλην χθόνα E.*Andr*.603.

ἐκκωπέω, *furnish with oars*, or generally, *equip, fit out*: ἐκκεκώπηται S.*Fr*.145 ap.Hsch.

ἐκκωφ-έω, *deafen, stun*, τὰς Ἀθήνας ἐκκεκώφηκας βοῶν Ar.*Eq*.312: —Pass., αἱ δέ μευ φρένες ἐκκεκωφέαται Anacr.81: metaph., ἐς τὸ κάλλος ἐκκεκώφηται ξίφη *are blunted* at the sight of.., E.*Or*.1288, cf. sq. —όω, *make quite deaf*, τὰ ὦτα Pl.*Ly*.204c:—Pass., *become* so, Luc.*Nav*.10, etc.; πρὸς τὸ κάλλος Ath.5.188c; ἐς κάλλος (v. foreg.) Ael.*NA*1.38, v.l. in E.*Or*.1288.

ἐκλᾰβή, ἡ, *amount contracted for*, *IG*12(5).647.19 (Ceos, ἐγλ—).

ἐκλαγχάνω, pf. ἐκλέλογχα condemned by Luc.*Sol*.5:—*obtain by lot* or *fate*, ὅπως πατρῴας τύμβον ἐκλάχῃ χθονός S.*El*.760; τὸν αὐτὸν δαίμον' ἐξειληχότες Id.*OC*1337; κακῶν μέρος ἐξέλαχον Ar.*Th*.1071.

ἐκλακτ-ίζω, *kick out, fling out behind*, σκέλος οὐράνιον Ar.*V*.1492; τὸ Φρυνίχειον ἐ. ib.1525: abs., Eup.411, Hp.*Art*.82. 2. metaph., *escape, run away*, Men.16; also εἰς κραιπάλην Procop.*Pers*.1.24. —ισμα, ατος, τό, *dance*, in which the legs are *thrown up behind, fling*, Poll.4.102. —ισμός, ὁ, = foreg., Hsch.

ἐκλᾰλ-έω, *blurt out, blab, divulge*, D.1.26, Ph.1.64, al., Aen.Gaz.*Ep*. 7; τὸ ἐκλαλοῦν *talkativeness*, E.*Fr*.219:—Pass., Hp.*Jusj*.1, Lib.*Or*. 18.213. —ησις, εως, ἡ, *uttering*, condemned by Poll.5.147. —ητικός, ή, όν, *capable of expressing*, Diocl.ap.D.L.7.49.

ἐκλαμβάνω, fut. -λήψομαι Isoc.12.194:—*receive from* others, ἀριστεῖ' ἐκλαβὼν στρατεύματος *having received* the meed of valour *from* them, S.*Ph*.1429; ἐ. νόμους *to accept* laws *from* another, Plb.2. 39.6. II. *seize and carry off*, βίᾳ τοὺς παῖδας Isoc.l.c.; ἐ. μέρος τι [τῆς μητρός] Arist.*GA*753ᵇ34: generally, *remove*, καρπὸν *PRev.Laws* 29.13 (iii B.C.), etc.: Medic., *evacuate*, πύον Heliod.ap.Orib.44.10.7; *dissect out*, Antyll.ap.Orib.7.14.5. III. *receive in full*, Isoc.*Ep*. 6.13; ἐ. τι παρά τινος E.*Ion*1335, Isoc.5.100, Pl.*Lg*.958d; τὸ τέλεον καὶ ἱκανόν τινων ib.807d. IV. ἔργα ἐ., = ἐργολαβέω, *contract to do* work, Hdt.9.95, cf. *PMagd*.10.1 (iii B.C.), *IG*12(5).647 (Ceos), etc.: c. inf., ἐ. παρὰ τῆς πόλεως πίνακα γράψαι Plu.*Pel*.25, cf. 2. 396e. 2. *hire*, ὀρχήστριαν *PGrenf*.2.67.5 (iii A.D.). V. *take in a certain sense, understand*, ἐ. τοὺς νόμους οὕτω Lys.11.6; ἐ. τι ἐπὶ τὸ χεῖρον Arist.*Rh*.1416ᵇ11; διχῶς Id.*APr*.32ᵇ26. 2. *take note of*, σηκώματα Nicom.*Harm*.6; ἐ. ἀντίγραφον *take* a copy, *PGen*.74.8 (iii A.D.). VI. *select*, τὰς προτάσεις Arist.*APr*.43ᵇ1; τὰ χαλεπώτατα Longin.10.3. VII. Med., ἐκλαμβάνομαι, = ὑπολογίζομαι, Din.*Fr*.16.4. 2. *take hold of*, c. gen., Ph.1.134. VIII. Pass., *to be picked out, adorned*, φιάλαις λιθοκολλήτοις Agatharch.102.

ἔκλαμπ-ρος, ον, *very bright*, φλόγες Lxx *Wi*.17.5, cf. Sch.Arat. 169: neut. as Adv., ἔκλαμπρον γελᾶν Ath.4.158d. Regul. Adv. -ρως *brilliantly*, *Annuario*3.151 (Pisidia, ἐγλ— lapis). —ρύνω, *polish up*, Herod.7.12 (tm.): *adorn*, τὸ ἱερὸν κατασκευῇ ἀναθημάτων J.*BJ*7.3.3, cf. Max.Tyr.22.2:—Pass., *to be adorned*, πόλιν τούτοις —υνθεῖσαν D.H. 2.3. —ω, *shine* or *beam forth*, Hdt.6.82, A.*Pr*.1083 (anap.); ὅπλα ὥστε κάτοπτρον ἐξέλαμπεν X.*Cyr*.7.1.2, etc.; ὀμμάτων ἐ. πόθος *APl*. 4.182 (Leon.); ὥσπερ ἀστραπήν Hp.*Epid*.7.88; πῦρ ἐκ λίθων ἐ. Arist. *HA*516ᵇ11: metaph., δίκας δ' ἐξέλαμψε θεῖον φάος *Trag.Adesp*.500; ὥσπερ ἐκ πυρείων ἐ. Pl.*R*.435a; ἐξ. ἡ δόξα Plb.31.23.2; of persons, Ph.1.326, al.; *burst forth violently*, of a fever, Hp.*VM*16; of sound, *to be clearly heard*, [ἐκ τῆς κραυγῆς] ἐξέλαμψε τὸ καλεῖν τὸν βασιλέα Plb.15.31.1. 2. *to be distinguished*, δι' εὐφυΐαν Plu.*Cic*.2; τῶν ἄλλων Lib.*Or*.62.37. II. c. acc. cogn., *flash forth*, πυρωπὸν γλῆνος ἐκλάμψαν φλόγα A.*Fr*.300.4; σέλας dub. l. in E.*Fr*.330, cf. Lyc.1091; πῦρ App.*Syr*.56, cf. Bias *Fr.Lyr*.: metaph., νοῦς ἐ. αἰσθήσεις Ph.1. 72; ἀπὸ τοῦ ἑνὸς ὁ θεὸς ἑαυτὸν ἐξέλαμψε Iamb.*Myst*.8.2. III. Astrol., = διαυγάζω III, *PLond*.1.132.95 (i/ii A.D.).

ἔκλαμψις, εως, ἡ, *shining forth, brightness*, Lxx 2*Ma*.5.3; ἡλίου Olymp.*in Mete*.49.9. II. metaph., *sudden development*, at puberty, Hp.*Epid*.6.114 (ἐκλάμψιας (acc. pl.) ap.Gal. ad loc.).

ἐκλανθάνω, *escape notice utterly*:—Med., *forget utterly*, c. gen. rei, ἐκ χόλω τῶδε λαθοίμεθα Alc.*Supp*.23.9; τοῦδ' ἐκλανθάνει thou *forgettest* this *entirely*, S.*OC*1005; ἐγλαθόμενος τῆς εὐθύνης *POxy*.1203.8 (i A.D.), cf. Ph.1.247, al.; ἐ. ὅτι.. Pl.*Ax*.369e. II. causal in pres.

ἐκληθάνω, with aor. 1 ἐξέλησα, Aeol. ἐξέλᾱσα (v. infr.): Ep. redupl. aor. 2 ἐκλέλᾰθον: 1. Act., *make one quite forgetful of* a thing, c. gen. rei, ἐκ δέ με πάντων ληθάνει ὅσσ' ἔπαθον Od.7.220; ἔκ μ' ἔλασας ἀλγέων Alc.95: c. acc. rei, ἐκλέλαθον κιθαριστύν made him *quite forget* his harping, Il.2.600: abs., Ἀΐδας ὁ ἐκλελάθων (redupl. pres.) Theoc. 1.63. 2. Med. and Pass., *forget utterly*, ὀϊζύος ἐκλελαθέσθαι Il.6. 285; ἀλκῆς ἐξελάθοντο 16.602; ὡς ἐκλέλησμαί γ' ἃ πάρος εἴπομεν E. *Ba*.1272: c. inf., ἐκλάθετο.. καταβῆναι Od.10.557; λελάθοντο.., οὐ μὰν ἐκλελάθοντ' Sapph.93.

ἐκλᾰπάζω, = ἐξαλαπάζω, *cast out from*, ἑδωλίων A.*Th*.456 (lyr.).

ἐκλάπτω, fut. -λάψομαι Ar.*Pax*885:—*drink off*, Id.*Ach*.1229, etc.

ἐκλᾱτομέω, *hew in stone*, Lxx *Nu*.21.18; *hew* or *hollow out*, ib.*De*. 6.11:—Pass., Str.7*Fr*.35. II. *quarry stones from*, τὴν γῆν Jul. *Gal*.135c.

ἐκλᾰχαίνω, *dig* or *hollow out*, A.R.1.374, Tryph.208.

ἐκλᾰχᾰνίζομαι, *cut vegetables*, Thphr.*HP*7.11.3.

ἐκλε-αίνω, *smooth out* or *away*, ῥυτίδας Pl.*Smp*.191a: hence, *abolish, cause to disappear*, Hp.*Prorrh*.2.20 (Pass.), Plu.2.567f. 2. *smooth* or *polish off*, [λίθον] Agatharch.82; ἐ. τὰ φαντάσματα *smooth* them *down*, Plu.2.83c. —ασμός, ὁ, *attrition*, ἐντέρων Orib.*Fr*.56, cf. Aët.9.43.

ἐκλέγω, fut. Pass. ἐκλεγήσεσθαι *IG*1².76.16: pf. Pass. ἐξείλεγμαι Pl.*Alc*.1.121e, and in med. sense, D.20.131, but ἐκλέλεγμαι Diph. 44, Posidipp.27.9 (prob.):—*pick* or *single out*, Th.4.59, etc.; esp. of soldiers, rowers, etc., X.*HG*1.6.19, Pl.*R*.535a; ἐκ πάντων κεφάλαια Id.*Lg*.811a:—Pass., Id.*Alc*.1.c.; ἐκλελεγμένος *select, recondite*, Diog. Oen.23:—Med., *pick out for oneself, choose*, Hdt.1.199, 3.38, D.l.c.; τὰ κάλλιστα Pl.*Smp*.198d, al.; ἐξ ἁπάντων Isoc.9.58. 2. Lit. Crit., *select*, λέξεις καλάς D.H.*Comp*.3; cf. ἐκλογή. 3. Med., of God, *elect, choose*, Lxx *De*.4.37, *Ep.Eph*.1.4, etc. 4. ἐκλέγειν τὰς πολιάς (sc. τρίχας) *pull out* one's grey hairs, Ar.*Eq*.908, *Fr*.410. II. *levy taxes* or *tribute*, χρήματα παρά τινος Th.8.44; τὰς ἐπικαρπίας And. 1.92, cf. *IG*1².76.8 (Pass., ib.16); ἔκ τινων D.49.49; *take toll of*, χαλκοῦς Thphr.*Char*.6.4: c. acc. pers., ἐ. τέλη τοὺς καταπλέοντας Aeschin.3.113: c. acc. et gen., τὴν δεκάτην τῶν πλοίων X.*HG*1.1. 22. III. *declare*, Prisc.p.294 D., *Gloss*.

ἐκλείανσις, εως, ἡ, = ἐκλεασμός, *Gloss*.

ἔκ-λειγμα, ατος, τό, *medicine that melts in the mouth, lozenge* or *jujube*, Aret.*CA*1.5, Dsc.2.158 (pl.), Archig.ap.Orib.8.2.27, Sor.1. 123. —λειγμᾰτώδης, ες, *of the consistency required for a lozenge*, Aët.3.111, 12.67. —λεικτικός, ή, όν, *made into a lozenge*, v.l. in Hp.*Acut.*(*Sp*.)30. —λεικτόν, τό, = ἔκλειγμα, Hp.l.c., Dsc.4.185.

ἐκλειοτρῑβέω, *to powder very fine*, Dsc.*Ther*.19 (Pass.).

ἐκλειόω, *rub down* or *to pieces*, Alex.Trall.7.5, Steph.*in Hp*.1. 156 D.

ἐκλειπ-ία, ἡ, *failure, lack*, πίστεως J.*AJ*19.4.6. —τέον, *we must omit*, Aristid.*Or*.43(1).3. —τικός, ή, όν, *of* or *caused by an eclipse*, σελήνης χρόνοι Hipparch.3.5.1a; πανσέληνοι Plu.2.145c; ἐπισκοτήσεις ib.932a; συγκρίσεις ἡλίου καὶ σελήνης Str.1.1.12; ἀριθμός dub. in Doroth.ap.Heph.Astr.3.20; ἐκλειπτικόν, τό, *part of moon's orbit in which eclipses take place*, Gem.11.6, cf. Paul.Al.*O*.2; ἐ. ζῴδιον, τόπος, Vett.Val.5.28, 7.10, al. II. ὁ ἐ. (sc. κύκλος) *ecliptic*, = ὁ ἡλιακός, so called because it is *the circle in the plane of which the sun and moon must be to produce eclipses*, interpol. in Cleom.2.5, Ach.Tat.*Intr.Arat*. 23. III. Gramm., *elliptical*, Pall.*in Hp*.2.145 D. —ω, *leave out, pass over*, πολλὰ δ' ἐκλείπω λέγων A.*Pers*.513; ἐ. ὅχλον λόγων Id.*Pr*. 827, cf. D.25.47; ἐ. Ἄνδρον *leave out, pass over* Andros, Hdt.4.33; ἐ. ὁτιοῦν τῆς παρασκευῆς Th.7.48; τὴν στρατιάν X.*HG*5.2.22; εἴ τι ἐξέλιπον, σὸν ἔργον ἀναπληρῶσαι Pl.*Smp*.188e:—Pass., ὄνειδος οὐκ ἐκλείπεται *fails* not *to appear*, A.*Eu*.97. 2. *forsake, desert, abandon*, τὰς πατρίδας, τὴν ξυμμαχίην, etc., Hdt.1.169, 6.13, etc.; θήρας μόχθον E.*Hipp*.52; τὸ ξυνώμοτον Th.2.74; τὸν ὅρκον E.*IT*750; *abandon, quit*, τὴν τάξιν Hdt.8.24, al.; τὴν χώρην Id.4.105, 118, al.; τὸν πλοῦν S.*Ph*. 911, cf. 58; *give up*, τὴν τυραννίδα Hdt.6.123; τὰ ὑπάρχοντα Th.1. 144; θρήνους E.*Ph*.1635; v. infr. II.2. 3. freq. in elliptic phrases, ἐκλείπειν τὴν πόλιν εἰς τὰ ἄκρα *abandon* the city *and go* to the heights, Hdt.6.100, cf. 8.50, X.*An*.7.4.2; ἐξέλειπον οἴκους πρὸς ἄλλον εὐνάτορα E.*Andr*.1040 (lyr.). 4. εἴ τις ἐξέλιπε τὸν ἀριθμόν (of the Persian immortals) if any one *left* the number *incomplete*, Hdt.7.83. 5. *fail* one, ἐκλελοίπασιν ὑμᾶς αἱ προφάσεις Lys.8.16, cf. Pl.*Lg*.657d. II. intr., of the Sun or Moon, *suffer eclipse*, Th.2.28; in full, ὁ ἥλιος ἐκλιπὼν τὴν ἐκ τοῦ οὐρανοῦ ἕδρην Hdt.7.37; ἐ. τὰς ὁδοὺς Ar.*Nu*.

584. 2. *die*, οἱ ἐκλιπόντες the *deceased*, Pl.*Lg*.856e; τῶν ἄλλων ἐκλελοιπότων Is.11.10, etc.; of trees, *BGU*1120.33 (i B.C.); more freq. in full, ἐ. βίον S.*El*.1131; ὑφ' ὧν ἥκιστα ἐχρῆν τὸν βίον ἐκλιπών (= ἀποθανών) Antipho 1.21; so ἐ. φάος E.*Ion* 1186, etc. 3. *faint*, Hp.*Prorrh*.1.71. 4. generally, *leave off, cease*, τῇ μοι [ὁ λόγος] ἐξέλιπε Hdt.7.239; ἐ. πυρετός Hp.*Aph*.4.56, cf. Th.3.87; ἐκλέλοιπεν εὐφρόνη, i.e. it is day, S.*El*.19; ὥστε μὴ 'κλιπεῖν κλέος ib.985, cf. 1149; [αἱ ἐργασίαι] ἐκλελοίπασιν Isoc.8.20: c. part., *leave off* doing, Pl.*Mx*.234b, cf. 249b: c. gen., θεραπείας Plu.*Marc*.17. 5. *fail, be wanting*, ῥώμη γὰρ ἐκλέλοιπεν ἣν πρὶν εἴχομεν E.*HF*230, cf. Pl.*R*.485d; τῶν ἐπιτηδείων ἐκλειπόντων D.S.16.75; ἡ φωνὴ ἐξέλιπε Luc.*Nigr*.35; περὶ ὧν ἐ. [ὁ νόμος] Arist.*Pol*.1286^{a}37: Gramm., of words in a sentence, A.D.*Synt*.11.17; of grammatical forms, ib. 168.21. 6. *remain, be left*, Lxx 4*Ki*.7.13. 7. *depart*, A.*Pers*. 128 (lyr.), *Th*.219. 8. ἐκλείπων σφυγμός *remittent* pulse, Gal. 9.66.

ἐκλείχω, *lick up*, of taking honey, Hp.*Acut*.56, cf. Ph.1.458, 527:—Pass., *to be taken as an* ἐκλεικτόν, Dsc.1.72, 2.158.

ἔκλειψις, εως, ἡ, (ἐκλείπω) *abandonment*, νεῶν, πολίων, Hdt.6.25, 7.37; τῆς πατρίδος D.C.41.13. II. (from intr.) of Sun or Moon, *eclipse*, ἡλίου ἐκλείψεις Th.1.23, cf. Arist.*Metaph*.1044^{b}10, etc.; ἔ. τελεία, μερική, Cleom.2.6; εἰλικρινής ib.5: metaph. (with play on I), βασιλέως Plb.29.16.1, cf. Plu.*Aem*.17. 2. *failing, cessation*, τῶν δυνάμεων Id.2.433f (pl.), cf. Aret.*SD*1.7; *extinction* of a race, Str.9.5.12. 3. *defect, omission*, Id.5.3.7. 4. in Law, *failing to appear in court*, *AB*259. 5. ἔκλειψις χορίου *retention* of the afterbirth, Paul.Aeg.6.75.

ἐκλεκτ-έος, α, ον, *to be picked out, selected*, Pl.*R*.456b, al. II. ἐκλεκτέον *one must select*, ib.412d, Arist.*APr*.43^{b}6, Sor.1.78. **-ικός**, ή, όν, *capable of exercising moral choice*, Chrysipp.*Stoic*.3.46. 2. ἐ. ἀξία value *deserving such choice*, Antip.ib.30, al. II. *picking out, selective*, δυνάμεις D.H.*Comp*.2 fin.; οἱ ἐ. *the Eclectics*, philosophers *who selected such doctrines as pleased them* in every school, Gal.14.684; ἐ. αἵρεσις D.L.*Prooem*.21, Gal.19.353. III. Adv. -κῶς Hierocl. p.41 A. **-ός**, ή, όν, *picked out, select*, Ibyc.22, Th.6.100; τὸ τῶν ἐ. δικαστήριον Pl.*Lg*.938b; ἐ. δικασταί, = Lat. *iudices selecti*, *OGI*499.3 (ii A.D.). Adv. -τῶς interpol. in Suid. s.v. ἐπίλεκτος. 2. *choice, pure*, σμύρνη Lxx*Ex*.30.23; βοήθημα Asclep.ap.Aët.9.12; ἀνδρῶν *PRein*.43.9 (ii A.D.); ἐκλεκτόν, = *corn*, Aq.*Ps*.64(65).14. II. *chosen of God, elect*, Lxx*Is*.43.20, *Ev.Marc*.13.20, etc. **-όω**, in Pass., *to be separated*, i.e. *purified*, Lxx*Is*.52.11.

ἐκλελᾰθεῖν, -θέσθαι, v. ἐκλανθάνω.

ἐκλελαμμένον· ἐξεστραμμένον, Hsch. **ἐκλελαπτημένον**· ἐκπεπονημένον, Id. **ἐκλελι(α)σμένος**· ἐξεστραμμένος, Id.

ἐκλελῠμένως, Adv. pf. part. Pass. of ἐκλύω, *loosely, carelessly*, Isoc.*Ep*.6.6; ἐ. καὶ ἀτόνως Plu.*Lyc*.18; *freely, licentiously*, Ath.12.519f.

ἔκλεμμα, ατος, τό, (ἐκλέπω) *peel, rind*, Hp.*Morb*.2.13.

ἔκλεξις, εως, ἡ, *selection, choice*, Pl.*Phdr*.231d

ἐκλεπεῖ· ἐκπορεύεται, Hsch.; cf. ἐκκληπεῖ.

ἐκλεπ-ίζω, = ἐκλέπω, Hp.*Nat.Puer*.29 (Pass.), Ph.1.345 (quoting *Ge*.30.37, where Lxx λεπίζω). **-ισις**, εως, ἡ, *taking off the shell*: *hatching*, Suid. s.v. νεοττεία.

ἐκλεπρόω, *make* λεπρός, in Pass., Sch.Theoc.1.40.

ἔκλεπτος, ον, *very thin*, οὖρον Hp.*Coac*.572.

ἐκλεπτόω, = sq., in Pass., *Gloss*.

ἐκλεπτύνω, *make very thin*, f.l. for -πλύνω, *Gp*.16.6.3; *reduce to a fine state*, τὰς οὐσίας Syn.Alch.p.58 B.

ἐκλεπῠρόω, *strip off the bark*: metaph., *strip*, Sophr.22.

ἐκλέπω, *free from shell* or *rind, peel*, κόκκους Hp.*Mul*.1.81, 84; of crocodiles and birds, *hatch* their young, Hdt.2.68, Cratin.108, cf. Ar.*Av*.1108; of serpents, Hdt.3.109; of insects and tortoises, Arist.*HA*553^{a}8, 558^{a}10:—Pass., fut. ἐκλᾰπήσομαι v.l. (ap.Erot.) in Hp.*Nat.Puer*.29: aor. ἐκλᾰπῆναι Ar.*Fr*.164.

ἐκλευκαίνω, ῥόθια δ' ἐκλευκαίνετε *dash the white* spray *off* the oar, E.*IT*1387. II. Pass., *become quite white*, Thphr.*CP*5.9.9, Thd.*Da*.12.10.

ἔκλευκος, ον, *quite white*, Hp.*Prog*.2, Arist.*HA*617^{a}12, *PCair.Zen*.129.18, Lxx*Le*.13.24: Comp., *inclining to white*, Arist.*HA*592^{b}7.

ἐκλήγω, *cease utterly*, δακρυρροοῦσα S.*El*.1312: abs., Herod.3.87.

ἐκ-ληθάνω, v. sub ἐκλανθάνω II. **-λήθομαι**, = ἐκλανθάνομαι, τῶν συγκειμένων App.*Mac*.11.5.

ἐκληπτ-έον, *one must select*, Arist.*APr*.43^{b}16. 2. *one must take in a certain sense*, Sch.Ar.*Nu*.298, etc. II. *one must evacuate*, κύστιν Orib.*Syn*.9.55.1. **-ωρ**, ορος, ὁ, later -λήμπτωρ, *contractor of works*, *PFay*.58.6 (ii A.D.), etc. 2. *tax-collector*, Just.*Nov*.130.3, al.

ἐκληρέω, *play antics, behave absurdly*, Plb.15.26.8.

ἔκλησις, εως, ἡ, *forgetting and forgiving*, Od.24.485.

ἐκλητουργέω, *undertake and complete a public burden*, Is.7.40.

ἔκληψις, εως, ἡ, *taking out, collecting*, Dsc.1.68.4; *removing*, Id.3.90. 2. *farming of taxes*, *BGU*897.1, Just.*Nov*.123.6; of any trade *enterprise*, *PTeb*.38.11 (ii B.C.). 3. *isolation, dissecting out*, of an aneurism, Antyll.ap.Orib.45.24.3; of a varicose vein, ib.4.36.7. 4. *taking of extract* from a document, Mitteis *Chr*.185 (ii A.D.), *Cod.Just*.10.11.8.4a, etc.

ἐκλῐθεύω, *clear of stones*, τὰς πέτρας *IG*11(2).199 *A*85 (Delos, iii B.C., ἐγλ-).

ἐκλῐθολογέω, *clear by picking off the stones*, Thphr.*CP*3.20.5.

ἐκλῐθόω, *turn into stone*, Tz.*H*.1.556.

ἐκλικμάω, *winnow, sift, empty*, Lxx*Ju*.2.27, *Wi*.5.23.

ἐκλικνίζω, = foreg., *Gloss*.

ἐκλῑμία, ἡ, (λιμός) *exceeding hunger, faintness*, Lxx*De*.28.20, Aq.*Jb*.41.14.

ἐκλιμν-άζω, *flood completely*, τὸ πεδίον ἐ. ὁ ποταμός App.*BC*4.107: pf. Pass. ἐκλελιμνάσθαι Sch.Th.*Oxy*.853 x 12:—also -λιμνιάζω, abs., of a river, *overflow its banks*, App.*Fr*.1.3. **-όομαι**, *become a complete swamp*, D.H.1.61.

ἔκλῑμος, ον, *emaciated*, Thphr.*CP*2.4.6.

ἐκλῑμώσσω, *faint with hunger*, Aq.*De*.28.65.

ἐκλιμπάνω, = ἐκλείπω, *abandon*, E.*Med*.800, *PHamb*.27.14 (iii B.C.), Ant.Lib.16.3. II. intr., *cease*, οὔποτ' ἐξελίμπανον θρυλοῦσα E.*El*.909. 2. *to be lacking*, Them.*in APo*.38.29. 3. *to be eclipsed*, Ascl.*in Metaph*.11.31.

ἐκλῐνάω, *escape out of the net*, Eust.574.30.

ἐκλῐπαίνω, in fut. -λιπανῶ, *make smooth as oil*, πέλαγος Posidipp. ap.Ath.7.318d:—Pass., *to be enriched, fertilized*, Plu.*Mar*.21.

ἐκλῐπᾰρέω, *entreat earnestly, move by entreaty*, Str.17.1.29: c. inf., Plu.*Them*.5, Jul.*Or*.7.220b: abs., Ph.2.521, J.*AJ*5.7.8, Apollon.*Mir*.3; πολλὰ ἐ. D.L.4.7:—Pass., D.H.7.10, Str.14.5.10, Memn.7.2.

ἐκλῐπής, ές, (ἐκλείπω) *failing, deficient*, ἡλίου ἐκλιπές τι ἐγένετο, = ἔκλειψις, Th.4.52: c. gen., *deficient in*.., Arist.*Xen*.980^{a}6. II. *omitted, overlooked*, Th.1.97, Arr.*An*.1.12.2.

ἐκλιστράω, *slap*, Eust.1119.59.

ἐκλιχάζει· ἐξορμᾶν ποιεῖ, ἐκσοβεῖ, Hsch.

ἐκλιχμάομαι, *absorb, exhaust*, Ph.1.124, Ael.*Fr*.82.

ἐκλογ-εύς, έως, ὁ, *collector of firstfruits, taxes*, etc., καρπῶν *IG*1^2.76.14; φόρου Lys.*Fr*.9, *IG*12(5).1001.14 (Ios, iv B.C., ἐγλ-), Ph.2.33, al. **-εύω**, *collect*, τὰ διάφορα *IG*5(1).1390.47 (Andania). **-έω**, *select*, *CPHerm*.p.80 (iii B.C.). II. mostly in Med., *excuse oneself*, ὑπέρ τινος App.*BC*5.77; ἐ. τὴν ἀνάγκην *plead in excuse*, ib.13: c. acc. et inf., *to state by way of excuse that*.., ib.3.48; μικρὰ ὑπὲρ ἐμαυτοῦ Them.*Or*.8.103d. **-ή**, ἡ, *choice, selection*, τῶν ἀρχόντων Pl.*R*.414a, 536c; ἐ. ποιεῖσθαι Id.*Lg*.802b; ἐ. [τῶν ἀρίστων νόμων] Arist.*EN*1181^{a}18; τῶν ἐναντίων Id.*Metaph*.1004^{a}2; ὀνομάτων Phld.*Rh*.1.162 S., D.H.*Comp*.1, etc.; ὀνόματος A.D.*Synt*.71.10; κατ' ἐκλογὴν ἀριστίνδην κεκριμένοι Plb.6.10.9; ἐπὶ ἐγλογῇ γεωργεῖν *PTeb*.5.166 (ii B.C.). 2. *levying of troops*, Plb.5.63.11. 3. *collection of tribute*, etc., κριθῶν Lex Attica ap.Ath.6.235c; χρημάτων D.C.42.6; σίτου Crates ap.Ath.6.235b. 4. Theol., *election*, *Ep.Rom*.9.11, etc.; σκεῦος ἐκλογῆς *Act.Ap*.9.15. 5. *balancing* of accounts, *PRyl*.157.6 (ii A.D.). II. *extract, quotation from a book*, Apollon.Cit.3, Ath.14.663c, Antig.*Mir*.15. 2. *choice collection* of passages, such as *the Eclogae* or '*Elegant Extracts*' of Stobaeus: ἐκλογαὶ Ἀρχιγένους *select prescriptions* of A., Gal.14.343. 3. διὰ τὴν ἐ. τῶν ἀνθρώπων because they were *picked* men, Plb.1.47.9, cf. Ph.2.362. 4. ἐκλογήν· κάλαθον (Lacon.), Hsch. **-ημα**, ατος, τό, *schedule of payments*, *PStrassb*.103.2 (iii B.C.). **-ίζομαι**, *compute, reckon*, τὰς εὐθύνας Harp. s.v. λογισταί; τὸ ἀργύριον *IG*9(1).694.104 (Corc.), cf. 2^2.1263.12:—Pass., ἀριθμὸν.. ἐκ τῶν ἀντιγράφων -λογισθέντα ib.7.3073.56 (Lebad.). 2. *consider, reflect on*, τι Hdt.3.1, E.*IA*1409, Th.4.10; περί τινος Id.2.40, And.1.57; ἐ. πρὸς οἵους.. ὁ ἀγὼν ἔσται Th.1.70; ἐ. ὅτι.. D.21.123; τίς ὢν πρὸς οὕστινας ἐπολέμει Aeschin.1.64: aor. ἐκλογισθῆναι in pass. sense, *to be calculated*, Plu.*Publ*.15. 3. *reckon on*, οὐδεὶς ἔθ' αὑτοῦ θάνατον ἐκλογίζεται E.*Supp*.482. 4. *reckon up, relate in detail*, Plb.3.99.3, 10.9.3, D.H.11.40. II. = ἐκλογέομαι, τινὶ περί τινος App.*BC*3.43. **-ισις**, εως, ἡ, *computation, reckoning*, Epicur.*Sent*.18. **-ισμός**, ὁ, *keeping of accounts*, in pl., *Inscr.Prien*.108.214 (ii B.C.), Phalar.*Ep*.24; *computation, calculation*, Haussoullier *Cinquantenaire* p.88 (Didyma, ii B.C.), Plu.*Cat.Mi*.36; *consideration, reckoning*, in pl., Plb.1.59.2, D.H.*Th*.3, Plu.*Oth*.9 (v.l.), etc.; *setting out* of grammatical paradigms, D.T.629.8; *conclusion* of an argument, Hp.*Nat.Puer*.12. **-ιστευω**, *to be* ἐκλογιστής, *CIG*3886 (Eumeneia), *PEdgar*44 (iii B.C.). **-ιστήριον**, τό, *office of* ἐκλογιστής, *PLond*.1.23.110. **-ιστής**, οῦ, ὁ, *accountant*, Lxx*To*.1.22; as public official, *Milet*.7.60 (Didyma), *PTeb*.72.449 (ii B.C.), *AJA*18.324 (Sardes, i B.C.), *CIG*4956.36 (Oasis Thebarum, i A.D.), etc. 2. = ἐκλογεύς, φόρων Ph.1.338. **-ιστία**, ἡ, *reckoning*: *accounts*, Lxx*To*.1.21, *Sammelb*.4423. **-ιστικός**, ή, όν, *capable of estimating*, τῶν οἰκῳ συμφερόντων Muson.*Fr*.3 p.10 H.: abs., Phld.*Herc*.1003. **-ος** (A), ὁ, *tale*, A.*Fr*.219. II. *balance of accounts*, *PLond*.1.131.6 (i A.D.), etc. **-ος** (B), ον, *picked out, choice*, Ph.2.479, 539; ᾠδή Max.Tyr.17.1. 2. ἔκλογον ὄν· μεταξὺ λόγων, Hsch.

ἐκλοιπάζω, *adjourn*, in Pass., *Gloss*.

ἐκλου-στρίς, ίδος, ἡ, *bathing-costume*, *PCair.Zen*.60.8 (iii B.C.). **-τήριος**, ον, *for washing out* or *rinsing*, χαλκίον ἐ. *IG*4.39.18 (Aegina). **-τρον**, τό, *washing-vessel*, Poll.10.46. **-ω**, *wash out*, Hp.*Steril*.241. II. *wash thoroughly*, Plb.3.88.1:—Pass., λουτροῖς ἐκλελουμένος δέμας A.*Fr*.32; ἐγλοηθείς *PPetr*.2 pp.72, 73 (iii B.C.).

ἐκλοφίζω, *quarry from a hill*, Anon.ap.Suid. s.v. ἐξελοφίζετο.

ἐκλόχ-ευμα, ατος, τό, *an offspring*, Suid. s.v. Πολύευκτος. **-εύω**, *bring forth*, Orph.*A*.129, *AP*9.602 (Even.):—so in Med., E.*Hel*.[258]: metaph., λόγον Orph.*A*.43:—Pass., *to be born*, E.*Ion* 1458 (anap.).

ἐκλοχίζω, *pick out of a cohort* or *troop*, Lxx*Ca*.5.10 (Pass.).

ἐκλοχμόομαι, Pass., *become bushy*, Thphr.*CP*3.19.1.

ἐκλῠγίζω, *twist exceedingly*, ἐκλελυγισμέναι ὀρχήσεις *mazy* dances, Porph.*Abst*.1.33.

ἔκλυρον· χλωρόν, δίυγρον, ἢ νοτερόν, ἔνικμον, ὑγρόν, Hsch.

ἔκλῠσις, εως, ἡ, *release, deliverance from* a thing, ἀφροσύνης Thgn. 590 (= Sol.13.70); ἄθλων A.*Pr.*264; τοῦδε τοῦ νοσήματος S.*OT*306; δεσμοῦ Theoc.24.33; Ἀΐδεω *AP*6.219.24 (Antip.(?)). 2. *weakening* of an opponent's case, Hdn.*Fig.*p.91 S., cf. Alex.*Fig.*1.2. II. *feebleness, faintness*, Hp.*Aph.*7.8, etc.; τῆς πόλεως ἔ. καὶ μαλακία D. 17.29; ψυχικῶν δυνάμεων Ph.1.154; φυσική Agatharch.55; ἐκλύσιες κοιλίης *relaxations*, Hp.*Coac.*625. 2. *laxity*, of style, [Longin.] *Rh.*12. III. *lowering of the voice through three quarter-tones* (διέσεις), Bacch.*Intr.*41, Aristid.Quint.1.10, Plu.2.1141b.

ἐκλυσσάω, Att. -ττάω, strengthd. for λυσσάω, Ph.1.430, J.*AJ*13. 16.3.

ἐκλῠτ-ήριος, ον, *bringing release*, S.*OT*392: -τήριον, τό, *expiatory offering*, E.*Ph.*969. -ικός, ή, όν, *calculated to weaken*, Arist.*GA* 726b13; ὥρα Aët.16.22: metaph., τῶν λόγων Herm.*in Phdr.*p.103 A. -ος, ον, *easy to let go, light, buoyant*, of missiles, E.*Andr.* 1133. II. *let loose, unbridled*, ἵμεροι Ti.Locr.102e; *lascivious*, φιλήματα Lyd.*Mag.*3.65; *unlimited, extreme*, βουλιμία Timocl.13.3; ἔ. καὶ βαρύ Olymp.*in Mete.*198.12. III. *relaxed, unnerved*, E.*Tr.* 1179, dub. in Eup.147; *exhausted*, Nic.Dam.p.98 D.; *deprived of force*, of an engine, Ph.*Bel.*85.10; *weak*, κίνησις Olymp.*in Mete.*169. 2; τόνος τοῦ φθέγματος Luc.*Im.*13; *diluted, watery*, οἶνος *Gp.*7.1.4, cf. Gal.12.278; *loose*, of proof, Eudem.ap.Theon.Sm.p.200 H.; *mild* (opp. σφοδρόν), γυμνάσιον Gal.6.156. Adv. -τως *by being relaxed*, Plu.*Lyc.*17; *weakly*, Agathin.ap.Gal.8.938. IV. *curing by* λύσις (opp. κρίσις), ἡμέραι Gal.9.817.

ἐκλυτρ-όομαι, Med., *redeem by payment of ransom*, *SIG*588.70 (Milet., ii B.C.), Sch.Od.4.33.—Act. only in Hsch. -ωσις, εως, ἡ, *redemption*, Lxx *Nu.*3.49.

ἐκλύω [ῡ, v. λύω], *set free*, πόνων *from* labours, A.*Pr.*328; *release*, ὕδατα *PTeb.*49.6 (ii B.C.):—Pass., *to be set free*, ἐκλέλυμαι πόθου Thgn. 1339; ἐκ δεσμῶν Pl.*Phd.*67d:—Med., *get one set free, release*, ἀλλ' ἄγε δή σε κακῶν ἐκλύσομαι Od.10.286; τοῦ φόβου σ' ἐξελυσάμην S.*OT* 1003; θανάτου νιν ἐκλύσασθε E.*Andr.*818; ἐξελυσάμην βροτοὺς τὸ μὴ μολεῖν A.*Pr.*237: c. acc. pers. only, ἐξελύσαντο τοὺς Ἀργείους X.*HG* 7.1.25: abs., ἐξελυσάμην I *delivered* him *from danger*, S.*Aj.*531. II. *unloose*, ἐ. τόξα *unstring* a bow, Hdt.2.173; ἐ. ἁρμοὺς E.*Hipp.*825; σκαιὸν ἐκλύσων στόμα *likely to let loose* a foolish tongue, S.*Aj.*1225. 2. *make an end of*, ἐξέλυσας... σκληρᾶς ἀοιδοῦ δασμόν *paid* it *off*, Id.*OT* 35; ἐπίπονον ἁμέραν Id.*Tr.*654; μόχθον E.*Ph.*695; ἔριν καὶ φιλονικίαν D.9.14; ἐξελύσατε (v.l. -λύσασθε) τὰς παρασκευάς Id.18.26. 3. *relax*, Arist.*HA*610a27; τῆς φροντίδος τὸ ἀκριβές Luc.*Dom.*17:—Pass., *to be faint, fail*, Hp.*Aph.*2.41, Isoc.15.59, D.19.224, Phld.*Ir.* p.69 W., etc.; πρὸς τὸν πόλεμον Isoc.4.150; ἐκλυθῆναι τοῖς σώμασι, τῇ ψυχῇ, Arist.*Fr.*144, Plb.29.17.4 (so intr. in Act., J.*BJ*1.33.5), etc.; of things, *to be unserviceable*, τὰ τῶν πλοίων ἐκλελυμένα Arist.*Pol.* 1320b37; ἐκλύεται ὁ ῥοῦς, τὰ ῥεύματα, *cease*, Plb.4.43.9, 4.41.5. 4. Medic., ἐ. κοιλίαν *relax* the bowels, Dsc.4.169. 5. *pay in full*, δάνειον Plu.*Caes.*12 (Pass.). b. *purchase*, Herod.6.91. 6. *resolve* a doubt, in Pass., A.D.*Synt.*176.24; also τὰ ὑπ' ἀμφιβολίαν πίπτοντα ἐκλύεται τοῦ ἀμφιβόλου ib.311.11. 7. *dissolve*, τι ὄξει Gal.11.106. III. intr., *to break up, depart*, Lxx 2*Ma.*13.16.

ἐκλωβάομαι, Pass., *sustain grievous injuries*, ἄγωγ' ὑπ' αὐτῶν ἐξελωβήθην S.*Ph.*330.

ἐκλωπίζω, (λῶπος) *lay bare*, ἐκ δ' ἐλώπισε πλευράν S.*Tr.*925. II. = λωποδυτέω, Hsch.

ἐκλωτίζομαι, = ἐξανθίζομαι, Achae.31:—Act. in aor. 1, Hsch. (prob.).

ἐκμᾰγεῖον, τό, (ἐκμάσσω) *napkin*, Pl.*Ti.*72c, Meyer *Ostr.*62.5 (ii B.C.). 2. *that which wipes off, gets rid of*, αἵματος μέλανος, of the spleen, Aret.*SD*1.15; *rough towel*, Archig.ap.Gal.12.621, Paul.Aeg. 1.57. II. *that on* or *in which an impression is made*, κήρινον ἐ. *lump* of wax, Pl.*Tht.*191c, cf. 196a; of *matter* (φύσις) *as a recipient of impressions*, Id.*Ti.*50c, Arist.*Metaph.*988a1; [σῶμα] ἐ. αὐτῆς τῆς γενέσεως Ocell.2.3. 2. *impress, mould*, Pl.*Tht.*194d,e, Ph.1.279: metaph., ἐκμαγεῖον πέτρης *impress* of the rocks, of a fisherman who is always wandering over them, *AP*6.193 (Flacc.). 3. *model*, Pl. *Lg.*800b, 801d; μηχανῆς Procop.*Aed.*2.3.

ἐκμᾰγεύω, *bewitch*, Iamb.*Bab.*9.

ἔκμαγμα, ατος, τό, *impression in wax*, etc., Poll.9.131. II. = κροκόμαγμα, Hp.*Steril.*235.

ἐκμάθησις [ᾰ], εως, ἡ, *thorough knowledge*, Phld.*Po.*5.2.

ἐκμαιεύομαι, *bring to the birth*, Simp.*in Ph.*786.21.

ἐκμαίνω, *drive mad* with passion, ἐκμήνας θυμὸν ἔρωτι Pl.*Epigr.* 7.6, cf. Theoc.5.91; ἐπί τινι *with love for* her, Ar.*Ec.*966; φόβῳ τέτρωρον ἐκμαίνων ὄχον E.*Hipp.*1229; πόθον ἐκμῆναι *to kindle mad* desire, S.*Tr.*1142; ἐκμῆναί τινα δωμάτων *to drive* one *raving from* the house, E.*Ba.*36:—Pass., with pf. 2 Act. ἐκμέμηνα, *go mad* with passion, ταῦτα ἐκμαίνεσθαι ἔς τινα *rage* so against one, Hdt.3.33, cf. 37, Paus. 1.11.15; ἔρωτι οὐρανίῳ ἐκμεμηνυῖα [διάνοια] Ph.1.482; of mania, Aret. *SD*1.6; ὑπὸ τοῦ ἀκράτου Luc.*Nigr.*5; of sexual passion, εἰς γυναῖκας ἐκμανείς J.*AJ*8.7.5: also, c. acc., ἐκμανῆναί τινα *to be madly in love with*.., *Anacreont.*11.4; τινί Aristaenet.1.15 tit.; of persons in delirium, Hp.*Epid.*3.17.ιγ'.

ἔκμακτος, ον, (ἐκμάσσω) *express*, εἴδη Emp.22.7.

ἔκμακτρον, τό, *impress*, ποδῶν E.*El.*535.

ἐκμᾰλάσσω, Att. -ττω, *relax, weaken*, τὰ σώματα Plu.*Fr.*20.1; *soften, mollify*, τραχύτητας γλώσσης Dsc.*Eup.*2.17: metaph., ὀργήν τινος J.*AJ*2.6.8.

ἐκμαλθᾰκόω, = foreg., Men.Prot.p.5 D.

ἐκμάλθαξις, εως, ἡ, *softening, enervating*, Erot. s. v. ἐκθήλυνσις.

ἐκμᾰνής, ές, *quite mad*, πρὸς τὰ ἀφροδίσια Nicias ap.Ath.10.437e; λύτται Ph.1.408. Adv. -νῶς Ath.13.603a.

ἐκμανθάνω, *learn thoroughly*, and, in past tenses, *to have learnt thoroughly, know full well*, ἐ. τὴν [Ἑλλάδα] γλῶσσαν Hdt.2.154; ἀνδρὸς ψυχήν S.*Ant.*175; ἐ. τι ἀπό τινος A.*Pr.*256; ἔκ τινος Pl.*Ax.*371a; παρά τινος S.*OT*286; τοῦ θεοῦ τί πρακτέον ib.1439, cf. *OC*114, Ar.*Ec.* 244; ἐ. ὅτι.. Hdt.3.134. II. *examine closely, search out*, Id.7. 28, E.*IT*667, X.*Cyr.*1.6.40. III. *learn by heart*, ὅλους ποιητάς Pl. *Lg.*811a, cf. Aeschin.3.135; ᾄσματα Thphr.*Char.*27.7; Σαπφοῦς ταρωτικά Epicr.4; Διονυσίου δράματα Ephipp.16; ἵνα πολλάκις ἀκούοντες τῶν ἐπῶν ἐκμανθάνωμεν τὴν ἔχθραν Isoc.4.159.

ἔκμαξις, εως, ἡ, *wiping*, Arist.*Insomn.*460a16.

ἐκμᾰραίνω, aor. -μάρᾱνα *AP*12.234 (Strat.):—*make to fade* or *wither away*, Thphr.*Ign.*11, *AP*l. c.:—Pass., *wither away*, Theoc.3.30.

ἐκμαργόομαι, *go raving mad*, ἐξεμαργώθης φρένας E.*Tr.*992.

ἐκμαρτῠρ-έω, *to bear witness to* a thing, c. acc., φόνον A.*Eu.*461; ἐκμαρτύρησον.. τό μ' εἰδέναι Id.*Ag.*1196; εἰς πολλούς before many persons, Aeschin.1.107:—Pass., Str.12.8.6. II. *make depositions out of court*, Is.3.21, Test.ap.D.35.20, Aeschin.2.19. -ησις, εως, ἡ, *deposition of absent witness*, *POxy.*1208.30 (iii A.D.). -ία, ἡ, *the deposition of a witness taken out of court*, -ίας ποιεῖσθαι Is.3.21 (pl.), D.46.7, Aeschin.2.19, *SIG*953.41 (Calymna, ii B.C., pl.). -ιον, τό, *evidence*, Anon.ap.Suid.; ἐν ἐκμαρτυρίοις Just.*Nov.*90.2. II. *official certificate*, *PMasp.*87.21 (vi A.D.), *BGU*1094.16 (vi A.D.).

ἐκμαρτύρομαι [ῠ], *prove by evidence*, τι Just.*Nov.*22.14. 2. abs., *give testimony*, ib.91.2.

ἐκμᾰσάομαι, *chew completely*, in aor. Pass. -μασήθην Ph.1.334.

ἐκμάσσατο, 3 sg. aor. 1, he *devised* or *invented*, τέχνην *h.Merc.* 511; cf. μαίομαι.

ἐκμάσσω, Att. -ττω, pf. ἐκμέμᾰχα (-κα codd.) cj. in D.H.*Dem.*4: aor. 2 Pass. -εμάγην [ᾰ] Pl.*Tht.*191d; also aor. 1 part. ἐκμαχθείς Hsch.:—*wipe off, wipe away*, κάρα κηλῖδας ἐξέμαξεν S.*El.*446; ἔκμασσε [τὸ αἷμα] E.*HF*1400; ἀλωπεκίας ὀθονίῳ Archig.ap.Gal.12.406:—Med., *wipe away one's tears*, *AP*5.42 (Rufin.). 2. *wipe dry*, ὑπὸ σπόγγου Hp.*Acut.*65 (Pass.), cf. Herod.6.9; [τοὺς ἔμπροσθεν πόδας] ἐ. εἰς τοὺς μέσους, of bees, Arist.*HA*624b1. II. of an artist, *mould* or *model* in wax or plaster, αὐτὸν ἐκμάττειν τε καὶ ἐνιστάναι εἰς τοὺς τῶν κακιόνων τύπους *to mould* and adapt oneself to.., Pl.*R.*396d; of pessaries, Hp.*Steril.*230:—so in Med., Id.*Nat.Mul.*109; ὧν ἔτι θερμὰ κονία.. ἐκμάσσεται ἴχνη of whose yet warm footsteps the dust *receives the impress*, Theoc.17.122; *express, imitate*, ἵππου γενεήν Nic.*Th.*740; τὸν Λυσιακὸν χαρακτῆρα ἐκμέμακται D.H.*Dem.*13 (so in Act., ib.4 codd., dub.); ἐς τὸ ἀκριβέστατον ἐξεμάξατο τὸν διδάσκαλον he *was the image of* his master, Alciphr.3.64:—Pass., μάλθης ἄναγνα σώματ' ἐκμεμαγμένοι (v.l. -μένα) S.*Ichn.*140; ἐκεῖνος αὐτὸς ἐκμεμαγμένος his very *image*, Cratin.255; βασιλέως.. εἰκόν' ἐκμεμ. *IGRom.*1.1190 (Memnon); ὃ ἂν ἐκμαγῇ whatever *be impressed*, whatever *impression be made* (cf. ἐκμαγεῖον), Pl.*Tht.*191d; τὴν ἰδέαν τοῦ παιδὸς ἐκμεμάχθαι *had impressed upon him* the image of the boy, Plu.*Cic.*44; ποιότης ἀπὸ μένοντος ἐκμαγεῖσα θείου λόγου Ph.1.548.

ἐκμαστεύω, *track out*, ὡς κύων νεβρὸν πρὸς αἷμα ἐ. A.*Eu.*247, Ph. Bybl.ap.Eus.*PE*1.9.

ἐκμαστῑγόω, *scourge*, in Med., Hsch. s. v. ἐκδέψηται.

ἐκμεθύσκω, *make quite drunk*: metaph., τὰς ῥίζας.. λίαν ἐ. *overcharge* them *with moisture*, Thphr.*CP*5.15.3; λύχνον ἐλαιηρῆς ἐ. δρόσου *AP*5.3 (Phld.).

ἐκμείλιξις, εως, ἡ, *appeasing, taming*, κυνῶν Eust.1749.43.

ἐκμειλίσσω, *soften*, Gal.11.317. II. mostly Med., *appease*, Corn.*ND*21, App.*BC*1.97, Plu.2.380c, D.C.79.19, Conon 18.

ἐκμείρομαι, *obtain for one's lot*, aor. 2 ἐξέμμορον Nic.*Th.*791; θεῶν ἐξέμμορε τιμῆς Od.5.335.

ἐκμελαίνομαι, *to be darkened, grow dark*, Heraclit.*All.*39; ὑπὸ [νυκτός] ib.45.

ἐκμελᾰνίζω, *lose colour*, Olymp.Alch.p.91 B.

ἐκμέλεια, ἡ, (ἐκμελής) *false note*, D.H.*Comp.*11: metaph., Corn. *ND*32. II. *carelessness*, Zos.1.23, al.

ἐκμελετάω, *train* or *teach carefully*, τινά Pl.*Hp.Ma.*287a. 2. *learn perfectly, con over, practise*, Antipho 3.2.7, Pl.*Hp.Ma.*286d; τὴν εἰς τὸ θεῖον ἐ. βλασφημίαν Men.715.

ἐκμελής, ές, (μέλος) *out of tune, dissonant*, Ph.1.375, al., Ti.Locr. 101b, Plu.*Demetr.*1; *unbridled*, φιλοτιμία Id.*Lys.*23; of persons, Just.*Nov.*136.6. Adv. -λῶς Poll.4.57.

ἐκμελίζω, *dismember*, Lxx 4*Ma.*10.5,8.

ἔκμελος· ἀδύναμος, Hsch. **ἐκμεταιωροῦνται**· μετεωρίζονται, Id.

ἐκμεταλλεύω, *empty of ore* or *metal*, Str.14.5.28 (Pass.).

ἐκμέταλλος, ον, *from a mine*, ἅλς Sch.Nic.*Al.*518 (s. v. l.).

ἐκμετρ-έω, *measure out, measure*, χρόνον E.*IA*816; κύκλος τις ὡς τόρνοισιν ἐκμετρούμενος Id.*Fr.*382; ἐ. τὸν βίον *to end* life, to die, Tz. *H.*3.800: abs., *measure a distance*, ἐπὶ τὰς πόλεις Lxx *De.*21.2:—freq. in Med., *measure for oneself, measure out*, ἄστροις.. ἐκμετρούμενος χθόνα *measuring, calculating its position* by the stars (for he was an exile), S.*OT*795; *take measure of*, τὰ ἐκείνου ὅπλα X.*Cyr.*6.4.2, cf. Plb.5.98.2:—Pass., *PTeb.*61(*b*).258 (ii B.C.), etc. -ησις, εως, ἡ, *measurement*, Plb.5.98.10, *BGU*432 ii 10 (ii A.D.). -ητής, οῦ, ὁ, *measurer, surveyor*, *PAmh.*2.79.16 (ii A.D.), etc. -ος, ον, *out of measure, measureless*, ὄλβος S.*Fr.*353, cf. Man.4.464,626; of a verse, *exceeding the due length*, Luc.*Pr.Im.*18.

ἐκμηκύνω, strengthd. for μηκύνω, D.H.1.56 (Pass.), 6.83, J.*BJ*7.8.3 (Pass.).

ἐκμηνίω, strengthd. for μηνίω, Hsch.

ἔκμηνος, ον, *of six months, half-yearly*, ἐκμήνους χρόνους (Pors. for ἐμμήνους) S.*OT*1137; βίος Arist.*HA*558^{a}17: Subst. ἔκμηνος, ὁ, *half-year*, ἐντὸς ἐκμήνου Pl.*Lg*.916b; ἐν ἐγμήνῳ *IG*12(9).207.52 (Eretria, iii B.C.), cf. D.C.59.6; ἔ. (sc. ἀρχή), ἡ, Plb.6.34.3. II. *six months old*, of an animal, Arist.*HA*562^{b}27; μὴ πρεσβύτερον ἐνιαυσίου καὶ ἐγμήνου *IG*12(5).647.8 (Ceos).

ἐκμηνύω, *inform of, betray*, Plu.*Pel*.9 (Pass.), Poll.5.154.

ἐκμηρύομαι, *wind off like a ball of thread*, Jul.*Gal*.135c; of an army, *make* it *defile out*, τὴν δύναμιν ἐκ τῶν δυσχωριῶν Plb.*Fr*.132; διὰ στενῆς θυρίδος.. ἐκμηρυόμενος αὐτόν Plu.*Aem*.26. II. intr., of the army, *defile*, X.*An*.6.5.22; τῆς χαράδρας Plb.3.53.5 (but τὰς δυσχωρίας ib.51.2). III. metaph., *evolve itself, develop*, Dam.*Pr*. 65, cf. eund.ap.Simp.*in Ph*.780.30.

ἐκμηχᾰνάομαι, aor. Pass. ἐξεμηχανήθην, *contrive*, J.*AJ*8.3.4, Hsch.

ἐκμῐαίνω, *pollute thoroughly, defile*, Opp.*H*.4.663:—Pass., *ejaculate semen*, Hp.*Superf*.31, Ar.*Ra*.753, Lxx *Le*.18.20.

ἐκμῑμ-έομαι, *imitate faithfully, represent exactly*, E.*HF*1298, Ar. *Av*.1285, X.*Mem*.3.10.1, Duris 89 J. **-ησις**, εως, ἡ, *imitation*, Arg.2 Ar.*Av*.

ἐκμῑσέω, *hate much*, Plu.*Phil*.12 (Pass.).

ἔκμισθος, ον, *receiving no pay*, Hsch.

ἐκμισθόω, *let out for hire*, ὁλκάδας X.*Vect*.3.14; χωρίον Lys.7.4; [τέμενος] *SIG*1044.30 (Halic.), etc.: c. inf., ἐ. τινὰ ἑταιρεῖν Aeschin. 1.13:—Med., *contract for*, ἔργον Them.*Or*.4.53a.

ἐκμολεῖν, inf. of aor. 2 ἐξέμολον, Ep. 3 sg. ἔκμολε, *go out, go forth*, Il.11.604; ἐξέμολεν A.R.1.845; cf. βλώσκω.

ἐκμολύνω, *pollute*, in Pass., Ar.*Ra*.753 cod.V.

ἐκμορφόω, *represent, express in form*, Plu.2.537d:—Pass., τὰς ἐκμεμορφωμένας διὰ τῶν αἰσθήσεων τέρψεις Phld.*D*.3.14. II. *bring into shape*, Ael.*NA*2.19.

ἐκμουσόω, strengthd. for μουσόω, *teach fully*, τινά τι E.*Ba*.825:—Pass., ἐκμουσωθῆναί τι Ael.*VH*14.34.

ἐκμοχθέω, *work out with toil*, κερκίσιν πέπλους E.*El*.307. 2. *struggle through*, πόνους Id.*IT*1455, cf. A.*Pr*.825, Porph.ap.Eus.*PE* 3.11. 3. *win by labour, achieve*, Ἑλένην ἐ. δορί E.*Tr*.873; ἐκμοχθῶν βίᾳ εὔκλειαν Id.*HF*1369. 4. *struggle out of*, τὰς τῶν θεῶν τύχας ib.309. 5. Pass., *to be worn out*, ὅσοι δεσμοῖς ἐκμεμόχθηνται βροτῶν Id.*Fr*.332.5 (s. v. l.).

ἐκμοχλ-εία, ἡ, *dislodgement*, φλέγματος Aët.16.21. **-ευσις**, εως, ἡ, f. l. for ἐκχόλωσις, Paul.Aeg.3.13. **-εύω**, *lift out with a lever*, Hp.*Art*.72 (and in Med., ib.76); πύλας ἐ. *to force* them *open with crow-bars*, Ar.*Lys*.429: generally, *force, compel*, τὴν φύσιν Plu.2. 662c; *dislodge*, τὰ λυποῦντα Gal.7.195, cf. Archig.ap.Orib.8.1.22; τὴν κακοχυμίαν τῶν σωμάτων Olymp.*in Grg*.p.143 J.

ἐκμῠελίζω, *suck the marrow out of, deprive of strength*, Lxx *Nu*.24.8.

ἐκμυζ-άω, *suck out*, αἷμ' ἐκμυζήσας Il.4.218, cf. Luc.*Tim*.8, Ael.*NA* 3.39, Gal.*UP*6.15, Q.S.4.398; *exhaust* air from a vessel, Hero *Spir*. 1 *Praef*.: metaph., *extort*, Lyd.*Mag*.3.67:—also in form **ἐκμύζω**, Dsc.*Eup*.1.62, Phlp.*in Mete*.115.18:—Pass., Antyll.ap.Orib.7.16. 16:—also **ἐκμυζέω**, Alex.Aphr.*Pr*.2.59: metaph., *drain, exhaust*, [στάσις] ἐ. τὰς δυνάμεις Aristid.*Or*.23(42).31. **-ηθμός**, ὁ, = sq., Alex.Trall.3.3. **-ησις**, εως, ἡ, *sucking out*, Sor.1.77, Philum.*Ven*. 7.3, Alex.Aphr.*Pr*.2.59. **-ησμός**, ὁ, = foreg., Archig.ap.Gal.12. 656, Aët.13.24.

ἐκμῡθόω, *make into a* μῦθος or *fable*, Philostr.*Im*.1.3 (Pass.).

ἐκμῡκάομαι, *bellow aloud*, τὰς ὀλοφύρσεις Phalar.*Ep*.122.2.

ἐκμυκτηρ-ίζω, *hold in derision, mock at*, Lxx *Ps*.2.4, *Ev.Luc*.16. 14. **-ισμός**, ὁ, *derision*, Hsch.

ἐκμῠσάττομαι, *abominate*, Ph.2.303.

ἐκμύσσομαι, Med., *blow the nose*, read by Gal. for ἀπο- in Hp.*Nat. Hom*.7.

ἐκναρκάω, *become quite torpid* or *sluggish*, Plu.*Cor*.31.

ἐκναυσθλόω, *cast on shore*, Lyc.726 (Pass.).

ἐκνε-άζω, *grow up afresh*, σπόρος κατ' ἔτος ἐκνεάζων Luc.*Am*. 33. II. *replace from fresh crop*, *PAmh*.2.147.9 (iv/v A.D.). **-ασμός**, ὁ, *renewal*, Simp.*in Ph*.4.36, *in Epict*.p.37 D.

ἐκνέμω, *pasture*, ἀγέλας Ph.2.233:—more freq. in Med. with aor. ἐξενεμήθην, *feed off* or *on*, τι Thphr.*HP*9.16.1, Nic.*Th*.571; *inhabit*, χώρας Ph.2.524: metaph., λύπης τὴν διάνοιαν ἐκνεμομένης Luc.*Am*. 25. II. *go forth to feed*: metaph. in Med., οὐκ ἄψορρον ἐκνεμῇ πόδα; S.*Aj*.369 (lyr., s. v. l.). III. Medic., -όμενον ἕλκος *rodent* ulcer, Alex.Trall.9.3. IV. ἐκνενεμήκασι· παραδεδώκασιν, and ἐκνενέμηται· ἐξῆλθεν, ἐξῆκται, Hsch.

ἐκνεοττεύω, *hatch*, Arist.*Mir*.842^{b}11, Antig.*Mir*.15.

ἐκνεύμυκτεν· κατέβαλλεν, Hsch.

ἐκνευρ-ίζω, (νεῦρον) *cut the sinews*, Plu.2.451d; ἐκνενευρισμένοι *broken down, enfeebled*, D.3.31; ἡ πόλις ἐκνενεύρισται Plu.2.755c, cf. Ph.1.258, al.; ἐκνευρισθεῖσα χώρα *exhausted* soil, Id.2.434. **-ισις**, εως, ἡ, *unnerving*, ψυχῆς Eustr.*in APo*.223.27. **-ος**, *enervus*, *Gloss*. **-όω**, = -ίζω, *Tab.Defix.Aud*.234.18 (Carthage, i A.D.).

ἔκνευσις, εως, ἡ, *turning the head aside to avoid*, βολῶν ἐκνεύσεσι Pl.*Lg*.815a. 2. ἐκνεύσεις τῶν ὁδῶν *deviations*, Sch.Ar.*Ra*.113; cf. ἔκνευσις ὁδοῦ, *diverticulum*, *Gloss*.

ἐκνεύω, aor. ἐξένευσα, *turn the head out of* its natural position, of a horse, ἐ. ἄνω *to toss* the head, X.*Eq*.5.4; τῇ κεφαλῇ ἐκνεύσας *by a side-movement* with the head, of the wild boar, Id.*Cyn*.10.12, cf. Lxx 4*Ki*.23.16. 2. c. acc., *shun, avoid*, Phld.*Sign*.27, Ph.1.146, Orph.*A*.458; ξίφος Hegesias ap.D.H.*Comp*.18; πληγήν D.S.17. 100. II. *fall headlong*, εἰς θάνατον E.*Ph*.1268; ἐ. πρός τι *to turn aside*, Ph.1.297: c. gen., τῶν παρόντων Plot.6.7.34. III. *motion away*, ἐξένευσ' ἀποστῆναι πρόσω E.*IT*1330.

ἐκνέφ-ελος, ον, *bursting forth from clouds*, ἥλιος Thphr.*HP*8.10. 3. **-ίας** (sc. ἄνεμος), ὁ, *a hurricane, caused by clouds meeting and bursting*, Alex.46.5, Arist.*Mete*.365^{a}1; νότος ἐ. D.S.20.88. 2. ἐ. ὄμβρος rain *with sunshine*, Hp.ap.Gal.19.96; ἐ. ἥλιος *seen through clouds*, Herod.Med.ap.Orib.10.9.1, cf. Philostr.*Gym*.58. 3. ἐ. πυρετός, perh. fever with sweating, Hp.ap.Gal. l. c. **-όομαι**, *become a cloud*, Thphr.*Vent*.7.

ἐκνέω, fut. -νεύσομαι: aor. 1 ἐξένευσα: pf. ἐκνένευκα Men.*Epit*. 355:—*swim out, swim to land*, E.*Hipp*.823; *escape by swimming*, Th.2.90: generally, *escape, get safely through*, Pi.*O*.13.114, E.*Hipp*. 470, Men. l. c., E.*IT*1186.

ἐκνῆναι· ἐξαπατῆσαι, Hsch.

ἐκνηπιόω, *rear from childhood*, Philostr.*VS*2.1.11:—Pass., *to be reared*, ὑπὸ λόγων Id.*VA*5.14.

ἐκνηστεύω, *continue fasting*, Hp.*Morb*.2.55, Plu.2.686e.

ἐκνήφω, fut. -ψω Lxx *Ge*.9.24:—*sleep off a drunken fit, become sober again*, l. c., Hippoloch.ap.Ath.4.130b, *AP*5.134, Plu.*Dem*.20: metaph., 1*Ep.Cor*.15.34: c. gen., *recover from*, χάρμῃ ἐ. τῆς δυσθυμίης Aret.*SD*1.5. II. trans., *carry off*, ἀρρώστημα ἐκνήψει ὕπνος Lxx *Si*.34(31).2 (dub.).

ἐκνήχομαι, aor. 1 ἐξενηξάμην Plb.38.16.12: pf. inf. ἐκνενῆχθαι Ath.7.315d:— = ἐκνέω, *swim out* or *away*, πρὸς τὴν γῆν Plb. l. c.; εἰς.. Arist.*Mu*.398^{b}32, Luc.*DMar*.8.2; πρός τινα Apollod.1.9.25; abs., Luc.*Merc.Cond*.2.

ἔκνηψις, εως, ἡ, *becoming sober* or *calm*, Lxx *La*.2.18.

ἐκνίζω, *wash out, purge away*, φόνον φόνῳ E.*IT*1224; of crimes, Pl.*Ep*.352c:—Med., *wash off from oneself*, οὐδέποτε ἐκνίψει τὰ πεπραγμένα σαυτῷ D.18.140; τὰ ἔθη γυναικῶν Ph.1.365; ἄγος φόνου Paus. 3.17.7; τὸ θνητόν Plu.2.499c. b. ἐκνενιμμένοι τόποι *washed away*, *POxy*.1469.6 (iii A.D.). II. *wash clean, purify*, ψυχήν *AP*14.74: metaph., *restore to clarity*, τὴν αἴσθησιν Aret.*CA*2.3:—Pass., ἐκνενιμμένη, of a cup, Eub.56.5; ἐκνιφθεὶς ὁ στόμαχος Philum.ap.Aët.9.3.

ἐκνῑκ-άω, *achieve by force*, ὁ χρυσὸς -νικᾷ τάδε E.*Ion*629; *carry one's point that*.., c. acc. et inf., Plu.*Ant*.63. 2. c. acc., ἐξενίκησε τὸν δῆμον καὶ τὸν εἴργοντα νόμον τῆς θέας τὰς γυναῖκας Ael.*VH*10.1:—Pass., ἄνεμος εἰς γαλήνην ἐξενικήθη Hld.5.23, cf. Ruf.ap.Orib.5.3. 9. II. intr., *win a complete victory*, Plb.15.3.6. 2. metaph., *gain the upper hand, come into vogue, prevail*, ἅπασι among all, Th. 1.3; ἐπὶ τὸ μυθῶδες ἐκνενικηκέναι *to have won its way to* the fabulous, ib.21; κακὸν εἰς τοὐμφανὲς ἐξενίκησε Luc.*Abd*.6; εἰς παροιμίαν Suid. s. v. Μάρας; εἰς δύναμιν Ph.1.420. **σις**, εως, ἡ, *eviction*, *Cod. Just*.1.3.38(39).

ἐκνίπτω, = ἐκνίζω, Hsch. s. v. ἐκλούηται (Pass.).

ἐκνιτρ-όω, *cleanse with* νίτρον, τἀκπώματ'.. ἐκνενιτρωμένα θεῖναι Alex.2.4, cf. *IG*7.3073.86 (Lebad.), Archig.ap.Gal.12.406. **-ωσις**, εως, ἡ, Orib.*Fr*.74.

ἔκνιψις, εως, ἡ, (ἐκνίζω) *washing*, Hsch.

ἐκνοέω, *think out, contrive*, D.C.*Fr*.73.3 codd.

ἔκνοια, ἡ, (ἔκνοος) *loss of one's senses*, Arist.*Somn*.455^{b}6 (pl.), 456^{b} 10.

ἐκνόμιος, ον (η, ον Orph.*Fr*.121), *unusual, marvellous*, Pi.*N*.1.56; *lawless*, Orph. l. c. Adv. -ίως Ar.*Pl*.981: Sup. ἐκνομιώτατα ib.992.

ἔκνομος, ον, *outlawed*, A.*Eu*.92. II. = foreg., Orph.*A*.60; *unlawful, monstrous*, τιμωρίαι D.S.14.112, cf. Ael.*Fr*.217, Ph.2.165, al.: Sup., ib.280. III. Adv. -μως *discordantly*, A.*Ag*.1473 (lyr.).

ἔκνοος, ον, contr. -νους, ουν, *senseless*, ὑπὸ γήρως Plu.*CG*19.

ἐκνοσηλεύω, *cure completely*, Ph.1.631, Gal.10.522:—Pass., -όμενοι *convalescents*, Gal.6.726, Orib.3.15.7.

ἐκνοσφίζομαι, *take for one's own*, *AP*15.24 (Simm.). II. ἐκνοσφίσαι· ἐκβαλεῖν, Hsch.

ἐκνοτίζω, *drip*, Hsch. s. v. ἀπολείβραξαι.

ἐκνυκτερεύομαι, *stand overnight*, *PLeid.X*.8.12.

ἐκνύσσω, *expungo*, *Gloss*.

ἐκξέω, *wipe off, erase*, *App.Anth*.7.56, 71, Tz.ad Lyc.874.

ἐκξῐφίζομαι, *unsheathe the sword*, Tz.*H*.3.134.

ἐκξῠλόομαι, *become woody*, Thphr.*HP*1.2.7.

ἐκξύω, *scrape out*, Herod.3.18.

ἑκοντ-ηδόν, Adv. = ἑκοντί, A.D.*Adv*.197.22. **-ήν**, Adv. = foreg., Theognost.*Can*.161.24, Arr.ap.Suid., *SIG*880.48 (Pizus).—The remark of Phryn.1 (ἑκοντὴν οὐ χρὴ λέγειν, ἀλλ' ἐθελοντήν) refers not to this Adv., but to a Noun **ἑκοντής**, οῦ, ὁ, used by Epict.*Gnom*.67; ἑαυτὸν ἑκοντὴν παρέχων *IPE*1^{2}.40.21 (Olbia, ii/iii A.D.). **-ί**, Adv. *willingly*, Ps.-Phoc.16, Them.*Or*.16.209a; but ἑκόντι may generally be read, Arist.*Rh.Al*.1431^{b}20, Plu.*Comp.Eum.Sert*.2.

ἑκοτόν, Arc. for ἑκατόν (q. v.).

ἑκουσι-άζομαι, *offer* or *be offered freely*, ἐν τῷ ἑκουσιασθῆναι λαὸν Lxx *Jd*.5.2; ὁ -όμενος τῷ νόμῳ ib.1*Ma*.2.42. **-ασμός**, ὁ, *free-will offering*, ib.2*Es*.7.16, Aq.*Jd*.5.2, etc. **-ος**, α, ον S.*Tr*.727, 1123, etc.; also ος, ον Id.*Ph*.1318, E.*Supp*.151, Antipho 2.2.3, Th.6.44, etc.: (ἑκών):—of actions, *voluntary*, πόνοι Democr.240; βλάβαι S.*Ph*. l. c.; φυγή E. l. c.; ἁμάρτημα Antipho 5.92, etc.; συμβόλαια Pl.*R*.556b; πράξεις ib.603c, al.; ἀδικήματα Id.*Lg*.860e, al., etc.; γυμνασιαρχία *undertaken voluntarily*, *POxy*.473.3 (ii A.D.); τὰ ἑ. *voluntary acts*, opp. τὰ ἀκούσια, *IG*1.1, X.*Mem*.2.1.18, Arist.*EN*1109^{b}31. 2. rarely of persons, *willing, acting of free will,* ἥμαρτεν οὐχ ἑκουσία S.*Tr.*1123; ἑ. ἀποθανεῖν Th.1.138. II. Adv. -ίως E.*Tr.*1037, etc.; also ἑκουσίῳ τρόπῳ Id.*Med.*751; ἐξ ἑκουσίας (sc. γνώμης) S.*Tr.*727; καθ' ἑκουσίαν Th.8.27.

ἑκουσιότης, ητος, ἡ, *willingness,* Memn.32.1.

ἐκπαγλ-έομαι, *to be struck with amazement, to wonder greatly,* only used in part., καί μιν ἐπεδείκνυσαν ἐκπαγλεόμενοι Hdt.7.181, cf. 8.92; ἐκπαγλεομένων ὡς.. Id.9.48. II. *wonder at, admire exceedingly,* c. acc., A.*Ch.*217, E.*Or.*890, *Tr.*929; rare in Prose, D.H.1.40. **-ος,** ον, Ep. and Ion. word, *terrible, violent*: I. of persons, ὧδ' ἔ. ἐών, of Achilles, Il.21.589; πάντων ἐκπαγλότατ' ἀνδρῶν, also of Achilles, 1.146, 18.170; of other heroes, 20.389, 21.452. 2. sts. of things, χειμὼν ἔ. Od.14.522; ἐκπάγλοις ἐπέεσσιν Il.15.198, Od.8.77; ἔδεισεν γὰρ ἐμὴν ἔ. ἐνιπήν 10.448, cf. 17.216. 3. mostly Adv. -λως *terribly, vehemently, exceedingly,* ἐ. ἀπόλεσσαν Il.1.268; κοτέοντο 2.223; ἐθέλει οἰκόνδε νέεσθαι ib.357; μαίνεται 9.238; ὠδύσατ' ἐ. Od.5.340; ἔχθαιρε 11.437; ὀδύρεται 15.355; αἴθεται Hp.*Mul.*2.171 (ἐκπατίως Erot.); ἐ. πονέει ib.1.3: neut. as Adv., ἔκπαγλον ἐπεύξατο Il.13.413, cf. Nic. *Th.*448, etc.; οὐ γὰρ ἐγώ σ' ἔ. ἀεικιῶ Il.22.256: neut. pl., ἔκπαγλα φιλεῖν to love *beyond all measure,* 3.415, 5.423; ἦν ἔ. χαλεφθῇ Nic. *Th.*445. II. in later Poets the word freq. signifies merely, *marvellous, wondrous,* ἀνὴρ ἔ. Pi.*P.*4.79; σθένει ἔ. Id.*I.*7(6).22; ἐν πόνοις ἔ. ib.6(5).54: not freq. in Trag., ἔ. κακόν, τέρας, A.*Ag.*862, *Ch.* 548; δείπνων ἀρρήτων ἔκπαγλ' ἄχθη S.*El.*204 (lyr.). Adv. ἔκπαγλα *marvellously,* Id.*OC*716 (lyr.): in early Prose only once, ὅπλα τὰ ἐκπαγλότατα X.*Hier.*11.3; in Com., Eup.8.14D.(Sup.). (Metath. for *ἔκπλαγος (ἐκπλήσσω) acc. to Eust.68.18; perh. dissim. from *ἔκπλαγλος.)

ἐκπαγλότης, ητος, ἡ, *enormity,* Hsch. (-πλαγ- cod.).

ἐκπάθεια [πᾰ], ἡ, *violent passion,* Longin.38.3.

ἐκπᾰθής, ές, (πάθος) *passionate, furious,* Plb.16.23.5, J.*AJ*15.3.4, etc.; ἐπί τινι Plb.1.7.8; ἐ. πρός τι *passionately eager* for a thing, Id. 1.1.6, etc. Adv. -θῶς Telesp.35 H., J.*BJ*2.18.4. II. *out of harm, unhurt,* Anon.ap.Suid.

ἐκπαιδ-ευμα, ατος, τό, *nursling, child,* E.*Cyc.*601. **-εύω,** *bring up from childhood,* ib.276; *train thoroughly,* ἐκθρέψαι καὶ ἐ. Pl.*Cri.* 45d, Luc.*Alex.*5. II. *teach* one a thing, τινά τι J.*Ap.*2.29, D.C. 45.2; but, III. ἐ. τινί τι *impress on* one *by education,* E.*Fr.*52.5 (lyr., s. v. l.).

ἐκπαίζω, *laugh to scorn, mock at,* Lxx 1*Es.*1.49(51), Phld.*Rh.*2. 216S.

ἐκπαιφάσσω, *rush madly to the fray,* Il.5.803.

ἐκπαίω, *throw* or *cast out of* a thing, με δόξης ἐξέπαισαν ἐλπίδες they *have dashed* me *from* my expectations, E.*HF*460. II. intr., *dash out, escape,* Anaxil.22.17 (Casaubon for ἐξέπεσε):—Med., Plu. *Brut.*51. (Cf. ἐμπαίω.)

ἔκπᾰλαι, Adv. for ἐκ πάλαι, *for a long time,* Ph.1.323, 2*Ep.Pet.* 3.5, J.*AJ*16.8.4, Plu.2.548d, Plot.6.4.14, *POxy.*938.3 (iii/iv A. D.), etc.

ἐκπάλαιστα (ἐκ- Meineke)· δεινά, ὑπερήφανα, Hsch.: **ἐκπάλαιστος·** ἄνανδρος, Id.

ἐκπᾰλαίω, *transgress the laws of wrestling,* Philostr.*Im.*1.6.

ἐκπᾰλ-εία, ἡ, *dislocation, PMed.Lond.*155.3.11. **-έω,** of a joint, *start out of the socket,* Hp.*Fract.*42, *Art.*55. **-ής,** ές, *out of joint,* ib.53, Hsch. **-ησις,** εως, ἡ, *dislocation,* Hp.*Fract.*42.

ἐκπᾰλιγκοτεῖν (prob.), = ἐναντιολογεῖν, Hsch. **ἐκπαλλακίδιοι·** οἱ νόθοι, Id.

ἐκπάλλω, *shake out*:—Pass., *spring* or *spurt out,* μυελὸς.. σφονδυλίων ἔκπαλθ' Il.20.483; also ἐκπάλη· ἐχωρίσθη, ἀπέστη, ἐξέπεσεν, Hsch.

ἔκπαλτος, ον, *excited,* dub. in Gal.19.543.

ἔκπᾱμον (-πάλιον cod.)· ἀκλήρωτον, Hsch.; cf. παμῶχος.

ἐκπᾰνουργέω, strengthd. for πανουργέω, Sch.Ar.*Eq.*270.

ἐκπαππόομαι, Pass., of seeds, *become plumous,* Thphr.*HP*3.16.6, 6.4.8, Dsc.3.118.

ἔκπαππος, ὁ, *great-great-grandfather, IGRom.*3.474.

ἐκπαραπίπτω, Astrol., *fail to combine,* Vett.Val.93.30.

ἐκπαρθενεύω, (παρθένος) *deflower,* Sch.Luc.*DMar.*7.1.

ἐκπᾰτάγέω, *deafen,* τὰ ὦτα Them.*Or.*21.253c: but aor. 1 ἐξεπατάγησαν· ἐξεφώνησαν, Hsch.

ἐκπᾰτάσσω, *strike, afflict,* τινὰ κακοῖσι E.*HF*890 (-πετάσουσιν codd.): metaph., γρηῦν βροντῆς ἐξεπάταξε φόβος *AP*9.309 (Antip. ⟨Thess.⟩):—Pass., φρένας ἐκπεπαταγμένος *stricken* in mind, Od.18. 327; ἐξεπατάχθη· ἐξεπλάγη, Hsch.

ἐκπᾰτ-έω, *withdraw from society,* D.L.1.112. II. pf. part. -πεπᾰτηκώς *having finished his walk,* Id.4.19. III. Pass., *to be avoided,* Metrod.60. **-ιος,** ον, (πάτος) *out of the common path*: *excessive,* ἄλγεα A.*Ag.*49 (anap.); expld. by Sch. as *lonely.* Adv. -ίως v.l. for ἐκπάγλως (ap.Erot.) in Hp.*Mul.*2.171. **-ος,** ὁ, = ἀπόπατος, Theognost.*Can.*24; cf. ὑσπέλεθος.

ἔκ-παυμα, ατος, τό, *total rest,* Hsch. **-παύω,** strengthd. for παύω, *set quite at rest, put an end to,* μόχθους E.*Ion* 144 (lyr.):—Med., *take one's rest,* Th.5.75.

ἐκπαφλ-άζω, *boil* or *bubble over,* Arist.*Pr.*936ᵇ23. **-ασμός,** ὁ, *boiling over,* ib.29.

ἐκπᾰχύνω, *make over-fat,* Thphr.*CP*4.1.4 (Pass.).

ἔκπεδος, ον, = ἔκπους, *IG*7.3073.75 (Lebad.).

ἐκπείθω, *persuade completely, over-persuade,* S.*OT*1024, *Tr.*1141, E.*HF*469, *PHal.*7.6 (iii B. C.), etc.

ἐκπειρ-άζω, *tempt,* c. acc., Lxx *De.*6.16, al., 1*Ep.Cor.*10.9. **-άομαι,** aor. ἐξεπειράθην [ᾱ], *make trial of, prove, tempt,* c. gen. pers., Hdt.3. 135: c. inf., ἐκπειρᾷ λέγειν; art thou *tempting* me to speak? S.*OT* 360 codd.: folld. by a relat., κἀξεπειράθην.. οἷον στέρεσθαι γίγνεται E.*Supp.*1089; ἐ. εἴτε.. Pl.*Ep.*362e. 2. *inquire, ask of another,* τί τινος Ar.*Eq.*1234.—Late in Act., Hld.7.19.

ἐκπεκτουμένη· κτενιζομένη, Hsch.

ἐκπέλει, impers., = ἔξεστι, *it is permitted* or *allowed,* S.*Ant.*478:—Hsch. has ἐξέπηλεν (leg. ἐξέπελεν)· ἐξεγένετο.

ἐκπελεκάω, *hew, cut away with an axe, IG*2.1054b9, Thphr.*HP*9.2. 7, *IG*11(2).144*A*64 (Delos, iv B. C.).

ἐκπελεύει· ἐξωθεῖ, Hsch.

ἐκπεμπτέος, α, ον, *that must be sent out,* Plu.2.595c. 2. ἐκπεμπτέον *one must reject,* Porph.*Abst.*2.31.

ἐκπέμπω: I. of persons, *send out* or *forth from,* c. gen. loci, ὅπως Πρίαμον... νηῶν ἐκπέμψειε Il.24.681; ὅς τίς σε.. δώματος ἐκπέμψῃσι Od.18.336, cf. S.*El.*1128; ἐ. ἐκ τῆς πόλεως Isoc.6.78:—Med., δόμου ἐκπέμψασθε θύραζε Od.20.361, cf. S.*Aj.*612 (lyr.), etc. 2. *bring out by calling, call* or *fetch out,* τινὰ ἐκτὸς πυλῶν Id.*Ant.*19:—so in Med., Id.*OT*951:—Pass., *go forth, depart,* Id.*OC*1664. 3. *send forth, dispatch,* πρέσβεις, στρατιάς, οἰκήτορας, Th.1.90, 141, 4.49; ἐ. συμπρεσβευτὰς τοὺς ἐχθρούς Arist.*Pol.*1271ᵃ24; ἐ. ἀποικίας οἷον σμήνη μελιττῶν Pl.*Plt.*293d, cf. Arist.*Pol.*1273ᵇ19:—Pass., τῶν -ομένων καὶ εἰσαγομένων ἐπιστολῶν Aen.Tact.10.6. 4. *send away,* τινὰ ἐς.. Hdt.1.160; ἐ. τινὰ ἄτιμον S.*OT*789; καθάρμαθ' ὥς τις ἐκπέμψας A.*Ch.* 98: in Prose, *divorce* a wife, ἐ. γυναῖκα Hdt.1.59, Lys.14.28, cf. D.59. 55:—also in Med., γῆς φυγάδας ἐκπέμψασθαι S.*OT*309. 5. c. dupl. acc., *conduct across,* τινὰ τὸν Ἰορδάνην Lxx 2*Ki.*19.31. II. of things, *send out, send abroad,* κειμήλια πολλὰ καὶ ἐσθλά.. ἵνα περ τάδε τοι σόα μίμνῃ Il.24.381; δῶρά τινι Hdt.1.136; σῖτόν τινι Th.4.16 (nisi leg. ἐσ-). 2. *export,* ἐ. ὧν ἐπλεόναζον Arist.*Pol.*1257ᵃ32:—Med., τὰ πλεονάζοντα τῶν γιγνομένων ἐκπέμψασθαι *export* their surplus products, ib.1327ᵃ27. 3. *send forth, give out,* σέλας A.*Ag.*281; πνεῦμα, [ὑγρόν], Arist.*PA*664ᵃ18, *HA*589ᵇ18; δυσοσμίαν Alciphr.3.28. 4. *utter, pronounce,* A.D.*Pron.*35.1 (Pass.).

ἔκπεμψις, εως, ἡ, *sending out* or *forth,* στρατιᾶς Th.4.85, cf. *SIG* 285.8. 2. *emission, expulsion,* πνεύματος Gal.*UP*6.2.

ἐκπεπαίνω, *make quite ripe* or *mellow,* καρπόν, χυλούς, Thphr.*HP* 5.1.1, *CP*1.16.2:—Pass., Medic., *to be concocted,* Hp.*Epid.*4.56.

ἐκπεπληγμένως, Adv., διακεῖσθαι to be in a state *of panic,* D.*Prooem.* 39.1.

ἐκπέποται, 3 sg. pf. Pass. of ἐκπίνω, Od.22.56.

ἐκπεπτᾰμένως, Adv., (ἐκπετάννυμι) *extravagantly,* X.*Cyr.*8.7.7.

ἐκπεραίνω, *finish off,* A.*Fr.*78; βίοτον E.*HF*428 (lyr.):—Pass., of oracles, *to be fulfilled,* Id.*Ion* 785, *Cyc.*696; of works, *to be accomplished,* X.*An.*5.1.13.

ἐκπεραιόω, *cross over,* Tz.*H.*3.494.

ἐκπέρᾱμα, ατος, τό, *coming out of,* δωμάτων A.*Ch.*655.

ἐκπερᾰτόομαι, *find one's limit,* Him.*Or.*1.13 (s. v. l.).

ἐκπεράω (Arc. ἐσ-, v. infr. I. 4), Ep. impf. ἐκπεράασκε *AP*9.381:—*go out over, pass beyond,* λαῖτμα μέγ' ἐκπερόωσιν Od.7.35; ἥ τ' ἐκπερᾷ μέγα λαῖτμα 9.323; χθόνα A.*Pr.*713; αὐλῶνα ib.731; χέρσον καὶ θάλασσαν Id.*Eu.*240; ἐ. βίον *go through* life, E.*IA*18 (anap.); ὀγδώκοντ' ἔτεα *AP*6.226 (Leon.); κῦμα συμφορᾶς E.*Hipp.*824. 2. abs., of an arrow, *pass through, pierce,* ὀϊστὸς ἀντικρὺ.. ὑπ' ὀστέον ἐξεπέρησεν Il. 13.652, cf. 16.346, etc.; of persons, *go forth,* X.*Cyn.*6.18; Ἀθήνας to Athens, Eub.10.5. 3. c. gen., *go* or *come out of,* μελάθρων E. *Cyc.*512 (lyr.). 4. *transgress,* ἐσπεράσαι πὰρ ἂν λέγῃ ἱεροθύτας *IG* 5(2).6 (Tegea, iv B. C.). II. *carry out* or *away,* Lxx *Nu.*11.31.

ἐκπερδῑκίζω, *escape like a partridge,* Ar.*Av.*768.

ἐκπέρθω, fut. -πέρσω, *destroy utterly, sack,* of cities, Il.1.19, al. (never in Od.), A.*Th.*427, etc.; also τὴν Διὸς τυραννίδ' ἐ. βίᾳ Id.*Pr.* 359: metaph., μὴ ἡμῖν.. τὸν Σιμωνίδην ἐκπέρσῃ Pl.*Prt.*340a. II. *take as booty from,* τὰ μὲν πολίων ἐξεπράθομεν Il.1.125.

ἐκπερι-άγω [ᾰ], *lead out round,* Plb.3.83.3; τοὺς ἀγκῶνας *tie behind the back,* Lys.ap.Iamb.*VP*17.78:—Pass., *to be passed round,* Porph. *Hist.Phil.Fr.*4. **-ειμι,** *go out and round, go all round,* X.*Cyn.*6.10, dub. in Hld.7.19; τὰ ὄρη Luc.*Rh.Pr.*5; τὴν κύκλῳ [ὁδόν] Jul.*Or.*7. 225c. **-έρχομαι,** = foreg., Plb.10.31.3, Onos.22.4, Plu.2.614c, Luc. *Asin.*18: c. acc., *traverse, include in one's survey,* τὰ φανερὰ πάντα Phld.*Sign.*19, cf. *Rh.*1.154S.; τὸν Πόντον Plu.*Caes.*58; πόλεις J.*AJ* 6.1.1. 2. *surround, envelop,* Hdn.3.3.8. II. *circumvent,* J. *AJ*5.1.14, al. **-οδεύω,** *go all round,* ib.3.6.8. II. metaph., *survey completely,* Phld.*Mort.*37, S.E.*M.*7.188. 2. *circumvent,* J. *AJ*17.2.4, Plu.2.705d. **-πλέω,** fut. -πλεύσομαι, *to sail out round,* so as to attack in flank, Plb.1.23.9; τὰς σχεδίας J.*BJ*3.10.9; *circumnavigate,* Λιβύην Arr.*An.*4.7.5: abs., ib.6.28.6; ταῖς ναυσί Plu.*Aem.* 15:—Ion. **-πλώω,** Arr.*Ind.*20.1. **-πορεύομαι,** *make a detour,* 'fetch a compass', of a boundary, Lxx *Jo.*15.3. II. *march round,* Ael.*Tact.*34.4. **-σπασμός,** ὁ, an evolution consisting of *a right-about-face* (περισπασμός) *followed by a wheel to r.* or *l.,* Plb.10.23.3, Ascl.*Tact.*10.8, etc. **-σπάω,** *execute this manœuvre,* ib.12.7, Arr. *Tact.*32.1:—Pass., Ascl.*Tact.*10.11.

ἐκπερισσεύω, *to be superfluous, Cod.Just.*10.27.2.4.

ἐκπερισσῶς, Adv. *more exceedingly, Ev.Marc.*14.31.

ἐκπεριτρέχω, *run all about,* Aristaenet.1.27: metaph., Procl.*in Prm.*p.781S.

ἐκπερονάω, *string together,* χρησμούς *Rev.Ét.Gr.*4.281 (Erythrae).

ἐκπέρῠσι, Adv. *more than a year ago,* Luc.*Sol.*7.

ἐκπέσσω, Att. **-ττω**, *cook thoroughly*: hence, 1. of animals, *digest* or *concoct* food *thoroughly*, Hp.*VM*22. 2. of plants, *ripen*, τὸν καρπόν Thphr.*HP*2.2.4:—Pass., of nourishment, *to be assimilated*, Arist.*Col.*799^{a}11. 3. of eggs, *hatch*, Id.*HA*562^{b}18 (Pass.), al. 4. *ripen, bring to a head*, of an abscess, Dsc.*Eup.*1.142.

ἐκπετάζω, = ἐκπετάννυμι, Lxx 2*Es.*9.5.

ἐκπέτᾰλος, ον, *outspread, flat*, ἀγγεῖον Mosch.ap.Ath.11.485e (Comp.), cf. Sch.Ar.*Ach.*1109.

ἐκπετ-άννῡμι, fut. -πετάσω, *spread out*, of a sail, E.*IT*1135 (lyr.); πώγωνα Luc.*Tim.*54; χεῖρας Lxx *Is.*65.2; of wings, *AP*5.178.10 (Mel.); τὰ ὦτα ἐξεπετάννυτο ὥσπερ σκιάδειον Ar.*Eq.*1348; of a net, τὸ δὲ δίκτυον ἐκπεπέταστα Orac.ap.Hdt.1.62; στέφος ἐξεπέτασσε *scattered* it *to the winds*, Bion 1.88. 2. metaph., ἐπὶ κῶμον ἐκπετασθείς *wholly given up to* the revel, E.*Cyc.*497 (lyr.): pf.part. Pass. ἐκπεπταμένος *wide open*, κοῖλα καὶ ἐ. Hp.*VM*22; of *gaping* wounds, Id.*Off.* 11; ἐ. τοῖς βλεφάροις Ael.*NA*2.12. **-ᾰσις**, εως, ἡ, *spreading out*, Plu.2.564c. **-ασμα**, ατος, τό, *that which is spread out* or *unfolded*: pl., title of a work by Democritus, D.L.9.47. II. *planisphere*, Ptol.*Geog.*7.7 tit.

ἐκπετήσιμος, ον, *ready to fly out of the nest, just fledged*, Ar.*Av.* 1355, Ael.*NA*2.43, Procop.*Vand.*1.4: metaph., of a *marriageable girl*, πρὸς ἄνδρας ἐ. Ar.*Fr.*582.

ἐκπέτομαι (**-πέταμαι** Arist.*HA*554^{b}1), fut. -πτήσομαι Ar.*V.*208: aor. ἐξεπτόμην, part. -πτόμενος Id.*Av.*788; also ἐξεπτάμην E.*El.*944, Pl.*Ti.*81e, ἐκπτάμενος Ἀθηνᾶ 20.249 (Chios): also in act. form ἐξέπτην Hes.*Op.*98, Batr.211, Ant.Lib.1.5, Palaeph.12: for aor. ἐξεπετάσθην, v. πέτομαι:—*fly out* or *away*, ll.cc.: metaph., ἔπαινοι Ἔρωσι μικροῖς ἐοικότες ἐκπετόμενοι Luc.*Rh.Pr.*6.

ἐκπετρίδδειν· παχύνειν ἱμάτιον (Lacon.), Hsch.

ἐκπεύθομαι, = ἐκπυνθάνομαι, A.*Pers.*955 (lyr.).

ἐκπεφῡυῖα, pf. part. of ἐκφύω.

ἔκπεψις, εως, ἡ, *cooking, baking*, *BGU*1.17 (iii A.D.), etc.

ἐκπήγνῡμι (-ύω Plu.2.978b), *make stiff* or *torpid*, l.c.; esp. of frost, *congeal, freeze*, Thphr.*CP*5.14.2:—Pass., *become stiff, congeal*, Str. 7.5.11; *to be frozen, frost-bitten*, Thphr.*HP*5.14.3.

ἐκπηδ-άω, fut. -πηδήσομαι Luc.*Zeux.*8, -ήσω App.*Hisp.*20: pf. -πεπήδηκα Men.*Pk.*277:—*leap out*, ἐς τὴν θάλασσαν Hdt.8.118 (v.l. ἐκπηδέειν, cf. 1.24); ἐπί τινα Lys.3.12. 2. *make a sally*, X.*An.* 7.4.16, App. l.c.; ἐκ τῆς ἐνέδρας *Hell.Oxy.*16.2; *escape*, ἐκ τῆς πόλεως Men.*Per.Fr.*3, cf. Wilcken *Chr.*1 ii 13 (iii B.C.), Plb.1.43.1: metaph., ἐ. ἐκ τῶν τεχνῶν εἰς τὴν φιλοσοφίαν Pl.*R.*495d. 3. *leap up, start*, εὕδουσαν ἐ. S.*Tr.*175; τοῦ ὕπνου Philostr.*VA*2.36; *throb*, of the heart, Aristaenet.2.5; λόγος ἐ. τοῦ στόματος ib.10. II. *start out of place*, σπόνδυλος ἐ. Hp.*Art.*46. **-ημα**, ατος, τό, *leap out*, ὕψος κρεῖσσον ἐκπηδήματος a height too great *for over-leap*, A.*Ag.*1376. **-ησις**, εως, ἡ, *leaping forth*, ἐν ὕψει Pl.*Lg.*815a (pl.). **-ητικός**, ή, όν, *bounding*, of the pulse, Gal.8.487.

ἐκπηκτικός, ή, όν, *freezing*, ἀήρ Thphr.*CP*5.14.7.

ἐκπηνίζομαι, fut. -ιοῦμαι, *spin a long thread*, [οἱ ἀράχναι] φερόμενοι ὑπὸ τοῦ πνεύματος πολὺ ἐ. Arist.*Pr.*947^{b}2: metaph., of an advocate, αὐτοῦ ἐκπηνιεῖται ταῦτα *will wind* these things *out of* him, Ar.*Ra.* 578.

ἔκπηξις, εως, ἡ, *stiffening, freezing*, Thphr.*CP*5.14.1 (pl.), al.

ἐκπῐ-άζω, = ἐκπιέζω, Lxx *Jd.*6.38, Str.16.2.43, *PHolm.*18.18. **-ασμα**, ατος, τό, = ἐκπίεσμα, Hsch. s. v. ἐπίτερα: **-ασμός**, ὁ, v. ἐκπιεσμός.

ἐκπῑδύομαι [ῡ], *gush forth*, A.*Pers.*815 (Schütz for ἐκπαιδεύεται).

ἐκπῐ-έζω, *squeeze out*, σπόγγους ἐξ ὕδατος ἐκπεπιεσμένος Hp.*Acut.* 21, cf. Dsc.1.50; *thrust* or *force out*, τοὺς προσβάλλοντας Plb.18.32. 3:—Pass., *to be squeezed out*, Arist.*Mu.*397^{a}23, Dsc.1.52; ἕλκος ἐκπεπιεσμένον a sore *that protrudes out of the skin*, dub. in Hp.*Fract.*25 (cf. ἐκπλίσσομαι). II. *oppress*, Lxx 1*Ki.*12.3: a form ἐκπιεζέω ib.*Ez.*22.29:—Pass., Plb.3.74.2. **-εσμα**, ατος, τό, *that which is squeezed out, juice*, Dsc.1.52, Archig.ap.Gal.12.551. II. false form for ἐμπίεσμα (q. v.), Gal.19.432, 14.782. **-εσμός**, ὁ, *squeezing out*, Hp.*Nat.Puer.*21, Arist.*Mu.*394^{a}28, Epicur.*Ep.*2p.45 U. (ἐκπιασμόν codd.). II. *exophthalmos*, Aët.7.2. **-εστήριον** (sc. ὄργανον), τό, *press*, Demioprat.ap.Poll.10.135. **-εστός**, ή, όν, *squeezed out*: ἐ. ξύλα logs *cleft by the wedge and mallet*, Arist.*Pr.* 915^{a}9.

ἐκπικρ-άζομαι, = ἐκπικρόομαι II, Hp.*Mul.*1.26. **-αίνομαι**, *to be embittered*, Nic.Dam.p.34 D.; πρὸς τὴν ἀπειλήν D.H.19.5; πρός τινα J.*AJ*5.7.1; ἐπί τινι D.H.4.38, Ath.8.351b, etc. 2. = sq. II, Hp. *Mul.*2.133. **-όομαι**, *become very bitter*, Arist.*Pr.*880^{a}29, Thphr. *CP*4.2.1. II. *have a bitter taste in the mouth*, Hp.*Aph.*4.17. **-ος**, ον, *very bitter*, Arist.*Pr.*880^{a}24. **-ωσις**, εως, ἡ, *making bitter*, Gal. 12.558.

ἐκπίμπλημι, *fill up*, κρατῆρα E.*Cyc.*388; ἐκ δ' ἐπίμπλαμεν δρόσου κρατῆρας *filled* them *full of*.., Id.*Ion*1194. 2. *satiate*, ὄμματ' ἐξεπίμπλαμεν Id.*Andr.*1087; ἐκπιμπλάναι τὴν αὐτίκα φιλονικίαν Th.3. 82; τὰς ἐπιθυμίας D.C.41.27:—Pass., ὡς ἐξεπλήσθη [τὸ νόσημα] S.*Ph.* 759. II. *fulfil*, ἐξέπλησε μοῖραν τὴν ἑωυτοῦ *fulfilled* his destiny, Hdt.3.142; ἐ. τοῦ ὀνείρου τὴν φήμην Id.1.43; ἐ. τὸν νόμον *to satisfy the requirements of* the law, Id.1.199, 4.117; πέμπτου γονέος ἁμαρτάδα ἐξέπλησε *paid the full penalty of* the sin of Gyges, Id.1.91. III. *accomplish*, ἐνιαυτὸν ἐξέπλησεν S.*Tr.*253; ἀρὰς..ἔοικεν ἐκπλῆσαι θεός E.*Ph.*1426; ἱερά τ' ἐξεπίμπλασαν Id.*Supp.*722; ἐ. πλῆθος κακῶν *to narrate in full*, A.*Pers.*430; μοχθήματα, etc., E.*Hel.*735, etc.; πανταχοῦ γὰρ ἄστεως ζητῶν νιν ἐξέπλησα I *have finished* seeking her in every part, Id.*Ion*1108. IV. *fill up* or *complete* a number, ἐ. τὸ ἐλλεῖπον (as v.l. for ἐκπληρώσατε) X.*Cyr.*4.5.39; τὸ ἱππικόν ib.6. 1.26, cf. Arr.*Tact.*14.2.

ἐκπίμπραμαι, *to be kindled*, Arist.*Mete.*346^{b}12.

ἐκπίνω [ῑ], fut. -πίομαι Amips.22.2, -πιοῦμαι Arist.*Rh.*1393^{b}31:—*drink out* or *off, quaff* liquor, Hom. only in Od., in Ep. aor., [ποτὸν] ἔκπιεν 9.353; ἔκπιον [οἶνον] 10.237: pf. Pass., ὅσσα τοι ἐκπέποται 22. 56, cf. Hdt.4.199; ἐκπίνουσ' ἀεὶ ψυχῆς..αἷμα S.*El.*785; δι' αἷματ' ἐκποθένθ' ὑπὸ χθονὸς A.*Ch.*66 (lyr.); ἐκπίνειν ὑστάτην πόσιν Antipho 1. 20; also of bugs, ticks, and the like, *drain*, τὴν ψυχὴν ἐ. Ar.*Nu.*712; τὸ αἷμα Arist.*Rh.*1393^{b}31:—Pass., σῶμα..ἐξεπόθη *IG*14.2002. 2. *drain* a cup *dry*, πλῆρες ἐ. κέρας S.*Fr.*483; μὴ 'κπιεῖν ἀλλ' ἢ μίαν (sc. κύλικα) Pherecr.143.9; ὅλην μύσας ἔκπινε Antiph.3, etc.; also ὡς ἔχιδν' ὑφειμένη λήθουσά μ' ἐξέπινες S.*Ant.*532. 3. metaph., ἐ. ὄλβον E.*Hipp.*[626]; τὰ χρήματα Pl.Com.9; ἀγρόν Alciphr.*Fr.* 6.2. 4. Pass., *to be absorbed*, Diog.Apoll.6.

ἐκπιπίζω or **-πινίζω**, *suck out*, *Gloss.* (perh. ff. ll. for -πιτύζω).

ἐκπιπράσκω, *sell off*, pf. Pass. ἐκπέπρᾱται D.9.39, cf. Poll.7.9.

ἐκπίπτω, fut. -πεσοῦμαι: aor. ἐξέπεσον: pf. ἐκπέπτωκα:—*fall out of*, δίφρου Il.5.585; ἵππων 11.179; ἀντύγων ἄπο E.*Ph.*1193, etc.: c. dat. pers., τόξον δέ οἱ ἔκπεσε χειρός Il.15.465; θαλερὸν δέ οἱ ἔκπεσε δάκρυ *fell from* his eyes, 2.266: abs., *fall out*, 23.467; *fall down*, of trees, Thphr.*HP*9.2.7; οἱ λεγόμενοι ἀστέρες ἐκπίπτειν *meteors*, Epicur. *Ep.*2 p.54 U.—After Hom., in various relations, freq. as Pass. of ἐκβάλλω: 1. of seafaring men, *to be cast ashore*, ἐκ δ' ἔπεσον θυμηγερέων Od.7.283; ἐ. τῇσι νηυσὶ ἐς Ἰηπυγίην Hdt.3.138; πρὸς τὰς πέτρας Id.8.13; πρὸς πέτραις E.*Hel.*1211; ναυαγὸν ἐ. ib.539; ἐ. πρὸς τὴν χώραν Pl.*Lg.*866d; of things, *suffer shipwreck*, X.*An.*7.5.13; of fish, *to be cast up*, Arist.*HA*601^{b}32. 2. *fall from* a thing, i. e. *be deprived of* it, ἐκ πολλῶν καὶ εὐδαιμόνων ἐς πτωχηΐην Hdt.3.14, cf. Lys.*Fr.*1.1; τυραννίδος, ἀρχῆς, A.*Pr.*756,757; [ἀπὸ] τῶν ἐλπίδων Th.8.81; ἐκ τῆς δόξης Isoc.5.64; τῶν ὑπαρχόντων Phld.*Ir.*p.51 W. 3. *to be driven out*, [ἐκ τῆς ἀκροπόλιος] Hdt.5.72; *to be banished*, ἐ. ἐκ τῆς πατρίδος Id. 1.150, cf. 6.121; ἐ. χθονὸς S.*OC*766, cf. *Aj.*1177; ἐ. πολέμῳ ἢ στάσει Th.1.2; γυμνὸς θύραζ' ἐξέπεσον Ar.*Pl.*244; ὑπό τινος by a person, ἐκ Πελοποννήσου ὑπὸ Μήδων Hdt.8.141; ὑπὸ τοῦ πλήθους Th.4.66, cf. *Inscr.Prien.*37.71; πρός τινος A.*Pr.*948, S.*Ant.*679:—in Th.7.50 the prep. ἐς is corrupt. 4. of limbs, *to be dislocated*, Hp.*Art.*8, etc.; of flesh, *mortify and separate itself*, Id.*Fract.*27; so ἐ. ὀδόντες, πτερά, Arist.*GA*745^{b}6, *HA*519^{a}26, etc.; of atoms, ἐκπεσοῦσαι κατέψυξαν Epicur.*Fr.*60. 5. *go forth, sally out*, Hdt.9.74; ἐκ τοῦ σταυρώματος X.*HG*4.4.11: abs., Id.*An.*5.2.17; of rays, *issue forth*, Alex. Aphr. *de An.*127.31. 6. *come out*, of votes, X.*Smp.*5.10; *turn out, happen*, Vett.Val.70.27, al. 7. *escape*, Th.6.95. 8. of oracles, *issue*, χρησμὸς ἐκπίπτει Luc.*Alex.*43, etc.; ἐκπεσεῖν φωνὴν ἐξ ἄλσους Plu.*Publ.*9; *to be published, become known*, εἰς ἀνθρώπους ἀπαιδεύτους Pl.*Ep.*314a; φήμη ἐ. ἐς τοὺς Ἕλληνας Plu.*Cleom.*5: abs., ἀπόκρισις ἐ. Plb.30.32.10. 9. *depart*, ἐκ τῆς ὁδοῦ X.*An.*5.2.31; ἐκ τοῦ ἐπιτηδεύματος Pl.*R.*495a. b. *digress*, Isoc.12.88; ἐ. ἐκ τοῦ λόγου Aeschin. 2.34; but ἐ. τῆς διανοίας *miss* the sense, Olymp.*in Mete.*7.26; *fall outside of* a class, Alex.Aphr. *de An.*169.17. 10. of things, *escape* one *unawares*, φασὶν ἐκπεσεῖν αὐτούς Arist.*EN*1111^{a}9, cf. Plu.*Per.*8; ἐ. τὴν αἴσθησιν Alex.Aphr. *in Sens.*147.18; of reason, *fail, be lacking*, Arist.*MM*1202^{a}3. 11. *degenerate*, εἰς ἀλλότριον ἦθος Pl.*R.*497b; εἰς τὴν Φρυγιστὶ ἁρμονίαν *slip* into.., Arist.*Pol.*1342^{b}11: abs., *come to naught*, *Ep.Rom.*9.6; *to be dilapidated*, *IG*2^2.204.74. 12. of actors or dramatic pieces, *to be hissed off the stage*, D.18.265, Arist.*Po.*1456^a 18, 1459^{b}31: so of orators, Pl.*Grg.*517a, cf. *Phlb.*13d. 13. ἐ. ἑαυτοῦ *lose* one's self-control, Philostr.*VA*3.36; ἐ. σκοποῦ *miss* the mark, ib.8.7. 14. of things, *arise from*, ἔκ τινος A.D.*Adv.*136.3. 15. of money, *cease to be current*, *IG*7.303.14 (Oropus, iii B.C.). 16. *run to excess*, δι' ἀοριστίαν Epicur.*Sent.Vat.*63; [ὁ πλοῦτος] εἰς ἄπειρον ἐ. Id.*Sent.*15, cf. Luc.*JConf.*7. b. Geom., as Pass. of ἐκβάλλω, *to be produced*, Archim.*Spir.*14. 17. *die*, χθὼν ἐκπιπτόντων *Not. Scav.*1923.35 (unless, = *rubbish* heap).

ἐκπίτνω, = ἐκπίπτω, θρόνων A.*Pr.*912.

ἐκπῑτ-ύζω, *eject* water under pressure, Hero *Spir.*1.28 (Pass.). **-υσμός**, ὁ, *jet* of water, ibid.

ἐκπλᾰγής, ές, (ἐκπλήσσω) *panic-stricken*, Plb.1.76.7, al.; ἐπί τινι Id.2.3.3; τῷ πράγματι Luc.*DMar.*15.2.

ἐκπλᾰνάω, *delude, cause to go astray*, Hsch. s. v. ἐξηπάτησεν.

ἐκπλάσσω, *model exactly*, Chaerem.1.6 (Pass.). 2. *make into a plaster*, *Hippiatr.*10.

ἔκπλαστο· ἐξεπήδησεν, Hsch. (leg. ἔκπαλτο).

ἐκπλᾰτύνω, *flatten out*, Sor.1.102; ἀγγεῖον -υσμένον *broad at the top*, Sch.Il.23.243.

ἐκπλεθρίζω, *run round and round, in a course which narrows every time*, Gal.6.133.

ἔκπλεθρος, ον, *six plethra long*, Phryn.387; in ἕ. ἀγών, = στάδιον, E.*El.*883, and κῶλον ἕ. δρόμου Id.*Med.*1181 (where Sch. expl. μέγα καὶ ὑπερβαίνον πλέθρου μέτρον) ἕ. is the better reading, *narrowing*.

ἐκπλέκω, *unfold*, διάνοιαν Alex.*Fig.*2.1.

ἐκπλεονάζω, strengthd. for πλεονάζω, Arist.*Pr.*882^{a}25.

ἔκπλεος, ον, neut. pl. ἔκπλεα D.C.38.20: poet. **ἔκπλειος**, α, ον: Att. **ἔκπλεως**, ων:—*quite full* of a thing, c. gen., δαιτός, βορᾶς, E.*Cyc.*247, 416. 2. *complete*, εὖρος τρίγυον *Tab.Heracl.*2.31; of a number of soldiers, ἱππεῖς ἔκπλεῳ..εἰς τοὺς μυρίους X.*Cyr.*6.2.7; *abundant, copious*, ἐπιτήδεια ib.1.6.7, cf. D.C. l.c.

ἔκπλευρος, ον, *six-sided*, Phryn.387.

ἔκπλευσις, εως, ἡ, = ἔκπλους, τῶν στόλων Procl.*Par.Ptol.*117 (pl.).

ἐκπλέω, fut. -πλεύσομαι: pf. -πέπλευκα *IG*2.793^{a}7: Ion. **ἐκπλώω**, aor. -έπλωσα: pf. πέπλωκα Lyc.1084:—*sail out* or *away*, τοῦ Πόντου Hdt.6.5; ἔξω τοῦ Ἑλλησπόντου Id.5.103; τῆσδ' ἐ. χθονὸς S.*Ph.*1375; ἐκ τῆσδε γῆς ib.577; ἐ. ἐς ἀποικίην Hdt.6.22; κατ' Εὐρώπης ζήτησιν, κατὰ ληΐην, Id.2.44,152; ἐπί τινα against.., Th.1.37; of fish, *swim out*, ἀγεληδὸν ἐ. ἐς θάλασσαν Hdt.2.93. 2. metaph., ἐκπλεῖν τῶν φρενῶν *go out of* one's mind, *lose* one's senses, Id.3.155, Ael.*Fr.*240. II. rarely c. acc. loci, *sail out past*, τὸ ἔθνος τῶν Ἰχθυοφάγων Arr.*Ind.*29.7, cf. Lyc.1084, A.R.2.645. 2. c. acc. cogn., ἐ. τὸν ὕστερον ἔκπλουν D.49.6. III. trans., ἐ. ἐς τὴν εὐρυχωρίαν τὰς τῶν πολεμίων ναῦς *outsail* them into the open sea, Th.8.102 (s.v.l.).

ἔκπλεως, v. ἔκπλεος.

ἐκπλήγδην, Adv. *terribly*, Suid.

ἐκπλήγνυμι, = ἐκπλήσσω, Th.4.125 (Pass.).

ἐκπληκτ-ικός, ή, όν, *striking with consternation, astounding*, θόρυβος Th.8.92; ἐ. τοῖς ἐχθροῖς X.*Eq.Mag.*8.18 (Comp.); ἐκπληκτικώτερον *more surprising* or *startling*, Arist.*Po.*1460^{b}25: Sup., Plb.3.4.5, Onos. 22.4. II. Adv. -κῶς *terribly*, D.S.14.25: Sup. -ώτατα Ael.*NA* 11.32. 2. *with enthusiasm*, ἀποδέξασθαί τινα Plb.10.5.2. -**ος**, ον, *terrifying*, Luc.*Herm.*18. II. *amazed, terror-stricken*, Orph. *H.*39.10, Man.4.81, Poll.5.72. III. Adv. -τως *rashly*, Ael.*NA*3. 22. IV. *astounding*, *Riv.Fil.*53.208 (Crete).

ἐκπλημμῡρέω, *gush out and overflow*, τοῦ γενείου Philostr.Jun.*Im.* 4:—also -πλημμύρω, ib.8.

ἐκπληξ-ία, ἡ, = sq., Callistr.*Stat.*14. -**ις**, εως, ἡ, *consternation*, ἐκπλήξιες τῆς γνώμης Hp.*Aër.*16, cf. Pl.*Phlb.*47a, etc.; ἔ. κακῶν *terror caused by* misfortunes, A.*Pers.*606; ἔ. παρέχειν Antipho 5.6, Th.4.55; ἐς ἔ. καθιστάναι, ἀγαγεῖν, Id.6.36, Philostr.Jun.*Im.*4; ἔ. ἐνέπεσεν ἀνθρώποις Th.4.34. II. *mental disturbance, passion*, Plb.3.81.6.

ἐκπληρ-όω, *fill up*, ἑκατὸν ἐχίδναις ἀσπίδ' ἐ. E.*Ph.*1135. 2. *make up* to a certain number, ἐκπληροῦσι τὰς ἴσας μυριάδας ἐκείνοισι Hdt.7.186; ἐξεπληροῦτο τὸ ναυτικὸν ἐς τὰς..τριηκοσίας ναῦς Id.8.82; δέκατον ἐκπληρῶν ὄχον *making up the number of* ten chariots, S.*El.* 708; ἐ. τοὺς ἱππέας εἰς δισχιλίους X.*Cyr.*5.3.24. 3. *man completely*, τριήρεις Arist.*Pol.*1327^{b}14. 4. *fulfil*, ἡ χάρις ἐκπεπλήρωται Hdt. 8.144; μοῖραν Hp.*Vict.*1.5; εὐαγγελίαν *Act.Ap.*13.33. 5. *pay off*, τὸ χρέος Pl.*Lg.*958b. II. ἐ. λιμένα πλάτῃ *make one's way over*, E. *Or.*54. -**ωμα**, ατος, τό, *filling up*, ἐ. ποιεῖν τοῦ κοίλου Hp.*Art.*9; *pad* or *cushion to fill up*, ἐνθεὶς μασχάλῃ ἐ. Id.*Mochl.*5 (pl.). -**ωσις**, εως, ἡ, *filling up*, Apollon.Cit.1; κλεψύδρας Marcellin.*Puls.*265; *completion*, Aesar.ap.Stob.1.49.27, Dsc.1.58; ἐνιαυτοῦ Str.17.1.46; *filling up the measure*, ἁμαρτιῶν Lxx 2*Ma.*6.14; *satisfaction*, τῶν ἐπιθυμιῶν D.H.6.86, cf. Ph.1.567. II. *fulfilment* of a cosmic cycle, *Cat. Cod.Astr.*1.163. -**ωτής**, οῦ, ὁ, *one who fulfils*, τοῦ τεταγμένου D.C.38.24. -**ωτικός**, ή, όν, *filling up, completing*, τοῦ πάθους Ph. 1.685.

ἐκπλήσσω, Att. -ττω, *strike out of, drive away from, expel*, ἐκ δ' ἔπληξέ μου τὴν αἰδῶ A.*Pr.*134; ὃς (sc. κεραυνὸς) αὐτὸν ἐξέπληξε τῶν.. κομπασμάτων ib.362, cf. E.*Ion*635: abs., *drive away*, ἡ τέρψις τὸ λυπηρὸν ἐκπλήσσει Th.2.38; φόβος μνήμην ἐ. ib.87. II. *drive out of one's senses by a sudden shock, amaze, astound*, Od.18.231 (tm.); κάλλει καὶ ὥρᾳ διενεγκόντες ἐ. τινάς Aeschin.1.134; ὁ φόβος ἐκπλήσσων.. Antipho 2.1.7; κακοὶ εὐτυχοῦντες ἐκπλήσσουσί με *Trag.Adesp.* 465; ὅ μ' ἐκπλήσσει λόγου *frightens* me in speaking, E.*Or.*549:— in this sense most freq. in aor. 2 Pass., Ep. ἐξεπλήγην (v. infr.), Att. ἐξεπλάγην [ᾰ] (also aor. 1 ἐξεπλήχθην Id.*Tr.*183: pf. part. ἐκπεπληγμένος A.*Pers.*290, S.*Tr.*386, etc.); *to be panic-struck, amazed*, esp. by fear, ἐκ γὰρ πλήγη φρένας Il.16.403, cf. 13.394; ἡνίοχοι ἔκπληγεν 18.225: c. part., ἐκπεπληγμένον κεῖνον βλέποντες S.*OT* 922, cf. *Ant.*433, etc.; ἐκπλαγῆναί τινι *to be astonished at* a thing, Hdt.1.116, etc.; ὑπό τινος Id.3.64; διά τι Th.7.21; ἐπί τινι X.*Cyr.* 1.4.27; πρός τι Plu.*Thes.*19, etc.: also c. acc., ἐκπλαγῆναί τινα *to be struck with panic fear of*.., S.*Ph.*226, *El.*1045; ἡμᾶς δ' ἂν..μάλιστα ἐκπεπληγμένοι εἶεν Th.6.11, cf. 3.82. 2. generally, of any sudden, overpowering passion, *to be struck with desire*, Ar.*Pl.*673; *with love*, E.*Hipp.*38, *Med.*8; χαρᾷ, ἡδονῇ, A.*Ch.*233, S.*Tr.*629; *with admiration*, Hdt.3.148, etc.: c. acc. rei, ἐκπλαγέντα τὰ προκείμενα ἀγαθά Id. 9.82. 3. εἰς ὁμολογίαν ἐκπλήττειν *frighten* one into.., f.l. in Plb. 23.4.11.

ἐκπλήωρον· ἐκπεπληρωκυῖαν ἑαυτήν, Hsch.

ἐκπλινθεύω, *take out bricks* or *tiles*, Is.*Fr.*19 S. II. *turn into bricks*, γῆν πᾶσαν Jul.*Gal.*135b.

ἐκπλίσσομαι, *gape*, of a wound, Hp.*Fract.*25; of the womb, Id. *Prorrh.*2.24.

ἐκπλοκή, ἡ, *unravelling*: metaph., *escape*, Artem.4.57 (pl.); τινός Vett.Val.183.32.

ἔκπλοος, contr. -**πλους**, ὁ, *sailing out, leaving port*, κρυφαῖον ἔ. καθίστατο A.*Pers.*385; ποιεῖσθαι ἔ., = ἐκπλεῖν, Th.1.65, etc.; βιάζεσθαι τὸν ἔ. to force one's *way out*, Id.7.70; εἴσπλους καὶ ἔ. the right of using a port, *IG*12(7).8.12 (Amorgos), *GDI*5687.8 (Chios). II. *entrance of a harbour*, A.*Pers.*367, X.*HG*1.6.18.

ἐκ-πλύνω [ῡ], fut. -πλυνῶ *IG*7.3073.87 (Lebad.):—*wash out*, esp. *wash out colours from* cloths, ἵνα..μὴ αὐτῶν ἐκπλύναι τὴν βαφὴν Pl.*R.* 430a; ἐκπλύναντας τὴν οἰσπώτην *having washed out* the grease and dirt, Ar.*Lys.*575:—Pass., τὰ δὲ ζῷα οὐκ ἐκπλύνεσθαι the pattern *is* not *washed out*, Hdt.1.203. II. *wash out*, i.e. *wash thoroughly*, ὄναιο μέντἄν εἴ τις ἐκπλύνειέ σε Ar.*Pl.*1062; τὸν σαπέρδην Id.*Fr.*686; ἔντερα *SIG*1025.35 (Cos); τὰ γράμματα *IG*1.c.:—Med., Hdt.4.73. III. Medic., in Pass., *to be evacuated*, Gal.16.158. -**πλῠσις**, εως, ἡ, *washing out*, Hsch. s.v. στρουθίον. -**πλῠτος**, ον, *to be washed out*, of colours, Pl.*R.*429e; χιτωνίσκον περιήγητον ἐκπλύτῳ ἁλουργεῖ *IG*2. 754.21: metaph., *washed out*, μίασμα δ' ἔ. πέλει A.*Eu.*281; ἔ. τὸ μιανθέν Pl.*Lg.*872e. II. a kind of νάρδος, Gal.14.74.

ἔκπλωτος, ον, *navigable*, ὁλκάσι καὶ κώπῃ Him.ap.Phot.*Bibl.* p.371 B.

ἐκπλώω, Ion. for ἐκπλέω. **ἐκπνείω**, Ep. for ἐκπνέω.

ἐκπνευμᾰτ-όω, *turn into vapour*, Arist.*Pr.*866^{a}3, Thphr.ap.Plu.2. 292d; *fan into wind*, prob. in Epicur.*Ep.*2 p.48 U.:—Pass., *to be so turned*, Arist.*Pr.*897^{b}1, al. II. *deflate*, metaph., οἴημα, τῦφον, Plu.2.39d. III. in Pass., *to be inflated*, Thphr.*CP*4.9.3: metaph., ὑπὸ κτήσεως Phld.*Vit.*p.27 J. -**ωσις**, εως, ἡ, *turning into wind*, Epicur.*Ep.*2 p.54 U. 2. *flatulence*, Aët.5.68.

ἔκ-πνευσις, εως, ἡ, *exhalation*, opp. ἀνάπν-, Arist.*HA*492^{b}9, al. -**πνέω**, Ep. -πνείω Q.S.1.349, impf. -είεσκον Id.13.148: fut. -πνεύσομαι or -οῦμαι:—*breathe out* or *forth*, κεραυνὸς ἐκπνέων φλόγα A.*Pr.* 361; ἐ. ἀράς τινι E.*Ph.*876; ἐ. θυμόν Id.*Ba.*620: abs., Emp.100.1, Pl.*Phd.*112b, Arist.*HA*492^{b}6. 2. βίον ἐ. *breathe one's last, expire*, A.*Ag.*1493 (lyr.), E.*Hel.*142; ἐ. ψυχήν Id.*Or.*1163; alone, ὑφ' οὗ φονέως ἄρ' ἐξέπνευσας S.*Aj.*1026; πρός τινος E.*HF*886 (anap.): abs., Id.*Hyps.Fr.*60 i 38, Parth.4.6: metaph., *lose power*, *Gp.*15.1.28; *lose lustre*, of pearls, *PHolm.*10.18. 3. *lose breath*, of a runner, Arist.*Rh.*1409^{a}32. II. abs., *cease blowing, become calm*, [ὁ δῆμος] ἴσως ἂν ἐκπνεύσειε E.*Or.*700; τὰ κατὰ τὸν πόλεμον ἐκπέπνευκε καὶ λελώφηκεν Sch.Ar.*Pax*942. 2. *blow out* or *outwards*, of a wind, ἔσωθεν ἐ. Hdt.7.36; ἐκ τοῦ κόλπου Th.2.84, cf. 6.104; *burst out*, σμικροῦ νέφους..ἐκπνεύσας μέγας χειμὼν S.*Aj.*1148; but simply, *blow*, of wind, Arist.*Mete.*365^{a}4, *Pr.*947^{a}31. -**πνοή**, ἡ, *breathing out, exhalation*, opp. ἀναπνοή, Pl.*Ti.*78e, Arist.*Sens.*436^{a}15; opp. εἰσπνοή, Id.*Resp.*471^{a}8; θανάσιμοι ἐ. E.*Hipp.*1438. 2. *death*, J.*AJ*19.8. 3. 3. *vent, blow-hole*, *Placit.*2.25.1; Τυφῶνος ἐκπνοαί, name of a marsh, Plu.*Ant.*3. II. *vapour*, Arist.*Mu.*394^{b}13 (pl.). -**πνοος**, ον, contr. -**πνους**, ουν, *breathless, lifeless*, Str.14.1.44. II. *breathing out, exhaling*, Hp.*Epid.*6.6.1; ἔ. μύρων *smelling of*.., Posidipp. ap.Ath.13.596c.

ἐκποδών, Adv., (ἐκ ποδῶν) opp. ἐμποδών, *away from the feet*, i.e. *out of the way, away*, ἐ. ἀπαλλάσσεσθαι depart and get *away*, Hdt.8.76; ἐ. σταθῆναι stand *aside*, A.*Ch.*20; ἀποστῆναι E.*Hel.*1023, etc.; ἐ. εἶναι Hdt.6.35; γενέσθαι X.*HG*6.5.38; ἐ. σαυτὸν ἔχειν, ἄγειν τινά, A.*Pr.* 346, S.*Ant.*1321 (lyr.); ἐᾶν Ar.*Ach.*305; ἄναγε σεαυτὸν ἐ. Id.*Ra.*853: abs., ἐκποδών *out of the way!* Id.*Ach.*240, *V.*1341: c. dat., ἐ. χωρεῖν τινί to get *out of* his way, E.*Hec.*52, etc.; ἐ. στῆναι ἀμφοτέροις Th.1.40; ἐκποδὼν εἶναι νέοις E.*Supp.*1113, cf. And.1.135; ἐκποδὼν τὰ ὄντα, τὰς ἐπιβουλὰς ποιεῖσθαι, X.*Cyr.*3.1.3, Isoc.4.173, etc.; ἐ. λέγειν declare *away* or *removed*, A.*Eu.*453: c. gen., ἐ. χθονός *far from* it, E.*Ph.* 978; ἐ. εἶναί or ἔχειν τινός, to be or keep *free from* a thing, X.*Cyr.*5.4. 34, E.*IT*1226; τὸ μὲν σὸν ἐ. ἔστω λόγου be thou *banished from* my words, Id.*Med.*1222.

ἔκποθεν, Adv. *from some place or other*, ἐ. ἀφράστοιο A.R.2.224, 824; ἐ. ἀπροφάτοιο Q.S.3.437: **ἔκποθε**, Id.9.420, 14.74.

ἐκποι-έω, *put out*: 1. *put out* a child, i.e. *give him to be adopted* by another, opp. εἰσποιέω, D.C.60.33:—Pass., *to be adopted*, ἂν ἐκποιηθῇ Is.7.25, cf. D.C.38.12. 2. *alienate*, Pherecr.65, *Cod. Just.*1.5.17.1, al. 3. *withdraw*, ἐμαυτὸν τοῦ δικαστηρίου Philostr. *VA*8.7. II. in Med., *produce, bring forth*, γαλᾶς, βότρυς, Ar.*Ach.* 255, *Pax*708, Epicur.*Nat.*2.5. III. *make complete, finish off*, Sophr.76, Hdt.2.125 (Pass.); οἰκίας *IG*12(5).252 (Paros, vi/v B.C.); τὰς ὁδοὺς γεφύραις ἐ. *furnish* them with.., D.C.68.15; πρὸς τὰ μεγέθη τὰ γεγραμμένα *IG*7.3073.101 (Lebad.): c. gen. materiae, Παρίου λίθου τὰ ἔμπροσθε ἐξεποίησαν they *made all* the front of Parian marble, Hdt. 5.62; ἱερὰ βασιλείοις -πεποιημένα τέλεσι Philostr.*VA*8.31. 2. *procure*, ὅπλα τινί Id.*Her.*19.4. IV. *cause*, βλαστάνειν οὐκ ἐ. τὸ τῆς ὥρας Thphr.*CP*1.14.2. 2. *permit*, τινί, c. inf., Lxx *Si.*18.4: impers., ἐκποιεῖ *it is allowable*, Hp.*Prorrh.*2.3; of the weather, *it is favourable*, Telesp.53 H.: intr., *to be sufficient*, Lxx 2*Ch.*7.7; ἐφ' ὅσους ἂν ἐκποιῇ μῆνας *SIG*976.57 (Samos, ii B.C.): impers., ἐκποιεῖ *it suffices*, Lys.*Fr.*57 S., cf. Chrysipp.*Stoic.*3.21: fut., περὶ τούτων ἐν τοῖς ἑξῆς σαφέστερον ἐκποιήσει κατανοεῖν Plb.2.24.17, cf. Ceb.8. -**ησις**, εως, ἡ, *putting forth*: *emissio seminis*, Hdt.3.109. II. *giving out a child in adoption*, Poll.6.178, D.C.37.51. III. *completion, erection*, ναοῦ Id.37.44, cf. 45.6. IV. *alienation*, *Cod.Just.*1.2.17.5, al. -**ητος** παῖς a child *given to be adopted by another*, ἐ. εἰς οἶκόν τινος Is.7.23, cf. Aeschin.3.21; cf. εἰσποίητος. 2. *alienated from*, μητρός, Is.7.25: metaph., κακίας Plu.2.562f.

ἐκποικίλλω, strengthd. for ποικίλλω, Max.Tyr.10.2 (Pass.).

ἐκποινίζομαι, fut. -ποινιοῦμαι, v.l. for ἐκπην- in Sch.Ar.*Ra.*586.

ἐκποκίζω, Att. fut. -ιῶ, *pull out wool* or *hair*, Ar.*Th.*567.

ἐκπολεμ-έω, *provoke to war*, ἵν' ἐκπολεμήσειε τοὺς Ἀθηναίους πρὸς τοὺς Λακεδαιμονίους X.*HG*5.4.20 (codd. and Harp.), cf. Th.6.91:—Pass., ἐκπεπολεμῆσθαι πρὸς τὸν ἑαυτοῦ οἶκον Philostr.*VA*5.35. II. *go to war with*, Lxx *De.*20.10, al. -**ιστής**, οῦ, ὁ, *warrior*, Hsch. s.v. εἴεω. -**όω**, *make hostile, involve in war*, Hdt.4.120, *Hell.Oxy.* 2.2, 13.1, D.1.7, 3.7, Plb.15.6.6; τινὰς πρὸς ἀλλήλους Th.6.77:—Pass., fut. Med. -ώσομαι (J.*BJ*7.10.2), *become an enemy to, be set at feud with*, τινί Hdt.3.66, 5.73: abs., Th.8.57. -**ωσις**, εως, ἡ, *making hostile*, Plu.*Aem.*13.

ἐκπολίζω, *make into a city*, in Pass., πεδίων νομοὺς ἐκπεπολισμένους Aristid.*Or.*26(14).6.

ἐκπολιορκ-έω, *force a besieged town to surrender, force to capitulate*, Th.1.94,134, X.*HG*2.4.3, etc.: metaph. of argument, ἐ. τινὰ λόγῳ Chio *Ep.*10:—Pass., *to be forced to surrender*, Th.1.117; ἐκ Βυζαντίου ἐκπολιορκηθεὶς ib.131, cf. *Inscr.Prien.*37.112; ὑπὸ τῶν τυράννων Arist.*Ath.*19.3: metaph., ἐκπολιορκηθέντος τοῦ σώματος ὑπὸ μακρᾶς νόσου Diog.Oen.39. **–ησις**, εως, ἡ, *reduction by siege*, Gloss.

ἐκπολῑτεύω, *change the constitution of a state, cause it to degenerate*, Lxx 4*Ma.*4.19.

ἔκπομα, = ἔκπωμα, Hsch.

ἐκπομπεύω, *conduct*, τὴν ἐπικηδείαν πομπήν Lib.*Decl.*40.15.

ἐκπομπή, ἡ, *sending out* or *forth*, λῃστῶν Th.3.51 (pl.); ἀποικιῶν Pl.*Lg.*740e. II. *divorce*, Antipho Soph.49 (pl.).

ἐκπονέω, *work out, finish off*, Sapph.98, Pi.*P.*4.236; ἄκη A.*Supp.* 367; τὸ εὐπρεπὲς τοῦ λόγου Th.3.38; δολιχὰν τρίβον *AP*7.212 (Mnasalc.), Ar.*Av.*379; also, *form by instruction*, as Chiron did Achilles, E.*IA* 209 (lyr.); ἐ. τινὰ πέπλοισιν *to deck* him *out*, Id.*Hipp.*632:—Pass., *to be wrought out, brought to perfection*, τὸ ναυτικὸν μεγάλαις δαπάναις ἐκπονηθὲν Th.6.31; τὰ σῖτα X.*Cyr.*8.2.5; ὅπλα ἐκπεπόνηται εἰς κόσμον Id.*HG*4.2.7, cf. Pl.*R.*529e. 2. *practise*, τὰ πρὸς τὸν πόλεμον X.*Cyr.*5.1.30; ὀρχήσεις Plb.4.20.12:—Med., Pl.*Lg.*834e:—Pass., of persons, ἐκπεπονῆσθαι τὰ σώματα *to be in good training* or *practice*, X. *Cyr.*3.3.57; ἐκπεπονημένοι, ὡς ἂν κράτιστοι εἶεν Id.*HG*6.4.28. 3. *work through, execute*, τἀντεταλμένα E.*Ph.*1648; ἐ. ἀέθλους *finish* hard tasks, Theoc.*Ep.*22.5; ἃ ἂν μάθωσιν, ἱκανώτεροι τῷ σώματι ἐ. X.*Cyr.* 4.3.11:—Med., E.*Med.*241:—Pass., ταῦτα δυοῖν ἐν ἐτοῖν.. μόλις ἐξεπονήθη Cratin.237. 4. *labour for, provide by labour, earn*, σωτηρίαν E.*Fr.*729; βίον Id.*Hipp.*467: c. acc. et inf., τοὺς θεοὺς ἐ. φράζειν *prevail on* the gods to tell, Id.*Ion* 375. 5. abs., *work hard*, σοὶ παρ' ἀσπίδ' ἐκπονῶν ὅπως.. Id.*Or.*653, cf. *Supp.*319. 6. *work out by searching*, Id.*Ion* 1355, *Andr.*1052; *search out*, Id.*Hel.*1514. 7. of food, *to digest*, X.*Mem.*1.2.4, *Cyr.*1.2.16: abs., Id.*Oec.*11.12. 8. *labour to shield off from*, τέκνων θάνατον E.*HF*581. 9. *work at, till*, γῆν *SIG*22.9; νειοὶ δ' ἐκπονέοιντο ποτὶ σπόρον Theoc.16.94, cf. Str.5. 4.5; αἱ [τὴν ὕλην] ἐκπονοῦσαι τέχναι Plu.*Per.*12. 10. Pass., *to be worn out, brought low*, ὑπό τινος Str.5.4.11; φροντίσιν ἐκπονούμενος Plu.*Oth.*9; τὰς ὄψεις ἐ. Id.2.854b.

ἐκπορ-ευτέον, *one must march out*, Aen.Tact.23.6. **–εύω**, *make to go out, fetch out*, E.*Ph.*1068, *HF*723:—Med., with fut. Med. (X. *An.*5.1.8) and aor. Pass., *go out* or *forth, march out*, X. l. c., etc.; ἐπὶ λείαν Aen.Tact.24.4; εἰς στρατείαν ἐ. *to march out* to a place.., Plb. 11.9.4: c. acc. loci, ἐ. τὸ βουλευτήριον ib.8; but ἐκ τοῦ χάρακος Id.6. 58.4; ἐκ τοῦ στόματος Lxx *Pr.*3.16, al.: more generally, ὅ θ' ὑγρὸς εἰς γῆν ὄμβρος ἐκπορεύεται Critias 25.36.

ἐκπορθ-έω, *pillage*, πόλεις E.*Tr.*95; οἰκίας Lys.12.83, cf. Herod. 3.5 (tm.), Plb.2.32.4, etc.:—Pass., of a person, *to be undone*, ὑπ' ἄτης ἐκπεπόρθημαι τάλας S.*Tr.*1104; γραῦς.. κρατ' ἐκπορθηθεῖσ' E.*Tr.*142 (lyr.). II. *carry off as plunder*, τὰ ἐνόντα Th.4.57. **–ησις**, εως, ἡ, *sacking, wasting*, Str.9.1.17, Ph.2.122, Onos.42.23. **–ητικῶς**, Adv. *with a view to plundering completely*, Eust.1490.65. **–ήτωρ**, ορος, ὁ, *waster, destroyer*, E.*Supp.*1223.

ἐκπορθμεύω, *carry away by sea*:—E. has pf. Pass. in pass. sense, [Ἑλένη] ἐκπεπόρθμευται χθονὸς *Hel.*1179; but in med. sense, Μενέλαος αὐτὴν ἐκπεπόρθμευται χθονὸς ib.1517.

ἐκπορ-ίζω, *invent, contrive*, ἄδικα E.*Ba.*1042 (anap.); φόνον εἴς τινα Id.*Ion* 1114; μηχανὴν Ar.*V.*365; ἐ. ὅπως.. Id.*Lys.*421. II. *provide, furnish*, στέγη.. πάντ' ἐ. S.*Ph.*299; ἀργύριον ὑμῖν And.2.17; ὅπλα τινὶ Th.6.72; χρήματα, μισθόν, X.*Cyr.*3.1.30, *An.*5.6.19; τὸ συμφέρον ἑκάστῳ Pl.*R.*341d, etc.; *procure*, βίον Ar.*V.*1113, cf. Pl.*Men.*78e:—so in Med., *provide for oneself*, τὰ αὑτῶν Th.1.82, cf. 125; ταῖς ἡδοναῖς πλήρωσιν Pl.*Grg.*492a; γράμματα παρά τινος Plb.22.3.2 (but Med., also, *supply* to others, *BCH*48.3 (Brusa)). III. *discharge* a cargo, *OGI* 521.27,30 (Abydos, v A.D.). **–ιστέον**, *one must bring about*, Gal. 10.389.

ἐκπορνεύω, *commit fornication*, Lxx *Ge.*38.24, *Ep.Jud.*7:—Pass., in same sense, Poll.6.126. 2. metaph., of idolatry, Lxx *Ex.*34. 15. II. c. acc., *prostitute*, τὴν θυγατέρα ib.*Le.*19.29; *cause to commit fornication*, ib.2*Ch.*21.11.

ἐκπόρπ-ῐσις, εως, ἡ, (πόρπη) lit., *unfastening*, hence μετ' ἐκπορπίσεως, of a compound fracture, Sor.*Fract.*24. **–όομαι**, = ἐκφιβλόομαι, Suid.

ἐκποτάομαι, Ion. **–έομαι**, = ἐκπέτομαι, *fly out* or *forth*, of snowflakes, Διὸς ἐκποτέονται Il.19.357; of a ghost, πεδ' ἀμαύρων νεκύων ἐκπεποτᾱμένα Sapph.68.4: metaph., πᾷ τὰς φρένας ἐκπεπότασαι; Theoc.11.72, 2.19.

ἐκποτέον, *one must drink to the dregs*, τὴν τρύγα Pherecr.249.

ἔκπους, ποδος, ὁ, ἡ, = ἐξάπους, *IG*1².313.93, al.

ἐκ-πράκτης, ου, ὁ, *tax-gatherer*, Aq.*Jb.*39.7. **–πραξις**, εως, ἡ, *exacting*, *IG*1².6.30; δανείων D.S.1.79:—Dor. **ἔσπραξις** *Foed.Delph. Pell.*2 *B* 16. **–πράσσω**, Att. **–ττω**, *bring about, achieve*, τι A.*Ag.* 582, etc.; τόδ' ἐξέπραξεν ὥστε.. Id.*Pers.*723; χρέος *perform* a service, Id.*Supp.*472; ὡς.. S.*Ant.*303; δόλιον εὐνὴν ἐξέπραξ' E.*Hel.*20; τὸν καλλίνικον.. ἐξεπράξατε ἐς γόον *ye have made* the hymn of triumph *end in* wailing, Id.*Ba.*1161; in later Prose, τὸ δέον Paul.Aeg.6. 118. II. *make an end of, kill, destroy*, A.*Ag.*1275, S.*OC*1659, E. *Hec.*515. III. *exact, levy*, αἵματος δίκην Id.*HF*43; καταδίκας *SIG* 554.19 (Thermon); τόκους ib.672.39 (Delph., ii B.C.): c. dupl. acc., χρήματα ἐ. τινά Th.8.108: abs., τοὺς ταμίας ἐ. Pl.*Lg.*774e, cf. *IG*1². 79:—Pass., *to be made to pay*, χρήματα ὑπό τινος Paus.7.12.1. 2. *exact punishment for* a thing, *avenge*, S.*OT*377; μητρῷον φόνον E. *Med.*1305:—Med., τὸν Δωριέος πρὸς Ἐγεσταίων φόνον ἐκπρήξασθαι Hdt.7.158.

ἐκπρᾱΰνω, strengthd. for πραΰνω, Plu.2.74d.

ἐκπρεμνίζω, *root out*, D.43.69, Philostr.Jun.*Im.*4.

ἐκπρέπ-εια, ἡ, *excellence*, Iamb.*VP*5.23. **–ής**, ές, *distinguished out of all, pre-eminent, remarkable*, ἐν πολλοῖσι Il.2.483; μία ἐ. [νίκα] Pi.*P.*7.12; μεγέθει ἐκπρεπεστάτα A.*Pers.*184; εὐγένειαν ἐκπρεπεῖς ib. 442; εἶδος ἐκπρεπεστάτη E.*Alc.*333; ῥόδα.. τιθήνημ' ἔαρος –έστατον Chaerem.13; ἐ. φύσιν Nausicr.2.6; κότταβος.. ἐκπρεπὲς ἔργον Critias 2.1; ἐ. [ἰδέα] Pl.*Phdr.*238a; –έστερα ζῷα Arist.*Phgn.*810ᵃ8. Adv. –πῶς *splendidly*, κεκόσμηται Plb.5.59.8: poet. –έως *IG*3.121: Comp. –έστερον *more conspicuously*, D.C.44.40. II. of things, = ἔξω τοῦ πρέποντος, *extraordinary*, οὐδὲν –έστερον παθεῖν Th.3.55. Adv. –πῶς *without reasonable grounds*, Id.1.38: Sup. –έστατα τιμωρῆσαι X.*Smp.*8.31. **–όντως**, Adv. = ἐκπρεπῶς, D.C.74.1. **–ω**, *to be excellent* in a thing, εὐψυχίᾳ E.*Heracl.*597.

ἐκπρεπώσοτον, dub. in *IGRom.*4.144 (Cyzicus: so the stone, perh. an error for ἐκπρεπῶς ἐτῶν).

ἔκπρησις, εως, ἡ, *setting on fire, inflaming*, Plu.*Lys.*12.

ἐκπρησμός, gloss on πάφλασμα, Sch.Ar.*Av.*1243 (pl.).

ἐκπρήσσω, Ion. for ἐκπράσσω.

ἐκπρίασθαι, aor. 2 (v. *πρίαμαι), *buy off*, χρήμασι.. κίνδυνον ἐ. Antipho 5.63, cf. Lys.27.6; ἐ. τοὺς κατηγόρους Id.20.15. 2. *buy*, ἐ. τι παρά τινος Isoc.3.22; μεγάλων χρημάτων τὴν σωτηρίαν D.C.62.28.

ἐκ-πρίζω, = ἐκπρίω, *Gp.*9.11.7, Heliod.ap.Orib.47.14.3, etc. **–πρῖσις**, εως, ἡ, *sawing out*, Paul.Aeg.6.84. **–πρισμα**, ατος, τό, *that which is sawn out*, Arist.*GC*316ᵃ34; *section sawn out of* cylinder, Hero *Deff.*97 (pl.). **–πριστέον**, *one must saw out, excise*, Antyll. ap.Orib.44.23.20. **–πρίω**, fut. –πρίσω [ῑ] Men.*Epit.*41:—*saw off*, Th.7.25, Men. l. c.; *excise*, τὸ ὀστέον Hp.*VC*21; of bonds, Herod.5. 25.

ἐκπροβάλλω, *expel*, βρέφος ἠλιτόμηνον Max.241.

ἔκπροθεν· ἐκ παλαιοῦ, Hsch.

ἐκπροθεσμ-έω, *to be later than the appointed day*, Ulp. ad D.21. 80. **–ος**, ον, *beyond the appointed day*, τοῦ ὀφλήματος *for* the debt, Luc.*Herm.*80; ἐ. τῶν ἑπτὰ ἡμερῶν *after* seven days have expired, Id.*Sat.*2; ἐ. τοῦ ἀγῶνος *past the time of*, i.e. *too old for*, the games, Id.*Anach.*39; ἐ. φιλοτιμήματα honours *deferred till too late*, Id.*Nav.* 40; πένθος Ph.2.169.

ἐκπροθρῴσκω, *spring out* or *forth*, aor. part. –θορών Orph.*A.*346, Man.6.33; ὅτ' ἂν βρέφος ἐκπροθόρῃσι Max.226.

ἐκπροθῡμέομαι, strengthd. for προθυμέομαι, E.*Ph.*1678.

ἐκπροΐημι, *send forth*, παγὰν ἐκπροϊεῖσαι E.*Ion* 119 codd. (lyr.).

ἐκπροικίζω, *portion off*, Phalar.*Ep.*131 (Pass.).

ἐκπρο-κᾰλέομαι, *call forth to oneself*, ἐκπροκαλεσσαμένη μεγάρων Od.2.400; ἀπὸ μεγάροιο *h.Ap.*111; νόσφιν A.R.4.353. 2. *invoke*, ἄστρων σέλας Orph.*H.*7.1. **–κρίνω** [ῑ], *choose out*, πόλεος ἐκπροκριθεῖσα E.*Ph.*214 (lyr.). **–λείπω**, *forsake*, κοῖλον λόχον ἐκπρολιπόντες Od.8.515, cf. Thgn.1136; βίον *IG*14.2123. II. *spare*, Ps.-Phoc. 85. **–μολεῖν**, aor. 2 (v. βλώσκω), *go forth from*, λίμνης A.R.4. 1587: abs., Orph.*L.*706. **–πίπτω**, *fall down from*, ὑψόθεν εἰς γαῖαν ib.324. **–πτωσις**, εως, ἡ, *prolapsus*, Sor.2.85 (pl.). **–ρέω**, *flow forth from*, c. gen., Orph.*L.*203, *AP*9.669 (Marian.).

ἐκπρο-τῑμάω, *honour above all*, S.*Ant.*913. **–φαίνω**, *show forth*, aor. 2 part. –φᾰνοῦσα Orph.*H.*71.7. **–φέρω**, *bring forth*, dub. in Man.6.733. **–φεύγω**, *flee away from*, τινός Hld.8.11; *escape*, τι Orph.*L.*397; μόρον *AP*6.218 (Alc.). **–χέω**, *pour forth*, ἰαχάν *AP*7.201 (Pamph.); πλοκάμους ib.22 (Simm.); ὅσσων δάκρυον *IG*14. 2123.

ἐκπτερόομαι, *to be furnished with wings*, Hp.*Vict.*1.25 (f.l. for ἐκπυρούμενα).

ἐκπτήσσω, *scare out of*, οἴκων με ἐξέπταξας (Dor.) E.*Hec.*179 (lyr.).

ἐκπτίσσω, *pound, bray*, f.l. in Ael.*NA*17.31 (Pass.).

ἐκπτοέω, = ἐκπτήσσω, Tz.*H.*5.484:—Pass., *to be struck with admiration*, E.*Cyc.*185; τὰς ψυχὰς ἐξεπτόηντο *were greatly excited*, Hdn. 5.4.1. 2. *to be scared*, Plb.5.36.3, 14.5.7. **ἔκπτοιος**, ον, *scared*, Phryn.*PS*p.15 B.

ἔκπτυξις, εως, ἡ, *spreading, parting* of the legs in riding, Aët.3.7.

ἔκπτῠσις, εως, ἡ, *expectoration*, αἵματος Alex.Trall.5.5.

ἐκπτύσσω, *unfold, spread out*, pf. part. Pass. ἐξεπτυγμένος, prob. for ἐξεστιγμ–, Erot. s. v. ἐκπεπταμένα.

ἐκπτύω, fut. –ύσομαι [ῠ] *AP*5.196 (Mel.):—*spit out*, στόματος δ' ἐξέπτυσεν ἅλμην Od.5.322, cf. *AP* l. c.; of the sea, *cast up*, ib.6.224 (Theodorid.): metaph., ὥσπερ χαλινὸν τὸν λόγον Plu.2.328c; so, of a ligature, Antyll.ap.Orib.45.24.7 (Pass.); *spit* or *blab out*, ἀπόρρητα Ael.*NA*4.44; of an abortion, ib.12.17 (Pass.). II. *spit* in token of disgust, Ar.*V.*792. 2. *spit at, abominate*, *Ep.Gal.*4.14.

ἔκπτωμα, ατος, τό, *dislocation*, Hp.*Art.*28. II. *collapse* of a dam, *PTeb.*72.78 (ii B.C.).

ἔκπτωσις, εως, ἡ, *breaking forth, escape*, [τοῦ θερμοῦ] Arist.*Mete.* 370ᵃ5; [ὑγροῦ] Id.*Resp.*480ᵃ1; ἡ τῶν ὄψεων ἐ. *projection* of rays from the sun, Id.*Pr.*911ᵇ5; *emission*, πυρός Epicur.*Ep.*2 pp.46, 54 U. 2. *banishment*, Plb.4.1.8, D.S.13.65, *PMag.Osl.*1.222. 3. *disappointment*, Ceb.7 (pl.); *falling off*, πρὸς τὸ χεῖρον Str.10.3.9; ἐ. ψυχῆς, *error*, Arr.*Epict.*2.17.21; *abandonment* of duty, *Stoic.*3.163; *missing*, τοῦ σκοποῦ Plot.6.1.10; *falling away from*, λόγου ib.3.7; [τοῦ ἀγαθοῦ] Simp. *in Epict.*p.74 D. 4. in argument, ἐ. εἰς ἄπειρον, *regressus ad infinitum*, Gal.5.79. 5. *shipwreck*, Hero *Aut.*22.6. 6. *loss*, χρημάτων *Cod.Just.*1.3.45.9. II. *dislocation of a joint*, Hp.

Fract.1 (pl.); ἐ. τῶν ὑστέρων *expulsion* of the afterbirth, Id.Aph.5.49; *decay* of flesh, sinews, etc., as result of erysipelas, Id.Epid.3.4; τῶν ἐσχαρέων ἐ. *detachment* of the eschars, Id.Art.11 (pl.); *prolapsus uteri*, Aret.SD2.11.

ἐκπτώσσω, *to be in fear of*, ἐχθρούς Man.5.237 (s. v.l.).

ἔκπτωτος, ον, *abject*, Paul.Al.O.1; *banished*, Vett.Val.86.14, al.

ἐκπῡ-έω, *suppurate*, Hp.Epid.1.20, Prog.15, Epid.2.1.7:—Med., Id. Aph.7.38, Fract.27:—Pass., Id.Aph.6.20. **-ημα**, ατος, τό, *sore that has suppurated*, Id.VM22, Prog.15, Coac.278. **-ησις**, εως, ἡ, *suppuration*, Id.Aph.7.20, etc. **-ητικός**, ή, όν, *bringing to suppuration*, ib.5.22. **-ΐσκομαι**, Pass., = ἐκπυέω, Id.Prog.15, v.l. ib.22:—later in Act., Gal.11.728.

ἐκπυκτεύω, *box*, Poll.2.147.

ἐκπυνθάνομαι, *search out, make inquiry*, Il.10.320; ἔκ τε πυθέσθαι ἠέ.. ib.308; ἵν' ἐκπυθώμεθα πόθεν.. E.Cyc.94, etc. 2. c. acc., *hear of, learn*, S.Aj.215 (anap.); τινός *learn from*.., E.HF529; τὸ πρᾶγμ' ὅπως ἔχει Ar.Ec.752; ἐ. τινός *question* him, Id.Pl.60: c. part., ἐ. τινὰ ἀφιγμένον E.Hel.817.

ἐκπῡόω, *cause to suppurate*, δοθιῆνας Dsc.2.155:—Pass., Erot.Fr.9.

ἐκπῠράκτωσις, εως, ἡ, *burning*, Tz.H.11.596 (pl.), Suid. s. v. φλογμός.

ἐκπῠρην-ίζω, (πυρήν) *squeeze out the stone*: generally, *squeeze out*, τὰ ἐνόντα Arist.Ph.214^{a}33, Steph. in Hp.1.82 D.:—Pass., Alex.Aphr. Pr.1.119, de An.132.29. **-ισις**, εως, ἡ, *squeezing out*, Olymp. in Mete.38.25, Mich. in PN117.15. **-ισμός**, ὁ, *squeezing out*, Steph. in Hp.1.82 D.

ἐκπῠρ-ιάω, *heat*, Hp.Aph.5.63 (Pass., v.l. for ἐκπυρόομαι), Aret. CA1.6. **-ος**, ον, *burning hot*, Str.15.1.26, v.l. in Hdt.4.73; σῶμα Sor.2.54: metaph., ἵππου βλέμμα Poll.1.192: neut. pl. as Adv., τί μ' ἔκπυρα λούεις; AP5.81 (v.l. for ἔμπ-). **-όω**, *burn to ashes, consume utterly*, E.IA1070 (lyr.); ὕδραν Id.HF421 (lyr.). 2. *set on fire*, Arist.Mete.341^{a}18. II. Pass., *catch fire*, ib.342^{b}2, Onos. 19.3: a term used in the Stoic philos. to express *the tendency* of all things *to pass into fire*, Zeno Stoic.2.182, etc. 2. *to be burnt up*, λαμπάσιν κεραυνίαις E.Ba.244, cf. Corn.ND17. 3. *to be much heated*, prob. in Hp.Vict.1.25, f.l. in Aph.7.38; *to become red-hot*, Plb.12.25.2. III. *heat, warm*, βαλανεῖα Philostr.VA1.16.

ἐκπυρσεύω, *kindle, inflame*: metaph., in Pass., τὴν ἐπιθυμίαν ὑπὸ φιλοσοφίας S.E.M.11.179 (Pass.). II. *give signals by a beacon-light*, J.BJ4.10.5. III. *give out* flame, τεῖχος ἐ. φλόγα ib.7.8.5.

ἐκπύρ-ωσις [ῠ], εως, ἡ, *conflagration*, Str.12.8.18 (pl.), Luc.Vit. Auct.14. 2. Philos., *conversion into fire*, Zeno Stoic.1.32, Chrysipp.ib.2.131, etc.; ἐ. πνεύματος Epicur.Ep.2 p.45 U. 3. *calcination*, Dsc.5.87. 4. *excessive heat, pyrexia*, in disease, Ptol.Tetr. 199. 5. *eruption*, τοῦ Βεσβίου ὄρους J.AJ20.7.2. 6. metaph., of anger, Phld.Ir.p.26 W. II. *catching fire*, Arist.Mete.342^{b}2. III. a kind of *dance*, Menipp.ap.Ath.14.629f. **-ωτικός**, ή, όν, *heating*, χρίσματα Aët.12.35. **-ωτός**, όν, *heated*, βαλανεῖον AP11.411 tit.

ἔκπυστος, ον, *heard of, discovered*, πρὶν ἐκπύστους γενέσθαι Th.3.30, cf. 4.70, 8.42, J.AJ19.1.7, Plu.Cam.3, etc.; ἔ. τι ποιεῖν Hdn.2.7.7, cf. 3.12.6.

ἐκπῠτίζω, *spit out*, Alex.141.12.

ἐκπωλεῖσθαι· προγυμνάζεσθαι, Hsch.

ἔκ-πωμα, ατος, τό, *drinking-cup, beaker*, Hdt.9.41,80, S.Ph.35, Th. 6.32, IG2.649.13, etc.:—Dim. **-πωμάτιον**, τό, Diph.19, Str.16.2. 25. **-πωμᾰτοποιός**, ὁ, *cup-maker*, name of a play by Alexis, Ath.15.691d. **-πωτάομαι**, poet. for ἐκποτάομαι, aor. 1 ἐξεπωτήθη Babr.12.1.

ἔκπωτις, ιδος, ἡ, = ἄμπωτις, Cat.Cod.Astr.1.137 (pl.).

ἐκράανθεν, v. κραίνω.

ἐκραβδίζω, *flog out, drive out with a rod*, Ar.Lys.576.

ἐκρᾰγή, ἡ, gloss on ἔκρηξις, Suid. (prob. f.l. for κραυγή, as in Zonar.).

ἐκράθην [ᾰ], v. κεράννυμι.

ἐκραίνω, *scatter out of, make to fall in drops from*, κόμης μυελὸν ἐ. S.Tr.781; ἐγκέφαλον ἐξέρρανε E.Cyc.402: metaph., τὴν χεῖρα καὶ τὴν ἄλυσιν ἐκ τῆς μηχανῆς dub. in Plb.8.6.3.

ἐκραίω, *destroy utterly*, Orph.L.604 (tm.).

ἐκρᾰπίζω, *expel, reject*, Phld.Po.5.1,29.

ἐκραστωνῆσαι· εὐχερῆ ἀποφῆναι, Hsch. **ἐκρέμω**, v. κρέμαμαι.

ἐκρευμᾰτιστέον, *one must allow to discharge*, ἕλκη Ruf.ap.Aët. 11.29.

ἔκρευσις, εως, ἡ, = ἐκροή I, Sch.Lyc.1012 (pl.), Hsch. s. v. ἔκκρισις.

ἐκρέω, pf. -ερρύηκα (v. infr.): aor. Pass. ἐξερρύην in act. sense, Hp. Aph.6.27, Pl.R.452d, Dor. 3 sg. -ερρύα IG4.952.3 (Epid.):—*flow out* or *forth*, ἐκ δ' αἷμα μέλαν ῥέε Il.21.119; ἔκ τινος Pl.Phd.112a; of streams, ἐ. ἐς θάλασσαν Hdt.2.20; ἐ. ἔξω ib.149. 2. of feathers, *fall off*, ἐξερρύηκε τὰ πτερά Ar.Av.104; of hair, Arist.HA518^{a}32. b. *shed fruit*, ἐκρυήσεται ἡ ἐλαία Lxx De.28.40. 3. metaph., *melt* or *fall away, disappear*, Pl.R.452d, Thg.130e; ἐξερρύησαν οἱ τοῦ Θεμιστοκλέους λόγοι τῶν Ἑλλήνων they *faded from* their *memory*, Plu. Them.12. II. c. acc. cogn., *shed, let fall*, χάριν ἐξέρρευσας AP11. 374 (Maced.).

ἐκρηγιάριος, *attonitus*, Gloss.

ἔκρηγμα, ατος, τό, *piece torn off*, ἐκρήγματα τρυχίων Hp.Art.78. 2. *broken bed of a torrent, ravine*, Plb.12.20.4. II. *breaking forth* of a stream, ὑδάτων Thphr.CP1.5.2. 2. *sluice*, PEdgar30.16 (ἐγρ-, iii B.C.), PSI5.488 (ἐχρ-, iii B.C.); cf. ἔκχρημα. 3. *eruption, bed-sore*, Hp.Epid.7.7 (pl.).

ἐκ-ρήγνῡμι, fut. -ρήξω S.Aj.775:—*break off, snap asunder*, νευρὴν δ' ἐξέρρηξε νεόστροφον Il.15.469: c. gen., ὕδωρ ἐξέρρηξεν ὁδοῖο the water *broke off* a piece of the road, 23.421:—Pass., *break, snap asunder*, of bows, εἰ τὸν πάντα χρόνον ἐντεταμένα εἴη, ἐκραγείη ἂν [τὰ τόξα] Hdt.2.173; of clothes, *to be rent asunder*, cj. in Chaerem.14. 9. II. c. acc. cogn., *let break forth, break out with*, νεφέλη ὄμβρον ἐκρήξει Plu.Fab.12; ἐ. ὀργήν Luc.Cal.23:—Pass., *break out*, of an ulcer, Hdt.3.133; *burst*, of an abscess, Hp.Aph.4.82; ἔνθεν ἐκραγήσονται.. ποταμοὶ πυρός A.Pr.369; of a quarrel, ἐξερράγη ἐς τὸ μέσον *broke out* in public, Hdt.8.74; of persons, *break out into passionate words*, ἐκραγῆναι ἔς τινα Id.6.129, cf. Th.8.84: pf. ἐξερρωγέναι *throw aside restraint, become dissolute*, Procop.Arc.1. III. sts. intr. in Act., οὔ ποτ' ἐκρήξει μάχη S. l. c.; ἐκρήξας ἄνεμος Arist.Mete.366^{b}32: pf. part. ἐξερρωγώς *precipitous*, ὄρη J.AJ14.15.5. **-ρηξις**, εως, ἡ, *breaking out, discharge*, Hp.Steril.213; *bursting* of an abscess, Hippiatr.20, al.; ἐ. τοῦ ὕδατος Sch.Theoc.7.5. II. *bursting asunder*, τοῦ νέφους Arist.Mu.395^{a}15. **-ρήσσω**, = ἐκρήγνυμι, Theano Ep. 6.4 (Pass.); *cause* an abscess *to burst*, Paul.Aeg.7.1.

ἔκρῑζ-ος, ον, neut. as Adv., *by the roots*, Et.Gud. **-όω**, *root out*, Lxx Je.1.10, al., Aesop.179, Ev.Matt.13.29:—Pass., Lxx Wi.4.4, Babr.36.8, etc.; ἁρπασθεῖσα ὑπὸ τοῦ δαίμονος ἐξεριζώθη IG12(7).405. 24 (Amorgos); in a form of execration, ἐκριζωθήσεται πανγενεί ib.3. 1424. **-ωτής**, οῦ, ὁ, *rooter out, destroyer*, Lxx 4Ma.3.5.

ἔκρῑν, ῑνος, ὁ, ἡ, *with prominent nose*, Aret.SD2.13.

ἐκρῑνέω, (ῥίνη) *file away, consume*, τὴν καρδίαν Alciphr.3.33.

ἐκρῑνίζω, (ῥίς) *smell out*, Ps.-Luc.Philopatr.22.

ἐκρῑπ-ίζω, *fan the flame, light up*, Arist.Mete.346^{a}9: metaph., *stir up, rouse*, θυμόν Theopomp.Hist.300, Com.Adesp.504; τὸ μάχιμον Plu.Pomp.8:—Pass., τοῖς θυμοῖς Id.Pel.15, cf. Lib.Or.51.125; εἰς πόλεμον J.BJ2.16.3. II. *blow away*, Aristid.Or.26(14).99. III. metaph., *fling away, cast out*, τινὰ ὥσπερ ἀπὸ σφενδόνης Ach.Tat.5. 9. **-ισμός**, ὁ, *blowing forth*, Epicur.Ep.2 p.45 U.

ἐκ-ριπτέω, = sq., f.l. for ἐκριπίζω, Plu.2.654e:—Pass., Agatharch. 48, Lib.Decl.31.33. **-ρίπτω**, *cast forth*, ἔξω με [γῆς].. ἐκρίψατε S.OT1412; ἔπη A.Pr.932; *discharge*, γάλα Sor.1.88:—Pass., δίφρων ἐκριφθεὶς S.El.512; of an orator, *to be hissed off*, μεταξὺ λέγων ὑφ' ὑμῶν ἐξερρίφη Aeschin.2.153. 2. Pass., *to be spread abroad*, Lxx Jd. 15.9. **-ριψις**, εως, ἡ, *throwing out* or *away*, Gloss.

ἐκροή, ἡ, (ἐκρέω) = ἔκροος I, Pherecyd.Syr.7, Pl.Grg.494b (pl.), Jul.Or.2.64d. II. = ἔκροος II, Hp.Epid.2.1.7 (pl.), Arist.Mete.356^{a}10, Pl.Phd.112d, al.; περὶ τὰς ἐκροάς *the places of efflux*, in the human body, Arist.PA688^{b}28.

ἔκροια, Ion. **ἐκροίη**, ἡ, Hsch., = ἔκρυσις II, Sor.2.47; αἵματος Aret. CD2.3 (pl.).

ἐκροιβδέω, *empty by gulping down*, in Pass., κρατὴρ ἐξερροίβδητ' οἴνου Mnesim.4.17.

ἐκροιζ-έω, *pour forth*, ἰδέας Dam.Pr.311. **-ησις**, εως, ἡ, *rushing forth*, φωτός ib.283.

ἐκρομβ-έω, *displace* air, of a falling weight, Ph.Bel.69.19. **-ίζω**, *excise*, v.l. in Dsc.4.170.

ἔκροος, contr. -ρους, ὁ, *outflow, issue*, ἔκροον ἔχειν ἐς θάλασσαν, of rivers, Hdt.7.129, cf. Arr.An.4.3.2 (pl.). 2. κατ' ἔκροον by *excretion*, Hp.Epid.2.1.7. II. *outlet*, Arist.Mete.351^{a}10; *means of escape*, Hp.Virg.

ἐκροφέω, *drink out, gulp down*, cj. in Ar.Eq.701, cf. Pl.Com.149, Arist.HA612^{a}30; *swill*, Jul.Caes.318c: metaph., ἐ. τὸν μισθόν Ar. V.1118.

ἔκρυθμος, ον, *out of tune*, S.E.M.11.186, Philostr.VA8.7. II. of the pulse, *irregular*, Gal.8.516.

ἐκρύομαι [ῡ], *deliver*, E.Ba.258, Fr.190, A.R.4.83 (tm.): c. gen., φασγάνων Lyc.190.

ἐκρῠπᾰρόω, perh. *reduce to ashes*, Theopomp.Hist.317.

ἐκρύπτω, *wash* or *rinse out*, Poll.1.44, 7.39:—Med., ἐκρύπτεσθαι τὸ ἀδικεῖν Ph.1.613.

ἔκρῠσις, εως, ἡ, = ἔκροος II, Arist.Mete.351^{a}5, IG11(2).144A73 ((ἐγρ-) Delos, iv/iii B.C.), Plb.4.39.8. II. *efflux, flooding*, differing from τρωσμός (miscarriage), Hp.Sept.9, Arist.GA758^{b}6 (pl.), HA583^{a}25 (pl.). III. ἐ. τριχῶν *loss* of hair, Thphr.HP7.14.1.

ἐκσᾰγηνεύω, *entangle in the toils*, Plu.2.52c.

ἐκσᾰλ-άσσω, *shake violently*, AP5.234 (Maced.), v.l. in Theoc. 2.85. **-εύω**, = foreg., Sammelb.4324.16, Hsch. s. v. ἐκβαβάξαι; *shake out*, Suid.

ἐκσᾰόω, Ep. for ἐκσῴζω, ἐξεσάωσεν ὀϊόμενον θανέεσθαι Il.4.12; ἐξεσάωσε θαλάσσης Od.4.501; ψυχὴν δ' ἐξ. v.l. in Archil.6; [πέδιλον] ὑπ' ἰλύος A.R.1.10.

ἐκσαρκ-ίζομαι, Pass., *have the flesh stripped off*, Lxx Ez.24.4. **-όω**, *make grow to flesh*:—Pass., *grow to flesh*: metaph., of olives, Thphr. CP1.19.5. II. intr., = Pass., Dsc.Eup.1.75:—hence **-ωμα**, ατος, τό, *fleshy excrescence*, Id.5.74. **-ωσις**, εως, ἡ, *formation of such an excrescence*, Gal.13.317.

ἐκσᾰρόω, *sweep out*, Eust.725.35 (Pass.), Gloss.

ἐκσβέννῡμι, in pf. part. intr. ἐξεσβηκώς, *run dry* at the source, ἐξ. τὸ γάλα Hsch. s. v. ἀμο⟨λ⟩γίδα.

ἐκσείω, *shake out* or *off*, τῆς κεφαλῆς ἐ. [τὸ δέρμα] Hdt.4.64; ἐ. τὴν ἐσθῆτα *shake out* one's clothes, Plu.Ant.79:—Pass., ἐκσέσεισται χαμᾶζ' (sc. ὁ τρίβων) Ar.Ach.344, cf. Gal.7.624. II. *drive out* or *forth*, τῶν λογισμῶν ἐ. τινά Plu.Ant.14; ἐ. τὴν ἀπολογίαν *reject* it, D.S.18.66.

ἐκσεμνύνω, strengthd. for σεμνύνω, Ath.14.661e.

ἐκσεύομαι, Pass., pf. ἐξέσσῡμαι: plpf. ἐξέσσῡτο with sense of impf. (Od.9.373), but usu. aor. (v. infr.): aor. 1 ἐξεσύθην [ῠ] :—*rush out* or *burst forth from*, πυλέων ἐξέσσυτο Il.7.1; φάρυγος δ' ἐξέσσυτο οἶνος Od.9.373; βλεφάρων ἐξέσσυτο νήδυμος ὕπνος sleep *fled away from* his eyelids, 12.366: abs., *rush out*, ἐκ δ' ἔσσυτο λαός Il.8.58; νομόνδ' ἐξέσσυτο.. μῆλα Od.9.438; αἰχμὴ δ' ἐξεσύθη the point *burst out*, Il.5.293 (v.l.); ἐξέσσυται ἄνθρωπος ἐξ ἀνθρώπου Democr.32.

ἐκσηκόω, *weigh in the balance, assay*, in Pass., Gloss.

ἐκσημαίνω, *disclose, indicate*, S.*El*.1191.

ἐκσήπομαι, *to be* or *become quite rotten*, Hp.*Aff*.5, Thphr.*CP*5.16.2.

ἐκσηπόω, f.l. for ἐξιπόω, Aët.15.13 (bis: ἐξυποῖ, ἐξυπεῖ, ἐξιπεῖ codd.).

ἐκσηπτόομαι, *to be decomposed*, Ps.-Democr.Alch.p.44 B. (v.l. ἐξιπωθείσης, quod fort. leg.). **ἔκσηψις**, εως, ἡ, *putrefaction*, Gal. 18(2).796.

ἐκσῑγάομαι, *to be put to silence*, *AP*7.182 (Mel., tm.).

ἐκσῑφωνίζω, *empty by a siphon*: metaph., *drain*, in Pass., ἐ. ἡ ἰσχύς Lxx *Jb*.5.5.

ἐκσῑωπάω, *put to silence*, in Pass., Plb.28.4.13. II. intr., *to be quite silent*, Arr.*An*.6.4.5.

ἐκσκᾰλεύω, *scoop out*, Ar.*Lys*.1028.

ἐκ-σκάπτω, *dig out*, *PTeb*.50.23 (ii B.C.); χοῦν *POxy*.1758.10 (ii A.D.) :—Pass., *to be hollowed out*, ἐξεσκαμμέναι κοιλότητες Gal.18(2). 618. **-σκᾰφή**, ἡ, *digging out*, *PTeb*.342.27 (iii A.D.).

ἐκσκεδάννῡμι, *scatter to the wind*, τὴν εἰρήνην ἐξεσκέδασας Ar.*Eq*. 795.

ἐκσκευάζω, *disfurnish of tools and implements*, ἡ γεωργία ἐξεσκευάσθη D.30.30 :—Med., *carry away with one*, χρήματα εἰς Σοῦσα Str.15. 3.9; *plunder*, οἴκους J.*BJ*4.7.2 :—Pass., ἐξεσκευασμένος f. l. for ἐν-, Plu.*Cleom*.37.

ἔκσκευος, ον, *without equipment, without mask*, Sch.Ar.*Av*.95. II. ἔ. πρόσωπα *special* masks, Poll.4.141; but ἔκσκευα· τὰ παρεπόμενα πρόσωπα ἐπὶ σκηνῆς, Hsch.

ἔκσκηνος, ον, (σκῆνος) *disembodied*, S.E.*M*.9.73 (ἡλίου is interpol.).

ἐκσκορπισμός, ὁ, *scattering abroad*, Plu.2.383d.

ἐκσκυζάω, = σκυζάω, Cratin.25 D.

ἐκσμάω, *wipe out*, τὰ ποτήρια Hdt.3.148.

ἐκσμήχω, = foreg., Ar.*Fr*.33a D. (Pass.).

ἐκσοβέω, *scare away*, ὄρνεις Men.168; πτῶκας *AP*6.167 (Agath.); νόον ἐκ στέρνων ib.5.259 (Paul. Sil.).

ἔκσπᾰσις, εως, ἡ, *plucking out*, τριχῶν Eust.1372.14.

ἐκσπαστέον, *one must draw out*, *Gp*.9.11.3.

ἐκσπάω, fut. -άσω, *draw out*, ἐξέσπασε μείλινον ἔγχος Il.6.65; σπάρτον Hero *Aut*.25.6; *pull up*, [χάρακα] Plb.18.18.14 :—and so Med., ἐκσπασσαμένω δολίχ' ἔγχεα *having drawn out their* spears, Il. 7.255 :—Pass., [τρίχες] ἐκσπῶνται Arist.*Pr*.893^{a}20, cf. Hero *Aut*.16. 2. II. *remove by force*, τοὺς ἐν τῷ ἱερῷ παστοφόρους *OGI*736.7 (Fayûm).

ἐκσπένδω, *pour out as a libation*, E.*Ion* 1193, Eub.71.

ἐκσπερμᾰτ-ίζω, *semen emitto*, ἐ. σπέρμα, of a woman, *conceive*, Lxx *Nu*.5.28. **-όω**, *convert into semen*, αἷμα Steph.*in Hp*.1.123 D. II. Pass., *run to seed*, Thphr.*HP*7.1.7.

ἐκσπεύδω, *hasten out* or *forth*, Ar.*Th*.277.

ἐκσπογγίζω, *wipe off with a sponge*, Eub.83, Aen.Tact.31.13.

ἐκσποδιάζω, *remove ashes*, Al.*Nu*.4.13.

ἔκσπονδος, ον, (σπονδαί) *out of the treaty, not a party thereto*, Th.3. 68, X.*HG*5.1.32, D.19.44; ἔ. τῶν συνθηκῶν Plb.21.30.5. II. *contrary to a treaty, violating it*, ἔ. τι παθεῖν D.H.2.72.

ἐκσπονδῠλίζω or **ἐκσφονδ-**, *break the vertebrae*, Lxx 4*Ma*.11.18: condemned by *EM*324.44.

ἔκσπουδος, *praeproperus*, Gloss.

ἐκστάδιος [ᾰ], ον, *six stades long*, Luc.*Nav*.39 (but prob. ἐκστ. shd. be read).

ἐκστάζω, *exude*, ὕδωρ Plot.2.7.2; *drain out*, αἷμα *PMag.Par*.1. 1545.

ἐκστᾰσιάζω, *provoke sedition*, Poll.6.130 :—Pass., Id.2.229.

ἔκστᾰσις, εως, ἡ, (ἐξίστημι) *displacement*, ἄρθρων Hp.*Art*.56; πᾶσα κίνησις ἔ. ἐστι τοῦ κινουμένου Arist.*de An*.406^{b}13: hence, *change*, εἰς ἀντικείμενα Id.*GA*768^{a}27; αἱ κακίαι ἐ. Id.*Ph*.247^{a}3; ἔ. ἐστιν ἐν τῇ γενέσει τὸ παρὰ φύσιν τοῦ κατὰ φύσιν Id.*Cael*.286^{a}19; ἔ. τῆς φύσεως *degeneracy*, Thphr.*CP*3.1.6; opp. στάσις, Plot.6.3.2; *movement outwards*, ἔ. ἀπὸ τοῦ παράγοντος Dam.*Pr*.97 bis; ἔ. εἰς τὸ ἔξω ib.401; [σῶμα] ἐν ἐκστάσει λαβὸν τὴν ὑπόστασιν Porph.*Sent*.36; *differentiation*, ἔ. καὶ πλῆθος Plot.6.7.17; αἱ εἰς πλῆθος ἐ. Procl.*in Ti*.2.203 D. II. *standing aside*, Arist.*Rh*.1361^{a}37 (pl.). b. = Lat. *cessio bonorum*, *CPR*20 ii 9 (iii A.D.); ἔ. χρημάτων Porph.*Abst*.1.53; *a tax on cessions*, *BGU*914.6 (ii A.D.), *PLond*.2.305.2 (*PTeb*. ii p.184). 2. *distraction* of mind, from terror, astonishment, anger, etc., Hp.*Aph*.7.5, *Prorrh*.2.9; ἔ. σιγῶσα Id.*Coac*.65; ἔ. μανική Arist.*Cat*.10^{a}1; ἔ. τῶν λογισμῶν Plu.*Sol*.8; νοῦ Plot.5.3.7; τὰ μηδὲ προσδοκώμεν' ἔκστασιν φέρει Men.149, cf. *Epit*.472, Epicur.*Fr*.113; εἰς ἔ. ἄγειν Longin.1. 4. 3. *entrancement, astonishment*, *Ev.Luc*.5.26, *Ev.Marc*.5.42. 4. *trance*, *Act.Ap*.10.10, 22.17; *ecstasy*, Plot.6.9.11; ἔ. καὶ μανία Herm. *in Phdr*.p.103 A. b. *drunken excitement*, Corn.*ND*30.

ἐκστᾰτικός, ή, όν, *inclined to depart from*, τοῦ λογισμοῦ Arist.*EN* 1145^{b}11; δόξης, opp. ἐμμενετικὸς δόξῃ, ib.1146^{a}18. 2. *excitable*, ἐ. διὰ τὸν θυμόν Id.*PA*650^{b}34; *out of one's senses*, of Ajax, Id.*Pr*.953^a 22, cf. Plu.2.2a. Adv. -κῶς, ἔχειν Id.*Dio* 55. II. Act., *able to displace* or *remove*, τινός Id.2.951c: abs., ἡ ἀλλοίωσις ἐ. κίνησις Plot. 6.3.21; *causing mental derangement*, Thphr.*HP*9.13.4.

ἐκστέλλω, *fit out, equip*, περόνας αἶσιν ἐξεστέλλετο S.*OT* 1269. II. *send out*, πολίτας *SIG*730.16 (Olbia).

ἐκστέφω, *take off the crown*: *empty* a full cup, opp. ἐπιστέφω (q.v.), Paus.Gr.*Fr*.159. II. *deck with garlands*, E.*Alc*.171; esp. of suppliants, τέκνα στολμοῖσι κρᾶτας ἐξεστεμμένα Id.*HF*526; but ἱκτηρίοις κλάδοισιν ἐξεστεμμένοι *with garlands* on the suppliant olive-branches, S.*OT*3, cf. 19. III. ἐξέστεψε θάλασσαν *he poured* it all round *like a garland*, Opp.*H*.2.33, cf. Sch.; but better, *crowned*, ὀφρύσι καὶ ῥηγμῖσι. IV. ἐκστέψας· λόγον γυμνώσας, Hsch.

ἐκστηθίζω, = ἀποστηθίζω, Eust.974.10.

ἐκστραγγίζω, *squeeze* or *strain out*, v.l. in Lxx *Ez*.23.34, Dsc.4.150 (leg. ἐκσπογγίσας).

ἐκστρᾰτ-εία, ἡ, *going out on service*, Luc.*Gall*.25, Anon.ap.Suid. s.v. ἀξιόλογος, D.C.41.39. **-ευμα**, ατος, τό, *expeditionary force*, Memn.15: metaph. of Nature, Steph.*in Hp*.2.418 D. **-εύσιμος**, η, ον, *fit to take the field*, Sch.Th.6.30. **-ευσις**, εως, ἡ, *expedition*, Tz.*H*.9.380, *EM*729.19. **-εύω**, *march out*, ἐς Λεῦκτρα Th.5.54; ὡς δουλωσόμενος.. X.*Ages*.7.7: trans., ἐ. τινά *march* him *out*, D.H. *Rh*.9.5,6. II. in Med., abs., *take the field*, Hdt.1.190; ἐς Ἴρασα Id.4.159: pf. Pass., *to be in the field*, Th.2.12; ἐπὶ τοῖς ὁρίοις And.1. 45. 2. in pf., *to have ended the campaign*, Th.5.55. b. pf. part. Pass. ἐξεστρατευμένοι *veterans*, App.*BC*3.46.

ἐκστρᾰτοπεδεύομαι, *encamp outside*, Th.4.129, X.*Cyr*.6.3.1 :—later in Act., J.*BJ*3.7.5.

ἐκστρέφω, *turn out of*, βόθρου τ' ἐξέστρεψε [δένδρον] *rooted up* a tree *from* the trench it stood in, Il.17.58. II. *turn inside out*, τὰ βλέφαρα Ar.*Pl*.721: metaph., *change* or *alter entirely*, τοὺς τρόπους Id. *Nu*.88; τοὺς ἡμετέρους Ἱππέας ib.554 :—Pass., ποσὶν ἐξεστραμμένοις πορευόμενοι with feet *turned outwards*, Arist.*Phgn*.813^{a}14; *to be distorted*, Gal.7.27. 2. metaph. in pf. part. Pass., γενεὰ ἐξεστραμμένη *perverse* generation, Lxx *De*.32.20. 3. *transmute* base metal, Zos. Alch.p.195 B.

ἐκστροφή, ἡ, *dislocation*, τῶν δακτύλων Alciphr.3.54; ἐ. τοῦ σφιγκτῆρος, *eversio ani*, *Hippiatr*.41: metaph., τοῦ λόγου Plu.2.1072c. II. *transmutation* of base metal, Zos.Alch.p.195 B. III. *inversion* of uterus, Sor.1.73. IV. *projection* of the eyes, Archig.ap.Orib.46. 26.2.

ἐκστρόφια (sc. φάρμακα), τά, *remedies for haemorrhoids*, Asclep. ap.Gal.13.313.

ἐκστροφόω, *force* a door *from its hinges*, Hsch. s.v. ἐξαγκυρῶσαι.

ἐκστρώννῡμι, *spread* :—Pass., κλῖναι ἐξέστρωντο Diog.*Ep*.37.3.

ἐκσῡριγγόομαι, Pass., of an abscess, *discharge itself by a fistulous opening*, Hp.*Coac*.389.

ἐκσῡρίζω, Att. -ττω, fut. ἐκσυριῶ Lxx *Si*.22.1: aor. 1 ἐξεσύρισα D.C.51.17 :—*hiss off the stage*, τινά D.19.337, Luc.*Nigr*.9 :—Pass., Antiph.191.21. 2. *hiss loudly*, D.C. l. c.

ἐκσυρτικός, ή, όν, *depilatory*, ἔμπλαστρον Hierocl.*Facet*.221.

ἐκσύρω [ῡ], *sweep away*, in aor. Pass. ἐξεσύρη [ῠ] *AP*9.56 (Phil.).

ἐκσφενδονάω, *throw as from a sling*, Hld.9.5, Mich.*in PN*93.32 (Pass.).

ἐκσφονδῠλίζω, v.s. ἐκσπονδ-.

ἐκσφρᾱγ-ίζομαι, Pass., *to be shut out from*, ἐκ γὰρ ἐσφραγισμένοι δόμων καθήμεθ' E.*HF*53. II. *to be sealed*, of a contract, *BCH*35. 43 (Delos). **-ισμα**, ατος, τό, *official copy*, ταύτης τῆς ἐπιγραφῆς *CIG*3276 (Smyrna), cf. *IGRom*.4.513 (Pergam.), *POxy*.1882 (vi A.D.): generally, Mich.*in PN*20.10.

ἐκσχίζω, *cleave asunder* :—Pass., *to be divided*, Arist.*Mu*.400^{b}4, *Mir*.846^{a}14.

ἐκσῴζω, Ep. **ἐκσαόω** (q.v.) :—*preserve from danger, keep safe*, Hdt. 9.107, S.*Aj*.1128, etc.; ἐ. Αἰγίσθου χερός E.*El*.28; ἐ. τινὰ ἐς φάος νεκρῶν πάρα *to bring* him *safe*.., Id.*HF*1222; τινὰ ἐκ κινδύνων Pl.*Grg*. 486b :—Med., *save oneself*, Hdt.2.107; also, *save for oneself*, ὡς.. βίοτον ἐκσωσοίατο A.*Pers*.360; κλῶνας ὡς ἐκσῴζεται [δένδρα] S.*Ant*. 713 :—Pass., ὅταν.. νῆσον ἐκσῳζοίατο when *they fled for safety to* the island, A.*Pers*.451; πῶς ἐξεσώθης E.*Supp*.751.

ἐκσωρεύω, *heap, pile up*, E.*Ph*.1195 (Pass.).

ἔκτᾰ, **ἔκτᾰμεν**, **ἐκτᾰν**, v. κτείνω.

ἐκτᾰγή, ἡ, (ἐκτάσσω) *delegation of powers*, *Cod.Just*.10.16.13.1 (pl.). II. *assessment of taxes*, *PGiss*.54.9 (iv A.D.), etc.

ἐκτᾰ-δά [δᾰ], = sq., Nonn.*D*.37.596, cj. ib.46.153. **-δην**, Adv., (ἐκτείνω) *outstretched*, ἐ. κεῖσθαι lie *outstretched*, i.e. dead, E. *Ph*.1698, Luc.*DMort*.7.2. **-διος**, η, ον, also ος, ον Opp.*C*.3.276 :—*outstretched*, χλαῖναν.. διπλῆν ἐκταδίην double, *with ample folds*, Il. 10.134; ἐ. ὅπλα Orph.*A*.359; οὔρεα D.P.643.

ἐκτᾰδόν, Adv. = ἐκτάδην, Lib.*Or*.11.215, Agath.5.12.

ἔκτᾰθεν, v. κτείνω. **ἐκτᾰθήσομαι**, v. ἐκτείνω.

ἐκταῖος, α, ον, (ἕξ) *on the sixth day*, ἐν τοῖσι πυρετοῖσι ἑκταίοισιν ἐοῦσι Hp.*Aph*.4.29, cf. *Coac*.15, X.*An*.6.6.38, D.S.17.65. II. = ἕκτος, μοῖρα *AP*14.119.10 (Metrod.). III. ἑκταῖον· αἱ δύο κοτύλαι, and ἑκταίους (sc. ἄρτους)· τοὺς ἐκ χοινίκων ἕξ, Hsch.

ἔκτακτος, ον, *detailed* for special duties, of soldiers, Ascl. *Tact*.6.3, Ael. *Tact*.9.4, 16.2,4. II. *special, reserved*, *POxy*.646 (ii A.D.); δι' ἐκτάκτου on *a separate sheet*, *PStrassb*.34.15.

ἐκτᾰλαιπωρέω, *endure*, ἄλλα Ant.Diog.6.

ἐκτᾰλαντόομαι, *to be stripped of money*, ἐκταλαντωθεὶς Sopat.19.

ἔκταλος· ἀκάνθης εἶδος, Hsch.

ἔκτᾰμα, ατος, τό, *extent, length*, Sch.Ar.*Nu.*2, Suid. s. v. πῆχυς. 2. gloss on ὄρεγμα, Sch.E.*Ph.*308.

ἐκτᾰμῐεύομαι, *dispense*, Agatharch.102. II. *receive from store*, *PRein.*15.16, al. (ii B.C.).

ἐκτάμνω, Ion. for ἐκτέμνω.

ἐκτανθαρύ(ζ)ω· τρέμω, Hsch.

ἐκτᾰνύω, = ἐκτείνω, βραχίονας Theoc.25.270:—Hom. has this form only, in the sense *to stretch out* (on the ground), *lay low*, ἐξετάνυσσ' ἐπὶ γαίῃ Il.17.58:—Pass., *lie outstretched*, ὁ δ' ὕπτιος ἐξετανύσθη 7.271; ἐξετανύσθη ἄμπελος it *spread out all ways*, *h.Bacch.*38. 2. *stretch tight*, ἐκ δ' ἐτάνυσσ' ἱμάντα βοός (f.l. for ἐν δ') Od.23.201; [δέρμα] Pi.*P.*4.242. 3. *extend*, ἐξετάνυσσας ὁδόν *Epigr.Gr.*1078.4 (Cilicia).—For S.*OC*1562, v. ἐξανύω.—Poet. word, used by Hp.*Fract.*43. [ῠ usu., but ῡ *Anacreont.*35.5 (s. v.l.).]

ἔκταξις, εως, ἡ, *array of battle*, ἔ. ποιεῖσθαι Plb.2.33.7, cf. D.S.11.17. II. *expedition*, ἔ. κατ' Ἀλανῶν, title of work by Arr. III. *disposal, distribution*, σίτου J.*AJ*15.9.2.

ἐκτᾰπεινόω, strengthd. for ταπεινόω, Plu.2.165b, *Cor.*14.

ἐκτᾰρ-ακτικός, ή, όν, *calculated to disturb*, v.l. in Hp.*Acut.*(*Sp.*) 50. **-αξις**, εως, ἡ, *agitation*, κοιλίης Hp.*Judic.*20. **-άσσω**, Att. **-ττω**, *throw into confusion*, τοὺς ἵππους Ascl.*Tact.*7.4, etc.; *agitate*, τὸν δῆμον Plu.*Cor.*19, cf. Jul.*Or.*2.97d:—Pass., *to be greatly troubled, be confounded*, ὑπό τινος Isoc.15.5, Ath.12.552f; πρός τι Luc.*Somn.*16. II. in Pass. also, *to have a bowel-complaint*, κοιλίη ἐκταραχθεῖσα Hp.*Aph.*4.60, *Epid.*1.15.

ἐκταρβέω, strengthd. for ταρβέω, in Pass., Hsch.

ἐκταρσόομαι, = ταρσόομαι, Hp.*Oss.*12.

ἔκτᾰσις, εως, ἡ, (ἐκτείνω) *stretching out, extension*, Hp.*Art.*19; σκέλους, κώλων, Arist.*IA*711ᵃ30, *PA*688ᵃ16; καμπὴ καὶ ἔ. Pl.*Lg.*795e: metaph., ἔ. ἄρρητος τῆς ἑαυτοῦ ⟨οὐσίας⟩ Porph.*Sent.*28; ἡ εἰς πλῆθος ἔ. Procl.*Inst.*128. 2. *extent*, φιλίας Max.Tyr.6.2; παμπληθῆ θεωρίας ἔ. Iamb.*VP*29.162. 3. mental *tension*, v.l. for ἔκστασις in D.H.*Comp.*15. 4. *making explicit*, κατ' ἔκτασιν, opp. κατ' ἐπίνοιαν, *Theol.Ar.*5, cf. 12. 5. *impulse*, τοῦ ὀρεκτικοῦ ἐπί τι Plot.1.1.5. 6. Tact., *extension, deployment*, συναγωγαὶ καὶ ἐκτάσεις στρατιᾶς Pl.*R.*526d, cf. Onos.10.2. II. *lengthening of a short syllable*, D.H.*Comp.*25 (pl.); κατ' ἔκτασιν παραλαμβάνεσθαι D.T.632.32; ἔστιν ἐν ἐκτάσει τοῦ ῑ A.D.*Adv.*161.6.

ἐκτάσσω, Att. **-ττω**, *draw out in battle-order*, of the officers, Plb.3.112.1, D.S.17.53; πρὸς μάχην Onos.1.13:—Med., *draw themselves out*, of the soldiers, X.*An.*5.4.12, etc.:—Pass., Plb.5.83.1. II. *keep muster-roll of*, λαόν Lxx 4*Ki.*25.19. 2. ἐκτάσσοντα· χαράσσοντα, γράφοντα, Hsch.

ἐκτᾰτέον, *one must pronounce long*, Sch.Il.21.262.

ἐκτᾰτικός, ή, όν, *given to lengthening*, Ἀθηναῖοι ἐ. τῶν φωνηέντων A.D.*Adv.*187.21. II. *preserving tension*, αὐτῶν δι' εὐτονίαν Chrysipp.*Stoic.*2.146 (codd. Plu., ἐκτικά Arnim).

ἐκτᾰτός, ή, όν, *capable of extension*, κῶλα ἐ. καὶ καμπτά Pl.*Ti.*44e.

ἐκταφρεύω, *to dig trenches*, in Pass., J.*BJ*5.2.2, App.*BC*3.65, Hsch.

ἐκτέατο, Ion. 3 pl. plpf. of κτάομαι.

ἐκτείνω, fut. -τενῶ A.*Pr.*325, etc.:—*stretch out*, χεῖρ' ἐπ' ἐκφορᾷ νεκροῦ Id.*Ch.*9; τὴν χ. ὑπτίαν Ar.*Ec.*782; τὰς χεῖρας ἐπί τι for something, Plb.1.3.6; πρός τινα, in sign of friendship, Id.2.47.2; πρὸς κέντρα κῶλον A.*Pr.*325; παῖδας ἐπὶ τὴν πυρήν Hdt.2.107; ἐκεῖσε κἀκεῖσ' ἀσπίδ' ἐ. E.*Andr.*1131; εἰς ἧπαρ ξίφος Id.*Ph.*1421: abs., *offer food*, Ath.5.186c; τὰ γόνατ' ἐ. *straighten* the knees, Ar.*V.*1212; ἐ. τὰ σκέλη X.*An.*5.8.14; νοῦ ἄπο μυρίον ὄμμα *IG*3.716; ἐ. νέκυν E.*Hipp.*786; ἓν γὰρ ἐκτενεῖ σ' ἔπος *will lay* thee *prostrate*, Id.*Med.*585:—Pass., *to be outstretched, lie at length*, of sleepers, etc., S.*Ph.*858 (lyr.); ἐκταθεὶς ὥσπερ Ὀδυσσεὺς ἀφικέσθαι εἰς τὴν Ἑλλάδα X.*An.*5.1.2, etc.; of countries, etc., *extend*, Id.*Vect.*4.3, D.P.40. 2. *stretch, spread out* a net, A.*Ch.*991; *extend the line of* an army, E.*Heracl.*801, Arr.*Tact.*5.6; λαὸν ἐκτείνοντ' ἄνω (sc. ἑαυτόν) E.*Supp.*654; στράτευμα X.*HG*6.5.19:—Pass., *to be unfolded, smoothed*, ὡς ἂν Διὸς μέτωπον ἐκταθῇ χαρᾷ S.*Fr.*902. II. *spin out, prolong*, πλεῦνα λόγον Hdt.7.51; φροίμιον θεοῖς A.*Ag.*829; μακρὰν ἐξέτεινας ib.916, cf. E.*Med.*1351; μῆκος λόγου A.*Eu.*201; μείζονα λόγον S.*Tr.*679, etc.; βίον E.*Supp.*1109; τοὺς περιπάτους X.*Mem.*3.13.5:—Pass., λόγος ἐκταθείς Pl.*Lg.*887a; of Time, πολὺς ἐκτέταται χρόνος S.*Aj.*1402 (anap.). III. *put to the full stretch*, ἵππον ἐ. X.*Cyr.*5.4.5; ἐ. πάντα κάλων Pl.*Prt.*338a; πᾶσαν προθυμίην ἐ. *put forth* all one's zeal, Hdt.7.10.η'; τὸν θυμόν And.3.31; ἅπασαν ἀγωνίαν D.60.30: metaph. in Pass., *to be on the rack*, ἐκτέταμαι S.*OT*153 (lyr.). IV. *lengthen* a short syllable, A.D.*Pron.*27.2 (Pass.), al., interpol. in D.H.2.58. V. intr., *draw along*, Lxx *Jd.*20.37.

ἔκτεισις, Arc. **ἐσ-**, εως, ἡ, later **ἔκτισις**, *payment in full*, *IG*5(2).6.37 (Tegea, iv B.C.), *SIG*279.17 (iv B.C.), *PCair.Zen.*1.18,44 (iii B.C.), *PPetr.*3p.160 (iii B.C.), etc.; ζημίας Pl.*Lg.*855a (pl.); ἐ. δεκαπλασία Din.2.17; ἡ ἔ. ἣν ἐπὶ τῆς ἐνάτης πρυτανείας And.1.73; προικός D.40.56; ἔ. ποιεῖσθαι, = ἐκτίνειν, Id.27.67; ἔγγυος εἰς ἔκτεισιν *PHib.*1.94 (iii B.C.), etc.; ἔ. δίκης, προστίμου, Iamb.*Myst.*4.5, *PLond.*1.113 (vi A.D.).

ἔκτεισμα, later **ἔκτισμα**, ατος, τό, *payment*, *IG*11(2).144*A*20 (Delos, iv B.C.), 162*A*41. II. *penalty*, Pl.*Lg.*868b, D.H.10.52 (pl.).

ἐκτειχ-ίζω, Att. fut. -ιῶ, *fortify completely*, Th.7.26, X.*HG*3.2.10, etc.:—Pass., τὸ τεῖχος ἐκτετείχισται ταχύ Ar.*Av.*1165. **-ισμός**, ὁ, *fortification*, Arr.*An.*6.20.1.

ἐκτεκμαίρομαι, aor. 1 part. Pass. ἐκτεκμαρθείς, *to be made out by guessing*, Orac.ap.Eus.*PE*5.23.

ἐκτεκνόω, *engender*, ἡ φύσις ἐ. πάθεα Hp.*Acut.*43:—Med., παῖδας ἐκτεκνούμενος λάθρᾳ E.*Ion*438.

ἐκτεκταίνομαι, aor. 1 ἐξετεκτηνάμην, *construct*, τὰς φλιὰς τῶν ὀνίσκων Hp.*Art.*47.

ἐκτελέθω, *spring from*, τινός Emp.17.10.

ἐκτελ-ειόω or **-εόω**, *bring to perfection*, Thphr.*CP*4.1.5, etc.; βίον Plu.*Publ.*23. **-είωσις**, εως, ἡ, *completion*, Thphr.*CP*1.9.3.

ἐκτελευτάω, *bring to an end, accomplish*, Pi.*P.*12.29 (tm.), Semon.1.5: c. inf., ἐ. γενέσθαι *to bring* it *at last* to be, Pi.*P.*4.19; ἐ. μῆκος χρόνου A.*Pr.*1020:—Pass., *to be the end of*, πόνων S.*Tr.*170. II. intr. in Act., *turn out*, καλῶς A.*Supp.*411.

ἐκτελ-έω, Ep. impf. ἐξετέλειον Il.9.493, Od.4.7: Ep. fut. -τελέω Il.2.286, 10.105: aor. part. ἐκτελέσσαντες Sapph.*Supp.*6.5: fut. Med. in pass. sense (v. infr.):—*bring to an end, accomplish, achieve*, ἐκτελέσας μέγα ἔργον Od.3.275; ὥς κεν.. ἐκτελέσειεν ἀέθλους 8.22; ὁδὸν ἐκτελέσαντες 10.41, etc.; *fulfil* a promise, etc., οὐδέ τοι ἐκτελέουσιν ὑπόσχεσιν Il.2.286; μή οἱ ἀπειλὰς ἐκτελέσωσι θεοί 9.245; οὔ θην Ἕκτορι πάντα νοήματα.. Ζεὺς ἐκτελέει 10.105, etc.; ἐπιθυμίην Hdt.1.32; ἔρωτα Pl.*Smp.*193c; τἀντεταλμένα E.*Ph.*1648 codd.; μυστήρια *PMag.Osl.*1.306: abs., Δαρείου ἐκτελέσας (sc. τὸ ἔργον) κατὰ νοῦν Epigr.ap.Hdt.4.88:—Pass., ὧδε γὰρ ἐκτελέεσθαι ὀΐομαι *will be accomplished*, Il.12.217, cf. 7.353; ἐκτελοῖτο δὴ τὰ χρηστά A.*Pers.*228. 2. of Time, Hes.*Op.*565, Hdt.6.69, Pi.*P.*4.104:—Pass., μῆνές τε καὶ ἡμέραι ἐξετελεῦντο Od.11.294. **-ής**, ές, (τέλος) *brought to an end, perfect*, ἀγαθ' ἐκτελῆ γενέσθαι A.*Pers.*218; of corn, *ripe*, Hes.*Op.*466; also of persons, ἤδη πεφυκότ' ἐκτελῆ νεανίαν E.*Ion*780, cf. A.*Ag.*105 (lyr., s. v.l.). Adv. -λῶς *in full, completely*, *BGU*1116.9 (i B.C.).

ἐκτέμνω, Ep. and Ion. **ἐκτάμνω** (as always in Hom.), fut. -τεμῶ: aor. 2 ἐξέταμον (v. infr.) or -έτεμον S.*Tr.*1196, Ar.*Ra.*575: fut. perf. ἐκτετμήσομαι Pl.*R.*564c, Ph.1.458:—*cut out*, μηροὺς ἐξέταμον Il.1.460, etc.; μηροῦ ἔκταμ' ὀϊστόν *cut* an arrow *from* the thigh, 11.829, cf. 515; ἐ. γλῶσσαν Hdt.9.112; ἐ. τὸν λάρυγγά τινος Ar.*Ra.*575; of a surgeon, *cut out* a diseased part, Pl.*R.*564c (Pass.); σχῆμα τῆς γῆς Arist.*Mete.*362ᵃ35. 2. *cut* trees *out* of a wood, *cut down*, Il.12.149, S.*Tr.*1196; also of planks, etc., *hew out, hew into shape*, ὅς ῥά τε τέχνῃ νήϊον ἐκτάμνῃσιν Il.3.62, cf. 4.486; ἐ. τὰ πρέμνα *to cut* the stumps *out of the ground*, Lys.7.19. 3. ἐ. ἶνας *cut away* the sinews, and so, *weaken*, Pi.*I.*8(7).57; ἐ. ὥσπερ νεῦρα ἐκ τῆς ψυχῆς Pl.*R.*411b; ῥόδον ἐ. ῥίζης *IG*14.2040: metaph., ἐλπίδας ἐξέταμες ib.1362; 'nip in the bud', πάθος Alex.Trall.1.17:—Pass., ἐκτέμνεσθαι νοῦν καὶ λόγον Ph.1.17. II. *castrate*, παῖδας Hdt.6.32, 8.105; ὄρχεις ἐ. S.*Fr.*620; οἱ ἐκτετμημένοι *eunuchs*, Arist.*HA*518ᵃ31; ἐ. τὰ θήλεα *circumcise* females, Str.17.2.5, cf. 16.4.9 (Pass.). III. = κείρειν, γῆς ἐκτεμνομένης D.H.9.57 (s. v.l.). IV. ἐκτέμνεσθαί τινας φιλανθρωπίᾳ *to disarm and deceive* by kindness, Plb.30.30.8.

ἐκτεμπροι· προσμένοντες, Hsch.

ἐκτέν-εια, ἡ, *zeal, assiduousness*, Molpis 3, *PPetr.*3p.18 (iii B.C.), Phld.*D.*3.2, etc.; '*gush*', '*empressement*', Cic.*Att.*10.17.1; ἐ. καὶ φιλοτιμία *IG*2².1343.28, cf. Hierocl.p.62A.; τὰν πᾶσαν ἐ. καὶ κακοπαθίαν παρεχόμενος *IG*12(1).1032.10 (Carpathos), cf. *Inscr.Prien.*107.20, al. (ii B.C.), *UPZ*110.12 (ii B.C.), etc.; ἐν ἐκτενείᾳ *eagerly*, *Act.Ap.*26.7, cf. Lxx *Ju.*4.9; μετὰ πάσης ἐ. ib.2*Ma.*14.38. II. *abundance*, ξύλων Hdn.7.2.4, cf. 8.2.6. III. *extension*, Dam.*Pr.*65. **-ής**, ές, *strained*: hence of persons, *warmly attached, friendly*, Plb.21.22.4 (Sup.), cf. D.S.34.2.39, Socr.ap.Stob.4.31.130; *assiduous*, περί τινα *Supp.Epigr.*2.277.5 (Delph., ii B.C.): Comp. -έστερος τῇ προθυμίᾳ *IGRom.*4.293ᵃii 38 (Pergam., ii B.C.): Sup. -εστάτη προθυμία Chrysipp.*Stoic.*2.293, cf. *Vit.Philonid.*p.9C.; πρόνοια *UPZ*110.46 (ii B.C.). 2. *extended*, Dam.*Pr.*64; *capable of extension*, ἐ. ἐστι τὸ μεταδίδον τῶν ἑαυτοῦ καὶ τοῖς ἄλλοις Herm.*in Phdr.*p.121A. 3. *abundant*, γάλα Sor.1.94. II. Adv. -νῶς (Elean ἐκτενέωρ *GDI* 1172.12; Cret. ἐκτενίως ib.5138.13; Ion. -έως Ps.-Hdt.*Vit.Hom.*7) *earnestly, zealously*, ἀγαπᾶσθαι Machoap.Ath.13.579e; ποιεῖν τι Arist.*MM*1210ᵃ27; συναγωνίζεσθαι *IG*2².945, cf. *SIG*538.17 (Delph., iii B.C.); εὐχὴ ἐ. γινομένη *Act.Ap.*12.5: Comp. -έστερον Cic.*Att.*13.9.1: Sup. -έστατα D.S.29.4. 2. in Adv. also, *eagerly, freely, splendidly* (condemned by Phryn.285), προσδέξασθαί τινα Plb.8.19.1, cf. D.S.2.24, etc.; of public duties, λαμπρῶς καὶ ἐ. τετελεκότα *CIG*2771 ii 14 (Aphrodisias): Comp., πολυτελῶς καὶ ἐκτενέστερον τῶν ἄλλων Agatharch.*Fr.Hist.*6J.—Not in early writers, corrupt in A.*Supp.*983.

ἔκτεξις, εως, ἡ, *child-birth*, Arist.*Mir.*847ᵇ6, Anon.Lond.18.21, Sor.2.54, S.E.*M.*5.55.

ἐκτέος, α, ον, (ἔχω) *to be held*, Ar.*Ach.*259. II. **ἐκτέον**, *one must have*, χάριν τινί X.*Mem.*3.11.2; πρόνοιαν Aen.Tact.*Praef.*3; πλέον ἑ., = πλεονεκτητέον, Pl.*Grg.*490c. 2. *one must behave, comport oneself*, πρὸς τοὺς κινδύνους εὐρώστως Iamb.*VP*30.173.

ἐκτετᾰμένως, Adv., (ἐκτείνω) *lengthened*, of a short syllable, Ath.3.105e, *AB*383, etc. II. = ἡπλωμένως, Hsch.

ἐκτεύς, έως, ὁ, (ἕκτος) *the sixth part* (*sextarius*) *of the* μέδιμνος, πυρῶν, κριθέων, *Schwyzer* 725 (Milet., vi B.C.), cf. *IG*1².76.6, Ar.*Ec.*547, Men.91.

ἐκτεύχω, *work out, produce*, Hp.*Ep.*23 (Ps.-Democr.).

ἐκτεφρ-όω, *burn to ashes, calcine*, in Pass., Str.5.4.9, Dsc.1.68.4, 5.81, Plu.2.696b: metaph., of bile, Alex.Trall.*Febr.*7. **-ωσις**, εως, ἡ, *burning to ashes*, Str.5.4.8.

ἐκτεχνάομαι, *devise a plan*, τοιόνδε τι ἐξετεχνήσαντο Th.6.46.

ἐκτεχνολογέω, *set forth in technical language, reduce to system*, Phld.*Rh.*1.203 S. (Pass.).

ἕκτη, ἡ, a silver coin, *the sixth of a stater*, *IG*1².310, al. II. *tax* *of one-sixth*, ἕ. παραδείσων *PTeb.*343.69 (ii A. D.), cf. *PHib.*1.109 (iii B. C.), *PRev.Laws* 36.9 (iii B. C.). **III.** *liquid measure*, ἕ. οἴνῳ *Schwyzer* 725 (Milet., vi B. C.).

ἐκτήκω, fut. -ξω E.*Or.*134:—*melt out*, Κύκλωπος ὄμματ' ἐ. πυρί Id.*Cyc.*459; τὰ γράμματ' ἐ. *melt out* the letters written on wax, Ar. *Nu.*772. **2.** metaph., *let melt, pine* or *waste away*, ὄμμα δακρύοις E.*Or.*134, cf. 529; δάκρυσι χρόα Id.*Hel.*1419; τὸν θυμόν Pl.*R.*411b; λῆστις δ' ἐ. μνημοσύνην πραπίδων Critias 6.12 D.; τὴν ὑπάρχουσαν ἐ. κρᾶσιν Plu.*Lyc.*5; ἐ. τινὰ εἰς δάκρυα Id.*Brut.*23; λύπῃ καὶ λιμῷ ἑαυτόν Ael.*NA*10.41. **II.** Pass., with pf. ἐκτέτηκα: aor. ἐξετάκην [ᾰ]:—*melt and ooze out*, Hp.*Coac.*629; τὸ ἐκτετηκὸς *flabby condition*, Id.*Aph.*2.35. **2.** metaph., *pine, waste away*, ἐκτέτηκα καρδίαν E. *Hec.*433; ἐξετηκόμην γόοις Id.*Or.*860, etc.; τὰς ὁράσεις ἐκτετηκυῖα ὑπὸ τῶν δακρύων D.H.8.45, cf. Luc.*Gall.*29,31; μάλα μοι τόδ' ἐμμένοι καὶ μήποτ' ἐκτακείη *may it* never *melt from* my remembrance, A.*Pr.* 535 (lyr.), cf. Critias l. c.

ἑκτημόρ-ιοι, οἱ, = ἕκτα τῶν γινομένων τελοῦντες, those *who paid a sixth* (or *five-sixths*) *of the produce* as rent, Plu.*Sol.*13:—also **ἑκτήμοροι**, Arist.*Ath.*2.2. **II.** ἑκτημόριον, τό, *a sixth part*, S.E.*M.*10. 140, Protag.Nicae.ap.Heph.Astr.3.30. **III.** ἑκτήμορος (sc. κύαθος), ὁ, a *liquid measure*, Herod.1.80. **-ίτης** [ῑ], ου, ὁ, = ἑκτημόριον, Gal.1.144.

Ἔκτηνες, οἱ, primitive inhabitants of Boeotia, Paus.9.5.1.

ἔκτηξις, εως, ἡ, *melting away*: hence, *attenuation*, φλεβῶν Hp. *Aër.*10 (v.l. ἔκτασιν). **II.** *cancelling* of contract, *BCH*37.91 (Beroea).

ἐκτῑθᾰσεύω, strengthd. for τιθασεύω, Poll.4.28.

ἐκτίθημι (inf. -τιθεῖν *IG*7.235.41), fut. -θήσω: pf. -τέθεικα *UPZ* 62.4 (ii B. C.):—*set out, place outside*, πυκινὸν λέχος Od.23.179; *expose* on a desert island, S.*Ph.*5; *expose* a new-born child, Hdt.1. 112, Ar.*Nu.*531, etc.; τὸν παῖδ'.. ἐξέθηκε δωμάτων E.*Ion* 344:—so in Pass., τέθνηκε.. θηρσὶν ἐκτεθείς ib.951; *expose*, ἑαυτὸν βέλεσι Polem.*Cyn.*7:—Med., ἐκτίθεσθαι λείαν εἰς Βιθυνούς *export* it thither, Plu.*Alc.*29. **II.** *set up, offer for a prize*, λέβητας ἐκτιθεὶς φέρειν S.*Fr.*378; ἆθλα Plb.15.9.4. **b.** *fix* or *grant* allowances, rates of pay, etc., *PSI*5.498 (iii B. C.), *PEdgar* 2.4 (Pass.), etc. **2.** *exhibit publicly, post up*, νόμους πρὸς τοὺς ἐπωνύμους Decr.ap.And.1. 83, cf. Lex ap.D.24.23; ἔκθεμα *PPetr.*2 p.44 (iii B. C.); ὀνόματα εἰς στοάν *SIG*577.28 (Milet., iii/ii B. C.):—Pass., ὅπως ἐκτεθῶσι [οἱ νόμοι] *IG*2².487.6, etc. **3.** *expose for sale*, D.C.46.14 (Pass.). **III.** *set forth, expound*, τὴν πρόθεσιν Arist.*Rh.Al.*1437b35; κατὰ γένος Thphr.*Char.Praef.*3:—also Med., λόγους καθόλου Arist.*Po.*1455b1; τὴν ἑαυτῆς ἐρημίαν D.S.12.18, etc. **2.** Philos., *predicate separate existence* of a thing, *explain by means of abstraction*, Arist.*Metaph.* 1086b10. **IV.** Med., *set forth, select* particular instances of a rule, [ποιεῖν τὴν ἀπόδειξιν] τῷ ἐκθέσθαι Id.*An.Pr.*28a23:—Pass., τὸ ἐκτεθέν ib.30a11. **2.** *set out* terms in syllogistic form, ib.48a1, al. **3.** *isolate* in thought, Id.*SE*179a3. **4.** *pick out for separate treatment*, Id.*Ph.*235a28. **5.** ἐ. καθόλου *set out* in general form, Id. *Po.*1455b1.

ἐκτῑθηνέω, *rear up, foster*, Plu.2.1070c (Med.).

ἐκτῐκεύομαι, *suffer from hectic fever*, Alex.Trall.*Febr.*4 (aor. part. -κωθέντας corrupt, ib.5).

ἐκτικός, ή, όν, (ἕξις) *formed by* or *forming habit*, τὸ βέβαιον καὶ ἐ. Chrysipp.*Stoic.*3.138; ἐ. δύναμις ib.2.149; ποιεῖν τι ἐκτικόν to do a thing *as a matter of habit, easily*, Arr.*Epict.*2.18.4; ἐ. πρὸς τὴν τέχνην Damocr.ap.Gal.13.1001. Adv. **-κῶς** *from habit, easily, fluently*, γράμματα ἀναγινώσκειν Artem.1.53, cf. D.S.3.4, Plu.2.802f: Comp. -ώτερον Arr.*Epict.*3.24.78; but also ἐ. διαμένειν [λίθον] remain *fixed in its nature*, Porph.*Abst.*4.20. **2.** ἐ. αἴτια *sustaining* causes, Chrysipp.*Stoic.*2.273 (s.v.l.). **3.** *capable of*, φύσις τινὸς ἐ. Phld.*Ir.* p.14 W. **II.** *hectic, consumptive*, f.l. in Arist.*Pr.*920b27; of fevers, Gal.7.315, Alex.Aphr.*Pr.*1.88; σφυγμός Gal.8.460. Adv. **-κῶς** Id. 10.603.

ἐκτίκτω, aor. 2 ἐξέτεκον Arist.*HA*621b20: pf. ἐκτέτοκα Pl.*Tht.* 210b:—*bring forth*, Arist.*HA*571b11, al.; of fish, *spawn*, ib.547a2, 621b20: metaph., Pl. l. c.

ἐκτῑλάω, *void* excrement, *Hippiatr.*90, Sch.Ar.*Av.*791.

ἐκ-τίλλω, fut. ἐκτιλῶ Hsch. s.v. ἐκποκιῶ: aor. inf. ἐκτῖλαι· ἐκτινάξαι, Id.:—Pass., fut. ἐκτιλήσομαι Lxx *Si.*40.16: aor. 2 ἐξετίλην [ῐ] Dsc.*Eup.*1.52, Thd.*Da.*7.4:—*pluck out*, τρίχας Arist.*HA*603b22; πτερόν ib.519a27 (Pass.); of a person, κόμην ἐκτετιλμένος Anacr.21. 11. **II.** *pluck, strip bare*, τὴν τράμιν Hippon.84; τὴν ῥοδωνιάν D. 53.16. **2.** *strip the leaves off*, ὀρίγανον, κρόμμυον, Arist.*Mir.*831a 30, *Pr.*924a32. **-τιλτέον**, *one must pluck out*, τὰς τρίχας Aët.9.8.

ἐκτῑμ-άω, *honour highly*, S.*El.*64 (Pass.), Plb.30.19.3, etc.; *honour too highly*, πλοῦτον Longin.44.7; ἐκτετιμημένος *overpriced*, Arist. *Oec.*1352b5. **II.** *estimate*, Pl.*Ep.*347b. **-ησις**, εως, ἡ, *high esteem*: *estimation*, Str.14.1.23, Porph.*Abst.*2.24. **II.** *valuation*, *PKlein.Form.*78 (v/vi A. D.). **-ητρα**, Dor. **-ατρα**, τά, *penalties*, *SIG*1146 (possibly, = *reward for redemption from slavery*). **-ος**, ον, (τιμή) *without honour*, γονέων ἐκτίμους ἴσχουσα πτέρυγας.. γόων restraining them *so that they show not the honour due* to parents, S. *El.*242 (lyr.). **II.** *highly priced*, Hsch.

ἐκτῐν-αγμός, ὁ, *shaking out, violent shaking*, Lxx *Na.*2.10(11), Ph. 1.415; perh. *winnowing* or *threshing*, *PFay.*114.22 (i A. D.). **-ακτρον**, τό, *winnowing-shovel*, *POxy.*1733.5 (iii A. D.). **-αξις**, εως, ἡ, = -αγμός, Heph.Astr.1.20, *EM*281.18. **-άσσω**, *shake out*, in cleaning, ἔρια, ἱμάτια, *BGU*827.22; *expel*, ἕλμινθας Diph.Siph.ap. Ath.2.51f, cf. Dsc.1.126; ἔμβρυα ib.76:—Pass., ἐκ δ' ἐτίναχθεν ὀδόντες Il.16.348, cf. Plu.*Cat.Ma.*14; [ὁ Φαέθων] ἐκτινάσσεται *is thrown out*, Palaeph.52, cf. Agath.4.20. **2.** *shake off*, τὸν κονιορτὸν τῶν ποδῶν *Ev.Matt.*10.14, etc.:—Med., *Act.Ap.*13.51. **3.** *search thoroughly*, τοὺς βαδίζοντας Diog.*Ep.*37.5. **II.** intr., *make a disturbance*, Hp. *Epid.*6.2.19; *make a thorough search*, *UPZ*5.12 (ii B. C.); *kick out*, of animals, εἰς τοὺς πλησίον ἵππους Ael.*Tact.*19.2.

ἐκτίννῡμι, = sq., v.l. in D.S.16.29, J.*BJ*3.8.5, Hermog.*Inv.*2.3, etc.: **ἐκτιννύω**, Cyr.

ἐκτίνω [ῑ], fut. -τείσω: aor. 1 ἐξέτεισα: pf. ἐκτέτεικα D.40.52:—*pay off, pay in full*, [ζημίην] χίλια τάλαντα Hdt.6.92; εὐεργεσίας Id. 3.47; Ἄργει δ' ἐκτίνων τροφάς *making a return for* bringing one up, A.*Th.*548; χάριτας πατρῴας E.*Or.*453, etc.; τροφεῖα Pl.*R.*520b; ἔκ τινα τῖσαι ἀμοιβήν Maiist.40; δίκην ἐ. *pay full* penalty, E.*El.*260, Lys. 23.14; τινός *for* a thing, Hdt.9.94; so τίσιν ἐ. τινί Id.6.72; ἄποινα ib.79; ἐ. βλάβην *to make* it *good*, Pl.*Lg.*936e, cf. A.*Ag.*1562 (lyr.), 1582; τὸ βλάβος D.21.43; δίκην ἐ. ὑπὲρ χρημάτων Is.10.15. **II.** Med., *exact full payment for* a thing, *avenge*, E.*HF*547; *take vengeance on*, τινά Id.*Med.*267. **2.** ἐ. ὕβριν *wreak* despite, S.*Aj.*304.

ἔκτισις, v. ἔκτεισις. **ἔκτισμα**, v. ἔκτεισμα.

ἐκτιστής· ἀποδότης, Hsch.

ἐκτιτθεύω, = ἐκτιθηνέω, *rear by suckling*, Arist.*HA*522a6.

ἐκτιτράω, fut. -τρήσω, *bore through*:—Pass., ἐκτιτρώμενος Orib. 46.20.10: pf. Pass. ἐκτετρῆσθαι Hero *Bel.*96.2, part. ἐκτετρημένος Poll.2.70.

ἐκτιτρώσκω, *bring forth untimely*, βρέφος D.S.3.64, 4.2, *PGoodsp. Cair.*15.15 (iv A. D.). **2.** abs., *miscarry*, Hdt.3.32, Hp.*Aph.*3.12, Arist.*HA*585a22:—so in Med., Hp.*Aër.*10. **3.** *attempt to procure abortion*, Id.*Mul.*1.78.—Ion. and later Prose for Att. ἐξαμβλόω, Phryn.184.

ἐκτλάω, *bear, sustain to the end*, aor. inf. ἐκτλῆναι Ph.2.464 (s.v.l.).

ἔκ-τμημα, ατος, τό, *section, segment*, τῆς γῆς ἐκτμήματα, of the zones, Arist.*Mete.*362b5. **-τμησις**, εως, ἡ, *castration*, Id.*Pr.*895a1; *excision*, *Gloss.* **-τμητέον**, *one must cut out*, Ph.2.212, Max.Tyr. 13.7, Philum.*Ven.*16.6.

ἔκτοθεν, Adv., (ἐκτός) Ep. for ἔξωθεν, = ἔκτοσθεν, *from without, outside*, c. gen., ἕ. ἄλλων μνηστήρων *outside* their circle, *apart from* them, Od.1.132; λίμνας ἕ. A.*Pers.*871 (lyr.); πύργων δ' ἕ. βαλών having struck them *from* the wall, Id.*Th.*629 (lyr.); ἕ. ἐρώτων *AP*5.301.7 (Agath.). **2.** abs., *outside, without*, οὐδ' ἀπ' ἄλλων ἕ. A.*Ch.*473 (lyr.); ἕ. βοᾶν S.*El.*802; ἕ. γαμεῖν marry *from an alien house*, E. *Andr.*975; τὰ ἕ. things *abroad*, Theoc.10.9:—ἕκτοθεν αὐλῆς is dub. in Od.9.239 (perh. *outside* in the court). **3.** *without, unaccompanied by*, τινός Nonn.*D.*11.428.

ἔκτοθι, Ep. Adv., (ἐκτός) *out of, outside, far from*, νηῶν, πυλάων, Il.15.391, 22.439, cf. A.R.1.243. **2.** simply, *from*, σέο δ' ἕ. μῆτις ὄρωρεν ib.1291. **3.** abs., *outside*, Id.3.255. **4.** *without*, i.e. *not having*, νίκης Nonn.*D.*22.252, al.

ἐκτοιχωρῠχέω, *break into a house and rob it*: generally, *pillage, plunder*, τοὺς βίους Plb.4.18.8; τὴν βασιλείαν Id.18.55.2.

ἐκτοκ-εύω, = sq., Aq.*Is.*66.9. **-ίζω**, *lend at interest*, *BGU*1246. 24 (iii B. C.); *exact interest*, Lxx *De.*23.19(20). **II.** *make to bring forth*, Sm.*Is.*66.9. **-ος**, ον, (τίκτω) = ἔκγονος, Ael.*NA*10.14.

ἔκτολμος, ον, *audacious*, f.l. in Suid. s.v. λαῖμα. Adv. **-μως** Man. 3.331.

ἑκτολογ-έομαι, (ἕκτη) *to be subject to a tax of one-sixth* of the produce, ἀμπελὼν -λογούμενος *Arch.Pap.*5.392. **-ία**, ἡ, *tax of one-sixth*, *PRyl.*225.52 (ii/iii A. D.).

ἐκτολῡπεύω, *wind off* a ball of wool: metaph., *bring to an end*, χαλεπὸν πόνον ἐκτολυπεύσας Hes.*Sc.*44; οὐδὲν.. καίριον ἐκτολυπεύσειν A.*Ag.*1032 (lyr.).

ἐκτομ-άζω, *castrate*, *Gloss.* **-άς**, άδος, ἡ, *wicket-gate*, Aen.Tact. 24.5, *Stud.Pal.*20.211.9. **II.** = περικεφαλαία, Hsch. **III.** a kind of *spear* (nisi leg. ἐκτομάδια), Id. **-εύς**, έως, ὁ, (ἐκτέμνω) *one that cuts out*, Id. **-ή**, ἡ, (ἐκτέμνω) *cutting out, excision*, Plu.*Alc.*16 (pl.): metaph., ἡδονῶν, λόγου, Ph.1.450,170; *cutting off*, καρπῶν Porph. ap.Eus.*PE*3.11. **2.** *castration*, Hdt.3.48,49, Pl.*Smp.*195c (pl.), etc. **b.** *circumcision* of women, Str.16.2.37. **II.** *segment*, Plu. *Num.*13; ἐ. γῆς *sod*, Id.*Pomp.*41 (pl.). **2.** *cutting*, κρημνώδης Id. *Flam.*3. **3.** *excision* in woodwork, Ph.*Bel.*64.27 (pl.). **-ιαῖος**, α, ον, = sq., σῦς *PMag.Par.*1.3118. **-ίας**, ου, ὁ, *one that is castrated, eunuch*, παῖδες ἐ. Hdt.3.92; ἐκτομίαν ποιεῖν τινα Id.6.9; βόες ἐ. Arist. *Pr.*897b27; κάπρος Antiph.133.5. **-ίζω**, = ἐκτέμνω, ἐκδομίζοντος (sic) αὐτοῦ τὴν ὅλην ἀλήθειαν *PMag.Par.*1.2452. **-ίς**, ίδος, ἡ, pecul. fem. of ἐκτομεύς, *cutting down*, δρεπάνη καυλῶν *AP*6.21.2. **II.** ἐ. (sc. μήτρα), = ἐκβολάς, Ath.3.101a. **-ον**, τό, *black hellebore*, Hp.*Mul.*1.78, Thphr.*HP*9.10.4, Diocl.*Fr.*151; but, *white hellebore*, Ps.-Dsc.4.148. **II.** ἔκτομος (sc. λίθος), ὁ, *stone forming interior angle*, *Rev.Phil.*29.240 (Didyma), 49.6 (ibid.).

ἐκτονίζομαι, *lose force*, -ιζομένου πνεύματος Herod.Med. in *Rh.Mus.* 58.99.

ἐκτοξεύω, *shoot out, shoot away*, τὰ βέλη ἐξετετόξευτο Hdt.1.214, etc.; ἐ. γραφήν Hld.9.5: metaph., τὸ σῶφρον ἐξετόξευσεν *has shot away all* its *arrows*, i.e. has no resource left, E.*Andr.*365; νομίζων ἐκτετοξεῦσθαι βίον Ar.*Pl.*34. **2.** metaph., *reject, banish*, ἀλήθειαν Ph.1.528:—Pass., ὑπερόριος ἐ. ib.252. **3.** abs., *shoot from* a place, *shoot arrows*, X.*An.*7.8.14, Arr.*An.*1.1.11. **4.** Pass., of the pulse, Gal.8.486.

ἐκτοπ-ίζω, *remove from* a place, *PTeb.*38.18 (ii B. C., Pass.), etc.; ἐ.

ἑαυτούς *take* themselves *off*, Arist.*Mir.*842^{b}12, Plb.1.74.7, Lxx 2*Ma.* 8.13; ἐκτετοπισμένα *remote regions*, Str.3.4.19; "Ομηρος ἐκτοπίζει τὸν Ἰάσονος πλοῦν Sch.Pi.*P.*4.370, cf. Max.Tyr.14.2; ἄνθρωποι -τετοπισμένοι τῆς καθ' ἡμᾶς οἰκουμένης *outside the bounds of* our world, Procl.*in Cra.*p.74 P. 2. metaph., ἐ. εἰς μῦθον *pervert* into a fable, Str.4.1.7. II. intr., *take oneself from a place, go abroad*, like ἀποδημέω, οἱ ἐκτοπίζοντες τύραννοι ἀπὸ τῆς οἰκείας Arist.*Pol.*1314^{b}9, etc.; of birds of passage and fish, *to migrate*, Id.*HA*600^{a}14. 2. metaph., of a speaker, *travel far*, Id.*Rh.*1414^{b}28. III. *avoid, shun*, τὸν πολιτισμόν D.L.4.39. **-ιος**, α, ον, = ἔκτοπος, ἀπάγετ' ἐ. με S.*OT*1340 (lyr.); ἐ. συθείς Id.*OC*119 (lyr.); ἠνύσατ' ἐκτοπίαν φλόγα, = ἐξετοπίσατε (as the Sch.), ye have *put away* the fire, Id.*OT*166 (lyr.). II. *foreign*, Ath.14.659a; *outlandish*, ὁρμαί Orph.*H.*58.10. **-ισις**, εως, ἡ, *removal from a place, deportation*, Gloss. **-ισμός**, ὁ, *migration*, τοὺς ἐ. ποιεῖσθαι Arist.*HA*599^{a}4. II. *being away, distance*, Str.4.5.5, prob. in Cic.*Att.*12.12.1. **-ιστικός**, ή, όν, *migratory*, ἐ. ζῷα, opp. ἐπιδημητικά, Arist.*HA*488^{a}14; βίος Id.*PA*694^{a}5. **-ος**, ον, *away from a place*, c. gen., τῶνδ' ἑδράνων πάλιν ἔ. ἔκθορε S.*OC*233 (lyr.); *distant*, ἄρουρα Id.*Tr.*32; ἔ. ἔστω let him *leave the place*, E.*Ba.* 69 (anap.). II. *foreign, strange*, [τέθνηκεν] αὐτὴ πρὸς αὑτῆς, οὐδενὸς πρὸς ἐκτόπου by no *strange* hand, S.*Tr.*1132. 2. *out of the way, strange, extraordinary*, δένδρον Ar.*Av.*1474 (lyr.); ὁτιοῦν τῶν ἐ. Pl. *Lg.*799c; χειμών Thphr.*CP*6.18.12; ἱστορία ἔ. Plu.2.977e; of persons, *eccentric*, Arist.*Pr.*954^{b}2. Adv. -πως *extraordinarily*, Id.*Mir.* 833^{a}14, *PPetr.*3 p.150, Plb.32.3.8: Comp. -ωτέρως Arist.*Metaph.*989^b 30 codd. 3. ἔκτοπον· ἔξοδον, Hsch.

'Εκτόρειος, 'Εκτόρεος, v. "Εκτωρ.

ἐκτορεύω, *chase*, Hld.2.11 (Pass.).

ἐκτορέω, *transfix*, αἰῶνα *h.Merc.*42.

ἐκτορμέω, (τόρμη) *turn from the way*, Paus.Gr.*Fr.*310.

ἐκτορνεύω, *carve*, Sm.*Ex.*25.35(36).

ἔκτορνος, ον, *rounded*, ἀξονίσκος Ph.*Bel.*76.25.

ἕκτος, η, ον, (ἕξ) *sixth*, Il.2.407, etc.; ἕκτος (sc. μήν), ὁ, Plu.2.268a; ἕκτη, ἡ, v. sub voc. (ϝέκτ- *Tab.Heracl.*2.106.)

ἐκτός, ή, όν, (ἔχω) ; ἐκτά, τά, the *qualities* of substances (opp. aggregates), *Stoic.*2.129,150; ἐκτά in Ath.10.420d appears to be corrupt.

ἐκτός (ἐχθός, *IG*9(1).333 (Locr., v B.C.), *Michel*995 *C*35 (Delph.), etc.), Adv., (ἐκ) *without, outside*, opp. ἐντός: 1. as Prep. with gen., which may either precede or follow, ἐ. κλισίης Il.14.13; τείχεος ἐ. 21.608; *out of, far from*, καπνοῦ καὶ κύματος ἐ. Od.12.219; esp. in prov. phrases (v. ἔξω I fin.), ἐ. κλαυμάτων ἔχειν πόδα S.*Ph.* 1260; ἐ. ἔχειν πόδα (sc. τῶν κακῶν) Pi.*P.*4.289; ἐ. τῶν ἐλαῶν *beyond* the olives, i.e. out of the course, Ar.*Ra.*995 (lyr.); Geom., *beyond*, τοῦ A σημείου Apollon.Perg.*Con.*1.8, al.; also ἐ. ἀτασθαλίης *outside of, free from*.., Thgn.754, cf. 744; ἐ. αἰτίης Hdt.4.133, A.*Pr.*332, etc.; ἐ. πημάτων S.*Ph.*504; ἄτας Id.*Ant.*614 (lyr.); τῶν κακῶν Id.*Fr.*724, cf. Pl.*Grg.*523b; ἐ. στρατειῶν *exempt from*.., Id.*R.*498c; ἐ. ἑωυτῆς *beside* herself, *out of* her wits, Hp.*Epid.*7.90, cf. S.*Aj.*640 (lyr.); ἐ. ἐλπίδος *beyond* hope, Id.*Ant.*330; ἡ ἐ. καὶ παρ' ἐλπίδας χαρά, i.e. ἡ ἐκτὸς ἐλπίδων καὶ παρ' ἐλπίδας, ib.392; δοκημάτων ἐ. E.*HF*771 (lyr.). 2. of Time, *beyond*, πέντε ἡμερέων Hdt.3.80. 3. *except*, *IG* l.c., etc.; ἐ. ὀλίγων X.*HG*1.2.3; *besides, apart from*, Pl.*Grg.* 474d, *PTeb.*19.7 (ii B.C.), etc.: abs., *besides, as well*, *GDI*1742.12; also ἐ. εἰ μή *unless*, 1*Ep.Cor.*15.2, Herod.Med.ap.Orib.7.8.1, Vett. Val.37.20, al., Luc.*Pisc.*6; ἐ. ἐὰν μή *Cat.Cod.Astr.*7.216; ἐ. ὅτι.. Hld.10.5. 4. *without the consent of*, τινός *PMag.Par.*1.356. II. abs., ἃ δ' ἐ. *external things*, E.*Ion*231 (lyr.), cf. Plb.2.4.8, etc.; οἱ ἐ. *strangers, foreigners*, Pl.*Lg.*629d, Plb.2.47.10, etc.; also, *the vulgar, the common herd*: *the Gentiles*, Lxx *Si.prol.*4. III. with Verbs of motion, ῥίπτειν ἐ. to throw *out*, S.*Tr.*269; ἧξας Id.*El.*1402 (lyr.); ἐκπέμπειν Id.*Ant.*18; ἕλκειν Pl.*R.*616a; οὐκ ἐ. εἶ; = ἔξιθι, S.*OT*676; χώρει ἐ. E.*IA*1117; εἰ δ' ἐ. ἔλθοις if thou *transgressest*, S.*Tr.*1189.

ἔκτοσε, Adv. *outwards*: c. gen., *out of*, ἔκτοσε χειρός Od.14.277.

ἔκτοσθε and **-θεν** (not only before vowels, cf. Il.7.341, al.), Adv., = ἔκτοθεν, *outside*, c. gen., τείχεος ἔ. 9.552; αὐλῆς, δόμων, Od.7. 112, 23.148; θεῶν ἔκτοσθεν ἁπάντων *out of the number of* the gods, Hes.*Th.*813; ἔ. παλαίστρας Theoc.2.51. 2. abs., ἔ... πάγοι ὀξέες *outside* are.., Od.5.411; ἔ. γενέσθαι to be *delirious*, Hp.*Epid.*5.85.—Ion. and late Prose, as Luc.*Merc.Cond.*41.

ἔκτοτε, Adv. for ἐκ τότε, *thereafter*, Socr.Rhod.1, Arr.*An.*1.26. 4, Plu.*Caes.*48, *POxy.*486.9 (ii A.D.), Vett.Val.168.28, Sm.*Is.*16.13, Sch.D.T.p.427 H.: condemned by Luc.*Sol.*7.

ἐκτότης, ητος, ἡ, *being* ἐκτός, *absence*, νόσου Gal.10.54.

ἐκτρᾰγῳδέω, *deck out in tragic phrase, exaggerate*, Plb.6.15.7, Agath. 4.8:—Pass., Plb.6.56.8. 2. *declaim tragically*, Ps.-Luc.*Philopatr.* 18; simply, *declaim*, Ath.9.403d. 3. *describe impressively*, Luc. *Tox.*11. II. *unmask*, Id.*Pisc.*38, *Merc.Cond.*41.

ἐκτρᾰνόω, *signify clearly*, Astramps.*Onir.*57.

ἐκτράπεζος [ᾰ], ον, *banished from the table*, Luc.*Gall.*4.

ἐκτρᾰπελόγαστρος, ον, *with an enormous paunch*, ὄνοι Epich.67.

ἐκτράπελος [ᾰ], ον, *turning from the common course, perverse, strange*, νόμοι Thgn.290, cf. Pherecr.145.23, Ael.*NA*14.9; ζῷα (i.e. Κύκλωπες) Hermog.*Id.*2.10; *monstrous*, of huge children, Plin.*HN*7. 76. Adv. -λως, ἔσθων *AP*11.402 (Luc.). II. *odious*, κέρδεα, ἔπος, prob. in Pi.*P.*1.92, 4.105.

ἐκτράπω, Ion. for ἐκτρέπω.

ἔκτρας· ἐν ῥυμῷ πάσσαλος, Hsch. (leg. ἔκτρα· ὁ).

ἐκτρᾰχηλ-ίζω, Att. fut. -ιῶ, prop. of a horse, *throw the rider over its head*, X.*Cyr.*1.4.8, Plu.2.58f: generally, *break* a person's *neck*, Ar. *Lys.*705; *overturn*, τὰ ὄρη *Tab.Defix.Aud.*271.26 (Hadrumetum, iii A.D.); κλίμακας Ph.*Bel.*85.38:—Pass., *break one's neck*, Ar.*Nu.*1501, *Pl.*70, Luc.*Merc.Cond.*42. 2. metaph., *ruin, pervert*, D.9.51, Luc. *Rh.Pr.*10, Alciphr.3.40, Porph.*Abst.*1.42; εἰς ὑπερηφανίαν Mich. *in EN*523.20:—Pass., εἰς ἀτόπους πράξεις Ph.*Fr.*102 H. II. metaph., *cause to lose control of one's language*, ἐ. τινὰς αἱ τραγῳδίαι Hermog. *Id.*1.6. III. *behead, Gloss.* **-ισμός**, ὁ, *beheading*, Id.

ἐκτρᾰχύνω [ῡ], *make rough*, τὴν ἐπιφάνειαν ἐκτετραχυσμένος Luc. *Pisc.*51. II. metaph., *exasperate*, Plu.*Alc.*14; τὸ πλῆθος App. *BC*2.12:—Pass., ἐκτραχύνεσθαι πρός τινα Plu.*Arat.*49: abs., App.*BC* 1.10.

ἐκτρέπω, Ion. **-τράπω** [ᾰ], *turn out of the course, turn aside*, τοῦ ποταμοῦ τὸ ῥέεθρον Hdt.1.186, cf. 2.11, Th.5.65; μηδ' εἰς 'Ελένην κότον ἐκτρέψῃς A.*Ag.*1464 (lyr.), cf. *Th.*628 (lyr.); τὸ δυστυχὲς δὲ τοῦτ' ἐς ἄλλον ἐκτρέπει E.*Supp.*483; ἑαυτοῦ μιαρίαν εἴς τινα ἐ. Antipho 2. 3.9; ἐ. [τινὰ] πρὸς ποίμνας S.*Aj.*53:—Pass. and Med., *turn off* or *aside*, ἐκτραπέσθαι ὁδὸν μακροτέρην Hdt.1.104: abs., Id.2.80, X.*HG*7. 4.22, etc.: c. gen., *turn aside from*, τοῦ πρόσθεν λόγου S.*OT*851; also ἐ. ἐκ.. Hdt.1.75; ἀπὸ.. ἐπί.. Pl.*Sph.*222a; πόθεν δεῦρο ἐξετραπόμεθα Id.*R.*543c. 2. *turn* a person *off the road, order* him *out of the way*, S.*OT*806:—Pass. (fut. -τραπήσομαι Luc.*Herm.*86) and Med., ἐκτρέπεσθαί τινα *get out of* one's *way*, D.19.225, cf. Ar.*Pl.*837, Luc.*Tim.* 5; *avoid*, τὸν ἔλεγχον Plb.35.4.14; τὴν φιλοσοφίαν Jul.*Or.*7.223d: c. inf., ὀφθῆναι *AP*10.56.10 (Pall.): abs., cj. in S.*OC*1541. 3. τὴν δρῶσαν ἐ. *prevent* her *from* acting, Id.*El.*350. 4. ἀσπίδας θύρσοις ἐ. *turn* shields *and flee before* the thyrsus, E.*Ba.*799. II. Med., *turn away*, φίλους Democr.101; also ἐκτρέπεσθαι τὰ ἐντὸς ἐκτός *turns itself* inside out, Arist.*HA*621^{a}7. III. Medic. in Pass., *to be diverted* or *everted*, Hp.*Steril.*213, *Off.*14, Dsc.2.15 (perh. *to be put out of joint*, *Ep.Hebr.*12.13, *Hippiatr.*26). IV. *turn* or *change*, εἰς ἄσπορον *PRyl.*133.22 (i A.D.), cf. Ael.*NA*14.28:—Pass., εἰς ὀλιγαρχίαν ἐκτραπῆναι Plb.6.4.9; ὑπ' ἀγεννείας εἰς μέμψεις Arr. *Epict.*1.6.42. V. Pass., *to be brought to birth*, Astrol. t.t., Vett. Val.50.27, al.

ἐκτρέφω, *bring up from childhood, rear up*, Hdt.1.122, A.*Ch.*750, etc.; ἐξέφυσε κἀξέθρεψέ με S.*OT*827; ἐκτεθραμμένοι σκύμνοι λεόντων *true-bred*.., E.*Supp.*1222; of plants, τὸ ἐκτρέφον τὴν ῥίζαν Hdt. 1.193; ἐκτρέφει ἡ γῆ τὸ σπέρμα X.*Oec.*17.10; ποταμοῦ πνεῦμα τραχύτερον ἐκθρέψαντος Plu.2.357d:—Med., *rear up for oneself*, τινά *h.Cer.* 166; ἤνεγκα κἀξέσωσα κἀξεθρεψάμην, says the παιδαγωγός, S.*El.*13, cf. *Fr.*387, Pl.*Lg.*929a:—Pass., εἴ σοί τις υἱός ἐστιν ἐκτεθραμμένος Ar.*Nu.*796; ἐγένου τε καὶ ἐξετράφης Pl.*Cri.*50e, cf. Lys.19.8. II. Med., of pregnant animals, *nourish*, [ζῷα] μεγάλα ἐντὸς ἐκθρέψωνται Pl.*Ti.*91d:—Act., *bring to birth*, τὰ κυήματα Arist.*GA*773^{a}34.

ἐκτρέχω, fut. -δρᾰμοῦμαι Diph.19.3: pf. ἐκδεδράμηκα Arist.*Aud.* 802^{a}21:—*run out* or *forth*, ἐκ δὲ θύραζε ἔδραμον ἀμφ' Ἀχιλῆα Il.18.30; τῆς συγκλήτου εἰς τὸν δῆμον Hdn.7.11.5; *make a sally*, ἐκ πόλεως Th. 4.25, etc.; ἐπὶ [σῦν] Arist.*Fr.*571, cf. *PGurob* 8.11 (iii B.C.). 2. *run off* or *away*, Ar.*Av.*991. 3. of horns, *spring up, grow*, ταχέως Arist.*Aud.* l.c.; of plants, *run* or *shoot up*, Thphr.*CP*2.15.5: c. gen., ἐ. τῶν ἄλλων Id.*HP*6.8.1. 4. c. acc., *exceed*, τὸν καιρόν Lycon ap. D.L.5.65: abs., of anger, *exceed bounds*, S.*OC*438. 5. *digress, wander from the point*, Corp.Herm.1.16. 6. c. gen., *escape from the clutches of*, δανειστοῦ App.*Fr.*22. b. *to be born of*, τῆς μητρός Lib. *Ep.*1036.9. 7. of Time, *expire, come to an end*, *PSI*4.444 (iii B.C.).

ἔκτρεψις, εως, ἡ, *displacement, distortion*, Hp.*Off.*3.

ἔκ-τρημα, ατος, τό, *hole made in trepanning*, Heliod.ap.Orib.46.11. 16. **-τρησις**, εως, ἡ, *hole*, Hp.*Steril.*222 (pl.), Aret.*SD*2.13 (pl.), Heliod.ap.Orib.46.11.26.

ἐκτρῐαινόω, *shake with the trident*, 'Ελλάδα Ps.-Theopomp.Hist.ap. Luc.*Pseudol.*29.

ἐκ-τρῐβή, ἡ, = ἔκτριψις, *destruction*, Lxx *De.*4.26. **-τρίβω** [ῑ], fut. Pass. -τρῐβήσομαι S.*OT*428:—*rub out*, i.e. *produce by rubbing*, πῦρ ἔκ τινος X.*Cyr.*2.2.15; φλόγα Poll.9.155 (but in S.*Ph.*296 ἐν πέτροισι πέτρον ἐκτρίβων.. ἔφην' ἄφαντον φῶς *rubbing hard*): metaph., λύπην Plu.2.610b:—Pass., τὰ ψυχικὰ προτερήματα διὰ τὰ ἔπαθλα οἷον ἐκτρίβεται Longin.44.3. II. *rub out*, i.e. *to destroy root and branch*, σφέας πίτυος τρόπον ἀπείλεε ἐκτρίψειν (cf. πίτυς) Hdt.6.37; ἐ. τινὰ πρόρριζον E.*Hipp.*684; τὴν ποίην ἐκ τῆς γῆς ἐκτρίβειν Hdt.4.120; αὕτη μ' ἡ γυνή ποτ' ἐκτρίψει Herod.6.27, dub. in E.*Cyc.*475; βίον ἐ. *bring* life *to a wretched end*, = Lat. *conterere vitam*, S.*OT*248, cf. 428:—Pass., πρόρριζος ἐκτέτριπται Hdt.6.86.δ'; ὁπλὰς ἐκτετριμμένος with the hoofs *worn off*, Luc.*Asin.*19. III. *rub constantly, wear out*, "Ατλας.. νώτοις οὐρανὸν ἐκτρίβων E.*Ion* 2 (s.v.l.). IV. *rub, thresh out*, f.l. in Nic.*Fr.*68.3. V. *polish*, Thphr.*HP*4.11.6, Plb. 10.20.2; ἀργυρώματα *Class.Phil.*19.234 (iii B.C.); cf. ἐξετρίβετο· σφόδρα ἐκοσμεῖτο, Hsch. 2. *wipe out*, Herod.1.79. **-τριμμα**, ατος, τό, *sore caused by rubbing, excoriation*, Hp.*Fract.*29 (pl.); ἐκτρίμματα ὑποδημάτων Dsc.2.151. II. *rubber, towel*, Philox.2.41. **-τριψις**, εως, ἡ, *violent friction*, νεφῶν D.L.2.9; πνεύματος Ruf.*Onom.*228. II. *destruction*, Lxx *Nu.*15.31.

ἔκτρομος, ον, *trembling*, v.l. for ἔντρ., *Ep.Hebr.*12.21; τὸν ποιοῦντα ἔ. τὴν γῆν ἅπασαν *Tab.Defix.Aud.*271.26 (Hadrumetum, iii A.D.).

ἐκτροπ-ή, ἡ, (ἐκτρέπω) *turning off* or *aside*, ἐ. ὕδατος *diversion* of water from its channel, Th.5.65; διὰ τὰς ἐ. τὰς ἐπὶ τὴν χώραν on account of [the river] *being turned off* over the country, Plb.9.43. 5. II. (from Med.) *turning aside, escape*, μόχθων *from* labours, A.*Pr.*913; ἐ. (sc. λόγου) *a digression*, Pl.*Plt.*267a, Aeschin.3.206

(pl.), D.Chr.7.128 (pl.); ἐπὶ τὴν ἐ. ἐπάνιμεν the *point from which we digressed*, Plb.4.21.12; ἡ ἐπὶ ταύτας τὰς αἰτίας ἐ. Arist.*Metaph.* 1089ᵃ1. 2. *fork, branch* in a road, Ar.*Ra.*113, E.*Rh.*881, X. *HG*7.1.29, Aen.Tact.15.6 (pl.); *bypath*, σκολιαὶ ἐ. D.S.3.15,26, cf. Varro *Sat.Men.Fr.*418 B. b. *branch* of a canal, *PPetr.*2 p.40 (iii B.C.). 3. ἐ. ὀνόματος *a collateral form*, Ath.11.490e. 4. ἐκτροπαὶ ποταμῶν *overflowings*, Lyd.*Ost.*55. 5. metaph., *change of life*, Philostr.*VA*6.36. 6. Astrol. t.t., *moment of birth*, Vett.Val. 51.37, al., Ptol.*Tetr.*108. b. = ὡροσκόπος, Paul.Al.*R.*1. 7. Medic., *eversion* of the eyelid, Antyll.ap.Aët.7.74, Id.ap.Orib.10.23. 24. **-ιάζομαι**, *expel as accursed*, Eust.1070 fin. **-ίας** οἶνος *turned* (i.e. *sour*) wine, Alciphr.1.20, Poll.1.248. **-ιον**, τό, *everted eyelid*, a disease in which the lid is turned outward, opp. τριχίασις, Cels.7.7, Antyll.ap.Aët.7.74, Dem.Ophth.ib.73. **-ος**, ον, *turning out of the way*. Adv. -πως Erot. s. v. ἐκπατίως.

ἐκτροφή, ἡ, *bringing up, rearing, nurture*, E.*Fr.*317.5 (pl.), Sor.1. 81, Arist.*HA*542ᵃ30 (pl.), *GA*754ᵃ8, al.; ἐ. καρπῶν J.*AJ*5.1.21: metaph., *breeding*, κακοδαιμονίας Phld.*Ir.*p.27 W.

ἔκτροφος, ἡ, *nursing mother*, *Epigr.Gr.*872.6 (Patmos).

ἐκτροφωλέων· σποδοειδῶν, Hsch. (Cf. τροφιωδέων· σποδιωδῶν, Erot.; ἐκ στροφωδέων Hp.*Prorrh.*1.156 codd.)

ἐκτροχάζω, *rush out*, Apollod.2.7.3. II. *treat summarily*, Dsc. *Ther.*2.

ἐκτρόχαλον· ἔκτροχον, Hsch.

ἐκτρῠγ-άω, *gather in the vintage*, *PGurob* 8.10 (iii B.C.), Lxx *Le.* 25.5. **-ίζω**, *clear from lees*, *Gp.*5.2.12 (Pass.); of molten silver, prob. in *PLeid.X.*20 (ἐκτροχιστῇ Pap.).

ἐκτρῡπ-άω, *bore* or *hollow out*, πρέμνον *Gp.*10.23.5, cf. Ph.*Bel.*92. 8. II. intr., *slip out through a hole*, Ar.*Ec.*337. **-ημα**, ατος, τό, *dust made by boring*, Thphr.*HP*5.6.3. II. pl., *holes* made in a wall, Ph.*Bel.*92.16. **-ησις**, εως, ἡ, *boring through*, Hp.*Ep.*22: pl., Ph.*Bel.*100.36.

ἐκτρῠφάω, *to be over-luxurious*, Clearch.39, Ath.12.519f.

ἐκτρῡχόω, *wear out, grind down, exhaust*, Th.3.93, 7.48:—Pass., ὑπὸ πόνων Luc.*Merc.Cond.*39; ῥάκη ἐκτετρυχωμένα *worn-out* rags, Id.*Tox.*30.

ἐκτρύχω [ῡ], = foreg., D.C.77.9.

ἐκτρύω, aor. -έτρῡσα, *wear out*, τινὰ ταῖς ἀπορίαις App.*BC*2.66; cf. ἐκτρυωθείς (sic)· φθαρείς, Hsch.

ἐκτρώγω, *eat up, devour*, Ar.*V.*155, Lxx *Mi.*7.4:—Pass., of a letter in a Ms., Demetr.Lac.*Herc.*1012.26 F.

ἔκ-τρωμα, ατος, τό, = παιδίον νεκρὸν ἄωρον, Hsch.; *untimely birth*, Arist.*GA*773ᵇ18 (pl.), Lxx *Jb.*3.16, al., 1*Ep.Cor.*15.8, Ph.1.59; as a term of contempt, Tz.*H.*5.515. **-τρωμᾰτιαῖος**, *abortive*, *Gloss.*:— also **-τρωμᾰτικός**, Id. **-τρωμᾰτισμός**, ὁ, = ἐκτρωσμός, Id. **-τρωσις**, εως, ἡ, *miscarriage*, Arist.*Pr.*860ᵃ18 (pl.); ἐκτρώσει ἐν τόκῳ v.l. in Hp.*Mul.*2.122, cf. Sor.2.49. **-τρωσμός**, ὁ, = foreg., Arist.*HA*583ᵇ 12, Aret.*SD*2.11, *Sammelb.*3451.5; *attempted abortion*, Hp.*Mul.*1.78, Ptol.*Tetr.*116. **-τρωτικός**, ή, όν, *abortive*, δύναμις Plu.2.974d.

ἐκτῠλίσσω, *unfold, develop*, ἕλικα Ti.Locr.97c.

ἐκτῠλ-όω, *excise a callosity*, Antyll.ap.Orib.44.23.32, Crito ap. Gal.13.794. **-ωσις**, εως, ἡ, *removal of callosity*, Paul.Aeg.4. 49. **-ωτέον**, *one must excise a callosity*, Id.3.75. **-ωτικός**, ή, όν, *removing callosities*, Antyll.ap.Orib.44.23.29, cf. Paul.Aeg.4.49.

ἐκτυμπάνωσις [ᾰ], εως, ἡ, *swelling out like a drum*, τῆς γαστέρος Str.16.4.13.

ἔκτῠπε, 3 sg. aor. 2 of κτυπέω. **ἐκτυπέω**, f.l. for ἐκκτυπέω (q.v.).

ἔκτῠπ-ος, ον, *worked in relief*, Ion Trag.42, Aristeas 58, D.S.18. 26, etc.; φιάλη.. ἔ. ζῷα ἔχουσα *IG*11(2).161 *B*76 (Delos, iii B.C.); ἔκτυπα, τά, Plin.*HN*35.152. 2. *distinct*, φαντασία *Stoic.*2.21: Comp., Hsch. Adv. -πως *with a distinct impression* or *character*, opp. συγκεχυμένως, S.E.*M.*7.171. II. *formed in outline*: ἔκτυπον, τό, *rough sketch*, δι' ἐκτύπων γεγραμμένη [ἱστορία] Marcellin.*Vit.Thuc.* 44. **-όω**, *model* or *work in relief*, ἐν τῷ βάθρῳ τὰ ἑαυτοῦ ἔργα ἐξετύπωσεν X.*Eq.*1.1:—Pass., οἱ ἐν στήλαις ἐκτετυπωμένοι Pl.*Smp.*193a, cf. *Ti.*50d; οἱ ἐκτυπωθέντες *these who are formed on this model*, Isoc. 13.18; *to be shaped*, ἐν τῇ διεξόδῳ Hp.*Prorrh.*2.4; εἰς τὸν Πρίαπον Porph.ap.Eus.*PE*3.11; of the foetus, Agath.4.25. II. metaph. in Med., ἐκτυποῦσθαί τι εἰς ὕδωρ, etc., *form an image* of a thing in.., Pl.*Tht.*206d, cf. *Lg.*775d. **-ωμα**, ατος, τό, *figure in relief*, Id.*Ti.* 50d, Apion ap.J.*Ap.*2.2, Philostr.*VA*2.33; ἐκτυπωμάτων πρόσωπα Men.24.4. II. *reflection*, of light, Olymp.*in Mete.*33.1. **-ωσις**, εως, ἡ, *modelling in relief*, Aesar.ap.Stob.1.49.27. II. *figure*, J. *AJ*12.2.9. 2. metaph., *allegory*, Ph.1.163. **-ωτός**, ή, όν, = ἔκτυπος, *IG*11(2).199 *B*7 (Delos, iii B.C.).

ἐκτυφλ-όω, *make quite blind*, τινά Batr.238, Hdt.4.2, 9.93, X.*Eq.* 10.2, Ar.*Pl.*301, etc.; ἐκτυφλοῦν τιν' ἀστραπή Antiph.195.4: abs., κονιορτὸς ἐκτυφλῶν Ar.*Fr.*569.2:—Pass., λαμπτῆρες ἐκτυφλωθέντες σκότῳ (expl. by σβεσθέντες in Sch.) A.*Ch.*536: metaph., Philostr. *VA*4.36; of buds destroyed by hail, Id.*Her.*2.11. **-ωσις**, εως, ἡ, *making blind*, Hdt.9.94.

ἔκτυφος [prob. ῠ], ον, *deluding, empty*, μοῦσα Oenom.ap.Eus.*PE* 5.11.

ἐκτῡφόω, *delude, deceive*, τὰ πλήθη Ph.1.1. 2. *puff up*, ἑαυτόν Id.2.569, cf. 215:—Pass., Plb.16.21.12. II. Pass., *vanish into smoke*, εἰς καπνὸν ἐκτυφοῦται Dsc.1.68.2; but perh. ἐκτύφεται shd. be read; ἐκτύφονται is v.l. for -τυφοῦνται in Id.1.68.5.

ἐκτύφω [ῡ], *burn in a slow fire*; cf. ἐξύθυψεν (sic, post ἐξήια)· ἐξέκαυσεν, Hsch.:—metaph. in Med., ἔρωτα ἐκτύφεσθαι *light a slow fire* of love, Alciphr.3.50:—Pass., aor. 2 ἐξετύφην [ῠ], ἐξ. κλαίουσα my face *swelled up* with weeping, Men.*Epit.Fr.*9.

ἕκτωρ, ορος, ὁ, ἡ, (ἔχω, cf. Pl.*Cra.*393a) *holding fast*, v.l. for ἕστωρ, Il.24.272, cf. *EM*383.25; epith. of Zeus, Sapph.157; of anchors, ἕκτορες πλημμυρίδος Lyc.100, cf. Luc.*Lex.*15: as Subst., = κροκύφαντος, *hair-net*, Leon.ap.Hsch.; also pl., = πάσσαλοι ἐν ῥυμῷ, Id. II. Hom. only as pr. n. Hector, *the prop* or *stay* of Troy, οἶος γὰρ ἐρύετο Ἴλιον Ἕκτωρ Il.6.403:—Adj. **Ἑκτόρεος**, α or η, ον, also ος, ον E.*Rh.* 1 (anap.):—*of Hector*, Hom., B.12.154, etc.: also **Ἑκτόρειος**, ον, Anaxil.38; κόμαι Lyc.1133.

ἔκυλος· εἶδος βοτάνης, Suid.

ἑκῠρ-ά, ἡ, Ep. for πενθερά, *mother-in-law*, Il.22.451, 24.770; also in Plu.2.143a, *CIG*(add.)3846*q* (Aezani). **-εύω**, Boeot. **ἑκουρεύω**, *to be a father-in-law*, Corinn.*Supp.*2.85. **-ός**, ὁ, Ep. for πενθερός, *father-in-law*, Il.3.172, 24.770, also *CIG*9136 (Cyrene), Jul.*Or.*3.127c. [ῡ only in *AP*14.9.] (I.-E. *swek̑uro-, cf. Skt. *śváśuras*, Lat. *socer*, etc.)

ἔκῠσα, aor. 1 of κυνέω; but **ἔκῡσα**, of κύω. **ἐκφᾰγεῖν**, v. ἐξεσθίω.

ἐκφαιδρύνω, strengthd. for φαιδρύνω, *make quite bright, clear away*, σταγόνα ἐκ παρηΐδων E.*Ba.*768.

ἐκφαίνω, fut. -φᾰνῶ, Ion. -φανέω in Luc.*Syr.D.*32: aor. ἐξέφηνα, Dor. -έφᾱνα Pi.*N.*4.68:—Pass., Ep. aor. 1 -εφαάνθην Il.13.278. I. of persons, *bring to light, reveal*, σήμερον ἄνδρα φόωσδε.. Εἰλείθυια ἐκφανεῖ 19.104; ἐ. τινά *produce* him, Hdt.3.36; εἰ μὴ τὸν αὐτόχειρα.. ἐκφανεῖτ' ἐς ὀφθαλμοὺς ἐμούς S.*Ant.*307, cf. *OT*329: c. part., ἐ. σεωυτὸν ἐόντα τοῦ πατρὸς οὐδὲν ἧσσω Hdt.3.71; κακοὺς θνητῶν ἐξέφηνε.. χρόνος E.*Hipp.*428:—Pass., οὕνεκ' Ἀχιλλεὺς ἐξεφάνη *showed himself, came forth to view*, Il.19.46, cf. Od.10.260, al.; Χαρύβδιος ἐξεφαάνθη he *came up from out* Charybdis, 12.441; ὅ τε δειλὸς ἀνὴρ ὅς τ' ἄλκιμος ἐξεφαάνθη *is revealed*, Il.13.278; δίκαιοι δ' αὖθις [ὄντες] ἐκφανούμεθα S.*Ph.*82; σὺ μέν.. ἐκφανεῖ κακή Id.*OT*1063; ἕκτον ἦμαρ ἐκπεφασμένος Id.*Ichn.*273. 2. *inform against*, τινά *Cod.Just.*1.5.16.5. II. of things, *bring to light*, δῶρα καὶ κράτος ἐγγενές Pi.*N.*4.68; *disclose, reveal*, τινὶ ἄρρητα ἱρά Hdt.6.135, al. (so abs., ὡς τὸ μαντεῖον ἐξέφηνεν.. ἐμοί S.*OT*243); ἐ. ἑωυτοῦ γνώμην Hdt.5.36; τὴν αἰτίην Id.6.3; τὴν ἀληθείην Id.1.117; λόγον E.*Hipp.*881; ἐ. ἐς φάος κακά ib.368; δειλίαν Pl.*Mx.*246e:—Pass., with fut. Med., *shine out*, οἱ ὄσσε δεινὸν ὑπὸ βλεφάρων, ὡς εἰ σέλας, ἐξεφάανθεν Il.19.17; *appear plainly*, πλευρὰ παρ' ἀσπίδος ἐξεφαάνθη 4.468, cf. Diog.Apoll.6; ἀστέρων ἐκφανέντων Th.2.28, cf. Phld.*Sign.*10: metaph., ταὶ Διωνύσου πόθεν ἐξέφᾰνεν (for -ησαν) χάριτες; Pi.*O.*13.18; ἐκφανήσεται *it shall be disclosed*, E.*Hipp.* 42, cf. Pl.*Hp.Ma.*295a; ἕως ἂν ἡμῖν ἐκφανῇ τὸν ἐφ' ᾧ αὐτὼ σπουδάζετον Id.*Euthd.*288c. 2. *exhibit*, κακότητα ἔς τινα Hdt.5.92.η'. 3. ἐ. πόλεμον πρός τινα *to declare*.., X.*An.*3.1.16.

ἐκφᾰλαγγίζω, *swerve from line*, Demetr.*Eloc.*84.

ἐκφάν-δην, Adv., = ἐκφανῶς, *openly*, Philostr.*VA*7.20. **-εια** [φᾰ], ἡ, *emergence above horizon*, Epicur.*Ep.*2 p.40 U. **-ής**, ές, *showing itself*, κάρυον ἐκφανὲς ἐκ λεπίδων *AP*6.102.4 (Phil.); *bright-shining*, ἀστέρες Artem.2.36; less freq. of persons, ἐ. γιγνόμενος *disclosing oneself*, Pl.*Ion* 535b; *plain, manifest*, τἀνδρὸς ἐκφανὲς τέκμαρ A.*Eu.*244, cf. Pl.*Phdr.*250d (Sup.); ἐκφανῆ γένοιτο ὅπῃ ἔχει Id.*R.* 528c; ἐ. ἰδεῖν A.*Pers.*398, etc. Adv. -νῶς Plb.5.1.3, Iamb.*Protr.*21. κϛ'. 2. *illustrious*, Artem.2.30. **-ίζω**, = ἐκφαίνω:—Pass., ἐκφανίζεται· μηνύεται, Hsch. **-όω**, pf. part. Pass. ἐκπεφανωμένος· ἀπόπληκτος, Id. **-σις**, εως, ἡ, *exhibition, manifestation*, Plot.3.5. 9, Jul.*Or.*7.220b, Olymp.*in Mete.*106.9, Dam.*Pr.*432, Procl.*Inst.*125.

ἐκφαντ-άζομαι, *form in imagination*, Alciphr.1.13. **-ικός**, ή, όν, = ἐκφαντορικός, Procl.*in Alc.Praef.* (s.v.l.). **-ορία**, ἡ, *revealing of secret things*, Suid. **-ορικός**, ή, όν, *revealing*, τῆς ἀληθείας Procl.*Theol.Plat.*6.12; τῆς οὐσίας Id.*in Cra.*p.16 P., al., cf. Dam.*Pr.* 367. **-ος**, ον, *shown forth, revealed*, Poll.5.147, Hsch. **-ωρ**, sine expl., Id.

ἐκφάσθαι, pres. inf. Med. of ἔκφημι.

ἔκφᾰσις, εως, Ion. ιος, ἡ, (ἔκφημι) *declaration*, Hdt.6.129. II. (ἐκφαίνω) *emergence, reappearance*, of an eclipsed body, Phld.*Sign.* 10 (pl.); *rising* of the sun, Agatharch.105; prob. f.l. for ἔκφανσις in Procl.*in Prm.*pp.480, 520 S.

ἐκφατν-ίζω, *throw out of the manger*: generally, *throw away*, Posidon.9(a) J. (Pass.); of teeth, Eust.1784.45 (Pass.). II. Med., *eat out of the manger*, Nic.Dam.p.3 D. **-ισμα**, ατος, τό, *that which is cleaned out of the manger*: mostly in pl., *scraps, remnants*, Philostr. *VA*1.19; ἄρτων Ath.6.270d. II. *a board of the manger taken out in cleaning it*, Poll.10.166. **-ώμα**, ατος, τό, = φατνώμα, Id.7.122.

ἔκφᾰτος, ον, *beyond power of speech*, Max.451. II. (ἔκφημι) Adv. -τως *with loud voice* or *ineffably, impiously*, A.*Ag.*706.

ἐκφαυλ-ίζω, *depreciate, disparage, pour contempt on*, J.*AJ*2.14.1, al., Arr.*An.*1.13.6, Luc.*Merc.Cond.*11, Hld.10.12; τινὰ τῆς ὀργῆς J. *AJ*5.8.6; *reject with scorn*, Ael.*VH*9.41, *NA*4.37 (Pass.): c. inf., *disdain* to do, ib.11.31. **-ισμός**, ὁ, *contemning*, τῶν θείων J.*AJ* 3.8.9. **-ως**, Adv., f.l. for -φύλως, Philostr.*VS*1.16.4.

ἐκφερομῡθέω, *reveal*, of secrets, Aen.Tact.22.5 (Pass.), *SIG*360.25 (Chersonesus, iii B.C.), Corn.*ND*30.

ἐκφέρω, fut. ἐξοίσω Hdt.3.71: Ion. aor. ἐξήνεικα:—Pass., ἐξοισθήσομαι E.*Supp.*561: fut. Med. ἐξοίσομαι in pass. sense, Hdt.8.49,76:— *carry out of*, τινὰ πολέμοιο Il.5.664, etc.; ὅπλα ἐκ μεγάρου ἐξενηνειγμένα Hdt.8.37, cf. E.*Ph.*779; ἐ. πεύκας Ar.*Fr.*599; γραμματεῖον Id.*Nu.* 19; ἐξένεγκέ μοι τὴν κοπίδ' ἔξω Men.*Pk.*332. 2. *carry out* a corpse for burial, ἐξέφερον θρασὺν Ἕκτορα δάκρυ χέοντες Il.24.786, cf. Hdt.7. 117, Antipho 6.21 (Pass.), etc.; also, *cause death*, εἰ ὑπερβάλλουσιν ἀλγηδόνες, ἐξοίσουσι Plot.1.4.8. 3. *carry away*, τρί' ἄλεισα Od.15.470, cf. *Test.Epict.*2.22, etc.; *carry off* as prize or reward, ἄεθλον Il.23.785:—more freq. in Med., τὠυτὸ (of a victory) ἐξενείκασθαι Hdt.6.103; κλέος, δόξαν, S.*El.*60, D.14.1, etc.; *accomplish*, Aeschin.2.66. 4. *carry ashore*, ἐπὶ Ταίναρον Hdt.1.24, etc.; *cast ashore*, πόντου νιν ἐξήνεγκε..κλύδων E.*Hec.*701:—Pass., with fut. Med., *come to land, be cast ashore*, ἐς τοὺς ἑωυτῶν ἐξοίσονται Hdt.8.49, cf. 76, 2.90. II. *bring forth*, in various senses: 1. of women, = φέρειν μέχρι τέλους, *bring to the birth*, Hp.*Nat.Mul.*19; εἰς φῶς κύημα Pl.*R.*461c, cf. Arist. *HA*577^{b}23, al.; of plants, *bear* seed, Id.*GA*731^{a}22; of the ground, *bear* fruit, Δήμητρος καρπὸν ἐ. Hdt.1.193, 4.198. 2. *bring about, accomplish*, μισθοῖο τέλος Il.21.451; τὸ μόρσιμον Pi.*N.*4.61; κακίας μεγάλας ὥσπερ ἀρετὰς αἱ μεγάλαι φύσεις ἐ. Plu.*Demetr.*1:—Pass., διὰ ἀνοήτων οὐδὲν ἂν καλῶς ἐξενεχθείη D.61.7. 3. *publish, deliver*, χρηστήριον Hdt.5.79; ἐ. λόγον S.*Tr.*741, Pl.*Mx.*236c, cf. Plu.*Them.*23; εἰς τοὺς Ἕλληνας τὰ τῆς πόλεως ἁμαρτήματα Isoc.8.14; of public measures, *refer*, ἐξενεῖκαι ἐς τὸν δῆμον Hdt.9.5; ἐς πολύφημον ἐξενείκαντας Id.5.79; ἐ. προβούλευμα εἰς τὸν δῆμον *bring* a project of law before the people, D.59.4 (so in Med., ἐκφέρεσθαι προβούλευμα εἰς τὴν ἐκκλησίαν Aeschin.3.125): abs., freq. in Att. Inscrr., ἡ δὲ βουλὴ ἐς τὸν δῆμον ἐξενεγκέτω ἐπάναγκες *IG*1^2.76.61, cf. 2^2.360.47; of authors, *publish* a work, Isoc.9.74, Arist.*Po.*1447^{b}17, D.H.*Comp.*1, Plu.2.10c, etc.:—Med., ἐκφέρεσθαι γνώμην *declare one's* opinion, Isoc.5.36:—Pass., εἰς Ἕλληνας ἐξοισθήσεται E.*Supp.*561. 4. *produce, exhibit*, Lys.19.30; *display*, δείγματα εἰς φῶς Pl.*Lg.*788c, cf. D.19.12; φανερῶς τὸ μῖσος εἴς τινας Plb.15.27.3; ἐ. τὴν ἰατρικὴν ἐπιστήμην D.S.5.74. 5. *disclose*, τι πρὸς τὸν μάγον Hdt.3.71; τὴν ἀπάτην ib.74; τὴν ἐπιχείρησιν Id.8.132. 6. *put forth, exert*, δύναμιν E.*Ion*1012:—and in Med., μέγα τι σθένος ἁ Κύπρις ἐκφέρεται νίκας S.*Tr.*497 (lyr.). 7. ἐ. πόλεμον *begin* war, D.1.21; ἐπί τινα Hdt.6.56; πρός τινα X.*HG*3.5.1; τινί Plb.2.36.4, etc. 8. *show the marks of, betray, reproduce*, ἐκφέρουσι γὰρ μητρῷ' ὀνείδη E.*Andr.*621. 9. ὅρον ἐ. *produce* a definition, Arist.*Metaph.*1040^{b}2; *express*, διάνοιαν Phld.*Po.*5.26, al.; '*word*' a sentence, D.H.*Comp.*3 (Pass.), 7; *utter*, Demetr.*Eloc.*94; *cite, adduce*, ib.142; πρὸς ἑαυτὸν ἐ. *soliloquize*, Sch.Pi.*O.*1.5. b. *pronounce*, Ath.3.94f; ὅταν μακρῶς ἐκφέρηται D.H.*Comp.*15, cf. Archyt.1, Str.9.5.17. 10. *pay as indemnity*, δισχίλια τάλαντα Plb.3.27.5, etc. b. Pass., of words, *to be formed*, κατὰ μίμησιν Demetr.*Eloc.*220; ἐπιρρηματικῶς A.D.*Adv.*175.28; διὰ τοῦ ε̄ ἐ. ib.193.5. 11. *exact*, ἀργύριον Lxx 4*Ki.*15.20. III. Pass., *to be carried beyond bounds*, ἔξω ὅρων ἐξενεχθὲν ἀκόντιον Antipho 3.2.4: mostly metaph., *to be carried away* by passion, ἀπαιδευσίᾳ ὀργῆς Th.3.84, cf. Chrysipp.*Stoic.*3.127; πρὸς ὀργὴν ἐκφέρει *givest way* to passion, S.*El.*628; ἐ. πρὸς αἰδῶ *is inclined* to feel respect, E.*Alc.*601 (lyr.); λέγων ἐξηνέχθην Pl.*Cra.*425a; ἐξενεχθεὶς ὥστε κωμῳδοποιὸς γενέσθαι Id.*R.*606c; πρὸς τὸ ἄγριοι πολῖται γενέσθαι X.*Cyr.*1.6.34; πάθος defined as ὁρμὴ ἐκφερομένη καὶ ἀπειθὴς λόγῳ *Stoic.*3.92:—later in Act., [θυμὸς] ἐ. τινὰ τοῦ λογισμοῦ Philostr. *Im.*2.21. IV. *bring to* one's end, *bring on* to the trail, εὖ δέ σ' ἐκφέρει..βάσις S.*Aj.*7; κινδυνεύει ὥσπερ ἀτραπός [τις] ἐκφέρειν ἡμᾶς [ἐν τῇ σκέψει] Pl.*Phd.*66b, cf. *IG*1^2.94.37:—Pass., ἐξηνέχθην εἰς ἅπερ Πρωταγόρας λέγει Pl.*Cra.*386a. V. intr. (sc. ἑαυτόν) *shoot forth* (before the rest), ὦκα δ' ἔπειτα αἱ Φηρητιάδαο..ἔκφερον ἵπποι· τὰς δὲ μέτ' ἐξέφερον Διομήδεος..ἵπποι Il.23.376, cf. 759; also, *to run away*, X.*Eq.*3.4. 2. *come to fulfilment*, ὁρᾷς τὰ τοῦδε..ὡς ἐς ὀρθὸν ἐκφέρει μαντεύματα S.*OC*1424; *come to an end*, Id.*Tr.*824 (lyr.).

ἐκ-φεύγω, fut. -ξομαι Ar.*V.*157, Pl.*Smp.*189b, and -ξοῦμαι Id.*R.*432d:—*flee out* or *away, escape*: abs., ἐκφυγέειν μεμαώς Od.19.231, cf. A.*Pers.*510, etc.; φεύγων ἐκφεύγειν Hdt.5.95. b. of persons accused, *to be acquitted*, Ar.*V.*157. 2. c. gen., *escape out of*, ἐξέφυγον πολιῆς ἁλὸς ἠπειρόνδε Od.23.236; νούσου *Epigr.Gr.*1041.9; of things, βέλος ἔκφυγε χειρός Il.5.18: with Prep., ματρὸς ἐκ κόλπων *APl.*4.182 (Leon.). 3. c. acc., *escape*, ἐξ αὖ νῦν ἔφυγες θάνατον Il.11.362; κῆρας Od.4.512; κακότητα 5.414; θανάτοιο τέλος Archil.6; νοῦσον Hdt.1.25; Σκύθας Id.6.40; τὴν πεπρωμένην A.*Pr.*518; τὰν θεῶν νέμεσιν S.*Ph.*518 (lyr.), etc. b. simply, *to have escaped, to be beyond*, οὐ πολλὰ ἐκφεύγεις παιδιὰς ἔτη Pl.*Plt.*268e. c. of things, ἐκπεφεύγασιν γάμοι με E.*Hel.*1622; ἐκφύγοι τὰ πράγματ' αὐτόν D.18.33, cf. 19.123; ἐ. τὰς αἰσθήσεις *escape* one's sense, Arist.*Fr.*208; also, *escape* one's lips, Pl.*Ly.*213d: abs., ἐκφεύγει τἀμελούμενον S.*OT*111, cf. Arist.*Metaph.*1090^{b}21. d. ἐκφεύγοντες τὴν χιόνα τόποι places *free from* snow, Plb.3.55.7. e. Astron., of stars, *emerge* from the Sun's rays, *become visible*, Autol.1.9, Gem.13.9, etc. f. *pass over, omit*, Apollon.Cit.1. 4. c. inf. (with or without Art.), Pl.*Sph.*235b; οὐκ ἐκφεύγει μὴ οὐκ εἶναι.. Id.*Phdr.*277e; τὸ μὴ ἕτερα εἶναι Id.*Prm.*147a; ἐ. τὸ ἀποθανεῖν Id.*Ap.*39a; μικρὸν ἐξέφυγε μὴ καταπετρωθῆναι X.*An.*1.3.2; ἐκφεύξεται τὰ δύο *will not admit of* duality, Plot.3.8.9. -**φευκτικός**, ή, όν, *of* or *for escape*, σύμβολον Sch.Ar. *Pl.*63:—also -**φεύξιμος**, ον, ὁδός Sch.A.R.1.246. -**φευκτος**, ον, *escapable*, cj. in Hsch. s.v. δυσάλωτος (cj. -νκτος). -**φευξις**, εως, ἡ, *escape*, Apollon.*Lex.* s.v. ἀλεωρή.

ἔκφημι, *speak out* or *forth, utter loudly*:—Ep. only in Med., ἐκφάσθαι ἔπος Od.10.246, cf. 13.308; νόον ἔκφατο A.R.1.439: later aor. 1 ἐξέφησε *EM*687.30.

ἐκφθέγγομαι, *utter*, *IGRom.*1.1192 (Memnon).

ἐκφθείρω, *destroy utterly*, Scymn.344, Str.17.1.44, etc.:—Pass., ἐκφθείρομαι *to be undone, ruined*, ἐξεφθαρμένη E.*Hec.*669: Com., 'go to the devil', ἐκφθαρεὶς οὐκ οἶδ' ὅποι Ar.*Pax*72; ἐκφθείρου Luc.*DMer.*15.2.

ἐκφθίνω, in Hom. only in 3 plpf. Pass., νηῶν ἐξέφθιτο οἶνος the wine *had all been consumed out of* the ships, Od.9.163; νηὸς ἐξέφθιτο ἤϊα πάντα 12.329; ἐξέφθινται they *have utterly perished*, A.*Pers.*679 (lyr.), 927 (anap.).

ἐκφιβλοῦσθαι, gloss on ἐκπορποῦσθαι, Suid.

ἐκφῐλέω, *kiss heartily*, *AP*12.250 (Strat.). 2. *love dearly*, prob. in *Epigr.Gr.*522.6.

*ἐκφλαίνω, = ἐκφλύω, only aor. inf. ἐκφλῆναι E.*Fr.*470.

ἐκφλαυρίζω, *make light of*, πρᾶγμα f.l. in Plu.2.680c, cf. *Pomp.*57, prob. in Sch.Ar.*Pl.*885.

ἐκφλεγμᾰτόομαι, Pass., *to turn into phlegm*, Hp.*Acut.*61.

ἐκφλέγω, *to set on fire*: metaph., τὴν πόλιν Ar.*Pax*608, Lxx 4*Ma.*16.3:—Pass., metaph., ἐκφλέγεσθαι τὴν διάνοιαν *to be inflamed..*, Plu.2.766a. 2. *warm up*, Aret.*SA*2.1.

ἐκφλίβω [ῑ], Ion. for ἐκθλίβω, Hp.*Loc.Hom.*9.

ἐκφλογ-ίζω, = ἐκφλέγω, Cleanth.ap.Stob.1.17.3 (Pass.). -όω, *scorch*, Phlp. *in Mete.*44.33:—Pass., *blaze up*, Arist.*Mir.*833^{a}9, Dsc.1.68.2. -ωσις, εως, ἡ, *upper part of a torch*, D.S.17.115.

ἐκφλοΐζω, *deprive of rind, peel*, *PHolm.*24.2 (Pass.).

ἐκφλοίομαι, f.l. for ἐκβδάλλομαι, Nic.*Al.*322.

ἐκφλύζω or **ἐκφλύσσω**, *spirt out*: c. acc. cogn., ἐκφλύξαι γόον *give vent to* a groan, A.R.1.275.

ἐκφλυνδάνω, *break out*, of sores, Hp.*Int.*13, 46 (-φινδάνω f.l. in Gal.19.96).

ἐκφλύω [ῠ], gloss on ἐκβράσσω, Gal.19.96.

ἐκφοβ-έω, *alarm*, φρένας A.*Pers.*606, cf. Pl.*Grg.*483c, etc.; τὸ ἐκφοβῆσαι so as *to cause alarm*, Th.2.87; ἐ. τινὰ ἐκ δεμνίων E.*Or.*312; ἐ. τινά τι *fright* one *with* a thing, Th.6.11:—Pass., *fear greatly*, c. acc., S.*El.*276; ὡς.. ib.1426; ὑπέρ τινος Id.*OT*989. -ημα, ατος, τό, *means of scaring*, Sch.A.*Th.*280. -ησις, εως, ἡ, *frightening*, Hdn.*Epim.*21, Sch.A.*Pr.*922, Hsch. s.v. ἔκπληξις. -ητικός, ή, όν, *terrifying*, Eust.1966.16. -ητρον, τό, *bogey*, Sch.Ar.*Pax*473. -ος, ον, *affrighted*, Arist.*Phgn.*812^{b}29, Lxx *De.*9.19, *Ev.Marc.*9.6, Plu.*Fab.*6.

ἐκφόδιος, dub. sens. in *POxy.*387 (i A.D.).

ἐκφοινίσσω, *make all red* or *bloody*, E.*Ph.*42:—Pass., *to be bloodshot*, ἐ. τοὺς ὀφθαλμούς Arist.*Phgn.*812^{a}37. II. ἐκφοινίξαι· ἀναγνῶσαι, Hsch.

ἐκφοιτ-άω, Ion. -έω, *go out constantly, be in the habit of going out*, ἐπὶ θήρην Hdt.4.116; simply, *go out*, ἐκ τῆς ἀκροπόλιος Id.3.68, cf. E.*El.*320. 2. of things, *to be spread abroad*, λόγοι παρὰ τῆς γυναικὸς ἐξεφοίτων Plu.*Lyc.*3. 3. ἐ. εἰς μανίαν *to end* in madness, Ael.*NA*11.32. 4. *issue*, κἂν μήπω τέλειον αὐτῆς ἐκφοιτήσῃ τὸ γέννημα, prob. for ἐμφ-, Ph.1.105. -ησις, εως, ἡ, *becoming public*, J.*AJ*19.1.7.

ἐκφορ-ά, ἡ, (ἐκφέρω) *carrying out*, esp. of a corpse to burial, A.*Th.*1029, *Ch.*9, 430 (lyr., pl.), Th.2.34; ἐπ' ἐκφορὰν βαδίζειν Ar.*Pl.*1008; ἐπ' ἐ. ἀκολουθεῖν τινί Lys.1.8; also of meats at a sacrifice, Theopomp. Com.70, Euphro 1.20, prob. in Ar.*Pl.*1138; τῶν κρεῶν μὴ εἶναι ἐ. ἔξω τοῦ τεμένεος *IG*7.235.32 (Orop.). 2. *blabbing, betrayal of secrets*, λόγων ἀπορρήτων ἐ. D.L.1.98. II. (from Pass.) of horses, *running away*, ἡ πρὸς οἶκον ἐ. X.*Eq.*3.5. 2. *passing out*, ἡ τοῦ πνεύματος ἐ. D.S.2.12. III. *projection in a building*, Vitr.3.5.1, 6.2.2 (pl.). IV. *utterance, pronunciation*, Phld.*Po.*994.24, Str.16.4.18, D.H.*Comp.*14. V. *expression, enunciation* of ideas, *Stoic.*2.58, al., D.H.*Comp.*8, Plu.2.1112e, Alex.Aphr.*in Metaph.*371.7; esp. *mode of expression, grammatical construction*, ἐ. προστακτική A.D. *Synt.*69.20; ἐνεργητική ib.150.19; ἐ. ἑνικαί, πληθυντικαί, Chrysipp. *Stoic.*2.6. VI. *digression*, εἰς ἐ. ἐκπίπτειν wander from the point, Gal.8.629. -έω, = ἐκφέρω, *carry out*, as a corpse for burial, Od.22.451, 24.417 (tm.). 2. generally, *carry out*, Hdt.1.197, 9.116, Is.6.42 (Pass., ib.41):—Med., *take out with one*, E.*Cyc.*234, etc.:—Pass., *move forth*, ὡς τότε ταρφειαὶ κόρυθες..νηῶν ἐκφορέοντο Il.19.360. 3. *dig out*, of earth dug from a trench, Hdt.2.150 (Pass.), 7.23; of metal from mines, X.*Vect.*4.2 (Pass.). 4. *sack, plunder*, πόλιν D.S.17.13 (Pass.). 5. in Pass., *to be cast on shore*, Hdt.8.12. 6. *blab, blurt out*, dub. in Hermesian.7.98. 7. Med., *distrain upon goods*, D.47.53, 75. 8. *make away with*, *PSI*5.463 (ii A.D.), *POxy.*1642.22 (iii A.D.). 9. ἐκφορεῖ· σπανίζει ὑπάρχοντα, Hsch. -ιαστής, οῦ, ὁ, *collector of* ἐκφόριον II, *IGRom.*3.576 (Lycia, ii A.D.). -ίζω, *exhaust by parturition*, Sch.Orib.3 p.681 D. (Pass.). -ικός, ή, όν, *belonging to* or *producing expression*: τὸ ἐ. *the power of expressing oneself in words*, Plu.2.1113c; but, *capable of being expressed*, νοήματα *Stoic.*2.77. Adv. -κῶς Plu.2.1112d. -ιον, τό, *that which the earth produces*, Hdt.4.198 (pl.), Lxx *Le.*25.19 (pl.), *Milet.*3.149 (ii B.C.), Poll.1.237. II. *payment assessed on produce*, = δεκάτη, Arist.*Oec.*1345^{b}33; esp. *rent paid in kind*, ἐ. ἀπότακτον *PAmh.*2.87 (ii A.D.), cf. *PTeb.*377.23 (iii A.D.), *OGI*669.30, etc. -όομαι, Pass., *to be worn into holes*, τῇ καύσει Thphr.*Lap.*14, cf. 15. -ος, ον, *exportable*, f.l. for ἐκφορά, Ar.*Pl.*1138. 2. *to be made known* or *divulged*, εἰ δ' ἐ. σοι ξυμφορὰ πρὸς ἄρσενας E.*Hipp.*295; οὐδεὶς γὰρ ἐ. λόγος Pl.*La.*201a; cf. ἐκφορά I. 2. 3. *carried astray*, Plu.2.424a; ἵππος ἐ. a *runaway* horse, Gal.5.510. 4. ἔκφορα, τά, *produce* of the earth, Antipho Soph.60. II. Act., *carrying out*:—in A.*Eu.*910 τῶν δυσσεβούντων ἐκφορωτέρα is not, *more ready to carry* them *out to burial* (v. ἐκφορά I), but rather, *more ready to weed* them *out*, as a gardener does noxious plants (ἀνδρὸς φιτυποίμενος δίκην, in next line). 2. *blabbing, betraying* secrets, Ar.*Th.*472. 3. = εὐέκφορος (quod fort. leg.), γυναῖκες Arist.*Fr.*283. 4. *expressive*, κίνησις ἐ. τινος Chrysipp.*Stoic.*3.112. III. as Subst., ἔκφοροι, οἱ, *reefing-ropes*, = τέρθριοι, Sch.Ar.*Eq.*438, Phot. s.v. ἡνιόχους.

ἐκφορτίζομαι, Pass., *to be sold for exportation*: metaph., *to be kidnapped, betrayed*, v.l. for ἐμφ-, S.*Ant.*1036.

ἐκφόρτιον, f.l. for ἐκφόριον I, Lxx *De.*28.33.

ἐκφούγιν, dub. in *Supp.Epigr.*2.727 (Pisidia, fort. = ἐκφύγιον, i.e. *place of refuge*).

ἐκφράζω, *tell over, recount*, A.*Pr.*950, dub. l. in E.*HF*1119; *denote*, δύναμιν τοῖς τῶν θεῶν ὀνόμασιν Plu.2.24a. II. *describe*, Hermog. *Prog.*10, *Id.*2.4, Men.Rh.p.373S.:—Pass., Theon *Prog.*2. 2. *express ornately*, τὸ ἐ. τὰ γέλοια ὅμοιόν ἐστι καὶ καλλωπίζειν πίθηκον Demetr.*Eloc.*165.

ἐκ-φρακτικός, ή, όν, (ἐκφράσσω) *for clearing obstructions*, ἐ. τῶν πόρων Gal.11.743; τὰ ἐ. *opening medicines*, *Hippiatr.*2; τροχίσκος Paul.Aeg. 7.12. **-φραξις**, εως, ἡ, *removal of obstructions*, Gal.1.391, 10.775.

ἐκφρᾰσείδιον, τό, Dim. of sq., Eust.1065.20.

ἔκφρᾰσις, εως, ἡ, *description*, D.H.*Rh.*10.17 (pl.), Luc.*Hist.Conscr.* 20, Hermog.*Prog.*10, Aphth.*Prog.*12, etc.; title of works *descriptive of works of art*, as that of Callistratus. II. = ἐπιθυμία, Hsch.

ἐκφράσσω, Att. -ττω, aor. 1 Pass. ἐκφραχθῆναι D.S.18.35:—*remove obstacles, open*, Gal.11.730, D.S. l. c.

ἐκφραστέον, *one must describe*, Aphth.*Prog.*12.

ἐκφραστικός, ή, όν, *descriptive*: τὸ ἐ. *the faculty of describing*, D.L. 5.65.

ἐκφρέω (v. εἰσφρέω), poet. impf. ἐξεφρίομεν (fort. -φρίεμεν) Ar.*V.* 125: fut. ἐκφρήσω ib.156: aor. ἐξέφρησα (v. infr.), also ἐξέφρηκα Hsch.: imper. ἔκφρες prob. for ἔκφερε Ar.*V.*162:—*let out, bring out*, μὴ.. οὐκ ἐκφρῶσιν restored in E.*Ph.*264 (for οὐ μεθῶσιν) from the Sch. and Phot. (leg. Εὐριπίδης), cf. Ar. ll. cc.; ἐξέφρησα ἐμαυτόν Luc.*Lex.*9:—Med., ἔκφρηται· ἐκφέρεται, Hsch.:—Pass., *go out*, ἐκφρησθῆναι Ael.*Fr.*89.

ἐκφρίττω, *tremble at*, Orac. in *App.Anth.*6.128.

ἐκφρονέω, *to be demented*, D.C.55.13, *Fr.*9.2. II. c. gen., = καταφρονέω, *AB*141.

ἐκφροντίζω, *think out, discover*, E.*IT*1323, Ar.*Nu.*695, Th.3.45, etc.

ἐκφροσύνη, Dor. -σύνα, ἡ, (ἔκφρων) *madness, nonsense*, Ti.Locr. 102e.

ἐκφρύγομαι [ῡ], *to be dried up, parched*, c. acc. cogn., ἅπασαν ἐ. τοῦ στόματος τὴν ἰκμάδα Gal.*UP*11.10, cf. 17(1).181: aor. 2 subj. ἐκφρῠγῇ Damocr.ap.eund.13.989. II. *to be consumed*, ἔρωτι Ael.*NA*14.18.

ἐκφρύττω, *dry, parch thoroughly*, Alex.Trall.12 (Pass.).

ἔκφρων, ον, gen. ονος, (φρήν) *out of one's mind, beside oneself*, Hp. *Mul.*2.117, Luc.*Nigr.*38, Plot.2.9.8; *senseless, stupid*, D.19.267; also, *frenzied, enthusiastic*, of poets, Pl.*Ion*534b; of Bacchantes, Luc. *Bacch.*1, *AP*6.220.2 (Diosc.), cf. Pl.*Lg.*790e. II. Adv. -φρόνως, ἥττων γίγνεσθαι τῶν προσπιπτόντων Hld.6.9.

ἐκφυάς, άδος, ἡ, = ἀποφυάς, Eratosth.26.

ἐκφυγγάνω, = ἐκφεύγω, A.*Pr.*525, Diph.7, Plb.18.15.11; *recover from* disease, Hp.*Morb.*2.26.

ἔκφῠγε, v. ἐκφεύγω.

ἐκφῠγή, ἡ, *escape*, Lxx 3*Ma.*4.19.

ἐκφυής, ές, *abnormally developed*, τοῖς ὀδοῦσιν ἢ τοῖς ὀφθαλμοῖς Vett. Val.110.15; *projecting*, Procl.*Hyp.*3.16. II. *eminent, extraordinary*. Adv. -ῶς App.*Ill.*25.

ἐκφυλάσαι· ἐκσπάσαι, Hsch.

ἐκφῠλάσσω, *guard* or *watch carefully*, S.*OC*285, E.*Or.*1259; ἴχνος ἐκφύλασσ' ὅπου τίθης Id.*Ion*741.

ἐκφυλλοφορ-έω, *expel* or *condemn by leaves*, used of the Athen. βουλή, which used olive-leaves as voting-papers, Aeschin.1.111, cf. *AB*248. **-ησις**, εως, ἡ, *sentence passed by leaves*, Tz.*H.*10.40. **-ία**, ἡ, = foreg., *EM*325.9.

ἔκφῠλος, ον, *foreign, alien*, Luc.*Lex.*24, *Sol.*11, Porph.*Abst.*1.4; ἔ. παρὰ τὴν γένεσιν *alien* to generation, Simp. *in Ph.*220.12: metaph., *strange, unnatural, horrible*, Str.4.4.5, Plu.*Brut.*36; ἀνὴρ ἔ. τὸ μέγεθος Id.*Caes.*69. Adv. -λως, ἀττικίζειν Philostr.*VS*1.16.4.

ἔκφῡμα, ατος, τό, *eruption of pimples*, v.l. in Hp.*Insomn.*89. 2. *outgrowth* of vine tendrils, *EM*330.29.

ἐκφῦναι, v. ἐκφύω.

ἐκφύρω [ῡ], strengthd. for φύρω, aor. 1 Pass. ἐξεφύρθην Lxx *Je.*3.2.

ἐκφῡσ-άω, *blow out*, ἔνθα ποταμὸς ἐκφυσᾷ μένος *pours forth* its strength, A.*Pr.*720; of elephants *spouting* water through their trunks, Plb.3.46.12: metaph., ἐ. πόλεμον *blow up* a war from a spark, Ar.*Pax*610; also ἐκπεφυσημένος a *puffed up, conceited* person, Plb. 3.103.7. 2. *blow away*, Lxx *Hg.*1.9:—Pass., Plb.1.48.8; *to be dissipated*, Aret.*SD*2.1. 3. *sublimate* volatile elements, Zos.Alch. p.148B., al.:—Pass., Dsc.5.75. II. *breathe out*, βαρὺν ὕπνον ἐ., i.e. snore loudly, Theoc.24.47; αἷμα Herod.2.72. III. intr., *snort*, Lyc.743; *burst forth*, φλόγες ἐκφυσήσασαι Arist.*Mu.*400ᵃ32. **-ημα**, ατος, τό, *pustule*, Poll.4.190. 2. *volcanic eruption*, Sch.A.R.3.41; πυρὸς ἐ. D.S.3.53 (pl.): pl., = πέτραι ὑπερέχουσαι τῆς γῆς, Hsch. **-ησις**, εως, ἡ, *emission of breath*, Gal.8.251, prob. in *EM*98.20. II. gloss on ἀποφύσιας, Hsch. **-ιάω**, poet. for ἐκφυσάω, A.*Ag.*1389.

ἔκφῠσις, εως, ἡ, (ἐκφύω) *growing out* or *forth*: *germination*, Thphr. *HP*8.1.5; *growth, increase*, Arist.*PA*658ᵇ5, Diog.Oen.28; ἐ. ἀρετῆς Pl.*Lg.*777e, cf. Hierocl. *in CA*24p.471M.; *manner of growth*, Thphr. *HP*1.14.2. II. *outgrowth*, A.*Fr.*252, Pl.*Phdr.*251b; γενύων Opp. *C.*2.497 (pl.). 2. *bony projection*, Hp.*Art.*45; *origin, attachment* of muscles, nerves, etc., Gal.8.61, al. 3. *shoot*, Thphr.*HP*1.10. 7: in pl., *suckers*, *Gp.*12.19.1; *seedlings*, Thphr.*HP*7.4.3 (so in sg., *crop of seedlings*, ib.3.3.7); *roots*, Plb.18.18.6.

ἐκφῠτεύω, *plant out*, πήγανον εἰς συκῆν Arist.*Pr.*924ᵇ36. II. *plant*, χώραν Heraclid.*Pol.*36; ἄλσος Philostr.*VS*1.23.2:—Pass., ib. 2.23.3.

ἔκφῠτον, τό, = ἔκφυσις II. 3, Alex.Aphr.*Pr.*2.16.

ἐκφύω, *generate*: mostly of the male, *beget*, S.*OT*437, 827, etc.; ὃς ἐξέφυσεν Ἀερόπης λέκτρων ἄπο Ἀγαμέμνον' E.*Hel.*391. 2. rarely of the female, *bear*, S.*OC*984. 3. generally, *produce*, ἡ γῆ κατὰ καιρὸν ἐκφύουσα πάντα Arist.*Mu.*397ᵃ26; ἐ. κέρατα Id.*HA*611ᵇ13: abs., of seed, *germinate*, D.24.154. II. Pass., with pf. and aor. 2 Act., *to be engendered, born from*, κεφαλαὶ τρεῖς ἑνὸς αὐχένος ἐκπεφυυῖαι (Ep. pf. part.) Il.11.40; πατρός, μητρὸς ἐκφῦναι, S.*Aj.*487, 1295, E. *Ion*542; λάλημα ἐκπεφυκός a *born* tattler, S.*Ant.*320. 2. *grow*, of hair, μέχρις ἂν [αἱ τρίχες] ἐκφυῶσι Archig.ap.Gal.12.407; *spring, take rise*, of muscles, ib.18(2).981. III. intr. in pres. Act., ἕλκεα ἐκφύουσιν Hp.*Epid.*6.5.15, cf. Arist.*Pr.*883ᵇ26.

ἐκφων-έω, *cry out*, Ph.2.49, Plu.*Caes.*66. II. *utter*, Id.2.1010a (Pass.), Demetr.*Eloc.*15; *pronounce*, D.H.*Comp.*14 (Pass.). 2. *publish, promulgate*, *POxy.*136.39 (vi A.D., Pass.), *Cod.Just.*10.16.13 (Pass.). **-ησις**, εως, ἡ, *pronunciation*, A.D.*Synt.*13.9, S.E.*M.*1. 102, al.; *exclamation*, Ph.1.618 (pl.), Plu.2.111d (pl.), A.D.*Synt.*4. 26 (pl.). 2. *acclamation*, *Sammelb.*3924.36 (i A.D.). II. *meaning, signification*, Marin.*Procl.*28 (pl.).

ἐκχᾰλάω, *let go from*, τεγέων δέμας *AP*11.354.18 (Agath.). 2. *relax*, τὴν ὀργήν Chor. in *Rev.Phil.*1.68. II. intr., *become loose* or *slack*, Hp.*Sept.*1.

ἐκχᾰλῑνόω, *unbridle*, Plu.*Pel.*33.

ἐκχαλκεύω, *work from brass*, J.*AJ*3.7.6.

ἐκχᾰραδρόω, strengthd. for χαραδρόω, Plb.4.41.9:—Pass., τόποι ἐκχαραδρούμενοι χειμάρροις Str.11.3.4.

ἐκχᾰράσσω, Att. -ττω, *erase*, Plu.2.873d, D.Chr.31.71, al.

ἐκχαρέων· μαγειρείων, Hsch. (Lacon. for ἐσχ-).

ἐκχᾰρυβδίζω, *swallow like Charybdis*, Pherecr.95 (s. v. l.); cf. ἐξεχαρυβδαάνθη (sic)· ἀνεπόθη, Hsch.

ἐκχάσκω, in pf. ἐκκέχηνα, *gape, gaze*, εἴς τινα Lxx 1*Es.*4.19.

ἔκχαυνος, ον, *very loose*, Erot. s. v. πλάδος.

ἐκχαυνόω, *puff up, make vain and arrogant*, ἐκ δὲ παίδων χαύνοις φρένας Alc.51; [πόλιν] ἐκχαυνῶν λόγοις E.*Supp.*412, cf. Phld.*Lib.* p.32O.; ἐ. τὸν πολὺν ὄχλον *to make* them *gape and stare*, Hp.*Art.*42.

ἐκχέζω, = Lat. *ecacare*, πεδία ὅλα Anon.ap.Demetr.*Eloc.*126, v.l. in Arist.*HA*551ᵃ7.

ἐκχερσεύω, *dry up*, Hsch. s. v. ἐκκεχιλωμένη (Pass.).

ἐκχεύω, = sq., Nic.*Fr.*74.34.

ἐκχέω (later -χύνω *Ev.Matt.*23.35 (Pass.), etc., condemned by Luc. *Pseudol.*29), fut. -χέω (v. χέω): aor. 1 ἐξέχεα (also imper. ἔκχυσον Hsch.); Ep. aor. Med. ἐκχευάμην Od.24.178: pf. ἐκκέχῠκα Men. 915:—*pour out*, prop. of liquids, οἶνον Il.3.296; αἷμ' ἐκχέας πέδοι A. *Eu.*653, cf. *Ev.Matt.*23.35 (Pass.); ἀναίτιον αἷμα *SIG*1181.5 (Jewish, ii B.C.); πηγάς E.*HF*941; δάκρυα Pl.*Smp.*215e (Pass.), Plu.*Alc.*6; ὁ οἶνος ἐκχεῖται *is spilt*, *Ev.Matt.*9.17: metaph., (in Med.) ταχέας δ' ἐκχεύατ' ὀϊστοὺς he *poured forth his* arrows, Od.22.3, 24.178; σοὶ.. δαίμονες ... ἐλπίδας ἐξέχεαν Pl.*Epigr.*7.4. b. *pour away*: hence, *spill*, a vessel, ποδάνιπτρον Ar.*Fr.*306; τὸν χόα Men. l. c.:—Pass., *to be drained*, εἰς [διώρυχα] *PRyl.*154.18 (i A.D.). 2. of words, *pour forth, utter*, Ar.*Th.*554; μολπάς E.*Supp.*773; πολλὴν γλῶσσαν ἐκχέας μάτην S.*Fr.*929, cf. A.*Ag.*1029 (lyr.). 3. *pour out like water, squander, waste*, ὄλβον Id.*Pers.*826; τὰ πάντα Id.*Ch.*520, cf. S.*El.* 1291; πλοῦτον ἐξέχεεν εἰς δαπάνας *AP*9.367 (Luc.); ἐ. τά τε αὑτοῦ καὶ ἑαυτόν Pl.*R.*553b; *spoil*, τὸ πᾶν σόφισμα S.*Ph.*13. 4. *spread out*, λίνα, ὀθόνας, A.R.2.902 (tm.), Luc.*Am.*6. 5. *throw down*, τινὰ κατὰ τοῦ κρημνοῦ D.H.13.8, cf. 4.7, 14.10. 6. ὕπνον ἐ. *shed*, i.e. *shake off* sleep, Herod.7.7. 7. = συγχέω, ὅρκια Hsch. s. v. ἐξέχεαν. II. Pass., used by Hom. mostly in plpf. ἐξεκέχυντο, as also in 3sg. Ep. aor. ἐξέχῠτο or ἔκχῠτο, part. ἐκχύμενος [ῠ]: later fut. ἐκχῠθήσομαι Hero *Aut.*4.1:—*pour out, stream out* or *forth*, prop. of liquids, Il.21.300, Od.19.504, etc.; ἐκ δ' ἄρα πᾶσαι χύντο χαμαὶ χολάδες Il.4.525; so ἐξεχύθη τὰ σπλάγχνα *Act.Ap.*1.18: metaph., of persons, σφήκεσσιν ἐοικότες ἐξεχέοντο Il.16.259; ἱππόθεν ἐκχύμενοι *pouring from* the [wooden] horse, Od.8.515; ἐκχυθέντες ἁλέες ἐκ τοῦ τείχεος Hdt.3.13: generally, *to be spread out*, πολλὰ δὲ [δέσματα].. μελαθρόφιν ἐξεκέχυντο Od.8.279; σάρκες εἰς ὑπέρογκον ἐκκεχυμέναι πιότητα Luc.*Am.*14. 2. metaph., ῥηθέντα ματαίως ἐκκέχυται στομάτων Emp.39.3; *to be cast away, forgotten*, ἐκκέχυται φιλότης Thgn. 110; αἱ πρόσθεν ὁμολογίαι ἐκκεχυμέναι εἰσίν Pl.*Cri.*49a. 3. *give oneself up to any emotion, to be overjoyed*, Ar.*V.*1469 (lyr.); ἐ. εἰς ἑταίρας, εἰς τὸν κίνδυνον, *give oneself up to*.., Plb.31.25.4, 3.19.1; ἐπὶ τὰ εὐτρεπισθέντα, of a glutton, Ph.1.38; ἁβρὰ γελῶν ὄμμασιν ἐκκέχυσαι *AP*12.156. 4. *lie languidly*, ib.5.54.8 (Diosc.). 5. metaph., of Time, ἐ. κατὰ τὴν χρονικὴν παράτασιν Procl.*Inst.*55. 6. *extend*, of a piece of land, *CPR*1.8, al. (i A.D.).

ἐκχῑλόω, *cover all over with grass* (χιλός): γῆ ἐκκεχιλωμένη land *that bears nothing but grass*, Paus.Gr.*Fr.*323.

ἐκχλευάζω, strengthd. for χλευάζω, τινά Sm.*Pr.*14.9, Lib.*Decl.*48.45.

ἐκχλοιόομαι, Pass., *to be* or *grow sallow*, Hp.*Coac.*480.

ἐκχοΐζω, *dig out*, *Ostr.Strassb.*677 (ii A.D.), Suid. II. Pass., *to be decanted into jars*, of wine, *PSI*5.517 (iii B.C.).

ἐκχοίρηξις· ἐκχοιρηλωμένος (Lacon.), Hsch.

ἐκχοιρῑλόω, only pf. part. Pass. ἐκκεχοιριλωμένη (sc. κωμῳδία) expld. by οὐ Χοιρίλου οὖσα, Hsch.

ἐκχολ-άω, *to be angry*, Lxx 3*Ma.*3.1. **-ίζω**, *purge of bile*, ὄρνεα *Gp.*14.19.3 (v.l. -χολῶσαι). **-όω**, *turn into bile*, Herod.Med. in *Rh.Mus.*49.555:—Pass., Gal.6.449, 626, Alex.Aphr.*Pr.*1.79. II. Pass., *to be charged with bile*, κοιλίαι ἐκχολοῦνται Dieuch.ap.Orib.4.7.

15. **-ωσις,** εως, ἡ, *turning into bile*, Alex.Trall.1.15, Steph.*in Hp.*1.130 D.

ἐκχονδρίζω, (χόνδρος) *cut away, remove cartilage*, Gal.14.791.

ἐκχορδόομαι, Pass., *to be deprived of strings*, Sopat.16.

ἐκχορεύω, *break out of the chorus*: generally, *break out*, ἐς ἄτην Opp.*H.*4.215; *exult*, Hld.10.38. II. Med., *drive out of the chorus*, ἄν τέ ποτ' Ἄρτεμις ἐξεχορεύσατο E.*Hel.*381 (anap.).

ἐκχράω (v. χράω c), *declare as an oracle, tell out*, τὰ πόλλ'.. ὅτ' ἐξέχρη κακά S.*OC*87. II. *suffice*, οὐκ ἐξέχρησέ σφι ἡ ἡμέρα Hdt.8.70: impers., c. inf., κῶς ταῦτα βασιλέϊ ἐκχρήσει περιυβρίσθαι; how *will it suffice* him, how *will he be content* to..? Id.3.137.

ἐκχρέμπτομαι, *cough up, bring up*, Hp.*Morb.*2.26.

ἔκχρημα, ατος, τό, misspelling of ἔκρηγμα, Wilcken*Chr.*11.10 (ii B.C.).

ἐκχρημᾰτίζομαι, *squeeze money from, levy contributions on*, τινά Th.8.87, D.C.53.10.

ἔκχρησις, εως, ἡ, *loan*, *SIG*742.52 (pl., Ephesus, i B.C.).

ἐκχρησμῳδέω, *deliver an oracle*, Sch.Pi.*O.*7.168 (v.l. ἐχρησμ-).

ἐκχρῡσόομαι, *turn to gold*, Tz.*H.*1.107.

ἐκχρώννῡμι, *impart a colour*, ἥλιος σκοτεινὸν ἄνθος ἐξέχρωσε λιγνύος εἰς σώματ' ἀνδρῶν Theodect.17.2.

ἐκχῠλ-ίζω, *squeeze out, express juice* or *liquor*, Hp.*Mul.*1.44; *suck out*, Arist.*HA* 596b12. **-όω,** in Pass., *to be squeezed out*, Gal.12.14.

ἐκχύμενος, v. ἐκχέω.

ἐκχῡμ-ίζω, = ἐκχυλίζω, Arist.*HA*594a15. **-όω,** *extract juice from*, σίδια Hp.*Morb.*2.47. II. in Pass., of the small veins, *shed the blood and leave it extravasated under the skin*, Id.*Fract.*11. **-ωμα,** ατος, τό, *ecchymosis*, ib.11 (pl.), *Art.*50:—also **-ωσις,** εως, ἡ, Id.*Liqu.* 1, Gal.10.232,al.

ἐκ-χύνω, v. ἐκχέω. **-χῠσιαῖος,** α, ον, *for a sluice*, ἧλοι *POxy.*1220.16 (iii A.D.). **-χῠσις,** εως, ἡ, *outflow*, Arist.*Mete.*354a26; *pouring out*, Thphr.*Vent.*50, Lxx *Le.*4.12; βαλανείου *PTeb.*86.9 (ii B.C.); *shedding*, αἵματος Porph.*Antr.*11. II. *effusion* of pus, Erasistr.ap. Gal.8.318. III. *sluice* or *drain*, *CPR*176.16 (iii A.D.), al. **-χῠτήριον,** τό, *drain*, *Gloss.* **-χύτης** [ῠ], ου, ὁ, *spendthrift*, Luc.*Vit. Auct.*24. 2. *drain*, *Gloss.* **-χῠτο,** v. ἐκχέω. **-χῠτος,** ον, (ἐκχέω) *poured forth, unconfined*, κόμη *AP*9.669.8 (Marian.); *outstretched*, ἔκχυτος ὕπνῳ κεῖτο ib.5.274 (Paul. Sil.). 2. *immoderate*, γέλως Suid. s. v. καγχασμός. II. Subst., ἔκχυτον, τό, dub. sens. in *AP*9.395 (Pall.; ποτόν tit., εἶδος βρώματος Sch.); title of dialogue on φοσκοπία by Hermagoras, *Stoic.*1.102.

ἐκχυτρίζω, *pour out of a pot*, Hsch.

ἔκχωνεν· ἔκκλινεν (Lacon.), Hsch.; cf. κωνάω.

ἐκχωνεύω, *melt down, coin anew*, D.C.68.15 codd.

ἐκχώννῡμι, *raise a mound*, Aq.*Ez.*17.17:—usu. in Pass., *to be raised on a bank* or *mound*, τῆς πόλιος ἐκκεχωσμένης ὑψοῦ Hdt.2.138; μάλιστα ἡ ἐν Βουβάστι πόλις ἐξεχώσθη ib.137. II. of a bay, *to be filled up by the deposit* of a river, v.l. ib.11. III. *to be removed*, of rubbish, *PFay.*110.5 (i A.D.).

ἐκχωρ-έω, *depart*, ἐκ χώρας *SIG*679.53; *leave a country, emigrate*, Hdt.1.56, Hecat.30 J.; *withdraw*, ἐκ τῆς οἰκίας *PAmh.*2.30.44 (ii B.C.), etc.: metaph., ἐ. ἐκ τοῦ ζῆν Plb.2.21.2: so abs., Id.7.2.1. 2. *slip out of*, ἀστράγαλος ἐξεχώρησε ἐκ τῶν ἄρθρων Hdt.3.129. 3. *give way, retire*, E.*IA*367, D.41.5; τῶν ὑπαίθρων Plb.1.15.7; τῶν ὑπαρχόντων Id.31.28.3; χειμῶνες ἐκχωροῦσιν εὐκάρπῳ θέρει S.*Aj.*671; ἐ. τινί τινος *give way* to a person in a thing, Hp.*Jusj.*; τινὶ περί τινος Plb. 21.20.1. 4. impers. of a *motion* of the bowels, Hp.*Epid.*5.33. II. trans., *give up, cede*, τινί τι *IG*12(3).324.15 (Thera), *PEleph.*15.2 (iii B.C.), *Sammelb.*4414.8, etc.; τῷ δαίμονί τι Vett.Val. 156.4:—Pass., *CIG*4268 (Xanthus). **-ησις,** εως, ἡ, *going out*, *Placit.*4.22.1. 2. *retirement, withdrawal from*, c. gen., τῶν πολλῶν Epicur.*Sent.*14; ἐκ τῶν οἰκητηρίων *BGU*1115.48 (i B.C.). II. *concession*, *CIG*3394 (Smyrna). 2. *deed of surrender*, *PSI*1.93 (iii A.D.). **-ητέον,** *one must retire*, πάντων τῶν τόπων Plb.18.45.9. **-ητικός,** ή, όν, *concessory*, *Gloss.*

ἐκχωρίζω, *cut off, separate*, *PRyl.*378.11 (ii A.D., Pass.). II. Pass., *to be voided*, of excrements, Arist.*HA*551a7.

ἔκψυξις, εως, ἡ, *cooling*, v.l. in Aret.*SA*2.2.

ἐκψύχω [ῡ], fut. -ξω, *lose consciousness, swoon*, Hp.*Morb.*1.5, Lxx *Jd.*4.21; ἐκ τάχα ψύξειν Herod.4.29; *give up the ghost, expire*, Babr. 115.11, *Act.Ap.*5.5, 12.23. II. *to be short of breath, gasp*, Arist. *Pr.*886b14. III. Pass., *to be thoroughly cooled, chilled*, ib.882a36, Plu.2.695d.

ἐκψωμίζω, of corn, *to be infested with grubs*, Hsch. s. v. ψώμηκες.

ἔκω, barbarism for ἔχω in Ar.*Th.*1197, 1220.

ἑκών, ἑκοῦσα, ἑκόν: (ϝέκ- *IG*9(1).334.12 (Locr.), *GDI*5131*b* (Crete), cf. γεκαθά; cf. Skt. *váśmi* 'wish'):—*readily*, Od.4.649, etc.; freq. contrasted with ἄκων, ἑ. ἀέκοντί γε θυμῷ Il.4.43; οὐ γάρ τίς με βίῃ γε ἑ. ἀέκοντα δίηται 7.197; ἑκόνθ' ἑκόντι Ζηνὶ συμπαραστατεῖν A.*Pr.*220; πάρειμι δ' ἄκων οὐχ ἑκοῦσιν S.*Ant.*276; ἑκόντα μήτ' ἄκοντα Id.*Ph.*771; βίᾳ τε κοὐχ ἑκών Id.*OC*935; ἑ. παρ' ἑκόντος λαμβάνειν, i.e. by mutual consent, D.21.44; τὴν φύσιν ἑκοῦσαν καὶ οὐ παθοῦσαν τὰ δέοντα ποιεῖν Gal.19.171. 2. *wittingly, purposely*, ἑκὼν δ' ἡμάρτανε φωτός Il.10.372, etc.; σφόδρ' ἑκὼν.. ἀγνοεῖν προσποιούμενος D.29.13. 3. in Att. Prose (cf. Phryn.241), ἑ. εἶναι *as far as depends on one's will, as far as concerns one*, with a neg., Hdt. 7.104, 8.116, Pl.*Ap.*37a, al.; also in oblique cases, ὑπὸ σοῦ ἑκόντος εἶναι Id.*Grg.*499c; or in a sentence implying a neg., θαυμάζοιμεν ἂν εἰ.. τις ἑκὼν εἶναι (fort. delendum) ... ἀφικνεῖται; Id.*Lg.*646b: once affirm., ἑκὼν εἶναι.. οἴχετο Hdt.7.164. II. rarely of things, κακὰ ἑ. κοὐκ ἄκοντα S.*OT*1230. III. for Adv. see ἑκοντήν, ἑκοντί: regul. Adv. ἑκόντως is dub. in Aristid.2.187, 226 J.

ἔλα· ἥλιος, αὐγή, καῦμα (Lacon.), Hsch. (ϝελ-, cf. βέλα, γέλαν). II. imper. of ἐλάω, v. ἐλαύνω. **ἐλάα,** Att. for ἐλαία. **ἐλάαν,** Ep. inf. pres. of ἐλάω, ἐλαύνω, Hom.: but fut. in Il.17.496.

ἐλᾴδιον, τό, Dim. of ἐλάα, *young olive-tree*, Alciphr.3.13 (pl.). II. *a little oil*, Teles p.41 H., Sotad.Com.1.7, Arched.2.11, *PSI*4.418.11 (iii B.C.). (Written ἐλαδ- in codd., but ἐλαιδ- *PSI* l. c.)

ἐλάεως· ἀμπέλου εἶδος, Hsch. **ἐλαθερής,** ές, = εἰληθερής, Id. **ἐλαθρά·** ἐλαφρά, ἢ ἐν ἐλαίῳ ἑφθά, Id.

ἐλαία, Att. **ἐλάα,** ἡ, *olive-tree*, Hom., esp. in Od., 11.590, al.; ἱερὴ ἐ. 13.372, cf. Pi.*O.*3.13, Hdt.8.55, S.*OC*701 (lyr.), etc.; ἡμέρη ἐλαίη Hdt.5.82 (opp. ἀγρία ἐ. or κότινος); φέρεσθαι ἐκτὸς τῶν ἐλαῶν to run beyond *the olives*, which stood at the end of the Athenian race-course, i.e. to go too far, Ar.*Ra.*995, ubi v. Sch.; of the Indian *Olea cuspidata*, Thphr.*HP*4.4.11. 2. variety of δάφνη III, ib.4.7.2, Str.16.3.6. II. *olive*, Ar.*Ach.*550, Pl.*R.*372c, D.18.262, Dsc. 1.119, etc.—Acc. to Gramm. ἐλάα was the proper form in this sense, ἐλαία in the first; but ἐλάα is simply the Att. form, cf. *IG*1^2.94.33, 2.476.21, 1055.36 (also *PHal.*1.98 (iii B.C.), etc.). III. *naevus on the skin*, Melamp.p.508 F. IV. = δίφρου Κυρηναϊκοῦ μέρος, Hsch. [In ἐλάα, the penult. is long, E.*Fr.*360.46, Ar.*Ach.*550, *Pax* 578, *Av.*617, etc.; but ἐλᾰῶν in Alex.261.3 (where perh. ἐλῶν—ἐλᾶς is acknowledged by Ael.Dion.*Fr.*162, and found in *PRyl.*97.7 (ii A.D.), ἐλᾶν in 130.11 (i A.D.)—should be restored), and ᾰ in ἐλάη, *AP*4.2.12 (Phil.), 6.102 (Id.).]

ἐλαί-αγνος or **ἐλέ-αγνος** (Hsch.), ὁ, *goat's willow, Salix Caprea*, Thphr.*HP*4.10.1,2. **-άεις** [ᾱ], Att. for ἐλαιήεις. **-ᾰκόνη,** ἡ, *whetstone used with oil*, Paul.Aeg.7.3 (s.v. λίθοι).

ἐλαιάω, = διεγείρω, Suid., Zonar.

Ἐλαιβάριος, epith. of Apollo at Isinda, *Jahresh.*18 *Beibl.*6.

ἐλαιεμπορία, ἡ, = ἐλαιωνία, prob. in *Dig.*50.4.18.19.

ἐλαιεύς, έως, ὁ, = ἐλαιών, Ἐφ.Ἀρχ.1902.31 (Chalcis).

ἐλαΐζω, *cultivate olives*, Ar.*Fr.*119. II. *to be olive-green*, Hsch.

ἐλαι-ήεις, Att. **-άεις,** εσσα, εν, *of the olive-tree*, φλοιός Nic.*Th.*676, etc.; *planted with olives*, ἐλαιήεντες ἄρουραι *IG*14.1389 i 50. II. *oily*, νηδύς S.*Fr.*457; *full of oil*, Nonn.*D.*5.226. **-ηρός,** ά, όν, *of* or *for oil*, κεράμια Hp.*Mul.*2.114; γόμος *OGI*629.48 (Palmyra, ii A.D.); *of oils*, εἶδος Pl.*Ti.*60a; ἐ. δρόσος, i.e. oil, *AP*5.3 (Phld.); κόλον ἐ. *PSI*5.535.46 (iii B.C.); ἐ. ἐν πεδίῳ *oil-producing*, *IG*14.933. 2. *oily*, λιβάς ib.12(2).129.6 (Mytil.), cf. Gal.6.547. 3. of bees, *honied*, dub. in Pi.*Fr.*123.8.

ἐλᾰ-ϊκός, ή, όν, *of olives* or *oil*, πλήθη Aristeas 117; καρπός *BGU* 603.10; εἴδη *PFay.*64.4 (ii A.D.); τόκος *IG*5(1).1208.22 (Gythium): -κή, ἡ, *oil monopoly*, *PPetr.*2 p.84 (iii B.C.), *PRev.Laws* 43.15 (iii B.C.), etc. Adv. -κῶς Arr.*Epict.*2.20.18. **-ΐνεος,** α, ον, = sq., ῥόπαλον Od.9.320; μοχλός ib.394. **-ϊνος,** η, ον, *of olive-wood*, ἐλαΐνῳ ἀμφὶ πελέκκῳ Il.13.612; στειλειόν Od.5.236, cf. Thphr.*HP* 5.3.7, *PLond.*3.1177 (ii A.D.), etc. b. *of olive-branches*, στέφανος D.Chr.31.110. c. *of the olive-tree*, φυλλάς Str.16.4.13. 2. *of olive-oil*, Orph.*L.*717. 3. *of olives*, ἔλαιον Lxx *Le.*24.2, J.*AJ*3.8.3. (Also spelt ἐλαίινος *IG*2.678 *B.*)

ἐλαιο-βᾰφής, ές, *dipped in oil*, Hsch. s.v. ἐλαιωτῷ (-θεῖ cod.). **-βρᾰχής,** ές, Antyll.ap.Orib.7.21.8, Sor.1.82:—and **-βρεχής,** ές, Gal. 13.581, = sq. **-βρεκτος,** gloss on ἐλαιόδευτον, Zonar. **-βροχος,** ον, *soaked in oil*, Clearch.44. **-γᾰρον,** τό, *fish preserved in oil*, Steph. *in Hp.*2.309 D. **-δευτος,** ον, = ἐλαιόβροχος, Suid., Zonar. **-δόκος** or **-δόχος,** ον, *holding oil*, Hdn.*Epim.*78, Suid. s.v. ληκύθιον. **-ειδής,** ές, = ἐλαιώδης, Aret.*SA*2.6; ἰχώρ Aët.13.23. **-θεσία,** ἡ, *provision of oil*, *IGRom.*3.484 (Oenoanda, ii A.D.), *BCH*11.399 (Attalia). **-θέσιον,** τό, *oiling-room* in the palaestra, Vitr.5.11.2. II. = foreg., *SIG*900.18 (Zeus Panam.). **-θετέω,** *provide oil* at the baths, ib. 12 (ibid.), *Ephes.*3 No.15 (iii A.D.). **-θέτης,** ου, ὁ, *official who supplied oil*, *IG*5(2).50 (Tegea, ii A.D.). **-θηλος,** ον, *nurturing olives*, νᾶμα ib.14.1374. **-θρεπτος,** ον, f.l. for ἐλεόθρεπτον, *Et.Gud.* s.v. Ἑλένη. **-κάπηλος** [ᾰ], ὁ, *oil-dealer*, *PLille*3.55 (iii B.C.), Lib. *Decl.*26.18. **-κομέω,** *cultivate olives*, Poll.7.141. **-κομία,** ἡ, *the cultivation of olives*, ib.140. **-κομικός,** ή, όν, *belonging to* ἐλαιοκομία: -κή, ἡ, ibid. **-κόμιον,** τό, *olive-yard*, *IG*14.352 i 69 (Halaesa). **-κόμος,** ον, *rearing olives*, *AB*248, perh. to be restored in Lys.*Fr.*28; but II. ἐλαιόκομος, ον, (κόμη) *olive-clad*, Μαραθών Nonn.*D.*13.184. **-κονία,** ἡ, *plaster made from lime and oil*, Eust. 382.37, Steph. *in Hp.*2.384 D.: -κόνιον, τό, = *malta*, *Gloss.* **-λογέω,** *pick olives*, Lxx *De.*24.20, Ph.2.390. **-λόγος,** Att. **ἐλαολόγος,** ον, (λέγω) *olive-gatherer*, Ar.*V.*712. **-μελι,** ιτος, τό, *sweet gum from the olive-tree*, Dsc.1.31, etc. **-μετρέω,** *provide oil for*, τοὺς βουλευτάς *IGRom.*4.216 (Ilium).

ἔλαιον, τό, (ἐλαία) *olive-oil*, in Hom. mostly *anointing-oil*, used after the bath, λοεσσαμένω καὶ ἀλειψαμένω λίπ' ἐλαίῳ Il.10.577, cf. 14.171, 18.350, etc.; before wrestling and other gymnastic exercises, πωλησεῦντι τὸ ἐ. εἰς τὸ γυμνάσιον *IG*12(1).3 (Rhodes); ἔ. θεῖναι to provide *oil* at the baths, ib.4.597, 606 (Argos): prov., πῦρ ἐλαίῳ κοιμίσαι *Lyr.Alex.Adesp.*8(*a*); ἐλαίῳ πῦρ κατασβεννύναι Luc.*Tim.*44; εὐῶδες ἔ. Od.2.339; ῥοδόεν (rose-scented) Il.23.186; ἔ. ῥόδινον Hp. *Mul.*2.135; ἔ. λευκόν ib.136; τοῦ λευκοτάτου πάντων ἔ. Σαμιακοῦ Antiph.331. II. *any oily substance*, ἔ. χήνειον Hp.*Mul.*2.194; κίκινον, ἀμυγδάλινον ἔ., etc., Dsc.1.32,33, etc.; ῥαφάνινον ἔλαιον *PAmh.*2.93 (ii A.D.), etc.; ἔ. ἀπὸ σελαχῶν, like our 'cod-liver *oil*',

Arist.*HA* 520ᵃ18; ἔ. ἀπὸ γάλακτος *butter*, Hecat.154 J. III. at Athens, *oil-market*, ἀναμενῶ σε..πρὸς τοὔλαιον Men.896.

ἐλαιο-πάροχος, ὁ, *purveyor of oil*, *IG* 5(2).47.5, al. (Tegea, i A.D.). **-πῑνής**, ές, *stained with* or *soaked in oil*, Hp.*Salubr.* 3. **-πλήθης**, ες, *full of oil*, Phryn.*PS* p.70 B. **-ποιΐα**, ἡ, *making of oil*, *PRyl.* 393, Poll.7.140. **-πράτης** [ᾰ], ου, ὁ, *oil-dealer*, *PKlein.Form.* 699, al. **-πρῳρος**, ον, *like an olive at top*, Arist.*Ph.* 199ᵇ12. **-πώλης**, ου, ὁ, *oil-merchant*, D.25.47, *PHib.* 1.53.6 (iii B.C.), Lib.*Or.* 58.5. **-πώλιον**, τό, *oil-shop*, *Gloss.* **-ροος**, ον, *flowing with oil*, παλαίστρη Man.1.100. **-ρῠτος**, ον, = foreg., Epic.*Oxy.* 1015.11.

ἔλαιος, ὁ, = κότινος, *wild olive*, ἄγριος ἔ. Pi.*Fr.* 46, S.*Tr.* 1197, Paus. 2.32.10. II. a *bird*, prob. a kind of *warbler*, Alex.Mynd.ap.Ath. 2.65b, cj. in *AP* 7.199 (Tymnes); cf. ἐλέα.

ἐλαιο-σπᾰράγος [σπᾰ], ὁ, *olive-shoots* used as a vegetable, *POxy.* 1849, 1861 (vi A.D.). **-σπονδα** (sc. ἱερά), τά, *drink-offerings of oil*, Porph.*Abst.* 2.20. **-στάφῠλος** [ᾰ], ὁ, *vine grafted on an olive*, *Gp.* 9.14 tit. **-τόκος**, = δίκταμνος, *Gloss.* **-τρίβιον** (or **-τριβεῖον**), *oil-press*, *Gloss.* **-τροπικός**, ή, όν, *for pressing olives*, ἅρμενα *CIG* 2694*b* (Mylasa). **-τρόπιον**, τό, *olive-press*, *Gp.* 6.1 tit., *BCH* 26.182 (Syria, iii A.D.). **-τρῠγον**, τό, *lees of oil*, = ἀμόργη, Hsch. (-τρωγ- cod.).

ἐλαιουργ-έω, *manufacture oil*, *PRev.Laws* 50.20, al. (iii B.C.), *PTeb.* 314.21 (ii B.C.). **-ία**, ἡ, *manufacture of oil*, *PFay.* 91.22 (i A.D.), etc. **-ιον** (-εῖον *Gloss.*), τό, *oil-press*, Arist.*Pol.* 1259ᵃ13, *PRev.Laws* 44.4, al., D.L.1.26, etc. **-ός**, ὁ, *manufacturer of oil*, *PRev.Laws* 44.8, etc.

Ἐλαιοῦς, epith. of Zeus in Cyprus, Hsch.

ἐλαιο-φᾰνής, ές, *resembling oil in appearance*, of urine, Gal.19.588. **-φῐλοφάγος** [ᾰ], ον, *fond of eating olives*, κιχῆλαι Epich.157. **-φόρος**, ον, *olive-bearing*, ὄχθος E.*HF* 1178 (anap.); χώρα ἐ. land *fit for olives*, Thphr.*CP* 2.4.4: -φόρον, τό, *oil-shop*, *Gloss.* **-φυής**, ές, *olive-planted*, πάγος E.*Ion* 1480 (anap.). **-φυλλον**, τό, = φύλλον, *Dog's Mercury*, *Mercurialis perennis*, Ps.-Dsc.3.125. **-φυτεία**, ἡ, *planting of olives*, St.Byz.s.v. Φελλεύς. **-φῠτος**, ον, *olive-planted*, A.*Pers.* 883 (lyr.), Str.12.7.1; ἐ. δένδρεσι *set with olive-trees*, Id.17.1.35. II. Subst. ἐλαιόφυτον, τό, *olive-yard*, Plu.2.524a. **-χρίστης**, ου, ὁ, *municipal official responsible for supply of oil*, *POxy.* 300 (i A.D.), *BGU* 576.14 (ii/iii A.D.). **-χριστία**, ἡ, *supply of oil* for anointing, D.L. 5.71 (codd. **ἐλαιοχρηστία**, *use of oil*):—also **-χρ(ε)ίστιον**, *IG* 12(9). 236.17 (Eretria), *Ath.Mitt.* 33.382 (Pergam.), *JHS* 9.231 (Paphos):—Boeot. **ἐληοχρίστιον**, *BCH* 26.156 (Thespiae); *tax* levied for this purpose, *Ostr.Strassb.* 178 (ii/i B.C.). **-χροος**, ον, contr. **-χρους**, ουν, *olive-coloured*, Hsch. s.v. ἐλαΐζων. 2. *of the colour of oil*, of urine, Gal.19.588. **-χῠτέω**, *anoint with oil*, Paul.Aeg.6.74, Sor.2.60. **-χύτης** [ῠ], ου, Dor. **-τας**, ὁ, = φαρμακεύς (Rhod.), Hsch. II. *attendant who served out oil in the gymnasium*, *CPHerm.* 57.9, 59.7. **-χύτησις** [ῠ], εως, ἡ, *anointing with oil*, Sor.2.61 (pl.). **-χῠτος**, ον, *oil-distilling*, κοτύλαι Epic.*Oxy.* 1015.14.

ἐλαιόω, *oil*:—only Pass., *to be oiled*, Arist.*HA* 605ᵇ20; σπόγγος ἠλαιωμένος Ph.1.433; ἐλαιοῦται θρίξ S.*Fr.* 624, cf. Pi.*Fr.* 305. 2. *bring to an oily consistency*, in Alchemy, Zos.Alch.p.163 B. II. *gather olives*, Poll.7.146.

ἐλαιρόν, τό, a kind of *vessel*, *IG* 7.3498.52 (Orop., iii/ii B.C.). (Perh. for ἐλαιηρόν (sc. ἀγγεῖον).)

ἐλαιρός, ὁ, *a liquid measure*, Hero *Geom.* 23.64.

ἐλᾱ-ΐς, ΐδος, ἡ, *olive-tree*, Att. pl. ἐλᾷδες Ar.*Ach.* 998, cf. *IG* 2.836ᵃᵇ 29. II. = αἰγίλωψ, Hsch. **-ϊστήρ**, ῆρος, and **-ιστής**, οῦ, ὁ, *olive-gatherer*, Poll.7.146, 10.130. **-ϊστήριον**, τό, *olive-press*, *CIG* 2694*b* (Mylasa).

ἐλαι-ώδης, ες, *oily*, Hp.*Epid.* 3.17.α', Philum.*Ven.* 17.1; *oleaginous*, λιπαρότης Arist.*HA* 522ᵃ22; τῇ γεύσει Dsc.1.39. **-ών**, ῶνος, ὁ, *olive-yard*, *PCair.Zen.* 57.2 (iii B.C.), Lxx *Ex.* 23.11, al., Str.16.4.14, Ph.2.289, *Gp.* 3.11.1. II. *the Mount of Olives, Olivet*, *Act.Ap.* 1.12, al., J.*AJ* 7.9.2. **-ωνέω**, *purchase oil for the state*, *Inscr.Cos* 113. **-ώνης**, ου, ὁ, *purchaser of oil for the state*, *IGRom.* 3.739 xix 17 (Lycia), *IG* 2².1100. **-ωνία**, ἡ, *purchase of oil for the state*, *Dig.* 27.1.6.8, *Cod.Just.* 10.(56)55.1. **-ωνίδιον**, τό, Dim. of ἐλαιών, *PBaden* 33.8 (ii A.D.). **-ωνικός**, ή, όν, *concerning* or *belonging to the* ἐλαιῶναι, *Sammelb.* 5126 (iii A.D.). **-ώνιον**, τό, = ἐλαιωνία, *IG* 5(1).1176 (Gythium, ἐλε- lapis). **-ωνοπαράδεισος**, ὁ, *garden and olive-yard*, *POxy.* 639 (ii A.D.), etc. **-ωσις**, εως, ἡ, *treatment with oil* or *reduction to an oily consistency*, in Alchemy, Zos.Alch. p.215 B. **-ωτός**, ή, όν, *oiled*, Hsch. (-ωτῷ cod.).

ἕλανδρος, ον, *man-destroying*, epith. of Helen, A.*Ag.* 689 (lyr.).

ἐλάνη (ἐλένη Hsch.), ἡ, *torch of reeds*, Neanth.4 J.; also, *bundle of reeds*, Nic.*Fr.* 89.

ἔλανος· ἰκτῖνος, Hsch. **ἐλαολόγος, ἐλαοφόρος**, v. ἐλαιο-. **ἐλάπεδον**· τέμενος, Id.

ἐλαπρός, όν, barbarism for ἐλαφρός, Ar.*Th.* 1180.

ἔλαρ (i.e. εἶλαρ)· βοήθεια Hsch. **ἔλαρα**, = ἄλαρα, *butt of spear-shaft*, Id.

ἔλᾰσα, ἐλάσασκε, ἐλασαίατο, v. ἐλαύνω.

ἐλασᾶς, ὁ, an unknown *bird*, Ar.*Av.* 886.

ἐλᾰσ-είω, (ἐλαύνω) Desiderat., *wish to march*, Luc.*Cont.* 9. **-ία**, ἡ, = ἔλασις, *riding*, X.*Eq.Mag.* 4.4; *march*, J.*AJ* 2.10.2. II. *striking* from a die, *Gloss.*

ἐλᾰσίβροντος, ον, *thunder-hurling*, Pi.*Fr.* 144 (dub., prob. -βροντᾰ, voc. of -βρόντᾱς). II. *hurled like thunder*, ἔπη ἐ. Ar.*Eq.* 626.

ἐλάσιος [ᾰ], α, ον, *driving away* epilepsy, Plu.2.296f.

ἐλάσιππος [ᾰ], ον, *horse-driving, horse-riding, knightly*, Pi.*P.* 5.85; ἁμέρα *Lyr.Adesp.* 97; of the sun, Orph.*H.* 8.18.

ἔλᾰσις, εως, ἡ, *driving away, banishing*, τῶν ἐναγῶν Th.1.139, Ph.1.140; ἔ. βοσκημάτων *driving* of them *away* as booty, Plu.*Rom.* 7. 2. (sc. στρατοῦ) *march, expedition*, ἐπὶ Σκύθας Hdt.4.1, etc.; ἔλασιν ποιέεσθαι Id.7.37; also, *procession*, X.*Cyr.* 8.3.34; ἡ ἅλαδε ἔ. *IG* 2².847.20. 3. (sc. ἵππου) *riding*, X.*Eq.* 9.6, *Eq.Mag.* 8.2, Aristaenet.1.8; *charge of horse*, D.H.6.12, Plu.*Sull.* 19. b. *driving* a chariot, Luc. *DDeor.* 25.2. 4. (ἐλαύνω II) *striking*, Apollon.*Lex.* s.v. ἐλαύνωσι.

ἐλᾰσίχθων, ονος, ὁ, *earth-striking*, Ποσειδῶν Pi.*Fr.* 18.

ἔλ-ασμα, ατος, τό, *metal beaten out, metal-plate*, Ph.*Bel.* 69.51, D.S.5.33, Dsc.5.81, Paus.10.16.1. 2. general name for *probes* and other surgical *instruments*, Gal.2.574; ἔ. ξύλινον ibid.: esp. *flat end* of a probe, Heliod.ap.Orib.44.11.3. II. = ἔλασις, Eust.1306.55. **-ασμάτιον** [μᾰ], τό, Dim. of foreg., Dsc.*Eup.* 2.168, Heliod. ap.Orib.49.4.59, Gal.19.148. **-ασμίη**· κυρία, Hsch. **-ασμός**, ὁ, = ἔλασμα I, Aristeas 65, D.C.46.36. II. = ἔλασις, *Hippiatr.* 1.

ἔλασσα, Ep. aor. 1 of ἐλαύνω.

ἐλασσονέω, *to be deficient, wanting*, *PMagd.* 26.2 (iii B.C.), *BGU* 1195.19 (i B.C.).

ἐλασσόνως, Adv. of ἐλάσσων, *in a lesser degree*, Hp.*Vict.* 1.35, etc.; ἐ. ἢ κατ' ἀξίαν Antipho 4.4.6.

ἐλασσ-όω, Att. **-ττόω**: aor. ἠλάττωσα Lys.13.9, Plb.16.21.5: pf. ἠλλάττωκα D.H.*Comp.* 6, etc.:—Pass., fut. -ωθήσομαι Th.5.34, D. 21.66: fut. Med. in same sense, Hdt.6.11, Th.5.104: aor. ἠλασσώθην, -ττώθην, Id.1.77, D.10.33: pf. ἠλάττωμαι Apollod.Com.7.3, Plb. 18.4.3:—*make less* or *smaller, diminish, reduce in amount*, *PTeb.* 19.11 (ii B.C.), *PLips.* 105.28 (i A.D.):—Pass., *POxy.* 918 xi 3 (ii A.D.). 2. in early writers, *lower, degrade*, τὴν πόλιν Lys.13.9, Isoc.8.17; ἠλάττωσας αὐτὸν βραχύ τι παρ' ἀγγέλους Lxx *Ps.* 8.6; *cut down, shorten*, συναλοιφαῖς τὰ ῥήματα D.H.*Comp.* 6: c. gen., *detract from*, μὴ προστιθέναι τιμήν, ἀλλὰ μὴ ἐλασσοῦν τῆς ὑπαρχούσης Th.3.42:—Med., *reduce the power of*, τινάς Plb.22.15.1. II. Pass., 1. abs., *to be lessened, suffer loss, be depreciated*, of things, Th.2.62; of persons, Id. 4.59, al., *OGI* 139.10 (ii B.C.), *PTeb.* 382.13 (i B.C.), Phld.*Lib.* p.32 O., al., *Ev.Jo.* 3.30, etc.; μέγα τοῦθ' οἱ πατέρες ἠλαττώμεθα Apollod.Com. 7.3; also, *take less than one's due, waive one's rights* or *privileges*, Th. 1.77, D.56.14; but, *fall short of one's professions, act dishonestly*, Isoc.1.49. 2. c. dat. rei, *have the worst of it*, Hdt.6.11, Th.5.104, etc.; τῷ πολέμῳ Id.1.115; *to be inferior*, τῇ ἐμπειρίᾳ Id.5.72; πολλαῖς ναυσί X.*HG* 1.5.15; πᾶσι τούτοις ib.6.2.28; ἠλαττωμένος τοῖς ὄμμασι, of a one-eyed man, Plb.18.4.3; πρός τινα *POxy.* 215 ii 18: c. gen., *fall short of*, τῶν ἀρχετύπων Ph.1.606. 3. c. gen. pers., *to be at a disadvantage with* a person, πολλὰ μὲν οὖν ἔγωγ' ἐλαττοῦμαι κατὰ τουτονὶ τὸν ἀγῶν' Αἰσχίνου D.18.3; ἐλαττοῦσθαί τινός τινι Pl.*Alc.* 1. 121b; μηδὲν τῶν δημιουργῶν Id.*Grg.* 459c. 4. c. gen. rei, *suffer loss in respect of*, κεφαλαίου, τόκων, *BGU* 155.10 (ii A.D.); *to be in want of*, Lxx 1 *Ki.* 21.15(16): also c. dat., ib. 2 *Ki.* 3.29. **-ωμα**, ατος, τό, = ἐλάττωμα, D.L.9.68; *reduction in amount* or *number*, *BGU* 20.8 (ii A.D.), etc. **-ων**, Att. **-ττων**, ον, gen. ονος: Sup. ἐλάχιστος (q.v.):—*smaller, less*, formed from ἐλαχύς (q.v.), but serving as Comp. to μικρός, δουρηνεκὲς ἢ καὶ ἔλασσον Il.10.357; τοὔλασσον ἔχειν to have the *worse, be worse off*, πάντη Thgn.269; οὐδὲν ἔλασσον ἔχειν τῇ μάχῃ Hdt.9.102; ἐ. ἔχειν παρά τινι D.21.187; ἐλάττων γίγνεσθαι Ar.*Eq.* 441, D.3.29; οὐκ ἐλάσσονα πάσχειν A.*Pers.* 813; ἐλάττω νομίσας τὴν ἀρχὴν ἢ κατὰ τὴν αὑτοῦ φύσιν εἶναι *too small* for.., Isoc.11.11: abs., *too small*, Thphr.*Char.* 23.9; *below the average in height*, *PLips.* 1.9, etc. 2. c. gen. pers., *worse than, inferior to*, Ar.*V.* 599, etc.: but c. gen. rei, *giving way to, subservient to*, σιτίων X.*Lac.* 5.8; πάθους Plu.*Cor.* 34: abs., *worse, inferior*, τόποι *Gp.* 2.48.1. 3. neut. with Preps., περὶ ἐλάσσονος ποιεῖσθαι to consider of *less account*, Hdt.6.6; ἐν ἐλάττονι θέσθαι Plb.4.6.12; παρ' ἔλαττον τοῦ δέοντος ἡγεῖσθαι Pl.*R.* 546d; ἐπ' ἔλαττον (sc. ἁρμοσθῆναι) Id.*Phd.* 93b; δι' ἐλάσσονος at *less distance*, Th.7.4; πάντ' ἐν ἐλάττονι ποιεῖσθαι τῆς ἡδονῆς Heraclid.Pont. ap.Ath.12.537c. II. of Number, *fewer*, οἱ ἐλάσσονες the *minority*, Hdt.3.121; ἐλάσσονες ἀριθμόν Id.8.66; ἐ. πλῆθος Th.1.49. III. of Time, *shorter*, Pl.*Pol.* 295c, etc. IV. of worth or rank, οἱ ἐ. the *meaner sort*, Isoc.2.13, Alex.116.12. V. neut. ἔλασσον, as Adv., ἐ. ἢ μηδὲν A.*Pr.* 938, cf. S.*El.* 598, Pl.*R.* 564d, etc.; ἐ. ἄπωθεν *less* far off, Th.4.67; πλείω ἔλαττον, with numbers, more or less, *PLips.* 28.10 (iv A.D.), etc.: neut. pl., as Adv., = ἐλαττονάκις, Pl.*Cri.* 53a, al.: regul. Adv. ἐλασσόνως (q.v.). VI. with indecl. Numerals, the ἤ of Comparison is often omitted, οὐκ ἐλάττους ὀγδοήκοντα D.S.14.8; esp. in Adv. ἔλασσον, as μὴ ἔ. δέκα ἔτη Pl.*Lg.* 856d, al. (Orig. ἐλάχ-yων, cf. ἐλάχ-ιστος, ἐλαχύς.) **-ωτέον**, *one must diminish*, Archig. ap.Aët.6.28.

ἐλασ-τής, οῦ, ὁ, = ἐλατήρ I, *EM* 325.38. **-τός**, = ἐλατός, *PLeid.X.* 36,70 (iii/iv A.D.). **-τρέω**, Ep. and Ion. for ἐλαύνω, πολλοὶ δ' ἀροτῆρες..ζεύγεα δινεύοντες ἐλάστρεον they *drove* the teams, Il.18.543; κατ' ἀμαξιτὸν ἦν ἠλάστρεις Thgn.600; ἐ. τινά *to drive about*, of the Furies, E.*IT* 971; in later Prose, δαιμονίοις χόλοις ἐλαστρηθέντες D.H.1.23; *row*, Ion. part. ἐλαστρεῦντας (-εύοντας codd.) Arr.*Ind.* 32.9:—Pass., of ships, *to be rowed*, Hdt.2.158, 7.24; cf. ἐλαστροῦται (sic)· ἐλαύνεται, Hsch.; -ιῶν· διαγινώσκων, Id. **-τρον**, τό, *that which drives*, *EM* 325.34. **-τωρ**, ορος, ὁ, = ἐλατήρ, *App.Anth.* 3.175.

ἐλάσω [ᾰ], fut. of ἐλαύνω. **ἐλᾶται**· ἡλιοῦται, Hsch.

ἐλάτ-ειρα [ᾰ], fem. of ἐλατήρ, ἵππων ἐ., of Artemis, Pi.*Fr.* 89; βοῶν ἐ. Σελήνη Nonn.*D.* 1.331. **-έον**, *one must ride*, X.*Eq.Mag.* 2.7.

ἐλάτη [ᾰ], ἡ, *silver fir*, *Abies cephalonica*, ὑψηλή Il.5.560; περιμήκετος 14.287; οὐρανομήκης Od.5.239, cf. Thphr.*HP*3.9.6, etc.; also, *Abies pectinata*, ib.5.8.3. II. *oar*, as *made of pine-wood*, λευκαίνον ὕδωρ ξεστῇς ἐλάτῃσιν Od.12.172, cf. Il.7.5; later, *ship* or *boat*, E.*Ph.*208 (lyr.), *Alc.*444 (lyr.). III. *the spathe of the date inflorescence*, Dsc.1.109.4 (but, = βόρασσος (q. v.), ib.5), cf. Epich.160, Gal.12.151. IV. *sea-weed* supposed to resemble the fir, *Cystoseira Abies-marina*, Thphr.*HP*4.6.2.

ἐλᾰτηΐς, ΐδος, ἡ, *like the pine*, σμῖλος Nic.*Al.*611.

ἐλᾰτ-ήρ, ῆρος, ὁ, (ἐλαύνω) *driver*, esp. of horses, *charioteer*, Il.4.145, 11.702, Alc.*Supp.*8.14, etc.; ἵππων ἐ. A.*Pers.*32 (anap.); ἐ. βροντᾶς *hurler* of thunder, Pi.*O.*4.1; ἐ. λύρας *striker* of the lyre, *AP*7.18 (Antip. Thess.). 2. *rower*, Luc.*Am.*6, Nonn.*D.*39.306. II. *one that drives away*, Call.*Jov.*3, Opp.*C.*1.119; [μυὼψ] βοῶν ἐ. Coluth.43. III. *a broad, flat cake* (ἀπὸ τοῦ ἐληλάσθαι εἰς μέγεθος, Hsch.), Ar.*Ach.*246, *Eq.*1183, Callias Com.21, *IG*2.841*b* 7, *SIG*1026.9 (Cos). IV. *hoop-stick*, Antyll.ap.Orib.6.26.4. **-ήριος**, ον, *driving, driving away*, c. gen., καθαρμοῖσιν ἀτᾶν ἐ. A.*Ch.*968 (lyr.). II. ἐλατήρια φάρμακα *purgatives*, Hp.*Acut.*2, cf. *Epid.*5.7, Erot. b. ἐ. ἀπόβαμμα *lustral* water, *IG*4.1607 (Cleonae). 2. Subst. -τήριον, τό, *squirting cucumber, Ecballium Elaterium*, Hp.*Steril.*238, *Epid.*6.5.15, Dsc. 4.150, Thphr.*HP*4.5.1; *drug prepared therefrom*, ib.9.9.4, 9.14.1. **-ης**, ου, ὁ, = ἐλατήρ, ποίμνας E.*Fr.*773.28 (lyr.), *Ostr.Strassb.* 649.2 (iii A.D.), Glauc.ap.*POxy.*1802.37. II. epith. of Poseidon at Athens, Hsch. **-ικός**, ή, όν, *of* or *for rowing*, ἐπίφθεγμα, i.e. ὠόπ, Sch.Ar.*Ra.*180. II. ἐ. κύνες *hounds*, Hsch.

ἐλατίνη, ἡ, *cankerwort, Linaria spuria*, Dsc.4.40, Plin.*HN*27.74.

ἐλάτινος [ᾰ], η, ον, also ος, ον Anaxil.22.17: Ep. **εἰλάτινος**, η, ον, as also E.*Hel.*1461 (lyr.), *Hec.*632 (lyr.):—*of the fir*, ὄζοι εἰ. Il.14.289, cf. E.*Ba.*1070; ὕλα εἰ. Id.*Hec.*632; [ῥητίνη] Thphr.*HP*9.2.2; ξύλα *SIG*135.11 (Olynthus, iv B.C.). 2. *made of fir* or *pine-wood*, ἱστὸς εἰ. Od.2.424; πλάται E.*Hel.*1461, cf. Anaxil. l. c. II. *of the date inflorescence*, ἔλαιον Dsc.1.44.

ἐλᾰτός, ή, όν, (ἐλαύνω) of metal, *ductile*, Arist.*Mete.*385ᵃ16, etc. II. *beaten*, *POxy.*85 ii 16 (iv A.D.); χαλκός Hero *Bel.*96.10, Heliod.ap.Orib.49.3.8; *of beaten work*, σάλπιγγες Lxx *Nu.*10.2; θώρακες Jul.*Or.*2.57b.

ἐλατρεύς, έως, ὁ, *thrice-forged iron*, Hsch.

ἔλατρον, τό, = ἐλατήρ III, *SIG*57.36 (Milet., v B.C.), *Inscr.Prien.* 174.11 (ii B.C.), Hsch. II. a *garment*, Eucrat.ap.eund.

ἐλαττον-άκις, Adv. *fewer times, multiplied by a less number*, opp. πλεονάκις, Pl.*Tht.*148a. 2. *less frequently*, Arist.*Mete.*368ᵇ25. **-έω**, *receive less*, Lxx *Ex.*16.18; but, *give less*, ib.30.15. 2. *waste, be consumed*, ib.3*Ki.*17.16; *to be missing, defective*, *PMagd.*26.12 (iii A.D.). 3. Med., *lack, want*, ib.11.22. **-ότης**, ητος, ἡ, *being less*, opp. μειζονότης, Iamb.*in Nic.*p.33 P. **-όω**, *diminish*, Lxx *Pr.* 14.34, al.:—Pass., ib.*Ge.*8.3, 18.28.

ἐλαττ-όω, v. ἐλασσόω. **-ωμα**, ατος, τό, *inferiority, disadvantage*, D.18.237, Phld.*Rh.*2.29 S.; ἐ. ποιεῖν Plb.6.16.3. 2. *loss, defeat*, *IPE* 1².32*B*15 (pl., Olbia, iii B.C.), Plb.1.32.2, Onos.32.8 (pl.), etc. 3. *defect*, κατὰ τὴν ὄψιν D.H.5.23; περὶ τὴν λέξιν Id.*Th.*35; τὰ τῶν παιδικῶν ἐ. Chor.in *Rh.Mus.*49.510; σωματικὰ ἐ. Hierocl.p.49A., cf. Phld.*Ir.*p.52 W., al., Iamb.*Protr.*20 (v. ἐλάσσωμα). **-ωμάτιον**, τό, Dim. of foreg. 3, *Gloss.* **-ων**, Att. for ἐλασσ-. **-ωσις**, εως, ἡ, *making smaller* or *less, lessening*, ἡ ἐπιείκεια ἐλάττωσις τῶν συμφερόντων καὶ δικαίων Arist.*Top.*141ᵃ16, cf. Pl.*Def.*412b; τροφῆς Epicur. *Fr.*428a: abs., *loss, diminution*, Diog.Oen.64. 2. *depreciation, disparagement*, Arist.*Rh.Al.*1436ᵇ34 (pl.), *VV*1251ᵃ5 (pl.). II. *defeat*, in peace or war, Antipho Soph.*Oxy.*1364.164, Plb.2.36.6, Onos.36.3. III. *fault, defect*, Phld.*Lib.*p.20 O. (pl.); τῆς φύσεως Plu.2.2c. 2. *loss* of health or property, ἐ. σωματικαὶ καὶ αἱ τῶν ἐκτὸς Hierocl.p.49 A. **-ωτικός**, ή, όν, *reducing, diminishing*, Sor. 1.42. II. *inclined to take less, not insisting on his full rights*, opp. ἀκριβοδίκαιος, Arist.*EN*1138ᵃ1, cf. 1136ᵇ21; τῶν δικαίων Id.*MM*1198ᵇ 26; ἐ. ἑαυτοῦ M.Ant.5.15, Porph.*Abst.*3.26.

ἐλαύνω, Il.12.62, etc.: Ion. impf. ἐλαύνεσκον (ἀπ-) Hdt.7.119: fut. ἐλάσω [ᾰ], part. ἐλάσοντας X.*An.*7.7.55 codd., cf. D.H.2.36, (ἐξ-) Hp.*Loc.Hom.*46, *Nat.Mul.*32 (ἐλάσσω (παρ-) is f. l. in Il.23.427, and ξυνελάσσομεν is subj. in Od.18.39); ἐλάω A.R.3.411; Att. ἐλῶ, ᾶς, ᾷ, inf. ἐλᾶν, also Hdt.1.207, etc., and so Hom. in the resolved form ἐλόω Il.13.315, Od.7.319: inf. ἐλάαν (though this is also inf. pres., v. infr.) Il.17.496, Od.5.290: aor. 1 ἤλᾰσα, Ep. ἔλᾰσα Il.5.80, ἔλασσα 18.564, Ion. 3 sg. ἐλάσασκεν 2.199: pf. ἐλήλᾰκα (ἀπ-, ἐξ-) X.*Cyr.*4.2.10, Ar.*Nu.*828: plpf. ἐληλάκειν (ἐξ-) Hdt.5.90:—**Med.** (v. infr. 1.2), fut. ἐλάσομαι (παρ-) dub. l. in Arr.*An.*3.30.3: aor. ἠλασάμην Il.11.682, rare in Att., as Pl.*Grg.*484b; 3 sg. ἠλάσατο Ibyc.55; Ep. ἐλάσαιο, -ασαίατο, -ασσάμενος, Od.20.51, Il.10.537, Od.4.637:—**Pass.**, fut. ἐλασθήσομαι (ἐξ-) D.H.4.9: aor. ἠλάθην [ᾰ] E.*Heracl.*430, Ar.*Ec.*4; later ἠλάσθην *AP*7.278 (Arch.), *Sammelb.*997 (iv A.D.), (ἐξ-, συν-) Plb.8.24.9, 18.22.6, etc. (in Hdt. the Mss. vary between the two forms, ἐξελαθείς 7.165, ἀπηλάσθησαν 3. 54): pf. ἐλήλαμαι Od.7.113, Hdt.7.84 (ἐξ-), etc.; ἐλήλασμαι Hp.*Mul.* 2.133, Aen.Tact.31.4 (prob.), (ἐξ-) Plb.6.22.4, (συν-) A.D.*Conj.*233. 30: plpf. ἠλήλατο Il.5.400; poet. also ἐλήλατο 4.135; 3 pl. ἠλήλαντο Hes.*Sc.*143, also ἐληλέδατ', ἐληλέατ', ἐληλάδατ' vv. ll. in Od.7.86.—The pres. **ἐλάω** is rare and mainly Poet., imper. ἔλα Pi.*I.*5(4).38, A.*Fr.* 332, E.*HF*819, *Fr.*779.1 (also non-thematic 3 pl. ἐλάντω *SIG*1025.8 (Cos)): inf. ἐλᾶν Canthar.4, X.*HG*2.4.32: inf. ἐλάαν as Ep. inf. pres. is freq. in Hom. (v. infr. 1.2): part. ἐλάουσα Emp.4.5: impf. 3 pl. ἔλων Od.4.2, 3 sg. ἔλαεν A.R.3.872; ἀπ-έλα X.*Cyr.*8.3.32; but ἀπ-ήλαον in Ar.*Lys.*1001 is prob. an error for -ήλα'αν, Dor. for -ήλασαν:—radic. sense, *drive, set in motion*, of driving flocks, εἰς εὐρὺ σπέος ἤλασε μῆλα Od.9.237; κακοὺς δ' ἐς μέσσον ἔλασσεν Il.4.299; aor. Med. ἠλασάμην in act. sense, 10.537, 11.682: freq. of horses, chariots, ships, *drive*, ἐλάαν (inf. pres.) ἅρμα καὶ ἵππους 23.334; ἐς τὴν ἀγορὴν τὸ ζεῦγος Hdt. 1.59; ἐ. ἵππον *ride* it, Id.4.64, al.; κέλητας καὶ ἅρματα ἐ. *ride* and *drive*, Id.7.86; ἐ. νῆα *row* it, Od.12.109, etc.; στρατὸν ἐ. Pi.*O.*10(11).66, Hdt. 1.176, 4.91, etc. b. with acc. omitted, intr., *go in a chariot, drive*, μάστιξεν δ' ἐλάαν (sc. ἵππους) he whipped them *on*, Il.5.366, al., cf. S.*El.*734, 739; βῆ δ' ἐλάαν ἐπὶ κύματα he *drove on* over the waves, Il. 13.27; διὰ νύκτα ἐλάαν *travel* the night through, Od.15.50; ἐς τὸ ἄστυ ἐ. *drive* into the city, Hdt.1.60; ἐπὶ ζευγέων ἐ. ib.199; *ride*, Id. 7.88, X.*Eq.Mag.*3.9, etc.; ἐλῶν ἐς Θρηΐκην *marching*.., Hdt.9.89, etc.; *row*, μάλα σφοδρῶς ἐλάαν Od.12.124; ἐλαύνοντες *rowers*, 13.22, etc. c. in this intr. sense, it sts. took an acc. loci, γαλήνην ἐλαύνειν *to sail* the calm sea, i.e. over it, 7.319; so τὰ ἕσπερα νῶτ' ἐ. E.*El.* 731 (lyr.); also ἐλαύνειν δρόμον *run* a course, Ar.*Nu.*28; ὁδόν D.P. 586. d. Pass., [νηῦς] ἐλαυνομένη a ship *under way*, Od.13.155 (but πλοῖα ὑπὸ σκληρῶν ἀνέμων ἐλαυνόμενα *Ep.Jac.*3.4); τὰ κατάντη ἐλαύνεσθαι, of horses, *to be ridden* on steep ground, X.*Eq.Mag.*8.3. 2. *drive away, carry off*, in Hom. of stolen cattle or horses, βοῶν ἀρίστας Od.12.353; ἵππους Il.5.236; ἐ. ὅ τι δύναιντο X.*HG*4.8.18:—Med., Od.4.637, 20.51; ῥύσι' ἐλαυνόμενος Il.11.674, etc. 3. *drive away, expel*, ἐ. [τινὰ] ἐκ δήμου 6.158; ἄνδρας ἀπ' Οἰνώνας Pi.*N.*5.16: freq. in Trag., ἐ. τινὰ γῆς E.*Med.*70; μύσος, μίασμα ἐ., A.*Ch.*967 codd., *Eu.* 283 (Pass.), cf. S.*OT*98; ἄγος ἐ., = ἀγηλατέω, Th.1.126; ἐ. λῃστάς Ar.*Ach.*1188, etc.:—Pass., γῆν πρὸ γῆς ἐλαύνομαι A.*Pr.*682. 4. *drive* (to extremities), *persecute, plague*, οἵ μιν ἅδην ἐλόωσι.. πολέμοιο who will *harass* him till he has had enough of war, Il.13.315; ἔτι μέν μίν φημι ἅδην ἐλάαν κακότητος I think I *shall persecute* him till he has had enough, Od.5.290; θεὸς ἐλαύνει πόλιν S.*OT*28; Ἰωνίαν ἤλασεν βίᾳ A.*Pers.*771; μή τι δαιμόνιον τὰ πράγματα ἐλαύνῃ D.9.54; σὺ δ' ἀπειλεῖς πᾶσιν, ἐλαύνεις πάντας Id.21.135, cf. 173:—Pass., ἐλαυνομένων καὶ ὑβριζομένων Id.18.48; λύπῃ πᾶς ἐλήλαται κακῇ S.*Aj.*275; κακοῖς πρός τινος E.*Andr.*31; ὑπ' ἀνάγκης καὶ οἴστρου Pl.*Phdr.*240d; τὴν ψυχὴν ἐρωτικῇ μανίᾳ Ael.*NA*14.18; ἐλαύνεσθαι τὴν γνώμην *to be out of one's* mind, Philostr.*VS*2.27.5. 5. = βινέω, Ar.*Ec.*39, Pl. Com.3.4. 6. intr. in expressions like ἐς τοσοῦτον ἤλασαν they *drove it* so far (where πρᾶγμα must be supplied), Hdt.5.50; ἐς πᾶσαν κακότητα Id.2.124; εἰς κόρον ἐλαύνειν *push matters* till disgust ensued, Tyrt.11.10; εἰς ἴσον (sc. τισί) Onos.*Praef.*4: hence, *push on, go on*, ἐγγὺς μανιῶν E.*Heracl.*904 (lyr.); ἔξω τοῦ φρονεῖν Id.*Ba.*853; πόρρω ἐ. σοφίας *go* far in.., Pl.*Euthphr.*4b, cf. *Grg.*486a, X.*Cyr.*1.6. 39. II. *strike*, ἐλάτῃσιν πόντον ἐλαύνοντες Il.7.6; κιθάραν πλήκτρῳ E.*HF*351 (lyr.). 2. *strike* with a weapon, but never with a missile, τὸν σκήπτρῳ ἐλάσασκεν Il.2.199; ξίφει ἤλασε κόρσην 5.584; κόρυθος φάλον ἤλασε 13.614; ὀδόντας ἐ. *knock out*, A.R.2.785: c. dupl. acc., τὸν μὲν.. μεταδρομάδην ἔλασ' ὦμον him he *struck* on.., Il. 5.80; χθόνα δ' ἤλασε παντὶ μετώπῳ *struck* earth with his forehead, of a falling man, Od.22.94: c. acc. cogn., *inflict* a wound, οὐλὴν τήν ποτέ με σῦς ἤλασε 21.219:—Pass., c. acc. νῶτον ὄπισθ' αἰχμῇ δουρὸς ἐληλαμένος Tyrt.11.20; ἐλαύνεται εἰς τὸν μηρόν Luc.*Tox.*61. 3. *strike* one thing against another, πρὸς γῆν ἐ. κάρη Od.17.237; of weapons, *drive through*, διαπρὸ χαλκὸν ἔλασσε 22.295; [δόρυ] διὰ στήθεσφιν ἔλασσε Il.5.57, cf. 20.269; ἤλασε Λυγκέος ἐν πλευραῖσι χαλκόν Pi.*N.*10.70:—Pass., *go through*, Il.4.135, 13.595; *to be fixed in*, ὀϊστὸς ὤμῳ ἐνὶ στιβαρῷ ἠλήλατο 5.400; διὰ [σφονδύλου] διαμπερὲς ἐληλάσθαι Pl.*R.*616e. III. metaph., 1. *beat out* metal, *forge*, ἀσπίδα.. ἣν ἄρα χαλκεὺς ἤλασεν Il.12.296; πέντε πτύχας ἤλασε *beat out* five plates, 20.270; περὶ δ' ἕρκος ἔλασσε κασσιτέρου *make* a fence *of beaten* tin (with a play on signf. 2), 18.564; εὐνὴ Ἡφαίστου χερσὶν ἐληλαμένη χρυσοῦ a bed of *beaten* gold, Mimn.12.6; σίδηρος λεπτῶς ἐληλ. Plu.*Cam.*41. 2. *draw a line of* wall, trench, etc., ἀμφὶ δὲ τάφρον ἤλασαν Il.7.450; ἀμφὶ δὲ τεῖχος ἔλασσε πόλει Od.6.9; σταυροὺς δ' ἐκτὸς ἔλασσε 14.11; τοῖχοι ἐληλέατ' 7.86; τεῖχος τοὺς ἀγκῶνας ἐς τὸν ποταμὸν ἐλήλαται the wall *has its* angles *carried down* to the river, Hdt.1.180, cf. 185, 191; ἐληλαμέναι πέρι πύργον *having* a wall *built* round, A.*Pers.*872 (lyr.); ὄγμον ἐλαύνειν *work one's way* down a ridge or swathe in reaping or mowing, Il.11.68; ἐ. αὔλακα Hes. *Op.*443; ἀμπελίδος ὄρχον ἐ. *to draw* a line of vines, i.e. *plant* them *in line*, Ar.*Ach.*995: generally, *plant, produce*, ἐλᾷ τέσσαρας ἀρετὰς αἰών Pi.*N.*3.74. 3. κολῳὸν ἐλαύνειν *prolong, keep up* the brawl, Il. 1.575. 4. ἐξ ὅσσων ἐς γαῖαν ἐ. δάκρυ E.*Supp.*96.

ἐλαύτατον· δεινότατον, Hsch.

ἐλάφειος [ᾰ], ον, *of a stag* or *hart*, κέρας *hart*shorn, Arist.*HA*534ᵇ 23; ἐ. κρέα *venison*, X.*An.*1.5.2, *PSI*6.594.15 (iii A.D.). b. ἐ. δίκτυα *for catching stags*, Aen.Tact.11.6, 38.7. 2. *deer-like, cowardly*, *EM*326.10. 3. ἐλάφειον, τό, = ὠκιμοειδές, Ps.-Dsc.4.28.

ἐλᾰφῆ, ἡ, *deerskin*, Poll.7.90.

ἐλᾰφη-βολία, Ep. -ίη, ἡ, *shooting of deer*, Call.*Dian.*262: in pl., S.*Aj.*178 (lyr.). **-βόλια** (sc. ἱερά), τά, *festival of Artemis*, *IG*9(1).90 (Phocis), Plu.2.660d. **-βολιών**, ῶνος, ὁ (sc. μήν), the ninth month of the Attic year, in which *the Elaphebolia* were held, Foed.ap.Th.4. 118, etc.; also at Iasos, *CIG*2675; at Apollonia in Chalcidice, Hegesand.40. **-βόλος**, ον, *shooting deer*, Il.18.319; of Artemis, *h.Hom.* 27.2, Anacr.1.1: Dor. ἐλαφᾱβ- S.*Tr.*213 (lyr.).

ἐλᾰφ-ίαι· οἱ τῶν ἐλάφων ἀστράγαλοι, Hsch. **-ικόν**, τό, = ἐλαφόβοσκον, Ps.-Dsc.3.69. **-ίνης**, ου, ὁ, *young deer, fawn*, Aq. 1*Ki.*24.3, Hsch. **-ιον**, τό, Dim. of ἔλαφος, Sm., Th.*Pr.*5.19, *Gp.*2.

18.5. II. = κώνειον, Hsch. **-ιος**, ὁ (sc. μήν), = Ἐλαφηβολιών, at Elis, Paus.5.13.11. **-ίς**, ἴδος, ἡ, a *bird*, perh. *heron* or *egret*, Dionys.*Av.*2.11.

ἐλᾰφό-βοσκον, τό, (**-βοσκός**, ὁ, Hsch.) *plant eaten by deer* as an antidote against the bite of snakes, *parsnip, Pastinaca sativa*, Dsc.3.69, Plin.*HN*22.79, Aët.13.21. II. = ἐλελίσφακον, Dsc.3.33; = σκόρδον, Ps.-Dsc.2.152. **-γενές**· τῆς ἐλάφου ὁ μυελός, Hsch. **-ειδής**, ές, *deer-like*, Plb.34.10.8. **-κρᾶνος**, ον, *deer-headed*, ἵπποι Str.15.1.56. **-κτόνος**, ον, *deer-killing*, θεά E.*IT*1113 (lyr.). **-πους**, ποδος, ὁ, ἡ, *deer-footed*, interpol. in *Hippiatr.*115.

ἔλᾰφος, ὁ and ἡ, *deer, Cervus elaphus*, whether male, *hart* or *stag*, Il.3.24, etc.; or female, *hind*, 11.113, etc.; κεραός, ὑψίκερως, ib.475, Od.10.158; κεροῦσσα S.*Fr.*89; ἔ. βαλιαί E.*Hipp.*218 (anap.); ἔ. ἀντὶ παρθένου Lib.*Ep.*785.1; κραδίην ἐλάφοιο [ἔχων] with heart *of deer*, i.e. a coward, Il.1.225; φυζακινῆς ἐλάφοισιν ἐοίκεσαν 13.102, cf. Pl.*La.* 196e. (Fem. as a generic term, in Trag. and X.*Cyn.*9.11, 10.22, cf. αἱ ἔ. τὰ κέρατα ἀποβάλλουσιν Arist.*HA*611a27.) II. κέρας ἐλάφου *hartshorn*, *Gp.*13.8.2. III. *deerskin*, ἐλάφου πήρα Longus 3.15. IV. a kind of *cake*, Ath.14.649e. V. *figure of a deer* used as a weight, *IG*5(2).125 (Tegea, ii A.D.). (-φος as in ἔρι-φος, etc., ἐλα- from ἐλn̥-, cf. ἐλλός (from *ἐλνός), Lith. *élnis* 'stag'.)

ἐλᾰφό-σκορδον, τό, a kind of *garlic*, Ps.-Dsc.2.152. II. = ἀπόκυνον, ib.4.80. **-σσοΐα**, Ep. -ίη, ἡ, (σεύω) *deer-hunting*, *AP*6.253.8 (Crin.). **-στικτος**, ον, *tattooed with figure of a deer*, Lys.13.19.

ἐλαφρ-ία, ἡ, *lightness*: *levity*, 2*Ep.Cor.*1.17. II. *alleviation*, Aret.*CD*2.2. III. = ὀλιγότης, Suid. **-ίζω**, *make light*: hence, *lift up, carry*, Coluth.29,156; Ep. 3 sg. impf. -ίζεσκε, κούρην Mosch.2.130; ἐ. ἑαυτὸν ὑψοῦ Ael.*NA*9.52; πτεροῖς ἑαυτήν Plu.2.317e. 2. *make light of, scorn*, Archil.87, cf. Hsch. II. intr., *to be light and nimble*, E.*Fr.*530.8, Call.*Del.*115, Anyt.ap.Poll.5.48, Opp.*C.*1.85. III. Pass., *to be relieved* of forced contributions, *IG*5(1).1146.28 (Gythium, i B.C.). **-ιος**, ὁ (sc. μήν), month at Cnidus, *SIG*953.85.

ἐλαφρό-γειος, ον, (γῆ) *of light soil*, *Gp.*3.3.11. **-νοος**, ον, *light-minded*, Phoc.9, Nonn.*D.*10.247.

ἐλαφρ-ός, ά, όν, and in Pi.*N.*5.20 ός, όν: (v. ἐλαχύς) :—*light in weight*, τόν οἱ ἐ. ἔθηκε (sc. λᾶαν) Il.12.450; ξύλου ἐλαφρότερα Hdt.3.23; πῦρ Parm.8.57; opp. βαρύς, Pl.*Ti.*63c, etc.; in Epitaphs, γαῖαν ἔχοις ἐλαφράν '*sit tibi terra levis*', *Epigr.Gr.*195 (Vaxos), cf. *Sammelb.* 315. Adv., τά (sc. δένδρεα) οἱ πλώοιεν ἐλαφρῶς Od.5.240. 2. *light to bear, easy*, καί κεν ἐλαφρότερος πόλεμος Τρώεσσι γένοιτο Il.22.287; συμφορὰν ἐλαφροτέραν καταστῆσαι Antipho 3.3.12; πόνος -ότερος ἑαυτοῦ συνηθείῃ γίνεται Democr.241: later, Comp. ἐλαφρώτερον ἄλγος Max.173; ἐλαφρόν [ἐστι] 'tis *light, easy*, Pi.*N.*7.77, *A.Pr.*265, etc.; *easy to understand*, [προβλήματα] ἐ. καὶ πιθανά Plu.2.133e, cf. D.Chr.18.11; ἐν ἐλαφρῷ ποιήσασθαί τι to make *light* of a thing, Hdt.3.154; οὐκ ἐν ἐ. ποιεῖσθαι Id.1.118; οὐκ ἐν ἐ. no *light matter*, Theoc.22.212. Adv. -ρῶς, φέρειν ζυγόν to bear it *lightly*, Pi.*P.*2.93. 3. *light of digestion*, Plu.2.137a. 4. *shallow*, διάπλους *Peripl.M.Rubr.*55; δῖναι ib.40. 5. Act., *ease-giving*, B.*Fr.*8, Theoc.2.92. II. *light in moving, nimble*, γυῖα δ' ἔθηκεν ἐ. Il.5.122; ἦ μάλ' ἐ. ἀνήρ 16.745; ἐλαφρότατος ποσσί 23.749; χεῖρες.. ἐπαΐσσονται ἐ. ib.628; κίρκος.. ἐλαφρότατος πετεηνῶν 22.139, Od.13.87; [ἵπποι] ἐλαφρότατοι θείειν 3.370; ἐλαφραῖς πτερύγων ῥιπαῖς *A.Pr.*125 (anap.); ἐ. ποδί ib.281 (anap.); γονάτων ἐλαφρὸν ὁρμάν Pi.*N.*5.20; ἐ. ποδῶν ἴχνι' ἀειράμεναι Call.*Fr.anon.*391; ἐλαφρὰ ἡλικία the age of *active* youth, X.*Mem.*3.5.27; ἐλαφροί, οἱ, *light troops*, Id.*An.*4.2.27 (restricted to cavalry who fight at close quarters, Ascl.*Tact.*1.3): metaph., πόλιας θῆκεν ἐλαφροτέρας made them *easier in condition*, *Epigr.Gr.*905 (Gortyn). Adv. -ρῶς *nimbly*, Ar.*Ach.*217; ὀρχεῖσθαι πυρρίχην X.*An.*6.1.12. III. metaph., *light-minded, unsteady, fickle*, πᾶν πλῆθός ἐστιν ἐ. Plb.6.56.11; ἐ. λύσσα *light-headed* madness, E.*Ba.*851. b. *gentle, mild*, σφᾶς αὐτοὺς -οτάτους τοῖς συνοῦσι παρέχοντας Isoc.12.31, cf. Pl.*Ep.*360c. 2. *small*, ποταμός Plb.16.17.7; *of small power or strength*, πόλεις Id.5.62.6. 3. *relieved* of a burden, ψυχὴ ἐ. καὶ δι' αὑτῆς Plot.4.3.32. IV. Ἐλαφρός· Ζεὺς ἐν Κρήτῃ, Hsch. **-ότης**, ητος, ἡ, = ἐλαφρία, *lightness, nimbleness*, Pl.*Lg.*795e, Plu.*Lyc.*17, al.

ἐλαφροτοκία, ἡ, *low rate of interest*, *IGRom.*4.292.4 (Pergam., ii B.C.).

ἐλαφρ-όω, = sq., Hsch. s. v. ἀλεγύνεται. **-ύνω**, *make light, lighten*, πόλεμον Jul.*Or.*1.18c, cf. Babr.111.6 (Pass.), Aq.*Jb.*39.34 (40.4). 2. *relieve*, ἀνίας Eus.Mynd.1; κεφαλήν Ruf.ap.Orib.8.47(*b*).1:—Pass., ἐλαφρυνθήσεται τοῦ ὄγκου *Hippiatr.*126. b. *relieve* of fiscal burdens, ἑαυτὸν ἐ. τῆς συντελείας Just.*Nov.*43.1.2:—Pass., ibid.

ἐλαχία· ἐδάφη (Cret.), Hsch. **ἐλαχίζει**· πλανᾶται, Id.

ἐλᾰχιστ-άκις, Adv. *fewest times, least often*, Hp.*Fract.*42. **-ιαῖος**, α, ον, *minute, infinitesimal*, μέγεθος Diog.Oen.2. **-ος** [ᾰ], η, ον, Sup. of ἐλαχύς: Comp. ἐλάσσων (q.v.):—*smallest, least*, freq. with a neg., γέρας, δύναμις οὐκ ἐ., *h.Merc.*573, Hdt.7.168, etc.; λόγου ἐλαχίστου of *least* account, Id.1.143; ἐλαχίστου ἐδέησε διαφθεῖραι *narrowly* missed destroying them, Th.2.77; περὶ ἐλαχίστου ποιεῖσθαι Pl.*Ap.*30a; παρ' ἐλάχιστον ἐποίησεν αὐτοὺς ἀφαιρεθῆναι D.17.22. 2. of Time, *shortest*, δι' ἐλαχίστου (sc. χρόνου) Th.3.39; δι' ἐλαχίστης βουλῆς with *shortest* deliberation, Id.1.138. 3. of Number, *fewest*, Pl.*R.*378a; ἐ. τὸν ἀριθμόν Arist.*Pol.*1312a30; ἐν ἐλαχίστοις δυσὶν between two *at least*, Id.*EN*1131a15. 4. Math., ἐλάχιστα καὶ μέγιστα *minima* and maxima, Apollon.Perg.*Con.*1 *Praef.* II. τὸ ἐλάχιστον, τοὐλάχιστον, *at the least*, Hdt.2.13, X.*An.*5.7.8, D.4.21; ἐλάχιστα *least* of any one, Th.1.70; ὡς ἐ. as *little as possible*, Pl.*Phd.*63d. III. from ἐλάχιστος came a new Comp. ἐλαχιστότερος *less than the least*, ἐ. πάντων ἁγίων *Ep.Eph.*3.8: Sup. ἐλαχιστότατος *very least of all*, S.E.*M.*3.54, 9.406. **-ότης**, ητος, ἡ, = *exiguitas*, *Gloss.*

ἔλαχος, ον, = ἐλαχύς, Call.*Fr.*349.

ἐλᾰχύ-νωτος [ῠ], ον, *short-backed*, prob. in Pi.*Pae.*4.14. **-πτέρυξ**, υγος, ὁ, ἡ, *short-finned*, of the dolphin, Id.*P.*4.17.

ἐλαχύς, ἐλάχεια (not -εῖα, Hdn.Gr.1.249), ἐλαχύ, *small, short, mean, little*: old Ep. Positive, whence ἐλάσσων, ἐλάχιστος are formed: in early Ep. only fem., *h.Ap.*197, v. l. in Od.9.116, 10.509 (v. λάχεια): in later Ep., Archyt.Amphiss.2, Euph.11, Nic.*Th.*324, Opp.*C.*3.480, Nonn.*D.*37.314: neut. ἐλαχὺ σκάφος *AP*7.498 (Antip.). (*legu̯h-* or *lengu̯h-*, cf. Lat. *levis*, Lith. *leñgvas* 'light'.)

ἔλαψ, = ἔλλοψ, *Gp.*20.7.1.

ἐλάω, Ion. **ἐλόω**, poet. pres. for ἐλαύνω; v. ἐλαύνω init.

ἐλᾱών, = ἐλαιών, *PLond.*5.1769 (vi A.D.).

ἔλδομαι and **ἐέλδομαι**, poet. Verb, only pres. and impf., *wish, long*, c. inf., Il.13.638, Od.4.162, Pi.*O.*1.4: c. gen., *long for*, σὴν ἄλοχον τῆς αἰὲν ἐέλδεαι Od.5.210; ἐλδόμεναι πεδίοιο (of mules) *eager to reach* it, Il.23.122: c. acc., *desire*, ἐὸν αὐτοῦ χρεῖος ἐελδόμενος Od.1.409, cf. Il.5.481: abs., νόστησας ἐελδομένοισι μάλ' ἡμῖν Od.24.400:—Pass. only once, νῦν τοι ἐελδέσθω πόλεμος *be* war now *welcome* to thee, Il.16.494.

ἔλδωρ, Hdn.Gr.2.770 (ἔλδ- ib.938 cod.), Ep. **ἐέλδωρ**, τό, *wish, longing, desire*, Il.1.41, Hes.*Sc.*36, etc.: fem., Ibyc.18 (s. v. l.).

ἐλεά· κάνεα, πλέγματα, Hsch.

ἐλέα, ἡ, perh. *reed-warbler, Salicaria arundinacea*, Arist.*HA*616b12: **ἔλεια**, Call.*Fr.*100c.14; cf. ἐλεᾶς.

ἐλέαγνος, v. ἐλαίαγνος.

ἐλεαίρω, Ep. impf. ἐλεαίρεσκον Il.24.23: aor. 1 ἐλέηρα A.R.4.1308, *Sammelb.*2134:—lengthd. form of ἐλεέω, *take pity on*, τινά Il.6.407, Od.10.399, etc.—Ep. word, used by Ar.*Eq.*793 (anap.), Luc.*Trag.*305.

ἐλεᾶς (**ἐλέας** Hsch.), ὁ, an unknown *bird*, perh. = ἐλέα, Ar.*Av.*302.

ἐλέατρος, ὁ, = ἐδέατρος, *seneschal* or *steward*, *PCair.Zen.*59.5, 71.1 (iii B.C.), dub. in Ath.4.171b: but, = μάγειρος, acc. to *Et.Gud.*, where it is distd. from ἐδέατρος (q. v.).

ἐλεάω, later form of ἐλεέω, *EM*327.29, Lxx *Pr.*21.26.

ἐλεγαίνω, *to be wrathful, wanton, violent*, *EM*152.50, 327.6.

ἐλεγ-εία, = ἐλεγεῖον, Str.13.1.48, Plu.*Sol.*8, Heph.1.5, al. **-ειακός**, ή, όν, *elegiac*, πεντάμετρον D.H.*Comp.*25, cf. Heph.1.5; *written in distichs*, ἐπίνικον Ath.4.144e, etc. **-ειδάριον**, τό, Dim. of ἐλεγεῖον, Petron.109: also **-είδιον**, τό, Pers.1.51.

ἐλεγεινή· χαλεπή, Hsch.

ἐλεγείνω, = ἐλεγαίνω, Suid.

ἐλεγειογράφος [ᾰ], ὁ, *writer of elegies*, *AP*9.248 tit.

ἐλεγεῖον, τό, *distich consisting of hexameter and pentameter*, Critias 4.3 D., Th.1.132, Arist.*Po.*1447b12. II. in pl., ἐλεγεῖα, τά, *elegiac poem* or *inscription*, merely in reference to the metre, not to the subject, Pl.*R.*368a, Arist.*Rh.*1375b32, Lycurg.142, D.59.98; even in two hexameters, Pherecr.153.7; sg., Ps.-Hdt.*Vit.Hom.*36. 2. later, *lament, elegy*, Paus.10.7.5, Luc.*Tim.*46; cf. ἐλεγεῖα· τὰ ἐπιτάφια ποιήματα, Hsch.: in sg., D.S.11.14, D.H.1.49, Plu.*Them.*8, etc. III. *a single line in an elegiac inscription*, prop. *the pentameter*, Id.2.1141a, Heph.15.14.

ἐλεγειοποιός, ὁ, *elegiac poet*, Arist.*Po.*1447b14, Ath.14.632d.

ἐλεγεῖος, α, ον, *elegiac*, δίστιχον Ael.*VH*1.17.

ἐλεγίαμβος, ὁ, the verse – ◡◡ – ◡◡ – ◡ – ◡ – ◡, Mar.Vict.p.145 K.

ἐλεγῖνος, ὁ, a *fish*, Arist.*HA*610b6.

ἐλεγκ-τέον, (ἐλέγχω) *one must refute*, Pl.*Lg.*905d; *one must reject, disapprove*, Ath.Med.ap.Orib.*inc.*23.13. b. *one must test*, Onos.1.19. c. *one must convict*, τινά τινος Them.*Or.*21.253a. 2. ἐλεγκτέος, α, ον, *to be refuted*, Str.2.1.35. **-τήρ**, ῆρος, ὁ, *one who convicts* or *detects*, τῶν ἀποκτεινάντων Antipho 2.4.3. **-τικός**, ή, όν, *fond of cross-questioning* or *examining*, Pl.*Sph.*216b, etc.; ὁ ἐ. ἐκεῖνος that *cross-questioner*, Id.*Tht.*200a; *fond of reproving, critical*, τῶν ἁμαρτανομένων Arist.*Rh.*1381a31, cf. Longin.4.1 (Sup.); ἐ. βίος Jul.*Or.*6.191a. Adv. -κῶς X.*Smp.*4.2, etc.: Sup., Luc.*Demon.*55. 2. *refutative*, of indirect modes of proof such as the reductio ad absurdum, ἐνθυμήματα Arist.*Rh.*1396b25. Adv. -κῶς Alex.Aphr. *in Metaph.*272.32. 3. -κά, τά, *means of detecting*, πάθους Alex.Trall.1.15. **-τός**, ή, όν, *fit to be refuted* or *worthy of reproof*, Hsch.

ἐλεγμός, ὁ, = ἔλεγξις, Lxx *Ps.*149.7 (pl.), al., 2*Ep.Ti.*3.16.

ἐλεγξίγᾰμος [ῐ], ον, *testing a wife's fidelity*, ποταμός *AP*9.125.

ἐλεγξῖνος, ὁ, *wrangler*, pun on the name of the philosopher Alexinus, D.L.2.109.

ἔλεγξις, εως, ἡ, *refuting, reproving*, Lxx *Jb.*21.4, al.; πικρὸς πρὸς τὰς ἐ. Philostr.*VA*2.22 (pl.). 2. *conviction*, παρανομίας 2*Ep.Pet.*2.16.

ἔλεγος, ὁ, *song, melody*, orig. accompanied by the flute, cf. ἄλυρος ἔ. E.*Hel.*185 (lyr.), *IT*146 (lyr.); Ἀσίας ἔ. ἰήιος Id.*Hyps.Fr.*3(1)iii 9; so Ἔλεγοι, title of a νόμος αὐλῳδικός, Plu.2.1132d; of the *song* of the nightingale, Ar.*Av.*218 (pl.); ἔλεγον οἶτον, of the halcyon, E.*IT*1091 (lyr.); later, *lament, song of mourning*, A.R.2.782. II. *poem in elegiac distichs*, Call.*Fr.*121; ἱλαροὶ ἔ. *AP*10.19 (Apollonid.). (Commonly derived from ἒ ἒ λέγειν, to cry woe! woe! *EM*326.49.)

ἐλεγχ-είη, ἡ, *reproach, disgrace*, Il.22.100, al., A.R.3.1114 (pl.),

Q.S.1.22. -ής, ές, *worthy of reproof*; of men, *cowardly*, ἐλεγχέες Il.4.242, 24.239: irreg. Sup. ἐλέγχιστος 2.285, etc. II. *reproachful*, μῦθος Nonn.*D*.40.35. -ιον, τό, Dim. of ἔλεγχος (B) IV, *Gloss*.

ἐλεγχοειδής, ές, *like a refutation*, Arist.*SE*174b18, 175a40.

ἔλεγχος (A), εος, τό, *reproach, disgrace, dishonour*, δὴ γὰρ ἔλεγχος ἔσσεται εἴ κεν νῆας ἕλῃ κορυθαίολος Ἕκτωρ Il.11.314; ἡμῖν δ' ἂν ἐλέγχεα ταῦτα γένοιτο Od.21.329, cf. Pi.*N*.3.15; of men, the abstr. being put for the concrete, κάκ' ἐλέγχεα base *reproaches* to your name, Il.5.787, al., Hes.*Th*.26; ἐλέγχεα alone, Il.24.260.

ἔλεγχος (B), ὁ, *argument of disproof* or *refutation*, πολύδηρις ἔ. Parm.1.36, cf. Pl.*Phdr*.276a; ὁ ἔ. συναγωγὴ τῶν ἀντικειμένων ἐστίν Arist.*Rh*.1410a22, cf. 1396b26; ἔ. δὲ συλλογισμὸς μετ' ἀντιφάσεως τοῦ συμπεράσματος Id.*SE*165a2, cf. *APr*.66b11; ἐλέγχου ἄγνοια, *ignoratio elenchi*, Id.*SE*168a18; ὅταν ὑπὸ τῶν ἐ. πιέζωνται Phld.*D*.3.8. II. generally, *cross-examining, testing, scrutiny*, esp. for purposes of *refutation*, οὐκ ἔχει ἔλεγχον does not admit of *disproof*, Hdt.2.23; τῶνδ' ἔλεγχον, abs., *as a test* of this, S.*OT*603; τὰ ψευδῆ ἔλεγχον ἔχει Th.3.53; ἔ. παραδοῦναί τινι to give him *an opportunity of refuting*, Pl.*Phdr*.273c; δόμεν τι βασάνῳ ἐς ἔ. to submit it to *scrutiny*, Pi.*N*.8.21; χρυσὸς νόθου ἀρετῆς ἔ. *Com.Adesp*.195; ἀρετῆς ἔ. δοῦναι *a proof* or *test* of it, And.1.150; ἔ. διδόναι τοῦ βίου to give *an account* of one's life, Pl.*Ap*.39c; οἱ ἔ. περὶ ὀρφανῶν Is.4.22; τὸ πρᾶγμα τὸν ἔ. δώσει D.4.15; ἔ. ποιεῖν τινός to *test* it, Ar.*Ra*.786; ἔ. ποιήσασθαι τῶν πεπραγμένων Antipho 1.7; ἔ. λαβεῖν τινός make *trial* of it, ib.12; ἐλέγχους ἀποδέχεσθαι to admit *tests*, Lys.19.6; ἐλέγχους προσφέρειν to allege them, Ar.*Lys*.484; διάπειρα βροτῶν ἔ. Pi.*O*.4.20; οὐδὲ ἔ. παρασχὼν οὐδὲ βάσανον Antipho 2.4.7; ἔ. διδόναι And.2.4; εἰς ἔ. πεσεῖν to be *convicted*, E.*Hipp*.1310, cf. *HF* 73; δεικνυμένων ἐ. Id.*Heracl*.905 (lyr.); οὔτ' εἰς ἔ. χειρὸς οὐδ' ἔργου μολών S.*OC*1297; εἰς ἔ. ἐξιέναι to proceed to the *proof*, put to the *test*, Id.*Ph*.98; or, to be put to the *proof*, Id.*Fr*.105; ἐξελθεῖν E.*Alc*.640; εἰς ἔ. ἰέναι περί τινος Pl.*Phdr*.278c; εἰς ἔ. ἔρχεσθαί τινος Philem.93.3; καταστῆναι εἰς ἔ. καὶ λόγον Isoc.12.150; ἔ. φεύγειν Antipho 5.38; οἱ περὶ Παυσανίαν ἔ. *the evidence on which he was convicted*, Th.1.135; πίστις πραγμάτων ἔ. οὐ βλεπομένων *Ep.Hebr*.11.1. III. Ἔλεγχος personified, Men.545, Luc.*Pseudol*.4. b. applied to *Conscience*, τὸ συνειδὸς ἔ. ἀδέκαστος Ph.1.236; ἔ. κατάλογον ποιεῖται τῶν ἁμαρτημάτων [τῆς ψυχῆς] ib.291. IV. *catalogue, inventory*, *Gloss*., Suet. *Gramm*.8 (pl.). V. *drop-pearl*, Plin.*HN*9.113, Juv.6.459.

ἐλέγχω, Od.21.424, etc.: fut. ἐλέγξω Ar.*Nu*.1043, etc.: aor. ἤλεγξα Il.9.522, etc.:—Pass., fut. ἐλεγχθήσομαι Antipho 2.4.10, X.*Mem*.1.7.2: aor. ἠλέγχθην Antipho l.c., Pl.*Grg*.458a, etc.: pf. ἐλήλεγμαι Id. *Lg*.805c: 3 sg. ἐλήλεγκται Antipho l.c. (ἐξ-ηλεγμένοι is f.l. in Lys. 6.44): plpf. ἐξ-ελήλεγκτο D.32.27:—*disgrace, put to shame*, μῦθον ἐ. *treat* a speech *with contempt*, Il.9.522; ἐ. τινά *put* one *to shame*, Od. 21.424.—This usage is only Ep. II. *cross-examine, question*, Hdt.2.115, Pl.*Ap*.18d, etc.; μὴ 'λεγχε τὸν πονοῦντα A.*Ch*.919; φύλαξ ἐλέγχων φύλακα S.*Ant*.260; τί ταῦτ' ἄλλως ἐλέγχεις; Id.*OT*333, cf. 783; ἔλεγχ', ἐλέγχου Ar.*Ra*.857; ἐ. τινὰ περί τινος Id.*Pl*.574; ἕνεκά τινος Antiph.207.10; τὰς ἀρχὰς βασάνοις χρώμενοι ἐλεγχόντων Pl. *Lg*.946c: c. acc. et inf., *accuse* one of doing, E.*Alc*.1058:—Pass., *to be convicted*, Hdt.1.24, 117; ἐλεγχόμενοι εἴ τι περιγένοιτο τῶν χρημάτων D.35.36, cf. Pl.*Prt*.331c,d: with part., ἐλεγχθεὶς διαφθείρας Antipho 2.3.9, cf. 2.4.10; ἐλεγχθήσεται γελοῖος ὢν X.*Mem*.1.7.2. 2. *test, bring to the proof*, ἀνδρῶν ἀρετὰν παγκρατὴς ἐλέγχει ἀλάθεια B.*Fr*.10.2; πρᾶγμ' ἐ. A.*Ag*.1351 (Pass., τὸ πρᾶγμ' ἐλεγχθέν Ar.*Ec*.485); λόγον Pl.*Sph*.242b (Pass., Id.*Tht*.161e): with subject. clause, ἐ. τινά, εἰ.., A.*Ch*.851, Ar.*Eq*.1232. 3. *prove*, τοῦτο ἐ. ὡς.. Pl.*Phdr*.273b, cf. *Sph*.256c: abs., *bring convincing proof*, ὡς ἡ ἀνάγκη ἐ. Hdt.2.22; αὐτὸ τὸ ἔργον ἐ. Th.6.86; περί τινος D.21.5. 4. *refute, confute*, τινά or τι, Pl.*Grg*.470c, al., D.28.2, Luc.*Nigr*.4:—Pass., Pl.*Tht*.162a; χρυσὸς κλῇδας ἐλέγχει *proves that* they *avail not*, *AP*5.216 (Paul. Sil.). b. *put right, correct, prove by a reductio ad impossibile*, ὅσα ἔστιν ἀποδεῖξαι, ἔστι καὶ ἐλέγξαι τὸν θέμενον τὴν ἀντίφασιν τοῦ ἀληθοῦς Arist.*SE* 170a24; παράδοξα ἐ. Id.*EN*1146a23. 5. *get the better of*, στρατιὰν ὠκύτατι ἐ. Pi.*P*.11.49, cf. D.P.750, Him.*Or*.1.16. 6. *expose*, τινὰ ληροῦντα Pl.*Tht*.171d, cf. X.*Mem*.1.7.2, M.Ant.1.17; *betray* a weakness, Democr.222. 7. *decide* a dispute, ἀνὰ μέσον τῶν δύο Lxx *Ge*. 31.37.

ἐλεδέμας, corrupt in A.*Th*.83.

ἐλεδώνη, ἡ, a kind of *octopus*, Arist.*HA*525a17, Henioch.3, Artem.2.14.

ἐλεεινολογ-έομαι, *speak piteously*, Hermog.*Stat*.3, *Id*.2.7, Herm. *in Phdr*.p.196 A. -ία, Att. **ἐλεινο-**, ἡ, *piteous appeal*, ἐ. καὶ δείνωσις Pl.*Phdr*.272a, cf. Hermog.*Id*.1.1; πρὸς -λογίαν λέγειν Agatharch.21.

ἐλεεινός, ή, όν, **ἐλεινός** *h.Cer*.284, Att. (Eup.25) and Trag. (v. infr.), but **ἐλεεινός** Men.*Sam*.156 Pap.: written **ἐλεηνός** in Lxx *Da*.9.23, 10.11: (ἔλεος):—*finding pity, pitied*, δός μ' ἐς Ἀχιλλῆος φίλον ἐλθεῖν ἠδ' ἐλεεινόν Il.24.309; *moving pity, piteous*, 23.110, etc.; ἐλεινὸς εἰσορᾶν *piteous* to behold, A.*Pr*.248; ἐλεινὸν ὁρᾷς thou lookest *piteous*, S.*Ph*. 1130 (lyr.); ἐσθῆτ' ἐλεινήν Ar.*Ach*.413; ἵν' ἐλεινοὶ τοῖς ἀνθρώποις φαίνοιντ' εἶναι Id.*Ra*.1063; ἐλεινοὶ οἱ ἀδικοῦντες Lys.24.7; ποιῶν ἑαυτὸν ὡς ἐλεινότατον D.21.186; -ότερος ἀνθρώποις τε καὶ θεοῖς Pl.*Lg*.729e. b. *having received mercy*, Lxx ll. cc. 2. *showing pity*, ἐ. δάκρυον a tear *of pity*, Od.8.531, 16.219, Men. l. c.; οὐδὲν ἐλεινόν no *feeling of pity*, Pl.*Phd*.59a, cf. *R*.606b. II. Adv. ἐλεεινῶς, Att. ἐλεινῶς, *pitiably*, S.*Ph*.870, Ar.*Th*.1063; ἐλεινῶς διακεῖσθαι D.19.81: neut. pl. ἐλεεινά as Adv., Il.2.314.

ἐλεεινότης, ητος, ἡ, = ἔλεος, Sch.E.*Or*.960.

ἐλε-έω, impf. ἠλέουν Apollod.Com.4.1: aor. ἠλέησα, Ep. ἐλέησα (v. infr.):—**Pass.**, pf. ἠλέημαι Men.595.2: (ἔλεος):—*to have pity on, show mercy to*, ὁ δ' ἐρύσατο καί μ' ἐλέησεν Od.14.279; σύ μ' ἐλέησον S.*Ph*.501, cf. Eub.1 D., etc.; ἐλέησον αὐτῶν τὴν ὄπα Ar.*Pax*400; ἐ. [τινα] ἐπὶ τοῖς ἀκουσίοις παθήμασι Antipho 1.27; τῆς τύχης τινά X. Eph.5.4:—Pass., Pl.*Ap*.34c, *R*.336e, *Ax*.368d; ἵνα.. ἧττον ὑφ' ὑμῶν ἐλεοίμην D.27.53; ἅμ' ἠλέηται καὶ τέθνηκεν ἡ χάρις Men.595.2, cf. 844. 2. abs., *feel pity*, Ar.*Ach*.706. -ημοποιός, όν, *giving alms*, Lxx *To*.9.6. -ημοσύνη, ἡ, *pity, mercy*, Call.*Del*.152. 2. *charity, alms*, Lxx *To*.4.7, *Ev.Matt*.6.2, D.L.5.17. -ήμων, ον, gen. ονος, *pitiful, merciful*, Od.5.191, D.21.101, Lxx *Ps*.111(112).4, *Ev.Matt*.5.7; of God, Lxx *Ex*.34.6, al.: c. gen., Ar.*Pax*425:—Comp. and Sup., ἐλεημονέστερος, -τατος, Arist.*HA*608b8, Lys.24.7. Adv. -μόνως, condemned by Poll.8.11. -ήσατο, prob. corrupt for ἐλῄσατο, Hsch. -ητικός, ή, όν, *merciful, compassionate*, Arist.*Rh*.1389b 8. -ητός, ή, όν, *to be pitied*, Sch.A.*Pr*.355. -ητύς, ύος, ἡ, Ep. and Ion. = ἔλεος, *pity, mercy*, Od.17.451.

ἐλεθαινομένη· ἀκολασταίνουσα, Hsch. **ἔλεια**, v. ἐλέα.

ἐλειήτης, ου, ὁ, *dwelling in marshes*, λέων Call.*Fr.anon*.88.

ἐλειθερεῖ· εὐδίᾳ, and **ἐλειθερεῖς** (ἐλειτεθ- cod.)· ἐν ἡλίῳ τιθέμενοι ἢ θερμοί, Hsch.; cf. εἱληθερής.

Ἐλείθυια, ἡ, v. Εἰλείθυια. **ἑλεῖν**, v. αἱρέω. **ἐλεινός**, v. ἐλεεινός.

ἐλειο-βάτης [ᾰ], ου, ὁ, *walking the marsh, marsh-dwelling*, A.*Pers*. 39 (anap.). -γενής, ές, *marsh-born*: τὸ ἐ., = ὄρυζα, Hsch. -δίακτος, ὁ, *conduit for draining marshes*, *CIG*2782.40 (Aphrodisias). -μᾰλάχη [ᾰχ], or -μολόχη, ἡ, *marsh-mallow*, Apul.*Herb*. 40, 38 (elaeo- codd.). -νόμος, ον, *dwelling in the marsh* or *meadow*, Νύμφαι A.R.2.821; ποίη Orph.*A*.1054; *situate there*, ib. 157. -ρριζον, τό, = κύπειρος, Hsch.

ἕλειος, ον (α, ον Ar.*Av*.244 (lyr.), Dsc.4.52): (ἕλος):—*of the marsh* or *meadow*, ἐ. ὕδωρ *marsh*-water, Hp.*Aër*.10; ἐ. δάπεδον the surface *of the meads*, Ar.*Ra*.352 (lyr.). 2. *growing* or *dwelling in the marsh*, δόναξ A.*Pers*.494; τῶν Αἰγυπτίων οἱ ἐ. Th.1.110; βίος ἐ. Arist.*PA* 693a15; [ζῷα] ἐ. ib.674b31; σχοῖνος Dsc. l.c.; ἀκτή Ps.-Dsc.4.173; ἕλειον, τό, = *asparagus*, *Gloss*. II. Ἑλεία, ἡ, title of Artemis in Cos, *Schwyzer* 251*B*5.

ἐλειός or **ἐλεῖος**, ὁ, a kind of *dormouse*, *Myoxus glis*, Arist.*HA*600b 12, Artem.3.65; μύες ἐ. *Edict.Diocl*.4.38. II. a kind of *hawk*, Hsch., prob. in Arist.*HA*620a21. III. *wood-worm*, Aristarch. ap.Hsch.

ἐλειο-σέλῑνον or **ἐλεο-**, τό, *marsh-celery*, *Apium graveolens*, Thphr. *HP*7.6.3, Dsc.3.64. -τροφος, ον, *bred in the marsh*, Archestr. *Fr*.15.7. -χρῡσος, = ἑλίχρυσος, Thphr.*HP*6.8.1, 9.19.3.

ἐλεϊσμός, ὁ, = ἔλεος, Aq.*Je*.36(43).7, 38(45).26 (leg. -ησμός).

ἐλείτης, ου, ὁ, *marsh-growing*, κάλαμος Dion.Byz.23. II. Ἑλείτας, ὁ, title of Apollo in Cyprus, *Schwyzer* 682.15.

ἔλεκτο, v. λέγω.

ἐλελεῦ, doubled ἐλελεῦ ἐλελεῦ, *a cry* of pain, A.*Pr*.877 (anap.); also an exclamation used at the ceremony of the ὠσχοφόρια, Plu.*Thes*. 22:—in form ἐλελελεῦ, *a war-cry*, Ar.*Av*.364, cf. Sch. ad loc.

ἐλελίζω (A), Ep. redupl. of ἑλίσσω (v. infr.), rare in pres., as Pi.*O*.9.13; impf. ἠλέλιζον Hsch., poet. ἐλέλιζον Maiist.42, Nonn.*D*. 2.525: mostly in aor. (v. infr.):—**Pass.**, impf. *h.Hom*.28.9: Ep. aor. ἐλέλικτο Il.13.558: pf. ἐλέλιγμαι Cerc.6.18:—*whirl round*, περὶ σχεδίην ἐλέλιξε [τὸ κῦμα] Od.5.314; ἡ δ' ἐλελίχθη [ἡ νηῦς] 12.416. 2. Med. and Pass., *move in coils* or *spires*, of a serpent, τὴν δ' ἐλελιξάμενος πτέρυγος λάβεν Il.2.316; ἐπ' αὐτοῦ (sc. τελαμῶνος) ἐλέλικτο δράκων 11.39, cf. A.R.4.143; σπείρας ὄφεων ἐλελιζομένη Ar.*Fr*. 500. II. in Il. of an army, *cause* it *to turn* and face the enemy, *rally* it, σφεας ὦκ' ἐλέλιξεν Αἴας 17.278:—in Pass., οἱ δ' ἐλελίχθησαν 5.497, 6.106; cf. ἑλίσσω II.1. III. *cause to vibrate*, μέγαν δ' ἐλέλιξεν Ὄλυμπον, of Zeus, ib.1.530, cf. 8.199; φόρμιγγα ἐ. *make* its strings *quiver*, Pi.*O*.9.13; ἀστεροπὰν ἐλελίξαις Id.*N*.9.19:—Med., ἵππον.. ἀγωνίῳ ἐλελιζόμενος ποδὶ μίμεο Simon.29:—Pass., *quake, tremble, quiver*, ἐλελίχθη γυῖα Il.22.448; ἐλέλικτο, of a *brandished* spear, 13.558; ἀμφὶ δὲ πέπλος ἐλελίζετο ποσσίν *h.Cer*.183; μέγας δ' ἐλελίζετ' Ὄλυμπος *h.Hom*. l.c.; φόρμιγξ ἐλελιζομένα Pi.*P*.1.4. (In Hom. ἐλελ- may have been substituted for ἐϝελ- (ϝεϝελ- in ἐλέλικτο); cf. ἑλίσσω.)

ἐλελίζω (B), aor. ἠλέλιξα X.*An*.5.2.14, Ep. ἐλ- Call.*Del*.137:—*cry* ἐλελεῦ, hence, *raise the battle-cry*, τῷ Ἐνυαλίῳ X.*An*.1.8.18: generally, *raise a loud cry*, E.*Ph*.1514 (lyr.); of a shield, *ring*, Call. l.c.:—Med., of the nightingale, *trill her lay of sorrow*, E.*Hel*.1111 (lyr.): c. acc., Ἴτυν ἐλελιζομένη *trilling her lament for* Itys, Ar.*Av*. 213 (lyr., but punctuation is dub.).

ἐλελίστροφε· εὔστροφε, ὁλόστροφε, Hsch.

ἐλελισφάκ-ίτης [ῑ] οἶνος wine *flavoured with sage*, Dsc.5.61. -ον, τό, = sq., Id.3.33, 4.103. II. = ψευδοδίκταμνον, Ps.-Dsc.3.32. -ος, ὁ, *salvia*, *Salvia triloba*, Thphr.*HP*6.1.4, 6.2.5.

ἐλελίχθ-ημα, ατος, τό, (ἐλελίζω A) *violent shaking*, Hsch. -ων, ον, gen. ονος, (ἐλελίζω A) *earth-shaking*, τετραορία Pi.*P*.2.4; Ἐλελίχθον, i.e. Poseidon, ib.6.50:—in S.*Ant*.153 Dionysus is called ὁ Θήβας ἐ. because *the ground shook* beneath the feet of his dancing bands.

ἐλελόγχειν, v. λαγχάνω.

ἐλελύζω, Aeol., = ὀλολ-, Sapph.*Supp*.20c.3.

ἔλεμα, ατος, τό, (ἑλεῖν) gloss on ἕλωρ, Sch.Il.17.667.

ἔλεμος· σπέρμα ὅπερ ἕψοντες Λάκωνες ἐσθίουσιν, Hsch.

ἑλέναυς, ἡ, *ship-destroying*, epith. of Helen, prob. for ἑλένας, A. *Ag*.689 (lyr.).

ἑλένη, ἡ, *torch*, Hsch.; cf. ἑλάνη. 2. *corposant, St. Elmo's fire*, Lyd.*Ost*.5. II. *wicker-basket*, to carry the sacred utensils at the feast of the Brauronian Artemis, Poll.10.191:—hence **ἑλενηφόρια**, *the feast itself*, ibid.

Ἑλένια (sc. ἱερά), τά, *feast in honour of Helen* in Laconia, Hsch.

ἑλένιον, τό, *calamint, Calamintha incana*, Chaerem.14.12, Thphr. *HP*6.6.2, Dsc.1.29. 2. *elecampane, Inula Helenium*, ib.28. 3. = σύμφυτον, Ps.-Dsc.4.9.

ἑλένιος· ἀγγεῖον χωροῦν τέταρτον, Hsch. **ἑλενοί**· κλήματα τὰ τῶν ἀμπέλων, Id.; cf. ἕλινος.

Ἑλενοφόντης, ου, ὁ, *slayer of Helen*, Sch.E.*Or*.1140.

ἐλεοδύτης [ῠ], ου, ὁ, *sacrificial cook* at Delos, Ath.4.173a.

ἑλεόθρεπτος, ον, (ἕλος) *marsh-bred*, σέλινον Il.2.776, Nic.*Th*.597.

ἐλεοκόπος, ὁ, dub. sens. in Lys.*Fr*.28. (Expld. either fr. ἐλεός I or as, = οἱ τὰ ἕλη κόπτοντες.)

ἐλεόν, Adv. *piteously*, Hes.*Op*.205: Comp. -ώτερον Hsch.

ἐλεός, ὁ, *kitchen-table, dresser*, in pl., Il.9.215, Od.14.432:—later **ἐλεόν**, τό, Ar.*Eq*.152,169. II. a kind of *owl*, Arist.*HA*592^{b}11.

ἔλεος, ὁ, *pity, mercy, compassion*, Il.24.44, etc.: also in pl., Pl.*R*. 606c, D.25.83; μ' ἔ. τινος ἐσῆλθε *pity for*.., E.*IA*491; ἔλεον ποιήσασθαι ἐπί τινι D.24.111; ἐλέου τυχεῖν παρά τινος Antipho 1.27:—later ἔλεος, τό, Plb.1.88.2, Lxx *Ge*.19.19, etc.: pl., ἐλέη, τά, ib.*Ps*.16(17).7; ἔ. ποιεῖν μετά τινος ib.*Ge*.24.12, al. (but masc. is also found, ib.*Ps*.83 (84).12, Plb.33.11.3, Agatharch.83, Phld.*Rh*.1.65 S., *Ep.Jac*.2.13, etc.). II. personified, worshipped at Athens, Sch.S.*OC*260; at Epidaurus, *IG*4.1282; Ἔ. ἐπιεικὴς θεός Timocl.31. III. *object of compassion, piteous thing*, E.*Or*.832.

ἐλεπόδιον· εἶδός τι βάναυσον (fort. βαλαυστίου), Hsch. **ἐλέποκες**· ἰχθὺς ὅμοιος φυκίδι, Id.

ἑλέπολις, poet. **ἑλέπτολις**, ι, εως, *city-destroying*, epith. of Helen, A.*Ag*.689 (lyr.); of Iphigenia, E.*IA*1476 (lyr.), 1511 (lyr.); of Lamia, *Com.Adesp*.303. II. fem. Subst., *engine for sieges*, invented by Demetrius Poliorcetes, D.S.20.48, Plu.*Demetr*.21, Ph.*Bel*.95.39, Vitr.10.16.4, etc.; ἄνευ μηχανῆς καὶ ἑ. Alciphr.3.45: pl., ἑ. μηχαναί D.H.9.68. 2. metaph., of a person, ἑ. τῆς Ἑλλάδος Hp.*Ep*.11; also ἡ τῶν ἀνοσίων ἑ. τοῦτο (sc. πένθος) Ph.2.191.

ἑλεσπίς, ίδος, ἡ, = ἕλος, *marsh-lands, meadow*, A.R.1.1266.

ἑλετός, ή, όν, (ἑλεῖν) *that can be taken* or *caught*, Il.9.409, Max.Tyr. 18.3. 2. = αἱρετός, Procop.*Pers*.1.16.

Ἐλευθεραί, αἱ, *Eleutherae*, on frontier of Attica and Boeotia:—hence **Ἐλευθερεύς**, έως, ὁ, title of Dionysus, Paus.1.38.8, etc.

ἐλευθ-ερία, Ion. -ίη, ἡ, *freedom, liberty*, Pi.*P*.1.61, Hdt.1.62,95; ἐλευθερίας φῶς A.*Ch*.809 (lyr.), cf. 863 (anap.); δι' ἐλευθερίας μόλις ἐξῆλθες, i.e. μόλις ἠλευθερώθης, S.*El*.1509 (anap.); ὑπῆρξαν ἐλευθερίας τῇ Ἑλλάδι And.1.142; *freedom from* a thing, ἀπὸ πασῶν ἀρχῶν Pl.*Lg*. 698a; τινός Id.*R*.329c, cf. *AP*6.228 (Adaeus). b. *manumission*, ἡ εἰκοστὴ τῶν ἐ., = Lat. *vicesima manumissionum*, *BGU*326 ii 11 (ii A.D.). 2. *licence*, ἀκολασία καὶ ἐ. Pl.*Grg*.492c; of Diogenes, Jul.*Or*. 6.185c. 3. later, = ἐλευθεριότης, *UPZ*62.7. 4. name of a *dance*, S.E.*M*.1.293. **-έρια** (sc. ἱερά), τά, *festival of Liberty*, held every four years at Plataea, in memory of the battle there, Posidipp.29, D.S. 11.29, Paus.9.2.6, etc.; at Syracuse, in memory of the restoration of the republic, D.S.11.72; at Samos, in honour of Eros, Erxias ap. Ath.13.562a: generally, ἐ. θύειν Henioch.5.10. II. *thanksgiving for liberty*, *IG*9(2).1034 (Thess.). **-εριάζω**, *speak* or *act like a freeman*, Pl.*Lg*.701e, Arist.*Pol*.1314^{a}8, Ph.1.380; ἐ. τοῖς λόγοις Plu.2.6e; πρός τινα Luc.*Cat*.1; ἐλευθεριάξαντας (Dor. aor.) Epimenid.ap.D.L. 1.113; *to be free*, ἀπὸ τοῦ πλούτου Crat.*Ep*.8; esp. from public burdens, *PFlor*.382.7 (iii A.D.): c. gen., πολυτελείας Chaerem.ap.Porph. *Abst*.4.8. **-ερικός**, ή, όν, *free*, πολιτεία Pl.*Lg*.701e (Sup.); τὸ ἐ. καὶ ἀνελεύθερον ib.919e. **-έριος**, ον, also α, ον X.*Smp*.8.16:—*speaking* or *acting like a freeman, free-spirited*, ἐ. καὶ δημωφελής Democr.282, etc.; ἀνδρεῖοι καὶ ἐ. Pl.*Lg*.635d; opp. δουλοπρεπής, X.*Mem*.2.8.4 (Comp.); of certain animals, as the lion, ἐ. καὶ ἀνδρεῖα καὶ εὐγενῆ Arist.*HA*488^{b}16. b. esp. *freely giving, bountiful*, ἐ. εἰς χρήματα X. *Smp*.4.15 (Comp.), cf. Arist.*EN*1120^{a}8, etc. 2. of pursuits, etc., *fit for a freeman, liberal*, πτηνῶν θήρας.. ἔρως οὐ σφόδρα ἐ. Pl.*Lg*.823e, cf. *Grg*.485b; ἐπιστήμη Id.*Ax*.369b (Sup.); τέχναι Plu.2.122d; βίος Men.408 (dub.); διαγωγή Arist.*Pol*.1339^{b}5; παιδεία ib.1338^{a}32; πρᾶξις, ἔργα, ib.1263^{b}12, *Oec*.1344^{a}28; ἡδοναί -ώταται, κινήσεις -ώτεραι, Id.*EN*1118^{b}4, *Pol*.1340^{b}10; τὸ ἐ., = ἐλευθεριότης, X.*Mem*.3.10.5: prov., ὕδωρ πίοιμι ἐ., i.e. may I become *free*, because slaves set free at Argos were then first allowed to drink of the spring Κυνάδρα, Antiph. 25. 3. of appearance, *frank, noble*, εὐπρεπής τε ἰδεῖν καὶ ἐ. X.*Mem*. 2.1.22, cf. *Lac*.11.3 (Comp.); ἵππος Id.*Eq*.10.17. II. Adv. -ίως, ζῆν Arist.*Pol*.1326^{b}31; τεθραμμένους Isoc.4.49, 7.43 (prob.): Comp. -ιώτερον, ζῆν X.*Mem*.1.6.3: Sup. -ιώτατα ib.4.8.1. III. Ζεὺς Ἐ. Zeus *the Deliverer*, Pi.*O*.12.1, Simon.140.4, Hdt.3.142, etc. IV. Ἐ., ὁ (sc. μήν), = Ἐλευθεριών, *SIG*1044.26. **-εριότης**, ητος, ἡ, *the character of an* ἐλευθέριος, esp. *freeness in giving, liberality*, Pl.*R*.402c, Arist.*EN*1119^{b}22, etc.; ἡ τῶν χρημάτων ἐ. Pl.*Tht*.144d: generally, *generosity*, ἡ ἐ. τῆς ὑπουργίας Plu.*Pomp*.73. **-εριών**, ῶνος, ὁ (sc. μήν), name of month at Halicarnassus, *Inscr.Cos*13. **-εριωτικός**, ή, όν, *claiming freedom*, λόγος Him.*Ecl*.7 tit.

ἐλευθερό-γλωσσος, ον, *free of speech*, Vett.Val.16.31. **-λάτομοι** [ᾰ], οἱ, *free quarrymen*, *PPetr*.3 p.105 (iii B.C.); δεκάταρχοι τῶν ἐ. ib. 2 p.33 (iii B.C.). **-παις**, ὁ, ἡ, gen. παιδος, *having free children*, Βενέτων δῆμος *APl*.5.359. **-ποιός**, όν, *making free*, θεός Ph.1.401; δόγμα Arr.*Epict*.4.1.176; *creating freedom*, Plot.6.8.12. **-πρᾱσίου** δίκη, ἡ, prosecution *for selling a freeman as a slave*, Poll.3.78. **-πρέπεια**, ἡ, *disposition of a freeman*, condemned by ib.119. **-πρεπής**, ές, *worthy of a freeman*, Pl.*Alc*.1.135c. Adv. -πῶς ibid.

ἐλεύθερος, α, ον (ος, ον A.*Ag*.328, E.*El*.868): later **ἐλαύθερος** *BCH*22.76 (Delph.); Elean **ἐλεύθαρος** *Schwyzer*416.3:—*free*, Hom. has the word only in Il. in two phrases, ἐλεύθερον ἦμαρ the day *of freedom*, i.e. *freedom*, Il.6.455, 16.831, al.; and κρητὴρ ἐλεύθερος the cup drunk *to freedom*, 6.528; ἐ. πιοῦσαν οἶνον ἀποθανεῖν Xenarch.5 codd. Ath. (fort. -ριον, cf. ἐλευθέριος I. 2); of persons, Alc.*Supp*.25. 11, Hdt.1.6, A.*Pr*.50, S.*Aj*.1020, Th.8.15, etc.: Comp., X.*Cyr*.8.3. 21: Sup., Id.*Hier*.1.16; τὸ ἐ. *freedom*, Hdt.7.103, etc.; τοὐλεύθερον E.*Supp*.438: c. gen., *free* or *freed from* a thing, φόνου, πημάτων, φόβου, A.*Eu*.603 codd., *Ch*.1060, E.*Hec*.869; αἰτίας Men.*Sam*.272; ἔξω αἰτίας ἐ. S.*Ant*.445; ἐ. ἀπ' ἀλλήλων *independent*, X.*Cyr*.3.2.23, Pl.*Lg*. 832d. b. ἐλευθέρα, ἡ, *married woman*, Ath.13.571d; *wife*, *POxy*. 1872.8 (v/vi A.D.); but, *freedwoman*, *IG*14.2490 (Vienne). c. *free*, of cities, in Roman Law, *BGU*316.3 (iv A.D.). 2. of things, *free, open to all*, ἀγορά X.*Cyr*.1.2.3; ἐ. φυλακή, = Lat. *libera custodia*, D.S. 4.46; περιωπή Ael.*NA*15.5; *unencumbered*, of property, D.35.21, *IG* 9(1).32.10 (Stiris), *SIG*364.36 (Ephesus, iii B.C.). 3. ἐλεύθερον εἶναί τινι, c. inf., *legally permissible, open to*.., ib.45.42 (Halic., v B.C.). II. = ἐλευθέριος, *fit for a freeman, free, frank*, φρήν Pi.*P*.2. 57; ἐλευθερωτέρη ὑπόκρισις Hdt.1.116; ἐλεύθερα βάζειν A.*Pers*.593 (lyr.); ὦ μηδὲν ὑγιὲς μηδ' ἐ. φρονῶν S.*Ph*.1006; δούλη μέν, εἴρηκεν δ' ἐ. λόγον Id.*Tr*.63, cf. *El*.1256; φρονήματα Pl.*R*.567a; βάσανοι ἐ. tortures *such as might be used to a freeman*, Id.*Lg*.946c (so φάσγανα E. *Fr*.495.38); τὸ ἐ. Pl.*Mx*.245c: freq. in Adv. -ρως, εἰπεῖν Hdt.5.93, al.; χαίρειν.. καὶ γελᾶν ἐ. S.*El*.1300; τεθραμμένους Isoc.7.43 codd. (fort. -ρίως); παιδευθεὶς ἐ. Aeschin.3.154 codd. (fort. -ρίως); ἐ. δούλευε, δοῦλος οὐκ ἔσει Men.857; ἐλεύθεροι ἐλευθέρως free and *like free men*, Pl.*Lg*.919e. (Cf. Lat. *līber*, fr. Ital. *loufero- (cf. Osc. *Luvfreis* 'Liberi'), I.-E. (*e*)*leudh-ero-*: the connexion with Slav. *liud*, OHG. *liut*, etc. 'people' is doubtful.)

ἐλευθεροστομ-έω, *to be free of speech*, A.*Pr*.182 (lyr.), E.*Andr*.153; in later Prose, Ph.1.474, al. **-ία**, ἡ, *freedom of speech*, D.H.6. 72. **-ος**, ον, *free-spoken*, γλῶσσα A.*Supp*.948.

ἐλευθερόψῡχος, ον, *free-souled*, Tz.*H*.10.620.

ἐλευθερ-όω, *set free*, τὰς Ἀθήνας Hdt.5.62; Ἰωνίην Id.4.137; πατρίδα A.*Pers*.403; πόλιν Id.*Ch*.1046, D.21.144; δούλους Th.8.15, etc.; ἐ. τὸν ἔσπλουν *set* the entrance *free, clear* it, Id.3.51; *release* a debtor, Hdt.6.59; τό γ' εἰς ἑαυτὸν πᾶν ἐλευθεροῖ στόμα he *keeps* his tongue altogether *free*, i.e. does not commit himself by speech, S. *OT*706; *free from blame, acquit*, τινά X.*HG*1.7.26:—Pass., *to be set free*, Hdt.1.95,127, al.; τυράννων Id.5.62; *indulge in licence*, Pl.*R*. 575a. 2. c. gen., *set free, release from*, φόνου E.*Hipp*.1449; χρεῶν Pl.*R*.566e; ἀρότρου βοῦν Hld.5.23; also ἐλευθεροῦντες ἐκ δρασμῶν πόδα, i.e. ceasing to flee, E.*HF*1010:—Pass., τῶνδε τῶν τόπων ἐ. Pl. *Phd*.114b; ἀπὸ τῶν πλουσίων Id.*R*.569a. **-ωμα**, ατος, τό, *release from*, κακῶν Procop.Gaz.p.141 B. **-ωσις**, εως, ἡ, *liberation*, Hdt. 9.45; ἀπό τινος Th.3.10; δούλων ἐ. ποιεῖσθαι Arist.*Pol*.1315^{a}37, cf. *POxy*.48.2 (i A.D.), etc.: pl., Plu.*Galb*.5. II. *licence*, Pl.*R*. 561a. **-ωτέον**, *one must set free*, Plb.18.45.9. **-ωτής**, οῦ, ὁ, *liberator*, Max.Tyr.21.6, Luc.*Vit.Auct*.8, D.C.41.57.

Ἐλευθία, Ἐλευθώ, v. Εἰλείθυια.

ἐλεύθω, causal of stem ἐλυθ- (cf. ἔρχομαι), *bring*, Dor. fut. ἐλευσίω· οἴσω, Hsch., Dor. 3 pl. aor. ἐλεύσαν Ibyc.*Oxy*.1790.18; cf. ἐπελεύθω.

ἐλευσέαν· τὴν βρυωνίαν, Hsch. (ἐλεψέαν poscit ordo).

Ἐλευσίνιος, α, ον, *of Eleusis*, *h.Cer*.266, Hdt.9.57, etc.; epith. of Zeus in Ionia, Hsch.; of Artemis in Sicily and Antioch, Id., Lib. *Or*.11.109; but mostly of Demeter, Antim.63, etc.; Δηὼ Ἐ. S.*Ant*. 1120 (lyr.); Ἐλευσείνιαι (sic) *Demeter and Cora*, *IG*4.955.14 (Epid.): hence, II. Ἐλευσίνιον, τό, *their temple at Eleusis*, And.1.110, *IG* 1^{2}.6.129. III. Ἐλευσίνια, τά, *their festivals*, ib.1^{2}.5, 2^{2}.847.24, Hyp.*Fr*.112, Paus.4.33.5, etc.: prov., Ἀττικοὶ τὰ Ἐ., of groups of persons confabulating, Duris 95 J.: Lacon. Ἐλευhύνια, τά, *IG*5(1). 213.11 (v B.C.). IV. Ἐλευσίνιος, ὁ (sc. μήν), name of month in Crete, *GDI*5183: also spelt Ἐλευσύνιος *SIG*712.8 (Olus), and so in Thera, *Test.Epict*.2.7, 3.3. [σῑ, exc. in *h.Cer*. l. c., S.*Ant*.1120 (lyr.).]

Ἐλευσίς, ῖνος, ἡ, *Eleusis*, an old city of Attica, sacred to Demeter and Cora, first in *h.Cer*.97; late Ἐλευσίν Str.9.1.12 codd. (but Ἐλευσίς 9.1.20), Corn.*ND*28. II. Advs. **Ἐλευσῖνι** *at Eleusis*, *IG*1^{2}.76. 10, al., And.1.111, Lys.6.4, etc.; later ἐν Ἐ. *IG*2^{2}.1028.11, al.: **Ἐλευσῖνάδε** *to Eleusis*, Lys.12.52, X.*HG*2.4.24: **Ἐλευσῖνόθεν** *from Eleusis*, And.1.111, Lys.6.45.

ἔλευσις, εως, ἡ, *coming, arrival*, εἰς βίον Corn.*ND*28, cf. Tz.*H*.7. 572, Sch.A.R.4.887, Hsch. 2. *the Advent* of Christ, *Act.Ap*.7.52.

ἐλευσίω, v. ἐλεύθω.

ἐλευστέον, (ἔρχομαι) *one must come*, Lxx 2 *Ma*.6.17.

ἐλεφαίρομαι, old Ep. Verb, perh. connected with ὀλοφώϊος (q.v.), *cheat with empty hopes*, said of the *false* dreams that come through the *ivory* gate (with play on ἐλέφας, cf. κραίνω), οἱ μέν κ' ἔλθωσι διὰ πριστοῦ ἐλέφαντος, οἵ ῥ' ἐλεφαίρονται Od.19.565: generally, *cheat, overreach*, ἐλεφηράμενος.. Τυδεΐδην Il.23.388. II. of the Nemean lion, ἐλεφαίρετο φῦλ' ἀνθρώπων he *used to destroy* them, Hes.*Th*.330. (Act. only in Hsch., who also has aor. 1 ἐλεφῆραι· ἀπατῆσαι.)

ἐλεφαντ-ᾰγωγός, ὁ, *elephant-driver*, Poll.1.140. **-άρχης**, ου, ὁ, *commander of a squadron of sixteen elephants*, Ascl.*Tact*.9, Phylarch.31 J., Plu.*Demetr*.25, Lxx 2 *Ma*.14.12. **-αρχία**, ἡ, *squadron of sixteen elephants*, Ael.*Tact*.23. **-ειος**, ον, *of an ele-*

phant, Dsc.2.76.17, Opp.*C*.2.500. **-εύς**, έως, ὁ, *ivory-worker*, *PPar.* 5 xliii. **-ηγός**, όν, *transporting elephants* (sc. νῆες), Agatharch. 83, cf. *PPetr.*2 p.135 (iii B.C.). **-ἴασις**, εως, ἡ, the disease *elephantiasis*, Cels.3.25, Dsc.2.70.3, Plu.2.731a. **-ιασμός**, ὁ, = foreg., *EM*561.4. **-ιάω**, *suffer from elephantiasis*, Phld.*Rh.*2.120 S., Dsc. 1.77, Ptol.*Tetr.*151, Antyll.ap.Orib.6.27.2. **-ίνεος**, α, ον, *of elephants*, ὀδόντες *IG*3.1376. **-ῐνος**, η, ον, *of ivory*, Alc.33.1, Ar. *Eq.*1169, *Pl.*815, al.; δίφρος ἐ., = Lat. *sella curulis*, Plb.6.53.9 (pl.), al.; οἶκοι ἐ. Lxx *Am.*3.15; τὸ ἐ. the *substance of ivory*, Pl.*Hp.Ma.* 290c. 2. *white as ivory*, μέτωπον *Anacreont.*15.12; τάριχος Crates 29. **-ίσκιον**, τό, Dim. of ἐλέφας, *young elephant*, Ael.*NA*8. 27. **-ιστής**, οῦ, ὁ, *elephant-driver*, Arist.*HA*497^{b}28 (cf. Demetr. *Eloc.*97), Porph.*Abst.*3.6. II. *shield of elephant-hide*, App.*Pun.*46.

ἐλεφαντό-βοτος, ον, *feeding elephants*, γαῖα Nonn.*D.*39.26. **-δετος**, ον, *inlaid with ivory*, δόμοι E.*IA*582 (lyr.); φόρμιγξ Ar.*Av.*219 (lyr.). **-θήρας**, ου, ὁ, *elephant-hunter*, Agatharch.54 (pl.), *Sammelb.* 4144, 4151. **-κομία**, ἡ, *care of elephants*, Ael.*NA*6.8. **-κωπος**, ον, *ivory-hilted*, ξιφομάχαιρα Theopomp.Com.25; ξίφη Luc.*Gall.* 26. **-μᾰχία**, ἡ, *battle of elephants*, Plu.*Pomp.*52. **-μάχος** [μᾰ], ον, *fighting against elephants*, ζῷον Str.16.4.15, cf. D.S.3.26. **-νωτος**, ον, *ivory-backed*, ἡνίαι Eust.583.44. **-πηχυς**, ὁ, ἡ, *ivory-armed*, Max.Tyr.14.6. **-πους**, ὁ, ἡ, gen. ποδος, *ivory-footed*, κλίνη Pl.Com. 208; τράπεζα Luc.*Gall.*14; ἐλεφαντόποδες τὰ ἐνήλατα καὶ κλιντῆρες Ph.1.666. **-τόμος**, ὁ, *ivory-cutter*, Opp.*C.*2.514.

ἐλεφαντ-ουργική (sc. τέχνη), ἡ, *the art of ivory-working*, Sch.Paul. Al.*P.*1. **-ουργός**, όν, *working in ivory*, ὄργανα Philostr.*VA*5.20: -γός, ὁ, *ivory-worker*, A.D.*Pron.*31.19, Them.*Or.*18.224b: **-ουργία**, ἡ, *ivory-working*, Vett.Val.3.23.

ἐλεφαντο-φάγος [ᾰ], ὁ, *elephant-eater*, Agatharch.55, Str.16.4. 10. **-φάνής**, ές, *like ivory*, ὀδόντες Eust.1877.42. **-χρως**, ὁ, ἡ, gen. -χρωτος, *ivory-coloured*, ὀδόντες ib.36.

ἐλεφαντ-όω, *inlay with ivory*, τράπεζα ἠλεφαντωμένη *IG*1^2.283. **-ώδης**, ες, *like an elephant*, ὦτα Aret.*SD*2.13. **-ωσις**, εως, ἡ, = *personacia* (i.e. ἄρκιον), *Gloss.* **-ωτός**, ή, όν, *inlaid with ivory*, *IG* 2.706*A*^{b}14.

ἐλέφας, αντος, ὁ (θήλεια ἐ. Phylarch.36 J.): irreg. gen. ἐλεφάντου *BCH*35.286 (Delos, ii B.C.): dat. pl. -τοις Lxx 1*Ma.*1.17 (v.l.):—*elephant*, first mentioned by Hdt. as a native of Africa, 3.114, 4.191; ἐλέφαντος ὀδόντες Id.3.97; of the Indian *elephant*, first in Arist. *Cael.*298^{a}13, *HA*610^{a}15, cf. Paus.1.12.4. II. in Hom. only of *elephant's tusk*, *ivory*, Il.5.583, cf. Hes.*Sc.*141, Pi.*O.*1.27, Pl.*R.*373a, *GDI*5500, etc.: Aeol. **ἐλέφαις** Sapph.*Supp.*20a10. III. = ἐλεφαντίασις, Aret.*SD*2.13, *IG*3.1423, Gal.15.331. IV. a *precious stone*, Thphr.*Lap.*37. V. a kind of *cup*, Damox.1.1. VI. = ἐλεφάντωσις, Apul.*Herb.*36.

ἐλεφιτίς, ὁ, a *fish*, corrupt in Hp.*Vict.*2.48 (ἀλφηστής Coraes).

ἐλέχει· ψηλαφᾷ, Hsch. **ἐλεών**· θάμνος, Id. II. the *snake* called σκυτάλη, Id.

ἐλέωτρις, ιδος, ἡ, a *fish of the Nile*, Ath.7.312b.

ἔλη, ἡ, = εἵλη, ἀλέα (B), Ar.*V.*772 (Sch. Rav.), Eust.667.22, 1573.45.

ἔλῃ, **ἔληαι**, v. αἱρέω.

ἐληγός, ὁ, *oil-merchant*, *OGI*521.25 (v/vi A.D.).

ἐληθερέω, = εἰλ–, Gal.19.97 (Pass.).

ἐλήλᾰκα, **ἐλήλαμαι**, **ἐληλέδατο** or **-άδατο**, v. ἐλαύνω. **ἐλήλεγμαι**, v. ἐλέγχω. **ἐλήλιγμαι**, v. ἑλίσσω. **ἐλήλῠθα**, **εἰλήλουθα**, **ἐλθεῖν**, **ἐλθέμεν**, **ἐλθέμεναι**, v. ἔρχομαι.

ἐλθετέον, = ἐλευστέον, Herod.Med.ap.Orib.10.4.1, Philum.ap.Aët. 9.12.

ἐλθετῶς· ἀντὶ τοῦ ἐλθέ, Σαλαμίνιοι, Hsch. **ἐλίβοτρυς**· ἄμπελός τις μέλαινα, Id.

ἑλίγ-δην, Adv., (ἑλίσσω) *whirling*, *rolling*, A.*Pr.*882 (anap.); cf. εἰλίγδην. **-μα**, ατος, τό, *fold*, *wrapping*, ἱμάντων ἑλίγμασι, of straps *bound round* the leg, Ephipp.14.9; στρουθωτὰ ἑ. Sophr.100. II. *bracelets*, in pl., Hsch., prob. in Sapph.*Supp.*20a.8. III. *curl*, *lock* of hair, *AP*6.211 (Leon.). IV. *depression of the skull without fracture*, = θλάσμα, Sor.*Fract.*1. V. *packet*, σμύρνης καὶ ἀλόης v.l. in *Ev.Jo.*19.39. **-μᾰτώδης**, ες, = ἑλικοειδής, *twisted*, *Lex. de Spir.* p.195 V. **-μός**, Ep. εἱλ–, ὁ, *winding*, *convolution*, of the Labyrinth, Hdt.2.148; πολλοὺς ἑ. ἄνω καὶ κάτω πλανᾶσθαι X.*Cyr.*1.3.4; of the gut, ἑ. ἔχει Arist.*HA*532^{b}7; of the Fallopian tubes, ib.510^{b}19; of the brain, Erasistr.ap.Gal.5.603; of a snake, Sch.Nic.*Th.*159; of dancers' feet, Orph.*H.*38.12: generally, *rotatory motion*, Plu.2. 404f; ὀφθαλμῶν ἑλιγμοί *rolling* of eyes, Procop.Gaz.p.151 B.; ἑ. καὶ ἀναστροφαὶ ὀργάνων Max.Tyr.19.4: pl., *the plies* of a knot, Plu.*Alex.* 18; ῥευμάτων ἑλιγμοί Id.*Caes.*19; ὀρῶν Lib.*Or.*61.8.

ἔλιγξ, v.l. for ὤλιγξ, Poll.2.67.

Ἑλιεύς, ὁ, title of Zeus at Thebes, Hsch.

ἑλῐκ-άμπυξ, ῦκος, ὁ, ἡ, *wreathed with a circlet*, Σεμέλα Pi.*Fr.*75.20; θεά Id.*Pae.*3.15. **-άστερος**, ον, *with circling orbit*, epith. of the moon, Man.4.224. **-αυγής**, ές, *with circling rays*, κύκλος, of the sun, Orph.*Fr.*236.1; of the moon, *Cat.Cod.Astr.*1.173. **-η**, ἡ, (ἑλίσσω) *winding*: hence, I. *the constellation of the Great Bear*, from its *revolving round* the pole, Arat.37, A.R.3.1195. II. *convolution* of a spiral shell, Arist.*HA*524^{b}12, *PA*680^{a}22, al.; of the bowels, ib.682^{a}15; of the ear, Id.*GA*781^{b}15. III. in Arcadia, *crack willow*, *Salix fragilis*, from its pliant nature, Thphr.*HP*3.13.7. **-ηδόν**, Adv. = ἑλίγδην, *spirally*, ib.1, Luc.*Hist.Conscr.*19. II. *revolving in a circle*, Nonn.*D.*1.195. **-ίας**, ου, ὁ, *forked lightning*, Arist.*Mu.* 395^{a}27 (pl.).

ἑλῐκο-βλέφᾰρος, ον, *with ever-moving eyes*, *quick-glancing*, epith. of Aphrodite, *h.Hom.*6.19, Hes.*Th.*16, Pi.*Fr.*123.5; of Alcmene, Id.*P.*4.172. **-βόστρῠχος**, ον, *with curling hair*, Ar.*Fr.*334 (lyr.). **-γρᾰφέω**, *describe a curve*, of the Nile, Anon.*Geog.Comp.* 31. **-δρόμος**, ον, *running in curves*, *twisting*, Orph.*H.*9.10; *circular*, E.*Ba.*1067 (cj. for ἕλκει δρόμον). **-ειδής**, poet. **εἱλικ–**, ές, *of winding* or *spiral form*, [σαυνία] D.S.5.30; γραμμή Plu.*Num.*13; of planetary orbits, Cleom.1.4; ἔντερον Aret.*SD*2.3; τόποι S.E.*P.*1. 126; σελήνη D.L.7.144. Adv. -δῶς Cleom.1.4, Dsc.2.165, Olymp. *in Mete.*13.9. **-κέρατος**, ον, *with curled horns*, Hsch. s.v. ἕλικας. **-πέτᾰλος**, ον, *with twining leaves*, prob. in Sacerd.p.540.1 K. **-ρροος**, ον, *with winding stream*, Orac.ap.Paus.4.20.1.

ἑλῐκός, ή, όν, *eddying*, of water, Call.*Fr.*290 (Sup.); χορεία *Hymn. Is.*155.

ἑλῐκοστέφᾰνος, ον, *with twisted diadem*, κούρα B.8.62.

ἑλικ-τήρ, ῆρος, ὁ, *anything twisted*: *ear-ring*, Ar.*Fr.*320.14, Lys. 12.19, *IG*2.747.5. **-τήριον**, τό, = foreg., Apollon.*Lex.Hom.* s.v. ἕλικας. **-τικός**, ή, όν, *coiled*, τὸ ἑ. τῆς οὐρᾶς Doroth. in *Cat. Cod.Astr.*2.158. **-τός** (or εἱλ–), ή, όν, *rolled*, *twisted*, *wreathed*, βοῦς κεράεσσιν ἑλικτάς *h.Merc.*192; δράκων S.*Tr.*12, cf. *Pae.Delph.*19; κισσός E.*Ph.*652 codd. (lyr.); στέφανος Chaerem.7; βόστρυχος Theodect.6.4; κλῖμαξ ἑ. *winding* staircase, Callix.1; ἑ. κύτος a *wheeled* ark, E.*Ion* 40; εἱλικτὸν κρούειν πόδα, of dancers (cf. ἑλίσσω I. 3), Id.*El.* 180 (lyr.); σῦριγξ περὶ χεῖλος ἑλικτά Theoc.1.129; ἑλικτά, of insects *that can roll* or *double themselves up*, Arist.*PA*682^{b}24, 692^{a}2: Comp. ἑλικτότερος Hsch. II. metaph., *tortuous*, *not straightforward*, ἑλικτὰ κοὐδὲν ὑγιές E.*Andr.*448; *obscure*, Lyc.1466. **-ώδης**, ες, = ἑλικοειδής, Plu.2.648f, Nonn.*D.*1.370. **-ων**, ωνος, ὁ, *thread spun from the distaff to the spindle*, Hsch. II. a *nine-stringed instrument*, Aristid.Quint.3.3, Ptol.*Harm.*2.2.

Ἑλῐκών, ῶνος, ὁ (ϝελ– Corinn.*Supp.*1.29), *Helicon*, a hill in Boeotia, the seat of the Muses, Hes.*Op.*639, etc.:—hence **Ἑλῐκωνιάδες** (sc. παρθένοι), αἱ, *dwellers on Helicon*, i.e. *Muses*, Pi.*Pae.Fr.*16.14, *I.*2.34; Μοῦσαι Hes.*Op.*658, *Th.*1, *CIG*3067.19 (Teos):—also **Ἑλῐκωνίδες** Νύμφαι S.*OT*1108 (lyr.); Μοῦσαι E.*HF*791 (lyr.), *IG*4.682. 13 (Hermione): sg., of a poet's *reed-pen*, *AP*9.162. II. Ἑλικωνιάς, άδος, ἡ, = ὑάκινθος, Ps.-Dsc.4.62.

Ἑλῐκώνιος, α, ον, *Heliconian*, *of Helicon*, παρθένοι Pi.*I.*8(7).63. II. title of Poseidon, Ἑ. ἄναξ Il.20.404: acc. to Sch., from Helice in Achaia, where he was especially honoured, 8.203 (but cf. Aristarch. ap.*EM*547.16, *h.Hom.*22.3).

ἑλῐκ-ωπός, όν, = ἑλικώψ, Orph.*H.*6.9. **-ωτός**, ή, όν, *threaded like a screw*, Orib.49.20.6. **-ωψ**, ωπος, ὁ, ἡ, fem. -ῶπις, ιδος, *with rolling eyes*, *quick-glancing*, as a mark of youth and spirits (not in Od.), ἑλίκωπες Ἀχαιοί Il.1.389, al.; ἑλικῶπις κούρη ib.98; νύμφη Hes.*Th.*298, cf. Sapph.*Supp.*20a.5; παρθένοι, Ἀφροδίτη, Pi.*Pae.*2.99, *P.*6.1.

ἕλῑνος, ὁ, (ἑλίσσω) *vine-tendril*, Philet.ap.*EM*330.39. 2. fem., *the vine*, Nic.*Al.*181, Opp.*C.*4.262, D.P.1157. [Later ἕλινος prob. in Nonn.*D.*12.299.]

ἑλῑνότροπος, ον, *like vine-tendrils*, *Hymn.Is.*18.

ἑλῑνοφόρος, Ep. εἱλ–, ον, *bearing vine-tendrils*, κόρυμβος Nonn.*D.* 16.278; Διόνυσος ib.17.333.

ἐλῑνύες, αἱ, *days of rest*, *holidays*: ἐλινύας ἄγειν, of the Roman *supplicatio*, Plb.21.2.1.

Ἐλινύμενος, title of Zeus at Cyrene, Hsch.

ἐλῑνύω, Hdt.1.67, Hp.*Acut.*47, A.*Pr.*53: impf. ἐλίνυον Hdt.8.71, ἠλ– App.*Mith.*43; Ion. ἐλινύεσκον A.R.1.589: fut. -ύσω [ῡ] Pi.*N.*5.1, *I.*2.46: aor. ἐλίνυσα Hdt.7.56, A.*Pr.*529 (lyr.), etc.:—Poet. and Ion. Verb, also used in Trag. and late Prose (as Plu.*Num.*14), *keep holiday*, *take rest*, *repose*, freq. in Hp., as *Acut.*47; μὴ ἐλινύειν Hdt.1.67; διέβη ὁ στρατὸς.. ἐλινύσας οὐδένα χρόνον without any *cessation*, Id.7. 56; ἐλινύσοντα.. ἀγάλματα *to stand unmoved* on their pedestals, Pi. *N.*5.1, cf. *I.*2.46; ὡς μή σ' ἐλινύοντα προσδερχθῇ πατήρ see thee *standing idle*, A.*Pr.*53; οὐκ ἐλινύειν ἐχρῆν Ar.*Th.*598; ἐ. μίαν ἡμέραν Orac. ap.D.21.53. 2. c. gen. rei, *rest from*, πλήθεος βρώμης Hp.*Acut.* 47 (v.l. ⟨ἐκ⟩); ἔργων D.H.1.33. 3. c. part., *rest* or *cease from* doing, ἐλίνυον οὐδένα χρόνον.. ἐργαζόμενοι Hdt.8.71, cf. A.*Pr.*529 (lyr.), Call.*Cer.*48, *Fr.*248. [υ of the impf. short in A.R.1.862, long ib.589, indeterminate in Trag.] (Written ἐλιννύω in some codd.)

ἕλιξ (A), ῐκος, ὁ, ἡ, as Adj., *twisted*, *curved*: in Hom. and Hes., as in S.*Aj.*374 (lyr.), Theoc.25.127, epith. of oxen, commonly understood of their *twisted*, *crumpled horns*, cf. ἑλικτός I; also expld. of the movement of their bodies as they walk, *rolling*: freq. coupled with εἰλίποδας, cf. Il.12.293 and Sch. ad loc., etc.; ἕλιξ abs., = βοῦς, E.*Ba.* 1170 (lyr.): later of various objects, ποταμός Pi.ap.Sch.Il.*Oxy.*221 ix 15; ἕλικα ἀνὰ χλόαν on the *tangled* grass, E.*Hel.*180 (lyr., cf. sq. III); δρόμος Nonn.*D.*2.263; σειρή Tryph.322.

ἕλιξ (B), poet. **εἷλιξ**, ῐκος, ἡ, (ἑλίσσω) *anything which assumes a spiral shape*: once in Hom., γναμπτάς θ' ἕλικας, of *armlets* or *ear-rings*, Il.18.401 (cf. ἑλικτήρ), cf. *h.Ven.*87, Arist.*Mir.*840^{b}20:—afterwards in various relations: II. *whirl*, *convolution*, ἕλικες στεροπῆς *flashes of forked* lightning, A.*Pr.*1083 (anap.); of *circular* or *spiral motion*, αἱ κινήσεις καὶ ἕλικες τοῦ οὐρανοῦ Arist.*Metaph.*998^{a}5; ἕλικα ἐκτυλίσσειν Ti.Locr.97c; *wreath* of smoke, A.R.1.438. III. *tendril of the vine*, Thphr.*CP*2.18.2; βοσκὰς εὐφύλλων ἑλίκων E.*Hel.*1331 (lyr.); βότρυος ἕλικα παυσίπονον the *clustering* grape, Ar.*Ra.*1321 (lyr.). 2. *tendril* of ivy, Id.*Th.*1000; also, *ivy*, *Hedera Helix*, Thphr.*HP*3.18.6, 7. 8.1. 3. *curl* or *lock of hair*, *AP*10.19 (Apollonid.), 12.10 (Strat.), *Anacreont.*16.6. 4. *coil* of a serpent, E.*HF*399 (lyr.): pl., *feelers* of the polypus, *AP*9.14 (Antiphil. Byz.). 5. *volute* on the capital of a column, Callix.1, Vitr.4.1.12. IV. *convolution* of a spiral shell (cf. ἑλίκη II), Arist.*HA*547^{b}11: pl., *convolutions* of the bowels, Id.*PA* 675^{b}24: sg., *colon*, ib.675^{b}20; also of the ear, Id. *de An.*420^{a}13, Ruf. *Onom.*44. V. *spiral* running round a staff, Ael.*VH*9.11, Ath.12. 543f; on a child's ball, A.R.3.139; *spiral strip* folded round the scytale, Plu.*Lys.*19. 2. Geom., *spiral*, Epicur.*Ep.*2p.40U., Hermesian.7.86; περὶ ἑλίκων, title of work by Archim.; also, = κύκλος, Hsch. b. of planets' *orbit*, Eudox.*Ars*5.3, Theo Sm.p.201 H.; but also of the sun's and moon's *orbits*, Eudox.*Ars*9.2. 3. *helix*, *screw-windlass*, employed in launching ships, invented by Archimedes, Moschio ap.Ath.5.207b. 4. *treadmill used to raise water*, Ph.1.410. VI. pl., *involved sentences*, D.H.*Th.*48. VII. Adj. *winding*, ὁ ῥοῦς φέρεται ἕλικα πορείαν Dion.Byz.3.

ἕλιξις, ιος, ἡ, *rolled bandage*, Hp.*Off.*10. 2. *convolution* of the bowels, Aret.*SA*2.6.

ἑλιξό-κερως, ωτος, ὁ, ἡ, *with crumpled horns*, κριός *AP*9.240 (Phil.). **-πορος**, ον, *revolving*, ἄτρακτος Procl.*H.*1.48.

ἕλις· μόνος καὶ ὅλος, Hsch.

ἑλίσσω or **ἑλίσσω** (the latter more freq. in codd. of Hom.), Att. **-ττω**, Ep. inf. -έμεν Il.23.309; Ion. **εἱλίσσω** or **εἱλίσσω** (εἱ. is found in codd. of Hdt. (v. infr.), but κατ-ελίσσειν Hp.*Acut.*(*Sp.*)37, κατ-ειλίξαι Id.*Morb.*2.18, al.): fut. ἑλίξω E.*Ph.*711: aor. εἵλιξα Pl.*Ti.*73a (εἵλ- codd., but κατ-ειλίξας *IG*2^2.204.32); part. ἑλίξας Il.23.466, Ion. εἱλίξας Hdt.4.34:—**Med.**, Il.23.320: fut. ἑλίξομαι 17.728: aor. ἑλιξάμην 12.467, 17.283:—Pass., fut. ἑλιγήσομαι Lxx *Is.*34.4: aor. 1 εἱλίχθην E.*Or.*358; part. ἑλιχθείς Il.12.74: pf. εἵλιγμαι Hes.*Th.*791, ἐλήλιγμαι Paus.10.17.12: plpf. εἵλικτο E.*HF*927; Ion. 3 pl. εἱλίχατο Hdt.7.90. —The Ion. form is found in Trag. (v. infr., codd. usu. εἱλ-; but τ' εἱ. A.*Pr.*138 (lyr., cod. Med.), cf. Ar.*Ra.*1314, 1348 (cod. Rav.)), in *IG* l. c., and codd. of Pl. (as *Ti.* l. c., ἀν-ειλίττων *Phlb.*15e); ἐπειλίξας is f. l. in D.23.161. (ϝελ-, ἐϝελ-, cf. εἴλω, ἐλελίζω ad fin.):—*turn round* or *about*: Act. in Hom. always of *turning* a chariot *round the doubling-post*, οἶσθα γὰρ εὖ περὶ τέρματ' ἑλισσέμεν [ἵππους] Il.23.309, cf. 466. 2. generally, *roll*, ἑ. βίου πόρον *roll* life's stream *along*, Pi.*I.*8(7).15; of the chariot of Day, αἰθὴρ κοινὸν φάος εἱλίσσων A.*Pr.*1092 (anap.); ἥλιος.. εἱλίσσων φλόγα E.*Ph.*3; εἱ. κόνιν *roll the eddying* dust, A.*Pr.* 1085 (anap.); ἑ. δίνας, of the Euripus, E.*IT*7, cf. 1103 (lyr.); ἑ. κόρας, βλέφαρα, Id.*HF*868 (troch.), *Or.*1266 (lyr.). 3. of any rapid motion, ἅλιον.. ἑ. πλάταν *ply* it *swiftly*, S.*Aj.*358 (lyr.); of the dance, ἑ. πόδα *move the swift* foot, cj. in E.*Or.*171 (lyr.), cf. *IA*215 (lyr.); εἱ. θιάσους *lead the dancing* bands, Id.*IT*1145 (lyr.); ἑ. χορούς Stratt.66.5: abs., *dance*, E.*Ph.*234 (lyr.), cf. *Or.*1292 (whence ἑ. τινά *dance in honour of* .., Id.*HF*690 (lyr.), *IA*1480 (lyr.)); ἑ. βωμόν *dance round* it, Call. *Del.*321. 4. *roll* or *wind round*, πλόκαμον περὶ ἄτρακτον Hdt.4.34, cf. 2.38; λίνον ἠλακάτᾳ δακτύλοις ἑ. E.*Or.*1432 (lyr.); χεῖρας ἀμφὶ γόνυ ἑ. *clasp* them round.., Id.*Ph.*1622. 5. metaph., *turn in one's mind*, *revolve*, τοιαῦθ' ἑ. S.*Ant.*231, cf. Pl.*Epin.*978d; μῆτιν A.R.1.463; ἑ. κακοὺς λόγους *speak wily* words, E.*Or.*892. 6. κόλπους ἑ. *form winding* reaches, of rivers, D.P.630; ἀγκῶνας Id. 979. II. Med. and Pass., *turn oneself round* or *about* (but in Il. 12.49 εἱλίσσεθ' ἑταίρους (as read by Nicanor) *rallied his* comrades), ἑλιχθέντων ὑπ' Ἀχαιῶν *when* they *turned to face* the foe, ib.74, cf. 408; so of a wild boar, ἑλιξάμενος *having turned to bay*, 17.283; of a serpent, *coil himself*, ἑλισσόμενος περὶ χειῇ 22.95; ἡ δέ τ' ἑλισσομένη πέτεται (sc. καλαῦροψ) the shepherd's staff flies *spinning through the air*, 23.846; κνίση.. ἑλισσομένη περὶ καπνῷ *rolling* with the smoke, 1.317; ἑλισσόμενοι περὶ δίνας *whirled round* in the eddies, 21.11; of a river, δίνῃς ἀργυρέῃς εἱλιγμένος Hes.*Th.*791, cf. D.S.1.32; of the waves, τὸ ἑλισσόμενον αἰεὶ κυμάτων Pi.*N.*6.55; of ocean, ἑλίσσεσθαι περὶ πᾶσαν χθόνα A.*Pr.*138; ὧραι ἑλισσόμεναι the *circling* hours, Pi. *O.*4.3. 2. *turn hither and thither*, *go about*, ἀν' ὅμιλον Il.12.49; καθ' ὅμιλον ib.467; ἑλίσσετο ἔνθα καὶ ἔνθα *turned himself* hither and thither, doubting what to do, Od.20.24. 3. metaph., *to be constantly in* or *about* a thing, περὶ φύσας Il.18.372; ἔν τινι, εἴς τι, Pl.*Tht.* 194b, Porph.ap.Eus.*PE*3.4: c. gen., μέλιτός τε καὶ ἔργων εἱλίσσονται (sc. μέλισσαι) Arat.1030. 4. *whirl in the dance*, E.*Ba.*569 (lyr.), *IA* 1055 (lyr.). 5. Med. in act. sense, ἧκε δέ μιν σφαιρηδὸν ἑλιξάμενος he threw it *with a whirl* like a ball, Il.13.204. 6. τὰς κεφαλὰς εἱλίχατο μίτρῃσι *have their* heads *rolled round* with turbans, Hdt.7.90.

ἑλίτροχος, ον, (ἑλίσσω) *whirling the wheel round*, σύριγγες ἑ. A.*Th.* 205 (lyr.).

ἑλιχάζει· πλανᾶται, Hsch.

ἑλίχρῡσος, ὁ, *gold-flower*, *Helichrysum siculum*, Alcm.16, Ibyc.6, Cratin.98; ξανθοτέρα ἑλιχρύσοιο Theoc.2.78.

ἑλῐχώνη, ἡ, *funnel* in an oil-press, *CPR*242i 10 (i A. D.).

ἑλκαίνω, (ἕλκανον) *fester*, A.*Ch.*843.

ἕλκᾰνον, τό, = ἕλκος, *wound*, Hsch., who also has **ἑλκανῶσα**, = ἑλκαίνουσα.

ἑλκείδιον, τό, Dim. of ἕλκος, Plu.300a (s. v. l.).

ἑλκεσί-πεπλος [ῐ], ον, *trailing the robe*, *with long train*, Il.6.442, al., Mus.286, Nonn.*D.*1.103. **-χειρος**, ον, *drawing the hand after it*, τρύπανα *AP*6.103 (Phil.).

ἑλκε-τρίβων [ῑ], ωνος, ὁ, *cloak-trailer*, nickname of a Laconian, Pl. Com.124. **-χίτων** [ῐ], ωνος, ὁ, *trailing the tunic*, *with a long tunic*, epith. of the Ionians, Il.13.685, *h.Ap.*147.

ἑλκ-έω, = ἕλκω, *drag about*, *tear asunder*, in impf. νέκυν.. εἵλκεον ἀμφότεροι Il.17.395: also in fut. and aor. κύνες ἑλκήσουσιν ib.558; σὲ μὲν κύνες ἠδ' οἰωνοὶ ἑλκήσουσ' 22.336; Λητὼ γὰρ ἥλκησε he *did violence to* Leto, Od.11.580; ἑ. τινὰ πέπλοιο Arat.638:—Pass., ἑλκηθείσας τε θύγατρας Il.22.62. **-ηδόν**, Adv. *by dragging*, *pulling*, ἐμάχοντο πύξ τε καὶ ἑλκηδόν Hes.*Sc.*302. **-ήεις**, εσσα, εν, *full of ulcers*, Man.1.162. **-ηθμός**, ὁ, *being carried off*, *violence suffered*, σῆς τε βοῆς σοῦ θ' ἑλκηθμοῖο πυθέσθαι Il.6.465. **-ηθρον**, τό, *stock of the plough*, Thphr.*HP*5.7.6. **-ηΐς**· ἡ λιθάργυρος, Hsch. **-ημα**, ατος, τό, *that which is torn in pieces*, *prey*, κυνῶν ἕ. E.*HF*568. **-ησί-στᾰχυς**, υ, *drawing the ears of corn*, νομῆες Orac.ap.Paus.8.42. 6. **-ητήρ**, ῆρος, ὁ, *one that drags*, κτένες ἑλκητῆρες, of a harrow, *AP*6.297 (Phan.).

ἕλκιμος, ον, = ἑλκύσιμος, Olymp. *in Mete.*320.37.

ἑλκίνα, = περδίκιον, Ps.-Dsc.4.85.

ἑλκο-ποιέω, *make wounds* or *sores*: metaph., *rip up old sores*, Aeschin.3.208. II. *make an incision in* a tree, πρέμνον *Gp.*5.38. 2. **-ποιός**, όν, *having power to wound*, A.*Th.*398; cf. ἑλκοποιόν· κανθαρίς, Hsch.

ἕλκος, εος, τό, *wound*, Il.4.190, al. (never in Od.), Pi.*P.*2.91, E.*Tr.* 1232 (pl.), etc. 2. *festering wound*, *sore*, *ulcer*, ἕ. ὕδρου *the festering bite* of a serpent, Il.2.723; *plague-ulcer*, Th.2.49, X.*Eq.*5.1, etc. (Gal. 10.232 defines ἕ. as ἡ τῆς συνεχείας λύσις ἐν σαρκώδει μορίῳ, and both I. 1 and I. 2 are treated in Hp.*Ulc.*; ἕ. is applied to amputations in *Art.*68.) II. metaph., *wound*, *loss*, Sol.4.17, S.*Ant.*652, al.; ἕ. δήμιον A.*Ag.*640; ὑποκάρδιον ἕ. Theoc.11.15; γίγνεται ἕ. ἐφ' ἕλκει Lib.*Ep.*1063.6. (Orig. *ἕλκος, cf. Lat. *ulcus*, Skt. *árśas* (n.) 'haemorrhoid': ἕ- by influence of ἕλκω.)

ἑλκόω, *wound*, *lacerate*, E.*Hec.*405; ἑ. ὄνυξιν Arist.*HA*630^{a}5, etc. 2. *ulcerate*, βλέφαρα Hp.*VM*19, al.:—Pass., of persons, *to suffer from wounds or sores*, Com.*Adesp.*106.8, *Ev.Luc.*16.20; of sores, *suppurate*, X.*Eq.*1.5. 3. *make an incision in* a tree, Thphr. *HP*4.16.1 (Pass.), *CP*3.2.2 (Pass.). II. metaph., ἑ. φρένας, οἴκους, E.*Alc.*878 (lyr.), *Supp.*223:—Pass., τὴν διάνοιαν ἑλκοῦσθαι Ph.2.551.

ἑλκ-τέον, *one must drag*, Pl.*R.*365c. **-τικός**, ή, όν, *fit for drawing*, *attractive*, πρός τι ib.523a, cf. Thphr.*CP*3.17.3 (Comp.), Ael.*NA* 17.6. **-τός**, ή, όν, *that can be drawn*, *tensile*, Arist.*GA*743^{b}5, *Mete.*385^{a}16. **-ύδριον**, τό, Dim. of ἕλκος, *slight sore*, Hp.*Art.*63, Ar.*Eq.*907. II. = κάδος, Dionys.Trag.12. **-υθμός**, ὁ, later form of ἑλκηθμός, Tryph.21. **-ύσιμος** [ῠ], ον, *that may be drawn*, Phot. s. v. ἐρύσιμον. **-ῦσις**, εως, ἡ, *attraction*, πύου Aret.*SD*1.10. 2. *drawing*, ἕ. τῆς σικύης, in cupping, Hp.*Loc.Hom.*22. **-υσμα**, ατος, τό, *that which is drawn*, i. e. *spun wool*, Hsch. s. v. ἀφρῖνον (pl.). 2. pl., κυνῶν ἑ. *bodies torn* by dogs, Man.4.200. 3. = σκωρία, *dross of silver*, because *drawn off with a hook*, Dsc.5.86, Gal.12.236, Orib.*Fr.* 90. **-υσμός**, ὁ, *attraction*; esp. of *idle fancy*, διάκενος ἑ. Chrysipp. *Stoic.*2.22, cf. Ph.1.151 (pl.). II. *dragging*, in pl., Anon.*Fig.*p.156 S. **-υστάζω**, Frequentat. of ἕλκω, *drag about*, ἵνα μή μιν ἀποδρύφοι ἑλκυστάζων Il.23.187, 24.21. **-υστέος**, α, ον, *to be dragged*, X.*Ag.*9. 4. II. ἑλκυστέον *one must draw*, αἷμα Gal.ap.Aët.8.50. 2. *one must drink*, οὐκ ἀθρόον πόμα Herod.Med.ib.4.47. **-υστήρ**, ῆρος, ὁ, *instrument for drawing*: surgeon's *crochet*, Hp.*Mul.*1.70; *a rein*, Sch. Il.16.475, Hsch. s. v. ῥυτήρ. II. as Adj., ἑ. πόνος toil *of dragging*, Opp. *H.*5.20. **-υστήριος**, α, ον, *fit for drawing*, ζῷα *draught* animals, Men.Prot.p.17 D. **-υστικός**, ή, όν, *drawing*: *extracting*, c. gen., σκολόπων Dsc.2.84. 2. *attractive*, ἑ. τι ἔχειν πρὸς φιλίαν Ath.5.185c; τὰ πιθανὰ καὶ ἑ. Arr.*Epict.*3.12.14. **-υστίνδα**, Adv. = διελκυστίνδα, Eust.1111.24. **-υστός**, ή, όν, *ductile*, Hsch. s. v. ῥύσιον, *Gloss.* 2. *drawn*, ἑ. ἅμαξα *transport*-wagon, *PMasp.*303.7 (vi A. D., -ιστή Pap.). II. ἑ. ἔλαιον *refined*, *fine-drawn* oil, *CIG*2719.21 (Stratonicea); cf. ἑλκυστῷ· λείῳ, Hsch. **-υστρον**, τό, *handle* or *lever* for raising a swing-beam, Apollod.*Poliorc.*162.10. 2. *halter*, Hsch. s. v. φορβε(ί)α.

ἕλκω (**ἑλκύω** late, Tz.*H.*6.621), Il.24.52, etc., impf. εἷλκον A.*Fr.*39, etc., Ep. ἕλκον Il.4.213, al. (never εἵλκυον): fut. ἕλξω A.*Supp.*909, etc., rarely ἑλκύσω [ῠ] Hp.*Fract.*2, Philem.174: aor. εἵλκῠσα Batr.232, Pi.*N.*7.103, Trag. and Att., E.*Ph.*987, Ar.*Nu.*540, *SIG*^{2}587.23, al., etc.; ἥλκυσα *IG*11(2).287 *B*61 (Delos, ii B. C.), *CIG*4993, 5006 (Egypt, iii A. D.); later εἷλξα, poet. ἕλξα *AP*9.370 (Tib. Ill.), Orph.*A.*258, Gal.*Nat.Fac.*1.12: pf. εἵλκῦκα D.22.59; pf. part. ἑολκώς prob. in Epich. 177:—**Med.**, fut. -ύσομαι (ἐφ-) Antyll.ap.Orib.6.10.9: aor. εἱλκυσάμην (ἀφ-) v. l. in Hp.*Art.*11, subj. ἀφελκύσωμαι Ar.*Ach.*1120; rarely εἱλξάμην Gal.4.534:—Pass., fut. ἑλκυσθήσομαι A.*Th.*614 (ξυγκαθ-), Lyc.358, ἑλχθήσομαι Gal.*UP*7.7: aor. εἱλκύσθην Hp.*Epid.*4.14, (ἐξ-) Ar.*Ec.*688, ἑλκ- Hdt.1.140, ἡλκ- *IG*12(7).115.11 (Amorgos); later εἵλχθην Ph.2.11, Philostr.*VA*8.15, D.L.6.91: pf. εἵλκυσμαι Hp.*Superf.*16, E.*Rh.*576, Ph.1.316, (καθ-) Th.6.50, ἕλκυσμαι (ἀν-) Hdt.9.98, ἥλκυσμαι *BGU*1256.11 (ii B. C.): plpf. εἵλκυστο Hp.*Epid.*4.36.—In Att., ἕλκω, ἕλξω were alone used in pres. and fut., while the other tenses were formed from ἑλκυ-; cf. ἑλκέω (q. v.), ἑλκυστάζω. In Hom., Aristarch. rejected the augm. (Cf. Lat. *sulcus*, Lith. *velkù* 'drag'):—*draw*, *drag*, with collat. notion of force or exertion, ὣς εἰπὼν ποδὸς ἕλκε *began to drag* [the dead body] by the foot, Il.13.383; ἣν περ.. ποδῶν ἕλκωσι θύραζε Od.16.276; τινὰ τῆς ῥινός Luc.*Herm.*73; Ἕκτορα.. περὶ σῆμ' ἑτάροιο ἕλκει Il.24.52; *drag away* a prisoner, 22.65 (Pass.); *draw* ships down to the sea, 2.152, etc.; *draw along* a felled tree, 17.743; of mules, *draw* a chariot, 24.324; ἑλκέμεναι νειοῖο.. πηκτὸν ἄροτρον *draw* the plough *through* the field, 10.353, cf. 23.518; ἕ. τινὰ ἐπὶ κνάφου Hdt.1.92; περιβαλόντας σχοινία ἕ. *haul at* them, Id.5.85. 2. *draw after one*, ἐν δ' ἔπεσ' Ὠκεανῷ.. φάος ἠελίοιο, ἕλκον νύκτα μέλαιναν Il.8. 486; πέδας ἕ. *trail* fetters *after one*, Hdt.3.129; ἕ. χλανίδα *let* one's cloak *trail behind*, Ephipp.19 (anap.); θοἰμάτιον Archipp.45. 3. *tear* *in pieces* (used by Hom. only in the form ἑλκέω), ὀνύχεσσι παρειάν E.*Tr.*280; *worry*, τὰς κύνας ὥλαφος ἕλκοι Theoc.1.135; ἑλκυσθῆναι ὑπὸ κυνός Hdt.1.140. **b.** metaph., *carp at*, Pi.*N.*7.103. **4.** *draw* a bow, ἕλκε.. γλυφίδας τε λαβὼν καὶ νεῦρα βόεια Il.4.122, cf. Od.21.419, Hdt.3.21, X.*An.*4.2.28, etc. **5.** *draw* a sword, S.*Ant.*1233, E.*Rh.*576 (Pass.):—Med., ἕλκετο δ' ἐκ κολεοῖο.. ξίφος Il.1.194. **6.** ἕ. ἱστία *hoist* sails, Od.2.426:—also in Med., *h.Bacch.*32. **7.** *lift up* scales, so as to poise them, ἕλκε δὲ μέσσα λαβών Il.8.72, 22.212. **II.** after Hom., **1.** *pull* a barge-pole, Hdt.1.194. **2.** *tow* a ship, Th.2.90, etc. **3.** *drag into court*, ἕλκω σε κλητεύσοντα Ar.*Nu.*1218, cf. 1004 (Pass.); εἰς ἀγοράν *Act.Ap.*16.19; *drag about*, esp. with lewd violence, ἕλκει καὶ βιάζεται D.21.150; μηδένα ἕλξειν μηδ' ὑβριεῖν ib. 221; ἕλκειν γυναῖκα Lys.1.12: metaph., ἄνω κάτω τοὺς λόγους ἕ. Pl.*Tht.*195c, cf. Arist.*SE*167ᵃ35; ἡμέας ὁ καιρὸς ἕλκει Herod.2.10; also ἥλκυσμαι λαμπαδάρχης *I have been compelled to serve as* λ., *BGU* l.c. **4.** *draw* or *suck up*, [ἥλιος] ἕλκει τὸ ὕδωρ ἐπ' ἑωυτόν Hdt.2.25; ἕ. τὸν ἀέρα *draw* it *in*, *breathe* it, Hp.*Aër.*19, Ti.Locr.101d (Pass.), cf. Philyll.20: ζωὴν φύσιν Archel.ap.Antig.*Mir.*89; esp. of persons drinking, *drink in long draughts, quaff*, μέθυ E.*Ion* 1200; ἀμυστιν Id.*Cyc.*417; τὴν.. τοῦ Πραμνίου [σπονδὴν] Ar.*Eq.*107; οἶνον ἐκ.. λεπαστῆς Teleclid.24(lyr.); ἀπνευστί Antiph.74.14, etc.: with acc. of the cup, δέπας μεστὸν.. ἕλκουσι γνάθοις ἀπαύστοις Id.237, cf. Eub. 56.7, al.; so ἕ. μαστόν *suck* it, E.*Ph.*987; *inhale*, ὀσμήν Antig.*Mir.* 89; of roots, *draw up* nourishment, Thphr.*HP*1.6.10: metaph., χανδὸν καὶ ἀμυστὶ τῶν μαθημάτων ἕ. Eun.*VS* p.474 D. **5.** *draw* from a receptacle, ἐξ ἑκάστου κιβωτίου πινάκιον ἕν Arist.*Ath.*64.1. **6.** ἕ. βίοτον, ζόαν, *drag out* a weary life, E.*Or.*207 (lyr.), *Ph.*1535 (lyr.); προφάσιας ἕ. *keep making* excuses, Hdt.6.86; πάσας τε προφάσεις.. ἕλκουσι Ar.*Lys.*727; ἕ. χρόνους *make long*, in prosody, Longin.*Proll. Heph.*p.83C.: hence intr., ἐπὶ τοσοῦτο λέγεται ἑλκύσαι τὴν σύστασιν.. that the conflict *dragged on, lasted*, Hdt.7.167, cf. *PHib.*1.83.9 (iii B.C.):—Pass., τῶν ἐγκλημάτων εἱκλυσμένων πλείονα χρόνον *Supp. Epigr.*2.281 (Delph., ii B.C.); also of a person, ἑλκόμενος καὶ μόγις Pl.*R.*350d. **7.** ἕ. κόρδακα *dance* in *long, measured* steps, Ar.*Nu.*540; ἐν τουτὶ (σχῆμα) Id.*Pax* 328. **8.** *draw to oneself, attract*, of the magnet, E.*Fr.*567; by spells, τινὰ ποτὶ δῶμα Theoc.2.17, cf. X.*Mem.*3.11.18, Plot.4.4.40, etc.; πείθειν καὶ ἕ. Pl.*R.*458d; ἐχθροὺς ἐφ' ἑαυτὸν D.22.59; *draw on*, ἐπὶ ἡδονάς Pl.*Phdr.*238a; εἰς τυραννίδας ἕ. τὰς πολιτείας Id.*R.*568c:—Pass., *to be drawn on* as by a spell, ἴυγγι δ' ἕλκομαι ἦτορ Pi.*N.*4.35; πρὸς φιλοσοφίαν Pl.*R.*494e. **9.** of things weighed, ἕ. σταθμὸν τάλαντα δέκα *draw down* the balance, i.e. *weigh* ten talents, Hdt.1.50, cf. Eup.116: abs., τὸ δ' ἂν ἑλκύσῃ whatever it *weigh*, Hdt. 2.65; πλεῖον ἕ. Pl.*Min.*316a. **b.** ἕ. τὰς ψήφους *cast up* the account, *PPetr.*2 p.37 (iii B.C.), *PHib.*1.17.25 (iii B.C.). **10.** *draw* or *derive* from a source, ἐντεῦθεν εἵλκυσεν ἐπὶ τὴν.. τέχνην τὸ πρόσφορον αὐτῇ Pl.*Phdr.*270a, cf. Jul.*Or.*7.207a; τὸ γένος ἀπό τινος Str.11.9.3; *assume*, μείζω φαντασίαν Plb.32.10.5; ὁ ἄρτος ἕλκει χρῶμα κάλλιστον Ath.3.113c. **11.** ἑλκύσαι πλίνθους *make* bricks, Hdt.1.179, cf. *PPetr.*3 p.137; ἕ. λάγανον Chrysipp.Tyan.ap.Ath.14.647e. **12.** αἱ θυρίδες ἕλκουσι the windows *draw in* air, Thphr.*Vent.*29. **13.** ἕ. ἑαυτόν, expressing some kind of athletic exercise, Pl.*Prm.* 135d.

B. Med., ἕ. χαίτας ἐκ κεφαλῆς *tear one's* hair, Il.10.15; ἀσσοτέρω πυρὸς ἕλκετο δίφρον *drew his* chair nearer to the fire, Od.19.506, cf. Semon.7.26. **2.** *draw to oneself, scrape up, amass*, τιμάς, ἄφενος ἕλκεσθαι, Thgn.30. **3.** ἕλκεσθαι στάθμας περισσᾶς in Pi.*P.*2.90, means lit., *to drag at* too great a line, i.e. *grasp* more than one's due—but whence the metaphor is taken remains unexplained.

C. Pass., *to be drawn* or *wrenched*, νῶτα.. ἑλκόμενα στερεῶς, of wrestlers, Il.23.715; of the nails, to be *curved*, Hp.*Morb.*2.48; *to close in* when the core is removed, of the timber of certain trees, Thphr.*HP*5.5.2. **2.** *to be drawn* or *to flow at a place*, of streams, Lyc.702; πρὸς ἀντολίην ἕ. αἶα D.P.1086. **3.** *to be drawn* or *contracted*, εἱλκύσθη ἐπὶ τὰ δεξιὰ τράχηλος Hp.*Epid.*4.14.

ἑλκ-ώδης, ες, *like a wound* or *sore, ulcerated*, στόματα Hp.*Epid.*3.7; χρώς E.*Hipp.*1359 (anap.); κνῆμαι Arist.*Pr.*895ᵃ31. **2.** *causing* or *accompanied by soreness*, ἁφή S.E.*M.*7.179; κόπος Gal.7.179; πόνος Archig.ap.eund.8.106; κονιορτός Lyd.*Ost.*1. **II.** metaph., *irritable*, Plb.32.11.8; θυμός Plu.2.454b. **-ωμα**, ατος, τό, *sore, ulcer*, Hp.*Epid.*3.7, *POxy.*1088.2,9 (i A.D.). **II.** *part wounded*, Thphr.*HP*9.2.1. **-ωμᾰτικός**, ή, όν, *causing sores, ulcerating*, Dsc.5.91. **-ωσις**, εως, ἡ, *ulceration*, Hp.*Aph.*3.21, Th.2.49, Ph.2.100; of plants, Thphr.*CP*1.14.2, al. **-ωτικός**, ή, όν, = ἑλκωματικός, Dsc.1.128.3: metaph., *exasperating*, δριμύτης Plu.2.854c.

ἑλλά, ἡ, Lacon. for καθέδρα, Hsch.:—also **Ἔλλα**· Διὸς ἱερὸν ἐν Δωδώνῃ, Id.

Ἑλλᾰδαρχ-έω, *hold office of* Ἑλλαδάρχης 3, *IGRom.*3.202 (Ancyra, ii A.D.). **-ης**, ου, ὁ, *president of the* κοινὸν τῶν Ἀχαιῶν, *IG*4.1600 (Corinth, ii A.D.), *SIG*846.5 (Delph., ii A.D.). **2.** *official of the Delphic Amphictyony*, Ἑ. ἀμφικτυόνων *IG*4.590 (Argos, ii A.D.). **3.** *official of the Greek community in the province of Galatia*, *IGRom.*3.211 (Ancyra, ii A.D.). **4.** as an honorary title, *OGI*528.10 (Prusias).

Ἑλλᾰδικός, ή, όν, *Hellenic*, ἀοιδαί Xenoph.6; κλίμα Herm.ap.Stob. 1.49.45; [ἵπποι] Str.11.13.7; οἱ Ἑ. Plu.2.676b. **II.** Ἑλλαδική, ἡ, name of a *plaster*, Alex.Trall.9.1; Ἑλλαδικὸν μάλαγμα Aet.15.11.

ἕλλᾱθι, = ἵληθι, B.10.8; Aeol. for ἵλαθι, *Et.Gud.* s.v. χίλιοι: pl., ἕλλατε Call.*Fr.*121.

ἐλλᾰλέω, *talk amongst*, μειρακίοις Pherecr.64 (prob.).

ἐλλαμβάνω, *receive*, *Supp.Epigr.*2.264.6 (Delph., ii B.C.). **II.** Med., aor. 2 ἐνελαβόμην *IG*12(5).1061.10 (Carthaea):—*seize hold of*, τῶν δένδρων ταῖς ἕλιξι Dsc.4.183, cf. Ph.1.21, al., J.*AJ*6.7.5, etc.

ἐλλαμπρύνομαι, Pass., *gain distinction*, ἰδίᾳ ἐ. τῷ τῆς πόλεως κινδύνῳ Th.6.12; *pride oneself*, Luc.*Dom.*1; ἔργῳ D.C.73.10; ἱππεῦσιν App.*BC*3.66; πρὸς τὰς φίλας ἐ. λόγοις J.*AJ*18.3.4.

ἐλ-λάμπω, *shine*, Σείριος.. ὀξὺς ἐ. Archil.61: c. dat., *shine upon, irradiate*, τῇ ψυχῇ Ph.1.273; πᾶσιν Procl.*Inst.*23; εἰς ψυχὴν Hierocl. *in CA* 10 p.433 M.; εἰς τὴν οἰκείαν ἕδραν Jul.*Or.*4.134b; *shine* or *be reflected in*, ἐν τοῖς ὄμμασι τῶν πλησίον Plu.2.40d: c. dat., Iamb.*Myst.* 2.3, al. **II.** trans., *illuminate*, ἐλλάμπουσα ἀεὶ ἐλλάμπεται Plot. 2.9.2, cf. Procl.*in Ti.*2.285 D., al.; ὅταν [ἡ ψυχὴ] οἷον ἐλλάμψῃ πρὸς ἑαυτήν Plot.6.4.16:—metaph. in Med., *distinguish oneself, gain glory in* or *with*, [τῷ ἱππικῷ] ἐπεῖχε ἐλλάμψεσθαι Hdt.1.80; τῇσι νηυσί Id.8. 74. **2.** *cause to shine upon*, καλλονὴν ἑκάστῳ Them.*Or.*4.52b; *cause to shine*, ἡ τῶν θεῶν παρουσία τὸ φῶς ἐ. Iamb.*Myst.*2.6. **-λαμψις**, εως, ἡ, *shining, flashing*, *Placit.*3.3.12 (v.l.), Plu.*Fr.inc.*150: metaph., *illumination, irradiation*, Plot.6.4.15, 5.8, al., Dam.*Pr.*34; τῆς ἀληθείας Hierocl.*in CA* 20 p.465 M. **II.** *radiation* of heat, Steph.*in Hp.*1.134 D., al.

Ἑλλάνιος, Dor. for Ἑλλήνιος.

Ἑλλᾱνοδίκ-αι [ῐ], ῶν, οἱ, *the chief judges at the Olympic games*, Pi.*O.*3.12 (sg.), Hellanic.113 J. (sg.), Paus.5.9.5 sq.; also, *at the Nemean games*, *IG*4.587 (Argos); at Epidaurus, ib.946 (iii B.C.). **II.** at Sparta, *court-martial to try cases arising among the allied troops*, X.*Lac.*13.11.—The Dor. form (Elean **Ἑλλανοζίκας** *Schwyzer* 409) is used in Att., but **Ἑλληνοδίκαι** is found in *SIG*1073.20, and is v.l. in Hdt.5.22, cf. Hsch. s.v. et s.v. Δίαρχοι. **-έω**, *to be a judge at the games*, Paus.6.1.5, 24.3. **-εών**, ῶνος, ὁ, *the place where the* Ἑλλανοδίκαι *held their meetings*, Id.6.24.1.

ἐλλαπίνα, Aeol., = εἰλ., *Et.Gud.*165.44.

Ἑλλάς, άδος, ἡ, *Hellas*, said to have been originally the name of the region round Dodona, Arist.*Mete.*352ᵃ34, Sch.Il.21.194. **2.** a city of Thessaly, founded by Hellen, οἵ τ' εἶχον Φθίην ἠδ' Ἑλλάδα Il.2.683. **3.** *part of Phthiotis*, inhabited by the Μυρμιδόνες, 9.395, al. **4.** *Northern Greece*, opp. Peloponnesus, D.19.303, Ptol.*Geog.* 3.14.1: sts. so expld. in the phrase καθ' Ἑλλάδα καὶ μέσον Ἄργος Od.1.344, 4.726, al. **5.** *Greece*, from Peloponnesus to Epirus and Thessaly inclusively, Hes.*Op.*653, Hdt.8.44, 47, A.*Pers.*50 (anap.), 234 (troch.): used collectively for Ἕλληνες, E.*Or.*648, Th.1.6, etc. **6.** as a general name for *all lands inhabited by Hellenes*, including Ionia, etc., Hdt.1.92, Th.1.3, X.*An.*6.5.23, etc.; οὔθ' Ἑ. οὔτ' ἄγλωσσος S.*Tr.*1060: hence ἡ ἀρχαία Ἑ. Old *Greece*, Plu.*Tim.*37; ἡ μεγάλη Ἑ. *Magna Graecia*, Plb.2.39.1, Ath.12.523e; including Sicily, Str.6.1.2. **7.** Ἑλλάδος Ἑ., Ἀθῆναι *AP*7.45 (Thuc.): pl., τὴν Ἑ. Ἑλλάσι πολλαῖς παραυξήσας Ph.2.567. **8.** (sc. φωνή) *the Greek language*, Ael.*VH*9.16. **II.** fem. Adj. *Greek*, γλῶσσα Hdt.6.98, al.; πόλις Id.5.93; χθών A.*Supp.*243; στολή S.*Ph.*223, etc.; masc., Id.*Fr.* 17; τίς Ἑ. ἢ βάρβαρος ἢ τῶν προπάροιθ' εὐγενετᾶν ἕτερος..; E.*Ph.*1509.

ἐλλάσαι· συγκλεῖσαι, κωλῦσαι, Hsch.

ἐλλεβορ-ιάω, *need hellebore*, i.e. *to be mad*, Call.Com.28. **-ίζω**, Ion. ἐλλ-, fut. -ιῶ Hp.*Ep.*20:—*dose with hellebore*, Id.*Mochl.*30, Plu.*Alex.*41, Archig.ap.Orib.8.1.1 (Pass.), etc.; and so, *to bring one to his senses*, τί σαυτὸν οὐχ ἐλλεβορίζεις; D.18.121: -όμενοι, title of play by Diph., *AB*100. **-ίνη**, ἡ, *rupture-wort, Herniaria glabra*, Thphr.*HP*9.10.2, Dsc.4.108. **-ισμός**, ὁ, *treatment with hellebore*, Hp.*Ep.* 21. **-ίτης** [ῑ] οἶνος wine *flavoured with hellebore*, Dsc.5.72. **II.** **-ίτης**, ου, ὁ, = κενταύρειον μικρόν, Ps.-Dsc.3.7.

ἐλλεβορο-δότης ἰατρός doctor *who prescribes hellebore*, Gal.*Thras.* 24. **-ποσία**, ἡ, *drinking of hellebore*, Hp.*Epid.*5.83.

ἐλλέβορος, Ion. ἐλλ-, ὁ, *hellebore*, Hp.*Acut.*23, *Aph.*4.13, Thphr.*HP*9.10.1, etc. (ἐ. λευκός white *hellebore*, *Veratrum album*, Dsc.4.148; ἐ. μέλας *hellebore*, *Helleborus orientalis* (or *cyclophyllus*), ib.162); given to the insane, Hp.*Vict.*1.35: hence, πῖθ' ἐλλέβορον, i.e. you are mad, Ar.*V.*1489; ἐλλέβορον ἤδη πώποτ' ἔπιες; Men.69 (prob. l.); ἐλλέβορον πῖσαι Hp.*Fract.*11, cf. Str.9.3.3, etc.; πικρότερον ἐλλεβόρου *AP*5.28 (Cillactor). **2.** = σησαμοειδὲς τὸ μέγα, Dsc.4.149. **II.** = ἐλλόβιον, of women, Ar.*Fr.*320.6, Nicostr.33, cf. Hsch.

ἐλλεβοροσήματα, = λειμώνιον, Ps.-Dsc.4.16.

ἐλλεδᾰνός, ὁ, *band for binding corn-sheaves*, in pl., Il.18.553, *h.Cer.* 456, Hes.*Sc.*291: sg., in Suid.

ἔλλειμμα, ατος, τό, *defect, deficiency*, Hp.*Praec.*9, Phld.*D.*3.2 (pl.), etc.; τὰ καθ' ὑμᾶς ἐλλείμματα *shortcomings* dependent on yourselves, D.2.27; *arrears*, Id.22.44; τοῦ γεγραμμένου νόμου ἔ. Arist.*Rh.*1374ᵃ 26; τὰ περὶ τὴν διάλεκτον ἐ. D.H.*Dem.*20. **2.** *remnant*, v.l. in Lxx 2*Ki.*21.2.

ἔλλειν· ἴλλειν, κατέχειν, Hsch.:—Pass., ἐλλόμενα· περικλειόμενα, Id.; cf. εἴλω.

ἐλλειπ-ασμός, f.l. for λοιπασμός (q.v.). **-ής**, freq. written for ἐλλιπής (q.v.). **-όντως**, Adv. *incompletely*, Plot.1.3.6; opp. σφοδρῶς, Hsch. s.v. ἀκραῆ. **-τικός**, ή, όν, in Gramm., *elliptic, defective*, σχῆμα Eust.66.24, cf. A.D.*Conj.*226.20: c. gen., τῶν μορίων Id.*Synt.* 141.14. Adv. -κῶς Phlp.*in APr.*316.30, Eust.1080.17. **b.** *summary, brief*, Gal.15.796. Adv. -κῶς Id.18(1).881. **-ω**, *leave in*, μόνον.. ἐλλελειμμένον *left in* a race, S.*El.*736; *leave behind*, οὐδ' ἐλλέλοιπας ἐλπίδα E.*El.*609; τοῖόν σφιν ἐνέλλιπε θέλκτρον ἀοιδῆς A.R.1.515. **2.** *leave out, leave undone*, freq. with neg. Pron. neut., μηδὲν ἐ. ὅσων χρὴ πονεῖν S.*Aj.*1379; οὐδὲν ἐλλείψουσι.. χειρουργίας Ar.*Lys.* 673; λέγε μηδὲν ἐλλείπων Pl.*Plt.*269c, cf. *Ti.*17b, X.*Mem.*4.3.17; ἐ. τι τῶν νομίμων Id.*Cyr.*1.2.14; τοῦτ' αὐτὸ ἐ. Pl.*Plt.*267c, cf. *R.*362d;

ἔνια, σμικρά, Id.*Cra.*431c,d, etc.:—Pass., Id.*Phlb.*18d; τῆς προθυμίας οὐδὲν ἐλλέλειπται Lys.12.99; εὑρήσει οὐδὲν ἐλλειφθέν D.18.303. b. *fail to pay, leave unpaid*, ἐλλελοιπότες εἰσφοράν Id.24.172, cf. Arist. *Ath.*48.1; τινὰ τῶν ὀψωνίων τοῖς μισθοφόροις Plb.4.60.2. 3. intr., *fall short, fail*, οὐ μὴν Τρίοπός γ' ἐνέλειπεν *h.Ap.*213; ἄτας οὐδὲν ἐλλείπει S.*Ant.*584 (lyr.); ἥνπερ μὴ 'λλίπωσιν αἱ δίκαι Ar.*Pl.*859; ἐ. ἐν τῷ ἔργῳ Th.1.120; τοῖς ἱππικοῖς Plb.15.3.5; opp. περιγίγνεσθαι, Pl. *Lg.*740d; opp. πλεονάζειν, Isoc.2.33; opp. ὑπερβάλλειν, Pl.*Lg.*719d, Arist.*EN*1108^{b}18; *fail in duty*, X.*HG*7.5.8, *Eq.*8.5; τὸ ἐλλεῖπον [τῆς ἐπιστήμης] *a deficiency* of.., Th.6.69; τὸ ἐ. ἐκπληρώσατε X.*Cyr.*4.5.39, etc.; *to be too small*, Id.*Cyn.*5.26; ἐλλείπων, ὁ, name of a *throw of the dice*, Eub.57.4. b. Geom., *fall short*, χωρίῳ *by* an area, Pl.*Men.* 87a, cf. Euc.6.27, al. 4. c. gen. rei, *to be in want of, fall short of, lack*, τὸν ἐλλείποντ' ἔτι ἥβης ἀκμαίας A.*Th.*10; ἐ. [χρημάτων] Th.1.80; τῆς δόξης Id.2.61; τὰ τῶν ἱκανῶν ἐλλείποντα X.*Hier.*4.8; τὸ τίμημα ἐνέλιπε τῶν ἑξακισχιλίων διακοσίοις ταλάντοις *fell short* of the 6000 by 200, Plb.2.62.7; τοσοῦτον ἐλλείπει τοῦ λυπεῖσθαι so far does he *fall short* of feeling pain, Arist.*EN*1108^{b}5; πολλοῦ γε καὶ τοῦ παντὸς ἐλλείπω (sc. τοῦ ταρβεῖν) A.*Pr.*961: with a neg., προθυμίας γὰρ οὐδὲν ἐλλείπεις ib.341, cf. Pl.*Ti.*20c; οὔτε ἀνοίας οὐδὲν ἐλλείπει οὔτε ἀναισχυντίας Id.*R.*571d: impers., ἐλλείπει πωμάτων *there is lack* of drink, Id.*Lg.*844b; οἷς ἂν τῆς γενέσεως ἐλλείπῃ ib.740c; ὧν δ' ἐνέλειπε τῇ πόλει.. D.18.302. 5. c. gen. pers., *to be inferior to*, Pl.*Alc.*1.122c; ἐμπειρίᾳ μηδὲν ἐκείνων ἐ. Id.*R.*484d: also c. gen. rei, τἀνθάδε τῶν ἐκεῖ ἐ. Id.*Alc.*1.122d. 6. folld. by μή c. inf., τί γὰρ ἐ. μὴ παραπαίειν; in what *does* it *fall short* of madness? A.*Pr.*1056 (anap.); οὐδὲν ἐλλείψω τὸ μὴ.. πυθέσθαι S.*Tr.*90. 7. c. part., ὅτι ἂν τις ἐλλείπῃ λέγων Pl.*Phdr.*272b; οὐκ ἐλλείψει εὐχαριστῶν *will* not *fail* to give thanks, Decr.ap.D.18.92: abs., οἱ ἐλλείποντες *defaulters*, Id.22.44. 8. of things, *to be wanting* or *lacking to*.., c. dat., X.*Mem.*2.1.8. II. c. acc. pers., ἐλλείπει τινά τι something *fails* one, Plb.9.41.11; ἵνα μηδὲν αὐτὰς ἐλλείπῃ τῶν ἐπιτηδείων Id.10.18.11. III. Pass., *to be surpassed*, ἐλλείπεσθαι εὖ ποιῶν X.*Mem.*2.6.5. 2. *to be wanting, fail*, Id.*Cyr.*6.2.37, *Eq.*3.8, etc.; *to be inferior*, Pl.*R.*484d: c. gen., τινὸς εἰς σύνεσιν Id.*Amat.*136a.

ἐλλείχω, *lick in, take one's fill of*, τινός *Com.Adesp.*125 Meineke.

ἔλλειψις, εως, ἡ, *falling short, defect*, opp. ὑπερβολή, Democr. 102, Pl.*Prt.*356a; opp. ὑπεροχή, Arist.*Ph.*187^{a}17, *Metaph.*1042^{b}25; ὑπερβολὴ καὶ ἔ. καὶ τὸ μέσον Id.*EN*1106^{b}17. 2. *the conic section ellipse*, Apollon.Perg.*Con.*1.13 (so called because the square on the ordinate is equal to a rectangle with height equal to the abscissa and applied to the parameter, but *falling short* of it). 3. ἐν ἐλλείψεσιν ἐνυπάρχειν to be present *in deficiency*, of the negative terms in an algebraical expression, Dioph.1*Praef.*p.14T. 4. Gramm., *ellipse*, Ath. 14.644a, A.D.*Synt.*117.19; *omission* of a letter, Id.*Pron.*56.28. 5. = ἔκλειψις, Olymp.*in Mete.*67.37 (s.v.l.). 6. Pythag. name for *two*, *Theol.Ar.*10.

ἔλλερος, dialectic for κακός, Call.*Fr.*434, cf. Eust.635.5, Hsch.

Ἑλλεσίη· ἡ Ἀθηνᾶ, Hsch.

ἔλλεσχος, ον, *talked of in the λέσχαι, commonly talked of*, Hdt.1. 153.

ἔλλετε, = ἔρρετε, Call.*Fr.*292; cf. ἔλλατε (v. ἔλλαθι).

ἔλλευκος, *albatus*, *Gloss.*

ἐλλήγω, *come to an end in*, *PLond.*1.98^{r}31.

ἐλληκέω, in aor. 1 ἐνελήκησα, = ἔπλησα, ἐψόφησα, Hsch. (dub.).

Ἕλλην, ηνος, ὁ, *Hellen*, son of Deucalion, Hes.*Fr.*7.1. II. Ἕλληνες, οἱ, *the Thessalian tribe of which Hellen was the reputed chief*, Il.2.684. 2. of all *Greeks*, Epigr.ap.Paus.10.7.6, Hdt.1.56, Th.1.3, etc.; cf. Πανέλληνες. 3. *Gentiles*, whether heathens or Christians, opp. Jews, Lxx *Is.*9.12, *Ev.Jo.*7.35, etc. 4. *non-Egyptian* (incl. Persians, etc.), *PTeb.*5.169 (ii B.C.). 5. *pagan*, Jul.*Ep.*114, Eun. *VS* p.524B., Dam.*Isid.*204, *Cod.Just.*1.11.10. III. as Adj., = Ἑλληνικός, στρατός Pi.*N.*10.25, etc.: with fem. Subst., Ἕλλην' ἐπίσταμαι φάτιν A.*Ag.*1254; στολὴν γ' Ἕλληνα E.*Heracl.*130; Ἕ. γυνή Philem.55; Ἕ. ἀληθῶς οὖσα, of fortune, Apollod.Car.5.10; Πυλῶν Ἑλλήνων D.18.304: with neut. Subst., ἐν χωρίῳ Ἕλληνι Them.*Or.*27. 332d. IV. *those who spoke* or *wrote Hellenistic Greek*, opp. Ἀττικοί, ἄρτι· οἱ μὲν Ἀ. τὸ πρὸ ὀλίγου, οἱ δὲ Ἕ. καὶ ἐπὶ τοῦ νῦν λέγουσι Moer. 68, al., cf. *POxy.*1012*Fr.*16; opp. οἱ παλαιοί, Moer.145.

Ἑλλην-άρχης, ου, ὁ, *chief of the Greek community*, title at Tanais, *IPE*2.423, al. **-ίζω**, impf. ἐλλήνιζον without augm., Charito4. 5 codd.: aor. Act. ἑλληνίσαι D.C.55.3: aor. Pass. without augm., Th.2.68 codd.: pf. Pass. ἡλλήνισται J.*AJ*1.6.1:—*speak Greek*, Ἕλλην μέν ἐστι καὶ ἑλληνίζει Pl.*Men.*82b, cf. *Chrm.*159a, *Prt.*328a, etc.; ἑ. τῇ φωνῇ, τὴν φωνήν, Aeschin.3.172, Charito l.c.; esp. *speak* or *write pure* or *correct Greek*, Arist.*Rh.*1407^{a}19, D.H.*Pomp.*2.5; ἄκρως ἑ. S.E.*M.*1.186; opp. βαρβαρίζω, ib.246. b. οὐδὲ γὰρ ἂν ἑλληνίζοι οὕτως τὸ ἐρώτημα λεχθέν *would* not *be Greek*, Arist.*SE* 182^{a}34. c. *speak common Greek*, opp. the Attic dialect, σὺ μὲν ἀττικίζεις.. οἱ δ' Ἕλληνες ἑλληνίζομεν Posidipp.28. II. trans., *make Greek, Hellenize*, τὴν βάρβαρον Lib.*Or.*11.103; *translate into Greek*, D.C. l.c.:—Pass., ἑλληνισθῆναι τὴν γλῶσσαν ἀπό τινος *acquire the Greek language* from.., Th. l.c.; τὰ ὀνόματα.. ἡλλήνισται *have assumed an Hellenic form*, J.*AJ*1.6.1. **-ικός**, ή, όν, *Hellenic, Greek*, Hdt.4.108, etc. 2. ἑλληνική (sc. γλῶσσα), ἡ, *the Greek language*, *Apoc.*9.11. 3. τὸ Ἑ. *the Greeks* collectively, Hdt.7.139, al.; *Greek soldiery*, X.*An.*1.4.13. b. *Greek culture*, D.H.1.89: pl., Hdt.4.78. 4. τὰ Ἑ. *the history of Greek affairs*, Th.1.97, etc.; title of works by X., Theopomp.Hist., etc.; *Greek literature*, App. *BC*4.67. II. *like the Greeks*, οὐ.. πατρῷον τόνδ' ἐδεξάμην νόμον, οὐδ' Ἑ. E.*Alc.*684, cf. Ar.*Ach.*115, Plu.*Luc.*41: Comp. -ώτερος Id. *Comp.Lyc.Num.*1; ἡ συγγνώμη τῆς τιμωρίας -ώτερον Lib.*Ep.*75.4: Sup. -ώτατος D.19.308, D.H.1.89. Adv. -κῶς *in Greek fashion*, Hdt.4. 108, E.*IT*660, Antiph.184. III. *pure Greek*, οὐχ Ἑ. λέξις Orusap. Eust.859.55, cf. Ael.Dion.*Fr.*207, S.E.*M.*1.187. Adv. -κῶς *in pure Greek*, opp. βαρβαρικῶς, Phld.*Lib.*p.13O., cf. S.E.*M.*1.243, Porph. *Abst.*3.3. 2. *in Hellenistic Greek*, opp. Ἀττικῶς, Moer.1, al.; but also, opp. κοινόν 'in common speech', Id.347, al. IV. *pagan*, Lxx 2*Ma.*4.10, al., Jul.*Ep.*84a, Suid. s.v. Διοκλητιανός. **-ιος**, Dor. **Ἑλλάνιος** [ᾱ] (also in Ar.*Eq.*1253), α, ον, = foreg., Ζεὺς Ἑ., Ἀθανᾶ Ἑ., Rhetra ap.Plu.*Lyc.*6 (Συλλ- codd.); Ζεὺς Ἑ. Hdt.9.7.α', cf. Pi.*N.*5.10, *IG*12(5).910 (Tenos), etc.; Ἀθηνᾶ Ἑ. E.*Hipp.*1121 (lyr.); θεοὶ οἱ Ἑ. Hdt.5.49, 92.η', Luc.*Herc.*2 codd., Hld.2.23. II. Ἑλλήνιον, τό, *Greek factory* (with temples of Θεοὶ Ἑλλήνιοι) at Naucratis, Hdt.2. 178; also of buildings at Arsinoe and Memphis, *BGU*133.6 (ii A.D.), Wilcken *Chr.*221 (iii B.C.). III. Ἑλλανία, ἡ, = Ἑλλάς, E.*Hel.* 1147 (lyr.), etc. **-ίς**, Dor. **Ἑλλανίς**, ίδος, ἡ, = fem. of Ἑλλήνιος, Pi.*P.*11.50; ἀρεταὶ ἀέθλων Id.*Pae.*4.23, cf. Cratin.293, Lys.30.18, Th. 1.35, D.18.304, etc.; Ἑ. διάλεκτος, γλῶττα, Phld.*D.*3.14. II. Ἑλληνίς (sc. γυνή), ἡ, *Grecian woman*, E.*El.*1076, Men.79. 2. *pagan woman*, Jul.*Ep.*112. **-ισμός**, ὁ, *imitation of the Greeks, Hellenism*, Lxx 2*Ma.*4.13. II. *use of a pure Greek style and idiom*, as an ἀρετὴ λόγου, Diog.Bab.*Stoic.*3.214, cf. Phld.*Po.*2.18, A.D.*Pron.*71.25, S.E.*M.*1.98; ἔνιοι λέγουσιν Ἑ. εἶναι τὸν ποιητήν (i.e. Homer), *Lex.Vind.*311; περὶ Ἑλληνισμοῦ, title of works by Seleucus, Ath.9.367a; by Ptolemy of Ascalon, Philoxenus and Tryphon, Suid.; κανόνες Ἑλληνισμοῦ, title of work by Irenaeus, Id. 2. *use of the* κοινή, opp. to strict Atticism, *POxy.*1012*Fr.*17. III. *paganism*, Jul.*Ep.*84a; ἡ τοῦ Ἑ. δυσσέβεια *Cod.Just.*1.11.9.1. **-ιστής**, οῦ, ὁ, *one who uses the Greek language*: *a Greek Jew*, *Act.Ap.*6.1, etc. II. *gentile, heathen*, Jul.*Ep.*84a. **-ιστί**, Adv. *in the Greek language*, Pl.*Ti.*21e, *PTaur.*1^{v}4 (ii B.C.), Ph.2.546, J.*AJ*14.10.2, etc.; Ἑ. ξυνιέναι to understand *Greek*, X.*An.*7.6.8; Ἑ. γινώσκεις; *Act.Ap.*21.37; *in Greek fashion*, Luc.*Scyth.*3.

Ἑλληνο-γαλάται [λᾰ], οἱ, = *Gallograeci*, D.S.5.32. **-δίκαι**, **-δικέω**, v. Ἑλλανο-. **-κοπέω**, *flatter the Greeks*, Plb.25.3.1; *affect Greek fashions*, Id.20.10.7. **-μεμφῖται**, οἱ, *Greeks resident at Memphis*, *PSI*5.531.6 (iii B.C.). **-τᾰμίαι**, ῶν, οἱ, *stewards of Greece*, i.e. *treasurers of the Confederacy of Delos*, *IG*1^2.191.1, al., Antipho 5. 69, And.3.38, Th.1.96, etc.:—hence **-τᾰμιεία**, ἡ, their *office*, X.*Vect.* 5.5 (-ταμία codd.). **-τρωοφθόρος**, ον, *destroying Greeks and Trojans*, μάχη Tz.*H.*5.772. **-φρων**, ονος, ὁ, ἡ, *with Greek tastes*, Dam.*Isid.*108.

Ἑλλησ-ποντιακός, ή, όν, *of the Hellespont*, X.*An.*1.1.9, etc.:— also **-πόντιος**, α, ον, Hdt.7.95, X.*HG*3.4.11. **-ποντίας**, Ion. **-ίης** (sc. ἄνεμος), ου, ὁ, *wind blowing from the Hellespont*, i.e. *from the NE.*, Hdt.7.188; = καικίας, Arist.*Mete.*364^{b}19, cf. *Pr.*946^{b}33, Thphr. *Vent.*62. **-ποντιάς**, άδος, ἡ, fem. Adj. *of the Hellespont*, θάλασσα Archestr.*Fr.*35.14B. **-πόντιος**, α, ον, *of the Hellespont*, Hdt.7. 95, X.*HG*3.4.11. II. Subst. -ποντία, ἡ, name of a *plaster*, Heras ap.Gal.13.914. **-ποντίς**, ίδος, fem. Adj., = -ποντιάς, πηλαμύς S. *Fr.*503. **-ποντος**, ὁ, *Hellespont* or *sea of Helle* (daughter of Athamas, who was drowned therein), now *the Dardanelles*, Il.2.845, Hdt. 4.38, etc.:—sts. taken to include the Propontis, Id.1.57, etc.:—*the adjacent country*, Th.2.9, etc.: in this sense without Art. in Att. Inscrr., *IG*1^2.106.16, al.: said to be used of the Aegean, Str.7 *Fr.* 58. **-ποντοφύλᾰκες** [ῠ], οἱ, *customs officials* established by Athens to control the trade of the Hellespont, *IG*1^2.57.36.

ἐλλίζων· τίλλων, Hsch.

ἔλλῐθος, ον, *containing a precious stone*, δακτυλίδιον *PLond.ined.* 2199 (iv A.D.).

ἐλλῐμεν-ίζω, *exact harbour-dues*, Ar.*Fr.*455. **-ικός**, ή, όν, only neut. pl. -ικά, τά (sc. τέλη), *harbour-dues*, Pl.*R.*425d. **-ιος**, α, ον, *in the harbour*, [πύργοι] Str.1.3.20. II. Subst. -ιον, τό, *harbour-dues, customs*, Eup.48, *SIG*524.6 (Crete, iii B.C.), *Milet.*3 No.37 *d*68, Arist.*Oec.*1350^{a}16, Plb.30.31.12: pl., *GDI*5018 (Cret.). **-ισις**, εως, ἡ, *coming into port*, Sch.rec.S.*OT*196. **-ιστής**, οῦ, ὁ, *farmer of harbour-dues* or *customs*, Aen.Tact.29.5, D.34.34.

ἐλλῐπαίνω, aor. 1 ἐνελίπᾱνεν, glossed by ἔπλησεν, ἔπληξεν, Hsch.

ἐλλῐπής, ές, (ἐλλείπω) Act., *leaving out, omitting*, τινός Pl.*Lg.* 924b. II. Pass., *wanting, defective*, μνήμης Th.7.8; ἐ. κάλλους, ἀκριβείας, Pl.*Lg.*669a, *R.*504b, etc.: c. dat., προθυμίᾳ ἐλλιπεῖς Th.6. 69; δεῖπνον.. μηδενὶ ἐλλιπές Euang.1.3; ἐν τοῖς πεζικοῖς τῷ καθοπλισμῷ Plb.18.22.5. 2. abs., *failing*, ἐ. καὶ μὴ δυνατὸς ἐπιμελεῖσθαι *negligent*, Pl.*Lg.*901c; τὸ μὴ ἐπιχειρούμενον ἀεὶ ἐλλιπὲς ἦν τῆς δοκήσεως whatever was not attempted was *so much lost* of their reckoning, Th.4.55, cf. 5.1; τὸ ἐ. τῆς γνώμης ὑν.. ᾠήθημεν πράξειν the *failure* of judgement in respect of.., Id.4.63; τὸ ἐ. *defect*, Arist. *Rh.*1371^{b}4; τὸ τῆς νομοθεσίας ἐ. Plb.6.49.6: Comp. -έστερος ib.11.3. Adv. -πῶς *inadequately, deficiently*, λέγειν Isoc.*Fr.*3.β'.5; πρός τι ἔχειν Aret.*CD*1.2; ἔχειν τινός *Cod.Just.*1.1.7.11; γεγραμμένα Gal. *Libr.Propr.*2; opp. περιττῶς, Philostr.*VS*1.11: Comp. -έστερον *OGI* 56.13 (iii B.C.); ἐ. τῆς ἀληθείας εἰρηκέναι Plb.5.32.2. III. of a number, *not equal to the sum of its factors*, opp. ὑπερτελής, Theo Sm. p.46H. Adv. -πῶς Iamb.*in Nic.*p.53P. IV. Gramm., *elliptical*, φωνή S.E.*P.*1.188, cf. Sch.S.*OT*324, etc. Adv. -πῶς Sch.A.R.1.252.

ἔλλῐπος, ον, *greasy*, τῇ γεύσει Vett.Val.4.3 (Sup.), cf. *Cat.Cod. Astr.*7.220 (Sup.).

ἐλλῐσάμην, v. λίσσομαι. **ἐλλῑτάνευε**, v. λιτανεύω.

ἐλλόβιον, τό, (λοβός) *that which is in the lobe of the ear, ear-ring*, Nic. Dam.p.5 D., Luc.*Gall.*29, S.E.*P.*3.203, Them.*Or.*13.167d.

ἐλλοβόκαρπος, ον, *bearing fruit in a pod*, Thphr.*HP*6.5.3. **ἔλλοβος**, ον, *in a pod*, καρπός ib.3.14.4, 4.2.8. **ἐλλοβοσπέρμᾰτος**, ον, *with its seed in a pod*, opp. γυμνοσπ., ib.7.3.2.

ἐλλοβώδης, ες, *with pods*, Thphr.*HP*8.2.5.

ἐλλογ-άω, v.l. for sq. in *Ep.Rom.*5.13, *Ep.Philem.*18. **-έω**, (λόγος) = ἐν λόγῳ τιθέναι, *reckon, put to an account*, *Ep.Philem.*18; τινί *PRyl.*243.11 (ii A.D.), etc.:—Pass., *to be reckoned in*, *IG*9(1).61.37 (Daulis, ii A.D.), *PStrassb.*1.32.10 (iii A.D.), etc. 2. metaph., *impute*, *BGU*140.32 (ii A.D.):—Pass., *Ep.Rom.*5.13. **-ιμος**, ον, *held in account* or *regard* (ἐν λόγῳ), *in high repute*, Hdt.2.176, Pl.*Prt.*327c, *Smp.*197a, al.; ἐ. ἐπὶ σοφίᾳ Id.*Prt.*361e: Sup., Plb.1.2.1, Philostr.*VS*1.9.1, al. Adv. -μως ib.2.11.1; ἔχειν τινός ib.33.2. II. *eloquent*, Men.Rh.p.354 S. (Sup.), Poll.2.125. Adv. -μως *Gloss.* III. = ἔλλογος, opp. ἄλογος, *Corp.Herm.*12.6. **-ιμότης**, ητος, ἡ, *capability of reasoning*, *Gloss.* **-ος**, ον, *endowed with reason*, opp. ἄλογος, Arist.*EN*1172ᵇ10, Plot.3.8.1.

Ἐλλοί· Ἕλληνες οἱ ἐν Δωδώνῃ, καὶ οἱ ἱερεῖς, Hsch.; cf. Σελλοί.

ἔλλοιπος, ον, = ἐλλιπής, *IG*1².373.48, 2².244.4.

ἐλλοξοτέρως, Adv. Comp. (λοξός) *rather obliquely*, Paul.Aeg.6.40.

Ἐλλοπία, Ep. -ίη, ἡ, (Ἔλλοψ, son of Ion) *the land of Dodona*, Hes.*Fr.*134.1. II. a *district in Euboea*, Hdt.8.23, etc.:—hence **Ἐλλοπιῆες**, its inhabitants, Hsch.

ἐλλοπιεύω, (ἔλλοψ) *fish*, Theoc.1.42: **ἐλλοπεύω** corrupt in *EM* 331.49.

ἐλλοπίης, ου, ὁ, name of a *fish*, cj. for ἀλλ- in Numen.ap.Ath.7.326a.

ἐλλόποδες (so *EM*331.53, -ιδες Hsch.), *the young of birds* or *serpents*, Cratin.408.

ἔλλοπος, ὁ, v. ἔλλοψ I. **ἐλλοπῶ**· ἀγαθήν, Hsch.

ἐλλός or **ἐλλός** (A), ὁ, *a young deer, fawn*, ποικίλος Od.19.228, cf. Ant.Lib.28.3, Eust.1863.40. (Prob. from *ἐλνός, cf. ἔλαφος.)

ἐλλός (B), ή, όν, = ἔλλοψ (q.v.); also variously expld. (ἀγαθόν, γλαυκόν, χαροπόν..ταχύ..ὑγρόν) by Hsch.

ἐλλοφόνος, ον, *fawn-slaying*, of Britomartis, Call.*Dian.*190.

ἐλλοχ-άω, *lie in ambush* (λόχος), Pl.*Tht.*165d:—Med., Phalar.*Ep.*5. II. *lie in wait for*, τινά Pl.*Smp.*213b, Ael.*NA*6.4. III. Pass., ἐλλοχᾶσθαι κακοῖς *to be filled with lurking* mischiefs, Alciphr. 2.3. **-ησις**, εως, ἡ, *lying in ambush*, Anon.ap.Suid. s.v. δεξιός. **-ίζω**, *lie in ambush*, E.*Ba.*722. II. *place in ambush*, ὁπλίτας Polyaen.3.1.2, cf. Plu.*Phil.*14.

ἔλλοψ, οπος, ὁ, ἡ, epith. of fish (exc. ἔλλοπι κούρᾳ, of Echo, Theoc. *Syrinx* 18), expld. as *dumb* by Hsch. (also by δασεῖς, τραχεῖς, ποικίλοι), but perh. rather, *scaly* (cf. λεπίς): ἔλλοπας ἰχθῦς Hes.*Sc.*212; ἔλλοπος μυνδοῦ δίκην Lyc.1375:—also **ἔλλοπος**, Emp.117: **ἐλλός**, ἰχθύες ἐλλοί Titanomach.*Fr.*4; ἐλλοῖς ἰχθύσιν S.*Aj.*1297. II. as Subst., *fish*, in general, Nic.*Al.*481, Lyc.600, Opp.*H.*2.658, 3.55, 89; fem., Lyc.796. 2. an unknown *sea-fish*, Arist.*HA*505ᵃ15, etc.; also **ἔλοψ**, Epich.71, Archestr.*Fr.*11.1, Matro *Conv.*69, Apio ap.Ath. 7.294f, Plu.2.979c; identified with ἱερὸς ἰχθῦς by Ael.*NA*8.28. 3. a *serpent*, Nic.*Th.*490.

ἔλλυες· ζῷα ἐν τῷ Σμαράγδῳ ποταμῷ, Hsch.

ἔλλῡπος, ον, *in grief, mournful*, Plu.2.621a.

ἔλλυσις, Cret. for ἔκλυσις, Hsch. **ἐλλύτατον**· οἰκτρότατον, Id.

ἐλλύτης, Dor. -ας, ὁ, a kind of *cake*, *Test.Epict.*5.35, al., Hsch.

ἐλλυχᾶται· πλανᾶται, διατρίβει, Hsch.

ἐλλυχν-ιάζω, *furnish* a lamp *with a wick*, *PMag.Par.*1.1099, *PMag.Lond.*121.376:—Pass., Dsc.1.72.4. **-ιον**, τό, *lamp-wick* (Att. θρυαλλίς), Hdt.2.62, Hp.*Nat.Mul.*26, *Mul.*2.203, Thphr.*Char.* 10.13, *Inscr.Délos* 316.76 (iii B.C.), Apollon.*Mir.*36, etc. 2. *surgical dressing*, Sor.2.11, Gal.10.954. **-ωτός**, ή, όν, *made of wick-cotton*, μοτός Gal.14.795, Paul.Aeg.3.24.

ἐλλωβάομαι, *commit an outrage*, εἰς τὸν οἶκόν τινος Ant.Lib.11.7.

Ἑλλωτία or **Ἑλλωτίς**, ίδος, ἡ, epith. of Athena, Sch.Pi.*O.*13.56. 2. Ἑλλωτίς, ἡ, *wreath worn at the* Ἑλλωτία, Seleuc.ap.Ath. 15.678a, cf. Hsch. II. Ἑλλώτια (sc. ἱερά), τά, *festival* of Athena at Corinth, Pi.*O.*13.40; of Europa in Crete, Hsch.

ἐλμακίνη λειμῶνος· ἡ λεπτὴ σχοῖνος, Hsch. **ἔλματα**· ὁμιλήματα, ἐνειλήματα, σανιδώματα, Id.

ἐλμινθ-ιάω, (ἕλμινς) *suffer from worms*, Arist.*HA*612ᵃ31. **-ιον**, τό, Dim. of ἕλμινς, *little worm*, Hp.*Epid.*4.16, Arist.*HA*570ᵃ14.

ἐλμινθοβότᾰνον, τό, a *herb used as a specific for worms*, Alex.Trall. *Verm.*2 p.595 P.

ἐλμινθώδης, ες, *like a worm*, Arist.*HA*538ᵃ5.

ἕλμινς (Hp.*Morb.*4.54), ινθος, ἡ, dat. pl. ἕλμινσι Choerob. *in Theod.* 1.299:—also nom. **ἕλμις**, Arist.*HA*602ᵇ26; acc. ἕλμιθα *IG*4.952.10, 18; nom. pl. ἕλμεις Dsc.*Eup.*2.67; dat. ἕλμῖσι Opp.*H.*3.180: also gen. ἕλμιγγος Hp.*Epid.*1.26.ιβ':—*worm*, I. *intestinal-worm*, either flat (πλατεῖα) or round (στρογγύλη), Id.*Morb.*4.54, cf. *Prog.*11, *Aph.* 3.26, Arist.*HA*551ᵃ8, Thphr.*HP*9.12.1. II. *parasitic worm* in sponges, Arist.*HA*548ᵇ15.

ἐλξίνη [ῐ], ἡ, (ἕλκω) *pellitory*, *Parietaria officinalis*, Dsc.4.85, Apollon.*Mir.*30. II. *bindweed*, *Convolvulus arvensis*, Dsc.4.39. III. = μῖλαξ τραχεῖα, Ps.-Dsc.4.142. IV. ἐ. μείζων, = περικλύμενον, ib.14.

ἕλξις, εως, ἡ, (ἕλκω) *dragging, trailing*, τὰς Ἕκτορος ἕλξεις Pl.*R.* 391b; ἱματίων ἕλξεις Id.*Alc.*1.122c. 2. *attraction, attractive power*, Id.*Ti.*80c, Hp.*Gland.*7; ἕλξει ἐκ γῆς ἀναδίδοται τὰ σπέρματα Porph. *Gaur.*3.3. 3. *drawing* of the bow, ἀπὸ τῆς χειρός Hero *Bel.*75.10, cf. Philostr.*Her.*11. 4. *retching*, Hp.*Coac.*55.

ἐλξῖτις, ιδος, ἡ, = ἐλξίνη, Ps.-Dsc.4.39.

ἔλοιμι, ἐλοίμην, ἑλόμην, ἕλον, v. αἱρέω.

ἐλονόμος, ον, *dwelling in marshes*, f.l. for ὑλο-, Hp.*Vict.*2.49.

ἕλος, εος, τό, *marsh-meadow*, ἵπποι ἕλος κάτα βουκολέοντο Il.20.221, cf. 4.483: generally, *marshy ground*, ἂν δόνακας καὶ ἕλος Od.14.474, cf. Hdt.1.191, Th.1.110, *Inscr.Cypr.*135.9 H. (Idalium), X.*HG*1.2.7, etc. 2. *backwater*, δάσκιον ἕ. A.R.2.1283.

ἔλοψ, v. ἔλλοψ. **ἐλόωσι**, v. ἐλαύνω.

ἐλπῐδο-δώτης, ου, ὁ, *giver of hope*, *AP*9.525.6, cj. in Timo 65. **-κοπέω**, *lead by false hopes*, ἐπιθυμίας S.E.*M.*6.26, cf. Eust. 1063.60 (Pass.). **-ποιέω**, *raise hopes*, Sch.Od.18.160, Hsch. s.v. ἔλπει.

ἐλπίζω, Att. fut. -ιῶ LXX *Ps.*43(44).7, *Ep.Rom.*15.12; ἐλπίσω Gal.10.656 (ἐλπίσω in A.*Ch.*187 is aor. subj.): aor. ἤλπισα Hdt.8.24, S.*Ph.*1175 (lyr.), etc. (ἤλπιζα (sic) *IG*3.1350): pf. ἤλπικα *Ev.Jo.*5.45, (προ-) Posidipp.27.8: plpf. ἠλπίκειν Plu.*Alc.*17, Luc.*Herm.*71, Hdn.8.5.1:—Med., App.*Pun.*115 (s.v.l.), *Supp.Epigr.*2.461 (Histria, i B.C.):—Pass., aor. ἠλπίσθην S.*OC*1105, *APl.*4.222 (Parmen.): pf. ἤλπισμαι D.H.5.40:—Att. form of ἔλπομαι, used also by Hdt., *hope for*, or rather (in earlier writers) *look for, expect*:—Constr.: c. acc., A.*Th.*589, *Ch.*539, etc., τι παρά τινος X.*Mem.*4.3.17, D.19. 102: freq. with a dependent clause in inf., *hope to* do, or *hope* or *expect that*..; c. fut. inf., ἐ. μιν ἀποθανέεσθαι Hdt.3.143, cf. Antipho 2. 3.6, Th.4.71, Lys.16.2; ἐ. τὴν Εὐρώπην δουλώσεσθαι (v.l. -ασθαι) Id. 2.21: c. aor. inf., ἐ. ποτὲ δεῖξαι S.*Ph.*629; ἤλπιζον ἑλεῖν X.*Ag.*7.6: also with ἄν, οὐδαμὰ ἐλπίζων ἂν ἡμίονον τεκέειν Hdt.3.151, Th.2.53; the inf. may be omitted, ἔκλυον ἄν..οὐδ' ἂν ἤλπισ' αὐδάν (sc. κλύειν) S. *El.*1281; also ἐ. ὅπως.., with fut., E.*Heracl.*1051, S.*El.*963:—Pass., τὸ μηδαμὰ ἐλπισθὲν ἥξειν Id.*OC*1105; ὁ ἐλπισθεὶς αὐτοκράτωρ *POxy.* 1021.6 (i A.D.). 2. of evils, *look for, fear*, in same constr., δύστανον ἐ. αἶσαν S.*Tr.*111 (lyr.); ἔξοδον ὀλεθρίαν Αἴαντος ἐλπίζει φέρειν Id. *Aj.*799, cf. Lys.12.70; τουτί..τὸ κακὸν οὐδέποτ' ἤλπισα Ar.*Av.*956; ἐ. πάγχυ ἀπολέεσθαι Hdt.8.12; θῆράς σφε τὸν δύστηνον ἐλπίζει κτανεῖν E.*Ion* 348: with μή folld. by aor. subj., οὐδαμὰ ἐλπίσας μή κοτε ἐλάσῃ Hdt.1.77; οὐκ ἂν ἤλπισε μή κοτέ τις ἀναβαίη Id.8.53. 3. c. pres. inf., *deem, suppose that*.., Emp.11.2; ἐλπίζων εἶναι..ὀλβιώτατος Hdt. 1.30; ἐλπίζων σιτοδείην τε εἶναι ἰσχυρὴν..καὶ τὸν λεὼν τετρῦσθαι ib. 22; οἰκότα ἐλπίζων ib.27, cf. A.*Th.*76, *Ch.*187; βοῦν ἢ λέοντ' ἤλπιζες ἐντείνειν βρόχοις; E.*Andr.*720; ἐλπίζει δυνατὸς εἶναι ἄρχειν Pl.*R.* 573c; ὅστις ἐλπίζει θεοὺς..χαίρειν ἀπαρχαῖς *Trag.Adesp.*118.2: sts. of future events, τίς ἂν ἤλπισεν ἁμαρτήσεσθαί τινα τῶν πολιτῶν τοιαύτην ἁμαρτίαν; Lys.31.27; οὐδὲν..ποιήσειν ἐλπίζων D.4.7. 4. c. dat., *hope in*.., τῇ τύχῃ Th.3.97; ὀνόματι *Ev.Matt.*12.21: also with Preps., ἔν τισι LXX 4 *Ki.*18.5; πρός τι ib.*Jd.*20.36; ἐ. εἴς τινα *Ev.Jo.*5.45, al.; ἐπί τινι *Ep.Rom.*15.12, al.; ἐπί τινα 1 *Ep.Pet.*3.5.

ἐλπ-ίς, ίδος, ἡ, (v. ἔλπω) *hope, expectation* (δόξα μελλόντων Pl.*Lg.* 644c), ἔτι γὰρ καὶ ἐλπίδος αἶσα Od.16.101, 19.84; personified, Hes. *Op.*96: pl., Pi.*P.*2.49, etc.; πολλῶν ῥαγεισῶν ἐλπίδων after the wreck of many *hopes*, A.*Ag.*505; ἔτι ἐν αὐτοῖς εἰσὶν ἐλπίδες, νέοι γάρ Pl.*Prt.* 328d; κεναῖσιν ἐλπίσιν θερμαίνεται S.*Aj.*478; *expectancy*, Id.*OT*771 (pl.), *OC*1749 (lyr., pl.), Pi.*N.*1.32 (pl.), etc.:—Constr., in Att., with gen. both of subject and object, as (where both are conjoined) Πελοποννησίων τὴν ἐλπίδα τοῦ ναυτικοῦ *the hope of* the P. *in* their navy, Th. 2.89; also αἱ τῶν Ἑλλήνων ἐς ὑμᾶς ἐλπίδες Id.3.14; ὑμέτεραι ἐλπίδες, = ἐς ὑμᾶς, Id.1.69; ἐλπίδ' ἔχω, = ἐλπίζω, with fut. inf., μὴ οὐ δώσειν δίκην Hdt.6.11, etc.: with aor. inf., κλέος εὑρέσθαι Pi.*P.*3.111: with ὡς and fut. inf., S.*OC*385; ὥστε μὴ θανεῖν E.*Or.*52; περὶ τῆς ἐμαυτοῦ ψυχῆς οὐ πολλὰς ἐλπίδας ἔχω D.H.5.27; ἐν ἐλπίδι εἰμί, c. fut. inf., Th.7.46; ἐν ἐλπίσι καλαῖς γενόμενος Plu.*Brut.*40; ἐλπίς [ἐστί] μοι with acc. and fut. inf. or aor., ἐλπίς τις αὐτὸν ἥξειν A.*Ag.*679; τοσοῦτόν γ' ἐστί μοι τῆς ἐλπίδος, τὸν ἄνδρα..προσμενεῖν S.*OT*836; πλείων ἐλπὶς φιλίαν ἢ ἔχθραν γενέσθαι Pl.*Phdr.*232e: c. pres. inf., Id.*Sph.*250e: folld. by ὡς.., E.*Tr.*487; ἐς ἐλπίδα ἐλθεῖν τινος Th.2.56; ἐπ' ἐλπίδας ἀφανεῖς καθίστασθαι Id.5.103; ἐλπίδα λαβεῖν X.*Cyr.*4.6.7; ἐλπίδας μεγάλας ἔν τινι ἔχειν ib.1.4.25, cf. Isoc.4.121; τίν' ὑπάγεις μ' ἐς ἐλπίδ'; E.*Hel.* 826; ἐλπίδας ἐμποιεῖν ἀνθρώποις, ὑποθεῖναί τισι, X.*Cyr.*1.6.19, *HG*4. 8.28; ἐλπίδας μεγίστας παρέχεται ποιῆσαι Pl.*Smp.*193d; ἐλπίδα or ἐλπίδας ὑπογράφειν, Epicur.*Ep.*3 p.65 U., Plb.5.36.1; ἀποκεκομμένης τῆς ἐλπίδος Id.3.63.8, cf. A.R.4.1272; ἐκτὸς ἐλπίδος *beyond hope*, S.*Ant.*330; ἀπ' ἐλπίδος πεσεῖν A.*Ag.*999; παρ' ἐλπίδα ib.899, S.*Ph.* 882: prov., πεινῶμεν ἐπὶ ταῖς ἐλπίσιν Antiph.123.7; κάπτοντες αὔρας ἐλπίδας σιτούμενοι Eub.10.7; αἱ δ' ἐλπίδες βόσκουσι τοὺς κενούς Men. *Mon.*42. 2. *object of hope, a hope*, Ὀρέστης, ἐ. δόμων A.*Ch.*776; ὑμεῖς, ἡ μόνη ἐ. Th.3.57; Εὔτυχος, ἡ γονέων ἐ. *IG*3.1311. 3. *reason to expect* or *believe*, πολλὴ ἐ. κτήσασθαι, νοητὸν εἶναι, Pl.*Phd.* 67b, *Lg.*898d. II. *anxious thought on the future, boding*, A. *Ag.*1434, Hp.*Coac.*267, E.*Or.*859, Pl.*Lg.*644c. **-ισμα**, ατος, τό, *hope, confidence*, Epicur.*Fr.*68 (= Metrod.*Fr.*5): pl., D.Chr.20. 24. **-ισμός**, ὁ, *expectation*, Phld.*Rh.*1.288 S. **-ιστέον**, *one must expect*, Lyd.*Ost.*24. **-ιστικός**, ή, όν, *producing expectation*, Arist.*Mem.*449ᵇ12. II. οἱ ἐ. a sect *who made hope the only stay of life*, Plu.2.668e. **-ιστός**, ή, όν, *to be expected*, Pl.*Lg.*853d; τὸ μέλλον ἐστὶ δοξαστὸν καὶ ἐ. Arist.*Mem.*449ᵇ11.

ἔλπος· ἔλαιον, στέαρ, εὐθηνία, Hsch.; cf. ἔλφος. (Cf. Skt. *sarpiṣ* 'melted butter', OHG. *salba*.) **ἐλπτέοντες**· ἐλπίζοντες, Id.

ἔλπω (ἐέλπω only Hsch. s.v. ἐέλποιμεν), causal, only found in pres.

(exc. ἔλπεον· ἤλπιζον, Id.), *cause to hope*, πάντας μὲν ἔλπει she *feeds* all *with hope*, Od.2.91, 13.380; perh. also, *cause to expect*, Max.178 (but may, = *expect*). II. elsewh. in Med., **ἔλπομαι**, Ep. **ἐέλπομαι**, ἠλπόμην Od.9.419, Alc.*Supp.*22.8, Pi.*P.*4.243, etc.: Ep. 3 sg. impf. ἔλπετο and ἐέλπ-, Od.3.275, Il.12.407 (ἔλπετο also in Luc.*Syr.D.*22): pf. ἔολπα Il.22.216, Od.5.379, Hes.*Op.*[273], A.R.2.147, etc.: 3 sg. plpf. ἐώλπει Il.19.328, Od.20.328, A.R.3.370, Theoc.25.115:—*hope* or *expect*, Ep., Lyr., Ion. (not in Hp.) for Att. ἐλπίζω (q.v.):—Constr., like ἐλπίζω: c. acc. and fut. inf., Il.13.8, B.*Fr.*12: c. aor. inf., Il.7.199, Pi.*P.*4.243 codd., *N.*4.92: c. pf. inf., Il.15.110: sts. the inf. must be supplied, ἐκτελέσας μέγα ἔργον ὃ οὔ ποτε ἔλπετο θυμῷ (sc. ἐκτελέειν) Od.3.275: c. acc. rei, Il.13.609, 15.539; ἅσσα οὐκ ἔλπονται Heraclit.27: later, c. gen. rei, πολυγλαγέος ἐνιαυτοῦ Arat.1100: ὡς.., dub. l. in Orph.*A.*846: abs., Heraclit.18: Homeric phrases, ἔλπετο θυμῷ Il.17.404, al.; also μάλα δέ σφισιν ἔλπετο θυμός 17.495; ἔλπετο θυμὸς ἐνὶ στήθεσσιν ἑκάστου 15.701; ἤλπετ' ἐνὶ φρεσί Od.9.419. 2. *expect anxiously, fear*, ἐλπόμενός τί οἱ κακὸν εἶναι *having a foreboding that*.., Hdt.9.113. 3. generally, *deem, suppose*, οὔ ποθι ἔλπομαι οὕτως δεύεσθαι πολέμοιο..Ἀχαιούς Il.13.309, cf. Theoc. 7.31; ἐπὴν ἡμέας ἔλπῃ ποτὶ δώματ' ἀφῖχθαι Od.6.297, cf. 23.345; ἔλπετο γὰρ κατὰ θυμὸν..ἑταίρους..ἰέναι (pres. inf.) Il.10.355; οὐ γὰρ ὅ γ' ἀθανάτων τιν' ἐέλπετο..Τρώεσσιν ἀρηξέμεν Il.13.8, cf. 7.199, 15.110, Orac.ap.Hdt.1.65, *AP*5.115 (Marc. Arg.); λάσην Alc. l.c. (ϝελπ-, ἐϝέλπομαι, ϝέϝολπα, cf. Lat. *volup.*)

ἐλπωρή, ἡ, Ep. form of ἐλπίς, c. fut. inf. et aor., ἐλπωρὴ..κακῶν ὑπάλυξιν ἔσεσθαι Od.23.287; ἐ. φίλους ἰδέειν 6.314: pl., A.R.3.1255. (Dissim. from *ἐλπωλή, cf. φειδωλή, etc.)

ἔλσαι, inf. and **ἔλσας**, aor. 1 part. of εἴλω (q.v.).

ἔλση, ἔλσοιμι, ἐλσών, Lacon. for ἐλθ-, Ar.*Lys.*105, 118, 1081.

ἐλσούς· τὰς μυίας, Hsch.

ἐλύδριον, τό, = χελιδόνιον, used to make yellow dye, *PHolm.*11.16, *PLeid.X.*68, Ps.-Democr.Alch.p.48 B., v.l. in Paul.Aeg.3.2.

ἔλῠμα, ατος, τό, (ἐλύω) *the stock of the plough*, Hes.*Op.*430, 436: also expld. by νύσσα, καὶ τὸ ἱμάτιον, καὶ ἡ ἀϊών, Hsch.

ἐλύμνιαι· δοκοὶ ὀροφῆναι, Hsch.

ἔλῠμος, ὁ, (ἐλύω) *case, quiver*, Hsch. II. a kind of Phrygian *pipe*, made of box-wood, with a horn tip and bend in the left pipe, ἔλυμοι αὐλοί S.*Fr.*450, 644, Call.Com.18; used by the Cyprians, Cratin.Jun.3. III. ἔλυμος, ἡ (masc. in pl., Procop.*Pers.*1.12), = μελίνη, *millet*, Hp.*Mul.*2.110, Ar.*Fr.*398, Plb.2.15.2, *OGI*55.16 (Telmessus, iii B.C.), Str.12.3.15, Dsc.2.98.

ἐλύσσει· εἰλεῖται, Hsch. **ἔλυστα**· ἄμπελος μέλαινα, Id.

ἐλυτροειδὴς χιτών, *tunica vaginalis testiculi*, Cels.7.18, Antyll.ap. Orib.44.23.75, Ruf.*Onom.*197 (written ἐρυτρο- Gal.18(2).998).

ἔλυτρον, τό, (εἰλύω) *covering*: 1. *bow-case*, S.*Fr.*1043 (pl.); *sheath* of a spear, Ar.*Ach.*1120; *mirror-case*, *IG*2.706 A^b13; χοᾶ ἐν ἐ. ib.11 (2).219 *B*76 (Delos, iii B.C.); *case* of a shield, D.S.20.11 (pl.). 2. *sheath* of the spinal cord, Hp.*Art.*45; the *shard* of a beetle's wing, Arist.*HA*532ᵃ23; *shell* of a crab, Ael.*NA*9.43; of the eye-*lids*, Arist. *de An.*421ᵇ29; of the umbilical cord, Id.*HA*586ᵇ23. 3. *husk* or *capsule* of seeds, J.*AJ*3.7.6; the flowering *glume* of ζέα δίκοκκος, Dsc. 2.89. 4. *the body*, as being *the case* or *shell* of the soul, Pl.*R.*588e, Poet.ap.Luc.*Demon.*44. 5. *reservoir for water*, Hdt.1.185, 4.173, Paus.2.27.7, al.; *tank* for fish, Palaeph.27. (Cf. Skt. *varūtram* 'cloak', *varūtár-* 'protector'.) [ῠ Ar. l.c.]

ἐλυτρόω, *cover, encase*, Hp.*Art.*45 (Pass.).

ἐλύω, *roll round* (cf. εἰλύω): only aor. 1 Pass., ῥυμὸς ἐπὶ γαῖαν ἐλύσθη the pole *rolled* to the ground, Il.23.393; προπάροιθε ποδῶν Ἀχιλῆος ἐλυσθεὶς *rolled up, crouching* before Achilles' feet, 24.510, cf. A.R.3.281, 1.1034; λασίην ὑπὸ γαστέρ' ἐλυσθεὶς *coiled* close *up*.., Od. 9.433; ἔρως ὑπὸ καρδίην ἐλυσθεὶς Archil.103. II. in later Ep., = εἰλύω, *wrap up, cover*, ἐνὶ κτερέεσσιν ἐλυσθεὶς *shrouded* in them, A.R. 1.254; ἐν πηλοῖσιν ἐλυσθεὶς Opp.*C.*3.418, cf. *H.*2.89; διὰ φλογὸς εἶθαρ ἐ. A.R.3.1313.

ἔλφος, εος, τό, Cypr., = βούτυρον, Hsch.; v. ἔλπος. **ἐλωγή**· ἔλεγον, Id.

ϝέλχανος, epith. of Zeus in Crete, *GDI*5118, Hsch. (Γελ-):—hence **ϝελχάνια**, τά, *BCH*13.61 (Βελχ-): **Ἐλχάνιος**, ὁ (sc. μήν), month at Cnossus, ib.29.204.

ἐλώδης, ες, *marshy, fenny*, ὕδατα Hp.*Aër.*1; χωρίον Th.7.47, cf. Arist.*HA*596ᵇ3, Onos.8.2 (v.l.); τὰ ἐ. Arist.*Pr.*910ᵃ4. II. *frequenting marshes*, of the elephant, Id.*PA*659ᵃ2. III. *bred in marshes*, πυρετὸς Gal.17(1).889.

ἔλωμα, ατος, τό, = ἕλος, prob. in Python 1.2.

Ἐλωός, epith. of Hephaestus among Dorians, Hsch.

ἔλωρ, τό, Ep. word (twice in Trag., v. infr.), only nom. and acc. sg. and pl.: (ἑλεῖν):—*spoil, prey*, in sg., of unburied corpses, ἀνδράσι δυσμενέεσσιν ἕ. καὶ κύρμα γενέσθαι Il.5.488, cf. 17.151; μὴ θήρεσσιν ἕ. κ. κ. γένωμαι Od.5.473, cf. 3.271, A.R.1.1251; of valuables, μή..ἕ. ἄλλοισι γένηται Od.13.208; κυσὶν πρόβλητος οἰωνοῖς θ' ἕ. S.*Aj.*830: pl., κυσὶν δ' ἕλωρα..πέλειν A.*Supp.*800 (lyr.). II. in pl. also, Πατρόκλοιο δ' ἕλωρα..ἀποτείσῃ may pay *penalty for the slaughter* of P., Il.18.93.

ἐλώρη· πελώρη, Hsch.

ἐλώριον, τό, = ἕλωρ, A.R.2.264: pl., ἑλώρια τεῦχε κύνεσσι Il.1.4.

ἐλώριος, ὁ, a *water-bird*, Clearch.73 (nisi leg. ἐρῳδιός).

ἐλώσθη· ἐφοβεῖτο, ἐμαλακίσθη, Hsch.

ἐμ, = ἐν, before labials.

ἐμαυτοῦ, ἐμαυτῆς, reflexive Pron. of first pers., *of me, of myself*: only gen., dat., and acc. sg., both masc. and fem.: not found in early Ep.; Aeol. ἔμ' αὔτῳ, ἔμ' αὔτᾳ, Alc.72, Sapph.*Supp.*15.11, cf. A.D. *Pron.*80.10; ἐμαυτόν is dub. in Xenoph. (*PLG*2 p.116 B.) and Anacr. 64; Ion. ἐμεωυτοῦ Hdt.4.97 (but ἐμωυτοῦ A.D.*Pron.*74.4), ἐμεωυτῷ Hdt.3.142, ἐμεωυτόν Heraclit.101; ἐμᾶτοῦ, ἐμᾶτόν, *Lyr.Alex.Adesp.*4.23, *SIG*741.12 (i B.C.): in pl. always separated, ἡμῶν αὐτῶν, etc.; ἐν ἐμαυτῷ συννοεῖσθαι in or with *oneself*, E.*Or.*634; πρὸς ἐμαυτόν Ar. *Ra.*53, etc.; strengthd., ἰσχυόν τ' αὐτὸς ἐμαυτοῦ Id.*V.*357, cf. *Lys.* 1125; but ἐν ἐμαυτοῦ (sc. οἴκῳ) εἶναι, metaph., to be *master of oneself*, Pl.*Chrm.*155d: nom. ἐμαυτός, com. formation in Pl.Com.78.

ἔμβᾱ, Poet. aor. 2 imper. of ἐμβαίνω.

ἐμβᾰβάζω, *interrupt*, ἐμβαβάξαντες prob. l. for ἐμβιβ-, Hippon.53.

ἐμ-βᾰδᾶς, ᾶ, ὁ, *cobbler*, name given to Anytus, Theopomp.Com.57, cf. Archipp.30. **-βᾰδεία**, ἡ, = ἐμβατεία, *POxy.*485.33 (ii A.D.), *BGU*832.12, etc. **-βάδευσις** [ᾰ], εως, ἡ, = foreg., prob. in *POxy.* 274.24 (i A.D.). **-βᾰδεύω**, = ἐμβατεύω, ib.1118.7 (i/ii A.D.), *BGU* 101.16 (ii A.D.). **-βᾰδίζω**, *walk on*, ὄχθαις Ael.*NA*10.24; simply, *walk, march*, Ph.1.232, D.C.79.14. **-βᾰδικός**, όν, *square*, πήχεις *PTeb.*472 (ii A.D.), cf. Hero *Mens.*23.2, al. II. -κόν, τό, *tax paid by tenants of land*, *Ostr.*1024. **-βάδιον** [ᾰ], τό, Dim. of ἐμβάς, Ar.*V.*600, *Pl.*847, 941. **-βᾰδομετρικός**, ή, όν, *belonging to the measuring of surfaces*, Hero *Deff.*133. **-βᾰδόν** (A), Adv. *by land*, = πεζῇ, Il.15.505; *wading*, Paus.10.20.8. **-βᾰδόν** (B), τό, *a surface, area* (opp. περίμετρος, Herm. *in Phdr.*p.108 A.), Plb.6.27.2, Phld.*Sign.*15, al., Hero *Deff.*117, *POxy.*505.6 (ii A.D.), Theo Sm. p.126 H., etc.: hence, in Arith., *product* of integers (opp. περίμετρος 'sum'), *Theol.Ar.*10. II. as Adj., δάκτυλος ἐμβαδὸς *square* inch, Hero *Mens.*23. **-βᾰδοποιός**, ὁ, *shoemaker*, *Gloss.*

ἔμβαθρα, ων, τά, a kind of *shoes*, Poll.7.93.

ἐμβαθρικὸν χωρίον, dub. sens. in *Inscr.Magn.*122 *b*6.

ἐμβαθύνους· σεσοφισμένους, σοφούς, Hsch.

ἐμβᾰθύνω, *make deep, hollow out*, βόθρια Alciphr.3.13; *cause to sink deep in*, κακίαν ἑαυτοῖς Plu.2.1128e. II. intr., *go deep into*, τοῖς νόμοις, ταῖς ἐπιστήμαις, Ph.1.18, 341; *sink deep in*, εἰς κάθισιν Lxx *Je.*30.8(49.30).

ἐμβαίνω, fut. -βήσομαι: pf. -βέβηκα; Ep. part. ἐμβεβαώς, -υῖα, Il. 5.199, Hes.*Th.*12, etc.: aor. 2 ἐνέβην; Ep. 3 sg. ἔμβη Od.4.656; dual imper. ἔμβητον Il.23.403:—*step in*, μή τις..ἐμβήῃ let none *step in* (so as to interfere), 16.94: c. dat., ποταμῷ οὐκ ἔστιν δὶς τῷ αὐτῷ ἐμβῆναι Heraclit.91; εἰς πηλόν Id.5; ἐμβέβακεν ἴχνεσιν πατρὸς Pi.*P.* 10.12. 2. *go on, go quickly*, ἔμβητον, says Antilochus to his horses, Il.23.403; ἔμβα *advance!* E.*El.*113 (lyr.). 3. *embark* on a ship, ἐρέται δ' ἐν ἑκάστῃ πεντήκοντα ἐμβέβασαν Il.2.720; τότε δ' ἔμβη νηῒ Πύλονδε Od.4.656, cf. Il.1.311; ἐς ἕτερον πλοῖον ἐ. (v.l. for ἐσβ-) Hdt.2.29, cf. Th.1.18 (v.l.), Lys.2.40, Pl.*Mx.*243c: c. acc., λέμβον ἐ. Plb.30.9.11: abs., *embark*, E.*Tr.*455 (troch.), Ar.*Ra.*188, etc.: generally, *step into, mount*, εἰς τὸ φορεῖον Plu.*Galb.*26: pf., *to be mounted on*, ἵπποισι καὶ ἅρμασιν ἐμβεβαῶτα Il.5.199; ἐπ' ἀπήνης ἐμβεβὼς S.*OT*803: also c. acc., Τροίαν Ἰλιάδ' ἐμβεβαῶτα E.*Hec.*922 (lyr.); στέγην τήνδ' ἐμβεβῶτες Id.*Cyc.*92. 4. *step upon*, τῷ δ' ἐγὼ ἐμβαίνων Od.10.164; πεδίλοις ἐμβεβαυῖα Hes.*Th.*12; τοιοῦδ' ἁλουργέσιν A.*Ag.*946; δαίμων ἐνέβη Περσῶν γενεᾷ *trampled upon* it, Id.*Pers.* 911 (anap.); μὴ 'μβαινε τῷ δυστυχοῦντι Men.*Mon.*356: abs., *tread on* one's *toes*, Thphr.*Char.*15.6; cf. βοῦς VIII. 5. *enter upon*, ἐς τόνδε χρησμὸν dub. in A.*Ag.*1567; εἰς κίνδυνον X.*Cyr.*2.1.15: c. acc., ἐ. κέλευθον E.*Supp.*989 (lyr.). b. metaph., *enter upon, embark in*, μεγαλανορίαις Pi.*N.*11.44; τῷ ἐπιτηδεύματι Pl.*Phdr.*252e; ἐν αὐτοῖς τοῖς δεινοῖς ἐμβεβηκὼς *embarked, engaged in*.., D.18.248; *light upon*, εἰς ἀρχήν τε καὶ τύπον τῆς δικαιοσύνης Pl.*R.*443c: abs., *enter upon office*, *IG*5(1).1390.31 (Andania). 6. rarely c. gen., *step upon*, νᾶος Alc.19; γῆς ὅρων S.*OC*400. 7. Poets, with acc. of the instrument of motion, ὄχοις..ἐμβεβὼς πόδα S.*Fr.*672; ἐς ἄντλον ἐμβήσει (2 sg.) πόδα E.*Heracl.*168. 8. *to be fixed* or *fastened*, κατά τι Il.24.81; *to be fixed in*, εἰς ἐμπνελίδας Hero *Aut.*2.3. 9. = ἐμβατεύω II, *SIG*364.75 (Ephesus, iii B.C.). II. causal in aor. 1 ἐνέβησα, *make to step in, put in*, ἐν δὲ τὰ μῆλα..ἐβήσαμεν Od.11.4; δίφρον ἐμβῆσαί τινα E.*Heracl.*845, cf. *Cyc.*467; ἐ. τὰν ἀρχάν *Schwyzer* 485.9 (Thespiae, iii B.C.): metaph., ἐμβῆσαί τινα ἐς φροντίδα *plunge* him into anxiety, Hdt.1.46. III. intr., *step, march* or *dance*, ὀρθῶς Pl. *Alc.*1.108c; πρὸς ῥυθμόν Luc.*Salt.*10.

ἐμβακανίτης· τὸ μετὰ τοῦ ταρίχους καὶ στέατος σκευαζόμενον βρῶμα, Hsch.

ἐμβακχεύω, *revel in*, τοῖς ἡμετέροις κακοῖς Hld.2.4.

ἐμβάλλω, fut. -βᾰλῶ: pf. -βέβληκα: aor. 2 ἐνέβᾰλον (Pass. is mostly supplied by ἐμπίπτω):—*throw in*, τινὰ πόντῳ Il.14.258; μιν.. χερσὶν Ἀχιλλῆος θεὸς ἔμβαλεν *let* him *fall into* Achilles' hands, 21.47; ἐ. νιν βροτοῦ ἀνέρος εὐνῇ 18.85; ἐ. τινὰ εἰς τὸ βάραθρον Ar.*Ra.*574, *Nu.* 1450; εἰς τὸ δεσμωτήριον D.53.14; ἐ. τινὰ εἰς συμφορὰς Antipho 3.4.10; εἰς ἀτυχίας Aeschin.3.79; εἰς αἰσχύνην καὶ ἀδικίαν Din.3.7; εἰς ὑποψίαν Plu.*Them.*23; ἐς γραφάς Ar.*Ach.*679, cf. Hdt.4.72, etc.; εἰς ἀπορίαν Pl.*Phlb.*20a; εἰς ἔχθραν D.18.70. 2. of things, ἵπποις χαλινοὺς ἐ. Thgn.551, X.*Eq.*6.7 (Pass.), 9.9, cf. Il.19.394; πώλοις ἡνίας E.*IT*1424; ἐ. ψῆφους εἰς τὸν καδίσκον D.57.13, cf. X.*Cyr.*2.2.21; ἐ. μοχλόν (sc. εἰς τὴν θύραν) Id.*An.*7.1.12; ἐ. σῖτον (sc. εἰς τὴν φάτνην) Id.*Cyr.*8.1.38; τοῖς ὑποζυγίοις ἐ. *throw* food *to*.., Thphr.*Char.*4.8; simply, *lay* or *put in*, [ἱμάντα] οἱ ἔμβαλε χερσίν *put* it *into* his hands, Il.14.218; ἐνέβαλον τῶν χρημάτων [εἰς τὸ κανοῦν] Arist.*Pol.*1304ᵃ3, cf. Ael.*VH*11.5; *hand in, submit* a petition, *PPetr.*3 p.39 (iii B.C.), etc.; ἐ. τὴν χεῖρά τινι *slide* one's hand *into* another's, Ar.*V.*554; ἔμβαλλε χεῖρα δεξιάν as a pledge of good faith, S.*Tr.*1181, cf. Ar.*Ra.*754; ἔμβαλλε χειρὸς πίστιν, to which Neoptolemus answers—ἐμβάλλω μενεῖν *I give my pledge* to remain, S.*Ph.*813 (troch.). **3.** freq. of the mind, ἐνὶ φρεσὶν ἐ. Od.19.10 (cf. infr. III. 2); εἰς νοῦν τινί Plu. *Tim.*3; ἐ. ἵμερον, μένος τινί, Il.3.139, 16.529; ἐ. νεῖκός τισι *to throw in* strife between them, 4.444; τισὶ λύσσαν ἐρισμοῦ Timo 28.3; ἐ. λόγον Pl.*R.*344d; βουλὴν ἐ. περί τινος X.*Cyr.*2.2.18 (and abs., ἐ. τινὶ περί τινος *to give* one *advice* on a thing, ib.5.5.43 (nisi addendum ⟨βουλήν⟩)); ἐ. πρᾶγμα εἰς γέλωτα καὶ λοιδορίαν D.10.75. **4.** *throw upon* or *against*, νηῒ κεραυνόν Od.12.415; δαλὸν νήεσσι Il.13.320; πέτρον στέρνῳ Pi.*N.*10.68; [Ἀχαιοὺς] πέτραις E.*Hel.*1129 (lyr.); πῆχυν στέρνοις Id.*Or.*1466 (lyr.); λίθον τινὶ εἰς κεφαλήν Antipho 5.26; πληγάς τινι X.*An.*1.5.11, cf. Plu.*Caes.*66; so ἐμβαλέτω ἰσχυρότατα (sc. πληγάς) *let him lay on..*, X.*Eq.*8.4; ἐ. ἕλκεα *to inflict* them, Pi.*Fr.*111; ἐ. πῦρ *set* fire *to..*, Th.7.53; ἐ. ῥήγεα *lay on* blankets, Od.4.298: metaph., ἐ. φόβον τινί *strike* fear into him, Hdt.7.10.ε΄; ἄταν A.*Th.*316 (lyr.); φροντίδας v.l. in Antipho 2.2.2; *impose*, ἔργα εἰς τὴν γῆν *PTeb.*37.7 (Pass., i B.C.); of a fine, *BCH*8.307 (Delos). **5.** ἐ. ὦμον *put* one's shoulder *to* the work, in archery, Hp.*Fract.*2. **6.** *put into* its place, *to set* a broken or dislocated limb, ib.24 (Pass.), *Art.*1, al., Arist.*PA*685ᵇ6. **7.** Medic., *put in*, ἀμυχάς, διαίρεσιν, Philum.*Ven.*7.4, Antyll.ap.Orib.45.24.4. **8.** *graft* a tree, D.53.15 (Pass.); but simply, *plant*, τὰ φυτά *IG*12(7).62.29. **9.** ἐ. τινί (sc. φάρμακον) *to throw at* another, Il.12.383. **10.** *insert* a word or a letter, Pl.*Prt.*343d, *Cra.*414c, al.; εἰς κωμῳδίαν στίχον Plu.2.334f. **11.** ἐ. οἰκίαν τινί *bring* it *down upon* him, Ar.*Ach.*511, cf. *Nu.*1489. **12.** τάφρον ἐ. *make* a trench, Plu.*Pyrrh.*27, *Mar.*15. **13.** *pay, contribute*, ἀργύριον *IG*7.235.13 (Oropus); τροφάν *GDI*1884.12 (Delph.). **14.** *denounce* an offender, ἐς τὰν βωλάν *SIG*527.103 (Dreros, iii B.C.). **15.** *intercalate* a month, *IG*1².76.53. **II.** intr. (sc. στρατόν), *make an inroad* or *invasion*, v.l. for ἐσβ. in Hdt.4.125, 5.15, 9.13, cf. X.*Ages.*1.29; in full, ἐ. στράτευμα A.*Th.*583, 1024: metaph., *attack*, Pl.*Tht.*165d. **b.** generally, *burst, rush in*, ἐμβάλλειν εἰς τὴν ἀγοράν Aeschin.2.164, Lycurg.5, etc.; *embark* upon, ἐμβάλωμεν εἰς ἄλλον λόγον E.*El.*962: c. dat., εἰκασίαις Hierocl.p.37 A.; βίβλοις μακραῖς καὶ δυσελίκτοις Jul.*Or.*7.227b. **2.** *strike* a ship *with the ram* (ἔμβολος I. 3), *charge* or *ram* it, νηΐ Hdt.8.84, al., cf. 7.10.β΄; ἐ. ταῖς λοιπαῖς (sc. ναυσί) Th.4.14; ξυνετύγχανε.. διὰ τὴν στενοχωρίαν τὰ μὲν ἄλλοις ἐμβεβληκέναι τὰ δὲ αὐτοὺς ἐμβεβλῆσθαι on one side *had charged* others, on the other *had been charged* themselves, Id.7.70. **b.** of water, ἐ. τοῖς ὄρεσι *to dash against* them, Hdt.2.28: abs., τὸ ὕδωρ ἐμβαλὸν τὰ χωρία ἐλυμήνατο D.55.11. **3.** κώπῃς ἐ. (sc. χεῖρας) *lay oneself* to the oars, Od.10.129, cf. Pi.*P.*4.201; ἐ. alone, *pull hard*, Ar.*Eq.*602, *Ra.*206, X.*HG*5.1.13. **4.** of a river, *empty itself*, εἰς.. Pl.*Phd.*113c. **III.** Med., *throw in what is one's own*, ὅρκον εἰς τὸν ἐχῖνον D.49.65, cf. 27.51: abs., *draw lots*, *SIG*1006.3 (Cos, iii B.C.). **2.** metaph., μή μοι φύξιν ἐμβάλλεο θυμῷ Il.10.447; μῆτιν ἐ. θ. 23.313; εἰς τὸν νοῦν ἐμβάλλεσθαί τι D.18.68 (later in Act., *PTaur.*4.9); τὸ καρτερὸν ἐμβαλόμενοι X.*Cyr.*4.2.21 (cf. supr. I. 3). **3.** c. gen., ἐμβάλλεσθε τῶν λαγῴων *fall upon* the hare's flesh, Ar.*Pax* 1312. **4.** *put on board ship*, *PHib.*1.152 (iii B.C.), *POxy.*1292.3 (i A.D.), Luc.*VH*1.5, etc. **5.** *set to work upon*, τῇ γεωργίᾳ *PStrassb.*111.3 (iii B.C.). **IV.** Pass., *to be dashed against*: of ships, *charge* (v. supr. II. 2), Th.7.34, 70.

ἔμβαμμα, ατος, τό, *sauce, soup*, X.*Cyr.*1.3.4, Theopomp.Com.8, Ath.Med.ap.Orib.*inc.*23.4, Aret.*CD*1.3, etc.

ἐμβαμμάτιον [μᾰ], τό, Dim. of foreg., Anaxipp.1.35.

ἐμβαπτίζω, = sq., Nic.*Fr.*70.12:—Pass., τοῖς τέλμασιν Plu.*Sull.*21.

ἐμβάπτω, *dip in*, τί τινι Hippon.36; τὴν χεῖρα ἐν τῷ τρυβλίῳ *Ev.Matt.*26.23; εἰς ἅλμην Cratin.143; ἐς τὸν κηρόν Ar.*Nu.*150:—Med., Id.*Fr.*151, Arched.2.10, Luc.*Asin.*6.

ἔμ-βᾰρος, ον, *of weighty sense*, Men.*Phasm.Fr.*3, Id.11 D. (where perh., = ἔμβαρος II), cf. Paus.Gr.*Fr.*163; but also, = ἠλίθιος, μωρός, Hsch. **II.** *pregnant*, Gloss. **-βᾰρύθω** [ῠ], *to be heavy upon*, κράατι Nic.*Th.*324: abs., of disease, ib.468, v.l. in *Al.*541. **II.** of smell, *to be offensive*, Id.*Th.*512.

ἐμβάς, άδος, ἡ, (ἐμβαίνω) *felt-shoe* or *slipper*, used by the Boeotians, Hdt.1.195; at Athens by old men, Ar.*Eq.*870, *Nu.*858, *V.*103, 275, 447, al.; by poor persons, Is.5.11; ἐ. Σικυωνία a woman's *shoe of white felt*, Luc.*Rh.Pr.*15; ἐ. ὠμοβοεῖς *AP*6.21. **2.** = κόθορνος, Callix.2, Plu.*Demetr.*41, v.l. in Luc.*Gall.*26; χρυσαῖ ἐ. Id.*Pseudol.*19, etc. **II.** *part of the* χελώνη, Hsch.

ἐμβᾰσᾰνίζω, *test, examine*, dub. l. in Hero *Bel.*73.10.

ἐμβᾰσί-κοίτας, ου, ὁ, name of a *cup*, Ath.11.469a, Petron.24. **-κοιτος**, ον, epith. of shepherds, *sleeping on the ground* (?), Man.4.247.

ἐμβᾰσῐλεύω, *to be king in* or *among*, c. dat., πόλεσι Od.15.413; Μολοσσίᾳ Pi.*N.*7.38; ἀνδράσιν A.R.1.173; οὐρανῷ Hes.*Th.*71, etc.; τοῖς ἀνθρώποις Iamb.*Protr.*20; ὅθ' ἄρ' Ἄδρηστος πρῶτ' ἐμβασίλευεν Il.2.572: c. gen., πάντων Theoc.17.85.

Ἐμβάσιος [ᾰ], ον, *favouring embarkation*, epith. of Apollo, A.R.1.359, 404.

ἔμβᾰσις, εως, ἡ, *embarkation*, Plb.4.10.3; *place of entering*, ποταμοῦ Id.3.46.1; *entrance*, τῆς πλατείας *Ephes.*3 No.71. **2.** *step*, εὐτακτος ἔ. τοῦ ποδός interpol. in Luc.*Salt.*10. **3.** ἐμβάσεις θαλάσσης sea-*bathing*, Herod.Med.ap.Orib.10.8.11, cf. Alex.Aphr.*Pr.*1.112; *bathing-place*, ποταμὸς παραρρεῖ χωρίον ἔ. ἔχον παγκάλην καὶ εὐειδῆ Aristid.*Or.*51(27).53. **4.** ἔ. Ὀσίριδος εἰς τὴν σελήνην Plu.2.368c; of planets, = ἐπέμβασις, Vett.Val.37.5 (pl.). **5.** *entering into possession*, *SIG*364.77 (Ephesus, pl.). **II.** *that on which one goes* or *steps*, πρόδουλος ἔμβασις ποδός, i.e. *a shoe*, A.*Ag.*945. **2.** *foot, hoof*, δίχηλος E.*Ba.*740. **III.** *bathing-tub, bath*, Arist.*Fr.*236, *AP*12.207 (Strat.), Ath.1.24c; εἰς τὴν ἔ. τοῦ ἐλαίου κατάβασις Dsc.*Eup.*1.223.

ἐμβᾰσίχυτρος [ῐ], ὁ, *pot-visitor*, name of a mouse in Batr.137.

ἐμβαστάζω, *bear in* or *on, carry*, Luc.*Ocyp.*14.

ἐμβᾰτ-εία, ἡ, *entering into possession*, *AB*249, *EM*334.35. **-έον**, *one must put into a bath*, Orib.*Fr.*131. **-εύω**, *step in* or *on, frequent, haunt*: c. acc., of tutelary gods, νῆσος.. ἣν ὁ φιλόχορος Πὰν ἐμβατεύει A.*Pers.*449, cf. E.*El.*595; Πὰν Πελασγικὸν Ἄργος ἐμβατεύων Cratin.321; ἵνα Διόνυσος ἐμβατεύει S.*OC*679 (lyr.): c. dat., ὁ -εύων τῷ χωρίῳ δαίμων D.H.1.77: c. gen., in simple sense, *set foot upon*, μήτ' ἐμβατεύειν πατρίδος S.*OT*825: abs., *enter* a sacred cave, *OGI*530.15 (Iasus). **II.** ἐ. κλήρους χθονὸς *enter on, come into possession of*, E.*Heracl.*876, cf. Lxx *Jo.*19.49: more freq. ἐ. εἰς τὴν ναῦν *enter on possession of* the vessel, D.33.6; εἰς τὴν οὐσίαν Id.44.19; εἰς τὸ χωρίον Is.9.3: abs., *enter on an inheritance*, *PEleph.*2.14 (iii B.C.). **2.** metaph., νέων ψυχάς Him.*Or.*4.5. **III.** *mount, cover*, of the male, Palaeph.39. **IV.** *to be initiated* into the mysteries, *Jahresh.*15.46 (Notium), cf. *Ep.Col.*2.18. **-έω**, = foreg., Nic.*Th.*147:—Med., Lyc.642. **II.** prob. f.l. for ἐμβοτ-, *lead to pasture*, *AP*7.657 (Leon.). **-ήρ**, ῆρος, ὁ, = βατήρ, prob. in *IG*4.481.2 (Nemea), cf. Hsch. **-ήριος**, ον, *of* or *for marching*, ἐ. παιάν Plu.*Lyc.*22, cf. Ath.14.630f; κινήσεις ἐ. Phillis 3. **II.** Subst., ἐ. (sc. μέλος), τό, *marching tune*, Plb.4.20.12, Polyaen.1.10; of the anapaests of Tyrtaeus, D.Chr.2.59. **2.** ἐ. (sc. ἱερά), τά, *offerings made on embarking, before weighing anchor*, ἐ. θύειν Philostr.*VA*5.43; ᾄδειν καὶ σπένδειν Hld.5.15; also ἐ. θυσία Id.4.16. **-ης** [ᾰ], ου, ὁ, a kind of *half-boot of felt*, X.*Eq.*12.10, Duris 14 J. **2.** = κόθορνος, Luc.*JTr.*41, Lib.*Or.*64.98, etc. **II.** *modulus* or *unit of measurement* in Greek architecture, Vitr.4.3.3. **-ικός**, = ἐμβαδικός, *PLond.*2.191.19 (ii A.D.). **II.** (ἐμβατός II) *for a bath*, θόλος *POxy.*896.11 (iv A.D.). **-ός**, όν (-ή, όν Lib.*Decl.*18.35), *passable, accessible*, Plb.34.5.2 (nisi leg. ἐμβαδόν), D.S.1.57 (nisi leg. εὐβ.), D.H.1.79. **II.** ἐμβατή, ἡ, *bath*, Dsc.*Eup.*2.59, Sch.Ar.*Eq.*1057, Hsch. s.v. πύελος.

ἐμβᾰφ-ίας· λοπάδες βαθεῖαι, Hsch. **-ιον**, τό, *flat vessel for sauces, saucer*, Hippon.112; τὰ δὲ λύχνα ἐστὶ ἐμβάφια ἔμπλεα.. ἐλαίου Hdt.2.62: as a measure, = ὀξύβαφον, Hp.*Loc.Hom.*13.

ἔμβαχον· ἔμβρυον, Hsch.

ἐμβέβᾰα, ἐμβέβᾰσαν, ἐμβεβᾰώς, v. ἐμβαίνω.

ἐμβεβαιόομαι, *confirm*, τὸ νίκημα τῇ φυγῇ τῶν πολεμίων Plu.*Lyc.*22 codd.

ἐμβεβρυττόμενος· ἀναίσθητος, ἐμβρόντητος, Hsch. **ἐμβεκανεῖται**· ἐμπέπλεκται, Id.

ἐμβελής, ές, *within range of missiles*, διάστημα, τόπος, Plb.8.5.2, D.S.20.44.

ἔμβη, ἔμβητον, ἐμβήῃ, v. ἐμβαίνω.

ἐμβῐβ-άζω, Att. fut. -βιβῶ, causal of ἐμβαίνω, *set in* or *on*, τινὰ ὡς εἰς ὄχημα Pl.*Ti.*41e; ἐ. εἰς ἴχνος Id.*Tht.*193c:—Pass., *to be put into, take* a bath, Herod.Med.ap.Orib.10.37.16. **2.** *put on board ship, cause to embark*, ἄνδρας ἐς κελήτιον (v.l. for ἐσ-) Th.1.53; εἰς πλοῖα X.*An.*5.3.1; ἐ. ναυσίν Plu.*Ant.*7, cf. Charito 8.3: abs., *put on board*, X.*An.*5.7.8, etc.:—Med., ἐμβιβασάμενος αὐτοὺς εἰς τὰς ναῦς Id.*HG*5.1.19. **3.** *lead, guide* to a thing, εἰς τὸ λῷστον E.*HF*856; εἰς τὴν δικαιοσύνην τοὺς οἰκέτας X.*Oec.*14.4; εἰς λόγους D.19.97; εἰς ἀπέχθειαν Plb.16.38.1; εἰς μέτρα ἐ. χρησμούς Philostr.*VA*6.11; τὴν ᾀδουσαν εἰς τὸ μέλος Id.*Im.*2.1; τοῖς ἀνθρωπίνοις πάθεσιν τὸν θεὸν ἐ. Plu.2.416f. **4.** *set* a dislocated joint, Hp.*Art.*7. **5.** ἐ. τινὰ εἰς... *put in possession of..*, *PFlor.*55.31 (i A.D.), etc. **6.** intr., οἱ τῆς σταδιαίας πάλης ἐμβιβάζοντες Philostr.*VS*1.22.4. **-άσκω**, = foreg., πρόβατα εἰς τὸ τέμενος *IG*12(7).62.36 (Amorgos). **-ασμός**, ὁ, *introduction*, Gloss. **-αστέον**, *one must cause to enter* (a bath), Herod.Med.ap.Orib.10.38.3. **II.** *one must set to hatch eggs*, τὰς ὄρνις *Gp.*14.7.18. **-αστής**, οῦ, ὁ, *introducer*, Gloss.

ἔμβῐ-ος, ον, *having life*, [Ζηνὸς] ἐργαζομένου ἔμβια τὰ ὑπὸ τῷ αἰθέρι Philostr.*Her.*2.19; *tenacious of life, established*, of trees which will bear transplanting, Thphr.*CP*5.6.5; of cuttings, ib.3.5.3 (Comp.); but εἰ σπέρμα ἔ. γένοιτο if the seed should *germinate*, ib.5.4.5, cf. Antipho Soph.15; τὸ ἔ. their *living and growing*, of trees, Ael.*VH*13.1. **2.** ἡ ἔ. ὑγρότης the moisture *necessary to life*, Thphr.*CP*1.1.3; αἷμα ἔ. τῇ γῇ πινόμενον Philostr.*Im.*1.24. **II.** *lasting one's whole life*, ἔ. τιμωρία D.C.78.12. **III.** ἔ. γενέσθαι *recover consciousness* after a swoon, Longus 2.30. **-οτεύω**, of epilepsy, *flourish in* certain conditions, Aret.*CD*1.4. **-όω**, fut. -ώσομαι Philostr.*Her.*2.3:—*live in*, ἐν νήσῳ D.S.5.19; ταῖς Ἀθήναις Lib.*Or.*18.31; ἐ. πέντε.. ἡγεμονίαις Plu.*Galb.*29, etc.; ἐ. πολιτικαῖς πράξεσιν Id.2.789a. **II.** of plants, *become established*, Thphr.*HP*3.6.4; simply, *take root*, ib.6.7.3; τῇ γῇ Philostr. l.c. **-ωσις**, εως, ἡ, *maintenance of life*, Lxx *Si.*38.14. **2.** *way of living*, ib.3*Ma.*3.23. **II.** *taking root*, Plu.2.640d. **-ωτήριον**, τό, *place to live in, dwelling*, D.S.5.19.

ἐμβλᾰκεύομαι, gloss on ἐνδιαθρύπτομαι, Sch.Theoc.3.36.

ἐμβλαστ-άνω, *grow on* a plant, as mistletoe, Thphr.*CP*5.15.4. **-ημα**, ατος, τό, = ἐλάτη III, Aët.1.412. **-ησις**, εως, ἡ, *growing on* a plant, Thphr.*CP*5.4.5 (pl.).

ἔμ-βλεμμα, ατος, τό, *looking straight at*, X.*Cyn.*4.4. **-βλέπω**, pf. ἐμβέβλοφα *PLond.*1.42.21 (ii B.C.):—*look in the face, look at*, τινὶ τοῖς ὀφθαλμοῖς Pl.*Chrm.*155c, cf. D.19.69; ἐ. εἰς τὸν ὀφθαλμόν Pl.*Alc.*

1.132e, etc.: c. acc., ἐμβλέπω σε, παῖ, *Com.Adesp.*17.7 D., cf. Herod. 2.68, *AP*11.3, *Ev.Marc.*8.25: abs., X.*Mem.*3.11.10, Arist.*EN*1175ᵃ 9. b. ἐ. εἰς *consider*, τὰ πετεινὰ τοῦ οὐρανοῦ *Ev.Matt.*6.26; *look into* a matter, *PTeb.*28.15 (ii B.C.). 2. simply, *look*, ποῖ ἐμβλέψασα ..; S.*El.*995; δεινὸν ἐ. Pl.*Ion* 535e, Plu.*Pyrrh.*34, etc.; πῦρ ἐ. Philostr.*Im.*1.28; ἱρὰ ἐς λῷον -οντα Herod.4.80. **-βλεψις**, εως, ἡ, *looking at*, Hp.*Epid.*7.7.

ἐμ-βλήθρα, ἡ, *place of lading*, *PPetr.*3 p.317. **-βλημα**, ατος, τό, *insertion*, τὸ εἰς τὸν σίδηρον ἔ. τοῦ ξύλου *the shaft fitting into* the spear-head, Plu.*Mar.*25. 2. *chased* or *embossed* ornament used in decoration of plate, τὰ ἀργυρᾶ τὰ χρυσοῦν τι ἔ. ἔχοντα D.C.57.15, cf. Cic.*Verr.*4.17.37, etc. 3. *graft*, Poll.1.241. 4. Lat. *emblema, mosaic*, Lucil.85 Marx, Varro *RR*3.2.4. 5. *inner sole put into the shoe in winter*, etc., Ph.*Bel.*102.39. 6. *sluice-gate*, *PThead.* 24.8 (iv A.D.). 7. *payment*, *PCair.Zen.*22.22 (iii B.C.), *BGU*1040.24 (ii A.D.); *fine*, *BCH*8.307 (Delos). **-βλησις**, εως, ἡ, (ἐμβάλλω II) *impaction*, Hp.*Loc.Hom.*47. II. *reduction* of dislocations, Paul. Aeg.6.114. **-βλητέον**, *one must put in*, Pl.*Phlb.*62b, Antyll.ap. Orib.46.27.8. II. ἐμβλητέος, α, ον, *to be put in, set*, Hp.*Mochl.*38.

ἐμβο-άω, *call upon, shout to*, τινί X.*Cyn.*6.17; ἑαυτοῖς D.H.11.38, etc.: abs., *shout aloud*, Th.2.92, 4.34; μέγα ἐμβοῶν Diog.Oen. 25. **-ησις**, εως, ἡ, *shouting*, Aret.*CA*1.2, Ruf.ap.Orib.*inc.*20.27, Antyll.ap.eund.6.6.5.

ἐμβοθρ-εύω, *make holes in* mud, Philostr.*VA*2.15. **-όομαι**, *to be embedded in* a cavity, Hp.*Cord.*5. **-ος**, ον, *like a pit* or *hole, sunken*, Thphr.*HP*9.3.1.

ἐμβολ-άδην, (ἐμβάλλω) *fitting in*, ἐ. ἐστραμμέναι ἀλλήλῃσι prob. in *h.Merc.*411 (ἀμβ- cod. Leid.). **-άδιον**, τό, Dim. of sq., *grafted tree*, prob. in *JHS*18.308 (Mopsuestia: lapis -άδιν). **-άς**, άδος, ἡ, fem. Adj. *grafted*, ἄπιοι v.l. in Arist.*Fr.*274: Subst., μορεῶν ἐμβολάδες Plu.2.640b. **-εύς**, έως, ὁ, *anything put in*: *piston*, Hero *Spir.*1.28, cf. Hsch. s.v. κίουρος; *peg*, Anthem.pp.151,152 W.; *dibble* or *stick for setting plants*, *AP*6.21.6. II. *model* (usu. wooden) for metal fittings or stone-work, Ph.*Bel.*70.13, Hero *Bel.*96.5. **-εύω**, *load a ship*, *POxy.*522.8 (ii A.D.), *BGU*14 iii 20. **-ή**, ἡ, *putting in*, Thphr.*Od.*26 (pl.): esp. *putting into* its place, *setting* or *reduction* of a fracture or a dislocated limb, ἐμβολὴν ποιεῖσθαι Hp.*Fract.*13; *mode of setting*, Id.*Art.*2. 2. *insertion* of a letter, ἐ. ποιεῖσθαι Pl.*Cra.* 437a. 3. *lading* of a cargo, *PStrassb.*111.16 (iii B.C.), *POxy.*62. 11 (iii A.D.): esp. *shipment* of corn to Rome and Constantinople, *BGU*15 ii 3 (ii A.D.), etc.; αἰτία ἐ. Just.*Edict.*13.4.1. II. *inroad into an enemy's country, foray*, X.*An.*[4.1.4], *HG*4.3.10; ἡ Θηβαίων ἐ. Arist.*Pol.*1269ᵇ37. 2. *charge*, of a bull, E.*HF*869; of an army, X. *Cyr.*7.1.18, Arr.*Tact.*12.10. b. esp. *ramming of one ship by another*, A.*Pers.*279 (lyr.), 336; ἀντιπρῴροις χρῆσθαι ταῖς ἐ. Th.7.36, etc. (opp. προσβολή, *collision*, ib.70); ἐμβολὰς ἔχειν to receive *such charges*, X.*HG*4.3.12; δοῦναι to make *them*, Plb.1.51.6, etc.; in A.*Pers.*415 ἐμβολαῖς χαλκοστόμοις with *shocks* of brazen beaks (nisi leg. ἐμβόλοις). c. *shock* of battering-ram, Onos.42.5 (pl.). 3. *stroke* or *discharge* of a missile, E.*Andr.*1130, Plb.8.7.3, Luc.*Nigr.*36, etc. 4. *entrance, pass*, X.*HG*5.4.48; in Hdt.1.191 ἡ ἐμβολὴ τοῦ ποταμοῦ is explained by the words τῇ ἐς τὴν πόλιν ἐσβάλλει; also, *mouth* of a river, Thphr.*HP*4.11.8. 5. pl., *gusts* of wind, πνευμάτων σφοδρῶν ἐ. Ascl.*Tact.*12.10. III. *battering-ram*, τὸ προέχον τῆς ἐ. Th. 2.76.

ἐμβολίδες· αἱ περιθεταί (sc. κόμαι), Hsch.

ἐμβολ-ῐμαῖος, α, ον, = sq., Aus.*Ecl.*16. **-ῐμος**, ον, *intercalated*, μὴν ἐ. *intercalary* month, Hdt.1.32 (without μήν, 2.4); ἐ. μῆνα ἄγειν *CIG*2693e (Mylasa); ἡμέρα *Inscr.Prien.*105.76, D.C.48.33. 2. τὰ ἐ. *choral interludes*, Arist.*Po.*1456ᵃ29. 3. ἐ. ἔπη *interpolated* lines, Hsch.; ἐ. παῖδες *supposititious* (nisi leg. ἐκβ-), Eup.103; ἐ. βασιλεύς *fictitious*, J.*Ap.*1.26. **-ίνη**, ἡ, = ἐπικακτίς, Plin.*HN*13.114. **-ιον**, τό, *missile discharged, javelin*, D.S.1.35. II. *interlude, episode*, Cic.*QF*3.1.7. III. *small net* used to fill a gap, Poll.5.35, 10. 141. IV. = ἔμβλημα 2, *IPE*1².105 (Olbia), *IG*11(2).128.44 (iii/ii B.C.); ποτήριον ἐ. ἔχον Πανίσκον *SIG*²588.126 (Delos, ii B.C.). V. *insertion*, ἐ. ξύλινον Ph.*Bel.*74.19. VI. *shoot* for lading corn, *PLond.*3.1164h 10 (iii A.D.). **-ισμα**, ατος, τό, *patch*, Aq., Thd. *Ez.*16.16. **-ῖται**, οἱ, *members of guild* meeting in an ἔμβολον 8, *Ephes.*3 No.59.

ἐμβολο-δέτης, ου, ὁ, = ὁ τοῦ παραξονίου δεσμός, Poll.1.146. **-ειδής**, ές, *wedge-shaped*, σχῆμα Ascl.*Tact.*7.2; τάξις ib.3, Arr.*Tact.*16.6.

ἔμβολος, ὁ, or **ἔμβολον**, τό, *anything pointed so as to be easily thrust in, a peg, stopper*, *CIG*2855.27, Poll.1.145; *linch-pin* (masc.), Pherecyd.37(a) J.: Com. for πέος, Ar.*Fr.*317 (masc.). 2. τῆς χώρης ἔμβολον *tongue* of land, Hdt.4.53; Ἀσίας ἔμβολον prob. the *headland* of Κυνὸς σῆμα in Caria, Pi.*O.*7.19 (ἔμβολος Ἀσίας ἡ Λυκία Sch. ad loc.). 3. *brazen beak, ram*, masc. in Hdt.1.166, *Tab.Heracl.*1. 166,182; neut. in *AP*6.236 (Phil.), Paus.6.20.10; gender doubtful in Pi.*P.*4.191, Th.7.36. b. οἱ ἔ., = Lat. *rostra, tribune* of the Roman forum, Plb.6.53.1, Plu.*Cat.Mi.*44. 4. *wedge-shaped order of battle*, neut. in X.*HG*7.5.22, Plb.1.26.16; of a march-formation, Ael.*Tact.*37.6, Arr.*Tact.*29.5; τὸ τρίγωνον σχῆμα ἔμβολόν τε καὶ σφηνοειδὲς ὀνομάζεται Ascl.*Tact.*7.6; ἡ ὅλη [τάξις] λέγεται ἔμβολος ib.11. 5. b. ἔμβολον, τό, *half a* ῥόμβος (q.v.) *of cavalry*, ib.7.3, Ael.*Tact.* 19.5. 5. *bolt, bar*, E.*Ph.*114 (neut., anap.). 6. λάϊνα κίοσιν ἔμβολα prob. = τὰ κίοσιν ἐμβεβλημένα, *architrave*, Id.*Ba.*591 (lyr.). 7. *graft*, *Gp.*10.77.4. 8. *portico*, *IG*11(2).161 D 118 (Delos, iii B.C.), *Ephes.*3 No.8, *CIG*4662b (Gerasa), interpol. in Hld.2.26; ἔ. τῆς κρατίστης βουλῆς *BCH*11.474 (Lydia). 9. ἔμβολος· εἶδος θηρίου ἐν λαχάνοις, Hsch.

ἐμβομβέω, *buzz in*, θεάτροις Him.*Or.*7.13.

ἐμβόσκομαι, *feed on* or *in*, Ph.2.289: metaph., τόποις ib.351.

ἐμβοτέω, v. ἐμβατέω.

ἐμβουκολέω, dub. sens. (perh. *deceive*) in *Com.Adesp.*25.35 D.

ἐμβράγχια, τά, = βράγχια, θύννου *Gp.*20.46.6.

ἐμβρᾰδύνω, *remain long in* or *on*, τῷ στόματι τῆς γαστρός Phlp.*in APo.*378.14: abs., Menemach.ap.Orib.10.14.2. 2. *dwell on*, τινί Luc.*Dom.*3,23, S.E.*M.*9.1, Herm.*in Phdr.*p.158 A. II. *go slowly* in winding-up a machine, Hero *Bel.*85.3.

ἐμβραμένα, ἡ, Sicil. for εἱμαρμένη, Sophr.119; cf. ἔμβραται· εἵμαρται, Hsch.

ἐμβράσσω, *cast up*, of the sea, in Pass., Aq., Sm., Thd.*Is.*57.20.

ἔμβρᾰχυ, Adv. *in brief, in fine*, in Att. with relat. such as ὅστις, ὅπου, etc.; in sense, *at all, soever*, παρέχειν ὅ τι τις εὔξαιτ' ἔ. Cratin. 254, cf. Ar.*V.*1120, *Th.*390, Hyp.*Fr.*41, prob. in Lys.13.92, Is.9.11; ἐρώτα ἔ. ὅτι βούλει Pl.*Hp.Mi.*365d, al.; later without relat., *in a word*, D.Chr.36.31. II. *slightly, somewhat*, ὑψηλότερον ἔ. Gal.18(2).410.

ἔμ-βρεγμα, ατος, τό, *lotion*, Dsc.2.124, Aret.*CA*1.1, Archig.ap. Gal.8.150. **-βρεκτέον**, *one must soak*, Herod.Med.ap.Aët.4.47, Id. in *Rh.Mus.*58.91. **-βρεκτός**, ή, όν, *soaked*, dub. in Hsch. s.v. ἔντριτον.

ἐμβρέμομαι, Med., *roar* or *bluster in*, ἀήτης ἱστίῳ ἐμβρέμεται Il.15. 627.

ἐμβρενθυόμενος, *infrendens*, *Gloss.*

ἔμβρεος· ἐνεός, μωρός, Hsch.

ἔμβρεφος, ον, *boy-like*, *AP*14.111.

ἐμβρέχω, *treat with embrocations*, Philum.ap.Aët.5.120, Plu.2. 74d. 2. *wet*, ἱμάτια J.*BJ*3.7.13:—Med., *soak*, Nic.*Al.*237:—Pass., *to be dipped, plunged*, Sotion p.183 W.; *to be soaked*, Dsc.*Eup.*1.1: aor. 2 part. Pass. ἐμβραχείς Paul.Aeg.3.43.

ἔμβρημα, ατος, τό, *abortion* (?), dub. in *PLond.*1821.

ἐμβρίθ-εια [ῑ], ἡ, *weight, dignity*, Suid., Zonar.; prob. in *Inscr. Prien.*108.65 (ii B.C.). II. *clumsiness of parts*, opp. λεπτομέρεια, Epicur.*Nat.*14.4. III. *severity*, μετὰ ἐμβριθείας κολαστέος Jul.*Ep.* 89a. **-ής**, ές, (βρίθω) *weighty*, of ropes, Hdt.7.36; ἐ. καὶ βαρύ Pl. *Phd.*81c; -εστέραν ποιεῖ τὴν πληγήν Arist.*PA*690ᵃ19. 2. metaph., *weighty, grave, dignified*, ἦθος Pl.*Ep.*328b; φρόνημα δημαγωγίας -έστερον Plu.*Per.*4; φύσις Id.*Brut.*1; τὸ ἐ. *dignity*, D.H.*Amm.*2.2; ἐ. καὶ στερρὸς τὰ ἤθεα Hp.*Ep.*11; σεμνὸς καὶ ἐ. Jul.*Or.*2.88a; οἱ -έστεροι *the more sedate*, opp. οἱ ὀξεῖς, Pl.*Tht.*144b. 3. *weighty, cogent*, τεκμήριον Phld.*Rh.*1.46 S.; διάνοια ib.2.209 S. (Comp.). Adv. -θῶς, opp. εὐτελῶς καὶ ἐλαφρῶς, Id.*Po.*5.4. 4. in bad sense, *heavy, grievous*, Parm.8.59; κακόν A.*Pers.*693; τῆς ἀνάγκης οὐδὲν -έστερον S.*Fr.*757; *difficult*, Pl.*Cra.*407a (Comp.); *burdensome*, φυλακή *SIG*731.8 (Comp., Tomi, i B.C.); of persons, *vehement*, Hdn.3.11.1. II. Adv. -θῶς *with severity*, D.C.69.6; *violently*, Hdn.4.3.3: Comp. -έστερον φέρειν to bear *with greater constancy*, Pl.*Phdr.*252c. **-ω**, *press heavily*, *AP*7.532 (Isid.). 2. *to be heavy*, ἀνίῃς Nic.*Th.*867.

ἐμβρῑμ-άομαι (Act. only in Hsch., Suid.), c. aor. Med. et Pass., *snort in*, ἵππους ἐν ἀμπυκτῆρσιν ἐμβριμωμένας, of horses, A.*Th.*461, cf. Luc.*Nec.*20. 2. of persons, *to be deeply moved*, τῷ πνεύματι, ἐν ἑαυτῷ, *Ev.Jo.*11.33,38. II. *admonish urgently, rebuke*, E.*Fr.* 1099: c. dat. pers., Lxx *Da.*11.30, *Ev.Matt.*9.30, *Marc.*1.43. **-ημα**, ατος, τό, *indignation*, Lxx *La.*2.6. **-ησις**, εως, ἡ, = foreg., Aq., Sm.*Ps.*37(38).4, Thd.*Is.*30.27, Eustr. *in EN*119.21, Steph. *in Hp.*1. 76 D. (pl.).

ἔμβριον· θεῖον, Hsch. **ἐμβρόνιον**· μικρὸν καὶ ἀπόρφυρον ἱμάτιον Τιβερικόν (leg. Ἰβηρικόν), Id.

ἐμβροντ-αῖος, α, ον, *struck by lightning*: τὸ ἐ. *place struck by lightning*, Lat. *bidental*, D.S.8.9. **-άω**, *dumbfounder*, τίς ἐνεβρόντησέ μοι; Eup.17 D.; τὸ κακὸν ἐνεβρόντησέ με Ach.Tat.3.15. II. Pass., *to be struck by lightning*, distd. fr. κεραυνῷ πληγῆναι, X.*HG*4.7. 7. 2. metaph., ἐμβεβροντῆσθαι, = ἐμβρόντητον εἶναι, D.19.231, Men.*Georg.Fr.*5. **-ησία**, ἡ, *sheer stupidity*, Id.*Sam.*196, S.E.*M.* 9.40. 2. *madness*, Plu.2.1119b, Philostr.*VS*2.27.5. **-ητος**, ον, *thunderstruck, stupefied, stupid*, ἐ. ποιεῖν τινά v.l. in X.*An.*3.4.12; ὦμβρόντητε σύ thou *gaping fool*, Ar.*Ec.*793; ἐγένετ' ἐ. Antiph.233.4; ἠλιθίους καὶ ἐ. Pl.*Alc.*2.140c, cf. Men.*Pk.*273; ἐμβρόντητε, εἶτα νῦν λέγεις; D.18.243. II. later of ideas, *crack-brained, mad*, ἐ. καὶ πεπλανημένον σόφισμα Porph.*Chr.*35; ἐμβρόντητα δὲ πάντα Orph.*Fr.* 47.

ἐμβροχ-άς, άδος, ἡ, *layer of the vine*, *Gp.*4.3.7. **-ή**, ἡ, (ἐμβρέχω) *infusion*, Dsc.1.43; *embrocation*, Antyll.ap.Orib.9.22.1, Plu.2. 42c. II. (βρόχος) *noose, halter*, Luc.*Lex.*11. **-ημα**, ατος, τό, = foreg. 1, Herod.Med. in *Rh.Mus.*58.83.

ἐμβρόχθιος, ον, (βρόχθος) *in the throat*, λίθος Tz.*H.*No.413 tit.

ἐμβροχίζω, (βρόχος) *catch in a noose*, Apollod.2.5.4.

ἔμβροχος (sc. γῆ), ον, (βρέχω) *inundated*, *PTeb.*74.38 (ii B.C.), al., *PLond.*2.256ʳ 6 (i A.D.).

ἐμβρύειον [ῠ], τό, *flesh of embryos*, Ar.*Fr.*569.4.

ἐμβρύκω [ῡ], *bite*, v.l. in Nic.*Th.*824:—Pass., Id.*Al.*338.

ἐμβρῠο-δόχος, ον, *receiving the foetus*, Luc.*Lex.*6. **-θλάστης**, ου, ὁ, *instrument to extract a foetus*, Gal.19.104.

ἐμβρύοικος [ῠ], ον, (ἐν, βρύον, οἰκέω) *dwelling in sea-weed*, ἄγκυρα *AP*6.90 (Phil.).

ἔμβρῠον, τό, *young one*, ὑπ' ἔμβρυον ἧκεν ἑκάστῃ put *a young one* under each dam (to be suckled), Od.9.245, al., cf. Arist.*PA*676ᵃ

17. II. *embryo, foetus*, A.*Eu.*945 (lyr.), Hp.*Aph.*5.52, Arist.*GA* 746^{a}1, al. (From βρύω; expld. as τὸ ἐντὸς τῆς γαστρὸς βρύον by Eust. ad Od. l. c.)

ἔμβρῠος, ον, (βρύω) *growing in*, βρέφος ἔ., = ἔμβρυον, Ps.-Phoc. 184. II. (βρύον) *grown with sea-weed*, Nonn.*D.*41.29.

ἐμβρῠο-σφάκτης, ου, ὁ, = -θλάστης, Herophil.ap.Tertull. *de An.* 25. **-τομέω**, *cut up the foetus in the womb*, c. acc., Olymp.*in Grg.*p.257 J., Aspasia ap.Aët.16.22 :—Pass., of the foetus, *to be cut up in the womb*, Vett.Val.53.27, Procl.*Par.Ptol.*214. **-τομία**, ἡ, *cutting up of the foetus*, Gal.19.107, Philum.ap.Aët.16.23, Olymp.*in Grg.*p.258 J., *PTeb.*676, Ptol.*Tetr.*149, etc. **-τόμος**, ὁ, *instrument for cutting up the foetus*, Sor.2.63.

ἐμβρῠουλκ-έω, *extract the foetus*, Colum.7.3.16 :—Pass., Sor.2.55. **-ία**, ἡ, *extraction of the foetus*, Id.1.68 (pl.), Archig.ap.Aët.16.91, Gal.19.107. **-ός**, ὁ, (ἕλκω) *crochet, hook*, Sor.2.61, Gal.19.97.

ἔμβρωμ-α, ατος, τό, *that which is eaten away*, ἔ. ὀδόντος *cavity in* a tooth, Dsc.1.77. II. *meal, snack*, ἔ. πρωϊνόν Ath.1.11c, cf. Sor.1.40. **-ᾰτίζω**, = ψίχω, ψίω, *EM*819.6, Suid. :—aor. Pass. in med. sense, *take a meal* or *snack*, Apollon.*Lex.* s. v. δειελιήσας. **-άτιον**, τό, Dim. of ἔμβρωμα, Sor.1.40.

ἔμβρωμος, ον, = βρωμώδης, Dsc.3.33, Aët.9.30.

ἐμβῠθίζω, *cause to sink to the bottom*, Plu.2.981a (Pass.).

ἐμβύθιος [ῠ], ον (η, ον *AP*9.227 (Bianor), 423 (Id.)), *at the bottom* of the sea, πέτρα ib.7.504 (Leon.); ἄγρη ib.9.227; κρηνῖδες D.H.1.32; πίννα Isid.Char.20.

ἐμβῠκᾰνάω, *blow with the trumpet*, κέρασι D.H.2.8.

ἐμβυρσόω, *sew up in skins*, Ps.-Plu.*Fluv.*5.2 (Pass.).

ἐμβύω [ῡ], *stuff in, stop with* a thing, Ar.*V.*128; ἔμβυσον τιμὴν εἰς τὴν χεῖρά τινι Herod.2.82.

ἐμβώμιος, ον, *on the altar*, σῦκον θυσίας ἁπάσης ἐ. Jul.*Ep.*180.

ἐμέθεν, ἐμεῖο, ἐμείω, etc., v. ἐγώ. **ἐμειάς**· διαχρήματα, ἑαυτούς, Hsch. **ἐμέμηκον**, v. μηκάομαι. **ἔμεν, ἔμεναι**, Ep. for εἶναι, v. εἰμί. **ἐμέν**, = ἐμέ, v. ἐγώ. **ἔμεν, ἔμεναι**, Ep. for εἶναι, v. ἵημι. **ἐμέο**, v. ἐγώ.

ἐμέρα, coined as etym. of ἡμέρα, Pl.*Cra.*418c.

ἐμ-εσία, ἡ, (ἐμέω) *disposition to vomit*, Hp.*Morb.*2.40, 43 (pl.). **-εσις**, εως, ἡ, *vomiting, being sick*, ib.74. **-εσμα**, ατος, τό, *vomit*, Id.*Prog.*13 (pl.).

ἐμετ-ηρίζω, *give an emetic*, Hp.*Loc.Hom.*33. **-ήριος**, ον, = ἐμετικός I: ἐ. φάρμακον *an emetic*, ibid.: pl. **-τήρια**, τά, Aret.*CD*1.3. **-ιάω**, *feel sick*, Arist.*Pr.*873^{b}24. **-ικός**, ή, όν, *provoking sickness*, ib.36. Adv. **-κῶς**, σπαραττόμενος Gal.13.155. II. *inclined to vomit*, Hp.*Acut.*67; of certain animals, Arist.*HA*632^{b}11. 2. *one who uses emetics*, like the Roman gourmands, Plu. *Pomp.*51. b. ἐμετικὴν (sc. δίαιταν) *agebat*, he was taking *a course of emetics*, Cic.*Att.*13.52.1.

ἐμετο-ποιέομαι, Med., *purge by vomiting*, τὴν ἄνω κοιλίην Hp.*Int.*38. **-ποιΐα**, ἡ, *causing to vomit*, Dionys.Aeg.ap.Phot.*Bibl.* p.130 B. **-ποιός**, όν, Dsc.2.9.

ἔμετ-ος, ὁ, *vomiting*, Hp.*Aph.*1.2 (pl.); ἐμέτοισι θηρώμενοι τὴν ὑγιείην Hdt.2.77; ἔ. ποιεῖσθαι Arist.*HA*612^{a}6; *disposition to vomit, sickness*, ναυτίαι καὶ ἔμετοι ib.584^{a}7. **-ός**, ή, όν, *vomited*, Suid. **-ώδης**, ες, *accompanied by sickness*, ὑποστροφαί Hp.*Coac.*560. Adv. Ion. **-δέως** *as in vomiting*, ἑλκόμενα Id.*Prorrh.*1.117.

ἐμεῦ, ἐμεῦς, v. ἐγώ.

ἐμέω Il.15.11, impf. ἤμουν Ar.*Fr.*351, X.*An.*4.8.20, Ion. ἤμεον Hdt.7.88: fut. ἐμέσω Hp.*Morb.*2.15, Att. ἐμῶ (ἐνεξ-) Polyzel.4: fut. Med. ἐμέομαι Hp.*Nat.Hom.*5, ἐμοῦμαι A.*Eu.*730: aor. ἤμεσα Hp. *Epid.*1.26.ε', etc., (ἐξ-) Ar.*Ach.*6, inf. ἐμέσαι Hdt.1.133; Ep. ἔμεσσα (ἀπ-) Il.14.437 (prob. ἐξήμεσσα should be restored for -ήμησα in Hes. *Th.*497; ὑπερ-έμησα occurs in the Mss. of Hp.*Morb.*2.17): pf. ἐμήμεκα Luc.*Lex.*21, Ael.*NA*17.37: plpf. ἐμημέκεε Hp.*Epid.*5.42, ἐμημέκει D.L.6.7 :—**Pass.**, fut. ἐμεθήσομαι (ἐξ-) Lxx *Jb.*20.15: aor. inf. ἐμεθῆναι Gal.7.219: pf. ἐμήμεσμαι Ael.*VH*13.22 :—*vomit, throw up*, αἷμ' ἐμέων Il.15.11, cf. Hdt.7.88; ἐμοῦσα θρόμβους A.*Eu.*184; ἰόν ib.730: abs., *vomit, be sick*, Hdt.1.133, X.*An.*4.8.20; ἐμέειν ἀπὸ συρμαϊσμοῦ Hp.*Art.*40; ἐ. πτίλῳ *to make oneself sick* with a feather, Ar. *Ach.*587. 2. metaph., *throw up a flood of words*, Eun.*VS* p.488 B. (ϝεμε-, cf. Skt. *vámiti* 'vomit', Lat. *vomo, vomitus*, Lith. *vémti*, etc.)

ἐμεωυτοῦ, Ion. for ἐμαυτοῦ. **ἔμηνα**, v. μαίνομαι II.

ἐμίας, ου, ὁ, *one who is inclined to vomit*, Eup.412.

ἐμίν, ἐμίνγα, ἐμίνη, v. ἐγώ.

ἔμμα, ατος, τό, Aeol. for εἷμα, Alc.*Supp.*4.21, Sapph.*Supp.*20a.8, *Lyr.Alex.Adesp.*9.

ἐμμᾰγεῖον, τό, *mould, matrix* (nisi leg. ἐκμ-), Procl. *in Cra.*p.104 P.

ἐμμαίνομαι, *to be mad at*, τινί *Act.Ap.*26.11, J.*AJ*17.6.5.

ἐμμᾰκεδονίζω, *play the Macedonian*, *Com.Adesp.*324.

ἐμμαλάξαι· ἐμμεῖναι, τῇ χειρὶ ἐπιλαβέσθαι, Hsch.

ἔμμαλλος, ον, *woolly, fleecy*, Luc.*Cyn.*5.

ἐμμᾰνής, ές, *frantic, raving*, Hdt.3.25, S.*Ichn.*15, etc.; ἐμμανεῖ σκιρτήματι A.*Pr.*675; ἀοίνοις ἐμμανεῖς θυμώμασιν *maddened by*.., Id. *Eu.*860; θεοῦ πνοαῖσιν ἐ. E.*Ba.*1094; ἐ. Ἥρας ὕπο Id.*Cyc.*3; ὥσπερ ἐ. ἐπεισπεσών Men.*Sam.*200; of elephants in the rutting season, Arist. *HA*571^{b}34; κῶμαι Lxx *Wi.*14.23: Comp. -έστερος Luc.*Am.*14: Sup. -έστατος, ἔρωτες Pl.*Lg.*734a, cf. Plu.*Arat.*17. Adv. -νῶς D.C.65.16; ἐρᾶν Eun.*VS* p.455 B.: Sup. -έστατα, ἐρῶν Men.336.

ἔμμᾰνις, v. ἔμμηνις.

ἐμμᾰπέως, Adv., (μαπέειν) *quickly, hastily*, ἐ. ἀπόρουσε Il.5.836; ὑπάκουσε Od.14.485, *h.Ven.*180; ὑπέδεκτο Hes.*Sc.*442.

ἐμμάρτῠρος, ον, *on testimony*, Them.*Or.*11.144b. Adv. -ρως Eust. 64.33.

ἐμμάσαι· ἐνερεῖσαι, Hsch.

ἐμμάσσομαι, Att. **-ττομαι**, aor. 1 ἐνεμαξάμην (v. infr.), *knead bread in*, ἐν θυείᾳ στρογγύλῃ 'νεμάττετο Ar.*Nu.*676 (cj. Dobr. for γ' ἀνεμάττετο). II. *press upon, inflict*, αὐχένι κέντρον Nic.*Th.*767; κῆρά τινι Opp.*H.*2.502; ὀργήν τινι Call.*Dian.*124; ἰδμοσύνην στέρνοις ἐνεμάξατο *APl.*4.273 (Crin.) :—late in Act., *smear*, ζωγραφίαν μέλανι *PMag.Lond.*121.230.

ἐμμᾰταιάζω, *talk idly*, Hsch. (leg. -ματάζω).

ἐμμᾰτέω, *put the finger down the throat to cause sickness*, Nic.*Al.* 138 (perh. f. l. for ἐμμαπέως, but cf. ἐμματέων· ψηλαφῶν, Hsch.). 2. *implant* a sting, of a bee, Nic.*Th.*809. 3. ἐμματούμενος, = μασώμενος, v.l. for ἐνδατούμενος in Sch.S.*Tr.*791.

ἐμμάχομαι [ᾰ], *fight a battle in*, πεδίον ἐπιτήδειον ἐ. Hdt.9.7.β', cf. D.C.50.12.

ἐμμέθοδος, ον, *according to rule* or *system*, S.E.*P.*2.21; τὸ ἐ. *systematic arrangement*, Ph.2.512. Adv. -δως *systematically*, Cleom.2.1, Hero *Deff.*138.5, A.D.*Synt.*155.21, S.E.*M.*1.188, etc.: Comp. -ώτερον Procl.*Hyp.*6.2.

ἐμμεθύσκομαι, Pass., *to be drunk in*, τοῖς ἁγίοις J.*BJ*4.4.3.

ἐμμείγνῡμι, *mingle*, ἄκρατον πρὸς τὸ κώνειον Plu.2.61b: metaph., τῇ σαρκὶ τὴν ψυχὴν ὁ θεὸς οἷον ἅλας ἐνέμιξεν Porph.*Abst.*3.20; ἐ. ἑαυτόν, ἑαυτούς τινι, *meddle* with.., Plu.2.805e, Just.*Nov.*124.4; εἴς τινα ib.117.15.1 :—more freq. in Pass., *to be mixed* or *mingled in*, ἐν δὲ γαίᾳ ζόα.. μέμεικται A.*Th.*937, cf. Plu.*Per.*4 (dub.); μικροῦ ἐμμειγνυμένου Arist.*GC*315^{b}13, cf. *Mete.*357^{a}16. II. of persons, *encounter*, ἔν τ' Ὠκεανοῦ πελάγεσσι μίγεν πόντῳ τ' ἐρυθρῷ Λαμνιᾶν τ' ἔθνει γυναικῶν Pi. *P.*4.251. 2. intr. in Act., ἔνθ' οἶμαι Θησέα καὶ τὰς.. ἀδελφὰς.. τάχ' ἐμμείξειν (sc. ἀλλήλοις) S.*OC*1057 (lyr.).

ἐμμειδιάω, *smile in*, ὀφθαλμοῖς καὶ παρειαῖς Philostr.*Ep.*51; *to be glad at*, πρὸς τὰ ἴχνη, of hounds, X.*Cyn.*4.3.

ἐμμέλεια, ἡ, (ἐμμελής) *harmony in music* or *the fit modulation of spoken words*, D.H.*Dem.*50: generally, *harmony, gracefulness*, ἀνασῴζειν τὴν ἐ. Plu.2.747b; ἐ. ἀγριοφανῆ καὶ αὐστηράν, of Pan, Corn. *ND*27; οὐ παρέργως, ἀλλὰ μετά τινος ἐ. Jul.*Or.*7.217a. II. *a tragic dance*, opp. πυρρίχη, Pl.*Lg.*816b; opp. σίκιννις and κόρδαξ, Ath.1.20e, 14.631d, Luc.*Salt.*26; *the tune of this dance*, Hdt.6.129. II. Com., ἐ. κονδύλου knuckle-*dance*, Ar.*V.*1503.

ἐμμελετ-άω, *exercise* or *train in* a thing, τινὰ ἀγῶσι Plu.*Cim.*18, etc.; ἐμαυτόν σοι ἐμμελετᾶν παρέχειν *to practise upon*, Pl.*Phdr.*228e; *give a lecture*, τισί Plu.2.932d. **-ημα**, ατος, τό, *that on which an art is practised*, χρυσὸν καὶ ἄργυρον, τέχνης ἐ. Lxx *Wi.*13.10; *instrument for practice*, τῆς πάρος ἁρμονίης *AP*6.83 (Maced.). **-ητέον**, *one must practise oneself in*, τινί Plu.2.531f.

ἐμμελής, ές, (μέλος) *in tune, harmonious*, opp. πλημμελής, ἐ. φωνή Ti.Locr.101b, Plu.2.1014c, etc.; προσόδιον *SIG*662.9 (Delos, ii B.C.); ἁρμονιῶν -εστάτη κρᾶσις Plu.*Phoc.*2; λέξις ἐ. D.H.*Comp.*25; also of a poet, *tuneful*, Theoc.*Ep.*21, cf. Philostr.*Im.*2.12. II. metaph., 1. of persons, *harmonious, orderly*, τὸν πλημμελοῦντα ἐμμελῆ ποιεῖν Pl. *Criti.*106b; ἵνα γένοιντο -έστεροι ib.121b; also -εστάτη καὶ κοσμιωτάτη πολιτεία Plu.*Pel.*19. b. *suitable, fit, proper*, κριτής Pl.*Lg.*876d; πρός τι Plu.*Demetr.*2 (Sup.). c. *witty*, ἐ. καὶ χαρίεσσα θεραπαινίς Pl.*Tht.*174a. 2. of things, *in good taste*, ἐμμελέστερόν [ἐστι], c. inf., Ar.*Ec.*807; ἐ. ὁμιλία Arist.*EN*1128^{a}1. 3. *well-proportioned*, κτήματα.. ποῖα ἄν τις κεκτημένος ἐμμελεστάτην οὐσίαν κεκτῇτο; Pl.*Lg.* 776b; *reasonable*, οὐκ ἐ. Id.*Sph.*259e: hence, *modest, small*, opp. μέγιστος, Id.*Lg.*760a (Sup.); πόλις μεγέθει ἐμμελεστέρα Arist.*Pol.* 1327^{b}15. b. *suitable*, λόγος ἐ. ἐπὶ τὴν χρείαν Plu.*Luc.*1. III. Adv. -λῶς, Aeol. and Ion. -λέως, *harmoniously*, opp. πλημμελῶς, Pl. *Lg.*816a; *in time*, πόδεσσιν ὠρχεῦντ' Sapph.54. 2. *elegantly*, ἐ. καὶ μουσικῶς Arist.*Cael.*290^{b}30; *in good taste*, παίζειν Id.*EN*1128^{a}9; δαπανῆσαι μεγάλα ἐ. ib.1122^{a}35. 3. *suitably, rightly*, οὐδέ μοι ἐμμελέως τὸ Πιττάκειον νέμεται Simon.5.8; ἐ. πάντων ἔχειν to be *suitably* provided with.., Pl.*Prt.*321c; ἐ. φέρειν τὰς τύχας Arist.*EN*1100^{b}21; ἐ. εἰρῆσθαι ib.1170^{b}21, etc.: Comp. -εστέρως, ἔχειν Pl.*Phdr.*278d; -έστερον Id.*R.*474a: Sup. -έστατα ib.581b. 4. *at a reasonable price*, διδάσκειν Id.*Ap.*20c.

ἐμμεμᾰώς, υῖα, ός, *in eager haste, eager*, of persons, Il.5.142, al., Plu.2.619e, etc.; of things, ἠχή (or πέτρη) Hes.*Sc.*439: later c. dat., ἐμμεμαὼς Βέβρυξι A.R.2.121. (Cf. *μάω, μέμονα.)

ἐμμέμονα, *to be lost in passion*, ἐμμέμονε φρήν S.*Tr.*982 (lyr.).

ἐμμεμφής, ές, Arc. ἰνμενφής, *liable to censure*, *IG*5(2).262 (Mantinea, v B.C.).

ἔμμεν, ἔμμεναι, Ep. for εἶναι, v. εἰμί.

ἐμμεν-ετέον, *one must abide by* or *endure*, D.L.7.93. II. ἐμμενετέος, α, ον, *to be endured*, Cleanth.*Stoic.*1.128; *to be maintained, held fast*, ὠφελήματα *Stoic.*3.22, cf. Chrysipp.ib.72. **-ετικός** or **-ητικός**, ή, όν, *disposed to abide by*, τῷ λογισμῷ, τῇ δόξῃ, Arist.*EN*1145^{b}11, 1151^{b}5; τοῖς ὀρθῶς κριθεῖσι *Stoic.*ap.Stob.2.7.5^{b2}: c. gen., ἕξις -ητικὴ νόμου Pl.*Def.*412b. Adv. -ητικῶς Chrysipp.*Stoic.*3.73. **-ετός**, ή, όν, *maintainable*, ἀγαθά *Stoic.*3.22. **-ής**, ές, *abiding in*: τὸ ἐ. *steadfastness*, Timo 58.1 (s. v. l.).—Hom. has only neut. ἐμμενές as Adv., always in phrase, ἐ. αἰεί *unceasing* ever, Il.10.361, Od.9.386, etc. (without αἰεί in later Ep., as Arat.83; ἐ. ἤματα πάντα Id.339): also Adv. -νέως, ἐμάχοντο Hes.*Th.*712.

ἐμμενύτρωτος· μέτριος, Hsch.

ἐμμένω, fut. -μενῶ S.*OC*648, etc.: pf. ἐμμεμένηκα Th.1.5 :—*abide in* a place, πολὺν χρόνον μελάθροις ἐμμένειν E.*Fr.*362.12; ἐν τῇ κεφαλῇ

Ar.*Ec.*1120; ἐν τῇ Ἀττικῇ Th.2.23, cf. X.*An.*4.7.17, Epist.Phil.ap. D.12.22: abs., Th.8.31. 2. *abide by, stand by, cleave to, be true to,* c. dat., τοῖς ὁρκίοις Hdt.9.106; πιστώμασι A.*Ch.*977, etc.; τῷ κηρύγματι S.*OT*351; ὀρθῷ νόμῳ Id.*Aj.*350; ἐ. ταῖς συνθήκαις καὶ ταῖς σπονδαῖς Th.5.18, cf. Isoc.7.81; τοῖς νόμοις X.*Mem.*4.4.16; τῷ τιμήματι Pl.*Ap.*39b; τῇ ὁμολογίᾳ Id.*Tht.*145c, etc.; ἐ. τοῖς Καρχηδονίοις *remain constant* to them, App.*Hisp.*24; ἐ. ἐν ταῖς σπονδαῖς τὸν ἐνιαυτόν Indut.ap.Th.4.118; ἐν τῇ τάξει Pl.*Lg.*844c; ἐν τῇ φιλοσοφίᾳ Isoc.9.89: abs., *stand fast, be faithful,* E.*Ph.*1241, *PTeb.*382.22 (i B.C.). 3. of things, *remain fixed, stand fast, hold good,* εἴ σοί γ' ἅπερ φῇς ἐμμενεῖ S.*OC*648; μάλα μοι τοῦτ' ἐμμένοι *may* it *remain fixed in* my mind, A. *Pr.*534 (lyr.); εἴ σφι ἔτι ἐμμένει [ἡ φιλίη] Hdt.7.151; τέσσαρα καὶ δέκα ἔτη ἐνέμειναν αἱ σπονδαί Th.2.2; ἐ. ὁ νόμος Pl.*Lg.*839c; ἐὰν.. [ὁ λόγος] ἐμμένῃ Id.*Phdr.*258b; τὸ σιδηροφορεῖσθαι τοῖς ἠπειρώταις ἐμμεμένηκεν *continued as a custom,* Th.1.5.

ἐμμερίζομαι, *to be divided, distributed,* J.*BJ*5.7.3.

ἐμμέριμνος, ον, *in anxiety, Cat.Cod.Astr.*2.210, Sch.E.*Or.*93. Adv. -νως Eust. ad D.P.*Praef.*

ἔμμεσος, ον, *intermediate,* [ψυχὴ] δεσμὸς ἐ. τυγχάνει τῶν ἄκρων Alex. Aphr.*Pr.*2.67; *having a mean,* ἐ. ἐναντία *having an intermediate term,* Simp.*in Cael.*340.33; ἔφη Πλάτων πάντα ἐ. Olymp.*in Mete.*242.28. II. *inserted,* μεταξυλογία ib.41.23. III. *mediate,* γνῶσις Eustr.*in EN*331.2. Adv. -σως *mediately,* Them.*in APo.*31.6.

ἐμμεστόομαι, Pass., *to be filled quite full,* S.*Ant.*420 (tm.), *El.*713 (tm.), unless in both passages ἐν be adverbial, v. ἐν B. 3.

ἔμμεστος, ον, *filled full of* a thing, τινός S.*Ichn.*282, Pl.*Ep.* 338d.

ἐμμετάβολος, ον, *admitting of modulation,* σύστημα Cleonid.*Harm.* 8, 11.

ἔμμεται· ὀρχεῖται, Hsch.

ἐμμετεωρίζομαι, Pass., *to be carried aloft,* τῷ αἰθέρι Philostr.*VA*1.5.

ἐμμετρ-έω, *measure by* or *according to,* τῇ προθυμίᾳ τὰ σιτία *AP*4. 3.18 (Agath.), v.l. for συμμ- in Luc.*Gall.*27. 2. simply, *measure out, provide, PMasp.*138 iv 1 (vi A.D.). -ία, ἡ, *fit measure,* opp. ἀμετρία, Pl.*R.*486d, *Phlb.*52c. -ος, ον, *in measure, proportioned,* opp. ἄμετρος, Id.*R.*486d, *Lg.*716c, al.; τὸ ἐ. *due measure, proportion,* Id.*Phlb.*26a, cf. 52d; πολιτεῖαι ἐ. *well-balanced,* title of work by Critias, Phlp.*in de An.*89.12. Adv. -τρως, πρός τι *proportionably* to.., Pl.*Plt.*282e. 2. *fitting, suitable,* ἔπαινος Id.*Lg.*823d; θεοῖσι ἀναθήματα χρεὼν ἔμμετρα τὸν μέτριον ἄνδρα.. δωρεῖσθαι ib.955e. Adv. -τρως Id.*Cra.*395c, M.Ant.1.16: Sup. ἐμμετρώτατα Pl.*R.*474d; also -ότατα *Lg.*674c, prob. in Aristaenet.1.18. 3. of persons, ἐμμετρότατος (v.l. -ώτατος) *reasonable, moderate,* Pl.*Lg.*926a; -ότερος (v.l. -ώτερος) Id.*Ti.*90e; ἐ. οἰνοχόος Aristaenet.1.3. II. *measuring, containing,* δέπας ἐ. ὡς τριλάγυνον Stesich.7. III. *in metre, metrical,* Pl.*Smp.*197c, *Phdr.*252b, Arist.*Rh.*1408^b21; ἔμμετρα λέγειν ἢ ἄμετρα Id.*Po.*1451^b1, cf. 1450^b14; φθόγγος ἐ. Phld.*D.*3.13; ἐ. ποιηταί poets *who use regular metres,* i.e. epic and tragic, opp. οἱ τῶν ᾀδομένων, D.60.9. Adv. -τρως, χρησμῳδεῖν Plu.2.623c.

ἐμμηλάδας· αἶγας· τὰς μετὰ τῶν προβάτων νεμομένας, Hsch.

ἐμμηναῖος, α, ον, epith. of the moon, *Gloss.*

ἐμμήνιος, ον, *monthly*: τὰ ἐ. *the menses* of women, Hp.*Nat.Mul.*7; ἐ. αἷμα γυναικῶν J.*BJ*4.8.4.

ἔμμηνις, ιος, ὁ, ἡ, Cret. -ᾱνις, *wroth,* θεός *SIG*527.78 (iii B.C.), cf. *GDI*5041.18, etc.

ἔμμηνος, ον, (μήν) *lasting a month,* ἔμμηνον τὰν περίοδον ἀποδίδωτι, of the moon, Ti.Locr.96d; περίοδος, of women, Plu.2.495e; ἔργον Pl.*Lg.*956a. II. *done* or *paid every month, monthly,* ἱερά S.*El.* 281, Pl.*Lg.*828c; σιτηρέσιον Plu.*Caes.*8; ἁρμαλιήν Theoc.16.35. 2. in Law, ἐ. δίκαι suits *in which judgement must be given within thirty days,* D.37.2, Arist.*Ath.*52.2; εἰσάγειν ἔμμηνα ib.3. 3. ἐ., τά, *the menses* of women, Dsc.3.36, al.: sg., Sor.1.19. III. neut. ἔμμηνα as Adv., *in the course of a month, IG*1^2.65.47.

ἔμμηρος, ὁ, poet. for ἐνόμηρος, *as a hostage,* Demetr.Com.Vet.2.

ἔμμητρος, ον, (μήτρα) *containing core,* ξύλον Antiph.220, Thphr.*HP* 1.6.5, Theoc.25.209.

ἔμμι, Aeol. for εἰμί.

ἐμμῐαίνω, *pollute,* Tz.*H.*1.665.

ἔμμιλτος, ον, *tinged with red,* Dsc.5.112.

ἐμμίμνω, poet. for ἐμμένω, Emp.35.11, Q.S.6.497.

ἐμμίσγω, = ἐμμείγνυμι, Ep. part. ἐνιμίσγων Opp.*H.*3.408.

ἔμμισθος, ον, *in receipt of pay, hired,* Th.6.22; ξένοι Pl.*Lg.*816e, al.; ἐ. τινος *paid for* a thing, Luc.*Merc.Cond.*13; ἐ. τινα ποιεῖν to make him *pensionary,* παῖδας ὀρφανούς Plu.*Alex.*71; ὅλην τὴν πόλιν Id.*Per.* 12. 2. of work, *paid,* ὀργάνων καὶ ἔργων γένεσις ἐ. Pl.*Lg.*920e. 3. metaph., *mercenary,* εἰ ἐ. ἡ θεραπεία Ph.2.19.

ἐμμογέω, *toil in,* ἄθλοις Sch.Pi.*Pae.*2.57.

ἔμμοιρος, ον, *partaking, sharing,* φύσεως ἀγαθοῦ Plot.4.8.6, cf. Porph.*Gaur.*6.2.

ἐμμολύνω, *pollute in* or *with,* in Pass., Lxx *Pr.*24.9(10).

ἐμμον-εύω, = ἐμμένω, ἐν τῷ γυμνασίῳ δι' ἐνιαυτοῦ *IG*12(9).235 (Eretria). -ή, ἡ, *continuance,* opp. ἀπαλλαγή, τοῦ κακοῦ Pl.*Grg.* 479d. -ίαι· συνθῆκαι, Hsch. -ος, ον, *abiding, lasting,* ψυχῇ βίαιον οὐδὲν ἐ. μάθημα Pl.*R.*536e; διάνοιαι X.*Cyr.*3.3.52; παρρησία Phld.*Lib.*p.34 O.; λύπη Them.*Or.*32.359c (Comp.); τῆς κακίας τὸ ἐ. Plot.1.5.6; of persons, *steadfast,* X.*Cyr.*3.3.55: c. dat., *abiding by,* Andronic.Rhod.p.578 M. Adv. -νως, ὑπομεῖναι βασάνους Plu.2. 208c. II. of disease, *chronic,* λέπρα Lxx *Le.*13.51; ἀρρώστημα ib. *Si.*30.17.

ἔμμορε, ἐμμόρμενος, ἔμμορον, v. μείρομαι.

ἔμμορος, ον, (μείρομαι) *partaking in, endued with,* τιμῆς.. ἔμμοροί εἰσι καὶ αἰδοῦς Od.8.480. II. ἔμμορον· εἱμαρμένον, Hsch.

ἔμμορφος, ον, *endued with form,* ἀρχαί Thphr.*Metaph.*14; ἄγαλμα Plu.*Num.*8, cf. 2.362d; ὕλην ἐ. ἀποτελεῖσθαι Plot.5.9.4.

ἐμμοτέω, *plug, stop,* σωλῆνας Steph.*in Hp.*2.384D.

ἔμμοτος, ον, *treated with tents* (μοτοί), Hp.*Aph.*5.47, *Art.*49, *Mochl.* 36. II. *used with such tents,* Dsc.1.68; ἐ. φάρμακα Gal.11.125; ἐ. σύστασις Id.13.500; ἐ. ἀγωγή treatment *by tents,* Paul.Aeg.6.3. 2. metaph., ἔμμοτον τῶνδ' ἄκος (Schütz for ἑκάς) *a salve* or *plaster to heal* these wounds, A.*Ch.*471 (lyr.).

ἔμμουσος, ον, = μουσικός, πράγματα Heph.Astr.2.32: Sup. -ότατον, θεώρημα Nicom.*Ar.*2.2; ἐμμούσοις γράμμασιν in literature, *IG*9(1). 235 (Larymna). Adv. -σως, παίζειν Plu.2.1119d.

ἔμμοχθος, ον, *toilsome,* βίοτος E.*Supp.*1004 (lyr.); δάχμα Nic.*Th.* 756.

ἐμμῠέω, *initiate in*: μῶν ἐνεμυήθης δῆτ' ἐν αὐτῷ τὰ μεγάλα; what, *were you initiated* at the great mysteries *in* that shabby coat? Ar.*Pl.* 845 cod. R.

ἐμμῡθόω, *form a myth,* ὡς.. Tz.*H.*3.248.

ἐμμῠχᾰτεύειν, = ἐγκεκλεῖσθαι, dub. cj. for ἐνμαχ-, Rhinth.p.189 K.

ἐμμύχιος, v. ἐννύχιος III.

ἔμμωμος, ον, *blemished,* Sm., Thd.*Ma.*1.14.

ἐμνιωβέλιον, v. ἡμιωβέλιον. **ἔμολον,** aor. 2 of βλώσκω.

ἔμος, εος, τό, = εἷμα, *Supp.Epigr.*2.710 (Pednelissus).

ἐμός, ή, όν, possess. Pron. of 1st pers.: (ἐγώ, ἐμοῦ):—*mine*; contr. with the Art., οὑμός, τοὐμόν, τοὐμοῦ, τὠμῷ, τἀμά, Trag. (not Com., τἀμὰ γὰρ διοίχεται is paratrag. in Ar.*Ec.*393), rarely in Prose, οὑμός Pl.*Ep.*354c; τἀμά Id.*Plt.*258b; οὑμός even in Il.8.360; and (acc. to some Gramm.) τὠμῷ 11.608, Od.4.71; τἠμῇ Il.9.654:—poet. **ἀμός** (q.v.): I. with a Subst.: 1. subjectively, *mine, of me,* ἐμὰ δάκρυα Il.1.42; χεῖρες ἐμαί ib.166; ἐμός τε πατὴρ καὶ σός Hes.*Op.*633: with the Art., τὸν ἐμὸν χόλον Il.4.42, etc.: in Poets sts. joined with gen., to strengthen the *possessive* notion, ἐμὸν αὐτοῦ *mine* own, 6. 446, Od.2.45; δαὴρ.. ἐμὸς ἔσκε κυνώπιδος Il.3.180; θρῆνον ἐμὸν τὸν αὐτῆς A.*Ag.*1323; τἀμὰ δυστήνου κακά S.*OC*344, cf. *El.*252; τὸν ἐμὸν αὐτοῦ.. βίον Ar.*Pl.*33. b. *mine,* i.e. *favourable to me,* τεκμήρια ἐμά, οὐ τούτων Antipho 2.4.10. 2. objectively, *relating to me, against me,* ἐμὴ ἀγγελίη Il.19.336; τὸν ἐμὸν γάμον Od.2.97; τὴν ἐμὴν αἰδῶ respect *for me,* A.*Pers.*699 (troch.); τἀμὰ νουθετήματα warnings *to me,* S.*El.*343; τὠμῷ πόθῳ by love *for me,* Id.*OT*969; αἱ ἐμαὶ διαβολαί slanders *against me,* Th.6.90; δωρεὰ ἐμή a gift *to me,* X.*Cyr.*8.3.32; sts. with another gen. added, τὰς ἐμὰς Λαΐου διαφθορὰς murder of L. *by me,* S.*OT*572; τοὐμὸν αἷμα πατρός his blood shed *by me,* ib.1400; τὰ ἐμὰ δῶρα Κύπριδος (Dind. for Κύπρις) her gifts *to me,* E.*Hel.*364 (anap.). II. without a Subst., *mine,* οὐ γὰρ ἐμὸν παλινάγρετον *my word,* Il.1.526; τὸ μὲν ἐμόν [ἐστι] 'tis *my counsel,* Pi.*I.*8(7).42: in Trag. and Prose, it is *my duty, my business,* E.*Ion* 1020, Pl.*Lg.* 664b. 2. ἐμοί *my friends,* Il.20.205; οἱ ἐμοί X.*Cyr.*3.2.28, etc.; ὁ ἐμὸς Ἡράκλειτος *my dear* Heraclitus, Arr.*Epict.*2.2.17. 3. τὰ ἐμά *my property,* Pl.*Prt.*310e, etc.; of children, S.*El.*538, *OC*922; τὸ τύπτειν καὶ ἐμὲ καὶ τὰ ἐμὰ ἀδίκως Pl.*Grg.*508e; of servants, *PEdgar* 4.6 (iii B.C.), etc.; but also τὰ ἐμά or τὸ ἐμόν, *my part, my affairs, my interest,* οὕτω τὸ ἐμὸν ἔχει things stand thus *with me,* Hdt.4.127; τὰ τούτου μᾶλλον ἢ τοὐμόν S.*Aj.*124; ἔρρει τἀμὰ παντελῶς X.*Cyr.*6.1.3; τὸ ἐμὸν εὖ πράττει Pl.*R.*463e, etc.; in full, τοὐμὸν μέρος S.*Tr.*1215: hence in Trag. and Att., *my conduct* (almost periphr. for ἐγώ), Id. *El.*1302, *Tr.*1068, Ar.*Th.*105; τὸ μὲν οὖν ἐμὸν οὐκ ἐμποδὼν ὑμῖν ἔσται Lys.8.19, cf. Pl.*Grg.*452c, etc.: abs., τό γε ἐμὸν *for my part, as far as concerns me,* Hdt.1.108, Pl.*Prt.*338c, *Sph.*237b. 4. ἡ ἐ. (sc. γῆ) *my country,* Th.6.78; also (sc. γνώμη) *my opinion,* ἐὰν ἡ ἐ. νικᾷ Pl. *R.*397d; κατά γε τὴν ἐ. Ar.*Ec.*153, Pl.*Plt.*277a.

ἐμοῦς, v. ἐγώ. **ἐμπᾶ,** v. ἐμπᾶς. **ἐμπᾰγή,** ἡ, *suretyship,* Sm. *Pr.*11.15.

ἐμπάζομαι, used only in pres. (and later impf., Bion *Fr.*7.9, Coluth. 113, Nonn.*D.*15.214), *busy oneself about, take heed of, care for,* c. gen., ἐμῶν ἐμπάζεο μύθων Od.1.271, al.; οὔτε θεοπροπίης ἐμπάζομαι Il.16.50, cf. Od.2.201; οὔτε ξείνων ἐμπάζομαι οὐθ' ἱκετάων 19.134; οὐκ ἐμπαζόμενον δόξης Timo 50: once c. acc. pers., οὐχ ἱκέτας ἐμπάζεαι Od.16. 422; also Ἔριν δ' ἀγέραστον ἐάσας οὐ Χείρων ἀλέγιζε καὶ οὐκ ἐμπάζετο Πηλεύς Coluth.38:—Ep. word, used in late Prose, οὐκ ἀλέγων Ἀδράστειαν οὐδὲ Νέμεσιν ἐμπαζόμενος Ael.*Fr.*325.

ἐμπάθ-εια [ᾰ], ἡ, physical *affection,* τῆς σαρκός Gal.18(1).447. II. *passion,* φυσικαὶ ἐ. Ptol.*Tetr.*92, cf. Hierocl.*in CA* 24 p.470 M. III. *partiality,* Mich.*in EN*61.28. -ής, ές, *in a state of emotion,* Arist. *Insomn.*460^b7 (Comp.); ἐ. τινι *much affected by* or *at* a thing, Plu. *Alex.*21; πρὸς τὰ θεῖα Id.2.1125d; ἐ. φιλία *passionate* affection, Alciphr.2.4.12; τὸ ἐ. *sentiment, emotion,* Plu.2.25d. Adv. -θῶς *with deep emotion,* [τὴν δεξιὰν] πιέσας Plb.31.24.9; *passionately,* αἰτιάσασθαί τινα J.*AJ*16.4.2: Comp. -έστερον ἔχειν πρός τι Plu.*Cic.*6; -εστέρως dub. in Phld.*Oec.*p.42 J.: Sup. -έστατα Plu.2.668c; -έστατα παρεστηκότες τῇ φιλοσοφίᾳ *Vit.Philonid.*p.9 C. II. opp. ἀπαθής, *subject to passivity,* Plot.4.7.13, 5.9.4; opp. ἐνδρανής, Procl.*Inst.*80. III. Rhet., *pathetic,* D.H.*Dem.*21. Adv. -θῶς, εἰρηκέναι Demetr.*Eloc.* 28. IV. Gramm., *modified, inflected,* A.D.*Synt.*47.16.

ἔμπαιγ-μα, ατος, τό, *jest, mocking, delusion,* Lxx *Is.*66.4; μαγικῆς ἐμπαίγματα τέχνης ib.*Wi.*17.7. -μονή, ἡ, *mockery, 2Ep.Pet.* 3.3. -μός, ὁ, *mockery, mocking,* Lxx *Si.*27.28, al., *Ep.Hebr.*11. 36 (pl.).

ἐμπαιδεύω, *lecture amongst*, τισί Philostr.*VS*1.21.3 :—Pass., *to be brought up in*, ἐλευθέροισι τρόποις E.*Fr.*413.

ἐμπαιδο-τρῐβέομαι, *to be brought up* or *educated in*, ὀρχήστρᾳ D.C. 77.21 ; βίβλοις J.*BJ*2.8.12. **-τροφέομαι**, Med., ἐ. τῇ τινὸς οὐσίᾳ *bring up one's children on* another person's property, D.44.23.

ἐμπαίζω, fut. -ξομαι Lxx*Hb.*1.10 : pf. ἐμπέπαιχα ib.*Nu.*22.29 :—*mock at, mock*, τινί Hdt.4.134 ; τινά *PCair.Preis.*3.10 (iv A. D.) : abs., S.*Ant.*799 :—Pass., ψυχὴ ὑπὸ..σωμάτων καὶ πραγμάτων ἐμπαιζομένη Ph.1.568, cf. Luc.*Trag.*333. 2. euphem. in mal. part., Lxx*Jd.* 19.25. 3. Pass., *to be deluded*, *Ev.Matt.*2.16, *AP*10.56.2 (Pall.), Vett.Val.16.14 ; *to be defrauded*, of the revenues, *Cod.Just.*1.34. 2. II. *sport in* or *on*, ὡς νεβρὸς χλοεραῖς ἐ. λείμακος ἡδοναῖς E.*Ba.* 866 (lyr.) ; τοῖς χοροῖσιν ἐ. *to sport in* the dance, Ar.*Th.*975 ; τῷ γυμνασίῳ Luc.*Lex.*5.

ἐμπαίκτης, ου, ὁ, *mocker, deceiver*, Lxx*Is.*3.4, *2Ep.Pet.*3.3, *Ep.Jud.* 18.

ἔμπαιος (A), ον, *knowing, practised in*, c. gen., οὐδέ τι ἔργων ἔμπαιον οὐδὲ βίης [penult. short] Od.20.379 ; κακῶν ἔμπαιος ἀλήτης 21. 400 ; ἐ. δρόμων Lyc.1321.

ἔμπαιος (B), ον, (παίω) *bursting in, sudden*, τύχαι A.*Ag.*187 (lyr.) ; πολλὰ δὲ δείλ' ἔμπαια prob. in Emp.2.2.

ἔμπαις, παιδος, ἡ, *with child*, ἡ παῖς ἔμπαις Cratin.287 (Kock cj. ἔκπαις *no longer a child*), cf. Hsch.

ἔμπαισ-μα, ατος, τό, *embossed work*, Eust.883.54 (pl.). **-τική** τέχνη the art *of embossing*, Ath.11.488b. **-τός**, όν, *embossed*, Eust.1357.40.

ἐμπαίτονται· ἐμπαίζουσιν, Hsch. (Fort.-παίττ-, Lacon. for -παίζ-.)

ἐμπαίω, *strike in, stamp, emboss*, σκίπων χρυσᾶς ἕλικας ἐμπεπαισμένος Ath.12.543f. II. intr., ἐμπαίει τί μοι ψυχῇ *bursts in upon* my soul, S.*El.*902.

ἐμπακτόω, *close by stuffing in* or *caulking*, τὰς ἁρμονίας ἐν ὧν ἐπάκτωσαν τῇ βύβλῳ Hdt.2.96.

ἐμπάλ-αγμα [πᾰ], ατος, τό, = ἐμπλοκή, *embrace*, A.*Supp.*296 (pl., cf. Sch. ad loc., Hsch., παλλαγμάτων codd.). **-άσσομαι**, Pass., *to be entangled in*, ἐν ἕρκεσι Hdt.7.85 ; τῷ ἀγκίστρῳ, of fish, Ael.*NA*15. 1 : abs., οἱ δὲ ἐμπαλασσόμενοι κατέρρεον *entangled one with another*, Th.7.84.—Act. ἐμπαλάξαι· ἐμπλέξαι, Hsch. (Cf. ἐμπελάζω III.)

ἔμπαλῐ, poet. for sq., Orph.*H.*73.5, *AP*7.421.5 (Mel.), 12.5 (Strat.), etc.

ἔμπαλιν, Adv., in Trag. and Prose freq. with Art., **τὸ ἔμπαλιν** or **τοὔμπαλιν, τὰ ἔμπαλιν** (as always in Hdt.) or **τἄμπαλιν** :—*backwards, back*, κατὰ δ' ἐ. αὐτὸς ἔβαινε *h.Merc.*78 ; δεδορκὼς Hes.*Sc.*145 ; ἐς τοὔ. δέδορκεν S.*Ichn.*113 ; πρόσωπον ἐ. στρέφοντα E.*Hec.*343 ; τοὔ. ὑποστρέψαντας X.*An.*6.6.38 ; τὰ ἐ. ἀπαλλάσσεσθαι Hdt.9.26 ; ἄπιμεν ἅπαντες τοὔ. X.*An.*1.4.15, etc. b. τὸ ἐ. καὶ ἀνάπαλιν *as before* and vice versa, Nech.ap.Vett.Val.154.28. II. *contrariwise, the opposite way*, τοὔ. σπεύδειν, κραίνειν, A.*Pr.*204, *Ag.*1424 ; λέγειν S.*Tr.* 358 ; ἀνατρέπειν ἐ. turn *upside down*, E.*Ba.*348 ; ἐ. ὑποδεῖσθαι to put on one's shoes *contrariwise* (i. e. on the wrong feet), Pl.*Tht.*193c ; ἐκ τοὔ. ἢ.. from *the opposite side* to.., Th.3.22. 2. c. gen., *contrary to*, τέρψιος, γνώμας ἐ., Pi.*O.*12.11, *P.*12.32 ; τὰ ἐ. πρήσσων τοῦ πεζοῦ doing the *opposite* thing to the army, Hdt.7.58 ; τἄ. τῶνδε *the reverse* of these things, A.*Pers.*223 ; τοὔ. πεσεῖν φρενῶν to be brought to *the opposite opinion*, E.*Hipp.*390 ; τοὔ. οὗ βούλονται X.*Cyr.*8.4.32 ; folld. by ἤ, Emp.100.20 ; γνώμην ἔχω τὰ ἐ. ἢ οὗτοι Hdt.1.207 ; ᾔσαν τὰ ἐ. ἢ Λακεδαιμόνιοι Id.9.56. 3. *on the contrary*, Nic.*Th.*288, Ph. 1.264, Porph.*Abst.*1.44 ; f.l. for ἔμπολιν in S.*OC*637 ; τοὔ. *on the other hand*, Epicur.*Ep.*3 p.63 U.

ἐμπάλλομαι, poet. ἐνιπ-, *shake* or *quiver in*, δόμοις ἐνιπάλλεται αἴγλη A.R.3.756. (Act. ἐμπάλλομεν apptly. occurs in Tyrt.1.64 Diehl.)

ἔμπᾱμα, ατος, τό, *property*, Boeot. ἔπη-, *IG*7.3172.163 (Orchom., iii B. C.).

ἐμπάμων, ον, gen. ονος, (πέπᾱμαι) = ἐπίκληρος, Hsch.

ἐμπᾰνηγυρίζω, *hold festal assemblies in*, Plu.*Comp.Per.Fab.*1 ; *make a display in*, Id.2.532b.

ἐμπαρα-βάλλομαι, *throw oneself into*, τιμωρίαις into punishment, Phalar.*Ep.*132 ; ἐ. τῇ ψυχῇ *to venture to believe* in one's heart, ib. 130. **-γίγνομαι**, *come in upon*, τινί Lxx*Pr.*6.11. **-θετος**, ον, *laid in* or *on*, Suid., cf. eund. s. v. Σέλευκος Ἐμεσηνός. **-λιμπάνω**, *pass over*, c. acc., Them.*in Ph.*11.29. **-σκευάζω**, *to prepare*, φόβον τοῖς ἀνδράσι Clin.ap.Stob.3.1.76, cf. Aen.Tact.9.3. **-σκευος**, ον, *prepared*, Sm.*Ps.*26(27).3 ; ἐμπαράσκευον, τό, a kind of *wind-screen* for engines, Ath.Mech.33.1. Adv. -ως Suid. s. v. ἑτοίμως.

ἐμπαρ-έχω, *hand over* to another, *put into* his *power*, τὴν πόλιν ἐμπαρασχόντες προκινδυνεῦσαι Th.7.56 ; μηδὲ τούτῳ ἐμπαράσχητε.. ἐλλαμπρύνεσθαι *put into* his *power, allow* him to gain distinction, Id. 6.12 ; ἐ. ἑαυτόν τινι *give* oneself *up* as his tool, App.*BC*5.68 ; but ἐμπαρασχεῖν ἑαυτὸν τοιούτῳ τινί (sc. δείπνῳ) *accept an invitation*, Luc. *Symp.*28 :—Med., ποτὶ τὸν θίασον.. εὔνουν ἑαυτὸν -εχόμενος *Rev. Arch.*22(1925).64 (Callatis), cf. Ph.2.127. II. *supply, furnish*, ψυχῇ τέρψιν, δυνάμεις τισί, Id.1.12, 2.383, al. ; ὄνομά τινι Plu.*Galb.* 29. **-ίσταμαι**, Pass. with aor. 2 Act., *stand by*, Hld.7.19.

ἐμπαροιν-έω, aor. ἐνεπαροίνησα J.*Ap.*1.8 :—*behave like one drunken*, Luc.*Tim.*14 ; *act offensively*, τινί to another, Ph.2.403, Luc.*DDeor.* 5.4 ; τοῖς πράγμασι J.*AJ*6.12.7 ; ἐ. ψεύσμασιν *indulge recklessly in* slanders, ib.20.8.3. **-ημα**, ατος, τό, *object of drunken treatment*, Longus 4.18.

ἔμπαρος· ἔμπληκτος, Hsch. [Prob. ᾱ, cf. ἔμπηρος.]

ἐμπαρρησιάζομαι, *speak freely against*, τινί Plb.38.12.7. II. τῇ προαιρέσει τῆς ἐπιβουλῆς -σάμενοι *drawing courage* from their purpose *to speak openly* of the plot, J.*AJ*15.8.4. III. abs., ἐ. ἔναντι Κυρίου Lxx*Jb.*22.26.

ἔμπαρσις, εως, ἡ, = διάπαρσις, Aët.8.50.

ἔμπᾱς (A), Pi.*P.*4.86, etc. (so always in Trag., exc. ἔμπᾰ S.*Aj.* 563) : Ep. **ἔμπης** also in late Ion. prose, Aret.*SA*2.8, *SD*2.11 : Dor. also **ἔμπᾱν**, Pi.*P.*5.55, *N.*6.4, 11.44 ; and **ἔμπᾰ** (v. supr.), Id.*N.*4.36, Call.*Ep.*14 :—poet. Adv. 1. = ὁμοίως, *alike*, Ζεὺς δ' ἐ. πάντ' ἰθύνει Il.17.632 ; ἐ. ἐς γαῖάν τε καὶ οὐρανὸν ἵκετ' ἀϋτμή 14.174 ; ἐ. τὰ καὶ τὰ νέμων Pi.*P.*5.55. 2. *in any case*, νῦν δ' ἐ. γὰρ κῆρες ἐφεστᾶσιν θανάτοιο, ἴομεν Il.12.326 ; οὐκ ἐφάμην ῥιγωσέμεν ἐ. Od.14.481 ; *anyhow, as things are*, σὺ δὲ χαῖρε καὶ ἐ. 5.205, cf. Il.19.308, v.l. for αὔτως in Od.16.143 ; ὄφρ' ἔτι μᾶλλον Τρωσὶ μὲν εὐκτὰ γένηται ἐπικρατέουσί περ ἐ. though they are victorious *as it is*, Il.14.98. 3. *in the same way, so*, ἐ. μοι τοῖχοι..φαίνοντ' ὀφθαλμοῖς ὡς εἰ πυρὸς αἰθομένοιο Od.19.37, cf. 18.354. II. = ὅμως, *all the same, nevertheless*, ἐ. δ' οὐκ ἐδάμασσα Il.5.191 ; πρῆξαι δ' ἐ. οὔ τι δυνήσεαι 1.562, cf. Od.19. 302, 2.199 ; after ἀλλά, ἀλλὰ καί, ἀλλ' ἐ. μιν ἐάσομεν 16.147, cf. Il. 8.33, Od.4.100, al. ; ἀλλὰ καὶ ἐ. αἰσχρόν but *even so*.., Il.2.297, cf. 19.422 ; ἐγὼ δ' αἰσχύνομαι ἐ. Od.18.12, cf. 15.214 ; following part. with περ, = καίπερ, Νέστορα δ' οὐκ ἔλαθεν πίνοντά περ ἐ. Il.14.1, cf. Od. 15.361, 18.165 ; rarely before the part., ἄλγεα δ' ἐ. ἐν θυμῷ κατακεῖσθαι ἐάσομεν ἀχνύμενοί περ Il.24.522. (Signff. I and II were distd. by Aristarch., cf. Sch.T Il.14.1.) III. in later Poets sts. in a milder sense, *at any rate, yet*, A.*Pr.*48, *Eu.*229, S.*Ant.*845, E.*Cyc.*535 (lyr.) ; after δέ, Pi.*P.*4.86 ; ἀλλ' ἔμπας A.*Pr.*189 (lyr.), E.*Alc.*906 (lyr.) ; ἀλλ' ἔμπαν Pi.*N.*6.4, 11.44 ; ἔμπα, καίπερ ἔχει.. ib.4.36, cf. S.*Aj.*563 : with a part., ib.1338 ; δύστηνον ἔμπας, καίπερ ὄντα δυσμενῆ ib.122 ; also with Adj., ἀφωνήτῳ περ ἔμπας ἄχει Pi.*P.*4.237.

ἔμπας (B), πασα, παν, *all*, dub. in *IG*7.2712.69 (Acraeph., i A. D.).

ἐμπασέντας· ἀρχεῖόν τι ἐν Λακεδαίμονι, Hsch.

ἔμπᾱσις, εως, ἡ, (πέπᾱμαι) = ἔγκτησις, *IG*5(2).11 (Tegea), 7.8.9 (Megara, iii B. C.), Hsch. (pl.) ; Boeot. **ἔππασις** *IG*7.3166 (Orchom., iii B. C.) ; also **ἔπασις** ib.3167, al. ; Arc. **ἴμπασις** ib.5(2).17 (Tegea), 394 (Lusi).

ἔμ-πᾰσις, εως, ἡ, *sprinkling, dusting*, εἰς ἔμπασιν *BKT*3 p.32. **-πασμα**, ατος, τό, *dusting-powder*, Antyll.ap.Orib.10.31.1, cf. 8.6. 7. **-πάσσω**, Att. -ττω, fut. -πάσω [ᾰ] :—*sprinkle in* or *on*, τι ἔς τι Thphr.*Lap.*67 ; τῆς τέφρας some *powder*, Pl.*Ly.*210a ; τί τινι Gal. 11.134 : in Hom. only metaph., *weave* rich patterns *in* a web of cloth, πολέας δ' ἐνέπασσεν ἀέθλους Il.3.126, cf. 22.441. **-παστέον**, *one must sprinkle*, Archig.ap.Aët.9.28.

ἐμπαστῆρας· μύθων· πιστωτάς, μάρτυρας, Hsch. ; cf. ἔμπαιος (A).

ἐμπαστήρια· μελίπη⟨κ⟩τα, Id.

ἐμπᾰτᾰγέω, *make a noise with*, μάστιξιν Them.*Or.*4.50b.

ἐμπάτακτος [πᾰ], ον, = ἐμβρόντητος, Ptol.*Tetr.*165.

ἐμπᾰτέω, *walk in* or *into*, c. acc., μέλαθρον A.*Ag.*1434. II. c. acc., *trample on*, νεκρούς J.*BJ*6.9.4 : metaph., τὰ κοινὰ τῶν ἀνθρώπων νόμιμα Agath.4.15 :—Med. or Pass., *tread* the wine-press, Poll. 7.151.

ἔμπατον· καταθύμιον, Hsch.

ἔμπεδα, v. ἔμπεδος.

ἐμπεδ-έω, = ἐμπεδόω, *Schwyzer* 414.3 (Elis). **-ής**, ές, = ἔμπεδος, *Trag.Adesp.*208. Adv. Ion. ἐμπεδέως *Scol.*25.

ἐμπέδιος, ον, *deep-rooted*, cj. in Numen.ap.Ath.9.371c.

ἐμπεδό-καρπος, ον, *ever-fruiting*, Emp.77. **-λώβης**, ου, ὁ, *ever-hurting*, Man.4.196. **-μοχθος**, ον, *ever-painful*, βίος Pi.*O.*1. 59. **-μῡθος**, ον, *steadfast to one's word*, Ἄτροπος, Πειθώ, Nonn.*D.* 12.141, 38.43.

ἐμπεδορκέω, *abide by one's oath*, Hdt.4.201, X.*Lac.*15.7 ; ταῦτα *IG*2[2].111.79 :—with a play on πέδη, Ar.*Fr.*772.

ἔμπεδος (A), ον, (πέδον) *in the ground, firm-set*, τεῖχος Il.12.12 ; λέχος Od.23.203. 2. mostly of qualities, etc., *steadfast*, μένος, ἴς, Il.5.254, Od.11.393 ; φρένες, ἦτορ, νόος, Il.6.352, 10.94, 11.813 ; χρὼς ἐ. 19.33 ; of a person, ἐ. οὐδ' ἀεσίφρων (of Priam) 20.183 ; λίσσεται ἔμπεδον εἶναι [τὴν πομπήν] prays that it may be *sure and certain*, Od.8. 30, cf. Pi.*N.*7.57 ; δίκη δέ τοι ἐ. ἔστω καὶ θέμις A.R.4.372, etc. ; once in A., ἐ. σίνος a *cleaving* or *clinging* mischief, *Ag.*561 ; ἐ. φρονήματα S.*Ant.*169 ; συντρόφοις ὀργαῖς ἐ. *continuing steadfast in*.., Id.*Aj.*640 (lyr.) ; ἔμπεδα φωνεῖν Nic.*Th.*4 : Comp. -ώτερος, νόος Luc.*Salt.* 85. 3. of Time, *lasting, continual*, φυλακή Il.8.521 ; κομιδή Od.8. 453 ; αἰών Emp.17.11 ; δουλοσύνα Pi.*P.*12.14 ; χρῆμα Simon.85.1 (s. v. l.) ; πόνος S.*OC*1674 (lyr.). II. neut. ἔμπεδον as Adv. (freq. in Hom.), στήλη μένει ἐ. stands *fast*, Il.17.434 ; Δαναοὶ Τρῶας μένον ἐ. *firmly*, 5.527 ; θέειν ἐ. run *on and on*, run *without resting*, 13.141 ; ἐ. βρύουσα B.12.178 ; strengthd., ἐ. αἰέν Il.16.107 ; ἐ. ἀσφαλὲς αἰεί 15.683 ; μάλ' ἀσφαλέως θέεν ἐ. Od.13.86 : pl., τίκτη δ' ἔμπεδα μῆλα the flocks bring forth *without fail*, 19.113 ; δρύες ἔμπεδα ῥίζαις ἑστᾶσιν *firmly*, *AP*9.291 (Crin.) : in Trag., ἴσθι τόδ' ἔμπεδον *of a surety*, S. *Ph.*1197 (anap.) ; more freq. regul. Adv. ἐμπέδως *continually*, Semon. 7.20 (nisi leg. -πεδῶς, cf. ἐμπεδής) : so in Trag., *constantly, firmly*, A.*Ag.*854,975, *Eu.*335 (lyr.), S.*Tr.*487 ; also in later Prose, ἐ. οἶδα *of a surety*, Pl.*Ax.*372a ; ἔτη τριάκοντα μείναντες ἐ. Plb.2.19.1, Porph. *Abst.*2.41. III. = χθόνιος, Hippon.113A.

ἔμπεδος (B), ον, (πέδη) *fettered*, Luc.*Lex.*10.

ἐμπεδο-σθενής, ές, *with force unshaken*, βίοτος *a settled, unruffled* life, Pi.*N.*7.98. **-φρων**, ον, gen. ονος, (φρήν) *steadfast of mind*, Phalar.*Ep.*37.2. **-φυλλος**, ον, *ever-green*, Emp.77.

ἐμπεδ-όω, impf. ἠμπέδουν X.*Cyr.*8.8.2: aor. ἐνεπέδωσα D.C.60. 28: (ἔμπεδος):—*confirm, ratify,* σὺ δ' ἐμπέδου δόσιν S.*Ichn.*50; ὅρκον E.*IT*790, cf. Ar.*Lys.*211,233, Polem.Hist.83; σπονδάς X.*HG*3.4.6; τὰ.. ὁρκωμόσιά τε καὶ ὑποσχέσεις Pl.*Phdr.*241b; ὅρκους καὶ δεξιάς τινι X.*Cyr.*5.1.22; συνθήκας Plb.29.24.4; ὁμολογίας D.H.4.79; ἀποδείξεσι δόγμα Gal.5.315; *uphold,* νόμους Plu.*Sol.*25:—Med., σπονδήν, ἀσφάλειαν ἐμπεδώσασθαι, Ph.1.439, Luc.*Hipp.*4. **-ωσις**, εως, ἡ, *making good,* ὅρκων D.H.5.10.

ἐμπειρ-άζω, *to make an attempt on,* c. gen. rei, v.l. for ἀπο-, Plb. 15.35.5. **-ᾰμος**, ον, poet. for ἐμπέραμος (q.v.). **-άομαι**, Dep., *make trial of,* τινός Hp.*Nat.Mul.*99. **-έω**, *to be experienced in, have knowledge of,* c. gen. rei, τῆς χώρας Plb.3.78.6, etc.; τῆς ὁδοῦ Lxx *To.*5.6. **-ία**, ἡ, *experience,* E.*Ph.*529, Th.4.10; opp. ἀνεπιστημοσύνη, Id.5.7; ἡ ἐκ πολλοῦ ἐ., opp. ἡ δι' ὀλίγου μελέτη, Id.2.85; ἡ μὴ 'μπειρία *want of experience,* Ar.*Ec.*115; δι' ἐμπειρίαν Pl.*Prm.* 137a; ἐπιστήμῃ, οὐκ ἐμπειρίᾳ οἰκείᾳ κεχρημένον Id.*R.*409b: pl., D. *Prooem.*45. 2. c. gen. rei, *experience in, acquaintance with,* τῶν πραγμάτων Antipho 5.1; μάχης ἐμπειρίᾳ τῆς ἐκείνων Th.3.95; ἀμφοτέρων τῶν ἡδονῶν Pl.*R.*582b; also ἐ. περί τι X.*HG*7.1.4; ἐ. ἡ κατὰ τὴν πόλιν Th.2.3; ἐ. ἡγεμονική Plb.10.24.4, etc. II. *practice,* without knowledge of principles, esp. in Medicine, *empiricism,* ἰατρὸς τῶν ταῖς ἐμπειρίαις ἄνευ λόγου τὴν ἰατρικὴν μεταχειριζομένων Pl.*Lg.*857c (hence οἱ ἀπὸ τῆς ἐ. ἰατροί S.E.*M.*8.191, Gal.*Sect.Intr.*1); κατ' ἐμπειρίαν τὴν τέχνην κτᾶσθαι *empirically,* Pl.*Lg.*720b; οὐκ ἔστιν τέχνη, ἀλλ' ἐ. καὶ τριβή Id.*Grg.*463b, cf. 465a, *Lg.*938a (whereas Plb. opposes ἐ. to ἀπειρία καὶ τριβὴ ἄλογος 1.84.6): but also, 2. *craft,* τοῖς περὶ τὰς ἐ. γεγυμνασμένοις Isoc.13.14; πραγμάτων ἐ., including τέχνη and ἐπιστήμη Metrod.61; αἱ ἄλλαι ἐ. καὶ τέχναι the other *crafts* and arts, Arist.*Pol.*1282^{a}1; αἱ περὶ τῶν τοιούτων ἐ. ib.1297^{b} 20; also, *experiments,* πολλαὶ τέχναι ἐκ τῶν ἐ. ηὑρημέναι Pl.*Grg.* 448c. **-ικός**, ἡ, όν, *experienced,* ἁλιεῖς Arist.*HA*532^{b}20. Adv. -κῶς, ἔχειν τινός Id.*GA*742^{a}17, cf. Alex.243, etc. 2. οἱ ἐμπειρικοί *the Empiric school of physicians,* Cels.1 *Praef.*, Gal.*Sect.Intr.*1, al., S.E.*M.*8.327, al.; ἡ -κή their doctrine, = Lat. *empirice,* Plin.*HN*29. 5; in full, ἐ. αἵρεσις Gal. l. c.; so ἐ. ἱστορία Phld.*Rh.*1.93 S. Adv. -κῶς *empirically,* ἰατρεύειν S.E.*M.*8.204, cf. Gal.15.8.

ἐμπειρο-θάλασσος [θᾰ], ον, = sq., Phot.ap.Sch.Aristid.p.185 F. **-πλους**, ουν, *experienced in navigation,* Tz. ad Hes.*Op.*687. **-πόλεμος**, ον, *experienced in war,* D.H.6.14, Ph.1.426: Sup., App.*BC*3.97. Adv. -μως ib.2.36. **-πράγμων**, ον, gen. ονος, *versed in affairs,* Suid. s. v. νόμος.

ἔμπειρος, ον, (πεῖρα) *experienced* or *practised in* a thing, *acquainted with* it, c. gen., τῆς θυσίης Hdt.2.49; τῶν χώρων Id.8.132; Βοιωτῶν Id.9.46; τῆς ἐκείνου διανοίης Id.8.97; κακῶν A.*Pers.*598; γάμων S. *OC*752; θαλάσσης Th.1.80 (Sup.); τοῦ ἀγωνίζεσθαι Antipho 5.7; ὁ περὶ τῶν νόμων ἔ. Pl.*Lg.*632d; οἱ μάλιστα περὶ ταῦτα τῶν ἱερέων ἔ. Id. *Ti.*22a: abs., οἱ ἔ. the *experienced,* S.*OT*44, *OC*1135; *experts,* Pl.*Lg.* 765b; ναυσὶν ἐμπείροις for ships *skilfully handled,* Th.2.89; τὸ ἐμπειρότερον αὐτῶν their *greater experience,* ib.87. II. Adv. -ρως, τινὸς ἔχειν to *know* a person or thing *by experience, by its issue,* X.*An.*2.6.1, Antiph.3, etc.; παιδεῦσαι D.59.18; διώκειν Aen.Tact.2.6; πόλεμον διενεγκεῖν Jul.*Or.*2.95a: Comp. -οτέρως Aeschin.1.82.

ἐμπειρότοκος, ον, *having borne a child,* Hp.*Mul.*1.4.

ἐμπείρω, *fix on* or *in,* ἥλους ἐκπώματι Ath.11.488d (Pass.); [δόρατος] ἐμπαρέντος ταῖς πύλαις Plu.2.298a; of fish bones in the throat, Aët.8.53 (Pass.); ἐμπεπαρμένος πόνος *fixed* pain, Archig.ap.Gal.8. 91. 2. *impale,* ὡς ἐμπαρείη ταῖς ἑαυτοῦ λόγχαις J.*AJ*16.10.3; ἥλοις ἐμπεπαρμένη βακτηρία *studded,* Alciphr.3.55. II. metaph., ψυχὴ τοῖς ἀλόγοις πάθεσιν ἑαυτὴν ἐ. Simp. *in Epict.*p.125 D.:—Pass., ibid.

ἐμπελᾰγίζω, *to be in* or *on the sea,* *IPE*1^{2}.35 (Olbia, i B.C.), Ach. Tat.5.9.

ἐμπελ-άδην [ᾰ], Adv. = sq., Nic.*Al.*215. **-ᾰδόν**, Adv. *near, hard by,* ἱστίῃ Hes.*Op.*734. **-άζω**, *bring near,* δίφρους ἐμπελάσαντες *having brought up* the chariots, Id.*Sc.*109:—Pass., *come near, approach,* κοίτης S.*Tr.*17. II. intr. in Act., *approach,* c. dat., ἐμπελάσσειν πυκινῷ δόμῳ *h.Merc.*523; εἴδωλα ἐ. τοῖς ἀνθρώποις Democr. 166; ποῦ δ' ἐμπελάζεις τἀνδρί..; S.*Tr.*748; τῇ ἀκοῇ Arist.*Mu.*395^{a} 19: abs., ib.^{b}28, Porph.*Abst.*2.22; κρήνης μηδὲ σχεδὸν ἐμπελάσειας Orph.*Fr.*32a. III. in Pass., wrongly used for ἐμπαλάσσομαι, τοῖσι αὐτοῖσι Hp.*Ep.*17; ἀλλήλοις D.C.36.49, 62.16; αὐτοῖς Id.72.19.

ἐμπέλᾱνα· πόπανα, Hsch.

ἐμπέλ-ᾰσις, εως, ἡ, *approaching,* S.E.*M.*9.393, 11.98. **-αστικῶς**, gloss on ἐμπελάδην, Sch.Nic.*Al.*215. **-άτειρα** [λᾰ], ἡ, = πελάτις, πλᾶτις, Call.*Fr.*170, Euph.9.11. **-άω**, imper. ἐμπέλα, *IG*14.271 (Selinus), Hsch.:— = ἐμπελάζω, Nic.*Al.*498:—Med., ib.356.

ἐμπέλιος, ον, *livid,* Nic.*Th.*782.

ἐμπέλωρος, ὁ, title of Laconian official, = ἀγορανόμος, Hsch.

ἐμπέπτας, ου, ὁ, *hollow wheaten cake,* Seleuc.ap.Ath.14.645d; Rhodian, acc. to Hsch.

ἐμπέρᾰμος, ον, = ἔμπειρος, *skilled in the use of,* νηῶν Call.*Jov.*71; πάσης ἐ. σοφίης *IG*14.1957, cf. 888 (Suessa), *Arch.Anz.*1904.8 (Milet.): abs., ἐμπέραμος φώς Androm.ap.Gal.14.37:—also **ἐμπειρᾰμος**, Lyc. 1196, Man.4.536, *AP*10.14 (Agath.), Nonn.*D.*39.181. Adv. ἐμπεράμως Call.*Lav.Pall.*25.

ἐμπερδολεκᾰνᾰρύταινα [ῠ], ἡ, dub. sens. in *Com.Adesp.*55 D.

ἐμπερής, ές, poet. for ἔμπειρος, S.*Fr.*464.

ἐμπερι-άγω [ᾰ], *bring round,* τὸν θεὸν κατὰ ἔθνος -άγοντα τὴν ἀρχήν J.*BJ*5.9.3. **-βάλλω**, *embrace, comprehend,* dub. in Phld.*Herc.*1251. 8. **-βολος**, ον, (περιβολή) *ornate, expanded,* Aristid.*Rh.*2 p.533 S.; λόγος Hermog.*Id.*1.11; προοίμια Men.Rh.p.400 S. **-γράφω** [ᾰ], *comprehend in a thing,* v.l. for συμπ-, S.E.*P.*1.206 (Pass.); *describe around,* κύκλον τηλίᾳ Poll.9.108. **-εκτικός**, ή, όν, *comprehending, inclusive,* c. gen., A.D.*Pron.*4.7, al.: abs., Id.*Synt.*231.3. **-έρχομαι**, *pass round,* prob. in Gal.2.826: metaph., μηδὲν ἐ. ἀκριβείᾳ λογισμοῦ Ph.2.61. **-έχω**, *encompass, surround, enclose,* Arist.*MM*1187^{a}3, *Mu.*395^{b}18, Thphr.*HP*1.11.1; *include,* A.D.*Adv.*124.22; *garrison,* τὸ βασίλειον τῷ μαχιμωτάτῳ J.*AJ*17.10.3:—Pass., *to be embraced, encompassed,* Arist.*Mu.*392^{a}9, Ph.1.385; *to be contained, included in,* λόφος -εχόμενος τῇ πόλει D.H.10.31; τῷ κόσμῳ Ocell.1.8: abs., Id.3.2: metaph., *to be contained* or *involved in,* ἔν τινι Plb.9.32.4, Corn.*ND*26; καθ' ἑκάστην ἰδέαν Longin.8.1. 2. Astrol., *blockade,* Vett.Val.268.20. **-ισχάνω**, = foreg., Nech.ap.eund.280.3 (Pass.). **-κλείω**, *enclose on all sides,* Eust.105.22. **-λαμβάνω**, *encompass, enclose,* Hp.*Ep.*23, Thphr.*CP*5.3.4; ὕδωρ ἐρύμασι Plu.*Ant.*63; τῇ αὐτοῦ οἰκίᾳ ψιλοὺς τόπους *Sammelb.*5233.7 (I A.D.); ὅρος J.*BJ*3.7.7; *comprehend,* ἑνὶ ὀνόματι [ἄμφω] Arist.*PA*644^{a}12; ψήφισμα πάσας ἐ. τὰς ἀρετάς τινος *Inscr.Prien.*105.27 (i B.C.):—Pass., Arist.*Mete.*388^{b}21; ἐμπεριείληπται ὁ διαβάλλων *is involved* in the charge, Id.*Rh.*1416^{a}20; τύποις -ειλημμένα Epicur.*Ep.*1 p.22 U.; ὑπὸ τοῦ κόσμου ib.2 p.38 U. **-ληπτικός**, ή, όν, *comprehending, inclusive,* τινός A.D.*Synt.*36.1, al.: abs., ἐ. τρόπος Epicur.*Nat.*28. 2. **-ληψις**, εως, ἡ, *encompassment,* τοῦ πυρός Arist.*Mete.*369^{b} 19; τοῦ φωτός Epicur.*Ep.*2 p.45 U.; *embracing,* χρόνων ἀξιολόγων D.H.*Dem.*38. **-νοέω**, *include in the thought of,* συνάψαι φάσμα τούτοις ἐμπερινενοημένον Epicur.*Nat.*11.9. **-οδος**, ον, *in periods, periodic,* of style, D.H.*Comp.*9. Adv. -δως Corn.*ND*27. **-οχή**, ἡ, *encompassing,* Cleom.1.3. **-πᾰτέω**, *walk about in,* [ἐμβάταις] Luc.*Ind.*6; μέσοις τοῖς ἁγίοις J.*BJ*4.3.10: metaph., ταῖς διανοίαις Ph.1.643, cf. 274; ἐ. ἐν ὑμῖν *tarry among* you, Lxx *Le.*26.12, cf. 2*Ep. Cor.*6.16: abs., *walk about,* ἅμα τῷ συμποσίῳ Luc.*Symp.*13: c. acc. cogn., ἐ. διαύλους τινάς *walk* several times to and fro, Ach.Tat.1. 6. II. *walk about upon,* τὴν ὑπ' οὐρανόν (sc. γῆν) Lxx *Jb.*1.7, al.; *trample on,* *PHolm.*18.30: metaph., *insult,* τινί Plu.2.57a. **-πείρω**, *impale upon*:—Pass., ἐμπεριπαρεὶς ταῖς σαρίσσαις Str.17.1.8 (prob. f.l. for περιπ-). **-πίπτω**, *fall upon,* ἔθνει ἐ. νοῦσοι Hp.*Flat.*6 (s.v.l.). **-πλέω**, prob. f.l. for ἐκπεριπλέω in J.*BJ*3.10.9. **-ποιέω**, *produce in,* δυνάμεις τισί Ptol.*Tetr.*50. **-ρρήγνῡμι**, *break all round,* v.l. in Arist.*HA*557^{b}26. **-σπούδαστος**, ον, *zealously frequented,* of temples, interpol. in J.*Ap.*2.35. **-στέγω**, *encase,* Sor.1. 57. **-σχεσις**, εως, ἡ, Astrol., *hemming in* of a planet by two others, Vett.Val.5.15, Porph. *in Ptol.*188, *Cat.Cod.Astr.*8(3).114.23, Heph.Astr.1.15.

ἐμπερκάζω, = περκάζω, Hsch.; cf. **ἐμπερ(καίν)ονται**· ἐμποικίλλονται, Id.

ἐμπερον-ατρίς, ίδος, ἡ, = ἐμπερόνημα I, Hsch. **-άω**, *fasten with a clasp, buckle on,* in Med., θώρακα.. ἐμπερονᾶται Hermipp.47, J.*BJ* 7.2.2. II. Pass., of nails, *to be fixed in,* Ath.11.488b. **-ημα**, Dor. **-ᾱμα**, ατος, τό, *a garment fastened with a brooch* on the shoulder, Theoc.15.34. II. *clasp, brooch,* Agath.3.15.

ἐμπερπερεύομαι, = περπερεύομαι, Cic.*Att.*1.14.4, Arr.*Epict.*2.1.34.

ἔμπεσον, Ep. aor. 2 of ἐμπίπτω.

ἐμπετᾰλίς, ίδος, ἡ, *dish consisting of cheese wrapped in a leaf* (ἐν πετάλῳ), Hsch.

ἐμπετ-άννῡμι or -ύω, fut. -πετάσω (v. infr.), *to unfold and spread in* or *on,* X.*Cyr.*1.6.40, J.*BJ*3.7.10: metaph., σφιν ἐμπετάσει λάθαν *will spread* oblivion, *Hymn.Is.*22:—Pass., *to be spread,* ἐπί τινος Callix.1. II. in Pass., ἐ. ὕφεσι *to be hung about with* cloths, Socr. Rhod.1. **-ασμα**, ατος, τό, *curtain,* *Inscr.Perg.*236, J.*AJ*15.11.3.

ἔμπετες, Dor. for ἐνέπεσες, aor. 2 of ἐμπίπτω, Pi.*P.*8.81.

ἐμπέτομαι, *fly into,* aor. inf. ἐμπτῆναι, εἰς τὸ στόμα Arcesil.ap.D.L. 4.32.

ἔμπετρος, ον, (πέτρα) *growing on rocks*: τὸ ἔ. *sea-heath, Frankenia pulverulenta,* Dsc.4.179, Gal.11.875.

ἐμπευκής, ές, (πεύκη) *bitterish,* ὀπός Nic.*Al.*202.

ἐμπεφῡκότως, Adv. *clinging firmly,* gloss on ἀπρίξ, Sch.Theoc.15. 68, cf. Hsch. s. v. φῦ χειρί.

ἐμπεφυρμένως, Adv. *confusedly,* Tz.*Trag.Poes.*150.

ἔμπη, Dor. for πῇ, *AP*13.5 (Phal.).

ἐμπήγνῡμι, *fix* or *plant in,* c. dat., μεταφρένῳ ἐν δόρυ πῆξε Il.5.40; ἐνέπαξαν ἕλκος ἑᾷ καρδίᾳ Pi.*P.*2.91; ἐ. τι εἴς τι Hp.*Art.*72, Arist.*Pr.* 889^{b}1; ὀδόντα εἴς τινα *AP*5.265 (Paul. Sil.), cf. 11.374 (Maced.):—Pass., with pf. and plpf. Act., *to be fixed* or *stuck in, stick in,* λόγχη τις ἐμπέπηγέ μοι δι' ὀστέων Ar.*Ach.*1226; ἔν τί σοι παγήσεται Id.*V.*437: abs., Thphr.*HP*1.8.3: metaph., ἐμπέπηγα τῷ διακονεῖν Diph.43.25; ταῖς ἑαυτῶν περιουσίαις ἐμπηγνύμενοι Just.*Nov.*98 *Pr.* II. *congeal, freeze,* Thphr.*CP*5.12.2 (v.l. for ἐκ-):—Pass., *to be congealed,* ib.1. 22.7 (v.l. for ἐκ-); *freeze to death,* Arist.*HA*603^{a}27.

ἐμπηδ-άω, *jump upon,* αὐτῇ ἐχούσῃ ἐν γαστρί Hdt.3.32: metaph. of sense-impressions, Archig.ap.Orib.8.2.5. 2. ἐ. εἰς.. *leap* or *spring into,* ἐς τὴν ναῦν Hermipp.54, cf. Plb.12.8.4. 3. abs., *beat,* of the heart, Ph.1.67: aor. part. ἐμπηδήσας *eagerly, greedily,* Luc. *Hist.Conscr.*20. **-ησις**, εως, ἡ, *leaping in* or *upon,* Hp.*Epid.*2.1.9.

ἐμπηκτέον, *one must stick in,* *Gp.*18.2.2.

ἐμπήκτης, ου, ὁ, *one who sticks up judicial notices,* Arist.*Ath.*64.2, al.

ἔμπηλος, ον, *muddy,* *Gp.*2.5.7, *Hippiatr.*22.

ἐμπηνός· ἧλος, Hsch.

ἔμπηξις, εως, ἡ, *impaction,* Gal.2.738. II. *solidification,* Meno

*Iatr.*15.33. 2. in concrete sense, ἐ. ὑμενώδης, of the χόριον, Porph.*Gaur.*10.3.

ἔμπηρος, ον, *crippled, maimed*, Hdt.1.167,196, Hp.*Morb.*1.1, etc.

ἔμπης, Adv., Ep. for ἔμπας.

ἐμπήσσομαι, = ἐμπήγνυμαι, Apollod.*Poliorc.*142.1, Sch.Il.4.535, *EM*709.9.

ἐμπῐ-έζω, *press, squeeze*, in Pass., Hp.*Gland.*13, Plu.2.1005a. **-εσις**, εως, ἡ, *pressure*, of massage, Sor.1.102 (pl.). **-εσμα**, ατος, τό, *depressed cranial fracture*, Id.*Fract.*6, Heliod.ap.Orib.46.14.1, Paul.Aeg.6.90.

ἐμπικραίνομαι, Med. or Pass., *to be bitter against*, τινί Hdt.5.62, D.C.47.8: abs., Eus.Mynd.54; of disease, *become virulent*, J.*AJ* 17.6.5.

ἔμπικρος, ον, *rather bitter*, Dsc.1.4, 2.122.

ἐμπῑλέομαι, Pass., *to be compressed*, Pl.*Ti.*74e, D.S.2.52.

ἐμπίλια [πῑ], τά, (πῖλος) *felt shoes*, Charis.p.552 K.; *bandage for horses' legs*, Hsch. s.v. νακτά.

ἐμπίμελος [ῐ], ον, *of a fatty substance*, Dsc.2.61, Xenocr.63.

ἐμπίμπλημι, Ion. 2 sg. pres. ἐμπιπλεῖς Hp.*Morb.*2.14, part. -πιπλῶν ib.12; 3 sg. ἐμπιπλέει Hdt.7.39 (with vv. ll. -πιπλεῖ, -πιπλᾷ): 1 sg. impf. ἐνεπίμπλων D.C.68.31: fut. -πλήσω Pl.*Lg.*875c: aor. ἐνέπλησα, Ep. subj. ἐνιπλήσῃς Od.19.117: pf. ἐμπέπληκα (v. infr.):—*fill quite full*, ἐν ὧν ἔπλησαν τοῦ νεκροῦ τὴν κοιλίην Hdt.2.87; τὸ πεδίον, τὴν ὁδόν, X.*HG*7.1.20, 2.4.11. 2. c. gen., *fill full of* a thing, ἐμπίπληθι ῥέεθρα ὕδατος Il.21.311, etc.; δέπας ὕδατος Od.9.209; [ἵππον] ἀνδρῶν ἐμπλήσας 8.495; μὴ.. θυμὸν ἐνιπλήσῃς ὀδυνάων 19.117; ἐ. [τὰ θυλάκια] τῆς ψάμμου Hdt.3.105, cf. 4.72, 5.114; τοὺς κοφίνους.. ἐμπίμπλη (imper.) πτερῶν Ar.*Av.*1310; ἐ. ἵππων τὸν ἱππόδρομον X.*Eq.Mag.*3.10: metaph., τὴν ψυχὴν ἔρωτος Pl.*Phdr.*255d; τινὰ ἐλπίδων κενῶν Aeschin.1.171. 3. *fill* a hungry man *with food*, Od.17.503. b. metaph., ἐ. τινὰ μύθων E.*Hel.*769; τοῦ πολεμεῖν Isoc.9.63; ἐκκεκώφωκε τὰ ὦτα καὶ ἐμπέπληκε Λυσίδος Pl.*Ly.*204c; ἐρώτων.. ἐμπίμπλησιν ἡμᾶς Id.*Phd.*66c; ἐμπιμπλὰς ἁπάντων τὴν γνώμην X.*An.*1.7.8. 4. *satiate*, τὴν ἀναιδῆ γνώμην αὐτοῦ D.21.91; ἵμερον A.R.4.429; ἕως νυκτὸς ἀλλήλους Longus 2.38. 5. *fulfil, accomplish*, τὴν αὑτοῦ μοῖραν Pl.*Lg.*959c. II. Med. (with aor. Pass.), ἐμπίμπλαμαι E.*Ion* 925; ἐμπιμπλάμενος Cratin.142, Pherecr.80, Epicur.*Nat.*117 G.: impf. ἐνεπιμπλάμην X.*An.*7.7.46, Aeschin.3.230, etc.: later 3 pl. ἐνεπιμπλῶντο D.S.34/5.2.29:—*fill for oneself* or *what is one's own*, ἐμπλήσατο νηδύν Od.9.296; μένεος ἐμπλήσατο θυμόν he *filled his* heart *with* rage, Il.22.312; θαλέων ἐμπλησάμενος κῆρ ib.504; τὸ ἄγγος τοῦ ὕδατος ἐ. Hdt.5.12. 2. abs., *eat oneself full, eat one's fill*, ἐνιπλησθῆναι ἀνώγει Od.7.221, cf. Hdt.8.117, Ar.*V.*911, X.*Mem.*1.3.6, etc.: metaph., ἐπειδὴ τάχιστα ἐνέπλητο (ἐνεπέπληντο codd.) Lys.28.6. III. **Pass.**, aor. 1 ἐνεπλήσθην (v. infr.): aor. 2 ἐνεπλήμην Ar.*V.*911, 1304, prob. in Lys.28.6; opt. ἐμπλήμην (v. infr.): plpf. ἐνεπεπλήμην f.l. in Lys. l.c., late ἐμπέπληστο Max.Tyr.18.7; ἐνέπλησθεν δέ οἱ.. αἵματος ὀφθαλμοί Il.16.348; δακρύων τὰ ὄμματα X.*Cyr.*5.5.10; ἔμπληντο βροτῶν ἀγοραί Od.8.16; πόλις δ' ἔμπλητο ἀλέντων Il.21.607; ἐνέπλητο πολλῶν κἀγαθῶν Ar.*V.*1304; φακῆς ἐμπλήμενος ib.984, cf. *Ec.*56: metaph., υἷος ἐνιπλησθῆναι.. ὀφθαλμοῖσιν *to take my fill of* my son with my eyes, i.e. *to sate myself with* looking on him, Od.11.452; ὀργῆς καὶ μένους ἐμπλήμενος Ar.*V.*424; πλεονεξίας ἐμπίμπλασθαι Pl.*Criti.*121b. 2. c. dat., ἀμπελίνῳ καρπῷ ἐ. *to be filled with*.., Hdt.1.212; ἐμπιπλάμενοι πυριάτῃ Cratin.142; ἐμπίπλαται.. αἵματι ὁ βωμός Paus.3.16.10. 3. c. part., μισῶν οὔποτ' ἐμπλησθήσομαι γυναῖκας E.*Hipp.*664, cf. *Ion* 925; βάλλων.. οὐκ ἂν ἐμπλήμην Ar.*Ach.*236; οὐκ ἐνεπίμπλασο ὑπισχνούμενος X.*An.*7.7.46; ἔμπλησο λέγων speak thy *fill*, Ar.*V.*603.—The two last constructions are post-Homeric. (Freq. written -πίπλ-, but the evidence of the best codd. of Att. writers is in favour of -πίμπλ-.)

ἐμπίμπρημι (pres. not in Hom. who has impf. ἐνέπρηθον, v. ἐμπρήθω), 3 pl. impf. ἐνεπίμπρασαν Th.6.94; also (as if from **ἐμπιπράω**) inf. ἐμπιπρᾶν Plu.*Cor.*26; part. ἐμπιπρῶν Plb.1.53.4: impf. ἐνεπίμπρων X.*HG*6.5.22: fut. ἐνιπρήσω Il.15.702, ἐμπρήσω Ar.*Th.*749, 3 pl. -πρήσοντι *Tab.Heracl.*1.145: aor. 1 ἐνέπρησα Hom., etc.: aor. 1 Med. ἐνεπρησάμην *PTeb.*61(*b*).289 (ii B.C.), Q.S.5.485:—Pass., part. ἐμπιπράμενος Hdt.1.19: fut. ἐμπεπρήσομαι (v.l. ἐμπρήσομαι, as in Id.6.9), Paus.4.7.10; Ep. inf. ἐνιπρήσεσθαι Q.S.1.494: aor. ἐνεπρήσθην Hdt.5.102, 6.25, Th.4.29, etc.: pf. ἐμπέπρησμαι Hdt.8.144 (v.l. -πέπρημαι), Ph.1.391:—*kindle, set on fire*, πυρὶ νῆας Il.8.182, al.; τῷ Λημνίῳ.. πυρὶ ἔμπρησον S.*Ph.*801; τὸν [νηὸν] ἐνέπρησαν Hdt.1.19, cf. 5.101, al.: c. gen., πυρὸς αἰθομένοιο νῆας ἐνιπρήσωσι *burn* them by force of fire, Il.16.82; ἐμπιμπράναι οἰκίαν Ar.*Nu.*1484, cf. Pl.*R.*471c:—Pass., *to be set on fire*, Hdt.1.19, etc.; ῥίζαι -πεπρησμέναι Ph. l.c.; *to be inflamed*, Aret.*SA*2.10: metaph. of anger, Luc.*Cat.*12. (Freq. written ἐμπίπρ- in codd., but cf. ἐμπιμπράντων Phld.*Ir.*p.53 W.)

ἐμπῐνής, ές, *soiled, dirty*, Antig.ap.D.L.5.67. II. = ἐξηρτισμένος, *Gloss.*

ἐμπίνω [ῑ], fut. -πίομαι: pf. -πέπωκα:—*drink*, πολλὰ καταφαγών, πόλλ' ἐμπιών Epich.35.7, cf. E.*Cyc.*336, X.*Cyr.*7.1.1: c. gen., ἐ. τοῦ αἵματος *to drink of* the blood, Hdt.3.11, 4.64, cf. Ph.1.324. 2. abs., *drink one's fill*, f.l. in Thgn.1129, cf. Ar.*Pax* 1143, 1156; ἐμπεπωκότες drunken, Id.*Ec.*142.

ἐμπῑπάσκομαι, = ἐμπάομαι, *acquire*, χρήματα *SIG*56.22 (Argos, v B.C.).

ἐμπῑπίσκω, aor. ἐνέπῑσα Pi.*Fr.*111.1:—Pass., aor. 1 ἐνεπίσθην:—causal of ἐμπίνω, *give to drink*, Pi. l.c., Nic.*Al.*519:—Med., *fill oneself*, ἐμπίσασθαι ὕδατι, ὄξει, Id.*Th.*573, *Al.*320:—Pass., of liquor, *to be drunk*, Νύμφαις ἐμπισθέν Id.*Th.*624.

ἐμπιπράσκω, *sell in*, Poll.7.9 (Pass.), Hsch. (Pass.).

ἐμπίπτω, fut. -πεσοῦμαι: aor. ἐνέπεσον, Ep. ἔμπεσον (v. infr.): lyr. aor. ἔμπετες Pi.*P.*8.81:—*fall in* or *on*, c. dat., τρύφος ἔμπεσε πόντῳ Od.4.508; ὁ δ' ὕπτιος ἔμπεσε πέτρῃ Il.4.108; ἐν δ' ἔπεσ' ὠκεανῷ, of the Sun, 8.485; πῦρ ἔμπεσε νηυσίν fire *fell upon* them, 16.113; αὐχένι.. ἔμπεσεν ἰός 15.451, cf. 624; with ἐν, ὡς δ' ὅτε πῦρ.. ἐν ἀξύλῳ ἐμπέσῃ ὕλῃ 11.155; κεραυνοὶ αὐτοῖσι ἐνέπιπτον Hdt.8.37; ἐμπέσοι γέ σοι (sc. ὁ πύργος) Ar.*Pl.*180, etc.: abs., ῥύμῃ ἐ. Th.2.76, cf. Hdt.1.34: c. gen., ὠκεανοῖο Arat.635. b. Geom., *meet*, of a line *meeting* another, Euc.1 *Post.*5, etc.; *to be placed*, ἐὰν εἰς τὸν κύκλον εὐθεῖα ἐμπέσῃ Archim.*Sph.Cyl.*1.9; ἡ ἐμπεσοῦσα ibid. c. of a dislocated limb, *fall into place*, Hp.*Art.*8. 2. *fall upon, attack*, ἐν δ' ἔπεσον προμάχοις Od.24.526, cf. Il.16.81; στρατῷ E.*Rh.*127; τοῖς πολεμίοις X.*Eq.Mag.*8.25, etc.; ἐμπεσόντες *having fallen on* them, Hdt.3.146, cf. 7.16.α': metaph., *insult*, ἄλλοισι δ' ἐμπίπτων γελᾷ Pi.*I.*1.68; so, 3. of evils, diseases, etc., *fall on* one, *attack*, κακὸν ἔμπεσε οἴκῳ Od.2.45; λὺγξ τοῖς πλέοσιν ἐνέπιπτε κενή Th.2.49; νόσημα ἐμπέπτωκεν εἰς τὴν Ἑλλάδα D.19.259; πρὶν ἐμπεσεῖν σπαραγμόν S.*Tr.*1253; ὕπνος ἐ. Pl.*Ti.*45e: of passions, of frames of mind, χόλος, δέος ἔμπεσε θυμῷ, Il.9.436, 17.625; ἔρως μή τις ἐμπίπτῃ στρατῷ A.*Ag.*341; Ἔρως, ὃς ἐν κτήμασι πίπτεις S.*Ant.*782 (lyr.); ἐμοὶ.. οἶκτος Id.*Ph.*965; τοῖς Ἀθηναίοις ἐνέπεσέ τι γέλωτος Th.4.28; μὴ λύσσα τις ἡμῖν ἐμπεπτώκοι X.*An.*5.7.26; ἔλεος ἐμπέπτωκέ τίς μοι Philippid.9.1; ἐ. εἰς.., Hdt.7.43, E.*IA*443, Th.2.48 codd., Lys.1.18, etc.: rarely c. acc., οὐδεὶς ποτ' αὐτοὺς.. ἂν ἐμπέσοι ζῆλος S.*OC*942; ἐμπέπτωκ' ἔρως ..Ἑλλάδα E.*IA*808. b. of words, καί μοι ἔπος ἔμπεσε θυμῷ *came into* my mind, Od.12.266; λόγος ἐμπέπτωκεν ἀρτίως ἐμοὶ *came to* my ears, S.*OC*1150; κἂν περὶ ἀνδρῶν γ' ἐμπέσῃ λόγος τις a report *arose*, Ar.*Lys.*858, cf. Pl.*R.*354b, *Lg.*799d, Thphr.*Char.*2.2; so τόποι ἐμπίπτοντες *available, suitable* topics, Hermog.*Prog.*7, etc., cf. Ph.1.179. 4. *light* or *fall upon*, πρὶν ἁλίῳ γυῖον ἐμπεσεῖν before his body *was exposed* to the sun, Pi.*N.*7.73; [θηρία] ἐμπίπτοντα ταῖς ὄψεσι Hdn.3.9.5; also εἰς τὴν ὄψιν, εἰς τὴν αἴσθησιν, Pl.*Ti.*67d, *R.*524d. b. *fall into*, ἐ. ἐν ἀπορίᾳ Id.*Euthd.*293a; ἐπὶ συμφορὴν Hdt.7.88; more freq. ἐ. εἰς.., ἐ. εἰς ἄτας S.*El.*216 (lyr.); εἰς βάρβαρα φάσγανα E.*Hel.*864; εἰς ἐνέδραν X.*Cyr.*8.5.14; εἰς ἔρωτα Antiph.235.3; εἰς νόσον Antipho 1.20; εἰς ὑποψίας Id.2.2.3; εἰς φαῦλον σκέμμα Pl.*R.*435c; εἴς τινα βυθὸν φλυαρίας Id.*Prm.*130d; εἰς πράγματα D.18.292; ἐ. εἰς τὰ πεπραγμένα, in speaking, *come upon* the exploits, ib.211; εἰς λόγους ib.42, cf. 59. 5. τῷ ἀκοντίῳ ἐ. τῷ ὤμῳ *throw oneself on* the javelin with one's shoulder, i.e. to give all one's force to the throw, Hp.*Aër.*20. 6. *break in, burst in*, στέγῃ S.*OT*1262; πύλαις E.*Ph.*1146; εἰς τὴν θύραν κρηδὸν Ar.*Lys.*309; *intrude*, εἰς τὸ ἀρχεῖον Arist.*Pol.*1270^{b}9: abs., A.*Ag.*1350; ἐμπεσών *violently, rashly*, Hdt.3.81. 7. εἴς τι *fall within* the province of, Pl.*Tht.*205d; εἰς τὰς εἰρημένας αἰτίας Arist.*Metaph.*986^{a}15, cf. *Rh.*1401^{b}29, *Ph.*196^{b}9; εἰς ἄλλο πρόβλημα Id.*Pol.*1268^{b}25. b. of income, εἰς τὸν λόγον τινὸς ἐ. *PLille* 16.5 (iii B.C.), cf. *POxy.*494.21 (ii A.D.). c. of suits, *come before*, εἰς δικαστῶν πλῆθος Arist.*Pol.*1300^{b}35, cf. Plu.*Sol.*18. 8. ἐ. εἰς δεσμωτήριον *to be thrown* into prison, Din.2.9, cf. D.25.60 (abs., *get into prison*, Luc.*Tox.*28); εἰς ζήτρειον Eup.19 D.; so ἐ. εἰς τὸν Τάρταρον Pl.*Phd.*114a: Com., εἰς τὸν οὐρανόν *Com.Adesp.*9 D. 9. of circumstances, *happen, occur*, Paus.7.8.4. 10. *desert*, πρός τινα Lxx 4*Ki.*25.11.

ἐμπίς, ίδος, ἡ, *mosquito, gnat*, Ar.*Nu.*157; ἐμπίδες ὀξύστομοι Id.*Av.*245, cf. Arist.*HA*490^{a}21, Porph.*Abst.*3.20; the gnat *Chironomus*, Arist.*HA*551^{b}27; prob. *may-fly*, ib.601^{a}4. 2. *larva of the* οἶστρος, ib.487^{b}5 (v.l.).

ἐμπῖσαι, ἐμπισθῆναι, v. ἐμπιπίσκω.

ἐμπίσιον· καὶ τὸ βραχὺ καὶ τὸ δαψιλῶς πιεῖν, Hsch. (Fort. **ἐμπιεῖν**.)

ἐμπιστ-ευσις, εως, ἡ, *trusteeship*, *Cat.Cod.Astr.*2.161. **-εύω**, *entrust*, τινί τι D.S.1.67, Plu.*Phoc.*32; Ἔρως ταῖς βολαῖς τῶν ὀμμάτων ἐ. τὴν τόξευσιν Lib.*Descr.*30.8:—Pass., τινί *PStrassb.*5.10; but also, *to be entrusted with*, τι Luc.*Demon.*51, *Gp.*2.44.1; ὁ ἐγκέφαλος.. ἀσφάλειαν ἐμπεπιστευμένος Hp.*Ep.*23. II. *trust in, give credence to*, τινί Lxx *De.*1.32, al., Nic.Dam.*Fr.*130.19 J.; ἔν τινι Lxx 2*Ch.*20.20; ἐπί τινι ib.3*Ma.*2.7.

ἐμπίτνω, poet. for ἐμπίπτω, *fall upon*, εἰς ὅμιλον B.9.24; τινί A.*Ag.*1468 (lyr.), *Supp.*120 (lyr.), cf. S.*Aj.*58.

ἐμπῑτῠάζομαι, *to be curdled*, of milk, Paul.Aeg.5.57.

ἐμπλάζω (A), *drive about in*:—hence in Pass., *wander about in* or *among*, ὕλῃ ἐνιπλαγχθείς Orph.*A.*645; πολλὴν ἀταξίαν τὰ σκευοφόρα τοῖς μαχομένοις -όμενα παρεῖχε Plu.*Oth.*12. 2. metaph., τεχνῖται -ονται μᾶλλον χρῆσθαι συνετωτέροις κριταῖς Phld.*Rh.*1.376 S. II. intr., *wander in*, ἀγυιαῖς Nic.*Al.*189.

ἐμπλάζω (B), poet. for ἐμπελάζω, Nic.*Th.*779.

ἐμπλᾰνάομαι, *wander in*, πολλοῖς τόποις Hld.2.29: abs., αἵματος περίττωμα ἐ. Plu.2.495e: metaph., δύναμις -πλανωμένη *erratic*, ib.336f.

ἔμ-πλασμα, ατος, τό, *plaster*, Phld.*Po.*2.66. **-πλάσσω**, Att. -ττω, *plaster up*, τὸν πατέρα ἐν σμύρνῃ ἐ. Hdt.2.73; ἀσφάλτῳ ἐμπλασθείς Str.16.1.15. 2. *stuff in*, κηρὸν εἴς τι Arist.*Pr.*919^{b}9. 3. *stop up*, τὰ φλέβια, Thphr.*Sens.*66; *clog* the teeth of a saw, Id.*HP*5.6.3:—Pass., -πλασσομένων τῶν πόρων Id.*Sens.*14. 4. *form in*, κηρία ἔν τινι D.C.78.25. 5. *cause to adhere*, τῇ γαστρὶ χυμόν Gal.6.428:—Pass., Id.15.204. b. abs., *to be viscous*, Id.6.495. II. Pass., *have an impression left* or *made*, Hp.*Mul.*2.116, al. **-πλαστέον**, f.l. for ἐμπαστέον, Archig.ap.Aët.9.28. **-πλαστικός**, ή, όν, *causing to adhere*, δύναμις Dsc.1.102. **-πλαστός**, ή, όν, *daubed on* or *over*:

ἔμπλαστον (with or without φάρμακον), τό, *plaster, salve*, Hp.*Hum.* 5:—also **ἔμπλαστος**, ἡ, Alex.Aphr. *de An.*25.1. **-πλάστριον**, τό, Dim. of ἔμπλαστρος, Paul.Aeg.4.48, 6.16. **-πλαστροποιΐα**, ἡ, *making of plasters*, Gal.13.898. **-πλαστρος**, ἡ, *salve* or *plaster*, Dsc.1.32; said to be later form of ἔμπλαστος, Gal.13.372; also **ἔμπλαστρον**, τό, Hierocl.*Facet.*221, *PSI*3.297 (v A.D.).

ἐμπλαστρώδης, ες, *like a plaster*, Dsc.*Eup.*1.196, Gal.12.512, 13.396; **-τώδης**, Antyll.ap.Orib.*Syn.*2.60.36.

ἐμπλᾰτ(ε)ιάσασα· ἐν πλατείαις τύπτουσα ταῖς χερσὶν ἢ τρυφερ(ευ)ομένη, Hsch.

ἐμπλᾰτής, ές, *square*, πούς Anon. *in Tht.*30.1.

ἐμπλατία, Arc. **ἰμπ-**, ἡ, a kind of *cake*, *IG*5(2).4 (iv B.C.).

ἐμπλᾰτύνω, *widen* or *extend*, τὰ ὅρια LXX *Ex.*23.18: metaph., δόμα ἀνθρώπου ἐ. αὐτόν ib.*Pr.*18.16:—Pass., λόγοις ἐμπλατύνεσθαι *to expatiate*, Str.8.7.3.

ἔμπλᾰτυς, υ, in Comp., *broader, more general*, εἴδη Plot.5.3.9.

ἐμπλέγ-δην, Adv. *by interlocking*: hence in Math. of proportion, *alternando*, Nicom.*Ar.*2.29. **-μα**, ατος, τό, *plait*: ἐ. γυναικεῖα Artem.4.83.

ἔμπλειος, v. ἔμπλεος.

ἐμπλέκ-της, ου, ὁ, *one who plaits hair*, *Gloss.*:—fem. **-πλέκτρια**, ib., *EM*528.5. **-τος**, ον, *inwoven*: ἔμπλεκτον, τό, *ashlar filled up with rubble*, Vitr.2.8.7. **-ω**, Ep. **ἐνιπλέκω**, pf. ἐμπέπλεχα Hp.*Oss.*17, ἐμπέπλεκα Call.*Iamb.*1.352, v.l. in Hp. l.c.: fut. Pass. ἐμπλᾰκήσομαι LXX *Pr.*28.18:—*plait* or *weave in, entwine*, χεῖρα ἐ. *entwine* one's hand *in* another's clothes, so as to hold him, E.*Or.*262; εἰς ἀρκυστάταν μηχανὰν ἐμπλέκειν παῖδα ib.1421 (lyr.); τῇ καλλίστῃ τέχνῃ τοὔνομα ἐ. *connect* the name *with*.., Pl.*Phdr.*244c; ποιηταὶ τοιαῦτα ἐμπλέκοντες καὶ συγκυκῶντες Id.*Lg.*669d; ἐ. τὴν ἡδονὴν εἰς τὴν εὐδαιμονίαν Arist.*EN*1153^{b}15; ποίῃ ἐνιπλέξω σε (sc. ἀοιδῇ); Call.*Del.*29; ἐ. τινὰ εἰς φιλίαν τινός Plb.27.7.11:—Pass., *to be entangled in* a thing, πλεκταῖσιν αἰώραισιν ἐμπεπλεγμένην S.*OT*1264; ἡνίαισιν ἐμπλακείς E.*Hipp.*1236; ἐν δεσμοῖσιν ἐμπεπλεγμένη Ar.*Th.*1032; εἰς δίκτυον ἄτης ἐμπλεχθήσεσθε A.*Pr.*1079: metaph., *to be involved*, ἐν πόνοις, ἐν κακοῖς ἐμπλακῆναι, Pl.*Lg.*814e, Isoc.8.112; εἰς ἀσχολίας βαθυτέρας τῶν ἐγκυκλίων Epicur.*Ep.*1 p.35 U.; εἰς τὰ κατὰ τὴν Σικελίαν Plb.1.17.3; *form a connexion with*, ἔθνει Id.24.6.1; γυναικὶ ἐμπλακείς D.S.19.2; εἴς τινα Vett.Val.118.4; of troops, *to be incorporated with* hoplites, Ascl.*Tact.*6.1; but also ἐμπλεκέντες τινί *having had a scuffle with*.., *PTeb.*39.17 (ii B.C.). 2. metaph., *weave by subtle art*, ἐ. αἰνίγματα A.*Pr.*610; ἐ. πλοκάς E.*IA*936.

ἔμπλεξις, εως, ἡ, *interweaving, entwining*, στήμονος Pl.*Plt.*282e.

ἐμπλεονάζω, *to be profuse in*, αἵματι Heraclit.*Ep.*7.6; ταῖς πυρίαις Sor.1.77.

ἔμπλεος, α, ον, Att. **-πλεως**, ων, Ep. **ἔμπλειος**, **ἐνίπλειος**, η, ον, Od. (v. infr.); later **ἐνίπλεος** A.R.3.119, Orph.*L.*192: heterocl. acc. ἔμπλεα (fem.) Nic.*Al.*164:—*quite full of* a thing, γαστέρα.. ἐμπλείην κνίσης τε καὶ αἵματος Od.18.118; φαρέτρην ἰῶν ἐμπλείην 22.3; σκύφος.. οἴνου ἐνίπλειον 14.113; δῶμα.. ἐνίπλειον βιότοιο 19.580; κύων.. ἐνίπλειος κυνοραιστέων 17.300; λέβητες κρεῶν.. ἔμπλεοι Hdt.1.59, cf. 2.62, Hp.*Epid.*6.4.8; γῆς ἢ κόπρου ἔμπλεων Pl.*Tht.*194e. 2. of persons, δυσκολίας ἔ. Id.*R.*411c; πάσης πονηρίας Plb.27.15.6, etc. 3. *in full measure, complete*, ἔμπλεα καὶ ὁλόκληρα καὶ τέλεα προσάγοντες Ph.1.185; f.l. for ἔμπεδος in Orph.*Fr.*261.

ἐμπλεύρια, τά, *pleural cavities*, *Hippiatr.*26.

ἐμπλευρόομαι, *dash against* one's *ribs, charge* him, S.*Fr.*53.

ἔμπλευρος, ον, *with large sides*, ἀθλητής Ph.1.70 (v.l. εὔπ-); τράγοι *Gp.*18.9.6.

ἐμπλέω, *sail in*, [πλοίοις] Hdt.7.184: abs., οἱ ἐμπλέοντες Th.3.77, X.*Oec.*8.8. 2. in Ion. form **-πλώω**, *float in* or *upon*, Nic.*Al.*426, Opp.*H.*1.260 (ἐνιπ-), Aret.*SD*1.9, 2.1: part. ἐμπλέων *loose*, πῶρος Heliod.ap.Orib.45.6.8. 3. Pass., of the sea, πελάγη ναυσὶν ἐμπλεόμενα Ph.1.28, cf. 2.514.

ἐμπλήγ-δην, Adv., (ἐμπλήσσω) *madly, rashly* (or *mightily*, or *capriciously*), Od.20.132. **-ής**, ές, = ἔμπληκτος, *mad, rash*, ἀφροσύνη Nic.*Al.*159.

ἐμ-πλήδην, Adv. *fully, as a whole*, Nic.*Al.*129. **-πληθής**, ές, = ἔμπλεος, Id.*Th.*948. **-πλήθομαι**, Ep. **ἐνιπλ-**, *to be filled*, Q.S.2.472. **-πληθύνομαι**, *to be filled with*, ἀλογιστίας LXX 3*Ma.*5.42.

ἐμπληκτᾰδοῦς, ὁ, = ἔμπληκτος, coined by Eust.971.43.

ἐμπληκτικός, ή, όν, (ἐμπλήσσω) *stupid*, θέατρα Plu.2.748d (sed leg. ἐμπλήκτων):—in Id.*Sull.*34 f.l. for ἐμπληκτότατον. Adv. **-κῶς** Apollon.*Lex.* s.v. ἐμπλήγδην.

ἔμπληκτος, ον, (ἐμπλήσσω) *stunned, amazed*, ὑπὸ τῶν κυνῶν γενέσθαι X.*Cyn.*5.9: hence, *stupid, senseless*, ἔ. καὶ μανικός Plu.*Rom.*28, Agath.3.24, etc.; ἔμπληκτα ληρεῖν Gal.8.693. 2. in Att., *impulsive*: hence, *unstable, capricious*, S.*Aj.*1358, Arist.*EE*1240^{b}17; αἱ τύχαι, ἔ. ὡς ἄνθρωπος, ἄλλοτ' ἄλλοσε πηδῶσι E.*Tr.*1205; [ἡ φιλοσοφία] τῶν ἑτέρων παιδικῶν πολὺ ἧττον ἔ. Pl.*Grg.*482a; ἐ. τε καὶ ἀσταθμήτους Id.*Ly.*214d; ἔ. ταῖς ἐπιθυμίαις Plu.*Dio* 18. II. Adv. **-τως** *rashly, madly*, Isoc.7.30, etc.; τὸ ἐ. ὀξὺ *frantic* vehemence, Th.3.82; *foolishly*, Gal.1.535.

ἐμπλημμῠρέω, *welter in*, πηγαῖς αἵματος Philostr.*Im.*1.29; ἐμπλημμυροῦντος αὐτοῖς (sc. τοῖς νηπίοις) τοῦ γάλακτος ib.2.3.

ἔμπλην (A), Adv. *near, next, close by*, c. gen., Βοιωτῶν ἔ. Il.2.526; before its case, Lyc.1029: abs., Hes.*Sc.*372 (cf. πλη-σίος).

ἔμπλην (B), Adv. strengtnd. for πλήν, *besides, except*, c. gen., Archil.111, Call.*Del.*73, Nic.*Th.*322.

ἔμπληντο, Ep. 3 pl. aor. 2 Pass. of ἐμπίμπλημι.

ἐμπληξία, ἡ, *amazement*: hence, *stupidity*, Aeschin.3.214, Aristid.1.413, 427 J., Gal.8.690; ἐ. ἡ ἄλογος φιλανθρωπία App.*Sam.*4.4. 2. πολιτείας ἐ. *capriciousness* of policy, Aeschin.2.164. 3. *frantic energy*, Plu.2.56c.

ἔμπληξις, εως, ἡ, = foreg., Ael.*VH*2.19.

ἐμπλήρ-ωμα, ατος, τό, *space filled up*, dub. l. in Gal.18(1).376. **-ωσις**, εως, ἡ, *quenching*, δίψους Herod.Med.ap.Orib.5.30.25.

ἔμπλησις, εως, ἡ, f.l. for ἔκ-, Epict.*Gnom.*17.

ἐμπλήσσω, Att. **-ττω**, in Hom. **ἐνιπλ-**: I. intr., *strike against, fall upon* or *into*, c. dat., ὡς ὅτ' ἂν ἢ κίχλαι.. ἠὲ πέλειαι ἕρκει ἐνιπλήξωσι Od.22.469; τάφρῳ Il.12.72; νηῒ ἐ. *fall upon* it, of a storm, Arat.423: abs., *dash*, A.R.1.1203, 2.602. II. c. acc. pers., *attack*, Id.3.1297. 2. ἐ. φόβον τινί *strike* terror *into*.., Opp.*H.*3.480. 3. pf. part. Pass. ἐμπεπληγμένος, = ἄνεως, Gal.*Lex.Hipp.* s.h.v.; cf. ἔμπληκτος.

ἐμπληστέος, α, ον, (ἐμπίμπλημι) *to be filled with*, ὄγκου Pl.*R.*373b.

ἔμπληντο, v. ἐμπίμπλημι.

ἐμ-πλοκή, ἡ, *braiding*, κόμης Str.17.3.7, cf. Nic.Dam.p.2 D., 1*Ep.Pet.*3.3. 2. *scuffle*, *PRyl.*124.28 (i A.D.), 150.12 (i A.D.). II. *interweaving*, Epicur.*Nat.*1420 (dub.); *entanglement*, Plu.2.916d (pl.); of the *matted* roots of trees, Ph.Byz.*Mir.*1.5 (pl.); τόποις ἐμπλοκὰς ἔχειν, of districts, *to run into one another*, Str.13.4.12. III. Math., κατ' ἐμπλοκήν, = ἐμπλέγδην, Iamb. *in Nic.*p.124 P., al. **-πλόκια**, τά, festival at Athens, Hsch. **-πλόκιον**, τό, *a fashion of plaiting women's hair*, Macho ap.Ath.13.579d. 2. *hair-clasp*, *BGU*1300.24 (iii/ii B.C.), LXX *Ex.*35.22, *Nu.*31.50.

ἐμπλούμος, ον, (Lat. *pluma*) = *plumatus, embroidered*, *PMasp.*6 ii 88 (vi A.D.), etc.

ἐμπνείω, poet. for ἐμπνέω.

ἐμπνευμᾰτοποιέομαι, *suffer from flatulence*, Alex.Aphr.*Pr.*2.43. II. *become gaseous*, ib.76.

ἐμπνευμᾰτ-όω, *inflate*, in Pass., Thphr.*Ign.*17, Anon.Lond.27.13, Sor.2.31, etc.; *to be filled by the wind*, of sails, Luc.*Lex.*15. II. *cause flatulence*, Diph.Siph.ap.Ath.2.54d, Dsc.2.173:—Pass., *suffer from flatulence*, Gal.16.833. III. Pass., *to be asthmatic*, Id.7.959. IV. *fill with the breath of life*, σῶμα *PMag.Leid.W.*7.15; ἐ. τινὰ θείου πνεύματος *PMag.Par.*1.966. V. intr., *to be inspired, show genius*, Apollon.Cit.3. **-ωσις**, εως, ἡ, *blowing up, inflation*, μήτρας *Placit.*5.6.1, cf. Sor.2.31, Ath.2.53c. 2. Medic., *flatulence*, Dsc.2.58 (pl.), Gal.*UP*4.9. **-ωτικός**, ή, όν, *causing flatulence*, Dsc.5.6.

ἔμ-πνευσις, εως, ἡ, *on-breathing*, LXX *Ps.*17(18).16. **-πνευστικὰ** ὄργανα *wind*-instruments, Luc.Tarrh.ap.Sch.D.T.p.111 H. **-πνευστός**, ή, όν, *blown into*: ἐ. ὄργανα *wind*-instruments, Aristocl.ap.Ath.4.174c, Ps.-Plu.*Vit.Hom.*148, Nicom.*Harm.*2; τὰ ἐ. alone, Theo Sm.p.57 H., Iamb. *in Nic.*p.122 P. II. = ἄφρων, Hsch.

ἐμπνέω, poet. **-πνείω**, fut. **-πνεύσομαι** E.*Andr.*555; later **-πνεύσω** Aen.Gaz.*Ep.*11:—*blow* or *breathe upon*, c. dat., πόντῳ Hes.*Op.*508; ἐμπνείοντε μεταφρένῳ, of horses so close behind as *to breathe upon* one's back, Il.17.502; of a lover, Hsch.; κατ' οὖρον, ὥσπερ ἱστίοις, ἐμπνεύσομαι τῇδε E. l.c.; ἄνεμος ἐμπνεύσας δορί Id.*Cyc.*19; [αὐλοῖς] ἐμπνεῖν *breathe into, play* the flute, *AP*9.266 (Antip.): c. acc. cogn., χείλεσι μοῦσαν ἐ., of Pan, *APl.*4.226 (Alc.):—Pass., ἐμπνεόμενα ὄργανα Poll.4.67; πνεῦμα -πνεόμενον τῷ αὐλῷ S.E.*P.*1.54. 2. abs., *breathe in, inhale*, Hp.*Flat.*4; but usu., b. *breathe, live, be alive*, A.*Ag.*671, Ar.*Th.*926, Pl.*Ap.*29d, etc.; τὰ ἐμπνέοντα, = ἔμψυχα, Call.*Iamb.*1.127; ἐ. τᾷ τέχνᾳ *AP*9.777 (Phil.); of one expiring, βλέποντα κἀμπνέοντ' ἔτι S.*Ph.*883; σμικρὸν ἐμπνέουσ' ἔτι E.*Alc.*205; βραχὺν δὴ βίοτον ἐμπνέων ἔτι Id.*Hipp.*1246. 3. c. gen., *breathe of, be laden with*, Ἀραβίης ὀδμῆς Perict.ap.Stob.4.28.19; ἐ. ἀπειλῆς καὶ φόνου *Act.Ap.*9.1. II. trans., *blow into*, ἄνεμος μέσον ἱστίον ἐ. *swell* the sail, *h.Bacch.*33, cf. Pi.*I.*2.40. 2. *breathe into, infuse into*, μένος, θάρσος τινί, Il.20.110, Od.9.381, al.; [Μοῦσαι] ἐνέπνευσαν δέ μοι αὐδήν Hes.*Th.*31; πατρὶ.. πατρὸς ἐνέπνευσεν μένος Pi.*O.*8.70: also c. inf. pro acc., φᾶρος ἐνέπνευσε φρεσὶν ὑφαίνειν *breathed into* my mind (i.e. *inspired* me *with the thought*) to weave it, Od.19.138:—Pass., *to be inspired*, ὑπὸ θεοῦ Longin.16.2; εἰς μαντικήν Plu.2.421b. **-πνοή**, ἡ, *force* of wind, Str.4.1.7. **-πνοια**, ἡ, *inbreathing, inhalation*, Luc.*Hes.*9. 2. *breath of life*, *Sammelb.*4127.16. **-πνοίησις**, εως, ἡ, *inspiration*, θεόμοιρος Ecphant.ap.Stob.4.6.22. **-πνοος**, ον, contr. **-πνους**, ουν, (πνοή) *with the breath in one, alive*, οὐκ ἀπέθανε, ἀλλ' ἦν ἔμπνοος Hdt.7.181; ἔτ' ἔμπνους E.*Ph.*1442; ἔμπνους ἔτι ἀρθείς Antipho 2.1.9; ἔτι ἔμπνουν ὄντα Th.1.134; ἔ. ἐγένετο *revived*, Pl.*Lg.*944a; μορφᾶς τύπος ἔμπνου, of a statue, *Epigr.Gr.*860.3; of pictures, τὸ ἔ. Philostr.*VA*2.20; also ἔ. νεκρός, of old age, Secund.*Sent.*12; θάλαττα πλωτὴ καὶ οἷον ἔ., of a sea which is *not a dead* calm, Philostr.*Im.*2.17. II. ἔ. μοῦσα, of a flute, Sopat.10. 2. *blown upon*, κόμη ὑπ. ἀνέμου ἔ. Philostr.*Im.*1.23: metaph., *inspired*, σεμνολογία ἔ., ὥσπερ ἐκ τρίποδος Id.*VS*1.25.10.

ἔμπνῡτο, read by Aristarch.Il.22.475, Od.5.458, al. for ἄμπνυτο; also ἐμπνύνθη for ἀμ- Il.5.697.

ἐμποδ-εία, ἡ, *impediment, hindrance*, Epicur.*Nat.*11.6 (pl.). **-έω**, = -ίζω, dub. in A.D.*Adv.*172.2, 185.16 codd. (leg. -ποδών). **-ιζομένως**, Adv. pres. part. Pass., *as if fettered*, Pl.*Cra.*415c. **-ίζω**, Att. fut. -ιῶ Id.*Ly.*210b, later -ίσω *Gp.*2.49.1:—Med. (v. infr. II.2):—Pass., fut. -ποδισθήσομαι Porph.*Abst.*1.17, Gal.ap.Orib.7.23.28, or (in med. form) -ίσομαι Antip.*Stoic.*3.256: pf. -πεπόδισμαι (v. infr.): (ἐν, πούς):—*put the feet in bonds*: hence, *put in bonds, fetter*, τοὺς μάντιας Hdt.4.69:—Pass., ἐμπεποδισμένος τοὺς πόδας ib.60; [ὀλιγοδρᾰνίᾳ] ἐμπεπ. A.Pr.550 (lyr.). II. generally, *hinder, thwart*, τὸ θεῖον ἐνεπόδιζέ με Ar.Av.965, cf. Lys.359, X.Cyr.2.3.10; τοὺς τῆς πόλεως καιροὺς Aeschin.3.223; ἐ. τοῦ ἰέναι *to hinder from*.., Pl.Cra.419c; πρός τι *in* a thing, Isoc.Ep.4.11, Arist.Pol.1341^{a}6, al., Ph.1.466:—Pass., χαὶ σοφαὶ γνῶμαι.. ἐμποδίζονται θαμά S.Ph.432; ἐμποδίζοιτο ἂν μὴ πράττειν *would be hindered from* doing, Pl.Smp.183a; τῆς εἰς τοὔμπροσθε πορείας D.S.14.28. 2. c. dat. rei, *to be a hindrance to, interfere with*, πολλαῖς ἐνεργείαις Arist.EN1100^{b}29; ἀλλήλαις Id.Pol.1299^{b}8; ταῖς χορηγίαις Plb.5.111.4: c. dat. pers., τοῖς γεωργοῖς Gp.2.49.1; τοῖς εἰς ἀρετὴν ἀφικνουμένοις Porph.Ep.Aneb.26: rarely c. acc. rei, ἐ. τὸ κοινὸν ἔργον Arist.Top.161^{a}37:—so in Med., ἐμποδίζεται δόσιν Philem.164. 3. abs., *to be a check* or *hindrance*, Arist.Pol.1288^{b}24. III. dub. in κέχηνεν ὥσπερ ἐμποδίζων ἰσχάδας Ar.Eq.755; prob. *playing bob-fig*, i.e. catching figs dangled by the stalk (πούς); Sch. and Lexx. also expl. as *stringing, chewing*, or *trampling figs*. -ιος, ον, *at one's feet*, Pl.Tht.201a; *coming in the way, meeting*, Eleg.ap.Plu.Rom.21. 2. commonly, *in the way, presenting an obstacle, impeding*, c. dat. pers. et rei, ἡ Βαβυλὼν οἱ ἦν ἐ. Hdt.1.153, cf. 2.158, 5.90; ἐ. κώλυμα E.Ion862 (lyr.); εἰ τοῦτ' ἐ. σοι Ar.Lys.531, etc.; ἐ. ταῖς ἐνεργείαις Arist.EN1175^{b}2; ἐ. τινὶ πρός τι Id.Mu.399^{b}12. 3. c. gen. rei, εἰρήνης Th.1.139; ἐ. γίγνεσθαι τοῦ μὴ ἀσκεῖν Pl.Lg.832b: c. inf., μὴ.. ἐ. γένηται θέσθαι τι Th.1.31. 4. ὅπῃ ταύτῃ ἀρετῇ ἀσκεῖται πάντῃ ἐ. Pl.R.407c. 5. ἐ. πρός τι Arist.EN1170^{b}27, Pol.1311^{a}18, Plb.4.81.4, Hierocl.in CA11p.441M. -ισις, εως, ἡ, = sq., IG3.49.14 (Epist. Plotinae). -ισμα, ατος, τό, *impediment, hindrance*, Pl.Plt.295b, D.3.4. -ισμός, ὁ, *hindering, impeding*, ταῖς βουλήσεσι Arist.Rh.1378^{b}18; τῶν συμπερασμάτων Id.Top.161^{a}15; ἡδονῶν Secund.Sent.10. -ιστής, οῦ, ὁ, *hinderer*, J.AJ17.10.3. -ιστικός, ή, όν, *trammelling*, Arist.EN1153^{b}2, Ph.215^{b}11, Plb.5.16.6, Phld.D.3.9, Lxx4Ma.1.4, M.Ant.8.41. -όομαι, = ἐμπεδόομαι, Hsch. -ος, ον, = ἐμπόδιος, dub. in Ascl.Tact.2.1.

ἐμποδοστᾰτ-έω, *to be in the way*, Epicur.Ep.1p.9U., PTeb.24.54 (ii B.C.), Ph.1.186:—also **ἐμποδιοστατέω**, v.l. LxxJd.11.35. -ης, ου, ὁ, (στῆναι) *in the way*, ib.1Ch.2.7, Suid.

ἐμποδών, Adv. perh. formed by anal. to ἐκποδών:—*before the feet, in the way, in one's path*, κτείνειν πάντα τὸν ἐ. γενόμενον every one that came *in the way*, Hdt.1.80; πᾶν ἔθνος τὸ ἐ. Id.2.102; τοὺς αἰεὶ ἐ. γινομένους Id.4.118, cf. 7.108; τὸ μὴ ἐ. those who are absent, Th.2.45; μή που λαθών τις ἐ. (sc. γενόμενος) Ar.V.247. 2. *in one's way*, i.e. *presenting an hindrance*, ὁ θεὸς.. [οἱ] ἐ. ἕστηκε Hdt.6.82; ὥς σφι τὸ ἐ. ἐγεγόνεε καθαρόν when *all impediments* had been cleared away, Id.7.183; τί τοὐμπ.; Ar.Lys.1161; οὐδὲν ἐ. [ἐστι] A.Pr.13; ἐ. ἔστη δορί Id.Th.1021; παρεῖναι S.OT445; οὐδεὶς ἐ. κεῖται νόμος E.Ion1047; καθῆσθαι Ar.Pax473; σὺ δ' ἡμῖν μηδὲν ἐ. γένῃ E.Hec.372; ἐ. τινι φῦναι Id.Or.605: c. inf., ἐ. εἶναι τῷ ποιεῖν X.HG2.3.23; ἐ. γενέσθαι, εἶναί τινι μὴ πράττειν, *prevent* a person's doing, Ar.Pax315, Th.6.28, etc.; τί ἐ. μοι μὴ οὐ..; what *prevents* my doing? X.Eq.11.13, cf. An.3.1.13; so ἐ. τὸ μὴ εἶναι ib.4.8.14; ἐ. γίγνεσθαι τοῦ μὴ δρᾶν Id.Cyr.2.4.23; ἐ. εἶναι ἀλλήλοις τινός to *hinder* each other from a thing, ib.8.5.24, cf. Plu.Them.4, etc.; λόγων τίς ἐ. ὅδ' ἔρχεται; E.Supp.395; ποιεῖσθαι ἐ. τι to regard it as *a hindrance*, suffer it to *hinder*, Lys.13.88, X.Cyr.4.2.46, D.21.104. 3. *in one's way, before one's eyes, manifest*, πόθεν ἄρξωμαι, ἐ. ἁπάντων ὄντων; And.4.10; Χαρίτων ἱερὸν ἐ. ποιοῦνται Arist.EN1133^{a}3; ἃ δ' ἐ. μάλιστα ταῦθ' ἥκω φράσων E.Ph.706; ἡ ἐ. παιδεία *everyday* education, Arist.Pol.1337^{a}39; πολλοῖς ἐ. εἶναι καὶ γνωρίζεσθαι Plb.2.17.1. 4. of Time, *immediately*, Polem.Hist.83.

ἐμποι-έω, *make in*, ἐν δ' αὐτοῖσι (sc. πύργοις) πύλας ἐνεποίεον Il.7.438, cf. Ar.Ec.154:—Med., Ἑλικῶνι χοροὺς ἐνεποιήσαντο Hes.Th.7, cf. PFlor.212.10 (iii A.D.):—Pass., χελιδὼν ἦν τις ἐμπεποιημένη *introduced by the poet's art*, Ar.Av.1301, v. Sch. 2. *put in*, ἐ. ἴχνεσιν ἴχνη, i.e. *put* their feet *in* the same tracks, X.Cyn.5.20. 3. *foist in*, ἐς τὰ Μουσαίου ἐ. χρησμόν Hdt.7.6; χρησμοὶ ἐμπεποιημένοι τοῖς Σιβυλλείοις D.H.4.62; simply, *insert*, opp. ἐξαγρέω, Schwyzer412.3 (Elis). II. *produce* or *create in*, ἡ χρεία καπήλων.. γένεσιν ἐ. τῇ πόλει Pl.R.371d; οἱ χρηματισταὶ.. πολὺν τὸν κηφῆνα καὶ πτωχὸν ἐ. τῇ πόλει ib.556a, etc.; δύναμιν (sc. τῇ πόλει) Isoc.9.47. 2. of states of mind, ἐπιθυμίαν ἐ. τοῖς Ἀθηναίων ξυμμάχοις ἐς τοὺς Λακεδαιμονίους Th.4.81; κακόν τι ἐ. ταῖς ψυχαῖς Pl.Phd.115e; ἐν αὐτῷ δειλίαν ἐ. Id.R.590b; ἐλπίδας ἐ. ἀνθρώποις X.Cyr.1.6.19; ψυχῇ ἐπιστήμην Id.Mem.2.1.20; ταραχήν τισι Men.Sam.9: without a dat., *produce, create*, μῖσος, λήθην, Pl.R.351d, Phlb.63e, D.19.3; ἡδονήν Arist.EN1126^{a}22; χρόνους [ψηφίσμασι] D.23.93; χαράν X.Hier.8.4; ὀργὰς καὶ λύπας ib.1.28: c. inf. pro acc., ἐ. τινὶ ἀκολουθητέον εἶναι *produce* in one's *mind the persuasion* that he must follow, Id.Oec.21.7; folld. by ὡς.., Id.An.2.6.8. 3. of conditions, *produce, cause*, ὀδύνην, σηπεδόνας, Hp.Acut.16, Aret.SD1.9; φθόρον Th.2.51; στάσεις Id.1.2; πολέμους καὶ στάσεις ἡμῖν αὐτοῖς ἐ. Isoc.4.168; χρόνου διατριβὴν ἐ. Th.3.38; κίνησιν Arist.Ph.250^{b}26. III. Med., ἐμποιεῖσθαι, = ἀντιποιεῖσθαι, *lay claim to*, ἱερωσύνης Lxx1Es.5.38, cf. AJA16.13 (Sardes, iv/iii B.C.), BGU13.13 (iii A.D.), etc.; τοῦ λαοῦ μου LxxEx.9.17. -ησις, εως, ἡ, *production*, δογμάτων Arr.Epict.4.11.8: f.l. for πτόησιν, D.C.37.16. II. (ἐμποιεῖσθαι) *laying claim to*, BGU94.14 (iii A.D.), etc. -ητέον, *one must create by means of* or *in*, τι ἐν τοῖς πράγμασιν Arist.Po.1453^{b}14; ἐλπίδα τοῖς ὑπηκόοις Them.Or.7.96a. -ητικός, ή, όν, *productive of* a thing *in*, ἄλλοις τῶν τοιούτων λόγων Arist.Metaph.1025^{a}4; πάθους S.E.M.7.191; δασείας A.D.Pron.78.11, cf. Andronic.Rhod.p.572M., Antyll.ap.Orib.6.7.1.

ἐμποικίλλω, *embroider upon*, νῖκαι ἐμπεποικιλμέναι Plu.Tim.8; γίγαντας ἐμπεποίκιλται [πέπλος] Sch.E.Hec.468, cf. 471.

ἐμποίνιμος, ον, (ποινή) *liable to punishment*, ὅρκος οὐκ ἐ. *that may be violated with impunity*, Trag.Adesp.525, cf. Corn.ND24. Adv. -μως Eust.1243.3.

ἐμποίνιος, ον, = foreg., Suid. **ἔμποιον**· τὸ γαλακτῶδες ὑγροῦν (leg. ὑγρόν), Hsch. (leg. ἔμπνουν).

ἔμποκος, ον, *unshorn*, of sheep, PThead.8.6 (iv A.D.).

ἐμπολ-αῖος, α, ον, *of* or *concerned in traffic*, epith. of Hermes as god of commerce, etc., Ar.Ach.816, Pl.1155, Corn.ND16. -άω, impf. ἠμπόλων Ar.V.444, (ἀπ-) E.Tr.973: fut. -ήσω S.Ant.1063: aor. ἠμπόλησα, but in Is.11.43 ἐνεπόλησα (Scaliger for ἐνέπωλ-): pf. ἠμπόληκα S.Aj.978, Ar.Pax367; late ἐμπεπόληκα Luc.Cat.1:—Med. (v. infr.):—Pass., aor. ἠμπολήθην S.Tr.250: pf. ἠμπόλημαι, Ion. ἐμπ- (ἐξ-) Hdt.1.1, S.Ant.1036:—*get by barter* or *traffic*, once in Hom., in Med., βίοτον πολὺν ἐμπολόωντο they *were getting* much substance *by traffic*, Od.15.456:—Act., *get by sale*, ἐξ ὧν [προβάτων etc.] ἐνεπόλησαν τετρακισχιλίας [δραχμάς] Is. l. c., cf. X.An.7.5.4: hence, *earn, procure*, τό γ' εὖ πράσσειν.. κέρδος ἐμπολᾷ S.Tr.93. 2. *deal* or *traffic in*, ἐμπολᾶτε τἀπὸ Σάρδεων ἤλεκτρον Id.Ant.1037; *purchase, buy*, Id.OT1025, Ar.V.444, Pax367,563, etc.; οὐκ ἐλεύθερος ἀλλ' ἐμποληθεὶς S.Tr.250:—Med., λαθραίαν ἐμπολωμένη Κύπριν E.Cret.7. 3. ἐ. τὴν ἐμὴν φρένα *make profit of* my mind *by dealing* with me, S.Ant.1063. II. abs., *traffic*, ἵν' ἐμπολᾷ βέλτιον Ar.Pax448; νυνὶ δὲ πεντήκοντα δραχμῶν ἐμπολῶ to the amount of 50 drachmae, ib.1201; οὐκέτ' ἐμπολῶμεν οὐδ' εἰς ἥμισυ Id.Th.452. 2. metaph., *deal* or *fare* in any way, ἠμποληκότα τὰ πλεῖστ' ἀμείνονα *having dealt in* most things with success, A.Eu.631; κάλλιον ἐμπολήσει *will fare* better *in health*, Hp.Morb.4.49; ἆρ' ἠμπόληκας ὥσπερ ἡ φάτις κρατεῖ; S.Aj.978. III. ἐμπολῶντο· ἐνεβάλλοντο, Hsch.

ἐμπολεμ-έω, *wage war in*, τὴν χώραν οὐ παρέχουσιν ἐ. And.3.27, cf. Plu.2.252a. -ιος, ον, *pertaining to war*, ταῦτα τὰ ἐ. Hdt.6.57; θεοί D.C.42.48. 2. *belonging to the forces*, ὅσον ἐ. Pl.Lg.755e; τὰ ἐ. *branches of the service*, ib.756a. 3. *warlike*, ἔθνη D.C.56.40. -ος, ον, = foreg., Hsch. -όω, *make enemies*, EM336.24, Suid.

ἐμπολ-εύς, έως, ὁ, *merchant, trafficker*, AP6.304 (Phan.). -έω, Ion. and late form for ἐμπολάω, Herod.6.63, Tz.H.1.820: Ion. part. Pass., δάπεδον ἐμπολεύμενον or -ευμένον dub. sens. in Keil-Premerstein *Erster Bericht* p.9 (Claros). -ή, ἡ, Arc. **ἰνπολά** IG5(2).3.27 (pl., Tegea, iv B.C.):—*merchandise*, Pi.P.2.67, Ar.Ach.930 (lyr.); ὁλκάδας γεμούσας.. ἐμπολῆς X.HG5.1.23: metaph., μέλεον ἐ. E.Hyps.Fr.41(64).87 (lyr.): pl., *wares*, IG l.c. II. *traffic, purchase*, E.IT1111 (lyr.), X.Cyr.6.2.39: pl., *ventures*, S.Fr.555.4. III. *gain made by traffic, profit*, ἀναθέμεν τῷ Ἀσκλαπιῷ τὰς ἐ. τῶν ἰχθύων Ἀρχ.Ἐφ.1918.168 (Epid., iv B.C.), cf. Palaeph.45; esp. *harlot's hire*, Artem.1.78 (pl.), D.C.79.13 (pl.). -ημα, ατος, τό, *matter of traffic, freight* or *cargo of a ship*, κόρην παρεισδέδεγμαι λωβητὸν ἐ. (metaph.) S.Tr.538: pl., *wares, merchandise*, E.Cyc.137. II. *gain made by traffic*, Thphr.Char.6.9. -ησις, εως, ἡ, *buying, trafficking*, Poll.3.124. -ητός, ή, όν, *bought*, οὑμπολητὸς Σισύφου Λαερτίῳ the son of Sisyphus *bought by* or *palmed off upon* L., S.Ph.417. -ίζω, *inclose within the city*, λόφον D.H.2.1 (Pass.). II. (πόλος) *insert at the pole*, Ptol.Alm.8.3, Procl.Hyp.6.7, al. -ιον, τό, *casing for a dowel*, ἐ. χαλκᾶ IG2.1054f4, 1054gA6.

ἐμπολῐορκέω, *besiege in* a place, in Pass., Str.6.2.6; ὑπό τινος Id.16.2.9:—Act., ἐνισχύσας πόλιν -ῆσαι LxxSi.50.4.

ἔμπολ-ις, εως, ὁ, ἡ, *belonging to the city* or *state*, = ἀστός, Eup.137; ὁ ἐ. τινι one's *fellow-citizen*, S.OC1156, prob. for ἔμπαλιν in ib.637. -ισις, εως, ἡ, *fixing of the pole*, Ptol.Alm.8.3.

ἐμπολῑτεύω, *to be a citizen, hold civil rights* in a place, Th.4.106; ἐ. ἐκεῖ ib.103:—Pass., οἱ ἐμπολιτευθέντες Isoc.5.5; τῇ πόλει καὶ τοῖς ἐμπολιτευομένοις Plb.5.9.9. 2. metaph., ἀφροσύνη ἐνεπολίτευσε τῷ ἔθνει J.AJ17.10.6; τὰς -ομένας ἡδονὰς ἐν Ῥώμῃ Philostr.VA5.36:—Med., ἐ. τῷ βίῳ Jul.Or.4.157b. 3. ἐμπολιτεύεσθαί τινι *to talk politics with* one, Cic.Att.7.7.7 codd. II. trans., *introduce into a state, naturalize*, ἐ. ἀκολασίαν οὐρανῷ Heraclit.All.69.

ἐμπολόωντο, v. ἐμπολάω I. 1.

ἐμπομπεύω, *walk in procession*: hence metaph., c. dat., *plume oneself upon*, Plu.2.527f; τῇ κιθάρᾳ Luc.Ind.10, cf. Arg.2D.20; ἐν πολλαῖς ῥάβδοις D.C.77.5; τῷ λόγῳ Procop.Gaz.Ep.69; γῇ ἐ. ἄνθεσιν Id.p.141B.; τοσούτοις δήμοις Hld.3.7.

ἐμπον-έω, *work on*, [τῇ γῇ] Alciphr.3.25, cf. JHS33.338 (Macedonia, ii A.D.). II. c. acc., *elaborate*, θεωρίαν Gal.4.760. -ημα, ατος, τό, in pl., *agricultural improvements*, Just.Nov.64.1, al.

ἔμπονος, ον, *patient of labour*, Hp.Aër.12; ἀρετῆς ἔργα φέρει ἔμπονος ἥβη Poet.ap.Sch.Heph.p.286C.; ἔμπονοι κόπῳ Ezek.Exag.208. II. *toilsome, painful*, τὰ ἔμπονα Aret.SA1.9; ἔ. κραυγή *vehement* outcry, Lxx3Ma.1.28.

ἐμπορ-εῖον, τό, later form of ἐμπόριον, Arist.Oec.1348^{b}21. -ευμα, ατος, τό, *merchandise*, in pl., X.Vect.3.4, Hier.9.11. II. *traffic*, Hsch. -εύομαι, fut. -πορεύσομαι: aor. 1 ἐνεπορεύθην:—Med., aor. 1 -ευσάμην Pl.Ep.313d:—*travel*, ξένην ἐπι.. γαῖαν S.OT456; ὡς τύραννον Id.Fr.873; ποῖ δ' ἐμπορεύῃ; Id.El.405; τηνῶθεν Ar.Ach.754. 2. abs., *walk*, Epich.53, Metag.10. II. *travel for traffic* or *business*, χρηματισμοῦ χάριν Pl.Lg.952e; εἰς Πόντον Chion Ep.7,8, cf. SIG1166 (Dodona): metaph., ἐ. εἰς ἰατρικὴν *inveigh against* the art of healing, Hp.de Arte1. 2. *to be a merchant, traffic*, Th.7.13, X.Vect.3.3, etc.; λόγοισιν Com.Adesp.269: c. acc., *trade in*, γῆν LxxGe.34.21. 3. c. acc. rei, *import*, Pl.Ep.313e; πολλὰς διὰ θαλάσσης ὠφελείας D.H.6.86; πορφύραν ἀπὸ Φοινίκης D.L.7.2; γλαῦκας Luc. *Nigr.Prooem.* b. metaph., δίαιταν ἥντιν' ἐμπορεύεται what manner of life he *leads*, E.*Fr.*812.6; ἐ. τὴν φιλοσοφίαν *to make a trade of* it, Ph.2.486, Them.*Or.*23.298d, cf. J.*AJ*4.6.8; πλήθη καλῶν γυναικῶν Ath.13.569f; in bad sense, *trade on*, τὴν λήθην τῶν δικαστῶν Ph.2.536. 4. c. acc. pers., *make gain of, overreach, cheat*, πλαστοῖς λόγοις ὑμᾶς 2*Ep.Pet.*2.3:—also in Act., Plb.38.12.10. -ευτέα, *one must tramp*, Ar.*Ach.*480. -ευτικός, ή, όν, *commercial, mercantile*, Pl.*Plt.*290a, Max.Tyr.36.2.

ἐμπορ-ία, Ion. -ίη, ἡ, (ἔμπορος) *commerce* (acc. to Arist.*Pol.*1258^{b}22, of three kinds, ναυκληρία, φορτηγία, παράστασις (qq.vv.)), mostly used of *commerce* or *trade by sea* (cf. ἔμπορος III), Hes.*Op.*646, Thgn. 1166, Simon.127, etc.; ἐμπορίαν ποιεῖσθαι Isoc.2.1; ἐμπορίας οὐκ οὔσης Th.1.2; ἐὰν κατὰ θάλατταν ἡ ἐ. γένηται Pl.*R.*371a; κατ' ἐμπορίην, Att. -ίαν, *for trade-purposes*, Hdt.3.139, Simon. l.c., Isoc.17.4, etc.; ἐμπορίας ἕνεκα or -κεν, Th.1.7, 6.2; πρὸς ἐμπορίαν Ar.*Av.*718: pl., τὰς ἐ. τὰς κερδαλέας ib.594 (anap.); περὶ τὰς ἐ. διατρίβειν Arist.*Pol.*1291^{a}5, cf. D.56.8. 2. *a trade* or *business*, *AP*6.63.8 (Damoch.), *Ev.Matt.* 22.5. 3. *errand, business*, E.*Hyps.Fr.*5.11 (anap.), Luc.*Scyth.*4; *journeying*, πενία ἀζημίωτος ἐ. Secund.*Sent.*10. II. *merchandise*, X.*Vect.*3.2, *AP*7.500 (Asclep.); αὐτοῦ τὴν ἐ. ἔφασκεν εἶναι Lys.32.25; ἐπὶ τῇ ἐμπορίᾳ ἣν ἦγεν ἐν τῇ..νηΐ Test.ap.D.35.23. -ιάρχης, ου, ὁ, *supervisor of trade*, *IGRom.*4.796 (Apamea). -ιζομαι, Pass., *to be provided*, Men.714. II. *acquire*, πολιτείας Procop.*Aed.*1 *Praef.* -ικός, ή, όν, *of* or *for commerce, mercantile*, οἶκος Stesich. 80; ἐ. τέχνη or ἐ. alone, = ἐμπορία I.1, Pl.*Euthphr.*14e, *Sph.*223d, al.; ἐ., τά, Id.*Lg.*842d; ἐ. δίκαι Arist.*Ath.*59.5, D.7.12; κατὰ τοὺς ἐ. νόμους Id.35.3; ἐ. συμβολαῖα ib.47; τὰ ἐ. χρήματα money *to be used in trade*, ib.49; ἡ μνᾶ ἡ ἐ. the mina *of commerce*, *IG*2^2.1013.34 (ii B.C.); ἐμπορικόν, τό, *the class of merchant-seamen*, Arist.*Pol.*1291^{b}24; *with an aptitude for trade*, παῖς Lib.*Decl.*33.7: Comp. -ώτερος Ptol.*Tetr.*66: -κοί, οἱ, *camp-traders, sutlers*, Arr.*Tact.*2.1. 2. *imported, foreign*, ἐ. χρήματα διεμπολᾶν Ar.*Ach.*974; φόρτος Plu. *Lyc.*9. 3. διήγημα ἐ. *a traveller's* tale, i.e. *a romance*, Plb.4.39. 11. II. Adv. -κῶς *in mercantile fashion*, Str.8.6.16. -ιον, τό, *trading-station, mart, factory*, Hdt.1.165, al., Th.1.100, Ar.*Av.* 1523, *IPE*1^2.47.9 (Olbia, i A.D.), etc.; προστάται τοῦ ἐ. Hdt.2.178; ἐ. παρέχειν, of Corinth, Th.1.13. b. *market-centre* for a district which had no πόλις, *SIG*880.22 (Macedonia, iii A.D.). 2. τὸ ἐ., at Athens, *the Exchange*, where the merchants resorted, δανείσασθαι χρήματα ἐν τῷ ἐμπορίῳ D.35.1, cf. 18.309; ἐκ τοὐμπορίου τινές foreign *merchants*, Diph.17.3, cf. 43.9. II. ἐμπόρια, τά, *merchandise*, X. *Vect.*1.7. -ιος, ὁ, = μέτοικος, Hsch. -ῖται· μέτοικοι, Id. (-ίσαι cod.). -ιωνήτας (-ιδον- cod.)· ἐνοικίου πρακτῆρας, i.e. those who *farm the tax paid by* ἔμποροι, Id. -ος, ον, *one who goes on ship-board as a passenger*, Od.2.319, 24.300. II. = ὁ ἐν πόρῳ ὤν, *wayfarer, traveller*, B.17.36, A.*Ch.*661, S.*OC*25,303, E.*Alc.*999 (lyr.). III. *merchant, trader*, Semon.16, Hdt.2.39, Th.6.31, etc.; distd. from *the retail-dealer* (κάπηλος) by his making voyages and importing goods himself, Pl.*Prt.*313d, *R.*371a, Arist.*Pol.*1291^{a}16, Sch.Ar.*Pl.*1156: metaph., ἐ. κακῶν A.*Pers.*598; ἐ. βίου *a trafficker* in life, E.*Hipp.*964; ἔ. περὶ τὰ τῆς ψυχῆς μαθήματα Pl.*Sph.*231d; ὥρης ἔ. *a dealer in* beauty, *AP*9.416 (Phil.); ἔ. γυναικῶν *IG*14.2000. 2. as Adj., = ἐμπορικός, ναῦς ἔ. D.S.5.12.

ἐμπορπ-άω, *fasten with a brooch* or *pin*:—Pass., εἵματα ἐνεπορπέατο (Ion. for -ηντο) they *wore* garments *fastened with a brooch upon the shoulder*, Hdt.7.77; ἐμπεπορπημένος διπλᾶ τὰ ἱμάτια Lycurg.40, cf. D.H.2.70, Plu.*Mar.*17: metaph., ἐμπεπορπημένοι ὠμότητα Lxx 3*Ma.* 7.5. -ημα, ατος, τό, *garment secured by a brooch*, Hsch. -όομαι, Pass., = ἐμπορπάομαι, Lxx 1*Ma.*14.44, Hsch. (Act. only *EM*336.6.)

ἐμπόρφυρος, ον, *inclining to purple*, Dsc.3.100, Orib.*Syn.*2.56.17, *Cat.Cod.Astr.*8(4).251.

ἔμποτος, ον, (ἐμπίνω) *drinkable*, Aret.*CD*1.13.

Ἔμπουσα, ἡ, *Empusa, a hobgoblin*, assuming various shapes, said to be sent by Hecate, Ar.*Ra.*293, *Ec.*1056, D.18.130; sts. identified with *Hecate*, Ar.*Fr.*500.

ἐμπρακτ-ικός, ή, όν, *efficacious*, Dsc.1.39 (Comp.), 2.78 (Sup.). -ος, ον, *within one's power to do, practicable*, μαχανά Pi.*P.*3.62: Comp. -ότερος, κένωσις Philum.ap.Orib.45.29.5, cf. Sor.2.9; χρόνος ἔ. εἰς πάντα *propitious*, Heph.Astr.2.30, cf. Vett.Val.205.32, al.; ἐ. ῥητορική *working* rhetoric, Phld.*Rh.*1.10S., al.; also of persons, *active*, ἀνὴρ τὰ περὶ τὸν πόλεμον ἔ. D.S.13.102; τόλμαν ἔχειν ἔμπρακτον πρός τι *ready for*.., ib.70; τὸ ἔ. *vigour*, of oratory, Longin.11.2. Adv. -τως *actively*, Plu.*Sert.*4; *effectively*, Phld.*Lib.*p.38O., Archig.ap.Aët.12. 1. b. *holding office*, ἄρχοντες *Cod.Just.*1.2.24.1. 2. ἔ. ἡμέρα day *on which legal business may be transacted*, *POxy.*1882.14 (vi A.D.). II. *under bond* to pay, = εἴσπρακτος, *IG*7.3171.54 (Orchom. Boeot.).

ἔμπραξις, εως, ἡ, *claim under a bond*, *IG*7.3172.156 (pl., Orchom. Boeot.).

ἔμπρεον· ἔμπειρον, Hsch.

ἐμπρεπής, ές, *conspicuous among* or *above* others, θύννος..πᾶσιν ἰχθύεσσιν ἐ. ἐν μυττωτῷ Anan.5.8. II. *conspicuous for*, ἰηλέμοισιν ἐ. A.*Supp.*115 (lyr.); cf. sq. III. *suitable, fitting*, Ph.1.501; ἐμπρεπές ἐστι, c. inf., it *is fitting*, ib.435, al.: Comp., ib.617: Sup., ib.695.

ἐμπρέπω, *to be conspicuous in*, πενταέθλοισιν B.8.27; αἰθέρι, of the stars, A.*Ag.*6; ἐπ' ὀμμάτων ἐ. (εὖ πρ. cod. Med.) *to be conspicuous* on the face, ib.1428 (lyr.); Βάκχαις ἐ. *among* them, Ar.*Nu.*605:—Med., Λύδαισιν ἐμπρέπεται γυναίκεσσιν Sapph.*Supp.*25.6. 2. *to be conspicuous* or *famous*, A.*Ch.*356 (lyr.), E.*Heracl.*407; ἀνδράσι *for* men, Pi.*P.*8.28; ἄλγεσι S.*El.*1187; ἐσθήμασι Id.*Fr.*769; ἐν ὅπλοις δεινῶς ἐ. D.C.40.41; ἐνέπρεπον ἔχοντες.. Hdt.7.67,83. 3. *suit*, τῇ φωνῇ καὶ τὴν τραυλότητα ἐμπρέψαι λέγουσι Plu.*Alc.*1: impers., *it is fitting* or *suitable*, c. inf., Hld.5.8.

ἐμπρήζω, = ἐμπρήθω II, *Gloss.*

ἐμ-πρήθω, *blow up, inflate*, of the wind, ἐν δ' ἄνεμος πρῆσεν μέσον ἱστίον Il.1.481:—Pass., *to be bloated* or *swollen*, ἐμπεπρησμένης ὑὸς Ar.*V.*36 (-πρημ- cod. R), cf. Gal.ap.Orib.8.19.7. II. *burn*, ἐνέπρηθον μέγα ἄστυ Il.9.589:—Pass., Ath.Med.ap.Orib.1.2.4; cf. ἐμπίμπρημι. -πρησις, εως, Ion. -ιος, ἡ, *burning*, Hdt.8.55, D.H.4.40; οἰκιῶν Pl.*R.*470a: pl., ἐμπρήσεις οἰκιῶν Aeschin.3.157. II. *inflammation*, Gal.12.693. -πρησμός, ὁ, = foreg., *SIG*679.85 (Magn. Mae., ii B.C.), Plu.2.824e, Gal.9.824, *BGU*163.6 (ii A.D.); opp. κατακλυσμός, prob. in Ph.2.515. -πρηστής, οῦ, ὁ, *one that burns*, Aq.*De.*8.15; *incendiary*, Ptol.*Tetr.*165.

ἐμπρίζω, = ἐμπρίω, Meges ap.Orib.44.24.19 (Pass.).

ἐμπρῑόεις, εντος, *pungent*, v.l. in Nic.*Al.*533, cf. Hsch. (-προιέντα cod.).

ἐμ-πριστικός, ή, όν, *like a saw*, of the pulse, Gal.8.478. -πρίω [ῑ], Ep. ἐνιπ-, *saw into*, ὀστέον, vulg. for ἐκ-, Hp.*VC*21; τὸ οὖς ἐνέπρισε τοῖς ὀδοῦσι *bit deep into* it, D.S.10.17. II. *gnash together*, ὀδόντας ἐμπεπρικώς *having* the teeth *fixed in a bite*, Id.17.92, v.l. in Luc.*Somn.*14; ἐ. γέννυν χαλινοῖς Opp.*H.*5.186, cf. *C.*2.261. III. intr., *bite, be pungent*, σίνηπυν, ὀνόγυρον, etc., Nic.*Al.*533 (dub. l.), *Th.*71, al. 2. ἐμπρίων σφυγμός *saw-like, hard* pulse, Gal.8.474, Alex.Trall.6.1.

ἐμπρόθεσμος, ον, *within* or *before the stated time*, opp. ἐκπρόθ., πένθος Ph.2.170; χρόνος Sor.1.33; ἀγῶνες Plu.2.502a; ἐμπρόθεσμόν (v.l. -μως) τινα πέμπειν Luc.*VH*2.27. Adv. -μως Ph.2.532, Sch.Ar.*Eq.* 392, *POxy.*61.12 (iii A.D.).

ἐμπροίκιος, ον, (προίξ) *given by way of dower*, ἐ. δοθῆναι, δεδόσθαι, App.*Mith.*75, *BC*1.10; δισμύρια τάλαντα ἐ. Anon.Hist. in *Rev.Ét.Gr.* 5.321:—also -ροικος, ον, *Gloss.*

ἐμπρό-κειμαι, *to be impending, imminent*, Carneisc.*Herc.*1027. 9. -μελετάω, *train oneself in beforehand*, θήραις Ph.2.90, cf. 1.521.

ἔμπροσθ-α, Adv., Aeol. and Dor. for sq., *Tab.Heracl.*1.57,101, A.D.*Adv.*153.17. -εν, sts. also ἔμπροσθε Hdt.5.62, 7.144, al., Isoc.*Ep.*4.10, in Poets metri gr., Hegesipp.Com.1.20, Nicom.Com. 1.14, A.R.4.590: neither form in Hom. or Trag., τοὔμπροσθεν dub. in E.*Hipp.*1228. I. Adv., 1. of Place, *before, in front*, Hdt.7. 126, X.*Cyr.*4.2.23; τὸ and τὰ ἔ. *the front, the foreside*, Id.*HG*2.3.55, Hdt.5.62, etc.; εἰς τὸ ἔ. *forwards*, Id.4.61; στὰς ἐκ τοῦ ἔ. *in front, opposite*, X.*Cyr.*2.2.6: metaph., εἰς τοὔμπ. προελθεῖν Isoc. l.c. 2. of Time, *before, of old*, Pl.*Phdr.*277d, etc.; τὰ ἔ. Id.*Grg.*448e; τὰ ἔ. τούτων ῥηθέντα Id.*Lg.*773e; οἱ ἔ. our *ancestors*, Id.*Plt.*296a, Hegesipp. l.c.; οἱ ἔ. χρόνοι *PPetr.*2 p.19 (iii B.C.), etc. II. as Prep. c. gen., *before, in front of*, 1. of Place, ἐ. αὐτῆς (sc. τῆς νηός) Hdt.8.87, cf. 2. 110, etc. 2. of Time, ἔ. ταύτης (sc. τῆς γνώμης) Id.7.144; ἔ. εἶναι τῶν πραγμάτων to be *beforehand with* events, D.4.39. 3. of Degree, ἔ. τοῦ δικαίου *preferred before* justice, Id.56.50. -ίδιος, α, ον, = sq., A.D. *Adv.*157.2, *PMag.Berol.*2.46. -ιος, ον, *fore*, like πρόσθιος, of the feet of a quadruped, opp. ὀπίσθιοι, ἐ. πόδες Hdt.4.60; σκέλη X.*Eq.*11.2, Arist.*PA*688^{a}12, *BCH*35.286 (Delos); κῶλα Arist.*PA*687^{b}28; οἱ ἐ. ὀδόντες Id.*Ph.*198^{b}25; ἐ. τραύματα wounds *in front*, D.H.10.37. II. Astron., *preceding* in the daily motion of the heavens, Cleom.1.1.

ἐμπροσθό-κεντρος, ον, *with a sting in front*, of dipterous insects, Arist.*HA*490^{a}18. -τονία, ἡ, *tetanic procurvation*, opp. ὀπισθοτονία, Cael.Aur.*CP*3.6. -τονικός, ή, όν, *suffering from* ἐμπροσθοτονία, ibid. -τονος, ον, *drawn forwards and stiffened*, opp. ὀπισθότονος, Aret.*SA*1.6.

ἐμπροσθουρητικός, ή, όν, (οὐρέω) *making water forwards*, opp. ὀπισθουρητικός, Arist.*HA*509^{b}2.

ἐμπροσθοφανής, ές, *showing on the front*, Gal.18(1).820.

ἐμπρόσοδος, ον, *furnishing revenue*, μέταλλον dub. in Str.6.2.10.

ἐμπρόσωπος, ον, *before the face of, in the presence of*, c. dat., Phalar. *Ep.*147.

ἔμπρῳρος, ον, *depressed towards the prow*, ἔ. τὰ σκάφη ποιεῖν Plb. 16.4.12.

ἐμπταίω, *fall into*, ἐς ἄρκυν Lyc.105.

ἐμπτίσσω, *pound in*, in Pass., Aq., Thd.*Pr.*27.22.

ἐμπτοέω, in Pass., *to be stirred by passion*, πρός τινα Procop.Gaz. p.156B.

ἔμ-πτῠσις, εως, ἡ, *spitting*, of blood, Aret.*SA*2.2. -πτυσμα, ατος, τό, *spitting on*, Lxx *Is.*50.6. -πτύω, *spit into*, ἐς ποταμόν Hdt.1.138; εἰς στόμα ἑρπετοῦ Dsc.4.25. II. *spit upon*, εἴς τι Ath. 8.345c; εἰς τὸ πρόσωπον *PMagd.*24.7 (iii B.C.), Plu.2.189a; ἐς τὸ πρόσωπόν τινος Herod.5.76, Lxx *Nu.*12.14, *Ev.Matt.*26.67; εἴς τινα *Ev. Matt.*27.30: c. dat., Arist.*Fr.*347, *Ev.Marc.*10.24, etc.:—Med., Lxx *De.*25.9:—Pass., *to be spat upon*, Muson.*Fr.*10p.52H.

ἔμ-πτωσις, εως, ἡ, *falling into*, Corn.*ND*22: generally, *falling*, [καρπῶν] *Cat.Cod.Astr.*7.186. 2. *falling upon, pressure*, D.H.9. 23. 3. *incidence, impact*, εἰδώλων Epicur.*Sent.Vat.*24, Cic.*Att.*2. 3.2 (pl.); τοῦ ἡλίου εἰς τὰ νέφη *Placit.*3.2.10. 4. *propensity*, διανοίας Onos.1.11. 5. *reduction* of dislocation, Gal.18(1).325. 6. *inundation* of the Nile, Heph.Astr.1.21. -πτωτος, ον, *falling into, inclined*, εἰς τὸ κακόν M.Ant.10.7; τῷ πάθει Aët.7.54.

ἐμπύγια [ῡ], τά, *region of the anus*, *PTeb.*1.18.

ἐμπῠελ-ίδιον, τό, Dim. of sq., Hero *Aut.*10.1. -ίς, ίδος, ἡ, (πύελος) *socket* or *bearing* to receive a κνώδαξ, ib.2.3.

ἐμπυ-έω, *suppurate*, Hp.*Prog.*18, Aret.*SD*1.8, etc. **-ημα**, ατος, τό, *gathering, abscess*, esp. internal, Hp.*Prog.*18, *Epid.*3.1.α', Arist. *HA*624ᵃ17; of the kidneys, Ruf.*Ren.Ves.*1.5; of the chest, Archig. ap.Aët.8.73, Gal.17(2).793. **-ημᾰτικός**, ή, όν, *suppurating*, Hp. *Art.*41. **-ησις**, εως, ἡ, *suppuration*, Id.*Aph.*5.65, Aret.*CA*1.7, etc. **-ητικός**, ή, όν, *causing suppuration*, Hp.*Acut.*22. **-ῐκός**, ή, όν, = ἐμπυηματικός, Aret.*SD*1.9. 2. *suffering from* ἐμπύημα, ἐ. καὶ φθισικοί Dsc.1.72, cf. Archig.ap.Aët.8.73, Alex.Aphr.*Pr.*2. 34. **-ῐ́σκω**, *cause suppuration*:—Pass., *suppurate internally*, Hp. *VC*2, *Morb.*3.16:—also intr. in Act., Aret.*SD*1.14.

ἐμπῠκάζω, *wrap up in*:—Pass., νόος οἱ ἐμπεπύκασται his mind *is shrouded, hard to make out*, v.l. for εὖ πεπ. in Mosch.1.15.

ἐμπύλαι· αἱ νύμφαι, Hsch.; cf. πιτύπαι.

ἐμπύλιος [ῠ], α, ον, *at the gate*, epith. of Artemis Hecate, Orph.*A.* 902: Boeot. **ἐμπύληος** (= -λαιος), epith. of Poseidon at Thebes, *IG* 7.2465 (iv/iii B.C.).

ἐμπυ-όομαι, Pass., *suppurate*, Hp.*Morb.*1.27. **-ος**, ον, (πύον) *suffering from an abscess* or *suppurating wound*, Id.*Prog.*18, *Aph.*5. 10, D.54.12, Isoc.19.26, Men.1009, *IG*4.952.57 (Epid.); τῷ ἐ. βέλτιον τὸ καίεσθαι τοῦ διαμένειν Iamb.*Protr.*2; ἵπποι Arist.*HA*604ᵇ 6. II. *festering, suppurating*, βάσις S.*Ph.*1378; στέρνων ἀπολύσεται ἔμπυον ἰλύν Androm.ap.Gal.14.35; ἐ. μοτός *tents*, Gal.19.97.

ἐμπύρ-ετος [ῠ], ον, *in fever heat*, Alex.Trall.5.4. **-ευμα**, ατος, τό, *a live coal covered with ashes*, so as to allow of the fire being rekindled (λείψανον, Hsch.; ἔναυσμα, Suid.), Arist.*Frr.*225,226, Gal.11. 629: metaph., Ph.2.59, al., Longus 1.29; ἀρετῆς Jul.*ad Ath.*269d: pl., ζωῆς ἐ. *embers, hidden sparks*, Simp.*in Cael.*677.11. **-εύω**, *set on fire*, Ar.*Lys.*372:—Med., *catch fire*, Thphr.*HP*5.9.6; *light a fire*, Philostr.*Im.*2.24:—Pass., Arist.*PA*649ᵃ26. 2. *set aglow*, τὴν ψυχὴν ἐμπεπύρευκεν Id.*Resp.*474ᵇ13, cf. *Juv.*469ᵇ16 (Pass.). II. *kindle in* the body, θερμότητα Id.*GA*739ᵇ10. III. *roast in* or *on the fire*, φηγόν Ar.*Pax*1137. **-ία** (leg. -εία), ἡ, *divination by fire*, in Boeotia, Hsch.; also, = ὅρκος δημόσιος, i.e. *ordeal by fire*, Id.

ἐμπῠρῐβήτης, ου, ὁ, (ἐν, πῦρ, βαίνω) *made for standing on the fire*, μέγαν τρίποδ' ἐμπυριβήτην Il.23.702.

ἐμπῠρ-ίζω, = ἐμπυρεύω, Lxx *Jo.*8.28, D.S.2.36, 12.43:—Pass., *Chron.Lind.*D.41, *PTeb.*5.135 (ii B.C.), Diog.Oen.8, Alex.Trall. *Febr.*2; [ψυχῇ] τοῖς πάθεσιν -ομένῃ Simp.*in Epict.*p.126 D. (In Thd. *Ge.*4.4,5 ἐ. is a mistranslation due to confusion of Hebr. *yiša'* and *'iššeh.*) **-ιος** [ῠ], ον, *belonging to the empyrean*, θεός (opp. αἰθέριος, ὑλαῖος) Procl.*Theol.Plat.*4.39, cf. Iamb.*Myst.*7.2, Lyd.*Mens.*4. 22. **-ισμός**, ὁ, = ἐμπρησμός (less Att., acc. to Phryn.313), Hyp. *Lyc.Fr.*4, Plb.9.41.5, Lxx *Le.*10.6, *Mon.Anc.Gr.*19.8, Ath.Mech.12. 6; *burning* of weeds, *PSI*4.338.7, al. (iii B.C.). **-ιστής**, οῦ, ὁ, *one who sets on fire*, ὁ ἐ. Ἕκτωρ Eust.1023.26.

ἐμπῠρισχησίφως [σῐ], ὁ, *deriving light from the empyrean*, *PMag. Par.*1.601.

ἐμπῠρίφοιτος [ῐ], ον, *dwelling in fire*, δαίμονες Orph.*H.*1.33 (prob.).

ἔμπῠρος, ον, (πῦρ) *in, on* or *by the fire*, σκεύη ἔ. implements *used at the fire*, opp. ἄπυρα, Pl.*Lg.*679a; ἡ ἔ. τέχνη the work *of the forge, smith's* art, Id.*Prt.*321e (but in E.*Ph.*954, *the art of divining by fire, soothsaying* trade (v. infr. III)); χειρώνακτες Ael.*NA*2.31. II. *exposed to fire* or *sun, burnt, scathed*, νεκρός E.*Ph.*1186; *roasted*, σάρξ *AP*6.89 (Maec.); *fiery hot, torrid*, χώρα Str.16.1.10; ἀήρ Thphr. *CP*1.13.5; [ἡ ὥρα] -ωτάτη ib.4; *feverish*, Hp.*Morb.*2.40 (v.l. ἐμπύρετος); λοιμοί Lxx *Am.*4.2; *inflammatory*, of a bite, Arist.*Mir.* 846ᵇ16; *heated*, of a cautery iron, *PMed.Lond.*155.3.2. 2. *burning, scorching*, ἥλιος *AP*9.24 (Leon.): metaph. of persons, *fiery*, Plu.*Num.*5. Adv. -ως, ἐρᾶν Poll.3.68. 3. *lighted*, λαμπάς *AP* 6.100 (Crin.); βωμός ib.10.7 (Arch.). III. *of* or *for a burnt-offering*, ὀρθοστάται E.*Hel.*547. 2. as Subst., ἔμπυρα (sc. ἱερά), τά, *burnt sacrifices*, opp. ἄπυρα, Pi.*O.*8.3, cf. A.*Ch.*485 (prob.); δι' ἐμπύρων σπονδὰς καθεῖναι to make libations at *the burnt-offerings*, E. *IA*59 (hence ἔμπυρα are improperly used for σπονδαί, S.*El.*405); κατάρας ἐπὶ ἐμπύρων ποιεῖσθαι swear upon *the sacrifice*, Plb.16.31.7, cf. App.*Hisp.*9; esp. of *burnt-offerings* as used *for purposes of divination* (v. supr. I), S.*Ant.*1005; εἰς ἔμπυρ' ἦλθε E.*IT*16; also ἐμπύρους ἀκμάς Id.*Ph.*1255; ἔμπυρα σήματ' ἰδέσθαι A.R.1.145: rarely sg., ἔμπυρον, τό, *PMag.Osl.*1.69, dub. sens. in *PCair.Zen.*14.17.

ἐμπῠρο-σκόπος, ὁ, *one who divines by* ἔμπυρα, Sch.Il.24.221, Eust. 1346.39. **-τέχνης**, ου, ὁ, *smith*, Arg.Man. (post Max.p.101 L.).

ἐμπῠρόω, = ἐμπυρεύω, *Inscr.Prien.*17.13 (iii B.C.), v.l. in Dsc.5.114 (Pass.), cj. in Hsch. s.v. πυρέας.

ἔμπυρρος, ον, *ruddy*, Arist.*Col.*797ᵇ13.

ἐμπυρσεύω, gloss on πυρακτῶ, Suid.

ἐμπύρωσις [ῠ], εως, ἡ, *kindling, heating*, Arist.*Resp.*478ᵃ30.

ἐμπῡτιάζω, *curdle with rennet*, γάλα Dsc.*Alex.*26 (Pass.); cf. ἐμπιτυάζομαι.

ἐμπῡτίζω, *spit into*, *Gp.*20.33.

ἐμπύωμα, ατος, τό, = ἐμπύημα, *Gloss.*

ἐμπωλέω, *dwell amongst*, [φθιμένοις] *Epigr.Gr.*316 (dub.).

ἔμσκεψις, εως, ἡ, *investigation*, *PSI*3.168.31 (ii B.C.).

ἐμύς or **ἐμύς**, ύδος, ἡ, *fresh-water tortoise*, esp. *Emys lutaria*, Arist. *HA*558ᵃ8, al.; also ὁ, ib.600ᵇ22.

ἐμφάατον (post ἔμφατον)· πλακοῦντα τετυρωμένον, Hsch.

ἐμφᾰγεῖν, inf. of aor. 2 ἐνέφαγον (no pres. ἐνεσθίω being in use), *eat*, Eub.89, J.*AJ*9.4.5, Plu.*Tim.*12, Ael.*NA*5.29, Luc.*Nigr.*22; esp. in X., *eat hastily*, 'snatch a bite', ἐμφαγόντες ὅ τι δύναιντο *HG* 4.5.8; ἐκέλευον αὐτοὺς ἐμφαγόντας πορεύεσθαι *An.*4.2.1, cf. *Cyr.*7. 1.1, 8.1.44. II. *eat in* or *upon*, χρυσὸς κοῖλος ἡμῖν ἐμφαγεῖν Luc. *Nav.*20.

ἐμφαίνω, *exhibit, display in*, οἷον ἐν κατόπτρῳ χρώματα Pl.*Ti.*71b:—Pass., τὸ -όμενον μέλαν (in the moon) *Stoic.*2.199. 2. *exhibit, display*, φαντασίαν μήκους Arist.*Mu.*395ᵇ6; τὴν ἰδέαν τοῦ σώματος Plu.*Alex.*4; εὐοδμίαν Thphr.*CP*6.5.2, cf. 6.3.4 (Pass.); αἱρέσεις καὶ διαλήψεις Plb.3.31.8; δυσχερασμόν Phld.*Lib.*p.8 O.; οὐδὲν τοιοῦτον ἐμφαίνει *presents* no such *appearance*, Luc.*DDeor.*26.1; ἡ φροντὶς ἐ. τινὰ ψυχρότητα ἤθους Demetr.*Eloc.*171. 3. *indicate*, ψυχρίαν Chrysipp.*Stoic.*3.50; εὔνοιαν Plb.22.7.9; ἐ. ὅτι.. D.S.1.87, Plu.2. 112f, al.; περί τινος ὡς περὶ ἰδίας Plb.3.23.5. 4. *lay information*, *IG*9(1).267 (Opus). II. Med. or Pass., with fut. ἐμφανήσομαι Phld.*Lib.*p.23 O.: 1. *to be seen in* a mirror, *reflected*, ἐν ὕδασι ἢ ἐν κατόπτροις Pl.*R.*402b, al., cf. Arist.*Mete.*345ᵇ26, *APo.*98ᵃ27 (where ἠχεῖ and ἐμφαίνεται are quasi-impersonal), Thphr.*Sens.*27; ἐν χαλκείῳ X.*Smp.*7.4; τῷ εἴδει Plu.*Alc.*4. 2. *become visible, to be manifested*, X.*Cyr.*1.4.3; τὰ ἤθη τὰ ἐπὶ τοῦ προσώπου -όμενα Arist. *Phgn.*806ᵃ30, cf. Lxx *Ps.*79(80).2, etc.; ἐν ἅπασιν ἐμφαίνεται τὸ ἄρχον καὶ τὸ ἀρχόμενον Arist.*Pol.*1254ᵃ30; ἐμφαίνεται impers., *it is manifest*, Plu.2.953e:—also in Act., ἐμφαίνει οὕτως Ceb.21. 3. *to be exemplified* or *implied in..*, ἐν τῇ κατηγορίᾳ τῇ τοιαύτῃ Arist.*Metaph.*1028ᵃ 28; ἐνυπάρχειν καὶ ἐ. Id.*de An.*413ᵃ15, *EN*1096ᵇ22. 4. *to be indicated*, τῆς ἡδονῆς -ομένης τέλους Chrysipp.*Stoic.*3.8, cf. Gal.10.126.

ἐμφαλκόομαι, dub. in Plb.*Fr.*136 (ap.Suid.).

ἐμφᾰν-εια [ᾰ], ἡ, *manifestation*, εἰς ἐ. ἄγειν bring to *light*, Thphr. *Ign.*2; τοῦ θεοῦ J.*AJ*15.11.7 (pl.); τὴν ἐ. τινων ποιεῖσθαι produce for *inspection*, *PLips.*52.9 (iv A.D.), etc. **-ερος**, ον, *designated*, *Gloss.* **-ής**, ές, *showing in* itself, *reflecting*, of mirrors, Pl.*Ti.* 46a. II. *visible to the eye, manifest*, a. of persons, S.*Tr.*199, etc.; esp. of the gods *appearing bodily* among men, E.*Ba.*22, Ar.*V.* 733, Pl.*Alc.*2.141a; so ὄψις ἐ. ἐνυπνίων A.*Pers.*518; τέκμαρ *Ch.*667; ἐ. τινὰ ἰδεῖν see him *bodily*, S.*Aj.*538, cf. Ar.*Th.*682; μαθεῖν S.*El.* 1454; πῶς ἂν ὑμῖν ἐμφανὴς.. γενοίμην; how could I make it *manifest?* Id.*Ph.*531; ἐμφανὴς τιμαῖσιν, = ἐμφανῶς τιμώμενος, Id.*OT*909 (lyr.); ἐ. ζῷα *familiar* animals, Epicur.*Ep.*2 p.43 U. b. as legal term, ἐμφανῆ παρέχειν τινά to produce a person or thing *in open court*, Antipho 5.36, cf. D.56.38; so ἐμφανῆ καταστῆσαι produce *in court*, either the property or the vouchers, Id.52.10; ἐμφανῶν κατάστασις, *actio ad exhibendum*, Is.6.31, D.53.14. c. of things, οὐ γάρ ἐστι τἀμφανῆ κρύπτειν S.*OC*755; ἐ. τεκμήρια *visible* proofs, Id.*El.*1109; ἄλγος ἐ. Pi.*Fr.*210; κλαυθμός Hdt.1.111; μεῖξις ib.203; χυμοί Thphr. *CP*6.3.4 (Sup.); ἐ. κόσμος *visible* sky, Vett.Val.8.12; τὰ ἐ. κτήματα the *actual* property, X.*HG*5.2.10; τοῦ μέλλοντος καὶ μὴ -οῦς Th.3.42; εἰς τοὐμφανὲς ἰέναι to come into *light*, come *forward*, X. *Mem.*4.3.13; εἰς τοὐ. ᾠοτοκεῖν, ζῳοτοκεῖν, Arist.*HA*510ᵇ20, 511ᵃ23; ἀεὶ ἐ. εἶναι to be constantly *in evidence*, X.*Ages.*9.1. 2. *manifest, palpable*, τυραννίς Ar.*V.*417; βία Th.4.86; ἐ. λόγος a *plain* speech, A.*Eu.*420; τῷ ἐμφανεῖ λόγῳ *openly*, Th.7.48; τὴν διάνοιαν ἐ. ποιεῖν διὰ φωνῆς Pl.*Tht.*206d; ἐμφανές ἐστιν ὅτι.. X.*Hier.*9.10. 3. *well-known*, τὰ ἐ. Hdt.2.33; ἐμφανῆ γὰρ ἦν S.*Ant.*448; *conspicuous, notable*, ἀνήρ D.S.1.68. III. Adv. -νῶς, Ion. -νέως, *visibly, openly*, Hdt.1.140, A.*Ag.*626, Th.7.48, etc.; λέγειν Ar.*Ach.*312; ἐ. ἐλευθεροῦν *without doubt*, Hdt.6.123; ἐ. ἠμύνατο *openly*, i.e. *not secretly* or *treacherously*, S.*Tr.*278; οὐ λόγοις, ἀλλ' ἐ. but *really*, Ar.*Nu.*611: Comp. -έστερον Pl.*Phlb.*31e. 2. neut. Adj., ἐκ τοῦ ἐ. Hdt.3.150, 4.120, al.; ἐν τῷ ἐ. Th.2.21, X.*An.*2.5.25. **-ία**, ἡ, *information laid*, *IG*9(1).267.10 (Opus). **-ίζω**, Att. fut. -ιῶ E.*Fr.*797: pf. ἐμπεφάνικα *PSI*4.400.2 (iii B.C.):—*show forth, manifest, exhibit*, αὐτὸς αὑτὸν E. l. c., cf. Philoch.20, Plb.30.17.2, etc.; ἐ. τινὰ ἐπίορκον, ἐχθρόν, *exhibit* or *represent* him as.., X.*Ages.*1.12, D.14.36; ἐ. οὐκ οὖσαν ἀγαθὸν τὴν ἡδονήν Arist.*EN*1173ᵇ31; πᾶν σύμπτωμα Metrod.10:—Med., *exhibit in court*, *PMasp.*32.33 (vi A.D.):—Pass., *to become visible, be manifested*, τινί Lxx *Wi.*1.2, *Ev.Matt.*27.53, Ph.1.107, J.*AJ* 1.13.1, D.L.1.7. 2. *make clear* or *plain*, Pl.*Sph.*244a, Men.*Sam.* 140, etc.; ἄστρα ἡμῖν τῆς νυκτὸς τὰς ὥρας ἐ. X.*Mem.*4.3.4: with a relat., τὰ παθήματα δι' ἃς αἰτίας γέγονε ἐ. Pl.*Ti.*61c; ἐ. τοῦτο ὅτι.. X. *Cyr.*8.1.26. 3. *declare, explain*, Arist.*APr.*46ᵃ24; *give orders*, τινὶ ποιεῖν τι Plb.6.35.8; *report*, περί τινος *SIG*412.4 (Delph., iii B.C.), cf. *UPZ*42.18 (ii B.C.), *IG*9(2).517.5 (Larissa), *Michel*431.6 (Iasus), etc.:—Pass., *GDI*2502 *B* 41 (Delph., iv B.C.). 4. *lay an information against*, τινά Arg.Ar.*Lys.*:—Pass., ὁ -ισθείς Charond.ap.Stob.4.2. 24. **-ίσιμα**, τά, *fees paid at installation* in a benefice, Just.*Nov.* 56.1 (but -ιστικά, τά, ib.*Praef.*). **-ισις**, εως, ἡ, *exposure*, ψευδοῦς συλλογισμοῦ Arist.*SE*176ᵇ29; πράξεων ἢ λόγων πρὸς ἄλληλα ἐναντιουμένων Id.*Rh.Al.*1427ᵇ14. 2. *indication*, A.D.*Synt.*67. 27. 3. *exhibition, production* in court, Just.*Nov.*15.3 (pl.). 4. *proof, demonstration*, *PMasp.*89.5 (vi A.D.). **-ίσκω**, = ἐμφανίζω, Iamb.*VP*35.260. **-ισμός**, ὁ, *manifestation*, Pl.*Def.*413e; *information, disclosure*, *PAmh.*2.30.2, al. (ii B.C.), Lxx *2Ma.*3.9, *BCH* 48.369 (Thessaly, i A.D.); *indication*, τινός A.D.*Synt.*50.27, al.; *explanation*, Ptol.*Tetr.*22. **-ιστέον**, *one must set forth, declare*, Pl. *Ti.*65c, Str.2.5.17. **-ιστής**, οῦ, ὁ, *informer*, Aristeas 167, *PTaur.* 1.8 (ii B.C.). **-ιστικός**, ή, όν, *declaratory*, λόγος Pl.*Def.*414e; *expressive*, Longin.31.1 (Comp.): c. gen., Porph.ap.Eus.*PE*3.11, Dam.*Pr.*350; τὸ -κὸν αὐτόθεν ἔχειν, of names which carry their own *meaning*, Ptol.*Tetr.*34. II. v. ἐμφανίσιμα. 2. -κόν, τό, *deposit paid on laying an information*, *PMasp.*89.5 (vi A.D.).

ἐμφανόν, *moechulus*, *Gloss.*

ἐμφαντ-άζομαι, Pass., *to be associated in idea with*, [τῷ ἀποθανεῖν]

M.Ant.2.12. 2. *to be imagined*, Dam.*Pr.*7. II. *to be mirrored in*, Plot.3.6.17; *take visible shape*, εἰς τὴν ὕλην Id.1.8.8, cf. Iamb. *Comm.Math.*14, al. III. *have visions*, Zos.Alch.p.110B. **-ἄσις,** εως, ἡ, *imagination*, Plot.3.6.17. **-ικός,** ή, όν, *expressive, indicative*, τινός of a thing, Ph.1.149, Plu.2.747e, 1010c, Demetr.*Eloc.*283, A.D.*Pron.*8.9, etc.; τῆς δικαιοσύνης -ωτάτη ἡ πεντάς *Theol.Ar.*27: abs., *expressive, vivid*, παράκλησις Plb.18.23.2, cf. Plu.2.1009e (Comp.), Ph.1.302 (Sup.). Adv. -κῶς *vividly, forcibly*, of a painter, Plu.*Arat.*32; ἐ. γράφεσθαι Plb.12.25^{g}.2; τρανοῦν Ph.2.140: Comp. -ώτερον Plb.12.27.10: Sup. -ώτατα Ph.1.50: also -κῶς τοῦ κινδύνου *setting forth* the danger *clearly*, Plb.11.12.1.—ἐμφατικός (q.v.) is a common v.l.

ἐμφαρμάσσω, *smear upon*, in Pass., τοὺς ἐμπεφαρμαγμένους τοῖς βέλεσιν [ἰούς] Gal.*Nat.Fac.*1.14.

ἐμφᾰρύγγομαι, aor. 1 part. -υξάμενος, *gulp down*, *Com.Adesp.*996, Dsc.*Ther.*19.

ἔμφᾰσις, εως, ἡ, (ἐμφαίνομαι) *appearing in* a smooth surface, *reflection*, as in a mirror or in water, Arist.*Mete.*373^{b}24, 377^{b}17; κατ' ἔμφασιν by *reflection*, Id.*Mu.*395^{a}29; ἔμφασιν ποιεῖν Thphr.*Lap.*30; ἀμυδραὶ ἐ. τῆς ἀληθείας faint *reflections* or *images*, Plu.2.354c: generally, ἔ. προσώπου (in the moon) Epicur.*Ep.*2 p.41 U., *Stoic.*2.198, cf. Plot.4.3.18; τοῦ ὄντος Dam.*Pr.*69; τῶν πρώτων ἐν τοῖς ἐσχάτοις Procl.*in Alc.*p.69C.; στερεοῦ πρώτη ἔ. ἐν τῇ τετράδι εὑρίσκεται Hierocl.*in CA* 20 p.465 M. 2. *outward appearance, impression, presentation*, τὰς ἔ. κρίνειν Arist.*Div.Somn.*464^{b}12; φαντασιῶν *Stoic.*2.24 (pl.); κατὰ τὴν ἔ. Plb.5.63.2; ποιεῖν ἔμφασίν τινος give *the appearance of..*, *suggest*, Chrysipp.*Stoic.*2.257; ποιεῖν ἔ. ὡς.. make as if.., Plb.5.110.6; ποιεῖν, c. fut. inf., Str.8.3.30; ἔ. λαβεῖν τινος Phld.*Ir.* p.95 W., al.; ἔ. ἔχειν τινός D.H.*Th.*16; ἔ. ἔχειν ὡς.. D.S.11.89; ἔ. γίγνεταί τινος Id.1.38; of taste, ἔ. ἁλυκότητος Dsc.5.87. II. (ἐμφαίνω) *setting forth, exposition, narration*, Plb.6.5.3, etc.; ποιεῖν ἐμφάσεις κατά τινος to make *statements* against, Id.28.4.8; συμβόλων -σεις *explanations*, Iamb.*VP*23.103. III. *meaning, significance*, Agatharch.21, Corn.*ND*15; esp. in Rhet., *significance, emphasis*, Quint.8.3.83, 9.2.3, Trypho *Trop.*p.199 S., Tib.*Fig.*14: coupled with δείνωσις, Demetr.*Eloc.*130. 2. *suggestion, hint*, ib.57, 171. IV. *moral* of a fable, Babr.116.15.

ἐμφᾰτικός, ή, όν, *forcible, expressive*, Phld.*Rh.*1.326 S.: Comp., Demetr.*Eloc.*51. Adv. -κῶς Phld.*Po.*5.1425.29, Gal.17(1).826: Comp. -ώτερον Hsch. (Freq. f.l. for ἐμφαντικός, as A.D.*Adv.*131.23: so in Adv. -κῶς S.E.*M.*1.194.)

ἔμφατον· αἰνιγματοειδῶς εἰρημένον, Hsch.

ἐμφέρβομαι, poet. **ἐνιφ-,** Pass., *feed in*, σταθμοῖς Mosch.2.80.

ἐμφέρ-εια, ἡ, *likeness*, Ps.-Dsc.1.1, Ph.1.15, Corn.*ND*9, Plu.*Num.*13; πρός τι Ph.1.433, al., Plu.*TG*2: pl., τὰς ἀριθμοῦ ἐ. καὶ ἀφομοιώσεις *Theol.Ar.*58. **-ής,** ές, *answering to, resembling*, ἀνθέμοισι Sapph.85, freq. in Hdt., as 2.76, al.: Sup., 3.37, al.; also in Trag. and Ar., as A.*Ch.*206, *Supp.*279 (Comp.), S.*Aj.*1152, Ar.*Nu.*502; ἐ. τινι τοὺς τρόπους Id.*V.*1103 (Sup.); also in Prose, X.*Cyr.*5.5.31, Arist.*HA*626^{a}6, Thphr.*HP*7.6.3, Phld.*D.*3 *Fr.*66, Ph.1.316 (Sup.), etc.; καὶ τὰ ἐ. 'and the *like*', Sor.1.2. Adv. -ρῶς *similarly*, D.L.6.103; ἐ. ἔχειν τινί Ath.1.27a: Sup. -έστατα Ar.*Fr.*68.

ἐμφέρω, *bear* or *bring in* (v. infr. II):—Pass., *to be borne* or *carried in*, ἔν τινι Hp.*Epid.*7.40 (vulg. ἐκφ.); δίναις A.R.4.613; βένθεσι πόντου Opp.*H.*1.81:—Med., *carry with oneself*, τι Arat.701. II. *enter in* an account, ἐν λήμματι *PEleph.*15.4 (iii B.C.):—Pass., ἐνεφέρετο *an account was given*, Gloss. ad Plb.14.12. III. Pass., *to be contained* in, εἴδος ἐ. γένει Ph.1.460, al.: abs., Id.2.1, al.; τὰ ἐμφερόμενα τῷ πράγματι *matters appertaining to* the subject, Longin.12.2, prob. in Id.10.1. 2. ἐμφέρεσθαι τῇ αἰτίᾳ, = ἐνέχεσθαι, *IG*12(3).174.12 (Astypalaea, Epist. Aug.); ὁ ἐμφερόμενος the party *concerned*, *CPHerm.*53.12 (pl., iii A.D.), etc. IV. ἐμφέρω, Thess., = εἰσφέρω, *IG*9(2).205.20 (Melitaea); also, = εἰσφέρω I.4, *Berl.Sitzb.*1927.8 (Locr., v B.C.).

ἐμφεύγω, *fly in* or *into*, εἰς.. Luc.*Pseudol.*27 (s.v.l.).

ἐμφθέγγομαι, = φθέγγομαι ἐν, *speak then* or *there*, Luc.*Eun.*7 (s.v.l.).

ἐμφθορής, ές, (φθορά) *lost* or *destroyed in..*, Nic.*Al.*176.

ἐμφῐληδέω, *delight in*, τινί Porph.*Abst.*2.47, M.Ant.5.5 (ἐμφιληδονοῦντι Casaub.).

ἐμφῐλο-δοξέω, *seek fame in*, πράγματι Phld.*Rh.*2.140 S. **-κᾰλέω,** *pursue honourable studies in..*, Plu.2.122e; ἐ. τινί *to be engaged in* such a pursuit, Id.*Phil.*4. **-νεικος,** ον, = φιλόνεικος, λόγοι Sch. E.*Med.*637. Adv. -κως Sch.E.*Andr.*289. **-σοφέω,** *study philosophy in*, τῇ Σικελίᾳ Philostr.*VA*5.18, cf. 1.7: abs., Porph.*Abst.*4.6, Lib.*Or.*18.187. **-σοφος,** *philosophical*, αἰσθήσεις Ph.2.22, cf. Ptol. *Tetr.*158, D.L.2.40; τέχνη Olymp.Alch.p.70B. **-τεχνέω,** *bestow pains on*, τῇ παρούσῃ φαντασίᾳ M.Ant.7.54. **-χωρέω,** *to be fond of dwelling in, haunt*, τῇ μνήμῃ Luc.*Hist.Conscr.*1; τοῖς ἀγροῖς Alciphr.3.15; τῇ οἰκήσει J.*AJ*2.7.2; ἐν δόμῳ Agath.5.7: abs., Archemach.1; of things, Gal.16.556. **-χώρως,** Adv., metaph., *dwelling upon*, φωνὴ ἀναστρέφεται ἐ. περὶ τὰς μέσας μελῳδίας Ptol. *Harm.*3.11.

ἔμφῑμος, ον, *closed*, opp. ἄπωμος, Zos.Alch.p.113B.

ἐμφλάω, Ion. for ἐνθλάω, Hp.*Prorrh.*2.14.

ἐμφλεβοτομέω, *split up veins into branches*, Hp.*Oss.*18.

ἐμφλέγω, *kindle in*, ἐν φρεσὶ πυρσόν *APl.*4.198 (Maec.):—Pass., *to be inflamed*, Nic.*Th.*338.

ἔμφλοιος, ον, *with a bark*, Thphr.*HP*5.1.2.

ἐμφλοιοσπέρμᾰτος, ον, *with the seed covered by an integument*, Thphr.*HP*7.3.2.

ἔμφλοξ, ογος, ὁ, ἡ, *with fire in it*, πέτρος *AP*6.5 (Phil.).

ἐμφοβ-έω, *terrify, intimidate*, *BGU*613.18 (ii A.D.):—Pass., *to be alarmed*, Ezek.*Exag.*82. **-ος,** ον, *terrible*, θεαί S.*OC*39. II. Pass., *in fear, timorous*, ὕπειξις τῆς ψυχῆς Thphr.*Char.*25.1; *terrified, frightened*, Lxx *Si.*19.24, *Ev.Luc.*24.5, al., *Bull.Soc.Alex.*6.45. Adv. -βως Hsch. s.v. ὀρρωδέως.

ἐμφοιτάω, *invade*: metaph., κόλλυβός τις ἐμπεφοίτηκεν εἰς [τὴν ἀγοράν] *OGI*515.50 (Mylasa).

ἐμφονεύω, *kill in..*, τι ἔν τινι *Gp.*16.19.

ἐμφορβιόομαι, Pass., *to have the mouth-band on* (cf. φορβειά II), Ar.*Av.*861.

ἐμφόρβιος, ον, *eating away, consuming*, τινός Nic.*Th.*629. II. ἐμφόρβιον, τό, *pasture-money*, Hsch.

ἐμφορβ-ίω, Arc. **ἰμφ-,** *muzzle* (or *impose a pasture-tax*), *IG*5(2).3 (Tegea, iv B.C.):—also **-ισμός,** ὁ, *muzzling* (or *imposition of a pasture-tax*), ibid.

ἐμφορ-έω, = ἐμφέρω:—Pass., *to be borne about in* or *on*, c. dat., κύμασιν ἐμφορέοντο Od.12.419; ὕδασι A.R.4.626. II. *pour in*, ἄκρατον D.S.16.93; *fill*, πολέμων καὶ ταραχῶν ἅπαντα Agath.1.1:—Med. and Pass., *fill oneself with* a thing, *take one's fill* or *make much use of it*, ἐνεφορέετο τοῦ μαντηΐου Hdt.1.55; *to be filled full of*, Duris 27 J.; οἴνου, ἀκράτου, Hdn.4.11.3, Plu.2.1067e; κακίας, ἀμαθίας, Ph.1.204, 97; ἀγαθῶν *PLips.*119 ii 6 (iii A.D.); ἐξουσίας, ὕβρεως, Plu.*Cic.*19, *Sert.*5, etc.; τοῦ τέλους Dam.*Pr.*288: c. acc. rei, ἄκρατον D.S.4.4, Ph.2.403, cf. Alciphr.1.35, Thrasym.4, Porph.*Abst.*1.23, Gal.6.243: abs., Alciphr.1.1:—Act. in this sense is dub. in Democr. 1^{a}. III. metaph., *put upon, inflict on*, πληγάς τινι D.S.19.70, Plu. *Pomp.*3; ἐ. ὕβρεις εἴς τινα Alciphr.1.9:—Med., App.*BC*3.28. 2. *cast in one's teeth*, φόνους ἐ. τινί S.*OC*989. **-ησις,** εως, ἡ, *greedy eating and drinking*, Ath.1.10b; σαρκῶν -σεις Plu.2.472b; τῶν ἀλλοτρίων σωμάτων Porph.*Abst.*1.34; *repletion*, Paul.Aeg.6.96.

ἔμφορος, ον, *productive, profitable*, γῆ *PLond.*3.882.13 (ii B.C.); περιστερεών *PEdgar*49.3 (iii B.C.). II. ἔμφορα προσβεβλημένα· ἀγέλη προβάτων (ad ἐμφόρβιον pertinens), Hsch.

ἐμφορτ-ίζομαι, Med., = sq., metaph., πολὺν τῇ γαστρὶ κόρον Onos.12.2. II. Pass., *to be laden*, ἱκανῶς ἐμπεφορτισμένος Timae.Astr. in *Cat.Cod.Astr.*1.98. **-όομαι,** Med., *load with a cargo, freight*, ναῦν Aesop.370b. **-ος,** ον, *laden with*, ἐδωδῆς Opp.*H.*2.212: abs., *laden*, πλοῖον D.L.1.31; σαγήνη Iamb.*VP*8.36.

ἔμ-φραγμα, ατος, τό, (ἐμφράσσω) *barrier, obstacle*, Isoc.7.40, Plu.2.745f (pl.). 2. *wooden framework, casing*, in pl., Ph.*Bel.*66.47. 3. pl., *impacted faeces*, Archig.ap.Aët.6.27. 4. *impaction* of foetus, Hp.*Oct.*10. **-φραγμός,** ὁ, = ἔμφραξις, Lxx *Si.*27.14. **-φρακτικός,** ή, όν, *likely to obstruct, stop*, Hp.*Acut.*(*Sp.*)9, Aët.1 p.5^{v} 20. **-φραξις,** εως, ἡ, *stoppage*, [τῶν πόρων] Arist.*Pr.*870^{b}19; τοῦ φάρυγγος ib.901^{a}1, cf. Str.16.1.10, Porph.*Antr.*19 (pl.); as a morbid condition, Diocl.*Fr.*40; ἔ. λίθων *impaction*, Aret.*CA*2.9. **-φράσσω,** Att. -ττω, pf. ἐμπέφρᾰκα Sch.Ar.*Nu.*1240: fut. Pass. -φραχθήσομαι Lxx *Mi.*5.1(4.14): aor. 2 part. Pass. ἐμφρᾰγείς Ph.*Fr.*41 H.:—*bar a passage, stop up, block up*, τὸ μεταξύ Th.7.34; τοὺς ἔσπλους Id.4.8; ἐ. συγκλείουσά τε Pl.*Ti.*71c; ἐ. τὸ στόμα D.19.208; ἐ. τὰς ὁδοὺς τῶν ἀδικημάτων Lycurg.124. 2. *bar the passage of, stop*, τὰς κατὰ σοῦ τιμωρίας Aeschin.3.223; πᾶσαν παρείσδυσιν Epicur.*Sent. Vat.*47 (= Metrod.49); τὰς βοηθείας D.S.14.56; τὴν περὶ τὰ αἰσθητήρια ἀκρίβειαν Ph.1.246; τὴν φωνήν Plu.2.606d. 3. Med. in act. sense, Nic.*Al.*191. II. *stuff in*, φύλλα εἰς τὰς ὀπάς (v.l. φύλλοις τὰς ὀ.) *Gp.*13.5.3; τινί τι v.l. in Nic.*Th.*79 (Med.).

ἐμφρονέω, *come to one's senses*, Hp.*Epid.*5.22.

ἐμφροντις, ιδος, ὁ, ἡ, *anxious*, Them.*Or.*18.219b, Sch.Od.13.421.

ἐμφρονώδης, ες, *showing intelligence*, Hp.*Epid.*7.7.

ἐμφρουρ-έω, *keep guard in* a place, Th.4.110, 8.60: c. acc. loci, D.C.47.30, 50.12:—Pass., *to be imprisoned*, τέχναις Phalar.*Ep.*122.4. **-ος,** ον, *on guard at a post*, X.*HG*1.6.13. 2. *liable to military duty* (cf. φρουρά), opp. ἄφρουρος, Id.*Lac.*5.7. II. Pass., *held by garrisons*, πόλεις ἐμφρούρους ποιεῖ Decr.ap.D.18.182, cf. Plb.2.41.10, etc. III. *shut up in*, τῷ ταύρῳ Phalar.*Ep.*147.3; οἷον ἔ. *kept* as it were *in prison*, Longin.44.4, cf. Jul.*ad Ath.*272d.

ἐμφρύγω, = φρύγω ἐν, Ael.*NA*14.18:—also **ἐμφρύττω,** Poll.6.64.

ἔμφρων, ον, gen. ονος, (φρήν) *in one's mind* or *senses, sensible*: opp., 1. to one mad, σε Ζεὺς τίθησιν ἔμφρονα brings thee *to thy senses*, A.*Pr.*848; ἔ. εἰμί Id.*Ch.*1026; ἔ. καθίσταμαι I come *to myself*, S.*Aj.*306; ποιητὴς.. οὐκ ἔ. ἐστίν Pl.*Lg.*719c; ἀντὶ μανικῶν.. ἕξεις ἔμφρονας ἔχειν ib.791b. 2. to one dead, ἔτ' ἔ. S.*Ant.*1237, cf. Antipho 2.3.2; ἔ. γίγνεσθαι to *recover from* a swoon or lethargy, Hp.*Coac.*136. 3. to one asleep, S.E.*M.*7.129. II. *rational, intelligent*, ζῷα ἔ., opp. εἴδωλα ἄφρ., X.*Mem.*1.4.4; also ζωή, βίος ἔ., Pl.*R.*521a, *Ti.*36e; ἡ πρεσβυτῶν ἔ. παιδιά Id.*Lg.*769a; τέχνη -εστέρα Arist.*Rh.*1359^{b}6; ὅταν ἐς ἥβην ἐξικώμεθ' ἔμφρονες when we come to years *of discretion*, prob. in S.*Fr.*583.6. 2. *sensible, prudent*, Thgn.1126, Pi.*O.*9.74, S.*OT*436; ἐ. σωφροσύνη Th.1.84; ἔ. περί τι *wise* about or in a thing, Pl.*Lg.*809d; τῶν δημιουργῶν ἢ τῶν ἄλλων τῶν ἐ. ἀνδρῶν *experts*, Id.*Hipparch.*226c. Adv. -όνως *sensibly, wisely*, Id.*R.*396d, al., Antiph.104: Comp. -έστερον Phalar.*Ep.*67.3: Sup. -έστατα Plu.*Ant.*14.

ἐμφυής, ές, *inborn*, ἦθος Pi.*O.*11(10).20; *engrafted*, Jul.*Ep.*180.

ἐμφύλιος, ον, = ἔμφυλος (q.v.).

ἐμφυλλ-ίζω, *engraft*, *Gp.*10.37.1 (Pass.). **-ιον,** τό, *graft*, Eust.1423.38. **-ισμός,** ὁ, *engrafting, side-graft*, *Gp.*10.75.1. **-ος,** ον, *leafy*, ib.4.15.4.

ἔμφῡλος and **ἐμφύλιος**, ον, the latter being preferred in Trag.: (φῦλον):—*in the tribe*, i. e. *of the same tribe* or *race*, ἀνὴρ ἔμφυλος Od. 15.273; ἐμφύλιοι *kinsfolk*, S.*Ant.*1264 (lyr.), Pl.*Lg.*871a; ἐμφύλιον αἷμα the guilt of *kindred* blood, i. e. the murder *of a kinsman*, Pi. *P.*2.32, Pl.*R.*565e, cf. S.*OT*1406; τοὐμφυλον αἷμα Id.*OC*407; στάσιές τε καὶ ἔμφυλοι φόνοι ἀνδρῶν Thgn.51; ἔμφυλοι παρ' ἑκατέροις *registered in a tribe*, *GDI*5040.15 (Hierapytna). 2. γῆ ἐμφύλιος *one's native* land, S.*OC*1385. II. *in* or *among one's people* or *family*, μάχα Alc.*Supp.*23.11; ἔμφυλος στάσις *intestine* discord, Sol. 4.19, Hdt.8.3, Democr.249; Ἄρης ἐμφύλιος A.*Eu.*863; μάχη Theoc. 22.200; πόλεμος Plb.1.65.2, cf. Plu.*Pomp.*24.

ἐμφῡρᾱμᾰτοπώλης, ου, ὁ, *seller of confectionery*, Gloss.

ἐμφύρω and **-άω** [ῡ], *mix up, confuse*, ἵπποι δ' ἐφ' ἵπποις ἐμπεφυρμένοι A.*Fr.*38, cf. Lyc.1380; Ep. aor. 1 ἐνιφυρήσαντες Opp.*H.*3.498: aor. Med. ἐνεφύραντο v.l. in Lxx*Ez.*22.6: also fr. ἐμφυράω, pf. part. Pass. ἐμπεφυραμένος Archig.ap.Orib.8.2.18.

ἐμφῡσ-άω, *blow in*, ἐς τὰς ῥῖνας Aret.*CA*1.2, cf. *POxy.*1088.37; αὐλητρὶς ἐνεφύσησε *breathed into* the flute, Ar.*V.*1219; οἴνῳ ἐ. *Hippiatr.*11. II. *breathe upon*, τινί, εἴς τινα, Lxx*Jb.*4.21, *Ez.*37.9, cf. *Ev.Jo.*20.22. III. *blow up, inflate*, τὸ μὲν [τῆς τροφῆς] ἐμφυσᾶν, τὸ δὲ σαρκοῦν Arist.*HA*603^{b}30; ἐ. τὰς φλέβας Id.*Pr.*881^{b}14:—Pass., *to be inflated* or, generally, *swollen*, Hp.*Coac.*154, Arist.*HA*524^{a}17, al.: metaph., τῇ κολακείᾳ ἐμφυσώμενος Clearch.25. **-ημα**, ατος, τό, *an inflation* of the stomach, peritoneum, or cellular tissue, mostly of the stomach, Hp.*Epid.*3.17.ιγ', Gal.19.132; *swelling* of the eye, Dem.Ophth.ap.Aët.7.14; of the knee, Gal.12.203. **-ημᾰτώδης**, ες, *like an* ἐμφύσημα, Id.7.609. **-ησις**, εως, ἡ, *inflation*, Plu.2.1077b; *flatulence*, Ath.1.32e (pl.). **-ητέον**, *one must blow in*, *Gp.*16.6.2; εἰς τὰς ῥῖνας ὄξος Herod.Med. in *Rh.Mus.*58.79. **-ητής**, οῦ, ὁ, *one who inflates*, Gloss. **-ητικός**, ή, όν, *inflating*, Gal.19.132 (Sup.).

ἐμφῡσιόω, (φύσις) *inspire, infuse life into*, τὴν ἀνάγνωσιν Lxx1*Es.* 9.48:—Pass., *to be inspired*, τοῖς ῥήμασιν ib.55. II. *implant, instil into*, τὸ αἰδεῖσθαι ἐμφυσιῶσαί τινι X.*Lac.*3.4; ἐνεφυσίωσαν τοῖς γινομένοις ἐξ ἑαυτῶν τὴν βούλησιν τοῦ θεοῦ *Michel*855.9 (Magn. Mae.):—Pass., μάθησις δεξιῶς ἐμφυσιωθεῖσα Hp.*Lex* 2; ἵνα ἐμφυσιῶται ἑκάστῳ τὸ κάλλιστον Charond.ap.Stob.4.2.24; ἐμπεφυσιωμένη κακία Diog. *Ep.*28.1.

ἔμφῠσις, εως, ἡ, *insertion* of a muscle, Gal.*UP*1.21, Orib.25.31.6.

ἐμφῠτ-εία, ἡ, *grafting*, in pl., Arist.*Juv.*468^{b}23, Thphr.*HP*1.6. 1, 2.1.4, al. **-ευμα**, ατος, τό, in Roman law, *hereditary leasehold held on cultivating tenure*, Just.*Nov.*7.3.2; *quitrent* paid on such property, *Cod.Just.*1.4.32, *PMasp.*298.40 (vi A. D.). **-ευσις**, εως, ἡ, *tenure of such a holding*, Just.*Nov.*7 *Pr.*1, al.; κατ' ἐμφύτευσιν ἔχειν *PMasp.*257.5 (vi A. D.). **-ευτής**, οῦ, ὁ, *holder of such an estate*, *PKlein.Form.*314 (v/vi A. D.), Just.*Nov.*7 *Pr.*1. **-ευτικός**, ή, όν, *concerning* ἐμφύτευσις or ἐμφυτεύματα, κανών, συγγραφή, ib.7.3.2; δίκαιον *PMasp.*298.39 (vi A. D.). **-εύω**, *implant, engraft*, Pl.*Ti.* 70c, *IG*12(7).62.34 (Amorgos):—Pass., Thphr.*CP*1.6.1, etc.; ἐλαίας ἐμπεφυτευμένας ἐν τοῖς κοτίνοις D.S.5.16: metaph., of souls, σώμασιν ἐμφυτευθῆναι Pl.*Ti.*42a. 2. metaph., ἐμφυτεύειν μονάρχους τοῖς Ἕλλησι Plb.2.41.10, cf. 9.29.6; ἐν τῇ ψυχῇ παράδεισον ἀρετῶν Ph. 1.335. II. Pass., of land, *to be granted on terms of* ἐμφύτευσις, *PMasp.*298.17 (vi A. D.), Just.*Nov.*7.3.3.

ἔμφῠτος, ον, *inborn, natural*, ἐ. μαντικὴν εἶχε Hdt.9.94; πατρὸς αἷμα S.*OC*1671 (lyr.); τοῖς πλουτοῦσι τοῦτο δ' ἐ. E.*Fr.*776.1, cf. Men. 15.1 D.; ἔρως ἐ. τοῖς ἀνθρώποις Pl.*Smp.*191d; ἡ μὲν [ἰδέα] ἐ. οὖσα, ἐπιθυμία ἡδονῶν Id.*Phdr.*237d, cf. D.60.1; αἰσχροκέρδεια, πονηρία, Din. 1.108; κακία Lxx*Wi.*12.10; ἐ. ἡ ἀρετή, opp. διδακτός, Pl.*Erx.*398c, cf. Lys.33.7; τὸ ἐ. θερμόν Hp.*Aph.*1.14; ἐ. θερμότης Arist.*Mete.*355^{b} 9; οὐκ ἦν ταῦτα τοῖς Ἀθηναίοις πάτρια.. οὐδ' ἐ. D.18.203; τὰν ἐ. αὐτοῖς ἀθεσίαν *IPE*1.185 (Chersonesus). Adv. -τως Ph.*Fr.*70 H. II. *planted*, χωρίον *PHamb.*23.16 (vi A. D.); ἐλαῖαι *BGU*241.28 (ii A. D.). 2. *implanted*, λόγος *Ep.Jac.*1.21.

ἐμφύω, *implant*, θεὸς δέ μοι ἐν φρεσὶν οἴμας παντοίας ἐνέφυσεν *planted* them *in* my soul, Od.22.348; ἐμφῦσαι ἔρωτά τινι X.*Mem.*1.4.7; νόον τινί Eleg.ap.Ath.7.337f, cf. Ph.1.631, al. II. Pass., with pf. ἐμπέφυκα and aor. 2 ἐνέφῡν: pf. subj. ἐμπεφύῃ Thgn.396: 1. *grow in* or *on*, τινί, ὅθι τε τρίχες ἵππων κρανίῳ ἐμπεφύασι (Ep. for ἐμπεφύκασι) Il.8.84; τὰ ἐμφυόμενα Hp.*Aër.*5; ἐμφύεσθαι ἐν [νήσῳ] Hdt.2.156: hence of qualities, φθόνος ἀρχῆθεν ἐμφύεται ἀνθρώπῳ *is implanted* in him, Id.3.80; ᾧ (sc. μάντει) τἀληθὲς ἐμπέφυκεν S.*OT*299; τὸ πιστὸν ἐμφῦναι φρενί Id.*OC*1488; πάντ' ἐμπέφυκε τῷ γήρᾳ κακά Id.*Fr.*949; τὸ μῶρον γυναιξὶν ἐμπέφυκε E.*Hipp.*967; οὐδεὶς χαρακτὴρ ἐμπέφυκε σώματι *is set by nature on* the body, Id.*Med.*519; κακία τῇ πόλει ἐμφύεται X.*Mem.*3.5.17, etc.: the pf. part. abs., *innate*, νόσημα πόλεως ἐ. Pl. *Lg.*736a, cf. 863b. 2. *to be rooted in, cling closely*, ὡς ἔχετ' ἐμπεφυυῖα (Ep. part.) she hung on *clinging*, Il.1.513; ἐν τ' ἄρα οἱ φῦ χειρί *clung fast* to his hand, *clasped* his hand *tight*, as a warm greeting, 6.253, etc.; ἔφυν ἐν χερσί Od.10.397; ἐν χείρεσσι φύοντο 24.410; so χεῖρες.. ἐμπεφυκυῖαι ἦσαν τοῖσι ἐπισπαστῆρσι *stuck fast* to the handles, Hdt.6.91; ἐμφύντε τῷ φύσαντι S.*OC*1113, cf. E.*Ion*891 (anap.); ὀδὰξ ἐν χείλεσι φύντες *biting* the lips *hard*, in suppressed anger, Od.1.381, 18.410, 20.268 (so ἐμφῦσαι ὀδόντας *to fix* the teeth *in*, Ael.*NA*14.8); ἀμὺξ ἐμφῦναι Nic.*Th.*131: c. gen., D.H.11.31 (s.v.l.): abs., ἐμφύς Hdt.3.109; ἐμφὺς ὡς βδέλλα Theoc.2.56; ἐμπεφυκὼς πόνος *fixed* pain, Archig.ap.Gal.8.110. 3. metaph., *cling to*, ταῖς ἐλπίσι καὶ ταῖς παρασκευαῖς Plu.2.342c; τοῖς ἠθικοῖς καὶ πολιτικοῖς δόγμασι Id.*Cat.Mi.* 4; τοῖς πολεμίοις Id.*Nic.*14; τὴν πόλιν ἀφέντας -φῦναι ταῖς ναυσίν Id. *Them.*9.

ἐμφωλεύω, *lurk in*.., Ph.1.315, al., Plu.2.314e, Dam.*Isid.*296, Just. *Nov.*80.9; ἡ κακηγορία -ευε τοῖς ὠσί Men.Prot.p.70 D.; esp. of disease, Aret.*SD*2.13, Gal.17(1).165. II. *dwell in caves* or *lairs*, *OGI*424.5 (Qanawât). III. Act., *hide, conceal*, Horap.2.90.

ἐμφωνέομαι, Pass., *to be expressed* in certain terms, *PMasp.*6 ii 118 (vi A. D.).

ἔμφωνος, ον, *vocal*, Ael.*NA*15.27.

ἔμφωτον, τό, *hollow* of a cone, Hero*Stereom.*1.55.

ἐμψάω, poet. ἐνιψ-, *wipe in* or *upon*, Call.*Fr.*121 (Med.).

ἐμψηφίζω, *enter* a debt in one's books, Hsch.; cf. ἐνιψηφίζομαι.

ἔμψηφος, ον, *adorned with gems*, φιάλη *IPE*1^{2}.107 (Olbia).

ἐμψίω, *feed with pap*, prob. in A.*Fr.*51, cf. Bgk. ad Hippon.33.

ἐμψοφ-έω, *make a noise in*, Hp.*Loc.Hom.*16. **-ος**, ον, *sounding*, *AP*5.243 (Paul. Sil.).

ἐμψῡκτικός, ή, όν, *cooling*, Gal.11.419; ἀγωγή Id.10.555; ἔμπλαστρος Orib.*Fr.*76. Adv. Comp. -ώτερον Aët.15.33.

ἔμψῡξις, εως, ἡ, *cooling, refreshing*, Aret.*SA*1.9, Ruf.ap.Orib.*inc.* 9.1, Gal.6.626.

ἐμψῡχ-ήϊος, v. l. for ἔμψυχος in Luc.*Vit.Auct.*6. **-ία**, ἡ, *having life in one, animation*, Epicur.*Fr.*310, Plu.2.1053b, S.E.*P.*2.25, Theo Sm.p.187 H., Dam.*Pr.*18, Simp.*in Ph.*638.2. **-ος**, ον, *having life in one, animate*, opp. ἄψυχος, Hdt.1.140, al., Simon.106.4, S.*OC* 1486, E.*Alc.*139, Pl.*Phdr.*245e, al.; ἐ. νεκρός '*a breathing* corpse', S. *Ant.*1167; γῦπες ἐ. τάφοι Gorg.*Fr.*5a D.; μὴ κτείνειν τὸ ἐ., of Empedocles, Arist.*Rh.*1373^{b}14, cf. E.*Fr.*472.18 (anap.); ἔμψυχον οὐδὲν ἐσθίει Alex.27.2, cf. 220.3; δοῦλος ἐ. ὄργανον Arist.*EN*1161^{b}4; εἶναι τὸν βασιλέα ἐ. νόμον Ph.2.135, cf. Diotog.ap.Stob.4.7.61; ἔμψυχα, τά, *animals*, Th.7.29, *PGiss.*40 ii 22 (iii A. D.): Sup., ὅσα ἐμψυχότατα.. ἦν *most full of vital fluid*, Pl.*Ti.*74e. 2. of diction, *animated, vivid*, λέξεις Arist.*Fr.*129 Bonitz, cf. Luc.*Dem.Enc.*14; so ἐ. ἄγαλμα *AP*12.56 (Mel.); πάθη Longin.34.4: Comp., ἡ ἀληθὴς εὐφημία -οτέρα τῶν Δαιδάλου ἔργων Them.*Or.*28.342d. Adv. -ως Plu.2.790f: Sup. -ότατα Herm.*in Phdr.*p.61 A. **-όω**, *animate*, ἐνεψύχωσε δ' ὁ γλύπτας τὸν λίθον *AP*9.774 (Glauc.):—Pass., *Gp.*15.2.28, Porph. *Gaur.*tit. **-ρία**, ἡ, *cold*, *Placit.*2.4.5. **-ρος**, ον, *cold*, Hp.*Epid.* 6.6.2: Comp., Thphr.*Sens.*53. **-ω**, *cool, refresh*, Philonid.ap.Ath. 15.676c, Antyll.ap.Orib.6.4.1, Aret.*CA*2.3, Gal.11.387: aor. 2 part. Pass. ἐμψῠγέντες S.E.*P.*1.51. **-ωσις**, εως, ἡ, *animating*, Gal.4. 763, Plot.4.3.9, Porph.*Gaur.*2.4, al.

ἐν, poet. ἐνί, εἰν, εἰνί (Il.8.199, etc.), forms used by Ep. and Lyric Poets as the metre requires, but only as f.l. in Trag., εἰν S.*Ant.* 1241; εἰνί E.*Heracl.*893: Arc. and Cypr. ἰν *IG*5(2).3.5, al., *Inscr. Cypr.*135.9 H., al.

PREP. WITH DAT. AND ACC. Radical sense, *in, into*.

A. WITH DAT.

I. OF PLACE, 1. *in*, νήσῳ ἐν ἀμφιρύτῃ Od.1.50; ἐν δώμασ' ἐμοῖσιν Il.6.221; ἐνὶ προθύροισιν 11.777; κοίλῃσ' ἐνὶ νηυσί Od.2.27; with names of cities or islands, as ἐν Ἀθήνῃς, ἐν Τροίῃ, Il.2.549, 162; ἡ ἐν Κερκύρᾳ ναυμαχία Th.1.57; ἡ ἐν Σαλαμῖνι μάχη Isoc.5.147 (but in Att. the Prep. is sts. omitted, as with Ἐλευσῖνι, Μαραθῶνι; where ἐν is used, it = *in the district of*.., ἐν Ἐλευσῖνι *IG*2^{2}.1028.11, ἐμ Μαραθῶνι ib.1243. 21): ἐν χερσὶν ἐμῇσι *in* my arms, Il.22.426; ἐνὶ θυμῷ Od.16.331, etc.; ἐν αὑτῷ εἶναι to be *in* one's senses, be oneself, ἔτ' ἐν σαυτῷ (v.l. -τοῦ) γενοῦ S.*Ph.*950; also ἐν αὑτοῦ, cf. signf. 2. b. ἐν τοῖς ἰχθύσιν *in* the fish-market, Antiph.125; ἐν τῷ μύρῳ Ar.*Eq.*1375; so ἐν τοῖν δυοῖν ὀβολοῖν ἐθεώρουν ἂν *in* the two-obol seats, D.18.28. 2. elliptic, in such phrases as ἐν Ἀλκινόοιο Od.7.132, cf. *Leg.Gort.*2.21, etc.; εἰν Ἀΐδαο Il.22.389, Att. ἐν Ἅιδου (v. Ἅιδης): later ἐν τοῖς τινός *PRev. Laws*38.1 (iii B. C.), *Ev.Luc.*2.49; ἐν ἡμετέρου Hdt.1.35, 7.8.δ'; ἐμ Πανδίονος *IG*2^{2}.1138.8; ἐν Δημοτιωνιδῶν ib.2.841^{b}21; ἐν τῶν πόλεων ib. 1^{2}.56.14: mostly with pr.n., but sts. with Appellatives, as, ἐν ἀφνειοῦ πατρός Il.6.47; ἐν ἀνδρὸς εὐσεβεστάτου E.*IA*926; ἐν παιδοτρίβου, ἐν κιθαριστοῦ, *at the school of*.., Ar.*Nu.*973, Pl.*Tht.*206a; ἐν γειτόνων (v. γείτων); ἐν αὑτοῦ (αὐτῷ cod. Rav.) Ar.*V.*642, cf. Men.*Sam.*125; οὐκέτ' ἐν ἐμαυτοῦ ἦν Pl.*Chrm.*155d; ἐν ὑμῶν αὐτῶν γένεσθε Lib.*Or.* 35.15. 3. *in, within, surrounded by*, οὐρανὸς ἐν αἰθέρι καὶ νεφέλῃσι Il.15.192; after Hom., of clothing, armour, etc., ἐν ἐσθῆτι Hdt.2.159; ἐν πεπλώματι S.*Tr.*613; ἐν ἔντεσι Pi.*O.*4.24; ἐν ὅπλοισι *in* or *under* arms, Hdt.1.13, etc.; also of particular kinds of arms, ἐν τόξοις, ἀκοντίοις, etc., *equipped with* them, dub. in X.*Mem.*3.9.2; ἐν μαχαίρῃ *PTeb.* 16.14 (ii B. C.); ἐν μεγάλοις φορτίοις βαδίζειν καὶ τρέχειν X.*Cyr.*2.3. 14; ἐν βαθεῖ πώγωνι Luc.*Salt.*5. 4. *on, at* or *by*, ἐν ποταμῷ Il. 18.521, Od.5.466; ἐν ὄρεσσιν 19.205; οὔρεος ἐν κορυφῇς Il.2.456; ἐν θρόνοις Od.8.422; νευρὴ ἐν τόξῳ the string *on* the bow, Il.15.463; ἐν [ξίφει] ἥλοι 11.29; κατεκλάσθη ἐνὶ καυλῷ ἔγχος was broken off *at* or *by* the shaft, 13.608; ἐν πέτροισι πέτρον ἐκτρίβων S.*Ph.*296; ἐν οἴνῳ *at* wine, prob. in Call.*Ep.*23, Luc.*Dem.Enc.*15. 5. *in the number of, amongst*, freq. in Hom., ἐν Δαναοῖσι, προμάχοισι, μέσσοισιν, νεκύεσσι, Il.1.109, 3.31, 7.384, Od.12.383, al.; οἵη ἐν ἀθανάτοισιν Il. 1.398; and with Verbs of ruling, ἐν δ' ἄρα τοῖσιν ἦρχ' 13.689; ἀνδράσιν ἐν πολλοῖσι.. ἀνάσσων Od.19.110; φῦλον ἐν ἀνθρώποισι παταιότατον Pi.*P.*3.21; ἐν τοῖς οἰκείοισιν ἀνὴρ χρηστός S.*Ant.*661; ἐν γυναιξὶν ἄλκιμος E.*Or.*754:—for ἐν τοῖς c. Sup., v. ὁ. b. *in the presence of*, ἐν πᾶσι Od.2.194; πτωχὸς ὢν ἐν ἐσθλοῖσιν λέγειν E.*Fr.* 703; λέγοντες ἐν τῷ δήμῳ Pl.*R.*565b; μακρηγορεῖν ἐν εἰδόσι Th.2.36; ἔλεγον ἐν τοῖς τριάκοντα Lys.12.6; ἐν τοῖς ὄχλοις εἰπεῖν Isoc.3.21; λέγειν ἐν ἀνδράσιν (of a woman) Lys.32.11; of a trial, διαγωνίζεσθαι, διαδικάζεσθαι ἔν τισι, Pl.*Grg.*464d, *Lg.*916b; προὐκαλούμην ἐν τοῖς αὐτοῖς δικασταῖς Antipho6.23. 6. *in one's hands, within one's reach* or *power*, νίκης πείρατ' ἔχονται ἐν ἀθανάτοισι θεοῖσι Il.7.102; δύναμις γὰρ ἐν ὑμῖν Od.10.69 (comp. the Homeric phrases θεῶν ἐν γούνασι κεῖται Il.17.514; ἐν γὰρ χερσὶ τέλος πολέμου 16.630); freq. in Hdt. and Att., ἔστιν ἔν τινι, c. inf., it depends *on* him to.., rests *with* him to.., ἔστιν ἐν σοὶ ἤ..ἤ.. Hdt.6.109, cf. 3.85, etc.; ταῦτα δ' ἐν τῷ δαίμονι καὶ τῇδε φῦναι χἀτέρᾳ S.*OC*1443; ἐν σοὶ γάρ ἐσμεν Id.*OT*314; ἐν σοὶ δ' ἐσμὲν καὶ ζῆν καὶ μὴ E.*Alc.*278; ἐν ταῖς ναυσὶ τῶν Ἑλλήνων τὰ πράγματα ἐγένετο Th.1.74; ἐν τῷ θεῷ τὸ τέλος ἦν, οὐκ ἐμοί D.18.193; also ἐν τούτῳ εἰσὶν πᾶσαι αἱ ἀποδείξεις depend *on* this, Pl.*Prt.*354e; ἐν τούτῳ λύεται ἡ ἀπορία ἢ ἄλλοθι οὐδαμοῦ ib.321e; ἔν γ' ἐμοί so far as rests *with* me, S.*OC*153 (lyr.); ἐν δὲ σοὶ λελείψομαι E.*Hipp.*324; also ἐν ἐμοί *in* my judgement, S.*OC*1214 (lyr.); ἐν θεοῖς καλά *in the eyes of* the gods, Id.*Ant.*925. **7.** *in respect of*, ἐν πάντεσσ' ἔργοισι δαήμονα φῶτα Il.23.671; ἐν γήρᾳ σύμμετρός τινι *in point of* age.., S.*OT*1112; ἐν ἐμοὶ θρασύς *in* my case, *towards* me, Id.*Aj.*1315; ἐν θανοῦσιν ὑβριστής ib.1092; ἡ ἐν τοῖς ὅπλοις μάθησις Pl.*La.*190d; also οὐδὲν δεινὸν μὴ ἐν ἐμοὶ στῇ stop *with* me, Id.*Ap.*28b. **8.** in a pregnant construction with Verbs of motion, *into*; implying both *motion to* and subsequent *position in* a place, ἐν κονίῃσι χαμαὶ πέσεν *fell* [to the dust and lay] *in* it, Il.4.482, etc.; βάλον ἐν κονίῃσι 5.588; νηῒ δ' ἐνὶ πρύμνῃ ἔναρα θῆκ' 10.570; ἐν χερσὶ τιθέναι 1.441, etc.; ἐν χερσὶ βαλεῖν 5.574; ἐν στήθεσσι μένος βαλεῖν ib.513; ἐν Τρωσὶν ὄρουσαν 16.258; ἐν χερσὶ πεσέειν 6.81; λέων ἐν βουσὶ θορών 5.161; ἐν δ' οἶνον ἔχευεν ἐν δέπαϊ χρυσέῳ Od.20.261; ἐν τεύχεσσιν ἔδυνον Il.23.131: in Trag. and Att., ἐν ποίμναις πίτνων S.*Aj.*184 (lyr.), cf. 374 (lyr.); ἐν χωρίῳ ἐμπεπτωκώς Th.7.87; ἡ ἐν τῷ Σπειραίῳ τῶν νεῶν καταφυγή Id.8.11; ἐν τόπῳ καταπεφευγέναι Pl.*Sph.*260c; ἐν ᾅδου διαπορευθείς Id.*Lg.*905b; ῥιπτοῦντες σφᾶς ἐν τῇ θαλάσσῃ Arr.*An.*1.19.4; later, with Verbs of *coming* and *going*, διαβάντες ἐν τῇ Σάμῳ Paus.7.4.3, cf. Lxx *To.*5.5, Arr.*Epict.*1.11.32, etc.: τὸν ἐν Σικελίᾳ πλοῦν is f.l. in Lys.19.43 codd. **9.** πίνειν ἐν ποτηρίῳ to drink *from* a cup, Luc.*DDeor.*6.2; ἐν ἀργύρῳ πίνειν Id.*Merc.Cond.*26; ἐν μικροῖς D.L.1.104. **10.** ἄργυρος ἐν ἐκπώμασι silver *in the form of* plate, Plu.2.260a; ἐμ φέρνῃ, ἐν θέματι, *as* a dowry, pledge, *PPetr.*1p.37, *PTeb.*120.125 (i B.C.). **11.** in citations, ἐν τοῦ σκήπτρου τῇ παραδόσει *in* the passage of the Il. describing this, Th.1.9, cf. Pl.*Tht.*147c, *Phlb.*33b.

II. Of State, Condition or Position: **1.** of outward circumstances, ἐν πολέμῳ Od.10.553; ἐν δαιτί Il.4.259; ἐν καρὸς αἴσῃ 9.378; ἐν μοίρῃ Od.22.54; οὐδὸς ἐν φάει βίος E.*Ph.*1281; ἐν γένει εἶναί τινι to be related to.., S.*OT*1016; of occupations, pursuits, ἐν φιλοσοφίᾳ εἶναι to be engaged *in* philosophy, Pl.*Phd.*59a, cf. *R.*489b; οἱ ἐν ποιήσι γενόμενοι poets, Hdt.2.82; οἱ ἐν τοῖς πράγμασι ministers of state, Th.3.28; οἱ ἐν τέλει the magistrates, Id.7.73, etc.; τοὺς ἐν ταῖς μοναρχίαις ὄντας Isoc.2.5; ὁ ἐν ταῖς προσόδοις *PPetr.*1p.62; ὁ μάντις ἦν ἐν τῇ τέχνῃ *in the practice of* it, S.*OT*562. **2.** of inward states, of feeling, etc., ἐν φιλότητι, ἐν δαΐ, Il.7.302, 9.230; ἐν φόβῳ γενέσθαι Pl.*R.*578e; οὐκ ἐν αἰσχύνῃ τὰ σά E.*Ph.*1276; ἐν σιωπῇ τἀμά Id.*Ion* 1397; ἐν ὀργῇ ἔχειν τινά to make him the object of one's anger, Th.2.21; ἐν ἔριδι εἶναι ibid.; ἐν αἰτίᾳ σχεῖν τινά to blame him, Hdt.5.106; ἐν αἰτίᾳ βαλεῖν S.*OT*656 (lyr.); ἐν αἰτίᾳ εἶναι to have the blame, X.*Mem.*2.8.9, etc.; οἱ ἐν ταῖς αἰτίαις D.*Ep.*2.14. **3.** freq. with neut. Adj., ἐν βραχεῖ, = βραχέως, S.*El.*673; ἐν τάχει, = ταχέως, Id.*OT*765, etc.; ἐν καλῷ ἐστί, = καλῶς ἔχει, E.*Heracl.*971; ἐν ἀσφαλεῖ [ἐστί] Id.*IT* 762; ἐν εὐμαρεῖ [ἐστί] Id.*Hel.*1227; ἐν ἐλαφρῷ ποιήσασθαι Hdt.3.154; ἐν ἴσῳ, = ἴσως, ἐν ὁμοίῳ, = ὁμοίως, Th.2.53: less freq. in pl., ἐν ἀργοῖς, = ἀργῶς, S.*OT*287; ἐν κενοῖς, = κενῶς, Id.*Aj.*971: with a Subst., ἐν δίκᾳ, = δικαίως, opp. παρὰ δίκαν, Pi.*O.*2.16, cf. S.*Tr.*1069, Ar.*Eq.*258, Pl.*R.*475c, al.; ἦσαν οὐκέτι ὁμοίως ἐν ἡδονῇ ἄρχοντες Th.1.99, cf. Pl.*Epin.*977b.

III. Of the Instrument, Means or Manner, ἐν πυρὶ πρήσαντες Il.7.429; δῆσαι ἐνὶ δεσμῷ 5.386, cf. Od.12.54, etc.; but in most cases the orig. sense may be traced, to put *in* the fire and burn, *in* fetters and bind, etc.; so ἐν πόνοις δαμέντα A.*Pr.*425 (lyr.); ἔζευξα πρῶτος ἐν ζυγοῖσι κνώδαλα ib.462; ἔργον ἐν κύβοις Ἄρης κρινεῖ Id.*Th.*414; also ἐν ὀφθαλμοῖσιν or ἐν ὄμμασιν ὁρᾶσθαι, ἰδέσθαι, to see *with* or *before* one's eyes, i.e. have the object *in* one's eye, Il.3.306, Od.10.385, etc.; ἔν τε τῇ ὄψει διαγιγνώσκειν καὶ ἐν τῇ ἀκοῇ Pl.*Tht.*206a; also ἐν ὠσὶ νωμῶν ὄρνιθας A.*Th.*25; also ἐν λιταῖς *by* prayers, S.*Ph.*60; ἐν δόλῳ *by* deceit, ib.102; ἐν λόγοις *by* words, A.*Ch.*613 (lyr.); ἀπέκτειναν ἐν τῇ προφάσει ταύτῃ Lys.13.12, cf. Antipho 5.59; ψαύειν ἐν κερτομίοις γλώσσαις S.*Ant.*961 (lyr.); ἐν τοῖς ὁμοίοις νόμοις ποιήσαντες τὰς κρίσεις Th.1.77; esp. with Verbs of showing, σημαίνειν ἐν ἱεροῖς καὶ οἰωνοῖς X.*Cyr.*8.7.3; τὰ πραχθέντα...ἐν..ἐπιστολαῖς ἴστε ye know *by* letters, Th.7.11; ἐν τῇδε ῥάβδῳ πάντα ποιήσεις Ezek.*Exag.*132, cf. *PMag.Osl.*1.108. **2.** of a personal instrument, ἐν τῷ ἄρχοντι τῶν δαιμονίων ἐκβάλλει τὰ δαιμόνια *Ev.Matt.*9.34.

IV. Of Time, ὥρῃ ἐν εἰαρινῇ Il.16.643; ἐν νυκτί Hdt.6.69, X.*Smp.*1.9; ἐν χρόνῳ μακρῷ S.*Ph.*235, *OC*88; ἐν τούτῳ (sc. τῷ χρόνῳ) *in* this space of time, Hdt.1.126, etc.; ἐν ᾧ (sc. χρόνῳ) *during the time* that, S.*Tr.*929, etc. (also ἐν οἷς Arist.*Mu.*391^{a}2); ἐν ὅσῳ Th.3.28; ἐν ταῖς σπονδαῖς *in the time of* the truce, X.*An.*3.1.1; ἐν τῇ ἑορτῇ Th.7.73 (but in some phrases the ἐν is omitted, as μυστηρίοισι *in the course of* the mysteries, Ar.*Pl.*1013; τραγῳδοῖς *at the performance of*.., Aeschin.3.36). **b.** ἐν ἄρχοντι Μητροδώρῳ *during* the archonship of M., *IG*7.1773 (Thebes, ii A.D.); ἐν ἄρχοντι Σύλλᾳ ib.3.113. **2.** *in*, *within*, ἐν ἡμέρῃ Hdt.1.126; ἐν ἔτεσι πεντήκοντα Th.1.118; ἐν τρισὶ μησί X.*HG*1.1.37, etc.; μυρίαις ἐν ἁμέραις *in*, i.e. *after*, countless days, E.*Ph.*305 (lyr.); ἐν ἡμέραις πολλαῖς νοσῆσαι Procop.*Arc.*9.35.

V. Of Numbers generally, ἐν δυσὶ σταδίοις *within* two stadia, D.S.20.74, cf. 19.39, dub. in Th.6.1. **2.** with gen. of price, ἐν δύο ταλάντων Lxx 3*Ki.*16.24. **3.** *amounting to*, προῖκα ἐν δραχμαῖς ἐννακοσίαις *BGU*970.14 (ii A.D.), etc.

B. With Acc., *into, on, for*, Arc. ἰν, νόμος ἰν ἄματα πάντα *IG*5(2).5; γράψαι ἐν χάλκωμα ib.511; ἐν πελτοφόρας ἀπεγράψατο ib.7.210 (Aegosthenae), etc.; also poet., ἐν πάντα νόμον Pi.*P.*2.86.

C. Without Case, as Adverb, in the phrase ἐν δέ.., **1.** *and therein*, Il.9.361; ἐν μέν..ἐν δέ Od.13.244. **2.** *and among them*, Il.2.588, etc.; in Hdt., mostly ἐν δὲ δή.. 3.39, 5.95; or ἐν δὲ καί.. 2.43, 172, 176. **3.** *and besides, moreover* (not in Att. Prose), S.*Aj.* 675, *OT*181 (lyr.), al.; ἐν δ' ὑπέρας τε κάλους τε πόδας τ' ἐνέδησεν ἐν αὐτῇ Od.5.260. **4.** ἔνι, = ἔνεστι, ἔνεισι, Il.20.248, etc.

D. Position: ἐν freq. stands between its Subst. and the Adj. agreeing therewith, Il.22.61, B.5.41, etc.: without an Adj., τῷ δ' ἐν ἐρινεὸς ἐστι μέγας Od.12.103: most freq. in Hom. in the form ἐνί, which is then written by anastrophe ἔνι, Il.7.221, Od.5.57; in Pi. between Subst. and gen., χόρτοις ἐν λέοντος *O.*13.44, al.—One or more independent words sts. come between the Prep. and its dat., as in Od.11.115; also in Prose, Hdt.6.69.

E. In Compos., **I.** with Verbs, the Prep. mostly retains its sense of being *in* or *at* a place, etc., c. dat., or folld. by εἰς.., or ἐν..: in such forms as ἐνορᾶν τινί τι, in translating, we resolve the compd., to remark a thing *in* one. **b.** also, *at* a person, ἐγγελᾶν, ἐνυβρίζειν τινί. **2.** with Adjs., it expresses **a.** a modified degree, as in ἔμπηλος, ἔμπικρος, ἔνσιμος, *rather* ... **b.** the possession of a quality, as in ἔναιμος *with* blood *in it*, ἐνάκανθος thorny: ἔμφωνος *with* a voice: ἔννομος *in accordance with* law, etc. **II.** ἐν becomes ἐμ- before the labials β μ π φ ψ; ἐγ- before the gutturals γ κ ξ χ; ἐλ- before λ; ἐρ- before ρ; rarely ἐσ- before σ; but Inscrr. and Papyri often preserve ἐν- in all these cases.

ἐναβρύνομαι, fut. -αβρῠνοῦμαι App.*BC*4.68:—*pride oneself on*, c. dat., D.H.*Dem.*5, App.l.c., etc.; χώρα ἐ. ὕδασιν Procop.*Goth.*4.20. **2.** *to be effeminate* in dress, Luc.*Salt.*2, D.C.43.43.

ἐνάγᾰμαι [ᾰγ], *admire in*, v.l. for ἐναυγάζομαι (q.v.), Ph.1.449.

ἐναγγειόσπερμος, ον, *having the seed in a capsule*, Thphr.*HP*1.11.3, *CP*4.7.5.

ἐνᾰγείρω, *gather together in* or *with*, Nic.*Th.*945 (tm.):—Med., A.R.3.347: Ep. aor. part. Pass. ἐναγρόμενος Opp.*H.*2.351.

ἐνᾰγελάζομαι, Pass., *assemble like a flock in*, πειρῶ φίλων ἀγέλας ἐ. σου τῇ οἰκίᾳ Epict.*Gnom.*41.

ἐνᾰγ-ής, ές, = ἐν ἄγει ὤν, *under a curse* or *pollution* because of bloodshed, of the Alcmeonidae, Hdt.1.61, 5.70 sq.; ἀπὸ τούτου ἐναγεῖς καὶ ἀλιτήριοι τῆς θεοῦ ἐκαλοῦντο Th.1.126; ἐναγὴς τοῦ Ἀπόλλωνος Aeschin.3.110: Sup., Hermog.*Inv.*1.4. **II.** in S.*OT*656 (lyr.), τὸν ἐναγῆ φίλον one *who has invoked a curse upon his head* (in case of treachery). **-ίζω**, fut. -ιῶ Is.6.51, 7.30:—*offer sacrifice to the dead*, opp. θύω (to the gods), τινί Hdt.1.167; ἐ. τινὶ ὡς ἥρωϊ, opp. θύειν τινὶ ὡς ἀθανάτῳ, Id.2.44, cf. Is.6.51, al., Plb.23.10.17; τοῖς κατὰ πόλεμον τελευτήσασιν *IG*2^{2}.1006.26 (ii B.C.): c. acc. rei, ἐ. ἀποπυρίδας τινί Clearch.16; κριόν Plu.*Thes.*4, etc. **-ικός**, ή, όν, *of an* ἐναγής, χρήματα Id.2.825c. **-ιος**, α, ον, *under a curse*, χρόνοι *PMag.Par.*1.844. **-ισμα**, ατος, τό, *an offering to the dead*, Ar.*Fr.*488.12, Arist.*Ath.*58.1, Epicur.*Fr.*217, Luc.*Merc.Cond.*28, D.C.67.9. **-ισμός**, ὁ, *offering to the dead*, *CIG*1976 (Thessalonica), 3645 (Lampsacus), J.*AJ*19.4.6 (pl.), Plu.*Pyrrh.*31, D.C.77.12. **II.** generally, *sacrifice*, in pl., J.*BJ*1.1.1, al. **-ιστήριον**, τό, *place for offering to the dead*, *IG*4.203.9 (Corinth).

ἐναγκᾰλ-ίζομαι, Med., *take in one's arms*, *AP*7.476.10 (Mel.), Lxx *Pr.*24.48; τέκνα Plu.*Cam.*5, *IG*12(7).395.25 (Amorgos): metaph., Νεῖλος [πόλιν] ἐ. Procop.Gaz.*Ep.*133; of a science, Apollon.Cit.3. **II.** Pass., *to be taken in the arms*, D.S.3.58. **-ισμα**, ατος, τό, *that which embraces*, ὠκεανὸς κόσμου ἐ. Secund.*Sent.*2.

ἐναγκοινέομαι, (ἄγκοινα) *hurl like a javelin*, κεραυνόν Eust.839.11.

ἐναγκῠλ-άω and **-όω**, *fit thongs* (ἀγκύλαι II. 2) *to* javelins, for the purpose of throwing them by, ἐναγκυλῶντες X.*An.*4.2.28 (D.S.14.27 has -οῦντες):—Med., Ach.Tat.2.34, Plu.2.180d (-ούμενον):—Pass., ἀκόντιον ἐνηγκύληται has a dart *ready to throw*, Ael.*NA*5.3. **-ίζω**, *fit as it were into a thong* (ἀγκύλη), εἴς τι Plb.27.11.5 (Pass.).

ἐναγκωνίζω, Att. fut. -ιῶ, *lean on the elbow*, Hsch.

ἐναγλᾰΐζομαι, Med., = ἐναβρύνομαι, Agath.3.28, Eust.9.43.

ἔναγμος, ον, *of a fracture*, περιφέρεια Sor.*Fract.*10.

ἐναγοράζειν· ἐναθροίζεσθαι, Hsch.

ἐναγρόμενος, v. ἐναγείρω.

ἔναγρος· ἔπαγρος, Hsch. **II.** epith. of Apollo at Siphnos, Id.

ἐναγρυπνέω, = ἐπαγρυπνέω, c. dat., Lyd.*Mag.*3.58, al.

ἔναγχος, Adv. *just now, lately*, Ar.*Nu.*639, Eup.181.2, Lys.19.50, Pl.*Grg.*462c, D.21.36; τὸ ἔ. Ar.*Ec.*823; opp. πάλαι, Isoc.19.43; τὸ ἔ. πάθος the *recent* misfortune, App.*BC*1.9: c. gen., ἔ. τοῦ χρόνου D.H.7.45.

ἐνάγω [ᾰ], *lead in*, Ti.Locr.99e; *bring in*, Anon.*in EN*225.3 (Pass.). **II.** *lead on, urge, persuade*, ἐνῆγόν σφεας οἱ χρησμοί Hdt.5.90; ἐνῆγε τῇ συμβουλῇ κελεύων.. Id.3.1, cf. 5.104, Th.4.21, etc.: mostly c. inf., μαίνεσθαι ἐνάγει ἀνθρώπους (sc. Bacchus) Hdt.4.79; ἐνάγει προθυμίη τινὰ ἀποθνήσκειν Id.5.49; ἐνῆγέ σφεας ὥστε ποιέειν Id.4.145; ἐ. τινὰ εἴς τι Plu.*Brut.*46, etc.:—Med., App.*Pun.*65. **2.** c. acc. rei, *urge on, promote*, τὸν πόλεμον Th.1.67, cf. 4.24; τὴν ἔξοδον Id.2.21; τὴν στρατείαν Id.6.15; περί τινος ib.61. **III.** *bring into court, accuse*, κλοπῆς of theft, J.*AJ*2.6.7 (Pass.); ἐ. πρός τινας δίκην CPR232.24 (ii/iii A.D.); ὁ ἐνάγων *the prosecutor*, Heph. Astr.3.34; ἐναγόμενος *defendant*, ibid., Cod.Just.4.21.16.

ἐνᾰγωγή, ἡ, *prosecution, suit, claim*, Sammelb.5357.13 (v A.D.), Cod.Just.3.10.2, etc.

ἐνᾰγων-ίζομαι, Ion. fut. -ιεῦμαι Hdt.3.83 :—*compete* in a contest *with*, τινί Id.2.160, 3.83. 2. *take part in*, ἡ τύχη ἐ. τοῖς τῶν ἀνθρώπων βίοις Plb.1.4.5, cf. 5.85.7. II. ἐναγωνίσασθαι εὐμενῆ τοῖς Ἕλλησιν favourable for them *to fight in*, Th.2.74; πεδιὰς ἱππεῦσιν ἐ. ἐπιτήδειος Jul.Or.2.63d. -ιος, ον, *of* or *for a contest, contending in the games*, παῖς Pi.N.6.13; freq. in later Prose, αἱ νῖκαι αἱ ἐ. Arist.VV 1250^{b}37; ἐ. κόσμος Duris 70 J.; ὄρχησις D.H.7.72, Luc.Salt.32. 2. ἐ. θεοί gods *who presided over the games*, esp. Hermes, Pi.P.2.10, Simon.18.1, A.Fr.384, cf. Ar.Pl.1161, IG2.1181; Ἀφροδίτη ib.3.189. II. *of, in* or *for battle*, πυκνώσεις ἐ. closing of the ranks *in battle*, Plb.18.29.2; παρακελευσμός Id.10.12.5; ἐνέργεια D.S.20.95; σχῆμα D.H.6.13; ἀρετή Onos.1.13 (v.l.). III. Rhet., *suited for forensic oratory* or *debate*, λόγος, πνεῦμα, λέξις, D.H.Is.20, Th.23, Dem.18, cf. Demetr.Eloc.193; *vehement*, κίνησις D.S.18.67; πάθος Longin.22.1. 2. of style, *energetic, vivid*, opp. διηγηματικός (as epith. of Il. compared with the Od.), Id.9.13, cf. Arg.Od. Adv. -ίως *incisively, vehemently*, Plu.2.771a, Longin.18.2. -ισις, εως, ἡ, *struggle*, Procop.Goth.4.32 (s.v.l.).

ἐνᾰδημονέω, *to be greatly afflicted in*, ἐρημίαις J.AJ15.7.7.

ἐνᾰδιαφορέω, *submit to*, τῇ αἰκίᾳ τοῦ Πατρόκλου Sch.Il.17.168.

ἐνᾰδικός, ή, όν, *pertaining to unity*, Dam.ap.AB1369. Adv. -κῶς Procl. in Prm.p.625 S.

ἐνᾰδολεσχέω, *prate about*, Ph.2.59.

ἐνάδοντες· ἐμπεσόντες, Hsch.

ἐνᾴδω, *sing among others*, Arist.Pr.918^{b}22.

ἐνᾰείρομαι, *lift up in*, κῶας χερσίν A.R.4.171.

ἐνάενος [ᾰ], ον, *of a year old*, Thphr.HP8.11.5, Stud.Pal.1.62.33, al. (i A.D.).

ἐνᾰέξω, aor. ἐνηέξησα, *produce in*, ἀρούραις Nic.Al.102; ἐν μὲν ἀέξειν ποίην, ἐν δὲ νομούς D.P.998.

ἐνᾰερίζω, *lift in air*, Hsch.

ἐνᾰέριος, ον, *in the air*, ζῷα Ti.Locr.101c, Gal.Thras.40; μεῖξις Luc.Musc.Enc.6; opp. ἔγγειος, Them.Or.13.168b, cf. Porph.Gaur.10.6.

ἐνάερος [ᾱ], ον, *tinted like the air*, χρῶμα Plu.2.915c.

ἐνᾰετία, ἡ, *period of nine years*, PSI4.281.40 (ii A.D.); cf. ἐνναετία.

ἐναθλέω, = ἀθλέω ἐν, τοῖς πολέμοις, ταῖς τοξείαις, D.S.1.54, 3.8; ἐν γυμνασίοις καὶ πόνοις Id.16.44; μαθήμασι Luc.Am.45; [ὑπολήψεσι] Arr.Epict.3.16.13 :—Med., ἐνηθλήσω προνοίᾳ AP7.117 (⟨Zenod.⟩). 2. *bear up bravely under*, ταῖς βασάνοις Ael.VH2.4; πρὸς τοὺς πόνους Iamb.Protr.20.

ἔναθλος, ον, *laborious*, πόνοι Ph.1.646. II. ἔναθλον, τό, *contest*, in pl., dub. in IG7.2532.

ἐναθρέω, = ἀθρέω ἐν, *to look searchingly on* or *in*, Hsch.

ἐν(α)θροίζομαι, gloss on ἐναγοράζειν, Hsch.

ἐναθύρω [ῠ], = ἀθύρω ἐν, χοροῖς καὶ μέλεσι Him.Or.21.8, cf. 4.9.

ἐναΐδιος, ον, (αἶα) *underground*, οἶκος Epigr.Gr.321.9; cf. ὑπαΐδιος.

ἐναιέτια, τά, (ἀετός III) *pediment-sculptures*, BSA16.193 (Parthenon), IG1^2.348.76, 4.1484.112 (Epid.).

ἐναιθέριος, ον, *in upper air*, M.Ant.12.24; θεοί Poll.1.23.

ἐναίθομαι, Pass., *burn in*, Q.S.11.94.

ἐναίθριος, ον, *fully exposed*, τόποι Thphr.CP5.14.2.

ἐναικίζω, *scourge*, Et.Gud.188.8, Suid.

ἐναιλέω, v. ἐναιρέω.

ἐναιμάσσω, = sq., Sch.S.Ph.1002.

ἐναιμ-ᾰτόω, *supply with blood*, Hp.Oss.18. -ήεις, εσσα, εν, = sq., κέντρα μύωπος AP6.233 (Maec.). -ος, ον, *with blood in one*, θεοὶ ἐ. καὶ σαρκώδεις *of* flesh and *blood*, Hdt.3.29; *charged with blood*, opp. ἄναιμος, ἔναιμον καὶ πυκνόν, οἷον ἧπαρ Hp.VM22; πλεύμων Arist.PA669^{a}25, al.; ἔναιμα *particles of blood*, Pl.Ti.81a; ἐναίμων κολλητικὰ *bleeding wounds*, Dsc.1.110; τὰ ἔ., of sacrifices, Ph.2.250. 2. τὰ ἔ. *red-blooded animals*, Arist.HA489^{a}30, PA690^{b}11, al. 3. χρῶμα ἔ. *blood*-colour, Pl.Ti.68b. 4. metaph., *full of blood, vigorous*, χλωρὰ καὶ ἔ. τὰ πράγματα Gorg.ap.Arist.Rh.1406^{b}9 (nisi leg. ἄναιμα). II. ἔναιμα (sc. φάρμακα) medicaments *for stanching blood*, Hp.Art.63: sg., Fract.24; φάρμακον ἔ. Thphr.HP4.7.2. 2. ἔ. ἀγωγή treatment *of bleeding wounds*, Orib.46.8.15, cf. 45.18.31. Adv. -μως ibid., Antyll.ib.44.23.46. -ότης, ητος, ἡ, *having blood in one*, Hp.VM22. -ώδης, ες, *bloody, like blood*, Antipho Soph. 35. -ων, ον, gen. ονος, = ἔναιμος, Hp.Oss.19.

ἐναιονάω, *foment*, Gal.18(2).838.

ἐναιρέω, *capture in* a place, Cret. aor. part. Pass. ἐναιλεθέντος Leg.Gort.2.30.

ἐναίρω, also ἐνναίρω v.l. in Batr.274: aor. 2 ἤνᾰρον Pi.Pae.6.114, E.Andr.1182 (lyr.), (κατ-)S.Ant.871 (lyr.); poet. ἔνᾰρον Pi.N.10.15, E.Supp.821 (hex.); inf. ἐναρεῖν (ἐξ-) Hes.Sc.329: later, aor. 1 ἔνηρα (κατ-) Orph.A.666 :—Med., Il.16.92: 3 sg. aor. 1 ἐνήρατο 5.43, Hes.Th.316 :—Pass. (v. infr.) :—poet. Verb (used by Trag. mostly in lyr. passages), *slay* in battle, freq. in Il.; ῥηΐτεροι ἐναιρέμεν easier *to kill*, 24.244; but also κατ' οὔρεα θῆρας ἐ. 21.485; θῆρα.. τόξοις ἐ. S.Ph.956; τοὺς εὐγενεῖς γὰρ κἀγαθοὺς.. φιλεῖ Ἄρης ἐναίρειν Id.Fr.724; of a hunter, κάπρους ἔναιρε Pi.N.3.47 (cf. ἔναρα) :—Med., much like Act., Ἰδομενεὺς δ' ἄρα Φαῖστον ἐνήρατο Il.5.43, cf. 59, 6.32, Od.24.424, Hes.Th.316; Τρῶας ἐναιρόμενος Il.16.92; once in the Od., of things, *to make away with, destroy*, μηκέτι νῦν χρόα καλὸν ἐναίρεο *destroy, disfigure* it not, 19.263 :—Pass., ἀδελφαῖς χερσὶν ἠναίρονθ' ἅμα A.Th.811; πόλις ἐναίρεται σθένει S.OC842 (lyr.).

ἐναίσαρι· στερεοῦ· οἱ δὲ ἐνάσαρι, Hsch. **ἐναίσασθαι**· φθαρῆναι, γηρᾶσαι, Id. **ἐναισιμία**· διοσημία, Id.

ἐναίσ-ιμος, ον, (αἶσα) Ep. Adj. (rare in Trag.) *ominous, fateful*, οὐδ' ἦλθον ἐναίσιμον (as Adv.) Il.6.519; ὄρνιθας γνῶναι καὶ ἐναίσιμα μυθήσασθαι Od.2.159; οὐδέ τε πάντες ἐναίσιμοι [ὄρνιθες] ib.182; esp. in good sense, *seasonable*, of omens, ἐ. σήματα φαίνων Il.2.353: generally, *favourable, boding good*, λιγνὺν ἐναίσιμον ἀΐσσουσαν A.R.1.438. II. of persons, their thoughts, etc., *righteous*, ἀνὴρ ὃς ἐ. εἴη Od.10.383; οἵ τινές εἰσιν ἐ. οἵ τ' ἀθέμιστοι 17.363; ᾧ οὔτ' ἂρ φρένες εἰσὶν ἐ. (of Achilles) Il.24.40, cf. Od.18.220; ἐμοὶ νόος ἐστὶν ἐ. 5.190; so τοῦτό γ' ἐναίσιμον οὐκ ἐνόησεν 2.122, 7.299; ἐ. τίει [βίον] A.Ag.775 (lyr.); γῆρας γὰρ ἐ. ἄνδρα τίθησιν makes him *honoured*, Opp.H.1.683. 2. of things, *fit, proper*, ἐ. δῶρα διδοῦναι ἀθανάτοις Il.24.425, cf. h.Cer.369. Adv. -μως *fitly, becomingly*, αἰνεῖν A.Ag.916; μή νυν ὑπέρβαλλ', ἀλλ' ἐ. φέρε E.Alc.1077. -ιος, ον, = foreg. I, opp. ἐξαίσιος, D.C.38.13. II. = foreg. II. 1, S.OC1482 (lyr.). 2. = foreg. II. 2, ὑβρισμοὺς οὐκ ἐ. A.Fr.179.

ἐναΐσσω, *rush in*, aor. part. ἐνᾴξας v.l. (POxy.2093) in S.Aj.305.

ἐναισχύνομαι, *to be ashamed*, c. inf., Sch.S.Tr.803, f.l. in D.C.38.38. (Act. is f.l. in Hsch. s.v. κυπτάζειν.)

ἐναιτέω, *claim* a penalty, = Lat. *petere*, prob. in Supp.Epigr.1.161.56.

ἐναιχμάζω, *fight in*, Lyc.546, AP12.147 (Mel.).

ἐναιωρ-έομαι, *float* or *drift about in*, θαλάσσῃ E.Cyc.700: abs., *to be always in motion*, ὀφθαλμοὶ ἐναιωρεύμενοι Hp.Prog.2. 2. οὖρα ἐνῃωρημένα *containing suspended matter*, Id.Prorrh.1.4. 3. -ούμεναι συστάσεις *movable* concretions, Sor.1.88. -ημα, ατος, τό, *suspended matter* in urine, Hp.Epid.1.26.ζ', Orib.Syn.6.4.7. II. *outer part of an extension apparatus for broken limbs*, Gal.18(2).581.

ἐνάκανθος [ᾰκ], ον, *spinous*, Thphr.HP3.10.1.

ἐνᾰκέομαι, *repair*, τοῖχον IG11(2).203A55 (iii B.C.).

ἐνᾰκηδεκᾰτος, ον, Boeot., *nineteenth*, IG7.3172.96, Schwyzer 485.41 (Thespiae, iii B.C.).

ἐνάκις, Ep. **εἰνάκις** [ᾰ], Adv. *nine times*, Od.14.230 :—usu. written **ἐννάκις** in codd.: **ἐννεάκις** is v.l. in Nicom.Harm.8: also **ἐννάκι** δ' ἐννέα Μοῦσαι AP14.120.8; **ἐνάκι** Iamb. in Nic.p.17 P.

ἐνᾰκισχίλιοι [χῑ], αι, α, *nine thousand*, Pl.Ti.23e (v.l. ἐνν-), OGI 214.57 (Milet., iii B.C.); Ion. **εἰνακισχίλιοι** Hdt.3.95, al. (Generally written ἐνν- in codd.)

ἐνακμάζω, = εἶναι ἐν ἀκμῇ, τὰ ἐνακμάζοντα ἄνθη Ael.VH3.1; of fire, *rage*, Id.NA2.8; of cold, ib.16.26: metaph., τῆς ἐπιθυμίας -ούσης αὐτῷ Chor. in Hermes 17.216: abs., Agath.5.18. II. *flourish in*, πάθος ἐ. τῇ Ἑλλάδι Max.Tyr.25.1; βασιλείοις ὅροις Him.Or.7.16; ταῖς Ἑλληνικαῖς Procop.Gaz.Pan.501.5.

ἔνακμος, ον, = ἐν ἀκμῇ, *in full bloom* or *strength*, Poll.2.10.

ἐνακολασταίνω, *indulge one's lust in* or *upon*, τινί Clearch.10.

ἐνᾰκοντίζω, *discharge a missile*, Gloss.

ἐνᾰκόσι-οι, αι, α, *nine hundred*, Th.5.12, SIG495.88 (Olbia, iii B.C.), IG5(1).1146.10 (Gytheion, i B.C.), ib.11(2).165.53 (Delos, iii B.C.); Ion. **ἐνακόσιοι** Hdt.2.13, 145. -οστός, v. ἐννακ-.

ἐνᾰκούω, *hear*, Lxx Na.1.12 (Pass.); *obey*, 1Es.4.10, Vett.Val.42.7 (Pass.), POxy.120.4 (iv A.D.); *listen to*, c. gen. rei, S.El.81. II. *take in* sounds, *be sensitive to*, ἰαχῆς Hp.Cord.8, cf. Liqu.2: metaph., ἐ. τῆς ξυμφορῆς *to be affected* by it, Id.Art.53; ἐνακούει ἐμβαλλόμενα, of dislocations, they *obey* the surgeon's hand, i.e. *are set*, Id.Fract.40; ἐ. ἰητρείης *yield to* treatment, Id.Art.62.

ἐνάκρα, ἡ, *promontory*, Dion.Byz.20.

ἐναλγής, ές, *painful*, Paul.Aeg.3.75.

ἐναλδαίνω, *cause to grow up on*, aor. 1 ἐνάλδηνα Nic.Al.409 (vv. ll. ἐναλδήσασα, ἐνανθήσασα): aor. Med. ἐναλδόμενος *growing in*, πρασιῇσι ib.532.

ἐνάλ-ειμμα [ᾰ], ατος, τό, *eyesalve*, Arist.Pr.876^{b}13. -ειπτος, ον, *anointed with*, Hp.Acut.(Sp.)65. -είφω, *anoint with*, τί τινι Id.Morb.2.36; ὀφθαλμοὶ ὀστρείῳ ἐναληλιμμένοι Pl.R.420c :—Med., *anoint onself*, AP11.112 (Nicarch.); ἐ. τὰς ῥῖνας *one's* nose, Alex. 190; τὴν κόμην φαρμάκῳ Plu.2.771b; τὼ ὀφθαλμώ Hld.7.14. II. *paint within* outlines, ὑπογράψαντες ταῖς γραμμαῖς οὕτως ἐναλείφουσι τοῖς χρώμασι τὸ ζῷον Arist.GA743^{b}24: generally, χύδην ἐ. Id.Po. 1450^{b}1 :—Pass., τὸ ἐναλειφθὲν *coat of stucco*, interpol. in Id.GA726^{b}27.

ἐνᾰλήθης, ες, *accordant with truth*, Longin.15.8. Adv. -θως *probably*, Luc.VH1.2.

ἐνᾰλίγκιος, ον, also η, ον A.R.3.857 :—*like, resembling*, c. dat., Il.5.5, al., Parm.8.43, Theoc.22.94, etc.: c. acc. rei, θεοῖς ἐναλίγκιος αὐδήν Od.1.371; χεῖρας Ἄρει Pi.I.8(7).41: neut. as Adv., Man.6.443.—Poet. word.

ἐνᾰλινδέομαι, Pass., *to be involved in*, συμφορῇσι v.l. in Hp.Ep.17; *wallow in*, ὥσπερ πορνείῳ τῇ πόλει J.BJ4.9.10. (Act. only Hsch. ἐναλῖσαι· ἐγκυλῖσαι.)

ἐνᾰλίνω, Cypr. ἰναλίνω, *engrave, inscribe*, pf. part. Pass. ἰναλαλισμένα Inscr.Cypr.135.26 H.

ἐνάλιος [ᾰ], α, ον, and ος, ον E.Andr.855 (nisi leg. ἐνάλου), Plu. Luc.39: Ep. and Lyr. also **εἰνάλιος**, α, ον (ος, ον E.Hel.526, lyr.): (ἅλς B):—*in, on, of the sea*, κῆτος, κορῶναι, Od.4.443, 5.67, etc.; νομός Archil.74.8; εἰνάλιον πόνον ἐχοίσας βαθὺν σκευᾶς ἑτέρας while the rest of the tackle is at work fishing deep *in the sea*, Pi.P.2.79, cf. Theoc.21.39; ἐ. πόροι A.Pers.453; ἐ. θεός, of Poseidon, S.OC888 (troch.), 1493 (lyr.); ἐ. λεώς seamen, Id.Aj.565; πόντου εἰναλία φύσις, i. e. the fish, Id.*Ant.*345 (lyr.); of islands, ἐ. Εὐβοὶς αἶα Id.*Fr.* 255; ἐ. χθών, of Tyre, E.*Ph.*6.—Poet. word, used in later Prose, ἐ. νῆσοι Arist.*Mu.*392b19; δίαιται Plu.*Luc.*39; ὄργανα Porph.*Antr.*35.

ἐνᾰλίσκομαι, *to be convicted in*, ᾠκοδόμηται τὰ δικαστήρια τοῖς πονηροῖς -ίσκεσθαι Lib.*Decl.*16.28; ἐναλόντα· συλληφθέντα, κρατηθέντα, Hsch.

ἐνᾰλῐταίνω, = ἀλιταίνω ἐν, aor. 2 ἐνήλῐτον Q.S.13.400, 14.436.

ἐναλλ-άδην, Adv. = ἐναλλάξ, *AP*5.301.16 (Agath.), Man.4.181, Doroth.ap.Heph.Astr.3.30, Agath.1.12, al. **-ᾰγή,** ἡ, *interchange*, κατ' ἐναλλαγὰν *alternando*, of proportion, Ti.Locr.99b. 2. Gramm., *interchange*, στοιχείων S.E.*M.*9.278; πτώσεως A.D.*Pron.*54.13; χρόνων D.H.*Th.*24; ἡμερῶν *POxy.*1413.22 (iii A.D.); κεφαλαίων Hermog.*Stat.*11: abs., *enallage*, A.D.*Synt.*157.12. II. *variation*, τῶν ὑποκειμένων Plot.2.6.3; τῶν ζῳδίων Ptol.*Tetr.*152 (pl.); *change*, Lyd. *Mag.*2.16. **-αγμα,** ατος, τό, *change*: in pl., *perverse actions*, Aq. *Is.*66.4. **-άκτης,** ου, ὁ, *perverse person*, ib.3.4. **-ακτικός,** ή, όν, *altering*, προαιρέσεως ἐ. σχέσις *Placit.*1.29.1: hence, *perverse, wanton*, Aq.*De.*22.14. **-άξ,** Adv. *crosswise*, οὐδ' ἴσχειν τὼ πόδ' ἐ. Ar.*Nu.*983, cf. Hp.*Mul.*2.144, *IG*2².463.80. 2. Math., *alternando*, Arist.*EN*1131b6, *APo.*74a18, 99a8; *permutando*, Euc.5 *Def.*12. 3. *alternately*, Pi.*N.*10.55, Pl.*Criti.*113d, 119d; [γέρανοι] καθεύδουσιν ἐπὶ ἑνὸς ποδὸς ἐ. Arist.*HA*614b25; ἐ. ἐναντίως *alternately* contrariwise, Id. *IA*712a13; of the teeth of carnivorous animals, ἐ. ἐμπίπτουσιν Id.*PA* 661b21; πρήσσειν ἐ. to have *alternations* of fortune, Hdt.3.40: c. dat., ἤν τε μὴ ἐ. αἱ εὐτυχίαι τοι τῇσι πάθῃσι προσπίπτωσι *alternately with* misfortunes, ibid.; ἐ. ἀλλήλοις Aen.Tact.26.1: c. gen., D.S.5.7. 4. *in inverted order, upside down*, Lib.*Descr.*13.8. **-αξις,** εως, ἡ, *crossing, interlacing*, φλεβῶν Arist.*PA*668b26, cf. Olymp. *in Mete.*31. 20. II. Gramm., = ἐναλλαγή, Longin.23.1 (pl.). **-ασσομένως,** Adv. *by enallage*, A.D.*Synt.*260.15. **-άσσω,** Att. -ττω, pf. ἐνήλλαχα Plb.6.43.2, Phld.*Mus.*p.73 K.:—*exchange*, φόνον θανάτῳ ἐ., i. e. *pay for* murder by death, E.*Andr.*1028 (lyr.); μεταβολὰς ἐ. *undergo* changes, Plb. l. c.; παντοίας μορφὰς ἐ. *to assume*., Apollod.2.5.11: c. inf., ἐνήλλαξεν θεὸς τὴν τοῦδ' ὕβριν πρὸς μῆλα..πεσεῖν *turned aside, diverted* his fury so as to fall upon the sheep, S.*Aj.*1060. 2. *cross*, τὼ πόδε Philostr.*Im.*2.7; also intr., *cross one another*, of veins and arteries, Arist.*PA*668b21. 3. Astrol., *exchange domicile*, of planets, Vett.Val.73.15. 4. ἐχρῆν ἐνηλλαχέναι one should *have reversed* the statement, Phld. l. c. II. *give in exchange*, τι ἀντί τινος App.*BC*3. 27, 5.12:—Med., *receive in exchange*, τί δ' ἐνήλλακται τῆς ἡμερίας νὺξ ἥδε βάρος; what heavy *change* from the day *hath* this night *received*? S.*Aj.*208, cf. Ph.2.638. III. Pass., *to be interarticulated*, ἄρθρα ἐνηλλαγμένα Hp.*Art.*46; also τὸ μέτρον τοῖς δισυλλάβοις ἐναλλάσσεται the metre *employs* the various disyllabic feet *interchangeably*, Anon.Metr.*Oxy.*220 iii 13. 2. *have commercial relations with*, ὅσοι Ἀθηναίοις ἤδη ἐνηλλάγησαν Th.1.120.

ἐναλλοι-όω, *alter*, *PSI*5.483 (iii B.C.):—Pass., Ph.2.659, Herm. ap.Stob.3.11.31. **-ωσις,** εως, ἡ, *alteration*, Ptol.*Tetr.*93.

ἐνάλλομαι, fut. -ᾰλοῦμαι Plu.2.1087b: aor. 1 -ηλάμην S.*OT*263, etc.: aor. 2 -ηλόμην (v. infr.):—*leap in* or *on*, ὡς ἄγαν βαρὺς ποδοῖν ἐνήλου..γένει A.*Pers.*516, cf. X.*HG*2.4.16, D.54.8; τινὶ τῷ σκέλει Philem.1.5 D.; εἰς τὸ κείνου κρᾶτ' ἐνήλαθ' ἡ τύχη S.*OT*263; εἰς τὸν ποταμόν Wilcken *Chr.*11 *A* 42; εἰς τὸν ἀσκόν Corn.*ND*30; εἰς τὴν γαστέρα Plu.*Luc.*11. 2. *rush at* or *against*, πύλαις ἐνήλατο S.*OT* 1261, cf. Ar.*Ra.*39. 3. abs., *jump about, dance*, Id.*V.*1305.

ἔναλλος, ον, *changed, contrary*, Theoc.1.134, *AP*5.298 (Agath.). Adv. -λως Plu.2.1045e.

ἔνᾰλος, ον, = ἐνάλιος, πόλις *h.Ap.*180, Critias *Fr.*2.7 D.; ἀκταί E. *Hel.*1130 (lyr.), Tim.*Pers.*109; πρῷραι E.*El.*1348 (anap.); ἔ. θρέμματα Arion 1.9; in later Prose, κώπη, opp. ἔξαλος, S.E.*M.*7.414.

ἐνᾰλύω, = ἀλύω ἐν, *revel in, exult over*, c. dat., ἐ. καὶ ἐνυβρίζειν Ph. 2.369, cf. 372; simply, *dwell upon*, ὅταν ἐναλύῃ αὐτοῖς ὁ λόγος Philostr. *Im.*2.8; θεραπείᾳ τῇ περὶ τὴν θεὸν ἐ. Hld.7.9; κόμη ἐναλύουσα τῷ μετώπῳ hair *hanging wildly over* the face, Philostr.*Im.*1.10.

ἐνᾰμάομαι, Med., *heap upon*, Sch.S.*Ant.*255 (nisi leg. ἐπ-).

ἐνάμαρτος [ᾰμ], ον, *faulty*, and Adv. -τως, *Gloss.*

ἐναμβλύνω, *deaden* or *discourage besides*, τοὺς συνάρχοντας Plu.*Nic.* 14.

ἐνᾰμείβω, *change, alter*, Lyd.*Mag.*3.39.

ἐνᾰμέλγω, *milk into*, γαυλοῖς Od.9.223.

ἐνᾰμιλλ-άομαι, = ἁμιλλάομαι, πρός τι Them.*Or.*21.254c. **-ος** [ᾰ], ον, (ἅμιλλα) *engaged in equal contest with, a match for*, τὴν φύσιν ἐ. τοῖς ἡλικιώταις Pl.*Prt.*316b, cf. Isoc.5.68; ἐ. τινὶ πρός τι Pl.*R.*433d, *Criti.*110e, cf. Arist.*Pol.*1283a5; τοῖς πολίταις ἐ. παρασκευάζων ἑαυτόν *IG*2².835.12, cf. Plu.*Comp.Ag.Gracch.*3; τὰ λοίπ' ἐ. τούτοις *on a par with*, D.25.54; τοῖς κρατίστοις ἐ. τὸν κυνισμὸν εἶναι Jul.*Or.*6.182c. Adv. -λως, τινὶ *equally with*, Isoc.12.7.

ἔναμμα, ατος, τό, (ἐνάπτω) *thing bound* or *tied on, thong*, ἔ. ἀγκύλης Plu.*Phil.*6. 2. *garment, covering*, ἔ. νεβρίδος a deerskin *cloak*, D.S.1.11.

ἐνᾰμοιβᾰδίς, Adv. = ἀμοιβαδίς, *alternately* or *one after another*, A.R.1.380, 4.1030.

ἐναμπέχομαι, Pass., *to be clad in*, τι Ph.1.635.

ἐναμπῠκίσαι· ἐγχαλινῶσαι, Hsch.

ἐνανάπτω, *tie*, dub. in Gal.18(1).750.

ἐναναστρέφομαι, Pass., *to be conversant with*, τινί Aristox.ap.Stob. 3.1.49, Hsch. s. v. ἐγκαλινδεῖται.

ἔνανδρον· κενὸν ἀνδρῶν, Hsch. (leg. ἄν- vel κέν-).

ἐνανειλέω, *roll back*, in Pass., dub. in Gal.6.177.

ἐνανθέω, f. l. for ἐναλδαίνω, Nic.*Al.*409.

ἐνανθρωπέω, *put on man's nature*, ψυχὴ -ήσασα Hld.2.31.

ἔναντα (ἐνάντᾳ Tim.*Pers.*11), Adv. *opposite, over against*, c. gen., ἔ. Ποσειδάωνος ἄνακτος ἵστατ' Ἀπόλλων Il.20.67; τοὶ δ' ἔ. στάθεν Pi. *N.*10.66; τὸν δ' ἔ. προσβλέπειν νεκρόν S.*Ant.*1299 (lyr.); ἔ. ἐλθεῖν E. *Or.*1478 (lyr.).

ἔναντι, Adv. *in the presence of*, c. gen., Lxx *Ge.*12.19, al., *IG*7.2225. 52 (Thisbe, ii B.C.), *Ev.Luc.*1.8, *GDI*2072.26 (Delph.); cf. ἔναντι.

ἐναντῐ-αῖος, α, ον, *of contrary nature*, Hp.*Liqu.*2. **-βῐος,** ον, *set against, hostile*, αἰθυίαις οὔποτ' ἐναντίβιος *AP*10.8 (Arch., Herm. for οὔποτε ἀντιβίας): elsewh. neut. as Adv., *face to face, against*, μαχέσασθαι, πολεμίζειν, Il.8.168, 10.451, etc.; ἐλθεῖν 20.130; στῆναι 21. 266: c. gen., Ἀχιλῆος ἐ. πολεμίζειν 20.85.—Only poet.

ἐναντῐο-βουλία, ἡ, *contrary purpose*, Vett.Val.201.13. **-βουλος,** ον, *of contrary purpose*, Polem.*Phgn.*66, Vett.Val.61.28, al. **-γνώμων,** ον, gen. ονος, (γνώμη) *of contrary opinion*, ib.29: gloss on ἀγνώμων, Sch.S.*OC*86. **-δρομέω,** *run opposite ways*: hence, *go the opposite way*, Thphr.*Vent.*28; ἐ. ἀλλήλοις Str.16.1.5. **-δρομία,** ἡ, *running contrary ways*, *Placit.*1.7.22: prob. for ἐναντιοτροπή, D.L. 9.7. **-δύνᾰμος** [ῠ], ον, *of opposite function* (as odd and even), Nicom.*Ar.*1.9. 2. gloss on ἀντίβιος, Eust.108.3. **-ζύγως** [ῠ], Adv. *in an opposite series*, *Theol.Ar.*11. **-θετος,** ον, Astrol., *in opposition*, *Cat.Cod.Astr.*8(4).148. **-λογέω,** *contradict*, αὐτὸν αὐτῷ Pl.*Sph.*268b: abs., Str.15.1.3. **-λογία,** ἡ, *contradiction*, -ίᾳ συνέχεσθαι Pl.*Sph.*236e, cf. Arist.*GC*323b17. **-λογικός,** ή, όν, *given to contradicting*, Gal.*Anim.Pass.*1.3.

ἐναντίον, Adv., v. ἐναντίος.

ἐναντῐό-ομαι, Ion. part. ἐναντιεύμενος Hdt.7.49: impf. ἠναντιούμην Th.1.127, etc.:—Med., fut. -ώσομαι A.*Pr.*786, Ar.*Pax* 1049, etc.:—**Pass.,** fut. ἐναντιωθήσομαι Lxx 4*Ma.*5.26, D.H.4.51: aor. ἠναντιώθην And.1.67, Pl.*Ap.*32b, etc.: pf. ἠναντίωμαι Th.2.40 codd., etc., but in Ar.*Av.*385 the metre requires ἐνηντίωμαι:—*set oneself against, oppose, withstand*, τινί And.1.67, cf. Hdt.7.49, Th.1.127, Ar.*Av.*385, *Pax* 1049; also ἐ. ὑπὲρ τῆς ἐλευθερίας Lys.13.17; ὑπὲρ ὑμῶν Id.20.8; τινί τινος Th.1.136, X.*An.*7.6.5: abs., Th.4.21: c. inf., οὐκ ἐναντιώσομαι τὸ μὴ οὐ γεγωνεῖν I *will* not *refuse* to speak, A.*Pr.*786; τοὺς χορευτὰς ἐναντιούμενος ἡμῖν ἀφεθῆναι τῆς στρατείας D.21.15. 2. *contradict, gainsay*, E.*Alc.*152; πρός τι Pl.*Cra.*390e, etc.: c. inf., τοῦτο..μοι ἐ. τὰ πολιτικὰ πράττειν Id.*Ap.*31d: with a neg., τίς ἐναντιώσεται μὴ οὐχὶ.. εἶναι; Id.*Smp.*197a. 3. of the wind, *to be adverse*, οὐκ ἔστι λῃσταῖς πνεῦμ' ἐναντιούμενον S.*Ph.*643; of circumstances, Th.8.23; ἄνεμοι ἐ. ἀλλήλοις Hp.*Aër.*8. 4. τὰ ἐς ἀρετὴν ἐνηντιώμεθα τοῖς πολλοῖς in respect of goodness we *are the opposite of* most men, Th.2.40; *behave in the opposite way*, Meno *Iatr.*15.41. 5. Astrol., *to be in diametrical aspect*, Vett.Val.126.5. (Act. only in doubtful form ἐναντιόωντα Man.4.473.) **-πᾰθέω,** *have contrary properties*, Nicom.*Harm.*4, *Theol.Ar.*10. **-πᾰθής,** ές, *of contrary properties.* Adv. -θῶς Nicom.*Harm.*10. **-πετής,** gloss on παλιμπετής, Hsch. **-ποιολογικός,** ή, όν, *of* or *for making contradictions*, -κή (sc. τέχνη), ἡ, Pl. *Sph.*268c. **-πρᾱγέω,** *oppose*, D.S.3.65, 4.49, al.

ἐναντίος, α, ον, *opposite*, = ἀντίος (which is rare in Prose): 1. of Place, *on the opposite side, opposite*, c. dat., ἀκταὶ ἐναντίαι ἀλλήλῃσιν Od.10.89; Πάτροκλος δέ οἱ..ἐ. ἧστο Il.9.190, cf. Od.23.89: hence, *fronting, face to face*, αὐτῷ οὔ πω φαίνετ' ἐναντίη 6.329; ὅττις ἐ. τοι ἰσδάνει Sapph.2.2; δεῖξον..τὸ σὸν πρόσωπον δεῦρ' ἐ. πατρί *before* him, E.*Hipp.*947; τἀναντία τινί *things open to* one's *sight*, X.*Cyr.*3. 3.45: abs., ἐ. στάνθ' E.*Hipp.*1078 (but ἐ. κεῖσθαι look *opposite* ways, Pl.*Smp.*190a). b. with Verbs of motion, *in the opposite direction*, ἔνθα οἱ..ἐναντίη ἤλυθε μήτηρ came *to meet* him, Il.6.251; ἐναντίοι ἀλλήλοισιν ὄγμον ἐλαύνωσιν 11.67; δύο ἅμαξαι ἐ. ἀλλήλαις Th.1.93; ἄνεμος ἐ. ἔπνει X.*An.*4.5.3. c. Astrol., *in diametrical aspect*, Vett.Val.70. 16, Man.3.360. 2. in hostile sense, *opposing, facing* in fight, c. gen., ἐναντίοι ἔσταν Ἀχαιῶν Il.5.497, cf. S.*Aj.*1284, X.*An.*4.3.28, etc.: c. dat., Il.5.12, E.*Supp.*856, *IT*1415; οἱ ἐ. *one's adversaries*, A. *Th.*375, Gorg.*Fr.*12 D., etc.; *the enemy*, Hdt.7.225, Th.4.64, etc. b. generally, *opposed to*, τινί X.*An.*3.2.10; τὸ ἐ. *the opposite party*, Id. *Ath.*1.4; *presenting obstacles, hindering*, τινί S.*Ph.*642. c. ὁ δι ἐναντίας the *opponent* in a lawsuit, *PFlor.*1.58.15 (iii A.D.), etc. 3. of qualities, acts, etc., *opposite, contrary, reverse*, τἀναντί' εἰπεῖν A.*Ag.* 1373; δίκαια καὶ τἀναντία S.*Ant.*667: mostly c. gen., τὰ ἐ. τούτων the *very reverse* of these things, Hdt.1.82, cf. Th.7.75, etc.; δείξας..ἄστρων τὴν ἐ. ὁδόν, i. e. τὴν τοῦ ἡλίου ὁδὸν ἐ. οὖσαν τοῖς ἄστροις E.*Fr.*861: also c. dat., Ὀρφεῖ δὲ γλῶσσαν τὴν ἐναντίαν ἔχεις A.*Ag.*1629; τἀναντία πρήσσειν [τῇ ὑγιείῃ] Democr.234; δύο τὰ -ώτατα εὐβουλίᾳ Th.3.42; ἀγαθῷ κακὸν -ώτερον ἢ τῷ μὴ ἀγαθῷ Pl.*R.*491d; ἐναντία λέγει αὐτὸς αὑτῷ Id.*Prt.*339b, cf. Ar.*Ach.*493; τἀναντία τούτοις Pl.*Prt* 323d; ἐναντία γνῶναι ταῖς πλείσταις [πόλεσιν] X.*Lac.*1.2; τὴν ἐ. τινὶ ψῆφον θέσθαι D.19.65; simply τὴν ἐ. θέσθαι τινί Pl.*La.*184d: folld. by ἤ, τοὺς ἐ. λόγους ἢ ὡς αὐτὸς κατεδόκεε Hdt.1.22; τοὐ. δρῶν ἢ προσήκ' αὐτῷ ποιεῖν Ar.*Pl.*14; τοὐ. ἔπαθεν ἢ τὸ προσδοκώμενον Pl.*Lg.*966e, cf. *R.*567c, etc.: freq. strengthd., πᾶν τοὐ., πάντα τἀ., quite *the contrary*, *Lg.* 967a, X.*Mem.*3.12.4; πολὺ τοὐ. Stratt.57; τὸ δὲ πολὺ ἐναντίον ἀποβήσεται Pl.*Ap.*39c. b. τὰ ἐ. *opposites* in Philos., Pherecyd.Syr. 3, Arist.*Metaph.*986b3, etc. 4. in the Philos. of Arist., τἀναντία (dist. fr. other ἀντικείμενα, *Metaph.*1018a25) are *contraries*, esp. the two attributes within the same genus which differ most widely from each other (as hot and cold), *Cat.*6a18, al. b. ἐ. ἀποφάνσεις, προτάσεις, *contrary* propositions (All *B* is *A*, No *B* is *A*), opp. *contradictory* (v. ἀντιφατικῶς), Id.*Int.*17b4, *APr.*63b28. II. freq. in Adv.

usages: 1. from Hom. downwds., neut. ἐναντίον as Adv., *opposite, facing*, ἐ. ὧδε κάλεσσον here *to my face*, Od.17.544; εἰς ὦπα ἰδέσθαι ἐ. to look one *in the face*, 23.107; ἐ. προσβλέπειν τινά E.*Hec.*968, etc.; γυναῖκας ἀνδρῶν μὴ βλέπειν ἐ. ib.975: abs., D.4.40, etc.: hence, like a Prep. c. gen., *in the presence of*, τῆς βουλῆς *IG*1^2.91; τῶνδ' ἐ. S.*OC*1002; μαρτύρων ἐ. Ar.*Ec.*448; ἐ. τοῦ παιδίου Id.*Lys.*907; ἐ. ἁπάντων λέγειν Th.6.25; ἐ. Διός Plb.7.9.2; also neut. pl., *IG*7.1779 (Thespiae). b. in hostile sense, *against*, c. gen., ἀνέσταν.. σφοῦ πατρὸς ἐ. Il.1.534; ἐ. ἰέναι τινός 21.574; ἐ. μάχεσθαί τινος 20.97; ἐ. ἵστασ' ἐμεῖο 13.448: abs., ἐ. μίμνειν stand one's ground *against*, ib. 106: c. dat., νεικεῖν ἀλλήλοισιν ἐ. 20.252; ἐ. θεοῖς E.*Or.*624; ἐ. τῷ ὅρκῳ πράττειν *IG*2^2.1258.2. c. *contrariwise*, in Att. also with the Art., τοὐναντίον *on the other hand*, τοὐ. δέ.. Antiph.80.4; ἢ πάλιν τοὐ. Men.460.5; *conversely*, Pl.*Men.*89e. d. neut. pl. ἐναντία as Adv., c. dat., Hdt.6.32, Th.1.29, etc. 2. with Preps., ἐκ τοῦ ἐ. *over against, opposite*, opp. ἐκ πλαγίου, X.*HG*4.5.15, etc.; ἐξ ἐναντίας, Ion. -ίης, Hdt.7.225, Th.4.33 (οἱ ἐξ ἐ. the *opposing parties*, prob. in *PGrenf.* 2.78.26 (iv A. D.)); ἐκ τῶν ἐ. *on the contrary*, Plb.5.9.9; ἀπ' ἐναντίας Ascl.*Tact.*1.2; ἀπ' ἐ. χωρεῖν Procop.*Arc.*4; κατὰ τὰ ἐ. Pl.*Ti.*39a: Geom., αἱ κατ' ἐναντίον τοῦ παραλληλογράμμου πλευραί the *opposite* sides of the parallelogram, Archim.*Aequil.*1.9; αἱ κατ' ἐ. τομαί *opposite* sections (i.e. branches) of the hyperbola, Apollon.Perg.*Con.* 3.23. 3. regul. Adv. -ίως *contrariwise*, c. dat., τούτοις οὐκ ἐ. λέγεις A.*Eu.*642; ἐ. διακεῖσθαί τινι Pl.*R.*361c; ἐ. ἀντικεῖσθαι Arist.*Int.*17^b 20; πικρῶς καὶ ἐ. *like an enemy*, D.19.339; ἐ. ἢ ὡς ἀνδραπόδοις τραφεῖσι Pl.*Tht.*175d; ἐ. ἔχειν to be *exactly opposed*, Id.*Euthd.*278a; πρός τι to be *contrary* in respect of.., D.1.4; in the Logic of Arist., *Metaph.*1057^{b}11, al., cf. Procl.*in Alc.*p.268 C.

ἐναντῐότης, ητος, ἡ, *contrariety, opposition*, Pl.*Phd.*105a, A.D.*Conj.* 253.16, Ph.1.7, etc.; πρὸς ἀλλήλω Pl.*Tht.*186b, etc.: pl., Ocell.2. 4. II. in the Philos. of Arist., *contrariety*, *Int.*21^{a}29, *EN*1108^b 27; v. ἐναντίος I. 4.

ἐναντῐο-τροπία, ἡ, *contrariety of character*, τῶν ἐθνῶν Aristid.Quint. 2.13. **-φᾰνής**, ές, *containing an apparent contradiction*, Sch.E.*Or.* 424. **-φημος**, ον, *contradicting oneself*, gloss on παλίγγλωσσος, Sch.Pi.*N.*1.88. **-φρων**, ον, gen. ονος, = ἐναντιογνώμων, *Cat.Cod. Astr.*8(4).194. **-φωνος**, ον, *contradicting*, Hsch. s. v. ἀντίφωνα.

ἐναντῐ-όω, v. ἐναντιόομαι. **-πέρᾱ**, Adv. *on the opposite side*, *Epigr. Gr.*981.6 (Philae). **-ωμα**, ατος, τό, *anything opposite* or *opposed, obstacle, hindrance*, Th.4.69, D.18.308, Plu.*Lys.*23; ἐχθροῖς ἐναντιώματα *opposition offered* to them, D.18.309. 2. *incompatibility*, Pl. *R.*524e: pl., *conflicting impulses*, ib.603d; *differences, discrepancies*, πρός τι Arist.*PA*695^{a}18. **-ωμᾰτικός**, ή, όν, *marking opposition*, σύνδεσμος D.T.643.14, A.D.*Conj.*251.3. Adv. -κῶς Eust.809. 36. **-ωνῠμέω**, *have an opposite name*, Nicom.*Ar.*1.10. **-ώνῠμος**, ον, *having an opposite name*, ib.9. **-ωσις**, εως, ἡ, *opposition*, Th. 8.50, Pl.*R.*454a; in social intercourse, Arist.*EN*1126^{b}34; *opposition*, *Sammelb.*5356.25 (iv A. D.). 2. *disagreement, discrepancy*, Isoc.12.203 (pl.), Pl.*R.*607c, etc.: pl., *contrarieties*, Arist.*Metaph.*986^b 1, al. **-ωτέον**, *one must answer, oppose*, τινί Id.*Top.*160^{b}16. **-ωτικός**, ή, όν, *opposing*, τινί Stob.2.7.11^k. Adv. -κῶς Thessal.ap.Gal.18 (1).288.

ἐναντλέω, *draw in*: metaph. in Pass., ἀκοὴ φωναῖς ἁπάσαις -ουμένη Ph.1.574 (v. l. ἐπ-).

ἔναξε, v. νάσσω.

ἐναξονίζω, *fit with an axle*, in Pass., γῆ τροχοῦ δίκην -ισμένη *Placit.* 3.13.3.

ἐνᾰολλής, ές, = ἀολλής, dub. l., Nic.*Th.*573, *Al.*236.

ἐνάπᾰλος [ᾰπ], ον, *somewhat soft*, Dsc.1.64.

ἐναπ-άρχομαι, Med., *make a beginning*, Aesop.291b. **-ασχολέω**, *to be wholly occupied in*, Steph.*in Hp.*1.134 D. **-ειλέω**, *threaten*, prob. f. l. for ἐπ-, τιμωρίας D.H.5.54.

ἐναπειροκᾰλέω, *show bad taste in*, διαλεκτικῇ S.E.*P.*2.245 (s. v. l.).

ἐναπ-ενῐαυτίζω, *dwell for a year in a strange* place, Parmenisc.ap. Sch.E.*Med.*273 (s. v. l.). **-εργάζομαι**, *produce in*, τινί τι Pl.*Plt.*273c, *Sph.*236a, v. l. in Isoc.7.38, etc. **-ερείδω**, *support* or *rest upon*, ὁ φωνῶν ἐ. αὐτὸν ἐν φθόγγῳ Plot.5.5.5:—Pass., *depend upon*, dub. in Phld.*Lib.*p.63 O. II. Med., ἐναπερείδεσθαι τὸ κέντρον ἐν νεύρῳ *fix it in*, Gal.8.196; ἐ. τὴν ὀργὴν εἴς τινα *vent* it *upon*.., Plb.22.13.2; τὸν ἀγῶνα τοῦ λόγου τινί J.*BJ*2.2.5; χρήματα ἐν ὑμῖν Phalar.*Ep.*69.2. 2. *fix attention upon*, τῇ τῶν νεῶν φροντίδι Plot.4.3.17:—Pass., *to be so fixed*, -ομένης ταύτῃ τῆς δυνάμεως ib.23. 3. *struggle with, resist*, τῇ μνήμῃ Plu.2.126e (s. v. l.). **-έρεισις**, εως, ἡ, *fixing of attention*, Plot.4.4.1. **-ερεύγω**, *vomit forth upon*, metaph. of lust, τὸ πάθος τινί Ph.2.393, cf. 202.

ἐναπεσφρᾱγισμένως, Adv., (ἐναποσφραγίζω, q. v.) *expressly, distinctly*, *Stoic.*2.31.

ἐναπῆκε, Ion. for ἐναφῆκε, 3 sg. aor. 1 of ἐναφίημι.

ἐναπῆπτε, Ion. for ἐναφῆπτε, 3 sg. impf. of ἐναφάπτω.

ἐναπηχέω, in Pass., *to be a faint echo* or *resonance*, τὸ οἷον -ηθὲν τοῖς σώμασιν Plot.4.4.22.

ἐνάπιγμα, ατος, τό, dub. in *Annuario* 4/5.483 (Tymnos, v/iv B. C.).

ἐναπιλλημένους· διακρατηθέντας, Hsch.

ἐνάπλωσις, εως, ἡ, *resolution into the elements*, Simp.*in Epict.* p.43 D.

ἐναπο-βάπτω, *dip quite in*, πρίονα ὕδατι Hp.*VC*21. **-βλέπω**, *look in and see*, *PHolm.*3.14. **-βρέχω**, *steep, soak in*, τινί τι Hp. *Haem.*4, *Gp.*12.19.2:—Pass., Heraclid.Tar.ap.Gal.14.187, Dsc.5. 35. **-γεννάω**, *beget in*, σώμασιν Plu.2.767d. **-γράφομαι** [γρᾰ], *inscribe for oneself*, [τὸ ἡγεμονικὸν] εἰς τοῦτο ἑκάστην τῶν ἐννοιῶν ἐναπογράφεται *Placit.*4.11.1. **-γρᾰφος**, ον, *registered*, esp. of cultivators or serfs, *POxy.*135.15, 137.12 (vi A. D.), *PAmh.*2.149.6 (vi A. D.), Just.*Nov.*54*Pr.*, al. **-δείκνῠμαι**, Med., *exhibit*, πίστιν τινί *to show one's* loyalty to a person, Plb.1.82.9; ἐ. εὔνοιαν, ἔχθραν εἴς τινα, Id.10.34.10, 3.12.4; ἡδονὴ ἐ. ἀλγηδόνας Diog.*Ep.*28.5:—Pass., εὔνοιαν ἴσην πᾶσιν ἐναποδεδεῖχθαι *IG*2^2.1042*b*18. II. ἐναπεδεικνύατο (Ion. impf. Pass.) *approved themselves, gained distinction among* others, Hdt.9.58. **-δείκτως**, Adv. *demonstrably*, *PMasp.*151. 180 (vi A. D.). **-δέω**, *bind up in* a thing, ἄχνην λόπῳ Hp.*Mochl.*2:—Pass., Pl.*Erx.*400a. II. ἐ. τὴν χεῖρα *fasten to* a bag, Hp.*Liqu.* 6. **-δύομαι**, Pass. with pf. Act., *strip in* a place, Him.*Or.*17.2, Men.Prot.p.1 D., Agath.*Praef.*p.132 D. **-ζέννῡμι**, *boil in* a thing, Gal.13.118: aor. 1 part. -ζέσας Dsc.4.176. **-θεσις**, εως, ἡ, *depositing*, καταλήψεων S.E.*P.*3.188. **-θησαυρίζω**, *store up in* a place, Iamb.*VP*29.162:—Pass., ὅσα δι' ὁράσεως -ίζεται Ph.1.278. **-θλίβω** [ῑ], *squeeze in*, ib.541 (s. v. l.), Archig.(?)ap.Gal.12.858:—Pass., Harp.Astr. in *Cat.Cod.Astr.*8(3).148. **-θνῄσκω**, *die in* a place, ἐν τῇ νήσῳ Th.3.104, cf. 2.52, Hdt.9.65; ἐν [λάροις] *among* the gulls, Phryn.Com.69: abs., *Schwyzer* 182.20 (Gortyn); *die in* or *during*, ἐναποθανεῖν ἐν τοῖς καλλίστοις ἔργοις Plb.18.41.9; ταῖς ὑπεροχαῖς Id. 15.35.5; τοῦτο εἴ τις φάγοι, ἐ. if he were to eat, he *dies of it*, Thphr. *HP*4.4.12; ἐ. βασάνοις *die under* torture, Ath.13.596f; ἀτυχίαις Ph. 2.192; ἱμάτιον ἐ. ἐπιτήδειον D.L.2.35. **-θραύω**, *break off in*, οἰστοὺς τοῖς τραύμασι Plu.*Crass.*25.

ἐναποικοδομέω, *enclose by a wall*, τινά Polyaen.8.51.

ἐναπο-κάμνω, *to be exhausted in*, ταῖς φυγαῖς J.*BJ*3.6.1. **-κειμαι**, Pass., *to be stored up in*, τόποις Plu.*Aem.*14, *CPHerm.*6.14 (iii A. D.): metaph., ψυχῇ, μνήμῃ, Ph.1.293, Porph.*Plot.*1, cf. Plot.3.6.2. **-κινδῡνεύω**, *run a hazard in* or *with*, στόλῳ D.C.49.2, cf. J.*AJ*2.9. 4. **-κίχραμαι**, Med., *contract a loan*, *PSI*4.317.21 (i A. D.). **-κλάω**, *break off short in*, τὰ δοράτια ἐναπεκέκλαστο Th.4.34. **-κλείω**, *enclose in*, Olymp.*in Mete.*315.20, Alex.Trall.2:—Pass., Alex.Aphr. *Pr.*1.53, Artem.2.2, Philum.ap.Aët.5.78. **-κλίνω** [ῑ], *lay down in*, ἑαυτὸν στιβάδι Philostr.Jun.*Im.*3. **-κλύζω**, in Pass., *to be stirred about in*, τινί Dsc.3.34. **-κρύπτω**, *conceal*, τὰς δυνάμεις Jul.*Or.*1.38c:—Pass., τῷ δάσει τῶν δένδρων Str.15.3.7, cf. Sch.Luc. *Cat.*14. **-κῠβεύω**, = ἐναποκινδυνεύω, ταῖς τῶν μισθοφόρων ψυχαῖς D.S.16.78. **-λαμβάνω**, *cut off and enclose, intercept*, [τὸν ἀέρα] ἐν ταῖς κλεψύδραις Arist.*Ph.*213^{a}27, cf. Onos.21.5; ἐξ ζῴδια Ph.2.153:—Pass., εἰς τὸ μέσον ἐ. Pl.*Ti.*84e; [μῦς] ἐναποληφθεῖσα ἐν ἀγγείῳ Arist. *HA*580^{b}11; [ἀὴρ] ἐ. Id.*Cael.*294^{b}27, cf. *Pr.*868^{b}25, Epicur.*Nat.*2.993. 1; ἐ. τῇ δίνῃ *to be involved in* it, D.S.1.7. II. Astrol., *annul by adverse influence*, Vett.Val.112.14 (Pass.). **-λαύω**, *enjoy*, *PLond.* 1727.26 (vi A. D.); προνομίῳ Just.*Nov.*111.1. **-λείπω**, *leave behind in* or *on*, ταῖς χερσὶ ποιότητα Xenocr.58; τι Plu.2.91b:—Pass., Arist. *Mete.*352^{b}35, Ph.1.8. **-λειψις**, εως, ἡ, *leaving* of empty spaces *within*, κενῶν Thphr.*Sens.*62. **-ληψις**, εως, ἡ, *intercepting, catching, retention*, Arist.*Mete.*370^{a}1, *Spir.*482^{b}31, Thphr.*CP*2.9.3, Dsc.*Eup.* 1.62. 2. *being caught up, involved in*, τὰς ἐ. τῶν συστροφῶν ἐν τῇ τοῦ κόσμου γενέσει Epicur.*Ep.*1 p.28 U.

ἐναπόλλῡμαι, *perish in* a place, X.*HG*3.1.4.

ἐναπο-λογέομαι, *defend oneself in*, τῇ πόλει Aeschin.1.122. **-λογίζομαι**, *account for before*, [τῷ κοινῷ] *IG*12(9).909 (Chalcis, iv/iii B. C.). **-λούομαι**, *wash oneself* or *bathe in*, Ath.2.43a. **-λύω**, *acquit*, *PLond.*2.425 (i B. C.). **-μαγμα**, ατος, τό, *impression, image*, Herm.*in Phdr.*p.68 A. **-μᾰραίνομαι**, *wither on*, τοὺς καρποὺς -ανθῆναι τοῖς φυτοῖς Lyd.*Ost.*23: metaph., οὐ γὰρ χρόνῳ ἡ τοῦ δημιουργοῦ δύναμις -μαραίνεται Aen.Gaz.*Thphr.*p.44 B. II. *shrivel up in*, ἐλαίῳ Orib.8.27.4. **-μάσσω**, *wipe off upon*, e. g. pigments, Plu. 2.99b:—Med., *receive an impression*, λογισμοὶ ἐ. τύπους φρονήσεως Ph.1.59, al.:—Pass., *to be stamped on*, κηροῖς Plu.2.3e, cf. D.L.7.46; *to be imaged in*, τῷ κατόπτρῳ Ach.Tat.5.13; also φαντασία κατ' αὐτὸ τὸ ὑπάρχον -μεμαγμένη Zeno *Stoic.*1.18. 2. Med., ἐναπομάξασθαι χεῖράς τινι *wipe one's* hands *on*, cj. in Alciphr.3.44; of a snake, λυσσᾶν ποῦ ἐναπομάξεται τὸν ἰόν Sch.Gen.Il.22.95. II. *rub, dry*, Alex. Trall.*Febr.*1. **-μειξις**, εως, ἡ, *intermixture*, Thphr.*CP*6.1.1, 6.3. 1. **-μεμαγμένως**, Adv. *by a distinct impression*, *Stoic.*2.31. **-μένω**, *remain in*, καρποὶ ἐ. τῇ χώρᾳ Lyd.*Mag.*3.61; τῷ αἰσθητῷ καὶ φαινομένῳ κάλλει Herm. *in Phdr.*p.100 A., cf. Aen.Gaz.*Thphr.*p.67 B.: abs., Hld.1.15.

ἐναπομόργνῡμι, *wipe off upon, impart*, e.g. colour *to* one, Iamb. ap.Stob.3.3.26:—Pass., ἐ. τύπος τῆς φαντασίας εἰς τὸ πνεῦμα Porph. *Sent.*29.

ἐναπόμορξις, εως, ἡ, *imbuing*, v. l. for -μειξις in Thphr.*CP*6.1.1.

ἐναπο-μύττομαι, *blow the nose upon*, ταῖς παροψίσιν Plu.2.1128b. **-νέμω**, *allot, assess*, Lyd.*Mens.*3.23. **-νίζω**, *wash clean in* a thing, τινί Polyzel.4:—Med., ἐναπονίζεσθαι τοὺς πόδας ἐν τῷ ποδανιπτῆρι *wash one's* feet in it, Hdt.2.172; χεῖρας Id.1.138. II. Med., *wash off from oneself in*, τῷ ποταμῷ τὸ αἷμα Paus.9.30.8. **-πᾰτέω**, *ventrem exonerare in*.., Ar.*Pax* 1228, Polyzel.4. **-πλύνω** [ῡ], *wash away in*, τὰ χρώματα ἐν τῷ ὑγρῷ Arist.*Sens.*441^{b}15; ἐσθῆτα Paus.3. 25.8. **-πνέω**, *expire in*, ταῖς πατρῴαις οἰκίαις D.S.13.89, cf. M.Ant. 5.4; ἱκεσίαις *expire in the act of*.., Plu.*Cor.*33; τῷ αὐλῷ Luc.*Harm.* 2. **-πνίγω** [ῑ], *suffocate, drown in*, in aor. 2 Pass. ἐναποπνῐγῆναι ἐν οἴνῳ Terpsicl.ap.Ath.7.325d, cf. Jul.*Ep.*82; καπνῷ Luc.*Peregr.* 24. **-πτύω**, *spit into*, Dsc.4.24.

ἐναπορέω, dub. l. for ἐπαπορέω, *to be in doubt*, Plb.29.27.6; πῶς.. Id.12.25^c.1.

ἐναπο-ρρίπτω, *throw aside*, Dsc.*Eup*.1.68 (dub.). **-σβέννῡμι**, aor. -έσβεσα, *quench in* a thing, Hp.*Mul*.1.78; τὴν θερμότητα Arist. *Pr*.937^{b}13; τι ὕδατι Gal.14.377; δᾷδας γλεύκει *Gp*.7.12.8:—Pass., Arist.*Mete*.369^{b}16, Cass.*Pr*.31, Hld.1.15. **-σημαίνω**, *indicate* or *point out in*, ἱστορίᾳ Plu.*Cim*.2:—Med., *impress* or *stamp on* a thing, σεισμοὶ τὴν ἁρμονίαν τῶν ὀρῶν ἐναπεσημήναντο τοῖς τμήμασι Philostr. *Im*.2.17, cf. Ph.1.291. **-σκηπτικός**, ή, όν, *supervening*, [πυρετός] Cass.*Pr*.15. **-σκήπτω**, *cause to descend*, θεὸς ἐ. νόσον τισί J.*AJ* 2.14.6. II. intr., *supervene, attack*, -σκηπτούσης τῆς φλεγμονῆς Cass.*Pr*.30, cf. Phlp. *in de An*.339.5. **-σκηψις**, εως, ἡ, *supervening*, *AB*435. **-σπάω**, *tear off*, βίᾳ τὸ χόριον Aët.16.20. **-στάζω**, *drip with*, λύθρου Lib.*Decl*.40*Intr*.1. **-στέγω**, *keep in*, Gal.7.709, 15.180. **-στηρίζομαι**, Med., *fix oneself in* or *on*, ἐς τὴν γλῶσσαν Hp.*Acut*.(*Sp*.).9, cf. *Placit*.2.20.10. **-σφάττομαι**, Pass., *to be slain among*, J.*BJ*4.6.3. **-σφρᾱγίζω**, *impress in* or *on*, ψυχῆς ὁμοιότητα εἰς παιδὸς χαρακτῆρα Lxx4*Ma*.15.4: abs., D.L.7.46:—Med., οὐ γὰρ ἂν -σφραγίσαιτο τὰ ἔξω τὴν ἑαυτῶν φύσιν Epicur.*Ep*.1 p.11 U.:—Pass., Zeno*Stoic*.1.18. **-τελέω**, in Pass., *to be produced*, Alex.Aphr.*Pr*.1.134. **-τέμνω**, in Pass., *to be cut off in*, Str.2.5.27. **-τήκω**, *dissolve in*, ἐλαίῳ στέαρ Gal.11.489. **-τίθεμαι**, *lay aside* or *store up in*, Id.*Nat.Fac*.3.12; ἐναποθέσθαι τὰ ξίφη εἰς τοὺς κολεοὺς D.C.73.10; τὸ γεγονὸς τῇ διανοίᾳ Ph.2.42; *deposit*, Gal.*Nat. Fac*.3.7; κηλῖδας τῇ ψυχῇ Jul.*Or*.1.15d; *include*, τι τοῖς γράμμασι Procop.Gaz.p.169 B.; but ἐναποτίθεσθαι τὴν ὀργὴν εἴς τι *vent one's anger upon*.., D.S.26.16; *produce in*, ψῦξιν τῷ σπλάγχνῳ Alex.Trall. 10:—Pass., Phld.*Herc*.862.14. **-τίκτω**, *produce in*, γνώμην τινί Procop.Gaz.*Ep*.31. **-τῑμάω**, *take in payment at a valuation*, τί τινι D.53.20:—Pass., D.C.41.37. **-τίνω**, *pay* or *spend in litigation in* a place, πόλις κοινῇ ἐναποτεῖσαι χρήματα Ar.*Av*.38. **-τῡπόομαι**, Pass., *receive impressions*, Thphr.*Sens*.53, Zeno*Stoic*.1.18; *to be impressed upon*, παιδίων ψυχαῖς Plu.2.3e. II. *express*, ὁ λόγος ἐ. τὴν τελειότητά τινος Hierocl. *in CA*26 p.480 M. **-φέρω**, in Med., *receive by heredity*, τι τῶν τεκόντων Lib.*Decl*.43.56. **-χράομαι**, *abuse*, τινί D.17.23. II. later in Act., *peculate*, *PAmh*.2.79 (ii A.D.). **-χρησις**, εως, ἡ, *peculation*, ibid. **-ψάω**, *wipe in* or *on*, Sch.Ar.*Ach*.843. **-ψύχω** [ῡ], *ease oneself in*, euphem. for ἐναποπατέω, Hes.*Op*.759. 2. *cool off*, *PHolm*.6.12 (Pass.). II. *give up the ghost*, *AP*9.1 tit., Hsch.

ἐνάπτω, *bind on* or *to*, σπάργανά τινι E.*Ion* 1490 (anap.); τι εἴς τι X. *Cyn*.6.8, cf. Aeschin.Socr.41 (Pass.):—Pass., θώρηκος κύτει ἐνημμένῳ κάλλιστα *fitted on, fitting* beautifully, Ar.*Pax*1225. 2. Pass., of persons, *to be fitted with, clad in*, c. acc., λεοντέας ἐναμμένοι (Ion. for ἐνημμ-) Hdt.7.69; διφθέραν ἐνημμένος Ar.*Nu*.72; παρδαλᾶς ἐνημμένους Id.*Av*.1250, cf. Str.15.1.71 (v.l.), Luc.*Herc*.1:—also in Med., ὁ χορὸς.. ἐναψάμενος δάπιδας Ar.*Fr*.253, cf. Luc.*Tim*.6. II. *kindle, set on fire*, Ar.*Pax*1032 (Pass.):—Med., *get oneself a light*, Lys.1.14. III. *lay hands on*, *GDI*1760.11, al. (Delph.).

ἔναρ, Lacon., = ἔνας, Hsch.; v. ἔνος (B).

ἔνᾰρα, ων, τά, (ἐναίρω) only pl., *arms and trappings of a slain foe, spoils*, φέρειν ἔ. βροτόεντα Il.6.480; φέρομαι 8.534; πόλλ' ἔ. Τρώων *taken from* them, 13.268; so ἔ. βροτόεντα Δόλωνος 10.570: generally, *spoil, booty*, τὴν [φόρμιγγα] ἄρετ' ἐξ ἐνάρων 9.188, cf. 6.68, Hes.*Sc*. 367.—Ep. word (used by S.*Aj*.177 (lyr.)) for Trag. σκῦλα, λάφυρα.

ἐνάραι· ὑγιᾶναι, Hsch. **ἐναράνει**· ἐντρυφᾷ, Id.

ἐνάραξις [ᾰρ], εως, ἡ, *beating*, τυμπάνων prob. in Plu.2.56e (pl.).

ἐνᾰράομαι, = ἐνεύχομαι, *adjure by*, ἐ. σοι τὴν ὑγίειαν τοῦ πατρὸς *PSI* 4.416.7 (iii B.C.).

ἐνᾰρᾰρίσκω, aor. 1 ἐνῆρσα, *fit* or *fasten in*, ἐν δὲ σταθμοὺς ἄρσε Od. 21.45. II. pf. ἐνάρηρα, intr., *to be fitted in*, εὖ ἐναρηρός 5.236; οὐρανῷ εὖ ἐνάρηρεν ἀγάλματα Arat.453.

ἐνᾰράσσω, *dash against*, κριοὶ ἐ. βίᾳ τὰ κέρατα Paus.4.13.1, cf. Dexipp.Hist.p.184 D.:—Pass., *to be dashed against*, ἐς τὰς πέτρας App.*BC*5.98.

ἐναράτιον, τό, = ἐνηρόσιον, *IG*12(1).924.20 (Rhodes, iii B.C.), dub. in ib.9(2).1229.10 (Phalanna, ii B.C.).

ἐνάργ-εια, ἡ, *clearness, distinctness, vividness*, Pl.*Plt*.277c. 2. Philos., *clear and distinct perception*, Epicur.*Ep*.1 p.11 U., al. 3. Rhet., *vivid description*, D.H.*Lys*.7; joined with συντομία, Phld. *Po*.5.3. II. *clear view*, Ἰταλίας Plb.3.54.2, etc. III. *self-evidence*, Phld.*Sign*.15, al.; ἡ ἐ. δείκνυσιν Diogenian.Epicur.4.10; παρὰ τὴν ἐ. contrary to *manifest facts*, Olymp. *in Mete*.215.12. **-ημα**, ατος, τό, *clearly perceived phenomenon, datum of experience*, Epicur. *Ep*.1 p.24 U., al.: pl., *evident facts*, opp. τὰ μὴ δῆλα, Phld.*Sign*.36, cf. *Po*.2.54. **-ής**, ές, *visible, palpable, in bodily shape*, esp. of the gods appearing in their own forms, χαλεποὶ δὲ θεοὶ φαίνεσθαι ἐναργεῖς Il.20.131; οὐ γάρ πως πάντεσσι θεοὶ φαίνονται ἐναργεῖς Od.16.161, cf. 3.420, 7.201; freq. of a dream or vision, ἐναργὲς ὄνειρον ἐπέσσυτο 4.841; [ὄναρ] A.*Pers*.179, etc.; ὄψιν ἐνυπνίου τῷ ἑωυτοῦ πάθει ἐναργεστάτην *most clearly relating to*.., Hdt.5.55, cf. 7.47; ἐνύπνια Hp. *Prorrh*.1.5; ἐ. ταῦρος *in visible form* a bull, a *very* bull, S.*Tr*.11; ἐ. τινὰ στῆσαι to set him *bodily before one*, Id.*OC*910; ἐ. βλεφάρων ἵμερος desire *beaming* from the eyes, Id.*Ant*.795 (lyr.). b. *prominent*, ἄρθρα Aret.*SD*1.8. 2. *manifest to the mind's eye*, τάδ' ἀντίπρῳρα δή σοι βλέπειν πάρεστ' ἐ. S.*Tr*.224; λῃστὴς ἐ. the *manifest* robber, Id.*OT*535, cf. *Ant*.263; τοῖς δρῶσιν ἐ. ἡ ὕβρις φαίνεται D.21.72. Adv. -γῶς *visibly, manifestly*, A.*Th*.136, S.*El*.878; ἐ. ἡ θεός σ' ἐπισκοπεῖ Ar. *Eq*.1173. 3. of words, etc., *clear, distinct*, ἐ. βάξις ἦλθεν A.*Pr*.663; freq. in Prose, ἐ. τεκμήριον, σημεῖον, ἀπόδειξις, etc., Pl.*Ion* 535c, *Ti*.72b (Comp.), D.18.300, etc.; -εστέρα γνῶσις Pl.*Tht*.206b, cf. Epicur.*Ep*.3 p.60 U.; -εστάτη αἴσθησις Arist.*Pr*.886^{b}35; ἐ. τοῦ πράγματος ἐπίνοια Epicur.*Fr*.255; καὶ τοῦτο ἐ. ὅτι.. (for δῆλον ὅτι) Pl.*Tht*.150d; ἐναργὲς τοῦτο συμβαλεῖν Ar.*V*.50. Adv. -γῶς, Ion. -γέως, λέγειν Hdt.8.77; παραστῆσαι Ael.*Tact*.1.5: Comp. -έστερον, εἰπεῖν, διόψεται, Pl.*Ti*.49a, *R*.611c: Sup. -έστατα, γνῶναι Id.*Alc*.1.132c. II. *brilliant, splendid*, βωμός Pi.*O*.7.42. **-ότης**, ητος, ἡ, = ἐνάργεια, Poll.4.97.

ἐναργῠρ-ίζω, *to be of silvery appearance*, Heph.Astr.1.24. **-όω**, in Pass., *to be silver-plated*, ἀργυρούμενα ἢ ἐνηργυρώμενα σκεύη Timae. Astr. in *Cat.Cod.Astr*.1.97.

ἐναργώδης, ες, = ἐναργής 1, ὄνειροι Aret.*SD*1.5.

ἐναρδ-εύω, *irrigate*, and **-ευτής**, οῦ, ὁ, *one who irrigates*, *Gloss*.

Ἐνάρεες or **-αρέες** (Ἐνάριες v.l. in Hdt.4.67, Ἀναριεῖς prob. in Hp.*Aër*.22), οἱ, prob. a Scythian word, = ἀνδρόγυνοι, Hdt.1.105, 4.67, cf. Hp. l. c.

ἐνάρετος [ᾰρ], ον, *virtuous*, Chrysipp.*Stoic*.3.72, Plot.1.3.3: interpol. in Epict.*Ench*.24.3; *valiant*, J.*BJ*6.1.8. Adv. -τως Aristo*Stoic*. 1.86, *IG*5(2).463 (Megalop.), *CIG*2771 i 7 (Aphrodisias), Alex.Aphr. *in Top*.331.11. II. *productive*, [γῆ] *PFlor*.50.4 (iii A.D.).

ἐνᾱρηρώς, v. ἐναραρίσκω. **ἐνάρης**· ἐνηρμοσμένος, Hsch.

ἐναρηφόρος (Dor. -ᾱφορος Hsch.), ον, *wearing the spoils*, *APl*.4.72.

ἐνάρθμιος, ον, *having an affinity with*, οἴνῳ Emp.91 (prob.).

ἐναρθρ-όομαι, *to be articulated by* ἐνάρθρωσις, Gal.2.735. **-ος**, ον, *jointed*: of speech, *articulate*, φωνὴ ἔ. Diog.Bab.*Stoic*.3.212, D.H. *Comp*.14, Babr.*Prooem*.1.7: Comp., Diog.Oen.18. Adv. -ρως, λέγειν Artem.4.19. II. *strong in limb*, Aret.*SD*2.5. **-ωσις**, εως, ἡ, a kind of *articulation*, when the ball is *deep set in* the socket, Gal.2.736.

ἐνᾰρίζω Il.1.191, etc.: impf. ἠνάριζον A.*Ag*.1644; Ep. ἐνάριζον (v. infr.): fut. -ίξω (ἐξ-) Il.20.339: aor. Ep. and Lyr. ἐνάριξα 22.323, Pi.*N*.6.52, later ἠνάριξα Lyc.486, ἠνάρισα *AP*7.226 (Anacr.):—**Med.**, aor. ἐναρίξατο Opp.*C*.2.20:—Pass., S.*Tr*.94 (lyr.): aor. ἠναρίσθην: pf. ἠνάρισμαι (v. κατ-):—*strip a slain foe of his arms* (ἔναρα), c. dupl. acc., ἔντεα.. τὰ Πατρόκλοιο βίην ἐνάριξα Il.17.187; ἀλλήλους ἐνάριζον ib.413: hence, *slay in fight*, Hes.*Sc*.194: generally, *slay*, Il.1.191, A. l. c.:—in Pass., νὺξ ἐναριζομένα *when dying*, i.e. *when yielding to* day, S. l. c.; cf. ἐναίρω.

ἐνᾰριθμ-έω, *reckon in* or *among*, in Pass., Arist.*SE*170^{a}8, *MM* 1204^{a}23, Luc.*Eun*.8. II. *account*, ἴσα καὶ τὸ μηδέν as nothing, S. *OT*1188 (lyr.):—Med., = ἐν ἀριθμῷ ποιεῖσθαι, *make account of, value*, E.*Or*.623. **-ησις**, εως, ἡ, *reckoning in*, v.l. for ἐξ- in Sch.Nic.*Th*. 156. **-ητέος**, α, ον, *to be reckoned in*, Plu.*Nob*.1. 2. -ητέον, *one must reckon in*, Eust.1719.7. **-ιος**, ον, (ἀριθμός) *in the number, making up the number*, ἄλλην ἐνίησι πατὴρ ἐναρίθμιον εἶναι Od.12.65; *counted among*, i.e. *among*, ζῴοις Theoc.7.86; ὑποχθονίοις A.R.1.647; ἐ. *among men, in the world*, *IG*7.2543.6 (Thebes, iii/iv A.D.); δήμου ἐ. f.l. in Epigr.ap.D.L.7.27; cf. ἀρίθμιος. II. *taken into account, valued*, οὔτε ποτ' ἐν πολέμῳ ἐ. οὔτ' ἐνὶ βουλῇ Il.2.202; ἐναρίθμια· φίλα, συνήθη, Hsch. **-ος**, ον, = foreg. 1, Pl.*Sph*.258c, Orph.*A*.109; τὰ ἐ., = αἱ μονάδες, Arist.*Metaph*.991^{b}22 (s. v.l.). II. *taken into account, esteemed*, οὐκ ἐλλόγιμον οὐδ' ἐ. Pl.*Phlb*.17e (with play on signf. 1).

ἐνᾰρῐκύμων [ῡ], ονος, ὁ, ἡ, f.l. for ἀρικύμων, Hp.*Aër*.5.

ἐνᾰρίμβροτος, ον, *man-slaying*, Μέμνων Pi.*P*.6.30; μάχα Id.*I*. 8(7).57.

ἐνᾰριστάω, *take breakfast in*..., Eup.250, Suid. s. v. Νικόλαος. II. *take a snack for breakfast* (cf. ἐμφαγεῖν 1), Hp.*Vict*.3.68, 80.

ἐναρκέω, *suffice, be able*, c. inf., Sch.Pi.*N*.6.97: ἐναρκεῖ· ἐνδέχεται, Hsch.

ἐναρκτεύει· φονεύει, κρίνει, Hsch.

ἐναρκτικός, ή, όν, *inchoative*, *Gloss*.

ἐναρμογή, ἡ, *fitting* of a surgical tube, Antyll.ap.Orib.10.19.4.

ἐναρμ-όζω and **-ττω**, Dor. aor. inf. -μόξαι Pi.*O*.3.5, *IG*4.952.68 (Epid.):—*fit* or *fix in*, ἔγχος σφονδύλοις E.*Ph*.1413; πλευροῖς βέλη Id. *HF*179, cf. Ar.*Lys*.413; ξύλα ἀλλήλοις Thphr.*HP*5.3.5; πήχεις Luc. *DDeor*.7.4:—Pass., *SIG*694.37 (Elaea, ii B.C.). b. Math., *insert* a mean term, Nicom.*Ar*.2.27:—Pass., Geom., *to be inserted*, Archim. *Fluit*.2.10. 2. metaph., *fit, adapt*, Δωρίῳ φωνὰν ἐ. πεδίλῳ Pi. l. c., cf. *I*.1.16; τι εἴς τι Pl.*Lg*.819c, D.H.*Isoc*.3; ἐ. αὑτόν *make* himself *popular*, Plu.*Alex*.52:—Pass., *to be fitted, adapted*, Plot.6.7.34:—Med., τὴν Δωριστὶ (sc. ἁρμονίαν) ἐναρμόττεσθαι.. τὴν λύραν *tune* it to the Dorian mode, v. l. in Ar.*Eq*.989 (lyr.). II. intr., *fit into*, ἐς τὸ κοῖλον τῆς ἀγκύλης Hp.*Art*.6; εἰς [γωνίαν] Archim.*Aren*.10, al.: metaph., *suit, be convenient*, εἰς τὴν πρόληψιν Epicur.*Sent*.37; ἔν τινι Ar.*Ra*.1202; τινί Pl.*Lg*.894c: abs., τὸ ἐναρμόττον μέγεθος Epicur.*Ep*. 1 p.12 U. 2. c. dat. pers., *please*, Plu.*Them*.5. **-όνιος**, ον, *of musical sound, musical*, ἔνρυθμος καὶ ἐ. αἴσθησις Pl.*Lg*.654a; ἐ. ἡ φωνὴ φερομένων κύκλῳ τῶν ἄστρων Arist.*Cael*.290^{b}22; ἐναρμόνιον μελῳδεῖν Luc.*DDeor*.7.4; νέκταρ, of music, *AP*7.29 (Antip. Sid.): metaph., *in harmony with*, ταῖς τῶν βίων ὑποθέσεσι Ti.Locr.103c. Adv. -ίως Ph.1.107, Corn.*ND*32, Eustr. *in EN*9.2, Eust.1422.19. 2. in Lit. Crit., *harmonious*, περίοδος D.H.*Dem*.24; μεταβολαὶ ἐ. changes *of harmony*, Id.*Comp*.19, cf. ib.6 (Comp.). II. in Music, *enharmonic*, συστήματα Aristox.*Harm*.p.17 M.; δίεσις ib.p.47 M.; ἐ. μέλη Arist.*Pr*.918^{b}22 (s. v. l.), cf. *POxy*.667.1, etc. **-οσις**, εως, ἡ, *fitting in*, Archim.*Stom*.1 (pl.), Procl.*Hyp*.6.9. **-οστος**, ον, *harmonious*, συμφωνίας Lxx4*Ma*.14.3; *concordant*, πρὸς ἄλλα Iamb. *Myst*.3.18. **-όττω**, v. ἐναρμόζω.

ἔναρξις, εως, ἡ, = καταρχή, Procl.*Par.Ptol*.131. II. *introduction*, τῶν λεχθησομένων Sch.E.*Hec*.313.

ἐνᾰροκτάντας, Dor. for -της, ου, ὁ, *spoiler and slayer*, of death, A. *Fr*.151 (lyr.).

ἔνᾰρος, ον, (ἀρά) *subject to a curse*, *Rev.Ét.Gr.*24.415 (Itanos, ii B.C.), Hsch.

ἐνᾰρόω, *plough in*, τῇ γῇ σπέρμα Antipho Soph.60.

ἐναρσφόρος, ον, = ἐναρηφόρος, Hes.*Sc.*192, prob. in Alcm.23.3.

ἐναρτάω, *fasten on*, σπάρτους Hero *Aut.*26.5 :—Pass., Sch.Arat.441.

ἐνάρχομαι, fut. -ξομαι prob. in E. (v. infr.) :—in sacrifices, *begin the offering*, by taking the barley from the basket, κανᾶ δ' ἐναρχέσθω τις E.*IA* 1470, cf. Men.*Sam.*7 ; προχύτας χέρνιβάς τ' ἐνάρξεται E.*IA* 955 : pf. in pass. sense, κανοῦν δ' ἐνῆρκται Id.*El.*1142 ; ἐνῆρκται τὰ κανᾶ Aeschin.3.120. 2. generally, *begin*, *Sammelb.*4369(b).23 (iii B.C.), etc. ; τῆς θερείας ἐναρχομένης Plb.5.30.7 : c. inf., πολεμεῖν ib.1.5 ; γενειᾶν D.H.6.13 : ἐ. τινός *make a beginning of*, τῆς ἐπιβολῆς Plb.5.1.3 ; τοῦ λόγου Plu.*Cic.*35 ; ὁμιλιῶν *engage in*, Ath.Med.ap.Orib.*inc.*21.9 ; ἐνῆρκται folld. by a quotation, Apollon.Cit.1 : abs., *begin to speak*, Plu.*Cam.*32. II. later, in Act., *hold office*, *IG*12(5).526.5 (Ceos).

ἔναρχος, ον, (ἀρχή) *in office, in authority*, App.*BC*1.14, Wilcken *Chr.*41 iii 10 (iii A.D.) ; οἱ ἔ. ὄντες ἀεί *GDI*2520.12 (Delph.) ; συνέδρους ἀεὶ τοὺς ἔ. those *who were in office* at the time, *CIG*3046.13 (Teos) ; ἔ. ἀρχιερεύς *IGRom.*1.1060.4 (Alexandria) ; ὑπομνηματογράφος *OGI* 715 (ibid.), etc. 2. *under authority*, Stob.2.7.3[a].

ἑνάς, άδος, ἡ, (ἕν) = μονάς, *unit*, Pl.*Phlb.*15a : pl., of an order of existences, Dam.*Pr.*40,99, al. ; οἱ νόες πλείους τῶν θείων ἑ. Procl.*Inst.* 62, cf. 6.

ἔνας, v. ἔνος (B).

ἐνασεβέω, = ἀσεβέω ἐν, Diog.*Ep.*28.4 ; τῇ Ἀρτέμιδι Sch.Gen.Il.21.401 :—Pass., ὑπό τινων Themist.*Ep.*8.

ἐνᾰσελγ-αίνω, *behave lewdly*, εἰς τὰς γυναῖκας D.S.34/5.2.12 :—Pass., *to be treated with insult in* a thing, cj. in Ar.*V.*61 (ἀνασελγ- codd.). **-έω**, = foreg., Aq.*Jd.*19.25.

ἐνάσθαι· φθαρῆναι, γηράσαι, Hsch. ; cf. ἐναίσασθαι.

ἐνασθενέω, prob. f.l. for ἐξ-, γήρᾳ Ph.2.493.

ἐνασκέω, *train* or *practise in* a thing, αὐτόν Plu.*Alex.*17 :—Pass. with fut. Med. (Luc.*Vit.Auct.*3), *to be trained*, c. dat., Ph.1.448, al., Luc. l.c. : c. acc., ἀτρεκίην *AP*11.354.10 (Agath.) :—Act. intr., like Pass., Plb.1.63.9. II. Pass., τῷ ὕφει ἐνησκῆσθαι *to be wrought in* it, J.*AJ*3.7.5.

ἐνασμενίζω, *take pleasure in*, τινί Ph.1.36.

ἐνασπάζομαι, *welcome*, Plu.2.987d.

ἐνασπίδ-ιος [πῐ], ον, = Lat. *clipeatus*, [εἰκόνες] *JRS*16.250 (Ancyra, ii A.D.). **-όομαι**, *fit oneself with a shield*, Ar.*Ach.*368.

ἐνασσα, v. ναίω II.

ἐναστεΐζομαι, = ἐνοικῶ, Hsch.

ἐναστράπτω, *flash in* or *on*, metaph., δικαιοσύνη ἐ. Them.*Or.*4.51d, cf. Iamb.*Myst.*3.11 ; πρὸς τὴν οὐσίαν Jul.*Or.*4.137b : c. acc. cogn., ἐ. φέγγος τινί Ph.1.448.

ἔναστρος, ον, *among the stars*, Achae.16 ; *starry*, ἰδέαι *Corp.Herm.* 3.2 (s.v.l.).

ἐνασχημονέω, *behave oneself unseemly in*, βαθεῖ πώγωνι καὶ ἀρετῇ Luc.*Icar.*21 ; ἀρχαῖς Plu.2.336b, cf. Id.*Sert.*27.

ἐνασχολέομαι, *to be engrossed with*, μαθήμασιν Phlp. *in GC*26.23 ; περί τινος Id. *in Mete.*18.1, cf. Men.Prot.p.80 D.

ἐνᾰταῖος, α, ον, (ἔνατος) *on the ninth day*, Hp.*Aph.*4.36, Th.2.49, *PSI*4.286 (iii/iv A.D.) ; of recurring fevers, Hp.*Epid.*1.24.

ἐνᾰτεν-ίζω, fut. -ιῶ Crates *Ep.*15 :—*fix steadfastly on*, τὰς ἀκοάς τινι Iamb.*VP*15.65 ; τὸ πρόσωπον εἰς.. Sor.1.70. II. intr., *look fixedly on* one, Lxx 3*Ma.*5.30, Hld.7.7, *PMag.Leid.W.*5.44 ; ἐ. δριμὺ καὶ τιτανῶδες Lib.*Decl.*51.10 : c. dat., [ἡδοναῖς] Crates l.c. ; ἡλίῳ S.E.*P.* 1.45, cf. Syrian. *in Metaph.*45.16 ; διαγράμματι Iamb. *in Nic.*p.88 P. **-ισις**, εως, ἡ, *gazing intently*, πρὸς τὸ πρᾶγμα Procl. *in Prm.* p.598 S.

ἐνᾰτεύω, in Pass., *have the ninth part removed for sacrifice*, *SIG* 1024.23 (Myconos), *Supp.Epigr.*2.505 (Thasos, v B.C.).

ἐνάτηρ, v. εἰνάτερες.

ἐνᾰτισταί, οἱ, members of a religious guild at Delos, *IG*11(4).1228, 1229.

ἔνατμος, ον, *full of vapour*, D.S.2.49.

ἔνᾰτος, η, ον, (ἐννέα) *ninth*, Il.2.313, Hes.*Op.*772, *IG*1[2].304.15, *PGrenf.*2.24.1 (ii B.C.), etc. ; Ep. **εἴνατος** Il.2.295, 8.266 ; Aeol. **ἔνοτος** *BCH*37.166 (Cyme, iii B.C.) ; τὰ ἔνατα (sc. ἱερά), *sacra novendialia*, Is. 8.39, Aeschin.3.225. (Freq. written ἔννατος in codd.)

ἐνατρεμέω, *to be at rest*, Them.*Or.*4.51d.

ἐναττῐκίζω : ἐναττικίζουσι τῷ χωρίῳ αἱ ἀηδόνες the nightingales *sing in* this place *just as in Attica*, Philostr.*Her.Prooem.*

ἐναυγ-άζω, *illuminate*, τὴν ἀχλὺν τῆς ψυχῆς Ph.1.52 :—Pass., Id. 2.300. 2. intr., *shine, be seen*, ἐναυγάζοντος λύχνου Ael.*NA*1.58. II. *behold*, Lyc.71 :—so in Med., Ph.1.449,471 :—Pass., ib. 422. **-ασμα**, ατος, τό, *illumination*, ἐ. θεῖον ib.88.

ἐναυγής, perh. f.l. for εὐαυγής, Pi.*Pae.Fr.*19.25.

ἔναυδος, ον, *speaking, living*, Hsch.

ἐναυλᾰκοφοῖτις, ιδος, ἡ, *wandering in the fields*, Ὧραι *AP*6.98 (Zon.).

ἐναύλ-ειον, τό, f.l. for ἔναυλος (A). II, E.*Hel.*1107 (lyr.). **-ήματα**, τά, *barley meal soaked in wine and oil*, *EM*338.8, *AB*259, Suid. (cf. θυλήματα). **-ίζω**, intr., *dwell* or *abide in* a place, S.*Ph.*33 ; νύκτ' ἐναυλίσαι μίαν prob. in E.*Hyps.Fr.*3(1).18. II. Med., *take up one's quarters* during the night, νύκτα οὐδεὶς ἐναυλίζεται [ἐν τῷ νηῷ] Hdt.1.181 ; ἐν Τανάγρῃ νύκτα ἐναυλισάμενος Id.9.15 ; esp. of soldiers, *take up night-quarters, bivouac*, Th.3.91, 4.54, 8.33, X.*An.*7.7.8, etc. ; ἐν τῇ γῇ *GDI*5597.14 (Ephesus, iii B.C.). III. metaph., of diseases, *lodge*, ἐν τῷ στήθει Hp.*Nat.Hom.*12. **-ιος**, α, ον, (αὐλή) *inside the court* : ἐναύλιος (sc. θύρα), ἡ, *the door leading into the house*, τὴν ἐναύλιον ὠθῶν pushing *it* open, *Com.Adesp.*1203.6. 2. ἐναυλίαν (sc. ζωήν) ἄγοντες the *inner life*, Zos.Alch.p.229 B. 3. ἐναύλιον, τό, *haunt, abode*, Ἀστερόποιο Euph.51.11 ; Ἰοχεαίρης Nonn.*D.*41.147. **-ισμα**, ατος, τό, *dwelling-place, abode*, Artem.4.47. **-ιστήριος**, ον, *habitable*, ἄντρον *AP*6.219.13 (Antip.(?)). **-ον**, τό, = sq. II, κατ' ἔναυλ' ὀρέων E.*Fr.*740, cf. *AP*9.102 (Anton. Arg.).

ἔναυλος (A), ὁ, Subst. : I. (αὐλός) *bed of a stream*, τάχα κεν.. ἐναύλους πλήσειαν νεκύων Il.16.71 ; *torrent, mountain-stream*, ὅν ῥά τ' ἔναυλος ἀποέρσῃ 21.283, cf. 312. II. (αὐλή) *dwelling, shelter* : pl., *haunts* of the country-gods, οὔρεα μακρὰ θεῶν χαρίεντας ἐναύλους Νυμφέων Hes.*Th.*129, cf. *h.Ven.*74,124, E.*Ba.*122 (lyr.), *HF*371 (lyr.) ; also ἁλὸς ἐναύλους, of the sea, Opp.*H.*1.305 ; Ποσειδάωνος ἐ. ib.3.5.—Ep. word, used by E. in lyr. III. Adv. -ως *by means of pipes*, διάγειν *AB*464.

ἔναυλος (B), ον, Adj. : I. (αὐλός) *on* or *to the flute, accompanied by it*, κιθάρισις Philoch.66 ; θροῦς Philostr.*Im.*1.2. 2. mostly metaph., λόγος, φθόγγος ἔ., words, voice *ringing in one's ears, still heard* or *remembered*, Pl.*Mx.*235c, Luc.*Somn.*5 ; ἔ. φόβος *fresh* fear, Pl.*Lg.*678c ; ἔναυλον ἦν πᾶσιν ὅτι.. all had it *fresh in memory* that.., Aeschin.3.191 ; ἔναυλα καὶ πρὸ ὀμμάτων D.H.9.7 ; ἔ. δύναμις Arist. *Pr.*928[b]7 ; ἔ. ἔχειν ὅτι to have it *fresh in one's mind*, that.., Plu.2.17d ; τὰ ὦτα ἔναυλος ὢν διαμέμνηται τοῦ μέλους Max.Tyr.7.7. II. (αὐλή) = ἐναύλιος, *dwelling in dens*, λέοντες E.*Ph.*1573 (anap.) ; *in one's den, at home*, opp. θυραῖος, S.*Ph.*158 (lyr.).

ἐναυλοστατέω, *make a fold in*, *SIG*685.82 (Itanos).

ἐναυξάνω, aor. 1 ἐνηύξησα, *increase*, ἐπιθυμίαν ἀρετῆς X.*Cyn.*12.9 :—Pass., c. dat., *grow in*.., τρυφῇ Hdn.2.10.6 ; **ἐναύξομαι**, v.l. for ἀέξομαι, Emp.106.

ἔναυρος, ον, (αὔρα) *exposed to the air*, Thphr.*HP*8.11.6. II. Ἔναυρος, epith. of Apollo, Hsch. **ἐναύρω·** πρωΐ (Cret.), Id.

ἔναυσις, εως, ἡ, *taking* from a neighbour, ὑδάτων τε πηγαίων καὶ πυρός Plu.*Cim.*10.

ἔναυσμα, ατος, τό, (ἐναύω A) *spark* : metaph., Max.Tyr.11.8 ; ζῳοῖσιν ἔ. *that which gives life* to animals, Orph.*H.*11.16 ; ἡ φύσις τοῖς σώμασιν ἐντίθησιν τῆς οἰκείας ἰδιότητος ἔ. Procl. *in Cra.*p.30 P., cf. Iamb.*Protr.* 21.ιζ'. 2. metaph., *spark, glimmer*, Plb.9.28.8, Plu.*Flam.*11 (pl.) ; ἐναύσματα εὐγενείας Ph.2.437 : pl., *slight indications* of a testator's wishes, Just.*Nov.*107 *Pr.* 3. *stimulus, incentive*, τῶν ἀρετῶν ἐ. D.S. 10 *Fr.*11.2 (pl.) ; τοιαῦτα ἔχων ἐ. ἐς βασιλείας ἐπιθυμίαν Hdn.2.15.2.

ἐναυχένιος, ον, *in* or *on the neck*, βρόχος *AP*7.493 (Antip. Thess.).

ἐναυχέω, *boast*, Ph.1.422, Hsch.

ἐναύω (A), impf. ἔναυον Hdt.7.231 : aor. 1 opt. ἐναύσειε Diph.62, inf. ἐναῦσαι Plu.*Phoc.*37 :—Med., Cratin.409 : fut. -σομαι *Com. Adesp.*25.23 D., Longus 3.6 : aor. ἐναύσασθαι Pl.*Ax.*371e, etc. :—*kindle*, ἐ. πῦρ τινί *light* one a fire, *give* him *a light*, as was the duty of a neighbour, X.*Mem.*2.2.12, cf. Hdt. l.c., Diph. l.c., Call.*Iamb.*1.191 ; τοῦτον μήτε πόλει δέχεσθαι μήτε πῦρ ἐ. Plb.9.40.5, cf. Din.2.9 :—Med., πῦρ ἐναύεσθαι *light oneself* a fire, *get* a light, ἐκ τῆς Αἴτνης Luc. *Tim.*6 ; ἀπὸ ἑτέρου πυρός Plu.*Num.*9 : metaph., ἐ. τὸ θάρσος *borrow* courage, Pl. l.c. ; τῆς ἐλευθερίας v.l. in Plb.18.11.7 ; of Poets, *draw inspiration*, Ἔφεσον ὅθεν πῦρ οἱ τὰ μέτρα μέλλοντες τὰ χωλὰ τίκτειν μὴ 'μαθῶς ἐναύονται Call.*Iamb.*1.335 ; ἐντεῦθεν ἐ. τὸν λόγον Ael.*Fr.* 246 ; ἐξ αὐτοῦ διδασκαλίαν ἐ. ib.89. 2. *apply fire* to smoke out a swarm of bees, Hsch. (Cf. αὔω, ἐπαύω ; the gloss ἔναυον (i.e. ἔναυ' ὄν for ἔναυσον)· ἔνθες (Cypr.), Id., belongs to this word.)

ἐναύω (B), *cry aloud in*, Sch.Il.5.333.

ἐναύω (C), = ἱκετεύω πρὸς τοῖς ναοῖς, Suid., Zonar.

ἐναφᾰνίζω, *cause to disappear, hide*, τῶν ἡδονῶν τὰς σωματικὰς αἱ πρακτικαὶ τῷ χαίροντι τῆς ψυχῆς ἐ. Plu.2.1099d :—more freq. in Pass., *to be lost in*, ἔν τινι Str.1.3.3 ; τινί Ph.2.118, Longin.17.2, Plu.2.489a, M.Ant.7.10, al. : abs., of the pulse, *die away, disappear in*, ταῖς ἀντιβάσεσιν Agathin.ap.Gal.8.936.

ἐναφάπτω, Ion. ἐναπ-, *tie up* or *hang in* a thing, ἐναπῆπτε τὴν κεφαλὴν ἐς τὸν ἀσκόν f.l. in Hdt.1.214 (cf. ἐναφίημι) ; *attach*, Arist.*Cael.* 301[b]26.

ἐναφέσιος, ὁ, *holder of land* ἐν ἀφέσει (cf. ἄφεσις I.1a), *PTeb.*352.6 (ii A.D.), etc.

ἐναφέψημα, ατος, τό, *decoction*, Aret.*CA*1.1.

ἐναφέψω, *boil down in*, Gal.6.291 : pf. Pass. εναφέψημαι Hp.*Mul.* 2.167, Orib.8.6.5 : aor. 1 part. ἐναφεψηθείς Dsc.1.7, 2.129.

ἐναφίημι, *let drop into, put in*, in aor. 1 ἐναπῆκε Hdt.1.214 (cf. ἐναφάπτω) ; *insert*, Arist.*GA*723[b]23. II. *discharge in* or *into*, γόνον Id.*HA*553[b]24 ; τῇ κοίτῃ (sc. κόπρον) Artem.2.26. III. of land in Egypt, *release*, i.e. *transfer to private tenure*, in Pass., *POxy.*918 xiii 9 (ii A.D.), etc. 2. *leave*, ἐναφῆκέν μου τὰ κτήματα ἀγεώργητα *PMasp.*5.20 (vi A.D.). IV. *permit*, διατρέχειν τὸ πνεῦμα ἐν αὐτοῖς (sc. τοῖς νεύροις) ἐ. Orib.*Fr.*37.

ἐναφροδῑσιάζω, *venerem exerceo in*.., κόρῃ Aristaenet.1.15, 2.1.

ἐνᾰχῶς, *in nine ways*, Syrian. *in Metaph.*171.4.

ἑνᾰχῶς, *in one way*, prob. in Simp. *in Ph.*399.24.

ἔναψις, εως, ἡ, *attachment*, Ph.*Bel.*82.39 (pl.) ; ἐνάψεις ἀγκυρῶν ib. 98.33.

ἔνβενος· ὑελοειδής, Hsch.

ἐνγεταυθί, in Ar.*Th.*646, com. tmesis for ἐνταυθί γε. **ἔνγλαυσιν·** ἐν γλαύκεσιν, Hsch. **ἐνδαγεῖ·** ἐμμανεῖ, Id.

ἐνδᾱδ-όομαι, Pass., of a pine, *suffer from resin-glut*, Thphr.*HP* 9.2.7. **-ος**, ον, (δᾴς) *resinous, full of resin*, ib.3.9.3.

ἔνδαες· ἐν διανοίᾳ ἑκάστου, Hsch.

ἐνδαίνῠμαι, Med., *feast on*, τι f.l. in Ath.7.277a.

ἔνδαις, αιδος, or **ἔνδᾳς**, ᾳδος, ὁ, ἡ, *with lighted torch*, σπονδαί A.*Eu.* 1044 (prob.).

ἐνδαίω (A), *light* or *kindle in*: metaph., ἐ. πόθον τινί Pi.*P.*4.184:— Med., *burn* or *glow in*, ἐν δέ οἱ ὄσσε δαίεται Od.6.131; βέλος δ' ἐνεδαίετο κούρῃ A.R.3.286.

ἐνδαίω (B), *distribute*, in Pass., ἐνδεδασμέναι ἡλικίαι Pyth.ap.Iamb. *VP*31.201; cf. ἔνδασαι· μέρισον, Hsch.

ἐνδάκνω, *bite into, seize with the teeth*, ἔχιδνα δ' ὥς μέ τις πόδ' ἐνδακοῦσ' ἔχει A.*Supp.*897 (dub.); ἐ. στόμια γνάθοις *take* the bit *between the teeth*, of runaway horses, E.*Hipp.*1223; ἐ. χαλινόν Pl.*Phdr.*254d; τὸ χεῖλος Luc.*Cal.*24: abs., Aret.*SA*1.7. 2. metaph., of sharp things, *fix themselves firm in*, τῇ γῇ Apollod.*Poliorc.*145.9; of mustard, *to be pungent*, Nic.*Fr.*70.16.

ἔνδακρυς, υ, gen. υος, *in tears, weeping*, J.*AJ*1.19.4, Luc.*Somn.*4.

ἐνδακρύω, *weep in* or *with*, ἐ. ὄμμασι *suffuse* them *with tears*, A.*Ag.* 541.

ἐνδᾰμάζω, *subdue*, σιδήρῳ Steph.*in Hp.*2.332 D. (Pass.).

ἐνδᾱμέω, ἐνδᾱμία, Dor. for ἐνδημ-.

ἐνδανδαίνει· ἀτενίζει, κατατολμᾷ, Hsch.

ἐνδάπιος [ᾰ], α, ον, *native of the country*, Mosch.2.11, Coluth.238, *AP*9.153 (Agath.); Ἕλλησι καὶ ἐνδαπίοισιν ἀμοιβήν *Bull.Inst.Egypt.* 1912.91; ἐ. Παλλάς Nonn.*D.*4.423: also in late Prose, Agath.2.15; cf. ἀλλοδαπός.

ἔνδᾰσυς, υ, *somewhat rough, hairy*, Dsc.2.142.

ἐνδᾰτέομαι, *divide*, δὶς . . τοὔνομ' ἐνδατούμενος *dividing* the name of Polynices (into πολὺ νεῖκος), A.*Th.*578 (v. Sch.); ἐ. λόγους ὀνειδιστῆρας *distribute* or *fling about* reproaches, E.*HF*218. 2. c. acc. objecti, a. *speak of in detail*, i.e., in bad sense, *reproach, revile*, τὸ δυσπάρευνον λέκτρον ἐ. S.*Tr.*791; in good sense, *dwell on, celebrate*, εὐπαιδίας A.*Fr.*350.1; βέλεα θέλοιμ' ἂν . . ἐ. S.*OT*205 (lyr.) (perh. *scatter* or *shower* them *abroad*). b. *tear in pieces, devour*, Lyc. 155. II. Pass., *to be ground small*, Nic.*Th.*509, acc. to Sch.

ἔνδαυλον· λοχ(μ)ῶδες, δασύ, Hsch.

ἐνδαύω, *sleep in*, Lyc.1354.

ἐνδαψῐλεύομαι, *to be liberal in*, Hld.8.14. II. ὀλίγης πρὸς τὸ πέρας [τῶν ξυνθηκῶν] αὐτῷ -ομένης παραδρομῆς ἡμερῶν when the lapse of a few days was all that it would have *cost* to complete the agreement, Men.Prot.p.102 D.

ἐνδέ-ημα, ατος, τό, *deficiency*, *PRyl.*214.23 (ii A.D.), *POxy.*71 i 15 (pl., iv A.D.). **-ής**, ές, neut. pl. ἐνδεᾶ: (ἐνδέω B):—*wanting* or *lacking in, in need of*, c. gen., ἐ. εἶναι or γεγενῆσθαί τινος, Hdt.1.32, Antipho 5.77; ἑνός μοι μῦθος ἐ. ἔτι E.*Hec.*835; πολλῶν ἐ., opp. αὐτάρκης, Pl.*R.*369b; ποιητοῦ δ' ἐστὶν ἐ. . . πρὸς τὸ ἐπιδεῖξαι, *caret vate sacro*, Id. *Smp.*195d, cf. *Lg.*697e; σμικροῦ τινος ἐ. εἰμι πάντ' ἔχειν Id.*Prt.* 329b. 2. abs., *in want, in need*, X.*HG*6.1.3 codd., etc. b. *lacking, deficient*, freq. in Comp., ἐνδεέστερα πράγματα Hdt.7.48; φαίνεται ἐνδεεστέρα [ἡ στρατεία] Th.1.10; -εστέρα παρασκευή Id.4.65; ἐνδεέστεροι ταῖς οὐσίαις Isoc.4.105; also in Posit., οὐδὲν ἐνδεὲς ποιεῖσθαι leave nothing *unsaid*, S.*Ph.*375; τοῦτο πολ. ᾧ τοῦ παρόντος ἐνδεές E.*Heracl.* 170; μηδὲν ἐνδεὲς λίπης Id.*Ph.*385; ἐνδεὲς φαίνεταί τι Th.5.9; ἐνδεές τι ἐν τῷ σώματι ἔχειν X.*Cyr.*8.1.40; ἐ. τὸν βίον Men.592; τὴν ὄψιν Luc.*DMar.*1.2; τὸ ἐ. *lack, want, defect*, = ἔνδεια, Th.1.77; τὸ αὐτῶν ἐ. their *deficiency*, Id.3.83. 3. *inferior*, τὰ κρείσσω μηδὲ τἀνδεᾶ λέγειν *the worse*, S.*OC*1430; γένει οὐδενὸς ἐνδεής X.*HG*7.1.23; τῆς δυνάμεως ἐνδεᾶ πρᾶξαι to act *short of* your real power, Th.1.70; τούτου ἐνδεᾶ ἐφαίνετο (sc. τὰ πράγματα) their power was *unequal to* the purpose, ib.102: Comp. ἐνδεέστερός τινος S.*Ph.*524; τῆς δόξης Th.2.11; αὐτοῦ Plu.*Cic.*35. 4. *inadequate, insufficient*, πρός τι Pl.*Prt.*322b; ἐ. ξυνθῆκαι Th.8.36. 5. Gramm., *defective*, A.D.*Synt.*239.18. 6. Adv. ἐνδεῶς *defectively, insufficiently*, opp. ἱκανῶς, Pl.*Phd.*88e, *R.*523e; ἐ. ἔχειν τινός to be *in want of*, E.*Fr.*898.8; τῶν ἀναγκαίων Plu.*Nic.*27; μὴ ἐνδεῶς γνῶναι judge not *insufficiently*, Th.2.40: Comp. ἐνδεεστέρως παρεῖχεν ἢ πρὸς τὴν ἐξουσίαν *less* than, Id.4.39; ἐ. πρὸς ὃ βούλεται δηλοῦσθαι Id.2.35; ἐ. ἔχειν Pl.*Phd.*74e; ἐ. ἢ προσῆκεν τιμωρήσασθαι Epist. Philipp.ap.D.12.12: rarely -έστερον A.D.*Synt.*209.21. **-ητικός**, ή, όν, *deficient*, περὶ τὸ τέλος Vett.Val.15.20.

ἔνδεια, ἡ, *want, lack*, δυνάμεως Th.4.18; τῆς ἀναγκαιοτάτης διαίτης Id.7.82; χρημάτων X.*Ath.*1.5, Pl.*Hp.Ma.*283d, etc. II. abs., *deficiency, defect*, opp. ὑπερβολή, Id.*Prt.*357b, Arist.*EN*1109ᵃ4: pl., opp. ὑπερβολαί, Isoc.2.33, cf. 8.90. 2. *want, need*, coupled with ἐπιθυμία, Pl.*Grg.*496d,e: pl., αἱ ἔνδειαι τῶν φίλων, τοῦ σώματος, X.*Cyr.* 8.2.22, Pl.*Erx.*401e, al. 3. *want of means, poverty*, ἀεὶ ἐνδείᾳ σύνοικος Id.*Smp.*203d; αἰσχρόν τι ποιεῖν δι' ἔνδειαν D.18.257; *famine*, Jul. *Or.*2.66c. 4. Gramm., *defect*, opp. πλεόνασμα, A.D.*Synt.*133.15.

ἔνδειγμα, ατος, τό, (ἐνδείκνυμι) *evidence*, ὅτι . . Pl.*Criti.*110b, cf. Iamb.*Myst.*1.11; *token*, εὐνοίας D.19.256, cf. Dam.*Pr.*46.

ἐνδείκ-νῡμι or -ύω, fut. -δείξω, *mark, point out*, τι Pi.*O.*7.58; πρίν γ' ἂν ἐνδείξω τί δρῶ S.*OC*48; ἐ. τῷ δικαστηρίῳ τἀδικήματα Antipho 6. 37, etc.; *indicate*, τοὺς καιρούς Gal.1.204: c. part., *show that* a thing is, Pl.*Plt.*278b; also ἑκάστοις ἐ. τὰ ἔργα ἀποτελεῖν ib.308e. 2. law-term, *inform against*, τινά Id.*Ap.*32b: abs., Isoc.18.20; ἐ. ταῖς ἀρχαῖς Pl.*Lg.*856c, cf. And.1.8, etc.; τῷ φήναντι ἢ ἐνδείξαντι *IG*2². 1128.18; ἐ. πρὸς τοὺς μαστῆρας ib.12(7).62.53 (Amorgos, iv B.C.):— Med., Plu.*Sol.*24:—freq. in Pass., κακοῦργος ἐνδεδειγμένος Antipho 5. 9; ἐνδειχθεὶς Lys.6.15, *OGI*669.45 (Egypt, i A.D.); ἐνδειχθέντα δικάζειν ὀφείλοντα τῷ δημοσίῳ D.21.182. 3. *exhibit, display*, ὑπερήφανον αἰχμάν A.*Pr.*406 (lyr.). 4. Med., *declare* the possession of goods to fiscal authorities, *PRev.Laws* 54.10 (iii B.C.). II. Med., *show forth oneself* or *what is one's own*, once in Hom., Πηλεΐδῃ ἐνδείξομαι I *will declare myself* to Achilles, Il.19.83; ἐνδεικνύμενοι τὴν ἑαυτῶν γνώμην Hdt.8.141; ἐ. περί τινος Plb.4.28.4; τι μετ' ἀποδείξεως Id.5. 16.7. 2. *show, make plain*, c. part., πῶς δ' ἂν . . μᾶλλον ἐνδείξαιτό τις πόσιν προτιμῶσ' . .; E.*Alc.*154, cf. *Ba.*47, X.*Cyr.*1.6.10; τὴν δύναμιν κρείττω οὖσαν ἐ. D.21.66; also ἐ. ὅτι . . Th.8.82, Pl.*Ap.*23b, X. *Cyr.*8.3.21; ἐ. ὁποῖα τούτων ἀληθῆ Pl.*Tht.*158e:—Pass., ἐνδεδεῖχθαι τὸ βούλεσθαι D.8.12. b. *prove, demonstrate*, *PMagd.*3.10 (iii B.C.), Phld.*Sign.*11, al. 3. c. acc. rei, *display, exhibit*, τὸ εὔψυχον Th.4. 126; εὔνοιάν τινα Ar.*Pl.*785; τῷ σώματι τὴν εὔνοιαν, οὐ χρήμασιν οὐδὲ λόγοις, ἐνεδείξατο τῇ πατρίδι D.21.145; τύπῳ τἀληθὲς ἐ. Arist.*EN* 1094ᵇ20; of a name, *denote*, Pl.*Cra.*394e. 4. ἐνδείκνυσθαί τινι *display oneself to* one, *make a set at* him, *court* him, D.19.113, Aeschin. 3.217, etc.; ἐνδεικνύμενοι καὶ ὑπερκολακεύοντές τινα D.19.160; *make a show, show off*, τινί Pl.*Prt.*317c, Arist.*Oec.*1352ᵇ13. **-της**, ου, ὁ, *informer, complainant*, *UPZ*69.4 (ii B.C.), Lxx 2*Ma.*4.1, Philostr. *VS*2.29. **-τικός**, ή, όν, *probative*, as the Protag. of Plato, D.L.3. 51. II. *indicative*, Gal.*Phil.Hist.*9, S.E.*P.*2.100, etc. Adv. -κῶς Id.*M.*8.155, 289, Gal.10.928, al. **-τός**, ή, όν, *liable to prosecution*, ποτὶ δραχμὰς ἑκατόν *IG*5(2).266.44 (Mantinea, i B.C.).

ἐνδείμᾰτος, ον, *accompanied by fear*, ὑποδοχή Iamb.*Protr.*20.

ἐνδεινῶς, Adv. *terribly*: Comp. -ότερον dub. in Them.*Or.*4.56a.

ἔνδειξις, εως, ἡ, *indication*, ἔνδειξιν τῷ λόγῳ ἐνδείκνυσθαι, opp. ἐννοεῖν, Pl.*Lg.*966b, cf. Plb.3.38.5, *Ep.Rom.*3.25, A.D.*Synt.*14.18, Ptol. *Phas.*p.10 H., D.C.62.23, etc.; esp. in disease, Gal.10.126, al., S.E. *P.*1.240. 2. as law-term, *laying of information against* one who discharged public functions for which he was legally disqualified, *writ of indictment* in such a case, And.1.10, D.20.156 (pl.), Arist.*Ath.* 52.1 (pl.), cf. Decr.ib.29.4, *IG*2².1128.35. II. *demonstration, display of one's good will* (cf. ἐνδείκνυμι II.4), ἡ εἰς Ἀλέξανδρον ἔ. Aeschin. 3.219. III. *proof, demonstration*, Phlp.*in Mete.*123.34.

ἕνδεκα, οἱ, αἱ, τά, indecl., *eleven*, Il.2.713, etc. II. at Athens, οἱ ἕ. *the Eleven, the Police-Commissioners*, Ar.*V.*1108, Antipho 5.70, Lys.14.17, Pl.*Phd.*59e, Arist.*Ath.*7.3, etc. 2. certain officers at Delos, *Hermes* 17.5.

ἑνδεκα-γράμμᾰτος, ον, *of eleven letters*, πούς prob. in Ath.10.455b. **-γωνος**, ον, *having eleven angles*, Hero *Metr.*1.24, al. **-ετής**, ές, *of eleven years*, χρόνος *IG*12(5).860.42 (Tenos).

ἑνδεκάζω, *celebrate the tenth* of the month, cited by Harp. fr. D.58. [40].

ἑνδεκᾰ-ήμερος, ον, *lasting eleven days*, Gal.7.510. **-κις** [ᾰ, parox.], Adv. *eleven times*, Arist.*HA*562ᵇ25, Theo Sm.p.126 H. **-κλῖνος**, ον, *with eleven couches*: κεφαλὴ ἑ. *big enough to hold eleven couches*, Telecl.44. **-κρούμᾰτος**, ον, *employing eleven notes*, μέτροις ῥυθμοῖς τε Tim.*Pers.*242. **-μετρον** μέτρον measure *of eleven μέτρα*, *PFay.*90.14. **-μηνος**, ον, *of eleven months*, Hp.*Oct.*13, Arist.*Fr.* 283. **-ούγκιον**, τό, *eleven ounces*, *Gloss.* **-πηχυς**, υ, gen. εος, *eleven cubits long*, ἔγχος Il.6.319; δοκός *IG*11(2).161 *D* 125 (iii B.C.); διάστημα S.E.*M.*10.160. **-πους**, ὁ, ἡ, πουν, τό, gen. ποδος, *eleven feet long* or *broad*, λίθος *Milet.*7.58 (Didyma), cf. Poll.1.72.

ἑνδεκάς, άδος, ἡ, *the number Eleven*, Pl.*Lg.*771c, Arist.*Metaph.* 1084ᵃ26.

ἑνδεκᾰσύλλᾰβος, ον, *eleven-syllabled*, ἑ. Πινδαρικόν (sc. μέτρον) Heph.14.2.

ἑνδεκᾰταῖος, α, ον, *on the eleventh day*, Hp.*Aph.*4.36, Th.2.97; ἔραμαι σχεδὸν ἑνδεκαταῖος *for* nearly *eleven days*, Theoc.10.12.

ἑνδέκᾰτος, η, ον, *eleventh*, Od.3.391, etc.; ἑνδεκάτη (sc. ἡμέρη), ἡ, *eleventh day*, 2.374.

ἑνδεκάχορδος [ᾰ], ον, *eleven-stringed*, λύρα Ion Eleg.3.1.

ἑνδεκᾰχῶς, *in eleven ways*, Simp.*in Ph.*553.2.

ἑνδεκ-έτης, ες, = ἑνδεκαετής, prob. in *CIG*(add.)3846 *z* 61 (Aezani): —fem. -έτις, ιδος, *AP*7.164.6 (Antip. Sid.). **-ήρης**, ες, *with eleven banks of oars*, Thphr.*HP*5.8.1, Callix.2.

ἐνδέκομαι, Ion. for ἐνδέχ-.

ἐνδεκτόν ἐστι, = ἐνδέχεται, A.D.*Synt.*148.4, al.

ἐνδελέχ-εια, ἡ, *continuity, persistency*, πέτρην κοιλαίνει ῥανὶς ὕδατος ἐνδελεχείῃ Choeril.10; πάντα γὰρ ταῖς ἐνδελεχείαις καταπονεῖται πράγματα Men.744.—Freq. confused with ἐντελέχεια (q.v.). **-έω**, *continue*, c. acc., μάστιγάς τινι Lxx *Si.*30.1:—Pass., *to be persistently afflicted* with a malady, Steph.*in Hp.*1.136 D. **-ής**, ές, (v. δολιχός) *continuous, perpetual*, μνήμη Pl.*Lg.*718a; λειτουργία Isoc.15.156 (Sup.); πῦρ Lxx 1*Es.*6.24; θυσίαι Ph.2.569, 587; πόλεμος Plu.*Per.*19; of persons, *plodding, persevering*, φροντισταὶ σύντονοι καὶ ἐ. Phld. *Oec.*p.52 J., cf. Plu.*Mar.*13; τὸ περὶ τοὺς πόνους ἐ. *perseverance*, ib.6. Adv. -χῶς Critias 19.5, Pl.*R.*539d, al., Diod.Com.1, Men.521, *IG*2². 1028.33, Lxx *Ex.*29.38, Plu.*Fab.*19, etc.—Freq. confused with ἐντελεχής in codd., as Ph. l.c. **-ίζω**, = ἐνδελεχέω, *persevere*, ἐν φιλοσοφίᾳ Epicur.*Fr.*195, cf. Lxx *Si.*9.4:—Pass., fut. -ισθήσομαι Hsch. **-ισμός**, ὁ, = ἐνδελέχεια, *persistence*, Philum.ap.Orib.45. 29.21; θυμίαμα -ισμοῦ *perpetual* incense, Lxx *Ex.*30.8; esp. of daily sacrifices, ib.29.38, al. (-ιστόν is f.l. in Thd.*Da.*11.31), cf. J.*AJ*11. 4.1 (pl.).

ἐνδελιπές· παντελές, Hsch.: **ἐνδελιστές**, sine expl. (Syrac.), Theognost.*Can.*162: **ἐνδελίτες** Epich.183.

ἔνδεμα, ατος, τό, (ἐνδέω A) *thing bound on*, *Gloss.*: pl., *amulets*, Dsc. *Eup.*2.136.

ἐνδέμω, *wall up*, τὰς διασφάγας Hdt.3.117. II. *build in* a place, τρεῖς μέν οἱ πολίων ἑκατοντάδες ἐνδέδμηνται Theoc.17.82:—Med., *build* or *make for oneself in*, κοῖτον θάμνῳ Nic.*Th.*419.

ἐνδενδίλλειν· ἐμβλέπειν, Hsch. **ἔνδενδρος**, epith. of Zeus in Paros, *IG*12(5).1027 (prob.); of Zeus at Rhodes, and of Dionysus in Boeotia, Hsch.

ἐνδεξιόομαι, *go round from left to right*, βωμόν E.*IA*1473.

ἐνδέξιος, α, ον, Hom. only neut. pl. ἐνδέξια, *towards the right hand, from left to right*, mostly as Adv., θεοῖς ἐνδέξια πᾶσιν οἰνοχόει he filled for all the gods *from left to right*, Il.1.597; δεῖξ' ἐνδέξια πᾶσιν 7.184; βῆ δ' ἴμεν αἰτήσων ἐνδέξια φῶτα ἕκαστον Od.17.365; τὴν ἐπὶ πυρκαῖῆς ἐ. φασι κέλευθον Ἑρμῆν τοὺς ἀγαθοὺς.. ἄγειν *AP*7.545 (Hegesipp.): regarded as lucky, hence ἐνδέξια σήματα *propitious* omens, Il.9.236, cf. *SIG* 1025.25 (Cos). 2. after Hom. without any sense of motion, *on the right*, v.l. in E.*Hipp.*1360 (anap.); ἐνδέξιος σῷ ποδὶ παρασπιστὴς *on* thy *right*, Id.*Cyc.*6; εἰσιόντων ἐνδέξια *on the right* as one enters, *PPetr.*3 p.203; ἡ παραστὰς ἡ ἐνδεξία *Inscr.Prien.*19.46 (iii B.C.): c. gen., ἐνδέξια τῆς εἰκόνος ib.53.74 (ii B.C.). II. *clever*, ἔργα *h.Merc.*454. Adv. -ίως Sch.Th.2.41.

ἐνδεόντως, Adv. *deficiently*, κατά τι ἐ. ἔχειν Gal.6.839.

ἐνδέρω, *wrap in skin*, of sacrificial offerings, in Pass., *SIG*1025.48 (Cos), 1026.8 (ibid.), cf. Hsch. s.v. ἔνδρατα.

ἐνδέρως, Adv. *after wrapping in skin* (cf. foreg.), θύεται Ἐφ.Ἀρχ. 1902.3 (Chalcis).

ἔν-δεσις, εως, ἡ, (ἐνδέω A) *binding on*, of the point of the *pilum*, Plb. 6.23.11: pl., *fastenings*, Ph.*Bel.*99.47; *junction*, τοῦ ποδός Hp.*Oss.* 16. 2. *swaddling*, Sor.1.84. II. *entanglement*, M.Ant.10. 28. 2. *cohesion* of superstructure and foundation, Ph.*Bel.*84. 20 (pl.). **-δεσμα**, ατος, τό, *amulet*, Dsc.2.114. **-δεσμεύω**, *bind to* or *in*, τινὰς εἰς καταπέλτας D.S.20.71:—Pass., Dsc.*Eup.*1.146; τῇ χέρσῳ D.S.3.40. **-δεσμέω**, = foreg., Aq.*Ex.*23.22, al., v.l. in Dsc.4.43 (Pass.): metaph., πρὸς ἃ -εῖται ἡ ψυχή Procl.*in Alc.* p.108 C. II. *tie up in*, τινί *Gp.*8.1.3. **-δεσμίς**, ίδος, ἡ, *fillet-band*, *IG*11(2).161*B*116 (pl., Delos, ii B.C.). **-δεσμος**, ὁ, *bundle, bag*, Dsc.3.83, Lxx 3*Ki.*6.10, al., Luc.*Lex.*10; ἐ. ἀργυρίου *purse*, Lxx *Pr.*7.20. II. Archit., *bonding*, τείχους *SIG*²587.308 (pl., written ἐνδέσζμων); ἐ. ποιεῖσθαι τοῦ ἔργου Procop.*Pers.*2.26.

ἔνδετος, ον, *bound to, entangled in*, πάγαις *AP*9.372.

ἐνδευκής, ές, *like, similar*, Hsch.

ἐνδεύω (A), Aeol. for ἐνδέω (B), *to be wanting*, *IG*12(2).6 (Mytilene).

ἐνδεύω (B), *soak* or *dye in*, βάμματι Nic.*Al.*414 (Med.).

ἐνδεχ[έτηρος], ον, = ἐνδεκέτης, *IG*9(1).882.13 (Corc., ii A.D.).

ἐνδέχομαι, Ion. **-δέκομαι**, fut. -ξομαι, *take upon oneself*, ταλαιπωρίας Hdt.6.11. II. *accept, admit, approve*, τὸν λόγον Id.1.60; τοὺς λόγους Id.5.92.α', 96, al., Ar.*Eq.*632; τὰ λεγόμενα Th.3.82; τὴν συμβουλίην Hdt.7.51; διαβολάς Id.3.80; ἀπόστασιν, = τὸν περὶ ἀποστάσιος λόγον, ib.128; so ἐ. [τὴν τοῦ Ἀλκιβιάδου κάθοδον] Th.8.50. 2. in Hdt. freq. *give ear to, believe*, mostly with a neg., ἀρχὴν.. οὐδὲ ἐ. τὸν λόγον 5.106; τοῦτο δὲ οὐκ ἐ. ἀρχὴν 4.25, cf. 3.73, 7.237: c. inf., *believe* that.., οὐ γὰρ ἔγωγε ἐ. Ἠριδανόν τινα καλέεσθαι ποταμόν 3.115. 3. abs., *give ear, attend*, σὺ δ' ἐνδέχου E.*Andr.*1238, cf. Pl.*Cra.*428b; περί τινος οὐδ' ὁπωσοῦν ἐ. *refuse to hear a word* about it, Th.7.49. III. of things, *admit, allow of*, τὸ προμηθὲς λογισμὸν οὐκ ἐνδέχεται περί τινος Id.4.92; μεταβολήν, ἀλλοίωσιν ἐ., Pl.*Phd.*78d; καθ' ὅσον φύσις ἐνδέχεται, *quantum recipit humana condicio*, Id.*Ti.*69a, cf. *Sph.*254c: c. inf., τὸ ναυτικὸν.. οὐκ ἐνδέχεται ἐκ παρέργου μελετᾶσθαι *does* not *admit of* being practised, Th.1.142, cf. Pl.*Ti.*90c, *Lg.*834d; ὅσων αἱ ἀρχαὶ μὴ ἐνδέχονται ἄλλως ἔχειν Arist.*EN*1139^{a}7. 2. abs., *to be possible*, ἃ πολλὰ ἐνδέχεται Th.4.18; ἐὰν ἐνδεχόμενον ᾖ if it be *possible*, *PGrenf.*2.14.4 (iii B.C.); freq. in Arist., *APr.*25^{a}38, al.; ἐνδέχεσθαι ἢ εἶναι οὐδὲν διαφέρει ἐν τοῖς ἀϊδίοις *Ph.*203^{b}30; ἐ. μέν, οὐ μὴν ἀναγκαῖον *Pol.*1275^{b}6: esp. in part. ἐνδεχόμενος, η, ον, *possible*, ἐκ τῶν ἐνδεχομένων by *all possible means*, X.*Mem.*3.9.4, D.S.1.54; αἱ ἐ. τιμωρίαι Lycurg.119; τὴν ἐ. ἀϊδιότητα Jul.*Or.*4.157b; εἰς τὸ ἐ. *so far as possible*, Hyp.*Epit.*41; and freq. in Arist., τὸ ἐ. ἀληθές *Metaph.*1009^{b}34; τῆς ἐ. αὐτοῖς εὐδαιμονίας μετέχειν *Pol.*1325^{a}10; ζωῆς τῆς ἐ. ἀρίστης ib.1328^{a}36, al.: freq. c. inf., τὰ ἐ. καὶ εἶναι καὶ μὴ εἶναι *contingent* events, *GA*731^{b}25, cf. *Metaph.*1050^{b}11; τὰ ἐ. ἄλλως ἔχειν *EN*1134^{b}31, al.; τὰ μὴ ἐ. αὐτῷ πρᾶξαι ib.1140^{a}32, al. 3. ἐνδέχεται impers., *it admits of* being, *it is possible that*.., c. acc. et inf., Th.1.124, 140, etc.; εἴπερ ἐνεδέχετο (sc. γράφειν) D.18.239; καθ' ὅσον ἐνδέχεται Pl. *Phdr.*271c; εἰς ὅσον ἐ. Id.*R.*501c; ὅσα ἐ. Arist.*Rh.*1354^{a}32; μέχρι οὗ ἐ. ib.1355^{b}13; ὡς ἐ. μάλιστα Plb.3.49.1: acc. abs., ὥσπερ ἐνδεχόμενον εἶναι, = ὥσπερ εἰ ἐνδέχοιτο, Arist.*GA*765^{b}23: gen. abs., ἐνδεχομένου *where possible*, Id.*PA*683^{a}20. b. c. dat. pers., *it is allowed*, X.*Hier.*4.9, D.29.50.

ἐνδεχομένως, Adv. of foreg., = ὅσον ἐνδέχεται, Decr.ap.D.18.165, Plb.1.20.4, al., D.S.20.26, Lxx 2*Ma.*13.26, etc.; ὡς ἐ. *PPetr.*2 p.53; ἀντέγραψεν ἐ. *to the best of his ability*, Aristeas 41.

ἐνδέω (A), fut. -δήσω (v. infr.), *bind in, on* or *to*, τι ἔν τινι Od.5. 260; εἰς σῶμα Pl.*Ti.*43a, cf. Dsc.3.83; more freq. τί τινι Ar.*Ach.* 929, etc.; ὅσα κατέρρωγεν τοῦ τείχους ἐνδήσει θράνοις *IG*2².463:—Med., ἐνεδήσατο δεσμῷ *bound* them *fast*, Theoc.24.27; ὥσπερ κέραμον ἐνδησάμενος *having packed* it *up*, Ar.*Ach.*905; πλίνθους εἰς ἄσφαλτον ἐνδησαμένη D.S.2.7:—Pass., ἱρὰ ἐνδεδεμένα ἐν καλάμῃ Hdt.4.33; ἐνδεθῆναι εἰς σῶμα, ἐν τῷ σώματι, Pl.*Phd.*81e, 92a; ἄστρα ἐνδεδεμένα τοῖς κύκλοις *fixed* stars, Arist.*Cael.*289^{b}33; also οὐρανὸς [ἀστράσιν] ἐνδέδεται *AP*9.25 (Leon.); Αἰγαῖον ὕδωρ Κυκλάδας ἐνδέδεται *App. Anth.*3.82.6 (Archim.). II. metaph., Ζεύς με.. ἄτῃ ἐνέδησε βαρείῃ *entangled* me *in* it, Il.2.111, cf. S.*OC*526 (lyr.); ἀναγκαίῃ ἐνδέειν τινά Hdt.1.11:—Pass., ἐνδεδέσθαι ὁρκίοισι Id.3.19; ἀναγκαίῃ Id.9.16; ἐνδεδεμένος εἰς τὴν πίστιν τῆς συγκλήτου Plb.6.17.8; τῇ χάριτι Id.20. 11.10; ἐ. κατὰ τὰς οὐσίας, i.e. in debt, Id.13.1.3; ἐνδεδέσθαι τὴν ἀρχὴν *to have* the government *secured*, Id.9.23.2:—Med., *bind to oneself*, ὅρκοις τὸν πόσιν E.*Med.*162; τινὰ εἰς τὴν τῶν Ῥωμαίων φιλίαν Plb. 10.34.1. III. Pass., *to be possessed by an evil spirit*, J.*AJ*8.2.5.

ἐνδέω (B), fut. -δεήσω Hdt.7.18, etc.:—*fall short*, c. inf., τίνος ἐνδέομεν μὴ οὐ χωρεῖν; what *do we lack* of going? E.*Tr.*797, cf. *IA*41 (anap.); ὅσον ἐνδέουσιν.. τὰ αὐτὰ ἔχειν how much they *fall short* of being indentical, Pl.*Cra.*432d; ἕως γ' ἂν μηδὲν ἐνδέῃ τοῦ ποιμενικὴ εἶναι Id.*R.*345d, cf. 529d, *Phd.*74d:—also in Med., *to be in want of, lack*, δριμύτητος ἐνδεῖται Id.*Plt.*311a, cf. X.*Cyr.*2.2.26, etc.:—so in aor. Pass., στρωμάτων ἐνδεηθέντες ib.6.2.30. 2. *to be wanting* or *lacking*, ποίεε.. ὅκως τῶν σῶν ἐνδεήσει μηδέν that nothing *may be wanting* on your part, Hdt.l.c.; ὁ σταθμὸς ἐνδεῖ App.*Mith.*47: c. dat., ἐνδεῖ τι τῷ ἔργῳ Luc.*Tyr.*10; οὐδὲν ὑμῖν ἐνδεήσει Hdn.2.5.8; ἐ. ταῖς παραγγελίαις *to be deficient* for.., App.*BC*1.21; ἐς βάθος τῷ ἀριθμῷ ἐνδέον Arr.*Tact.*16.12; τὸ ἐνδέον the *deficiency*, *POxy.*1117.8 (ii A.D.). 3. impers., ἐνδεῖ *there is need* or *want*, c. gen. rei, τοῦ ἴσου ἡμῖν ἐνδεῖ πρὸς τὸ εἰδέναι Pl.*Euthd.*292e; πολλῶν ἐνέδει αὐτῷ ὥστε.. he *had need of, was wanting* in much, X.*An.*7.1.41; ἅπαντος ἐνδεῖ τοῦ πόρου *there is a deficiency* of all revenue, D.1.19; ἐνδεῖ κωπῶν *IG* 2.789^{a}6.

ἐνδηΐδες· αἱ Νύμφαι ἐν Κύπρῳ, Hsch.

ἔνδηλος, ον, *visible, manifest, clear*, ἔνδηλα καὶ σαφῆ λέγειν S.*Ant.* 405; ἔ. τι ποιεῖν Th.4.132. 2. *manifest, discovered, known*, mostly of persons, Ar.*Eq.*1277, Th.6.36; τινί Id.4.41: with a part., ἔνδηλοι ἔστε.. βαρυνόμενοι Id.2.64, cf. Pl.*Phd.*88e, *Tht.*174d, D.21.198; of things, τί τὸ ὑποκείμενον, οὐκ ἔστιν ἔνδηλον Arist. *de An.*422^{b}34. II. Adv. -λως: Sup. -ότατα, προλέγειν Th.1.139.

ἐνδημ-έω, Dor. **ἐνδᾱμέω**, *live at* or *in* a place, Lys.9.5, *IG*12(5). 534.6 (Ceos, ii B.C.); simply, *stay, remain in* a place, μέχρις ἂν ἐνδημῶσιν οἱ πρέσβεις Aen.Tact.10.11; ἐνδημῶν καὶ ἀποδημῶν Mitteis *Chr.*284.3 (ii B.C.), etc.: metaph., ὁ θεὸς ἐνδεδήμηκεν εἰς τὴν ἐμὴν ψυχήν Chariton 6.3; ἐ. ἐν τῷ σώματι, πρὸς τὸν Κύριον, 2*Ep.Cor.*5.6, 8. **-ία**, Dor. **ἐνδᾱμία**, ἡ, *dwelling in* a place, *lodging, sojourning*, τὴν ἐ. ποιεῖσθαι *IG*12(5).533.5 (Ceos, ii B.C.), cf. 4.679.18 (Hermione), 5(1).7 (Sparta), Hsch. **-ιος**, ον, = ἔνδημος, Opp.*H.*4.264. **-ιουργέω**, *manufacture, produce*, φάσματα Plu.2.17b; τι ἔν τινι ib.664f:—Pass., ib.636c. **-ος**, ον, *dwelling in* a place, *native*, Hes.*Op.*225, Thgn. 794, etc.; ἔ. πάρων being here *at home*, A.*Ch.*570; ἐνδημότατοι *the greatest 'stay-at-homes'*, opp. ἀποδημηταί, Th.1.70. 2. of things, βοὴ ἔ. *intestine* war, A.*Supp.*683 (lyr.); πόλεμοι D.H.8.83; τὰ ἔ. *home-affairs*, opp. τὰ ὑπερόρια, Arist.*Pol.*1285^{b}14; ἀρχαί (opp. ὑπερόριοι) Id.*Ath.*24.3, cf. Aeschin.1.45, Foed.ap.Th.5.47; *endemic*, νοσήματα Gal.15.429, 17(1).11; also τὰ ἔ. βιβλία applied to the surgical treatises of Hippocrates, Pall.*in Hp.Fract.*12.271 C.

ἔνδια· ὀδύνη, λεῖψις πράγματος, ἡ μεσημβρία, διατριβή, Hsch.

ἐνδιαβάλλω, *calumniate*, Ctes.*Fr.*29.10, Lxx *Ps.*108(109).4, Luc. *Cal.*24 (Act. and Pass.). 2. *stand in the way as an adversary*, Lxx *Nu.*22.22.

ἐνδιάβολος, ον, *containing a slander*, *PMag.Par.*1.2572.

Ἐνδίαγρος, epith. of Artemis, Hsch.

ἐνδιάγω [ᾰ], *pass one's life in*, ἐν τοῖς στρατιωτικοῖς καταλόγοις Heph.Astr.1.1; f.l. for ἐνδιάω in *AP*5.291 (Agath.).

ἐνδῖαεριαυερί(-αυρι- Dind., prob.)**νήχετος**, ον, *floating in midday airy breezes*, dithyrambic parody in Ar.*Pax*831.

ἐνδιάζω, (ἔνδιος I. 1) *pass the noon, take a siesta*, Plu.*Rom.*4, 2. 726f. II. *weave in*, in Pass., Hsch.

ἐνδιά-θεσις, εως, ἡ, only in phrase ὁ κατὰ -θεσιν λόγος, = λ. ἐνδιάθετος, *Placit.*4.11 tit. **-θετος**, ον, *residing in the mind* (ἐν τῇ διαθέσει, opp. ἐν τῇ προφορᾷ, Porph.*Abst.*3.3), ἐ. λόγος *conception, thought*, opp. προφορικὸς λ. (expression), *Stoic.*2.43, etc.; of the *immanent* reason of the world, Ph.1.598; ἕξις ib.36, Plu.2.48d; ὁ ἐ. ἄνθρωπος the *inner* man, *Corp.Herm.*13.7 (s.v.l.). 2. *innate*, περιαυτολογία Plu.2.44a: hence, *unaffected, spontaneous*, Hermog.*Id.*2. 7; τὸ ἐ. ib.1.11, al. 3. τὸ σὸν εἰς ἡμᾶς ἐ. your *disposition* towards us, *PAmh.*2.145.12 (iv/v A.D.). Adv. -τως λέγειν speak *from the heart*, Hermog.*Id.*2.7; βοᾶν Sch.Arat.968; εὔχεσθαι Eust. ad D.P. 739. II. *deep-seated*, opp. ἐπιπόλαιον, ἄλγημα Gal.14.739. 2. Adv. *fixedly*, opp. προσκαίρως, Sor.1.92. **-θηκος**, ον, *committed to writing*, λόγος Hsch. **-θρύπτομαι**, *play the prude towards*, τινί Theoc.3.36.

ἐνδῐαιτ-άομαι, Ion. -έομαι, *live* or *dwell in* a place, ἐν τῷ ἱρῷ Hdt. 8.41; μνήμη παρ' ἑκάστῳ ἐ. Th.2.43; οἰκία ἥδιστη ἐνδιαιτᾶσθαι X.*Mem.* 3.8.8, cf. Crates Theb.15; ἐπίνοια ἐ. ἡμῖν Plu.2.608e; ἡδονὴ ἐ. τῇ γνώμῃ Lib.*Or.*64.116. **-ημα**, ατος, τό, *dwelling-place*, D.H.1.37, Ph.1.52, al., Plu.2.968b, Phalar.*Ep.*34 (pl.), Agath.3.23; ἐ. δαιμόνων τὴν ψυχὴν κατασκευάσας Porph.*Marc.*11. **-ησις**, εως, ἡ, *dwelling in* a place, Ph.1.334 (pl.), 2.234, Them.*Or.*27.334a.

ἐνδιά-κειμαι, Pass., *to be set in*, λίθοι σχοινίσιν ἐ. J.*AJ*12.2. 9. **-κειμένως**, Adv. = ἐνδιαθέτως, λέγειν τι Hermog.*Id.*2.7. **-κοσμέω**, = διακοσμέω ἐν.., Ocell.3.1. **-λαμβάνω**, in pf. part. Pass. ἐνδιειλημμένος *divided at intervals*, γόνασιν Dsc.2.94.

ἐνδιαλλάσσω, Att. -ττω, *alter*, Arist.*Phgn.*806^{a}13:—Pass. **-αγμένος**, ὁ, *sodomite*, Lxx 3*Ki.*22.47, Aq.*Ge.*38.21.

ἐνδιαλύω, *loosen, disperse* a clot of blood, Sor.2.32.

ἐνδιάλῳ· μεσημβρίας ὥρᾳ, Hsch. (Fort. ἐν δειέλῳ, vel ἐν διάλῳ, = δεάλῳ, δήλῳ.)

ἐνδια-μένω, *remain in* (sc. the body), dub. l. in D.H.8.62. **-περονάω**, *transfix with a pin*, *Gloss.* (Pass.). **-πράττω**, f.l. for δια-,

Pl.*Phdr.*253c (Med.). **-πρέπω,** *to be distinguished in,* γυμνασίαις πολεμικαῖς D.S.36.4.5.

ἐνδιαρκής, ές, *sufficient, adequate, PStrassb.*40.32 (vi A.D.).

ἐνδια-σκευάζω, *work up,* in literary composition, Sch.Ar.*Ra.*1488 (Pass.), Sch.Il.3.393. **-σκευος** διήγησις, in Rhet., *elaborate, highly wrought* statement, Hermog.*Inv.*2.7. Adv. -ως ib.3.15, Eust. 177.31. **-σπείρω,** *sprinkle, Gp.*6.8.1:—Pass., *to be dispersed in,* τινί Arist.*Fr.*217: abs., ἔθνος -εσπαρμένον Lxx *Es.*3.8 (v.l.); *to be distributed,* of nerves, Gal.2.370. II. [σπέρματα] πᾶσι χυμοῖς καὶ ὀσμαῖς -εσπαρμένα *impregnated* with, Epicur.*Fr.*250. **-στέλλομαι,** *distinguish clearly,* Stob.2.7.4^{a}. **-στροφος,** ον, *perverted,* Phlp. *in de An.*21.24. **-τάσσω,** *draw up in,* χῶρος ἐπιτήδειος ἐνδιατάξαι (sc. τὸν στρατόν) Hdt.7.59. **-τίθεμαι,** Med., *dispose*: hence, *set forth in,* οἷς -θήσονται τὸ εὐχάριστον Ph.2.524. II. = ἐν διαθέσει εἶναι, ἐνδιάθετος εἶναι, ἀεὶ -θέμενος Plot.5.3.11. **-τρίβω** [ῐ], pf. -τέτρῐφα Arist.*Mete.*357^{a}4:—*spend* or *consume in* doing, χρόνον Ar.*Ra.*714, Th.2.18,85. II. abs. (sc. χρόνον or βίον), *spend time in* a place, αὐτόθι D.33.5; τῇ χώρᾳ Plb.3.88.1, etc.; ἐν τόπῳ D.S. 5.44; ἀνθρωπίσκοις *among* them, Luc.*Alex.*33. 2. *waste time by staying in* a place, *linger* there, Th.5.12, 7.81, etc. 3. *continue in* the practice of a thing, τοῖς ἤθεσι..τοῖς ἀρχαίοις Ar.*Ec.*585, cf. Pl. *Grg.*484c, *R.*487d; ἐὰν ἐνδιατρίβειν τὴν ὄψιν ἔν τινι let one's eyes *linger on* it, X.*Cyr.*5.1.16; ἐ. λόγοις καὶ ἔργοις *linger fondly on* them, Luc.*Nigr.*7; τῇ περὶ τοὺς βίους ἀναγραφῇ Plu.*Per.*2; κατὰ φιλοσοφίαν Epicur.*Fr.*217; περὶ μουσικήν Ath.14.623e; ἐ. ὅθεν ἡσυχιεῖ Epicur. *Nat.*27 G.; esp. *dwell upon a point* (in speaking), Aeschin.3.201, cf. Arist.*Pol.*1258^{b}35, Jul.*Or.*1.45b; περί τινος Arist.*Metaph.*989^{b}27; τῷ χρησίμῳ Hermog.*Prog.*7, etc. **-τριπτέον,** *one must dwell upon,* τινί Luc.*Hist.Conscr.*6; *one must stay in* a place, Ath.Med.ap. Orib.*inc.*23.13; ἐ. τούτοις *one must continue the treatment,* Sor.1. 46. **-τριπτικός,** ή, όν, *fondly dwelling in,* τόποις καὶ πράγμασι τοῖς αὐτοῖς M.Ant.1.16.7. **-τριπτος,** ον, *spent, consumed* in a process, ἐνιαυτός, ὁ ἐ. χρόνος *EM*342.34, cf. *Et.Gud.* s. v. ἐνιαυτός.

ἐνδιαυγέω, *shine through,* Pass., νέφη -εῖσθαι Sch.Arat.858.

ἐνδια-φθείρω, fut. -ερῶ, *to destroy in,* dub. in Plu.2.658c; *destroy* a child *in* the womb, Hp.*Carn.*19. **-φορος,** ον, *differing, varying,* στηριγμοί Paul.Al.*G.*1; περὶ τὸ γένος Vett.Val.105.33. 2. *containing differences,* νοῦς *Corp.Herm.*12.6. **-χειμάζω,** *winter in,* νήσῳ Str.2.3.4.

ἐνδῐάω, (ἔνδιος) *stay in the open air*: generally, *linger in* or *haunt* a place, c. dat., βάτοις *AP*5.291.6 (Agath.); ἔνθα δ' ἀνὴρ..ἐνδιάασκε Theoc.22.44: also c. acc., πάγους καὶ πρῶνας Opp.*C.*3.315: abs., περὶ σπήλυγγας ib.4.81: metaph., [ὄμμασιν] ἐλπὶς ἐνδιάει *AP*5.269.10 (Paul. Sil.); ἐ. εἰς κενεὰς εἰκόνας ib.4.4.10 (Agath.):—abs. in Med., ἀκτῖνες ἐνδιάονται *are bright as day* (of the moon), *h.Hom.*32.6; but ἐνδιῶνται· μεσημβριάζουσι, Hsch. II. trans., ποιμένες μῆλα ἐνδιάσκον shepherds *drove* their sheep *afield,* Theoc.16.38 (s. v. l.).

ἐνδιδομένως, Adv., (ἐνδίδωμι) *remissly,* Phot., Suid. s. v. ὑφειμένως.

ἐνδῐδύσκω, *put on,* τινά τι Lxx 2*Ki.*1.24, *Ev.Marc.*15.17:—Med., *put on oneself, Ev.Luc.*8.27, J.*BJ*7.2.2 (Act. is v.l.): written ἐνδυδισκόμενος *SIG*^{2}857.13 (Delph.). II. *clothe,* τινὰ ἱματίῳ *Gp.*16.21.9.

ἐνδίδωμι, *give in*: hence, I. *give into* one's *hands, give up to,* ἀσκὸν ἔνδος μοι E.*Cyc.*510 (lyr.), etc.; ἑαυτόν τινι Pl.*R.*561b, cf. Ar.*Pl.*781 (v.l.); τινὰ τοῖς πολεμίοις Pl.*R.*567a; ἐ. πόλιν *surrender* a city, esp. by treachery, Th.4.66, cf. X.*HG*7.4.14, etc.; τοῖς Ἀθηναίοις τὰ πράγματα ἐ. Th.7.48, cf. 2.65:—Pass., τῷ Ἱπποκράτει τὰ ἐν τοῖς Βοιωτοῖς ἐνεδίδοτο Id.4.89: impers., οὐδὲν ἐνεδίδοτο ἀπὸ τῶν ἔνδον no *sign of surrender was made,* Arr.*An.*1.20.6. 2. *put in, apply to,* ἅρμασι κέντρον E.*HF*881 (lyr.). 3. *hand in* a report, ἐ. ἀναφοράν Mitteis *Chr.*68.2 (i A.D.). 4. Pass., *to be interposed,* ἐνδοθεισῶν ὀλίγων ἡμερῶν Aët.13.121. II. *lend, afford,* ἐνδιδόναι τινὶ χερὸς στηρίγματα *lend* him a supporting hand, E.*IA*617; ἐ. ἀφορμάς *give* an occasion, Id. *Hec.*1239; λαβήν Ar.*Eq.*847; πρόφασίν τινι κακῷ γενέσθαι Th.2.87, cf. D.18.158; καιρόν Id.4.18; ἐ. ὑποψίαν ὡς.. *give ground for* suspicion that.., Pl.*Lg.*887e; ἐλπίδας τινί τινος Plu.*Alc.*14:—*cause, excite,* λύγξ σπασμὸν ἐνδιδοῦσα Th.2.49; ποθήν, δίψαν, Aret.*SA*2.1, *CA* 1.10; τάδε τῆς ψυχῆς τοῦ στομάχου -όντος εἶναι δεῖ τὴν πάθην Id.*SD* 2.6. III. *show, exhibit,* δικαιοσύνην καὶ πιστότητα ἐνέδωκαν, ἄχαρι δὲ οὐδέν Hdt.7.52; μαλακὸν ἐνδιδόναι οὐδέν *show* no *sign* of flagging, Id.3.51,105, Ar.*Pl.*488; ἣν δ' ἐνδιδῷ τι μαλθακόν E.*Hel.*508; ἵνα σοὶ μηδὲν ἐνδοίην πικρόν Id.*Andr.*225. IV. *grant, concede,* εἰ δ' ἐνδιδοίης, ὥσπερ ἐνδίδως, λόγον ib.965; ἐ. οὐδέν *make* no *concession,* Th. 2.12; ἐ. τι *make a concession,* ib.18; ἐ. ὁποσονοῦν Id.4.37; κἂν παίζων τίς σοι ἐνδῷ ὁτιοῦν Pl.*Grg.*499b. V. intr., *allow, permit,* ὅσον ἐνέδωκαν αἱ μοῖραι Hdt.1.91; *give in, give way,* οὐ πρότερον ἐνέδοσαν ἤ.. Th.2.65; ὡς εἶδον αὐτοὺς ἐνδόντας ib.81; *flag, fail,* ἐνδόντες τύχῃ παρεῖσαν αὐτούς E.*Tr.*692; τὸ ἐνδιδόν the *weak spot,* Luc.*Anach.*26; ἐ. τινί *yield to..,* οἴκτῳ Th.3.37; ἀλλήλοις Id.4.44; τῇ τῶν πλειόνων γνώμῃ D.*Prooem.*34; τῇ διακρίσει Dam.*Pr.*303; πρὸς ὕπνον Plu.*Sull.* 28; ἐ. πρὸς τὰς διαλύσεις *show an inclination* towards.., Id.*Flam.* 9. 2. of ailments, *abate,* Aret.*SA*1.10; but ἢν τὸ οὖρον μὴ ἐνδῷ does not *pass,* Hp.*Prog.*19:—in S.*OC*1076, Elmsl. restored ἐνδώσειν from Sch. 3. of elastic substances, *give way, yield,* οἰσοφάγος ἐ. Arist.*PA*664^{a}34; of the air, Id.*Pr.*937^{b}34; of trees, *be flexible,* Thphr. *HP*5.6.1; of the flanks and eyes, *fall in,* Arist.*Pr.*876^{a}37, cf. *GA*747^{a} 16; of a corpse, *decompose,* Parth.31.2; of a funeral-pile, Thphr. *HP*9.3.3; ἐρείσματα ἐ. the props *give way,* Plb.5.100.5. 4. εἴσω ἐνδιδοῖ τὸ ἄλγος *penetrates* inwardly, Aret.*CA*1.10. 5. of a river, *disembogue, empty itself,* Hdt.3.117 codd., but prob. ἐσδ-; cf. ἐκδίδωμι. VI. *give the key-note* of a tune, *strike up,* τοῖς ἵπποις τὸ ὀρχηστικὸν μέλος Arist.*Fr.*583: abs., ἡγεῖτο.. εἷς ἀνήρ, ὃς ἐνεδίδου τοῖς ἄλλοις τὰ τῆς ὀρχήσεως σχήματα D.H.7.72, cf. Luc.*Rh.Pr.*13; τὰ ἐνδιδόμενα *orders, words of command,* Arr.*Tact.*31.6: metaph., *give the key-note,* of a speech, Arist.*Rh.*1414^{b}26; cf. ἐνδόσιμος (but ἐ. φωνήν *cry aloud,* Lxx *Nu.*14.1): τοῖς μεθ' ἑαυτὸ τὴν γόνιμον ἐ. πρόοδον Procl.*Inst.*152.

ἐνδιές· ἔνυδρον, Hsch. **ἐνδίες** ἵπποι, f.l. for Ἐνετίδες, Id.

ἐνδι-εσπαρμένως, Adv., (σπείρω) *in scattered passages,* τὸν βίον ἀναγράφειν τοῖς βιβλίοις Eun.*VS*p.454 B. **-ηθέω,** *strain,* οἶνον Plu.2.692b tit. **-ήκω,** *pervade,* as the essence pervades the individuals of a class, αἱ ἐνδιήκουσαι ἐν τοῖς κατὰ μέρος κοινότητες S.E. *M.*8.41. **-ημερεύω,** *pass the day in,* cj. in Thphr.*Char.*8.14.

ἐνδίημι, *chase, pursue,* only 3 pl. impf. ἐνδίεσαν Il.18.584.

ἐνδῐκ-άζομαι, *to be a litigant, sue, IG*5(2).6.34 (Tegea). **-ία,** ἡ, = ἐκδ-, *Michel*459.14 (Telmessus). **-ος,** Arc. ἴνδικος, ον, (δίκη): I. of things, *according to right, just, legitimate,* Pi.*P.*5.103; γόος ἔ. A.*Ch.* 330 (lyr.); ὀνείδη Id.*Eu.*135; λέκτρα *IG*12(5).675.4 (Syros); κρίμα *Ep.Rom.*3.8: τὸ μὴ 'νδικον, = τὸ ἄδικον, S.*OT*682 (lyr.); τὰ πάντων ἐνδικώτατα Id.*OC*925; μὴ λέγων γε τοὔνδικον not speaking *truth,* Id. *OT*1158. 2. *legal,* ἔ. ἡμέρα a *court*-day, Poll.8.25. b. *having a locus standi,* μή οἱ ἔστω ἴνδικον μηδέποθι ἀλλ' ἤ.. he shall not have *the right to sue, IG*5(2).6.33 (Tegea, iv B.C.), cf. *Foed.Delph.Pell.*2 A 16, Pl.*Lg.*915d, *IG*2^{2}.46c56. c. = ἔνοχος δίκᾳ, *Leg.Gort.*3.23, 11. 22. d. ἔ. πόλις a city *in which justice is done,* Pl.*Hp.Ma.*292b; *in which sales may be publicly registered, Milet.*3.140. II. of persons, *upright, just,* A.*Eu.*699, S.*Ant.*208; πρὸς ἐνδίκοις φρεσίν A.*Ag.*996 (lyr.); δῆμος ἐνδικώτατος Id.*Fr.*196: c. dat., ἔ. γάμοις *favourable* to them, Id.*Supp.*82 (lyr.). 2. *possessed of right,* τίς μᾶλλον ἐνδικώτερος; who *has a better right?* Id.*Th.*673. III. Adv. -κως *right, with justice, fairly,* Id.*Pr.*63, *Ch.*462 (lyr.), etc.; ὀρθῶς ἐ. τ' ἐπώνυμος Id.*Th.*405: Sup. -ώτατα Pl.*Ti.*85b. 2. *justly, naturally, as one has a right to expect,* S.*OT*135, E.*Andr.*920.

ἔνδῑνα, τά, *entrails,* ὁππότερός κε φθῆσιν.., ψαύσῃ δ' ἐνδίνων Il.23. 806.

ἐνδῑν-ευτής, οῦ, ὁ, *one who evades, 'shuffler', Gloss.* **-εύω,** = sq., Longus1.23. **-έω,** *roll,* ἐνδεδινημένα ὄμματα Hp.*Epid.*5.99, cf. Gal.16.610. II. *revolve, go about,* ἐνδινεῦντι, Dor. for ἐνδινοῦσι, Theoc.15.82.

ἐνδίολκος, ον, (ἕλκω) *attractive,* Ph.1.517 (v.l.).

ἔνδῐον, τό, *place of sojourn in the open air,* ἔνδια πέτρης, of a grotto, Opp.*H.*4.371; ἔνδιον εὐφροσύνης *seat* of joyousness, epith. of a wine-cask, *AP*11.63 (Maced.); ἔ. Ἁμαδρυάδων ib.9.668 (Marian.); σοὶ δὲ ..ἔνδιον ᾗ Πιτάνη *IG*5(1).730.14 (Sparta, ii A.D.).—Poet. word.

ἐνδιορθόομαι, *correct,* κακίαν τῆς φύσεως Porph.*Marc.*35.

ἔνδιος, ον, *at midday, at noon* (but ἔνδιον τὸ δειλινόν Plu.2.726e), ἔνδιος δ' ὁ γέρων ἦλθ' Od.4.450; ἔνδιοι ἱκόμεσθα Il.11.726; ποιμένας ἐνδίους πεφυλαγμένος Theoc.16.95; ἔνδῑον Κυνὸς ἆσθμα *AP*10.12; ἄλκαρ ἴδεος ἐνδίοιο Call.*Fr.*124; ἐνδῑον ἦμαρ ἔην A.R.4.1312; but also ἐνδίοις· ὀρθρίοις (ὀρθηνίοις cod.), Hsch. 2. *in the daytime,* Arat.498; ἔ. οἰνοπότης *AP*7.703 (Myrin.). 3. *from the sky,* ὕδωρ Arat.954; *hanging in mid-air,* ἀκρεμόνες *AP*9.71 (Antiphil.). II. Subst. ἔνδιον, τό, *noon,* ποτὶ τὤνδιον Call.*Cer.*39 (also in masc., δείελος ἀλλ' ἢ νὺξ ἢ ἔνδιος ἢ ἔσετ' ἠώς Id.*Hec.*1.4.1). 2. *evening,* ἐς ἔνδῐον A.R. 1.603, cf. Plu. l. c. [ῐ Hom.; ῑ and ῐ later (v. supr.).] (From ἐν δι*F*ι, cf. Skt. *div-* 'daylight, sky', Lat. *diu* 'by day'.)

ἐνδιόω, Dor., pf. part. ἐνδεδῐωκότα: πεφυτευμένα καὶ ἐ., perh. *established,* of plants, *Tab.Heracl.*1.121; perh. cf. ἐμβιόω.

ἐνδιπλ-ᾰσιάζω, = sq., Hp.*Epid.*2.2.22 (Pass.). II. Gramm., *reduplicate, EM*499.11 (Pass.). **-όω,** *fold in two,* Gal.*UP*14.6, 7. 12 (Pass.), Sor.1.14; *fold in* at the edge, Paul.Aeg.6.65:—hence **-ωμα,** ατος, τό, and **-ωσις,** εως, ἡ, *folding,* Gal.11.508.

ἐνδίσματα· ἐναλίσματα, Hsch.

ἐνδίφριος, ον, (δίφρος) *sitting on the same seat,* ἐκαθεζόμην ἐνδίφριος αὐτῷ X.*An.*7.2.33, cf. 38.

ἐνδογεν-ής, ές, *born in the house,* = οἰκογενής, *SIG*^{2}854.5, al. (Delph.), Lxx *Le.*18.9. **-ικός,** ή, όν, = foreg., *PFlor.*294.52 (vi A.D.).

ἔνδοθεν, Adv. *from within,* Od.20.101, Ar.*Nu.*1164 (lyr.), etc.; ὑπό τινων ἔνδοθεν πρασσόντων Th.2.79: c. gen., ἔ. στέγης *from inside* the tent, S.*Aj.*741. 2. *of oneself, by one's own doing,* A.*Th.*194; οὔτ' ἔ. οὔτε θύραθεν neither *of oneself* nor by help of others, S.*Tr.* 1021 (lyr.). II. *within,* c. gen., αὐλῆς Il.6.247; οἴκου v.l. in Hes. *Op.*523. 2. abs., θυμὸν τέρπεται ἔ. Pi.*P.*2.74, cf. Hdt.2.68, *Com. Adesp.*21.31 D., etc.; εἴ οἱ φρένες..νοήμονες ἔ. ἦσαν Theoc.25.80; οἱ ἔ. the *domestics,* Ar.*Pl.*228,964; also, the *citizens,* Pl.*Ti.*17d; ὁ ἔ. θόρυβος Th.8.71; τἄνδοθεν ibid. (but, *the inner man,* Pl.*Phdr.*279b); ὁ καρπὸς ὁ ἔ. the produce *of* her *own property, Leg.Gort.*3.27.

ἔνδοθι, Adv. *within, at home,* Od.5.58; τά τ' ἔ. καὶ τὰ θύρηφι 22. 220; σὺ δ' ἔ. θυμὸν ἀμύξεις Il.1.243, etc.; rare in Att., ἔ. μέν ἐστι Πρωταγόρας Eup.146a codd., cf. Posidipp.24. 2. c. gen., ἐελμένοι ἔ. πύργων Il.18.287; ἔ. νήσου Hes.*Fr.*76.4; οἴκου Id.*Op.*523.

ἐνδοθίδιος, α, ον, *belonging to the house, Leg.Gort.*2.11.

ἔνδοι (not ἐνδοῖ, A.D.*Adv.*197.10, Hdn.Gr.1.502), Dor. for ἔνδοθι, Theoc.15.1,77, Call.*Cer.*77, *IG*4.1484.66 (Epid.).

ἐνδοι-άζω, aor. ἐνεδοίασα Hermog.*Id.*2.6, App.*Mith.*33, Luc.*Gall.* 11: (ἐν δοιῇ):—*to be in doubt, at a loss,* c. inf., ὅταν..ἐνδοιάζῃ χωρίον προσλαβεῖν Th.1.36: abs., οἱ ἐνδοιάζοντες the *waverers,* Id.6.91; μηδὲν ἐνδοιάσας Luc.*Herm.*25; ἐ. τῇ γνώμῃ Plu.*Sull.*9; ὑπέρ τινος Id.*Cat. Mi.*17; περί τινος Luc.*Phal.*2.2; ἐ. εἰ.. D.H.4.58:—Pass., of things, *to be matter of doubt*, λόγῳ ἐνδοιασθῆναι Th.1.122; ἐνδοιαζόμενον D.H. 7.59, cf. Ph.1.622; ἐνεδοιάζετο δὲ πότερον.. Luc.*VH*2.21: aor. 1 also in act. sense, Parth.9.6. **-άσιμος** [ᾰ], ον, *doubtful*, J.*AJ*16. 11.7, Luc.*Scyth.*11. Adv. -μως, ἔχειν περί τινος J.*AJ*16.10.4. **-ασις**, εως, ἡ, *doubt, uncertainty*, Hermog.*Id.*1.6. **-ασμός**, ὁ, = foreg., ibid., Ph.2.67, al., Eust.146.18. **-αστής**, οῦ, ὁ, *doubter*, Ph.1.459, 2.582. **-αστικός**, ή, όν, *expressing doubt* or *ambiguous*, ὀνόματα Id.*Fr.*15 H.; ἐπίκρισις Hermog.*Id.*2.7,8: Gramm., *dubitative*, σύνδεσμος Ammon.*in APr.*68.10. Adv. -κῶς Eust.1080.69. **-αστός**, ή, όν, *doubtful*, Hp.*Prorrh.*2.15, J.*AJ*19.1.4. Adv. -τῶς *doubtfully*, προθύμως, οὐδ' ἔτι ἐ. Hdt.7.174, cf. Th.8.87; ἐ. ἀκροᾶσθαι Id.6.10.

ἐνδοιΐτιναι, οἱ, *those who can trace citizen-ancestry through seven generations*, Hsch. **ἐνδοκία**· ἡ μήτηρ, παρὰ Ἀθηναίοις, Id. **ἔνδοκος**· ἐνέδρα, Id.

ἔνδομα, ατος, τό, (ἐνδίδωμι) *diminution* of fever, Gal.19.398.

ἐνδομαρία· ἡ κτῆσις, ἡ παροικία (κτίσις ἡ παροιμία cod.), Hsch.

ἐνδομᾰτικά, τά, *court-fees*, *Cod.Just.*10.19.9.6, Lyd.*Mag.*3.70, *PLips.*28.15 (iv A.D.). 2. *douceurs, gratuities*, Just.*Edict.*13.7.

ἐνδομάχας [μᾰ], α, ὁ, *fighting* or *bold at home*, epith. of a dunghill-cock, Pi.*O.*12.14.

ἐνδομεν-ία (-εία Corn.*ND*14, *POxy.*[v. infr.]) or **ἐνδυμενία** (Phryn.312, *PAmh.*2.152.16 (v/vi A.D.)), ἡ, *household goods*, Plb.4. 72.1, Olympias ap.Poll.10.12, Paul.Al.*L.*4; freq. in wills, as *POxy.* 493.17 (ii A.D.); *furniture supplied to public guests, Gloss.* **-ικός**, ή, όν, *belonging to household stock*, *PGiss.*35.2 (iii A.D.), *PLips.*28.15 (iv A.D.).

ἐνδομ-έω, *build in*, ἐνδεδόμηται Hp.*Cord.*6; κίονες ἐνδεδομημένοι J. *AJ*15.11.5. **-ησις**, εως, ἡ, *thing built in, structure*, τοῦ τείχους *Apoc.*21.18; esp. *mole* or *breakwater*, J.*AJ*15.9.6; cf. ἐνδώμησις.

ἐνδο-μῠχέω, *lurk in the recesses* of a house, Sch.Ar.*V.*964; *lie hidden*, φλὸξ -οῦσα *Gp.*2.3.9; *to be latent*, of περιττώματα, Steph. *in Hp.*1.164 D. **-μῠχί**, Adv. *in secret*, Hsch. **-μῠχος**, ον, *in the inmost part of a dwelling, lurking within*, S.*Ph.*1457 (anap.), Call. *Cer.*88, Nonn.*D.*8.329. 2. *insidious*, νόσημα Gal.9.837. II. of persons, *treacherous*, Ptol.*Tetr.*158. 2. *stay-at-home*, Paul.Al. *M.*4, Vett.Val.18.20.

ἔνδον, Adv. *within*, Il.11.98, etc.; ἦσαν ἡμῖν ἔ. ἑπτὰ μναῖ Lys.19. 22, cf. D.27.10; φρένες ἔ. εἶσαι Od.11.337, al.; κραδίη ἔ. ὑλάκτει 20. 13; τἄνδον οὐχ οὕτω φρονῶν *in one's heart*, E.*Or.*1514 (troch.; but lit. τἀ. ἀνακάλλυνον Phryn.Com.2 D.); *at home*, Pl.*Prt.*310e, etc.; οἱ ἔ. those *of the house*, the *family*, esp. the *domestics*, S.*El.*155 (lyr.), *Tr.* 677, Pl.*Smp.*213c; τἄνδον *family matters, household affairs*, S.*Tr.* 334, etc.; also, = οἱ ἔ., E.*Hec.*1017; οἱ ἔ. καθήμενοι the βουλή, And.1. 43. 2. c. gen., Διὸς ἔ., Ζεφύροιο ἔ., *in the house* of Zeus, of Zephyrus, Il.20.13, 23.200; μὴ κεύθετ' ἔ. καρδίας A.*Ch.*102; σκηνῆς ἔ. S.*Aj.* 218 (anap.); γῆς ἔ. Pl.*Prt.*320d. b. ἔ. ὢν αὑτοῦ *master of* oneself, self-possessed, Antipho 5.45; so σῶν φρενῶν οὐκ ἔ. ὤν E.*Heracl.*709: abs., ἔ. γενοῦ A.*Ch.*233 (οὐκ ἔ. ἔ. ἐστίν with a play on signf. 1, Ar. *Ach.*396). 3. Pi. uses it c. dat. as strengthd. for ἐν, *N.*3.54, 7.44, cf. E.*Fr.*203. 4. *below*, in a book, ἔ. γέγραπται D.L.5.4. 5. with Verbs of motion, = εἴσω, D.Chr.7.56, Ael.*NA*9.61. II. Comp. and Sup., v. ἐνδοτέρω.

ἐνδοξ-άζομαι, Pass., *to be glorified*, ἔν τινι Lxx *Ex.*14.4, al., 2*Ep. Thess.*1.10, *PMag.Leid.W.*4.17. **-ασμός**, ὁ, *glorifying*, Sm.*Ps.* 45(46).4, Al.*Is.*24.14.

ἐνδοξο-κοπέω, *covet fame for*, θαυμαστὸν ἔργον Vett.Val.4.20. **-λογέω**, *speak for fame*, D.L.6.47. **-πωλος**, gloss on κλυτόπωλος, Hsch.

ἔνδοξ-ος, ον, (δόξα) *held in esteem* or *honour, of high repute*, πρός τινος by one, X.*Oec.*6.10 codd. (Sup.); -ότατοι ποιηταί Id.*Mem.*1.2. 56; πόλις -οτέρα εἰς τὰ πολεμικά ib.3.5.1; νέοι πλούσιοι καὶ ἔ. Pl.*Sph.* 223b; μὴ πλουσιώτερος ἀλλ' -ότερος Isoc.1.37; ὀλίγοι καὶ ἔ. ἄνδρες Arist.*EN*1098^{b}28, cf. Epicur.*Sent.*7, etc. 2. of things, *notable*, πράγματα Aeschin.3.231, cf. Diod.Com.2.21; *generally approved*, τὸ καλόν, = τὸ ἔ., Epicur.*Fr.*513; *glorious*, ταφαί Plu.*Per.*28; ἡδὺ καὶ ἔ. καὶ ὠφέλιμον Id.2.99f. Adv. -ξως, freq. in Inscrr., *SIG*442.7 (Erythrae, iii B.C.), etc., cf. *Vit.Philonid.*p.12 C., Plu.*Alc.*1, etc.: Comp. -οτέρως, τὰ ἔνδοξα ἐ. λέγειν Hermog.*Id.*1.9; also στῆλαι ἔχουσαι ἐπιγραφὰς -ξως *conspicuously* placed, *Sammelb.*6152.22 (i B.C.): Sup. -ότατα, ἐβουλεύσασθε D.18.65. II. *resting on opinion, probable, generally admitted*, ἔ. τὰ δοκοῦντα πᾶσιν ἢ τοῖς πλείστοις ἢ τοῖς σοφοῖς, opp. to what is necessarily true (τὰ πρῶτα καὶ ἀληθῆ), Arist.*Top.*100^b 21, cf. *EN*1145^{b}5, *Rh.*1355^{a}17, al.; ἡ ἔ. διδασκαλία *popular* teaching, Gal.2.247. 2. Adv. -ξως, συλλογίζεσθαι *plausibly*, opp. ἀληθῶς, Arist.*SE*175^{a}31. III. *conceited*, οὐκ ἔνδοξοι πρὸς τὸ μαθεῖν ἃ μὴ ἴσμεν not *too proud* to learn, Erot.*Fr.*60. **-ότης**, ητος, ἡ, *distinction, glory*, Hsch. s.v. εὔκλεια, Eust.1279.44. II. as a honorific address, Just.*Nov.*41 *Pr.*, *Sammelb.*4736.1, etc.

ἐνδόπυος, ὁ, ἡ, *having an internal abscess*, Theognost.*Can.*162 (misprinted -πυρος by Cramer).

ἔνδορα, τά, (ἐνδέρω) *offerings wrapped in hide*, *SIG*1025.48 (Cos), 1026.8 (ibid.).

ἔνδορχις, ὁ, *with concealed testicles*, Theognost.*Can.*162.

ἐνδόρωμα, ατος, τό, perh. *ornament in plaster* of a sarcophagus, Μουσ.Σμυρν.1884/5 p.24 No.241; cf. δόρωσις.

ἔνδος, Dor., = ἔνδον, *GDI*1752.4 (Delph.), Theognost.*Can.*162. 9. **ἔνδοσε**, = εἴσω, *IG*12(5).593^{A}14 (Iulis, v B.C.).

ἐνδόσ-θια, τά, (ἔνδον) = ἐντόσθια, Lxx *Ex.*12.9, al. **-θίδια**, τά, = foreg., *IG*4.914.15 (Epid.), and prob. for -ιαῖα, v.l. in Lxx *Le.*6.33 (7.3).

ἐνδόσιμος, ον, *serving as a prelude*, ᾆσμα Artem.2.66; ψαλμὸς ἐ. τῇ ᾠδῇ, Suid.: but usu. neut. ἐνδόσιμον, τό (τὸ πρὸ τῆς ᾠδῆς κιθάρισμα, Hsch.); *that which gives the key to the tune*, in music, Arist.*Rh.*1414^b 24, *Mu.*399^{a}19, Hld.3.2, Ael.*NA*11.1, Poll.1.210: metaph., *key-note* of a speech, Arist.*Rh.*1415^{a}7, *Pol.*1339^{a}13, cf. Max.Tyr.7.7, Jul.*Ep.* 186: generally, *signal* for a race, Hld.4.3; [πρόβατα] πρὸς τὰ ἐ. τῆς σύριγγος ποιμαινόμενα Id.5.14: metaph., τὸ τοῦ καιροῦ καὶ τῆς ὥρας ἐ. Id.4.16; τοῦ φιλοσοφεῖν ἐ. ἔδωκαν Phld.*Acad.Ind.*p.5 M.; ὥσπερ ἐ. ἕξει πρός τι Plu.2.73b; τοῦ λογισμοῦ τὸ ἐ. παρεσχηκότος Porph.*Sent.* 32, cf. Luc.*Symp.*30 (also ἐ. παρασχέσθαι Dam.*Pr.*415); λαβεῖν Luc. *Alex.*19; μέχρις ἂν τὸ ἐ. τῆς διαλύσεως σημήνῃ M.Ant.11.20; ἐ. τοῖς στρατιώταις ἔργῳ διδούς Hdn.3.6.10 (so prob. as Adj., [σιτία] ἐ. τῇ πέψει *giving the signal* for digestion, Plu.2.131c). II. *yielding*, τὸ ἐ. καὶ πειθήνιον ib.442c, cf. Max.Tyr.1.2, Hld.9.4; of arguments, *easily refuted*, κατηγόρησεν ἐνδόσιμα Hyp.*Fr.*241; ἐνδόσιμα προτείνειν D.H.*Rh.*8.15.

ἔνδοσις, εως, ἡ, *striking of the key-note* (cf. foreg. 1), Arist.*Mu.*398^{b}26, Anon.ap.Suid. s.v. ἐνδόσιμον. 2. *imparting*, τῆς ὑγρότητος Thphr. *CP*1.15.3; τοῦ εἴδους Simp.*in Ph.*440.8; τὰς πολλὰς οὐσίας ἐνδόσεις εἶναι κατὰ ἔλλαμψιν ἀπὸ τῆς μιᾶς οὐσίας προϊούσας εἰς πάντα ὄντα Dam. *Pr.*100. II. *giving in, alleviation, remission*, Hp.*Ep.*1. 2. *relaxation*, τόνου Plu.*Lys.*12. 3. *yielding, giving way*, of pillars, Str.15.3.10; of sand, D.S.1.30, cf. Ph.*Bel.*78.3: metaph., Plu.*Per.*31; πρός τι Id.2.457a; *way out* of a difficulty, Simp.*in Ph.*137.21; *retirement*, of troops, Plb.5.100.2.

ἐνδοτάτω, v. sq.

ἐνδοτέρω, Adv. Comp. of ἔνδον, *more within, quite within*, ἐ. συστέλλειν ἑαυτόν to draw himself *within* his means, Plu.*Cat.Ma.*5; ἐ. τῆς χρείας προσαγαγέσθαι to unite into greater intimacy, Id.*Arat.*43; *within*, *Placit.*5.21.2; (sc. κόσμου) ib.1.18.4; ἐ. τείχους J.*AJ*15.11.3; *farther on, below*, in a book, D.L.10.43, etc. 2. of Time, *within* a certain limit, *sooner*, Hp.*Fract.*33. 3. Sup. ἐνδοτάτω *quite within*, Luc.*Am.*16; *innermost*, Procl.*Hyp.*6.12; οἱ ἐνδοτάτω Θρᾷκες Hdn.6.8.1: c. gen., *very far in*, Plu.2.918f. II. Adj. ἐνδότερος, ον, *inner*, *PLond.*4.1768.2 (vi A.D.): Sup. ἐνδότατος *inmost*, Ἀρμενία Just.*Nov.*31.1 *Intr.*; τόποι Hsch. s.v. μυχοί.

ἐνδοτικός, ή, όν, *yielding, soft*, Alex.Aphr.*in Mete.*201.14: metaph., ὀφθαλμοί Aristaenet.1.4 (s.v.l.). Adv. -κῶς Chrysipp.*Stoic.* 3.124. II. Subst. -κόν, τό, *suppository*, Ruf.ap.Orib.8.39.9.

ἐνδουπέω, *fall in with a heavy sound*, μέσσῳ ἐνδούπησα Od.12.443; ἄντλῳ δ' ἐνδούπησε πεσοῦσα 15.479.

ἐνδουχία, ἡ, (ἔχω) = ἐνδομενία, Plb.18.35.6.

ἐνδοχεῖον, τό, = δοχεῖον, Hp.*Ep.*23.

ἐνδρᾱν-εια [ρᾱ], ἡ, (δραίνω) *activity*, *Gloss.* **-ής**, ές, *active*, opp. ἐμπαθής, Procl.*Inst.*80, Suid.

ἐνδράσσομαι, pf. part. Pass. ἐνδεδραγμένος, *grasp*, *PMag.Par.*1. 2137.

ἔνδρατα· τὰ ἐνδερόμενα σὺν τῇ κεφαλῇ καὶ τοῖς ποσί, Hsch.; cf. ἔνδορα. **ἐνδριώνας**· δρόμος παρθένων ἐν Λακεδαίμονι, Id. (ἐν δριῶνας Mein.). **ἔνδροια**, written for ἔνδρυα II, Id.

ἐνδρομ-έω, *run into*, τινί Max.282 (v.l. ἐπι-). II. *run through*, Λιβυκῶν πόρων *AP*7.395 (Marc. Arg.). **-ή**, ἡ, *air played during the pentathlon*, Plu.2.1140d. **-ίς**, ίδος, ἡ, a sort of *high shoe*, worn by Artemis in the chase, Call.*Dian.*16, *Del.*238, *APl.*4.253; soldier's *high boot*, Ph.*Bel.*100.8. II. Adj., *used in the foot-race*, ἀσπίδες *GDI*2517.11 (Delph.). 2. Subst., *bath-wrapper* or *draw-sheet*, Herod.Med.ap.Orib.10.37.5, 38.1; also, *thick wrapper worn by runners*, after exercise, for fear of cold, Mart.4.19, Juv.3.103, 6. 246. **-ος**, ον, *running on, hastening*, εἰς Ἀΐδαν *IPE*2.197 (Panticapaeum, ii A.D.).

Ἐνδρομώ, ἡ, epith. of Demeter at Halicarnassus, Hsch.

ἔνδροσος, ον, *bedewed, dewy*, εὐνή A.*Ag.*12, cf. Str.6.1.9, Dion. Byz.29, Alciphr.*Fr.*6.6· αὖραι Ph.2.292, cf. Dsc.5.53; λειμῶνες Jul. *Or.*7.236a.

ἔνδρῠον, τό, (δρῦς) *oaken peg* or *pin* by which the yoke is fixed to the pole, Hes.*Op.*469. II. *heart-wood* of trees, Hsch.

ἐνδυ-άζω, -ασμός, written for ἐνδοι-, Hsch.

ἔνδυδαν· ἔωθεν, Hsch. (Fort. ἐνδύλαν· ἔσωθεν, cf. ἐνδύλω.)

ἐνδῠκέως, Adv. *sedulously, kindly*, freq. in Hom. (esp. in Od.), with Verbs expressing friendly actions, as πέμψαι Od.14.337; ὁμαρτεῖν Il.24.438; φιλέειν καὶ τιέμεν Od.15.543; παρέχειν βρῶσίν τε πόσιν τε ib.491; so ἐ. δέκεσθαι θυσίαισιν Pi.*P.*5.85; ῥύεσθαι Theoc.25.25, etc.; ἔχραεν A.R.2.454. II. *steadfastly*, μαρνάμεθ' ἐ. B.5.125, cf. 112. 2. *greedily, ravenously*, ἐσθίειν Od.14.109; ἐ. ῥινὸν σχίσσας, of a lion tearing his prey, Hes.*Sc.*427.—No Adj. ἐνδυκής occurs: but neut. ἐνδυκές, as Adv., is prob. l. in A.R.1.883; used for συνεχές, Nic.*Th.*263; expld. by συνεχές, συνετόν, ἀφελές, ἀσφαλές, γλυκύ, κτλ., Hsch. (Etym. dub.: for sense 1 perh. cf. ἀ-δευκής.)

ἐνδύκιον· πιστόν, φίλον, κτλ., Hsch. **ἐνδύλω**· ἔνδοθεν, Id.

ἔνδῡμα, ατος, τό, (ἐνδύω) *garment*, *IG*12(5).593^{A}4 (Iulis, v B.C.), Men.*Pk.*269, Lxx 4*Ki.*10.22, al., *BCH*6.25 (Delos, ii B.C.), *PFay.*12. 20 (ii B.C.), Str.3.3.7, *Ev.Matt.*7.15, Plu.*Sol.*8, Porph.*Abst.*1.31, etc.; *covering*, τῶν ἀστῶν Gal.19.367, prob. in Hp.*Cord.*8.

ἐνδῡμάτια, τά, name of a musical festival at Argos, Plu.2.1134c.

ἐνδυμενία, v. ἐνδομενία.

ἐνδύμιος, v.l. for ἐνδόμιος, Thd.*Pr.*26.22.

ἐνδῠνᾰμ-ος [ῠ], ον, *mighty*, Ps.-Ptol.*Centil.*38, Them.*Or.*34 p.446 Dind. Adv. -ως *Gloss.* **-όω**, *strengthen, confirm*, Lxx *Jd.*6.34, 1*Ep.Ti.*1.12, al.:—Pass., ἐπὶ τῇ ματαιότητι Lxx *Ps.*51(52).9; τῇ πίστει

*Ep.Rom.*4.20, al. II. *endow with vitality*, in Pass., metaph. of scientific theorems, Plot.4.9.5.

ἐνδῠναστεύω, *to have power* or *exercise dominion in* or *among*, τισί A.*Pers.*691; παρά τισι Pl.*R.*516d; ἐ. ἐν τῷ σώματι Hp.*VM*20, cf. Iamb.*Myst.*3.28: abs., Eus.Mynd.39. II. *procure by one's authority* or *influence*, ἐνδυναστεύει Ἐπαμεινώνδας ὥστε μὴ φυγαδεῦσαι τοὺς κρατίστους X.*HG*7.1.42. **ἐνδυνέω, ἐνδύνω**, v. ἐνδύω.

ἔνδῠο, Adv. *one-two*, i.e. *quickly*, Men.198.

ἔνδῠσις, εως, ἡ, (ἐνδύω) *entry*, coined by Pl.*Cra.*419c; [σελήνη] ἐν Κρόνου ἐνδύσει Alex.Trall.12. 2. = κατάδυσις, Hsch. II. *putting on*, ἱματίων 1*Ep.Pet.*3.3; *dressing, dress*, Lxx *Es.*5.1, Aristeas 96, Agatharch.57.

Ἐνδυσποιτρόπιος, ὁ (sc. μήν), name of tenth month at Delphi, *SIG*672.40 (ii B.C.).

ἐνδυστῠχέω, *to be unlucky in* or *with*.., ἐνδυστυχῆσαι τοὔνομ' ἐπιτήδειος εἶ in name thou art fit *to be luckless*, E.*Ba.*508, cf. *Ph.*727; τῇ πόλει Plu.*Comp.Per.Fab.*3.

ἐνδύτας· αὐλωτὸς στάμνος, Hsch.

ἐνδῠτ-έον, *one must put on*, χιτῶνάς τισι Herod.Med. in *Rh.Mus.* 58.103. **-ήρ**, ῆρος, ὁ, *for putting on*, πέπλος S.*Tr.*674. **-ήριος**, α, ον, = foreg., χιτὼν ἄπειρος ἐ. κακῶν Id.*Fr.*526. **-ης**, ου, ὁ, *garment*, Aq.1*Ki.*17.38. **-ός**, όν, *put on*, ἐσθήματα A.*Eu.*1028 codd.; στέφη E.*Tr.*257 (anap.); στολαί Antiph.36. 2. ἐνδυτόν (sc. ἔσθημα). τό, *garment, dress*, Simon.179.10, Call.*Ap.*32, dub. in Herod.8.65; ἐ. νεβρίδων *a dress* of fawn-skin, E.*Ba.*111 (lyr.), cf. 138 (lyr.); ὅπλων ἐνδυτά Id.*IA* 1073 (lyr.): metaph., ἐ. σαρκός the skin, Id.*Ba.*746; τοὔνδυτον τῆς κοιλίας Alex.98.14. II. *clad in, covered*, στέμμασιν E.*Ion* 224 (lyr.).

ἐνδύω or **ἐνδύνω** (ἐνδυνέω v.l. in Hdt.3.98), with Med. **ἐνδύομαι**, fut. -δύσομαι: aor. 1 -εδυσάμην; Ep. aor. or impf. -εδυσόμην: aor. 2 Act. -έδυν: pf. -δέδῠκα: I. c. acc. rei vel loci, *go into*, 1. of clothes, *put on*, ἔνδυνε χιτῶνα Il.2.42; ἔνδυνε περὶ στήθεσσι χιτῶνα 10.21; χιτῶν' ἐνδῦσα 5.736; τι ὡς θώρηκα ἐνδύνουσι Hdt.3.98; ἐνδύντες τὰ ὅπλα Id.1.172; τὴν σκευὴν ib.24; πέπλον ἐνδύς S.*Tr.*759, etc.: pf. ἐνδέδῠκα, *wear*, κιθῶνας λινέους Hdt.2.81, cf. 7.64, 9.22; λεοντῆν ἐνδέδυκα Pl.*Cra.*411a:—Med., ἐν δ' αὐτὸς ἐδύσετο χαλκόν Il.2.578, 11.16; ἐνδύεσθαι ὅπλα v.l. in Hdt.7.218; σκευάς Th.1.130; ἐνδύσεται στολὴν E.*Ba.* 853: metaph., ἐνδυόμενοι τόλμημα Ar.*Ec.*288; also τὸν Ταρκύνιον ἐνδύεσθαι *assume* the person of T., D.H.11.5; τὸν καινὸν ἄνθρωπον *Ep.Eph.* 4.24:—Pass., *to be clothed in, have on*, ἐσθῆτα ἐνδεδύσθαι Hp.*Insomn.* 91, cf. Men.432. 2. *enter, press into*, c. acc., ἐν δέ οἱ ἦτορ δῦν' ἄχος ἄτλητον Il.19.367; ἀκοντιστὺν ἐνδύσεαι thou *wilt enter* the contest (Aristarch. ἐσδύσεαι), 23.622; τὴν τοῦ Θερσίτου [ψυχὴν] πίθηκον ἐνδυομένην Pl.*R.*620c; εὔνοια ἐνδύεταί τινα Id.*Lg.*642b; ἔρως δεινὸς ἐνδέδυκέ τινος Id.*Tht.*169c; also ἐ. εἰς.. Ar.*V.*1020, Arist.*HA*609b21; εἰς τὴν ἐπιμέλειαν ἐνδῦναι *enter upon* it, *undertake* it, X.*Cyr.*8.1.12: abs., *enter*, Pl.*Phd.*89d: c. dat., ἐ. ταῖς ψυχαῖς τῶν ἀκουόντων *insinuate oneself into* their minds, X.*Cyr.*2.1.13; τοῖς ταύροις τὸν οἶστρον ἐνδύεσθαι Plu.2.55e, etc.; ἐνὶ χροῒ δύετο ῥινὸς ἐντυπάς Epic. in *Arch.Pap.*7. 3: pf. Pass., φυσικαῖς ἐνδεδυμένος αἰτίαις dub. in Plu.2.435f (leg. -δεδεμένος): abs., *creep in*, v.l. for ἐσ-, Hdt.2.121.β'; ἐ. διά τινος *slip through*, Plu.2.38a, etc. 3. *sink in*, hence τρίβος ἐνδεδυκὼς *sunken* path, Id.*Arat.*22; ῥὶς *sunken* nose, Id.*Publ.*16. II. causal in pres. ἐνδύω, fut. -δύσω: aor. 1 -έδυσα:—*put on* another, *clothe in*, c. dupl. acc., τὴν ἐξωμίδ' ἐνδύσω σε Ar.*Lys.*1021; ὃς ἐμὲ κροκόεντ' ἐνέδυσεν Id. *Th.*1044, cf. X.*Cyr.*1.3.3. 2. *clothe*, ἐνδύουσι τὤγαλμα Hdt.2.42; ἐὰν .. πένητα γυμνὸν ἐνδύσῃς Philem.176; σύ με ἐνδέδυκας [prob. ῠ] *PGiss.*77.8 (ii A.D.).

ἔνδω, = ἔνδον, *GDI*1767 (Delph.), *Michel*995*D*31 (ibid.).

ἐνδώμησις, εως, ἡ, *enclosing with a wall*, τεμένους *SIG*996.30 (Smyrna), cf. *BCH*28.78 (Tralles), J.*AJ*15.9.6 (v.l.), *Apoc.*21.18 (v.l.).

ἐνδωσείω, *to be inclined to yield*, D.C.46.37 (cj.), Agath.1.9.

ἐνεάζω, (ἐνεός) *strike dumb, astonish*, *AB*251, *EM*340.50.

ἐνεᾰρίζω, = ἐαρίζω ἐν.., c. dat., Plu.2.770b.

ἔνεγγυς, f.l. for ἐγγύς, Q.S.4.326.

ἐνέγκαι, ἐνεγκεῖν, v. φέρω. **ἐνεγλαύκως**· φοβερὸς ἰδεῖν, Hsch. **ἐνεγύησα**, irreg. aor. of ἐγγυάω.

ἐνέδρ-α, ἡ, *sitting in*: hence, *lying in wait, ambush*, Th.5.56 (pl.), etc.; ἐ. ποιεῖσθαι Id.3.90; ἐνέδραι κατασκευάζονται X.*Eq.Mag.*4.10; ἐνέδραν τιθέναι D.S.19.108; θέσθαι Plu.*Rom.*23; εἰς ἐ. ἐμπίπτειν X. *Cyr.*8.5.14; ἐκ τῆς ἐ. ἀνίστασθαι ib.5.4.4; θέειν ἐκ τῆς ἐ. Th.4.67. b. *men laid in ambush*, τὴν ἐ. ἐξανιστάναι X.*HG*4.8.37. 2. metaph., *trickery, treachery*, δόλου καὶ ἐνέδρας πλήρης Pl.*Lg.*908d, cf. D.19.77; ἐνέδρας ἕνεκα Antiph.124.7; ἐξ ἐνέδρας, opp. φανερῶς, Ph.2.422; μετ' ἐνέδρας App.*BC*1.30, cf. Archig.ap.Orib.8.2.20. II. *position*, ναρθήκων Hp.*Fract.*16, 27. III. *delay*, περί τι *POxy.*62.10 (iii A.D.), etc. **-άζω**, *to be firmly established*, pf. part. ἐνηδρακώς Gal. *UP*3.8. **-εία**, ἡ, = ἐνέδρα, Epich.103. II. *creation of difficulties, obstruction*, *POxy.*900.19 (iv A.D.). **-ευτής**, οῦ, ὁ, *ensnarer, plotter*, Sm.1*Ki.*22.8, Ptol.*Tetr.*159. **-ευτικός**, ή, όν, *fit for ambush*, χωρία Aen.Tact.1.2, cf. Str.3.3.6; *tricky, deceitful*, Ph.2.269, Gal.9.217, 19.138. **-ευτος**, ον, f.l. for -ευτής, Timae.Astr. in *Cat. Cod.Astr.*1.98. **-εύω**, impf. ἐνήδρευον X.*Cyr.*1.6.39: fut. ἐνεδρεύσω Plu.*Ant.*63: aor. ἐνήδρευσα Th.4.67, X.*An.*4.1.22, etc.:—Med., fut. -σομαι (in pass. sense) Id.*HG*7.2.18:—Pass., aor. ἐνηδρεύθην D.28.2: pf. ἐνήδρευμαι Luc.*Cal.*23: (ἐνέδρα):—*lie in wait for, lay snares for*, τινά D.40.10, Men.*Kol.*44:—Pass., *to be caught in an ambush, to be ensnared*, of animals, X.*Mem.*2.1.5; μέλιτι Porph. *Antr.*16; of persons to whom poison has been given, Phylarch.10 J.: metaph., ὑπὸ νόμων τοὺς πολίτας ἐνεδρεύεσθαι Lys.1.49; εἰ .. μὴ τῷ χρόνῳ ἐνηδρεύθημεν if we *had* not *been deceived* by time, D.28.2. 2. abs., *lay* or *set an ambush*, ἐς τὸ Ἐνυάλιον Th.4.67, cf. X.*An.*1.6.2, 4.1.22, etc. II. *place in ambush*, πεζούς App.*BC*2.76, v.l. in J.*AJ*5.8.11:—Med., abs., *set an ambush*, X.*HG*4.4.15:—Pass., metaph., οἱ ἐνηδρευμένοι τῇ δημηγορίᾳ λόγοι Hld.10.17. III. *hinder, obstruct*, τινάς *POxy.*1773.33 (iii A.D.); διάπρασιν *PGiss.*105.24 (v A.D.):—Pass., *PAmh.*2.143.9 (iv A.D.). **-ιον**, τό, *row of reserved seats* in a theatre, *IGRom.*4.1414 (Smyrna). **-ον**, τό, = ἐνέδρα 1, Lxx *Jo.* 8.2, 12, al. II. *hindrance, obstruction*, *POxy.*892.11 (iv A.D.). **-ος**, ὁ, *inmate, inhabitant*, S.*Ph.*153 (lyr.). II. ἔνεδρος, α, ον, *anal*, σύριγγες Meges ap.Orib.44.24.1, 11.

ἐνεείσατο, v. ἐνίζω.

ἐνέζομαι, *sit in* or *upon*, Arist.*Pr.*881b36. II. *have one's seat* or *abode in*, c. acc. loci, τόδ' ἐ. στέγος A.*Pers.*140 (lyr.).

ἐνεθίζω, *accustom to* a thing, τινὰ φιλοσοφίᾳ Socr.*Ep.*27.2:—Pass., ἐνεθίσθαι ταῖς παρατηρήσεσι Ptol.*Tetr.*5, cf. D.L.3.23; ἀέρι Hdn.6.6.2.

ἐνειδέσσιν· ἐν διαφοραῖς, Hsch. **ἐνειδημένους**· πορθήσαντας, Id.

ἐνεῖδον, aor. 2 with no pres. in use, ἐνοράω being used instead, *see* or *observe in*, τι ἔν τινι Th.1.95; τί τινι X.*An.*7.7.45: c. acc., *observe, remark*, S.*Ph.*854 (lyr.): c. part., πλέον ἐνεῖδον σχήσοντες Th. 7.36: c. inf., ἃ ἀρωγὰ ἐνείδομεν .. ἔσεσθαι ib.62: c. dat., *gaze at*, ἀτενὲς ἐ. αὐγῇ Orib.*Eup.*4.13.1.

ἐνειδοφορέω, of a sculptor, *work into shape*, πέτρον ἐνειδοφορῶν *AP* 12.57 (Mel.).

ἐνεῖκαι, ἔνεικας, ἔνεικε, ἔνεικαν, v. φέρω.

ἐνεικονίζω, *impart form to*, τὰς ἀμόρφους ὕλας *Placit.*1.10.1:—Med., *have portrayed in* a thing, τοὺς ἑαυτοῦ [λόγους] τοῖς ἑτέρων ἐνεικονίζεσθαι Plu.2.40d; *represent as by an image*, Simp.*in Ph.*1355.11; τὸ θεῶν κάλλος δι' ἐγκοσμίων εἰδῶν Hierocl.*in CA*23 p.468 M., cf. Procl.*Inst.*152:—Pass., *find a place in a metaphor* or *piece of symbolism*, Id.*in Prm.*pp.480, 503 S.

ἐνειλάσιμος, dub. in *Sammelb.*4116 (fort. εὐιλάσιμος, = εὐίλαστος).

ἐνειλ-έω, *wrap in*, τι ὀθονίῳ Dsc.5.72:—Med., τινὰ κακοῖσι Q.S. 14.294:—Pass., *to be enwrapped*, ἐν [τῇ γῇ] Arist.*Mu.*396a14; ἐν τῷ ἱματίῳ Lxx 1*Ki.*21.9(10); τῃ λεοντῇ Philostr.*Her.*12a.1; ῥάκεσι Artem.1.13; ἱστίοις δοράτια ἐνειλημένα Aen.Tact.29.6, cf. 31.7; φύλλοις Dsc.2.80. II. metaph., *engage*, ἐνίων αὐτοὺς ἐνειληκότων οἰκονομίαις *PTeb.*24.62 (ii B.C.):—Pass., *to be engaged, entangled in* or *with*, τοῖς πολεμίοις Plu.*Art.*11; ὅπλοις Id.*Brut.*45; ὥσπερ θηρίον ταῖς πάντων χερσίν Id.*Caes.*66; ὥσπερ ἄρκυσιν ἐνειλημένους prob. for -λημμ-, J.*BJ*6.2.8; βρέφη -ημένα τὰς χεῖρας Artem.l.c.; *come to blows with*, *PRyl.*144.18 (i A.D.). **-ημα**, ατος, τό, *wrapper, cover*, J.*AJ*12.2. 11, Artem.1.74 (pl.). **-ησις**, εως, ἡ, *wrapping, bandaging*, Herod. Med.ap.Orib.10.18.7. II. *confinement* of intestinal gases, Ruf. ap.eund.8.24.9. **-ητέον**, *one must enwrap*, Herod.Med. in *Rh. Mus.*58.85.

ἐνειλινδέομαι, v.l. for ἐναλ- (q.v.), J.*BJ*4.9.10.

ἐνειλίσσω, Ion. for ἐνελίσσω.

ἐνείλλω, *wrap up in*, πηλὸν ἐν ταρσοῖς καλάμου Th.2.76 (ἐνιλλ- codd.).

ἐνειματιῶν· ὃ τὰ ἐνπάσματα τοῖς ἀνδράσιν ἐκτιθείς, Hsch.

ἔνειμεν, Ep. 1 pl. of ἔνειμι, Il.5.477:—but **ἔνειμεν**, 3 sg. aor. 1 of νέμω.

ἐνειμένος, η, ον, pf. part. Pass. of *ἐν-έννυμι (which is not found), *clad*, c. acc., θώρακας Agath.2.8; χλαμύδα Id.4.1.

ἔνειμι (εἰμί, *sum*), 3 sg. and pl. ἔνι freq. for ἔνεστι, ἔνεισι (v. infr.): inf. ἐνεῖμεν *IG*2².1126.24 (Amphict. Delph.): 3 sg. ἔνι freq. for fut. ἐνέσομαι:—*to be in*, ἄργυρος ἀσκῷ ἔνεστι Od.10.45; ἔνι (for ἔνεστι) κήδεα θυμῷ Il.18.53; ἔνι τοι φρένες οὐδ' ἠβαιαί Od.21.288; εἰ .. χάλκεον .. μοι ἦτορ ἐνείη Il.2.490; εἴ τι ἐνέοι (sc. τοῖς χρησμοῖσι) Hdt.7.6; νοῦς ἔνεστιν ὑμῖν ἐγγενής S.*El.*1328; τοῖς λόγοις ἐ. κέρδος ib.370; πόλλ' ἔ. τῷ γήρᾳ κακά Ar.*V.*441; πλήθη, ἐν οἷς τὸ ἓν οὐκ ἔνι Pl.*Prm.*158c; στάσιν ἐνέσεσθαι τῇ γνώμῃ Th.2.20; ἔνεστ' ἐν τῷ τρόπῳ Ar.*Eq.*1132; ἐνῆν ἄρ' .. κἂν οἴνῳ λόγος Amphis 41; ἀγαθὸς βαφεὺς ἔνεστιν ἐν τῷ παιδίῳ Diph.72; ἔνι τις καὶ ἐν ἡμῖν παῖς Pl.*Phd.*77e; also ἐν τοῖσιν οὔρεσι δένδρεα ἔνι ἄγρια Hecat.292 J.; ἐν [ὄρει] ἔνι μέταλλα Hdt.7.112; ἐν τῷ προθυμεῖσθαι ἐνοῦσαν ζημίαν A.*Pr.*383, etc. b. c. dat. pl., *to be among*, Thgn.1135, Hdt.3.81, al.; οὐκ ἔνι ἐν ὑμῖν οὐδεὶς σοφός 1*Ep.Cor.*6.5. c. c. Adv. loci, οἴκοι ἔνεστι γόος Il.24.240; ἔνεστιν αὐτόθι *is in* this very place, Ar.*Eq.*119; ἐνταῦθα Id.*Nu.*211, etc. 2. abs., *to be present in* a place, οἶνος ἐνέην Od.9.164; οὐδ' ἄνδρες νηῶν ἔνι τέκτονες ib.126; οὐδ' ἔνι στάσις A.*Pers.*738 (troch.); Ἄρης οὐκ ἔνι χώρᾳ Id.*Ag.*78 (anap.); σίτου οὐκ ἐνόντος *as there was* no corn *there*, Th.4.8; τὰ ἐνόντα ἀγαθά the good *that is therein*, ib.20; ἱερῶν τῶν ἐνόντων the temples *that were in the place*, ib.97; ἀμέλειά τις ἐνῆν καὶ διατριβή Id.5.38; πόλεμος οὐκ ἐνῆν Pl.*Plt.*271e; μηδὲ μύλαν ἐνεῖμεν μηδὲ ὅλμον *IG*2². l.c.; also, *to be mentioned in* a treaty, Th.8.43, cf. Ar.*Av.*974; χρόνος ἐνέσται time *will be necessary*, Th.1.80; ἡ βὴξ ἔνι the cough *is persistent*, Hp.*Epid.*7.12. II. *to be possible*, ἄρνησις οὐκ ἔ. ὧν ἀνιστορεῖς S.*OT*578; τῶνδ' ἄρνησις οὐκ ἔ. μοι Id.*El.*527; τίς δ' ἔνεστί μοι λόγος; what plea *is possible* for me [to make]? E.*IT*998; οὐκ ἐνῆν πρόφασις X.*Cyr.*2.1.25; οὐκ ἐνέσται αὐτῷ λόγος οὐδὲ εἷς D.21.41; εἴ τι ἄλλο ἐνῆν Id.18.190; ἐνούσης οὐδεμιᾶς ἔτ' ἀποστροφῆς Id.24.9. 2. impers., c. dat. pers. et inf., *it is in one's power*, S.*Tr.*296, *Ant.*213, etc.: c. inf. only, οὔκουν ἔ. καὶ μεταγνῶναι; Id.*Ph.*1270; οὐ γὰρ δὴ τοῦτό γ' ἔνεστιν εἰπεῖν D.29.14; πῶς ἔ. ἢ πῶς δυνατόν; Id.57.24, etc.;

οὐκ ἔνεστι *it is not possible*, Anaxil.22.7; ὃ μὴ νεώς γε τῆς ἐμῆς ἔνι which *it is not possible* [to get] from my ship, S.*Ph*.648 (sed leg. ἔπι): ἔνι is freq. in this sense, ἃ δὲ ἔνι [λέγειν] D.2.4; δι' ὀργήν γ' ἔνι φῆσαι πεποιηκέναι Id.21.41; ὡς ἔνι ἥδιστα in the pleasantest way *possible*, X. *Mem*.4.5.9, cf. 3.8.4; ὡς ἔνι μάλιστα Plb.21.4.14, Ph.1.465, Luc. *Prom*.6, Jul.*Or*.7.218c: impf., ὡς ἐνῆν ἄριστα Luc.*Tyr*.17. b. ἔνεστιν ὑμᾶς εἰδέναι *it is relevant, pertinent*, *BGU*486.12 (ii A.D.). 3. part. ἐνόν, abs., ἐνὸν αὐτοῖς σῴζεσθαι *since it was in* them, *was possible for* them, Hdn.8.3.2, cf. Luc.*Anach*.9. 4. τὰ ἐνόντα *all things possible*: τὸ πλῆθος τῶν ἐ. εἰπεῖν the *possible materials* for a speech, Isoc. 5.110, cf. 11.44; τῶν ἐ.. ἐν τῷ πράγματι Pl.*Phdr*.235b; τῶν φαινομένων καὶ ἐ. τὰ κράτιστα ἑλέσθαι D.18.190; ἐκ τῶν ἐ. *as well as one can under the circumstances*, ib.256; τὰ ἐ. καὶ τὰ ἁρμόττοντα Arist.*Po*. 1450^b5: in sg., πᾶν τὸ ἐνὸν ἐκλέγων Th.4.59. b. τὰ ἐνόντα *cargo* or *stores* in a ship, Pl.*R*.488c; *contents* of a basket, *PTeb*.414.20 (ii A.D.).

ἐνείργω, aor. ἐνεῖρξα, *shut up in*, εἰς κιβωτόν Sch.Pi.*P*.10.72; τῷ ταύρῳ Phalar.*Ep*.136.1:—Pass., χοῖρος ἐνειρχθεὶς σιρῷ Tz.*H*.6.250.

ἐνείρω, aor. 1 ἐνεῖρα (v. infr.), *entwine, enwreath*, τέττιγας ταῖς θριξί Ael.*VH*4.22:—Pass., ἀνθερίκων ἐνειρμένων περὶ σχοίνους Hdt.4.190. 2. *thread, pass through*, Aen.Tact.31.18; also καρίδα ἀγκίστρῳ Ael.*NA*1.15; ὀστέοις καὶ νεύροις τινά Lxx *Jb*.10.11; ῥίζαν λίνῳ Dsc.2.166. 3. *string together*, Thphr.*HP*9.9.1, 9.12.1 (Pass.). II. *insert*, πῆχυν μεταξὺ τῶν μηρίων Hp.*Art*.70; χεῖρας εἰς σφαίρας Dionys. Eleg.3.3; ἐνεῖραι [πεύκῃ] σφῆνας Babr.38.2.

ἐνειρωνεύομαι, *employ irony in* a matter, Procl.*in Prm*.p.728S.

ἕνεκα, Il.1.110, etc., or **ἕνεκεν** (twice in Hom., Od.17.288,310, rare in Trag., as E.*Med*.999 (lyr.), and early Prose, Th.6.2, X.*HG*2.1.14, Pl.*Smp*.210e; in Com., Men.*Epit*.330; twice in fourth-cent. Att. Inscrr., *IG*2.987^{A}2, 611*b*13, but prevalent in later Inscrr., cf. *SIG* 577.7 (Milet., iii/ii B.C.); in late Prose, Sch.Pi.*O*.7.10), Ep., Ion., and poet. **εἵνεκα** (also in Pl., *Lg*.778d, al.), or **εἵνεκεν** (both forms in Hdt. and Hp. and not uncommon in codd. of later writers; εἵνεκεν B.12.136, Pi.*I*.8(7).35 codd.; **εἵνεκε** Aret.*CA*1.2, f.l. in Hdt.7.133): **ἕνεκε** *SIG*333.14 (Samos, iv B.C.), *Supp.Epigr*.1.351.10 (ibid.), *CIG* 3655.18 (Cyzicus, iii/ii B.C.): Aeol. **ἕννεκα** Alc.*Supp*.9.1, *IG*12(2). 258.8 (Lesbos, i A.D.), but **ἕνεκα** ib.11(4).1064*b*32 (Delos), 12(1). 645*a*38 (Nesus): late **ἕνεκον** *JHS*37.108 (Lydia), etc.:—Prep. with gen., usu. after its case; also before, Il.1.94, B.12.136, Hdt.3.122, etc. When it follows its case, it is sometimes separated from it by several words, as in Hdt.1.30, D.20.88, etc. 1. *on account of*, Τρώων πόλιν.. ἧς εἵνεκ' ὀϊζύομεν κακὰ πολλά Il.14.89, etc.; ὕβριος εἵνεκα τῆσδε 1.214; τοῦδ' ἕνεκα *for* this, ib.110; ὧν ἕ. *wherefore*, 20. 21; τίνος ἕ. βλάβης; A.*Fr*.181; παῖσαι ἄνδρας ἕνεκεν ἀταξίας X.*An*. 5.8.13; στεφανοῦσθαι ἀρετῆς ἕνεκα Aeschin.3.10; *for the sake of*, τοῦ ἕ.; Pl.*Prt*.310b; τῶν δὲ εἵνεκα, ὅκως.., or ἵνα.., Hdt.8.35,40; κολακεύειν ἕ. μισθοῦ X.*HG*5.1.17; διὰ νόσον ἕ. ὑγιείας by reason of sickness *for the sake of* health, Pl.*Ly*.218e, cf. *Smp*.185b; τὸ οὗ ἕ. the *final cause*, Arist.*Ph*.194^a27, *Metaph*.983^a31; τὸ οὗ ἕνεκεν Id.*Ph*.243^a3, *Metaph*.1059^a35. 2. *as far as regards*, ἐμοῦ γ' ἕνεκα *as far as depends on* me, Ar.*Ach*.386, D.20.14; τοῦ φυλάσσοντος εἵνεκεν Hdt. 1.42; εἵνεκεν χρημάτων *as for* money, Id.3.122, etc.; ἕνεκά γε φιλονικίας Pl.*R*.548d, cf. 329b; ἐμπειρίας μὲν ἄρα ἕ. ib.582d; ὅμοιοι τοῖς τυφλοῖς ἂν ἦμεν ἕνεκά γε τῶν ἡμετέρων ὀφθαλμῶν X.*Mem*.4.3.3. 3. *in consequence of*, εἵνεκα τέχνας *by force of* art, *AP*9.729. 4. pleon., ἀμφὶ σοὔνεκα S.*Ph*.554 codd.; ὅσον ἀπὸ βοῆς ἕ. *as far as* shouting *went*, Th.8.92, X.*HG*2.4.31; τίνος χάριν ἕ.; Pl.*Lg*.701d, cf. *Plt*.302b. II. Conj., for οὕνεκα (q.v.), *because*, h.*Ven*.199, Call.*Aet*.3.1.6, *Fr*.287. 2. εἵνεκεν, = ὁθούνεκα, *that*, Pi.*I*.8(7).35 codd.

ἐνεκέχειρον, τό, = ἐκέχειρον, *travelling allowance for* θεωροί, *Inscr. Magn*.38 (Megalopolis): pl., ib.40 (Argos), 41 (Sicyon):—also **-χηρον**, ib.35 (Same), 42 (Corinth).

ἐνεκπλύνω [ῡ], *wash off* (dirt) *in* a thing, Polyzel.4.

ἐνελαύνω, *drive in* or *into*, c. dat., ἐν δεινῷ σάκει ἤλασεν ἔγχος Il.20. 259, cf. Pi.*N*.10.70: metaph., καρδίᾳ κότον Id.*P*.8.9:—Med., *drive in* or *on*, D.C.49.30.

ἐνελίσσω or **-ειλ-**, *roll up in*, σίλφιον μέλιτι Aret.*CA*1.6; τι εἰς ὀθόνην Gal.15.713:—Med., *wrap oneself in*, ἐν ἱματίῳ Hdt.2.95:—Pass., *to be wrapped in*, ὀλίγῳ ὄγμῳ Nic.*Al*.287; ἐπιστολὴ *POxy*. 1153.23 (i A.D.); ἐνειλιγμένος τοὺς πόδας εἰς πίλους *having* one's feet *wrapped in*.., Pl.*Smp*.220b. 2. *wrap round*, λήνεα ἠλακάτῃ Nonn. *D*.6.147.

ἐνέλκω, in Pass., *to be charged, imposed upon* an estate, τοῦ ἐνελκομένου σοι φόρου ἢ ἐνελκυσθησομένου τὸ ἥμισυ *PFlor*.370.14 (ii A.D.), cf. *PLond*.5.1695.12 (vi A.D.), etc.; of land, *to be assigned for forced cultivation*, *PFlor*.50.75 (iii A.D.).

ἔνελος· νεβρός, Hsch.

Ἐνελυσκίς, title of Demeter at Samos, Hsch.

ἔνεμα, ατος, τό, (ἐνίημι) *injection, clyster*, Dsc.2.118 (pl.), Gal.13. 295, Orib.*Fr*.60, etc.

ἐνεμᾰτίζω, *treat with a clyster*, τινά Hierocl.*Facet*.176.

ἐνεμέω, *vomit in*, ἔς τι Hdt.2.172: metaph., Πιερίδεσσιν ἀπλυσίην ἐλέγων *AP*7.377 (Eryc.).

ἐνεμπορεύομαι, *trade with one in*, σοι ἐν ψυχαῖς Lxx *Ez*.27.13.

ἐνενήκοντα, οἱ, αἱ, τά, indecl., *ninety*, Il.2.602, etc.; cf. ἐνήκοντα, ἐννήκοντα. (ἐννεν- freq. in codd., but Inscrr. have ἐνεν- *IG*1^2.324. 109, *Hermes* 17.5 (Delos), etc.:—also gen. pl. ἐνενηκόντων *GDI*5653*c* 26 (Chios).)

ἐνενηκοντᾰ-εννέα, *ninety-nine*, Lxx *Ge*.17.1. **-έξ**, *ninety-six*, ib. 1 *Es*.8.63(66). **-ετής**, ές, *ninety years old*, ib.2*Ma*.6.24, Ph.1.606 (dub. l.):—contr. **-ούτης**, ου, Luc.*DMort*.27.7, App.*Pun*.106, D.C. 69.17. **-μερίς**, ίδος, ἡ, *ninetieth degree* from the ὡροσκόπος, Firm. 8.2.1. **-μοιρία**, ἡ, *arc of ninety degrees*, Pancharius ap.Heph. Astr.2.11. **-πέντε**, *ninety-five*, Hero *Geom*.17.5. **-πηχυς**, ὁ, ἡ, *ninety cubits long*, θύρσος Callix.2. **-πλάσιος** [πλᾰ], ον, *ninety times as large*, c. gen., Gem.6.38.

ἐνενη-κοστός, ή, όν, *ninetieth*, interpol. in X.*HG*1.2.1, cf. Aët.1. 112: **-κοστογδοαῖος**, α, ον, *on the ninety-eighth day*, Gal.7.501: **-κοστόπρωτος**, η, ον, *ninety-first*, Tz.*H*.13.530: **-κοστοτέταρτος**, η, ον, *ninety-fourth*, ib.10.479: **-κοστότρῐτος**, η, ον, *ninety-third*, ib.11.838.

ἐνενίαυτα [ῐ], Adv., (ἐνιαυτός) *in the course of the year*, *BGU*920. 18 (ii A.D.).

ἐνένῑπε, v. ἐνίπτω.

ἐνένωτο, -νωκασι, Ion. for ἐνενόητο, -νοήκασι, v. νοέω.

ἐνεξεμέω, *vomit in*, λεκανίῳ Polyzel.4.

ἐνεξουσιάζω, *show independence in*, τοῖς ῥυθμοῖς D.H.*Comp*.19; τῇ γραφῇ Id.*Th*.8; ἐν τοῖς συνθετικοῖς μορίοις ib.24. 2. *exert authority, be supreme in*, ἔστι τούτων τῶν θεῶν -άζειν τοῖς ὅλοις Procl.*Theol. Plat*.6.15, cf. ib.2, Id.*in Cra*.p.98P.; περὶ τὸν κόσμον Iamb.*Myst*.2.3: abs., ib.3.18. II. Med., *usurp authority*, Lxx *Si*.20.8. III. Pass., *to be brought into subjection*, ἐν τῷ σώματι ib.47.19.

ἐνεορτ-άδια [ᾰδ], τά, *dues paid at festivals*, *OGI*484.30 (Pergam.). **-άζω**, *keep holiday in*, τόπῳ Str.12.3.36, cf. Plu.*Comp.Per.Fab*.1, *OGI*383.98 (Antioch. Commag.).

ἐνεός (in codd. sts. **ἐννεός** *Act.Ap*.9.7, etc.), ά, όν, *dumb, speechless*, freq. joined with κωφός, as Pl.*Tht*.206d, Arist.*HA*536^b4, *Pr*. 961^b14, *Sens*.437^a16; without κωφός, ἐνεοῖς ἀνθρώποις ὁμοίους Epicur. *Fr*.356, cf. Lxx *Is*.56.10, Plu.*Num*.8, D.C.62.16: acc. to Hsch., ὃς οὔτε ἀκούει οὔτε λαλεῖ *deaf and dumb*, as in X.*An*.4.5.33. Adv. **-εῶς** dub.l. in Orac.ap.Polyaen.6.53. 2. *senseless, stupid*, ἀπείρους καὶ ἐ. Pl.*Alc*.2.140d. 3. of things, *useless*, Hp.*Off*.8; ἐς τὸ ἐ. κεῖσθαι ibid. 4. *dumbfounded, astonished*, εἱστήκεισαν ἐ. *Act.Ap*. l.c.

ἐνεοστᾰσία, Ep. **-ίη**, ἡ, *standing dumb*, A.R.3.76.

ἐνεότης, ητος, ἡ, *dumbness*, Arist.*Pr*.895^a16. 2. *stupidity*, dub. in Cratin.188.

ἐνεόφρων, ον, gen. ονος, *stupid*, prob. in Panyas.12.11.

ἐνεπαγγελία, ἡ, *token, sign*, ἡ ῥὶς ἐ. θυμοῦ Hld.2.35.

ἐνεπάγομαι [ᾰ], Med., *attack*, Aesop.234.

ἐνέπαλτο, v. ἐνεφάλλομαι.

ἐνεπηρεάζω, = ἐπηρεάζω, Poll.8.30:—Pass., ὑπό τινος Phld.*Ir*. p.9W.

ἐνεπι-δείκνῠμαι, Med., *display in*, τὴν εὔνοιαν ἔν τισι Isoc.19.24; σύνεσιν πράγμασι Ph.1.398, cf. Plu.2.90e. II. abs., *show off, make a display*, Ph.2.28, Lib.*Decl*.16.28. **-δημέω**, *sojourn in*, Ael.*VH* 12.52, Ath.6.233a; opp. κατοικέω, Id.8.361f, D.C.51.17. **-μένω**, *remain in* or *about*, ἐπί τινα τόπον *Peripl.M.Rubr*.65. **-ορκέω**, *forswear oneself by*, [Ἀθηνᾶ] Aeschin.3.150. II. Pass., *have false witness given against one*, ὑπό τινων Themist.*Ep*.8. **-πεδος**, ον, *flat*, ὀροφή Gal.18(1).518. **-σημος**, gloss on ἀριφραδής, Sch.Il. 23.206. **-σκημμα**, ατος, τό, *claiming of property alleged to belong to the state* (cf. ἀπογράφω III.2), Harp. **-σκήπτομαι**, Med., *claim property alleged to belong to the state*, ἐνεπισκήψασθαι ἐν τῇ οὐσίᾳ τῇ ἐκείνου ἐνοφειλόμενον αὐτῷ ἀργύριον D.49.45, cf. Harp., Poll.8.61. 2. generally, *take proceedings to enforce a claim*, *PGurob* 2.28 (iii B.C.). **-τρέπω**, *impose* a contribution *upon*, τινί *PLond*.5.1677.15 (Pass.).

ἐνέπω, lengthd. **ἐννέπω**, both forms in Hom. and Pi. (ἐνν- *P*.9. 96, ἐν- *N*.6.59), ἐνν- Sapph.*Supp*.4.2; in Trag. only ἐνν-, exc. E. in lyr., as *Hipp*.572,580 (anap.), *Heracl*.95 (lyr.), al.: pres. is used by Hom. only in imper. ἔννεπε, opt. ἐνέποιμι Od.17.561, part. ἐνέπων, also 3 sg. impf. ἔννεπε; pres. ind. not before Pi. ll. cc.; inf. Boeot. ἐνέπιν Corinn.*Supp*.2.73: impf. ἤνεπον Pi.*N*.10.79, Call.*Fr*. 1.58P.: aor. 2 ἔνισπον, ἔνισπες Il.24.388, ἔνισπε 2.80; imper. ἐνίσπες Il.11.186, 14.470, Od.3.101, A.R.1.487, ἔνισπε Od.4.642, A.R.3.1; subj. ἐνίσπω Il.11.839; opt. ἐνίσποις, -οι, Od.4.317, Il.14.107; inf. ἐνισπεῖν Od.4.323: fut. ἐνισπήσω 5.98, ἐνίψω 2.137, al. Pres. **ἐνίσπω** in later Poets, as Nic.*Th*.522, D.P.391:—*tell* or *tell of*, Διὸς δέ σφ' ἔννεπε μῦθον Il.8.412; τὸν Ἕκτορι μῦθον ἐνίσπες 11.186; νημερτέα πάντ' ἐνέποντα Od.17.549; εἴ τινά μοι κληηδόνα πατρὸς ἐνίσποις if thou *couldst tell* me any tidings of my father, 4.317; ἄνδρα μοι ἔννεπε *tell* me *the tale of*.., 1.1; τίς.. ἄριστος ἔην, σύ μοι ἔννεπε, Μοῦσα Il.2.761; μνηστήρων.. θάνατον καὶ κῆρ' ἐνέπουσα Od.24.414: abs., *tell news* or *tales*, πρὸς ἀλλήλους ἐνέποντε 23.301, cf. S.*El*.1439 (lyr.): freq. in Tragg., who use ἐννέπω as a pres. to the aor. εἰπεῖν (aor. ἔνισπον only in imper. ἔνισπε A.*Supp*.603, inf. ἐνισπεῖν E.*Supp*.435); ἐνν. τινί ὅτι .. S.*El*.1367. 2. simply, *speak*, μύθοισι σκολιοῖς ἐνέπων Hes.*Op*. 194, cf. A.*Ch*.550; πρὸς τίν' ἐννέπειν δοκεῖς; S.*Tr*.402. 3. c. acc. et inf., *bid* one *do* so and so, Pi.*P*.9.96, S.*OT*350, *OC*932. 4. *call, name*, ἀγώνων, τοὺς ἐνέποισιν ἱερούς Pi.*N*.6.59; ἐνν. τινὰ δοῦλον E.*HF*270. 5. *address, accost*, τινά S.*Aj*.764. (In Hom. ἐνέπω, ἐννέπω, ἐνισπεῖν (Subst. ἐνοπή), = *tell, relate*; ἐνίπτω and ἐνίσσω (qq. vv., cf. ἐνιπή), *reprove, upbraid*; Pi. and later Ep. used ἐνίπτω, = ἐνέπω.) (For the root, v. ἔσπον.)

ἐνεραδνούμιον, τό, dub. sens. in *PMasp*.151.168 (vi A.D.).

ἐνεργ-άζομαι, *make* or *produce in*, ἡ φορὰ τῆς τοξίτιδος ἐ. τῷ βέλει κίνησιν Ph.*Bel*.68.41; τι ἐν τῷ σώματι v.l. for ἀπ- in Hp. *VM*22; τι τοῖς ἀνδριᾶσιν X.*Mem*.3.10.6; τὸ πείθεσθαι τοῖς νόμοις [τῇ Σπάρτῃ] ib.4.4.15; πολλοῖς ἔρωτα Gorg.*Hel*.18; [δόξαν] ib.13;

ἔκπληξιν Pl.*Phlb.*47a; ἐπιστήμην Chrysipp.*Stoic.*2.39; δέος τοῖς πολίταις D.60.25; μοχθηρὰς συνηθείας τινί Id.61.3; εὔνοιαν ἐν πᾶσι Plb. 6.11ᵃ.7, cf. Ph.2.89, etc.: aor. 1 ἐνειργάσθην in pass. sense, *to be made* or *placed in..*, X.*Mem.*1.4.5. 2. *work for hire in*, of harlots, αἱ ἐνεργαζόμεναι παιδίσκαι Hdt.1.93; ἐ. τῇ οὐσίᾳ *trade* with the property, D.44.23; ἁλιεῖς ἐνειργασμένοι τοῖς τόποις Plb.10.8.7. **–εια**, ἡ, *activity, operation*, opp. ἕξις (disposition), Arist.*EN*1098ᵇ33, al.; ζῴου Plb.1.4.7; ἡ χαρὰ καὶ ἡ εὐφροσύνη κατὰ κίνησιν ἐνεργείᾳ βλέπονται Epicur.*Fr.*2; opp. ἀργία, Hierocl. *in CA*19 p.461 M.: pl., παντοδαπαὶ ἐ. Polystr.p.30 W.; ἐ. καὶ σπουδή *PTeb.*616 (ii A. D.); physiological *function*, Gal.6.21; *performance*, τῶν καθηκόντων Ph.1.91; *activity*, of drugs, Gal.6.467; *force*, of an engine, D.S.20.95 (but, *mechanism*, '*action*', Hero *Aut.*1.7). b. *workmanship*, Aristeas 59. 2. esp. of divine or supernatural *action*, *Ep.Eph.*1.19, al., Aristeas 266; ἐ. θεοῦ Διὸς Βαιτοκαίκης *OGI*262.4 (Syria, iii A. D.); magical *operation*, ἱερὰ ἐ. *PMag.Par.*1.159. 3. pl., ἐνέργειαι *cosmic forces*, Herm.ap.Stob.1.41.6. 4. Gramm., *active force*, opp. πάθος, D.T.637.29, A.D.*Synt.*9.9 (pl.), al.; ἐνέργειαι καὶ πάθη *active* and *passive forms*, Alex.*Fig.*2.14. 5. Rhet., *vigour of style*, Arist. *Rh.*1411ᵇ28. II. in the philos. of Arist., opp. δύναμις, *actuality*, *Metaph.*1048ᵃ26, al.; opp. ὕλη, ib.1043ᵃ20; ἡ ὡς ἐ. οὐσία, substance in the sense of *actuality*, ib.1042ᵇ10; opp. ἐντελέχεια, as *actuality* to *full reality*, ib.1050ᵃ22, 1047ᵃ30; ἐνεργείᾳ *actually*, opp. δυνάμει, ib.1045ᵇ19, al., etc. **–είς**· ἡ εἰς γλουτοὺς κάθεσις τῶν χειρῶν, Hsch. **–έω**, *to be in action* or *activity, operate*, Arist.*Rh.*1411ᵇ26; εὐδαίμων ὁ κατ' ἀρετὴν τελείαν –ῶν Id.*EN*1101ᵃ15: c. acc., ἐνεργεῖς ποσὸν καὶ δυάδα Plot.6.6.16; esp. of divine or supernatural *action*, freq. in *NT.*, τινί, ἔν τινι, *Ep.Gal.*2.8, *Ev.Matt.*14.2:—Med., *Ep. Rom.*7.5, al. 2. *to be efficacious*, of drugs, Diocl.*Fr.*147, Dsc.1. 98, al.; ἐοικότα ἐ. ib.106; ἐνήργησε τὸ φάρμακον Plot.6.1.22; *to be effective*, of troops, ταῖς σαρίσαις Ael.*Tact.*14.6:—Pass., *to be the object of action*, Arist.*de An.*427ᵃ7, *Ph.*195ᵇ28; ὁ ἐνεργούμενος λίθος *IG*7.3073.108 (Lebad.); also, *to be actualized*, Plot.3.7.11. II. trans., *effect, execute*, πάντα κατὰ δύναμιν Plb.18.14.8; τὰ τοῦ πολέμου Id.7.5.8; χρείαν Ath.Mech.14.2, cf. Aristid.Quint.2.9:—Pass., *to be actively carried on*, ὁ πόλεμος ἐνηργεῖτο Plb.1.13.5, cf. D.S.20.95; τὰ κατὰ πρόθεσιν ἐνεργούμενα *things executed*, Plb.9.12.7; μηδὲν ἐνέργημα... ἐνεργείσθω M.Ant.4.2. III. Medic., of sexual intercourse, τὴν τοιαύτην πρᾶξιν –οῦσι μετρίως Diocl.*Fr.*141, cf. *Cat.Cod.Astr.*8(4). 176: euphem. for βινεῖν, *in opere esse*, Theoc.4.61; ἐ. τινά Alciphr. 3.55; ἐρωτικόν τι Id.1.39. IV. *operate*, in surgery, Orib.45.18.5, Paul.Aeg.6.73; ὁ ἐνεργῶν, ὁ ἐνεργούμενος, the *surgeon*, the *patient*, Gal.18(2).626,683. **–ημα**, ατος, τό, *action, activity, operation*, Plb. 4.8.7, D.S.4.51 (of the labours of Heracles), Ph.1.213, M.Ant.4.2, Procl.*Inst.*158, al.: pl., φύσεων Iamb.*Myst.*4.13; opp. πάθος, *Stoic.* 2.59, cf. 3.134, Chrysipp.ib.2.295. 2. *realized object*, [νοῦς] αὐτοῦ ἐ. Plot.6.8.16, cf. 6.9.2. 3. dub. for ἐνάργημα, Epicur.*Ep.*1 p.4 U.; τὸ κατὰ φιλοσοφίαν ἐ. Metrod.*Herc.*831.8, cf. Phld.*Po.*2.68. **–ής**, ές, later form of ἐνεργός, *active, effective*, μηχανὰς ἐνεργεῖς ποιοῦντες D.S. 17.44, etc.; of medicines, *strong*, *POxy.*1088.56 (i A. D.), Dsc.5.88, etc.: Comp. –έστερος *more effective*, πρός τινα Arist.*Top.*105ᵃ19: Sup. –έστατος, πρός τι D.S.1.88, cf. Dsc.1.19, A.D.*Synt.*291.9. **–ητέος**, α, ον, *to be done*, dub. l. in Zeno *Stoic.*1.49. **–ητικός**, ή, όν, *able to act upon, acting upon*, τοῦ κινητοῦ Arist.*Ph.*202ᵃ17. 2. *productive*, τινός *Gp.*12.35.1. II. *active*, Arist.*EE*1220ᵇ3; αὐτοπάθεια Plb. 12.28.6. Adv. –κῶς *actively*, S.E.*M.*7.223,293. 2. Gramm., ἐ. ῥῆμα an *active* verb, D.H.*Amm.*2.7; of Nouns, A.D.*Adv.*161.18; ἐκφορά, διάθεσις, Id.*Synt.*150.19, 210.19. Adv. –κῶς ib.276.20, Phryn. *PS* p.9 B. III. *efficacious, stimulating*, *Gp.*2.33.4 (Sup.). **–ήτρια**, ἡ, *effectrix*, *Gloss.* **–ίς**, epith. of Demeter, Hsch. **–μός**, ὁ, *a way of playing on the lyre*, Phryn.Com.6. 2. *peg* on the κιθάρα for tuning the strings, Euphron.ap.*EM*340.3.

ἐνεργο-βᾰτέω, *step vehemently, pass wonderfully* from one thing to another, εἴς τι Ps.-Luc.*Philopatr.*3. **–λᾰβέω**, *exploit*, Aeschin.3. 150, Procop.*Arc.*20,25; τοὺς ἑτέρων βίους Just.*Nov.*17.13.

ἐνεργός, όν, *at work, active, busy*, Hdt.8.26, etc.; ζῷα ἐ., opp. εἴδωλα ἀκίνητα, X.*Mem.*1.4.4; δικασταί, κυβερνῆται, ἐ. ὄντες *on duty*, Pl.*Lg.*674b; ὅπως ἂν ἐ. ὦσι that they may *begin business*, D.35.7; ἐ. περί τι γίγνεσθαι Plb.3.17.4; *effective, fit for service*, νῆες, στράτευμα, Th.3.17, X.*Cyr.*2.2.23; πεζὸν σὺν ἵπποις –ότατον Id.*Eq.Mag.*9.7; ἐ. προσβολή *vigorous* attack, Plb.4.63.8; ἐ. ὑσσοί *effective* javelins, Id.1.40.12; πελέκεις D.S.5.39; ἐ. ποιεῖσθαι τὴν πορείαν march *with rapidity*, Plb.5.8.3; τὸ τῆς ὥρας πρὸς τὰς νόσους –ότατον D.S.14. 70; τόποι (in logical sense) –ότατοι *most effective*, Arist.*Top.*154ᵃ16; ἡ γεωργία ἐ. ποιεῖ τὴν τροφήν calls *into action* the nutritive properties (of the soil), Id.*Pr.*924ᵃ17. 2. *actual*, opp. *potential*, *Theol.Ar.*6, 12. II. of land, *productive*, opp. ἀργός, X.*Cyr.*3.2.19, cf. 5.4.25, *HG*4.4.1, Plu.*Sol.*31 (Comp.); simply, *tilled*, *SIG*685.72 (Itanos); πεδίον πολλαῖς ἐνεργὸν μυριάσι *producing enough* for multitudes, Plu. *Caes.*58; μυλαῖον ἐ. *in working order*, *PRyl.*167.10 (i A. D.); also of mines, X.*Vect.*4.2; ἐνεργά (sc. χρήματα) *employed capital, which brings in a return*, D.27.7,10, cf. X.*Hier.*11.4; θησαυρὸς ἐ. *PLond.*2.216 (i A. D.); τὸ δάνειον ἐ. ποιεῖν to put out *to interest*, D.56.29. III. Adv. –γῶς *with activity*, μαχεῖται X.*Mem.*3.4.11; γυμνάζειν Plb.1.9.7, al.: Comp., Id.4.59.3.

ἐνερείδω, *thrust in*, μοχλὸν.. ὀφθαλμῷ ἐνέρεισαν Od.9.383; δακτύλους Hp.*Art.*34; βέλος ἐνερεισθὲν τοῖς ὀστέοις Plu.2.344c; *apply*, ἐν δὲ πλατὺν ὦμον ἔρεισεν A.R.1.1198: metaph., μὴ ἐνέρειδε μηθένα *Sammelb.*5905; *fix upon*, τὴν ὄψιν τινί Plu.2.586d; τοὺς ἄκμονας τῷ τραχήλῳ Ant.Lib.28.4; τὸν θυμόν τισι Oenom.ap.Eus.*PE*5.34; τὴν ψυχήν Luc.*Nigr.*7:—Med., ἐνερεισάμενος πέτρᾳ γόνυ *his own* knee, Theoc.7.7, cf. Orph.*A.*1090. II. intr., *lie in* or *on*, τὰ ἐνηρεικότα στομάχῳ *adherent to...*, Dsc.3.23:—Med., πεσὼν ἐνερείσατο γαίῃ A.R. 1.428.

ἐνέρεισις, εως, ἡ, *pressure*, Hp.*Off.*12: pl., Arr.*Tact.*16.13.

ἐνερεύγομαι, *belch on*, γυίοις ἰόν Nic.*Th.*185: also aor. 2 Act., ἔμοιγε ... τυροῦ κάκιστον ... ἐνήρῠγεν Ar.*V.*913.

ἐνερευθ-ής, ές, *somewhat red*, ἄστρον Str.3.1.5; ἀφρός Dsc.1.100: Comp., Sor.1.13; of the countenance, *flushed*, Phld.*Ir.*p.5 W., Cic. *Att.*12.4.1; τῷ χρώματι γενόμενος ἐ. *blushing*, Plb.31.23.8; παρειῶν τὸ ἐ. Luc.*Im.*7, cf. Antyll.ap.Orib.7.16.3. **–ομαι**, *to be somewhat ruddy*, Nic.*Th.*511,871.

ἔνερθε and **–θεν**; Dor. ἔνερθα A.D.*Adv.*153.17; also **νέρθε** and **–θεν**: I. Adv. *from beneath, up from below*, αὐτὰρ νέρθε Ποσειδάων ἐτίναξε Il.20.57; πέμψατ' ἔνερθεν ψυχὴν εἰς φῶς A.*Pers.*630; τήνδ' ἔπεμψας νέρθεν ἐς φάος E.*Alc.*1139, cf. 985 (lyr.); ν. ἀνακαλούμενον Id.*Hel.*966. 2. without sense of motion, *beneath, below*, ἐ. πόδες καὶ χεῖρες ὕπερθε Il.13.75, cf. 78; ῥαίνοντο δὲ νέρθε κονίῃ [ἵπποι] 11.282, cf. 535, etc.; πρόσωπά τε ν. τε γοῦνα Od.20.352; esp. of the nether world, οἱ ἐ. θεοί the gods *below*, Il.14.274; τοῖς ἐ. νεκροῖς S.*Ant.*25 (lyr.), cf. *El.*1068; κοίταν ἔχει ν. Id.*OC*1707 (lyr.); ἔνερθ' ὑπὸ γῆς, ὑπὸ γᾶν, Hes.*Th.*720, Pi.*P.*9.81; τοῖς .. ν. κἀπὶ γῆς ἄνω S.*OT*416; *below*, i.e. in the vale, E.*Ba.*752; βαιὸν δ' ἐ. S.*Ph.*20. II. as Prep. with gen., before or after its case, *beneath, below*, ἀγκῶνος ἐ. Il.11.252, cf. 234; γαίης ν. καὶ.. θαλάσσης 14.204; ν. γῆς Od.11.302; ἔνερθ' Ἀΐδεω Il.8.16; γῆς ἔνερθ' ᾤχου θανών S.*Fr.*686, cf. E.*Ph.* 505. b. *from below*, γῆς ἔνερθεν ἐς φάος A.*Pers.*222 (troch.). 2. *subject to, in the power of*, ἐχθρῶν ἐ. ὄντα S.*Ph.*666.—Never in Att. Prose; used by Hdt., ἐ. τῆς λίμνης 2.13 (abs. in metaph. sense, *inferior*, τοῖς ἅπασι 1.91); also in *IG*4.1485.57 (Epid.), Aret.*CD*1.3, Luc.*Rh.Pr.*4; in form ἐνέρθε, *IG*12(2).74b21 (Mytil., iii B. C.).

ἕνερμα, ατος, τό, = ὅρμος, Sch.Pi.*O.*2.135.

ἔνερξις, εως, ἡ, = ἐνεργμός, *EM*340.2, Hsch.

ἔνεροι, οἱ, *those below, those beneath the earth*, of the dead and the gods below, ἐνέροισιν ἀνάσσων Il.15.188, Hes.*Th.*850; ἄναξ ἐνέρων Il.20.61, etc.; βασιλεῦ ἐνέρων A.*Pers.*629 (anap.); ἐνέρων ἀρωγός, i.e. of the murdered Agamemnon, S.*El.*1391 (lyr.); οἱ ἔνεροι Pl.*R.* 387c, cf. *Tab.Defix.*99.9. (Perh. fr. ἔρα.)

ἐνερόχρως, ωτος, ὁ, ἡ, *cadaverous*, Alciphr.1.3, Agath.2.23, *EM* 340.10.

ἔνερσις, εως, ἡ, (ἐνείρω) *fitting in, fastening*, ἐνέρσει χρυσῶν τεττίγων, used by old men at Athens to fasten up their hair, Th.1.6.

ἐνέρτερος, α, ον, Comp. of ἔνεροι, *lower, of the nether world*, οἵ περ ἐ. εἰσὶ θεοί Il.15.225; οἱ ἐ., = ἔνεροι, A.*Ch.*285; ἱστός *Lyr.Adesp.*132: c. gen., ἦσθα ἐ. Οὐρανιώνων *below* them, Il.5.898. 2. simply, *lower*, Nonn.*D.*44.164.—After Hom. usu. in form νέρτερος (q. v.). II. Sup., ἐνέρτατον βένθος *lowest*, Emp.35.3; cf. νέρτατος.

ἐνέρυθρος, ον, = ἐνερευθής, *reddish*, ὀφθαλμοί Aret.*SD*1.6.

ἐνεσία, ἡ, (ἐνίημι) *suggestion*, used only in Ep. form **ἐννεσίη**: dat. pl., with gen. pers., once in Hom., κείνης ἐννεσίῃσι *at* her *suggestion*, Il.5.894; Γαίης, Διός, Ἥρης ἐνν., Hes.*Th.*494, *h.Cer.*30, Call.*Dian.* 108; ὑπ' ἐννεσίῃσι A.R.1.7, prob. in Q.S.3.475: gen. pl., ἐννεσιάων A.R.3.1364.

ἔνεσις, εως, ἡ, (ἐνίημι) *injection*, φύσης ἐνιεμένης ἐς τὴν κοιλίην Hp. *Art.*48, cf. Hero *Spir.*2.18, Orib.*Syn.*9.14.1.

ἐνεστιάομαι, *give an entertainment in*, Luc.*Am.*12.

ἐνέστιος, ον, *offered at the public hearth*, τὸ ἐ. θῦμα οἶν *Inscr.Magn.*36. 20 (Ithaca):—also **ἐνίστιος**, ον, ib.72.40 (Syrac.):—Subst. **ἐνέστιον** (sc. θῦμα), τό, ib.42.12 (Corinth):—Arc. **ἰνίστιον** ib.38.41 (Megalop.).

ἐν-ετέον, (ἐνίημι) *one must treat with injections* or *clysters*, Sor.2.44, Orib.*Fr.*60, Herod.Med. in *Rh.Mus.*58.85. **–ετή**, ἡ, (ἐνετός) = περόνη, *pin, brooch*, Il.14.180, Call.*Fr.*149, *Mus.Belg.*16.71 (Attica, ii A. D.). **–ετήρ**, ῆρος, ὁ, *clyster-syringe*, Cass.Fel.48, Alex.Trall. 8.2; περὶ ἐνετήρων on *clysters*, Sever.*Clyst.*tit., cf. Steph. *in Gal.*1.331 D. II. *siege-engine of war for hurling projectiles*, Ph.*Bel.*91.45, 100.18. **–ετήρια**, τά, *taxes on admission* to citizenship, *IG*9(1). 334.9 (Locr., v B. C.). **–ετός**, ή, όν, *inserted*, σκυταλίδες J.*AJ*3. 6.5; *for injection*, τροχίσκοι Paul.Aeg.7.12 (v. l. ἐνετικῶν). II. *suborned*, X.*Cyr.*1.6.19, *An.*7.6.41, App.*BC*1.22, *Mith.*59.

ἐνευδαιμονέω, *to be happy in*, Th.2.44, D.S.34.3; τῷ καιρῷ Lib.*Or.* 14.43.

ἐνευδιάω, *float in the clear sky*, ἐνευδιόων πτερύγεσσι A.R.2.935.

ἐνευδοκῐμέω, *gain glory in*, ὅτῳ τὰ τῶν Ἑλλήνων ἀτυχήματ' ἐνευδοκιμεῖν ἀπέκειτο D.18.198, cf. D.S.34.2.18, J.*Ap.*1.5, Plu.2.71a; περί τι *Cod.Just.*1.2.25.1. 2. *enjoy repute with* another, Ael.*VH*8.12.

ἐνεύδω, *sleep in* or *on*, χλαῖναν.. καὶ κώεα, τοῖσιν ἐνεῦδεν Od.20.95, cf. 3.350, al., Theoc.5.10; τρίβωνι D.L.6.22.

ἐνευεργετέω, in Pass., ἐνευεργετημένος *well-treated*, dub. in *PLond.* 2.177.26 (i A. D.).

ἐνευημερέω, *to be lucky in*, τοῖς θεάτροις, τοῖς ὕδνοις, Plu.2.289d, 665d.

ἐνευθηνέομαι, *abound in*, Sch.Ar.*Pl.*586.

ἐνευκαιρέω, *pass one's time in*, διαβολαῖς Ph.2.522, cf. 1.387.

ἐνευλογέομαι, Pass., *to be blessed in*, τῷ σπέρματί σου *Act.Ap.*3.25, ἐν σοί Lxx *Ge.*12.3, *Ep.Gal.*3.8:—Med., *take a blessing to oneself*, ἀπαρχῆς Lxx *1Ki.*2.29.

ἐνευν-άζομαι, Med., aor. 1 ἐνευνάσσαντο, *sleep in*, Nic.*Fr.*19. **–αιος**, ον, *on which one sleeps*, ἐστόρεσεν δ' ἐπὶ δέρμα.. ἐνεύναιον a skin *to* *sleep on*, Od.14.51; χήτει ἐνευναίων for want *of bed-furniture*, 16.35; τὰ ἐ. *bed-clothes*, Hierocl.p.25 A. **-οι**· ἐπιτήδειοι τόποι εἰς Κύπριοι, Hsch.

ἐνευπᾰθέω, = εὐπαθέω ἐν.., Lib.*Or.*11.257,268.

ἐνευρίσκω, *discover in*, J.*BJ*5.13.5 (Pass.), cf. Aristid.*Or.*28(49).13 (dub. l.).

ἐνευστομέω, *sing sweetly in*, τοῖς ἄλσεσι Philostr.Jun.*Im.*6.

ἐνευσχημονέω, = εὐσχημονέω ἐν.., Hierocl.*in CA*5 p.427 M.

ἐνευσχολέω, *have leisure for*, λογισμοῖς Luc.*Am.*35.

ἐνευτῠχέω, = εὐτυχέω ἐν.., Aristid.1.111 J.

ἐνευφραίνομαι, = εὐφραίνομαι ἐν..., Lxx *Pr.*8.31, Ph.1.232, al.

ἐνεύχομαι, *adjure, implore*, *Test.Epict.*1.13, Herod.6.46; ἐνεύχομαι ὑμῖν θεοὺς καὶ θεάς *IG*5(1).1208.50 (Gythium): c. dat., of god invoked, *PMag.Par.*1.2258; also ἐνεύχομαί σοι τὴν Ἀφροδίτην μὴ ἀποκνήσῃς I *adjure* you by A. not to.., *PBaden* 51 (ii A. D.).

ἐνευωχέομαι, = εὐωχέομαι ἐν..., abs., Str.17.1.15.

ἐνεφάλλομαι, aor. 2 ἐνέπαλτο, *leap upon*, Q.S.10.467.

ἐνέφει· ἐρείδει, Hsch.

ἐνεχθήσομαι, ἐνέχθητι, ἐνεχθείην, ἐνεχθῶ, ἐνεχθῆναι, v. φέρω.

ἐνεχῠρ-άζω, fut. -άσω D.47.79 (but -χυρῶ Lxx *De.*24.17):—*take a pledge from* one, τινός Lexap.D.21.10: metaph., ἡ φύσις ἐ. τοῦ μὲν ὄψιν, τοῦ δὲ ἀκοήν Pl.*Ax.*367b. 2. c. acc. rei, *take in pledge*, D.24.197; ἐ. ὁ νόμος τὰς οὐσίας τῶν ὑπευθύνων Aeschin.3.21, cf. Lxx *De.*24.6, al., D.H.6.29, *PPetr.*3 pp.56,69: abs., Plb.6.37.8 (ἐνεχυριάζων codd.):—Pass., τὰ χρήματα ἐνεχυράζομαι I *have my* goods *seized for debt*, Ar.*Nu.*241:—Med., *have security given one, take it for oneself*, τόκου *for* interest, ib.35; *seize as a pledge*, Id.*Ec.*567. **-ᾰσία**, ἡ, *taking* property *in pledge, security* taken, *pledge*, Pl.*Lg.*949d, *IG*2.1055.7 (iv B. C.), *PSI*4.288 (ii A. D.), etc.; ἐ. ποιήσασθαι D.47.76, 80. **-ασμα**, ατος, τό, *pledge, thing pawned*, Lxx *Ex.*22.26(25), al., *PHamb.*10.42 (ii A. D.). **-ασμός**, ὁ, = ἐνεχυρασία, Lxx *Ez.*18.7, Plu.*Cor.*5 (pl.). **-αστής**, οῦ, ὁ, *one who distrains*, *Schwyzer* 177.8 (Crete, v B. C.), Hsch. s. v. δήμαρχον. **-αστός**, ή, όν, *seizable for debt*, *Test.Epict.*5.19. **-ιάζω, -ιασμός**, later forms for ἐνεχυράζω, -ασμός, Just.*Nov.*134.7, 52.1, *Gloss.*:—also **-ιασία, -ίασις, -ιαστής**, ib. **-ιμαῖον**, = ἐνέχυρον, censured by Phryn.342. **-ιος**, ον, *pledged*, Socr.*Ep.*9.1 (Aristippus). II. Subst. ἐνεχύριον, τό, = sq., *BGU*907.11 (ii A. D.). **-ον**, τό, (ἐχυρός) *pledge, security*, ἐ. ἀποδεικνύναι and ὑποτιθέναι to offer *a pledge*, Hdt.2.136; ἐνέχυρα ἀποδιδόναι And.1.39; λαμβάνειν ibid., X.*An.*7.6.23; ἐνέχυρα βίᾳ φέρειν Antipho 6.11; ἐνέχυρον φέρειν τῶν γειτόνων Hermipp.29; τὰ ἐ. τινων *PHib.*1.46 (iii B. C.), etc.; ἐ. τιθέναι τι make a thing *a pledge*, put it *in pawn*, Ar.*Pl.*451, cf. *Ec.*755; ἐ. κεῖται Pl.*Lg.*820e; ἐπ' ἐνεχύρῳ δοῦναι give on *security*, D.49.2; ἐπ' ἐνεχύροις δανείζειν Ph.1.634; ἐκ τῶν ἐ. τῶν ὠφληκότων τὴν δίκην from the forfeited *pledges*, *IG*2.814ᵃ *A* 26 (iv B. C.): metaph. in pl., *hostages*, of wives and children, Aen.Tact.5.1, cf. Ph.1.323 (sg.). **-όω**, *pledge*, *POxy.*729.44 (Pass., ii A. D.). **-ωμα**, ατος, τό, = -ασμα, *EM*706.41 (pl.). **-ως**, Adv. *safely*, *Peripl.M.Rubr.*43.

ἐνέχω, *hold* or *keep fast within*, χόλον ἐνέχειν τινί *harbour* a grudge against one, Hdt.1.118, 6.119 (v. II. 2). II. Pass., with fut. and aor. Med. (v. infr.), *to be held, caught, entangled in*, c. dat., τῇ πάγῃ Id.2.121.β'; ἐνεχομένων τῶν πελτῶν τοῖς σταυροῖς X.*An.*7.4.17; ἐν τοῖς τῆς νεὼς σκεύεσι Pl.*La.*183e. 2. metaph., ἐ. ἀπορίῃσι Hdt.1.190; φιλοτιμίᾳ E.*IA*527; ὀργαῖς πολυχρονίοις Phld.*Ir.*p.63 W.; ἐν ἄγεϊ Hdt.6.56; ἐν ταῖς αὐταῖς δυσχερείαις Arist.*Cael.*309ᵃ29; ἐν θώματι ἐνέσχετο *was seized with* wonder, Hdt.7.128. 3. *to be liable* or *subject to*, οὐ δικαίοις Ζεὺς ἐνέξεται λόγοις A.*Supp.*169 (Pors. for ἐνεύξεται, lyr.), cf. And.1.44; πράγμασιν, λειτουργίαις, *BGU*473.7 (ii A. D.), *PFlor.*382.31 (iii A. D.), etc. b. in legal formulae, ἐν ἐπιάρῳ κ' ἐνέχοιτο *SIG*9.9 (Elis, vi B. C.); ἐ. ἀρᾷ Διός Pl.*Lg.*881d (in tmesi, ἐν τήπαρῇ ἔχεσθαι *SIG*38.34 (Teos, v B. C.)); ζημίᾳ, αἰτίᾳ, Pl.*Lg.*935c, *Cri.*52a; τοῖς ἐσχάτοις ἐπιτιμίοις D.51.11; ἐν τοῖς αὐτοῖς ἐπιτιμίοις Aeschin.3.175; νόμῳ *Schwyzer* 634 *B* 49 (Nesus, iv B. C., prob.), Plu.*TG*10; ἐν τοῖς αὐτοῖς νόμοις Pl.*Lg.*762d; νοθείᾳ *in an imputation of* bastardy, Plu.*Them.*1; ἱεροσυλίαις *PTeb.*5.5 (ii B. C.): abs., ἐὰν ἐνσχεθῶσι *PSI*3.168 (ii B. C.). 4. in good sense, ἐνέχεσθαι ἀγγελίᾳ *meet with* a message, Pi.*P.*8.49. 5. in aor., *come to a standstill*, ἔν τινι Pl.*Tht.*147d. III. intr., *enter in, pierce*, εἴς τι X.*Cyn.*10.7. 2. *to be urgent against*, τινί Lxx *Ge.*49.23, *Ev.Marc.*6.19, *Ev.Luc.*11.53.

ἐνέψ-ημα, ατος, τό, *a thing boiled* or *infused*, Aret.*CA*1.1. **-ητέον**, *one must boil in, infuse*, ibid.

ἐνεψίημα, ατος, τό, *plaything*, Nic.*Al.*233. [ῑ metri gr.]

ἐνέψω, *boil in* or *among*, Aret.*CA*1.1: pf. Pass., ἐνήψηται ib.6: aor. 1 Pass., ἐνεψηθέντα.. καμάτοισι μελίσσης Nic.*Al.*71.

ἐνέωρα, Adv. *up* (cf. μετέωρος), *Philol.*65.637 (Milet.).

ἐνέωσα, aor. 1 of ἐνωθέω, A.R.4.1243.

ἐνϝοικέω, = ἐνοικέω, *Leg.Gort.*4.34.

ἐνζάω, *live in*, f. l. in Ph.1.65: metaph., ἐν τῇ τινῶν μνήμῃ prob. in *IGRom.*4.146 (Cyzicus, i A. D.).

ἐνζεύγνῡμι, *yoke*, ἐνιζευχθέντες βόες A.R.1.686; *bind fast*, ἄρθρα ποδοῖν S.*OT*718. II. metaph., *involve in*, ἀνάγκαις ταῖσδ' ἐνέζευγμαι A.*Pr.*108; τί ποτέ μ'.. ἐνέζευξας.. ἐν πημοσύναις; ib.578 (lyr.).

ἐνζέω, *boil in*, πήγανον ἐνεζέσθη Aret.*CA*1.2.

ἐνζύμιον, = κώνειον, Ps.-Dsc.4.78.

ἐνζωγρᾰφέω, *paint in* or *on*, Pl.*Phlb.*40a (Pass.), Tz.*H.*12.560.

ἐνζώννῡμι, aor. 1 -έζωσα, *gird*, ἑαυτόν Plu.*Sull.*28:—Med., ἐνεζωσμένοι κῴδια Dicaearch.2.8.

ἔνζῳος, ον, *full of beasts*, ἄλση dub. in Nic.*Fr.*31.2.

ἕνη, v. ἕνος (B). **ἕνη καὶ νέα**, v. ἕνος 2.

ἐνηβ-άω, *spend one's youth in*, Longus 3.13. II. of plants, *flourish in*, νάπαισι δ' ἀνθέρικος ἐνηβᾷ Cratin.325, cf. Nic.*Fr.*85.2. III. intr., ἐνηβώσαις ἵπποις mares *in the prime of youth*, *IG*5(1).213.15, al. (Sparta, v B. C.). **-ητήριον**, τό, *place of amusement*, Hdt.2.133, Ael.*NA*11.10. **-ος**, ον, *in the prime of youth*, from fifteen upwards, Sch.Theoc.8.3.

ἐνήδ-ομαι, Pass., *rejoice in*, τινί Mich.*in EN*532.4, Sch.Il.8.51, Hsch.: abs., Gal.16.566. **-ονος**, ον, *full of joy, delightful*, Sch.E.*Hec.*828; ἐ. ὀφθαλμός *'glad eye'*, Heph.Astr.1.1. **-ύνω**, *cheer, gratify*, τὰς ἀκοάς Ps.-Luc.*Philopatr.*3. **-ῠπᾰθέω**, = ἡδυπαθέω ἐν.., Ph.2.326.

ἐνη-είη, ἡ, *kindness, gentleness*, νῦν τις ἐνηείης Πατροκλῆος.. μνησάσθω Il.17.670, cf. Opp.*H.*5.519. **-ής**, ές, Ep. Adj. *kind, gentle*, ἑταῖρον... ἐνηέα τε κρατερόν τε Il.17.204; ἑτάροιο ἐνηέος ὀστέα λευκά 23.252; ἑταῖρον ἐ., of Athena, Od.8.200; μευ αἰεὶ μέμνησαι ἐνηέος Il.23.648; φιλότητος ἐνηέος Hes.*Th.*651: later in nom. ἐνηής *IG*14.1648.8; etym. of Ἐνυώ, Corn.*ND*21: pl., ἐνηῆες Opp.*C.*2.89; ἐνηέες Id.*H.*2.644; of stars, *propitious*, Max.262, al. (ἐν and -ής, cf. Skt. *ávas* 'help', 'favour', *ávati* 'he helps'.)

ἐνήκοντα, indecl. *ninety*, *IG*11(2).199 *B* 32 (Delos, iii B. C.).

ἐνήκω, *appertain, belong*, *PMasp.*124.10 (vi A. D.).

ἐνηλάσιον [ᾰ], τό, *rent*, *GDI*5661.5, al. (Chios, iv B. C.).

ἐνήλᾰτον, τό, (ἐνελαύνω) *anything driven in*: as Subst. mostly pl., ἐνήλατα (sc. ξύλα), τά, I. *the four rails*, which make the frame *of a bedstead*, ἐ. ξύλα S.*Fr.*315, cf. Ph.1.666 (Att. κραστήρια, acc. to Phryn.155): later in sg., ἐνήλατον, τό, *bedstead*, Sor.2.61; τὸ τῆς κλίνης ἐ. *PSI*6.616.17 (iii A. D.). II. *rungs* of a ladder, which are *fixed in* the poles or sides, κλίμακος ξέστ' ἐνηλάτων βάθρα E.*Ph.*1179; ἄκρα κλιμάκων ἐνήλατα Id.*Supp.*729. III. ἀξόνων ἐνήλατα *the pins driven into the axle, linchpins*, Id.*Hipp.*1235. IV. ἐνήλατον· μέρος νεώς, Hsch.

ἐνηλεγής (-είς cod.)· ἐν ἐπιθυμίᾳ ὤν, Hsch. **ἐνηλεῦσαι**· δογματίσαι, Id. **ἐνηλίαζ**· ἑορτὴ τοῦ Ἐνυαλίου, Id.

ἐνήλῐκος, ον, = sq., *Sammelb.*4638.11 (ii B. C.), *IG*7.2712.70 (Acraeph.), Plu.*Cat.Ma.*24, etc.

ἐνῆλιξ, ῐκος, ὁ, ἡ, *of age, in the prime of manhood*, *OGI*338.21 (Pergam., ii B. C.), Lxx 4 *Ma.*18.9, *POxy.*646 (ii A. D.), etc.

ἐνηλῐόομαι, *to be exposed to the sun*, Aët.8.16; ἐνηλιωμένα *sunlit* objects, Gal.17(2).396.

ἐνηλλαγμένως, Adv. pf. part. Pass. of ἐναλλάσσω, *reversely, in reverse order*, Meno *Iatr.*17.42; *inverting the true order*, Plot.3.7.13. 2. *crosswise*, = ἐναλλάξ, τοῖς ποσὶν ἵστασθαι Procop.Gaz.p.163 B.

ἔνηλος, ον, *clavatus*, *Gloss.*

ἐνηλόω, *nail to*, in Pass., Cels.ap.Orig.*Cels.*6.34,36.

ἐνηλύσιος [ῠ], ον, (ἠλύσιον II) *struck by lightning*: ἐνηλύσια, τά, *places set apart from worldly uses*, because a thunderbolt has fallen there, A.*Fr.*17, cf. *EM*341.5, Hsch.

ἐνήλωσις, εως, ἡ, *ornamental nail*, Callix.1.

ἐνῆμαι, used as pf. of ἐνέζομαι, *to be seated in*, ἵν' ἐνήμεθα πάντες Od.4.272, cf. Theoc.22.44; θάκοις.. ἐνήμενοι E.*Fr.*795.

ἐνημερεύω, *spend the day in*, ἁρπαγαῖς D.S.17.70; μελέταις Id.32.16, cj. in Thphr.*Char.*8.14.

ἐνημμένος, η, ον, pf. part. Pass. from ἐνάπτω.

ἐνήνοθε, only found in compds.: v. ἐπ-, κατ-, παρ-ενήνοθε.

ἐνήνοχα, ἐνήνεγμαι, v. φέρω.

ἐνηρεμέω, = ἠρεμέω ἐν.., Ph.2.140, Hld.1.18.

ἐνήρης, ες, *with a single bank of oars*, ναῦς Plu.*Brut.*28, *Sull.*24, etc.

ἐνηρόσιον, τό, *rent for corn-land*, ἐ. τῶν ἱερῶν χωρίων *Inscr.Délos* 314.168 (iii B. C.): also in pl., ἐνηρόσια, τά, *IG*11(2).142.20, 144 *A* 9, al. (Delos, iv B. C.); cf. ἐναράτιον. II. *right of tillage*, *SIG*1044.18 (Halic., iv/iii B. C.). III. gloss on γαλάσιον, Hsch.

ἐνηρυθμοί, v. ἐνιαυθμός.

ἐνησῠχάζω, = ἡσυχάζω ἐν.., *to be quiet in*, Chio *Ep.*16.7, Ph.2.140.

ἐνήφαιστος, ον, *volcanic*, Tz.*H.*10.502.

ἐνηχ-έω, *to be resonant*, Aret.*SA*1.6: c. dat., *ring in the ears of*, Plu.2.589d; in full, τοῖς ὠσί τισιν Id.*Lib.*4; ἐ. ἀκοαῖς σάλπιγξ Onos.1.13. 2. *teach by voice, word of mouth*, Eustr.*in EN*112.19 (Pass.). **-ημα**, ατος, τό, *a sound in* one's ears, Iamb.*VP*15.65 codd. **-ησις**, εως, ἡ, *musical accompaniment* of a song, *Et.Gud.*576.34. **-ος**, ον, *sounding within*, of wind-instruments, opp. ἔγχορδος, Phillis ap.Ath.14.636c: generally, *sounding, noisy*, ἀναπνοή Herod.Med. in *Rh.Mus.*58.77; ἐ. ὕδατα Philostr.*VA*6.26. II. c. gen., *acquainted, conversant with*, Lxx *Si.prol.*9 (s. v. l.).

ἔνθᾰ, Adv.: I. Demonstr., 1. of Place, *there*, Il.14.216, etc.: also with Verbs of motion, *thither*, 13.23, 14.340, Od.3.297, 6.47, 12.5; ἔ. καὶ ἔ. *hither* and *thither*, 2.213, etc.; διηρέθη τὸ ὕδωρ ἔ. καὶ ἔ. Lxx 4 *Ki.*2.8; also ᾗ ἔ. ᾗ ἔ. Od.10.574: rare in Trag. and Com., A.*Supp.*33 (anap.); ἔ. καὶ Πείσανδρος ἦλθε Ar.*Av.*1556: in Prose in such phrases as ἔ. μὲν.. ἔ. δὲ.. *in one place.. in another..*, Pl.*Smp.*211a; later γενόμενοι ἔ. *POxy.*896.32 (iv A. D.). 2. of Time, *thereupon, then*, Il.5.1, etc.; ἔ. δ' ἔπειτα and *there*upon, Od.7.196, 10.516; ἔ. δή *hereupon, and so*, Hdt.1.59, X.*HG*2.4.39. II. Relat., 1. of Place, *where*, Il.1.610, 9.194, Alc.*Supp.*25.5, etc.; repeated, Hes.*Sc.*334, Theoc.8.45; also ἔνθα τε Il.2.594, 5.305; in later Prose, Ph.2.580, Wilcken *Chr.*41 iii 11 (iii A. D.); ἔνθα περ, v. ἔνθαπερ: c. gen., γαίας ἔ... *in that spot of* earth *in which*.., S.*Aj.*659; ἔ. πημάτων κυρῶ *at what point* of misery I am, E.*Tr.*685, cf. A.R.3.771: with Verbs of motion, *whither*, Od.1.210; ὁδοιποροῦμεν ἔ. χρῄζομεν S.*El.*

1099, cf. *Ph.*1466 (anap.), Th.4.42,75; *to the place where*, S.*OT*796; *at the place whence*.., Id.*El.*436, X.*Oec.*18.1: rarely in indirect questions, Αἴγισθον ἔνθ' ᾤκηκεν ἱστορῶ S.*El.*1101. 2. of Time, *when*, interpol. in X.*An.*5.1.1; ἔστιν ἔ. *sometimes*, S.*El.*1042, cf. X.*Cyr.* 7.4.15; ἔ. τοῦ χρόνου *at which point* of time, Ael.*VH*10.18.

ἐνθάδε [ᾰ], Adv.: I. of Place, *thither, hither*, Od.15.492, S.*Ph.*304, Th.6.36, etc. 2. after Hom. more freq., = ἔνθα, *here* or *there*, ἐνθάδε αὐτοῦ μένων Ar.*V.*765; *in this world*, opp. the nether-world, Pi.*O.*2. 57, Pl.*Grg.*525b; ὁ δ' εὔκολος μὲν ἐνθάδ' εὔκολος δ' ἐκεῖ Ar.*Ra.*82; οἱ ἐ., opp. οἱ κάτω, A.*Supp.*923, S.*Ant.*75; also, the people *of this country*, Id.*OC*42; τοῖς ἐνθάδ' αὐτοῦ ib.78; τις τῶν ἐνθάδ' αὐτοῦ Eup.357; τὰ ἐνθάδε, opp. τὰ ἐκεῖ, Th.6.17. II. of circumstances, *in this case* or *state*, X.*Cyr.*2.4.17; ἐνθάδ' ἥκων having come *to this point*, S. *Ph.*377: c. gen., ἐ. τοῦ πάθους *at this stage* of my suffering, ib. 899. 2. of Time, *here, now*, οὔτ' ἐνθάδ' ὁρῶν οὔτ' ὀπίσω neither *the present* nor the future, Id.*OT*488 (lyr.); αὐτίκ' ἐ. Id.*OC*992.

ἐνθαδί [ῑ], Att. strengthd. for foreg., Ar.*Pl.*54, *Lys.*1010, Eup.2, etc.

ἐνθάδιος [ᾰ], α, ον, = ἐντόπιος, Hsch.: σεῦτλον ἐ. *Gp.*12.1.3.

ἐνθᾰκ-έω, *sit in* or *on*, θρόνοις τοῖσιν πατρῴοις S.*El.*267, cf. *OC* 1293. **–η**, ἡ, = ἐνέδρα, *LW*1471 (Pompeiopolis). **–ησις**, εως, ἡ, *sitting in*, ἡλίου διπλῆ πάρεστιν ἐ. a twofold *seat in* the sun, i.e. both at morn and evening, S.*Ph.*18.

ἐνθαλάμια· πλάσματα ἐκ μήκωνος καὶ σησάμης, Hsch.

ἐνθᾰλασσ-εύω, Att. **–ττεύω**, *live at sea*, Ael.*NA*9.63; *to be at sea*, Longus 2.12; πρὸς ἐναντία πνεύματα νῆες –εύουσαι Ph.1.287. **–ιος**, ον, = sq., νεῶν ποιμαντῆρσιν ἐνθαλασσίοις S.*Fr.*432.10. **–ος**, Att. **–ττος**, ον, *in the sea*, σπιλάδες D.S.3.44; *by the sea*, πόλις Ath.Mech.32.3.

ἔνθαλλος, ον, *sprouting*, κριθή *PAmh.*2.133.4 (ii A.D.).

ἐνθάλλω, pf. part. ἐντεθηλώς, = θάλλω, Hsch., Suid.

ἐνθάλπω, *warm in*, D.S.2.52.

ἐνθαλύξας· σφοδρῶς πατάξας, Hsch.

ἐνθᾰνᾰτόω, *condemn to death*, ψήφῳ Philoch.144.

ἔνθᾰπερ, Adv. *there where, where*, stronger form of ἔνθα, Il.13.524, Hdt.1.14, Th.6.32, X.*Lac.*5.7, al.; *to the place where*, S.*El.*1495, *Ph.* 515 (lyr.).

ἐνθάπτω, *bury in* a place, *CIG*2839.10 (Aphrodisias), al.:—Pass., aor. 2 ἐνετάφην Aeschin.1.99, D.S.1.66, *IG*12(8).114 (Imbros), *CIG* 2824 (Aphrodisias); part. ἐνθαφεὶς (sic) ib.2839.11 (ibid.): fut. 2 ἐνταφήσομαι ib.2826 (ibid.), Ph.2.108, Plu.*Dio*43.

ἐνθαυθοῖ, = ἐνταυθοῖ (q.v.). **ἐνθαῦτα**, v. ἐνταῦθα.

ἐνθεάζω, *to be inspired*, Hdt.1.63, Luc.*DDeor.*18.1:—Med., Id. *Alex.*13, Plu.2.623c, etc.

ἐνθέακτος, gloss on ἐνθρίακτος, Hsch. (fort. –θέαστος).

ἐνθεάομαι, *behold*, *Sammelb.*4127.9.

ἐνθεαστικός, ή, όν, *inspired*, Pl.*Lg.*682a; ψυχαί, μέλη, Procl.*in Prm.*p.742 S., *in Ti.*1.355 D. Adv. –κῶς Luc.*Am.*14, Procl.*in Prm.* p.530 S., Syrian.*in Metaph.*42.14: Sup. –ώτατα Procl.*in R.*1.133 K. II. *neurotic*, ἴλιγγος Ruf.ap.Orib.7.26.177; πνιγμός Mnesith. Cyz.ib.*inc.*15.3; πάθος Praxag.ap. Herod.Med. in *Rh.Mus.*49.549 (–ατικόν codd.).

ἐνθεάτης (leg. –αστής), ου, ὁ, *seer, prophet*, *Gloss.*

ἔνθεμα, ατος, τό, *thing put in, graft*, Thphr.*CP*1.6.8. II. *deposit*, of money in a bank, *CIG*3599.15 (Ilium). III. *ornament*, ἐ. τῶν τραχήλων Lxx *Ca.*4.9. IV. *reservoir*, *POxy.*1830.9, al. (vi A.D.). (Cf. ἔνθημα.)

ἐνθεμᾰτίζω, *engraft*, *Gp.*10.23.4.

ἐνθεμέλιοι θεοί gods *who make foundations secure*, prob. in *Milet.* 1(7).298 (ii A.D.).

ἐνθέμεν, poet. aor. 2 inf. of ἐντίθημι.

ἐνθέμιον, τό, *cabin on the poop of a ship*, Poll.1.90. II. *socket* of a lampstand, Lxx *Ex.*38.16(37.19).

ἔνθεν, Adv.: I. Demonstr., *thence*, 1. of Place, Il.10.179, etc.: also in tracing pedigrees, γένος δέ μοι ἔ. ὅθεν σοί 4.58; ἔ. μὲν .. ἑτέρωθι δὲ.. *on the one side* and on the other, Od.12.235, cf. 59; αἱ μὲν ἐξ ἀριστερᾶς, αἱ δ' ἔ. E.*Hec.*1152; ἔ. καὶ ἔ. *on this side* and *on that*, Hdt.4.175, Th.7.81, Pl.*Prt.*315b, etc.; ἔ. μὲν.., ἔ. δὲ.., *on one side .. on the other*.. X.*An.*3.5.7; ἔ. μὲν.., ἐξ εὐωνύμου δὲ.., Hdt.1. 72; ἔ. μὲν.., ἑτέρωσε δὲ.., Pl.*Sph.*224a: c. gen., ἔ. καὶ ἔ. τῶν τροχῶν *on both sides of*.., X.*Cyr.*6.1.30, cf. *An.*4.3.28. 2. of Time, *thereupon, thereafter*, Il.13.741; τὰ δ' ἔ. *what follows*, A.*Ag.*248 (lyr.); τὸ δ' ἔ. S.*OC*476. 3. of occasion, *thence, from that point*, ἔ. ἑλών [τὴν ἀοιδήν], Lat. *inde exorsus*, Od.8.500, cf. D.L.1.102; *from that cause* or *circumstance*, E.*Tr.*951. II. Relat., for ὅθεν, 1. of Place, *whence*, δέπα ἔ. ἔπινον *from which*.., Od.19.62, cf. 4.220; freq. answering to ἔνθα, ὁ μὲν ἔνθα καθέζετ' ἐπὶ θρόνου ἔ. ἀνέστη Ἑρμείας *from which*.., 5.195, etc.; of origin, τὸ κέρδος ἔ. οἰστέον S.*Ant.*310; ἔ. ἦν γεγώς Id.*OT*1393, cf. 1485; *to the place whence*, ἄξουσιν ἔ. ἔξουσι τὰ ἐπιτήδεια X.*An.*2.3.6; in speaking, ἐπάνειμι ἔ... ἐξέβην Id.*HG*6. 5.1, cf. *Oec.*6.1. 2. of occasion, *whence*, Ἄρει.. ἔ. ἔστ' ἐπώνυμος πέτρα πάγος τ' Ἄρειος A.*Eu.*689, cf. E.*El.*38, etc.

ἐνθενᾰρίζω, (θέναρ) = ἐγχειρέω, Hsch.

ἐνθένδε, Adv. *hence*, Il.8.527, Od.11.69, etc.; *from this quarter*, i.e. *from people here*, S.*OT*125; ἐ. τὰ δίκαια ἀρξόμεθα λαμβάνειν, i.e. *from you*, X.*An.*7.7.17; καλῶς τά γ' ἐ. all 's well *on this side*, E.*Or.* 1278; opp. κάτωθεν, Pl.*Phdr.*229b; ὡς ἐ. ἰδεῖν Id.*Plt.*289d; ἦρξατο ἐ. ποθέν Id.*Euthd.*275d, cf. *Smp.*178a; ἐνθένδ' αὐτόθεν *from this* very *city*, Ar.*Ach.*116: with Verbs of motion, τοὺς ἐ. ἐκεῖσε πορεῦσαι carry those *here*, i.e. *in this world*, thither, Pl.*Phd.*107e, cf. *Ap.*40c; ὁ ἐ. στρατός the army *from this place*, i.e. the Athen. army, E.*Supp.*695; οἱ ἐ. ἑταῖροι X.*Cyr.*2.4.16. 2. of Time or Consequence, *from that time*, Th.2.1; τὸ ἐ. or τοὐνθ. *thereafter*, S.*Ph.*895, E.*IT*91; τοὐνθ. or τἀνθ. *what followed*, the *event*, τοὐνθ. δεινὸν ἦν θέαμ' ἰδεῖν Id.*Med.*1167, cf. S.*OT*1267, *El.*1307. 3. ἐ. *from the following point of view*, Pl. *Tht.*178a; ἐ. ἂν γίγνοιτο γνώριμον Jul.*Or.*4.136c.

ἐνθενδί, Att. strengthd. for foreg., Ar.*Lys.*429.

ἔνθενπερ, *from the point whence*, Arr.*An.*1.2.3.

ἐνθεόομαι, *to be inspired*, Sch.D.T.p.61 H.

ἔνθεος, ον, in later Prose contr. **ἔνθους** Ph.2.542, App.*Hisp.*18, Aen.Gaz.*Thphr.*p.12 B.:—*full of the god, inspired, possessed*, ἔ. γυναῖκες, of the Bacchantes, S.*Ant.*964 (lyr.); ἔ. Ἄρει *possessed* by him, A.*Th.*497; ἐκ Πανός E.*Hipp.*141; ὑπὸ τοῦ ἔρωτος X.*Smp.*1.10: c. gen. rei, τέχνης νιν Ζεὺς ἔνθεον κτίσας φρένα A.*Eu.*17; also ἔ. πρὸς ἀρετήν *inspired with a love for* it, Pl.*Smp.*179a: Sup. –ωτάτη, φύσις, of Homer, Max.Tyr.32.4. II. of divine frenzy, *inspired by the god*, τέχναι A.*Ag.*1209; μαντική Pl.*Phdr.*244b; μαντεῖαι Id.*Ti.*72b; ἔνθεον ἡ ποίησις Arist.*Rh.*1408ᵇ19; ἔ. φιλία Plu.2.752c; τὰ ἔ. *frenzied rites*, prob. in Herod.8.70. Adv. ἐνθέως Men.*Mon.*229, App.*Hisp.*26, Jul.*Or.*7.215b, Iamb.*VP*32.216.

ἐνθερίζω, *spend summer in* a place, Poll.1.62; πόλις ἐνθερίσαι οἵα βελτίστη Dicaearch.1.21.

ἐνθερμαίνω, *heat*, in Pass., ἐντεθέρμανται πόθῳ *is heated by* passion, S.*Tr.*368.

ἔνθερμος, ον, *hot*, φύσις Hp.*Epid.*6.4.13; αἷμα Arist.*Pr.*898ᵃ6; πνεῦμα Zeno *Stoic.*1.38, Antip.ib.3.251; Λιβύη Plu.2.951f. 2. metaph., *passionate*, μειράκιον prob. in *Com.Adesp.*24.10 D.; *hot, fervid*, διάνοια Arist.*Phgn.*806ᵇ26, cf. Ph.1.605, al.

ἐνθεσίδουλος [ῐ], ὁ, = ψωμόδουλος, *Com.Adesp.*999.

ἔνθεσις, εως, ἡ, (ἐντίθημι) *putting in, insertion*, τοῦ νῦ Pl.*Cra.*426c; εἴδους Plot.5.9.3, cf. Porph.*Abst.*4.20; *putting into the mouth*, τῆς τροφῆς Aret.*CA*1.4. II. *that which is put in the mouth, mouthful*, Ar.*Eq.*404 (troch.), Pherecr.108.6, Telecl.1.10, Hermipp.41, etc. 2. *grafting, graft*, Ph.1.301, *Gp.*10.37.1.

ἔνθεσμος, ον, *lawful*, λιτανεία Lxx 3 *Ma.*2.21, cf. Plu.*Nic.*6; βασιλεύς *Peripl.M.Rubr.*23; *authorized*, τράπεζα *BGU*1127.30 (i B.C.); *valid*, συγχωρήσεις *POxy.*271.21 (i A.D.). Adv. –μως, βασιλεύειν Gal.14.216.

ἐνθετ-έον, (ἐντίθημι) *one must insert*, Plot.1.3.1, *Gp.*6.1.4, Antyll. ap.Orib.44.23.42; *one must dip* in water, Archig.ap.Aët.9.6. **–ικός**, ή, όν, *fit for implanting*, τινός Stob.2.7.2. 2. ἡ –κὴ τῶν σιτίων προθυμία the *swallowing* impulse, Orib.*Fr.*74. **–ος**, ον, *capable of being put in*, εἰ.. ἦν ἔ. ἀνδρὶ νόημα Thgn.435; ἐξαίρετα καὶ ἔ. Orib. 49.4.80. 2. *grafted*, τὰ ἔ. τῶν δένδρων Hp.*Nat.Puer.*26.

ἐνθεττᾰλίζομαι, *become a Thessalian*, i.e. *wear the large Thessalian cloak* (Θετταλικὰ πτερά), Eup.201.

ἐνθεῦτεν, Ion. for ἐντεῦθεν, Hdt.

ἐνθεωρέω, *observe in*, in Pass., τὰ –ούμενα τοῖς ἀριθμοῖς Nicom.*Ar.* 1.16, cf. Eust.1722.62; ἔν τινι Eustr.*in EN*281.25.

ἐνθηκάριος, ὁ, *factor, broker*, *Gloss.*

ἐνθήκη, ἡ, *store*, Ph.2.525 (pl.), Sm.*Ge.*41.36, Artem.2.37, *Cod. Just.*9.49.7.1 (pl.), Just.*Nov.*128.8 (pl.). II. *capital*; late word for ἀφορμή, Phryn.199, Arg.D.36. III. *insertion*, λίθων Procop.*Aed.* 2.1. IV. *enclosure*, *BGU*890.11 (ii A.D.).

ἐνθηλῠπᾰθέω, *to be effeminate*, J.*BJ*4.9.10.

ἔνθημα, ατος, τό, = ἔνθεμα II, *IG*12(1).937.11 (Rhodes). II. f.l. for σύνθ., Iamb.*Myst.*1.21 (pl.).

ἔνθηρος, ον, (θήρ) *full of wild beasts, haunted, infested by them*, δρυμός E.*Rh.*289; πάγος S.*Ichn.*216; [ὗλαι] [Arr.]*Peripl.M.Eux.*12. II. metaph., *wild, rough*, τιθέντες ἔ. τρίχα A.*Ag.*562; ἔ. πούς '*angry*', of the ulcerated foot of Philoctetes, S.*Ph.*698 (not = θηρόδηκτος, as Sch.); τὸ ἔ. *savagery*, Ael.*NA*6.63.

ἔνθῑνος, ον, Cret., = θεῖος (in the sense of εὐσεβής), ἔνορκον τε ἔστω καὶ ἔ. *GDI*5039.11 (Hierapytna), cf. 5041.7 (ibid.); cf. θῖνος.

ἔνθῐος, = ἐνθάδιος, prob. in *GDI*3087.33 (Cherson.).

ἔν-θλᾰσις, εως, ἡ, *dint* or *injury caused by pressure*, Ael.*NA*16.22, Gal.7.39. **–θλασμα**, ατος, τό, = foreg., Id.14.81. **–θλάω**, Ion. **ἐμφλάω**, *indent by pressure*, Hp.*Int.*44, Aristid.*Or.*47(23).13; *impress* (on coin), σημεῖον Ael.*NA*6.15.

ἐν-θλίβω [ῑ], *press in*, Nic.*Al.*454, Aret.*SA*1.9, Gal.*UP*5.15, S.E. *P.*3.68:—Pass., Arist.*HA*599ᵇ20, *Pr.*927ᵃ25; ἄνθρωποι ἐντεθλιμμένοι τὴν ῥῖνα *Peripl.M.Rubr.*62. **–θλιπτικός**, ή, όν, *pressing*. Adv. –κῶς *by pressure*, S.E.*P.*3.69. **–θλιψις**, εως, ἡ, *pressing in*, Archig.ap.Gal.8.110, Aret.*SA*1.6, etc.; *pressure*, Apollon.Cit.2.

ἐνθνήσκω, *die in*, χθονὸς.. τοσοῦτον, [ὥστε] ἐνθανεῖν μόνον S.*OC* 790, cf. E.*Rh.*869; σῇ χερί Id.*Heracl.*560. 2. of the hand, *grow rigid* or *torpid in*, τινί Id.*Hec.*246.—Dub. in Prose, Lys.16.15 (ἐναπο– Markland), Plu.2.357d (ἐκθ– Reiske).

ἐνθολή· ἰσόρροπον, Hsch. (Fort. ἀνθολκή.) **ἐνθοργάζει**· πονεῖ, Id. **ἐνθορίσκει**· ἐνθρύπτει, Id.

ἔνθορος, ον, (ἐνθορεῖν) *impregnated*, of animals, v.l. in Nic.*Th.*99.

ἐνθορῠβέω, *disturb*, Tz.*H.*13.494 (Pass.).

ἔνθους, ουν, contr. for ἔνθεος (q.v.).

ἐνθουσί-α, ἡ, = ἐνθουσιασμός, Procl.*in Alc.*p.198 C., Hsch., Zonar. **–άζω**, in Trag. always **ἐνθουσιάω** (also in Ph., 1.148, al.); in Pl. both forms occur (v. infr.):—*to be inspired* or *possessed by a god, to be in ecstasy*, ἐνθουσιᾷ δὴ δῶμα A.*Fr.*58; ὥσπερ ἐνθουσιῶν X.*Cyr.*1.4.8; ἡ ψυχὴ.. ἐνθουσιάζουσα Pl.*Ion* 535c, cf. 536b; ἐνθουσιάζοντες Id.*Ap.* 22c; ἐνθουσιῶντες Id.*Phdr.*253a; ἐνθουσιάσας Id.*Tht.*180c; ὑπὸ τῶν

Νυμφῶν.. ἐνθουσιάσω Id.*Phdr.*241e; ὑφ' ἡδονῆς ἐνθουσιᾷ Id.*Phlb.*15e; ἐνθουσιάσαι ποιεῖν τοὺς ἀκροατάς Arist.*Rh.*1408^{b}14: c. dat., ἐνθουσιᾷς τοῖς σαυτοῦ κακοῖς E.*Tr.*1284; ταῖς φωναῖς -άζοντες Phld.*Lib.*p.4 O.; περὶ φιλοσοφίαν Plu.*Cat.Ma.*22; εἴς τι Ael.*NA*4.31; πρὸς τὴν ἀλήθειαν Jul.*Or.*4.136b. II. c. acc., *inspire*, ἔρωτας ἐνεθουσίασε θεοῖς Herm.ap.Stob.1.49.44 codd. **-ασις**, εως, ἡ, = sq., Pl.*Phdr.*249e (pl.), Ph.2.344 (pl.), Iamb.*Myst.*3.6. **-ασμός**, ὁ, *inspiration, enthusiasm, frenzy*, Democr.18, Pl.*Ti.*71e, Ph.1.535 (pl.), S.E.*M.*9.20 (pl.); ἄλογος ἐ. Phld.*Ir.*p.67 W.; produced by certain kinds of music, Arist.*Pol.*1340^{a}11, 1342^{a}7. **-αστής**, οῦ, ὁ, *person inspired, possessed*, Ptol.*Tetr.*180, Eust.47 fin. **-αστικός**, ή, όν, *inspired*, φύσις Pl.*Ti.*71e; esp. by music, Arist.*Pol.*1340^{a}11; ἡ ἐ. σοφία *divination*, Plu.*Sol.*12; ἐ. ἔκστασις Iamb.*Myst.*3.8; τὸ ἐ. *excitement*, Pl.*Phdr.* 263d: Sup. -ώτατος Sch.Iamb.*Protr.*p.129 P. Adv. -κῶς, διατιθέναι τινά Plu.2.433c: Comp. -ώτερον Marin.*Procl.*6. II. Act., *inspiring, exciting*, of certain kinds of music, Arist.*Pol.*1341^{b}34; νοσήματα μανικὰ καὶ ἐ. Id.*Pr.*954^{a}36: Comp. -ώτερα, ἀκούσματα Pl.*Ep.* 314a. **-άω**, v. ἐνθουσιάζω. **-ώδης**, ες, *ecstatic*, ὁρμαί D.H. *Comp.*1, cf. Plu.*Lyc.*21; φοραί Id.*Pyrrh.*22, etc.; τὸ ἐ. Ph.1.689. Adv. -δῶς Hp.*Ep.*17, Sch.Il.*Oxy.*1086.41.

ἐνθραδές· ἐμμανές, Hsch.

ἐνθράσσω, *prick*, τὰ ὀστέα τὰ κατεηγότα ἐ. τὸν χρῶτα Hp.*Art.*46 (= ἐγκείμενον νύττει, Gal.19.98); = ὑποκινεῖν, ταράττειν, Tim.*Lex.* post ἕδος.

ἐνθρεῖν· φυλάσσειν, Hsch.

ἐνθρην-έω, = θρηνέω ἐν.., Aristid.*Or.*18(20).9. **-ος**, ον, *mournful*, ἀνθυπήχησις Schubart *Papyruskunde* p.42.

ἔνθρι-α· ζῴδια, Hsch. **-άζειν**· παρακινεῖν, ἀπὸ τῶν μαντικῶν θριῶν, Id. **-ακτος** [ῐ], ον, (θριάζω) *inspired*, S.*Fr.*544.

ἐνθρίζειν· ἐνατενίζειν, νύσσειν, and **ἐνέθριξε**· προσωρμίσθη, Hsch.

ἐνθριμματίς, a spelling of ἐνθρυμματίς, Id.

ἐνθρῑόω, (θρῖον) *wrap in a fig-leaf*: *muffle up*, in pf. Pass., ἐντεθριῶσθαι Ar.*Lys.*664. II. metaph., *deceive, cozen*, Men.*Sam.*241; cf. ἐντεθρίωκεν· ἐνείληκεν, ἐσκεύακεν, Hsch.

ἐνθρίτης, = ἐνθρύπτης, and ἐνθρίτας· *intritas*, *Gloss.*

ἐνθρομβ-όομαι, *become clotted*, of blood, Aspasia ap.Aët.16.72; *become full of clotted blood*, Gal.8.409. **-ωσις**, εως, ἡ, = θρόμβωσις, Antyll.ap.Orib.7.11.2.

ἐνθρον-ιαστικά, τά, *fees* paid by bishops *on enthronization*, Just. *Nov.*123.3. **-ίζω**, *place on a throne*, metaph., τὸν ἡγεμόνα νοῦν Lxx 4 *Ma.*2.22:—in lit. sense only Pass., ib.*Es.*1.2; τοῖς βασιλείοις D.S.33.13. **-ισμα**, ατος, τό, *consecrated seat*, θεῶν *OGI*383.46 (Nemrud Dagh). **-ιος**, ον, *enthroned*, Poll.10.52. **-ισμός**, ὁ, *enthroning*, title of προσόδια by Pindar, Suid.

ἐνθρύβω, = ἐνθρύπτω, Harp. s. v. ἔνθρυπτα.

ἐνθρυμμᾰτίς, ίδος, ἡ, *sop*, Anaxandr.41.42 (anap.).

ἔνθρῠος, ον, *reedy*, *CPHerm.*7 ii 16, *PRyl.*207 *a* 7.

ἐνθρύπ-της, = *intritio* (fort. *intritor*), *Gloss.* **-τος**, ον, *crumbled and put into liquid*: τὰ ἔ. *sops* or perh. a kind of cake, D.18.260, cf. *SIG*1016.4 (Iasos), Poll.6.77, Hsch. s. v. ἀττανίδες, *AB*250. II. Ἔνθρυπτος, title of Apollo at Athens, Hsch. **-τω**, poet. ἐνιθρ-, *crumble into liquid, make sop*, ἄρτος ἐν οἴνῳ ἐντεθρυμμένος Hp.*Salubr.*7, cf. Lxx, Thd.*Bel*33; κεδρίδας ἐς ὄλπην Nic.*Th.*81; βάρος οἴνης ib.655: —Med., ἕλικας νύμφαις Id.*Al.*266:—Pass., Lynceus ap.Ath.3.109e.

ἔνθρυσκον, τό, = ἄνθρυσκον (q. v.).

ἐνθρῴσκω, aor. 2 ἐνέθορον, Ep. ἔνθορον:—*leap in, on*, or *among*, c. dat., ἔνθορε μέσσῳ [ποταμῷ] Il.21.233; ἔνθορ' ὁμίλῳ 15.623; ὡς δὲ λέων ἐν βουσὶ θορών 5.161, cf. 20.381; ὄρει πῦρ ἐνθορόν Pi.*P.*3.37; ἐνθρῴσκει τάφῳ E.*El.*327; λὰξ ἔνθορεν ἰσχίῳ *kicked* him on the hip, Od.17.233; λὰξ ἐ. τινί D.C.74.14: metaph., κόσμοις Orac.Chald.ap.Dam.*Pr.*182.

ἐνθυίων· ἐρωτικόν, Hsch. **ἐνθυλήματα**, cj. for ἐναυλήματα (q. v.).

ἐνθῡμ-άζω· ἐμπίπτω, καὶ ἐνορμῶ, Hsch. **-έομαι**, fut. -ήσομαι Lys.12.45, later -ηθήσομαι Philostr.*VS*2.26.3, Epict.*Ench.*21, etc.: aor. ἐνεθυμήθην Ar.*Ra.*40, Th.2.62, Lys.31.27, etc.: pf. ἐντεθύμημαι Th.1.120: plpf. ἐνετεθύμητο Lys.12.70:—*lay to heart, ponder*, ἤτοι κρίνομέν γε ἢ ἐνθυμούμεθα ὀρθῶς τὰ πράγματα Th.2.40; ἄξιον ἐνθυμηθῆναι Antipho 6.20; πρὸς ἐμαυτόν And.1.50; ἐ. καὶ λογίζεσθαι freq. joined in D., as 1.21, al. b. c. gen., ἐνθυμεῖσθαί τινος *think much* or *deeply of*, τοῦ θανόντος Semon.2; τούτων οὐδὲν ἐ. Hermipp.41; τῶν λεγομένων Antipho 5.6; ὧν ἐνθυμηθέντες Th.1.42, cf. Pl.*Mx.*249c, X.*Mem.*1.1.17; τῶν προγόνων ἐ. ὅτι... Lys.16.20; also περί τινος Pl.*R.*595a. c. folld. by a relat., ἐ. ὅτι.. *notice* or *consider* that .., Ar.*Nu.*820, Th.5.111, etc.; ὡς.. how.., Ar.*Ra.*40, X.*Mem.*4. 3.3, etc.; εἰ.. Isoc.15.60; μή... Pl.*Euthd.*279c, *Hp.Ma.*300d. d. c. part., οὐκ ἐντεθύμηται ἐπαιρόμενος *is* not *conscious* that he is becoming excited, Th.1.120, cf. 6.78, X.*HG*4.4.19. 2. *take to heart, be concerned* or *angry at*, τι A.*Eu.*222; ξυμφοράν Th.7.18, cf. 5.32 (v. ἐνθυμίζομαι); εἰ μηδεὶς ὑμῶν μήτ' ἐνθυμεῖται μήτ' ὀργίζεται D. 4.43: abs., *to be concerned*, Hp.*Aër.*22; = ἐνθύμιον ποιεῖσθαι, D.C. 57.4. 3. *form a plan*, κράτιστος ἐνθυμηθῆναι Th.8.68, cf. 2.60; *take care, see to it*, ἐ. ἵνα μηθεὶς ἀδικῇ *PSI*4.436.9 (iii B.C.). 4. *infer, conclude*, τί οὖν ἐκ τούτων.. ἐνθυμεῖσθαι δεῖ; D.21.54. II. Act., ἐνθυμέω Epich.99.4, Aen.Tact.37.6 (s. v. l.); ἐνθυμέομαι, in pass. sense, *to be in a person's thoughts, to be desired*, κρατεῖν τῶν ἐνθυμουμένων App.*BC*5.133: pf. (cf. 1.3), ταυτὶ μὲν ἡμῖν ἐντεθύμηται καλῶς Ar.*Ec.*262; εὖ ἐντεθυμημένον Pl.*Cra.*404a (nisi leg. φιλοσόφου.. καὶ εὖ ἐντεθυμημένου). **-ημα**, ατος, τό, *thought, piece of reasoning, argument*, S.*OC*292,1199, Isoc.9.10 (pl.), Aeschin.2.110. 2. *meaning, sense*, opp. λέξις, Olymp.*in Mete.*4.23. 3. in Aristotle's Logic, *enthymeme, rhetorical syllogism drawn from probable premises* (ἐξ εἰκότων ἢ σημείων), opp. ἀποδεικτικὸς συλλογισμός, *APr.*70^{a}10, cf. *Rh.* 1355^{a}6, etc.; ἐ. δεικτικά, ἐλεγκτικά, ib.1396^{b}24. II. *invention, device*, X.*HG*4.5.4, 5.4.52, *An.*3.5.12, *Cyn.*13.13 (pl.), Men.*Epit.* 295. **-ημᾰτικός**, ή, όν, *determined, resolute*, πρός τι Hp.*Decent.* 3. 2. *skilled in the use of enthymemes*, Arist.*Rh.*1354^{b}22. II. *consisting of* or *in the form of enthymemes*, ῥητορεῖαι ib.1356^{b}21; θόρυβοι Epicur.*Nat.*14.9: Comp. -ώτερον, [σχῆμα] Corn.*Rh.*p.397 H. Adv. -κῶς Arist.*Rh.*1418^{b}36, Theon *Prog.*5, etc. **-ημᾰτίζομαι**, *form an enthymeme*, Steph. *in Rh.*265.29. **-ημάτιον**, τό, Dim. of ἐνθύμημα, v. l. in Gell.7(6).13.4. **-ημᾰτώδης**, ες, *enthymematic*, Arist. *Rh.Al.*1439^{a}5. **-ησις**, εως, ἡ, *consideration, esteem*, E.*Fr.*246. II. *consideration, reflection*, Th.1.132, *Ev.Matt.*9.4 (pl.), Sm.*Jb.*21.27, Vett.Val.301.8, etc. 2. *idea, conception*, εἰς ἐ. ἐσθήτων ἦλθον Diog. Oen.10; τὰς ἐ. ὀξύς Luc.*Salt.*81. III. *anxiety, worry*, Hp.*Praec.* 4. IV. *resolution*, *BGU*1024 iv 12 (iv A.D.). **-ητέον**, *one must reflect*, νυκτός Epich.270; τόδε, ὅτι.. And.1.7; ἐ. [ὑμῖν].. παρ' ἄλλων ἀκούουσι D.4.3. **-ία**, ἡ, *cause of misgiving*, ἐς ἐνθυμίαν τινὶ προβάλλεσθαι Th.5.16. **-ιάζομαι**, = sq., Nic.Dam.*Fr.*130.30 J., *EM* 341.22 (*Et.Gen.*):—Act., ἐνεθυμίαζον Hsch. **-ίζομαι**, later form of ἐνθυμέομαι, D.C.*Fr.*57.80b, Poll.2.231 (citing Th.5.32), Hsch. II. = ἐπιθυμέω, τι App.*Mith.*120.—Act. **-ίζω** only in Hsch. **-ιος**, ον, (θυμός) *taken to heart, weighing upon the mind*, μὴ δή τοι κεῖνός γε λίην ἐνθύμιος ἔστω let him not lie too *heavy on* thy *soul*, take not too *much thought for* him, Od.13.421; ἐνθύμιόν οἱ ἐγένετο ἐμπρήσαντι τὸ ἱρόν he had *pricks of conscience* for having done it, Hdt.8.54; ἐνθύμιόν τί τινι προσθεῖναι Antipho 3.1.2; τί δ' ἐστί σοι τοῦτ'.. ἐ.; what is't *that weighs upon* thy *heart?* S.*OT*739; ἐπειδή σοι τόδ' ἐστ' ἐ. if this matter causes thee *any scruple*, E.*HF*722; ἐ. γίγνεταί τινί τις Antipho 2.3.10, cf. App.*BC*5.133; ἐνθύμιον ποιεῖσθαί τι, = ἐνθυμεῖσθαι, to take *to heart*, to have a *scruple about* it, Th.7.50; ἐ. ποιεῖσθαί τινος D.C.58.6; ἐ. τιθέναι τί τινι to make him have *scruples about* it, E.*Ion*1347; ἐ. ἔχειν ὡς, c. part., *Inscr.Cos*319.10; ἐ. ὑπολείπεσθαί τι Antipho 3.4.9; ἐ. εὐναί a couch *full of care*, S.*Tr.*110 (lyr.); ἐνθύμιον ἔστω Δάματρος, formula in a curse, *GDI*3541.7 (Cnidos): ἐνθύμιον, τό, *wrath*, Lxx *Ps.* 75(76).10. II. ἐνθύμια, τά, *meaning*, Ph.2.484; *ideas*, Iamb.*VP*5. 20; ἐνθύμιον ποιεῖσθαι *reflect*, c. acc. et inf., Alciphr.3.10; λαμβάνω τὸ ἐ. I take the *hint*, Ach.Tat.2.7. **-ιστός**, ή, όν, *taken to heart*, ἐ. ποιεῖσθαι make *a scruple of* a thing, Hdt.2.175 (nisi leg. -ητόν). **-ος**, ον, *spirited*, Arist.*Pol.*1327^{b}30.

ἐνθύριον· μέρος τι τῆς νεώς, Hsch.

ἐνθῡσιάζω, *sacrifice in..*, Lxx *Si.*34(31).7.

ἐνθύσκει· ἐντυγχάνει, Hsch. **ἐνθύσκος**· ὁ ἀσφαλός, τὸ ὄρνεον, Id. **ἐνθύω**, = θύω, τῇ Ἀρτέμιδι χοῖρον *IG*11.153.11. **ἔνθω, ἔνθοι, ἐνθών**, Dor. for ἔλθω, etc.; v. ἔρχομαι. **ἐνθωκεῦσαι**· ἐμφωλεῦσαι, ἐγκρύπτεσθαι, Hsch.

ἐνθωρᾱκίζω, *arm*: pf. part. Pass. ἐντεθωρακισμένος *mailed*, X.*An.* 7.4.16.

ἐνί, poet. for ἐν, both Ep. and Att., also in Ion. prose.

ἑνί, dat. from εἷς.

ἔνι, for ἔνεστι, ἔνεισι, ἐνέσται; v. ἔνειμι.

ἑνιαῖος, α, ον, (ἕν) *single, unitary*, λόγος Aristid.Quint.1.3; αἰτία Iamb.*Myst.*8.3; οὐσία ἑ. καὶ ἀμέριστος Procl. *in Prm.*p.564 S., etc.: pl., ἑνιαῖα *individual elements*, Iamb. *in Nic.*p.81 P.; *concerned with unity*, γνῶσις Dam.*Pr.*25 bis. Adv. -αίως Ptol.*Tetr.*1, Iamb.*Comm. Math.*10, Procl. *in Prm.*p.589 S., Dam.*Pr.*1, etc.

ἑνιάκις, *sometimes*, Sor.*Fract.*2.

ἐνιαυθμός, ὁ, (ἐνιαύω) *abode*, *EM*342.35, prob. in Call.*Fr.*127 (ἐνηρυθμοί [-μοῖ] codd. Stob.). [ῐ metri gr.]

ἐνῐ-αυσιαῖος, α, ον, = sq. III, Arist.*Cat.*5^{b}5, D.S.11.69 (s. v. l.); κύκλος Jul.*Or.*4.155b; χρόνος *PMasp.*159.20 (vi A.D.); ζῴδιον, = ἐνιαυτοῦ κύριον, Balbillus in *Cat.Cod.Astr.*8(4).240. II. = sq. I, ἄρνες J. *AJ*3.10.1; ἄμπελοι *Gp.*3.2.1. III. = sq. II, J.*BJ*2.16.4, *Gp.*2.44. 2. **-αύσιος**, α, ον, Hdt.4.180, E.*Hipp.*37, X.*Ages.*2.1, *SIG*167 (Mylasa, iv B.C.), etc.; also ος, ον Th.4.117, 5.1, Arist.*Mu.*400^{b}21 (v. l.): (ἐνιαυτός):—*of a year, one year old*, σῦς Od.16.454, cf. D.27. 63, etc.; τίκτει ἡ θήλεια [ὗς] ἐ. Arist.*HA*545^{a}29. II. *annual*, Hom.*Epigr.*15.11; ὁρτή Hdt.4.180, etc.; τῇ τρίτῃ ἐπὶ τοῖς ἐνιαυσίοις *IG*12(5).593 *B*5 (Ceos, v B.C.): neut. pl. as Adv., Hes.*Op.*449. Regul. Adv. -ίως Sch.Arat.462, *PLond.*1.113(4).11 (vi A.D.). III. *lasting a year*, Hp.*Aph.*6.45; ἐ. φυγή *a year's* exile, E.*Hipp.*37; χρόνος Id.*Hel.*775 (dub.); ἐκεχειρία Th.4.117, 5.15; ὁδὸς X. l. c.; κἀνιαύσιος βεβὼς gone, absent *for a year*, S.*Tr.*165. **-αυτίζομαι**, *spend a year*, Pl.Com.113: late in Act., Sch.E.*Or.*1645, Suid. **-αύτιος**, α, ον, = ἐνιαύσιος, *IG*2^2.1126.44 (Amphict. Delph.), *SIG*1025.37 (Cos). **-αυτοκράτωρ** [ρᾰ], ορος, ὁ, zodiacal sign *presiding over the year according to the Chaldean dodekaeteris*, Serapio in *Cat.Cod. Astr.*8(4).231. **-αυτός**, ὁ, (ἐνί, αὐτός) prop. *anniversary*, μηδὲ τᾷ ὑστεραίᾳ μηδ' ἐν ταῖς δεκάταις μηδ' ἐν τοῖς ἐνιαυτοῖς *Michel*995 *C*49 (pl., Delph.): hence πρὸ τῶ ἐ. before the *lapse of a year*, *Leg.Gort.*9.29; ἐνιαυτῷ *on the expiry of a year*, ib.1.35; and so, *any long period of time, cycle, period*, ἔτος ἦλθε περιπλομένων ἐνιαυτῶν as *times* rolled on the year came, Od.1.16; ἐπιπλομένων ἐ. Hes.*Th.*493, *Sc.*87; χρονίους ἐτῶν παλαιῶν ἐνιαυτοὺς Ar.*Ra.*347; πόλιν ἐνιαυτόν τινα ἔδοσαν ἐνοικεῖν Th.3.68; ὁ μέγας ἐ., of a Pythagorean *cycle*, Eudem.ap.Theon.Sm. p.198 H.; also of *the Metonic Cycle* of nineteen years, D.S.12.36; of a period of 600 years, J.*AJ*1.3.9:—ἀΐδιος ἐ. Apollod.3.4.2. 2. = ἔτος, *a year*, εἴνατος ἐστι περιτροπέων ἐ. Il.2.295; δεκάτους περιτελλομένους ἐ. 8.404; Διὸς ἐνιαυτοί 2.134; μῆνές τε καὶ ἐνιαυτῶν περίοδοι

Pl.*Ti.*47a; ἐ. ἡμερῶν Lxx*Le.*25.29; ἐνιαυτόν *during a year*, Od.1.288; αἱ σπονδαὶ ἐνιαυτὸν ἔσονται Indut.ap.Th.4.118; ἐπεί κε ὠνίαυτος ἐξέλθῃ *IG*12(2).1.12 (Mytil., iv B.C.); τὸν πρῶτον ἐ. Lys.32.8; ὁπηνίκα..τοὐνιαυτοῦ at what time *in the year*, Ar.*Fr.*569.7; δὶς τοῦ ἐ. twice *a year*, Pl.*Criti.*118e; τοῦ ἐ. *every year*, X.*Vect.*4.23; ἑκάστου ἐ. Id.*Ath.*3.4; but ἕκαστον τὸν ἐ. *IG*2.1055.4: with Preps., δι' ἐνιαυτοῦ Antipho *Fr.*28; δι' ἐ. πέμπτου *every* five *years*, Pl.*Criti.*119d; θητεύσαμεν εἰς ἐ. for *a year*, Il.21.444; τελεσφόρον εἰς ἐ. 19.32; κατ' ἐνιαυτὸν ἄρξαι for *a year*, Th.1.93; or, *every year*, Isoc.3.17, Diph.38.5; καθ' ἕκαστον ἐ. Id.89; ἐπ' ἐ. for *a year*, Pl.*Lg.*945b, etc.; μετὰ τὸν ἐ. at the end of *the year*, Th.1.138; παρ' ἐνιαυτὸν ἄρχειν in alternate *years*, D.S.4.65; πρὸ ἐνιαυτοῦ *a year* before, Plu.2.147e; ἐς τὸν σᾶτες ἐ. for the current *year*, *IG*14.256 (Phintias); ἐν τῷ καθ' ἔτος ἐ. in the current *year*, *CIG*3641*b* 5 (Lampsacus). 3. Ἐνιαυτός, personified, Ael.*Fr.*19, Orph.*Fr.*127.3 (s. v. l.), Procl. *in Ti.*3.41 D. II. name for a *Cornucopiae*, Callix.2, cf. Ath.11.783c.

ἐνῐαυτο-φᾰνής, ές, *yearly seen*, Ptol.*Phas.*p.9 H. **-φορέω**, *bear fruit a year* before it ripens, Thphr.*HP*3.4.1.

ἐνῐαύω, *sleep among*, [ταῖς ὑσί] Od.15.557, cf. 9.187; *sleep in*, [φάρεσι] Bion 1.72.

ἐνῐάχ-ῆ, Adv., (ἔνιοι) *in some places*, c. gen., τοῦ Λιβυκοῦ χωρίου Hdt.2.19; τῆς Κύπρου Id.1.199. II. *sometimes*, Plu.2.427f, Ath.11.478b. **-οῦ**, Adv., (ἔνιοι) *in some places*, Arist.*HA*545ᵃ32, D.H.*Rh.*5.7, etc.; *in some cases*, Pl.*Phd.*71b, Jul.*Gal.*152d; *sometimes*, *BGU*747ii9 (ii A.D.).

ἐνιβάλλω, ἐνιβλάπτω, poet. for ἐμβ-.

ἔνιγμα, ατος, τό, (ἐνίσσω) *rebuke*, *Et.Gud.*

ἐνίγυιος [ῐ], ον, *joined in one body*, Ibyc.16.3. II. *lame of one foot*, Suid. (ἐνίγυος codd.).

ἐνῐδεῖν, v. ἐνεῖδον.

ἐνιδρόω, *sweat in*, *labour hard in*, X.*Smp.*2.18.

ἐνίδρ-ῡσις, εως, ἡ, *settling*, *establishment*, ἐν τοῖς αἰτίοις Herm.*in Phdr.*p.145 A. **-ύω**, *set in* a place, Plu.2.745c; *establish in*, ἕνωσις τὸ πᾶν κῦρος ἐνιδρύουσα τοῖς θεοῖς Iamb.*Myst.*5.26:—Med., *found*, *establish*, ἐνιδρύσασθαι πόλιας, βωμοὺς καὶ τεμένεα, Hdt.1.94, 2.178:—Pass., *to be established in*, ἐν.. Id.4.53: c. dat. loci, Συρακούσσαις Theoc.*Epigr.*18.5, cf. 17.102, *AP*10.9; κόρσῃ (v.l. κόρσην)..ἐνιδρυθεῖσα ἀλώπηξ Call.*Dian.*79; ταῖς ψυχαῖς, τοῖς θεοῖς, Iamb.*Myst.*1.5, 15; *frequent*, ταῖς ὁμιλίαις αὐτῆς Σειρῆνες ἐνίδρυντο Alciphr.1.38: abs., prob. cj. in E.*Hipp.*33. II. Act. intr., *settle in*, Plot.1.3.4; ταῖς μακάρων ἐνιδρῦσαι νήσοις Hierocl. *in CA*27p.483 M.

ἐνιζάνω, *sit* or *settle in* or *on*, αἰθούσῃσιν Il.20.11; of food, τοῖς ὀδοῦσιν Alciphr.1.22, cf. Lib.*Or.*60.11: metaph. of ψυχή and its object, Plot.4.6.3.

ἐνιζεύγνῡμι or **-ύω**, poet. for ἐνζ-.

ἐνίζ-ησις, εως, ἡ, *sitting in*, ἔς τι Aret.*CA*1.4. **-ω**, *to set in*, Ep. aor. 1 Med. ἐνεείσατο he *placed upon*, πρύμνῃ κούρην A.R.4.188. II. intr., = ἐνιζάνω, pf. ἐνίζηκα, *sit in* or *on*, c. acc., θάκους ἐνίζουσαν E.*Hel.*1108 (lyr.), prob. in A.*Ch.*801 (lyr.): c. dat., σώματι καὶ ψυχῇ..ἐνίζει Ἔρως Pl.*Smp.*196b; νεῦρα τοῖς μυσὶν -ηκότα Gal.2.691; ἡ -ηκυῖα τοῖς μορίοις ποιότης τοῦ φαρμάκου Id.11.354:—Med., ἐς ἕψημα τῶν βοτανῶν Aret.*CA*2.8.

ἐνίζω, *to be a partisan of the One*, i.e. *teach a monistic doctrine*, Arist.*Metaph.*986ᵇ21, Procl. *in Prm.*p.597 S. II. *treat as a unity*, τι τῇ διανοίᾳ Plot.6.9.6:—Pass., ὡς μονὰς καὶ σημεῖον -ίζεται ibid. III. *unite*, ἑαυτὸν τῷ ἐραστῷ Procl. *in Alc.*p.33 C.; *unify*, τὰς ἐμφύτους ἐννοίας Porph.*Marc.*10; τὰ ὄντα Procl.*Inst.*13:—Pass., Porph.*Sent.*11; πλῆθος -ιζόμενον *reduced to unity*, ib.36; τὸ -ιζόμενον, opp. τὸ ἑνίζον, Dam.*Pr.*13. IV. Med., *concentrate*, Hero *Deff.*136.25.

ἐνῆλαι· κωλῦσαι, Hsch.; cf. εἴλω. **ἐνιηλίζειν**· τὴν Ἐνυάλιον ἑορτὴν ἄγειν, Id. **ἐνίηλος**· ἀνόητος, Id.

ἐνίημι, fut. -ήσω Th.4.115: aor. -ῆκα, Ep. -έηκα: [mostly ἐνῑημι in Ep., always ἐνῑημι in Trag.; but ἐνῐετε Il.12.441]:—*send in* or *into*, ἄλλους δ' ὀτρύνοντες ἐνήσομεν *will send into the battle*, ib.14.131; ἄλλην ἐνίησι πατὴρ ἐναρίθμιον εἶναι Od.12.65. 2. *implant*, *inspire*, c. acc. rei et dat. pers., ἐνῆκε δέ οἱ μένος ἠΰ Il.20.80; καί οἱ μυίης θάρσος ἐνὶ στήθεσσιν ἐνῆκε 17.570; τοῖσιν κότον αἰνὸν ἐνήσεις 16.449; ἐνεὶς ἐλαφρὰν λύσσαν E.*Ba.*851; ἐ. τισὶ δαπάνην *involve* them *in* expense, *PAmh.*2.133.9 (ii A.D.):—Pass., κίνησις παρ' ἄλλου ἐνιεμένη *introduced from* without, Plot.6.3.23. 3. reversely, c. acc. pers. et dat. rei, *plunge into*, τὸν..Ζεὺς ἐνέηκε πόνοισι Il.10.89; νῦν μιν μᾶλλον ἀγηνορίῃσιν ἐνῆκας *plunged* him *in*, *inspired* him *with* pride of soul, 9.700; so ἥδε δ' ὁδὸς καὶ μᾶλλον ὁμοφροσύνῃσιν ἐνήσει (sc. ἡμᾶς) *shall bring us* yet more *to* harmony, Od.15.198. 4. generally, *throw in*, ἐπεί ῥ' ἐνέηκε (sc. φάρμακον οἴνῳ) ib.4.233; τάμισον [τυρῷ] Theoc.11.66; νηυσὶν ἐνίετε θεσπιδαὲς πῦρ Il.12.441, cf. E.*Tr.*1262 (so in Pass., πῦρ ἐνίετο ταῖς ἀσπίσιν Jul.*Or.*1.27d); also ἐς τὰς πόλις ἐ. πῦρ Hdt.8.32, cf. Th.4.115; of ships, *launch* them *into* the deep, ἐνήσομεν εὐρέϊ πόντῳ (sc. νῆα) Od.2.295, 12.293. 5. *send into* the assembly, *employ*, ἄλλους ῥήτορας Th.6.29; ἐ. διαβολάς Plb.28.4.10. 6. *inject* poison, of spiders, X.*Mem.*1.3.12; ἰὸν ἐ. τινί A.R.4.1508; also of clysters, Nic.*Al.*197, Aret.*CA*1.6, Dsc.1.30, etc. b. *infuse*, in Pass., ἐνήσθω ἐν αὐτέῳ ἄνηθον Aret.*CA*1.1; κάνναβις ἐνεσμένη (ἐνεεσμένη Geronthr.) ἐς χόλῃ *soaked* (?), *Edict.Diocl.*32.17. 7. *urge on*, *incite*, πόθος μ' ἐνέηκε v.l. for ἀν- in Mosch.2.157. 8. Med., of trumpets, *begin to sound*, D.S.17.106. II. intr., *press on*, X.*Cyr.*7.1.29, *HG*2.4.32:—Med., *plunge into*, ὑδάτεσσι Arat.943.

ἐνιθνήσκω, ἐνιθρύπτω, Ep. for ἐνθ-.

ἐνῑθύνω, *direct by*, [δόγμασι] οἴακα βιοτῆς *App.Anth.*4.48.2.

ἐνι-κάββαλε, -κάππεσε, Ep. aor. 2 of ἐγκαταβάλλω, -πίπτω. **-κάτθανε**, Ep. 3 sg. aor. 2 of ἐγκαταθνῄσκω. **-κάτθεο, -κάτθετο**, Ep. aor. 2 of ἐγκατατίθημι.

ἐνικλάω, poet. for ἐγκ- (q.v.), *break off*: metaph., ἔωθεν ἐνικλᾶν ὅττι κεν εἴπω is wont *to frustrate* what I devise, Il.8.408, cf. 422; ἐνέκλασσας (Ep. aor. 1) δὲ μενοινήν Call.*Jov.*90; γάμον βαρὺς ὅρκος ἐνικλᾷ Id.*Aet.*3.1.22; τίς ἄτη σωομένους μεσσηγὺς ἐνέκλασε; A.R.3.307.

ἐνικλείω, Ep. for ἐγκ-, A.R.2.1029.

ἔνικμος, ον, (ἰκμάς) *with wet in it*, *humid*, γῆ Arist.*HA*570ᵃ17, Thphr.*CP*1.2.1; διαφύσεις Ph.1.8; δένδρα *Gp.*10.75.2, cf. Dsc.2.101; τὸ ἔ. τῶν ἄντρων Porph.*Antr.*5; of young pigs, Ar.Byz.ap.Ath.9.375a; of perspiring patients, Orib.*Fr.*116.

ἐνικνέομαι, *arrive at*, τοὺς ἐνικομένους ταῖς ἡλικίαις *IG*9(1).32.16 (Phocis).

ἐνικνήθω, ἐνικνώσσω, poet. for ἐγκ-, Nic.*Th.*911 (Med.): divisim, Mosch.2.6.

ἑνῐκός, ή, όν, (ἕν) *single*: Gramm., ἀριθμὸς ἑ. the *singular* number, opp. δυϊκός, πληθυντικός, Chrysipp.*Stoic.*2.99, D.T.635.30, A.D.*Pron.*12.11, al.; τὰ -κά Longin.24.1. Adv. -κῶς D.H.*Comp.*6, A.D.*Synt.*258.24, St.Byz. s.v. Ἄγρα. II. *exhibiting unity*, *individual*, in Comp., Plot.6.9.6, Syrian. *in Metaph.*34.17, Procl. *in Prm.*p.581 S.: Sup., ib.p.820 S., *in Alc.*p.255 C. Adv. -κῶς Theo Sm.p.21 H., Plot.2.4.13.

ἐνικρίνω, Ep. for ἐγκ-, A.R.1.48 (Pass.).

ἐνῑλάσιμος [ᾰ], ον, *propitious*, *Sammelb.*4116.5 (-ειλ- lapis).

ἐνίλλω, *look askance*, Paus.Gr.*Fr.*209:—also **ἐνιλλώπτω**, Ael. Dion.ibid.

ἐνῑοβολέω, *cast venom upon*, βοτάναις Hp.*Ep.*16.

ἔνιοι, αι, α, *some*; never in Ep., Lyr., or Att. Poets before Men., exc. Ar.*Pl.*867 (cf. however ἐνίοτε); first used in Ion. Prose, as Hdt.1.120, 8.56, Hp.*Praec.*6; πολλοὶ μὲν..ἔνιοι δὲ.. Lys.25.19; ἔνιοι μὲν..ἔνιοι δὲ.. Pl.*Tht.*151a, X.*Mem.*4.2.38; ἔνιοι μὲν..οἱ δὲ... Pl.*Mx.*238e; ἔνιοί τινες Isoc.15.258: later in sg., οὐ πᾶσα κίνησις θερμαίνει, ἀλλ' ἐνία ψύχει Arist.*Pr.*884ᵇ13, cf. Thphr.*Vert.*1; περὶ ψυχῆς ἐνίας θεωρῆσαι Arist.*Metaph.*1026ᵃ5: neut. pl. as Adv., συμμανῆναι ἔνια δεῖ Men.421; ἔστι καὶ ταὐτόματον ἔνια χρήσιμον Id.486.

ἐνίοκα, Dor. for sq., Archyt.ap.Stob.3.1.114.

ἐνίοτε, Adv. *at times*, *sometimes*, E.*Hel.*1213, Ar.*Pl.*1125, Hp.*Praec.*14, etc.; ἐ. μὲν.., ἐ. δὲ.. Pl.*Grg.*467e; ἐ. μὲν..ἔστι δ' ὅτε.. Id.*Tht.*150a; ἐ...τότε δὲ.. Id.*Phlb.*46e; ἐ. μὲν..ὅτε δὲ.. Arist.*Mete.*360ᵇ2.

ἐνιπάζων· τύπτων, Hsch.:—also **ἐνιπῆσαι** (as if from ἐνιπάω)· ἀπειλῆσαι, βοῆσαι, Id.

ἐνῑπή, ἡ, (ἐνίπτω, v. ἐνέπω fin.) poet. Noun, *rebuke*, *reproof*, Il.4.402, etc.; κρατερὴν δ' ἀποθέσθαι ἐνιπήν 5.492; ἐνιπῇ ἀργαλέῃ 14.104; ἔδδεισεν γὰρ ἐμὴν ἔκπαγλον ἐ. Od.10.448; *abuse*, *contumely*, ἐπίσχετε θυμὸν ἐνιπῆς 20.266: pl., *angry threats*, φεύγων..Ποσειδάωνος ἐνιπάς 5.446, cf. *h.Merc.*165; ψευδέων ἐνιπᾶ *reproach* of lying, Pi.*O.*10(11).6. 2. later, of any *violent attack*, as of the sun's rays or thirst, Opp.*C.*1.133, 299.

ἐνί-πλειος, ον, Ep. for ἔμπλεος. **-πλήσασθαι, -σθῆναι, -σωσι**, v. ἐμπίπλημι. **-πλήσσω**, Ep. for ἐμπλήσσω. **-πλώω**, v. ἐμπλέω.

ἐνιππ-άζομαι, = sq., Arr.*An.*2.6.3, Plu.*Mar.*25. **-εύω**, *ride in*, χωρίον ἐπιτήδεον ἐνιππεῦσαι Hdt.6.102. **-ομᾰχέω**, *fight a cavalry action in*, ἐπιτήδειον πεδίον -ῆσαι D.H.2.13.

ἐνιπρῆσαι, Ep. for ἐμπρ-, v. ἐμπίμπρημι.

ἐνιπρίω [ῑ], Ep. for ἐμπρίω, Opp.*C.*2.261.

ἐνιπτάζω, lengthd. for ἐνίπτω, A.R.1.492, 864.

ἐνιπτύω, Ep. for ἐμπτύω.

ἐνίπτω, fut. ἐνίψω Il.7.447: aor. ἠνίπαπε [ῐ] 2.245, al., also ἐνένιπε 15.546, al. (with vv.ll. ἐνένισπεν, ἐνένιπτεν, Od.18.321, Il.23.473):—Ep. Verb (once in A. (v. infr.)), *reprove*, *upbraid*, freq. with words added to strengthen the sense, χαλεπῷ ἠνίπαπε μύθῳ Il.2.245; χαλεποῖσιν ὀνείδεσι θυμὸν ἔνιπτε 3.438; ἐνένιπεν ὀνειδείοις ἐπέεσσιν Od.18.326; τὸν δ' αἰσχρῶς ἐνένιπε ib.321, Il.23.473; or simply πόσιν δ' ἠνίπαπε μύθῳ 3.427; κραδίην ἠνίπαπε μύθῳ *reproved* his soul with words, Od.20.17: without a modal word, εἴ τίς με καὶ ἄλλος ἐνίπτοι were another *to attack* me, Il.24.768; τόν ῥ' Ἕκτωρ ἐνένιπεν 15.552, cf. 546; καί τίς μ' ἐνίπτων εἶπε A.*Ag.*590: without acc., Od.18.78, cf. 24.161. II. after Hom., = ἐνέπω, *tell*, *announce*, ἀδείας ἐνίπτων ἐλπίδας Pi.*P.*4.201, cf. Nonn.*D.*27.59. Cf. ἐνίσσω.

ἐνισκέλλω, ἐνισκήπτω, ἐνισκίμπτω, Ep. for ἐνσ-.

ἔνῑσον, Adv. *equally*, dub. l. in Iamb.*Comm.Math.*25.

ἐνῑσόω, *mix in equal proportions*, *Gp.*6.6.1 (Pass.).

ἐνισπεῖν, v. ἐνέπω. **ἐνισπείρω**, Ep. for ἐνσπ-. **ἐνισπέσθαι**· ὁ νῦν μὴ καταπίνων, Hsch. **ἐνισπήσω, ἐνίσπω**, v. ἐνέπω.

ἐνίσσω, Ep. collat. form of ἐνίπτω, *attack*, *reproach*, ἐκπάγλοις ἐπέεσσιν ἐνισσέμεν Il.15.198; ὀνειδείοισιν ἐνίσσων 22.497; ἔπεσσ' αἰσχροῖσιν ἐνίσσων 24.238: also generally, *maltreat*, ἔπεσίν τε κακοῖσιν ἐνίσσομεν ἠδὲ βολῇσιν Od.24.161:—Pass., βαλλόμενος καὶ ἐνισσόμενος ib.163.

ἐνίστημι, causal in pres., fut. and aor. 1 Act., and aor. 1 Med.:—*put*, *place in*, ἵππον ἐν λίθοις ἐνιστάναι X.*Eq.Mag.*1.16; στήλας ἐνίστη ἐς τὰς χώρας Hdt.2.102; εἰς αὐτὴν (sc. τὴν πόλιν) ἡνίοχον ἐνστῆσαι Pl.*Plt.*266e; τοὺς ἱπποκόμους εἰς (i.e. amongst) τοὺς ἱππέας ἐ. X.*Eq.Mag.*5.6: c. dat., ἱστὸν ἐνεστήσαντο μεσόδμῃ A.R.1.563. 2. in Law, *institute* an heir, ἐ. κληρονόμους τοὺς υἱούς *PMasp.*151.75 (vi A.D.). 3. aor. 1 Med., also, *begin*, ὅσαι τὸ πρᾶγμα τοῦτ' ἐνεστήσαντο Ar.*Lys.*268; οὐδὲν πώποτε τῶν πραγμάτων ἐνεστήσασθ' ὀρθῶς D.10.21; ὁ τοιοῦτον ἀγῶν' ἐνστησάμενος Id.18.4; ἐ. τὸ πρᾶγμα, Lat. *rem instituere*, Arist. *Pr.*951^{a}28; ἀρχὰς τῆς γενέσεως Thphr.*HP*7.10.4; ὀργὴν καὶ μῖσος πρός τινα ἐνστήσασθαι *to begin to show*.., Plb.1.82.9; πρᾶξιν Plu. *Arat.*16: c. inf., D.S.14.53. **4.** ἐνστήσασθαι τὸ μέγεθος *determine* the size, Ph.*Bel.*50.29.

B. Pass., with aor. 2, pf., and plpf. Act.:—*to be set in, stand in*, λόχοις E.*Supp.*896; ἐν τῷ νηῷ Hdt.2.91: abs., πύλαι ἐνεστᾶσι ἑκατόν Id.1.179, cf. Pl.*Ti.*50d, etc. **2.** *enter upon, take possession of*, ὁ νικάσας ἐν τὰν οὐσίαν ἐνίσταται τὰν τοῦ ἁλόντος *Foed.Delph.Pell.*2 *B* 14. **II.** *to be appointed*, σοῦ ἐνεστεῶτος βασιλέος Hdt.1.120, cf. 6.59; ἐς ἀρχήν Id.3.68; ἐς τυραννίδας Id.2.147. **III.** *to be upon, threaten*, c. dat. pers., τοιούτων τοῖσι Σπαρτιήτῃσι ἐνεστεώτων πρηγμάτων Id.1.83; τὸν πόλεμον τὸν ἐνστάντα σοὶ καὶ τῇ πόλει Isoc.5.2; in war, *press hard*, τινί Plb.3.97.1: abs., *begin*, [τοῦ θέρους] ἐνισταμένου Thphr.*HP*9.8.2; ἐνισταμένου τοῦ ἐνιαυτοῦ Lxx 3*Ki.*12.24; *to be at hand, arise*, ὁ τότ' ἐνστὰς πόλεμος D.18.89, cf. 139, Plb.1.71.4; τοῦ πολέμου πρὸς Φίλιππον ὑμῖν ἐνεστηκότος Aeschin.2.58: esp. in pf. part., *pending, present*, μιᾶς ἐνεστώσης δίκης Ar.*Nu.*779, cf. Is.11.45, D.33.14; ὁ νῦν ἐνεστηκὼς ἀγών Lycurg.7; so οὐδενὸς ἡμῖν ἐνεστῶτος πρὸς αὐτούς *PStrassb.*91.21 (i B.C.); of Time, *instant, present*, τοῦ ἐνεστῶτος μηνός Philipp.ap.D.18.157; ἡ ἐνεστῶσα κακία, ἀνάγκη, *PPetr.*2 p.60, 1*Ep.Cor.*7.26; κατὰ τὸν ἐ. καιρόν Arist.*Rh.*1366^{b}23; ἀγαθὸν ἐνεστὼς ἢ μέλλον *Stoic.*3.94; cf. ἐνεστάναι τὸν πάντα χρόνον ὡς τὸν ἐνιαυτὸν ἐνεστηκέναι λέγομεν Apollod.*Stoic.*3.260. **2.** esp. Gramm., ὁ ἐνεστὼς (sc. χρόνος) the *present tense*, *Stoic.*2.48, D.T.638.22, A.D.*Pron.*58.7, al.; also ἐνεστῶσα συντέλεια *the state of completion expressed by the perfect tense*, Id.*Synt.*205.15: also in aor., τοῦ ποτὲ ἐνστάντος *when* the moment *has arrived*, Plot.4.3.13; τὰ ἐνεστηκότα πράγματα *present* circumstances, X.*HG*2.1.6; so τὰ ἐνεστῶτα Plb.2.26.3. **IV.** *stand in the way, resist, block*, τοῖς ποιουμένοις Th.8.69; τῇ φυγῇ Plu.*Luc.*13; τῇ αὐξήσει Id.*Rom.*25; πρὸς πᾶσάν τινι πολιτείαν Id.*Arist.*3, cf. *Marc.*22: abs., *stand in the way*, Th.3.23; in argument, ἐνέστηκεν ὁ νυνδὴ Κέβης ἔλεγε Pl.*Phd.*77b; ὁ ἐνεστηκὼς *the opponent* in a lawsuit, *SIG*45.28 (Halic., v B.C.). **2.** in Logic, *object*, τῷ καθόλου Arist.*Top.*157^{b}3; πρὸς τὸν ἔξω λόγον Id.*APo.*76^{b}26: abs., Id. *Rh.*1402^{b}24, al.; ἐ. ὅτι.. Id.*APr.*69^{b}6; ὡς.. Id.*EN*1172^{b}35, A.D. *Synt.*176.23. **3.** of the Roman tribunes, *exercise the right of intercessio, veto*, Plb.6.16.4, Plu.*TG*10, al. **V.** of fluids, *congeal, freeze*, ὕδωρ ἐνεστηκός Thphr.*CP*5.13.1; *become impacted in*, ἐνιστάμενον ἐπὶ τὰ τοῦ στομάχου στενά (sc. γάλα) Dsc.*Alex.*26.

ἐνίστιος, v. ἐνέστιος.

ἔνισχνος, ον, *somewhat thin, slight*, Nic.*Al.*147, *Cat.Cod.Astr.*7.196.

ἐνισχῡρίζομαι, *rely upon*, τινί D.44.8.

ἐνισχύω, *strengthen, confirm*, ὁ χρόνος ταῦτα -ύσει πάντα Hp.*Lex* 3; ἄγγελος ἐνισχύων αὐτόν *Ev.Luc.*22.43:—Pass., Jul.*Gal.Fr.*7. **II.** intr., *prevail in* or *among*, ἐν ταῖς πόλεσι ἐνισχύει τὰ νόμιμα Arist.*EN* 1180^{b}4: abs., Id.*PA*653^{a}31 al.; τοῦτ' ἐνισχύειν ἑκάστῳ Thphr.*Sens.* 63, cf. 67; παρά τισιν ἐ. ἐν παροιμίας μέρει D.S.20.58; ἐνίσχυσεν ὡς.. *the opinion prevailed* that.., Id.5.57.

ἐνίσχω, = ἐνέχω:—Med., ἐνίσχεσθαι τὴν φωνήν *to keep in one's* voice, Plu.*Cic.*35:—Pass., *to be held fast*, Hdt.4.43; προχοῇσιν A.R. 1.11; ἔν τινι v.l. for ἐνεχ- in X.*An.*7.4.17; of phlegm, etc., *to be impacted*, χυμοὶ ἐνισχόμενοι Gal.15.221

ἐνιτελέω, *complete*, τὰ κατάλοιπα τῶν ἔργων *BCH*20.323 (Lebad.).

ἐνιτρέφω, -τρίβω, Ep. for ἐντ-. **ἐνιφέρβομαι, -φύρω**, Ep. for ἐμφ-

ἐνίχνιον, τό, *footprint* (?), Prisc.*Inst.*14.36, *Gloss*

ἐνιχραύω, -χρίμπτω, Ep. for ἐγχ-. **ἐνιψάω**, poet. for ἐμψάω.

ἐνιψηφίζομαι, *put to the vote*, Maiuri *Nuova Silloge* 443.

ἐνίψω, v. ἐνίπτω. **ἔνκομον**· ἐν τῷ μαρίῳ ἴσον θείας κελεύσεως, Hsch.

ἐνλαξευω, *carve in* or *on*, pf. Pass. ἐνλελάξευνται *AP*3.9 Arg.

ἐνλᾰπῐθάζεσθαι· μαχέσασθαι Λαπίθαις, ἢ ἐνθυμηθῆναι, Hsch.

ἔνλῐθος, ον, *adorned with jewels*, μασχαλιστήρ *CPR*22.5 (ii A.D.).

ἐνλῐμενίζειν, *exact harbour-dues*, Hsch.

ἐνμαχατεύειν, v. ἐμμαχατεύειν.

ἐνμεντευθενί, Com. tmesis for ἐντευθενὶ μέν, Metag.6.5.

ἐννάγωνον [ᾰ], τό, *nonagon*, Hero *Metr.*1.22

ἐννᾰετήρ, ῆρος, ὁ, (ἐνναίω) *inmate, inhabitant*, *AP*9.495 (Arch.), v.l. in Mosch.2.123:—fem. **ἐννᾰέτειρα**, *APl.*4.94 (Arch.).

ἐννᾰ-ετηρίς, v. ἐννεετηρίς. **-έτηρος**, ον, = sq., *nine years old*, Hes.*Op.*436. **-έτης** (A), ες, *nine years old*, Theoc.26.29: Ep. neut. εἰνάετες, as Adv., *for nine years*, Hes.*Th.*801:—fem. **-έτις**, poet. **εἰν-**, ιδος, *AP*7.643 (Crin.). **-έτης** (B), ου, ὁ, = ἐνναετήρ, Isyll. 38, A.R.2.517, *APl.*4.331 (Agath.), etc.:—fem. **-έτις**, ιδος, A.R.1. 1126. **-ετία**, ἡ, *period of nine years*, Sch.Il.1.1; cf. ἐναετία. **-ετίζομαι**, v. εἰνα-.

ἔνναιον, τό, f.l. for ναιὸν (= ναόν, cf. Hsch.), Cliniasap.Sch.A.R. 2.1085, cf. Suid., Zonar.

ἐνναίω, *dwell in*, τοιοῖσδ' ἐνναίει δόμοις E.*Hel.*488; ὅσοισι [κακοῖσι] ..ὁρᾷς ἐνναίοντά με S.*Ph.*472, cf. *Lyr.Alex.Adesp.*35.22; ἐκεῖ S.*OC* 788: c. acc. loci, *inhabit*, Mosch.4.36, A.R.1.1076: in later Prose, [Κόρινθον] ἐ. ἐν μέσοις τοῖς ἀγαθοῖς Aristid.*Or.*46(3).27: 3 pl. fut. Med. ἐννάσσονται A.R.4.1751: 3 pl. aor. 1 Med. ἐννάσσαντο ib.1213, Call.*Del.*15: 3 sg. aor. 1 Pass. ἐννάσθη A.R.3.1181.

ἐννάκις [ᾰ], **ἐννᾰκόσιοι, ἐννᾰταῖος, ἔννᾰτος**, v. ἐνακ-, ἐνατ-.

ἐννάσσω, *bung up*, πίθον *Gp.*6.6.1.

ἐνναυλοχέομαι, Dep., = ναυλοχέω ἐν.., D.C.50.12.

ἐνναυμᾰχέω, = ναυμαχέω ἐν.., Plu.2.1078d.

ἐνναυπηγέομαι, Pass., *have ships built in it*, of a place, v.l. in Th. 1.13.

ἐννέᾰ, Dor. also **ἐννῆ** (q.v.), indecl., *nine*, Il.6.174, Od.8.258, etc.; Μοῦσαι ἐννέα Hes.*Th.*917, Od.24.60; τρὶς ἐννέα κλῶνας, in a religious ceremony, S.*OC*483; τρὶς ἐ. ἔτη Orac.ap.Th.5.26. **2.** as a round number for, *many*, τρὶς ἐννέα φῶτας ἔπεφνεν Il.16.785, cf. Od.11.577, Sch.Nic.*Th.*781. (Cf. Lat. *novem*, Skt. *náva*, etc.)

ἐννεά-βοιος [ᾰ], ον, *worth nine beeves*, Il.6.236, *Eleg.Alex.Adesp.*1. 3:—but also glossed by ἐνν(ε)άβυρσος, Hsch. **-γηρα** κορώνη *nine times*(as) *old*(as a man), Arat.1022 (ἐννεάνειρα cj. Lobeck). **-γράμμᾰτον**, τό, *word of nine letters* (λιθάργυρα), Olymp.Alch.p.71 B. (-γραμμον codd.). **-γωνος**, ον, of a class of figurate numbers, *enneagonal*, Theo Sm.p.40 H. **-δάκτῠλος**, ον, *with nine fingers*, Ptol.Heph.ap.Phot.*Bibl.*p.147 B. **-δεσμος**, ον, *with nine joints, many-jointed*, Nic.*Th.*781. **-δικός**, ή, όν, *based on* or *calculated by division by nine*, ἀγωγή, [κλιμακτήρ], Vett.Val.147.31, 148. 14. **-ετηρικός**, ή, όν, *nine-yearly*, ἀγών *BSA*16.117 (Pisidia, ii/iii A.D.). **-έτης**, ου, ὁ, *nine years old*, *IG*9(2).639 (Larissa), *Annales du Service* 19.223. **-ετία**, ἡ, *period of nine years*, *EM*343.28.

ἐννεάζω, *spend one's youth in*, μεγέθει σώματος ἐννεάσαι *to be of* great stature *in one's youth*, Hp.*Aph.*2.54; τῇ τῶν πραγμάτων ἀκριβεστέρᾳ καταλήψει Ph.1.622; ἐ. [τῇ βασιλείᾳ] καὶ ἐγγηράσκει, of one crowned in his mother's womb, Agath.4.25; ῥόδον ἐννεάσαν τῷ ἦρι *having bloomed* in spring, Philostr.*Ep.*51.

ἐννεᾰκαίδεκα, indecl., *nineteen*, Il.24.496, etc.

ἐννεᾰκαιδεκα-ετηρίς, ίδος, ἡ, *cycle of nineteen years*, D.S.12.36, *Placit.*2.32.2, Ptol.*Tetr.*205. **-έτης**, ου, ὁ, *of nineteen years*, χρόνος D.S.2.47. **-μηνος**, ον, *nineteen months old*, *IG*14.1970. **-πλάσιος** [πλᾰ], α, ον, = sq., Procl.*Hyp.*4.110. **-πλᾰσίων**, ον, gen. ονος, *nineteen times as large as*, τῆς γῆς *Placit.*2.25.1, cf. Ach.Tat. *Intr.Arat.*20.

ἐννεᾰκαιδεκ-άς, άδος, ἡ, = sq., Vett.Val.339.2, Tz.*H.*2.885. **-ατος**, η, ον, *nineteenth*, Hp.*Epid.*3.1.γ', *CIG*2220 (Chios), *IG*3.677.6 (ii A.D.). **-έτης**, ες, = ἐννεακαιδεκαέτης, poet. gen. -τευς *AP*7.11 (Asclep.), 9.190:—fem. **-έτις**, *IG*3.1370: written -δεχέτις *Epigr.Gr.*205.

ἐννεᾰκαιεικοσῑ-καιεπτᾰκοσιοπλᾰσιάκις, Adv. *seven-hundred-and-twenty-nine times*, Pl.*R.*587e. **-χοίνῑκος**, ον, *containing twenty-nine* χοίνικες, *PHib.*1.85.18 (iii B.C.).

ἐννεᾰκέφᾰλος, ον, *nine-headed*, Sch.Hes.*Th.*313, Tz.*H.*2.237.

ἐννεάκις, Adv. = ἐνάκις, v.l. in Nicom.*Harm.*8.

ἐννεᾰκισχίλιοι [χῐ], αι, α, *nine thousand*, D.S.17.66, Ael.*VH*6.12.

ἐννεά-κλῑνος, ον, *with nine dining-couches*, Phryn.Com.66, D.S.31. 9, Them.*Or.*18.223a. **-κότῠλος** [ᾰ], ον, *containing nine* κοτύλαι, *PCair.Zen.*61.3 (-κυτ- Pap.). **-κροσσον**· πολλοὺς κροσσοὺς ἔχον, Hsch. **-κρουνος**, ον, *with nine spouts*, name of a well at Athens, in earlier times (as at this day) called Καλλιρρόη, Hdt.6.137, Th.2. 15, Polyzel.2: metaph. of an orator, *copious*, Lib.*Ep.*1493.4. **-κυκλος**, ον, *in nine circles*, Coluth.214, Nonn.*D.*4.317. **-λῐνος**, ον, *of nine threads*, ἄρκυς X.*Cyn.*2.4. **-μηνιαῖος**, α, ον, = sq., *Theol. Ar.*47. **-μηνος**, ον, *of* or *in nine months*, τίκτειν Hdt.6.69, cf. Hp.*Septim.*8; χρόνος Gal.*Nat.Fac.*3.3; λόγος *BGU*977.13 (ii A.D.). **-μορφος**, ον, *of nine forms*, *PMag.Leid.W.*10.1, 21. **-μυκλος**, ον, (μύκλος) *having nine stripes* or *folds*, hence, *nine years old*, ὄνος Call.*Fr.*180, cf. Hsch.

ἐννεάνειρα, v. ἐννεάγηρα.

ἐννεά-πηχυς [ᾰ], υ, *nine cubits broad* or *long*, ζυγόδεσμον Il.24.270, al.; cf. εἰνάπηχυς. **-πλάσιος** [πλᾰ], α, ον, *ninefold*, dub. in Ibyc. 33. **-πνεύμων**, ον, gen. ονος, '*nine winds strong*', ζάλη Secund. *Sent.*8 (prob.). **-πολις**, *having nine cities*, Πύλος Sch.Od.3. 7. **-πον**· λοξόν, Hsch. **-πους**, ποδος, ὁ, ἡ, *nine feet long*, λίθος *Milet.*7.57 (Didyma).

ἐννεάρμενος, ον, *having nine sails*, Tz. ad Lyc.101.

ἐννεάς, άδος, ἡ, *body of nine*, Theoc.17.84 (pl.), *AP*7.17 (Tull. Laur.); ἡ ὑμνουμένη ἐ. ἐν τῷ νοητῷ Dam.*Pr.*117: Porph. divided the works of his master Plotinus into six enneads, *Plot.*24. **II.** *the number nine*, Plu.2.726d, 744a, Nicom.*Ar.*1.19, etc. **III.** *the ninth day of the month*, v. εἰνάς.

ἐννεάστεγος, ον, *of nine stories*, κατασκεύασμα D.S.20.91.

ἐνν(ε)άστερος, ον, *containing nine stars*, δορά Sch.Arat.322.

ἐννεά-σύλλᾰβος, ον, *nine-syllabled*, Steph.*in Rh.*321.16, *AP*13.19 tit.: -σύλλαβον (sc. μέτρον), τό, Σαπφικόν Heph.10.2. **-σφαιρος**, ον, *having nine spheres*, Phlp.*in Mete.*110.23.

ἐννεατηρίς, v. ἐννεετηρίς.

ἐννεά-φάρμᾰκος, ον, *consisting of nine ingredients*, of remedies, Heraclid.Tar.ap.Gal.14.186, Cels.5.19.10, Androm.ap.Gal.13.310, Orib.*Fr.*142. **-φθογγος**, ον, *of nine notes*, μέλος *Trag.Adesp.*546. 11. **-φωνος**, ον, = foreg., σῦριγξ Theoc.8.18. **-χειλος** (A), ον, *with nine lips*, Nicom.*Ar.*1.14. **-χειλος** (B), ον, Ion. for sq., read by Aristarch. in Il.5.860, and mistranslated as, = ἐννεάχειλος (A). **-χῑλοι**, αι, α, Ep. for ἐνάκις χίλιοι, *nine thousand*, Il.5.860 (v. foreg.); ἄνδρες Ps.-Luc.*Philopatr.*6: sg., κτύπος -χιλος noise *as of* 9,000, Nonn.*D.*8.45. **-χορδος**, ον, *of nine strings*: Subst. ἐννεάχορδον (sc. ὄργανον), τό, Phillisap.Ath.14.636b. **-χρονος**, gloss on ἐννέωρος, Sch.Od.11.311. **-χωρος**, ον, *containing nine terms* or *places*, στίχος *Theol.Ar.*28. **-χῶς**, *in nine ways*, Procl. *in Prm.*p.961 S. **-ψῡχος**, ον, *with nine lives*: prov., ἐ. ὁ κύων (as we say of the cat) Hsch.

ἔννεεν· ἐξέτεινεν, Hsch.

ἐννεετηρίς, ίδος, ἡ, *nine-year period*, Pl.*Min.*319e, *IG*2.985^{A}2, *Delph.*

3(2).48.8; written ἐννεατηρίς in Vett.Val.337.17; ἐνναετ- Plu.2.293b; ἐννετ- (v.l. ἐννεατ-) Thphr.*HP*4.11.2: v. ἐννεαετ-.

ἔννεκα, Aeol., = ἕνεκα (q.v.).

ἐννεκρόομαι, Pass., *die in*, ταῖς γαλήναις Plu.2.792b.

ἐννεμέθομαι, Pass., *feed in*, Opp.*H*.1.611, 3.546.

ἐννεμέσιμος, ον, *just, righteous*, Cyr.

ἐννέμω, *feed* cattle *in* a place, *SIG*685.82 (Itanos), D.C.72.3:—Med., of the cattle, Ph.2.118 (prob.); of fish, Opp.*H*.1.5; also, *live amongst*, Lxx 3*Ma*.3.25.

ἐννενή-κοντα, -κοστός, -κονταετής, ff.ll. for ἐνεν-.

ἐννενώκασι, Ion. for ἐννενοήκασι, 3 pl. pf. of ἐννοέω.

ἐννεόβολον, τό, *sum of nine obols*, *IG*7.235.22 (Orop.).

ἔννεον, Ep. for ἔνεον, impf. of νέω *swim*, Il.21.11 (v.l. νῆχοντ').

ἐννεόργυιος, ον, *nine fathoms long*, Od.11.312, Matro *Conv*.45.

ἐννεοσσεύω, Att. -ττεύω, later **ἐννοσσεύω** Lxx *Je*.22.23, *Gp*.5.48. I:—*make a nest in* a place, ἔν τινι Ar.*Av*.1108: metaph., Pl.*Lg*.949c; as etym. of νόσος, Anon.Lond.3.22:—Med., D.S.5.43. II. c. acc., *hatch as in a nest*, ἔρωτα Pl.*Alc*.1.135e; παιδείας ψυχαῖς Them.*Or*.24. 307d:—Pass., *to be hatched*, ἐπιθυμίαι ἐννενεοττευμέναι Pl.*R*.573e.

ἐννεόω, *break up* land, *Gp*.3.1.9.

ἐννέπω, v. ἐνέπω. **ἐννεσία**, ἡ, v. ἐνεσία.

ἔννευμα, ατος, τό, *signal, wave of the hand*, δακτύλων ἐννεύμασι Lxx *Pr*.6.13.

ἐννευρόκαυλος, ον, *with fibrous stalk*, Thphr.*HP*6.1.4.

ἐννεύω, *nod* or *make signs to*, ἐννεύει με φεύγειν Ar.*Fr*.75, cf. Luc. *DMeretr*.12.1; ἐ. τινὶ τὸ τί ἂν θέλοι.. *ask* him *by signs* what.., *Ev.Luc*.1.62.

ἐννέω, *swim in*, Aristid.*Or*.48(24).21.

ἐννέωρος (cf. ὥρος), Ep. Adj. *in the ninth season*: hence, 1. Μίνως ἐννέωρος βασίλευε Διὸς .. ὀαριστής perh. *at nine years old* or *after nine years*, Od.19.179, cf. Apollon.*Lex*.; Pl.*Min*.319b couples ἐ. ὀαριστής taking counsel with Zeus *every ninth year*. 2. *nine years old*, of the Aloidae, Od.11.311; βοῦς 10.19 (unless, = πενταέτηρος, ὥρος meaning a *season*, i.e. half-year, cf. Arist.*HA*575^{b}6); σίαλοι Od.10.390; ἄλειφαρ Il.18.351. (Perh. = *of full age*, ἐννέα being taken as a round number, cf. Sch.Il.l.c.) 3. (ὥρα) *nine hours long*, νύκτες Herod.8.5.

ἐννῆ, = ἐννέα, *SIG*240*E*43 (Delph., iv B.C.); also at Cyrene, Hsch.

ἐνν-ήκοντα, Ep. for ἐνενήκοντα, Od.19.174. **-ῆμαρ**, Ep. Adv. *for nine days*, Il.1.53, al. **-ήρης**, ες, *of nine banks of oars*, ναῦς Plb. 16.7.1, Ath.5.203d.

ἐννησιάδες Νύμφαι *island*-Nymphs (Lesb.), Hsch.

ἐννήυσκλοι· ὑποδήματα Λακωνικῶν ἐφήβων, Hsch. (ἐννήϊσκλοι cod.): fr. ἐννῆ and ὕσκλος.

ἔννηφιν, v. ἔνος (B).

ἐννήφω, *to be sober in*, ἑκατέρῳ (sc. good and evil fortune), M.Ant. 1.16.10.

ἐννήχομαι, *swim* or *float in*.., τινί Ph.1.385, Plu.2.994b, Antyll. ap.Orib.6.27.5: metaph., νοήματα ἐ. ὡς ἐν ποταμῷ τῷ λόγῳ Ph.1.693:—later in Act., Gal.*UP*15.5, prob. in Lib.*Decl*.32.20: metaph., Gal. 2.461.

ἔννιον, τό, *handle of an oar*, Hsch.

ἐννιτρόγεως, ων, *with soil impregnated with nitre*, Hero *Geom*.23.68.

Ἐννοδία, v. ἐνόδιος.

ἐννο-έω, Ion. aor. 1 part. ἐννώσας Hdt.1.68,86: pf. ἐννένωκα Id.3.6:—Att. also Dep. **ἐννοοῦμαι**, with aor. 1 Pass. ἐνενοήθην:—*have in one's thoughts, consider, reflect*, ἐ. ὅτι.. Id.1.86, etc.; ἐ. ὡς.. Pl.*Ap*. 40c; εἴτε.. Id.*Phd*.74a; ἐ. μή.. *take thought, be anxious* lest.., X. *An*.4.2.13, etc.; ἐννοούμενοι μὴ οὐκ ἔχοιεν ib.3.5.3; ἐννοούμενοι (v.l. -οῦντες) οἷα πεπονθὼς ἢ Lys.9.7: abs., ὧδε γὰρ ἐννόησον Pl.*Prt*.324d; also τέκνων ἐννοουμένη πέρι E.*Med*.925. 2. c. acc., *reflect upon, consider*, τὰ λεγόμενα Hdt.1.68, cf. 3.6; τοῦτ' ἐννοοῦμαί πως ἐγὼ Eup. 11.6D.; ἐ. τὸ γιγνόμενον, ὅτι.. Pl.*Tht*.161b, cf. S.*Ant*.61; τοῦτ' ἐννοεῖσθ', ὅταν πορθῆτε γαῖαν, εὐσεβεῖν Id.*Ph*.1440; ταῦτ' ἐννοήσασ' (v.l. ἐννοηθεῖσ') E.*Med*.882, cf. 900; γένος ἐπιεικὲς ἀθλίως διατιθέμενον Pl.*Criti*.121b. 3. c. gen., *take thought for*, μητρὸς οὐδὲν ἐννοούμενοι κακῶν E.*Med*.47; ἐνενόησεν αὐτῶν καὶ ὡς.. he *took note of* them that.., X.*Cyr*.5.2.18; *notice*, ἐννενόηκας τῶν λεγομένων πονηρῶν, σοφῶν δέ, ὡς.. Pl.*R*.519a; ἐννενόηκά σου λέγοντος ὅτι.. Id.*Hp.Mi*. 369e, cf. *Tht*.168c; ἔκ τινος ἐννοεῖσθαι *draw conclusions* from.., Id. *Hp.Ma*.295c. II. *understand*, εἰ σὺ μὴ τόδ' ἐννοεῖς, ἐγὼ λέγω σοι A.*Ag*.1088 (lyr.); οὐ γὰρ ἐννοῶ S.*OT*559, *Ph*.28: c. part., ἐννοοῦμαι φαῦλος οὖσα E.*Hipp*.435. III. *intend* to do, c. inf., ἐννοεῖς ἡμᾶς προδοῦναι S.*OT*330, cf. Lxx *Ju*.9.5, Aristeas 133: c. acc. rei, S.*Aj*. 115. IV. *think of, invent*, Id.*Tr*.578; ὁδόν X.*An*.2.2.10; μηχανήν Pl.*Lg*.798b. V. *form a notion of*, τι Id.*Phd*.73c sq.; *suppose*, ὃ δ' ὑμεῖς ἐννοεῖτε, ὅτι.. X.*An*.6.1.29. VI. of words, *mean, signify*, τί σοι ἄλλο ἐννοεῖ.. τὸ ῥῆμα; Pl.*Euthd*.287c codd. **-ημα**, ατος, τό, *notion, concept*, Arist.*Metaph*.981^{a}6, Epicur.*Ep*.1 p.5 U., Lxx *Si*.21.11, Aristeas 189, D.H.*Comp*.25, Plot.6.6.12, etc.; *object of thought*, Zeno *Stoic*.1.19, etc. **-ημᾰτικός**, ή, όν, *notional*, *Stoic*. 2.75; *subjective*, Ascl.*in Metaph*.106.26; opp. οὐσιώδης, Gal.1.306. Adv. -κῶς Ascl.*in Metaph*.106.27, Procl.*in Prm*.p.632 S.; gloss on ἐμφαντικῶς, *EM*336.53. II. *inventive*, Vett.Val.42.33. Adv. -κῶς Id.166.7. **-ησις**, εως, ἡ, *consideration*, Pl.*R*.407c. **-ητέον**, *one must consider*, Id.*Lg*.636c. **-ητικός**, ή, όν, *thoughtful*, Arist.*Phgn*. 813^{a}29.

ἔννοια, ἡ, (νοῦς) *act of thinking, reflection, cogitation* (συντονία διανοίας Pl.*Def*.414a): ἄξιον ἐννοίας Id.*Lg*.657a, al. 2. *notion, conception*, χρόνου ἔννοια Id.*Ti*.47a; ἐν ταῖς περὶ τὸ ὂν.. ἐννοίαις Id.*Phlb*. 59d; ἔ. λαβεῖν to form *an idea*, opp. αἴσθησιν λαβεῖν, Id.*Phd*.73c; τοῦ καλοῦ ἔ. ἔχειν Arist.*EN*1179^{b}15; ἐννοίας χάριν λέγειν Id.*Metaph*. 1073^{b}12; ἔννοιαι, opp. φαντασίαι, αἰσθήσεις, Id.*MA*701^{b}17; κατὰ ἀθρόαν ἔ. Epicur.*Ep*.1 p.23 U. (but κατὰ πᾶσαν ἔ. θυμοῦ every *kind, variety* of anger, Phld.*Ir*.p.90 W.); δοξαστικαὶ ἔ. Epicur.*Sent*.24; εἰς ἔ. ἔρχεσθαί τινος Plb.1.57.4; εἰς ἔ. τινὸς ἄγειν τινά ib.49.10; ἡ κοινὴ ἔ. the common *notion*, Id.10.27.8; κοιναὶ ἔ. *axioms*, heading in Euc.; general *ideas*, Chrysipp.*Stoic*.2.154, etc.; ψιλὴ ἔ. mere, i.e. vague, *notion*, Simp.*in Ph*.18.1. 3. *intent*, E.*Hel*.1026; ἔννοιαν λαβεῖν form *a design*, Id.*Hipp*.1027; *intention* of a testator, Is.1.13; ἔ. ἔχειν περί τι Pl.*Lg*.769e; ἔ. ἐμποιεῖν put an *idea* into one's head, Isoc.5.150; ἔ. ἐμπίπτει τινί X.*An*.3.1.13. 4. *good sense, better judgement*, παρὰ τὴν ἔννοιαν Plu.2.1077d. II. *sense* of a word, D.C.69.21. III. Rhet., *thought*, opp. *diction* (λέξις), Hermog.*Id*.2.4, cf. *Prog*.6.

ἐννοιάδες αἶγες, αἳ μὴ κορύπτουσιν, Hsch. (post ἐνοῖ).

ἐννόμιος, ον, *of* or *for pasturage*, ὅσ' ἄλλα ἐ. (sc. χωρία) *IG*2.1059. 13 (iv B.C.), cf. *OGI*55.14 (Telmessus, iii B.C.); τὸ ἐ. *dues paid for pasturage*, *IG*2.584c7, 7.3171.49 (Orchom. Boeot.), *Inscr.Délos* 353*A* 34 (iii B.C.), *PSI*4.368.4 (iii B.C.), *OGI*629.173 (Palmyra, ii A.D.), etc.

ἐννομολέσχης, ου, ὁ, *prater about laws*, Timo 25.

ἔννομος, ον, *ordained by law, lawful, legal*, Pi.*O*.7.84; [χθονὸς αἶσα] Id.*P*.9.57; δίκα A.*Supp*.384 (lyr.), cf. E.*Ph*.1651, etc.; ἔννομα πείσονται they will suffer *lawful punishment*, Th.3.67; ἔ. ὁμολογία, πολιτεία, Pl.*Lg*.921c, Aeschin.1.5; σὺμ ψάφοις ταῖς ἐ. *Supp.Epigr*.2. 277 (Delph., ii B.C.); ἐκκλησία *IG*9(1).3 (Locr.), *Act.Ap*.19.39; ἡλικία, χρόνοι, *POxy*.247.12 (i A.D.), *Michel* 468.29 (ii B.C.). Adv. -μως, ζημιοῦσθαι, διοικεῖσθαι, Lys.9.12, 30.35, cf. D.C.56.7: Comp. -ώτερον *POxy*.1204.24 (iii A.D.). 2. of persons, *keeping within the law, upright, just*, A.*Supp*.404 (lyr.), Pl.*R*.424e; also, *subject to the law*, μὴ ὢν ἄνομος Θεοῦ, ἀλλ' ἔ. Χριστοῦ 1*Ep.Cor*.9.21. II. (νέμομαι) *feeding in*, i.e. *inhabiting*, οἳ γᾶς τότ' ἦσαν ἔννομοι A.*Supp*.565 (lyr.).

ἔννοος, ον, always contr. **ἔννους**, ουν, *thoughtful, shrewd, sensible*, νηπίους ὄντας τὸ πρὶν ἔννους ἔθηκα A.*Pr*.444, cf. S.*OT*916; οὐδεὶς ἔ. ἐφάπτεται μαντικῆς ἐνθέου Pl.*Ti*.71e; ἔ. γίγνομαι I come *to my senses*, E.*Ba*.1270, D.31.2; ἔ. γεγονέναι ὅτι.. to be *aware* that.., Lys.10. 20: Sup. ἐννούστατος Hsch. II. *intellectual*, ζωή Plot.6.2.21.

ἔννος, v. ἔνος (B).

ἐννοσία· ἀλογία, ἀργία, Hsch.

Ἐννοσίγαιος [σῐ], ὁ, Ep. for Ἐνοσίγ-, *Earth-shaker*, as a name of Poseidon, Il.13.43, al., Mosch.2.149, Nonn.*D*.36.126, etc.: **ἐνοσί-**, Luc.*JTr*.9.

Ἐννοσίδᾱς [ῐ], α, ὁ, Dor. for Ἐννοσίγαιος, Pi.*P*.4.33, *Pae*.4.41.

ἔννοσις, v. ἔνοσις.

ἐννοσίφυλλος [ῐ], ον, = εἰνοσίφυλλος, Ep. for ἐνοσιφ-: ἀήτα Simon. 41.

ἐννοσσεύω, v. ἐννεοσσεύω.

ἐννοσσοποιέομαι, Med., *make oneself a nest on*, Lxx 4*Ma*.14.16.

ἐννότιος, α, ον, *wet, moist*, Call.*Fr*.350.

ἐννοχλέω, poet. for ἐνοχλέω, Theoc.29.36.

ἔννυθεν· ἐκέχυντο, Hsch.

ἐννυκτερεύω, *pass the night in*, ἐν τῇ χώρᾳ Plb.3.22.13: abs., Hld. 3.4. 2. *stand for a night*, of preparations, Dsc.2.76.9, Philum.ap. Orib.45.29.7, Gal.13.1046.

ἕννῡμι or **ἐννύω** (Hsch., cf. ἀμφι-, καθ-), Ion. **εἵνυμι, εἱνύω** (cf. ἐπι-, κατα-): fut. ἕσω (ἀμφι-) Od.5.167, Ep. ἕσσω 16.79, etc.: Ep. aor. ἕσσα Il.5.905 (the common form only in compd. ἀμφι-έσαιμι, ἀμφι-έσασα):—**Med.**, ἕννῡμαι Od.6.28; impf. ἕννῦτο 5.230: Ep. fut. ἕσσομαι (ἐπιϝ-, ἐφ-) Pi.*N*.11.16, A.R.1.691: aor. (ἀμφι)..ἕσατο Il. 14.178, Ep. (ἐπὶ)..ἕσσαντο ib.350: Ep. 3 sg. (ἀμφὶ)..ἑέσσατο 10.23, Od.14.529:—**Pass.**, pf. εἷμαι, εἷται, 19.72, 11.191, but 2 sg. ἕσσαι 24. 250, 3 sg. ἕσται (ἐπι-) Orac.ap.Hdt.1.47: plpf. 2 sg. ἕσσο Il.3.57, Od. 16.199, 3 sg. ἕστο Il.23.67, Ep. ἕεστο 12.464, 3 dual ἕσθην 18.517, 3 pl. εἵατο ib.596; part. εἱμένος (v. infr.). (ves-, cf. Lat. *vestis*, Skt. *váste* 'clothes himself': ϝεσ- in βέστον, γεστία, γέστρα (qq.vv.), cf. ϝῆμα *Leg.Gort*.3.38.):—*put clothes on* another, c. dupl. acc., κεῖνός σε χλαῖνάν τε χιτῶνά τε ἕσσει he *will clothe* thee in cloak and frock, Od. 15.338, cf. 16.79; χαρίεντα δὲ εἵματα ἕσσε Il.5.905. II. Med. and Pass., c. acc. rei only, *clothe oneself in, put on, wear*, κακὰ δὲ χροῒ εἵματα εἷμαι Od.23.115; χλαίνας εὖ εἱμένοι 15.331; freq. of armour, ἕσσαντο περὶ χροῒ νώροπα χαλκόν Il.14.383, etc.; [ἀσπίδας] ἑσσάμενοι, of tall shields which *covered* the whole person, ib.372; [ξυστὰ] κατὰ στόμα εἱμένα χαλκῷ shafts *clad* with brass at their point, 15.389; of any covering, *wrap, shroud oneself in*, χλαίνας.. καθύπερθεν ἕσασθαι, of bed-clothes, Od.4.299; ἐπὶ δὲ νεφέλην ἕσσαντο Il.14.350; ἠέρα ἑσσαμένω ib.282; εἱμένος ὤμοιιν νεφέλην 15.308: metaph., λάϊνον ἕσσο χιτῶνα thou *hadst been clad* in coat of stone, i.e. stoned, 3.57; τὸν ἀεὶ κατὰ γᾶς σκότον εἱμένος S.*OC*1701; τρυχηρὰ περὶ τρυχηρὸν εἱμένην χρόα λακίσματ' E.*Tr*.496: metaph. also, φρεσὶν εἱμένος ἀλκήν Il.20.381.—Twice in Trag., elsewh. in Compds., as always in Prose.

ἐννῠχ-εύω, *to sleep in* or *on*, τῷ σηκῷ Plu.2.434e: metaph., Ἔρως, ὃς ἐν μαλακαῖς παρειαῖς νεάνιδος ἐννυχεύεις S.*Ant*.784 (lyr.). II. *sink*, of a star, Babr.124.16. **-ιος** [ῠ], α, ον Hes.*Th*.10, etc.; ος, ον S.*Aj*.180 (lyr.): (νύξ):—*by night, at night*, ἐ. προμολών Il.21.37; [νῆες] ἐννύχιαι κατάγοντο Od.3.178; ἐννύχιαι στεῖχον Hes.l.c.; ἐ. μέλπεσθαι Pi.*P*.3.79; ἐ. τέρψις S.*Aj*.1203 (lyr.); Ῥιπαὶ *gloom-encompassed*, Id.*OC*1248 (lyr.); φροντίδες Ar.*Eq*.1290, etc.: neut. as Adv., dub. in Parrhas.3. II. ἐννυχίων ἄναξ Ἀϊδωνεῦ king *of those who dwell in the realms of Night*, S.*OC*1558 (lyr.); cf. sq. II. III.

ἐννύχιον κρύπτεις· σκοτεινῶς καὶ δολίως, τινὲς δὲ ἐμμύχιον ἐν τῷ μυχῷ Hsch., cf. Call.*Aet*.3.1.21. **-ος**, ον, = foreg., ἄγγελος ἦλθε..ἔννυχος Il.11.716, cf. Maiist.16; ἔ. κοῖται Pi.*P*.11.25; ὄψεις A.*Pr*.645: neut. pl. as Adv., ἔννυχα λίαν ἀναστάς *Ev.Marc*.1.35: Comp. -ώτερον Aesop.110. II. epith. of Hades, S.*Tr*.501 (lyr.).

ἔννωθρος, ον, *dazed*, Dsc.1.31.

ἐννῶσαι, -νώσας, Ion. aor. 1 inf. and part. of ἐννοέω (q.v.).

ἐννωτίζομαι, *carry on one's back*, Tz.*H*.4.5.

ἐνό, ἔνο, Dor. and Aeol., = ἔνι, Axiop.1.5, cf. *An.Ox*.1.176.

ἐνόβρυζος, ον, *pure, assayed*, χρυσός dub. in *POxy*.1430.16 (iv A.D.).

ἔνογκος, ον, *swollen*, φλέβες Steph. *in Hp*.1.206 D. II. *possessing bulk, corporeal*, Porph.*Sent*.27; τὸ ἔ. καὶ διαστατόν Iamb.*Comm. Math*.8.

ἐνόδιος, α, ον, Ep. **εἰνόδιος**, η, ον Il.16.260, and so Trag. in lyr., in fem. εἰνοδία: Thess. **Ἐννοδία** *IG*9(2).358,1286; later ος, ον Paus. 3.14.9:—*in* or *on the way*, σφήκεσσιν ἐοικότες..εἰνοδίοις like wasps *that have their nests by the way-side*, Il.16.260; ἐ. σύμβολοι omens *seen on the way*, portending good or ill success, A.*Pr*.487; πόλεις Plu.*Aem*.8; στάσεις σκηνῶν Id.*Ant*.9; ὅπλα *for use by the way*, D.H. 4.48. 2. Subst. ἐνόδια, τά, *nets for stopping the pathways*, X.*Cyn*. 6.9. b. *blisters caused by walking*, Thphr.*Sud*.15. II. epith. of divinities, who had their statues *by the way-side* or *at cross-roads*, most freq. of Hecate, εἰνοδίας Ἑκάτης S.*Fr*.535.2; also of Persephone, ἐνοδία θεός Id.*Ant*.1199; εἰνοδία θυγάτηρ Δάματρος E.*Ion* 1048; δαίμων ἐνοδία *IG*14.1390; and Ἐνοδία alone, Hp.*Morb.Sacr*.1, E.*Hel*.570, *AP*6.199 (Antiphil.), *IG* ll. cc.; ἡ Ἐνόδιος Paus. l. c., v.l. in Hp. l. c.; also of Hermes, Theoc.25.4, etc.

ἐνοδῖτις, εως, ἡ, = ἐνοδία, Orph.*H*.72.2.

ἔνοδμος, ον, (ὀδμή) *sweet-smelling, fresh*, Nic.*Th*.41.

ἔνοδος, ἡ, *visit*, *PLond*.3.1159.4 (ii A.D.).

ἑνο-είδεια, ἡ, *singleness*, Steph. *in Rh*.318.28. **-ειδής**, ές, *single, simple*, φωνή Nicom.*Harm*.12. II. *resembling, having the form of unity*, Plot.6.9.5, Jul.*Or*.4.139b, al., Procl. *in Prm*.p.540 S., etc.; opp. πληθοειδής, Dam.*Pr*.45: Comp., ib.38, Procl.*Inst*.62: Sup., Id. *in R*.1.177. Adv. -δῶς Jul.*Or*.4.143b, Nicom.*Ar*.1.6, Iamb.*Myst*. 1.3, Dam.*Pr*.237. **-ζῠγος**, ον, *of single pairs* of gladiators matched with beasts, κοντοκυνηγέσιον *IGRom*.4.1632.

ἐνοιδ-έω, *swell up in*, Hp.*Hum*.8 vulg., Antyll.ap.Orib.7.16.6: metaph. of the wounds of love, Plu.*Fr*.25.4. **-ής**, ές, *swollen*, Nic.*Al*.422. **-ίσκομαι**, = ἐνοιδέω, of vine-buds, Gal.12.187.

ἐνοικ-άδιος, ον, = ἐνοικίδιος, γαλεοί Aret.*CD*1.4. **-ειος**, ον, *contained in a house*: τὰ ἐ. *furniture, contents of a house*, *Rev.Ét.Gr*. 32.171 (Delos, iv/iii B.C.). **-ειόω**, *introduce among*, τὴν ἐπιείκειαν...τοῖς ἀνθρώποις D.S.1.93:—Pass., *creep in*, τὰ κατὰ μικρὸν -ούμενα πάθη Plu.2.960a. II. *to be related*, τινί Lxx *Es*.8. 1. **-έτις**, ιδος, ἡ, *she who inhabits*, ἐ. τῶν νήσων ἡ Ἀφροδίτη Suid. **-έω**, *dwell in*, c. dat. loci, Θήβαις E.*HF*1282, etc.; χώρα καλὴ ὥστε ἐ. X.*An*.5.6.25; κατὰ στέγην E.*Alc*.1051; ἐνταῦθα Ar.*Nu*. 95: abs., οὔ τι γὰρ κεκτήμεθ'... αὐτό (sc. τὸ σῶμα), πλὴν ἐνοικῆσαι βίον.. we possess it not, save *to dwell in* during life, E.*Supp*.535, cf. *Leg.Gort*.4.34, *IG*12(5).568,1100 (Ceos, v B.C.); [Θυρέαν] ἔδοσαν ἐνοικεῖν *dwell in*, Th.4.56, cf. Hdt.2.178. 2. *to be present at*, συνελεύσει *PMasp*.3.10 (vi A.D.). 3. metaph., *dwell upon*, '*be at home in*', ἐν τοῖς φυσικοῖς Arist.*GC*316ᵃ6; τοῖς συγγράμμασιν Clearch. 45. II. c. acc., *inhabit*, Th.1.18, S.*OC*1533, etc.: abs., οἱ ἐνοικοῦντες *the inhabitants*, Hdt.2.66, cf. 1.4, Th.1.91, Arist.*Pol*.1330ᵇ 8. **-ήσιμος**, ον, *habitable*, Sch.S.*OC*27. **-ησις**, εως, ἡ, *dwelling in* a place, Th.2.17, D.H.2.1. II. *right of occupation*, οἴκου *BGU*1115.39 (i B.C.), etc. **-ητήριον**, τό, *abode*, Poll.1. 73. **-ήτωρ**, ορος, ὁ, *inhabitant*, St.Byz. s.v. Πικεντία. **-ί**, Adv. *in the house, at home*, Hdn.*Epim*.255. **-ίδιος**, ον, or α, ον, *domestic*, ὄρνιθες Poll.10.156. **-ίζω**, *settle in* a place, *plant, fix in*, A.*Fr*.252; παρά τισί τι ἐ. Pl.*Epin*.978c:—Med., ἀλλοεθνεῖς -ισάμενοι γυναῖκας J.*AJ*11.5.4:—Pass., *take up one's abode in* a place, Hdt.1. 68 (so in aor. Med., Th.6.2); also, = ἐνοικέω 1. 3, ἐπιτηδεύμασι Pl. *Ax*.371c. 2. *introduce* a tenant into premises, ἐ. καὶ ἐξοικίζειν *BGU* 1116.18 (i B.C.). **-ιολόγος**, ὁ, *rent-collector*, Artem.3.41, *BGU*3, etc. **-ιος**, ον, *in the house, keeping at home*, ἐ. ὄρνις *dunghill* cock, A.*Eu*.866. II. as Subst., 1. ἐνοίκιον, τό, *house-rent*, Lys.*Fr*. 27, Is.6.21, D.48.45, *AP*11.251 (Nicarch.), Plu.*Sull*.1: pl., *BCH*6. 10 (Delos, ii B.C.), Ps.-Luc.*Philopatr*.20, *POxy*.104.15 (i A.D.): metaph., τῷ σώματι τελεῖ ἐ. ἡ ψυχή Thphr.ap.Plu.2.135e; *rent* in general, ἀποθήκης, θησαυροῦ, *BGU*32.3, *PTeb*.520. b. *allowance in lieu of quarters*, *IG*11(2).144.27 (Delos, iv B.C.). 2. ἐνοίκιον, τό, *dwelling*, D.P.668. **-ισμα**, ατος, τό, *dwelling*, Suid. s.v. ἐναύλισμα. **-ισμός**, ὁ, *right of occupation*, οἰκίας *POxy*.104.21 (i A.D.), cf. 1641.7 (i A.D.).

ἐνοικο-δομέω, *build in* a place, [τῇ νήσῳ] πύργον Th.3.51; [ἐν τῇ Λακωνικῇ] τείχισμα Id.8.4; θύρετρον *BCH*6.24 (Delos, ii B.C.):—Pass., ἐν τῇ Μιλήτῳ φρούριον Th.8.84:—Med., ἐ. τεῖχος *build oneself* a fort *there*, Id.3.85. II. *build up, block up*, τὰς θύρας τῶν οἰκιῶν *PPetr*.2p.28; θυρίδα Arr.*An*.6.29.10; εἴσοδον D.S.11.45; πυλίδα τινὰ ἐνῳκοδομημένην Th.6.51 (or perh. *built into* the wall), cf. Polyaen. 1.40.4; φάραγξ -ημένη D.S.3.37. **-δομία**, ἡ, *walling*, φρέατος *Jahresh*.11.63 (Theangela). **-λογέω**, *receive rent*, *PFlor*.1.7 (ii A.D.): c. acc., *receive rent for*, οἰκίας *PLond*.5.1708.39 (vi A.D.). **-λόγος**, ὁ, *rent-collector*, *POxy*.2008.1, *PKlein.Form*.87.2. **-νομέω**, *supply, furnish*, τῆς φύσεως τὸ γάλα ἐ. Sor.1.87.

ἔνοικος, ον, *inhabitant*, A.*Supp*.611, etc.; ἔ. θεός Hierocl. *in CA*11 p.441 M.: mostly c. gen. loci, *inhabitant of* a place, A.*Pr*.415 (lyr.), S.*Tr*.1092, Th.4.61, etc.: c. dat., *dweller in* a place, Pl.*Criti*.113c; ἑσμὸς τεχνιτῶν ἔνοικος πόλει Limen.20. 2. Pass., *dwelt in*, Παλλάδος ἔνοικα μέλαθρα E.*Ion* 235 (lyr.) (nisi leg. Παλλάδι συν-)

ἐνοικουρέω, *keep house*, of a garrison, ἐν.. D.H.6.3: metaph., ἡ μνήμη ἐνοικουροῦσα Luc.*Philops*.39.

ἔνοινος, ον, *full of wine*, Longus 2.1.

ἐνοινο-φλύω, *prate in one's cups*, Luc.*Lex*.14 (dub. l.). **-χοέω**, *pour in wine*, c. acc. cogn., οἶνον ἐνοινοχοεῦντες v.l. in Od.3.472; νέκταρ ἐνῳνοχόει v.l. ant. in Il.4.3.

ἐνοκλάζω, *squat upon*, τοῖς ὀπισθίοις, of a dog, Philostr.Jun.*Im*.3.

ἔνολβος, ον, *prosperous, wealthy*, Man.4.85.

ἐνολισθάνω, later **-αίνω**, aor. 2 ἐνώλισθον, *fall in*, of the ground, χάσμασι πολλοῖς Plu.*Cim*.16; *slip and fall*, of birds, Id.*Pomp*.25.

ἔνολμος, ον, (ὅλμος) *sitting on the tripod*, epith. of Apollo, S.*Fr*. 1044 (ἐνολμίς *Et. Gen*.).

ἐνομήρης, ες, = ὁμήρης ἐν..., *joined*, Nic.*Al*.238; cf. Hsch. s.v. ἐμπήρους.

ἐνομῑλέω, = ὁμιλέω ἐν.., D.C.43.15; τοῖς ἀνθρωπείοις καὶ φθαρτοῖς Ph.1.363, al. II. *to be well acquainted with*, πολλὰ τοῖς Πάρθων ἤθεσιν ἐνωμιληκώς Plu.*Ant*.41. III. Pass., *to be made familiar*, εὐθὺς ἐκ παιδίων -ημέναι δόξαι Polystr.p.32 W.

ἐνομμᾰτόω, *to furnish with eyes*, Ph.1.586, al.:—Pass., ib.540, al.

ἐνόμνῡμαι, Med., *make an affidavit*, ὑπέρ τινων *PHal*.1.71 (iii B.C.):—Pass., μαρτυρίαι ἐνομωμοσμέναι *sworn* depositions, ib.77. (Act. dub. in *Schwyzer* 167ᵃ(3).)

ἐνομόργνῡμι, *wipe on*:—Med., *impress*, τῷ ἐπιπέδῳ γραμμήν Plu. 2.1081b; ἐνομόρξασθαι [τῇ ψυχῇ] τὰ τῶν πολλῶν πάθη *impress* the feelings of the vulgar *upon* it, Id.*Cic*.32.

ἐνονυχίζει· ἀποδέχεται *EM*344.41, *AB*258.

ἐνόπη, ἡ, *ear-ring*, S.*Fr*.54.

ἐνοπή, ἡ, (ἐνέπω) *crying, shouting*, as of birds, Τρῶες μὲν κλαγγῇ τ' ἐνοπῇ τ' ἴσαν, ὄρνιθες ὥς Il.3.2; esp. *war-cry, battle-shout*, μάχη ἐνοπή τε 12.35, 16.246, etc. (hence, *battle*, *AP*6.163 (Mel.)); also, *cry* of sorrow, ἐνοπήν τε γόον τε Il.24.160; *wild cry*, ἐν Φρυγίαισι βοαῖς ἐνοπαῖσί τε E.*Ba*.159 (lyr.). 2. generally, *voice*, ἐνοπήν τε πυθοίμην Od.10. 147; Φοίβου..γλώσσης ἐνοπαί E.*El*.1302 (anap.), cf. *Hyps.Fr*.11(9). 13 (lyr.); νύχιοι ἐ. Id.*IT*1277 (lyr.); ταύρων ἐ. Nic.*Th*.171. 3. of things, *sound*, αὐλῶν συρίγγων τ' ἐνοπήν Il.10.13; ἰαχήν τ' ἐνοπήν τε, of thunder, Hes.*Th*.708; κιθάρας ἐ. E.*Ion* 882 (anap.); σαρκῶν ἐ. ἠδ' ὀστέων *crushing*, Pi.*Fr*.168.—Ep. and Lyr. word, used by E. in lyr.

ἐνόπιος, v. ἐνώπιος.

ἐνοπλ-ίζω, *adapt to*.., ὠλέναις πλάτην Lyc.205. II. Med., *arm oneself*, Ath.1.16a:—Pass., pf. part. -ωπλισμένος *armed*, Aq.*Ex*. 13.18. **-ιος**, ον, (ὅπλον) = ἔνοπλος, ἔρις Gorg.*Fr*.6; πρύλις Call. *Dian*.241; ἐπιστήμη D.H.20.2; πυρρίχη Anon.Vat.64: neut. as Adv., ἐλέλιξεν ἐνόπλιον Call.*Del*.137. II. ἐνόπλιος (with or without ῥυθμός), ὁ, '*martial*' *rhythm*, X.*An*.6.1.11, etc.; ῥυθμὸς κατ' ἐνόπλιον Ar.*Nu*.651; ἐ. σύνθετος Pl.*R*.400b; also νόμος Epich.75; ἀγωνία Phld.*Hom*.p.28 O.; ἐ. μέλη Ath.14.630f; Κουρήτων ἐ. παίγνια Pl. *Lg*.796b; θεῖν τὸν ἐ. Him.*Or*.2.20: hence ἐνόπλια παίζειν Pi.*O*.13. 86.—On the ῥυθμὸς κατ' ἐνόπλιον, v. Sch.Pi.*P*.2.127, Sch.Ar.*Nu*. 651. III. ἐνόπλιον, τό, *contest in arms*, of a race of war-chariots, *SIG*802*A* 10 (i A.D.). **-ισμός**, ὁ, mistranslation of Hebr. *ḥōmeš* 'belly' (*ḥāmuš* = 'in battle-array'), Aq.2*Ki*.2.23, 3.27. **-ος**, ον, *in arms, armed*, Tyrt.16, S.*OT*469 (lyr.), E.*HF*1164, *PGurob*1.7 (iii B.C.), D.H.5.28, Heraclit.*Incred*.19, etc.; κινήσεις τῶν ἐ. δραματικῶν Phld.*Mus*.p.15 K. II. *containing arms* or *armed men*, of the Trojan horse, E.*Tr*.520 (lyr.). III. εἰκὼν ἔ., = Lat. *imago clipeata*, portrait-statue *in armour*, *IPE*1.185 (Cherson., ii B.C.). IV. Adv. -ως Hsch. s.v. περιχορίζειν.

ἑνοποι-έω, *combine in one, unite*, Arist.*de An*.410ᵇ11:—Pass., Plb. 8.4.11. II. *unify*, τὸ διακεκριμένον Dam.*Pr*.391:—Pass., ὑπό τινος Procl. *in Prm*.p.541 S. **-ός**, όν, *combining in one, uniting*, λόγος Arist.*Metaph*.1045ᵇ17, cf. Porph.*Intr*.6.23. II. *creating unity*, Procl.*Inst*.13, Dam.*Pr*.33, cf. 298. Adv. -ῶς Ascl. *in Metaph*.439.25.

ἐνοπτιλίζειν· ἐμβλέπειν, Hsch.

ἔνοπτος, ον, *visible in* a thing, Arist.*Pr*.865ᵇ17.

ἐνοπτρ-ίζω, *reflect*, Damian.*Opt*.10:—Pass., *to be seen as in a mirror*, Porph.*Marc*.13, Olymp. *in Mete*.230.17:—Med., *see as in a mirror*, ἑαυτούς Ph.1.451, cf. Plu.2.696a; τὸ τῆς ἀληθείας κάλλος Hierocl. *in CA Praef*.p.416 M. **-ικοί**, οἱ, *optical geometers*, Olymp. *in Mete*. 69.18. II. neut. pl. ἐνοπτ⟨ρ⟩ικά, τά, title of work by Philip of Opus, Suid. s.v. φιλόσοφος. **-ισις**, εως, ἡ, *representation as in a mirror, reflection*, Plot.3.6.17. **-ον**, τό, *mirror*, E.*Hec*.925 (lyr.), *Or*.1112, *Not.Scav*.1920.328: generally, *reflecting surface*, ἐν ὕδατι καὶ τοῖς τοιούτοις ἐ. Arist.*Mete*.345ᵇ26, cf. 372ᵃ33.

ἐνόρ-ᾱσις, εως, ἡ, *beholding*, θεοῦ Porph.*Marc*.13. **-άω**, fut. ἐνόψομαι Iamb. *in Nic*.p.38 P.: aor. ἐνεῖδον (q.v.): aor. 1 Pass. ἐνώφθην *Theol.Ar*.30:—*see, remark, observe* something *in* a person or thing, τί τινι Th.3.30, X.*Cyr*.1.4.27, etc.; τι ἔν τινι Hdt.1.89, Th.1.95, Lys. 33.9 codd.; ἐν γὰρ τῷ οὐκ ἐνεώρα (sc. τὸ τυραννικόν) Hdt.3.53; ἐν τῷ χαλκίῳ ἐνορῶ γέροντα δειλίας φευξούμενον Ar.*Ach*.1129: c. acc. et fut. part., ἐνεώρα τιμωρίην ἐσομένην he *saw* that vengeance would come, Hdt.1.123, al.: c. dat. pers. et part., ἐνορῶ ὑμῖν οὐκ οὖσι τοῖς ἐσομένοισι πολεμεῖν Id.8.140.β':—Pass., Iamb. *in Nic*.p.43 P. II. *look at, behold*, Arist.*Fr*.153; δεινὸν ἐ. τοῖς παισί Plu.*Publ*.6; ἐνορῶντες ἐς ἀλλήλους δεινόν Paus.4.8.2.

ἐνοργείας· τὰς νεοσσείας (Cret.), Hsch.

ἐνόρειος, ον, (ὄρος) *in the mountains*, prob. for ἐνόριον, Scymn.832.

ἐνορθιάζω, *raise up*, πλέον τῆς φύσεως ἑαυτήν Ph.2.265 (dub.).

ἐνόριος, ον, (ὅρος) *within the boundaries*, Poll.9.8; *on the boundaries*, θεοί Hld.10.1: Subst. ἐνορία, ἡ, *territory* of a city, πόλις καὶ ἐ. *POxy.*1101.5 (iv A.D.), cf. *Cod.Just.*1.2.25.1, etc.

ἐνορκ-ίζομαι, Med., *make* one *swear*, ἐ. τινὶ ποιεῖν τι *IG*12(5).697.4 (Syros); ἐ. τινὶ ὅρκον ib.9(1).643 (Cephallenia), cf. J.*AJ*8.15.4 (v.l. ἐνωρκήσατο):—later in Act., ἐνορκίζω ὑμᾶς τὸν κύριον ἀναγνωσθῆναι τὴν ἐπιστολήν 1*Ep.Thess.*5.27; ἐ. ὑμῖν τὸν βασιλέα τῶν δαιμόνων *Tab. Defix.Aud.*26.15 (Cyprus, iii A.D.). **-ιος**, ον, = ἔνορκος, λόγος Pi. *O.*2.92. 2. Subst. ἐνόρκιον, τό, *oath*, Lxx *Nu.*5.21. II. = ἔνσπονδος, *GDI*3045 (Olympia). **-ος**, ον, *having sworn, bound by oath*, ἔνορκόν τινα θέσθαι to bind one *by oath*, S.*Ph.*811; ἔ. λαμβάνειν τὸν Ἀθηναίων δῆμον Aeschin.3.90, cf. 2.116, Arist.*Rh.*1396^{b}19: c. dat. pers., ἔ. οὐδενί S.*Ph.*72. 2. = ἔνσπονδος, *included in a treaty*, Th.2.72. II. *that whereto one is sworn*, θεῶν ἔ. δίκη S.*Ant.*369 (lyr.); ἔνορκον [εἶμεν] τοῖς ἐπιϝοίκοις μὴ ποσταμεν *IG*9(1).334.11 (v B.C.); παρακαταθήκην ἔνορκον εἰληφὼς παρὰ τῶν νόμων, of the jurors, D.25.11; ἔ. προσφώνησις *Stud.Pal.*22.184.88 (ii A.D.); ἔνορκόν τι καταστῆσαι Aeschin.2.176; τῷ μὴ βουλομένῳ μὴ εἶναι ἔνορκον συμμαχεῖν X.*HG*6.3.18; of a decree, *Rev.Ét.Gr.*24.415 (Itanos, ii B.C.); ἔνορκον ποιεῖσθαι to bind oneself *by oath*, Pl.*Phd.*89c; ἔνορκον ἐποίσει τὴν ψῆφον, Lat. *juratus feret sententiam*, D.H.7.45. Adv. **-κως** Lxx *To.*8.20, Ath.6.274e, Poll.1.39. b. *consecrated by oath*, λίθος Pl. *Lg.*843a. **-όω**, *adjure*, *BGU*836.9 (vi A.D.), etc.; ἐνορκῶ σε κατὰ τοῦ πατρός Sch.Luc.*Cat.*23.

ἐνορμ-άω, *rush in*, εἴς τι Plb.16.28.8 (prob. for ἐνήρμοσεν); ἐνορμῶντα, τά, = πνεύματα (viz. φυσικόν and ψυχικόν), Hp.ap.Gal.7.597 and Pall.*in Hp.*2.200 D. (v.l. in Hp.*Epid.*6.8.7). **-έω**, *ride at anchor in* a harbour, Plb.16.29.13: metaph., Ph.1.523:—Med., J.*AJ*15.9.6. **-ίζω**, *bring* a ship *to land*: hence metaph., κύρτον ῥοθίοισι Opp.*H.*3.409:—Med., *enter harbour*, Str.5.4.6, D.H.1.56, Ph.2.8, etc.: metaph., λιμέσιν ἀρετῆς Id.1.688, al.:—also in Pass., ἐκ θυελλῶν ἐνωρμίσθην Thgn.1274. **-ιον** (ἐνόρμιν ostr.), τό, *harbour-dues*, *Ostr.*263,304, Hsch. s. v. ἀγκυροβόλῳ δείπνῳ. **-ισμα**, ατος, τό, *anchorage, roadstead*, App.*BC*4.106. **-ίτης** [ῑ], ου, poet. **-τας**, αο, ὁ, *in harbour*, *AP*10.2 (Antip. Sid.), 10.14.9 (Agath.). **-ος**· ἡ ὥρα παρὰ Θετταλοῖς, Hsch.

ἐνόρνῡμι, aor. 1 ἐνῶρσα: Ep. aor. 2 Pass. ἐνῶρτο:—the only two tenses used by Hom.:—*arouse, stir up in* a person, τῇσιν γόον ἐνῶρσεν Il.6.499; [Ἀχαιοῖς] ἀνάλκιδα φύζαν ἐνόρσας 15.62; ἐν δὲ σθένος ὦρσεν ἑκάστῳ 2.451; φόβον τινί 11.544; [μάχαν] (sc. ἄμμιν) Alc.*Supp.*23.12; θάρσος δ' ἐνῶρσε.. στρατῷ E.*Supp.*713:—Pass., *arise in* or *among*, ἐνῶρτο γέλως θεοῖσιν Il.1.599.

ἐνορούω, *leap in* or *upon*, usu. of an assault, c. dat., Τρωσὶ.. ἐνόρουσεν Il.16.783; ὡς δὲ λέων.. αἴγεσιν ἢ ὀΐεσσι.. ἐνορούσῃ 10.486: abs., ἐν δ' Ἀγαμέμνων πρῶτος ὄρουσε 11.217; ὕδωρ ἀνέδην ἐνοροῦον prob. in Hp.*Cord.*2; of fish, νήεσσιν ἐ. Opp.*H.*2.516.

ἐνορύσσω, *dig*, plpf. Pass. ἐνωρώρυκτο, κολυμβήθρα Philostr.*VA*2.27.

ἐνορχέομαι, = ὀρχέομαι ἐν.., Alciphr.3.65.

ἐνόρχ-ης, ου, ὁ, = ἔνορχος, Ar.*Eq.*1385, al., Arist.*HA*632^{a}20; **ἐνορχής**, ές, *SIG*57.20 (Milet., vi B.C.). 2. Dor. τὸν ἐνόρχᾶν (acc.), *he-goat*, Theoc.3.4 (ἐνόρχαν v.l. ap.Sch.). 3. title of Dionysus at Phigalia, Lyc.212; at Samos, Hsch. **-ις**, ιος, ὁ, ἡ, Ion. for foreg., Hdt.6.32, 8.105, Luc.*DDeor.*4.1. **-ος**, ον, (ὄρχις) *with the testicles in, uncastrated, entire*, ἔνορχα.. μῆλ' ἱερεύσειν, i.e. *rams*, Il.23.147; τὰ ἔ. *entire animals*, Hp.*Vict.*2.49; also of palm-trees, Arist.*Fr.*267 codd. Ath.

ἔνος (A), ὁ, *year*, Lyd.*Mens.*4.1, Hsch.

ἔνος (B), η, ον, found only in oblique cases of fem., gen. ἕνης, Ep. ἔνηφι, dat. ἕνῃ, acc. ἕνην, in the sense of εἰς τρίτην, *the day after tomorrow*: ἔς τ' αὔριον ἔς τ' ἔνηφιν Hes.*Op.*410 (v.l. ἔς τ' ἔννηφι); gen. ἕνης Ar.*Ec.*796, Dor. ἕνας Theoc.18.14; εἰς ἕνην Ar.*Ach.*172; αὔριον ⟨καὶ⟩ τῇ ἕνῃ Antipho6.21; ἐς ἕνης ἢ prob. l. (for ἐς ἐν ᾗ σῇ) in D.C. 47.41; cf. ἕναρ· ἐς τρίτην (Lacon.), Hsch., and v. ἐπέναρ. (Demonstr. stem *eno-* (*ono-*), cf. Umbr. *enom* 'tum', Slav. *onŭ* 'he'.)

ἔνος (C), η, ον (so Att. Inscrr., Ar.*Nu.*1134, Pl.*Cra.*409b; in codd. freq. written ἕνος, as Hes.*Op.*770, etc.), *belonging to the former of two periods* (τὸ ἕνον..· τὸ πρότερον καὶ παρεληλυθὸς δηλοῖ, Harp.; ἕνην· τὴν παλαιάν, Suid.), ὁ νόμος ἐπὶ Κρόνου ἕνος (opp. νεωστί) Dam. *Pr.*348: hence, *last year's*, ἕναι ἀρχαί *last year's* magistrates, D.25.20, prob. in Arist.*Pol.*1322^{a}12; στρατηγοὶ ἕνοι Id.*Ath.*4.2; Ἑλληνοταμίαι ἕνοι *IG*1^2.324.26; ἕνης ἐπιφορᾶς ib.2181138; ἕνος [καρπός] *last year's* fruit, Thphr.*HP*3.4.6; also ἕνος ὄνος *a year old*, *BGU*806: generally, *old, by-gone*, νέον δέ που καὶ ἕνον ἀεί ἐστι περὶ τὴν σελήνην τοῦτο τὸ φῶς Pl.*Cra.*409b:—in Ar.*Ach.*610 ἤδη πεπρέσβευκας σὺ πολιὸς ὢν ἕνη, the Sch. takes ἕνη as an Adv. = ἐκ πολλοῦ, *long ago*; but the passage is prob. corrupt. 2. ἕνη καὶ νέα (sc. ἡμέρα) *the old and new day*, i.e. *the last day of the month*, *IG*1^2.374.276, Ar.*Nu.*1134sq., Lys.23.6: first used by Solon, acc. to D.L.1.57; Σκιροφοριῶνος ἕνῃ καὶ νέᾳ *IG*2^2.916.10, cf. Decr.ap.D.18.29; ἕνη alone, Hes. *Op.*770. (Cf. Lith. *sẽnas* 'old', Lat. *senex*, etc.)

ἐνοσίζεται· τρέμει, σείεται, Cyr.

ἔνοσις, εως, ἡ, *shaking, quake*, Hes.*Th.*681,849; αἰθερίαι ἐ. E.*Hel.*1363 (lyr.), cf. Orph.*Fr.*285.24; ἔννοσις· κίνησις, Hsch. II. personified in poet. form Ἔννοσις, prob. in E.*Ba.*585 (lyr.).

Ἐνοσίχθων, ονος, ὁ, *Earth-shaker*, epith. of Poseidon, Il.7.445, al.; Ἐ. alone, 13.89, al. II. later, as Adj., *earth-stirring*, ἄροτρον Euph.152; σίδηρος Nonn.*D.*2.67.

ἑνότης, ητος, ἡ, (εἷς) *unity*, Arist.*Metaph.*1018^{a}7, *Ph.*222^{a}19, Plot. 6.6.16, etc.; ἡ ἑ. ἐν ἑτερότητι Porph.*Sent.*36; τοῦ αἵματος Arist.*PA*667^{b}30. II. *union*, συμπάθεια πρὸς ἀλλήλους καὶ ἑ. ἰδιότροπος Epicur.*Ep.*1 p.13 U.; τοῦ πνεύματος τῆς πίστεως *Ep.Eph.*4.3,13; ἑνότητα ποιεῖν Plu.2.769f. III. in concrete sense, ἀπογεγεννημένη ἑ. Epicur.*Nat.Herc.*1634.1; τῶν αἰσθητῶν ἑ. Demetr.Lac.1055.7 F., cf. Phld.*Piet.*80 (pl.).

ἔνοτος, Aeol., = ἔνατος (q.v.).

ἔνουλα, τά, (οὖλον) *gums inside the teeth*, Poll.2.94.

ἐνουλίζομαι, Pass., *to be curly*, of hair, Aristaenet.1.1, Alciphr.*Fr.*5.4.

ἔνουλον, τό, *wound*, Phld.*D.*1.24.

ἔνουλος, ον, *curled, curly*, πλόκαμοι ἔ. Callistr.*Stat.*3.

ἐνουράνιος [ᾰ], ον, *in heaven, heavenly*, *AP*9.223 (Bianor), Poll. 1.23; ἀνάγκη *Sammelb.*5620.9.

ἐνουρ-έω, aor. 1 ἐνεούρησα Eup.45:—*make water in*, ἔς τι Hdt.1.138, 2.172; εἰς τὰ ὦτα Porph.*Abst.*3.3; ἔν τινι Hermipp.82.1: abs., ὥσπερ ἐνεουρηκότες like *piss-a-beds*, Ar.*Lys.*402, cf. Arist.*Pr.*876^{a}15, Dsc.*Eup.*2.106, Paul.Aeg.3.45. **-ήθρα**, ἡ, or **-ηθρον**, τό, *chamber-pot*, S.*Fr.*485. **-ητής**, οῦ, ὁ, = *submeiolus*, *Gloss.*, Sch.Ar.*Eq.*399.

ἐνουσι-ακῶς, Adv. dub. sens. in *BGU*277 ii 10 (ii A.D., fort. ἐν οὐσιακοῖς). **-όομαι**, *acquire substance*, τῇ φύσει τῆς γῆς Dam.*Pr.*74, cf. 81; ὁ τοῦ χρόνου λόγος ἀΐδιος [φύσει] ἐνουσιωμένος Id.ap.Simp.*in Ph.*780.5. II. *subsist in*, ὁ τοῖς λογικοῖς γένεσιν ἐνουσιωμένος ὅρκος Hierocl.*in CA*2 p.422 M. **-ος**, ον, = συμφυής, Hsch. 2. = πολυκτήμων, Id. 3. Adv. **-ίως** *on the security of one's property*, *CPR*40.15 (iv A.D.).

ἐνοφείλω, *owe on security*, *IG*14.956^{B}16 (iv A.D.): generally, *owe*, *POxy.*986:—Pass., *to be due upon a security*, τινί to one, D.53.10; ἐν οὐσίᾳ *secured on* property, Id.49.45: generally, *to be due, owing*, εἴ τι -οφείλεται *PRev.Laws*18.17, al. (iii B.C.), cf. *IG*2.1134, *PTeb.*17.6 (ii B.C.), etc.

ἐνοφθαλμ-ιάζομαι, Pass., *admit of being inoculated*, Plu.2.640b tit. **-ιάω**, *cast longing eyes upon*, v.l. for ἐπ-, Poll.2.62. **-ίζω**, *inoculate, bud*, δένδρον ἐν ἀπὸ πλειόνων Thphr.*CP*5.5.4, cf. *Gp.*10.77.1:—Pass., *Inscr.Délos*366*B*20, Procl.*in Cra.*p.39 P. **-ισμός**, ὁ, *budding*, *Gp.*10.77.1: pl., Thphr.*CP*1.6.1,2, Plu.2.640b.

ἔνοφρυς, υ, *with bushy eyebrows*, *Gloss.* (dub.).

ἐνοχή, ἡ, *liability, obligation*, *PLand.*48.11 (vi A.D.), etc.; ἀγωγὴ καὶ ἐ. conduct and *responsibility* of a transaction, *POxy.*133.7 (vi A.D.).

ἐνοχία, ἡ, dub. in *PTeb.*112.10 (ii B.C.).

ἐνοχλ-έω, Aeol. and poet. 2 sg. ἐννοχλεῖς Theoc.29.36: impf. with double augm. ἠνώχλουν X.*Cyr.*5.3.56, Isoc.5.53, etc.: fut. ἐνοχλήσω Id.15.153: aor. ἠνώχλησα D.19.206: pf. ἠνώχληκα Id.21.4:—Pass., fut. -ηθήσομαι D.H.10.3, Polystr.p.8 W.; also -ήσομαι (in pass. sense) Id.p.6 W., App.*BC*1.36, Gal.*UP*11.19 (as v.l.): aor. part. ἐνοχληθείς Hp.*Coac.*510: pf. ἠνώχλημαι (παρ-) D.18.50:—*trouble, annoy*, τινά Pl.*Alc.*1.104d, Diod.Com.2.18, X.*Mem.*3.8.2, etc.; simply, *address*, *PMag.Leid.W.*3.34:—Pass., *to be troubled* or *annoyed*, X.*Cyr.*5.4.34, D.19.20; ἡ ἐκκλησία ἠνωχλεῖτο Aeschin.3.43; *to be unwell*, Lxx *Ge.*48.1, al.; of a horse, *PPetr.*3 p.73 (iii B.C.); *to be overburdened with work*, *PHamb.*27.18 (iii B.C.), etc. 2. c. dat., *give trouble* or *annoyance to*, Lys.24.21; τοῖς ἀκούουσιν Isoc.4.7; τῇ ὑμετέρᾳ εὐδαιμονίᾳ X.*An.*2.5.13, cf. Amphis 15, Epicur.*Nat.*11.10; ἠνώχλει ἡμῖν D.3.5, etc. 3. abs., *to be a trouble, a nuisance*, Hp.*Aph.*2.50, Ar.*Ra.*708, Epicur.*Ep.*3 p.61 U., etc.: with neut. Adj., ὅσα.. ἠνώχλησεν *all the trouble he has given*, D.21.15: c. part., τὸ δὲ μὴ οὐκ ἠνώχλει λέγων X.*Cyr.*5.3.56. II. *worry about, fuss over*, τὰς ἀρετὰς τὰς ὑπὸ τούτων ἐνοχλουμένας Diog.Oen.25.—Prose word, sts. used in Com., never in Trag. **-ημα**, ατος, τό, *trouble, worry*, Epicur.*Fr.*154. II. Medic., *distress, malaise*, Apollon.ap.Orib.7.20.3. **-ησις**, εως, ἡ, *annoyance*, Philem.92.3 (pl.), *PLond.*3.971.4 (iv A.D.); ἐ. σοφιστικαί Arist.*Int.*17^{a}37, cf. D.L.7.14,112, Procl.*in Alc.*p.333 C. **-ητέον**, *one must annoy*, οὐκ ἐ. τῷ θεῷ Max.Tyr.11.4.

ἐνοχο-ποιέω, *convict*, τινα ἐπί τινι Anon.*in Rh.*237.25. **-ποιός**, όν, *creating obligations*, *Gloss.*

ἔνοχος, ον, = ἐνεχόμενος, *held in, bound by*, τοιαύταις δόξαις Arist. *Metaph.*1009^{b}17; ταῖς εἰρημέναις βλάβαις Id.*Pol.*1337^{b}17; [ἔθεσι γεροντικοῖς] Apollod.Com.7.2. 2. c. gen., *connected with*, κοιλίης Hp.*Ep.*23. II. as law-term, *liable to, subject to*, νόμοις, δίκαις, Pl.*Lg.*869b; τῇ γραφῇ X.*Mem.*1.2.64; τῇ κρίσει *Ev.Matt.*5.22; τῷ ὅρκῳ *PRyl.*82.14 (ii A.D.), etc.; τοῖς ἐπιτιμίοις τοῦ φόνου Antipho 4.1.6; ζημίαις Lys.14.9; ταῖς ἀραῖς D.19.201; δεσμῷ Id.51.4; ὅρκῳ *PHib.*1.65.22 (iii B.C.), etc.; ἔ. ἀνοίαις *liable to the imputation of* it, Isoc.8.7; ἁμαρτήμασι Aeschin.2.146; τοῖς αἰσχίστοις ἐπιτηδεύμασιν Id.1.185. 2. ἔνοχος ψευδομαρτυρίοις *liable to action for..*, Pl.*Tht.*148b: c. gen., ἔ. τοῦ φόνου Antipho6.46; βιαίων, λιποταξίου (sc. δίκῃ, γραφῇ), Pl.*Lg.*914e, Lys.14.5; ἱεροσυλίας Lxx 2*Ma.*13.6; μοιχείας Vett.Val.117.10; ἔ. θανάτου *liable to the penalty of* death, D.S.27.4, *Ev.Matt.*26.66 (but θανάτῳ Wilcken *Chr.*13.11 (i A.D.)): c. inf., ἔ. ἔστω ἀποτῖσαι *CIG*2832.8 (Aphrodisias). 3. less freq. with Preps., ἔ. ἐν τοῖς αὐτοῖς Decr.ap.And.1.79; περὶ ταὐτά Arist.*Rh.*1384^{b}2; ἔνοχοι ἔντω ἐνς Ἀθαναίαν *IG*4.554 (Argos, vi/v B.C.). 4. *guilty, liable to the penalty for*, ἔ. τῷ φόνῳ Antipho 1.11, Arist.*Pol.*1269^{a}3, cf. *Rh.*1380^{a}3: abs., Antipho4.1.1, 6.17, Pl.*Sph.*261a, etc. b. of property, *subject to liability*, *PMasp.*312.86 (vi A.D.).

ἔνοψις, εως, ἡ, (ὄψομαι) = ἔποψις, Them.*Or.*13.177d.

ἑνόω, (εἷς) *make one, unite*, λίαν τὴν πόλιν Arist.*Pol.*1261^{b}10; τὰ ἐναντιώτατα Archyt.ap.Stob.1.41.2; τὰ πολυμιγῆ Herm.ap.eund.1.49.3; τὸ ἀκούειν τῷ πράττειν Ph.1.609: ἑνοῦν τινὰ τῇ γῇ to bury him, Philostr.*Im*.2.29; of *mixing* drugs, ἀκριβῶς ἕνωσον Dsc.*Eup*.1.13, cf. 1.31 (Pass.):—Pass., Ph.1.471, al., Cleom.2.1, etc.; ἡνῶσθαι τὰ πάντα Arr.*Epict*.1.14.2; λίμνη.. ἡνωμένη τῇ θαλάσσῃ Ath.7.311d; τὰ φύσει ἡνωμένα *things united* by nature, Longin.22.3; τὰ ἡ. *propositions couched in the singular number*, Id.24.1; ἡνωμένοι, opp. ἀσύντακτοι, of troops, J.*BJ*3.2.2; esp. in Philos., *unified*, τὸ μὲν ὂν ἀριθμὸς ἡνωμένος Plot.6.6.9; τὸ ἡ., = τὸ ὄν, Dam.*Pr*.20, cf. 68, al.

ἐνρ–, see also ἐρρ–.

ἐνραβῶς· ἐγγράψας, Hsch.

ἐνράπτω, *sew up in*, βυβλίον εἰς ἡνίαν χαλινοῦ Aen.Tact.31.9, Plu.*Arat*.25:—Med., Διόνυσον ἐνερράψατο ἐς τὸν μηρόν into *his* thigh, Hdt.2.146, cf. *IG*14.1285,1292:—Pass., *to be sewed up in*, ἐνερράφη Διὸς μηρῷ E.*Ba*.286; ἱμάντα ἐν ᾧ ἐπιστολὴ ἐνέρραπτο Aen.Tact.31.32; λίθοι ἐνερραμμένοι τῷ ἐσσῆνι J.*AJ*3.8.9.

ἐνράσσω, *dash against*, ταῖς πύλαις J.*AJ*5.8.10.

ἔνρειθρον, *endoriguum*, *Gloss.*

ἐνρήγνῡμι, *break into*:—Pass., *discharge itself into*, ἐς ἔντερον Aret.*SA*1.10. II. intr. in pf. part. Act. ἐνερρωγώς, υῖα, ός, *broken*, κλῖναι *IG*11(2).199*B*90 (iii B.C.).

ἔνρηξις, εως, ἡ, *impact*, *Gloss.* **ἐνρήσσω**, = ἐνρήγνυμι, Apollod.*Poliorc*.141.2.

ἐνρητορεύω, *show eloquence in*, πατρῴοις λόγοις Heraclit.*All*.63.

ἐνρῑγισκάνω, *shiver in*, τριβώνιον πονηρὸν οἷον -ειν *Com.Adesp*.10D.

ἐνρῑγόω, = ῥιγόω ἐν, *shiver* or *freeze in*, Ar.*Pl*.846.

ἔνριζ-ος, ον, *with a root*, *Gp*.3.4.6. **-όω**, *implant*, τῷ ἐγκεφάλῳ Hp.*Oss*.12; -οῦσα τὸ νεῦρον ὡς εἰς γῆν τὰ μόρια Gal.*UP*7.15; Εὔβοιαν θαλάσσῃ Nonn.*D*.42.411:—Pass., Gal.*UP*11.14: so metaph., *to be rooted*, *grounded in*, τῇ οἰκείᾳ ἀκρότητι Dam.*Pr*.258; τῇ σφῶν αἰτίᾳ ib.34; of conditions, *become firmly established*, ἡ διάθεσις ἐνερριζῶσθαι φαίνεται Orib.*Syn*.9.12.1. **-ωσις**, εως, ἡ, *rooting in*, Simp.*in Ph*.637.1.

ἐνρίπτω, *throw in*, αὐτὸν ἐς τὴν πόλιν Arr.*An*.6.10.4; λίθον D.C.74.14.

ἔνρυθμος, ον, *of rhythm*, αἴσθησις Pl.*Lg*.654a; *possessing rhythm* (opp. εὔρυθμος), D.H.*Comp*.11; διάλεκτος Ephor.6J.; opp. ἔκρυθμος, S.E.*M*.11.186. Adv. -μως Ath.5.179f, 14.631b (prob.).

ἐνρῡσόομαι, *become wrinkled*, ἐνερρυσωμένος *rugose*, Meges ap.Orib.44.24.2.

ἐνς ἄς· αὔριον, Hsch. (ἔνσας cod.: Cretan or Argive form); cf. εἰς, ἄας.

ἐνσαλπίζω, *sound a trumpet in*, τοῖς ὠσί Gal.12.656.

ἔνσαρκος, ον, *of flesh*, ἔ. βορά *flesh* meat, Porph.*Abst*.1.1, cf. *Gaur*.3.2.

ἐνσᾰρόομαι, Pass., *to be swept about in..*, πόντου.. ἐνσαρούμενος μυχοῖς Lyc.753.

ἐνσάττω, *stuff in*, of one eating sausages, Alciphr.3.7.

ἐνσᾰφῶς, Adv. *clearly*, *BGU*713.

ἐνσβέννῠμαι, Pass., *to be quenched in*, ὕδατι Dsc.5.80.2.

ἔνσειμι, Cret. for εἴσειμι, *enter*, 3 sg. pres. subj. ἐνσείη *Leg.Gort*.5.36.

ἐν-σεισμός, ὁ, *attack*, of engines of war, Thd.*Ez*.26.9. **-σείω**, pf. ἐνσέσεικα *BGU*136.11 (ii A.D.):—*brandish* or *hurl at*, c. acc. rei, ἐ. βέλος κεραυνοῦ S.*Tr*.1087; ὀξὺν δι' ὤτων κέλαδον ἐ. πώλοις *drive* a shrill sound into their ears, Id.*El*.737; ἐνέσεισε.. μεταниπτρίδα Philetaer.1. 2. c. acc. pers., *plunge in*, *drive into*, ἐ. τινὰ ἀγρίαις ὁδοῖς S.*Ant*.1274; ἑαυτοὺς τῇ ἐπιτροπῇ *BGU*l.c.; ἑαυτὸν τῇ ἑστίᾳ Luc.*Asin*.31; σπινθῆρας πυρὸς ὑγιαίνοντι σώματι Gal.7.182; οἱ κακῶν σαυτὴν ἐνέσεισας Alciphr.3.27; τὸν Ἀρχίαν εἰς τὸν πότον Plu.2.588b; εἰς βάραθρον ἐ. τινά Luc.*Merc.Cond*.30; ἐ. τὴν πόλιν εἰς πόλεμον Plu.*Phoc*.23; ἐ. χιόνα εἰς τὸν ἄκρατον Macho ap.Ath.13.579f:—Pass., εἰς ὠνήν *to be jockeyed* into a purchase, Hyp.*Ath*.26. b. c. acc. rei, *loosen*, *damage*, μέρος τοῦ χάρακος *BGU*1215.15 (iii B.C.). 3. Pass., *to be interpolated*, Sch.Il.23.104. 4. *shake*, *jar*, Hp.*Off*.25 (Pass.); ἐ. βάσιν *jar* one's foot, Luc.*Ocyp*.9. 5. *dash to the ground*, νήπια Lxx 4*Ki*.8.12. 6. Pass., ἐνσεσεισμένη *broken by age*, *Com. Adesp*.1001. 7. metaph., *shake thoroughly*, Pass., ἐνσείσθητι Arr.*Epict*.3.14.3. II. intr., *rush upon*, *attack*, [τινὶ ναυσὶ] πλαγίαις D.S.13.40; εἰς τὰς ναῦς Id.14.60; τοῖς πολεμίοις κατὰ τὸ δεξιὸν κέρας D.H.9.16, cf. Plu.*Alex*.60; πόνοι ἐ. εἰς ὀσφύν *shoot*, Ruf.*Ren.Ves*.1.3:—Med., *jostle*, Arr.*Epict*.4.4.24, v.l. in Epict.*Ench*.4:—Pass., τοῖς κιόσιν ἐνσεισθείς J.*AJ*5.8.12.

ἐνσεμνύνομαι, Pass., *glory in*, προγόνοις Onos.1.24.

ἐνσήθω, *sift in*, Aret.*CA*1.1.

ἐνσημαίνω, *contain a signification*, *imply*, ὅτι ἀγαστὸς.. ἐνσημαίνει τὸ ὄνομα Ἀγαμέμνων Pl.*Cra*.395b. 2. *report*, *signal*, τὴν αἴσθησιν Arist.*de An*.423ᵃ4:—Pass., *to be indicated* or *expressed*, ἐ. ἡ ἀναίδεια ἐν τοῖς ὀφθαλμοῖς Longin.4.4. 3. *show in*, Philostr.*VA*2.22. II. Med., *give notice of*, *intimate*, τινὶ τὴν ὀργήν Isoc.20.22, cf. Arist.*Ath*.18.2; τοῦτο, ὅτι.. X.*Cyr*.8.2.3:—Pass., *POxy*.396 (i A.D.). 2. *give signs one to another*, X.*Cyn*.6.22. 3. *impress* or *stamp upon*, σημεῖα Pl.*Tht*.191d, cf. 209c; τύπον ἐ. ἑκάστῳ Id.*R*.377b:—Pass., *to be imprinted*, εἴς τι Id.*Tht*.194c, cf. Ph.1.242; ὑπὸ τῶν ἐννοιῶν ἐνσεσημασμένον.. λόγον Diog.Bab.*Stoic*.3.216.

ἔνσημος, ον, *significant*, *important*, Hp.*Superf*.17: f.l. for ἐπίσημος, κώμη *Peripl.M.Rubr*.54. II. *coined*, νόμισμα Tz.*H*.1.928.

ἐνσήπομαι, Pass., *putrefy within*, Hp.*Morb*.1.18, Lyd.*Mag*.3.61.

ἔνσηστρον, τό, *sieve*, *Gloss.* (prob.).

ἔνσῑμος, ον, *somewhat snub-nosed*, *PPetr*.3p.21 (iii B.C.), etc.: f.l. for ἔνσημος, Hp.*Superf*.17:—written ἔσσιμος, *PCair.Zen*.76.11. II. *concave*, of surfaces, Ruf.*Anat*.40,52.

ἐνσῑνής, ές, (σίνος) *injured*, Man.2.445; *in ill-health*, *BGU*560.22 (iv A.D.).

ἐνσῑτ-έομαι, Med., *feed upon*, Lxx *Jb*.40.25(30). **-ος**, ον, *public guest*, a title of honour at Sparta, *IG*5(1).53.35, al. II. *fed*, *replete*, *Hippiatr*.111.

ἐνσκέλλω, Ep. ἐνισκ–, *dry* or *wither up*, μή τοι ἐνισκήλῃ.. Nic.*Th*.694:—Pass., with pf. Act. ἐνέσκληκα, *to be dry*, *withered*, Hp.*Morb*.1.28; ἐνεσκληκὼς γὰρ ἀνίαις *AP*12.166 (Asclep.): also of timber, *to be dry*, *seasoned*, A.R.3.1251.

ἐνσκέπαρνος, ον, *oblique*, of bandages, Heliod.ap.Orib.48.64.2.

ἐνσκευ-άζω, *get ready*, *prepare*, δεῖπνον Ar.*Ach*.1096; *harness*, ἵππους Polyaen.7.21.6:—Med., *contrive*, διαβολάς J.*BJ*1.3.2. 2. *dress in*, ἱματίῳ τινά Plu.*Lyc*.15, cf. Luc.*Nec*.8; ὅτιή σε.. Ἡρακλέα 'νεσκεύασα *dressed* you *up* as Hercules, prob. l. in Ar.*Ra*.523:—Med., *dress oneself up*, Id.*Ach*.384, Pl.*Cri*.53d; δουλικῶς Phryn.Com.2D.; *arm oneself*, X.*Cyr*.8.5.11; ἱππεῖς -σάμενοι τοὺς ἵππους *having put trappings on their* horses, Jul.*Or*.2.76d:—but Med. just like Act., Luc.*Asin*.37:—Pass., *to be equipped*, ἐνεσκεύαστο γὰρ οὕτως Hdt.9.22; ἀναξυρίσι καὶ χειρῖσιν ἐ. Plu.*Oth*.6; εἰς εἰκόνα τοῦ δημιουργοῦ, τοῦ ἡλίου, Porph.ap.Eus.*PE*3.12: metaph., σωφροσύνην ἐνεσκευασμένος Ph.1.682. **-ος**, ον, *with a mask on*, v.l. for ἔκσκευος, Poll.4.141.

ἔνσκεψις, in form ἔμσκεψις, q.v.

ἐνσκηνοβᾰτέομαι, Pass., *to be brought on the stage*, Alciphr.2.4.6.

ἔνσκην-ος, ον, *furnished with an awning*, *PLond*.5.1714.32 (vi A.D.). **-όω**, *encamp*, dub. in Lxx *Ge*.13.12.

ἐνσκήπτω, Ep. ἐνισκ–, *hurl*, *dart in* or *upon*, ὁ θεὸς ἐνέσκηψε βέλος [ἐς οἰκίην] the god *darted* his lightning *on* it, Hdt.4.79; τούτων ἐκγόνοισι ἐνέσκηψε ἡ θεὸς.. νοῦσον Id.1.105; ἐνισκ. ἰόν v.l. in Nic.*Th*.140, cf. 336 (v. ἐνσκίμπτω). II. intr., *fall in* or *on*, ἐνέσκηψαν οἱ λίθοι ἐς τὸ τέμενος Hdt.8.39; ἐν οἷς ἂν [δένδροις] ἐνσκήψῃ ἡ ἶρις Arist.*Pr*.906ᵇ24; κεραυνὸς ἐνσκήψας εἰς τὸν βωμόν Plu.*Aem*.24; τινί Ael.*NA*14.27; ὁκόσα κύστι καὶ νεφροῖσι ἐνσκήπτει Aret.*SD*2.2; εἰς κεφαλήν D.C.53.29: abs., Ruf.*Fr*.118; of love, εἴς τινα Alciphr.1.13.

ἔνσκηψις, εως, ἡ, *falling*, κεραυνῶν Lyd.*Ost*.41 (pl.).

ἐνσκῐατροφέομαι, Pass., (σκιά, τρέφω) *to live in the shade*, ἐ. ἐλπίσι *to feed* on *sickly* hopes, Plu.2.476e.

ἐνσκιμβέω, in pf. ἐνεσκίμβηκα, = ἐνσκιρρόομαι, Hsch.

ἐνσκίμπτω, poet. ἐνισκ–, Ep. and Lyr. form of ἐνσκήπτω, *lean upon*, οὔδει ἐνισκίμψαντε καρήατα, of horses *hanging* their heads *in grief* for their master's loss, Il.17.437; *fix*, *plant in*, βέλος ἐνισκ. τινί A.R.3.153; ἐ. βολῇσι *smite* with its beams, of dawn, Id.4.113:—Pass., *stick in*, δόρυ οὔδει ἐνεσκίμφθη Il.16.612. II. *hurl upon* one, κεραυνὸς ἐνέσκιμψε μόρον Pi.*P*.3.58 (v.l. ἐνέσκηψε); ὁππότ' ἀνίας.. πραπίδεσσιν ἐνισκίμψωσιν Ἔρωτες A.R.3.765; of a snake, ἐνισκ. ἰόν Nic.*Th*.140; βλοσυρὸν δάκος ib.336.

ἔνσκῐος, ον, (σκιά) *tarnished*, Ps.-Democr.Alch.p.53B.

ἐνσκιρρόω, *harden*:—Pass., *become callous*, *inveterate*, of diseases, X.*Eq*.4.2, Thd.*Is*.27.1, Sch.Ar.*V*.920.

ἐνσκολιεύομαι, *catch in a snare*, Lxx *Jb*.40.19(24).

ἐνσκοπέομαι, *consider the while*, Hld.8.10 (perh. f.l. for ἐπισκ–).

ἐνσοβέω, *step proudly in*, πεδίλῳ Philostr.*VA*6.10. II. *agitate*:—Pass., τὸ ἐνσεσοβημένον *agitation*, Chrysipp.*Stoic*.3.127.

ἔνσομφος, ον, *spongy*, οἴδημα [Gal.]14.384.

ἐνσόριον, τό, (σορός) *place for a sarcophagus*, *IGRom*.4.1452 (Smyrna), *AJA*18.68 (Sardes, iii A.D.), etc.

ἐνσοφιστεύω, = σοφιστεύω ἐν.., ἀκακωτάτοις ἤθεσι Ph.1.315: abs., Id.2.59.

ἔνσοφος, ον, *wise in* a thing, Man.4.549: abs., ἔ. ἄνδρες *IG*14.1020.

ἐνσπᾰθάω, = σπαθάω ἐν.., ταῖς τοῦ θεοῦ δωρεαῖς Ph.2.372.

ἐνσπᾰθίζω, *stir* boiling liquid, Orib.*Fr*.133.

ἐνσπαργᾰνόω, *wrap as in swathing bands*, in Pass., ἔθεσι καὶ ἐπιτηδεύμασι Longin.44.3; ἔπεσι Heraclit.*All*.1.

ἐνσπειράομαι, Pass., *to be coiled up in*, φωλεῷ S.E.*M*.7.410: metaph., *to be involved*, *wrapped up in*, ἔπεσιν Heraclit.*All*.2.

ἐνσπείρω, Ep. ἐνισπ–, *sow in*, ἐνισπείρας [ὀδόντας] πεδίοισιν A.R.3.1185:—Pass., ἡμῖν οὐδέν τι παραπλησία ψυχὴ τοῖς ἄλλοις ἐ. ζῴοις Jul.*Or*.6.194c; ὑπὸ φύσεως Iamb.*Myst*.3.27.

ἐνσπερμᾰτος, ον, *possessing seed*, Phan.Hist.31.

ἔνσπερμος, ον, *prolific*, of a plant, Dsc.3.23.

ἔνσποδος, ον, *ashen*, τῇ χροᾷ Dsc.5.88.

ἔνσπονδος, ον, (σπονδή) *included in a truce* or *treaty*, opp. ἔκσπονδος, ἔ. ποιεῖσθαι Th.3.10; ἔ. τινι *in alliance with* one, E.*Ba*.924, Th.1.40, 3.65, al.: as Subst., *ally*, οὐδενὸς Ἑλλήνων ἔ. Id.1.31; οἱ ἔ. *the allies*, ib.35. 2. of animals, *gently disposed*, πρός τινα Ael.*NA*1.3; ἔνσπονδα εἶναί τινι πρός τινα ib.57. II. *under truce* or *safe-conduct*, E.*Ph*.171.

ἔνσπορος, ον, = ἔνσπερμος, *Corp.Herm*.3.3.

ἐνσπουδάζω, *employ oneself actively in*, τῇ Σμύρνῃ Philostr.*VS*1.25.2, al.; πόλις ἐνσπουδάσαι ἀγαθή Lib.*Or*.11.268.

ἐνστάζω, fut. -ξω, *drop in* or *into*, τινί τι Ar.*V*.702, Pi.*P*.9.63 (tm.); [χάριν] B.12.229; ἁπαλὰς τροφάς Ph.2.470:—Pass., εἰ δή τοι σοῦ πατρὸς ἐνέστακται μένος ἠΰ *is instilled into* thee, Od.2.271; ἀλλά οἱ δεινός τις ἐνέστακτο ἵμερος Hdt.9.3, cf. Dsc.*Eup*.1.35, Plu.*Ages*.11, Paus.4.32.4.

ἐνστακτέον, *one must instil*, Philum.ap.Aët.5.120, Paul.Aeg.3.23.

ἔνστακτον, τό, *instillation* for the eyes, Gal.12.782.

ἐνστᾰλάζω, = ἐνστάζω, τι εἴς τι Ar.*Ach.*1034, Luc.*Tox.*37 : aor. 2 part. Pass. ἐνσταλαγεῖσα v.l. for ἐνσταγεῖσα in Dsc.1.77.

ἐνστᾱλόω, Dor. for ἐνστηλόω, *set upon a pillar*, *IGRom.*1.1295 (Philae).

ἐν-στᾰσία, ἡ, = sq., Hp.*Ep.*23. **-στᾰσις**, εως, ἡ, (ἐνίσταμαι) *origin, beginning*, τῶν ὅλων πραγμάτων Aeschin.2.20 ; τοῦ πολέμου Plb.4.62.3; πραγμάτων Ph.2.75 ; *institution* of legal proceedings, τὴν ὅλην ἔ. τοῦ ἀγῶνος Aeschin.1.132. 2. ἔ. βίου *a way* of life, D.L.6.103, cf. Jul.*Or.*6.201a. 3. *institution* of an heir, *Cod.Just.*1.2.25 *Intr.*, *PMasp.*151.274 (vi A.D.); *inheritance*, ib.312.55 (vi A.D.). II. in Medic., *lodgement*, λίθων Aret.*CD*2.3. 2. *impaction, obstruction*, ὄγκων Asclep.ap.Gal.10.101, Herod.Med.ap.Orib.5.30.5, etc. : generally, *interference*, ὀνύχων Iamb.*Protr.*21.ιθ'. III. in Logic, *objection* to an argument, ἔ. πρότασις προτάσει ἐναντία Arist.*APr.*69ᵃ37, cf. *Top.*157ᵃ35, *Rh.*1402ᵃ31, Hermog.*Inv.*3.6, etc. 2. generally, *opposition*, Plb.6.17.8 (pl.), Ph.2.60. 3. *prosecution*, ἐν μολποῖς *SIG* 633.66 (Milet., ii B.C.). 4. χαλεπὴ ἔ. difficult *situation*, *IG*12(5).509.4 (Seriphos, iii/ii B.C.). IV. (ἐνίστημι) *winding up* an engine, Ph.*Bel.*61.21, 57.41 (nisi leg. ἔντασις). V. *impact, interference* of an object of vision, *Placit.*4.13.2, Plot.4.5.2. **-στᾰτέον**, *one must oppose, resist*, ταῖς ἐπιθυμίαις Sor.1.53. **-στάτης** [ᾰ], ου, ὁ, *adversary*, S.*Aj.*104, Ael.*Fr.*248. **-στᾰτικός**, ή, όν, *setting oneself in the way, stubborn, savage*, of beasts, Arist.*HA*488ᵇ13. II. *opposing, checking*, Plu.2.975a ; ἐ. ταύτης τῆς ὁδοῦ *hindering from* this course, M.Ant.5.20. Adv. -κῶς, gloss on διασταδόν, Sch.Opp.*H.*1.502. III. *able to find objections*, Arist.*Top.*164ᵇ3, *Cael.*294ᵇ11 ; *controversial*, ἐνέργεια Procl.*in Prm.*p.502 S. ; *addicted to controversy*, Id.*in Alc.*p.23 C. ; οἱ ἐνστατικοί Grammarians *who started difficulties* in Homer, opp. λυτικοί or ἐπιλυτικοί, Eust.1166 fin. : -κόν, τό, Hermog.*Inv.*3.6. Adv. -κῶς ibid.

ἐνστείνω, *straiten, coop up in*, Q.S.9.179 (Pass.).

ἐνστέλλω, *dress in* :—Pass., ἱππάδα στολὴν ἐνεσταλμένος *clad in* a horseman's dress, Hdt.1.80. II. νομίσματα -στελλόμενά τινι *paid over*, *PMasp.*6 ii 32 (vi A.D.).

ἐνστερνισάμενος· περιπτυξάμενος, Hsch.

ἐνστερνομαντίαις· ἐγγαστριμύθοις, f.l. in Hsch., cf. S.*Fr.*59.

ἐνστηλῑτόω, *record*, in Pass., ἱεροῖς γράμμασιν *OGI*666.21.

ἐνστηλόω, v. ἐνσταλόω.

ἔνστημα, ατος, τό, *objection*, εἴς τι Epicur.*Ep.*2 p.39 U. II. *check, obstacle*, Chrysipp.*Stoic.*2.268, M.Ant.8.41, S.E.*M.*7.253, al.

ἐνστηρίζω, *fix* or *press in*, πρίονα ἔς τι Hp.*VC*21 : metaph., τινὶ τὸ ὅραμα Plot.3.5.2 :—Pass., γαίῃ ἐνεστήρικτο it *stuck fast in* earth, Il.21.168 ; πόντῳ, of Delos, Call.*Del.*13 :—the Med. in A.R.4.1518.

ἐνστίζομαι, Pass., *to be embroidered in* a web, D.C.63.6.

ἐνστοιβάζω, *pack, stuff in*, *Gloss.*

ἐνστομ-ίζω, *put into one's mouth*, *PMag.Par.*1.2144, cf. Suid. **-ιος**, ον, *in the mouth*, ἕλκος Dsc.1.96 ; τραύματα Antyll.ap.Orib.45.16.4 ; χυλός Ph.1.373 ; θερμασία *PMed.Lond.*155.2.5. **-ισμα**, ατος, τό, *bit, curb*, metaph., J.*AJ*18.9.3 (s.v.l.).

ἐνστόρνῡμι, *lay*, τραπέζας Ἐφ.Ἀρχ.1902.29 (Chalcis) :—Pass., ἐνεστρωμένοι ὑμένες *spread over*, Antyll.ap.Orib.45.2.5.

ἐνστρᾰτοπεδεύω, *encamp in*, Th.2.20 ; ἐν τῇ πόλει Plu.*Thes.*27 :—Med., χῶρος ἐπιτηδεότερος ἐνστρατοπεδεύεσθαι Hdt.9.2, D.C.50.12.

ἐνστρέφω, *turn in* :—Med., ἄρθρα ἐνστρέφεσθαι *turn* or *move one's* limbs, Hp.*Dieb.Judic.*8 :—Pass., *turn* or *move in*, μηρὸς ἰσχίῳ ἐνστρέφεται Il.5.306. 2. c. acc. loci, σηκοὺς ἐνστρέφειν *visit* them, f.l. in E.*Ion* 300.

ἐνστρηνές· ἰσχυρόν, ἢ σαφές, Hsch.

ἐνστροβῑλίσας (or -ήσας)· συνστρέψας, Hsch., Suid.

ἐνστροφή, ἡ, in pl., *haunts*, Aristid.*Or.*27(16).15.

ἔνστροφος, ὁ, a kind of *ear-ring*, Poll.5.97.

ἐνστρωφάομαι, Frequentat. of ἐνστρέφομαι, Hp.*Art.*58, Q.S.1.308.

ἐνστύφω [ῡ], *to be bitter, astringent*, πόμα, ποτόν, Nic.*Al.*299, 321.

ἐνσυγκαταζέω, *make to boil together*, Mnesith.ap.Orib.4.4.4.

ἐνσύζῠγος, ον, in choric lyrics, *assigned to* συζυγίαι, Sch.Ar.*Ra.*357.

ἐνσύνθηκος, ον, *ratified by treaty*, φιλία App.*Mith.*14.

ἐνσφαιρόω, *spread all round*, Nonn.*D.*32.77.

ἐνσφηκόομαι, v. sq.

ἐνσφηνόομαι, Pass., *to be wedged in, fit close*, Dsc.5.21, Paul.Aeg.3.77, Procl. ad Hes.*Op.*425 ; πιθάκνη ἐνεσφηνωμένη καλάμῳ *stoppered* with a reed, Dsc.5.31 (v.l. -σφηκ-).

ἐνσφίγγω, *bind tight to* a thing, τινί Luc.*Am.*15.

ἐνσφονδύλια [ῠ], τά, *bones of the* ὀσφύς, Poll.2.179.

ἐνσφρᾱγ-ίζω, Ion. **ἐνσφρηγ-**, *stamp, impress as with a seal*, Ph.1.661 ; ἐνεσφρήγισσεν Ἔρως εἰκόνα βένθεϊ σῆς κραδίης *AP*5.273 (Paul. Sil.) :—Med. freq. in Ph., as τύπον ψυχῇ 2.353 :—Pass., *to be impressed upon*, τινί Luc.*Am.*5, 14 ; ἔν τι -ιζόμενον ἐν πολλοῖς Plot.6.5.6. II. Pass., *to be kept under seal*, *CPR*18.37 (ii A.D.). **-ισις**, εως, ἡ, *imprint*, in pl., Plot.4.3.26, 4.6.1.

ἐνσχέδιος, ον, *superficial, perfunctory*, κάθαρσις f.l. in Aret.*SD*2.10.

ἐνσχερώ, Adv. *in a row*, A.R.1.912, prob. in Antim.16.5.

ἐνσχημᾰτίζω, *arrange* or *set* a fracture, Gal.18(2).333.

ἐν-σχίζω, *split* or *rend asunder*, λεοντῆν Tz.*H.*7.63. **-σχισμός**, ὁ, *incision*, *Gloss.* (pl.). **-σχιστος**, ον, *split, cleft*, Thphr.*CP*5.17.2.

ἐνσχολάζω, *spend one's leisure in* a place, Arist.*Pol.*1331ᵇ12 : metaph., *reside in*, φρόνησις ἐ. ψυχῇ Ph.1.358. 2. *spend time upon*, θεωρήμασι Id.2.428, cf. Them.*Or.*2.39b : abs., *theorize, in his molestiis* Cic.*Att.*7.11.2.

ἐνσωμᾰτ-ίζω, = -όω, Herm.ap.Stob.1.49.69 (Pass.). **-ος**, ον, *corporeal*, opp. ἀσώματος, Ph.1.43. **-όω**, *embody*, ψυχήν Porph.*Abst.*4.20 :—Pass., ibid., Herm.*in Phdr.*p.167 A., Anon.*in Tht.*53.7. **-ωσις**, εως, ἡ, *incarnation, embodiment*, τῶν ψυχῶν Iamb.ap.Stob.1.49.40, cf. Anon.*in Tht.*57.30, Herm.ap.Stob.1.49.44.

ἔνσωμος, ον, = ἐνσώματος, ἐ. φράσις *materialistic* language, Zos. Alch.p.228 B.

ἔνσων· ἕλκων, Hsch.

ἐνσωρεύω, *heap on* or *in*, τῷ κολπώματι χρυσόν Sch.Pi.*P.*7 *Intr.* :—Pass., σῖτος εἰς τὰ δώματ' -εύεται [Emp.]*Sphaer.*123.

ἐντᾰγ-ής, ές, *duly authorized*, κουφισμός *PLond.*5.1646.47 (vi A.D.). **-ιον**, τό, *order for delivery*, esp. *requisition* by the state, τὰ ἐ. τῶν ἀννωνῶν, τῆς ἐσθῆτος, *PGiss.*54.15 (iv A.D.), *PLips.*58.13 (iv A.D.) ; private *order for payment* or *delivery*, *PKlein.Form.*988, 1065 (v A.D.). 2. *receipt*, *PSI*1.36 (iv A.D.), etc. II. *entrance-fee*, *PLond.*3.1178 (ii A.D.), *BGU*1074.15 (iii A.D.).

ἐντάδε, = ἐνθάδε, *Schwyzer* 105 (Methana, vi B.C.).

ἐντακτ-έον, *one must introduce, place next in order*, Dam.*Pr.*44. **-ος**, ον, *ordered, rhythmical*, κίνησις Herod.Med. in *Rh.Mus.*58.70.

ἐντᾰλαιπωρέομαι, *persevere*, ταῖς ζητήσεσιν Olymp.*in Alc.*p.64 C.

ἔνταλμα, ατος, τό, = ἐντολή, Lxx *Is.*29.13, *Ev.Matt.*15.9, al.

ἐντᾰμῐευόμενον· ἐνθησαυριζόμενον, Hsch.

ἐντᾰμίευτος [ῐ], ον, *fitted for* a purpose, πρός τι Gal.18(1).224.

ἐντάμνω, Ion. for ἐντέμνω.

ἐντάν-ῠσις [ᾰ], εως, ἡ, *stretching*, Eust.1913.37. **-υσμός**, ὁ, gloss on τανυστύς, Sch.Od.21.112. **-ύω**, poet. and Ion. for ἐντείνω, *stretch tight*, of the bow-string, νευρὴν ἐντανύσαι Od.19.587, al. ; also, *stretch* a bow *tight*, i.e. *bend* or *string* it, 21.306, al. ; τὰ τόξα ἐντανύουσι *string* their bows, opp. ἐκλύουσι, Hdt.2.173, cf. Theoc.24.107 :—Med., δυνήσεται ἐντανύσασθαι *string* the bow, Od.21.403 :—Pass., fut. inf. ἐντανύεσθαι ib.92. 2. *stretch* or *strain tight* with cords or straps, ἐντανύσας [τὸν θρόνον ἱμᾶσιν] *cover* it *with stretched* straps, Hdt.5.25. 3. ἐ. αὔλακας *draw long* furrows, Pi.*P.*4.227.

ἐντάξιμος· *inserticius*, *Gloss.*

ἔνταξις, εως, ἡ, *putting in, insertion*, Ptol.*Geog.*2.1.7. II. *placing of light-armed soldiers alternately with hoplites in the phalanx*, Ael.*Tact.*31.3, Arr.*Tact.*26.6, Suid.

ἐντᾰράσσω, Att. -ττω, Ion. **ἐνθράσσω** (q.v.), *toss about*, τὴν στρωμνήν Aristaenet.2.22 :—Med., *cause confusion in*, τῷ ὁμίλῳ Philostr.*VA*3.20 :—Pass., -ταραγμένοι ὀφθαλμοί Arist.*Phgn.*812ᵇ8.

ἐντᾰρῑχεύω, *pickle in the sun*, Paul.Aeg.3.18 (Pass.).

ἔντᾰσις, εως, ἡ, (ἐντείνω) *inscribing*, εἰς τὸν κύκλον Pl.*Men.*87b. II. *tension, straining*, τοῦ ὑποχονδρίου Hp.*Epid.*3.1.β' ; τοῦ σώματος Id.*Aër.*4 ; τῶν ῥάβδων Id.*Fract.*30 ; ὀφθαλμῶν *fixed stare*, prob. in Aret.*CD*1.3 (pl.) ; *distension*, αἰδοίων Gal.7.728. 2. *exertion*, Plu.2.948b, Aret.*SA*2.2 ; pl., *retchings*, Id.*CD*2.13. 3. ἡ τοῦ προσώπου ἔ. *the assumption of a serious* face, Luc.*Symp.*28 ; *earnestness*, περὶ ἑκάστου Porph.*Abst.*1.54 ; *strictness*, νόμων *PSorb.*675.14 (iii A.D.). 4. Arch., *swelling* in the outline of a column, Vitr.3.3.13.

ἔντᾰσις, ιος, ἡ, Thess. for ἔγκτησις, *IG*9(2).511 (iii B.C.), al.

ἐντάσσω, Att. -ττω, *insert* or *register in*, ἐν τοῖς δημοσίοις γράμμασι *CIG*2737 *a*50 (Aphrodisias, M. Antonius), cf. *PFay.*91.46 (i A.D., Pass.), etc. ; ἐ. τινὰ τῇ ἀρχαίᾳ κωμῳδίᾳ Ath.1.5b :—Pass., τῷ σφενδονᾶν ἐντεταγμένῳ *who takes post* to use the sling, X.*An.*3.3.18 (as v.l.) : in lit. sense, *insert*, πυρὴν -έσθω μήλης Paul.Aeg.6.66. 2. *arrange light-armed troops and hoplites alternately*, Ael.*Tact.*31.3, Arr.*Tact.*26.6 : generally, *insert* men *alternately*, ib.25.4 (Pass.). II. = ἀντιτάσσω, τινὶ δόρυ E.*Rh.*492. III. *issue orders*, ἐντεταχέναι τὸν στρατηγόν *PCair.Preis.*32.3 (ii A.D.).

ἐντᾰτ-ικός, ή, όν, *stimulating, aphrodisiac*, Xenocr.16, cf. Gal.12.341, Aët.11.35. 2. *sexually vigorous*, [ζῷον] -ώτερον πρὸς τὴν μεῖξιν *Gp.*19.5.4. II. ἐντατικόν, τό, = σατύριον, Ps.-Dsc.3.128. **-ός**, ή, όν, (ἐντείνω) *stretched* : ἐ. ὄργανα *stringed* instruments, Str.7.5.7, Ps.-Plu.*Vit.Hom.*148, Ath.4.182e, Nicom.*Harm.*2.

ἐνταῦθα, Ion. **ἐνθαῦτα** (also **ἐντοῦθα**, q.v.), Elean **ἐνταῦτα** *SIG*9 (Olympia, vi B.C.) : Adv., formed from ἔνθα, but more common in Prose : I. of Place, *here, there*, Hdt.1.76, A.*Pr.*82, etc. ; ἐνταῦθά που *here*abouts, Ar.*Av.*1184 : folld. by ἵνα, ὅπου, etc., S.*Ph.*429, *Tr.*800, etc. b. *in this material world*, opp. ἐκεῖ (in the ideal world), Arist.*Metaph.*990ᵇ34, etc. 2. *hither, thither*, Il.9.601 ; παριέναι ἐνθαῦτα Hdt.5.72 ; ἐνταῦθα πέμπειν A.*Pers.*450, etc. ; ἐ. πέμψειν ἔνθα μήποθ' ἡλίου φέγγος προσόψῃ S.*El.*380 ; ὅθεν δ' ἕκαστον ἐς τὸ φῶς ἀφίκετο, ἐνταῦθ' ἀπελθεῖν E.*Supp.*533 ; φέρε δεῦρο.. ἐ. Ar.*Ec.*739 ; ἐ. προεληλύθας Pl.*Tht.*187b ; μέχρι ἐ. Id.*Cra.*412e. 3. freq. c. gen., ἐ. τοῦ οὐρανοῦ X.*Mem.*4.3.8 ; ἐ. τῆς ἠπείρου Th.1.46 ; ἐ. τοῦδ' ἀφικόμην κακοῦ A.*Ch.*891 ; ἐ. που ἦμεν τοῦ λόγου Pl.*Tht.*177c ; ἐνταῦθ' ἑαυτὸν τάξας τῆς πολιτείας *in that department of*.., D.18.62. II. of Time, *at the very time, then*, A.*Pr.*206 ; in apodosi, ἡνίκα.., ἐνταῦθα δὴ μάλιστα.. S.*Tr.*37 ; after ὅτε, Id.*OT*802 ; after ἐπειδή, ἐπεί, Th.1.11, X.*An.*3.4.25 ; ἐ. δή Id.*Cyr.*4.5.9, etc. 2. c. gen., ἐ. ἤδη εἶ τῆς ἡλικίας Pl.*R.*328e. III. of Sequence, *thereupon*, Hdt.1.61, 62. IV. generally, *herein*, S.*OT*582, *Fr.*77, Pl.*Ap.*29b, etc. ; *in this position*, ἐ. ἕστηκε τὸ πρᾶγμα D.21.102 ; ἐνταῦθ' ἔνι depends upon *that circumstance*, S.*OT*598.—In Att. also strengthd. **ἐνταυθί** [ῑ], Pl.Com.173.8 (prob.), Pl.*Prt.*310a, D.15.22, al.

ἐνταυθοῖ (**ἐνθαυθοῖ** *IG*1².76.13), Adv. *hither*, ἐ. νῦν κεῖσο *come and lie down here*, Il.21.122 ; ἐ. νῦν ἧσο Od.18.105, 20.262 ; *here*, ἡ ἐ. μονή Arist.*Ph.*229ᵇ28, cf. D.27.54 : freq. with or without v.l. ἐνταυθί in

Com. and Prose, Cratin.37, Ar.*Ra.*273, *Lys.*568, al., Pl.*Ap.*18d, 33d, al., Antipho 5.2,10.—Once in Trag., E.*IT*1010 (s. v.l.).

ἐντᾰφ-ή, Dor. **-ά**, *burial*, *IGRom.*4.1302.10 (Cyme), *GDI*3502.9 (Cnidos), *SIG*1234.5 (Lycia). **-ήϊα**, v. ἐντοφήϊα. **-ιάζω**, *prepare for burial, lay out*, Lxx *Ge.*50.2, *Ev.Matt.*26.12, Plu.2.995c, *AP* 11.125: metaph., τὴν τυραννίδα τῇ πόλει Plu.*Dio* 44:—Med., τὸ λοιπὸν ἐντεταφιασμένος περιπατεῖ Phld.*Mort.*38. **-ιασις**, εως, ἡ, = sq., Suid. **-ιασμός**, ὁ, *laying out for burial*, *Ev.Marc.*14.8, Sch.Ar.*Pl.* 1009, etc. **-ιαστής**, οῦ, ὁ, *undertaker, embalmer*, Lxx *Ge.*50.2, *POxy.* 476.8 (ii A.D.), *PPar.*7.6 (i B.C.), Ptol.*Tetr.*180, *AP*11.125, etc.; of the Bactrian dogs, Str.11.11.3. **-ιαστικός**, ή, όν, *of an* ἐνταφιαστής, τάξις *PSorb.*675.14 (iii A.D.). **-ιεύω**, = -ιάζω, Charis.p.566 K.

ἐντᾰφιοπώλης, ου, ὁ, *undertaker*, *Dialex.*1.3, Artem.4.56.

ἐντάφιος [ᾰ], ον, *of, belonging to* or *used in burial*, κόσμοι D.H.2.67. II. as Subst., 1. ἐντάφιον, τό, *shroud, winding-sheet*, *AP* 11.125; ἐ. δὲ τοιοῦτον οὔτ' εὐρὼς οὔτε.. ἀμαυρώσει χρόνος Simon.4.4; καλὸν ἐ. ἡ τυραννίς Isoc.6.45; κάλλιστον ἐ. ἕξουσι τὸν ὑπὲρ τῆς πατρίδος θάνατον Plb.15.10.3; ὁ πλοῦτος δ' οὐκ ἐμὸν ἐ. *AP*9.294 (Antiphil.). b. μηδ' ἐντάφια καταλιπόντι *money for funeral expenses*, Plu.*Arist.*27: later in sg., *funeral expenses*, *PLond.*5.1708.205 (vi A.D.). 2. ἐ. (sc. ἱερά), τά, *offerings to the dead, obsequies*, S.*El.*326, Is.8.38, *Epigr. Gr.*313.13 (Smyrna): Cyren. ἐντόφιον *Notiz.Arch.*4.96.

ἐντᾰχύ, *quickly, presently*, *Sammelb.*365: Comp. ἐντάχιον *as soon as possible*, *BGU*826 (ii/iii A.D.), etc.

ἔντε, = ἔστε, *until*, *GDI*2561 *B* 44, *C* 18 (Delph.); **ἔντε** ib.1707.7 (ibid.); ἔντε κ' ἀποτείσῃ *IG*9(1).334.15 (Locr., v B.C.); of numbers, *up to*, τὰς ὑπὲρ πέντε μνᾶς ἔντε δέκα *Foed.Delph.Pell.*1 *A* 4.

ἔντεα, τά, *fighting gear, arms, armour*, ἔ. ἀρήϊα Il.10.407, Od. 23.368; ἔ. πατρός 19.17; esp. *coat of mail, corslet*, Il.10.34; ἔντε' ἔδυνεν 3.339, etc. II. *furniture, appliances, tackle*, ἔ. δαιτός Od. 7.232; ἔ. νηός *rigging*, *h.Ap.*489, Pi.*N.*4.70; ἔ. ἵππεια *trappings, harness*, ib.9.22, cf. *P.*4.235; ἔντη δίφρου *harness*, A.*Pers.*194 (but ἔντεα alone for *chariots*, Pi.*O.*4.24); ἔντεα αὐλῶν periphr. for αὐλοί, ib.7.12; also ἔντεα alone, *musical instruments*, Id.*P.*12.21; of the *instruments* of the Γάλλαι, *Lyr.Adesp.*121; ἔντεα Φοίβου Call.*Ap.* 19.—Ep. and Lyr. word, once in Trag. (v. supr.):—sg. ἔντος only in Archil.6.

ἐντείνω, *stretch* or *strain tight*, esp. of any operation performed with straps or cords, 1. ἐνέτεινε τὸν θρόνον [ἱμᾶσι] Hdt.5.25 (cf. ἐντανύω):—more freq. (as always in Hom.) Pass., δίφρος.. ἱμᾶσιν ἐντέταται *is hung on tight-stretched* straps, Il.5.728; [κυνέη] ἔντοσθεν ἱμᾶσιν ἐντέτατο στερεῶς *was* strongly *lined* inside *with tight-stretched* straps, 10.263; so [τὰς γεφύρας] ἐδόκεον ἐντεταμένας εὑρήσειν expected to find the bridge *with the mooring-cables taut*, Hdt.9.106; σχεδίαι ἐντετ. Id.8.117; κλίνη ἐντετ. Polyaen.7.14.1; εἰ ἡ ἔντασις τῶν ῥάβδων χρηστῶς ἐνταθείη Hp.*Fract.*30; τράχηλος ἐντετ. *with sinews taut*, Phld.*Ir.*p.5 W.: metaph., ἐντεταμένου τοῦ σώματος *being toned, tempered*, Pl.*Phd.*86b, cf. 92a. 2. *stretch* a bow *tight*, *bend* it for shooting, A.*Fr.*83, cf. E.*Supp.*886: metaph., καιροῦ πέρα τὸ τόξον ἐ. ib.745:—Med., *bend one's* bow, Id.*IA*549 (lyr.), X.*Cyr.*4.1.3:—Pass., τόξα ἐντεταμένα bows *ready strung*, Hdt.2.173, Luc.*Scyth.*2: hence, com., κέντρον ἐντέταται *is ready for action*, Ar.*V.*407. b. of the strings of the lyre, τῆς νεάτης ἐντεταμένης Arist.*Pr.*921^{b}27. 3. ἐ. ναῦν ποδί *keep* a ship's sail *taut* by the sheet, ναῦς ἐνταθεῖσα ποδὶ ἔβαψεν E.*Or.*706. 4. ἐ. ἵππον τῷ ἀγωγεῖ *hold* a horse *with tight* rein, X.*Eq.*8.3. 5. *tie tight*, βοῦν.. ἐ. βρόχοις E.*Andr.*720. II. metaph., *strain, exert*, τὰς ἀκοάς Polyaen.1.21.2; ἑαυτόν Plu.2.795f:—Med., φωνὴν ἐντεινάμενος Aeschin.2.157; ἐντεινάμενοι τὴν ἁρμονίαν *pitching* the tune *high*, Ar.*Nu.*968:—Pass., πρόθυμοι καὶ ἐντεταμένοι εἰς τὸ ἔργον *braced up* for action, X.*Oec.*21.9; τῇ διανοίᾳ περί τι Plb.10.3.1; ἐνταθῆναι περί τινος *PSI*4.340 (iii B.C.); ἐντεινόμενος *on the stretch, eager*, opp. ἀνιέμενος, X.*Mem.*3.10.7, cf. *Cyn.*7.8; μᾶλλον ἐντεινάμενος εἶπον Pl.*R.*536c; πρόσωπον ἐντεταμένον a *serious* face, Luc.*Vit. Auct.*10. 2. *intensify, carry on vigorously*, τὴν πολιορκίαν Plu.*Luc.*14; *excite*, θυμὸν ἀνόητον Plu.2.61e, cf. 464b. III. intr. in Act., *exert oneself, be vehement*, E.*Or.*698, *Fr.*340. 2. intr. in Act., *penem erigere*, Arist.*Pr.*879^{a}11:—Pass., εἰκόνες ἐντεταμέναι D.S.1.88. IV. *stretch out at* or *against*, πληγὴν ἐ. τινί *lay* a blow *on* him, X.*An.*2.4.11, cf. Lys.*Fr.*75.4; without πληγήν, *attack*, Pl.*Min.* 321a; πύξ τινι D.C.57.22. V. *place exactly in*, ἐς κύκλον χωρίον τρίγωνον *inscribe* an area as a triangle in a circle, Pl.*Men.*87a (Pass.). 2. esp. *put into verse*, ἐ. τοὺς Αἰσώπου λόγους Id.*Phd.* 60d; ἐ. εἰς ἐλεγεῖον Id.*Hipparch.*228d; τοὺς νόμους εἰς ἔπος Plu.*Sol.* 3; ἔπεσιν ἐ. τὴν παραίνεσιν Jul.*Or.*6.188b; *set to music*, ποιήματα εἰς τὰ κιθαρίσματα Pl.*Prt.*326b:—Med., Ἰθάκην ἐνετείνατο.. Ὅμηρος ᾠδῇσιν Hermesian.7.29.

ἐντείρω, = τείρω ἐν.., Q.S.1.671 (Pass.).

ἐντειχ-ίδιος, ον, = ἐντείχιος, Luc.*Par.*42, Onos.42.12. **-ίζω**, *build* or *fortify in* a place, ἀκροπόλεις ἐν ταῖς πόλεσιν Isoc.4.137, cf. X.*HG*4.8.1; φρούρια Id.*Cyr.*3.1.27; πόλιν ἐν τῷ ἀγκῶνι D.H.3.44; φρουροὺς τοῖς χωρίοις J.*AJ*9.10.3:—Pass., τὰ τείχη ἃ ἐνετετείχιστο X.*Ages.*2.19. II. Med., *wall in*, i.e. *blockade*, Th.6.90; but also, *fortify*, Nic.Dam.*Fr.*66.32 J., Plu.*Pomp.*28: plpf. ἐνετετείχιστο D.C. 42.38. **-ιος**, ον, *enclosed by walls*, οἰκήσεις D.H.1.26.

ἐντεκμαίρομαι, *infer*, τοῖς ἄλλοις σημείοις f.l. in Hp.*Superf.*10.

ἐντεκν-όομαι, *beget children in*, Plu.*Cat.Mi.*25. **-ος**, ον, *having children*, opp. ἄτεκνος, Luc.*DMort.*6.3.

ἐντεκταίνομαι, *build* or *fix in*, v.l. for ἐκ-, Hp.*Art.*47, cf. Apollon. Cit. ad loc.

ἐντελέθω, = τελέθω ἐν.., Nic.*Th.*660.

ἐντέλεια, ἡ, (ἐντελής) *completeness*, τοῦ λόγου A.D.*Synt.*186. 15. II. *full rights*, *GDI*1339.11 (Dodona).

ἐντελετέω, *to be inspired, frenzied*, Hsch. s.v. κορυβαντιᾷ.

ἐντελευτάω, *end one's life in*.., Th.2.44, Lib.*Or.*18.31.

ἐντελέχ-εια, ἡ, (ἐντελής, ἔχειν) *full, complete reality*, opp. δύναμις, ψυχή ἐστιν ἐ. ἡ πρώτη σώματος φυσικοῦ δυνάμει ζωὴν ἔχοντος Arist.*de An.*412^{a}27; ὑπὸ τοῦ ἐντελεχείᾳ ὄντος τὸ δυνάμει ὂν γίνεται Id.*GA*734^a 30; distd. fr. ἐνέργεια, *actuality*, opp. *activity*, Id.*Metaph.*1050^{a}23, *Ph.*257^{b}8, cf. Ph.1.625 (ἐνδ- codd.), Plot.4.7.8; later, τὸ ᾠὸν κατὰ δύναμιν μέν ἐστι νεοσσός, κατ' ἐντελέχειαν δὲ οὐκ ἔστιν S.E.*M.*10.340, cf. Theo Sm.p.37 H.: confused with ἐνδέλεχεια (q.v.) by Cic.*Tusc.* 1.10.22, Luc.*Jud.Voc.*10. **-ής**, ές, only as f.l. for ἐνδ-, e.g. Thphr. *CP*5.1.10, Ph.2.587; and so Adv. -ῶς Pl.*Lg.*905e.

ἐντελ-έω, dub. in Phld.*Ir.*p.12 W. **-ής**, ές, (τέλος) *complete, full*, τὸν μισθὸν ἀποδώσω 'ντελῆ Ar.*Eq.*1367, cf. Th.8.45; δώσειν ἐ. τὴν δραχμήν ib.29; τροφὴν ἐ. δοῦναι ib.78; δεῖπνον ἐ. καὶ μηδὲν ἐλλιπές Euang.1.2 (but τὸ ἐ. ὀνομαζόμενον δεῖπνον the *last* course, Luc.*Symp.* 38); ἵν' ἐ. ὦσι [οἱ λόγοι] Phld.*Herc.*1251.13; opp. ἐλλιπής, A.D. *Synt.*38.9, al.: Sup. -έστατος, βάσανος Ael.*Tact.*21.3; ἐντελὲς τρίγωνον ∴ Luc.*Vit.Auct.*4. 2. of victims, *perfect, unblemished*, δώδεκ' ἐντελεῖς ἔχων βοῦς S.*Tr.*760, cf. Luc.*Sacr.*12. 3. of military equipment, *in good condition*, Th.6.45; τριήρεις Aeschin.2.175. 4. of men, οὐ γὰρ ἐντελής.. προσφέρειν *full-grown* so as to offer, A.*Ch.* 250; ἐ. τὴν ἡλικίαν Ael.*NA*3.40; *finished, accomplished*, ἐ. καὶ ἔνδοξοι Artem.2.35, cf. Sch.Hes.*Th.*242; also ἐντελῆ τὴν ἀνδρείαν εἰσφέρονται Onos.4.2: Comp. -έστερος Hsch.: Sup., Id. 5. Adv. -λῶς, Ion. -λέως, *entirely, completely*, Arist.*Rh.Al.*1436^{a}12, Herod.4. 79, Plb.10.30.3, etc.; *perfectly*, J.*AJ*19.6.2: Comp. -έστερον Marin. *Procl.*15. II. *possessing full rights*, ἱππεῖς ἐ. Ῥωμαίων D.S.34.2. 31; *qualified to hold public office*, opp. ἀτελής, *SIG*286.10 (Milet., iv B.C.):—dub. cj. in A.*Ag.*105. **-ικός**, ή, όν, f.l. for ἐντολικός, A.D.*Synt.*112.27.

ἐντέλλω, *enjoin, command*, Act. only in Pi.*O.*7.40, S.*Fr.*269:—mostly in Med., τινί τι Hdt.1.47, etc.; in a will, φίλοις ταῦτα ἐντέλλομαι Diog.Oen.66: c. dat. pers. et inf., Hdt.1.53, Pl.*R.*393e, etc.; ἐντείλασθαι ἀπὸ γλώσσης *command* by word of mouth, Hdt.1.123: so in pf., ἐντέταλται Lxx 3*Ki.*13.17; ἐντεταλμένοι εἴησαν Plb.18.2.1, cf. Hdn.1.9.9:—Pass., τὰ ἐντεταλμένα *commands*, Hdt.1.60, 5.73, S. *Fr.*462, X.*Cyr.*5.5.3. II. *invest with legal powers, authorize to act*, ἐ. σοι καὶ ἐπιτρέπω *PLips.*38.5 (iv A.D.), cf. *PMasp.*124.6 (vi A.D.).

ἐντελόμισθος, ον, *receiving full pay*, D.50.18.

ἐντεμεν-ίζω, *place within a precinct*, Poll.1.11. **-ιος**, ον, *having statues in the* τέμενος, θεοί *SIG*1037.4 (Milet.), *Inscr.Prien.*123.10 (i B.C.).

ἐντέμνω, Ion. **-τάμνω**, *cut in, engrave upon*, ἐν τοῖσι λίθοισι γράμματα Hdt.8.22; of a map, χάλκεον πίνακα, ἐν τῷ γῆς.. περίοδος ἐνετέτμητο Id.5.49: *cut* or *scoop* a hollow in a thing, in Pass., ἐντετμέαται Hp.*Art.*72; ἐντετμημένου τοῦ σπληνίου Orib.46.25.4. II. *cut up a victim, sacrifice*, ἥρωϊ to a hero, Th.5.11, cf. Luc.*Scyth.*1; ἐ. σφάγιά τινι Plu.*Sol.*9:—Med., εἰ.. ἵππον τόμιον ἐντεμοίμεθα *should get* it *cut up*, Ar.*Lys.*192:—Pass., ἐντέμνεται σφάγια Dion.Byz.14. 2. *cut in, shred in*, of herbs in a remedy, metaph., A.*Ag.*16. 3. *cut*, ναῦς ἐ. κύματα Ph.1.352, cf. Luc.*Tim.*22 (Pass.), *Tox.*37, *Hist.Conscr.*25.

ἐντενής, ές, *on the stretch, intent*: only neut. ἐντενές as Adv., A.R. 2.933.

ἐντεομήστωρ, v. ἐντεσιμήστωρ.

ἐντερ-επιπλοκήλη, ἡ, *intestinal and omental hernia*, Gal.19.448. **-εύω**, *gut* fish, Archipp.25. **-ίδια**, τά, Dim. of ἔντερα, Alex. 84. **-ικός**, ή, όν, *intestinal*, ἀποφυάδες Arist.*PA*675^{a}17. **-ινος**, η, ον, *made of gut*, Sch.Ar.*Ra.*233. **-ιον**, τό, *privy parts*, M.Ant. 6.13. **-ιώνη**, ἡ, *inmost part, pith* or *heart-wood* of plants, Hp.*Mul.* 1.78, Thphr.*HP*3.17.5, 1.2.6, Porph.*Gaur.*3.3, Luc.*VH*2.37.

ἐντερο-ειδής, ές, *like intestines*, Arist.*HA*508^{b}11. **-κήλη**, ἡ, *intestinal hernia, rupture*, Dsc.1.74 (pl.), Gal.7.36, Cels.7.18. **-κηλήτης**, ου, ὁ, *one who suffers from rupture*, *Gloss.*:—hence **-κηλικός**, ή, όν, *suffering from intestinal hernia*, Dsc.1.110.2, Gal.14.789.

ἐντερόμφᾰλον, τό, *umbilical hernia*, Gal.14.786. II. **-όμφαλος**, ὁ, *patient suffering therefrom*, Id.19.444.

ἔντερον, τό, *piece of the guts* or *intestines*, ἐΰστρεφὲς ἔντερον οἰός a string of sheep's *gut*, Od.21.408: elsewh. in Hom. always pl., ἔντερα *guts, bowels*, Il.13.507, al., cf. A.*Ag.*1221, Ar.*Eq.*1184, *Ra.* 476, Pl.*Ti.*73a: in sg., *gut, bowel*, Arist.*HA*524^{b}13; τοὔντερον τῆς ἐμπίδος Ar.*Nu.*160; collectively, *bowels*, Arist.*HA*514^{b}13, al.; *womb, belly*, Archil.142, cf. Luc.*Lex.*6; ἐπὶ μετρίῳ ἐντέρῳ for moderation *in eating*, Lxx *Si.*34.20, cf. *AP*9.170 (Pall.): metaph., *inside* of fruit, ib.14.57. II. ἔντερα γῆς earth-*worms*, Arist.*IA*705^{b}28, 709^{a}28, Arat.959, Numen.ap.Ath.7.305a; but *worm-casts*, Arist.*HA*570^{a}16, Thphr.*Sign.*42, Nic.*Th.*388. III. *bag made of gut*, Hp.*Morb.*3. 1. (I.-E. *en-tero-, Comp. of *en 'in'.)

ἐντερόνεια, ἡ, = ἐντεριώνη, Hsch., Suid.; ἐ. εἰς τριήρεις *timber for the ribs* of a ship, *belly-timber*, Ar.*Eq.*1185 (with a pun on τοῖς ἐντέροις), v. Sch.

ἐντερο-πράτης [ᾱ], ου, ὁ, = sq., Sch.Ar.*Eq.*155. **-πώλης**, ου, ὁ, *tripe-seller*, *AB*379. **-φύλαξ** [ῠ], ακος, ὁ, name of a *surgical instrument*, *Hermes* 38.282.

ἔντεσα· ἔσωθεν, Hsch. (cf. ἔξεσα).

ἐντεσῐ-εργός, όν, *working in harness*, ἡμίονοι ἐ. *draught*-mules, Il. 24.277. **-μήστωρ**, ορος, ὁ, *skilled in arms*, Hsch. (also ἐντεομ-).

ἐντέταμαι, ἐντεταμένος, pf. Pass. from ἐντείνω.

ἐντεταμένως, Adv., (ἐντείνω) *vehemently, vigorously*, Hdt.1.18, 4.14, J.*AJ*11.4.5.

ἐντετριμμένως, Adv., (ἐντρίβω) *adroitly, 'like an old hand'*, Poll. 5.144.

ἐντετυπωμένως, gloss on ἐντυπάς, Eust.1343.55.

ἔντευγμα, ατος, τό, = ἔντευξις, D.S.39.9.

ἐντεῦθεν, Ion. **ἐνθεῦτεν**, Adv., (related to ἔνθεν, as ἐνταῦθα to ἔνθα): I. of Place, *hence* or *thence*, Od.19.568, Hdt.1.2, al., A.*Pr.* 836, *Pers.*488, Th.8.42, etc.; τὸ γένος ἐ. ποθεν ἐκ Χίου Pl.*Euthd.*271c; *τἀντεῦθεν matters there*, i.e. in the house, S.*El.*1339; ἐ. καὶ ἐ. Lxx *Nu.*22.24, *Ev.Jo.*19.18; ἐ. κἀκεῖθεν Sch.D.T.p.29 H.; ἐντεῦθεν εἰς τυχόν *'go to Jericho'*, Men.*Pk.*184. II. of Time, *henceforth, thereupon*, S.*El.*728, *Ph.*384 (lyr., dub. l.), etc.; also τὸ ἐ. Hdt.1.9, 27, al., Pl.*Tht.*198b; Att. also τοὐντεῦθεν E.*Med.*792, al.; τἀντεῦθεν A.*Eu.* 60; τὸ ἐ. ἐπὶ τούτοις Ael.*NA*8.17. III. causal, *thence, from that source*, τὸν βίον ἐ. ἐποιοῦντο Th.1.5; ἐ. αἱ μάχαι Arist.*EN*1131ᵃ23; ἐ. ποθεν Id.*Pol.*1286ᵇ15; *therefore, in consequence*, E.*Andr.*949, Pl.*Cra.* 399c.—Att. strengthd. **ἐντευθενί** [ῑ], Ar.*Av.*10, *Lys.*92, etc.; cf. ἐνμεντευθενί.

ἐντευκτικός, ή, όν, *affable*, Plu.*Alc.*13, 2.9f.

ἐντευξίδιον, τό, Dim. of sq. 4, *little petition*, Arr.*Epict.*1.10.10.

ἔντευξις, εως, ἡ, (ἐντυγχάνω) *lighting upon, meeting with*, c. dat., αἱ τοῖς λῃσταῖς ἐντεύξεις Pl.*Plt.*298d. 2. *converse, intercourse*, πρὸς τοὺς πολλούς Arist.*Rh.*1355ᵃ29: c. gen., *Vit.Philonid.*p.7C.; ἐντεύξεις ποιεῖσθαί τισι hold *converse with*.., Isoc.1.20; [ἡ πραγματεία] χρήσιμος πρὸς τὰς ἐ. Arist.*Top.*101ᵃ27, cf. *Metaph.*1009ᵃ17, etc.; τὴν ἡλικίαν τῇ ἐντεύξει γνωρίζομεν Sor.2.8. b. *manners, behaviour*, Aeschin.2.47, Thphr.*Char.*5.1, 20.1. c. esp. *sexual intercourse*, Epicur.*Sent.Vat.*51, *Fr.*61. 3. ἐντεύξεις ὀχλικαί *speeches* to the mob, D.H.*Th.*50. 4. *petition*, *PSI*4.383.6 (iii B.C.), *PFlor.*55.18 (i A.D.), Plu.*TG*11, etc.; *intercession* for a person, D.S.16.55, Nic. Dam.*Fr.*130.7 J., 1*Ep.Ti.*2.1 (pl.). 5. *reading, study*, ἡ ἐ. τῆς πραγματείας Plb.1.1.4, etc.

ἐντευτενί, for ἐντευθενί, barbarism in Ar.*Th.*1212.

ἐντευτλᾰνόομαι, Pass., *to be stewed in beet* (v. τεῦτλον), of eels, Ar. *Ach.*894 (prob. ἐντετευτλιωμένης), Aret.*CA*1.2.

ἐντεύχω, *produce*, ἐρυθήματα Archig.ap.Orib.8.1.1 (Pass.).

ἔντεφρος, ον, (τέφρα) *ash-coloured*, Dsc.5.74, Ath.9.395e.

ἐντεχν-άζω λόγον *introduce an elaborate* argument, Lib.*Eth.*6.5. **-ής**, ές, f.l. for ἔντεχνος, Sch.Pi.*N.*8.24. **-ος**, ον, *within the range* or *province of art*, αἱ πίστεις ἔντεχνόν ἐστι μόνον Arist.*Rh.* 1354ᵃ13. 2. *furnished* or *invented by art, artificial, artistic*, Pl. *Prt.*321d, al.; opp. ἄτεχνος, πίστεις Arist.*Rh.*1355ᵇ36; ἡ ἐ. μέθοδος the *regular* method, ib.ᵃ4. Adv. -ως Id.*SE*172ᵃ35 (condemned by Phryn.327 (who however cites Adv. -ῶς from Lys.*Fr.*314S.)). II. of persons, *skilled*, ἐ. δημιουργός a *cunning* workman, Pl.*Lg.*903c, cf. *Plt.*300e.

ἔντηκτος, ον, *liquefied*, αἷμα Aret.*CD*2.13.

ἐντήκω, *pour in while molten*, μόλιβδον D.S.2.8; ἐ. μόλιβδον [τῇ κεφαλῇ] Plu.*CG*17: metaph., ἐ. τέτανον τερπνόν v.l. in Ar.*Lys.* 553. II. Pass., with pf. Act. ἐντέτηκα, *to be dissolved in*, ὕδατι Aët.9.42. 2. *to be cast*, ἀνδριάντα χαλκῷ ἐντετηκότα D.Chr.64.4: but usu., 3. metaph., of feelings, *sink deep in*, μῖσος ἐντέτηκέ μοι S.*El.*1311, cf. Pl.*Mx.*245d; τὸ δέος ἐντετηκὸς ταῖς ψυχαῖς D.H.6.72; ἐν ταῖς ψυχαῖς ἐντέτηκεν ἡ δεισιδαιμονία D.S.1.83; ἐντήκεται γὰρ πλευμόνων ὅσοις ἔνι ψυχή (sc. Κύπρις) *sinks in*..as the breath of life, S.*Fr.* 941.7. 4. of persons, οὐδ' ἂν εἰ κάρτ' ἐντακείη τῷ φιλεῖν *should be absorbed by* love, Id.*Tr.*463; θρήνοισιν ἐντακεῖσα Lyc.498.

ἐντηρέω, *guard*, Procop.*Arc.*4, *PGrenf.*1.61.13 (vi A.D.).

ἐντί, v. εἰμί.

ἐντίθημι, fut. ἐνθήσω: poet. aor. 1 inf. ἐνθέμεν Thgn.430:—*put in* (esp. *put on board* a ship), οἶνον ἐρυθρὸν ἐνθήσω Od.5.166; ἐνθείς τινα εἰς τὸ πλοῖον Antipho 5.39:—freq. in this sense in Med., κτήματά τ' ἐντιθέμεσθα Od.3.154, cf. X.*An.*1.4.7, *Oec.*20.28; ἐν δ' ἱστὸν τιθέμεσθα.. νηΐ Od.11.3; ἐνθέσθαι εἰς τὴν ναῦν φορτία D.34.6. 2. generally, *put in* or *into*, ἐνέθηκε δὲ χερσὶν ἅρπην Hes.*Th.*174; χειρὶ δ' ἔνθες ὀξύην E.*Heracl.*727; σε μήτηρ ἐνθεμένη λεχέεσσι Il.21.123; ἐντιθέναι αὐχένα ζυγῷ E.*Hec.*376, cf. 1045; also ἔς τι Hdt.2.73, Ar. *Ach.*920; ἐς τὼ κοθόρνω τὼ πόδ' ἐνθείς Id.*Ec.*346, cf. *V.*1161:—Med., ἐνθεμένης τὸ κυμβίον εἰς τὸν κόλπον D.47.58. b. metaph., ἐνθέμεν φρένας ἐσθλάς Thgn.430; ἄρτι μοι τὸ γῆρας ἐντίθησι νοῦν Pherecr. 146.6; ἐ. ἀθυμίαν Pl.*Lg.*800c; ἰσχύν D.3.33; ἐνθεῖναι φόβον *inspire* fear, X.*An.*7.4.1, etc.; ἐ. ταῖς χορδαῖς τὴν ἁρμονίαν Plot.4.7.8:—so in Med., χόλον ἔνθεο θυμῷ thou *hast stored up* wrath *in thy* heart, Il.6.326; κότον ἔνθετο θυμῷ Od.11.102; opp. ἵλαον ἔνθεο θυμόν Il. 9.639; τὴν εἴς τινα εὔνοιαν *PMag.Lond.*125.26; μῦθον πεπνυμένον ἔνθετο θυμῷ *laid* it *to his* heart, Od.21.355; μή μοι πατέρας.. ὁμοίῃ ἔνθεο τιμῇ *put* not *our* fathers *in* like honour, Il.4.410. 3. *put in the mouth*, τινί τι Ar.*Eq.*717; ψώμισμα (sc. τῶν νηπίων στόματι) Plu. 2.320d:—Med., ἐνθοῦ *put in*, i.e. *eat*, Ar.*Eq.*51; cf. ἔνθεσις II. 4. *insert*, δέλτα ἀντὶ τοῦ νῦ Pl.*Cra.*417b. 5. *put on*, χλαίνας Il.24.646; κόσμον τάφῳ E.*IT*632:—Med., σάκος ἔνθετο νώτῳ A.R.3.1320. 6. *engraft, bud*, ἀφ' ἑτέρων δενδρέων ὀφθαλμοὶ ἐνετέθησαν Hp.*Nat.Puer.* 26. 7. of cautery, ἐνθεῖναι ἐσχάρας Id.*Art.*11, cf. Paul.Aeg.6.44.

ἐντίκτω (for ἐντέξῃ v. infr. I. 2), *bear* or *produce in*, δόμοις τοῖσδ' ἄρσεν' ἐντίκτω κόρον E.*Andr.*24; ᾠὰ ἐ. ἐς τὴν ἰλὺν *drop* eggs into the mud, Hdt.2.93: abs., *bear children in* a place, Th.3.104; ἐντίκτουσιν ἐνταῦθα Arist.*HA*552ᵇ29; ἐν τῇ τῶν ἐλαττόνων ὀρνίθων νεοττιᾷ ἐ., of the cuckoo, ib.563ᵇ31. 2. *create* or *cause in*, τὸ κακοῦργον.. ἐντίκτει Κύπρις ἐν ταῖς σοφαῖσιν E.*Hipp.*642; ἐ. ἔρωτας, ἔχθρας ὄγκον, φθόνους, ἀνελευθερίαν, εὐχέρειαν τοῖς νέοις πονηρίας, σωφροσύνην, Pl.*Lg.*870a, 843b, 870c, *Phdr.*256e, *R.*392a, 410a; τοῖς νέοις ζῆλον Plb.12.26ᶜ.4; ἐντέξῃ is dub. in Ar.*Lys.*553. II. pf. part. ἐντετοκώς, intr., *inborn, innate*, νόσον.. ἐν τῇ πόλει ἐντετοκυῖαν Id.*V.*651.

ἐντῑλάω, *void excrement upon*, τινί τι Ar.*Ach.*351.

ἔντιλτος πλακοῦς, ὁ, prob. a cake *seasoned with* τιλτόν (q.v.), Clearch.65 (s.v.l.).

ἐντῑμ-άω, *value in* or *among*, ἐν ταῖς μ' μναῖς ἐνετιμᾶτο τὰ χρυσία καὶ τὰ ἱμάτια τῶν χιλίων [δραχμῶν] D.41.27; ἐς τὰς προῖκας ἐντετιμῆσθαι D.C.48.8; ἐντετιμημένος *highly valued, valuable*, Sophr.100 codd. Ath. (ἐντετμαμένα Meineke):—Med., *value* in giving a dowry, Poll. 8.142. **-όομαι**, Pass., *to be held in honour*, Lxx 4*Ki.*1.13. **-ος**, ον, (τιμή), 1. of persons, *in honour, honoured*, opp. ἄτιμος, Pl. *Euthd.*281c, etc.; τινί by another, S.*El.*239 (lyr.), *Ant.*25, etc.; παρά τινι Pl.*Ti.*21e: c. dat. rei, *honoured with*, σπονδαῖς E.*Or.*1688 (anap.); *in office*, Pl.*R.*564d; of *men of high rank* in Persia, X.*Cyr.*3.1.8, al.; opp. ἄδοξοι, D.3.29; = ἐπίτιμος, Decr.ap.eund.59.104. 2. of things, τὰ θεῶν ἔ. *what is honoured in* their sight, their *ordinances* or *attributes*, S.*Ant.*77; ἔ. ποιῆσαι τὴν τέχνην hold it *in honour*, Isoc.4.159; ἔ. ποιεῖν τι Arist.*Pol.*1286ᵇ15; ἔργα -ότερα (opp. ἀναγκαιότερα) ib. 1255ᵇ28; δαπανήματα -ότατα Id.*EN*1122ᵇ35; χώρα ἔ. place *of honour*, Pl.*Epin.*985e; ἔ. ἀπόλυσις, = Lat. *honesta missio*, *PHamb.*1.31.19 (ii A.D.). 3. Adv. -μως, ἄγειν τι Pl.*R.*528c, cf. Satyr.*Vit.Eur.Fr.* 39xviii 27 (Pass.); ἔχειν τι Pl.*R.*528b; also ἐ. ἔχειν to be *in honour*, X.*An.*2.1.7: Sup. -ότατα D.C.63.17; -μως ἀπολελυμένος, = Lat. *missus honesta missione*, *POxy.*1471.6 (i A.D.), al. II. *doing honour, honourable* (to a person), λόγος Pl.*Lg.*855a. III. *valuable, highly valued*, [χώρα] Arist.*Mete.*352ᵃ12 (Comp.), cf. *PLond.*5. 1708.33 (vi A.D.); of currency, *accepted* in exchange, opp. ἀδόκιμον, νόμισμα Pl.*Lg.*742a. **-ότης**, ητος, ἡ, *honour, rank*, Arist.*Rh.* 1390ᵇ19.

ἐντῐν-αγμός, ὁ, *shaking*, Lxx *Si.*22.15 (v.l. ἐντίναγμα, as in Sch. Od.17.231). **-άσσω**, *hurl against*, δοκόν τινι D.L.6.41, cf. Lxx 1*Ma.*2.36, 2*Ma.*4.41, Aesop.357:—Pass., *to be shaken*, aor. 2 ἐνετινάγῃ *PFlor.*163.3 (iii A.D.). II. intr., *collide with* (nisi leg. ἐκτ- (q.v.)), εἰς τοὺς πλησίον ἵππους Ael.*Tact.*19.2.

ἐντιτός, όν, *liable to be sued*, αὐτῷ ἐντιτὸν ἔστω ἐπὶ τᾷ δόσει *GDI* 5087ᵃ6 (Crete); cf. ἐντιτόν· ἔνδικ[τ]ον, Hsch.

ἐν-τμήγω, Ep. for ἐντέμνω, Nic.*Fr.*82. **-τμημα**, ατος, τό, *cut in* a thing, *incision, notch*, X.*Cyn.*2.7. **-τμησις**, εως, ἡ, = foreg., Apollon.*Lex.* s.v. ἁρματροχιή.

ἔντο, 3 pl. aor. 2 Med. of ἵημι, Hom.

ἔντοθεν, v. ἔντοσθεν.

ἐντοίχιος, ον, *on the walls*, γραφαί D.H.16.3; τὰ ἐ. γράφειν prob. cj. in X.*An.*7.8.1; ἐ. ὄρυγμα Ruf.ap.Orib.49.32.5.

ἔντοκος, ον, *with young*, Lyc.185, *PTeb.*53.20 (ii B.C.). 2. *bearing interest*, *PStrassb.*92.8 (iii B.C.), etc.

ἐντολ-εύς, έως, ὁ, = ἐντολικάριος, *agent, representative*, *Cod.Just.*4. 20.16.1, *PGrenf.*1.62.8 (vi A.D.). **-ή**, ἡ, *injunction, order, command*, freq. in pl., *orders, commands*, Pi.*Fr.*177, Hdt.1.22, 3.147, A.*Pr.*12, etc.; ἐντολαὶ θεοῦ 1*Ep.Cor.*7.19; ἐντολὰς δοῦναι Decr.ap.D.18.75; ἐντολὴν ἐπιτελέειν Hdt.1.157; royal *ordinance*, *PTeb.*6.10 (ii B.C.); θεῖαι ἐ., of Imperial *ordinances*, *SIG*888.51 (iii A.D.); ἀπ' ἐντολῆς by *proxy*, Luc.*Pr.Im.*16.—Rare in Trag. and Att. Prose. **-ίδιον**, τό, Dim. of foreg., *POxy.*1767.17 (iii A.D.). **-ικάριος**, ὁ, *mandatory*, *IG*14.956*B*15 (iv A.D.), Mitteis *Chr.*78.8 (iv A.D.), etc. **-ικός**, ή, όν, *of* or *for a command*, νόμος prob. in *CIG*2712.8 (Mylasa, v A.D.); ἐπιστολίδιον *POxy.*1677.5 (iii A.D.). II. Subst. -κόν, τό, *authorization, power of attorney*, *PFlor.*142.2 (iii A.D.), etc. 2. *prescription, recipe*, *BGU*953.1 (iii/iv A.D.), dub. sens. in *POxy.*1775.13 (iv A.D.). **-ιμαῖον** γράμμα power *of attorney*, *PMasp.*161.14, al. (vi A.D.). **-ιος**, ὁ, dub. sens. in *CRAcad.Inscr.*1905.158 (Egypt).

ἐντολμάομαι, Dep., = τολμάω ἐν.., Ael.*Fr.*212.

ἐντομ-ή, ἡ, *slit, groove*, Hp.*Art.*33, 47; in insects, *notch, incision*, Arist.*HA*487ᵃ33 (pl.), 523ᵇ14 (pl.); ἐντομαὶ κτενός Luc.*Am.*44. 2. *hewing* of masonry, λίθοι ἐντομῇ (v.l. ἐν τομῇ) ἐγγώνιοι Th.1.93. 3. *narrow gorge, cleft*, D.S.1.32. **-ίας**, ου, ὁ, *eunuch*, Hsch.; *castrated animal*, Sch.Il.9.539. **-ιος**, ον, dub. sens. in *PLond.*5.1656 (iv A.D.). **-ίς**, ίδος, ἡ, *incision, gash*, Lxx *Le.*19.28, 21.5. II. *grave, burial-vault*, *Ath.Mitt.*16.368 (Thessalonica). III. ἐντομίδας· μαμιλάρι (leg. σμιλάρια), ψαλίδια, Hsch. **-ος**, ον, *cut in pieces*, esp. in neut. pl. ἔντομα *victims* offered to the dead, ἱερεῖα being prop. used in reference to gods (Eust.1671 fin., cf. ἐναγίζω), ἔ. ποιεῖν offer *as victims*, Hdt.2.119, cf. 7.191; ἔ. μήλων A.R.1.587, cf. Call. ap.Sch.Th.*Oxy.*853 x 38. II. ἔντομα (sc. ζῷα), τά, *insects*, καλῶ δὲ ἔντομα ὅσα ἔχει κατὰ τὸ σῶμα ἐντομάς Arist.*HA*487ᵃ33, cf. 523ᵇ13, Ant.Lib.4.7. III. ἔντομοι· ἔνορκοι, Hsch.

ἐντον-ία, ἡ, = Lat. *distentio penis*, Horap.1.46 (v.l. εὐτ-). **-ιον**, τό, *apparatus for stretching the* τόνοι *of a torsion-engine*, Ph.*Bel.*57.46, 61.12, Hero *Bel.*107.1. **-ος**, ον, (ἐντείνω) of persons, *sinewy*, v.l. for εὐ-, Hp.*Aër.*4; τὰ μέλη ἐντόνοις ὅμοια Zeno *Stoic.*1.58. 2. *violent*, of wind, etc., νότος Olymp.*in Mete.*195.39; ἀκτῖνες -ώτεραι ib.259. 23: metaph., *intense, eager, vehement*, γνώμη Hdt.4.11; σπλάγχνον E.*Hipp.*118; Μοῦσα.. ἔ. Ἀχαρνική Ar.*Ach.*666; ἔ. καὶ δριμεῖς Pl.*Tht.* 173a; -ώτατος πρός τι S.*Fr.*842; δρᾶν ἔ. χέρες E.*Fr.*291 (s.v.l.). Adv. -νως *eagerly*, χωρεῖν Th.5.70; ἀπαιτεῖν X.*An.*7.5.7; ζητεῖσθαι Pl.*R.*528c: Comp. -ώτερον *PPetr.*3 p.111 (prob.). II. Subst.

ἔντονος, ὁ, dub. l. for τόνος, Pl.*Lg*.945c.—Freq. confounded with εὔτονος.

ἐντοπ-ίζω, sine expl., Suid. **-ιος**, ον, *local*, θεοὶ ἐ., = ἐγχώριοι, Pl.*Phdr*.262d; νόμισμα, πλοιάρια, *Peripl.M.Rubr*.49,36; πόλεμοι ἐ. *civil* wars, D.H.8.83; ἡ ἐ. ἱστορία D.L.7.35; ἐντόπιοι *local residents*, opp. ξένοι, *IG*5(2).491 (Megalopolis, ii/iii A.D.); opp. Ἀλεξανδρεῖς, *PLond*.2.192.94 (i A.D.). 2. Medic., *local*, βάρος Antyll.ap.Aët.9.40. **-ος**, ον, *in* or *of a place*, S.*Ph*.212 (lyr.), 1171 (lyr.), *OC*1457, Pl.*Lg*.848d, prob. in Nausicr.1; ἔλαιον prob. in *OGI*629.70 (Palmyra, ii A.D.).

ἐντορεύω, *carve in relief on*.., Plu.*Cic*.1:—Pass., Id.2.164a, 399f, Luc.*Ind*.8.

ἐντορν-εύω, *turn by the lathe*, in pf. Pass. ἐντετορνεύσθω Hero *Aut*.16.2. **-ία**, ἡ, *raised rim* or *flange*, Id.*Bel*.97.5. **-ος**, ον, *turned with the lathe*, Pl.*Lg*.898a; [ὁ κόσμος] κατ' ἀκρίβειαν ἔ. perfectly *rounded*, Arist.*Cael*.287^{b}15, cf. *IG*2.1054*f*24; πρὸς τὴν ἔ. (sc. γραμμήν) στρογγύλα *IG*2^{2}.244.101 (Piraeus). Adv. -νως Hero *Aut*.23.3.

ἔντος, τό, v. ἔντεα, τά.

ἐντός, (ἐν) *within, inside*, opp. ἐκτός: I. Prep. c. gen., which mostly follows, but may precede, τείχεος ἐ. Il.12.380, al., cf. Ἀρχ. Ἐφ. 1920.33 (Boeot., v B.C.); ἐ. Ὀλύμπου Hes.*Th*.37; στέρνων ἐ. A.*Ag*.77 (anap.); σ' ἔθρεψεν ἐ. . . ζώνης Id.*Eu*.607; ἐ. ἐμεωυτοῦ *in* my *senses, under* my own *control*, Hdt.7.47; ἐ. ἑωυτοῦ γίνεσθαι Id.1.119, cf. Hp.*Epid*.7.1; ἐ. ὧν εἰπεῖν αὐτοῦ D.34.20; ἐ. τῶν λογισμῶν Plu.*Alex*.32; ἐ. ὑμῶν *in* your *hearts*, *Ev.Luc*.17.21; τῶν μαθημάτων ἐ. Dicaearch.1.30; γραμμάτων ἐ. Sor.1.3; ἐ. εἶναι τῶν συμβαινόντων παθῶν *acquainted with*, Chrysipp.*Stoic*.3.120; ἐ. τοξεύματος *within* shot, E.*HF*991, X.*Cyr*.1.4.23; οὐδ' ἐντὸς πολλοῦ πλησιάζειν not *within* a great distance, Pl.*Smp*.195b, cf. Th.2.77; ἐ. ποιεῖν put *within*, τῶν τειχῶν Id.7.5; ἐ. ποιεῖσθαι τῶν ἐπιτάκτων Id.6.67; ἐ. πλαισίου ποιησάμενοι X.*An*.7.8.16; of troops, ἐ. αὐτῶν *within* their own *lines*, ib.1.10.3: also with Verbs of motion, τείχεος ἐ. ἰόντες Il.12.374; πύργων ἔπεμψεν ἐντός E.*Tr*.12. 2. *within*, i.e. *on this side*, ἐ. Ἅλυος ποταμοῦ Hdt.1.6, cf. 8.47, Th.1.16; ἡ ἐ. Ἱσπανία, = Lat. *Hispania Citerior*, Plu.*Cat.Ma*.10; ἐ. τοῦ Πόντου Hdt.4.46; ἐ. ὅρων Ἡρακλείων Pl.*Ti*.25c; ἐ. τῶν μέτρων τετμημένον μέταλλον *within* the bounds of the adjacent property, an encroachment, Hyp.*Eux*.35; τῶν μέτρων ἐ. D.37.36; also ἐ. τῶν πρῳρέων . . καὶ τοῦ αἰγιαλοῦ *between*.., Hdt.7.100. 3. of Time, *within*, ἐ. οὐ πολλοῦ χρόνου Antipho 5.69; ἐ. εἴκοσιν ἡμερῶν Th.4.39, cf. *IG*1^{2}.114.40, etc.; ἐ. ἑξήκοντ' ἐτῶν Amphis 20.2; ἐ. ἑσπέρας *short of*, i.e. *before*, evening, X.*Cyn*.4.11; ἐ. ἑβδόμης *before* the seventh of the month, Hsch.; οἱ τῆς ἡλικίας ἐ. γεγονότες *short of* manhood, Lys.2.50; τῆς πρεπούσης ἐ. ἡλικίας *within* the fitting limits of age, Pl.*Ti*.18d. 4. with Numbers, ἐ. εἴκοσιν [ἐτῶν] *under* twenty, Ar.*Ec*.984; ἐ. δραχμῶν πεντήκοντα *within*, i.e. *under*.., Pl.*Lg*.953b. 5. of Degrees of relationship, ἐ. ἀνεψιότητος *within* the relationship of cousins, *nearer than* cousins, ib.871b, Lexap.D.43.57. II. Adv. *within*, ἐ. ἐέργειν Il.2.845, Od.7.88; χώρην ἐ. ἀπέργειν Hdt.3.116; ἐ. ἔχειν τινάς Th.7.78; ἐ. ποιῆσαι or ποιήσασθαι, Id.5.2, 6.75: freq. with the Art., ἐκ τοῦ ἐ., = ἔντοσθε, Id.2.76; τὰ ἐ. the *inner parts* of the body (of ᾗ τε φάρυγξ καὶ ἡ γλῶσσα), ib.49, cf. Pl.*Prt*.334c, etc.; τοὐντός, opp. τοὔξω, S.*Ichn*.302; ἐ. *in the Mediterranean*, Arist.*Mu*.393^{a}12.

ἐντόσαρκες· ἐντὸς τοῦ σώματος, Hsch.

ἔντοσθε and **ἔντοσθεν** (the latter both before vowels, as Il.12.455, al., and before consonants, as ib.296, al.), Adv. *from within*, Od.2.424; also, = ἐντός, abs., Il.22.237: c. gen., ἔντοσθε χαράδρης 4.454, etc.; after its case, δόμων ἔ. Od.1.380: never in Att. or Trag., unless read metri gr. for ἔνδοθεν in A.*Pers*.991 (lyr.): rare in Prose, Hp.*Medic*.11, D.S.1.35, Luc.*VH*1.24.—The form **ἔντοθεν**, mentioned in Sch.D.T.p.278 H., *An.Ox*.1.178, is sts. found in codd., as Luc.*Vit.Auct*.26, and is conjectured in Od.9.239,338.

ἐντοσθίδια, τά, = ἐντόσθια, Hp.*Steril*.230, Arist.*PA*684^{b}32; cf. ἐνδοσθίδια. II. as Adj., ἐντοσθίδιον πάθος *intestinal* complaint, Androm.ap.Gal.14.42.

ἐντόσθιος, ον, *intestinal*, ἕλμιθες Lyd.*Ost*.32: but mostly, II. Subst. **ἐντόσθια**, τά, *inwards, entrails*, Arist.*PA*685^{a}3, Ti.Locr.100b:—also **ἐνδόσθια**, Lxx *Ex*.12.9, al., Hsch., *EM*345.21.

ἐντότερος, α, ον, *inner*, τὴν αὐλὴν τὴν ἐ. Lxx *Es*.4.11.

ἐντοῦθα, = ἐνταῦθα, *Schwyzer* 792 (Cumae), 811.17 (Oropus).

ἐντουρίων, ωνος, ὁ, dub. sens. in *OGI*262.7 (Syria).

ἐντοφήϊα, τά, Delph., = ἐνταφ-, *offerings buried in tombs*, *Michel* 995 *C*20. **ἐντόφιον**, v. ἐντάφιος.

ἐντρᾰγεῖν, prop. aor. 2 inf. of ἐντρώγω, used in Att. as regul. aor. of τρώγω (q.v.), *eat dessert*, ἔντραγε τουτί Ar.*V*.612, cf. *Eq*.51, Phryn.Com.25, Alciphr.1.22, etc.: c. gen., ἰσχάδων, μήλου, καρύων, Luc.*Merc.Cond*.24, Plu.2.279f, Hld.2.23.

ἐντραγεῖ· ἐντρυφᾷ, Hsch. **ἐντραγούμενοι**· μασώμενοι, Id.

ἐντρᾰγῳδέω, *come the hero over*, τισί Luc.*Sat*.19.

ἐντρᾱν-ής, ές, *clear, manifest*, *PMasp*.32.54 (vi A.D.). II. ἐντρανῆ· τόνον· ἰσχυρόν, Hsch. (ἐντραγήτονον cod.). **-ίζω**, *look keenly at*, Eust.259.8, Sch.Theoc.10.18; τῷ ἀγαθῷ Eustr. *in EN* 312.1.

ἐντρᾰπεζίτης [ῑ], ου, ὁ: fem. **-ῖτις**, ιδος, *parasite*, Suid., Zonar.

ἐντράπελος [ᾰ], ον, (ἐντρέπω II. 4) *shameful*, dub. l. in Pi.*P*.4.105, Thgn.400 cod. A.

ἔντρᾱχυς, εια, υ, *somewhat rough*, Dsc.5.159. II. of music, *somewhat harsh*, S.E.*M*.6.50.

ἐντρεπ-τικός, ή, όν, *fit to put one to shame*, Ael.*NA*3.1; τὸ ἐ. the *sense of shame*, Arr.*Epict*.1.5.3,9. II. *commanding respect*, Herm. *in Phdr*.p.72 A. III. Adv. -κῶς· ἐλεγκτικῶς, Hsch. **-ω**, *turn about*, τὰ νῶτα Hdt.7.211; ἐξεστραμμένην ἕδραν ἐ. *reduce* prolapsed anus, Gal.12.365; of a muscle, *turn* the eye *in*, Id.*UP*10.9 (Pass.). 2. mostly metaph., *make* one *turn*, *put* him *to shame*, 1*Ep.Cor*.4.14, Ael.*VH*3.17, S.E.*P*.3.135, D.L.2.29. 3. *alter*, Luc.*Hist.Conscr*.15; τὴν φωνὴν εἰς μέλος Id.*Pseudol*.7. 4. Med., ἐντρέψασθαι· τὸ εἴσω τρέψαι τὸ ἱμάτιον, Hsch. II. Med. or Pass., fut. ἐντραπήσομαι Lxx *Le*.26.41, al.; *turn about, hesitate*, esp. *feel misgiving* or *compunction*, στείχωμεν ἤδη μηδ' ἔτ' ἐντρεπώμεθα (where Sch. compares ἐντροπαλιζόμενος) S.*OC*1541; ἐνετρέποντο . . ἐν ἑαυτοῖς Plb.31.2.6 (prob. cj.). 2. c. gen. pers., *turn towards, give heed* or *regard to, respect, reverence*, οὐδέ νυ σοί περ ἐντρέπεται φίλον ἦτορ ἀνεψιοῦ κταμένοιο; Il.15.554, cf. Od.1.60; συμμάχου S.*Aj*.90; δωμάτων Id.*OT*1226; νόμων Pl.*Cri*.52c, etc.; ὧν ἐντρέπου σὺ μηδέν S.*OT*724: c. inf., *take heed to*.., φεύγειν ὀλεσήνορας ὅρκους ἐντρέπευ cj. in Thgn.400: aor. 2 Pass., ⟨οὐκ⟩ ἐντρεπέντος τοῦ Ἀμώσιος since A. *paid* no *attention*, *UPZ*5.24 (ii B.C.). 3. later c. acc., *reverence, feel regard for*, τὴν πολιάν Alex.71, cf. Plb.3.10.3, al., *Ev.Marc*.12.6. b. *feel shame on account of*, Plb.2.49.7. 4. abs., *feel shame* or *fear*, *UPZ* 62.29 (ii B.C.), 2*Ep.Thess*.3.14, *Ep.Tit*.2.8.

ἐντρέφω, poet. ἐνιτ-, = τρέφω ἐν, *bring up* or *train in*, τέκνα E.*Ion* 1428; ἐνιθρέψασ' ὀροδάμνοις βότρυας *AP*9.231 (Antip.):—Med., φυτὰ ἐνθρέψασθαι Hes.*Op*.781, cf. Hp.*Aër*.12 (Pass.):—Pass., *to be raised* or *bred in*, γυμνάσια οἷσιν ἐνετράφην E.*Ph*.368, cf. Call.*Iamb*.1.184; νόμοις Pl.*Lg*.798a; ποιήμασι, ἤθει, Plu.2.32e, 38b; διαλογισμοῖς Arr.*Epict*.4.4.48; τοῖς λόγοις τῆς πίστεως 1*Ep.Ti*.4.6.

ἐντρέχ-εια, ἡ, *skill, aptitude*, Corn.*ND*18, M.Ant.1.8, Vett.Val.61.15, S.E.*M*.1.141, etc.; ἐ. φυσική Gal.14.213, cf. 306: in pl., ἐ. τῶν ζῴων *instincts*, Antig.*Mir*.26, cf. 60: so generally, *instinct*, Anon.Lond.1.24. b. concrete, *an industry*, Str.17.1.15. **-ής**, ές, *skilful, ready*, ἐν πόνοις καὶ μαθήμασι καὶ φόβοις ἐντρεχέστατος Pl.*R*.537a: abs., Longin.44.1, M.Ant.6.14, etc.; τὸ ἐ. Perseusap.Philetaer.Gramm. in *Rh. Mus*.43.416. Adv. -χῶς Iamb.*Protr*.5: Comp. -έστερον M.Ant.7.66; -εστέρως *An.Ox*.3.188. II. ἐντρεχέστερον· γοργότερον, Hsch. **-ω**, aor. -έδραμον, *run in, be active in*: hence, *fit, suit*, once in Hom., εἰ ἐντρέχοι ἀγλαὰ γυῖα if his limbs *moved freely in* [the armour], Il.19.385. 2. *to be current among*, λόγος ἀνθρώποις Arat.100. II. *slip in, enter*, Luc.*Am*.24; πόντῳ *AP*9.370.3 (Tib. Illustr.). III. *come in the way, intervene*, Phld.*D*.3.8, *Ir*.p.75 W.; εἴ τις ἐ. νῆσος Str.17.1.4; *occur*, τὰ ἐντρέχοντα Philostr.*VA*2.36; ἐ. τοῖς Τυρρηνοῖς ἰδέαι δελφίνων Id.*Im*.1.19; ἄχρι ἂν μηδὲν ἐντρέχῃ μολυβδῶδες *is met with*, Dsc.5.81; κεφαλαιώματα τοῦ ἐντρέχοντος κοινοῦ τοῖς πολλοῖς Procl. *in Prm*.p.564 S. IV. c. dat. pers., *apply to*, *BGU*1197.11 (i A.D.).

ἐν-τριβάσαι· ἐναντίαν τύψαι, Hsch. **-τρῑβής**, ές, metaph. from the touchstone, *proved by rubbing, versed* or *practised in*, ἀρχαῖς τε καὶ νόμοισιν ἐ. S.*Ant*.177; τέχνῃ Pl.*Lg*.769b; περί τι Isoc.15.187; πληγῶν Sch.Il.11.559. 2. ἐ. ὁδὸς *beaten* track, App.*Hann*.4. **-τρίβω** [ῑ], *rub in*, esp. unguents or cosmetics, ψιμύθιον τῷ προσώπῳ Luc.*Hist.Conscr*.8; οἴνῳ λίθον ἐ. *crumble* a stone *into* wine, Orph.*L*.344. 2. metaph., ἐ. κόνδυλόν τινι *give* him *a drubbing*, Plu.*Alc*.8, Luc.*Prom*.10:—Med., ἐντρίβεσθαί τινι πληγάς *cause* them *to be given* him, D.H.7.45; ἐ. κακόν τινι Luc.*DDeor*.20.2. II. c. acc. pers., *rub* one *with* cosmetics, ὑποχρίουσι καὶ ἐντρίβουσιν αὐτούς X.*Cyr*.8.8.20:—Med., ἐ. τὰ πρόσωπα Ath.12.523a:—Pass., *have* cosmetics *rubbed in, to be anointed, painted*, Ar.*Lys*.149, *Ec*.732, X.*Cyr*.8.1.41; ἐντετριμμένη ψιμυθίῳ Id.*Oec*.10.2; ἀλφίτοισιν Hermipp.26: also c. acc. rei, ἐντετρ. χρῶμα Luc.*DDeor*.20.10: metaph., παιδέρωτ' ἐ. Alex.98.18. III. *rub away, wear by rubbing*, Ar.*Ra*.1070. IV. Pass., *to be familiar with*, γυναικῶν ἐντριβεῖσα παθήμασιν Procop.Gaz. p.163 B., cf. *Cod.Just*.10.27.3*Intr*. **-τριμμα**, ατος, τό, *cosmetic*, Plu.*Crass*.24 (pl.), Them.*Or*.13.167c (pl.).

ἔντριτον· τὸ διονίου ἔμβρωμα, ὃ Γαλάται ἐμβρεκτόν φασιν, Hsch. (Fort. ἔντριπτον.)

ἔντρῐτος, ον, *of three strands, threefold*, σπαρτίον Lxx *Ec*.4.12. II. = Lat. *sequester*, *Gloss*.

ἐντρῐτωνίζω, Com. word in Ar.*Eq*.1189, *to third* with water, i.e. *to mix three* parts of water with two of wine, with a pun on Τριτογενής.

ἔντρῐχ-ος, ον, *hairy*, *AP*14.62, Sm.*Ps*.67(68).22; *with the hair on*, δέρμα Tz. ad Lyc.634. II. Subst., τὸ ἔ. *wig*, Poll.2.30. III. ἔντριχον· ἀσθενές, Hsch. **-ωμα**, ατος, τό, *edges of the eyelids, eyelashes*, Poll.2.69. II. *hair-sieve*, also ἠθμός, Plu.2.912e. **-ώσεις**· αἱ βλεφαρίδες τῶν ὀφθαλμῶν, Hsch.

ἔντριψις, εως, ἡ, *rubbing in*, of cosmetics, X.*Cyr*.1.3.2; ἀσβόλου Hld.6.11. II. *cosmetic*, Ael.*VH*12.1.

ἔντρομος, ον, *trembling*, Plu.*Fab*.3, *AP*5.203 (Mel.); γῆ Lxx *Ps*.17(18).8, *Act.Ap*.7.32, Sor.1.89, *PMag.Par*.1.3076.

ἐντροπάδην· ἐναλλὰξ μεταβολὴ χειρῶν, Hsch.

ἐντροπᾰλ-ίζομαι, Pass., Frequentat. of ἐντρέπω, only pres. part., *often turning round*, ἄλοχος δὲ φίλη οἶκόνδε βεβήκει ἐντροπαλιζομένη Il.6.496; esp. of men retreating with their face to the enemy, θηρὶ ἐοικώς, ἐντροπαλιζόμενος 11.547, cf. 17.109, 21.492, Q.S.12.583. **-ισμός**, ὁ, *turning round*, Sch.Aristid.3 p.213 D.

ἐντροπ-ή, ἡ, *turning towards*: only metaph. (cf. ἐντρέπω II. 2), ἐντροπήν τινος ἔχειν *respect for* one, S.*OC*299, cf. Plb.4.52.2, *OGI*323.7 (Pergam., ii B.C.), etc.: abs., *modesty*, Hp.*Decent*.5, 1*Ep.Cor*.6.5, etc.; ἐ. καὶ αἰδώς Iamb.*VP*2.10. 2. *humiliation*, Lxx *Ps*.34(35).26, al. **-ημᾰτικός**, ή, όν, gloss on δεινός, Apollon.*Lex.* **-ία**, Ion. **-ίη**, ἡ, = ἐντροπή, Hp.*Decent.*2. II. δόλιαι ἐντροπίαι subtle *twists, tricks, dodges*, *h.Merc.*245. **-ίας** οἶνος, ὁ, = τροπίας, Hsch., Suid.; cf. ἐκτροπίας. **-ίδες**· ὑποδήματα, Hsch. (before ἐντροπάδην: fort. leg. ἐνδρομίδες). **-ικός**, ή, όν, = αἰδήμων, Hdn.*Epim.*28. **-ον**, τό, an *ornament*, Poll.5.96. **-όω**, *fasten* the oars *with thongs*, Hsch.:—Med., Agath.5.22; cf. τροπωτήρ.

ἔντροφος, ον, (ἐντρέφω) *living in* or *acquainted with*, σὺ γάρ με μόχθῳ τῷδ' ἔθηκας ἔ. S.*OC*1362; παλαιᾷ μὲν ἔ. ἁμέρᾳ, λευκῷ δὲ γήρᾳ Id.*Aj.* 622 codd.; ἔ. ὕλῃ *reared in*.., A.R.1.1117. 2. as Subst., ἔ. τινος *nursling* of.., E.*IA*289 (lyr.), cf. Arist.*Fr.*675, *AP*9.242 (Antiphil.).—Poet. word.

ἐντροχ-άζω, = ἐντρέχω, *intervene, occur*, κοινότητος ἐντροχαζούσης φωνῶν Demetr.Lac.*Herc.*1014.48, cf. 57,62 F., al. II. *exercise* a horse *in a ring*, *Hippiatr.*33. **-ος**, ον, = ἐντρεχής, *EM*762.29.

ἐντρῠγ-άω, *gather grapes in*, Moeris s. v. ἄρριχος. **-ηφάνιον**· ὁ δεύτερος οἶνος, Hsch. **-ος**, ον, *containing sediment* or *lees*, *Hippiatr.*34.

ἐντρυλλίζω or **-τρῡλίζω**, *whisper in one's ear*, Ar.*Th.*341; term used in quail-baiting, Poll.9.109.

ἐντρῠφ-άω, *revel in, delight in*, c. dat., ἐξουσίᾳ E.*Fr.*362.24; γαμηλίῳ λέχει Men.535.8; ἡδοναῖς D.S.19.71, cf. Luc.*JTr.*21; in good sense, δικαιοσύνῃ Ph.2.258; of persons, Πελοπίδᾳ Plu.*Pel.*30; ἔν τινι D.C.65.20; in bad sense, ἐν ταῖς ἀγάπαις 2*Ep.Pet.*2.13; κόμαι ἀνέμοις ἐνετρύφων it was *playing in* the wind, Chaerem.1.7: abs., X.*HG*4.1.30, Ph.1.666. II. *treat haughtily* or *contemptuously*, τινί E.*Cyc.* 588, Plu.*Them.*18, Alciphr.1.35; *exult over*, τινὸς συμφοραῖς Jul.*ad Ath.*279c; ἔν τινι Lxx*Hb.*1.10: abs., Plu.*Alc.*23:—Pass., *to be made a mock of*, Id.*Lys.*6, *Caes.*64. III. *use* or *abuse at pleasure*, τοῖς νόμοις, τοῖς συνοῦσι, Luc.*Abd.*10, *Merc.Cond.*35, al. **-ημα**, ατος, τό, *thing to take pleasure in, a delight*, Lxx*Ec.*2.8 (pl.), Ph.1.690. **-ής**, ές, *luxurious, wanton*, Man.4.85.

ἐντρύχομαι [ῡ], Pass. or Med., *waste away*, D.C.38.46 codd.

ἐντρώγω, v. ἐντραγεῖν.

ἔντῠβον, τό, *endive*, *Gp.*12.1.7.

ἐντυγχάνω, fut. -τεύξομαι: aor. 2 ἐνέτῠχον: pf. ἐντετύχηκα Ph. 1.395, also ἐντέτευχα *Klio* 15.35 (Delph., i B. C.): aor. 1 Pass. ἐνετεύχθην Ph.2.170, Plu.*Cat.Ma.*9:—*light upon, fall in with, meet with*, c. dat. pers., Hdt.1.134, al., Ar.*Nu.*689, etc.; ὀλίγοι τινὲς ὧν ἐντετύχηκα (i. e. τούτων οἷς...) Pl.*R.*531e, cf. *Grg.*509a, *Prt.*361e; κατ' ὄψιν ἐ. τινί Plu.*Lyc.*1. 2. c. dat. rei, κακοῖς ἐ., = τυγχάνω ὢν ἐν κακοῖς, S.*Aj.*433; οὐντυγχάνων (sc. τοῖς πράγμασιν) cj. Valck. in E.*Fr.*287; ἐ. τῷ νώτῳ, of the crocodile, Hdt.2.70; ὁ ἐ. τοῖς ...τοξεύμασι *he who fell in* their *way*, Th.4.40; of obstacles, ἐ. τάφροις X.*An.*2.3.10; λόφῳ ib.4.2.10. 3. abs., E.*Alc.*1032, Ar.*Ach.*848, Thphr.*Char.*24.8; οἱ ἐντυχόντες *chance persons*, Th.4.132; οἱ ἐντυγχάνοντες Isoc.18.36; τὴν ὠμότητα, ᾗ καθ' ἁπάντων χρῆται τῶν ἐντυγχανόντων D.21.88, cf. 183: sg., ὁ ἐντυχών Isoc.3.61, Pl.*Alc.*2.144b. b. ἐν δὲ μηνὸς πρῶτον τύχεν ἆμαρ it *chanced to be*.., Pi.*Pae.*2.75. 4. *obtain an audience* or *interview*, S.*Fr.*88.8, Thphr.*Char.*1.3:—Pass., *to be appealed to, consulted*, περί τινων Ph.2.170. 5. of thunder, *strike*, κεραυνὸς οἷς ἂν ἐντύχῃ X.*Mem.*4.3.14; but hardly so in S.*Ph.*1329, παῦλαν ἴσθι.. μήποτ' ἐντυχεῖν νόσου (ἂν τυχεῖν Pors.). 6. rarely c. gen., λελυμένης τῆς γεφύρης ἐντυχόντες *having found* the bridge broken up, Hdt.4.140; τῶν παρ' ἡμῖν ἐντυχὼν Ἀσκληπιδῶν *having falling in with* them, S.*Ph.* 1333. II. *converse with, talk to*, τινί Pl.*Ap.*41b, *Phd.*61c, etc.; οὐκ ἄχαρις ἐντυχεῖν Id.*Ep.*360c; οὐκ ἀηδὴς ἐ. Men.*Pk.*112. 2. *have sexual intercourse with*, τινί Plu.*Sol.*20. 3. *petition, appeal to*, τινὶ περί τινος (masc.) *Act.Ap.*25.24; τῷ βασιλεῖ περὶ τούτων Plb.4.76.9; ὁ ἐντυγχάνων the *petitioner*, *OGI*669.5; ἐ. κατά τινος *plead* against, *PGiss.*1.36.15 (ii B. C.), Lxx1*Ma.*8.32, *Ep.Rom.*11.2; τῷ βασιλεῖ τὴν ἀπόλυσιν Lxx3*Ma.*6.37; τῷ διοικητῇ *PTeb.*58.43 (ii B. C.): c. inf., *entreat* one *to* do, Nic.Dam.*Fr.*47 J., Plu.*Pomp.*55; ἐ. ὅπως.. Id.*Ages.* 25:—Pass., ὑπὲρ φυγάδων ἐντευχθείς Id.*Cat.Ma.*9. III. of books, *meet with*, βιβλίῳ ἀνδρὸς σοφοῦ Pl.*Smp.*177b, cf. *Ly.*214b; οἱ ἐντετυχηκότες ταῖς ἱερωτάταις βίβλοις Ph.1.395: hence, *read*, Luc. *Dem.Enc.*27, Plu.*Rom.*12, Jul.*Or.*7.210d, etc.; οἱ ἐντυγχάνοντες *readers*, Plb.1.3.10, Longin.1.1; ἐντυχὼν ὑμῶν τῷ ψηφίσματι *IG*12(3). 176 (Epist. Hadriani), cf. 5(1).1361.7 (Epist. Commodi).

ἐντύλ-η [ῠ], ἡ, *rug* (or *cushion*), *PLond.*2.402ᵛ 15 (ii B. C.). **-ίσσω**, *wrap up*, Ar.*Pl.*692, *Nu.*987 (Pass.), Diocl.Com.13, Gal.10.541; σῶμα σινδόνι *Ev.Matt.*27.59. **-όομαι**, Pass., *grow hard*, of callous lumps, dub. l. for -τυπ-, Dsc.2.43.

ἐντυμβεύω, *entomb*, in Pass., ψυχὴ ἐ. ὡς ἂν ἐν σήματι τῷ σώματι Ph.1.65, cf. 2.367.

ἐντύνω [ῡ], fut. ἐντυνῶ Lyc.734: aor. 1 ἔντῡνα Il.14.162, E.*Hipp.* 1183; imper. ἔντῡνον Il.9.203:—also **ἐντύω** [ῠ], Thgn.196; imper. ἔντυε *AP*10.118; impf. ἔντυον Il.5.720:—Med., Call.*Ap.*8: aor. ἐντῡνάμην Hom. (v. infr.):—Pass., A.R.1.235: (ἔντεα):—*equip, deck out, get ready*, ἔντυεν ἵππους *was harnessing* them, Il.5.720 (so once in Trag., ἐντύναθ' ἵππους ἅρμασιν E.*Hipp.*1183); ἔντυον εὐνὴν *were getting* it *ready*, Od.23.289; δέπας δ' ἔντυνον (aor. 1 imper.) ἑκάστῳ *prepare* the cup, i. e. mix the wine, for each, Il.9.203; λιγυρὴν δ' ἔντυνον ἀοιδὴν *raise* the loud strain, Od.12.183; εὖ ἐντύνασαν ἑ αὐτὴν *having decked* herself well *out*, Il.14.162; θοίνας ἐντῦον B.*Fr.*18; ἐ. ὑπόσχεσιν *make* it *good, implement* it, A.R.3.737; ὑποσχεσίην ib. 510:—Med., ὄφρα τάχιστα ἐντύνεαι (trisyll.) *may'st get thee ready*, Od.6.33; ἦλθ' ἐντυναμένη 12.18; μολπήν τε καὶ ἐς χορὸν ἐντύνεσθε Call.*Ap.*8, cf. Mosch.2.30: more freq. in Hom. c. acc., *prepare for oneself*, only in the phrases ἐντύνεσθαι ἄριστον, δαῖτα, δεῖπνον, Il.24. 124, Od.3.33, 15.500, al.; ἄρμενον ἐντύνασθαι *provide one* what is needful, Hes.*Op.*632; ἀγλαΐην A.R.4.1191:—Pass., *to be furnished with*, τι Id.1.235. II. c. acc., *make* one *ready, urge* him *on*, κρατερή μιν ἀνάγκη ἐντύει Thgn.196, cf. Pi.*O.*3.28: also c. inf., *urge to* do a thing, Id.*P.*9.66, *N.*9.36.

ἔντυνος· κόσμος, Hsch.

ἐντῠπ-άδεια (-δία cod.)· ὅταν τῷ ἱματίῳ τὴν χεῖρα πρὸς πρόσωπα κατειλημμένος στήσῃ, Hsch. **-άζω**, pf. Pass. ἐντετύπασται, *enwrap, shroud*, *BSA*16.107 (Pisidia). **-άς**, Adv., once in Hom., Il.24.163 ἐντυπὰς ἐν χλαίνῃ κεκαλυμμένος (of Priam in his grief) lying wrapt up in his mantle so closely *as to show the contour of his limbs* (τύπος), cf. Sch. ad loc., Hsch.; ἐ. ἐν λεχέεσσι καλυψάμενος A.R.1.264, cf. 2.861, Q.S.5.530, Epic. in *Arch.Pap.*7 p.3. **-ές**· πύκτην, ἔμπληκτον, Hsch. **-ή**, ἡ, *plan, scheme*, *PSI*5.502.20 (iii B. C.). II. *pattern*, *PGiss.*12.6 (ii A. D.). **-ος**, ον, *coined*, ἀργύριον Poll.3.86. II. *receiving impressions, impressible*, Plot. 4.6.3 (Sup.). **-όω**, *carve* or *mould in* or *upon*, τῷ νομίσματι ἐνετύπωσεν ἀηδόνην Arist.*Fr.*568; ἐς τὰ νομίσματα ξιφίδια δύο D.C.47.25; ἄγαλμα Plot.5.8.6; also of a painter, *APl.*4.282 (Pall.): metaph., σχῆμα τῇ ψυχῇ ἐντετύπωκεν ὁ θεός Ph.1.106:—Med., Φειδίαν ἐν μέσῃ τῇ ἀσπίδι τὸ ἑαυτοῦ πρόσωπον ἐντυπώσασθαι Arist.*Mu.*399ᵇ35:—Pass., Aristeas 67; τύλοι ἐντετυπωμένοι Dsc.2.43; *to be imprinted*, of a birth-mark, Jul.*Or.*2.81c; also, *to be flattened* by pressure, Gal.*UP* 4.7, *Hippiatr.*38: metaph., ἐντετύπωται ταῖς θύραις *is like a piece of carving on* the doors, Philostr.*VA*8.7.11. II. metaph., τὸ ἰδίωμα τῇ λέξει ἐ. Longin.10.6. **-ωδῶς**, gloss on ἐντυπάς, Eust.1343. 56. **-ωμα**, ατος, τό, *that which is graved*, χηλῆς ἐ., of a pier, Agatharch.92. **-ωσις**, εως, ἡ, *impression, dint, pit*, Thphr.*Sens.* 51, Antyll.ap.Orib.45.2.1: metaph., Gal.10.74.

ἐντῠραννέομαι, Pass., *live under a tyranny*, Cic.*Att.*2.14.1.

ἐντῡρ-εύω, = ἐνταράσσω, *Com.Adesp.*998. **-ίτης** (sc. ἄρτος), ὁ, *cheese-cake*, *Gloss.* **-όω**, in Pass., *to be turned into cheese*, prob. in Nic.*Al.*364.

ἐντυφλόω, *blind*, Al.*Le.*26.16.

ἐντύφω [ῡ], fut. -θύψω, *smoke* as one does wasps, Ar.*V.*459:—Pass., *smoulder, be on fire*, Ph.1.455, al. II. ἐντεθυμμέναι ἄμπελοι *frost-bitten*, *EM*458.42.

ἐντῠχ-αλός· ἐντευκτική, Hsch. **-ημα**, ατος, τό, = sq., in pl. prob. for εὐτ., Plu.*Phoc.*5, cf. Him.*Ecl.*32.4. **-ία**, ἡ, = *conversation, intercourse*, Plu.2.67c, 582e. 2. *meeting*, Plb.6.11ᵃ.4; *interview*, πρός τινα Aristeas 1. II. *petition*, *PTeb.*61(*b*).26 (ii B. C.), Lxx3*Ma.*6.40, J.*AJ*16.9.4, Heph.Astr.3.20, Seren.ap.Stob.3.13.48; *prayer*, ἐ. πρὸς ἥλιον *PMag.Par.*1.1930, cf. *PMag.Leid.W.*4.10. III. pl., *records* of verdicts, etc., Lyd.*Mag.*3.8. **-ικά**, τά, *petitions*, Heph.Astr.3.20.

ἐντυψίω· ἐντινάξω, Hsch.

ἐντύω, v. ἐντύνω.

ἐνυαίνειν· τρυφᾶν, Hsch.

Ἐνυαλία, ἡ, name of a tribe at Mantinea (fr. sq.), *IG*5(2).271.

Ἐνυάλιος [ᾰ], ὁ, *the Warlike*, in Il. as epith. of the War-god, Ἄρης δεινὸς Ἐνυάλιος 17.211, 20.69: written Ἐνοιάλιος *IG*4.717 (Hermione), Ἐνυιάλιος *JRS*15.254 (Antioch. Pisid.): abs., as his name, ἀτάλαντος Ἐνυαλίῳ ἀνδρειφόντῃ Il.2.651, 7.166, cf. Archil.1, S.*Aj.* 179 (lyr.), E.*Andr.*1015 (lyr.), Aen.Tact.24.2; ξυνὸς Ἐ. Il.18.309: in later authors, distinct from Ares, Ar.*Pax*457, cf. Alcm.104; object of a special cult, *SIG*1014.34 (Erythrae), cf. Plu.*Sol.*9, etc.; Ἐνυαλίῳ ἐλελίζειν, ἀλαλάζειν, X.*An.*1.8.18, 5.2.14: Ἐνυάλιον, τό, *temple of Ἐνυάλιος*, Th.4.67. 2. *battle*, κοινὸν Ἐ. μαρναμένους E.*Ph.*1572 (anap.); ὁ Ἐ. *the battle-cry*, Hld.4.17; also τὸν Ἐ. παιᾶνα τῶν στρατοπέδων ἐπαλαλαξόντων Jul.*Or.*1.36b. 3. = Lat. *Quirinus*, Plb.3.25. 6, D.H.2.48: hence ὁ Ἐ. λόφος, = *Collis Quirinalis*, Id.9.60. II. after Hom. generally (in Opp.*C.*2.58, ίη, ιον), *warlike, furious*, ἰωχμός Theoc.25.279; ἀϋταί Opp. l. c.; epith. of Dionysus, *Lyr.Adesp.*108. [ῠ *Lyr.Adesp.* l. c.; elsewh. ῡ, prob. metri gr.]

ἐνυβρ-ίζω, *insult* or *mock* one *in* a thing, τινά τινι S.*Ph.*342; τινὰ ἐν κακοῖς E.*El.*68; μή μου ἐνυβρίξῃς ἁγνὸν τάφον *Epigr.Gr.*195 (Vaxos). 2. c. dat. pers., *insult*, γυναιξίν Plb.10.26.3, cf. *POxy.*237 vi 17 (ii A. D.); εἴς τινα D.S.34.2. 3. abs., Ar.*Th.*720. 4. in Pass., Medic., of ulcers, *to be irritated*, Sor.1.120. **-ισμα**, ατος, τό, *victim of outrage*, J.*Vit.*42, Plu.2.350c.

ἐνυγρ-αίνω, *moisten*, Gal.12.692, Alex.Trall.7.4. **-αντέον**, *one must moisten*, Aët.7.20.

ἐνυγρό-βῐος, ον, = ἐνυδρόβιος, *EM*232.45. **-θηρευτής**, οῦ, ὁ, *one who seeks his prey in the water, fisherman*, Pl.*Lg.*824b. **-θηρικός**, ή, όν, *of* or *for fishing*, Id.*Sph.*220a, 221b.

ἔνυγρος, ον, *in the water, aquatic*, of animals, Arist.*Spir.*482ᵃ21: = ἔνυδρος, of plants, Thphr.*CP*1.21.6, 6.11.13, v.l. in Ps.-Dsc.4. 134. II. *wet, damp*, τόποι Arist.*Mete.*351ᵃ19; ἔτος Id.*HA*569ᵇ 21. III. *watery*, καρπός D.S.12.58. IV. Astrol., *involved in* loss at *sea*, πραγμάτων φθορεὺς καὶ ἔνυλος τε καὶ ἔνυγρος Rhetor. in *Cat.Cod.Astr.*1.151 (cf. ἕξει.. χρημάτων ἀποβολὴν καὶ ἐμπρήσεις καὶ ναυαγίας Heph.Astr.1.1).

ἐνυδρ-έονται· καθυγραίνονται, Erot. (not found in text of Hp.). **-ίας** ἄνεμος *rainy* wind, Call.*Fr.*39. **-ιος**, ον, = ἔνυδρος, Orac.ap. Lyd.*Mens.*3.5; [θεοί] Iamb.*Myst.*1.9. Adv. -ίως ibid.

ἔνυδρις, ἡ, gen. ιος, Hdt.: **ἐνυδρίς**, ίδος, Arist.*HA*594ᵇ31:—*otter*, *Lutra vulgaris*, Hdt.2.72, 4.109, Arist. l. c. II. *water-snake*, *Enhydris*, Plin.*HN*32.82.

ἐνυδρόβῐος, ον, *living in the water*, χῆνες *AP*6.231 (Phil.).

ἔνυδρος, ον, (ὕδωρ) *with water in it, holding water*, ἔ. τεῦχος, i.e. a bath, A.*Ag.*1128 (lyr.); of countries, *well-watered*, Ἄργος ἔ. Hes. *Fr.*24; Αἴγυπτος ἐοῦσα.. ὑπτίη τε καὶ ἔ. Hdt.2.7 (ἄνυδρος codd.), cf. X.*Cyr.*3.2.11; opp. χερσαῖος, *PMasp.*188.5 (vi A.D.); τὸ ἔ. *abundance of water*, Hdn.6.6.4. **2.** *of water, watery*, νάματα, λίμνη, E.*Ph.*659 (lyr.), *Ion*872 (anap.). **3.** *living in* or *by water*, νύμφαι ἔ. λειμωνιάδες who haunt the *watery* meads, S.*Ph.*1454 (anap.); of plants, *growing in water*, δόναξ Ar.*Ra.*234, cf. Thphr.*HP*1.14.3, 5.3.4; of animals, Pl.*Sph.*220b, *Plt.*264d; of fish, Arist.*IA*713a10, Ti. Locr.104e; of birds, Arist.*HA*559a21; τὰ ἔ. (sc. ζῷα) ib.487a26. **4.** of land, *in the water, submerged*, Id.*Mete.*352a22.

ἐνυδρώθη· ὑδρωπικὸς ἐγένετο, Hsch.

ἐνύει· ἔνδον (Lacon.), Hsch.

Ἐνύειον [ῡ], τό, *the temple of Bellona* (Ἐνυώ) at Rome, D.C.42.26, 50.4.

ἐνῡλισμένον· κεκαθαρμένον, Hsch.

ἔνῡλος, ον, (ὕλη) *involved* or *implicated in matter*, τὰ πάθη λόγοι ἔ. εἰσιν Arist. *de An.*403a25, cf. Procl.*Inst.*195, etc.; ἡ ἔ. καὶ γεννητικὴ ψυχή Plot.2.3.17, cf. Dam.*Pr.*126 bis: Comp., ib.414. Adv. -λως Iamb.*Myst.*6.3, Syrian. *in Metaph.*50.5. **II.** *wooded*, f.l. for ἔναυλος in Ar.Did.*Epit.*11. **III.** Astrol., *involved in* loss by *wood*, i.e. by *fire*, v. ἔνυγρος IV.

ἐνῡμενόσπερμος, ον, *with seeds enclosed in a membrane*, i.e. *husk*, Thphr.*HP*8.3.4.

ἔνυον· ἔφορον, Hsch.

ἐνυπάλλαγμα, ατος, τό, *pledge*, *PLond.*3.1166.17 (i A.D.).

ἐνυπάρχω, *exist* or *be present in*, τὸ ἔμβρυον τὸ ἐνυπάρχον Arist.*HA* 577a14; -άρχουσα ψυχή Epicur.*Ep.*1 p.21 U. **2.** *to be immanent* or *inherent*, τὸ πρῶτον ἐ., = ὕλη, Arist.*Ph.*193a10, cf. 194b24; ἐν ἅπαντι χρόνῳ τὸ [νῦν] ἐ. ib.233b35; ἐξ ὧν (sc. στοιχείων) ἐστὶ τὰ ὄντα ἐνυπαρχόντων *the inherence* whereof is the cause of existences, Id.*Metaph.* 998a31, cf. 1014a26, Plot.5.3.11, Jul.*Or.*4.140c, etc. **3.** in Logic, *to be contained in, inhere*, ἐνυπάρχειν τοῖς κατηγορουμένοις ἢ ἐνυπάρχεσθαι, of the predicates, *to be contained in* the subjects or *to have* them *inhering*, Arist.*APo.*73b17; ἐ. ἐν τῷ τί ἐστι ib.84a25; ἐν τῷ λόγῳ Id. *Metaph.*1022a29; τοῖς ὅροις Id.*APr.*28a6.

ἐνυπνι-άζω, *dream*, Arist.*Insomn.*459a21, *Somn.Vig.*453b19, *HA* 537b13, al.:—in Med. and Pass. c. acc., ἐνυπνιάζεσθαι θορυβώδεα Hp. *VM*10, cf. Arist.*HA*587b10, Ph.1.672, Plu.*Cat.Ma.*23: so in fut. Pass. -ασθήσομαι Lxx *Jl.*3.1, Lyd.*Ost.*33: aor. Med. -ασάμην Lxx *Jd.* 7.13, Pass. -άσθην ib.*Ge.*37.5,6,10. **-αστής**, οῦ, ὁ, *dreamer*, ib.37.19, Ph.1.664. **-άστρια**, ἡ, *she who dreams*, title of book, prob. in *IG*2.992 ii 6.

ἐνυπνίδιος, ον, = ἐνύπνιος, φαντασία S.E.*M.*9.43.

ἐνυπνιο-κρίτης [κρῐ], ου, ὁ, *interpreter of dreams*, *UPZ*84.79. **-μαντις**, εως, ὁ, *one who divines by dreams*, Hsch. s.v. βριζόμαντις.

ἐνύπν-ιον, τό, (ὕπνος) *thing seen in sleep*, in appos. with ὄνειρος, θεῖός μοι ἐνύπνιον ἦλθεν ὄνειρος a dream from the gods, *a vision in sleep*, came to me, Od.14.495, Il.2.56; ἐ. τὰ ἐς ἀνθρώπους πεπλανημένα Hdt.7.16.β'; ἐ. παιδός *the vision* of a boy, *AP*12.125 (Mel.): used adverbially, ἐ. ἑστιᾶσθαι 'to feast with the Barmecide', Ar.*V.*1218; κακοδαίμον' οὕτω δεσπότην οὐδ' ἐ. ἰδών Men.*Pk.*169; later κατ' ἐνύπνιον *AP*11.150 (Ammian.); cf. sq. **2.** after Hom., = ὄνειρος, *dream*, ὄψις ἐνυπνίου the vision *of a dream*, Hdt.8.54; ὄψις ἐμφανὴς ἐνυπνίων A. *Pers.*518, cf. 226, Pl.*R.*572b; ἐνυπνίῳ πιθέσθαι Pi.*O.*13.79; ἐ. ἰδεῖν Ar.*V.*25, Pl.*Plt.*290b; τέλεον τὸ ἐ. ἀποτετέλεσται Id.*R.*443b; ἐνύπνια κρίνειν Theoc.21.29, *Sammelb.*685 (ii B.C.):—Artem. (1.1 b) distinguishes ἐνύπνιον *a mere dream*, and ὄνειρος *a significant, prophetic one*; but the distn. is not generally observed, exc. by Philo. **-ιος**, ον, *in sleep, in dreams appearing*, φαντάσματα A.*Th.*710; ἐνύπνιος ἦλθε *AP*12.124 (inc. or Artemon). **-ιώδης**, ες, *dreamlike*, ὑπολήψεις Str.15.1.59; κινήσεις Plu.2.1024b; ἀσήμαντα καὶ ἐ. Artem. 1.10. **-ος**, ον, = ἐνύπνιος, φάντασμα *Trag.Adesp.*375 (anap.); ὄψις (prob. for ἐνύπνιον) E.*Hec.*703 Herm. **-όω**, *sleep on*, ἄντλῳ ἐνυπνώοντα (Ep. part.) Nic.*Th.*546.

ἐνυπο-γρᾰφή, ἡ, *description*, Dexipp. *in Cat.*2.13. **-γρᾰφος**, ον, *executed and signed*, ὁμολογία *PFlor.*323.9 (vi A.D.). **-δύομαι**, *slip into*, λόγοις S.E.*M.*2.49. **-κειμαι**, *subsist in*, ἐ. καὶ τῇ ὄψει καὶ τῷ ἀέρι τὸ δυνάμει διαφανές Aristombr.ap.Stob.1.52.21, cf. Hierocl. *in CA*11 p.438 M. **-κρίνομαι** [ῐ], *play the hypocrite*, τῷ νόμῳ Lxx *Si.*36(33).2. **-κρῐτος** ὑποστιγμή a stop *put after the protasis*, Sch.D.T.p.24 H.; cf. ἀνυπόκριτος.

ἐνύποπτος, ον, *suspicious*, Sor.1.79. **2.** Act., *suspecting*: Adv. -τως Ps.-Callisth.1.9.

ἐνυπό-σαπρος, ον, *partly putrid*, Hp.*Coac.*437 (ἦν ὑποσ. Littré). **-στᾰτος**, ον, *substantial*, Phlp. *in Ph.*4.20, Eustr. *in EN*40.23. **-τάσσω**, fut. Pass. ἐνυποταγήσομαι, *to be made subject*, τισί Lxx *To.*14.9 cod. Alex.

ἐνυπτιάζω, *throw back upon*, ἑαυτὸν τῇ γῇ Philostr.*Im.*2.16; ἐ. τῇ σεμνότητι *glorying in* his pomposity, Id.*VS*1.10.

ἔνυρεν· ἔτρισεν, Hsch. **ἐνυρήσεις**· θρηνήσεις, Id.

ἔνυστρον, τό, = ἤνυστρον, Lxx *De.*18.3, *Ma.*2.3, J.*AJ*4.4.4.

ἐνῠφ-αίνω, *weave in as a pattern*, [πιλήματι] χρυσοῦ ποικιλίαν Duris 14 J.; τῆς σκιᾶς τὴν πορφύραν Men.561; ἐν τοῖς ἐπομένοις ἐνυφήνας τὰ Τρωικὰ πάθη Jul.*Or.*8.240c:—Pass., *to be inwoven*, ζῷα ἐνυφασμένα θώρηκι Hdt.3.47, cf. 1.203; γράμματα *IG*2.754.9, cf. Arist.*Mir.*838a22; αὐλαία ἔχουσα Πέρσας -ασμένους Thphr.*Char.*5.9; [χιτῶνα] ἀρετῶν ποικίλμασιν ἐνυφασμένον Ph.1.654: metaph., ἅπαν καλὸν ὄνομα ἐνύφανται τῇ ποιήσει [τῆς Σαπφοῦς] Demetr.*Eloc.*166. **II.** *weave in* a place, *Leg.Gort.*2.51. **-άντης**, ου, ὁ, *embroiderer*, prob. in *PAmh.*2.131.12 (ii A.D.). **-αντός**, όν, *inwoven*, Theoc.15.83. **-ασμα**, ατος, τό, *pattern woven in*, D.S.17.70, Antyll.ap.Orib.9.14.7.

ἐνυφ-ίζω, aor. 1 ἐνυφίζησα, *settle down in*, *Gp.*6.5.7. **-ίσταμαι**, *subsist in*, M.Ant.4.14; ἐν τῷ ἑνί Id.6.25. **II.** *withstand*, τὸν πόλεμον J.*BJ*4.1.5.

ἐνυψόω, *exalt, excite*, in Pass., -ούμενος ὑπὸ τοῦ οἴνου Lxx *Da.*5.1.

Ἐνῡώ, οῦς, ἡ, *Enyo*, goddess of war, Il.5.333; companion of Ares, ib.592, A.*Th.*45, etc.; daughter of Phorcys and Ceto, Hes.*Th.* 273. **II.** = Lat. *Bellona*, Plu.*Sull.*9.

ἐνφέρνιοι θεοί, dub. sens. in *Tab.Defix.Aud.*155 *B* 3 (Rome, iv/v A.D.; perh. for Lat. *inferni*).

ἐνωδάς· ἐν ᾧ ὁ ἴουλος ἐπιγίνεται, Hsch.

ἐνώδιον, τό, = ἐνώτιον, *IG*2.652a17, 11(2).199*B*46 (Delos, iii B.C.), *PPetr.*3 p.37 (iii B.C.), *PRyl.*124.30 (i A.D.).

ἔνῳδος, ον, *musical*, Nicom.*Harm.*2, al. Adv. -δως ibid.

ἐνωθέω, aor. 1 ἐνέωσα A.R.4.1243:—*thrust in* or *upon*, τινὰ ἠιόνι l.c.; τοὺς ἵππους εἰς τὰ ὅπλα Plu.*Luc.*28.

ἔνωμα, ατος, τό, *concrete unity*, Dam.*Pr.*53,107 (pl.).

ἐνωμένως, Adv., f.l. for ἡν–, Hero *Geom.*12.8.

ἔνωμος, ον, *rather raw*, κρέας Archestr.*Fr.*57.5 (Comp.); μόρα Diph.Siph.ap.Ath.2.51f; of bread, *under-baked*, Hp.*VM*14; *not too much cooked*, Id.*Mul.*2.211 (Comp.); of fruit, *rather crude, unripe*, Dsc.1.115, cf. *Gp.*8.20 (Comp.), Ruf.ap.Orib.45.11.2; of swellings, *hardish*, opp. χαῦνος, Hp.*Aph.*5.67.

ἐνωμοτ-άρχης, ου, ὁ, *leader of an* ἐνωμοτία (q.v.), Th.5.66 codd., X.*Lac.*11.4, Ascl.*Tact.*2.2:—also **-αρχος**, X.*An.*3.4.21 (v.l.), Arr. *Tact.*6.2. **-ία**, ἡ, (ἐνώμοτος) prop. *band of sworn soldiers*: hence, *division of the Spartan army*, Hdt.1.65, Th.5.68, X.*HG*6.4.12, *Lac.*11.4, etc. **II.** later, = λόχος, cj. in Ascl.*Tact.*2.2; also, *a quarter of a* λόχος, Arr.*Tact.*6.2. **-ίς**, ίδος, ἡ, = foreg., *EM*345.1c. **-ος**, ον, (ὄμνυμι) *bound by oath*, ὅρκων οἷσιν ἦν ἐνώμοτος S.*Aj.*1113; μάρτυρες Luc.*Deor.Conc.*15. Adv. -τως *on oath*, Plu.*Caes.*47. **2.** *confirmed by oaths*, συνθῆκαι *PLond.*1.113.1 (vi A.D.). Adv. -τως *POxy.*904.3 (v A.D.). **II.** Subst., *conspirator*, Plu.*Sert.*26.

ἐνωνά, ᾱ, *right of purchase in* a state, γᾶς κὴ ϝυκίας (Boeot., = γῆς καὶ οἰκίας) *IG*7.3287 (Chaeronea).

ἐνωπ-ᾰδίς, Adv. = sq., A.R.4.354. **-ᾰδίως**, Adv., (ἐνωπή) *in one's face, to one's face*, Od.23.94 (v.l. ἐνωπιδίως). **-ᾰδόν**, Adv. = foreg., Q.S.2.84.

ἐνωπάλιζεν· ἐνέτεινεν, ἐνεδίδου, Hsch.

ἐνωπ-ή, ἡ, (ὤψ) *face, countenance*, used by Hom. only in dat. ἐνωπῇ, as Adv., *before the face, openly*, Il.5.374, [21.510]; later ἐνωπῆς γλήνεα Nic.*Th.*227. **-ια**, τά, perh. *face* of a wall, ἐ. παμφανόωντα Il.8.435, Od.22.121, al.; perh. *façade*, A.*Supp.*146 (lyr.): later in sg., ἑκατέρῳ ἐνωπίῳ τῶν στοῶν *SIG*2588.245 (Delos, ii B.C.). **-ίδες**, αἱ, = θεράπαιναι, Did.ap.*EM*345.3. **-ιδίως**, v. ἐνωπαδίως. **-ιος**, ον, (ὤψ) *facing, to the front*, πρό τ' ἐνώπια Alc.*Supp.*4.17; ἐνώπιος ἐνωπίῳ λαλεῖν *face to face*, Lxx *Ex.*33.11; ἄρτοι ἐ. *shew*bread, ib.25.29(30); διαστολῶν γεγονυιῶν ὑμῖν καὶ ἐνοπίοις (sic) καὶ διὰ γραμμάτων *in person*, *UPZ*110.36 (ii B.C.), cf. *Sammelb.*3925.6 (ii B.C.). **II.** neut. ἐνώπιον as Adv., *face to face*, Theoc.22.152; *in person*, *IG*12(5).1061.10 (Carthaea), *PTeb.*14.13 (ii B.C.): as Prep. c. gen., Aeschin.3.43 codd., *PCair.Zen.*73.14 (iii B.C.), *PGrenf.*1.38.11 (ii/i B.C.), *Ep.Rom.*12.17, *Ep.Gal.*1.20, Hermog.*Inv.*1.1; ἐ. θεῶν *SIG*2843.7 (Delph., ii A.D.). Regul. Adv. -ίως Suid. **-ῶς**· ἐμφανῶς, Hsch.

ἐνωραΐζομαι, *beautify oneself for the benefit of*, τοῖς γυναίοις Luc.*Am.* 9. **II.** *give oneself airs in*, τῷ βασιλείῳ θάκῳ Agath.2.26.

ἔνωρος, ον, *early*, in Adv. Comp. -ότερον, Epist.Hadrian. in *Gloss.* iii p.37, Gem.12.5, 13.9: irreg. Comp. **ἐνωρίστερος**, *earlier*: Adv. -τερον, τοῦ κατειθισμένου καιροῦ Phylarch.44 J.

ἐνῶρσε, ἐνῶρτο, v. ἐνόρνυμι. **ἐνῶσα**, Ion. contr. from ἐνόησα.

ἕνωσις, εως, ἡ, (ἑνόω) *combination into one, union*, Philol.10, Archyt. ap.Stob.1.41.2, Arist.*Ph.*222a20, *GC*328b22, Phld.*Po.*2.17, Ph.1.45, al.; τοῦ συμφραζομένου A.D.*Synt.*175.16, cf. Hermog.*Id.*2.11: pl., Procl.*Inst.*63. **II.** *compression*, Heliod.ap.Orib.46.11.20.

ἐνωτ-άριον, τό, *ear-ring*, Hsch. s.v. βοτρύδια. **-ίδιον**, τό, = foreg., *IG*11(2).287*B*19 (Delos, iii B.C.), *Rev.Ét.Gr.*12.71 (Tanagra).

ἐνωτίζομαι, (οὖς) *give ear, hearken to*, λόγους Lxx *Ge.*4.23; ῥήματα *Act.Ap.*2.14: c. dat., ἐντολαῖς Lxx *Ex.*15.26.

ἑνωτικός, ή, όν, (ἑνόω) *serving to unite* or *unify*, δύναμις Ph.1.31; εὔνοια Id.2.219, cf. Plu.2.428a; τινῶν Procl.*Inst.*13, al., Dam.*Pr.*47. Adv. -κῶς *EM*54.10.

ἐνώτιον, τό, (οὖς) *ear-ring*, A.*Fr.*102, Testamentum Platonis ap. D.L.3.42, Aen.Tact.31.7, *IG*11(2).161 *B*26 (Delos, iii B.C.), Hedyl. ap.Ath.8.345b, etc.; cf. ἐνώδιον.

ἐνώτισις, εως, ἡ, = σύνεσις, ἡ σύνοψις τῶν ῥημάτων, Zonar.

ἐνωτοκοίτης, ου, ὁ, *with ears large enough to sleep in*, Str.2.1.9, 15.1.57.

ἔνωχρος, ον, *yellowish*, Arist.*PA*673b29, *Phgn.*812b10, Dsc.3.2.

ἐξ, v. ἐκ.

ἕξ, οἱ, αἱ, τά, indecl., *six*, Il.5.270, al.: dat. pl. ἑξάσιν *OGI*200.28 (Axum); ϝέξ *Tab.Heracl.*2.34, al., *GDI*1267.27 (Pamphyl.), 4968 (Gortyn); ἑκ ποδῶν is written in *IG*12.372.175; cf. ἕκπους. **2.** ἕξ, τό, *the six* in ἀστράγαλοι used as dice, = Κῷον, Ruf.*Oss.*38. (Cf. Skt. *ṣáṭ*, Avest. *xšvaš*, Lat. *sex*, Welsh *chwech*, etc.)

ἑξά-βιβλος [ᾰ], ον, *in six books*, πραγματεία Erot.*Praef.* **-βρᾰχυς** πούς foot *of six short syllables*, Sch.Ar.*Av.*738, etc.

ἐξαβρύνω, *make delicate*, ναςμοῖς δέμας Aristonous 1.43.

ἐξᾰνακτέω, *to be very wroth*, πρός τινα J.*AJ*4.2.1.

ἐξάγαστον· ἄξιον θαύματος, Hsch.

ἐξαγγ-ελία, ἡ, *secret information sent out* to the enemy, X.*Cyr*.2.4.23 (pl.). II. *expression*, of style, Longin.*Rh*.p.186 H. **-έλλω**, *tell out, proclaim, make known*, freq. with collat. sense of *betraying* a secret, εἰ μὴ μητρυιῇ.. Ἑρμέα ἐξήγγειλεν Il.5.390; εἰσὶ γάρ, εἰσὶν οἱ πάντ' ἐξαγγέλλοντες ἐκείνῳ D.4.18, cf. Th.4.27, Lys.20.9, v.l. in X. *An*.1.6.5; ἐ. τινὶ ὅτι.. Hdt.5.33; ἐ. τινὶ προσιὸν τὸ στράτευμα X.*HG*7.5.10; τινὶ οὕνεκα.. S.*OC*1393; τινὶ περί τινος Pl.*R*.601d; τινὶ τὰ περί τι ib.359e; ἐ. κατά τινος Arist.*Pol*.1313b34; of traitors and deserters, X.*Cyr*.6.1.42, etc.; cf. sq.:—Med., *cause to be proclaimed*, Hdt.5.95, 6.10, S.*OT*148: c. inf., *promise to* do, E.*Heracl*.531:—Pass., *to be reported*, Hdt.5.92.β', al.; ἐξηγγέλθη βασιλεὺς ἀθροίζων the king *was reported to be* collecting, X.*Ages*.1.6: impers., ἐξαγγέλλεται *it is reported*, c. acc. et inf., Id.*HG*3.2.18; πολιορκεῖσθαι τοὺς.. στρατιώτας ἐξηγγέλλετο D.21.162. II. *express*, ἔννοιαν Hermog.*Id*.2.5:—Pass., ἐ. λέξει *to be expressed*, Arist.*Po*.1460b11; ὀνόμασι Ti.Locr.102e. III. *narrate*, Them.*Or*.15.184b. **-ελος**, ὁ, ἡ, *messenger who brings out news* from within: hence, *one who betrays a secret, informer*, ἐ. γίγνεται ὡς.. Th.8.51; ἐ. γίγνεσθαί τινος Pl.*Lg*.964e, etc. II. on the Greek stage, *messenger* who told what was doing *in the house* or *behind the scenes* (opp. ἄγγελος, who told news from a distance); first used by Aeschylus, Philostr.*VS*1.9. **-ελσις**, εως, ἡ, *statement*, Arist.*Rh.Al*.1426b26. **-ελτέον**, *one must report*, τί τινι Agatharch.21. **-ελτικός**, ή, όν, *conveying information*, Arist.*Pr*.903a24. 2. *expressive*, c. gen., ὀνόματα τῶν θείων διακόσμων Procl.*in Cra*.p.72 P. 3. *apt to tell tales, gossiping*, Arist.*Rh*.1384b5. **-ελτος**, ον, *told of*, τοῦ μὴ ἐξάγγελτοι γενέσθαι Th.8.14.

ἐξαγγίζω, (ἄγγος) *pour out of a vessel*, Hp.*VM*22; cf. ἐξαλίζω.

ἐξαγέτης· καλαμίνθη, Hsch.

ἐξᾰγῐάζω, *assay*, *Gloss.*:—Pass., of measures, *to be fixed*, Hero *Stereom*.2.54.3.

ἐξᾰγίζω, (ἄγος) *drive out as accursed*, ἐξαγισθέντας δόμων.. διπλῇ μάστιγι A.*Ag*.641: or perh. fr. ἁγίζω, *taken as victims from* many homes.

ἐξᾰγῐνέω, Ion. for ἐξάγω, *lead forth*, τινὰ ἐς γυμνάσια Hdt.6.128.

ἐξάγιον, τό, *assaying, testing*, ποιεῖσθαί τινος *Gp*.2.32 tit.

ἐξάγιον, τό, weight of 1½ dr., Orib.*Fr*.1,67.

ἐξάγιστος [ᾰ], ον, (ἐξαγίζω) *devoted to evil, accursed, abominable*, usu. of persons, D.25.93, D.H.6.89, Ph.1.265, etc.; of things, λιμήν Aeschin.3.113; βουλεύματα Jul.*Or*.2.99b. II. in S.*OC*1526 ἃ δ' ἐξάγιστα μηδὲ κινεῖται λόγῳ what things are *matters of religion*: cf. Hsch.

ἐξαγκῠλόω, *fasten by an* ἀγκύλη, Poll.5.56 (Pass.):—Med., *take* a spear *by the* ἀγκύλη, Sch.Nic.*Th*.170.

ἐξαγκυρῶσαι· θύραν· ἐκστροφῶσαι, Hsch. (ἐξανκιρῶσαι cod.).

ἐξαγκωνίζω, *nudge with the elbow*, Ar.*Ec*.259. II. *bind* one's *hands behind his back*, D.S.34.2, Ph.2.564; ἐξηγκωνισμένος D.S.13.27: metaph., ἐξηγκωνισμένος τὸν λογισμὸν Ph.2.128.

ἐξαγμός, ὁ, *selected portion*, *POxy*.1917.124,127 (vi A.D.).

ἐξάγνῡμι, *break and tear away, rend*, ὡς δὲ λέων.. ἐξ αὐχένα ἄξῃ πόρτιος Il.5.161; ἐξ αὐχέν' ἔαξε 17.63: aor. 2 part. Pass. ἐξεαγεῖσα A.R.4.1686 (nisi leg. ἐξαγεῖσα).

ἐξᾰγορ-άζω, *buy from*, τι παρά τινος Plb.3.42.2; *buy up*, Plu.*Crass*.2; *buy off*, μικροῦ διαφόρου τὸν ἀδικηθέντα Dicaearch.1.22; *redeem*, D.S.36.2; ἐκ τῆς κατάρας τοῦ νόμου *Ep.Gal*.3.13:—Med., ἐξαγοράζεσθαι τὸν καιρόν *Ep.Col*.4.5, cf. *Ep.Eph*.5.16 (but -άζειν τὸν κ. Lxx *Da*.2.8). **-ᾰσία**, ἡ, *ransom, redemption*, *Gloss.* **-εία** or **-ία**, ἡ, *excantation* of disease, *cure by confession*, Ptol.*Tetr*.170. **-ευσις**, εως, ἡ, *telling out, betrayal*, D.H.*Rh*.8.14. II. = ἐξαγορεία, Ptol.*Tetr*.154. **-ευτής**, οῦ, ὁ, *one who confesses* his sins, ib.158. **-ευτικός**, ή, όν, *fit to tell* or *explain*, τινός Luc.*Salt*.36. **-εύω**, fut. ἐξαγορεύσω *Epic.Alex.Adesp*.2.55: aor. supplied by ἐξειπεῖν, fut. and pf. (exc. in late authors) by ἐξερῶ, ἐξείρηκα:—*tell out, make known, declare*, ἑκάστη ὃν γόνον ἐξαγόρευεν Od.11.234; *betray* a secret or mystery, Hdt.2.170; τι πρός τινα Id.9.89; ἐ. ἀπόρρητα Luc.*Pisc*.33; *confess*, τὰς ἁμαρτίας Lxx *Le*.5.5, Plu.2.168d: abs., Rhetor.in *Cat.Cod.Astr*.8(4).148:—Pass., -εύεσθαι τὸ πάθος Sch.Ptol.*Tetr*.142.

ἐξαγρέω, = ἐξαιρέω, *Schwyzer*412.3 (Elis), cf. Hsch.

ἐξαγρι-αίνω, *make savage*, Pl.*Ly*.206b; λέοντα Ph.1.670; τινὰ πρός τινα Plu.*Dio*7; τινὰ ἐπί τινι J.*AJ*17.6.5:—Pass., *to be made* or *become savage*, Pl.*R*.336d, Arist.*HA*571b31; πρός τινα Thd.*Da*.8.7. II. intr. in Act., = Pass., App.*Ill*.23. **-όω**, *make wild* or *waste*, χώραν, opp. ἐξημερόω, D.S.20.69:—Pass., *to be made so*, Isoc.9.67; ὑπό τινος Aeschin.1.98, cf. Porph.*Abst*.4.21. II. = foreg., *make savage*, Hdt.6.123, E.*Ph*.876:—Pass., *to be brutalized*, ὑπὸ πόθων Pl.*Lg*.870a, cf. Ph.1.584, al. III. intr., *become* or *be savage*, J.*AJ*17.6.1; ἐπί τινι, κατά τινος, ib.19.1.15, 17.6.4.

ἐξαγροικίζω, *barbarize*, Eust. ad D.P.875 (Pass.).

ἐξάγω, pf. -ῆχα D.42.19, -αγήγοχα *PHib*.1.34.10 (iii B.C.):—*lead out, lead away*: I. of persons, mostly c. gen. loci, μεγάροιο, πόληος, ὁμίλου, Od.22.458, 23.372, Il.5.353; μάχης ib.35: with ἐκ.., Od.8.106, 20.21; ἐ. ἐκ τῆς χώρης Hdt.4.148, al.; Ἄργεος ἐξαγαγόντες *having brought* her *out from* Argos, Il.13.379; *bring out of* prison, *release*, *PHib*.1.34.4, al. (iii B.C.), *Act.Ap*.16.39; *bring forth into the world*, τόν γε.. Εἰλείθυια ἐξάγαγε πρὸ φόωσδε Il.16.188; νεοττοὺς *lead out of the nest*, Arist.*HA*613b12; ἐ. Λυδοὺς ἐς μάχην Hdt.1.79, etc.; ἐπὶ θήραν τινά Ar.*Fr*.2 D., cf. X.*Cyr*.1.4.14; *lead out* to execution, Hdt.5.38, X.*An*.1.6.10, etc.: c. acc. cogn., με τήνδε τὴν ὁδὸν.. ἐξήγαγε S.*OC*98. b. seemingly intr., *march out* (sc. στρατόν), X.*HG*4.5.14, 5.4.38, etc.: generally, *go out*, ὡς εἰς θήραν Id.*Cyr*.2.4.18; εἰς προνομάς ib.6.1.24: once in Hom., τύμβον.. ἕνα χεύομεν ἐξαγαγόντες let us *go out* and pile one tomb for all, Il.7.336 (Aristarch.); also, *come to an end*, οἱ μεγάλοι πόνοι συντόμως ἐ. soon *pass away*, Epicur.*Fr*.447, cf. M.Ant.7.33. 2. *draw out from, release from*, ἀχέων τινά Pi.*P*.3.51; ἐ. τινὰ ἐκ τοῦ ζῆν, i.e. put him to death, Plb.23.16.13; ἑαυτὸν ἐκ τοῦ ζῆν commit suicide, Id.38.16.5; τοῦ ζῆν Plu.2.1076b; τοῦ σώματος Id.*Comp.Demetr.Ant*.6; simply ἐ. ἑαυτόν Chrysipp.*Stoic*.3.188, cf. Paul.Aeg.5.29; ὅταν ἡμᾶς τὸ χρεὼν ἐξάγῃ Metrod.49. 3. *eject* a claimant from property (cf. ἐξαγωγή II), D.30.4, 32.17, 44.32, etc.:—Pass., *to be turned out*, ὑπὸ τοῦ παιδοτρίβου Aeschin.Socr.37. II. of merchandise, etc., *carry out, export*, ῥῶπον χθονός A.*Fr*.263, cf. Ar.*Eq*.278,282, etc.; εἴ τις ἐξαγαγὼν παῖδα ληφθείη *exporting* him as a slave, Lys.10.10, cf. 13.67:—Pass., And.2.11, Th.6.31, X.*Vect*.3.2, etc.; τὰ -όμενα *exports*, Arist.*Rh*.1359b22; οὔτε γὰρ ἐξήγετο.. οὐδὲν οὔτ' εἰσήγετο D.18.145:—Med., X.*Ath*.2.3. 2. *draw off* water, Id.*Oec*.20.12 (Pass.), D.55.17; *draw out*, of perspiration, ὑπὸ τοῦ ἡλίου Hp.*Aër*.8 (Pass.); so, *carry off* by purgative medicines, ἕλμινθας *Gp*.12.26.1, cf. Dsc.2.152.2, Plu.2.134c, Aret.*CA*2.5: generally, *get rid of*, Thphr.*HP*5.6.3. 3. of building, *draw* or *carry farther out*, αἱμασιάν D.55.22:—Pass., ὁ περίβολος πανταχῇ ἐξήχθη τῆς πόλεως Th.1.93. 4. of expenses, ἐπὶ πλεῖστον ἐξάγεσθαι D.C.43.25. III. *bring forth, produce*, οὐκ ἐξάγουσι καρπὸν οἱ ψευδεῖς λόγοι S.*Fr*.834; ᾠά *hatch*, Arist.*HA*564b8; *call forth, excite*, δάκρυ τινί E.*Supp*.770:—Med., γέλωτα ἐξαγαγέσθαι X.*Cyr*.2.2.15; μικρὰ ἆθλα πολλοὺς πόνους ἐξάγεται *elicit, induce*, Id.*Hier*.9.11. IV. *lead on, carry away, excite*, τινά E.*Alc*.1080, *Supp*.79; τινὰ ἐπ' οἶκτον Id.*Ion*361, cf. *HF*1212 (anap.); ἐς τοὺς κινδύνους Th.3.45; in bad sense, *lead on, tempt*, οὐδέ με οἶνος ἐ. ὥστε εἰπεῖν Thgn.414; ἐ. ἐπὶ τὰ πονηρότερα τὸν ὄχλον Th.6.89:—Med., E.*HF*775 (lyr.); εἰς τὸ διδόναι λόγον Plu.2.922f:—Pass., *to be led on to* do a thing, c. inf., ἐξήχθην ὀλοφύρασθαι Lys.2.61; ταῦτα.. ἐξήχθημεν εἰπεῖν Pl.*R*.572b, cf. X.*An*.1.8.21; ἃ μὲν ἄν τις ἐξαχθῇ πρᾶξαι D.21.41, cf. 74; εἰς ἅμιλλαν Plu.*Sol*.29: abs., *to be carried away* by passion, Din.1.15; ὑπὸ τοῦ θυμοῦ Paus.5.17.8, etc.; ἐξάγουσα ὀδύνη *distracting* pain, Herod.Med.ap.Orib.7.8.1. 2. *lead away*, [λόγον] εἰς ἄλλας ὑποθέσεις Plu.2.42e; προβλήματα ἐ. εἰς ὀργανικὰς κατασκευάς *reduce*, Id.*Marc*.14 (also εἰς ἔργον πρόβλημα ibid.); ἐ. εἰς τὸ ἀνώτερον, Lat. *altius repetere*, Id.2.639e; πρὸς τὴν Ἑλληνικὴν διάλεκτον ἐξάγειν τοὔνομα *express* in Greek, Id.*Num*.13. V. *exercise*, τὴν ἀρχὴν οὐκέτι βασιλικῶς, ἀλλὰ τυραννικώτερον D.H.2.56, cf. *IG*2².1304.4,14; *carry out* instructions, *Michel*409.18 (Naxos, iii B.C.). VI. *give directions* in a will, ἐμαυτὸν οὕτως ἐξάγω Lycon ap.D.L.5.72. VII. intr., *pass one's life*, D.S.3.43.

ἐξαγωγ-εύς, έως, ὁ, *one who leads out* troops, D.S.15.38, also of the queen-bee, Arist.*HA*625a22. II. = ἐξαγωγίς, *Gloss.* **-ή**, ἡ, *leading out* of troops, X.*Eq.Mag*.4.9 (pl.), Plb.5.24.4 (pl.). 2. *drawing out* of a ship from shallows, Hdt.4.179. 3. *carrying out, exportation*, πωλεῖν ἐπ' ἐξαγωγῇ Id.5.6, cf. 7.156; ἐξαγωγὴν δοῦναι, παρέχεσθαι, grant *a right of exporting*, Isoc.17.57, Pl.*Lg*.705b; ἐ. λαβεῖν τοῦ σίτου receive *an export licence*, D.34.36, cf. *PCair.Zen*.93.13 (iii B.C.); ἐπ' ἐξαγωγῇ for *removal from the country*, for *deportation*, ἀδελφὴν ἐπ' ἐ. πέπρακε D.24.203, cf. 25.55; ἐ. σίτου, σιτική, Plb.28.2.2, 28.16.8. 4. *evacuation*, Arist.*Pr*.869b28; αἱ κατὰ φύσιν ἐ. Plu.2.134c. 5. intr., *going out*: hence, *ending* of a thing, τῶν παρόντων κακῶν Plb.2.39.4, etc.; ἐ. ἐκ τοῦ ζῆν, ἐ. βίου, *departure from* life, Epicur.*Sent*.20, *Sent.Vat*.38; ἐ. alone, *suicide*, Chrysipp.*Stoic*.3.188, Varro *Sat.Men*.p.227 B., etc. 6. *the Exodus*, Ph.1.438, al.; title of poem by Ezekiel. II. as law-term, *ejectment*, Is.3.22, D.44.34. **-ικός**, ή, όν, *of* or *for exports*, τέλη ἐ. *export* duties, opp. εἰσαγωγικά, Str.17.1.13. **-ιμος**, ον, *exportable*, ἐξαγώγιμον ποιεῖν τι Lycurg.26; τὰ ἐξαγώγιμα *exports*, Arist.*Oec*.1345b21. 2. *unsettled, migratory*, of people, v.l. for εἰσ-, E.*Fr*.360.10. II. *for drawing off* water, αἱ ἐ. τῶν ὑδάτων τάφροι D.H.4.44. **-ιον**, τό, *duty on exports*, *Inscr.Prien*.3.28 (iv B.C.), Decr.ap.J.*AJ*14.10.6, Just.*Edict*.13.15. **-ίς**, ίδος, ἡ, *drain*, *IG*11(2).287*A*50 (Delos, iii B.C.), Ph.*Bel*.100.32 (pl.). **-ός**, ὁ, *waste-pipe* for letting off water, Timarch.ap.Ath.11.501f, *PLond*.3.1177.315 (ii A.D.). II. *overflow drain*, *PPetr*.2 p.14 (iii B.C.), etc.

ἐξᾰγωνίζομαι, *fight, struggle hard*, E.*HF*155; περί τινος D.S.13.73 codd.

ἐξᾰγων-ίζω, (ἑξάγωνος) *to be in sextile aspect*, Ptol.*Tetr*.115. **-ικός**, ή, όν, *hexagonal*, Procl.*Hyp*.1.16, Simp.*in Ph*.419.14; *of a hexagon*, πλευραί ib.57.16; ἐ. ἀριθμοί, of a kind of figurate numbers, Iamb.*in Nic*.p.60 P.: Astrol., *sextile*, Paul.Al.*R*.3; also of the moon's phase, Gal.9.902.

ἐξᾰγώνιος, ον, (ἀγών) *beside the mark, irrelevant*, Aeschin.ap.*AB*260; ἐ. καὶ πόρρω τοῦ σκοποῦ Luc.*Anach*.19; cf. ἀγών I.2. II. *excluded from competition*, Ph.2.60; = ἔξω τοῦ ἀγῶνος ὤν, Hsch.

ἑξάγωνος [ᾰ], ον, *hexagonal*, Arist.*Cael*.306b7, *HA*554b25; δακτύλιος *SIG*²588.189: Math., ἀριθμός Nicom.*Ar*.2.11. II. Astrol., *in sextile aspect*, Vett.Val.20.2.

ἑξαδακτῠλ-ία, ἡ, *possession of six fingers*, Phlp.*in GA*.194.4. **-ιαῖος**, α, ον, *six inches long*, Heliod.ap.Orib.49.4.41. **-ος**, ον, = foreg., *six inches long*, Hp.*Nat.Mul*.32,109, Dsc.4.43, Orib.8.6.15, D.L.4.34, Ammon.*in APr*.46.1. II. *having six fingers*, Gal.19.454, Eustr.*in EN*376.1, Tz.*H*.7.902.

ἐξάδαρχος [ᾰδ], ὁ, (ἑξάς) *leader of a body of six*, X.*Cyr*.3.3.11.

ἐξάδελφος [ᾰ], ὁ, ἡ, *cousin-german*, *TAM*2.224 (Sidyma): fem. also ἐξαδέλφη *CIG*3891 (Eumenia). II. *nephew*, Lxx *To*.1.22(25), J.*AJ*20.10.3.

ἐξαδιαφορ-έω, *to be utterly indifferent to*, Ph.1.214, 2.279. **-ησις**, εως, ἡ, *utter indifference to*, τῶν ἀδιαφόρων Id.1.509.

ἐξᾰδικός, ή, όν, (ἑξάς) *consisting of six* or *sixes*, εἰδοποίησις *Theol. Ar*.34. 2. *sixfold*, Dam.*Pr*.264.

ἐξαδραχμ-ία, ἡ, *tax of six drachmae*, *POxy*.1457.2 (i B.C.), 1438.19 (ii A.D.). **-ον**, τό, *sum of six drachmae*, Arist.*Oec*.1347^{a}34, 1353^{a}18.

ἐξαδρ-όομαι, = sq., f.l. in *Gp*.4.8.5. **-ύνομαι**, Pass., *come to maturity*, Hp.*Septim*.1.

ἐξαδῠνᾰτέω, *to be quite unable* or *incapable*, c. inf., Arist.*Pol*.1282^{b}4, Plu.*Alc*.23; πρός τι Arist.*GA*785^{a}10: abs., Id.*HA*575^{a}21, Plb.1.58.5; τῷ σώματι Plu.*Mar*.33; ἐ. τὸ γεννᾶν generation *becomes impossible*, Thphr.*CP*1.16.3.

ἐξᾴδω, *sing out, sing one's last song*, of the swan, Pl.*Phd*.85a; of Arion, Plu.2.161c; ἐξᾴσας τὸ κύκνειον Plb.31.12.1. 2. *sing the* ἔξοδος, of a chorus, Plot.6.9.8. II. trans., *sing away by means of a spell*, Luc.*Philops*.16; *disenchant*, Id.*Trag*.173:—Pass., ὑπό τινος J.*AJ*6.8.2. 2. *sing of, laud*, E.*Tr*.472.

ἑξά-εδρος [ᾰ], ον, *with six surfaces*, *Theol.Ar*.25. II. Subst. ἑξάεδρον, τό, *hexahedron*, Gal.5.669. **-ειδος**, ον, (εἶδος IV) *composed of six ingredients*, Phlp.*in GC*192.29, 269.34; cf. τετράειδος, τρίειδος.

ἐξᾰείρω, v. ἐξαίρω.

ἐξᾰερ-ίζω, = sq., Simp.*in Cael*.571.8 (Pass.). **-όω**, Ion. -ηερ-, *make into air, volatilize*, τι Arist.*Pr*.938^{b}34, Luc.*Peregr*.30:—Pass., *evaporate*, Hp.*Nat.Puer*.25, Arist.*Pr*.933^{a}36; *to be dissipated in perspiration*, Aret.*SD*2.1. **-ωσις**, εως, ἡ, *evaporation*, Id.*CD*2.2.

ἑξᾰ-έτηρος, ον, = sq. 1, Nonn.*D*.38.14. **-ετής**, ές, or -έτης, ες, (ἔτος) *six years old*, *IG*3.1336, *BGU*983.18, J.*AJ*19.9.1, etc.:—fem. -έτις, ιδος, Theoc.14.33 (v.l.). II. *of six years*, χρόνος Plu.*Pyrrh*.26. Adv. ἑξάετες *for six years*, Od.3.115; cf. ἑξέτης. **-ετία**, ἡ, *term of six years*, Ph.2.371, J.*AJ*16.1.1, *POxy*.101.17 (ii A.D.), etc. **-ήμερος**, ον, *of* or *in six days*, ἡ ἑξαήμερος (sc. περίοδος) *the six days* of creation, Ph.1.69: also -ον, τό, Id.2.197.

ἐξαηρμένον· ἐξηρημένον, Hsch.

ἐξᾰθέλγω, *draw* or *drain off*, in Pass., Hp.*Oss*.19, Hsch.

ἐξᾰθερ-ίζω, *scorn*, Eust.1046.58. **-ισις**, εως, ἡ, *scorning*, Id. 1910.2.

ἔξαθλος, ον, *past athletic exercise*, Luc.*Lex*.11. II. *disqualified*, in an athletic competition, Sch.Od.21.76.

ἐξαθρέω, *look at carefully*, dub. in Thesp.(*Fr*.2)ap.Chrysipp.*Stoic*. 2.55.

ἐξαθροίζομαι, Med., *seek out and collect*, E.*Ph*.1169.

ἐξαθῡμέω, strengthd. for ἀθυμέω, *PSI*4.418.25 (iii B.C.), Plb.11.17.6, Plu.*Cic*.6.

ἑξάθυρος [ᾰ], ον, *having six sluices*, *PLond*.2.139*b*, 166*b* (i A.D.), *PFay*.365 (ii A.D.).

ἐξαιάζω, strengthd. for αἰάζω, E.*Tr*.198 (lyr.).

ἐξαιγειρόομαι, Pass., of the white poplar (λεύκη), *degenerate into a black poplar* (αἴγειρος), Thphr.*CP*2.16.2.

ἐξαιθᾰλόω, *turn into soot*, Zos.Alch.p.168 B. (Pass.).

ἐξαιθερόω, *change into ether*, Chrysipp.*Stoic*.2.184 (Pass.).

ἐξαιθραπεύω, *to be a satrap*, *SIG*167.2 (Mylasa, iv B.C.); cf. ἐξαιτραπεύω.

ἐξαιθριάζω, *expose to sun and air*, Hp.*Int*.35, Dsc.5.16, Apollon. ap.Gal.12.478:—Pass., *Com.Adesp.* in *PLond.ined*.2294 (iii/ii B.C.).

ἐξαιμάσσω, Att. -ττω, *make quite bloody*, τοὺς πόδας *IG*4.952.134 (Epid.); τὸν ἵππον τῷ κέντρῳ X.*Cyr*.7.1.29:—Pass., τῇ μάστιγι Philostr.Jun.*Im*.11, prob. in Paul.Aeg.6.110. 2. metaph., ἐ. τὰς λύπας *open* one's griefs *afresh*, D.H.6.81.

ἐξαιμᾰτ-ίζω, *take blood from*, φλέβας *Hippiatr*.1. **-όω**, *change into blood*, Gal.8.359:—Pass., Arist.*Somn.Vig*.456^{b}4, Ph.2.244. **-ωσις**, εως, ἡ, *conversion into blood*, of food, ibid., Alex.Aphr.*Pr*.2.63, Gal. 11.139. **-ωτικός**, ή, όν, *blood-producing*, δύναμις Alex.Aphr.*Pr*. 2.63.

ἔξαιμ-ος, ον, (αἷμα) *bloodless, drained of blood*, Hp.*VC*16, *Epid*.5.6, D.S.3.35, etc. **-ων**, ον, gen. ονος, = foreg., Poll.4.186, 8.79.

ἐξαίνῠμαι, *take out* or *away*, νηῒ δ' ἐνὶ πρύμνῃ ἐξαίνυτο κάλλιμα δῶρα *took out* (*and placed*), Od.15.206: in Il. always in phrase ἐξαίνυτο θυμόν, *animam eripuit*, 5.155, al.; νάρθηκος νηδὺν ἐ. Nic.*Al*.272.

ἐξαιονάω, *spray, douche*, *EM*348.24 (Pass.).

ἑξάϊππος [ᾰ], ον, *with six horses*, Sch.A.*Pers*.48.

ἐξαιρ-έσιμος, ον, (ἐξαιρέω) *that can be taken out*, ἡμέραι ἐ. days *taken out of the calendar*, Arist.*Oec*.1351^{b}15, cf. Cic.*Verr*.2.2.52. 129. **-εσις**, εως, ἡ, *taking out* the entrails of victims, Hdt.2.40: pl., *the entrails* themselves, *offal*, Dionys.Com.3.12; *extraction* of teeth, Arist.*Mech*.854^{a}25, Paul.Aeg.6.28; of weapons, Gal.2.283; *taking out* of patients from a bath, Philum.*Ven*.15.8. b. *removal, purgation*, τῶν παθῶν Porph.*Abst*.2.43. 2. *way of taking out*, τὴν ἐ. τοῦ λίθου Hdt.2.121.α'. 3. Rhet., *taking exception, questioning of* an adversary's arguments, Ulp. ad D.24.66. b. in Law, = Lat. *exceptio*, Just.*Nov*.136.2. 4. *transcendence*, τοῦ ἐνδεοῦς Dam.*Pr*.13. II. *place where cargoes are landed, wharf*, Hyp.*Fr*.186, *PTeb*. 5.26 (ii B.C.). III. as law-term, ἐξαιρέσεως δίκη action against one who has asserted the free birth of a slave, Is.*Fr*.70. IV. *killing*, ὑός Str.8.6.22. **-ετέος**, α, ον, *to be taken out* or *removed*, ἐκ τῆς στρατιᾶς X.*Cyr*.2.2.23. II. ἐξαιρετέον *one must take out, remove*, τὴν ἀναρχίαν ἐκ παντὸς τοῦ βίου Pl.*Lg*.942c, cf. *Tht*.157b. 2. *one must pick out, select*, X.*Cyr*.4.5.52. **-έτης**, Lacon. -έταρ· ἁρπάγη, ἢ ἅρπαξ ὁ πρὸς τὰ ἀντλήματα, Hsch.; cf. ἐξαι⟨ρέ⟩της· ἀφαιρέτης, Suid. **-ετός**, ή, όν, *removable*, Hdt.2.121.α'; βάλανοι Aen.Tact. 20.3; στελεοί J.*AJ*3.6.6; ἐξαίρετα, τά, *removable parts* of a machine, Orib.49.5.81. II. ἐξαίρετος, ον, *taken out*, and so, 1. *picked out, chosen, choice*, κοῦροι Ἰθάκης ἐξαίρετοι Od.4.643; γυναῖκες Il.2. 227; ἕνα ἐ. ἀποκρίνειν Hdt.6.130; esp. of booty and things *given as a special honour, not assigned by lot*, χρημάτων ἐ. ἄνθος A.*Ag*.954; δώρημα Id.*Eu*.402, etc.; ἐ. τι ἐκτῆσθαι Hdt.8.140.β'; ἐ. οἰκόπεδον *SIG* 141.5 (Issa, iv B.C.); διδόναι X.*Cyr*.8.4.29; δίδοσθαι Hdt.2.98, 3. 84. 2. *excepted*, ἐ. τίθημι τὴν ἀκουσίαν S.*Fr*.746; ποιεῖσθαι Th.3. 68, cf. D.40.14; ἐ. μοι δὸς τόδ' E.*IT*755; οὐδ' ἔστιν ἐ. ὥρα τις ἣν διαλείπει D.9.50, cf. D.H.6.50; τριήρεις ἑκατὸν ἐξαιρέτους ἐψηφισάμεθα εἶναι to be *set apart for special service*, And.3.7; χίλια τάλαντα ἐ. ποιήσασθαι Th.2.24. 3. *special, singular, remarkable*, ἐ. μόχθος Pi.*P*. 2.30; οὐδὲν ἐ. οὐδ' ἴδιον πεποίημαι D.18.281; ἐ. αὐτῷ τυραννίδα περιποιεῖσθαι Aeschin.3.89; βασιλείαν ἐ. αὐτοῖς παρ' ἐκείνων ἔλαβον Isoc. 6.20; στρατηγία ἐ. *extraordinary* praetorship, Plu.*Cat.Mi*.39; τούτῳ μόνῳ ἐξαίρετόν ἐστι ποιεῖν ὅτι ἂν βούληται he alone has *the special privilege*.., Lys.10.3, cf. D.19.247; κατ' ἐξαίρετον *specially*, *POxy*.907.10 (iii A.D.), etc.; *par excellence*, Eustr. *in EN*348.1; ἐ. τινος *peculiar to*, Jul.*Or*.1.5c; ἰδιότητος Procl.*Inst*.21. III. ἐξαίρετα, τά, = ἀναλώματα, *Ath.Mitt*.13.249 (*CR*40.18), Heberdey-Wilhelm *Reisen in Kilikien* p.161. IV. Adv. -τως *specially*, φίλανδρος *IG*12(7).395.14 (Amorgos), cf. Plu.2.667f, *POxy*.1675.6, etc.; *in a special degree*, Arr. *Epict*.1.6.12; ὃν ἐ. τῶν φίλων στέργω *BMus.Inscr*.481*.393 (Ephesus, ii A.D.); *exclusively, characteristically*, A.D.*Synt*.194.1; *for choice, for preference*, *PMag.Lond*.121.652. **-έω**, fut. -ήσω, later ἐξελῶ D.H.7. 56, etc.: aor. 2 ἐξεῖλον, Ep. and Lyr. ἔξελον Il.16.56, Pi.*O*.1.26; inf. ἐξελεῖν:—Med., fut. ἐξαιρήσομαι A.*Supp*.924; later ἐξελοῦμαι Alciphr. 1.9: aor. 2 ἐξειλόμην, rarely 1 ἐξηρησάμην Ar.*Th*.761 (perh. interpol.):—Pass., pf. -ήρημαι, Ion. -αραίρημαι Hdt.:—*take out*, ἔνθεν.. ἔξελε πέπλους Il.24.229; ἐπεί νιν καθαροῦ λέβητος ἔξελε Κλωθώ Pi.l.c.; τὸ δέλτα τοῦ ὀνόματος Pl.*Cra*.413e; simply, *take out*, τὴν κοιλίην, τὴν νηδύν, Hdt.2.40 (tm.), 87; πρὶν ἀνταράξας πῖαρ ἐξεῖλεν γάλα Sol.36. 21:—Pass., εἰ τὸ ἔαρ ἐκ τοῦ ἐνιαυτοῦ ἐξαραιρημένον εἴη Hdt.7.162, cf. Pericl.ap.Arist.*Rh*.1365^{a}33. 2. Med., *take out for oneself*, φαρέτρης ἐξείλετο πικρὸν ὀϊστόν from *his* quiver, Il.8.323; ἐξελέσθαι τὰ μεγάλα ἱστία *their* large sails, X.*HG*1.1.13; ἐ. τὰ φορτία *discharge their* cargoes, Hdt.4.196; τὰ ἀγώγιμα X.*An*.5.1.16; τὸν σῖτον ἐς [τὴν στοὰν] ἐξαιρεῖσθαι Th.8.90: abs., Syngr.ap.D.35.13, etc.:—Pass., *to be discharged*, of a cargo, Hdt.3.6, D.34.8. II. *take from* a common stock, *reserve*, κούρην, ἣν ἄρα μοι γέρας ἔξελον υἷες Ἀχαιῶν Il.16.56; Ἀλκινόῳ δ' αὐτὴν γέρας ἔξελον Od.7.10, cf. Il.11.627; βασιλέϊ τεμένεα ἐξελὼν καὶ ἱερωσύνας Hdt.4.161; Νίσῳ ἐ. χθόνα S.*Fr*.24.5; θεοῖσιν ἀκροθίνια E.*Rh*.470; κλήρους τοῖς θεοῖς Th.3.50:—Med., *choose for oneself, carry off as booty*, τὴν ἐκ Λυρνησσοῦ ἐξείλετο Il.2.690, cf. 9.130; *choose*, μενοεικέα Od.14.232; μίαν ἕκαστος σιτοποιὸν ἐ. Hdt.3.150, cf. X.*An*.2.5.20; ταύτας ἐξείλεθ' αὑτῷ κτῆμα S.*Tr*.245; δῶρον.. πόλεος ἐξελέσθαι *to have accepted* as a gift, Id.*OC*541 (lyr.):—Pass., *to be given as a special honour*, τινί to one, Th.3.114; ἐξαραιρημένος Ποσειδέωνι *dedicated* to him, Hdt.1.148; γέρεα.. σφι ἦν τάδε ἐξαραιρημένα Id. 2.168; ἐ. αὐτοῖς *set apart* for them, Pl.*Criti*.117c; τὰ τεμένη τὰ ἐξῃρημένα *IG*1^{2}.45.10; of funds, *to be set apart, ear-marked*, *SIG*577.64 (Milet., iii/ii B.C.); but τοῦ ἀργυρίου τοῦ ἐκ τοῦ λιθοτομείου ἐξαιρουμένου moneys *received* from.., *IG*2^{2}.47. 2. *take out of* a number, *except*, μητέρας ἐξελόντες Hdt.3.150; Σιμμίαν ἐξαιρῶ λόγου Pl.*Phdr*.242b, cf. X.*Mem*.1.4.15. III. *remove* people from their country, Hdt.2. 30; τοὺς ἐν τῇ λίμνῃ κατοικημένους Id.5.16; στρουθούς (sc. ἐκ τοῦ νηοῦ) Id.1.159: generally, *remove*, τὸν λίθον Id.2.125; ἐκ τοῦ λυχνούχου τὸν λύχνον Alex.102; πατρὸς φόβον E.*Ph*.991, cf. Isoc.2.23; ὀδυρμούς, ἄγνοιαν, ἔρωτα, Pl.*R*.387d, *Lg*.771e, *Smp*.186d; ἀλλήλων τὴν ἀπιστίαν X.*An*.2.5.4:—Med., νεῖκος E.*Med*.904; ὑμῶν ἐ. τὴν διαβολὴν.. ταύτην *remove* this prejudice from your minds, Pl.*Ap*.19a, cf. 24a. 2. *get rid of*, [ὗν] ἐκ τῆς χώρας Hdt.1.36; θῆρας χθονὸς E.*Hipp*.18; *make away with*, παῖδας, θῆρα, Id.*HF*39, 154; Ἀθηναίους X.*HG*2.2.19. b. *destroy*, πόλιν Hdt.1.103, al., cf. Th.3.113, 4.69, D.18.30; χωρία Id.23. 115; οἰκίδιον Men.*Pk*.199, cf. 278; φρούριον D.H.8.86. c. *annul, bring to naught*, θέσφατα S.*OT*908 (lyr.), cf. D.23.36. 3. Med., ψυχήν, θυμόν, φρένας ἐξελέσθαι, either c. acc. pers., *bereave* a person *of* life, etc., as μιν ἐξείλετο θυμόν Il.15.460, 17.678 (so in Trag., E.*Alc*. 69, *IA*972): or c. gen. pers., as μευ φρένας ἐξέλετο Ζεύς Il.19.137, cf. Hes.*Sc*.89; σεῦ ψυχὴν χαλκῷ Il.24.754; μου τέρψιν ἐξείλου βίου E.*Alc*. 347, etc.: rarely, c. dat. pers., Γλαύκῳ φρένας ἐξέλετο Ζεύς Il.6.234; [οἰωνοῖς] τέκνα Od.16.218: in tmesi, ἐκ δέος εἵλετο γυίων 6.140; ἐκ θυμὸν ἕλοιο 20.62, cf. Il.11.381:—Med., *take away from one*, τὰ φίλτατα S.*El*.1208:—Pass., ἐξαιρεθέντες τὸν Δημοκήδεα *having had* him *taken out of their hands*, Hdt.3.137; τὸ ἐπιθυμοῦν τοῦ πλοῦ οὐκ ἐξῃρέθησαν Th.6.24, cf. Pl.*Grg*.519d, etc. 4. Pass., *to be removed from*, i.e. *transcend*, τοῦ ὄντος πλήθους Procl. *in Prm*.p.546 S.; ἑνάδες ἐξῃρημέναι *transcendent*, ib.p.547 S., cf. Dam.*Pr*.7; τὸ μᾶλλον -μένον μᾶλλον καὶ χωρεῖ διὰ τῶν ἄλλων ib.325. Adv. ἐξῃρημένως *transcendently*, ib.270; *ultimately*, opp. προσεχῶς, Phlp. *in de An*.270.14. IV. Med., *set free, deliver*, τινά A.*Supp*.924, Ar.*Pax*316; ἐκ τῶν κινδύνων τινά Decr.ap.D.18.90; ἐκ τῆς ἀνάγκης *PPetr*.3p.74; ἐκ τῶν θλίψεων *Act.Ap*.7.10; ἐξαιρεῖσθαι εἰς ἐλευθερίαν *claim* as a freeman, Lys.23. 9, D.8.42, 10.14. 2. *bring to an end, accomplish*, πᾶν γὰρ ἐξαιρεῖ λόγος E.Ph.516.— Freq. confounded with ἐξαίρω. —ημα, ατος, τό, sum deducted, SIG1106.78 (Cos, iv/iii B.C., pl.). II. reserved portion of an estate, AJA16.13 (iv/iii B.C.). —ῖτις, ιδος, ἡ, ladder, Ath.Mech.36.7.

ἐξαιρόομαι, Pass., (αἶρα) turn into darnel, Thphr.CP2.16.2.

ἐξαίρω, Ep. **ἐξᾰείρω** Hom. (v. infr.), also in Ion. Prose, Hp.Fract. 21, cf. ἀείρω, αἴρω: aor. 1 ἐξῆρα S.OC358, etc.:—lift up, lift off the earth, ἐκ μὲν ἄμαξαν ἄειραν Il.24.266; ἐκ δὲ κτήματ' ἄειραν Od.13.120 (elsewh. Hom. uses only Med., v. infr.); ἐξάρας [αὐτὸν] παίει ἐς τὴν γῆν Hdt.9. 107; ἐ. χεῖρας in prayer, Plb.3.62.8; κοῦφον ἐξάρας πόδα S.Ant.224; βάθρων ἐκ τῶνδέ μ' ἐξάραντες having bidden me rise (from suppliant posture), Id.OC264, cf. Tr.1193; τίς σ' ἐξῆρεν οἴκοθεν στόλος; made thee start, Id.OC358; ἡδοναῖς ἄμοχθον ἐ. βίον Id.Tr.147; ἐ. θώρακα take it out (of its case), Ar.Ach.1133; πυρσόν Hero Aut.22.5:—Pass., ib.22. 6. b. seemingly intr., rise from the ground, of a bird, D.S.2.50; ἐ. τῷ στρατεύματι start, Plb.2.23.4, cf. LxxNu.2.9. 2. raise in dignity, exalt, magnify, Κλεισθένης [τὴν οἰκίην] ἐξῆρε (v.l. -ήγειρε) Hdt.6.126; ἐξάρας με ὑψοῦ καὶ τὴν πάτρην Id.9.79; ἄνω τὸ πρᾶγμα ἐ. exaggerate it, Aeschin.2.10; ἐπὶ μεῖζον ἐ. τὰ γενόμενα D.H.8.4; ὑψηλὸν ἐ. αὐτὸν ἐπί τινι Pl.R.494d; ἐ. ὑπόθεσιν Procl. in Prm.p.522S.; Rhet., treat in elevated style, Hermog.Id.2.3; τὸν τῆς ἑρμηνείας τύπον ἐ. παρὰ τὸ εἰωθὸς Procl. in Prm.p.484S.; ἐπιστολαὶ μικρὸν ἐξηρμέναι Demetr.Eloc.234; of music, ἐξηρμένον καὶ τεθαρρηκὸς Heraclid.Pont.ap.Ath.14.624d. 3. arouse, stir up, θυμὸν ἐς ἀμπλακίην Thgn.630; μηδὲν δεινὸν ἐξάρῃς μένος S.Aj.1066; ἐ. σε θανεῖν excites thy wish to die, E.Hipp.322; ἐ. φρένα λακεῖν Id.Alc.346; ἐ. χάριν χορείας Ar.Th.981. 4. pervert, λόγους δικαίων LxxDe.16.19. 5. remove, ἔπιπλα PLond.1.177.21 (i A.D.); make away with, get rid of, ἐξάρατε τὸν πονηρὸν ἐξ ὑμῶν αὐτῶν 1Ep.Cor.5.13:—Pass., to be carried away, of a dam, PRyl.133.19 (i A.D.). II. Med. (Hom. only in 3 sg. aor. ἐξήρατο), carry off for oneself, earn, δοιοὺς μισθοὺς Od.10.84; ὅσ' ἂν οὐδέ ποτε ἐκ Τροίης ἐξήρατ' Ὀδυσσεὺς 5.39; ἐξάρατο ἕδνον won it as a dower, Pi.O.9.10; θοῶν ἐξῆρατ' ἀγώνων.. κειμήλια Theoc.24.122. (In Hom. ἐξήρατο may have displaced ἐξήρετο, aor. of ἐξάρνυμαι, v. ἀείρω.) 2. ἐξαίρεσθαι νόσον take a disease on oneself, catch it, S.Tr.491. 3. carry off, Pl. Prt.319c. III. Pass., to be raised, [τὸ τεῖχος] ἐξήρετο διπλήσιον τοῦ ἀρχαίου Hdt.6.133; rise up, rise, ἐξαιρόμενον νέφος οἰμωγῆς E.Med. 106; φλὸξ Plb.14.5.1; κονιορτός Id.3.65.4. 2. swell, dub. in Hp. VC15; ἐξαειρόμενα (-εύμενα codd.) ὑπὸ τῆς πιέξιος swellings caused by compression, Id.Fract.21. 3. to be excited, agitated, ἐλπίδι S.El. 1461; ἐξαρθεὶς ὑπὸ μεγαλαυχίας puffed up, Pl.Lg.716a: c. part., ἐξήρθης κλύων E.Rh.109. 4. ἐξηρμένος prob. f.l. in Plb.4.4.5.

ἐξαίσι-ος, ον, also α, ον X.HG4.3.8:—beyond what is ordained or fated, opp. ἐναίσιος: hence, 1. outstepping right, lawless, ῥέξας ἐξαίσιον having done some lawless act, Od.4.690; ἤ τινά που δείσας ἐ... fearing some lawless man, 17.577; Θέτιδος.. ἐ. ἀρήν Il.15.598; ἀφροσύναι B.14.58. 2. of omens, portentous, opp. ἐναίσιος, D.C. 38.13: Sup., Id.45.17. 3. of things, extraordinary, ἐ. τὸ θερμόν Hp.Epid.7.94; violent, of a wind, Hdt.3.26, X.HG5.4.17; χειμών, σεισμοί, Pl.Ti.22e, 25c; ὄμβροι X.Oec.5.18; ἐ. δεῖμα A.Supp.514; γέλωτες καὶ δάκρυα Pl.Lg.732c: ἐ. φυγὴ headlong flight, X.HG4.3.8; ἐ. βρονταί Plb.18.20.7, cf. J.BJ4.4.5; ὑπουργία Vit.Philonid.p.5C.; κάλλος Ph.2.166; χελῶναι ἐ. τοῖς μεγέθεσιν D.S.3.21; ἐ. τὸ μέγεθος καὶ τὸ ὕψος Id.13.82. Adv. -ίως Them.Or.26.312d. —ότης, gloss on ἐκπαγλότης, Hsch.

ἐξαΐσσω, contr. -ᾴσσω, Att. -ᾴττω, rush forth, start out, ἐκ δὲ τὼ ἀΐξαντε πυλάων Il.12.145; ἐξηξάτην οὖν δύο δράκοντ' ἐκ τοῦ νεὼ Ar.Pl. 733; ὁ δ' ᾤχετ' ἐξάξας γε Id.Ra.567; ἐ. ἐν τοῖς ὕπνοις start, Arist.Pr. $957^{a}32$; ἐξᾳττούσης [τῆς ψυχῆς] καὶ φερομένης πρός τι Phld.Mus.p.12 K., cf. Max.Tyr.37.5; τὸ ἐξᾷττον αὐτῶν the violence of these passions, Plu.2.83e:—Pass., ἐκ δέ μοι ἔγχος ἠΐχθη παλάμηφιν Il.3.368.

ἐξαϊστόω, bring to naught, destroy, A.Pr.668.

ἐξαισχύνομαι [ῡ], to be ashamed, c. inf., Procl. in Prm.p.648S.

ἐξαιτ-έω, demand or ask for from another, c. dupl. acc., τήνδε μ' ἐξαιτεῖ χάριν S.OC586, cf. E.Or.1657, Supp.120; ἐ. τινὰ πατρός ask her in marriage from.., S.Tr.10; ἐ. τινὰ demand the surrender of a person, esp. a criminal, Hdt.1.74, cf. D.18.41 (Pass.), IG2^{2}.457b17 (iv B.C.); demand a slave for torture, Antipho6.27, Lys.7.36; τὸν ἐλεύθερον ἐ. D.29.14 (also ἐ. τὴν βάσανον ib.13); ἐ. [τινὰ] βασανίζειν Id.37.51; σμικρὸν ἐ. ask or beg for little, S.OC5; ἐ. τινὰ ποιεῖν τι Id. OT1255, E.Rh.175. II. Med., ask for oneself, demand, Act., Hdt. 1.159, 9.87, S.El.656, etc.; χάριν παρά τινος Lys.20.31; τινὰ Ev.Luc. 22.31; πέμψον τὸν δαίμονα ὃν ἐξῃτησάμην for whose aid I prayed, PMag.Par.1.434, cf. 1290. 2. in Med. also, = παραιτοῦμαι, beg off, gain his pardon or release, A.Ag.662, X.An.1.1.3, Lys.20.15 (Pass.), Plu.Per.32, etc.; αὐτὸν ἐξαιτήσεται D.21.99; also ἐ. ὑπέρ τινος make intercession for.., E.Ba.360: c. inf., τοὺς κάτω.. ἐξῃτησάμην τύμβου κυρῆσαι I begged of them to allow me to obtain, Id.Hec. 49, cf. Med.971. 3. c. acc. rei, avert by begging, τὰ πρόσθεν σφάλματα Id.Andr.54; τὰς γραφὰς παρανόμων Aeschin.3.196. —ησις, εως, ἡ, demanding one for punishment or torture, D.49.55, IG2^{2}.457b 19 (iv B.C.), Inscr.Prien.121.26 (i B.C.). II. intercession, ἡ τῶν φίλων ἐ. D.59.117. III. demand for satisfaction, D.S.8Fr.25. IV. petition, prayer, PMag.Par.1.434. —ητέον, one must beg off, τινὰ παρά τινος Lycurg.135.

ἐξαιτιολογέω, explain fully, τὸ ὅθεν ὁ φόβος ἐγίνετο ἐ. Epicur.Ep.1 p.31 U.

ἔξαιτος, ον, (ἐξαίνυμαι) picked, choice, excellent, οἶνόν τ' ἔ. μελιηδέα Il.12.320; νῆα καὶ ἐ. ἐρέτας Od.2.307; ἐ. ἑκατόμβας 5.102: in later Poets like ἐξαίρετος, A.R.4.1004, AP6.332.5 (Hadr.), Man.2.226, 3. 354, Mus.Belg.16.71 (Attica, ii A.D.).

ἐξαιτρᾰπ-εύω, = ἐξαιθραπεύω, to be a satrap, prob. in SIG134.3 (Milet., iv B.C.). —ης, ου, ὁ, satrap, Ἰωνίης ib.30.

ἐξαίφν-ης, Adv. on a sudden, Il.17.738, 21.14, Pi.O.9.52, A.Pr. 1077 (anap.), S.OC1610, etc.: c. part., ψυχὴν θεωρεῖν ἐ. ἀποθανόντος ἑκάστου the moment that he is dead, Pl.Grg.523e; ἀκούσαντι ἐ. at first hearing, Id.Cra.396b: c. Art., τό γ' ἐ. D.18.153; but τὸ ἐ. the instantaneous, that which is between motion and rest, and not in the time-series, Pl.Prm.156d; but, = τὸ ἐν ἀναισθήτῳ χρόνῳ διὰ μικρότητα ἐκστάν, Arist.Ph.$222^{b}15$. —ίδιος, ον, also α, ον Pl.Cra. 414a, Gal.6.185:—sudden, αὔξη Pl. l.c.; μεταβολή Gal. l.c.; ἐπιδρομαὶ τῆς τύχης Hierocl.p.60A.

ἐξαιχμᾰλωτεύω, make captive, Hsch. s.v. ἐλεήσατο.

ἐξαΐω, hear, εὐχῆς ἐξάϊων Klio15.46 (Delph., iii B.C.).

ἐξαιωρέομαι, Pass., to be suspended from a thing, Hp.Art.70.

ἐξᾰκανθ-ίζω, pick out thorns: metaph., 'pick holes in', Cic.Att. 6.6.1. —όομαι, Pass., become prickly, prob. in Thphr.HP6.4.2 (ἐξανθ- codd.).

ϝεξακάτιοι, v. ἑξακόσιοι.

ἐξᾰκ-έομαι, heal completely, Hp.Vict.3.67: hence, make amends, αἳ δ' ἐξακέονται ὀπίσσω (sc. Λιταί) Il.9.507, cf. Pl.Lg.885d. II. c. acc., appease, τότε κεν χόλον ἐξακέσαιο Il.4.36, cf. Od.3.145; quench, δίψος D.C.60.9; make up for, τὰς ἐνδείας φίλων X.Cyr.8.2.22; τὰ δεινὰ Iamb. Myst.1.11. 2. in common language, mend, ἱμάτια Pl.Men.91d; δίκτυον Men.863.—Late in aor. Act. ἐξακέσας, Carm.Aur.66. —εσις, εως, ἡ, thorough cure, νόσων Ar.Ra.1033 (pl.). —εστήριος, α, ον, remedying evil, Ζεύς Lex Solonis ap.Poll.8.142; epith. of Hera, Hsch.; θεοί D.H.10.2. 2. expiatory, θυσία Id.5.54.

ἑξάκῐς [ᾰ], Adv., (ἕξ) six times, Pi.O.7.86, Pl.R.337b, etc.:—also **ἑξάκι**, cj. in Simon.156, Call.Fr.120, AP14.129 (Metrod.), 141 (Id.), CIG2834.4 (Aphrodisias).

ἑξᾰκισ-μύριοι [ῡ], αι, α, sixty thousand, Hdt.4.86, X.Cyr.2.1. 6. —μῡριοτετρᾰκισχῑλιοστός, ή, όν, 64,000th, Theo Sm.p.126 H. —χίλιοι [χῑ], αι, α, six thousand, Hdt.1.192, al., Th.2.13, etc.: also **ἑξᾰκῐχήλιοι**, Abh.Berl.Akad.1925 No.5 p.25 (Cyrene).

ἑξάκλῑνος, ον, with six couches, also **ἕξκλινος**, EM346.14:—as Subst. **ἑξάκλινον**, τό, couch to hold six, Mart.9.59.9.

ἐξακμάζω, to be gone by, of an opportunity, Sch.S.Aj.594.

ἑξάκνημος, ον, of a wheel, six-spoked, Sch.Pi.P.2.73.

ἐξᾰκολουθέω, follow, of persons, τοῖς φίλοις Plb.18.10.7, cf. Lxx Jb.31.9; μύθοις 2Ep.Pet.1.16, J.AJProoem.4. 2. of things, follow, result from, c. dat., Epicur.Fr.181; attend, c. dat., εὔνοια, φήμη ἐ. τινί, Plb.4.5.6, 5.78.4; ἔπαινοί τισι κατορθουμένοις D.H.Comp.24; esp. of penalties, ἐ. πρόστιμά τισι UPZ112v10 (ii B.C.), PTeb.5.132 (ii B.C.); also of obligations, fall on one, CPR5.15, etc. 3. abs., follow, result, Ph.Bel.58.5, Antyll.ap.Orib.45.15.4; also of logical consequences, πάντα ταῦτα ἐ. Arr.Epict.1.22.16, cf. Polystr.p.5W.

ἐξακολουθοῦσαι· ἐκθρούζεσθαι, Hsch.

ἐξᾰκονάω, strengthd. for ἀκονάω, LxxEz.21.11(16).

ἑξᾰκονταμοιρία, ἡ, arc of sixty degrees, Heph.Astr.2.11 cod.

ἐξᾰκοντ-ίζω, dart or hurl forth, launch, ἐ. τὰ δόρατα X.HG5.4.40; φάσγανον πρὸς ἧπαρ ἐ. strike it home, E.HF1149: c. dat., ἐ. τοῖς δόρασι, τοῖς παλτοῖς, X.HG4.6.11, An.5.4.25; ἐ. ἐπί τινα Plu.Art.9; κατὰ συὸς D.S.9Fr.29; -ίζεται τὸ αἷμα Gal.4.708. b. intr., dart away, [ὁ κάραβος] μακρὰν -ίζει Arist.HA$590^{b}29$. 2. metaph., freq. in E., ἐ. κῶλον τῆσδε γῆς, i.e. flee precipitately, Ba.665; ἐ. χεῖρας γενείου γονάτων τε dart out the hands towards his chin and knees [in supplication], IT362; τοὺς Ὀδυσσέως πόνους ἐ. shoot forth, i.e. proclaim loudly, Tr.444 (troch.); ταῦτα πρὸς τὰ σὰ Supp.456; so γλώσσῃ ματαίους ἐ. λόγους Men.1091; τοσαύτην ἐ. πνοήν Antiph. 217.7. —ισις, εως, ἡ, ejaculation, emission, σπέρματος Gal.19. 168. —ισμα, ατος, τό, jet, αἵματος Sch.Od.22.19. —ισμός, ὁ, = foreg., Gal.4.523, Antyll.ap.Orib.7.10.2; shooting of a shooting star, Arist.Mu.$395^{b}5$.

ἑξᾰκοσί-αρχος [ῐ], ὁ, captain of six hundred men, Polyaen.Prooem. 2. —οι, αι, α, six hundred, Hdt.1.51, etc.: Dor. **ϝεξακάτιοι** Tab. Heracl.2.41. —οστός, ή, όν, six hundredth, Lxx Ge.7.11.

ἑξᾰκοτῠλιαῖος, α, ον, of six cotylae, πλῆθος S.E.P.3.95.

ἐξᾰκου-στέον, Gramm., one must understand (a word), Sch.Pi.O. 1.157 (v.l.), Sch.Str.7.3.2. —στος, ον, heard, audible, Ph.Bel.93.51; κραυγή D.S.20.67; λόγος D.H.10.41; ἦχος, ψόφος, Ath.8.361e, Porph. Abst.3.3; of persons, J.AJ4.8.12. 2. famous, Sch.D.P.13, Hsch. —ω, hear or catch a sound, esp. from a distance, give ear to, c. acc. rei, κληδόνος βοήν A.Eu.397; σοῦ τάδ' ἐξήκουσ' ὕπο S.El. 553: c. part., ὅσοισι [κακοῖς].. ἐξήκουσας ἐνναίοντά με Id.Ph.472: abs., λόγῳ μὲν ἐξήκουσ', ὅπωπα δ' οὐ μάλα ib.676: c. gen., τῶν ῥητόρων ἵν' ἐξακούω Ar.Th.293, cf. X.Cyr.4.3.3 (v.l.): c. gen. rei, Plu.Fab.6:—Pass., to be audible, Arist.Pr.$901^{a}7$, D.L.8.82. II. understand in a certain sense, Id.7.89.

ἐξακρῑβ-άζω, know accurately, τὰ νόμιμα J.AJ19.7.4:—Med., Lxx Nu.23.10, al. —ολογέομαι, = sq., Sch.D.T.p.109H. (Pass.). —όω, make exact, precise, or accurate, ἐ. λόγον make a distinct or precise statement, S.Tr.426; τὸ τρανὸν τῆς κλήσεως J.BJ4.1.1; ἐ. τι ἐπὶ πλεῖον labour after too great exactness, Arist.EN$1102^{a}25$, cf. $1101^{b}34$; ἕκαστα.. ἐξακριβοῦσιν οἱ μεθ' ἡδονῆς ἐνεργοῦντες achieve each activity more completely, ib.$1175^{a}31$; κατὰ μέρος ἐ. work out in detail, Epicur. Ep.1 p.31 U.:—Med., ἐξακριβώσομαί σοι λόγῳ shall describe it exactly, Philostr. Jun. Im.10:—Pass., Arist.EN$1180^{b}11$, Thphr.HP9.16.6,

Epicur.*Ep.*1 p.4 U., al. II. intr., *speak accurately*, ὑπέρ τινος Arist. *EN*1096^{b}30; περί τινος Plb.2.56.4, cf. Porph.*Abst.*1.39. 2. *observe the exact interval*, Arist.*HA*583^{a}30. **-ωσις**, εως, ἡ, *strict observance*, τοῦ νόμου J.*AJ*17.2.4. II. *exact statement*, Eustr.*in EN* 108.6.

ἐξακρίζω αἰθέρα *skim the upper* air, E.*Or.*275; cf. ὑπεξακρίζω.

ἔξακρος Μενεκρίτου (physician of Tiberius), name of a *bandage for the wrist and hand*, Heliod.ap.Orib.48.53.

ἐξακ-τέον, (ἐξάγω I. 2) *one must put out of the way, kill*, αὐτόν M. Ant.3.1. 2. *one must lead out*, Aët.9.8. II. (ἐξάγω I. 1 b) *one must march out*, X.*HG*6.5.18. **-τέω**, *collect revenue*, Hsch. **-της**, ου, ὁ, title of an official, *BGU*849.2 (iv A. D.).

ἐξάκτ-ωρ, ορος, ὁ, = Lat. *exactor*, *BGU*21 ii 17, Tz.*H.*5.607:—hence **-ορία**, ἡ, *his office*, *PLond.*2.378.8, *PGen.*56.32.

ἐξάκυκλος [ᾰ], ον, *six-wheeled*, ἅμαξαι Hp.*Aër.*18.

ἐξάκωλος [ᾰ], ον, *of six members*, περίοδος Sch.Ar.*Ach.*836.

ἐξᾰλάομαι, *migrate*, πανοικεσίᾳ Antipho Soph.108.

ἐξᾰλάω, *blind utterly*, υἱὸν φίλον Od.11.103; ὀφθαλμὸν.. τὸν ἀνὴρ κακὸς ἐξαλάωσεν *put* it *quite out*.., 9.453, cf. 504. 2. *make blind and useless*, ὅλον δέμας Opp.*C.*3.228.

ἐξᾰλᾰπ-άζω, *sack, storm*, πόλιν Il.4.40, 1.129, etc.; also, *empty* a city *of its inhabitants, clear* it *out*, so as to plant new settlers in it, μίαν πόλιν ἐξαλαπάξας Od.4.176: generally, *destroy utterly*, νῆας, τεῖχος, Il.13.813, 20.30: metaph., ἀλλά με νόσος ἐξαλάπαξεν Theoc. 2.85.—Ep. word, used by X.*An.*7.1.29. **-ίζω**, (Lat. *alapa*) *slap in the face*, Gloss.

ἐξαλγέω, c. acc., *suffer pain in*, τοὺς πόδας Ps.-Callisth.3.27.

ἐξαλδαίνει· ἐκβλαστάνει, Hsch.

ἐξᾰλεείνω, = ἐξαλέομαι, Opp.*H.*5.398.

ἐξᾰλειπ-τέον, *one must wipe out, erase*, τοὺς νόμους Lys.6.8. **-της**, ου, ὁ, = κονιάτης, Gal.19.98. **-τικός**, ή, όν, *obliterating*, τύπος ἐ. τοῦ προτέρου S.E.*M.*7.373. **-τρον**, τό, *unguent-box*, Ar.*Ach.* 1063, Antiph.208, Lxx *Jb.*41.22(23), *IG*2.751 *B* ii *d*4, 11(2).161 *B*125 (Delos, iii B. C.), etc.

ἐξᾰλείφω, pf. Pass. ἐξαλήλιμμαι (v. infr.): subj. aor. 2 Pass. ἐξαλιφῇ v.l. in Pl.*Phdr.*258b:—*plaster* or *wash over*, τοῦ σώματος τὸ ἥμισυ ἐξηλείφοντο γύψῳ Hdt.7.69; ᾗ ἔτυχε.. οὐκ ἐξαληλιμμένον τὸ τεῖχος where it was not *whitewashed*, Th.3.20; τοὺς βωμοὺς ἐξαλείψαντι *IG*11.161 *A* 103 (Delos, iii B. C.):—Med., *anoint*, μύρῳ βρενθείῳ ἐξαλείψαο Sapph.*Supp.*23.20. II. *wipe out, obliterate*, ἐξαλειφθεῖσ' ὡς ἄγαλμα E.*Hel.*262: metaph., *wipe out of one's mind*, πάντα τὰ πρόσθεν Pl.*Tht.*187b; τὸ γιγνώσκειν D.37.34; [ὑπόνοιαν] Men.*Pk.*310 (prob.); *cancel*, ἐ. ψηφίσματα And.1.76; νόμους Lys.1.48; αἰτίας Arist.*Ath.*40. 3; ἐξαλειφόντων (sc. τὸ ὀφείλημα) *IG*1^{2}.91.10; esp. at Athens, ἐ. τινὰ ἐκ τοῦ καταλόγου *strike* his *name off* the roll, X.*HG*2.3.51, cf. Arist. *Ath.*36.2; so ἐ. τινά Ar.*Eq.*877, cf. D.39.39; opp. ἐγγράφω, Ar.*Pax* 1181, Lys.30.2, etc.; ὑμᾶς ἐκ παντὸς τοῦ Ἑλληνικοῦ Th.3.57:—Med., ἐξαλείψασθαι τὰς ἀπογραφάς *to get* one's inventory *cancelled*, Pl.*Lg.* 850d: metaph., ἐ. πάθος φρενός *blot* it *out from* one's mind, E.*Hec.* 590. 2. metaph., *wipe out, destroy*, μὴ 'ξαλείψῃς σπέρμα Πελοπιδῶν A.*Ch.*503, cf. E.*Hipp.*1241:—Pass., ἡ Σπάρτης εὐδαιμονίη οὐκ ἐξηλείφετο Hdt.7.220; τιμὰς μὴ 'ξαλειφθῆναι A.*Th.*15; οὐδ' ἄπαις δόμος.. ἐξαλειφθείη ποτ' ἄν E.*IT*698.

ἐξάλειψις [ᾰ], εως, ἡ, *whitewashing*, τοῦ ἀποδυτηρίου *BCH*23.566 (Delph., iii B. C.). II. *blotting out, destruction*, Lxx *Mi.*7.11, al.

ἐξᾰλέομαι, *beware of, avoid, escape*, ἐκ τ' ἀλέοντο Il.18.586; mostly in Ep. aor. 1 inf., Διὸς νόον ἐξαλέασθαι Hes.*Op.*105, cf. 758, 802, Orac. ap.Ar.*Eq.*1080: abs., τάων οὔτινά φημι διαμπερὲς ἐ. A.R.2.319, cf. 3.466: pres. ἐξαλέονται Q.S.2.385.—Ep. word, cf. sq.

ἐξᾰλεύομαι, = foreg., ὡς ἂν.. μῆνιν.. ἐξαλεύσωμαι θεᾶς S.*Aj.*656 codd., but ἐξαλύξ- (Hsch.) is prob. l.

ἐξαληθίζομαι, *to be truly recorded*, *EM*327.44.

ἐξαλίζω, *evacuate*, in Pass., Hp.*VM*22 ap.Gal.19.98 (v. l. ἐξαγγ-). II. ἐξαλίζεται· συναθροίζεται, Hsch. [ᾱ.]

ἐξᾰλίνδω, only aor. part. ἐξαλίσας [ῑ], pf. ἐξήλικα:—*roll out* or *thoroughly*, ἄπαγε τὸν ἵππον ἐξαλίσας οἴκαδε take him away *when you have given* him *a good roll on the* ἀλινδήθρα, Ar.*Nu.*32 (cf. X.*Oec.*11. 18); to which Strepsiades retorts, ἐξήλικας ἐμέ γ' ἐκ τῶν ἐμῶν you *have rolled* me *out of* house and home, Ar.*Nu.*33.

ἐξᾰλίπτης, f.l. for ἐξαλείπτης (q.v.).

ἐξᾰλίστρα, ἡ, = ἀλινδήθρα, Poll.1.183.

ἐξαλλ-αγή, ἡ, *complete change, alteration*, τῶν εἰωθότων νομίμων Pl. *Phdr.*265a; ἐ. εἰς ἕτερον γένος Thphr.*CP*4.4.5; τῶν κρεῶν ἐ. *variety*, Ath.1.25e; ποικίλων μαθημάτων Iamb.*Protr.*21.κα'. 2. ἐξαλλαγαὶ τῶν ὀνομάτων *variations in the forms* of nouns, Arist.*Po.*1458^{b}2: generally, *variation*, Procl.*Inst.*162, 175 (pl.). **-αγμα**, ατος, τό, *recreation, amusement*, in pl., Anaxandr.20, Parth.24.1 (dub.). **-ακτέον**, *one must change*, Sor.2.24. **-άκτης**, ου, ὁ, = ἀλαζών, Hsch. s.v. διαμέσταν, cf. *PSI*4.392.7 (iii B. C.). **-αξις**, εως, ἡ, = ἐξαλλαγή, Str.2.3.1, Gal.7.52, al., Longin.*Fr.*3; λόγου Alex.*Fig.*1.2. **-άσσω**, Att. -ττω, *change utterly* or *quite*, strengthd. for ἀλλάσσω, ἐσθῆτα E.*Hel.*1297; τινὰς κοσμήσεσι Plu.*Thes.*23; αἰὼν.. ἄλλ' ἄλλοτ' ἐξάλλαξεν Pi.*I.*3.18. b. intr., of evolution, τὰ δὲ.. ἐξαλλάσσει ἐς τὴν μέζω τάξιν Hp.*Vict.*1.6; ἐ. γένος εἰς ἕτερον *degenerate*, Thphr.*HP*8. 8.3:—Pass., ἐξηλλαγμένος πρός τι ib.4.4.14. c. Med., κακοῖσιν ὅστις μηδὲν ἐξαλλάσσεται who *sees no change take place* in his miseries, S.*Aj.*474:—Pass., ἰδιωτικῆς ἑστίας ἐξηλλαγμένη ἡγεμονία D.S.10 *Fr.* 20. 2. Rhet., *vary* common words and phrases, ἐ. τὸ εἰωθός Arist. *Rh.*1406^{a}15, cf. 1404^{b}8; ἐ. τὸ ἰδιωτικόν *vary* the common idiom, Id. *Po.*1458^{a}21; ἐξηλλαγμένον [ὄνομα] *altered* form, ib.1458^{a}5: c. gen., ἐξηλλαγμένος τινός *different from*, Isoc.8.63. b. pf. part. Pass. ἐξηλλαγμένος *extraordinary, strange*, Plb.2.37.6, D.S.1.94, Ant.Lib. 41.8, etc.; *varied*, ὄφεις ταῖς ποικιλίαις ἐ. D.S.17.90. 3. c. acc. loci, *withdraw from, leave*, Εὐρώπαν E.*IT*135 (lyr.). II. ἐ. τί τινος *withdraw* or *remove from*, τὴν ἑαυτοῦ γύμνωσιν ἐ. τῶν ἐναντίων Th.5.71. 2. intr., *change from*, τῆς ἀρχαίας μορφῆς Arist.*GA* 766^{a}26; μικρὸν ἐ. *exceed the limit* by a little, Id.*Po.*1449^{b}13; ἐ. ἀπὸ τῆς νεώς Philostr.*Her.Prooem.*3; ἐς ἄνδρας Id.*VA*3.28: abs., ἐξαλλάσσουσα χάρις *unusual, rare* grace, E.*IA*564 (lyr.); *to be different from*, πάντων τῶν παρ' ἡμῖν Phld.*Sign.*9. b. ἐξαλλάσσουσαι στολαί *changes of* raiment, v.l. in Lxx *Ge.*45.22. 3. *turn another way, move back and forward*, κερκίδα E.*Tr.*200 (lyr.); ἐ. δρόμου *change* one's course, X.*Cyn.*10.7; ποίαν (sc. ὁδόν) ἐξαλλάξω; which *other* way *shall* I *take*? E.*Hec.*1060 (lyr.). 4. *divert, amuse*, Men.747, Philippid.35; *coax, win over*, ὀψαρίοις *POxy.*531.18 (ii A. D.).

ἐξαλλοι-όω, *change, alter*, Lxx 3 *Ma.*3.21:—Pass., *change utterly*, πρὸς τὸ χεῖρον Thphr.*CP*2.15.2, cf. Ph.1.674. **-ωσις**, εως, ἡ, *metabolism*, of food, prob. for -αλλάττωσις, Gal.15.250.

ἐξάλλομαι, fut. -ᾰλοῦμαι Lxx *Mi.*2.12: aor. -ηλάμην S.*OT*1311 (lyr.), -ηλάμην Luc.*Asin.*53, Dor. -άλατο Theoc. (v. infr.); Ep. aor. part. -άλμενος (v. infr.):—*leap out of* or *forth from*, ἐξάλλεται αὐλῆς, of a lion, Il.5.142: elsewh. used by Hom. only in aor. part. ἐξάλμενος, abs., 15.571: c. gen., προμάχων ἐξάλμενος, τῶν ἄλλων ἐ. *springing out from the midst* of.., 17.342, 23.399 (not in Od.); ἐξάλατο ναός Theoc.17.100; ἐ. κατὰ τοῦ τείχους *leap down off*.., X. *HG*7.2.6: abs., *jump, hop off*, Ar.*V.*130, *Act.Ap.*3.8; ὦ δαῖμον, ἵν' ἐξήλου; to what point *didst thou leap forth*, i. e. to what misery hast thou come? S.*OT*1311 (lyr.); of fish, *leap out of* the water, Arist. *HA*602^{a}29, cf. 528^{a}32. 2. *start from its socket, be dislocated*, of a limb, ἐ. ἔξαλσιν Hp.*Art.*46; of a broken bone, Plu.2.341b; of wheels, *start from the axle*, X.*Cyr.*7.1.32. II. *leap up*, Id.*An.* 7.3.33; μήκιστα ἐ. Ph.1.318; of horses, *rear*, X.*Cyr.*7.1.27. 2. ἐξάλλετο γαστήρ *swelled, became distended*, Call.*Cer.*88 (s. v. l.). 3. metaph., ἐ. πρός τι *fly off* to, *have recourse* to, Plu.2.382e.

ἔξαλλος, ον, *special, distinguishing*, ἐσθῆτες Plb.6.7.7, cf. Lxx 2 *Ki.* 6.14; στέφανος *OGI*737.19 (ii B. C.); στολαί Ph.1.468; τὰ ἐ. τοῦ βαρβαρικοῦ κόσμου Plu.2.330a. Adv. -ως *strangely*, of superstitious veneration, Plb.32.15.7.

ἐξαλλοτρι-όω, *export*, Str.5.1.9. II. *divert, alienate*, πόρον εἰς ἑτέρας χρείας *BSA*17.229 (Pamphyl.), cf. *PGiss.*2.24 (ii B. C.). 2. *alienate, estrange*, τὸν πολιτικὸν ὄχλον D.H.11.39; τοὺς πολλοὺς πρὸς τοὺς ἀρίστους S.E.*M.*2.42:—Pass., *to be estranged*, Lxx 1 *Ma.*12. 10. **-ωσις**, εως, ἡ, *alienation*, *POxy.*94.7 (i A. D.), etc.

ἔξαλμα, ατος, τό, (ἐξάλλομαι) = πήδημα, Hsch. II. *distance, interval*, τὸ μέγιστον ἔ. οὐρανὸς καὶ γῆ A.D.*Adv.*209.2 (s. v. l.), cf. Sch. D.P.30 (nisi leg. ἔξαρμα); ἐ. ἀπὸ ζῳδίου ἐπὶ ζῴδιον, of the sun or moon, Paul.Al.*S.*1, cf. Barbill. in *Cat.Cod.Astr.*8(3).104 (pl.).

ἐξαλμίζω, *deprive of saltness*, Bilabel Ὀψαρτ. p.11.

ἐξαλμός, ὁ, = ἔξαλσις, opp. ἄφαλσις, Antyll.ap.Orib.6.31.1.

ἐξαλμῠρ-όομαι, *become salt*, *PTeb.*72.11 (ii B. C.). **-ος**, ον, *having lost its saltness*, of earth, Thunell *Sitologenpapyri* 1^{v} iii 11.

ἐξᾰλογόομαι, *become irrational*, Eustr. *in EN*276.6.

ἔξᾰλος, ον, (ἅλς B) *out of the sea*, ἐ. ἰχθὺς *leaping out of the sea*, Emp. 117; ἔ. τὸ σκάφος ἀνασπᾶν Luc.*Am.*8; ἔ. ἀΐσσειν Opp.*H.*2.593; πληγὴ ἔ. a blow on a ship's hull *above water*, Plb.16.3.8; τὰ ἔ. τῆς νεώς Luc.*JTr.*47; *rising high out of the water*, of islands, Str.17.1.52.

ἔξαλσις, εως, ἡ, *leaping with the legs held together* (κομιδῇ σκελῶν συνεχής) for exercise, Aret.*CD*1.2. II. *dislocation, displacement*, Hp.*Art.*46.

ἐξάλυξις [ᾰ], εως, ἡ, *escape*, Eustr. *in APo.*221.22.

ἐξᾰλύσκω, aor. ἐξήλυξα, *flee from*, c. acc., E.*El.*219, *Hipp.*673 (lyr.): abs., *escape*, A.*Eu.*111, E.*Hec.*1194: c. gen., Opp.*H.*3.104; cf. ἐξαλεύομαι.

ἐξᾰλύω, = ἐξαλέομαι, μόρον *h.Bacch.*51.

ἐξάλφεις· εὑρίσκεις, Hsch.; ἐξαλφήσεις· ἐκτ(ι)μηθήσῃ μεγάλως,... τινὲς δὲ ἐκλάμψεις, Id.

ἐξᾰμαρτ-άνω, fut. -ήσομαι (-ήσω Hp.*Acut.*(*Sp.*)13):—*miss the mark, fail*, c. part., ἐ. παίοντες X.*Cyr.*2.1.16: abs., *miss one's aim*, S.*Ph.*95; opp. κατορθοῦν, Isoc.7.72. 2. *err, do wrong*, abs., A. *Pr.*1039, etc.; τοῖς πᾶσι κοινόν ἐστι τοὐξ. S.*Ant.*1024, cf. Men.15.1 D.; opp. εὖ ποιεῖν, Lys.25.16; ἔς τινα Hdt.1.108, Lys.12.20; εἰς τοὺς οἰκέτας Isoc.2.5; εἰς θεούς A.*Pr.*945; περί τινα Isoc.4.110, 9.24; ἔν τινι in a thing, Pl.*R.*336e; περὶ τὰ μέγιστα X.*An.*5.7.33: c. part., ἐ. διατρίβων Id.*Cyr.*3.3.56: c. acc. cogn., ἐ. τι *commit a fault*, Hdt. 3.145, S.*Ph.*1012, etc. II. Pass., *to be mismanaged, to be a failure*, ἡ ἐξαμαρτανομένη πρᾶξις Pl.*Prt.*357d; ἐξημαρτήθη τὰ νοσήματα X.*Eq.* 4.2; πολιτεῖαι ἐξημαρτημέναι Arist.*Pol.*1289^{b}9. III. trans., *cause to sin*, Lxx 3 *Ki.*15.26, al. **-ία**, ἡ, *error, transgression*, S.*Ant.*558, Them.*Or.*32.362c.

ἐξᾰμάρτῠρος, ον, *attested by six witnesses*, συγγραφή *UPZ*124.11; δάνεια *BGU*813.10 (ii A. D.); ἀποχή *PHaw.*303.20 (ii A. D.), *BGU*260. 7 (*Arch.Pap.*5.205, i A. D.): neut. as Subst., *BGU*1239.20 (ii B. C.).

ἐξᾰμαυρ-όω, *obscure utterly*, E.*Fr.*781.64 (lyr., Pass.):—Pass., of a plant, *lose its natural character*, Thphr.*CP*2.16.4: metaph., ἐ. ὅσον ἐν τῷ γένει λαμπρόν Ph.2.438; τὰ χείρονα τοῖς βελτίοσι Plu.2.469a; τὰ σοφίσματα ἐ. τὸ μέγεθος Longin.17.2, dub. l. in Hp.*Alim.*6. **-ωσις**, εως, ἡ, *disappearing*, μετάλλων Plu.2.434a (pl.).

ἐξαμάχανα· ἐξαίφνης, Hsch. (before ἐξαμαρτάνει).

ἐξᾰμάω (A), *mow* or *reap out, finish mowing* or *reaping*, ἐξαμᾷ θέρος A.*Pers*.822, cf. *Ag*.1655 (troch.), E.*Ba*.1315; σπείρων.. κἀξαμῶν ἅπαξ sowing and *reaping*, S.*Tr*.33; χρυσοῦν θέρος ἐξαμησάμενος Plu.*Demetr*. 4:—Pass., γένους ἅπαντος ῥίζαν ἐξημημένος (pf. part.) *having* all the race *cut off* root and branch, S.*Aj*.1178, cf. Paus.8.7.7.—Poet. and later Prose. [On the quantity, v. ἀμάω.] (ἐξαμοῦν· ἐκθερίζειν is corrupt in Hsch.)

ἐξᾰμάω (B), = ἐξαφύσσω (cf. ἀμάω B), τἄντερ' ἐξαμήσω Ar.*Lys*. 367:—Med., τὰ σπλάγχν' ἔφασκον ἐξαμήσεσθαι E.*Cyc*.236; ἐξαμησάμενος τὴν λατύπην *IG*2².244.81 (iv B.C.).

ἐξαμβλ-έομαι, Pass., *miscarry*, Hp.*Mul*.1.25 (s.v.l.); cf. ἐξαμβλέβει· διαφθείρει, ἐγκυμονεῖ, Hsch. **-ίσκω**, = sq., Ael.*Fr*.49, Hsch. (-ύσκω Procop.*Arc*.9 is f.l.). **-όω** (ἐξαναβλ- is dub. in Hsch.), aor. 2 inf. -αμβλῶναι prob. f.l. for -ῶσαι in Them.*Or*.2.33b:—*make to miscarry*, νηδὺν ἐξαμβλοῦμεν E.*Andr*.356:—Pass., of the foetus, *miscarry*, βρέφος ἐξαμβλωθέν Apollod.3.4.3: metaph., αὕτη ἡ ἐλπὶς ἐξήμβλωτο αὐτῇ Ael.*Fr*.57. 2. *make abortive*: metaph., φροντίδ' ἐξήμβλωκας you *have made* a notion *miscarry*, Ar.*Nu*.137; to which Strepsiades retorts, εἰπέ μοι τὸ πρᾶγμα τοὐξημβλωμένον your *abortive thought*, ib.139, cf. Pl.*Tht*.150e; ἐ. θείας γονάς Ph.1.219:—Pass., ὁ πυρὸς ἐξαμβλούμενος Thphr.*CP*4.5.3; σώματος ἰσχὺς ἐξαμβλοῦται Plu. 2.2e. II. intr., *prove abortive*, Ael.*NA*2.25: impers., ἐξαμβλοῖ *a miscarriage follows*, Arist.*HA*577b6. **-ύνω**, *blunt, weaken*, τὰς τῶν ὑγρῶν διαφθοράς Dsc.1.88:—Pass., Plu.*Fab*.23. **-ωμα**, ατος, τό, *abortion*, Artem.1.51 (pl.). **-ωσις**, εως, ἡ, *miscarriage*, Hp. *Nat.Puer*.18 (pl.), Thphr.*HP*9.9.2, Gal.19.178. **-ώσκω** (v.l. **-ώττω**), = ἐξαμβλόω, Dsc.2.164.

ἐξαμβρακοῦται· ἐκλύεται, Hsch.

ἐξαμ-βρόσαι and **-βρῦσαι**, v. ἐξαναβρύω.

ἐξᾰμείβω, *exchange, alter*, σαρκὸς ἐξαμείψασαι τρόμον *having put away* fear *from* one, E.*Ba*.607 (troch.); ἄλλην ἄλλοτε χρόαν Plu.2. 590c:—Med., *exchange places with*, i.e. *take the place of*, ἔργου δ' ἔργον ἐξημείβετο one labour *came hard upon* another, E.*Hel*.1533. 2. intr. in Act., φόνῳ φόνος ἐξαμείβων Id.*Or*.816 (lyr.). II. of Place, *change one for another, pass over*, c. acc., A.*Pers*.130 (lyr.), E.*Ph*. 131; so ἐξαμείψας Μακεδονίαν εἰς Θετταλίαν ἀφίκετο X.*Ages*.2.2: abs., *withdraw, depart*, E.*Or*.272:—so in Med., *pass*, διά τινος Id.*Fr*.781. 45; τηνεῖ πρὸς τὴν σχοῖνον ἐξαμείβεο *APl*.4.255. III. Med., *requite, repay*, τινὰ ποιναῖς A.*Pr*.225 (v.l. ἀντημείψατο).

ἐξάμειψις [ᾰ], εως, ἡ, *alternation*, Plu.2.426d (pl.).

ἐξᾰμέλγω, *milk out, suck out*, γάλα A.*Ch*.898:—Pass., f.l. for ἐξαθελγ-, Erot. II. *press out*, πλήρωμα τυρῶν ἐξημελγμένον E.*Cyc*.209.

ἐξᾰμελέω, *to be utterly careless of*, τινός Hdt.1.97: abs., *show no care, be negligent*, ἐπὶ τῶν γυναικῶν Arist.*Pol*.1269b22:—Pass. impers., ἐξημέληται περὶ τῶν τοιούτων *no care is taken*..., Id.*EN*1180a27; ἐξημέλητο τὰ τῶν θεῶν αὐτοῖς Plu.*Cam*.18; ἐξαμελουμένων [τῶν παίδων] *being uncared for*, Arist.*EN*1180a30; -ούμενον ἅπαν χεῖρον γίγνεται Thphr.*HP*3.2.2.

ἐξᾰμέρ-εια, ἡ, *division into six parts*, Stob.2.7.2. **-ής**, ές, *in six parts*, of the hexameter, Orph.*Fr*.356.

ἑξάμετρος [ᾰ], ον, *of six metres*, ἐν ἑ. τόνῳ in *hexameter* measure, Hdt.1.47; ἐν ἔπεσι ἑ. Id.7.220, cf. Pl.*Lg*.810d; ἑξάμετρα (sc. ἔπη) Arist.*Rh*.1404a34, *Po*.1449a27, Demetr.*Eloc*.1, etc.

ἐξαμεύω, in pf. Pass. ἐξήμευσαι· ἀπο(κε)κίνησαι, Hsch.

ἑξᾰμηνιαῖος, α, ον, = ἑξάμηνος, Apollod.3.4.3; ἡμέρα Gem.6.15. II. = ἑξάμηνος II, πῶλος *Hippiatr*.20.

ἑξᾰμηνόβῐος, ον, *living six months*, σαῦρος v.l. in Arist.*HA*558a17.

ἑξᾰμηνος, ον, *of, lasting six months*, ἀρχαί Arist.*Pol*.1299a6, 1308a 15; ἀνοχαί Plb.21.5.11. 2. Subst. ἑ. (sc. χρόνος), ὁ, *half-year*, X. *HG*[2.3.9]; ἑξαμήνου σῖτος a *half-year's* supply, ib.3.4.3; ἑξάμηνον διαλείπειν Arist.*HA*573a13; ἐν -μήνῳ Thphr.*HP*8.2.7 also ἡ ἑ. (sc. ὥρη) Hdt.4.25. II. *six months old*, ὕες Arist.*HA*545b2.

ἐξαμηχᾰνέω, *get out of a difficulty*, εἰ μή τι τούτων -ήσομεν E. *Heracl*.495.

ἐξᾰμιλλάομαι, aor. 1 part. ἐξαμιλλησάμενος and -ηθείς, E.*Hel*.1471 (lyr.), 387: imper. ἐξαμίλλησαι Id.*Hyps.Fr*.2:—*struggle vehemently*: c. acc. cogn., τὰς τεθρίππους Οἰνομάῳ.. ἁμίλλας ἐξαμιλληθεὶς *having contested* the chariot-race with him, Id.*Hel*.387: abs., ib.1471; διαφόροις ὁδοῖς πρὸς ἓν καὶ ταὐτὸν ἄκρον Constantius in Them.*Or*.p.22 D. II. *drive out of*, ἐξαμιλλῶνταί σε γῆς E.*Or*.431; *drive out of his wits*, τινὰ φόβῳ ib.38. III. aor. 1 in pass. sense, *to be rooted out*, of the Cyclops' eye, πυρί Id.*Cyc*.628.

ἑξάμῐτος [ᾰ], η, ον, *of six strands*, θρίξ prob. in *AP*7.702 (Apollonid.).

ἔξαμμα, ατος, τό, (ἐξάπτω) *handle*, Them.*Or*.13.166a. II. ἔξαμμα πυρός, = ἄναμμα (q.v.), *Stoic*.2.196,199.

ἐξαμμᾰτίζω, gloss on ἐπαλλάξαντες, Apollon.*Lex*.

ἑξα-μν(α)ιαῖος, = ἑξάμνους, Hsch. s.v. πέλεκυς. **-μναῖος**, α, ον, *owning six minae*, *SIG*363.9 (Ephesus, iii B.C.). **-μνους**, ουν, *worth* or *weighing six minae*, Eust.1878.57.

ἐξαμοιβάς· ἑτέροις καὶ ἑτέραις, Hsch.

ἑξαμοιρία, ἡ, *arc of six degrees*, Vett.Val.356.30.

ἑξάμορος [ᾰ], ον, for *ἑξάμοιρος, *one-sixth*, Nic.*Th*.594.

ἐξαμοῦν· ἐκθερίζειν, Hsch.; cf. ἐξαμάω (A).

ἐξαμπρεύω, *haul out*, Ar.*Lys*.289.

ἔξαμπρον, τό, *team of oxen*, *Gloss*.

ἐξᾰμυγδᾰλίζω, *make like an almond*, Aq.*Ex*.25.32(33):—also -όω, ib.35(36).

ἐξᾰμύνομαι [ῡ], Med., *ward off from oneself, drive away*, νόσους A. *Pr*.483; αἶθρον θεοῦ E.*Supp*.208; τινά Id.*Or*.269:—Act. is dub. l. in Them.*Or*.23.284b.

ἐξᾰμυστίζω, *drink off at a draught*, Pl.Com.189.

ἐξαμφοτερίζω, *make ambiguous*, ἐξημφοτέρικεν τὸν λόγον has *led* the argument *into a contradiction* (by answering 'neither and both'), Pl.*Euthd*.300d; ἐξαμφοτερίσας· τὸ ἀμφίβολον ποιῆσαι, καὶ τὸ δύο πραγμάτων ἐκπεσεῖν, Hsch., cf. *EM*347.7.

ἐξάμφω, *both*, *PMasp*.311.14 (vi A.D.). **ἔξαν**, v. ἑξῆς.

ἐξανα-βαίνω, *get to the top of*, Artem.2.28; ἀτραπὸν ἐξανάβα *Epigr. Gr*.782 (Halic.). **-βλύζω**, *gush forth*, *PMag.Par*.1.942 (Pap. -βλύδω). **-βρύω**, causal of foreg., τύχας ὀνησίμους γαίας ἐξαμβρῦσαι (Pauw for ἐξαμβρόσαι) *cause* happiness *to spring forth from* the earth, A.*Eu*.925 (lyr.). **-γεννάομαι**, Pass., *to be born again*, Jul.*Ep*.61c. **-γιγνώσκω**, *read through*, Plu.*Cat.Mi*.68, *Cic*.27, etc.

ἐξᾰναγκάζω, fut. -άσω S.*Ichn*.212:—*force* or *compel utterly*, τινὰ δρᾶν τι Id.*El*.620, cf. E.*Or*.1665, etc.: with the inf. omitted, S.*OC* 603, Ar.*Av*.377:—Pass., ὑπὸ τοῦ λόγου Hdt.2.3. 2. *force out*, ἕδρην Hp.*Haem*.2. 3. *enforce*, τὸν ταγὸν.. ἐξξανακάδην *IG*9(2).257 (Thess., v B.C.). II. *drive away*, τὴν ἀργίαν πληγαῖς X.*Mem*.2.1.16.

ἐξαναγνωρίζω, gloss on ἐπαναγνῶναι, Hsch.

ἐξανάγω [ᾰγ], *bring out of* or *up from*, ἐ. τινὰ Ἅιδου μυχῶν E. *Heracl*.218:—Pass., *put out to sea, set sail*, of persons, Hdt.6.98, al., S.*Ph*.571, Th.2.25, etc.; of ships, Hdt.7.194: metaph., τῆς τῶν ψευσμάτων καὶ σοφισμάτων χώρας -αναχθησόμεθα Ph.1.517.

ἐξανα-δείκνῡμι, *show forth, declare*, ἀρετὴν κρήνης.. ἐξανέδειξεν *IPE* 2.37 (Panticapaeum). **-δοσις**, εως, ἡ, *eruption, scab*, Aq.*Le*.13.6, 18. **-δύομαι**, aor. 2 Act. ἐξανέδυν, *rise out of, emerge from*, as a diver from the water, c. gen., ἁλός, κύματος ἐξαναδύς, Od.4.405, 5.438; ἰλύος Them.*Or*.20.240c; ἀφ' ὕδατος Batr.133; γενέσεως ἐ. *arise from, emerge from*, Pl.*R*.525b. 2. *escape from*, c. gen., ἐξαναδύεσθαι φανερᾶς μάχης Plu.*Sert*.12: c. acc., Ἀΐδεω μέγα δῶμ' Thgn.1124; λόχον Orac.ap.Paus.4.12.4. **-ζέω**, *boil up with*: c. acc. cogn., metaph., τοιόνδε.. ἐξαναζέσει χόλον *will let* such fury *boil forth*, A.*Pr*.372. **-θλίβω** [ῑ], *squeeze out, express*, *Placit*.2.13.2.

ἐξαν-αιρέω, *take out of*, πυρός *h.Cer*.254, cf. A.R.3.867:—Med., ἦ καί σφ' Ἀθάνα γῆθεν ἐξανείλετο; E.*Ion* 269. **-αισθητέω**, *to be utterly without feeling*, Porph.*Abst*.1.39 codd.

ἐξανα-κᾰλύπτομαι, Med., *uncover oneself*, Sch.Ar.*Nu*.3. **-κολυμβάω**, *rise again after diving*, Arist.*HA*591a27. **-κρούομαι**, Med., *retreat from* a place *by backing water*, τῇσι λοιπῇσι [νηυσί].. ἐξανακρουσάμενοι Hdt.6.115. **-κτίζω**, *rebuild*, πόλιν Tz.*H*.13.7. **-λαμβάνω**, cited in error from Th. by *AB*93.

ἐξανᾱλίσκω, pf. Pass. ἐξανήλωμαι Hp.*Nat.Puer*.30, but -ανάλωμαι Pl.Com.175:—*spend entirely*, τὰ πλεῖστα τῶν ἰδίων ἐ. Plu.*Pomp*.20:—Pass., τὰ ἀλλότρι'.. ἐξανάλωται Pl.Com. l.c.; τὰ παρ' ἐμοῦ ἐξανηλωμένα D.50.15. 2. *exhaust*, ἐξανήλωσεν ὁ ἥλιος [τὸ ὑγρόν] Thphr. *Vent*.15, etc.; ἐ. δύναμιν ἔν τινι Plu.*Cat.Mi*.20:—Pass., *to be used up, exhausted*, Arist.*GA*750a34; εἴς τι Hp.*Nat.Puer*. l.c.; διὰ τῆς καθάρσεως Sor.1.31; πόνος ἐξανηλώθη Babr.95.44. 3. *destroy utterly*, ἐξαναλῶσαι γένος A.*Ag*.678:—Pass., ἐξανήλωνται δ' οἵ τ' ἴδιοι πάντες οἶκοι καὶ τὰ κοινὰ τῇ πόλει D.13.27, Aeschin.3.103.

ἐξανᾱλόω, = foreg., Max.Tyr.13.3:—Pass., Ph.2.511.

ἐξαναλύω, *set quite free*, ἄνδρα.. θανάτοιο δυσηχέος ἐξαναλῦσαι Il. 16.442; Μοιρᾶν μίτον ἐ. *IG*14.1449. II. *resolve into its elements*, *PMag.Par*.1.439.

ἐξανάλωσις [ᾰλ], εως, ἡ, *entire consumption*, τῆς δυνάμεως Plu.*Marc*. 24.

ἐξανα-νεόομαι, Med., *renew*, συγγένειαν Str.9.4.2. **-πείθω**, *win over*, θεούς Hermesian.7.8. **-πληρόω**, *supply, replace*, D.51.6:—Pass., *be renewed*, of the bark of trees, Thphr.*HP*3.17.1. **-πνέω**, *recover breath*, Pl.*Phdr*.254c, *Sph*.231c. **-πτύσσω**, *unfold, explain*, Tz.*H*.6.41.

ἐξαν-άπτω, *hang from* or *by*, τί τινος E.*IT*1351, cf. 1408:—Med., *attach to oneself*, δύσκλειαν Id.*Or*.829 (lyr.). II. *kindle*, πυρσὸν τοῖς νέοις *AP*5 *Prooem*. (Cephalas); σβεννυμένην φύσιν Plu.2. 752a. **-ᾰριθμέω**, *reckon, number*, *IGRom*.4.661.34 (Pass., Acmonia). **-αρπάζω**, *snatch away*, E.*Hel*.1565, *IA*75.

ἐξανα-σπάω, *tear away from*, ἐκ τῶν βάθρων Hdt.5.85; βάθρων E. *Ph*.1132: *tear up from*, [ἐλάτην] χθονός Id.*Ba*.1110. **-στᾰσις**, εως, ἡ, *removal, expulsion*, Plb.2.21.9, al. II. intr., *emigration*, τινῶν ἐκ τῆς οἰκείας Str.2.3.6. 2. *rising from bed to go to stool*, Hp. *Prog*.11; later simply, *going to stool*, Aret.*SD*2.9 (pl.), Sever.*Clyst*. pp.3,34 D., etc. b. *rising from bed in the morning*, Porph.*VP*40; ἐ. ὕπνου Gal.7.96. 3. ἡ ἐ. ἡ ἐκ νεκρῶν *resurrection* from the dead, *Ep. Phil*.3.11. 4. woman's *ornament*, *BGU*717.11 (ii A.D.). **-στᾰτόομαι**, = ἐξανίσταμαι, *PTeb*.2(*d*).16 (Poet. Alex.). **-στέφω**, strengthd. for ἀναστέφω, E.*Ba*.1055. **-στημα**, ατος, τό, *erection*, Eust.1719.39 (pl.).

ἐξαναστράπτω, *lighten*, [Emp.]*Sphaer*.66.

ἐξανα-στρέφω, *turn upside down*, μακέλλῃ Ζηνὸς ἐξαναστραφῇ S. *Fr*.727: c. gen. loci, *hurl headlong from*.., δαιμόνων ἱδρύματα.. ἐξανέστραπται βάθρων A.*Pers*.812. **-τέλλω**, *cause to spring up from*, ποίην χθονὸς A.R.4.1423: metaph., θόρυβον ἐκ κεφαλῆς Telecl. 44. 2. intr., *spring up from*, χθονὸς Emp.62.4; ἀφ' αἵματος Mosch. 2.58. **-φαίνω**, *bring up and show*, Orph.*A*.1357 (tm.), Man.2. 153. **-φανδόν**, Adv. *openly*, ἐρέω δέ τοι ἐ. Od.20.48. **-φέρω**, *bear up*, of buoyant sea-water, Arist.*Fr*.217. 2. ἐ. λόγχης τύπον *exhibit* the form of a spear, Plu.2.563a. II. intr., *weather the storm*, Id.*Pyrrh*.15: metaph., ἐν νοσήματι κατειλημμένος ἐ. Id.2.

147c; πρὸς τὴν ἀδηλότητα Id.*Oth.*9: abs., ἐ. καὶ διωθεῖσθαι τὸ πάθος Id.2.446b, cf. 541a, 550c. 2. *rise in the scale*, ἐπὶ ζυγοῦ πρὸς τὰ βελτίονα ib.469b. **-φορά**, ἡ, *recovery*, Phld.*D*.3*Fr*.43. **-φύομαι**, aor. 2 ἐξανέφυν, *grow up from*, γαίης Orph.*Fr*.285.36. **-χωρέω**, *go out of the way, withdraw, retreat*, ἐπὶ τὸν ποταμόν, πρὸς τὸ ὄρος, Hdt.1.207, 5.101, cf. Ph.1.229, al.; ἀπὸ τῶν φορτίων Hdt.4.196; of a plant, [γῆς] συνημερουμένης ἐ. Thphr.*HP*6.3.3. II. c. acc., ἐξανεχώρει τὰ εἰρημένα *sought to back out of* his words, Th.4.28. **-ψήχω**, *corrode*, interpol. in Stob.*Flor*.38.53 Meineke.

ἐξανδήριστον· ἐκπέρασον, Hsch.

ἐξανδρᾰποδ-ίζω, *reduce to utter slavery*, Ἀθήνας Hdt.6.94, cf. X.*HG*2.1.15:—mostly in Med. **-ίζομαι**, τοὺς Τεγεήτας Hdt.1.66, cf. And.4.22, X.*HG*2.2.16, etc.; τῶν τεθνεώτων ἐ. τοὺς βίους *confiscate* the substance of the deceased, Plb.32.5.11.—The Att. fut. ἐξανδραποδιοῦμαι, Ion. -ιεῦμαι, which is mostly trans. (as in Hdt.1.66), takes a pass. sense in Id.6.9: so aor. 1 ἐξηνδραποδίσθην ib.108, D.50.4: pf. part. ἐξηνδραποδισμένος Plu.*Ant*.3, Luc.*Cal*.19. **-ισις**, εως, ἡ, *selling into slavery*, Hdt.3.140. **-ισμός**, ὁ, = foreg., Plb.6.49.1. **-ιστής**, οῦ, ὁ, *enslaver, kidnapper*, *Gloss*.

ἐξανδρόομαι, *come to man's years*, ἐξανδρωμένος Hdt.2.63, cf. Antipho Soph.61; ἐξανδρούμενος E.*Ph*.32, Ar.*Eq*.1241. II. λόχος δ' ὀδόντων ὄφεος ἐξηνδρωμένος the host *having grown to men* from teeth, E.*Supp*.703. III. ἐξηνδρωμένον· ὀρθιάζοντα, Hsch.

ἐξαν-εγείρω, *raise* a cry, Aq.*Is*.15.5. **-ειμι**, *go forth from*, Ἑλλάδος A.R.2.459; αἴγλη ὕδατος ἐξανιοῦσα *being reflected from..*, Id.3.757; ἐ. οὐρανοῦ *go up* the sky, of stars, Theoc.22.8 codd. II. *come back from*, ἄγρης *h.Pan*.15.

ἐξᾰνεμ-ίζω, strengthd. for ἀνεμίζω, Sch.Il.20.440. **-όω**, *blow out with wind, inflate*:—Pass., *to be inflated*, Hp.*Mul*.1.34; *to be impregnated by the wind*, of mares, Arist.*HA*572ᵃ13, cf. Ael.*NA*4.6: metaph., Ἥρα ἐξηνέμωσε τἄμ' Ἀλεξάνδρῳ λέχη E.*Hel*.32:—Pass., ἐξηνεμώθην μωρίᾳ *I was puffed up*, Id.*Andr*.938, cf. Ph.1.698. II. Pass., of corn, *to be parched by wind*, '*wind-bitten*', Thphr.*HP*8.10.3. 2. of hair, *float in the wind*, Apollod.1.6.3. III. metaph., *excite*, εἰς δρόμον ἐ. τινά Ael.*NA*13.11:—Pass., τὴν διάνοιαν ἐξηνεμώθη ib.15.29.

ἐξαν-ερευνάω, *search*, τὴν πήραν Tz.*H*.5.83. **-έρχομαι**, *come forth from*, γῆς ἐξανελθών E.*Tr*.753. **-ερωτάω**, *inquire*, Tz.*H*.6.596. **-έσασα**· ἐπιστρέψασα, Hsch. **-ευρίσκω**, *invent*, S.*Ph*.991; *discover*, Plu.*Sol*.20, *Arat*.22. **-έχω**, *hold up from*: mostly intr., *jut out from, stand up upon*, ἀγκὼν ἐ. γαίης A.R.2.370; στήλη ἐ. τύμβου Theoc.22.207. II. Med. (impf. and aor. 2 with double augm. ἐξηνειχόμην, ἐξηνεσχόμην, cf. ἀνέχω), *bear up against, endure, suffer*, with part., οὐ λόγων ἄλγιστ' ἂν ἐξανασχοίμην κλύων S.*OC*1174, cf. *Ph*.1355, E.*Alc*.952; οὐ γὰρ ἐξηνέσχετο ἰδών Ar.*Pax*702; ταῦτα παῖδας ἐξανέξεται πάσχοντας; E.*Med*.74, cf. *Andr*.201; ταῦτα δόξανθ'.. ἐξηνέσχετο that these things should be decreed, Id.*Heracl*.967.

ἐξανέψιοι, οἱ, *children of* ἀνεψιοί, *second cousins*, Plb.6.11ᵃ.4, Ar. Byz. post Hdn.*Epim*.286, Hsch.: fem., ἐξανέψιαι Men.1010 (*children of* ἀνεψιαδοῖ (-δαῖ) Poll.3.29, wrongly): sg., ἐξανέψιος *Inscr.Mus. Alex*.72.16, *POxy*.270.4 (i A.D.), 502.14 (ii A.D.): proparox., Trypho ap.Ammon.*Diff*.p.53 V.

ἐξανηλ-ίσκω, -ωσις, later forms for ἐξανᾱλ-, *PSI*4.400 (iii B.C.), 6.604 (iii B.C.).

ἐξανήσας· ἐξαντήσας, Hsch. (leg. ἐξαμήσας· ἐξαντλήσας).

ἐξανθ-έω, *put out flowers*, γῆ ἐξανθοῦσα X.*Cyn*.5.5; *bloom*, of flowers, Thphr.*HP*4.7.2; of the growth of hair, ἐ. ἡ τῆς ἥβης τρίχωσις Arist.*GA*728ᵇ27: c. acc. cogn., ἐ. ποικίλα *put forth* varied *flowers*, Luc.*Pisc*.6; ἐ. φλόγα, σφῆκας, Plu.*Alex*.35, *Cleom*.9; μέλι Alciphr.3.23. 2. metaph., *burst forth from* the surface, like an efflorescence, ὡς αἱματηρὸν πέλαγος (v.l. πέλανον) ἐξανθεῖν ἁλὸς E.*IT*300; ὕβρις γὰρ ἐξανθοῦσ' ἐκάρπωσε στάχυν ἄτης *bursting into flower, breaking out*, A.*Pers*.821; ἐκ ταύτης τῆς ὑπολήψεως ἐξήνθησεν ἡ δόξα Arist.*Metaph*.1010ᵃ10; κακίαι Plu.*Thes*.6. 3. of ulcers, etc., *break out*, Hp.*deArte*9; ἐ. λευκή Arist.*Col*.797ᵇ15; ὡς φλυκταίνας -ῆσαι *IG*4.955.25 (Epid.); also of the skin, τὸ ἔξωθεν σῶμα.. φλυκταίναις καὶ ἕλκεσιν ἐξηνθηκός *breaking out* with boils and ulcers, Th.2.49, cf. Luc.*DMort*.20.4; τὸ ἔδαφος σκόλοψι ἐξηνθήκει Luc.*VH*2.30; also πλῆθος μυῶν ἐξανθῆσαν Str.13.1.48. II. *to be past its bloom, lose its bloom*, of colour, Plu.2.287d; of wine, ib.692c; ἐξηνθηκυῖα ἐλαία, i.e. when the flower has dropped and the fruit is forming, Dsc.3.125. 2. metaph., *degenerate, run wild*, πέφυκεν ἀνδρεία... κατὰ μὲν ἀρχὰς ἀκμάζειν ῥώμῃ, τελευτῶσα δὲ ἐξανθεῖν... μανίαις Pl.*Plt*.310d; τὸν ἐγγύτατα χρόνον ἀεὶ τῆς ἀφέσεως κάλλιστα πάντα διάγει... τελευτῶντος δὲ ἐξανθεῖ τοῦ χρόνου (sc. ὁ κόσμος) ib.273d. **-ημα**, ατος, τό, *efflorescence, eruption, pustule*, Hp.*Aph*.6.9, *Epid*.1.9, cf. Arist.*HA*518ᵃ12, Ph.2.225: metaph., [πάθη] χρηστῆς φύσεως οἷον ἐ. Plu.2.528d. **-ησις**, εως, ἡ, = foreg., Hp.*Aph*.3.20, Ph.2.101, Archig. ap.Gal.12.468; *growth of young hair*, Sch.A.R.1.972, etc. II. *fading*, ὥσπερ ἐ. τις τῆς προϋπαρχούσης ὀσμῆς Thphr.*CP*6.15.2 codd. **-ίζω**, *deck as with flowers, paint in various colours*, γυναῖκες... αἱ καθήμεθ' ἐξηνθισμέναι Ar.*Lys*.43; ἄνωθεν ἐξηνθισμένον, of a fish, Philem.79.6; παντοίᾳ κομμωτικῇ.. ἐξηνθισμένη Hld.7.19; ἐλέφας φοίνικι -ισμένος Max.Tyr.40.2. II. Med., *gather flowers*, Plu.2.661f. **-ισμα**, ατος, τό, f.l. for ἐξάνθημα, Hp.*Coac*.435. **-ισμός**, ὁ, = ἐξάνθημα, v.l. in Dsc.2.82.3.

ἐξανθρᾰκόω, *burn to ashes*, Ion Trag.28.

ἐξανθρωπ-ίζω, *humanize, bring down to men*, τὰ θεῖα Plu.2.360a; φιλοσοφίαν, of Socrates, ib.582b. II. [πνεύμασι καὶ χυμοῖσι] χρῆται (sc. the new-born child) ἧσσον -ισμένοισι less *humanized* (than those enjoyed by the foetus), Hp.*Oct*.12. **-ος**, ον, *unsociable*, of epileptics, Aret.*SD*1.4. II. ἐ. ἡ συμφορή it (epilepsy) is an *inhuman* calamity, Id.*SA*1.6.

ἐξαν-ίημι, poet. impf. ἐξανίεσκον A.R.4.622: fut. ἐξανήσω, also -ήσομαι E.*Andr*.718: pf. part. Pass. -ειμένος Orib.46.19.20:—*send forth, let loose*, εὔπρηστον ἀϋτμὴν ἐξανιεῖσαι Il.18.471; [ὀδμήν] A.R.l.c.; ἐξανῆκε γᾶ ὄψιν E.*Ph*.670 (lyr.); κρήνην ἐξανῆκ' οἴνου θεός Id.*Ba*.707; ἐ. αἷμα *make it spout forth*, Id.*IT*1460; [ῥόον] Call.*Del*.207; ἀρὰς σφῷν ἐξανῆκα *I have sent forth* curses against you, S.*OC*1375. b. c. gen., *send forth from*, τίς σε πολιᾶς ἐξανῆκεν γαστρός; Pi.*P*.4.99; θύρσους ἐξανιεῖσαι χερῶν E.*Ba*.762; νάματ' ὅσσων μηκέτ' ἐξανίετε Id.*HF*625. 2. *let go*, Id.*IA*372; τὴν ἀρετὴν ἐ. *relax, slacken*, Plu.*Cat. Ma*.11:—Pass., *to be set free from*, πόνων Hp.*Nat.Hom*.12: abs., Ph.2.371. 3. *loosen, undo*, στροφίδας E.*Andr*.718:—Pass., Plu.2.788b. 4. *dilute*, Heras ap.Gal.13.795:—Pass., pf. part. -ειμένος Orib. l.c. II. intr., *slacken, relax*, Hp.*Nat.Hom*.7; ἀνίκ' ἐξανείη.. ἄτα (Herm. for ἐξανίησι) S.*Ph*.705: c. gen., ὀργῆς ἐξανεὶς κακῆς E.*Hipp*.900. 2. *burst forth from*, γῆς, of a river, A.R.4.293: abs., of seed, *spring up*, Arist.*Mir*.833ᵇ2. **-ῐμάω**, *draw up*, ποτόν Ph.1.296. **-ιστάνω**, = sq., *drive out of one's senses*, Dsc.4.73. **-ίστημι**: I. causal in pres., impf., fut., and aor. 1: 1. *raise up*, τοὺς θανόντας S.*El*.940; *make* one *rise from his seat*, Pl.*Prt*.310a; *bid* one *rise* from suppliant posture, ἐγώ σ' ἕδρας ἐκ τῆσδε.. ἐξαναστήσω E.*Andr*.263, cf. 267; ἐ. τὴν ἐνέδραν *order* the men in ambush *to rise*, X.*HG*4.8.37. 2. *make* a tribe *emigrate, remove* or *expel*, ἐ. τινὰς ἐκ τῶν νήσων, ἐξ ἠθέων, etc., Hdt.1.171, 5.14, etc.; ἄνδρας δόμων S.*Ant*.297; ἐ. πόλεως *bid* one *depart from..*, Id.*OC*47; simply ἐ. τινάς Hdt.6.127, Th.4.98, etc. (v. infr. II. 2). b. *challenge* a juror, *PHal*.9.5 (iii B.C.), *PGurob*2.10 (iii B.C.), etc. 3. *depopulate, destroy*, πόλιν Hdt.1.155, al.; Ἰλίου ποτ' ἐξαναστήσας βάθρα E.*Supp*.1198; Ἑλλάδα Id.*Tr*.926. 4. ἐ. θηρία *rouse* them *from their lair*, X.*Cyr*.2.4.20. 5. τουτὶ ἐ., *erigere penem*, E.*Cyc*.169. II. intr. in Pass., with aor. 2, pf. and plpf. Act.: 1. *stand up from one's seat*, Hdt.3.142; ἐκ τοῦ θρόνου Id.5.72, cf. Pl.*Ly*.211a; θάκων X.*Hier*.7.7; ὁδῶν τινί, in courtesy, Id.*Smp*.4.31; *rise* to speak, S.*Ph*.367; *rise* from ambush, λόχου E.*El*.217: without λόχου, Th.3.107; *rise* after dinner, Pl.*R*.328a, etc.; πρὸ μέθης Isoc.1.32; from bed, λέχους E.*El*.786; ἐξ εὐνῆς X.*Oec*.10.8; ἐξαναστῶμεν εἰς τὴν αὐλὴν *let us rise and go* into.., Pl.*Prt*.311a; εἰς περίπατον X.*Smp*.9.1. 2. c. gen., *arise and depart from, emigrate from*, Λακεδαίμονος Pi.*P*.4.49, cf. E.*Andr*.380; ἐκ τῆς γῆς τῆσδε Hdt.4.115: abs., *break up, depart*, Th.7.49, etc. 3. *to be driven out* from one's home, *to be forced to emigrate*, ἐξ ἠθέων ὑπό τινος Hdt.1.15, cf. 56, al.; πρὸς δάμαρτος ἐξανίσταται θρόνων A.*Pr*.767. 4. of places, *to be depopulated*, ἐξαναστάσης πάσης Πελοποννήσου ὑπὸ Δωριέων Hdt.2.171; Τροίης ἐξανεστάθη βάθρα E.*Hel*.1652, cf. D.16.25. 5. *rise to go to stool*, Hp.*Epid*.1.26.δ', etc. 6 *rise from the plain*, of a mountain, Plb.1.56.4. b. so of ulcers, *rise*, Aret.*SD*2.13; of an excrescence, κέρχνος ἐ. S.*Fr*.279. **-ίσχω**, = ἐξανέχω, *rise*, of the sun, Eust.419.17. **-οίγω**, *lay open*, μηχανὰς Σισύφου Ar.*Ach*.391; διάφραγμα D.S.1.33:—Pass., Str.16.1.10, Ath.Mech.36.9: pf. inf. ἐξανεῷχθαι *to be exposed*, of high ground, Ath.Med.ap.Orib.9.12.1. **-οιδέω**, *swell up*, Arist.*Mete*.367ᵃ3. **-οιξις**, εως, ἡ, *opening*, Str.16.1.10.

ἐξανόμεναι· ἐκκενούμεναι, Hsch.

ἐξαντάω, v. ἐξαντῶν.

ἐξάντες· ἐξεναντίας, ὅτε δὲ τὸ ὑγιές, Hsch.

ἐξάντης, ες, of patients, *out of danger, healthy*, ἐ. γίνεται Hp.*Morb*.3.3, *Mul*.1.41; ἐξάντη ποιεῖν τινα Pl.*Phdr*.244e. b. *harmless*, ἐξάντη φάσκοντες ποιήσειν (sc. μῆνιν Ἑκάτης) D.Chr.4.90. 2. c. gen., *free from*, κακοῦ Ael.*NA*3.5; νούσου Hp.*Morb*.1.14, cf. *Com.Adesp*.1279 (= *Trag.Adesp*.151); δειλίας Jul.*Or*.6.192b. 3. = ἐξεστηκώς, μαινόμενος, *EM*346.42.

ἐξαντίαι, Adv. = *opposite*, *SIG*306.12 (Tegea, iv B.C.).

ἐξάντιον, τό, Dim. of ἐξᾶς, Epich.10.

ἐξαντλ-έω, *drain* or *draw off*, Pl.*Lg*.736b, *PTeb*.123.6 (i B.C.), Aret.*SA*2.4:—Pass., Arist.*HA*570ᵃ8. 2. metaph., *endure to the end, see out*, ἐκείνων μείζον' ἐ. πόνον E.*Cyc*.10; τὸν αὐτὸν δαίμον' ἐ. ἐμοί ib.110; τὸν αὐτὸν ἐ. βίον Id.*Fr*.454; βίον οἰκτρὸν ἐ. Men.74; στρατῷ γόους E.*Supp*.838. 3. *empty out*, Hld.1.3; *squander*, [πλοῦτον] Luc.*Tim*.18, cf. 17 (Pass.); δύναμιν πόνοις Id.*Anach*.35, cf. Alciphr.1.21. **-ημα**, ατος, τό, *douche*, Aret.*CD*2.12 codd. **-ησις**, εως, ἡ, *douching*, Sor.1.99, Antyll.ap.Orib.10.30.6. **-ητέον**, *one must douche*, ib.13.19.

ἐξαντῶν· ἀντιάζων τῆς κόρρης καὶ τοῦ πώγωνος, οἷον ὑπογεν⟨ε⟩ιάζων, Hsch. (with a second and less prob. expl.).

ἐξάν-ῠσις [ᾰ], εως, ἡ, *exaction in full*, *PMon*.7.26 (vi A.D.); *exaction*, τῶν δημοσίων Just.*Nov.App*.4.1, cf. *Cod.Just*.10.19.9 *Intr*. **-ύω**, Att. -ύτω [ῠ], fut. -ύσω [ῠ] (v. infr.), but Ep. fut. -ύω Il.11.365: pf. inf. ἐξηνῦκέναι Critias 16.14:—*accomplish, make effectual*, Θέτιδος δ' ἐξήνυσε βουλάς Il.8.370; θεῶν θέσμι' ἐξήνυσε S.*Aj*.712 (lyr.); ἔμελλες ἐξανύσειν κακὰν μοῖραν ib.926 (lyr., -ύσσειν cod. Med.); τί μοι ἐξανύσεις χρέος; Id.*OT*156 (lyr.); πάθεα E.*Ion*1066 (lyr.); λειτουργίαν *POxy*.904.8 (v A.D.):—Med., *accomplish* or *finish for oneself*, κακῶν μῆχος E.*Andr*.536 (lyr.); τέκνοις τάφον Id.*Supp*.285 (dact.). 2. *finish, dispatch*, i.e. *kill*, ἦ θήν σ' ἐξανύω (fut.) Il.11.365; κενταυροπληθῆ πόλεμον E.*HF*1273. b. *conquer*, ἔθνη App.*Ill*.15. 3. of Time and Distance, *bring to an end, finish, accomplish*, βίοτον S.*Tr*.1022 (dact.); ἁμέραν τάνδε E.*Med*.649 (lyr.); δρόμον, ἴχνος, πόρον, Id.*Ph*.163 (lyr.), *Tr*.232 (lyr.), *IT*897 (anap.): abs. (like ἀνύω I. 6), *finish* *one's way to* a place, *arrive at* it, ἐς or ἐπί.., Hdt.6.139,7.183: also c. acc. loci, ἐξανύσαι τὰν νεκρῶν πλάκα (Vauvill. for ἐκτανύσαι) S.*OC* 1562; πόλον ἐξανύσας E.*Or.*1685 (anap.). 4. c. inf., *manage* to do, ἐ. κρατεῖν Id.*Hipp.*400. 5. Med., *obtain, borrow*, τι παρά τινος Id.*Ba.*131 (lyr.).

ἐξάνω· ἄνωθεν ἐξάγει, ἐξενέγκει, Hsch.

ἐξά-ξεστος, ον, *containing six* ξέσται, μέτρον Hero *Geom.*23.66, cf. *Gloss.* **-ούγκιον**, τό, *six ounces*, ib.

ἐξαπ-ᾰείρω, *carry away*, Philox.2.39. **-αιολεῖσθαι·** παραλογίζεσθαι, prob. in Hsch. (ἐξαποίνασθαι cod.). **-αιτέω**, strengthd. for ἀπαιτέω, dub. in Jul.*Mis.*349b (ἐξαπατῶσι codd.).

ἐξᾰπάλαστος [πᾰ], ον, *of six hands-breadth*, Hdt.1.50, 2.149 (v.l. -αιστος).

ἐξαπ-αλλάσσω, Att. **-ττω**, *set free from, remove from*, τινὰ κακῶν E.*IA*1004; (sc. ἑαυτόν) ταλαίνης ζόης Id.*Hec.*1108:—Pass., *get rid of, escape from*, κακῶν ἐξαπαλλαχθείς Hdt.5.4; ἄλυπος ἄτης ἐξαπαλλαχθήσεται S.*El.*1002; τῶν εἰρημένων ἐξαπαλλαγῆναι *escape from* his own words, Th.4.28. **-αντάω**, *meet*, v.l. in X.*Cyr.*3.3.24.

ἐξᾰπᾰτάω, Ep. iter. ἐξαπάτασκον Ar.*Pax*1070 (hexam.):—Pass., fut. -απατηθήσομαι Pl.*Grg.*499c; but -απατήσομαι in pass. sense, X.*An.*7.3.3:—*deceive* or *beguile, deceive thoroughly*, εἴ τινά που.. ἔτι ἔλπεται ἐξαπατήσειν Il.9.371, cf. Od.9.414, Pi.*O.*1.29, Hdt.1.153, Ar.*V.*901, etc.; ἐ. τινὰ φρένας Id.*Pax*1099 (hexam.); ἐ. καὶ φενακίζειν D.21.204; *seduce* a woman, Hdt.2.114: c. dupl. acc., ἐ. τινά τι *in* a thing, X.*Cyr.*3.1.19; also ἐ. ἐπὶ τοῖς ἰδίοις συμβολαίοις Isoc.10.7; περὶ σαυτὸν ποιεῖσθαι.. ἐφ' οἷς ἐξαπατᾷς ἔλεον surround yourself with compassion for your *swindling tricks*, D.21.196; ἐ. τινὰ ὡς.. *cheat* him *into believing* that.., X.*An.*5.7.6, cf. Pl.*Cra.*413d; ἐ. νόσον *beguile* or *assuage* it, Luc.*Nigr.*7:—Pass., ὡς ἐξαπατηθείς Hdt.9.94; ἐνόμιζον ἐξηπατῆσθαι Th.5.42; ᾔδει ὑπὸ τῆς μητρυιᾶς ἐξαπατωμένη Antipho1.19; τὸ δεῖπνον ἐξαπατώμενος Ar.*V.*60; ἐ. ἀπάτην Plot.2.9.6:—Med. like Act., f.l. in Pl.*Cra.*439c.

ἐξαπάτερθεν· ἐκ τοῦ ἑτέρου, Hsch.

ἐξᾰπάτ-η [πᾰ], ἡ, *deceit*, Hes.*Th.*205 (pl.), Thgn.390 (pl.), X.*An.*7.1.25, App.*BC*5.22. **-ημα**, ατος, τό, gloss on φήλωμα, *EM*791.32. **-ησις**, εως, ἡ, strengthd. for ἀπάτησις, Ath.9.387e. **-ητέον**, *one must deceive*, Pl.*Cri.*49e. **-ητήρ**, ῆρος, ὁ, *deceiver*, Hom.*Cercop.* **-ητής**, οῦ, ὁ, = foreg., Ptol.*Tetr.*165. **-ητικός**, ή, όν, *calculated to deceive*, τῶν πολεμίων X.*Eq.Mag.*4.12, S.E.*M.*2.93. Adv. -κῶς Poll.4.24. **-ύλλω**, Com. Dim. of ἐξαπατάω, *cheat a little, humbug*, Ar.*Ach.*657, *Eq.*1144.

ἐξᾰπᾰφίσκω, Ep., = ἐξαπατάω, Hes.*Th.*537: aor. ἐξήπᾰφον Od.14.379; subj. ἐξαπάφω 23.79; part. ἐξαπαφών, -οῦσα, *h.Ap.*379, *h.Ven.*38, E.*Ion*704 (lyr.), Alex.Aet.3.19, etc.: Hom. also has 3 sg. aor. opt. Med. ἐξαπάφοιτο in act. sense, Il.9.376, 14.160: later aor. 1 ἐξαπάφησε *h.Ap.*376, Q.S.1.137, Opp.*H.*3.94.

ἐξά-πεδος [ᾰ], ον, *six feet* long, Hdt.2.149, *IG*14.352.1.62 (Halaesa). **-πεζος**, ον, *six-footed*, Lyc.176.

ἐξαπ-εῖδον, inf. ἐξαπιδεῖν: aor. without any pres. ἐξαφοράω in use, *observe from afar*, only in S.*OC*1648 (lyr.). **-ειλέω**, *menace*, dub. in Chor. in *Rev.Phil.*1.71. **-ελαύνω**, *drive away out of*, δόμων μ' ἐμῶν ἐ. *IG*12(5).564.3 (Carthaea).

ἐξᾰπέλεκυς, εως, ὁ, ἡ, *with six axes*, ἐ. ἀρχή, = Lat. *sexfascalis, of the praetor*, Plb.3.40.9; ἐ. ἡγεμών or simply ἐ. *a praetor*, Id.2.24.6, 3.40.11; στρατηγός ib.106.6, D.S.31.42: pl., App.*Syr.*15.

ἐξαπ-ελευθερόω, *manumit*, *POxy.*722.13, al. (Pass., i A.D.). **-εύχομαι**, strengthd. for ἀπεύχομαι, Tz.*H.*13.606. **-ηλιωτικός**, ή, όν, *easterly*, *PFlor.*50.105 (iii A.D.).

ἐξάπηχυς [ᾰ], υ, *six cubits long*, Hdt.2.138, Hp.*Art.*72, X.*An.*5.4.12 codd.; ξύλα ἐξαπήχη *PCair.Zen.*112.6; cf. ἕξπηχυς.

ἐξάπῑν-ᾰ [ᾰπ], later form of ἐξαπίνης, Lxx*Nu.*4.20, *Ev.Marc.*9.8, *PGiss.*1.68.6 (ii A.D.), Procop.*Aed.*2.11. **-αιος**, proparox., or -αῖος, α, ον, or ος, ον, = ἐξαιφνίδιος, Hp.*Acut.*28, X.*Hier.*10.6, Plb.25.2.1, Call.*Jov.*50, Ruf.ap.Orib.6.38.25. Adv. -ως Hp.*Art.*43, Th.3.3, al. **-ης**, Dor. and Aeol. **-ας**, = ἐξαίφνης, Il.15.325, Alc.27, Pi.*P.*4.273, Hdt.1.74, 87, Hp.*Acut.*28, Epicur.*Nat.*14.8; never in Trag., sts. in Att., as Ar.*Pl.*336, 339, 815, Th.1.50, Nicol.Com.1.6:—with a Subst., ἔαρ ἐξαπίνας *sudden* spring, Theoc.9.34. **-ον**, dub. l. in Hp.*Aff.*4, for ἄπνουν or ἐξαίφνης.

ἐξαπλάσι-άζω, *multiply by six*, in Pass., *Theol.Ar.*48, *EM*595.15. **-επίτρῑτος**, ον, *six and one-third times as much*, Procl.*Hyp.*4.109. **-ος**, α, ον, Ion. **-πλήσιος**, η, ον, *six times as large as*, τινός Hdt.4.81: abs., Plu.2.1020a, 1028f: neut. -πλάσιον κηροῦ *six times as much* wax, Orib.*Fr.*99. **-ων**, ον, gen. ονος, = foreg., χρόνος Arist.*Mu.*399ᵃ10.

ἐξά-πλεθρος, ον, *of six* πλέθρα, *six* πλέθρα *long*, Hdt.2.149. **-πλευρος**, ον, *with six sides*, Plot.6.3.14. **-πλήσιος**, v. ἐξαπλάσιος. **-πλόος**, όη, όον, *sixfold*, *GDI*5075.38 (Crete). **-πλόω**, = ἐξαπλασιάζω, *multiply by six*, Paul.Al.*E.*1.

ἐξαπλ-όω, *unfold, roll out*, οὐρανὸν ὡς δέρριν ἐξαπλῶσαι Ps.-Luc.*Philopatr.*17; ἐ. τὴν χεῖρα S.E.*M.*2.7: metaph., πᾶσαν τὴν ἔννοιαν εἰς τὰ πάντα Dam.*Pr.*1:—Pass., *to be unfolded, spread out*, ὕπτιος ἐξήπλωτο νεκρὸν δέμας Batr.106; ἀϊδιότης -ωθεῖσα κατὰ τὴν χρονικὴν παράτασιν *unrolled* successively, Procl.*Inst.*55. 2. *unfold, explain*, ἀμφιβόλους λέξεις Ph.1.302:—Pass., Demetr.*Eloc.*254, S.E.*M.*7.233. 3. Medic., *open out* a fistula, Heliod.ap.Orib.44.23.50 (Pass.). **-ωσις**, εως, ἡ, *unfolding*, δακτύλων S.E.*M.*2.7; τῶν ὑμένων εἰς πλάτος Aret.*SA*1.8; opp. πίλησις, Ph.1.385 (pl.). 2. *opening out*, of roots, Archig.ap.Orib.8.2.12. II. *explanation*, Erot.*Prooem.* III. *expansion* or *paraphrase* of an expression, S.E.*M.*7.51. b. Math., *expansion*, εἰς μονάδας Nicom.*Ar.*2.10. **-ωτέον**, *one must explain*, Gal.18(2).669.

ἐξαποβαίνω, *step out of*, νηός Od.12.306; νηὸς χέρσονδε A.R.3.199, etc.

ἐξᾰποδία, ἡ, *hexapody, hexameter*, Anon. *in Rh.*190.31.

ἐξαποδύνω, *put off*, εἵματα Od.5.372. **ἐξαποίνασθαι**, v. ἐξαπαιολεῖσθαι.

Ἑξάπολις [ᾰ], εως, ἡ, *league of six cities*, of the Asiatic Dorians, Hdt.1.144, Sch.Ar.*Pl.*385.

ἐξαπόλλῡμι (-ύων prob. cj. in A.*Ch.*837 (lyr.)), *destroy utterly*, A. l.c., S.*El.*588, E.*Heracl.*950, Thphr.*HP*8.7.2, etc. II. Pass., with pf. 2 ἐξαπόλωλα: aor. 2 ἐξαπωλόμην:—*perish utterly out of*, c. gen., Ἰλίου ἐξαπολοίατ' Il.6.60; ἐξαπόλωλε δόμων κειμήλια 18.290; ἠέλιος δὲ οὐρανοῦ ἐξαπόλωλε Od.20.357; σπέρμα πάσης ἐξαπόλλυται χθονός A.*Ag.*528: abs., *perish utterly*, Hdt.4.173, S.*Fr.*236.

ἐξαπο-λογία, ἡ, title of three speeches of Antipho, *second defence, rejoinder* (nisi scribendum ἐξ ἀπολογίας: cf. ἐκκατηγορία). **-νέομαι**, *return out of*, Il.16.252, 20.212 (or ἐξ ἀ.). **-νίζω**, *wash thoroughly*, πόδας Od.19.387.

ἐξαποξύνω, *sharpen well*, E.*Cyc.*456 (s.v.l.).

ἐξαπο-πᾰτέω, strengthd. for ἀποπατέω, Hp.*Morb.*4.43. **-πειρῆσθαι·** πειρᾶσθαι, Hsch. (ἐξαπειρῆσθαι cod.). **-πέμπω**, *send quite away*, Tz.*H.*3.887. **-πνέω**, *breathe quite away*, τὸν βίον ib.364, 6.185. **-πτύω**, *spit quite out*, ib.7.

ἐξαπορέω, strengthd. for ἀπορέω, to be in *great doubt* or *difficulty*, Plb.4.34.1; τοῖς πράγμασι Arist.*Ath.*23.1:—Med., ἀπορούμενοι, ἀλλ' οὐκ ἐ. 2*Ep.Cor.*4.8: so in aor. Pass. ἐξηπορήθην Lxx*Ps.*87(88).15, D.S.24.1, Plu.*Alc.*5; ἐξαπορηθῆναι ἀργυρίου *to be without* money, D.H.7.18; τῶν κοινῶν ἐξηπορημένων *SIG*495.12 (Olbia, iii B.C.), cf. *PEleph.*2.10 (iii B.C.).

ἐξαπο-σταλτέος, α, ον, *to be dispatched*, *Gloss.* **-στέλλω**, fut. -στελῶ Lxx4*Ki.*8.12: pf. ἐξαπέσταλκα Attal. (v. infr.):—*dispatch*, πρεσβευτάς Plb.3.11.1; στρατηγόν D.S.19.102; θεωρούς *SIG*629.8 (Delph., ii B.C.); βιβλίον τινί Attal.ap.Hipparch.1.3.3:—Pass., *to be dispatched*, Philipp.ap.D.18.77, *OGI*90.20 (Rosetta, ii B.C.); ὑπό τινων *Vit.Philonid.*p.7 C.; ἐξαπεσταλμένοι μάχεσθαι Aristeas 13; also ἡμῶν ὁ λόγος -εστάλη *Act.Ap.*13.26. 2. *send forth*, [δαίμων] -στέλλων ὕδατα καὶ ἀνέμους *Sammelb.*4324.16. 3. of prisoners, *send* before a tribunal, ἐ. τινὰ δέσμιον πρός τινας *PTeb.*22.18 (ii B.C.), etc.:—Pass., *PTaur.*1 iii 13 (ii B.C.). II. *send away, dismiss*, e.g. a prisoner, Plb.4.84.3; ἐ. τινὰ κενόν *send away* empty-handed, *Ev.Luc.*1.53; *divorce* a wife, Lxx*De.*24.4; *expel*, ἐκ τοῦ παραδείσου ib.*Ge.*3.23. III. *discharge* a projectile, Hero *Bel.*81.4 (Pass.). IV. *destroy*, ὀχυρώματα ἐν πυρί Lxx4*Ki.*8.12. V. *emit, display*, φαντασίαν Procl.*Hyp.*5.72. **-στολή**, ἡ, *sending away*, *IG*2.985 *A* 1 (ii B.C.), Plb.1.66.2, Lxx3*Ma.*4.4; ἐ. θανάτου Ph.1.233: pl., Plb.9.5.5. II. *discharge* of an engine or projectile, Ph.*Bel.*53.46, Hero *Bel.*79.4, 110.10. **-στολος**, ὁ, = πρεσβευτής, *PAmh.*2.138.10 (iv A.D.). **-τίνω** [ῑ], *satisfy in full*, Ἐρινύας ἐξαποτίνοις Il.21.412.

ἑξάπους [ᾰ], ὁ, ἡ, πουν, τό, gen. ποδος, *six-footed*, Arist.*PA*683ᵇ2. II. = ἐξάπεδος, Luc.*Sat.*17; κολοσσός Plu.*Luc.*37; λίθος *Milet.*7.57 (Didyma). 2. of metre, *of six feet*, D.H.*Comp.*4. Cf. ἕξπους.

ἐξαπο-φαίνω, strengthd. for ἀποφαίνω, Luc.*Hes.*1. **-φθείρω**, *destroy utterly*, A.*Pers.*464, S.*Tr.*713. **-χέω**, in Pass., *pour forth from*, Tz.*H.*3.327.

ἑξά-πρυμνος, ον, *with six stems*, i.e. *ships*, Lyc.1347. **-πτέρῠγος**, ον, *six-winged*, *Gloss.*

ἐξαπτίς, ἡ, *cloak*, *Gloss.*

ἑξάπτῠχος, ον, *with six folds*, Sch.Il.12.295, Hsch. s.v. ἑξήλατον.

ἐξάπτω, *fasten from* or (as we say) *to*, πεῖσμα νεὸς.. κίονος ἐξάψας μεγάλης *having fastened* it to a pillar, Od.22.466, cf. Il.24.51; ἐ. τι χροός E.*Tr.*1220; τὴν πόλιν τοῦ Πειραιῶς Plu.*Them.*19; ἐ. τι ἔκ τινος Hdt.4.64; ἀπό τινος X.*Cyn.*10.7; also ἐ. ἐκ τοῦ νηοῦ σχοινίον ἐς τὸ τεῖχος Hdt.1.26; ἐξάψας διὰ τῆς θυρίδος τὸ καλῴδιον Ar.*V.*379:—Pass., περὶ τὴν κεφαλὴν ἐξῆμμαι πηνίκην τινά I *have* a wig *fastened* on my head, Id.*Fr.*898 (s.v.l.). 2. metaph., ἐ. στόματος λιτάς *let* prayers *fall from* one's mouth, E.*Or.*383; τῆς τύχης ἐ. τὰ πραττόμενα *consider* actions *as dependent upon* chance, Plu.*Sull.*6; ἐ. τὴν διαδοχὴν τῶν ἀξίων λόγου *continue* the narrative, D.L.8.50; ἐξαμμένος ἐκ σώματος *dependent on* it, Ti.Locr.102e. 3. ἐ. τινί τι *place upon*, ἱκετηρίαν γόνασιν E.*IA*1216; κόσμον νεκρῷ Id.*Tr.*1208; ἐ. βρόχον ἀμφὶ δειρήν Id.*Ion*1065 (lyr.). II. Med., *hang by, cling to*, πάντες ἐξάπτεσθε all *hang on*, Il.8.20; ἐ. τῆς οὐραγίας, τῆς πορείας, *hang on* the enemy's rear, *on* his line of march, Plb.4.11.6, 3.51.2; τῶν πολεμίων, τῆς μάχης, D.S.11.17, 13.10; τῶν Ἑλληνικῶν ἐ. *attend to*.., Plu.*Them.*31; τοῦ πολέμου D.H.6.25; *cling to* an authority, Plu.2.1111f. 2. *hang* a thing *to oneself, carry it suspended about one, wear*, κώδωνας D.25.90; πέπλους χροός E.*Hel.*1186; σφραγίδια Ar.*Th.*428; also ἐ. ναῦς *fasten* them *to one's own ship, take in tow*, D.S.14.74; ἐ. τοὺς ἐραστάς *have* them *hanging about one*, Philostr.*VA*8.7.6, cf. Luc.*Am.*11.

B. Act. also, *set fire to*, [ὕλαν] Ti.Locr.97e, cf. Thphr.*HP*9.8.6, App.*Hisp.*5. II. *kindle, inflame*, πόλεμον Ael.*NA*12.35; πυρετόν Gal.6.240; of love, Chor. in *Rh.Mus.*49.495; νόσημα *aggravate*, Id. in *Hermes*17.234:—Pass., πῦρ ἐ. ἐκ λίθων Arist.*PA*655ᵃ15; ὑπὸ φιλοσοφίας ὥσπερ πυρὸς *to be inflamed* by.., Pl.*Ep.*340b; αὖθις οὐκ -ονται they *are* not *rekindled* (like Heraclitus' sun), Id.*R.*498b; ὑπ' ὀργῆς ἐξαφθέντες D.H.5.38; πόλεμος ἐξήφθη Str.9.3.8; ψυχαὶ -ονται *are turned to flame*, M.Ant.4.21.

ἐξά-πτωτος, ον, (πτῶσις) *with six cases*, Prisc.*Inst*.5.77. **-πῦλα**, τά, a gate at Syracuse, Plb.8.3.6, D.S.14.18, Plu.*Marc*.18.

ἐξαπωθέω, *thrust away*, E.*Rh*.811.

ἐξάπωλος [ᾰ], ον, *with six colts* or *horses*, ἅρμα Hdn.5.6.7.

ἐξάραγμα [ᾰρ], ατος, τό, = σύντριμμα, Hp.ap.Gal.19.98.

ἐξαραι-όω, -ωσις, strengthd. for ἀραι-όω, -ωσις, Aret.*CA*2.6, *SA* 2.2.

ἐξαραιρημένος, ἐξαραίρηται, v. ἐξαιρέω.

ἐξᾰράομαι, *utter curses*, ἐκ δ' ἀρὰς ἠρᾶτο S.*Ant*.427. II. *dedicate with solemn prayers*, νεών Aeschin.3.116.

ἐξᾰράσσω, Att. -ττω, *dash out*, ἐκ δέ οἱ ἱστὸν ἄραξε Od.12.422; ἐ. λίθῳ ὀδόντας Semon.7.17; ἐ. αὐθαδίαν τινός *knock* his self-will *out* of him, Ar.*Th*.704; *shatter*, τὴν ῥῖνα Hippon.60; τὴν κιγκλίδα Ar.*Eq*. 641; πεφραγμένην ἔξοδον Ael.*NA*15.16; in cookery, *beat up*, Ruf.ap. Orib.4.2.6. II. c. acc. pers., ἐ. τινὰ κακοῖς καἰσχροῖσι *assail* him *furiously* with abuse, Ar.*Nu*.1373.

ἐξαργέω, *to be quite torpid*, ἐξηργηκώς Arist.*EN*1099ᵃ2; τὴν δύναμιν ἐξηργηκέναι Id.*Pol*.1312ᵃ13. II. Pass., *to be quite neglected*, ἔργα δρώμεν', οὐκέτ' ἐξαργούμενα S.*Ph*.556; [γῆ] ἐξαργηθεῖσα Plu.2.2e.

ἐξάργματα, τά, (ἐξάρχομαι) *the first pieces cut from the victim's flesh*, = μασχαλίσματα, A.R.4.477.

ἐξαργῠρ-ίζω, *turn into money*, v.l. for ἐξαργυρόω in Th.8.81; ἐ. τὴν οὐσίαν D.5.8, cf. Mitteis*Chr*.88iv23 (ii A. D.):—Med., ἐξαργυρίσασθαι τὸν οἶκον Is.5.43, cf. D.S.22.1, Plu.2.850d. II. ἐξαργυρίζεσθαί τινα *plunder* him, Plb.32.6.1. **-ισμός**, ὁ, = Lat. *adaeratio, conversion of payment in kind into money payment*, *PFlor*.95.9, *Cod. Just*.12.37.19.3, etc. **-όω**, *turn into money*, τὰ ἡμίσεα πάσης τῆς οὐσίης Hdt.6.86.α', cf. Th.8.81.

ἐξάρδω, *water*, πεδία E.*Antiop*.B58 p.21 A.

ἐξᾶρεν· ἐκτός ἐστιν, Hsch. **ἐξαρέσασθαι**· διῶξαι, Id. (cf. eund. s.v. ἀραχθείς).

ἐξᾰρεσκ-εύομαι, v.l. for sq. (q.v.). **-ομαι**, *make oneself acceptable, make offerings*, τοῖς θεοῖς X.*Oec*.5.3,19 (with v.l. -ευομένους, nisi leg. θεούς). 2. c. acc. pers., ἐξαρέσασθαί τινα δώροις *win* him *over* by gifts, D.60.25, cf. 26.

ἐξαρῆξαι· ἐκφορῆσαι, Hsch.

ἐξαρθρ-έω, *dislocate the joints of*, οἱ Ἀμαζόνες ἐ. τὸ ἄρσεν γένος τὸ ἑωυτῶν Hp.*Art*.53:—Pass., ἐξαρθρέεται τὰ τοιαῦτα ib.58, cf. Gal.6. 876. II. intr., *to be dislocated*, ἐξαρθρήσαντα ὀστέα Hp.*Art*.29; *suffer from dislocations*, ib.8,53. **-ημα**, ατος, τό, *dislocation*, ib.58, Gal.6.876. **-ησις**, εως, ἡ, = foreg., Hp.*Art*.53, Gal.6.876. **-ος**, ον, (ἄρθρον) *dislocated*, Lxx 4*Ma*.9.13, Gal.6.10; τοῦ σκέλους ἔξαρθρος γενέσθαι J.*AJ*3.11.6. II. *with distorted, clumsy joints*, Hp.*Art*. 10; *loose-jointed*, Gal.1.178. **-όω**, *dislocate*, Lxx 4*Ma*.10.5. II. ἐξηρθρωμένος, = foreg. II, ἐπωμίδες Arist.*Phgn*.810ᵇ35. **-ωμα**, ατος, τό, **-ωσις**, εως, ἡ, = ἐξάρθρημα, -ησις, Gal.18(2).323.

ἐξαριθμ-έω, *enumerate, count*, τὸν στρατόν Hdt.7.59,60, etc.; *reckon up*, πᾶν τὸ λυποῦν Phld.*Ir*.p.25 W.:—Pass., μυριάδες ἐξηριθμήθησαν Hdt.4.87. II. *count out*, ἐ. χρήματα *pay in ready* money, D.27.58. III. *recount*, κινδύνους Isoc.4.66:—later in Med., τὰ κατὰ μέρος D.H.5.72, cf. D.C.44.48: pf. Pass. in med. sense, Plb.9. 2.1:—Pass., Arist.*Rh*.1410ᵇ2. **-ησις**, εως, ἡ, *numbering, enumeration*, J.*AJ*7.13.1, App.*BC*2.82, D.C.43.46, A.D.*Conj*.244.21, Plot.6.3.19, etc.; προβάτων *PLond*.2.376.7 (ii A. D.). II. *reckoning up, recounting*, τῶν πεπραγμένων Plb.16.26.5.

ἐξάριθμος [ᾰ], ον, *supernumerary*, τῆς τάξεως Ascl.*Tact*.2.9.

ἐξάριθμος [ᾰ], ον, *sixfold*, Pi.*O*.10(11).25, cf. Sch.

ἐξαρκ-έω, I. of objects, *to be quite enough for, suffice for*, τινί Heraclit.114, S.*OC*6, 1116, *Ph*.459, etc.; ἔμοιγ' ἐ. ὃς ἂν μὴ κακὸς ᾖ Pl.*Prt*.346c; ὁ βίος μοι δοκεῖ τῷ μήκει τοῦ λόγου οὐκ ἐξαρκεῖν Id.*Phd*. 108d; ἐ. εἴς τι Lys.19.55, 30.20; πρός τι Pl.*R*.526d, X.*Mem*.4.1.5: c. inf., μία μεσότης ἂν ἐξήρκει.. συνδεῖν Pl.*Ti*.32a: abs., *suffice*, μέτρια δ' ἐξαρκεῖν ἔφη E.*Supp*.866, cf. And.4.15; βραχὺς.. ἐξήρκει λόγος D. 18.196. 2. impers., ἐξαρκεῖ *it is enough for, suffices for*, c. dat. pers., Pl.*Prt*.336c, al.: with inf. added, ἐ. ἡμῖν ἡσυχίην ἄγειν Hdt.7.161; ἐ. σώματι εἶναι σώματι Pl.*R*.341e; also ἐξαρκέσει σοι τύραννον γενέσθαι Id.*Alc*.2.141a; ἐξαρκέσει εἰπεῖν D.27.12; οὐκ ἐξαρκεῖ περὶ τούτου μόνον αὐτῷ ψεύσασθαι Lys.3.25, cf. Isoc.19.47: c. dat. pers. et part., ταῦτα ἔχουσιν οὐκ ἐξήρκεσεν αὐτοῖς D.47.52: abs., οὐκ ἂν ἐξαρκέσειεν Id.21. 129; ἐξαρκεῖ *enough!* Pl.*Grg*.503a, *Hp.Ma*.302b; ὡς ἐξαρκέσαν, εἰ.. Is.6.13. II. of the subject, *to be satisfied* or *content with*, κτεάτεσσι Pi.*O*.5.24; ἐ. διαίτῃ *to be strong enough* for it, Hp.*Aph*.1.9; πᾶσιν ἐ. *to be a match* for all, E.*Supp*.574: abs., ἐξαρκέσας ἦν Ζεύς Zeus was *strong enough*, ib.511: c. part., τὸν νοῦν διδάσκαλον ἔχουσα ἐξήρκουν ἐμοί I *contented myself, was satisfied* with having, Id.*Tr*.653, cf. Ar.*Eq*.524; πῶς ἂν.. ἐξαρκέσειε.. ἐκτίνων; how *could* he pay *enough?* X.*Hier*.7.12:—Pass., οὐκ ἐξηρκεῖτο φυγαδεύειν dub.l. in Plb. 13.6.6. III. *assist, succour*, φίλοις Pi.*N*.1.32: c. acc., ταῦτα ὁ φίλος πρὸ τοῦ φίλου ἐξήρκεσεν X.*Mem*.2.4.7. **-ής**, ές, *enough, sufficient*, πλοῦτος ἐ. δόμοις A.*Pers*.237 (troch.); τἄνδον ἐξαρκῆ τιθέναι put *in order*, S.*Tr*.334. **-ούντως**, Adv. pres. part. of ἐξαρκέω, *enough, sufficiently*, Ar.*Ra*.377 Isoc.12.8; -ως ἔχει is *content with*.., Pl.*Grg*.493c.

ἔξαρμα, ατος, τό, (ἐξαίρω) *rising, swelling*, Hp.*Epid*.4.31; of the *tragus* of the ear, Ruf.*Onom*.44. II. *meridian height* or *elevation* of the heavenly bodies, τοῦ ἡλίου Str.2.1.18, cf. 1.1.21; τοῦ πόλου Hipparch.1.3.6, Gem.6.24, Plu.*Mar*.11, Ptol.*Alm*.2.3,6, *Tetr*.76; opp. ἀντέξαρμα, *Theol.Ar*.25; τοῦ ἐξάρματος ὃ ἐξῆρται Plu.2.410f.

ἐξαρμόζω, in Pass., *to be displaced, wrenched out*, τὰ πλευρὰ ἐξηρμοσμένα τῶν σπονδύλων Philostr.*Her*.1.3; ἐξηρμοσμέναι πέτραι Id.*Im*. 2.17; ἐξήρμοσται τὰς κνήμας ib.4.

ἐξαρμόνιος, ον, *out of harmony, discordant*, καμπαί Pherecr.145.9, cf. ib.26.

ἔξαρμος, ον, *with dislocated limbs*, v.l. in Lyd.*Mag*.3.57.

ἐξαρν-έομαι, aor. 1 ἐξηρνησάμην Hdt.3.74, Att. ἐξηρνήθην Pl.*Smp*. 192e, *Lg*.949a, Cret. aor. subj. ἐξαννήσεται *Leg.Gort*.3.6:—*deny utterly*, τὸν φόνον Hdt. l. c.; οὔ τοι τοῦτό γ' ἐξαρνήσομαι E.*Hel*.579, etc.; ἤν τις ὀφείλων ἐξαρνῆται *should deny a debt*, Ar.*Ec*.660; μὴ λαβεῖν ἐξαρνούμενος D.27.16; οὐκ ἐ. πράττειν Aeschin.3.250. **-ησις**, εως, ἡ, *denial*, Pl.*R*.531b. **-ητικός**, ή, όν, *apt at denying*, Ar.*Nu*. 1172. **-ος**, ον, *denying*: ἔ. εἰμι or γίγνομαι, = ἐξαρνέομαι, abs., Ar. *Nu*.1230, Antipho 5.51, And.1.12, etc.; οὐ πώποτε ἔ. ἐγενόμην Pl. *Hp.Mi*.372c; ἔ. γίγνεσθαι περί τινος D.23.176; ὑπέρ τινος D.H.7.34; also ἔ. εἶναί τι Lys.3.27, cf. Pl.*Chrm*.158c; ἔ. ἦν τοῦ φόνου J.*AJ*14. 11.4: freq. folld. by μή c. inf., ἔ. ἦν μὴ.. ἀποκτεῖναι Σμέρδιν Hdt.3.67, cf. Ar.*Pl*.241; ἔ. γεγονέναι τὸ παράπαν μηδ' εἶναι ψεῦδος Pl.*Sph*.260d; τὸ καλὸν μὴ καλὸν εἶναι Id.*Hp.Ma*.288c; by μὴ οὐ.., Luc.*DMort*.14.1; also ἔ. ἦ μὴν οὐκ ἐγερεῖσθαι τὸ τεῖχος Polyaen.1.30.5; ἔ. ἐγένετο ὡς οὐ.. D.34.49.

ἐξάρνυμαι, v. ἐξαίρω II. 1.

ἐξαροτριάω, *plough up*, Gloss.

ἐξαρπάζω, fut. -άσομαι Ar.*Eq*.708: aor. 1 ἐξήρπαξα Hom. (v. infr.), ἐξήρπασα Hdt.8.135, Plu.*Comp.Per.Fab*.2:—*snatch away from*, φῶτ' ἐξαρπάξασα νεός Od.12.100; ἐ. τι παρά τινος Hdt. l. c.; τι ἐκ χερῶν τινος E.*IA*315; *rescue*, τὸν δ' ἐξήρπαξ' Ἀφροδίτη Il.3.380, cf. 20.443, 21.597; τῆς πολιορκίας Μάριον Plu.*Sull*.29:—Pass., *to be carried off*, οἱ μὲν ἐξηρπασμένοι σπεύδουσιν *the captured ones* are speeding on their way, S.*OC*1016 (s. v. l.): c. acc., ἐξαρπάζεσθαι τὸ νοτερόν *to have* the moisture *forcibly drawn out*, Pl.*Ti*.60d. II. *tear out*, ἐ. σου.. τἄντερα Ar.*Eq*.708; *tear off*, Asclep.ap.Gal.12.418.

ἔξαρσις, εως, ἡ, (ἐξαίρω) *removal*, κακῶν ἁπάντων Ἀρχ.'Εφ.1919.52 (Pharsalus, v/iv B. C.); *destruction*, Lxx *Je*.12.17. II. (from Pass.) *setting out*, ib.*Nu*.10.6. 2. *rising, height* of water in a vessel, Cleom.1.1.

ἐξαρτ-άω, *hang upon*, τι ἔκ τινος Plb.18.18.4; ἀπό τινος Arr.*An*. 2.19.2; τί τινος Longus 1.32: metaph., *make dependent upon*, ἐπαίνων ἐ. τὴν δόξαν Plu.*Arat*.1; πρᾶξιν τῆς προδοσίας Id.*Fab*.22; τὴν ποίησιν μέθης Ath.10.429b, cf. Plot.6.7.42:—Med., E.*Tr*.129, cf. Gal.*Anim.Pass*.1.9 (prob. l.). 2. *stretch out*, Ael.*NA*4.21. II. Pass., mostly in pf. ἐξηρτῆσθαι: fut. Med. in pass. sense, ἐξαρτήσομαι X.*Cyr*.5.4.20:—*to be hung upon, hang upon*, χειρός E.*Hipp*. 325; περὶ σὸν γένειον Id.*IA*1226: abs., Ar.*Pax*470; *to be attached to*.., ἔκ τινος Arist.*HA*495ᵇ33; ἐ. τινί ib.496ᵃ26. 2. *depend upon, be attached to*, σοῦ γὰρ ἐξηρτήμεθα E.*Supp*.735, etc.; τῆς ἰσχύος X. *Cyr*.5.4.20; ἑνός Plu.*Galb*.8; ἔκ τινος Pl.*Ion* 536a, *Lg*.732e, etc.; τῶν ἐλπίδων Isoc.8.7. 3. of countries, *be adjacent to*, πεδία τῶν λόφων ἐ. Plu.*Ant*.46. 4. abs., *to be elevated*, ἐξήρτηται τὸ χωρίον Th.6.96; ἐξήρτηται ἡ χώρα πρὸς Νότον (Casaub. ἐξῆρται) Str.7.1.3. 5. *hang upon oneself*, πήραν ἐξαρτήσασθαι Luc.*Fug*.15 (s. v. l.): esp. in pf. part. Pass., c. acc. rei, *having* a thing *hung on one*, ἐπιστολὰς.. ἐξηρτημένος ἐκ τῶν δακτύλων Aeschin.3.164; παιδίον ἐξηρτημένη τοῦ τραχήλου Plu. *Brut*.31: hence, *equipped* or *furnished with*, πώγωνας ἐξηρτῆσθαι Ar. *Ec*.494; τοιοῦτον ἐξηρτῆσθαι στρατόπεδον D.9.49. **-ηδόν** (ἐξαρτιδῶν cod.)· μετὰ τοῦ ἐκκρεμάσθαι, Hsch. **-ημα**, ατος, τό, *that which is suspended from*, τῶν νεῶν Sch.Ar.*Eq*.759; *weight*, Theo Sm.p.65 H., Iamb.*VP*26.117, Nicom.*Harm*.6; of the ligaments of the uterus, Sor.2.84. II. *that which is attached* or *dependent*, Dam.*Pr*.130 (pl.). **-ησις**, εως, ἡ, *attachment of parts* of the body *one to another*, νεύρων Hp.*Fract*.37; ἡ τῶν ἐμβρύων ἐ. Arist.*HA*511ᵃ33; τὴν ἐ. ἔχειν ἔκ τινος ib.519ᵇ9; τινί ib.497ᵃ19. II. *suspension* of a weight, μολύβδου Sor.1.72. **-ία**, ἡ, *equipment*, *PFlor*.241.6 (iii A. D.), etc.: pl., σὺν πάσαις ἐ. ib.285.13 (vi A. D.). **-ίζω**, *complete, finish*, τὰς ἡμέρας *Act.Ap*.21.5; *finish* a building, *IG*12(2).538 (Mytilene); [βιβλία] *POxy*.296.7 (i A. D.):—Pass., πόδες (sc. τραπέζης) ἕως τῶν κάτω τελέως -ισμένοι J.*AJ*3.6.6. II. *equip and dispatch*, σκάφας εἰς.. *Peripl.M.Rubr*.33:—Pass., πλοῖα, γένη, ib.19, 14; simply, *equip*, ναῦς -ισμένας D.S.19.77; *furnish, supply*, Wilcken*Chr*.176.10 (i A. D.):—Pass., ἐξηρτισμένον ἅπασι *completely furnished*, *PAmh*.2.93.8 (ii A. D.); πρὸς πᾶν ἔργον ἀγαθὸν ἐξηρτισμένος 2*Ep.Ti*.3.17: c. acc., *provide oneself with*, τὰ ἄλλα ἐξήρτιστο Luc.*VH*1.33. **-ιος**, ον, *for suspension*, σχοινία *Et.Gud*. II. Subst. ἐξάρτιον, τό, = ἐξαρτία, *PLond*.3.994. 12 (vi A. D.). **-ιόω**, = ἐξαρτύω, πτέ]ρυγη.. σ]φην[ίσκ]οις ἐξηρτίωται Herod.7.23. **-ισις**, εως, ἡ, of an engine, *preparation* for discharge, '*gun-laying*', Ph.*Bel*.56.45, 57.40 (-ῦσις codd. in both passages), Hero *Bel*.74.2 (-ήσεως v.l.). **-ισμός**, ὁ, *equipment* of a ship, *Peripl.M.Rubr*.21 (pl.): pl., *fittings*, *PRyl*.233.13 (ii A. D.): metaph., τρόπων Aristeas 144. **-ιστήριον**, τό, *place of equipment*, *Gloss*. **-ῦσις**, εως, ἡ, *equipment*, esp. of *musical arrangement*, Callicrat.ap.Stob.4.28.16, Eurypham.ib.39.27; of the soul, Iamb. *VP*15.64 (pl.), 25.114. **-ύω** [ῡ], *get ready*, τἄνδον ἐξάρτυε E.*El*. 422; *equip thoroughly, fit out*, ἐπίπλουν Th.2.17:—more freq. in Med., *get ready for oneself, fit out*, ναυτικόν Id.1.13, al.; τὰ ἡμέτερα ib.82; φόνον γε μητρὸς ἐξαρτύσομαι *will set about it*, E.*El*.647: c. inf., οἷον ἐξαρτύεται γάμον γαμεῖν A.*Pr*.908:—Pass., *to be got ready*, πάντα σφι ἐξήρτυτο ἐς τὴν κάτοδον Hdt.1.61; πόλεμος ἐξαρτύεται *is preparing*, E.*Heracl*.419: esp. in pf. part. Pass., *equipped, harnessed*, Id.*Hipp*. 1186: c. dat. rei, *furnished* or *provided with*, ἐξηρτυμένος νεηνίῃσι καὶ κυσί Hdt.1.43; ὕδατι καὶ σιτίοισι εὖ ἐ. Id.2.32; τόξοισιν ἐξηρτυμένοι (ἐξηρτημένοι cod. Med.) A.*Pr.*711; ναυτικὰ πλοίοις μακροῖς ἐ. Th.1.14; τοῖς ἄλλοις ἅπασιν ἄριστα ἐ. ib.80; καὶ ναυσὶ καὶ πεζῷ ἅμα ἐξαρτυθεὶς Id.6.31; τὰ πρὸς τὴν χρείαν D.S.20.4. II. Med., *train musically*, Plu.2.973d. III. ἐξαρτύειν· παιδεραστεῖν, Hsch.

ἐξάρῠσις, εως, ἡ, = ἀπάντλησις, Gal.19.98.

ἐξᾰρύω [ῠ], *draw* or *drain off*, Hp.*Fract.*48 (vulg.), Plu.2.637f:— ἐξαρ(υ)όμεναι· ἐξ ἀγκῶνος φλεβοτομούμεναι, Hsch. (ἐξαρώμεναι cod.).

ἐξαρχῆς, Adv., more correctly ἐξ ἀρχῆς, *from the beginning*, v. ἀρχή.

ἐξαρχ-ίδιος, ον, = ἐξ ἀρχῆς γενόμενος, ἐπιτροπά *SIG*712.3 (Delos, ii B.C.), dub. in *CIG*5235, Ps.-Philol.21. **-ος**, ὁ, ἡ, (ἄρχω) *leader, beginner*, c. gen., ἀοιδοὶ θρήνων ἔξαρχοι Il.24.721. 2. *leader of a chorus*, D.18.260: generally, *leader, chief*, τῶν ἱερέων (= *pontifex maximus*) Plu.*Num.*10; τῆς ἀποστάσεως, τῆς στάσεως, Polyaen.4.6.6 (pl.), 2.1.14(pl.): *military commander*, Ael.*Tact.*9.2, Arr.*Tact.*10.1: ἐ. Παλμυρηνῶν, title of Odaenathus, *OGI*643; Συβαριτῶν Iamb.*VP* 17.74: metaph., δικαιοσύνην τὴν ἐ. καὶ ἡγεμονίδα τῶν ἀρετῶν Ph.1.347. **-ω**, *begin, take the lead in, initiate*, c. gen., Θέτις δ' ἐξῆρχε γόοιο Il.18.51; μολπῆς ἐξάρχοντες Od.4.19, Il.18.606; ἐξῆρχον ἀοιδῆς Μοῦσαι Hes.*Sc.*205; ἐξάρχετε φωνᾷ (sc. τῆς μολπῆς) Pi.*N.*2.25; πτολέμω Corinn.26; ἐ. πετροβολίας X.*An.*6.6.15; παιᾶνος Plu.*Lyc.*22; δόγματος Id.*Galb.*8, etc.:—Med., κακῆς ἐξάρχετο βουλῆς Od.12.339. 2. c. acc., βουλὰς ἐξάρχων ἀγαθάς Il.2.273; χορούς *h.Hom.*27.18; ἐ. παιήονα Archil.76; ᾠδάν Theoc.8.62; παιᾶνα X.*Cyr.*3.3.58 (so in Med., 4.1.6):—Med., ἐξάρχου κανᾶ (cf. ἐνάρχομαι) E.*IA*435: c. dupl. acc., εἰ δέ μ' ὧδ' ἀεὶ λόγους (v.l. λόγοις) ἐξῆρχες S.*El.*557; μολπὰν.. οἵαν ἐξῆρχον θεούς E.*Tr.*152 (lyr.). 3. *teach*, οἱ λόγων ἁπτόμενοι ἀσεβῶν ἄλλοις τε ἐξάρχοντες Pl.*Lg.*891d; ἐ. ὅρκον *dictate*.., E.*IT*743: also, = διδάσκω III, οἱ -οντες τὸν διθύραμβον Arist.*Po.*1449ᵃ11. 4. *hold office*, Polem.*Cyn.*18; *rule*, c. gen., Eustr.*in EN*2.32. 5. c. part., ἐξάρχεσθαι ἀεθλεύων A.R.1.362. **-ων**, οντος, ὁ, *ruler, president*, τῶν Ἑβραίων Müller-Bees *Inschriften der jüdischen Katakombe am Monteverde* No.14 (ii/iii A.D.).

ἐξᾶς, ᾶντος, ὁ, a coin, Lat. *sextans*, as adopted by the Sicil. Greeks, Arist.*Fr.*510, cf. Hsch.; cf. ἑξάντιον.

ἑξάς, άδος, ἡ, (ἕξ) *the number six*, Ph.1.3, Luc.*Sat.*4, Plu.*Lyc.*5, etc.: pl., ἑξάδες ἄρτων, υἱῶν, Ph.2.239,418.

ἐξασελλάνωμεν· ἀναπληρώσωμεν, Hsch.

ἑξάσημος [ᾰ], ον, *of six times*, συζυγία Heph.14.1; ῥυθμοί Aristid. Quint.1.14.

ἐξασθεν-έω, *to be utterly weak*, Hp.*Morb.*4.43, Arist.*MM*1203ᵇ11; of plants, *to be exhausted*, Thphr.*CP*5.9.11: metaph., τοῖς λογισμοῖς Agatharch.*Fr.Hist.*20(a) J., cf. D.S.20.78; *to be in financial straits*, *PTeb.*50.33 (ii B.C.), etc.: c. inf., *to be too weak to*.., ὁσάκις ἂν ὁ λόγος -ήσῃ ἐναργῶς παραστῆσαι Ael.*Tact.*1.5. **-ής**, ές, *financially weak*, *PMasp.*151.12 (vi A.D.).

ἐξασθμαίνω, *exhale, pant*, *Gloss.*

ἑξασκελής, ές, *six-tailed*, of a bandage, Heliod.ap.Orib.48.22 tit., Gal.18(1).774, Paul.Aeg.6.60.

ἐξασκ-έω, *adorn, deck out, equip*, ἐσθῆτί τινα S.*OC*1603: c. dupl. acc., ἀγώ νιν ἐξήσκησα *in* which.., E.*Hel.*1383 codd.; πλόκαμον ἐ. κόμης *arrange* or *dress* it, Id.*El.*1071:—Pass., *to be adorned* or *furnished with*, ὀργάνοισιν ἐξησκημένος Id.*Rh.*922; φυτοῖσιν Lyc.858; παισίν Luc.*Am.*10: abs., [ἡ χώρα] ὑπὸ τῶν Ἀθηναίων ἐξήσκητο καὶ διεπεπόνητο *Hell.Oxy.*12.5; πώλους.. ἐξησκημένας *decked out, ready*, Eub.84; μνῆμα εἰς κάλλος ἐξησκημένον beautifully *wrought*, Luc.*DMort.*24.1. II. *train thoroughly*, τινά Pl.*Clit.*407b; τὸ ναυτικόν D.C.48.49:—Pass., *to be trained* or *practised in*, τι X.*Eq.Mag.*2.1; περί τι ὑπό τινος Plu.*Nic.*5. 2. *practise*, ἕξιν Id.*Per.*4; τέχνην Them.*Or.*18.217c. **-ητέον**, *one must practise*, σωφροσύνην Nicostr.ap.Stob.4.23.65.

ἑξασσός, ή, όν, *in six copies*, *POxy.*908.38 (ii A.D.), *PStrassb.*29.46; cf. δισσός, τρισσός, τετρασσός.

ἑξαστάδιος [στᾰ], ον, *of six stades*, χῶμα Str.5.3.7.

ἑξάστερον, τό, *the six stars*, i.e. the Pleiades, Sch.Hes.*Op.*383, Eust.870.26.

ἔξαστις, ιος, ἡ, *selvage* of linen or cloth, Hp.*Off.*11, Heliod.ap. Orib.46.19.2 (pl.): **ἔξεστις** in Gal.18(2).791. II. *fringe*, Michel 832.15 (Samos, iv B.C.).

ἑξά-στῐχος, ον, *of six lines*, σχῆμα Sch.D.T.p.191 H. **-στοιχος** κριθή barley *with six rows of grain on the ear*, Thphr.*HP*8.4.2: **-στῐχος** in Colum.2.9.14.

ἐξαστράπτω, *flash as with lightning*, Lxx *Na.*3.3, *Ev.Luc.*9.29; of the sun's light, Zos.Alch.p.111 B.; φόβῳ καὶ κάλλει Tryph.103.

ἑξά-στῡλος, ον, *with six columns in front*, of temples, Vitr.3.3.7. **-σύλλᾰβος**, ον, *of six syllables*, πόδες Aristid.Quint.1.22; χορίαμβος Sch.Ar.*Av.*738.

ἐξασφᾰλίζω, *make secure*, Cic.*Att.*6.4.3, Archig.ap.Aët.6.50, Gal.14.298: more freq. in Med., τὰ καθ' αὑτόν Phld.*Rh.*2.141 S.; τὸν τόπον Str.17.1.54; τὰ κύκλου σάνισιν *Ath.Mitt.*32.259 (Pergam.); *secure the allegiance of* persons, ὅρκοις τινάς J.*BJ*2.8.7.

ἐξατῑμ-άζω, *dishonour utterly*, S.*OC*1378, v.l. in Lxx 1*Ki.*17.42:— also **-ατιμάω** (s.v.l.) Phld.*Rh.*2.174S. **-όομαι**, Pass., *to be utterly dishonoured*, Lxx *Ez.*16.61.

ἐξατμ-ιάω, = sq., Hp.*Morb.*4.49:—also **-ιδόω**, ibid., Olymp. *in Phd.*p.240 N. **-ίζω**, *turn into vapour, draw up as vapour*, ἐκ τῆς γῆς τὸ ὑγρόν Arist.*Mete.*347ᵇ27, cf. 355ᵃ18, Aret.*SD*1.16:—Pass., *evaporate*, Arist.*Mete.*388ᵃ29, Ph.2.508, Gal.6.536. II. intr. in Act., = Pass., Arist.*Mete.*383ᵃ16, al., *GA*782ᵃ29. **-ισμός**, ὁ, *evaporation*, Epicur.*Nat.Herc.*908.6.

ἑξατον-έω, *to be tired out*, Arist.*HA*630ᵇ8; *to be weakened*, ἐκ νηστείας Ph.2.672. **-ίζομαι**, *become relaxed*, Sor.1.46.

ἑξάτονος [ᾰ], ον, *in* or *of six tones*, Plu.2.1028e, Aristid.Quint.1.9, Alex.Eph.ap.Theon.Sm.p.141 H.

ἐξατράπης, v. σατράπης. ***ἐξαττάομαι**, v. ἐξηττημένη.

ἐξαττῐκίζω, *express in Attic form, Atticize*, Phryn.*PS*p.19 B.

ἐξάττω, Att. for ἐξαΐσσω.

ἐξαυ-άζω, (αὖος), = sq., Thphr.*Fr.*172.2. **-αίνω**, *dry up*, ὁ νότος..τὰ ἔλυτρα τῶν ὑδάτων ἐξηύηνε (aor. 1) Hdt.4.173:—Pass., τὰ δένδρεα..ἐξαυάνθη ib.151, cf. Hp.*Carn.*11, Ar.*Fr.*612, Arist.*GA* 750ᵃ22, Hsch. s.v. ἐξευασμένου.

ἑξαυγ-ής, ές, (αὐγή) *dazzling white*, in Comp., χιόνος E.*Rh.*304. **-ος**, ον, *not ὕπαυγος*, i.e. more than fifteen degrees from the sun, Olymp. *in Mete.*56.2, Porph.ap.Heph.Astr.2.18, Steph. *in Hp.*2.363 D.

ἐξαυδάω, *speak out*, ἐξαύδα, μὴ κεῦθε νόῳ Il.1.363; τόδ' ἐξαύδασ' ἔπος Pi.*N.*10.80, cf. S.*Fr.*210.71; οὐδὲν ἐξαυδᾷς σοφόν Id.*Ph.*1244:— Med., A.*Ch.*151, 272. (Com. only paratrag., Ar.*Ach.*1183.)

ἐξαυθᾱδίζομαι, strengthd. for αὐθαδίζομαι, J.*AJ*15.10.4.

ἐξαῦθις, Adv., v. ἐξαῦτις.

ἐξαυλᾰκίζω, *pour forth*, πλοῦτον Lyd.*Mag.*2.8; ἑστίαν ib.3.65.

ἐξαυλέω, *pipe away, wear out*, of the mouthpieces of clarionets, Poll.4.67.

ἐξαυλίζομαι, *leave one's quarters*, ἐ. εἰς κώμας *go out of camp* into villages, X.*An.*7.8.21; -ισάμενοι ἀνεμένομεν v.l. in Luc.*VH*1.37.

ἔξαυλος, ον, *piped away, worn out*, of a flute, Poll.4.73.

ἐξαύξω, *increase*, Thphr.*CP*1.22.1:—Pass., *grow too fast*, Id.*HP* 6.6.6.

ἔξαυος, ον, *dry, parched, thirsty*, Alc.*Supp.*4.11 (dub. l.).

ἐξαυσ-τήρ, ῆρος, ὁ, *flesh-hook for taking meat out of a pot*, A.*Fr.* 2, Poll.6.88, *EM*346.56, Hsch.; [ἐξ]αυστήρ *IG*2.818.27; ἐξ[αυστήρ] ib.689. **-τριον**, τό, Dim. of foreg., ib.11(2).161 *C*70 (Delos, iii B.C.).

ἐξαυτῆς, Adv., for ἐξ αὐτῆς [τῆς ὁδοῦ], *at once*, Thgn.231, Cratin. 34, Aen.Tact.22.29, Arat.641, Plb.2.7.7, *Ev.Marc.*6.25, *POxy.*64.3 (iii/iv A.D.), etc.

ἐξαῦτις, Ep. Adv. *once more, anew*, Il.1.223, etc., Archil.6, *PLips.* 27.25 (ii A.D.). II. of place, *back again, backwards*, Il.16.654, A.R.3.482. III. = ἔπειτα, Rhian.25.

ἐξαυτομολέω, *desert from* a place, πρός τινα Ar.*Nu.*1104. II. Pass., *to be betrayed by deserters*, τὸ σύνθημα Aen.Tact.24.16.

ἐξαυχενισμός, ὁ, *rebellion*, Aq.*Na.*3.1.

ἐξαυχέω, *boast loudly, profess*, c. part., ἐξηύχει λαβών A.*Ag.*872 codd.: c. inf. fut., S.*Ant.*390; c. inf. pres., E.*Supp.*504: c. acc. rei, τοῦτ' ἂν ἐξηύχησ' ἐγώ S.*Ph.*869.

ἐξαυχμέω or **-άω**, *suffer from drought*, ὅταν -ῶσι Thphr.*CP*5.9.8. II. **ἐξαυχμόω**, in Pass., *to be dried up*, ἐξαυχμοῦται D.L.7.141.

ἐξαύω (A), *take out*, esp. *dressed meat* (cf. ἐξαυστήρ), τὸν ἐγκέφαλον..ἐξαύσας καταπίνει Pl.Com.38, cf. Hsch. ἐξαῦσαι· ἐξελεῖν.

ἐξαύω (B), *heat*, aor. 1 Med., ἐξαύσατο βαυνόν Eratosth.24.

ἐξαύω (C), *cry out*, ἐκ δ' ηὖσ' ἐγώ S.*Tr.*565.

ἐξαφάζων· ἐξ ἑαυτοῦ γιγνόμενος, καὶ περιβλέπων, Hsch.

ἐξαφαιρέω, *take away*:—Med., εἰσόκε πασέων ψυχὰς ἐξαφέλησθε Od.22.444, cf. S.*El.*1157; ἐ. φρενῶν τὸν νοῦν τὸν ἐσθλόν *Trag.Adesp.*296; f.l. in D.8.42.

ἐξαφᾰνίζω, *destroy utterly*, παίδων ἀγόνων γόνον ἐ. Eub.107.11; γένος J.*AJ*3.15.1; τι τῆς μνήμης ἐκκάθαιρε καὶ ἐ. Iamb.*Protr.*21.κθ':—Pass., *disappear utterly*, Pl.*Plt.*270e, Sor.1.34.

ἑξάφαρμᾰκον, τό, *remedy containing six ingredients*, Orib.*Fr.*89.

ἐξαφεδρόομαι, Pass., *to be excreted*, νοστίμου αἵματος -ουμένου dub. in Herm.ap.Stob.1.42.7 codd.; v. ἐξαφρόομαι.

ἐξᾰφή, ἡ, *contact*, *Gloss.*

ἐξαφ-ίημι, *send forth, discharge*, [παλτόν] X.*Eq.*12.12; *dispatch*, γροσφομάχους Plb.10.39.1; *let go* an elastic board, Aët.6.87. II. *set free from*, ἐξαφεῖται τοῦδε (sc. τοῦ πονεῖν) S.*Tr.*72, cf. J.*AJ*18.1.1; *set free*, ἐ. σῶον Lxx 2*Ma.*12.24; *let loose*, ἀγέλας εἰς καρπούς *PLips.* 35.8 (iv A.D.):—Pass., *to be allowed to escape*, J.*BJ*4.6.3. III. *squander*, πλοῦτον S.*Ichn.*156. **-ινα**, = ἐξαίφνης, Bell *Jews and Christians in Egypt*, No.1914.3 (iv A.D.). **-ίστημι**, *remove*, αἱ ἁμαρτίαι..ἐξαπέστησαν τὰ ἀγαθὰ ἀφ' ὑμῶν v.l. in Lxx *Je.*5.25. 2. *dispatch*, ἐφ' οὓς καθήκει *BGU*1253.16 (ii B.C.). II. Pass., with aor. 2, pf., and plpf. Act., *depart* or *withdraw from*, τινός S.*OC*561, E.*IA*479; *grow out of*, ἡλικίας *PLond.*5.1708.263 (vi A.D.).

ἐξαφολέκτης, sine expl., Hsch. **ἐξαφορήσωσιν**· εὐπορίσωσιν, Id.

ἑξάφορον [ᾰ], τό, at Rome, *litter borne by six men*, Mart.2.81.1. II. **ἑξάφοροι**, οἱ, *bearers of such a litter*, Vitr.10.3.7.

ἐξαφρ-ίζω, *remove the froth* by boiling, τὸ ἐξηφρισμένον [μέλι] *despumated*, Dsc.2.82.3:—Med., metaph. from a horse, αἱματηρὸν ἐξαφρίζεσθαι μένος *exhaust by foaming*, A.*Ag.*1067. **-όομαι**, Pass., *turn into foam*, cj. in Herm.ap.Stob.1.42.7 (-αφεδρ- codd.).

ἐξᾰφύω [ῠ], *draw forth*, οἶνον..ἐξαφύοντες Od.14.95: poet. aor., ἰὸν ἐξήφυσσεν ὀδόντων Opp.*H.*1.573: Ep. fut. 3 pl., ἐξαφύουσιν· ἐξαντλήσουσιν, Hsch.

ἑξά-χαλκος [ᾰ], ὁ, *coin of the value of six* χαλκοῖ, *IG*5(1).1433.29 (Messene). **-χειρ**, χειρος, ὁ, ἡ, *six-handed*, Luc.*Herm.*74, *Tox.*62:— also **-χειρος**, ον, Ps.-Callisth.3.28. **-χῆ**, Adv. *in six parts*, σχίσας Pl.*Ti.*36d; *in six ways*, κινεῖσθαι Ph.1.44:—also **ἕξαχα**, Hdn.Gr.1.496. **-χοίνῐκος**, ον, *containing six choenices*, Ar.*Fr.*640. **-χοος**, οον, contr. **-χους**, ουν, *holding six* χόες, Arist.*Ath.*67.2, Plu.*Sol.*

23. -χρονος, ον, *of six times*, [πούς] Heph.3.2, cf. Procl. *in Prm.* p.990 S.

ἐξᾰχῠρόω, *clear of husks*, Hsch. s. v. λεπυριῶσαι.

ἑξᾰχῶς, Adv. *in six ways*, Arist.*Top.*112ᵇ27, Gal.9.702.

ἔξαψις, εως, ἡ, *fastening*, TheoSm.p.72 H. (pl.), Iamb. *in Nic.*p.112 P. (pl.). II. *heating*, σιτίων ἔξαψιν ποιεῖν Hp.*Acut.*(*Sp.*)46 (v.l. ἐφ-). 2. *lighting, kindling*, Arist.*Mu.*395ᵇ3, Ph.2.256, Plot.3.6.15, Anthem.p.152 W.: pl., *Placit.*3.3.9: metaph., θερμασίης καὶ τόλμης Aret.*CA*2.11.

ἑξάωρος [ᾰ], ον, *of six* equinoctial *hours*, *Theol.Ar.*52; ἑξάωρον, τό, *period of six* such *hours*, Balbill.(?)in *Cat.Cod.Astr.*8(4).243.

ἕξ-γυον, said to be a town in Sicily with six streets (ἓξ ἀγυιαί), Eust.450.48. -δάκτῠλος, ον, *six digits long*, *IG*2.807 *a* 117; cf. ἑκ-, ἑγ-δάκτυλος.

ἐξεᾱγείς, v. ἐξάγνυμι.

ἐξεγγῠ-άω, *give up* a slave *on security* to be examined, Antipho 5.47; *free* one *by giving bail for* him, D.24.73:—Pass., *to be bailed*, ἐξεγγυηθέντες κριθῆναι And.1.44, cf. D.19.169; ἐφ' οἷς ἐξηγγυήθη [to fulfil the conditions] on which *security was given*, Lys.23.10. -η, ἡ, f.l. for ἐγγύη, Is.5.3. -ησις, εως, ἡ, *giving of bail* or *surety*, esp. to take one out of prison, -ησιν ποιεῖν D.24.77.

ἐξεγ-είρω, *awaken*, S.*OT*65, *Tr.*978:—Pass., *to be awaked*, ὑπαὶ κώνωπος A.*Ag.*892; *wake up*, Hdt.1.34, E.*Or.*1530: aor. 2 Med. ἐξηγρόμην Ar.*Ra.*51; Ep. 3 pl. ἐξέγροντο Theoc.24.21; 3 sg. ἐξέγρετο Hsch.; inf. ἐξεγρέσθαι Pl.*Smp.*223c; ἐξεγρόμενος ibid.: so also pf. Act. ἐξεγρήγορα Ar.*Av.*1413: 2 sg. aor. 2 Pass. ἐξέγρης· ἐξηγέρθης, Hsch. 2. *raise from the dead*, 1*Ep.Cor.*6.14:—Pass., A.*Ch.*495. 3. metaph., *awake, arouse*, εὕδοντα φόνον E.*El.*41; ἄνθρακα Ar.*Lys.*315; τὸν ἵππον X.*Eq.*11.12; πόλεμον D.S.14.44; ὁ ἄνεμος τὸ πῦρ ἐ. Arist.*Pr.*866ᵃ18. -ερσις, εως, ἡ, *awakening*, Plb.9.15.4 (pl.). 2. *waking up*, D.H.3.70, Plu.2.909d. -έρτης, ου, ὁ, *one who arouses*, *PMag.Leid.V.*7.13.

ἐξεγκᾰτίζω, *disembowel*, *Gloss.*

ἐξεγκεφᾰλίζω, *remove the brains*, *Gloss.*

ἐξεδᾰφισθέν, *desolatum*, *Gloss.*

ἐξέδοντα, τά, *erosion*, dub. in Gal.18(2).573.

ἐξεδούαζεν· ἐξήνεγκεν, Hsch. post ἐξεκοδόαξεν.

ἐξ-έδρα, ἡ, *hall* or *arcade furnished with recesses and seats*, in the gymnasia, E.*Or.*1449 (anap.), Men.*Kon.*10, *IPE*1².182 (Olbia), *IG* 12(3).1091 (Melos), *BGU*931.26 (i A.D.), etc.; in the schools of Philosophers, Phld.*Acad.Ind.*p.100 M., Str.17.1.8, Cic.*Fin.*5.2.4, Vitr.5.11.2; in a private house, Gal.14.18. 2. *bench, seat*, in front of a house, D.L.4.19; any *public bench*, Str.13.4.5, D.Chr.28.2; *belvedere*, Nic.Dam.*Fr.*1 J. 3. *parlour* or *saloon*, Lxx *Ez.*40.44, Cic. *de Orat.*3.5.17, *ND*1.6.15, Vitr.6.7.3, 7.3.4, *POxy.*912.13 (iii A.D.); *the hall in Pompey's theatre at Rome*, where the Senate met, Plu. *Brut.*14, 17. -έδριον, τό, Dim. of foreg., *IG*12(9).907.27 (Chalcis, iv A.D.), *GDI*5075.58 (Latos), Roussel *Cultes Égyptiens* 224 (Delos, ii B.C.), Cic.*Fam.*7.23.3. -εδροποιός, όν, *driving out of*, φρενῶν, gloss on ἔξεδροι φρενῶν, Sch.E.*Hipp.*934. -εδρος, ον, (ἕδρα) *away from home*, opp. ἔντοπος, S.*Ph.*212 (lyr.); πνεῦμα ἔ. γενόμενον ἐκ τῶν οἰκείων τόπων Arist.*Mu.*395ᵇ32: metaph., *strange, extravagant*, Id.*Rh.*1406ᵃ31. 2. c. gen., *out of, away from*, χθονὸς E.*IT*80: metaph., ἔξεδροι φρενῶν λόγοι insensate words, Id.*Hipp.*935. II. of birds of omen, ἔ. χώραν ἔχειν to be *out of a good* (i.e. *in an unlucky*) quarter, Ar.*Av.*275 (nisi leg. χρόαν cum Sch.); ἔ. ὄρνιθες D.C.37.25.

ἐξεζητημένως, Adv., (ἐκζητέω) *exquisitely, in a recherché manner*, *Gloss.*

ἐξεθίαζε· χορείας ἐπετέλει, and **ἐξεθιασθέν**· λαμπρυνθέν, Hsch.

ἐξεθ-ίζομαι, Pass., *to be habituated, accustomed*, c. inf., Ph.2.363, 391. -ισμός, ὁ, *change of habit*, Ath.Med.ap.Orib.*inc.*1.7.

ἐξεῖ· ἔξω (Lacon.), Hsch. **ἐξεῖα**· τὰ ἑξῆς, Id.

ἑξείδιον, τό, Dim. of ἕξις, *EM*347.54, *Et.Gud.*

ἐξείη· ἔξοδος, κέρδος, Hsch. (fort. ἐξεσίη et ⟨πλεον⟩εξίη).

ἐξεῖδον, inf. ἐξιδεῖν, aor. in use of pres. ἐξοράω:—*look out, see far*, μέγ' ἔξιδεν ὀφθαλμοῖσιν he *saw far, saw well*, Il.20.342: also aor. imper. Med. ἐξιδοῦ *see well to* it! S.*Ph.*851 (lyr.).

ἑξείης, Adv., poet. for ἑξῆς (q.v.).

ἐξεικάδιοι· οἱ ἐκτὸς⟨τῆς⟩ αὐτῆς εἰκάδος, καὶ τάγματος τοῦ αὐτοῦ, Hsch.

ἐξεικ-άζω, *make like, adapt*, αὐτὸν ταῖς τῶν φιλούντων ὑπουργίαις X.*Hier.*1.38:—Pass., ἐξείκαστό τινι *was like* it, Id.*Cyr.*1.6.39: mostly in pf. part., οὐδὲν ἐξῃκασμένα not *mere semblances*, but the things themselves, A.*Ag.*1244; κεραυνὸν οὐδὲν ἐξῃκασμένον.. θάλπεσιν τοῖς ἡλίου Id.*Th.*445; στέρνα τ' ἐξῃκασμένα *portrayed*, E.*Ph.*162; οὐ γὰρ ἐστιν ἐξῃκασμένος he is not *represented by a portrait-mask*, Ar.*Eq.*230. -ασμα, ατος, τό, *representation, copy*, dub.l. in Jul.*Or.*8.247d.

ἐξεικάττιοι, Thess., = ἑξακόσιοι, *Supp.Epigr.*2.264.4 (ii B.C.).

ἐξεικονίζω, *explain by a simile*, Plu.2.445c. II. Pass., *to be fully shapen* or *formed*, Lxx *Ex.*21.22 sq., Hsch. 2. *to be exactly like*, τῷ φύσαντι Aristaenet.1.19; μητρῴῳ γένει.. -ισθέν *formed in the image of*.., Ph.1.661.

ἐξειλεγμένως, Adv., (ἐκλέγω) *elegantly*, *Gloss.*

ἐξειλ-έω, *slip out* from its cover, ἢν ἐξειλήσῃς [βιβλίον] Luc.*Merc. Cond.*41; τὸ ψυχάριον ἀπὸ τοῦ σώματος ἐξειλεῖται the soul *slips out* of [its envelope], M.Ant.10.36. II. intr., *escape*, aor. ἐξείλησα *PAmh.*2.142.9 (iv A.D.), cf. *EM*348.12. -ησις, εως, ἡ, *release, escape* from, αὐχένων καὶ χειρῶν καὶ πλευρῶν, in wrestling, Pl.*Lg.*796a.

ἐξείλλω, = ἐξειλέω, *disentangle*, τὰ ἴχνη, of hounds at a check, X.*Cyn.*6.15. 2. *keep forcibly from, debar from*, ἐάν τις ἐξείλλῃ τινὰ τῆς ἐργασίας D.37.35, cf. Sol.*Oxy.*221 xiv 13; αἰ δέ χ' ὑπὸ πολέμω ἐγϝηληθίωντι (= ἐξειληθῶσι) *Tab.Heracl.*1.152. 3. *force* a stone *from* the urethra, prob. in Gal.19.659 (ἐξιλεῶσαι '*relieve the patient*', Kühn).—ἐξίλλω is a v.l.

ἐξειλύω, *unfold*:—Pass., ἐξειλυσθέντες ἐπὶ χθονὶ γαστέρας, of serpents *gliding* along the ground, Theoc.24.17.

ἔξειμι (A), (εἶμι *ibo*) Ep. 2 sg. ἔξεισθα (v. infr.); ἔξει wrongly expld. as imper. by Sch.Ar.*Nu.*633; Dor. 3 sg. ἔξειτι Hsch.; inf. ἐξιέναι, also ἐξίναι Macho ap.Ath.13.580c: serving as Att. fut. of ἐξέρχομαι, but with impf. ἐξῄειν, Ion. ἐξήϊα Hdt.2.139:—*go out, come out*, esp. out of the house, Hom. mostly in Od., ἔξεισθα θύραζε 20.179: c. gen. loci, ἐξιέναι μεγάρων 1.374; τῆς χώρας S.*OC*909; so ἐκ τῆς χώρης Hdt.1.94; but ἐ. ἐκ τῶν ἱππέων *leave* the knights, *quit service* as one, ib.67; ἐκ τῆς ἀρχῆς ἐ. D.C.60.10. 2. εἰς ἔλεγχον ἐξιέναι *come forth* to apply the test, S.*Ph.*98; but, *submit* to the test, Id.*Fr.*105; λόγων.. εἰς ἅμιλλαν ἐξιών E.*Fr.*334. 3. abs., ἔξει Ar.*Nu.*633; esp. *march out with an army*, Th.5.13, X.*Cyr.*3.3.20, etc.; οἱ ἐξιόντες Th.1.95: c. acc. cogn., ἐκδήμους στρατείας οὐκ ἐξῇσαν ib.15; πολλοὺς ἀγῶνας ἐ. S.*Tr.*159; ἐξόδους ἐ. *go out* in procession, D.48.55; ἐ. ὑστάτην ὁδόν E.*Alc.*610; ἐ. τὴν ἀμφίαλον (sc. ὁδόν) X.*HG*4.2.13; τὰς πύλας Ath.8.351d. 4. *come forward on the stage*, οὐξιὼν πρώτιστα Ar.*Ra.*946. II. of Time or incidents, *come to an end, expire*, Hdt.2.139; ὅταν περ τὸ κακὸν ἐξίῃ S.*Ph.*767; ἐξιούσης τῆς ἀρχῆς Lys.9.6; ὅποι ἔξεισι τὰ ἴχνη where they *cease*, X.*Cyn.*8.3.

ἔξειμι (B), (εἰμί *sum*), only used in impers. forms (v. ἔξεστι), exc. in αἰ ἐλεύθεροι μὴ ἐξεῖεν if [a woman] shall leave no free-born *issue*, *Leg.Gort.*7.9.

ἔξειον· ἐπιζήμιον τὸ καταδικάζειν τοῖς ἑκουσίοις, οἱ δὲ ἀπόλυσιν ἐγκλήματος, Hsch.

ἐξεῖπον, inf. ἐξειπεῖν, aor. 2 in use of ἐξαγορεύω; ἐξερῶ (q.v.) being the fut.: also aor. 1 ἐξεῖπας S.*El.*521:—*tell out, declare*, ἐξείπω καὶ πάντα διίξομαι Il.9.61; αὐτίκ' ἂν ἐξείποι Ἀγαμέμνονι 24.654, cf. Od.15.443; ἐ. ὅτι μοι παρορᾷς Ar.*Av.*454 (lyr.); ἀκριβείᾳ χαλεπὸν ἐ. Th.7.87. 2. c. dupl. acc., κακὰ ἐ. τινά *tell* evil *tales of* a person, D.21.79; τίν' ἀρχήν σ' ἐξείπω κακῶν; E.*El.*907; πολλὰ πρὸς πολλούς με δὴ ἐξεῖπας, ὡς.. S.*El.*521, cf. 984.

ἔξειρα· σκορπίος, ὁ ἰχθύς, Hsch.

ἐξειργασμένως, Adv. pf. part. Pass. of ἐξεργάζομαι, *carefully, accurately*, Plu.*Alex.*1.

ἐξείργω, Att. for ἐξέργω (q.v.).

ἔξειρξις, εως, ἡ, *exclusion, expulsion*, Eust.1769.35.

ἐξείρομαι, Ion. for ἐξέρομαι. **ἐξειρύω**, v. ἐξερύω.

ἐξείρω, *put forth*, τὴν χεῖρα Hdt.3.87; τὴν γλῶσσαν Hp.*Int.*7 codd.; τὸ κέντρον Ar.*V.*423. II. *pull out*, τὴν γλῶσσαν Id.*Eq.*378 (lyr.), Hermipp.Hist.43.

ἐξειρωνεύομαι, *turn into jest, ridicule*, τοὺς λόγους J.*AJ*15.3.6; τοῦτ' ἐκεῖνος -όμενος ἔφερεν ἐγκρατῶς ib.15.7.4.

ἔξεισθα, v. ἔξειμι (A). **ἐξεκᾰτέρωθεν**, Adv. *on either side*, Procl. *Par.Ptol.*188.

ἐξεκελέμησεν, sine expl., Hsch. **ἐξεκηρύωσας**· ἐξέστησας, Id. (fort. ἐξεκηρίωσας· ἐξέσμησας).

ἐξεκκλησιάζω, = ἐκκλησιάζω, Arist.*Oec.*1348ᵃ11.

ἐξεκοδόαξεν· ἐξέχεεν, Hsch.

ἐξελάαν, Ep. pres. inf. of ἐξελαύνω: **ἐξελᾶν**, Att. fut. inf.

ἐξελαιόω, *make into oil*, Thphr.*CP*6.8.1:—Pass., *become oily*, ib.6.7.4.

ἐξελ-ᾰσία, ἡ, *driving out* cattle, Plb.12.4.10. II. intr., *expedition*, Ps.-Hdt.*Vit.Hom.*9. -ᾰσις, εως, ἡ, *driving out, expulsion*, τῶν Πεισιστρατιδέων Hdt.5.76; τινὸς ἐκ τῆς νήσου Id.6.88. II. intr., *marching out, expedition*, βασιλέος ἐκ Θέρμης Id.7.183, cf. X.*Cyr.*8.3.1, etc.; *charge of cavalry*, Plu.*Art.*16 (pl.). -ᾰτέος, α, ον, *to be driven out*, Jul.*Ep.*89b. II. ἐξελατέον *one must expel*, Epicur.*Ep.*1 p.24 U.; ψεῦδος ψυχῆς Them.*Or.*21.259a. -αύνω, fut. -ελῶ Hdt.4.148, 5.63, *IG*1².39.4: pf. -ελήλακα:—Ep. pres. part. ἐξελάων Od.10.83; inf. ἐξελάαν Il.8.527, Od.11.292, Hes.*Th.*491 (v.l. -άειν): Arc. 1 sg. pres. opt. ἐξελαύνοια *IG*5(2).343.65 (iv B.C.):—*drive out*, ἄντρου ἐξήλασε μῆλα Od.9.312, cf. 227, 11.292: abs., *drive afield*, of a shepherd, 10.83. 2. esp. *drive out, expel from* a place, μήτι.. ἡμέας ἐξελάσωσιν γαίης ἡμετέρης 16.381; ἐξήλασέν με κἀπέκλῃσε δωμάτων A.*Pr.*670; πάτρας, χθονός, S.*OC*376, 823; γῆς ἐκ πατρῴας ἐξελήλαμαι ib.1292; ἐκ τῆς πατρίδος Hdt.5.91; ἐκ τῆς οἰκίας Ar.*Nu.*123; ἐκ τῶν πόλεων Pl.*Grg.*466d; Τιτῆνας ἀπ' οὐρανοῦ Hes.*Th.*820; τὸ βάρβαρον ἐκ τῆς θαλάττης Pl.*Mx.*241d; ἐξεληλαμένος τῆς βουλῆς Plu.*Cic.*17; ἐ. τινά *banish*, Hdt.1.60, Ar.*Ach.*717, Pl.*Ap.*30d:—Med., Th.4.35, 7.5. 3. *drive out* horses, etc., ἵππους ἐξέλασε Τρώων *out of* the ranks of the Trojans, Il.5.324, cf. 10.499; ἁρμάτων ὄχους E.*Ph.*1190:—Med., *drive out one's* horses, ἵππους ἐξελάασθαι ὑφ' ἅρματι Theoc.24.119 (but, *drive off* captured cattle, Plb.4.75.7); ἐ. στρατόν, στρατιήν, *lead out* an army, Hdt.1.76, 7.38; ἐ. νῆα ὅρμου A.R.1.987; *lead out* a procession, ἐ. τὸν Ἴακχον Plu.*Alc.*34; θρίαμβον Id.*Marc.*22: hence, b. freq. with the acc. omitted, as if intr., ἐς δίφρον ὀρούσας ἐξέλασ' ἐς πληθὺν he *drove out*, Il.11.360, etc.; *ride out*, Th.7.27, X.*Cyr.*1.3.3, etc.; ἐ. ἐκ τῶν ἄλλων ἱππέων Lys.20.28; *march out*, Hdt.4.80, 8.113, etc.; *go out*, X.*Cyr.*8.3.1. 4. *expel, banish, get rid of* a thing, τῶν ὀμμάτων τὸ αἰδούμενον Plu.2.654d; by washing, κόνιν λαγόνων Call.*Lav.Pall.*6. 5. metaph., *reject*, Jul.*Caes.*306c. II. *knock out*, χαμαὶ δέ κε πάντας ὀδόντας γναθμῶν ἐξελάσαιμι Od.18.29. III. *beat out* metals, ἐ. ἡμιπλίνθια ἐκ χρυσοῦ Hdt.1.50; ἐθηεῖτο σίδηρον ἐξελαυνόμενον ib.68, cf. 7.84; κέντρον ἐπὶ λεπτὸν ἐξεληλασμένον Plb. 6.22.4.

ἐξελ-εγκτέος, α, ον, *to be refuted*, Pl.*Grg.*508a. **-έγχω**, strengthd. for ἐλέγχω, *convict, confute, refute*, Simon.75, S.*OT*297, *Ant.*399, Ar. *Nu.*1062; τοῖς ἔργοις τοὺς λόγους ἐ. Antipho 6.47; ἐν τῷ δήμῳ ἐ. [τινά] D.21.16:—Pass., ἐπ' αἰσχραῖς αἰτίαις ἐξελήλεγκται Lys.6.44; ὑπὸ τῶν εἰκότων Antipho 2.1.9; ἔκ τινος Ar.*Ra.*960; ἐξελεγχόμενος περί τινος Pl.*Hp.Ma.*304d; ὑπ' ἐμοῦ ἐξελεγχθήσονται ἔργῳ Id.*Ap.*17b. 2. c. dupl. acc. pers. et rei, *refute* one in a point, ib.23a, *Ly.*222d:—Pass., τοσοῦτον.. ἡλίκον οὗτος νῦν ἐξελήλεγκται *has been convicted of* .., D.21.147; οὐ τοῦτό γ' ἐξελέγχομαι I *am* not *to blame* in this, E. *El.*36. 3. with predicate added in part., *convict* one *of* being .., ἐ. τινὰ ἀδύνατον ὄντα Pl.*Grg.*522d; ἐ. τινὰ τεχνάζοντα D.29.19; ἐ. τινὰ ὡς οὐ.. Pl.*Grg.*482b:—Pass., ἵν' ἐξελέγχοισθε πονηρευόμενοι Heraclit.125a; κἀξελέγχεται.. κάκιστος ὤν E.*Hipp.*944; ἐξελέγχεται συμβεβουλευκώς D.19.5, etc. II. *put to the proof, bring to the test*, ὁ ἐξελέγχων.. ἀλάθειαν χρόνος Pi.*O.*10(11).53; in a court of justice, A.*Eu.*433; τὴν ποίησιν Ar.*Ra.*1366; ἐ. τὴν τύχην, τὰς ἐλπίδας, Plb. 21.14.4, 1.62.4; ἐ. τοὺς Θηβαίους εἰ διαμαχοῦνται Plu.*Ages.*19:—Pass., πάντες ἦσαν ἐξεληλεγμένοι all had *had their sentiments well ascertained*, D.18.23; ἃ δ' ἡ φύσις ἀεὶ ἐβούλετο, ἐξηλέγχθη ἐς τὸ ἀληθές *was fully proved* to be true, Th.3.64; χρυσὸς μὲν οἶδεν ἐξελέγχεσθαι πυρί Men.691. 2. Medic., *find out one's weak points*, Gal.15.902:—Pass., Id.6.323. III. *compute*, χαλκὸν μυρίον Pi.*N.*10.46. IV. *establish a claim to*, ὀγδοήκοντα τάλαντα D.38.20.

ἐξελευθερ-ικός, ή, όν, *of the class of freedmen* or *their offspring*, φῦλον D.H.4.22; οἱ ἐ. Plu.*Ant.*58. II. νόμοι ἐ. laws *concerning freedmen*, D.ap.Poll.3.83; καθάρματα ἐ. the refuse *of the freedmen*, Plu.*Sull.*33; φιάλαι ἐ. *presented by freedmen* on manumission, *IG*2. 720*A*15,15. **-ος**, ὁ, *freedman*, Hyp.*Fr.*197, Cic.*Att.*6.5.1: fem. **-έρα** *IG*14.1907.—The special application of ἐ. to a *released* debtor (cf. Ammon.p.23V., Eust.1751.2) is not confirmed by usage; ἐξ– and ἀπελεύθερος are used of the same person by D.C.39.38. **-οστομέω**, strengthd. for ἐλευθ–, S.*Aj.*1258. **-όω**, *set at liberty*, D.C.36.42, Hsch.

ἐξέλευσις, εως, ἡ, later word for ἔξοδος, Lxx 2*Ki.*15.20.

ἐξελεύσομαι, ἐξελθεῖν, fut. and aor. inf. of ἐξέρχομαι.

ἐξελθεῖν· ἐξωθεῖν, Hsch.

ἐξελ-ιγμός, ὁ, *countermarching*, ἐ. Μακεδονικός, Λακωνικός, Κρητικός, Ascl.*Tact.*10.13,14,15, cf. Arr.*Tact.*23.2,3,4; οἱ ἐπὶ τῶν ἵππων ἐ. Them.*Or.*1.2b. II. *doubling*, of the hare, Arr.*Cyn.*16.3 (pl.); so of *turning* movements in walking or driving a hoop, Antyll.ap.Orib. 6.21.18, 26.1. III. *revolution* of the heavenly bodies, Nicom.*Ar.*1. 6. 2. esp. of the *shortest period containing a whole number of synodic months, days, and* ἀποκαταστάσεις of the moon, Gem.18.1, Ptol.*Alm.* 4.2. **-ίκτρα**, ἡ, *roller, cylinder*, of a windlass, Hero *Aut.*5.3: **-ικτρον**, τό, *bobbin*, Ph.*Bel.*67.38. **-ιξις**, εως, ἡ, *evolution*, λόγων Plot.5.7.3; of troops, ἐξελίξεις ἐπ' ἀσπίδα, ἐπὶ δόρυ, Aristid.Quint.2.6.

ἐξέλιπον· ἐξώλισθον, Hsch.

ἐξελίσσω, Att. **-ττω**, *unroll, unfold*, περιβολὰς σφραγισμάτων E. *Hipp.*864; ταρσούς Aen.Tact.29.8; χάρτην Hero *Aut.*26.8: metaph., *unfold*, θεσπίσματα, λόγον, E.*Supp.*141, *Ion* 397; θεῖον νόμον Porph. *Marc.*26; οὐδ' ἄρα [τὸν αἰῶνα] ἐξελίξεις Plot.3.7.6; προσελθοῦσα ἡ πηλικότης ἐξελίττει εἰς μέγεθος τὴν ὕλην; Id.2.4.9:—Pass., ὁ.. κύκλος ..ἴσην ἐξελίττεται γραμμὴν *is unrolled so as to form* a line, Arist.*Mech.* 855ᵃ29, cf. *Pr.*914ᵃ30, Hero *Aut.*25.3. 2. of any rapid motion, ἴχνος ἐ. ποδός *evolve the mazy* dance, E.*Tr.*3; χορείαν Aristid.1.97J.; ἐ. τινὰ κύκλῳ *hunt* one round and round, E.*HF*977; ἐ. κύκλους περί τινα *wheel* in circles round him, Hld.5.14; ἐ. τὸν αὐτῆς κύκλον [ἡ σελήνη] Plu.2.368a; of the hare, δρόμον ἐ. *double*, Arr.*Cyn.*17.3:—Pass., -ιχθῆναι τοὺς ἑλιγμοὺς ib.21.3; *wheel about*, ἐπὶ δεξιά Plu.*Cam.* 5, cf. *Tim.*27: c. acc. loci, τοὺς κόλπους ἐ. *follow the windings of* the bays, App.*BC*5.84; ἐ. τὴν τάφρον Plu.*Pyrrh.*28. b. intr. in Act., Arr.*Cyn.*25.2; ἐξελίττει τῇ καὶ τῇ Ael.*NA*13.14 (also ἐ. ἑαυτόν *escape*, ib.3.16); of ships, παρὰ τὴν γῆν -ξασαι διέφυγον Plb.1.28.12, cf. 1.51. 11. 3. *evolve*, in Pass., ζωὴ ἐξελιττομένη εἰς τέλος Plot.1.4.1; ὅσα τὰ πολλά, τοσαῦτα τὸ ἕν, ἀφ' οὗ ἐξελίττεται Dam.*Pr.*4. II. as military term, = ἀναπτύσσειν, *extend* the front by bringing up the rear men, *deploy*, τὴν φάλαγγα X.*Cyr.*8.5.15, *HG*4.3.18; ἐξελίττεται ὁ στίχος Id.*Lac.*11.8. b. *countermarch*, Ascl.*Tact.*10.13, etc. c. generally, *manœuvre*, Arr.*Tact.*25.6:—Med. or Pass., ib.16.8. 2. *extricate*, τὴν δύναμιν τῶν στενῶν Plu.*Alex.*20.

ἐξελκόω, *cause sores in*, [τὴν σάρκα] Arist.*Pr.*883ᵇ31; τὸ πρόσωπον D.S.14.88:—Pass., *break out into sores*, ἐξελκοῦται τὸ χωρίον Hp.*VM* 18; ἐξήλκοῦτο τὰ σώματα J.*AJ*2.14.4.

ἐξελκ-τέον, *one must drag along*, γόνυ πρός τι E.*El.*491. **-υσμός**, ὁ, *pulling out, removal*, Ruf.ap.Orib.8.39.13. II. *extension*, Heliod. ap.Orib.49.10.6. **-ω**, fut. -έλξω Ar.*Eq.*365 (Pors.): aor. 1 -είλκυσα; inf. -ελκύσαι Id.*Pax* 315, 506:—Pass., -ελκυσθῇ Hdt.2.70:—*draw, drag out*, Il.23.762: c. gen. loci, Od.5.432 (Pass.); φάσγανον ..ἐ. κολεοῦ E.*Hec.*544; Ἑλλάδ' ἐ. δουλίας *rescue from* slavery, Pi. *P.*1.75; δύστηνον ἐ. πόδα, of a lame man, S.*Ph.*291: abs., without πόδα, of one wounded, E.*Andr.*1121; ἐξέλξω σε τῆς πυγῆς θύραζε Ar. *Eq.*365 (Pors. for ἐξελῶ); ἐξελκύσαι τὴν πᾶσιν Εἰρήνην φίλην *drag* her *out of the* cave, Id.*Pax* 294, cf. 315, 506; rare in Prose, as Pl.*R.* 515e; ἐξελκυσθεὶς Arist.*Pol.*1311ᵇ30; τέχναι τινὰ ἐ. τῆς πενίας Lib. *Or.*39.14.

ἐξέλκωσις, εως, ἡ, *causing of sores in* or *on*, τῶν χειρῶν D.S.3.29 (pl.).

ἐξελληνίζω, *turn into Greek*: ἐ. ὄνομα *trace* it *to a Greek origin*, Plu. *Num.*13; *put* it *in a Greek form*, J.*AJ*1.6.1. II. intr., *to be good Greek*, Anon.*in SE*63.37.

ἐξελυτρόω, (ἔλυτρον) in aor. ἐξελύτρωσας· ἐγύμνωσας, Hsch.

ἐξέμεν, Ep. aor. 2 inf. of ἐξίημι, Il.11.141.

ἐξέμεν, Ep. fut. inf. of ἔχω, Il.5.473.

ἐξεμέω, pf. ἐξεμήμεκα Aristid.*Or.*50(26).5 (v.l. ἐξημεκώς), Hsch.:—*vomit forth, disgorge*, of Charybdis, ὅτ' ἐξεμέσειε.. Od.12.237; ὄφρ' ἐξεμέσειεν ὀπίσσω.. ib.437: aor. 1 ἐξήμησε Hes.*Th.*497 codd.; ἐ. τὸ νόσημα Pl.*R.*406d; πάντα ἐ. ἀκριβῶς Diocl.*Fr.*139; λώπιον μεστὸν ὢν ἐξήμεσε κακῶν *IG*4.952.128 (Epid.): metaph., *disgorge* ill-gotten gains, τὰ τάλαντα Ar.*Ach.*6; ἅττ' ἂν κεκλόφωσί μου Id.*Eq.*1148: abs., Lib.*Or.*63.22; also νειόθεν ἐξεμέσαι Cerc.4.55; also of *rejecting* an opinion, Gal.5.325. 2. abs., *vomit, be sick*, Ar.*Ra.*11.

ἐξέμμορον, v. ἐκμείρομαι.

ἐξέμπαλιν· ἐπαριστέρως, Hsch.

ἐξεμπεδόω, *keep firm, observe strictly*, τὰς συνθήκας X.*Cyr.*3.1.21 codd. II. *unfetter*, Hsch.

ἐξεμπολάω, Ion. (and later Prose, J.*AJ*8.7.2) **-έω**, *gain by trading*, κέρδος ἐ. *drive* a gainful *trade*, S.*Ph.*303:—Pass., pf. ἐξημπόλημαι I *am bought and sold, betrayed*, Id.*Ant.*1036. II. *sell off*, τὸν φόρτον D.H.3.46:—Pass., ἐξεμπολημένων σφι σχεδὸν πάντων Hdt.1.1.

ἐξεναίρω, strengthd. for ἐναίρω, aor. inf. ἐξεναρεῖν Hes.*Sc.*329.

ἐξέναντι, Adv. *right opposite*, τοῦ μνημείου *BMus.Inscr.*918 (Halic.), cf. *TAM*2.210 (Sidyma).

ἐξενᾰρίζω, *strip* or *spoil* a foe slain in fight, τινά Il.4.488, etc.; also τεύχεα ἐ. *strip off* his arms, 13.619, etc. 2. *kill, slay*, Od.11.273; ἔγχεϊ Il.6.30, cf. Hes.*Th.*289, B.5.146, Lyc.50, etc.—In Hom. more freq. than the simple Verb.

ἐξενεῖκαι, -νειχθῆναι, Ion. aor. 1 Act. and Med. of ἐκφέρω.

ἐξενέπω, *speak out, proclaim*, τι Pi.*N.*4.33; ἐξένεπεν Αἴγιναν πάτραν *declared* Aeg. [to be] his country, Id.*O.*8.20:—Pass., Nic.*Fr.*73. 2. abs., *speak*, A.R.1.764.

ἐξενεχῠριάζω, strengthd. for ἐνεχυριάζω, D.L.6.99.

ἐξενῐαυτ-ίζω, *spend a year in exile*, Sch.E.*Or.*1645. **-ος**, ον, *in arrears, carried over from one year to the next*, *PLond.*1.17.19 (ii B.C.), *UPZ*21.12 (ii B.C.). II. Adv. -ίαυτα *yearly*, *PAmh.*2.85.14 (i A.D.).

ἐξεντερίζομαι, Pass., *have the entrails taken out*, Dsc.2.62; of plants, *have the pith taken out*, Id.4.162:—also **-όομαι**, *Gloss.*

ἐξεντισμέναι· κεκοσμημέναι, Hsch. (Cf. ἐντεσμέναι Id., and Ar. *Lys.*43.)

ἐξεόω, v. ἐξωθέω.

ἐξεπ-ᾴδω, *charm away*, Pl.*Phd.*77e, Plu.2.384a:—Pass., ἐξεπᾴδεσθαι φύσιν *to be charmed out of* their nature, S.*OC*1194. **-αίρω**, *stir up, excite* one to do, c. inf., Ar.*Lys.*623; ὅ σ' ἐξεπαρεῖ (fut.) μεῖζον ἢ χρεὼν φρονεῖν E.*Fr.*963.

ἐξεπείγω, *to be urgent, pressing*, *PPetr.*3 p.143.

ἐξέπερεν· ἐξεῖλεν, ἐπόρθησεν (-σαν cod.), Hsch. (fort. ἐξέπερσεν).

ἐξεπερώτησις, εως, ἡ, *formal question* put to a contracting party, *PMasp.*243.22 (vi A.D.).

ἐξεπεύχομαι, *boast loudly that*.., c. inf., S.*Ph.*668.

ἐξέπηλεν· ἐξεγένετο, Hsch. (fort. ἐξέπελεν).

ἐξεπικαιδέκᾰτος, η, ον, = ἑκκαιδέκατος, *AP*12.4 (Strat.).

ἐξεπιπολῆς, v. ἐπιπολή.

ἐξεπίσταμαι, *know thoroughly*, τι Hdt.2.43, 5.93: c. part., *know well that*.., ἐ. τὸν Κῦρον οὐκ ἀτρεμίζοντα Id.1.190, cf. S.*OC*1584; τὸν θεὸν τοιοῦτον (sc. ὄντα) ἐ. Id.*Fr.*771: c. inf., *know well how* to do, Id. *Ant.*480: with εὖ, Hdt.3.146, A.*Ag.*838; καλῶς S.*OC*417, etc.: c. acc. et inf., *know that*, Id.*Ant.*293. II. *know by heart*, τὸν λόγον Pl.*Phdr.*228b.

ἐξεπισφρᾱγίζομαι, Pass., *to be stamped deep on* a thing, Chaerem. 14.10.

ἐξεπιτάξ· ἐξεπίτηδες, Hsch. (ἐξεπίταξεν cod.).

ἐξεπίτηδες, Adv. = ἐπίτηδες, *on purpose*, Hp.*Art.*47, Ar.*Pl.*916, Pl.*Grg.*461c, al., Men.*Epit.*328. 2. *with malice prepense*, D.21.56, 187, Phld.*Lib.*p.62 O.

ἐξεπομβρέω, *rain on*, S.*Fr.*524.4: c. acc., τὰς δρόσους Tz.*H.*3.59.

ἐξέπτη, 3 sg. aor. 2 Act. of ἐκπέτομαι, Hes.*Op.*98.

ἐξέρ-ᾱμα, ατος, τό, *vomit, thing vomited*, 2*Ep.Pet.*2.22. **-ᾱσις**, εως, ἡ, *vomiting*, Eust.1856.5. II. *dye-extract*, *PHolm.*15.39.

ἐξεραυνάω, v. ἐξερευνάω.

ἐξεράω, aor. ἐξήρᾶσα (v. infr.):—Pass., aor. 1 part. ἐξερᾱθείς Hp. *Mul.*2.121:—*evacuate*, esp. by *purge* or *vomit*, Id.*Morb.*4.49; *draw off* a patient's water from the chest, ib.2.61:—Pass., *to be vomited*, Dsc. *Eup.*2.160; ὡς μὴ.. ἐξερῆται that (the wound) *may* not *keep on discharging*, Hp.*VC*15 (prob. cj.). II. *disgorge*, τὴν χύτραν χρὴν ἐξερᾶν τὰ τεῦτλα Crates Com.14.8; μαλάχας ἐ., = ἐξερυγγάνειν, Pherecr. 131.1. 2. *pour out, let fall*, τοὺς λίθους.. χαμᾶζε πρῶτον ἐξεράσατε Ar.*Ach.*341; φέρ' ἐξεράσω [τὰς ψήφους] *let me pour out* the ballots *from* the urn (in order to count them), Id.*V.*993; ἐξέρα τὸ ὕδωρ *pour* it *out*, D.36.62, cf. Aen.Tact.31.13, D.H.2.69; ὥσπερ ἐ. [τὸν ἀέρα] *drive forth* air from the lungs, Arist.*Pr.*960ᵇ26, cf. *Placit.*4.22.3. III. *give out* a dye, *PHolm.*15.37, al.; ὅταν δόξῃ ἐξερακέναι τὰ φάρμακα ib. 18.16.—Cf. συνεράω: the simple ἐράω is not found.

ἐξεργ-άζομαι, fut. -άσομαι: aor. -ηργασάμην, Dor. -ηργάξατο *IG* 1.423: pf. -είργασμαι, Ion. -έργασμαι, both in act. and pass. sense (v. infr.): aor. -ειργάσθην always Pass., Isoc.5.7, Plu.*Num.*9: so fut. -εργασθήσομαι Isoc.*Ep.*6.8:—*work out, bring to completion*, Hdt.1.93, 4.179 (Pass.), etc.; τίς βλέποντα σώματ' ἐξεργάζεται; E. *Hel.*583; οὐδὲ.. μελετῶντες αὐτὸ (i.e. seamanship) ἐξείργασθέ πω Th.1.142; τὰ ἐπιμαχώτατα ἐ. *finish* [fortifying] the most assailable points, Id.4.4, cf. 5.75, 6.101 (Pass.); τέχνην ἐ. X.*Smp*.4.61, cf. *Cyr*.8.2.5 (Pass.); τοιούτους ἐ. τινάς *make* them *exactly* such, Id.*Smp*.4.60. 2. *accomplish, achieve*, ἦδ' ἔστ' ἐκείνη τοὔργον ἡξειργασμένη S.*Ant*.384, cf. Men.*Epit*.474; ἐ. τάραχον *work utter* confusion, X.*Eq*.9.4; πήματα E.*Heracl*.960; ἐ. συμμαχίαν *bring* it *about*, Aeschin.3.239; πραγματικῶς ἐ. τὴν ὑπόθεσιν Plb.5.26.6: c. dupl. acc., κακὸν ἐ. τινά *work* him mischief, Hdt.6.3, cf. Pl.*Ep*. 352d, etc.:—Pass., σφιν ἔργον ἐστὶν ἐξειργασμένον A.*Pers*.759, cf. Hdt.9.75; ἐπ' ἐξεργασμένοισι after *the deed had been done*, usu. of crimes or acts of violence, Id.4.164, 8.94, cf. A.*Ag*.1379, S.*Aj*.377; ἐπ' ἐ. κακοῖσι E.*Ba*.1039; τοὐξειργασμένον S.*Aj*.315. 3. *contrive* or *manage that..*, ἐξειργάσατο βασιλεὺς προσαγορευθῆναι Plb.31.33.3, cf. Luc.*Tox*.32, Plu.*Cat.Ma*.3. 4. *work at*, esp. in Pass., ἀγροὶ εὖ ἐξεργασμένοι well-*cultivated* lands, Hdt.5.29, cf. 6.137; [ἡ γῆ] ὅσῳ ἄμεινον ἐξείργασται Th.1.82; of plants, *train*, Thphr.*CP*5.3.5. 5. of an author, *work out*, D.H.*Th*.15: abs., *treat fully*, ἐ. κατὰ μέρος περί τινος Plb.3.26.5:—Pass., τὰ κατ' ἐπιτομὴν ἐξειργασμένα Phld.*Lib*. p.10. II. *undo, destroy*, esp. of men, *ruin*, Hdt.4.134, 5.19, E.*Hel*.1098, etc.; in Trag., also ἐ. αἷμα μητρός Id.*Or*.1624:—Pass., ἐξειργάσμεθα we *are undone*, Id.*Hipp*.565; ὡς μή τι ἐξεργάσωνται that they may *do* no *harm*, Hp.*Morb*.3.16 as cited by Gal.19.182, cf. 212 (ἐξ- [or κατ-]εργάσηταί τι κακόν codd. Hp.). **-ἄσία**, ἡ, *working out, completion*, Plb.10.45.6. II. *labour at a thing*, ἡ πεπονημένη ἐ. [τῆς γῆς] high *state of cultivation*, App.*BC*1.11: abs., ἀκριβὴς καὶ πολλὴ ἐ. Thphr.*CP*3.1.6: *treatment, discussion* of a subject by an author, D.H.*Isoc*.4, Gal.5.664, etc.; ἡ καθ' ἕκαστον ἐ. Plu.2.1004e, cf. Phld.*Rh*.1.121 S.; ποιητικὴ ἐ. Id.*Po*.5.1: pl., ib.2.47; ἐ. λογικὴ Iamb.*Comm.Math*.24. **-ασμός**, ὁ, = ἐξεργασία I, Simp.*in Cat*.240.26. **-αστέον**, *one must treat, discuss*, Gal.15.467, al. **-αστικός**, ή, όν, *able to accomplish*, τινός X.*Mem*.4.1.4 (in Sup.), Plb.15.37.1; τὸ ἐ. τοῦ λόγου *diligent inquiry*, A.D.*Synt*.312.9. II. Adv. **-κῶς** *elaborately, in detail*, Phld.*Rh*.1.156 S., *Piet*.19: Comp. -ώτερον Corn. *ND*35, A.D.*Synt*.282.10. **-άτης** [ᾰ], ου, ὁ, *workman*, *PBasel* 19.6 (vi A.D.).

ἐξέργω, Att. **ἐξείργω**, fut. -είρξω Ar.*Ach*.825:—*shut out from* a place, *debar*, ἐξέργειν τινά Hdt.3.51, etc.; ἐξείργειν τινὰ χθονός, γῆς, E.*Heracl*.20, 25; ἐξ ἀγορᾶς, ἐκ τοῦ ἄστεος, Pl.*Lg*.936c; ἀπὸ τοῦ βήματος Aeschin.1.32; ἐκ τῶν ἱερῶν Lys.6.16; ἐκ τοῦ θεάτρου D.21.178; ἐ. θύραζε *drive away and shut* him *out* of doors, Ar.*Ach*.825, cf. D.18. 169:—Pass., ἐξείργεσθαι πάντων Th.2.13; ἐξειργόμενοι δίκης Plu.*Rom*. 23. 2. *prevent, preclude*, καιρὸν ἐ. λόγος S.*El*.1292; τῶνδ' οὐδὲν ἐξείργει νόμος E.*Andr*.176; ἐ. δέει τὸ δίκην λαμβάνειν D.21.124: abs., ὅταν μὴ ἡ ὥρα τοῦ ἔτους ἐξείργῃ X.*Oec*.4.13:—Pass., πολέμοις ἐξειργόμενοι Th.1.118; ἐὰν μὴ χρόνῳ ἐξείργηται Arist.*Cat*.13ᵃ31: c. inf., *to be hindered from* doing, D.H.*Th*.15. 3. *constrain, compel*, τινὰ πληγαῖς Pl.*Lg*.935c:—Pass., ἀναγκαίῃ ἐξέργεσθαι ἔς τι *to be constrained* by necessity to undertake a thing, Hdt.7.96: c. inf., ἀναγκαίῃ ἐ. γνώμην ἀποδέξασθαι ib.139; ὑπὸ τοῦ νόμου ἐξεργόμενος Id.9.111; νόμῳ Th.3.70.

ἐξερεείνω, Ep. Verb, 1. c. acc. rei, *inquire into*, ἐξερέειν ἕκαστα Od.10.14. 2. c. acc. pers., *inquire after*, ἢ... φίλον πόσιν ἐξερεείνοι 23.86; *inquire of*, ἄλλος ἄλλον ἐ. A.R.4.1250: abs., *make inquiry*, Il. 9.672, etc.:—Med., ἐξερεείνετο μύθῳ 10.81. II. *search thoroughly*, πόρους ἁλὸς ἐξερεείνων Od.12.259; μυχοὺς *h.Merc*.252: metaph. of a harp, *try* its *tones, tune* it, ib.483.

ἐξερεθ-ίζω, strengthd. for ἐρεθίζω, Pi.*P*.8.13, Ph.2.359, Plu.*Aem*. 30, etc.; of a plaster, *stimulate*, Crateuas *Fr*.8. **-ιστής**, οῦ, ὁ, *one who provokes*, *AB*251. **-ω**, strengthd. for ἐρέθω, *AP*5.243 (Paul. Sil.).

ἐξερείδω, *prop firmly*, ταῖς ἀντηρίσι Plb.8.4.6; *support*, ἐ. μου βάσιν τρέμουσαν Luc.*Trag*.55; ἐ. ἀτονίαν σώματος Dsc.1.69.4:—Pass., *to be underpinned*, Plb.16.11.5, Sor.1.47.

ἐξερείπω, *strike off*, ὄζους δρυὸς πελέκει Pi.*P*.4.264. II. more freq. intr. in aor. 2 ἐξήριπον, inf. ἐξεριπεῖν:—*fall to earth*, ὡς δ' ὅθ' ὑπὸ ῥιπῆς πατρὸς Διὸς ἐξερίπῃ δρῦς Il.14.414; χαίτη ζεύγλης ἐξεριποῦσα the mane *streaming downwards from* the yoke-cushion, 17.440; [κάπροι] αὐχένας ἐξεριπόντες *letting* their necks *fall on the ground*, Hes.*Sc*. 174; *fall down*, Id.*Th*.704.—Mostly Ep., but ᾗ ἐξήριπε τὸ κάτηγμα where the fractured part *projects*, Hp.*Off*.12.

ἐξέρ-εισις, εως, ἡ, *fixing firmly*, αἱ πρὸς τὴν γῆν ἐ. Plb.6.23.4. **-εισμα**, ατος, τό, *prop, support*, metaph., Longin.40.4 (pl.). **-ειστικός**, ή, όν, *resistent, tense*, of the pulse, πληγή Archig.ap.Gal.8. 651, cf. 938; dub. l. in Epicur.*Sent*.14.

ἐξέρεκτα· ἐκπέσῃ, Hsch.

ἐξερεύγομαι, *vomit forth*, πλῆθος βατράχων Lxx *Wi*.19.10, al.; ἀφρόν, of honey when boiled, Gal.6.273: metaph., λόγον ἀγαθόν Lxx *Ps*.44(45).1. II. of a tumour, *break out*, Hp.*Prorrh*.1. 168. III. Med. or Pass., of rivers, *empty themselves*, Hdt.1.202, Arist.*HA*603ᵃ14, D.H.1.9, etc.; of veins, *discharge*, Hp.*Oss*.14. (Cf. ἐξερυγγάνω.)

ἐξερευν-άω (later -εραυν- Lxx *Ps*.118(119).2, al.), *search out, examine*, S.*OT*258, *El*.1100; τὰ περὶ τὴν πόλιν Aen.Tact.28.4; λογισμὸς τὰς αἰτίας ἐ. Epicur.*Ep*.3 p.64 U.; τὰς προσόδους Plb.14.1.13, cf. Lxx l.c., al.; τὰ πρόσφορ' ἤν πως ἐξερευνήσας λάβω E.*Hel*.429:—Med., D.C.52.6; τόπους Plb.9.5.8, cf. 18.21.1. **-ησις**, εως, ἡ, *inquiry, investigation*, Lxx *Ps*.63(64).7 (in form -εραυν-), cj. in Lyd.*Ost*. 16. **-ητικός**, ή, όν, *good as a spy* or *scout*, Str.3.3.6.

ἐξέρευξις, εως, ἡ, *belching*, Aret.*SA*2.2 (pl.).

ἐξερεύω, = ἐξερευνάω, Hsch.

ἐξερέω (A), Att. contr. ἐξερῶ, fut. of ἐξεῖπον (q.v.):—I *will speak out, tell out, utter aloud*, Hom. always abs. in sg., ἐξερέω Il.8.286, 12. 215, Od.9.365, al.; in tmesi, ἔκ τοι ἐρέω Il.1.204, 233, al.: c. acc. in Trag., τἀληθὲς ἐξερῶ S.*OT*800, cf. 219, etc.: c. dupl. acc., τοιαῦτά τοι νὼ πᾶς τις ἐ. Id.*El*.984; ἐ. ὅτι.. Id.*Ant*.325:—after Hom., also pf. Act. ἐξείρηκα Id.*Tr*.350, 374: 3 sg. plpf. Pass. ἐξείρητο Id.*OT*984: 3 sg. fut. Pass. ἐξειρήσεται Id.*Tr*.1186.

ἐξερέω (B), Ep. pres., = ἐξέρομαι (of which it is an Ep. form) and ἐξερεείνω: 1. c. acc. rei, *inquire into* a thing, Od.3.116, 14.375:—Med., πάντα.. ἐξερέεσθαι 13.411, cf. 4.119. 2. c. acc. pers., *inquire of* a person, 10.249, etc.:—Med., 3.24, 19.99. II. *search through*, κνημοὺς ἐξερέησι 4.337. 2. *search for*, ὕδωρ A.R.4.1443.

ἐξέρημα, sine expl., Hsch.

ἐξερημόω, *make quite desolate*, ἐ. οἶκον *leave* it *destitute of heirs*, D. 43.76, cf. Lxx *Le*.26.31, al.; ἐξερημῶσαι γένος S.*El*.1010 (but ἐ. δόμους *abandon* them, E.*Andr*.597, 991); πόλεις -ωμένας Pl.*Ep*.332e; ἐ. τὰ ἑαυτῶν *leaving* their own places *destitute* (of troops), X.*Vect*.4. 47; δράκοντος γένυν ἐ. *making* it *destitute* of teeth, E.*HF*253:—Pass., *to be left destitute*, Ἑλλὰς ἐξερημωθεῖσα Ar.*Pax* 647; εἰς τὸν ἐξηρημωμένον.. οἶκον Pl.*Lg*.925c.

ἐξερίζω, *to be contumacious*, Plu.*Pomp*.56, App.*BC*2.151.

ἐξερῑθεύομαι, *bind to oneself by party ties*, τοὺς νέους διὰ [τῆς στρατηγίας] Plb.10.22.9.

ἐξερῑνάζω, strengthd. for ἐρινάζω: metaph., *fertilize*, ἐρινὸς... ἀχρεῖος ὢν ἐς βρῶσιν ἄλλους ἐξερινάζεις λόγῳ S.*Fr*.181.

ἐξέρ-ισμα, ατος, τό, f.l. for ἐξορισμός, Porph.*Abst*.1.10. **-ιστής**, οῦ, ὁ, *stubborn disputant*, τῶν λόγων E.*Supp*.894. **-ιστικός**, ή, όν, *captious, disputatious*, dub. l. in Epicur.*Sent*.14; cf. ἐξερειστικός.

ἐξερμηνεύω, *interpret, translate*, εἰς τὴν Ἑλλάδα γλῶσσαν τοὔνομα D.H.1.67, cf. Jul.*Or*.2.77d:—Pass., Plb.2.15.9, D.H.4.67, Plu.2. 383d, etc. II. *describe accurately*, Luc.*Hist.Conscr*.19.

ἐξέρομαι, Ion. **-είρομαι**, fut. -ερήσομαι: aor. 2 -ηρόμην, inf. -ερέσθαι: 1. c. acc. rei, *inquire into* a thing, Διὸς ἐξείρετο βουλήν Od. 13.127; so also ἀναξίου μὲν φωτὸς ἐξερήσομαι... τί νῦν κυρεῖ *will inquire concerning* him, what he is now about, S.*Ph*.439. 2. c. acc. pers., *inquire of*, Ζῆν' ὕπατον.. ἐξείρετο Il.5.756; ἢ τοὐπίτριπτον κίναδος ἐξήρου μ' ὅπου; S.*Aj*.103; ἐ. καὶ προσέειπε Il.24.361.—Ion. pres. ἐξείρομαι A.R.3.19: in Hom. more freq. ἐξερέω, ἐξερεείνω, ἐξερέομαι.

ἐξέρπω, aor. ἐξείρπῠσα Arist.*HA*599ᵃ26, Aret.*SD*2.13:—*creep out of*, ἔκ τινος Ar.*Nu*.710. 2. abs., *creep out* or *forth*, of a lame man, S.*Ph*.294; εἴ τις ἐξέρποι θύραζε Ar.*Eq*.607; of insects, Arist.*HA* 550ᵃ5, 599ᵃ26. II. generally, *go out*, Hp.*Vict*.1.24; *go forth*, of an army or general, οὐ ταχὺ ἐξέρπει X.*An*.7.1.8, cf. Chilo ap.D.L.1. 73. 2. *go away*, ὑγιὴς ἐξῆρπε *IG*4.951.97 (Epid.). III. trans., *make to come forth, produce*, βατράχους Lxx *Ps*.104(105).30.

ἐξέρρω, in imper., ἔξερρε γαίας *away out of* the land! E.*Hipp*.973: impf. ἐξέρρον· ἐξεπορεύοντο, Hsch. (ἐξέρον cod.).

ἐξέρρωσας· ἐπ' ἐμὲ ἀφῖξαι, ἤτοι ἐπὶ τῶν νεύρων, Hsch.

ἔξερσις, εως, ἡ, *unthreading*, [λίνου] prob. cj. in Aen.Tact.31.19.

ἐξερυγγάνω, *utter*, aor. 2 (in tmesi) ἐξ ἂν ἐπεὶ καὶ τῶν ἤρυγες ἱστορίην Call.*Aet*.3.1.7; cf. ἐξερεύγομαι.

ἐξερυθρ-ιάω, *to be very red*, Hp.*Nat.Mul*.9. **-ος**, ον, *very red*, κατακαύματα Id.*Coac*.154; χρῶμα Thphr.*HP*4.6.10; τὸ πρόσωπον *red* in the face, Arist.*Pr*.869ᵃ8, cf. 903ᵃ3.

ἐξερυθρώδης, ες, *very red*, Hp.*Prorrh*.1.127.

ἐξερύκω [ῡ], *ward off, repel*, τὰ κακὰ S.*Ph*.423.

ἐξερύω, Ion. **ἐξειρύω**, aor. 1 ἐξείρῠσα, Ep. ἐξέρῠσα and ἐξείρυσσα; also ἐξερύσασκον (v. infr.):—*draw out of*, βέλος.. ἐξέρυσ' ὤμου Il.5.112; ἰχθύας, οὕς θ' ἁλιῆες... πολιῆς ἔκτοσθε θαλάσσης δικτύῳ ἐξέρυσαν Od.22. 386, cf. Hdt.1.141; τοῖο δ' ἅμα ψυχήν τε καὶ ἔγχεος ἐξέρυσ' αἰχμήν Il. 16.505; *snatch out of*, ἐξείρυσε χειρὸς τόξον 23.870; but τὸν.. λαβὼν ποδὸς ἐξερύσασκε *by* the foot, 10.490; *draw out*, τοὺς δ' ἐξείρυσσαν Ἀχαιοί 13.194; *tear out*, μήδεά τ' ἐξερύσας Od.18.87; τὴν γλῶσσαν ἐξειρύσας Hdt.2.38. (Pres. supplied by ἐξέλκω.)

ἐξέρχομαι, fut. -ελεύσομαι (but in Att. ἔξειμι (A) supplies the fut., also impf. ἐξῄειν): aor. 2 ἐξῆλθον, the only tense used in Hom.:—*go* or *come out of*, c. gen. loci, τείχεος, πυλάων, πόληος, Il.22.237, 413, 417; ἐκ δ' ἦλθε κλισίης 10.140; ἐ. δωμάτων, χθονός, etc., A.*Ch*.663, S.*El*. 778, etc.; ἐ. ἐκ.. Hdt.8.75, 9.12, S.*OC*37, etc.; ἔξω τῆσδ'.. χθονός E.*Ph*.476; of an actor, *come out* on the stage, Ar.*Ach*.240, *Av*.512: abs., *come forth*, ἐ. καὶ ἀμῦναι Il.9.576. b. rarely c. acc., ἐξῆλθον τὴν Περσίδα χώραν Hdt.7.29; ἐ. τὸ ἄστυ Id.5.104, cf. Arist.*Pol*.1285ᵃ5, Lxx *Ge*.44.4. c. abs., *march out, go forth*, Th.2.11, etc.; ἐπί τινα Hdt.1.36. d. of an accused person, *withdraw from the country* to avoid trial, opp. φεύγω, D.23.45. e. ἐ. ὑπηρέτης to be commissioned to carry out an order of the court, Mitteis *Chr*.89.36 (ii A.D.), etc. f. c. acc. cogn., *go out on* an expedition, etc., ἐ. ἐξόδους X.*HG*1.2.17; στρατείαν Aeschin.2.168; so παγκόνιτ' ἐ. ἄεθλ' ἀγώνων *went through* them, S.*Tr*.506 (lyr.); νίκης ἔχων ἐξῆλθε.. γέρας Id.*El*.687. g. with Preps., ἐ. ἐπὶ θήραν, ἐπὶ θεωρίαν, etc., X.*Cyr*.1.2.11, Pl.*Cri*.52b, etc.; ἐπὶ πλεῖστον ἐ. *pursue their advantages* to the utmost, Th.1.70; εἰς τόδ' ἐ. ἀνόσιον στόμα *allow oneself to use* these impious words, S. *OC*981; also ἐ. εἴς τινας *come out of* one class into another, as εἰς τοὺς τελείους ἄνδρας, opp. ἔφηβοι, X.*Cyr*.1.2.12. h. of disease, *pass off*, ἣν ἐκ τοῦ ἄλλου σώματος ἡ νοῦσος ἐξεληλύθῃ Hp.*Morb*.2.13. i. of offspring, *issue from* the womb, τὰ μὲν τετελειωμένα, τὰ δὲ ἀτελῆ ἐ. Arist.*Pr*.896ᵃ18; ἐκ τῆς γαστρός M.Ant.9.3. 2. ἐ. εἰς ἔλεγχον *stand forth and come* to the trial, E.*Alc*.640; ἐς χερῶν ἅμιλλαν ἐ. τινί Id.*Hec*.226: abs., *stand forth, be proved to be*, ἄλλος S.*OT*1084; *come forth* (from the war), Th.5.31. 3. c. acc. rei, *execute*, ἃ ἂν.. μὴ ἐξέλθωσιν (v.l. for ἐπεξ–) Id.1.70; τὸ πολὺ τοῦ ἔργου ἐξῆλθον (v.l. for ἐπεξ–) Id.3.108. 4. abs., *exceed all bounds*, Pl.*Lg*.644b; so ἐ. τὰ νόμιμα Nymphis 15. 5. with acc. of the instrument of motion, ἐ. οὐδὲ τὸν ἕτερον πόδα Din.1.82. II. of Time, *come to an end, expire*, Hdt.2.139, S.*OT*735, *PRev.Laws* 48.9 (iii B.C.), etc.; τοῦ ἐξελθόντος μηνός Hyp.*Eux*.35; ἐπειδὰν.. ὁ ἐνιαυτὸς ἐξέλθῃ Pl.*Plt*.298e; ἐλέγοντο αἱ σπονδαὶ ἐξεληλυθέναι X.*HG*5.2.2. 2. of magistrates, etc., *go out of office*, ἡ ἐξελθοῦσα βουλή Decr.ap.And.1.77, cf. Arist.*Pol*.1273^{a}16. III. of prophecies, dreams, events, etc., *to be accomplished, come true*, ἐς τέλος ἐ. Hes.*Op*.218: abs., τὴν ὄψιν συνεβάλετο ἐξεληλυθέναι Hdt.6.108, cf. 82; ἐξῆλθε (sc. ἡ μῆνις) *was satisfied*, Id.7.137; ἰσόψηφος δίκη ἐξῆλθ' ἀληθῶς A.*Eu*.796; κατ' ὀρθὸν ἐ. *come out* right, S.*OT*88; ἀριθμὸς οὐκ ἐλάττων ἐ. X.*HG*6.1.5; of persons, μὴ ..Φοῖβος ἐξέλθῃ σαφὴς *turn out* a true prophet, S.*OT*1011. 2. of words, *proceed*, παρά τινος Pl.*Tht*.161b; of goods, *to be exported*, Id.*Alc*.1.122e.

ἐξερῶ, v. ἐξερέω (A).

ἐξερωέω, *swerve from the course*, of shy horses, αἱ δ' ἐξηρώησαν Il.23.468; ἐξηρώησε κελεύθου Theoc.25.189.

ἐξερωτάω, *search out, inquire*, Pi.*P*.9.44. 2. c. acc. pers., *question*, E.*Fr*.579, *BGU*1141.34 (i B.C.).

ἔξεσα· ἔξωθεν (Lacon.), Hsch. (ἐξέσας cod.; cf. ἔντεσα).

ἐξεσθίω, fut. ἐξέδομαι: pf. ἐξεδήδοκα: aor. ἐξέφαγον:—*eat away, eat up*, ἐξέδεταί σου τοὔψον Ar.*Eq*.1032, cf. Epimenid.10; ἐκ τῶν πόλεων τὸ σκίρον ἐξεδήδοκεν Id.*V*.925; ἐὰν μή σ' ἐκφάγω ἐκ τῆσδε τῆς γῆς Id.*Eq*.698; ἐξεσθίουσι αὐτὰ (the grubs) αἱ μέλιτται Arist.*HA*554^{b}4, cf. Dsc.*Eup*.1.150.

ἐξέσθω, = foreg., A.*Ch*.281.

ἐξεσίη, ἡ, (ἐξίημι) *sending forth, mission, embassy*, Hom. only in phrase, ἐξεσίην ἐλθόντι Il.24.235, cf. Od.21.20: acc. pl. in Hsch.

ἔξεσις, εως, ἡ, *dismissal, divorce*, γυναικός Hdt.5.40.

ἐξέσσυτο, v. ἐκσεύω.

ἔξεστι, imper. ἐξέστω, subj. ἐξῇ, inf. ἐξεῖναι, part. ἐξόν: impf. ἐξῆν: fut. ἐξέσται, opt. ἐξέσοιτο X.*Ages*.1.24, part. ἐξεσόμενον (v. infr.): impers. (v. ἔξειμι B):—*it is allowed, is possible*, c. inf., Hdt.1.183, etc.: c. dat. pers. et inf., ib.138, A.*Eu*.899, etc.; ἔ. σοι ἀνδρὶ γενέσθαι X.*An*.7.1.21; ἔ. εὐδαίμοσι γενέσθαι '*licet esse beatis*', D.3.23: with acc. instead of second dat., ἔ. ὑμῖν φίλους γενέσθαι Th.4.20: c. acc. pers. et inf., Ar.*Ach*.1079, Pl.*Plt*.290d: neut. part. abs., ἐξεόν τοι.. ἕτερα ποιέειν *since it was possible* for thee to.., Hdt.4.126; ἐξόν σοι γάμου τυχεῖν A.*Pr*.648; ἐξὸν κεκλῆσθαι S.*El*.365; ὡς οὐκ ἐξεσόμενον τῇ πόλει δίκην.. λαμβάνειν Lys.14.10.

ἔξεστις, ιος, ἡ, v. ἔξαστις.

ἐξετ-άζω, fut. ἐξετάσω, rarely ἐξετῶ Isoc.9.34, cf. *AB*251: aor. ἐξήτασα Ar.*Th*.438, S.*OC*211 (lyr.), etc., Dor. ἐξήταξα Theoc.14.28: pf. ἐξήτακα Pl.*Tht*.154d, etc.:—**Pass.**, fut. –ετασθήσομαι D.2.20: aor. –ητάσθην (v. infr.): pf. –ήτασμαι (v. sub fin.):—*examine well* or *closely, scrutinize, review*, ἐ. φίλους, ὅντιν' ἔχουσι νόον Thgn.1016, cf. Ar. l. c., etc.; τὴν ὑπάρχουσαν ξυμμαχίαν ἐ. Th.2.7; βίον αὐτοῦ πάντα ἐξετάσω D.21.21; ἐκ τοῦ εἰκότος ἐξετασθῆναι δεῖ τὸ πρᾶγμα Antipho 5.37; ἐ., opp. ὑπέχειν λόγον, Arist.*Rh*.1354^{a}5; τὸ δι' ἀκριβείας –αζόμενον exactly *weighed* words, Pl.*Tht*.184c; ἐ. τι (διὰ) τῶν εἰδότων *make inquiries into* a thing *from*.., Plb.10.8.1: folld. by Relat., ἐ. ὅστις ἦν D.45.82; ἐ. τί καὶ πῶς λέγουσι Pl.*Phdr*.261a; ἐ. τινά, τίνος ἐστὶ γένους Epicr.11.17. 2. of troops, *inspect, review*, Th.7.33,35, etc.; στρατιώτας σὺν τοῖς ὅπλοις *Hell.Oxy*.10.1:—Pass., στρατὸς δὲ θάσσει κἀξετάζεται E.*Supp*.391, cf. Th.6.97. 3. ἐ. τὴν βουλήν, τὸ βουλευτικόν, = Lat. *legere senatum, revise the roll of* the Senate, D.C.52.42, 54.13. 4. *examine, approve*, *PRev.Laws*40.19 (Pass., iii B.C.), etc. 5. *pass in review, enumerate*, ἁμαρτήματα ἀκριβῶς ἐ. Isoc.7.63, cf. D.20.52,58. II. *examine* or *question* a person *closely*, Hdt.3.62, S.*Aj*.586, *OC*211; τινὰ περί τινος Pl.*Phdr*.258d; τινά τι Id.*Grg*.515b, X.*Cyr*.6.2.35; δικαίως αὐτὸν ἐξετάσω D.21.154, cf. 18.20; τὸν δεσπότην ὁ δοῦλος ἐξετάζει Id.45.76:—Pass., Men.*Epit*.65. III. *estimate*, τι πρός τι one thing with reference to another, D.6.7; πρὸς ἐκείνους ἐ. καὶ παραβάλλειν ἐμέ Id.18.314; ἰσοστάσιος ἦν ἡ πορφύρα πρὸς ἄργυρον ἐξεταζομένη Theopomp.Hist.114, cf. Jul.*Or*.3.119a; ἐ. τινὰ παρ' ἄλληλα D.18.265, cf. Isoc.8.11; *compare*, πρὸς Ἀριστογείτονα ἐμαυτόν D.*Ep*.3.43. IV. *prove by scrutiny* or *test*, of gold, Chilo 1 (Pass.); ἐ. τοὺς κακούς τε κἀγαθοὺς X.*Oec*.20.14; τοὺς χρησίμους D.34.38: c. part., ἐξητακὼς στερεοὺς ὑπάρχοντας τοὺς τόπους Plb.3.79.1:—more freq. in Pass., ἐὰν μὴ παρὼν ἐ. unless he is *proved* to have been present, Pl.*Lg*.764a; καὶ λέγων καὶ γράφων ἐξηταζόμην τὰ δέοντα D.18.173; ἐξήτασαι πεποιηκὼς ib.197; ἐξετάζεσθαι φίλος (sc. ὤν) E.*Alc*.1011; ἐχθρὸς ἐξεταζόμενος D.21.65; κατήγορος Id.22.66; μέτριοι ἐν τοῖς ἀνηκέστοις Plu.2.74b; of things, τὰ φοβερὰ ἐξετασθήσεται μέχρι λόγου τοιαῦτα ὄντα D.H.6.63. V. Pass., *to be numbered, counted*, c. gen., ὧν εἷς ἐγὼ βουληθεὶς ἐξετάζεσθαι And.4.2; τῶν ἐχθρῶν εἷς ἐξετάζεσθαι *to be found in the number of*.., D.19.291; μετὰ τῶν ἄλλων ἐξητάζετο he *appeared among*.., Id.18.217; ἔν τισι D.H.6.59; *to be placed on a roll*, ἐν τοῖς ἱππικοῖς among the *Equites* at Rome, Plu.*Pomp*.14; of the census, ἐξητάσθησαν αἱ πᾶσαι πεντεκαίδεκα [μυριάδες] Id.*Caes*.55. 2. Pass., *present oneself, appear*, D.21.161; πρὸς τὸν ἄρχοντα.. οὐδέπω.. ἐξήτασται Id.37.46, cf. 18.277. **–ᾱσία**, ἡ, = sq., τῶν δούλων *IG*12(3).174.29 (Astypalaea, Epist. Aug.). **–ᾰσις**, εως, ἡ, *close examination, scrutiny, test*, Pl.*Ap*.22e, *Tht*.210e; ἡδονῆς ἐ. πᾶσαν ποιήσασθαι Id.*Phlb*.55c; ἐ. ποιεῖσθαι περί τινος Lycurg.28; ἐ. λαμβάνειν undertake *an inquiry*, D.18.246; ἐ. τινος ἔχειν Th.6.41; ἔσχον τὸ ἴσον εἰς ἐ. I received the copy for *examination*, *PLond*.2.338.24 (ii A.D.), etc.; ἐ. γίγνεταί πρός τι *comparison* is made with.., Luc.*Prom*.12. 2. *a military inspection* or *review*, ἐ. ὅπλων, ἵππων ποιεῖσθαι, hold *a review of*.., Th.4.74, 6.45,96; τῶν Ἑλλήνων καὶ τῶν βαρβάρων ποιεῖσθαι X.*An*.1.2.14; ἐ. σὺν τοῖς ὅπλοις ἐγίγνετο ib.5.3.3. b. at Rome, ἐ. ἱππέων, = Lat. *transvectio equitum*, Plu.*Aem*.38, D.C.55.31; ἐ. ἐτησία Id.63.13. c. ἐ. τῶν βουλευτῶν, = Lat. *lectio Senatus, revision* of the Senatorial roll, Id.54.26. d. ἐ. βίων, of the Roman *Census*, Plu.*Aem*.38, cf. J.*AJ*3.12.4. e. *inspection* of articles, *IG*2^2.333.11. 3. *arrangement, order*, Nicom.*Harm*.6. **–ασμός**, ὁ, = foreg., ἐ. ποιεῖσθαι D.18.16, cf. *Hell.Oxy*.10.1,2, *IG*2^2.500.12 (pl.), Plu.2.1060b; ψυχῶν ἐν Ἅιδου D.H.*Pomp*.6. II. *visitation*, Lxx *Wi*.4.6. **–αστέον**, *one must examine carefully*, ὅπως.. Jul.*Or*.7.226d. **–αστήριον**, τό, *office of public auditor*, *SIG*976.61 (Samos, ii B.C.). **–αστής**, οῦ, ὁ, *examiner, inquirer into*, τινός D.H.2.67, Plu.*Ages*.11. 2. *auditor of public accounts*, Arist.*Pol*.1322^{b}11, *SIG*284.10 (Erythrae), 976.77 (Samos), 1015.32 (Halic.). 3. at Athens, *officer who checked payments to* ξένοι, etc., Aeschin.1.113, *IG* 2^2.641 (iii B.C.). **–αστικός**, ή, όν, *capable of examining into*, τῶν ἔργων X.*Mem*.1.1.7; ἐ. καὶ κριτικός Luc.*Herm*.64; ἐ. πρὸς ἀκρίβειαν *exacting*, Hierocl.*in CA*7 p.429 M.: abs., *fitted for inquiry*, of Dialectic, Arist.*Top*.101^{b}3 (in *Po*.1455^{a}34 ἐκστατικοί is prob. l.). Adv. **–κῶς** D.17.13. II. ἐ. (sc. ἀργύριον), τό, *salary of an* ἐξεταστής, Id.13.4.

ἐξέτειον· ἐκ τούτου τοῦ ἔτους, οἷον ἐπέτειον, Hsch.

ἐξέτεροι, αι, α, later form of μετεξέτεροι, Nic.*Th*.412,744.

ἐξέτης, ες, *six years old*, ἵππον.. ἐξέτε' ἀδμήτην Il.23.266, cf. 655, Pi.*N*.3.49, Ar.*Nu*.862:—fem. **ἐξέτις**, μετὰ τὸν ἑξέτη καὶ τὴν ἑξέτιν Pl.*Lg*.794c. II. *lasting six years*, ἀρχή Lys.30.2.

ἐξέτι, Prep. with gen., ἐξέτι τοῦ ὅτε.. *ever since* the time when.., Il.9.106; ἐ. πατρῶν *from* our fathers' time, Od.8.245; ἐ. νηπυτίης A.R.4.791; ἐ. κεῖθεν Call.*Ap*.104; ἐ. παίδων *IG*14.1549: also in late Prose, ἐ. νέου, νεαροῦ, App.*BC*2.86, Ael.*NA*5.39; ἐ. σπαργάνων Ph.2.94.

ἐξευασμένου· τεθνεῶτος, γενομένου, Hsch. (v. ἐξαυαίνω).

ἐξευγεν-ίζω, = ἐλευθεροποιέω, Hsch.; τινάς *produce noble offspring*, Vett.Val.119.26; *make noble*, Sophon.*in de An*.145.14:—but **–ισμός**, ὁ, apptly., = *degeneration*, *Gloss*. (pl.).

ἐξευδιάζω, *calm utterly*, τοὺς χειμῶνας τῶν πραγμάτων Ph.2.345, cf. Hsch.

ἐξευθετίζω, *set in order*, prob. in S.*Ichn*.270.

ἐξευθύνω [ῡ], *straighten*, δακτύλους *IG*4.951.29 (Epid.), cf. Gal.*UP* 14.3 (Pass.). II. *examine*, τοὺς ἄρχοντας Pl.*Lg*.945d.

ἐξευ-κρῑνέω, *handle with discrimination*, Hp.*Fract*.15; ἐ. τὰς διαφορὰς *treat* them *systematically*, Plb.35.2.6. **–λᾰβέομαι**, *guard carefully against*, τι Pl.*La*.199d, al.; ἐ. τοῦτο μή.. E.*Andr*.644; ἐ. μή.. A.*Fr*.205. **–λῡτέω**, *discharge* a debt, *POxy*.271.22 (Pass., i A.D.). **–μᾰρίζω**, *make light* or *easy*, συμφοράς E.*HF*18; ᾠδῇ ἐ. τὴν ἔνδειαν Ph.2.477; θεὸς ἐ. πάντα ib.83, cf. 426 (Pass.), Babr.[46a], Simp.*in Cael*.667.25. II. Med., *prepare*, E.*HF*81:—Pass., ἐξευμαρίσθη· παρεσκευάσθη, Hsch.

ἐξευμεν-ίζω, *propitiate*, θεόν J.*AJ*8.13.8:—Med., ib.12.2.14, Lxx 4*Ma*.4.11, Plu.*Fab*.4, Ph.2.2, al., Herm.*in Phdr*.p.89 A.:—Pass., ὑπό τινος, περί τινος, Ph.2.520,533, cf. Porph.*Abst*.2.37. **–ισις**, εως, ἡ, *propitiation*, *Gloss*. **–ιστέον**, *one must propitiate*, Eust.676.16. **–ισμός**, ὁ, '*friendship's offering*', Nicom.*Harm*.12. **–ιστήριον**, τό, *propitiatory offering*, *Gloss*.

ἐξευνουχίζω, strengthd. for εὐνουχίζω, metaph., τὸν ἄκρατον Plu.2.692c:—Pass., Ph.1.224; –ισμένη ψυχή ib.389.

ἐξευπορέω, *supply abundantly*, ἐπικουρίαν ταῖς χρείαις Pl.*Lg*.918c. II. abs., *find a way out*, περί τι ib.861b.—The form ἐξευπορίζω, in X.*An*.5.6.19, is prob. f. l. for ἐκπορίζω.

ἐξεύρ-εσις, εως, ἡ, *searching out, search*, Hdt.1.67. 2. *finding out, invention*, ib.94. 3. *discovery*, τοῦ ὄντος Pl.*Min*.315a. **–ετέος**, α, ον, *to be discovered*, νοῦς Ar.*Nu*.728 (v.l. for εὑρητέος). II. ἐξευρετέον αὐτοῖς they *must find out*, Pl.*R*.380a. **–ετικός**, ή, όν, *inventive, ingenious*, M.Ant.1.9:—written **–ητικός**, Sch.E.*Med*.408. **–ημα**, ατος, τό, *thing found out, invention*, Hdt.1.53,94,171, A.*Th*.649, Metrod.*Fr*.7 (pl.); ἐ. σοφόν Ar.*Ec*.578 (lyr.); Παλαμηδικὸν.. τοὐξεύρημα Eup.351.6; τὰ καλὰ τῆς ψυχῆς ἐ. Metrod.*Fr*.6; *stratagem*, Phryn.Com.22 (pl.). **–ίσκω**, fut. –ευρήσω: aor. 2 ἐξηῦρον, Med. –ηυρόμην or –ηυράμην (Men.161.4 codd. Stob.):—*find out, discover*, Il.18.322, Th.8.66, Pl.*R*.566b, etc.; ἐ. ὁπόθεν *find out* from what source.., Ar.*Eq*.800; *invent*, Hdt.1.8, etc.; βωμολόχον τι Ar.*Eq*.1194; ἀριθμόν, μηχανήματ' ἐ., A.*Pr*.460, 469; ἐ. ἐπ' ἐμοὶ δεσμόν ib.97; simply, *find*, [πόλεως] σε σωτῆρα ἐ. (sc. ὄντα) S.*OT*304; αὐτὸν ἐ. ἐχθίω Φρυγῶν Id.*Aj*.1054; ποῦ τὸν ἄνδρα.. ἐξευρήσομεν; Ar.*Eq*.145: c. inf., ἄλλο τι ἐξευρήκασι.. γενέσθαι Hdt.1.196; οὐκ ἐξευρίσκω τι ἄλλο ποιεῖν *POxy*.1588.10 (iv A.D.); ἓν γὰρ πόλλ' ἂν ἐξεύροι μαθεῖν *would lead* one on to learn, S.*OT*120:—Pass., Hdt.1.94, al.: impers., ὧδέ σφι ἐς τὴν ἔψησιν τῶν κρεῶν ἐξεύρηται *this invention has been made*.., Id.4.61. 2. *seek out, search after*, Id.7.119, 5.33. 3. *win, get, procure*, ἀέθλων κράτος Pi.*I*.8(7).4; τὸ κάλλος ἄλγος ἐ. S.*Tr*.25; γαστρὶ μὲν τὰ σύμφορα τόξον τόδ' ἐ. Id.*Ph*.288; νόμους σεαυτῷ Antipho 5.12; ἄνδρα ἐ., of a girl, Phoen.2.11:—Med., τὴν τέχνην Men. l. c.; παλαίσματα Theoc.24.114. II. *search* a place, ἄλὸς θέναρ Pi.*I*.4(3).56.

ἐξευτελ-ίζω, strengthd. for εὐτελίζω, Acus.28 J., J.*AJ*6.5.3, Plu.*Alex*.28, Ath.11.494d. II. ἐ. τὴν δίαιταν *reduce* one's standard of living, J.*AJ*18.1.3. **–ισμός**, ὁ, *disparagement*, D.H.*Th*.3, Sm.*Ps*.122(123).3. **–ιστής**, οῦ, ὁ, *disparager*, τῶν ἄλλων ἀνθρώπων Phld.*Vit*.p.14 J., cf. p.42 J.

ἐξευ-τονέω, strengthd. for εὐτονέω, Arr.*Epict.*4.1.147. **-τρεπίζω**, strengthd. for εὐτρεπίζω, E.*El.*75. **-φραίνομαι**, *to be delighted*, *Corp.Herm.*1.30. II. *show rejoicing*, Lxx *Ez.*23.41 (v.l.).

ἐξεύχομαι, *boast aloud, proclaim*, ἐ. τι [εἶναι] *boast* that.., Pi.*O.* 13.61, A.*Ag.*533; Ἀργεῖαι γένος ἐξευχόμεσθα we *boast to be* Argives by race, Id.*Supp.*275; also ἐ. γένος *boast of* it, ib.272. II. *pray earnestly for*, ἐς ὄψιν ἥκεις ὥνπερ ἐξηύχου Id.*Ch.*215: c. acc. et inf., E. *Med.*930. III. ἐξεύχομαι· ἀφίξομαι, Hsch.

ἐξευωνίζω, *cheapen*, *Dacia* 2.127 (Callatis).

ἐξεφάλλομαι, only in Hsch., ἐξέπαλτο (-τον cod.)· ἐξεπήδησεν (-σαν cod.), but cf. ἐκπάλλομαι.

ἐξέφᾰνεν, poet. for -φάνησαν, Pi.*O.*13.18.

ἐξέφηβος, ὁ, *one who is beyond the age of an* ἔφηβος, *a youth of seventeen*, Censorin.*Nat.*14.8.

ἐξεφίημι, = ἐφίημι:—only Med. ἐξεφίεμαι, *enjoin, command*, c. inf., ἐκεῖνον εἴργειν Τεῦκρος ἐξεφίεται S.*Aj.*795, cf. E.*IT*1468.

ἐξεχαρυβδαάνθη· ἀνεπόθη, Hsch.; cf. ἐκχαρυβδίζω.

ἐξεχέ-βρογχος, *having the thyroid cartilage* (*Adam's apple*) *prominent*, Hp.*Art.*41, Aret.*SD*1.8. **-γλουτος**, ον, *with prominent buttocks*, Hp.*Art.*56.

ἐξεχέμεναι· χωρὶς ἐμοῦ (Lacon.), Hsch.

ἐξεχής, ές, *gradual*: neut. as Adv., dub. l. in Aret.*CD*1.8.

ἐξέχω, *stand out* or *project from*, τινός Ar.*V.*1377; πέτρα ἐξέχουσα ὑπὲρ κοιλάδος *SIG*827 iii 11 (ii A.D.). 2. abs., *stand out, be prominent*, Hp.*VC*1; ἐξέχοντα ὦτα Corn.*ND*27; ἐξέχοντα *convexities*, opp. κοῖλα, Pl.*R.*602c; τὸ ἐξέχον in painting, Philostr.*VA*2.20:—Pass., τὰ ἐξεχόμενα *projecting* panels, Lxx 3*Ki.*7.16(29). b. of the sun, *shine out, appear*, ἣν ἐξέχῃ ἕλη κατ' ὄρθρον Ar.*V.*771; ἔξεχ', ὦ φίλ' ἅλιε *shine out*, fair sun, Id.*Fr.*389; πρὶν ἥλιον ἐ. before sun*rise*, Lex ap. D.43.62. c. metaph., *to be prominent, distinguished*, ἀρετῇ Ascl. *Tact.*7.2; ὁ ἐξέχων ἀνήρ Demetr.*Eloc.*146; οἱ τῶν στρατιωτῶν ἐξέχοντες Hdn.2.7.7; ἐξέχει ἐν ἑκάστῳ ἄλλο each *has* its own *distinction*, Plot.5.8.4. II. *to be attached to, depend on, cling to*, τοῦ θείου Porph. *Marc.*11:—but usu. Med., τινός D.H.1.79, *POxy.*1027.6 (i A.D.), D.Chr.45.5; σώματα ψυχῶν ἐξέχεται Dam.*Pr.*99, cf. Procl.*Inst.*100 (but prob. corrupt in sense *give up, withdraw from*, J.*AJ*3.12.3).

ἐξεψάμενος· κατασχών, περιπλακείς, Hsch. (leg. ἐξαψ-).

ἐξέψω, *boil thoroughly*, Hdt.4.61:—Pass., *to be boiled out*, v.l. in Arist.*Mete.*384ᵃ2.

ἔξζευξις, εως, ἡ, *team of six*, *Gloss.*

ἔξηβος, ον, (ἥβη) *past one's youth* (acc. to Hsch., thirty-five years old), A.*Th.*11.

ἐξηγ-έομαι, *to be leader of*, c. gen. pers., τῶν δ' ἐξηγείσθω Il.2.806 (for And.1.116, v. II. 3). 2. c. acc. pers., *lead, govern*, in Th., τὰς πόλεις 1.76; τὴν Πελοπόννησον ib.71. b. abs., Hdt.1.151, 9.11. 3. c. dat. pers. et acc. rei, *show* one *the way to*, τοῖσι ἐχθροῖσι τῆς πατρίδος ἄλωσιν Hdt.6.135; ἃ δ' ἐξηγεῖσθε τοῖς ξυμμάχοις Th.3.55: c. dat. pers. only, *go before, lead*, ἡμῖν S.*OC*1589, etc.: c. acc. loci only, *lead the way to*, χῶρον ib.1520. 4. c. gen. rei, ἐ. τῆς πράξεως X.*Cyr.*2.1.29; with dat. pers. added, πᾶσι κάλλους τε καὶ τελειότητος Jul.*Or.*4.132d. 5. ἐ. εἰς τὴν Ἑλλάδα *lead an army* into Greece, X.*An.*6.6.34. II. *dictate* a form of words, ἐ. τὸν νόμον τῷ κήρυκι D.19.70; ἐξηγοῦ θεοὺς *dictate, name* them, E.*Med.*745. 2. generally, *prescribe, order*, ποιήσουσι τοῦτο τὸ ἂν κεῖνος ἐξηγέηται Hdt. 5.23; ὅ τι χρὴ ποιέειν ἐξηγέο σύ Id.4.9, cf. 7.234; ᾗ ὁ νόμος ἐξηγεῖται Pl.*R.*604b: of a diviner, c. inf., *order* one to do, A.*Eu.*595; τἄλλα δ' ἐξηγοῦ φίλοις Id.*Ch.*552; esp. freq. of religious forms and ceremonies, οἷς τῶν ἄλλων θεῶν οἱ Μάγοι ἐξηγοῦντο, = τοῖς ἄλλοις θεοῖς οὓς .. X.*Cyr.*8.3.11, cf. 4.5.51, 7.3.1; τί φῶ; δίδασκ' ἄπειρον ἐξηγουμένη A.*Ch.*118, cf. S.*OC*1284, etc.; οὗτος ὁ θεὸς περὶ τὰ τοιαῦτα .. ἐ. Pl.*R.* 427c, cf. 469a. 3. *expound, interpret*, ἐ. τὸ οὔνομα καὶ τὴν θυσίην Hdt.2.49; τὸν ποιητήν Pl.*Cra.*407a; ἃ Ὅμηρος λέγει Id.*Ion* 531a; ὁ τὸν Ἡράκλειτον .. ἐξηγούμενος Antiph.113.3; τὰ νόμιμα D.47.69: abs., ἄγραφοι νόμοι καθ' οὓς Εὐμολπίδαι ἐξηγοῦνται according to which they *expound* things, Lys.6.10, cf. And.1.116 (leg. κηρύκων ὧν); cf. ἐξηγητής II. III. *tell at length, relate in full*, Hdt.2.3, A.*Pr.*216, 702, Th.5.26; *set forth, explain*, τὴν ἔλασιν the line of march, Hdt. 3.4, 7.6; ἃ μετὰ χεῖρας ἔχοι καὶ -ήσασθαι οἷός τε Th.1.138; τὰ τοῦ νομοθέτου βουλήματα Pl.*Lg.*802c, cf. *R.*474c: c. acc. et inf., *explain* that.., S.*Aj.*320: folld. by relat., ἐ. ὁτέῳ τρόπῳ .. Hdt.3.72, etc.; ἐ. περί τινος X.*Lac.*2.1. **-ημα**, ατος, τό, *explanation*, D.H.*Rh.* 9.8. **-ηματικός**, ή, όν, = ἐξηγητικός, ὕμνοι Men.Rh.p.337 S. 2. *having a gift for exposition*, Olymp.*Proll.*10.25. 3. Adv. Comp. -ώτερον, λέγειν τῆς λέξεως Id. *in Alc.*p.205 C. **-ησις**, εως, ἡ, *statement, narrative*, ἐ. ποιήσασθαι Th.1.72; ὑπέρ τινος Plb.6.3.1. II. *explanation, interpretation*, περὶ τοὺς νόμους Pl.*Lg.*631a; ἐνυπνίων D.S. 2.29; Ἐ. τῶν Ἐμπεδοκλέους, title of a work by Zeno Eleaticus; so in Gramm., Sch.Il.8.296. **-ητεία**, ἡ, *office of* ἐξηγητής, *PRyl.*77.35, al. (ii A.D.). **-ητέον**, *one must relate, set forth*, Plb.3.4.6. **-ητεύω**, *hold the office* of ἐξηγητής, *PLond.*2.153.14 (ii B.C.), *Sammelb.*176 (ii A.D.), *PFay.*85.1 (iii A.D.). **-ητής**, οῦ, ὁ, *one who leads on, adviser*, πρηγμάτων ἀγαθῶν Hdt.5.31 codd.; οὑτοσὶ δὲ .. ἁπάντων ἦν τούτων ὁ ἐ. D.35.17. II. *expounder, interpreter*, esp. of oracles, dreams, or omens, Hdt.1.78; at Athens, of sacred rites or customs, modes of burial, expiation, etc., *spiritual director*, Pl.*Euthphr.*4d, 9a, *Lg.*759c, e, 775a, D.47.68, Is.8.39, Thphr.*Char.*16.6: as an official title, ἐ. Πυθόχρηστος *IG*3.241; ἐ. ἐξ Εὐπατριδῶν ib.267; ἐ. ἐξ Εὐμολπιδῶν Lys.6.10, etc., cf. Suid. s.v.; πάτριος ἐ., of Apollo, Pl.*R.*427c. b. at Rome, of the *pontifices*, D.H.2.73. 2. *guide, cicerone*, to temples, etc., Paus.5.15.10, *SIG*1021.20 (Olympia). 3. *commentator*, Gal. 15.518, Mich. *in EN*50.8. **-ητικός**, ή, όν, *of* or *for narrative*, Diom. p.428 K.: Comp. Adv. -ώτερον Antig.*Mir.*60. 2. *explanatory*, Hermog.*Id.*1.6, Alex.Aphr. *in Metaph.*358.13, S.E.*M.*9.132, etc. Adv. -κῶς ib.7.28. II. ἐξηγητικά (sc. βιβλία), τά, title of work on religious rites by Anticlides, Plu.*Nic.*23: -κόν, τό, work by Timosthenes, Sch.A.R.3.847. **-ορέω**, = ἐξειπεῖν, in pf. part., Hsch. **-ορία**, ἡ, *utterance*, Lxx *Jb.*33.26. 2. *confession*, ib. 22.22.

ἐξηέρωσις, v. ἐξαέρωσις.

ἐξηθέω, *filter out, purify*, in Pass., Arist.*Pr.*967ᵃ15, Thphr.*CP*6. 13.1.

ἐξήια· θυμιάματα, Hsch.

Ἐξηκεστῖδαλκίδαι, = κιθαρῳδοί, called after Ἐξηκεστίδης and Ἀλκίδας, Hsch.

Ἐξήκεστος· ἡταιρηκώς, ὅθεν καὶ τοὺς πρωκτοὺς ὁμωνύμως ἐξηκέστους ἔλεγον, Hsch.

ἐξηκονθ-ημερισία, ἡ, *sixty days' crop*, *PCair.Zen.*54(c).5 (iii B.C.). **-ήμερος**, ον, *on the sixtieth day*, ἀπόφθαρμα Hp.*Epid.*2.2. 13.

ἑξήκοντα (ϝεξ- *SIG*56.30 (Argos, v B.C.)), οἱ, αἱ, τά, indecl., *sixty*, Il.2.587, etc.; οἱ ἑ., a college of γελωτοποιοί at Athens, Telephan. ap. Ath.14.614d.

ἑξηκοντά-βιβλος [ᾰ], ον, *consisting of sixty books*, Suid. s. v. Ἱπποκράτης. **-δύο, -τέσσᾰρες, -πέντε, -έξ, -επτά, -οκτώ, -εννέα**, 62, 64, 65, 66, 67, 68, 69, Thd.*Da.*5.31, Ph.1.21, Lxx *Nu.*3.50, *Ge.*46.26, 1*Es.* 5.15, *Ne.*11.6, 1*Es.*2.14. **-έτης**, ες, *sixty years old*, Mimn.6, Hp. *Epid.*5.25; also -ετῶν λυκαβάντων *IG*12(7).290 (Amorgos). **-ετία**, ἡ, *the age of sixty*, Ph.2.276, Plu.*Cic.*25. **-κις**, poet. -κι, Adv. *sixty times*, Pi.*O.*13.99. **-κλῖνος**, ον, *with sixty couches*, οἶκος D.S. 16.83. **-λιθος**, ὁ, *precious stone of many colours*, Plin.*HN*37. 167. **-μοιρία**, ἡ, *arc of sixty degrees*, Heph.Astr.2.11 (ἑξακ- cod.). **-μοιρος**, ον, *consisting of sixty degrees*, Sch.Arat. 644. **-πηχυς**, υ, *sixty cubits long*, Callix.2. **-πους**, ὁ, ἡ, -πουν, τό, gen. ποδος, *sixty feet square*, Gal.10.33.

ἑξηκοντάρουρος [ᾰ], ον, *possessing sixty* ἄρουραι, *PCair.Zen.*1.24, 57 (iii B.C.).

ἑξηκοντάρχιον, τό, name of an eyesalve, Aët.7.103.

ἑξηκοντάς, άδος, ἡ, *the number sixty*, Vett.Val.300.17, al., Iamb. *Myst.*5.8. II. *sixtieth part*, Str.2.5.7.

ἑξηκοντα-στάδιος [στᾰ], ον, *of sixty stades*, δίαρμα Str.6.2.3. **-τᾰλαντία**, ἡ, *sum of sixty talents*, D.14.19.

ἑξηκοντ-όργυιος, ον, *sixty fathoms high*, Tz.*H.*9.587. **-ούτης**, ες, = ἑξηκονταέτης, Pl.*Lg.*755a, 812b, Luc.*Alex.*35, *Philops.*5.

ἑξηκοσταῖος, α, ον, *on the sixtieth day*, Hp.*Art.*69.

ἑξηκοστός (Aeol. **ἐξήκοιστος** *IG*11(4).1064b15), ή, όν, *sixtieth*, Hdt.6.126, etc. II. ἑξηκοστή, ἡ, *customs duty* or *tax of* $\frac{1}{60}$, *IG*12 (2).3 (Mytil.), *PEleph.*14.11 (iii B.C.). III. ἑξηκοστόν, τό, $\frac{1}{60}$ *of a degree, second*, Gem.18.7; but, $\frac{1}{60}$ *of a grand circle*, Id.16.6, al. IV. τόκοι ἑ. ἐφ' ἔτη δέκα interest *at the rate of* $\frac{1}{60}$, *OGI*444.14 (Ilium).

ἑξηκοστοτέταρτος, ον, *sixty-fourth*, Nicom.*Ar.*1.8, Hero *Geom.*12. 68, al.

ἐξήκω, *to have reached* a certain point, ἐξήκεις ἵνα φανεῖς *hast reached* a point at which thou wilt show, S.*Tr.*1157; ἅλις ἵν' ἐξήκεις δακρύων Id.*OT*1515 (troch.); ἀτελές τι καὶ οὐκ ἐξῆκον ἐκεῖσε οἷ πάντα δεῖ ἀφήκειν Pl.*R.*530e; δεῦρ' ἐ. Id.*Epin.*987a; ἐπειδὰν αἱ κλήσεις ἐξήκωσιν εἰς τὸ δικαστήριον Plu.2.833f, etc.: c. acc. cogn., ἐ. ὁδὸν S.*El.* 1318. II. of Time, *to have run out* or *expired*, Hdt.2.111, S.*Ph.* 199, Lys.7.11, X.*An.*6.3.26, *IG*2².682.69, etc.; πρίν μοι μοῖραν ἐξήκειν βίου S.*Ant.*896; ἐξήκει ἡ ἀρχή, ἡ προθεσμία, Pl.*Lg.*766c, Lex ap. D. 43.16. 2. of prophecies, dreams, etc., *to have come to an accomplishment, turn out true*, Hdt.1.120, 6.80; τὰ πάντ' ἂν ἐξήκοι σαφῆ S. *OT*1182; of magical operations, *succeed*, *PMag.Par.*1.1273.

ἐξήλᾱσα, Ep. **ἐξήλασσα**, v. ἐξελαύνω.

ἐξήλᾰτος, ον, *beaten out*, ἀσπίδα χαλκείην ἐξήλατον Il.12.295.

ἐξηλέκατα· φανερῶς γενόμενα, Hsch. (leg. ἐξέλεγκτα). **ἐξῆλθον**, v. sub ἐξέρχομαι.

ἐξηλιάζω, *hang in the sun*, as a form of torture, Lxx 2*Ki.*21.6, 13:—Pass., *to be burnt by the sun*, Hsch.

ἐξηλίμβωρ· ἔβλεπε (Lacon.), Hsch.

ἐξηλιόομαι, Pass., *to be sunny, light*, Plu.2.929d.

ἐξηλίφαμεν· ἐξεκαθάραμεν, Hsch.

ἐξηλλαγμένως, Adv., (ἐξαλλάσσω) *strangely, unusually*, D.S.2.42, Plu.2.745f, S.E.*M.*8.187, Iamb.*Protr.*5, etc.

ἐξηλόω, *remove nails from, unfasten*, θύρας *PTeb.*332.15 (ii A.D.), cf. *PFlor.*69.21 (iii A.D.):—Pass., -ωμένος *unfastened*, *POxy.*1272.8 (ii A.D.).

ἐξήλῠσις, εως, ἡ, *way out, outlet*, τοῦ πυρὸς οὐκ ἔχοντος (nisi leg. -τες) ἐξήλυσιν ἐκ τοῦ ἄστεος Hdt.5.101; of a river, ἔχοντος οὐδαμῇ ἐ. Id.3.117; ἐ. ἐς θάλασσαν κατήκουσα Id.7.130.

ἐξῆμαρ, Adv. *for six days, six days long*, Od.10.80, 14.249.

ἐξήμαρε· ἐπέρασεν, Hsch.

ἐξημαρτημένως, Adv., (ἐξαμαρτάνω) *wrongly, to no purpose*, Pl.*Lg.* 891d.

ἑξήμερος, ἡ, *space of six days*, Vett.Val.369.24, Procl.*Hyp.*3.56.

ἐξημερ-όω, *tame* or *reclaim entirely*, χῶρον [ἀκανθώδη] Hdt.1.126; ἐ. γαῖαν *free* the land *from wild beasts*, etc., E.*HF*20, 852; *reclaim* wild plants, κοτίνους εἰς συκᾶς ἐ. Plu.*Fab.*20, cf. Thphr.*HP*2.2.12 (Pass.), al.: metaph., *soften, humanize*, τὸ τῆς ψυχῆς ἀτέραμνον Plb.4.

21.4; διανοίας Ph.2.402; τὰς τῶν ἠθῶν καὶ παθῶν ὕλας Lxx 4*Ma.*1.29; αὐτὸν διὰ παιδείας Plu.*Num.*3; τὴν νῆσον ἐξηγριωμένην ὑπὸ κακῶν... ἐξημέρωσε Id.*Tim.*35, cf. Parth.20.1; ἡ ἐξημερωμένη ἐν τοῖς νῦν χρόνοις ἀναστροφή our present *civilized* life, Phld.*Sto.*339.19. **-ωσις,** εως, ἡ, strengthd. for ἡμέρωσις, Plu.*Num.*14, Porph.*Abst.*3.18, etc.

ἐξήμευσαι, v. ἐξαμεύω. **ἐξήμησε,** v. ἐξεμέω.

ἐξημμένως, Adv., (ἐξάπτω B) *angrily*, Sch.Il.9.512.

ἐξημοιβός, όν, (ἐξαμείβω) *serving for change*, εἵματα δ' ἐξημοιβά *changes of* raiment, Od.8.249; τεύχεα Q.S.7.437; ἐξημοιβαί· ἕτεραι, Hsch.

ἐξήνεγκα, ἐξήνεγκον, v. ἐκφέρω.

ἐξηνθισμένως, *carptim*, *Gloss.*

ἐξήνιος, ον, (ἡνία) *unbridled, uncontrollable*, Plu.2.510e.

ἐξήπᾰφον, v. ἐξαπαφίσκω.

ἐξηπειρόω, *join to the mainland*, of rivers which form deposits at their mouths, πόρον, νήσους, Str.1.3.7, 10.2.19:—Pass., νησῖδες Id. 11.4.2.

ἐξηπεροπεύω, *cheat utterly*, Ar.*Lys.*840.

ἐξηπέτριπται· δεδαπάνηται (Lacon.), Hsch.

ἐξηπῐᾰλόομαι, Pass., *change into an* ἠπίαλος, Hp.*Judic.*11.

ἐξηπλωμένως, Adv., (ἐξαπλόω) *fully, diffusely*, Sch.Opp.*H.*2.113.

ἐξήρᾰτο, v. ἐξαίρω 11.1.

ἐξήρετμος, ον, *of six banks of oars*, ἐξηρέτμοις πτέρυξιν ἠγλαϊσμένος, i.e. in command of a ἑξήρης, *Epigr.Gr.*337 (Cyzicus).

ἐξηρημένως, Adv. *transcendentally*, v. ἐξαιρέω.

ἑξ-ήρης, ες, *with six banks of oars*, ναῦς Plu.*Cat.Mi.*39. II. Subst. **ἑξήρης** (sc. ναῦς), ἡ, Plb.1.26.11, etc. **-ηρικὸν** πλοῖον, = foreg. 11, Id.*Fr.*39.

ἐξηρώησα, aor. 1 of ἐξερωέω (q.v.).

ἑξῆς, Ep. **ἑξείης,** Adv., Dor. **ἑξᾶν** (accent unknown), *IG*12(1). 155.108 (Rhodes, ii B.C.), *SIG*1023.80 (Cos, iii/ii B.C.), al.:—*one after another, in order, in a row*, ἑξῆς εὐνάζοντο Od.4.449; ἑξῆς δ' ἑζόμενοι ib.580 (elsewh. Hom. uses the form ἑξείης, Il.6.241, Od.4.408); πάντας ἑ....κτείνοντες Th.7.29, cf. E.*Fr.*657.2; τὰ ἑ. v.l. in Arist. *Cael.*310^{b}12. b. Math., ἑ. ἀνάλογον in *continued* proportion, Euc. 8.1, al.; οἱ ἑ. ἀριθμοί *successive* numbers, Archim.*Spir.Praef.*; γραμμαὶ ἑ. κείμεναι placed *in order*, ib.11; τούτου ἑ. γινομένου if this be done *continually*, Id.*Sph.Cyl.*1.11. 2. ἑ. διεξελθεῖν, λέγειν, *in a regular, consequential manner*, Pl.*Plt.*257b, 286c; τοῦ ἑ. ἕνεκα περαίνεσθαι τὸν λόγον Id.*Grg.*454c; ὁ ἑ. λόγος the *following* argument, Id.*Ti.*20b; ἐν ἅπασι τούτοις ἑ. Longin.9.14, cf. 4.4. 3. Gramm., τὸ ἑ. *grammatical sequence*, opp. ὑπερβατόν, A.D.*Pron.*41.3, al.; καὶ τὰ ἑ., Lat. *et cetera*, *PTeb.*319.34 (iii A.D.), etc. 4. of Time, *thereafter, next*, A.*Fr.*475, Ar.*Ec.*638; τὸν ἑ. χρόνον Pl.*Plt.*271b; ἡ ἑ. ἡμέρα *Ev.Luc.* 9.37; ἐν τῷ (v.l. τῇ) ἑ. *next day*, ib.7.11; εἰς τὸ ἑ. for the *future*, *POxy.*474.28 (ii A.D.), etc. b. of Place, *next*, E.*IA*249, Arist. *Mu.*392^{a}26. II. c. gen., *next to*, τινός Ar.*Ra.*765; τὰ τούτων ἑ. Pl.*R.*390a; τούτων ἑ. *next after*.., D.18.102; of logical connexion, Pl.*Phlb.*42c: c. dat., *next to*, Λάχητι...τὴν ἑ. θύραν Ephipp.16; τούτοις ἑ. *next in order to*, Pl.*Cra.*399d, al.; τὸ ἑ. τῇ γεωμετρίᾳ *what comes next to*..., Id.*R.*528a; τὸ ἑ. ἔργον τοῖς Μαραθῶνι *next after*, Id. *Mx.*241a; ἑ. Ἀριστογείτονι *beside* A., Ar.*Lys.*633; παρὰ τὸ ἑ. τῷ νοερῷ ζῴῳ *that which befits*.., M.Ant.4.5; ἐπεχορήγησα αὐτῇ τὰ ἑ. made *suitable* provision for her, *POxy.*282.7 (i A.D.).

ἐξητασμένως, Adv., (ἐξετάζω) *after full investigation, deliberately*, M.Ant.1.16, Them.*Or.*16.203c; *with deliberate precision* (in the choice of words), Ph.1.605, al., Aristid.*Or.*45(8).4.

ἐξητριάζω, *filter*: pf. Pass. ἐξητρίασμαι Hp.ap.Gal.19.98.

ἐξηττάομαι, strengthd. for ἡττάομαι, τῆς σπουδῆς Plu.*Alex.*14; διαβολῶν Arr.*An.*7.12.5; ὑπὸ κακοῦ ib.4.9.1; ὑπὸ λόγου Ph.1.179.

ἐξηττημένη, pf. part. Pass., *sifted*, Antiph.34.5: pres. not found, cf. διαττάω: fort. ἐξεττημένη.

ἐξηχ-ευη, *stupes*, *Gloss.* (leg. -εύη). **-έω,** *sound forth*, Lxx *Jl.* 3(4).14, Nech.ap.Vett.Val.241.17: c. acc. cogn., τὸ κύκνειον ἐξηχεῖν *sound forth* the swan's song, i.e. *give vent to* dying prayers, Plb.30. 4.7, cf. Ph.2.24:—Pass., Id.2.107, 1*Ep.Thess.*1.8, Hsch., etc. II. *utter senseless sounds*, of idiots, Polem.*Phgn.*51. **-ησις,** εως, ἡ, *unpleasant sound*, Ael.Dion.*Fr.*298. 2. *mode of utterance*, *PMag. Par.*1.923. **-ία,** ἡ, *stupidity, nonsense*, Porph.*Chr.*35, Hsch. s.v. ἀφραδίησι. **-ος,** ον, *rudely sounding*: hence, *absurd, stupid*, Porph.*Chr.*35, *EM*696.39.

ἐξῐάλλω, = ἐκβάλλω, Suid.

ἐξῐ-άομαι, fut. -άσομαι, Ion. -ήσομαι:—*cure thoroughly*, Hdt.3. 132,134, E.*Rh.*872, Ph.1.541; φόβους Pl.*Lg.*933c; πείνην ἢ δίψαν Id.*Phlb.*54e; *make full amends for*, τὴν βλάβην Id.*Lg.*879a; πόλεως ἅλωσιν E.*El.*1024. **-ᾱτέον,** *one must heal*, τὴν ἕλκωσιν Aët.16. 36. **-ατρός·** ἐκθυτικός, Hsch.

ἐξῐδῐ-άζομαι, Med., *appropriate to oneself*, Diph.42, *SIG*1106.46 (Cos), *Klio* 16.163 (Delph.), *Sammelb.*4638.10, D.S.1.23, etc. 2. *win over*, Plb.8.25.7, al. 3. *receive for one's own use*, παρά τινος *PRein.*14.18 (ii B.C.). **-ασμός,** ὁ, *winning over*, τῶν πόλεων Plb. 22.6.1; *appropriation*, Str.17.1.8. **-όομαι,** = ἐξιδιάζομαι 1, Isoc. 12.43, X.*HG*2.4.8.

ἐξῐδῐοποι-έομαι, = ἐξιδιάζομαι, D.S.5.57, Ath.2.50f, Aesop.12, A.D.*Synt.*199.6. **-ησις,** εως, ἡ, *appropriation*, *Gloss.*

ἐξιδίω [δῐ], *exude*: in Ar.*Av.*791 euphem. for τιλάω.

ἐξιδρόω, *perspire*, Hp.*Vict.*4.89, D.S.4.78, Dsc.*Eup.*1.97: c. acc. cogn., ὕδωρ ἐ. Alex.Aphr.*Pr.*1.119.

ἐξιδρύω, fut. -ύσω [ῡ], *make to sit down*, S.*OC*11:—Med., βίοτον ἐξιδρυσάμην I *have settled*, E.*Fr.*884.

ἐξίδρωσις, εως, ἡ, *violent sweat*, Plu.2.949e (pl.), Sor.1.46.

ἐξιερ-ιστεύω (fort. -ιερατ-), *vacate a priesthood*, *IG*12(1).701 (Rhodes, i B.C.). **-όω,** *consecrate*, Hsch.

ἐξίημι (v. ἵημι), *send out, let* one *go out*, ἱππόθεν ἐξέμεναι (Ep. aor. 2 inf. for ἐξεῖναι) Od.11.531; μηδ' ἐξέμεν ἂψ ἐς Ἀχαιούς Il.11.141; ἐπὴν γόου ἐξ ἔρον εἵην *had dismissed, satisfied* it, 24.227; πόθον prob. in Sapph.*Supp.*23.23; [τοὺς ἐπικούρους] ἐξῆκε ἐπὶ τοὺς Πέρσας Hdt.3. 146; ἐ. ἱστίον *let out* the sail, Pi.*P.*1.91; ἐξιέναι πάντα κάλων (v. sub κάλως); ἐ. ἀφρόν *throw out* or *forth*, E.*Ba.*1122; ἐ. ἐκ τῆς κοιλίης τὴν κεδρίην *take* it *out*, Hdt.2.87; ἐ. τι εἴς τι *discharge* it into..., Pl.*Ti.* 82e. 2. intr., of rivers, *discharge themselves*, ἐς θάλασσαν Hdt. 1.6 (in 3 sg. ἐξίει, cf. ib.180), al., Th.4.103. II. Med., *put off from oneself, get rid of*, freq. in Hom. in the phrase πόσιος καὶ ἐδητύος ἐ. ἔρον ἕντο Il.1.469, al.; ἱμερτῶν ἔργων ἐξ ἔρον ἱέμενος Thgn.1064. 2. *send from oneself, divorce*, τὴν ἔχεις γυναῖκα ἔξεο Hdt.5.39 (ἐκσέο codd.).

ἐξίθμη (-ίθνη cod.)· ἔξοδος, Hsch. **ἐξιθυίω·** ἔξω καθίσω, Id.

ἐξῐθύνω, *make straight*, στάθμη δόρυ νήϊον Il.15.410; εἰ ἱκανῶς ἐξιθυνται Hp.*Fract.*3, cf. *Art.*42. 2. *direct aright*, πηδάλιον A.R.1.562.

ἐξῐκᾰνόω, *suffice*, τῇ χώρᾳ Procop.*Aed.*4.2.

ἐξῐκάνω [ᾰ], *arrive at*, impf. ἐξίκανε [ῐ] Orph.*A.*194; cf. ἐξίκω.

ἐξῐκετεύω, *entreat successfully, persuade by entreaty*, S.*OT*760, Parth.17.5, J.*AJ*3.11.3, Polyaen.6.16.5.

ἐξικμ-άζω, (ἰκμάς) *send forth moisture, cause to exude*, ἡ θερμότης ἐ. τὸ ὑγρὸν ἐκ τοῦ γεώδους Arist.*GA*718^{b}19; τὸ σπέρμα ib.727^{b}24, cf. *HA*583^{a}11:—Pass., *to be exuded* or *evaporated*, Id.*Mete.*385^{b}8, *Sens.* 443^{a}14. 2. intr. in Act., = Pass., Id.*Mete.*384^{b}9, *Pr.*930^{b}34. II. *deprive of moisture, suck dry*, Id.*HA*594^{a}13; ἐ. τὴν ὑγρότητα Thphr. *CP*4.8.4 (cod. Urb.):—Pass., ἐξικμασμένη τροφή *digested*, Pl.*Ti.*33c, Arist.*PA*675^{b}31; τὰ παλαιὰ σπέρματα ἐξίκμασται τὴν δύναμιν Id.*Pr.* 924^{b}30; *lose all moisture*, Thphr.*HP*5.7.4, 7.5.1; of athletes, τοῦ περιττοῦ -άζεσθαι Philostr.*Gym.*58. III. in E.*Andr.*398, ἐξικμάζω seems to be corrupt (perh. for ἐξιχμάζω). **-ᾰσις,** εως, ἡ, *drying*, Gal.17(2).496. **-αστέος,** α, ον, *that must have moisture removed*, c. acc., -τέοι τοὺς ἱδρῶτας Philostr.*Gym.*52. **-αστικός,** ή, όν, = ἀναποτικός, *sucking up*, τῶν ὑγρῶν Procl.*Par.Ptol.*27.

ἐξικνέομαι, poet. aor. ἐξῐκόμην Il.9.479, augm. ἐξίκοντο [ῑ] Sapph. 1.13:—*reach, arrive at* a place, Hom. always in aor. and mostly c. acc. loci, ἄλλων ἐξίκετο δῆμον Il.24.481, etc.; Φθίην δ' ἐξῐκόμην ἐριβώλακα ...ἐς Πηλῆα ἄνακτα 9.479; δεῦρο Simon.171, cf. Pi.*P.*3.76, A.*Pr.*810: abs., Sapph. l.c.: with Preps., ἐ. ἐς βυσσόν Hdt.2.28; ἐς ἥβην S. *Fr.*583.6; ἐπ' ὄρος A.*Ag.*303; πρὸς πεδία Id.*Pr.*792; μέχρι γάμου καὶ γενεᾶς Plu.2.149d. II. *come to* as a suppliant, c. acc. pers., Od. 13.206, 20.223, Pi.*P.*11.35; πρός τινα Ant.Lib.38.2. 2. c. acc. rei, *arrive at, reach* an object, σοφίας ἄωτον ἄκρον Pi.*I.*7(6).19; ἔργῳ οὐδὲ τἀναγκαῖα ἐ. *complete, accomplish*, Th.1.70; τεθνηκόσιν γὰρ ἔλεγεν, οἷς οὐδὲ τρὶς λέγοντες ἐξικνούμεθα (by attract. for οὕς) Ar.*Ra.*1176, cf. Plu.2.347e: c. gen., E.*El.*612; ἀλλήλων X.*HG*7.5.17; also πρός τι Plb.1.3.10, etc. 3. abs., *reach* to a distance, of an arrow, ὅσον τόξευμα ἐξικνέεται Hdt.4.139; of sight, ἐπὶ πολλὰ στάδια ἐ. X.*Mem.* 1.4.17, cf. 2.3.19, E.*Ba.*1060; of mental operations, ὅσον δυνατός εἰμι ⟨ἐπὶ⟩ μακρότατον ἐξικέσθαι ἀκοῇ so far as I can *get* by inquiry, Hdt. 1.171; ἐπ' ὅσον μακρότατον ἱστορεῦντα ἦν ἐξικέσθαι Id.2.34, cf. 4.16, 192; ἐ. φρονήσει ἐπ' ἀμφότερα Pl.*Hp.Ma.*281d; περαιτέρω τῆς χρείας ἐ. τῇ θεωρίᾳ Plu.*Sol.*3. b. *suffice*, of persons, πρὸς τὸν προκείμενον ἄεθλον Hdt.4.10; ἐπί τι Plu.*Pomp.*39; of things, ἂν ἐξικνῆται τὰ ἡμέτερα χρήματα Pl.*Prt.*311d: prov., ἂν μὴ λεοντῆ γ' ἐξίκητ', ἀλωπεκῆν πρόσαψον *Com.Adesp.*49 D.

ἐξικόρ· ἐκτικός, Hsch.

ἐξίκω [ῑ], = ἐξικάνω, Orph.*A.*392.

ἐξῑλᾰρόω, *cheer*, Ath.10.420e.

ἐξῐλ-ᾰσις [ῐ], εως, ἡ, *propitiation, atonement*, Lxx *Nu.*29.11, D.L. 1.110, Iamb.*Myst.*1.13 (pl.). **-άσκομαι,** fut. -άσομαι [ᾰ], *propitiate*, Δία Orac.ap.Hdt.7.141; Ἀπόλλωνα X.*Cyr.*7.2.19; τὴν θεόν Men.544.6, cf. J.*AJ*12.2.14; τὴν ὀργήν τινος Plb.1.68.4; τὸ μήνιμα Plu.2.149d. 2. *atone for*, ἁμαρτίαν *IG*2^2.1365, 1366:—Pass., τὸ ἀποίνοις ἐξιλασθὲν *that which is atoned for* by..., Pl.*Lg.*862c. 3. abs., *make atonement*, περὶ τῶν ψυχῶν, περὶ τῆς ἁμαρτίας, Lxx *Ex.*30. 15, 32.30; ὑπὲρ τοῦ οἴκου Ἰσραήλ ib.*Ez.*45.17. [ῐ in Orac.ap.Hdt. l.c.] **-ασμα,** ατος, τό, *ransom, propitiatory offering*, Lxx 1*Ki.*12. 3, *Ps.*48(49).8. **-ασμός,** ὁ, = ἐξίλασις, ib.*Le.*23.27, al., Procl.*Par. Ptol.*24. **-αστήριος,** ον, *propitiatory*, in neut. pl., Sch.A.R.2. 485. **-αστικός,** ή, όν, = foreg., Corn.*ND*32 (v.l. -κῶς), Sch.A. *Th.*268. **-εόω,** *appease*, Hld.4.15, 1.8 (Pass.):—Med., Str.4.4. 6 (s.v.l.), Onos.5 tit., Hermog.*Stat.*3, Zen.4.93, Jul.*Or.*2.68b.—Cf. ἐξείλλω 3. **-έωμα,** ατος, τό, = ἐξίλασμα, Hsch. s.v. ἀποτροπίασμα (ἐξιλέωσμα cod.). **-έωσις,** εως, ἡ, = ἐξίλασις, Sch.A.*Pers.*229, *Gloss.* **-εωτός,** ή, όν, *appeasable*, ib.

ἐξίλλω, v. ἐξείλλω. **ἐξίμεναι,** poet. inf. of ἔξειμι (A).

ἐξῐν-ιάζω, (ἶνες) *take out the fibres from*, καλάμους *Peripl.M.Rubr.* 65:—Pass., Ath.9.406a. **-ίζω,** = foreg. (wh. shd. perh. be restored), Ruf.ap.Orib.8.47.4, Gal.12.672, al. **-όω,** *strip of fibre* and *sinew, destroy*, Lyc.841 (Pass.); but ἐξινώμενος (from ἐξινάω), = ἐκκενούμενος.., Hsch.; = κεκαθαρμένος, dub. in *Com.Adesp.*1004.

ἐξιονθίζω, (ἴονθος), τρίχα *shoot out* hair, S.*Fr.*729.

ἐξιόω, (ἰός) *clean from rust*, Arr.*Epict.*4.11.13, *PLeid.X.*6:—Pass., *to be freed from rust*, ib.10; *from poison*, Aët.8.16. II. *make poisonous*, τοὺς χυμούς Herod.Med. in *Rh.Mus.*58.104.

ἐξῑπόω, *press* or *squeeze out*, Hp.*Art.*50 (Pass.); ἰόν Aët.15.14. 2.

dry thoroughly, ἥλιος ὄρος ἐ. Aristid.*Or.*36(48).69 :—Pass., prob. l. in Ps.-Democr.Alch.p.44 B. II. *press heavily upon*, Ar.*Lys.*291.

ἐξιππ-άζομαι, *ride out* or *away*, Lxx *Hb.*1.8, J.*AJ*9.3.2. **-εύω**, = foreg., Plu.*Arat.*42 ; πρός τινας D.S.17.78 ; ἔς τινας App.*Hann.* 35.

ἔξιππον, τό, *six-horsed chariot*, *Com.Adesp.*1281 (pl.), Plb.30.25.11 (pl.), *Gloss.*

ἐξίπταμαι, later form of ἐκπέτομαι, Arist.*Fr.*346, Lxx *Pr.*7.10, Plu.2.90c, Jul.*Or.*2.101a.

ἐξιπωτικός, ή, όν, *fit for squeezing out, expressive*, φάρμακα Gal.13. 993, cf. Aët.12.31.

ἕξις, εως, ἡ, (ἔχω): I. (ἔχω trans.) *having, being in possession of, possession*, ἐπιστήμης ἕ., opp. κτῆσις, Pl.*Tht.*197b ; νοῦ Id.*Cra.* 414b ; ἡ τῶν ὅπλων Id.*Lg.*625c, cf. *R.*433e, *Sph.*247a, al., Arist. *Metaph.*1022^{b}4 ; opp. *στέρησις*, ib.1055^{b}13, S.E.*P.*3.49. 2. in surgery, *posture*, Hp.*Off.*3 ; ἕ. ἢ θέσις ib.15. II. (ἔχω intr.) *a being in a certain state, a permanent condition* as produced by practice (πρᾶξις), diff. from σχέσις (which is alterable) (v. infr.): 1. *state* or *habit* of body, Id.*Aph.*2.34, cf. Pl.*Tht.*153b ; ἕ. ὑγιεινή (so also X.*Mem.*1.2.4), opp. διάθεσις ἀθλητική, Hp.*Alim.*34 ; σχέσις καὶ ἕ. καὶ ἡλικίη Id.*Mochl.*41 ; ἡ φύσις καὶ ἡ ἕ. Id.*Acut.*43 : pl., Thphr. *Sens.*69 : generally, *condition*, ἐν ἕξει τοῦ δρᾶν D.H.*Comp.*25 ; ἕ. λεπτὴ κατὰ τοῦτο τὸ μέρος Hp.*Art.*12 ; τῷ θερμὴν ἕ. ἔχοντι Polystr. p.26 W. ; *outward appearance*, ἡ ἕ. τοῦ σώματος κρείσσων Lxx *Da.* 1.15, cf. *1Ki.*16.7, Sm.*La.*4.7 ; *habit* of a vine, Thphr.*CP*3.14.5 ; of material objects, ὑπὸ μιᾶς ἕξεως συνέχεσθαι S.E.*M.*7.102, cf. Ph.2. 511, *Stoic.*2.124, al. b. Medic., *the system*, Ath.2.45e, Mnesith. ib.54b, Paul.Aeg.3.59. 2. *state* or *habit of mind*, ἕ. κακίης Democr. 184 ; τὰς φύσεις τε καὶ ἕξεις τῶν ψυχῶν Pl.*Lg.*650b, etc. ; ἡ ἐν τῇ ψυχῇ ἕ., opp. ἡ τῶν σωμάτων ἕ., Id.*Tht.* l. c. ; πονηρᾶς ψυχῆς ἕξει ib.167b; λαμβάνειν ἕξιν τιμιωτέραν Id.*R.*591b. b. esp. *acquired habit*, opp. ἐνέργεια, Arist.*EN*1098^{b}33, al. 3. *trained habit, skill*, Pl.*Phdr.* 268e, Arist.*Pr.*955^{b}1, Plb.10.47.7, D.S.2.29 ; τέχνη defined as ἕ. ἢ διάθεσις ἀπὸ παρατηρήσεως Phld.*Rh.*1.69 S. ; ἄκρα ἕ. D.H.*Comp.*11 : c. gen., τὴν τῶν Ἰουδαϊκῶν γραμμάτων ἕξιν Aristeas 121 ; ἕ. πολιτικῶν λόγων Phld.*Rh.*2.35 S. (Almost confined to Prose, but cf. Orph.*A.* 391.)

ἐξισ-άζω, *make equal*, τοῖς ἐνθυμήμασι τὴν λέξιν Steph. *in Hp.*1.57 D. ; σεαυτὸν τῷ θεῷ *Corp.Herm.*11.20, cf. Sch.Il.13.745 :—Med., *make oneself equal*, Lxx *Si.*35(32).9(13).—Pass., *to be equal*, τῇ Ἰνδικῇ Str.2.1.31. II. Act. intr., *to be equal*, Id.17.3.1, Hermog.*Stat.*1, Olymp. *in Mete.*158.15. 2. *to be coextensive*, Ascl. *in Metaph.*381. 31, Procl. *in Prm.*p.857 S., Dam.*Pr.*144 ; ταῦτα ἀλλήλοις ἐξισάζει Procl. *in R.*1.29 K. **-ασμός**, ὁ, *equalization*, Simp. *in Epict.*p.8 D., *in Cael.*162.28. **-όω**, *make equal* or *even, bring to a level with*, τινί τινα S.*OT*425 ; μηδ' ἐξισώσῃς τάσδε τοῖς ἐμοῖς κακοῖς ib.1507 ; ἐ. τοῖς μεγίστοις ἐγκλήμασι τὸ πρᾶγμα Antipho 4.2.1 ; ἐ. ζυγὰ *bring* the teams *abreast*, S.*El.*738 :—Med., *make oneself equal*, δράκοντι μῆκος ἐξισουμένην σαύραν Babr.41.2 :—Pass., *to be* or *become equal*, c. dat., Hdt. 2.34, 6.111, Pl.*R.*563a, etc. ; *to be reduced to a level with*, τινί Hdt.8. 13 ; *to be a match for, rival*, Th.2.97, D.S.2.52 ; πρός τινα Plu.*Agis* 7. 2. *put on a level*, τοὺς πολίτας Ar.*Ra.*688, cf. Isoc.4.91, Arist. *Mu.*397^{a}8 (Pass.). 3. Pass., φύλοπις οὐκέτ' ἐξισοῦται *is levelled, equalized*, i. e. *resolved in harmony*, S.*El.*1072 (lyr.) ; lit., ἐξισωθέντος τοῦ μέχρι τῶν τειχῶν διαστήματος *levelled*, J.*BJ*5.3.5. II. intr., *to be equal* or *like*, μητρὶ δ' οὐδὲν ἐξισοῖ *acts* in no way *like* a mother, S. *El.*1194 ; ἐ. τοῖς ἄλλοις Th.6.87 ; τισὶ *make* a line of battle *equal* to the enemy's, Id.5.71.

ἐξιστάνω, later form of ἐξίστημι, Lxx *3Ma.*1.25, Dsc.4.73 :—also **ἐξιστάω**, *Act.Ap.*8.9.

ἐξίστημι, A. causal in pres., impf., fut., aor. 1 :—*displace* : hence, *change, alter utterly*, τὰν φύσιν Ti.Locr.100c, Arist.*EN*1119^{a} 23, cf. Plot.6.2.7 ; τὴν πολιτείαν Plu.*Cic.*10 ; ἐ. τῆς ποιότητος τὸν οἶνον Id.2.702a. 2. metaph., ἐξιστάναι τινὰ φρενῶν *drive* one *out of* his senses, E.*Ba.*850 ; νοῦ οἶνος ἐξέστησέ με E.*Fr.*265 ; τοῦ φρονεῖν X.*Mem.*1.3.12 ; ταῦτα κινεῖ, ταῦτα ἐξίστησιν ἀνθρώπους αὐτῶν D. 21.72 ; simply ἐ. τινά *drive* one *out of his senses, confound, amaze*, Hp.*Coac.*429 ; ἐξιστάντα καὶ φοβοῦντα τοὺς ἀνθρώπους Muson.*Fr.*8 p.35 H. ; ἐξίστησι *diverts the attention*, Arist.*Rh.*1408^{b}23 ; *excite*, ib. 36, *Ev.Luc.*24.22 ; τὸν λογισμόν, τὴν διάνοιαν, Plu.*Sol.*21, *Crass.*23 ; also ἐ. τινὰ τῶν λογισμῶν Id.*Fab.*5 ; εἰς ἀπάθειαν ἐ. τὴν ψυχὴν Id.*Publ.* 6. 3. *get rid of, dispose of the claims* of a person, *Sammelb.*5246. 14 (i B.C.), etc. 4. ἐξεστᾰκότα (ἐξεστηκότα cod.)· εἰς δίκην κεκλη-κότα, Hsch.

B. intr. in Pass. and Med., with aor. 2, pf., and plpf. Act. : 1. of Place, *arise out of, become separated*, ἐξ . . ἵστατο Νεῖκος Emp.36, cf. 35.10 ; *stand aside from*, ἐκστάντες τῆς ὁδοῦ *out of* the way, Hdt.3.76 ; ἐκ τοῦ μέσου X.*An.*1.5.14 ; θάκων καὶ ὁδῶν ἐ. [τινί] *stand out of* the way *for* him, *make way for* him, Id.*Smp.*4.31 ; ἐκστῆναί τινι S.*Ph.*1053, *Aj.* 672, Ar.*Ra.*354, etc. : abs., in same sense, E.*IT*1229 (troch.), Ar. *Ach.*617, etc. : metaph., ἐξ ἕδρας σοι πλόκαμος ἐξέστηχ' *is displaced, disordered*, E.*Ba.*928 ; οὐδὲ μένει νοῦς . . ἀλλ' ἐξίσταται S.*Ant.*564. 2. c. acc., *shrink from, shun*, νιν οὐκ ἂν ἐξέστην ὄκνῳ Id.*Aj.*82 ; οὐδέν' ἐξίσταμαι D.18.319 ; οὐδένα πώποτε κίνδυνον ἐξέστησαν Id.20.10. 3. *go out of joint*, ἐ. ἰσχίον Hp.*Aph.*6.59, cf. *Fract.*14,6. II. c. gen. rei, *retire from, give up possession of*, τῆς ἀρχῆς Th.2.63, 4.28 ; ἐκστῆναι τῆς οὐσίας, ἁπάντων τῶν ὄντων, become bankrupt, Antipho 2.2.9, D.36.50 ; τῶν ὑπαρχόντων *BGU*473.11 (ii A. D.). 2. *cease from, abandon*, τῆς φιλίας, τῶν μαθημάτων, Lys.8.18, X.*Cyr.*3.3.54 ; τῶν σπουδασμάτων Pl.*Phdr.*249c, etc. ; οἱ τῶν πολιτικῶν ἐξεστηκότες Isoc. 4.171 ; τῆς ὑποθέσεως D.10.46 ; τῶν πεπραγμένων, i. e. *disown* them, Id.19.72 ; ἐ. τινὸς εἴς τι Pl.*Lg.*907d ; also ἐ. ἄθλου τινί, στρατηγίας τινί, *abandon* it in his favour, Nic.Dam.73 J., Plu.*Nic.*7 ; τῆς Σικελίας τινι Id.*Pomp.*10. 3. ἐκστῆναι πατρός *lose* one's father, *give* him *up*, Ar.*V.*477 ; καρδίας ἐξίσταμαι τὸ δρᾶν I *depart from* my heart's purpose, S.*Ant.*1105 ; esp. φρενῶν ἐκστῆναι *lose* one's senses, E.*Or.* 1021, etc. ; διὰ τὸ γῆρας τοῦ φρονεῖν Isoc.5.18 ; ἐμαυτοῦ Aeschin.2.4, Men.*Sam.*276 ; ψυχὴ ἐξεστηκυῖα τῶν λογισμῶν Plb.32.15.8 : abs., *to be out of one's wits, be distraught*, ἐ. μελαγχολικῶς Hp.*Prorrh.*1.18, cf. Men.*Sam.*64, etc. ; ἐξέστην ἰδών Philippid.27 ; ἐ. ὑπὸ γήρως *Com. Adesp.*860 ; ταῖς διανοίαις Vett.Val.70.25 ; ἐξίστασθαι καὶ μαίνεσθαι πρὸς τὴν ὀσμήν Arist.*HA*577^{a}12 ; of anger, εὐθέως ἐξεστησόμενος Phld. *Ir.*p.78 W. ; *to be astonished, amazed*, *Ev.Matt.*12.23, *Ev.Marc.*2.12, etc. ; *lose consciousness*, of Sisera, Lxx *Jd.*4.21. 4. ἐξίστασθαι τῆς αὑτοῦ ἰδέας *depart from, degenerate from* one's own nature, Pl.*R.*380d; ἐκ τῆς αὑτοῦ φύσεως Arist.*HA*488^{b}19 ; [δημοκρατία] ἐξεστηκυῖα τῆς βελτίστης τάξεως Id.*Pol.*1309^{b}32 ; αἱ δημοκρατίαι ἐ. εἰς τὰς ἐναντίας πολιτείας *degenerate* into . . ., ib.1306^{b}18, cf. *Rh.*1390^{b}28 : abs., ἐ. μὴ μεταφυτευόμενον Thphr.*HP*6.7.6, etc., cf. Plu.2.649e ; χυμὸς ἐξιστάμενος *changing its properties, turning*, Hp.*VM*24 ; οἶνος ἐξεστηκὼς or ἐξιστάμενος *changed, sour* wine, D.35.32, Thphr.*CP*6.7.5 ; πρόσωπα ἐξεστηκότα *disfigured* faces, X.*Cyr.*5.2.34. 5. abs., *change one's position, one's opinion*, ἐγὼ μὲν ὁ αὐτός εἰμι καὶ οὐκ ἐξίσταμαι Th.2.61 : opp. ἐμμένειν τῇ δόξῃ, Arist.*EN*1151^{b}4. 6. of language, *to be removed from common usage*, Id.*Rh.*1404^{b}13. III. *stand out, project*, ἐξεστηκὸς *convex*, opp. κοῖλον, Id.*HA*493^{b}4.

ἐξίστιον· ἔχθιστον, Hsch. **ἔξιστον**· ἱερεῖον, Id.

ἐξιστορέω, *search out, inquire into*, τι A.*Th.*506, *Ch.*678, E.*Hec.* 744, J.*AJ*3.14.2, Porph.*Abst.*2.49. 2. *inquire of*, τινά τι Hdt.7. 195, E.*Hec.*236 ; ἐ. τινα εἰ . . Id.*Or.*289. 3. *roam about*, πόλιν X. Eph.1.12. II. *explain, set forth*, τὴν τοῦ πράγματος διάθεσιν *POxy.* 486.12 (ii A. D.).

ἐξίστως, ων, *fringed*, χιτωνίσκος *IG*2^{2}.1514.30, 1516.9 ; cf. ἔξαστις.

ἐξίσχιος, ον, *projecting at the hip*, σκέλος Hp.*Art.*58.

ἐξισχν-αίνω, strengthd. for ἰσχναίνω, βόας Them.*Or.*1.10a :—Pass., ἐξισχνάνθη τὸ σῶμα D.C.*Fr.*17.11. **-όομαι**, Pass., *dry up*, Hp.*Mul.*1.27 codd. **-ωσις**, εως, ἡ, *thinning, refining*, χαλκοῦ Zos. Alch.p.169 B.

ἐξισχύω [ῡ], *have strength enough, be able*, ὥστε ποιεῖν Str.17.1.3 : c. inf. only, Lxx *Si.*7.6, *Ep.Eph.*3.18, J.*BJ*1.23.2 ; ἐξίσχυσεν τὰ βιβλείδια ἀθετηθῆναι *procured* the rejection of the petition, *POxy.*1120. 7 (iii A. D.) : abs., *prevail*, Str.16.1.15, Jul.*Or.*5.160c ; ἐξισχῦσαι καὶ κρατῆσαι τῶν πολλῶν Plu.2.801e. II. c. gen., τὸ δαιμόνιον παίδων ἐξισχῦον fate *prevailing over* the children, Ael.*VH*6.13, cf. Steph. *in Hp.*1.71 D. III. Med., of flames, *gather force*, Thphr.*Ign.*71.

ἐξίσχω, = ἐξέχω, once in Hom., ἐξίσχει κεφαλὰς δεινοῖο βερέθρου *puts forth* her heads *from* . ., Od.12.94. II. intr., *stand out, project*, Paus.5.12.1 ; ἐξίσχοντες ὀφθαλμοί *prominent* eyes, Hp.*Prog.*2, cf. Ruf.ap.Orib.45.30.27 ; of bones, Aret.*SA*2.8.

ἐξίσ-ωσις [ῐ], εως, ἡ, *equalization*, *CIG*3546.18 (Pergam.) ; κτημάτων Plu.*Cleom.*18 ; πρός τι Id.2.1078a, cf. Aq.*Za.*4.7. 2. = Lat. *peraequatio*, *Cod.Just.*10.16.13 *Intr.* II. *filling up, levelling* of hollow ulcers, Sor.1.122. **-ωτέον**, *one must claim an equal right*, S.*OT*408. **-ωτής**, οῦ, ὁ, *officer* (of the empire) *who apportioned and equalized the taxes* among the payers, Lat. *peraequator*, ἐπόπτης ἢ ἐ. *Cod.Just.*10.16.13 *Intr.* (v A. D.), cf. Ps.-Luc.*Philopatr.*19 ; ἐξισωτής· ἐπόπτης, Suid.

ἐξίταλα· ἀναλώματα, Hsch. ; cf. ἐσσίταλα.

ἐξιτέον, *one must go forth*, Artem.3.34.

ἐξιτηλία· μωρία, Hsch.

ἐξίτηλος [ῐ], ον, (ἐξιέναι) *going out* : hence, *losing colour, fading, evanescent*, πορφυρίδες ἐξίτηλοι X.*Oec.*10.3 ; of paintings, *faded*, ἐ. ὑπὸ τοῦ χρόνου Paus.10.38.9, cf. Poll.1.44 ; γράμματα Id.5.150. 2. metaph., ἐ. τροφή food *that has lost its properties during assimilation*, Hp.*Alim.*4 ; so of seed sown in alien soil, Pl.*R.*497b ; of a drug or wine *that has lost its power*, Phylarch.10 J., Dsc.5.6 ; ἐ. γενέσθαι, of a family, to become *extinct*, Hdt.5.39 ; οὔπω σφιν ἐ. αἷμα δαιμόνων is not yet *extinct*, A.*Fr.*162.4, cf. Pl.*Criti.*121a ; ἐξιτήλου ἐόντος where *attenuation* takes place, Hp.*Praec.*9 ; of acts, *extinct, obsolete*, τῷ χρόνῳ ἐ. Hdt.*Prooem.*, cf. Isoc.5.60, 7.47, Plu.2.68b, Max.Tyr.16.2, etc. ; τρίχας ἐ. ποιεῖν *eradicate*, Dsc.2.76.19.

ἐξιτήριος, ον, *of* or *for departure*, ἐξιτήρια εὐωχεῖσθαι *IG*3.1184.21 (iii A. D.) : -τήρια, τά, *day of leaving office*, at Athens, Hsch.

ἐξίτης [ῑ], ου, ὁ, (ἕξ) *the throw of six* on the dice, = Κῷος, *Epigr. Gr.*1038.2 (pl., Attalia), Poll.9.100.

ἐξιτ-ητέον, (ἔξ-ειμι *ibo*) *one must go forth*, X.*Mem.*1.1.14. **-ητήρια**, τά, = ἐξιτήρια, *IG*2^{2}.1039.57. **-ητός**, όν, = ἐξιτός, οὐδενὶ -ητὸν Alciphr.3.30 ; ἐξιτητὰ εἶναι ἐπὶ τοὺς πολεμίους Procop.*Goth.*1. 19. **-ός**, ή, όν, *to be come out of*, τοῖς οὐκ ἐξιτόν ἐστι for whom there is no *coming out*, Hes.*Th.*732.

ἐξίχν-ευσις, εως, ἡ, *tracking out*, *Gp.*2.6.22, Vett.Val.242.1. II. *reduction* of copper ore, Syn.Alch.p.66 B. **-ευτέον**, *one must track out*, Luc.*Fug.*26, Vett.Val.276.12. II. Adj. -τέος, α, ον, Iamb.*Protr.*21.ιζ'. **-ευτής**, οῦ, ὁ, *one who tracks out*, *Gloss.* **-εύω**, *track out*, τινά E.*Ba.*352, 817 ; τὰς βοῦς ὅπῃ βεβᾶσι S.*Ichn.*160 ; τοὺς λανθάνοντας Plu.*Pomp.*27 ; [κύνες] ἐ. τοὺς πολεμίους Polyaen.4.2.16 : metaph., τι A.*Ag.*368 (lyr.) ; τὴν ἀλήθειαν Arg.Men.*Oxy.*1235.49 ; ἐ. Ἑλλάδα γλῶσσαν *'feel for', try to talk* Greek, Tim.*Pers.*161. **-ιάζω**,

= ἐξιχνεύω, Lxx *Jd.* 18.2, *Jb.* 5.27, 10.6, al. -**ιασμός**, ὁ, = ἐξίχνευσις, ib. *Jd.* 5.16 (v.l.), Aq. *Jb.* 11.7.

ἐξιχνοσκοπέω, *seek by tracking*, ἵππους S. *Tr.* 271 :—so in Med., τὸν σὸν μόρον διώκων κἀξιχνοσκοπούμενος Id. *Aj.* 997.

ἐξῑχωρίζω, (ἰχώρ) *cleanse from humours*, Suid. (Pass.), prob. in Aët. 6.50.

ἐξίωσις [ῐ], εως, ἡ, (ἰός) *reduction to metallic state*, χαλκοῦ Syn. Alch. p.66 B., cf. Maria ap. Zos. Alch. p.148 B.

ἑξκαί-δεκα, *sixteen*, Hp. *Acut.* (*Sp.*) 8, Plu. 2.367f: -**δέκᾰτος**, *sixteenth*, Hp. *Epid.* 1.26.ϛʹ.

ἑξκαιδεκά-εδρος [ᾰ], ον, *with sixteen surfaces*, Ps.-Ptol. *Centil.* 222. -**κροτος**, ον, *with sixteen oars*, ναῦς Ael. *Tact.* [4]. -**σύλλᾰβον**, v.l. for ἑκκ., Heph. 10.6.

ἑξκαιπεντηκονταπλάσιος [πλᾰ], ον, *fifty-sixfold*, Plu. 2.925c.

ἑξκαιτεσσᾰρᾰκοντάμετρος [τᾰ], ον, *of forty-six measures*, περίοδος Sch. Ar. *Pax* 974.

ἔξκλῑνος, ον, = ἑξάκλινος, *EM* 346.14.

ἑξμέδιμνος, ον, *holding six medimni*, Ar. *Pax* 631.

ἔξμετρα· ἑξάμετρα, Hsch.

ἐξό, Dor., = ἔξεστι, *An.Ox.* 1.160.20.

ἐξογκ-έω, (ὄγκος) *form a prominence*, Hp. *Art.* 11; *swell*, Aret. *CA* 1.7 bis. -**ος**, ον, *prominent*, ὀφθαλμοί Plu. *Fr.inc.* 149, cf. Steph. *in Hp.* 1.187 D. -**όω**, *heap up*, σπλῆνας (compresses), Hp. *Art.* 14: metaph., μητέρα τάφῳ ἐξογκοῦν *honour* her *by raising* a tomb, E. *Or.* 402, cf. ἐξόγκωμα:—Pass., *to be swelled out*, πάντα ἐξώγκωτο, of Alcmeon with his garments stuffed with gold-dust, Hdt. 6.125, cf. Arr. *Tact.* 35.4; τραπέζαις ἐξογκοῦσθαι *to be a luxurious liver*, E. *Supp.* 864: metaph., *to be puffed up, elated, proud*, πάτρη ἐξωγκωμένοι Hdt. 6.126; σύ σός τ' ἀδελφὸς ἐξωγκωμένοι E. *Andr.* 703; τὰ ἐξωγκωμένα *full-sailed* prosperity, Id. *IA* 921; ὑπὸ φθόνου καὶ λύπης πρὸς τὸν ἐμφύλιον ἐξώγκωτο πόλεμον Eun. *Hist.* p.222 D.:—Med., fut., E. *Hipp.* 938: aor., ἐξωγκώσατο Ath. 7.290a. -**ῡλόω**, = -ογκόω, Tz. *H.* 11.731. -**ωμα**, ατος, τό, *anything raised* or *swollen*, ἐ. λάϊνα cairns, E. *HF* 1332; *swelling*, Hp. *Epid.* 2.2.24. -**ωσις**, εως, ἡ, *raising, elevation*, Eust. ad D.P. 285. II. *swelling*, Antyll. ap. Orib. 6.1.6, Aret. *CA* 1.7; σώματος *corpulence*, Ruf. *Fr.* 62: metaph., τῶν μετρίων Phld. *Rh.* 1.219 S. (pl.).

ἐξοδ-άω, *sell*, E. *Cyc.* 267. II. ἐξοδῆσαι· ἐξοδεῦσαι, Hsch. -**εία**, ἡ, prob. for ἐξοδία, *expedition*, Plb. 4.54.3, Str. 5.4.11. II. ἐ. τῶν ναῶν *procession from* the shrines, *OGI* 90.42 (pl., Rosetta, ii B.C.). -**εύω**, *march out*, Plb. 5.94.7, Lxx 1 *Es.* 4.23, D.S. 19.63, Nic.Dam. 92 J., etc.; simply, *depart*, εἰς Τεβτῦνιν *PTeb.* 55.3 (ii B.C.); εἰσοδεύειν καὶ ἐ. ingress and *egress*, *CPR* 187.13 (ii A.D.). II. *depart this life*, Lxx *Jd.* 5.27 (Pass.). -**ία**, Ion. -**ίη**, ἡ, *marching out, expedition*, Hdt. 6.56, Lxx *De.* 16.3, *Sammelb.* 293. 2. *journey*, *PSI* 4.406.27 (iii B.C.). -**ιάζω**, *scatter*, [ὀστᾶ] πρὸς τὸν ἄνεμον Nic.Dam. 118 J. 2. *pay in full, defray, discharge*, τὸ ἀνάλωμα *IG* 5(1).1167 (Gythium); τινὶ τὸ διάφορον ib. 1390.52 (Andania); τὰ γεγραμμένα τισί *Test.Epict.* 7.8, cf. *IG* 12(3).168.7 (Astypalaea):—Pass., Lxx 4 *Ki.* 12.12(13): metaph. in Act., Gal. *Anim.Pass.* 1.2 (dub.). -**ιάριος**, ὁ, at Rome, *actor in the Atellana* (cf. ἐξόδιος II. 2), Lyd. *Mag.* 1.40. -**ιασμός**, ὁ, = ἐξοδία, f.l. for ἐξιδιασμός, Plb. 22.6.1. II. *payment*, *Sammelb.* 4425 vi 1 (ii A.D.), Artem. 1.57, etc. -**ιαστής**, οῦ, ὁ, *spendthrift*, Anon. *in Rh.* 119.6. -**ικός**, ή, όν, *belonging to departure*: τὰ ἐ., = ἐξόδιος II. 1, Sch. Ar. *V.* 270. II. = διεξοδικός, θεωρίαι Syrian. *in Metaph.* 24.15. Adv. -κῶς *from beginning to end*, D.L. 9.64. -**ιος**, ον, *of* or *belonging to an exit*, ἐ. νόμοι *finale* of a play, Cratin. 276. II. as Subst., ἐξόδιον (sc. μέλος), τό, *finale of a tragedy*, Philist. 42, Plu. *Alex.* 75: metaph., *catastrophe, tragical conclusion*, Id. *Crass.* 33; also ἦν ὁ χειμὼν ἐπ' ἐξοδίοις ἤδη Jul. *Or.* 1.26b. 2. Lat. *exodium, after-piece*, Liv. 7.2 (pl.), Juv. 3.175, Suet. *Tib.* 45 (pl.). 3. among the Jews, *a feast to commemorate the Exodus*, Lxx *Le.* 23.36, *De.* 16.8. 4. *gateway*, *POxy.* 243.16 (i A.D., -ωδ- Pap.).

ἐξοδοιπορέω, *go out of*, στέγης S. *El.* 20.

ἐξοδοντίζομαι, *have one's tusks removed*, Sch. Od. 18.29.

ἔξοδος (A), ἡ, *going out*, opp. εἴσοδος, S. *Aj.* 798, 806, etc.; ἐκ τῆς χώρης Hdt. 1.94; ἔστι.. λήθη μνήμης ἔ. Pl. *Phlb.* 33e; λήθη ἐπιστήμης ἔ. Id. *Smp.* 208a; ἔ. τοῦ βίου *PLond.* 1.77.57 (vi A.D.). 2. *marching out, military expedition*, Hdt. 9.19; κοιναὶ ἔ. ib. 26; ἔ. ποιεῖσθαι Th. 3.5, etc., cf. Ar. *Nu.* 579; τὴν ἐπὶ θανάτῳ ἔ. ποιεῖσθαι, of Leonidas, Hdt. 7.223; ἔ. ἐξελθεῖν X. *HG* 1.2.17; ἐξόδους ἕρπειν κενάς S. *Aj.* 287; τὴν ἐπ' Ὠρεὸν ἔ. D. 18.79; ἔ. πεζαί ib. 100 (s.v.l.). 3. *procession*, Hdt. 3.14; esp. of women of rank with their suite, ἔ. γυναικεῖαι Pl. *Lg.* 784d, cf. Thphr. *Char.* 22.10; ἐξόδους λαμπρὰς ἐξιοῦσαν D. 48.55, cf. Lex Solonis ap. Plu. *Sol.* 21. 4. *divorce*, *BGU* 1105.24 (i B.C.). II. *way out, outlet*, διὰ τῶν στεγέων Hdt. 2.148 (pl.), cf. Th. 1.106, 2.4 (sg.); πυλῶν ἐπ' ἐξόδοις A. *Th.* 33, cf. 58, 285; πρὸς θυρῶνος ἐξόδοις S. *El.* 328; εἴσοδοι καὶ ἔ. entrances and *exits*, *POxy.* 241.20 (i A.D.); of a river, ἔ. ἐς θάλασσαν Hdt. 7.130; ἡ Ἀρκαδία οὐκ ἔχει ἐξόδους τοῖς ὕδασιν εἰς θάλατταν Arist. *Pr.* 947ª19. b. esp. of the Jewish *Exodus*, Lxx *Ex.* tit., etc. 2. *way out* of a difficulty, Pl. *R.* 453e. 3. of *orifices* in the body, ἡ ἔ. τοῦ περιττώματος, of the vent or anus, Arist. *PA* 675ᵇ9; τῆς τροφῆς Id. *HA* 507ª32, cf. 532ᵇ6; so of other *orifices* in the body, ib. 511ª27, etc. 4. *delivery*, ἡ τοῦ ἐμβρύου ἔ. Id. *GA* 777ª27, cf. 752ᵇ12; πρὸς ἔξοδον ἔχειν Lyd. *Ost.* 44. 5. *emission* of semen, Arist. *HA* 586ª15, al.; κοιλίης ἔξοδοι *discharges* from the bowel, Aret. *SD* 2.3. III. *end, close*, ἐπ' ἐξόδῳ εἶναι (of a truce) Th. 5.14; ἐπ' ἐ. τῆς ἀρχῆς X. *HG* 5.4.4; ἐπ' ἐ. (-ου vulg.) τοῦ ζῆν J. *AJ* 4.8.2; ἔ. τοῦ βίου *PLond.* 1.77.57: abs., *departure, death*, *Ev.Luc.* 9.31, 2 *Ep.Pet.* 1.15, Arr. *Epict.* 4.4.38. 2. *end, issue* of an argument, Pl. *Prt.* 361a. b. *decision* of a court, *BGU* 168.15 (ii A.D.). 3. *end of a tragedy*, i.e. all that follows the last choral ode, Arist. *Po.* 1452ᵇ21; ἔξοδον αὐλεῖν play the chorus *off the stage* (their exit being led by an αὐλητής), Ar. *V.* 582, cf. Sch. IV. *outgoing, payment of money*, *IG* 14.422 (Tauromenium), 5(1).1390.50 (Andania, i B.C.), Plb. 6.13.2; opp. εἴσοδος, *Test.Epict.* 6.34: pl., D.H. 10.30. V. *street*, Lxx 2 *Ki.* 22.43.

ἔξοδος (B), ον, *promoting the passage*, λίθων Aret. *CD* 2.3.

ἐξοδῠνάω, strengthd. for ὀδυνάω, E. *Cyc.* 661 (Pass.).

ἐξόζω, intr., *smell*, κακὸν ἐξόσδειν (Dor.) *smell* foully, Theoc. 20.10, cf. Gal. 7.76, al., Artem. 5.33. II. c. gen., *smell* of a thing, σησάμου Thphr. *Od.* 20. 2. ἐ. τῶν ἄλλων *smells stronger than*.., ib. 47.

ἐξόθεν, Adv. for ἐξ οὗ (sc. χρόνου), *since when*, Nic. *Th.* 318.

ἔξοθεν, = ἔξωθεν (cf. ἔνδοθεν), Stesich. 81, Ibyc. 30 Diehl, *Foed.Delph.Pell.* 2 A 14, *PCair.Zen.* 21.28, 42 (iii B.C.).

ἔξοι, Dor. for ἔξω (cf. ἔνδοι), τᾶς πόλεως *SIG* 527.67 (Crete, iii B.C.), cf. *Schwyzer* 176 (ibid.), Eust. 140.15.

ἐξοίγνῡμι, *open, cut open*, Hermipp. 30 (Pass.):—also -**οίγω** Hp. *Loc.Hom.* 25 (Act. and Pass.).

ἔξοιδα, pf. in pres. sense, plpf. ἐξῄδη as impf., S. *Ant.* 460, dub. in *Tr.* 988 (lyr.): Ep. inf. ἐξίδμεναι A.R. 3.332:—*know thoroughly, know well*, S. *OT* 129, E. *Ph.* 95, etc.: with part. agreeing with the subject, ἔξοιδ' ἔχουσα S. *Tr.* 5; ἐ. ἀνὴρ ὢν Id. *OC* 567; with the object, ἔ. σε οὐ ψιλὸν ἥκοντα ib. 1028, cf. *Ph.* 79, 407; ὑφ' ἡμῶν οὐδὲν ἐξειδώς *having learnt*, Id. *OT* 37: c. gen., ὧν γ' ἂν ἐξειδὼς κυρῶ, as if it were an Adj., Id. *Tr.* 399: abs., Id. *El.* 222 (lyr.), etc.

ἐξοιδ-αίνω, = sq., Aret. *CA* 1.1: metaph., Porph. *Marc.* 7. -**έω**, *swell* or *be swollen up*, πληγαῖς πρόσωπον.. ἐξῳδηκότα E. *Cyc.* 227; νεκρὸς ἐξῳδηκώς Luc. *DMort.* 14.5, cf. Aristid. *Or.* 24(44).44: metaph., *swell beyond its proper size*, of a body in the state, Plb. 6.18.7. -**ησις**, εως, ἡ, *swelling*, Herod.Med. in *Rh.Mus.* 58.86, Gal. 12.875. -**ίσκομαι**, Pass., = ἐξοιδέω, Hp. *Morb.* 2.57, Gal. 6.790.

ἐξοικ-ειόω, *appropriate, assimilate*, μένε μέχρι -ειώσῃς σεαυτῷ καὶ ταῦτα, ὡς ὁ ἐρρωμένος στόμαχος πάντα -ειοῖ M.Ant. 10.31, cf. Sor. 1.46 (Pass.):—Med., *appropriate*, χώραν Str. 4.1.8; *conciliate, win over*, Id. 5.4.12; ἀνθρώπους μεταδόσει Id. 2.3.4, cf. J. *BJ* 1.8.9; ὄχλον εἴς τι Ph. 2.529. 2. Pass., ἐξοικειοῦσθαί τινι *adapt oneself to* one, Plu. 2.649e. II. *reduce to its proper nature*, Gal. 14.298. -**είωσις**, εως, ἡ, = Lat. *emancipatio*, *Gloss.* -**έω**, *emigrate, remove*, εἰς τὴν ὑπερορίαν Lys. 31.9, cf. Hyp. *Ath.* 29; Μέγαράδε D. 29.3, cf. *PLond.* 2.391.17 (v A.D.): abs., Arist. *Ath.* 39.1. II. Pass., *to be completely inhabited*, Th. 2.17. -**ήσιμος**, ον, *habitable, inhabited*, S. *OC* 27. -**ησις**, εως, ἡ, *emigration, deportation*, Pl. *Lg.* 704c, 850b, Arist. *Ath.* 39.4, 40.4. -**ίζω**, *remove* one *from his home, eject, banish*, Th. 1.114, 6.76; ἐξῴκισέν [με] γάμος οἴκων E. *Hec.* 948 (lyr.); τινὰς εἰς Ῥώμην Plu. *Pom.* 24; *give notice to quit*, *BGU* 1116.18 (i B.C.); ἐ. χρυσὸν τῆς Σπάρτης Plu. *Comp.Arist.Cat.* 3:—Pass. and Med., *go from home, emigrate*, φροῦδοι... εἰσιν ἐξῳκισμένοι Ar. *Pax* 197; ἐξῳκίσαντο ib. 203; *quit a house* or *shop*, opp. εἰσοικ-, Aeschin. 1.124; *to be deported*, εἰς ἄλλην χώραν Pl. *Lg.* 929a; τὸν πόλεμον τῆς Ἑλλάδος -ισμένον Plu. *Ages.* 15: metaph., ἡ ἀλήθεια τοῦ νόμου διὰ τὸν φόβον ἐξῳκίσθη *was banished*, cj. in Gorg. *Hel.* 16. II. *dispeople, empty*, Λῆμνον ἀρσένων ἐξῴκισαν E. *Hec.* 887; *lay waste*, πόλεις D.H. 5.77:—Med., Plu. *Comp.Ages.Pomp.* 3. -**ισμός**, ὁ, *expulsion of inhabitants*, Sm. *Ez.* 3.11, dub. l. in Ph. 2.526. -**ιστής**, οῦ, ὁ, *one who expels*, δαίμονες Charond. ap. Stob. 4.2.24. -**ιστος**, ον, *expelled from home*, Ps.-Callisth. 2.21.

ἐξοικοδομ-έω, *build*, Hdt. 2.176, 5.62; *make a building good*, *IG* 2².463.48: metaph., τέχνην μεγάλην ἐ. Pherecr. 94:—Med., Plb. 1.48.11:—Pass., ἐξῳκοδόμηταί σοι τὸ τεῖχος *is finished*, Ar. *Av.* 1124. 2. ἐ. κρημνὸν *build up a road along* it, Plb. 3.55.6. II. *unbuild, lay open*, τὰς πύλας D.S. 11.21, cf. Plu. *Dio* 50. -**ησις**, εως, ἡ, *building up*, τειχῶν J. *AJ* 19.7.2. -**ητον**, τό, *tomb-chamber*, *IGRom.* 4.798 (Apamea).

ἐξοικονομ-έω, *eliminate*, Sor. 1.107, Philum. ap. Orib. 45.29.48 (Pass.). II. *alienate, dispose of*, *BGU* 184.21 (i A.D.), *PFay.* 31.14 (ii A.D.). III. *handle, treat* a subject, Phld. *Lib.* p.47 O. -**ησις**, εως, ἡ, *alienation*, *CPR* 220.6 (i A.D.), *PHamb.* 14.24 (iii A.D.).

ἔξοικος, ον, *houseless*, Lxx *Jb.* 6.18.

ἐξοιμώζω, *wail aloud*, οἰμωγάς S. *Aj.* 317; γόοισιν Id. *Ant.* 427.

ἐξοιν-έω, (οἶνος) *to be tipsy*, Hegesand. 21, Poll. 6.21. II. *get sober*, Paul.Aeg. 1.33. -**ία**, ἡ, *drunkenness*, Antig.Car. ap. Ath. 12.547f. -**ίζω**, *become sober*, Orib. *Syn.* 5.34.2. -**όομαι**, Pass., *to be drunk*, ἐξῳνωμένος (Elmsl. for ἐξοιν-) *drunken*, E. *Ba.* 814, Ath. 2.38e. -**ος**, ον, *drunken*, Alex. 63, Plb. *Fr.* 40, Macho ap. Ath. 8.349a, Alciphr. 1.39; λογισμὸς ὥσπερ ἔ. ὤν Ph. 1.382. Adv. -νως, censured by Poll. 6.21.

ἔξοισις, εως, ἡ, *bringing out, divulging*, λόγων J. *AJ* 17.4.1 (pl.).

ἐξοιστ-έος, α, ον, (ἐξοίσω, fut. of ἐκφέρω) *to be brought out*, Ar. *Lys.* 921. II. ἐξοιστέον, *one must bring out*, E. *Ph.* 712, Pl. *Prm.* 128e, Aen.Tact. 2.7. -**ικός**, ή, όν, *extravagant*, χαρά Ptol. *Tetr.* 11, cf. Heph.Astr. 1.1. -**ός**, ή, όν, *to be uttered*, S.E. *M.* 7.122.

ἐξοιστρ-άω or -**έω**, *make wild, madden*, -εῖν Luc. *DMar.* 10.2:—Pass., -ᾶται Ael. *NA* 15.19; ἐξοιστρημένοι Vett.Val. 356.6. II. intr., *rave*, -ᾶν (v.l. -εῖν) Ph. 1.380; *go mad*, -εῖν Sch. Od. 22.299: aor. -ήσασα v.l. in Palaeph. 42.1. -**ηλᾰτέομαι**, Pass., *to be driven to madness*, ὑπό τινος Ps.-Plu. *Fluv.* 18.1.

ἐξοίσω, fut. of ἐκφέρω.

ἐξοιχ-νέω, *go out* or *forth*, ἐξοιχνεῦσι (Ion.) Il.9.384. **-ομαι,** *to have gone out, to be quite gone*, Il.6.379,384, S.*OC*867; ἐ. θύραζε Pl.Com.69.11: metaph., ἐκ τῆς γνώμης ἐ. Antipho Soph.49; τὸ βέβαιον αὐτῶν ἐξοίχεται Pl.*R*.503c.

ἐξοιωνίζομαι, *avoid as ill-omened*, τὸν ἴδιον δαίμονα Plu.*Dem*.21; τὸ γαμεῖν Id.2.289b.

ἐξοκέλλω, intr., of a ship, *run aground*, ἐς τὰς ἐκβολὰς τοῦ Πηνειοῦ Hdt.7.182; πρὸς κραταίλεων χθόνα A.*Ag*.666; also [δελφῖνες] ἐ. εἰς τὴν γῆν Arist.*HA*631^{b}2. 2. metaph., *drift into*, ἐ. εἰς τραχύτερα πράγματα Isoc.7.18; εἰς λόγου μῆκος Id.*Ep*.2.13; εἰς ἀσέλγειαν Plb.18.55.7; πρὸς ἀπληστίαν Ph.1.686; ἐς ἐπιθυμίας ἀνοήτους Paus.8.24.9; εἰς κύβους Plu.2.5b; εἰς ὕβριν Phylarch.45 J.; εἰς τρυφήν ibid., Plb.7.1.1, Ath.12.523c (= Arist.*Fr*.584); μέχρι τῶν ἐσχάτων Phld.*Ir*.p.35 W.: abs., *to be ruined*, Plb.4.48.11. II. trans., *run* (a ship) *aground*: metaph., *drive headlong*, τινὰ εἰς ἄτην E.*Tr*.137 (lyr.); ὁ πλοῦτος ἐξώκειλε τὸν κεκτημένον εἰς ἕτερον ἦθος Men.587:—Pass., metaph., δεῦρο δ' ἐξοκέλλεται things *are coming* to this *pass*, A.*Supp*.438.

ἐξολεθρ-ευμα, ατος, τό, *destruction*, Lxx 1*Ki*.15.21. **-ευσις,** εως, ἡ, *destruction*, ib.*Jd*.1.17, al., interpol. in J.*AJ*11.6.6. **-ευτικός,** ή, όν, *destructive*, Sch.Ar.*Pl*.443 (Comp.). **-εύω,** *destroy utterly*, Lxx *Ge*.17.14, al., *Act.Ap*.3.23, v.l. in J.*AJ*8.11.1. (The spelling -ολοθρ- in this group of words is freq. in later codd. and Pap., as *PMasp*.2 iii 28 (vi A.D.).)

ἐξολῐγωρέω, *hold of slight account*, τύφῳ τὰ θεῖα -ώρηται Ph.2.181.

ἐξολισθάνω, later **-αίνω** Epicur.*Ep*.2 p.45 U., Sm.*Ps*.35(36).3: aor. 2 -ώλισθον:—*glide off, slip away*, ἐκ δέ οἱ ἧπαρ ὄλισθεν Il.20.470; *glance off*, as a spear-point from a hard substance, E.*Ph*.1383; αὐτῶν *away from* them, Arist.*HA*590^{b}17; of leaves, *drop off*, Ael.*NA*12.18; *slip out, escape*, Hippon.37, Ar.*Pax*141; of things, Epicur. l.c., *Fr*.383 bis; of a bandage, Diocl.*Fr*.188; ἐ. εἰς ἡδονάς *slip imperceptibly* into.., Hdn.1.3.1: c. acc., *slip out of*, διαβολάς Ar.*Eq*.491; ὡς μήποτ' ἐξολίσθῃ ἡμᾶς *slip from* our *memory*, Id.*Ec*.286.

ἐξολκή, ἡ, *extraction*, Sor.1.69, Antyll.(?) ap.Orib.45.18.21, Paul.Aeg.3.72.

ἐξόλλῡμι and **-ύω,** fut. -ολῶ: aor. 1 ἐξώλεσα: pf. ἐξολώλεκα:—*destroy utterly*, τοὺς Ζεὺς ἐξολέσειε Od.17.597, cf. E.*Hipp*.725, Pl.*Euthd*.285a, Men.*Pk*.230, etc. II. Med., with pf. 2 ἐξόλωλα, *perish utterly*, Emp.11.3, S.*Tr*.84, Ar.*Pax*366, Pl. l.c., etc.; ὑπὸ τοῦ γε λιμοῦ.. ἐξολωλότες Ar.*Pax*483: opt. in imprecations, ἐξολοίμην Id.*Fr*.105; ἐξόλοιο Alex.120.

ἐξολοθρ-, v. ἐξολεθρ-.

ἐξολολύζω, *howl aloud*, Batr.101, Hld.10.19.

ἐξομᾰλίζω, *make quite smooth*, πρὸς τὸν κανόνα τὸν λίθινον *IG*1^{2}.373.209; τὴν ῥάχιν Sor.1.102, cf. Herod.Med.ap.Orib.10.37.9 (Pass.) (also in Med., τὰ σώματα Str.15.1.54); *level*, τὸν τῆς πόλεως περίβολον J.*BJ*7.1.1:—Pass., ἔδαφος -ισμένον D.S.2.10. 2. *render homogeneous*, Hp.*Medic*.10. 3. *smooth away*, κακά Babr.60 ad calcem. II. *form according to rule*, A.D.*Synt*.310.5 (Pass.), al.

ἐξομβρ-έω, *pour out like rain*, γνῶσιν, βδέλυγμα, Lxx *Si*.1.19, 10.13. **-ιστήριον,** τό, perh. *overflow-tank*, *Gloss*.

ἐξόμειννος, Thess., = ἐξάμηνος, *IG*9(2).506.4 (Larissa, ii B.C.).

ἐξομήρ-ευσις, εως, ἡ, *demand for hostages*, Plu.*Rom*.29, *Cam*.33. **-εύω,** *bind by taking hostages*, [τοὺς δούλους] ταῖς τεκνοποιΐαις ἐ. *bind* slaves *to one's service by the pledges* of wives and children, Arist.*Oec*.1344^{b}17, cf. Phld.*Oec*.p.33 J.:—Med., νήπιοι ψυχῆς φίλτρα -εύσασθαι δυνάμενα στρατηγὸν πρὸς πατρίδα Onos.1.12; also, *produce by hostages*, φιλίαν Str.6.4.2; *bind to oneself*, D.S.27.7; *win over*, *SIG*656.21 (Abdera, ii B.C., found at Teos).

ἐξομῑλ-έω, *have intercourse, live with*, τισί X.*Ages*.11.4: metaph., *bear* one *company*, στεφάνων οὐ μία χροιὰ.. τάχ' ἐξομιλήσει E.*Cyc*.518 (lyr.); φιλανθρώπως ἐ. Plu.*Cim*.6. II. c. acc., *win over, conciliate*, τινά Plb.7.4.6, Plu.2.824d, etc. III. Med., *to be away from one's friends, be alone in the crowd*, E.*IA*735. **-ος,** ον, *out of one's society, alien*, S.*Tr*.964 (lyr.).

ἐξόμμᾰτ-ος, ον, = ἐξόφθαλμος, Poll.5.69. **-όω,** *open the eyes of*, τὰ τέως μεμυκότα καὶ τυφλά Ph.1.455:—Pass., *to be restored to sight*, ἀντὶ τυφλοῦ ἐξωμμάτωται S.*Fr*.710, cf. Ph.1.109, Ael.*NA*17.20. 2. metaph., *make clear* or *plain*, φλογωπὰ σήματα ἐξωμμάτωσα A.*Pr*.499. II. *bereave of eyes*, E.*Fr*.541. **-ωσις,** εως, ἡ, *clearing* or *cleansing of the eyes*, interpol. in Poll.2.48.

ἐξόμνῡμι and **-ύω,** fut. ἐξομοῦμαι: aor. ἐξώμοσα:—*swear in excuse*, ἐξώμοσεν ἀρρωστεῖν τουτονί D.19.124. II. mostly, *swear in the negative*, ἐξομῇ τὸ μὴ εἰδέναι; S.*Ant*.535; μαρτυρεῖν ἢ ἐξομνύειν D.29.20:—mostly in Med., aor. ἐξωμοσάμην, *deny* or *disown upon oath, swear formally that one does not know* a thing, *abjure*, τὰς διαβολάς Id.57.36; ἃ μὲν οἶδεν ἐξόμνυσθαι Is.9.19: abs., ib.18, Pl.*Lg*.949a, etc.; οὐκ ἂν ἐξομόσαιτο μὴ οὐκ εἰδέναι D.57.59, cf. *PHal*.1.230 (iii B.C.); *forswear, renounce*, συγγένειαν ἐξόμνυσθαι Lxx 4*Ma*.4.26, 10.3. 2. *decline* or *refuse* an office *by an oath* that one has not means or health to perform it, ἐξομόσασθαι τὴν πρεσβείαν Aeschin.2.94, cf. D.19.124; [τὴν ἀρχήν] Arist.*Pol*.1297^{a}20, Plu.*Marc*.6, 12, cf. Thphr.*Char*.24.5. 3. *forswear, renounce*, τὴν ἐλευθερίαν Luc.*Apol*.6; τὴν ἐπικουρίαν Jul.*Or*.2.60d. III. later, simply, *swear, make affidavit*, *PFlor*.32 *A* 12 (iii A.D.).

ἐξομοι-άζω, = sq., Callicrat.ap.Stob.4.22.101. **-όω,** *make quite like, assimilate*, τὸ εἶδος Hdt.3.24; αὑτὸν τῇ πολιτείᾳ Pl.*Grg*.512e; ἐ. τοὺς καρποὺς *produce* fruit *exactly like*, Thphr.*HP*2.2.4; *adapt*, τοῖς ἤθεσι τῶν λεγόντων καὶ τῶν ἀκουόντων τοὺς λόγους Anon.*Oxy*.1012 i 28; *compare, liken*, τί τινι Str.2.5.22, Ph.2.11, al.:—Pass., *become* or *be like*, ἄνδρας γυναιξὶν ἐξομοιοῦσθαι φύσιν E.*Andr*.354, cf. S.*Aj*.549, X.*Oec*.7.32; ὁ Ἄψος σχῆμα ἐ. πρὸς τὸν Πηνειόν Plu.*Flam*.3. **-ωσις,** εως, ἡ, *assimilation*, Thphr.*CP*4.3.1, Gal.7.225. II. *becoming like*, Ph.1.35, Plu.*Per*.2, Dam.*Pr*.341, Procl.*in Ti*.3.200 D. **-ωτικός,** ή, όν, *causing similitude*, παρουσία οὐ τοπική, ἐ. δέ Porph.*Sent*.35.

ἐξομολογ-έομαι, *confess*, τὰς ἁμαρτίας Lxx *Da*.9.20, *Ev.Matt*.3.6, al., J.*AJ*8.4.6; *admit, acknowledge*, μυθογραφίαν Str.1.2.35; ἧτταν Plu.*Eum*.17; πίστεις *PGnom*.18; ὅτι.. *Ep.Phil*.2.11, Luc.*Herm*.75; διότι.. Lxx 2*Ma*.7.37; esp. in legal formulae, ἐ. εἰληφέναι *PAvrom*.1.7 (i B.C.); *acknowledge*, υἱόν *POxy*.1473.9 (iii A.D.): abs., *acknowledge a liability*, *PHib*.1.30.18 (iii B.C.). 2. *make grateful acknowledgements, give thanks, sing praises*, Lxx 2*Ki*.22.50, al., Ph.1.59, al., *Ev.Matt*.11.25: c. acc., τοῦτο τῷ Κυρίῳ Lxx *Ge*.29.35. II. later in Act., *agree, consent*, *Ev.Luc*.22.6:—Pass., ἐξωμολογημέναι ἀποδείξεις *agreed, admitted* proofs, *SIG*685.95 (Magn. Mae., ii B.C.). **-ησις,** εως, ἡ, *admission, confession*, ἥττης Plu.2.987d; ἄρτου, i.e. of the possession of a loaf, J.*BJ*5.10.3; *confession of gratitude*, Ph.1.60, al. **-ητικός,** ή, όν, *giving thanks, thankful*, ibid.; τρόπος ib.84.

ἐξομόρ-γνῡμι, fut. ἐξομόρξω, *wipe off from*, ἐκ δ' ὄμορξον στόματος πέλανον E.*Or*.219:—Med., *wipe off from, purge away a pollution*, νασμοῖσι with water, Id.*Hipp*.653; αἷμα ἐξομόρξασθαι πέπλοις *wipe off* blood *on your* garments, Id.*HF*1399, cf. *El*.502. II. metaph., ἐξομόρξασθαί τινι μωρίαν *wipe off one's* folly *on* another, i.e. give him part of it, Id.*Ba*.344, parodied by Ar.*Ach*.843. 2. = ἀπομάττομαι, *stamp* or *imprint upon*, ἃ ἑκάστη ἡ πρᾶξις αὐτοῦ ἐξωμόρξατο εἰς τὴν ψυχήν Pl.*Grg*.525a, cf. *Lg*.775d, prob. in Chaerem.14.15. **-ξις,** εως, ἡ, *wiping off*: metaph., *impression*, Pl.*Ti*.80e.

ἐξομπλάριον, τό, in form ἐξονπλάριν, *sample*, *POxy*.1066.7 (iii A.D.).

ἔξομπλον· ἴσον, Hsch. (Lat. *exemplum* 'copy'.)

ἐξόμφᾰλος, ον, *with prominent navel*, as in umbilical hernia, Gal.7.730. II. as Subst., ἐξόμφαλος, ὁ, *prominent navel*, Dsc.4.69, Gal.19.444, Paul.Aeg.6.51.

ἐξονειδ-ίζω, strengthd. for ὀνειδίζω: 1. c. acc. rei, *cast in one's teeth*, κακά, ὄνειδος, S.*El*.288, E.*IA*305; τισὶ τὸν φόβον J.*AJ*5.1.18; ἐξονειδισθεὶς κακά *having* foul *reproaches cast upon* one, S.*Ph*.382. b. simply, *bring forward*, Lat. *objicere*, τὸ τόλμημ' οἷον ἐξωνείδισεν E.*Ph*.1676. 2. c. acc. pers., *reproach*, abs., S.*OC*990; τινά D.S.5.29. **-ισμός,** ὁ, *reproach*, ἁμαρτημάτων J.*BJ*2.16.4 (pl.). **-ιστικός,** ή, όν, *throwing reproach on*, τοῖς ἄλλοις M.Ant.1.16.5.

ἐξονειρ-ιασμός, ὁ, = ἐξονειρωγμός, Diocl.*Fr*.141 (pl.). **-όω,** = ἐξονειρώττω, Hp.*Mul*.2.175. **-ωγμός,** ὁ, = ὀνειρωγμός, Arist.*Pr*.877^{a}9 (pl.), Thphr.*Lass*.16. **-ωκτικός,** ή, όν, *subject to* ὀνειρωγμοί, Arist.*Pr*.884^{a}7, Thphr.*Lass*.16. **-ωξις,** εως, ἡ, = ἐξονειρωγμός, Phlp.*in GA*96.29. **-ώσσω,** Att. **-ττω,** = ὀνειρώττω, Hp.*Genit*.1, Arist.*GA*739^{a}23, *IG*4.951.105 (Epid.).

ἐξονομ-άζω, *utter aloud, announce*, γενεήν *h.Merc*.59; freq. in Hom. in the phrase ἔπος τ' ἔφατ' ἔκ τ' ὀνόμαζε he spoke the word and *uttered* it *aloud*, Il.1.361, al.; cf. E.*IA*1066 (lyr.). II. *call by name*, Plu.*Cic*.40:—Pass., *to be referred to by name*, *PTeb*.28.17 (ii B.C.), etc. **-αίνω,** *name, speak of by name*, ἄνδρα Il.3.166; αἴδετο.. γάμον ἐξονομῆναι *name, tell* it, Od.6.66, cf. *h.Ven*.252; τὸ πλῆθος τοῦ ἀργυρίου *SIG*527.122 (Crete, iii B.C.). **-ακλήδην,** Adv. *by name*, ἐ. ὀνομάζων Il.22.415; ἐκ δ' ὀ. Od.4.278; ἐμὲ δὲ φθέγγοντο καλεῦντες ἐ. 12.250; προκαλεῖσθαι Critias 6.8 D.

ἐξονῠχίζω, *try* a thing's smoothness *by drawing the nail over* it: hence, *scrutinize closely*, Ath.3.97d, Artem.1.16, Jul.Laod. in *Cat.Cod.Astr*.4.103; μὴ λίαν ἐξακριβοῦν ταῦτα μηδ' ἐ. τὰ τοιαῦτα Jul.*Or*.7.216a, cf. Phryn.256. II. *deprive of the base of the petal*, ῥόδα Orib.5.33.1; of lilies, in Pass., Aët.1.115. 2. *trim the hoof*, *Hippiatr*.123.

ἐξοξύνομαι, Pass., *turn sour*, Thphr.*CP*6.7.7.

ἐξοπάζω· ἐκπέμπω, Hsch.

ἐξοπίζω, *squeeze out the juice*, ὀπὸς εἰς ἔριον ἐξοπισθείς Arist.*HA*522^{b}3.

ἐξόπ-ῐθεν and **-ῐθε,** Adv., Ep. for ἐξόπισθεν, *behind, in rear*, Il.4.298, al., Hes.*Sc*.130. II. Prep. with gen., *behind*, ἐ. κεράων Il.17.521. **-ιν,** Adv., = foreg. I, A.*Ag*.115 (lyr.). **-ισθεν,** poet. **-ισθε,** Adv., Att. for ἐξόπιθεν, Ar.*Eq*.22, Pl.*Lg*.947d, Lxx 1*Ch*.19.10, etc.; εἰς τὸ ἐ. *backwards*, Pl.*Ti*.84e, etc.; τὸ ἐ. τῆς κεφαλῆς Arist.*HA*512^{b}14. II. Prep. with gen., Ar.*Ach*.868, Lxx 3*Ki*.19.21; τὰ ἐ. χειρὸς ἐς τὰ δεξιά S.*Fr*.598. **-ισθίως,** Adv. *backwards*, Tz.*H*.5.104. **-ιστο** (-θο cod. Rav.), barbarism for -ισθεν, Ar.*Th*.1124. **-ίσω,** Adv., I. of Place (as always in Il.), *backwards, back again*, Il.11.461, 13.436; ἀποπέμπειν ἐ. Hes.*Op*.88. II. as Prep. with gen., *behind*, ἐ. νεκροῦ χάζεσθαι Il.17.357; ἐ. χερὸς ὄμμα τρέπουσ' S.*Fr*.534. III. of Time (as always in Od.), *hereafter*, Od.4.35, al., Hes.*Th*.500, Tyrt.12.30, Pi.*O*.7.68, *Pae*.2.27.

ἐξοπλ-ᾰσία, ἡ, = -ισία, Arist.*Ath*.15.4, *IG*12(5).647.39 (Ceos), *SIG*410.10 (pl., Erythrae, iii B.C.), v.l. in D.S.16.3, 19.3. **-ίζω,** *arm completely*, Hdt.7.100, X.*Cyr*.4.5.22, al.; poet., ἐ. Ἄρη A.*Supp*.683, 702, cf. 99 (all lyr.):—Med. and Pass., *arm oneself*, στολὴν.. λέοντος, ἧπερ.. ἐξωπλίζετο, of Hercules, E.*HF*466; *get under arms, stand in armed array*, Id.*IT*302; ὄπισθεν τῶν ἁρμαμαξῶν ἐξοπλίσθητε X.*Cyr*.6.3.32; ἐξωπλισμένος *fully armed*, Ar.*Lys*.454, Pl.*R*.555d, etc. 2. generally, ἐξωπλισμένος *fully prepared, ready*, Ar.*Pax*566; μᾶζα.. πρὸς εὐτέλειαν ἐξωπλισμένη Antiph.226.2, cf. 217.19. II. *disarm*, *deprive*, Καίσαρα τῆς στρατιᾶς App.*BC*2.28, cf. Max.Tyr.29.3, 40. 5. **-ῐσία**, ἡ, *muster of troops under arms, review*, Aen.Tact.10. 13 (pl.); ἐν τῇ ἐξοπλισίᾳ *under arms*, X.*An*.1.7.10, Plb.11.9.4, Str. 15.3.18, etc. **2.** *field-day, manœuvres*, Ael.*Tact*.24.1 (pl.); ταῖς ἐ. γυμνάζειν Man.Hist.42. **-ισις**, εως, ἡ, *getting under arms*, πολλοῦ χρόνου δέονται εἰς ἐξόπλισιν X.*Cyr*.8.5.9, cf. Arist.*Pr*.922^{b}14. **-ος**, ον, *unarmed*, Plb.3.81.2.

ἐξοπτ-άω, *bake thoroughly*, ἐν τῇ καμίνῳ τοὺς ἀμφορέας Hdt.4.164; σάρκας πυρί E.*Cyc*.403, cf. Ar.*Ach*.1005:—Pass., τεμάχη ἐξωπτημένα Pherecr.108.10, cf. Eub.15.8; ἐ. τὴν κάμινον *heat it violently*, Hdt. 4.163. **II.** metaph., of love, ἐξοπτᾷ δ' ἐμέ S.*Fr*.474.3. **-ος**, ον, *well-baked*, Hp.*VM*14; of bricks, *PGrenf*.1.21.8 (ii B.C.).

ἐξοράω, *see from afar*:—Pass., ὥστ' ἐξορᾶσθαι E.*Heracl*.675, *Hel*. 1269; cf. ἐξεῖδον. **II.** *have the appearance*, ὡς ἀγχόμενος Hp. *Morb*.2.68.

ἐξοργ-άω, strengthd. for ὀργάω, Plu.2.652d:—hence **-ησις**, εως, ἡ, Herm.*in Phdr*.p.62 A. (pl.).

ἐξοργῐάζω, *excite to mystic frenzy*, χρῆσθαι τοῖς ἐξοργιάζουσι τὴν ψυχὴν μέλεσι Arist.*Pol*.1342^{a}9; *stir to frenzy*, Phld.*Mus*.p.49 K. **II.** intr., *become frenzied*, ib.p.26 K.

ἐξοργίζω, *enrage*, ἵππον X.*Eq*.9.2; τινάς Aeschin.1.192; τὰς ψυχὰς πρὸς τοὺς πολεμίους X.*Mem*.3.3.7:—Pass., *to be enraged, furious*, Batr.[184a], Satyr.*Vit.Eur.Fr*.39 x 33 (prob.), Plb.6.57.8, al., Phld. *Mus*.p.78 K., Aristaenet.2.20.

ἐξορθιάζω, *lift up the voice, cry aloud*, A.*Ch*.271. **II.** intr., *stand erect*, Plu.2.371f.

ἐξόρθ-ιος, ον, = sq., Sch.Arat.161. **-ος**, ον, *upright*, Ath.11. 496d. **-όω**, *set upright*, τὸ πεσόν Pl.*Lg*.862c. **2.** metaph., *set right, correct*, τὸν σὸν ἐξόρθου πότμον S.*Ant*.83; διεφθαρμένας περιόδους Pl.*Ti*.90d; ἥν τι μὴ καλῶς ἔχῃ, γνώμαισιν ὑστέραισιν ἐξορθούμεθα E.*Supp*.1083, cf. 1086.

ἐξορθρίζω, in pf. part. Pass., μήτρα -ισμένη womb *of the morning*, Aq.*Ps*.109(110).3.

ἐξορία, ἡ, v. ἐξόριος.

ἐξορίζω (A), (ὅρος) (3 sg. aor. subj. ἐξορύξη [from *ἐξορϝίξ-] *Inscr. Cypr*.135.11 H.):—*send beyond the frontier, banish*, E.*Heracl*.257, Pl. *Lg*.874a, etc.; γαθέν τινα E.*Tr*.1106 (lyr.); τὸ σῶμά τινος ἐ. (cf. ἐξόριστος) Plu.*Phoc*.37:—Pass., ἐξορισθῆναι καὶ ἀποθανόντα, μηδὲ ἐν τῇ πατρίδι ταφῆναι Hyp.*Lyc*.20. **2.** *expose* a child, E.*Ion* 504 (lyr.). **3.** *banish, get rid of*, ἀγριότητα Pl.*Smp*.197d; αἰσχρολογίαν ἐκ τῆς πόλεως Arist.*Pol*.1336^{b}5; τοὺς ἀνιάτους Id.*EN*1180^{a}10: c. gen., τι τῆς ἀκοῆς Jul.*Or*.6.186b. **II.** c. acc. loci only, ἄλλην ἀπ' ἄλλης ἐ. πόλιν *pass* from one to another, E.*Heracl*.16. **III.** Pass., *come forth from*, τινός Id.*Hipp*.1380 (lyr.).

ἐξορίζω (B), (ὀρός) *press out the whey from cheese*, *EM*349.29, Hsch.

ἐξορίνω [ῑ], *exasperate*, τινὰ ὑλάγμασιν A.*Ag*.1631.

ἐξόρ-ιος, α, ον, (ὅρος) *out of the bounds of one's country*, Poll.6. 198. **II.** Subst., **ἐξορία** (sc. ζωή), ἡ, *exile*, Marcellin.*Vit.Thuc*. 47, Eust.1161.35. **-ισιμαῖος**, gloss on δηπορτᾶτος (*deportatus*), Hsch. **-ισμός**, ὁ, *sending beyond the frontier*, ἐ. καὶ φυγή D.H.5.12; νεκρῶν Plu.2.549a; ζῴων prob. cj. in Porph.*Abst*.1.10. **-ιστέον**, *one must expel*, Id.*Sent*.32, Them.*Or*.23.300a. **-ιστος**, ον, *expelled, banished*, ἐξόριστος ἀνῃρῆσθαι to be ruined *by banishment*, D. 21.105: c. gen., τῆς Ἰταλίας Plb.2.7.10; οἰκείων Porph.*Abst*.1. 30. **2.** *put beyond the borders*, of the dead body of a criminal, τὸν ..ἀλιτήριον ἀποκτείναντες ἐ. ἐκ τῆς πόλεως ποιῆσαι Din.1.77.

ἐξορκ-ίζω, = ἐξορκόω, D.54.26 (codd., -οῦντες Harp.), *PRev.Laws* 56.12 (iii B.C.), Plb.3.61.10, *GDI*5075.25 (Crete, i B.C.), etc.: c. dupl. acc., *SIG*524.29 (Crete, iii B.C.):—Pass., ib.46.6 (Halic., v B.C.), Plb.6.26.4, *IG*2^2.1346. **2.** *conjure*, ἐ. σε κύριον τὸν θεόν Lxx *Ge*. 24.3, cf. *PMag.Lond*.121.269; ἐ. [τινὰ] τοῖς μεγάλοις ὀνόμασιν ib. 892; ἐ. σε κατὰ τοῦ θεοῦ *Ev.Matt*.26.63; also τινὰ κατά τινος *PMag. Par*.1.356. **II.** *exorcise* an evil spirit, *Tab.Defix*. in *Rh.Mus*.55. 248. **-ισμός**, ὁ, *administration of an oath*, Plb.6.21.6. **-ιστής**, οῦ, ὁ, *exorcist*, *Act.Ap*.19.3, Luc.*Epigr*.23, Ptol.*Tetr*.182. **-ος**, ον, *bound by oath*, Pi.*O*.13.99. **-όω**, earlier form of ἐξορκίζω, *administer an oath to* one, c. acc. pers., or abs., ἐξορκούντων οἱ πρυτάνεις Foed.ap.Th.5.47, cf. D.21.65, *IG*2^2.1174.15: c. fut. inf., ib.2. 841 b 35: folld. by ἦ μήν (Ion. ἦ μέν) Hdt.3.133, 4.154: later, c. pres. inf., J.*AJ*9.7.4: c. acc. pers. et rei, *make one swear by*, ἐ. τινὰ τὸ Στυγὸς ὕδωρ Hdt.6.74. **-ωσις**, εως, ἡ, *binding by oath*, Id.4.154. **II.** *exorcism*, J.*AJ*8.2.5 (pl.).

ἐξορμάω, *send forth, send to war*, A.*Pers*.46, E.*IT*1437; πάλιν ἐ. *bring quickly* back, Id.*IA*151 codd. (anap.); ἐ. τὴν ναῦν *start* the ship, *set* it *agoing*, Th.7.14; κοῦφον ἐ. πόδα Ar.*Th*.659:—Pass., *set out, start*, Hdt.9.51, etc.; πρὸς ἔργον E.*Or*.1240; ἐπ' ἔργον Men.*Epit*.162; of arrows, *dart from* the bow, γλυφίδες τόξων ἐξορμώμεναι E.*Or*.274, cf. A.*Eu*.182; *move rapidly, rush*, S.*OC*30; τὸ κεῖσε δεῦρό τ' ἐ. Id. *Tr*.929. **2.** *excite to action, urge on*, E.*Rh*.788, Th.6.6,88; ἐ. τινὰ ἐπὶ τὴν ἀρετήν X.*An*.3.1.24. **II.** intr., like Pass., *set out, start*, esp. in haste, μή σε λάθῃσιν κεῖσ' ἐξορμήσασα (sc. νηῦς) Od.12. 221; δεῦρο ἐξωρμῶμεν πεζῇ X.*An*.5.7.17: c. gen., *set out from*, χθονός E.*Tr*.1131, etc.: metaph., *break out*, ἤνθηκεν, ἐξώρμηκεν [ἡ νόσος] S. *Tr*.1089.

ἐξορμενίζω, (ὅρμενος) *shoot forth, sprout*, S.*Ichn*.275: metaph., ῥήτορες ἐξωρμενικότες Nicostr.Com.34. **2.** *run to seed*, Poll.6. 54.

ἐξορμ-έω, *to be out of harbour, run to sea*, Lycurg.17, And.1.11, Is. 6.27: metaph., ἐ. ἐκ τῆς πόλεως Aeschin.3.209; ἐ. ἐκ τοῦ νοῦ *to be out of* one's senses, Paus.3.4.1. **-ή**, ἡ, *going out, expedition*, ἐπὶ στρατείαν Pl.*Thg*.129d. **-ησις**, εως, ἡ, *urging on*, ἐς τὰ καλά Arr.*An*. 3.9.7, cf. J.*AJ*19.1.10. **II.** *rushing forth*, κύματος ἐπὶ τὴν γῆν Sch.Th.3.89; *vehement attack*, ἡ δι' ὀλίγου ἐ. D.C.75.6; *setting out, start*, οἴκοθεν Arr.*An*.1.11.5. **III.** *cutaneous eruption*, Gal.17(1). 366 (= 9.138 Chart.). **-ητικός**, ή, όν, *stimulating*, εἰς πόλεμον Sch. Pl.*R*.400b. **-ίζω**, *bring out of harbour*, τὴν ναῦν ἐξορμίσαι ἐκ τοῦ λιμένος D.33.9:—Pass., *put out to sea*, Sophr.52, Ph.1.670. **2.** *let down*, ἐς πόντον E.*Hel*.1247: pf. Pass. in med. sense, ἐξώρμισαι σὸν πόδα thou *hast come forth*, Id.*Ph*.846. **-ιστόν**, τό, a *fish* similar to the μύραινα, Cassiod.*Var*.12.4,14. **-ος**, ον, *sailing from a harbour*, c. gen., Κρήτας E.*Hipp*.156 (lyr.), prob. in Id.*IA*149 (anap.). **II.** (ὁρμή) *issuing forth*, dub. l. in Arist.*PA*694^{a}23.

ἐξόρνῡμι, in Med., *rush out*, aor. ἐξῶρτο (or ἐξ ὦρτο), A.R.1.306.

ἐξοροθύνω, *excite greatly*, Cypr.*Fr*.7.9, Q.S.2.431.

ἔξορος, ον, (ὅρος) = ἐξόριος, Poll.6.198.

ἐξορούω, *leap forth*, Πάριος δὲ θοῶς ἐκ κλήρος ὄρουσεν Il.3.325; ἄνεμοι δ' ἐκ πάντες ὄρουσαν Od.10.47.

ἐξορύξη, v. ἐξορίζω.

ἐξορύσσω, Att. -ττω, *dig out* the earth from a trench, τὸν ἀεὶ ἐξορυσσόμενον χοῦν Hdt.7.23; τόποι ἐξορυσσόμενοι Arist.*Mir*.833^{b}4:—Med., ἐξορύξασθαι χάρακας *make oneself* a vallum, D.H.9.55. **II.** *dig out* of the ground, *dig up*, τοὺς νεκρούς Hdt.1.64, cf. *BGU*1024 iv 4 (iv/v A.D.); ἄγλιθας Ar.*Ach*.763; [μορίαν] Lys.7.26:—Pass., τοῦ χοὸς τοῦ -ομένου *PHal*.1.109 (iii B.C.); φυτά X.*Oec*.19.4. **2.** *gouge out*, ἐ. αὐτῶν τοὺς ὀφθαλμούς Hdt.8.116, cf. Lxx *Jd*.16.21, Plu. *Art*.14. **3.** metaph., τὸν ἐξορύσσοντα λόγον τὰ κεκρυμμένα τῶν πραγμάτων Ph.1.72.

ἐξορχέομαι, *dance away, hop off*, αὐταῖς πέδαις D.22.68. **II.** c. acc. cogn., ἐ. ῥυθμόν *dance out* a figure, *go through* it, Philostr.*Im*. 2.12; ἀσελγήματα Suid. s. v. Ἀστυάνασσα. **III.** c. acc. rei, *dance out*, i.e. *let out, betray*, ἐ. τὰ ἀπόρρητα, prob. of some dance which burlesqued those ceremonies, Luc.*Salt*.15; τὰ μυστήρια Id. *Pisc*.33, Alciphr.3.72, Ach.Tat.4.8, Anon.*Oxy*.411.25; ἐξαγγέλλεις αὐτὰ καὶ ἐ. παρὰ καιρόν Arr.*Epict*.3.21.16. **2.** ἐ. τινά *disgrace* him *by one's conduct*, Plu.*Art*.22; πολιτείαν Id.2.1127b; and ἐ. τὴν ἀλήθειαν *scorn* it, ib.867b; ἐ. τοὺς Σαλαμινίους 'dance out of their graves', Philostr.*VA*4.21. **3.** πόλεμον *dance away*, i.e. *lose*, Ael. *NA*16.23. **4.** *celebrate with dances*, ἱερωσύνην Hdn.5.5.3.

ἔξος, Delph., = ἔξω, *SIG*244 ii 43 (iv B.C.), cf. *An.Ox*.2.164.

ἐξόσδω, Dor. for ἐξόζω (q. v.).

ἐξοσιόω, *dedicate, devote*, Plu.*Cam*.20, prob. in E.*Ba*.70:—Med., Plu.*Arat*.53. **II.** Med., *avert by expiation*, D.S.15.9 (nisi leg. -ιάσατο), Plu.2.586f. **III.** ἐξοσιοῦν· δικαιοῦν, Hsch.

ἐξοστεΐζω, *take out the bones*, prob. l. in Horap.2.38, cf. Suid. s. v. ἔξαρθρος; *take out of the bone*, μυελόν Dsc.2.77: metaph., of fruits, *remove the seeds* or *kernels*, μῆλα.. ἐξωστεϊσμένα Id.5.75; ἐλαιῶν -ισμένων Ruf.ap.Orib.8.47.7.

ἐξοστρᾰκ-ίζω, *banish by ostracism*, Hdt.8.79, And.4.32, Lys.14. 39, Pl.*Grg*.516d; ἐκ τοῦ οὐρανοῦ Luc.*Sacr*.4:—Pass., Themist.*Ep*. 2; also (with a play on *broken pots*, ὄστρακα) ἀμφορεὺς ἐξοστρακισθεὶς Ar.*Fr*.593; ἐξωστράκισται πᾶν τὸ χρήσιμον ἐκ τῶν πραγμάτων Demad. 53; ἐξωστρακίσθησαν τῆς ἀληθείας Anon.Alch. in *Gött.Nachr*.1919. 14. **-ισμός**, ὁ, *banishment by ostracism*, ἐ. ποιεῖσθαι κατά τινος Plu.*Them*.22, cf. Themist.*Ep*.1. **II.** ἐ. τῆς γῆς *formation of any external shell*, interpol. in Corn.*ND*17 (nisi leg. ἐξοστεϊσμόν).

ἐξόστωσις, εως, ἡ, (ὀστέον) *diseased excrescence on the bone, node*, esp. on the temples, Gal.7.728, 10.1013.

ἐξότε, Adv., (ἐξ ὅτε) = ἐξ οὗ, Ar.*Av*.334, Call.*Ap*.48, *AP*11.383 (Pall.), *IG*3.171.

ἐξότολον· φανερόν, Hsch.

ἐξοτρύνω, *stir up, urge on, excite*, σ' ἵμερος ἐ. τελεῖν A.*Th*.692 (lyr.), cf. E.*Supp*.24; τινὰ ἐπί τι Th.1.84, etc.:—Pass., Ph.2.564.

ἐξουδεν-έω, = sq., Lxx 4*Ki*.19.21, al., *BGU*1117.31 (i B.C.). **-ίζω**, = ἐξουδενόω, Plu.2.308e, 310c. **-ισμός**, ὁ, *scorn, contempt*, Aq. *Ps*.122(123).4. **-όω**, *set at naught*, Lxx *Jd*.9.38. **-ωμα**, ατος, τό, *contempt*, ib.*Ps*.89(90).5, Hsch. s. v. προπηλακισμός. **-ωσις**, εως, ἡ, *contempt*, Lxx *Ps*.30(31).19. **-ωτής**, οῦ, ὁ, *one who sets at naught*, Phld.*Vit*.p.42 J.

ἔξουθα, dialectic form for ἔξωθε(ν), Hsch.

ἐξουθεν-έω, = ἐξουδενόω (cf. οὐ σὲ ἐξουθενήκασιν, ἀλλ' ἢ ἐμὲ ἐξουδενώκασιν Lxx 1*Ki*.8.7), ib.*Wi*.4.18, al., *Ev.Luc*.23.11, *Ep.Rom*.14.10, J.*BJ*6.5.4. **-ημα**, ατος, τό, *object of contempt*, ἐ. λαοῦ Lxx *Ps*.21 (22).6. **-ητικός**, ή, όν, *inclined to set at naught*, τοῦ θείου D.L.7. 119. **-ία**, ἡ, *scornfulness*, *Gloss*. **-ίζω**, = ἐξουδενόω, Decr.ap.J.*AJ* 19.5.3, Sch.Ar.*Ach*.443; τὰ μυστήρια Ps.-Plu.*Fluv*.12.1. **-ισμός**, = ἐξουδενισμός, *Gloss*. **-όω**, = ἐξουδενόω, v.l. in *Ev.Marc*.9.12 (Pass.), *Ev.Luc*.23.11 (Act.). **-ωσις**, εως, ἡ, *extinction*, Phld.*Rh*. 2.63 S. (s.v.l.).

ἐξούλης δίκη, ἡ, (ἐξείλλω) action *of ejectment*, brought by a plaintiff alleged to have been unlawfully ejected from or dispossessed of property, Phryn.Com.42, *Com.Adesp*.652, D.30 and 31 tit., cf. Harp. ap.Suid. s. v. **II.** action *of ejectment* brought by one who claims property in consequence of a judgement of court and is excluded (ejected) from it by the former defendant or his agent, against a defendant who has seized or refused to surrender property, D.21. 81,91, 52.16. **III.** metaph., of an action brought to *expel* or *eject* an interloper or trespasser, νόμων [? νόμῳ] ἐξούλης λαχεῖν Aristid.*Or*.

54 p.688 D.; also ἐξούλης ὑμῖν οὐδ' ἂν εἷς λάχοι τῆς γῆς Id.1.103 J. (Mostly found in gen., but τὴν ἐξούλην D.21.44 (codd. opt.); ἐξούλας ἢ γραφὰς ὦφλον And.1.73.)

ἐξουρ-έω, *pass with the urine,* Arist.*HA* 577^{a}22; ⟨λίθον⟩ Dsc.*Eup.* 2.118:—Pass., Mnesith.ap.Orib.*inc.* 15.12. II. abs., *make water,* Ael.*NA* 11.18; *finish making water,* Hierocl.*Facet.* 118. **-ησις,** εως, ἡ, *passing with the urine,* αἵματος Aët.ap.Phot.p.179 B. **-ικός,** ή, όν, *cleared of whey,* γάλα Ps.-Democr.Alch.p.54 B. (cf. ἐξορίζω (B)). **-ισμός,** ὁ, *drawing forth of urine,* Dsc.*Eup.* 2.113.

ἔξουρος, ον, (οὐρά) *conical,* πρόσθετα Hp.*Mul.* 2.133; *contracted,* αἰδοῖα v.l. ib.148.

ἐξουσ-ία, ἡ, (ἔξεστι) *power, authority* to do a thing, c. inf., χαίρειν καὶ νοσεῖν ἐ. πάρεστι S.*Fr.* 88.11 codd.; αὐτῷ ἐ. ἦν σαφῶς εἰδέναι Antipho 1.6, cf. Th.7.12; ἐξουσίαν ὁ νόμος δέδωκε *permission* to do.., Pl. *Smp.* 182e; ἐ. ποιεῖν Id.*Cri.* 51d, etc.; ἐ. λαβεῖν And.2.28, X.*Mem.* 2.6.24, etc.; λαβὼν ἐ. ὥστε.. Isoc.3.45; ἐπὶ τῇ τῆς εἰρήνης ἐ. with the *freedom permitted* by peace, D.18.44: c. gen. objecti, ἐ. ἔχειν θανάτου *power* of life and death, Poll.8.86; πρᾶγμα οὗ τὴν ἐ. ἔχουσιν ἄλλοι *control* over.., Diog.Oen.57; ἐ. τινός *power over, licence in* a thing, τοῦ λέγειν Pl.*Grg.* 461e; ἐν μεγάλῃ ἐ. τοῦ ἀδικεῖν ib.526a, cf. *R.* 554c; κατὰ τὴν οὐκ ἐ. τῆς ἀγωνίσεως from want of *qualification for*.., Th.5.50: abs., *power, authority,* E.*Fr.* 784. 2. *abuse of authority, licence, arrogance,* ὕβρις καὶ ἐ. Th.1.38, cf. 3.45, D.19.200; ἡ ἄγαν ἐ. ib.272; ἄμετρος ἐ. *OGI* 669.51 (i A.D.). 3. Lit. Crit., ἐ. ποιητική poetic *licence,* Str.1.2.17, Jul.*Or.* 1.10b. II. *office, magistracy,* ἀρχαὶ καὶ ἐ. Pl.*Alc.* 1.135b; οἱ ἐν ταῖς ἐ. Arist.*EN* 1095^{b}21; οἱ ἐν ἐ. ὄντες Id.*Rh.* 1384^{a}1; οἱ ἐπ' ἐξουσιῶν Lxx *Da.* 3.2; ἡ ὑπατικὴ ἐ. the *consulate,* D.S.14.113, etc.; also ἡ ὕπατος ἐ. D.H.7.1; ἡ ταμιευτικὴ ἐ. the *quaestorship,* Id.8.77; δημαρχικὴ ἐ., v. δημαρχικός; ἡ τοῦ θαλάμου ἐ., in the Roman empire, *lordship* of the bedchamber, Hdn.1.12.3. 2. concrete, *body of magistrates,* D.H.11.32; αἱ ἐ. (as we say) the *authorities,* *Ev.Luc.* 12.11, al., Plu.*Phil.* 17. b. ἡ ἐ. as an honorary title, *POxy.* 1103 (iv A.D.), etc. III. *abundance of means, resources,* ἐξουσίας ἐπίδειξις Th.6.31; πλοῦτος καὶ ἐ. Id.1.123, cf. D.21.138; ἐνδεεστέρως ἢ πρὸς τὴν ἐ. Th.4.39; τῶν ἀναγκαίων ἐ. Pl.*Lg.* 828d; *excessive wealth,* opp. οὐσία, *Com.Adesp.* 25a.5 D. IV. *pomp,* Plu.*Aem.* 34. **-ιάζω,** fut. -άσω Phld. (v. infr.):—*exercise authority,* Lxx *Ec.* 8.4: c. inf., *have power,* Phld.*Rh.* 1.6 S., D.H.9.44. 2. *exercise authority over,* τοῦ μνήματος *CIG* 4584 (Palestine); τινῶν *Ev.Luc.* 22.25, cf. 1 *Ep.Cor.* 7.4; τῶν ἑαυτῆς ἐδνῶν *PMasp.* 15.170 (vi A.D.):—Med., ἐπὶ τὸν λαόν Lxx *Ne.* 5.15; ἔν τινι ib.*Ec.* 8.9:—Pass., *to be held under authority,* 1 *Ep.Cor.* 6.12. 3. *enjoy licence,* Arist.*EE* 1216^{a}2. **-ιαστής,** οῦ, ὁ, *mighty one, person in authority,* Lxx *Is.* 9.6(5), *Cat.Cod.Astr.* 5(3).86, *PGen.* 53.2 (iv A.D.). **-ιαστικός,** ή, όν, *authoritative, powerful,* Vett.Val.6.3, al., Sm.*Ec.* 8.4, Eustr. *in EN* 119.21; πράξεις Heph.Astr.3.4; [θεάματα], ἐνεργήματα, Iamb. *Myst.* 2.4. Adv. -κῶς Id.*VP* 32.217: Comp. -ώτερον Plb.5.26.3. II. *free, self-determining,* δύναμις Diogenian.Epicur.3.65. **-ιος,** ον, (οὐσία) *stripped of property,* Ph.2.528, *EM* 323.45.

ἐξοφέλλω, *increase exceedingly,* ἐξώφελλεν ἔεδνα *offered higher and higher* dowry, Od.15.18.

ἐξοφθαλμ-ιάζω, *have no eye for, disregard,* τοῖς ἐμοῖς καμάτοις *PGoodsp.Cair.* 15.22 (iv A.D.). **-ίσας,** *occaecatus, Gloss.* **-ος,** ον, *with prominent eyes,* opp. κοιλόφθαλμος, X.*Eq.* 1.9, Pl.*Tht.* 209c. II. *manifest,* Plb.1.10.3. Adv. -μως Diog.Oen.36. III. *having a keen eye for,* [ὑποθήκης] *PRyl.* 119.21 (i A.D.).

ἐξοφρυόω, in pf. part. Pass. ἐξωφρυωμένος *supercilious,* Hsch., *EM* 350.22.

ἔξοχα, v. ἔξοχος.

ἐξοχάδες, ων, αἱ, (ἔξοχος) *external piles, haemorrhoids* (the internal being called ἐσοχάδες), Paul.Aeg.3.59.

ἐξοχετ-εία, ἡ, *drawing into channels* or *sluices,* Str.4.6.7. **-ευσις,** εως, ἡ, *drawing off,* αἵματος Paul.Aeg.6.79. **-ευτέον,** *one must draw off,* τὸ οὖρον *Gp.* 18.2.1. **-εύω,** *draw off,* ποταμοὶ ἐ. τὸ ὕδωρ ἐκ τῶν πεδίων Hp.*Aër.* 18; εἰς τὸ στόμα τὸ σίαλον ἐ. οἱ ἀδένες Gal.*UP* 10.11: metaph., λόγου λόγον -εύων Emp.35.2; ὑψόθεν ἁρμονίης ῥύμα Procl.*H.* 1.4.

ἐξοχ-ή, ἡ, (ἐξέχω) *prominence,* ἐ. κεράτων *elevated nature,* Arist.*PA* 663^{a}8; πέτρας Lxx *Jb.* 39.28; ζῴων ἐξοχαὶ *embossed figures* on shields, D.S.5.30; εἰσοχαὶ καὶ ἐ. S.E.*P.* 1.120, cf. Simp. *in Cael.* 409.13; *wart,* Dsc.2.104; ἐ. ἀκανθώδεις Id.3.16; also, = ἐξοχάδες, ib.80; *extremities* of animals, J.*AJ* 3.10.3. II. metaph., *pre-eminence, ἐ. in nullo est,* Cic.*Att.* 4.15.7; ἀπεργάσασθαι τὴν ἐ. Longin.10.3; δι' ἐξοχὴν μορφῆς Hierocl.p.55 A.; κατ' ἐξοχὴν *par excellence,* Str.1.2.10, Ph.1.65, A.D.*Synt.* 26.15, *OGI* 764.52 (ii B.C.), etc.; οἱ κατ' ἐξοχὴν τῆς πόλεως *leading* men, *Act.Ap.* 25.23. **-ία,** ἡ, *eminence, EM* 384.28. **-ος,** ον, *standing out, jutting,* πρῶνες Pi.*N.* 4.52; ἁφαί Sch.E.*Hipp.* 530: c. gen., ἔξοχος Ἀργείων κεφαλὴν *prominent above* them, Il.3.227. II. more freq. metaph., *eminent, excellent,* ἔξοχον ἄνδρα Il.2.188; αἶσα Pi.*N.* 6.47: Comp. -ώτερος ib.3.71: Sup. -ώτατος ib.2.18, A.*Ag.* 1622, E.*Supp.* 889; τῶν φίλων τὸν -ώτατον Phld.*Lib.* p.20 O.; ἐξοχώτατος, = Lat. *eminentissimus,* ἔπαρχος *OGI* 640.16 (iii A.D.), *POxy.* 1469.1 (iii A.D.), cf. *IG* 14.2433 (Massilia, iii A.D.); οἱ -ώτατοι τῆς βουλῆς Hdn.2.12.6. b. c. gen., *standing out from, raised above,* freq. used like a Sup., *most eminent, mightiest,* ἔξοχος ἡρώων Il.18.56; τέμενος τάμον ἔ. ἄλλων 6.194, etc.; βοῦς ἀγέληφι μέγ' ἔ. ἔπλετο πάντων 2.480; ἀριθμὸν ἔ. σοφισμάτων A.*Pr.* 459; οὐδεὶς ἔ. ἄλλος ἔβλαστεν ἄλλου S.*Fr.* 591; ἁπάσης νοῦν τε καὶ ἀνορέαν ἔξοχος ἡλικίας *beyond* all his contemporaries, *IG* 1².1021. c. c. dat., αἶγας.. αἳ πᾶσι μέγ' ἔξοχοι αἰπολίοισιν Od.21.266, cf. 15.227; also ἐκπρεπέ' ἐν πολλοῖσι καὶ ἔξοχον ἡρώεσσιν Il.2.483. 2. freq. in Hom. in pl., ἔξοχα as Adv. (cf. ὄχα), *especially, above others,* ὅς κ' ἔ. μὲν φιλέῃσιν, ἔ. δ' ἐχθαίρῃσιν Od.15.70, cf. Il.5.61; ἔ. λυγρὰ ἰδυῖα Od.11.432; ἐμοὶ δόσαν ἔ. gave me *as a high honour,* 9.551: with Sup., ἔξοχ' ἄριστοι *beyond compare* the best, Il.9.638, Od.4.629, al. b. c. gen., ἔ. πάντων *far above* all, Il.14.257, etc.; ἔξοχ' ἑταίρων Pi.*P.* 5.26; ἔ. πλούτου *above all* wealth, Id.*O.* 1.2.—Regul. Adv. -χως ib.9.69, E.*Ba.* 1235, Lyc.1195, Arist.*Mu.* 400^{b}1, Lxx 3 *Ma.* 5.31: Comp. -ώτερον Sor.1.99: Sup. -ώτατα Pi.*N.* 4.92. **-ότης,** *eminentia, Gloss.*

ἐξοχυρόω, strengthd. for ὀχυρόω, J.*AJ* 13.5.11, Plu.*Cam.* 10 (Pass.).

ἐξπελευστής, οῦ, ὁ, = *compulsor, Cod.Just.* 10.19.9.1, al.

ἔξπηχυς, = ἔκπηχυς, prob. in S.*Fr.* 1045 (ἐξπηχυστί codd. *EM*).

ἐξποδιαῖος, α, ον, *six feet high* or *broad, CIG* 2860i9 (Didyma).

ἔξπους, ὁ, ἡ, = ἑξάπους, Pl.Com.242.

ἐξυβρίζω, *break out into insolence, wax wanton,* Pherecyd.Syr.5, Hdt.4.146, 7.5; εὐπραγίαις Th.1.84; ὑπὸ πλούτου X.*Cyr.* 8.6.1; ἐ. ἐς τόδε *come to this pitch of insolence,* Th.3.39: with neut. Adj. or Pron., παντοῖα ἐ. *commit* all kinds of *violence* or *extravagance,* Hdt.3.126; τάδ' ἐ. S.*El.* 293; ἐ. πλείω περὶ τοὺς θεούς Lys.2.9; τι εἴς τινα Luc. *Fug.* 18; εἴς τινα Plu.*Phoc.* 2, Eus.Mynd.54, Ant.Lib.21.3. 2. c. acc. pers., *treat with insolence* or *violence,* Id.12.2; also ἐ. τοὺς ἔρωτας Conon 24.2:—Pass., ἡ πόλις ὑφ' ὑμῶν -ίζετο Hyp.*Phil.* 9; τὰ -ισμένα *despised* things, Longin.43.5. II. of the body, *break out* from high feeding, Pl.*Lg.* 691c; of plants, *to be over-luxuriant,* Arist. *GA* 725^{b}35, Thphr.*CP* 2.16.8; ὥσπερ ἐξυβρίσαντα τὸν δῆμον ἀναφῦσαι πλῆθος συκοφαντῶν Plu.*Arist.* 26.

ἐξυγι-άζω, *heal thoroughly,* Plb.3.88.2:—Pass., αὐτὰ ὑφ' ἑωυτοῦ ἐ. Hp.*de Arte* 8. **-αίνω,** *recover health,* Id.*Fract.* 9:—Pass., Id.*de Arte* 4.

ἐξυγρ-αίνω, *saturate,* Arist.*Pr.* 877^{a}33, al.:—Pass., *to be full of moisture,* τοῦ ἀέρος -ομένου ib.944^{a}21, etc. 2. *make watery,* of the blood, Id.*HA* 521^{a}12 (Pass.), cf. Plu.2.97b (Pass.): metaph., ἐ. τὰ σώματα ταῖς ἡδοναῖς ib.136b:—Pass., *to be so,* of plants, Thphr.*CP* 6.6.4. II. Pass., *to be deprived of moisture,* Id.*Lap.* 10. III. Pass., of liquid purgations, τὰ τῆς κοιλίης ἐξυγρασμένα ἦν ἰσχυρῶς Hp. *Prog.* 2; so -αίνεσθαι τὴν κοιλίαν Plu.*Arat.* 29, cf. 2.914e. **-ος,** ον, *watery, liquid,* Hp.*Acut.*(*Sp.*)1.

ἐξυδαρόω, *make watery,* Aët.4.10 (unless = *wash off*): metaph., ἐ. τὴν τῶν γινομένων δύναμιν ἡ τοῦ ποιοῦντος ῥαθυμία Simp. *in Epict.* p.94 D.:—Pass., *become water,* Arist.ap.Ath.10.434f, Alex.Aphr.*Pr.* 1.81.

ἐξυδατ-ίζω, = sq., Hsch. **-όω,** *make into water* or *make watery,* τὸ ἁλμυρόν Hp.*Fist.* 7; ὥσπερ ἐ. τὰς ὀσμάς Thphr.*Od.* 66; τὸ γάλα Sor.1.93:—Pass., Corn.*ND* 17, Archig.ap.Orib.44.26.6, etc.; *become dropsical,* Hp.*Epid.* 4.49. **-ωσις,** εως, ἡ, *changing into water,* Herod.Med. in *Rh.Mus.* 49.556 (= Diocl.*Fr.* 46), Zos.Alch. p.202 B. **-ωτικός,** ή, όν, *tending to make watery,* Sor.1.98.

ἐξυδραργυρ-όω, *cleanse of mercury,* Zos.Alch.p.123 B. (Pass.). **-ωσις,** εως, ἡ, *expulsion of mercury,* Id.pp.122, 123 B.

ἐξυδρίας ἄνεμος *rainy* wind, Arist.*Mu.* 394^{b}19, Ach.Tat.*Intr.* p.68 M.

ἐξυδρωπιάω, *become dropsical,* ὄμματα Arist.*HA* 553^{a}16.

ἐξυθλέω, in Pass., *to be foolishly spoken,* Phld.*Rh.* 1.249 S.

ἐξυλακτέω, *bark out*: *burst out in rage,* Plu.*Arat.* 50; πρός τινα Aeschin.Socr.38: c. acc. cogn., ἐ. γόον *yell* it *out,* Lyc.764.

ἐξυλίζω, *filter out* or *through,* Gal.19.673.

ἐξυμεν-ίζω, (ὑμήν) *strip off the skin* or *membrane,* Dsc.2.76.1; τὸ στέαρ Archig.ap.Aët.16.48. **-ιστέον,** *one must strip off the coat* or *membrane,* Dsc.2.76.5. **-ιστήρ,** ῆρος, ὁ, *flaying* or *dissecting knife,* Paul.Aeg.6.5.

ἐξυμνέω, strengthd. for ὑμνέω, Plb.6.47.7, Phld.*Rh.* 1.219, 2.148 S., D.S.9 *Fr.* 26, Procl. *in Alc.* p.84 C.:—Pass., Lyc.1195.

ἐξυνῆκα, ἐσύνηκα, = ξυνῆκα, poet. aor. c. dupl. augm. of συνίημι, Anacr.146 (ἐξ-), Alc.131 (ἐσ-).

ἐξυπ-άγω [ᾰ], *go over thoroughly, coat,* [λίθους] πηλῷ ἠχυρωμένῳ *IG* 2².463.42. **-ακουστέον,** *one must supply, understand* a word, Sch.Pi.*O.* 9.131. **-άλυξις** [ᾰ], εως, ἡ, *escape,* Orph.*A.* 684 codd. **-αλύσκω,** *escape from,* τι or τινά, Q.S.12.502, Orph. *L.* 584. **-ανίστημι,** only in intr. aor. 2, σμῶδιξ μεταφρένου ἐξυπανέστη a weal *started up from under* the skin of the back, Il.2.267, cf. Pythag.ap.Porph.*VP* 40. **-ειπεῖν,** = ὑπειπεῖν, *advise,* E.*Ba.* 1265.

ἐξυπερ-ζέω, aor. part. -ζέσας, *boil over,* τῷ θυμῷ Tz.*H.* 3.267. **-θε,** Adv., = ὕπερθε, *above,* S.*Ph.* 29. **-οπτάω,** *bake* or *dry extremely,* Gal.19.626, 649. **-όπτησις,** εως, ἡ, *over-heating,* ξανθῆς χολῆς Pall. *in Hp.* 1.139 D.

ἐξυπέρχομαι, aor. ἐξυπῆλθον, *withdraw,* S.*Ichn.* 205.

ἐξυπηρετ-έω, *assist to the utmost,* S.*Tr.* 1156; τῇ ἑαυτοῦ παρανομίᾳ Lys.12.23, cf. Chrysipp.*Stoic.* 3.123; ταῖς σαῖς χρείαις J.*AJ* 13.3.1: abs., Phld.*Sto.* 339.9:—later in Med., ἀρχὰς καὶ λιτουργίας τῇ πατρίδι ἐ. *IG* 12(7).406 (Amorgos):—Pass., οὕτω πᾶσα περίστασις -ηθήσεται every emergency *will be provided for,* Ael.*Tact.* 35.1. **-ησις,** εως, ἡ, *service, provision,* ἔργων *BGU* 1159.7 (i A.D.), cf. Vett.Val.355.17 (pl.). **-ητέον,** *one must supply,* Theano *Ep.* 6.3.

ἐξύπισθα, Aeol. for ἐξόπισθεν, *Lyr.Adesp.* 67.

ἐξυπν-ίζω, (ὕπνος) *awaken from sleep,* οἱ κόρεις εὐχρήστως -ίζουσιν ἡμᾶς Chrysipp.*Stoic.* 2.334, cf. *Ev.Jo.* 11.11:—Pass., *wake up,* Lxx *Jd.* 16.14, Plu.*Ant.* 30, M.Ant.6.31. (Condemned by Phryn.200, etc., dub. in *Com.Adesp.*43.) **-ος,** ον, *awakened out of sleep*, ἐ. γενέσθαι Lxx 1*Es.*3.3, *Act.Ap.*16.27, J.*AJ*11.3.2, Zos.Alch.p.118 B. Adv. -ως *PGiss.*1.19.4 (ii A.D.). **-όω,** *wake out of sleep*, τινά Sm., Al.*Ps.*138(139).18: also intr. metaph., ἀπὸ φιλοσοφίας Lxx 4*Ma.*5.10.

ἐξυπονοέω, *suspect*, J.*AJ*15.7.7 (s.v.l.).

ἐξυπτιάζω, *turn* a person *quite on the back*, ὄμμα (ὄνομα codd.) *throw* his eyes *upwards* or *backwards*, A.*Th.*577; ἐ. ἑαυτόν *throwing back* his head haughtily, Luc.*Cat.*16: abs., Id.*Gall.*12, *Herc.*3, *Ind.*21:—Med., ἐξυπτιάζεσθαι τὴν κεφαλὴν *throw* it *back*, Arist.*Fr.*106. II. intr., *lie back*, of the horns of wild cattle, Id.*HA*499ᵃ7.

ἐξυφ-αίνω, *weave*, φᾶρος Hdt.2.122, 9.109, cf. *PCair.Zen.*44.3 (iii B.C.); [πέπλον] Batr.182; of bees, ἐ. κηρία X.*Oec.*7.34 (Pass.); σάγους ἀπ' ἐρέας Str.4.4.3:—Med., Nicopho 5, Them.*Or.*21.250d:—Pass., ἐξύφανται ὑμέσι *are tissues of* membranes, Aret.*SA*2.7; -ασμένη πάπυρος, of rolls, Porph.ap.Eus.*PE*3.7. 2. *finish weaving*, ἱστὸν ἐξυφαγκέναι Artem.4.40; πρὶν ἐξυφῆναι (sc. τὰ κηρία) *Gp.*15.5.2. II. metaph., *finish*, ἐ. μέλος Pi.*N.*4.44; τὶν χάριτες ἐξυφαίνονται Id.*P.*4.275; of speech or writing, βύβλους τεσσαράκοντα καθαπερανεὶ κατὰ μίτον ἐξυφασμένας Plb.3.32.2, etc.; τὸ συνεχὲς τῆς ἐπιβολῆς ἐ. Id.18.10.3. **-ασμα,** ατος, τό, *finished web*, κερκίδος ἐ. σῆς E.*El.*539.

ἐξυφηγέομαι, = ὑφηγέομαι, S.*OC*1025.

ἐξυψόω, *exalt*, σεαυτόν Lxx *Si.*1.30; τὸν θεόν ib.*Da.*3.(51); *elevate*, παίγνια καὶ κώμους Αἰσχύλος -ωσεν *AP*7.411 (Diosc.).

ἔξω, Adv. of ἐξ, as εἴσω of εἰς: I. of Place, 1. with Verbs of motion, *out* or *out of*, ἐ. ἰών Od.14.526; χωρεῖν ἐ. Hdt.1.10; πορεύεσθαι Pl.*Phdr.*247b; βλέπειν D.18.323; ἐ. τοὺς Χριστιανούς (sc. φέρε) Luc.*Alex.*38, etc. b. as Prep., c. gen., ἐ. χροὸς ἕλκε Il.11.457; ἐ. βήτην μεγάροιο κιόντε Od.22.378; ἐ. or γῆς ἐ. βαλεῖν, A.*Th.*1019, S.*OT*622, etc.: pleon. with ἐκ, κραδίη δέ τοι ἐ. στηθέων ἐκθρῴσκει Il.10.94; ἐκ τῆς ταφῆς ἐκφέρειν ἐ. Hdt.3.16, cf. E.*Hipp.*650: ἐκπλώσαντες ἐ. τὸν Ἑλλήσποντον sailing *outside* the H., Hdt.5.103; ἐ. τὸν Ἑλλ. πλέων 7.58. 2. without any sense of motion, *outside*, Od.10.95, etc.; τὸ ἐ. the *outside*, Th.7.69; τὸ ἐ. τῶν ὀμμάτων their *prominency*, Pl.*Tht.*143e; τὰ ἐ. *things outside* the walls or house, Th.2.5, X.*Oec.*7.30; *external things*, Pl.*Tht.*198c; τὰ ἐ. πράγματα *foreign* affairs, Th.1.68; οἱ ἐ. those *outside*, Id.5.14; of exiles, Id.4.66, cf. S.*OC*444 (but in *NT*, the *heathen*, 1*Ep.Cor.*5.12); ἡ ἐ. στηλέων θάλασσα ἡ Ἀτλαντὶς καλεομένη Hdt.1.202, cf. Pl.*Criti.*108e; ἡ ἐ. θάλασσα, opp. ἡ εἴσω, Aristid.*Or.*40(5).9; ἐ. τὴν χεῖρα ἔχειν keep one's arm *outside* one's cloak, Aeschin.1.25. b. as Prep., c. gen., οἱ ἐ. γένους, opp. τὰ ἐγγενῆ, S.*Ant.*660; ἐ. τῶν κακῶν οἰκεῖν Id.*OT*1390; ἐ. τοξεύματος *out of range of* arrows, Th.7.30; ἐ. βελῶν, τῶν β., X.*Cyr.*3.3.69, *An.*5.2.26; ἐ. τοῦ πολέμου *unconcerned with* the war, Th.2.65; τοῦ πάσχειν κακῶς ἐ. γενήσεσθε D.4.34; τῶν ἐ. τοῦ πράγματος ὄντων persons *unconcerned in* the matter, Id.21.45, cf. ib.15; πράξεις ἐ. τῆς ὑποθέσεως λεγομένας *away from* the subject, Isoc.12.74; ἐ. τοῦ πράγματος Arist.*Rh.*1354ᵃ22; ἐ. τοῦ δικαστηρίου [ἔπαινοι] Luc.*Hist.Conscr.*59; ἐ. λόγου τίθεσθαι, θέσθαι, Plu.2.671a, *Tim.*36; ἐ. πάτου ὀνόματα *out-of*-the-way words, Luc.*Hist.Conscr.*44; ἐ. πίστεως *beyond* belief, Id.*DMar.*4.1; ἐ. φρενῶν *out of* one's senses, Pi.*O.*7.47; ἐ. ἐλαύνειν τοῦ φρονεῖν E.*Ba.*853; ἐ. σαυτοῦ γίγνῃ Pl.*Ion* 535b; ἐ. γνώμης E.*Ion*926; οὐδὲν ἐ. τοῦ φυτεύσαντος δρᾷς *unlike* thy sire, S.*Ph.*904; ἐ. τῆς ἀνθρωπείας...νομίσεως *alien to* human belief, Th.5.105: prov., αἴρειν ἐ. πόδα πηλοῦ keep *clear* of difficulties, Suid.; so ἐ. κομίζων πηλοῦ πόδα A.*Ch.*697; πημάτων ἐ. πόδα ἔχειν Id.*Pr.*265; ἐ. πραγμάτων ἔχειν πόδα E.*Heracl.*109. II. of Time, *beyond, over*, ἐ. μέσου ἡμέρας X.*Cyr.*4.4.1; ἐ. τῆς ἡλικίας D.3.34; ἐ. πέντ' ἐτῶν Id.38.18. III. *without, except*, c. gen., ἐ. σεῦ Hdt.7.29, cf. 4.46; ἐ. ἤ.. Id.2.3, 7.228; ἐ. τοῦ πλεόνων ἄρξαι *besides*.., Th.5.97, cf. 26; ἐ. τοῦ ἐφθακέναι ἀδικοῦντες *except* the being first to do wrong, Epist. Philipp.ap.D.18.39, cf. *PSI*6.577.17, *PCair.Zen.*225.4. IV. τὰ κατὰ τὸν Φίλιππον ἐ. τελέως ἐστί, Philip is 'played out', Plb.5.28.4.—Cf. ἐξωτέρω, -τάτω.

ἔξω, fut. of ἔχω.

ἐξω-βάδια· ἐνώτια (Lacon.), Hsch. **-βλητος,** ον, *outcast*, Id.

ἐξώγλουτοι, gloss on ῥοικοὶ μηροί, Bacchius ap.Erot.*Fr.*43.

ἐξώδων, οντος, ὁ, ἡ, *with prominent teeth*, *Hippiatr.*115.

ἔξωθεν, rarely **ἔξωθε** Diog.Oen.18, Adv., (ἔξω) *from without* or *abroad*, ἔ. εἴσω A.*Th.*560, cf. Pl.*Plt.*293d, etc.; ἔ. εἰστρέχειν Men.*Sam.*37. II. = ἔξω, Hdt.1.70, Pl.*Ti.*33c, etc.; οἱ ἔ. those *outside*, Hdt.9.5, etc. (but *heathen* in 1*Ep.Ti.*3.7); οἱ ἔ. περιεστηκότες Aeschin.2.5; τὰ ἔ. *matters outside the house*, opp. τἄνδον, A.*Th.*201, cf. E.*El.*74, etc.; αἱ ἔ. πόλεις *foreign* states, Pl.*Plt.*307e; οἱ ἔ. λόγοι *foreign to the subject*, D.18.9; ἀκαταξέστους ἐκ τοῦ ἔ. *IG*1².372.61. b. c. gen., ἐντὸς ἢ ἔ. δόμων; E.*Med.*1312; ἔ. ὅπλων συγκαθήμενοι X.*An.*5.7.24; *free from*, ξυμφορᾶς S.*El.*1449; δειμάτων E.*HF*723. c. c. gen., *besides, apart from*, Gal.6.409, 16.502. III. Gramm., ἔ. προσλαμβάνειν *supply* or *understand* a word, A.D.*Synt.*107.3; προσνεῖμαι ib.92.1; ὑπακούεσθαι ib.22.21. 2. *initially*, Id.*Pron.*58.5, al.; *finally*, ib.60.6, al.

ἐξωθ-έω, aor. 1 ἐξέωσα (v. infr. II), *thrust out, force out*, ἐκ δ' ὦσε γλήνην Il.14.494, cf. 17.618; even by pulling, *wrench out*, ἐκ δ' ἄρα οἱ μηροῦ δόρυ μείλινον ὦσε θύραζε 5.694; *displace*, Hp.*Art.*46 (Pass.); *expel, eject, banish*, γῆς τινά S.*OC*1296; πάτρας ib.1330; *put away* a wife, *PSI*1.41.16 (iv A.D.); *thrust back*, τοὺς δίκῃ νικῶντας S.*Aj.*1248; *drive*, τοὺς Λακεδαιμονίους ἐς τὰς ἁμάξας Th.5.72; πλοῖον εἰς αἰγιαλὸν *Act.Ap.*27.39, cf. Jul.*Or.*2.60c; τὴν πόλιν εἰς χαλεπὸν Plu.*Nic.*12; ἐ. εἰς ἅπαν ἀπὸ τῆς ὄχθης Arr.*An.*1.15.4; ἐ. νόμον Plu.*Comp.Ag.Gracch.*5:—Pass., ἐξωθέεσθαι ἐκ τῆς χώρης Hdt.4.13, cf. 5.124; μάχῃ Id.6.83; πατρίδος ἐξωθούμενος S.*OC*428; ἐξωσθήσομαι εἰπεῖν *shall be debarred* from.., D.24.61. 2. ἐ. γλώσσας ὀδύναν *put forth* painful words, *break forth into* cruel words, S.*Ph.*1142 (lyr.). II. *drive out of the sea, drive on shore*, τὰς ἄλλας [ναῦς] ἐξέωσαν πρὸς τὴν γῆν Th.2.90, cf. 8.104; ἐς τὴν γῆν Id.7.52:—Pass., πνεύμασιν ἐξωσθέντες E.*Cyc.*279 (cf. ἐξώστης II): metaph., ἐξωσθῆναι τῇ ὥρᾳ ἐς χειμῶνα Th.6.34. (Late inf. ἐξεοῦν Just.*Nov.*59.4 *Intr.*, pres. ind. Pass. ἐξεοῦται *Cod.Just.*1.2.24.6, formed fr. ἐξέωσα.) **-ησις,** εως, ἡ, *expulsion*, Alex.Aphr.*Pr.*1.90, Aët.8.53. 2. Gramm., *expulsion* of a letter, Eust.378.3, 1542.32.

ἐξώκαρπος πάλη a form of wrestling, Eust.1572.39.

ἐξωκεαν-ίζω, Geog., *represent as placed out in the ocean*, Str.1.2.17, 7.3.6:—Pass., Eust.1050.64. **-ισμός,** ὁ, *a placing out in the ocean*, Κίρκης, Μηδείας, Str.1.2.10.

ἐξωκέλης, ητος, ὁ, *barebacked horse*, Suid. II. *piratical craft*, Id.

ἐξώκοιτος, ον, *sleeping out*, Hsch.:—as Subst., **ἐξώκοιτος,** ὁ, *a fish which comes upon the beach to sleep*, = ἄδωνις, Clearch.73, Thphr.*Fr.*171.1, Ael.*NA*9.36, Opp.*H.*1.158.

ἐξωλαίμας· οὐκ αἰσίους, Hsch.

ἐξώλ-εια, ἡ, (ὄλλυμι) *utter destruction*, ἐπαρώμενον ἐξώλειαν ἑαυτῷ ἐπιορκοῦντι *IG*1².10.15, cf. Antipho 5.11, Lys.12.10, Jusj.ap.D.24.151; κατ' ἐξωλείας ὀμόσαι, ἐπιορκεῖν, D.21.119, 57.22; ὑπόχον ἐξωλείας αὑτὸν ποιεῖν ib.53. **-ης,** ες, *utterly destroyed, ruined*, ἐ. γίνεσθαι Hdt.7.9.β'; ἐξώλεις καὶ προώλεις ποιεῖν τινας ἐν γῇ καὶ ἐν θαλάσσῃ D.18.324, cf. 19.71; freq. in imprecations, ἐ. ἀπόλοιο Ar.*Pax*1072, Men.*Sam.*152; ἐξώλη αὐτὸν εἶναι καὶ γένος Lex ap.And.1.98, cf. 126; ἐξώλη γίνεσθαι καὶ αὐτὸν καὶ τοὺς ἐκείνου πάντας *SIG*167.15 (Mylasa, iv B.C.); ἐ. ἀπολοίμην καὶ προώλης D.19.172. II. metaph., of persons, *pernicious, abominable*, Αἰγύπτου γένος A.*Supp.*741; γέρων Eup.45; οὐδὲν πέφυκε ζῷον -έστερον Ar.*Pl.*443, cf. *Ec.*1053, 1070, D.58.63, Antiph.159.12, etc.

ἐξώμαλλος, ον, *with the nap outside*, Sch.D.Chr.72.1 p.789 Emp.

ἐξωμ-εύς, έως, ὁ, *one who wears an* ἐξωμίς, Diog.*Ep.*29.2. **-ίας,** ου, ὁ, *one with arms bare to the shoulder*, Luc.*Vit.Auct.*7.

ἐξωμῐδοποι-ΐα, ἡ, *manufacture of* ἐξωμίδες, X.*Mem.*2.7.6. **-ός,** ὁ, *maker of* ἐξωμίδες, Poll.7.159.

ἐξωμ-ίζω τὸν ἕτερον βραχίονα *bare* one arm *up to the shoulder*, *as when wearing an* ἐξωμίς, Ar.*Ec.*267. **-ίς,** ίδος, ἡ, (ὦμος) = χιτὼν ἑτερομάσχαλος, *tunic with one sleeve*, leaving one shoulder bare, worn by slaves and the poor, Id.*V.*444 (cf. Sch. ad loc.), *Lys.*662, X.*Mem.*2.7.5, etc.; by Laconizers, Ael.*VH*9.34; by Cynics, S.E.*P.*1.153; by the rich when not on ceremony, Suid. s. v.; by women, Ar.*Fr.*8; at Rome, *sleeveless tunic*, Plu.*Cat.Ma.*3, Gell.6(7).12.3.

ἔξωμος χιτών, = foreg., Hsch., cf. Aq.*Is.*15.4.

ἐξωμοσία, ἡ, *denial on oath that one knows anything* of a matter, Ar.*Ec.*1026, *PEleph.*34.1 (iii B.C.). II. *declining an office*, D.19.129. III. *vow*, Al.*Le.*22.18.

ἐξωνέομαι, *buy off, redeem*, c. gen. vel dat. pretii, χρημάτων τινὰς ἐ. Arist.*Oec.*1352ᵃ13; χρήμασι τοὺς κινδύνους Lys.24.17; ἀτιμίας μείζοσι τιμαῖς Arist.*Pol.*1315ᵃ24, cf. *PFay.*21.20 (ii A.D.); τρισχιλίων ἐ. παρὰ τῶν γονέων..μὴ ἀπαχθῆναι Luc.*Peregr.*9, cf. J.*BJ*1.18.4; *redeem*, ἅπαντα τὰ σφάλματα ἑνὶ ὕψει καὶ κατορθώματι Longin.36.2. 2. generally, *buy* (in impf., *bid for*, Hdt.1.196), ὁ ἐξωνούμενος the *purchaser*, Aeschin.3.66; *bribe*, Paus.4.17.3.

ἐξώνῠχον, τό, = λιθόσπερμον, Dsc.3.141, Id.*Eup.*2.118.

ἐξώπιος, ον, (ὤψ) *out of sight of*, hence, *out of*, freq. in E., δόμων ἐ. βέβηκε *Supp.*1038; δωμάτων *Med.*624, *Alc.*546; used in parody by Ar.*Th.*881.

ἐξώπροικα, τά, = ἕδνα, *EM*316.40, Sch.Od.2.195.

ἐξωπῠλ-ῖται, οἱ, *dwellers outside the gates*, as an organized body, *BGU*34 ii 21 (ii A.D.), etc. **-ος,** ον, *out of doors*, Sch.A.R.1.1174.

ἐξωραϊσμένον· κεκοσμημένον, κεκαλλωπισμένον, Hsch.

ἐξωριάζω, (ὥρα) *leave out of thought, neglect*, f.l. for εὐωριάζω, A.*Pr.*17.

ἔξωρος, ον, (ὥρα) *untimely, out of season, unfitting*, ἔξωρα πράσσω S.*El.*618. 2. *too late, too old, superannuated*, Aeschin.1.95, Plu.*Sull.*36, Luc.*Herm.*78, al. (also glossed by ἐξαέτης as though ἔξωρος, *EM*350.2): c. gen., *too old for*.., τοῦ ἐρᾶν Luc.*Merc.Cond.*7. Adv. -ρως, ἔχειν τοῦ ἀποδημεῖν Philostr.*VS*1.21.8.

ἐξώροφος, ον, (ὄροφος) *with* or *of six stories*, πύργοι D.S.14.51.

ἐξῶρτο, v. ἐξόρνυμι.

ἔξ-ωσις, εως, ἡ, *putting out, displacement*, Hp.*Art.*46, Gal.14.778. 2. *thrust*, ἡ κατὰ τὴν ἔ. βία Marcellin.*Puls.*99. II. *purgation, evacuation*, Sever.*Clyst.*25 D. **-ωσμα,** ατος, τό, *banishment*, Lxx *La.*2.14 (pl.). **-ώστης,** ου, ὁ, *one who drives out*, Ἄρης E.*Rh.*322. 2. ἐ. ἄνεμοι violent winds *which drive ships ashore* (cf. ἐξωθέω II), Hdt.2.113, Hp.*VM*9, Aeschin.*Ep.*1.3. 3. ὁ ἐ. (sc. σφυγμός), term coined by Archig.ap.Gal.8.662. 4. = ἐξώστρα III, *Cod.Just.*8.10.12.5b (pl.), *Gloss.* **-ωστικός,** ή, όν, *expulsive*, τρόπος Epicur.*Nat.*2.5. **-ώστρα,** ἡ, *stage-machine* identified with the ἐκκύκλημα (q.v.) by Hsch. and Poll.4.127, but distd. from it, ib.129: metaph., τῆς τύχης ἐπὶ τὴν ἐ. ἀναβιβαζούσης τὴν ὑμετέραν ἄγνοιαν Plb.11.5.8:—also **-ωστρον,** τό, *IG*11(2).199 *A* 95 (pl., Delos, iii B.C.). II. *bridge thrust out* from the besiegers' tower against the walls of the besieged place, Lat. *exostra*, Veget.*de Re Milit.*4.21. III. *balcony*, Sm.4*Ki.*1.2; = Lat. *maenianum*, *Gloss.*

ἐξωστῷον, τό, *outer porch*, Hdn.*Epim.*267.

ἐξω-τάτω, Adv., Sup. of ἔξω, *outermost*, Pl.*Phd.*112e, Arist.*Cael.*

279a20, Ph.2.331, etc.:—later, Adj. **ἐξώτατος**, Lxx 3*Ki*.6.30; τὸ ἐ. Ph.1.95. **-τεριαῖος**, α, ον, *external, superficial*, λίθοι *POxy*.498.18 (ii A.D.). **-τερικός**, ή, όν, opp. ἐσωτερικός, *external, belonging to the outside*, τὰ ἐ. *the exterior members*, such as hands and feet, Arist. *GA*786a26; ἐ. ἀρχή *foreign* dominion, Id.*Pol*.1272b19; ἐ. πράξεις *external* activities, ib.1325b22; ἐ. ἀγαθά ib.1323b25; οἱ ἐ. *persons outside* the Pythagorean school, Iamb.*VP*32.226. II. οἱ ἐ. λόγοι *popular* arguments or treatises, opp. οἱ κατὰ φιλοσοφίαν, Arist.*EE* 1217b22, *Pol*.1278b31, *Metaph*.1076a28, *EN*1102a26, al.; ταῦτα-κωτέρας σκέψεως Id.*Pol*.1254a33; ἐ. λόγοι, opp. ἀκροαματικοί or ἐσωτερικοί (q.v.), Gell.20.5.2; ἐ. διάλογοι, opp. τὰ ἠθικά, τὰ φυσικὰ ὑπομνήματα, Plu.2.1115b; cf. ἐσωτερικός. **-τέρω**, Adv., Comp. of ἔξω, *more outside*, δρόμου ἐ. A.*Ch*.1023, cf. Arist.*Metaph*.1055a25, Lxx *Jb*.18.17, etc.:—hence later, Adj. **ἐξώτερος**, *outer*, Lxx *Ex*.26.4, etc., *Ev.Matt*.8.12; ξυστός *POxy*.896.14 (iv A.D.). **-τικός**, ή, όν, *foreign*, οἰκονομίαι Iamb.*VP*21.97; of a plant, *PHolm*.17.31; *outlying*, κτήματα *PMasp*.21 ii 1 (vi A.D.); *alien*, opp. συγγενής, *CIG* 2686 (Iasos); of heirs, Just.*Nov*.22.20.2; ὑμνῳδοί *IGRom*.4.353c11 (Pergam.); ἐ. ἑστιάσεις banquets *in other men's houses*, opp. ἰδιωτικαί, Epict.*Ench*.33.6 (v.l.). 2. *uninitiated*, c. gen., τῆς θρησκείας Porph.*Abst*.4.6. 3. Adv. -κῶς f.l. in Democr.179. **-φανής**, ές, *convex*, of mirrors, Phlp.*in Mete*.28.17. **-φορος**, ον, *brought out, published*, ἐ. ποιήσασθαι Iamb.*VP*34.247, cf. Stob.2.7.11k. II. *tending outwards*, πνεῦμα Marcellin.*Puls*.65. **-χείριον** ποιῶ, = Lat. *emancipare*, *Gloss*. **-χειριότης**, = Lat. *emancipatio*, ibid.

ἔξωχρος, ον, *very pale*, Arist.*HA*631b28, Thphr.*HP*4.6.3, Aret.*SD* 2.6.

εὀ-, written for εὐ- in Ion. Inscrr., *SIG*168.5, etc.

ἔο, Ep. for οὗ: **ἑοῖ**, Ep. for οἷ. **ἔοι**, Ep. for εἴη, 3 sg. pres. opt. of εἰμί.

ἔοικα, ας, ε, etc., pf. with pres. sense, *to be like*: rarely in other tenses, 3 sg. impf. εἶκε *it was opportune*, Il.18.520 (unless fr. εἴκω III): fut. εἴξω *will be like*, Ar.*Nu*.1001; pf. 3 dual ἔϊκτον Od.4.27; 1 pl. ἔοιγμεν S.*Aj*.1239, *Ichn*.95, E.*Cyc*.99; ἐοίκαμεν Pl.*La*.193d; 3 pl. εἴξασι E.*Hel*.497, Ar.*Av*.96, Pl.*Plt*.291a, *Sph*.230a, Pl.Com.22, 153, Eub.98.8; ἐοίκασι Pl.*R*.584d; inf. εἰκέναι E.*Fr*.167, Ar.*Nu*.185 (cf. προσέοικα); part. εἰκώς (also εἰκώς Il.21.254, v. sub εἰκός); εἰοικυῖαι 18.418: Ion. (not Ep.) οἶκα, ας, ε, Hdt.4.82, 5.20, 106, part. οἰκώς Id. 6.125; but ἔοικα, ἐοικώς are found in other Ionic writers, as Semon. 7.41, Anacr.84, Heraclit.1, Hp.*Aër*.6, Democr.266, and codd. of Hdt. vary; 2 sg. εἶκας (v.l. οἶκας) Alcm.80: plpf. ἐῴκειν, εις, ει, Od. 1.411, etc.; 3 pl. ἐῴκεσαν Th.7.75, etc., Ep. ἐοίκεσαν Il.13.102; Ep. 3 dual εἴκτην 1.104, Od.4.662, Hes.*Sc*.390 codd.: Att. plpf. ᾔκειν Ar. *Av*.1298 (Dawes from Sch.):—**Pass.**, 3 sg. pf. ἤϊκται Nic.*Th*.658: plpf. ἤϊκτο Od.20.31, al., ἔϊκτο Il.23.107. I. *to be like, look like*, c. dat., Il.14.474, etc.; Μαχάονι πάντα ἔοικε 11.613; κεφαλήν τε καὶ ὄμματα καλὰ ἔοικας κείνῳ Od.1.208; so εἶδός τε μέγεθός τε, δέμας, etc., Il.2.58, 21.285, etc.; εἰς ὦπα ἔοικεν, ἄντα ἐῴκει, 3.158, 24.630, al.; μελαίνῃ κηρὶ ἔοικε *is considered like*, i.e. *hated like*, death, Od.17.500: c. part., αἰεὶ γὰρ δίφρου ἐπιβησομένοισιν ἐΐκτην *seemed* always just about to set foot upon the chariot, Il.23.379; ἔοικε σημαίνοντι *seems* to indicate, Pl.*Cra*.437a; τοὐναντίον ἔοικεν σπεύδοντι *seems* to urge the opposite, Id.*Prt*.361b, cf. X.*Mem*.1.6.10, 4.3.8, Arist.*Sens*.437b 24; ἔοικεν τοῦτο ἀτόπῳ this *is like* an absurdity, *seems* absurd, Pl.*Phd*. 62d; δαιμονίᾳ ἔοικεν εὐεργεσίᾳ D.2.1: used by A. in this sense only in part. εἰκώς *like*, c. dat., *Ag*.760 (lyr.), *Ch*.560 (cf. IV. 1). 2. ἐοικέναι κατά τι *to be analogous to*, Plot.4.4.39. II. *seem*, c. inf. (where we make the Verb impersonal): c. inf. pres., *methinks*, ἔοικα δέ τοι παραείδειν ὥς τε θεῷ I *seem* to sing (i.e. *methinks* I sing) to thee, as to a god, Od.22.348; χλιδᾶν ἔοικας *methinks* thou art delicate, A.*Pr*.971; ἔοικα θρηνεῖν μάτην Id.*Ch*.926, cf. 730; ἔοικα ... οὐκ εἰδέναι S.*OT*744; ἔοικα .. ἐποικτίρειν σε Id.*Ph*.317: c. fut. inf., θέλξειν μ' ἔοικας *it seems likely* that thou wilt .., A.*Eu*.900; ἐρεῖν ἔοικας Id.*Pr*.984; ἔοικα θεσπιῳδήσειν Id.*Ag*.1161; κτενεῖν ἔοικας Id.*Ch*.922; τὸν ἄνδρ' ἔοικεν ὕπνος ἐξειν S.*Ph*.821; ἔοικα πράξειν οὐδέν E.*Hec*.813, cf. *Cyc*.99: c. aor. inf., πικροὺς ἔοιγμεν .. ἀγῶνας κηρῦξαι *methinks* we proclaimed, S.*Aj*.1239: c. pf. inf., ἔοικεν ἐπωνομάσθαι Pl.*Cra*.419c: c. part., ἔοικε κεκλημένῃ *seems* to be called, ibid.; ἐοίκατε ἡδόμενοι X.*HG*6.3.8; κατακεκομμένῃ ἔοικεν ἡ σύνθεσις καὶ εὐκαταφρόνητος Demetr.*Eloc*.4. 2. impers., ἔοικε *it seems*: ὡς ἔοικε as *it seems*, S.*Ant*.576, 740, *El*.772, 1341, E.*Andr*.551, etc., used by Pl. merely to modify a statement, *probably, I believe*, *Phd*.61c, *R*.332b, al.; ἔοικεν in answers, *so it seems*, ib.334a, 346c, al. 3. personal in the same sense, ὡς ἔοικας S.*El*.516, *Tr*.1241; ὡς εἴξασιν E.*Hel*.497. III. *beseem, befit*, c. dat. pers., τὸ μὲν ἀπιέναι ... οὐδενὶ καλῷ ἔοικε X.*An*.6. 5.17 (unless οὐδενὶ κ. is neut.); ἀνδράσι ἔοικεν τὰ τῆς γεωργίας *POxy*. 899.18 (200 A.D.): c. dat. et inf., τὰ μὲν οὔ τι καταθνητοῖσιν ἔοικεν ἄνδρεσσιν φορέειν Il.10.440; cf. III. 2 fin. 2. most freq. impers., ἔοικε *it is fitting, reasonable*, mostly with neg. and folld. by inf., οὐκ ἔστ' οὐδὲ ἔοικε τεὸν ἔπος ἀρνήσασθαι Il.14.212; οὐ γὰρ ἔοικ' ὀτρυνέμεν 4.286: freq. c. acc. et inf., 12.212, al.; in Od.22.196 an inf. must be supplied, εὐνῇ ἔνι μαλακῇ καταλέγμενος, ὥς σε ἔοικεν (sc. καταλέξασθαι); ἐπεὶ οὐδὲ ἔοικε (sc. εἶναι) Il.1.119:—rare in Att., ἔοικεν νέῳ .. ὀργὴν ὑποφέρειν Pl.*Lg*.879c. IV. part. ἐοικώς, εἰκώς, Ion. οἰκώς, υῖα, ός, 1. *seeming like, like*, Il.3.449, etc.:—the longer form is found in Att. Prose, φόβος οὐδενὶ ἐοικώς Th.7.71; εἰκώς A.*Ag*.760 (lyr.), *Ch*.560, E.*Cyc*.376, Ar.*V*.1321. 2. *fitting, seemly*, μῦθοί γε ἐοικότες .., ὧδε ἐοικότα μυθήσασθαι, Od.3.124, 125, cf. 4.239; ἐοικότι κεῖται ὀλέθρῳ 1.46; εἰκυῖαν ἄκοιτιν *a suitable* wife, 'a help *meet for him*', Il.9.399. 3. *likely, probable*, εἰκός ἐστι, = ἔοικε, S.*El*.659, 1488, etc.; esp. ὡς εἰκός, Ion. ὡς οἰκός, = ὡς ἔοικε, Hdt.1.45 (sc. ἦν), S.*Ph*.498, etc.; οἷον εἰκός Pl.*R*.406c; καθάπερ εἰκός Id.*Ti*.24d; also ὡς τὸ εἰκός Id.*Phd*.67a, *R*.407d, etc.; οἱ εἰκότες λόγοι, μῦθοι, Id.*Ti*. 48d, 59c; ἀδύνατα εἰκότα *plausible* miracles, opp. δυνατὰ ἀπίθανα, Arist.*Po*.1460a27. 4. καὶ τὰ ἐοικότα and *the like*, αἶγες, αἴλουροι, καὶ τὰ ἐ. S.E.*P*.1.47, cf. 3.180; ἄρτιον, περιττόν, τέλειον, τὰ ἐ. Nicom. *Ar*.1.3. 5. neut. Subst. εἰκός (q.v.).

ἐοικότως, Att. **εἰκότως**, Ion. **οἰκότως**, Adv. of part. ἐοικώς, *similarly, like*, τινί A.*Ag*.915. 2. *reasonably, fairly, naturally, as was to be expected*, Hdt.2.25, A.*Supp*.403 (lyr.); οὐκ εἰ. *unfairly*, Th.1.37; freq. emphat. at the close of a sentence or clause, ib.77, 2.93, Isoc. 1.48, etc.

ἑοῖο, Ep. gen. of ἑός. **ἔοις**, Ep. 2 sg. opt. of εἰμί. **ἔοισα**, Aeol. for ἐοῦσα, οὖσα, part. fem. of εἰμί.

ἐόλει, *caused to waver*, πῦρ δέ νιν οὐκ ἐόλει (3 sg. impf.), as Böckh for αἰόλλει in Pi.*P*.4.233:—Pass., ἐόλητο (3 sg. plpf.) *was troubled*, ἐόλητο νόον μελεδήμασι A.R.3.471; ἐόλητο θυμὸν ... ὑποδμηθεὶς βελέεσσι Κύπριδος Mosch.2.74; cf. ἐόληται· τετάρακται, ἐπτόηται, ὠδύνηται, Hsch. (Perh. cf. εἴλω.)

ἔολον· πρόσφορον, χρηματιστόν, Hsch. (fort. ἐσλόν).

ἔολπα, ας, ε, poet. pf. with pres. sense of ἔλπομαι (q.v.).

ἔον, Ep. (Il.23.643) and Aeol. for ἦν, 1 sg. impf. of εἰμί (q.v.):— but ἐόν, Ion. for ὄν, part. neut. of εἰμί.

ἔορ· θυγάτηρ, ἀνεψιός, and **ἔορες**· προσήκοντες, συγγενεῖς, Hsch. (Cogn. with Skt. *svasar*-, Lith. *seser*- 'sister', etc.)

ἔοργα, ας, ε, poet. pf. of ἔρδω, Il.3.57, al., Hecat.6 J., Hdt.3.127; 3 pl. ἔοργαν for ἐόργασι, Batr.179; part. ἐοργώς Il.9.320, Od.22.318: Ion. 3 sg. plpf. ἐόργεε Hdt.1.127.

ἐόργη, ἡ, = τορύνη, Poll.6.88 (cf. εὐέργη). **ἐοργῆσαι**· τορυνῆσαι, ibid.

ἑορτάζω, in Ion. Prose **ὁρτάζω**: impf. ἑώρταζον (with irreg. augm.) Isoc.19.40, Paus.4.19.4: fut. -άσω Luc.*Merc.Cond*.16, Alciphr.3.18, etc.: aor. ἑώρτασα D.C.48.34, etc.; inf. ἑορτάσαι Ar.*Ach*.1079, Pl. *R*.458a; cf. διεορτάζω: (ἑορτή):—*keep festival* or *holiday*, Hdt.2.60, 122, E.*IT*1458, etc.; ἑορτὰς ἑ. *celebrate* festivals, X.*Ath*.3.2; ἡμέρας τέτταρας Plu.*Cam*.42; τὴν γενέθλιόν τινος *OGI*493.26 (Ephesus, ii A.D.); ἑ. τῷ θεῷ Luc.*Anach*.23. II. *celebrate as a festival*, νίκην ἑ. *celebrate it by a festival*, Plu.2.349f, cf. *Ant*.56; at Rome, *celebrate by a triumph*, D.C.51.21.

ἔορται· ἔδοξε, Hsch. II. = κρεμνᾶται (cf. αἰωρέω), Id. III. **ἑόρτας**· ἀρεσκούσας, καλάς, Id.

ἑορτ-αῖος, α, ον, *festal*, καιροί D.H.4.74. **-άσιμος** [ᾰ], ον, *of a festival*, ἡμέρα J.*AJ*11.6.13, cf. Plu.2.270a, *OGI*524.8 (Thyatira); ἐμαυτῷ οὐχ ἑορτάσιμα ὄντα though I was *in no holiday mood*, Luc.*Sat*. 11. **-άσιος** [ᾰ], ον, perh. = Lat. *sollemnis*, *Arch.Anz*.38/39.154 (Antioch). **-ασις**, εως, ἡ, *holiday-keeping*, Pl.*Lg*.657d. **-ασμα**, ατος, τό, *festival, holiday*, Lxx *Wi*.19.16. **-ασμός**, ὁ, = ἑόρτασις, Plu. 2.1101e (nisi leg. -ασίμων), *Gloss*. **-αστής**, οῦ, ὁ, *reveller*, Poll.1. 34, Max.Tyr.6.8 (pl.), Procop.*Aed*.1.10. **-αστικός**, ή, όν, *fit for a festival*, μάχαι (i.e. tourneys) Pl.*Lg*.829b; ἡμέρα Luc.*Am*.1, Alciphr. 3.57; θυσία Ael.*VH*3.37. **-ή**, in Ion. Prose **ὁρτή** (so *Schwyzer*726. 21 (Milet., v B.C.), prob. in Ion Trag.21, but ἑορτή *Schwyzer* 725.12 (Milet., vi B.C.)), ἡ, *feast, festival, holiday*, ἐπεὶ καὶ πᾶσιν ἑ. Od.20.156; ἑ. τοῖο θεοῖο 21.258; ἐούσης ὁρτῆς τῇ Ἥρῃ τοῖσι Ἀργείοισι Hdt.1.31; ὁρτὴν ἄγειν keep *a feast*, ib.147, cf. Th.4.5, etc.; ἄξεις τότ' ἀμελιτῖτιν ὁρτὴν ἐξ ὁρτῆς Herod.5.85; ὁρτὴν ποιευμένους Hdt.1.150; ὁρτὴν ἀνάγειν Id.2.40, 48, al.; ἑορτὰς ἑορτάσαι X.*Ath*.3.2; ἑορτὴν τῇ θεῷ ποιεῖν Th.2.15; ἡ τῶν Παναθηναίων ἑ. D.4.35: metaph., οἵας ἑορτῆς ἔστ' ἀπόπτυστοι θεοῖς στέρηθρ' ἔχουσαι, of the Eumenides, A.*Eu*. 191; ἑορτὴ ὄψεως Ael.*VH*13.1. 2. generally, *holiday-making, amusement, pastime*, παιδιᾶς καὶ ἑορτῆς χάριν Pl.*Phdr*.276b, etc.; so ἑορτὴν ἡγεῖσθαι τὸ τὰ δέοντα πρᾶξαι Th.1.70. 3. prov., κατόπιν ἑορτῆς ἥκειν to have come the day after *the fair*, Pl.*Grg*.447a; ἀεργοῖς αἰὲν ἑορτά every day's *a holiday* to those who don't work, Theoc. 15.26, cf. Herod.6.17; ἄγουσιν ἑ. οἱ κλέπται Suid. 4. *assembled multitude at a festival*, ὄχλος καὶ ἑ. καὶ στρατὸς καὶ πλῆθος Plot.6.6. 12. **-ικός**, ή, όν, = ἑορταῖος, *PStrassb*.40.49 (vi A.D.): ἑορτικά, τά, *presents given at festivals*, *POxy*.724.6 (ii A.D.). **-ίς**, ίδος, ἡ, = ἑορτή, Sch.Il.5.299; coined to expl. ἔροτις. **-ολόγιον**, τό, *calendar of holidays*, Suid. **-ώδης**, ες, *festal, solemn*, J.*AJ*16.2.1, Ph.1.450, al., Sch.Th.5.54. **-ών**, μὴν Ἀττικός Eust.1698.35 (misunderstanding Hdn.Gr.ap.Choerob.*in Theod*.1.280: ἡμερῶν καὶ ἑ., εἰ τύχοι, ὤφειλον λέγεσθαι).

ἑός, ἑή, ἑόν, dat. written εἱῷ [⏑ –] Maiist.10; Boeot. **ἰός** Corinn. *Supp*.2.73; possess. Adj. of 3 pers. sg., *his, her own*, Hom., Pi., Dor., Thess. (*IG*9(2).250); not in Att. Prose (unless in A.*Fr*.350 the word is Plato's), dub. in Trag., E.*El*.1206 (lyr.):—τὸν ἑόν τε Πόδαργον *his own* Podargus, Il.23.295; strengthd., ἑῷ αὐτοῦ θυμῷ in *his own inmost* soul, 10.204; ἑοὶ αὐτοῦ θῆτες *his own* labourers, Od.4. 643. II. after Hom. (also v.l. Il.1.393, al.), of other persons, 1. as Adj. 3 pers. pl., *their*, Hes.*Op*.58, Pi.*P*.2.91, freq. in later Ep., as Batr.103, A.R.1.1113, etc. 2. in Alex. Poets, = ἐμός, A.R.2. 226. 3. also, = σός, Batr.23, A.R.2.634, 3.140, Theoc.17.50. 4. = ἡμέτερος, A.R.4.203. 5. = ὑμέτερος, Id.2.332, 3.267, *AP*7.730 (Pers.), Q.S.1.468. (I.-E. *sewo*-, Lat. *suus*; cf. ὅς.)

ϝέος, Locr. gen. sg., = οὗ (ἕο), *IG*9(1).334.32.

ἑοσσητήρ· ἐπίκουρος, τιμωρός, ἀντὶ τοῦ ἀοσσητήρ, Hsch.

ἑοῦ, = ἕο, read by Zenod. in Il.2.239, cf. A.R.4.803. **ἑοῦς**,

Boeot. for ἕο, οὗ, gen. of pers. Pron. 3 pers., Corinn.2. **ἐοῦσα,** Ion. and Ep. for οὖσα, pres. part. fem. of εἰμί.

ἐπᾰβελτερόω, *make a yet greater ass of,* ἐπαβελτερώσας τόν ποτ' ὄντ' ἀβέλτερον Men.*Per.Fr.*1.

ἐπάγᾰθος [ᾰγ], ον, = χρηστός, used in προσκυνήματα, *CIG*4991, 5020 (Nubia); also τὸ ἐ. γόνιμον νέον ὕδωρ, of the Nile, *Sammelb.* 991.4 (iii A.D.).

ἐπᾰγαίομαι, Pass., *exult in,* κάρτεϊ A.R.3.1262; *feel a malignant joy in,* ἄτῃ ib.470: Ep. aor. ἐπαγάσσατο Epic.ap.Parth.21; ἐπαγασσαμένη· ἐκπλαγεῖσα, Hsch. (ἐπαταssομένη cod.).

ἐπαγαλλιάζων, v. ἐπαγγαλιάζων.

ἐπᾰγάλλομαι, Pass., *glory in, exult in,* c. dat., πολέμῳ καὶ δηϊοτῆτι Il.16.91, cf. Q.S.7.327, Tryph.671; πόρνησ' ἐπαγαλλόμενος πυγῇσιν CratesTheb.4; ἁμίλλῃ Them.*Or.*11.151c; εἰκόσιν Artem.3.31; ἐπί τινι X.*Oec.*4.17.

ἐπᾰγᾰνακτέω, *to be indignant,* abs., J.*BJ*2.13.3, Plu.*Alc.*14, *Ages.* 19.

ἐπᾰγάνωσις [γᾰ], εως, ἡ, *polishing* (with oil or wax), ἀγαλμάτων *IG*7.4149.18 (Ptoön); cf. γάνωσις, ἐπιγανόω.

ἐπαγγαλιάζων· ἐπιχαίρων, Hsch. (leg. ἐπαγαλλιάζων).

ἐπαγγ-ελία, ἡ, *command, summons,* Plb.9.38.2. b. *announcement, notice, IG*2².1235.7 (iii B.C.); τοῦ ἀγῶνος *SIG*561.9 (Chalcis), prob. in LXX 1*Ma.*10.15; v.l. in 1*Ep.Jo.*1.5. 2. as law-term, ἐ. (sc. δοκιμασίας) *summons to attend* a δοκιμασία τῶν ῥητόρων (v. ἐπαγγέλλω 3), ἐ. τινὶ ἐπαγγέλλειν Aeschin.1.64, cf. 81; πρὸς τοὺς θεσμοθέτας ἔσθ' ἡμῖν ἐ. D.22.29: generally, *notification, summons, Sammelb.* 4434 (ii A.D.). 3. *offer, promise, profession, undertaking,* D.21.14; τὰς ὑπερβολὰς τῶν ἐ. Arist.*EN*1164ᵃ29, cf. Phld.*Herc.*1251.20; ἐπαγγελίας ποιεῖσθαί τινι Plb.1.72.6; ἐν ἐπαγγελίᾳ καταλιπών having left it as *a promise,* Id.18.28.1; τὴν ἐ. ἐπὶ τέλος ἀγαγεῖν ibid., cf. *SIG*577. 11 (Milet., iii/ii B.C.); ὤμων ἐπαγγελίᾳ *the promise* of his shoulders, Philostr.*Im.*1.4; ἐξ ἐ., = ἐπαγγειλάμενος, *BCH*11.12 (Lagina); ἐ. ποιησάμενος ἐκ τῶν ἰδίων *Michel*473.10 (Mylasa); ἐβεβαίωσεν τὴν ἐ. *Inscr.Prien.*123.9, cf. *GDI*3624*a*34 (Cos). 4. *indication,* τοῦ ἐσομένου A.D.*Synt.*205.13. 5. pl., *canvassing,* = Lat. *ambitus,* prob. f.l. for παρ–, Plu.2.276d. 6. = ἐπάγγελμα 2, *subject* of a treatise, Gal.*Libr.Propr.Prooem.* 7. the *curative property claimed* for prescriptions or drugs, ταῖς τῶν φαρμάκων ἐ. their *advertised properties,* Herod.Med.ap.Orib.10.5.1, cf. Gal.13.504,al.; ἐ. ἐπιτηδεύματος *public exercise* of a profession, Men.Prot.p.1 D. **–έλλω,** aor. Pass. –ηγγέλθην *IG*1².188.25, –ηγγέλην ib.1².76.19:—*tell, proclaim, announce,* Od.4.775, Ar.*Lys.*1049(lyr.); τινὶ ὡς... Hdt.3.36; τῷ δήμῳ ὑπέρ τινος ὅτι... *Inscr.Prien.*5.17 (iv B.C.); esp. *proclaim by authority, notify publicly,* ἐ. [τὴν ἐκεχειρίαν] Th.5.49; ἐ. πόλεμον Pl.*Lg.*702d:—Pass., *to be proclaimed, IG* ll.cc., etc.; μὴ ἐπηγγέλθαι πω τὰς σπονδάς Th.5.49, cf. 8.10; βουλῆς –θείσης a meeting *having been summoned,* D.C.56.29:—Med., *cause proclamation to be made,* Hdt.2.121.ζ'. 2. *give orders, command,* abs., Id.1.70: c.acc.etinf., *give orders that...,* ἐπαγγείλας τοὺς Λακεδαιμονίους παρεῖναι ib.77, cf. Th.6.56: c. dat. et inf., *order* one to do, D.42.7, etc.: c. acc. rei, στρατιὰν ἐς τοὺς ξυμμάχους ἐ. *send* them *orders* to furnish their contingents, Th.7.17; κατὰ πόλεις τεσσαράκοντα νεῶν πλῆθος ἐ. Id.3.16: abs., βοηθεῖν... καθ' ὅ τι ἂν –ωσιν αἱ πόλεις Foed.ap.Th.5.47:—Med., ἐπαγγέλλεσθαί τινι ἑτοιμάζειν στρατιήν Hdt.7.1, cf. 4.200; ἐ. τινί E.*HF*1185 (lyr.); ἐ. τισὶ ὅκως ἂν ἀπέλθοιεν Hdt.5.98:—Pass., τὸ ἐπαγγελλόμενον Id. 2.55. 3. as law-term, prop. δοκιμασίαν ἐ. *denounce and summon to* a δοκιμασία τῶν ῥητόρων one who, having incurred ἀτιμία, yet takes part in public affairs (v. ἐπαγγελία 2), ἐπήγγειλα αὐτῷ τὴν δοκιμασίαν ταυτηνί Aeschin.1.2, cf. ib.32; πρὸς τοὺς θεσμοθέτας D.22.23 (but ἐπηγγέλθη αὐτοῖς ὅτι ἐπεξίοιμι is f.l. for ἀπ– in Antipho 1.11). 4. *promise, offer,* ξείνοις δεῖπνα Pi.*P.*4.31; θεοῖς εὐχάς A.*Ch.*213:—more freq. in Med., *promise unasked* (opp. ὑπισχνέομαι) or *offer of one's free will,* ἐ. τι ἐς τὴν δωρεὴν τοῖσι ἀδελφεοῖσι Hdt.3.135; ἐ. καταγωγὴν καὶ ξείνιά τινι Id.6.35; παίδων... ἐ. γονάς E.*Med.*721; ἀπηγγελλόμην what I *was proposing,* S.*El.*1018, cf. D.4.15; ἐ. τάδε, ὡς.. Hdt.6.9: c. inf., *promise* or *offer,* ξυμπολεμεῖν Th.6.88; διαθήκας ἀποφαίνειν (–φανεῖν Dobree) Is.1.15; ἐ. τῇ βουλῇ μηνύσειν And.1.15; τισὶν τριήρεις ἔχων ἐκπλεύσεσθαι Lys.28.4, cf. D.18.132, etc.; τινὶ ὥστε βοηθεῖν Th.8.86; ἐ. ὅ τι χρὴ δρᾶν *offering* (to do) what in justice he ought to do, Pl.*Lg.*915a. 5. Med., *profess, make profession of,* c. acc., ἀρετήν X.*Mem.*1.2.7; θεοσέβειαν 1*Ep.Ti.*2.10; esp. of Sophists, as in Pl.*Euthd.*273e; τί ἐστιν ὃ ἐ. τε καὶ διδάσκει Id.*Grg.*447c; τοῦτό ἐστι τὸ ἐπάγγελμα ὃ ἐπαγγέλλομαι Id.*Prt.*319a; ἐπαγγελλόμενος πάντα ..οὐδὲν ἐπιτελεῖ Arist.*EN*1164ᵃ5; [γνῶσιν] 1*Ep.Ti.*6.21: c. inf., ἐ. ἀποκρίνεσθαι ὅ τι ἄν τίς σε ἐρωτᾷ Pl.*Grg.*447d; ἐ. οἷός τε εἶναι ποιῆσαί τι Id.*La.*186c, *Thg.*127e; ταῦτα ἐπαγγέλλεται δεινὸς εἶναι D.35.41; οἱ σοφισταὶ ἐ. διδάσκειν τινά Arist.*EN*1180ᵇ35; παιδεύειν D.35.41: and abs., *profess* an art, Pl.*R.*518b, Arist.*SE*172ᵃ32. 6. *demand, require,* cj. in D.H.5.65:—Med., D.19.193; but, *ask a favour,* ib. 41. **–ελμα,** ατος, τό, *promise, profession,* D.19.178 (pl.); τὸ Πρωταγόρου ἐ. Arist.*Rh.*1402ᵃ25, cf. Pl.*Prt.*319a; ὑπὸ τοῦ μεγέθους τοῦ ἐ. οὐδὲν θαυμαστὸν ἀπιστεῖν Id.*Euthd.*274a: pl., Metrod.ap.Phld. *Rh.*1.88 S.; ἐπαγγέλματι, opp. κατ' ἀλήθειαν, S.E.*M.*1.182. 2. *subject* of a treatise, that which it *purports* to contain, τὸ ἐ. τοῦ λόγου D.H.*Dem.*33; τὸ ἐ. τοῦ συγγράμματος Ael.*Tact.Praef.*7. 3. = ἐπαγγελία 7, Crito ap.Gal.13.878, Id.ap.Aët.15.16. 4. *art, profession,* τὸ ἐ. τῆς ἀρτοποιΐας M.Ant.3.2. **–ελτήρ,** ῆρος, ὁ, *envoy who announces a festival,* etc., *SIG*558.5 (Ithaca). **–ελτής,** *promissor, sponsor, Gloss.* **–ελτικός,** ή, όν, *given to promising,* ἐπεκλήθη Δώσων ὡς ἐ. Plu.*Aem.*8; also [λόγος] πρὸς τοὺς πολλοὺς ἐ. Phld.*Rh.*2.2 S., cf. Iamb.*Myst.*3.30. Adv. –κῶς Ath.Mech.15.9: Comp. –κώτερον, εἰπεῖν *too professorially,* Arist.*Rh.*1398ᵇ30. 2. *promised,* οὐ δύνασθαι τελεῖν τὸ ἐ. ἀργύριον *SIG*832.7 (Epist. Hadr.). **–ελτος,** η, ον, *voluntary,* παραγενηθεὶς ἐπάγγελτος coming forward *voluntarily,* ib. 708.21 (Istropolis, ii B.C.).

ἐπᾰγ-είρω, *gather together, collect,* of things, Il.1.126:—Pass., of men, *assemble,* πρὶν ἐπὶ ἔθνε' ἀγείρετο Od.11.632, cf. Pi.*P.*9.54 (Act.). **–ερσις,** εως, ἡ, *mustering* of forces *against* an enemy, Ξέρξης τοῦ στρατοῦ ἐ. ποιέεται Hdt.7.19.

ἐπάγην [ᾰ], v. πήγνυμι.

ἐπᾰγῑνέω, Ion. for ἐπάγω, *bring to,* Hdt.2.2, Q.S.6.235.

ἐπαγκᾰλίζομαι, *embrace,* Pall.*in Hp.Fract.*12.278C.

ἐπαγκρούω, v. ἐπανα–.

ἐπαγκῠλ-έω, *furnish with a thong,* ἐπηγκυλημένα ξύλα Suid. (Pass.). **–ίζομαι,** Pass., *to be fitted with an* ἀγκύλη, Sch.E.*Or.* 1476. **–ωτός,** όν, *fitted with a thong,* βρόχος Heraclas ap.Orib. 48.14.1.

ἐπαγκων-ίδιον, τό, *cushion,* Aët.16.108(98). **–ισμός,** ὁ, a kind of *dance,* Ath.14.630a.

ἐπαγλαΐζω, *honour, grace,* δῆμον ὠφελίαισι βίου Ar.*Ec.*575, cf. *Fr.*682; ὃν σοφίας μῦθος ἐ. *IG*12(9).954.7 (Chalcis), cf. 7.2532 (Thebes). II. Med., *pride oneself on* a thing, *glory* or *exult in* it, οὐδέ ἕ φημι δηρὸν ἐπαγλαϊεῖσθαι (fut. inf.) Il.18.133. 2. Pass., ἐπηγλαϊσμέναι..τράπεζαι *dressed out,* Cratin.301.

ἐπάγνῡμι, *break,* οὗ τ' ἐπὶ νῶτα ἔαγε (intr. perf.) Hes.*Op.*534.

ἐπᾰγορ-άζω, *purchase a title to the next vacancy* of a priesthood, *SIG*1014.17 (Erythrae, iii B.C.). **–ευσις,** εως, ἡ, *funeral oration,* Them.*Or.*20 p.285 D. **–εύω,** = ἀν–, *proclaim,* στεφάνους *IG*7.21.33 (Megara, iii/ii B.C.).

ἐπᾱγορία, v. ἐπηγ–.

ἐπαγρ-ος, ον, (ἄγρα) *in quest of prey,* Arist.*HA*616ᵇ34; οὐκέτι χεῖρες ἔπαγροι φιλητέων Call.*Hec.*1.4.10. **–οσύνη,** ἡ, *good luck in hunting, fishing,* etc., Theoc.*Beren.*1.

ἐπαγρυπν-έω, *keep awake and think over, keep a watchful eye on,* τινί Luc.*Tim.*14; πράξεσι Onos.1.4: abs., Luc.*Gall.*31, Plu.*Brut.*37; ὡς... *PTeb.*27.75 (ii B.C.). 2. *watch for,* ἀπωλείᾳ τινὸς –ηκὼς D.S. 14.68: abs., Aristaenet.1.27. **–ησις,** εως, ἡ, *watching for,* ibid.; εἴς τι Aristeas 167; *watchfulness,* Phld.*Lib.*p.7 O. **–ία,** f.l. for εὐαύγεια, Iamb.*VP*3.13. **–ος,** ον, *wakeful, sleepless,* κηδεμονία Mitteis *Chr.*77.11 (Sup., iv A.D.), cf. Vett.Val.11.16, Aristaenet.1.27.

ἐπαγχάζομαι, in aor. ἐπαγχάσασθε· ἐπαναχωρήσατε, Hsch.

ἐπαγχάλιξον· ἄκρατον ἐπίχεον, prob. in Hsch. (ἐπαγλαΐζον cod.).

ἐπάγχιστος, ον, *next of kin, IG*9(1).334.17; neut. pl. as Adv., οἱ ἐπάγχιστα πεπαμένοι *GDI*4986 (Gortyn).

ἐπαγχωνίζω, dub. sens. in *Tab.Defix.Aud.*155*B*11 (Rome, iv/v A.D.).

ἐπάγω [ᾰ], *bring on,* οἷον ἐπ' ἦμαρ ἄγῃσι πατήρ Od.18.137; ἐ. πῆμά τινι Hes.*Op.*242; νύκτ' Id.*Th.*176; ἐλεύθερον ἦμαρ Bacis ap.Hdt.8. 77; ἄτην ἐπ' ἄτῃ A.*Ch.*404 (lyr.), cf. S.*Aj.*1189 (lyr.); κινδύνους τινί Is.8.3; πόλεμον ἐπὶ τὰς Θήβας Aeschin.3.140; νόσους γῆράς τε ἐ. Pl. *Ti.*33a; πάθος ἐ. Hp.*Morb.Sacr.*3. 2. *set on, urge on,* as hunters do dogs, ἐπάγοντες ἐπῆσαν (sc. κύνας) Od.19.445, cf. X.*Cyn.*10.19:—in Med., ib.6.25. b. *lead on* an army *against* the enemy, Ἄρη τινί A.*Pers.*85 (lyr.); τὴν στρατιήν Hdt.1.63, cf. 7.165; τὸ δεξιὸν κέρας Ar. *Av.*353; στρατόπεδον Th.6.69; τινὰ ἐπί τινα Id.8.46: intr., *march against,* τισί Plb.2.29.2: abs., dub. in Luc.*Hist.Conscr.*21: metaph., Diph.44 (nisi leg. ἐπῆττε). c. *quicken* the pace, Ar.*Eq.*25, *Nu.*390, Pl.*Cra.*420d; θᾶττονα ῥυθμὸν ἐ. X.*Smp.*2.22. 3. *lead on by persuasion, influence,* Od.14.392, Th.1.107; ἐλπὶς ἥ σ' ἐπήγαγεν E.*Hec.* 1032: c. inf., *induce* one to do, ib.260, Isoc.14.63:—Pass., οἷς ἐπαχθέντες ὑμεῖς D.5.10 (cod. S). 4. *bring in, invite* as aiders or allies, τὸν Πέρσην Hdt.9.1, cf. 8.112; τὸν Π. ἐπὶ τοὺς Ἕλληνας Epist. Phil.ap.D.12.7; Μήδους Ar.*Th.*365 (v. infr. II. 2). 5. *bring to* a place, *bring in,* S.*Tr.*378, E.*Ph.*905; ἅμαξαι...τοὺς λίθους ἐπῆγον Th. 1.93:—Med., *draw in* nourishment, of roots, Thphr.*HP*1.1.9:—Pass., τροφὰ ἐπάγεται τῷ σώματι Ti.Locr.102b. 6. *bring in, supply,* ἐπιτήδεια Th.7.60; τὰ ἐκ τῶν διωρύχων ἐ. νάματα Pl.*Criti.*118e; λίμνην... εἰς τὴν ἅλμην Ephipp.5.12: metaph., ἐπάγει ἡ ψυχὴ τὸ ἓν ἄλλῳ Plot.6.9.1. 7. *lay on* or *apply* to one, ἐ. κέντρον πώλοις, of a charioteer, E.*Hipp.*1194; ἐ. πληγὴν ἐπί τινα LXX *Is.*10.24; ἐ. ζημίαν, = ἐπιτιθέναι, Luc.*Anach.*11; ἔπαγε τὴν γνάθον *lay* your jaws *to it,* Ar. *V.*370; ἐ. τὴν διάνοιάν τινι *apply* it, Plu.*Per.*1. 8. *bring forward,* ἐ. ψῆφον τοῖς ξυμμάχοις *propose* a vote to them, like ἐπιψηφίζειν ἐς.. Th.1.125, cf. 87; ψῆφος ἐπῆκτό τινι περὶ φυγῆς *against* him, X.*An.*7. 7.57, cf. D.47.28; ἐ. ὅρκον τισί Paus.4.14.4, cf.*IG*9(1).334.13 (Locr.); also ἐ. δίκην, γραφήν τινι, *bring* a suit *against* one, Pl.*Lg.*881e, D.18. 150; γραφάς, εὐθύνας, εἰσαγγελίας ib.249; λεγέτω πρότερος ὁ ἐπάγων τὰν δίκαν *Foed.Delph.Pell.*1*A*10; ἐ. αἰτίαν τινί D.18.141; αἰτίαν ἐπήγαγέ μοι φόνου ψευδῆ Id.21.110, cf. 114. b. *introduce* a person before the assembly, *IG*12(7).389.5, *BCH*50.251, etc. 9. *bring in over and above,* παροψώνημα A.*Ag.*1446; τῷ λόγῳ τὸ ἔργον Plu.*Lyc.*8:—Pass., τὸ ἐπαγόμενον φωνῆεν the vowel *which follows, EM*176.55; ὁ ἐ. ἀγών *extraordinary, CIG*3491 (Thyatira). b. *intercalate* days in the year, Hdt.2.4, D.S.1.50; αἱ ἐπαγόμεναι, with or without ἡμέραι, *intercalated* days, ib.13, Plu.2.355e, *Inscr.Cypr.*134 H., *PStrassb.*91. 6, Vett.Val.20.26, 36.9, etc. 10. in instruction or argument, *lead on,* τινὰς ἐπὶ τὰ μήπω γιγνωσκόμενα Pl.*Plt.*278a:—Pass., ἐπαχθέντων αὐτῶν Aristox.*Harm.*p.23 M. b. esp. in the Logic of

Aristotle, *teach* or *convince by induction*, ἐπάγοντα ἀπὸ τῶν καθ' ἕκαστον ἐπὶ τὸ καθόλου καὶ τῶν γνωρίμων ἐπὶ τὰ ἄγνωστα *Top*.156^{a}4:—Pass., ἐπαχθῆναι μὴ ἔχοντας αἴσθησιν ἀδύνατον *APo*.81^{b}5, cf. 71^{a}21,24: abs., συλλογιζόμενον ἢ ἐπάγοντα by syllogism or *by induction*, *Rh*.1356^{b}8, cf. *Top*.157^{a}21, al.; οὐδ' ὁ ἐπάγων ἀποδείκνυσιν *APo*.91^{b}15. c. also ἐ. τὸ καθόλου *bring forward, advance*: hence, *infer* the general principle, τῇ καθ' ἕκαστα ἐπὶ τῶν ὁμοίων ἐπαγωγῇ ἐ. τὸ καθόλου *Top*.108^{b}11, cf. *SE* 174^{a}34; so later, *adduce the argument*, ὅτι.. Alex.Aphr.*in SE* 6.2; *conclude, infer*, Arr.*Epict*.4.8.9. II. ἐ. τὴν κοιλίαν *move* the bowels, v.l. for ὑπ-, Dsc.4.157. II. Med., *bring to oneself, procure* or *provide for oneself*, ἐκ θαλάσσης ὧν δέονται ἐπάξονται Th.1.81, cf. 6.99: metaph., Ἅιδα φεῦξιν ἐ. *devise, invent* a means of shunning death, S. *Ant*.362 (lyr.); τὴν τῶν ξυμμάχων δούλωσιν Th.3.10; τῶν.. κακῶν ἐ. λήθην Men.467. 2. of persons, *bring into* one's country, *bring in* or *introduce* as allies (v. supr. I. 4), Hdt.2.108, Th.1.3, 2.68, 4.64, al.; οἰκιστὴν ἐ. Hdt.6.34, cf. 5.67; ἐπιϝοίκους ἐ. *Berl.Sitzb*.1927.8 (Locr., v B.C.). 3. μάρτυρας ποιητὰς ἐ. *call* them *in* as witnesses, Pl.*R*. 364c, cf. *Lg*.823a, Arist.*Metaph*.995^{a}8; ἐ. ποιητὰς ἐν τοῖς λόγοις *introduce* by way of quotation, Pl.*Prt*.347e; τὸν Ἡσίοδον μάρτυρα Id.*Ly*. 215c; ἐ. μαρτύρια *adduce* testimonies, X.*Smp*.8.34; εἰκόνας ἐ. Id. *Oec*.17.15; ὅρκον ἐ. πάντα τὰ ζῷα Porph.*Abst*.3.16. 4. *bring upon oneself*, νύκτα ἐν μεσημβρίᾳ Pl.*Lg*.897d; φθόνον X.*Ap*.32; συμφορὰν ἐμαυτῷ Lys.4.19; αὐθαίρετον αὑτοῖς δουλείαν D.19.259; πράγματα Id.54.1; ἑαυτοῖς δεσπότην ἐ. τὸν νόμον Pl.*Grg*.492b; μητρυιὰν ἐ. κατὰ τῶν ἰδίων τέκνων D.S.12.12. 5. *bring with one*, προῖκα πολλήν Nicostr.ap.Stob.4.22.102. 6. *bring over to oneself, win over*, τὸ πλῆθος Th.5.45; τινὰ εἰς εὔνοιαν Plb.7.14.4: c. acc. et inf., ἐ. τινὰς ξυγχωρῆσαι *induce* them to concede, Th.5.41. 7. *put in place*, λίθον *Princeton Exp.Inscr*.1175 (iii A.D.).

ἐπαγωγ-εύς, έως, ὁ, *coat of clay* on a wall, *IG*2^2.1672.61 (fort. pro ὑπ- legendum, Ar.*Av*.1149, sed cf. ἐξυπάγω). **-ή**, ἡ, *bringing on* or *to*, τῶν ἐπιτηδείων Th.5.82, 7.24. 2. *bringing in to one's aid, introduction*, τὴν τῶν Ἀθηναίων ἐ. Id.3.100, cf. 82 (pl.); *introduction* of food through the gullet, Arist.*Spir*.483^{a}9. 3. *invasion, attack*, ἐπὶ τοὺς ἐναντίους Plb.10.23.7: abs., Id.11.15.7. 4. *allurement, enticement*, ταῖς ἐλπίσι καὶ ταῖς ἐ. D.19.322. b. *incantation, spell*, in pl., Pl.*R*.364c, *Lg*.933d; Ἑκάτης φάσκων ἐπαγωγὴν γεγονέναι saying that Hecate had put it under a *spell*, Thphr.*Char*.16.7. 5. *process of reasoning*, Aristox.*Harm*.pp.4,53 M. b. esp. in the Logic of Aristotle, *argument by induction* (cf. ἐπάγω I. 10b), ἐ. ἡ ἀπὸ τῶν καθ' ἕκαστον ἐπὶ τὰ καθόλου ἔφοδος *Top*.105^{a}13; μανθάνομεν ἢ ἐπαγωγῇ ἢ ἀποδείξει *APo*.81^{a}40; διδασκαλία.. ἡ μὲν δι' ἐπαγωγῆς ἡ δὲ συλλογισμῷ *EN* 1139^{b}27; ἔστι τὸ μὲν παράδειγμα ἐ., τὸ δ' ἐνθύμημα συλλογισμός *Rh*.1356^{b}3; so later συλλογισμοὺς ἢ ἐπαγωγὰς περαίνοντας Polystr.p.11 W., cf. Plot.2.4.6, etc.; also of *dialectical argument* which leads an opponent into a trap, Gell.6(7).3.34, D.L.3.53. 6. in Tactics, *sequence formation*, one wing following the other, opp. παραγωγή, Ascl.*Tact*.10.1, 11.2,4. 7. *leading away into captivity, captivity*, Lxx *Is*.14.17: generally, *distress, misery*, ib.*Si*.23.14 (pl.), cf. Hsch. 8. ἡ τῆς τριχὸς ἐ. *direction of growth*, D.S.3.35. **-ικός**, ή, όν, *inductive*, τρόπος S.E.*P*.2.196, cf. Asp.*in EN* 2.25. Adv. -κῶς S.E.*P*.2.195, Sch.Pi.*O*.1.20. II. (from Med.) *attractive*, v.l. for ὑπαγωγικός in D.H.*Comp*.4. **-ιμος**, ον, *imported*, Plu.*Lys*.17, *IG* 14.422 iii 46,60 (Tauromenium). **-ιον**, τό, *foreskin, prepuce*, Dsc. 3.22. **-ίς**, *femella*, Gloss. **-ός**, όν, *bringing on*, μανίας A.*Fr*.57.5 (anap.); ἡδονῆς Gorg.*Hel*.10; ὕπνου Pl.*Ti*.45d; κίνησις ἐ. ὁράσεως Ph.2.359. II. *attractive, alluring*, τὰ ἐπαγωγότατα λέγειν Hdt.3. 53, cf. Th.4.88; ἀκούσαντες.. ἐπαγωγὰ καὶ οὐκ ἀληθῆ, of ex-parte statements, Id.6.8, cf. 5.85; ὀνόματος ἐπαγωγοῦ δυνάμει ἐπισπᾶσθαι ib. 111; ἐ. πρός τι X.*Oec*.13.9; λόγοι ἐ. D.59.70; of *dainty* dishes, ὄψον .. ἐ. πάνυ Antiph.242: Sup., δελέατα καὶ φίλτρα -ότατα Ph.1.396: c. gen., ἐ. ἡδονῇ τῶν ἀκροωμένων D.H.*Isoc*.3; τοῦ δήμου Plu.*Publ*.2; also ἔμφασιν κάλλους ἐπαγωγὸν εἶναι τοῦ ἔρωτος Chrysipp.*Stoic*.3.181; ἐπαγωγόν ἐστι, c. inf., it is a *temptation* to.., X.*Mem*.2.5.5; τὸ ἐ. *seductiveness*, Pl.*Phlb*.44c: neut. as Adv., ἐπαγωγὸν μειδιᾶν Luc. *DMeretr*.1.2, 6.3. Adv. -γῶς Poll.4.24: Sup. -ότατα Paus.9.12.5.

ἐπάγων· ἠφφήδιος, κασάνδρα, Hsch.

ἐπᾰγωνίζομαι, *contend with*, τινί Plu.*Fab*.23; *continue to attack*, Aeschin.*Ep*.2.2. 2. c. dat. rei, *contend in*, εὐνοίᾳ *IG*12(5).860.19 (Tenos); *contend for*, τῇ πίστει *Ep.Jud*.3: *lay stress on*, ἐ. τῷ λόγῳ Gal.14.246; τεκμηρίοις ἐ. Plu.*Num*.8; ἐ. τῇ λέξει τὰ ἰσοδυναμοῦντα παρατιθείς Aristid.*Rh*.1 p.500 S.: abs., S.E.*M*.3.93; *exert oneself*, *IG*2^2. 1343.16. 3. *contend again*, in games, D.H.*Rh*.7.6. b. *speak after* a person, *follow* him, Philostr.*VS*1.25.7; ἐ. τῷ λόγῳ Lib.*Arg.D*.22.

ἐπάει· ἐπαίρει ἀρᾷ, Hsch.

ἐπᾰείδω, contr. Att. **ἐπᾴδω**, fut. -ᾴσομαι Ar.*Ec*.1153, etc.; -ᾴσω Ach.Tat.2.7:—*sing to* or *in accompaniment*, μάγος ἀνὴρ.. ἐ. θεογονίην Hdt.1.132; ᾠδὰν χορῷ E.*El*.864 (lyr.):—Pass., Arr.*An*.2.16.3. 2. *sing as an incantation*, ἃ αἱ Σειρῆνες ἐπῇδον τῷ Ὀδυσσεῖ X.*Mem*.2.6.11; χρὴ τὰ τοιαῦτα ὥσπερ ἐπᾴδειν ἑαυτῷ Pl.*Phd*.114d, cf. 77e; ἐ. ἡμῖν αὐτοῖς τοῦτον τὸν λόγον Id.*R*.608a; ἐ. τινί *sing to* one *so as to charm* or *soothe* him, Id.*Phdr*.267d, *Lg*.812c, al.:—Pass., Porph.*Chr*.35: abs., *use charms* or incantations, Pl.*Tht*.157c; ἐπαείδων *by means of charms*, A.*Ag*.1021 (lyr.), cf. Pl.*Lg*.773d, *Tht*.149d.

ἐπᾰείρω, poet. for ἐπαίρω (q.v.).

ἐπᾰέξω, *make to grow, prosper*, θεὸς δ' ἐπὶ ἔργον ἀέξῃ Od.14.65:—Pass., *increase, grow*, Semon.7.85 (κἀπ- may be for καὶ ἀπ-), Nic. *Th*.449.

ἐπαεσσούριον· κατήγορον, Hsch.

ἐπαθλοκομέω, *train for contest*, φῶτας *IG*7.3226 (Orchom. Boeot., i B.C.).

ἔπαθλον, τό, *prize of a contest*, mostly in pl., E.*Ph*.52, etc.; τὰ ἔ. τοῦ πολέμου Plu.*Flam*.15; *rewards*, ἀρετῆς D.S.28.4, cf. *OGI*455.3 (Aphrodisias, M.Antonius), Hdn.1.17.11; οὐδ' ἐπὶ σαφέσι τοῖς ἐ. not even if the *advantages* (of taking an emetic) were obvious, Archig. ap.Orib.8.23.2: also in sg., δοὺς ἑκάστῳ τὸ ὑπὲρ τῆς φιλοπονίας ἔ. *Inscr.Prien*.113.31 (i B.C.); προτιθεμένου ἐ. τῷ λύσαντι γαμεῖν τὴν Ἰοκάστην D.S.4.64; ἔ. πόνων Plu.*Cor*.23.

ἔπᾰθον, v. πάσχω.

ἐπαθρέω, = εἰσαθρέω, *look with favour on*, B.12.227, prob. l. in Id. 5.8; simply, *behold*, v.l. in Q.S.1.111.

ἐπαθροίζομαι, Pass., *assemble besides*, *Ev.Luc*.11.29, Plu.*Ant*.44.

ἐπαιάζω, *cry* αἰαῖ *over, mourn over*, τῷ νεκρῷ Luc.*DDeor*.14.2; *bewail*, μόρον Nic.*Al*.303. II. *join in the wail*, Bion 1.2, etc.; ἐ. πρὸς τὸ μέλος Luc.*Luct*.20.

ἐπαΐγδην, Adv. *impetuously*, Opp.*H*.2.616.

ἐπαιγῐᾰλῖτις, ιδος, ἡ, *on the beach*, χηλή *AP*10.8 (Arch.).

ἐπαιγίζω, (αἰγίς II) *rush upon*, twice in Hom. of a stormy wind, Ζέφυρος.. λάβρος ἐπαιγίζων Il.2.148; οὖρον.. λάβρον ἐπαιγίζοντα δι' αἰθέρος Od.15.293; λάβρως ἐ. ὁ βορρᾶς Alciphr.3.42: metaph., Ἔρως λάβρον ἐπαιγίζων *AP*5.285 (Paul. Sil.): c. dat., *rush over*, ἐπαιγίζει πεδίοισι, of a stream that has burst its banks, Opp.*C*.2.125: c. acc., πόντον ἐπαιγίζει, of the dolphin, Id.*H*.2.583.

ἐπαιδέομαι, fut. -αιδεσθήσομαι E.*IA*900 (troch.): aor. -ηδέσθην Pl. *Lg*.921a:—*to be ashamed*, c. inf., E. l.c.; σὺ δ' οὐκ ἐπαιδῇ.. εἰ..; *te non pudet si..?* S.*Ant*.510: c. dat., *to be ashamed of*, Babr.43.14: abs., *feel compunction*, E.*Hyps.Fr*.60.21. II. c. acc., *reverence*, A. *Fr*.135, Antipho Soph.*Oxy*.1364.270, Pl. l.c., Herod.2.39.

ἐπαιθύσσω, *flash at*, σπινθῆρας Ὀλύμπῳ Nonn.*D*.2.322, etc.:—Pass., *to be blown over*, πλόκαμοι.. ἐ. προσώπῳ ib.11.247. 2. intr., *rush violently on*, Opp.*C*.4.176.

ἐπάϊκλα, τά, *additions to the ordinary meal* (αἶκλον), Dor. for ἐπιδείπνια, ἐπιδόρπια, Pers.*Stoic*.1.101, Sphaer.ib.142: sg., Molpis 3:—also **ἐπαΐκλεια**, ibid., Apion ap.Ath.14.642e.

ἐπαίμονες· ἀγχόγονοι, Hsch.

ἐπαίν-εσις, εως, ἡ, *praise*, E.*Tr*.418 (pl.). **-ετέον**, *one must praise*, Pl.*R*.390e, Luc.*Hist.Conscr*.9. 2. Adj. **-ετέος**, έα, έον, Philostr.*VS*1.15.1: -τέοι οἱ θεοὶ τῆς διανοίας Id.*VA*2.33, cf. S.E.*M*. 2.104. **-ετέω**, = ἐπαινέω, Phld.*Rh*.1.83 S. (s.v.l.). **-έτης**, ου, ὁ, *praiser, commender*, Hp.*Acut*.6, Th.2.41, Pl.*R*.366e, Timocl. 8.9, etc.:—fem. **-έτις**, ιδος, φιλοσοφία -έτις παμβασιλείας Them.*Or*. 18.219d. II. *rhapsodist*, Pl.*Ion* 536d; cf. ἐπαινέω IV. **-ετικός**, ή, όν, *given to praising, laudatory*, Arist.*EN*1125^{a}7; λόγος ἐ. Luc.*Pr. Im*.19. Adv. -κῶς Eust.102.37. **-ετός**, ή, όν, *to be praised, praiseworthy, laudable*, Pl.*Cra*.416c, *Lg*.660a, etc.; τὸ ἐ. *the object of praise*, Arist.*EN*1101^{b}13: Comp., Theon *Prog*.12. Adv. -τῶς Phld. *Po*.2.26, Ph.1.682, al.

ἐπαιν-έω, Aeol. **ἐπαίνημι** Simon.5.19; Lacon. **ἐπαινίω** Ar.*Lys*. 198: impf. ἐπῄνεον Il.3.461 (tm.): fut. -έσω Semon.7.29, S.*El*.1057, E.*Andr*.465 (lyr.), *Heracl*.[300], Pl.*Smp*.214e (dub. l.), X.*An*.1.4. 16, 5.5.8: but more freq. -έσομαι E.*Ba*.1195 (lyr.), Pl.*Smp*.199a, *R*. 379e, 383a, X.*HG*3.2.6, D.2.31, etc.; poet. -ήσω Thgn.93 codd., Pi. *P*.10.69: aor. 1 ἐπῄνεσα S.*Aj*.536, Th.1.86, etc. (v. infr.); poet. (not Trag.) ἐπῄνησα Il.2.335, 18.312, Thgn.876, Pi.*P*.4.168,189: also Aeol. prose, *Schwyzer*622.21, 623.31, 636.17 (but -έσαι 623.34): pf. ἐπῄνεκα Isoc.12.207,261, Pl.*Plt*.307a, etc.:—**Med.**, aor. ἐπηνησάμην Them.*Or*.16.200c; -εσάμην Phalar.*Ep*.147:—Pass., fut. ἐπαινεθήσομαι And.2.13, Pl.*R*.474d; later ἐπαινηθήσομαι Longus 4.4 codd.: aor. ἐπῃνέθην Th.2.25, Isoc.12.146, etc.; but ἐπῃνήθην *SIG*708.20 (Istropolis, ii B.C.): pf. ἐπῄνημαι Hp.*Acut*.51, Isoc.12.233: = αἰνέω (for which it is regularly used in Att.):—*approve, applaud, commend*, in Hom. mostly abs., ἐπὶ δ' ᾔνεον ἄλλοι Ἀχαιοί Il.3.461, etc.: c. acc. rei, μῦθον ἐπαινήσαντες Ὀδυσσῆος 2.335; μῦθον ἐ. πρεσβυτέροισι *h.Merc*.457; σύνθεσιν Pi.*P*.4.168: c. dat. pers., *agree with, side with*, Ἕκτορι μὲν γὰρ ἐπῄνησαν Il.18.312: abs., *assent, agree*, Ar.*Av*.1616; ἐπαινεσάντων δ' αὐτῶν on their *assent*, Th.4.65. 2. *praise, commend* in any way (the usu. sense in Att. and Trag.), τινά or τι, Alc. 37A, Hdt.3.34, 6.130; τὸ λίαν ἧσσον ἐ. τοῦ μηδὲν ἄγαν E.*Hipp*.264; ἐ. τινά τι *commend* one *for* a thing, but in this case the thing is always a neut. Pron. or Adj., τὰ μέν σ' ἐπαινῶ A.*Pr*.342 (cf. III); πάντ' ἔχω σ' ἐπαινέσαι S.*Aj*.1381, cf. Pl.*Smp*.222a; in Din.3.22 ἐπαινεῖσθαι ταῖς ζητήσεσιν, (ἐπί) shd. be read; ἐπί τινι.. καὶ διότι *Inscr.Prien*. 44.17 (ii B.C.); εἴς τι Pl.*Alc*.1.111a; κατά τι D.S.1.37; πρός τι Pl. *Tht*.145b; also ἐ. τινά τινος Plu.2.1c, Luc.*Herm*.42 (but ἐ. τί τινος *praise* something in some one, Pl.*Prt*.361d): c. acc. cogn., ἔπαινον ἐ. Id.*La*.181b: c. part., ἐπαινέσεσθαί τινα ἀνασχόμενον D.21.73; ἐ. τινὰ ὅτι.. Pl.*Grg*.471d; ἐ. τινὰ πρός τινα *praise* one man to another, Id.*R*. 501c; esp. *compliment publicly*, [Βρασίδας] πρῶτος τῶν κατὰ τὸν πόλεμον ἐπῃνέθη ἐν Σπάρτῃ Th.2.25; freq. in honorary Inscrr., cf. *IG*2^2.102, *Inscr.Prien*. l.c., etc.: c. dat. pers., τῷ δήμῳ τῷ Σαμίων *IG*1^2.101.2, cf. *SIG*604.11 (Delph., ii B.C.). 3. of things, [πολιτεία] ὑπὸ πάντων -ουμένη Isoc.12.118, cf. Arist.*Pol*.1289^{a}1; νόμοι -ούμενοι Id.*Rh*.1375^b 24; *approve*, πόλις ἄλλως ἄλλοτ' ἐ. τὰ δίκαια A.*Th*.1077. 4. *agree to* or *undertake to do*, ῥώμην μ' ἐπαινῶ λαμβάνειν E.*Andr*.553; ἐ. εἰς τὸ λοιπόν *PTeb*.8.18 (iii B.C.). 5. aor. ἐπῄνεσα in Att. in pres. sense, ἐπῄνεσ' ἔργον I *commend* it, S.*Aj*.536: abs., *well done!* Id.*Fr*. 282, Ar.*Ach*.485, cf. E.*Alc*.1095, *Med*.707. II. = παραινέω, *recommend, advise*, τοιούσδ' ἐπαινεῖς δῆτα σὺ κτᾶσθαι φίλους; S.*Aj*.1360, cf.

A.*Th.*596, *Supp.*996: c. dat. et inf., ὑμῖν δ' ἐπαινῶ γλῶσσαν εὔφημον φέρειν Id.*Ch.*581; σιγᾶν ἐπῄνεσ' (cf. I. 5) S.*El.*1322, cf. *OC*665. III. as a civil form of declining an offer or invitation, I *thank you*, I *am much obliged*, κάλλιστ', ἐπαινῶ Ar.*Ra.*508 (ubi v. Sch.), cf. A.*Pr.*342; so ἐ. τὴν κλῆσιν *decline* it, X.*Smp.*1.7, cf. *An.*7.7.52. IV. of Rhapsodists, *recite, declaim publicly*, Pl.*Ion* 536d, 541e. -**ος**, ὁ, *approval, praise, commendation*, Simon.4.3, Pi.*Fr.*181; ἔ. ἔχειν πρός τινος Hdt.1.96; πολλῷ ἐχρᾶτο τῷ ἐ. Id.3.3: freq. in Trag. and Att., ἐπαίνου τυχεῖν ἔκ τινος S.*Ant.*665, etc.; κλεινὴ καὶ ἔπαινον ἔχουσα meriting *praise*, ib.817; ἔπαινον ἐπαινεῖν Pl.*La.*181b: pl., *praises*, S.*OC*720, *El.*976, X.*Mem.*2.1.33; τιμαὶ.. καὶ ἔ. Pl.*R.*516c, etc. 2. *complimentary address, panegyric* (but distd. fr. ἐγκώμιον, as the general from the particular, Arist.*EE*1219^{b}15, *Rh.*1367^{b}27); ἔ. ποιεῖσθαι περί τινος Pl.*Phdr.*260c; λόγον εἰπεῖν ἔπαινον Ἔρωτος Id.*Smp.*177d; συντιθεὶς λόγον ἔ. κατά τινος Id.*Phdr.*260b; οἱ κατὰ Δημοσθένους ἔ. Aeschin.3.50; εἴς τινα Pl.*Lg.*947c; ὑπέρ τινος Plb.1.1.1, D.S.13.22, D.H.10.57.

ἐπαινός, ή, όν, only in fem. ἐπαινή, *awesome*, epith. of Περσεφόνεια in Il.9.457, Od.10.491, al., Hes.*Th.*[768]; of Hecate, Luc.*Nec.*9; of Demeter, prob. in *AP*11.42 (Crin.).

ἐπαινουμένως, Adv. pres. part. Pass., *praiseworthily*, D.S.16.88.

ἐπαιονάω, *bathe, foment* (trans.), Ath.2.41c:—Med., *bathe* (intr.), λοετροῖς Nic.*Al.*463:—also -έω, τῷ ἐλαίῳ Philostr.*Gym.*42.

ἐπαίρω, Ion. and poet. **ἐπᾰείρω** Hdt.1.204 and always in Hom.: fut. ἐπᾱρῶ (contr. from -ᾰερ-) E.*IA*125 (anap.), *Supp.*581 (prob. l.), X *Mem.*3.6.2: aor. ἐπῆρα, part. ἐπάρας Hdt.1.87, etc.: pf. ἐπῆρκα Amphis 13, Them.*Or.*8.114b:—Pass., aor. ἐπήρθην, part. ἐπαρθείς: *lift up and set on*, [αὐτὸν] ἁμαξάων ἐπάειραν *lifted and set* him *upon* .., Il.7.426; ὀβελοὺς.. κρατευτάων ἐπάειρας 9.214. 2. *lift, raise*, κεφαλὴν ἐπαείρας 10.80; καί μ' ἔπαιρε S.*Ph.*889; ἐπαίρων βλέφαρα Id.*OT*1276 codd.; ἐπάειρε δέρην E.*Tr.*99 (anap.); ἔπαιρε σαυτόν Ar.*V.*996; σεμνῶς ἐπηρκὼς τὰς ὀφρῦς Amphis l. c.; πάντες ἐπῆραν (sc. τὴν χεῖρα) *SIG*1109.24; οὐδεὶς ἐπῆρε *IG*3.1132; ἐπάρας τὴν φωνὴν D.18.291; ἐπαιρόμενα ἱστία, opp. ὑφιέμενα, Plu.*Luc.*3:—Med., με τεῷ ἐπαείραο μαζῷ *didst lift and put* me *to* thy breast, A.R.3.794; [λόγχην] E.*IT* 1484; ὅπλ' ἐπαίρεσθαι θεῷ Id.*Ba.*789; ἱστοὺς Plb.1.61.7; βακτηρίαν Plu.2.185b: metaph., τί.. στάσιν γλώσσης ἐπήρασθε; S.*OT*635; πολλοὺς καὶ θρασεῖς τῇ πόλει λόγους ἐπαιρόμενος D.18.222; κοινὸν ἡ πόλις ἐπήρατο πένθος D.S.34.17. 3. *exalt, magnify*, ἐπαείρειν Λοκρῶν ματέρ' Pi.*O.*9.20; ἐπαρεῖς τὸν πατρῷον οἶκον X.*Mem.*3.6.2. 4. intr., *lift up one's leg* or *rise up*, Hdt.2.162; *rise from table*, Euang.1.10. 5. Pass., *swell up*, Hp.*Liqu.*2, Gal.6.264, 18(2).119; ἐπῆρται τοῦτό γε, in mal. part., Ar.*Lys.*937; ὁ καυλὸς ἐπαίρεται *Hippiatr.*54. 6. Gramm., ἐ. τὴν προσῳδίαν *make* the accent *acute*, Sch.Il.11.636. II. *stir up, excite*, πολλά τέ μιν καὶ μεγάλα τὰ ἐπαείροντα.. ἦν Hdt.1.204; τίς σ' ἐπῆρε δαιμόνων; S.*OT*1328; πέρα τοῦ καιροῦ τοὺς ἑτέρους ἐ. D.16.23; ἐ. θυμόν τινι E.*IA*125; τοῦτό σε ψυχὴν ἐπαίρει Id.*Heracl.*173; ἑαυτὸν ἐπί τινι Diog.Oen.64; ἵππον *urge on*, Them.*Or.*1.13c; *induce, persuade* to do, c. inf., εἰρωτᾶν εἰ οὔτι ἐπαισχύνεται ἐπάρας Κροῖσον στρατεύεσθαι Hdt.1.90, cf. Isoc.4.108, Aeschin.1.192; ἥτις με γῆμ' ἐπῆρε Ar.*Nu.*42, cf. *Ra.*1041; ἐ. τινὰ ὥστε.. E.*Supp.*581; ὅστις μ' ἐπάρας ἔργον (sc. πρᾶξαι) Id.*Or.*286:—Pass., *to be roused, led on, excited*, τῷ μαντηΐῳ Hdt.1.90, cf. 5.91; τοῖσι δωρήμασι Id.7.38; τοῖς τῆς πόλεως κακοῖς And.1.37; ὑπὸ τῆς τύχης Lys.2.10; πλούτῳ, τιμῇ, Pl.*R.*434b, 608b; ὑπὸ λόγων Ar.*Av.*1448; τῇ ἐλπίδι ὡς.. Th.1.81, cf. Lys.9.21; τοῖς λόγοις Th.4.121; δεινότητι καὶ ξυνέσεως ἀγῶνι Id.3.37 (so τὸ ἐπαιρόμενον τοῦ λόγου τῇ δεινότητι Plu.*Cic.*25); ὑπὸ μεγάλου μισθοῦ Th.7.13; ἐ. ἐς τὸ νεωτερίζειν Id.4.108; ἐπὶ τὴν βασιλείαν Lxx 3*Ki.*12.[24]: c. inf., ἐπήρθην γράψαι Isoc.5.10; τῷ or τὸ λέγειν (dub. l.) Pl.*Phdr.*232a (but ναυτικῷ προύχειν -όμενοι *flattering themselves* that they were superior.., Th.1.25): abs., *to be excited, on tiptoe*, Ar.*Nu.*810; and so Ἑλλὰς τῇ ὁρμῇ ἐπῆρται Th.2.11. 2. Pass., also, *to be elated at* a thing, εὐδαιμονίῃ μεγάλῃ Hdt.5.81; ψυχρῇ νίκῃ Id.9.49, cf. 1.212, 4.130; ἐπὶ πλούτῳ X.*Mem.*1.2.25; πρός τι Th.6.11, 8.2; ἐκ τοῦ γεγονότος προτερήματος Plb.1.29.4: abs., Th.4.18.

ἐπαισθ-άνομαι, *have a perception* or *feeling of*, c. gen. objecti, μῶν Ὀδυσσέως ἐπῃσθόμην; S.*Ph.*1296; ὀμφῆς τῆς ἐμῆς Id.*OC*1351, cf. *Ant.*1183; διαφορᾶς Epicur.*Nat.*14.10; esp. of symptoms of disease, τῶν καθ' ἕκαστα σαθρῶν D.11.14: hence abs., ἐ. τι τῷ σώματι *to be indisposed*, D.C.52.24. 2. c. acc., *perceive*, τι A.*Ag.*85 (anap.); οὐδέν S.*Aj.*553, D.2.21; τὸν σὸν μόρον ἐ. *hear of* it, S.*Aj.*996: c. part., ἐπῄσθετ' ἐκ θεοῦ καλούμενος Id.*OC*1629; ᾔσθέντα δ' αὐτὸν ὡς ἐπῃσθόμην E.*Cyc.*420. 3. abs., *become sensible, recover one's senses*, Hp.*Morb.*3.8. -**ημα**, ατος, τό, *perception*, Epicur.*Fr.*36, *Placit.*4.8.2, Phld.*Mus.*p.66 K. -**ησις**, εως, ἡ, *perception*, τὴν ἐ. τὴν ἐπί τινος ποιεῖν Epicur.*Ep.*1 p.13 U., cf. Phld.*Mus.*p.42 K., al., Sor.2.19; τινός Epicur.*Nat.*125 G., Porph.*Abst.*1.57, 3.15.

ἔπαισοι· καθήκοντες, ἐπιβάλλοντες, Hsch. (cf. ἐπάσιοι: fort. ἐπάσιστοι, v. ἆσσον I, ἐπάγχιστος).

ἐπαΐσσω, Ep. aor. ἐπήϊξα Od.10.322, Iterat. ἐπαΐξασκε Il.17.462: contr. **ἐπᾴσσω**, Att. -ττω, fut. -ᾴξω:—*rush at* or *upon*: c. gen. (never in Od.), ἵππων ἐπαΐξαι *rush at* them, Il.5.263; νεῶν 13.687. 2. c. dat. pers., Κίρκῃ ἐπαΐξαι *rush upon* her, Od.10.295: in Il. only c. dat. instrum., ξίφει, δουρὶ ἐ., 5.584, 10.369, etc.; so μοι.. ἐπήϊσσον μελίῃσιν Od.14.281. 3. c. acc., *assail, assault*, Ἕκτορα Il.23.64; τεῖχος 12.308 (never so in Od.):—Med., ἐπαΐξασθαι ἄεθλον *rush at* (i.e. *seize upon*) the prize, Il.23.773. 4. abs. (so usu. in Hom.), of a hawk, ταρφέ' ἐπαΐσσει *makes* frequent *swoops*, 22.142; of the wind, ἐπαΐξας.. ἐκ νεφελάων 2.146, etc.; σῦς ἐπαΐσσων βίᾳ B.5.116, cf. Ar.*Ach.*1171 (lyr.); ἐπᾴξας ἐς δόμους S.*Aj.*305; rare in Prose, as Pl.*Tht.*190a (metaph.), Arist.*HA*629^{b}25:—also Med., χειμῶνος μέλλοντος ἐπαΐσσεσθαι ὅδοῖο Arat.1139. 5. τὰ νεῦρα ἐπαΐσσεται ἀμφὶ τὰς φύσιας τῶν ἄρθρων (in the development of the embryo), dub. in Hp.*Nat.Puer.*17. II. later, with acc. of the Instrument of motion, ἐ. πόδα *move with hasty* step, E.*Hec.*1071 (lyr.); ἐ. ξίφος A.R.1.1254:—Pass. even in Hom., χεῖρες ὤμων ἀμφοτέρωθεν ἐπαΐσσονται ἐλαφραί they *move lightly*, Il.23.628 (v. l. ἀπ-). [ᾱ- Ep., ᾰ- Att.]

ἐπάϊστος, ον, (ἐπαΐω) *heard of, detected*, usu. c. part., ἐ. ἐγένετο ἐργασμένος Hdt.2.119; ἐ. ἐγένετο προδιδούς Id.8.128, cf. 6.74; ἐ. ἐγένετο ὑπὸ Καμβύσεω Id.3.15, cf. 7.146; *perceived*, Ant.Lib.34.4. Adv. -τως Onat.ap.Stob.1.1.39 (dub.).

ἐπαισχ-ής, ές, (αἶσχος) *shameful*, Nic.Dam.5 J., D.C.56.13. -**ρος**, ον, = foreg., Antioch.Astr.in *Cat.Cod.Astr.*7.115, Vett.Val.11.17, al. 2. in physical sense, *ugly*, Id.110.23. -**ύνομαι**, fut. -αισχυνθήσομαι, *to be ashamed at* or *of*, τῷ οὐνόματι Hdt.1.143; τινά or τι, X.*HG*4.1.34, Pl.*Sph.*247c: c. inf., *to be ashamed* to do, A.*Ag.*1373: c. part., *to be ashamed of* doing or having done a thing, Hdt.1.90, S.*Aj.*1307, *Ph.*929, etc.: abs., *feel shame, show a sense of shame*, Pl.*R.*573b, Men.625. II. late in Act., *make ugly, mar*, Nonn.*D.*20.61, 42.421.

ἐπαιτ-έω, *ask besides*, εἰ καί νύ κεν.. ἄλλο μεῖζον ἐπαιτήσειας Il.23.593; ὧν ἐπαιτεῖς S.*OT*1416: abs., *ask for more*, φαγὼν ἔτ' ἐπῄτεον Posidipp.ap.Ath.10.412e:—so in Med., S.*El.*1124. 2. *beg as a mendicant*, ἄλλους ἐ. τὸν καθ' ἡμέραν βίον Id.*OC*1364, cf. E.*Rh.*715: abs., Vett.Val.68.30, Luc.*Asin.*35. 3. simply, *demand*, *PTeb.*26.13 (ii B. C., Pass.), etc. -**ης**, ου, ὁ, *beggar*, Teles p.14 H., Nech.ap. Vett.Val.290.2, Ath.5.192f, D.C.66.8 codd. -**ησις**, εως, ἡ, *begging*, Lxx *Si.*40.28, 30. -**ητάριον**, τό, *little beggar*, name of an amulet, *PMag.Par.*1.2378.

ἐπαιτιάομαι, fut. -άσομαι [ᾱ], Ion. -ήσομαι, *bring a charge against, accuse*, τινά Hdt.2.121.β', etc.; θεὸν ἐ. Hp.*Aër.*22; ἐ. τινά τινος *accuse* one of a thing, Th.6.28, D.21.114; ἡ κἀμὲ γάρ τι ξυμφοραῖς ἐπαιτιᾷ; for your mishaps, A.*Pr.*974; also κείνην ἐπαιτιῶμαι τοῦδε βουλεῦσαι τάφου I *accuse* her of this burial, that she planned it, S.*Ant.*490: c. inf., ὧν ἐπαιτιᾷ με δρᾶν Id.*OT*645; ὃν.. με.. τρέφειν μιάστορα ἐπῃτιάσω Id.*El.*604; Αἴσωπον.. φιάλην ἐπῃτιῶντο κλέψαι Ar.*V.*1447, etc.; τὴν πρόμαντιν ἐ. αὐτὸν πεῖσαι Th.5.16; so ἐ. τινὰ ὅτι.. Hdt.6.30, Th.2.70: c. acc. rei, *lay the blame upon*, τὴν ξυμφορὰν τῆς φυγῆς Id.8.81; τὸ μῆκος τῆς πορείας Pl.*Ep.*329a: also c. acc. cogn., μέζονα ἐπαιτιώμενος *bringing* heavier *accusations*, Hdt.1.26; τοῦτο ἐπαιτιῶμαι, c. acc. inf., I *complain of* this, viz. that.., Pl.*R.*497b: also c. dupl. acc., ἃ ἐπαιτιῶμαι τὴν γυναῖκα ταύτην the charges which I *bring against* her, Antipho 1.10; τῷ μὲν νῷ οὐδὲν χρώμενον οὐδέ τινας αἰτίας ἐπαιτιώμενον nor *ascribing* any *causes* to it, Pl.*Phd.*98b.

ἐπαιτίνδα παίζειν play *at beggars*, Hdn.Gr.1.495.

ἐπαίτιος, ον, (αἰτία) *blamed for* a thing, *blameable, blameworthy*: 1. of persons, οὔ τί μοι ὔμμες ἐπαίτιοι Il.1.335; τινός *for* a thing, A.*Eu.*465, E.*Hipp.*1383 (lyr.); *accused of* a thing, Th.6.61; ἐ. τινὰ ποιεῖν πρός τινας Plu.*Comp.Dion.Brut.*2. 2. of things, ἀναχώρησις Th.5.65; ἐπαιτιώτατοι τῶν κινδύνων Lys.7.39. II. ἐπαίτια, τά, *legal punishments*, = προστιμήματα, Solon ap.Poll.8.22, Lex ap.D.24.105.

ἔπαιτον, τό, dub. sens. in *PFay.*81.13 (ii A. D.), *BGU*792.12, etc.

ἐπαιτοσύνη, ἡ, = ἐπαίτησις, Charis.p.554 K.

ἐπαΐω, contr. ἐπᾴω E.*HF*773 (lyr.): aor. 1 ἐπήϊσα Hdt.9.93, A.R. ll. cc.: (v. ἀΐω, εἰσαΐω):—*give ear to*, θεῶν οὐδὲν ἐπαΐοντες A.*Supp.*759 (lyr.), cf. E. l. c.; *hear*, τῆς φωνῆς Plu.*Brut.*16. 2. *perceive, feel*, τι Pi.*Fr.*75.15 (v. l. ἐπάγοισιν); θεοὶ ἔναιμοί τε καὶ σαρκώδεες καὶ ἐπαΐοντες σιδηρίων Hdt.3.29; δηγμάτων Ael.*NA*1.5; τῶν ὄντως ἀγαθῶν Hierocl. *in CA*24 p.472 M.: c. part., καταγελώμενος οὐκ ἐπαΐεις Ar.*V.*516; ὥστε μηδὲ θιγγανόμενος ἐπαΐειν Hp.*Prorrh.*2.16; ἄψ ἀνιόντας, αὐτοὺς παριόντας, A.R.1.1023, 2.195: abs., ὡς ἐπήϊσε when *he perceived it*, Hdt.9.93. 3. *understand*, c. acc., τὴν βάρβαρον γὰρ γλῶσσαν οὐκ ἐπαΐω S.*Aj.*1263; esp. of persons under instruction, ἐπαΐονθ' ὁποῖός ἐστι τῶν ῥυθμῶν κατ' ἐνόπλιον κτλ., Ar.*Nu.*650; ἐ. τό τε καλὸν καὶ μή Pl.*Lg.*701a; ἐ. τίς πολιτεία συμφέρει Arist.*Rh.*1360^{a}31; ἐ. τι τῆς Ῥωμαίων γλώσσης Luc.*Laps.*13, etc. 4. *to have knowledge of* any subject, *to be an expert in* such subjects, οὓς ἂν οἴωμαί τι τούτων ἐπαΐειν Pl.*Tht.*145d; τοὺς μηδὲν αὐλήσεως ἐπαΐοντας Id.*Prt.*327c; ὁ ἐπαΐων περὶ τῶν δικαίων καὶ ἀδίκων, i.e. a moral philosopher, Id.*Cri.*48a; ἐπαΐεις οὐδὲν περὶ γυμναστικῆς Id.*Grg.*518c, cf. *Ap.*19c, *R.*598c, *Hp.Ma.*289e: abs., ὁ ἐπαΐων Id.*Prt.*314a, *Phdr.*275e; τὸ εἰδέναι καὶ τὸ ἐ. Arist.*Metaph.*981^{a}24.

ἐπαιώνιος, ον, *ruling over the* αἰῶνες, θεός *Tab.Defix.Aud.*271.9 (Hadrumetum, iii A. D.).

ἐπαιωρέω, *keep hovering over* another, στέφανον καρήνῳ, πέτρον καρήνων, Nonn.*D.*5.132, 4.456; *keep floating in*, ἐ. πτερὸν ἠέρι πολλῷ *Epigr.Gr.*312.5 (Smyrna): metaph., ἐ. [εὐτυχίαις] βίον *AP*7.645 (Crin.). II. Pass., *hover over* or *on the surface, float upon*, ἐπανθισμὸς ἐ. χαλκείοις Dsc.5.92, cf. 75; ἐλπίσιν ἐπαιωρούμενοι *buoyed up* by .., Luc.*Alex.*16; ἐπαιωρεῖσθαι πολέμῳ *hang over it, conduct* it *remissly*, Plu.*Pel.*29; in Hp.*Art.*75, of one who *throws his whole weight upon* another, during a surgical operation. 2. *overhang, threaten*, σφιν ἐπὶ δέος ἠωρεῖτο A.R.1.639; Σκύθαι τοῖς μέσοις ἐπαιωροῦντο Them.*Or.*8.119c; ξίφος αὐχένι ἐ. Hdn.5.2.1: c. gen., τῶν πολεμίων Plu.*Fab.*5: abs., τὰ ἐκτὸς ἐπῃωρημένα Ph.1.650. 3. *rise, swell*, ὄγκος -εύμενος ἔξω Aret.*CA*1.7.

ἐπᾰκανθίζω, in pres. part., *pointed*, Thphr.*HP*3.10.1, al.; *thorny, set with thorns*, ib.4.8.8, 6.4.1, al.

ἐπᾰκέομαι, Delph. ἐφακ-, *repair*, τὸν δρόμον, τὰς γεφύρας, *IG*2^{2}.1126.37,41 (Amphict. Delph.).

ἐπακμ-άζω, *to be in one's prime*, Ph.1.33; also of things, Id.2.434, Aristaenet.2.1, Hld.7.8: metaph., *come to its height*, Luc.*Abd.*17, Ath.1.18e; ἐπήκμασαν οἱ ἐτησίαι *were blowing hard*, Str.15.1.17. II. of persons, *flourish in succession to*, τινί D.H.*Pomp.*4; οἱ ἐπακμάσαντες ib.1; also νέα ἐ. παλαιοῖς, of animals and crops, Ph.1.28, 2.424. **-αστικός**, ή, όν, *coming to a height* or *crisis*, opp. παρακμαστικός, πυρετός Gal.10.615.

Ἐπακμόνιος, epith. of Poseidon in Boeotia, Hsch.

ἔπακμος, ον, (ἀκμή) *in the bloom of age*, κόραι D.H.4.28 (v.l.). II. *pointed*, ἄκανθα Dsc.1.90; ὀδοὺς Plu.2.966c; *sharp-edged*, Sor.1.80; σμιλίον Gal.ap.Orib.*inc.*12.1.

ἐπᾰκολουθ-έω, *follow close upon, follow after, pursue*, τινί Ar.*V.*1328, Pl.*Ap.*23c, al.; *move with*, τῷ ἄλλῳ σώματι Hp.*Fract.*16; ἐ. ἡ χεὶρ τοῦ νεκροῦ X.*Cyr.*7.3.8. 2. *pursue* as an enemy, Th.4.128, 5.65, X.*An.*[4.1.1], etc. 3. *attend to, follow* mentally, *understand*, τῷ λόγῳ Pl.*Phd.*107b; τοῖς λεγομένοις Id.*Lg.*861c; αὐτοῖς λέγουσι Id.*Sph.*243a; κάλλιστ' ἐπακολουθεῖς Id.*Lg.*963a, etc. 4. *attend to, follow*, i.e. *obey* or *comply with*, ταῖς τῶν συμμάχων γνώμαις Isoc.6.90; τοῖς πάθεσι D.26.18; αὐτῶν τῇ προαιρέσει Philipp.ap.D.18.167; ταῖς τῶν ποιητῶν βλασφημίαις ἐ. *follow* them (as authorities), Isoc.11.38: c. dat. pers., Arist.*EN*1096^{b}7. 5. *attend to*, i.e. *execute*, a task, τῷ πραττομένῳ Pl.*R.*370c; *wait upon*, of bees, τοῖς βασιλεῦσι Arist.*GA*760^{b}15. 6. *supervise, attend to*, τῇ ἐγχύσει τοῦ γλεύκους *PPetr.*2 p.136 (iii B.C.), cf. *PAmh.*2.40.24 (ii B.C.), etc.: abs., *POxy.*1024.33 (ii A.D.), etc. 7. *concur*, *PFay.*24.19 (ii A.D.). 8. *verify, check*, *PEleph.*10.8 (iii B.C.), *PGen.*22.1 (i A.D.), etc. II. *accompany, result, accrue*, τινί Phld.*Ir.*p.59 W., al.; βλάβος, ζημία ἐ., *PRyl.*126.19 (i A.D.), *BGU*3.14 (iii A.D.). 2. τὰ ἐπακολουθοῦντα σημεῖα *confirmatory, authenticating* signs (cf. I.7), *Ev.Marc.*16.20. 3. of the offspring of cattle, πρόβατα σὺν τοῖς -οῦσι ἄρνασι *POxy.*245.11 (i A.D.), cf. 244.9 (i A.D.). **-ημα**, ατος, τό, *consequence*, τινός Plu.*Nic.*4, Plot.6.2.9, Iamb.*in Nic.*p.38P. (pl.); κατ' ἐπακολούθημα *consequentially*, Alex.Aphr.*Fat.*178.13, S.E.*M.*7.34; τὰ κατ' ἐ. πάθη Anon.Lond.1.29. II. *secondary consideration*, Him.*Ecl.*3.19. **-ησις**, εως, ἡ, *cognizance, concurrence*, *PRyl.*233.14 (ii A.D.), etc.; γράμματα ἐπακολουθήσεως documents in proof of *compliance*, i.e. *settlement* of debts, *POxy.*1473.8 (iii A.D.). 2. *consequence*, κατ' ἐ. *consequentially*, opp. προηγουμένως, *Stoic.*2.333, Stoic.ap.Plu.2.1015c, M.Ant.6.44, S.E.*M.*1.194; *result*, εὐεξία κατ' ἐ. τῆς ὑγιείας συνισταμένη Gal.19.382. **-ητέον**, *one must follow*, τινί D.61.4. **-ητικός**, ή, όν, *capable of following*, δύναμις Plu. *in Hes.*21. **-ήτρια**, ἡ, *concurring party*, *PLips.*9.6 (iii A.D.), etc. **-ος**, ον, *following*, τὸ ἐ. τῆς ἐπαγγελίας Aristid.*Rh.*2 p.522 S.: Comp., *PMag.Par.*1.1536. Adv. **-θως** *agreeably to*, τῷ ἑαυτῶν τρόπῳ Antip.ap.Stob.4.22.103, cf. *PMasp.*97 ii 68 (vi A.D.).

ἐπᾰκονάω, *whet*, in Pass., *IG*7.3073.104,119 (Lebadea). II. *whet against*, δημίου ξίφος ἑαυτῷ Lib.*Decl.*40.35.

ἐπᾰκοντ-ίζω, *dart* a thing *at* a person, Socr.*Ep.*30.13 codd. **-ισμός**, ὁ, *casting of dice* (βόλου ὄνομα), Hsch. **-ιστής**, οῦ, ὁ, *dicer*, Poll.7.204.

ἐπάκοος, Dor. for ἐπήκοος (q.v.).

ἐπᾰκου-ός, όν, *attentive to*, c. gen., ἀγορῆς ἐπακουὸν ἐόντα Hes.*Op.*29, cf. Call.*Fr.*236; cf. ἐπήκοος. **-σις**, εως, ἡ, *hearing*, μαρτυριῶν *GDI*3591.43 (Cnidus). **-στός**, όν, *to be listened to*, Emp.2.7. II. *to be obeyed*, Lxx 1*Es.*4.12. **-ω**, fut. ἐπακούσομαι ib. *Ge.*30.33, later ἐπακούσω *Psalm.Solom.*18.3:—*hear*, c. acc. rei, ὃς πάντ' ἐφορᾷς καὶ πάντ' ἐπακούεις, of the Sun, Il.3.277, cf. Od.11.109; prov., ὁπποῖόν κ' εἴπῃσθα ἔπος, τοῖόν κ' ἐπακούσαις as thou speakest, so *wilt* thou *be answered*, Il.20.250; φωνὴν ἐ. Hes.*Op.*448; χρησμόν Ar.*Eq.*1080: c. acc. rei et gen. pers., ἔπος ἐμέθεν Od.19.98: c. gen. rei, εὐχῆς Ar.*Nu.*263; τῆς φωνῆς Hdt.2.70: abs., Th.1.53, Hdt.9.98, etc. 2. *overhear*, μή τις τῶν ἀμυήτων ἐπακούσῃ Pl.*Tht.*155e, cf. Ar.*Th.*628. 3. *hear about, hear tell of*, μόχθων E.*Tr.*165 (lyr.); c. part., οἷον γᾶς Ἀσίας οὐκ ἐπακούω.. βλαστὸν φύτευμα S.*OC*695 (lyr.); τινά τι δρῶντα Pl.*Lg.*729b. 4. *give ear, listen*, A.*Ch.*725 (anap.): c. gen. pers., ἐμοῦ 'πάκουσον S.*OT*708, cf. Pl.*Prt.*317d; ἐ. μοι 'pray *attend*', Id.*Sph.*227c: esp. of *giving ear* to one who prays, of God, Lxx *Is.*49.8, *UPZ*78.24 (ii B.C.); or to advice, commands, etc., i.e. *obey*, βουλῆς Il.2.143; δίκης Hes.*Op.*275; ἐμῶν μύθων S.*Ph.*1417 (anap.): c. dat. rei, τῷ κελεύσματι Hdt.4.141; ταῖς εὐχαῖς D.H.13.6, cf. Lxx *Ho.*2.21(23). 5. later, like ἐπαΐω, *perceive, understand*, τῶν ᾀδομένων Luc.*Salt.*64, cf. Plu.*Flam.*10 (or, *hear distinctly*). 6. ἐπακούσεταί μοι ἡ δικαιοσύνη μου *shall answer for* me, Lxx *Ge.*30.33.

ἐπακρῑβ-ής, ές, *accurate*: neut. as Adv., -ὲς πάντα ἐπεξιέναι Aps.*Rh.*p.316 H. **-όω**, *develop in detail*, Epicur.*Ep.*1 p.27 U.:—Med., D.S.37.8.

ἐπακρ-ίδες πόλεις, (ἄκρα) cities *on the hills*, *EM*353.1. **-ίζω**, *reach the top of* a thing, πολλῶν αἱμάτων ἐπήκρισε (= ἐπ' ἄκρον ἦλθε, Sch., τέλος ἐπέθηκεν, Hsch.) he *reached the farthest point* in deeds of blood, of Orestes, A.*Ch.*932. **-ιος**, α, ον, *on the heights*, epith. of Zeus, Polyzel.7. II. ἡ ἐπακρία (sc. χώρα), a district in Attica, Str.9.1.20.

ἐπακρο-άομαι, = ἐπακούω, abs., Pl.Com.16, Nic.Dam.*Vit.Caes.*29: c. gen. pers., *Act.Ap.*16.25, Luc.*Icar.*1: c. gen. rei, Hld.2.17: c. acc. rei, πάντ' ἐπακροάσει Men.*Epit.Oxy.*1236^{v}16; τὸν λόγον Ant.Lib.11.6. **-ᾱσις**, εως, ἡ, *hearkening, obedience*, Lxx 1*Ki.*15.22. **-ᾱτής**, οῦ, ὁ, *hearer, listener*, Gloss.

ἔπακρος, ον, (ἄκρα) *pointed at the end*, Hp.*Morb.*2.61.

ἐπακταῖος, α, ον, = ἐπάκτιος, Opp.*H.*2.127, 4.273. II. epith. of Poseidon at Samos, Hsch.

ἐπακ-τέον, *one must bring upon*, πόλεμον τῇ χώρᾳ Cic.*Att.*9.4.2. 2. *one must apply*, μέτρον τινί Luc.*Hist.Conscr.*9, cf. D.H.*Rh.*2.6; τοῦτο ἐ., ὅτι.. S.E.*P.*3.135. **-τήρ**, ῆρος, ὁ, Ep. word, = ὁ κύνας ἐπάγων, *hunter, huntsman*, ἐς βῆσσαν ἵκανον ἐπακτῆρες Od.19.435; ἄνδρες ἐ. Il.17.135; later, *fisherman*, A.R.1.625. **-τήρεσιν**· ἀλλεπαλλήλοις, συνεχέσιν, Hsch. (Leg. ἐπασσυτέροισιν.) **-τικός**, ή, όν, *leading on*: 1. in Logic, *inductive*, πρότασις, λόγοι, Arist.*APo.*77^{b}35, *Top.*108^{b}7, *Metaph.*1078^{b}28, Phld.*Rh.*1.11 S. Adv. -κῶς, σκοπεῖν Arist.*Ph.*210^{b}8. 2. *conducive*, εἰς εὔνοιαν Hld.4.3; *stimulating*, πρὸς πότον Ath.2.52d (Sup.). 3. *attractive*, ἐν τῇ ὀσμῇ Dsc.1.26; διὰ τὴν ἡδονήν Id.4.83; ἀκρόασις Vett.Val.260.26; of persons, Id.250.22.

ἐπάκτιος, ον, E.*Fr.*670.2, and ία, ιον S.*Tr.*1151, *Fr.*549, E.*Andr.*853 (lyr.): (ἀκτή):—*on the strand* or *shore*, ll.cc., S.*Aj.*413 (lyr.); epith. of Apollo, A.R.1.403 codd.; of Hermes at Sicyon, Hsch.

ἐπακ-τός, όν, or ή, όν (cf. III infr.), (ἐπάγω) *brought in*, ὕδατα Hp.*Aër.*9; esp. *brought in from abroad, imported*, ἐ. σῖτος Th.6.20; πάντων ἐπακτῶν δεῖσθαι Id.7.28; *acquired*, τῇ Ἑλλάδι πενίη μὲν.. σύντροφός ἐστι, ἀρετὴ δὲ ἐ. Hdt.7.102; ὕδωρ εἴτ' ἐ. εἴτε συμφυές Arist.*Mete.*382^{b}11, cf. *GA*750^{a}9; ἐ. πημονή E.*Hipp.*318; κακόν Philem.93.5; ἐ. παρ' ἄλλων δίκαιον Pl.*R.*405b; ὅρκος ἐ. an oath *imposed* by the other party, Lys.*Fr.*251 S., Isoc.1.23; *adventitious*, ἐ. χρώμασι κοσμεῖσθαι Socr.*Ep.*6.3, cf. Plot.1.4.3. 2. of persons, ἐ. ποιμήν an *alien* lord, Pi.*O.*10(11).89; ἐ. δικασταί dub. in *IG*11(4).1065*b*20 (Delos); ἱκέσιος ἐ. *Notiz.Arch.*4p.98 (Cyrene); esp. of *foreign* allies or mercenaries, ἐ. στράτευμα, στρατός, A.*Th.*583, S.*Tr.*259; δόρυ Id.*OC*1525; ἐπακτῷ δυνάμει with an *alien, mercenary* force, Isoc.10.37, cf. Pl.*R.*573b; also λαβὼν ἐπακτὸν ἄνδρα, i.e. an adulterer, S.*Aj.*1296; ἐ. πατήρ a *false* father, E.*Ion*592: metaph., ὄμβρος ἐ. ἐλθών rain coming *as an invader*, Pi.*P.*6.10. II. like αὐθαίρετος, *brought upon oneself*, νόσος S.*Tr.*491; γάμων ἐ. ἄταν E.*Ph.*343 (lyr.). III. ἐπακταί (sc. ἡμέραι), αἱ, *intercalary days*, Isid.*Etym.*6.17.29, Zonar. IV. ἐπακτόν, τό, *charm, spell*, *GDI*3545 (Cnidus). V. ἐ. ὅρκος oath *administered*, *PMon.*6.8 (vi A.D.). **-τρεύς**, έως, ὁ, = ἐπακτήρ, Hsch., Eust.1539.25. **-τρίς**, ίδος, ἡ, *light vessel, skiff*, X.*HG*1.1.11, Aul.Gell.10.25.5. **-τροκέλης**, ητος, ὁ, *light piratical skiff*, Aeschin.1.191, Arist.*Int.*16^{a}26. **-τρον**, τό, = ἐπακτρίς, Nic.*Th.*824.

ἐπᾰλαζονεύομαι, *boast over*, τινί J.*BJ*2.18.4.

ἐπᾰλᾰλάζω, *raise the war-cry*, A.*Th.*497, 951 (lyr.), D.S.19.30; τῷ Ἐνυαλίῳ X.*Cyr.*7.1.26; τὸν ἐνυάλιον παιᾶνα Jul.*Or.*1.36b.

ἐπᾰλαλκέμεν, v. ἐπαλέξω.

ἐπᾰλάομαι, *wander about* or *over*, πόλλ' ἐπαληθείς Od.4.81; Αἰγυπτίους ib.83: subj. aor. ἐπαληθῇ 15.401.

ἐπᾰλαστέω, *to be full of wrath at* a thing, τὸν δ' ἐπαλαστήσασα προσηύδα Od.1.252, cf. A.R.3.369, 557.

ἐπαλγ-έω, *grieve over*, φθιμένων E.*Supp.*58 (lyr.); δουλώσει πατρίδος J.*AJ*19.1.9. **-ής**, ές, *painful*, Aristeas 167, Str.11.13.2, Philum.ap.Aët.5.127, Aët.15.13, Opp.*H.*4.508: Comp., Lxx 4*Ma.*14.10, Onos.42.19, Aret.*SD*2.3. Adv. **-γῶς** Poll.3.99. **-ύνω**, *give pain*, Nic.*Al.*335; *afflict*, τινά Q.S.4.416:—Med., *feel pain at*, ταῖς συμφοραῖς Tz.*H.*4.398.

ἐπάλ-ειμμα [ᾰλ], ατος, τό, *unguent*, ἐκζεμάτων Dsc.1.43.4, cf. *Inscr.Prien.*112.90, al. (i B.C.), *Michel* 544.20 (Themisonium, ii B.C.). **-ειπτέον**, *one must anoint*, Orib.*Syn.*5.53.17, Paul.Aeg.2.46. **-είφω**, *smear over*, ἐπὶ δ' οὔατ' ἀλεῖψαι ἑταίρων Od.12.47; ἐπ' οὔατα πᾶσιν ἄλειψα ib.177; κηρὸν.. ὅν σφιν ἐπ' ὦσιν ἄλειψ' ib.200; ὁπόταν.. λεαίνῃ ἐπαλείφουσα τὰ τραχυνθέντα Pl.*Ti.*66c; ἐ. χρόαν ἑτέραν ἐφ' ἑτέραν Arist.*Sens.*440^{a}9: prov., τοὺς τοίχους τοὺς δύο ἐ. 'run with the hare and hunt with the hounds', Paus.6.3.15:—Pass., τὸ ἐπαλειφθὲν Pl.*Ly.*217c; ἐπαλήλιπται ὁ κύτταρος Arist.*HA*555^{a}6; χρυσὸς ἐπαληλιμμένος J.*AJ*17.10.2. 2. metaph., from anointing athletes, *prepare for contest, stir up, irritate*, τινὰ ἐπί τινα Plb.2.51.2; ἐ. τινάς τινι *set* them *upon* him, D.L.2.38; μέθυσμα ἐ. θυμοὺς Ph.1.680; so perh. in physical sense, *irritate*, Hp.*Mul.*1.99, *Epid.*5.20. **-ειψις**, εως, ἡ, *painting over* of colours, Alex.Aphr.*in Sens.*63.5. 2. *smearing over, anointing*, *EM*69.41 (pl.).

ἐπᾰλέξ-ησις, εως, ἡ, etym. of ἔπαλξις, *EM*353.22. **-ω**, Ep. Verb, *defend, succour*, τινί Il.8.365, 11.428, v.l. in Batr.174; κακῇ ἐπαλαλκέμεν ἄτῃ (Ep.aor. 2 inf.) *lend aid against*.., Nic.*Th.*352. II. *ward off, keep off*, ἐπὶ Τρώεσσιν ἀλεξήσειν κακὸν ἦμαρ Il.20.315.

ἐπᾰλετρεύω, *grind at*, μύλης πελάνους A.R.1.1077.

ἐπαληθείς, v. ἐπαλάομαι.

ἐπαληθ-εύω, *prove true, substantiate, verify*, τὴν αἰτίαν, τὸν λόγον, Th.4.85, 8.52; ἔργοις τὴν προσηγορίαν J.*BJ*7.8.1:—Pass., D.H.1.58. 2. *prove one's right to*, τοὔνομα, τὴν πρόσρησιν, Ph.2.6, 263. II. intr., *to be true, genuine*, ἐπαληθεῦον καὶ παγίως ἐνιδρυμένον ib.311, cf. Dam.*Pr.*31 bis, Sch.Pi.*O.*10.17. 2. ἐ. τῷ ὀνόματι *use* the name *correctly*, Plot.5.9.5; *assert truly*, Dexipp.*in Cat.*50.24 (Pass.); but οὐ γὰρ -εύει τῷ ἐξῃρημένῳ τὸ οἰκεῖον ὄνομα κατ' ἀκρίβειαν the transcendent *is* not strictly *entitled* to its own name, Dam.*Pr.*7. **-ίζω**, = foreg., Hsch.

ἐπάλης, ές, (ἀλέα B) *open to the sun, sunny*, λέσχη Hes.*Op.*493 (nisi leg. ἐπ' ἀλέα, cf. ἀλής).

ἐπαλθ-έω, *heal, cure*, fut. ἐπαλθήσουσιν Nic.*Al.*395: aor. ἐπαλθήσειε ib.614:—Med., aor. ἐπαλθήσαιο Id.*Th.*654. **-ής**, ές, *healing*, ib.500. II. *healed*, Id.*Al.*156.

ἐπᾰλινδέομαι, Pass., lit., *roll on*: hence ἴχνια ἐπηλίνδητ' ἀνέμοισιν *had been effaced*, A.R.4.1463:—also **ἐπᾰλίνδομαι**, Nic.*Th*.266.

ἐπαλίνω [ῑ], = ἐπαλείφω, aor. 1 inf. ἐπαλ[ε]ῖναι, Hsch.

ἐπαλκής, ές, *strong*, dub. in A.*Ch*.415 (lyr.).

ἐπαλλ-ᾰγή, ἡ, = ἐπάλλαξις, γάμων ἐπαλλαγή, = ἐπιγαμία, Hdt.1.74; τὰς ἐ. τῶν σωμάτων their *fitting into one another*, Democr.ap.Arist.*Fr*.208; *crossing*, νεύρων Aret.*SD*1.7. II. *premium on exchange* of currency, *PCair.Zen*.22.2 (iii B.C.). **–ακτικῶς**, gloss on ἐπαμοιβαδίς, Sch.Od.5.481. **–άξ**, Adv., = ἐναλλάξ, *crosswise*, Hp.*Nat. Mul*.5, X.*Eq*.1.7; *alternately*, D.S.19.30. **–αξις**, εως, ἡ, *interweaving* or *dovetailing*, Antipho Soph.20 (pl.); αἱ ἐ. τοῦ χάρακος Plb. 18.18.11; ἡ ἐ. τῶν δακτύλων *crossing* of two fingers so as to feel double, Arist.*Metaph*.1011a33, *Insomn*.460b20, *Pr*.958b14; *linking together*, Id.*Mete*.387a12. 2. *overlapping* of species, Id.*GA*732b 15; *confusion* of different things, Str.12.8.2. b. *alternation*, Pl. *Sph*.240c. 3. *change*, θέσεως Hierocl.*in CA* 1 p.419 M.; διαιτημάτων Gal.6.59 (pl.); *varieties* of abnormal constitutions, ib.385 (pl.). **–άσσω**, Att. **–ττω**, *change over*: once in Hom., τῶ... ὁμοιΐου πτολέμοιο πεῖραρ ἐπαλλάξαντες ἐπ' ἀμφοτέροισι τάνυσσαν *crossing*, i.e. *tying*, the rope-end of balanced war, Il.13.359 (vv. ll. τοί, ἀλλήλοισι, in which case the metaph. is from a tug of war, *pulling alternately this way and that*); ἐ. ἅλματα ἐμποιοῦντες ἴχνεσιν ἴχνη *interchange* leaps, i.e. one to leap into the other's steps, X.*Cyn*.5.20 (cf. ἐπηλλαγμένα [ἴχνη] 8.3); of καρχαρόδοντα, ἐ. τοὺς ὀδόντας *have* their teeth *fitting in* like two saws, Arist.*HA*501a18:—Med., [νεῦρα] ἀλλήλοισι ἐπαλλαξάμενα ἐς χιασμὸν σχήματος Aret.*SD*1.7:—Pass., *cross one another*, δόρατα.. ὡς ἥκιστα ἂν ἀλλήλοις ἐπαλλάττοιτο X.*Eq.Mag*.3.3; ἐπηλλαγμέναις δι' ἀλλήλων ταῖς χερσίν with the arms *crossed*, Plu. *Luc*.21; θώρακες ἁλύσεσι λεπταῖς σιδηραῖς ἐπηλλαγμένοι Arr.*Tact*.3. 5; ποὺς ἐπαλλαχθεὶς ποδί *closely joined*, E.*Heracl*.836: metaph., μή πῃ ὁ λόγος ἐπαλλαχθῇ that it be not *entangled*, X.*Mem*.3.8.1; of permutations and combinations, –όμεναι συζυγίας ἀποτελοῦσιν ἐννέα Gal.6.112. II. intr., *alternate*, ὀδόντες ἐπαλλάσσοντες *interlocking* teeth, Arist.*PA*661b18; of leaves, dub. in Thphr.*HP*4.6.10. 2. *overlap*, of classes or species, ib.1.3.2; ἀλλήλοις Arist.*GA*733a 27; τοῦτο μόνον ἐ. *overlaps* both classes, ib.774b17; ἡ φώκη ἐ. τῷ γένει τῶν ἰχθύων *forms a link with*.., Id.*HA*501a22; ταῦτα συνδυαζόμενα ποιεῖ τὰς πολιτείας ἐπαλλάττειν causes them to *overlap*, Id.*Pol*.1317a2; so διὰ τὸ τὴν δύναμιν ἐπαλλάττειν αὐτῶν (sc. two species of τυραννίς) καὶ πρὸς τὴν βασιλείαν ib.1295a9; ὃ ποιεῖ τοὺς λόγους ἐ. makes the arguments *confused*, ib.1255a13, cf. 1257b 35. b. *become confused* or *intermixed*, ἐ. τὰ μόρια Id.*GA*769b34; *to be interchangeable with*, τὰ νοσώδη ἐ. τοῖς βραχυβίοις Id.*Long*.464b 28. 3. ἐ. τοῦτο τὸ σύμπτωμα τοῖς τοιούτοις this accident *invades*, *makes its way into* this class, Id.*GA*770b6. **–ηλία**, ἡ, *sequence*, *unbroken series*, φωνηέντων Eust.11.32 (pl.), cf. *EM*576.2; ἐ. τῶν φαρμάκων *taking one* drug *after another*, '*mixing* medicines', Gal.19. 679. **–ηλος**, ον, also η, ον D.C.74.10, al.:—*one close after another*, *in close order*, φάλαγξ, τάξεις, Plb.2.69.9, 11.11.7; ἄρτοι κατὰ ἓξ ἐ. J.*AJ*3.6.6; θυρίδας πέριξ ἐ. D.C.74.10; γυμνασίαι, φθοραί, κτλ., Ph.2.288,175, al.; *continuous*, βοή Hdn.2.7.6; δαπάναι *IG*7.2712. 54 (Acraephia); ἐ. πληγαί *given in quick succession*, Alciphr.3. 6. b. Gramm., τὸ ἐ. τῶν δύο εὐθειῶν *succession*, *sequence* of two nominatives, A.D.*Synt*.179.13, al. II. ἐπαλλήλοιν χεροῖν by *one another's* hands (Hermann for ἐπ' ἀλλ–), S.*Ant*.57. 2. γόμφοι ἐ. *mortised into one another*, Longin.41.3. III. Adv. –λως *again and again*, δι' ὅλου τοῦ ἔτους Dsc.1.115.5; Rhet., ἐ. ῥῆμα ἐπιτιθέναι *repeat* (e.g. μικρὸν μικρόν), Alex.*Fig*.2.2. 2. ἐ. ἔχειν τὰ ἔμπροσθεν *lean against one another*, Ath.10.456e. 3. *in alternate succession*, Ph.1.397. **–ηλότης**, ητος, ἡ, *repetition*, *duplication*, ἐν –τητι ἔχει ἕνα σύνδεσμον τὸν δή A.D.*Conj*.257.5.

ἐπαλλόκαυλος, ον, *clinging to another plant*, *quasi-parasitic*, prob. cj. in Thphr.*HP*3.18.9, 11.

ἐπάλμενος, v. ἐφάλλομαι.

ἐπάλξ-ιον, τό, *parapet*, *IG*2².463.56; cf. sq. **–ις**, εως, ἡ, (ἐπαλέξω) *means of defence*: mostly in pl., *battlements*, Il.12.263, Hdt.9.7, A.*Th*.30,158 (lyr.), E.*Ph*.1158, etc.; τὰς ἐ. ἀπώσαντες Th.3.23; αἱ οἰκίαι.. ἐπάλξεις λαμβάνουσι Id.4.69, cf. 115. b. in sg., mostly, *line of battlements*, *parapet*, Il.12.381, al. (never in Od.); οἱ παρ' ἔπαλξιν the defenders of the wall, Th.2.13, cf. 7.28, Ar.*Ach*.72: pl., of individual *crenellations*, Th.3.21. 2. generally, *defence*, *protection*, πλούτου A.*Ag*.381 (lyr.); σωτηρίας E.*Or*.1203, etc. 3. court for trial of homicide, *EM*353.26, *AB*243. **–ίτης** [ῑ] λίθος *copingstone*, *EM*353.28.

ἔπαλπνος, ον, (v. ἄλπνιστος) *cheerful*, *happy*, Pi.*P*.8.84 codd.; expld. by ἡδύς, προσηνής, Sch.

ἐπαλφῐτόω, *add meal* to wine, prob. in Ath.10.432b.

ἐπᾰλωστής, οῦ, ὁ, (ἀλοάω) *one who threshes with oxen*, X.*Oec*.18.5.

ἐπαμ–, before labials poet. or dial. for ἐπανα– (q.v.).

ἐπᾰμαξεύω, = ἐφαμ–, *traverse with cars*, γῆ.. ἐπημαξευμένη τροχοῖσι *marked with the tracks* of wheels, S.*Ant*.251.

ἐπᾰμάομαι, *scrape together for oneself*, εὐνὴν ἐπαμήσατο χερσί *heaped him up* a bed (of leaves), Od.5.482; γῆν ἐπαμησάμενον Thgn. 428, cf. Thphr.*HP*4.13.5, *AP*7.446 (Hegesipp., tm.); γῆν ἐπαμησάμενος *having heaped up* a grave or barrow, Hdt.8.24; so ἐ. κόνιν Polyaen.2.1.23; ἐ. τινί τι Plu.2.982b; γῆν εἰς τοὺς ὀφθαλμούς Porph. *Abst*.4.9:—later in Act., κόνιν ἐπαμῆσαι D.L.6.79, cf. Iamb.*VP*31. 192: written ἐφαμᾶν in Hld.2.20.

ἐπαμ-βαίνω, poet. for ἐπαναβαίνω, Opp.*H*.3.638. **–βᾰτήρ**, ῆρος, ὁ, poet. for *ἐπαναβάτης, *one who mounts upon*, *assailant*: metaph., νόσοι σαρκῶν ἐπαμβατῆρες, of leprous eruptions, A.*Ch*.280. **–βλήδην**· ἀναβαλλόμενος, ἀνακρουόμενος, Hsch.; cf. ἐπαναβληδόν.

ἐπαμβλύνω, v.l. for ἀμβλύνω in Artem.3.38.

ἐπᾰμείβω, *exchange*, *barter*, τεύχεα δ' ἀλλήλοις ἐπαμείψομεν Il.6. 230; φύσεις ἐ. Orph.*A*.422:—Med., *come one after another*, *come in turn to*, νίκη δ' ἐπαμείβεται ἄνδρας Il.6.339; ἐξαῦτις δ' ἑτέρους ἐπαμείψεται (sc. κήδεα) Archil.9.9.

ἐπᾱμέριος, = sq., Pi.*Fr*.182.

ἐπάμερος [ᾱ], ον, Dor. and Aeol. for ἐφήμερος, Pi.*P*.8.95, Theoc. 30.31: neut. ἐπάμερον, as Adv., = αὐθημερόν, *IG*4.800 (Troezen).

ἐπαμέτραιον· μέτρον τι παρὰ Κνιδίοις, Hsch.

ἐπαμμένος, Ion. for ἐφημμένος, pf. part. Pass. of ἐφάπτω.

ἐπαμμένω, poet. for ἐπαναμένω, A.*Pr*.605 (lyr.).

ἐπᾰμοιβ-ᾰδίς, Adv., (ἐπαμείβω) *interchangeably*: hence ὣς ἄρα πυκνοὶ ἀλλήλοισιν ἔφυν ἐ. so thick they grew *with interwoven boughs*, Od.5.481, cf. A.R.4.1030 (v.l.):—in Hsch. also **–ᾰδόν**. **–ή**, ἡ, *dovetailing*, *BCH*35.43 (pl.). **–ῐμος**, ον, = sq.; ἐ. ἔργα *barter*, *h.Merc*. 516 (ἐπ' ἀμοίβημα cod. M, ἐπαμοίβια cett.). **–ός**, όν, *one upon another*, *continuously*, of tiles, A.R.2.1075; cf. ἐπημοιβός.

ἐπαμπέχω and **–ίσχω** (v. infr., cf. ἐπαμφίσκω), *put on over*, *overwrap*, ἐπαμπίσχοντες γῆν τινι E.*Tr*.1148; *enwrap*, αἴσχιστα ἔργα εὐπρεπέσι κλήσεσιν Ph.2.379; ὕβρει καὶ κόμπῳ ἐπαμπέχειν τι Plu.*Oth*. 5:—Med., Ph.1.358, al., D.Chr.6.26; διὰ φόβον δόξας Plu.2.1102d:— Pass., φύσις λογισμῷ –ομένη Id.*Sert*.10.

ἐπαμπήγνῡμι, poet. for ἐπαναπ– (q.v.).

ἐπᾰμύν-τωρ, ορος, ὁ, *helper*, *defender*, Od.16.263; as fem., Orph.*L*. 587. **–ω**, *come to aid*, *succour*, τινί Il.6.361, 18.99, al., Th.3.14, al., Lys.12.99, etc. 2. abs., Il.16.540, al. (never in Od.), Hdt.1.82, Th.1.25, 101, Lys.3.16, etc.; τῶν ἐπαμυνούντων λόγων ὡς εἰσὶ θεοί *apologetic* arguments *to prove* that.., Pl.*Lg*.891b. 3. *ward off*, δολίην v.l. for ἀπ– in *AP*5.6 (Asclep.).

ἐπαμφέρω, poet. for ἐπαναφέρω (q.v.).

ἐπαμφι-βάλλω, *use ambiguous terms*, Gal.17(2).24. **–έννῡμι**, *cloak* or *veil*, ἐπαμφιέσαι [τὴν ἀτυχίαν] χρήμασιν prob. l. in Men.404.5; in later form ἐπαμφιασαμένη Aristid.*Or*.30(10).18:—Pass., ἐπημφιεσμένος πτίλον [S.]*Fr*.1127.2. **–λλογος**, ον, *disputed*, *SIG*683.51 (ii B.C.).

ἐπαμφισβητέω, *dispute a claim*, *CPR*188.21 (ii A.D.).

ἐπαμφίσκω, = ἐπαμπίσχω, Hsch.

ἐπαμφόδιος, ἡ, (ἄμφοδος) *street-walker*, prob. in Luc.*Rh.Pr*.24.

ἐπάμφορος δίκα, (ἐπ-ανα-φέρω) suit *sent for retrial* after conviction of witnesses for perjury, *Foed.Delph.Pell*.i*A* 14, ii*B* 5.

ἐπαμφοτερ-ής, ές, *double-dealing*, διχόνους καὶ ἐ. Ph.*Fr*.20 H. (sed leg. **–ιστής**). **–ιζόντως**, Adv. *ambiguously*, Sch.Ar.*Pax* 854. **–ίζω**, *to be double*: hence, *play a double game*, 'run with the hare and hunt with the hounds', Pherecr.19, Th.8.85; *halt between two opinions*, Pl.*Phdr*.257b, Arr.*Epict*.4.2.4; ἐ. τὴν γνώμην Ph.2.170; τοῖς λογισμοῖς Plu.*Mar*.40; τὸ –ίζον τῆς διανοίας Ph.1. 346. 2. of statements or arguments, *to be ambiguous*, *susceptible of two interpretations*, λόγους ἀμφιβόλους καὶ –ίζειν δυναμένους Isoc.12. 240, cf. Pl.*R*.479b; λοξὰ καὶ –ίζοντα.. ἀποκρινόμενος Luc.*DDeor*.16. 1. b. of fevers, *partake of both kinds*, Gal.10.749. 3. of vowels, *to be doubtful* in quantity, Aristid.Quint.1.20. II. *lie half-way between*, of *intermediate* species, e.g. seals and bats, Arist. *PA*697b1, *HA*589a21; of apes, ἐ. ἀνθρώπῳ καὶ τετράποσι *share the properties of*.., ib.502a16; ἐ. τὴν μορφὴν *to be intermediate* in shape, Id.*PA*689b32; ὁ ἄνθρωπος ἐ. πᾶσι τοῖς γένεσι Id.*GA*772b1; of amphibious animals, Thphr.*Fr*.171.1. III. abs., *suffice for both*, Arist. *GA*777a16. **–ισμός**, ὁ, *inclination both ways*, *wavering*, ἐνδοιασμὸς καὶ ἐ. Ph.1.409, cf. Arr.*Epict*.4.2.5. II. *uncertainty* of parentage, τῶν τέκνων Ph.2.202. **–ιστής**, οῦ, ὁ, *waverer*, ἐνδοιαστὰ καὶ ἐ. Id.1.459, cf. 176. **–ος**, ον, *ambiguous*, τὸ ἐ. Philostr.*VS*1.25.10. Adv. –ρως, εἰπεῖν ib.21.5.

ἐπάμων, ονος, ὁ, (ἕπομαι) = ὀπάων, *attendant*, restored in Clitarch. Gloss.ap.Ath.6.267c, cf. Hsch. (pl.).

ἐπάν, Conj., later form of ἐπήν (v. ἐπεί A. II), Arist.*Ath*.42.2, Thphr.*Char*.24.10, *IG*2².1298.18 (iii B.C.), Plb.2.2.9, Agatharch.32, Str.10.4.20, etc.: cf. ind. in late Greek, ἐπὰν ἑάλω Sch.Luc.*Peregr*. 9. [ᾰ Men.223.2, Alex.269.]

ἐπανα-βαθμός (v.l. **–βασμός**), ὁ, *step of a stair*, Pl.*Smp*.211c (pl.). **–βαίνω**, poet. **ἐπαμβ–**, Opp.*H*.3.638:—*get up on*, *mount*, ἐπί τι Ar.*Nu*.1487, *Eq*.169; ἐπαναβεβηκότες *mounted* (on horseback), Hdt.3.85; of a star, *rise above the horizon*, Arist.*Mete*.342b 34. 2. of animals, *cover*, Id.*HA*540a22, Clearch.36. 3. *come upon*, τὸ γῆρας ἐπαναβάν *Com.Adesp*.612. II. *go up* inland, Th. 7.29. III. *to be promoted*, εἰς τὰς τῶν ταξιάρχων χώρας X.*Cyr*.2.1. 23. 2. of αἰτίαι and ἀρχαί, *mount upwards*, ἐπὶ τὰ ἀνωτέρω Arist. *Metaph*.990a6, cf. *Ph*.257a22; τὸ ἐπαναβεβηκὸς *higher* or *more ultimate principle*, S.E.*P*.1.174; *the genus*, Sor.2.6; [ἀρχῆς] οὐδεὶς ἂν εὕροι ἁπλουστέραν οὐδὲ ἐπαναβεβηκυῖαν ἡντινοῦν Plot.2.9.1; *search for higher principles*, ἐ. ἀεὶ εἰς ἄπειρον Id.3.6.1; ἐπαναβεβηκότα τῇ ψυχῇ [νοῦν] Id.6.9.5. b. *transcend*, c. gen., Anon.*in Prm*. in *Rh. Mus*.47.617; also c. dat., ἐνέργεια –βεβηκυῖα πάσαις καὶ χρωμένη αὐταῖς ὡς ὀργάνοις ibid. **–βάλλω**, *throw on* or *over*:—Med., ἐπαναβάλλεσθαι θαἰμάτια (cf. ἐπαναβληδόν) Ar.*Ec*.276. II. *lift up*, τὰ λευκὰ τῶν ὀφθαλμῶν Ath.12.529a. III. Med., *put off*, *defer*, τρία ἔτεα ἐ. τὴν Σαρδίων ἅλωσιν Hdt.1.91, cf. Phalar.*Ep*.95 (prob.). **–βάσις**, εως, ἡ, *search for higher principles*, Plot.6.7.27. II. *rise*, *diastole* of the pulse, Gal.7.430. **-βασμός**, v. -βαθμός. **-βιβάζω**, causal of ἐπαναβαίνω, *make to mount upon*, ἄνδρας (sc. τοῖς πύργοις) Th.3.23, cf. D.C.50.23. **-βιβασμός**, ὁ, in pl., *ascending steps* in argument, Herm.*in Phdr*.p.64A. **-βλαστάνω**, *grow upon*, Choerob. in *An.Ox*.2.198.30, Sch.Dsc.p.362 Matth. **-βληδόν**, Adv. *thrown over*, ἐπὶ [τοῖς κιθῶσι] εἰρίνεα εἵματα... ἐ. φορέουσι Hdt.2.81; cf. ἐπαμβλήδην. **-βοάω**, *cry out*, Ar.*Pl*.292 (lyr.). **-γιγνώσκω**, *read over, read out*, f.l. in Lys.10.18, cf. Plb.31.13.10; ἐ. τινὶ ἔντευξιν *PPetr*.2p.3 (iii B.C.); of a teacher, S.E.*M*.10.19, Porph.*Chr*.58:—Pass., D.7.19.

ἐπᾰναγκ-άζω, *compel by force, constrain*, c. acc. et inf., A.*Pr*.671, Ar.*Av*.1083, *PHib*.1.34.3 (iii B.C.), etc.:—Pass., ἀροῦν ἐπαναγκασθείς Ar.*Pl*.525, etc.: freq. with inf. omitted, οὐδ' ἐπηνάγκαζε οὐδὲ εἷς (sc. αὐτοὺς προϊέναι) Hdt.8.130, cf. Ar.*Pl*.533, Th.5.31. **-αστέον**, *one must constrain*, Dam.*Pr*.74. **-αστής**, οῦ, ὁ, *taskmaster*, Sm.*Jb*.3.18. **-αστικός**, ή, όν, *coercive, potent*, *PMag.Par*.1.2567. **-ης**, used only in neut.: 1. ἐπάναγκές [ἐστι] *it is compulsory, necessary*, c. inf., And.1.12, Pl.*Lg*.878e, etc.; μηδὲν ἐ. ἔστω let there be no *compulsion*, ib.765a, cf. *Smp*.176e. 2. as Adv., *on compulsion*, ἐ. κομῶντες wearing long hair *by fixed custom*, Hdt.1.82; ἐ. λέγειν, ἐντίθεσθαι, Aeschin.1.24, D.34.7; ἐ. λαβεῖν Men.576; ἐ. βουλὴν ἀθροισάτω *IG*2^{2}.1100.50, etc.; τὰ ἐπάναγκες *Act.Ap*.15.28. **-ος**, ον, = foreg., *Leg.Gort*.4.28, *SIG*1219.17 (Gambreum, iii B.C.), *PGen*.20.17 (ii B.C.), *POxy*.270.38 (i A.D.). II. = ἐπαναγκαστικός, *PMag.Par*.1.2574, etc.

ἐπανᾰγορεύω, *proclaim publicly*:—impers. in Pass., ἐπαναγορεύεται *proclamation is made*, Ar.*Av*.1071.

ἐπαν-άγω [ᾰγ], *bring up*: hence, 1. *stir up, excite*, τὸν θυμόν Hdt.7.160. 2. *exalt, elevate*, εἰς ἡρωϊκὴν ἐπανῆκται τάξιν D.60.9. II. *bring up*, πρὸς τὸ φῶς Pl.*Lg*.724a. 2. *lead* or *draw back*, τὸ στρατόπεδον ἐς τὴν εὐρυχωρίαν Th.7.3; ἐ. τὰ δεξιά X.*Eq*.12.13; τὸν ἄνθρωπον ἐπανήγαγεν ὡς ὑμᾶς D.18.133; σύαγρον εἰς τὴν οἰκίαν Antiph.42 (s.v.l.). 3. *bring back*, τινὰ εἰς τὸν περὶ τοῦ πράγματος λόγον Pl.*Lg*.949b; τὸν λόγον ἐπὶ τὴν ὑπόθεσιν X.*Mem*.4.6.13; ἐ. ἐμαυτὸν ἀπὸ τῶν κακῶν Pl.*Ep*.325a; εἰς ἐλευθερίαν τὰ πράγματα v.l. in D.15.19; *restore*, τὰς αἱρέσεις τῶν ἱερέων εἰς τὸν δῆμον D.C.37.37; τὸν οἶκον Philostr.*VA*1.28; τὰ ἱερά ib.2 (Pass.); τὰ ἀδικήματα εἰς τὰ κοινὰ δικαστήρια ἐ. *refer* them to.., Pl.*Lg*.846b, cf. Epicur.*Ep*.3p.62 U.; ἐ. τὸ διστοζόμενον εἰς τὸν κανόνα *UPZ*110.57 (ii B.C.); but τῷ Διὶ ἐ. *make acknowledgements* to Zeus, ib.6:—Pass., *to be referred back*, ἐπαναγέσθω πάλιν ἐπὶ τοὺς ἄρχοντας Arist.*Pol*.1298^{b}37; *to be restored*, ἐπὶ ἀρχὰς καὶ στρατηγίας App.*BC*4.15. 4. ἐ. ἐπί τι *lead to, entail*, ἐπ' ἀλγοῦν Epicur.*Sent*.26,30. III. intr., *withdraw, retreat*, X.*Cyr*.4.1.3; *revert*, ἐπὶ τὴν ἀρχήν Plb.3.5.9, etc.; *recur*, in argument, ὅθεν ἐξέβην Jul.*Or*.7.226c; *return*, ἐπὶ ὕψιστον Lxx*Si*.17.26; *turn back*, ἀπὸ δικαιοσύνης εἰς ἁμαρτίαν ib.26.28. 2. ἐ. τῷ σώματι *recover one's health*, Apollon.Perg.*Con*.1*Praef*. IV. *put out to sea*, τὸ κέρας ἀπὸ τῆς γῆς X.*HG*6.2.28: abs., *Ev.Luc*.5.3:—Pass., *put to sea against*, τινί Hdt.9.98; ἐπανάγεσθαι ταῖς ναυσί with one's ships, Th.8.42: abs., Hdt.7.194, X.*HG*2.1.24; ἐπὶ τὴν Χίον ib.1.6.38; *sail up* the Nile, *PStrassb*.102.19 (iii B.C.). V. Pass., also, *to be carried to* a place, ἐπαναχθέντας Hdt.4.103, where however the v.l. ἐπαναχθέντες (in signf. IV) is to be preferred. **-ᾰγωγή**, ἡ, *sailing against, naval attack*, Th.7.34; ἐπανήγαγεν τὰς ἐ. καθ' ἕκαστον μῆνα ποιούμενος perh. held the monthly naval *manœuvres*, *IG*2^{2}.1227.12 (Salamis, ii B.C.). II. *leading up, exalting*, τοῦ βελτίστου πρὸς τὴν τοῦ ἀρίστου θέαν Pl.*R*.532c. 2. Rhet., *return to the point*, Corn.*Rh*.p.397 H. (pl.). **-ᾰγωγὸς Τύχη**, = Lat. *Fortuna Redux*, D.C.54.10.

ἐπαναδέρω, *strip off the scalp*, Hp.*Vid.Ac*.8.

ἐπανα-δίδωμι, intr., *increase more and more*, πυρετὸς ἐ. καθ' ἡμέρην ἑκάστην Hp.*Epid*.1.25. **-διπλάζω**, poet. **ἐπανδ-**, *reiterate questions*, A.*Pr*.817. **-διπλᾰσιασμός**, ὁ, *doubling*, τοῦ αὐτοῦ συμφώνου *EM*605.17; *repetition*, Elias*in Porph*.20.22. **-διπλόω**, *repeat yet again*, Arist.*Pr*.910^{b}25, Gal.15.879:—Pass., *to be repeated*, Arist.*APr*.49^{a}11, *Metaph*.1003^{b}28. **-δίπλωμα**, ατος, τό, *fold, double*, Id.*HA*506^{b}14. **-δίπλωσις**, εως, ἡ, *doubling, folding*, of the intestines, ib.507^{b}30 (pl.); of the spermatic glands, Id.*GA*717^{a}33; τοῦ δέρματος Leonid.ap.Aët.15.5. II. *repetition*, Arist.*APr*.49^{a}26. 2. Rhet., = ἀναστροφή (q.v.), Tib.*Fig*.25. III. Medic., '*reduplication*', i.e. *combination* of two kinds of fevers, Gal.7.433. **-δοσις**, εως, ἡ, *restitution*, Just.*Nov*.97.5. **-ζεῦξαι**· ἐπανελθεῖν, Hsch. **-ζευξις**, εως, ἡ, *return*, Ascl.*in Metaph*.399.19. **-ζώννῦμαι**, Med., *gird on one's clothes*, Ph.2.479. **-θαρρέω**, = ἀναθαρρέω, ἐπί τινι Onos.14.4: abs., Id.33.5. **-θεάομαι**, *contemplate again*, X.*Cyr*.5.4.11. **-θερμαίνομαι**, *receive warmth again*, v.l. in Hp.*Epid*.1.26.α'. **-θέω**, *run up against*, τινί Onos.18: abs., Id.6.1.

ἐπαν-αίρεσις, εως, ἡ, *slaughter, destruction*, Plb.2.37.8: pl., μεγάλαι ἀνθρώπων ἐ. Nech. in *Cat.Cod.Astr*.7.140. **-αιρέω**, *make away with, destroy*, D.S.19.51; *remove*, τὰ γεῖσα *IG*2^{2}.463.54:—Med., Plb.2.19.9, etc.; ἐπαναιρεῖσθαί τινα φαρμάκῳ Id.8.12.2; ἐ. τὰς Συρακούσας Id.1.10.8:—Pass., ἐπανῄρηται φαρμάκῳ *PTeb*.43.19 (ii B.C.). 2. *kill after* or *together with*, App.*BC*4.15, al.; μετά τινα ἑαυτόν ib.4.26. II. Med. (pf. Pass., f.l. in Pl.*Ly*.219a, cf. Plu.*Comp.Alc.Cor*.2), *take upon one, enter into*, φιλίαν Pl. l.c.; esp. into a profession, τέχνην, λατρείαν, Luc.*Bis Acc*.1, *Apol*.4; [βίον] Men.Rh.p.376S., Just.*Nov*.149.2; ἐ. πόλεμον *enter upon* a war, Plb.9.29.8:—Pass., of cures, *to be employed*, Aret.*SD*2.12. b. *gain*, δόξαν Vett.Val.173.24; in bad sense, *incur*, ἔχθραν Jul.*Mis*.355a. c. *receive* as one's share in a division of property, *BGU*234.7 (ii A.D.), etc. 2. *withdraw*, τὸν φιλάνθρωπον νόμον Plu.*TG*10, cf. *CG*4. **-αίρω**, *lift up, raise high*, τὰς κεφαλάς X.*Cyn*.6.23:—Med., κἀπαναίρονται δόρυ (Herm. for κἀπαναιροῦνται) *raise* the spear *one against the other*, S.*OC*424; but ἐπανήρατο τὴν βακτηρίαν *raised his* staff *against* him, Th.8.84, cf. Hsch. s.v. ἐπανήραντο:—Pass., *rise up*, ἀλλ' ἐπαναίρου Ar.*Eq*.784. **-αίσθητος**, f.l. for ἀνεπ-, Aret.*SD*1.14. **-αιτέω**, *demand*, dub. in *BGU*330.6 (ii A.D.). **-αιώρημα**, ατος, τό, f.l. for ἐναιώρημα (q.v.) ap.Erot.

ἐπανα-καινίζω, *renew, revive*, Lxx *Jb*.10.17, Phld.*Acad.Ind*.p.4 M.:—also **-καινόω**, Herod.Med.in *Rh.Mus*.49.549. **-κᾰλέω**, *invoke besides*, A.*Ag*.145. II. *recall*, Aret.*SD*2.13 (Pass.):—Med., τινὰς ὡς ἐπὶ τὸ στρατόπεδον Arr.*An*.4.27.1, cf. Dam.*Pr*.245, Procl.*in Alc*.p.182C.:—Pass., πρὸς τὸ δέον Hierocl.*in CA*7p.429M. **-κάμπτω**, intr., *come back again*, ἐπὶ τὴν ἀρχήν Arist.*Pr*.916^{a}32: abs., *bend back*, of ducts or veins, Id.*HA*510^{a}21, 514^{a}11; *return*, Aq., Sm., Thd.*Is*.35.10. **-καμψις**, εως, ἡ, *return*, ἐπὶ τὴν πρώτην ἡλικίαν Ocell.1.14. **-κειμαι**, *to be imposed upon* as punishment, τινί X.*Cyr*.3.3.52. II. *to be superadded*, κακὸν κακῷ -κείμενον Numen.ap.Eus.*PE*14.8. 2. *to be entered as well* in a register, *Stud.Pal*.1.62.33 (i A.D.). **-κεφᾰλαιόομαι**, = ἀνακεφαλαιόω, Hermog.*Stat*.3, Olymp.*in Mete*.319.25. **-κεφαλαίωσις**, εως, ἡ, *recapitulation*, ib.30. **-κλαγγάνω**, *give tongue again and again*, X.*Cyn*.4.5, 6.23. **-κλησις**, εως, ἡ, *recall, reaction*, ἐπανάκλησιν θέρμης ποιέεσθαι Hp.*Aph*.5.21, Aret.*CA*2.3: metaph., ἡ ἐ. τῶν ἀπορρεόντων μερῶν ἀπὸ τοῦ ὅλου εἰς αὐτὸ τὸ ὅλον Dam.*Pr*.241; *call to repentance*, Hierocl.*in CA*7p.429M. II. *double inspiration*, Hp.*Epid*.2.3.7, Gal.7.899. **-κλίνω** [ῑ], *make to lie down*, τινά Hp.*Acut.*(*Sp*.)37, cf. Sm.*Ca*.2.5; *incline* one valve of the heart *towards* the other, Hp.*Cord*.10. **-κοινόω**, *communicate*, τινί τι Pl.*Lg*.918a. **-κομίζω**, *bring back*:—Pass., *return*, D.C.40.44. **-κράζω**, *call out to*, in aor. imper. ἐπανακραγέτω, Poll.5.85. **-κρεμάννῦμαι**, *to be dependent*, Arist.*Pol*.1318^{b}38. **-κρουσις**, εως, ἡ, *putting back*, Sch.Ar.*Av*.649. **-κρούω**, poet. **ἐπαγκρ-**, *put* a ship *back* (v. ἀνακρούω), Hsch.: metaph., πάλιν ἐπαγκρούων Isyll.6:—Med., *put back*, Ar.*Av*.648. **-κτάομαι**, *recover*, *SIG*799.10 (Cyzicus, i A.D.).

ἐπανακτ-έον, *one must recall*, τὸν λόγον ἐπί τι Him.*Ecl*.36.7, cf. Jul.*Or*.6.190a. **-ικός**, ή, όν, *indicating return*, πρός τινας Phld.*D*.3*Fr*.75.

ἐπανα-κτῠπέω, dub. l. in Arr.*Tact*.41.2. **-κυκλέω**, *recur*, of intermittent fevers, Gal.7.412. II. Pass., *make a counter revolution*, Pl.*R*.617b; but simply, *revolve*, ἀπὸ τοῦ αὐτοῦ πρὸς ταὐτόν Dam.*Pr*.23. **-κύκλησις**, εως, ἡ, *return* of a circle *into itself*, Pl.*Ti*.40c. **-κύπτω**, *have an upward slope*, X.*Eq*.12.13. II. *rise up to thwart*, ταῖς ἐλπίσιν τινός J.*BJ*1.31.1. 2. ἐπανέκυψε λόγος *a new* argument *rose up*, Plu.2.725c. **-λαμβάνω**, *take up again, resume, repeat*, πῶς, ὡς..., Pl.*Grg*.488b, X.*Lac*.13.2; εἴπωμεν ἐπαναλαβόντες Arist.*Metaph*.1035^{b}4, cf. Pl.*Tht*.169e: the part. may be best rendered by an Adv., πολλάκις ἐπαναλαμβάνων ἐκέλευέν οἱ λέγειν he ordered him *repeatedly*, Id.*Phdr*.228a. II. *revise, correct*, Id.*Lg*.781b; τῇ τροφῇ τὴν κακοπάθειαν Thphr.*CP*3.7.8. III. *undertake*, *PMasp*.151.136 (vi A.D.). **-λέγω**, *repeat*, Alex.*Fig*.1.13 (Pass.).

ἐπανᾰλείφω, *plaster on*, Gal.6.577 (f.l. for ἐπαλ-).

ἐπανα-ληπτέον, *one must resume*, Jul.*Gal*.351a. **-ληπτικῶς**, Adv. *by repetition*, Eust.624.46. **-ληψις**, εως, ἡ, in Rhet., *resumption, repetition*, Demetr.*Eloc*.196, Hermog.*Id*.1.4 (pl.), *Meth*.9, Alex.*Fig*.1.13, etc. II. = ἐπαναδίπλωσις III, Gal.7.433.

ἐπανᾱλίσκω, *consume still more*, [χρόνον] D.50.42: aor. 1 ἐπανάλωσα Hadr.Rh.p.45 H. II. *spend in addition*, τὸ ἐπανᾱλωθέν *IG*12(7).24 (Amorgos); but ἐπανηλωθέντος *PCorn*.1.88.

ἐπανά-λῠσις, εως, ἡ, = ἀναποδισμός, *retracing one's steps*, Hsch. **-λύτης**, = Lat. *remeabilis*, *Gloss*. **-λύω**, *return*, *POxy*.942.3 (vi (?) A.D.).

ἐπανᾱλωτής, οῦ, ὁ, *spendthrift*, Lat. *sumptuarius*, *Gloss*.

ἐπανα-μένω, poet. **ἐπαμμένω**, *wait longer*, Hdt.8.141, Ar.*Ec*.790. II. *wait for* one, τινά Id.*Nu*.803; ἐ. τινὰ ἐλθεῖν Id.*Lys*.74: impers., ὅ τι μ' ἐπαμμένει παθεῖν what *there is in store* for me to suffer, A.*Pr*.605 (lyr.); οὗ σφιν κακῶν ὕψιστ' ἐπαμμένει παθεῖν Id.*Pers*.807; τίς ἄρα με πότμος..ἐπαμμένει; (Herm. for ἐπιμένει) S.*OC*1718. **-μιμνήσκω**, *remind* one *of, mention again to* one, τινά τι Pl.*Lg*.688a, cf. Arist.*Mem*.451^{a}12, Porph.*Abst*.1.30; ἕκαστον ὑμῶν, τίς.. D.6.35. **-μνησις**, εως, ἡ, *mentioning again*, τῶν προαποδεδειγμένων πραγμάτων D.H.*Rh*.10.18, cf. Corn.*Rh*.p.370H. **-νεάζω**, *to be recrudescent*, Gal.19.210. **-νεόομαι**, Med., *revive*, τὸν λόγον Pl.*R*.358b; *renew*, τὰ διαστρώματα *POxy*.237 viii 41 (ii A.D.). **-νέωσις**, εως, ἡ, *renewal*, Just.*Const*.Δέδωκεν init. **-παυσις**, εως, ἡ, *lighting down, descent*, Sm.*Is*.30.30 (Auct.p.30F.). **-παύω**, *rest upon*, τῇ λαβῇ τοῦ ξίφους τὴν χεῖρα Procop.Gaz.p.170B., cf. Ael.*NA*5.56:—Med. (fut. -παύσομαι, later -παήσομαι v.l. in *Ev.Luc*.10.6), *rest upon*, ταῖς χερσί J.*AJ*8.3.6, Hdn.2.1.2; *rest in* or *upon*, τινί Lxx 1*Ma*.8.12; *rest one's hopes on*, νόμῳ *Ep.Rom*.2.17; *rest content with, rely on*, ταῖς παλαιαῖς ἀποβάσεσιν Artem.4.65; τῇ ἐφημέρῳ τροφῇ Trypho *Trop*.p.194S.; ταῖς διωρισμέναις ἐννοίαις Dam.*Pr*.37: in Logic, *to be based on*, ὁ δεύτερος συλλογισμὸς ἐ. τῇ ἐννοίᾳ τοῦ ἑνός ib.321. II. Med., *come to rest*, of a machine, Hero *Aut*.24.4: metaph., ἐ. ἔν τινι *come to rest* in, Iamb.*Comm.Math*.8; ἐπαναπαύσεται ἐπ' αὐτὸν (sc. τὸν οἶκον) ἡ εἰρήνη ὑμῶν *Ev.Luc*.10.6; ἐπανεπαύσατο ἐπ' αὐτοῖς πνεῦμα Lxx *Nu*.11.26. **-πέμπω**, *send back to* a point, Hp.*Mul*.2.133, prob. in *PPetr*.2p.64 (iii B.C.). **-περάω**, *cross over again*, Nic.Dam.

*Vit.Caes.*6 codd. **-πέτομαι,** aor. 2 inf. -πτῆναι *fly up,* Hsch. s.v. ἐπαναπτήσιμον. **-πήγνῡμι,** *fix in* or *on* :—Med., δούρατ' ἐπαμπήξασθαι *fix their* spears *in the ground,* Orph.*A.*319. **-πηδάω,** *leap upon,* Ar.*Nu.*1375. **-πιπράσκω,** *put up to sale again* :—Pass., aor. part. -πραθέν *PPetr.*3p.120 (iii B.C.): fut. -πραθήσομαι *PTheb. Bank* 1.24 (ii B.C.), cf. *UPZ*112iii 12 (ii B.C.). **-πίπτω,** *lie down on,* φύλλοις ῥόδων Ael.*VH*9.24. **-πλάσσω,** Att. -ττω, = ἀναπλάσσω, Axionic.8. **-πλέω,** *put to sea against,* ἐπί τινα Hdt.8.9, cf. 16; ἐπ' ἀργυρολογίαν X.*HG*4.8.35. 2. *sail back again,* ib.24, D. 56.29, Plb.1.28.10. II. *rise to the surface*: metaph., ἐπαναπλέει ὑμῖν ἔπεα κακά ill language *rises to* your *tongue,* Hdt.1.212, cf. Ph.2. 174. **-πληρόω,** *fill up, supply,* Thphr.*Sens.*8 (Pass.). **-πνέω,** *have a double inspiration* (cf. ἐπανάκλησις II), ἐ. διπλόον Hp.*Epid.*7. 92. **-ποδίζω,** *retrace one's steps* in argument, Alex.Aphr.*in Metaph.*813.20. **-ποδιστέον,** *one must re-examine,* Arist.*GC*317^b 19. **-πολέω,** *repeat yet again,* Pl.*Phlb.*60a, *Lg.*723e. **-πόλησις,** εως, ἡ, *repetition,* Ph.1.254. **-πορεύομαι,** *return, PSI*4.353. 3 (iii B.C.). **-πρίασθαι,** aor., *buy at a re-sale,* ὁ ἐπαναπριάμενος τὰ παλίμπωλα *IG*7.3073.26 (Lebad.). **-πτήσιμος,** ον, *ready to fly, Com.Adesp.*1006. **-πωλέω,** = -πιπράσκω, *PPetr.*3p.120 (iii B.C.):—Pass., *UPZ*112v 22 (ii B.C.). **-ρρήγνῡμι,** *tear open again,* τὸ τραῦμα Plu.*Cat.Mi.*70 :—Pass., *burst open afresh,* Hp.*Loc.Hom.* 14. **-ρριπίζω,** = ἀναρριπίζω, J.*AJ*19.2.2. **-ρρίπτω** or -έω, *throw up in the air*: seemingly intr. (sc. ἑαυτόν), *spring high in the air,* X.*Cyn.* 5.4. **-ρρύεται·** μετὰ κρίσιν θύει, κρέα δίδωσιν, Hsch. **-ρρυμα,** ατος, τό, = τὸ ἐν Ἀρείῳ πάγῳ ἐπίθυμα, *AB*417, cf. Phot. s.v. κρέας. **-ρρύσις,** εως, ἡ, = foreg., Suid. s.v. ἀναρύει. **-σεισις,** εως, ἡ, *brandishing against,* τῶν ὅπλων Th.4.126. **-σείω,** *lift up and shake,* Hp.*Foet.Exsect.*4 : metaph., ἐ. τὴν δημαρχικὴν ἐξουσίαν *threaten* one *with it,* D.H.11.6 ; κατηγορίαν Procop.*Arc.*23 :—Pass., of soldiers, -όμενοι τοῖς κρατίστοις *being used to overawe..,* J.*AJ*19. 1.16, cf. 17. **-σκοπέω,** *consider yet again,* Pl.*Cra.*428d, *Hp.Mi.* 369d ; πάλιν ἐπανασκεψώμεθα Id.*Tht.*154e. **-σπείρω,** *sow again* ; and **-σπορά,** ἡ, *second sowing,* Tz.ad Hes.*Op.*444. **-στᾰσις,** εως, ἡ, *rising up* to go to stool : hence in pl., concrete, *stools,* Hp.*Prorrh.* 1.146. 2. *rising up again,* D.S.18.31. 3. *rising up against, insurrection,* Hdt.3.44,118, Th.2.27, etc.; ἐγένετο ἡ ἐν Σάμῳ ἐ. ὑπὸ τοῦ δήμου τοῖς δυνατοῖς Id.8.21 ; ἐ. μέρους τινὸς τῷ ὅλῳ τῆς ψυχῆς Pl.*R.*444b ; παθῶν Hierocl.*in CA*1p.418M. ; opp. ἀπόστασις, D.H. 3.8, Sch.Th.3.39. b. concrete, ἐπαναστάσεις θρόνων *rebellions* (i.e. *rebels*) *against* the throne, S.*Ant.*533. II. *rising up, swelling,* Hp.*Coac.*216 ; *prominent growth,* Thphr.*HP*3.7.4 ; *prominence* on the head, Arist.*HA*500^{a}5 ; φλυκταινῶν Dsc.*Ther.*9, cf. Sor.2.18, Antyll.ap.Orib.8.17.2. III. metaph., *rise in* rhetorical *tone,* Demetr.*Eloc.*278. **-στέλλω,** *check, resist,* αἱ γενέσεις ἐ. τὰς φθορὰς Arist.*Mu.*397^{b}3 (v. ἀνασηκόω). **-στημα,** ατος, τό, *rising, blister,* Sch.Ar.*Ra.*238. 2. *eminence, hill,* ἐ. γῆς Phlp.*in de An.*311. 24. 3. *crest* of a helmet, Hsch. s.vv. λόφος, χαλκόλοφον, *EM*570. 4. **-στρέφω,** intr., *turn back upon* one, *wheel round and return to the charge,* Ar.*Ra.*1102, Th.4.130, 8.105, X.*HG*6.2.21 :—Pass., Ar. *Eq.*244, X.*Eq.Mag.*8.25 ; εἴς τι Porph.*Marc.*13. II. Pass., *return to the surface,* Arist.*Fr.*335. III. Pass., *to be charged upon,* τῇ ἐμῇ περιουσίᾳ *PMasp.*151.136 (vi A.D.). **-στροφή,** ἡ, = ἀναστροφή, *return,* of the chorus, Sch.Ar.*Nu.*596. 2. Rhet., *repetition* of the last word or words of a sentence at the beginning of the next, Hermog.*Id.*1.12 ; of the syllables -μια in Σαμία μία ναῦς Eust.1751. 40. **-σχίζω,** *split open,* Philum.*Ven.*7.12 (Pass.). **-σωστικός,** ή, όν, *bringing safely home,* Τύχη Ἐ., = Lat. *Fortuna Redux,* Inscr.ap. Lyd.*Mens.*4.132. **-τᾰσις,** εως, ἡ, *stretching upwards, holding up,* τοῦ σκήπτρου Arist.*Pol.*1285^{b}12 ; μάστιγος S.E.*M.*8.271. II. metaph., *threatening,* Ph.1.282 (pl.), al., *POxy.*237 viii 10 (ii A.D.), Iamb.*Myst.* 6.6 ; *brandishing,* σιδήρου *PHal.*1.186 (iii B.C) ; misspelt ἐπάντασις). **-τείνω,** poet. ἐπαντ-, Orph.*A.*61, 332 :—*stretch out and hold up,* τὸν τράχηλον, f.l. for ὑπερανα-, X.*An.*7.4.9 ; ἐ. τὰς χεῖρας, as in prayer, D.S.32.6, cf. Orph.*A.* ll.cc.; ἐ. ἐλπίδας τινὶ *hold out* hopes, X.*Cyr.*2.1.23 (Pass.). II. freq. in Med., ἐπανατείνεσθαι σίδηρόν τινι *brandish threateningly, PHal.*1.186 (iii B.C.) ; βάκτρον τινὶ Luc.*Cat.* 13, cf. Jul.*Or.*6.196b ; ἐ. φόβους τινὶ Plb.2.44.3 : c. inf., ἐ. τι πράξειν *threaten* to do, Id.15.29.14 :—Pass., *POxy.*1408.17 (iii A.D.). 2. *speak with prolixity,* D.H.*Rh.*8.14. 3. *set oneself up, rebel,* Philostr. *VA*7.14. **-τέλλω,** poet. **ἐπαντέλλω,** *raise,* ποδὸς ἴχνος E.*Ph.*105 (anap.) ; ἐ. κέρας ἐκ μετώπου *send forth,* Opp.*C.*2.97. II. intr., *rise,* [τὸν ἥλιον] ἐπανατεῖλαι Hdt.2.142 ; ἡλίου ἐπανατείλαντος Id.3. 84; ὡς ἐπανέτελλε ὁ ἥλιος Id.7.54 ; ἐπαντέλλων ἀστράσιν ἠέλιος *AP*12. 178 (Strat.) ; ἐπανατεταλκέτω τὸ Η Arist.*Mete.*376^{b}29; of a star, *Sammelb.*2134.7 ; *rise again,* Gem.6.10 ; εὐνῆς ἐπαντείλασαν *having risen* from bed, A.*Ag.*27 ; ἐκ τοῦ χάρακος Plu.*Aem.*18 ; *show oneself, appear,* λευκὰς δὲ κόρσας τῇδ' ἐπαντέλλειν νόσῳ A.*Ch.*282 ; φόνος -τέλλει E.*HF*1053 (anap.); ὁ ἐπαντέλλων χρόνος the time *coming to light, the future,* Pi.*O.*8.28. **-τέμνω,** Ion. -τάμνω, *cut open further,* Hp.*VC* 13; *cut open again,* Aret.*CA*1.4. **-τίθημι,** *lay upon,* ἐπαναθῶ σοι καὶ ξύλον Ar.*V.*148: metaph., *shift* a burden, *PSI*4.286.7 (iii/iv A.D.): —Pass., μείζων δύναμις ἐ. τινὶ *is entrusted* to him, Pl.*Lg.*926d. II. Med., *shift one's position,* of patients under operation, Gal.18(2). 425. III. Med., *bequeath, PLips.*29.7 (iii A.D.). IV. *shut,* σανίδας Il.21.535 (Aristarch.). **-τολή,** ἡ, invisible *rising* of stars just *after* sunrise or sunset, Ptol.*Alm.*8.4. **-τρέπω,** *overturn, upset,* Hdn.3.8.5. II. intr., *return,* εἰς τὸν λόγον Cratin.181 (dub.). **-τρέφω,** *feed up, recruit, nourish,* Hp.*Aph.*2.7, Aret.*CD* 1.5. **-τρέχω,** aor. 2 ἐπανέδραμον, *return, recur,* Phld.*Ir.*p.63 W., *return to,* τὴν ἀρετὴν J.*AJ*18.9.6 ; ἐπὶ τοὺς κυρίους D.S.36.8. II. of property rights, *pass,* ἐπί, εἴς τινα, *PLond.*3.1044.14 (vi A.D.), 5. 1727.46 (vi A.D.). **-τρίβω** [ῑ], *scrub again,* Asclep.ap.Gal.12. 412. **-τροπιάζω,** *relapse* (Lat. *recidit*), Gloss. **-τρῠγάω,** *glean after the vintage,* c. acc., Lxx *De.*24.21, *Le.*19.10. **-φέρω,** poet. **ἐπαμφέρω,** fut. ἐπανοίσω Epicur.*Sent.*25 : aor. 1 -ήνεγκα :—*throw back upon* : hence, *ascribe, refer,* μή τι θεοῖς τούτων μοῖραν ἐπαμφέρετε Sol.11.2 ; τι εἴς τινα or εἴς τι, Ar.*Nu.*1080, Pl.*R.*434e, D.5.11, 27. 49 ; ἐπί τι Pl.*Lg.*680d ; ἐπί τι αἴτιον Arist.*Ph.*196^{a}13 ; ἐπὶ τὸ τέλος Epicur.*Sent.*25 ; πρός τι Hp.*VM*1 (v.l.) ; ἐπί τινα, of an analogous case, ib.10 : abs., πάλιν ἐ. And.3.33 ; ἐ. τινὶ ὑπέρ τινος, Lat. *referre alicui de re,* Plb.21.4.14 :—Pass., ἐπανενεχθεισῶν τῶν συνθηκῶν εἰς τὴν Ῥώμην Id.1.17.1. b. intr. in Act., *rise* or *be referred* to a cause, ἐπί τι Pl.*Ly.*219c. 2. *put into the account,* D.41.20, cf. *IG*2^2.1607a 7. 3. *bring back a message,* X.*HG*2.2.21 (Act. with Med. as v.l.) ; ὥς τινα Plu.*Art.*29. 4. *vomit,* Aret.*SA*2.2. II. intr., *recover consciousness,* ἐπανενέγκαντες θνήσκουσι Hp.*Coac.*1 (unless = *sigh,* cf. ἀναφέρω I. 2). 2. of disease, *abate,* Aret.*SA*2.1. III. Pass., *rise,* as an exhalation, X.*Cyn.*5.2 ; as stars or the sun, Gem.7.11, Plu.2.19e, cf. 735a ; esp. in Astrol., *occupy the position following a* κέντρον, Ptol.*Tetr.*115. 2. *move in counter revolution,* Ti.Locr. 96d. IV. Rhet., *repeat* a word (cf. sq.), Demetr.*Eloc.*59 :—Pass., ib.268, D.H.*Dem.*40. **-φορά,** ἡ, *referring, reference,* ἐπί τι Arist. *EN*1130^{a}29; πρός τι Thphr.*HP*1.2.4. 2. *reference* of a question to an assembly, And.3.33 ; to the people, Harp. II. Rhet., *repetition* of a word at the beginning of several clauses, Longin.20.2 (pl.), Demetr.*Eloc.*61, Hermog.*Id.*1.12, Ps.-Plu.*Vit.Hom.*33. III. *rising,* ἀτμῶν Aret.*CA*1.6. IV. Astrol., τόπος *which follows a* κέντρον (q.v.), Ptol.*Tetr.*112, S.E.*M.*5.14, Paul.Al.*L.*2. **-φορικός,** ή, όν, *of* or *for* ἐπαναφορά, σχῆμα Sch.Ar.*Pl.*545, cf. Eust.67.35. **-φορος,** v. ἐπάμφ-. **-φῡσάω,** *play on the flute in accompaniment,* Ar.*Th.* 1175. **-φύω,** *put forth again,* Ael.*NA*10.13. **-φωνέω,** *pronounce in addition* or *after,* opp. προαναφωνέω, S.E.*M.*1.130 (Pass.). **-χάζομαι,** v. ἐπαγχ-. **-χέω,** *pour out upon, EM*329.17 (Pass.). **-χρεμπτήριος,** ον, *promoting expectoration,* Hp.*Loc.Hom.*17. **-χρέμπτομαι,** *expectorate,* ib.14. **-χρεμψις,** εως, ἡ, *expectoration,* ib.17, 18. **-χωρέω,** *retreat, return,* Charon *Fr.*2, Ar.*Lys.*461, Th.6.49 ; δεῦρο Pherecr.59 ; ἐς τὰς Θήβας Hdt.9.13 ; ἐς τὸ τεῖχος Th.1.63, cf. 3.96 ; πρὸς τὰ μετέωρα Id.4.44 ; ἐπὶ τὰ πρῶτα λεχθέντα Pl.*Lg.*781e ; εἰς θεοὺς ἐ. τῆς τῶν πράξεων ἀρχῆς *return from..,* Plu.2.580a ; ἐ. τῶν πραγμάτων *withdraw from, PLond.*5.1727.16 (vi A.D.). **-χώρησις,** εως, ἡ, *return,* κύματος Th.3.89 ; *retreat,* D.S.25.6.

ἐπανδιπλάζω, poet. for ἐπαναδιπλάζω (q.v.).

ἔπανδρ-ος, ον, (ἀνήρ) *manly,* Demad.37, Phld.*Ir.*p.65 W., Vett. Val.14.24, al. ; πρᾶξις D.S.4.50 ; ἐργασία *IG*14.951 (i B.C.) ; τὸ ἔ. *masculine spirit,* Corn.*ND*20 ; ἔργα Hierocl.p.63 A. (Comp.). Adv. -δρως S.E.*M.*11.107 ; ἀγωνίσασθαι *CIG*4239 (Tlos), cf. *SIG*709.6 (Cherson., ii B.C.). **-όω,** *make manly,* ψυχὰς νέων Lxx 2 *Ma.*15.17.

ἐπαν-εγείρω, = ἀνεγείρω, Hp.*Prorrh.*2.4, Plu.2.101a. **-έγερσις,** εως, ἡ, gloss on ἐπανάστασις, Hsch. **-ειλέω,** *unroll,* Gal.19. 91. **-ειμι,** (εἶμι *ibo*) used as fut. of ἐπανέρχομαι, *go back, return,* Th.6.102, etc. ; αὐλὸς.. ἐπάνεισιν the music of the flute *will rise again,* S.*Tr.*642 (lyr.) ; in writing or speaking, *go back* or *return* to a point, ἐπὶ τὸν πρότερον λόγον Hdt.7.138; ἐγὼ δ' ἔνθεν ἐξέβην ἐπάνειμι X.*HG*7. 4.1 ; μικρὸν ἐ. Id.*Cyr.*1.2.15 ; ἐ. δὴ πάλιν ἐπὶ τὰς ἀποδείξεις D.18.42, cf. 21.196 ; περὶ φύσεως πάσης ἐπανιόντα τῆς τῶν σώματων *recurring* to first principles of physiology, Pl.*Lg.*857d. 2. c. acc. rei, *return to, recapitulate,* τοὺς λόγους ib.693c ; τὰ ὑποτεθέντα ἐ. αὖθις Id.*Ti.* 61d. II. *rise,* [ὕδωρ] κάτωθεν ἐ. πέφυκεν ib.22e; *go up,* Ὀλυμπίαζε Id.*Hp.Mi.*363d; *ascend,* ἀπὸ.. Id.*Smp.*211b,c; ἡ νόησις ἐπὶ τὸ εἶναι ἐ. Dam.*Pr.*81 ; *rise up,* Hp.*VC*17. **-ειπεῖν,** *offer publicly besides,* ἀργύριον τῷ ἀποκτείναντι Th.6.60. **-είρομαι** or **-έρομαι** (Hp.*Prog.*7), *question again and again,* Hdt.1.91, 3.32 : Trag. and Att. only in aor. 2 ἐπανηρόμην, τάδε σ' ἐπανερόμαν A.*Pers.*973 (lyr.) ; μηδ' αὖθις ἐπανέρῃ με Ar.*Ra.*439 ; *inquire further,* Hp. l.c. 2. *ask again,* εἰ ἐπανέροιτό τινά τι Pl.*Prt.*329a, cf. *Grg.*451b ; ὅντινα.. J.*AJ*18.6. 6. **-έλευσις,** εως, ἡ, (ἐπανέρχομαι) *return,* Eust.1393.8. **-ελευστέον,** *one must return, recur,* ἐπί τι Apollon.Cit.3. **-ελίττω,** *roll up again,* Eust.1688.40. **-έλκω,** *draw up* on shore, τὴν ναῦν Arr. *An.*2.19.3. **-εμέω,** *vomit thereafter,* ἰώδεα Hp.*Epid.*1.12. II. of ruminants, *bring back into the mouth,* Gal.2.545.

ἐπάνεμος [ᾰ], ον, *windy,* ὥρη Hp.*Epid.*6.8.13.

ἐπαν-ερεύγομαι, = ἀνερεύγομαι, Hp.*Acut.*67 ; ἅλμαν Tim.*Pers.*95. **-έρχομαι,** *go back, return,* ἐκ ποταμοῦ Anacr.23 ; ἐκ Πειραιέως And. 1.81, cf. Th.4.16 ; ἐς τὴν Κόρινθον ib.74; θάλασσα -ελθοῦσα ἀπὸ τῆς γῆς Id.3.89 ; in writing or speaking, *go back* or *return* to a point, ἐκεῖσε δὴ 'πάνελθε, πῶς.. E.*IT*256; ἐπί τι X.*HG*1.7.29; ἐπανελθεῖν ὁπόθεν.. ἐξέβην βούλομαι D.18.211 ; ἀλλ' ἐκεῖσε ἐπανέρχομαι ib.66 ; εἰς τὰ γράμματα ταῦτα ἐπανελθεῖν *refer to..,* Id.28.5. b. *recur,* of intermittent fevers, etc., Gal.7.412, 16.711. 2. c. acc. rei, *return to, recapitulate,* Pl.*Ti.*17b, X.*Oec.*6.2, *Ages.*11.1. II. *go up, ascend,* εἰς ὄρη Id.*HG*4.8.35 ; δοκέει.. ἐνθεῦτεν γεωμετρίη.. ἐς τὴν Ἑλλάδα ἐπανελθεῖν *to have gone up, passed over,* Hdt.2.109. 2. *rise up* (cf. ἐπάνειμι II), Hp.*VC*17. **-έρομαι,** v. ἐπανείρομαι. **-ερωτάω,** of persons, *question again,* v.l. in Id.*Prog.*7 ; τινά Pl.*Cra.*413a, X.*Mem.* 3.1.11 :—Pass., Pl.*Clit.*409d. 2. of things, *ask over again,* Id.*Grg.* 454c, *Lg.*645d. **-εσις,** εως, ἡ, (ἐπανίημι) *abatement,* of fevers, Aret.*CA*1.1 (pl.). II. name of a *bandage,* Heliod.ap.Orib.48.43.

1. -έχω, *hold up, support*, τὰ οἰκεῖα πάθη τοῖς δημοσίοις ἐπανέχων Plu.*Dem.*22:—Med., *take upon oneself*, τὸν πρὸς Γέτας πόλεμον Anon. ap.Suid. s.v. ἐπανέσχετο. 2. *hold*, χώραν D.S.17.115. II. seemingly intr. (sc. ἑαυτόν), *rest upon*, ἐπὶ ταῖς ἐλπίσιν v.l. in D.19.51; *to be contented with*, τινί Alciphr.1.38; *rely on, rest contented with*, τοῖς βιβλίοις Artem.1.12; cf. ἐπαναπαύομαι. 2. c. dat., *attend to*, *POxy.*1033.6 (iv A.D.). -ήκω, pf. ἐπάνηκα *PAmh.*2.50.5 (ii B.C.):—*to have come back, return*, E.*IA*1628 (anap.), Pl.Com.68 (cj.), Ph.2.117; ὥς τινα D.47.55; πρός τινα Plb.6.58.3; ἐκ νόσου πρὸς εὐδαιμονίαν Paus.3.9.2; εἰς τὸν οἶκον Lxx *Pr.*7.20. -ηλογέω, f.l. in Hdt.1.90 ἐπανηλόγησε πᾶσαν τὴν ἑωυτοῦ διάνοιαν (leg. ἐπαλιλλόγησε from Poll. 2.120, cf. Hdt.1.118). -ήλωμα, ατος, τό, *additional expense*, *PPetr.* 2 p.113 (iii B.C.).

ἐπάνθεμα, ατος, τό, in pl., *additional offerings*, *IG*4.526 (Heraeum).

ἐπανθεμίζω, metaph., *flit* like a bee from flower to flower, S.*Ichn.* 323 (lyr.).

ἐπανθερεών, ῶνος, ὁ, *chin*, dub. (fort. ἀνθερεών) in Gal.18(1).831.

ἐπάνθετα, τά, things *dedicated in addition*, *IG*7.3498.29, al. (Oropus), *Schwyzer* 462 *B* 28 (Tanagra, iii B.C.).

ἐπανθ-έω, *bloom, be in flower*, Theoc.5.131, Lxx *Jb.*14.7. II. metaph., of any thing that *forms on the surface*, ἅλμην ἐπανθέουσαν [τοῖσι ὄρεσι] Hdt.2.12, cf. Str.11.13.2; χνοῦς ὥσπερ μήλοισιν ἐπήνθει Ar.*Nu.*978; τὸ τρυφερὸν.. ἐπὶ τοῖς μήλοις ἐπανθεῖ Id.*Ec.*903; τὴν ἐπανθοῦσαν τρίχα ib.13; also of hair turning grey, κύκνου... πολιώτεραι δὴ αἵδ' ἐπανθοῦσιν τρίχες Id.*V.*1065, cf. X.*Cyn.*4.8. 2. generally, *to be upon the surface*, τρηχύτης ἐπήνθει Hp.*Epid.*7.43; ἐμοὶ... ἐπάνθεεν ἁδύ τι κάλλος Theoc.20.21; ἐπὶ σμικρῷ ἰκτέρῳ ἡ χροιὴ μέζων ἐπανθέει Aret.*SD*1.15. b. abs., *show itself, appear plainly*, τοὐπιχώριον ἐπανθεῖ Ar.*Nu.*1174; ὅπερ... παισὶ καὶ θηρίοις... σύμφυτον ἐπανθεῖ Pl. *Lg.*710a; τῷ Ἰσοκράτει πολλαὶ χάριτες ἐπήνθουν D.H.*Comp.*19; πᾶσιν ἐπανθεῖ... ἡ χάρις Luc.*Im.*9, cf. *Hist.Conscr.*55; τῷ προσώπῳ τὸ θηριῶδες ἐ. Callistr.*Stat.*12; τὰ -οῦντα τῇ αἰσθήσει τῶν ζῴων θελκτήρια ib.7. III. *to be bright*, περίσκοις πορφυροῖς ἐπανθούντων Babr. 118.5. -ημα, ατος, τό, *efflorescence*, [γέλως] ὥσπερ τι ἐ. ὑπάρχων Iamb.*Protr.*21.κς'; *fine flower*, Id.*in Nic.*p.39 P., al.; ἀριθμῶν ἑκάστου ἐπανθήματα *special virtues*, ib.p.118 P. -ησις, εως, ἡ, *flowering, bloom*, Plot.4.3.13 (pl.). -ιάω, poet. for ἐπανθέω, Ep. part. ἐπανθιόωντας ἰούλους A.R.3.519. -ίζω, *deck as with flowers, make bright-coloured*, ἐ. τινὶ ἐρύθημα *give* one a red *tint*, Luc.*Hist. Conscr.*13; ἐλέφαντα ἐ. τῷ χρυσῷ ib.51; *brighten, give lustre to* a dye, *PHolm.*17.9, al.:—Pass., χρώμασιν ἐπηνθισμένος D.S.1.49. 2. metaph., *deck as with flowers, decorate, adorn*, κωκυτοῖς ἐ. παιᾶνα A.*Ch.*150; πολλοῖς ἐ. πόνοισι γενεάν Id.*Th.*949:—Pass., ἀπαγγελία ἐπηνθισμένη ὀνόμασι ποιητικοῖς Philostr.*VS*1.15.4.—The aor. Med. ἐπηνθίσω is prob. corrupt in A.*Ag.*1459 (lyr.). -ισμα, ατος, τό, lit. *efflorescence*: hence ἀφρῶδες ἐ. *coloured froth*, Hp.*Prorrh.*1.21, cf. Aret.*SD*1.11. -ισμός, ὁ, *efflorescence, scum*, πορφύρας Dsc.5.92. II. name for a *vein*, Dionys.ap.Ruf.*Onom.*205.

ἐπανθοπλοκέω, *plait of flowers*, κόρυμβον *AP*12.8 (Strat.).

ἐπανθρᾰκ-ίδες, ων, αἱ, (ἀνθρακίς) *small fish for frying, small fry*, Ar.*Ach.*670, *V.*1127. -ίζω, *broil on the coals*, Cratin.143 (cod. A Ath.). II. *blacken with charcoal*, ὦπας *AP*11.66 (Antiphil.). -όομαι, Pass., *to be broiled on the coals*, Poll.6.55.

ἐπανῐάομαι, *to be annoyed at* a thing, X.Eph.1.15, Poll.5.129.

ἐπαν-ίημι, *let loose at*, σοὶ δ' ἐπὶ τοῦτον ἀνῆκε Il.5.405. II. *let go, give up*, c. acc., ταῦτ' ἐπανέντας D.2.30; *dismiss*, τὸν παρόντ' ἐπανεῖναι φόβον Id.18.177; *remit*, τοῖς νέοις τὰ σκληρότατα τῆς ἀγωγῆς Plu.*Lyc.*22; *release from*, τὰς κύνας ἐ. τῶν πόνων X.*Cyn.*7.1; *relax*, τῆς ὀργῆς Ruf.ap.Orib.6.38.5. 2. *relax*, τὸν δακτύλιον (v. δακτύλιος II. 2) Dsc.*Eup.*2.56: more freq. intr., *relax, leave off*, τέμνων οὐκ ἐπανῆκεν πρὶν... Pl.*Phdr.*266a: abs., of spasms, σιηγῶν ἐπανῆκε Hp. *Epid.*3.17.β'; μὴ ἐπανιείς without *slackening speed*, X.*Cyn.*4.5; ἐπανῆκεν ὁ σῖτος corn *became easier* in price, D.32.25; ἐπανέντα *lukewarm*, opp. θερμά, Sosip.1.53. -ίπτᾰμαι, = ἐπαναπέτομαι, Man. 5.220. -ῐσόω, *make equal, balance evenly*, τινας πρὸς ἀλλήλους Th.8.57; ἐ. τὰ μέτρα *IG*2^2.1013.15; τοῖς ἀδελφοῖς τὸ διαφέρον Just. *Nov.*92.1 *Intr.*; τὰς τῆς κράσεως πλεονεξίας Ruf.(?)ap.Orib.*inc.*4.2; τὸ ἐλαττούμενον Polyaen.7.16.2; *reduce*, εἰς τὸ μέτριον τὴν ὑπερβολήν Arist.*Resp.*478^{a}3; τἆλλα οὕτως ἐπανισῶν ἔνεμε the others likewise he *made equal* to one another, distributing to them their faculties, Pl.*Prt.*321a:—Pass., *to be made equal*, τινί Id.*Lg.*745d. -ίστημι, *set up again*, τὰ τείχη ib.778d. 2. *make to rise against*, ἄνδρας ἐκ χαράδρας ἐ. τινί Plu.*Sert.*13; *raise in revolt against*, Ἰβηρίαν Ῥωμαίοις App.*Hisp.*101. 3. *cause to arise*, Plu.2.654f. II. Pass., with fut. Med. (Hdt.3.62, 1.89), aor. 2 and pf. Act., *stand up after* another or *at* his *word*, once in Hom., αἱ δ' ἐπανέστησαν Il.2.85. b. *rise from bed, rise*, Ar.*Pl.*539; ἐπὶ τοῦ καταστρώματος X.*HG*1.4.18; *rise* to speak, Id.*Smp.*4.2, D.19.46; of buildings, in pf., *to be raised* or *built*, ἣν τοῦτ' ἐπανεστήκῃ Ar.*Av.*554: c. gen., *rise above*, ἱερῷ -στηκότι τῆς ἀγορᾶς D.H.2.50; ταῖς -ισταμέναις (ἐκ add. cod. unus) τῶν ὑδάτων πομφόλυξιν Dsc.5.75. 2. *rise up against, rise in insurrection against*, τινί Hdt.1.89, 130, 3.62; τῷ δήμῳ Th.1.115, etc.; τοῖς πράγμασι Din.1.19: abs., *rise in insurrection*, opp. ἀφίσταμαι, Th.3.39, al.; οἱ ἐπανεστεῶτες *the insurgents*, Hdt.3.63: c. inf., ἐάν τις τυραννεῖν ἐπαναστῇ if any one *aim at* tyranny, Lex ap.And.1.97; in mal. part., ἐ. ἀλλήλοις πώγωνας ἔχουσι Theopomp.Hist.217c; παρθένοις Ael.*Ep.*15. 3. Medic., of tumours, etc., *rise, swell*, Hp.*Prorrh.* 1.165; [ὦτα] ἐπανεστηκότα *projecting, prominent*, Arist.*PA*691^{a}13; λόφος αὐτῶν τῶν πτερῶν ἐ. crest *which sticks up* and is composed of feathers, Id.*HA*504^{b}10. -ίσωσις [ῐσ], εως, ἡ, *making equal, equalizing*, Ph.2.479. -ῑτάω, pf. part. ἐπανιτακώρ, = ἐπανεληλυθώς, *Schwyzer* 425.8 (Elis). -ῑτέον, *one must return* to a point, Pl.*R.*532d, Arist.*PA*682^{a}31, etc. -οδευτέον, gloss on ἐπανιτέον, Hsch. -οδος, ἡ, *rising up*, ἐκ τοῦ καταγείου εἰς τὸν ἥλιον Pl.*R.* 532b, cf. 521c; of phlegm from the lungs, Hp.*Acut.*17. II. *return*, Lxx *Si.*17.24, etc.; εἰς τὴν Ἑλλάδα Plu.*Tim.*38; ὥς ἐπί τινα νύσσαν Iamb.*in Nic.*p.76 P.; *to one's country*, ταχυτέραν ποιήσασθαι τὴν ἐ. E.*Ep.*2.2, cf. Hdn.8.7.7: metaph., *ascent* of the soul, Dam.*Pr.*75; simply, *journey*, *PLips.*45.17 (iv A.D.). 2. in speaking, *recapitulation*, Pl.*Phdr.*267d, Arist.*Rh.*1414^{b}2. b. *fuller statement* of a point, Alex.*Fig.*2.7, Tib.*Fig.*45, etc. -οίγω, *open*, τὸ ἡρῷον *CIG*4259 (Pinara): in aor. Med., *cause to be opened*, *Epigr.Gr.*340. -οιδέω, *swell up, rise on the surface*, Hp.*Nat.Mul.* 2, Arist.*HA*531^{b}3:—Pass., -οιδίσκομαι in same sense, Hp.*VC* 13. -οίκτης, ου, ὁ, = sq., Arg.Man.post Max.p.102 L., *EM*459.5. -οίκτωρ, ορος, ὁ, *one who bursts open*, θυρέτρων Man.1.310. -οιξις, εως, ἡ, *breaking into, forcible entry*, τοῦ ταμιείου *PHib.*1.31.12, 23 (iii B.C.). -οιστέον, (ἐπαναφέρω) *one must refer*, Plb.1.37.3.

ἐπανορθ-όω, impf. with double augm., ἐπηνώρθουν Isoc.12.200: aor. ἐπηνώρθωσα Lys.1.70: pf. ἐπηνώρθωκα Iamb.*Comm.Math.*23:—Med., fut. ἐπανορθώσομαι Pl.*La.*200b, D.15.34 (but in pass. sense, D.C.73.1): impf. ἐπηνωρθούμην Pl.*Tht.*143a: aor. ἐπηνωρθωσάμην Isoc.4.165, D.7.18:—Pass., fut. ἐπανορθωθήσομαι Aeschin.3.177: aor. ἐπηνωρθώθην D.9.76: pf. ἐπηνώρθωμαι Id.18.311:—*set up again, restore*, τὴν δύναμιν... καίπερ πεπτωκυῖαν Th.7.77; τὰ δυστυχηθέντα Lys. l. c.; τὴν πολιτείαν Isoc.7.15; τὸ ἱππικόν Din.1.96, etc. 2. *correct, amend, revise*, νόμους Pl.*Lg.*769e; τὰς διαθήκας Is.1.18; τὸ ἁμάρτημα Pl.*Prt.*340d; ἐ. τινά *correct* one, *teach* him *better*, Ar.*Lys.* 528, cf. Isoc.1.3, Iamb. l. c.; εἰς τὸ ψήφισμα τὸ πρότερον *IG*1^2.108.49:—Med. in proper sense, *correct oneself*, Pl.*R.*361a: but more freq. trans., *correct, amend*, Id.*Euthphr.*9d, *Tht.*143a, Isoc.4.165, D. 1.11, etc. 3. *supply*, χρείας Jul.*Ep.*89b. -ωμα, ατος, τό, *correction*, Pl.*Prt.*340a, d, *Tht.*183a, D.25.16, Arist.*EN*1135^{a}13, 1137^{b}12. -ωσις, εως, ἡ, *setting right, correcting*, τᾶς ψυχᾶς Ti.Locr. 104b; κόλασις εἰς -σιν φέρουσα Jul.*Or.*2.80c; ἐδεσμάτων Diocl.*Fr.* 138; *revision*, νόμων Lexap.D.24.22; ἐ. ἔχειν to be capable of *improvement*, opp. ἀνίατον εἶναι, Arist.*EN*1165^{b}18; of circumstances, *amendment*, Plb.1.66.12, 1.11.2, etc. -ωτέος, α, ον, *to be corrected*, Pl.*Lg.*809b. II. ἐπανορθωτέον *one must correct*, Plu.2.24a, Gal.6.226. -ωτής, οῦ, ὁ, *corrector, restorer*, τοῦ κάμνοντος D.H.8.67; of writings, Gal.7.894; τῶν τρόπων, = Lat. *corrector morum*, D.C.54.30; also, = Lat. *corrector civitatis*, *IG*4.1417 (Epid.), 5(1).541 (Sparta), 7.91 (Megara). -ωτικός, ή, όν, *corrective, restorative*, τῶν ἠθῶν Str.1.2.3; τὸ ἐ. δίκαιον Arist.*EN*1132^{a}18; τέχνη Gal. 1.303. Adv. -κῶς Sch.D.3.33.

ἐπαντέλλω, poet. and Ion. for ἐπανατέλλω.

ἐπάντης, ες, rare form for ἀνάντης, *steep*, Th.7.79.

ἐπαντιάζω, *to be present*, prob. in *h.Ap.*152.

ἐπαντίθετος, ον, *reversed*, ἐπείλησις Sor.*Fasc.*12.515 C.

ἐπαντλ-αῖος, ον, = ἱμαῖος, Hsch. s. h. v. (ἐπανταῖος cod.). -έω, *pump over* or *upon, pour over*, Pl.*Phd.*112c (Pass., ib.d.); ἐπί τι Id. *Phdr.*253a; λόγους τινὶ ἐ. *pour a flood* of words *over*, E.*Fr.*899.4, cf. Ael.*NA*6.51; κακά Diph.107; *irrigate*, ἐ. καὶ ἄρδειν τὰ φυτά Plu. 2.688e: metaph., μυριάδας χιλιάδας τῇ Σμύρνῃ Philostr.*VS*1.25.2; ἑσμὸν ἡδονῶν Id.*VA*6.11: abs., Luc.*Tim.*18:—Pass., *to be irrigated*, D.S.1.33, *Stud.Pal.*17 p.13 (ii A.D.), etc.; νάμασι λόγων Ph.2.345; *overflowed*, φροντίσιν ἐπηντλημένος Plu.2.107a. -ημα, ατος, τό, *fomentation*, γαγγραίνης Dsc.2.109. -ησις, εως, ἡ, *pouring over*, as of water over a person bathing, Hp.*Acut.*65 (pl.), D.S.2.10 (v.l. ὑπ-, pl.). 2. *pumping*, ὑδάτων *Stud.Pal.*10.259.15 (v. A.D.). -ησμός, ὁ, = foreg., *PLond.ined.*2179 (iii A.D.). -ητέον, *one must douche*, Dem.Ophth.ap.Aët.7.75. -ητός, ή, όν, *artificially irrigated*, *PRev. Laws* 24.8 (iii B.C.), *PCair.Zen.*176.230 (iii B.C.).

ἐπᾰνύω, fut. -ύσω [ῠ], *complete, accomplish*, οὐδέ ποτέ σφιν νίκη ἐπηνύσθη, ἀλλ' ἄκριτον εἶχον ἄεθλον Hes.*Sc.*311:—Med., *procure*, οἵαν .. ἐπί μοι μελέῳ χάριν ἠνύσω codd. in S.*Tr.*995 (lyr.); *carry into effect*, Ph.1.77.

ἐπάνω [ᾰ], Adv., (ἄνω) *above, on the upper side* or *part*, Ar.*Lys.* 773, Pl.*R.*514b, etc.; with Art., ὁ ἐ. πύργος the *upper* tower, Hdt. 3.54, etc. 2. as Prep., c. gen., Id.1.179 (in tmesi, ἐπὶ τοῦ σήματος ἄνω ib.93), Pl.*Phd.*109d; ἐ. τῆς χώρας *IG*12(5).872.32 (Tenos, iii B.C.); ἐ. γεγονότες κακίας having risen *superior to*.., Plu.2.1063c; γίγνεται ἐ. τῆς πληγῆς J.*BJ*1.4.2; ἐ. χρημάτων εἶναι D.L.6.28 (but ἐ. χρημάτων τεταγμένος set *over*, Vett.Val.48.5). 3. *before, in front of*, c. gen., Lxx *Ge.*18.2, 2 *Ki.*24.20; *in the presence of*, τινός *POxy.* 903.14, 20 (iv A.D.). II. *above*, in a book, ἐν τοῖς ἐ. εἴρηται X.*An.* 6.3.1 (interpol.), cf. Arist.*Metaph.*1012^{b}6; τὰ ἐ. λεχθέντα Str.2.5.8; καθὼς ἐ. γέγραπται *IG*9(1).694.131 (Corc.), cf. *CIG*3059.3 (Teos), Polystr.p.22 W. III. of Time, ἐν τοῖς ἐ. χρόνοις in *former* times, D.S.16.42, 18.49; ἐν τῷ ἐ. μηνί *OGI*764.40 (Pergam.). IV. of Relationship, πατέρες καὶ τούτων ἐ. D.60.7; οἱ ἐ. πρόγονοι J.*Ap.*1.7; ἐ. ὄντες Εὐρωπαῖοι citizens of Europus *in unbroken descent*, Cumont *Fouilles de Doura-Europos* p.300. V. in Logic, τὸ ἐ. γένος the genus or species *above*, opp. τὰ ὑποκάτω, Arist.*Top.*122^{a}4, 143^{a}21; τὰ ἐ. τοῦ γένους ib.122^{a}34. VI. of Number, *above, more*, ἀπὸ εἰκοσαετοῦς καὶ ἐ. Lxx *Ex.*30.14, al.; *above, more than*, ἐ. τριακοσίων δηναρίων *Ev.Marc.*14.5; ὤφθη ἐ. πεντακοσίοις 1 *Ep.Cor.*15.6.

ἐπάνωθεν or **-ωθε,** Adv. *above, on top,* κοῦφα σοι χθὼν ἐπάνωθε πέσοι E.*Alc.*463: c. gen., Pl.*Ti.*45a, Luc.*Epigr.*39. 2. *up country, inland,* Th.2.99. II. of Time, *of old,* χαῶν τῶν ἐ. prob. in Theoc.7.5; τῶν ἐπάνωθε μουσοποιῶν Id.*Ep.*22.3; ἐν τοῖς ἐ. in *former times, CPR*188.19 (ii A.D.).

ἐπαξῐ-έραστος, ον, *amiable,* Ph.2.166. **-ος,** α, ον, *worthy, deserving* of.., πάντων Pi.*N.*7.89; τῆς δίκης ἐπάξια A.*Eu.*272 (lyr.), cf. *Ch.*95; θαυμάτων ἐπάξια E.*Ba.*716; σπουδῆς οὐ..πολλῆς τινος ἐ. Pl. *Sph.*218e: c. inf., ἐ. [εἶ] κατοικτίσαι *deserving* of pity, S.*OC*461: abs., ἐ. φύσει καὶ τροφῇ *worthy, qualified* by birth and breeding, Pl. *Lg.*961b. 2. *deserved,* στεφάνωμα Pi.*I.*4(3).44; *worthy, meet,* ἄλγος A.*Th.*865 (lyr.); γάμοι S.*El.*971, etc.; κυρεῖν τῶν ἐπαξίων meet with *one's deserts,* A.*Pr.*70. Adv. -ίως S.*OT*133, Iamb.*Myst.*3.20. 3. *worth mentioning, notable,* Hdt.2.79, 7.96 (sed v. ἀπαξοί); *worth while* to do a thing, Hp.*Art.*72. **-όω,** *think right, deem it right,* c. inf., τοῦτ' ἐπηξίωσα δρᾶν S.*Ph.*803, cf. *El.*1274 (lyr.). 2. *expect, believe,* c. acc. et inf., τὰ δ' ἄλλα.. ἐπαξιῶ σε.. ἐξειδέναι ib.658; but ὁ γὰρ ξένος σε.. ἐπαξιοῖ δικαίαν χάριν παρασχεῖν *deems* thee *worthy of honour,* so as to render thee a due return, Id.*OC*1497 (lyr.). **-ωσις,** εως, ἡ, *valuing, estimation,* D.H.19.15 (v.l. ἀπ-).

ἐπαξον-έω, (ἄξων I) *place on axles,* Orph.*Fr.*49.39. 2. (ἄξων II) *enroll in tablets, register,* Lxx *Nu.*1.18. **-ιος,** ον, (ἄξων I) *upon an axle,* δίφρῳ Theoc.25.249 (v.l. ἐν ἀξ-).

ἐπαοιδ-έω, = ἐπᾴδω, Steph. *in Hp.*2.458 D. **-ή,** ἡ, Ion. and poet. for ἐπῳδή (q.v.). **-ία,** ἡ, later form of foreg., Ps.-Luc.*Philopatr.* 9, Hsch. **-ός,** ὁ, = ἐπῳδός, Lxx *Ex.*7.11, 22, al., Ph.1.449 (pl.), Arr. *Epict.*3.24.10, Man.5.183 (pl.). Adv. -ῶς *by way of a charm,* Steph. *in Hp.*2.458 D.

ἐπᾰπειλέω, *hold out as a threat to* one, λῆγ' ἔριδος, τὴν πρῶτον ἐπηπείλησ' Ἀχιλῆϊ Il.1.319; ἀπειλάων τὰς -ησε Od.13.127, cf. Hdt.6.32; δεῖν' ἐ. ἔπη S.*Aj.*312, etc. 2. c. dat. only, *threaten,* ἐπαπειλήσας Ἑλένῳ Il.13.582. 3. c. fut. inf., *threaten* to do, Hdt.1.189, S.*El.* 779, Ar.*Av.*630: but the inf. is freq. omitted, ὥς ποτ' ἐπηπείλησεν as he *threatened,* Il.14.45, cf. S.*Ant.*752, Antim.24. 4. ἐ. εἰ μή.. X. *An.*6.2.7. 5. Pass., πρὸς σοῦ τὰ δείν'.. ἐπηπειλημένοι *threatened,* S.*Ant.*408.

ἐπαπερείδομαι, Pass., *lean upon,* δυσίν Posidon.26 J.:—Med., τὸν ἀγῶνα τοῦ λόγου ἐ. τινί *rest* the weight of the argument *on..,* J.*BJ* 2.2.5. II. *support,* τοῖς βάρεσι τῶν μελλόντων Ph.Byz.*Mir.*6.2.

ἐπαπηχεῖαι (sic)· ἀπηχῆσαι, καὶ ἐπὶ πολὺ ἐξικέσθαι, ἔνιοι δὲ καὶ ἐπὶ ἀπεχθείᾳ καὶ ἔχθρᾳ ἀπέδοσαν, *AB*253.

ἐπαπογᾰμέω, *marry again,* dub. in *Cat.Cod.Astr.*8(3).188.

ἐπαπο-δίδωμι, *make good,* τοῦ πλείονος χρόνου *GDI*1832.24 (Delph.). **-δρόμιον·** ἡ ἱέρεια παρὰ Κρησίν, Hsch. **-δύω,** *strip* one *for combat against* another, *set* him *up as a rival to,* τινά τινι Plu. 2.788d:—Med., *strip and set to work at* a thing, τῷ πράγματι Ar.*Lys.* 615; πολυοινίᾳ Ph.1.360; *set upon, attack,* τοῖς νενικηκόσιν Plu.*Marc.* 3. **-θνήσκω,** *die after* another, τινί Pl.*Smp.*180a, 208d, J.*BJ*5.12. 3; ἐ. λόγοις *die while* yet speaking, Id.*AJ*13.11.3: abs., Plu.*Aem.*35.

ἐπαποικίζω, *colonize anew,* Καρχηδόνα D.C.52.43.

ἐπαπο-κτείνω, *kill besides,* D.C.49.23:—also **-κτιννύω,** Aristid. *Or.*25(43).23. **-λαύω,** *revel in,* ἡδοναῖς D.S.37.3: c. gen., ἡλίου σελασμάτων Tz.*H.*9.315; *profit by,* τινός Anon. *in Rh.*111.28.

ἐπαπόλλῡμι or **-ύω,** *kill in addition,* Ael.*NA*10.48, Luc.*Merc.Cond.* 42:—Med., *die after,* τινί D.C.60.34: abs., Aristid.*Or.*25(43).22.

ἐπαπο-λογέομαι, = ἀπολογέομαι, v.l. in Plu.*Marc.*27. **-λογος,** ον, in Arc. form ἐπαπύ-, *requiring defence, SIG*306.34 (iv B.C.).

ἐπαπολύω, *discharge against,* Hsch. s.v. ἐπαφῆκεν.

ἐπαπονίνᾰμαι, Pass., *enjoy besides,* Ph.1.327.

ἐπαποπνίγω [ῑ], *choke besides*:—Pass., aor. 2 ἐπαποπνῐγείης *may you be choked besides,* Ar.*Eq.*940 (Elmsl. for ἀποπν-).

ἐπαπορ-έω, *raise a new doubt* or *question,* πότερον... Plb.6.3.6; δύο ταῦτα, εἰ.., τί.. Ph.2.216, cf. S.E.*P.*1.225, Ph.Byz.*Mir.*4.2, Procl. *in Prm.*p.529 S.:—Pass., ἐπαπορεῖταί τι *a new doubt is raised,* Thphr. *Vert.*9; τὰ ἐπαπορηθέντα Plb.6.5.3. II. c. dat., *criticize,* Diog. Oen.18. **-ησις,** εως, ἡ, = ἀπορία, Hsch. **-ητικός,** ή, όν, *dubitative*: -κόν, τό, a kind of rhetorical question, *Stoic.*2.61, cf. D.L. 7.68; σύνδεσμος Gal.16.722. Adv. -κῶς Phlp. *in APo.*359.15, Eust. 1114.30.

ἐπαπο-στέλλω, *send after,* γράμματα ἐπαπεστάλη αὐτοῖς Plb.31.2. 14; ἐ. στρατηγὸν ἕτερον *send* another general *after him* (to supersede him), Id.6.15.6. II. *send to attack,* Id.32.5.11; τινάς τισι Id.2.8. 12; συκοφάντην ἐπί τινα D.S.12.24, cf. Lxx *Jb.*20.23. **-στολή,** ἡ, *sending against,* Sm.*Ps.*77(78).49; δαιμόνων Heph.Astr.1. 23. **-σφάζω,** aor. 2 Pass. -εσφάγην [ᾰ], *slay afterwards,* D.C. 57.2. **-τίνω,** *repay,* Thd.*Is.*59.18.

ἐπάπτω, Ion. for ἐφάπτω.

ἐπαρά, Ion. **ἐπαρή,** ἡ, *solemn curse, imprecation,* θεοὶ δ' ἐτέλειον ἐπαράς Il.9.456, cf. Thebaïs *Fr.*2.7; ἐπαρὴν ποιῆσαι *SIG*38.30 (Teos); ἐπαρὰς ἐποιήσαντο ib.167.28 (Mylasa). [ἐπᾱρ- in Hom.]

ἐπαράμενοι· οἱ παρὰ μοῖραν ἀπολλύμενοι, Hsch.

ἐπᾰράομαι, Cret. part. ἐπαριόμενον *Leg.Gort.*, Cyren. ἐπαρεώμενοι *Abh.Berl.Akad.* (v. infr.):—*imprecate curses upon,* Πέρσῃσι πολλὰ ἐπαρησάμενος Hdt.3.75; ἐ. ἐξώλειαν (q.v.) ἑαυτῷ *IG*1².10.15, Antipho 5.11, Lys.12.10; τῶν ἱερῶν *by* the temples, Isoc.4.156. 2. c. dat. only, *curse solemnly,* Pl.*Lg.*931b, Jul.*Or.*2.50b, *Leg.Gort.*2.40, etc. 3. c. acc. rei only, τίνα.. τόνδ' ἐπηράσω λόγον; what *imprecation* is this *that thou didst utter?* S.*El.*388; τί ταῦτ' ἐπήραμαι; D.18.142: c. acc. et inf., *Abh.Berl.Akad.*1925(5).23 (Cyrene). 4. with κατά τινος, *Schwyzer*688 *C*7 (Chios, v B.C.). 5. c. acc. pers., Pl.*Lg.*684d. 6. c. fut. inf., *swear, vow,* ἐ. τάδε.., τούτῳ ξυναμυνεῖν E.*IA*60; *vow in addition,* βοῦν προσάξειν, εἰ.. Babr.23.7.

ἐπᾰρᾰρίσκω, aor. 1 -ῆρσα: aor. 2 -ήρᾰρον:—*fit to* or *upon, fasten,* θύρας σταθμοῖσιν ἐπῆρσεν *on* or *to* the posts, Il.14.167; ἐπὶ δὲ ζυγὸν ἤραρεν ἀμφοῖν *h.Merc.*50. II. intr. in Ion. pf. ἐπάρηρα [ᾰρ], plpf. ἐπᾰρήρειν:—*fit tight* or *exactly,* μία δὲ κληῒς ἐπαρήρει a cross-bolt *was fitted therein,* Il.12.456; part. ἐπαρηρώς, υῖα, ός, *close-fitting, well fixed,* εὖ ἐπαρηρὼς ποσσίν *firm on* his feet, Arat.83: also ἐπάρμενος, η, ον, Ep. aor. part. Pass., *well-fitted, prepared, ready,* βίον, ὅπλα, Hes. *Op.*601, 627:—also in form ἐφάρμ-, *suited,* c. dat., Nonn.*D.*12.35.

ἐπαράσαι· κουφίσαι, ἐπαράσασθαι, Hsch.

ἐπᾰράσιμος [ρᾱ], ον, *abominable,* Ps.-Phoc.18.

ἐπᾰράσσω, Att. -ττω, *dash* or *clap to,* τὴν θύραν Pl.*Prt.*314d, cf. Plu.*Art.*29; τὸν πῆχυν τῷ αὐχένι ὥσπερ μοχλόν Hld.10.31; ναρθήκια κατὰ τῶν ἰσχνῶν μορίων ἐ. *strike* rods *against* the thin parts, Gal.10. 998.

ἐπάρᾱτος [ᾰρ], ον, (ἐπαράομαι) *accursed, laid under a curse,* ἐ. ποιεῖσθαι Th.8.97; ὃ ἐπάρατον ἦν μὴ οἰκεῖν which it was *accursed* to inhabit, Id.2.17; τῷ δὲ ἐπάρατον τύχην [γενέσθαι] Pl.*Lg.*877a; of persons, Arist.(?)*Fr.*148, *Ev.Jo.*7.49, J.*AJ*6.6.3: Sup., γενεά Ph.1. 516; used in imprecations on those who violated graves, *CIG*2824 (Aphrodisias), etc.

ἐπάργεμος, ον, *having a film over the eye,* Arist.*HA*609^{b}16, 620^a 1. II. metaph., *dim, obscure,* σήματα, θέσφατα, λόγοι, A.*Pr.*499, *Ag.*1113, *Ch.*665.

ἐπάργματα, τά, = ἀπαρχαί, *IG*12(3).436.14 (Thera).

ἐπαργῠρ-όομαι, *to be overlaid with silver, IG*2².1485.48: metaph., of costly dinners, μὴ πόλλ' ἄγαν.. μηδ' ἐπηργυρωμένα Mnesim.3. 2. **-ος,** ον, *overlaid with silver,* κλῖναι Hdt.1.50, 9.80, cf. *IG*1². 276, *BMus.Inscr.*4.481*.472; πανοπλίαι Onos.1.20.

ἐπάρδ-ευσις, εως, ἡ, *watering*: hence, *shower,* of rain, Epicur.*Ep.* 2p.44 U.: metaph., in pl., *influx,* ib.p.38 U. 2. *irrigation, POxy.* 1631.14 (iii A.D.), al. **-ευτής,** οῦ, ὁ, *irrigator, PTeb.*120.137 (i B.C.), al. **-εύω,** = -ω, Nonn.*D.*11.166; γῇ ἐ. τοῖς φυτοῖς τροφήν Gal.4.625. **-ια,** τά, *irrigated land, PAmh.*2.36.11 (ii B.C.). **-ω,** *irrigate,* Arr.*An.*4.6.5: metaph., ἐ. ἀρεταῖς τὴν ψυχήν Luc.*Am.*45, cf. Lxx 4*Ma.*1.29, Plot.6.7.33; ὁ δικαστὴς τὰ δίκαια ἐ. τοῖς ἐντευξομένοις Ph.2.345; Ἀττικὰ ἐ. τὰ νάματα [τῇ ψυχῇ] Him.*Ecl.*32.6:—Pass., J.*BJ*4.8.3; of the body by nourishment, Ti.Locr.102b.

ἐπᾰρέσκομαι, *to be satisfied,* ὡς.. Eustr. *in EN*270.16: aor. Med., ἐπηρέσσατο· εὐαρέστους ἐποίησεν, Hsch.

ἐπᾰρ-ήγω, *come to aid, help,* τινί Il.23.783, Od.13.391, E.*El.*1350 (anap.), Ar.*V.*402: abs., νῦν ἐπάρηξον A.*Ch.*725 (anap.); οὐπαρήξων S.*El.*1197; also in Prose, X.*Cyr.*6.4.18, Lxx 2*Ma.*13.17. **-ηγών,** όνος, ὁ, ἡ, *helper,* A.R.1.1039, *Milet.*1(7).205*a* (pl., ii A.D.): c. gen., ἄθλων, νίκης, Orph.*A.*348, *L.*677. **-ηξις,** εως, ἡ, *help, aid,* Eust. 52.38.

ἐπάρην [ᾰ], v. πείρω.

ἐπᾰρήρει, ἐπᾰρηρώς, v. ἐπαραρίσκω.

ἐπᾰριθμέω, *count in addition,* Paus.10.5.8; ἐ. ταῖς ἡμέραις τὰς πόλεις *count* the cities by the days, i.e. visit a city a day, Aristid.*Or.* 26(14).93.

ἐπάρισμα· ἀφανῆ, ἄσημα, Hsch. (fort. ἐπάργεμα).

ἐπᾰριστερ-εύομαι, *to be awkward, clumsy,* Hsch. s.v. σκανεύεσθαι. **-ος,** ον, *towards the left, on the left hand,* τὰ ἐπαρίστερα (nisi scrib. ἐπ' ἀρ-) Hdt.2.36, 93, 4.191; but ἐπὶ τὰ ἀριστερά Id.2.36. 2. *written from right to left, Tab.Defix.*67*a*8 (iii B.C.). II. *left-handed,* D.C.72. 19: usu. metaph., '*gauche*', Ephipp.23; ἐ. ἔμαθες γράμματα *at the wrong end,* Theognet.1.7; βουλεύματα D.S.8*Fr.*5; ἐ. Κάτωνες *awkward* imitators of Cato, Plu.*Cat.Ma.*19. Adv. -ρως, λαμβάνειν τι Men.325.2; τὴν τύχην δεξιὰν παρισταμένην ἐ. λαμβάνειν Plu.2. 467c. **-ότης,** ητος, ἡ, *awkwardness,* Arist.*VV*1251^{a}2.

Ἐπάριτοι, οἱ, the soldiers of the Arcadian Federation (371 B.C.), X.*HG*7.4.33–6, Ephor.215 J., Androt.54. (Arc. ἐπᾱριτοι 'picked', 'selected' (= ἐπίλεκτοι, D.S.15.62), cf. pr. nn. Ἐπήριτος, Πεδάριτος: fr. root of ἀριθμός.) (Ἐπαρῖται is a misquotation of Ephor. l.c. by St.Byz., Ἐπαρόητοι f.l. in Hsch.)

ἐπάρκ-εια, ἡ, *help, support,* Plb.1.48.5, al.: pl., αἱ τῶν συμμάχων ἐ. Id.6.52.5; ἐ. καὶ χορηγίαι ib.49.7. **-εσις,** εως, ἡ, *aid, succour,* γένους S.*OC*447, cf. E.*Hec.*758. **-έω,** fut. -έσω (v. infr.): Ep. aor. inf. ἐπαρκέσσαι A.R.2.1161, cf. *IG*5(1).730.18:—*to be strong enough for* a thing, in Hom. always of cases of danger or injury: 1. c. acc. rei et dat. pers., *ward off* something from one, οὐδέ τί οἱ τό γ' ἐπήρκεσε λυγρὸν ὄλεθρον Il.2.873; οὔτε τι Τηλέμαχος τό γ' ἐπήρκεσεν Od.17.568; οὐδὲν γὰρ αὐτῷ ταῦτ' ἐπαρκέσει τὸ μὴ οὐ πεσεῖν *prohibebit quominus..,* A.*Pr.*918. 2. c. acc. rei, *ward off, prevent,* ἐπαρκέσσαι κακότητα A.R.2.1161; σέ τοι μόνον δέδορκα πημονάν (Reiske for ποιμένων) ἐ. S.*Aj.*360 (lyr.). 3. c. dat. pers. only, *help, assist,* Thgn.871, Hdt.1.91, Lys.13.93, 1*Ep.Ti.*5.10, etc.: rarely c. acc. pers., E.*Or.*803 (troch.): abs., τίς ἄρ' ἐπαρκέσει; who *will aid?* A. *Th.*91 (anap.), cf. S.*OC*777. II. *supply, furnish,* ἄκος δ' οὐδὲν ἐπήρκεσαν, τὸ μὴ πόλιν.. παθεῖν A.*Ag.*1170 (lyr.); ἐ. τινί τι Pl.*Prt.* 321a, cf. Ar.*Pl.*830, Lxx 1*Ma.*11.35, etc.; also ἐ. τινὶ τῶν ἑαυτοῦ *impart* to him *a share of..,* X.*Mem.*1.2.60: c. dat. rei, *supply with,* πέπλοις E.*Cyc.*301. III. abs., *to be sufficient, enough,* ὅσσον ἐπαρκεῖ Sol.5.1 (v.l. ἀπαρκεῖ); ἐπαρκέσει νόμος ὅδ' this law *shall prevail,* S.*Ant.*612 (lyr.). 2. *stand to the credit of,* c. dat., γενεᾷ Pi.*N.*6. 60. **-ής,** ές, *helpful,* κρᾶσις Emp.22.4; of remedies, *effective,* Nic.

*Al.*564. II. *sufficient*, οὐσία ταῖς δαπάναις ἐ. Plu.*Cic.*7, cf. D.P. 1101. Adv. -κῶς *IG*4.491 (Cleonae). -ιος, ον, *sufficient*, Opp. *H.*4.377, *AP*10.76 (Paul. Sil.); [ἀγαθῶν] χρῆσιν ἐπάρκιον ἡμερίοισιν *Inscr.Perg.*324.8. -ούντως, Adv. pres. part., *sufficiently*, S.*El.* 354.

ἔπαρμα, ατος, τό, (ἐπαίρω) *something raised, a swelling*, Hp.*Epid.* 1.1; τῶν ἀγγείων Sor.1.48; τὰ τῶν φολίδων ἐ. Ach.Tat.3.7. II. metaph., *elation, vanity*, ἔ. τύχης Sotad.9.4. b. in good sense, *elevation*, πόσον ἔ. ψυχῇ λαμβάνει Ath.Med.ap.Orib.*inc.*21.21. 2. *height*, Lxx 2*Es.*6.3.

ἐπάρμενος, v. ἐπαραρίσκω.

ἔπαρμον· σῶμα κάθυγρον, Hsch.

ἐπαρνέομαι, *deny*, Phld.*Rh.Supp.*p.13 S.

ἔπαρξις, εως, ἡ, f.l. for ἔπαρσις, Lxx *Za.*12.7.

ἐπαρότης, ου, ὁ, = ἀροτήρ, *PLond.*1.131ʳ262 (i A.D.).

ἐπᾰρούρ-ιον (sc. τέλος), (ἄρουρα) *land-tax*, *Ostr.*332, al. (ii B.C.), *BGU*1422 (ii A.D.). -ος, ον, *attached to the soil* as a serf, βουλοίμην κ' ἐ. ἐὼν θητευέμεν ἄλλῳ Od.11.489.

ἔπαρσις, εως, ἡ, (ἐπαίρω) *rising, swelling*, κοιλίης Hp.*Coac.*85; τῶν μαστῶν Arist.*HA*581ᵃ27; ἐ. ἰονθώδεις *eruptions* accompanying the sprouting of the beard, Thphr.*Sud.*16. 2. *lifting up*, χειρῶν Lxx *Ps.*140(141).2. 3. *devastation*, ib.*La.*3.47; in concrete, *heap of ruins*, ib.4*Ki.*19.25 (pl.). 4. *raising, erection* (?), τοῦ θυρέτρου *IG* 11(2).287 *A* 116, *B* 153 (Delos, iii B.C.). b. αἰδοίων Arist.*HA*572ᵇ 2. 5. *elevation, projection*, of a machine, Hero *Aut.*28.2. II. *elation*, ψυχῆς Zeno *Stoic.*1.51 (pl.), cf. Chrysipp.ib.3.116; ἡδονή, = ἄλογος ἔ. *Stoic.*3.95, al., Andronic.Rhod.p.570 M., cf. Lxx *Za.*12. 7. 2. *elevation* of style, τοῦ λόγου Thom.Mag.p.175 R.

ἐπαρτ-άω, *hang on* or *over*, φόβους τοῖς ἀκροωμένοις Aeschin.1.175, cf. Porph.*Abst.*1.2; τισὶν ὀχλήσεις Polystr.p.30 W.; τιμωρίαν τινί Ael.*VH*7.15:—Med., lit., *hang upon*, τινί τι Orph.*A.*1337:—Pass., *hang over, impend*, τοσοῦτος ἐπήρτηται φόβος D.23.140; ἀπαλλαγὴν τῶν ἐπηρτημένων φόβων Id.18.324; ἀγών τινι -ημένος Hdn.2.3.7; κίνδυνος *IGRom.*4.151 (Cyzicus), *BGU*1027.23 (iv A.D.). II. τὸ ἐπηρτημένον [τοῦ ζυγοῦ] *the elevated part* of the beam, Arist.*Mech.* 850ᵃ23. -είνη· εὐπρεπίνη, Hsch. (fort. ἐπαρτέϊ νηΐ· εὐτρεπεῖ νηΐ). -ηίαν· παρασκευήν, Id. (fort. ἀπαρτίην). -ής, ές, (cf. sq.) *ready-equipped*, ἐπαρτέες εἰσὶν ἑταῖροι Od.8.151, cf. 14.332; νῆες, ἐδωδή, A.R.1.235, 3.299. II. (ἐπαρτάω) *depending*, ἐπαρτέες ἐκ νεφελάων... πηγυλίδες Orph.*Fr.*270.1 (s. v. l.). -ίζω, *get ready*, in Ep. aor. ἐπαρτίσσειεν A.R.1.1210:—Med., c. inf., ib.877. II. intr., *fit in*, ἐς τὸν μυκτῆρα Hp.*Morb.*2.33. -ικός, ή, όν, (ἐπαίρω) *making to rise* or *swell*, τοῦ στομάχου Aret.*CD*1.2. -ύω and -ύνω [ῡν], *fit* or *fix on*, αὐτίκ' ἐπήρτυε πῶμα Od.8.447. II. *prepare*, ἐπὶ γὰρ Ζεὺς ἤρτυε πῆμα Od.3.152; ὄλεθρόν τινι Opp.*C.*2.443:—Med., δεῖπνον ἐπηρτύνοντο they *prepared them* a meal, *h.Cer.*128.

ἐπᾰρ-υστήρ, ῆρος, ὁ, (ἀρύω) *vessel for pouring* oil into a lamp, Lxx *Ex.*25.37(38). -υστρίς, ίδος, ἡ, = foreg., ib.*Nu.*4.9, al. -ύτω [ῠ], *draw* a liquid from one vessel *into* another, metaph. in Med., ἐκ τῶν ἀγαθῶν τοῖς κακοῖς Plu.2.600d:—Act., dub. in D.Chr.12.70.

ἐπαρχ-εία, ἡ, *office of praefectus*, *IG*12(3).336.22 (Thera). II. = ἐπαρχία I, *SIG*683.65 (ii B.C.), *IG*14.951 (i B.C.), etc. -εῖον, τό, = ἐπαρχία I, ἄρξαντι -είου Νουμιδίας *IG*14.911:—also -ειος (sc. χώρα), ἡ, *IPE*1².54 (Olbia), *IG*14.1078*a*, *IGRom.*1.580 (Nicopolis ad Istrum), *Ath.Mitt.*48.113 (ibid.). -έω, *to be an* ἔπαρχος, *CIG*2047 (Philippopolis). -ή, ἡ, = ἀπαρχή, *IG*2².1672.182, 263, 2².1215.13, 7.235. 20 (Oropus), *Delph.*3(2).88. -ία, ἡ, *the government of an* ἔπαρχος, or *the district governed by him*, = Lat. *provincia*, Plb.2.19.2, *SIG*888. 45 (Scaptopara, iii A.D.), Str.3.4.20, 17.3.25 (pl.), D.S.37.10, 38. 8, al., *Act.Ap.*23.34, Plu.*Caes.*4; of Carthage, *empire*, Phleg.*Mir.* 18. II. military '*command*', *force occupying a district*, Ph.*Bel.* 96.49 (pl.). -ικός, ή, όν, *of* or *for an* ἔπαρχος, ἐ. ἐξουσία the office of *praefectus urbi*, D.C.75.14. II. ἐπαρχικοί, οἱ, *provincials*, Plu.*Cic.*36, *IG*2².1121.33 (iv A.D.). -ιώτης, ου, ὁ, *a provincial*, Hadrian.Epist.ap.Justin.M.*Apol.*1.68, Jul.*Ep.*14, *BGU*1024 vi 24 (iv A.D.):—also written -εώτης, Just.*Nov.*128.21, al., *Cod.Just.*1.3. 4. -ος, ον, *commander*, Κιλίκων A.*Pers.*327; νεῶν Id.*Ag.*1227 (Canter for ἄπαρχος); *governor of a country*, Plb.5.46.7. 2. = Lat. *praefectus* (in all senses), Id.11.27.2, Plu.*Flam.*1, etc.; ἔ. τεκτόνων or τεχνιτῶν, *praef. fabrum*, Id.*Cic.*38, *Brut.*51; ἔ. τῆς πόλεως, *praef. urbi*, D.H.4.82, etc.; ἐ. παρεμβολῶν, *praef. castrorum*, *Gloss.*; ἔ. Αἰγύπτου *PFay.*21 (ii A.D.); ἔ. τῆς αὐλῆς, *praef. praetorio*, Plu.*Galb.*2, cf. ib.8, 13; ἔ. Ἑῴας *prefect* of the East, *Epigr.Gr.* 919.4 (Sidyma); ἀπὸ ἐπάρχων, *ex praefecto*, *CIG*2593 (Gortyn, iv A.D.). II. as Adj., ἀρχὴν ἔπαρχον στόλου the office of admiral, *IG*14.873 (Misenum, iii A.D.). -ότης, ητος, ἡ, = ἐπαρχία, Lyd. *Mag.*1.15, al., Just.*Nov.*38*Pr.*3.

ἐπάρχω, *rule over*, χώρας πολλῆς X.*Cyr.*4.6.2; τῶν ὁμόρων Isoc.4. 140; τῶν ἔξωθεν Pl.*Criti.*116e; [νήσων] prob. in Thphr.*HP*9.4.10; *to be governor, commandant of* a place, *Hell.Oxy.*16.6: c. dat., Epigr. ap.Paus.6.19.6: abs., ὁ ἐπάρχων, = ἔπαρχος, Hdn.4.12.1; of consular authority, Plu.*Sull.*8. 2. *rule besides* one's hereditary dominions, X.*Cyr.*1.1.4. II. Med., ἐπάρξασθαι δεπάεσσιν *pour the first drops* before a libation, freq. in Hom.:—οἰνοχόος μὲν ἐπαρξάσθω δεπάεσσιν, ὄφρα σπείσαντες κατακείομεν *let* him *begin by pouring* wine into the cups, Od.18.418, cf. 7.183; κοῦροι.. κρητῆρας ἐπεστέψαντο ποτοῖο, νώμησαν δ' ἄρα πᾶσιν ἐπαρξάμενοι δεπάεσσιν Il.1.471, al. 2. generally, *serve, offer*, νέκταρ τε καὶ ἀμβροσίην χερσὶν ἐπήρξατο *h.Ap.*125; ἐπάρχεσθαι δὲ τοὺς χοροὺς [χορ]είας (dub.) τῷ Διονύσῳ *IG*12(9).192.10 (Eretria, iv B.C.). 3. = ἀπάρχομαι, τῇ ἐπαρχῇ ἣν ἐπάρχονται οἱ δημόται ib. 2².1215.13. 4. *begin*, c. inf., *PTeb.*27.34 (ii B.C.).

ἐπᾰρωγ-ή, ἡ, (ἐπαρήγω) *help, aid*, A.R.1.302; ἐπαρωγὴν ποιεῖσθαί τινι Charond.ap.Stob.4.2.24. II. ἐ. τινος *aid against* a thing, Orac.ap.Luc.*Alex.*28: hence, *opposition*, *IG*14.2012 *A* 5. -ής, ές, *efficacious*, of remedies, Nic.*Al.*110. -ός, ὁ, *helper, aider*, Od.11. 498, E.*Hec.*164 (lyr.), etc.: also fem., A.R.4.196: neut., τὸ ζωὰς ἐπαρωγόν *AP*6.219.21 (Antip., v.l. τὸν).

ἐπασθμαίνω, *breathe hard, pant in working*, Lxx 4*Ma.*6.11; μαντικὸν ἐ. Philostr.Jun.*Im.*5.

ἐπάσιοι, v. ἐπαισοι. **ἔπᾱσις**, ἁ, v. ἔμπᾱσις.

ἐπασκ-έω, *labour* or *toil at, prepare* or *finish carefully*, ἐπήσκηται δέ οἱ αὐλὴ τοίχῳ καὶ θριγκοῖσι Od.17.266. II. *adorn, exalt*, τινὰ τιμαῖς Pi.*N.*9.10, cf. *Fr.*194.4; τινὰ μήδεσι Id.*Parth.*2.71. III. *practise, cultivate*, τέχνην, τὰ ἐς πόλεμον, Hdt.2.166; πεντάεθλον, μουνομαχίην, Id.6.92; τὰ ἄλλα κατὰ ταὐτὰ Σκύθῃσι ἐ. Id.4.17; ἀρετήν Id. 3.82; δι' ἐμπύρων τέχνην E.*Hyps.Fr.*34(60).59; σοφίαν Ar.*Nu.*517; παγκράτιον Aeschin.3.179; μνήμην ἐ. *cultivate* memory, Hdt.2.77; δύναμίν τινος ἐ. *increase* his strength, Aeschin.2.136: abs., *to be in training as an athlete*, Achae.3:—Pass., ταῦτα Ῥωμαίοις ἐκ παλαιοῦ ἐπήσκηται Arr.*An.*5.8.1. 2. *set on* one *against* another, τινὶ τοὺς ἐχθρούς D.C.46.40. 3. *train for* the contest, ἀέθλοισιν... ἐφήβους *IG*3.121.4: also c. inf., τινὰς τάξει χρῆσθαι Arr.*Tact.*16.6. -ημα, ατος, τό, *method of fighting*, ib.22.6 (pl., v.l.). -ητέον, *one must practise*, ib.9.3. -ητής, οῦ, ὁ, *athlete*, Hsch.

ἐπάσκιον, τό, = χώνη (Sicilian), Hsch.

ἔπᾳσμα, ατος, τό, (ἐπᾴδω) *enchantment*, Elias *in Porph.*31.14, Zonar., Tz.*H.*13.262.

ἐπασπαίρω, *pant over* or *at*, μόχθῳ Opp.*H.*5.407.

ἐπασπῐδόομαι, Pass., *take as a shield*, εὐλάβειαν cj. in Ph.1.669 (ἐπασπιδήσεται cod. unicus); cf. ἐνασπιδόομαι.

ἐπασσύτερος [ῠ], α, ον, Ep. Adj. *one upon another, one after another*, mostly in pl., ἐπασσύτεραι κίνυντο φάλαγγες Il.4.427; πάντας ἐπασσυτέρους πέλασε χθονί 8.[277]; σκοποὶ ἷζον αἰὲν ἐπασσύτεροι watchers sat *one after another*, i.e. at short distances, Od.16.366; τριηκοσίας πέτρας πέμπον ἐ. Hes.*Th.*716; ἐ. ποσὶν ἕρπον Nic.*Th.*717: and in sg., κῦμα... ὄρνυτ' ἐπασσύτερον wave *upon* wave, Il.4.423. II. *frequent, repeated*, λυγμοί Nic.*Th.*246: with sg. word, ἐ. οὖρος, perh. *following* breeze or *ever-freshening*, A.R.1.579; and so ἐ. βιότοιο χρησμοσύνη *ever-growing* penury, Id.2.472. (Perh. from ἐπ-αν(α)-σ(ε)υ-.)

ἐπασσυτεροτρῐβής, ές, *following close one upon another*, τὰ χερὸς ὀρέγματα A.*Ch.*426 (lyr.).

ἐπᾳστέον, *one must recite a charm*, Pl.*Chrm.*158c, Plot.5.3.17.

ἐπαστράπτω, *lighten upon*, ἐνίοις ἐπήστραψε δεξιόν Plu.2.594e: metaph., βασίλειον ἐ. τῷ κόλπῳ Lib.*Or.*61.10: abs., *AP*7.49 (Bianor): c. acc. cogn., ἐ. πῦρ *flash* fire, *APl.*4.141 (Phil.); σπινθῆρας Nonn.*D.* 18.74.

ἐπασφᾰλίζω, *shore up*, *PLond.*1.131ʳ44 (i A.D.). 2. *close up* a wound, -ισάμενος ῥαφαῖς Paul.Aeg.6.67.

ἐπασχάλλω, *to be indignant at*, ἐφ' ὕβρει Man.3.86.

ἐπᾰτενίζω, *gaze steadfastly at*, εἴς τι Thphr.*Vert.*9.

ἐπατρεμέω, *remain quiet after* a thing, Hp.*Art.*34.

ἐπάττω, Att. for ἐπαΐσσω.

ἐπαυγάζω, *illumine on the surface*, Max.26. 2. Med., *look at by the light, examine carefully*, ἕκαστον ἀκριβέστερον Ph.2.412; simply, *behold*, *AP*9.58.8 (Antip.): Ep. aor., ἐπηυγάσσασθε ib.12.91 (Polystr.). II. intr., *shine*, Them.*Or.*4.52b; f.l. for ὑπ-, Polyaen. 1.39.1.

ἐπαυδάω, *call to* or *say in addition*, Hsch., Suid.:—Med., *call upon, invoke*, τινά S.*Ph.*395 (lyr.).

ἐπαυλ-έω, *accompany on the flute*, τῇ θυσίᾳ Luc.*Sacr.*12: abs., Id. *Salt.*10. 2. c. acc. cogn., ἐ. τινὶ τὸν ἐνόπλιον Epich.75:—Pass., μέλος ἐπαυλεῖται *is played on the flute*, E.*HF*897 (lyr.). -ημα, ατος, τό, *musical phrase played on the flute*, *EM*757.32.

ἐπαυλ-ία, Ion. -ίη, epith. of Artemis, *IG*12(8).359 (Thasos, v B.C.). -ίζομαι, Dep. with aor. Med., *encamp on the field*, Th. 3.5, 4.134; cf. αὐλίζομαι. 2. *encamp near*, τῇ πόλει Plu.*Sull.* 29. 3. *pass the night*, Hsch. 4. of birds, *roost in*, [αἰγείρῳ] A.R.3.929. -ιον, τό, Dim. of sq. 2, *SIG*344.98 (Teos, iv B.C.), *OGI*765.13 (Priene), Call.*Fr.*131.4, Plb.4.4.1, Plu.2.508d, Alciphr. *Fr.*6.4. II. τὰ ἐπαύλια or ἡ ἐπαυλία (sc. ἡμέρα) *the day after the wedding*, Id.3.49, Poll.3.39, Hsch., Suid.; also, *presents given to the bride*, Poll. l. c. III. ἐπαύλιος· ἡ τῆς αὐλῆς ὁδός, Suid., Zonar. -ις, εως, ἡ, *steading*, Hdt.1.111; οὐκ ἀσφαλὲς λέοντι καὶ προβάτοις ὁμοῦ ποιεῖσθαι τὴν ἔπαυλιν Plb.5.35.13, cf. *IG*14.1284, etc. 2. *farm-building, country house*, D.S.12.43, Plu.*Pomp.*24, Alciphr.*Fr.* 6.1, etc. 3. in military language, *quarters*, ἐ. ποιεῖσθαι encamp, Pl.*Alc.*2.149c; ἐπὶ στρατοπεδείᾳ Plb.16.15.5. 4. *unwalled village*, Lxx *Le.*25.31, al. -ισμα, ατος, τό, gloss on ἔπαυλα, Sch.A.*Pers.* 870. -ισμός, ὁ, *passing the night*, Sch.S.*Ant.*356. -ος, ὁ, (αὐλή) mostly in pl., ἔπαυλοι Od.23.358, A.R.1.800; ἔπαυλα S.*OT* 1138, *OC*669 (lyr.):—*fold* for cattle at night, Od. l. c., S.*OT* l. c. 2. generally, *dwelling, home*, A.*Pers.*870 (lyr.), S.*OC* l. c.

ἐπαυλόσυνος, f.l. for ἀπ-, *AP*6.221.8 (Leon.).

ἐπαυξ-άνω (Pl.*Ti.*19a (Pass.), D.3.33, etc.) or -αύξω (X.*Oec.*7.43 (Pass.), *OGI*90.38 (Rosetta, ii B.C.)): fut. -αυξήσω:—*increase, enlarge*, Emp.17.32; τὴν πατρίδα νικήσαντας ἐπαυξῆσαι Th.7.70, cf. 2.36, D. l. c.; τὰμ βασιλείαν *SIG*629.5 (Delph., ii B.C.); τὸν ἔρανον *IG*12 (1).155 iii 84 (Rhodes); τὴν φιλαγαθίαν ib.12(7).232.6 (Amorgos):—

Pass., *grow, increase*, X. l. c., Pl. l. c., etc. II. intr., *grow, increase*, Aristaenet.1.16. -η, ἡ, = ἐπαύξησις, Pl.*Lg*.815e. -ημα, ατος, τό, = foreg., Dosith.p.381 K., *PMasp*.26*B*8 (pl., vi A.D.). -ής, ές, *increasing, growing*, νόσοι Hp.*Epid*.6.5.15 (but perh. = diseases *of adolescence*, cf. Gal.17(2).288); πάθεα Aret.*SA*2.7. -ησις, εως, ἡ, *increase, increment*, τῶν δικαίων Pl.*Lg*.957d; τῆς φορολογίας *PTeb*. 27.47 (ii B.C.); τῶν μέτρων Plu.*Sol*.15; εἰς τὴν ἐ. τῶν πολιτῶν to their *profit*, Plb.5.88.6. -ω, v. ἐπαυξάνω.

ἐπαύρ-εσις, εως, ἡ, *enjoyment of the fruit* of a thing, *fruition*, μεγάλαι.. ἐπαυρέσιες Hdt.7.158; ταχείας τὰς ἐ. ποιεῖσθαι Th.2.53; ἐ. γίγνεται ἀπό τινος Democr.278. -έω and -ίσκω, ἐπαυρεῖ Hes.*Op*.419, ἐπαυρίσκουσι Thgn.111: aor. ἐπαῦρον Pi.*P*.3.36, subj. ἐπαύρω, ῃς, ῃ (v. infr.), inf. ἐπαυρεῖν, -έμεν, Hom. (v. infr.):—**Med.**, ἐπαυρίσκομαι Il.13.733, Democr.172, Hp.*Nat.Puer*.12, *Morb*.4.39: fut. ἐπαυρήσομαι Il.6.353: 2 sg. aor. 1 ἐπηύρω (ἐπηύρου Elmsl.) A.*Pr*.28, inf. ἐπαύρασθαι Hp.*Jusj*.fin., *Ep*.27, Plb.18.11.7: aor. 2 ἐπηυρόμην E.*Hel*. 469, poet. 2 sg. ἐπαύρεο Pi.*N*.5.49, 3 sg. ἐπηύρετο prob. in Arist.*EN* 1163ᵃ20; Ep. 2 sg. subj. ἐπαύρηαι Il.15.17, -ῃ (cf. II. 3), 3 pl. -ωνται 1.410; inf. ἐπαυρέσθαι E.*IT*529, And.2.2 (v. infr. II):—Pass., aor. ἐπαυρεθέντα· ἐπιβάλλοντα, Hsch. I. Act., *partake of, share*, c. gen. rei, τῶν.. βέλτερόν ἐστιν ἐπαυρέμεν Il.18.302; αὐτὸν .. σε βούλομ' ἐπαυρέμεν (gen. omitted) Od.17.81; πλεῖον νυκτὸς ἐπαυρεῖ *enjoys* a greater *share* of night, of Sirius, Hes.*Op*.419; γειτόνων πολλοὶ ἐπαῦρον many *have had enjoyment of* (i.e. *suffered loss from*) neighbours, Pi.*P*.3.36; τὸ μέγιστον ἐπαυρίσκουσι *have enjoyment* in the highest degree, Thgn.111; *obtain, meet with*, εἴ κε.. κυβερνητῆρος ἐπαύρῃ A.R.2.174. 2. of physical contact, *touch, graze*, esp. of slight wounds, c. acc., παρος χρόα λευκὸν ἐπαυρεῖν (sc. τὰ δοῦρα) Il.11.573; μή τις χρόα χαλκῷ ἐπαύρῃ 13.649: c. gen., λίθου δ' ἀλέασθαι ἐπαυρεῖν take care not *to touch*, 23.340: abs., καὶ εἴ κ' ὀλίγον περ ἐπαύρῃ if the spear *touch* ever so little, 11.391, cf. Nic.*Th*.763. II. Med., *reap the fruits, enjoy the benefit of* a thing, whether good or bad: 1. c. gen., in good sense, τοῦ πολλοὶ ἐπαυρίσκονται Il.13.733; μόχθων ἀμοιβὰν ἐπαύρεο Pi.*N*.5.49; τοῦδ' ἐπαυρέσθαι θέλω E.*IT*529, cf. A.R. 1.677, 4.964; μικροῦ δὲ βιότου ζῶντ' ἐπαυρέσθαι χρεών *Trag.Adesp*. 95.4 (= *Com.Adesp*.1207.4); τῆς ζόης ἐ. Herod.3.2, cf. 7.26; τῆς ἐλευθερίας Plb.18.11.7; οὐδὲ φάους.. πολλὸν ἐπαυράμενον *IG*12(7). 302.5 (Amorgos), cf. *Epigr.Gr*.839 (Lebena): rare in Prose, εἰ.. χρὴ ἀγαθὸν ἐμοῦ ἐπαυρέσθαι And.2.2; ἀποδοτέον.. ὅσον ἐπηύρετο Arist.*EN* 1163ᵃ20; τάχα δ' ἄν τι καὶ τοῦ οὐνόματος ἐπαύροιτο *may have got* his fate from his name, Hdt.7.180; τίν' αἰτίαν σχὼν ἧς ἐπηυρόμην ἐγώ; E. *Hel*.469. b. more freq. in bad, though not ironical, sense, ἵνα πάντες ἐπαύρωνται βασιλῆος that all *may enjoy their* king, i.e. feel what it is to have such a king, Il.1.410; οὐ μὰν οἶδ' εἰ αὖτε κακορραφίης.. ἐπαύρηαι 15.17: c. acc. et gen., τοιαῦτ' ἐπηύρω τοῦ φιλανθρώπου τρόπου such *profit didst* thou *gain from*.., A.*Pr*.28: abs., τῷ καί μιν ἐπαυρήσεσθαι ὀΐω I doubt not he *will feel* the consequences, Il.6.353; ἀπό τινος κακὰ ἐ. Democr.172. 2. ἐ. ἀπό τινος *get nourishment from*.., Hp.*Morb*.4.39. 3. c. acc. rei, *bring upon oneself*, μή πού τι κακὸν καὶ μεῖζον ἐπαύρῃ Od.18.107 (v.l. ἐπαύρῃς, but perh. better taken as 3 sg. aor. Act., lest a greater evil *reach* thee).—Mainly poet. and Ion.

ἐπαυρίζω, (αὔρα) *breathe* or *blow gently*, J.*BJ*1.21.5.

ἔπαυριν· ἀπολέσαι, Hsch. (Leg. ἐπαυρεῖν· ἀπολαῦσαι.)

ἐπαύριον, Adv. *on the morrow*, τῇ ἐ. ἡμέρᾳ *PLille*1.15 (iii B.C.); ἡμέρα ἡ ἐ. Lxx *Nu*.11.32; usu. τῇ ἐ. *on the morrow*, Plb.3.53.6, al., *Ev. Matt*.27.62, al.; εἰς τὴν ἐ. Plb.8.13.6, al. (Sts. written ἐφ–, *PHamb*. 1.27.4 (iii B.C.), *PTeb*.119.17 (ii B.C.).)

ἐπαῦσας, ἐπάϋσον [ῡ], v. ἐπαύω.

ἐπᾰϋτέω [ῡ], *make a noise* or *creak besides*, ἐπὶ δὲ πλῆμναι μέγ' ἀΰτευν Hes.*Sc*.309. II. = ἐπευφημέω, ἐπηΰτησε δὲ λαός Call.*Ap*.102, Q.S.4.262; Βέβρυκες δ' ἐπαΰτεον Theoc.22.91; of horses, Q.S.11. 327: c. acc. cogn., ἐ. βοήν Call.*Dian*.58.

ἐπαυτίκα [ῐ], Adv. *immediately*, Orph.*L*.334.

ἐπαυτομολέω, *pass over*, πρὸς τὸ ἥμερον Ael.*NA*2.11.

ἐπαυτοφάδες· ἐπ' αὐτοφώρῳ, Hsch.

ἐπαυτόφωρος, ον, = αὐτόφωρος, *palpable*, Sch.Il.24.556.

ἐπαυχένιος, ον, (αὐχήν) *on* or *for the neck*, ζυγόν Pi.*P*.2.93; κύναγχα *AP*6.34 (Rhian.).

ἐπαυχέω, aor. -ηύχησα Ar.*Av*.629:—*exult in* or *at*, c. dat. rei, S. *Ant*.483, Ar. l. c. 2. c. acc. et inf., *to be confident that*.., S.*El*.65.

ἐπαυχμέω, *send drought upon*, τυραννίδι Ζεὺς ἐπαυχμήσας S.*Fr*. 524.4.

ἐπαύω, *shout over*, ἐπαῦσας πατρὸς ἔργῳ A.*Ch*.828 codd. (lyr.); in Theoc.23.44 τρὶς ἐπάϋσον [ῡ], ὦ φίλε, κεῖσαι is dub.

ἐπαφαίρ-εσις, εως, ἡ, *a fresh taking away* of blood, Aret.*CA*1.1, Archig.ap.Gal.8.150, Philum.ap.Orib.45.29.1; of a beard, Mart.8. 52. -ετέον, *one must let blood again*, Herod.Med. in *Rh.Mus*.58. 81. -έω, *take away again*, esp. blood, Aret.*CA*2.10, Gal.6.299.

ἐπαφανίζω, *make to disappear besides*, Lysis ap.Iamb.*VP*17.77.

ἐπαφαυαίνομαι, Pass., *to be withered*: hence ἐπαφαυάνθην γελῶν I *was quite spent* with laughing, Ar.*Ra*.1089 (anap.).

ἐπᾰφάω (v. ἀφάω), *touch on the surface, touch lightly*, Hecat.22 J., A.*Pr*.849, *Trag.Adesp*.458.7, Pl.*Cra*.404d:—also in Med., abs., τῷ δακτύλῳ Hp.*Mul*.2.165: c. gen., ἐ. χερσί τινος Mosch.2.50; κιθάρης *AP*5.221.1 (Agath.); μουσικῆς Alciphr.3.12: c. acc., παλάμῃ κρᾶτ' ἐπαφησάμενος *IG*14.2123.

ἐπαφετέον, *one must admit*, [τοὺς κριοὺς] ταῖς θηλείαις *Gp*.18.3.1, cf. *Hippiatr*.14.

ἐπᾰφ-ή, ἡ, (ἐπαφάω) *touch, touching, handling*, A.*Supp*.17, Pl.*Ti*. 46b, al.; σφυγμοῦ Marcellin.*Puls*.114, al.; ἐ. μωσικὰ [τῆς λύρας] Euryph.ap.Stob.4.39.27: pl., ἐπαφαὶ χειρῶν Plu.2.2d. 2. *severe handling, punishment*, ἐ. καὶ νουθεσία ib.46d; esp. of Pythagorean *treatment*, Iamb.*VP*15.64 (pl.), 25.114. 3. *touch, contact*, ἡδεῖα ἐ. *IGRom*.4.503.11 (Pergam.). b. metaph., of *apprehension*, Epicur.*Fr*.250; ἡ τοῦ ἀγαθοῦ εἴτε γνῶσις εἴτε ἐ. Plot.6.7.36, cf. Iamb. *Comm.Math*.8; τοῦ μέλλοντος Id.*Myst*.3.26. 4. Geom., *point of contact*, Euc.*Phaen*.p.68 M., Procl.*Hyp*.2.7; περὶ ἐπαφῶν, on the theory of *tangents*, title of work by Apollonius of Perga, Papp.636. 21, al. II. *the sense of touch*, Pl.*Tht*.186b. III. in phrases such as ἐκτὸς ἱερᾶς νόσου καὶ ἐ. *PLips*.4.20 (iii A.D.), πλὴν ἐ. καὶ ἱ. ν. *POxy*.94.11 (i A.D.), etc., prob. *external claim*, cf. *PStrassb*.79.7 (i B.C.). -ημα, ατος, τό, *a touch*, Diog.*Ep*.10.1 (pl.). -ητός, όν, *capable of being touched*, χερσὶ μὲν οὐδαμῶς ἐ., διανοίᾳ δὲ μόνῃ κρατητός Porph.*Marc*.8.

ἐπαφίημι, *throw at, discharge at*, τὰ παλτὰ X.*Cyr*.4.1.3; κεραμίδα τινί Plu.2.241b; *let loose upon*, πρόβατα *allow* them *to graze*, Thphr. *HP*8.7.4, cf. *BGU*1251.11 (iii/ii B.C.), etc.; τοὺς ἱππεῖς τοῖς ἱππεῦσι Plb.11.22.8; τοὺς εὐζώνους Id.10.39.3; ἐλέφαντας ἐ. τινί Paus.1.12. 3, etc.; ἐμαυτόν τισι Alciphr.1.22:—Pass., εὐθὺ τὸν λίθον ἐπαφίεσθαι Aen.Tact.32.6. 2. *let in upon*, ὕδωρ τῷ σίτῳ Thphr.*CP*2.5.5:—Pass., Jul.*Or*.1.30a. 3. *discharge, emit*, ἐ. ὑγρότητα Arist.*HA* 550ᵃ13; ἐ. φωνήν *utter*, Id.*Mir*.847ᵇ2.

Ἐπάφιος, epith. of Dionysus, Orph.*H*.50.7, 52.9.

Ἔπᾰφος, ὁ, a son of Zeus and Io, A.*Pr*.851 (v. ἀφή); the Hellenic representative of the Egyptian god Apis, Hdt.2.153, 3.27,28.

ἐπαφρ-ιάω, *foam against*, Ep. part. -όωσα Nonn.*D*.43.318 (v.l. ὑπ–). -ίζω, *foam up* or *on the surface*, Mosch.*Fr*.1, Nic.*Al*. 32. 2. c. acc., *foam out*, αἰσχύνας *Ep.Jud*.13.

ἐπαφροδ-ισία, ἡ, *loveliness, elegance*, Lync.ap.Ath.6.242c, Ptol. *Tetr*.86, Vett.Val.160.13; περὶ τοὺς λόγους D.Chr.37.33; ἐν τοῖς πρασσομένοις Artem.2.20; *charm*, *PSI*4.328.6 (iii B.C.), *UPZ*33.9 (ii B.C.), *PMag.Osl*.1.224, *PMag.Lond*.122.5, etc. -ῖτος, ον, (Ἀφροδίτη) *lovely, fascinating, charming*, of persons, Hdt.2.135, Aeschin.2.42; of things, ἔπη καὶ ἔργα X.*Smp*.8.15 (Comp., codd.); ποίησις Isoc.10. 65: Sup. -ότατος X.*Hier*.1.35. Adv. -τως, γράφειν D.H.*Lys*.11, cf. Alciphr.2.1, Philostr.*VA*6.3. II. used to translate Sulla's epithet *Felix, favoured by Venus*, i.e. *fortune's favourite* (metaph. from the dice), Plu.*Sull*.34, App.*BC*1.97. III. *gracious*, ἡγεμονία *PRyl*.77.36 (ii A.D.).

ἔπαφρος, ον, *frothy*, Hp.*Epid*.1.26.β', Aret.*SA*2.1.

ἐπᾰφύσσω, *pour over*, θερμὸν ἐπήφυσεν Od.19.388.

ἐπᾰχθ-εια, ἡ, *trouble, annoyance*, Just.*Nov*.115.3.14, al.: pl., *onerous charges*, *Cod.Just*.1.3.38.2. -έω, *load, burden with*, τινί Tryph. 690:—Pass., *to be overloaded* (?), Sor.1.84. -ής, ές, (ἄχθος) *heavy, ponderous*, ῥήματα Ar.*Ra*.940. II. metaph., *burdensome, grievous*, ἅπαντ' ἐπαχθῆ (so Stanley for ἐπράχθη) A.*Pr*.49; εἰ μὴ ἐπαχθές ἐστιν εἰπεῖν Pl.*Phd*.87a; ἐπαινεῖν ἐπαχθέστερόν [ἐστι] Id.*Lg*.688d; ἵνα μηδὲν ἐπαχθὲς λέγω not to say anything *offensive*, D.18.10; ἐπαχθεῖς αἱ ὑπερβολαί Arist.*EN*1127ᵇ8: Sup. -έστατος, θάνατος Phalar. *Ep*.1; κακά Ph.2.402; τὸ ἐ. τῶν λόγων *invidiousness, offence*, Pl. *Euthd*.303e; τὸ ἐ. [τῆς σοφιστικῆς τέχνης] Id.*Prt*.316d. Adv. -θῶς, ἐνέγκαι, = Lat. *aegre ferre*, D.H.*Th*.41. 2. of persons, ἐ. ἦν ἐς τοὺς πολλούς Th.6.54, cf. Pl.*Men*.90a; κινδυνεύει τὸ λίαν εὐτυχεῖν.. ἐπαχθεῖς ποιεῖν D.21.205. Adv. Comp. -έστερον, τισὶ βιῶναι Pl.*Ep*. 327b. -ίζομαι, *to be burdened with*.., λείαν, ἀγγεῖα, Ph.2.103, 113; βάρος πραγματειῶν ib.288: abs., ἐπηχθισμένοι ib.450. -ομαι, *to be annoyed at*.., κακοῖς E.*Hipp*.1260.

ἐπαχλύω, *to be obscured* or *dim*, A.R.4.1480, Q.S.14.462, Ant. Lib.9.2. II. trans., *darken*, Them.*Or*.11.144c:—Pass., -ύεται ὁ λογισμὸς ὑπὸ πάθους ib.19.232d. [ῡ even in pres., A.R. l. c.; in Arat.906 Schneider restored ἐπαχλύων (signf. I) for -ύόων.]

ἐπαχνίδιος, α, ον, (ἄχνη) *lying like down upon*, κόνις *AP*9.556 (Zon.).

ἐπάχνυμαι, Pass., *grieve over*, τινί Tryph.424.

ἐπὰψ θέμεναι· πάλιν ἐπικλεῖσαι καὶ ἐπιθεῖναι *EM*354.25 (leg. ἐπ' ἄψ θ., v.l. in Il.21.535).

ἐπέβρᾰχε, v. ἐπιβραχεῖν.

ἐπεάν, v. ἐπεί A.II.

ἐπεγ-γελάω, fut. -άσομαι, Ep. iterative ἐπεγγελάασκε Q.S.14.397:—*laugh at, exult over*, τινί S.*Aj*.989, X.*An*.2.4.27; κατά τινος S.*Aj*. 969; ταῖς συμφοραῖς τινῶν J.*AJ*11.6.10: abs., S.*Aj*.454, Aeschin.2. 182, Phld.*Mort*.20; ἐπεγγελόωσα Opp.*H*.2.303: c. acc. cogn., ὑβριστήν τινα γέλωτα Aristaenet.2.6. -γρᾰφος, ον, *added to the list*: of non-citizens who were *admitted* to contend for prizes, *IG*3.1092 (i/ii A.D.), al.

ἐπεγγυάω, = ἐγγυάω, Lex ap.Lys.10.17; 3 pl. impf. ἐπενεγύων *SIG* 705.43 (ii B.C.):—Pass., Dor. pres. part. ἐπεγγυάμενοι Sophr.60.

ἐπεγ-είρω, *awaken, rouse up*, τινά Od.22.431, Thgn.469, Ar.*Av*. 83:—Pass., *to be roused from sleep, wake up*, Hom., only in aor. forms ἐπέγρετο, ἐπεγρόμενος, Il.10.124, 14.256, Od.20.57; μέχρι ἐπέγρωνται Hp.*Morb.Sacr*.1; φεύγετε.. ἄνδρ' ἐπεγειρόμενον E.*HF*1083 (anap.); δόξαι, αἳ ἐρωτήσει ἐπεγερθεῖσαι ἐπιστῆμαι γίγνονται Pl.*Men*. 86a: pf. ἐπήγερται is dub. l. in Luc.*Zeux*.4. II. metaph., *awaken, excite*, πόλεμον εὕδοντ' Sol.4.19; διωγμόν *Act.Ap*.13.50; τὸ πάλαι κείμενον κακόν S.*OC*510 (lyr.); ἐπὶ.. θρῆνον ἐ. ib.1778 (anap.); ὅσον ἐσμὸν λόγων ἐπεγείρετε Pl.*R*.450b; *stir up*, τὸ Ἑλληνικόν Hdt.7.139; τὰς ψυχάς *Act.Ap*.14.2; ἡμᾶς εἰς τὴν νεότητα μνήμῃ ἐ. Pl.*Lg*.657d; τοῦ ἐπεγείροντος ὥσπερ μύωπος δεήσει Socr.*Ep*.1.6:—Pass., ἐπηγέρθη [ἡ Ταλθυβίου μῆνις] Hdt.7.137; ἐπηγείροντο ταῖς ψυχαῖς D.S.

14.52. III. *erect, raise,* τὰς ἀκάνθας -ων *erecting* his prickles, like certain fish when irritated, *Com.Adesp.*1338 (=[S.]*Fr.*1121); ὅταν ἐπεγερθῶσιν φλύκταιναι Philum.*Ven.*17.5. -ερσις, εως, ἡ, *being roused, awaking,* Hp.*Prorrh.*1.112, Max.Tyr.16.6. -ερτικός, ή, όν, *awakening,* Arist.*Pr.*886ᵃ9. II. *stimulating,* ἐ. ὁρμῆς Plu.2.138b; ἐ. εἰς τὰ ἀφροδίσια *Cat.Cod.Astr.*2.197.

ἐπεγ-κᾰλέω, *bring a charge against,* τινί Lys.8.1; τυραννίδα τινί Procop.*Arc.*18; τινὶ ὡς ψευσαμένῳ Gal.18(2).295; τισί c. inf., Hierocl. *in CA*25 p.477 M.:—Med., πολιτείαν Olymp. *in Alc.*p.155 C. -κᾰνάσσω, *drink* or *pour in besides,* Hsch. (-κενάξαι cod.). -κάπτω, *eat up besides, gulp down,* Ar.*Eq.*493. -κᾰχάζω, *laugh at,* τινί Lyc.285. -κειμαι, *press hard,* Sch.Il.24.657. -κέλευμα, ατος, τό, gloss on ἐπίσιγμα, Hsch. -κελεύω, *give an order* or *signal to* others, E.*Cyc.*652; *exhort, encourage,* τινί prob. in Id.*El.*1224 (lyr.). -κεράννῡμαι, Med., *mix in with,* Pl.*Plt.*273d, Nic.*Al.*166, etc.; τινί τι Plu.2.1025b. -κλάω, *turn towards,* τὰ βλέφαρα εἴς τινα D.C.51.12; τοὺς ὀφθαλμούς Id.79.16. -κλημα, ατος, τό, *accusation,* Sopat. in Rh.5.209 W. -κλίνω [ῑ], *incline, turn towards* either side, v.l. in Gal.*UP*12.9. -κολάπτω, *engrave upon* or *besides,* Lyc.782. -κρᾰνίς, ίδος, ἡ, *cerebellum,* Erasistr. ap.Gal.*UP*8.13. -κρεμάννῠμαι, Med., *hang up in,* καπνῷ Nic.*Fr.*72.2. -κυκλέω, in Pass., *to be introduced* into a speech, of parallels, etc., Aristid.*Rh.*2 p.538 S. -κύκλιος, ον, *circular,* of bandages, Sor.*Fasc.*12.512,516 C., Gal.18(1).815.

ἐπεγνωσμένως, Adv., (ἐπιγιγνώσκω) = ᾠκειωμένως, Zonar.

ἐπεγρόμην, part. **ἐπεγρόμενος,** Ep. aor. Pass. of ἐπεγείρω.

ἐπεγ-χᾰλάω, *loose,* δέσμα Nic.*Al.*439. -χάσκω, *make mouths at,* in aor. 2 inf. ἐπεγχανεῖν, τινί Ael.*Fr.*69: abs., S.*Fr.*210.49. -χειρέω, *attack,* Gal.2.221. -χέω, poet. -χεύω Nic.*Fr.*72.5:—*pour in upon* or *besides,* A.*Ag.*1137 (lyr.), Philox.2.40; ἄλλην [κύλικα] ἐπ' ἄλλῃ E.*Cyc.*423; *pour in fresh water,* Hp.*Int.*1. -χῡμᾰτίζω, *wash out* the throat *afterwards, Hippiatr.*22. II. *give a clyster afterwards,* γάλακτι Dsc.5.15. -χύνω, late form for -χέω, Hero *Spir.*2.28 (Pass.). -χύτης [ῠ], ου, ὁ, *cup-bearer,* so called by the Hellespontines, Demetr.Sceps.ap.Ath.10.425c.

ἐπέδρᾰμον, v. ἐπιτρέχω. **ἐπέδρη,** ἡ, Ion. for ἐφέδρα.

ἐπέην, Ep. for ἐπῆν, 3 sg. impf. of ἔπειμι (A), Il.20.276.

ἐπεθίζομαι, *to be accustomed to* a thing, Aristox.*Harm.*p.33 M.

ἐπεί, Conj., both temporal and causal; also **ἐπειδή, ἐπείτε.**

A. OF TIME (ἐπειδή is more freq. in this sense in Prose), *after that, since, when,* from Hom. downwds.: I. with Ind., 1. of a definite occurrence in past time, mostly c. aor., ἐπεὶ δ' εὔξαντο *after* they had prayed, Il.1.458; ἐπειδὴ ἐτελεύτησε Δαρεῖος καὶ κατέστη Ἀρταξέρξης *after* D. had died and A. had succeeded, X.*An.*1.1.3: rarely c. impf., ἐπειδὴ εἰστιώμεθ' Ar.*Nu.*1354; ἐ. πόντον εἰσεβάλλομεν E.*IT*260; ἐ. ἠσθένει Δαρεῖος X.*An.*1.1.1: c. plpf., ἐπειδὴ ἐξηπάτησθε.. *after* you had been deceived.., D.18.42; but generally the aor. is found, the plpf. being used only for special emphasis: c. impf. to express an action not yet complete, ἐπεὶ ὑπηντίαζεν ἡ φάλαγξ καὶ ἡ σάλπιγξ ἐφθέγξατο *after* the phalanx began to advance and the trumpet had sounded, X.*An.*6.5.27. 2. with implied reference to some later time, ἐ. or ἐπειδή, = ἐξ οὗ, *from the time when, since,* mostly c. aor., πολλὰ πλάγχθη, ἐ. ἔπερσε Od.1.2; ἐπείτε παρέλαβον τὸν θρόνον, τοῦτο ἐφρόντιζον *ever since* I came to the throne, I had this in mind, Hdt.7.8.α'; ἐπειδήπερ ὑπέστη Th.8.68; δέκατον μὲν ἔτος τόδ' ἐ... ἦραν A.*Ag.*40: sts. c. pres. (used in pf. sense) and pf., ἐ. δὲ φροῦδός ἐστι στρατός *since* the army is gone, S.*Ant.*15; ἐπείτε ὑπὸ τῷ Πέρσῃ εἰσί, πεπόνθασι τοιόνδε *ever since* they have been, *now that* they are.., Hdt.3.117. II. with Subj., ἄν being always added in Att. Prose, and ἄν or κε generally in Poetry: ἐπεί with ἄν becomes ἐπήν (so in Com., Ar.*Lys.*1175, *Av.*983), later ἐπάν (q.v.), Ion. ἐπεάν *Schwyzer* 800 (vi B.C.), Hdt.3.153, al., ἐπήν Hp.*Fract.*6, al., and ἐπειδή with ἄν ἐπειδάν (q.v.); Hom. has ἐπεί κε, ἐπήν (once ἐπεὶ ἄν Il.6.412): 1. referring to future time with fut. apodosis, τέκνα ἄξομεν.. ἐπὴν πτολίεθρον ἕλωμεν *when* we shall have taken the city, Il.4.238; ἐ. κ' ἀπὸ λαὸς ὄληται 11.764, cf. Od.17.23; ἐπεάν περ ἡμίονοι τέκωσι, τότε τὸ τεῖχος ἁλώσεσθαι Hdt.3.153; ταῦτ', ἐπειδὰν περὶ τοῦ γένους εἴπω, τότ' ἐρῶ I will speak of this, *when* I have spoken.., D.57.16, cf. X.*An.*2.3.29; ἐ. ἂν σύ γε πότμον ἐπίσπῃς Il.6.412; χρὴ δέ, ὅταν μὲν τιθῆσθε τοὺς νόμους, ..σκοπεῖν, ἐπειδὰν δὲ θῆσθε, φυλάττειν whenever you are enacting your laws, .. and *after* you have enacted them.., D.21.34. 2. of repeated action, with a pres. apodosis, *whenever, when once,* δαμνᾷ, ἐ. κε λίπῃ ὀστέα θυμός Od.11.221, cf. Il.9.409; ἐπειδὰν ἡ ἐκφορὰ ᾖ.. ἄγουσι *whenever* the burial takes place they bring, Th.2.34; ἐπειδὰν κρύψωσι γῇ..λέγει *when* they have covered them with earth, ibid.: sts. without ἄν or κε in Poets, ἐ. ἂρ βλέφαρ' ἀμφικαλύψῃ Od.20.86; ἐ. δὴ τόν γε δαμάσσεται..ὀϊστός Il.11.478, cf. S.*OC*1225 (lyr.), *Ant.*1025. 3. like A. I. 2, δέκα ἡμερῶν ἐπειδὰν δόξῃ within ten days *from* the passing of the resolution, *IG*1².88.7. III. with Opt. (without ἄν): 1. referring to future time, ἐπειδὴ πρὸς τὸ φῶς ἔλθοι, ὁρᾶν οὐδ' ἂν ἓν δύνασθαι (sc. οὐκ οἴει); *after* he had come into the light.., Pl.*R.*516a: Hom. sts. uses ἐπήν with opt. in same sense as ἐπεί, Il.24.227, Od.2.105 (codd.), etc. 2. more freq. of repeated action, with a past apodosis, ἐ. ζεύξειεν.., δησάσκετο Il.24.14; ἐπειδὴ δέ τι ἐμφάγοιεν, ἀνίσταντο X.*An.*4.5.9; ἐ. πύθοιτο, ἐπήνει Id.*Cyr.*5.3.55, cf. Th.8.38, Pl.*Phd.*59d, *Prt.*315b. 3. in orat. obliq. after past tenses, representing a subj. in orat. rect., αὐτὸς δὲ ἐπεὶ διαβαίης, ἀπιέναι ἔφησθα (the direct form being ἐπὴν διαβῶ) X.*An.*7.2.27, cf. 3.5.18, *Cyr.*1.4.21; after opt. in a final clause, ἐπορεύοντο, ὅπως ἐπειδὴ γένοιντο ἐπὶ τῷ ποταμῷ..ἴοιεν Th.7.80. 4. by assimilation to opt. in principal clause, ἤ τ' ἂν..νῦν μὲν ἀνώγοιμι πτολεμίζειν.. ἐπὴν τεισαίμεθα λώβην Il.19.208; ὃς τὸ καταβρόξειεν ἐπεὶ κρητῆρι μιγείη Od.4.222. 5. ἐπειδάν c. opt. is f.l. in some passages of early authors, as X.*Cyr.*1.3.11, D.30.6 (c. ind., Plb.13.7.8): found in later Gr., Agath.2.5, al., Zos.5.18.10. IV. with Inf., only in orat. obliq., ἐπειδὴ δὲ κατὰ σχολὴν σκέψασθαι, κόπτεσθαι (sc. ἔφη) Pl.*R.*619c, cf. *Smp.*174d, Hdt.4.10, 7.150. V. with other words: 1. ἐ. τάχιστα *as soon as,* freq. separated by a word, ἐ. ἦλθε τάχιστα, .. ἀπέδοτο X.*An.*7.2.6; ἐ. δὲ τάχιστα διέβη Id.*Cyr.*3.3.22; ἐ. θᾶττον Arist.*Pol.*1284ᵃ40; ἐ. εὐθέως X.*HG*3.2.4; ἐ...αὐτίκα Pi.*N.*1.35; ἐπειδὴ τάχιστα Pl.*Prt.*310c, D.27.16; ἐπειδὰν τάχιστα Hdt.8.144, X.*An.*3.1.9; rarely ἐπειδὴ θᾶττον D.37.41; ἐπειδὰν θᾶττον Pl.*Prt.*325c. b. ἐ. τὰ πρῶτα Il.12.420; ἐ. τὸ πρῶτον A.*Ag.*1287. 2. with emphatic Particles, ἐπεὶ ἄρα *when* then, in continuing a narrative, Il.6.426; ἐπεὶ οὖν *when* then, in resuming a narrative, 1.57, 3.4; ἐπεὶ ὦν Hdt.3.9; ἐπεὶ γὰρ δή Id.9.90, etc.

B. CAUSAL (ἐπεί more freq. in this sense in early Prose: ἐπειδή *whereas* is used in preambles of decrees, *IG*2².103, etc.; ἐπειδήπερ *inasmuch as, Ev.Luc.*1.1), *since, seeing that,* freq. from Hom. downwards: 1. with Ind. (after both present and past tenses), ἐ. οὐδὲ ἔοικε Il.1.119, cf. 153, 278, Pi.*O.*4.16, X.*Mem.*2.3.4; ἐπειδή Th.8.80; ἐπειδὴ οὐκ ἐθέλεις Pl.*Prt.*335c; νίκῃ δ' ἐπείπερ ἔσπετ', ἐμπέδως μένοι A.*Ag.*854; freq. with past tenses with ἄν, ἐπεὶ οὔποτ' ἂν στόλον ἐπλεύσατ' ἂν S.*Ph.*1037; ἐπεὶ οὔ κεν ἀνιδρωτί γ' ἐτελέσθη Il.15.228, cf. D.18.49; οὐ γὰρ ἂν σθένοντά γε εἷλέν μ'· ἐπεὶ οὐδ' ἂν ὧδ' ἔχοντ' (sc. εἷλεν) S.*Ph.*948: esp. in the sense, *for otherwise..,* Pi.*O.*9.29, S.*OT*433, X.*Mem.*2.7.14, Herod.2.72, etc.: so c. fut., ἐξέστω δὲ μηδενὶ..τεθῆναι.., ἐ. ἀποδώσει.. *otherwise* he shall pay.., *Rev.Ét.Anc.*4.261 (near Smyrna): c. imper., ἐ. δίδαξον *for* teach me, S.*El.*352, *OC*969, cf. *OT*390, Ar.*V.*73, Pl.*Grg.*473e: with an interrog., ἐ. πῶς ἂν καλέσειας; *for* how would you call him? Ar.*Nu.*688, cf. Pi.*P.*7.5, A.*Ch.*214, S.*Tr.*139 (lyr.); ὦ Ἀλκιβιάδη, ἐπειδὴ περί τίνος Ἀθηναῖοι διανοοῦνται βουλεύεσθαι, ἀνίστασαι συμβουλεύσων; Pl.*Alc.*1.106c. 2. c. Opt., ἐ. ἂν μάλα τοι σχεδὸν ἔλθοι Il.9.304, cf. S.*Aj.*916; so after past tenses on the principle of orat. obliq., ἐπείπερ ἡγήσαιντο *since* (as they said) they believed, X.*Mem.*1.4.19. 3. c. Inf. in orat. obliq., ἐ. γιγνώσκειν γε αὐτά Pl.*Prt.*353a, cf. Hdt.8.111, Th.2.93. 4. in elliptical expressions, ἀδύνατος [εἰμι], ἐ. ἐβουλόμην ἂν οἷός τ' εἶναι I am unable (and yet I am sorry), *for* I should like to have the power, Pl.*Prt.*335c; so εἶμι· ἐ. καὶ ταῦτ' ἂν ἴσως οὐκ ἀηδῶς σου ἤκουον ibid. (here the sense may be given by *and yet, although,* cf. ib.333c, 317a, *Ap.*19e, *Smp.*187a, Arist.*EN*1121ᵃ19); ἐ. ὅ γε ἀποθανὼν πελάτης τις ἦν ἐμός *and yet* (*moreover*) the murdered man was my own hired man, Pl.*Euthphr.*4c. b. sts. after a voc., where 'listen' may be supplied, Ἕκτορ, ἐ. με κατ' αἶσαν ἐνείκεσας Il.3.59, cf. 13.68, Od.3.103, 211. 5. with other Particles, ἐ. ἄρα, ἐ. ἂρ δή *since* then, Od.17.185; ἐ. γε (ἐπεί..γε Il.1.352, Hes.*Th.*171), more emphatic than ἐ., *since* indeed, E.*Cyc.*181, *Hipp.*955; ἐπειδή γε ib.946, Pl.*Phd.*77d, D.54.29; sts. separated, ἐπειδή..γε S.*El.*631, Pl.*Phd.*87c; ἐ. γε δή Hdt.3.9, S.*Ant.*923; ἐπειδή γε καί Th.6.18; ἐ. ἦ *since* in truth, ἐ. ἦ πολὺ φέρτερόν ἐστι Il.1.169, cf. 156, Od.9.276; ἐπείπερ (ἐ...περ Il.13.447, Od.20.181) in Trag. and Prose, A.*Ag.*822, S.*OC*75, Pl.*Phd.*114d; ἐπειδήπερ in Com. and Prose, Ar.*Ach.*437, 495, *Nu.*1412, Th.6.18, Pl.*R.*350e; ἐ. τοι *since* surely, S.*OC*433; ἐ. νύ τοι Il.1.416; ἐ. τοι καὶ E.*Med.*677, Pl.*R.*567e. [ἐ. sts. begins a verse in Hom., Il.22.379, Od.4.13, 8.452, 21.25; sts. coalesces by synizesis with οὐ, οὐδέ, etc., S.*Ph.*446, 948, etc.]

ἐπείγω, Il.12.452, etc., Aeol. **ἐποίγω** Hdn.Gr.2.436: impf. ἤπειγον Pi.*O.*8.47, S.*Ph.*499, Ep. ἔπειγον Od.12.205: aor. ἤπειξα Hp.*Ep.*17, Plu.*Pomp.*21, etc.:—**Med.** and **Pass.,** Hom. (v. infr.), etc.: fut. Med. ἐπείξομαι A.*Pr.*52: aor. ἠπείχθην Th.1.80, Pl.*Lg.*887c: pf. ἤπειγμαι J.*BJ*1.8.7, Aristid.*Or.*17(15).9, Gal.6.177: the compd. κατ-επείγω is more freq. in Att. Prose:—*press by weight,* ὀλίγον τέ μιν ἄχθος ἐπείγει the weight *presses* lightly *on* him, Il.12.452:—Pass., *to be weighed down,* ἐπείγετο γὰρ βελέεσσι 5.622; θάμνοι..ἐπειγόμενοι πυρὸς ὁρμῇ *overpowered,* 11.157, cf. 21.362. 2. *press hard* (in pursuit), ἀναγκαίη γὰρ ἐπείγει 6.85, Od.19.73: c. acc., δύω κύνε.. κεμάδ' ἠὲ λαγωὸν ἐπείγετον Il.10.361:—in a current phrase, οὐδεὶς ἡμᾶς τὸ λεγόμενον ἐπείγων διώκει Pl.*Lg.*887b. II. *drive on, urge forward,* ἐρετμά..χερσὶν ἔπειγον Od.12.205; freq. of a fair wind, ἔπειγε γὰρ οὖρος 12.167; ὁππότ' ἐπείγῃ ἲς ἀνέμου Il.15.382; καιρὸς καὶ πλοῦς ὅδ' ἐπείγει κατὰ πρύμναν S.*Ph.*1451 (anap.). III. generally, *urge on, hasten,* ἐπείγετε δ' ὦνον Od.15.445; τὸν οἴκαδ' ἤπειγον στόλον *urged* the homeward course, S.*Ph.*499; ἐ. τινά Id.*OC*1540:—Pass., of a ship, ἐπείγετο χέρσ' ἐρετάων Od.13.115; Διὸς οὔρῳ 15.297, cf. E.*IT*1393, Th.3.49; of persons, θορύβοις ἠπειγμένος J.l.c. 2. Med., *urge on for oneself,* μίμνετ' ἐπειγόμενοι τὸν ἐμὸν γάμον Od.2.97; so τὴν παρασκευήν, τὸν πλοῦν ἐπείγεσθαι, Th.3.2, 4.5, al.: abs., ἐπειγομένων ἀνέμων *by the force of* winds, Il.5.501; ὀπὸς γάλα.. ἐπειγόμενος συνέπηξεν the fig-juice *by its power* curdles the milk, ib.902. 3. Pass., *hurry oneself, haste to do,* c. inf., μή τις..ἐπειγέσθω οἰκόνδε νέεσθαι Il.2.354, cf. Hes.*Sc.*21, Hdt.8.68.γ', Th.8.46, etc.: abs., *make haste,* ἐπειγέσθω δὲ καὶ αὐτὸς Il.6.363; ὧραι ἐπειγόμεναι Pi.*N.*4.34; ἐπειχθῆναι πᾶν πρῆγμα τίκτει σφάλματα Hdt.7.10.ζ'; δρόμῳ ἐπείγεσθαι Id.6.112; νυκτὸς ἅρμ' ἐπείγεται A.*Ch.*660; δεῦρ' ἐπείγονται E.*Ion*1258; ὥσπερ τι δεινὸν ἀγγελῶν ἐ. Ar.*Ach.*1070; οὐ τῶν ἐπειγομένων ἀλλὰ τῶν εὖ βουλευομένων Antipho 5.94, cf. Th.8.82; ἐπείγεσθαι ἐπί.. Hdt.4.135; ἐς πύλας, πρὸς τὴν γέφυραν, E.*Ph.*1171, Th.6.101;

ἠπείγετο οἴκαδε Pl.*Tht.*142c, etc.: in Hom. mostly in part., like an Adv. with Verbs, ἐπειγομένη ἀφικάνει *in eager haste* she comes, Il. 6.388; ψυχὴ.. ἔσσυτ' ἐπειγομένη 14.519; τάμνον ἐπειγόμενοι 23.119, etc.; so in Att., εἴσω ᾔει ἐπειγόμενος Pl.*Prt.*310b. b. Pass., also, *to be eager for* a thing, esp. in part.: c. inf., πρὸς ἠέλιον κεφαλὴν τρέπε.. δῦναι ἐπειγόμενος *eager for* its setting, Od.13.30, cf. A. *Pr.*52: c. gen., ἐπειγόμενός περ ὁδοῖο *longing for* the journey, Od.1.309, etc.; ἐ. περ Ἄρηος *eager for* the fray, Il.19.142; ἐ. περὶ νίκης 23.437,496. IV. intr., = Pass., *hasten* to a place, Pi.*O.*8.47, S.*El.* 1435, E.*Or.*799, Ar.*Pax* 943, etc. 2. *to be pressing, urgent*, ἐν ταῖς ἐπειγούσαις χρείαις Ph.*Bel.*56.47; τὰ ἐπείγοντα *pressing* matters, Plu. *Sert.*3, Aristid.1.119 J., cf. *BGU* 1141.4 (i B.C.), etc.; χρείαν τινὰ ἐπείγειν λέγων App.*Mith.*79; τῆς ὥρας -ούσης since time *was pressing*, Plu.2.108f; τῶν ἀρχαιρεσίων ἐπειγόντων Id.*Marc.*24. 3. impers., οὐκ ἐπείγει διαριθμεῖν *there's no pressing need* to count, Longin.43.6: part. abs., ἐπεῖξαν *the need being urgent*, Aristid.*Or.*36(48).10.

ἐπειγωλή, ἡ, *haste*, *EM* 356.34.

ἐπειδάν, i.e. ἐπειδὴ ἄν (v. ἐπεί A. II, ἄν B. I. 2), *whenever*, with Subj., of Time, once in Hom., Il.13.285, freq. in Att. 2. for ἐπειδάν c. opt. v. ἐπεί A. III. 5. [-ᾱν is prob.; ἐπεὶ δ' ἄν is to be read in A. *Th.*734, E.*Rh.*469.]

ἐπειδέ, once = ἐπειδή before a vowel, *IG* 7.15 (Megara, ii B.C.).

ἐπειδή, ἐπειδήπερ, v. ἐπεί.

ἐπεῖδον, aor. 2, inf. ἐπιδεῖν, with no pres. in use, ἐφοράω being used instead, *look upon, behold, see*, of evils, κακὰ πόλλ' ἐπιδόντα Il.22.61:—Med., ἐπιδόμενοι A.*Supp.*646 (lyr.); ἐπιδέσθαι E.*Med.*1414 (anap.); ἐπιδώμεθα Ar.*Nu.*289 (lyr.). 2. esp. of the gods, *look upon* human affairs, Ζεὺς ἐπίδοι προφρόνως στόλον A.*Supp.*1 (anap.), cf. 145 (lyr.), 1030 (lyr.); νιν Ζεὺς ἐπίδοι κοταίνων Id.*Th.*485 (lyr.); Κύριε, ἔπιδε ἐπὶ τὰς ἀπειλὰς αὐτῶν *Act.Ap.*4.29. 3. *remain seeing*, i.e. *live to see*, τὰ τέκνα Hdt.6.52, cf. X.*Vect.*6.1; *experience*, χαλεπά Id.*An.*3.1.13: with part. added, μηδ' ἐπίδοιμι τάνδ' ἀστυδρομουμέναν πόλιν A.*Th.*220 (lyr.), cf. *Ag.*1539 (lyr.); ἐπιδεῖν ἐρήμην τὴν πόλιν γενομένην Isoc.4.96; τὴν πατρίδα ἐπιδεῖν δουλεύουσαν D.18.205; αὐτὸς λωβηθεὶς καὶ τοὺς αὑτοῦ ἐπιδὼν παῖδας [λωβηθέντας] Pl.*Grg.*473c.

ἐπεὶ ἤ, v. ἐπεί B. 5.

ἐπεικάδες, ων, αἱ, (εἰκάς) *the days between the 20th and the end* of the month, *EM* 131.15; cf. εἰκάς.

ἐπεικ-άζω, *surmise, guess*, ἦ καὶ δάμαρτα τήνδ' ἐπεικάζων κυρῶ κείνου; am I right in *surmising* that she is his wife? S.*El.*663; τάσδ' ἐπεικάσας τύχω χοὰς φερούσας; A.*Ch.*14, cf. 567; ὡς ἐπεικάσαι πάθη πάρεστι as one may *read the riddle of* their fates, ib.976; ὡς ἐπεικάσαι as far as *one may guess*, Hdt.9.32; ὅσ' ἐπεικάσαι (Bothe for ὡς) S.*OC* 152 (lyr.); ὥς γ' ἐπεικάζειν ἐμέ Id.*Tr.*1220. **-ασμός**, ὁ, *conjecture*, Gal.14.339.

ἐπείκεια, ἐπεικής, v. ἐπιεικ-.

ἐπείκελος, dub. l. for ἐπιείκελος, Opp.*C.*2.167.

ἐπείκοστον, τό, a sum *greater by* $\frac{1}{20}$ than another, *PPetr.*2 p.156 (ii B.C.):—also **ἐφ-** *PRev.Laws* 56.15 (iii B.C.).

ἐπεικ-τάς· ὑπόσχεσις, σπουδή, Hsch. **-τέον**, *one must hurry*, Pl.*Lg.*687e. **-της**, ου, ὁ, *one who urges* or *presses*, *EM* 356.34, *Gloss.*; coupled with ἐκβιβαστής, *Cod.Just.*7.51.5.1. **-τικός**, ή, όν, *urgent*, Sch.Il.11.165.

ἐπεικώς, Att. part. of ἐπέοικα (q.v.).

ἐπειλ-έω, *wind up*, Hero *Aut.*6.2:—Pass., Id.*Bel.*84.10. **-ησις**, εως, ἡ, *winding up*, ἐ. ποιεῖσθαι ib.85.2. II. *rolling*, of a bandage, Sor.*Fasc.*12.506 C., al. **ἐπείλικτο, ἐπειλίξας**, v. ἐφελίσσω.

ἔπειμι (A), (εἰμί *sum*) inf. ἐπεῖναι: Ep. impf. ἔπεσαν Od.2.344: fut. ἐπέσομαι, Ep. and Lyr. -έσσομαι, 4.756, Pi.*O.*13.99:—*to be upon*, c. dat. loci, κάρη ὤμοισιν ἐπείη Il.2.259; σῆμα δ' οὐκ ἐπῆν κύκλῳ A. *Th.*591; in Prose mostly with Prep., ἐπὶ τοῦ καταστρώματος ἐ. Hdt. 8.118; ἐπὶ [τῷ ποταμῷ] πύλαι ἔπεισι Id.5.52, cf. 7.176; ἐπὶ ταῖς οἰκίαις τύρσεις ἐπῆσαν X.*An.*4.4.2: abs., κώπη δ' ἐλέφαντος ἐπῆεν Od.21.7, cf. 2.344, Il.5.127, A.*Ag.*547, etc. 2. *to be upon, be set upon*, of names, οὐκ ἔπεστι ἐπωνυμίη Περσέϊ Hdt.6.53; so ψεύδεσι σεμνὸν ἔπεστί τι Pi.*N.*7.23; τοῖσι λόγοις σῶφρον ἔ. ἄνθος Ar.*Nu.*1025; *to be attached*, μελέτη δ' ἔπεστι παντί *Anacreont.*58.3; οὔτε τις τάξις οὔτε ἀνάγκη ἔπεστιν αὐτοῦ τῷ βίῳ Pl.*R.*561d; esp. of rewards and penalties, ποινά, κέρδος ἐπέσται, A.*Eu.*543 (lyr.), Ar.*Av.*597; ἔπεστι νέμεσις S.*El.*1467; ἔσχαται τιμωρίαι ἐπὶ ταῖς ἐπαγγελίαις ἔπεισιν Is.3.47, cf. Pl.*Lg.*943d: abs., Ταραντίνων οὐκ ἐπῆν ἀριθμός no count *was taken*, no number *was attached*, Hdt.7.170, cf. 191; *to be at hand, be present*, τίς τέρψις ἐπέσται; S.*Aj.*1216 (lyr.); αἰσχύνη X.*Cyr.*6.2.33; πιεῖν δὲ θάνατος οἶνον, ἢν ὕδωρ ἐπῇ Cratin.273 (s.v.l.); τὰ ἐπόντα *accidents* or *characteristics*, opp. τὸ ὑποκείμενον, Plot.2.4.10. 3. *to be in* one's *possession*, ἀνέρες οἷσιν ἔπεστι μέγα κράτος *h.Cer.*150. 4. *to be imminent*, ἐπόντος τοῦ φόβου τούτου D.21.9; εἰ μηδεὶς ἐπῆν ἀγὼν μηδὲ κίνδυνος ibid. 5. ἔπι for ἔπεστι (v. ἐπί E. II). II. of Time, *to be hereafter, remain*, ἀλλ' ἔτι πού τις ἐπέσσεται Od.4.756; *to be at hand*, οὐδέ τι δειλὸν γῆρας ἐπῆν Hes.*Op.*114; ἐπεσσόμενοι ἄνθρωποι generations *to come*, Orac.ap.Hdt.6.77, Epigr.ap.Aeschin. 3.184; ἐπεσσόμενοι alone, Theoc.12.11. III. *to be set over*, τισί Hdt.7.96, 8.71; ἔπεστί σφι δεσπότης νόμος Id.7.104; τίς δὲ ποιμάνωρ ἔ.; A.*Pers.*241 (troch.), cf. 555 (lyr.). IV. *to be added, be over and above*, of numbers, χιλιάδες ἔπεισι ἐπὶ ταύτῃσι ἑπτά Hdt.7.184, cf. 185; ἐπόντων τεσσάρων *plus* four, Arr.*Tact.*10.8; τὰ ἐπεσόμενα τούτοις (sc. προβάτοις) *Arch.Pap.*1.64 (ii B.C.). V. *to be added* as confirmation, ἔξορκος ἐπέσσεται Pi.*O.*13.99. 2. *belong in addition*, τὰν περὶ αὐτὸ χώραν ἐπείμειν Πριανέων *Schwyzer* 289.27 (ii B.C.).

ἔπειμι (B), (εἶμι *ibo*) inf. ἐπιέναι, serving in Att. as fut. of ἐπέρχομαι: Ep. 3 sg. impf. ἐπήϊεν Il.17.741; 3 pl. ἐπήϊσαν Od.11.233, ἐπῇσαν 19.445; Att. ἐπῇα, 3 pl. ἐπῇσαν: ἐπιείσομαι, -εισαμένη (qq.v.) belong to a different word: I. *come upon* (in fut. sense, though this is not so fixed in Hom. as in Att.): 1. of persons, *come upon, approach*, Od. 16.42, etc. b. mostly in hostile sense, *come against, attack*, c. dat., Il. 13.482, etc.; τῷ λόφῳ ἐ. Th.4.129; in Prose also with Preps., ἐ. ἐπὶ τὴν Ἑλλάδα, ἐπὶ τοὺς ἀδικοῦντας, Hdt.7.157, Th.1.86 (v.l. πρός), etc.; πρὸς τὸ τεῖχος Id.7.4: abs., Αἰνείαν ἐπιόντα Il.13.477, cf. 5.238; ἐπάγοντες ἐπῇσαν Od.19.445; οἱ ἐπιόντες the *invaders, assailants*, Hdt.4.11, etc.; ὡς ἐπιὼν *by assault*, D.1.21; but ὁ ἐπιών in Trag., = ὁ τυχών, the *first comer*, τό γ' αἴνιγμ' οὐχὶ τοὐπιόντος ἦν ἀνδρὸς διειπεῖν S.*OT* 393, cf. *OC* 752. c. *get on the* βῆμα to speak, v.l. for παριέναι in Th.1.72; *come on*, of performers, dub. l. in X.*An.*6.1.11. d. *approach, attack* a question, Arist.*Ph.*186^{a}4. 2. of events, *come upon* or *over* one, *overtake*, c. acc., πρίν μιν καὶ γῆρας ἔπεισιν Il.1.29 (but ἔπειμι γῆρας ἔς τε τὸν μόρσιμον αἰῶνα Pi.*I.*7(6).41); οἷός σε χειμὼν καὶ κακῶν τρικυμία ἔπεισι A.*Pr.*1016: c. dat., *come near*, ὀρυμαγδὸς ἐπήϊεν ἐρχομένοισιν Il.17.741; δεινῶν ἐπιόντων πᾶσι Ἕλλησι *threatening* them, Hdt.7.145: abs., χειμὼν ἐπιών Hes.*Op.*675; νὺξ ἐπῄει A.*Pers.*378, cf. X.*Mem.*4.3.14, *An.*5.7.12; τὸ ἐπιόν the (madness) which *threatens* me, Pl.*Phdr.*238d. b. c. dat. pers., *come into* one's *head, occur* to one, εἰ καὶ ἐπίοι αὐτῷ λέγειν if it so much as *occurred* to him to say.., Id.*R.*388d, cf. 558a; ὅ τι ἂν ἀπὸ ταὐτομάτου ἐπίῃ μοι X.*Mem.*4.2.4; ἄν.. ὑμῖν ἐπίῃ σκοπεῖν D.21.185: abs., τὸ ἐπιόν *what occurs to one*, Pl.*Phdr.*264b. II. of Time, *come on* or *after*: mostly in part. ἐπιών, οῦσα, όν, *following, succeeding, instant*, ἡ ἐπιοῦσα ἡμέρα the *coming* day, Hdt.3.85, Ar.*Ec.*105, Pl.*Cri.*44a; ἡ 'πιοῦσα λαμπὰς θεοῦ E.*Med.*352; ἡ ἐπιοῦσα (sc. ἡμέρα) Plb.2.25.11, LXX *Pr.*27.1, *Act. Ap.*16.11; τῆς ἐ. νυκτός Pl.*Cri.*46a; τῇ ἐ. νυκτί *Act.Ap.*23.11; ὁ ἐ. βίοτος E.*Or.*1659; τοῦ ἐ. χρόνου Pl.*Lg.*769c; ἐν τῷ ἐ. χρόνῳ X.*Cyr.* 2.1.23; ἡ ἐ. ὥρα τοῦ ἔτους D.8.18; εἰς τὴν ἐ. ἐκκλησίαν Id.21.162, *IG* 2^2.717.16; εἰς τὴν ἐ. Πυλαίαν D.18.151; τοὐπιόν the *future*, E.*Fr.*1073.6; τῆς ἐ. ἐλπίδος Ar.*Th.*870; περὶ τῶν ἐπιόντων D.*Ep.*4.3; τῶν ἐ. ἕνεκα because of the *consequences*, Id.19.258. 2. generally, *come after, succeed*, κύματα.. βάντ' ἐπιόντα τε S.*Tr.*115 (lyr.); ὁ ἐπιών the *successor*, Id.*OC* 1532; αὐτόματα ἔπεισιν ἐκ τῶν ἔμπροσθεν ἐπιτηδευμάτων Pl.*R.*427a; τὰ ἐπιόντα the words *which follow*, Id.*Prt.*344a, cf. *Sph.*257c. 3. rarely, *pass, elapse*, ἐπιόντος τοῦ χρόνου Id.*Ti.* 44b. III. *go over* a space, *traverse, visit*, ἀγρόν Od.23.359; χώρους Hdt.5.74; of an officer, ἐ. πύλας E.*Ph.*1164; τὸ στράτευμα Th.7.78, etc. 2. *go over*, i.e. *count over*, φώκας.. ἀριθμήσει καὶ ἔπεισιν Od.4.411; *think over*, τῇ μνήμῃ ἕκαστα Luc.*Herm.*1; *read*, Hld.2.6.

ἐπείνυσθαι, Ion. for ἐφέννυσθαι, *put on* clothes, Hdt.4.64.

ἐπείξ-ιμος, ον, *pressing*, ἔργα *POxy.*531.9 (ii A.D.). **-ις**, εως, ἡ, *haste, hurry*, J.*AJ* 18.6.5, Plu.*Rom.*29, Ruf.ap.Orib.8.24.23, Aristid. *Or.*48(24).61, Luc.*DMeretr.*10.3, etc. 2. *emergency*, Antyll.ap. Orib.10.23.30. II. *urging, pressing*, *Gloss.*: pl., App.*BC* 1.19 (s.v.l.).

ἐπείπερ or **ἐπεί περ**, v. ἐπεί B. 1, 2, 5.

ἐπεῖπον, aor. 2, inf. ἐπειπεῖν, pf. ἐπείρηκα Plu.2.1054f: pres. ἐπιλέγω (q.v.):—*say besides* or *afterwards*, Hdt.1.123, Th.1.67, Aeschin. 2.157, etc. 2. ψόγον ἐ. τινί *say* it *of* one, A.*Supp.*972 (anap.), cf. Luc.*Hist.Conscr.*26; σκωπτικόν τι εἴς τινα Id.*Dem.Enc.*33. 3. *quote* as apposite, τὰ ἐξ Ἰλιάδος ἐκεῖνα Ael.*VH* 4.18; ἐ. τὸ κοινὸν ἀρχὴ δέ τοι ἥμισυ παντός Luc.*Somn.*3; cf. ἐπιλέγω. 4. *utter, pronounce* a spell, ἐ. ἐπῳδήν Id.*Philops.*35. 5. *make a speech at*, τάφῳ Polem.*Cyn.*2.

ἐπείρομαι, inf. -είρεσθαι v.l. in Hdt.7.101, al.: impf. -είρετο Id. 3.22, al.: fut. -ειρήσομαι Id.1.67, al.: used by Att. only in fut. -ερήσομαι Ar.*Lys.*98, *Pl.*32, and aor. -ηρόμην, inf. -ερέσθαι, S.*OC* 557 (prob.), Th.8.29, etc.; Ion. ἐπειρέσθαι Hdt.1.19, al.:—*ask besides* or *again*, τοῦτο X.*Cyr.*6.3.10. II. c. acc. pers., *ask* or *question* him *besides*, τι *about* a thing, Ar.*Lys.*98, v.l. in Hdt.7.101; περί τινος Id. 1.158; with relat., ἐ. ὅ τι σιτέεται ὁ βασιλεύς Id.3.22; ὅντινα τρόπον Id.4.161. 2. esp. *inquire of* a god, τὸν θεόν Id.1.19; ἐπήροντο τὸν θεόν, εἰ παραδοῖεν.. Th.1.25; ἐπερησόμενος ᾠχόμην ὡς τὸν θεόν Ar.*Pl.* 32; ἔπεμπον τὴν ἐς θεὸν ἐπειρησομένους τὸν χῶρον Hdt.1.67; *question* a person, S. l.c. 3. *ask* the people *for* their opinion, τὴν γνώμην Pl.*Ax.*368d, cf. D.22.5.

ἐπειρύω, Ep. and Ion. for ἐπερύω.

ἐπειρωνεύομαι, *speak ironically*, App.*BC* 4.70, J.*BJ* 5.13.1: c. dat., *mock at*, τὸ δαιμόνιον ἐ. ταῖς ἐκ τῶν ἐμῶν σπλάγχνων χοαῖς ib.1.3.6.

ἐπειρωτάω or **-έω, ἐπειρώτημα, -ησις**, Ion. for ἐπερ-.

ἐπεισ-άγω [ᾰ], *bring in besides* or *over*, esp. of bringing in a second wife, ὁ παισὶν αὑτοῦ μητρυιὰν ἐπεισάγων *Com.Adesp.*110.3; ἐ. [τὴν Κλεοπάτραν] τῇ Ὀλυμπιάδι Satyr.5; ἐ. ἑταίρας εἰς τὴν οἰκίαν (i.e. besides one's wife), And.4.14 (so in Med., γυναῖκα ἄλλην ἐπεισάγεσθαι ἐφ' ὕβρει Δημητρίας *PEleph.*1.8 (iv B.C.)); τινὰς εἰς τὸ δικαστήριον dub. in *CIG* 5187 a 25 (Ptolemais):—Pass., οἱ ἐπεισαχθέντες the *newly made citizens*, D.H.2.56, cf. Luc.*Nav.*33:—Med., *introduce besides*, νέους ἑταίρους Pl.*R.*575d, cf. *Plt.*293d. 2. *bring in* something *new* or *strange*, ἔξωθεν Aeschin.1.166, etc.; ἐ. ἄλλην μηχανήν Plb.32.5.11; νόμον *introduce*, Jul.*Or.*2.88d:—Med., ὕδωρ ἐπὶ τόπους Plb.10.28.3. 3. *bring on besides*, χορείαν ἢ τράπεζαν δευτέραν Antiph.174.1; *bring next upon the stage*, Aeschin.3.231; δρᾶμα Plb. 23.10.12. 4. Med., *draw in*, τὸν οὐρανὸν ἐπεισάγεσθαι ἐκ τοῦ ἀπείρου χρόνου τε καὶ πνοὴν καὶ τὸ κενόν Arist.*Fr.*201. **-ἀγωγή**, ἡ, *bringing* *in besides*, ἑτέρων ἰητρῶν Hp.*Praec.*7; esp. of a second wife, J.*AJ*11.6.2; προσώπων ἐ. *introduction of new* characters, D.H.*Vett.Cens.*2.10 (pl.), cf. 3.3 (pl.); κρείττονος ἐλπίδος *Ep.Hebr.*7.19. 2. *means of bringing* or *letting in*, ἐπεσαγωγὰς τῶν πολεμίων Th.8.92. **-ἀγώγιμος,** ον, *brought in* from abroad, τὰ ἐ. *imported* wares, Pl.*R.*370e. **-ακτέον,** *one must introduce*, Herod.Med. in *Rh.Mus.*58.102. **-ακτος,** ον, *brought in from outside*, opp. οἰκεῖος, [Ἔρως] διὰ τῶν ὀμμάτων Pl.*Cra.*420b; *alien*, opp. αὐτόχθων, E.*Ion* 590; σῖτος D.18.87, 20.31; τροφή Hdn.8.5.4, cf. *Ostr.*757.4 (ii B.C.); ἡδονή Arist.*EN* 1169^{b}26; κακόν *Com.Adesp.*110.5; γάμοι J.*AJ*8.7.5; βασιλεύς Hdn.1.5.5; θύραθεν ἐ., opp. φύσει ὑπάρχον, Arist.*PA*659^{b}19; εἰ ἐπείσακτον τὸ τῆς ἀρετῆς ἦν, καὶ μηδὲν αὐτοῦ φύσει ἡμῖν μετῆν Muson.*Fr.*2 p.6 H.: fem. [ἐπει]σάνκτην (sic) is prob. l. in *SIG*1231 (Nicomedia). 2. *capable of import*, Aristid.*Or.*36(48).17,18. **-βαίνω,** *go into upon*, ἵππῳ εἰς θάλασσαν X.*HG*1.1.6; ἐ. ἐς τὴν θάλασσαν *go into* the sea *so as to board* ships, Th.2.90, 4.14. **-βάλλω,** *throw into besides*, ποτῷ E.*El.*498. II. intr., *invade again*, Th.3.13; of a *double attack* of fever, Gal.7.352; simply, *attack*, τῇ ἀγέλῃ Palaeph.1. **-βάτης** [ᾰ], ου, ὁ, *additional passenger, supernumerary on board* ship, E.*Hel.*1550. **-βῐάζομαι,** *force one's way in besides, intrude*, ὃς δ' ἂν ἕτερος ἐπεισβιάσηται, Inscrr. on grave-stones, *CIG*3996 (Iconium), etc. **-δέχομαι,** *admit besides*, *Placit.*4.22.2. **-ειμι,** (εἶμο *ibo*) *come in besides*, τῷ οὐρανῷ Arist.*Ph.*213^{b}23; θύραθεν Id.*GA*736^{b}28; *come on* (in battle) *besides*, v.l. in Hdt.7.210; *come next upon the stage*, Aeschin.3.153; *go on into*, X.*Cyn.*10.9; *enter into*, σώματα Hierocl. *in CA*4p.425 M. 2. *come in after*, Hp.*Prorrh.*2.1; ἔξωθεν Pl.*Ti.*81d. b. *impinge*, of external stimuli, Democr.9, Pl.*Ti.*50e, Epicur.*Nat.*84,129 G.; ἀπὸ τῶν ἔξωθεν Id.*Ep.*1p.11 U. **-έλευσις,** εως, ἡ, *additional incursion* (?), Eustr. *in EN*19.34. **-ενεκτέον,** *one must bring in besides*, Stob.2.7.2. **-έρπω,** *enter into*, εἴς τι Iamb.*Myst.*8.6. **-έρρω,** *rush in with ill luck to* one, Poll.9.158, Suid. **-έρχομαι,** *come in besides*, τινί *to* one, Th.8.35; esp. into a family as stepmother, Hdt.4.154; *rush in and attack*, ἐπεισήλθοσαν τῷ Σίμωνι εἰς τὸ συμπόσιον Lxx 1 *Ma.*16.16, cf. *UPZ*13.19 (ii B.C.). 2. *come in after*, Hdt.1.37; κατόπιν τινός Pl.*Prt.*316a; and freq. in Att.; τινί D.H.*Dem.*8. 3. *come into besides*, c. acc., ξένος ἐ. πόλιν E.*Ion*813: c. dat., δόμοις ib.851 (nisi leg. δόμους); εἰς τὸ χωρίον D.47.53; of things, *to be imported*, ἐ. ἐκ πάσης γῆς τὰ πάντα Th.2.38. II. metaph., 1. of customs, *to be introduced later*, Plu.2.676f, etc. 2. *come into* one's *head, occur to* one, c. dat., ib.585f: c. acc., Luc.*VH*2.42. **-ηγέομαι,** *introduce besides into*, τὴν τῶν ἱστίων χρείαν τοῖς ναυτικοῖς D.S.5.7. **-θεσις,** εως, ἡ, *further 'indentation'*, in Kolometry, Sch.Ar.*Eq.*381. II. *insertion*, Anon.*Prog.* in Rh.1.605 W. **-θρῴσκω,** aor. 2 ἐπείσθορε, *spring in after*, *AP*6.219.7 (Antip.).

ἐπείσιον, v. ἐπίσιον.

ἐπεισ-κᾰλέω, *co-opt*, Decr.ap.Arist.*Ath.*30.4. **-κλητος,** ον, *co-opted*, ibid. II. Subst., ἐπείσκλητος (sc. ἐκκλησία), ἡ, *specially convened meeting*, *Inscr.Magn.*44.10. **-κομίζω,** *bring in besides*, ἕτερον σῶμα ἐ. *CIG*(add.)3882*i* (Afium Kara Hissar), cf. *Rev.Phil.*36.53. **-κρίνομαι** [ῑ], Pass., *to be overcharged with food*, Hp.*Alim.*5. 2. *replace losses*, οὐσία ἀεὶ ῥεῖ τε καὶ ἑτέρα ἀνθ' ἑτέρας ἐπεισκρίνεται S.E.*P.*3.82. **-κυκλέω,** *roll* or *bring in one upon another*, 'pile up', τὰ μηδὲν προσήκοντα Luc.*Hist.Conscr.*13; ἀσάφειαν ἡμῖν τοσαύτην S.E.*P.*2.210; πλῆθος σημαινομένων Gal.8.575; ἄλλ' ἐπ' ἄλλοις Longin.22.4:—Pass., ἕτερα ἑτέροις -ούμενα Id.11.1; ὁ Ἄττις καὶ ὁ Κορύβας πόθεν ἡμῖν -ήθησαν; Luc.*Deor.Conc.*9, cf. *Philops.*29. **-κύκλησις,** εως, ἡ, = ἀνακύκλησις, ἐπισύναξις, Zonar. **-κωμάζω,** *rush in like disorderly revellers*, Pl.*R.*500b; of tyrants, *Stoic.*3.191: metaph. of arguments, Pl.*Tht.*184a, cf. Luc.*Pseudol.*11: c. acc., Σωφροσύνην καὶ Ἐγκράτειαν -εκώμασαν (nisi leg. -εκόμισαν) Aristox.*Fr.Hist.*15: c. dat., *make an inroad upon*, Κελτοὶ ἐ. τῇ Ἑλλάδι Aristid.*Or.*22(19).8.

ἐπεισοδ-ιάζω, *import, introduce* from without, ὁ τῶν αἰσθήσεων ὄχλος ἐπεισωδίασεν [τῇ ψυχῇ] κηρῶν ἀμήχανον πλῆθος Ph.1.134:—Pass., ib.592. **-ιος,** ον, *coming in besides, adventitious*, σύμφυτον .., οὐκ ἐ. Plu.2.451c, cf. 584e; ἐ. ἀκροάματα Id.*Luc.*40; ἐπιθυμίαι Id.*Cat.Ma.*18; φύκους ἄνθος ἐ. *AP*5.18 (Rufin.). II. **ἐπεισόδιον,** τό, *addition for the purpose of giving pleasure*, Plu.2.629c, 710d; ἐ. γαστρός, of dessert, *AP*6.232.6 (Crin.(?)). 2. in Poetry, *parenthetic addition, episode*: a. in Ep. poems, as the Catalogue in the Iliad, Arist.*Po.*1459^{a}36. b. in Tragedy, the portions of dialogue between two choric songs, ib.1452^{b}20: then of all *underplots* or *parenthetic narratives* in poetry, which might themselves form distinct wholes, ib.1451^{b}34; also in prose speeches, etc., D.H.*Comp.*19, *Isoc.*4, *Th.*7. c. in Comedy, *interlude, intermezzo*, Metag.14. 3. metaph., ἐπεισόδια τύχης Plb.2.35.5; ὅτι μὴ ἐ. τὸ σὸν τῷ παντί Plot.3.3.3. **-ιόω,** *vary by introducing episodes*, Arist.*Po.*1455^{b}1; τὸν λόγον ἐ. ἐπαίνοις Id.*Rh.*1418^{a}33. **-ιώδης,** ες, *episodic, incoherent*, μῦθος Id.*Po.*1451^{b}34: metaph., οὐκ ἔοικεν ἡ φύσις ἐ. οὖσα ὥσπερ μοχθηρὰ τραγῳδία Id.*Metaph.*1090^{b}19, cf. Dam.*Pr.*279. Adv. -δῶς Ascl. *in Metaph.*142.28. II. = ἐπεισόδιος I, *adventitious*, οὐ γὰρ ἔξωθεν ἐπίκτητος οὐδ' ἐ. Porph.*Sent.*36; ἐ. καὶ δευτέραν συνεπομένην ὑπόστασιν Iamb.*Protr.*3; ἐ. καὶ συμβεβηκός Dam.*Pr.*14; ἐ. καὶ ἀλλαχόθεν ἐφῆκον Procl.*Inst.*19. **-ος,** ἡ, *coming in besides, approach*, S.*OC*730, *Fr.*273; *entrance from without*, Epicur.*Nat.*21 G., *Placit.*4.22.1; ἀέρος ψυχροῦ Orib.*Fr.*38; ἀθέων λογισμῶν Ph.1.76.

ἐπεισ-παίω, *burst in*, ἐς τὴν οἰκίαν Ar.*Pl.*805; εἰς τὰ συμπόσια *Com.Adesp.*439: abs., Luc.*DMeretr.*15.1. **-πέμπω,** *send in* or *to*, D.C.67.17. **-πηδάω,** *leap in upon*, τοὺς εἰς τὰς τάφρους ἐμπίπτοντας -ῶντες ἐφόνευον X.*Cyr.*3.3.64; τῷ ἄρχειν *usurp*, Philostr.*VA*2.31, cf. Just.*Nov.*42 *Pr.*: abs., Ar.*Eq.*363, D.47.56, D.C.67.17. **-πηδητής,** οῦ, ὁ, *house-breaker, burglar*, *Gloss.* **-πίπτω,** *fall* or *burst in upon*, c. dat., ναυστάθμοις E.*Rh.*448; ἐ. αὐτοῖς πίνουσι X.*Cyr.*7.5.27: also c. acc., ἐ. πόλιν E.*HF*34: abs., τὰ ἐπεσπίπτοντα Hp.*Vict.*1.10; *burst in*, S.*OC*915, E.*Hec.*1042, J.*BJ*6.9.4. 2. *fall upon*, βρονταὶ καὶ πρηστῆρές τινι ἐπεσπίπτουσι Hdt.7.42. 3. metaph., ἐπεισπίπτει οἰκοτριβὴς δαπάνη Critias 6.14. **-πλέω,** *sail in after*, Th.6.2, X.*HG*1.1.5; θύννων.. ἐπεισέπλει ὑπογάστρι' Eub.37. II. *sail against, attack*, Th.4.13. **-πνέω,** *breathe in again* (cf. ἐπανάκλησις II), Hp.*Epid.*2.3.7. **-πράττω,** *exact besides*, D.C.74.8. **-ρέω,** *flow in upon* or *besides*, *Trag.Adesp.*89, Ph.*Fr.*73 H., Plu.*Num.*20, Luc.*Alex.*49. **-ροή,** ἡ, *influx*, τῆς νοητῆς λαμπηδόνος *Corp.Herm.*10.4. **-ρῦσις,** εως, ἡ, v. ἐπέκρυσις. **-τρέχω,** aor. -έδραμον Jul.*Caes.*309c:—*run in upon* or *after*, τινί l. c.: abs., Ph.2.128. **-φέρω,** *bring in besides* or *next*, [ἅρμενον] Hp.*Art.*4 (Pass.); κακοῦ κάκιον ἄλλο πῆμα A.*Ag.*864; τέκνον δόμοισι Id.*Ch.*649 (lyr.); ἐ. λόγον *bring in a new* argument, Ar.*Th.*1164; in Inscrr. on grave-stones, *bring in another* body, *CIG*3384 (Smyrna), al.:—Med., *bring in for oneself*, μαρτύρια Th.3.53:—Pass., *rush in besides*, Aen.Tact.39.3; τὸ αἰεὶ ἐπεσφερόμενον πρῆγμα whatever *comes upon us, occurs*, Hdt.7.50; ὁ ἐ. [νόμος] the law *newly brought in*, Arist.*Top.*151^{b}13. **-φοιτάω,** *to be in the habit of coming in*, ἔξωθεν Ph.1.615. **-φορέω,** = ἐπεισφέρω, in Pass., ib.468. II. Med., abs., *take food afterwards*, Archig.ap.Orib.8.1.7. **-φρέω,** *bring in* or *introduce besides*, πῶς ἐπεσφρῶ τήνδε τῷ κείνης λέχει; E.*Alc.*1056; λέκτροις τ' ἐπεισέφρηκε Id.*El.*1033; ὄφεις ἐπεισέφρησε σπαργάνοις Id.*HF*1267: aor. part. ἐπεισφρείς (as if from ἐπεισπίφρημι) Id.*Fr.*781.50. II. intr., *come in besides*, Suid. **-χέω,** *pour in besides*, φῶς ἐς νοῦν Ph.1.150; ποιότητας τῇ διανοίᾳ ib.194:—Pass., ib.174, al.; of a crowd, *pour in one after another*, J.*BJ*1.18.2, 4.3.3 (v.l. ἐπιχ-).

ἔπειτα, Ion. and Dor. **ἔπειτε(ν)** (q.v.), Adv., (ἐπί, εἶτα): I. of mere Sequence, without any notion of cause, *thereupon, thereafter, then*, freq. from Hom. downwds., as Il.1.48, 2.169, etc.: when in strong opposition to the former act or state, with past tenses, *thereafter, afterwards*; with future, *hereafter*, ἢ πέφατ' ἢ καὶ ἔ. πεφήσεται Il.15.140; opp. αὐτίκα νῦν, 23.551; ὃς δ' ἔπειτ' ἔφυ, opp. ὅστις πάροιθεν ἦν, A.*Ag.*171 (lyr.): in Hom. freq. with other Advs., αὐτίκ' ἔ. Il.5.214; αἶψα, ὦκα ἔ., 24.783, 18.527; even ἔνθα.. ἔ. Od.10.297; δὴ ἔ. 8.378: usu. with reference to a former act, *just then, at the time*, 1.106; freq. in narrative, πρῶτα μὲν.., αὐτὰρ ἔ. Il.16.497; πρῶτον μέν.., folld. by ἔ. δέ.., Th.2.55, Pl.*Ap.*18a, etc.; by ἔ. alone, Th.1.33, etc.; by ἔ. δέ.. ἔ. δέ.. ἔ..., X.*Cyr.*1.3.14; ἐπεὶ δέ.. ἔ... ἔ... ἔ. δέ, ib.8.3.24, al.; πρὶν μέν.., ἔ. δέ.. S.*El.*724; ἔ. γε Pl.*Tht.*147c, etc., f.l. in Ar.*Th.*556; κἄπειτα, freq. in Trag., S.*Aj.*61, 305, etc. 2. c. Art., τὸ ἔ. *what follows*, τό τ' ἔ. καὶ τὸ μέλλον καὶ τὸ πρίν Id.*Ant.*611 (lyr.); τά τε πρῶτα, τά τ' ἔ., ὅσα τ' ἔμελλε τυχεῖν E.*IT*1265 (lyr.); οἱ ἔ. *future generations*, A.*Eu.*672; ὁ ἔ. βίος Pl.*Phd.*116a; εἰς τὸν ἔ. χρόνον Id.*Phlb.*39e, X.*Cyr.*1.5.9, *OGI*90.43 (Rosetta, ii B.C.); ἡ ἐς τὸ ἔ. δόξα Th.2.64; ἐν τῷ ἔ. Pl.*Phd.*67d; ἐκ τοῦ ποτὲ εἰς τὸ ἔ. Id.*Prm.*152b. 3. like εἶτα, with a finite Verb after a participle, μειδήσασα δ' ἔ. ἑῷ ἐγκάτθετο κόλπῳ she smiled and *then* placed it in her bosom, Il.14.223, cf. 11.730, etc.: freq. in Trag. and Att., A.*Th.*267, *Eu.*29, Pl.*Phd.*82c: so freq. when part. and Verb are opposed, marking surprise or the like, *and then, and yet, nevertheless*, τὸ μητρὸς αἷμα.. ἐκχέας πέδοι ἔ. δώματ' οἰκήσει πατρός; A.*Eu.*654, cf. 438; χὤταν ἐν κακοῖσί τις ἁλοὺς ἔ. τοῦτο καλλύνειν θέλῃ S.*Ant.*496; ὅστις ἀνθρώπου φύσιν βλαστὼν ἔ. μὴ κατ' ἄνθρωπον φρονῇ Id.*Aj.*761; εἰ πτωχὸς ὢν ἔπειτ' ἐν Ἀθηναίοις λέγειν μέλλω Ar.*Ach.*498, cf. *Av.*29, Pl.*Grg.*519e, *Prt.*319d: adversatively, answering μέν, πολλάκις μὲν ὥρμα.., ἔ... διεκωλύετο Id.*R.*336b; ἔτι μὲν ἐνεχείρησα.., ἔ... Id.*Prt.*310c, etc.; also κἄπειτα after a part., Ar.*Nu.*624, *Av.*536; cf. εἶτα I. 2. 4. in apodosi (never at the beginning of the clause; in Hom. freq. strengthd. by other Particles): a. after a Temporal Conj., *then, thereafter*, ἐπεὶ δὴ σφαίρῃ πειρήσαντο, ὀρχείσθην δὴ ἔ. when they had done playing at ball, *then* they danced, Od.8.378; after ἐπεί, Il.16.247; ἐπὴν ..δὴ ἔ. Od.11.121; ὁπότε, Il.18.545; ὅτε, 3.223; ὡς..ἄρ' ἔ. 10.522; ἦμος..καὶ τότ' ἔ. 1.478. b. after a Conditional Conj., *then surely*, εἰ δ' ἐτεὸν δὴ.. ἀγορεύεις, ἐξ ἄρα δή τοι ἔ. θεοὶ φρένας ὤλεσαν if thou speakest sooth, *then of a surety* have the gods infatuated thee, 7.360, cf. 10.453, Od.1.290, etc.; so after ἤν, Il.9.394; also when the apodosis takes the form of a question, εἰ μὲν δὴ ἕταρόν γε κελεύετέ μ' αὐτὸν ἑλέσθαι, πῶς ἂν ἔ. Ὀδυσῆος λαθοίμην; how can I *in such a case?* 10.243; when a condition is implied in relat. Pron., ὃν (= εἴ τινα) μέν κ' ἐπιεικὲς ἀκουέμεν, οὔ τις ἔ. τόν γ' εἴσεται 1.547; ὃν (= εἴ τινα) δέ κ' ἐγὼν ἀπάνευθε μάχης ἐθέλοντα νοήσω μιμνάζειν, οὔ οἱ ἔ. ἄρκιον ἐσσεῖται 2.392. II. of Sequence in thought, i.e. Consequence or Inference, *then, therefore*, ξεῖν', ἐπεὶ ἂρ δὴ ἔ.... μενεαίνεις Od.17.185, cf. Il.15.49, 18.357; οὐ σύ γ' ἔ. Τυδέος ἔκγονός ἐσσι 5.812; rarely at the beginning, ἔπειθ' ἑλοῦ γε θάτερα S.*El.*345. 2. in telling a story, νῆσος ἔ. τις ἔστι *now*, there is an island, Od.4.354, cf. 9.116. 3. in Att. freq. to introduce emphatic questions, *why then ..?* ἔ. τοῦ δέει; Ar.*Pl.*827, cf. *Th.*188, *Nu.*226; mostly to express surprise, or to sneer, *and so forsooth..? and so really..?* ἔ. οὐκ οἴει φροντίζειν [τοὺς θεοὺς τῶν ἀνθρώπων]; X.*Mem.*1.4.11; so κἄπειτα E.*Med.*1398 (anap.), Ar.*Ach.*126, *Av.*963, X.*Smp.*4.2; freq. with δῆτα added, ἔ. δῆτα δοῦλος ὢν κόμην ἔχεις; Ar.*Av.*911, cf. 1217, *Lys.*985, E.*Alc.*822.

ἐπείτε or **ἐπεί τε**, *when* or *since*, Il.11.87, 12.393, Hdt.1.14,48, etc.: **ἐπεί τε ἄν, ἐπεί τ' ἄν**, Hdt.1.200,202, *OGI*213.24,35, *SIG*577.30 (Milet., iii/ii B.C.).

ἔπειτε, Ion. for ἔπειτα, *thereafter*, prob. in Hdt.1.146, 2.52, al., cf. *SIG*^{2}660.2 (Milet., iv B.C.), but ἔπειτεν is Ion. acc. to Ael.Dion.*Fr.* 158; Dor. **ἔπειτεν** Pi.*P.*4.211, *N.*3.54, al., Ar.*Ach.*745, *IG*5(1).1390.28 (Andania).

ἐπέκ, v. ἐπές.

ἐπεκ-βαίνω, *go out upon, disembark*, ἐς γῆν Th.8.105: abs., Id.1.49: c. acc., ἐ. χέρσον, of waves, *go out over*, *AP*7.393 (Diocl., χέρσῳ codd.), 9.276 (Crin.). **–βάλλω**, *prolong* an incision, Antyll.ap. Orib.45.26.3. II. Geom., *produce*, Archim.*Spir.Praef.* (Pass.); τὸ μῆκος Iamb.*in Nic.*p.57 P. **–βοάω**, *cry out against*, D.C.43.24 codd. **–βοηθέω**, *rush out to aid*, Th.7.53, 8.55. **–δῐδάσκω**, *teach* or *explain besides*, τι Pl.*Prt.*328e; ὡς.. Id.*Euthphr.*7a; ὅπως.. Plu.*Sol.*25; ὁ -διδάσκων λόγος Plb.15.35.7:—Pass., Gal.*Libr.Propr.* 1. **–δῐδᾰχή**, ἡ, *added explanation*, Choerob.Rh.22. **–δίδωμι**, *farm out a contract again*, *IG*7.3073.38 (Lebad.). II. *publish again*, Sch.Il.19.365 (Pass.). **–διηγέομαι**, *explain besides*, Pl.*Phd.* 97e. **–δῐκέω**, *avenge*, τινί Tz.*H.*10.428. **–δρομή**, ἡ, *sally, sortie*, Th.4.25, Procop.*Vand.*2.8, al.; *raid*, D.C.46.38.

ἐπέκεινα, Adv., for ἐπ' ἐκεῖνα, opp. ἐπὶ τάδε (Pl.*Phd.*112b), *on yonder side, beyond*, c. gen., Hecat.ap.Str.12.3.23; τοῦ Ἡρακλείου ἐ. X. *HG*5.1.10; οἱ ἐ. Τίγριδος καὶ Εὐφράτου Hdn.2.8.8; ἐ. ἐλθεῖν Διονύσου *farther than..*, Arr.*An.*5.2.1: metaph., ἐ. τῆς οὐσίας ὑπερέχειν Pl. *R.*509b; ἐλπίδος ἐ. Hld.9.5. 2. with Art., τὸ ἐ., Att. τοὐπ., or τὰ ἐ., Att. τἀπ., the *part beyond*, the *far side*, τὰ ἐ. τῆς Εὐρώπης Hdt.3.115, cf. Th.6.63, etc.; τοὐπέκεινα τῆσδε γῆς *beyond* it, E.*Hipp.*1199; Πίνδου τε τἀπ. A.*Supp.*257, cf. X.*HG*5.1.10: abs., οἱ ἐκ τοῦ ἐ. Id.*An.* 5.4.3; ἐν τῷ ἐ. Th.7.58; τῶν νόθων [ἡδονῶν] εἰς τὸ ἐ. ὑπερβάς Pl.*R.* 587c; τὸ ἐ. τοῦ νοῦ Porph.*Sent.*25, Jul.*Or.*4.132c. II. of past Time, οἱ ἐ. χρόνοι the times *beyond* or *before, earlier* times, Isoc.6.41; οἱ ἐ. (sc. τῶν Τρωϊκῶν γενόμενοι) Id.9.6. 2. of future Time, *henceforth*, Lxx 1*Ma.*10.30, Thd.*Su.*64.

ἐπεκέκλετο, v. ἐπικέλομαι. **ἐπεκήκατο**· ἐπωνείδιστο, Hsch.

ἐπέκ-θεσις, εως, ἡ, *further* ἔκθεσις, Sch.Ar.*Nu.*456. **–θέω**, = ἐπεκτρέχω, Th.4.34, 5.9, X.*HG*5.3.6; ἐς τὰς τάξεις Arr.*An.*5.17.3; τῷ τάγματι Plb.*Fr.*122. **–θύομαι**, *offer sacrifice for*, Arr.*Epict.* 2.7.9, Gal.9.833. **–κουφίζω**, *lighten*, τὰς ἐτησίους εἰσφοράς J.*BJ* 1.21.12. **–κρῐσις**, εως, ἡ, *secretion* or *expulsion* of bodies, cj. in Leucipp.ap.D.L.9.32 (ἐπέκρυσιν codd.). **–λέγομαι**, *choose, select*, Procop.*Arc.*6. **–πίνω** [ῑ], *drink off after*, E.*Cyc.*327. **–πλέω**, *sail out against*, v.l. in Th.7.37. **–πλοος**, contr. **–πλους**, ὁ, *sailing out against, attack by sea*, ἐ. ποιεῖσθαι Id.8.20. **–πνέω**, *breathe out twice*, opp. ἐπεισπνέω, Gal.10.700. **–ρηξις**, εως, ἡ, *outbreak, bursting out*, Epicur.*Ep.*2 p.54 U. **–ροφέω**, *swallow up*, dub. l. in Ar.*Eq.*701; v. ἐκρ–. **–ρῠσις**, εως, ἡ, *influx from without*, Leucipp.ap.D.L.9.32 (nisi leg. ἐπείσρυσις vel ἐπέκκρισις). **–τᾰσις**, εως, ἡ, *extension*, Arist.*Cael.*305^{b}18; ἔχειν ἐ. to be capable of *extension*, Id.*LI*971^{b}1. b. of Time, Just.*Nov.*111.1. 2. *explication, evolution*, εἰς ἐνέργειαν καὶ ἐ. προχωρεῖν *Theol.Ar.*14. 3. *stretching* of a rope, Hero *Aut.*2.4; of strands of gut, Ph.*Bel.*58.13; of hernia, κατ' ἐπέκτασιν Heliod.ap.Orib.50.42. 4. οἱ κατ' ἐπέκτασιν παραλελυμένοι patients suffering from *creeping* paralysis, Herod.Med.ap. Orib.10.8.1. II. *lengthening* of a word, Arist.*Po.*1458^{b}2 (pl.), 1458^{a}23, A.D.*Pron.*6.14, al.; of a vowel, Id.*Adv.*144.19. **–τᾰτικός**, ή, όν, *lengthening*, Eust.1393.14. **–τείνω**, *stretch*, Sor.1.10 (Pass.), al.; *extend*, [τὸ αὔταρκες] ἐπὶ τοὺς ἀπογόνους Arist.*EN*1097^{b}12:—Pass., *to be extended, extend*, Id.*Ph.*217^{b}9, etc. 2. intr., *extend*, ἐπὶ πλέον Id.*APo.*96^{a}24; of a people or country, μέχρι.. Str.8.3.11: c. dat., *extend over*, Olymp.*in Mete.*75.12. 3. Pass., *extend beyond*, τῆς οἰκείας ὥρας Thphr.*HP*6.8.4; *reach out towards*, τοῖς ἔμπροσθεν *Ep.Phil.*3.13. 4. Tact., *extend*, τοὺς ἱππέας Ascl.*Tact.* 10.20. 5. *expand*, ἓν νόημα Hermog.*Inv.*4.4. II. *lengthen, prolong*, λόγους Plu.2.1147. 2. *pronounce* a syllable *as long*, Arist. *Metaph.*1014^{b}17. 3. *lengthen* a word, by inserting a vowel or otherwise (as πόληος for πόλεως), ἐπεκτεταμένον, opp. ἀφῃρημένον, Id.*Po.*1457^{b}35; also by adding a syllable, in Pass., A.D.*Pron.* 34.5, al. III. *make more burdensome*, τὰς προσόδους Str.17.1.15. **–τετᾰμένως**, Adv., (ἐπεκτείνω) *vehemently*, θρηνεῖν Sch.A.*Pers.* 1051. **–τίνω**, Cret. aor. inf. ἐπεσ-τεῖσαι, *pay up*, τὸ ἁπλόον *GDI* 4993 (Gortyn). **–τρέχω**, aor. 2 -έδρᾰμον, *sally out upon* or *against*, πελτασταῖς ἐκ τοῦ τείχους X.*HG*4.4.17: abs., ib.6.2.17: c. acc., *raid*, Paus.1.20.5. **–φέρω**, *carry out*, f.l. for ὑπ– in Plu.*Alex.*26. II. *seek to enforce* a contract, *PEleph.*1.14,16 (iv B.C.). **–φώνησις**, εως, ἡ, *exclamation*, Anon.*Fig.* in *Rhet.Lat.Min.*p.66 Halm. **–χέω**, *pour out upon*, Anon.ap.Suid. s.v. θραυλοτέρας:—Pass., *rush upon*, τοῖς πολεμίοις Lxx *Ju.*15.4, cf. *PTeb.*39.24 (ii B.C.); *to be stretched upon*, τινί Q.S.10.481. **–χράομαι**, *abuse, misuse*, *PRyl.*75.18 (ii A.D.). **–χωρέω**, *advance next* or *after*, A.*Pers.*401.

ἐπελ-ᾰσία, ἡ, *driving away*, 'lifting', [ἵππων] D.S.36.4. **–ᾰσις**, εως, ἡ, *charge*, of cavalry, Arr.*Tact.*16.10 (pl.), al.; ποιεῖσθαι τὰς ἐ. Plu.*Tim.*27, cf. Jul.*Or.*2.60b, Agath.1.14, al.; of elephants, Luc. *Hist.Conscr.*31.

ἐπελαύνω, *drive upon*, τὰς ἁμάξας ἐπελαύνουσι, i.e. *upon* the ice, Hdt.4.28. b. *drive to* a place, ἐπελάντω (non-thematic 3 pl. imper.) βοῦς τρεῖς *SIG*1025.11 (Cos). 2. in Hom., *lay* metal *beaten out into plates over* a surface (cf. ἐλαύνω III. 1), ἐπὶ δ' ὄγδοον ἤλασε χαλκόν Il.7.223; πολλὸς δ' ἐπελήλατο χαλκός 13.804, cf. 17.493. 3. metaph., ὅρκους ἐπελαύνειν τινί *force* an oath *upon* one, Hdt.1.146, cf. 6.62. II. *drive* or *ride against*, ἵππον τινί X.*Eq.*8.11; *lead against*, τὴν στρατιήν Hdt.1.164; *push forcibly against*, στέρνα θ' ὁμοῦ καὶ χεῖρας A.R.1.381. 2. intr., *march against*, Hdt.1.17, al.; τινί X. *HG*7.1.21; ἐπὶ Βαβυλῶνα Hdt.3.151, cf. 7.9.α'; ἐπήλασαν οἱ ἱππόται *charged*, Id.9.49, cf. 18, Arr.*Tact.*4.7, al.; τρεῖς [νῆες] ἐπήλασαν περὶ τὸ ἕρμα *drove upon* the rock, Hdt.7.183: c. acc. loci, *march over*, Luc.*Rh.Pr.*5. III. Pass., *to be driven in after*, τὸ -όμενον [τοῦ τομέως] X.*Eq.Mag.*2.3. IV. Med., 3 pl. aor. imper., ἐπελασάσθων οἱ ἁλιασταί *let* them *impose a fine*, *IG*5(2).6.23 (Tegea): 3 pl. pres. imper. (non-thematic), ἐπελάσθω (fr. *ἐπελάνσθω) τὰ ἐπιζάμια *Tab.Heracl.*1.127.

ἐπελαφρ-ίζω, *lighten, make easy to bear*, ἀτυχήματα, etc., Ph.2.339, al.:—Med., metaph. of persons, ἔχοντες παραμύθιον ἐ. τὰς ἀνίας ib.420; of birds, κακοπαθείας τῷ εὐσεβεῖν ib.200:—Pass., *to be made lighter*, ib.621: metaph., ψυχὴ ἐ. ὑπὸ πενθείας Id.1.351. **–ύνω**, *lighten*, τὸν δεσμόν τινι Plu.2.165e; πόνον J.*AJ*18.1.1, cf. D.Chr.3.123, Max.Tyr.37.5, Hierocl.*in CA*15 p.454 M.

ἐπέλδομαι, v. ἐπιέλδ–.

ἐπελέγχω, = ἐλέγχω, D.L.6.97, *POxy.*64.4 (Pass., iii/iv A.D.).

ἐπελευθεριάζω, *act with free will*, Ph.2.328.

ἐπελ-εύθω, aor. 1 ἐπήλευσα, *bring* a child *to* its father, *Leg.Gort.*3.45, al. **–ευσις**, εως, ἡ, *coming on* or *to, arrival*, ὄχλων *Cat.Cod. Astr.*7.132, cf. Eust.1574.59; *touching on* a thing, *survey* of it, Id. ad D.P.*Prooem.*p.71 B.; so [μέγεθος] ἐν διεξόδῳ καὶ ἐ. καθ' ἕκαστον μέρος αἰσθανόμεθα Plot.2.8.1, cf. Them.*in de An.*30.33. 2. *adventitious impulse*, Chrysipp.*Stoic.*2.282. 3. in Law, *prosecution*, *PFay.* 26.14 (ii A.D.), *POxy.*1638.13 (iii A.D.). **–ευστικός**, ή, όν, *coming on* or *to, touching on* a thing: hence, of casual mention, Eust.ad D.P. *Prooem.*p.69 B. Adv. -κῶς Eust.1440.18, 7.26 (Comp.). 2. *of the nature of* ἐπέλευσις 2, κίνησις Chrysipp.*Stoic.*2.282. 3. *occurring casually*, εἶδος ἐν τοῖς λόγοις Str.12.3.27. 4. *liable to prosecution*, *POxy.*1120.10 (iii A.D.).

ἐπελήλατο, 3 sg. plpf. Pass. of ἐπελαύνω. **ἐπέλησε**, v. ἐπιλήθω. **ἐπέλι⟨γ⟩ξεν**· ἐπέδραμεν, Hsch.; cf. πελίγξαι. **ἐπελίσσω, ἐπέλκω**, Ion. for ἐφελ–. **ἐπέλλαβε**, poet. for ἐπέλαβε, 3 sg. aor. 2 of ἐπιλαμβάνω.

ἐπελλύχνιον, τό, *lamp-oil*, *PRev.Laws* 40.10, 55.9 (iii B.C.).

ἐπελπίζω, *buoy up with hope*, αὐτοὺς θειάσαντες ἐπήλπισαν, ὡς λήψονται Th.8.1, cf. Anon.ap.Suid. s.v. Πυθαγόρας, Longin.44.2, Luc. *DMort.*5.2. II. intr., ἐ. τινί *pin one's hopes upon, hope in*, Hld.7.26; ἐπί τινι D.C.41.11: abs., Luc.*Tim.*21; but also, 2. merely, = ἐλπίζω, E.*Hipp.*1011, Ph.1.74, al.; *hope besides*, Th.8.54 (v.l. ἐλπίζων).

ἐπέλπομαι, Ep. **ἐπιέλπομαι**, poet. Verb, *have hopes of, hope*, c. inf. fut., μὴ δὴ.. ἐμοὺς ἐπιέλπεο μύθους εἰδήσειν Il.1.545; ἐπιελπόμενος τό γε θυμῷ, νευρὴν ἐντανύειν (fut. inf., v.l. –σειν) Od.21.126; οὐδὲν ἐπελπομένα.. ἐκτολυπεύσειν A.*Ag.*1031 (lyr.): generally, *expect*, Telest.1.1.

ἐπεμ-βᾰδόν, Adv. *step upon step*, *AP*9.668 (Marian.). **–βαίνω**, *step* or *tread upon*, in pf., *stand upon*, c. gen., οὐδοῦ ἐπεμβεβαώς Il. 9.582; σῆς ἐπεμβαίνων χθονός S.*OC*924; δίφρου ἐπεμβεβαώς *mounted on* a chariot, Hes.*Sc.*324; ὄχθων ἐπεμβάς E.*Ba.*1061 codd.: abs., ἐπεμβεβαώς Pi.*N.*4.29: also c. dat., *approach, attack*, πύργοις ἐπεμβάς A.*Th.*634, etc.; τῷ δήμῳ Hyp.*Phil.Fr.*10; ἐ. ἀλλοτρίαις ἕδραις Gal. *UP*14.14: c. acc., ῥάχιν E.*Rh.*783: with a Prep., εἰς πέτραν ὅτι ποτ' ἐπεμβάσῃ Id.*IT*649 (lyr.). 2. *embark* on ship-board, D.50.25. II. c. dat. pers., *trample upon*, ἐχθροῖσιν.. ἐπεμβῆναι ποδί S.*El.*456: metaph., παισὶν ἐπεμβαίνειν E.*Hipp.*668; κατ' ἐμοῦ.. μᾶλλον ἐπεμβάσει S.*El.*836 (lyr.); ἁμαρτήμασί τινων Plu.2.59d. 2. τῷ καιρῷ ἐπεμβαίνων *taking advantage of* the opportunity, D.21.203. **–βάλλω**, *put on*, πῶμα πίθοιο Hes.*Op.*98; στόμι' ἐ. ἐμοί E. *IT*935; γιγνώσκοντι ἐ. *heap words on* one who already knows, Arist. *Rh.*1406^{a}34. 2. *throw down upon*, δόμους ἐπεμβαλῶ *will throw* them *on* [the inmates], E.*HF*864: c. acc. loci, ὄχθον ὡς ἐπεμβάλῃ *that* she *may dash* [her] *upon* it (dub. constr.), Id.*IT*290. 3. *intercalate*, Hdt.2.4; *insert*, Pl.*Cra.*399a; πολλὰ ἐπὶ τὰ πρῶτα ὀνόματα ib. 414d; of parentheses, Hermog.*Id.*1.12 (Pass.), cf. 1.4, al.; of ingredients in a salad, Gal.6.539: metaph., γῆς σωτῆρα σαυτὸν τῷδ' ἐπεμβάλλεις λόγῳ by this story thou *foistest* thyself *in, intrudest* thyself, as saviour of the land, S.*OC*463: in Inscrr. on grave-stones, *put in another* corpse, *IGRom.*4.1284, al. (Thyatira):—Med., *make fresh additions*, of sculptors, Pl.*Plt.*277a:—Pass., of fruit-trees, *to be engrafted*, Ath.14.653d; cf. ἐπεμβολάς. 4. *thrust on*, X.*Cyn.*10.11. II. intr., *flow in besides*, of rivers, Id.*HG*4.2.11. III. ἐπεμβάλλεται· τρώγει, Hsch. **–βᾰσις**, εως, ἡ, *attack, advance*, D.H.3.19 (pl.). 2. pl., *steps*, τῶν κρηπίδων *IG*2^2.1671.10,13 (iv B.C.). II. Astrol., *commencement of* χρονοκρατορία, Man.5.80, Ptol.*Tetr.*141, al., Paul.Al.*R.*3. **–βᾰτήρ**, ῆρος, ὁ, = sq.; v. ἐπαμβατήρ. **–βάτης** [ᾰ], ου, ὁ, *one mounted*, ἵππων ἐπεμβάται E.*Ba.*782: abs., *horseman*, Anacr.75.6; also ἁρμάτων ἐ. E.*Supp.*585: abs., ib.685. II. *one who walks on* or *in*, ἐπεμβάται ἴχνεσι κούφοις Orph.*H.*31.3. **–βᾰφίζω**, *bathe again*, Hsch. s.v. κἀπεμβαφίζων: glossed by **–βάπτω**. **–βιβάζω**, *put into* a bath *again*, Antyll.ap.Orib.10.13.19. 2. *place on top*, Mich.*in PN*68.5. **–βλέπω**, *gaze at*, τινί prob.l. in D.Chr.4.95. **–βλημα**, ατος, τό, in pl., *the upper* ἀποστηρίγματα (q.v.), Gal. 18(2).919. **–βλητέον**, *one must insert*, Pl.*Ti.*51d. **–βοάω**, *raise* a shout, μακρὸν ἐπεμβοάᾳ γλώσσῃ θρόον Nic.*Al.*219. **–βολάς**, άδος, ἡ, of fruit-trees, *grafted*, Arist.*Fr.*274. **–βολέω**, Astrol., =

μεσεμβολέω, *Cat.Cod.Astr.*1.107. **-βολή**, ἡ, *insertion, parenthesis*, Hermog.*Id.*1.1, al., Eust.48.46, etc. 2. *placing over* so as to fasten, Heliod.ap.Orib.48.33.4. **-βόλιμος**, ον, *intrusive*, θεός Lyd. *Mag.*2.3. 2. = ἐμβόλιμος, *intercalary*, Gloss. **-βολος**, ον, = foreg. 2, *CIG*2722.3 (Stratonicea). **-βρίθω** [ῑ], *bear heavily on*, c. acc., *PFlor.*93.14 (vi A.D.):—Med., *overcome*, ἀηδία ἐ. τινάς *PMasp.* 153.13 (vi A.D.). **-βρῑμάομαι**, *to be indignant, rage against*, Sch. rec.A.*Pr.*73. **-μηνος**, ον, *in menstruation*, γυναιξὶν -οις (v.l. ἐπ' ἐμμ.) J.*BJ*6.9.3. **-πηδάω**, *trample upon*, τινὶ κειμένῳ Ar.*Nu.* 550. II. *make a second throb*, of the pulse, Gal.8.556. **-πίνω** [ῑ], gloss on ἐπεγκανάσσω, Hsch. **-πίπτω**, *fall upon, attack furiously*, ἀλλήλοις Ph.2.109; ποίμναις ἐπεμπίπτειν βάσιν S.*Aj.* 42. 2. *fall to, set to work*, Ar.*Pax*471. 3. *fit in*, of cogs, v.l. in Heliod.ap.Orib.49.4.65.

ἐπεμφέρω, *bring in besides, add*, ἀνάγκην τινί Hippodam.ap.Stob. 4.39.26:—Pass., Nic.*Al.*28.

ἐπέναρ· εἰς τετάρτην (Lacon.), Hsch.; cf. ἔναρ.

ἐπενᾰρίζω, *kill one over another*, S.*OC*1733 (Elmsl. for ἐνάριξον).

ἐπεν-δίδωμι, *give over and above*, ἐ. τρίτην *I put in yet a third blow*, A. *Ag.*1386. **-δίημι**, = ἐπαφίημι, Ep. 3 pl. aor. 2 ἐπενδίεσαν, Hsch. **-δῐκάζω**, *contest a claim in court*, *BGU*1105.31 (i A.D.). **-δῠμα**, ατος, τό, *upper garment*, Aq.*Ex.*28.26, al., f.l. in Plu.*Alex.*32. **-δύνω** [ῡ] or **-δύω**, *put on over*, ἐπὶ τοῦτον ἄλλον κιθῶνα Hdt.1.195:—Med., -σάμενος χιτῶνα J.*AJ*3.7.4; πολλὰ σώματα Aen.Gaz.*Thphr.*p.60 B.:—Pass. (with aor. 2 part. -δύντες J.*AJ*5.1.12), *have on over*, ἐσθῆτας ἐπενδεδυμένοι γυναικείας τοῖς θώραξι Plu.*Pel.*11. **-δύτης** [ῠ], ου, ὁ, *robe* or *garment worn over* another, Ps.-Thesp.1, S.*Fr.*439, Lxx 1*Ki.* 18.4; ἐ. χιτών Nicoch.5, cf. Ael.Dion.*Fr.*325, Poll.7.45. **-δῠτοπάλλιον**, τό, = foreg., *CIG*2663 (Halic.). **-δύω**, v. ἐπενδύνω.

ἐπένε(γ)ξις, εως, ἡ, (ἐπενεγκεῖν) *adding*, *EM*354.30.

ἐπένερθε, Adv. *below*, *Ath.Mitt.*49.15 (Argos).

ἐπενέχῠρον, τό, *deed giving security*, *BGU*993iii 11 (ii B.C.).

ἐπενήνεον, impf. of ἐπινηνέω (q.v.). **ἐπενήνοθε**, 3 sg. plpf. and pf., thrice in Hom.; of Thersites' head, ψεδνὴ ἐ. λάχνη a thin coat of downy hair *grew thereon*, Il.2.219; of a cloak, οὔλη ἐ. λάχνη a thick pile *was on* it, 10.134: c. acc., of the ambrosial unguent, οἷα θεοὺς ἐ. αἰὲν ἐόντας such as *is on* the gods, Od.8.365, *h.Ven.*62: c. dat., *stick to*, στομίοισι πέριξ ἐ. γαστρός, of leeches when swallowed, Nic. *Al.*509: perh. related to ἐπανθέω. 2. of Time, πουλὺς ἐ. αἰών *had passed*, A.R.4.276. (Cf. κατ-, παρ-; also ἀνήνοθε: ἐπανήνοθε shd. perh. be restored in signf. 1.)

ἐπεν-θάπτω, *bury as well in* a tomb, *Anatolian Studies* 204 (Termessus). **-θεσις**, εως, ἡ, *insertion*, as of a letter, A.D.*Pron.*82.4; of a word, Id.*Synt.*78.24, Phlp.*in APo.*186.26; *application* of a drug, Paul.Aeg.6.42. **-θετικός**, ή, όν, *inserted*, Sch.Il.13.137 (cod. Basil.ap.Valck.Hdt.5.92). **-θήκη**, ἡ, = ἐπένθεσις, Eust.1349. 31. **-θρῴσκω**, *leap upon*, (sc. βωμῷ) Pi.*Pae.*6.115; σέλμασι ναῶν A.*Pers.*359; ἐ. ἄνω (sc. τῇ εὐνῇ) S.*Tr.*917; ἐ. ἐπί τινα *leap forth after* or *upon* one, as an enemy, Id.*OT*469 (lyr.). **-θῡμέομαι**, *support, corroborate* a conclusion by additional argument, Hermog. *Inv.*3.9. **-θύμημα** [ῡ], ατος, τό, *added enthymeme* in support of a position, Arist.*Rh.Al.*1438^{b}34, Hermog.*Inv.*3.9. **-θύμησις** [ῡ], εως, ἡ, *insertion of a corroborative argument*, Id.*Meth.*5 (pl.), Greg. Cor. in Rh.7.1147 W. (pl.). **-ίημι**, *compress* the pulse, Gal.8.887.

ἐπεννάτος λόγος ratio *of* 10 : 9, Iamb.*in Nic.*p.84 P.

ἐπεννεάκαιδέκᾰτος [λόγος] ratio *of* 20 : 19, Aristid.Quint.3.1.

ἐπεννέπω, *utter over* a victim, ἐπὶ δ' ἔννεπεν εὐχωλῇσιν A.R.4.1596.

ἐπεννοέω, *invent in addition*, in Pass., ἐνθύμημα Hermog.*Inv.*3.9.

ἐπένποι, ἐπενπέτω, opt. and imper. forms of doubtful origin, *pronounce a sentence* or *inflict a fine*, *Schwyzer* 409 (Elis).

ἐπεν-σᾰλεύω, v. ἐπισαλεύω. **-σείω**, *reduce by succussion*, Hp. *Art.*47. **-τᾰνύω** [ῠ], = ἐπεντείνω, *bind tightly to*, πεῖσμα νεὸς.. ὑψόσ' ἐπεντανύσας Od.22.467. **-τάσις**, εως, ἡ, *stretching*, of the τόνοι of an engine, Ph.*Bel.*67.24 (pl.), 25. **-τείνω**, *stretch tight*, ἐπενταθεὶς *stretched upon* his sword, S.*Ant.*1235. II. intr., *press on amain*, ἐπεντείνωμεν ἀνδρικώτερον Ar.*Pax* 514 (lyr.); *gain strength, increase*, of a report, Thphr.*Char.*8.7. **-τέλλω**, *command besides*, S.*Ant.*218:—Med., *enjoin*, *PMag.Par.*1.2075.

ἐπεντεῦθεν, perh. f.l. for ἀπ-, *henceforward*, *PMag.Par.*1.2011.

ἐπεν-τίθημι, *insert* a letter, A.D.*Adv.*148.8 (Pass.); a word, Id. *Synt.*88.5; a drug into a cavity, Paul.Aeg.6.14:—Pass., *to be put in besides*, *CIG*4429 (Seleucia). **-τρίβω** [ῑ], *rub in besides*, Poll.5. 102; *inflict*, πληγήν Eust.219.18. **-τρῠφάω**, *treat with wanton insolence*, c. dat., Men.Prot.pp.34, 102 D., cf. Suid. II. *revel in*, διηγήμασι Procop.Gaz.*Ep.*31. **-τρώγω**, *eat besides*, τῶν ὀστέων Ph. 2.479. **-τρώματα**, τά, Epicur.*Fr.*413, and **-τρώσεις**, αἱ, Ph.1. 115:—*dainties, delicacies*, expld. by Eust.1910.40 (sg.) as ἐρεθισμὸς τρυφητικός, but as τὰ ἐγκοίλια τῆς ἡδονῆς by Ph.: perh. ἐπικεντρώματα.

ἐπεντύω and **-ύνω** [ῡν], *set right, get ready*, ἐπέντυε νῶϊν ἵππους Il. 8.374; χεῖρα ἐπεντύνειν ἐπί τινι *arm* it for the fight, v.l. in S.*Aj.* 451:—Med., *prepare* or *train oneself for* a thing, ἐπεντύνονται ἄεθλα Od.24.89: c. inf., ἐπεντύνοντο νέεσθαι A.R.1.720.

ἐπεξ-άγω [ᾰ], *lead out* an army *against* the enemy, Th.2.21. II. *extend, lengthen*, τὴν διήγησιν Plu.2.855c; esp. *discuss at length*, D.C.46.8; περί τινος ἀκριβῶς Id.55.28. 2. seemingly intr. (sc. τάξιν), ἐ. ἀπὸ σφῶν *extend the line of battle* (by taking ground to right or left), Th.5.71; of ships, ἐ. τῷ πλῷ πρὸς τὴν γῆν *extend his line* by sailing towards land, Id.7.52. **-ᾰγωγή**, ἡ, *extension of a line of battle*, τοῦ κέρως Id.8.105. **-ᾰμαρτάνω**, *sin* or *err yet more*, D.H.2.35; δύο ἕτερα Ph.2.346; εἴς τινα against one, J.*AJ*14.16. 4. **-ᾰμαρτητέον**, *one must err yet more*, D.22.6. **-ανίστημι**, Pass. with aor. 2 Act. -ανέστην, *rise up, stand up*, Ph.2.582. **-ᾰπᾰτάω**, *deceive yet more*, Mnesim.3.5. **-άπτω**, *kindle*, πῦρ Diog.Oen. 38 (Pass.). **-αρκέω**, *supply in full*, Tz.*H.*12.220. **-αρτίζω**, *equip, furnish*, *PFay.*95.10 (ii A.D., Pass.). **-ειμι**, (εἶμι *ibo*) serving as Att. fut. to ἐπεξέρχομαι, to which it also supplies the impf. -ῄειν, Ion. 3 pl. -ῄϊσαν Hdt.7.223:—*go out against* an enemy, l.c., Th.2. 21, etc.; τισί Id.6.97; πρὸς πολεμίους X.*Eq.Mag.*7.3; ἐ. τινὶ ἐς μάχην Th.2.23, etc. 2. *get out, escape*, Arist.*Pr.*937^{a}28. II. *proceed against, take vengeance on*, Hdt.8.143; esp. in legal sense, *prosecute*, τινί D.21.216, Men.*Epit.*140; ἐ. τινὶ φόνου *for* murder, Pl. *Lg.*866b, *Euthphr.*4e; ἐ. τινὶ ὑπὲρ φόνου ib.b, cf. e: c. acc. pers., ἐπεξῄμεν τοῦ φόνου τὸν Ἀρίσταρχον Test.ap.D.21.107, cf. Antipho 1.11, etc.: c. dat. rei, *visit, avenge*, τῷ παθήματι Pl.*Lg.*866b (and c. acc., τὸν τῶν πατέρων θάνατον D.S.4.66); also ἐ. δίκῃ, γραφῇ, *prosecute* at law, Pl.*Lg.*754e, *Euthphr.*4c, Aeschin.2.93; *attack*, τῷ λόγῳ μεγαλοπρεπέστερον Pl.*Ly.*215c. III. c. acc., *go over, traverse*, δρυμοὺς Clearch.37. 2. in writing, *traverse, go through in detail*, σμικρὰ καὶ μεγάλα ἄστεα Hdt.1.5; πάντα Ar.*Ra.*1118; πάσας τὰς ἀμφισβητήσεις Pl.*R.*437a. 3. *go through with, execute*, παρασκευὰς λόγῳ καλῶς μεμφόμενοι ἀνομοίως ἔργῳ ἐπεξιέναι Th.1.84; ἐ. τὰς τιμωρίας ἔτι μείζους Id.3.82. **-ελαύνω**, *send on to the attack*, τοὺς ἱππέας X. *HG*5.3.6. **-έλεγχος**, ὁ, *additional* ἔλεγχος, Pl.*Phdr.*267a, Arist. *Rh.*1414^{b}15. **-έλευσις**, εως, ἡ, *visitation, punishment*, Ph.2.569, *POxy.*67.15 (iv A.D.), etc.; *vengeance*, Eust.120.38. II. *traversing of ground* in argument, Eustr.*in EN*316.23. **-ελευστικός**, ή, όν, *avenging*, Eust.18.18. **-έλκω**, *draw off besides*, Hp.*Ulc.* 27. **-εργάζομαι**, *effect besides*, ἓν δ' ἐπεξειργάσατο D.18.140; *accomplish*, βουλὴ μὲν ἄρχει, χεὶρ δ' ἐ. Ion Trag.63. 2. *slay over again*, ὀλωλότ' ἄνδρ' ἐπεξειργάσω S.*Ant.*1288 (lyr.). 3. *work anew*, ἀγρόν Luc.*Tim.*37. 4. *investigate*, τὴν αἰτίαν A.D.*Synt.*82.7, cf. 122.7. **-εργᾰσία**, ἡ, *investigation*, Ptol.*Tetr.*117; *elaboration*, Eustr.*in EN*135.16, Sch.Il.11.226; *carrying into effect* of a law, Just. *Nov.*99 *Pr.* **-εργαστικός**, ή, όν, *conclusive*, -κώτερον τιθέναι τὸν λόγον S.E.*M.*9.144. 2. Adv. Comp. -κώτερον *in greater detail*, ἑρμηνεύει Eust.104.3. **-έρπω**, *creep out into*, c. acc., ἡ ψυχὴ -ουσα τὰ μέρη τοῦ σώματος Hp.*Insomn.*86. **-έρχομαι** (v. ἐπέξειμι), *march out, make a sally*, Hdt.3.54, 6.101, Th.3.26, etc.; ἐ. τινὶ ἐς μάχην Id.5.9; of a message, ἐ. τινί *reach* him, Hdt.8.99 codd. (ἐπεσ– Reiske). 2. *proceed against, prosecute*, τινί Antipho 1.1: generally, τῷ δράσαντι Th.3.38; *attack*, Pl.*Prt.*345d; ἐ. τινὶ φόνου *proceed against* one *for* murder, Id.*Euthphr.*4d; also ἐ. τινὶ δίκην Id.*Lg.* 866b; [γραφὴν] *follow* it *up*, Lex ap.D.21.47; ἐ. φόνον Antipho 2.1.2: abs., ἐπεξέρχῃ λίαν thou *visitest* with severity, E.*Ba.*1346: c. acc. pers., *prosecute*, Lys.31.18; *punish*, Plu.*Caes.*69; τὴν πόλιν E.*Andr.* 735: c. dat., *take vengeance for*, Nic.Dam.130.18 J. 3. *proceed to an extremity*, κἀπαπειλῶν ὧδ' ἐπεξέρχῃ; S.*Ant.*752; ἐ. πρὸς τέλος ἁπάσης πολιτείας Pl.*Lg.*632c. 4. *follow up*, τῇ παρούσῃ τύχῃ Th.4.14; *pursue, develop*, an argument, τῷ λόγῳ Pl.*R.*361d, *Grg.*492d. II. c. acc., *go through* or *over*, πάντα τῆς χώρης Hdt.4.9; τὸ πᾶν γὰρ ἐ. διζήμενον Id.7.166. 2. *carry out, accomplish*, ἔργῳ τι (opp. ἐνθυμεῖσθαι) Th.1.120; opp. ἐπινοεῖν, ib.70; πᾶν πρὸ τοῦ δουλεῦσαι ἐ. *try* every course, Id.5.100: abs., opp. παραινέσαι, ib.9; νίκην App.*BC* 5.91; ἐ. τι εἰς τέλος Luc.*JTr.*17. 3. *discuss, relate* or *examine accurately* or *fully*, οὐδ' εἰ πάντ' ἐ. σκοπῶν S.*Fr.*919, cf. A.*Pr.*870, Th. 3.67, Pl.*Lg.*672a; ἀκριβείᾳ περὶ ἑκάστου· ἐ. Th.1.22; τι δι' ὀλίγων Pl.*Lg.*778c. **-ετάζω**, *pass in review, feast one's eyes upon*, Men.*Pk.*414. **-έτᾰσις**, εως, ἡ, *fresh review* or *muster*, Th.6. 42. **-ευρίσκω**, *devise* or *discover besides*, Hdt.2.160; τι πρὸς ἀσφάλειαν J.*AJ*15.8.5:—Pass., ἐπεξευρημέναι χρεῖαι Arist.*Pol.*1331^a 14. **-ηγέομαι**, *recount in detail*, Plu.*Art.*8, Sch.Ar.*Eq.*714. 2. *explain besides*, Asp.*in EN*48.20, Sch.Il.13.281. **-ηγημᾰτικός**, ή, όν, *epexegetical*, Sch.Pl.*Phd.*64d. **-ήγησις**, εως, ἡ, *detailed account*, Phoeb.*Fig.*1.3, Sch.Il.11.221. 2. *explanation*, Corn.*ND*9.

ἐπεξῆς, Ion. for ἐφεξῆς.

ἐπεξ-ῐακχάζω, *shout in triumph over*, παιᾶνα A.*Th.*635. **-όδιος**, ον, *of a march* or *expedition*: ἐπεξόδια (sc. ἱερά), τά, sacrifices *before the march of an army*, v.l. in X.*An.*6.5.2. **-οδος**, ἡ, *march out against* an enemy, ἐ. ποιήσασθαι πρός τινα Th.5.8; *sortie*, Aen.Tact. 23.1 (pl.), D.C.39.4. II. *attack* for the purpose of revenge, Nic. Dam.130.17 J., Ph.2.314; for punishment, Id.1.283. **-οιωνίζομαι**, *take auguries afresh*, Gal.9.833. **-ορκίζω**, *compel to swear a second time*, Plb.15.25.11. **-ορύσσω**, *dig further*, in Pass., *IG*4.823.37 (Troezen). **-ουσιαστής**, gloss on Μαῖος, Philox.Gramm.11.

ἐπέοικα, *to be like, suit*, c. dat. pers., ὅς τις οἷ τ' ἐπέοικε Il.9.392: elsewh. impers., *it is fit, proper*, c. dat. pers. et inf., σφῶϊν μέν τ' ἐπέοικε.. ἑστάμεν 4.341; νέῳ δέ τε πάντ' ἐπέοικε.. κεῖσθαι *'tis a seemly thing* for a young man to lie dead, 22.71, cf. Pi.*N.*7.95: c. acc. pers. et inf., λαοὺς δ' οὐκ ἐπέοικε.. ταῦτ' ἐπαγείρειν Il.1.126; ὅν τ' ἐπέοικε βουλὰς βουλεύειν 10.146: with inf. understood, ἀποδάσσομαι ὅσσ' ἐπέοικε [ἀποδάσσασθαι] 24.595; οὔτ' οὖν ἐσθῆτος δευήσεαι οὔτε τευ ἄλλου, ὧν ἐπέοιχ' ἱκέτην.. ἀντιάσαντα [μὴ δεύεσθαι] Od.6.193. II. part. pl., ἐπεικότα *seemly, fit*, τινί A.*Ch.*669, cf. S.*Ichn.*271. III. *resemble*, c. dat., Arr.*An.*1.12.2, 2.7.8; ἀριθμῷ πάντ' ἐ. Pythag.ap. S.E.*M.*4.2.

ἐπέπιθμεν, v. πείθω. **ἐπέπλως**, v. ἐπιπλέω. **ἐπεποίθει**, v. πείθω. **ἐπεπόνθει**, v. πάσχω. **ἐπέπταρε**, v. ἐπιπταίρω. **ἐπέπτᾰτο,** v. ἐπιπέτομαι. **ἐπέπω,** Ion. for ἐφέπω.

ἐπέραστος, ον, *lovely, lovable,* Lyr.Alex.Adesp.4.18, D.S.4.7, Ph. 1.671, Vett.Val.18.29, Luc.*Tim.*17, *Im.*10; ἱερὸς ὁ κόσμος καὶ ἐ. Porph.*Antr.*12; ἐ. ὀφθαλμός Heph.Astr.1.1.

ἔπεργα, gloss on ἐπικέλια, Hsch.

ἐπεργ-άζομαι, *cultivate besides, encroach upon,* τὰ τοῦ γείτονος Pl. *Lg.*843c. 2. esp. *encroach upon* sacred ground, Lys.7.24, Aeschin. 3.113; αἴ τις τὰν γᾶν ἐπιεργάζοιτο ἂν Ἀμφικτίονες ἱάρωσαν...ἀποτεισάτω..στατῆρας..καὶ πρασσόντων τὸν ἐπιεργαζόμενον *IG*2².1126.15 (Delph.). 3. generally, *cultivate,* Luc.*Tim.*37. 4. *dress* the upper surfaces of blocks of masonry, *IG*1².372.86, *SIG*970.11 (Eleusis, iii B.C.), etc. 5. *discuss, inquire into,* Ptol.*Tetr.*117 (nisi leg. ἐπεξ–): c. dat., *work up, pursue in detail,* Men.Rh.p.442S. II. pf. in pass. sense, *to be wrought* or *sculptured upon,* τῷ χαλκῷ Paus.3. 17.3, cf. 8.31.1. **–ασία,** ἡ, *cultivation of another's land, encroachment upon* sacred ground (cf. foreg. 1.2), τῆς γῆς τῆς ἱερᾶς Th.1.139, cf. Pl.*Lg.*843c. II. *right of mutual tillage* in each other's territory, X.*Cyr.*3.2.23. III. *treatment, discussion,* Steph.*in Hp.*1. 107 D. **–αστικός,** prob. f.l. for ἐπηρεαστικός, *AP*5.177 tit. (Mel.).

ἔπεργος, ὁ, *assistant, Sammelb.*5680.3 (iii B.C.). 2. ἔπεργον, τό, *work done in addition* to payment of rent, τοῦ μισθώματος καὶ τῶν ἐ. ἀπάντων ἀπότεισμα *IG*12(7).62.15 (Amorgos). 3. as Adj., *useful, PSI*6.619.8 (iii B.C.).

ἐπερεθ-ίζω, *stimulate, urge on,* Plu.*Eum.*11; ἐ. πηκτίδα χερσίν *touch* the lyre, *AP*9.270 (Marc. Arg.). **–ισμός,** ὁ, *irritation, stimulation,* Plu.2.908e.

ἐπερ-είδω, *drive against,* ἐπέρεισε δὲ Παλλὰς Ἀθήνη [ἔγχος] νείατον ἐς κενεῶνα *drove* it *home,* Il.5.856, cf. 17.48; ἐπέρεισε δὲ ἶν' ἀπέλεθρον *put* vast strength *to* it, 7.269, Od.9.538; *thrust* a door *to, shut* it *close,* Q.S.12.331; ἐ. γένειόν τινι *lean* it *upon*..., Ael.*NA*5.56: metaph., ἐ. τὸν νοῦν *attend to* a thing, A.D.*Synt.*148.20; τὴν διάνοιαν Plu.2.392b; ἐ. τῷ φιλεῖν ἐμαυτόν *give* oneself *up to,* ib.463c; *direct,* πρὸς τὴν θεὸν τὸν λόγον Sch.Pi.*N.*7.1:—Med., *rest in* or *upon,* βαυκάλη ἐπὶ διαγωνίων λίθων ἐπηρεισμένη Sor.1.109: metaph., ψυχαὶ -όμεναι πνεύματι Porph.*Abst.*2.38; οὐσίᾳ Plot.6.1.3; ἄλλῳ Id.5.5.7; ἐπ' ἄλλου Iamb.*Comm.Math.*8. 2. ἐ. τὴν φάλαγγά τινι *bring the whole force of* the phalanx *against,* Plu.*Flam.*8: abs., ἐ. τοῖς ἀντιτεταγμένοις Id.*Pyrrh.*21, cf. Arr.*Tact.*16.13:—Med., Ael. *Tact.*14.5. 3. Med., λαίφη προτόνοις ἐπερειδομένας *staying their* sails with ropes, E.*Hec.*112:—Pass., *lean* or *bear upon,* βακτηρίαις Ar.*Ec.*277, cf. Pl.*Lg.*789e: metaph., *lean upon,* ἡμετέρῃ ἐ. Ἑλλὰς ἐφορμῇ A.R.4.204: abs., *resist with all one's force,* Ar.*Ra.*1102. 4. Pass., *to be leaned on,* J.*AJ*9.4.4. b. *to be subject to pressure* or *impact,* Chrysipp.*Stoic.*2.142. II. intr. in Act., τῇ χειρὶ ἐπερείδειν *press heavily* with the hand, Hp.*Art.*11. **–εισις,** εως, ἡ, *pressure,* Dsc.5.77, Sor.2.10, Heliod.ap.Orib.10.37.7, Gal.2.386; of the objects of sense, *impact,* Chrysipp.*Stoic.*2.233, al. **–εισμα,** ατος, τό, *support, foundation,* τὰ μαθηματικὰ ἐπὶ ταῖς ἰδέαις ἔχειν τὸ ἐ. Iamb.*Comm.Math.*8. **–εισμός,** ὁ, *impact,* Epicur.*Ep.*1 p.12 U. **–ειστικός,** ή, όν, *for support,* βακτηρία Sch.E.*Hec.*64. II. *pressed home, vigorous,* ἐπιβολή Procl.*in Prm.*p.845 S.

ἐπερέομαι, Ion. for ἐπείρομαι, Luc.*Syr.D.*36.

ἐπερεύγομαι, Pass., *to be disgorged upon*: of water, *to be poured upon,* ἀκτάς A.R.4.631; δισσὰς ἠπείρους D.P.95.

ἐπερέφω, *put a cover upon, roof,* εἴ ποτέ τοι χαρίεντ' ἐπὶ νηὸν ἔρεψα Il.1.39.

ἐπέρομαι, v. ἐπείρομαι.

ἔπερος, ον, *woolly,* of sheep, *Schwyzer*644.15 (Lydia).

ἐπερρώπτης· ὑπηρέτης, Hsch. **ἐπέρτερα·** μείζω καὶ ὑψηλότερα, Id. (leg. ὑπ–).

ἐπερύω, Ep. and Ion. **–ειρύω,** *pull to,* θύρην δ' ἐπέρυσσε κορώνῃ Od. 1.441; ἐπὶ στήλην ἐρύσαντες *having dragged* a stone *to the top* [of the tumulus], 12.14; *draw* to one, A.R.3.149:—Med., *draw on one's* clothes, ἐπειρυσάμενον τὴν λεοντέην Hdt.4.8.

ἐπέρχομαι, impf. ἐπηρχόμην Th.4.120 (unless fr. ἐπάρχομαι: Att. impf. is ἐπῄα (but v. ἔρχομαι) and fut. ἔπειμι): aor. 2 ἐπῆλθον, Ep. -ήλυθον: pf. -ελήλυθα: I. *come upon*: 1. of persons, *approach,* c. dat., Il.12.200, 218, etc.; esp. *come suddenly upon,* Od.19.155, Hdt. 6.95: c. acc., ἐ. πόλιν E.*HF*593 codd. (nisi leg. ἐσ–); *come to for advice,* μάντεις, μοῦσαν, Id.*Supp.*155, *Hel.*165, cf. Pl.*Lg.*772d: with Preps., ἐ. ἐς ποταμόν Od.7.280, cf. S.*Aj.*438: metaph., ἐ. ἐς λόγου στάσιν Id.*Tr.*1180; ἐ. ἐς πόλεμον Th.3.47; ἐ. ἐνθάδε Il.24.651. b. freq. in hostile sense, *go* or *come against, attack,* abs., 12.136, al., Th. 1.90, etc.: c. dat., Il.20.91, E.*Ba.*736, Th.6.34, etc.: rarely c. acc., τμήδην αὐχέν' ἐπῆλθε Il.7.262; τὴν τῶν πέλας ἐ. *invade* it, Th.2.39: hence, *visit, reprove,* ταῦτα μέν σε πρῶτ' ἐπῆλθον E.*IA*349, cf. *Andr.* 688: with a Prep., *invade,* ἐπὶ τὴν οἰκίαν *PFay.*12.12 (ii B.C.). c. *come forward to speak,* E.*Or.*931, Th.1.119, Pl.*Lg.*850c; ἐ. ἐπὶ τὸν δῆμον, ἐπὶ τοὺς ἐφόρους, Hdt.5.97, 9.7; ἐπὶ τὸ κοινόν Th.1.90; τοῖς Λακεδαιμονίοις ib.91. d. in Law, *proceed against,* ἐπί τινα *PEleph.*3. 3 (iii B.C.); ἐπί τινα περί τινος *PAmh.*2.96.8 (iii A.D.); τινὶ περί τινος *POxy.*489.11 (ii A.D.); ἐπὶ πιττάκιον *impugn, BGU*1167.14 (i B.C.): also in aor. 1 ἐπελεύσασθαι *PStrassb.*35.25 (ii B.C.), etc. (ἐπιπορεύομαι (q.v.) is more common in the pres. in the Hellenistic period.) 2. of events, conditions, etc., *come upon,* esp. *come suddenly upon,* c. acc., μιν..ἐπήλυθε νήδυμος ὕπνος Od.4.793, al., cf. Hdt.2.141; ἔρως γὰρ ἄνδρας οὐ μόνους ἐπέρχεται E.*Fr.*431: c. dat., τοῖσιν ἐπήλυθε νήδυμος ὕπνος Od.12.311, cf. 5.472; μοι νοῦσος ἐπήλυθεν 11.200; βροτοῖσιν.. ὅταν κλύδων κακῶν ἐπέλθῃ A.*Pers.*600, cf. *Ag.*1256; ἐπῆλθέ μοι πάθος Pl.*Lg.*811d, etc. 3. c. dat. pers., *come into* one's *head, occur to* one, ἵμερος ἐπειρέσθαι μοι ἐπῆλθε Hdt.1.30; ὅ τι ἂν ἐπέλθῃ, Lat. *quicquid in buccam venerit,* Isoc.12.24: impers. c. inf., καί οἱ ἐπῆλθε παρεῖν Hdt.6.107, cf. S.*Tr.*134 (lyr.); ἐμοὶ τοιαῦτ' ἄττα ἐ. λέγειν Pl. *Grg.*485e, etc.; also ἐπέρχεταί με λέγειν Id.*Phd.*88d. 4. *come in,* of revenues, etc., ἐπερχόμενοι τόκοι, ἐπιβολαί, *BGU*155.11 (ii A.D.), 1049.16 (iv A.D.). II. of Time, *come on,* ἐπήλυθον ὧραι the season *came round again,* Od.2.107, etc.; also, *come on, be at hand,* νὺξ δ' ἄρ' ἐπῆλθε 14.457; γῆρας ἐ. Thgn.528, 728; ἕκαθεν ἐπελθὼν ὁ μέλλων χρόνος Pi.*O.*10(11).7; τὸ παρὸν τό τ' ἐπερχόμενον πῆμα and *that which is coming, the future,* A.*Pr.*98. 2. *come in after* or *over* another, of a second wife, Hdt.5.41. III. *go over* or *on* a space, *traverse,* mostly of persons, c. acc., πολλὴν γαῖαν Od.4.268; ἀγρόν 16.27; ἄγκεα πολλά Il.18.321, cf. Od.14.139, Hdt.1.30; *go the round of, visit,* δόμους S.*El.*1297; ναοὺς χοροῖς Id.*Ant.*153 (lyr.); πόλιν, of a god, Maced.*Pae.*29; of an officer, πύλας φυλακάς τ' ἐπῆλθον E.*Ph.* 699; τὰς ξυνωμοσίας ἐπελθών Th.8.54; *walk on* ice, Id.3.23; also of water, ἐπέρχεται ὁ Νεῖλος τὸ Δέλτα *overflows* it, Hdt.2.19, cf. A.*Supp.* 559 (lyr.), Th.3.89. 2. *go through* or *over, discuss, recount,* c. acc., Hes.*Fr.*160.4 codd. Str., Ar.*Eq.*618; *review,* τὰ εἰρημένα περί τινος Arist.*EN*1172ᵇ8; also ἐ. περί τινος Id.*Ph.*189ᵇ31, al.; folld. by an interrog., πειρατέον ἐπελθεῖν τίνες.. Id.*Pol.*1289ᵇ24; πῶς δεῖ..ἐπέλθωμεν συντόμως ib.1317ᵃ15. 3. *accomplish,* πολέμῳ καὶ διαχειρίσει πραγμάτων Th.1.97. IV. *come up to, imitate,* πάτρῳ Pi.*P.*6.46.

ἐπερωτ-άω, Ion. **ἐπειρ–,** *consult, inquire of,* c. acc. pers., τὸ χρηστήριον, τὸν θεόν, εἰ.. Hdt.1.53, Th.1.118, etc.; τινὰ περί τινος Hdt. 1.32, cf. Orac.ap.D.43.66; later, ἐν τῷ θεῷ Lxx *Jd.*18.5:—Pass., *to be questioned, asked* a *question,* Th.5.45, Pl.*Sph.*250a. 2. c. acc. rei, *ask* a question, ταῦτα, τάδε, Hdt.1.30, 55, cf. Antipho 1.10; also, *ask about* a thing, [τὰς ναῦς] καὶ τὸν πεζόν Hdt.7.100; σμικρόν τι τῶν ῥηθέντων *call* it *in question,* Pl.*Prt.*329a; ἐ. θυσίαις καὶ οἰωνοῖς ὅ τι χρὴ ποιεῖν *inquire* what.., X.*Oec.*5.19; ἐ. ἐς.. *inquire* about, Lxx 2*Ki.*11. 7:—Pass., τὸ ἐπερωτηθέν *the question asked,* v.l. in Pl.*Tht.*146e. 3. c. acc. pers. et rei, ἐ. τοὺς προφήτας τὸ αἴτιον Hdt.9.93 codd.; ἐπηρώτα ὑμᾶς τὸ ἐκ τοῦ νόμου κήρυγμα Aeschin.1.79. 4. abs., *put a question,* esp. of a chairman putting a question to the vote, D.22.9, *SIG*898.17 (Chalcis, iii A.D.), al. 5. in Roman Law, *put a formal question* in *stipulatio,* most freq. in Pass., *POxy.*905.19 (ii A.D.), etc.: also in Act., ib.1273.41 (iii A.D.). b. hence later, *guarantee, PLand.*48.9 (vi A.D.). 6. *ask a further question, SIG*953.49 (Calymna, ii B.C.), al. **–ημα,** Ion. **ἐπειρ–,** ατος, τό, *question,* Hdt. 6.67, Th.3.53, 68, Epicur.*Sent.Vat.*71. 2. *answer to inquiry* put to higher authority: hence, *sanction,* κατὰ τὸ ἐ. τῶν Ἀρεοπαγιτῶν *SIG* 856.6 (ii A.D.), cf. 1008.4 (iii A.D.). 3. = Lat. *stipulatio, PCair. Preis.*1.16 (ii A.D.), *Cod.Just.*8.10.12.3 (pl.): hence prob., *pledge,* συνειδήσεως ἀγαθῆς ἐ. εἰς θεόν 1*Ep.Pet.*3.21. **–ησις,** Ion. **ἐπειρ–,** εως, ἡ, *questioning, consulting,* Hdt.6.67; χρησμῶν Id.9.44, cf. *IG*12 (3).248.3 (Anaphe): pl., Th.4.38. 2. = foreg. 3, *POxy.*1205.9 (iii A.D.), *Cod.Just.*8.10.12.1a. **–ητής,** οῦ, ὁ, *inquirer, Gloss.*

ἐπές, Prep. (Arc. for ἐπέκ), c. dat., *as far as relates to,* ταῖς οἰκίαις *SIG*306.9 (Tegea, iv B.C.), cf. *IG*5(2).6.54 (ibid., iv B.C.).

ἔπεσα, v. πίπτω. **ἔπεσαν,** Ep. for ἔπεσον, 3 pl. impf. of ἔπειμι (A).

ἐπεσ-βολέω, *use violent language,* Lyc.130, Max.101. **–βολία,** ἡ, *hasty speech, scurrility,* ἐπεσβολίας ἀναφαίνειν Od.4.159, cf. Man.6. 625, Q.S.1.748: later in sg., Max.65; φοβερῆς ἰὸς -ίης, of Archilochus' satires, *AP*9.185, cf. 7.70 (Jul.). **–βόλος,** ον, (ἔπος, βάλλω) *throwing words about, rash-talking, scurrilous,* λωβητῆρα ἐ., of Thersites, Il.2.275, cf. Them.*Or.*21.262a; νεῖκος ἐ. A.R.4.1727; of satires, ἐ. ἦχος ἀοιδῆς *AP*4.3b.82 (Agath.).

ἐπεσθίω, *eat after* or *with* (cf. ἐπί B.1.1 d, and v. ἐπιπίνω), κρέασι βοείοις χλωρὰ σῦκ' ἐπήσθιεν E.*Fr.*907; μικρῷ σίτῳ πολὺ ὄψον X.*Mem.* 3.14.3; *eat* cheese *with* wine, Telecl.25, cf. *Com.Adesp.*722. 2. *eat as an antidote,* ὅταν ἔχεως φάγῃ, ἐπεσθίει τὴν ὀρίγανον Arist.*HA* 612ᵃ24, cf. Thphr.*CP*6.4.7, Trophil.ap.Stob.4.36.28, Dsc.*Eup.*1. 25. II. *eat up,* dub. in Pherecr.156. III. *chew the cud,* Ael. *NA*2.54.

ἐπέσθω, Dor. and poet. for foreg., Epich.42.6, Call.*Epigr.*48.

ἐπεσκεμμένως, Adv., (ἐπισκέπτομαι) *carefully, circumspectly,* Hierocl.*in CA*10p.436M.

ἐπεσκοτισμένως, Adv. *obscurely,* Vett.Val.331.9.

ἐπεσπευσμένως, gloss on ἐπιτροπάδην, Hsch. **ἐπέσπον,** aor. of ἐφέπω.

ἐπέσσηθον· ἐπέλεκον, ἐπελέπτυνον, Hsch. (v. ἐπισήθω).

ἐπεσσῠμένως, Adv., (ἐπισεύομαι) *violently,* v.l. in Q.S.3.443. 2. *hastily, promptly,* Aret.*CA*2.3.

ἐπεστεῖσαι, v. ἐπεκτίνω. **ἐπεστεώς,** Ion. pf. part. of ἐφίστημι.

ἐπεστραμμένως, gloss on ἐπιστροφάδην, Eust.819.52.

ἐπεσχάρ-ιος [ᾰ], ον, (ἐσχάρα) *on the hearth,* δαλός *AP*7.648 (Leon.). II. Subst. **–ίη,** ἡ, *hearth,* ἀελίου, of the earth, dub. in *Epigr.Gr.*149 (Rhenea). **–ωσις,** εως, ἡ, *scarring over,* Orib.*Fr.*143.

ἐπετειό-καρπος, ον, *bearing fruit annually,* Thphr.*HP*1.2.2. **–καυλος,** ον, *changing its stalk every year,* ib.6.2.8, 7.2.1.

ἐπέτειος, ον, Dor. gen. pl. ἐπετειᾶν A.*Ag.*1015 (lyr.): Ion. **ἐπέτεος** *GDI* iv p.876, v.l. in Hdt.3.89:—*annual,* θυσίαι Id.6.105; ὁ ἐ. καρπός Id.8.108; ὁ ἐ. φόρος the *yearly* revenue, Id.5.49; πρόσοδος Id. 3.89; βύβλον τὴν ἐ. γινομένην Id.2.92; τὸ ὕδωρ τὸ ἐ. the water drawn up by the sun *every year,* ib.25; γενήματα *PTeb.*27.33 (ii B.C.); ἐπέτεια, τά, *yearly additions to treasure, IG*1².242, 244; ἐ.

ἐπικαρπία Pl.*Lg.*955d; ἐ. ἄλοκες A.*Ag.* l. c.; ἐ. νοσήματα *recurring annually*, Pl.*R.*405c: metaph., ἐπέτειοι τὴν φύσιν *changeful* as the seasons, or like birds *of passage*, Ar.*Eq.*518. 2. *lasting for a year*, ἐ. τὰ πολλὰ τῶν ἐντόμων Arist.*Long.*466ᵃ2; τῶν φυτῶν τὰ μὲν ἐπέτειον ἔχει τὴν ζωήν ib.464ᵇ25, cf. Thphr.*HP*1.1.2; ἐ. ψηφίσματα *having force for a year*, D.23.92; τὰ κατὰ τὰς ἀρχάς Plb.6.46.4. 3. *this year's*, ῥόδα Dsc.5.27; = ἐπὶ τοῦ νῦν ἔτους, Hsch.

ἐπετειο-φορέω, *bear fruit every year*, Thphr.*CP*1.20.3. **-φόρος**, ον, *fruiting every year*, ibid. **-φυλλος**, ον, *deciduous*, Id.*HP*7.11.3.

ἐπέτεος, Ion. for ἐπέτειος.

ἐπέτης, ου, Dor. **-ας**, ὁ, (ἕπομαι) *follower, attendant*, Pi.*P.*5.4: fem. **ἐπέτις**, ιδος, A.R.3.666.

ἐπετήσιος, ον, = ἐπέτειος, *from year to year, yearly*, καρπός Od.7.118, cf. *PSI*4.320.12 (i A. D.); προστατεία Th.2.80; θυσίαι Jul.*Or.*4.131d; *lasting the whole year*, τελεσφορίη Call.*Ap.*78; ἐγχρονίσας ἐπετήσιον *for a year*, *Epigr.Gr.*815.

ἐπετίνη, ἡ, name of a plant, dub. in Thphr.*HP*7.8.1 (prob. πιτυίνη, = χαμαίπιτυς).

ἐπετινός, ή, όν, *of the year*, χόρτος *POxy.*1482.12 (ii A. D.).

ἔπετον, v. πίπτω.

ἐπέτοσσε, poet. aor. (no pres. in use), = ἐπέτυχε, *fell in* or *met with*, c. gen., Pi.*P.*4.25; also in part., ἐπιτόσσαις ῥέζοντας *having come upon* them as they were sacrificing, ib.10.33.

ἔπεττον· ἐπιτίνων, Hsch.

ἐπεύαδε, Ep. aor. 2 of ἐφανδάνω, Musae.180.

ἐπευάζω, *shout over*, τινά Orph.*H.*79.9.

ἐπευδοκέω, *approve*, *PMasp.*151.225 (vi A. D.).

ἐπευθῡμέω, *rejoice at* a thing, τινί Lxx *Wi.*18.6.

ἐπευθύνω, *guide, direct*, X.*Cyn.*5.32; τὸν δρόμον Plu.2.980f; *direct, administer*, πολίσματα A.*Pers.*860 codd. (lyr.); τὰ κοινά Aeschin.3.158 (v.l.).

ἐπευκλεΐζω, *glorify, make illustrious*, πατρίδ' ἐπευκλεΐσας Simon.125.2; πολλά σ' ἔπαινος ἐ. *IG*12(9).1195.1 (Oreus).

ἐπευκτ-αῖος, α, ον, = sq., *PMag.Par.*1.271. **-ός**, ή, όν, *longed for, to be longed for*, ἡμέρα Lxx *Je.*20.14.

ἐπευλᾰβέομαι, *shrink from*, c. inf., Lxx 2 *Ma.*14.18.

ἐπευλογέω, *bless*, Tz.*H.*9.206.

ἐπευνάζω, *sleep on*, βοείαις Nonn.*D.*17.117.

ἐπεύνακτοι, ων, οἱ, (εὐνάζω) name for the Helots who were adopted into their lords' places during the Messenian wars, Theopomp.Hist.166:—D.S.8*Fr.*21 writes **ἐπευνακταί**, and seems to identify them with the παρθενίαι (q.v.): Hsch. has ἐνεύνακτοι· οἱ παρθενίαι, and ἐπευνακταί· οἱ συγκοιμηταί.

ἐπευσχημονέω, *conduct in due order*, πομπήν *IG*12(8).666.4.

ἐπευφημ-έω, *assent with a shout of applause*, c. inf., πάντες ἐπευφήμησαν Ἀχαιοὶ αἰδεῖσθαί θ' ἱερῆα Il.1.22; cf. A.R.4.295: abs., Ph.2.28, Plu.*Galb.*14. II. c. acc. pers., Ἥρην ἐ. *glorify, sing praises to* her, Musae.275. 2. c. acc. et dat. rei, *sing over* or *in furtherance of*, χοαῖσι..ὕμνους ἐπευφημεῖτε A.*Pers.*620; ἐπευφήμησαν εὐχαῖσιν..παιᾶνα E.*IT*1403. 3. c. dupl. acc., ἐμὰς τύχας παιᾶν' ἐπηυφήμησεν *sang* a paean *over* my fortunes, A.*Fr.*350.4; folld. by dat., ἐ. παιᾶνα τῇμῇ συμφορᾷ Ἄρτεμιν *sing* the paean *in praise of* her over my fate, E.*IA*1467. 4. c. acc. et dat., ἐ. νόστον τινί *wish* them *a happy* return, A.R.1.556. 5. c. dupl. acc., *call for the sake of good omen*, Heraclit.*All.*68:—Pass., θεῶν παῖδες οἱ ἥρωες -οῦνται Hierocl. *in CA* 3p.425 M. **-ίζομαι**, *use a euphemism*, Sch.Ar.*Ra.*1421, Hsch. s.v. καταίσια. (Act. only as f.l. for -ησεν, Hld.10.41.) **-ισμός**, ὁ, *shout of approval*, Eust.120.18.

ἐπευφραίνομαι, *delight in*, c. dat., Jul.*Gal.*347c, Olymp. *in Phlb.* p.239 S.

ἐπευφρᾱτίδιος, ον, *dwelling on Euphrates*, Luc.*Pisc.*19.

ἐπευχ-άδιος [ᾰ], ον, *votive*, βωμός *JRS*2.93 (Antioch Pisid.). **-ή**, *prayer*, Pl.*Lg.*871c (pl.). 2. [ἐ]πευχά, = ἐπαρά, *SIG*360.42 (Cherson., iii B. C.). **-ιον**, τό, prop. *praying-carpet* or *rug*: hence, generally, *rug*, Eust.1056.64, Sch.Ar.*Pl.*528. **-ομαι**, *pray* or *make a vow to* a deity, c. dat., θεοῖς, Διΐ, Od.11.46, Il.6.475, etc.; but in S.*OC*1024, ἐ. θεοῖς *give thanks to* them: c. dat. et inf., *pray to* one *that..*, ἐπεύχετο πᾶσι θεοῖσι νοστῆσαι Ὀδυσῆα Od.14.423, 20.238, cf. S.*Ph.*1470, Ar.*Pax*1320 (anap.), etc.: without a dat., κατθανεῖν ἐπηυχόμην S.*Tr.*16; ἐ. εὐορκοῦντι εἶναι ἀγαθά Lexap.And.1.98, cf. Aeschin.3.111: c. acc. rei, *pray for*, θανάτου μοῖραν A.*Ag.*1462 (lyr.): c. acc. cogn., ἐ. λιτάς S.*OC*484; τοιαῦτα θεοῖς A.*Th.*280: later, c. acc. pers., ἐ. θεούς Aristaenet.2.2. II. *vow*, c. fut. inf., ἐ. θήσειν τροπαῖα A.*Th.*276. III. *imprecate upon*, μόρον..Πελοπίδαις Id.*Ag.*1600, cf. 501, *Ch.*112; ἀρὰς τοῖς ἀπειθοῦσιν Pl.*Criti.*119e: c. inf., ἐπεύχομαι [αὐτῷ] παθεῖν S.*OT*249: abs., *utter imprecations*, μὴ 'πεύξῃ πέρα Id.*Ph.*1286, cf. *Tr.*809: rarely in good sense, ἐ. εὐτυχίαν τινί Plu.*Galb.*18; ἐ. τινὶ εὐτυχεῖν A.*Th.*481. IV. *exult over*, δοιοῖσιν ἐπεύξεαι Ἱππασίδῃσι Il.11.431: abs., 5.119. 2. c. inf., *boast that..*, c. aor. inf., μιγῆναι *h.Ven.*287; fut., A.*Ag.*1262; pres., Id.*Eu.*58, etc.; Ἄργος πατρίδ' ἐμὴν ἐ. (sc. εἶναι) E.*IT*508: c. part., ἐ. ἐκφυγόν *boast* that it has escaped, Pl.*Sph.*235c, cf. E.*Rh.*693 (reading θρασύς).

ἐπευων-ίζω, *lower the price of* a thing, D.23.201; ἐ. τοῖς πένησι τὴν ἀγοράν Plu.*CG*5, cf. *Cic.*8, dub. in Luc.*Nigr.*23:—Pass., [ἡ πολιτεία] ὑπὸ τῆς εὐχερείας ἐπευωνίσθη D.C.60.17. **-ισμός**, ὁ, *cheapening*, ἐλαίου *BCH*11.473 (Lydia).

ἐπευωχέομαι, Med., *feast upon*, ἐπὶ στρωμάτων D.C.62.15.

ἐπέφαντο, 3 sg. plpf. Pass. from φαίνω, Hes.*Sc.*166. **ἔπεφνον**, Ep. redupl. aor. 2 from root of θείνω. **ἐπεφόρβει**, plpf. of φέρβω. **ἐπέφρᾰδον**, Ep. redupl. aor. 2 of φράζω. **ἐπέφῡκον**, Dor. for ἐπεφύκεσαν, 3 pl. plpf. of φύω, Hes.*Op.*149, *Th.*152.

ἐπέχερον· ἀκόλουθον, Hsch.

ἐπεχές, Adv., = ἐφεξῆς, *following, next*, ἁ ἐ. ἁμέρα, ὁ ἐ. ἐνιαυτός, *IG*4.841.30,32 (Calauria): Delph. **ἐπεχεῖ** *GDI*2642.47 (ii B. C.).

ἐπέχυντο, Ep. 3 pl. aor. 2 Pass. of ἐπιχέω, Hom.

ἐπέχω, fut. ἐφέξω (v. infr. IV. 1,2) and ἐπισχήσω E.*Andr.*160, D.45.88: aor. ἐπέσχον, imper. ἐπίσχες, inf. ἐπισχεῖν; poet. ἐπισχέθοι A.*Th.*453 (lyr.), ἐπέσχεθον A.R.4.1622: pf. ἐπέσχηκα *Supp.Epigr.*1.362.12 (Samos, iv B. C.):—*have* or *hold upon*, θρῆνυν.., τῷ κεν ἐπισχοίης (v.l. ἐπίσχοιας) λιπαροὺς πόδας Il.14.241, cf. Od.17.410; ποτῷ κρωσσὸν ἐ. *hold* it *to* or *for*..., Theoc.13.46; λόγον ζωῆς ἐπέχοντες (sc. κόσμῳ) *holding it out* like a torch, *Ep.Phil.*2.16:—Med., *hold by*, χειρός A.R.4.751. II. *hold out to, present, offer*, οἶνον ἐπισχών Il.9.489; ἐπέσχε τε οἶνον ἐρυθρόν Od.16.444; κοτύλην..ἐπέσχε Il.22.494; εἴ ποτέ τοι..μαζὸν ἐπέσχον ib.83, cf. E.*Andr.*225; also γάλακτι δ' οὐκ ἐπέσχον οὐδὲ μαστῷ τροφεῖα ματρός I *offered* not mother's food *with* my breast, Id.*Ion*1492: c. inf., πιεῖν ἐπέσχον Ar.*Nu.*1382: abs., Id.*Pax*1167:—Med., ἐπισχόμενος (sc. τὴν κύλικα) ἐξέπιεν *having put* it *to his lips*, Pl.*Phd.*117c, cf. Stesich.7, A.R.1.472, Luc.*Tox.*37; ἐπὶ χείλεσι..μαστὸν ἐπισχομένη Euph.92; *present* a sum of money, τῇ πόλει *Supp.Epigr.* l. c. 2. *extend, spread out*, τὴν πλεκτάνην Arist.*HA*550ᵇ6. 3. simply, *hold*, σκῆπτρα *IPE*2.37 (Panticapaeum); of writings, *contain*, Philostr.*VS*2.24.2, cf. 2.9.1. 4. *enjoin, impose* a task, c. dat. pers., Procop.*Arc.*17, *Vand.*1.8. III. *hold* or *direct towards*, ἔπεχε τόξον σκοπῷ Pi.*O.*2.89; ἄλλῳ ἐπεῖχε τόξα E.*HF*984:—Med., abs., ἐπισχόμενος βάλεν ἰῷ *having aimed at him* he hit him, Od.22.15. b. intr., *aim at, attack*, τί μοι ὧδ' ἐπέχεις; why thus *launch out against* me? 19.71; in tmesi, ἐπὶ αὐτῷ πάντες ἔχωμεν 22.75; ἀλλήλοις ἐ. Hes.*Th.*711; ἄνδρα ἐπέχοντα τῷ Πύρρῳ Plu.*Pyrrh.*16; ἐπέχειν ἐπί τινα Hdt.9.59; τὰς ἐπὶ σφίσι ναῦς ἐπεχούσας Th.8.105; πρός τι Plu.*Ant.*66: c. dat., ἀκτῇσιν ἐπέσχεθον *held straight for* the beach, A.R.4.1766: abs., E.*Ba.*1131. 2. ἐπέχειν τὴν διάνοιαν ἐπί τινι *direct* one's mind to a thing, Pl.*Lg.*926b; τῷ πολέμῳ τὴν γνώμην Plu.*Aem.*8, etc.; also ἐ. ἑαυτόν τινι *attend* to him, Pl.*R.*399b codd. b. abs., ἐπέχειν (sc. τὸν νοῦν) *intend, purpose*, c. inf., ἐπεῖχε ἐλλάμψεσθαι Hdt.1.80, cf. 153, 6.96: c. dat. rei, *to be intent upon*, ταῖς ἀρχαῖς, διαβάσει, etc., Ar.*Lys.*490, Plb.3.43.2, etc. 3. *stand facing, face* in a line of battle, οὗτοι (sc. οἱ Μῆδοι) ἐπέσχον Κορινθίους Hdt.9.31. IV. *hold back, keep in check*, ἐπέσχε δὲ καλὰ ῥέεθρα Il.21.244; καὶ πῶς ἐπέσχε χεῖρα μαιμῶσαν φόνου; S.*Aj.*50; ἐπισχὼν ἡνίαν ib.847; ἐπίσχωμεν τὸ πλεῖν Id.*Ph.*881; ὀργάς E.*Hel.*1642; οὐκ ἐφέξετε στόμα; Id.*Hec.*1283; χρησμοὺς ἐ. *withhold* them, Id.*Ph.*866; ἐπέχειν τινὰ τῷ ξύλῳ *keep* him *down* with the stick, Ar.*Pax*1121; τὸ εὐθέως ἐπιχειρεῖν Th.7.33; *confine*, as the earth a corpse, *AP*7.461 (Mel.); ἐ. τῇ χειρὶ τὸ στόμα *cover*, Plu.*Cat.Mi.*28; ἐπέχομεν τὴν ἐκπνοήν Gal.6.172; τὰς διαχωρήσεις ἐ. Id.*Vict.Att.*12:—Med., ἐπισχόμενος τὰ ὦτα Pl.*Smp.*216a:—Pass., τοῦ βάθους ἐπεσχημένου J.*AJ*5.1.3; *to be prevented, hindered*, ὑπό τινος *PFreib.*11.13 (iv A. D.); of the menses, Gal.1.184. b. *stay* or *adjourn* proceedings, τὰ πρὸς Ἀργείους Th.5.46; τὴν ζημίαν καὶ τὴν κατασκαφήν ib.63; τὴν δίαιταν D.21.84; *suspend* payments, in Pass., *PTeb.*337.4 (ii/iii A. D.), cf. *PGiss.*48.11 (iii A. D.). c. ἐ. τινά τινος *stop, hinder from*, E.*Andr.*160, Ar.*Lys.*742, D.S.13.87: c. inf., σε μήτε νὺξ μήτε ἡμέρα ἐπισχέτω ὥστε ἀνεῖναι.. *let* them not *stop* thee so that thou neglect.., Th.1.129; ἐ. τινὰ μὴ πράσσειν τι S.*El.*517, *Ph.*349; κλαυθμυρίζον τὸ βρέφος ἐπισχεῖν μὴ δυνάμεναι Sor.1.88:—Pass., μηδενὸς ἐπεχομένου no *objection being taken*, *PTeb.*327.37 (ii A. D.). d. impers., ἐπέχει *there is a hindrance*, Astramps.*Orac.*97.3. 2. abs., *stay, pause*, Ἀντίνοος δ' ἔτ' ἐπεῖχε Od.21.186; *refrain*, Hdt.1.32, 5.51, 7.139; εἰ δ' ἐφέξετον if you *tarry*, S.*El.*1369, etc.: folld. by a Conj., esp. in imper., ἐπίσχες ἤν.. *wait and see* whether..., E.*Supp.*397; ἐπίσχες ἔστ' ἂν..προσμάθῃς A.*Pr.*697; ἐ. ἕως.. D.4.1; μέχρι τοσούτου ἕως.. Th.1.90; ἐπίσχες, abs., *hold! stop!* A.*Ch.*896, S.*OC*856, etc.; ἐπίσχετε, μηδὲ συρίξητε Timocl.2.6D.; ἐπίσχετον, μάθωμεν S.*Ph.*539, cf. E.*Hipp.*567; in part., ἐπισχὼν ὀλίγον χρόνον Hdt.1.132, al.; τὸ ἐπισχεῖν, opp. τὸ παραχρῆμα, Antipho 5.73; οὐ πολὺν χρόνον ἐπισχὼν ἧκεν came *after* a short *interval*, Pl.*Phd.*59e; μικρὸν ἐπισχόντα διεφθείροντο they very *shortly* died, Thphr.*HP*4.4.13, cf. Diocl.*Fr.*43; in Th.2.81 οὐκ ἐπέσχον τὸ στρατόπεδον καταλαβεῖν *did* not *halt* for the purpose of occupying a camp (unless it, = '*had* no *intention* of occupying'). b. c. gen. rei, *stop* or *cease from*, ἐπίσχες τοῦ δρόμου Ar.*Av.*1200; τῆς πορείας X.*Cyr.*4.2.12; τούτου Th.8.31; also ἐ. περί τινος Id.5.32, cf. 8.5: so c. inf., *leave off, cease* to do, X.*Mem.*3.6.10: c. part., *cease* doing, ἀναλῶν οὐκ ἐφέξεις Ar.*Eq.*915 (lyr.), cf. E.*Ph.*449. c. as technical term of the Sceptics, *suspend judgement, doubt*, Str.2.1.11, Ph.1.387, S.E.*P.*1.196; ἐ. ἐν τοῖς ἀδήλοις Plu.2.955c; ⟨πρὸς⟩ τὰ ἄδηλα Arr.*Epict.*1.7.5. 3. Med., *maintain reserve*, ἐπείχετο [ἡ σύγκλητος] κατὰ τοὺς Ἀθηναίους Plb.30.19.17 (s.v.l.). V. *reach* or *extend over* a space, ἑπτὰ δ' ἐπέσχε πέλεθρα Il.21.407; ὁππόσσον ἐπέσχε πυρὸς μένος so far as the fire *reached*, 23.238, cf. Hdt.7.19, Th.2.77, f.l. in Hp.*Aër.*5, etc.: aor. Med., ἐπέσχετο he *lay outstretched*, Hes.*Th.*177; βούβρωστις ἐπέσχετο κόσμον *prevailed over..*, *Epigr.Gr.*793.5 (Apollonia); ἀφορία ἐ. τὸν βίον Longin.44.1. VI. *have power over, occupy* a country, οἱ Σκύθαι τὴν Ἀσίην πᾶσαν ἐπέσχον Hdt.1.104, cf. 108, 8.32, Th.2.101, 7.62, etc.; of things, ἐπ' ὀκτὼ μῆνας Κυρηναίους ὀπώρη ἐ. *occupies* or *engages* them, Hdt.4.199; τὴν πόλιν ἐπεῖχε κλαυθμός Plu.*Oth.*17; ὧν τὰς χρόας τὸ ἡμερινὸν φῶς ἐ. *overspreads*, Pl.*R*.508c: κραυγῆς ἐπεχούσης τὴν ἐκκλησίαν D.S.13.87; πρὸ τοῦ τὰ σώματα τὰς ὠδῖνας ἐπισχεῖν Sor.2.53: generally, *occupy*, τὴν κρατίστην μοῖραν ἐ. *hold* the foremost place, Longin.9.1, cf. 44.12; ὕλης ἐ. τάξιν *Stoic*.3.27; τὴν γῆν κέντρου λόγον ἐπέχουσαν D.L.7.155, cf. *Placit*.3 *Praef*.; τὸν τέλειον ἐ. λόγον Gal.19.160; δίκην ἐπέχειν ἡμᾶς φυτῶν we *are like* plants, Meno *Iatr*. 6.18. 2. abs., *prevail, predominate*, ἢν μὴ λαμπρὸς ἄνεμος ἐπέχῃ Hdt.2.96; σεισμοὶ ἐπέσχον ἐπὶ πλεῖστον μέρος γῆς Th.1.23; πάντῃ ἐπεῖχε γαλήνη Timo 63; [τῶν νεῶν] ἐπὶ πολὺ τῆς θαλάσσης ἐπεχουσῶν *being spread over*.., Th.1.50; τὴν [τύχην].., ἣ νῦν ἐπέχει D.18.253; ἐτησίων ἐπεχόντων Plb.5.5.6. b. of Time, *continue*, τὴν θύραν ἐπεῖχε κρούων Ar.*Ec*.317; ἐπέχων καὶ οὐκ ἀνιείς *continuously*, Pl.*Tht*.165e; ἐπὶ πλείους ἡμέρας ὁ σεισμὸς ἐπεῖχεν D.C.68.25; σκότος, νὺξ ἐπέσχε, *came on*, Plu.*Mar*.20, *Crass*.30, etc. VII. Med., fut. ἐπιέξομαι, *meet*, Orac. in *Michel* 855.39 (Magn. Mae.).

ἐπηβάω, Ion. for ἐφηβάω, Hdt.6.83.

ἐπηβολ-ή, Dor. **ἐπαβολά**, ἡ, *part, share*, *Leg.Gort*.5.50, Hsch. -**ία**, ἡ, = συνηβολία, *EM*357.29. -**ος** (Aeol. **ἐπάβ-** dub. in Sapph. *Supp*.10.2), ον, *having reached, achieved*, or *gained* a thing, c. gen., οὐ νηὸς ἐ. οὐδ' ἐρετάων γίγνομαι Od.2.319; τούτων ἐ. Hdt.9.94; ἱματίου ἐ. γενέσθαι *PSI*4.418.22 (iii B.C.); τούτων τῶν θεῶν ἐ. *in possession of*.., Hdt.8.111; τερπνῆς..τῆσδ' ἐ. νόσου A.*Ag*.542; ἐ. φρενῶν, Lat. *compos mentis*, Id.*Pr*.444, S.*Ant*.492; ἐπιστήμης, παιδείας ἐ., Pl. *Euthd*.289b, *Lg*.724b, cf. Hp.*Lex* 2; μήτε πόλεως μήτε πολιτείας Hyp. *Fr*.78; μεγάλων καὶ καλῶν Arist.*EN*1101^{a}13; νόος οἰκωφελίας αἶσιν ἐπάβολος whose mind is *skilled in* housewifery, Theoc.28.2; τῶν ὄντων ἐ. γενόμενος having become *acquainted with* the true facts, Hld. 10.20: c. inf., *most dexterous at*.., κλέψαι -ώτατος Plu.*Arat*.10. 2. *pertaining to, befitting*, κλήροισιν ἐ. *belonging to* our fields, Nic.*Al*. 232; πάντεσσιν ἐ. ἥνδανε μῆτις A.R.4.1380. II. Pass., *to be reached* or *won*, ἐπήβολος ἅρματι νύσσα Id.3.1272. (ἐφήβολος *CIG* (add.)4303*a* 20 (Myra).)

ἐπηγκενίδες [ῐ], αἱ, *long planks* bolted to the upright ribs (σταμίνες) of the ship, Od.5.253. (Prob. from ἀγκών: ἐπηγανίδες (sic)· ἐπηνύγματα, Hsch.: ἐπητανίδεσσι (ἐπιτανίδες cod.) was read by Rhian.ap. Sch.Od. l.c.)

ἐπηγορ-εύω, *say against* one, *cast in* his *teeth*, τινί τι Hdt.1.90 codd.:—also part. -**έων** (ἐπιγ- cod.) Hsch. (prob. in Hdt. l.c.). -**ία**, ἡ, *accusation, blame*, D.C.55.18, al., Them.*Or*.11.152b; cj. in Pi.*Fr*. 122.

ἐπηέριος, ον, *through the air*, φορέεσθαι Q.S.2.573.

ἐπηετᾰνός, όν, also ἡ, όν (v. infr.), *abundant, ample, sufficient* (Hom. only in Od.); παρέχουσιν ἐπηετανὸν γάλα θῆσθαι 4.89; πρασιαὶ..ἐπηετανὸν γανόωσαι (as Adv.) 7.128; σῖτον..ἐ. παρέχοιμι 18. 360; πλυνοὶ ἐ. troughs *always full*, 6.86, cf. 13.247; ἐπεὶ οὐ κομιδὴ κατὰ νῆα ἦεν ἐπηετανός 8.233; ἐπηετανὸν γὰρ ἔχεσκον for they had *great store*, 7.99, cf. 10.427; ἐ. βίος Hes.*Op*.31, Pi.*N*.6.10; ἐπηεταναὶ τρίχες *thick, full* fleeces, Hes.*Op*.517; [Ἀμαζόνες] ἐπηετανὸν κομέουσαι A.R.2.1176; ἐπηεταναὶ πλατάνιστοι Theoc.25.20, cf. Orph. *Fr*.280. [In *h.Merc*.113, Hes.*Op*.607, quadrisyll.]

ἐπήκοος, Dor. **ἐπάκοος** [ᾱ], ον, *listening, giving ear to*, c. gen., ἐμῶν ἔργων A.*Ag*.1420; κακῶν, δίκης, Id.*Ch*.980, *Eu*.732; ἐ. καὶ θεαταὶ δικῶν Pl.*Lg*.767d; λόγων Id.*R*.499a: less freq. c. dat., εὐχαῖς Id. *Phlb*.25b; ἐ. εἶναι γονεῦσι πρὸς τέκνα θεοὺς Id.*Lg*.931c; ὧν ηὔχοντο τὰ μέγιστα αὐτοῖς οἱ θεοὶ ἐ. γεγόνασι Id.*Mx*.247d; γυναιξὶν *AP*9.303 (Adaeus): abs., *listening to prayer*, of gods, Pi.*O*.14.14 codd., Ar.*Th*. 1157 (lyr.), *BGU*1216.50 (ii B.C.); Ἀσκληπιῷ ἐ. θεῷ *IG*12(8).366 (Thasos); epith. of Artemis, *IG*14.963, 12(9).1262 (Attica), etc. 2. *obedient*, ψυχαί J.*BJ*3.8.5. II. *within hearing, within ear-shot*, εἰς ἐπήκοον στῆσαί τινα, καλέσασθαι, X.*An*.2.5.38, 3.3.1; ἐν ἐπηκόῳ εἶναι, στῆναι, J.*BJ*5.9.3, 3.10.2; ἐξ ἐπηκόου Luc.*Cont*.20; ἐς τὸ ἐπηκοώτατον τοῦ οὐρανοῦ Id.*Icar*.23; ἀναγνῶναι ἐς ἐ. ἅπασι Id.*Symp*. 21 III. Pass., *heard, listened to*, ἃ πᾶς ὑμνεῖ ἐπήκοα γενέσθαι παρὰ θεῶν Pl.*Lg*.931b; ἐ. αἱ τοῦ θεοφιλοῦς εὐχαί Ph.1.296. IV. Subst. ἐπήκοος, Dor. ἐπάκοος, ὁ, *witness* to a transaction, *IG*5(1). 1228 (Taenarum), al., dub. in *Foed.Delph.Pell*.1 *A* 15; ἐπήκοοι *delegates*, *IG*11(4).1065. (Dual ἐπακόω ib.5(1).1230, ἐπάκω 1231, 1233, ἐπάκοε 1232.)

ἔπηλις (not ἐπηλίς Hdn.Gr.1.91), ιδος, ἡ, Ion. for ἔφηλις, *cover, lid*, S.*Fr*.1046, Posidipp.41. II. *freckle*, Ael.Dion.*Fr*.57.

ἐπηλλαγμένως, Adv., (ἐπαλλάσσω) *crosswise*, Hp.*Oss*.16. II. *changeably*, Hierocl.*Prov*.p.462 B.

ἐπηλῠγ-άζω or -**ίζω**, *overshadow, cover*, τινὰς ἱματίοις Ael.*NA*4.7, cf. 3.16, al.:—Med., τῷ κοινῷ φόβῳ τὸν σφέτερον ἐπηλυγάζεσθαι *throw a shade over*, i.e. *disguise, conceal* one's *own* fear by.., Th.6.36; ἐ. τὴν χεῖρα *hold* one's hand *as a shade over one's eyes*, Arist.*GA*780^{b} 19; and (without χεῖρα) ἐ. πρὸ τῶν ὀμμάτων ib.781^{b}12, cf. Aristocl. ap.Eus.*PE*14.18; ἐπηλυγισάμενός τινα *putting* him *as a screen before one*, Pl.*Ly*.207b; ἐ. ὕλην Arist.*HA*559^{a}1, cf. 613^{b}9; *use as a lurking place*, ὀπήν ib.623^{a}29:—Pass., *to be concealed*, ὑπὸ τῆς ἀγνωσίας Dam.*Pr*.26; τινί ib.29; *to be suppressed*, Hp.*Mul*.2.156. (Both -άζω and -ίζω are found in codd.) -**αιος**, ον, (ἠλύγη) *shady, dark*, *AB*243, Hsch. -**ισμός**, ὁ, = ἐπισκιασμός, Hsch. s. v. ἠλύγη.

ἐπῆλυξ, ῠγος, ὁ, ἡ, *overshadowing*, τὴν πέτραν ἐπήλυγα λαβεῖν take the rock *as a screen*, E.*Cyc*.680.

ἔπηλ-ῠς, ῠδος, ὁ, ἡ, ἔπηλυ, τό, (ἐπήλυθον) *one who comes to* a place, ἔλθετ' ἐπήλυδες αὖθις *come* back *to me* (for they were going away), S. *Ph*.1190 (anap.). II. *incomer, stranger, foreigner*, opp. αὐτόχθων, Hdt.1.78, 4.197; ἄνδρας πολεμίους ἐ. A.*Pers*.243 (troch.), cf. *Th*.34, *Supp*.195, Th.1.29: Adj., ἔ. γένεσις Pl.*Mx*.237b; ἔ. βίος J.*AJ*8.12. 2: also in neut. pl., ἐπήλυδα ἔθνεα Hdt.8.73: neut. sg., ἐπήλυδος γένους D.H.1.60; ὕδωρ ἔπηλυ Paus.2.5.3. -**ῠσία**, Ep. -**ίη**, ἡ, *coming over one*, esp. by spells, *bewitching*, *h.Cer*.228, *h.Merc*. 37. II. *approach*, Διονύσου Nonn.*D*.14.328. -**ῠσις**, εως, ἡ, *approach, assault*, Opp.*H*.4.228; πτερύγων *AP*5.267 (Paul. Sil.); βαρβάρων Heph.Astr.1.21. -**ύτης** [ῠ], ου, ὁ, = ἔπηλυς, Th.1.9 codd., f.l. in X.*Oec*.11.4, cf. Poll.3.54, Philostr.*VA*2.9, Procop.*Vand*.2.10: —also -**ῠτος**, ον, D.H.3.72, Ph.1.160.

ἐπημάτιος [ᾰ], η, ον, (ἦμαρ) *day by day*, A.R.3.895, Opp.*H*.3.229.

ἐπημοιβός, όν, late ή, όν Opp.*H*.5.135:—*crossing*, ὀχῆες ἐ. (unless = *shifting to and fro*) Il.12.456; τελαμῶνες ἐ. *cross*-belts, Opp.*C*. 1.98. 2. *alternating, serving for change*, χιτῶνες ἐ. Od.14.513; ἀστέρες Arat.190; πρηδόνες Nic.*Th*.365.

ἐπημύω, *bend* or *bow down*, ἐπὶ δ' ἠμύει ἀσταχύεσσιν (sc. τὸ λήϊον) Il.2.148, cf. Nic.*Th*.870, Opp.*H*.1.228, *C*.4.123. **ἐπήν**, v. ἐπεί.

ἐπηνέμιος, ον, *windy*: metaph., *vain*, πλοῦτος Suid.

ἐπηνύγματα, v. ἐπηγκενίδες.

ἐπηόνιος, ον, (ἠών) *on the shore*, κύκνος *AP*5.124 (Bass.).

ἐπήορος, ον, *uplifted*, δούρατα A.R.2.1065, cf. Nonn.*D*.37.47: c. dat., *lifted upon*, καυλοῖσιν ἐ. ἄνθος A.R.3.856, cf. Nonn.*D*.10.205.

ἐπηπύω, *shout in applause*, λαοὶ δ' ἀμφοτέροισιν ἐπήπυον Il.18.502: abs., *shout*, Orph.*A*.528.

ἐπήρᾰνος, = ἐπιήρανος, dub. in Orph.*A*.823, prob. in *Epigr.Gr.* 1013.5 (Memnon).

ἐπηρᾰσία, ἡ, = ἐπήρεια, *Supp.Epigr*.2.710.8 (Pednelissus).

ἐπήρατε· καλέσατε, Hsch.

ἐπήρᾰτος, ον, (ἔραμαι) *lovely, delightsome*, δαίς Il.9.228; εἵματα Od.8.366; freq. of places, [Ἰθάκη] μᾶλλον ἐ. ἱπποβότοιο 4.606; νῆσος Hes.*Fr*.76.4; also καλὸν εἶδος ἐπήρατον Id.*Op*.63; ἐπήρατον ὄσσαν ἱεῖσαι Id.*Th*.67; ἐπήρατον ἴαχον ὄρθιον Sapph.*Supp*.20c.4; κῦδος Alc. *Supp*.23.13; later of persons, ἐ. νεάνιδες A.*Eu*.958 (lyr.); παρθενική A.R.3.1099.

ἐπηρε-άζω, *threaten abusively*, λέγειν ἐπηρεάζοντες Hdt.6.9: c. acc., *speak disparagingly of*, τὴν ἀγαθὴν ἀναστροφήν 1*Ep.Pet*.3.16. II. *deal despitefully with, act despitefully towards*, c. dat. pers., X.*Mem*. 1.2.31; ἐ. μοι συνεχῶς καὶ μικρὰ καὶ μείζω D.21.14, etc.; ἐ. ψηφίσμασι καὶ νόμοις *oppose* them *insolently*, Id.18.320; τινός Luc.*Nav*.27; τινά Arist.*Pol*.1311^{a}37, *Ev.Luc*.6.28, etc.; εἰ δ' ἄν τις..ἐπηρεάζεν δέατοι ἰν τὰ ἔργα *IG*5(2).6.46 (Tegea, iv B.C.): abs., *to be insolent*, Antipho 6.8; ὑψηλὴ ῥὶς ὥσπερ -άζουσα διατετείχικε τὰ ὄμματα X.*Smp*.5.6:— Pass., *to be insulted*, Lys.29.7, D.21.15, D.S.36.11, Ph.2.52, *PGen*. 31.18 (ii A.D.):—later Med. in act. sense, τινί *PLond*.3.846.6 (ii A.D.). III. of the action of disease, διάφορα ἐ. μόρια Steph.*in Hp*. 1.204 D. -**ασμός**, ὁ, *despiteful treatment*, defined as ἐμποδισμὸς ταῖς βουλήσεσιν, οὐχ ἵνα τι αὐτῷ, ἀλλ' ἵνα μὴ ἐκείνῳ Arist.*Rh*.1378^{b}18, cf. 1382^{a}2, *PTeb*.28.4 (ii B.C.); τύχης ἐ. D.S.20.54. -**αστής**, οῦ, ὁ, *insolent person*, Sm.*Ps*.56(57).2, Vett.Val.104.8, *PAmh*.2.134. 12 (ii A.D.). -**αστικός**, ή, όν, *insolent*, *Com.Adesp*.202, Alex. Aphr.*in Metaph*.308.13. Adv. -κῶς Gal.*Anim.Pass*.1.12, al.

ἐπήρεια, ἡ, (ἐπί, ἄρος) *insulting treatment, abuse*, ἐχθροῦ D.18.12, cf. Is.4.5, etc.; περὶ τὸν χορόν D.21.25; κελεύειν κατ' ἐπήρειαν order *haughtily* or *by way of insult*, Th.1.26; κατ' ἐ. τινος γεγένηταί τι is done to *insult* him, Amips.9; κατ' ἐπήρειαν *BGU*180.8 (ii A.D.); φθόνον τ' ἐ. τε Philem.92.2; ἐν ἐπηρείας τάξει D.18.13; πολλὰ πρὸς ἐπήρειαν καὶ χάριν πράττειν Arist.*Pol*.1287^{a}38; εἰς ἐ. τὴν ἐμήν ib. 195.20 (ii A.D.); χωρὶς ἐ. *OGI*262.24 (iii A.D.): pl., Man.4.331; λῃστρικαὶ ἐ. Chor. in *Rev.Phil*.1.73; ἐ. δαίμονός τινος his *capricious dealing*, Luc.*Laps*.1, cf. Philostr.*Ep*.18:—later spelt **ἐπήρια**, *BGU* 340.21 (ii A.D.), Melamp.(?) in *PRyl*.28.139 (iv A.D.).

ἐπηρεμ-έω, *rest after*, τοῖς καμάτοις Luc.*Am*.45, cf. Paul.Aeg.6.60 (dub.), Marcellin.*Puls*.192. -**ησις**, εως, ἡ, *pause* between systole and diastole of pulse, ib.184, al.

ἐπηρέσιον· τὸ προσκεφάλαιον, Hsch. (cf. ὑπ-).

ἐπήρετμος, ον, *at the oar*, ἑταῖροι ἧατ' ἐπήρετμοι Od.2.403; ἐ. πόνοι Opp.*H*.4.76. 2. *equipped with oars*, νῆες Od.5.16, 14.224, al.

ἐπηρεφής, ές, *overhanging, beetling*, ἐπηρεφέας φύγε πέτρας νηῦς ἐμή Od.10.131, cf. 12.59; κρημνοὶ ἐ. Il.12.54; κότινος Theoc.25.208. II. Pass., *covered, sheltered*, σίμβλοι Hes.*Th*.598; ἐ. φολίδεσσι, of a dragon, A.R.4.144; σπέος πέτρῃσιν ἐ. Id.2.736; νήσους ἐ. δονάκεσσιν Simm.1.8; κόρυμβοι ἐ. πετάλοισι Nic.*Fr*.74.24, cf. Hld.8.14.

ἐπήρης, ες, *equipped*, esp. of ships, πλοῖα Agatharch.83; ἐ. κελήτιον a boat *furnished with oars*, Arr.*An*.5.7.3: generally, ἐ. πτερύγεσσιν Max.415.

ἐπήριστος or -**ῖτος**, ον, (ἐρίζω) *contended for*, coined by Eust.725. 16, 1962.7, to expl. Ἐπήριτος (v. Ἐπάριτοι).

ἐπῆρσε, Ep. 3 sg. aor. 1 of ἐπαραρίσκω. **ἐπησθείεν**, Ion. 3 pl. aor. 1 opt. of ἐφήδομαι.

ἐπησῠχάζω (sic), *acquiesce in*, πράσει *PLond*.1.113 (vi A.D.).

ἐπητᾰνός, v. ἐπηετανός.

ἐπήτεια, ἡ, = ἐπητύς, A.R.3.1007 (pl.).

ἐπητής, οῦ, ὁ, *courteous, gentle*, opp. rude and barbarous, Od.13. 332; ἐπητῇ ἀνδρὶ ἔοικας 18.128: pl. ἐπητέες as fem., A.R.2.987 (ἐπήτιδες Lobeck); cf. ἐπητύς.

ἐπητικός, ή, όν, *given to following*, Metop.ap.Stob.3.1.115.

ἐπήτρῐμος, ον, (ἤτριον) prop. *woven to, closely woven*: hence, generally, *close, thronged*, πυρσοί τε φλεγέθουσιν ἐπήτριμοι torch *upon* torch, Il.18.211; δράγματα..ἐ. πῖπτον ἔραζε ib.552; λίην γὰρ πολλοὶ καὶ ἐπήτριμοι..πίπτουσι too many *one after another*, 19.226, cf. A.R.

1.30,etc.: later in sg., κῦμα Q.S.14.248; ὄχλος Opp.*C*.3.382: neut. pl. as Adv., ib.1.322,al.

ἐπήτριος· λόγιος, πανοῦργος, Hsch.

ἐπητύς, ύος, ἡ, *courtesy, kindness*, Od.21.306. (This and ἐπητής perh. from ἕπω; for the form cf. ἐδ-η-τύς.)

ἐπηύρον, -όμην, v. ἐπαυρίσκομαι.

ἐπηχ-έω, *resound, re-echo*, E.*Cyc*.426, Pl.*R*.492c: c. acc., ἐπαίνους καὶ ὕμνους Ph.1.348: c. dat., ἐπηχοῦντα [τοῖς κύκνοις] τὰ δένδρα Jul. *Or*.7.236a. II. *accompany* one *in shouting*, E.*IA*1584. **-ησις**, εως, ἡ, *playing upon*, τοῦ αὐλοῦ Callistr.*Stat*.1. 2. abs., *resonance*, St. Byz. s.v. Δωδώνη.

ἐπηῷος, ον, (ἠώς) f.l. for ὑπηῷος in Orph.*A*.658.

ἐπήωρα· κρεμάμενα, μετέωρα, Hsch. (cf. ἀπήωρος).

ἐπί, Thess. (before τ) ἐτ *IG*9(2).517.14 (iii B.C.), Prep. with gen., dat., and acc., to denote the *being upon* or *supported upon a surface* or *point*.

A. WITH GEN.: I. of Place, 1. with Verbs of Rest, *upon*, καθέζετ' ἐ. θρόνου Il.1.536; ἧστο.. ὑψοῦ ἐπ' ἀκροτάτης κορυφῆς 13.12; ἐ. πύργου ἔστη 16.700; κεῖται ἐ. χθονός 20.345: without a Verb expressed, ἔγχεα ὀρθ' ἐ. σαυρωτῆρος (sc. σταθέντα) ἐλήλατο 10.153; ἔκλαγξαν ὀϊστοὶ ἐπ' ὤμων the arrows *on* his shoulders, 1.46; ἐ. γῆς, opp. ὑπὸ γῆς, Pl.*Lg*.728a: also with Verbs of Motion, where the subject rests *upon* something, as *on* a chariot, a horse, a ship, φεύγωμεν ἐφ' ἵππων *on* our chariot, Il.24.356; οὐκ ἂν ἐφ' ὑμετέρων ὀχέων.. ἵκεσθον 8.455; ἄγαγε.. δῶρ' ἐπ' ἀπήνης 24.447; ἐπὶ τῆς ἁμάξης.. ὠχέετο Hdt.1.31; ἐπὶ τῶν ἵππων ὀχεῖσθαι X.*Cyr*.4.5.58; οὓς κῆρες φορέουσι.. ἐ. νηῶν Il.8.528; πέμπειν τινὰς ἐ. τριήροιν X.*HG*5.4.56, etc.; ἐπ' ὤμου.. φέρειν Od.10.170; τὴν κλεῖδα περιφέρειν ἐφ' ἑαυτοῦ to carry the key about *on* his person, Numen.ap.Eus.*PE*14.7; βαδιοῦνται ἐ. δυοῖν σκελοῖν, ἐφ' ἑνὸς πορεύσονται σκέλους, Pl.*Smp*.190d; ἐπ' ἄκρων ὁδοιπορεῖν walk *on* tiptoe, S.*Aj*.1230; of places, *upon*, if the place is an actual *support*, νέρθε κἀπὶ γῆς ἄνω Id.*OT*416; ἐ. τοῦ εὐωνύμου *on* the left, ἐ. τῶν πλευρῶν *on* the flanks, X.*An*.1.8.9,3.2.36; but most freq., *in*, rarely in Hom., ἐπ' ἀγροῦ *in* the country, Od. 1.190; γᾶς ἐ. ξένας S.*OC*1705 (lyr.); νήσου τῆσδ' ἐφ' ἧς ναίει Id.*Ph*. 613; ἐ. ξένας δμωὶς ἐπ' ἀλλοτρίας πόλεος E.*Andr*.137 (lyr.); οἱ ἐ. Θρᾴκης σύμμαχοι Th.5.35; τοὺς ἐ. τῆς Ἀσίας κατοικοῦντας Isoc.12. 103; ἐπ' οἰκήματος κατίσαι, καθῆσθαι, *in* a brothel, Hdt.2.121.ε', Pl. *Chrm*.163b; τοὺς ἐ. τῶν οἰκημάτων καθεζομένους Aeschin.1.74; ἐ. τῶν ἐργαστηρίων καθίζειν Isoc.7.15; μένειν ἐ. τῆς αὐτῶν (sc. χώρας) remain *in* statu quo, Indut.ap.Th.4.118; οἱ ἐπ' ἐρημίας λῃστεύοντες Jul. *Or*.7.210a; later of towns, ἐπ' Ἀλεξανδρείας *BGU*908.16 (ii A.D.), etc.; sts. also, *at* or *near*, ἐπ' αὐτάων (sc. τῶν πηγῶν) Il.22.153; κόλπος ὁ ἐ. Ποσιδηΐου Hdt.7.115; αἱ ἐ. Λήμνου ἐπικείμεναι νῆσοι *off* Lemnos, ib.6 codd.; τὰ ἐ. Θρᾴκης the Thrace-*ward* region, Th.1.59, cf. *IG*1[2]. 45.17, etc.; ποταμοὶ ἐφ' ὧν ἔξεστιν ἡμῖν ταμιεύεσθαι.. *on*, i.e. *near* which.., X.*An*.2.5.18; ἐ. τῶν τραπεζῶν *at* the money-changers' tables, Pl.*Ap*.17c; in Geom., αἱ ἐφ' ὧν ΑΑ ΒΒ [γραμμαί] the lines ΑΑ ΒΒ, Arist.*EN*1132[b]6, etc.; ἕλιξ ἐφ' ἧς τὰ ΑΒΓΔ a spiral ABCD, Archim.*Spir*.13 (cf. B.I.1k); also ἐ. τοῦ βάτου *in the passage concerning* the bush, *Ev.Marc*.12.26. 2. in various relations not strictly local, μένειν ἐ. τῆς ἀρχῆς remain *in* the command, X.*Ages*.1. 37; μένειν ἐ. τινος abide *by* it, D.4.9; ἐ. τῶν πραγμάτων, ἐ. τοῦ πολεμεῖν εἶναι, to be engaged *in*.., Id.15.11, *Prooem*.1; ἐ. ὀνόματος εἶναι bear a name, Id.39.21; ἔχεται πόλις ἐ. νόσου S.*Ant*.1141 (lyr.). b. of ships, ὁρμεῖν ἐπ' ἀγκύρας ride *at* (i.e. *in dependence upon an*) anchor, Hdt.7.188; ἐ. προσπόλου μιᾶς χωρεῖν *dependent upon* an attendant, S.*OC*746. c. with the personal and reflexive Pron., once in Hom., εὔχεσθε.. σιγῇ ἐφ' ὑμείων Il.7.195; later mostly with 3rd pers., ἐπ' ἑωυτῶν κεῖσθαι *by* themselves, Hdt.2.2, cf. 8.32; οἰκέειν κώμην Id. 5.98; ἐ. σφῶν αὐτῶν αὐτόνομοι οἰκεῖν Th.2.63; ἵζεσθαι Hdt.9.17; ἐφ' ἑαυτῶν πλεῖν Th.8.8; ἐπ' ὑμέων αὐτῶν βαλέσθαι consider it *by* yourselves, Hdt.3.71, etc.; αὐτὴ ἐφ' αὑτῆς σκοποῦσα Th.6.40; ἐφ' ἡμῶν αὐτῶν τὸν ἐξετασμὸν ποιεῖσθαι D.18.16; ἐπ' ἑωυτῶν διαλέγονται speak *in* a dialect of their own, Hdt.1.142; also αὐτοὶ ἐφ' ἑαυτῶν χωρεῖν X. *An*.2.4.10; πράττειν Pl.*Prt*.326d, cf. *Sph*.217c; τὸ ἐφ' ἑαυτῶν μόνον προορώμενοι considering their own *interest* only, Th.1.17. d. with numerals, to denote the *depth* of a body of soldiers, ἐ. τεττάρων ταχθῆναι to be drawn up four *deep*, four *in file*, X.*An*.1.2.15, etc.; ἐ. πεντήκοντα ἀσπίδων συνεστραμμένοι, of the Thebans at Leuctra, Id.*HG* 6.4.12; ἐπ' ὀλίγων τεταγμένοι, i.e. *in* a long thin *line*, Id.*An*.4.8.11; οὐκ ἐπ' ὀλίγων ἀσπίδων στρατιὰν παρατεταγμένην Th.7.79; ἐφ' ἑνὸς ἄγειν *in* single *file*, X.*Cyr*.2.4.2, cf. *An*.5.2.6; rarely of the *length* of the line, ἐ. τεσσάρων ταξάμενοι τὰς ναῦς Th.2.90; in X., ἐγένοντο τὸ μέτωπον ἐ. τριακοσίων.. τὸ δὲ βάθος ἐφ' ἑκατὸν *Cyr*.2.4.2; πλεῖν ἐ. κέρως, ἐ. κέρας, v. infr. C.I.3; ἐ. φάλαγγος γίγνεται τὸ στράτευμα is formed *in* column, *An*.4.6.6, etc. (but in E.*Ph*.1467, ἀσπίδων ἔπι is merely *in* or *under* arms): hence, generally, ἐ. ὀκτὼ πλίνθων τὸ εὖρος eight bricks *wide*, X.*An*.7.8.14. e. c. gen. pers., *before, in presence of*, ἐ. μαρτύρων.. πράσσεταί τι Antipho 2.3.8; ἐξελέγχεσθαι ἐ. πάντων D.25.36; so, *before* a magistrate or official, ἐ. τοῦ στρατηγοῦ *POxy*. 38.11 (i A.D.), cf. *UPZ*71.15 (ii B.C.), *Ev.Matt*.28.14; γράφομαί σε ἐ. Ῥαδαμάνθυος Luc.*Cat*.18; τινὰ εἰς δίκην καὶ κρίσιν ἐ. τῶν στρατοπέδων προκαλεῖν Jul.*Or*.1.30d; πίστεις δοῦναι ἐ. θεῶν D.H.5.29; but ἐπὶ δικασταῖς is f.l. in D.19.243 (leg. ἔπη). f. with Verbs of perceiving, observing, judging, etc., *in the case of*, ἐπὶ νούσων παντοίων ἐπύθοντο Emp.112.10; ὁρᾶν τι ἐ. τινος X.*Mem*.3.9.3; αἰσθάνεσθαί τι ἐ. τινος Pl.*R*.406c, etc.; τὴν γνώμην ἔχειν ἐ. τινος Hyp.*Eux*.32; τὰ συμβόλαια ἐ. τῶν νόμων σκοπεῖν D.18.210; ἐπ' αὐτῶν τῶν ἔργων ἂν ἐσκόπει ib.233, cf. 25.2 (v.l.); ἐφ' ἑνός τι παριδεῖν Lycurg.64; τὰς ἐναντιώσεις ἐ. μὲν τῶν λόγων τηροῦντες, ἐ. δὲ τῶν ἔργων μὴ καθορῶντες Isoc.13.7; οὐδεὶς ἐφ' αὑτοῦ τὰ κακὰ συνορᾷ Men.631; ἀγνοεῖν τι ἐ. τινος X.*Mem*.2.3.2; also with Verbs of speaking, *on* a subject, λέγειν ἐ. τινος Pl.*Chrm*.155d, *R*.524e, etc.; ἐπιδεῖξαί τι ἐ. τινος Isoc.8.109; ἵνα τοὺς ἐπαίνους ἐπ' αὐτῶν κοινοὺς ποιήσωμαι D.60.12. 3. implying Motion: a. where the sense of motion is lost in the sense of being supported, ὀρθωθεὶς.. ἐπ' ἀγκῶνος having raised himself *upon* his elbow, Il.10.80; ἐ. μελίης.. ἐρεισθεὶς 22.225; τὴν μὲν.. καθεῖσεν ἐ. θρόνου 18.389. b. in a pregnant sense, denoting the goal of motion (cf. εἰς A.I.2, ἐν A.I.8), νῆα.. ἐπ' ἠπείροιο ἔρυσσαν drew the ship *upon* the land *and left it there*, 1.485; περάαν νήσων ἔπι carry *to* the islands *and leave there*, 21.454, cf. 22.45; ἐ. τῆς γῆς καταπίπτειν X.*Cyr*.4.5.54; ἀναβῆναι ἐ. τῶν πύργων ib.7.1.39; ἐπ' Ἀβύδου ἀφικομέναις Th.8.79 (v.l.); freq. of motion *towards* or (in a military sense) *upon* a place, προτρέποντο μελαινάων ἐ. νηῶν Il.5.700; τρέσσε.. ἐφ' ὁμίλου 11.546 (but νήσου ἔ. Ψυρίης νέεσθαι to go *near* Psyria, Od.3.171); ἐπ' οἴκου ἀπελαύνειν, ἀναχωρεῖν, ἀποχωρεῖν, home*wards*, Hdt.2.121.δ', Th.1.30,87, etc.; also with names of places, ἰέναι ἐ. Κυζίκου Hdt.4.14; πλεῖν ἐ. Χίου Id. 1.164, cf. 168; ἀποπλεῖν ἐπ' Αἰγύπτου ib.1; ἀπαλλάσσεσθαι ἐ. Θεσσαλίης Id.5.64; ὁ κόλπος ὁ ἐ. Παγασέων φέρων the bay that leads *to* Pagasae, Id.7.193; ἡ ἐ. Βαβυλῶνος ὁδός the road *leading to* B., X.*Cyr*. 5.3.45, cf. *An*.6.3.24. c. metaph., ἐ. γνώμης τινὸς γίγνεσθαι come *to* an opinion, D.4.7; ἐπ' ἐλπίδος γενέσθαι Plu.*Sol*.14; ὡς ἐ. κινδύνου as if *to meet* danger, Th.6.34; ἐ. τοῦ ἀλύπως ζῆν *with a view to*.., Pl.*Prt*. 358b; cf. infr. B.III.2. II. of Time, *in the time of*, ἐ. προτέρων ἀνθρώπων Il.5.637, 23.332; ἐ. Κρόνου Hes.*Op*.111; ἐ. Κέκροπος, ἐ. Δαρείου, etc., Hdt.8.44, 6.98, etc.; ἐ. τῶν τριάκοντα Lys.13.2; ὀλιγαρχία ἡ ἐ. τῶν τετρακοσίων κατάστασα Isoc.8.108; ἐ. τούτου τυραννεύοντος, ἐ. Λέοντος βασιλεύοντος, ἐ. Μήδων ἀρχόντων, etc., Hdt.1.15,65, 134, etc.; ἐ. τῆς ἐμῆς βασιλείας Isoc.3.32; ἐπ' ἐμεῦ *in* my *time*, Hdt.1.5, 2.46, etc.; ἡ εἰρήνη ἡ ἐπ' Ἀνταλκίδου D.20.54, cf. X.*HG*5.1.36; αἱ ἐπ' Ἀσδρούβα γενόμεναι ὁμολογίαι Plb.3.15.5; ἐπ' εἰρήνης *in time of* peace, Il.2.797, 9.403; ἐπ' ἐμῆς νεότητος Ar.*Ach*.211 (lyr.); ἐ. Λάχητος καὶ τοῦ προτέρου πολέμου Th.6.6; ἐπ' ἡμέρης ἑκάστης v.l. for -η -τῃ in Hdt.5.117. b. later ἐ. δείπνου *at* dinner, Luc.*Asin*.3; ἐ. τῆς τραπέζης, ἐφ' ἑκάστης κύλικος, Plu.*Alex*.23; ἐ. τῆς κύλικος, ἐ. τοῦ ποτηρίου, Luc.*Pisc*.34, Plu.*Alex*.53. III. in various causal senses: 1. *over*, of persons in authority, ἐπ' οὗ ἐτάχθημεν Hdt.5.109; οἱ ἐ. τῶν πραγμάτων the public officers, D.18.247; freq. in forged decrees, ὁ ἐ. τῶν ὅπλων στρατηγός ib.38; ὁ ἐ. τῶν ὁπλιτῶν, τῶν ἱππέων, ib.116; ὁ ἐ. τῆς διοικήσεως ib.38 (but cf. C.III.3); τοῦ ἐ. τῶν ὁπλιτῶν is f.l. in Lys. 32.5; ὁ ἐ. τῆς χώρας στρατηγός Plu.*Phoc*.32; οἱ ἐ. τῶν σιτοποιῶν καὶ μαγείρων Id.*Alex*.23; ὁ ἐ. τοῦ οἴνου Id.*Pyrrh*.5; ὁ ἐ. τῶν ἐπιστολῶν τοῦ Ὄθωνος, = Lat. *ab epistulis*, his secretary, Id.*Oth*.9; cf. B.III. 6. 2. κεκλῆσθαι ἐ. τινος to be called *after* him, Hdt.4.45; ἐ. τινος μετονομασθῆναι Id.1.94: ἐ. τινος τὰς ἐπωνυμίας ἔχειν Id.4.107; ἐ. τινος ἐπώνυμος γίγνεσθαι ib.184; also ἐπ' ὀνόματος καλεῖν Plb.5.35. 2. 3. of occasions, circumstances, and conditions, οὐκ ἐ. τούτου μόνον, ἀλλ' ἐ. πάντων, *on* all occasions, D.21.38, cf. 183; ἐφ' ἑκάστων Pl.*Phlb*.25e; ἐφ' ἑκατέρου Id.*Tht*.159c; ἐφ' ἑκάστης μαντείας D.21. 54; ἐπ' ἐξουσίας καὶ πλούτου πονηρὸν εἶναι *in*.. ib.138; ἐ. τῆς ἀληθείας καὶ τοῦ πράγματος ib.72, cf. 18.17; τὴν ἐ. τῆς πομπῆς καὶ τοῦ μεθύειν πρόφασιν λαβών Id.21.180; ἐ. σχολῆς Aeschin.3.191; ἐπ' ἀδείας Plu. *Sol*.22; ἐπ' ἀληθείας *Ev.Marc*.12.14, *POxy*.255.16 (i A.D.): hence in adverbial phrases, ἐπ' ἴσας (sc. μοίρας) *equally*, S.*El*.1062 (lyr.); ἐ. καιροῦ D.20.90; ἐπ' ἐσχάτων *at* the last, Lxx*De*.17.7 (v.l. ἐσχάτῳ); ἐπὶ τοῦ παρόντος *for* the present, *SIG*543.6 (Epist. Philipp.). 4. *in respect of*, ἐ. τῶν πραγμάτων Arist.*Pol*.1280[a]17, cf. *EN*1131[b]18; *concerning*, τὰ ἐπ' αὐτῶν ἐνεστηκότα *PTeb*.7.6 (ii B.C.).

B. WITH DAT.: I. of Place, *upon*, just like the gen. (hence Poets use whichever case suits the metre, whereas in Prose the dat. is more freq.): 1. with Verbs of Rest, ἕζεο τῷδ' ἐ. δίφρῳ Il.6.354; ἧντ' ἐ. πύργῳ 3.153; στῆ δ' ἐ.. νηῒ 8.222; κεῖσθαι ἐ. τινι X.*An*.1.8. 27; καίειν ἐ. πᾶσι (sc. βωμοῖς) Il.8.240; ἔβραχε χαλκὸς ἐ. στήθεσσι 4.420; ἐ. χθονὶ δέρκεσθαι 1.88, etc.: also with Verbs of Motion, where the subject rests *upon* something, νηυσὶν ἐπ' ὠκυπόροισιν ἔβαινον 2. 351 (v.l. for ἐν); ἐπ' ὤμοις φέρειν E.*Ph*.1131 (but ἐφ' ἵππῳ, ἐφ' ἵπποις and the like are never used for ἐφ' ἵππου, etc.); of places, mostly *in*, ἐ. τῇ χώρῃ Hdt.5.77; τἀπὶ Τροίᾳ πέργαμα S.*Ph*.353; ἐπ' ἐσχάτοις τόποις Id.*Tr*.1100; ἐ. τῇ ψυχῇ δάκνομαι Id.*Ant*.317; also, *at* or *near*, ἐ. κρήνῃ Od.13.408; ἐ. θύρῃσι Il.2.788, etc.; of rivers, etc., *by, beside*, ἐ. ὠκυρόῳ Κελάδοντι.. 7.133, etc.; ἐπ' ἐσχάρῃ Od.7. 160; ἐ. νηυσί Il.1.559, etc.; of persons, οὐ τἀπὶ Λυδοῖς οὐδ' ἐπ' Ὀμφάλῃ λατρεύματα *in* Lydia, *in the power of* O., S.*Tr*.356. b. *on* or *over*, ἐπ' Ἰφιδάμαντι *over* the body of Iphidamas, Il.11.261, cf. 4.470; τοιόνδ' ἐπ' ἀνδρὶ κομπάζεις λόγον A.*Ag*.1400; also, *over* or *in honour of*, ἐ. σοὶ κατέθηκε.. ἄεθλα Od.24.91; [βοῦς] ἐ. Πατρόκλῳ πέφνεν Il. 23.776; κειράμενοι χαίτας ἐπ' Ἀδώνιδι Bion 1.81, cf. Lys.2.80; in Dor. and Aeol. sepulchral Inscrr., *Schwyzer*348,al. c. in hostile sense, *against*, Hdt.1.61, 6.74,88, S.*Ph*.1139 (lyr.), etc.; *as a check upon*, οἱ πρόβουλοι καθεστᾶσιν ἐ. τοῖς βουλευταῖς Arist.*Pol*.1299[b]37, cf. 1271[a] 39; also, *towards, in reference to*, ἐ. πᾶσι χόλον τελέσαι Il.4.178; ἐπ' ἔργοις πᾶσι S.*OC*1268; δικαιότερος καὶ ἐπ' ἄλλῳ ἔσσεαι Il.19.181, cf. S.*Tr*.994 (anap.), etc.; ἐ. τοῖς δυνατοῖς ἔχειν τὴν γνώμην Democr. 191; τὸ ἐ. πᾶσιν τοῖς σώμασι κάλλος *extending over* all bodies, Pl. *Smp*.210b; ἡ [παιδεία] ἡ ἐ. σώμασι, ἐ. ψυχῇ, Id.*R*.376e; τἀπὶ σοὶ κακά the ills which lie *upon* thee, S.*Ph*.806: in Att. also, νόμον τίθεσθαι, θεῖναι ἐ. τινι, make a law *for his case*, whether *for* or *against*, Pl.*Grg*.

488d, Lex ap.And.1.87; νόμους ἀναγράψαι ἐ. τοῖς ἀδικοῦσι D.24.5; νόμος κεῖται ἐ. τινι ib.70; τἀπὶ τῷ πλήθει νενομοθετημένα ib.123, cf. 142; τί θεσμοποιεῖς ἐ. ταλαιπώρῳ νεκρῷ; E.*Ph.*1645. d. of accumulation, *upon, after*, ὄγχνη ἐπ' ὄγχνῃ one pear *after* another, pear *on* pear, Od.7.120; ἐ. κέρδεϊ κέρδος Hes.*Op.*644; ἄτη ἑτέρα ἐπ' ἄτῃ A. *Ch.*404 (lyr.); πήματα ἐ. πήμασι, ἐ. νόσῳ νόσος, S.*Ant.*595, *OC*544 (both lyr.). e. *in addition to, over and above, besides*, οὐκ ἄρα σοί γ' ἐ. εἴδεϊ καὶ φρένες ἦσαν Od.17.454, cf. 308; ἄλλα τε πόλλ' ἐ. τῆσι παρίσχομεν Il.9.639, cf. Od.22.264; ἐ. τοῖσι *besides*, 24.277; ἐ. τούτοις Him.*Or.*14.10; so of Numerals, τρισχιλίους ἐ. μυρίοις Plu.*Publ.*20, cf. Jul.*Or.*4.148c, etc.; γυναῖκ' ἐφ' ἡμῖν..ἔχει E.*Med.*694: with Verbs of eating and drinking, *with*, ἐ. σίτῳ πίνειν ὕδωρ X.*Cyr.*6.2.27; νέκταρ ποτίσαι ἐπ' ἀμβροσίᾳ Pl.*Phdr.*247e; esp. of a relish, κάρδαμον μόνον ἐ. τῷ σίτῳ ἔχειν X.*Cyr.*1.2.11; παίειν ἐφ' ἅλι τὰν μᾶδδαν Ar.*Ach.*835: metaph., ἐ. τῷ φάγοις ἥδιστ' ἄν; ἐ. βαλλαντίῳ; Id.*Eq.*707; later ἐ. γογγυλίσι διαβιῶναι live *on* turnips, Ath.10.419a. f. of position, *after, behind*, of soldiers, X.*Cyr.*8.3.16–18. g. *in dependence upon, in the power of*, τὰ δ' οὐκ ἐπ' ἀνδράσι κεῖται Pi.*P.*8.76; ἐ. τινί ἐστι it is *in* his *power* to do, c. inf., Hdt.8.29, etc.; ἐ. σοί ἐστιν ἀναζωπυρεῖν M.Ant.7.2; ἐ. ἑτέροις γίγνεσθαι Th.6.22; ἐ. τῷ πλήθει *in* their *hands*, S.*OC*66, cf. Th.2.84; τὸ ἐπ' ἐμοί, τὸ ἐ. ἐκείνῳ, etc., as far as is *in* my *power*, etc., X. *Cyr.*5.4.11, Isoc.4.142, etc.; τὸ ἐ. τούτοις εἶναι Lys.28.14; ἐ. τοῖς υἱάσι their *property*, *Leg.Gort.*4.37. h. *according to*, ἐ. τοῖς νόμοις Lex ap.D. 24.56; ἐ. πᾶσι δικαίοις ποιούμεθα τοὺς λόγους Id.20.88; ἐ. προφάσει θηρός S.*Tr.*662 codd. (lyr.). i. of condition or circumstances *in* which one is, ἀτελευτήτῳ ἐ. ἔργῳ Il.4.175, etc.; ἐπ' ἀρρήτοις λόγοις S.*Ant.*556; ἐπ' ἀσφάκτοις μήλοισι E.*Ion* 228 (lyr.); ταύταις ἐ. συντυχίαις Pi.*P.*1.36; ἐπ' εὐπραξίᾳ S.*OC*1554; ἐ. τῷ παρόντι Th.2.36; ἐπ' αὐτοφώρῳ λαβεῖν, v. αὐτόφωρος; also ἐ. τῷ δείπνῳ *at* dinner, X.*Cyr.*1.3.12, Thphr.*Char.* 3.2; ἐ. τῇ κύλικι Pl.*Smp.*214b; ἐ. θαλίαις E.*Med.*192 (anap.). k. Geom., of the point, etc., *at* which letters are written, κέντρον ἐφ' ᾧ K Hippocr.ap.Simp.*in Ph.*64.14; ἡ [γραμμὴ] ἐφ' ᾗ HK the line HK, Arist.*Mete.*375ᵇ22. 2. with Verbs of Motion: a. where the sense of motion merges in that of support, ἐ. χθονὶ βαίνει Il.4.443; θεῖναι ἐ. γούνασιν 6.92; καταθέσθαι ἐ. γαίῃ 3.114; ἱστὸν ἔστησεν ἐ. ψαμάθοις 23.853; ἐ. φρεσὶ θῆκε 1.55; δυσφόρους ἐπ' ὄμμασι γνώμας βαλεῖν S.*Aj.*51, etc. b. in pregnant construction, πέτονται ἐπ' ἄνθεσιν fly *on to* the flowers *and settle there*, Il.2.89; ἐκ..βαίνον ἐ. ῥηγμῖνι θαλάσσης Od.15.499; καθεῖσεν ἐ. Σκαμάνδρῳ Il.5.36; ἦλθε δ' ἐ. Κρήτεσσι 4.251, cf. 273; νῆες εἰρύατ'..ἐ. θινὶ θαλάσσης 4.248. c. rarely for εἰς c. acc., νηυσὶν ἔ. γλαφυρῇσιν ἐλαυνέμεν 5.327, 11.274. d. in hostile sense, *upon* or *against*, ἐ. τινι ἔχειν, ἰθύνειν ἵππους, 5.240, 8.110; ἐ. τινι ἱέναι βέλος, ἰθύνεσθαι ὀϊστόν, 1.382, Od.22.8; ἐ. τοι Ἀκράγαντι τανύσαις Pi.*O.*2.91; ἐ. Τυδεΐδῃ ἐτιταίνετο..τόξα Il.5.97; ἐφ' Ἕκτορι..ἀκοντίσσαι 16.358; κύνας..σεύῃ ἐπ' ἀγροτέρῳ συΐ 11.293; ὡρμήθησαν ἐπ' ἀνδράσιν Od.10.214, cf. E.*Ph.*1379, etc.: also ἐ. τινι τετάχθαι Th.2.70, 3.13; ὅστις φάρμακα δηλητήρια ποιοῖ ἐ. Τηΐοισιν *SIG*37.2 (Teos, v B.C.). II. of Time, rarely, and never in good Att., exc. in sense of succession (infr. 2), ἐ. νυκτί *by* night, Il.8.529; ἐφ' ἡμέρῃ, αἱ δ' ἐ. νυκτί Hes.*Op.*102; ἐπ' ἤματι τῷδε *on* this very day, Il.13.234; ἐπ' ἤματι *for* to-day, 19.229, 10.48, Od.2.284; αἰεὶ ἐπ' ἤματι every day, 14.105; ἐπ' ἡμέρῃ ἑκάστῃ Hdt.4.112, 5.53, cf. D.S. 34/5.2.1; ὁ ἥλιος νέος ἐφ' ἡμέρῃ ἐστίν Heraclit.6; ἐ. τρὶς *Act.Ap.*10. 16, *PHolm.*1.18. 2. of succession, *after*, ἕκτῃ ἐ. δέκα on the 16th of the month, Chron.ap.D.18.155, Decr.ib.181 (δεκάτῃ codd.); τετράδι ἐ. δέκα *IG*1².304.62; πρὸ τῆς ἕκτης ἐ. δέκα ib.2².1361.19; ἐπ' ἐξεργασμένοισι, = Lat. *re peracta*, Hdt.4.164, etc.; ἐ. τινι ἀγορεύειν, ἀνίστασθαι, E.*Or.*898, 902, X.*Cyr.*2.3.7, etc.; ἐ. διεφθαρμένοισι Ἴωσι Hdt.1. 170; τὰ ἐ. τούτοισι, = Lat. *quod superest*, Id.9.78, cf. Th.1.65, A.*Ag.* 255, etc.; τοὐπὶ τῷδε πῆμα E.*Hipp.*855 (lyr.), etc. 3. *in the time of* (cf. A. II) only in Arc., ἐπὶ Χαιριάδαι *Schwyzer* 665 *A* 21, cf. 666 (Orchom.). III. in various causal senses: 1. of the occasion or cause, τετεύξεται ἄλγε' ἐπ' αὐτῇ *for* her, Il.21.585; ἐ. σοὶ μάλα πόλλ' ἔπαθον *for* thee, 9.492: freq. with Verbs expressing some mental affection, ἐπὶ παντὶ λόγῳ ἐπτοῆσθαι Heraclit.87; μέγα φρονεῖν ἐ. τινι to be proud *at* or *of* a thing, Pl.*Prt.*342d, X.*HG*3.4.11, etc.; χλιδᾶν ἐ. τινι S.*El.*360; ἀγάλλεσθαι, ἀγανακτεῖν ἐ. τοῖς παροῦσι, X.*An.*2.6.26, Isoc.4.122; ὀνομαστὸς ἐ. τινι γεγονέναι X.*Mem.*1.2.61; also ἐφ' αἵματι φεύγειν to be tried *on* a capital charge, D.21.105; πληγὰς λαμβάνειν ἐ. τινι X.*Cyr.*1.3.16; ζημιοῦσθαι ἐ. τινι D.24.122, etc.: in adverbial phrases [δικάσσαι] ἐπ' ἀρωγῇ *with* favour, Il.23.574; δολίῃ ἐ. τέχνῃ Hes.*Th.*540; ἐ. μιῇ αἰτίῃ ἀνήκεστον πάθος ἔρδειν Hdt.1.137, etc.; ἐ. κακουργίᾳ καὶ οὐκ ἀρετῇ *for* malice, Th.1.37; ἐπ' εὐνοίᾳ, ἐπ' ἔχθρᾳ, D. 18.273, 21.55; ἐπ' ἀγαθῇ ἐλπίδι *with*.., X.*Mem.*2.1.18, cf. *Ep.Rom.* 4.18; ἐφ' ἑκατέροις *in* both cases, Pl.*Tht.*158d, cf. Xenoph.34.4; ἐ. δάκρυσί τινα καταστένειν E.*Tr.*315 (lyr.); ἐ. τῇ πάσῃ συκοφαντίᾳ καὶ διασεισμῷ Mitteis *Chr.*31 vi (ii B.C.), etc. 2. of an end or purpose, υἱὸν ἐ. κτεάτεσσι λιπέσθαι Il.5.154, cf. 9.482; ἐ. δόρπῳ *for* supper, Od.18.44; ἐ. κακῷ ἀνθρώπου σίδηρος ἀνεύρηται Hdt.1.68; ἐ. διαφθορῇ Id.4.164; ἐ. σῷ καιρῷ S.*Ph.*151 (lyr.); ἐ. τῷ κέρδει X.*Mem.*1.2.56; δῆσαι ἐ. θανάτῳ or τὴν ἐ. θανάτῳ, Hdt.9.37, 3.119, cf. 1.109, X.*An.*1.6. 10; ἐ. θανάτῳ συλλαβεῖν Isoc.4.154; ἐπ' ἐξαγωγῇ *for* exportation, Hdt.5.6; χρηστηριάζεσθαι ἐ. τῇ χώρῃ *with a view to gaining*.., Id.1. 66; ἐ. τούτοις ἐθύσαντο X.*An.*3.5.18; ἐ. τῷ ὑβρίζεσθαι Th.1.38, cf. 34, etc.; τι κακοτεχνεῖν ἐ. αἰσχύνῃ τοῦ ἀνδρός *PEleph.*1.6 (iv B.C.). 3. of the condition *upon* which a thing is done, ἐ. τούτοισι *on* these terms, Hdt.1.60, etc.; ἐ. τοῖσδε, ὥστε.. Th.3.114; ἐ. τούτῳ, ἐπ' ᾧτε *on condition that*.., Hdt.3.83, cf. 7.158: in orat. obliq., ἐπ' or ἐφ' ᾧτε folld. by inf., Id.1.22, 7.154, X.*HG*2.2.20; ἐφ' ᾧ μηδὲν κακὸν ποιήσουσιν Th.1.126 (but ἐφ' ᾧ = *wherefore*, *Ep.Rom.*5.12); ἐπ' οὐδενί *on* no condition, *on* no account, Hdt.3.38; but, *for* no adequate *reason*, D. 21.132; ἐπ' ἴσῃ τε καὶ ὁμοίῃ, ἐπὶ τῇ ἴσῃ καὶ ὁμοίᾳ, *on* fair and equal *terms*, Hdt.9.7, Th.1.27; ἐ. ῥητοῖς, v. ῥητός; also of a woman's dowry, τὴν μητέρα ἐγγυᾶν ἐ. ταῖς ὀγδοήκοντα μναῖς D.28.16; γῆμαί τινα ἐ. δέκα ταλάντοις And.4.13; τὴν θυγατέρα ἔχειν γυναῖκα ἐ. τῇ τυραννίδι Hdt.1.60; *on the principle of*.., ἐ. τῷ μὴ λυπεῖν ἀλλήλους Th.1. 71. 4. of the price *for* which.., ἔργον τελέσαι δώρῳ ἔ. μεγάλῳ Il.10. 304, cf. 21.445; ἐ. τίνι χρήματι; Hdt.3.38; ἐ. πόσῳ; Pl.*Ap.*41a; ἐ. ταλάντῳ χρυσίου Ar.*Av.*154; ἐπ' ἀργυρίῳ λέγειν, πράττειν, D.19.182, 24.200; ἐ. χρήμασι λυμαίνεσθαι Id.19.332; ἐ. πολλῷ ἐρρᾳθυμηκότες Id.1.15; also of money lent *at* interest, δανείζεσθαι ἐ. τοῖς μεγάλοις τόκοις ibid.; ἐ. δραχμῇ δανείζειν lend *at* 12 per cent., Id.27.9; ἐπ' ὀκτὼ ὀβολοῖς τὴν μνᾶν τοῦ μηνὸς ἑκάστου δανείζειν, i.e. *at* 16 per cent., Id.53.13; ἐ. διακοσίαις εἴκοσι πέντε τὰς χιλίας *for* 225 per mille, i.e. 22·5 per cent., Syngr.ap.eund.35.10; also of the security *on* which money is borrowed, δανείζειν ἐ. ἀνδραπόδοις Id.27.27; ἐπ' οἴνου κεραμίοις τρισχιλίοις Id.35.18; ἐ. νηΐ Id.56.3; δανείζειν ἐ. τοῖς σώμασιν Arist.*Ath.*9.1, cf. 2.2, D.H.4.9. 5. of names, φάος καὶ νὺξ ὀνόμασται..ἐ. τοῖσί τε καὶ τοῖς Parm.9.2; ἐ. τῇ τοῦ οἰκείου ἔχθρᾳ στάσις κέκληται Pl.*R.*470b; so ὄνομα κεῖται ἐ. τινι X.*Cyr.*2.2.12; ὄνομα καλεῖν ἐ. τινι Pl.*Sph.*218c, cf. 244b; πότερον ταῦτα, πέντε ὀνόματα ὄντα, ἐ. ἑνὶ πράγματί ἐστι Id.*Prt.*349b (v. supr. A. III. 2). 6. of persons in authority, ὅς μ' ἐ. βουσὶν εἶσεν who set me *over* the kine, Od.20. 209, cf. 221; ποιμαίνειν ἐπ' ὄεσσι Il.6.25; οὖρον κατέλειπον ἐ. κτεάτεσσιν Od.15.89; σημαίνειν ἐ. δμῳῇσι 22.427; πέμπειν ἐ. τοσούτῳ στρατεύματι Th.6.29; ἐ. ταῖς ναυσίν X.*HG*1.5.11; οἱ ἐ. ταῖς μηχαναῖς Id.*Cyr.*6.3.28; οἱ ἐ. ταῖς καμήλοις ib.33; οἱ ἐ. τοῖς πράγμασιν ὄντες D. 9.2; ἐ. θυγατρὶ..γαμεῖν ἄλλην γυναῖκα Hdt.4.154. 7. *in possession of, possessing*, ἐ. τοῖς ἑαυτοῦ μένειν Th.4.105, cf. 8.86; ζῆν ἐ. παιδίοις, τελευτᾶν ἐ. παιδὶ γνησίῳ, Alciphr.1.3, Philostr.*VS*2.12.2; ἐ. παισὶ διαδόχοις Hdn.4.2.1; ἀποθανεῖν ἐ. κληρονόμοις ταῖς θυγατράσι Artem.1.78, cf. *PMeyer* 6.22 (ii A.D.); ἐ. μόνῳ παιδὶ σαλεύειν Hld. 1.9.

C. WITH Acc.: I. of Place, *upon* or *on to* a height, with Verbs of Motion, ἐ. πύργον ἔβη Il.6.386, cf. 12.375; ἐ. τὰ ὑψηλότατα τῶν ὀρέων ἀναβαίνειν Hdt.1.131; προελθεῖν ἐ. βῆμα Th.2.34; ἀναβιβαστέον τινά, ἀναβαίνειν ἐ. τὸν ἵππον, Pl.*R.*467e, X.*An.*3.4.35; also ἐξ ἵππων ἀποβάντες ἐ. χθόνα Il.3.265; ἐξεκυλίσθη πρηνὴς ἐ. στόμα *upon* his face, 6.43; ἐ. θρόνον..ἕζετο 8.442; ὤμω..ἐ. στῆθος συνοχωκότε drawn together *upon* his breast, 2.218; Ὀδυσσῆ' εἷσαν ἐ. σκέπας Od.6.212; θέσθαι ἐ. τὰ γόνατα X.*An.*7.3.23; ἐπ' ἀμφότερα τὰ ὦτα καθεύδειν Aeschin.Socr.54; ἐ. κεφαλήν head-*foremost*, Pl.*R.*553b, Luc.*Pisc.*48 (v. κεφαλή): less freq. than ἐπί with gen. or dat. b. Geom., αἱ ἐ. τὰς ἁφὰς ἐπιζευγνύμεναι εὐθεῖαι *joining* the points of contact, Archim.*Sph.Cyl.*1.8; κάθετος ἐ. perpendicular *to* (v. κάθετος). 2. *to*, ἦλθε θοὰς ἐ. νῆας Il.1.12, etc.; ἐ. βωμὸν ἄγων ib.440; ἴθυσαν δ' ἐ. τεῖχος 12.443; ἐ. τέρμ' ἀφίκετο S.*Aj.*48; ἡ [ὁδὸς] ἐ. Σοῦσα φέρει X. *An.*3.5.15; ἡ ὁδὸς ἡ ἀπὸ τῶν Πυλῶν ἐ. τὸ Ποσειδώνιον Th.4.118; ἐ. τὸ αὐτὸ αἱ γνῶμαι ἔφερον Id.1.79: c. acc. pers., βῆ δ' ἄρ' ἐπ' Ἀτρεΐδην Il.2.18, cf. 10.18, 85, 150, etc.: sts. in pregn. constr. with Verbs of Rest, ἐπιστῆναι ἐ. τὰς θύρας Pl.*Smp.*212d; παρεῖναι ἐ. τὸν τάφον Th.2.34, cf. X.*Cyr.*3.3.12. b. metaph., ἐ. ἔργα τρέπεσθαι, ἰέναι, Il.3.422, Od.2.127; ἰέναι ἐ. τὸν ἔπαινον Th.2.36; ἐ. συμφορὴν ἐμπεσεῖν Hdt.7.88 codd.; also ἐ. τὴν τράπεζαν ἀποδιδόναι, ὀφείλειν, pay, owe *to* the bank, D.33.12, Docum.ap.eund.45.31; ἡ ἐγγύη ἡ ἐ. τὴν τράπεζαν D.33.10; τὸ ἐ. τὴν τράπεζαν χρέως ib.24; also εἰσποιηθῆναι ἐ. τὸ ὄνομά τινος to be entered *under* his name, Id.44.36. c. *up to, as far as* (μέχρι ἐ. X.*An.*5.1.[1]), παρατείνειν ἐπ' Ἡρακλέας στήλας Hdt.4.181; ἐ. θάλασσαν καθήκειν Th.2.27, 97: metaph., ἐ. πεῖρατ' ἀέθλων ἤλθομεν Od.23.248; ἐ. διηκόσια ἀποδιδόναι yield 200-*fold*, Hdt. 1.193; in measurements, πλέον ἢ ἐ. δύο στάδια X.*Cyr.*7.5.8, *An.*6.2. 2; ὅσον ἐ. εἴκοσι σταδίους ib.6.4.5, cf. 1.7.15: freq. with a neut. Adj. or Pron., τόσσον τίς τ' ἐπιλεύσσει ὅσον τ' ἐ. λᾶαν ἵησιν Il.3.12; ὅσσον ἐφ' 2.616, cf. 15.358; ἐ. τοσοῦτό γε φρονέω,..ταύτην μηδὲν σίνεσθαι I am prudent *enough*, not to.., Hdt.6.97; ἐ. ὅσον δεῖ Th.7.66; ἐ. πάντ' ἀφίξομαι S.*OT*265; ἐ. πᾶν ἐλθεῖν X.*An.*3.1.18; ἐ. τὸ ἔσχατον ἀγῶνος ἐλθεῖν Th.4.92; ἐ. μεῖζον χωρεῖν, ἔρχεσθαι, ib.117, S.*Ph.*259; ἐ. μέγα χωρεῖν δυνάμεως Th.1.118; ἐ. μακρότερον, ἐ. μακρότατον, Id. 4.41, 1.1, Hdt.4.16, 192; ἐ. σμικρόν, ἐ. βραχύ, a little *way*, a little, S. *El.*414, Th.1.118; ἐπ' ἔλαττον, ἐπ' ἐλάχιστον, Pl.*Phd.*93b, Th.1.70; ἐπ' ὀλίγον, ἐ. πολλά, Pl.*Sph.*254b; ἐ. πλέον *still* more, Hdt.2.171, 5. 51, Th.2.51; rarely with Advs., ἐ. μᾶλλον Hdt.1.94, 4.181. d. *before, into the presence of* (cf. A. I. 2e), ἦγον δή μιν ἐ. τὰ κοινά Id. 3.156 (but στὰς ἐ. τὸ συνέδριον standing *at the door of* the council, Id.8.79); ἐ. ἡγεμόνας καὶ βασιλεῖς ἀχθήσεσθε *Ev.Matt.*10.18. e. in Military phrases (cf. A. I. 2d), ἐπ' ἀσπίδας πέντε καὶ εἴκοσιν ἐτάξαντο, i.e. twenty-five *in file*, Th.4.93; dub. in X., as ἐ. πολλοὺς τεταγμένοι many *in file*, *An.*4.8.11 codd.; ἐπ' ὀλίγον τὸ βάθος γίγνεσθαι *Cyr.*7.5.2 codd.; for ἐ. κέρας v. infr. 3. 3. of the quarter or direction *towards* or *in* which a thing takes place, ἐ. δεξιά, ἐπ' ἀριστερά, *to* the right or left, Il.7.238, 12.240, Od.3.171, Hdt.6.33, etc.; ἐ. τὰ ἕτερα or ἐ. θάτερα, Id.5.74, Th.1.87, etc.; ἐ. τὰ μακρότερα, βραχύτερα, *on* the longer, shorter *side*, Hdt.1.50; ἐπ' ἀμφότερα νοέων both *ways*, Id.8.22; ἐπ' ἀμφότερα μαχᾶν τάμνειν τέλος Pi.*O.*13. 57, etc.; ἐ. τάδε Φασήλιδος *on* this *side*, Isoc.7.80; ἐ. ἐκεῖνα, v. ἐπέκεινα; ἐφ' ἕν, ἐ. δύο, ἐ. τρία, of space, *in* one, two, three *dimensions*, Arist.*de An.*404ᵇ23, Plot.6.3.13; in Military phrases, ἐ. δόρυ ἀναστρέψαι, ἐ. ἀσπίδα μεταβαλέσθαι, *to* the spear or shield *side*, i.e. *to* right or left, X.*An*.4.3.29, *Cyr*.7.5.6; ἐ. πόδα ἀναχωρεῖν, etc., retire *on* the foot, i.e. facing the enemy, Id.*An*.5.2.32; so ἐ. κέρας or ἐ. κέρως πλεῖν, etc., sail *towards* or *on* the wing, i.e. *in* column (v. κέρας VII): metaph., ἐ. τὸ μεῖζον κοσμῆσαι, δεινῶσαι, etc., *with* exaggeration, Th.1.10, 8.74, etc.; ἐ. τὸ πλέον ἀγγέλλεσθαι Id.6.34; ἐ. τὸ φοβερώτερον ib.83; ἐ. τὰ γελοιότερα ἐπαινέσαι so as to provoke laughter, Pl. *Smp*.214e; ἐ. τὰ καλλίω, ἐ. τὰ αἰσχίονα, Id.*Plt*.293e; ἐ. τὸ βέλτιον καὶ κάλλιον, ἐ. τὸ χεῖρον καὶ τὸ αἴσχιον, Id.*R*.381b; ἐ. τὸ ἄμεινον Orac.ap.D.43.66. 4. in hostile sense, *against*, ἰέναι ἐ. νέας Il. 13.101; ὦρτο δ' ἐπ' αὐτούς 5.590; στρατεύεσθαι or -εύειν ἐ. τινα, Hdt. 1.71,77, Th.1.26, etc.; ἰέναι ἐ. φάτιν S.*OT*495 (lyr.); πλεῖν ἐ. τοὺς Ἀθηναίους Th.2.90; πέμπειν στρατηγὸν ἐ. τινας Hdt.1.153; θύεσθαι ἐ. τινα offer sacrifice *on going against*.., X.*An*.7.8.21; ἐφ' ὑμᾶς *to* your *prejudice*, D.6.33, 10.57. 5. of extension *over* a space, πουλὺν ἐφ' ὑγρὴν ἤλυθον *over* much water, Il.10.27: ἐπ' εὐρέα νῶτα θαλάσσης 2.159; ἐ. κύματα 13.27; δρόων ἐπ' ἀπείρονα πόντον 1.350; πλέων, λεύσσων ἐ. οἴνοπα πόντον, 7.88, 5.771; ἐ. πολλὰ δ' ἀλήθην Od. 14.120; ἄγοισι..Ἀνδρομάχαν..ἐπ' ἅλμυρον πόντον Sapph.*Supp*.20a. 7: also with Verbs of Rest, ἐπ' ἐννέα κεῖτο πέλεθρα *over* nine acres he lay stretched, Od.11.577; τόσσον ἔπ' *over* so much, 5.251, cf. 13.114; διώκοντες ἐ. πολύ *over* a large space, Th.1.50, cf. 62, etc.; ἐ. πλεῖστον ib.4; ὡς ἐ. πλεῖστον 2.34, etc.; freq. to be rendered *on*, δράκων ἐ. νῶτα δαφοινός Il.2.308; ἵππους..ἐ. νῶτον ἐΐσας ib.765; ὅσσα τε γαῖαν ἔπι πνείει 17.447; ἐ. γαῖαν εἰσὶ δύω [γένη] Hes.*Op*.11; ἀοιδοὶ ἔασιν ἐ. χθόνα *Th*.95; ἐ. γᾶν μέλαιναν ἔμμεναι κάλλιστον Sapph. *Supp*.5.2; also, *among*, κλέος πάντας ἐπ' ἀνθρώπους Il.10.213, cf. 24.202,535; δασσάμενοι [κτήματ'] ἐφ' ἡμέας Od.16.385, cf. Pl.*Prt*. 322d. II. of Time, *for* or *during* a certain time, ἐ. χρόνον Il.2. 299, Od.14.193: πολλὸν ἐ. χρόνον 12.407; παυρίδιον..ἐ. χρόνον Hes. *Op*.133; ἐ. δηρόν Il.9.415; ἐ. πολὺν χρόνον Pl.*Phd*.84c, etc.; ἐπ' ὀλίγον χρόνον Lycurg.7; ἐ. χρόνον τινά, ἐ. τινα χρόνον, Pl.*Prt*.344b, *Grg*.524d; γῆν ἀπεμίσθωσαν ἐ. δέκα ἔτη Th.3.68; ἐ. διετές Lex ap.D. 46.20; ἐ. τρεῖς ἡμέρας X.*An*.6.6.36; τὸ ἐφ' ἡμέραν ἀρκέσον enough *for* the day, Id.*Cyr*.6.2.34, cf. D.50.23, Hdt.1.32; ἐ. πολύ *for* a long time, Th.1.6, etc. 2. *up to, until* a certain time, εὗδον παννύχιος καὶ ἐπ' ἠῶ καὶ μέσον ἦμαρ Od.7.288; οὐδ' ἐ. γῆρας ἵκετ' 8.226. III. in various causal senses: 1. of the object or purpose *for* which one goes, ἀγγελίην ἔπι Τυδῆ στεῖλαν sent him *for* (i.e. *to bring*) tidings of.., Il.4.384 (dub.); ἐ. βοῦν ἴτω let him go *for* an ox, Od.3.421; ἐ. τεύχεα δ' ἐσσεύοντο Il.2.808; ἐλθεῖν πρός τινα ἐπ' ἀργύριον X.*Cyr*.1. 6.12; πέμπειν εἴς τινα ἐ. στράτευμα ib.4.5.31; ἴτω τις ἐφ' ὕδωρ ib.5. 3.49; ἥκειν ἐ. τοὺς τόκους *for* (i.e. *to demand*) the interest, D.50.61: less freq. c. acc. pers., ἐπ' Ὀδυσσῆα ἤϊε Od.5.149, cf. S.*OT*555; κατῆλθον ἐ. ποιητήν Ar.*Ra*.1418; κατέρχονται ἐ. τὸν Ἀγόρατον Lys. 13.23: with acc. of a Noun of Action, ἐξιέναι ἐ. θήραν go out hunting, X.*Cyr*.1.2.9; ἔπλεον οὐχ ὡς ἐ. ναυμαχίαν (v.l. for -μαχίᾳ) Th.2. 83; ἐ. μάχην ἰέναι X.*An*.1.4.12; ἔρχεσθαι, ἵζειν ἐ. δεῖπνον, Il.2.381, Od.24.394; ἐ. δόρπον ἀνέστη 12.439; κληθεὶς ἐ. δεῖπνον Pl.*Smp*.174e, etc.; καλεῖν ἐ. ξείνια Hdt.2.107, 5.18; ἐ. τὴν θεωρίαν *to see* the sight, *Ev.Luc*.23.48, cf. *PTeb*.33.6 (ii B.C.): freq. with neut. Pron. or Adj., ἐ. τοῦτο ἐλθεῖν *for* this *purpose*, X.*An*.2.5.22, cf. Th.5.87; ἐπ' αὐτὸ τοῦτο Pl.*Grg*.447b, etc.; ἐ. τί; *to* what *end*? Ar.*Nu*.256; ἐφ' ὅ τι Id. *Lys*.22,481; ἐφ' ἃ ἤλθομεν *for* which *purpose*, Th.7.15, etc.; ἐπὶ ἴσα *for* like *ends*, Pi.*N*.7.5 (but ἐ. ἴσα μάχη τέτατο, = ἴσως, Il.12.436); ἐ. τὸ βέλτιον *to* a better *result*, X.*An*.7.8.4; ἀναστῆσαί τινα ἐ. χριστὸν Θεοῦ set up *as* God's anointed, Lxx *2Ki*.23.1: after an Adj., ἄριστοι πᾶσαν ἐπ' ἰθύν Il.6.79, cf. Od.4.434; ἄπορος ἐ. φρόνιμα S.*OT*691 (lyr.); χρήσιμος ἐ...οὐδέν D.25.31: after a Noun, ὁδὸς ἐ. τι X.*Cyr*.1.6.21; ὄργανα ἐ. τι ib.6.2.34. 2. *so far as regards*, τοὐπὶ τήνδε τὴν κόρην S.*Ant*.889; ὅσον γε τοὐπ' ἐμέ E.*Or*.1345; τοὐπί σε, τὸ ἐ. σέ, Id.*Hec*. 514, X.*Cyr*.1.4.12; τὸ ἐ. σφᾶς εἶναι Th.4.28; ὡς ἐ. τὸ πολύ *for* the most part, Arist.*Top*.100b29, etc.; ἐ. πᾶν Th.2.51; τὸ πρὸς ἅπαν ξυνετὸν ἐ. πᾶν ἀργόν Id.3.82; κρείσσων ἐπ' ἀρετήν Democr.181; ἐ. μέγα Call.*Dian*.55. 3. of persons set *over* others, ἐ. τοὺς πεζοὺς καθιστάναι ἄρχοντα X.*Cyr*.4.5.58, cf. *HG*3.4.20; στρατηγὸς ἐ. τοὺς ὁπλίτας, ἐ. τὴν χώραν, Arist.*Ath*.61.1, *IG*2².682.24; ἐ. τὸν Πειραιέα Arist.*Ath*. l.c.; ἐ. Ῥαμνοῦντα *IG*2.1206*b* (cf. A. III. 1); οἱ θεσμοθέται οἱ ἐ. τοὺς νόμους κληρούμενοι D.20.90. 4. *according to, by*, ἐ. στάθμην *by* the rule, Od.5.245, 21.44, etc.

D. Position:—ἐπί may suffer anastrophe (ἔπι) and follow its case, as in Il.1.162; it may likewise follow its Verb, ἤλυθ' ἔπι ψυχή Od.24.20, cf. Il.9.539. II. in Poets it is sts. put with the second of two Nouns, though in sense it also governs the first, ἢ ἁλὸς ἢ ἐ. γῆς Od.12.27, cf. S.*OT*761, *Ant*.367 (lyr.).

E. Abs., used adverbially, without anastrophe, καὶ ἐ. σκέπας ἦν ἀνέμοιο Od.5.443; κτεῖνον δ' ἐ. μηλοβοτῆρας *as well*, Il.18.529; esp. ἐ. δέ... and *besides*.., Hdt.7.65,75, etc.; πολιαί τ' ἐ. ματέρες S. *OT*182 (lyr.). II. ἔπι, for ἔπεστι, *there is*, Il.1.515, 3.45, Od.16. 315; οὐ γὰρ ἔπ' ἀνήρ.. *there is* no man.., 2.58; σοὶ δ' ἔ. μὲν μορφὴ ἐπέων 11.367; ἔ. δέ μοι γέρας A.*Eu*.393 codd. (lyr.).

F. Prosody: in ἐπιόψομαι, ι is not elided before a vowel; also in some words where σ or ϝ has been lost, as ἐπιάλμενος, ἐπιείκελος, ἐπιεικής, ἐπιέξομαι (v. ἐπέχω VII), Dor. ἐπιεργάζομαι (v. ἐπεργάζομαι).

G. In Composition: I. of Place, denoting, 1. Support or Rest *upon*, ἔπειμι (A), ἐπίκειμαι, ἐπικαθίζω, ἐπαυχένιος, ἐπιβώμιος, etc. 2. Motion, a. *upon* or *over*, ἐπιβαίνω, ἐπιτρέχω. b. *to* or *towards*, ἐπέρχομαι, ἐπιστέλλω, ἐπαρίστερος, ἐπιδέξιος. c. *against*, ἐπαΐσσω, ἐπιπλέω II, ἐπιστρατεύω, ἐπιβουλεύω. d. *up to* a point, ἐπιτελέω. e. *over* a place, as in ἐπαιωρέομαι, ἐπαρτάω. f. *over* or *beyond* boundaries, as in ἐπινέμομαι. g. implying reciprocity, as in ἐπιγαμία. 3. Extension *over* a surface, as in ἐπαλείφω, ἐπανθίζω, ἐπιπέτομαι, ἐπιπλέω I, ἐπάργυρος, ἐπίχρυσος. 4. Accumulation of one thing *over* or *besides* another, as in ἐπαγείρω, ἐπιμανθάνω, ἐπαυξάνω, ἐπιβάλλω, ἐπίκτητος. 5. Accompaniment, *to, with*, as in ἐπᾴδω, ἐπαυλέω, ἐπαγρυπνέω: hence of Addition, ἐπίτριτος one *and* $\frac{1}{3}$ *more*, $1+\frac{1}{3}$; so ἐπιτέταρτος, ἐπίπεμπτος, ἐπόγδοος, etc. 6. with Adjs., *somewhat, slightly*, as in ἐπίξανθος, ἐπίπικρος. II. of Time and Sequence, *after*, as in ἐπιβιόω, ἐπιβλαστάνω, ἐπιγίγνομαι, ἐπακόλουθος, ἐπίγονος, ἐπιστάτης I. 2. III. in causal senses: 1. Superiority felt *over* or *at*, as in ἐπιχαίρω, ἐπιγελάω, ἐπαισχύνομαι. 2. Authority *over*, as in ἐπικρατέω, ἔπαρχος, ἐπιβουκόλος, ἐπιποιμήν. 3. Motive *for*, as in ἐπιθυμέω, ἐπιζήμιος, ἐπιθάνατος. 4. to give force or intensity to the Verb, as in ἐπαινέω, ἐπιμέμφομαι, ἐπικείρω, ἐπικλάω.

ἐπιαλές· τερπνόν, Hsch.; so prob. ἐ]πιαλῆ οἰωνόν *IG*4.760 (Troezen).

ἐπιάλλομαι, Ep. for ἐφάλλομαι, aor. 2 part. ἐπιάλμενος Il.7.15, Od.24.320.

ἐπιάλλω, fut. ἐπιαλῶ: aor. ἐπίηλα [ῐ]:—*send upon*, ἑτάροις ἐπὶ χεῖρας ἴαλλε *laid* hands *upon* them, Od.9.288; ἐπὶ δὲ Ζεὺς οὖρον ἴαλλεν 15.475; οὗτος γὰρ ἐπίηλεν τάδε ἔργα for this man *brought* these deeds *to pass*, 22.49; also in Com., ἐπιαλῶ (sc. τὸ κέντρον) I *will lay it on*, Ar.*Nu*.1299, cf. *Fr*.552 (dub. l.), Phryn.Com.1 (dub. l.).

ἐπίαλος, = sq., Alc.129.

ἐπιάλτης, ου, ὁ, Aeol. for ἐφιάλτης, Alc.129, Macrob.*Somn*.1.3.7.

ἐπιανδάνω, v. ἐφανδάνω. **ἐπιανέω**· ἐπιτρέπω, Hsch.

ἐπιάομαι, *cure*, *BCH*25.235 (Amphissa).

ἐπίᾰρον, τό, = ἐφίερον, *sacred penalty*, *SIG*9 (Elis, vi B.C.).

ἐπιαύω, *sleep among*, c. dat., v.l. (ed. Steph.1566) for ἐνιαύω, Od. 15.557. 2. *sleep upon*, ἠϊόσιν *AP*6.192 (Arch.).

ἐπιάχω [ᾰ], *shout out, shout applause* after a speech, ὣς ἔφαθ'· οἱ δ' ἄρα πάντες ἐπίαχον Il.7.403. 2. *shout*, ὅσσον τ' ἐννεάχιλοι ἐπίαχον 5.860.

ἐπιβάδαι, f.l. for ἐπίβδαι, Hsch. **ἐπιβάδες** (sc. ἡμέραι), αἱ, gloss on ἐπίβδαι, Sch.Pi.*P*.4.247a.

ἐπιβάθρα, ἡ, *ladder* or *steps to ascend by*: *scaling ladder*, Ph.*Bel*. 91.48, Ath.Mech.25.3, J.*BJ*7.9.2, Arr.*An*.4.27.1; *ship's ladder, gangway*, D.S.12.62. 2. metaph., *means of approach, stepping-stone*, Plb.3.24.14 (pl.); ἐ. ἔχειν τὴν Ἄβυδον Id.16.29.2; γάμον ἐ. τισὶ γενέσθαι J.*AJ*11.8.2; τῆς Ἑλλάδος *towards*.., Plu.*Demetr*.8; τῷ ἑξῆς λόγῳ Arr.*Epict*.1.7.22, cf. Plot.1.6.1; εἰς τὸ ἐξευρεῖν Gal.9.149. 3. *platform* for engines of war, J.*BJ*7.8.5; *base, foundation*, γῆ..τοῖς ἐπ' αὐτῆς βεβηκόσιν ἑδραία ἐ. Plot.2.1.7: metaph., γεῦσις ἐ. τῶν αἰσθήσεων Ph.1.665.

ἐπίβαθρον, τό, *fare of an* ἐπιβάτης, *passenger's fare*, καὶ δέ κεν ἄλλ' ἐ...δοίην Od.15.449, cf. D.S.1.96; so of Charon's *fare*, νεὼς Ἀχεροντείας ἐ. Call.*Fr*.110: generally, *rent, payment for* anything, γῆς Plu.2.727f; *toll*, Call.*Del*.22 (pl.). II. τὰ ἐ., of a sacrifice, regarded as a *fare* paid on embarking, A.R.1.421. III. ἐ. ὀρνίθων *roosting-place, perch*, *AP*9.661 (Jul.); ἐ. ἀοιδῆς *stool* for a singer, ib.140 (Claud.), cf. *PLond*.1821.283. 2. = foreg. 1, *PSI*2.171.27 (pl., dub., ii B.C.).

ἐπιβαίνω, rarely -βάω, imper. ἐπίβα Thgn.847, Dor. inf. ἐπιβῆν (infr. IV): fut. -βήσομαι: pf. -βέβηκα: aor. 2 ἐπέβην: aor. 1 Med. ἐπεβησάμην (of which Hom. always uses the Ep. form ἐπεβήσετο, imper. ἐπιβήσεο Il.8.105, al.; later ἐπεβήσατο A.R.3.869, Dor. -βάσατο Call.*Lav.Pall*.65). A. in these tenses, intr., *go upon*: I. c. gen., *set foot on, tread, walk upon*, γαίης, ἠπείρου, Od.9.83, *h.Cer*. 127; πόληος, πατρίδος αἴης, Τροίης, Il.16.396, Od.4.521, 14.229; ἀδύτων ἐπιβάς E.*Andr*.1034 (lyr.); ἐ. τῶν οὔρων *set foot on* the confines, Hdt.4.125, cf. Th.1.103, Pl.*Lg*.778e; τῆς Λακωνικῆς ἐπὶ πολέμῳ X. *HG*7.4.6; πυρῆς ἐπιβάντ' ἀλεγεινῆς, of a corpse, *placed upon*.., Il.4. 99; πλατεία τῇ ῥινὶ ἐ. τοῦ χείλους Philostr.*Im*.2.18; also ἐ. ἐπί τινος Hdt.2.107. 2. *get upon, mount on*, πύργων Il.8.165; νεῶν ib. 512; ἵππων 5.328, 10.513; δίφρου 23.379; εὐνῆς 9.133; τοῦ τείχεος Hdt.9.70; λέκτρων ἐ. A.*Supp*.39; also ἐ. ἐπὶ νεός Hdt.8.118: freq. in Hom., in aor. Med., ἐπεβήσετ' ἀπήνης Od.6.78, al. b. Archit., *to be superposed*, τὰ ἐπιβαίνοντα πάντα ἐπὶ τοὺς κρατευτάς *IG*7.3073. 104, cf. 111 (Lebad.). 3. of Time, *arrive at*, τετταράκοντα ἐ. ἐτῶν Pl.*Lg*.666b; δεκάτω (sc. ἔτεος) ἐ. Theoc.26.29; δωδεκάτου ἐπιβὰς *IG* 14.1728; τῆς μειρακίων ἡλικίας Hdn.1.3.1. 4. metaph., ἀναιδείης ἐπέβησαν *have trodden the path of* shamelessness, Od.22.424; εὐφροσύνης ἐπιβῆτον *enter into* joy, 23.52; τέχνης ἐπιβήσομαι, -βήμεναι, *h.Merc*.166, 465; ὁσίης ib.173; εὐσεβίας S.*OC*189 (lyr.); ἐ. δόξης *entertain* an expectation, Id.*Ph*.1463 (anap.); ἐ. σοφίας *undertake* it, Pl.*Epin*.981a; λόγου Luc.*Astr*.8; ἐ. τῆς ἀφορμῆς, τῆς προφάσεως, *seize upon* it, App.*Syr*.2, *Samn*.11, etc.; *preside over*, τῆς ἀνθρωπίνης ψυχῆς Iamb.*Myst*.9.8, al. II. c. dat., *get upon, board*, ναυσί Th.7. 70; *land on*, ἐ. τῇ Σικελίᾳ D.S.16.66: metaph., ἐ. ἀνορέαις Pi.*N*.3.20; also, *make forcible entry into*, τινὸς οἰκίαις, γῇ, *PHamb*.10.6 (ii A.D.), *PAmh*.2.142.7 (iv A.D.). b. with a Prep., ἐπὶ πύργῳ ἄλλος πύργος ἐπιβέβηκε Hdt.1.181. 2. c. dat. pers., *set upon, assault*, τινί X.*Cyr*. 5.2.26, Plu.*Cim*.15, etc.; simply, *approach*, dub. in Pi.*Fr*.88.2. 3. *trample on*, λὰξ ἐπίβα δήμῳ Thgn.847. III. c. acc. loci, *light upon*, in Hom. twice of gods *lighting upon* earth after their descent from Olympus, Πιερίην ἐπιβᾶσα, ἐπιβάς, Il.14.226, Od.5.50; so πολλῶν ἐ. καιρόν *light on* the fit time, Pi.*N*.1.18; then simply, *go on to* a place, *enter* it, γῆν καὶ ἔθνος Hdt.7.50; λειμῶν' S.*Aj*.144 (anap.): with Prep., ἐ. ἐπὶ χώραν Decr.Amphict.ap.D.18.154; εἰς Βοιωτίαν D.S.14.

84. 2. rarely c. acc. pers., *attack*, only poet., S.*Aj.*138 (anap.): metaph., of passion or suffering, Id.*El.*492 (lyr.), *Ph.*194 (anap.). 3. *mount*, νῶθ' ἵππων ἐπιβάντες Hes.*Sc.*286: more freq. with Prep., ἐπὶ τὸν ἵππον Hdt.4.22; ἐπὶ νέα Id.8.120, cf. Th.1.111; but ἐ. ἐπὶ τὸ θῆλυ, of male quadrupeds, *cover* a female, Arist.*HA*539ᵇ26; so abs., ib. 574ᵃ20, al.: c. dat., Luc.*Asin.*27: c. gen., Horap.1.46, 2.78. 4. ἐ. ἐπὶ τὸ σκέλος *use, put one's weight on*, a broken leg, Hp.*Fract.* 18. 5. with acc. of the Instr. of Motion (cf. βαίνω A. II. 4), ἐπιβῆναι τῷ ἀριστερῷ ἐκείνης τὸν ἐμὸν δεξιόν Luc.*DMeretr.*4.5, cf. *Tox.*48. IV. abs., *get a footing, stand on one's feet*, Il.5.666, Od.12.434; μὴπιβῆν it is forbidden to *set foot* here, *IG*12(3).1381 (Thera). 2. *step onwards, advance*, Τρώων δὲ πόλις ἐπὶ πᾶσα βέβηκε Il.16.69, cf. Hes.*Op.* 679, f.l. in Pi.*N.*10.43; ἐπίβαινε πόρσω S.*OC*179 (s. v. l., lyr.): metaph., *advance in one's demands*, Plb.1.68.8. 3. *mount on a chariot* or *on horseback, be mounted*, Hdt.3.84; *go* or *be on board ship*, Il.15.387, S.*Aj.*358 (lyr.), Hdt.8.90, Th.2.90, etc.

B. Causal in fut. -βήσω Luc.*DMort.*6.4, Ep. inf. -βησέμεν Il.8.197, Hes.*Th.*396, but usu. in aor. 1 Act. (ἐπιβιβάζω, ἐπιβάσκω serve as pres.):—*make* one *mount, set* him *upon*, ὅν ῥα τόθ' ἵππων.. ἐπέβησε Il.8.129; πολλοὺς δὲ πυρῆς ἐπέβησ' ἀλεγεινῆς 9.546; ὥς κ' ἐμὲ.. ἐμῆς ἐπιβήσετε πάτρης Od.7.223; ἐ. τινὰς σκάφεσιν J.*BJ*4.7.6; πλοίων ib. 11.5, cf. Luc. l. c.; ὁπλίτας ὁλκάσιν App.*BC*5.92; τινὰς ἐπὶ τὰς ναῦς ib.2.59: also in aor. 1 Med., νιν ἕω ἐπεβάσατο δίφρω Call.*Lav.Pall.* 65. b. of things, νευρὰν ἐπέβασε κορώνας *set* the string *on* his bow's tip, B.5.73. 2. metaph. (cf. A. I. 4), εὐκλεῖης ἐπίβησον *bring to* great glory, Il.8.285; τιμῆς καὶ γεράων Hes.*Th.*396; χαλιφρονέοντα σαοφροσύνης ἐπέβησαν they *bring* him *to* sobriety, Od.23.13; λιγυρῆς ἐπέβησαν ἀοιδῆς Hes.*Op.*659; δουλοσύνας (prob.) E.*Hyps.Fr.*41(64). 86; εἴ σε τύχη.. ἡλικίας ἐπέβησεν *had brought thee to* full age, *IG*2. 2263. 3. [ἠὼς] πολέας ἐπέβησε κελεύθου dawn *sets* them *on* their way, Hes.*Op.*580.

ἐπιβακχεύω, *rush on like a bacchanal*, Nicostr.Com.4.

ἐπιβάλλον, τό, a kind of *ephemeron* (insect), Sch.[Arr.]*Peripl.M. Eux.*60 (p.417 M.), Sch.Antig.*Mir.*85(92).

ἐπιβάλλω: I. trans., *throw* or *cast upon*, θριξὶ.., ἃς ἐπέβαλλον (sc. πυρί) Il.23.135; ἐπὶ δὲ χλαῖναν βάλεν αὐτῷ Od.14.520, cf. 4.440; ἑωυτὸν ἐς τὸ πῦρ v.l. in Hdt.7.107; φάρη κόραις E.*El.*1221 (lyr.); ἐ. τινὰς ἐπὶ ἁμάξας Th.4.48, cf. Hdt.4.75, 5.112; ἐπιβάλλοντας (sc. χοῦν) *throwing on more and more*, Th.2.76. 2. *lay on*, [ἡμιόνοις] ἐπέβαλλεν ἱμάσθλην Od.6.320; ἐ. πληγάς τινι X.*Lac.*2.8; Ζεὺς ἐπὶ χεῖρα βάλοι A.*Ch.*395 (lyr.), cf. Ar.*Nu.*933 (anap.); ἐ. τὴν χεῖρά τινι Id.*Lys.* 440 (but τῷ καρπῷ τοῦ νοσοῦντος τὴν χεῖρα, of feeling the pulse, Gal. 18(2).40; so τὴν ἁφήν Id.8.821, Marcellin.*Puls.*119); τὰς χεῖρας τοῖς κατ' Αἴγαιον Plb.3.2.8; Ῥωμαίοις Id.18.51.8; ἐπί τινα *Ev.Matt.*26.50; *impose* as a tax, tribute, τινί τι Hdt.1.106, Th.8.108; as a fine or penalty, ζημίην, φυγὴν ἐ. τινί, Hdt.6.92 (Pass.), 7.3; ἀργύριον Lys.9.6; ἐπιβολάς Id.20.14, cf. Arist.*Ath.*61.2; λύτρα Lxx *Ex.*21.30 (Pass.); *inflict*, θνατοῖς ἐ. ἀνάλγητα, λύπην, etc., S.*Tr.*128 (lyr.), E.*Med.*1115 (anap.), etc. 3. ἐ. σφρηγῖδα, δακτύλιον, *affix* a seal, Hdt.3.128, 2.38; σφραγῖδ' ἐπί τι Ar.*Av.*559; σύμβολόν τινι ib.1215. 4. *add, contribute*, μικρὸν [ἀληθείᾳ] Arist.*Metaph.*993ᵇ2; ἐ. ἐπὶ τὸ ὕδωρ Thphr.*Ign.*49; νέον [φῶς] Pl.*Cra.*409b: metaph., *throw in, mention*, τι dub. in S.*El.*1246 (lyr.) (in Med., "χαίρειν" τεοῖς προθύροις ἐπιβάλλομαι Theoc.23.27); Φαῖστος.. ἐπιβάλλων φησί Sch.Pi.*P.*4.28: abs., *bid higher*, Arist.*Pol.*1259ᵃ14. 5. *place next in order*, Plb.1.26. 15. 6. *let grow*, κλήματα Thphr.*HP*4.13.5; βλαστούς ib.3.5. 1. 7. *let loose*, πρόβατα ἐπὶ κνῆκον *PRyl.*69.6 (i B.C.). 8. causal of ἐπιβαίνω A. III. 3, D.Chr.7.134. II. *throw oneself upon, go straight towards*, c. acc., ἡ δὲ Φεὰς ἐπέβαλλεν Od.15.297: later c. dat. loci, Plb.5.18.3, D.S.1.30, Plot.3.7.12, etc.; νήσοις Rhian.39; εἰς Ἰταλίαν, ἐπὶ τὸν τόπον, Plb.2.24.17, 5.6.6, cf. *PAmh.*2.31.5 (ii B.C.), etc. 2. *fall upon*, ὅπου ἂν ὁ ἥλιος ἐ. Arist.*HA*598ᵃ3; esp. in hostile sense, *set upon*, c. dat., ib.623ᵇ1, etc.; τοῖς Ἀρβήλοις D.S.17.64: abs., ἐ. λῃστρικῷ τρόπῳ *PRyl.*127.10 (i A.D.); ἐπιβάλλουσαι *jostling, trampling*, Pl.*Phdr.*248a; sens. obsc., Ar.*Av.*1216. 3. (sc. τὸν νοῦν) *set* to a thing, *devote oneself to* it, c. dat., M.Ant.10.30; τοῖς αὐλοῖς D.S.3.59; τοῖς κοινοῖς πράγμασιν Plu.*Cic.*4 (in full τὴν διάνοιαν ἐ. πρός τι D.S.20.43): generally, *give one's attention to, think on*, *Ev.Marc.* 14.72. b. *apprehend*, Epicur.*Fr.*423; *attain by intuition*, c. dat., Dam.*Pr.*54. 4. *fall in one's way*, ὅταν ἐπιβάλλῃ περὶ τῆς τοιαύτης πολιτείας ἡ σκέψις Arist.*Pol.*1266ᵃ25; κατὰ τὸν ἐπιβάλλοντα λόγον Id.*GA*716ᵃ3. 5. *follow, come next*, Plb.11.23.2; τισί Plu.*Aem.* 33; ἐφ' ὃν ἐπιβαλὼν ἔφη said *thereupon*, Plb.1.80.1; *interrupt*, ἀποκρινομένῳ Thphr.*Char.*7.2. 6. *belong to, fall to the share of*, μόριον ὅσον αὐτοῖσι ἐπέβαλλε Hdt.7.23, cf. Diph.43.16; εἰ μὴ τὸ ὅλον, μέρος γε, ἐπιβάλλει τῆς βλασφημίας ἅπασι D.18.272; ὅσον ἐπιβάλλει αὐτοῖς Arist.*Pol.*1260ᵃ19; ἑκάστῳ τῆς εὐδαιμονίας ἐπιβάλλει τοσοῦτον ὅσονπερ ἀρετῆς ib.1323ᵇ21; τῶν κτημάτων τὸ ἐπιβάλλον (sc. μέρος) *the portion that falls to one*, Hdt.4.115, cf. Lxx *To.*3.17, 6.12; so τὸ ἐ. ἐφ' ἡμᾶς μέρος D.18.254; τὸ ἐ. μέρος τῆς οὐσίας *Ev.Luc.*15.12, cf. *PGrenf.* 1.33.33 (ii B.C.), etc.; *fall due*, of payments, *PLond.*1.3.21 (ii B.C.); τόκον ὃν ἔφη ἐπιβάλλειν αὐτῷ which *was payable by* him, *BCH*6.21 (Delos, ii B.C.). b. part. ἐπιβάλλων, in Law, *next-of-kin*, ὁ ἐ., οἱ ἐ., *Leg.Gort.*7.36, 11.42, al. 7. impers. c. acc. et inf., τοὺς Δελφοὺς δὴ ἐπέβαλλε.. παρασχεῖν *it concerned* them to provide, Hdt.2.180: or c. dat. et inf., ἐπιβάλλει τινὶ ποιεῖν τι Chrysipp.*Stoic.*2.39, al., Plb.18. 51.1; ἐπιβάλλοντος ἡμῖν εὐεργετικοῖς εἶναι Corn.*ND*15; κοινῇ πᾶσιν ἐπιβάλλει *UPZ*112.10 (ii B.C.); καθότι ἐπέβαλλεν ἀνδρὶ καλῷ καὶ ἀγαθῷ *IG*12(7).231.5 (Amorgos): freq. in part., ἐπιβάλλουσαν ἡγεῖσθαι τὴν στρατείαν τινὶ *incumbent* upon.., Teles p.61 H.; τὸ ἐπιβάλλον Cleanth. *Stoic.*1.128, Arr.*Epict.*2.11.3, etc.; τὰς -ούσας τάσεις τῆς φωνῆς Chrysipp.*Stoic.*2.96; τὸ τῇ φύσει ἐ. Antip.*Stoic.*3.255; *appropriate*, ὑποδοχαί Teles p.41 H.; ἱμάτια *IG*2².1121.15; ἁρμονία Iamb.*Comm. Math.*30; ἡ στέρησις ἐπιβάλλοντός ἐστι παρεῖναι εἴδους τινός a specific form which *ought* to be present, Plot.1.8.11. 8. *shut to, close*, of the larynx, Arist.*PA*664ᵇ26. 9. in Logic, λόγοι ἐπιβάλλοντες, -όμενοι, *overlapping* and *overlapped*, of syllogisms in a sorites, Chrysipp.*Stoic.*2.85; so of Time, ἐπέβαλε τοῖς χρόνοις Ἰουλιανῷ Eun.*VS* p.497 B.:—Med., γηραιῷ τῷ Κυρηναίῳ ἐπεβάλετο Anon.*Intr.Arat.* p.326 M. 10. in Alchemy, *make a 'projection'* (cf. ἐπιβολή), Syn.Alch.p.68 B. III. Med., mostly like the intr. usages, but also: 1. c. gen., *throw oneself upon, desire eagerly*, ἐνάρων ἐπιβαλλόμενος Il.6.68; παρθενίας ἐπιβάλλομαι Sapph.102; τοῦ εὖ ζῆν ἐπιβάλλονται Arist.*Pol.*1258ᵃ3. 2. c. acc., *put upon oneself*, ἐπιβαλλομέναν.. πλόκον ἀνθέων E.*Med.*840; ἐπιβάλλεσθαι *put on more wraps*, Thphr.*Char.*2.10 (cf. IV. 1); ὕπνον ἡδὺν -όμενος D.Chr.12.51: metaph., *take possession of*, καὶ ἐπὶ κλήρους ἐβάλοντο Od.14.209; αὐθαίρετον δουλείαν ἐπιβαλεῖται *will take upon himself*, Th.6.40. b. of trees, *make fresh growth*, Thphr.*HP*3.5.1. 3. c. acc., also, *attempt, undertake*, ἔργον Pl.*Sph.*264b, *Ti.*48c; μέθοδον Arist.*Pol.* 1260ᵇ36: c. inf., Decr.ap.D.18.164, Zeno *Stoic.*1.68, Plb.1.43.2, etc.: abs., πολλῶν -ημένων though many have *made the attempt*, Agatharch.76. 4. c. dat., *put one's hand to*, ἐχέτλῃ *AP*7.650 (Phal.(?)): metaph., *apply* or *devote oneself to*, τόλμῃ καὶ πράξει Plb.5.81.1; ἐγχειρήματι μεγάλῳ D.H.5.25, etc. 5. *arrive at*, [πολίεσσι] Call.*Del.*68; ὅταν ἐπὶ τοὺς χρόνους ἐπιβαλώμεθα D.S.19. 55. 6. ἐπὶ πᾶσι -εβάλοντο *brought up the rear*, Id.18.33. IV. in Pass., *lie upon, be put upon*, ἐπιβεβλημένοι τοξόται archers *with their arrows on the string*, X.*An.*4.3.28, cf. 5.2.12; λάσιον ἐπιβεβλημένος *having* a rough cloak *on*, Theopomp.Com.36; τὸ ἐν ψύχει κεῖσθαι -ημένον Hp.*Epid.*2.3.1, cf. 6.4.14; διφθέραν -ημένη D.Chr.5.25. 2. *to be set over*, ὁ τελώνης ὁ ἐπιβεβλημένος τῷ Ζεύγματι Philostr.*VA*1. 20. 3. Rhet., *ornate* (v. ἐπιβολή), ἰδέα λόγων οὔτ' ἐπιβεβλημένη οὔτ' αὖος Id.*VS*1.20.2.

ἐπίβαλμα, ατος, τό, = ὑποπόδιον, Hsch. (leg. **ἐπίβαμα**). **ἐπίβαλος,** ὁ, *heel*, Id.

ἐπιβαπτίζω, metaph., *sink, overwhelm*, J.*BJ*1.27.1, 3.7.15.

ἐπίβαπτος, ον, *covered with* (lit. *steeped in*), τινί Thphr.*HP*3.7.4.

ἐπιβάπτω, *dip into*, τι ἔς τι Hp.*Morb.*3.16. II. *tan*, Arist.*Pr.* 898ᵇ18; *dye*, Alex.Trall.2; *gild* or *silver*, Ps.-Democr.p.46 B.

ἐπιβάρ-εσις [ᾰ], εως, ἡ, *burden imposed* on a person, *PLond.*5. 1674.24 (vi A.D.). **-έω,** *weigh down*: hence, *be a burden to*, τινά 1*Ep.Thess.*2.9; *overload*, of food, τὸν ὄγκον Sor.1.108: c. dat., *press heavily upon*, τοῖς ἠτυχηκόσι App.*BC*4.31, cf. 15, 5.107:—Med., *lay a burden on oneself, trouble oneself*, c. inf., *POxy.*1481.12 (ii A.D.):—Pass., with fut. Med. ἐπιβαρήσομαι D.H.4.9, 8.73; ὑπό τινος *SIG* 807.16 (Magn. Mae., i A.D.); ὑπὸ τῶν δανείων *IG*12(5).860.9 (Tenos). 2. Pass., of a bandage, *to be found irksome*, *PMed.Lond.*3. 39. (Cf. ἐπιζαρέω.) **-ής,** ές, *heavy*, Hero *Bel.*102.9. **-ησις,** εως, ἡ, *burden*, *IG*12(5).860.32 (Tenos). **-ύνω,** *press heavily on* the enemy, App.*Mith.*25. **-υς,** εια, υ, *oppressive*, εὐωδία Thphr. *HP*3.13.6.

ἐπι-βᾰσία, ἡ, = sq., -βασίαν ποιεῖσθαι D.C.80.3, *Fr.*37.2; πρὸς τὴν ὑπατείαν εἰληφέναι Id.37.54: concrete, in pl., ἵνα αἱ ἐ. διὰ [τῆς γεφύρας] διεξίωσιν Id.68.13. 2. ἐ. τῇ δίκῃ, sine expl., Hyp.*Fr.* 242. 3. *wrongful entry*, interpol. in Poll.2.200. **-βᾰσις,** εως, ἡ, *stepping upon*, ἐς τὴν ναῦν Luc.*Nav.*12; *advent*, *Annuario* 6/7.417 (Phaselis); αἱ ἐ. τῆς θαλάσσης *risings*.., Plb.34.9.6. 2. *means of approach, access*, ἔχειν ἐ. *IG*7.167 (Megara); τοῦ νοητοῦ -σεις Plot.6.7. 36; ἐ. τοῦ ἐραστοῦ Them.*Or.*13.163d: hence concretely, *rungs, steps*, Pl.*R.*511b (pl.). 3. ἔς τινα ποιεῖσθαι ἐ. make *a handle against, a means of attacking* one, Hdt.6.61; ἐ. τι τίθεσθαι εἴς τι App.*BC*1.37; *attack*, Luc.*Hist.Conscr.*49; ἀμφισβητούμενον ἢ ἐπίβασιν ἔχον liable *to be impugned*, *IG*2².1051a14. 4. *getting on one's feet*, of a child beginning to walk, Sor.1.114; esp. in recovery after a broken leg, Hp. *Fract.*18 (pl.); τῇ ἐ. χρῆσθαι Id.*Art.*58; *foothold*, in snow, Plb.3.54. 5. 5. *resting of one thing on another*, e.g. of a bone, Hp.*Art.*51. 6. Rhet., κατ' ἐπίβασιν *by gradation*, Longin.11.1. 7. *that on which one stands*, Ph.1.125, 332. 8. *entry* into office, *PLond.*3.1170.3 (iii A.D.). II. of the male, *covering*, Plu.2.754a (pl.). **-βάσκω,** causal of ἐπιβαίνω, c. gen., κακῶν ἐπιβασκέμεν υἷας Ἀχαιῶν *lead* them *into* misery, Il.2.234. (Perh. by haplology from ἐπιβιβάσκω.)

ἐπιβαστάζω, *weigh in the hand*, E.*Cyc.*379.

ἐπιβᾰτ-έον, *one must tread*, ἐπὶ [ἴχνη] Arist.*Mir.*838ᵃ34. **-εύω,** *set one's foot upon, occupy*, c. gen., Συρίας Plu.*Ant.*28, cf. Luc.*Cont.* 2: metaph., *take one's stand upon*, τοῦ Σμέρδιος οὐνόματος ἐπιβατεύων *usurping* it, Hdt.3.63, cf. 67, 9.95; τῆς ἡγεμονίας D.C.79.7; τὸ τῆς οὐσίας ἐν -εῦον Dam.*Pr.*88; τούτου ἐ. τοῦ ῥήματος *rely upon*.., Hdt.6.65. II. *to be an* ἐπιβάτης, *passenger* or *soldier on board ship*, ἐ. ἐπὶ [νεῶν] ib.15, al., Luc.*Par.*46; ἐπὶ νηί Pl.*La.*183d: c. dat., Ar.*Ra.*48 (with an obscene allusion, cf. ἐπιβαίνω A. III. 3). 2. *mount*, τοῦ θρόνου Philostr.*VS*2.8.2. **-ηγός** (sc. ναῦς), ἡ, *conveying marines*, Ulp.ap.*Dig.*14.1.12. **-ήριος,** ον, *fit for scaling*, μηχαναί J.*BJ*3.7.23. 2. *belonging to the entry* of a place, ᾠδή Him.*Ecl.*13. 38. II. a name of Apollo at Corinth, Paus.2.32.2. III. ἐπιβατήριον, τό, *festival to celebrate the advent* of a god, *CIG*4352–5 (Side). 2. ἐπιβατήρια (sc. ἱερά), τά, *sacrifices on disembarkation*, Lib.*Decl.*6.37. 3. λόγος ἐ. speech delivered *on disembarka-*

tion, Men.Rh.p.377 S., al. —**ης**, ου, ὁ, *one who mounts* or *embarks*: 1. ἐπιβάται, οἱ, *soldiers on board ship, fighting men*, opp. the rowers and seamen, *marines*, Hdt.6.12, 7.100, Th.3.95, Plb.1.51.2, etc. b. *merchant on board ship, supercargo*, D.34.51, 56.10. c. *passenger* on ship, D.Chr.1.29, al., Plu.*in Hes.*8. d. subordinate officer in the Spartan navy, Th.8.61, X.*HG*1.3.17, *Hell. Oxy.*17.4. 2. *fighting man* in a chariot, Pl.*Criti.*119b; on an elephant, Arr.*An.*5.17.3. 3. *rider*, Arist.*EN*1106ᵃ20, Luc.*Zeux.*10. 4. *male quadruped*, *Gp.*16.21.9. 5. *heel*, Hsch. 6. *middle finger*, [Ruf.]*Onom.App.*p.600 R. —**ικός**, ή, όν, *of* or *for the* ἐπιβάται, ἡ ἐ. χρεία *their* service, Plb.3.95.5; τὸ ἐ. *the complement of* ἐπιβάται on board ship, Arist.*Pol.*1327ᵇ9, Plb.1.47.9 (pl.) (but also, *payment for the ἐ.*, *IG*1².127.20, 37, cf. 35). II. ἐπιβατικά, τά, = παρενθήκη II, *EM*357.45, Hsch. —**όριος** ἵππος *stallion*, interpol. in Suid. s.v. κηλώνιον. —**ός**, ή, όν (D.C.44.42), *that can be climbed, accessible*, Hdt.4.62; ἐξ ἧς ἐπιβατὸν..τοῖς τότε ἐγίγνετο πορευομένοις there was *a passage* for them, Pl.*Ti.*24e; τὴν Κελτικὴν ἐπιβατὴν ποιῆσαι D.C. l.c.: metaph., χρυσίῳ ἐ. *accessible* to a bribe, Plu.*Dem.*14. II. παίων ἐ. foot consisting of five long syllables, Id.2.1143b.

ἐπιβάφια [βᾰ], τά, in Alchemy, *powders* for gilding and silvering, Zos.Alch.p.218 B.

ἐπίβδᾰ, ἡ, *the day after a festival*, Sch.Pi.*P.*4.249, *EM*357.54 (pl.); esp. *the day after* the three days of *the Apaturia*, Hsch. s.v. ἐπιβάδαι: proverb., ἕρπειν πρὸς τραχεῖαν ἐπίβδαν come to hard *reckoning* (on the day after the feast, when the guests suffer from excess), Pi.*P.*4.140; χαῖρε..ταῖς ἐπίβδαις Cratin.323. 2. *new-year's day*, Aristid.*Or.*51(27).26 (pl.).

ἐπιβδάλλω, *milk a second time*, Sch.Pi.*P.*4.249.

ἐπιβεβαι-όω, *add proof*, Thphr.*CP*5.14.4; *confirm*, ὑποψίαν J.*BJ*1.22.5; *ratify*, νόμον Plu.*Cat.Mi.*32, cf. *PLond.*3.1157ᵛ*b*4 (iii A.D.): —Pass., *to be further confirmed*, Arist.*APr.*47ᵃ6. —**ωσις**, εως, ἡ, *further confirmation*, Id.*Rh.Al.*1438ᵇ29 (pl.); *guarantee*, *Sammelb.*5240.17 (i A.D.).

ἐπιβελτίωσις, εως, ἡ, *amelioration*, *Gloss.*

ἐπιβήματα· εἴδη χορικῆς ὀρχήσεως, Hsch.

Ἐπιβήμιος, ὁ, epith. of Zeus at Siphnos, Hsch.

ἐπιβήτ-ης, ου, ὁ, *one who sets foot on* or *dwells in*, Orph.*Fr.*353. —**ωρ**, ορος, ὁ, *one who mounts*, ἐ. ἵππων Od.18.263, Simm.1.3; νεὼς ἐπιβήτορα λαόν, = ἐπιβάτας, *AP*7.498 (Antip.(?)); ἐ. κύκλων, of the Trojan horse, Tryph.307. 2. of male animals, e.g. a boar, συῶν ἐπιβήτωρ Od.11.131; of a bull, Theoc.25.128. II. as Adj., *springing*, Nonn.*D.*20.113. 2. metaph., *at home in, master of* a thing, θηροδιδασκαλίης Man.4.245; *dwelling in*, ὕλης οὐρανίας κτλ. Orph.*Fr.*353.

ἐπιβῐ-άζομαι, *constrain besides*, *CIG*(add.)4325*k* (Olympus), *Rev. Phil.*36.56 (Iconium). —**αστικός**, ή, όν, *exercising constraint*, Epicur.*Nat.Herc.*1420.3.

ἐπιβιβ-άζω (fut. -βιβῶ Lxx *Ho.*10.11, *Hb.*3.15), causal of ἐπιβαίνω, *put* one *upon*, ἐπ' ὀλίγας ναῦς τοὺς ὁπλίτας Th.4.31; τινὰ ἐπὶ τὸ ἴδιον κτῆνος *Ev.Luc.*10.34:—Pass., Apollod.3.1.1. —**άσκω**, = foreg., *put the male to the female*, Arist.*HA*573ᵇ1.

ἐπιβιβρώσκω, *eat with* a thing, ἐπὶ δὲ γλυκὺ κηρίον ἔβρως (aor. 2) Call.*Jov.*49; ἐπιβεβρωμένος *eaten off at the top*, Gal.14.74; -βρωθέντα *eaten afterwards*, Dsc.*Eup.*2.140.

ἐπίβῐος, ον, *surviving*, παιδίον Is.*Fr.*156 (nisi leg. -βιόν).

***ἐπιβῐόω**, only in aor. 2 -εβίων:—*live over* or *after, survive*, ἐπεβίω δύο ἔτη Th.2.65; ἐπεβίων διὰ παντὸς [τοῦ πολέμου] Id.5.26; ἐπιβιόντος..πένθ' ἡμέρας D.41.18, cf. Is.2.45; but αἷς ἂν..ἐπιβιῶ *live to see married*, Pl.*Ep.*361d. (Freq. corrupted to -βιοῦντα, etc. in codd.)

ἐπιβλᾰβής, ές, *hurtful*, Aret.*CD*1.2; τῇ ψυχῇ Hierocl.*in CA*13 p.448 M.; τὸ ἐ. Procl.*Par.Ptol.*166. Adv. -βῶς Poll.5.135.

ἐπιβλαί· περόναι, Hsch.

ἐπιβλάπτω, *damage, mar*, εἰς τὸ κάλλος ὑπὸ τῆς λύπης J.*AJ*7.8.5 (Pass., v.l.).

ἐπιβλάς· συννεφὲς νιφετῷ, Hsch.; cf. ἐπιβλύξ.

ἐπιβλαστ-άνω, *grow* or *sprout on*, τοῖς γεώδεσι Plu.2.325b. II. *grow in addition* or *after*, Thphr.*CP*1.10.6, *HP*7.2.3; τοῖς πρώτοις (sc. φύλλοις) ἀπορρέουσιν ἑτέρων -όντων Plu.2.723f. —**ησις**, εως, ἡ, *after-growth*, Thphr.*HP*3.5.5, *CP*1.10.6, 1.13.6. —**ικός**, ή, όν, *able to grow afresh*, ib.8 (Comp.).

ἐπιβλασφημέω, *load with reproaches*, App.*BC*1.115 (Pass.). II. abs., *use blasphemous language*, J.*AJ*20.5.4.

ἐπι-βλεπτέον, *one must look at*, Arist.*APr.*45ᵇ28. —**βλέπω**, fut. -ψομαι, later -ψω Lxx *Le.*26.9:—*look upon, look attentively*, εἴς τινα Pl.*Phd.*63a; ἐπὶ πόλιν Din.1.72; ἐφ' ἑαυτόν v.l. in Arist.*EN*1120ᵇ6; πρός τινα Lxx *Ho.*11.4; τινί Luc.*Astr.*20. 2. c. acc., *look well at, observe*, λόγους ἀθρόους Pl.*Lg.*811d; αἰτίαν Arist.*EN*1147ᵃ24; κοινωνίαν Id.*Metaph.*991ᵃ8: c. acc. dupl., ἄφθαρτον τὸν θεὸν ἐπεβλέψαμεν Phld.*D.*3 *Fr.*39; τῆς κατὰ τὴν γαστέρα ταραχῆς -ομένης *being taken into consideration*, Gal.15.673. 3. *face* upwards or downwards, Dsc.5.120. II. *eye with envy*, τύχαις S.*OT*1526. III. Astrol., *to be in aspect with*, Heph.Astr.3.20. —**βλεψις**, εως, ἡ, *looking at*, τοῦ θεάτρου εἴς τινα Plu.*Phil.*11; *view*, ἔργου Id.*Nic.*25, al. 2. of the mind, *inquiry*, Arist.*APr.*45ᵇ19, 45ᵃ17 (pl.), Epicur.*Ep.*1 p.3 U., Porph.*Abst.*1.41. 3. Astrol., *being in aspect*, Procl.*Par.Ptol.*166.

ἐπιβλήδην, Adv. *laying on*, ἐλάοντες, of hammers, A.R.2.80.

ἐπί-βλημα, ατος, τό, *that which is thrown over, covering*, Nicostr. Com.15; *coverlet, bedspread*, *IG*12(5).593.4 (Iulis, v B.C.), Gal.14.638, Sor.1.85; *head-covering*, Gal.*UP*11.12. 2. *tapestry, hangings*, Plu.*Cat.Ma.*4, Arr.*An.*6.29.5. II. *that which is put on, piece of embroidery*, ἐ. ποικίλον *IG*1².387.28, 2².1514.31; *mantle*, Lxx *Is.*3.22. 2. *patch*, *Ev.Matt.*9.16, etc. 3. *outer bandage*, Paul. Aeg.6.92. —**βλημᾰτικός**, ή, όν, *introductory*, τρόπος Ptol.*Tetr.*107. —**βλής**, ῆτος, ὁ, *bolt* or *bar fitting into* a socket, Il.24.453; sens. obsc., *AP*5.241 (Eratosth.). II. *cover*, ib.7.479 (Theodorid.). III. ἡ ἐ. (sc. δοκός) *cross-beam*, Lys.*Fr.*175 S., *IG*11.144 *A*58 (Delos, iv B.C.), 2².463.62, 1672.193. —**βλητέον**, *one must apply*, ἀμυχάς Antyll.ap.Orib.7.18.3; ἐμβροχάς Paul.Aeg.3.43; προσθέτοισι ἐς τὴν χώρην Aret.*CA*2.10; *one must make an attempt*, τινί Artem.1.11. 2. -τέον, τό, *accessory reagent*, Ps.-Democr. p.47 B. —**βλήτιον**, τό, = ἐπίβλημα I, *SIG*102*b*24, al. (pl., Athens, v B.C.). —**βλητικός**, ή, όν, *apprehending directly* (v. ἐπιβολή I. 2b), τρόπος Epicur.*Nat.*28.6; νοήσεις Iamb.*Protr.*4; *quick to apprehend*, τοῦ ἀληθοῦς Alex.Aphr.*in Top.*584.13, cf. Herm.*in Phdr.*p.113 A. Adv. -κῶς *by direct apprehension*, Epicur.*Ep.*1 p.12 U., Phlp.*in de An.*547.9, Id.*in APo.*332.14. II. Adv. -κῶς, gloss on ἐπιβλήδην, Sch. A.R.2.80. —**βλητος**, ον, *put upon*, Sm.*Ez.*27.20. II. *imposed, levied*, *Gloss.*

ἐπι-βλύζω, *pour forth*, *AP*9.349 (Leon.). —**βλύξ**, Adv. *abundantly, redundantly*, Pherecr.130.4. II. ἐπιβλύξ· συννεφής, Hsch. (-βληξ cod.). —**βλυσμός**, ὁ, *gushing forth*, Aq.*Ge.*2.6, al. —**βλύω**, *flow over*, A.R.4.1238.

ἐπιβο-άω, fut. -βοήσομαι, Ion. and Ep. -βώσομαι (v. infr.):—*call upon* or *to, cry out to*, ἐ. τινὶ ὅτι.. Th.5.65; ἐ. τινί, c. inf., *call on* one to do.., Id.4.28, 7.70: c. acc., *invoke*, θεόν *AP*9.334 (Pers.): abs., of hounds, *give tongue*, X.*Cyn.*6.19; *cry out*, Arr.*Epict.*4.1.14; of *calling upon* the dead at funerals, *BMus.Inscr.*791, al. (Cnidus). 2. *utter* or *sing aloud over*, τινί τι, μέλος χέρνιβι ἐπιβοᾶν Ar.*Av.*898; *shriek out besides*, στέρν' ἄρασσε κἀπιβόα τὸ Μύσιον A.*Pers.*1054 codd. (lyr.); ἔγχει, κἀπιβόα τρίτον παιῶνα Pherecr.131.5. 3. Med., *cry out against*, Luc.*DMeretr.*12.1:—Pass., τὰ ἴδια ἐπιβοώμενος *cried out against* in regard to private matters, Th.6.16. 4. *applaud, acclaim*, Arr.*Epict.*3.23.10, M.Ant.10.34. II. Med., *invoke, call upon*, θεοὺς ἐπιβώσομαι Od.1.378; σὲ γὰρ πρώτην..ἐπιβωσόμεθ' (v.l. for ἐπιδωσόμεθ') Il.10.463; τὸν Ἀπόλλωνα ἐπιβώσασθαι Hdt.1.87; ἐπιβοᾶται Θέμιν E.*Med.*168 (lyr.); θεοὺς..ἐπιβοώμενοι, πατέρων τάφους ἐ., Th.3.59, 67; ὅρκους καὶ πίστεις D.H.11.49; *call to aid*, τὴν ἄλλην στρατιὴν ἐπεβώσαντο Hdt.9.23, cf. 5.1: c. inf., ἐ. [τινὰ] μὴ ἀπολέσαι τὴν πατρίδα Th.8.92. 2. c. acc. rei, *call out*, Id.7.69. —**ή**, ἡ, = ἐπιβόησις, D.L.5.90.

ἐπιβοήθ-εια, ἡ, *coming to aid, succour*, Th.3.51, X.*Cyr.*5.4.47. —**έω**, Dor. -βοᾱθέω, *come to aid, succour*, τινί Hdt.3.146, 7.207, Th.1.73, 4.29, al., *SIG*398.7 (Cos, iii B.C.): abs., Th.3.69, *PPetr.*2 p.143 (iii B.C.), etc. II. *come to aid against*, τινί Th.3.26; ἐπὶ τὸ ἐχόμενον X.*HG*7.5.24. —**ητέον**, *one must take protective measures*, Ath. Med.ap.Orib.*inc.*23.7.

ἐπιβό-ημα, ατος, τό, *a call* or *cry to* one, Th.5.65: pl., D.C.42.19, al. —**ησις**, εως, ἡ, *applause*, D.H.*Rh.*7.3: pl., J.*Vit.*48, Plu.*Arat.*23, D.Chr.40.29, M.Ant.1.16, Chariton6.2. 2. *shouting*, Str.10.3.15. —**ητος**, Ion. -**βωτος**, ον, *cried out against, ill spoken of*, περί τινος Th.6.16; ἐπίβωτος ἀνθρώποις Aeschrio 8, cf. Anacr.60. Adv. -τως *notoriously*, Poll.5.160. II. in good sense, *famous*, D.C.60.28, Themist.*Ep.*11.

ἐπιβόθριος, ον, *in* or *at the trench*, Aristid.*Or.*48(24).27.

***ἐπίβοιον**, τό, = τὸ ἐπὶ βοῒ θῦμα, *sacrifice* of a sheep to Pandrosos *after an ox offered* to Athena, Philoch.32, Lycurg.*Fr.*35.

ἐπιβόλ-αιον, τό, *covering, wrapper, garment*, Lxx *Ez.*13.18, 21, Herod.Med.in *Rh.Mus.*58.100, Ar.Byz.*Epit.*9.10. —**εύς**, έως, ὁ, epith. of Heracles at Thurii, Hsch. —**ή**, ἡ, *throwing* or *laying on*, ἱματίων Th.2.49 (pl.); χειρῶν σιδηρῶν, of grappling-irons, Id.7.62 (pl.); τῶν χρωμάτων Luc.*Zeux.*5; σημείων *affixing* of seals, Id.*Tim.*13; χειρῶν ἐπιβολαὶ ἐγίνοντο *a fray* arose, D.H.10.33. b. χειρῶν ἐπιβολή *massage*, Gal.6.92; without χειρῶν, σκληρὰ ἐ. ib.101, cf. 176. 2. metaph., ἐ. τῆς διανοίας *application* of the mind to a thing, Epicur.*Ep.*1 pp.5, 12 U. (pl.), Ph.1.230 (pl.), Plot.2.4.10; αἱ ἐ. τῶν νοημάτων Philostr.*VS*2.18; ἐξ ἐπιβολῆς πάνυ very *scrupulously*, Antyll.ap.Orib.45.25.5. b. *act of direct apprehension*, Epicur.*Ep.*1 p.3 U.: pl., ib.p.4 U.; ἡ ἐκ τῶν ἐ. ταραχή Phld.*D.*1.14; ἐπί τι Epicur.*Fr.*255, cf. Plot.1.6.2; *intuition*, [τῇ ψυχῇ] τὴν ἐπιβολὴν ἀθρόαν ἀθρόων γίνεσθαι Id.4.4.1; [γνῶσις] ἐφάψεται τοῦ ἑνὸς κατὰ ἐπιβολήν Dam.*Pr.*25bis; opp. συλλογισμός, ibid. c. *conception, notion*, Iamb.*Comm. Math.*1, cf.9, Dam.*Pr.*258 (pl.); *point of view*, ib.201, 396, al.; *doctrine*, ἡ τοῦ Συριανοῦ θαυμασία ἐ. ib.270: pl., *principles*, Ael.*Tact.*21.1. d. *impulse*, *Stoic.*3.41, 149; ἐ. φιλοποιίας ib.96. 3. *setting upon* a thing, *design, attempt, enterprise*, v.l. in Th.3.45: c. gen., ἡ ἐ. τῆς ἱστορίας *writing* history, Plb.1.4.2; τῶν ὅλων *acquisition* of empire, Id.1.3.6, cf. 5.95.1; κατασκευασμάτων ἐπιβολαί *designs*, Plu.*Per.*12; ἐξ ἐπιβολῆς *designedly*, D.S.13.27. b. of surgical operations, οὐδεμία ὄνησις τῆς ἐ. Philum.*Ven.*4.7; μὴ κατακολουθεῖν ἀδυνάτοις ἐπιβολαῖς Hegetor ap.Apollon.Cit.3. 4. *hostile attempt, assault*, Plb.6.25.7 (pl.), cj. for -βουλάς in Th.1.93. 5. *application* of name to thing, Procl.*in Cra.*p.109 P., al. II. *that which is laid on*, ἐπιβολαὶ πλίνθων *courses* of bricks, Th.3.20; βυρσῶν *layers* of hide, Luc.*Nav.*4; *superstructure, gallery*, Ph.*Bel.*80.36 (pl.); λεπιδοειδεῖς ἐπιβολαί the squamous *commissures* of the skull, Gal.10.452. 2. *penalty, fine*, *IG*1².84.29 (pl.), Ar.*V.*769; ἐπιβολὴν ἐπιβάλλειν Lys.20.14 (pl.), X.*HG*1.7.2, etc.; ἐπιβολὰς ὀφλεῖν And.1.73; ἡ ἐ. τῆς βουλῆς *the penalty imposed* by the council, Aeschin.2.93; ἐξ ἐπιβολῆς in consequence of infliction of a *fine*, Lys.6.21. 3. *requisition, number of men required*, Plb.3.106.3; *impost, public burden*, Plu.*Cat.Ma.*18 (pl.), cf. Procop.*Arc.*23; τῆς λαογραφίας *PTeb.*391.19 (i A.D.); *requisition* of corn, *PFay.*81.9 (ii A.D.). b. *additional quantity*, *IG*2^2.1672.285,297. c. κατ' ἐπιβολήν τινος *in proportion* to.., *pro rata*, *CPR* 28.17 (ii A.D.), etc. III. *a thing put over for shelter* or *protection*, Thphr.*CP*3.16.4. 2. ἐ. χώματος *embankment*, *PPetr.*3 p.80 (iii B.C.). 3. *cloak*, *POxy.*298.9 (i A.D.), etc. IV. Rhet., = ἐπαναφορά, Phoeb.*Fig.*2.4, Rut.Lup.1.7. 2. *introduction, approach* to a subject, Hermog.*Id.*1.3; ἐ. τοῦ ῥυθμοῦ ib.2.1. 3. *power, 'grasp'*, of style or treatment, χάρις καὶ ἐ. D.Chr.18.14; *general survey, consideration*, Ptol.*Tetr.*204; Ἀλεξάνδρου τὴν ἐν ταῖς παρατάξεσιν ἐ. Ael.*Tact.Praef.*6. 4. *'trimmings', ornament*, τὸ ἀφαιρεῖν τὰς ἐ. καὶ αὐτοῖς χρῆσθαι τοῖς ὀνόμασι Aristid.*Rh.*p.522S. V. in Alchemy, *'projection'*, i.e. chemical reaction intended to produce transmutation, Syn.Alch.p.58B. (pl.). –ος, ον, f.l. for ἐπήβολος (q.v.), Vett.Val.11.16, 39.35. Adv. –βόλως, = φρονίμως, Hsch.

ἐπιβομβέω, *make a booming noise with*, τυμπάνῳ Luc.*DDeor.*12.1. 2. *ring*, οὔασι Nonn.*D.*40.503. II. trans., *cause to sound*, ἠχώ ib.21.230.

ἐπιβόσκ-ησις, εως, ἡ, *feeding upon*, Thphr.*CP*5.17.6 (pl.). –ίς, ίδος, ἡ, of insects, = προβοσκίς, Arist.*PA*678^{b}13. –ομαι, of cattle, *graze* or *feed upon*, σεύτλοις Batr.54:—Pass., *to be fed upon, eaten down*, τὰ ἐπιβοσκόμενα Thphr.*HP*3.6.3. 2. *feed on, draw its nutriment from*, αἶαν Nic.*Th.*68: metaph., *devour*, of poison, ib.430; of fire, Hdn.1.14.5. 3. metaph., *haunt, visit*, θεοὶ ἐ. γῆν Max.Tyr.19.6. II. *feed among*, ποίμνης Mosch.2.82.

ἐπιβουκόλος, ὁ, = βουκόλος, Od.3.422, al., usu. in pleon. phrase, βοῶν ἐ. ἀνήρ: without ἀνήρ, 22.292.

ἐπιβούλ-ευμα, ατος, τό, *plot, scheme*, Th.3.45, J.*AJ*17.12.2, Plu.*Caes.*4 (pl.), D.C.61.13. –ευσις, εως, ἡ, *plotting, treachery*, Pl.*Lg.*872d, prob. in A.*Th.*29. –ευτής, οῦ, ὁ, *one who plots against*, ἐ. στρατοῦ S.*Aj.*726. –ευτικός, ή, όν, *treacherous*, Ptol.*Tetr.*66. Adv. –κῶς ib.191. –εύω, Dor. –βωλεύω *SIG*527.145 (Dreros, iii B.C.):—*plot, contrive against*, c. dat. pers. et acc. rei, ἐ. ⟨κακὸν⟩ πόλει Tyrt.4.8; ἐπανάστασίν τινι Hdt.3.119; θάνατόν τινι ib.122, And.4.15; τοὺς θανάτους τοῖς πέλας Antipho 1.28; κατάλυσιν τῇ τυραννίδι Th.6.54. b. c. dat. only, *plot against, lay snares for*, τῇ πόλει A.*Th.*29 codd., *SIG* l.c.; τῷ πλήθει Ar.*Pl.*570, Th.6.60; θεοῖς Pl.*R.*378c; τῇ πολιτείᾳ D.8.40: c. dat. rei, *tamper with*, σφραγῖδι *Cat.Cod.Astr.*2.193: abs., οὑπιβουλεύων *the plotter*, S.*OT*618, cf. Pl.*Lg.*856c, Arist.*EN*1135^{b}33: also in aor. 1 Med., *plot*, Arr.*Epict.*4.1.160. c. c. acc. rei only, *plan secretly*, τὸν ἔκπλουν Th.7.51; ἀπόστασιν Id.8.60, etc. 2. c. dat. rei, *form designs upon, aim at*, πρήγμασι μεγάλοισι Hdt.3.122; ἀνδριάντι Id.1.183; τυραννίδι Pl.*Grg.*473c, etc.; ἔργοις τοιούτοις Lys.28.8. 3. c. inf., *purpose* or *design to* do, Ἀρίονα ἐκβαλόντες ἔχειν τὰ χρήματα Hdt.1.24; ἐπιχειρήσειν Id.6.137; ποιεῖν Ar.*Pl.*1111; ἐξελθεῖν Th.3.20; καταλῦσαι τὴν δημοκρατίαν Lys.13.12; ἀποκτεινύναι Pl.*R.*566b; also ἐ. ὅπως.. X.*Cyr.*1.4.13: abs., Th.3.82. 4. *to be injurious*, δριμύτητα τοῖς ὀφθαλμοῖς –εύουσαν Paul.Aeg.6.9. II. Pass., with fut. Med. –εύσομαι (in pass. sense) X.*Cyr.*5.4.34: fut. Pass. –ευθήσομαι D.C.52.33: aor. –εβουλεύθην Antipho 4.2.6, Th.1.82, D.22.1, Men.481.15, etc. (but v. supr. I.1b):—*to have plots formed against one, to be the object of plots*, Antipho l.c.; ὑπό τινος Th.4.60,64, Isoc.4.140; εἰς χρήματα D. l.c. 2. of things, *to be designed against*, πρᾶγμα.., ὃ τοῖς θεοῖς..ἐπιβουλεύεται Ar.*Pax* 404: abs., Antipho 2.1.1, Th.3.96; τὰ ἐπιβουλευόμενα *plots*, X.*Eq.Mag.*9.8. –ή, ἡ, *plan formed against* another, *plot, scheme*, Hdt.1.12, Th.4.77,86, Isoc.4.148, etc.; ἐπιβουλὴν ἐπιβουλεύειν Lys.13.18; πρός τινα against one, X.*An.*1.1.8; ἐξ ἐπιβουλῆς *by treachery, treacherously*, ἐξ ἐ. ἀποθανεῖν, ἐξ ἐ. φονεὺς εἶναι, Antipho 2.1.5,1.3, cf. Th.8.92, X.*An.*6.4.7, etc.; μετὰ ἐπιβουλῆς *designedly*, Pl.*Lg.*867a, al. –ία, ἡ, *treachery*, Pi.*N.*4.37, D.S.26.15. –ος, ον, *plotting against*, τοῖς καλοῖς Pl.*Smp.*203d: abs., *treacherous*, νόσοι A.*Supp.*587 (lyr.); of persons, X.*Cyr.*1.6.27, Thphr.*Char.*1.7; [θηρίον] (i.e. παῖς) Pl.*Lg.*808d; δεινὸς καὶ ἐ. a deep *designing fellow*, Lys.*Fr.*75.2; γένος Diph.66.4; πίθηκον, ἐ. κακόν Eub.115; ζῷα ἐ. Arist.*HA*488^{b}16,18; τὰ ἐ. τῶν ἀνθρώπων creatures *which prey on* man, Plu.2.727f; τὰ ἐ. τῆς ψυχῆς Porph.*Antr.*34; ἐ. ἀνέμων *PMag.Leid.V.*7.22: Comp. –ότερον, ζῷον Pl.*Tht.*174d: Sup. –ότατος D.Chr.10.7. Adv. –λως, γίγνεσθαι D.H.11.49, cf. Plu.2.715b, etc.; πράσσειν J.*AJ*17.5.7.

ἐπιβρῑδ-ύνω, *tarry* or *loiter at* a place, Luc.*Tim.*46 (nisi leg. ἔτι βρ.). 2. *to be late* or *in default*, *PFlor.*278ii 13 (iii A.D.), etc. II. trans., *slacken*, opp. ἐπιταχύνειν, τὸν τόνον τῆς ἀπαγγελίας Aristid.*Rh.*p.545S.; of planetary influence, Vett.Val.219.23; intr., of the pulse, Gal.8.492. –υς, εια, υ, *slow, hesitating*, Hsch. s.v. μελλονικιᾶν.

ἐπιβρᾰχεῖν, aor. 2 inf. with no pres. in use, *echo, resound*, ἐπέβραχε Q.S.5.498, 8.408; in tmesi, A.R.4.642, Orph.*A.*995.

ἐπί-βρεγμα, ατος, τό, *wet application, lotion*, Philonid.ap.Ath.15.692; *affusion, douche*, Dsc.4.170, Gal.19.720; *decoction*, Ruf.*Ren.Ves.*7.3. –βρεκτέον, *one must foment*, Id.*Sat.Gon.*45.

ἐπιβρέμω, *make to roar*, τὸ δ' (sc. πῦρ) ἐπιβρέμει ἶς ἀνέμοιο Il.17.739:—Med., *roar*, χείλεσιν δεινὸν ἐ. χελιδών (comicé) Ar.*Ra.*680 (lyr.), cf. Opp.*C.*4.171. II. *roar out*, [ἐπ'] εὐάσμασι τοιάδ' ἐπιβρέμει E.*Ba.*151: abs., *ring*, οὔασιν ἠχῇ Musae.193; στεροπῇσιν Q.S.14.458.

ἐπιβρέχω, *pour water on*, *water*, cj. for ἀποβρίθουσι in Thphr.*HP* 5.3.3; *rain upon*, παγίδας ἐπί τινας Lxx *Ps.*10(11).6. II. impers., *it rains*, Simp. *in Epict.*p.92 D.

ἐπιβρῑθ-ής, ές, *falling heavy upon*, A.*Eu.*965 (lyr.). –ω, *fall heavy upon, fall heavily*, of rain, ὅτ' ἐπιβρίσῃ Διὸς ὄμβρος Il.5.91, 12.286; in good sense, ὁππότε δὴ Διὸς ὧραι ἐπιβρίσειαν ὕπερθεν when the seasons *weigh down* [the vines], i.e. make the clusters heavy, Od.24.344; *press down*, μένος τῆς πορθμίδος Ael.*NA*13.19; of winds, Thphr.*Vent.*34; ἐπ' ἄλσεα Q.S.3.326: c. dat., ἐλάτῃσι Id.12.124, cf. 2.371, al.: metaph., μή ποτ' ἐπιβρίσῃ πόλεμος Il.7.343; of persons, ἐπέβρισαν.. ἀμφὶ ἄνακτα *pressed closely, thronged* around him, 12.414, cf. Theoc.22.93, App.*BC*4.25; esp. in Tactics, *exert pressure*, τοῖς σώμασι Ascl.*Tact.*5.2, cf. Arr.*Tact.*12.10; τοῖς πεζοῖς Jul.*Or.*1.36d: generally, ᾗ ἂν ἐπιβρίσῃ Porph.*Abst.*1.43; also of wealth, ὄλβος εὖτ' ἂν ἐπιβρίσαις ἕπηται follows *in full weight*, Pi.*P.*3.106; of love, Opp.*C.*1.392; of wine, ib.4.351; of sleep, *AP*9.481 (Jul.). II. trans., *press on*, τὸν κριὸν ἐπὶ τὰ γέρρα J.*BJ*3.7.23; *press home*, ἀκωκὴν ἐ. Opp.*H.*2.467.

ἐπιβρῑμάομαι, *to be angry at*, *Gloss.*; cf. ἐπιβρωμάομαι: also ἐπιβριμεῖ (sic)· ἐπιφωνεῖ, Hsch.

ἐπιβρομέω, *roar upon* or *over*, of the sea, σπιλάδεσσιν A.R.3.1371; of sea-birds, *scream over*, πελάγεσσιν Id.4.240. 2. c. acc. cogn., βρύχημα, of lions, Opp.*C.*3.36; κτύπον Nonn.*D.*6.115. 3. Pass., ὄφρ'.. ἐπιβρομέωνται ἀκουαί *may be filled with the sound*, A.R.4.908.

ἐπιβροντ-άω, *thunder in response*, Plu.*Marc.*12: impers., *it thunders as well*, Ps.-Gem.*Calend.*p.183W. –ητος, ον, = ἐμβρόντητος, *frantic*, S.*Aj.*1386.

ἐπιβροχέω, *tie with a noose* or *ligament*, τὸ περιτόναιον Gal.14.789.

ἐπιβροχή, ἡ, *wetting, bathing*, Gal.14.732, Sor.1.67 (pl.).

ἐπίβροχος, ον, *rainy*, ἑσπέρα Lyd.*Ost.*62.

ἐπιβρύκω [ῡ], *snap at* another, dub. for ἀπο–, Archipp.35. II. ἐ. ὀδόντα *gnash* the teeth, *AP*7.433 (Tymn.):—also in form **ἐπιβρύχω**, abs., *gnash the teeth*, Herod.6.13.

ἐπιβρῡχάομαι, *roar at*, Nonn.*D.*2.245: abs., λέων –ώμενος Aristid.*Or.*28(49).124.

ἐπιβρύχω, v. ἐπιβρύκω.

ἐπιβρύω, fut. –ύσω [ῠ], *burst over*, as water: of flowers, *burst forth*, Theoc.22.43; ἐ. σκώληξι *to be overrun by*.., Alciphr.1.17.

ἐπιβρωμάομαι, *bray at*, λεχωῖσιν Call.*Del.*56 (nisi leg. ἐπεβριμᾶτο).

ἐπιβρωτέον, *one must eat afterwards*, Philum.*Ven.*21.4.

ἐπιβύστρα, ἡ, *stopper, stoppage*, ὤτων Luc.*Lex.*1.

ἐπιβύω, fut. –ύσω [ῡ], *stop up*, εἰ μὴ.. ἐπιβύσει τις αὐτοῦ τὸ στόμα Cratin.186; τὸ στόμ' ἐπιβύσας κέρμασιν τῶν ῥητόρων Ar.*Pl.*379:—Med., ἐπιβύσασθαι τὰ ὦτα Luc.*Tim.*9, *Pr.Im.*29.

ἐπιβωθέω, Ion. for ἐπιβοηθέω (q.v.).

ἐπιβωμ-ίζω, *sacrifice at an altar*, *PSI*4.435.8, *PCair.Zen.*34.8 (iii B.C.), cf. Hsch. –ιος, ον, *on* or *at the altar*, ψόλος A.*Fr.*24; πῦρ E.*Andr.*1024 (lyr.); βοῦς *AP*9.453 (Mel.); ἐπιβώμια μῆλ' ἐρύσαι drag them *to the altar*, A.R.4.1129; θεοῖς ἐπιβώμια ῥέζειν Theoc.16.26; ἐ. δᾷδες Hld.10.16; ἐπιβώμιος (sc. λόγος), ὁ, Hp.*Ep.*26; Δημοσθένης ἐ. *seated on an altar*, *IG*14.1146. II. Subst., *priest of an altar*, *Ath.Mitt.*35.457 (Pergam.). –ιοστᾰτέω (as if from a Subst. ἐπιβωμιοστάτης), *stand suppliant at the altar*, E.*Heracl.*44. –ίς, = Lat. *altarium*, *Gloss.* –ίτης [ῑ], ου, ὁ, *one who attends the altar, a sacrificing priest*, Lysim.ap.J.*Ap.*1.34 (pl.).

ἐπιβώσομαι, Ion. for ἐπιβοήσομαι, fut. of ἐπιβοάω, Hom.

ἐπιβωστρέω, Ion. and Dor. for ἐπιβοάω, *shout to, call upon*, τινά Theoc.12.35 (nisi leg. ἐπιβῶται).

ἐπίβωτος, ον, Ion. for ἐπιβόητος.

ἐπιβώτωρ, ορος, ὁ, *shepherd*, ἐπιβώτορι μήλων Od.13.222.

ἐπίγαιος, ον, *upon the earth*, τὰ ἐ. *the parts on* or *near the ground*, Hdt.2.125; cf. ἐπίγειος.

ἐπιγαιόω, *make into land*, Zos.2.35.2 (Pass.).

ἐπιγαμβρ-εία, ἡ, *connexion by marriage*, *Peripl.M.Rubr.*16 (–βρίαν codd.), dub. in J.*BJ*1.8.9. –ευμα, ατος, τό, = foreg., Sch.E.*Or.*477. –ευσις, εως, ἡ, = foreg., Anon. *in Rh.*78.31 (–γάμευσις codd.). –ευτής, οῦ, ὁ, *one connected by marriage*, Aq.*De.*25.7. –εύω, *become son-in-law*, τῷ βασιλεῖ Lxx 1*Ki.*18.22, cf. Lyd.*Mens.*1.13. 2. *become father-in-law*, τινί Lxx 1*Ma.*10.54,56. II. ἐ. γυναῖκα *take* a woman *to wife as her husband's next of kin*, ib.*Ge.*38.8 (v.l.), *Ev.Matt.*22.24. III. Med., *intermarry with*, Lxx *Ge.*34.9, 2*Ch.*18.1.

ἐπιγᾰμ-έω, *marry besides*, ἐ. πόσει πόσιν *wed one* husband *after* another, E.*Or.*589; τῇ θυγατρὶ ἐ. τὴν μητέρα *marry* the mother *after* the daughter, And.1.128; ἐ. τέκνοις μητρυιάν *marry and set* a stepmother *over* one's children, E.*Alc.*305, cf. Plu.*Cat.Ma.*24; ἡ ἐπιγαμηθεῖσα γυνή *the second* wife, D.S.16.93, cf. Plu.*Them.*32. –ία, ἡ, *additional marriage*, Ath.13.560c. 2. *connexion by marriage*, J.*AJ*17.1.1, al.; πρός τινα Id.*BJ*1.12.13. II. *right of intermarriage* between states, ἐπιγαμίας..καὶ ἐπεργασίας καὶ ἐπινομίας X.*Cyr.*3.2.23; Ἀθαναίοις δόμεν ἐπιγαμίαν Decr.Byz.ap.D.18.91, cf. *GDI*5040 (Hierapytna), Wilcken *Chr.*27 (ii A.D.). b. = Lat. *conubium*, *BGU*265.7 (ii A.D.), etc.: generally, *intermarriage*, mostly pl., ἐπιγαμίας ποιεῖσθαι Hdt.2.147; ἀλλήλοις X.*Cyr.*1.5.3, cf. Decr.ap.D.18.187 (sg.); Εὐβοεῦσιν Lys.34.3; παρ' ἀλλήλοις X.*HG*5.2.19; πρὸς ἀλλήλους Arist.*Pol.*1280^{b}16, Str.5.3.4; ἐπιγαμίαις χρῆσθαι Arist.*Pol.*1280^{b}36. –ιος, ον, *nuptial*, εὐχαί Ph.2.301. –ος, ον, *marriageable*, masc. in Hdt.1.196; more freq. as fem., D.40.4, Pl.*Ep.*361d, Men.658, *Epit.*575, etc. II. = πατρῷος, Hsch. (fort. ἐπίπαμος· πατρῷχος).

ἐπιγᾰν-όω, *varnish, glaze*, σιλφίῳ Alex.186.10; cf. ἐπαγάνωσις.

ἐπιγάνῠμαι [ᾰ], *exult in*, τινί Hsch.

ἐπιγάστριος, ον, *over the belly*: τὸ ἐ. the *covering of the abdominal* *cavity* from thorax to pubes, Ruf.*Onom.*97, Sor.2.55, Gal.17(2).534, Aret.*SA*2.10, Plu.2.559f, *PSI*3.252.37 (iii A.D.): esp. of *the part above the navel*, Poll.2.170, Ps.-Gal.14.705.

ἐπίγαυρον· ἰσχυρόν, Hsch.

ἐπιγαυρόω, *make proud*, ἑαυτούς Plu.2.78c; τινὰς τιμαῖς καὶ ἀρχαῖς D.C.56.3:—Pass., *to be proud of, exult in*, ἐπιγαυρωθεὶς τῇ ἐντολῇ X.*Cyr.*2.4.30, cf. Them.*Or.*11.143c: abs., Plu.*Oth.*17, 2.760f.

ἐπιγδουπέω, Ep. for ἐπιδουπέω, *shout at* or *in applause*, ἐπὶ δ' ἐγδούπησαν Ἀθηναίη τε καὶ Ἥρη Il.11.45: abs., *sound aloud*, *AP*9.662 (Agath.): c. acc. cogn., καναχὴν ἐ. Nonn.*D.*1.243.

ἐπιγεΐζω, *live on earth*, ψυχὴ ἀνθρωπευομένη καὶ ἄλλως ἐπιγεΐζουσα Herm.ap.Stob.1.49.68.

ἐπιγείνομαι, = ἐπιγίγνομαι, Pi.*P.*4.47 (nisi metri gr. pro ἐπιγενομένων).

ἐπιγειόκαυλος, ον, *with procumbent stem*, Thphr.*HP*6.4.5, cj. in 7.8.1.

ἐπίγειος, ον, *on* or *of the earth, terrestrial*, ζῷα Pl.*R.*546a; βροτοί *IG*14.1571; opp. ὑπόγειος, *PMag.Par.*1.3043 (iii A.D.), etc. 2. *creeping*, of plants, Thphr.*HP*3.18.6, 6.2.2, al.; but *land*-plants, opp. water-plants, Arist.*PA*681^{a}21; *living on the ground*, [ὄρνιθες], τετράποδα, Id.*HA*633^{b}1, *PA*657^{b}24. 3. neut. pl., ἐπίγεια *ground-floor*, opp. πύργος διώρυφος, *PPetr.*2 p.20 (iii B.C.). II. Subst. ἐπίγειον, τό, misspelling of ἐπίγυον, v.l. in Ar.*Fr.*80,426. (Cf. ἐπίγαιος.)

ἐπιγειόφυλλος, ον, *with radical leaves flat on the ground, rosulate*, Thphr.*HP*7.8.3, 9.10.1.

ἐπιγεισόω, *put on a coping-stone*, Hsch. s. v. ἐθρίγκωσεν.

ἐπιγειτνιάω, *border upon*, Hsch. s. v. ἐπιχωρεῖ.

ἐπιγελαστάρ· ὁ καταγελῶν (Lacon.), Hsch.

ἐπιγελάω, fut. -άσομαι [ᾰ] Lxx*Pr.*1.26:—*laugh approvingly*, γέλασσαν δ' ἐπὶ πάντες Ἀχαιοί Il.23.840, cf. Pl.*Phd.*62a, X.*Ap.*28, etc.; ἐ. χορείαις *smile upon*, Ar.*Th.*979 (lyr.); τινὶ σκώψαντι Thphr.*Char.*2.4: abs., κύματα ἐπιγελᾷ *break with a plashing sound*, Arist.*Pr.*931^{a}35; στόματα ἐπιγελῶντα, of the mouths of rivers, Str.1.4.2 (s. v.l.); λόγοι ἐπιγελῶντες *pleasant* words, Plu.2.27f. 2. metaph., *sparkle on the surface*, ἐπεγέλασέ τις ὕλη τῷ μίγματι Herm.ap.Stob.1.49.44. II. = ἐπεγγελάω, Lxx*Pr.*1.26, Gal.6.234, Luc.*Bis Acc.*5; τῷ δυστυχοῦντι Chilo ap.Stob.3.1.172.

ἐπιγεμ-ίζω, *lay as a burden*, ἐπὶ ὄνους Lxx*Ne.*13.15, cf. *AB* 94. **-ισις,** εως, ἡ, perh. *straining, spiritus cohibitio* κατ' ἐπιγέμισιν *vocata*, Gal.4.222 Chart.

ἐπιγέν-ημα, ατος, τό, *excess of price realized over cost, profit*, *PPetr.*2 p.2 (iii B.C.); opp. ἔκδεια, *PRev.Laws*17.2 (iii B.C.). **-ής,** ές, *growing after* (opp. συγγενής), φακός Poll.4.194.

ἐπιγενν-άω, *generate after*, *Theol.Ar.*64:—Pass., κοινὸν πάντων εὐτύχημα ἐπεγεννήθη Καῖσαρ *Inscr.Prien.*105.9 (i B.C.), cf. Ath.14.653d: metaph., *spring up*, Phld.*D.*1.16. **-ημα,** Dor. **-ᾱμα** (Ps.-Archyt.ap.Stob.3.1.112), ατος, τό, *that which grows upon*: hence, *coating* of the tongue, Hp.*Coac.*225. 2. *superfetation*, Steph.*in Hp.*2.470 D. II. *that which is produced after*, Plu.2.637e, Longin. 6; κατὰ ἐ. *accidental*, opp. congenital, Antyll.ap.Orib.50.2.1. 2. *result, consequence*, Plb.*Fr.*41 (pl.), Phld.*Ir.*p.40 W., al.; ἡ ἑβδόμη ἐ. ἐξάδος Ph.1.237; as philosoph. term of the Stoics, *subsequent manifestation*, *Stoic.*3.19, Chrysipp.ib.3.43. 3. Medic. (καθάπερ ἐν ταῖς ἀρρωστίαις Plb. l. c.), *after-symptom*, Gal.7.43, Erasistr.ap.eund.14.729; σύμπτωμά ἐστι τοῦ πάθους ἐ. Gal.19.395. **-ημᾰτικός,** ή, όν, *of the nature of an* ἐπιγέννημα, *resulting, consequential*, *Stoic.*3.137; ἐν τῇ ψυχῇ τὸ ἓν οὐκ ἐ. ὡς ἐπὶ τοῦ σώματος Dam.*Pr.*237. Adv. **-κῶς** Chrysipp.*Stoic.*2.247. **-ησις,** εως, ἡ, *increase of population*, *BGU* 111.21 (ii A.D.), etc. II. *extra growth*, τῶν τοπικῶν σαρκῶν Leonid. ap.Aët.15.5. **-ητός,** όν, *formed above, adnate*, ὑδροκήλη, of encysted hydrocele, Heliod.ap.Orib.50.31 tit.; καλοῦσι..τοῦτο τὸ πάθος "ἐν ἐπιγεν⟨ν⟩ητῷ (sc. χιτῶνι)" Paul.Aeg.6.62 (in tunica superagnata vocamus, Leonid.ap.Aët.14.22).

ἐπιγεοῦχος, ὁ, *landowner*, *CPR*36.21 (iii A.D.).

ἐπιγεραίρω, *give honour to*, τινά X.*Cyr.*8.6.11.

ἐπιγεύομαι, *taste of*, τινός cj. in Ael.*NA*4.15.

ἐπιγεώμοροι, οἱ, *those next to the* γεώμοροι, *artisans*, *AB*257.

ἐπιγεωργέω, *continue cultivating*, *PFrankf.*1.38 (iii B.C.), *PTeb.* 105.50 (ii B.C.).

ἐπιγηθέω, *rejoice, triumph over*, ὡς μήτε θεὸς μήτε τις ἄλλος τοῖσδ' ἐπεγήθει A.*Pr.*157; *exult in*, γάμῳ ἐπιγηθήσαντες Opp.*H.*1.570:—also in form **-γήθω,** τοῖς γινομένοις Simp.*in Epict.*p.88 D.

ἐπιγηράσκω, *grow old one upon another*, Jul.*Ep.*180 (citing Od.7.120).

ἐπιγίγνομαι, Ion. and later **-γίνομαι** [γῑ], fut. ἐπιγενήσομαι: aor. 2 ἐπεγενόμην: pf. ἐπιγέγονα: I. of Time, *to be born after, come into being after*, ἔαρος δ' ἐπιγίγνεται ὥρῃ (sc. φύλλα, nisi leg. ὥρη) Il.6.148; of persons, Hdt.7.2; οἱ ἐπιγινόμενοι ἄνθρωποι *posterity*, Id.9.85; οἱ ἐπιγενόμενοι τούτῳ σοφισταί *who came after* him, Id.2.49; ἀνάγκη τὰ -όμενα κρατεῖν the *new* must prevail over the old, Th.1.71, cf. Pl.*R.*574a; ἀντὶ τῶν ἀποθανόντων ἕτεροι..[ἐπιγενήσονται] X.*Cyr.*6.1.12, cf. Th.6.26; τῇ ἐπιγιγνομένῃ ἡμέρᾳ the *following*, the *next*.., Id.3.75; τοῦ ἐπιγιγνομένου θέρους Id.4.52; χρόνου ἐπιγενομένου as time *went on*, Ht.1.28, cf. Th.1.126 (v.l.); χρόνος..παρὰ λόγον ἐπιγιγνόμενος Id.4.26; τὰ ἐπὶ τούτῳ ἐπιγενόμενα *that happened after*.., Hdt.8.37. 2. *follow*, of a fleet, Th.3.77. II. of things, *come at the end, come as fulfilment*, c. dat., βουλαῖς οὐκ ἐπέγεντο τέλος Thgn.640; τὸ τέλος, ἡ τελευτὴ ἐ. τινί, Hdt.3.65, 7.157; esp. of sudden changes of weather and the like, *supervene*, καί σφι..ἅμα τῇ βροντῇ σεισμὸν ἐπιγενέσθαι Id.5.85; πλέουσι αὐτοῖσι χειμὼν..ἐπεγίνετο Id.8.13, cf. Th.4.3; ἐ. σφι τέρεα Hdt.8.37; νὺξ ἐ. ib.70; νὺξ ἐ. τῷ ἔργῳ Th.4.25; ἄνεμος ἐπεγένετο τῇ φλογί *seconded* the flame, Id.3.74: abs., τοσαύτη ἡ ξυμφορὰ ἐπεγεγένητο Id.8.96, cf. 1.16; ἐπιγενομένου νότου *Act.Ap.*28.13; τὴν ἐπιγινομένην ἡδονὴν..τοῖς ἔργοις the *supervening* pleasure, Arist.*EN*1104^{b}4; μέμψις καὶ μετάνοια ἐ. πράξεσι Plu.*Tim.*36. 2. *come in after*, ἐπὶ τῇ ναυμαχίῃ ἐ. Ἱστιαῖος Hdt.6.27, cf. Ar.*Eq.*136; *come upon, assault, attack*, τινί Th.3.30, 4.93; ἀφυλάκτοις καὶ ἐξαίφνης ἐ. Id.7.32, cf. 3.108; of disease, ἀρρωστία ἐ. D.36.7: freq. in Hp. of additional symptoms, *supervene*, *Aph.*5.2, *Art.*69, al. 3. *befall, come to pass*, Th.5.20. 4. *fall to* one, *become due*, μισθώσεις ἐ. D.36.9; τὰ ἐπιγινόμενα *the accruing interest*, Arist.*Pol.*1280^{a}30, cf. *IG*1^2.236, al., *BGU*8 ii 4 (iii A.D.), etc. 5. *to be incident to*, δόξῃ ἐ. ψεῦδός τε καὶ ἀληθές Pl.*Phlb.* 37b. 6. *to be added*, πρός τι Arist.*Cael.*297^{a}32.

ἐπιγιγνώσκω, Ion. and later **-γῑνώσκω,** *look upon, witness, observe*, ἵνα πάντες ἐπιγνώωσι..μαρναμένους Od.18.30; τινὰ ὀργιζόμενον X.*Cyr.*8.1.33, cf. S.*Aj.*18: rarely c. gen., Pi.*P.*4.279. II. *recognize*, αἴ κέ μ' ἐπιγνώῃ Od.24.217; ὅπως μήτηρ σε μὴ 'πιγνώσεται φαιδρῷ προσώπῳ by thy glad face, S.*El.*1296, cf. Pl.*Tht.*192e (v.l.). 2. of things, *find out, discover*, ἔργον A.*Ag.*1598, cf. Th.1.132, etc.; τὰ γεγονότα Plb.2.11.3; ἐπιγνοίης ἂν αὐτὴν [τὴν σοφίαν]..οἰκείαν γενομένην; *would you recognize* when it became your own?, Pl.*Euthd.*301e; ἐπιγνοὺς ἄνδρα δίκαιον *IG*9(2).313 (Tricca); ἐ. ὅτι.. Arist.*HA*631^{b}11; τὸν πόλεμον ἐ. τίνα φύσιν ἔχει Plb.1.65.6, cf. *POxy.*930.14 (ii/iii A.D.); ἐ. εἰ.. Lxx*Ge.*37.32, *PFay.*112.14 (i A.D.):—Pass., Phylarch.10 J. b. *find out too late*, ἐπιγνώσῃ τί σπάνις ἐστὶ φίλων *AP*12.186 (Strat.). 3. *learn to know*, θεόν S.*Ant.*960 (lyr.). 4. *take notice of*, Lxx*Ru.*2.10. b. *show favour to*, πρόσωπον ib.*De.*16.19. III. *come to a judgement, decide*, τι περί τινος Th.3.57; τὰ πρόσφορα τοῖς οἰχομένοις Id.2.65; ἐπιγνῶναι μηδέν *come to* no *new resolve*, Id.1.70; ἐ. τι εἶναί τινος *adjudicate* it as his property, D.H.11.52. IV. *recognize, acknowledge, approve*, 1*Ep.Cor.*16.18; ἐ. σε τῆς ἐπιμελείας Chio *Ep.*6. 2. *recognize* an obligation, *undertake* to discharge or deliver, *PLips.*22.14 (iv A.D.), etc.

ἐπιγλισχραίνω, *make still more viscid*, Hp.*Acut.*17.

ἐπιγλῠκ-αίνω, *sweeten*, Dion.Byz.2, Gal.14.277, Philum.ap.Orib. 45.29.8. II. intr., *to be sweetish*, Thphr.*CP*6.15.4. **-υς,** εια, υ, *somewhat sweet*, Id.*HP*3.18.10.

ἐπιγλῠφ-ίς, = Lat. *cala* (?), *Gloss.* **-ω,** *carve on the surface*, Lxx 1*Ma.*13.29; τύπον δακτυλίῳ Iamb.*Protr.*21.κγ'.

ἐπιγλωσσ-άομαι, Att. **-ττάομαι,** *utter abuse*, μηδ' ἐπιγλωσσῶ κακά A.*Ch.*1045; περὶ τῶν Ἀθηνῶν οὐκ ἐπιγλωττήσομαι τοιοῦτον οὐδέν Ar.*Lys.*37. II. c. gen., *vent reproaches against*, ταῦτ' ἐπιγλωσσᾷ Διός A.*Pr.*928. **-ίς,** Att. **-ττίς,** ίδος, ἡ, *valve which covers the larynx, epiglottis*, Hp.*Cord.*2, Arist.*HA*492^{b}34, etc. 2. of the *vocal chords*, Gal.8.50.

ἐπιγναμπτ-ός, ή, όν, *curved, twisted*, ἕλικες *h.Ven.*87. **-ω,** *curve, bend*, ἆξαι ἐπιγνάμψας δόρυ Il.21.178; ἐπεγνάμπτοντο δὲ κῶπαι A.R. 2.591. II. metaph., *bow, bend to one's purpose*, ἐπέγναμψεν ἅπαντας Ἥρη λισσομένη Il.2.14; ἐπιγνάμψασα φίλον κῆρ 1.569; ἐπιγνάμπτει νόον ἐσθλῶν 9.514:—Med., Nic.*Al.*363.

ἐπιγνάπτω, *clean* clothes: *smarten up*, ἑαυτόν Luc.*Fug.*28.

ἐπιγνᾰφεῖον and **-ῆϊον,** τό, (γνάφος) *angle-stone of a* γεῖσον, so called from its resemblance to a carding comb, *SIG*245*G*21,22 (Delph., iv B.C.).

ἐπίγνᾰφος, ον, *cleaned*, of clothes, Poll.7.77; cf. δευτερουργός II.

ἐπι-γνώμας, α, = ἐπιγνώμων, title of magistrate at Mantinea, *IG* 5(2).269.32 (i B.C.; nom. -γνώμα appears to occur, ib.265.34): **-γνωμονεύω,** *hold this office*, ib.275.7. **-γνώμη,** ἡ, = συγγνώμη, διάγνωσις, Hsch. **-γνωμοσύνη,** ἡ, *prudence*, Lxx*Pr.*16.23. **-γνώμων,** ονος, ὁ, ἡ, *arbiter, umpire, judge*, c. gen. rei, Pl.*Lg.*828b, Lxx *Pr.*12.26, *CIG* (add.) 3641*b* 27 (Lampsacus); αἰτιῶν Plu.*Cam.*18; ὀσφρήσιος, of the nose, Hp.*Ep.*23; ἐ. τῆς τιμῆς *appraiser*, D.37.40: abs., Luc.*Deor.Conc.*15. 2. in pl., *inspectors*, Lys.7.25 ap.Harp. (γνώμονας codd.). II. = συγγνώμων, *pardoning*, τινί Mosch.4.70. III. *acquainted with*, φύσεως, γυναικῶν, Ph.1.29, 2.274; τέχνης S.E.*M.*7.56. **-γνωρίζω,** *make known, announce, signify*, ἀληθῆ εἶναι ταῦτα X.*Cyn.*6.23:—Pass., Sm.*Pr.*20.11. II. *recognize*, J.*AJ*19.3.1. **-γνωσις,** εως, ἡ, *recognition*, c. gen., Phld.*Lib.* p.49 O.; σφραγίδων Hdn.7.6.7; [τινῶν] διὰ βοῆς, δι' ὀμμάτων, J.*BJ*6.2.6; ἐς ἐπίγνωσιν App.*Praef.*13; *recognition* of a mistake, D.S.17.114; *determination* of a fact, *PTeb.*24.23 (ii B.C.). 2. *knowledge*, τινός Plb.3.7.6, 3.31.4, Attal.ap.Hipparch.1.8.10, cf. Ph.*Bel.*59.2; τοῦ μέλλοντος Ph.2.222; μουσικῆς Plu.2.1145a; θεοῦ Lxx*Pr.*2.5, cf. *Ep. Rom.*10.2, etc.; τὸν θεὸν ἔχειν ἐν ἐπιγνώσει ib.1.28, etc.; λαβὼν κανόνας εἰς ἐπίγνωσιν τῆς ἀληθείας Arr.*Epict.*2.20.21, cf. S.E.*M.*7.259; ἐ. ἐπιστημονική scientific *theory*, *Theol.Ar.*17. II. *decision*, πρὸς -σιν κεκαθίκασιν *SIG*826*D*16; θεῶν ἐ. Him.*Or.*1.17. **-γνωστέον,** *one must know*, ὅτι.. Nicom.*Ar.*2.6; *one must recognize, discern*, Aristid.Quint.1.21. **-γνωστικός,** ή, όν, *able to discern*, c. gen., Arr. *Epict.*2.3.4. **-γνωστος,** ον, *known*, Lxx*Jb.*18.19. **-γνώωσι,** Ep. 3 pl. aor. 2 subj. of ἐπιγιγνώσκω.

ἐπιγογγύζω, *murmur at*, Hsch. s. v. ἐπιτρύζουσιν.

ἐπιγομφόω, *nail, rivet on*, ἀστράγαλον *IG*1^2.372*E*.

ἐπιγονᾰτίς, ίδος, ἡ, *knee-pan*, Ruf.ap.Orib.25.1.50, Sor.1.103, Gal. 2.303; cf. ἐπιγουνατίς. II. *garment reaching to the knee*, Paus. Gr.*Fr.*144.

ἐπιγόνειον, τό, Egyptian harp, with forty strings arranged in pairs as in the μάγαδις, named from the inventor Epigonus, Juba ap. Ath. 4.183c, Poll. 4.59.

ἐπιγονή, ἡ, *increase, growth*, ἐ. λαμβάνειν become *larger*, Plu. 2.506f; μείζονος κακίας Luc. *Tim.* 3; ἐνιαυτοῦ αἰγῶν κτλ. ἐ. the year's *produce*, Plu. *Fab.* 4; τὴν ἐ. μακαρίαν [γίνεσθαι] *SIG* 695.48 (ii B.C.); θρεμμάτων Ph. 2.234; ζῴων Porph. *Abst.* 1.16; ἐξ ἐπιγονῆς ἐπιγεγενημένοι πῶλοι *BGU* 353.14 (ii A.D.). 2. *offspring, breed*, ἵππων D.S. 4.15; of men, Lxx 2*Ch.* 31.16. II. in Egypt, *descendants of foreign military settlers*, Μακεδών, Ἰουδαῖος τῆς ἐ., Wilcken *Chr.* 241 (iii B.C.), Mitteis *Chr.* 21.13 (iii B.C.), etc.; later apptly. used in legal fictions of a category of persons, Πέρσης τῆς ἐ. *PStrassb.* 83.12 (ii B.C.), *BGU* 1134 (i B.C./i A.D.), etc.

ἐπίγονος, ον, *born besides*, of superfetation, Hp. *Vict.* 1.31. II. as Subst., ἐπίγονοι, οἱ, *offspring, posterity*, A. *Th.* 903 (lyr.); *breed*, of bees, prob. in X. *Oec.* 7.34. 2. οἱ Ἐπίγονοι *the Afterborn*, sons of the chiefs who fell in the first war against Thebes, title of Cyclic Epic ascribed to Homer, Hdt. 4.32, cf. Pi. *P.* 8.42, D.S. 4.66, etc. b. of the Heraclids, Hecat. 30 J. c. *descendants* of the successors to Alexander's dominions, περὶ Ἀλεξάνδρου καὶ τῶν διαδόχων καὶ ἐ., title of work by Nymphis, Suid. s.v. Νύμφις, cf. D.S. 1.3, D.H. 1.6, Str. 15.3.24; τῷ Ἐπιγόνου κούρῳ, of Antigonus Gonatas, *BMus. Inscr.* 797.8 (Cnidus). d. corps of barbarian youths in Alexander's army, Arr. *An.* 7.6.1. e. in Egypt, *belonging to the* ἐπιγονή II, *PSI* 6.588.7 (iii B.C.), *UPZ* 14.70 (ii B.C.). 3. *after-born*, i.e. *born after* or *besides the presumptive heir*, Pl. *Lg.* 740c, 929d. b. *issue of second marriage*, Poll. 3.25.

ἐπιγουν-ἄτίς, ίδος, ἡ, Ion. for ἐπιγονατίς, Hp. *Oss.* 17. **-ίδιος** [ῐδ], ον, *upon the knee*, βρέφος ἐ. κατθηκάμενος Pi. *P.* 9.62. **-ίς**, ίδος, ἡ, *part above the knee, great muscle of the thigh*, taken as a sign of strength and vigour, κεν.. μεγάλην ἐπιγουνίδα θεῖτο he would grow a stout *thigh-muscle*, Od. 17.225; οἵην ἐπιγουνίδα φαίνει 18.74, cf. Theoc. 26.34, Alciphr. 3.19, Philostr. *Im.* 2.24; prob. in this sense in A.R. 3.875. II. = ἐπιγονατίς, *knee-pan*, Hp. *Art.* 70, 77, Philostr. *Gym.* 35; *knee*, Arat. 254, 614.

ἐπιγράβδην, Adv., (ἐπιγράφω) *scraping the surface, grazing*, Il. 21.166. II. *like lines*, Orph. *L.* 365.

ἐπίγραμμ-α, ατος, τό, *inscription*, E. *Tr.* 1191; esp. of the name of the maker on a work of art, or of the dedicator on an offering, Hdt. 5.59, 7.228, Th. 6.54, 59. b. *sepulchral inscription in verse, epitaph*, *IG* 14.1746, etc. c. *commemorative inscription*, D. 20.112: hence, = ἐπιγραφή I.4, App. *Pun.* 94. 2. *short poem*, usu. in elegiac verse, *epigram*, Hieronym. Rhod. ap. Ath. 13.604f, Callistr. ap. eund. 3.125c, etc. 3. *title* of a work, Alex. 135.4, 10, D.H. *Rh.* 8.8, Gal. 6.372, etc.; of a picture, Ael. *VH* 9.11. 4. *written estimate* or *demand* of damages, D. 38.2; *title* or *label* of a criminal charge, Arist. *Rh.* 1374^{a}1. 5. *mark branded* on a slave's forehead, Herod. 5.79. **-άτιον**, τό, Dim. of ἐπίγραμμα, Plu. *Cat. Ma.* 1, Antig. *Mir.* 89. **-ἄτιστής**, οῦ, ὁ, = sq., Sidon. Apoll. *Ep.* 4.1. **-ἄτογράφος** [γρᾰ], ὁ, *writing epigrams*, prob. in *AP* 7.715 (lemma), cf. Sch. Theoc. 7.40. **-ἄτοποιός**, ὁ, *epigrammatist*, Phld. *Po.* 5.35.9, D.L. 6.14. **-ἄτοφόρος**, ὁ, f.l. for -γράφος in *AP* 7.715 (lemma), Tz. *H.* 8.425. **-ή**, ἡ, in pl., *markings*, καθ' ὅλον τὸ σῶμα Aët. 13.20. **-ος**, *superpostum* (?), *Gloss.*

ἐπιγρἄφ-εύς, έως, ὁ, *inscriber*: at Athens, *registrar* of property, etc. (cf. sq. II. 2), Antipho Soph. 112, Poll. 8.103, *AB* 254, Harp.; prob. for -φῶν in Isoc. 17.41. II. = ζωγράφος, Hsch. **-ή**, ἡ, *inscription*, στηλῶν on stones, Th. 2.43, cf. Arist. *Mir.* 843^{b}17, J. *AJ* 15.8.1; on a vase, *BCH* 6.6 (Delos, ii B.C.); on statues, Plb. 5.9.3. 2. *title* of a work, Id. 3.9.3, Luc. *Hist. Conscr.* 30, etc. 3. *name* of a ship, *OGI* 447 (i B.C.). 4. *ascription* of a deed to its author, *credit* or *honour* of a thing, τὴν ἐ. τινος λαβεῖν Plb. 1.31.4, cf. *PSI* 4.424.9 (iii B.C.); ἀπενέγκασθαι D.S. 16.50, cf. Jul. *Caes.* 322d. 5. *insertion, interlineation* in a document, *PLond.* 2.178.13 (ii A.D.), *PRyl.* 316.2 (pl., ii A.D.). II. *description* of parties in pleadings, Is. 4.2. 2. *registration of property for taxation*, in pl., Isoc. 17.41 codd. (v. foreg.). 3. *impost, tax*, *PSI* 5.510.11 (iii B.C.); *assessment*, *POxy.* 1445.8 (ii A.D.), etc. 4. *requisition*, ὑποζυγίων *BCH* 46.309 (Teos). **-ικός**, ή, όν, *concerning assessments* (?), *IG* 11(2).159 *A* 64 (Delos, iii B.C.). **-ω**, *mark the surface, graze*, ὀϊστὸς ἐπέγραψε χρόα φωτός Il. 4.139, cf. 13.553, Poll. 4.179; μιν ἐπιγράψας having *put a mark on* the lot, Il. 7.187; ἄκροις δακτύλοις ἐ. *trifle with* dishes, Luc. *Am.* 42.—In Hom. the word has not the sense of *writing*. II. *write upon, inscribe*, γράμματα Hdt. 3.88; τάδε Id. 4.88; ἐ. ὀνομαστὶ τὰς πόλεις Th. 1.132, cf. D. 59.97; ἐπίγραμμα ὃ.. προείλεθ' ἡ πόλις αὐτοῖς ἐπιγράψαι Id. 18.289: abs., ἐ. τοῖς ἀναθήμασι *IG* 1^{2}.76.43; esp. *write* or *place an epitaph* on a tomb, ib. 14.1835, al., 7.2543.9:—Med., *have inscribed*, ἐπεγράφου τὴν Γοργόνα Ar. *Ach.* 1095 (with play on III. 5); ἐλεγεῖον Th. 1.132:—Pass., of the inscription, *to be inscribed upon*, ἐπιγέγραπταί οἱ τάδε Hdt. 5.77, cf. 7.228; τῶν τῷ χρυσέῳ ἐπιγέγραπται "Λακεδαιμονίων" Id. 1.51; [ἐπίγραμμα] ὃ Μίδᾳ φασὶν ἐπιγεγράφθαι *over* or *on the tomb of* Midas, Pl. *Phdr.* 264c; ἐπιστολὴ -γεγραμμένη *addressed*, of a letter, Plb. 16.36.4, cf. Plu. *Cic.* 15; also, *to have* something *inscribed upon one*, ἐπεγράφοντο ῥόπαλα, ὡς Θηβαῖοι ὄντες *used to bear* clubs *upon their shields*, X. *HG* 7.5.20; so ἀσπὶς ἐπιγεγραμμένη τὰς ὁμολογίας *having* the articles *inscribed upon it*, D.H. 4.58. 2. *entitle*, τοῦτο τὸ δρᾶμα Καλλίμαχος ἐ. Εὐνοῦχον Ath. 11.496f; αἱ -όμεναι Μαιανδρίου ἱστορίαι *Inscr. Prien.* 37.104 (ii B.C.). 3. *sign, append a signature to*, ἄφεσιν *PSI* 4.392.6 (iii B.C.); ἐ. τὸν Ἀντώνιον *sign* Antonius' *name*, App. *BC* 5.144; αὑτοῦ ποιήματα ἐπέγραψεν (sc. τοῖς Ἑρμαῖς) *inscribed* poems *signed* by himself, Pl. *Hipparch.* 228d. 4. *write subsequently*, αἱ ἐπιγραφεῖσαι διαθῆκαι J. *AJ* 17.9.4. 5. *write over* an erasure, *POxy.* 34.14 (ii A.D.). III. freq. as law-term: 1. *set down* the penalty or damages *in the title* of an indictment (cf. ἐπίγραμμα 4), τί δῆτά σοι τίμημ' ἐπιγράψω τῇ δίκῃ; Ar. *Pl.* 480; μέχρι πεντήκοντα δραχμῶν καθ' ἕκαστον ἀδίκημα ἐ. Lex ap. Aeschin. 1.38; τὰ ἐπιγεγραμμένα the *damages claimed*, D. 29.8, cf. Pl. *Lg.* 915a; τιμημάτων -μένων Isoc. 16.47:—Med., Lex ap. Aeschin. 1.16. b. of a lawgiver, *assign* a punishment, τὰ μέγιστα ἐπιτίμια Aeschin. 1.14:—Pass., Din. 2.12. c. *make note of, enter*, τὴν πρόφασιν, in inflicting a fine, Arist. *Ath.* 8.4. 2. *register* the citizens' names and property, with a view to taxes, *lay a public burden upon* one (cf. ἐπιγραφή II. 2), ἐμαυτῷ.. τὴν μεγίστην εἰσφοράν Isoc. 17.41, cf. Arist. *Oec.* 1351^{b}2; ἐ. δήμοις καὶ δυνάσταις στρατιωτῶν καταλόγους Plu. *Crass.* 17, cf. *PHib.* 1.44.3 (iii B.C., Pass.), etc.; but ἐ. τινὰ προστίμοις *visit* with penalties, D.S. 12.12 (s.v.l.). b. *assess*, τὸ τρίτον μέρος *PEdgar* 38.3:—Pass., τὸ τίμημα τὸ -γεγραμμένον τοῖς χρήμασιν Lys. 17.7. 3. generally, *register* or *enter in a public list*, ἐπιγράψαι σφᾶς αὐτοὺς ἐπιτρόπους Is. 6.36; ἐ. τινὰ εἰς τοὺς πράκτορας *register* his *name* among the πράκτορες, Decr. ap. And. 1.77 (Pass.):—Med., ἐπεγράψαντο πολίτας *enrolled fresh* citizens, Th. 5.4; ξένην καὶ ξένον γονέας -ψάμενος D. 57.51; πῶς οἷόν τε τῷ ἀνδρὶ δύο πατέρας -ψασθαι; Is. 4.4 (later in Act., ἑαυτῷ τινὰ πατέρα -γράφων *claiming* as his father, App. *BC* 1.32). 4. Med., ἐπιγράφεσθαι μάρτυρας *cause to be endorsed on a deposition as* witnesses, D. 54.31; κλητῆρα οὐδ' ὀντινοῦν ἐπιγραψάμενος Id. 21.87; but ἐπιγράφεσθαι τίμημα τῷ κλήρῳ *set one's* valuation on the property, Is. 3.2. 5. προστάτην ἐπιγράψασθαι *choose* a patron, *and enter his name as such* in the public register (as μέτοικοι at Athens were obliged to do), Ar. *Pax* 684; so prob. ἐπεγράφοντο shd. be restored for -γραφον in Luc. *Peregr.* 11; ἐπιγράψασθαί τινα κύριον D. 43.15; οἱ τὸν Πλάτωνα ἐπιγραφόμενοι, i.e. the Platonists, Luc. *Herm.* 14:—Pass., κύριος ἐπιγεγράφθαι D. 43.15, cf. *POxy.* 251.32 (i A.D.), al. b. metaph., Ὅμηρον ἐπιγράφεσθαι *attribute* one's fluency to Homer, Luc. *Dem. Enc.* 2; πρεσβυτέρους ἐ. χρόνους *claim the authority of* greater antiquity, Id. *Am.* 35. IV. ἐπιγράψαι ἑαυτὸν ἐπί τι *claim credit for*, Aeschin. 3.167; ἀλλοτρίοις ἑαυτὸν πόνοις Ael. *NA* 8.2, cf. Plu. *Pomp.* 31; αὐτὸς ἐ. τὴν νίκην *claim* as his own, J. *AJ* 7.7.5:—so Med. and Pass., τοιούτων ῥητόρων ἐπὶ τὰς τοῦ δήμου γνώμας ἐπιγραφομένων *inscribing their names* on.., Aeschin. 1.188; ἐπιγράφεσθαι ἀλλοτρίαις γνώμαις D. 59.43; τὸν ἐπὶ τοῖς τῆς πόλεως ἀτυχήμασιν ἐπιγεγραμμένον Din. 1.29; οἱ ἐπιγεγραμμένοι ἢ φυλάττοντες the parties *whose names were endorsed* upon the συνθῆκαι as securities, Arist. *Rh.* 1376^{b}4; οἱ ἐπιγραφόμενοι τοῖς δόγμασι D.H. 6.84; ἡμεῖς δ' ἐσμὲν ἐπιγεγραμμένοι we are merely *the endorsers*, Men. 482.8. V. *ascribe to*, τοῖς θεοῖς τὸ ἔργον Hld. 8.9 (but θεὸν τῇ πομπῇ Philostr. *VA* 8.12):—Med., Φοίβῳ τὰς ἀνίσους χεῖρας *AP* 9.263 (Antiphil.). 2. *claim credit for*, τὰ ὑπὸ ἄλλων εὑρημένα J. *AJ* 3.4.2; *assume*, προσωνυμίαν Plu. *Demetr.* 42; ἐπεγράψατο τὴν ἑαυτοῦ προσηγορίαν Id. *Tim.* 36:—Pass., of books, *to be ascribed*, τινί Gal. 15.25. 3. *predicate of*, φυγὴν οὐ φυγόντι Philostr. *VS* 2.1.12.

ἐπίγρῡπος, ον, *somewhat hooked*, of the beak of the ibis, Hdt. 2.76; of the muzzle of the βοῦς ἄγριος, Arist. *HA* 499^{a}7; of horses and men, *somewhat hook-nosed*, Pl. *Phdr.* 253d, *Euthphr.* 2b, *PPetr.* 3 p.7, al. (iii B.C.), etc.

ἐπιγύᾰλος [ῠ], ον, *hollow on the surface*, dub. l. in S. *OC* 1492 (lyr.).

ἐπίγυιον or **ἐπίγῠον**, τό, *stern-cable*, Ar. *Fr.* 80, cf. 426: written -γυιον in Aristid. *Or.* 23(42).17, Zonar., -γυον in *IG* 2^{2}.1611.255–8 (iv B.C.), Plb. 3.46.3, Harp. s.v. ἐπίγυον (v.l. ἀπόγυιον): scanned ⏑ ⏑ – ⏑ in Ar.

ἐπιγυμν-άζω, *exercise excessively*, Philostr. *Gym.* 51; *exercise again*, ib. 53:—Pass., *take exercise at* or *in*, τοῖσι γυμνασίοισι Hp. *Insomn.* 88: abs., dub. in Ph. 1.467. **-όω**, *lay bare*, [ὀστοῦν] σμίλῃ Pall. *in Hp. Fract.* 12.286C.

ἐπιγώνιος, α, ον, *at the angle*, μονάδες Nicom. *Ar.* 1.19. II. ἐπιγώνια, τά, *corner-stones* or *-columns*, Aq. *Ps.* 143(144).12.

ἐπιδαίομαι (A), Pass., (δαίω A) *to be kindled at*: metaph., *delight greedily in*, κίχλης -δαίεται ἦτορ Opp. *H.* 4.173, cf. Sch. ad loc.

ἐπιδαίομαι (B), (δαίω B) *distribute*, ἐπιδαίομαι ὅρκον dub. sens. in *h. Merc.* 383:—Pass., δεκάτη δ' ἐπὶ μοῖρα δέδασται Hes. *Th.* 789.

ἐπιδαίσιος, ον, (δαίω B) *assigned, allotted*, οἶκος Call. *Jov.* 59.

ἐπίδαιτρον, τό, *additional dish, dainty*, Philem. ap. Ath. 14.646c; = ὄψον, Hsch.

ἐπιδάκν-ω, *bite*: hence, of anything pungent, *sting, cause to smart*, ὁ καπνὸς ἐ. τὰς ὄψεις Arist. *Fr.* 660; of urine, Ath. 1.32e; ἐ. τὴν γεῦσιν Dsc. 2.166: metaph., Satyr. *Vit. Eur. Fr.* 39 xvi 27:—Med., Nic. *Al.* 19, 121:—Pass., οἱ -όμενοι τὴν κύστιν Dsc. 1.112; of hunger, Apollod. ap. Suid. s.v. καρδιώττειν. **-ώδης**, ες, *gnawing*, dub. l. in Philagr. ap. Orib. 5.21.10.

ἐπίδακρ-υς, υ, *tearful*, Hsch. and Suid. s.v. μυδαλέον. **-ῡσις**, εως, ἡ, *oozing*, of blood, Heliod. ap. Orib. 50.52.5. **-ύω**, *weep over* or *for*, πτώματι Ph. 2.44; τῇ μνήμῃ τινός Plu. 2.583c: abs., Ar. *V.* 882, Aeschin. 2.85:—Pass., ἐπιδακρυνθέντα· ἐπιγραφέντα (i.e. in a tomb inscription), Hsch. 2. *ooze, exude*, Heliod. ap. Orib. 50.49.1.

ἐπίδαλον· λοιμικόν, Hsch.

ἐπιδᾰμι-ασταί, οἱ, *those enjoying the privilege of* ἐπιδαμία (v. ἐπιδημία) at Rhodes, *IG* 12(1).157. **-οργέω**, *hold office of* ἐπιδαμιοργός, prob. in *IG* 9(1).330.2 (*Supp. Epigr.* 2.354). **-οργός**, ὁ, *official* at Delphi, ib. 263.35 (iii/ii B.C.), al.; at Sparta, *IG* 5(1).5 (iii/ii B.C.); at Ithaca, *SIG* 558.30 (iii B.C.); cf. ἐπιδημιουργός.

ἐπιδάμνᾰμαι, *subdue*, ἠϊθέους *AP* 12.96.5.

ἐπίδᾱμος, ἐπιδάμιος, Dor. for ἐπιδημ-.

ἐπιδᾰνείζω, *lend money on property already mortgaged*, D.35.22, *PPetr.* 3 p.41 (iii B.C.); ἐ. ἐπὶ κτήμασι Arist.*Oec.* 1347^{a}1; ἱερατικὰς προσόδους ἐ. *PGnom.* 184 (ii A.D.):—Med., *borrow on property already mortgaged*, D.34.6, Syngr.ap.eund.35.11: metaph., ἐπιδανείζεσθαι χρόνον παρὰ τῆς τύχης εἰς ἄδοξον βίον Plu.*Brut.* 33.

ἐπιδᾰπᾰν-άω, *exhaust, consume as well*, Pall.*Febr.* 23. **-ητής**, οῦ, ὁ, *steward*, *Gloss.*

ἐπιδασμός, ὁ, *assessment*, *PSI* 8.901.11 (i A.D.).

ἐπίδᾰσυς, εια, υ, *hairy*, Thphr.*HP* 3.18.5.

ἐπιδαψῐλεύω, intr., *abound, be abundant*, Ister 43, Hsch. s.v. Συβαριτικοὶ λόγοι: but more commonly, II. Med., *lavish upon* a person, *bestow freely*, τὰς ἑωυτῶν μητέρας καὶ τὰς ἀδελφεὰς ὑμῖν Hdt. 5.20, cf. Ph.1.400; [τὰν δαπάναν] *Supp.Epigr.* 1.327.7 (Callatis, i A.D.); ἐ. τινί τοῦ γέλωτος *give* him *freely of* it, X.*Cyr.* 2.2.15: metaph., *illustrate more richly*, Luc.*DMort.* 30.2. 2. intr., *to be lavish*, Arist. *VV* 1250^{b}25, Ph.2.170; ἔν τινι D.H.*Rh.* 6.2, Luc.*Pr.Im.* 14.

ἐπιδέδρομα, poet. pf. 2 of ἐπιτρέχω.

ἐπιδεής, poet. **ἐπιδευής** (q.v.), ές, *in need of*, τινός Pl.*Ti.* 33c, v.l. in X.*Cyr.* 8.7.12, etc.: pl., -δεέες v.l. in Hdt.4.130: Comp. -έστερος ἐκείνων *inferior to*.., Pl.*Plt.* 311b: Sup. -έστατος *most in need*, πλείστων Id.*R.* 579e. Adv. -εῶς *inadequately*, Id.*Lg.* 899d.

ἐπιδεῖ, v. ἐπιδέω (B).

ἐπίδειγμα, ατος, τό, *pattern, example*, X.*Smp.* 6.6, *PTeb.* 25.18 (ii B.C.); σοφίας πλείστης Pl.*Hp.Mi.* 368c; προνοίας Gal.*UP* 15.4. 2. *display*, ἐ. ἐπιδεικνύναι X.*Cyr.* 8.2.15; τὰ τῶν πλουσίων ἐ. *show-pieces, gauds*, Demetr.*Eloc.* 108. II. *memorial*, χειμῶνος μεγάλου Epigr. ap.Str.2.1.16.

ἐπιδείδω, 3 pl. plpf. (= impf.) ἐπεδείδισαν, *fear*, κτύπον Nonn.*D.* 28. 330.

ἐπιδείελος, ον, *at even, about evening*: neut. pl. ἐπιδείελα as Adv., Hes.*Op.* 810, 821 (nisi leg. ἐπὶ δείελα).

ἐπιδείκ-νῡμι (-νύω *PPetr.* 2 p.110 (iii B.C.)), fut. -δείξω: aor. ἐπέδειξα, Ion. ἐπέδεξα Hdt.2.42:—*exhibit as a specimen*, Ar.*Ach.* 765: generally, *display, exhibit*, βίαν Pi.*N.* 11.14; τεκμήρια A.*Supp.* 53 (lyr.), etc.; ἑωυτόν τινι Hdt.2.42; πᾶσαν τὴν Ἑλλάδα τινί Id.3.135, cf. 6.61; ἐ. τὸ στράτευμά τινι *parade* it before.., X.*An.* 1.2.14, cf.*Cyr.* 5.5.5; of speeches, compositions, etc., ἐπιδειξάτω τῇ βουλῇ he *shall exhibit* his draft, *IG* 1^{2}.76.60; ἐ. λόγον Ar.*Eq.* 349; ῥαψῳδίαν Pl.*Lg.* 658b, cf. Isoc.2.7 (Pass.); σοφίαν Pl.*Euthd.* 274a, X.*Smp.* 3.3. 2. more freq. in Med., *show off* or *display for oneself* or *what is one's own*, μουσικὰν ὀρθὰν ἐ. *give a specimen of his* art.., Pi.*Fr.* 32; ἐμὲ ἐπεδέξατο γυμνήν *exhibited* me naked, Hdt.1.11; πάντα τὸν στρατόν *showed* all *his* army, Id.7.146; ἐ. τὸν Ἀλέξανδρον *recall* Alexander, Plu.*Pyrrh.* 8; esp. of one's personal qualities, ἐπιδείκνυσθαι τὴν αὑτοῦ δύναμιν And.4.14; σοφίαν, πονηρίαν, Pl.*Phdr.* 258a, Isoc.20.4, cf. X.*An.* 1.9. 16; ἐπιδείξασθαι αὐτὸν ἀβέβηλον *Inscr.Prien.* 113.66 (i B.C.). b. ἐπιδεῖξαι.. ἅττ' ἐδίδασκες *give a specimen of*.., Ar.*Nu.* 935; τὰ γυμνικά *POxy.* 42.5 (iv A.D.): abs., *show off, make a display of one's powers*, ἐπεδείκνυντο τοῖς λωποδύταις Ar.*Ra.* 771; ὃν.. ἐθεάσασθε ἐπιδεικνύμενον *giving a display* (of fighting in armour), Pl.*La.* 179e; of a rhetorician lecturing, Id.*Phdr.* 235a; πολλὰ καὶ καλά Id.*Grg.* 447a; of epideictic orators, Arist.*Rh.* 1391^{b}26; of a musician, Ael.*VH* 9.36: c. part., ἐ. ὑπερθέων Pl.*Lg.* 648d. II. *show, point out*, τινὶ τὴν αἰτίαν Id.*Phd.* 100b, cf. Aeschin.1.177; τὴν πονηρίαν Pl.*Prt.* 346a; ἐ. αὐτήν, ἥτις ἐστίν Pl.Com.173.5; ἐ. τὸν ἀλεκτρυόν' ὡς ἐτυράννει *show, prove* that.., Ar.*Av.* 483, cf. Lys.1.4; ὅτι.. Pl.*R.* 391e, etc.: c. part., ἐ. πάντα ἐόντα μεγάλα Hdt.1.30; ἐ. τινὰ φονέα ὄντα *show* that one is a murderer, v.l. in Antipho 1.3, cf. Th.3.64 (where perh. ἐπ- '*as an afterthought*'); ἐ. τινὰ δωροδοκήσαντα *prove* that one took bribes, Ar.*Eq.* 832 (anap.); ἐπιδείξω σε ταῦτα ὁμολογοῦντα Pl.*Euthd.* 295a, cf.*Chrm.* 158d; ψυχὴν ἐ. πρεσβυτέραν οὖσαν τοῦ σώματος Id.*Lg.* 892c; ἐ. αὐτὸν φοβερὸν (sc. ὄντα) καὶ μέγα δυνάμενον And.4.11: c. acc., ἐ. ὅ τι ἂν ἐγκαλῇ ἐναντίον ἀνδρῶν τριῶν *PEleph.* 1.7 (iv B.C.), etc.:—Pass., ἐπιδείκνυται αὐθέντης (sc. ὤν) Antipho 3.4.9; ἐπεδείχθησαν οὐδὲν βελτίους ὄντες Isoc.4.145, cf. 18.56; κινδυνεύσεις ἐπιδεῖξαι χρηστὸς εἶναι X.*Mem.* 2.3.17 (ἐπιδεῖξαι secl. Cobet). 2. Med., τῆς αἰτίας τὸ εἶδος Pl.*Phd.* 100b; ἔργῳ ἐπεδείκνυτο, ὅτι.. X.*An.* 1.9.10, cf. Is.5.30. **-τέον**, *one must display*, τὴν εὐψυχίαν Id.*Cyn.* 10.21, etc. 2. *one must point out*, Gal.10.222; *one must prove*, ὅτι.. Porph.*Abst.* 3.9. **-τιάω**, Desiderat., *wish to display oneself*, *Com.Adesp.* 1008. **-τικός**, ή, όν, *fit for displaying* or *showing off*, ἤθους καὶ πάθους Luc.*Salt.* 35; ἡ ἐπιδεικτική *display*, Pl.*Sph.* 224b. 2. ἐ. λόγοι speeches *for display*, *set* orations, D.61.2; ἐ. γένος λόγων Arist.*Rh.* 1358^{b}8; ὁ ἐ. *declamatory* speaker, ib.1359^{a}15, cf. Plu.*Comp.Dem.Cic.* 1. Adv. -κῶς, πολεμεῖν Id.*Luc.* 11; ἐ. ἔχειν Isoc.4.11: Comp. -ώτερον, γράφειν Plu.2. 28e.

ἐπιδεῖν, v. ἐπεῖδον.

ἐπιδεινοπᾰθέω, gloss on ἐπαλαστήσασα, Apollon.*Lex.*

ἐπίδειξις, Ion. **ἐπίδεξις**, εως, ἡ, *showing forth, making known*, τοῦτο ἐς ἐ. ἀνθρώπων ἀπίκετο became *notorious*, Hdt.2.46. 2. *exhibition, display, demonstration*, τῆς δυνάμεως Th.6.31; ἐ. ποιεῖσθαι, of a military *demonstration*, Id.3.16; ἐν τοῦτ' ἦν τῆς ἐ. *showing off*, Pl. *Grg.* 447c: generally, ἐ. ποιήσασθαι ἢ.. *exhibit* how.., Id.*Phd.* 99d; ἐλθεῖν εἰς ἐπίδειξίν τινι come to *display* oneself to one, Ar.*Nu.* 269; ἡ ἐ. (sc. τοῦ κάλλους) X.*Mem.* 3.11.2; ἐ. ποιήσασθαι τῆς σοφίας Arist. *Pol.* 1259^{a}19. 3. esp. λόγων ἐ. ποιεῖσθαι D.18.280: abs., *set speech, declamation*, Th.3.42; ἐ. ποιήσασθαι Pl.*Grg.* 447c, cf. Isoc.4.17, 5.17: pl., *SIG* 577.53 (Milet., iii/ii B.C.), 775.3 (Delph., i B.C.). b. name of a trireme at Athens, *IG* 2^{2}.1623.144. 4. *proof*, Men.161.2 (pl.), *PTaur.* 1.1 vii 7 (pl., ii B.C.), etc. II. *example*, ἐπίδειξις Ἑλλάδι *an example* to Greece, E.*Ph.* 871; ἐπίδειξιν ποιεῖσθαί τινι ὡς.. *give a sign* or *proof* that.., Aeschin.1.47.

ἐπιδειπν-έω, *eat a second meal*, Hp.*VM* 10, *Acut.* 28. II. *dine, sup off*, Ar.*Eq.* 1140, *Ec.* 1178 (both lyr.); τῶν πράσων Alex.242. III. *sup at* or *upon*, σκεῦος ᾧ τις ἐ. Artem.1.74. **-ιος**, ον, *after dinner*, ἐ. ἀφῖχθαι Luc.*Lex.* 9. II. *convivial*, βασιλεύς Them.*Or.* 2.36a (prob.). **-ίς**, ίδος, ἡ, = sq., Ph.2.479 (pl.), Petron.69, Mart.11. 31.7 (pl.); said to be Maced. by Ath.14.658e. **-ον**, τό, *second course, dessert*, ib.664e (pl., s.v.l.).

ἐπιδεκᾰτ-εία (-ία Thrasyll. in *Cat.Cod.Astr.* 8(3).101), ἡ, Astrol., = καθυπερτέρησις, Vett.Val.102.33. **-εύω**, = καθυπερτερέω, Heph. Astr.1.16, Thrasyll. l.c., Vett.Val.102.27 (Pass.), Porph.*in Ptol.* 188. **-ος**, ον, *containing an integer and one-tenth*: hence ἐ. λόγος ratio *of* 11 : 10, Iamb.*in Nic.* p.54 P. II. *one in ten*: hence Subst. -δέκατον, τό, 1. *tenth, tithe*, Lex ap.And.1.96, X.*HG* 1.7.10, Lex ap.D.43.71; ἐ. τόκοι interest *of* 10%, *IG* 1^{2}.377, Arist.*Rh.* 1411^{a}17, *Oec.* 1346^{b}32. 2. *payment of* 10% *on account*, *IG* 11.161 *A* 79 (Delos, iii B.C.). 3. *payment of* 10% as παρακαταβολή (q.v.), ib.5(2).357 (Stymphalus), *PHal.* 1.63 (iii B.C.); προδικία ἄνευ ἐπιδεκάτων *IG* 12 (8).640 (Peparethus, ii B.C.). 4. *additional, extra payment of one-tenth*, *PHib.* 1.32.9 (iii B.C.), *PAmh.* 2.33.32 (ii B.C.).

ἐπιδεκ-τέον, *one must acquiesce in*, τὸ παραγγελλόμενον Plb.36.5. 4. **-τικός**, ή, όν, *capable of containing* πόλεων Str.3.4.13. 2. *capable of*, c. gen., Chrysipp.*Stoic.* 2.64, Phld.*Ir.* p.81 W.; *admitting*, ἄρθρου A.D.*Pron.* 63.19; γύμνασμα ἐ. ἠθῶν καὶ παθῶν Theon *Prog.* 10; *receptive*, ἐ. αἴτιον, opp. ποιητικόν, Alex.Aphr.*Febr.* 25. **-τος**, ον, *accepted*, Sm., Thd.*Is.* 60.7; also gloss on ἐπιδεκτικός, Hsch. **-τωρ**, ορος, ὁ, Adj., = -τικός 2, δίκας Aesara ap.Stob.1.49.27.

ἐπιδελεάζομαι, in pf. part. Pass., *to be put on as a bait*, D.S.1.35.

ἐπιδέμνιος, ον, *on the bed* or *bed-clothes*, ἐπιδέμνιος ὡς πέσοιμ' ἐς εὐνάν E.*Hec.* 927 (lyr.).

ἐπιδέμομαι, Med., *build upon*, τινί τι Opp.*C.* 4.121.

ἐπιδένδρ-ιος, ον, *on* or *in the tree*, [σῦκον] Jul.*Ep.* 180 p.393b. **-ος**, ον, = foreg., ὄφις Teucr.ap.Boll *Sphaera* p.17.

ἐπιδέννω, = ἐπιδέω, Sm.*Is.* 1.6 (Pass.).

ἐπιδεξῐ-ελεύθερος, f.l. in Pl.*Tht.* 175e ap.Suid. s.v. ἀναλαμβάνειν. -όομαι, Med., *entertain one another*, Anaximen.ap.D.L.2.4. **-ος**, ον, *towards the right*, i.e. *from left to right*: I. used by Hom. only in neut. pl. as Adv., ὄρνυσθ' ἑξείης ἐπιδέξια rise in order, Od.21.141, cf. Pl.*Smp.* 214b; περίθι τὸν βωμὸν ἐ. Ar.*Pax* 957; πίνειν τὴν ἐ. (sc. κύλικα) Eup.325, cf. Anaxandr.1.4, Critias 33 D.; without idea of motion, ἕστηκεν ἐ. Lys.*Fr.* 94; sts. as two words, ἐπὶ δεξιά, opp. ἐπ' ἀριστερά, Il.7.238, cf. Eust. ad Od. l.c.; ἐπὶ δ. χειρός Pi.*P.* 6.19, Theoc. 25.18; τὰ ἐπὶ δ., opp. τὰ ἐπ' ἀριστερά, Hdt.2.93, 4.191, 6.33. 2. *auspicious, lucky*, ἀστράπτων ἐ. Il.2.353. II. later as Adj., = δεξιός, *on the right hand*, X.*An.* 6.4.1, etc.; τἀπιδέξια *the right side*, Ar.*Av.* 1493 (lyr.); οἱ ἐ. ἄνεμοι Arist.*Pr.* 941^{b}12. 2. *clever, dexterous, tactful*, Aeschin.1.178, Arist.*EN* 1128^{a}17, Thphr.*Char.* 29.4; λαβὴ φιλοσόφων ἐπιδέξιος ἡ διὰ τῶν ὤτων Zeno *Stoic.* 1.64: c. inf., Arist.*Rh.* 1381^{a}34; ἐ. πρὸς τὰς ὁμιλίας Plb.5.39.6; περί τι Plu.*Aem.* 37, D.C.69.10: Sup., Ἀφροδίτην -ωτάτην θεῶν Plu.2.739e: neut. pl. as Adv., ἐπιδέξια *dexterously, cleverly*, Anaxandr.53.5, Nicom.Com.1.27; *elegantly*, ἀναβάλλεσθαι ἐ. Pl.*Tht.* 175e: Regul. Adv. -ίως Erasistr.ap.Gal.7.539, Plb.3.19.13, 4.35.7, Corn.*ND* 14, Plu.2.439e. 3. *lucky, prosperous*, τύχη D.S.8.4. **-ότης**, ητος, ἡ, *handiness, cleverness, tact*, Pittac.ap.Stob.3.1.172, Aeschin.2.47, Arist.*EN* 1128^{a}17: pl., Plu. 2.441b. II. *position on the right*, Paul.Al.*E.* 3.

ἐπιδεξιπολίης· ἐκ τῶν δεξιῶν μερῶν περιστρέψας, Hsch.

ἐπίδεξις, εως, ἡ, Ion. for ἐπίδειξις.

ἐπίδερις, ιδος, ἡ, = ὑποδορίς, Poll.2.174.

ἐπιδέρκομαι, *look upon, behold*, τι, τινάς, Hes.*Op.* 268, *Th.* 760, etc.; Hom. only as v.l., Od.11.16.

ἐπιδερκτός, όν, *to be seen, visible*, τινί Emp.2.7.

ἐπί-δερμα, ατος, τό, = sq. II, *Gloss.* **-δερμᾰτίς**, ίδος, ἡ, gloss on λέμμα, *peel*, Erot. II. *skin*, αἰγός Alex.Trall.1.15. **-δερμίς**, ίδος, ἡ, *outer skin, epidermis*, Hp.*Nat.Puer.* 20, etc. II. *web of water-birds' feet*, Arist.ap.Sch.Il.2.460.

ἐπί-δεσις, εως, ἡ, *bandaging*, Hp.*Art.* 14, *VC* 13, Gal.14.793. 2. *binding*, κεραμίδων *PLond.* 1.177.164 (ii A.D.). **-δεσμα**, ατος, τό, = ἐπίδεσμος, Hp.*Fract.* 21, *Art.* 14, etc. **-δεσμεύω**, *bind up*, *AP* 11.125. **-δεσμέω**, *bind up* or *on*, Pall.*in Hp.Fract.* 12.284 C., Paul.Aeg.3.35, *Hippiatr.* 11. **-δέσμια**, τά, gloss on δέσματα, Hsch. **-δεσμίς**, ίδος, ἡ, = sq., Gal.14.794, Cass.*Pr.* 57. **-δεσμος**, ὁ, *upper* or *outer bandage*, Hp.*Off.* 9, Ar.*V.* 1440, Arist.*HA* 630^{a}6, Ph. *Bel.* 96.19: metaph., of fortresses as the '*fetters*' of Greece, Str.9. 4.15: heterocl. pl. ἐπίδεσμα Ael.*NA* 8.9:—also -δεσμον, τό, Gal.13. 686. **-δεσμοχᾰρής**, ές, *bandage-loving*, of gout, Luc.*Trag.* 198.

ἐπιδεσπόζω, *to be lord over*, στρατῷ A.*Pers.* 241.

ἐπιδετέον, *one must bind on*, Antyll.ap.Orib.7.21.9, Gal.18(2).897.

ἐπιδετόν, τό, *application under a bandage*, Hp.*Mul.* 1.78.

ἐπιδευής, ές, poet. for ἐπιδεής, *in need* or *want of, lacking*, c. gen., δαιτὸς ἐΐσης, κρειῶν, γάλακτος, etc., Il.9.225, Od.4.87, etc.; βιότου Hes.*Th.* 605; λώβης τε καὶ αἴσχεος οὐκ ἐπιδευεῖς *lacking* not scathe nor scorn, Il.13.622; τῶν πάντων ἐπιδευέες (v.l. -δεέες) Hdt.4.130: abs., ὅς κ' ἐπιδευὴς whoever be *in want*, Il.5.481, cf. Parm.8.33. II. *lacking, failing*, ἵνα μή τι δίκης ἐπιδευὲς ἔχησθα that thou may'st have no point of right *wanting*, Il.19.180: c. gen., βίης ἐπιδευέες *failing* in strength, Od.21.185; ἐ. θέσφατα μαντοσύνης A.R.2.315: as Comp., βίης ἐπιδευέες εἰμὲν ἀντιθέου Ὀδυσῆος *inferior to* Ulysses in strength, Od.21.253, cf. *h.Ap.*338: and abs., πολλὸν δ' ἐπιδευέες ἦμεν far *too weak* were we, Od.24.171: c. inf., τεθνάκην ὀλίγω 'πιδεύης cj. in Sapph.2.15.

ἐπιδεύομαι, Ep. for ἐπιδέομαι (v. ἐπιδέω (B) II), *to be in want of, lack,* c. gen. rei, χρυσοῦ ἐπιδεύεαι Il.2.229, cf. Od.15.371, Nic.*Th.*57; *need the help of,* c. gen. pers., σεῦ ἐπιδευομένους Il.18.77. II. *to be lacking in, fall short of,* c. gen. rei, μάχης ἐπιδεύομαι 23.670, cf. 17.142: also c. gen. pers., πολλὸν κείνων ἐπιδεύεαι ἀνδρῶν *fallest* far *short* of them, 5.636; or both together, οὔ τι μάχης ἐπιδεύετ' Ἀχαιῶν 24.385: later c. acc. rei, ἀλκήν A.R.2.1220.—The Act. occurs only in Aeol. fut. inf. ἐπιδεύσην, f.l. in Sapph.2.15 (v. ἐπιδευής).

ἐπιδεύτερ-ος, ον, *secondary, of minor rank,* of a dramatist, Suid. s.v. Ἀριστομένης. **-όω,** *repeat, AB*93. **-ωσις,** εως, ἡ, *repetition,* Sm.*Ps.*76(77).11.

ἐπιδεύω, *moisten, AP*7.208 (Anyte, tm.):—Pass., αἵματι κρητήρ Orph.*A.*1076.

ἐπιδέχομαι, Ion. etc. **-δέκομαι** Hdt. (v. infr.), *Leg.Gort.*11.25:—*admit besides* or *in addition,* Hdt.8.75. 2. *receive besides,* Men. 583. 3. *receive, welcome,* τινὰς φιλανθρώπως Plb.21.18.3; ἐ. εἰς τὰ οἰκητήρια *POxy.*281.9 (i A.D.). II. *take on oneself, undertake,* πόλεμον Plb.4.31.1; τὴν στεφανηφορίαν *Inscr.Prien.*108.255 (ii B.C.), cf. *POxy.*498.6 (ii A.D.), etc.: c. inf., ib.102.7 (iv A.D.): abs., *agree, admit liability, PAmh.*2.31.12 (ii B.C.). 2. of things, *allow of, admit of,* κατηγορίαν D.10.28; λόγον Arist.*Cat.*3^{b}2; τὸ μᾶλλον καὶ τὸ ἧττον ib.6^{a}19; ἐναντιότητα ib.11^{b}1; τὴν μεσότητα Id.*EN*1107^{a}8; τἀκριβές ib.1094^{b}25; δόξαν αἰτίας Aeschin.1.48, cf. Hero *Aut.*1.7: c. inf., ὁ χρόνος οὐκ ἐπιδέχεται μακρολογεῖν Din.1.31. 3. *expect, await,* βαρεῖαν ἐπιδέγμενοι ἀνάγκαν B.16.96. 4. *accept* a term *as applying to,* ἐπί τινος Ascl.*Tact.*11.2 (v.l. ἐκδ-).

ἐπιδέω (A), fut. -δήσω, *bind, fasten on,* τὸν λόφον Ar.*Ra.*1038:—Med., ἐπὶ τὰ κράνεα λόφους ἐπιδέεσθαι *have* crests *fastened* on . ., Hdt. 1.171: for Od.21.391, v. πεδάω. II. *bind up, bandage,* Hp.*VC*13, *Fract.*21, *Art.*14:—Pass., ἐπιδεδεμένος τραύματα *with one's* wounds *bound up,* X.*Cyr.*5.2.32, al.; ἐπιδεδεμένοι ἀντικνήμιον, χεῖρα, ib.2.3.19.

ἐπιδέω (B), fut. -δεήσω, *want* or *lack of* a number, τετρακοσίας μυριάδας . ., ἐπιδεούσας ἑπτὰ χιλιάδων Hdt.7.28: generally, *to be in need of,* Ocell.1.8; τῆς τέχνης ἂν μόνον ἐπιδέοι would *need* nothing *further* but his skill, Pl.*Lg.*709d: impers., ἐὰν δὲ καὶ ἄλλης ἐπιδέῃ βοηθείας D.H.6.63. II. Med., *to be in want of,* τινός Hdt.1.32, Pl.*Smp.* 204a, X.*Smp.*8.16, etc.; ἀρχὴν τριάκοντα ἐπιδεομένην ἡμερῶν *lacking* thirty days of its expiry, Pl.*Lg.*766c. 2. *request, PMag.Lond.* 121.546.

ἐπίδηλ-ος, ον, *seen clearly, manifest,* Thgn.442; ἐ. εἶναί τινι Hdt. 8.97; ἐ. ποιεῖν τισί, ἦν . . Ar.*Eq.*38: c. part., ἐ. ἐστι κλέπτων is *detected* stealing, Id.*Ec.*661. 2. ἐ. μάλιστα γίνεται [ἄνθρωπος] ἀπὸ ἑπταετέος μέχρι τεσσαρεσκαιδεκαετέος *formed,* Hp.*Carn.*13. II. *indicative* of a crisis to come, Id.*Aph.*2.24, cf. Gal.17(2).510: so in neut. pl., σῆς ἀρετῆς ἐπίδηλα *as a witness of . ., IG*12(7).286 (Amorgos). 2. *distinguished, remarkable,* X.*Oec.*21.10. 3. *like, resembling,* τινί Ar.*Pl.*368. III. Adv. -λως Hp.*Acut.*45, Arist. *Cael.*297^{b}34, etc.: Comp. -ότερον Id.*GA*728^{b}29, -οτέρως Id.*HA* 604^{a}2: Sup. -ότατα ib.510^{a}5, -οτάτως Id.*GA*727^{a}23. (Cf. also ἐπίζηλος.) **-όω,** *indicate,* Id.*Mete.*373^{a}31; νεύματί τι Philostr.*VA*5.34.

ἐπίδημα, ατος, τό, *cushion* (?), dub. in Paul.Aeg.2.48.

ἐπιδημ-εύω, = sq., *live among the people, live in the throng,* opp. live in the country, Od.16.28. **-έω,** *to be at home, live at home,* opp. ἀποδημέω, Th.1.136, Pl.*Tht.*173e, etc.; παρόντες καὶ ἐπιδημοῦντες Antipho 6.46; ἐ. τρία ἔτη And.1.132; ἐ. Ἀθήνησι *stay at home* at Athens, D.35.16; so ἐν αὐτῇ (sc. τῇ πόλει) ἐ. Pl.*Cri.*52b; opp. στρατεύομαι, Is.9.3. 2. of diseases, *to be prevalent, epidemic,* Hp.*Prog.*25. II. *come home,* X.*Mem.*2.8.1; ἐνθάδε ἐ. Pl.*Smp.* 172c; εἰ νῦν ἐξ ἀγροῦ ἐνθάδ' ἐπιδημεῖ Men.*Georg.*19. III. of foreigners, *come to stay in a city, reside in* a place, οἱ -οῦντες ἐν Λακεδαίμονι ξένοι X.*Mem.*1.2.61; ἐ. εἰς Μέγαρα *come* to Megara *to stay* there, D.59.37, cf. Aeschin.2.154; ἐκ Κλαζομενῶν Pl.*Prm.*126b; ἐ. τοῖς μυστηρίοις *to be present at, attend* them, D.21.176; τοὺς ἐπιδημήσαντας ἅπαντας τῶν Ἑλλήνων all *who were present* [at the festival], ib. 217; Φοίβου ἐπιδημήσαντος Call.*Ap.*13: later c. dat., ταῖς Σάρδεσιν Philostr.*VS*1.22.4; also ἐν Μέμφει *UPZ*42.14 (ii B.C.). 2. abs., *stay in a place, be in town,* ὅσοι ξένοι ἐπιδημοῦσιν Lys.12.35, cf. *Inscr.Prien.*108. 286 (ii B.C.), *Act.Ap.*17.21; Πρωταγόρας ἐπιδεδήμηκεν; Pl.*Prt.*309d: metaph., ἐ. θίασος Μουσῶν Ar.*Th.*40. 3. ἐ. τινί *visit* a person, *PLond.*2.416.5 (iv A.D.). **-ηγορέω,** *harangue over* a person, App. *BC*1.96. **-ησις,** εως, ἡ, = ἐπιδημία 2, f.l. in Pl.*Ep.*330b. **-ητικός,** ή, όν, *staying at home, non-migratory,* ζῷα, opp. ἐκτοπιστικά, Arist. *HA*488^{a}13. II. ἐπιδημητικά, τά, *expenses of* a governor's *visit, Cod.Just.*12.40.12. **-ία,** ἡ, *stay in a place,* Pl.*Prm.*127a; αἱ ἐ. αἱ τῶν συμμάχων X.*Ath.*1.18; of an Emperor, *visit, OGI*517.7 (Thyatira, iii A.D.), Hdn.3.14.1. 2. ἐ. εἰς . . *arrival* at . . *IG*3.1023. 3. *prevalence of an epidemic,* νουσήματος Hp.*Nat.Hom.*9; of rain, Ael. *NA*5.13. 4. Dor. **ἐπιδαμία,** ἡ, *right of residence, IG*12(1).43 (Rhodes). **-ιακός,** ή, όν, *epidemic,* νοσήματα Pall.*in Hp.*2.2 D. **-ιος,** ον (but α, ον *IG*9(1).333.7 (Locr.)), *among the people,* ἐπιδήμιοι ἁρπακτῆρες plunderers *of one's own countrymen,* Il.24.262; πόλεμος ἐ. *civil* war, 9.64; ἐπιδαμίᾳ δίκᾳ χρήστω *IG* l.c.; ἔφαντ' ἐ. εἶναι σὸν πατέρ' that he was *at home,* Od.1.194; ἐ. ἔμποροι *resident* merchants, Hdt.2.39; οὐδ' εὐνῆς αἰδὼς ἐ. A.R.2.1023: generally, *common, commonplace,* τοῦτο τοὐπιδήμιον Plu.2.735a. 2. *sojourning among,* ψυχὴ . . ἐ. ἄστροις *IG*12(8).609.3 (Thasos); *settling in* a place, A.R.1.827. 3. of diseases, *prevalent, epidemic,* ἴκτερος Hp.*Int.*37. 4. ἐπιδήμια θύειν sacrifice *in honour of a visit* or *arrival,* Him.*Ecl.*36.1.

ἐπιδημιουργ-έω, *order perfectly,* of the stars, Hp.*Ep.*18 (Pass.). II. v. ἐπιδαμιοργέω. **-οί,** οἱ, magistrates sent annually by Doric states to their colonies, Th.1.56. II. = δημιουργοί, Procop.*Arc.* 25, al. III. v. ἐπιδαμιοργός.

ἐπίδημος, Dor. **-δᾱμος,** ον, = ἐπιδήμιος, Antiph.11; οὐ τυγχάνει ἐ. ὤν not *at home,* Ar.*Fr.*390; ἐπίδᾱμος φάτις Οἰδιπόδα *the popular current* report concerning, S.*OT*495 (lyr.). 2. *sojourning in* a place, Call.*Dian.*226; Δήλῳ δ' ἦν ἐπίδημος, of Artemis, Id.*Aet.*3.1.26; οἱ ἐπίδᾱμοι *GDI*5040 (Hierapytna), cf. *Milet.*3.149 (ii B.C.). 3. of diseases, *prevalent, epidemic,* Hp.*Epid.*1.14. b. ἐ. βιβλία writings *on epidemic diseases,* Pall. *in Hp.Fract.*12.271 C.

ἐπιδια-βαίνω, *cross over after* another, Hdt.4.122, 6.70; ἐ. τάφρον Th.6.101; [ποταμόν] X.*HG*5.3.4, etc.; ἐ. ἐπί τινα, τινί, *cross a river* to attack an enemy, force the passage, Plb.3.14.8, Str.2.5.8, cf. D.C. 60.21. II. *pass all bounds,* ταῖς ἐλπίσιν J.*AJ*15.7.9. 2. *spread,* of diseases, ἄχρι τῆς καρδίας Gal.8.297; ἐπὶ γόνατα Aët.12.2. **-βάλλω,** *criticize,* Philostr.*VS*2.9.3. **-γιγνώσκω,** Ion. **-γῑνώσκω,** *consider afresh,* Hdt.1.133. **-γράφω** [γρᾰ], *pay in addition, PRev.Laws* 34.14 (iii B.C.); -γραφήσω f.l. in Vett.Val.348.11. **-θήκη,** ἡ, *additional will, codicil,* J.*AJ*17.9.4. II. *pledge, security,* Lys.*Fr.*110 S.

ἐπιδιαίρ-εσις, εως, ἡ, *further incision,* Heliod.ap.Orib.46.8.4, Gal. 1.386. **-ετέον,** *one must make a further incision,* Antyll.ap.Orib. 7.12.3, cf. Gal.17(1).434. **-έω,** fut. -ελῶ *PPetr.*2 p.10 (iii B.C.):—*divide, distribute,* ἑκάστῳ ἄρτους ἑξήκοντα l.c., cf. Plb.1.73.3; κρέα *Schwyzer*726.33 (Milet., v B.C.); πολίτας ταῖς φράτραις D.H.2.55; τοὺς στρατιώτας εἰς τὴν σατραπείαν D.S.19.44; αὐτοῖς . . τοὺς ἱππέας ἐπιδιῄρει *divided and sent against* them, App.*Hisp.*25:—Med., of several, *distribute among themselves,* Hdt.1.150, 5.116. II. *make a cross-incision in,* ὑμένα Gal.12.522.

ἐπιδιαίτησις, εως, ἡ, *an after-course of dietetic,* Dsc.4.148.3.

ἐπιδια-κατέχω, *control afterwards,* Vett.Val.246.21. **-κειμαι,** *to be staked upon* a throw at dice, used as Pass. of ἐπιδιατίθημι, Poll. 9.96. 2. *to be laid upon,* καλάμοις, of vegetables, Sor.1.51. **-κινδῡνεύω,** τινί *share in one's danger,* J.*AJ*14.14.3 (s.v.l.). **-κλύζω,** *rinse out afterwards,* Gal.12.876 (Med.).

ἐπιδιᾱκονέω, *render service, PStrassb.*5.11 (iii A.D.).

ἐπιδια-κρίνω [ρῑ], *decide as umpire,* Pl.*Grg.*524a, prob. in Id.*La.* 184c. II. *confirm a sentence,* D.C.57.20. III. *estimate carefully,* Vett.Val.277.17. IV. f.l. in Aristid.*Or.*26(14).30 (ἔτι δ. cj. Reiske). **-κρῐσις,** εως, ἡ, *exact estimate,* χρόνων Vett.Val.37. 10 (pl.). **-λείπω,** *allow to elapse,* ὀλίγας ἡμέρας Alex.Trall.1.17.

ἐπιδιαλλ-ᾰγή, ἡ, *reconciliation,* dub.l. in J.*AJ*18.9.9 (pl.). **-άσσω,** *bring to reconciliation,* ib.16.6.8.

ἐπιδια-λύω, *come as a relief to,* c. acc., Antyll.ap.Orib.6.8.5. **-μένω,** *remain after,* D.L.*Prooem.*11, Dsc.1.12, Artem.1.45; *continue to exist,* Diog.Oen.36. **-μονή,** ἡ, *continued existence, Stoic.* 2.182, M.Ant.4.21. **-νέμω,** *distribute,* ἄρτους ἱερεῦσι Ph.2.240; τινί τι J.*BJ*2.6.3:—Pass., αἱ τρεῖς μναῖ ἐ. τῷ στατῆρι Arist.*Ath.*10. 2. **-νοέομαι,** *think on, devise besides,* Hp.*Praec.*14. **-πέμπω,** *send over besides,* D.C.60.20. **-πλέω,** *sail across after* or *besides,* Id.47.47.

ἐπιδιαρθρ-όω, *articulate further,* Procl.*Inst.*177, Ammon.*in Int.* 195.22, Prisc.Lyd.36.8:—hence **-ωσις,** εως, ἡ, Dam.*Pr.*431.

ἐπιδια-ρρέω, *flow through* or *melt away besides,* Erot. s.v. ἐπίδυεν. **-ρρήγνῡμαι,** aor. -διερράγην [ᾰ], Pass., *burst at* or *because of* a thing, Ar.*Eq.*701. **-σάφέω,** *declare further,* Vett.Val.87.20, al.; *make more explicit,* Hdn.*Fig.*p.95 S.:—Pass., *become clearly understood,* Plb.32.16.5. **-σκευάζω,** *revise again, prepare a new edition of* a work, Hp.*Acut.*3. **-σκοπέω,** *consider further,* D.C. *Fr.*46.2 codd. (nisi leg. ἔτι δια-). **-σύρω** [ῡ], *carry ridicule further,* Sch.Ar.*Pax*201. **-σχίζω,** *subdivide further, Proll.Hermog.* in Rh.7.214 W. **-τάσσομαι,** *make additions to a will, Ep.Gal.* 3.15. **-τείνω,** *stretch* by inflation *yet further,* Gal.2.17. 2. intr., *spread far,* of fame or rumour, Plb.31.23.3; *extend* so as to include, ἐπί . . Phld.*Rh.*2.209 S. **-τίθημι,** *arrange besides* or *afterwards,* D.C.62.15:—Med., *deposit as security for* one's doing a given act, Lys.*Fr.*110 S.; ἀργύριον D.33.13; cf. ἐπιδιαθήκη II; also, *stake on* a throw at dice, Poll.9.96; cf. ἐπιδιάκειμαι. II. Med., *make a second* or *later will, Pap.Erzherzog Rainer*723 (ined., cf. Kreller *Erbrechtl.Untersuch.*p.298). **-τρίβω** [ρῑ], *spend time on,* χρόνον τῇ γεύσει Thphr.*Od.*11; *spend,* ἡμέρας τρεῖς J.*AJ*11.5.2, cf. Hdn.2.11.1; ἐπιδιατρίψας *dwelling on it,* Arist.*Mete.*371^{a}23. **-φέρομαι,** *go across after,* Th.8.8 (v.l. διαφ-). **-φθείρω,** *destroy, ruin besides,* in Pass., Ph.ap.Eus.*PE*8.14; *become corrupt,* Gal.8.42.

ἐπιδῐδάσκω, *teach besides,* X.*Cyr.*1.3.17, *Oec.*10.10, *Sammelb.* 5656.10 (vi A.D.).

ἐπιδιδῠμίς, ίδος, ἡ, (δίδυμος II) in Anatomy, *epididymis,* Gal.4.565.

ἐπιδίδωμι, *give besides,* τινί τι Il.23.559, Hdt.2.121.δ', al., E.*Med.*186 (anap.), *Ba.*1128, etc.: abs., Hes.*Op.*396, etc. b. of a physician, *administer,* ὅσων τῷ κάμνοντι δεῖ Ph.1.253; *give afterwards,* τροφὴν προδόντες ἐπιδιδόασι τὸν ἐλλέβορον Dsc.4.148. 2. *give in dowry,* ὅσσ' οὔ πώ τις ἑῇ ἐπέδωκε θυγατρί Il.9.148, cf. Lys.16.10, Pl.*Lg.*944a (Pass.), X.*Cyr.*8.5.19. b. esp. *contribute as a 'benevolence',* for the purpose of supplying state necessities, opp. εἰσφέρειν (which was compulsory), Is.5.37; ἐκ τῶν ἰδίων ἐ. Din.1.80; τριήρη ἐπέδωκεν D.21.160; ἐπέδωκα τὰ χρήματα Id.18.113; τὸ κοινὸν ἐπέδωκε τῷ θεῷ *SIG* 489.9 (Delph., iii B.C.); but also, c. *offer money* as a bribe or consideration, X.*Ath*.3.3. 3. *give freely, bestow*, Th.4.11, Ar.*Pax* 333; ὑμῖν τῶν ἑαυτοῦ τι Lys.30.26; ἐ. τοῦ ἑαυτοῦ μέρους X.*Cyr*.1.5.1; τὸν ἑαυτοῦ [ζῆλον] εἰς τὴν φιλοδοξίαν *Inscr.Prien*.114.12 (i B.C.). 4. ἐπιδιδόναι ἑαυτόν *give* oneself *up, devote* oneself, τινί to one, Ar.*Th*. 213, cf. Luc.*Peregr*.13; εἴς τι *SIG*495.124 (Olbia, iii B.C.), cf. Hdn. 3.4.1; εἰς πᾶν τό σοι χρήσιμον ἐμαυτὸν ἐ. *UPZ*62.9 (ii B.C.); also (sc. ἑαυτὸν) ἐπιδιδόναι εἰς τρυφήν Ath.12.525e; εἰς ὑπερηφανίαν Nymphis 15; ἐ. ἑαυτὸν τῇ πνεούσῃ Luc.*Herm*.28: abs., ἐπιδόντες ἐφερόμεθα ran *before the wind*, *Act.Ap*.27.15. 5. *give into* another's *hands, deliver*, ἐπιστολήν τινι D.S.14.47 (dub. l.), *Act.Ap*.15.30; χρηματισμόν Lxx 2*Ma*.11.17; γραμματεῖον Luc.*Peregr*.16: abs., of petitions, freq. in Pap., *BGU*45, etc.; of reports or returns, *POxy*.255.16 (i A.D.), etc.:—Pass., *OGI*515.37 (Mylasa, iii A.D.), Just.*Nov*.53.3.1. 6. ἐ. ψῆφον τοῖς πολίταις *give* them *power to* vote, Plu.*Num*.7. 7. *dictate*, opp. γράφειν, D.Chr.18.18. II. Med., *take as one's witness*, θεοὺς ἐπιδώμεθα '*give each other our* gods', Il.22.254:—in Il.10.463, Aristarch. read σὲ γὰρ πρώτην.. ἐπιδωσόμεθ', perh. in the same sense, though Apollon. and Scholl. explain it by δώροις τιμήσομεν: cf. περιδίδωμι. III. in Prose, freq. intr., *increase, advance*, ἐς ὕψος Hdt.2.13; καθ' ἡμέραν ἐς τὸ ἀγριώτερον Th.6.60; ἐς τὸ μισεῖσθαι Id. 8.83; ἐπὶ τὸ μεῖζον ib.24; ἐπὶ τὸ βέλτιον Hp.*Aph*.1.3, Pl.*Prt*.318a; εἰς ὄγκον πρὸς ἀρετήν *increase* in virtue Id.*Lg*.913b; πρὸς εὐδαιμονίαν Isoc.3.32: and abs., *grow*, Pl.*Euthd*.271b; *advance, improve*, Th.6. 72, 7.8; βελτίων ἔσται καὶ ἐ. Pl.*Prt*.318c, cf. *Cra*.410e, *Tht*.146b,150d, Isoc.9.68, etc.; ἐ. πάμπολυ [ἡ μάχη] *waxes* great, Pl.*Tht*.179d. 2. = ἐνδίδωμι v, *give in, give way*, ἐ. ἐπίδοσιν τοῖσι ἕλκουσι Hp.*Art*.72, cf. Gal.6.5, Sor.1.103.

ἐπιδιεξέρχομαι, *to be excreted afterwards*, opp. προδιεξ–, Gal.16. 699.

ἐπιδιέρχομαι, *pass along the line*, σύνθημα Poll.1.163.

ἐπιδιευγάζω, dub. sens. in *BGU*1143.16 (i B.C.).

ἐπιδίζημαι, *inquire besides, go on to inquire*, Hdt.1.95. 2. *seek for* or *demand besides*, Id.5.106: so **ἐπιδίζομαι** Mosch.2.28.

ἐπιδιηγ-έομαι, *relate again, repeat*, Lxx*Es*.1.17, Aristid.*Or*.48 (24).35. **-ησις**, εως, ἡ, *after-* or *repeated narration*, Arist.*Rh*. 1414^{b}14, Corn.*Rh*.p.364H.

ἐπιδιήκω, *extend through*, Sor.*Fract*.2.

ἐπιδιιστάω, = sq., *dilate*, τὸ στόμα τῆς ὑστέρας Aspasia ap.Aët.16. 22.

ἐπιδιίστημι, *let an interval elapse*, σύμμετρον ἐπιδιαστήσαντες Philum.ap.Orib.45.29.48. 2. Pass., ἐπιδιίσταμαι *have a second diastole*, of the pulse, Ruf.*Syn.Puls*.8.7. 3. -αμένων τῶν βραχιόνων *getting more separated*, Sor.2.62.

ἐπιδῐκ-άζω, *adjudge property in dispute to* one, of the judge, ἐ. κλῆρόν τινι Is.11.26, D.48.26:—Pass., ἐπιδεδικασμένου καὶ ἔχοντος τὸν κλῆρον *having had* it *adjudged to one* and being in possession, Id.43. 7: abs., Lexib.16. II. Med., of the claimant, *go to law to establish one's claim*, Pl.*Lg*.874a, *PGnom*.28,40 (ii A.D.); ἔχω.. τὸν κλῆρον ἐπιδικασάμενος I have obtained it *by a lawsuit*, Is.11.19. 2. c. gen., *sue for, claim at law*, ἐπιδικάζεσθαι τοῦ κλήρου Lys.*Fr*.32, Is.3.41, D. 43.3; ἐ. τῆς ἐπικλήρου *claim the hand of* the heiress, ib.55, cf. And.1. 120, Is.10.5; Ἐπιδικαζόμενος, ὁ, title of plays by Philem., Diph., and Apollod.; later ἐ. τῆς ἀρχῆς J.*AJ*19.2.1: metaph., ἐ. τῆς μέσης χώρας Arist.*EN*1107^{b}31:—Pass., *to be assigned*, of an heiress, D.S.12. 18. **-ᾰσία**, ἡ, *process at law to obtain an inheritance*, Is.3.41,61 (pl.), Lex ap.D.43.16, Ph.2.443; τῆς θυγατρὸς *for* her *hand* as heiress, Is.3.72. **-άσιμος** [ᾰ], ον, *to be claimed as one's right*, J.*AJ*4.2.4; *much sought for*, Luc.*Somn*.9. **-ατοί**, οἱ, *those to whom property is adjudged*, *IG*5(2).159.6 (Tegea, v B.C.).

ἐπιδῐκεῖν (cf. δικεῖν), *throw upon*, δίκον φύλλ' ἔπι Pi.*P*.9.124.

ἐπιδῐκ-έω, *render justice*, τινί *Schwyzer*366*A* 23 (Tolophon, iii B.C.). II. = ἐπιδικάζομαι, *Mon.Ant*.23.85 (Adalia). **-ος**, ον, *disputed at law, liable to be made the subject of a process at law* (cf. ἀνεπίδικος), ἐ. τινί ἐστιν ὁ κλῆρος Is.3.3,43, cf. 11.10; μὴ ἐ. εἶναι τὸν κλῆρον D.44.46. Adv. -κως, ἀνυέσθω Petos.ap.Vett.Val.128.27. II. Subst. ἐπίδικος, ἡ, *an heiress for whose hand her next of kin are claimants at law*, Is.3.64; ἐ. τινα καταλιπεῖν ib.73. 2. generally, *subject to a judicial decision*, δίδωμι ἐμαυτὸν ἐπίδικον τοῖς δημόταις I commit myself *to* the people's *decision*, D.H.7.58 codd.; *disputed*, of territory, πρός τινας Plu.*Cleom*.4; ἐ. νίκη *a disputed* victory, Id.*Fab*.3.

ἐπιδῐμερής, ές, *containing* 1⅔, Nicom.*Ar*.1.20, al.

ἐπιδῖν-εύω, later form for sq., Opp.*H*.4.218, Hld.3.3. **-έω**, *whirl for* the throw, *swing round* before throwing, ῥῖψ' ἐπιδινήσας Il. 3.378, cf. Od.9.538, etc.:—Med., *turn over in one's mind, resolve*, ἐμοὶ τόδε θυμὸς πόλλ' ἐπιδινεῖται 20.218:—Pass., *wheel about*, as birds in the air, 2.151; Σιληνοὶ.. ὅθμασι δινήθησαν ἔπι Nic.*Al*.33; so ἐπιδινεῖν αὐτούς, of drones, Arist.*HA*624^{a}24.

ἐπιδιόγκωσις, εως, ἡ, *swelling up*, Sor.1.48 (pl.), 2.31.

ἐπιδίομαι, = -διώκω, inf. -δίεσθαι, part. -διόμενος *GDI*4998 (Gortyn).

ἐπιδιορθ-όω, *correct afterwards*, *GDI*5039.9 (Hierapytna, ii B.C.): —Med., ἐ. τὰ λείποντα *to have* deficiencies *set right also, complete* unfinished *reforms*, *Ep.Tit*.1.5; simply, *correct*, Syrian. *in Metaph*.167. 11. **-ωσις**, εως, ἡ, *correction of a previous expression*, Hermog.*Id*. 2.7, Tib.*Fig*.9. 2. *excusing* of an unpleasant statement (opp. προ–, q.v.), Alex.*Fig*.1.4, Longin.*Rh*.p.194H. 3. simply, *correction*, Eustr. *in APo*.173.27. **-ωτικός**, ή, όν, *corrective*, Hermog.*Id*.2.4, Alex.Aphr. *in Top*.454.3. Adv. -κῶς Sch.Ar.*Pl*.493.

ἐπιδιορ-ίζω, *define* or *determine further*, Arist.*Cael*.303^{a}13, Gal.7. 706, al. **-ιστέον**, *one must define further*, Arist.*Top*.149^{a}31.

ἐπιδιουρέω, *pass along with the urine*, Hp.*Prorrh*.2.4.

ἐπιδιπλ-ᾰσιάζω, *make double*, σιτηρέσια v.l. in Hdn.6.8.8:—Pass., J.*AJ*19.1.5. **-οΐζω**, *redouble*: prob. f.l. for ἐπανδιπλάζω, A.*Eu*.1014 codd. (lyr.). **-όω**, *make double*, τὴν δέρριν Lxx*Ex*.26.9; ἐ. τὰ φύλλα *fold* them *double*, *Peripl.M.Rubr*.65. 2. *multiply by two*, Paul.Al.*H*.4:—Pass., Vett.Val.223.34. **-ωσις**, εως, ἡ, *redoubling, double fold*, Ph.2.479 (pl.).

ἐπιδισκεύω, *throw away*: hence, *discard*, in Pass., prob. in Phld. *Herc*.1251.17.

ἐπιδιστ-άζω, *doubt about* a thing, Thphr.*Od*.45; περί τινος Porph. *Marc*.19. **-ασις**, εως, ἡ, *ambiguity*, v.l. in Gal.6.136.

ἐπιδίτρῖτος, ον, *containing* 1⅔, Nicom.*Ar*.1.21.

ἐπιδιφρι-άς, άδος, ἡ, *breastwork of a chariot*, Il.10.475. **-ος**, ον, *on the car*, εἰς ὅ κε δῶρα φέρων ἐπιδίφρια θήῃ Od.15.51, cf. 75. II. *one who sits at his work, plies a sedentary* or *humble trade*, D.H.*Th*.50, *PLond*.5.1708.21 (vi A.D.), Just.*Nov*.90.1 *Intr*.; ἐ. τεχνίτης Iamb. *VP*34.245; τέχνη ἐ. *a sedentary* trade, D.H.2.28; ἐργασία Artem.2. 14. 2. Adj., *belonging to daily life*, λέξις, opp. πολιτική, δημηγορική, Phld.*Rh*.1.199S.

ἐπίδιχα· σκύφον τὸν μὴ κενόν, Hsch.

ἐπιδίψιος, ον, = δίψιος, Nic.*Th*.436.

ἐπιδῐ-ωγμός, ὁ, *continued pursuit*, ἐναντίων Plb.11.18.7. **-ώκτης**, ου, ὁ, *pursuer*, *Gloss*. **-ώκω**, *pursue after*, τινά Hdt.4.1,160, Lys. 3.35, etc.; *seek for*, Alex.Aphr.*Pr*.1.103. II. *prosecute again*, Is. *Fr*.157. III. *recite afterwards*, *PMag.Leid.V*.11.16. **-ωξις**, εως, ἡ, = ἐπιδιωγμός, Str.10.4.21, Hld.1.32.

ἐπιδοιάζω, *entertain doubts over, turn over and over*, πολέας ἐπεδοίασσα βουλάς A.R.3.21; cf. δοιάζω, ἐνδοιάζω.

ἐπίδοκα· προσδοκία, Hsch. **ἐπιδοκέω**, f.l. in And.4.29. **ἐπιδοκίδες**· προσδοκίαι, Hsch.

ἐπίδομα, ατος, τό, *contribution* to a feast, Ath.8.364f (pl.).

ἐπιδομέω, v. ἐπιδωμάω.

ἐπιδονέω, *sound* or *rattle atop*, Antiph.185.

ἐπιδοξ-άζω, *form an opinion about* a thing:—Pass., ἐπιδοξαζόμενον *matter of opinion*, Thphr.*CP*1.5.5. **-ος**, ον, *likely*, of persons, ἐ. γενέσθαι ἐπιεικεῖς *likely* to turn out well, Pl.*Tht*.143d; ἐ. τοῦτο πείσεσθαι *in danger* of suffering.., Hdt.6.12; ἐ. ὢν πάσχειν Antipho 2.1.5, cf. 2.4.9; ἐ. ὢν τυχεῖν being *expected* to gain.., Isoc.6.8; τοὺς ἐ. γενήσεσθαι πονηρούς Id.20.12; ἐπιδοξοτέρου ὄντος (sc. αἱρεθῆναι) App.*BC*1.32: sts. c. fut. part., ἐ. ἦσαν ἐμβαλοῦντες Plu.*Agis* 13; of things, ἐ. ἡ ἀπόστασις παρασχίδων ὀστέων ἀπιέναι Hp.*Fract*.24; ἐ. γενέσθαι Hdt.1.89; πρὸς οὓς ἐ. [ἐστι] πολεμεῖν Arist.*Rh*.1359^{b}39: abs., ὅσα..κακὰ ἐπίδοξα καταλαμβάνειν (-λαμβάνει codd.) Hdt.4. 11. II. of repute, *glorious*, κῦδος Pi.*N*.9.46; and in late Prose, as Lxx*Si*.3.18, D.S.13.83, Plu.2.239d, etc. Adv. -ξως Lxx1*Es*.9. 45, *IG*12(7).117,288 (Amorgos), Artem.2.30. **-ότης**, ητος, ἡ, *glory*, Aq.*Za*.6.13, al.

ἐπιδορᾰτίς, ίδος, ἡ, *tip, point of a lance, spear-head*, Demad.20, Plb. 6.25.5, al., Corn.*ND*30, Plu.2.217e. II. = σαυρωτήρ (q.v.), *AB* 303. III. *spear-shaft*, gloss on χάρμη, Sch.Pi.*Dith.Oxy*.3. 13. IV. *dewlap*, *Gloss*. (nisi leg. ἐπιδορά τις vel ἐπιδορίς).

ἐπίδορπ-α, τά, *second course*: hence, of a small offering, Herod. 4.13. **-ίδιος**, ον, = ἐπιδόρπιος, *AP*6.299 (Phan.). **-ίζομαι**, *eat in the second course* or *for dessert*, τι Diph.79, Sophil.4.5: in Poll. 6.102 ἐπιδορπήσασθαι is f.l. for -ίσασθαι, cf. ib.79. **-ιος**, ον (α, ον Ath.4.130c), *for use after dinner*, ὕδωρ (cf. προσδόρπιος) Theoc.13. 36; *for dessert*, τράπεζαι Ath. l.c.; also τεῦχος ἐ., of the stomach, Nic.*Al*.21. **-ίς**, ίδος, ἡ, old name for δεῖπνον, Philem.ap.Ath.1. 11d. **-ισμα**, ατος, τό, *second course, dessert*, Philippid.20 (pl.), *Com.Adesp*.141 (pl.), Ath.14.664f. **-ισμός**, ὁ, = foreg., *dessert*, Arist.*Fr*.104.

ἐπι-δόσιμος, ον, *given over and above*, ἐ. παρὰ τἄλλα τοῦτ' ἔσται Alex.65; ἐ. [δεῖπνα] *to which unexpected luxuries have been added*, Crobyl.5. II. *contributed freely*, τριήρης *IG*2^{2}.1629.960, cf. 950, *Inscr.Prien*.112.100 (i B.C.). III. ἐπιδόσιμον, τό, *return* handed in, *PLond*.1.131^{r}.348. 2. ἐπιδόσιμος (sc. λόγος), ὁ, *section* of a document, *PRyl*.233.11 (ii A.D.). **-δοσις**, εως, ἡ, *free giving*, ἐν ἐπιδόσει καὶ χάριτι τὴν ἀλλαγὴν ποιοῦνται τούτων Plb.34.8.10. II. *free gift*, esp. *voluntary contribution* to the state, '*benevolence*', *benefaction*, οἱ τὰς μεγάλας ἐπιδόσεις ἐπιδόντες D.18.171; ἐγένοντ' εἰς Εὔβοιαν ἐπιδόσεις παρ' ὑμῖν πρῶται κτλ. Id.21.161, cf. Thphr.*Char*.22.3; ἐπιδόσεις πεποιῆσθαί τισι *Histria* 7.23 (i B.C.); *charitable endowment*, *POxy*.705.59 (iii A.D.). 2. *largess* given to soldiers, Lat. *donativum*, Hdn.1.5.1, al. III. *handing in* of a petition, return, etc., *BGU*1193.11 (i B.C.), etc. IV. (ἐπιδίδωμι III) *increase, advance, progress*, ἐ. ἐς πλῆθος τοῦ ῥυφήματος Hp.*Acut*.12; *progress* of disease, Gal.1.198; ἐ. ἔχειν to be capable of *progress* or *improvement*, Pl.*Tht*. 146b, *Smp*.175e, cf. Plb.1.20.2; ἐ. λαμβάνειν πρός τι Isoc.15.267, cf. Arist.*Cat*.10^{b}28; ἐ. ποιῆσαι τοῖς πράγμασι Plb.1.36.2; ἡ ἐ. γίγνεται πρός τι Arist.*EN*1109^{a}17; τῶν τεχνῶν αἱ ἐ. ib.1098^{a}25; ἡ τρίτη ἐ. τῆς ὀλιγαρχίας *stage*, Id.*Pol*.1293^{a}27. b. *devotion, addiction*, τινός *to* a thing, D.H.*Comp*.4 codd.; ἐ. μὲν εἰς τιμὴν πλούτου.., ὀλιγωρία δὲ τῶν καλῶν Gal.10.172. 2. *giving way, relaxation*, of sinews, Hp. *Art*.8 (pl.); ἐ. ἐπιδοῦναι ib.72. 3. ἐ. αὐτοῦ self-*surrender*, Plot.6. 9.11. **-δοτήρ**, ῆρος, ὁ, *giver of more*, τέκνων, opp. ἀφαιρέτης, of planets, Ptol.*Tetr.*189. **-δοτικός**, ή, όν, *ready to give to those who need*, distd. from μεταδοτικός by Ammon.*Diff.*p.56 V. II. *ready to give way*, Hp.*Mochl.*41.

ἐπιδουλεύω, *to be a slave*, παρά τινι Jul.*Ep.*198.

ἐπιδουπέω, *make a noise* or *clashing*, ταῖς σαρίσαις Plu.*Eum.*14; ἠχείοις Id.*Crass.*23.

ἐπιδούριτον· ἐπιπαραστροφίδα, Hsch.

ἐπιδοχή, ἡ, *reception in addition*, πολιτῶν Th.6.17 (pl.). II. *undertaking*, *POxy.*102.18, 103.16 (iv A.D.).

ἐπιδράγματα, τά, *offerings plucked*, πυρῶν καὶ καρπῶν Orac. in *App.Anth.*p.602 (Tralles).

ἐπιδρᾰμεῖν, ἐπιδρᾰμέτην, v. ἐπιτρέχω.

ἐπιδράσσομαι, Att. **-ττομαι**, *lay hold of*, τινός Plu.*Alex.*25, Gal. 4.537, etc.; τι Alciphr.3.60: metaph., τινός Phld.*Rh.*2.266S.; ἀληθείας Jul.*Or.*6.188c; παντὸς πολιτεύματος Plu.2.793c; τὸ ἀκόλαστον ἐ. τινός Id.*Oth.*2.

ἐπιδράω, *perform over* a person, of purificatory rites, τινί τι Philostr.*VA*6.5.

ἐπιδρέπω, *pluck*, σταφυλήν Hp.*Mul.*1.105.

ἐπιδρομ-άδην, Adv., = ἐπιτροχάδην, Orph.*A.*561, *H.*21.5; *rapidly*, Nic.*Th.*481; *cursorily*, ἱστορῆσαι Str.2.1.6. **-έω**, = ἐπιτρέχω, cj. for ἐνι- in Max.282. **-ή**, ἡ, *running over, inroad*, κυμάτων Arist. *Mu.*400ᵃ26 (pl.); *onward motion*, *IGRom.*4.503.34 (Pergam.). 2. metaph., *brief notice*, Phld.*Rh.*2.268S.; ἐν τῇ ἐ. τῶν φιλοσόφων in his *summary notice* of them, D.L.7.48; *summary*, προειρημένων λόγων Corn.*Rh.*p.389H.; ἀποδείξεων Dam.*Pr.*369; ἐπιτομὰς ἢ συνάψεις ἢ ἐπιδρομάς Gal.9.431; ὡς ἐν ἐπιδρομῇ δεδείχθω Iamb.*in Nic.* p.72P. II. *inroad, raid, attack*, Th.4.34,56; τῷ τειχίσματι ib. 23; ἐξ ἐπιδρομῆς ἁρπαγή plundering by means of *an inroad*, Hdt. 1.6: hence ἐξ ἐπιδρομῆς on *the spur of the moment*, ἐξ ἐ. αἱρέσεις ποιεῖσθαι Pl.*R.*619d; εἰπεῖν Plu.*Ant.*80, cf. Men.*Pk.*148; *cursorily*, μνήμην ποιήσασθαι φαύλως καὶ ἐξ ἐ. D.H.*Pomp.*3 (so κατ' ἐπιδρομήν Aps.*Rh.*p.258H.); μηδὲν ἐξ ἐ. παθεῖν by *a sudden attack*, D.21. 138, cf. D.H.2.3. III. *office of inspector*, τῆς μητροπόλεως *PFay.* 23.2 (ii A.D.). IV. *a place to which ships run in, landing-place*, Λιβύης.. ἐρήμους ἀξένους τ' ἐπιδρομάς E.*Hel.*404; πλοῦν οὔριον..'Ιλίου τ' ἐπιδρομάς Id.*IA*1597; τὰς ἐ. τῆς θαλάσσης διαχῶσαι Phalar.*Ep.* 62. V. *flow* of blood (to an atrophied part), Hp.*Off.*24. **-ία**, ἡ, = foreg. II, *assault*, A.R.3.593 (pl.). **-ικός**, ή, όν, *hasty, cursory, summary*, S.E.*M.*5.3 (Comp.). **-ίς**, ίδος, ἡ, *pulley*, *Gloss.* **-ος**, ον, *that may be overrun*, τεῖχος ἐ. a wall *that may be scaled*, Il.6.434 (but τεῖχος ἅρμασιν ἐ. *on which* chariots *can run*, *AP*9.58 (Antip.(?))); ἐ. Ζεφύροισι *overrun* by the W. winds, ib.10.13 (Satyr.), cf. Opp.*H.* 3.635; νηυσὶν ἐ. ἐστι θάλασσα Mosch.2.137; τὰ ἐ. καὶ ταπεινά, of countries, Plu.*Eum.*9. 2. metaph., *intelligible*, τοῖς ἀμυήτοις Them.*Or.*13.162c. 3. *fatally easy*, πρᾶγμα Just.*Nov.*72.6. II. Act., *running over, spreading*, of sores, Nic.*Th.*242. 2. metaph., *over-hasty*, rash, γνώμη, ὅρκος, Paus.9.21.6, 33.3. 3. *following freely* or *easily*, A.*Supp.*124 (lyr.); τὸ σὸν κατὰ χειρὸς ἐ. καὶ λεῖον Luc. *Dem.Enc.*10. III. Subst. ἐπίδρομος, ὁ, *cord which runs along the upper edge of a net*, X.*Cyn.*6.9, Poll.5.29, cf. Plin.*HN*19.11; so δι' ὀργάνων ἐπιδρόμων (prob.) by *running ropes*, Plu.*Sert.*22. 2. *a small sail at the stern*, like the *mizzen-sail* of a yawl (or, acc. to Poll.1.91, *the mast of such a sail*), Isid.*Etym.*19.3.3.

ἐπίδροσος, ον, *catching the dew*, prob. cj. in Thphr.*HP*7.14.1.

ἐπιδυσφημέω, *give an ill name to*, τινά Arist.*EN*1145ᵃ33.

ἐπιδυσ⟨ω⟩χεῖν· ἐπιτωθάζειν, Hsch.

ἐπιδύτης [ῠ], ου, ὁ, = ἐπενδύτης, Thd.1*Ki.*2.19, *Is.*59.17.

ἐπιδύω (**-δύνω** [ῡ] Man.6.642), aor. 2 ἐπέδυν, *set upon* or *so as to interrupt* an action, μὴ πρὶν ἐπ' ἠέλιον δῦναι Il.2.413; ὁ ἥλιος μὴ ἐ. ἐπὶ τῷ παροργισμῷ ὑμῶν *Ep.Eph.*4.26, cf. Lxx *De.*24.15, Ph.2.324.

ἐπιδωμάω, *build upon*, pf. Pass. ἐπιδεδώμηται Ph.Byz.*Mir.*4.4: written ἐπιδεδομ- ib.2.3 (teste Bast *Ep.Cr.*p.45); cf. δωμάω, ἐνδώμησις.

ἐπιδωρέομαι, *give besides*, Gal.14.305.

ἐπιδώτης, ου, ὁ, *the Bountiful*, epith. of gods, esp. Zeus at Mantinea, Paus.8.9.2, cf. Plu.2.1102e:—hence **'Επιδώτειον**, τό, temple at Epidaurus, *IG*4.1492.24.

ἐπιέβδομος λόγος ratio *of* 8:7, Ptol.*Harm.*1.15.

ἐπιεθανίς· λεπτὸν πρόβατον, Hsch. post ἐπηετα(ν)ῶν.

ἐπιείκεια, ἡ, *reasonableness*, ἔχει τινὰ οὗτος ὁ λόγος ἐπιείκειαν Hp. *Fract.*31. 2. *equity*, opp. strict law, Arist.*Top.*141ᵃ16, etc.; κατ' ἐπιείκειαν, opp. κατὰ τοὺς ὅρκους, Isoc.18.34; ἄκαμπτον εἰς ἐ. Plu.*Cat. Mi.*4. 3. of persons, *reasonableness, fairness*, Th.3.40,48, 5.86, Pl.*Lg.*735a, etc.; ἐ. καὶ πρᾳότης Plu.*Per.*39, cf. 2*Ep.Cor.*10.1; also, *goodness, virtuousness*, Lys.16.11, D.21.207, Arist.*EN*1175ᵇ24: pl., joined with χάριτες, Isoc.4.63, cf. 15.149. II. personified, *Clemency*, Plu.*Caes.*57.

ἐπιείκελος, ον, = εἴκελος, *like*, τινί, the masc. freq. in Hom. (esp. in Il.), but only in phrases ἐ. ἀθανάτοισιν, θεοῖς ἐ., Il.1.[265], 4.394, Od.24.36, etc.; so θεοῖς ἐπιείκελα τέκνα Hes.*Th.*968.

ἐπιεικ-εύομαι, *to be* ἐπιεικής, Lxx 2*Es.*9.8 (cod. A, cf. Hsch.). **-ής**, ές, *fitting, meet, suitable*, τύμβον οὐ μάλα πολλὸν.., ἀλλ' ἐπιεικέα τοῖον not very large but *meet* in size, Il.23.246; τείσουσι βοῶν ἐπιεικέ' ἀμοιβήν a *fair* recompense for them, Od.12.382.—Elsewh. Hom. has only the neut. ἐπιεικές, either in the phrase ὡς ἐπιεικές as is *meet*, Il.19.147, 23.537, Od.8.389: or c. inf., ὅν κ' ἐπιεικὲς ἀκουέμεν whom it may be *meet* for you to hear, Il.1.547; ὅπλα.. οἷ' ἐπιεικὲς ἔργ' ἔμεν ἀθανάτων such as is *meet* they should be, 19.21, cf. 23.50, Od.2.207. II. after Hom., 1. of statements, rights, etc., a. *reasonable, specious*, ἡ δὲ τρίτη τῶν ὁδῶν πολλὸν ἐπιεικεστάτη ἐοῦσα μάλιστα ἔψευσται Hdt.2.22; ἐ. πρόφασις Th.3.9; λόγος Pl.*Ti.*67d; ἐπιεικῆ λέγειν Id.*Ap.*34d; ἐ. ὁδός a *tolerable* road, Plu.*Crass.*22. b. opp. δίκαιος, *fair, equitable, not according to the letter of the law*, ἐπανόρθωμα νομίμου δικαίου Arist.*EN*1137ᵇ11, cf. *Rh.*1374ᵃ26; τῶν δικαίων τὰ ἐπιεικέστερα προτιθεῖσι Hdt.3.53; οὔτε τοὐπ. οὔτε τὴν χάριν οἶδεν, μόνην δ' ἔστερξε τὴν ἁπλῶς δίκην S.*Fr.*770, cf. E.*Fr.*645; συγχωρεῖν τἀπιεικῆ τινι Ar.*Nu.*1438; ἐπιεικέστερον ἢ δικαιότερον Antipho 2.2.13; ἐ. ὁμολογία Th.3.4; γνώμη Ar.*V.*1027; τὸ ἐ. καὶ σύγγνωμον Pl.*Lg.* 757e; πρὸς τὸ ἐ., = ἐπιεικῶς 3, Th.4.19. 2. of persons, *able, capable*, παῖς τὰ μὲν ἄλλα ἐ., ἄφωνος δέ Hdt.1.85; οἱ ἐπιεικέστατοι τῶν τριηράρχων X.*HG*1.1.30; τίνες.. τῶν νέων ἐπίδοξοι γενέσθαι ἐ. may be expected to turn out *well*, Pl.*Tht.*143d, cf. *Lg.*957a; τοὺς ἐ. καὶ τοῦ δήμου καὶ τῶν εὐπόρων Arist.*Ath.*26.1. b. in moral sense, *reasonable, fair, good*, ἐ. τὴν ψυχήν, φύσει, Pl.*Smp.*210b, *R.*538c: abs., Th.8. 93, Isoc.1.48, *Ep.Jac.*3.17, etc.; ἐ. ἄνδρες, opp. μοχθηροί, Arist.*Po.* 1452ᵇ34; ἐ. περὶ τὰ συμβόλαια D.34.30; τοὐπιεικές *fairness, goodness*, S.*OC*1127. c. with social or political connotation, the *upper* or *educated classes*, λέγω ἀντικεῖσθαι τοὺς ἐ. τῷ πλήθει Arist.*Pol.* 1308ᵇ27, cf. *Ath.*28.1. III. Adv. **-κῶς**, Ion. **-κέως**, *fairly, tolerably, moderately*, ἐγγλύσσει ἐ. Hdt.2.92; ἐ. δάκνειν, παρρησίαν ἄγειν, Phld.*Lib.*pp.13,45O.; ἐ. ἔχειν to be *pretty well*, Hp.*Coac.*368; ἐ. ἐξεπίστασθαι Ar.*V.*1249; ἔστι τὸ χωρίον ἐ. ἰσχυρόν *Hell.Oxy.*13.5; ἐ. ἀναίσθητον Arist.*GC*319ᵇ20; ἐ. πλατύ Id.*HA*495ᵇ27, cf. 497ᵃ23; οἱ πυρετοὶ ἐς τεταρταῖον ἐ. μεθίστανται *about* the fourth day, Hp.*Coac.* 140, cf. Alex.281; ἐ. τὸ τρίτον μέρος *pretty nearly, about*, Plb.6.26.8; ἐ. οἷοί τε ἦσαν κατέχειν were *fairly well* able.., Pl.*Phd.*117c; ἐ. μὲν.. *perhaps*, Id.*Grg.*493c. 2. *probably, reasonably*, Id.*R.*431e, etc.: Sup. **-έστατα**, γενέσθαι *most suitably*, Id.*Lg.*753b. 3. *with moderation, mildly, kindly*, οὐκ ἐ. ἐντυγχάνων οὐδὲ πρᾴως Plu.*Pyrrh.*23; ἐ. ἔχειν πρός τινα Isoc.15.4: Comp. **-έστερον**, διακείμενοι Id.8.61. 4. *generally, usually*, Plu.*Pel.*18, Jul.*Mis.*348c, Lib.*Or.*11.19, al.

ἐπιεικοσθέβδομος λόγος ratio *of* 28:27, Ptol.*Harm.*1.13.

ἐπιεικοστόμονος λόγος ratio *of* 22:21, Ptol.*Harm.*2.1.

ἐπιείκοστος λόγος ratio *of* 21:20, Ptol.*Harm.*1.15.

ἐπιεικοστο-τέταρτος λόγος ratio *of* 25:24, Ptol.*Harm.*2.14. **-τρίτος** λόγος ratio *of* 24:23, ib.1.15.

ἐπιεικτός, ή, όν, *yielding*, Ep. word, in Hom. always with neg., σθένος οὐκ ἐ. *unyielding, dauntless* might, Il.8.32; μένος ἔμπεδον οὐδ' ἐ. Od.19.493; μένος.. ἀάσχετον, οὐκ ἐ. Il.5.892; πένθος ἄσχετον, οὐκ ἐ. *ceaseless*, 16.549. 2. ἔργα γελαστὰ καὶ οὐκ ἐπιεικτά not *tolerable*, Od.8.307; ὀστέον οὐκ ἐ. Opp.*H.*1.526. 3. *permissible*, οὐκ ἐπιεικτὰ ζητῶν Anon.*Incred.*15(14) = Luc.*Astr.*15: c. dat., *befitting*, βροτοῖσιν Man.6.402.

ἐπιειμένος, v. ἐπιέννυμι.

ἐπιείσομαι, ἐπιεισάμενος, only fut. and aor., *rush, hasten to* or *against*, τοὺς ἄλλους ἐπιείσομαι, ὅν κε κιχείω Il.11.367; ἀγροὺς ἐπιείσομαι ἠδὲ βοτῆρας Od.15.504; ἐπιεισαμένη πρὸς στήθεα χειρὶ παχείῃ ἤλασε Il.21.424 (v.l. ἐπερεισαμένη). (Cf. εἴσομαι II: perh. fut. and aor. of (ἐπι-)(ϝ)ίεμαι.)

ἐπιεκᾰτοστοεικοστόγδοος λόγος ratio *of* 129:128, Ptol.*Harm.* 1.10.

ἐπίεκτος λόγος ratio *of* 7:6, Ptol.*Harm.*1.15.

ἐπιέλδομαι, poet. for ἐπέλδομαι, *desire*, ἐνισπεῖν A.R.4.783.

ἐπιελίκτωρ, ορος, ὁ, *one who rolls round*, coined to explain the Homeric ἠλέκτωρ, Sch.Il.19.398.

ἐπιέλπομαι, Ep. for ἐπέλπομαι (q.v.).

ἐπίελπτος, ον, *to be hoped* or *expected*, Archil.74.5, Opp.*H.*4. 311.

ἐπιένᾰτος λόγος ratio *of* 10:9, Ptol.*Harm.*1.15.

ἐπιενδέκᾰτος λόγος ratio *of* 12:11, Ptol.*Harm.*2.14.

ἐπιεννεᾰκαιδέκᾰτος λόγος ratio *of* 20:19, Ptol.*Harm.*2.1.

ἐπιέννῡμι, *put on besides* or *over*, χλαῖναν δ' ἐπιέσσαμεν we threw a cloak *over* him, Od.20.143: elsewh. Hom. has only pf. part. Pass. ἐπιειμένος (Aeol. ἐπέμμενος Sapph.70): in metaph. sense c. acc., ἀναιδείην, ἀλκήν, *clad in* shamelessness, strength, Il.1.149, 8.262, etc.; ἐ. ἀχλὺν *AP*7.283 (Leon.); λευκοῖσι κόμας ἐ. ὤμοις covered *with* hair *over* her white shoulders, A.R.3.45; χαλκὸν ἐπίεσται *has* brass *upon* or *over it*, Orac.ap.Hdt.1.47:—Med., *put on oneself besides, put on* as an *upper* garment, χλαίνας ἐπειννυσθαι Hdt.4.64: metaph., ἐπὶ δὲ νεφέλην ἕσσαντο Il.14.350; γᾶν ἐπιεσσόμενος (fut.), i.e. to be buried, Pi.*N.*11.16; so γῆν ἐπιέσασθαι X.*Cyr.*6.4.6; γῆν ἐπιεννύμεθα *AP*7.480 (Leon.), cf. Theoc.*Epigr.*9.4: also, c. acc. rei, ἐπιεσσάμενοι νώτων κρόκαις *having wrapt one's* shoulders *with* it, Pi.*N.*10.44.—Old Ep. Verb, not found till late (exc. Sapph. l.c.) in the form **ἐφέννῡμι**, because of the digamma, v. ἕννυμι, καταέννυμι; ἐπιέσασθαι is retained even in X. l.c.; ἐφέσσεσθαι, ἐφέσσατο, A.R.1.691, 1326; ἐφεσσάμενος Theoc. l.c., *AP*7.299 (Nicom.), 446 (Hegesipp.).

ἐπιεξηκοστοτέταρτος λόγος ratio *of* 65:64, Ptol.*Harm.*1.11.

ἐπιεπτᾰκαιδέκᾰτος λόγος ratio *of* 18:17, Ptol.*Harm.*1.10.

ἐπιεργάζομαι, v. ἐπεργάζομαι.

ἐπίεργος, ον, perh., = ἔπεργος, θησαυρός *PLond.*2.216.8 (i A.D.).

ἐπιέτ-εια, ἡ, *annual college of magistrates*, *IG*5(2).6.61 (Tegea, iv B.C.). **-ής**, ές, *of this year*, ἀγών *SIG*690 (Delph., ii B.C.); χιών v.l. in Plb.3.55.1.

ἐπιέψεται, v. ἐφέπω. **ἐπιϝοικία, ἐπίϝοικος**, v. ἐποικ-. **ἔπιζα**· ὄρνεα (Cypr.), Hsch. **ἐπιζάνω**, Ion. for ἐφιζάνω. **ἐπιζάξ**· ἐπὶ τὰ ἀριστερὰ καὶ ἐπ' εὐθείας, Hsch. (with other expll., cf. ἐπιτάξ).

ἐπιζᾰρέω, = ἐπιβαρέω, E.*Rh.*441 (prob., -ζάτει codd.), *Ph.*45: said to be Arc. by Eust.909.28.

ἐπιζάφελος [ᾰ], ον, *vehement, violent*, χόλος Il.9.525. Adv. -λῶς (as if from ἐπιζαφελής, which never occurs, v. Eust.769.22) *vehemently, furiously*, ἐ. χαλεπαίνειν, μενεαίνειν, Il.9.516, Od.6.330; ἐρεείνειν *h.Merc.*487: also neut. as Adv., ἐπιζάφελον κοτέουσα A.R. 4.1672.

ἐπιζάω, Ion. -ζώω, *survive*, εἰ ἐπέζωσε Hdt.1.120; ἂν ὡς ὀλίγιστον χρόνον ἐπιζώῃ Pl.*Lg.*661c (-ζώιη cod.), cf. Eus.Mynd.38, etc.: metaph. of envy, Plu.*Num.*22.

ἐπιζείω, poet. for ἐπιζέω, Orph.*A.*459.

ἐπίζεμα, ατος, τό, *boiling* or *boiled liquid*, Sm.*Ho.*10.7.

ἐπιζέννῡμι, = ἐπιζέω, *boil in*, οἴνῳ Gal.13.319 (Pass.).

ἐπι-ζεύγνῡμι and -ύω, *join at top*, Hdt.7.36; τοὺς κίονας τοῖς ἐπιστυλίοις Plu.*Per.*13; τοὺς δακτύλους τῆς ἑτέρας χειρὸς ἐπὶ τὴν ἑτέραν ἐ. Arist.*Pr.*912^{b}14; simply, *bind fast*, χεῖρας ἱμᾶσι Theoc.22.3. 2. *join to*, πώλοις..τόνδ' ἐπιζεύξασ' ὄχον A.*Eu.*405: metaph., ἐπέζευκται κοινὸν ὄνομά [τινι καί τινι] Arist.*HA*531^{b}22, cf. *Rh.*1407^{b}19; θνητὸν βίον ἀθανάτῳ ἐ. Ph.1.209; μηδ' ἐπιζευχθῇς στόμα φήμῃ πονηρᾷ nor *let* thy mouth *be joined to* evil sayings, A.*Ch.*1044: Math., ἐπεζεύχθω ἀπὸ κτλ. *let* the point A *be joined to* the point B, Arist.*Mete.*376^{a}17. II. *enclose, join up*, of hills, Plb.1.75.4, 3.49.7. III. ἐπεζευγμένον, τό, *minor premise of a disjunctive syllogism*, Chrysipp.ap.S.E.*P.*2.158. -ζευκτήρ, ῆρος, ὁ, *strap, trace*, Hsch. -ζευκτικός, ή, όν, *connective*, [σύνδεσμος] A.D.*Synt.*272.3, cf. Sch.A.R.1.1349. -ζευξις, εως, ἡ, *fastening together, joining*, Thphr.*HP*2.6.1, prob. for ἐπίδεσις in Paul.Aeg.6.97. II. Gramm., *repetition* of a word, Hdn.*Fig.*p.99 S., Phoeb.*Fig.*1.3. III. *addition*, τοῦ τόπου A.D.*Synt.*336.10, cf. Ptol.*Tetr.*1.

ἐπιζέφῠρος, ον, *towards the west, western*, Euph.121: the Italian Locrians were called **Ἐπιζεφύριοι**, Hdt.6.23, etc., f.l. in Pi.*O.*10.13.

ἐπιζέω, *boil over*, πυρὸς καὶ κλύδωνος ἐπιζέσαντος Plu.2.399d; *bubble up*, πομφόλυγες -ζέουσαι Arr. in Stob.*App.*p.9 G.; *effervesce*, Dsc.5.74: metaph., ἀκούσαντί μοι ἡ νεότης ἐπέζεσε my youthful spirit *boiled over* when I heard, Hdt.7.13; οὐ θαυμάσιον ἐπιζεῖν τὴν χολήν Ar.*Th.*468; θυμάλωψ ἐπέζεσεν (as if he had said θυμός) Id.*Ach.*321; κέντρ' ἐπιζέσαντα of the poison *working out* of the skin, S.*Tr.*840 (lyr.): c. dat., δεινόν τι πῆμα Πριαμίδαις ἐπέζεσεν E.*Hec.*583. II. Act., *cause to boil, heat*, c. acc., ἐπιζεῖν λέβητα πυρί Id.*Cyc.*392: metaph., δεινή τις ὀργὴ δαιμόνων ἐπέζεσε τὸ Ταντάλειον σπέρμα Id.*IT*987.

ἐπίζηλος, Dor. -ζᾶλος, ον, *enviable, happy*, τύχα B.5.52, cf. A.*Ag.*939, Ptol.*Tetr.*186: written ἐπίδηλα in *TAM*2(1).245.12 (Lycia).

ἐπιζήμι-ος, Dor. etc. -ζάμιος [ᾱ], ον, *bringing loss upon, hurtful, prejudicial*, Charon 12, Th.1.32, Isoc.2.18, etc.; τινί X.*Mem.*2.7.9, cf. Aeschin.1.45. Adv. -ίως Poll.8.147, D.Chr.14.18. 2. *penal*: ἐπιζήμια, τά, *punishments, penalties*, Pl.*Lg.*784e, 788b; -ζάμια *Tab. Heracl.*1.127; χρησόμεθα ἐπιζημίοις, = ἐπιζημιώσομεν, Epist.Philipp. ap.D.18.157: sg., -ζάμιον, τό, *fine*, *IG*5(2).6.36 (Tegea), 5(1).1498 (Messenia). II. *liable to punishment*, of persons, Pl.*Lg.*765a; of acts, Arist.*Pol.*1297^{a}33, cf. *PRev.Laws*7.6 (iii B.C.). -όω, *mulct*, στατῆρι κατὰ τὸν ἄνδρα τῆς ἡμέρας X.*HG*5.2.22. -ωμα, Dor. -ζᾱμίωμα, ατος, τό, *penalty*, *Tab.Heracl.*1.155, Poll.8.149. -ωσις, εως, ἡ, *infliction of penalties*, Arist.*Ath.*45.1 (pl.).

ἐπιζητ-έω, *seek after, wish for, miss*, τινά Hdt.3.36, Plu.*Sull.*19; οὐδὲν ἄλλο χρῆμα οὕτω ἐν βραχεῖ ἐπεζήτησα ὡς.. Hdt.5.24; μηδὲν ἐπιζητείτω *let* her *lack* nothing, *PTeb.*416.20 (iii A.D.); ἐ. τὸν ἄνθρωπον *make further search for*.., D.18.133; τῆς αἰτίας αἰτίαν ἐπιζητούσης *requiring*, Plb.1.5.3, cf. Ph.1.18: abs., οἱ ἐπιζητοῦντες *the beaters* (for game), X.*Cyr.*2.4.25:—Pass., τὰ ἐπιζητούμενα περὶ τὴν εὐδαιμονίαν Arist.*EN*1098^{b}22, cf. 1172^{b}35, Diog.Oen.23; οἱ -ούμενοι criminals '*wanted*', *POxy.*80.15 (iii A.D.). b. *request*, πρός τινας ὁμολογίαν *Anatolian Studies* 38, cf. *PMasp.*156.16 (vi A.D.). 2. *seek for besides*, μηδ' ἕτερ' ἐπιζήτει καλά Antiph.44.5; *inquire further*, περὶ.. Sor.1.2, cf. Gal.16.490. 3. Pass., ἐπιζητεῖται *is matter of question*, ἐ. πότερον.. Arist.*EN*1169^{b}13, cf. Phld.*D.*1.22, *Rh.*1.194 S., al. 4. *demand, require*, *PLille*7.6 (iii B.C.):—Pass., *POxy.*1194.2 (iii A.D.). -ημα, ατος, τό, *requirement, demand*, Phld.*D.*1.16 (pl.); τὰ φυσικὰ ἐ. Id.*Oec.*p.14 J. -ησις, εως, ἡ, *seeking after, craving*, X.Eph.2.12; τροφῆς Gal.19.372; δεινὴ τἀνδρὸς ἐ. ἦν he was sorely *missed*, J.*AJ*13.6.3, cf. 4.8.3; *desire, craving* (for drink), Herod.Med.ap.Orib.5.30.4: in pl., *cravings*, Id. in *Rh.Mus.*58.87. 2. *inquiry*, *PSI*4.386.40 (iii B.C.), Phld.*Sign.*21, 28 (pl.), J.*Ap.*1.22, Iamb.*Myst.*1.18. 3. *rendering of account for examination*, ἐ. πρός τινας θέσθαι *PLond.*5.1708.158 (vi A.D.). -ητέος, α, ον, *to be looked for, required*, Arist.*EN*1094^{b}13; *to be sought for*, Chor. in *Rh.Mus.*49.502. -ητικός, ή, όν, *apt to crave* or *miss*, τῶν κενώσεων -κὸν γίγνεσθαι τὸ σῶμα Erasistr.(?) ap.Gal.*Consuet.*5. 2. *interrogative*, σύνδεσμος Suid. s.v. μῶν.

ἐπιζῠγ-έω, in pass. sense, *to be joined*, Nic.*Fr.*74.22. -ιον, τό, = ὑποζύγιον, *IG*5(2).3.13 (Tegea, iv B.C.). II. μέρος τῆς νεώς, Hsch. -ίς, ίδος, ἡ, *iron pin* upon which the strands of the torsion-engine were wound, Ph.*Bel.*53.27, Hero *Bel.*83.5. II. *cross-beam*, Apollod.*Poliorc.*172.7.

ἐπιζυγκ(λ)-εῖν· ἐπισκαρδαμύττειν, ἐπιστένειν, ἐπικατακλᾶν, and -οῦσα· ἐπικλείουσα, μύουσα, Hsch.

ἐπίζῠγ-ος, ον, of tiles, dub. sens. in *Inscr.Délos* 366 *A* 21, 23. -όω, *shut to*, τὰς θύρας Artem.1.4, cf. Poll.10.26. -ωμα, ατος, τό, *part of the latch of a door*, *Et.Gud.*288.36.

ἐπιζώνιον, τό, *over-girth*, *Gloss.*

ἐπι-ζώννῡμι, *gird on*:—Pass., ἐπεζωσμέναι *with their clothes girt on* so as to leave the breast bare, v.l. for ὑπεζωμέναι in Hdt.2.85; ἐπεζωσμένος ἐγχειρίδιον *girt with*.., Plu.*CG*15 codd.; ταινίαις τὸν χιτῶνα ἐπιζωσθείς Paus.9.39.8. -ζώστρα, ἡ, = ζωστήρ, *girdle*, S.*Fr.*342.

ἐπιζώω, Ion. for ἐπιζάω (q.v.). **ἐπίηλε** [ῑ], v. ἐπιάλλω. **ἐπιήνδανε**, v. ἐφανδάνω.

ἐπίηρα φέρειν, = ἦρα φέρειν or ἦρα ἐπιφέρειν, bring one *acceptable gifts*, render *service*, ἐπίηρα φέροντα S.*OT*1094 (lyr.), cf. Rhian.1.21; ἐπίηρα φέρεσθαι A.R.4.375; δέχθαι *AP*13.22 (Phaedim.); ἐπίηρα, as Adv., = χάριν, *for the sake of*, Antim.87; ὃς κακὰ πόλλ' ὑπέμεινε μιῆς ἐ. θυγατρός *PHamb.*22.2 (iv A.D.). II. sg. **ἐπίηρος** *pleasant, grateful*, χθών Emp.96.1; γέρας Simm.6.3: Comp. ἐπιηρέστερος Epich.186. Cf. ἦρα, ἐπιήρανος.

ἐπιήρᾰνος, ον, *pleasing, acceptable*, οὐδέ τί μοι ποδάνιπτρα ποδῶν ἐπιήρανα θυμῷ Od.19.343. II. after Hom., *helping, assisting*, Μινύαις ἐπιήρανος Orph.*A.*98 (prob.). 2. *ruling, governing*, Ἀθηνάων ἐπιήρανε *IG*14.1389 ii 1, cf. Nonn.*D.*2.683; σοφῶν ἐ. ἔργων Emp.129.3; καλῶν ἐ. ἔργων, of Dionysus, Ion Eleg.1.15. 3. *warding off, repelling*, ἐπιήρανος ἀσπὶς ἀκόντων *AP*9.41 (Theon). 4. νεύρων ἐπιήρανος *strengthening, giving tension*, Pl.Com.173.19.

ἐπίηρος, ον, v. ἐπίηρα.

ἐπιθᾰλᾰμ-ιογράφος [γρᾰ], ὁ, *writer of epithalamia*, Tz. ad Lyc.p.1 S. -ιος, ον, *belonging to a bridal, nuptial*, ἐπιβουλή Luc.*Salt.*44; ἐ. ᾠδαί D.H.*Rh.*4.1. II. Subst. ἐπιθαλάμιος (sc. ὕμνος or ᾠδή), ὁ or ἡ, *bridal song*, sung in chorus before the bridal chamber, Theoc. 18 tit., Luc.*Symp.*40, Him.*Or.*1.1. -ίτης [ῑ], ου, ὁ, epith. of Hermes in Euboea, Hsch.

ἐπιθᾰλασσ-ίδιος, Att. -ττίδιος, ον, = sq., Th.4.76, X.*HG*3.4.28, Pl.*Lg.*704b, etc.; ἐπιθαλαττιαῖος is prob. f.l. in Str.2.1.16, 3.4.20. -ιος, Att. -ττιος, α, ον Pl.*Lg.*704d, *PRev.Laws*93.5 (iii B.C.), also ος, ον X.*HG*3.1.16:—*lying* or *dwelling on the coast*, Hdt.1.154; τὰ ἐ. Id.5.30; ἐ. τῆς Πελοποννήσου Th.2.56; *marine*, Epich.90:—in App.*Hisp.*12 **ἐπιθάλασσος** is prob. f.l.

ἐπιθαλέωσις, εως, ἡ, perh. *celebration of the festival of the Corybantes* Θάλειοι, *SIG*1014.95 (Erythrae, iii B.C.).

ἐπιθάλλω, *flourish*, prob. in Nonn.*D.*3.254 (ἔτι θ. codd.).

ἐπι-θαλπής, ές, = τερπνός, Hsch. -θάλπω, *warm on the surface*, γαῖαν Xenoph.31, cf. Plu.2.780d (Pass.); [ᾠά] Ael.*NA*10.35. II. *comfort afterwards*, *BCH*47.284 (Macedonia, Pass.). -θαλψις, εως, ἡ, *warming*, δακτύλων prob. in Paul.Aeg.6.40.

ἐπιθαλύνω, *warm, chafe*, dub. in Hsch. (ἐπιθαλάμοντι cod., fort. ἐπιθάλποντι).

ἐπιθαμβέω, *marvel at*, Nonn.*D.*1.60.

ἐπιθᾰνάτ-ιος [νᾰ], ον, *condemned to death*, D.H.7.35, Lxx *Bel* (ο') 31, 1 *Ep.Cor.*4.9; ἐ. μέλος, of Arion, Tz.*H.*1.400. Adv. -ίως, ἔχειν, = ἐπιθανάτως ἔχειν, Ael.*VH*13.27. II. αἱ ἐ. δᾷδες the *funeral* torches, Lib.*Decl.*40.15; but ἐ. ἐπιστολή *deadly*, ib.2.28. -ος, ον, *sick to death, hard at death's door*, D.50.60. Adv. -τως, ἔχειν to be *sick to death*, Poll.3.106. II. *deadly*, ὕβωσις Hp.*Mochl.*36; of poisons, Thphr.*CP*6.4.5.

ἐπιθᾰνής, ές, = foreg., Ael.*Fr.*102.

ἐπιθάπτω, *bury again*, Philostr.*Her.*1.3. II. *bury another in the same grave*, *CIG*4341 *d* (Attalia), 4366 *k* (Termessus), sqq.

ἐπιθαρσ-έω, Att. -ρρέω, *put trust in* or *on*, θεῶν ἀρωγαῖς Plu.*Brut.*37, cf. S.E.*M.*1.270. II. *take heart to resist*, τοῖς ἐχθροῖς App.*BC*3.10, cf. Ael.*NA*4.34, 9.1; ἐ. τῷ πελάγει *venture on*.., ib.5.56: abs., *take courage*, D.C.41.50, al. -ύνω, Att. -ρρύνω, *cheer on, encourage*, τινά Il.4.183, D.H.10.41, Plu.*Mar.*36.

ἐπιθαυμάζω, *pay honour to*, ἐ. τι τὸν διδάσκαλον by giving him a fee, Ar.*Nu.*1147; ἐπιθαυμάσας τὸ παράλογον *in wonder at*.., Plu.*Marc.*30: abs., Arr.*Epict.*1.26.12.

ἐπιθεάζω, = ἐπιθειάζω, *invoke the gods against*, τῷ πατρί Pherecr.118: abs., ἀγανακτῶν καὶ ἐ. *with imprecations*, Pl.*Phdr.*241b. II. v. ἐπιθοάζω.

ἐπιθεάομαι, *survey, examine*, Sch.Ar.*Nu.*499; *look at*, τὸν οὐρανόν Agath.5.3; *reflect on* a thing, Poll.6.115.

ἐπιθέατρον, τό, *building adjoining a theatre*, *IG*11(2).287 *A* 94, 120 (Delos, iii B.C.).

ἐπιθει-άζω, *call upon in the name of the gods, adjure, conjure*, τοσαῦτα ἐπιθειάσας Th.2.75; ἐ. μὴ κατάγειν Id.8.53; τῷ λόγῳ Plu.*Them.*28. II. *inspire*, τινί Id.2.580d, 589d, Max.Tyr.37.5. b. abs., *to be inspired, prophesy*, D.H.1.31: c. acc. cogn., τοιαῦτα J.*AJ*4.6.5. 2. *ascribe to divine influence*, τὰς πράξεις Plu.2.579f, cf. Philostr.*VS*1.10; *treat with reverence*, Arr.*Epict.*4.1.108, Porph.*Chr.*39. -ᾰσις, εως, ἡ, = sq. 1, Plu.2.1117a (pl.). -ασμός, ὁ, *appeal to the gods*, Th.7.75 (pl.). 2. *inspiration*, Poll.1.16, Ph.2.299. -αστικός, ή, όν, *given to appeals to heaven*, in Sup., Plu.*Prov.*2.14. II. *frenzied, inspired*, Hsch. s.v. νυμφόληπτοι.

ἐπιθέλγω, *soothe, assuage*, τὴν ὀργήν Plu.2.456a.

ἐπίθεμ-α, ατος, τό, = ἐπίθημα, *cover*, Arist.*HA*529^{b}8 (v.l. -θημα), Lxx *Ex.*25.16(17), J.*AJ*3.6.5, *IG*3.14.18, Ruf.ap.Orib.4.2.6, Gal.12.889. 2. *capital* of a column, Lxx 3 *Ki.*7.4 sq. 3. *remedy for external application*, Ruf.*Ren.Ves.*10, Dsc.*Ther.*19. 4. *addition*, *POxy.*500.14 (ii A.D.); *higher bid*, *PAmh.*2.85.21 (i A.D.). 5. *shaft* of an arrow, Paul.Aeg.6.88. -άτιον, τό, Dim. of ἐπίθεμα 3, *Gloss.* -ᾰτισμός, ὁ, = Lat. *augmentum*, ib.

ἐπίθεος· σημεῖον ἐν θυτικῇ, Hsch.

ἐπιθεράπ-εία, ἡ, *care* of a statue, *IGRom.*4.293 *a* i 43, ii 62 (Pergam.). -ευσις, εως, ἡ, Rhet., *indignant reiteration of a charge*,

Ps.-Ascon. *in Verr.Act.*i § 27. **-εύω**, *to be diligent about, work zealously for*, τὴν κάθοδον Th.8.47; *court* one's *favour*, ib.84:—Pass., πρός τινος D.C.*Fr.*68.3. II. *apply after-treatment*, Hp.*Mochl.*41 (Pass.). 2. *repeat an application*, *Gp.*17.23.2.

ἐπιθερμαίνομαι, Pass., *become feverish*, Hp.*Epid.*1.1, 3.17.ιγ΄. II. later in Act., *warm up*, *PHolm.*17.40.

ἐπιθεσία, ἡ, *plot*, Aq.*Ps.*34(35).20 (pl.).

ἐπίθεσις, εως, ἡ, *setting on its base*, τοῦ ἀνδριάντος *CIG*3124 (Teos). 2. *laying* or *putting on*, opp. ἀφαίρεσις, Arist.*Juv.*470^{a}11; τῶν χειρῶν *Act.Ap.*8.18, etc.; *application*, περιχρίστων Plu.2.102a, cf. Luc.*DDeor.*13.1 (prob.). 3. *application of epithets*, τὰς ἐ. ποιεῖσθαι Arist.*Rh.*1405^{b}22. 4. *imposition of increased burdens*, *Cat.Cod.Astr.*7.134. II. (from Med.) *setting upon, attack*, Antipho 2.2.13; ἐ. γίγνεταί τινι X.*An.*4.4.22; ἡ Περσῶν ἐ. τοῖς Ἕλλησι Pl.*Lg.*698b; τῶν ἐ. αἱ μὲν ἐπὶ τὸ σῶμα γίγνονται τῶν ἀρχόντων *attempts*, Arist.*Pol.*1311^{a}31; ἐ. συστῆσαι ἐπί τινα ib.1306^{b}35; ποιεῖσθαι ib.1312^{a}20; λῃστῶν *PPetr.*3p.60 (iii B.C., prob.); κατά τινος D.H.5.7; ἡ διὰ τοῦ πυρὸς ἐ. τοῖς ἔργοις Plb.1.45.2; of disease, *aggravated attack*, Sor.2.49 (pl.). 2. c. gen., *attempt to gain*, τῆς τυραννίδος D.S.13.92, etc. 3. *small urn placed on a* σορός, *IGRom.*4.1284 (Thyatira). 4. *imposture, deception*, Aq.*Pr.*11.1, al. 5. Pythag. name for *two*, Hsch.

ἐπιθέσοντας· ἐποξύνοντας, ἐπιφέροντας, Hsch.

ἐπιθεσπ-ίζω, of Triton, *prophesy* or *divine upon*, τῷ τρίποδι Hdt.4.179. II. of an oracle, *give sanction*, τινί D.H.2.6; ἐ. βασιλείαν τινί Id.3.35. III. *apply a prophecy*, τὰ Τειρεσίου ἑαυτῷ Philostr.*VA*7.4. **-ισμός**, ὁ, *sanction of an oracle*, Arr.*An.*6.19.4.

ἐπιθετ-έον, *one must impose*, δίκην Pl.*Grg.*507d; *one must set on*, σφραγῖδα τῷ λόγῳ Jul.*Or.*4.141c; *one must put on, apply*, Herod.Med. ap.Aët.9.2; ἐπίπλασμα Aret.*CA*1.4. II. (from Med.) *one must set upon*, τινί Pl.*Sph.*231c; τῷ ἀνδρί Id.*Smp.*217c. **-ης**, ου, ὁ, *plotter, impostor*, Luc.*Trag.*172, Sm.*Ps.*1.1, Ptol.*Tetr.*165, Vett.Val.16.11. II. *official of a religious association*, *IG*3.1280*a*. **-ικός**, ή, όν, *ready to attack*, θηρίοις X.*Mem.*4.1.3; *enterprising*, στρατηγός ib.3.1.6, Str.3.4.5; ἐπιθετικώτατον περὶ πάσας τὰς πράξεις Arist.*Pol.*1315^{a}11: **-κόν**, τό, *enterprise*, Corn.*ND*21. 2. = ἐπιθέτης 1, Ptol.*Tetr.*165. II. *added*: τὸ ἐ. *the adjective*, A.D.*Synt.*81.17 (pl.); ἐ. σύνταξις, προσηγορίαι, ib.18.7, D.S.4.5. Adv. **-κῶς** Corn.*ND*35, Sch. Il.13.29: Comp. -ώτερον A.D.*Synt.*81.15. **-ος**, ον, *additional*, φυλαί D.H.3.71; esp. at Athens, opp. πάτριος, *relatively modern*, ἑορταί Isoc.7.29; τὰ ἐ., opp. τὰ πάτρια, the *acquired powers* of the Areopagus, Lys.*Fr.*178 S., cf. Arist.*Ath.*25.2, 3.3; so ἐ. ἐξουσία *usurped* authority, Plu.*Cleom.*10: generally, *adventitious*, τὰ μὲν τῶν νόμων ἐπίθετα, τὰ δὲ τῆς φύσεως ἀναγκαῖα Antipho Soph.*Oxy.*1364.25; ἐπιθυμίαι, opp. κοιναί, Arist.*EN*1118^{b}9; ἐ. τῇ φύσει κακά Men.534.13. 2. *fictitious*, Thphr.*HP*9.8.8; opp. ἀληθινός, D.H.4.70, cf. 68. 3. of letters, *entrusted for conveyance*, Lys.*Fr.*116 S. II. ἐ. [ὄνομα] *adjectival*, D.T.636.9, cf. Plu.*Cor.*11. III. Subst. **ἐπίθετον**, τό, *epithet*, Arist.*Rh.*1406^{a}19, D.H.*Comp.*5, A.D.*Synt.*41.15; *adjective*, ib.81.24 (so Adv. **-τως**, λέγειν indicate *by epithets*, Str.1.2.29, al.). 2. = ἐπίθημα 5, Aret.*CA*1.1. 3. ἐπίθετος, ὁ, a throw of the dice, Eub.57.4.

ἐπιθέω, *run upon, at* or *after*, Hdt.9.107, X.*Cyn.*6.10: abs., App.*Hisp.*90; ἐ. πρὸς τὴν μάχην Hdn.6.7.8. 2. metaph., ἡ ἐπιθέουσα εἰς ἀνθρώπους ἀπάτη Plot.2.9.6; *to be diffused over*, πᾶσι τοῖς ἀληθέσι Id.5.3.17, al. II. *run upon the surface* of water, Arist.*HA*551^{b}22.

ἐπιθεωρ-έω, *examine over again* or *carefully, ascertain*, τι Hp.*Acut.*(*Sp.*)8, Philem.138, D.H.*Rh.*3.2, Plu.*Demetr.*1, Iamb.*Comm.Math.*14:—Pass., Thphr.*Metaph.*34. b. *consider next in order*, πάθος Epicur.*Nat.*13 G. 2. *inspect*, μόσχον Wilcken *Chr.*89.3 (ii A.D.); νεκρόν *POxy.*475.6 (ii A.D.). 3. *look at, behold*, τινά J.*AJ*15.7.5. 4. Pass., *to be observed in, to be an aspect of*, ἑκάστῃ οὐσίᾳ Plot.6.6.5. 5. Astrol., *aspect from the right*, Vett.Val.44.31, Gal.19.541. **-ησις**, εως, ἡ, *contemplation*, τῆς τῶν ὅλων φύσεως M.Ant.8.26. 2. *inspection*, *CPHerm.*7 ii 23 (iii A.D.). 3. Astrol., *aspect*, Ptol.*Tetr.*193. **-ητέον**, *one must consider*, πότερον.. Sor.1.97, cf. Gal.8.165, Herod.Med.ap.Orib.7.8.3. II. *one must take care*, μή.. Gal.16.134. **-ία**, ἡ, Astrol., *aspecting from the right*, Rhetor.in *Cat.Cod.Astr.*1.155.15.

ἐπιθήγω, *whet* or *sharpen yet more*, τὰ κέντρα Ael.*NA*5.16: metaph., *stimulate yet more*, τὰς ἐπιθυμίας Plu.786b.

ἐπιθήκη, ἡ, *addition, increase*, Hes.*Op.*380; κἀπιθήκην τέτταρας and 4 loaves (or perh. obols) *over*, Ar.*V.*1391; adponam epithecam insuper, cj. for apo- in Plaut.*Trin.*1025. II. *cover* put over a statue, *CPR*27.10 (ii A.D.). III. *sum allowed to cover expenses*, *POxy.*1158.24 (iii A.D.), etc.

ἐπιθηλέω, = ἐπιθάλλω, Nonn.*D.*3.151.

ἐπίθημα, ατος, τό, *something put on* (cf. ἐπίθεμα): hence, 1. *lid, cover*, φωριαμῶν ἐπιθήματα *lids* of chests, Il.24.228, cf. Hippon.56, Hp.*Morb.*2.26, Hdt.1.48, Arist.*Ath.*68.3, *IG*2^{2}.1408; ἀσπίδα ἐ. τῷ φρέατι παράθες Ar.*Fr.*295; τοὐπ. τῆς χύτρας ἀφελών Hegesipp.Com.1.13; *slab*, used as the top of a table, Ath.2.49a. 2. *monument, sepulchral figure*, Is.2.36, Paus.1.2.3. 3. *head* of a spear, D.S.5.30. 4. *device* on a shield, Paus.5.25.9. 5. Medic., *application*, Aret.*CA*1.1, 2.2.

ἐπιθημᾰτ-ικός, ή, όν, *concerned with* ἐπιθήματα, -κή (sc. τέχνη) Poll.7.208. **-ουργία**, ἡ, *making of lids* or *covers*, Pl.*Plt.*280d. **-όω**, *put a lid upon*, τι Anticl.13.

ἐπιθηραρχ-ία, ἡ, *contingent of four elephants*, Ascl.*Tact.*9, Ael.*Tact.*23. **-ος**, ὁ, *officer commanding such a contingent*, ll. cc.

ἐπιθιγγάνω, aor. 2 ἐπέθῐγον, *touch*, Thphr.*Od.*11, Agath.2.24; τῆς κεφαλῆς Plu.*TG*19. 2. *reach as far as*, ὄψις ἐ. τῆς θαλάσσης Id.2.921d. 3. c. dat., = ἐφάπτομαι, *IG*5(2).429 (Phigalea).

ἐπιθλάσας· συντόμως εἰπών, Hsch.

ἐπίθλᾰσις, εως, ἡ, *fracture*, v.l. for περίθλασις, Orib.46.5.2.

ἐπι-θλίβω [ῑ], *press upon the surface*, D.S.3.14; *tread*, ὀπώρην Nonn.*D.*7.91; *crowd round*, App.*BC*4.45: metaph., *repress, check*, Plu.2.782d. **-θλιψις**, εως, ἡ, *pressure on the surface*, Aret.*CA*1.9 (pl.); *crushing*, τοῦ δακτύλου Orib.*Fr.*74.

ἐπιθοάζω, *sit as suppliant at an altar*, τάδ' ἐπευχομένη κἀπιθοάζουσ' A.*Ch.*856 (οα in litura); τάδε καὶ θρηνῶ κἀπιθοάζω E.*Med.*1409; cf. θοάζω II; but κἀπιθεάζουσ' *invoking the gods*, and κἀπιθεάζω shd. prob. be read.

ἐπιθολ-ος, ον, *turbid*, ὕδωρ Lyd.*Ost.*8. **-όω**, *make turbid*, Luc.*Ind.*7, Max.Tyr.33.5: metaph., τὴν φιλίαν Plu.*inHes.*66; σοφίας κρατῆρα Philostr.*VA*6.11; τῆς ψυχῆς τὰς καθαρότητας Iamb.*VP*24.107; τὸ κρῖνον Agath.3.11:—Pass., *become turbid*, *Placit.*3.5.8, Gal.6.57, Luc.*Lex.*4: metaph., ἡ ψυχὴ -οῦται οὔτε φόβοις οὔτε ἐλπίσιν Artem.4 *Prooem.*; τὰ θεωρήματα μηδὲν -ούμενα ὑπ' ἀλλοτρίων δοξασμάτων Iamb. *in Nic.*p.4 P., cf. *Myst.*5.4, Just.*Nov.*22.20.2.

ἐπιθόρνῠμαι, *cover*, of the male, βουσί Luc.*Am.*22, etc.; ἐ. ταῖς γεγαμημέναις Philostr.*VA*5.29, cf. *Im.*2.3: abs., Ael.*NA*10.2, al.

ἐπιθορῠβ-έω, *shout to*: 1. in token of approval, X.*HG*2.3.50, Pl.*Prt.*339e, D.H.6.39. 2. in token of displeasure, X.*HG*1.7.13, Luc.*Asin.*54. **-ως**, Adv. *agitatedly, in turmoil*, διάγειν Vett.Val.184.31.

ἐπιθράνιον· μέρος τι τῆς νεώς, Hsch.

ἐπίθρᾱνοι, οἱ, *binding timbers* in brick construction, Poll.10.49.

ἐπιθράσσω, aor. 1 ἐπιθρᾶξαι· ἐπιθρύξαι, ἐπινύξαι, Hsch.; cf. ἐνθράσσω.

ἐπιθραύω, *break besides*, τρύφος ἄρτου *AP*6.105 (Apollonid.).

ἐπιθρέξας, v. ἐπιτρέχω.

ἐπίθρεπτος, ον, *well-nourished*, σάρξ Hp.*Prorrh.*2.24.

ἐπιθρην-έω, *lament over*, συμφοράς Babr.118.8: abs., τὸ -θρηνεῖν Plu.2.123c, Diog.Oen.61: c. acc. cogn., γοώδες τοῖς εἰρημένοις Hld.10.37. **-ησις**, εως, ἡ, *lamentation over*, Plu.2.611a (pl.). **-ητος**, ον, *lamentable*, Hsch. s. v. περίσφατα.

ἐπιθρίαμβος [ῐ], ὁ, *subsequent triumph*, Suid. s. v. θρίαμβος.

ἐπιθριδάκια [ᾰκ], τά, (θρίδαξ) *festival of Apollo*, Hsch.

ἐπίθροισις, εως, ἡ, prob. f.l. for -θλιψις, Gal.17(1).51.

ἐπιθρομβόομαι, Pass., *curdle*, Nic.*Al.*364 (v.l. ἐπιτυρ-).

ἐπιθρῡλέω, *disturb with noise*, *EM*456.40. 2. *proclaim noisily*, Agath.2.2.

ἐπιθρύπτω, *enfeeble, enervate*, Philostr.*VA*1.37:—Pass., *practise affectations*, Aristaenet.1.28; ἐπιτεθρυμμένος *effeminate*, Plu.*Dio*17.

ἐπιθρῴσκω, *leap upon*, c. gen., νηὸς ἐπιθρῴσκων Il.8.515, cf. E.*Rh.*100: c. dat., *leap* (contemptuously) *upon*, τύμβῳ ἐπιθρῴσκων Μενελάου Il.4.177. II. *leap over* a space, τόσσον ἐπιθρῴσκουσι so far *do* [the horses] *spring at a bound*, 5.772; μακρὰ ἐ. Hes.*Sc.*438. 2. *jut out*, of a rock, Orph.*A.*1266. III. *rise*, ὀμίχλη Musae.113.

ἐπιθυλλίς, ίδος, ἡ, f.l. for γηθυλλίς in Ath.9.371f, cf. Eust.1155.20.

ἐπίθυμα, ατος, τό, *that which is burnt* in magic, *PMag.Par.*1.1308, al.; *sacrificial victim*, Hsch. s. v. ἱεράθετα.

ἐπιθυμελίας ἀγῶνα· τὴν τῶν διαφραγμάτων στάσιν, Hsch.

ἐπιθῡμ-έω, *set one's heart upon* a thing, *long for, covet, desire*, c. gen. rei, Hdt.2.66, A.*Ag.*216, etc.: also c. gen. pers., Lys.3.5, X.*An.*4.1.14 (later c. acc. pers., [Men.] ap.Clem.Al.*Strom.*5.119, *Tab.Defix.Aud.*271.45 (Hadrumetum, iii A.D.)); of political attachments, τῶν ἡμετέρων πολεμίων And.4.28; ὀλιγαρχίας Lys.20.3: c. inf., *desire to* do, πλῶσαι Hdt.1.24; ἀπικνέεσθαι ib.116; περισσὰ δρᾶν S.*Tr.*617, etc.: abs., *desire, covet*, Th.6.92; ὁ ἀεὶ -ῶν Pl.*Prt.*313d, etc.; τὸ ἐπιθυμοῦν τοῦ πλοῦ, = ἐπιθυμία, *eagerness for* it, Th.6.24:—Pass., *to be desired*, τὰ ἐπιθυμούμενα Pl.*Phlb.*35d. **-ημα**, ατος, τό, *object of desire*, Id.*Lg.*687c (sg.), Arist.*EN*1118^{a}13, X.*Hier.*4.7 (pl.). II. *yearning, desire*, Hp. *de Arte* 1, Antipho Soph.110, Epicur.*Fr.*141: pl., Philyll.30. **-ησις**, εως, ἡ, *longing, desire*, κακῶν Is.*Fr.*158. **-ήτειρα**, ἡ, fem. of sq., Call.*Dian.*237. **-ητής**, οῦ, ὁ, *one who longs for* or *desires*, νεωτέρων ἔργων Hdt.7.6; [δογμάτων] And.4.6; ἔργων Lys.12.90; τιμῆς, σοφίας, Pl.*R.*475b, etc.; φύσει πολέμου ἐ. Arist.*Pol.*1253^{a}6; κακῶν 1*Ep.Cor.*10.6; ἀλλοτρίων *BGU*531 ii 22 (ii A.D.). 2. abs., *lover, follower*, X.*Mem.*1.2.60. b. *one who lusts*, Lxx *Nu.*11.34. **-ητικός** (hyperdor. -ᾱτικός Diotog.ap.Stob.4.7.62), ή, όν, *desiring, coveting, lusting after*, τινός Pl.*R.*475b, al.; τὸ ἐ. *that* part of the soul *which is the seat of the desires and affections*, ib.439e, Arist.*EN*1102^{b}30, etc. Adv. -κῶς, ἔχειν τινός, = ἐπιθυμεῖν, *Hell.Oxy.*16.4, Pl.*Phd.*108a, Isoc.15.244, D.L.8.1; ἐ. διακεῖσθαι Palaeph.23. **-ητός**, ή, όν, *desired, to be desired*, -τὸν τὸ φαινόμενον καλόν Arist.*Metaph.*1072^{a}27, cf. *Rh.*1371^{a}33, etc.; of the *cravings* of pregnant women, Sor.1.53. Adv. -τῶς *EM*148.7. **-ία**, Ion. -ίη, ἡ, *desire, yearning*, ἐ. ἐκτελέσαι Hdt.1.32; ἐπιθυμίᾳ *by passion*, opp. προνοίᾳ, Th.6.13: generally, *appetite*, Pl.*Cra.*419d, etc.; αἱ κατὰ τὸ σῶμα ἐ. Id.*Phd.*82c; esp. *sexual desire, lust*, Democr.234 (pl.), Pl.*Phdr.*232b, etc.; αἱ πρὸς τοὺς παῖδας ἐ. X.*Lac.*2.14. 2. c. gen., *longing after* a thing, *desire of* or *for* it, ὕδατος, τοῦ πιεῖν, Th.2.52, 7.84, etc.; τοῦ πλέονος Democr.224; τῆς τιμωρίας Antipho 2.1.7; τῆς μεθ' ὑμῶν πολιτείας And.2.10; τῆς παρθενίας Pl.*Cra.*406b; εἰς ἐ. τινὸς ἐλθεῖν Id.*Criti.*113d; ἐν ἐ. τινὸς εἶναι Id.*Prt.*318a, *Tht.*143e; γεγονέναι Id.*Lg.*841c; εἰς ἐ. τινὸς ἀφικέσθαι θεάσασθαι Id.*Ti.*19b; ἐ. τινὸς ἐμβαλεῖν τινί X.*Cyr.*1.1.5;

ἐ. ἐμποιεῖν ἔς τινα *an inclination* towards.., Th.4.81. II. = ἐπιθύμημα, *object of desire*, ἐπιθυμίας τυχεῖν Thales ap.Stob.3.1.172, cf. Lync.ap.Ath.7.295a; ἀνδρὸς ἐ., of woman, Secund.*Sent*.8; πενήτων ἐ., of sleep, prob. in ib.13.

ἐπιθῡμί-ᾱμα, ατος, τό, *incense-offering*, S.*OT*913, prob. in *BGU*1.10 (ii/iii A.D.). **-ᾱσις**, εως, ἡ, *offering of incense*, *CIG*3068*A*24 (Teos). **-ατρός**, ὁ, *one who burns incense*, ib.2983 (Ephesus). **-άω**, *offer incense*, Plu.*Alex*.25, *CIG*2715.6 (Stratonicea): c. acc., τῷ Βορέᾳ λιβανίδιον prob. in Men.260 (-ίσας codd. Ath.), cf. Plu.2.372d; λιβανωτόν *Milet*.3.145 (iii/ii B.C.), *SIG*694.43 (Pergam., ii B.C.), Artem.4.2:—Pass., λίβανος ἐπιθυμιασθεὶς Dsc.1.68.

ἐπιθύμιος [ῡ], ον, = ἐπιθυμητικός, Man.4.565.

ἐπιθῡμίς, ίδος, ἡ, *wreath of flowers* for the neck, Hsch. (pl.). II. **ἐπιθῡμίς**, ίδος, ἡ, = θύμος, Ps.-Dsc.3.36.

ἐπιθῡμόδειπνος, ον, *eager for dinner*, Plu.2.726a.

ἐπίθῡμον, τό, *a parasitic plant growing on thyme, Cuscuta Epithymum*, Dsc.4.177, Gal.6.414, 11.875, Artem.1.77.

ἐπίθῡμος, ον, *desirous*, *Gloss*.

ἐπῑθύνω, = ἐπευθύνω, S.*Ph*.1059: Ep. Iterat. -εσκεν A.R.3.1325: c. dat., ἔργοις Man.2.340.

ἐπιθύρ-ιος [ῠ], ον, *over a door*, ἀσπίδες *IG*4.1488.22 (Epid.). II. *fixed on a door*, ἧλοι ib.2^2.1408.20. III. Subst. ἐπιθύριον, τό, *lintel*, ib.11(2).165.11 (Delos, iii B.C.). **-ον**, τό, = foreg. III, *BCH*6.34 (Delos, ii B.C.), *Princeton Exp.Inscr*.1177.

ἐπι-θῡσιάω, *offer incense*, Sophr.120. **-θύσιμα** [ῠ], τά, *sacrificial victims*, *IG*2^2.1672.295. **-θῡσις**, εως, ἡ, *burning of incense*, *BMus.Inscr*.789 (Cnidus), Ph.Bybl.ap.Eus.*PE*1.10 codd.; λιβανωτοῦ καὶ ἀρωμάτων *OGI*383.142 (pl., Nemrud Dagh, i B.C.). **-θύτης** [ῠ], ου, ὁ, *one who burns incense*, *Gloss*.; so prob. in *CIG*3663*A*15 (Cyzicus).

ἐπῐθύω, (θύω A) *sacrifice upon*, *h.Ap*.491 (tm.); *sacrifice besides* or *after*, τέλεον νεαροῖς ἐπιθύσας A.*Ag*.1504; ἐπὶ δ' ἔθυσα μητέρα E.*Or*.562:—Med., Νέρωνι Γάλβαν ἐ. Plu.*Galb*.14, cf. *Marc*.29, Artem.1.12. II. *burn incense*, Lxx 3*Ki*.12.33, J.*BJ*7.3.3, D.S.12.11, 18.60, Porph.*Abst*.2.59; λιβανωτόν D.S.18.61, v.l. in Ar.*Pl*.1116: generally, *offer on*, ἐπὶ τοῦ βωμοῦ τὰς δεκάτας D.H.1.40 codd.

ἐπῑθύω, *rush eagerly at*, ὥς ἂν ἐπιθύσαντες ἑλοίμεθα Od.16.297: c. gen., ἐπιθύουσι βοῶν λίες Euph.35a: c. dat., Opp.*C*.1.281,385. 2. c. inf., *strive vehemently to* do a thing, ἐρύσσασθαι.. Τρῶες ἐπιθύουσι Il.18.175; θυμὸς ἐπιθύει κιθαρίζειν *h.Merc*.475; δεδαῆσθαι A.R.2.1154; κύσσαι.. στόμα Id.1.1238:—Med., *rush upon, flood*, Νεῖλος ἐπεθύσατο (sic) αὔλακι γαίης Epic.Anon. in *BKT*5(1).119. (Prob. a compound of ἰθύω [ῠ], with ῡ metri gr.: taken as ἐπῐ-θύω by Epic.Anon. l.c.)

ἐπιθώϊος, ον, (θωή) *under penalty of a fine* for non-attendance, βουλὴ ἀγειρέσθω ἢ δημοσίη ἐ. *Schwyzer*687 *B*6 (Chios, vii/vi B.C.).

ἐπιθωρᾱκ-ίδιον, τό, *tunic worn over the* θώραξ, Plu.*Art*.11. **-ίζομαι**, *put on one's armour*, v.l. for θωρακ- (q.v.).

ἐπιθωτάζω, = ἐπιχλευάζω, Hsch.; cf. τωθάζω.

ἐπιθωΰσσω, *shout* or *call out, give loud commands*, A.*Pr*.73; οὐκ ἀκούσαις ἐπεθώϋξας τοῦτο thou *didst urge* this *upon* not unwilling ears, ib.279; κάλαμος.. κώπαις ἐπιθωΰξει E.*IT*1127.

ἐπιΐδμων, ον, gen. ονος, = ἐπιΐστωρ, τινός *AP*6.175 (Maced.).

ἐπιιερουργέω, *preside at sacrifice*, *Gloss*.

ἐπιιζάνω, *sit on*, ἑῇ ἕδρῃ Q.S.6.38.

ἐπιίζομαι, Ion. for ἐφέζομαι, Luc.*Epigr*.47.

ἐπιΐστωρ, ορος, ὁ, ἡ, *privy to* a thing: c. gen., μεγάλων ἔργων ἐ. *privy to* great works (i.e. the robbery of the mares), Od.21.26; so τεῶν μύθων ἐ. A.R.4.89: abs., ib.16. 2. *acquainted with, practised in*, δίσκων, γεωμετρίης, *AP*11.371 (Pall.), *App.Anth*.7.2 (Euc.); σοφίης *IG*3.946, cf. Doroth. in *Cat.Cod.Astr*.2.172.

ἐπικαγχάζω, *laugh loud*, *PMag.Leid.W*.11.50, Hsch.

ἐπικαγχᾰλάω, *exult in*, τινί Q.S.1.161; *exult over*, ib.643: abs., Id.2.374.

ἐπικᾰδεία, ἡ, (κάδος) *fixing of buckets on* a water-wheel, *PLond*.3.1177.178, al. (ii A.D.).

ἐπικαθαιρέω, *pull down* or *destroy besides*, Th.8.20.

ἐπικᾰθ-αίρω, *purge yet more*, Hp.*Judic*.11, Ruf.ap.Orib.7.26.169 (Pass.); of *supplementary menstruation*, Sor.1.28 (Pass.). **-αρσις**, εως, ἡ, *cleaning*, τοῦ ναοῦ *IG*4.1484.109 (Epid.).

ἐπικαθ-έζομαι, *sit down upon*, ἐπί τινι Ar.*Pl*.185; [ἐλέφαντι] Gal.*UP*17.1: aor. 1 part. ἐπικαθεσθεὶς Artem.2.20. II. *to be supported, rest on*, ἐπιζυγίδα -ομένην τῷ διαπήγματι Hero *Bel*.83.11, cf. J.*AJ*8.3.5. **-εύδω**, *sleep upon*, τινί Luc.*Ind*.4; *sit on eggs*, Arist.*HA*542^{b}20: metaph., *go to sleep over*, i.e. *neglect*, τινί Just.*Nov*.88.2.1. **-έψω**, *boil in as well*, Philum.*Ven*.14.6 (Pass.). **-ηλόω**, *nail fast to*, Apollod.*Poliorc*.146.7 (Pass.). **-ημαι**, Ion. **-κάτημαι**, *sit upon*, τινί Hdt.6.72, Ar.*Eq*.1093; *press upon, be heavy upon*, ἐπί τινι Id.*Ra*.1046: also c. acc., ἐ. καμήλους App.*Syr*.32; πόλις.. λόφον ἐπικαθημένη D.H.1.14: abs., *sit upon eggs, incubate*, Arist.*HA*558^{a}19, 619^{b}14; of bees, ἐ. ἐπὶ τοῖς κηρίοις ib.625^{a}5. 2. ἐ. ἐπὶ τῆς τραπέζης (v.l. ἐπὶ τῇ τρ.) *sit at* his counter, of a banker's clerk or money-changer, D.49.17, cf. 33: abs., ὁ ἐπικαθήμενος Id.36.7. 3. of rain, *cling to* a flower, Thphr.*CP*3.24.4. II. *sit down against* a place, *besiege* it, abs., Th.7.27: c. dat., App.*Mith*.78. III. ἐπικαθήμενοι, οἱ, *settlers, residents*, *PTeb*.391.11 (i A.D.). **-ιζάνω**, = ἐπικαθίζω II, ἐπὶ τὴν κεφαλήν Antiph.202.12. **-ίζω**, *set upon*, τινὰ ἐπί τι Hp.*Art*.78: abs., (sc. κλίμακι) ibid.; τινὰ ἐν ἅρματι Lxx 4*Ki*.10.16; ἐν ὅπλοις ἀφανῶς ἐ. τὸ στρατιωτικόν J.*AJ*18.3.1:—Med., φυλακὴν ἐπεκαθίσαντο *had* a guard *set*, Th.4.130 (ἐπικαθίσταντο Poppo). II. intr., *sit upon*, πειθώ τις ἐπεκάθιζεν ἐπὶ τοῖς χείλεσι Eup.94.5; τοῖς καρχησίοις ἐ. *light upon*, Plu.*Them*.12, cf. Thphr.*CP*6.10.5. 2. *sit down against, besiege*, πόλει Plb.4.61.6. **-ίημι**, *let down, set upon*, τι βακτηρίᾳ Ephipp.14.11; *insert*, Heliod.ap.Orib.44.23.53. 2. *let down, shut*, πύλας App.*Hann*.51. 3. *put down* the foot, Hp.*Art*.60. 4. *incise* or *prick again*, Gal.ap.Orib.7.5.12. **-ικνέομαι**, Dor. 3 sg. fut. -καθιξεῖται, *impose a surcharge* or *penalty*, *IG*5(1).1421.15 (Cyparissia, iv/iii B.C.). **-ισμα**, ατος, τό, = Lat. *insessus*, *Gloss*. **-ίστημι**, *set upon, establish*, φυλακάς D.C.41.50; cf. ἐπικαθίζω. 2. *set over*, κριτάς Pl.*Ti*.72b. 3. *establish besides*, τὴν τῶν ἐφόρων ἀρχήν Arist.*Pol*.1313^{a}27; ἐ. τινὰ στρατηγόν *appoint as successor* in command, Plb.2.19.8, cf. J.*AJ*17.2.4:—Pass., ἐπικατασταθεὶς στρατηγός Plb.2.2.11, cf. *IG*5(1).1390.12 (Andania). 4. *pay in addition*, *Leg.Gort*.1.47; but simply, *deliver*, σῖτον ἐπὶ τοὺς ὅρμους *PLille*53 (iii B.C.). 5. *perform the manœuvre of* ἀντικατάστασις, Ascl.*Tact*.12.11:—Pass., of troops executing the manœuvre, ib.10.11. **-οράω**, v. ἐπικατεῖδον. **-υγραίνομαι**, *to be kept moist*, Sor.1.44, Orib.*Fr*.144, Paul.Aeg.3.63.

ἐπικαιν-ίζω, *renew, restore*, Lxx 1*Ma*.10.44 (Pass.). **-ουργέω**, *contrive novelties*, Democr.191. **-όω**, *introduce innovations into*, μὴ 'πικαινούντων νόμους A.*Eu*.693 (Steph. for μὴ 'πικαινιζόντων).

ἐπικαίνῠμαι, *surpass, excel* (v. καίνυμαι), πάντας ἐπ' ἀνθρώπους ἐκέκαστο ὄλβῳ τε πλούτῳ τε Il.24.535. II. Pass., *to be adorned* or *furnished with*, ἐπὶ φρεσὶ πευκαλίμῃσι κέκασται 20.35 (unless in signf. 1); οἷς ἐπικαίνυνται ἵππος (cj. for ἐπικίνυνται) Q.S.12.145.

ἐπικαιρ-ία, ἡ, *opportunity*, Hp.*Gland*.4; αἰτίαι περὶ ἀκαιριῶν καὶ ἐ., title of work by Democr., D.L.9.48. **-ιος**, ον, = sq., Sup. -ώταται, πράξεις X.*Oec*.5.4, cf. Vett.Val.293.22. Adv. -ίως *conveniently*, ἵδρυται Str.9.2.15, cf. 10.1.7. 2. *important*, τὰ -ώτατα τῆς τέχνης X.*Oec*.15.11; of persons, οἱ ἐ. the *most important persons* of the army, Id.*Cyr*.3.3.12, cf. *HG*3.3.11: c. inf., οἱ θεραπεύεσθαι ἐπικαίριοι those whose cure is *all-important*, Id.*Cyr*.8.2.25. 3. of parts of the body, *vital*, τόποι ἐ. Ti.Locr.102d. **-ος**, ον, *in fit time* or *place, seasonable, opportune*, S.*OT*875 (lyr.), Th.6.34; νίκη -οτάτη Id.8.106; of places, -ότατον χωρίον πρὸς τὰ ἐπὶ Θρᾴκης ἀποχρῆσθαι Id.1.68; τὰ ἐ. *advantageous* positions, X.*Hier*.10.5; τοὺς ἐ. τῶν τόπων D.18.27, cf. Arist.*Pol*.1331^{a}21; Κόρκυρα ἐν -οτάτῳ κειμένη Isoc.15.108; τὰ ἐνδεχόμενα καὶ -ότατα Arist.*Rh*.1396^{b}5; τοῦ πάθους τὸ ἐ. *spontaneous outburst* of passion, Longin.18.2: also c. gen., τρίποδα.. λουτρῶν ἐπίκαιρον, = καιρὸν ἔχοντα λουτρῶν, *convenient for*.., S.*Aj*.1406 (anap.); ἰατὴρ -ότατος *helping in time of need*, Pi.*P*.4.270. Adv. -ως Sm.*Ps*.9.10, Sup. -οτάτως Anon.in *Rh*.132.8. 2. *serious, important*, ἐ. σημεῖα *important* symptoms, Hp.*Epid*.1.25; ἐς τεκμαρσιν Id.*Acut*.1. 3. of parts of the body, *vital*, ἐν τῷ -οτάτῳ ἀφύλακτον X.*Eq*.12.7, cf. Arist.*GA*766^{a}24; ἐ. τοῦ ζῆν *necessary* for life, ib.719^{a}16; of wounds, *dangerous*, ἐ. τρῶμα Hp.*Fract*.11; ἕλκος Id.*Acut*.46. Adv. -ρως, τετρῶσθαι Paus.4.8.4. 4. *susceptible* to disorders, Gal.*Nat.Fac*.2.8. II. *for a time, temporary*, opp. ἀΐδιος, Epict.*Gnom*.8; ἡ τῆς δόξης ἐ. εὐδαιμονία Vett.Val.130.30.

ἐπικαίω, *light up* or *kindle on* a place, πῦρ *h.Ap*.491; *burn on an altar*, ὅς μοι πολλὰ βοῶν ἐπὶ μηρί' ἔκηεν Il.22.170, cf. Od.3.9, 17.241. II. *burn on the surface, scorch*, Hp.*Aër*.17 (Pass.); οἱ τὰ σώματα ὑπὸ τῶν ἡλίων ἐπικεκαυμένοι Pl.*Ep*.340d; τῷ χρώματι παρὰ φύσιν -κεκαυμένος Plb.38.8.7, cf. Apollon.*Mir*.23; ἀέρα -όμενον Antipho Soph.26; of lightning, Arist.*Mete*.371^{b}14; of hot iron, Id.*HA*631^{b}26; of cold, Hp.*Aër*.20, Thphr.*CP*2.1.6 (v.l.); of a caustic drug, Dsc.3.35. 2. *burn on the top*, of stumps, Plu.2.529b; of pruning trees by *burning*, Thphr.*HP*6.6.6; *cauterize*, τὰ χείλη τῶν τραυμάτων Aët.13.4, cf. Philum.*Ven*.3.5, al. 3. *brand*, ἵππον *PCair.Zen*.93.4 (iii B.C.).

ἐπικακτίς, ίδος, ἡ, prob. f.l. for ἐπιπακτίς, Plin.*HN*13.114, 27.76.

ἐπικᾰλᾰμ-άομαι, *glean after* the reapers, Luc.*Tox*.16. **-εια**, τά, *fields whose corn is in stalk*, *PTeb*.115.4, al. (ii B.C.). **-ίς**, ίδος, ἡ, f.l. for ἐπισκαλμίς, Agath.5.22. **-οι** πυροί wheat *in the stalk*, *AB*291 (cf. καλάμη); αἱ ἀπὸ ἐπικαλάμου ἄρουραι fields *whose corn is in stalk*, *POxy*.499.10 (ii A.D.).

ἐπικᾰλέω, *summon* a god to a sacrifice or as witness to an oath, etc., *invoke*, θεόν Hdt.2.39, 3.8, al.; ἐπὶ δὲ κάλεσον Ἄρτεμιν Ar.*Lys*.1280, cf. *Act.Ap*.7.59, etc.; ἐ. θεόν τινι *invoke* a god *over* one, *to be gracious to* him, Hdt.1.199; or, *watch over* his good faith, Id.3.65:—Med., Id.1.87, al., X.*HG*2.3.55, al.; ἐπικαλεσάμενος τὸν θεόν *OGI*194.18 (Egypt, i B.C.). b. *pray for*, πρὸ καιροῦ τὸν θάνατον *PLond*.5.1676.24 (vi A.D.). 2. *invite*, γέροντας ἐπὶ πλέονας καλέσαντες Od.7.189:—Med., Hdt.1.187, al. II. Med., *call in* as a helper or ally, ἐπικαλεῖσθαί τινα σύμμαχον Id.8.64, cf. Th.1.101: c. inf., Hdt.1.87; ἐ. τοὺς κεκμηκότας μὴ γενέσθαι Th.3.59; ἐ. ἐκ Θεσσαλίης ἐπικουρίην Hdt.5.63. 2. *call in* as witness, μάρτυρας ἐ. τινάς Antipho 1.30, cf. Pl.*Lg*.664c: c. inf., ἐ. θεοὺς.. καθορᾶν τὰ γιγνόμενα X.*HG*2.3.55: with neut. Adj., ταῦτα ἐ. Hdt.9.62. b. *appeal to*, σύνεσιν καὶ παιδείαν D.18.127 (hence, = Lat. *appello, provoco*, Plu.*Marc*.2; τὸν δῆμον ἀπὸ τῶν δικαστῶν Id.*TG*16; Καίσαρα *Act.Ap*.25.11). 3. *call before one, summon*, of the Ephors, Hdt.5.39. 4. *challenge*, ib.1. III. *call by surname*, Δίων ὃν ἐπεκάλουν Χρυσόστομον Eun.*VS*p.454B.:—more freq. Pass., *to be called by surname*, ἐπεκλήθησαν Κεκροπίδαι Hdt.8.44; *to be nicknamed*, Ἀριστόδημον τὸν μικρὸν ἐπικαλούμενον X.*Mem*.1.4.2, cf. *HG*2.3.31; also τὸ ὄνομα ἐπικέκληταί σοι Lxx *De*.28.10; ἐπικληθήσεται ἐν αὐτοῖς τὸ ὄνομά μου ib.*Ge*.48.16. IV. *bring as an accusation against*, τινί τι Th.1.139, 4.133, cf. Isoc.12.9; ἐ. τινί, c. inf., *accuse* one of doing, Th.2.27, cf. Antipho 3.1.1; ἐ. τὴν ἀπόστασιν ὅτι.. ἐποιήσαντο Th.3.36; ἐ. τινὶ πάντα ὅσα ἠδίκητο D.C. 37.6; ταῦτ' ἐπικαλεῖς; *is this your charge?* Ar.*Pax* 663; ἐ. ἀρχαιότητα *objecting to* its obsoleteness, Pl.*Lg.*657b: abs., ἐπικαλείτω *let him bring his action*, *SIG*45.17 (Halic., v B.C.); ὁ ἐπικαλῶν *the plaintiff*, *PHal.*1.216 (iii B.C.):—Pass., τὰ ἐπικαλεύμενα χρήματα the money *imputed to him*, i.e. *which he was charged with having*, Hdt.2.118 (but τὰ ἐπικαλούμενα the *sums claimed*, *PPetr.*2 p.108 (iii B.C.), and so in Act. λείαν ἐ. ib.3 p.185); περὶ δανείου *PGrenf.*2.31.15 (ii B.C.). 2. c. dat. pers. only, ἐπικαλεῖν τινί *quarrel, dispute with*, ἀλλήλοις Pl.*Lg.*766e.

ἐπικαλλύνω, *deck out*, Them.*Or.*32.359b; τὴν ἀκοσμίαν τῆς φύσεως Chor.*Zach.*15. **ἐπικαλλωπίζοντες**, *illinentes*, *Gloss.*

ἐπικάλυμμα [κᾰ], ατος, τό, *cover, veil*, πλοῦτος πολλῶν ἐ. ἐστιν κακῶν Men.90. II. in animals, *covering* of any orifice, of the *gills* of fish, Arist.*HA*505a1, *PA*696b3; of the *opercula* of crabs and other crustacea, Id.*HA*527b26, 541b26, cf. 530a21.

ἐπικᾰλυπτ-ήριον, τό, *covering*, Arist.*PA*687b24. **-ος**, ον, *covered*, Thd.*Ez.*27.20. **-ω**, *cover over, cover up, shroud*, κακὸν δ' ἐπὶ κῶμα καλύπτει v.l. in Hes.*Th.*798; of snow *covering* a track, X.*Cyn.*8.1; ἐ. τὴν ἀπορίαν Pl.*Chrm.*169d; τοὺς ὀφθαλμούς Sor.1.106:—Pass., *to be covered over, veiled*, ἡ ἐπωνυμία ἐπικεκάλυπται Pl.*Cra.*395b; ἐπικαλύπτεσθαι τὸν νοῦν πάθει ἢ ὕπνῳ *is darkened, obscured*, Arist.*de An.*429a7. II. *put as a covering over*, βλεφάρων φᾶρος E.*HF*642 codd. (lyr.):—Pass., τῶν βλεφάρων -κεκαλυμμένων when the eyelids *are drawn down*, Arist.*Sens.*437a25.

ἐπικάμισον, τό, = ἐπενδύτης, Tz. ad Hes.*Op.*534, cf. *An.Ox.*3.359.

ἐπικάμνω, *suffer at* or *after*, τοῖς παρελθοῦσιν Ael.*VH*14.6.

ἐπικαμπ-ή, ἡ, *bend, return* or *angle* of a building, Hdt.1.180 (pl.), *IG*2^2.1666*B*54. 2. ἐ. ποιεῖσθαι draw up their army *angular-wise*, i.e. with the wings thrown forward at an angle with the centre, so as to take the enemy in flank, X.*Cyr.*7.1.6; ἐς ἐ. τάττειν Arr.*An.*2.9.2, cf. 3.12.2. **-ής**, ές, *curved, curling*, ὠτάρια *BGU*781 ii 4 (i A.D.); [οὐραῖον] Luc.*Gall.*28; ξύλον Plu.*Cam.*32; *convex*, Pall. in Hp.*Fract.*12.284C.; of hammer-toes, Heph.Astr.1.1. Adv. -πῶς Sch.rec.A.*Th.*384. **-ία**, ἡ, *bend, curve*, σπᾶσθαι πρὸς -ίαν *EM*722.35. **-ιος**, ον, = ἐπικαμπής, *curved*, τοῖχοι, τείχη, Ph.*Bel.*80.11, 82.3; ἐ. τάξις an order of battle in which one or both wings *formed an angle* with the centre, being either thrown forwards to attack the enemy in flank (cf. ἐπικαμπή), or backwards so as to meet a flank attack, Plb.6.31.2, D.S.17.57; also as a march formation, Ascl.*Tact.*11.1. II. Subst. ἐπικάμπιον, τό, = ἐπικαμπή, Arr.*Tact.*26.7; ἐπικαμπίου τάξις Ael.*Tact.*31.4; ἐν ἐπικαμπίῳ, opp. ἐν μετώπῳ, Polyaen.4.3.22, cf. Plb.5.82.9; also of fleets in naval warfare, Id.1.27.4. 2. of buildings, *wing*, τὸ ἐ. τῆς στοᾶς Plu.2.594b; τῇ ἐξέδρᾳ τῇ ἐν τῷ ἐ. *IG*12(9).234 (Eretria, i B.C.), cf. 12(8).266 (Thasos), *AJA*19.333 (Atalante). 3. ἐπικάμπια, τά, *nodal points* of the moon's orbit, Ptol.*Tetr.*167, Doroth. in *Cat.Cod.Astr.*6.91. **-τω**, *bend into an angle*, τὸν δάκτυλον Arist.*HA*556b17; [κλάδους] χερσί Them.*Or.*21.249a; Archit., *make an angle* or *return*, *IG*2^2.1668.75:—Pass., *bend* or *turn*, ἐς τὰ ἀριστερά Hp.*Oss.*10; *arch*, ὀφρὺς ἐπικεκαμμένη Arist.*PA*671b33; of troops, *advance the wings, so as to form angles* with the centre and take the enemy in flank, X.*Cyr.*7.1.5, *HG*4.2.20, *An.*1.8.23; τὸ στόμα ἐπικεκαμμένον ἔχουσα [φάλαγξ] Ascl.*Tact.*11.1; also of a fleet, *form a curved line* so as to envelop the enemy, D.C.50.31. 2. Act., ἐ. πρὸς ἔλεόν τινας *move* to pity, Lib.*Decl.*46.13:—Pass., abs., Ctes.*Fr.*29.56, Lib.*Or.*6.38; πρὸς τὸν ὀδυρμόν Id.*Loc.Comm.*1.31. II. intr., *to be bent*, Arist.*HA*529a12. **-ύλος** [ῠ], ον, *crooked, curved*, ὤμους *in* the shoulders, *h.Merc.*90; ἐ. κᾶλα Hes.*Op.*427.

ἐπίκαμψις, εως, ἡ, *enveloping movement* in naval warfare, D.C.50.31. II. *curvature*, [τοῦ ῥάμφους] Ael.*Fr.*76, cf. Paul.Aeg.6.30. III. *bend* in a road, τῆς ὁδοῦ Nic.Dam.47 J.

ἐπικανθίς, ίδος, ἡ, = ἐγκανθίς, *Hippiatr.*34, v.l. in Poll.2.71.

ἐπικᾱπίς (Dor. for -κηπίς), ίδος, ἡ, *plot by a garden*, *IG*4.823.29 (Troezen).

ἐπίκᾰρ, Adv. *head-foremost*, better divisim ἐπὶ κάρ, v. κάρ II.

ἐπικαρδιάω, = καρδιάω, Nic.*Al.*19.

ἐπικαρπ-ία, ἡ, *produce, crop*, ἡ ἐπέτειος ἐ. Pl.*Lg.*955d, cf. *IG*1^2.328.11, *Rev.Ét.Gr.*10.29 (Thespiae, iii B.C.). 2. *harvest-rights*, *Tab.Heracl.*1.108, *BGU*101.19 (ii A.D.); *usufruct*, αἱ ἐκ τῆς γῆς ἐ. D.H.3.58. 3. *revenue* from property, *Leg.Gort.*7.33; τὰς ἐκ ταύτης (sc. τῆς ὠνῆς) ἐπικαρπίας .. ἐνενήκοντα μνᾶς ἐκλέξας having collected 90 minae as the *revenue* from this tax, And.1.92. 4. *profit*, Arist.*Pol.*1258b24; αἱ ἐ. the *profits*, opp. the principal (τὰ ἀρχαῖα), D.27.50; ἐπικαρπίας λαμβάνειν Isoc.8.125; γῆθεν ἀναμένοντι τὴν ἐ. looking to the land for his *profits*, *Com.Adesp.*133.3; ἡ ἐ. τῶν ἁδρῶν the *profits* on the full-grown animals, Antiph.20. 5. *tithe* paid for the pasturage of cattle, Arist.*Oec.*1346a3. 6. metaph., παρρησίας ἐπικαρπίαι D.C.39.10; κινδύνων Onos.34.4; τοῦ πόνου Ael.*NA*2.8. **-ίδιος** [ῐδ], ον, *on fruit*, χνοῦς *AP*9.226 (Zon.). **-ίζομαι**, *draw the nutriment from, exhaust*, γῆν, of crops, Thphr.*HP*8.9.3. **-ιος**, ον, (καρπός I) *bringer* or *guardian of fruits*, epith. of Zeus, Corn.*ND*9, Arist.*Mu.*401a19, Plu.2.1048c, etc.; of Hermes, *IG*12(7).252 (Amorgos); θεοί Max.Tyr.30.4; *fruit-bearing*, ὧραι Arat.552. 2. τὸ ἐ. *pedicle* or *fruit-stalk*, Phanias ap.Ath.2.68c, cf. 51c. II. (καρπός II) *on* or *for the wrist*, ἐ. ὄφεις *bracelets* in the shape of snakes, Philostr.*Ep.*22. 2. Subst. ἐπικάρπιον, τό, *part of the hand near the wrist*, Sor.1.84.

ἐπικαρπολογέομαι, *glean*, τοὺς ἀμητούς Lxx *4Ma.*2.9.

ἐπίκαρπος, ον, *fruit-bearing*, ἐλαιών *Sammelb.*5126.19 (iii A.D.).

ἐπικάρσιος, α, ον, later ος, ον Plb.6.29.1, 6.30.6, Opp.*C.*2.169:— = ἐγκάρσιος, *cross-wise, at an angle*, esp. *at a right angle*, as of the *cross-streets* of Babylon, Hdt.1.180; ῥύμη ἐ. πρὸς τὴν .. εὐθεῖαν Plb.6.29.1, cf. 6.30.6; τῆς Σκυθικῆς τὰ ἐ. the country *measured along the coast*, opp. τὰ ὄρθια (inwards, at right angles to the coast), Hdt.4.101; opp. κατ' ἰθύ, Q.S.5.81: c. gen., τριήρεας .. τοῦ μὲν Πόντου ἐπικαρσίας, τοῦ δὲ Ἑλλησπόντου κατὰ ῥόον *forming an angle* with the current of the Pontus, but.., Hdt.7.36; ἐπικάρσιαι σανίδες *cross*-planks, Plb.1.22.5; ἐπικάρσιος ἐπείλησις Sor.*Fasc.*12.506C.: neut. pl. as Adv., ἐπικάρσια δὴ προπεσοῦμαι *athwart*, *Com.Adesp.*640. Regul. Adv. -ίως *transversely*, Antyll.ap.Orib.44.8.2, Paul.Aeg.6.40. 2. *striped*, *CPR*21.19 (iii A.D.), etc. II. in Od.9.70 αἱ μὲν [νῆες] ἔπειτ' ἐφέροντ' ἐπικάρσιαι, either (ἐπὶ κάρ), *plunging*, cf. Eust. ad loc., or (as Sch.) = πλάγιαι, i.e. *making leeway, drifting*. III. Subst. ἐπικάρσιον, τό, *striped garment*, *Ostr.*64 (ii A.D.), *POxy.*921.14 (iii A.D.).

ἐπικαρυκεύεται· ἀρτύει, Hsch.

ἐπικατα-βαίνω, *go down to* a place, ἐς Πλαταιάς Hdt.9.25; πρὸς τὴν πόλιν Th.6.97; πρὸς τὴν θάλασσαν Id.7.23,35; *extend downwards*, ὀδύναι ἐς τὰς χεῖρας ἐ. Hp.*Prorrh.*2.40: metaph., [θεοὶ] ψυχῶν προέστησαν -βάντες Dam.*Pr.*130. 2. *go down after* or *against* an enemy, Hdt.8.38, Th.4.11, 7.84. **-βάλλω**, Ep. aor. 2 ἐπικάββαλον, τῷ δ' ἐπὶ φᾶρος κάββαλε A.R.4.187, cf. Q.S.14.583:—*cast over*, ll. cc.; *throw down upon*, ἐ. τὸν οἶκόν τισι, of Samson, J.*AJ*5.8.12, cf. 14.15.5; *throw down at*, πέτρους D.C.50.33. 2. *let fall down* or *droop at* a thing, τὰ ὦτα X.*Cyn.*4.3. 3. *impose a fine*, *Tab.Heracl.*1.134, where for ἐπικαταβάνοντι Ahrens corrected -βαλίοντι (fut. part.). 4. Pass., *to be distrained upon* by a creditor, Meyer *Juristische Papyri* p.224 (i B.C.). **-βολή**, ἡ, *distraint*, *PMagd.*31.9 (iii B.C.); ἐ. ποιήσασθαι *PBasel* 7.19 (ii B.C.).

ἐπικατ-άγνυμαι, *to be broken upon*, of eggs, Arist.*Pr.*889b11. II. pf. part. Pass. ἐπικατηγμένος, perh. = ἐπικεκλασμένος, *weak*, *Cat.Cod.Astr.*8(3).188. **-άγω** [ᾰγ], *work out* a calculation, Vett.Val.304.20. II. usu. in Pass., of ships or persons at sea, *come to land along with* or *afterwards*, Th.3.49, 8.28, J.*AJ*18.7.2, D.Chr.37.4, D.C.42.7, etc.

ἐπικατα-δαρθάνω, aor. 2 -έδαρθον, *fall asleep afterwards*, Th.4.133, Pl.*R.*534d. **-δεσμέω**, *swaddle*, σανίσι βρέφη Sor.1.85. **-δέω**, *bind upon* or *to*, Hp.*Epid.*5.58, Luc.*Asin.*16,34. **-δύνω** [ῡ], *dive after*, Poll.1.108. II. of stars, *set after*, Procl.*Hyp.*5.52; τῷ ἡλίῳ Gem.9.1:—also Med., -δύομαι Cleom.1.3, Theo Sm.p.138 H. **-δῦσις**, εως, ἡ, *setting of a star just after sunrise* or *after sunset*, Ptol.*Alm.*8.4, Vett.Val.50.12, etc. II. Astrol., name of eighth τόπος, Antioch.Astr. in *Cat.Cod.Astr.*8(3).117.11. **-θέω**, *run down upon, attack*, D.C.40.36. **-θλάω**, *crush*, Sch.Il.19.93.

ἐπικατ-αιγίζω, gloss on ἐπαιγίζω, Sch.Il.2.148. **-αιόνησις**, εως, ἡ, *additional fomentation*, Aët.3.172. **-αίρω**, intr., *swoop down upon*, νεκροῖς ὥσπερ ὄρνιν Plu.*Pomp.*31.

ἐπικατα-καίω, *burn over*, τοῖς ἀποθανοῦσιν ἱερά Lib.*Decl.*13.59. **-κλάω**, *bend*, Apollon.*Lex.* s.v. ἐπιγνάμψασα, Hsch. s.v. ἐπέγκαψαν. **-κλίνω** [κλῐ], *make bend down upon*, τί τινι *EM*431.4, Sch.Il.2.148. II. *introduce as a concubine*, J.*AJ*1.10.4. **-κλύζω**, *overflow besides*, τὴν Ἀσίην πᾶσαν Hdt.1.107. **-κλώθω**, gloss on ἐπεκλώσαντο, Hsch. **-κοιμάομαι**, *sleep upon*, Hdt.4.172. **-κοιμίζομαι**, gloss on ἐπικαταδαρθάνειν, Sch.Pl.*R.*534d.

ἐπικατᾰκολουθέω, *attend to*, φωνῇ Sch.Pi.*O.*6.108: abs., *comply*, *PLille* 4.6 (iii B.C.).

ἐπικατα-λαμβάνω, *follow and catch up, overtake*, τὰς ναῦς Th.2.90; τινά Id.3.111, Plb.1.66.3, etc.; σελήνη ἥλιον ἐ. Pl.*Ti.*39c: abs., μεταξὺ δὲ ἁμέρα -λαμβάνει *IG*4.952.14 (Epid.):—Pass., Arist.*HA*611b33. b. of fruit which forms before the last year's fruit is ripe, *overtakes* it, Thphr.*HP*2.6.10. 2. *fasten, bind on*, κατάπλασμα ταινιδίῳ Gal.13.357. 3. Gramm. in Pass., of σημεῖα, *to be understood after*, S.E.*M.*8.166. **-λείπω**, *bequeath in addition*, Ramsay *Studies in the Eastern Rom.Emp.*345. **-ληψις**, εως, ἡ, *overtaking*, Procl.*Hyp.*4.39.

ἐπικαταλλαγή, ἡ, *money paid for exchange, discount*, Thphr.*Char.*30.15, *SIG*252.7 (Delph., iv B.C.).

ἐπικατα-λύω, *reduce yet further*, τὴν δύναμιν Gal.15.721. **-μένω**, *tarry longer*, X.*Cyr.*1.2.11, *HG*7.4.36. **-μωκάομαι**, = καταμωκάομαι, Poll.8.77; gloss on ἐπιλλίζω, Sch.A.R.3.791. **-ξύω**, *graze, scratch*, Apollon.*Lex.* s.v. ἐπιγράβδην. **-πάσσω**, *sprinkle on*, Dsc.*Eup.*2.37 (Pass.). **-πηδάω**, *leap down after*, εἰς τὰ σκάφη J.*BJ*3.10.9. **-πίμπρημι**, *set fire to over*, βουλευτήριόν τινι App.*BC*2.22. **-πίπτω**, *fall upon*, Luc.*Anach.*1; γαίῃ Q.S.3.399. 2. metaph., *fall to the lot of*, λυγρῷ ἐπικάππεσεν ὄλβος Id.7.78. **-πλάσσω**, *put on a plaster as well*, Hp.*Fract.*25. **-πλέω**, *bear down upon*, of ships, D.S.16.66, Chariton 8.6. **-πνέω**, *blow against*, *EM*554.1.

ἐπικατ-άράομαι, *bring curses*, Lxx *Nu.*5.19,22; *call down curses upon*, λαόν ib.22.17. 2. *curse* (of God), ib.*Ma.*2.2. **-αράσσομαι**, Pass., *fall with a crash*, D.H.10.16, 11.26. **-άρᾱτος** [ᾰρ], ον, *accursed*, Lxx *Ge.*3.14, *Ep.Gal.*3.10,13, *IG*12(9).955 (Euboea); ταῖς ἀραῖς *BMus.Inscr.*918.6 (Halic.).

ἐπικατα-ρρέω, *run down*, of humours, from the head to other parts, Hp.*Aër.*3. II. *fall down upon*, νεκροῖς Plu.*Pel.*4. **-ρρήγνυμι**, *tear, rend*, στολάς J.*AJ*2.6.7:—Pass., *fall violently down upon*, τινί D.H.10.16; of rain, Plu.*Mar.*21. 2. Pass., *to be violently purged*, κοιλία -ερρηγνυμένη Gal.16.691. **-ρριπτέω**, *throw down after*, ἑαυτάς X.*An.*4.7.13. **-σείω**, *bring down on*, ἑαυτῷ ἐλέφαντα J.*BJ*1.1.5; ὀρόφους τισί ib.17.6. **-σκάπτω**, *destroy*, τῇ καλαύροπι τὸ σπήλαιον D.H.1.39; *throw down upon*, ἔτι ζῶντος τὴν γῆν Id.4.48; τὴν πόλιν τισί J.*AJ*13.13.3; *destroy as well*, App.*Ill.*8, al. -σκευάζω, *build upon*, πύργους ἐπὶ σκάφη D.C.50.23. 2. *bring about in addition*, πρὸς τῷ πολέμῳ στάσιν ἑαυτοῖς καὶ λιμόν J.*BJ* 4.3.3. 3. Med., *establish by additional arguments*, Arg.D. 46. -σκοπέω, *supervise*, Procop.*Goth.*1.7. -σπάω, *draw down after*, Arist.*Pr.*901^{a}2:—Pass., *to be drawn in afterwards*, Hp.*Vict.*3. 70. -σπένδω, *pour besides as a libation over*, J.*BJ*1.3.6. -σσω, late form of ἐπικατάγνυμι, Sch.Od.2.355 (Pass.). -στᾰσις, εως, ἡ, in Tactics, wheeling through four right angles and *return to original point*, Ascl.*Tact.*10.1,9. -στρέφω, *invert and put over*, ποτήριον σύκοις *Gp.*10.56.6, cf. Dsc.5.79; τῷ Ταντάλῳ ἡ Σίπυλος -εστράφη Sch.S.*Ant.*134. -σφάζω, later -σφάττω Phld.*Ir.*p.36 W.:—*slay upon* or *over*, τινὰ τῷ νεκρῷ, τῷ τύμβῳ ἑωυτόν, Hdt.1.45; τῇ παρθένῳ Plu.2.772c: without dat., Parth.31.2, Plu.*Cleom.*37; αὐτούς Phld.l.c.:—Pass., τινί J.*AJ*19.1.13. 2. *slay in succession* or *after*, D.H.3.20, App.*Hann.*59, al. -τέμνω, *carry the workings of a mine beyond one's boundaries*, D.37.36. -τρέχω, *rush down on*, D.H.9.21, D.C.36.32. -φέρω, *fell, knock down on top of*, Lib. *Descr.*1.7:—Pass., *fall down upon*, τινί J.*AJ*12.9.4. II. Pass., of stars, *follow the sun*, Nech.ap.Vett.Val.279.22, Anon. *in Ptol. Tetr.*22; -φερόμενον, τό, name of eighth τόπος, Thrasyll. in *Cat.Cod. Astr.*8(3).101. III. metaph., *to be brought* or *come to* the use of an expression, ἐπικατενεχθήσεται Aristid.*Rh.*2p.544S. -φορά, ἡ, Astrol., name of eighth τόπος, Firm.2.19.9, 7.6.8, al.; cf. ἐπικαταφέρω II. -φορος, ον, *prone to*, ἐπί or πρός τι, Terpsicles ap.Ath.9. 391e, Ath.13.608d. -χέω, *pour upon*, Jul.*Mis.*346d. -χρίω, in Med., *smear oneself with*, Orib.*Fr.*85. -ψάω, *harrow lightly*, χώραν Str.17.3.11. -ψεύδομαι, *tell lies besides*, Hdt.3.63, Th.8.74, D.H. 3.2. II. *accuse falsely*, J.*AJ*17.5.5. 2. ἐ. θηλύτητα τῆς ὄψεως *give a false* appearance of femininity, ib.19.1.5. -ψήχω, *smooth down*, metaph., τὴν βουλήν App.*BC*2.145 (v.l. -ψύχων).

ἐπικατ-εῖδον, aor. 2 (no pres. in use), *look at besides*, τι Hp.*Prog.* 7. -ειμι, *go down into*, ἐς τὴν κοιλίαν Th.2.49: abs., of persons, J.*AJ*1.19.3: metaph., *descend in the scale*, Dam.*Pr.*87. -εράω, *pour off liquid on* a thing, Heras ap.Gal.13.39, Orib.*Fr.*88. -εργάζομαι, dub. sens. in *Tab.Defix.Aud.*83. -έρχομαι, = ἐπικάτειμι, Hp.*Nat.Puer.*30. -έχω, *detain*, D.H.9.60, Luc.*Herm.*23, Arg. Cratin. in *POxy.*663.39; *restrain*, ὀργήν D.Chr.3.34.

ἐπικατηγορ-έω, *predicate of* a thing *besides*, τί τινος S.E.*M.*9.334; *attribute to..*, τί τινι Plu.2.1113b; ἐπικλήσει τὸ σχῆμα ἐπικατηγοροῦσῃ D.H.1.66 (L.Dind. for ἐπικατηγορήσει):—Pass., *to be added to the predicate*, Arist.*APr.*49^{a}25; *to be predicated of*, c. dat., τῷ αὐτῷ ἀριθμῷ ποικίλα Iamb.*in Nic.*p.34P. -ημα, ατος, τό, *accusation*, f.l. in Plu. 2.1127d. -ία, ἡ, *further predication* or *characterization*, τὰς ἰδιότητας τῶν ἐ. Demetr.Lac.*Herc.*1012.41 F., al., cf. S.E.*M.*10.297.

ἐπικατ-οικέω, *live at, inhabit*, Ceb.15. -ορθόω, *adjust again*, ὀστέα Hp.*Fract.*16. -ορύσσομαι, Pass., *to be buried after*, ἐπὶ τῇ ἀπαιδίᾳ Antipho 3.2.10 (sed leg. ἔτι κατ-).

ἐπικαττύω, *mend* shoes, Poll.7.82; τὰ σαπρὰ τῶν χιτωνίων Lib. *Decl.*33.10. 2. metaph., *vamp up* old plays, *Com.Adesp.*46.

ἐπικάτω [ᾰ], *downwards*, Hsch. s.v. ἐπιπρηνές.

ἐπικαυλόφυλλος, ον, *with cauline leaves*, Thphr.*HP*7.8.3.

ἐπί-καυμα, ατος, τό, *blister caused by a burn*, Apollod.ap.Sch.Ar. *Pl.*535, Dsc.*Eup.*1.36. 2. *ulcer on the eye*, esp. *the cornea*, Gal.12. 758, 14.774, 19.434. -καυσις, εως, ἡ, *burning*, ἐξ ἐ. Str.13.4.11; *scorching*, of the sun's heat, Id.15.1.24. II. *inflammation of the surface, scorching up*, joined with ἐρυσίβη, Pl.*Ax.*368c. III. = foreg. 2, Dsc.2.136 (pl.). -καυστέον, *one must cauterize*, τὰ ῥήγματα Aët.13.12. -καυτος, *burnt at the tip*, ἀκόντια Hdt.7.71,74.

ἐπικαχλάζω, *plash against*, κῦμα πέτραις ἐ. A.R.4.944, cf. Aesop. 381.

ἐπίκειμαι, serving as Pass. to ἐπιτίθημι, *to be laid upon*, and so, I. of doors, *to be put to* or *closed* (cf. ἐπιτίθημι II), θύραι δ' ἐπέκειντο φαειναί Od.6.19: metaph., γλώσσῃ θύραι οὐκ ἐπίκεινται Thgn.421. 2. generally, *to be placed, lie in* or *on*, c. dat., ἐπισκύνιον ἐπέκειτο προσώπῳ Theoc.24.118; of troops, ὄχθαις Ἴστρου ἐ. Hdn.2.9.1. 3. of islands, νῆσοι ἐπὶ Λήμνῳ (—ου codd.) ἐπικείμεναι *lying off* Lemnos, Hdt. 7.6; so ἐ. τῇ Θρηΐκῃ ib.185; ἐπὶ [τῇ Λακαίνῃ χώρῃ] ib.235, cf. Th.4. 53: abs., αἱ νῆσοι αἱ ἐπικείμεναι the islands *off the coast*, Id.2.14, cf. 4.44; πάσῃ ἐ. τῇ θαλάσσῃ *lies* right *across* the sea, of Crete, Arist. *Pol.*1271^{b}34; ἡ ἐπικειμένη τινὸς γῆ *PTeb.*50.6 (ii B.C.). II. *to be laid upon*, ἐμοὶ σφρηγὶς ἐπικείσθω τοῖσδ' ἔπεσι Thgn.19 (so lit., σφραγὶς οὐκ ἐ. *BGU*361 iii 29 (ii A.D.), etc.); ἐπίκειται ἀγνώμων σῇ κεφαλῇ στέφανος Thgn.1259, cf. X.*Oec.*19.13; ἐ. ἐπί τινος Hero *Spir.*1. 38, al., D.C.67.16: metaph., κρατερὴ δ' ἐπικείσετ' ἀνάγκη Il.6.458, cf. 1*Ep.Cor.*9.16; of a duty, οἷς ἐπέκειτο φροντίζειν Plu.2.786f. 2. *press upon, be urgent* in entreaty, Hdt.5.104; *press upon* a retreating enemy, *attack*, Βοιωτοῖσι ib.81; *to be urgent against*, Id.6.49; ἐπεκείμην αὐτοῖς ἐνοχλῶν *PLips.*36.7 (iv A.D.): abs., κἀπικείσομαι βαρύς E. *Rh.*101; κἀπικείμενος βόα Ar.*Eq.*252; Κλέων μ' ὑπεταράττεν ἐπικείμενος Id.*V.*1285; ἐ. λαμπρῶς Th.7.71; πολὺς δ' ἐπέκειτο Theoc.22. 90; of a crowd, ἐ. τινί *Ev.Luc.*5.1. 3. *hang over*, τηλικούτων ἐπικειμένων τῷ μοιχεύοντι κακῶν X.*Mem.*2.1.5; of penalties, θάνατος ἢ ζημίη ἐπίκειται the penalty *imposed* is death, Hdt.2.38, cf. 6. 58, Arist.*Pol.*1297^{a}18; τῷ ἄρξαντι μεγάλα ἐπιτίμια ἐ. Antipho 4.4.7; ζημία.. ἐπέκειτο στατήρ Th.3.70; ὁ ἐπικείμενος κίνδυνος Hdn.1.13. 4. 4. of a name, *to be imposed*, Pl.*Cra.*411c, *Prt.*349c. 5. metaph., σκώμματα ἐπικείμενα *suitable to the purpose, pointed*, Longin. 34.2. 6. *to be set in authority*, ἐπὶ τοῦ πυρός *Corp.Herm.*1.13; ἐπικείμενος Ἀλεξανδρείας *PLips.*102 i 8, etc. III. c. acc. rei, esp. in part., κἀπικείμενον κάρα κυνέας head *with* helmet *set thereon*, E.*Supp.* 716 (dub. constr.); ἐ. κυνῆν τῆς κεφαλῆς Hld.5.22; στέφανον ἐπικείμενος *with* a crown *on one's head*, Plu.*Marc.*22; ἅπικας ἐπικείμενοι ταῖς κεφαλαῖς D.H.2.70; σεμνὸν ἐπικειμένη τὸ κάλλος J.*AJ*11.6.9; ἀγγέλου ἢ θεράποντος ἐπικείμενος πρόσωπον Plu.*Lys.*23; ἐπέκειτο ὠτειλάς he *bore* scars *upon* him, App.*Mith.*6; ἱερὰν ἐσθῆτα ἐ. Id.*BC*4. 134; φθίμενος τήνδ' ἐπίκειμαι κόνιν *Epigr.Gr.*622.6; κιθάραν.. κόλλοπας ἐπικειμένην *fitted with* pegs, Luc.*Ind.*10: metaph., οἱ κίνδυνον ἐπικείμενοι *exposed to..*, App.*BC*4.124.

ἐπικείρω, Ep. aor. 1 ἐπέκερσα, *cut off, cut down*, πρώτας ἐπέκερσε φάλαγγας Il.16.394; ὄρχους ὀδόντι B.5.108; *cut down* growing corn, τὸν σῖτον ἐ. Thphr.*HP*8.7.4. II. metaph., *cut short, baffle*, μάχης ἐπὶ μήδεα κείρει Il.15.467, cf. 16.120.

ἐπικεκρυμμένως, Adv., (ἐπικρύπτω) *mysteriously*, Plot.3.9.1, Porph. *Plot.*15.

ἐπικελᾰδέω, *shout at* or *to*, esp. *in applause, cheer*, ἐπὶ δὲ Τρῶες κελάδησαν Il.8.542.

ἐπικέλευ-σις, εως, ἡ, *cheering on, exhortation*, Th.4.95, D.H.2. 41. -σμα, ατος, τό, = foreg., Hsch. s.v. ἐπιστίγματα. -σμός, ὁ, = foreg., Sch.Luc.*Cat.*19. -στής, οῦ, ὁ, v.l. for κελευστής, D.S. 20.50. -στικός, ή, όν, *cheering on*: τὸ ἐ. the *signal for attack*, Polyaen.5.16.4. -ω, *exhort, encourage, cheer on*, c. dat., ἐπεκέλευσά σοι E.*El.*1224 codd.: abs., Id.*Ba.*1088: c. acc. pers., ἐ. τὸν μὴ διανοούμενον Th.3.82: c. acc. rei cogn., πρὸς τοῖς ἄλλοις κελεύσμασιν ἐ. τόδε "εὖ κύνες" X.*Cyn.*6.20; joined with παρακελεύομαι (which prop. means *cheer* one *on to an act not begun*, ἐ. *to one already begun*), Pl.*Phd.*61a:—Med., τινὶ παραδιδόναι τὴν ἀρχήν Th.4.28: abs., Plu. *Ant.*77. II. *give consent* or *authorization*, *PPetr.*3 p.133 (iii B.C.), *PTeb.*201 (i B.C.).

ἐπικέλια· ἔπεργα, ἱμάτια, Hsch.

ἐπικέλλω, aor. 1 ἐπέκελσα, also ἐπέκειλα *Act.Ap.*27.41: fut. part. acc. ἐπῑκέλσοντα Numen. (v. infr.):—*bring* ships *to shore*, νῆας ἐπικέλσαι Od.9.148, cf. *Act.Ap.* l.c. 2. abs., *run ashore*, Od.9.138; χέρσῳ ἐ. ἐρετμοῖς A.R.3.575: c. acc., γῆν ἐ. Id.2.352; also of the ship itself, ἡ μὲν ἔπειτα ἠπείρῳ ἐπέκελσεν Od.13.114; of a fish, *rush into* the net, Numen.ap.Ath.7.321b (cj. for ἐπιτέλσοντα).

ἐπικέλομαι, *call upon*, στυγερὰς δ' ἐπεκέκλετ' Ἐρινῦς (redupl. aor. 2) Il.9.454; ἐπικεκλομένα Δῖον πόρτιν A.*Supp.*40 (lyr.): c. dat., παιδί A.R.3.85.

ἐπικεντρ-ίζω, *apply the spur*, *AP*9.777 (Phil.). II. *graft vines*, *Gp.*5.17.11. -όομαι, Astron., *occupy a cardinal point*, -ούμενος cj. for ἐπικεντρόμερος, Antioch.Astr. in *Cat.Cod.Astr.*8(3).115. -ος, ον, Astron., *occupying a cardinal point*, Vett.Val.9.19, Man.1.34, Doroth.ap.Heph.Astr.2.5, S.E.*M.*5.40: Comp., Ptol.*Tetr.*79. -ωσις, εως, ἡ, *occupation of a cardinal point*, Paul.Al.*P.*1.

ἐπικεράννῡμι, *mix in addition*, οἶνον ἐπικρῆσαι (aor. 1 inf.) *mix fresh* wine, Od.7.164, cf. Gal.18(1).169:—Med., Damocr.ap.eund.14.10c.

ἐπίκερας, τό, = τῆλις, Hp.ap.Gal.19.99.

ἐπικεραστικός, ή όν, *tempering the humours*, Gal.6.260; ἀγωγή Alex.Trall.7.7.

ἐπικερδ-αίνω, *gain besides*, ἐνιαυτὸν τῇ ἀρχῇ Plu.*Flam.*3. -εια, ἡ, = ἐπικέρδια (q.v.), *Peripl.M.Rubr.*49, Philostr.*Her.*19.14: pl., Ph. 2.11. II. *interest*, *PGiss.*53.4 (iv A.D.), etc. -ής, ές, *profitable, advantageous*, *TAM*2(1).245 (Lycia), Aesop.137, Vett.Val.189. 30, al., Heph.Astr.2.30, App.*BC*1.57. -ια, τά, *profit on traffic* or *business*, Hdt.4.152, Philostr.*VS*2.21.2. -ιον, *compendium*, *Gloss.*

ἐπικέρνης, ου, ὁ, *cupbearer*, Ps.-Callisth.3.31 (v.l.). (Cf. *pincerna*.)

ἐπικερτομ-έω, *mock*, used by Hom. only in part., τὸν δ' ἐπικερτομέων προσέφης *in mockery*, Il.16.744, Od.22.194, cf. Luc.*DMort.*14. 5, Hld.8.9; in milder sense, *laughingly*, Il.24.649 (or, *in mockery* of Agamemnon). II. c. acc., ἐπεκερτόμησε he *reproached* him, Hdt. 8.92; τινός *for* a thing, Agath.5.22; *tease, banter*, Theoc.20.2, cf. Luc.*Bis Acc.*12. -ημα, ατος, τό, *sarcasm, taunt*, Demetr.*Eloc.* 111. -ησις, εως, ἡ, = foreg., Hdn.*Fig.*p.92S., Trypho *Trop.*p.206 S. -ος, ον, *mocking, cheating*, Q.S.1.136.

ἐπικεύθω, *conceal, hide*, always with a neg., ἐρέω ἔπος οὐδ' ἐπικεύσω Il.5.816; πρόφρων ὑποθήσομαι οὐδ' ἐπικεύσω Od.5.143; εἰπέ μοι.. νημερτέα μηδ' ἐπικεύσῃς 15.263; μῦθον δέ τοι οὐκ ἐπικεύσω 4.744, cf. 17. 141: and in A.*Ag.*800 (anap.), c. acc., οὔ σ' ἐπικεύσω I *will* not *hide* it *from* thee, cf. A.R.3.332.

ἐπικέφᾰλ-α, Adv. *mouth downwards*, of jars, Aët.1.138. -αιος, α, ον, *of* or *for the head*, κόσμος Suid. s.v. τιάρα, *EM*758.4. II. Subst. -αιον, τό, = ἐπικεφάλιον, Arist.*Oec.*1346^{a}4, *POxy.*1157.14 (iii A.D.); -αιον τέλος *SIG*1009.4 (Chalcedon, iii/ii B.C.). 2. *list, register*, *PTeb.*174 (ii B.C.), etc. 3. measure of weight, = two δίδραγμα, Hero *Mens.*60.4. III. Adv. -αίως *with brief headings, summarily*, Gal.17(2).207. -αιόω, *add up*, Vett.Val.260.21:—Med., *sum up*, Plb.2.40.4; τὸ ἀρκοῦν Phld.*D.*1.15. II. Pass., *to be summed up*, D.C.52.28. -ιον, τό, *poll-tax*, *IGRom.*4.181 (Lampsacus), *IG*12(5).724.11, *POxy.*1438.14 (ii A.D.), Ἀρχ.Δελτ.2. 148 (Beroea, ii A.D.): more freq. in pl., Cic.*Att.*5.16.2, *BGU*833, Wilcken *Chr.*28 (ii A.D.), *POxy.*2131.10 (iii A.D., v.l. -κεφάλαια), etc. -ον, τό, *head of battering-ram*, Ath.Mech.23.8. II. *money distributed at so much a head, head-money*, *IG*12(5).946.22 (Tenos); = ἐπικεφάλιον, Hsch.

ἐπικεχοδώς, ὁ, pf. part. of ἐπιχέζω, used as a mock-name for a bird, *Shitterling*, Ar.*Av.*68.

ἐπικηδ-εία, ἡ, (κῆδος) *funeral*, *EM*326.56. **-ειος**, ον (α, ον Lib. *Decl.*40.15), *of* or *at a burial*, *funeral*, ᾠδά E.*Tr.*514 (lyr.), cf. Pl.*Lg.* 800e (pl.); πόνοι E.*Alex.* in *Gött.Nachr.*1922.9; μοῦσα Ael.*NA*5.34; λόγοι D.H.*Rh.*6.1; ἐ., τό, *dirge*, *elegy*, Plu.*Pel.*1, al. (sung before burial, opp. ἐπιτάφιον, Serv. ad Virg.*Ecl.*5.14; opp. θρῆνος, Ptol. Ascal.p.404 H.). **-εύω**, γάμους ἀλλήλοις *form connexions* by marriage, Procop.*Aed.*3.3. II. *bury*, Hsch. s. v. ψέγος. **-ομαι**, *take thought for*, μερόπων Nonn.*D.*7.60: c. inf., Steph. *in Hp.*1.157 D. (fort. ⟨οὐκ⟩ ἐ.).

ἐπικηκ-άζω, *revile*, Hsch. in Pass., ἐπεκήκα⟨σ⟩το· ἐπωνείδιστο. **-αστος**, ον, = ἐπονείδιστος, Eust.1402.53.

ἐπικηραίνω, *to be hostile to* one, Hsch.

ἐπικήριος, ον, = sq., Heraclit.ap.Luc.*Vit.Auct.*14.

ἐπίκηρος, ον (α, ον Hsch., hyperdor. **-κᾶρος** Ecphant.ap.Stob.4.7. 65), (κήρ) *subject to death*, *perishable*, *mortal*, Hp.*Morb.Sacr.*1 (Sup.), Arist.*GA*753ᵃ7 (Comp.); φθαρτή τε καὶ ἐ. [φύσις] Id.*Mu.*392ᵃ34; βίος Call.*Ep.*59; τὸ τῆς φύσεως ἐ. Pl.*Ax.*367b; τὸ θνητὸν καὶ ἐ. Phld. *Mort.*38, etc. b. of plants, *delicate*, Thphr.*HP*6.7.3, 7.5.1. 2. *subject to disaster*, *hazardous*, ἐ. πρᾶγμα ἡ περίφρασις Longin.29.1; κοινωνία Plot.4.4.18: Sup. -ότατος Hsch. Adv., τῆς φιλοσοφίας -ρως διακειμένης Isoc.11.49.

ἐπικηρόω, *wax over*, *rub with wax*, Polyaen.2.20.

ἐπικήρ-υγμα, ατος, τό, *proclamation*, *Inscr.Prien.*109.162 (pl., ii B.C.). **-ῡκεία**, ἡ, *sending an embassy to treat for peace*, *entering into negotiation*, διὰ τὴν πρὸς Λακεδαιμονίους ἡμῖν ἐ. D.5.18, cf. Plb.14. 2.13, Theopomp.Hist.209 (pl.). **-ύκευμα** [ῡ], ατος, τό, *demand by herald*, E.*Med.*738. **-ῡκεύομαι**, Med. (Act. only *AB*141,153), *send a message by a herald*, πρός τινα Hdt.9.87: πρός τινα ὥστε.. Th.7. 49; ὥς τινα ib.48; περί or ὑπέρ τινος, D.S.14.75, Paus.4.8.13; τινὶ εἰ.. *send a message proposing to ask* whether.., Hdt.1.60; ἐ. ταῦτα δι' ἀγγέλων ib.69:—perh. Pass. in Th.8.44 ἐπικηρυκευομένων *messages being sent*. 2. *send ambassadors to treat for peace*, *make proposals for a treaty of peace*, τινί to one, Ar.*Th.*336, Th.4.27; ταῦτά τινι Hdt.4.80, 6.97; ταῦτ' ἐπικηρυκεύομαι Ar.*Th.*1163. 3. of private affairs, *negotiate*, τινί *with* one, D.32.24. II. abs., *go as a herald* or *ambassador*, παρά τινος Plb.21.16.1. **-υκτος**, ον, *denounced*, ᾧ θάνατος ἐ. ἦν App.*Pun.*93. **-υξις**, εως, ἡ, *proclamation of a reward*, Ulp. ad D.19.21. 2. generally, *proclamation*, Ph.*Bel.*98. 36. **-ύσσω**, Att. -ττω, pf. -κεκήρυχα D.19.21:—*proclaim*, ἐπικηρυχθεὶς χθονὶ *proclaimed king*, A.*Th.*634; ἐ. πόλεμόν τινι D.C.78.38 (Pass.). 2. esp. of penalties, ἐ. θάνατον τὴν ζημίαν ὃς ἂν.. *proclaim* death as the penalty, X.*HG*1.1.15; ἐ. ἀργύριον ἐπί τινι *set* a price *on* his head, Hdt.7.214 (but ἀργύριον, of a money penalty, Arist.*Oec.* 1351ᵇ31); χρήματά τινι ἐ. D. l. c.; λάφυρον κατά τινων *issue* letters of marque, Plb.4.26.7:—Pass., καὶ οἱ φυγόντι... ἀργύριον ἐπεκηρύχθη Hdt.7.213; τὰ ἐπικηρυχθέντα χρήματα the price *set upon one's head*, Nymphod.12, cf. Plu.*Them.*26; but also ὁ ἐπικηρυχθεὶς the *proscribed person*, *outlaw*, D.C.37.10 (pl.). 3. *offer as a reward*, χρημάτων πλῆθος τοῖς ἀνελοῦσι D.S.14.8, cf. D.C.56.43; τὸ -κηρυχθὲν τῷ ἀγαγόντι Plu.*Them.*29: c. inf., τάλαντον δώσειν τῷ ἀπαγαγόντι Lys.6. 18. II. *put up to public auction*, τὰς ὠνὰς *PEdgar*64.4 (iii B.C.), cf. *PRev.Laws*48.13 (iii B.C.), *SIG*975.6 (Delos, iii B.C., Pass.), v.l. for ἀποκ. in Plu.*Cam.*8.

ἐπικίδνημι, *spread over*, κακοῖς ἐπικίδνατε θυμόν *spread* a brave spirit *over* your ills, Orac.ap.Hdt.7.140:—in Hom. always Pass. (only in Il.), ὕδωρ ἐπικίδναται αἶαν *is spread over* the earth, Il.2.850, cf. A.R.2.978; ὅσον τ' ἐπικίδναται ἠώς far as the morning light *is spread*, Il.7.451,458; ἐπεκίδνατο οὐρανὸν ἄστρα Q.S.5.347.

ἐπικῐθάρισμα [ᾰρ], ατος, τό, *piece performed after a play*, Tertull. *Valent.*33.

ἐπικίνδῡν-ος, ον, *in danger*, *insecure*, Hdt.6.86.α'; ἐ. ἦν μὴ λαμφθείη Id.7.239; πρόσοδοι D.36.11; ἐν ἐπικινδύνῳ, opp. ἐν τῷ ἀσφαλεῖ, Th.1.137. 2. *dangerous*, διδάσκαλοι Gorg.*Pal.*4 (Comp.); στρατεῖαι Pl.*R.*467d; ἀρρωστίαι Phld.*Ir.*p.29 W.; δεινὴ καὶ ἐ. ἔρις Pl.*Lg.* 736c, cf. X.*Mem.*4.6.10; -οτέρα πρᾶξις Id.*An.*1.3.19; τινί to one, Hp.*Aph.*4.16, Th.3.54; ἐπικίνδυνόν [ἐστι] *there is danger*, Arist.*HA* 588ᵃ10. 3. Adv. -νως *with danger*, τίκτειν Hp.*Aph.*5.55; *at one's risk*, Th.3.37; *in a precarious* or *critical state*, κεῖσθαι S.*Ph.*502; ἔχειν E.*Fr.*682. **-ώδης**, ες, = foreg., Sch.S.*El.*222.

ἐπικῑν-έω, Act. only as f.l. for ἐπινέω (B) or -νηνέω (q.v.), Iamb.*VP* 3.17:—Pass., *to be moved*, ὀσφὺς -κινεῖται Luc.*Asin.*6; *gesticulate at* a thing, v.l. Epict.*Ench.*33.10: metaph., *to be moved*, *zealous*, ἐπί τινι Lxx 1*Es.*8.69(73); also, *to be moved* to passion, τοὺς οὐδ' ἐπικινηθῆναι δυναμένους Phld.*Piet.*21. **-ημα**, ατος, τό, *onward motion*, Procl. *Hyp.*3.53. **-ησις**, εως, ἡ, = foreg., τοῦ ἡλίου Simp. *in Ph.*701. 29. **-ῡμαι**, *move on*, Q.S.12.145 codd.

ἐπικιρνάω, = sq., Dsc.*Ther.Praef.*, Alex.Trall.*Febr.*7.

ἐπικίρνημι, Ion. for ἐπικεράννυμι, Heraclit.*All.*35, Philum.ap. Orib.45.29.8:—Pass., ἐπικίρναται [ὁ κρητήρ] Hdt.1.51, Plu.2.270a, cf. Heraclit.*All.*40.

ἐπικιχλίδες, αἱ, a poem ascribed to Homer, so called because he was rewarded by a present of κίχλαι, *fieldfares*, Clearch.ap.Ath.14. 639a, Menaechm.3 J.

Ἐπικιχράδας, title of Zeus at Cos, Hsch.

ἐπικίχρημι, aor. 1 ἐπέχρησα, *lend*, τινὶ τάγματα πρὸς τὸν πόλεμον Plu.*Pomp.*52; ἐπιχρήσας ἑαυτὸν εἰς ἀπαλλοτρίωσιν *CIG*3281 (Smyrna).

ἐπικλάζω, *sound to*, θαλάσσῃ Opp.*H.*5.295; ἐπί οἱ ἔκλαγξε βροντάν *made* thunder *sound in answer to* him, Pi.*P.*4.23.

ἐπικλαίω, Att. **-κλάω**, *weep in answer*, Ar.*Th.*1063; τινί at a thing, Nonn.*D.*30.114.

ἐπίκλᾱρος, -κλᾱρόω, Dor. for ἐπικληρ-.

ἐπί-κλασμα, ατος, τό, *weakening*, *Gloss.* **-κλασμός**, ὁ, = foreg., ib., dub. in *BGU*920.22 (ii A.D.).

ἐπίκλαυτος, ον, *tearful*, νόμος Ar.*Ra.*684 (lyr.).

ἐπικλάω, *bend*, in lit. sense only Pass., *bend double*, ἡ δεξιὰ περὶ τὴν κεφαλὴν ἐπὶ τὸ ἄνω ἐπικεκλασμένη Luc.*DDeor.*11.2; ἐπικεκλ. τὸν αὐχένα Id.*Rh.Pr.*11; ὕδωρ ἐπικλώμενον *broken* water, Id.*Tox.*20; ἐπ' ἀλλήλων -κλωμένων τῶν κυμάτων Alciphr.1.1; also, *to be bruised*, Paul.Aeg.6.117. II. metaph., *move to pity*, Plu.*Per.*37; ἐ. τινὰ εἰς οἶκτον Ael.*NA*10.36:—Pass., Th.3.67; ἐ. τῇ γνώμῃ ib.59; ὑπ' εὐνοίης Hp.*Ep.*13; πρὸς οἶκτον Jul.*Or.*2.90d. 2. *shake the resolution of*, τινά Plu.*Oth.*15:—Pass., ἐπικλασθῆναι τῇ γνώμῃ *to be broken in spirit*, *lose courage*, Th.4.37; τὸ ἐπικεκλασμένον τῶν μελῶν *effeminate*, *unmanly* music, Luc.*Demon.*12.

ἐπικλεής, ές, *famous*, A.R.4.1472; ὄνομα *CIG*2613 (Cyprus): Comp., Max.Tyr.29.1. 2. *named*, *called after*, τινί Opp.*H.*2.130. (Ep. acc. ἐπικλεᾶ.)

Ἐπικλείδια, τά, festival of Demeter at Athens, Hsch.

ἐπίκλειθρον, τό, = ἐπίκλιντρον II, dub. in Gal.*UP*11.13 (vv.ll. ἐπικαίρων, ἐπικλήρων, ἐπικλήθρων): fort. ἐπίκλιθρον, cf. ἀνάκλιθρον.

ἐπικλείω (A), Ep. **-κληΐω**, Att. **-κλῄω**, *shut to*, *close*, τοὺς πρωκτοὺς Ar.*Pax*101 (anap.); ἐπεκλῄϊσσε θύρην Tryph.200:—Med., Luc.*Tox.* 50:—Pass., *to be shut to*, opp. ἀναπτύσσομαι, X.*Eq.*12.6: c. dat., *to be covered* by.., Gal.18(1).429.

ἐπικλείω (B), *extol* or *praise the more*, τὴν γὰρ ἀοιδὴν μᾶλλον ἐπικλείουσι Od.1.351. 2. *relate* or *recount that*.., c. acc. et inf., A.R. 1.18, Opp.*C.*3.78. 3. *call*, *name*, τόν ῥ' ἄνδρες ἐ. Βοώτην Arat.92, cf. A.R.2.1156. 4. *call upon*, *invoke*, Ἀπόλλωνα Id.2.700: c. inf., Κυθέρειαν ἐ. ἀμύνειν Id.3.553.

ἐπικλέπτοιτο· ἐπιθυμοίη, Hsch. **ἐπικλεσαιδόνα**· ἐπικληδόνα, Id.

ἐπικλήδην, Adv., = ἐπίκλην, formed like ὀνομακλήδην, Opp.*C.*1.471.

ἐπικλῄζω, = ἐπικλείω (B) 3, Ἀνάφην νῆσον -κλῄζουσι Orph.*A.*1359, cf. Poet. *de herb.*154:—Pass., Poet.ap.D.L.6.100, App.*Syr.*17.

ἐπικληΐω, v. ἐπικλείω (A).

ἐπίκλημα, ατος, τό, *accusation*, *charge*, S.*OT*227,529, E.*Or.*570, X. *Oec.*11.4, D.C.*Fr.*23.1.

ἐπίκλην, Adv. *by surname*, *by name*, Pl.*Sph.*221c; ἐπίκλην αἰθὴρ καλούμενος Id.*Ti.*58d; ἔξεώς τινος ἐ. λεγομένη called *after*..., Id. *Phlb.*48c; Σαραπίων ἐ. βουκόλος *PLips.*6.7 (iv A.D.), cf. Luc.*Symp.*6, *IG*12(8).529 (Thasos); ὁ τοῦ Αὐγούστου ἐ. λιμήν D.C.75.16. 2. *nominally*, Apollod.3.13.4.—Prop. acc. from an obsolete nom. ἐπίκλη, = ἐπίκλησις, ἐπωνυμία (Hsch.); ἐπίκλην (acc.) ἔχειν, occurs in Pl.*Ti.*38c, *IG*14.1018.6.

ἐπικληρ-ικός, ή, όν, *concerning an* ἐπίκληρος, λόγος D.H.*Din.* 12. **-ῖτις**, ιδος, ἡ, = ἐπίκληρος, ἡ, Is.*Fr.*91 S. **-ος**, Dor. **-κλᾶρος**, ἡ (ὁ only in Thom.Mag.p.138 R.), *heiress*, Ar.*Av.*1653, *V.* 583, And.1.121, Lys.26.12, Pl.*Lg.*630e, Arist.*Ath.*9.2, *Pol.*1270ᵃ27, *IG*2².1165, *Test.Epict.*3.31, etc.; ὥσπερ ἐπικλήρου.. ἀμφισβητησόντων ἧκει Lys.24.14. 2. c. dat., ἐ. τῇ ἀρχῇ (so codd.: prob. τῆς ἀρχῆς) *heiress to* the kingdom, D.H.1.70: c. gen., ἐ. οὐσίας μεγάλης Plu. *Cleom.*1. 3. Astrol., perh. f. l. for ἔγκληρος, *Cat.Cod.Astr.*8(4). 225. **-όω**, Dor. **-κλᾱρόω**, *assign by lot*, τοῖς χοροῖς τοὺς αὐλητάς D.21.13; ἐ. ταῖς ἀρχαῖς τὰ δικαστήρια Arist.*Ath.*59.5; τὰς διαίτας ib. 53.5; εἰς τὰς φυλὰς τὰ ὀνόματα *OGI*229.52 (Smyrna, iii B.C.); τινὰ ἐπὶ φυλὴν καὶ χιλιαστὺν καὶ ἑκατοστὺν καὶ γένος *Supp.Epigr.*1.352.19 (Samos, iv B.C.); ἐ. τινά c. inf., *appoint* one to do, Call.*Dian.*23:—Pass., *to be assigned by lot*, τῷ μορίῳ ἑκάστῳ Pl.*Lg.*760b, *Inscr.Prien.* 37.103; τῶν δικαστηρίων -κεκληρωμένων *having been settled by lot*, D. 37.39. 2. *have assigned* one *by lot*, ἔθνος D.C.37.50. **-ωσις**, εως, ἡ, *assignment by lot*, *SIG*333.29 (Samos, iv B.C.), *Milet.*3 No. 143.31 (iii B.C.). **-ωτικοὶ** νόμοι laws *governing the treatment of heiresses*, Sch.Patm.D. in *BCH*1.153. **-ωτός**, όν, *assigned by lot*, δικαστήριον *AB*260.

ἐπί-κλησις, εως, ἡ, *surname*, *additional name*; used by Hom. only in acc. abs., like ἐπίκλην, and mostly ἐπίκλησιν καλέειν, as Ἀστυάναξ, ὃν Τρῶες ἐπίκλησιν καλέουσιν Astyanax, as they call him *by surname* (his name being Scamandrius), Il.22.506; Ἄρκτος, ἣν καὶ Ἅμαξαν ἐ. καλέουσι which they *call also* the Wain, 18.487, cf. 7.138, 22.29; Τιτῆνας ἐ. καλέεσκεν.. τιταίνοντας ἀτασθαλίῃ μέγα ῥέξαι ἔργον *named* them Titans, *after* their endeavouring.. (ἐπὶ τῷ τιταίνειν), Hes.*Th.* 207; so in Hdt., ἐ. δὲ ἡ κρήνη ἐπικαλέεται Ἡλίου 4.181; Ἀθηναίης ἐ. Ἀσσησίης 1.19; also, *in name only*, *nominally*, [Μενέσθιον] τέκε Πολυδώρη Σπερχειῷ, αὐτὰρ ἐ. Βώρῳ she bare him to Spercheius (really), but *nominally* to Borus, Il.16.177; τὸν τοῦ βουκόλου ἐπίκλησιν παῖδα Hdt.1.114; κατ' ἐ. Apollod.1.3.2; opp. ὄνομα, D.H.5.21. 2. after Hom., in other cases, *surname*, *name*, Th.1.3, etc. 3. *imputation*, *charge*, Id.7.68, *PLille*29.27 (iii B.C.); ἐ. ἔχει κακὸς εἶναι X.*Lac.*9. 4. 4. *title*, D.C.37.6, etc.; βασιλέα ἄξιον τῆς ἐ. Jul.*Or.*2.70c. 5. *announcement* of result of an election, *OGI*458.82 (i B.C., pl.). II. *calling upon*, *invocation*, Ἀφροδίτης Luc.*Salt.*11; δαιμόνων D.C.78.4: abs., *prayer*, ἐ. καὶ εὐχαί Lxx 2*Ma.*15.26; μεμιγμένας ἀπειλαῖς ἐπικλήσεις D.H.5.21. 2. *call* to an office, Astramps.*Orac.*84.9. 3. judicial *appeal*, Vett.Val.281.14; esp. = Lat. *appellatio*, *appeal* to the Tribunes, Plu.*Marc.*2, *Cat.Mi.*33, al. **-κλητος**, ον, *called upon*, *called in as ally*, Hdt.5.75, 7.203, Th.4.61. 2. *specially summoned*, σύλλογον ἐ. Περσέων τῶν ἀρίστων ἐποιέετο held a *privy* council, Hdt.7.8 (so Subst. ἐπίκλητος, ἡ, *convocation*, *assembly*, Lxx *Nu.*28.18, al.); ἐπίκλητοι *privy councillors*, among the Persians, Hdt.8.101, 9.42; *committee* of a council, *SIG*353.2 (Ephesus, iv B.C.), Str.14.1.21. 3. *called to* an office, D.H.2.76; ἐ. τῆς συναγωγῆς Lxx *Nu.*1.16. b. *appointed, designated*, πόλεις ib.*Jo.*20.9. 4. *summoned before* a court, *accused*, D.C.78.21. II. *invited in addition, supernumerary guest*, Ar.*Pax* 1266, Plu.2.707a. 2. *alien, foreign*, ὄχλος, opp. ἐπιχώριος, D.H. 6.53. b. *irrelevant*, λοιδορία Plb.8.11.2.

ἐπικλῐβάνιος [ᾰ], ον, *at* or *presiding over the oven*, θεά Carnead.ap. S.E.*M.*9.185.

ἐπικλίν-εια [κλῐ], ἡ, *inclination, bend*, Heliod.ap.Orib.49.13. 3. 2. *tendency*, πρὸς φθίσιν Gal.17(1).726. **-ής**, ές, *sloping*, χωρίον Th.6.96; λόφοι Plu.*Ant.*45; ἐ. τῷ στάχυϊ καὶ μὴ ὀρθά *inclining, bending*, Thphr.*CP*3.22.1; ἐπικλινές ἐστι τάλαντον Call.*Fr.* 312. 2. *prone, inclined*, πρὸς τὸν Ἄρην Them.*Or.*15.187b; οἰκείωσις ἐ. πρός τινα Ph.1.252. Adv. -νῶς, ἔχειν πρός τι ib.37, al.

ἐπικλῑνοπάλη [ᾰ], ἡ, *wrestling on the couch*, in mal. part., Mart.14. 201.

ἐπικλίν-της, ου, ὁ, *moving sideways*, [σεισμοὶ] ἐπικλίνται earthquakes *that move at acute angles*, Arist.*Mu.*396^{a}1 (v.l. ἐπικλῖται: ἐπικλινίαι (sic) Lyd.*Ost.*53 codd.). **-τρον**, τό, *couch, arm-chair*, Ar.*Ec.*907 (lyr.), *Fr.*44, *IG*2^2.1541.26 (iv B.C.); but, *straight-backed chair*, Gal.18(1).344. II. *back* of a couch or chair, *IG*11(2).144 *A* 66, *B* 8 (Delos, iv B.C.), *Gp.*13.14.9.

ἐπι-κλίνω, *put to, shut* a door: hence, in Pass., once in Hom., ἐπικεκλιμέναι σανίδες *closed* doors, Il.12.121. II. *bend towards*, τὰ ὦτα ἐ. *prick* the ears, X.*Cyn.*6.15; ἐ. αὑτὸν πρός τι *lean against*.., Paus.9.30.10; ξίφει ἑαυτὴν Philostr.*Her.*19.11; ἐ. τὸ στόμα *pull* it *open*, Arist.*PA*660^{b}22:—Pass., κεραῖαι ἐπικεκλιμέναι spars *leaning on* the wall *and inclined at an angle* to it, Th.2.76. 2. *cause to incline*, πρὸς ταῦτα τὰ πράγματα D.3.8. 3. intr., *lean upon*, τοῖν χεροῖν Pl.*Amat.*132b; *incline towards*, ἐπί τι Chrysipp.*Stoic.*3. 175; πρὸς τὸ χεῖρον Dam.*Pr.*400. 4. = ἐπικατακλίνω, J.*AJ*1.10. 4. III. in Pass., *lie over against* or *near*, Σαλαμῖνος τᾶς ἐπικεκλιμέναις ὄχθοις ἱεροῖς (sc. of Attica), E.*Tr.*801 (lyr.), cf. A.R.2.418. IV. Pass., also, *recline upon*, τύλῃ *AP*11.14 (Ammian.). **-κλῐσις**, εως, ἡ, *slope*, ἐδαφῶν Str.1.3.7. II. *inclination towards*, Antip. ap.Stob.4.22.25, Chrysipp.*Stoic.*3.175. III. *lying in bed*, Gal. 18(2).456 (pl.). **-κλῐτέον**, *one must fold in, turn in*, Orib.46.25.5.

ἐπικλονέω, *urge violently on*, [τινά] A.R.3.687; δῆριν Q.S.8.426:—Pass., *rush like a tide upon*, of persons, A.R.1.783; of storms, Q.S. 14.501.

Ἐπικλόπ-ειος, title of Zeus, Hsch. **-ίη**, ἡ, *trickery*, Nonn.*D.* 8.121. **-ος**, ον, *thievish, tricky, wily*, ἠπεροπῆά τ' ἔμεν καὶ ἐ. Od. 11.364; κερδαλέος κ' εἴη καὶ ἐ. 13.291; ἐ. ἦθος, of women, Hes.*Op.*67, cf. A.*Eu.*149 (lyr.); ἐπικλοπώτερον.. τὸ θῆλυ Pl.*Lg.*781a; ἐ. λόγοις χρῆσθαι Corn.*ND*16. Adv., Comp. -ώτερον Procop.*Arc.*25, *Goth.*4. 30. 2. c. gen., ἐ. ἔπλεο μύθων *cunning* in speech, Il.22.281; ἐ. ἔπλετο τόξων *cunning* in archery, Od.21.397.

ἐπι-κλύζω, pf. -κέκλῠκα Aeschin.3.173:—*overflow, flood*, ὅθι κύματ' ἐπ' ἠϊόνας (v.l. -όνος) κλύζεσκον Il.23.61, cf. Th.3.89, *PLond.*2.267. 112 (ii A.D.); ἐπέκλυζε τὸ πᾶν.. θάλασσα Anon.*Oxy.*1014.16; τοὺς χυμοὺς οἷον ἐπικλύζοντας τὸ δέρμα, in blushing jaundice, Gal.7.267; ἐ. χρυσῷ τὴν λεωφόρον Ps.-Luc.*Philopatr.*21, cf. *Tim.*18:—Pass., *to be overwhelmed*, κύμασι v.l. in Batr.69; πλημυρίσιν Arist.*Mu.*397^{a}29. 2. metaph., *deluge, swamp*, πόλιν E.*Tr.*1327 (lyr.), cf. Theoc.25.201; ἐπέκλυσε θυμὸν ἀνίῃ δείματι A.R.3.695; ψυχὴν Ph.1.91; ἐ. τινὰ κακοῖς Luc.*Pseudol.*25; φωναῖς ῥητόρων Lib.*Decl.*50.44; τῷ πλούτῳ πάντα Jul.*Or.*1.8b:—Pass., ὑπὸ τῶν δυσπραγιῶν Id.*ad Them.*257c. 3. *sweep away in the flood*, A.R.1.257: metaph., τὸ βασιλικὸν χρυσίον ἐπικέκλυκε τὴν δαπάνην *has merged*, i.e. *liquidated*, the expenses, Aeschin. l.c. 4. Pass., *to be poured over*, Eun.*VS* p.476 B. II. intr., *overflow, abound*, D.S.3.47; πλοῦτος -κλύζων Eun.*Hist.*p.257 D., cf. D.H.6.17; τινί with a thing, Id.*Isoc.*14. **-κλῠσις**, εως, ἡ, *overflow, flood*, Th.3.89; ποταμοῦ Thphr.*Fr.*171.11: pl., Them. *Or.*13.167b. **-κλυσμός**, ὁ, = foreg., Poll.1.114, 116, Hld.9.3, Aq. *Jb.*21.17. **-κλυστος**, ον, *flooded*, D.S.1.10, Str.1.2.25.

ἐπι-κλῠτός, όν, *famed*, ἐ. ἀνδράσι Φινεὺς ὄλβῳ A.R.2.236. **-κλύω**, *listen to, hear*, c. acc., ἐπεὶ πάντ' αἶνον ἐπέκλυε Νηλεΐδαο Il.23.652, cf. A.R.3.598; σοῦ φωνήμαθ' ὡς ἐπέκλυον βοῶντος S.*Ichn.*39: c. gen., ἐπεὶ δὴ Ζηνὸς ἐπέκλυεν ἀγγελιάων Od.5.150, cf. A.R.1.1240, Eratosth. 19.

ἐπι-κλώθω, *spin upon*, ῥάμμα (q.v.) Hermipp.48; elsewh., II. *spin to* one, *assign*, prop. of the Fates who spun the thread of destiny; also of all powers which influence men's fortunes, οὔ μοι τοιοῦτον ἐπέκλωσαν θεοὶ ὄλβον Od.3.208, cf. 4.208, etc.; ὁππότε κεν Μοῖραι ἐπικλώσωσ' (sc. θάνατον) Callin.1.9, cf. Them.*Or.*32.356d:—Med., ὁππότε [θεοὶ] βασιλεῦσιν ἐπικλώσωνται ὀϊζύν Od.20.196, cf. 8.579: sts. c. inf. pro acc., τῷ οἱ ἐπεκλώσαντο θεοὶ οἶκόνδε νέεσθαι 1.17; ὡς γὰρ ἐπεκλώσαντο θεοὶ δειλοῖσι βροτοῖσι, ζώειν ἀχνυμένοις Il.24.525 (here only in Il.):—so in Act., φιτρὸν τὸν Μοῖρ' ἐπέκλωσεν ζωᾶς ὅρον ἔμμεν B.5.143; τοῦτο γὰρ λάχος.. Μοῖρ' ἐπέκλωσεν ἐμπέδως ἔχειν A. *Eu.*335 (lyr.); ἐπεί τό γε (sc. θανεῖν) Μοῖρ' ἐ. *CIG*3136 (Erythrae), al.—Poet. word, used by Pl.*Tht.*169c τὴν.. εἱμαρμένην, ἣν ⟨ἂν⟩ σὺ ἐπικλώσῃς, cf. *Stoic.*2.319, Luc.*Cont.*16, *DMort.*30.2, Jul.*Or.*7. 229c:—Pass., τὰ ἐπικλωσθέντα *its destiny*, Pl.*R.*620e, cf. *Lg.*957e, Plu.2.22b, 114d; ἐξ ἀρχῆς -κεκλωσμένην ἀπόβασιν *Com.Adesp.*295 (troch.). **-κλωσις**, εως, ἡ, *spinning*, τῶν Μοιρῶν *EM*495.25 (pl.). **-κλωσμα**, ατος, τό, *spun yarn*, Diogenian.Epicur.2.53.

ἐπικνάω, *scrape* or *grate over*, ἐπὶ δ' αἴγειον κνῆ (impf.) τυρόν Il.11. 639; ἐ. τυρόν, σίλφιον, Ar.*Av.*533 (anap.), 1582; τί τινι ib.1586: Att. inf. ἐπικνῆν *Com.Adesp.*722. 2. *scratch*, τὴν παρειάν Hld.2.8.

ἐπικνέομαι, Ion. for ἐφ-.

ἐπικνήθω, = ἐπικνάω, Nic.*Th.*698.

Ἐπικνημίδιοι, οἱ, name of a tribe of Locrians, who lived *on the slopes of Mount Cnemis*, Str.9.2.42.

ἐπικνήμιον, f.l. for ἀντι-, X.*Cyr.*2.3.19.

ἐπι-κνίζω, *scratch the surface*, Thphr.*HP*4.2.1, *CP*5.2.4 (Pass.); of the plough, *AP*6.238 (Apollonid.). **-κνῐσις**, εως, ἡ, *scratching on the surface*, Thphr.*CP*5.2.4.

ἐπικοιλ-αίνω, *make hollow*, [τὴν ῥάχιν] Sor.1.102. **-ίς**, f.l. for ἐπικυλίς, Poll.2.66. **-ος**, ον, *porous, spongy*, ὀστέον Hp.*VC*1 (Comp.); ἕλκη cj. for ποικίλα in Sor.1.122.

ἐπικοιμ-άομαι, *fall asleep after* a thing, Hp.*Aph.*5.27; or, *over* a thing, [τοῖς βιβλίοις] Luc.*Alex.*49: abs., *fall asleep*, δοκεῖς οὐ καθεύδων ἐπικεκοιμῆσθαι Pl.*Euthd.*300a. 2. ἐ. ἐπί τινα *overlay*, Lxx 3*Ki.* 3.19; τῷ αὐτῆς παιδίῳ J.*AJ*8.2.2. II. metaph. in pf. part. Pass., *sleepy* or *negligent about* a thing, Plb.2.13.4. **-ησις**, εως, ἡ, *sleeping upon* one ear, Hp.*Art.*40. **-ητηριάσασθαι**· ὑπηρετικὸν ὄνομα, Hsch. **-ίζω**, *lull to sleep*, Nonn.*D.*4.307.

ἐπικοινάομαι, *consult* an oracle, *GDI*1557, 1563 (Dodona).

Ἐπικοίνιος, title of Zeus at Salamis, Hsch.

ἐπίκοιν-ος, ον, *common to many, promiscuous*, ἐπίκοινον τῶν γυναικῶν τὴν μεῖξιν ποιεῖσθαι Hdt.4.104, cf. 172, 180; *sharing equally in*, λέκτρων E.*Andr.*124 (lyr.): c. dat., *in common with*, ἀρχὴν ἐ. αὐτῷ ἔχειν D.C.42.44; ἐ. ἀμφοῖν *belonging equally*, Plu.2.368e, cf. 1018f, *BGU* 906.21 (i A.D.): neut. pl. Adv., *in common*, [γυναιξὶν] ἐπίκοινα χρέωνται Hdt.1.216; χρηστήριον, τὸ ἐ. ἔχρησε ἡ Πυθίη Id.6.77 (but ἐχρήσθη ἐπίκοινον χρ. ib.19). Regul. Adv. -νως Orph.*Fr.*256. II. Gramm., *common*, of gender, D.T.634.19, Gell.13.7.3. Adv. -νως A.D.*Conj.* 253.20. III. ἐπίκοινος, ἡ, a game, = ἐπίσκυρος, Sch.Pl.*Tht.*146a, Eust.1601.34, Poll.9.104. **-όω**, *communicate*, περί τινος D.C.66.10, etc.:—Med., *consult with*, τινὶ περί τινος Pl.*Prt.*313b; *communicate*, τινί τι D.C.52.21, Procop.*Aed.*2.3. II. Med., *share*, ib.1.4:—Pass., *to be shared with*, γάμους ἀλλήλοις ἐπικοινουμένους Pl.*Lg.* 631d. **-ωνέω**, *communicate with*, τῷ ἔξω χωρίῳ Hp.*Prog.*7; ἀλλήλοις Pl.*Sph.*251d; of troops in order of battle, *to be in touch with*, τοῖς ἄκροις Ascl.*Tact.*1.3; ἐ. πᾶσαι αἱ ἐπιστῆμαι ἀλλήλαις κατὰ τὰ κοινά Arist.*APo.*77^{a}26; τίνι οὐκ ἐ. [τὸ μάθημα] τῶν ἐπικαιροτάτων ἐν ἰητρικῇ; Hp.*Fract.*31, cf. Pl.*Grg.*464c: c. dat. pers., D.29.36. 2. *share in* a thing *with* one, τῶν γραμμάτων τί ἐπικοινωνεῖ; what letters *has* it *in common?* Pl.*Cra.*394c; νόμος οὐδὲν ἐπικοινωνῶν τῷ περὶ τῶν στεφανουμένων νόμῳ *having* nothing *in common with*.., Aeschin.3.44: generally, *share in*, c. gen., Ph.1.561. 3. *to be in partnership with*, c. dat., *POxy.*1280.6 (iv A.D.). **-ωνία**, ἡ, *interrelation*, Pl. *Sph.*252d, Thphr.*Od.*67. **-ωνός**, όν, = κοινωνός, Hp.*Decent.*5.

ἐπικοίρᾰνος, ὁ, = κοίρανος, Orph.*A.*294 (better ἔπι κ.).

ἐπικοιτ-άζομαι, *pass the night*, Arist.*HA*599^{a}30. **-έω**, *keep watch over*, ἐπὶ τῶν ἔργων Plb.21.27.6. **-ιος**, ον, *at bedtime*, ᾆσμα ἐ., of self-examination, Hierocl.*in CA*19 p.460 M.

ἐπικοκκάστρια, ἡ, *mocker*, ἠχὼ λόγων ἀντῳδὸς ἐ. Ar.*Th.*1059: Ar. Byz.ap.Eust.1761.26 refers it to a verb **ἐπικοκκάζω**: masc. **ἐπικοκκαστής** cj. in Timo 43.

ἐπικόκκουρος· ὁ παρατηρητὴς ἐν σταδίῳ (Lacon.), Hsch.

ἐπικολάπτω, *carve on stone*, γράμματα *IG*2^2.1672.6; ὅρον ἐπὶ πέτρας *Inscr.Prien.*37.162 (ii B.C.).

ἐπικολλ-αίνω, *smear on*, πηλόν τινι Thphr.*CP*1.6.6. **-ημα**, ατος, τό, *that which is glued on, tessellated work*, Id.*HP*4.3.4 (pl.).

ἐπικόλπιος, ον, *in* or *on the bosom*, Ael.*NA*2.50, Nonn.*D.*8.78 codd.

ἐπικολπόω, *bend round*, τὰ κέρα, of troops, Agath.3.22.

ἐπικόλωνος, ον, *on* or *over a hill*, ὁδός f.l. in D.S.19.19.

ἐπικομάω, *wear long hair*, Poll.2.25; ξανθῇ κόμῃ ἐ. Id.4.136.

ἐπικομίζω, *bring* or *carry to*, ἐπὶ τοὺς ἔξω τόπους Str.11.2.17, cf. Arist.ap.D.L.5.14 (Pass.):—Med., *bring with one*, τὰ τοῦ Ἰωσήπου ὀστᾶ J.*AJ*2.15.2; τὴν τροφὴν ἑαυτοῖς D.C.50.11, cf. *PLips.*41.10 (iv A.D.).

ἐπικομμόω, *adorn with cosmetics*, Them.*Or.*13.167d.

ἐπικομπ-άζω, *add boastingly*, E.*HF*981; ἀληθεῖ λόγῳ τι Plu.*Cam.* 22: abs., *boast*, Ph.1.550. **-έω**, = foreg., Th.8.81. 2. *boast of*, τι Id.4.126.

ἐπικομψεύω, *deck out*, λόγον J.*AJ*20.12.1 (cod. A).

ἐπικονέω, pf. Pass. ἐπικεκόνημαι (-ιμαι cod.)· ἐξέφθαρμαι, ἀπόλωλα, Hsch.

ἐπικονιάω, *whitewash*, στοιάν *IG*11(2).229 *A* 10 (Delos, iii B.C.).

ἐπι-κόπᾰνον, τό, *chopping-block, billet*, Men.33, *IG*11(2).199 *B* 89 (Delos, iii B.C.), Poll.10.101. **-κοπάς** (sc. γῆ), άδος, ἡ, *land cleared of trees*, *PLond.ined.*2316 (iii B.C.). **-κοπή**, ἡ, *cutting close, pollarding*, of trees, Thphr.*CP*5.17.3. 2. *cutting down, felling*, μιᾶς ἐπικοπῆς εἶναι fall by a single *blow*, D.C.38.50, 49.29 (owing to f.l. in Th.5.103). 3. in building, *dressing, trimming* face of blocks of masonry, ἐπικόπτων τὰς ἐπικοπὰς *BCH*35.43 (Delos), cf. *IG* 7.3073.71 (Lebad.); ἐ. στρωτήρων ib.4.1484.235 (Epid.). II. *interruption*, Philostr.*VS*2.30. **-κοπος**, ον, of coins, *re-stamped*, *EM* 360.41, Hsch. II. Act., *for cutting*: as Subst., ἐπίκοπον, τό, = ἐπικόπανον, Luc.*DMort.*10.9, Eust.1476.33; *support for cutting upon*, in surgery, Heliod.ap.Orib.44.23.66, Antyll.ib.18, Gal.2.685.

ἐπικοπρίζω, *manure*, *Gp.*2.23.5.

ἐπικόπτ-ης, ου, ὁ, *satirist, censor*, Timo 60 (v. ἐπισκώπτης). **-ω**, pf. -κέκοφα Phld.*D.*1.15:—*strike upon* (i.e. *from above*), *fell*, βοῦν ἐπικόψων Od.3.443. 2. later, of trees, *lop, pollard*, Thphr.*CP*5.17.3; *cut down* brushwood, *PLond*.3.1170*B*26 (iii A.D.): metaph., *cut short, bring down from high estate*, τοὺς πεφρονηματισμένους Arist.*Pol*.1284^{b}2; φιληδονίαν ἀκόλαστον Plu.2.529b; *check, impede*, πράξεις ib.975b; στάσιν J.*BJ*2.17.4 (Pass., Hp.*Ep*.13); *reprove, censure*, τινά Timo 4, Myro 2 J., Plu.*Cic*.24, Philostr.*VA*5.35, al.; *refute*, Phld. l.c.; δόξας Id.*Po*.5.26. 3. ἐ. χαρακτῆρα *stamp, coin*, Arist.*Oec*.1349^{b}31. 4. *cut anew*, [τὸν] ἀποτριβέντα [μύλον] Str.15.2.2. b. Archit., *dress* blocks of stone, etc., κατὰ κεφαλήν *IG*7.3073.183 (Lebad.), cf. ib.4255.15 (Oropus); πλίνθον *Milet*.7 p.59 (Didyma). 5. Med., *smite one's breast, wail for*, τινά E.*Tr*.627. 6. of disease, *afflict*, βαρύτερον Aret.*SD*2.13. 7. *injure*, αἱ ἡδοναὶ ἐ. τὴν ἰσχύν Philostr.*Gym*.52:—Pass., -κοπεὶς τοὺς ὀφθαλμοὺς ὑπό τινος Id.*VS*2.25.2.

ἐπικόρμιον, τό, = ἐπικόπανον, Eust.1476.34: written **ἐπικόρμον** Id.1692.62.

ἐπίκορον· ἐπίκοπον, Πάμφιοι (sic), Hsch.

ἐπικορρ-ι· ἐπὶ κονδυλίῳ, Hsch. **-ίζω**, (κόρρη) *strike* or *peck on the head*, Arist.*HA*614^{a}10 (-κορίζω codd.). **-ιστος**, η, ον, *with one's ears boxed* (ἐπὶ κόρρης), Hsch.

ἐπικορύσσομαι, *arm oneself against*, τινί Luc.*Alex*.57.

ἐπικορύφ-ωμα [ῠ], ατος, τό, gloss on ἐπικτόλωμα, Hsch. **-ωσις**, εως, ἡ, *culmination, terminal number* of an arithmetical series, Nicom.*Ar*.2.3.

ἐπικός, ή, όν, *epic*, ποίησις D.H.*Comp*.22; ἐγκώμιον *IG*9(2).531.45 (Larissa); στίχοι Sch.Ar.*Pax*1288; ἐ. κύκλος (v. κύκλος); παροιμίαι Heph.8.6. Adv. -κῶς, = λογίως, Suid. s.v. Μαρῖνος.

ἐπικοσμ-έω, *add ornaments to, decorate after* or *besides*, τὰ ἱρά Hdt.1.184; *adorn*, ἄγαλμα, ἕδος, Hyp.*Eux*.24,25; τὴν θεόν *IG*2^2.1277; [κέρκους] ἐπικεκόσμηκεν ἡ φύσις θριξί Arist.*PA*658^{a}32; ἐ. τινὰς ἐπιγράμμασι *honour* them with.., Hdt.7.228; θεὰν ἐ. *honour, celebrate*, Ar.*Ra*.385; of funeral honours, X.*Cyr*.7.3.11: abs., λέξις -οῦσα Demetr.*Eloc*.106:—Pass., Arist.*Pol*.1263^{a}23; ἱερὸν ἐ. ὅπλοις *SIG*398.9 (Cos, iii B.C.), cf. *Sammelb*.996.4 (i A.D.). **-ημα**, ατος, τό, *ornament*, Asp.*in EN*109.14. **-ησις**, εως, ἡ, *adornment, decoration*, τραπέζης *IG*2^2.1245; τῆς Ἥρας *BCH*35.285 (Delos); τῶν κοινῶν *IG*2^2.1228.16. II. *perfecting* of matter by form, Syrian.*in Metaph*.38.21.

ἐπικοτ-έω, = κοτέω, ἐπὶ ζαμενὲς κοτέουσα Nic.*Th*.181. **-ος**, ον, *wrathful, vengeful*, στάσις Pi.*Fr*.109.4; μήδεα A.*Pr*.601 (lyr.); ἐπικότους τροφᾶς.. ἀράς *in wrath at* the sons he had bred, Id.*Th*.786 (lyr.). Adv. -τως *wrathfully*, Id.*Pr*.163 (lyr.). II. Pass., *hateful*, S.*Fr*.428.

ἐπικοττᾰβίζω, *throw the cottabus on* or *at*, Poll.6.110, prob. f.l. for ἀποκοττ-.

Ἐπικούρειος, ον, *of Epicurus, Epicurean*, ἄτομα *AP*11.93 (Lucill.); φιλόσοφος *Act.Ap*.17.18, etc., cf. Str.14.2.20; Ἐπικούρειον, τό, '*utilitarian*' doctrine, Cic.*Fam*.3.9.2; οἱ Ἐ. the *Epicureans*, Luc.*Herm*.16.

ἐπικουρ-έω, *to be an* ἐπίκουρος, *act as an ally*, once in Hom., ἑ Μοῖρα ἦγ' ἐπικουρήσοντα μετὰ Πρίαμον Il.5.614, cf. Th.7.57; φίλοις, χθονί, E.*Rh*.937,956; *render aid*, Foed.ap.Th.5.23, etc. 2. *serve as allies* or *mercenaries*, Isoc.4.168; μισθοῦ ἐ. Pl.*R*.575b. II. generally, *aid* or *help at need*, τινί E.*IA*1452, Ar.*V*.1018, Lys.12.98; [τῇ δικαιοσύνῃ] Pl.*R*.368c; also τῇ ἀναγκαίᾳ τροφῇ ἐ. *provide for* it, Aeschin.1.27; νόσοις ἐπικουρῆσαι *remedy* them, *aid* one *against* them, X.*Mem*.1.4.13; ἐ. τῷ λιμῷ, τῷ γήρᾳ, τῇ πενίᾳ, Id.*Lac*.2.6, 10.2, *Vect*.1.1 (Pass.); ἐσθὴς ἐπικουρεῖ τινι πολλά '*does him yeoman's service*', Id.*Cyr*.6.2.30. 2. c. acc. rei, ἐπικουρεῖν τινι χειμῶνα *keep* it *off from* one, Id.*An*.5.8.25. 3. c. acc. et dat., *furnish, supply*, *POxy*.1630.5 (iii A.D.). **-ημα**, ατος, τό, *protection*, τοῖς ὀφθαλμοῖς χιόνος X.*An*.4.5.13; *remedy*, Gal.6.171: pl., *aids, succours*, τῇ ζωῇ Iamb.*Protr*.20. **-ησις**, εως, ἡ, *succour, protection*, Antipho Soph.*Oxy*.1364.158; τὰς ἐκ τῶ θήω γινομένας ἐ. Euryph.ap.Stob.4.39.27; κακῶν *against* evils, E.*Andr*.28; τῆς ἀπορίας Pl.*Lg*.919b. **-ητικός**, ή, όν, = ἐπικουρικός, Pl.*R*.441a, Aen.Tact.38tit. **-ία**, Ion. -ίη, ἡ, *aid, succour*, Hdt.6.100,108, A.*Pers*.731 (troch.), etc.; ἐπικουρίας δεῖσθαι Th.1.32, X.*Oec*.17.13; τῆς ἐνδείας ἐ. τὸ κέρδος Arist.*EN*1163^{b}4; ἐ. ποιεῖσθαί τινι Th.1.33; ἐ. λαβεῖν, ἔχειν, E.*Or*.266, Pl.*Grg*.492c; ἀπολογίας *towards* one's defence, D.49.50; σκυτίνη 'πικ., = ὄλισβος, Ar.*Lys*.110. II. *auxiliary force*, A.*Supp*.721, Th.7.59 (pl.), Hdt.5.63. 2. *position of the* ἐπίκουροι (in Plato's Republic), Pl.*R*.415c. III. *prayer for aid, entreaty*, *SIG*1015.24 (Halic., iii B.C.). **-ικός**, ή, όν, *serving as* ἐπίκουροι 1.3, γένος Pl.*R*.434c, 441a. 2. mostly of troops, *auxiliary, mercenary*, ἐπικουρικὸν μισθώσασθαι Th.4.52; *dependent on* ἐπίκουροι, πράγματα Id.7.48; τὸ ἐ. Ph.2.98. **-ιος**, ον, *succouring*, epith. of deities, Paus.8.41.7. **-ος**, ὁ, *helper, ally*, Hom. only in Il., mostly in pl. of the barbarian *allies* of Troy, Τρῶες.. ἠδ' ἐ. 2.815; Τρῶες καὶ Δάρδανοι ἠδ' ἐ. 3.456, al., cf. Hdt.2.152, 3.91, al. 2. *mercenary troops*, opp. citizen-soldiers, ἐπικούρους προσμισθοῦσθαι Th.2.33, cf. Hdt.1.154, 2.163, 3.145, Lys.12.94, X.*HG*7.1.12, etc.; ἀπὸ Ἀρκαδίας ἐπίκουροι Hermipp.63.18; used as body-guard by tyrants, Hdt.1.64, 6.39, Th.6.55,58. 3. οἱ ἐ. the *guards*, the military class in Plato's Republic, *R*.414b, 415a, 545d. II. as Adj., *assisting, aiding*, c. dat. pers., Ἀφροδίτη ἦλθεν Ἄρῃ ἐπίκουρος Il.21.431; βῆναι ἐ. τινι Pi.*O*.13.97; ταῖς νήσοις ἐ. Ar.*Eq*.1319; τοῖς ἀδικουμένοις ἐ. Th.3.67: c. gen. pers., ἐπίκουρε βροτῶν their *defender*, *h.Mart*.9; τῶν ἀνθρώπων, of Eros, Pl.*Smp*.189d: abs., *patron, protector*, δεσπότης ἐ. X.*Cyr*.7.5.61. 2. c. gen. rei, *defending* or *protecting against*, νόσου E.*Or*.211 (troch.); πῦρ ἐ. ψύχους, σκότους, X.*Mem*.4.3.7; Λαβδακίδαις ἐ. θανάτων *protecting* them *against* deaths, S.*OT*496 (lyr.); πατρὶ αἱμάτων ἐ. E.*El*.138 (lyr.).

ἐπικουφ-ίζω, *lighten* a ship by throwing out part of its cargo, Hdt.8.118 (Pass.): metaph., ἐ. ἡ τιμὴ τοὺς πόνους τῷ ἄρχοντι *lightens* his labours, X.*Cyr*.1.6.25; τὰς συμφοράς D.23.70; λειτουργίας *IG*14.1078*a*; τὴν ταλαιπωρίαν Jul.*adThem*.253b: c. gen. rei, *relieve of* a burden, μόχθου E.*El*.72; τοῦ δέους D.C.43.18:—Med., ταῖς διὰ τὴν ἀρετὴν ἡδοναῖς τὸν πόνον -ίζομαι Lxx 4*Ma*.9.31. II. *lift up, support*, πατρὸς πλευρὰς σὺν ἐμοὶ τάσδ' ἐπικούφιζ' S.*Aj*.1411 (anap.); ἐ. τὴν γῆν *lift up* the soil, X.*Oec*.17.13. 2. metaph., *lift up, encourage*, ἐλπίσι Id.*Cyr*.7.1.18. b. ἐ. νόον ἀνδρὸς *puff up*, in bad sense, Thgn.629. **-ισμός**, ὁ, *relief*, *IGRom*.4.1523.9 (Sardes); τῆς ὀχλήσεως Sor.2.38.

ἐπικρᾰδ-αίνω, *wave on high*, πέλεκυν Hld.3.1; *quiver*, τὸ σῶμα πᾶν ἐ. Poll.5.61. **-άω**, = foreg., ἐρετμά A.R.1.552, cf. Opp.*C*.1.91.

ἐπικράδιον· ἐπικάρδιον, Hsch.

ἐπικράζω, *shout to* or *at*, τινί Luc.*Anach*.16 (pf. part. ἐπικεκρᾱγότες): aor. 1 inf. ἐπικράξαι Ps.-Luc.*Philopatr*.1.

ἐπικραίνω, Ep. -κραιαίνω, 3 sg. fut. ἐπικρᾰνεῖ dub. in A.*Ag*.1340 codd. (anap.): aor. 1 -έκρᾱνα, Ep. -έκρηνα, -εκρήηνα (v. infr.):—Med., 3 pl. aor. 1 ἐπεκρήναντο Q.S.14.297:—*bring to pass, accomplish*, ἀρὴν πᾶσαν ἐπικρήνειε *may* he *fulfil* it, Il.15.599; οὔ σφιν ἐπεκραίαινε he *fulfilled* it not for them, 3.302, cf. 2.419 (v.l. -άαινε); νῦν μοι τόδ' ἐπικρήηνον ἐέλδωρ *grant* me this prayer, *fulfil* it, 1.455, etc.; μῦθον ἐπεκρήηνε καρήατι by a nod, Call.*Dian*.40; ἐ. τέλος A.*Supp*.624; ἀληθῆ Id.*Th*.887 (lyr.); γάμου πικρὰς τελευτάς Id.*Ag*.744 (lyr.); ποινὰς θανάτων ib.1340 (anap.); χάριν ἀντ' ἔργων ib.1546 (anap.), cf. S.*Ph*.1468 (anap.); τὸ δέον Archyt.ap.Iamb.*Protr*.4:—Pass., χρυσῷ δ' ἐπὶ χείλεα κεκράαντο *were finished off* with gold, Od.4.132, cf. 616.

ἐπικρανής· ἐπιμελητής, Hsch. (fort. -κράντης).

ἐπικρᾱν-ίς, ίδος, ἡ, *membrane of the brain*, Erasistr.ap.*Placit*.4.5.3, dub. in Gal.2.728 (fort ἐπεγκρ-). **-ισμα**, ατος, τό, = ἐπίκρανον, Hsch. s.v. ἰανοκρήδεμνος. **-ῖτις**, ιδος, ἡ, pl. -ίτιδες, πλίνθοι *top course* of a wall, *IG*1^2.372.16, al. **-ον**, τό, *that which is put on the head, head-dress, cap*, E.*Hipp*.201 (anap.), Ph.2.309. II. = κιονόκρανον, *capital*, Pi.*Fr*.88.5, E.*IT*51, *IG*1^2.313.89, 2^2.1668.44, etc.

ἐπίκρᾱσις, εως, ἡ, (ἐπικεράννυμι) *mixing* of wine, Διοσκούροις *IG*11(2).159*A*7 (iii B.C.), al.; *tempering*, Diph.Siph.ap.Ath.3.91f; of humours, Herod.Med.ap.Orib.5.30.3, Gal.10.640; φαυλοτήτων Dsc.2.49.

ἐπικρᾰτ-αιόω, *add strength to, confirm*, Lxx *Ec*.4.12 (Pass.). **-εια**, ἡ, *mastery*, σωφροσύνη ἐστὶν ἐ. τῶν ἐπιθυμιῶν ib.4*Ma*.1.31; *possession*, X.*Cyr*.5.4.28; *rule*, Plb.12.25.3, etc.; *victory, superiority*, Id.2.1.3. 2. *predominance*, in heredity, *Placit*.5.7.6; διάφορος τῶν χυμῶν ἐ. S.E.*P*.1.80; τὸ κατ' ἐπικράτειαν ὠνομασμένον αἷμα named *from its dominant element*, opp. εἰλικρινὲς αἷμα, Gal.15.74, cf. 5.672, 17(2).216; παρὰ τὰς ἐ. *Placit*.4.9.9: Gramm., *prevalence, authority*, A.D.*Synt*.256.26, al.; numerical *superiority*, ib.326.14. 3. *prevailing opinion*, ἐν τοῖς συμβαίνουσιν.. κατὰ τὴν ἐ... στροβοῦνται Polystr.p.22 W.; αἱ κατ' ἐπικράτειαν δόξαι Epicur.*Nat*.1431.8. II. of a country, *realm, dominion*, ἄπιμεν.. ἐκ τῆς τούτων ἐπικρατείας X.*An*.7.6.42, cf. *Hier*.6.13; ὑπὸ τῇ ἐ. τοῦ χωρίου within *the country subject to* the place, Id.*An*.6.4.4; ἡ Καρχηδονίων ἐ. Pl.*Ep*.349c; of a Roman *province*, Ph.2.518,583 (pl.). **-έω** (Aeol. -κρετέω prob. in Alc.82), *rule over*, c. dat., νήεσσιν ἐπικρατέουσιν ἄριστοι Il.10.214; νήσοισιν Od.1.245: abs., *have* or *hold power*, εὖτ' ἂν μηκέτ' ἐπικρατέωσιν ἄνακτες 17.320, cf. 14.60, Archil.69. II. *prevail in battle, be victorious*, ἐπικρατέουσί περ ἔμπης [to them] though they *are victorious* as it is, Il.14.98, cf. Ar.*Lys*.767; ἐ. ἢ ἀπόλλυσθαι *conquer* or die, Hdt.7.104; ἐ. τῇ στάσι Id.1.173; ἐ. τὰ πλείω τοῦ πολέμου *gain the advantage* in most points in the war, Th.4.19. 2. freq. c. gen., *prevail over, get the mastery of* an enemy, ἐ. μάχῃ τῶν Γελῴων Hdt.7.155; τῶν ἐχθρῶν Id.8.94, Lys.34.4; τῆς τινων πονηρίας Id.22.16; ἐ. αὐτῶν (-οῦ codd.) παρὰ τῷ βασιλεῖ, in a suit at law, Hdt.4.65; ἰσχυρὰ ἐ. ἀνδρὸς Ἀνάγκη Philet.8; ἐ. τοῦ πυρός Hdt.1.86; γήρως Pl.*Lg*.752a; ὑμῶν -ήσω τῷ κοάξ Ar.*Ra*.267. 3. rarely c. acc., *master, conquer*, τὰς τῆς φύσεως ἁμαρτίας Isoc.1.52; δύο βασιλέας D.C.36.16:—Pass., -ηθεῖσα (sc. ἡ δεξιά), in left-handed persons, Sor.1.111. 4. c. gen., *become master of*, τῶν πραγμάτων Hdt.4.164; τῆς θαλάσσης Id.1.17, al.; τῶν πολίων, τῶν νεῶν, Id.6.32,115; τῆς ἀναγκαίου τροφῆς, τῆς ἀναβάσεως, Th.1.2, 7.42; τῶν ἐρώτων Pi.*N*.8.5, etc. b. *to be in possession of*, [οἰκίας] *PRyl*.160.3 (i A.D.), etc. 5. generally, *prevail, be superior*, πλήθεϊ Hdt.5.2; πολὺ τῷ ναυτικῷ Th.2.93; τὰ πλείω τῷ πεζῷ Id.7.63; κατὰ θάλασσαν X.*HG*7.1.6: c. inf., *they carried the point that*.., Th.5.46; ἐπεκράτουν μὴ δέχεσθαι τοὺς Ἀθηναίους Id.6.74. b. metaph., *prevail*, τὸ ἀνθρώπινον ἦθος ἐπεκράτει Pl.*Criti*.121b; τὸ δίκαιον Men.*Epit*.16; τὸ ψῦχος, τὸ ὑγρόν, Arist.*Mete*.347^{b}26, *MM*1210^{a}20; τὸ ὄνομα Plb.2.38.1; ὁ λόγος D.S.5.62; ὁ τραχὺς ἦχος Phld.*Po*.994.33. 6. c. part., ἐ. διαιροῦντες *succeed* in keeping it open, Arist.*GA*773^{a}29. **-ής**, ές, *master* of a thing: only Comp. -έστερος, τῇ μάχῃ *superior* in.., Th.6.88; -έστερός τινος γενόμενος having *the upper hand of*.., D.C.55.30; τὸ -έστερον φέρειν Memn.34.3; κατὰ τὸ -έστερον with *success*, D.S.37.2.—Hom. only in Adv. -τέως *with overwhelming might, impetuously*, Il.16.67,81, 23.863 (never in Od.); so Hes.*Sc*.321, A.R.1.367, etc. **-ησις**, εως, ἡ, *mastering, conquest of*, Αἰγινητῶν Th.1.41. II. *supreme power*, ἡ τοῦ Καίσαρος ἐν τῇ Ῥώμῃ D.C.47.21. III. of things, *prevalence*, Gal.4.629, 19.488; ἡ οὐκ ἴση ἐ. Plot.5.7.2; ἐ. αἰθέρος, name given to the *predominance* of πῦρ τεχνικόν at the ἐκπύρωσις, *Stoic*.2.185. **-ητικός**, ή, όν, *astrin-*

gent, Gal.12.361. **-ήτωρ,** ορος, ὁ, ἀστήρ *ruling* star, Ps.-Ptol.*Centil.* 25, cf. Vett.Val.132.15, etc.

ἐπικρᾰτ-ίδες, ίδων, αἱ, (κράς, κρατός) a kind of *head-dress* (cf. ἐπίκρανον) or *towel*, Hp.*Praec.*10. **-ίδιον,** τό, Dim. of foreg., = στημονικὸν κάλυμμα [χωρὶς] τῆς κεφαλῆς, Hsch.

ἐπικρᾱτικός, ή, όν, (ἐπικεράννυμι) v.l. for ἐπικεραστικός, Gal.6.260, 582, Orib.1.42.3.

ἐπικρᾰτύνω, *strengthen*, Hsch.

ἐπικραυγάζω, *cry out to* or *at*, Arr.*Epict.*1.21.3, 4.1.19.

ἐπικρεμάννῡμι and **-ύω,** *hang over*, ἄτην τινί Thgn.206 codd.; κίνδυνον Plb.2.31.7; φόβον D.S.16.50. II. Pass., ἐπικρέμαμαι, aor. ἐπεκρεμάσθην, *overhang*, of a rock, *h.Ap.*284; οἰκία ἐπικρεμαμένη τῇ ἀγορᾷ Plu.*Publ.*10: metaph., *hang over, threaten*, θάνατος Simon.39.3; δόλιος αἰών Pi.*I.*8(7).14 (tm.); τιμωρία Th.2.53; ἐπικρεμάμενος κίνδυνος *impending* danger, Id.7.75, cf. 3.40: c. dat. pers., ἐπικρέμαθ' ἧμιν ὄλεθρος A.R.3.483; Ep. 3 pl. impf. ἐπεκρεμόωντο Nonn.*D.*20.173.

ἐπικρήδιος, ὁ, a *Cretan dance*, Ath.14.629c.

ἐπικρήηνον, -κρήνειε, v. ἐπικραίνω.

ἐπίκρημνος, ον, *precipitous, steep*, Pherecyd.82(b) J., Dicaearch.2.6 (v.l. ἀπόκρ-).

ἐπικρῆναι· ἑορτὴ Δήμητρος παρὰ Λάκωσιν, Hsch. (leg. -κρήναια). **ἐπίκρηνον·** κεφαλόδεσμον, Id.; cf. ἐπίκρανον.

ἐπικρηπῖδες, αἱ, *goloshes*, Thphr.*Char.*2.7 (s.v.l.).

ἐπικρῆσαι, v. ἐπικεράννυμι.

ἐπικρητηρίδιος ἠθμός strainer *for a mixing bowl*, Demioprat.ap. Poll.10.108.

ἐπι-κρῐδόν, Adv., (ἐπικρίνω) *choosing out*, A.R.2.302. **-κρῖμα,** ατος, τό, = Lat. *decretum*, *OGI*453.23 (Aphrodisias, M. Antonius), 669.28 (Egypt, i A.D.); Καίσαρος Epist.ap.J.*AJ*19.6.3. **-κρίνω** [κρῐ], fut. -κρῐνῶ (v. infr.):—*decide, determine*, τι Pl.*Lg.*768a; τὸ πλεῖον καὶ τοὔλαττον D.H.3.29; περί τινος Decr.ap.D.18.38; τοῦ ἐπικρινοῦντος δέοι ἄν Pl.*R.*524e: c. inf., ἐπέκρινε γενέσθαι τὸ αἴτημα αὐτῶν *Ev. Luc.*23.24; ἐ. τί διαφέρει what is the difference, Arist.*de An.*431^{a}20; τὸ ἐπικρῖνον *the deciding power*, Id.*Insomn.*461^{b}25; also, *principle of selection*, rule of life, Epicur.*Nat.*125 G.; *adjudge, inflict*, θάνατόν τινι Lxx 2*Ma.*4.47:—Pass., μέχρις ἂν ἐπικριθῇ αὐτῷ ὑπὸ τῶν ἱερέων ἢ ἀποδοῦναι αὐτὸν ἢ εἰσέρχεσθαι until the judges *determine* whether he shall pay up or enter (without payment), *SIG*1109.71, cf. *PTeb.*284.2 (i B.C.). 2. c. acc. pers., *judge*, τινά Ph.2.380:—Pass., ib.309. II. *select, pick out*, ἐξ ἑαυτῶν τὸν ἄριστον D.S.1.75; ἐ. τινὰ ἴσον ἀδελφοῖς *distinguish, esteem*, Hp.*Jusj.* 2. in Egypt, *select by* ἐπίκρισις II (q.v.), *PGen.*19 (ii A.D.):—Pass., *POxy.*39 (i A.D.). 3. *consider*, πάντα ταῦτα Phld.*Oec.*p.63 J. III. Med., *choose for oneself, pick out*, βοῦν *SIG*1025.17 (Cos, iv/iii B.C.).

ἐπίκριον, τό, (ἴκρια) *yard-arm*, Od.5.254, 318, A.R.2.1262, etc.

ἐπί-κρῐσις, εως, ἡ, *determination*, τῶν ἐκλειπτικῶν τηρήσεων Str. 1.1.12; συνημμένων Plu.2.43c (pl.), cf. D.L.9.92, A.D.*Adv.*151.14, Plot.5.3.2; *discrimination* of scents, Dsc.1.14. 2. *verification*, Gal. 17(2).354, cf. 1.117. II. in Egypt, revision of lists and *selection* of privileged persons, *POxy.*288.35 (i A.D.), *PFay.*27.24 (ii A.D.), *BGU*324.2, 19 (ii A.D.), etc. III. *judgement*, Ph.1.38, al.; arbitrator's *award*, *SIG*364.6 (Ephesus, pl.). **-κρῐτέον,** *one must select*, Ph.1.564. **-κρῐτήριον,** τό, *court of appeal*, *GDI*5040.67 (Hierapytna), 5024.52 (Gortyn). **-κρῐτής,** οῦ, ὁ, *adjudicator, arbiter*, τῶν λεγομένων Plb.14.3.7. II. in Egypt, *examining magistrate* (cf. ἐπίκρισις II), *PFay.*27.3 (ii A.D.), *PTeb.*320.2 (ii A.D.). **-κρῐτικός,** ή, όν, *adjudicatory, determinative*, τινός D.L.9.47, A.D.*Conj.*222.25. **-κρῐτος,** ον, *approved*, J.*BJ*3.5.5 (v.l. ἔκκριτοι). II. oxyt., ἐπικριτός, ή, όν, *capable of determination* or *resolution*, διαφωνία S.E.*P.*1.170.

ἐπίκροκον· ἐπανθητόν, Hsch.; cf. Lat. *epicrocum*, Paul. ex Fest. p.72 L., etc.

ἐπικροτᾰλίζω, = sq., Nonn.*D.*17.29, 37.34.

ἐπικροτ-έω, *rattle on* or *over*, τὰ δ' ἐπικροτέοντα πέτοντο ἅρματα flew *rattling over* the ground, Hes.*Sc.*308. 2. c. acc., *strike with a rattling sound, clash*, κύμβαλα Alciphr.1.12; κρόταλα Luc.*Syr.D.* 44; γένειον Opp.*C.*2.244. 3. *clap, applaud*, Men.887, Plu.*Ant.* 12; τινί Luc.*Cont.*8. 4. c. dat. instr., ἐ. ὀδοῦσι *chatter* with one's teeth, Ps.-Luc.*Philopatr.*21; ἐ. τοῖς δακτύλοις *snap* the fingers, Eust. 1602.16: abs., Aristobul.9 J. codd. Ath. **-ησις,** εως, ἡ, = Lat. *increpatio*, *Gloss.* **-ος,** ον, *beaten* or *trodden hard*, esp. of ground, ἐν τῷ ἐπικρότῳ ἱππεύειν X.*Eq.Mag.*3.14; ἐ. ποιεῖν Arist.*HA*558^{a}6: metaph., τὸ ἐ. τῶν λόγων their *sonorousness*, Philostr.*VS*1.25.7.

ἐπί-κρουμα, ατος, τό, *beating* with the foot, χθονὸς Ἀργείας S.*Fr.* 287 (anap.). **-κρουσις,** εως, ἡ, treatment with rods as counter-irritants, Gal.10.998. 2. medical *percussion*, Paul.Aeg.3.69, 6. 51. **-κρουσμα,** ατος, τό, *forcible blow*, ib.91. **-κρουστήριον,** τό, *hammer*, *Gloss.* **-κρουστίκιον,** τό, a surgical instrument, = sq., Aët.6.8 (s.v.l.). **-κρούστιον,** τό, a surgical instrument, perh. *slasher*, *Hermes* 38.282. **-κρούω,** *hammer in*, ἧλον Ar.*Th.*1004, cf. *IG*2^2.463.64; τὸν ἵππον καὶ τὸν ἄνδρα τὸν -κρούοντα ib.1^2.374.173; χθόνα βάκτροις *striking* the ground.., A.*Ag.*202 (lyr.); ἐ. τῇ χειρὶ τὸ ξίφος *clap* one's hand *on* one's sword, Plu.*Pomp.*58: metaph., *jeer at*, εἴς τινα Macho ap.Ath.13.579b. II. = ἐπικροτέω 4, Lxx *Je.*31 (48).26. III. Medic., use *percussion*, Aret.*SA*1.6.

ἐπι-κρύπτω, poet. aor. 2 ἐπέκρῠφον Q.S.7.235 (v.l. ἀπ-):—*throw a cloak over, conceal*, χεῖρας φονίας A.*Eu.*317 (lyr.); τὴν βούλησιν τοῦ ὀνόματος Pl.*Cra.*421b; f.l. for ἔτη κρύπτειν, E.*Supp.*296:—freq. in Med., *disguise*, κἀπικρύψασθαι κακά S.*Fr.*88.12 (v.l.); τὰς αὑτοῦ τύχας.. τοὐπικρύπτεσθαι σοφόν E.*Fr.*553; ἐ. τὴν αὑτοῦ ἀπορίαν Pl.*La.*196b, cf. *Prt.*346b; τἀληθῆ D.17.17: abs., ἐπικρυπτόμενος *with concealment* or *secrecy*, X.*An.*1.1.6; ἐπικρύπτεσθαί τι τῷ μεγέθει τῶν ἄλλων ἔργων D. 61.45; πρὸς τοὺς πολλοὺς τὴν δεινότητα Plu.*Per.*4; ἐ. τινά τι *conceal* a thing *from* one, Plb.3.75.1; also ἐ. τινὰ ὡς.. Pl.*Tht.*180d; ὅτι οὐχ ὑγιαίνει Id.*R.*476e; *disguise, conceal one's purpose*, τῶν πεντακισχιλίων τῷ ὀνόματι Th.8.92; ἐσθῆτι θεράποντος Plu.*Caes.*38:—Pass., *to be concealed*, Arist.*Pol.*1278^{a}39. **-κρῠφος,** ον, *unknown, inglorious*, οἶμος Pi.*O.*8.69, Max.21; *concealed*, πράξεις Plu.*Arat.*10. **-κρυψις,** εως, ἡ, *concealment*, Str.2.3.8, Plu.*Nic.*23; νούσων *latencies, quiescences*, Aret.*CD*1.5 (pl.).

ἐπικρώζω, *caw* or *croak at*, Orac.ap.Ar.*Eq.*1051; τισὶ ὅτι.. Them. *Or.*4.61d.

ἐπικτάομαι, *gain* or *win besides*, φίλους A.*Eu.*901; πατρίοισι νόμοισι ἄλλον οὐδένα ἐπικτῶνται Hdt.2.79; ἐ. ἀρχὴν *extend one's* empire, Th.1.144; ἐ. τὰ μὴ προσήκοντα Id.4.61; τριήρεις κέκτησθε πολλὰς καὶ πάτριον ὑμῖν ἐστι ναυτικὸν ἐπικτᾶσθαι *add to those* you have, X.*HG* 7.1.3; τόνδ' ἐ. σύμμαχον *as* an ally, A.*Eu.*671; ξυμμάρτυρας ὔμμ' ἐ. S.*Ant.*846 (lyr.); *acquire additional* property, *PGiss.*108.3 (ii B.C.), etc.:—late in Pass., Agath.1.2, Just.*Nov.*123.4.

ἐπικτείνω, *kill besides* or *again*, τὸν θανόντ' ἐ. *slay* the slain *anew*, S.*Ant.*1030; f.l. for ἔτι κτ-, Plu.*Caes.*46.

ἐπικτένιον, τό, (κτείς) *tow which remains in the heckle*, ἐ. ὠμοῦ λίνου (v.l. ὠμόλινον) Hp.*Mul.*1.74, cf. Gal.19.99. II. *the pubes*, Hp.*Mul.*1.60. 2. *instep* of the foot, Hsch.

ἐπικτέρεα· ἐντάφια, Hsch. (sed cf. κτέρεα).

ἐπικτερεΐζω, *perform funeral rites over*, Nonn.*D.*47.241.

ἐπίκτημα, ατος, τό, *property held in a foreign country*, Ammon. *Diff.*p.83 V., Ptol.Ascal.p.399 H. II. *acquisition, improvement*, τὸ τῆς τέχνης ἐ. *PMasp.*20.18 (vi A.D.).

ἐπικτηνίτης [νῑ], ὁ, (κτῆνος) *drover*, *PFlor.*126.13 (iii A.D.), *Gloss.*

ἐπί-κτησις, εως, ἡ, *further acquisition, fresh gain*, S.*Ph.*1344; χρημάτων Arist.*HA*522^{a}18: pl., D.H.9.53. **-κτητικός,** ή, όν, *acquisitive*, Nech.ap.Vett.Val.278.36. **-κτητος,** ον, *gained besides* or *in addition*, ἐ. γῆ *acquired* land, which was formerly under water, as the Delta of Egypt, Hdt.2.5, cf. 10; property *added to one's hereditary property*, Pl.*Lg.*924a, cf. Lycurg.48; ἐ. γυνή *a foreign* wife (like ἐπακτός), or *newly acquired*, Hdt.3.3; ἐ. φίλοι *newly acquired* friends, opp. ἀρχαῖοι, X.*Ages.*1.36; ἐ. δόξα, opp. ἔμφυτος ἐπιθυμία, *acquired* perception, Pl.*Phdr.*237d; τὰ ἐ., opp. τὰ φύσει ὄντα, Id.*R.*618d; opp. σύμφυτα, Arist.*GA*721^{b}30; τὸ αὐτοφυὲς τοῦ ἐ. αἱρετώτερον Id. *Rh.*1365^{a}29; γίνεται.. ἐξ ἐπικτήτου, of an *acquired* deformity, Paul. Aeg.6.29; τὰ ἐ. *property acquired after* a certain date, Edict.Aug. in *Notiz.Arch.*4.21, *PGnom.*126 (ii A.D.). Adv. -τως Prisc.Lyd.21.15.

ἐπικτίζω, *found in addition* or *anew*, Str.14.1.12, 10.1.10 (Pass.). II. *found in* or *among*, πόλεις ἀγρίοις ἔθνεσι Plu.2.328b codd.

ἐπικτόλωμα· ἐπικορύφωμα, Hsch.

ἐπικτόριον, τό, *lid* of a pot, Hsch. (leg. ἐπικύθριον, cf. χύτρα).

ἐπικτός, = ἐφικτός, prob. cj. for ἑρκτός in Arr.*Ind.*20.11.

ἐπικτῠπέω, aor. 1 (v. infr.): aor. 2 ἐπέκτῠπον A.R.1.1136:—*make a noise upon*, τοῖν ποδοῖν ἐπικτυπῶν *stamp on the ground* with the feet, Ar.*Ec.*483; σάκεα ξιφέεσσιν ἐ. *clashed on* their shields with.., A.R. l.c.; σακέεσσιν ἐ. Id.2.1081; *strike*, ἄντυγα χηλαῖς Nonn.*D.*38.397: abs., *re-echo, respond*, πᾶς δ' ἐπεκτύπησ' Ὄλυμπος Ar.*Av.*780; of a chorus, Plb.30.22.9.

ἐπικῡδ-αίνομαι, *exult in*, τινί D.C.71.2. **-ής,** ές, only in Comp. -έστερος (unless the Posit. is to be restored in Sapph.*Supp.*8.11), *glorious, distinguished*, X.*HG*5.1.36; *brilliant, successful*, -έστερα τὰ πράγματα ἐποίησεν Isoc.4.139; -έστεραι ἐλπίδες Plb.16.4.3; and of persons, -έστερος ταῖς ἐλπίσι *more sanguine*, Id.5.69.11, cf. Ph.1. 252, al., Onos.23.2. Adv. Comp. -εστέρως, ἀγωνίζεσθαι Plb.5.23. 2. **-ιάω,** *vaunt oneself*, τινί A.R.4.383 (nisi leg. ἢ ἔπι κυδιάει).

ἐπικῠ-έω, = ἐπικυΐσκομαι, Hp.*Epid.*5.11, Arist.*HA*585^{a}17:—Pass., ib.11. II. simply, *become pregnant again*, *BGU*1058.30 (i B.C.), al. **-ημα,** ατος, τό, *a superfetation*, Hp.*Superf.*1, Arist.*GA*773^{b}7. **-ησις,** εως, ἡ, *superfetation*, Id.*Fr.*259, 260 Bonitz; title of treatise by Hp. **-ΐσκομαι,** *become doubly pregnant*, i.e. *pregnant again before the first foetus is born*, Hdt.3.108, Hp.*Superf.*1, Arist. *GA*773^{b}28.

ἐπικυκλ-έω, intr., *come round in turn upon*, ἐπὶ πῆμα καὶ χαρὰ πᾶσι κυκλοῦσι S.*Tr.*130:—Pass., D.H.*Rh.*10.17. **-ησις,** εως, ἡ, *return in a cycle*, Alex.Aphr.*de An.*30.26. **-ίδιος,** epith. of Zeus, Hsch. **-ιος,** ον, *circular*: ἐ. (sc. πλακοῦς), ὁ, *a round Sicilian cake*, Epich.26 codd. Ath.; of a bandage, *in a circle*, Gal.18(1).820. **-ος,** ὁ, Astron., *epicycle*, Plu.2.1028b, Theo Sm.p.162 H., Ptol.*Alm.*3.3, Iamb.*VP*6.31 (pl.), etc. **-όω,** *circle round*, τὸν δῆμον Lyd.*Ost.*8.

ἐπικῠλίδες, ίδων, αἱ, *upper eyelids*, Poll.2.66; cf. κύλα.

ἐπικῠλίκειος or **-ίκιος,** ον, *said* or *done over* one's *cups*, λόγοι Ath. 1.2a, Plu.2.1146d, cf. D.L.4.42, Poll.6.108.

ἐπικῠλινδέω or **-κυλίω** (Plb.3.53.4, D.S.19.19), fut. -κυλίσω [ῑ]:—*roll down upon*, πέτρους ἐπί τινας X.*HG*3.5.20; τοῖς ὁδοιπoροῦσι πέτρας D.S. l.c., cf. Plb. l.c.:—Pass., τὰ τμήματα τοῦ πελάγους -ισθέντα Ph.2.109; τόκων τόκοις -κυλισθέντων interest *being heaped on* interest, Plu.2.831e; τὸ σιτίον εἰς τὸν στόμαχον -ινδεῖσθαι *is slipped into*.., ib.699c; -ισθεῖσα *overlaying* the infant, Sor.1.106. 2. Pass., *to be applied by rolling*, ταῖς σαρξί Gal.11.757. 3. Pass., *degenerate*, εἰς χρόνια πάθη Id.19.560: metaph., [νοήσεις] δι' ἀρρωστίαν -ούμεναι καὶ ἐπιτρέχουσαι τοῖς εἴδεσιν Dam.*Pr.*88. 4. intr., *roll on*, κύματα Ps.-Luc.*Philopatr.*3.

ἐπικῠλινδρόομαι, Pass., *to be flattened by rollers*, Thphr.*CP*5.6.7.

ἐπικύλιον [ῠ], τό, *upper eyelid* (cf. ἐπικυλίδες), Eust.1951.20.

ἐπικῠλισμός, ὁ, *turning round*, Sor.2.64, Sm.*Pr*.2.9, Thd.*Pr*.2.15.

ἐπικυλλόω, *mould* a cake of dough, prob. for ἐπεκώλυσεν, Hsch.

ἐπικύλλωμα, ατος, τό, *lameness*, Eust.1599.13.

ἐπικῡμ-αίνω, *flow in waves over*, τῇ θαλάττῃ Philostr.*Im*.2.17: metaph., of hair, ὤμοις καὶ νώτοις Hld.3.4; τοῖς ἱππεῦσιν ἐ. ἡ φάλαγξ Plu.*Alex*.33:—Pass., ὥσπερ ἐν βυθῷ ἄνθρωπος ἐ. Herm.ap.Stob.1.49.45. II. trans., *cause to rise in waves*, τὴν θάλασσαν J.*AJ*4.3.2. **-ᾰτίζω**, *float upon the waves*, Ph.1.455, Ael.*Ep*.18: metaph., -ίζουσα φορὰ τῶν πραγμάτων (cf. foreg.), Ph.1.553; also of persons, ὑπόπτερος ἐ. Id.2.300; of a runner, -ίζων αἴρεται Philostr.*Her*.2.3:—Pass., τοὺς διὰ φιλοκερδίαν τὸν ἅπαντα βίον -ομένους Phld.*Mort*.33; opp. ἐν τῇ γῇ διατρίβειν, Id.*Rh*.2.55 S. **-ᾰτωσις** [ᾰ], εως, ἡ, *fluctuation*, τῶν μεταβολῶν M.Ant.9.28 (pl.).

ἐπικῠνέω, *kiss on the lips*, *EM*361.11.

ἐπικύπτω, pf. (v. infr.):—*bend oneself over, stoop over, bow down*, Hp.*Art*.52, Ar.*Th*.239; ὀρθὸς ἕστηκεν, μικρὸν ἐπικύπτων Arist.*HA* 522^{b}18; of the horn of the moon, Thphr.*Sign*.27; ἐ. ἐπί τι *stoop down* to get something, X.*Cyr*.2.3.18; ἐ. ἐς βιβλίον *pore over* a book, Luc.*Herm*.2; *lean upon*, τινί Id.*DMort*.6.2; ἐ. τῷ συνεδρίῳ *bend over towards* it, Id.*JTr*.11: pf. part. ἐπικεκῡφώς *habitually stooping*, Anaxandr.37.

ἐπικύρβιος, ον, *registered on* κύρβεις, ἐνέχυρα *IG*12(7).58.5 (Amorgos).

ἐπικῡρόω, *confirm, sanction, ratify*, τὴν γνώμην Th.3.71, cf. S.*El*. 793, X.*An*.3.2.32, D.15.34, *SIG*167.20, etc.: c. inf., τίνες..λόγοι καθεῖλον ἡμᾶς κἀπεκύρωσαν θανεῖν; E.*Or*.862:—Pass., πρίν τι ἐπικυρωθῆναι Th.5.45; ἐπικυρωθέντων τῶν νόμων Arist.*Ath*.37.1, cf. *Sammelb*.1161.17 (i B.C.).

ἐπίκυρτ-ος, ον, *arched*, S.*Ichn*.294; *round-shouldered*, Πλάτωνος τὸ ἐ. Plu.2.53c. **-όω**, *bend forward*, κάρηνα Hes.*Sc*.234:—Pass., *to be arched*, Luc.*Am*.14.

ἐπικύρω [ῡ], Ep. impf. ἐπίκῡρον, Ep. aor. 1 ἐπέκυρσα and ἐπεκύρησα [ῠ] (v. infr.):—*light upon, fall in with*, c. dat., μεγάλῳ ἐπὶ σώματι κύρσας Il.3.23; ἱεροῖσιν ἐπ' αἰθομένοισι κυρήσας Hes.*Op*.755; αἰὲν ἐπ' αὐχένι κῦρε φαεινοῦ δουρὸς ἀκωκῇ (v.l. ἀκωκήν) *kept* always *touching* his neck with.., Il.23.821; ἐπὶ ξίφος αὐχένι κύρσαι *let* his sword *touch* her neck, Q.S.13.394; ἐ. μετατροπίαις Pi.*P*.10.21: c. gen., *meet with, obtain*, ἐπικύρσαις ἀφθόνων ἀστῶν Id.*O*.6.7; μεγάλας ἀγαθὰς τε..βιοτᾶς ἐπεκύρσαμεν A.*Pers*.853, cf. A.R.3.342.

ἐπικύρ-ωσις [ῡ], εως, ἡ, *ratification, confirmation*, χειροτονίας Arist. *Ath*.41.3, cf. D.H.9.51, Just.*Nov*.42.1.1. **-ωτέον**, *one must confirm*, τινὶ τὴν βασιλείαν dub. in J.*AJ*17.9.7.

ἐπικυστίς, ίδος, ἡ, = ἐφήβιον, *Gloss*.

ἐπίκῡφος, ον, *bent over, crooked*, Lxx 3*Ma*.4.5, Sch.Opp.*H*.1.342, Suid. (Comp.).

ἐπικύψ (-κύς cod.)· ἐπικύψας, Hsch.

ἐπικυψέλιος, ὁ, (κυψέλη) *guard of beehives*, Πάν *AP*9.226 (Zon.).

ἐπίκυψις, εως, ἡ, of the head, *stooping*, Hp.*Epid*.2.1.8, Antyll. and Heliod.ap.Orib.44.8.4 (pl.); *bending forward*, Sor.1.93, prob. cj. in Ruf.*Sat.Gon*.34 (pl.).

ἐπικωθωνίζομαι, *go on drinking*, Critias 59 D.

ἐπικωκύω, *lament over*, πατρὸς δαῖτα S.*El*.283; τὸν υἱόν ib.805: abs., Hld.1.13.

ἐπικωλύω, *hinder, check*, ἀλλήλους X.*Oec*.8.4; τίς..μ' οὐπικωλύσων τάδε; S.*Ph*.1242; τὸ ἔργον *IG*7.3073.35 (Lebad.); τὸν ἐργώνην ib.45: abs., *to be a hindrance*, Th.6.17:—Pass., *PPetr*.3p.109 (iii B.C.), etc.

ἐπικωμ-άζω, *rush on* or *in with a party of revellers*, Plb.26.1.4, Call. *Ep*.43: generally, *make a riotous assault*, ἐπί τινα Ar.*Ach*.982; τινί Men.881; *go careering about*, εἰς τὰς πόλεις Pl.*Lg*.950a; ἐπὶ τὴν οἰκίαν τινός Plu.2.772f: metaph., ἀτύχημα Σπαρτιάταις -εκώμασεν Chor.in *Jahrb*.9.177:—Pass., *to be visited by a reveller*, Plu.*Pyrrh*. 13. **-ασία**, ἡ, *revelling*, *Gloss*. **-αστής**, οῦ, ὁ, *reveller*, Id.

ἐπικωμ-ιαστικός, ή, όν, = ἐγκωμ- (q. v.), Arg.Theoc.3. Adv. **-κῶς** Sch.Pi.*N*.8.1. **-ιος**, α, ον, *of, at*, or *for a* κῶμος or *festal procession*, ὄψ, ὕμνος, Pi.*P*.10.6, *N*.8.50; epith. of Apollo, *IGRom*.4.1539 (Erythrae); ἐπικώμια, τά, = ἐγκώμια, *praises*, Pi.*N*.6.32: sg., **-κώμιον** *revel*, *Gloss*. **-ος**, ον, *revelling*, Aristias 3 (L.Dind. for ἐπίκωπος); εἰς οἰκίαν ἐμβαλεῖν ἐ. Plu.2.128d; ἐ. φοιτᾶν Alciphr.1.37.

ἐπικωμῳδέω, *make a jest of, caricature*, Pl.*Ap*.31d.

ἐπικωπ-αστήρ, ῆρος, ὁ, = sq., *EM*360.44. **-ητήρ**, ῆρος, ὁ, = τροπωτήρ, Hsch. **-ος**, ον, *at the oar, rower*, Men.Eph.ap.J.*AJ*9. 14.2. 2. of a boat, *furnished with oars*, κέρκουρος Moschio ap.Ath. 5.208f, cf. D.H.3.44, D.S.3.40; *phaselus epicopus*, *dispatch*-boat, Cic. *Att*.14.16.1, cf. 5.11.4. 3. of a weapon, *up to the hilt, through and through*, Ar.*Ach*.231 (lyr.); cf. ἐπίκωμος.

ἐπιλᾰβή, ἡ, *taking hold of, grasping*, πέπλων τ' ἐπιλαβὰς ἐμῶν A. *Supp*.432 (lyr.). 2. *handle, hold*, ἐ. ἔχειν οὐδεμίαν Hp.*Art*.47.

ἐπιλαγχάνω, pf. (v. infr. II):—*succeed* another in an office on a vacancy, οὔτε λαχὼν οὔτ' ἐπιλαχών Aeschin.3.62, D.58.29; ἐ. τινὶ βουλῆς *succeed* him in the Council, Pl.Com.167, cf. 166.5. 2. *obtain, have allotted to one*, εὐδαιμονίας Ph.1.629, al. II. *fall to one's lot next*, ἐπιλέλογχε πύματον..γῆρας S.*OC*1235 (lyr.); ἐπιλαχόντα τινὶ πράγματα *PMon*.6.50, cf. 7.45 (vi A.D.).

ἐπῑλᾰδόν, Adv., = ἰλαδόν, *in troops*, D.P.763.

ἐπιλάζῠμαι, *hold tight, stop*, ἐ. στόμα, i.e. to be silent, E.*Andr*. 250.—Poet. word for ἐπιλαμβάνω.

ἐπιλαΐς, ΐδος, ἡ, name of a bird (v. l. ὑπολαΐς), Arist.*HA*592^{b}22.

ἐπίλακκος, ον, *forming a hollow*, τὸ ἐ. μέρος, = βρόχθος, Sch.Theoc. 3.54.

ἐπιλᾰλ-έω, *interrupt in speaking*, Sm.*Ps*.122(123).4. 2. *charm* (v.l. ἐπᾴδω), Lxx *Je*.8.17. 3. Pass., *to be said of*.., ἀλόγοις -εῖται Eust.773.26. **-ημα**, ατος, τό, *incantation*, *PMag.Lond*.121.290.

ἐπιλαμβάνω, *take* or *get besides*, ἐπὶ τοῖς πεντήκοντα ταλάντοις ἑκατὸν Arist.*Pol*.1259^{a}28: c. gen. partit., ἐ. τοῦ χρόνου *take a little more* time, M.Ant.1.17; τῆς ἀρχῆς Paus.9.14.5. 2. simply, *take, receive*, *PEleph*.10.1 (iii B.C.), *OGI*179.18 (Egypt, i B.C.), etc. II. *lay hold of, seize, attack*, as a disease, Hdt.8.115, Hp.*Aph*.6.51, Th.2.51; of an enemy, Luc.*Nav*.36:—Pass., ἐπείληπται νόσῳ S.*Ant*.732; τὴν αἴσθησιν ἐπιληφθεὶς *becoming unconscious*, Plu.*Flam*.6; ἐπελήφθη *had an epileptic fit*, Gal.11.859. b. of events, *overtake, surprise*, μὴ.. χειμὼν τὴν φυλακὴν ἐπιλάβοι Th.4.27; νυκτὸς ἐπιλαβούσης τὸ ἔργον ib. 96; ταχὺ ἐπιλαβὸν γῆρας Pl.*Epin*.974a: impers., ἐπιλαμβάνει, c. acc. et inf., *it befalls* one *that*.., Paus.6.22.4, 7.21.1. 2. *attain to, come within reach of, reach*, X.*An*.6.5.6; ἔτη ὀκτὼ ἐ. πολέμου *live over* eight years, Th.4.133; ἡμέρας ἑπτακαίδεκα τῆς ἑβδόμης ὑπατείας Plu.*Mar*. 46: c. gen. partit., ἐ. τετάρτου μηνὸς *arrive at*, of the foetus, Arist.*HA* 583^{b}22 (but ἐ. τοῦ ἑνδεκάτου μηνός, of the mother, ib.584^{a}37); ὥστε καὶ τοῦ χειμῶνος ἐ. Thphr.*HP*1.9.6. 3. *seize, stop*, esp. by pressure, τὴν ῥῖνα Ar.*Pl*.703; ἐ. τὸ κλύσμα τῆς ὀπίσω ὁδοῦ Hdt.2.87; ἐ. τὸ ὕδωρ *stop* the water-clock in court, Lys.23.4, Is.3.76; τὸν αὐλίσκον Arist.*Ath*.67.3, cf. *Pr*.866^{b}13, Plb.10.44.12; τὸ στόμα τοῖς ἐπικαλύμμασιν Arist.*HA*527^{b}21. 4. *occupy* space, μηδὲν τῶν τῆς πόλεως.. οἰκοδομήμασι ἐ. Pl.*Lg*.779c (Med.); πλείω τόπον Arist.*Cael*.305^{b}19; πλατύτερον τόπον Plu.*Cat.Ma*.5: metaph., πολὺν χῶρον ἐ. *get over* much ground, *traverse* it rapidly, Theoc.13.65. 5. c. gen., *undertake*, τῆς κινήσεως, τῆς νήξεως, Ael.*NA*5.18, 13.19. 6. c. dat., *assist*, App.*BC*4.96 (nisi leg. ⟨συν⟩επιλ.). 7. intr., *succeed, follow*, Arist.*Pr*.860^{a}7. 8. of food or drink, *take extra*, οἰνάριον Plu.*Cat. Ma*.1; *take after* other food, Dsc.2.112. III. Med. (with pf. ἐπείλημμαι Pl.*Cra*.396d, D.3.27), *hold oneself on by, lay hold of*, c. gen., τῶν νεῶν Hdt.6.113, Th.4.14, etc.; τῶν ἀφλάστων νεός Hdt. 6.114; τῶν ἐπισπαστήρων ib.91; τῆς ἴτυος X.*An*.4.7.12; τῶν ἁμαξῶν Plu.*Oth*.3; ὅτου ἐπιλάβοιτο τὰ δρέπανα whomsoever the scythes *caught*, X.*Cyr*.7.1.31; ἐπιλαμβάνεταί μου τῆς χειρὸς τῇ δεξιᾷ Pl. *Prt*.335c; ἐπιλαβόμενός [τινος] τῇ χειρί D.21.60; τῶν τριχῶν by the hair, Aeschin.3.150; μὴ 'πιλαμβάνου *hold* me not! E.*Ph*. 896. 2. *attack*, τινός X.*HG*4.2.22; esp. with words, Pl.*Phdr*. 236b; of things, τῆς θερμασίας πόρων -ομένης Epicur.*Ep*.2 p.52 U.; of diseases, Luc.*Nigr*.29. 3. *make a seizure of, arrest*, τῶν παίδων D.33.9; *seize* goods in default of payment, Id.21.133. b. *lay hands on in assertion of a claim*, Pl.*Lg*.954c, *POxy*.1707.15 (iii A.D.), etc. 4. *lay hold of, get, obtain*, προστάτεω a chief, Hdt.1.127; προφάσιος ἔς τινα Id.3.36, cf. 6.49; δυνάμιος Id.9.99; καιροῦ Ar.*Lys*. 596; ἐξουσίας, γαλήνης, Pl.*R*.360d, *Plt*.273a, cf. *PTeb*.48.20 (ii B.C.), etc.; ἐ. λογισμῷ, Lat. *ratione assequi*, Pl.*Phd*.79a. 5. of Place, *reach*, δασέος Arist.*HA*629^{b}15; τῶν ὀρῶν Plu.*Ant*.41: metaph., of a state or condition, ἐρημίας ἐπειλημμένοι *having found* an empty field, i.e. an absence of all competitors, D.3.27, cf. Arist.*Pol*.1305^{b}16. 6. *attempt*, πράξεων μεγάλων Plu.*Mar*.7. b. c. inf., *undertake*, γεωργεῖν *IG*7.2446 (Thebes). 7. *touch on*, τινός Pl.*R*.449d. 8. *take up, interrupt* in speaking, Id.*Grg*.506b, *Smp*.214e; *object to*, τοῦ ψηφίσματος X.*HG*2.1.32; ἐ. ὅτι.. *object* that.., Pl.*R*.490c. 9. rarely c. acc., *seize*, τὰς 'Αθήνας (leg. λήψονται) Lycurg.84.

ἐπιλαμπάδιον, τό, a surgical instrument used as a *trocar*, *Mulomed. Chironis* 64.

ἐπίλαμπρ-ος, ον, *brilliant, illustrious*, Artem.3.61, Sch.Arat.156. **-ύνω**, *make splendid, adorn*, τὴν οἰκίαν, τὸν οἶκον, Phld.*Piet*.74, Plu. *Lys*.30; γένος τιμαῖς D.H.6.41. 2. of sound, *make loud and clear, raise high*, τὸν ἦχον Id.*Comp*.14; τὴν φωνήν, of frogs, Plu.2.912c.

ἐπίλαμπτος, ον, Ion. for ἐπίληπτος.

ἐπι-λάμπω, *shine after* or *thereupon*, ἠέλιος δ' ἐπέλαμψε *thereupon* the sun *shone forth*, Il.17.650; of the moon, *h.Merc*.141, Plu.2.944d, etc.; ὥς σφι ἡμέρη ἐπέλαμψε Hdt.8.14, cf. 3.135; ἡμέρης ἐπιλαμψάσης when day *had fully come*, Id.7.13; also ἔαρος ἐπιλάμψαντος Id.8. 130. 2. *shine upon* (a place), abs., Hp.*Aër*.6, X.*Cyn*.8.1: c. dat., φλόγες ἐ. ἄκροις τοῖς κέρασι Plu.*Fab*.6; ὁ ἥλιος ἐπέλαμπε τῷ ἔργῳ Id. *Arat*.22, cf. Theo Sm.p.121 H.: metaph., οὔριος..ἐπίλαμψον ἐμῷ ἔρωτι, Κύπρι *AP*5.16 (Gaet.); τοῖς ἀπελπίζουσιν ἐ. *bring* them *new light*, *OGI*194.20 (Egypt, i B.C.), cf. ib.669.7 (ibid., i A.D.). II. trans., *make to shine*, μόχθοι νεόταт' ἐπέλαμψαν μυρίοι (so L.Dind. for μυρίοις) Pi.*Fr*.172 (dub. l.); τὸ ἀγαθὸν πᾶσιν ἐ. τοῖς νοητοῖς ἀλήθειαν Plot.4.7. 10:—Pass., *shine upon*, λόφῳ -ελάμπετο πήληξ A.R.2.920. 2. *illumine*, κολώνας ib.164. **-λαμψις**, εως, ἡ, *shining*, of heavenly bodies, Ph.1.24, al.; ἀστραπῶν Id.2.7 (pl.); *illumination*, Iamb.*Myst*. 5.26, also cj. for ἔκλ. in Hp.*Epid*.6.1.4.

ἐπιλανθάνω, v. ἐπιλήθω.

ἐπιλάρκισμα, ατος, τό, (λάρκος) *cover of a basket*, *EM*361.22.

ἐπῑλάρχ-ης, ου, ὁ, *commander of an* ἐπιλαρχία, *PPetr*.3 p.21 (iii B.C.). **-ία**, ἡ, *double* ἴλη, i.e. *two* ἶλαι or 128 *horse*, Ascl.*Tact*.7. 11, Arr.*Tact*.18.2.

ἐπίλᾱσις, Dor. for ἐπίλησις.

ἐπιλᾰφύσσω, *devour in addition*, Tim.Gaz.*Epit*.103.29.

ἐπιλε-αίνω, *smooth over*, Plu.2.74d; τὰ ἄκρα τῶν βλεφάρων, of light sleep, Hld.2.16: metaph., ἐπιλεήνας τὴν Ξέρξεω γνώμην, i.e. *making* it *plausible*, Hdt.7.10; τὸ φαῦλον καὶ ἀγεννὲς τῶν διηγημάτων Jul.*Or*.3.111d. II. *chew*, τροφήν Ph.1.63, al.: metaph., λόγον ib.

180. **-ανσις**, εως, ἡ, *chewing small, rumination*, τροφῆς ib.254: metaph., ἡδονῶν ib.115 (pl.).

ἐπιλέγδην, Adv. *by selection*, Eust.955.8.

ἐπίλεγμα, ατος, τό, *extract* from a document, *PGrenf.*1.37.15 (ii B.C.).

ἐπιλέγω, *say in connexion with* an action, etc., Hdt.2.35,64, etc.; ποιεῖν τι καὶ ἐπιλέγειν *say while* or *after* doing it, Id.4.65; παίζουσιν ἐπιλέγοντες Id.5.4; ἐ. λόγον τόνδε, ὡς.. Id.2.156, 8.49; ἐξηπάτων... ἐπιλέγων τοιαυτί Ar.*Eq.*418; ἐ. τεκμήρια τὴν ἄλλην αὐτοῦ... παρανομίαν *citing* it as proof, Th.6.28, cf. Alciphr.3.56. 2. *say besides*, ἑκάστῳ "σοὶ μέν κτλ." X.*Cyr.*1.3.7, cf. Arist.*Rh.*1395ª27, Ph.1.512; τὴν αἰτίαν ἐ. Arist.*Rh.*1417ª28:—Med., *repeat*, D.H.*Rh.*11.5:—Pass., [τὰ] ἐπιλεγόμενα Arist.*Rh.*1394ª13. 3. *call by name*, Hdt.5.70; ἐπέλεγον δὲ κιθαρῳδικούς (sc. νόμους) Pl.*Lg.*700b:—Med., A.*Supp.*49 (lyr.):—Pass., *to be surnamed*, J.*AJ*13.10.4. 4. *utter, pronounce* a spell (cf. ἐπεῖπον), ῥῆσιν μυστικήν Ath.11.496b; ῥῆσίν τινα μακράν Luc.*Nec.* 7; τοὺς ἀνθρώπους ἐπιλέγειν τῷ λοιμῷ "φεῦγ' ἐς κόρακας" Arist.*Fr.* 496, cf. *Pr.*926ᵇ23, *EN*1109ᵇ11. 5. *attribute*, τινὶ τὸ καλόν, τὸ χρήσιμον, Id.*Pol.*1323ᵇ12; ἐ. τοῖς εὖ ἔχουσιν ἔργοις, ὅτι... Id.*EN*1106ᵇ 10. 6. *say against* one, App.*BC*3.18. II. *pick out, select*, Hdt. 3.44,81; ἔκ τινων πεζούς Wilcken *Chr.*11 *A* 35 (ii B.C.):—freq. in Med., τῶν Βαβυλωνίων ἐπελέξατο he *chose him* certain of the Babylonians, Hdt.3.157, cf. 6.73, Th.7.19, Arist.*Fr.*151, Wilcken *Chr.*11 *A* 49 (ii B.C.), D.S.3.74:—Pass., ἐπιλελεγμένοι or ἐπειλεγμένοι *chosen men*, X.*Cyr.*3.3.41, Isoc.4.146, *POxy.*1210.4 (i B.C.), etc.; οἱ ἐπιλεγέντες *SIG*577.72 (Milet., iii/ii B.C.). III. Med., *think upon, think over*, ταῦτα Hdt.1.78, 2.120, al., cf. Ant.Lib.5.4; μὴ ἐ. *not to care*, Hdt. 7.236, al.; οὐδαμὰ ἐ. μή κοτε... *to have no fear* lest..., Id.3.65, cf. 7. 149: c. inf., πᾶν ἐπιλεγόμενος πείσεσθαι *expecting*..., Id.7.49, cf. 52: rare in Trag., μηδ' ἐπιλεχθῇς Ἀγαμεμνονίαν εἶναί μ' ἄλοχον *deem* me not to be..., A.*Ag.*1498 (anap.). 2. in Hdt. also, *con over, read*, τὸ βυβλίον, τὰ γράμματα, 1.124,125, 2.125, al., cf. Paus.1.12.3, al., Hld.4.8: so in Act., Them.*Or.*11.153a. 3. *recount*, in speaking, τὴν αἰσχύνην καὶ τὸν κίνδυνον D.H.9.57.

ἐπιλείβω, also **ἐπιλλ-**, *pour* wine *over* a thing, ἐπὶ δ' αἴθοπα οἶνον λεῖβε Il.1.462; ἐπιλλείβειν ἱεροῖσιν A.R.1.1133: abs., ἀνιστάμενοι δ' ἐπέλειβον Od.3.341.

ἐπίλειμμα, ατος, τό, αἰθέρος Sch.Arat.786 (pl., v.l. ἐπιλήμματα, leg. πιλήματα).

ἐπίλειος, ον, = ἐπίλεπτος, Steph. *in Gal.*1.272 D.

ἐπιλειόω, *smooth off, shave smooth*, τὸ γένειον D.C.48.34 (Med.).

ἐπιλείπω, *leave behind*, ἐπὶ δὲ πλεῖον ἐλέλειπτο Od.8.475, cf. X.*An.* 1.8.18 codd.:—Med., *leave behind*, of gleanings, v.l. in Lxx *Ob.*1.5:—Pass., c. gen., *fall short of*, παντὸς ἀριθμοῦ Pl.*Epin.*978b: c. dat., τῇ δυνάμει, τῇ οὐσίᾳ, Arist.*Ath.*20.2, 27.4. 2. *leave untouched*, ὡς οὔτ' ἂν τῶν ἐμῶν ἐπιλίποιμι οὐδὲν οὔτε τῶν φίλων Pl.*Prt.*310e: c. part., μυρία ἐ. λέγων Id.*Phlb.*26b, cf. 52d. II. of things, *fail* one, c. acc. pers., ἥβην.., ἥ μ' ἐπιλείπει Thgn.1131; ὕδωρ [μιν] ἐπέλιπε Hdt.7.21, cf. 2. 174; so τῶν ὄμβρων ἐπιλιπόντων αὐτούς (sc. τοὺς ποταμούς) Id.2.25; γλαῦκες ὑμᾶς οὔποτ' ἐπιλείψουσι Ar.*Av.*1106; ἐπειδὰν αὐτοὺς ἐπιλίπωσιν ἐλπίδες Th.5.103: c. inf., [ὁ νόμος] ἐμοὶ μόνῳ ἐπέλιπε μὴ ὠφελῆσαι Antipho 5.17; ἐπιλίποι ἂν ἡμᾶς ὁ χρόνος time would *fail* me, Isoc.1.11, cf. Lys.12.1, *Ep.Hebr.*11.32; τὸ ὕδωρ ἡμᾶς ἐ. Isoc.15.320; ἐπιλείψει με λέγονθ' ἡ ἡμέρα D.18.296: later, c. dat., Plu.*Cic.*42, Ael.*NA*8. 17. 2. Hdt., freq. of rivers, ἐ. τὸ ῥέεθρον *leave* their stream *unfilled, run dry*, Hdt.7.43,58, al.; without ῥέεθρον, *fail, run dry*, ib. 127; τὰς κρήνας καὶ τὰ φρέατ' ἐπιλείπειν πέφυκεν D.14.30. 3. generally, *fail, be wanting*, ἵνα μὴ ἐπιλίπῃ κατεσθιόμενα Hdt.3.108; σῖτος ἐπιλιπών *a deficiency* of it, Th.3.20 codd.; τὰ ἐπιτήδεια ἐ. X.*An.*4.7.1; ὥστε τὸν λόγον μηδέποτε ἐ. Pl.*Prt.*334e; opp. περιγίγνεσθαι, Ar.*Pl.* 554: c. gen., *fall short*, σπουδῆς οὐθὲν ἐ. *Michel* 332.9 (Odessus).

ἐπιλείχω, *lick over, lick*, *Ev.Luc.*16.21.

ἐπίλειψις, εως, ἡ, *deficiency, lack*, ὀρνίθων Th.2.50; τῆς δυνάμεως Plu.2.695d; τελῶν *CIG*2695*b* (Mylasa).

ἐπιλεκτ-άρχης, ου, ὁ, *commander of a picked band*, Plu.*Arat.*32:—hence **-αρχέω**, *SIG*421.18 (Aetolia, iii B.C.). **-έον**, *one must select*, τόπους Ath.Med.ap.Orib.*inc.*23.8; χῆνας *Gp.*14.22.1; *one must approve*, Just.*Nov.*6.5. **-ης**, ου, ὁ, *collector*, τῶν ἐθνικῶν Eust.367. 23. **-ος**, ον, *chosen*, τὸ ἐ. γένος Ἰσραήλ Ph.1.242; ξύλα πρὸς εὐωδίαν ἐ. Ael.*VH*5.6; ἐ. σμύρνα *choice*, J.*AJ*3.8.3; ἐλκασίαι Callix.2. 2. esp. of soldiers, οἱ ἐπίλεκτοι X.*An.*3.4.43, *HG*5.3.23, *IG*2².680.12, *IPE*1².352.39 (Cherson.); in Egypt, *OGI*731 (ii B.C.), *UPZ*110.21 (ii B.C.). b. = ἔκτακτος (q.v.), Arr.*Tact.*10.4. c. = Lat. *extraordinarii*, Plb.6.26.6, etc. 2. Adv. -τως, = λογάδην, Sch.Th.4.4.

ἐπιλελογισμένως, Adv., (ἐπιλογίζομαι) *with consideration*, Phld. *Rh.*1.218 S.

ἐπίλεξις, εως, ἡ, *choice, selection*, App.*BC*3.5.

ἐπίλεπτ-ος, ον, *somewhat light*, γῆ *Gp.*2.21.3; σιδήρια Arr.*Alan.* 16. **-ουργέω**, *refine still further*, Dam.*Pr.*354, cf. 341 (v.l. **ἐπιλεπτολογέω**). **-ύνω**, *smear over with a thin coat*, τιτάνῳ Poll.7. 124. 2. *sift finely*, Hsch. s.v. ἐπέσηθον.

ἐπιλέπω, *strip of bark*, ὄζον ἐ. σιδήρῳ *h.Merc.*109.

ἐπιλευκ-αίνω, *to be whitish*, Arist.*PA*676ª32; of a plant, τὴν χρόαν ξανθὸς ἐπιλευκαίνων Thphr.*HP*3.12.9, etc. **-ία**, ἡ, = λευκή, *leprosy*, Plu.2.670f. **-ος**, ον, *white on the surface, whitish*, Thphr.*HP*3.7.5.

ἐπιλεύσσω, *look towards* or *at*, τόσσον τίς τ' ἐπιλεύσσει one can only *see* so far *before* one, Il.3.12.

ἐπιλήγω, *end in* or *at*, αἰγιαλῷ J.*BJ*3.9.3, cf. 3.10.7; τῇ τοπαρχίᾳ prob. l., ib.3.3.4.

ἐπιλήθ-ης, ες, v.l. for sq., Od.4.221. **-ος**, ον, *causing to forget*, c. gen., φάρμακον..., νηπενθές τ' ἄχολόν τε κακῶν ἐπίληθον ἁπάντων Od.4.221 (Aristarch.; ἐπιλῆθον Ptol.Ascal.); ἴυγγα δέους ἐπίληθον παντός Ael.*NA*15.19, cf. 4.41. **-ω**, *cause to forget*, ὁ γάρ τ' [ὕπνος] ἐπέλησεν ἁπάντων *laps one in forgetfulness* of all, Od.20.85; ἡδονὴ σφέας ἐπιλήθουσα τῶν πάρος Aret.*CD*2.12; ἐπιλήσει σε ἀφροδισίων Philostr.*Ep.*68:—Pass., *to be forgotten*, in pf. part. ἐπιλελησμένος Lxx *Is.*23.16, *Ev.Luc.*12.6: fut. -λησθήσομαι Lxx *Wi.*2.4. II. Med., **ἐπιλανθάνομαι**, or more commonly **ἐπιλήθομαι**, Aeol. and Dor. **-λᾱθ-** Alc.*Supp.*25.6, S.*El.*146 (lyr.), fut. -λήσομαι: aor. 2 -ελᾰθόμην Pl.*Ap.*17a: late aor. 1 -ελήσατο Nonn.*D.*48.969: with pf. Act. λέληθα Hdt.3.46, Pi.*O.*(v. infr.), but more freq. Pass. -λέλησμαι E.*Ba.*188, Ar.*Nu.*631, Lys.26.1, Pl.*Phd.*75d, al.: plpf. -ελελήσμην Ar.*V.*605, Pl.*Phd.*73e, al.:—*let a thing escape one, forget, lose thought of*, c. gen., ὅπως Ἰθάκης ἐπιλήσεται (Ep. aor. subj.) Od.1.57; οὐδ' ὁ γέρων δολίης ἐπελήθετο τέχνης 4.455, cf. Hes.*Th.*560; οὐδ' ὣς σχεδίης ἐπελήθετο Od.5.324; γονέων ἐπιλάθεται (Dor.) S.*El.*146 (lyr.), cf. Hdt.4.4, Lys.26.1, etc.; ὑπ' αὐτῶν ὀλίγου ἐμαυτοῦ ἐπελαθόμην Pl.*Ap.* l.c.: prov., Μαλέας δὲ κάμψας ἐπιλάθου τῶν οἴκαδε Str.8.6.20: c. acc., Hdt.3.46, E.*Hel.*265, Ar.*Nu.*631; ὑπὸ χρόνου τι Pl.*Phd.*73e: c. inf., Ar.*V.*853, Pl.*R.*563b, Hyp.*Lyc.*8: c. part., ὀφείλων ἐπιλέλαθα I *forgot that* I owed, Pi.*O.*10(11).3, cf. E.*Ba.*188: with a Prep., ἐ. περὶ τῶν πεπραγμένων And.1.148; περὶ οὗ..., περὶ ὅτου..., Pl.*Prt.*334d, 336d; *leave disregarded, neglect*, πρόσταγμα Ceb.24. 2. less freq., *forget wilfully*, τῶν ἐντολέων μεμνημένος ἐπελανθάνετο Hdt.3.147; ἑκὼν ἐπιλήθομαι Id.4.43, cf. 3.75, Aeschin.1.158.

ἐπιληΐς, ΐδος, ἡ, (λεία) *obtained as booty* or *plunder, gained in war*, πόλεις X.*HG*3.2.23.

ἐπιληκέω, *clap the hands in applause*, or *beat time to* the dancers, Od.8.379.

ἐπιλήκητος· ὁ τετυφλωμένος, Hsch.

ἐπιληκυθίστρια, Dor. **-λᾱκ-**, ἡ, comic nickname of the muse of Mnasalcas, *the bombastical*, *AP*13.21 (Theodorid.); cf. λήκυθος.

ἐπιλήνιος, ον, (ληνός) *of* or *at a wine-press* or *the vintage*, μέλος Callix.2; ὕμνοι *Anacreont.*57.8; ὄρχησις Longus 2.36; ἐπιλήνια χαίρειν Opp.*C.*1.127; epith. of Dionysus, Orph.*H.*50.1:—also **ἐπιλήναιοι** θεοί Max.Tyr.30.4. II. ἐπιλήνιον, τό, *commission on the vintage*, *PLond.ined.*2135 (iv A.D.). 2. ἐπιλήνια, τά, *vintage-festival*, Ph.1.323, *PFlor.*369.14 (ii A.D.).

ἐπιληπτ-έον, (ἐπιλαμβάνω) *one must take into account*, ὁμοιότητα Arist.*Col.*792ᵇ25. **-εύομαι**, = sq., Lxx *1Ki.*21.15(16). **-ίζω**, *have an epileptic fit*, Plu.2.290b:—Pass., Alex.Trall.1.15. **-ικός**, ή, όν, *subject to epilepsy, epileptic*, Hp.*Aph.*2.45, Arist.*Pr.*953ª16, Dsc.2.78, al. II. νόσοι, νοσήματα ἐ., *epileptic* complaints, Arist.*EN*1149ª11, 1150ᵇ34. Adv. -κῶς, ἀποθνήσκειν, σπᾶσθαι, Hp.*Coac.*339, Agathin. ap.Orib.10.7.10. III. Adv. -κῶς *by intuition* or *apprehension*, βλέπειν τὰ πράγματα Gal.5.90. **-ος**, Ion. **-λαμπτος**, ον, *caught* or *detected in* anything, ἐ. ηὑρέθη S.*Ant.*406: c. part., ἐπίλαμπτος ἀφάσσουσα *caught* in the act of feeling, Hdt.3.69. 2. *culpable, censurable*, πάθος Ph.2.348; βίος Id.2.4, al., cf. Porph.*Chr.*23; of errors in metre, Heph.4.6. 3. *disabled*, ἀνδράποδον Hyp.*Ath.*15 (unless in signf. II); of a hen-partridge, Arist.*HA*613ᵇ18. II. *suffering from epilepsy*, Hp.*Aph.*3.16:—D.25.80 puns on the two senses, τοὺς ἐπιλήπτους φησὶν ἰᾶσθαι, αὐτὸς ὢν ἐ. πάσῃ πονηρίᾳ; so ἐ. ὑπὸ πάθους Plu.2. 798f. **-ωρ**, ορος, ὁ, *censurer*, Ζήνωνος πάντων ἐπιλήπτορος Timo 45.2.

ἐπίλησις, Dor. **-λᾱσις**, εως, ἡ, *forgetting, forgetfulness*, καμάτων Pi.*P.*1.46.

ἐπιλησμ-ονή, ἡ, *forgetfulness*, Cratin.410 ap.Sch.Ar.*Nu.*788, Lxx *Si.*11.27; ἀκροατὴς -λησμονῆς *Ep.Jac.*1.25:—also **ἐπιλησμονείη** (sic), Hsch., and **ἐπιλήσμη** Alex.315. **-οσύνη**, ἡ, = foreg., Cratin.410 ap.Suid. (v. -λησμονή), *IG*12(8).561 (Thasos), Archig.ap. Gal.8.149, D.C.56.41. **-ων**, ον, gen. ονος, *apt to forget, forgetful*, Cratin.154, Ar.*Nu.*129, al., Lys.12.87, Pl.*R.*486d, etc.: Comp. -έστερος X.*Mem.*4.8.8: c. gen. rei, Id.*Ap.*6: Sup. -έστατος Lys.34. 2, Phalar.*Ep.*30: irreg. Sup. ἐπιλησμότατος (as if from ἐπίλησμος) Ar.*Nu.*790. II. Act., *causing forgetfulness*, ἐ. ἐπῳδή Chio *Ep.*3.6.

ἐπι-ληψία, ἡ, = ἐπίληψις I.4, *stoppage*, Arist.*Pr.*866ᵇ14. II. = ἐπίληψις II, Hp.*Aph.*3.22 (pl.), Arist.*Fr.*370. **-λήψιμος**, ον, *reprehensible*, Luc.*Rh.Pr.*22, Philostr.*VA*4.42, Max.Tyr.24.6, Hermog. *Inv.*4.13. II. *liable to seizure*, Polem.*Call.*34. **-ληψις**, εως, ἡ, *taking hold of, clasping*, Epicur.*Fr.*141; *taking besides*, τετάρτου τυράννου App.*BC*5.77. 2. in Law, *claiming* property *by seizing*, Pl.*Lg.*954e. 3. *reprehension, censure*, εἰκῇ τὰς ἐ. ποιεῖσθαι Isoc.8. 61; -λήψεως δεόμενος Plu.2.35d; ἔχει ἐπιλήψεις admits *room for censure*, Ath.5.187f. 4. *stoppage*, Mich. in *PN*49.14. II. *epileptic fit*, Hp.*Coac.*587, *Morb.Sacr.*10, Arist.*Pr.*960ª18, etc. (but, *invasion, attack* of disease, Hp.*Morb.*3.16).

ἐπιλίγδην, Adv. *grazing*, Il.17.599, Luc.*Nigr.*36. [ἐπῑ-, v.l. ἐπιλλ-, Il. l.c.]

ἐπιλίζω, *whizz*, of arrows, Nic.*Fr.*100 (cited as from Men. by *An. Ox.*1.267).

ἐπίλιημι· ἐπιτρέπω, Hsch.

ἐπιλιμνάζομαι, Pass., *to be overflowed*, Plu.*Caes.*25.

Ἐπιλίμνιος, ὁ, *by the lake*, title of Poseidon, Hsch.

ἐπιλιμπάνω, = ἐπιλείπω, Gramm., *to be wanting*, of a tense, *An. Ox.*4.393, etc.

ἐπιλιν-άω, *visit nets*, Hsch. **-ευτής**, οῦ, ὁ, *one who catches with nets*, prob. in *AP*6.93 (Antip. ⟨Thess.⟩).

ἐπιλῐπαίνω, *make fat* or *sleek*, τὸ δέρμα Plu.*Alex.*57.

ἐπιλῐπᾰρέω, *make earnest entreaty*, Them.*Or.*34 p.457 D.

ἐπιλῐπής (A), ές, = ἐπίλοιπος, Plu.*Sull*.7. II. *defective, wanting*, interpol. in Sor.2.53, Hsch.

ἐπιλῐπής (B), ές, (λίπος) *fatty*, Heliod.ap.Orib.46.22.4.

ἐπιλιχμάω, *lick up*, Babr.48.6:—Med., *lick up, devour*, Ph.1.550: metaph., ἐπιθυμία ἐ. τι πυρὸς δίκην ib.305, cf. 527.

ἐπιλιχνεύω, *desire eagerly*, Ph.1.38,137.

ἐπιλλείβω, v. ἐπιλείβω.

ἐπιλλ-ίζω, (ἰλλός) *make signs to* one *by winking*, οὐκ ἀΐεις ὅτι δή μοι ἐπιλλίζουσιν ἅπαντες Od.18.11; *wink roguishly*, *h.Merc*.387; *look askance*, A.R.1.486: c. dat., *mock at*, Id.4.389: c. acc. et dat., τινὶ κερτομίας Id.3.791. 2. *blink*, when drowsy, Nic.*Th*.163. **-ος**, ον, *leering, squinting*, Eust.206.29. **-όω**, = sq., ib.31. **-ώπτω**, *wink* or *leer*, ἐξ ὀφρύος Plu.2.51c.

ἐπιλοβίς, ίδος, ἡ, (λοβός) *lobe of the liver*, *PAmh*.2.14 (iii/iv A.D.), Hsch. (-βολίς cod.).

ἐπιλόγεον (fort. -λώγεον), *coarse chaff*, Hsch.

ἐπιλόγ-ευσις, εως, ἡ, *levying of arrears of taxation*, *PRev.Laws* 19. 12 (iii B.C.). **-εύω**, *levy arrears of taxation*, ib.6.1 (iii B.C.), *PPetr*. 3 p.69 (iii B.C.), etc. **-ή**, ἡ, *picking out, choice*, τῶν ἀκαθάρτων Lysim.ap.J.*Ap*.1.34, cf. *Cod.Just*.1.5.16.2; *selection*, ἀνδρῶν Plb.7. 16.7, etc.; ἵππων Simon *Eq*. tit.; ἡμερῶν Ps.-Ptol.*Centil*.6. **-ίζομαι**, Att. fut. -λογιοῦμαι Pl.*Ax*.365b: aor. -ελογισάμην X. (v. infr.), D. (v. infr.), -ελογίσθην Hdt. (v. infr.): pf. -λελόγισμαι D.H.3.15:—*reckon over, conclude, consider*, ὅτι.. Hdt.7.177, D.44.34, Pl. l. c., Phld.*Sign*.8, al.; τὰ ἄλλα ὀρθῶς ἐ. D.H. l. c.; *take into account*, οὐδὲν τοῦτο ἐπελογίσαντο X.*HG*7.5.16; οὐκ ἐπιλογίζεται τὸ τέταρτον, of the Egyptian year of 365 days, Procl.*Hyp*.3.56; ἐ. δείγμασιν οὐκ ἀμφιβόλοις *Theol.Ar*.33:—Pass., τὰ βουλαῖς -λογισθέντα Ph.1.428, cf. Phld.*D*.1.15. II. *address the peroration*, πρὸς ὀργὴν ἢ ἔλεον Theodect.ap.Rh.7.33 W. **-ικός**, ή, όν, *of, belonging to the epilogue* or *peroration*, οἶκτοι Ath.13.590e; ἔννοιαι, νοήματα, Hermog.*Id*.2.9. Adv. -κῶς Arg.Aeschin.3. **-ιον**, τό, perh. *epilogue*, Phld.*Lib*. p.65 O. **-ισις**, εως, ἡ, = ἐπιλογισμός, Epicur.*Fr*.423, *Nat*.28. 8. **-ισμα**, ατος, τό, *a reflection*, Id.*Nat*.123 G. **-ισμός**, ὁ, *reckoning, calculation*, Arist.*Pol*.1322^{b}35 codd. (pl.); of dates, D.H.1.74 (pl.); τῆς αἰτίας Plu.2.435b; τῶν φαινομένων Phld.*Sign*.22; ἐξ ἐπιλογισμοῦ Ph.1.168, al., J.*AJ*15.10.2: generally, *reflection, consideration*, opp. ἀπόδειξις, Epicur.*Ep*.1 p.25 U., cf. *Sent*.20, Phld.*Ir*.p.92 W. (pl.); κατ' ἐπιλογισμὸν οὐδένα on no *fixed* or *reasoned principle*, Heph. 16.1; μηδεμίαν ἐπιστροφὴν μηδ' ἐ. ἔχων Chrysipp.*Stoic*.3.187; ἐπιλογισμός defined as a *generally accepted inference*, *Stoic*.2.89, cf. Gal. *Sect.Intr*.5, Menodot.ap.eund.*Subf.Emp*.12: practically, = συλλογισμός, ὃ διὰ τοιούτου τινὸς ἐ. συνεβίβαζον οἱ Πυθαγορικοί *Theol.Ar*.47; but perh. of *inductive reasoning*, opp. συλλογισμός, Phld.*Herc*.1003; *higher reasoning*, opp. λογισμός, Plot.1.3.6. 2. *signification*, Iamb. *Protr*.21.ιʹ. 3. *description, account*, Apollod.*Poliorc*.138.13 (pl.), Erasistr.ap.Gal.8.317. II. *afterthought, later consideration*, opp. προλογισμός, Hierocl. *in CA* 18 p.460 M. **-ιστέον**, *one must reckon*, ὡς.., ὅτι.., Plu.2.40b, S.E.*M*.8.322, Epicur.*Ep*.1 p.25 U., al. **-ιστικός**, ή, όν, *able to calculate* or *take into account*, θεωρία ἐ. τῶν ὑπαρχόντων Phld.*Rh*.2.47 S.; τοῦ ἑξῆς Arr.*Epict*.2.10.3; *calculating, prudent*, Ptol.*Tetr*.155. Adv. -κῶς Phld.*Rh*.1.254 S., Gal.18(2).26. II. *inferential, illative*, [σύνδεσμος] A.D.*Conj*.257.18. **-ος**, ὁ, *reasoning, inference*, only Ion., Hdt.1.27; τῆς γνώμης ποιέεσθαι ἐπίλογον give a *reason* for their opinion, Hp.*Nat.Hom*.1. II. *peroration* of a speech, Arist.*Rh*.1414^{b}12, Chrysipp.*Stoic*.2.96, Phld.*Rh*.1.202 S., Longin.12.5, etc. 2. *the concluding portion of a play*, = ἔκθεσις, Sch. Ar.*Ra*.1548: metaph., ἐ. τῆς κοσμοποιίας Ph.1.237. 3. *subjoined* or *explanatory sentence*, Arist.*Rh*.1394^{b}8, cf. ^{a}11.—In E.*El*.719 (lyr.), ἐπίλογοι is corrupt.

ἐπίλογχος (A), ον, (λόγχη) *barbed*, βέλος E.*Hipp*.221 (anap.).

ἐπίλογχος (B), ὁ, (λαγχάνω) *reserve candidate* for an office, *PRyl*. 77.43, al. (ii A.D.).

ἐπιλοιβή, ἡ, *drink-offering*, *Epic.Alex.Adesp*.9 vi 26 (pl.), Orph.*A*. 547,603 (both pl.).

ἐπιλοιδορέω, *cast reproaches on*, cj. in Plb.15.33.4:—Med., Suid. s.v. ἐπιτωθάζων.

ἐπιλοίμια (sc. ἔπη), τά, (λοιμός) *incantations to drive away pestilence*, Poll.4.53.

ἐπίλοιπος, ον, *still left, remaining*, μῆνας ἑπτὰ τοὺς ἐπιλοίπους Καμβύσῃ ἐς τὰ ὀκτὼ ἔτεα τῆς πληρώσιος Hdt.3.67: freq. in pl., c. gen., αἱ ἐ. τῶν πολίων Id.6.33; τὰ ἐ. τοῦ λόγου Id.4.154; τἀπ. τῶν λόγων S. *Ph*.24, etc.; τἀπίλοιπ' ἄκουσον E.*Tr*.923, cf. Pl.*Cra*.397a; ἡ 'πίλοιπος ὁδός E.*Ph*.842; τί οὖν ἦν ἐπίλοιπον; And.1.87. 2. of Time, *future*, χρόνος Hdt.2.13, Pl.*Lg*.628a, etc.; ἁμέραι ἐ. Pi.*O*.1.33; βίος Antipho *Fr*.67, Lys.2.71, Pl.*Lg*.929e.

ἐπιλοξόω, *look askance*, τῇ ἑτέρῃ κούρῃ Herod.4.71.

ἐπίλουτρον, τό, *price of a bath*, Luc.*Lex*.2.

ἐπιλούω, *bathe*, ἐν ὕδασί τινας Alex.*Fig*.2.21.

ἐπιλοχᾱγός, ὁ, *commander of the* λοχαγοί, *PPetr*.3 p.47 (iii B.C.).

ἐπιλῠγάζω, -λῠγαῖος, -λῠγίζω, ff. ll. for ἐπηλ-.

ἐπιλύζω, Ep. ἐπιλλ-, *have the hiccough besides*, Nic.*Al*.81.

Ἐπιλύκειον [ῠ], τό, at Athens, *office of the polemarch* (because built or restored by Epilycus), Arist.*Ath*.3.5.

ἐπιλῡμαίνομαι, *infest, ruin*, τὸν ἀνθρώπινον βίον Plu.2.881d.

ἐπιλῡπ-έω, *trouble, annoy, offend besides*, τινά v.l. in Hdt.9.50, Lxx 2 *Ma*.8.32:—Pass., *to be troubled at*, ἀγαθοῖς ἀλλοτρίοις Iamb.*Protr*. 21.λʹ; ὅτι.. S.E.*M*.11.127. **-ία**, ἡ, *trouble, grief*, *Stoic*.3.25. **-ος**, ον, (λύπη) *sad*, γένος Ph.2.29; *in low spirits*, Aret.*SA*2.12, *SD*1.6, Ruf.*Fr*.70.21. Adv. -πως *sadly*, ἀπολαύειν Ph.1.136. II. *painful*, ἐπίλυπον ἡ ἀνδρεία Arist.*EN*1117^{a}34; τὸ ἐ. *a thing that causes pain*, ib.1110^{b}19; ἐ. γῆρας Plu.2.13a. Adv. -πως, καταστρέψαι τὸν βίον D.S.17.118.

ἐπί-λῠσις, εως, ἡ, *release from*, ἐ. φόβων δίδου A.*Th*.134 (lyr.): abs., *exemption* from banishment, *SIG*306.51 (Arc., iv B.C.). 2. *solution*, σοφισμάτων S.E.*P*.2.246; *explanation*, 2*Ep.Pet*.1.20, Vett. Val.172.3 (pl.), Hld.1.18, 4.9, Iamb.*Protr*.21 (pl.). 3. *discharge*, of a debt, δοῦναί τισιν ἐ. *PEleph*.27.23 (iii B.C.), cf. *PGrenf*.2.26.27 (ii B.C.). 4. *spell*, *PMag.Leid.W*.25.11, al. 5. Medic., *change of dressing*, Sor.1.28 (pl.), Gal.18(2).838 (pl.), Paul.Aeg.4.48. **-λῠτικός**, ή, όν, *good at solving difficulties*, [γραμματικοὶ] οἱ ἐ. καλούμενοι Suid. s. v. Σωσίβιος, cf. Gal.*Subf.Emp*.12. **-λῠτος**, ον, *manumitted*, *Delph*.3(2).233 (ii B.C.).

ἐπίλυτρος, ον, *set at liberty for ransom*, Str.11.2.12.

ἐπίλυχνος, ὁ, or -ον, τό, *oil for lamps*, Arist. or Thphr.ap.Ath.4. 173f (prob. f.l. for ἔτι λύχνον).

ἐπιλύω, *loose, untie*, δεσμά Theoc.*Adon*.42; ἐ. κύνας *let slip* dogs, X.*Cyn*.7.8: generally, *set free, release*, τοὺς κακούργους τῷ πολέμῳ Luc.*Par*.50:—Med., ἐπιλύεσθαί τινα τὸ μὴ οὐχὶ ἀγανακτεῖν Pl.*Cri*. 43c; ἐπιλύεσθαι ἐπιστολάς *open* them, Hdn.4.12.8; Ἐπιλυσαμένη, epith. of various divinities, Hsch. 2. *solve, explain*, πάντα τοῖς μαθηταῖς *Ev.Marc*.4.34:—Pass., S.E.*P*.2.246, Sch.Od.9.106:—Med., J.*AJ*8.6.5, Vett.Val.259.4, Ath.10.450f, al.: pf. part. Pass. ἐπιλελυμένος *lucid*, of writings, Vett.Val.329.25. 3. *confute* an accusation, Luc.*BisAcc*.30. 4. Med., *manumit*, *Delph*.3(2).233 (ii B.C.). 5. *release, discharge* a debtor, ἀπὸ τᾶν κοινᾶν ποθόδων ἐπιλυθῆμεν (inf. Pass.) τοὺς ἐρρυτιασμένους *Schwyzer* 104.7 (Troezen, ii B.C.): *pay*, c. dat. pers., ib.12:—Med., *discharge* a debt, δάνειον *PGrenf*.1.26.2 (ii B.C.). II. fut. Med. in pass. sense, *lose strength, give in*, Lys.25.33 (dub. l.).

ἐπιλωβ-εύω, (λώβη) *make mockery of* a thing, Od.2.323. **-ής**, ές, *injurious, mischievous*, Nic.*Th*.35,771. **-ητος**, ον, *insulted, degraded*, Lyc.1173. **-ος**, ον, *calamitous*, ἔτος Vett.Val.180.23.

ἐπιμάζιος, ον, (μαζός) = ἐπιμαστίδιος, *AP*9.548 (Bianor), 5.275.5 (Agath.).

ἐπιμαθής, ές, v.l. for εὐμαθής, *Cat.Cod.Astr*.8(4).140.

ἐπιμαιμάω, *long earnestly after*, τινός Lyc.301.

ἐπιμαίνω, *make madly in love with*, τινά τινι Anon.ap.Suid. s.v. Ἀναγυράσιος. II. Pass., with aor. 2 ἐπεμάνην [ᾰ], but also aor. 1 Med. ἐπεμηνάμην Il.6.160, *AP*6.309 (Leon.), Luc.*Syr.D*.21: pf. -μέμηνα:—*to be mad after*, c. dat., τῷ δὲ γυνὴ Προίτου ἐπεμήνατο Il. l. c., cf. Anacr.3, Mosch.*Fr*.2.2, Plu.*Bru*.5; θεὰ ἐ. χώρῳ Call.*Cer*.30; τὰ πράγμαθ', οἷς τότ' ἐπεμαίνετο Ar.*V*.744 (lyr.), cf. 1469 (lyr.), Luc. *Am*.22; [ἀστραγάλαις] *AP*6.309 (Leon.): abs., *to be mad, rage*, A. *Ag*.1427, *Th*.155 (both lyr.). 2. *fly madly at, fall upon*, πύργοις *APl*.4.106.

ἐπιμαίομαι, Ep. fut. -μάσσομαι (also perh. in S.*Fr*.55): aor. -εμασσάμην:—*strive after, seek to obtain, aim at*, mostly c. gen., σκοπέλου ἐπιμαίεο *make for* (i.e. *steer for*) the rock, Od.12.220: metaph., ἐπιμαίεο νόστου *strive after* a return, 5.344; δώρων ἐπεμαίετο θυμὸς his mind *was set upon* presents, Il.10.401; λουτρῶν Theoc.23.57; φυγῆς Timo 5.7: c. dat., *to be set upon*, Orph.*A*.932.—Ep. word, dub. in S. l. c. II. c. acc., *lay hold of, grasp*, ξίφεος δ' ἐπεμαίετο κώπην he *clutched* his sword-hilt, Od.11.531; τῶν ὁπότ' ἰθύσειε.. ἐπὶ χερσὶ μάσασθαι ib.591; χείρ' (i.e. χειρί) ἐπιμασσάμενος *having clutched* [the sword] with my hand, 9.302, cf. 19.480; τὴν ἐπεμάσσατο χειρὸς *took* her by the hand, A.R.3.106. 2. *touch, handle, feel*, ὀΐων ἐπεμαίετο νῶτα Od.9.441; τὸν δ' ἐπιμασσάμενος προσέφη.. Πολύφημος ib. 446; τὴν (sc. οὐλὴν) γνῶ ῥ' ἐπιμασσαμένη 19.468; ἐπὶ νῶτ' ἐπεμαίετο Hes.*Fr*.166; ἕλκος δ' ἰητὴρ ἐπιμάσσεται ἠδ' ἐπιθήσει φάρμαχ' Il.4.190; ὣς ἄρα μιν... ῥάβδῳ ἐπεμάσσατ' Ἀθήνη Od.13.429, cf. 16.172; μάστιγι θοῶς ἐπεμαίετ' ἄρ' ἵππους she *touched* the horses sharply with the whip, Il.5.748, etc.; κεφαλὰν ἐπεμάσσατο *stroked*, *AP*7.730 (Pers.): metaph., πυρὸς δ' ἐπεμαίετο τέχνην, Lat. *artem tractavit*, *h.Merc*.108; νόῳ ἐ. ἕκαστα A.R.3.816. III. later abs., of night, *come slowly on*, Orph.*A*.121.

ἐπίμακρος, ον, *oblong*, Hp.*Art*.79 (v.l. ὑπόμακρος).

ἐπιμάλθα (leg. ἐπιμάλθακα)· ἀγαθά, προσηνῆ· ἢ μαλακά, ἢ ἀσθενῆ λίαν, Hsch.

ἐπιμανδᾰλωτόν, τό, (μανδαλωτός) *a lascivious kiss*, like καταγλώττισμα, Ar.*Ach*.1201.

ἐπιμᾰνής, ές, *mad after* a thing, τὸ ἐ. εἰς τὰς γυναῖκας Paus.1.6.8; so πρός τινα Ach.Tat.8.1. Adv. -νῶς, ἔχειν πρός τι Ath.7.276e. 2. abs., *raving, mad*, parody of Ἐπιφανής, Plb.26.1^a.1; νόσημα Plu.*Dio* 47: Comp. -εστέρα, αἰσχρουργία Luc.*Pseudol*.21.

ἐπιμανθάνω, *learn besides* or *after*, opp. προμανθάνω, Th.1.138: c. inf., Hdt.1.131; εἰ.. Id.2.160.

ἐπιμαντεύομαι, *prophesy*, c. acc. et inf., App.*BC*4.127; τινί τι ib. 138, Philostr.*VA*5.19.

ἐπιμαργαίνω, *to be raving-mad after*, σύες φορυτῷ ἐ. Arat.1123.

ἐπίμαργος, ον, *mad after* a thing, Suid.

ἐπιμάρναμαι, *go on fighting*, μείζονι πέτρῳ Nonn.*D*.21.8.

ἐπιμάρπτω, *clutch*, Hsch.

ἐπιμαρτῠρ-έω, *bear witness to* a thing, *depose to*, ἐ. ἡμῖν τὰ ὀνόματα μὴ.. κεῖσθαι Pl.*Cra*.397a; ἐ. τι πρός τινας Plu.*Lys*.22; τὰ χρήματα ἅ κα ἐπιμαρτυρήσωντι of which they *admit the possession*, *Tab.Heracl*. 1.156: c. inf., τῶν πραγμάτων -ούντων τὴν δύναμιν αὐξάνεσθαι Plu. *Sert*.12, cf. 1*Ep.Pet*.5.12; ὅτι.. Luc.*Alex*.42: abs., Plu.*Nic*.6:—

Pass., *to be confirmed by evidence*, S.E.*M*.7.211, Polystr.p.31 W. 2. *bear witness in favour of*, τινί Phld.*Oec*.p.57 J. II. Astrol., *support by aspect*, Vett.Val.111.31, *PMag.Leid.W*.24.16 (ii/iii A. D.). III. in Med., *adjure*, τισὶ μὴ ποιέειν τι Hdt.5.93 (as v.l. for ἐπιμαρτύρομαι). **–ησις,** εως, ἡ, *confirmation, corroboration*, Epicur.*Sent*.24, al.; –ήσεως δεῖσθαι M.Ant.7.62; ἡ ἐκ τῶν φαινομένων ἐ. S.E.*P*.1.181. II. Astrol., *supporting by aspect*, Paul.Al.*O*.4, Ptol.*Tetr*.200. **–ητής,** οῦ, ὁ, *one who calls to witness, Gloss*. **–ία,** ἡ, *a calling to witness*, ἐς ἐ. καταστῆναι Th.2.74; τῶν θεῶν D.C.59.11. II. *supporting by aspect*, ἄστρων Man.2.400 (pl.), cf. 3.314 (pl.), al.

ἐπιμαρτύρομαι [ῡ], *call to witness, appeal to*, in case of a treaty, θεούς X.*Cyr*.8.5.25, *An*.4.8.7, etc.; in case of history, Id.*HG*3.4.4: abs., Plb.24.11.8; also, *call* a person *to appear as one's witness*, Ar.*Nu*.495, *V*.1437, etc.; folld. by ὅτι.., *call* bystanders *to witness* that.., D.34.28. 2. *call on earnestly, conjure*, Hdt.5.92.η', Th.6.29. 3. *adduce as evidence, appeal to fact*, ὅτι.. Pl.*Phdr*.244b: c. acc. rei et inf., Plu.*Luc*.35. II. = ἐπιμαρτυρέω I, *PLille* 3.8 (iii B. C.), etc. 2. = ἐπιμαρτυρέω II, Vett.Val.292.10.

ἐπιμάρτῠρος, ὁ, *witness to* one's word, etc., Ζεὺς δ' ἄμμ' ἐ. ἔστω Il.7.76; θεοὶ δ' ἐ. ἔστων Od.1.273 (nisi scrib. ἐπὶ μ., et sic Hes.*Sc*.20): fem., Orph.*A*.351. II. Astrol., *supporting by aspect*, Man.6.231 (fem.), Doroth.ap.*Cat.Cod.Astr*.6.113.1.

ἐπίμαρτυς, ῠρος, ὁ, = foreg., Ar.*Lys*.1287 (lyr., dat. pl.): acc. –μάρτυρα Musae.1, *Epigr.Gr*.905: pl., nom. –μάρτυρες Call.*Aet*.3.1.48; acc. –μάρτυρας A.R.4.229: in Astrol. sense (v. foreg.), Man.3.285, Doroth.ap.*Cat.Cod.Astr*.6.101.12.

ἐπιμᾰσάομαι, *chew*, Alciphr.3.51; *chew after* other food, *Gp*.12.30.9:—Pass., Dsc.3.45.

ἐπιμαστεύω, *search for*, Sch.Od.20.377, *EM*361.53.

ἐπιμαστίδιος, ον, (μαστός) *on* or *at the breast, not yet weaned*, of infants, A.*Th*.349 (lyr.), E.*IT*231 (lyr.), Nic.Dam.13 J., Luc.*Tox*.61; of birds, γόνος ὀρταλίχων S.*Fr*.793 (anap.).

ἐπιμάστιος, ον, (μαστός) = foreg., A.R.4.1734, Poll.2.8.

ἐπιμαστίω, *whip* or *beat besides*, Nonn.*D*.1.80, al.

ἐπίμαστος, ον, (ἐπιμαίομαι) *sought out, brought in* (like ἐπακτός), ἀλήτης Od.20.377 (variously expld. by Gramm.).

ἐπιμᾰχ-έω, (μάχομαι) *stand by, help one in battle*, ὥστε τῇ ἀλλήλων ἐπιμαχεῖν *for* the mutual *defence* of their countries, Th.5.27. **–ία,** ἡ, *defensive alliance*, opp. συμμαχία (both offensive and defensive), Id.1.44, 5.48, D.12.7: metaph. of the state, Arist.*Pol*.1280^{b}27. **–ιμος,** ον, f.l. for –ος, Arr.*An*.4.25.2. **–ομαι,** *fight after, act as a reserve*, Ael.*Tact*.17, Arr.*Tact*.15.5. **–ος,** ον, *that may easily be attacked, assailable*, of fortified places, opp. ἄμαχος, Hdt.1.84; ἐκ τῆς γῆς ἐ. Th.4.31, cf. 35; τὰ –ώτατα ib.4; τῇ τὸ –ώτατον ἦν τοῦ χωρίου Hdt.9.21, cf. 6.133, X.*An*.5.4.14. II. *contended for, contested*, Hld.8.1. III. *equipped for battle*, Thom.Mag.p.113 R.; epith. of Πλούτων, *GDI*3520 (Cnidus), cf. *SIG*1014.61 (Erythrae, iii B. C.). IV. *ally, helper*, Ph.1.659, Hsch.; ἐ. χωρία *impregnable*, Ph.2.383 (v.l. ἀπο–), cf. Hsch.

ἐπιμείγνῡμι and **–ύω,** *add by mixing*, μέθυος πολιοῦ ἐπιμείξας Nic.*Th*.582: metaph., ἀθανάταν χάριν Θήβαις –μείξων Pi.*Parth*.2.5; κόλακι.. ἐπέμειξεν ἡ φύσις ἡδονήν τινα *added a mixture of* pleasure to.., Pl.*Phdr*.240b; ἀγλαΐαισιν ἐ. λαόν *make* them *acquainted with* festal enjoyments, Pi.*N*.9.31; ἐμφύλιον αἷμα ἐπέμειξε θνατοῖς *brought* domestic murder *among* them, Id.*P*.2.32; ἐ. τισὶ χεῖρας to fight with them, Id.*N*.3.61. II. intr., *mingle with* others, *have intercourse* or *dealings*, ἀδεῶς Th.1.2; πρός τινας X.*An*.3.5.16; τισί Hld.6.13; χωρίῳ ἐ. *come to* it, Id.5.33; πολλῶν ἐπιμειγνύντων δεῦρο Philostr.*VA* 5.24:—Pass., τοῦ ἠέρος –υμένου τῷ θερμῷ Hp.*Morb*.1.11; ἐπιμείγνυσθαι ἀλλήλοις φιλικῶς X.*Cyr*.7.4.5; παρ' ἀλλήλους Th.2.1: abs., Id.1.146; also ἐ. τισί *join* them, Plu.*Aem*.12; ταῖς πράξεσι *mingle in*.., Id.*Flam*.2; of sexual *intercourse*, ἐ. ἀνδρί D.59.75, cf. Luc.*Am*.22, Artem.1.80. Cf. ἐπιμίσγω.

ἐπιμειδ-άω, *smile at* or *upon*, in Hom. always in phrase, τὸν δ' ἐπιμειδήσας προσέφη he addressed him *with a smile*, Il.4.356, al.; in 10.400, of a scornful smile; but ἦκ' ἐπιμειδήσας Hes.*Th*.547: c. dat., *AP*6.345 (Crin.). **–ίᾱσις,** εως, ἡ, *smiling upon*, Plu.2.1009e: pl., –σεις τῆς ψυχῆς ib.1092d. **–ιάω,** *smile at*, X.*Cyr*.2.2.16, A.R.3.129; τῷ λόγῳ Arr.*An*.5.2.3.

ἐπιμείζων, ον, gen. ονος, strengthd. for μείζων, *still larger* or *greater*, Democr.211 (sed leg. ἔτι μείζ– vel μέζ–).

ἐπιμεικτέον, *one must mix*, Herod.Med.ap.Orib.10.38.2.

ἐπίμεικτος, ον, *common to*, Λυδοῖς καὶ Καρσί Str.14.1.38. 2. *mixed*, Nic.*Th*.528, Gal.7.433; φάσηλοι ἐ. ἐκ φορτίδων νεῶν καὶ μακρῶν *combining the features* of.., App.*BC*5.95: ὁ ἐ. (sc. ὄχλος) Lxx *Nu*.11.4. 3. in Metric, of metres in which different feet are combined, Heph.9.1, cf. Sch.adloc. 4. *sociable, gregarious*, Timo 47. 5. Adv. –τως *in combination*, Paul.Aeg.3.48.

ἐπιμείλια, v. μείλια.

ἐπιμειλίσσομαι, *placate*, τινὰ δώροις J.*BJ*1.20.3:—Act., aor. 1 inf. ἐπιμειλίξαι, prob. for ἐπιμελύξαι· δοῦναι, Hsch.

ἐπιμειξία, Ion. **–ίη,** ἡ, *mixing with* others, *intercourse, dealings*, ἐούσης ἐπιμειξίης πρὸς τοὺς Τεγεήτας Hdt.1.68; ἐπιμειξίᾳ χρῆσθαι πρός.. X.*HG*5.1.1; ἐπιμειξίας οὔσης παρ' ἀλλήλους Th.5.78; ἐπιμειξίαι ἦσαν τοῖς Ἀθηναίοις καὶ Πελοποννησίοις ib.35; ἡ πόλεων ἐ. πόλεσιν Pl.*Lg*.949e; κατὰ τὰς ἐπιμειξίας τὰς τοῖς πολλοῖς Phld.*Ir*.p.73 W.; κατ' ἐπιμειξίαν τοῖς ἄλλοις *in common with*.., opp. ἰδίᾳ, D.L.10.2; of sexual *intercourse*, Vett.Val.48.19 (pl.). 2. *mixture, combination* of elements, Id.162.20, Aret.*SD*2.1, Gal.6.587.

ἐπίμειξις, εως, ἡ, = foreg., Thgn.297, Babr.12.23: pl., Chor. in *Rev.Phil*.1.73. (ἐπιμιξ– codd.)

ἐπιμείρομαι, *to be assigned by fate*, Vett.Val.346.6.

ἐπιμελαίνομαι, *to become black on the surface*, a symptom of mortification, Hp.*Fract*.35; of the tongue, Id.*Morb*.3.6. II. of fruit, *blacken in ripening*, Thphr.*HP*3.15.6.

ἐπιμέλᾱς, αινα, ᾰν, *blackish*, Thphr.*HP*3.8.7, 6.5.3, etc.

ἐπιμελεδαίνω, *attend to*, –ομένη δὲ ὑγιαίνει Hp.*Mul*.1.9 (vv. ll. –μελαινομένη, –μελομένη).

ἐπιμέλ-εια, ἡ, written –εα *IG*2^{2}.483.24 (iv B. C.), Aeol. gen. –ηΐας ib.12(2).243 (Mytilene); Ion. gen. –λίης Ps.-Hdt.*Vit.Hom*.5 (s. v. l.):—*care bestowed upon* a thing, *attention paid* to it, and abs., *attention, diligence*, Prose word, once in Hdt. (v. infr.), freq. in Th., X., etc.: in pl., *pains*, X.*Cyr*.1.6.4, etc.: c. gen. objecti, ἐ. τοῦ ναυτικοῦ, οἰκείων καὶ πολιτικῶν, Th.2.39, 40; τῶν ἔργων Id.3.46; τῶν πραγμάτων And.2.13; τῶν κοινῶν Isoc.7.25; τῶν καμνόντων Pl.*Lg*.720d (hence, of medical *treatment*, S.E.*P*.2.240); πλήθους γεννημάτων Pl.*Lg*.740d; also περί τινος τὴν ἐ. ποιεῖσθαι Th.7.56; περὶ τοὺς νέους Lycurg.106; πρὸς τοὺς θεούς, πρὸς τὴν πόλιν, D.22.78, Pl.*Lg*.754b; εἰς τὰ ἀναγκαῖα Posidon.8 J.; ἐπιμέλειάν τινος ποιεῖσθαι, ἔχειν, Hdt.6.105, Th.6.41, Arist.*Pol*.1330^{b}11, D.61.43, cf. Pl.*R*.451d; opp. ἐπιμελείας τυγχάνειν to have *attention paid* to one, Isoc.6.154, cf. *POxy*.58.22 (iii A. D.), etc.; ἐ. παρὰ τοῦ δαιμονίου Hyp.*Epit*.43; δι' ἐπιμελείας ἔχειν τινά Is.7.14; ἐπιμελείᾳ, κατ' ἐπιμέλειαν, *with diligence*, X.*Cyr*.5.3.47, *HG*4.4.8; δι' ἐπιμελείας θεοῦ ἡ ἀτυχία γίγνεται Antipho 3.3.8; μετὰ πάσης ἐ. X.Eph.2.10. 2. *a commission* or *charge*, Aeschin.3.13, Arist.*Pol*.1299^{a}20 (pl.); ἡ περὶ τοὺς θεοὺς ἐ. ib.1322^{b}18, cf. ib.30 (pl.); ἡ τῶν ἐφήβων ἐ., a special office at Athens, Din.3.15; so πρὸς τῇ ἐ. τῶν χρηματιστῶν, = ἐπιμελητὴς τῶν χρ., *POxy*.281.2 (i A. D.). 3. *any employment* or *pursuit*, interpol. in X.*Cyr*.1.6.13, etc.: pl., ἐ. καὶ σπουδαί *pursuits* which demand zeal, Arist.*Rh*.1370^{a}11, cf. *EN*1138^{b}26. **–έομαι,** also **–μέλομαι** Hdt.1.98, 2.2, 174, al., Th.6.54 (v. l. in 7.39), Lys.7.25 (cod. M), Pl.*Grg*.516b, *PEleph*.13.7 (iii B. C.), *PCair.Zen*.44.17 (iii B. C.), etc.; the contr. form prevails in codd., e. g. Ar.*Pl*.1117, X.*An*.5.7.10, Pl.*Mx*.248e, and in Att. Inscrr. from 380 B. C. (older Att. spellings are ambiguous), and is required by the metre in E.*Ph*.556: fut. ἐπιμελήσομαι Hdt.5.29, Th.3.25, etc.; –μεληθήσομαι v.l. in X.*Mem*.2.7.8, Aeschin.3.27 (Dor. 3 sg. –θησεῖ *IG*12(3).170.25 (Astypalaea), pl. –θησεῦντι ib.12(1).694 (Rhodes)): aor. ἐπεμελήθην Hdt.8.109, Th.8.68, Isoc.4.38, X.*Mem*.1.3.11, etc. (ἐπεμελησάμην only late, *IGRom*.4.684.14 (i A. D.), *SIG*875 (ii A. D.), Gal.*Protr*.9): pf. ἐπιμεμέλημαι Th.6.41: Act. only in *SIG*1044.31 (Halic.):—*take care of, have charge* or *management of*, rare in Poets, as E.*Ph*.556, freq. in Prose: c. gen. objecti, Hdt.1.98, 5.29, Ar.*V*.154, *Pl*.1117, Th.3.25, Isoc.4.38, Pl.*R*.331d, etc.; περί τινος X.*An*.5.7.10; [ὑπὲρ] τῆς στρατηγίας Id.*Cyr*.1.6.12; περί τινα Pl.*Mx*.248e: later, c. dat., παιδίῳ *POxy*.744.6 (i B. C.), cf. *PTeb*.58.62 (ii B. C.): c. acc. et inf., *take care that*.., Th.6.54: c. gen. et inf., X.*Oec*.20.9: folld. by ὅπως with ind. fut. or subj. aor., Foed.ap.Th.4.118, X.*Mem*.2.10.2, etc.: with opt. after an aor., Id.*HG*6.5.37; by ὅπως c. inf., Id.*Cyr*.4.2.37 (s. v. l.); by ὡς with opt. (after past tenses), Id.*An*.1.1.5, etc.; also ἐ. τινὸς ὅπως ἔσται Pl.*Euthphr*.2d; by ἵνα c. subj., *Inscr.Prien*.44.35 (ii B. C.): with neut. Adj. in acc., *take care with respect to* a thing, Th.6.41: c. acc. et dat., τὰ ἄλλα τοῖς πολεμάρχοις X.*HG*5.4.4, cf. *IG*2^{2}.233.20 (in E.*Ph*.556 the acc. belongs to ἔχοντες): c. acc. cogn., ἐ. πᾶσαν ἐπιμέλειαν Pl.*Prt*.325c, cf. *IG*2^{2}.1261.5: abs., *give heed, attend*, Hdt.2.2. 2. of public commissions, *have charge of, be inspector* or *curator of*, τῶν μοριῶν ἐλαῶν Lys.7.29; τῶν δεκαδέων X.*Cyr*.8.1.14; δρόμου Id.*An*.4.8.25; ὁδῶν (of the Roman *cura viarum*) *CIG*4011 (Ancyra): c. acc. cogn., Pl.*Lg*.812e:—in Att. Inscrr., ἐπιμεληθῆναι (inf. = imper.) is usual of a definite commission, ποιήσεως *IG*2^{2}.555, etc. (so –ηθέντων ib.1^{2}.70); ἐπιμελεῖσθαι, of matters requiring permanent attention, ib.1^{2}.56, etc. 3. *to be engaged in, cultivate* any pursuit, art, etc., δυοῖν τέχναιν D.27.31; τῆς ἀρετῆς X.*Cyr*.7.5.71, cf. *Mem*.4.5.10. **–ημα,** ατος, τό, *care, business*, in pl., Id.*Oec*.4.4, 7.22, 37. **–ής,** ές, *careful* or *anxious about*, ἀγαθῶν Pl.*Smp*.197d; τῶν φιλῶν X.*Mem*.2.6.35, etc.; also ἐ. περὶ τὰ αὑτῶν ἔργα ib.3.4.9. 2. abs., *careful, attentive*, Ar.*Nu*.501, X.*Mem*.2.6.38, etc.: Comp. –εστέρα ψυχή S.*Fr*.472, cf. X.*An*.3.2.30: Sup., Isoc.4.142; –εστέραν ἔχειν ἑτέρου θεραπείαν Men.223.9. Adv. –λῶς *carefully*, X.*Mem*.2.4.2, Pl.*Ti*.88c, Men.*Pk*.32, etc.; Ion. –λέως Hp.*Art*.55; Cret. –λίως *SIG*685.118 (Itanos): Comp. –έστερον X.*Mem*.3.5.14; –έστερα *SIG*785.9; –εστέρως Ath.14.629b: Sup. –έστατα Pl.*Alc*.1.104d. II. Pass., *cared for, an object of care*, οἷ τοῦτ' ἦν ἐπιμελές Hdt.3.40; οἷς ἁγνεῖαι.. ἐπιμελεῖς Pl.*Lg*.909e; τὸ ἐ. τοῦ δρωμένου *the charge* of the execution of orders, Th.5.66: mostly in neut. ἐπιμελές, c. dat. pers., Κύρῳ ἐπιμελὲς ἐγένετο τὰ Κροῖσος εἶπε made him *anxious*, Hdt.1.89, cf. 5.12, 7.37; ἐ. μοι ἦν it was my *business*, Id.2.150: c. inf., οὐδενὶ ἐ. ἦν σκοπεῖν it was no one's *business* to see, Antipho 2.4.6; οἷς ἐ. εἴη εἰδέναι who made it their *business* to know, Th.1.5, cf. D.18.249; ἐ. πεποίημαι εἰδέναι Pl.*Smp*.172c; τοῖς ἄρχουσιν ἐ. ἔστω μή.. Id.*Lg*.932d: c. dat. et gen., οἷς τούτων ἐ. ib.763e, cf. 824; δεῖ περὶ ἀρετῆς ἐ. εἶναι τῇ πόλει Arist.*Pol*.1280^{b}7. 2. *suitable*, τόπος *POxy*.1412.11 (iii A. D.). **–ησις,** εως, ἡ, *further precaution*, Gal.19.108. **–ητεία,** ἡ, *office of* ἐπιμελητής, *IG*2^{2}.1338.30 (pl., i B. C., –ειτ– lap.); *term of such office*, *SIG*825 *A* 5 (Delph., ii A. D.). **–ητέον,** *one must take care of, pay attention*, ἐ. ὅπως... Pl.*R*.618c; τινός X.*Mem*.2.1.28; περί τι Arist.*Pol*.1334^{b}31. **–ητεύω,** *to be an* ἐπιμελητής, *PTeb*.61(*b*).71 (ii B. C.), *IG*3.393, *SIG*829 *A* 7 (Delph., ii A. D.), 855.6 (Ceos, ii A. D.), etc. **–ητής,**

οῦ, ὁ, *one who has charge of* a thing, *manager, curator*, τῶν τῆς πόλεως πραγμάτων Ar.*Pl.*907; ὄνων καὶ ἵππων Pl.*Grg.*516a; τῶν εἰς τὴν δίαιταν ἐπιτηδείων X.*Cyr.*8.1.9; also ὁ περὶ τῆς παιδείας ἐ. Pl.*Lg.*951e: abs., φύλαξ καὶ ἐ. X.*Mem.*2.7.14; of a bailiff, Theoc.10.54; of a governor, X.*HG*3.2.11; τῆς Τριφυλίας Plb.4.80.15, cf. Plu.*Alex.*35; Δήλου *SIG*^{2} 508 (Delos, ii B.C.), etc.; in Salamis, *IG*2^2.1008.77, etc. **2.** *military commander*, τῆς οὐραγίας Plb.3.79.4. **II.** as an official title, *curator*, **1.** of sacred matters, Lys.7.29; τῶν περὶ τὰ ἱερά Arist.*Pol.* 1322^{b}19; μυστηρίων D.21.171, *IG*2^2.1672.246, etc.; of the Dionysia, D.21.15; [τῆς πομπῆς] Arist.*Ath.*56.4, *IG*2^2.668; of the shrine of Amphiaraus at Oropus, ib.7.4255.32. **2.** financial officers at Athens, ib.1^2.65.46; of the Eleven, ἐ. τῶν κακούργων Antipho 5.17. **3.** of the *chiefs* of the φυλαί or Tribes, D.21.13, *IG*2^2.1139, etc.; ἐ. τῆς συμμορίας D.47.22. **4.** τῶν νεωρίων Id.22.63, *IG*2^2.1629.179; ἐ. ἐμπορίου *clerk* of the market, Din.2.10; ἐ. ἐπὶ τὸν λιμένα harbour-*master*, *IG*2^2.1012.19; *inspector* of weights and measures, ib.2^2.1013.47; *curator* of the gymnasia, ib.2^2.1077.12; of the πρυτανεῖον, ib.3.90; κρηνῶν Arist.*Pol.*1321^{b}26, *Ath.*43.1; ἐ. ὁδοῦ Ἀππίας, = Lat. *curator viae Appiae*, *CIG*4029 (Ancyra, ii A.D.); πυλῶν τε καὶ τειχῶν φυλακῆς Arist.*Pol.*1322^{a}36, cf. *SIG*707.18 (ii B.C.); τῶν ξένων *IG*12(1).49.50 (Rhodes, ii B.C.). **5.** title of a magistrate at Epidaurus, Ἀρχ.Ἐφ.1918.117 (ii B.C.), cf. *IG*4.490 (Cleonae), 4.840, 841 (Calauria), 4.2 (Aegina). **6.** *financial officer* in Egypt, *Arch.Pap.* 2.83 (iii B.C.), *PAmh.*2.33.7 (ii B.C.), etc. **7.** *deputy* of an Emperor holding honorary local office, *SIG*872 (Eleusis, ii A.D.). **–ητικός**, ή, όν, *able to take charge, managing*, X.*Oec.*12.19; ἡ –κή (sc. τέχνη), = ἐπιμέλεια, Pl.*Plt.*275e sq.; αἴσθησις ἐ. τῶν τέκνων Arist.*GA*753^{a}8; τὸ τοῦ ἰδίου σώματος ἐ. M.Ant.1.16. **–ήτρια**, ἡ, fem. of ἐπιμελητής, Hsch. s.v. κομίστρια. **–ία**, v. ἐπιμέλεια. **–ομαι**, v. ἐπιμελέομαι.

ἐπιμέλπω, *sing to*, Ἀΐδα παιᾶνα A.*Th.*870 (anap.).

ἐπιμελῳδ-έω, *sing over* or *at* a person, τοιαῦτα Aristid.*Or.*29(40).30. **–ημα**, ατος, τό, *refrain*, Sch.Theoc.1.64.

ἐπιμέμβλεται, late Ep. redupl. form, = *ἐπιμέλει, σοὶ οὐ Τρώων ἐ. thou *carest* not *for* the Trojans, Q.S.3.123; cf. μέμβλεται.

ἐπιμεμιγμένως, gloss on ἐπιμίξ, Apollon.*Lex.*

ἐπιμέμονα, poet. pf. 2 with pres. sense, *desire* (sc. πορεύεσθαι), S. *Ph.*515 (lyr.); cf. μέμονα.

ἐπιμεμπτ-έον, *one must condemn*, Sor.1.28. **–ος**, ον, = sq., of persons or actions, Ph.1.260, Ptol.*Tetr.*157, A.D.*Pron.*86.2, Doroth. ap.Heph.Astr.3.30, App.*BC*2.148, al. **2.** *blaming*, Sch.S.*Tr.*446. Adv. –τως Arg.Aeschin.3.

ἐπιμεμφής, ές, = ἐπίμομφος II, Nic.*Fr.*74.15, *AP*6.260 (Gem.), Sext.*Sent.*610.

ἐπιμέμφομαι, *cast blame upon*, c. dat. pers., ἦ τι κασιγνήτοις ἐπιμέμφεαι Od.16.97, etc.: c. gen. rei, *find fault for* or *because of* a thing, *complain of* it, εὐχωλῆς ἐπιμέμφεται *complains of* a vow [neglected], Il.1.65, cf. 2.225; ἕνεκ' ἀρητῆρος 1.94; ἐ. τινί τινος *blame* one *for* a thing, Luc.*DMort.*27.2; rarely ἐ. τινά τινος, ὧν ἐπιμεμφομένα σε S. *Tr.*122 (lyr.): c. acc., *blame*, νῆσον Call.*Del.*163; γηραλέην χεῖρα *AP*6.83 (Maced.); *find fault, complain*, μηδὲν ἐ. Hdt.1.116, etc.; ἐ. ὅτι... Hp.*Aër.*22. **b.** c. inf., *to be unwilling*, Hld.1.9. **2.** c. acc. rei, *impute as matter of blame*, τὰ Κροῖσος ἐπιμεμφόμενος τῷ Κύρῳ Hdt. 1.75, cf. 2.161, etc.

ἐπίμεμψις, εως, ἡ, = ἐπιμομφή, ἐπίμεμψιν φέρειν D.H.3.11.

ἐπιμενετέον, *one must persist in*, c. dat., Archig.ap.Aët.9.35:— more freq. **–ητέον**, Philum.ib.8.84, Herod.Med.in*Rh.Mus.*58.89, Aët.16.107(97).

Ἐπιμενίδειος σκίλλη *Bath asparagus, Ornithogalum pyrenaicum*, Thphr.*HP*7.12.1, cf. Plin.*HN*19.93; called Ἐ. φάρμακον 'iron ration' in Ph.*Bel.*88.29 (ἐπιμο[νι]δίου codd.).

ἐπιμένω, *stay on, tarry*, abs., Il.19.142, Od.17.277; ἐπιμεῖναι ἐς αὔριον 11.351; ἄγε νῦν ἐπίμεινον, Ἀρήϊα τεύχεα δύω do you *wait*, and I will put on my armour, Il.6.340; also ἐ. ἐνὶ μεγάροισιν... ὄφρα.. Od. 4.587; ἐ. ἵνα.. *h.Cer.*160, Ar.*Nu.*196; so ἐ. ἔς τε.. X.*An.*5.5.2: after Hom., *remain in* a place, ἐ. ἐν τῇ πόλει And.1.75, etc.; ἐπὶ τῇ στρατιᾷ X.*An.*7.2.1. **2.** abs., *remain in place, continue as they are*, of things, Th.4.4, Pl.*Phd.*80c, X.*Cyn.*6.4; *keep one's seat*, of a horseman, Id.*Cyr.*1.4.8; *stay behind* in a place, Str.10.2.24. **3.** *continue* in a pursuit, ἐπὶ τῇ ζητήσει, ἐπὶ λόγῳ, Pl.*La.*194a, *Tht.*179e; ἐπὶ τοῖς δοξαζομένοις Id.*R.*490b; ἐπὶ τοῦ κακουργήματος D.24.86; ἐπὶ τῆς πολιορκίας Plb.1.77.1: c. dat., *persist in*, τῇ ἀπονοίᾳ *PTeb.*424.4 (iii A.D.); *continue* treatment, ἐ. βοηθήματι Herod.Med. in *Rh.Mus.*58.83; *cleave to*, μιᾷ γυναικί *PSI*3.158.26 (iii A.D.): also c. part., ἐ. ἐπὶ τῶν ἵππων ὀρθὸς ἑστηκώς Pl.*Men.*93d, cf. *Ev.Jo.*8.7; *spend time over*, ὑποδείγμασι A.D.*Synt.*166.14. **4.** *abide by*, ταῖς σπονδαῖς dub. l. in X.*HG*3.4.6. **5.** *endure*, τοῖς συμβεβηκόσι Sor.1.3. **II.** c. acc., *await, be in store for*, τινά E.*Supp.*624 (lyr.), v.l. in Id.*Ph.*223 (lyr.), cf. Pl.*R.* 361d: c. aor. inf., ἐ. τι τελεσθῆναι Th.3.2; μὴ 'πιμεῖναι τοὐμὸν ὀξῦναι στόμα not *to wait* so as to.., S.*Tr.*1176: c. fut. inf., Th.3.26.

ἐπιμερ-ής, ές, *superpartient*, of numbers of the form $1+\frac{2}{x}$, $1+\frac{3}{x}$, etc., Theo Sm.p.76 H., Nicom.*Ar.*1.17, al.; cf. ἐπιμόριος. **–ίζω**, *impart, give a portion*, v.l. in Lxx *Jb.*31.2, 39.17. **b.** Astrol., *assign* a number of years to life, Vett.Val.164.9. **2.** *distribute*, τινὰς τοῖς φράτραις D.H.2.50; esp. in Gramm., πρόσωπα A.D.*Synt.*92.21; ἐπιμεριζόμενον ὄνομα *distributive*, D.T.637.15; also γενικὴ –ομένη *partitive* genitive, A.D.*Synt.*35.1:—Pass., *to be distributed*, εἰς πλείονας ἡμέρας Sor.1.21. **3.** *mention severally, enumerate*, Str.13.1.10, Hdn.*Epim.*157. **–ισις**, εως, ἡ, *distribution*, *Gloss.* **–ισμός**, ὁ, *distribution*, Hsch. s.v. ἐπινέμησις; esp. in Gramm., προσώπων A.D. *Synt.*96.1; ἐθνικῶν ib.192.10: abs., *division* of a sentence into words (μέρη λόγου), *parsing*, ib.340.17. **b.** Astrol., *assignment*, Vett.Val. 97.9, Critodem. in *Cat.Cod.Astr.*8(3).102.4. **2.** ἐ. τῶν ἀπόρων *allocation of irrecoverable contributions* to wealthier taxpayers, *PFay.*53.5 (ii A.D.), cf. *PAmh.*2.96.8 (pl., iii A.D.), etc. **3.** as title of gramm. works: ἐπιμερισμοὶ τῆς Α Ἰλιάδος *parsings* of words in Il.1, *An.Par.* 3.294; ἐ. Ὁμήρου κατὰ ἀλφάβητον *parsings* arranged alphabetically, *An.Ox.*1.1; but ἐ. κατὰ ἀλφ. τοῦ Ἡρωδιανοῦ alphabetical *arrangements* of (not 'by') Herodian, title of a spelling-list, Hdn.*Epim.*1, 157; later still ἐ. τῶν ἐννέα μέτρων *analysis, digest*, Trichas in Heph. p.365C.; the nature of the lost Ἐπιμερισμοί of Hdn. (*EM*779.27, Sch. Il.4.66) is conjectural. **–ιστής**, οῦ, ὁ, *distributor*, *Gloss.* **–ος**· μοιχεύεται, Hsch. **–ότης**, ητος, ἡ, *the quality of being* ἐπιμερής, Iamb.*in Nic.*pp.44, 70 P.

ἐπίμεσος, ον, *middle*, ἡλικία *AB*108; ῥῆμα ἐ. a *middle* verb, *Gloss.*

ἐπιμεσουράνημα [ᾰν], ατος, τό, *culmination* of a star just after sunrise or just after sunset, Ptol.*Alm.*8.4.

ἐπιμεσόω, *to be at the middle*, ἐπιμεσούσης τῆς ἡμέρας dub. l. in Lxx *Je.*15.9.

ἐπίμεστος, ον, *filled up, in full measure*, δωσεῖ πάντ' ἐπίμεστα Call. *Cer.*134, Poll.4.170: neut. pl. as Adv., Pherecr.190, Phryn.*PS* p.70 B.

ἐπιμεταλλάσσω, *die subsequently*, *POxy.*265.30 (i A.D.), etc.

ἐπιμετα-πέμπομαι, *send for a reinforcement*, Th.6.21, 7.7. **–φέρω**, *undergo a change*, J.*AJ*19.1.2.

ἐπιμετρ-έω, *measure out to*, οὐκ ἐπιδώσω οὐδ' ἐπιμετρήσω Hes.*Op.* 397:—Pass., ὁ ἐπιμετρεόμενος σῖτος the corn *paid by measure* to the Persians, Hdt.3.91. **II.** *add to the measure, give over and above*, ἐ. ὀβολὸν τοῖς ναύταις Plu.*Lys.*4, cf. *Alex.*42; ἄλλα τοσαῦτα [ἔτη] Luc.*DMort.*5.1; ἐ. στρατηγίας χρόνον *prolong* one's magistracy, Plu. *Comp.Ages.Pomp.*3, etc.; *add*, in speaking, πολλά Plb.28.17.2, etc.: c. gen. partit., ἐ. σκωμμάτων *add* some jests, Luc.*Nav.*19; ἐ. τινί *add to* it, ib.18, Plb.3.118.6: abs., 'add insult to injury', Id.5.15.8; so τὸ ἐπιμετροῦν τῆς ἀπεχθείας Id.12.15.12. **III.** ἐ. τὸν οὐρανόν *measure* it, v.l. in Luc.*Icar.*6. **2.** *reduce to measure* or *order*, τὸν ἀνθρώπινον βίον Hierocl.*in CA*20p.462M. **IV.** intr., ὁ ἐπιμετρῶν λόγος, *of superfluous* additions, Plb.7.7.7, al. **–ησις**, εως, ἡ, *means of measuring*, τοῦ μᾶλλον καὶ ἧττον Dam.*Pr.*50. **–ίδα**· τὸ ἐπίμετρον, ὃ προσάπτεται τῷ χιτῶνι, Hsch. **–ον**, τό, *something added to make good measure, excess*, Theoc.12.26, *PTeb.*91.11 (ii B.C.); ἐ. ποιεῖν make *an increase*, Thphr.*CP*4.13.7, Plu.2.676b; πολὺ ποιεῖ τοῦ ψεύδους ἐ. ib.503d; λόγον ἐν ἐπιμέτρῳ διατίθενται *into the bargain*, Plb.6.46. 6; ἐξ ἐπιμέτρου λέγειν S.E.*P.*2.47, cf. Gal.8.493.

ἐπιμήδιον, τό, an unidentified plant, Dsc.4.19, etc.

ἐπιμήδομαι, *imagine* or *contrive* a thing *against* one, δόλον δ' ἐπεμήδετο πατρί Od.4.437, cf. Q.S.14.479.

ἐπιμήθ-εια, ἡ, *second thoughts, afterthoughts*, opp. προμήθεια, Corn. *ND*18. **–εύομαι**, *think of afterwards* or *too late*, Eust.67.27:— also **–έομαι** Corn.*ND*18.

Ἐπιμηθεύς, έως, ὁ, *Epimetheus, Afterthought*, brother of *Prometheus, Forethought*, Hes.*Op.*85, Pl.*Prt.*320d; Ἐ. ἁμαρτίνοος Hes. *Th.*511; ὀψίνοος Pi.*P.*5.27; τὸ μεταβουλεύεσθαι Ἐπιμηθέως ἔργον, οὐ Προμηθέως Luc.*Prom.Es*7.

ἐπιμηθής, ές, *thoughtful*, Theoc.25.79. Adv. –θέως *carefully*, Herod.3.94.

ἐπιμήκης, ες, *longish, oblong*, Democr.164, Plb.1.22.6, *Placit.*4.19. 3. **2.** *long*, μάχαιραι, ταινία, App.*Syr.*32, *Pun.*95, cf. Arist.*Mu.* 393^{b}5, Bito 52.3, v.l. in Hdt.7.36: Comp. –έστερος Dsc.1.7, Luc. *DDeor.*10.1; *far-stretching, extensive*, τόπος Lxx *Ba.*3.24; ἐ. ἐξ... ἐπί ... *extending* from...to..., App.*Ill.*22; also of Time, Vett.Val.344.5: Sup. –έστατος Hdn.8.1.5; irreg. ἐπιμηκιστος dub. in Ph.1.291.

ἐπιμηκύνω, *lengthen, prolong*, μάχην Paus.4.10.4.

ἐπιμηλάδες αἶγες she-goats *of the flock*, Call.*Ap.*51 codd.

Ἐπιμηλίδες Νύμφαι, αἱ, (μῆλα) *protectors of sheep* or *flocks*, Ant. Lib.31.5, Longus 2.39, Alciphr.3.11, Nonn.*D.*14.210, Epic. in *Arch. Pap.*7 p.7: **Ἐπιμηλιάδες** in Paus.8.4.2.

ἐπιμήλιος, ὁ, *guardian of flocks*, epith. of Apollo at Camirus, Macrob.1.17.45; of Hermes at Coronea, Paus.9.34.3.

ἐπιμηλίς, ίδος, ἡ, (μῆλον) *a kind of medlar, mespilus germanica*, Dsc. 1.118; or *pear*, Pamphil.ap.Ath.3.82d, cf. Hsch. **II.** = πόρπη, Id.

ἐπιμηνάω, 3 pl. pf. –μεμηνάκαντι, = ἐπιμεμενήκασι, they *have been content to wait*, *Schwyzer*91.11 (Argos, iii B.C.).

ἐπιμηνίδιον, τό, *monthly allowance*, *PGiss.*16.3 (ii A.D.), *PMich.* in *Class.Phil.*22.250 (pl., ii A.D.), *POxy.*1070.45 (pl., iii A.D.).

ἐπιμηνι-εία, ἡ, *the office of* ἐπιμήνιος, *Test.Epict.*4.31, *SIG*241.121 (Delph., iv B.C.). **–εύω**, *hold the office of* ἐπιμήνιος, ib.241.90 (ibid.), 495.180 (Olbia, iii B.C.), *BCH*17.555 (Lampsacus), *Test.Epict.* 4.15, 35, etc.; τῆς ἐκκλησίας *hold monthly chairmanship*, *SIG*708.2 (Istropolis). **–η**, Ion., = ἐπιμηνιεία, ib.58.11 (Milet., v B.C.). **–ος**, ον, *monthly*, χρεῶν –ίων τόκοι Hondius *Novae Inscriptiones Atticae* 91; *holding office for a month*, πολέμαρχος, προμνήμων, at Chios, *SIG*402.1, 443.1, 2 (iii B.C.); ἐπιμήνιοι, οἱ, *monthly officers*, ib.58.5 (Milet., v B.C.), *OGI*229.30 (Smyrna, iii B.C.): sg., *IG*12(2).645b38 (Nesos); ἐ. τῶν ταμιῶν *SIG*426.27 (Bargylia, iii B.C.). **2.** *priests who offered the* ἐπιμήνια, Hsch.; ἐπιμηνίους.. οἵτινες ἐχθυσεῦνται τὰ ἱερὰ μετὰ τοῦ ἱερέως *SIG*1106.63 (Cos), cf. 1044.24 (Halic.), *Test.Epict.*2.33. **II.** ἐπιμήνια, τά, **1.** (sc. ἱερά) *monthly offerings*, Hdt.8.41, Inscr.ap.Ath. 6.234e. **2.** *provisions, monthly ration*, *POxy.*531.17 (ii A.D.), etc.; also ἐ. ὀψώνια *PLond.*2.190.16 (iii A.D.); ὁ ἐ. σῖτος Plu.*Flam.*5; ὁ λόγος ὁ ἐ. the *monthly* account, *SIG*578.54 (Teos, ii B.C.). b. simply, *provisions*, for a ship, Plb.31.12.13, Sor.1.19. 3. *monthly courses of women*, Hp.*Nat.Mul.*13, Sor.1.19 (sg.); ἐπιμήνιον (sc. αἷμα), τό, Dsc.2.79; κάθαρσις ἐπιμηνίων Aret.*SA*1.9.

ἐπιμηνίω, *to be angry with*, Πριάμῳ ἐπεμήνιε δίῳ Il.13.460, cf. App. *BC*3.55; τινὶ τῶν γεγονότων Id.*Mith.*55.

ἐπιμηνῦτής, οῦ, ὁ, = μηνυτής, τοῦ ἔργου Arr.*An.*3.26.2.

ἐπιμηρύομαι, *wind* a layer of gut *on top of* others, Ph.*Bel.*65.43.

ἐπιμητιάω, Ep. part. -όωσα, *consider how* to do, c. inf., A.R.3.668.

ἐπιμηχᾰν-άομαι, *devise plans against, take precautions*, Hdt.1.94, 6.91; πᾶν Phld.*Ir.*p.30 W.; δεινόν τινι Luc.*DDeor.*3.1, cf. Q.S.14.427. II. *devise besides*, ἄλλα ἀεὶ καινὰ ἐ. X.*Cyr.*8.8.16; σιτία πονηρά τισι D.Chr.6.11, cf. App.*BC*4.120. **-ημα**, Dor. **-μᾱχάνᾱμα**, ατος, τό, *a means towards* a thing, Hippod.ap.Stob.4.1.94. **-ησις**, εως, ἡ, *device, contrivance*, ἐξ -ήσεως *on purpose, artificially*, Chrysipp. *Stoic.*2.153. **-ητέον**, *one must devise besides*, Herod.Med. in *Rh. Mus.*58.105, Gal.14.169. **-ος**, ον, *craftily devising*, κακῶν ἐπιμήχανε ἔργων *contriver* of ill deeds, Orac.ap.Hdt.6.19.

ἐπιμῐγή, ἡ, *intermixture*, S.E.*P.*1.124 (pl.).

ἐπιμίγνυμι, ἐπίμικτος, late spellings of ἐπιμείγνυμι, etc. (qq. v.).

ἐπιμῑμέομαι, *imitate further*, Thphr.*Metaph.*33.

ἐπιμιμνήσκομαι, fut. -μνήσομαι Hdt.1.5, etc., rarely -μνησθήσομαι (Hdt.2.3, D.19.276): aor. -εμνήσθην Od.1.31, Hdt.1.85, etc., -εμνησάμην Il.17.103, A.*Ch.*623 (lyr.), etc.: pf. ἐπιμέμνημαι, late -μέμνησμαι *POxy.*791 (i A.D.):—*bethink oneself of, remember, think of*, c. gen., ἐπὶ δὲ μνήσασθε ἕκαστος παίδων Il.15.662; κ᾽.. ἐπιμνησαίμεθα χάρμης we would *think of* battle, 17.103; τοῦ ὅ γ᾽ ἐπιμνησθεὶς Od.1.31, 4.189 (the only parts of the Verb used by Hom.). 2. *make mention of*, ἐπιμνησαίμεθα σεῖο ib.191, cf. Hdt.1.5, 85, A.*Ch.* l. c., S.*Ph.*1400, etc.; οὗ δ᾽ ἐπεμνήσθην 'but, by the way', Herod.5.53, cf. 6.42; also ἐ. περί τινος Hdt.2.101, X.*Cyr.*1.6.12, Pl.*Mx.*239c, etc.: with neut. pron. in acc., τοσαῦτα ἐπιμνησθέντες Hdt.1.14, cf. 2.3; with gen. and acc., τῆς μάχης τε πολλὰ ἐπιμεμνημένοι καὶ τὴν Λῆμνον αἵρεσιν Id.6.136; also ἐ. ὅτι.. X.*HG*3.2.8; ἐ. περὶ γυναικῶν, ὡς.. Pl.*Ti.*18c.

ἐπιμίμνω, poet. for ἐπιμένω, *abide* or *continue in*, [ἔργῳ] Od.14.66, 15.372.

ἐπιμίξ, Ep. Adv. *mixedly, confusedly, pell-mell*, ἐ. ἵπποι τε καὶ αὐτοί Il.11.525, cf. 21.16; ἐ. δέ τε μαίνεται Ἄρης Ares rages *without respect of persons*, Od.11.537; ἐ. κτείνονται Il.14.60: in later Prose, Lxx *Wi.*14.25.

ἐπι-μιξία, -μιξις, v. ἐπι-μειξία, -μειξις.

ἐπιμίσγω, older poet. and Ion. form (found also in *PRev.Laws* 28.17 (iii B.C.)) of ἐπιμείγνυμι, intr., *have intercourse*, παρ᾽ ἀλλήλους Th. 1.13. II. mostly Pass., in Il. always in hostile sense, αἰεὶ μὲν Τρώεσσ᾽ ἐπιμίσγομαι I *have* always *to be dealing with* the Trojans, *am* always *clashing with* them, Il.10.548; ἂψ -ομένων *as the fight was joined* again, 5.505; in Od. of peaceful relations, commerce, etc., οὐδέ τις ἄμμι βροτῶν ἐπιμίσγεται ἄλλος Od.6.205, cf. 241; so in Prose, *have dealings with*, Αἰγύπτῳ, τῇ Ἑλλάδι, Hdt.2.104, cf. 151; ἀλλήλοις X.*Ath.*2.7; πρὸς ἀλλήλους Arist.*Pol.*1327ᵃ39; ἐ. ἐς τὴν ξυμμαχίαν πρός τινας Foed.ap.Th.4.118: abs., Hdt.1.185; ἐ. μηδετέρωσε Foed.ap.Th. l. c.; of sexual *intercourse*, Vett.Val.75.13. 2. of Place, οὐδέ ποτ᾽ ἐς βουλὴν ἐπιμίσγεται οὐδ᾽ ἐπὶ δαῖτας Hes.*Th.*802: later c. acc. loci, *draw nigh to* a place, Call.*Jov.*13. III. Med., *cross*, in breeding, Ἀρκάδας Ἠλείοις Opp.*C.*1.395.

ἐπιμίσθ-ιος, ον, *engaged for hire*, χρηματισμός Dam.ap.Suid. s. v. Σεβηριανός, cf. Hsch. s. v. ἐπάρουρος (ἔπταμ- cod.):—pecul. fem. **ἐπιμισθίς**, ίδος, ἑταῖραι *AP*7.403 (Marc. Arg.). **-όω**, *contract for*, in Pass. of bricks, *Michel*1512 (Piraeus, iv B.C.), cf. *IG*12(9).189.30 (Eretria), 11.165.36, 199*A*106 (Delos, iii B.C.), *PPetr.*3 p.109 (iii B.C.); v. l. in Ael.*VH*3.14.

ἐπιμνημονεύω, *bear in mind*, *POxy.*264.5 (i A.D.).

ἐπί-μνησις, εως, ἡ, *recollection*, Aristeas 154, *EM*357.57. 2. *mention*, Aristeas 31, Orph.*Fr.*49.17. **-μνηστέον**, *one must mention*, Pl.*Ti.*90e.

ἐπιμοιρ-άομαι, *receive by lot, receive as one's share*, c. acc., ἐ. κόνιν get earth *enough* for a grave, Moschio Trag.6.31, cf. Ps.-Phoc.99 (ἐπῑ- metri gr.): c. gen., *have a share of*, ταφῆς Ph.2.178. **-ιος**, ον, *fated*, νήματα *AP*7.504 (Leon.). **-ος**, ον, *partaking in*, c. gen., στεφάνων B.1.48, cf. Euryph.ap.Stob.4.39.27.

ἐπιμοιχ-εύω, *commit adultery besides*, τινά *with* one, Ps.-Luc. *Philopatr.*6. **-ίδιος**, ον, *adulterine*, Olymp. *in Alc.*p.153C.

ἐπιμολεῖν, aor. 2 inf. of ἐπιβλώσκω, *come upon, befall*, ἐπέμολε πάθος S.*Tr.*855 (lyr.).

ἐπίμολος, ὁ, *invader*, γᾶς A.*Th.*629 (lyr.).

ἐπιμολύνω, *defile on the surface*, Sor.1.22.

ἐπιμομφ-ή, Dor. **-φά**, ἡ, *complaint*, Pi.*O.*10(11).9. **-ος**, ον, *inclined to blame*, φίλοις E.*Rh.*327. II. *blameable, unlucky*, A.*Ag.* 553; ἐπίμομφον ἄταν dub. l., Id.*Ch.*830 (lyr.).

ἐπιμον-ή, ἡ, *tarrying, delay*, Th.2.18; *residence*, *Sammelb.*5343.42 (ii A.D.). 2. *steadfastness*, Pl.*Cra.*395b, Plu.*Sert.*16; *persistence*, Sor.2.16, 40; of fruit, Thphr.*CP*2.9.8. 3. *staying still, inactivity*, of a patient confined to bed, Phld.*Ir.*p.29 W. 4. Rhet., *dwelling on a point, treating it elaborately*, Longin.12.2, Demetr.*Eloc.*280, Hermog.*Id.*1.11, Alex.*Fig.*1.10, etc. II. ἐν ἐπιμονᾷ τινος, of a balance left in the *hands* of the treasurer, *IG*14.423 ii 5. **-ίδιος**, v. Ἐπιμενίδειος. **-ος**, ον, *staying on, lasting long*, Plb.6.43.2; ἐ. ποιεῖν τὸν στρατηγόν *continue* him in his command, ib.15.6; ἐπιμόνους ποιεῖν ἐράνους *delay* their payment, Id.38.11.10; ὁ ὦνος ἐ. ἔστω *Hermes*17.5 (Delos); κράτησις ἐπίμονος σπέρματος Sor.1.43; ἐ. τινι or ἔν τινι *persevering* in it, Plb.29.26.2, Plu.*Flam.*1; ἐπί τινος *Stoic.*3.32. Adv. -νως *constantly, permanently*, Pl.*Ax.*372a, Ph.1.179; *persistently*, cj. in Gal.19.220: Comp. -ώτερον *more permanently*, *Gp.*2.5.7.

ἐπιμορῐ-ασμός, ὁ, *formation of a number of the form* $1+\frac{1}{x}$, Iamb. *in Nic.*p.108 P. **-ος**, ον, (μόριον) *containing a whole + a fraction with* 1 *for its numerator* $(1+\frac{1}{x})$, *superparticular*, ἐ. [ἀριθμοί] Arist.*Pr.* 921ᵇ5; λόγοι Ph.2.183 (v. l. for ὑποεπιμερῶν), Plu.*in Hes.*59; of the rhythm of the pulse, Gal.8.516; also ἐπιμόριον, τό, Arist.*Metaph.* 1021ᵃ2. Adv. -ίως Nicom.*Ar.*2.20; opp. ἐπιμερής (q. v.), ib.1.20; τῶν ἀριθμῶν οἱ μὲν ἐν πολλαπλασίῳ λόγῳ λέγονται, οἱ δὲ ἐν ἐπιμορίῳ, οἱ δὲ ἐν ἐπιμερεῖ Euc.*Sect.Can.Praef.*, cf. Theo Sm.p.76 H. **-ότης**, ητος, ἡ, *the property of being* ἐπιμόριος, Iamb. *in Nic.*p.44 P.

ἐπιμορμύρω [ῡ], *murmur*, as a wave, D.P.82 (tm.).

ἐπίμορτος γῆ *farmed on the métayer system*, Sol.ap.Poll.7.151.

ἐπιμορφ-άζω, *pretend*, c. inf., Ph.1.387; ὅτι.. ib.96; ὡς, c. part., ib.193: abs., ib.363. II. c. acc., *simulate*, εὐσέβειαν, τὸ ἀδέσποτον, ib.340, 698:—Med., Hsch. **-όω**, prob. f. l. for foreg., Ph.2.520.

ἐπιμοτόω, *apply a* μοτός (q. v.), in imper. Pass. -μοτούσθω, τιλτοῖς Heliod.ap.Orib.44.10.9.

ἐπιμοχθ-έω, *work* or *toil at*, Hsch. **-ητος**, ον, *always toilsome*, *CIG*3816 (Dorylaeum). **-ος**, ον, *toilsome*, ἀρετά B.1.71, cf. Man. 4.248: gloss on πόνηρος, Sch.Ar.*Pax*383; γῆ Hp.*Ep.*17. Adv. -θως *with toil*, App.*Pun.*72; so neut., Lxx *Wi.*15.7.

ἐπιμοχλεύω, *bolt, bar*, κλεῖθρα Hld.4.17 (Pass.).

ἐπιμύζω, *murmur* or *mutter at* another's words, αἱ δ᾽ ἐπέμυξαν Il. 4.20 (also expld. as = ἐμυκτήρισαν, Trypho *Trop.*p.205 S.):—Med., ἐπεμύξατο Hsch.

ἐπιμῡθ-έομαι, *say besides*, v. l. for ἀπομ-, Il.9.109. **-εύομαι**, *to be added fabulously*, Arist.*HA*605ᵃ5, Ant.Diog.5. **-ιος**, ον, *coming after the fable*: τὸ ἐ. the *moral*, Luc.*Bacch.*8, Aphth.*Prog.*1, Herm. *in Phdr.*p.92 A.

ἐπιμυκτηρ-ίζω, *turn up the nose, mock at*, Men.562.4. **-ισμός**, gloss on ἐπισμυκτόν, Hsch.

ἐπίμυκτος, ον, (ἐπιμύζω) *scoffed at*, Thgn.269.

ἐπιμῠλ-ίδιος, ον, = sq. I, δαίμων Hsch. s. v. διαλαός (post διαλυγίσαντες). **-ιος**, ον, *at* or *in the mill*, epith. of Artemis, S.E.*M.*9. 185. 2. *of a millstone*, κλάσμα Lxx *Jd.*9.53 (s. v. l.). II. as Subst., 1. ἐπιμύλιον, τό, *the upper millstone*, ib.*De.*24.6. 2. ἐπιμύλιος (sc. ᾠδή), ἡ, *song sung while grinding*, Trypho ap.Ath.14. 618d, Ael.*VH*7.4, Hsch. s. v. ἱμαλίς.

ἐπιμῠλίς, ίδος, ἡ, *knee-pan*, Hp.*Mochl.*1.

ἐπίμυξις, εως, ἡ, (ἐπιμύζω) *sniffing*, Choerob.*Rh.*p.254 S. 2. = στεναγμός, Hsch.

ἐπιμῠρίζω, *smear*, τινί with.., Thphr.*Od.*45.

ἐπιμύρομαι [ῡ], *to be washed* by the sea, A.R.1.938; but ῥισὶν ἐπιμύρεται κόρυζα *dribbles*, *An.Ox.*3.220 (ἐπιμυρμύρεται cod.).

ἐπίμῠσις, εως, ἡ, *closing*, βλεφάρων Philum.*Ven.*16.3 (pl.), cf. Erot. s. v. καρδαμύσσειν, *EM*490.54; of the *os uteri*, Sor.2.18.

ἐπιμύσσω, *laugh at*, cj. in Luc.*DMort.*6.3: aor. 1 ἐπέμυξα Hsch.

ἐπιμυχθίζω, gloss on foreg., Hsch.

ἐπιμύω, pf. -μέμῡκα Sor.2.27:—*close* the eyes, τοὺς ὀφθαλμούς D.S. 1.48; τὰ βλέφαρα Aret.*SA*1.5; ὄμματα Opp.*H.*2.110: abs., *close the eyes*, Plb.4.27.7, Theoc.21.4 (cj.), Alex.Aphr. *in Sens.*17.14: metaph., *die*, Call.*Ep.*41.5. 2. *wink at*, in token of assent, Ar.*V.*934. II. intr., *close over*, τὰ βλέφαρα τοῖσι ὀφθαλμοῖσι ἐπιμύει *close over* the eyes, Aret.*CA*1.6, cf. *SA*1.5, Sor. l. c.; *close up*, of wounds, Opp.*C.* 2.290; ταχὺ τὸν ὄγκον ἐπιμύειν Onos.19.3; ἐπῑμύοντας ὀλόσχους, prob. l. for ἐπημ-, Nic.*Th.*870, cf. Sch. ad loc.

ἐπιμωκάομαι, *mock at*, Sch.S.*OT*970, Sch.A.R.1.486:—also -μωκεύω, v. l. in Luc.*JTr.*16.

ἐπιμωλέω, (μῶλος) *claim at law*, *Leg.Gort.*9.28.

ἐπιμωμ-άομαι, *find fault with*, τινί D.P.896. **-ητός**, Dor. **-ᾱτός**, ἡ, όν, *blameworthy*, [ἔρις] Hes.*Op.*13; ἔργον Theoc.26.38. **-ος**, ον, *blameworthy*, τὸν βίον Hld.7.2; *blemished*, Artem.5.67: opp. ἄμωμος, Herm.ap.Stob.1.41.1.

*ἐπιναίω, aor. Pass. ἐπενάσθην, = ἐπῳκίσθη (sic), Hsch.

ἐπινάσσω, fut. -ξω, *stuff up, close up*, Hsch.; cf. ἐπινέω (B) fin. II. *pour, heap over*, *Gp.*6.6.2. III. in Pass., *to be blocked*, of too thick milk, Sor.1.87.

ἐπινάστιος, ον, (ναίω) *taken as a stranger into a country, sojourning in a country*, A.R.1.795.

ἐπιναυμᾰχία, ἡ, *battle beside the ships*, Ps.-Plu.*Vit.Hom.*192 (pl.).

ἐπιναυπηγέω, *build upon the ship*, Poll.1.92 (Pass.). II. *build in addition*, καινὰς τριήρεις Anon.Argent.p.75 Keil.

ἐπιναυσίος, ον, (ναυσία) *feeling nausea, sickish*, Plb.31.14.1; *subject to vomiting*, Hp.*Dent.*3.

ἐπινάχομαι, Dor. for ἐπινήχ-, Theoc.23.61.

ἐπινάω, *send forth emanations* or *influences*, ὁ θεὸς ἀεὶ ἐ. Ascl. *in Metaph.*23.5:—Pass., ἐνέργειαι ἐπινάονται ib.120.2, cf. 186.1.

ἐπινεάζω, *take youthful pleasure in*, τινί Poll.10.53.

ἐπινεᾱνιεύομαι, *behave like a youth*, in good sense, Poll.3.121; ὁ νοῦς ἐ. καλὴν καὶ ὁσίαν νεανιείαν Ph.1.258; also in bad sense, ἐπινεανιευόμενός φησι *with youthful audacity*, Plu.2.1079d, cf. Ph.1.203, 298. 2. *commit further outrages*, Lib.*Decl.*13.9, 56.

ἐπινεικής, ές, *contentious*, Them.*Or.*13.166c.

ἐπίνειον, τό, (ναῦς) *sea-port* where the fleet of a country lies, Hdt. 6.116, Th.1.30, 2.84; ἐπίνεια καὶ λιμένας the *harbours* and roadsteads, Arist.*Pol.*1327ᵃ33; πολίχνη ἢ ἐ. καὶ ἀγορὰ ἐχρῶντο D.H.9.56, etc. II. Adj. ἐπίνειος, ον, *at a port*, φρουραί, φρούριον, App.*Praef.* 15, *Pun.*100.

ἐπινείσομαι, = ἐπινίσσομαι, Hsch.

ἐπινείφω, *snow upon*, Thphr.*HP*4.14.6 (Pass.), *CP*5.9.13 (Pass.); θεὸς ἐπινείφει δρόσον (i.e. manna) Ph.2.112: metaph., οἷς δ' ὁ θεὸς ἐπινείφει καὶ ἐπομβρεῖ τὰς ἀγαθῶν πηγάς Id.1.296, cf. 2.383:—Pass., ἐνθυμήματα *are dropped, distilled into* the mind, Id.1.441. 2. impers., ἐπινείφει *fresh snow falls*, or *it keeps snowing*, X.*Cyn.*8.1.

ἐπινεμεσάω, *to be wroth against*, οἴκῳ τινός J.*AJ*13.16.2 (v.l.).

ἐπινέμ-ησις, εως, ἡ, *appropriate apportioning* of medical treatment, Hp.*Praec.*8; of a bandage, = ἐπινομή II, Gal.18(1).775. II. (from Med.) *spreading*, πυρός Plu.*Lys.*12, Epicur.*Ep.*2 p.40 U.; of disease, Antyll.ap.Orib.50.8.3. III. = Lat. *indictio*, *IG*12(9).907.4 (Chalcis, iv A.D.), prob. in ib.7.24 (Megara, v A.D.), Jul.*Ep.*73, Lyd.*Mens.* 3.23, *Cod.Just.*10.16.13.5, etc. **-ητέον**, *one must assign*, Pl.*Lg.* 737c. **-ω**, *allot, distribute*, σῖτον ἑλὼν ἐπένειμε τραπέζῃ Il.9.216, 24. 625: c. dat. pers., σῖτον δέ σφ' ἐπένειμε Od.20.254; ἐφ' ἑκατέρῳ τὸ μέρος ἑ. ἑκάτερον Pl.*Plt.*264d. II. *turn* one's cattle *to graze on another's land*, ἐάν τις βοσκήματα ἐπινέμῃ Id.*Lg.*843d; τὰ κτήνη παρὰ τὸν ποταμόν Arist.*Pol.*1305ᵃ26, cf. D.55.11; *enjoy right of pasturage*, *Berl. Sitzb.*1927.7 (Locr., v B.C.). b. ἐ. σῖτον *graze* a crop, Thphr.*HP* 8.7.4. 2. metaph. in Med., *encroach*, of fire, πῦρ ἐ. τὸ ἄστυ *spreads over* the town, Hdt.5.101; πῦρ ἐ. τὴν γραφήν Plu.*Demetr.*22: abs., τὸ πῦρ ταχέως -νέμετο Plb.14.5.7; τὸ πῦρ ἐκώλυσαν.. ἐπινεμηθῆναι D.S.17.26; also of disease, *spread*, τὸ ἐρυσίπελας ταχὺ πάντοθεν ἐπενέμετο Hp.*Epid.*3.4; ἡ νόσος ἐπενείματο Ἀθήνας Th.2.54, cf. Plu. 2.776f: abs., Aret.*SA*1.7: generally, of a piratical force, ἐπενείματο τὴν θάλασσαν Plu.*Pomp.*25; of an army, ἐ. τὴν Γαλατίαν Id.*Caes.*19; of a custom, *spread among*, τινάς Id.*Demetr.*18; *approach*, Μοισᾶν ἀπὸ τόξων Δία .. βέλεσσιν Pi.*O.*9.6. b. *feed after*, i.e. *on the leavings of*, τινί Arist.*HA*591ᵇ19. c. *feed on, consume*, κόμην Call. *Dian.*79; δαῖτα Nic.*Al.*510, cf. Plu.2.980d: abs., ib.293a. d. *inhabit*, Luc.*Bacch.*6. 3. metaph. in Pass., *to be encroached upon*, as if by cattle straying over the bounds of their pasture, θῆλυς ὅρος ἐπινέμεται A.*Ag.*485 (lyr.).

ἐπινεόω, *renew*, *PMasp.*24 *C*44 (Pass., vi A.D.).

ἐπί-νευμα, ατος, τό, *nodding* of the head, Gal.5.227 (pl.). **-νευσις**, εως, ἡ, *nodding assent*, τῆς κεφαλῆς Ath.2.66c: abs., *assent*, Καίσαρος J.*AJ*17.9.1; ἡ ἑαυτοῖς ἐ. Polystr.p.16 W. II. *inclination* of the head, Gal.2.461; *movement down*, opp. ἀνάνευσις, Ath.Mech.26.2; ἐ. ἐπὶ τὸ ἀριστερὸν πλευρόν, of patients in bed, Philum.(?)ap.Aët.9. 23. **-νευστάζω**, *incline forwards*, opp. ὑπτιάω, of the crescent moon, Arat.789. **-νεύω**, fut. -νεύσω Luc.*Sat.*4, -νεύσομαι Aristaenet.2.1:—*nod to*, in token of command or approval, *nod assent*, opp. ἀνανεύω, ἐμῷ δ' ἐπένευσα κάρητι Il.15.75; ἐπ' ὀφρύσι νεῦσε Κρονίων 1.528, etc.; ἐπὶ γλεφάροις νεῦσαν Pi.*I.*8(7).49; σύ.. ἐπένευσας τάδε *did'st approve, sanction* these acts, E.*Or.*284, cf. D.18.324; ἐπένευσεν ἀληθὲς εἶναι he *nodded in sign that* it was true, Aeschin.3.59; σιγῇ δὲ τὰ ψευδῆ.. ἐπινεύουσι they *indicate* falsehoods without speaking, D.21.139: abs., Antipho 2.2.7; Ἑλληνικὸν ἐ. *give a Greek nod*, Ar.*Ach.*115: c. acc., *grant* or *promise*, τινά τινι E.*Hel.*681 (lyr.); τι Id.*Ba.*1349; ὑπέρ τινος Plb.21.5.3: c. dat., ἐ. τῇ δεήσει τινός *PGiss.* 1.41 ii 9 (ii A.D.): c. dat. pers., ἐ. τισὶ δεομένοις *SIG*888.13 (Macedonia, iii A.D.): c. dat. pers. et inf., *permit*, κῴδια ἐ. ἡμῖν ἐργάζεσθαι *PPetr.*2 p.108 (iii B.C.). 2. *make a sign* to another to do a thing, *order* him to do, c. inf., ἐπ' ὀφρύσι νεῦσε σιωπῇ.. στορέσαι λέχος Il.9. 620: abs., Od.16.164 (tm.), *h.Cer.*169,466, X.*Cyr.*5.5.37. 3. *nod forwards*, κόρυθι ἐπένευε φαεινῇ he *nodded* with his helmet, i.e. it *nodded*, Il.22.314; λόφων ἐπένευον ἔθειραι Theoc.22.186; ἐ. ἐς τὸ κάταντες Luc.*DDeor.*25.2; πέτραι ἐπινενευκυῖαι *overhanging*, Id.*Prom.*1. 4. *incline towards*, εἴς τινα Ar.*Eq.*657. 5. *roll down* an inclined plane, Hero *Aut.*2.1. 6. trans., *elevate, point upwards*, Id.*Bel.*78. 8, 89.14:—Pass., *to be inclined downwards*, opp. ἐξυπτιάζεσθαι, S.E. *P.*1.120. b. *tilt*, [κεράμιον] *Gp.*7.9. 7. ἐπινενευκὼς σφυγμός, name coined by Archigenes, Gal.8.479.

ἐπινεφελ-ίς, ίδος, ἡ, *cloudiness* in the eye, Alex.Trall.2. **-ος**, ον, *clouded, overcast*, Hp.*Epid.*3.2, Pl.Com.65; ἐπινεφέλων ἐόντων the weather being *cloudy*, Hdt.7.37, cf. Arist.*Pr.*939ᵇ15; τὰ ἐ. ib.33; ὅταν ἐπινέφελον ᾖ, opp. αἰθρίας οὔσης, Id.*Mete.*369ᵇ23, cf. *Pr.*939ᵇ39; ἐ. οὖρον *clouded* urine, Hp.*Aph.*4.71, cf. Gal.17(1).494. II. *bringing clouds*, οἱ βορέαι Arist.*Pr.*947ᵇ5.

ἐπινεφής, ές, *clouded, dark*, [ἀήρ] Arist.*Pr.*941ᵃ5, Thphr.*CP*5.12.2; ἐπινεφῆ *a clouded sky*, Id.*Vent.*51. II. *bringing clouds*, [ἄνεμος] ib.4.

ἐπινεφρίδιος, ον, *upon the kidneys*, δημός Il.21.204.

ἐπινέφω, *bring clouds over the sky*, Arist.*Pr.*944ᵇ26; ἐπινέφει ὁ Ζεύς Alex.29; ἐ. [ἄνεμος] Thphr.*Vent.*61: or impers., ἐπινέφει *it is cloudy*, Id.*CP*3.24.4. (In codd. freq. accentuated as if from ἐπινεφέω.)

ἐπίνεψις, εως, ἡ, *clouding over*, Arist.*Pr.*944ᵇ25.

ἐπινέω (A), *spin to*, esp. like ἐπικλώθω, of the Fates, γιγνομένῳ ἐπένησε λίνῳ *span* for him with her thread at his birth, Il.20.128, 24.210: —Pass., ὁ ἐπινησθεὶς αὐταῖς μόχθος Ael.*NA*7.1, cf. *Fr.*260; ἐπινενησμένα ἐς ἅπαντας Ps.-Luc.*Philopatr.*14.

ἐπινέω (B), *heap upon*, γῆν πολλήν Longus 1.31: elsewhere in Ep. form ἐπινηνέω, q.v. II. *heap up* or *load with*, c. gen. rei, ἁμάξας.. ἐπινέουσι φρυγάνων Hdt.4.62: pf. part. Pass., τράπεζαι ἐπινενησμέναι ἀγαθῶν ἁπάντων Ar.*Ec.*838 (-νενασμέναι codd.).

ἐπινέω (C), fut. -νεύσομαι, *float on the top*, Alex.33.5; ἐπὶ λεκάνης Ath.15.667e. 2. *swim upon*, τινί Aristid.2.94 J.; *swim over*, Arist. *HA*620ᵇ22.

ἐπίνηθρος, ὁ, = *iniclaris* (?), *Gloss.*

ἐπινήϊος, ον, *on board ship*, *AP*9.82 (Antip. Thess.).

ἐπινηνέω, Ep. for ἐπινέω (B), only in impf., *heap* or *pile upon*, c. gen. loci, νεκροὺς πυρκαϊῆς ἐπενήνεον Il.7.428; perh. to be read in Iamb. *VP*3.17. (Fort. -νήεον, cf. νηέω.)

ἐπινήσιος, α, ον, *on an island*, ἄκρα *Stad.*182 (s.v.l.).

ἐπίνητρον, τό, *distaff*, Poll.7.32, 10.125, *EM*362.20.

ἐπινήφω, *to be sober at* or *in*, τῷ βίῳ Plu.2.87e; τῇ πράξει *for* it, Luc.*Am.*45.

ἐπινήχομαι, Dor. -νάχ- [ᾱ], *swim upon*, πόντῳ Batr.107, cf. Cerc. 17.11; *flow over*, τοῖς πεδίοις Hdn.8.4.3; παιδὸς ἐπενάχετο φωνά *floated on* the stream, Theoc.23.61; *float*, ὑγρὸν -όμενον ταῖς κρήναις Dsc.1.73, cf. Sor.1.115, Alex.Aphr.*Pr.*1.22; opp. καταδύεσθαι, *Gp.* 7.8.2; of Noah, Ph.1.455; ἀέρι ib.602: metaph., ib.166, Dam.*Pr.* 270. 2. *swim to* or *over to*, c. acc., Call.*Del.*21. 3. *swim against, attack*, ἄλλῳ ἐ. ἄλλος πότμον ἄγων Opp.*H.*2.46.

ἐπινήχυτος, ον, = νήχυτος, *abundant*, δῶρα Orph.*A.*39,312.

ἐπινίκ-ειος [ῐ], ον, = sq., S.*OC*1088 (lyr.). **-ιος**, ον, *of victory*, ἀοιδαί Pi.*N.*4.78; ὕμνος D.S.5.29; ἀγῶνες ἐ. games *to celebrate victory*, Plb.30.22.1, cf. *IGRom.*4.1268 (Thyatira); ἐ. πομπή, ἑορτή, D.H.3. 41, Plu.*Rom.*29; ἐ. τιμαί the honours *of a triumph*, Id.*Aem.*31; ἡμέρα Id.*Cor.*3; στολή D.C.37.21. Adv. -ίως Hsch. s.v. ἀλαλάζει. II. as Subst., ἐπινίκιον (sc. ᾆσμα, μέλος), τό, *song of victory, triumphal ode*, such as Pindar's, cf. Ath.1.3e; Ζῆνα.. ἐπινίκια κλάζων A.*Ag.*174 (lyr.). 2. ἐπινίκια (sc. ἱερά), τά, *sacrifice for a victory* or *feast in honour of it*, Ar.*Fr.*433, And.4.29, D.21.55, etc.; τὰ ἐ. θύειν Pl.*Smp.*173a, etc.; ἑστιᾶν D.59.33; ἐ. πέμψαι, πεμφθῆναι, of a Roman *triumph*, D.C.36.25, 37.21. b. (sc. ἆθλα) *prize of victory*, S.*El.* 692, D.H.3.27, *IG*7.3195,3196 (Orchom. Boeot.). **-ος**, ον, = foreg., ἄωτος Pi.*O.*8.75, cf. Stratt.40 (dub. l.): Subst. ἐπίνικος (sc. ὕμνος), ὁ, Aristid.*Or.*28(49).34, 61 (pl.).

ἐπινιπτρὶς κύλιξ cup handed round at table *after washing hands, grace*-cup, Poll.6.31.

ἐπινίσσομαι, *go over*, c. gen., πεδίων S.*OC*689 (lyr.). 2. c. acc., *come upon, visit*, A.R.4.817, Nic.*Th.*470, *Pae.Delph.*6: abs., Theoc. 8.43, A.R.4.281. (Written with single -σ-, *Pae.Delph.* l.c.)

ἐπινίφω, misspelling of ἐπινείφω, q.v.

ἐπινο-έω, *think on* or *of, contrive*, τι Hdt.1.48, Hp.*Art.*42,77, Ar. *Eq.*884, Pl.*Lg.*677b; φάρμακον τῇ ψύξει Ael.*NA*9.7, etc.: c. inf., πῶς ἐπενόησας ἁρπάσαι; Ar.*Eq.*1202, cf. *Nu.*1039: abs., *form plans*, opp. δρᾶν, Antipho 3.2.7; opp. ἐπεξελθεῖν, Th.1.70; opp. ἐξεργάσασθαι, Ph.*Bel.*58.43. 2. *have in one's mind, intend, purpose*, ὀλίγον οὐδέν Th.2.8, cf. X.*An.*2.5.4, etc.: c. pres. inf., Hdt.1.27, Ar.*Th.*338, X. *An.*6.4.9, etc.: fut., Hdt.3.134: aor., Id.2.152, 5.24,65, E.*Rh.*195 (lyr., nowhere else in Trag.), Pl.*Ti.*37c:—Pass., Philostr.*Her.*10. 6. 3. *note, observe*, Phld.*Po.*5.11; *perceive*, Plu.*Per.*6. 4. *conceive*, Epicur.*Ep.*1 p.23 U.:—Pass., ib.p.6 U., S.E.*M.*8.381. II. *invent, contrive*, κατασκευήν Gal.*UP*12.6, etc.:—Med., aor. -ησάμην Luc. *Astr.*17:—Pass., ὀνόματα ὑπὸ τῶν φιλοσόφων ἐπινοηθέντα Id.*Deor. Conc.*13, etc.; but aor. Pass. ἐπινοηθῆναι in act. sense in Hdt.3.122, 6.115, Luc.*Am.*16,31. **-ημα**, ατος, τό, *thought, purpose, contrivance*, Hp.*Art.*42, Antipho Soph.101; esp. in Rhet., Ruf.Rh.p.404 H., Aristid.*Rh.*2 p.521 S., al. 2. *conception*, Epicur.*Nat.*130,137 G. **-ημᾰτικός**, ή, όν, = ἐπινοητικός, Vett.Val.49.6. **-ήμων**, ον, gen. ονος, = foreg., Id.72.19, Zonar. **-ησις**, εως, ἡ, *thought, conception*, Phld.*Mort.*36. **-ητέον**, *one must contrive, devise means*, c. inf., Nicom.*Harm.*4; τί πρακτέον Hld.10.38; *one must devise* a remedy, Philum.ap.Aët.5.119. **-ητής**, οῦ, ὁ, *inventive person*, περὶ τὰς ἐδωδάς M.Ant.1.16. **-ητικός**, ή, όν, *inventive*, of a writer, Longin.4.1; ἐ. τοῦ διασῴζειν ἑαυτόν Ath.7.310f. 2. *due to reflection*, φάσμα Epicur. *Nat.*362. **-ητός**, ή, όν, *conceivable*, *Vit.Philonid.*p.10 C., Phld.*Mus.* p.92 K.; *object of thought, existing in the mind*, S.E.*M.*8.38.

ἐπίνοια, ἡ, *thinking on* or *of* a thing, *thought, notion*, οὐδ' ἐς ἐπίνοιαν ἰέναι τινός Th.3.46; ὡς.. Id.4.92; οὐδ' ἐπίνοιαν ποιήσασθαί τινος Plb.1.20.12; τὰς ἐ. εἴς τι φέρειν D.H.*Pomp.*1; πάσαις ταῖς ἐ. γίγνεσθαι περί τι Plb.5.110.10; *conception, idea*, ἐναργὴς τοῦ πράγματος ἐ. Epicur.*Fr.*255, cf. Phld.*D.*3.8, al.; κατ' ἐπίνοιαν in *idea*, opp. κατὰ περίπτωσιν (q.v.), *Stoic.*2.29; κατ' ἐ. ψιλὴν ὑφεστάναι ib.159; πᾶσαν ἐ. ἀτοπίας ὑπερβάλλειν Plu.2.1065d. 2. *power of thought, inventiveness*, οἷνον σὺ τολμᾷς εἰς ἐ. λοιδορεῖν; Ar.*Eq.*90, cf. X.*Cyr.*2.3.19; κατὰ τέχνην καὶ ἐ. γίγνεσθαι Thphr.*Od.*7. 3. *invention, device, conceit*, ἐ. ἀστειοτάται Ar.*Eq.*539; ζητεῖν καινὴν ἐ. Id.*V.*346; θαυμαστὰς ἐξευρίσκων ἐ. Id.*Eq.*1322, etc.; τέχνης ἐπίνοιαι Arist.*Mu.*399ᵇ 17; πενία ἐπινοιῶν διδάσκαλος Secund.*Sent.*10. 4. *purpose, design*, τίν' ἐ. ἔσχεθες; E.*Ph.*408, cf. *Med.*760 (lyr.); τίς ἐ.; Ar.*Th.*766, cf. *Av.*405 (lyr.); ἥτις ἡ 'πίνοια τῆς ἐγκεντρίδος Id.*V.*1073, cf. *Pl.*45; κατὰ τὴν ἐκφορὰν καὶ τὴν ἐ. *Stoic.*2.128; ἡ ἐ. τῆς καρδίας *Act.Ap.*8.22: pl., ἐξ οἰκείων ἐ., = *sua sponte*, *OGI*580.7 (Cilicia, iv A.D.). II. *afterthought, second thoughts*, ψεύδει γὰρ ἡ 'πίνοια τὴν γνώμην S.*Ant.* 389. III. *intelligence*, κοινὴ ἐ. Plb.6.5.2, cf. Longin.ap.Eus.*PE* 15.20. 2. Psychol., *reflection on experience, retrospection*, Plot.2. 9.1, 6.8.7.

ἐπινομ-ή, ἡ, (ἐπινέμομαι) *a grazing over the boundaries*: metaph., ἐ. πυρὸς the *spread* of fire, Plu.*Alex.*35; of poison, Ael.*NA*12. 32. 2. *right of pasturage*, *Schwyzer* 197.33 (Itanos, iii B.C.). 3. *grazing after* mowing, *POxy.*730.11 (ii A.D.), al. II. pl., *final turns of a bandage*, Heliod.ap.Orib.48.51.2 (pl.), Gal.18(2).563. **-ία**, ἡ, *a grazing over the boundaries*: *right of pasture*, X.*Cyr.*3.2.23 (pl., cf. Poll.7.184), *Berl.Sitzb.*1927.7 (Locr., v B.C.), *IG*9(2).61.7 (Lamia),

5(2).511 (Arc., iii/ii B.C.); ἐ. ἐν τᾷ Δελφίδι SIG534.15 (Delph., iii B.C.). -ιον, τό, payment for pasturage, IG5(2).456 (Megalop.), prob. in GDI4647 (Messenia). II. (νόμος) = sq. 1, title of work ascribed to Plato, Theo Sm.pp.7,84,178 H. -ίς, ίδος, ἡ, addition to a law, appendix, name of a work ascribed to Plato; applied to Deuteronomy by Ph.1.495. II. new-year's gift, Ath.3.97d. III. part of a trireme, Apollonius ἐν Τριηρικῷ ibid.

ἐπινομοθετέω, make additional laws, Pl.Lg.779d.

ἐπίνομος, ον, visiting the land, ἐ. ἡρώων στρατός Pi.P.11.7. II. legal, formal, App.BC3.94 (Sup., s.v.l.). III. Subst. ἐ., ὁ, possessor of right of pasturage, Berl.Sitzb.1927.8 (Locr., v B.C.). 2. = κληρονόμος, IG9(1).694.36 (Corc.), Delph.3(2).243 (ii B.C.), Schwyzer 335.18, al., Hsch.

ἐπινοσέω, to be ill after, μετὰ τοὺς τόκους Hp.Epid.1.16, cf. Phryn. PSp.120 B.

ἐπίνοσος, ον, subject to sickness, unhealthy, σῶμα Arist.EN1113^{a}28, cf. Thphr.Fr.20.48 Schneider, D.S.2.48; γενεά Ph.1.516. Adv. -σως like one who is sick, διάγειν Hp.Epid.1.5, Crates Ep.20; ἐ. διακειμένου τοῦ σώματος Sor.1.117, cf. POxy.939.21 (iv A.D.). II. unwholesome, χωρίον Porph.Abst.1.36; θέρος Gp.1.12.34; τόπος Hierocl. Facet.73; κατομβρία Lyd.Ost.37.

ἐπινοσσοποιέομαι, Med., build their nests upon, ὄρεσιν Ps.-Democr. Symp.Ant.p.6 G.

ἐπίνοστος, ον, for a return, ᾠδή Hsch. s. v. ἱμαῖος.

ἐπινοτίζω, sprinkle on the surface, Dsc.2.83.2. II. Pass., perspire slightly, Philum.ap.Aët.5.78.

ἐπινυκτ-ερεύω, pass the night at or in, ναυσί Heraclit.All.9; of water, stand for a night, Plu.2.690c. -ίδιος, ον, = sq., Procop.Aed. 1.7. -ιος, ον, by night, ἐ. μῆλα νομεύων AP6.262 (Leon.). -ίς, ίδος, ἡ, pustule which is most painful by night, Hp.Aër.3, Diocl.Fr. 82, Ruf.ap.Orib.44.20.1, Antyll.ib.10.24.10, etc. II. (-νεκτίς cod.)· φυλακὴ δοκοῦντι ἀδικεῖν, Hsch.

ἐπινύμφ-ειος, ον, bridal, ὕμνος prob. in S.Ant.814 (lyr.): fem. -είη Supp.Epigr.2.874 (nisi ἐπὶ νυμφείην). -εύομαι, contract a second marriage, of a woman, GDI3721.5 (Cos). -ίδιος, ον, bridal, Ἀΐδας AP7.182 (Mel.).

ἐπινύσσω, prick on the surface, Antyll.ap.Orib.10.19.5; -οντες πόνοι stabbing pains, Archig.ap.Gal.8.110:—Pass., Sor.Fract.24, f.l. in Luc.Lex.11.

ἐπινυστάζω, drop asleep over, τοῖς σιτίοις Plu.Brut.36: abs., Luc. Bis Acc.2, Agath.4.18.

ἐπινωμάω, bring or apply to, παιῶνα κακῶν τινί S.Ph.168 (anap.); σώματα.. ὄμματος αὐγαῖς ἐπενώμας didst survey.., E.Ph.1564 (anap.). II. distribute, apportion, λάχη τὰ κατ' ἀνθρώπους A.Eu. 311 (anap.); κλήρους Id.Th.727 (lyr.), cf. S.Ant.139 (lyr.).

ἐπινῶς, = λίαν, Suid.; read by Sch. for ἐπιμανῶς in Luc.VH2.25.

ἐπινωτ-ιδεύς, έως, ὁ, = νωτιδανός, Epaen.ap.Ath.7.294d. -ίδιος, ον, on the back, AP6.21.3. -ίζω, attack from behind, E.HF362 (lyr.); = ἐφορμάω, Archipp.5:—Med., take on one's back, Paus.Gr.Fr. 143. -ιος, ον, on the back, Batr.80, Luc.Am.26, Alciphr.3. 68. II. ἐπινώτιοι, οἱ, shoulder-blades, Poll.2.133 (v.l. ἐπινώτια).

ἐπιξαίνω, scratch, τὴν κατάποσιν Sor.1.86.

ἐπιξανθ-ίζω, brown over by toasting, πλευρὰ δελφάκεια Pherecr.108. 16 (Pass.). -ος, ον, inclining to yellow, tawny, of hares, X.Cyn. 5.22; of deer, Poll.5.76; of the open lime-flower, Thphr.HP3.10.4, cf. 4.2.7.

ἐπιξενᾱγ-ία, ἡ, = four ξεναγίαι, i.e. 2048 men, Ascl.Tact.6.3, etc. -ός, ὁ, officer attached to an ἐπιξεναγία, Ascl.Tact.6.3, Ael.Tact.16.4, Arr.Tact.14.6.

ἐπιξενοδίκη· ἡ συνηγορή, καὶ ἡττηθεὶς ἀπόλλυται, Hsch.

ἐπιξεν-όομαι, Ep. -ξειν- A.R.2.764:—Pass., to be entertained as a guest, dwell abroad, Isoc.Ep.6.2, Arist.Pol.1327^{a}13; πόλει Luc. Am.7; to be on a visit, εἰς Ὀξύρυγχα Mitteis Chr.8.2 (iii B.C.); ἐ. τινί to be entertained by one, A.R.l.c., Plu.2.250a; Σοφοκλεῖ ζῶντι Ἀσκληπιὸν ἐ. Id.Num.4; παρά τισι Sammelb.6262 (iii A.D.). 2. have hospitable relations with, be intimate with, ἐπεξενῶσθαι πολλοῖς D.50.56, cf. D.S.1.23; ἡ ἐπιξενωθεῖσα σώμασι μοῖρα lent to or communicated with, Heraclit.ap.S.E.M.7.130. II. as Med., in A.Ag.1320 ἐπιξενοῦμαι ταῦτα δ' ὡς θανουμένη I appeal to thee in these matters, as one at death's door, cf. S.Fr.146. -ος, ὁ, = ἐπιχθόνιος, Hsch. 2. stranger, POxy.480.11 (ii A.D.), etc. -ωσις, εως, ἡ, hospitable relations, pl., D.S.31.13, SIG888.140 (iii A.D.).

ἐπιξέστ-ης, ου, ὁ, (ἐπιξέω) workman who dresses blocks of masonry, IG2^2.1672.31. -ικῶς, gloss on ἐπιγράβδην, Sch.Il.21.166, Hsch.

ἐπιξέω, scrape or graze on the surface, Hp.VC14 (v.l. for ἐπιξύω), Aret.CD1.2; ἅλμασιν ἀκρωνύχοις τὴν πέτραν Hld.5.14: metaph., polish a poem, Vit.Apollon.Rhod.

ἐπίξηνον, τό [not -ος, ὁ, as Suid.], (ξηνός) chopping-block, Eust. 1443.16; executioner's block, A.Ag.1277, Ar.Ach.318, 355, 359, 365.

ἐπιξηρ-αίνω, dry on the surface, Hp.Fract.33, Arist.Pr.928^{a}9:—Pass., to be so dried, Hp.Prorrh.2.6; have an interval of dryness, Id. Acut.28: generally, to be dried up, Ruf.Ren.Ves.6.5; to be constipated, Aret.CA1.1. -ᾰσία, ἡ, dryness on the top, Hp.Epid.6.2.6. -ος, ον, very dry, γλῶσσα ib.1.26.β', cf. Aret.SD1.15: Comp., more arid, Id.CA1.1.

ἐπιξοά, ἡ, Archit., dressing of blocks, IG4.1484.84 (Epid.).

ἐπιξῠλία, ἡ, right of cutting timber, IG5(2).510 (Thisoa, iii/ii B.C.).

ἐπίξυλον· τὸ ἐπὶ παραστροφίδα τοῦ ὑφαινομένου ἱματίου, Hsch.

ἐπίξῠν-ος, ον, poet. for ἐπίκοινος, ἐ. ἄρουρα a common field, in which several persons have rights, Il.12.422. -όω, poet. for ἐπικοινόω, impart τινί τι Nonn.D.26.290:—Med., A.R.3.1162, 4.435.

ἐπιξῡρ-άω, shave, ἐπιξύρα τὸν τόπον Cleopatra ap.Gal.12.404. -ητέον, one must shave, τὸν τόπον Menemach.ap.Orib.10.15.4.

ἐπιξύω, grate over, τυρὸν ἐπιξυσθέντα Pl.R.406a, cf. Arist.HA612^{b}17; scrape the surface of the skull, Hp.VC14. 2. skim over, γαῖαν Arat.650. 3. Pass., to be carved, εἰκόνες λίθῳ Procop.Aed.1.11.

ἐπιογδοηκοστὸς λόγος ratio of 81 : 80, Ptol.Harm.1.16.

ἐπιόγδοος λόγος ratio of 9 : 8, Porph. in Harm.p.310 W.

ἐπιοικοδομά, ἡ, v. ἐποικοδομή. **ἐπίϝοικος**, v. ἔποικος.

ἐπιοίνιος, ον, at or over wine, ἆθλον Thgn.971.

ἐπιοινοχοεύω, pour out wine for, θεοῖς h.Ven.204.

ἐπιοκτωκαιδέκᾰτος λόγος ratio of 19 : 18, Ptol.Harm.2.1.

ἐπιοπτ-εύω, inspect, overlook, Schwyzer 701 C (Erythrae, v B.C.). -ης, ου, ὁ, poet. for ἐπόπτης, βοτῶν Hom.Epigr.11. -ος, ον, poet. for ἔποπτος, observed, Opp.H.1.10; visible, Arat.25.

ἐπιοραντές· τερπνόν, ἁρπαλέον, Hsch.

ἐπιορκ-έω, also **ἐφιορκέω** IG2^2.1126.9 (Delph. Amphict.), OGI 229.69 (Smyrna, iii B.C.), etc.: fut. -ήσω Il.19.188, Ar.Lys.914, etc., -ήσομαι (κατ-) D.54.40: aor. ἐπιώρκησα Id.49.67, inf. -ορκῆσαι Hdt. 4.68 (v.l. ἐφ-): pf. ἐπιώρκηκα Pl.Lg.948e, X.An.3.1.22, Din.1.47 (ἐπιόρκηκα is v.l. in Hdt. l. c.):—swear falsely, forswear oneself, οὐδ' ἐπιορκήσω πρὸς δαίμονος Il.19.188: also, c. acc., of things sworn by, τὰς βασιληΐας ἱστίας ἐπιώρκηκε has sworn falsely by the royal hearth, Hdt.4.68; θεάς Din.1.47; [θεούς] Ar.Av.1609, X.An.2.4.7, D.49.67, etc.: mostly abs., Ar.Eq.298, 428, Nu.402, Pl.Phlb.65c, etc.; οὐδὲν ἐφρόντιζ' ἐπιορκῶν D.21.119: c. acc. cogn., ἐ. ὅρκους τινί Id.49.65, cf. Aeschin.1.115; opp. εὐορκέω, Lex ap.And.1.98, Cleanth. Stoic.1.131, Chrysipp.ib.2.63, who distinguishes betw. εὐορκεῖν and ἀληθορκεῖν, and betw. ἐπιορκεῖν and ψευδορκεῖν. II. simply, = ὄμνυμι, swear, Sol.ap.Lys.10.17. -ία, ἡ, false swearing, perjury, X.An.3.2.4, etc.; ἐ. οἴκαδ' εἰσενέγκασθαι D.19.220: pl., Pl.Grg.525a; πρὸς θεούς X.An.2.5.21. -ίζω, prob. = ἐξορκ-, Tab.Defix.Aud. 41 B1. -ος, ον, sworn falsely, of oaths, εἰ δέ τι τῶνδ' ἐπίορκον Il. 19.264: freq. in the phrase ἐπίορκον ὀμόσσαι take a false oath, swear falsely, 3.279, 19.260, Hes.Op.282, Th.232; in full, ἐπίορκον ὅρκον ὤμοσε Ar.Ra.150; and so ἐ. ἐπομνύναι (v. ἐπόμνυμι); but in Il.10.332 ἐ. ἐπώμοσε he swore a bootless oath, i.e. one which he meant to fulfil, but the gods willed otherwise. II. of persons, forsworn, perjured, Hes.Op.804, Schwyzer 179^a (Crete), E.El.1355 (anap.), Ar.Nu. 399, al.: Sup. -ότατος Antipho 6.48. Adv. -κως Hdn.6.9.2. -οσύνη, ἡ, = ἐπιορκία, AP12.250.6 (Strat.). **ἐπίορος**, v. ἐπίουρος II.

ἐπιόσσομαι, have before one's eyes, ἐπιοσσομένω θάνατον καὶ φύζαν ἑταίρων Il.17.381; gaze on, A.R.2.28 (tm.); ἐ. αὐγὰς ἠελίοιο, i.e. live, Nic.Th.276.

ἐπιουδίς, Adv. on the floor, Theognost.Can.163. **ἐπίουρα**, v. οὖρον.

ἐπιούριον, τό, Dim. of sq. II, Hero Aut.28.6.

ἐπίουρος, ὁ, = οὖρος (B), guardian, watcher, ward, c. gen., ὑῶν ἐ. Od. 13.405; βοῶν Theoc.8.6, 25.1; Οἰχαλίης A.R.1.87; ναυτιλίης v.l. in Id.4.652: less freq. c. dat., Μίνωα τέκε Κρήτῃ ἐ. Il.13.450; κρήνῃ A.R. 3.1180. II. wooden peg, pin, IG4.1484.63 (Epid.), Hero Aut.16.2, al., Hippiatr.26, Gp.10.61, prob. l. in Arist.Pr.915^{a}11; nickname of Secundus (son of a joiner), Philostr.VS1.26: Lat. epiurus, Pall.Agr. 12.7.15, prob. in Sen.Ben.2.12, Aug.Civ.Dei 15.27, Isid.Etym.19. 19.7: also **ἐπίορος**, Ath.Mitt.51.154 (Delos).

ἐπιούσιος, ον, either, sufficient for the coming (and so current) day, (ἐπιοῦσα (sc. ἡμέρα)), or, for the day (ἐπὶ τὴν οὖσαν (sc. ἡμέραν)), ἄρτος Ev.Matt.6.11, Ev.Luc.11.3; τὰ ἐ. dub. sens. (cf. Phil.Woch.47.889) in Sammelb.5224.20. (Very rare word in Origen's day, De Orat. 27.7.)

ἐπιόψομαι, fut. (or Ep. aor. subj.), I will choose, Il.9.167, Od.2. 294: aor. 1 ind. ἐπιωψάμην chose, IG2.948.1 (iv B.C.), cf. Pl.Lg.947c (ἐπόψ- codd.), Hsch., Suid.: aor. 1 Pass., τοὺς ἐπιοφθέντας IG2.949.2 (iv/iii B.C.). (From ὀπ- 'choose', cf. Lat. optare.)

ἐπίπᾰγος, ὁ, (ἐπιπήγνυμι) congealed or hardened crust on the top of a thing, Dsc.1.101.2, Aret.SA1.9, Gal.Lex. s. v. σύναγμα; ἐ. ὑμενώδης capsule of lens, Ruf.Anat.17; ἁλώδης Plu.2.627f; = γραῦς II, scum, Hsch., cf. Gal.6.252.

ἐπίπαγχῠ, Adv., strengthd. for πάγχυ, Theoc.17.104, Maiist.13.

ἐπιπᾰθής, ές, liable to diseases, Cat.Cod.Astr.8(4).132, Paul.Al.L. 2: Comp., Id.O.

ἐπιπαιᾱν-ίζω, sing a paean over, D.S.5.29: c. acc. cogn., πομπήν Plu.Marc.22. (The form -παιωνίζω is found in Hsch.) -ισμός, ὁ, song of victory, ἐπὶ νίκῃ Str.9.3.10 (v.l. -ωνισμός).

ἐπιπαίζω, mock at, τινί Hld.10.13: abs., Alex.172.16, with reference to the preceding line, where ἐπιπαίζεται means are an after-play, in allusion to things eaten at a second course. 2. sport upon, θαλάττῃ Philostr.Im.2.17.

ἐπίπαιμα, ατος, τό, = ἐπίπταισμα, πρόσκομμα, Hsch.

ἐπιπαιστικός, ή, όν, (ἐπιπαίζω) droll, πρόβλημα Clearch.63.

ἐπιπακτίς, ίδος, ἡ, rupture-wort, Herniaria glabra, Dsc.4.108 (cf. ἐπικακτίς).

ἐπιπακτόω, shut close, τὰς θύρας Ar.Fr.721.

ἐπιπᾰλᾰμάομαι, = ἐπιμηχανάομαι, dub. in Luc.Tox.16 (v.l. -καλαμ-).

ἐπιπάλλω, brandish at or against, βέλη A.Ch.162 (lyr.).

ἐπιπᾱμᾰτίς, ίδος, ἡ, = ἐπίκληρος, prob. in Delph.3(1).294 V7, GDI 4969 (Gortyn), cf. Sch.Ar.V.581, Hsch.

ἐπιπαμφᾰλάω, glance over, A.R.2.127.

ἐπίπαν or **ἐπὶ πᾶν**, v. ἐπί. II. Adj. ἐπίπαντες, v. ἐπίπας.

ἐπιπάξ· *συντόμως..*, ἢ ἐπὶ τὰ ἀριστερά, Hsch. (cf. ἐπιτάξ, ἐπιζάξ).

ἐπίπαππος, ὁ, *grandfather's grandfather*, Poll.3.18, Sch.rec.S.*OT* 183; or, *grandfather's father*, Jul.*Or*.2.82b, Hsch.; *grandfather*, Lib. *Or*.1.3, al., prob. l. in *BCH*17.532 (Mysia).

ἐπιπαραγίγνομαι, *arrive on the scene*, Satyr.*Vit.Eur.Fr*.39xxi 25, Mitteis *Chr*.8.3 (iii B.C.), etc.; of generals, *succeed in a command*, Plb.1.31.4; of troops, *come up*, ἀτάκτως καὶ σποράδην Id.4.12.7; of events, *come also upon*, τινί Junc.ap.Stob.4.50.27.

ἐπιπαράγω [ᾰγ], *bring round upon*, τὴν χεῖρα ἐπὶ τὸ στῆθος Hp. *Mochl*.5.

ἐπιπαρα-δέχομαι, Gramm., *take besides*, ἄρθρον A.D.*Synt*.170.13. **-κειμαι**, *to be adjacent*, Steph. *in Hp*.1.209 D. **-μένω**, *continue to stay with* some one, Phld.*Herc*.1041.1. **-νέω**, *heap up still more besides*, Th.2.77.

ἐπιπαρᾰριθμέω, *reckon in comparison*, *PRev.Laws* 76.2 (iii B.C.).

ἐπιπαρασκευάζομαι, *provide oneself with besides*, X.*Cyr*.6.3.1.

ἐπιπάρειμι (A), (εἰμί *sum*) *to be present besides* or *in addition*, Th. 1.61 codd. (leg. -ιόντας), Luc.*Merc.Cond*.26; *to be present to*, τινί Id. *Symp*.20, Ach.Tat.2.7. 2. Astrol., *occupy a position as well*, Nech. ap.Vett.Val.279.16.

ἐπιπάρειμι (B), (εἶμι *ibo*) *march on high ground parallel with* one below, X.*An*.3.4.30, Plb.10.13.3, etc. 2. c. dat., *proceed to attack*, ἐπιπαριὼν τῷ δεξιῷ Th.5.10. 3. *come to one's assistance*, Id.4.108, etc.; εἰ δέοι τι..., ἐπιπαρῇσαν οὗτοι X.*An*.3.4.23; ἐπιπαριόντες ib. 30. 4. *pass along the front of* an army, so as to address it (cf. πάρειμι IV. 2), Th.4.94, 6.67, 7.76; ἐ. κατὰ πρόσωπον Plb.5.83.1. 5. *visit in passing*, Φρυγίαν, Μυσίαν, App.*BC*5.7.

ἐπιπαρ-εμβάλλω, *re-form*, ἐ. φάλαγγα Plb.12.19.6. II. intr., *fall into line with others*, Id.3.115.10, 11.23.5. **-έξειμι**, *pass farther along*, of the sun (relatively to the moon), Arist.*Pr*.912ᵃ11. **-έρχομαι**, *go past on the way to* a place, παρὰ τὴν ὄχθην D.C.40.35; κατὰ τὰ μετέωρα Id.47.35. 2. Astrol., *intervene as well*, ἐπὶ τόπον Vett. Val.291.9. **-οδος**, ἡ, *second* πάροδος (q.v.), Poll.4.108. **-οινέω**, in Pass., *to be further intoxicated* (with anger), prob. in Phld.*Ir*.p.33 W. **-οξύνω**, *incite still more*, D.C.44.35, Ach.Tat.1.8:—Pass., of persons in fever, *suffer from successive accesses*, v.l. in Hp.*Epid*. 1.2, cf. Gal.7.306; of a sore, *become more inflamed*, Hp.*Prorrh*.1. 162 (dub.). **-ορμάω**, *stir up yet more*, πρὸς τὸν πόλεμον Plu.2.118f.

ἐπιπαρουσία, ἡ, *presence* of a planet in a τόπος, *Cat.Cod.Astr*.5(3). 88.5, Paul.Al.*O*.4.

ἐπιπαρρησιάζομαι, abs., *apply plain-speaking*, Phld.*Lib*.p.3 O.

ἐπίπας, πασα, παν, = σύμπας, Cret. fem. ἐπίπανσα *Schwyzer* 176.2: pl. ἐπίπαντες ib.198.15 (Crete, ii B.C.), *AP*12.87 (Strat.).

ἐπιπᾰσῐμάχη [ᾰχ], ἡ, *general engagement*, *IG*14.1296.

ἐπί-πασμα, ατος, τό, *powder for sprinkling*, ῥοὸς Aret.*CA*2.2; ἄρτων Sch.Theoc.15.114, cf. Alex.Trall.*Febr*.3. **-πάσσω**, Att. -ττω, Dor. inf. ἐπιπῆν *IG*4.951.119 (Epid.), cf. πῆν:—*sprinkle upon* or *over*, ἐπ' ἄρ' ἤπια φάρμακα πάσσε Il.4.218, cf. 5.401, *IG* l.c., Euphro 11.10; τι ἐπί τι Hdt.4.172; τινί τι Orph.*L*.455, Luc.*DMar*.15.3: c. partit. gen., τῆς εἰρωνείας Id.*Pisc*.22: abs., Theoc.2.18:—Pass., ἐπ' οἶνον ἄλφιτα ἐπιπασθέντα Pl.*R*.405e, cf. *PTeb*.1.19. **-παστέον**, *one must sprinkle* or *spread*, Antyll.ap.Orib.7.21.8. **-παστος**, η, ον, *sprinkled over*, ἐπίπασται τευθίδες Philox.2.16. II. ἐπίπαστον, τό, a kind of *cake with comfits* (or the like) *upon it*, Ar.*Eq*.103, 1089, Pherecr.130.3; but (sc. φάρμακον), = ἐπίπασμα, Hp.*Hum*.5, Theoc. 11.2, Aret.*CA*2.2.

ἐπιπᾰτᾰγέω, *make a noise with*, κώδωνι καὶ τυμπάνῳ Men.Prot. p.50 D.

ἐπιπατρόφιον, τό, *patronymic*, *Schwyzer* 462 *A* 28 (Tanagra, iii B.C.).

ἐπιπάτωρ [ᾰ], ορος, ὁ, (πατήρ) *stepfather*, Poll.3.26.

ἐπιπαφλάζω, *boil upon* or *over*, κύματα ἐ. αἰγιαλοῖσιν Q.S.11.229, cf. Nonn.*D*.7.34; *boil, foam in*, c. dat., ib.1.237.

ἐπιπᾰχύνω, *make still thicker*, Alex.Trall.*Febr*.1 and 7.

ἐπιπεδάω, f.l. for πεδάω, Corn.*ND*7.

ἐπιπεδ-ικός, ή, όν, *two-dimensional*: κύκλοι *two-dimensional* cyclic numbers, Simp. *in Ph*.59.17. **-όομαι**, *to be made plane*, Iamb. *in Nic*.p.27 P., al. **-ος**, ον, *on the ground, on the ground-floor*, στοαὶ ἐ., opp. ὑπερῷοι, D.H.3.68, cf. *PFlor*.376.7 (iii A.D.); σηκὸς Aret.*CA*2. 2. II. *level, flat*, Pl.*Criti*.112a; χωρίον X.*HG*7.1.29, etc.; οὐκ ἐν ἐπιπέδῳ, ἀλλὰ πρὸς ὀρθίῳ not *on a level*, but.., ib.6.4.14; ἐξ ἐπιπέδου *PThead*.20 i 3 (iv A.D.); = Lat. *de plano*, J.*AJ*19.5.3: irreg. Comp. -πεδέστερος X.*HG*7.4.13. 2. στεγνὰ ἐπίπεδα an accurately fitting *pavement*, *SIG*996.27 (Smyrna, i A.D.). III. in Geom., *plane, superficial*, opp. στερεός (solid), Pl.*Phlb*.51c, *Ti*.32a; ἐ. γωνία a *plane* angle, ib.54e; ἡ τοῦ ἐ. πραγματεία *plane* geometry, Id.*R*.528d; μήκους καὶ ἐ. καὶ βάθους one-, *two-*, and three-*dimensional magnitude*, Id. *Lg*.817e; εἰ κῶνος τέμνοιτο ἐπιπέδῳ Democr.155. 2. of numbers, *representing a surface*, Plu.2.367f, Nicom.*Ar*.2.7; ὁ ἰσόπλευρος καὶ ἐ. ἀριθμός a *square* number, Pl.*Tht*.148a. Adv. -δως Nicom.l.c. **-ωσις**, εως, ἡ, *formation of a plane surface*, Iamb. *in Nic*.p.59 P.

ἐπιπειθ-εια, poet. -είη or -ίη, ἡ, *confidence*, Semon.1.6, Porph. *Gaur*.6.4. **-ής**, ές, *obedient*, λόγῳ Arist.*EN*1098ᵃ4; τινί Hierocl. *in CA*24 p.473 M. **-ομαι**, *to be persuaded*, εἴ τις ἐμοὶ ἐπιπείσεται... οἴκαδ' ἴμεν Il.17.154; ἐπεπείθετο θυμὸς ἀγήνωρ Od.2.103. 2. *trust to, put faith in*, μαρτυρίοισι A.*Ag*.1095 (lyr.), cf. *IG*14.1389 ii 32. 3. *comply with, obey*, τινί Il.1.218, Hes.*Sc*.369; εὖ παραινεῖς, κἀπιπείσομαι S.*El*.1472.

ἐπιπειράομαι, *do violence to* a woman, c. acc., *Leg.Gort*.2.17, cf. Hsch. ἐπιπείρει (sic)· μοιχεύεται, ἢ μοιχεύει.

ἐπιπελάζω, *bring near to*, ξίφος αἵματι σῷ E.*IT*880 (lyr., tm.).

ἐπιπελανίαι· ὀλαί, καὶ πόπανα, Hsch.

ἐπιπέλομαι, *come to* or *upon*, οὐδέ τις ἄλλη νοῦσος ἐπὶ στυγερὴ πέλεται.. βροτοῖσι Od.15.408, cf. 13.60: elsewh. only in Ep. aor. 2 part. ἐπιπλόμενος *rolling on, approaching*, ἀλλ' ὅτε δὴ ὄγδοόν μοι ἐπιπλόμενον ἔτος ἦλθεν when the eighth *revolving* year had come, 7.261; ἐπιπλομένων ἐνιαυτῶν Hes.*Sc*.87, *Th*.493 (v. ἐνιαυτός); ἐπιπλ. νυκτί, ἐπιπλ. ἠοῦς A.R.2.1231, 4.670, etc.; of persons, Id.3.25, 127; in hostile sense, *attacking, assaulting*, Id.1.465; so of a storm, νέφος.. ἐπιπλ. ἄφατον S.*OT*1314 (lyr.). (Cf. περιτέλλομαι, ἐπιτέλλω (B).)

ἐπίπεμμα, ατος, τό, *sacrificial cake*, *Inscr.Prien*.362.15 (iv B.C.), al.

ἐπιπεμπτέον, *one must send*, Alex.*Fig*.1.1.

ἐπίπεμπτος, ον, Math., = 1 + ⅕, Nicom.*Ar*.1.22, etc. 2. of loans *bearing interest at the rate of* ⅕ *of the principal*, i.e. 20 per cent., ναυτικὸν ἐ. X.*Vect*.3.9. II. = πέμπτος, Eup.65, Lxx *Le*.5.16, al.; τοὐπίπεμπτον *one-fifth* of the votes in a trial, Ar.*Fr*.201.

ἐπιπέμπω, pf. -πέπομφα *POxy*.743.30 (i A.D.):—*send after* or *again*, ἀγγελίας, ἀγγέλους ἐ., c. inf., Hdt.1.160, 4.83 (nisi leg. περι-). 2. *send to*, τοὺς ὁριστὰς ἐπιπέμψαι ὁρίσαι τὰ ἱερά *IG*1².94; of the gods, *send upon* or *to*, [ὄνειρον] Hdt.7.15; χάριν Pi.*Fr*.75.2 (tm.); ἔρως τινί Pl.*Phdr*.245b (Pass.); esp. by way of punishment, *send upon* or *against, let loose upon*, generally of the gods, γένναν ἂν...ʽΑιδας Καδμείοις ἐ. E.*Ph*.811 (lyr.); δέῃ καὶ κινδύνους τινί Lys.6.20; δεσμοὺς καὶ θανάτους Pl.*Cri*.46c; ἀνάγκην τινά Id.*Phd*.62c; τισὶ πλῆθος ἄρκων Lxx *Wi*.11.17; *send against*, κατασκόπους τοῖς Ῥωμαίοις App.*Pun*. 39; τῇ Καρχηδόνι τινά prob. ib.49, cf. Hdn.3.3.4. II. *send besides*, ἄλλην στρατιάν Th.7.15; πρὸς τὸ στράτευμα ὠφελίαν ἄλλην Id.6. 73. 2. *send* by way of supply, σιτία Ar.*Ec*.235, cf. Plb.6.15.4; digested food, etc., to various parts of the body, Gal.6.301, 427, 15.112.

ἐπίπεμψις, εως, ἡ, *a sending to* a place, διὰ τὴν.. ἐπὶ πολλὰ ἡμῶν αὐτῶν ἐ. Th.2.39, cf. Luc.*Phal*.1.3. 2. *visitation*, Epicur.*Ep*.2 p.44 U. (pl.).

ἐπιπένθεκτος, ον, = ἐπιπενταμερής, Nicom.*Ar*.1.21.

ἐπιπεντᾰκοσῐοτέταρτος, ον, 1 + 1/54, Aristid.Quint.3.1.

ἐπιπεντᾰμερής, ές, = 1 + 5/8, Nicom.*Ar*.1.21.

ἐπιπεντεκαιδέκᾰτος λόγος ratio *of* 16 : 15, Porph.*in Harm*.p.310 W.

ἐπιπεντένᾰτος, ον, = 1 + 5/9, Nicom.*Ar*.1.23.

ἐπιπερι-ελίσσω, *wrap round a second time*, τι περὶ τὴν κεφαλήν Hp. *Art*.38. **-τρέπω**, *convert to a purpose*, M.Ant.8.35 (s.v.l.).

ἐπιπερκ-άζω, *turn dark*, of grapes ripening: ἐπιπερκάζειν τριχί *begin to get a dark* beard, *AP*11.36 (Phil.). **-νος**, ον, *somewhat dark*, of grapes ripening: hence, of the colour of certain hares, X. *Cyn*.5.22, Poll.5.67.

ἐπιπέσσω, Att. -ττω, *bake*, ἔλατρα *SIG*57.36 (Milet., v B.C.). II. Pass., *to be concocted*, Gal.*UP*14.11.

ἐπιπετάννῡμι, *spread over*, τὰ ὦτα ἐπὶ τὰς ὠμοπλάτας X.*Cyn*.5.10, cf. Aret.*CA*1.10:—Pass., τέφρη ἐπεπέπτατο Q.S.14.25; ἐπίπαγος ἐπιπετάννυται Aret.*SD*2.9.

ἐπιπέτομαι, fut. -πτήσομαι Hdt.7.15: aor. ἐπεπτάμην or -όμην (v. infr.); later, also in act. form ἐπέπτην, part. ἐπιπτάς *AP*11.407 (Nicarch.), Alciphr.3.59, Porph.*Abst*.1.25:—*fly to* or *towards*, καθ' ὅμιλον ἐπιπτέσθαι μενεαίνων Il.4.126; οἱ..ἐπέπτατο δεξιὸς ὄρνις 13. 821; ἐ. σοὶ τὠυτὸ ὄνειρον Hdt.7.15; ἣ 'πέπτετο Ar.*Av*.48; ἀετὸς ἐπιπτόμενος αἴσιος X.*Cyr*.2.4.19. 2. c. acc., *fly over*, πεδία E.*Hel*.1486 (lyr.); γῆν καὶ θάλατταν Ar.*Av*.118; ἐ. ἀρούραις Ael.*NA*17.16: metaph., καινὰ καὶ θαυμαστὰ ἐ. *fly over to, run eagerly after*, Ar.*Av*. 1471 (lyr.); ἐπὶ πάντα τὰ λεγόμενα ὥσπερ ἐπιπτόμενοι *flitting* from one to another, Pl.*R*.365a. 3. *fly at* or *on to*, of a male bird, Arist. *HA*564ᵇ4.

ἐπίπετρον, τό, *a rock-plant*, a kind of *sedum*, Hp.*Ulc*.11 (vulg. ἐπίπτερον), Arist.*PA*681ᵃ23, cj. for ἐπίμετρον in Thphr.*HP*7.7.4.

ἐπίπηγμα, ατος, τό, in pl., *cross-rods* connecting parts of a torsion-engine, Ph.*Bel*.54.5. II. *second cover*, Heliod.ap.Orib.49.4.39.

ἐπιπήγνῡμι or -ύω, *make to freeze on the top*, X.*Cyn*.5.1:—Pass., with intr. pf. ἐπιπέπηγα, *congeal, coagulate*, Thphr.*CP*5.13.2, Gal. 18(1).597. II. Pass., *to be fastened on*, ὀργάνῳ Heliod.ap.Orib. 49.4.39. (Cf. ἐπιπήσσομαι.)

ἐπιπηδ-άω, fut. -ήσομαι Pl.*Ly*.216a:—*leap upon, rush at, assault*, ἀγρίως ἐ. τινί Ar.*V*.705, cf. Pl. l.c., *PTeb*.44.18 (ii B.C.); ἐ. τῷ λόγῳ Plu.2.512d: c. gen., σκάφους J.*BJ*2.21.6; ἐπὶ τὴν τιμωρίαν ib.10; of male animals, ἐπιπηδῶν ὀχεύει Arist.*HA*539ᵇ32, cf. Pl.*Phdr*.254a: metaph., *rush in, plunge in*, τῇ τέχνῃ Gal.18(1).635. **-ησις**, εως, ἡ, *springing upon, assault*, Plu.2.916d (pl.): metaph., ὁρμαὶ καὶ -σεις ib.76c, etc.; of the male animal, ib.768e, 1095a (pl.).

ἐπιπῆν, v. ἐπιπάσσω.

ἐπίπηξ, πηγος, ὁ, = ἐπίπηγμα, Apollod.*Poliorc*.188.4. 2. *graft*, *Gp*.4.12.8.

ἐπίπηξις, εως, ἡ, *bracing up, constriction*, τοῦ σώματος Agathin.ap. Orib.10.7.25. II. = ἐπίπαγος, *capsule* of lens, Gal.*Anat.Adm*.10 (Arabic version).

ἐπιπήσσομαι, = ἐπιπήγνυμαι I, Dsc.5.101. 2. = ἐπιπήγνυμαι II, Apollon.Cit.3.

ἐπίπηχυς, υ, *above the elbow*, Poll.2.140, Hsch.

ἐπιπῐ-έζω, *press upon*, ἐπὶ μάστακα χερσὶ πίεζε Od.4.287; λαῖον ἐπὶ στιβαρῷ πιέσας ποδὶ A.R.3.1335, cf. Dsc.2.4. **-εσμός**, ὁ, *pressing upon*, Gal.8.509, Archig.ap.eund.8.931.

ἐπίπιθον, *seria* (= πιθάκνη), *Gloss*.

ἐπιπικρ-αίνω, *make still more keen*, δίψαν Hp.*Acut.*62. **-ος**, ον, *somewhat bitter*, Thphr.*HP*6.4.10.

ἐπιπίλναμαι, only pres., Ep. for ἐπιπελάζομαι, *come near*, οὔτε χιὼν ἐπιπίλναται Od.6.44 (v.l. ἐπικίδναται); ἐπ' οὔδει πίλναται Il.19.92.

ἐπιπίμπλημι, *fill full of*, σπλάγχνων χεῖρ' ἐπιπλῆσαι Ar.*Av.*975.

ἐπιπίνω [πῐ], *drink afterwards* or *besides*, Hp.*Acut.*56, Ar.*Pax* 712; opp. προπίνω, Ctes.*Fr.*57.25; ἐ. τοῦ οἴνου *drink* some wine *with their food*, Pl.*R.*372b; ὅταν τὸ ὕδωρ πνίγῃ, τί δεῖ ἐπιπίνειν; Arist.*EN* 1146^{a}35: esp. *drink after* eating, κρέ' ἔδων καὶ ἐπ' ἄκρητον γάλα πίνων Od. 9.297; θύννεια.. καταφαγών, κᾆτ' ἐπιπιὼν ἀκράτου.. χοᾶ Ar.*Eq.*354, cf. *Pl.*1133, Philem.85.3; ἐ. μετὰ τὸν σῖτον οἶνον X.*Cyr.*6.2.28: abs., τὸ πρῴ 'πιπίνειν Eup.351 (Elmsl. for πρῶτ' ἐπ.).

ἐπιπιπράσκω, *sell the right of succession to* a priesthood, *SIG*1014.8 (Erythrae, iii B.C., Pass.); to an inheritance, dub. in *PLond.*1.113 (1).88 (vi A.D.).

ἐπιπίπτω, *fall upon* or *over*, ἐπέπιπτον ἀλλήλοις Th.7.84; ἐπί τι X.*Oec.*18.7, cf. Thphr.*CP*5.4.5: metaph., ἐπέπεσε μοῖρα Pi.*Pae.*2.64; ἐπί τι Isoc.5.89; διαλογισμοὶ ἐπιπίπτουσί τινι Plu.*Oth.*9. 2. of money, *accrue*, τὸ μέρος ὃ εὑρίσκομες ἐπιπῖπτον ἐπὶ τὸ χρέος τὸ ὀφειλόμενον *SIG*953.66 (Cnidus, ii B.C.). II. *fall upon* in hostile sense, *attack, assail*, τινί Hdt.4.105, Th.3.112; ἀφυλάκτῳ αὐτῷ ἐ. Hdt.9. 116; ἀφάρκτῳ τῷ στρατοπέδῳ Th.1.117; ἀπαρασκεύοις τοῖς ἐναντίοις X.*Cyr.*7.4.3; also ἐς τοὺς Ἕλληνας, v.l. for ἐσ-, Hdt.7.210; of storms, τοῖσι βαρβάροισι ὁ βορῆς ἐπέπεσε ib.189; χειμὼν ἐπιπεσὼν Pl.*Prt.* 344d; of winds *meeting* one another, Arist.*Mete.*364^{b}3; of diseases, Hp.*Aër.*3; ἡ νόσος ἐ. τοῖς Ἀθηναίοις Th.3.87; so of grief, misfortunes, etc., οὐχὶ σοὶ μόνᾳ ἐπέπεσον λῦπαι E.*Andr.*1043 (lyr.), etc.; ἐπέπεσε πολλὰ καὶ χαλεπὰ κατὰ στάσιν ταῖς πόλεσι Th.3.82, etc. 2. *come on after*, ἐ. ῥῖγος πυρετῷ Hp.*Aph.*4.46. 3. *accumulate*, πλήθη σίτου ἐπιπεπτωκέναι *PPetr.*2p.62 (iii B.C.).

ἐπιπίσσω· ἐπιπάσσω, Hsch.

ἐπιπίστωσις, εως, ἡ, *further* πίστωσις, in Rhet., Theod.Byz.ap. Pl.*Phdr.*266e, cf. Herm.*in Phdr.*p.191 A.

ἔπιπλα, τά, *implements, utensils, furniture, movable property* (ἡ κούφη κτῆσις, τὰ ἐπιπολῆς ὄντα τῶν κτημάτων, Poll.10.10; σκεύη τὰ μὴ ἔγγεια ἀλλ' ἐπιπόλαια, Hsch.); opp. fixtures, Hdt.1.150,164, 7.119, al., S.*Fr.*8, Th.3.68, Is.8.35, X.*Oec.*9.6, Arist.*Pol.*1267^{b}12, etc.; *fittings* of a ship, *PCair.Zen.*242 (iii B.C.): rarely sg., ἔπιπλον Is.(*Fr.* 28) ap.Poll.10.11, Asp.*in EN*96.30. (The form ἐπίπλοα occurs in Mss. of Hdt.1.94 (cf. Poll.10.10), and late Pap., as *BGU*483.6 (ii A.D.), but ἔπιπλα *PCair.Zen.* l.c., *PGrenf.*1.12.18 (ii B.C.), etc.)

ἐπιπλᾰδάω, *to be loose, flabby on the surface*, Ph.2.418 codd.

ἐπίπλαδον· φέρεσθαι, Hsch.

ἐπιπλάζομαι, fut. -πλάγξομαι: aor. 1 ἐπεπλάγχθην:—*wander about over*, πόντον ἐπιπλαγχθεὶς Od.8.14; πόντον ἐπιπλάγξεσθαι A.R.3. 1066:—later in Act., Nic.*Al.*127.

ἐπιπλάζω, Aeol., = ἐπιπλήσσω, Sapph.17.

ἐπιπλᾰνάομαι, = ἐπιπλάζομαι, γῆν Democr.[299]; δακρύων τοῖς ὄμμασιν ἐπιπλανωμένων Hld.7.17, cf. 3.5: abs., κιττὸς ἐπιπλανώμενος Longus 1.2.

ἐπί-πλᾰσις, εως, ἡ, *application* of a σικύη, Aret.*CA*2.3; of plasters, ib.1.9 (pl.). **-πλασμα**, ατος, τό, *plaster*, Hp.*Art.*40, Aret.*CA*1.1, Lyc.ap.Orib.9.25.1, etc. **-πλάσσω**, Att. -ττω, *spread* or *plaster on*, γῆν σημαντρίδα ἐπιπλάσας Hdt.2.38; τι ἐπὶ δῆγμα Thphr.*HP*9. 13.3; τί τινι Gal.11.86. II. *plaster up*, τὰ ὦτα Arist.*Pr.*875^{a}36; τοὺς πόρους Thphr.*Sens.*8. III. *mould upon*, ποτάνοις ἵππον ποτάμιον Plu.2.371d, cf. 362f:—Pass., ναστὸς ἐπιπεπλασμένος *moulded*, *IG*2^2.1367. IV. Med., *plaster over*, νηδύν Ael.*Fr.*89. **-πλαστέον**, *one must plaster over*, *Gp.*16.18.3. **-πλαστος**, ον, *plastered over*, πρόσωπον Alciphr.3.11; ἐπίπλαστα, τά, *poultices* or *plasters*, Artem.4. 22, Asclep.ap.Gal.12.415. 2. metaph., *feigned, false*, λόγοι J.*BJ*4. 4.3; ὀλοφυρμός, δάκρυα, ib.1.32.2, Luc.*DMort.*27.7; ὑπόκρισις Id.*Am.* 3; φιλία Hdn.3.15.7. Adv. -τως M.Ant.2.16. **-πλαστώδης**, ες, *suitable for a plaster*, Orib.9.55.1.

ἐπιπλᾰτᾰγέω, *applaud by clapping*, τινί Theoc.9.22; χεῖρας *Epic. Alex.Adesp.*2.72.

ἐπιπλᾰτ-ής, ές, *flat, broad*, only in Adv. -τῶς, Aët.7.31. **-ορ**· πλακοῦντος εἶδος, Hsch. **-ύνω**, *expand yet more*, Arist.*Mu.*393^a 20 (Pass.). **-ύς**, ύ, *broad at the top, flat*, ἐπιπλατὺ σφαιροειδές an *oblate* spheroid, Archim.*Con.Sph.Praef.*; λοβοί Thphr.*HP*8. 5.3.

ἐπιπλεκ-τέον, *one must weave*, Orph.*Fr.*49.62. **-ω**, *wreathe into* a chaplet, *AP*12.256.5 (Mel.); νάρκισσον ὑακίνθῳ Nonn.*D.*10. 338. 2. *bind*, αὐχένα δεσμῷ ib.18.189; *bind upon*, ταρσῷ γυιοπέδην ib.36.365:—Pass., Luc.*Cont.*16. II. metaph., *interweave, combine*, αὐτὰ τῷ τῆς παραλείψεως σχήματι Arist.*Rh.Al.*1438^{b}5; τὸ διὰ τῶν αὐτῶν ὀνομάτων ἐπιπλέξαι Aristid.*Rh.*2p.544S.; ἐ. ἑαυτοὺς ταῖς προσόδοις *concern* themselves *with*, *PTeb.*6.39 (ii B.C.):—Pass., τὰς ἐπιβολὰς τὰς Ἀννίβου ταῖς.. πράξεσιν ἐπιπεπλέχθαι Plb.4.28.2, cf. Luc.*Dem.Enc.*8; τοῖς Ἕλλησιν ἐ. *to have dealings with*.., Str.14.2. 28; ξένοις ἐπιπλᾰκέντες ἔθεσιν J.*AJ*8.7.5; also, *to have sexual intercourse with*, Posidon.36 J., D.S.36.2a; ἐπιπεπλεγμένος *mixed*, Gal. *Sect.Intr.*6; *complex*, πυρετοί Id.7.432.

ἐπιπλεοναστέον, *one must increase the quantity*, Herod.Med.ap. Orib.5.30.39.

ἐπίπλεος, έα, Ion. έη, εον, *quite full of*, κρεῶν Hdt.1.119, 3.18; ἀγαθῶν πάντων Id.6.139:—Att. -πλεως, ων, Plu.*Ant.*85.

ἐπίπλευρα, τά, = τὰ παρὰ τοῖς μαστοῖς ὑπὸ τὰς μασχάλας, Hsch. II. ἐπίπλευρος φέρεται *sideways*, Sch.Nic.*Th.*268.

ἐπίπλευσις, εως, ἡ, *sailing against*, ἐ. ἔχειν to have *the power of attacking* (the *weather gage*), opp. ἀνάκρουσις, Th.7.36.

ἐπιπλέω, Ion. -πλώω (both in Hom.), fut. -πλεύσομαι Th.3.16: aor. 1 -έπλευσα ib.80, Ion. -έπλωσα Hdt.1.70: Ep. 2 sg. aor. 2 ἐπέπλως, part. ἐπιπλώς, but (Il.3.47) ἐπιπλώσας:—*sail upon* or *over*, ἐπέπλεον ὑγρὰ κέλευθα Il.1.312, Od.4.842; πόντον ἐπιπλώων 5.284; πόντον ἐπέπλως 3.15; ἐπιπλὼς εὐρέα πόντον Il.6.291; ἐπιπλεῖν ἁλμυρὸν ὕδωρ Od.9.227, etc. II. *sail against, attack by sea*, νηυσὶ ἐ. τινί Hdt.5.86; τῇ Κερκύρᾳ Th.3.76; ἐπὶ τὰς Μινδάρου ναῦς X.*HG*1.5.11, etc.; ἐπὶ τὴν Σαλαμῖνα D.S.20.50: abs., Hdt.1.70, 6.33; also of the ships, Th.3.80: generally, *sail on*, Plb.1.25.4, etc. III. *sail on board* a ship, Hdt.7.98, 8.67, Th.2.66; of commanders, τοὺς ἐπὶ τῶν νεῶν ἐ. στρατηγούς Hdt.5.36; [ναύαρχος] Th.3.16; ξύμβουλος ib.76; ταμίας D.49.14; also ἐ. ταῖς ἐμπορίαις *sail in charge of*, Id.56.8; and ὁ ἐπιπλέων the *supercargo*, Id.32.12; οἱ ἐπιπλεύσαντες ἐπὶ τοῦ ἐλαίου *PCair.Zen.*77.2 (iii B.C.). IV. of a naval commander, *sail past* (in order to address, cf. ἐπιπάρειμι (B) 4), τοὺς κυβερνήτας καὶ τριηράρχους Plu.*Lys.*11. V. *sail after*, ἐπὶ παντὶ τῷ στόλῳ Plb.1.50.5; *sail up afterwards*, ib.25.4. VI. *float upon*, ἐπ' αὐτοῦ (sc. τοῦ ὕδατος) Hdt.3.23; ἐπὶ τῆς θαλάσσης Arist.*HA*622^{b}6; ἐπὶ τῷ ὕδατι Id.*Mete.* 384^{b}17; *slip, slide upon* ice, Plb.3.55.2,4. VII. *overflow* (of a river), gloss on ἄρδειν, interpol. in App.*BC*2.153; μέχρι ἐπιπλεύσῃ until (the water) *covers* the substance, *PHolm.*21.29.

ἐπίπλεως, ων, Att. for ἐπίπλεος (q.v.).

ἐπίπληγμα, ατος, τό, gloss on ἔνιγμα, *rebuke*, *Et.Gud.*

ἐπιπληθύνω, *increase*, Lxx *Ge.*7.17 (Pass.):—Pass., **-ύομαι**, *superabound*, χάριτες Demetr.*Eloc.*156.

ἐπιπλήκτ-ειρα, ἡ, = fem. of ἐπιπλήκτης, *AP*6.233 (Maec.). **-έος**, α, ον, *worthy of reproof*, Ph.1.242. **-ης**, ου, ὁ, (ἐπιπλήσσω) *corrector*, *Gloss.* **-ικός**, ή, όν, *given to rebuking*, D.L.4.63. Adv. -κῶς D.S. 17.114, Sch.E.*Med.*967.

ἐπιπλημμύρω [ῡ], *overflow*, τι Opp.*H.*1.465:—also **-έω**, τῇ θαλάττῃ Philostr.*Im.*2.17.

ἐπίπληξις, Dor. -πλαξις, εως, ἡ, *blame, rebuke*, Ti.Locr.103e (pl.), D.61.18 (pl.); τυγχάνειν τῆς καθηκούσης ἐ. *SIG*630.9 (Delph., ii B.C.); ἐ. ἔχειν incur *criticism*, Aeschin.1.177; ἐ. πρός τι or τινα, Hp. *Decent.*12, Plu.*Sol.*3 (pl.). 2. in strong sense, *punishment*, Lxx 2*Ma.*7.33, *PSI*5.542.30 (iii B.C.), Mitteis *Chr.*31 iii 14 (ii B.C.): pl., of *plagues*, Ph.2.100.

ἐπιπληρ-όω, *fill up*, συμπόσιον Ephipp.4 (Casaub., -κληρ- codd. Ath.); κακοῖς ἐ. κακά S.E.*M.*1.68:—Med., οὐδ' ὁπόθεν ἐπιπληρωσόμεθα τὰς ναῦς no resources whence we *shall man our* ships *afresh*, Th.7. 14:—Pass., Gal.15.781. **-ωσις**, εως, ἡ, *refilling, keeping full*, Id. 4.471.

ἐπιπλήσσω, Att. -ττω, *strike*, τόξῳ ἐπιπλήσσων Il.10.500; ὑπέροισιν Nic.*Th.*952. II. *punish, chastise*, esp. with words, *rebuke, reprove*, c. acc. pers., καί μ' οὔ τινά φημι ἄλλον ἐπιπλήξειν Il.23.580, cf. Pl.*Prt.*327a: c. dat., Ἕκτορ, ἀεὶ μέν πώς μοι ἐπιπλήσσεις Il.12.211, cf. Isoc.1.31; ἐμαυτῷ Pl.*Lg.*805b, cf. 1*Ep.Ti.*5.1, etc.; ἐπί τινι for a thing, Pl.*Plt.*286b:—Pass., *to be rebuked*, Id.*Grg.*478e. 2. ἐ. τινί τι *cast* a thing *in* one's *teeth*, Hdt.3.142, 7.136; τὴν.. αὐθαδίαν.. μὴ 'πίπλησσέ μοι A.*Pr.*80; ἐ. τινὶ τοῦτο, ὅτι.. Pl.*Prt.*319d: c. acc. rei only, τί τόδ' ἐπέπληξας; S.*OC*1730 (lyr.): abs., Id.*Aj.*288, X.*Oec.*13.12, etc. III. intr., *fall upon*, ἀρούραις Arat.1095.

ἐπιπλινθοβολέω, *lay courses of bricks above*, *IG*2^2.463.58.

ἐπίπλοα, v. ἔπιπλα ad fin.

ἐπιπλοεντεροκήλη, ἡ, *hernia of omentum and intestines*, Paul.Aeg. 6.65.

ἐπίπλοιον, v. ἐπίπλοον.

ἐπιπλοκή, ἡ, *plaiting together*, ῥίζαι κατ' ἐπιπλοκὴν δασεῖαι *matted* roots, Dsc.4.187; ἐπιπλοκαὶ ἀτόμων *entanglements*, Ph.2.489: metaph., τῶν αἰτίων πρὸς ἄλληλα Plot.3.1.2. 2. *union, intercourse*, πρὸς ἀλλήλους Plb.5.37.2; τῶν βαρβάρων Str.14.2.28; εἰς τοὺς τόπους Plb.2.12.7 (but ἐ. εἰς Πελοπόννησον *intermeddling* with the affairs of P., Id.4.3.3): c. dat., Phld.*Ir.*p.47 W.; *connexion* of people with one another, *Stoic.*3.90,161 (pl.); φίλων ἐπιπλοκαὶ ἑστιατικαί friendly *relations*.., ib.254; *sexual intercourse*, D.S.4.9, Plu.*Sol.*20 (pl.), etc. 3. *combination* of styles, in pl., D.H.*Dem.*37, Hermog.*Stat.* 5; *concatenation* of cause with effect, Chrysipp.*Stoic.*2.293,265. 4. *complexity, confusion, muddle*, τοῦ βίου Men.16.8 D.; ἐ. σοφιστικαί *involved arguments*, Alex.Aphr.*in Metaph.*270.30. 5. Gramm., *insertion* of a letter, Ath.7.324d, Hdn.Gr.2.928; *combination*, στοιχείων, λέξεων, A.D.*Synt.*3.11, 4.10. b. *alloying* of metals, Ps.-Democr.p.54 B. c. *mixed nature* of disease, Gal.*Sect.Intr.*6; esp. of fevers, Id.7.370, al. 6. in Metre, *conversion* of rhythms by change in order of syllables, Mar.Vict.p.63 K.; also, *a group of rhythms thus related*, ἐ. δυαδικὴ τετράσημος, τρίσημος, ibid., cf. Juba ib.p.94 K., Sch.Heph.p.110 C., al.

ἐπιπλο-κήλη, ἡ, *hernia of the omentum*, Gal.7.36:—hence **-κηλικός**, ὁ, *one who suffers from it*, Id.14.789. **-κομιστής**, οῦ, ὁ, *possessing an omentum*, Id.2.556.

ἐπιπλόμενος, v. ἐπιτέλομαι. **ἔπιπλον**, τό, v. ἔπιπλα.

ἐπιπλοόμφαλον, τό, *umbilical hernia of omentum*, Gal.19.444.

ἐπίπλοον, τό, = Homer's δέρτρον, *fold of the peritoneum, omentum*, Hp.*Aph.*5.46, Arist.*HA*495^{b}29, 519^{b}7, *PA*677^{b}12, etc.:—also **ἐπίπλοος**, ὁ, Hdt.2.47; contr. **ἐπίπλους** Epich.80 codd. Ath., Ion Hist. 3; and **ἐπιπόλαιον**, τό, Eub.95.3, Hsch.: **ἐπίπλοιον** Philetaer.17 (s.v.l.).

ἐπίπλοος (A), ον, contr. **ἐπίπλους**, ουν, (ἐπιπλέω) *sailing against* *the enemy*, νῆες 'ships of the line', Plb.1.50.6, cf. 1.27.5, Ph.*Bel.*104.16. 2. *sailing after*, D.S.20.50.3. 3. *on board ship*: as Subst., = ἐπιβάτης, Arr.ap.Suid., cf. *POxy.*276 (i A.D.), etc. II. for ἐπίπλοα, τά, v. ἔπιπλα ad fin.

ἐπίπλοος (B), contr. **ἐπίπλους**, ὁ, *sailing against, bearing down upon, attack* or *onset* of a ship or fleet, Th.2.90, X.*HG*4.3.11, Plu.*Lys.*11, etc.; ποιεῖσθαι ἐπίπλουν, = ἐπιπλεῖν, Th.8.79; ἐ. ἐποιοῦντο τῇ Μιλήτῳ ib.30; ἐπὶ τὴν Σάμον ib.63; τοῖς Ἀθηναίοις Id.3.78; τῇ Πελοποννήσῳ ἑκατὸν νεῶν ἐπίπλουν ἐξαρτύοντες fitting out 100 ships for *the expedition against*.., Id.2.17, cf. 56; ἐ. θέσθαι Plu.*Aem.*9; rarely of friends, *sailing towards, approach*, ἐ. φίλιος Th.8.102.

ἐπίπλοος (C), contr. **ἐπίπλους**, ὁ, v. ἐπίπλοον.

ἐπιπλώω, Ion. and Ep. for ἐπιπλέω.

ἐπί-πνευσις, εως, ἡ, *spasmodic inspiration*, Gal.17(2).750. II. *divine inspiration*, ἐ. θεία Str.10.3.9. **-πνευστικός**, ή, όν, *depending on inspiration*, εἶδος μαντικῆς Sch.A.*Pr.*484. **-πνεύων**· ἐπιβλέπων (Aeol.), Hsch. (citing Alc.66).

ἐπιπνέω, Ep. **-πνείω** (as always in Hom., cf. Call.*Del.*318, A.R.3.937), *breathe upon, blow freshly upon*, περὶ δὲ πνοιὴ.. ζώγρει ἐπιπνείουσα Il.5.698; τινί *on* one, Ar.*V.*265; *blow fairly for*, νηῦς.., ᾗ.. οὖρος ἐπιπνείῃσιν ὄπισθεν Od.4.357: abs., εἰς ὅ κε.. ἐπιπνεύσωσιν ἀῆται 9.139; ἄνεμος..ἥδιστος ἐπέπνει Plu.*Sert.*17, etc. 2. *blow furiously upon*, τινί Hdt.3.26: metaph., μαινόμενος δ' ἐπιπνεῖ..Ἄρης A.*Th.*343 (lyr.), cf. S.*Ant.*136 (lyr.). 3. c. acc., *blow over*, θάλασσαν Hes.*Th.*872; ἀγρούς Luc.*Charid.*1. 4. c. acc. cogn., *blow forth*, πυρὸς σέλας A.R.3.1327. 5. *blow afterwards*, Arist.*Pr.*945^{b}1. 6. *blow against*, of one wind *against* another, Thphr.*Vent.*53. II. metaph., 1. *excite, inflame* against, Ἀργείοις Σπαρτῶν γένναν E.*Ph.*794 (lyr.); στρατὸν αἵματι *to* slaughter, ib.789 (lyr.). 2. *inspire into, grant*, Μουσῶν προφῆται ἐπιπεπνευκότες ἡμῖν τὸ γέρας Pl.*Phdr.*262d; ὄλβον Orph.*H.*84.8. 3. *favour*, λαμπρᾶς ἐπιπνεούσης τῆς τύχης, metaph. from the wind, Plb.11.19.5: c. acc., of love, A.R.3.937, Nonn.*D.*3.121: abs., Plu.2.759f. III. Pass., *to be inspired*, ὑπό τινος Longin.13.2; πρὸς αὐτῶν τῶν Μουσῶν Jul.*Or.*2.78b.

ἐπίπνοια, ἡ, *breathing upon, inspiration*, ἐ. πρᾳότητος Pl.*Ti.*71c; ἐξ ἐπιπνοίας Διός A.*Supp.*17 (anap.), cf. 43 (lyr.); θείαις ἐ. ib.577 (lyr.); οὐκ ἄνευ τινὸς ἐπιπνοίας θεῶν Pl.*Lg.*811c, cf. *Cra.*399a; μαντικὴν..ἐπίπνοιαν Ἀπόλλωνος θέντες κτλ. Id.*Phdr.*265b; ἐπιπνοίᾳ δαιμονίου ἐνθουσιάζειν Arist.*EE*1214^{a}24; ἐ. πρὸς τὸ καλὸν κατασχεθῆναι Plu.*Agis* 7. II. pl., *winds blowing opposite ways*, Thphr.*Vent.*55.

ἐπίπνοος, ον, contr. **-πνους**, ουν, *breathed upon*, Poll.5.110. 2. *inspired*, παρά τινος Pl.*Cra.*428c; ἐ. καὶ κατεχομένους ἐκ τοῦ θεοῦ Id.*Men.*99d; ἐ. ἐκ τούτου τοῦ ἔρωτος Id.*Smp.*181c; σὺν τῷ ῥυθμῷ Ael.*NA* 11.10; ἐ. καὶ φοιβόληπτος Plu.*Pomp.*48. Adv. -πνως Poll.1.16.

ἐπιπόδιος, α, ον, *upon the feet*, S.*OT*1350 (lyr.).

ἐπιποθ-έω, *desire besides* or *yearn after*, c. acc., Hdt.5.93, Ph.2.598; *feel the want of*, Pl.*Lg.*855e; ἐ. τινός Lxx *Ps.*118(119).20; ἐπί τι ib.61(62).11. **-ημα**, ατος, τό, *object of desire*, Aq.*Ps.*139(140).9. **-ησις**, εως, ἡ, *longing after*, τινός 2*Ep.Cor.*7.7, Aq.*Ez.*23.11, Dam.*Pr.*38. **-ητος**, ον, *longed for, desired*, *Ep.Phil.*4.1; *missed, found wanting*, ὅρκοι App.*Hisp.*43. **-ία**, ἡ, = ἐπιπόθησις, *Ep.Rom.*15.23.

ἐπιποι-έω, *superadd*, τινί τι Philostr.*VS*2.5.2; *produce*, ξενιτείαν Vett.Val.97.13; τὸ λίαν ἐπιποιεῖν, perh. *exaggeration*, Phld.*Piet.*27. 2. = ἐπιτίθημι v, τὰ δίκαια *Schwyzer* 409.4 (Elis). **-ησις**, εως, ἡ, *production*, κάλλους Eust.1843.15,37.

ἐπιποιμήν, ένος, ὁ, ἡ, = ποιμήν, θεαὶ δ' ἐπιποιμένες εἰσί Od.12.131.

ἐπίποκος, ον, *covered with wool, woolly*, dub. l. in Lxx 4*Ki.*3.4, cf. *GDI*3731.6 (Cos).

ἐπίπολα, τά, = ἔπιπλα, *GDI*1365 (Dodona).

ἐπι[πολ]-ᾷ, = ἐπιπολῆς (cf. ἐπιπολή II), *Mnemos.*42.332 (Argos, iv B.C.). **-άζω**, fut. -άσω Isoc.5.64: pf. ἐπιπεπόλακα Ph.1.365: (ἐπιπολή):—*to be at the top, come to the surface, float on the surface*, ὕλη ἐ. X.*Oec.*16.14; αἱ ἐγχέλεις οὐκ ἐ. Arist.*HA*592^{a}10, cf. 547^{b}22; ἡ ἀτμὶς ἐ. Id.*Mete.*341^{b}11; τὸ ἐπιπολάζον, opp. τὸ ὑφιστάμενον, Id.*Cael.*312^{a}6: c. dat., ὕδατι ἐ. ib.311^{a}28; [τὸ ἔλαιον] ἐν τῷ ὕδατι ἐ. Id.*Mete.*383^{b}25; of birds, *hover over*, Theopomp.Hist.76; of food, *remain crude* in the stomach, Hp.*Vict.*2.54, Arist.*APo.*94^{b}13, Gal.6.433, 15.63. II. metaph., *have the upper hand, prevail*, [Epich.]282; Φίλιππος ἐπιπολάζει D.9.25, cf. Isoc.5.64, 8.107; ἐ. ἐν πᾶσι τοῖς πολιτεύμασιν Plb.30.13.2. 2. *to be prevalent, fashionable, current*, τοῖς τηλικούτοις..ὕβρις ἐ. X.*Lac.*3.2; ἐκ τῆς ἐπιπολαζούσης τὰ νῦν λεσχηνείας Pl.*Ax.*369d; αἱ μάλιστα ἐπιπολάζουσαι [δόξαι] Arist.*EN*1095^{a}30; ἐπιπολάζοντος τοῦ γελοίου ib.1128^{a}12. 3. *to be common, abound*, ὁ χυμὸς ἐπεπόλασεν Hp.*Epid.*1.15; οἱ ἐπιπολάζοντες μύες Arist.*HA* 580^{b}14; τὴν..ἄνοιαν ἐ. Alex.45.7 (with play on 1); of habits, Plb.13.3.1, etc.; of poems, Sch.Ar.*Th.*169; γένος -άζον τῷ βίῳ *abounding* in the world, Luc.*Icar.*29. 4. *to be 'uppish'* or *insolent*, D.H.11.6, App.*Mith.*75; ἐ. ὑπεροψίᾳ Id.*BC*3.76: c. dat. pers., *behave insolently to*, Plu.2.634c. III. *wander over*, τὴν Αἴγυπτον Hld.2.25, cf. 8.8. IV. *overflow*, of the sea, Luc.*Asin.*34. 2. ἐ. τῇ ῥητορικῇ *to be engaged upon* it, Id.*Rh.Pr.*26. **-αιόρριζος**, ον, *with roots which run along the surface*, Thphr.*HP*1.6.4, 2.5.1 (Comp.). **-αιος**, ον, *on the surface, superficial*, Hp.*Art.*69 (Comp.); ῥίζα Dsc.4.184, cf. Thphr.*HP*3.6.4 (Sup.), al.; λεπτὸν καὶ ἐ. δέρμα Arist.*Pr.*890^{a}13; τραῦμα Luc.*Nav.*37. 2. ὀστέον *shallow* (of the skull), Hp.*VC*21; ὀφθαλμοί, i.e. not deep-set, X.*Smp.*5.5. 3. metaph., *superficial, shallow, commonplace*, παιδεία Isoc.15.190; ἐ. ἡδοναὶ καὶ διατριβαί D.61.56; ἐ. πιθανότης Dsc.*Ther.Praef.*; -ότατος πυρετός *slight* fever, Diocl.*Fr.*107; ἐ. ὕπνος *light* sleep, Luc.*Gall.*25; ἔρως Id.*DMeretr.*8.2; ἐπιστήμης..φύσις (compared to a well) οὐκ ἐ. ἀλλὰ πάνυ βαθεῖα Ph.1.621. b. *on the surface, manifest*: hence, *obvious*, ἐ. λέγομεν τὰ παντὶ δῆλα Arist.*Rh.*1410^{b}22, cf. 1412^{b}25; ἐπιπολαιότερον τοῦ ζητουμένου Id.*EN*1095^{b}24; ἡ -οτάτη..ζήτησις the *most obvious* method of inquiry, Id.*Pol.*1276^{a}19; ἐπιπόλαιον τὸ ψεῦδος ib.1282^{b}30. II. Adv. -ως *on the surface*, τιτρώσκειν J.*BJ*3.7.22. 2. *slightly*, Hp.*Aph.*2.28; *superficially*, Arist.*Metaph.*987^{a}22: Comp. -οτέρως ib.993^{b}13. III. ἐπιπόλαιον, τό, v. ἐπίπλοον. IV. ἐπιπόλαια χρήματα, = ἔπιπλα, *Leg.Gort.*5.41, cf. *GDI*5016.15 (Gortyn). **-ἄσις**, εως, ἡ, *being on the surface, coming to the surface*, Hp.*Hum.*3, Arist.*Sens.*440^{b}16. **-ασμός**, ὁ, = foreg., ἐ. τῆς ζέσεως Id.*Pr.*930^{b}31; λιποθυμώδεις ἐ. *retchings* with faintness, Archig.ap.Orib.8.1.26. 2. metaph., *arrogance, insolence*, D.H.6.65. **-αστικός**, ή, όν, *apt to rise to the surface, floating on the stomach*, of undigested food, Hp.*Acut.*62, Arist.*Pr.*873^{b}26. 2. *insolent*: in Adv. -κῶς *violently*, χρώμενος τῇ κραυγῇ Plb.4.12.9. **-έομαι**, v. ἐπιπωλέομαι. **-εύω**, = ἐπιπολάζω I, Ael.*NA*9.61. **-ή**, ἡ, (ἐπιτέλλω (B)) pl. Ἐπιπολαί, αἱ, the *Rise*, a triangular plateau near Syracuse which rises from its base (the wall of Achradina) to its apex (Euryalus), Th.6.96, etc. 2. sg., *surface*, *Schwyzer* 89.15 (Argos, iii B.C.), Aret.*SD*2.7, Gal.2.626. II. elsewh. only in gen., ἐπιπολῆς, as Adv., *on the top*, Hdt.2.62, Arist.*GA*747^{a}5, etc.; κάτω μὲν καὶ ἐ..., ἐν μέσῳ δέ.. X.*Mem.*3.1.7; λίαν ἐ. πεφυτευμένα Id.*Oec.*19.4; ἐ. τὸ σιναρὸν σκέλος ἔχοντα *uppermost*, Hp.*Art.*77; τά ἐ. τε καὶ ἐντός Pl.*Phlb.*47c, cf. 46e; of arguments, ἐ. εἶναι to be *superficial*, Arist.*Rh.*1400^{b}31; but τὰ παντελῶς ἐ. quite *simple* tasks, D.61.37; πᾶσίν ἐστιν ἐ. ἰδεῖν Arist.*HA*622^{b}25, cf. *Rh.*1376^{b}14. 2. as Prep., c. gen., *on the top of, above*, τῶν πυλέων Hdt.1.187, cf. Ar.*Ec.*1108, *Pl.*1207. 3. with other Preps., κατύπερθε ἐπιπολῆς τῶν ξύλων Hdt.4.201; ἐξ ἐ. εὑρίσκεσθαι D.S.5.38; οὐκ ἐξ ἐ. ὁ λόγος ἡμῶν καθίκετο made a *deep* impression, Luc.*Nigr.*35, etc. (condemned by Phryn.*PS* p.67 B., Luc.*Sol.*5); δι' ἐ. τῶν λέξεων Seleuc.ap.Ath.9.398a; so ἐν ἐπιπολῇ, = ἐπιπολῆς, Str.12.7.3. **-ῆδες**· περόναι, Hsch. **-ιαῖος**, epith. of Hermes at Rhodes, Gorgon 2; of Zeus at Miletus, Hsch. (prob.).

ἐπιπολίζω, *build upon*, Hsch.

ἐπιπολῐ-όομαι, *begin to grow grey*, τρίχες ἐ. Arist.*GA*785^{a}18. **-ος**, ον, *growing grey, grizzled*, D.54.34.

ἐπίπολος, ὁ, = πρόσπολος, *companion*, S.*OT*1322 (lyr.).

ἐπιπολύ, Adv. for ἐπὶ πολύ, v. πολύς.

ἐπιπομπ-εύω, *triumph over*, ταῖς τῆς πατρίδος συμφοραῖς Plu.*Caes.*56. **-ή**, ἡ, *visitation, punishment*, Aristeas 131 (pl.). 2. *enchantment*, Poet. *de herb.*22 (pl.), 165 (pl.), 175, *PMag.Par.*1.2159. **-ός**, ὁ, *one who sends visitations*, *PMag.Leid.V.*7.10.

ἐπιπον-έω, *toil on*, X.*Cyr.*5.4.17, *Lac.*2.5, Pl.*Lg.*789e. II. c. dat., *labour on* or *at*, τῇ γῇ J.*AJ*18.8.5, cf. 19.2.5. **-ία**, ἡ, *continued toil*, Hsch. s.v. πονηρία. **-ος**, ον, *painful*, οὖρα f.l. for πέπονα in Hp.*Prorrh.*59 (ap.Gal.); θάνατοι Phld.*Ir.*p.30 W.; ἐπιθυμία Epicur.*Fr.*457; *toilsome, laborious*, λατρεία S.*Tr.*829 (lyr.); ἀσχολία, ἄσκησις, φυλακή, Th.1.70, 2.39, 8.11; γῆρας *wearisome*, Pl.*R.*329d (but in good sense, ἔργα ἐξειργασμένοι καλὰ καὶ ἐ. Id.*Lg.*801e, cf. X.*Cyr.*8.1.29 (Sup.)); βίος ib.2.3.11; μαθήσεις καὶ μελέται Id.*Cyn.*12.15; ἁμέρα day *of sorrow*, S.*Tr.*654 (lyr.): Comp. πρᾶξις -ωτέρα καὶ ἐπικινδυνοτέρα X.*An.*1.3.19; -ώτερον ⟨ἔργον⟩ οὐκ εἴληφ' ἐγώ Alex.195; οὐδὲν διαβολῆς ἐστιν -ώτερον Men.576: Sup. παιδεία -ωτάτη Pl.*R.*450c; τὸ ἐπίπονον *toil*, X.*Cyn.*l.c.; τὰ ἐ. Arist.*EN*1116^{a}14; ἐπίπονόν [ἐστι] τὴν δύσκλειαν ἀφανίσαι 'tis *a hard task* to..., Th.3.58. 2. of persons, *laborious, patient of toil*, Ar.*Ra.*1370 (lyr.), Pl.*Phdr.*229d; also, *sensitive to fatigue, easily exhausted*, Thphr.*Sens.*11. 3. of omens, *portending suffering*, X.*An.*6.1.23. II. Adv. -νως *with suffering*, Hp.*Epid.*1.1; *with difficulty*, εὑρίσκεσθαι Th.1.22; ζῆν (opp. τρυφᾶν) Arist.*Pol.*1265^{a}34; ἐ. καὶ καλῶς τινα θεραπεύειν Isoc.19.11; βιώσεται X.*Mem.*1.7.2, etc.: Comp. -ώτερον, διακονεῖν Arched.3.8: Sup. -ώτατα, ζῆν X.*Cyr.*7.5.67.

ἐπιποντία, ἡ, *Goddess of the Sea*, epith. of Aphrodite in Hsch.

ἐπιπορ-εία, ἡ, *coming on the scene*, of marionettes, opp. ἀποπορ., Hero *Aut.*19.1. **-εύομαι**, *travel*, ψυχῆς πείρατα οὐκ ἂν ἐξεύροιο πᾶσαν -όμενος ὁδόν Heraclit.45; *march*, Plb.1.12.4, al.: c. acc., τὴν χώραν *traverse*, ib.30.14: c. dat., τοῖς ἀγροῖς Plu.*Lyc.*28 (s.v.l.); ἐπὶ τοὺς τόπους *PLille* 3.78 (iii B.C.). 2. = ἐπιπάρειμι (B) 4, of a general, -όμενος τὰ συστήματα παρεκάλει Plb.11.12.1, cf. 15.10.1, Plu.*Tim.*12; also ἐ. ἐπὶ τὸ πλῆθος *come before* the assembly, Plb.4.9.2; πρός τινα *Ev.Luc.*8.4: metaph., *go* or *run through*, τῇ διανοίᾳ, τῇ ὄψει, Plu.2.470a. 3. Astron., *reach*, τινὶ τῶν κέντρων Ptol.*Tetr.*99: c. acc., ἥλιος τὸν Κριὸν ἐ. *begins to traverse* the Ram, Jul.*Or.*5.172c. 4. ἐ. τὸν ἱστόν, = ἐποίχομαι (q.v.), Ephor.5 J. 5. *take legal proceedings against* a person, *PHib.*1.96.10 (iii B.C.), etc. **-ευσις**, εως, ἡ, *course*, of planets, Ptol.*Phas.*p.11 H.; of the moon, Id.*Tetr.*98. 2. name for *the fifth* τόπος, *Cat.Cod.Astr.*8(4).152.

ἐπιπορθμεύομαι (v.l. -πορευ-), *spread*, of a morbid condition, Sch.Nic.*Al.*544.

ἐπιπορπ-άομαι, *buckle on oneself, buckle on*, πορφυρίδα Plb.38.7.2. **-ημα**, Dor. -ᾱμα, ατος, τό, *garment buckled over the shoulders, cloak, mantle*, part of the dress of a musician, Pl.Com.10, App.*Pun.*109. **-ίς**, ίδος, ἡ, = foreg., Call.*Ap.*32; νυμφᾶν *AP*6.274 (Pers.). **-όομαι**, = ἀόομαι, σάγους D.S.5.30.

ἐπιπόρρω, Adv. *yet further*, Arc.190.20, Sch.Pi.*O.*3.79.

ἐπιπορσ-αίνω, *prepare for* one, *offer, supply*, Nic.*Fr.*74.54 codd. Ath. **-ύνω**, = foreg., Q.S.7.712.

ἐπιπορφῠρ-ίζω, *have a tinge of purple*, Arist.*Col.*796^{b}14, Thphr. *HP*3.18.2, 6.2.1, al. **-ος**, ον, *with a purple tinge*, ib.4.6.7.

ἐπιποτάμ-ιος [ᾰ], α, ον, *on a river*, πόλις Hellanic.54 J. **-ίς**, ίδος, ἡ, *river-nymph*, Sch.Il.20.8.

ἐπιποτάομαι, lengthd. for ἐπιπέτομαι, *fly* or *hover over*, τοῖον ἐπὶ κνέφας ἀνδρὶ μύσος πεπόταται A.*Eu.*378; Στυγία τις ἐπ' ἀχλὺς πεπόταται Id.*Pers.*668; γῆν καὶ θάλατταν Ph.2.200. II. *float upon*, ἀέρι Dsc.5.75; τῷ ὑγρῷ Porph.*Antr.*10.

ἐπιπότια ᾄσματα (πότος), = σκόλια, Sch. Aristid.p.488 Dind.

ἐπιποτ-ίζω, *water*, *PCair.Zen.*286 (iii B.C.). **-ισμός**, ὁ, *watering*, *PHamb.*62.11 (ii A.D.).

ἐπιπράττομαι, *exact over and above from*, τινά τι Anon.ap.Suid.

ἐπιπρείγιστος (Cret. = ἐπιπρέσβιστος), *next-eldest*, *Leg.Gort.*7.20.

ἐπιπρέπ-εια, ἡ, *congruity, suitableness*, Arist.*Phgn.*809^{a}13, Adam. 2.2: in pl., Plb.3.78.2; of literary effect, Phld.*Po.*2.19,47. II. *appearance*, ἐναντία ἐ. τᾶς ἀλαθινᾶς διαθέσιος Archyt.ap.Stob.3.1.114, cf. Simp.*in Cael.*661.10. **-ής**, ές, *becoming*, Diotog.ap.Stob.4.7. 62; τὸ ἐ., = foreg. 1, Luc.*Im.*7. **-ω**, *to be conspicuous*, οὐδέ τί τοι δούλειον ἐπιπρέπει εἰσοράασθαι εἶδος καὶ μέγεθος Od.24.252; φυᾷ τὸ γενναῖον ἐπιπρέπει ἐκ πατέρων παισὶ λῆμα Pi.*P.*8.44, cf. Theoc.25. 40, D.H.*Din.*7; ὁ ὀφθαλμὸς ἐ. τῷ μετώπῳ Luc.*DMar.*1.1. II. *beseem, suit*, c. dat., Plu.2.794a: impers., ἐπιπρέπει *it is fitting*, c. inf., Xenoph.26.

ἐπιπρεσβεύομαι, *go as ambassador*, D.H.2.47. II. *send an embassy*, πρός τινα Id.6.56; τινί Plu.*Sert.*27, *Ant.*68. 2. *send a second embassy*, App.*Gall.*18.

ἐπιπρηνής, ές, *sloping downwards*, A.R.1.939; = ἐπὶ στόμα, Hsch.

ἐπιπρητήν· αἰγὸς ἡλικία, Hsch.

ἐπιπρηΰνω, Ion. for ἐπιπραΰνω, *soothe*, D.P.1052.

ἐπιπρίω [ρῑ], *grind with rage at*, τὸ γένειον *AP*7.531 (Antip. Thess.), cf. Hsch.

ἐπιπρό, Adv. *right through, onwards*, A.R.2.133, D.P.276.

ἐπιπρο-βαίνω, pf. -βέβηκα, *stretch forward, project*, D.P.128, Ruf. *Oss.*37. **-βάλλω**, *throw forward*, ὅπλα ἐπί τινι Simyl.ap.Plu.*Rom.* 17. **-έηκα, -έμεν**, v. ἐπιπροΐημι. **-έχομαι**, *stand forward, project*, A.R.4.524. **-θέω**, *run on farther*, Id.1.582, Nic.*Th.*382: *rush into*, κύρτον Opp.*H.*3.379 (nisi divisim). **-ϊάλλω** [ῐ], poet. Verb, *set out* or *place before one*, σφωῒν ἐπιπροΐηλε τράπεζαν Il.11.628. II. *send on one after another*, θεοὺς ἐπιπροΐαλλεν *h.Cer.*326; ἄλλον ἐπ' ἄλλῳ ἰόν Q.S.6.231. **-ΐημι**, poet. Verb, *send forth*, τὸν μὲν νηυσὶν ἐπιπροέηκα.. Ἴλιον εἴσω *on board* ship to Ilium, Il.18.58; but κεῖνον.. νηυσὶν ἐπιπροέηκα θοῇσιν, ἐλθεῖν.. *to* the ships, to go.., 17.708; ἄνδρας δὲ λίσσεσθαι ἐπιπροέηκεν ἀρίστους *sent* them *forth* to supplicate, 9.520; Μενελάῳ ἐπιπροέμεν ταχὺν ἰόν (Ep. aor. 2 inf.) *shoot* an arrow *at* him, 4.94; νημερτέα βάξιν ἐ. A.R.4.1185; φρῖκας Nic.*Th.*778; πότμον Orac.ap.Luc.*Alex.*27; λιγὺν οὖρον Orph.*A.*361; τινὰ θαλάσσῃ *into* the sea, A.R.4.1617, etc.; ῥέεθρον θαλάσσῃ, of a river, D.P.49, cf. 794: hence, seemingly intr., νήσοισιν ἐπιπροέηκε (sc. νῆα) he *made straight for* them, Od.15.299.

ἐπί-προικα· τὸ δεύτερον ἐπὶ προικὶ δῶρον, Hsch. **-προικος**, ἡ, (προΐξ) *woman who inherits a charge upon a property as her dowry*, *AB* 256; but simply, *dowered*, opp. ἄπροικος, Poll.3.35, cf. Hsch.

ἐπιπρό-κειμαι, *project*, Sch.Ruf.*Onom.*p.240 R. **-μολεῖν**, aor. 2 inf. of -βλώσκω, *go forth towards*, A.R.3.665, Maiist.27. **-νέομαι**, = foreg., A.R.4.1588. **-νεύω**, *lean forward over*, Nic.*Th.*374, Opp. *C.*4.122. **-πίπτω**, *fall forwards*, A.R.4.1449, Nic.*Al.*496; *project*, Sor.1.69.

ἐπιπροσ-βάλλω, *direct one's course to*, Ἀβύδῳ A.R.1.931. **-γίγνομαι**, *to be added besides*, A.D.*Synt.*260.28, Herm.ap.Stob.1.49.69, *POxy.*1725.18 (iii A.D.). **-ειμι**, Astrol., *to be present as well*, Nech.ap.Vett.Val.279.18.

ἐπίπροσθεν, rarely **-θε** Antiph.250, *SIG*493.12 (Delos, iii B.C.), Adv.: I. of Place, *before*, ἐ. τίθεσθαι, ποιεῖσθαί τι, put *before one* as a screen, E.*Or.*468, X.*Cyr.*1.4.24; ἐ. γίγνεσθαι to be *in the way, intercept the view*, Pl.*Grg.*523d, cf. *Ti.*40c; κώμας καὶ γηλόφους ἐ. ποιεῖσθαι take *cover behind*, X.*Cyr.*3.3.28. 2. c. gen., ἐ. τῶν ὀφθαλμῶν ἔχειν Pl.*Smp.*213a; ταῖς νήσοις οὐδὲν ἐ. τῆς φορᾶς Thphr.*Vent.*30; εὐθὺ οὗ ἂν τὸ μέσον ἀμφοῖν τοῖν ἐσχάτοιν ἐ. ᾖ Pl.*Prm.*137e. II. of Degree, θεῖναί τι ἐ. τινος prefer one *before* another, E.*Supp.*514; ἐ. εἶναί τινος to be *better* than.., Id.*Or.*641; ἐ. τάσσειν.. τῶν καλῶν Antiph. l.c.; ἐ. τι θέσθαι τινός J.*AJ*2.4.3; γίγνεται ἐ. τοῦ δικαίου τὰ τριακόσια τάλαντα Id.*BJ*1.6.3. III. of Order, *first, prior*, τὰ ἐ. αὐτῶν.. τάξαντες αὐτὰ ἐ. ποιησόμεθα Pl.*Lg.*783b,c.

ἐπιπρόσ-θεσις, εως, ἡ, *occultation*, Aristarch.Sam.8. **-θετέω**, *occult*, τὰ -οῦντα Phld.*Sign.*10. 2. metaph. of nutriment, τροφὴ -ηθεῖσα Hp.*Alim.*4. **-θέτησις**, εως, ἡ, *occultation*, Epicur.*Ep.*2 p.40 U. 2. pl., of *objects casting a shadow* by which measurements are taken, Hero *Deff.*135.8. 3. name of a *bandage*, Nicet.ap.Gal. 18(1).792. **-θέω**, *to be before* or *in the way*, Thphr.*Vent.*32; of *occultations* or *eclipses*, Zeno *Stoic.*1.34, Chrysipp.ib.2.199, Procl.*Hyp.* 5.14, al.; but τούτοις ἐ. ⟨ἡ⟩ ἡλίου ἀνταύγεια Ascl.*Tact.*12.10; μηδὲν ἔχειν τὸ -προσθοῦν τοῖς πνεύμασι *protection from* the wind, Ath.Med. ap.Orib.9.12.1: c. dat., Hp.*Medic.*7, etc.; τὸ μέσον ἐ. τοῖς πέρασι *stands before, intercepts the view of*, Arist.*Top.*148^{b}27; ἐ. τοῖς πύργοις *is in a line with* them, *so as to cover* one with the other, Plb.1.47.2: metaph., ἡ ὀργὴ.. πολλάκις τοῖς καταλαμβανομένοις -προσθεῖ Chrysipp. *Stoic.*3.95; τὸν χρόνον -προσθοῦντα τῇ γνώσει τῶν πραγμάτων Plu. *Per.*13; *veil*, Longin.32.1:—Pass., *to be occulted*, Theo Sm.p.193 H.: metaph., ὑπὸ τῶν σαρκῶν -ουμένη [ψυχή] Max.Tyr.15.6; περισπασμοῖς Hierocl.p.53 A.; ὑπ' αἰδοῦς Parth.17.3; [τὴν τραγῳδίαν] ὑπὸ τῶν ὀνομάτων ἐπιπροσθουμένην *obscured*, Melanthius ap.Plu.2.41d. **-θησις**, εως, ἡ, *being before, covering*, Thphr.*Vent.*30; esp. of *eclipses* or *occultations*, Arist.*Cael.*293^{b}22, Procl.*Hyp.*5.15, etc.; *superposition* of colour, Arist.*Mete.*342^{b}9 (pl.); of objects that serve as *cover*, Plb.3. 71.3 (pl.). **-πλέω**, *sail to* or *towards*, τῷ τόπῳ Str.1.3.16. **-τίθημι**, *add besides*, Longin.44.1:—Med., corrupt in Artem.4.82. **-φθέγγομαι**, f.l. in Him.*Or.*14.32.

ἐπιπρόσω, *in front*, ἡ ἐ. πτέρνη Aret.*SD*2.12.

ἐπιπρόσωπος, ον, *with a face represented on it*, φιάλη *Annuario* 4/5. 463 (Halic., iii B.C.).

ἐπιπροτέρωσε, Adv. *still farther*, θέειν A.R.2.940.

ἐπιπρο-φαίνομαι, Pass., *to appear before one*, of οἰωνοί, A.R.3. 917. **-φέρω**, *move on forwards*, ταρσὸν ποδός Id.4.1519. **-χέω**, *pour forth*, θρῆνον *h.Pan.*18:—Pass., *gush forth, burst loose*, Nonn.*D.* 21.69. **-ωθέω**, *push farther forward*, Luc.*Asin.*10.

ἐπίπρῳρος, ον, (πρῷρα) *at the prow of a ship*, Hsch.

ἐπιπταίρω, *sneeze at*, υἱός μοι ἐπέπταρε πᾶσιν ἔπεσσιν he *sneezed* as I spoke the words (a good omen), Od.17.545, cf. *h.Merc.*297, Nonn. *D.*7.107: metaph., *to be gracious to, favour*, Ἔρωτές τινι ἐπέπταρον Theoc.7.96; ἀγαθός τις ἐ. ἐρχομένῳ Id.18.16.

ἐπίπταισμα, ατος, τό, *snap of the fingers*, Ar.*Fr.*773 (pl.).

ἐπιπτάρνυμαι, = ἐπιπταίρω, Hsch. (glossed by μετακαλῶ, κατέχω· ἐπισχετικὸν γὰρ ὁ πταρμὸς πολλάκις).

ἐπίπτερον, τό, = φακός, Ps.-Dsc.4.87; cf. ἐπίπετρον.

ἐπίπτησις, εως, ἡ, *flying down upon*, Jul.*Gal.*358e.

ἐπιπτήσσω, *crouch for fear*, ἐν τείχει Aristid.ap.Philostr.*VS*2.9.3.

ἐπιπτίσσομαι, *to be shelled, freed from the husk*, *Gp.*3.7.1.

ἐπί-πτυγμα, ατος, τό, (ἐπιπτύσσω) *over-fold, flap*, such as covers the orifices in animals, *operculum*, Arist.*PA*679^{b}18, *HA*526^{b}29, 528^b 7: pl., *opercula*, of crustaceans, Id.*Resp.*477^{a}4. **-πτυξις**, εως, ἡ, *application* to one another of vocal cords, Gal.*UP*7.13. **-πτύσσω**, *fold up, fold*, γραμματεῖον Luc.*Dem.Enc.*25; ἱμάτιον περὶ τὰς ῥῖνας Dam.*Isid.*131: abs., *produce folds*, Gal.11.508:—Pass., *to be folded over*, Hp.*Epid.*6.8.28; of the epiglottis, ἐ. ἐπὶ τὸ τῆς ἀρτηρίας τρῆμα Arist.*HA*495^{a}28, cf. *PA*664^{b}28; of the vocal cords, Gal.*UP*7. 13. **-πτῠχή**, ἡ, = ἐπίπτυγμα, *flap*, χιτῶνος J.*AJ*17.5.7, Plu.2. 979c; τοῦ θώρακος Id.*Pomp.*35; αἱ ἐ. τῶν ῥακίων *rags* and tatters, Luc.*DMort.*1.2.

ἐπιπτύω, *spit upon*, τινί Call.*Fr.*235, Gal.6.754.

ἐπί-πτωμα, ατος, τό, *accident*, *PSI*3.252.28 (iii A.D.). **-πτωσις**, εως, ἡ, *onslaught*, αἰφνίδιον ποιεῖσθαι τὴν ἐ. J.*AJ*18.9.2. 2. *falling upon*, φωνῆς ἐπὶ μίαν τάσιν Nicom.*Harm.*12. b. *falling over* the forehead, τριχῶν Antyll.ap.Orib.44.8.1. 3. *falling to* one, κλήρων Plu.2.740d (pl.). b. *chance*, ἐ. τυχική Phld.*Rh.*1.211 S., cf. Theag. ap.Stob.3.1.117, Str.2.3.7.

ἐπιπυκνόομαι, Pass., *to become dense*, Arist.*Col.*794^{a}14, Sor.2.29.

ἐπιπυνθάνομαι, *learn after*, τὰ γεγενημένα D.H.*Th.*29. 2. *inquire again*, Diogenian.3.34.

ἐπιπυργῐδία, ἡ, *on the tower*, epith. of Hecate at Athens, Paus.2. 30.2; of Artemis, ibid., *IG*3.268: so **ἐπιπυργῖτις**, of Athena at Abdera, Hsch.

ἐπιπῠρέσσω, aor. 1 -επύρεξα, *have fever afterwards*, Hp.*Prorrh.*1. 15, Gal.18(1).568; after drinking wine, Herod.Med.ap.Orib.5.27.23.

ἐπιπῠρεταίνω, = foreg., Hp.*Septim.*3, Aret.*CA*2.2.

ἐπιπῠριάω, *foment as well*, Paul.Aeg.3.77; gloss on ἐπιτυφῶσαι, Hsch.

ἐπίπῠρον, τό, (πῦρ) *hearth* of an altar, Hero *Spir.*2.21, Hsch. s.v. θυμέλη. II. *brazier* of a censer, *IG*11.199*B*16 (Delos, iii B.C.), al., *PCair.Zen.*13.34 (iii B.C.).

ἐπίπυρρος, ον, *reddish*, Arist.*Phgn.*807^{b}32, Thphr.*HP*4.10.4, *PLond.*3.1207.17 (i B.C.), Poll.5.68.

ἐπιπυρσεία, ἡ, *counter-signal by fires*, Polyaen.6.19.2.

ἐπιπωλέομαι, *go about, go through*, c. acc., ἐ. στίχας ἀνδρῶν, of the general *inspecting* his troops, Il.3.196, etc.; but in 11.264, of *reconnoitring* an enemy.—Them. has **ἐπιπολεῖσθαι** *visit*, Βόσπορον *Or.*6.75c: c. dat., Σύροις ib.11.152b (nisi leg. ἐπιπωλ-).

ἐπιπωλέω, *sell the right of succession to* a priesthood, in Pass., *SIG* 1014.85,107 (Erythrae, iii B.C.).

ἐπιπώλησις, εως, ἡ, *going round, visitation*, a name given by Gramm. to the latter half of Il.4, *IG*14.1290.59 (prob.), cf. Str.9.1. 10, Plu.2.29a.

ἐπίπωμ-α, ατος, τό, *cover*, Heliod.(?)ap.Orib.49.4.39, Gal.4.636. **-άζω**, *cover with* or *as with a lid*, Hero *Spir.*1 *Praef.*p.150, Simp. *in Cael.*520.15, al., Sm.*Ps.*68(69).16:—Pass., *to be so covered*, Hp. *Loc.Hom.*47, Anthem.p.151 W.—So **ἐπιπωμάννῡμι** Hero *Spir.*1.28 (Pass.). **-ασμός**, ὁ, *covering with a lid* or *cover*, of an arrow, Eust. 1630.63. **-ᾰτίζω**, *cover as with a lid, close up*, Arist.*Cael.*294^{b}15, Thphr.*Ign.*59:—Pass., ib.49; τὸ πῦρ -όμενον σβέννυται Alex.Aphr. *Pr.*1.16; [ἐγχέλεις] ὑπὸ τοῦ θολοῦ τοὺς πόρους -ίζονται Arist.*Fr.*311; of the epiglottis, Gal.14.716. **-ατικός**, ή, όν, *serving to close up the pores*, of oil, Sch.Ar.*Pl.*616. **-άτισις**, εως, ἡ, *covering with a lid*, Phlp. *in APo.*420.13.

ἐπιπωρ-όομαι, *become callous on the surface*, Hp.*Art.*29; or *afterwards*, Id.*Fract.*38. **-ωμα**, ατος, τό, *callus formed over* the fracture of bone, Id.*Art.*36. 2. *gouty concretion*, ἀμφὶ τοῖσιν ἄρθροισιν Id. *Prorrh.*2.8. **-ωσις**, εως, ἡ, *formation of a callus*, -ωσιν ποιεῖσθαι Id.*Art.*14; -ώσιες ἄρθρων γίγνονται Aret.*SD*2.12. 2. *callus*, *Placit.*5.13.1 (pl.); of projections on renal stones, Aret.*SD*2.3.

ἐπιπωτάομαι, lengthd. form of ἐπιποτάομαι, *AP*9.88 (Phil.).

ἐπιρραβδ-ίζω, *smite*, κράδαις καὶ θρίοις Hsch. s. v. κραδίης νόμος. **-οφορέω**, *urge* a horse *by shaking the whip*, X.*Eq*.7.11, Poll.1.220.

ἐπιρραθυμέω, *to be careless about* a thing, Luc.*BisAcc*.1.

ἐπιρραίνω, aor. 1 -έρρᾶνα, *sprinkle upon* or *over*, ὕδωρ τινί Theoc. 24.98, cf. Arist.*GA*758ᵃ16; καρποὺς ταῖς κεφαλαῖς D.H.7.72; ἐπὶ τὰ ᾠὰ τὸν θορόν Arist.*HA*567ᵇ5, cf. Dsc.5.78 (Pass.). II. *besprinkle*, c. acc., Arist.*HA*567ᵇ9; βωμὸν κατέχριεν ἐπιρραίνων ἑπτάκις Ph.2. 157:—Pass., Arist.*GA*756ᵃ24.

ἐπιρρακτός, ή, όν, *dashed on* or *down*, θύρα ἐπιρρακτή *trap*-door, Plu.2.781e; ποτὸν *forced down* the throat, ib.699d.

ἐπίρραμμα, ατος, τό, *that which is sewn on*, *Gloss.*; dub. cj. for ἐπίρρημα in Poll.4.119 (v. ἐπίρριμμα 1 b).

ἐπιρραντίζω, = ἐπιρραίνω, Lxx *Le*.6.27(20) (Pass.), *Hippiatr*.16.

ἐπιρρᾰπ-ίζω, *smite*, τινὰ κατὰ κόρρης Aristaenet.1.4; ἐ. τὸ πῦρ *beat* it *out*, D.H.1.59. 2. metaph., *rebuke*, Diog.Bab.*Stoic*.3.221 (Pass.), Sosicr.ap.Ath.10.422c, Herm. *in Phdr*.p.85 A. 3. Pass., *to be checked*, of motion, Olymp. *in Mete*.24.20. **-ιξις**, εως, ἡ, *reproof*, Ion Hist.1. **-ισμός**, ὁ, = foreg., Plb.2.64.4.

ἐπιρράπτω, aor. 2 ἐπέρρᾰφον Nonn.*D*.9.3, al.:—*sew* or *stitch on*, τι ἐπὶ ἱμάτιον *Ev.Marc*.2.21: metaph., δόλον δόλῳ Nonn.*D*.42.315. 2. *sew up*, in Pass., Gal.18(2).579.

ἐπιρράσσω, Ep. -ρρήσσω, *dash to, shut violently, slam to*, θύρην δ' ἔχε.. ἐπιβλὴς..., τὸν τρεῖς μὲν ἐπιρρήσσεσκον Ἀχαιοί, τρεῖς δ' ἀναοίγεσκον Il.24.454, cf. 456; πύλας ἐπιρράξασ' ἔσω (with v.l. ἐπιρρήξασ') S.*OT*1244; τὸ πῶμα prob. in Plu.2.356c; λίθον (at the door of a cave) Id.*Phil*.19:—Pass., *to be dashed to*, of gates, D.H.8.18. 2. *dash against*, ἐ. αὐτοῖς τὴν ἵππον *throw* the cavalry *upon* them, Id. 3.25; ἴχνος κολώναις Nonn.*D*.11.195; *strike*, πέδον ὁπλῇ ib.41. 189. II. intr., *beat upon* one, of a storm, μή τις Διὸς κεραυνὸς ἤ τις ὀμβρία χάλαζ' ἐπιρράξασα; S.*OC*1503; of winds, Arat.292, Opp. *H*.1.634, App.*BC*2.59, Ph.1.507; ἐ. τισί *attack* them, D.S.15.84, cf. D.H.8.67, Ph.2.173, etc.

ἐπιρραψῳδέω, *recite in accompaniment*, ἔπη Luc.*Nec*.4; ἐ. ἔπη τινί *upon* him, Philostr.*Her*.2.9.

ἐπιρρέζω, *offer sacrifices at* a place, ὅθι πάντες ἐπιρρέζεσκον ὁδῖται (Ion. impf.) Od.17.211. 2. *sacrifice afterwards* or *besides*, Ζηνὶ χοῖρον Theoc.24.99, cf. *AP*6.157 (Theodorid.); ὄϊν *GDI*3639ᵃ5 (Cos): abs., *IG*12(1).677.29 (Ialysus).

ἐπιρρεμβῶς, Adv. *aimlessly, desultorily*, Herm.ap.Stob.1.49.69.

ἐπιρρεπ-ής, ές, *inclining the balance*, μνᾶς -έστερον βραχύ rather *more than* a mina *in weight*, Damocr.ap.Gal.13.919. II. *leaning towards, prone to*, πρός τι Luc.*Hist.Conscr*.60, Ath.13.576f (Comp.); ἐς τὸ φιλάνθρωπον Hdn.6.9.8; εἰς κακίαν Hierocl. *in CA*3p.425 M.; -εστέρας τὰς γνώμας πρός τινα ἔχειν Hdn.5.8.2: abs., ἐλπίδες -έστεραι *favourable*, Plb.1.55.1. Adv. -πῶς, ἔχειν πρός τι Arr.*Epict*.3.22.1; τῆς τύχης ἐ. κινουμένης Chor.*Milt*.61: Comp. -έστερον S.E.*M*.1.280: Sup. -έστατα Men.Prot.p.119 D. **-ω**, *lean towards*, ὄφρα... ἡμῖν δ' αἰπὺς ὄλεθρος ἐπιρρέπῃ, metaph. from the balance, Il.14.99: hence, generally, *fall to one's lot*, [ὑμέναιος] ἐ. γαμβροῖσιν ἀείδειν A.*Ag*.707 (lyr.): abs., ib.1042. 2. metaph., *incline*, πρὸς ἔλεον Ph.2.582. II. trans., ἐ. τάλαντον *force down* one scale, Thgn.157. 2. *weigh out to* one, *allot*, esp. of ill fortune, ἐ. μῆνιν πόλει A.*Eu*.888; Δίκα τοῖς παθοῦσι μαθεῖν ἐπιρρέπει Id.*Ag*.251 (lyr.).

ἐπιρρευμᾰτ-ίζομαι, *have a further flow* of morbid humours, Gal. 19.664. II. *have a further attack of rheumatism*, Alex.Trall. 12. **-ισμός**, ὁ, *flow* of humours *to* a wound, *Hippiatr*.10; ἰχώρων Harp.Astr. in *Cat.Cod.Astr*.8(3).150.20.

ἐπίρρευσις, εως, ἡ, = -ρρυσις, Sch.Opp.*H*.1.116.

ἐπιρρέω, late fut. -ρρεύσω Hero *Spir*.1.9: aor. 1 Act. -έρρευσα Procop.*Aed*.4.6: pf. -έρρευκα Gal.ap.Orib.51.36.17: aor. 2 Pass. -ερρύην Hp.*Nat.Hom*.1, etc.:—*flow upon the surface, float*, καθύπερθεν ἐπιρρέει ἠΰτ' ἔλαιον Il.2.754. 2. *flow in besides, keep on flowing*, ποταμοῖσι.. ἐμβαίνουσιν.. ἕτερα ὕδατα ἐπιρρεῖ Heraclit.12; ἐπιρρεόντων ποταμῶν (into the sea), Ar.*Nu*.1294; χολὴ πλείων ἐπιρρέουσα Pl.*Ti*.85e; ἄνωθεν ἐπὶ τὰς ἀρούρας ib.22e: metaph. of large bodies of men, *stream on*, ἐπέρρεον ἔθνεα πεζῶν Il.11.724; ἐπιρρεόντων τῶν Ἑλλήνων καὶ γινομένων πλεύνων Hdt.9.38; ἐ. ὄχλος Γοργόνων Pl.*Phdr*. 229d; of a flood of topics, Id.*Tht*.177e; ὄχλος πολὺς ἄμμιν ἐπιρρεῖ Theoc.15.59; of the ἀπόρροιαι of Democritus, Plu.2.733d: c. inf., τὸ πλῆθος τῶν εἰπεῖν ἐπιρρεόντων Isoc.12.95: metaph. also, οὑπιρρέων χρόνος *onward-streaming* time, i.e. the future, A.*Eu*.853; ὄλβου ἐπιρρυέντος if wealth *accumulates*, E.*Med*.1229; ἀγαθῶν ἐπιρρεόντων X. *Ap*.27; πολλὴ αὔξη ὅταν ἐ. πόνων Pl.*Lg*.788d; τὰ ἐπιρρέοντα the *stream* of wealth, Aen.Gaz.*Thphr*.p.27 B. 3. c. gen., [τρίποδες] οἴνου ἐπέρρεον *flowed with* wine, Philostr.*VA*3.27. II. Pass., *to be watered*, ὕδασι Paus.9.8.6.

ἐπιρρήγνῡμι, *rend*, πέπλον δ' ἐπέρρηξ' ἐπὶ συμφορᾷ A.*Pers*.1030 (lyr.); *split*, Heliod.ap.Orib.48.21.3; *break*, νάρθηκας Alciphr.3.51.

ἐπι-ρρήδην, Adv., (ἐρέω, ῥηθῆναι) *by name* or *surname*, ἐ. καλέονται Arat.261. II. *explicitly, openly*, A.R.2.640; *directly*, τινὰ ἱλάεσθαι ib.847; *clearly*, Arat.191. **-ρρημα**, ατος, τό, *that which is said afterwards*: I. in Old Comedy, a *speech*, commonly of trochaic tetrameters, *spoken* by the Coryphaeus *after the Parabasis* (as in Ar.*Nu*.575, *Eq*.565), Hsch., Suid. II. *adverb*, D.H.*Comp*.2, etc.; περὶ ἐπιρρημάτων, title of work by Apollonius Dyscolus. III. *surname, nickname*, Macho ap.Ath.13.578d. IV. v. ἐπίρραμμα, ἐπίρριμμα. **-ρρημᾰτικός**, ή, όν, *adverbial*, A.D.*Adv*.169.11, al., Sch.Ar.*Pl*.244, etc. Adv. -κῶς Phryn.*PS*p.10 B., A.D.*Synt*.10.9.

ἐπίρρηξις, εως, ἡ, *fissure*, χειλῶν Dsc.2.76; *tearing*, τῆς ἐπιφανείας Paul.Aeg.6.89.

ἐπίρρησις, εως, ἡ, *rebuke, reproach*, δειλοῦ -ρρησιν μελεδαίνων Archil.8, cf. Plu.2.19c (pl.), Hsch. II. *invocation*, θεῶν Phld.*Piet*. 74 (pl.); *spell, charm*, Luc.*Philops*.31, Jul.Afric.*Oxy*.412.46. III. *comment*, Phld.*Rh*.2.55 S.; opp. πρόρρησις, ib.1.31 S.

ἐπιρρήσσω, v. ἐπιρράσσω.

ἐπιρρητέον, *one must say concerning*, τῷ τοῦ Αἰσχύλου.. ὅτι.. Plu.2.36b.

ἐπιρρητορεύω, *declaim over*, τί τινι Luc.*Hist.Conscr*.26; τι κατά τινος Ach.Tat.8.8. II. *introduce besides*, τοὺς ἐπιλογικοὺς οἴκτους Ath.13.590e.

ἐπίρρητος, ον, *exclaimed against, infamous*, τέχναι X.*Oec*.4.2; πλοῦτος Philostr.*VA*7.23. Adv. -τως Poll.3.139. II. ἐ. διαιτητής *agreed upon*, Sch.Patm.D. in *BCH*1.153.

ἐπιρρῑγέω, *shiver afterwards*, Hp.*Epid*.1.14:—also -ριγόω, Id. *Prorrh*.1.61.

ἐπιρρίζ-ιον, τό, *side-root*, v.l. in Dsc.1.11. **-όω**, prob. f.l. for ἐνριζόω, Nonn.*D*.40.532.

ἐπίρρικνος, ον, '*fine*', *wiry*, σκέλη X.*Cyn*.4.1 (περικνά codd.), Poll. 5.58.

ἐπίρριμμα, ατος, τό, *winding-sheet*, dub. in Lyd.*Mag*.3.60. b. *slave's outer garment*, dub. cj. in Poll.4.119 (v. ἐπίρραμμα). 2. (ἐπιρρίπτω I. 2) *poultice*, Alex.Trall.8.2 (ἐπιρρίματα codd.), *Febr*.2 (ἐπιρρήματος codd.).

ἐπιρρίν-ιον [ῐν], τό, Dim. of sq., Sm.*Ez*.16.12. **-ον**, τό, *nose-ring*, Id.*Jb*.42.11. **-ος**, ον, (ῥίς) *with a long nose*, Heph.Astr.2.2, Ps.-Luc.*Philopatr*.12: so **ἐπίρρις**, in acc. pl. -ρρινας, *Cat.Cod.Astr*.7.196.4.

ἐπιρριπίζω, dub. sens. in Nonn.*D*.30.187 (s. v. l.).

ἐπιρριπτ-έον, *one must apply* a plaster, Paul.Aeg.2.47. **-έω**, = sq., only in pres. and impf., X.*An*.5.2.23, Plb.18.46.12, Ph.*Bel*.100. 13, Sor.2.32:—Pass., Ph.*Bel*.99.48, Parth.9.8. 2. intr., *throw oneself upon* the track, X.*Cyn*.6.22. **-ω** (ἐπῐρίπτω *AP*5.128 (Autom.)), *cast at*, ὅτε μοι χαλκήρεα δοῦρα Τρῶες ἐπέρριψαν Od.5.310; διώκων ἐ. ἑαυτόν *throw* himself *upon* his prey, Arist.*HA*629ᵇ20; Βρούτῳ τὴν αὑτοῦ φοινικίδα ἐ. Plu.*Ant*.22; χεῖρα ἐ., Lat. *manum injecit*, *AP*9.84 (Antiphan.): metaph., ἐ. πλάνας τινί A.*Pr*.738; ψευδεῖς αἰτίας ἐ. D.S. 14.12; τὴν μέριμναν ἐπὶ [θεόν] 1*Ep.Pet*.5.7; *inflict*, πολλὰ σκληρὰ... ἐπιρριφήσεται, c. dat., Nech. in *Cat.Cod.Astr*.7.146. 2. *apply* a plaster or fomentation, Sor.1.50 (Pass.), 69; σκεπάσματα Dsc.5.88. 3. Pass., -όμενα σκιρρώματα *spreading over the surface*, Id.1.42. 4. *requisition*, ἔργα *PTeb*.5.249 (ii B.C.); ἱερεῖα τρέφειν ib.183. 5. metaph. in Pass., *to be imminent*, οὐ βραχὺς ἐπέρριπτο κίνδυνος Ph.2. 594. II. *throw out opinions*, ἀδιορίστως ἐ. περὶ τῶν λοιπῶν, v.l. for -, Arist.*Metaph*.986ᵃ34.

ἐπίρρις, v. ἐπίρρινος.

ἐπίρριψις, εως, ἡ, *casting upon*, Aq.*Hb*.2.15.

ἐπιρρόγανον· ἀπόμακτρον, Hsch. (Prob. -ροχ-, cf. ῥόχανον.)

ἐπιρροή, ἡ, (ἐπιρρέω) *afflux, influx*, κακαῖς ἐ. ὕδωρ μιαίνων A.*Eu*. 694; ἐπιρροαῖσιν αἱμάτων Id.*Ag*.1510 (lyr.); δακρύων ἐπιρροαί E.*Fr*. 573; ἐ. αἵματος *determination* of blood *to*.., Hp.*VC*13; opp. ἀπορροή (efflux), Ti.Locr.102b; τῆς τροφῆς Thphr.*CP*5.4.6; κατ' ἐπιρροάν Ti. Locr.101d: metaph., αὔξην τε καὶ ἐ. (sc. νοσημάτων) Pl.*Lg*.783b; ἐ. κακῶν E.*Andr*.349 (pl.); ἀνάμνησίς ἐστιν ἐ. φρονήσεως ἀπολιπούσης Pl. *Lg*.732b. 2. *stream* of a river, A.*Fr*.143 (pl.), A.R.4.623 (pl.). 3. *channel, duct*, Hp.*Gland*.12 (pl.). 4. *irrigation*, Ph.1.249.

ἐπιρροθ-έω, *shout in answer* or *in approval*, στάσις πάγκοινος ἅδ' ἐπιρροθεῖ A.*Ch*.458 (lyr.); χορὸς.. ἰχθύων ἐπερρόθει S.*Fr*.762, cf. E.*Hec*. 553; ἐ. ὡς.. Id.*Or*.901; ἐ. κτύπῳ *answer to, ring with* the sound, A.*Ch*. 427 (lyr.); *applaud*, D.H.6.83. 2. c. acc., λόγοις ἐπιρροθεῖν τινα *rage against, abuse* him, S.*Tr*.264. **-ητος**, ον, *blamed*, Hsch. **-ος**, ον, *coming to the rescue*; as Subst., *helper*, τοίη οἱ ἐ. ἦεν Ἀθήνη Il.4. 390; θεὰ..., μοι ἐ. ἐλθὲ ποδοῖιν 23.770; μακραὶ ἐπίρροθοι εὐφρόναι εἰσίν Hes.*Op*.560; ἐπίρροθοι ἄμμι πέλεσθε A.R.2.1193: also as Adj., μῆτις, πύργος ἐ., ib.1068, 4.1045: c. gen., *giving aid against*, νύκτερον τέλος .. ἀλγέων ἐ. A.*Th*.368 (lyr.); cf. ἐπιτάρροθος. 2. [ὁδὸς] λείη καὶ ἐ. *easy* (?), *AP*7.50 (Archim.). II. ἐ. κακά reproaches *bandied backwards and forwards, abusive* language, S.*Ant*.413. 2. δῶμαθ' .. ἐ. *full of fault-finding*, Id.*Fr*.583.10.

ἐπίρροια, ἡ, = ἐπιρροή, Thphr.*Sud*.20; τῶν χυμῶν Ael.*NA*12.20: pl., *Placit*.4.22.1, Ph.2.151, Archig.ap.Orib.47.13.12; of rivers, D.S. 5.25: metaph., ἡ ἐ. τῶν ἀγαθῶν Id.33.18.

ἐπιρροιβδ-έω, *croak so as to forbode rain*, of a raven, Thphr.*Sign*. 16. 2. c. acc. cogn., ἐ. ἰὸν λαιμῷ *shoot a whizzing* arrow at.., Q.S. 8.322; cf. ἐπιρροιζέω. **-ην**, Adv. *with noisy fury*, E.*HF*860 (troch.).

ἐπιρροιζέω, = ἐπιρροιβδέω, Thphr.*Sign*.16, Arat.969. 2. c. acc. cogn., ἐ. φυγάς τινι *shriek* flight at him, A.*Eu*.424, cf. Lyc.585. II. *make a rustling* or *whirring sound*, Nonn.*D*.48.940, 37.688. III. v. ἐπιρρύζω.

ἐπιρρομβέω, *make a buzzing noise*, ἐπιρρόμβεισι δ' ἄκουαι Sapph.2. 11. 2. *swoop down upon*, of an eagle, Sch.Pi.*I*.4(3).77.

ἐπίρροος, contr. -ρους, ὁ, *influx, redundance*, Hp.*Ulc*.24. 2. *accessory flux*, Orib.8.36.3.

ἐπίρροπος, ον, *inclining*, Serapio in *Cat. Cod. Astr*. 1.100.3 (Comp.), Eustr. *in EN*33.16.

ἐπιρροφ-άνω, = sq., Hp.*Int*.6. **-έω**, Ion. -ρυφέω, *swallow besides*, Id.*Acut*.24; *take draughts* (of an actor), Arist.*Pr*.948ᵃ2; ἐπιρροφεῖν τοῦ ὕδατος Plu.*Phoc*.9; τῆς κύλικος Ael.*NA*14.5; ὅταν τὸ ὕδωρ πνίγῃ, τί ἐπιρροφήσομεν; (cf. ἐπιπίνω) Archig.ap.Gal.8.577. II.

swallow greedily, gulp down, Clearch.Com.1; ἐ. ἀγαθοῦ δαίμονος Theopomp.Com.76.

ἐπιρρόχανον, v. ἐπιρρόγανον.

ἐπιρρυγχίς, ίδος, ἡ, (ῥύγχος) hook of a bird's beak, Ar.Byz.Epit.4.11, Suid.

ἐπιρρύζω, set a dog on one, ἐπί τινα Ar.V.705, acc. to Sch. and Hsch. (where also -ρροίζειν); cf. ῥύζω.

ἐπιρρυθμίζω, remould, amend, [ποιήματα] Pl.Lg.802b; ἐ. ἐς τὸ ἀφελὲς ἑαυτήν dress oneself simply, v.l. in Luc.Pisc.12.

ἐπιρρύομαι, save, preserve, A.Th.165 (lyr.).

ἐπιρρῠπαίνω, soil on the surface, ὥσπερ ἰοῦ -αίνοντος τὴν πολυτέλειαν Plu.2.828a, cf. Philum.Ven.3.2 (Pass.). II. Pass., become foul again, of a wound, Archig.ap.Orib.46.26.3.

ἐπιρρύπτω, clean, Herod.Med. in Rh.Mus.58.85.

ἐπίρρῠσις, εως, ἡ, = ἐπιρροή, Hp.Loc.Hom.21; αἵματος Arist.PA $653^{a}13$. II. perh. **ἐπίρρῡσις** (ῥύομαι) means of saving, Id.GA $745^{a}28$.

ἐπιρρυσμίζω, Ion. for ἐπιρρυθμίζω, Hsch.

ἐπιρρύσμιος, η, ον, (ῥυσμός) in-flowing, Hsch.; ἐπιρρυσμίη ἑκάστοισιν ἡ δόξις adventitious, Democr.7.

ἐπιρρῠτής, οῦ, ὁ, = ἐπαρυστρίς, Aq.Za.4.2 (pl.).

ἐπίρρῠτος, ον, (ἐπιρρέω) running, ὕδατα Thphr.CP3.8.3, HP5.9.5; of food, infused into the body, τροφῆς νάματα ἐ. Pl.Ti.80d; of sight, infused from the sun, Id.R.508b; ψυχαί Ti.Locr.99e; ἡδοναὶ δι' αἰσθήσεων ἐπίρρυτοι Max.Tyr.31.7; ἐ. δύναμις, opp. σύμφυτος, Gal.1.319. 2. metaph., overflowing, abundant, καρπός A.Eu.907. II. Pass., flowed into, subject to influx, opp. ἀπόρρυτος, Pl.Ti.43a. 2. overflowed, moist, πεδίον X.An.1.2.22. III. as Subst., perh. oil-vessel or pipe, ἀλείψασαν δρακτοῖς καὶ ἐπιρύτοις JRS16.90, cf. OGI479.10 note. **ἐπιρρῠφέω**, Ion. for -ρροφέω (q.v.).

ἐπιρρωγολογέομαι, (ῥώξ, ῥάξ) glean grapes off the vines, Lxx 4Ma.2.9.

ἐπιρρώννῡμι and -ύω: aor. ἐπέρρωσα:—add strength to, strengthen or encourage in a thing, αὗται [αἱ νέες].. σφέας ἐπέρρωσαν Hdt.8.14; τοὺς μὲν ἐξέπληξε, τοὺς δὲ πολλῷ μᾶλλον ἐπέρρωσεν Th.4.36, cf. 8.89; εἰς τὸ ἐπιρρῶσαι αὐτοὺς X.HG7.5.6; ἐ. τινὰ πρὸς τὸν πόλεμον Plu.Lys.4; ἐπίρρωσον σαυτήν collect your strength, Luc.Tim.41; ἐ. τὴν γνώμην, τὰ πάθη, Plu.2.62a,681f. II. Pass. (in which the pf. ἐπέρρωμαι, plpf. ἐπερρώμην serve as pres. and impf.), fut. ἐπιρρωσθήσομαι Luc.Somn.18: aor. 1 ἐπερρώσθην (v. infr.):—recover strength, pluck up courage, Th.6.93, 7.2; οἱ Κορίνθιοι.. πολλῷ μᾶλλον ἐπέρρωντο Id.7.17; ἐς τἆλλα πολὺ ἐπέρρωντο ib.7; ἐπερρώσθη ἄν τις ἰδὼν X.HG3.4.18; ἐπερρώσθησαν ταῖς ὁρμαῖς πρὸς τὸν πόλεμον Plb.1.24.1; τὰς ψυχὰς Hdn.3.3.8; κείνοις.. ἐπερρώσθη λέγειν (impers.) they took courage to speak, S.OC661.

ἐπιρρώομαι, old Ep. pres.: aor. 1 Med. ἐπερρώσαντο:—apply one's strength to a thing, work lustily at it, c. dat., [μύλαις] δώδεκα πᾶσαι ἐπερρώοντο γυναῖκες worked with might and main at the mill, Od.20.107; ἐπερρώοντ' ἐλάτῃσι A.R.2.661. 2. move nimbly, ποσσὶν ἐπερρώσαντο Hes.Th.8, cf. A.R.1.385 (tm.): c. acc. cogn., ἐπίρρωσαι δὲ χορείην urge the rapid dance, AP9.403 (Maec.). 3. follow rapidly, ἐπερρώοντο τιθήνῃ Coluth.101. II. flow or stream upon (one's head), χαῖται ἐπερρώσαντο ἄνακτος κρατὸς ἀπ' ἀθανάτοιο his locks flowed waving from his head, Il.1.529; πλοχμοὶ.. ἐπερρώοντο κιόνι A.R.2.677.

ἐπιρρώπια· ἐπιτελῆ, Hsch. (Prob. ἐπὶ ῥώπια· ἐπ' εὐτελῆ.)

ἐπίρρωσις, εως, ἡ, strengthening, Ael.NA6.1; ῥώμης Lib.Decl.48.60. II. Rhet., intensification, Longin.11.2.

ἐπιρρωστέον, one must arouse, πᾶσαν σπουδήν Nicom.Harm.1.

ἐπίρῠτος, ὁ, or -ον, τό, v. ἐπίρρυτος III.

ἐπίσαγμα, ατος, τό, (ἐπισάττω) pack-saddle, Lxx Le.15.9; load, ὄνων Sch.Ar.Nu.449: metaph., δεινὸν τοὐπίσαγμα τοῦ νοσήματος the burden of the disease, S.Ph.755.

ἐπίσαθρος, ον, infirm, τὰς ὑπάρξεις ἐ. καὶ ἐπικινδύνους ποιεῖν Vett.Val.90.3: Sup., Hsch. s.v. ἐπικηρότατοι.

ἐπισᾰλ-εύω, ride at anchor off, τοῖς ἀκρωτηρίοις Philostr.Her.19.14: metaph., ἐ. τοῖς ὤμοις (cf. σαλεύω) Arist.Phgn.$813^{a}11$. II. float over, ἡ κόμη ἐπισαλεύει τῷ μετώπῳ Philostr.Im.1.23:—Med., Luc.Am.40. -ος, ον, tossed on the sea, πρᾶγμα Secund.Sent.17. II. rough, ὅρμος Peripl.M.Rubr.8,12; τόπος Stad.55.

ἐπισαλπίζω, accompany on the trumpet, τοῖς ὑμνῳδοῦσιν J.AJ9.13.3. II. ἐ. τοῖς κέρασιν blow the horns, ib.7.14.5.

ἐπίσᾱμα, v. ἐπίσημα.

ἐπισανδᾰλίς, ίδος, ἡ, sandal-strap, Schwyzer 462 B 29 (Tanagra, iii B.C.).

ἐπίσαξις, εως, ἡ, heaping on or up, τῆς γῆς Thphr.CP5.6.3. II. stuffing, filling, Erasistr.ap.Gal.7.538.

ἐπίσαπρος, ον, rotten, dub. l. in Thphr.HP3.7.5.

ἐπισαρκάζω, grin, sneer at, Ph.1.587; τινί Sch.Il.11.110: abs., Sch.S.El.1457.

ἐπισαρκ-ίδιον, τό, v.l. for ὑποσαρκ- (q.v.) in Hp., Gal.15.891. **-ος**, ον, covered with flesh, ὀστέον Hp.Fract.18.

ἐπισάττω, pile a load upon, τι ἐπὶ ὄνους, ἐπὶ καμήλους, Hdt.1.194, 3.9; τι ὄνῳ J.AJ1.13.2; ἵππον ἐ. saddle it, X.Cyr.3.3.27, An.3.4.35: c. dupl. acc., load with, τὴν ὄνον σῦκα Alciphr.3.20. 2. heap up, τὴν ἐπισεσαγμένην γῆν Thphr.HP7.2.5. 3. Pass., to be filled full, Gal.7.541.

ἐπισαχθής· χρεωφειλέτης, Hsch.

ἐπισβέννῡμαι, Pass., go out upon, τῷ ἄνθρακι Luc.JTr.15.

ἐπίσειον, v. ἐπίσιον.

ἐπίσειστος, ον, shaking or waving over the forehead, κόμη Luc.Gall.26. 2. ἐπίσειστος, ὁ, a comic mask with hair hanging on the forehead, Poll.4.146 sq.

ἐπισείω, Ep. **ἐπισσ-** (as always in Hom.), shake at or against, τί τινι, esp. with the view of scaring, ὅτ' ἂν.. Ζεὺς.. αὐτὸς ἐπισσείῃσιν ἐρεμνὴν αἰγίδα πᾶσι Il.4.167, cf. 15.230; ἐπισείουσα τὸν λόφον ἐκπλήττει με Luc.DDeor.19.1, cf. 2.2, etc.; τὰ δόρατα Hdn.2.13.4; ἐ. πόλεμον τῇ πατρίδι stir up.., J.BJ2.17.3; Πέρσας ἐ. hold them out as a threat, Plu.Them.4; but ἐ. τὴν χεῖρα, in token of assent or applause, Luc.Pr.Im.4, Bis Acc.28; ἐπὶ δ' ἔσεισεν κόμαν E.IT1276 (lyr.): abs., τόσσον ἐπισσείει so she seems to threaten, of a statue, AP9.755:—Pass., κόμαι ἐ. τοῖς κροτάφοις Lib.Decl.12.27: metaph., τὸν ἐπισεισθέντα τῶν παθῶν σκηπτόν Ph.1.210. 2. urge on, [ἵππον] S.Fr.147; ἐ. τινὶ τὰς δρακοντώδεις κόρας set them upon one, E.Or.255; ἐ. πόλιν σοί ib.613; μὴ 'πίσειέ μοι τὸν Μισγόλαν Alex.3; hurl at, τινὶ πέτρον Parth.14.4. 3. intr., assault, τοῖς τείχεσι D.S.13.94 codd. 4. shake so as to touch, Callistr.Stat.6, cf. Poll.4.147.

ἐπισείων, οντος, ὁ, streamer of a ship (cf. παράσειον), Poll.1.90, 91. 2. = μακροπώγων, Id.4.143.

ἐπισέληνος, ον, (σελήνη) moon-shaped: ἐπισέληνα, τά, cakes of this shape, Pl.Com.174.10 (nisi leg. -σέλινα); = πόπανα μηνοειδῆ, Hsch.

ἐπισεμνολογέω, gloss over, πρᾶξιν Anon.Prog. in Rh.1.599 W.

ἐπίσεμνος, ον, rather proud, Cat.Cod.Astr.8(4).137.

ἐπισεμνύνομαι, pride oneself on a thing, Ph.1.599, al., J.Ap.2.3.

ἐπισεσυρμένως, (ἐπισύρω II) carelessly, perfunctorily, Epict.Ench.31, Simp. in eund. p.53 D., EM191.34.

ἐπισεύω, Ep. **ἐπισσ-** (as always in Hom.), put in motion against, set on, μή.. μοι κῆτος ἐπισσεύῃ μέγα δαίμων Od.5.421; δμῶας ἐπισσεύας 14.399: metaph., τόσα γάρ μοι ἐπέσσευεν κακὰ δαίμων 18.256; ὀνείρατ' ἐπέσσευεν κακὰ δαίμων 20.87; κῆρας AP7.439 (Theodorid.). II. mostly Pass., hurry or hasten to or towards, ἐπεσσεύοντο δὲ λαοί Il.2.86; ἔς τινα 13.757; ἐπεσσεύοντο νομόνδε to pasture, 18.575; νῆάδ' (so Aristarch.) ἐπεσσεύοντο Od.13.19; in hostile sense, rush upon or at, c. dat., νηυσὶν ἐπισσεύεσθαι Il.15.347. 2. freq. in pf. part. Pass. ἐπεσσύμενος, with 3 sg. plpf. ἐπέσσῠτο (used as an aor.): 3 pl. aor. 1 ἐπεσσύθεν Opp.C.4.136:—mostly in hostile sense, charge, ἐπέσσυτο δαίμονι ἶσος Il.5.438, al.; τῷ ἐπεσσύμενον βάλε τείχεος ὑψηλοῖο struck him with an arrow from the wall as he rushed on, 12.388: c. dat., αὐτῷ μοι ἐπέσσυτο 5.459, cf. 21.227: c. acc., τεῖχος ἐπεσσύμενοι 12.143: c. gen., ἐπεσσύμενος πεδίοιο rushing, hurrying over the plain, 14.147, 22.26 (cf. διαπράσσω); also of fire, etc., ἠΰτε πῦρ, τό τ' ἐπεσσύμενον πόλιν ἀνδρῶν.. φλεγέθει 17.737; κῦμα δεινὸν ἐπεσσύμενον Od.5.314, cf. 431: also, without any hostile sense, to express rapid motion, c. dat., ὥς οἱ.. ὄνειρον ἐπέσσυτο 4.841: c. acc., ὡς πνοιὴ ἐπέσσυτο δέμνια swept over them, 6.20: c. inf., ἐπέσσυτο διώκειν he hasted on to follow, Il.21.601, cf. A.R.1.758: abs., χερσὶν ἐπεσσύμενος λάβε πέτρης Od.5.428; ἐπεσσύμενος λάβε γούνων 22.310. 3. metaph., to be in excitement or agitation, εἴ τοι θυμὸς ἐπέσσυται Il.1.173; θυμὸς ἐ. ὄφρ' ἐπαμύνω 6.361: c. inf., μοι ἐπέσσυτο θυμὸς.. τέρπεσθαι 9.398.—Ep. word, used occasionally by Trag., only in lyr. (exc. S.Ichn.21,43), πέδον ἐπισύμενος A.Eu.786; ἐπέσυτο τάνδε γᾶν.. ἄτα E.Ph.1065; τείχεα.. ἐπέσυτο φλόξ Id.Hel.1162; so τίς ὄρεα... τάδ' ἐπέσυτο; Ar.Fr.698 (parody of dithyramb).

ἐπισήθω, sprinkle upon, ψῆγμα χρυσοῦ ταῖς κόμαις J.AJ8.7.3: impf. ἐπέσηθον Hsch.

ἐπισηκρητεύω, (Lat. secretum) perform secretarial duties as well, Lyd.Mag.3.27.

ἐπί-σημα, ατος, τό, device on a coin, Simon.157; on a shield, τοὐπίσημ' A.Th.659; ἐ. ἔχων.. ἐν μέσῳ σάκει E.Ph.1107, cf. 1125: also in form -σᾱμα, Schwyzer 607 (Thess., v B.C.). **-σημαίνω**, Dor. -σᾱμαίνω SIG953.31 (Calymna, ii B.C.):—mark, γράμματα Aen.Tact.31.3 (Med.):—Med., seal, μαρτυρίας τᾷ δαμοσίᾳ σφραγῖδι SIG l.c.:—Pass., to have a mark set on one, κἀπισημανθήσεται κείνου κεκλῆσθαι λαὸς E.Ion1593. 2. of a disease, τῶν ἀκρωτηρίων ἀντίληψις αὐτοῦ ἐπεσήμαινεν the seizure of his extremities set a mark upon him, Th.2.49:—Pass., ἣν ἅπαξ ἐπισημανθῇ if once he has the mark of the disease upon him, Hp.Morb.Sacr.8. b. indicate as a symptom, πολλὰ τοῦ νοσώδους Philostr.Gym.30: as a weather-sign, αὐχμοὺς Id.Her.2.9:—Pass., show symptoms of disease, Gal.14.661. II. indicate, c. acc. et inf., ὁ θεὸς ἐπεσήμαινεν αὐτῷ ὅσιον εἶναι X.HG4.7.2. III. intr., give signs, appear as a symptom in a case, Hp.Epid.1.18; ἄρθρον ἐ. συντεταμένον Id.Art.30; of puberty, show itself, Arist.GA$727^{a}8$, $728^{b}24$; of weather-signs, indicate a change of weather, Thphr.Sign.10, etc.; of omens, τῷ Ῥώμῳ γῦπες ἐ. ἐξ D.H.1.86, etc.; εἰς τὸ δημόσιον Paus.3.12.7; of the gods, δαιμόνιον αὐτοῖς ἐ. D.S.19.103, cf. 5.3, Plu.Num.22, Sull.14: impers., ἐπισημαίνει symptoms appear, Arist.HA $572^{b}32$; ἐ. περὶ τοὺς μαστούς Id.GA$728^{b}29$. IV. Med. (pf. Med. in act. sense, Phld.Mus.p.82 K., Ir.p.5 W., aor. Pass., Id.Rh.1.58 S., al.), assign as a distinguishing mark, μίαν τινὰ φύσιν Pl.Phlb.25a, cf. Plt.258c; distinguish, τί βούλομαι Id.Lg.744a; ἐάν τε ἰάσιμος ἐάν τε ἀνίατος δοκῇ εἶναι Id.Grg.526b: abs., D.S.13.28; τοσοῦτον -σημηναμένους having added so much by way of explanation, Gal.17(1).800. 2. signify, indicate, ὃ.. Ὅμηρος ἐπεσ. Pl.Lg.681e; ἐ. ἐν τοῖς ὅρκοις ὅτι "οὐκ ἀδικήσω" Arist.Pol.$1310^{a}11$; τῷ μειδιάματι.. τὴν διαμαρτίαν Luc.Laps.1; remark, "ὀρθῶς" Thphr.Char.2.4. 3. set one's name and seal to a thing (in token of approbation), ἐπισημαίνεσθαι τὰς εὐθύνας D.18.250: generally, applaud, signify approval, Isoc.12.

2, Aeschin.2.49, Men.*Phasm.Fr.*1, etc.: rarely in bad sense, *disapprove*, M.Ant.6.20, App.*BC*5.15; of a historian, Plb.2.61.1. 4. *distinguish* by reward or punishments, ἐπισημαίνεσθαί τινα δώροις Id.6.39.6; τοὺς μὲν χάρισι, τοὺς δὲ κολάσεσιν Id.*Fr.*148; τὰ καλὰ τῶν ἔργων *OGI*116.13 (Delos, ii B.C.), cf. 51.12 (Ptolemais, iii B.C.). **-σήμανσις**, εως, ἡ, *marking*, ἀπὸ ἐπισημάνσεως κεραυνῶν where lightning *has left its mark*, Arist.*Pr.*937ᵇ26. **-σημαντέον**, *one must signify*, Id.*Top.*160ᵃ3, Phld.*Rh.*2.72 S., cf. Antig.Nicae. ap.Heph.Astr.2.18. **-σημαντικός**, ή, όν, *indicative*, *portending*, Ptol.*Tetr.*94,101, *Cat.Cod.Astr.*4.84.1. **-σημᾰσία**, ἡ, *marking*, *notice*, ἄξιος ἐπισημασίας Plb.39.1.1; τυχεῖν -ασίας Id.30.1.2, cf. Phld.*Rh.*1.12 S., al., etc.; ὑπὸ τοῦ πλήθους ἐ. εὐνοϊκῆς τυγχάνειν Plb.6.6.8; pl., *acclamations*, Cic.*Att.*1.16.11, cf. 14.3.2 (sg.): in bad sense, -ασίας ἔτυχεν ὑπὸ τοῦ δαιμονίου κεραυνωθείς D.S.16.83. II. *marking* of letters in a cipher, Aen.Tact.31.3. III. *symptom*, and hence *access* of an illness, Gal.7.426, 10.604, Alex.Aphr.*Pr.*1.130; *signs of the seasons*, Epicur.*Ep.*2 p.43 U., Plb.1.37.4, D.S.1.49, *Placit.*2.19.1 (pl.); *indication of weather to be expected*, Ptol.*Phas.*p.11 H. (pl.), al. 2. pl., *changes in the weather*, *Stoic.*3.184, *Gp.*7.10. **-σημειόομαι**, = ἐπισημαίνομαι, *distinguish*, *observe*, τὸ ἀνίσχον ζῴδιον S.E.*M.*5.68; κρότῳ by applause, Plu.2.235c (nisi leg. -σημην-). 2. *observe*, *remark*, ὅτι.. Asp.*in EN*139.6, cf. Anon.Lond.21.21. **-σημείωσις**, εως, ἡ, *note* or *comment*, Zeno *Stoic.*1.68. **-σημον**, τό, *distinguishing mark*, *device*, *badge*, Hdt.1.195; *badge* or *bearing* on a shield, v.l. in Id.9.74; *ensign* or *flag* (or *figurehead*) of a ship, Id.8.88, cf. Hp.*Ep.*17; *device* on a coin, Plu.*Thes.*6; on a signet, *SIG*²588.3 (Delos, ii B.C.); *serial number*, *PPetr.*3 p.203 (iii B.C.); ἐπίσημα, τά, *hieroglyphics*, *OGI*56.64 (Canopus, iii B.C.). II. generally, *mark*, *imprint*, τῶν ὅπλων S.*Ichn.*102. **-σημόομαι**, = ἐπισημειόομαι, στεφάνωσίν τινος *IGRom.*4.159.27 (Cyzicus). **-σημος**, Dor. **-σᾱμος**, ον, (σῆμα) *serving to distinguish*, τοῖς δ' ὄνομ' ἄνθρωποι κατέθεντ' ἐ. ἑκάστῳ Parm.19.3. II. *having a mark*, *inscription* or *device on* it, esp. of money, *stamped*, *coined*, χρυσὸς ἐ., opp. ἄσημος, Hdt.9.41; ἀργύριον Th.2.13; χρυσίον X.*Cyr.*4.5.40, cf. *IG*1².301, al.; so ἀναθήματα οὐκ ἐ. offerings *with* no *inscription on them*, Hdt.1.51; ἀσπίδες ἐ., opp. λεῖαι, *IG*1².280, cf. Men.526. 2. of epileptic patients, *bearing the marks of the disease*, Hp.*Morb.Sacr.*8; of cattle, *spotted* or *striped*, Lxx *Ge.*30.42. 3. *notable*, *remarkable*, μνῆμ' ἐ. *a speaking* remembrance, S.*Ant.*1258 (anap.); ξυμφοραὶ E.*Or.*543; εὐνή, λέχος, Id.*HF*68, *Or.*21; τύχη Id.*Med.*544; χαρακτήρ Id.*Hec.*379; τάφος ἐπισημότατος Th.2.43; τιμωρία Lycurg.129; τόποι *IG*12(3).326.42 (Thera, Sup.); of garments, *fine*, *SIG*695.39 (Magn. Mae., ii B.C.); and of persons, ἐ. σοφίην *notable* for wisdom, Hdt.2.20; ἐ. ἐν βροτοῖς E.*Hipp.*103; ἐ. ξένοι Ar.*Fr.*543: in bad sense, *conspicuous*, *notorious*, ἐς τὸν ψόγον E.*Or.*249; δέσμιος ἐ. *Ev.Matt.*27.16; διὰ δημοκοπίαν Plu.*Fab.*14; ἐπὶ τῇ μοχθηρίᾳ Luc.*Rh.Pr.*25. 4. *significant*, οὐκ ἐ. Artem.1.59, 3.32. III. Adv. -μως Plb.6.39.9, Sm.*Ps.*73(74).4, J.*BJ*6.1.8: Comp. -ότερον Gal.9.762; -οτέρως Artem.2.9: Sup. -ότατα Luc.*Hist.Conscr.*43. **-σημότης**, *nobilitas*, *Gloss.*

ἐπίσης, for ἐπ' ἴσης (sc. μοίρας), v. ἴσος.

ἐπισθενέω, *have strength enough*, c. inf., Q.S.4.567, 14.177.

ἐπίσθμιος, ον, *on the neck*: ἐπίσθμιον, τό, *collar*, Hsch.

ἐπίσιγμα, ατος, τό, *hounding on* of a dog, prob. l. in S.*Fr.*9 (pl.).

ἐπισίζω, *hound on*, *set on*, as a dog, Ar.*V.*704, cf. Hsch. s.v. ἐπιρροίζειν.

ἐπίσιμον, f.l. for ἐπίσημον, S.*Ichn.*102.

ἐπισῑμόω, *bend inwards*, τὴν προβοσκίδα Ael.*NA*8.10: seemingly intr., *turn aside one's course*, X.*HG*5.4.50.

ἐπισῐνής, ές, (σίνομαι) *liable to be injured by*, *infested with*, ὄρνισιν ἢ ἄλλοις θηρίοις cj. in Thphr.*HP*8.6.1: abs., Id.*CP*4.10.3 (Comp.). II. Act., *injurious*, τινί ib.2.3.2, *HP*9.8.6; ἐχθροὶ καὶ ἐ. Vett.Val.76.29. III. abs., *blemished*, *feeble*, *diseased*, Chaerem.ap.J.*Ap.*1.32, Vett.Val.18.22, al., *Cat.Cod.Astr.*2.166.13.

ἐπισίνιος, ον, *plotting mischief*, Hsch.

ἐπισίνομαι [σῐ], aor. 1 -σινάμην, *do hurt to*, Nic.*Al.*413.

ἐπίσιον [ῐσῐ], or **ἐπείσιον**, τό, *pubic region*, Hp.*Carn.*14, *Mul.*1.64, 2.113,120,177, Arist.*HA*493ᵃ20, Lyc.1385, Gal.*UP*14.13, al., Poll. 2.170,174, Hsch., Suid., *EM*363.55, Choerob. in *An.Ox.*2.200, cj. in Archil.140. [Both spellings in codd.; also ἐπίσειον, which is disproved by the metre in Lyc. l.c.]

ἐπίσιστον, τό, *a cry to urge on dogs*, *AB*252, *EM*363.54.

ἐπισιτ-ίζομαι, fut. Att. -ιοῦμαι Philostr.*VA*6.15, Ion. -ιεῦμαι Hdt. 9.50:—*furnish oneself with food* or *provender*, Id. l.c., Th.8.101, cf. X.*Vect.*4.48; ἐ. ἐκ τῆς κώμης Hdt.7.176; ἐκεῖθεν Th.6.94; εἶχον οὐδὲν ὅτου ἂν ἐπισιτίσαιντο D.50.53, cf. Arist.*Rh.*1411ᵃ9. 2. c. acc. rei, ἐ. ἄριστον *provide oneself with*.., Th.8.95; ἀργύριον ἐ. εἰς τὴν πορείαν X.*An.*7.1.7; κλεψύδραν Philostr.*VS*2.10.1. 3. metaph., ἐ. πρὸς σοφιστείαν *store oneself* for sophistry, Plu.2.78f. II. = παρασιτέω, Pherecr.32. **-ικός**, ή, όν, in neut. -κόν, τό, *provision of food*, *BGU*362 viii 2 (iii A.D.). **-ιος**, ον, (σῖτος) *working for his victuals alone* (without wages), of slaves, Crates Com.33.1, Pl.*R.*420a, Eub. 21; applied to παράσιτοι, Ar.*Fr.*437, Timocl.29. II. ἐπισίτια, τά, *provision-money*, Lys.*Fr.*75 S. **-ισις**, εως, ἡ, = sq. 2, δέκα ἡμερῶν D.S.20.73:—also **-ισμα**, ατος, τό, Polyaen.3.10.11. **-ισμός**, ὁ, *furnishing oneself with provisions*, *foraging*, X.*HG*3.2.26, *An.*1.5.9. 2. *stock* or *store of provisions*, ib.7.1.9, D.34.7, J.*BJ*3.5.3, *Ev.Luc.*9.12; ἔχοντες ἐπισιτισμὸν ἡμερῶν μ' Philipp.ap.D.18.157; ἐ. ἀννώνης *OGI*200.15 (Axum, iv A.D.): in pl., Hdn.6.7.1.

ἐπισίττω, = ἐπισίζω, Hsch. **ἐπισίφλιον**· αἰσχρόν, μωμητόν, Id.

ἐπισῐωπάω, *cease speaking at* a point, τὰ ῥήματα οἷς -ησα Philostr. *VA*8.26.

ἐπισκάζω, *limp upon*, μηρῷ Lxx *Ge.*32.31(32); πόδεσσι A.R.1.669: abs., τὸ σκέλος ἐ. Hp.*Nat.Mul.*47, cf. *Mul.*2.140, Nic.*Th.*294, Corn. *ND*18: written -σχάζω *BGU*997 ii 5 (ii B.C.).

ἐπισκαίρω, *leap*, *bound*, Ael.*NA*14.8, Nonn.*D.*48.902: c. dat., *leap at* or *on*, Id.2.657, al.: c. acc., Id.22.36 (s.v.l.).

ἐπισκαλμίς, ίδος, ἡ, (σκαλμός) *the part of the rowlock on which the oar rests*, Hsch., Poll.1.87.

ἐπισκάπτω, *dig superficially*, *AP*9.52 (Carph.). II. *harrow in* seed, *Gp.*2.24.1 (Pass.).

ἐπισκαρδᾰμύσσω, *wink at*, Hsch. s.v. ἐπιζυγκλεῖν.

ἐπισκᾰφ-εῖον, τό, *mattock*, *hoe*, *BCH*23.566 (Delph., iii B.C.). II. -εῖα, τά, festival at Rhodes, Hsch. (-άφια cod.). **-εύς**, έως, ὁ, *one who harrows in the seed*, Id.

ἐπισκεδάννῡμι, *scatter* or *sprinkle over*, τι ἐπί τι Pl.*Ti.*85a (Pass.), cf. Alex.186.9:—Pass., *to be sprinkled over*, τινί Plu.*Cat.Mi.*32.

ἐπισκέλῐσις, εως, ἡ, (σκέλος) *first spring* or *bound*, in a horse's gallop, X.*Eq.*7.12.

ἐπισκέλλω, *dry up*: intr. pf. ἐπέσκληκα Epich.155 codd. Ath.

ἐπισκεπ-άζω, *cover over*, τινά Lxx *La.*3.43; *put over*, νεφέλην σεαυτῷ ib.44. **-ής**, ές, (σκέπη) *covered over*, *sheltered*, Arist.*HA*616ᵇ14, Thphr.*Vent.*30.

ἐπισκεπτ-έος, α, ον, *to be considered* or *examined*, Th.6.18, Pl.*Phd.* 107b (s.v.l.). II. neut. -τέον, *one must consider*, Id.*R.*598d, Aen.Tact.10.20, etc. **-ης**, ου, ὁ, *inspector*, *PLond.*3.1171.63 (i B.C.); ἐλαϊκῶν καρπῶν *Sammelb.*4416.8 (ii A.D.): generally, *one who inquires into*, φήμης App.*BC*3.25; = ἐπίσκοπος, *AB*254; = *salutigerulus*, *Gloss.* **-ικός**, ή, όν, *fit for examining*, τινός Arr.*Epict.*1.17.10; μέθοδος S.E.*M.*5.3. Adv. -κῶς Ptol.*Tetr.*171. **-ομαι**, = ἐπισκοπέω, Hp.*Prorrh.*2.1, Men.710, S.E.*M.*5.89, Plu.2.129c, etc. 2. *pass in review*: hence, *number* a host, Lxx 1 *Ki.*15.4. **-ος**, ον, *considered*, *An.Ox.*3.208.

ἐπισκέπω, = ἐπισκεπάζω, Apollod.1.6.2, Longus 1.21, Iamb.*Protr.* 21:—Med., *AP*6.62 (Phil.).

ἐπισκευ-άζω, fut. -σκευῶ *PSI*4.382.3 (iii B.C.):—*get ready*, δεῖπνον Ar.*Ec.*1147 (Pass.); ἐ. ναῦν *refit*, Th.1.29, etc.; ἐ. ἵππους *saddle*, *equip* them, X.*HG*5.3.1 (s.v.l.):—Med., ἐπισκευάσασθαι ναῦς *have* them *refitted*, Th.7.36; ἐ. ὑποζύγια *have* them *packed*, *pack* them, X. *HG*7.2.18. 2. τὰ χρήματα ἐφ' ἁμαξῶν ἐπισκευάσαι *pack* them upon .., Id.*Cyr.*7.3.1. 3. Med., *provide oneself with necessaries* for a journey, *Act.Ap.*21.15. II. *make afresh*, *repair*, *restore*, τὰ τείχη Th.7.24; τὸν ναόν Inscr.ap.X.*An.*5.3.13; τὰς τριήρεις And.3.14, cf. Lys.*Fr.*34; τὰς ὁδοὺς D.3.29:—Med., πόλιν παλαιὰν ἐ. διεφθαρμένην Pl.*Lg.*738b:—Pass., *PPetr.*2 pp.34,62 (iii B.C.). 2. metaph., *reconstruct*, [τὴν διαλεκτικήν] Arist.*Rh.*1359ᵇ15. **-άσιμος** [ᾰ], ον, *needing repair*, *OGI*483.92 (Pergam.). **-αστής**, οῦ, ὁ, *one who equips* or *repairs*, πομπείων D.22.78, etc.; τῶν ἱερῶν Lex ap.Ath.6.235d, Arist.*Ath.*50.1, Ἀρχ.Ἐφ.1923.39 (Oropus, iv B.C.). **-αστικός**, ή, όν, *preparatory*, prob. in Procl. *in Alc.*p.8 C.; *artificial*, χάρις Id. *in Prm.*p.493 S. **-αστός**, ή, όν, *repaired*, *restored*, ἀθανασία Pl.*Plt.* 270a. **-ή**, ἡ, *repair*, *restoration*, τῶν ἱρῶν Hdt.2.174, cf. 175; τειχῶν D.18.311, etc.; τὰς ἐ. καὶ κατασκευὰς τῶν δημοσίων Plb.6.17.2. 2. *means of repairing*, Th.1.52. II. pl., *materials for repair* or *equipment*, *stores*, ἐλέφαντα καὶ μαχαιρῶν λαβὰς καὶ ἄλλας ἐ. D.27.20; χορηγίας καὶ ἐ. Plb.1.72.3. **-όω**, = -άζω, *IG*4.558.20 (Argos, ii B.C.), Ἐφ.Ἀρχ.1908.200 (Crete).

ἐπίσκεψις, εως, ἡ, *inspection*, *visitation*, X.*Oec.*8.15; τῶν ἱερῶν Pl. *Lg.*849a; τῶν ἱππέων Plu.*Crass.*13; ἐν ἐπισκέψει *from the observer's point of view* (opp. ἐν ὑποκειμένοις), Alex.Philalethes ap.Gal.8.726; *visiting* of the sick, Plb.5.56.8, Gal.*Libr.Propr.*1. 2. *investigation*, *inquiry*, Hp.*Prorrh.*2.4, etc.; ἡ ἐ. ἦν, εἰ.. Pl.*R.*456c: pl., Phld. *Oec.*p.71 J. 3. *numbering*, *census*, Lxx *Nu.*1.21, al.

ἐπίσκημμα, ατος, τό, = ἐπίσκηψις, *Lex.Rhet.Cant.*

ἐπισκήν-ιος, ον, *stagy*, *theatrical*, λέξις Porph.*Chr.*71. 2. ἐπισκήνιον, τό, in a theatre, *the upper story of the σκηνή*, Vitr.7.5.5; but τὸ ἐπὶ τῆς σκηνῆς καταγώγιον, Hsch. **-ος**, ον, *at* or *before the tent*, i.e. *public*, γόοι S.*Aj.*579. 2. οἱ ἐ. *the soldiers quartered* (in the towns), Plu.*Sert.*24, Ἀρχ.Ἐφ.1917.2; cf. sq. II. *on the stage*: ἡ ἐ., as Subst., = ἐπισκήνιον, Vitr.5.6.6. III. *external*, *adventitious*, ὄχλος D.H.6.53, cf. 9.53. IV. ἐπίσκηνα, τά, festival at Sparta, Hsch. **-όω**, *to be quartered in*, ταῖς οἰκίαις Plb.4.72.1; ἐπὶ τὰς οἰκίας ib.18.8: metaph., *dwell upon*, ἡ δύναμις ἐ. ἐπί τινα 2 *Ep.Cor.*12.9.

ἐπισκήπτω, pf. ἐπέσκηφα D.L.1.117:—*make to lean upon*, ἐς δὲ παῖδ' ἐμὸν Ζεὺς ἐπέσκηψεν τελευτὴν θεσφάτων *made* it *fall upon* him, A.*Pers.*740 (troch.); ἐ. χάριν τινί *impose* it *upon*, S.*Aj.*566. 2. intr., *fall upon*, like lightning, πρᾶγμα δεῦρ' ἐπέσκηψεν it *came to* this point, A.*Eu.*482; νόσος ἐπέσκηψεν πολλή (v.l. ἐν-) Plu.*Thes.*15; ᾧ ἂν ἔρως ἐπισκήψῃ Id.2.767d, cf. 701c; αὐτῷ ὁ θάνατος Philum.*Ven.*31.3. II. *lay it upon* one to do a thing, c. dat. pers. et inf., μοῖρ' ἐπέσκηψε Πέρσαις πολέμους διέπειν A.*Pers.*103 (lyr.), cf. S.*OT*252: folld. by imper., ib.1446: less freq. c. acc. et inf., E.*Alc.*365; τοῖσι πλησιοχώροισι ἐ. κελεύοντας προπέμπειν Hdt.4.33: inf. can freq. be supplied, τοσοῦτον δή σ' ἐπισκήπτω (sc. ποιεῖν) thus much I *command* thee to do, S.*Tr.*1221; so πρὸς δεξιᾶς σε τῆσδ' ἐπισκήπτω τάδε E.*IT*701: pers. is freq. omitted, ἐ. (sc. ὑμῖν) τὸν ... φόνον ἐκπρήξασθαι Hdt.7.158; βάξις ἐπισκήπτουσα .. ἔξω δόμων .. ὠθεῖν ἐμέ A.*Pr.*664; ἐπέσκηψε .. εἶρξαι Αἴαντα S.*Aj.*752, cf. Antipho 1.1; also ἐ. περί τινος E.*IT*1077. 2. esp. *conjure* a person to do a thing, ὑμῖν τάδε ἐπισκήπτω ... μὴ περιδεῖν

Hdt.3.65; τινὶ πρὸς τῶν θεῶν And.1.32; κλαίοντας, ἱκετεύοντας.. ἐπισκήπτοντας μηδενὶ τρόπῳ τὸν ἀλιτήριον στεφανοῦν Aeschin.3.157, cf. Th.2.73, etc.; of the curses or orders of dying persons, μέμνησθε τὰ ἐπέσκηψε Πέρσῃσι.., μὴ πειρωμένοισι Hdt.3.73, cf. Lys.13.92, D.28. 15, 36.32. 3. γᾳ ἐπισκήπτων χέρα *resting* hand on earth, i.e. *calling* earth *to witness*, B.7.41: abs., γᾳ -σκήπτων πιφαύσκω Id.5.42. III. as Att. law-term, generally in Med., *denounce* a person, so as to begin a prosecution for perjury (cf. ἐπίσκηψις II), διεμαρτύρησε οὑτοσί..· ἐπισκηψαμένων δ' ἡμῶν..ἡ..δίκη τῶν ψευδομαρτυριῶν εἰσῄει, i.e. a διαμαρτυρία was entered..: we *replied by an* ἐπίσκηψις.., and the action for false witness was brought on, Is.5.17; in full, ἐ. τινὶ ψευδομαρτυριῶν D.29.7; ᾗ (sc. τῇ θεῷ) οὐδὲ ψ. θέμις ἐστὶν ἐ. Aeschin.1.130; ἐ. ταῖς μαρτυρίαις D.47.1, cf. Is.3.11; ἐ. [τῇ μαρτυρίᾳ] ὡς ψευδεῖ οὔσῃ *denounce* it as false, Din.1.52:—also in Act., Pl.*Tht.*145c codd., Jul. *Or.*6.186b:—hence Pass., ἐὰν ἐπισκηφθῇ τὰ ψευδῆ μαρτυρῆσαι Pl.*Lg.* 937b: generally, πρὸς τῆς θανούσης..ἐπεσκήπτου *wast denounced, accused*, S.*Ant.*1313:—so in Act., *blame*, τινί Jul.*Or.*7.239a.

ἐπισκηρίπτω, = ἐπισκήπτω, Hsch. s. h. v.

ἐπίσκηψις, εως, ἡ, *injunction*, τὰς Εὐθυκράτους ἐπισκήψεις Is.9.36, cf. Ph.1.362 (pl.), Plu.*Dio*11. II. as law-term, *denunciation*, the first step in a prosecution, esp. in a δίκη ψευδομαρτυριῶν, brought against the witness of a διαμαρτυρία (q.v.), τῇ ἐ. τῶν ψευδομαρτυριῶν D.47.51; Charondas πρῶτος ἐποίησε τὴν ἐ. Arist.*Pol.*1274^{b}7; τούτων τὰς ἐ. εἶναι theirs shall be the right of ἐ., D.47.72.

ἐπισκῐ-άζω, *throw a shade upon, overshadow*, τῇ [πτέρυγι] τὴν Ἀσίην Hdt.1.209, cf. Arist.*GA*780^{a}30, Thphr.*CP*2.18.3, *Ev.Matt.*17.5: c. dat., Thphr.*Sens.*79, *Ev.Marc.*9.7:—Pass., Ph.1.262, al.; opp. φωτίζειν, S.E.*P.*1.141:—Med., -σκιάζεσθαι τὸν ἥλιον *to ward off* the sun's rays, *Gp.*5.29.3: metaph., *conceal, obscure*, ἀλήθειαν πλάσμασι μυθικοῖς Ph.1.41, etc.; τὰ δεινὰ ἑτέροις ὀνόμασιν ἐ. Junc.ap.Stob.4.50. 95; τὴν θωπείαν, τὸν βίον, Luc.*Hist.Conscr.*11, v.l. in *Cal.*1:—Pass., τῇ εὐγενείᾳ Hdn.2.10.3; λαθραῖον ὄμμ' ἐπεσκιασμένη *keeping a hidden* watch, S.*Tr.*914. 2. *darken, obscure*, Ph.2.223 (Pass.): metaph., ἀφροσύνη ἐ. ψυχήν Id.1.685, al. 3. of the Divine presence, *overshadow* for protection, etc., τινί Lxx*Ps.*90(91).4; ἐπὶ τὴν κεφαλήν τινος ib.139(140).8; δύναμις ὑψίστου ἐπισκιάσει σοι *Ev.Luc.*1.35. 4. Pass., *to be weak-sighted*, Vett.Val.111.1. **-ασμα**, ατος, τό, *shadow thrown in eclipses*, Ptol.*Tetr.*76. **-ασμός**, ὁ, *shading, covering*, Hsch. II. *weak sight*, Vett.Val.110.36 (pl.), al. **-άω**, = ἐπισκιάζω, Arat.736, Q.S.2.479; of peacocks, ἑὸν δέμας.. ἐπισκιάουσιν Opp.*C.*2. 590. **-ος**, ον, (σκιά) *shaded, dark*, τόπος Pl.*R.*432c, Arist.*HA*569^b 10; οἴκημα Plu.*Mar.*39; ἀκτῖνες Arat.870: metaph., βίος ἐ. *a retired* life, Lat. *vita umbratilis*, opp. a public life, Plu.2.135b. II. Act., *shading*, c. gen., χεῖρ ὀμμάτων ἐπίσκιος S.*OC*1650. Adv. -ίως Poll.4.51.

ἐπισκιρρόομαι, *become coagulated*, of blood, Poet. *de herb.*33.

ἐπισκιρτ-άω, *leap upon*, τινί Nonn.*D.*2.29: metaph., τῷ νεκρῷ Plu.*Dem.*22: abs., ἐπισκιρτῶσιν ἔθειραι, ἴουλος, *AP*5.102 (Rufin.), 12.10 (Strat.). **-ημα**, ατος, τό, *spring, bound*, Nonn.*D.*19.154.

ἐπίσκληρος, ον, *somewhat hard*, κοιλίη Hp.*Prorrh.*1.138: Comp., J.*AJ*17.12.2.

ἐπισκληρύνομαι, Pass., *become somewhat hard*, Gal.16.800.

ἐπισκοπ-εία, ἡ, *inspection*, *PTeb.*5.189 (pl., ii B.C.). **-εύω**, = sq., Sm.*Ps.*65(66).7. **-έω**, fut. -σκέψομαι, later -σκοπήσω Babr. 103.8: aor. -εσκεψάμην, later -εσκόπησα Luc.*Herm.*44, 59: pf. ἐπέσκεμμαι Hp.*VM*14, Pl.*Epin.*990a; also in pass. sense, Arist.*Cael.*299^a 10, *PA*692^{a}18:—*look upon* or *at, inspect, observe*, ἱστορίας καὶ τἆλλα ἔγγραφα *Milet.*3.155 (ii B.C.) (also in Med., ἐ. τὸ περίχωμα *PLille* 1^v 27 (iii B.C.), etc.); *regard*, τἀμ' ἐ. κακά E.*Heracl.*869; of tutelary gods, Θηβαίας ἐπισκοποῦντ' ἀγυιάς, of Bacchus, S.*Ant.*1136 (lyr.); Ἴλιον .. ἐπισκοπεῖ σεμνὸς Ποσειδῶν E.*IT*1414, cf. *Ph.*661 (lyr.); ὦ Δῆμ', ἐναργῶς ἡ θεός σ' ἐπισκοπεῖ Ar.*Eq.*1173, cf. 1186; also of a ruler, ἐ. τὴν πολιτείαν Pl.*R.*506b, cf. X.*Oec.*4.6 (so in Med., θαμὰ ἐπεσκοπεῖτο ἡμᾶς *observed*, Pl.*Ly.*207a): folld. by Relat., ἐ. καὶ ἀναμετρήσαντες ὅσῳ ἐλάσσων ὁ χῶρος γέγονε Hdt.2.109; ἐ. πῶς ἔχει Pl. *Grg.*451c; τόδε ἐπίσκεψαι εἴ τι λέγω Id.*Phd.*87b, cf. X.*Mem.*2.1.22; πότερον .. ἢ .. Pl.*R.*518a; τίς εἴη.. X.*Mem.*3.2.4, cf. *Smp.*1.12; ἐ. μή.. *take care* lest, *Ep.Hebr.*12.15. 2. *visit*, ὦ θάνατε, νῦν μ' ἐπίσκεψαι μολών S.*Aj.*854; *visit* as a friend (ironically), D.9.12; esp. *visit* the sick, X.*Cyr.*8.2.25, *Mem.*3.11.10; of the physician, Hdn.4.2.4:—Med., D.59.56, Gal.11.2, 14.633:—Pass., εὐνὴν ὀνείροις οὐκ ἐπισκοπουμένην *visited* not by dreams, i.e. sleepless, A.*Ag.* 13. 3. of a general, *inspect, review*, τὰς τάξεις X.*An.*2.3.2; τὰ ὅπλα Id.*Cyr.*6.3.21, cf. A.*Eu.*296. 4. *consider, reflect, meditate*, ὅ τι ἂν μέλλῃς ἐρεῖν, πρότερον ἐπισκόπει τῇ γνώμῃ Isoc.1.41; also ἐ. πρός τι Pl.*Lg.*924d; περί τινος Id.*Prt.*348d, al., Ceb.35.5; ὑπέρ τινος Plb.3.15.2; σαυτὸν ἐ. ὅστις εἴης X.*Mem.*4.2.24; ἐ. τίς.., ποῖα τις.. Arist.*Pol.*1274^{b}32; πότερον.. ib.1276^{b}16:—Med., *examine with oneself, meditate*, Pl.*Phd.*91d; εἰς τὸ ἀληθὲς ἐ. τι Id.*Phlb.*61e, cf. Alex. 219.8, Philem.46:—Pass., pf. (v. supr.). 5. *exercise the office of* ἐπίσκοπος, v.l. in 1*Ep.Pet.*5.2. **-ή**, ἡ, *watching over, visitation*, of God, Lxx*Nu.*16.29, *Ev.Luc.*19.44. II. *office of* ἐπίσκοπος, 1*Ep. Ti.*3.1, *Cod.Just.*1.3.35 *Intr.*, etc.: generally, *office*, Lxx*Ps.*108(109). 8. 2. = ἐπίσκεψις 3, ib.*Nu.*14.29, al. **-ησις**, εως, ἡ, *inspection, examination*, Aen.Tact.10.6. **-ητέον**, *one must consider*, εἰ.. Sch.Luc.*Dem.Enc.*43, cf. Heph.Astr.3.1. **-ία**, ἡ, = εὐστοχία, condemned by Poll.6.205. **-ικός**, ή, όν, *episcopal*, *Cod.Just.*1.4.29. 3. **-ος** (A), ὁ, (σκοπός I) *one who watches over, overseer, guardian*, ἣ γὰρ ὄλωλας ἐπίσκοπος, ὅς τέ μιν αὐτὴν ῥύσκευ (sc. τὴν πόλιν), of Hector, Il.24.729, ἐ.. ὁδαίων Od.8.163; ἐπίσκοποι ἁρμονιάων *watchers over* compacts, of the gods, Il.22.255; νεκροῦ S.*Ant.*217; σῆς ἕδρας Id.*OC*112; ἐ. ὀϊστῶν, of an archer, v.l. in Theoc.24.107; in education, *tutor*, Pl.*Lg.*795d; ἐ. σωφροσύνης καὶ ὕβρεως ib.849a: c. dat., ἀγυιαῖς ἔσσῃ καὶ λιμένεσσιν ἐ. Call.*Dian.*39; esp. of tutelary gods (cf. ἐπισκοπέω), Παλλὰς ἐ. Sol.4.3; Δίκη Pl.*Lg.*872e; Κλειὼ ἐ. χερνίβων Simon.45; Χάριτες Μινυᾶν ἐ. Pi.*O.*14.3; θεοὶ ἐ. ἀγορᾶς A.*Th.*272; πατρῴων δωμάτων ἐ. Id.*Ch.*126; τὸ δεινὸν..φρενῶν ἐπίσκοπον *guardian* of the mind, Id.*Eu.*518 (lyr.); νυχίων φθεγμάτων ἐ., of Bacchus, S.*Ant.* 1148 (lyr); Ἐρινύες *IG*12(9).1179.33 (Euboea, ii A.D.); [Χριστὸς] ἐ. τῶν ψυχῶν 1*Ep.Pet.*2.25: rarely c. dat., πᾶσι γὰρ ἐ. ἐτάχθη..Νέμεσις Pl.*Lg.*717d. 2. *scout, watch*, c. dat., ἐ. Τρώεσσι, νήεσσιν ἡμετέρῃσιν, *one set to watch* them, Il.10.38, 342. 3. *supervisor, inspector*, sent by Athens to subject states, Ar.*Av.*1023, *IG*1^2.10, 11; of *municipal officials* at Rhodes, ib.12(1).49.42 (ii/i B.C.): generally, *PPetr.*3 p.75 (iii B.C.), etc. 4. *ecclesiastical superintendent*, ἐπίσκοποι καὶ διάκονοι *Ep.Phil.*1.1, cf. *Act.Ap.*20.28, 1*Ep.Ti.*3.2, etc. **-ος** (B), ον, (σκοπός II) *hitting the mark, successful*, βάλλειν ἐ. Them.*Or.*11.143a (Sup.); τοξότης Him.*Ecl.*14.3; ἠχῇ Opp.*C.*1.42; *reaching, touching*, νίκης μὴ κακῆς ἐπίσκοπα A.*Eu.*903; ἄτης τῆσδ' ἐ. μέλος *having regard to* the calamity, S.*Aj.*976: neut. pl. ἐπίσκοπα, as Adv., *successfully, with good aim*, ἐ. τοξεύειν Hdt.3.35, Jul.*Or.*1.11c: regul. Adv. -πως, ἀκοντίζειν ἢ τοξεύειν Alcid.*Soph.*7, cf. Poll.6.205: Comp. -ώτερα, βάλλειν Them.*Or.*8.116b: Sup. -ώτατα Poll.1.215. Cf. εὔστοχος, εὔσκοπος.

ἐπισκορπίζω, *scatter over*, Suid. s. v. ἐπικίδναται (Pass.).

ἐπισκοτ-άζω, = sq., Hp.*Off.*3. **-έω**, (σκότος) *throw a shadow over*, οἰκίαν ᾠκοδόμησεν τοσαύτην ὥστε πᾶσιν ἐπισκοτεῖν τοῖς ἐν τῷ τόπῳ D.21. 158; ἐ. τινὶ τῆς θέας *to be in the way* of his seeing, Pl.*Euthd.*274c, cf. Plu.2.538e; τῷ βωμῷ Judeich *Altertümer von Hierapolis* 339: abs., Plb.24.4, Polyaen.8.23.2; *form a roof*, Hero *Aut.*28.2. 2. metaph., *throw darkness* or *obscurity over*, τῇ κρίσει Sor.*Vit.Hippocr.*13, Arist. *Rh.*1354^{b}11; ταῖς τῆς ψυχῆς ἐπιμελείαις Isoc.1.6; τὸ πρὸς χάριν ῥηθὲν ἐ. τῷ καθορᾶν Id.8.10, cf. D.2.20; οἶνος τῷ φρονεῖν ἐπισκοτεῖ Eub.135 = Ophelio4; ἐ. γὰρ τῷ φρονεῖν τὸ λαμβάνειν Antiph.250; τὸ δ' ἐρᾶν ἐ. ἅπασιν, ὡς ἔοικε Men.48; ἡ ὀργὴ ἐ. τοῖς λογισμοῖς Phld.*Ir.*p.78 W.:—Pass., *to be in the dark* or *in uncertainty*, ἐπισκοτεόμενος τῇ ἀπειρίῃ Hp. *Praec.*8; ἐπισκοτεῖσθαι καὶ κωλύεσθαι Plb.2.39.12; *to be obscured*, ὑπό τινος Id.12.25^d.7; *to be blinded*, τὰς ὄψεις ὑπὸ θεοῦ J.*AJ*9.4.3, cf. Ph. 2.62. **-ησις**, εως, ἡ, *darkening, obscurity*, of the sun or moon in eclipse, Plu.*Per.*35, *Nic.*23, Ptol. *Tetr.*76, etc.: metaph., οὗ λέγουσιν εἰς -ησιν Plot.2.9.10. **-ίζω**, = ἐπισκοτέω, Plb.13.5.6 (Pass.), Lib.*Decl.* 48.38; *to be overshadowed*, Ps.-Democr.*Symp.Ant.*p.3 G. **-ισις**, εως, ἡ, and **-ισμός**, ὁ, = ἐπισκότησις, Procl.*Par.Ptol.*112, 119. **-ος**, ον, *in the dark, darkened*, ἐπίσκοτον ἀτραπὸν ἐσσυμένα, of the sun, prob. in Pi.*Pae.*9.5, dub. l. in Plu.*Aem.*17.

ἐπισκύζομαι, *to be indignant at* a thing, ὄφρα καὶ ἄλλοι ἐπισκύζωνται Ἀχαιοί Il.9.370; μή σοι θυμὸς ἐπισκύσσαιτο ἰδόντι (Ep. aor.) Od.7.306:—Act., aor. ἐπισκύσαι *EM*364.10.

ἐπισκῠθίζω, *pour out drink in Scythian fashion*, i.e. with unmixed wine, Hdt.6.84, Chamael.ap.Ath.10.427c.

ἐπισκυθρωπάζω, *look gloomy* or *stern*, of hounds, X.*Cyn.*3.5; of men, Plu.2.375a.

ἐπισκύλλω, in Pass., aor. 2 part. -σκυλέντες, παροδικῶς *after being* temporarily *distressed*, Vett.Val.171.18.

ἐπισκύνιον [ῠ], τό, *skin of the brows* which projects over the eyes and is knitted in frowning (Arist.*GA*780^{b}28), πᾶν δέ τ' ἐπισκύνιον κάτω ἕλκεται ὄσσε καλύπτων, of a lion, Il.17.136; δεινὸν ἐ. ξυνάγων, of Aeschylus, Ar.*Ra.*823 (hex.); τοῖον ἐ. βλοσυρῷ ἐπέκειτο προσώπῳ Theoc.24.118, cf. *APl.*4.100; ῥυσὸν ἐ., πολιὸν ἐ., *AP*6.64 (Paul. Sil.), 7.117 (Zenod.); even φαιδρὸν ἐ. ib.12.159 (Mel.); ἐπιστρέψας γυρὸν ἐ., of one who puts on a wise face, ib.11.376.8 (Agath.): in pl., Posidipp.ap.Ath.10.414e: hence, II. *superciliousness*, γυμνώσαντο βίου παντὸς ἐ., of Diogenes, *AP*7.63, etc.; but in Plb.25.3.6, simply, *austerity, gravity of deportment.* III. Adj. ἐπισκύνιος, ον, *supercilious*, Gloss.

ἐπίσκῡρος, ὁ, *ball-game* (= ἐπίκοινος III) resembling Rugby football, Hsch., Poll.9.103, Sch.Pl.*Tht.*146a. II. *governor*, Call.*Fr.* 231, cf. Hsch.

ἐπισκῠφισμός, ὁ, *operation* performed on the scalp for eye-affections, Aët.7.93.

ἐπί-σκωμμα, ατος, τό, *jest*, gloss on σιλλοί, *EM*713.7. 2. *term of derision*, Gramm.ap.Gaisf.*Choerob.*1 p.43 (pl.). **-σκώπτης**, ου, ὁ, *mocker*, v.l. for ἐπικόπτης (q.v.). **-σκώπτω**, *laugh at, make fun of*, τινά X.*Mem.*4.4.6; τι ib.3.11.16; τινὰ ὡς.., ὅτι.., Pl.*Euthphr.*11c, X.*Smp.*1.5; εἴς τι Plu.*Lyc.*30; *cast in one's teeth*, τινὶ τὴν δεισιδαιμονίαν J.*Ap.*1.22:—Pass., πρός τινων Gal.6.307. 2. abs., *jest, make fun*, Ar.*Ra.*375; ἔφη ἐπισκώπτων X.*Mem.*1.3.7. **-σκωψις**, εως, ἡ, *mocking, raillery*, Plu.*Ant.*24 (pl.).

ἐπισμᾰρᾰγέω, *rattle* or *echo again*, Opp.*C.*2.78, Q.S.2.546 (ἀπεσμ- codd.), etc.: c. acc. cogn., ἐ. ὕμνον τινί Nonn.*D.*48.965.

ἐπισμάω, *rub, smear* something *over* a person, c. acc. pers. et rei, τί γὰρ οὗτος ἡμᾶς οὐκ ἐπισμῇ τῶν κακῶν; Ar.*Th.*389, cf. Cratin.90: **ἐπισμήχω** is a less Att. form, Opp.*C.*1.501 (v.l. ἐπισμύχω).

ἐπισμῠγερός, ή, όν, *gloomy, sad*, Ἀχλύς Hes.*Sc.*264; αἶσα A.R. 4.1065.—Hom. has only the Adv. -ρῶς, ἀπέτεισεν *sadly* did he pay for it, Od.3.195; ἐ. ναυτίλλεται *at his peril, to his misfortune* doth he sail, 4.672, cf. A.R.1.616.

ἐπισμυκτόν (fort. leg. ἐπιμυκτόν)· ἐπιμυκτηρισμόν, Hsch.

ἐπισμύχομαι [ῡ], Pass., *to become more and more inflamed* with passion, Zos.4.44.3.

ἐπισοβέω, *urge on*, τινά Them.*Or*.4.50b; *push on*, τι Hld.6.11, 4.5; ἐ. κώθωνά τινι *send whizzing at*, Alex.176. II. intr., *glory in*, τιάρᾳ Philostr.*Im*.1.30.

ἐπίσογκος [ῐ], ον, (ἴσος, ὄγκος) *of equal bulk*, Str.13.1.67.

ἔπῐσος, ον, = ἴσος, Plb.3.115.1, Lxx*Si*.9.10.

ἐπισοφίζομαι, *devise in addition*, c. inf., Hp.*Art*.14, Iamb.*VP*18. 86.

ἐπισπάδην [ᾰ], Adv., (ἐπισπάω) *at one draught*, πίνειν Hp.*Int*.26.

ἐπισπαίρω, *pant, struggle*, ἐπί τινι Plu.2.327c.

ἐπί-σπᾰσις, εως, ἡ, *drawing in*, τῆς τροφῆς Arist.*Spir*.482ᵃ15, cf. Thphr.*CP*1.17.6, etc.; ἡ ἐ. τοῦ στόματος, in sucking in liquid, Alex. Aphr.*Pr*.2.59. **-σπασμός**, ὁ, *rapid respiration*, Hp.*Epid*.6.5. 15. II. *trailing*, of a serpent, Sch.Nic.*Th*.160. III. *inducement* (to inference), *hint*, Phld.*Sign*.13, Demetr.Lac.*Herc*.1055. 13 F. IV. *traction* of the foetus, Sor.2.62. V. *suction* of cupping instruments, ib.11. **-σπαστήρ**, ῆρος, ὁ, *latch* or *handle by which a door is pulled to*, Hdt.6.91: spelt **-σπατήρ** *IG*2².1672.123. II. τρίκλωστον ἐπισπαστῆρα βόλοιο, of the fowler's *line*, *AP*6.109 (Antip.). **-σπαστικός**, ή, όν, *drawing to oneself, drawing in*, τοῦ ὑγροῦ Arist.*Pr*.966ᵃ4; ἀτμοὶ ἐ. πρὸς ἑαυτούς Str.15.1.38; αἵματος Gal.*Nat. Fac*.2.3: abs. of drugs, Id.11.761, cf. Dsc.2.85,109; ἔμπλαστροι Orib. *Fr*.85; ῥυφήματα ἐ. dub. sens. in Hp.*Acut*.(*Sp*.)2. 2. metaph., *attractive*, Plb.4.84.6, *Stoic*.3.46. Adv. -κῶς, κινεῖν S.E.*P*.3.69. **-σπαστός** or **ἐπίσπαστος**, ή, όν, *drawn upon oneself*, Ἶρος.. ἐπίσπαστον κακὸν ἕξει Od.18.73, cf. 24.462; λύπη Hld.2.6; δεσποτεία D.C.62.3; ἐπισπαστοί, of the suitors in the Od., Paus.8.12.6. II. ἐ. βρόχοι *tight-drawn* nooses, E.*Hipp*.783. **-σπαστρον**, τό, *rope for pulling*, D.S.17.90; also, a fowler's *net*, Dionys.*Av*.3.12. 2. = ἐπισπαστήρ I, Poll.10.22. II. *that which is drawn over, curtain, hanging*, Lxx*Ex*.26.36. **-σπάω**, *draw* or *drag after one*, Hdt.2.121.δ'; ἦγ' ἐπισπάσας κόμης by the hair, E.*Hel*.116, cf. *Tr*.882, *Andr*.710:—Med., X.*An*.4.7.14:—Pass., ἐπισπασθῆναι τῇ χειρί with the hand, Th.4.130. 2. metaph., *bring on, cause*, τοσόνδε πλῆθος πημάτων A.*Pers*.477. 3. *pull to*, τὴν θύραν X.*HG*6.4.36; cf. ἐπισπαστήρ: ἐπισπασθέντος τοῦ βρόχου *being drawn tight*, D.24.139. 4. *attract, gain, win*, πέποιθα τοῦτ' ἐπισπάσειν κλέος S.*Aj*.769:—freq. in Med., ἐπισπᾶσθαι κέρδος Hdt.3.72; εὔνοιαν Plb.3.98.9; χάριν *SIG*685.40 (Magn. Mae., ii B.C.); ἔχθραν *AP*11.340 (Pall.); *welcome*, Ph.1.384; ἐπισπᾶσθαι πώγωνα *get one* a beard, Luc.*JTr*.16; *induce*, ὕπνον ἐκπώμασιν Lib.*Or*.56.26; *attract*, σίδηρον Phld.*Sign*.1. 5. *draw on, allure, persuade*, τὴν ψυχήν Pl.*Cra*.420a:—Med., ὁ λόγος... ἂν ἐπισπάσαιτο Th.3.44, cf. 5.111; ἐ. ἡ πέρδιξ [τὸν θηρεύοντα] Arist.*HA*613ᵇ19; θάτερον παρεμπῖπτον ἐπεσπάσατο...τὸ ἕτερον ἐπινόημα *induced, provoked*, Epicur.*Nat*.137 G.: c. inf., *induce* to do, ἐπισπάσασθαι [ἂν] αὐτοὺς ἡγεῖτο προθυμήσεσθαι he thought it would *induce, invite* them to make the venture, dub. l. in Th.4.9; ἐπισπᾶσθαί τινα ἐμπλησθῆναι δακρύων τὰ ὄμματα X.*Cyr*.5.5.10; ἐ. τοὺς πολεμίους ἐφ' ἑαυτόν Plu.*Phil*. 18, cf. *Mar*.11, 21, 26; but τοὺς πολεμίους εἰς τόπους *allure, entice*, Plb. 3.110.2, etc.:—Pass., ἐπισπώμενον εἰς τἀναντία πολλάκις ἅμα though often he *is being drawn* in opposite directions at once, Pl.*Lg*.863e; φοβοῦμαι μὴ πάντες.. ἐπισπασθῶσιν πέρα τοῦ συμφέροντος [πολεμῆσαι] D. 5.19; πολύ τι μᾶλλον ἐπεσπάσμεθα *OGI*223.18 (iii B.C.); ἐπεσπάσθην φιλονεικεῖν Demetr.Lac.*Herc*.1055.23 F. 6. Med., *absorb*, τὰ σιτία -σπᾶται τὴν ὑγρότητα Arist.*Pr*.868ᵇ30; τὰ ἐρινεαστὰ [σῦκα] ἐ. τὸν ὀπόν Thphr.*CP*2.9.12; *quaff*, of a drinker, ἀπνευστὶ ἐ. Gal.15.500, cf. Luc. *DDeor*.5.4; of infants, *suck*, γάλα Sor.1.88; of cupping instruments, Hp.*VM*22; *draw in*, πνεῦμα Phld.*D*.3.13:—Pass., of air, *to be sucked in*, Arist.*Pr*.931ᵇ22. 7. Med., *draw in, call in*, Πύρρον Plb.1.6.5; φυλακὴν καὶ βοήθειαν παρά τινος ib.7.6; μάρτυρας -ᾶται τοὺς μουσικούς Phld.*Po*.5.1425.8:—Pass., *to be called in, forced to work*, εἴς τι *PTeb*. 27.4 (ii B.C.). 8. in Pass., of the sea, ἐπισπωμένη βιαιότερον *returning with a rush* after having retired, Th.3.89. II. *overturn*: hence proverb., ὅλην τὴν ἅμαξαν ἐπεσπάσω you have 'upset the apple-cart', Luc.*Pseudol*.32. III. Med., *draw the prepuce forward, become as if uncircumcised*, μὴ ἐπισπάσθω 1*Ep.Cor*.7.18; of the nurse, ἐπισπάσθω τὴν ἀκροποσθίαν Sor.1.113.

ἐπισπεῖν, ἐπισπών, v. ἐφέπω (A).

ἐπισπείρω, *sow with seed*, ὁδόν Hdt.7.115; *sow upon* or *among*, τι ἐπὶ τὰ ἄνδηρα Thphr.*CP*3.15.4, cf. *HP*7.5.4; τινί τι Id.*CP*.2.17.3 (Pass.): metaph., ἐ. μομφὰν ἀλιτροῖς Pi.*N*.8.39; σοφιστικὰ ζητήματα ταῖς ἐξηγήσεσι Gal.15.519 (v.l.). 2. *sow again, with fresh seed*, Thphr.*CP*2.17.10 (Pass.); *sow after*, ζιζάνια *Ev.Matt*.13.25.

ἐπίσπεισις, εως, ἡ, *libation poured over* a sacrifice, Hdt.2.39.

ἐπί-σπεισμα, ατος, τό, *a last libation over*: metaph., ἐ. τῶν ἐκκεχυμένων βίων cj. in Demetr.ap.Plu.2.349b. **-σπένδω**, *pour upon* or *over*, esp. as a drink-offering, ἐπὶ τοῦ βωμοῦ οἶνον κατὰ τοῦ ἱρηΐου ἐ. Hdt.2.39; οἶνον ἐ. κατὰ τῶν κεφαλέων Id.4.62; τοῖσι ἱροῖσι Id.7.167; νεκρῷ A.*Ag*.1395; τοιαῖσδ' ἐπ' εὐχαῖς τάσδ' ἐ. χοάς *after* the vows I *pour* these libations, Id.*Ch*.149: abs., Hdt.4.60; οὐδ' ἄν τι θύων οὐδ' ἐπισπένδων ἄνοις A.*Fr*.161; also ἐ. δάκρυ Theoc.23.38. 2. *promise, pledge*, *Leg.Gort*.4.52, 6.11:—Med., *accept in pledge*, ib.6.13, al. II. Med., *make a fresh treaty*, Th.5.22.

ἐπισπερχ-ής, ές, *hasty, hurried*, μὴ ἐ. ἀλλ' ἀγαθὸς φαινέσθω Arist. *Phgn*.808ᵃ7, cf. 807ᵇ5. Adv. -χῶς X.*Cyr*.4.1.3: Comp. -εστέρως Aen. Tact.26.10. **-ω**, *urge on*, Od.22.451; [ἵππους] κέντρῳ ἐπισπέρχων Il.23.430; [νῆα] ἐρετμοῖς A.R.3.346; τὸ πρᾶγμα κάρτ' ἐπισπέρχει θεός A.*Th*.689; τοὺς ἄλλους τοιαῦτα ἐπέσπερχε Th.4.12: c. inf., *urge* one to do, A.R.1.525, Plu.2.347b. 2. ἐ. ἴχνος *follow close upon* the track, Opp.*C*.4.96: abs., Nic.*Th*.144. II. intr., *rage furiously*, ἐπισπέρχουσιν ἄελλαι Od.5.304, cf. Pi.*Parth*.2.18; εἴ τι ἡ πνὶξ ἐπισπέρχοι Aret.*CA*1.8. 2. *hasten* in flight, Tim.*Pers*.98.

ἐπισπέσθαι, v. ἐφέπω (B).

ἐπισπεύδω, *urge on, further* or *promote* an object, opp. ἀποσπεύδω, Hdt.7.18; ἐ. τὸ δρᾶν S.*El*.467; τὴν στρατείαν Isoc.4.138, etc.; of persons, *urge on, hasten*, X.*HG*5.1.33; ὁδίταν Theoc.16.93: metaph., οἷς (attracted for οὕς) μὴ φύσις ἐπέσπευσεν whom Nature *has not matured quickly*, Pl.*Lg*.810b. II. intr., *hasten onward*, E.*Tr*. 1275; πρός τινα X.*Vect*.3.4; ἐ. εἰς ταὐτόν τινι Id.*Smp*.7.4: part. ἐπισπεύδων *in haste*, A.R.3.1389; τὸ -σπεῦδον τῆς πορείας Hld.8.17.

ἐπισπευστικός, ή, όν, *urgent*, Eust.831.29.

ἐπισπῑλόω, *make spotty*, *Cat.Cod.Astr*.8(4).154.

ἐπισπλαγχν-ίδιος, ὁ, apptly. a sacrificial implement, dub. sens. in *IG*11(2).153 (Delos, iii B.C.), *BCH*6.25 (ibid., ii B.C.). **-ίζομαι**, *to have compassion*, Lxx*Pr*.17.5.

ἐπίσπληνος, ον, *diseased in the spleen, splenetic*, Hp.*Epid*.7.107.

ἐπισπόμενος, v. ἐφέπω (B).

ἐπι-σπονδή, ἡ, in pl., *treaty made after another*, Th.5.32. **-σπονδον**, τό, *libation*, οἴνου *Inscr.Prien*.195.26 (iii/ii B.C.). **-σπονδορχηστής**, οῦ, ὁ, = ὑποσπ-, *SIG*1021.28 (Olympia, i B.C.).

ἐπισπορ-ά, ἡ, *second sowing*, Thphr.*CP*2.17.10, *PTeb*.375.14 (ii A.D.). **-ία**, Ep. -ίη, ἡ, = foreg., Hes.*Op*.446, Poll.1.223. **-ος**, ον, *sown afterwards*, οἱ ἐ. *posterity*, A.*Eu*.673; τὰ ἐ. *secondary crops*, of vegetables, Thphr.*HP*7.1.2, *PTeb*.27.37 (ii B.C.).

ἐπισπουδ-άζω, *urge on, further*, Lxx*Ge*.19.15, *Pr*.13.11 (Pass.). II. intr., *haste* or *make haste in* a thing, Luc.*Pisc*.2. III. *study over*, τι τῷ οἴνῳ Philostr.*VS*2.10.1. **-ασμός**, ὁ, *transport, dispatch*, πυροῦ *PGrenf*.2.23.17 (ii B.C.), cf. *Annales du Service* 13.224 (Crocodilopolis, iii A.D.), prob. in *PStrassb*.93.2 (ii B.C.). **-αστής**, οῦ, ὁ, *one who presses on a work*, Lxx*Is*.14.4. II. ἐ. τῆς Θηβαΐδος, name of an official in Egypt, *PBodl.ined*.31218. 2. *transport-master*, *PRyl*.183 (i A.D.).

ἐπίσπω, -σποιμι, -σπών, v. ἐφέπω (A).

ἔπισσαι, αἱ, Ion., = ἐπιγινόμεναι τοῖς προγόνοις, Hecat.363 J.; cf. μέτασσαι. **ἔπισσον**· τὸ ὕστερον γενόμενον, Hsch.

ἐπισσείω, ἐπισσεύω, Ep. for ἐπισείω, ἐπισεύω.

ἐπίσσοφος, ὁ, an official at Thera, *Test.Epict*.8.15. (Perh. fr. ψέφω, lit. *supervisor*):—the Verb [**ἐπισ**]**οφεύω** is prob. in *IG*9(1).691.15 (Corc., iii B.C.).

ἐπίσσῠτος, ον, (ἐπισεύω, ἐπέσσυμαι) *rushing, gushing*, κλαυμάτων πηγαί A.*Ag*.887; *violent, sudden*, δύαι ib.1150 (lyr.); βίου τύχαι Id. *Eu*.924 (lyr.); φήμα E.*Hipp*.574 (lyr.).

ἐπίσσωτρον, τό, Ep. for ἐπίσωτρον (q. v.).

ἐπίστᾳ, for ἐπίστασαι, 2 sg. of ἐπίσταμαι.

ἐπί-σταγμα, ατος, τό, *anything dropped on* or *in*, Gal.19.118. **-σταγμός**, ὁ, = κόρυζα, Id.13.61, v.l. in Dsc.3.20 (pl.).

ἐπισταδόν, Adv., (ἐφίστημι, ἐπιστῆναι) *standing over each in turn* (ἐφιστάμενος ἑκάστῳ *EM*364.35), i.e. *one after another, successively*, νείκεον ἄλλοθεν ἄλλον ἐ. Od.12.392; νώμησεν δ' ἄρα πᾶσιν ἐ. 13.54; *standing by*, A.R.1.293; ἐ. οὐτάζοντες *standing up to* each other, Id. 2.84.—The words of Od.16.453, δόρπον ἐ. ὡπλίζοντο, seem to have given rise to the other expl. of the Sch., ἐπισταμένως, ἐμπείρως (as if from ἐπίσταμαι).

ἐπιστάζω, *let fall in drops upon* or *into, instil*, τινί τι Arist.*Pr*.871ᵇ 18, Orib.46.19.13, cf. Herod.1.81: metaph., ἐ. χάριν *shed* delight or honour, Pi.*I*.4(3).72; ὀλίγον τοῦ μέλιτος Luc.*VH*1.24:—Pass., *to be dropped on*, ἐπειδὰν ἐπισταγῇ ὄνυχι Dsc.2.70, cf. Sor.1.91. II. intr., *bleed at the nose again*, Hp.*Prorrh*.1.148, *Coac*.337.

ἐπισταθμ-άομαι, *weigh well, ponder*, A.*Ag*.164 (lyr.). **-εία** or **-ία**, ἡ, *lodging*, ἐ. ποιεῖσθαι παρά τινι take up one's *quarters* with him, D.S.17.47 (v.l. -είαν), cf. 34.17. II. *liability to have persons quartered on one*, Cic.*Att*.13.52.2, Plu.*Sert*.6 (pl.). **-εύω**, *to be billeted* or *quartered upon* another, Id.*Sull*.25; τινί Id.*Demetr*.23, cf. 2.828f. II. Pass., *to have others quartered upon one*, *PPetr*.2 p.36 (iii B.C.), *UPZ* 146 ii 27 (ii B.C.), Plb.21.6.1. 2. *to be assigned as quarters*, οἰκία Plu.*Ant*.9. III. trans., *occupy with*, in metaph. sense, τὰ ὦτα διαλέξεσιν Id.2.778b. **-ησις**, *interpondium*, *Gloss*. **-ος**, ον, *quartered on another*, *PPetr*.3 p.41 (iii B.C.); στρατιῶται *SIG*880.61 (Pizus, iii A.D.): neut. pl. as Subst., ἐπίσταθμα, τά, *quarters*, Poll.4.173. II. as Subst., ἐπίσταθμος, ὁ, *quartermaster, satrap*, Isoc.4.120; ἐ. Καρίας ib.162, cf. *AB*253. b. *image placed at a door*, Call.*Epigr*.26, dub. in *POxy*.2146.9 (iii A.D.). 2. = συμποσίαρχος, Plu.2.612c.

ἐπιστάκτης, ου, ὁ, *wool used for dropping oil*, Heliod.(?) ap.Orib. 46.19.13.

ἐπιστᾰλάζω, = ἐπιστάζω, τι ἐπί τι Mnesith.ap.Orib.*inc*.15.11:—also **-στᾰλάω**, *drop over*, ἱδρὼς.. στῆθος ἐ. *AP*9.322 (Leon.).

ἐπίσταλ-μα, ατος, τό, (ἐπιστέλλω) *commission*, Thphr.*Char*.5. 8. II. *official communication* or *order*, *PFay*.26.4 (ii A.D.), Wilcken *Chr*.42.3, 8 (iv A.D.), *Cod.Just*.7.37.3.1c: pl., of Imperial *letters*, Just. *Nov*.167.1. **-σις**, εως, ἡ, *order*, in pl., Hsch. s. v. ἐπιστολαί. **-τικός**, ή, όν, *epistolary*, ἀπαρέμφατα A.D.*Synt*.239.24, al.; of the dative case, D.T.636.6; ἐ. ὅσα κατὰ ἐντολὰς πρός τινας ποιοῦντες διέπεμπον Procl.*Chr*.ap.Phot.p.322 B.

ἐπίστᾱμα, v. ἐπίστημα.

ἐπίστᾰμαι, 2 pers. -ασαι A.*Pr*.376, 982, S.*El*.629, Pl.*Euthd*.296a, but ἐπίστᾳ Pi.*P*.3.80, A.*Eu*.86, 581, ἐπίστῃ Thgn.1085, *PCair.Zen*. 41.19 (iii B.C.), Ion. ἐπίστεαι (ἐξ-) Hdt.7.135; imper. ἐπίστασο ib. 29, 209, A.*Pr*.840, 967, *PCair.Zen*.57.4 (iii B.C.), etc., but ἐπίσταο v.l. in Hdt.7.209, contr. ἐπίστω S.*OT*658, etc.; subj. Ion. ἐπιστέωμαι

Hdt.3.134, Att. ἐπίστωμαι Pl.*Euthd.*296a: impf. ἠπιστάμην A.*Pr.*267, etc.; without augm. ἐπίστατο Il.5.60: Hdt. has ἐπ- 5.42 (v.l. ἠπ-), ἠπ- 3.139; Ion. 3 pl. ἠπιστέατο or ἐπιστέατο 8.132: fut. ἐπιστήσομαι Il.21.320, etc.: aor. 1 ἠπιστήθην Hdt.3.15, Pl.*Lg.*687a. I. *know* how to do, *be able* to do, *capable* of doing, c. inf., οὐδέ οἱ ὀστέ' ἐπιστήσονται Ἀχαιοὶ ἀλλέξαι Il.21.320, cf. Od.13.207, Sapph.70, etc.: Hom. has it both of intellectual power, ὅς τις ἐπίσταιτο ᾗσι φρεσὶν ἄρτια βάζειν Il.14.92; ἐπισταμέναι σάφα θυμῷ Od.4.730; and of artistic skill, ὃς χερσὶν ἐπίστατο δαίδαλα πάντα τεύχειν Il.5.60: freq. in Trag. and Att., οὔπω σωφρονεῖν ἐπίστασαι A.*Pr.*982, cf. 1032, S.*OT* 589; πένεσθαι δ' οὐκ ἐ. δόμος A.*Ag.*962; ἐ... θεοὺς σέβειν E.*Hipp.*996, cf. *Alc.*566; κιθαρίζειν οὐκ ἐ. Ar.*V.*989, cf. Pl.*Smp.*223d, *R.*420e, al.: without inf., σῷζ' ὅπως ἐπίστασαι as best you *can*, A.*Pr.*376, cf. *Eu.* 581. 2. *to be assured, feel sure* that.., τοῦτον ἐπίστανται πλεῖστα εἰδέναι Heraclit.57, cf. Hdt.3.134,139, 6.139, al.: folld. by ὡς, Id. 1.122. II. c. acc., *understand* a matter, *know, be versed in* or *acquainted with*, πολλὰ δ' ἐπίστατο ἔργα Il.23.705, cf. Od.2.117; Μουσέων δῶρον Archil.1; τὴν τέχνην Hdt.3.130; τὸ μέλλον A.*Pers.* 373; ἐμπειρίᾳ ἐ. τὴν ναυτικήν Th.4.10; τὰς φύσεις ὑμῶν Id.7.14; πάσας τὰς δημιουργίας Pl.*R.*598c; ἔγωγε γράμματ' οὐδ' ἐ. Cratin.122; τὸ μὴ ἐ. γράμματα illiteracy, *PRyl.*73.19 (i B.C.), etc.; ἐ. ἱερατικὰ καὶ Αἰγύπτια γράμματα *PTeb.*291.41 (ii A.D.); ἐ. μύθους τοὺς Αἰσώπου *know* them *by heart*, Pl.*Phd.*61b, cf. *Grg.*484b: also with an Adv., Συριστὶ ἐ. *know* Syrian, X.*Cyr.*7.5.31; with acc. and inf. conjoined, A.*Eu.*276; with inf. to expl. the acc., ἔργον δὲ μοῦνον ἐσθίειν ἐ. Semon.7.24, cf. Archil.65. 2. after Hom., *know* as a fact, *know for certain*, ἐπισταμένοισι εὖ οὐκ ἂν τις λέγοι Hdt.7.8.α', etc.; used convertibly with εἰδέναι, Pl.*Tht.*163b, Arist.*APr.*66^b31, *Ph.*184^a10; even χάριν ἐ., = χάριν εἰδέναι, Jul.*Or.*8.246c (but sts. εἰδέναι is general, ἐπίστασθαι being confined to *scientific knowledge* (ἐπιστήμη), διὰ τὸ εἰδέναι τὸ ἐπίστασθαι ἐδίωκον Arist.*Metaph.*982^b21): freq. strengthd., εὖ ἐ. Hdt. l. c.; σαφῶς ἐ. A.*Pr.*840, etc.: most freq. c. acc., τὰ διαφέροντα ἐ. And.4.19, etc.; also ἐ. περί τινος Hdt.2.3, Th.6.60; περὶ θεῶν E.*Fr.*795.4: folld. by a dependent clause, τί σφιν χρήσηται ἐ. Thgn. 772; ἐ. ὅτι.., or ἐ. τοῦτο, ὅτι.., Hdt.1.3,156, etc.; ὡς.. A.*Pers.*599; τοῦτ' ἐπίστασ', ὡς S.*Aj.*1370; ἐ. αὐτὸν οἷς ψωμίζεται Ar.*Eq.*715, etc. 3. rarely, *know* a person, Ἀρίγνωτον γὰρ οὐδεὶς ὅστις οὐκ ἐ. Ar.*Eq.*1278, cf. Muson.*Fr.*3 p.12 H., Luc.*Asin.*1; τὸν Ἰησοῦν γινώσκω καὶ τὸν Παῦλον ἐ. *Act.Ap.*19.15; but ὁ παῖς τοὺς τεκόντας οὐκ ἐ. *does* not *know who* they *are*, E.*Ion* 51. III. c. part., in Prose and Trag., *know that* one is, has, etc., εὖ ἐ. αὐτὸς σχήσων Hdt.5.42; ἐσθλὸς ὢν ἐπίστασο S.*Aj.*1399, cf. Th.2.44; also ὡς ὧδ' ἐχόντων τῶνδ' ἐ. σε χρή S.*Aj.*281; ὡς φανέν γε τοὔπος ὧδ' ἐ. Id.*OT*848: c. dupl. acc., ἑαυτοὺς Φαυστύλου ἠπιστάμεθα παῖδας (sc. ὄντας) Plu.*Rom.*7: c. acc. et inf., S.*Ant.*1092, Lys.*Fr.*53.1. IV. pres. part. ἐπιστάμενος, η, ον, freq. as Adj., *knowing, understanding, skilful*, ἀνδρὸς ἐ. Od.14.359; χαλεπὸν ἐ. περ ἐόντι Il.19.80; καὶ μάλ' ἐ. Od.13.313; even of a dancer's feet, θρέξασκον ἐπισταμένοισι πόδεσσι Il.18.599: also c. gen., φόρμιγγος ἐ. καὶ ἀοιδῆς *skilled, versed in* them, Od.21.406: and c. dat., ἄκοντι Il.15.282: hence, 2. Adv. ἐπισταμένως *skilfully, expertly*, 7.317, Hes.*Th.*87, etc.; εὖ καὶ ἐ. Il.10.265, Od.20.161, Hes.*Op.*107; ἐ. πίνειν Thgn.212; also in Prose, X.*Cyr.*1.1.3, A.D.*Adv.*146.7, Vett. Val.298.2: c. inf., *with knowledge* how to.., Epicur.*Nat.*14.4. (Since ἐφίστημι τὸν νοῦν is used in the sense of ἐπίσταμαι, *attend, observe*, it is prob. that ἐπίσταμαι is merely an old med. form of ἐφίστημι, cf. Arist. *Ph.*247^b11 τῷ γὰρ ἠρεμῆσαι καὶ στῆναι τὴν διάνοιαν ἐπίστασθαι.. λέγομεν, and v. ἐπίστασις II. 2.)

ἐπίσταξις, εως, ἡ, f.l. for στάξις in Hp.*Prorrh.*1.148.

ἐπιστᾰσία, Ion. -ίη, ἡ, = ἐπίστᾰσις II. 2, *attention, care*, ἐ. ποιεῖσθαί τινος Ph.1.192, cf. Phld.*Rh.*2.149 S. (prob.); ἐ. ἔχειν deserve *attention*, Ath.2.66b. 2. *recognition*, ἐς ἐ. τῆς νούσου ἀφικνεόμενοι Aret. *SD*1.6. II. *authority, dominion*, πρὸς τὴν ἐ. αὐτῶν *dominion over* them, Str.8.5.5; τὰς πόλεις ἠλευθέρου τῆς τῶν Καρχηδονίων ἐ. D.S. 20.32: abs., Plu.*Luc.*2, *Nic.*28; ἀρχικὴ ἐ. *Stoic.*3.158, cf. 2.339 (pl.).

ἐπιστᾰσιάζω, *to be at variance further*, S.E.*M.*11.37.

ἐπιστᾰσίδια, τά, title of work by Archimedes, Tz.*H.*12.974 (cod. Par. in *Rh.Mus.*4(1836).18).

ἐπιστάσιον [ᾰ], τό, *office of* ἐπιστάτης, *IG*2².1635.71, 1651.10, 1672.74.

ἐπιστάσιος [ᾰ] Ζεύς, = Lat. *Jupiter Stator*, Plu.*Rom.*18. (From ἐφίστημι, *he that makes to stand firm.*)

ἐπίστᾰσις, εως, ἡ, (ἐφίστημι) *stopping, stoppage*, [τῆς κοιλίης], οὔρου, Hp.*Coac.*480, *Prorrh.*1.110; ἐ. αἵματος *sluggishness* of the flow of blood, Id.*Insomn.*93, cf. Arist.*GA*718^a21; of the growth of trees, Thphr.*CP*2.9.1; πρὸς ἐπίστασιν τῶν ἄλλων as a *deterrent* to others, *PAmh.*2.134.9 (ii A.D.). 2. *violence, vehemence*, ἐπαινεῖ τὴν Ζήνωνος πραγματείαν μετὰ δή τινος λαμπρᾶς ἐ. Procl. *in Prm.*p.604 S. II. (ἐφίσταμαι) *stopping, halt*, τοῦ στρατεύματος X.*An.*2.4.26, cf. Plb.8. 28.13; φροντίδων ἐπιστάσεις *haltings* of thought, *anxious* thoughts, S.*Ant.*225; ἐπιστάσεις καὶ διατριβαί Plu.2.48b (following quot. of S.*Ant.*232); opp. κίνησις, Arist.*de An.*407^a33, cf. *LI*969^b3. b. ἐπίστασιν ἔχει, πῶς.. there is a *difficulty*, as to how.., Id.*Metaph.* 1089^b25. 2. *stopping* to examine a thing, *observation, attention*, τοῦτ' ἄξιον ἐπιστάσεως, εἰ.. Id.*Ph.*196^a36; μετὰ ἐ. Plb.2.2.2; μετὰ πολλῆς ἐ. καὶ φιλοτιμίας D.S.29.32; ἄξιος ἐπιστάσεως Plb.11.2.4, Phld. *Rh.*1.31 S.; ἄγειν τινὰ εἰς ἐ. Plb.9.22.7; ἐξ ἐ. ῥητέον *carefully*, Id.3. 58.3; ἐπίστασίν τινων λαμβάνειν Aristeas 256; medical *treatment, care*, πρὸς φλεγμονήν Sor.1.76: generally, *care, attention*, Phld.*Lib.* p.5 O., *Mus.*p.84 K. 3. = ἐπιστασία II, D.S.14.82, Ph.1.143 codd.; κατὰ τὴν ἐ. during his *term as* ἐπιστάτης, *SIG*10 (Samos, vi B.C.); ἐ. ἔργων *superintendence* of works, X.*Mem.*1.5.2; ἡ ἐ. μοι ἡ καθ' ἡμέραν 2*Ep.Cor.*11.28; *oversight* of students, D.H.*Comp.*1. 4. *beginning*, ἐ. ποιεῖσθαι ἀπό.. Plb.1.12.6; ἡ ἐ. τῆς ἱστορίας *introduction*, Id.2.71.7; ἀρχὴ καὶ ἐ. τῆς κατασκευῆς *method of setting about* construction, Ph.*Bel.*50.35. 5. *scum* on urine, Hp.*Aph.*7.35. 6. *position* in rear, τὴν ἐ. ἐπ' ἀλλήλοις ἔχειν one behind the other, of ships, Plb.1.26.12. 7. = μέρος τι τῆς νεώς, Hsch.; cf. ἐπιστατήρ. III. *onset*, Lxx 2*Ma.*6.3; ὄχλου *Act.Ap.*24.12 (nisi leg. ἐπισύστασις). IV. ἐν ἐπιστάσει καὶ ἐν ἀπολογισμῷ, perh. of land *of which the rent has been raised*, *PTeb.*61(*a*).163 (ii B.C.), al. V. Cypr. ἐπίσταις, = ἐπιστασία II, *Inscr.Cypr.*144 H.

ἐπιστᾰτ-εία, ἡ, (ἐπιστατεύω) *authority, rule*, Iamb.*VP*30.174, Porph.*VP*9, *PFay.*104.25 (iii A.D.). II. *office of* ἐπιστάτης, *Klio* 12. 365 (Alexandria, ii B.C.). III. *watchfulness*, Diog.Oen.65. **-έον**, *one must consider*, τί.. A.D.*Synt.*18.22; τῷ "ἐρίπω" ῥήματι, εἰ... ib.280.16; πρὸς ἕκαστον τῶν λεχθέντων Plot.6.6.12. **-εύω**, = sq., Eus.Mynd.41 codd. Stob., *BMus.Inscr.*1100 (Italy), *CIG*5142 (Cyrene). **-έω**, pf. ἐπεστάτηκα *Michel* 164.10 (Delos):—*to be* ἐπιστάτης, *to be set over*, ποιμνίοις S.*OT*1028, E.*Fr.*188.4; ἡ ψυχὴ ἐ. τῷ σώματι Pl.*Grg.*465d; ἐπιστήμη ἐ. τῇ πράξει Id.*R.*443e; τῷ τοῦ νομοθέτου ἔργῳ Id.*Cra.*390c, cf. 405d (but τέχνῃ according to art, Id.*Plt.* 293b): abs., Durrbach *Choix d'inscrr. de Délos* 159, *PCair.Zen.*34.7; εἰ μὴ ἐπιστατοῖ τὸ τάττον Plot.4.4.16. 2. c. gen., *to be in charge of, have the care of*, τοῦ ἔργου Hdt.7.22; ἔργων X.*Mem.*2.8.3; ζῴων Id. *Cyr.*1.1.2; τοῦ εἶναι οἵους δεῖ ib.8.1.16; τῆς παιδείας Pl.*R.*600d; οὐκ ὀρθῶς ἂν ἔχοι τὸν χείρω τῶν βελτιόνων ἐπιστατεῖν Id.*Prt.*338b; ὅλων τῶν πραγμάτων Isoc.4.104; τῶν λαῶν σκληρῶς ἐ. Mnaseas 32; ἐ. νοσεόντων Hp.*Praec.*6. 3. *stand by, aid*, οὐ ψεῦδις μάρτυς ἔργμασιν ἐ. Pi.*N.*7.49; Παιὼν τῷδ' ἐπεστάτει λόγῳ A.*Ag.*1248. 4. rarely c. acc., *attend, follow*, τίς γάρ με μόχθος οὐκ ἐπεστάτει; S.*Fr.*150. 5. *stand in the rear rank*, Ascl.*Tact.*10.15. 6. *notice, observe*, Sch.Pi. *O.*3.81. II. at Athens and elsewhere, *to be* ἐπιστάτης or *president* (in the βουλή and ἐκκλησία), freq. at the head of decrees, ἔδοξεν τῷ δήμῳ·.. Νικιάδης ἐπεστάτει Th.4.118, cf. Ar.*Th.*374, Lex ap.And.1. 96, *IG*1².10, al., Arist.*Ath.*44.3; in other cities, *SIG*279.1 (Zelea, iv B.C.), *OGI*219.1 (Ilium, iii B.C.), etc.; προέδρων *Inscr.Magn.*2, al.: generally, *preside over*, δικαστηρίων *OGI*556.13 (Tlos). 2. *exercise the office of* ἐπιστάτης III. 2, τοῦ Καίσαρος ναοῦ ib.555.2 (Oenoanda): abs., *SIG*707.21 (Olbia, ii B.C.). **-η**, ἡ, = ἐπιστάτης IV, Sch.Ar. *Av.*437. **-ήρ**, ῆρος, ὁ, = τὸ στόμα τῆς νεώς, Hsch.: and in pl., = οἱ τῶν πλοίων νομεῖς, Id. II. pl., = ἀγορανόμοι, Id. **-ήριος**, ὁ, title of Zeus in Crete, Id. **-ης**, ου, ὁ, (ἐφίσταμαι) *one who stands near* or *by*: hence, like ἱκέτης, *suppliant*, οὐ σύ γ' ἄν.. σῷ ἐπιστάτῃ οὐδ' ἅλα δοίης Od.17.455. 2. in battle-order, *one's rear-rank man*, X.*Cyr.* 3.3.59, 8.1.10, al. b. also, *even numbers* in a λόχος, Ascl.*Tact.*2.3, Arr.*Tact.*6.6. II. *one who stands* or *is mounted upon*, ἁρμάτων ἐ., of a charioteer, S.*El.*702, E.*Ph.*1147; ἐλεφάντων ἐ., of the driver, Plb.1.40.11. 2. *one who is set over, chief, commander*, A.*Th.*816 (815); ὅπλων Id.*Pers.*379; ποιμνίων ἐ. S.*Aj.*27; ἐρετμῶν ἐ. E.*Hel.* 1267; θύματος ἐ. Id.*Hec.*223; but ταύρων πυρπνόων ζεύγλῃσι *mastering* them with.., Id.*Med.*478; ἐνόπτρων καὶ μύρων, of the Trojans, Id.*Or.*1112; ἐ. Κολωνοῦ, of a tutelary god, S.*OC*889; [καιρὸς] ἀνδράσιν μέγιστος ἔργου παντὸς ἔστ' ἐ. Id.*El.*76; also in Prose, ἐ. γενέσθαι τῶν λόγων ἴσους καὶ κοινούς *judges*, And.4.7; ποίας ἐργασίας ἐ.; Answ. ἐ. τοῦ ποιῆσαι δεινὸν λέγειν (where it = ἐπιστήμων) Pl.*Prt.*312d; πραγμάτων Isoc.4.121; ἐπιστάται ἄθλων *stewards* of games, Pl.*Lg.*949a, cf. X.*Lac.*8.4; of a pilot, Id.*Oec.*21.3; *supervisor* of training, Pl. *R.*412a, X.*Mem.*3.5.18 (pl.); ἐ. τῶν παίδων *IG*12(1).43 (Rhodes); τῶν ἐφήβων *Inscr.Prien.*112.73 (i B.C.): voc. ἐπιστάτα, = *Rabbi*, *Ev. Luc.*5.5, al. III. *president* of a board or assembly: at Athens, ἐ. τῶν πρυτάνεων *chairman* of βουλή and ἐκκλησία in cent. v, Arist. *Ath.*44.1, later, *keeper* of Treasury or Archives, *IG*3.841, etc.; ἐ. τῶν προέδρων *chairman* of βουλή and ἐκκλησία from cent. iv, Aeschin. 3.39, D.22.9, etc.; ἐ. ὁ ἐκ τῶν προέδρων *IG*2².204.31 (iv B.C.); in other Greek states, ib.12(1).731 (Rhodes), 12(7).515.116,125 (Amorgos), etc.; ἐ. τῶν νομοθετῶν ib.2².222; τῶν δικα[στῶν] *LW*1539 (Erythrae). 2. *overseer, superintendent*, in charge of any public building or works, τοῦ νεὼ τοῦ ἐν πόλει, i.e. of the temple of Athena Polias, *IG*1².372; ἱεροῦ *UPZ*42.22 (ii B.C.); ἐ. τῶν ἔργων *clerk* of the works, D.18.114, Lxx *Ex.*1.11 (pl.); τῶν δημοσίων ἔργων Aeschin.3. 14; τοῦ ναυτικοῦ ib.222; τῆς Ἀκαδημείας Hyp.*Dem.Fr.*7; τοῦ Μουσείου *OGI*104.4 (ii B.C.); τῶν κοπρώνων D.25.49. 3. *governor, administrator*, τῆς πόλεως *OGI*254.3 (Babylon, ii B.C.), cf. *IG*12(3). 320.7 (Thera, iii B.C.), *OGI*479.7 (Dorylaeum, ii A.D.); κώμης local *magistrate*, *Arch.Pap.*4.38. 4. = προστάτης, Lat. *patronus*, *IG*14. 1317. IV. in Ar.*Av.*437, = χυτρόπους, Ar.Byz.ap.Eust.1827.45; other explanations, ibid., cf. Sch.Ar. l. c.: τοὐπιστάτου is fr. ἐπίστατος, = πυρίστατος, Anon.ap.Eust.1827.56: dub. sens. in *BpW*1892.514; cf. ἐπίστατον. **-ητέον**, *one must oversee, superintend*, c. dat., Pl.*R.* 377b, 401b: c. gen., X.*Oec.*7.35. **-ικός**, ή, όν, *of* or *for government*: ἡ -κή (sc. ἐπιστήμη) Pl.*Plt.*292b, 308e; δυνάμεις ἐ. τῆς φύσεως Iamb. *Myst.*2.1. 2. *concerning an* ἐπιστάτης, γραφή Arist.*Ath.*59.2. b. -κόν, τό, *tax levied for the support of an* ἐ., *BGU*337.2 (iii A.D.); ἐ. ἱερέων *PFay.*42(*a*) ii 8 (ii A.D.). 3. *careful, attentive*, Syrian. *in Metaph.*13.6. Adv. -κῶς ib.6.6, S.E.*M.*7.182. 4. ἐ. πρός τι *giving an impulse* towards, Phld.*Mus.*p.84 K. 5. *scientific*, κατάλημμα D.L.7.45. II. *steady, calm*, Aët.6.8. Adv. -κῶς, gloss on ἐπισταδόν, Sch.A.R.2.84. **-ις**, ιδος, ἡ, fem. of ἐπιστάτης, οὐ γὰρ μουσικὴ τούτων ἐ. Aristid.Quint.2.6, cf. Corn.*ND*20, Sch.Ar.*Th.* 380. -ον, τό, *support, stand, SIG*2 *B*4 (Sigeum, vi B.C.), Ar.*Av.* 437, *IG*11(2).161 *C*94 (Delos, iii B.C.), *PGrenf.*1.14.6 (ii B.C.), Hsch. s.v. λάανα; cf. ἐπιστάτης IV. II. ἐπιστᾰτός, v. ἐπιστητός.

ἐπιστᾰχύω, (στάχυς) *shoot* or *sprout* forth, prop. of corn: metaph. of the beard, A.R.1.972.

ἐπιστέαται, Ion. for ἐπίστανται.

ἐπιστεγ-άζω, *roof over*, οἴκημα δοκοῖς Ctes.*Fr.*20. -η, ἡ, *roof-timber*, Ath.Mech.13.6. -νόω, *close up, block*, τρύπημα Hero*Spir.* 2.37. -ωσις, εως, ἡ, *roofing over*, *POxy.*1450.8 (iii A.D.).

ἐπιστείβω, *tread upon, stand upon*, τόπον S.*OC*56, cf. Nic.*Th.*32, 570; γαῖαν Rhian.1.11; αἰγιαλόνδε Orph.*A.*1120; ἐ. ἔργον *set about*, ib.943.

ἐπιστείριον· τὸ τῆς νηός, Suid.

ἐπιστείχω, *approach*, νᾶσον Pi.*I.*6(5).21; ἀήματα.. ἐ. χθόνα A.*Eu.* 906: abs., τὴν ἐπιστείχουσαν ἡμέραν E.*Fr.*816.7.

ἐπιστέλλω, *send to*, γράψας ἐς βυβλίον τάδε ἐπέστειλε ἐς Σάμον Hdt. 3.40; τοῖσι Ἕλλησι Id.7.239; ἠδίω.. ἂν εἶχον ὑμῖν.. ἐπιστέλλειν Th. 7.14; ἐ. ἐπιστολάς τινι D.4.37, cf. Pl.*Ep.*363b; *send a message*, τάδε E.*IT*770; esp. by letter, *write word*, τοιαῦτα Lys.20.27; περί τινος ὡς ἀδικοῦντος Th.8.38; ἐ. ὅτι.. ib.50,99; τὰ ἐπισταλέντα ἐκ τῆς Σάμου the *news received* from Samos, ib.50; τὰ ὑπό τινος ἐπεσταλμένα Plu.*Art.*21. 2. *enjoin, command*, τισί τι Th.5.37; τὸν ἄγγελον ἐπιστείλας ταῦτα ἔπεμψε X.*Cyr.*2.4.32; τινὶ περί τινος ib.4.5.34: c. inf., ἐ. τινὶ ἀπίστασθαι Hdt.6.3; τινὶ ἐκμαθεῖν E.*Ph.*863; ὁ Κῦρος αὐτῷ ἐπέστελλε πρὸς Πέρσας λέγειν X.*Cyr.*4.5.26; also ἐ. τινὰ ποιεῖν τι S.*OT*106, X.*Cyr.*5.5.1: without any case, *give orders* to do, A. *Eu.*205, Th.8.72, etc.; *give orders in writing*, Thphr.*Char.*24.13:— Pass., ἔφη οὐδέν οἱ ἐπεστάλθαι ἄλλο ἢ ἀπαλλάσσεσθαι he *had received orders* to.., Hdt.4.131; καί μοι ἐκ βασιλέος ὧδε ἐπέσταλται Id.6.97; αἷς ἐπέσταλται τέλος to whom the office *has been committed*, A.*Ag.* 908, cf. *Eu.*743; τἀπεσταλμένα Id.*Ch.*779; κατὰ τὰ ἐ. ὑπὸ Δημοσθένους Th.4.8; ἀξιῶ ἐπισταλῆναί τισι c. inf., *PRyl.*121.13 (ii A.D.): with personal construction, ταῦτα ἐπεσταλμένοι *having received* these *instructions*, Th.5.37: in later writers, usu. of *orders given in writing*, *Act.Ap.*15.20, 21.25, *SIG*837.14 (ii A.D.), etc.; of *orders* for payment, *POxy.*1304 (ii A.D.), etc.

ἐπιστεν-αγμός, ὁ, *groaning*, Gloss. -άζω, *groan over*, τινί A. *Pers.*727 (troch.), Plu.*Brut.*51, etc.: abs., E.*IT*283. -ακτος, ον, *uttered in lament over*, Sch.E.*Ph.*1301. -ᾰχίζω, = ἐπιστένω, Hes. *Th.*843 (v.l. -στοναχ-), Nonn.*D.*8.204. -άχω [ᾰ], = ἐπιστένω, τινί A.*Ag.*790 (anap.): aor., ἐπεστενάχησε θανόντι *IPE*2.171 (Panticapaeum): abs., S.*OT*185 (lyr.):—Med., ἐπεστενάχοντο δ' ἑταῖροι Il.4. 154, cf. 19.301 (tm.).

ἐπίστενος, ον, *contracted*, Arist.*HA*514^{b}23 (Comp.).

ἐπιστένω, *groan* or *sigh at* or *in answer*, ἐπὶ δ' ἔστενε δῆμος Il.24. 776; ἐπέστενε δ' οὐρανὸς εὐρύς Hes.*Th.*679; *lament over*, τέκνοις E. *Med.*929, cf. Plu.*Caes.*21, etc. 2. c. acc., *lament*, S.*Tr.*947 (lyr.).

ἐπιστέρησις, εως, ἡ, *secondary negation* (cancelling a first), *EM* 97.11, *Et.Gud.*51.57.

ἐπιστεφᾰν-όω, *deck with a crown*, βωμόν Pi.*O.*9.112; μνάματα *Schwyzer*491 (Thespiae); τινά *IG*3.713.7, Ph.2.6. -ωμα, *corollarium*, Gloss.

ἐπιστεφ-ής, ές, Hom. only in phrase κρητῆρας ἐπιστεφέας οἴνοιο bowls *full of* wine, Il.8.232, Od.2.431; ἐγκέρασον Χαρίτων κρατῆρ' ἐ. *Lyr.Alex.Adesp.*19. II. *garlanded*, Εὐμενίδες ναρκίσσου -στεφέες πλοκαμῖδας Euph.94; ὕλης ἀγρίης ἐ., either *full of* jungle or *crowned with*.., Archil.21.2. -ω, in Hom. always in Med., κρητῆρας ἐπεστέψαντο ποτοῖο *filled* them with wine, Il.1.470, Od.1.148, etc. (variously expld., cf. Ath.1.13d, 15.674e, and ἐκστέφω I). II. *to be full of* or *covered with*, τράπεσδαι μακωνίδων ἄρτων ἐπιστέφοισαι Alcm.74 B. III. χοὰς ἐ. τινί *pour* libations *as an honour to* the dead, S. *El.*441. IV. Med., *wreathe*, ἄνθεϊ χαίτην Nonn.*D.*47.11:—also in Act., *crown, surround*, κύμασι Παταλήνην ib.27.158.

ἐπιστέωνται, ἐπίστῃ, v. ἐπίσταμαι.

ἐπιστηθίδιος, ον, *on the breast*, τιτθοί *EM*760.48.

ἐπιστηλόομαι, *to be set up as a column upon*, θινὸς -ωμένον ἄχθος *AP*7.503 (Leon.).

ἐπίστημα, Dor. -ᾱμα, ατος, τό, (ἐφίστημι) *anything set up*, e.g. *monument over* a grave, Pl.*Lg.*958e, Is.*Fr.*159, *IG*12(3).87 (Nisyrus, iii B.C.), D.H.2.67; *ornament on* the prow of ships, D.S.13.3 (nisi leg. ἐπισήμασι).

ἐπιστήμη, ἡ, (ἐπίσταμαι) *acquaintance with* a matter, *understanding, skill*, as in archery, S.*Ph.*1057; in war, Th.1.121, 6.72, 7.62; ἐ. πρὸς τὸν πόλεμον Lys.33.7 (fort. leg. περί); περὶ τὰ μαθήματα Pl. *Phlb.*55d; τοῦ νεῖν Id.*Grg.*511c; ἐπιστήμῃ *skilfully*, οἱ μὴ ἐ. τοὺς ἐπαίνους ποιούμενοι Plot.5.5.13. 2. *professional skill*: hence, *profession*, οἱ τὴν ἰατρικὴν ἐ. μεταχειριζόμενοι *PFay.*106.22 (ii A.D.); ζωγράφος τὴν ἐ. painter *by profession*, *POxy.*896.5 (iv A.D.). II. generally, *knowledge*, ἐπιστήμη σύ μου προὔχοις ἂν S.*OT*1115; πάντ' ἐπιστήμης πλέως full *of knowledge* in all things, Id.*Ant.*721, cf. *Tr.* 338; ἐκ τῆς ἐ. E.*Fr.*522.3; ἐ. δοξαστική, opp. ἀλήθεια, Pl.*Sph.*233c: pl., *kinds of knowledge*, μυρίαι ἀνδρῶν ἐπιστᾶμαι πέλονται B.9.38, cf. Pl.*Smp.*208a. 2. *scientific knowledge, science*, opp. δόξα, Pl.*R.*477b sq., Hp.*Lex*4, Pl.*Plt.*301b, Arist.*APo.*88^{b}30, *EN*1139^{b}18: coupled with ἐμπειρία and τέχνη, Pl.*R.*422c, cf. *Ion* 536c, Arist.*Metaph.*981^{a} 2: pl., *the sciences*, freq. in Pl.(*R.*522c, al.), etc.

ἐπιστημον-ίζω, *make wise*, Al.*Is.*52.13 (Pass.). -ικός, ή, όν, *capable of knowledge*, τὸ ἐ. τῆς ψυχῆς Arist.*de An.*431^{b}27; opp. βουλευτικός, Id.*MM*1196^{b}17, cf. *EN*1139^{a}12; θεὸς.. πάντων -ώτατον Id. *Fr.*10 (= S.E.*M.*9.21): Comp. -ώτερος Arist.*Top.*141^{b}16, Ph.*Fr.*70 H. II. *of* or *for science, scientific*, ἀρχαί Arist.*Top.*100^{b}19; ὁ ὁρισμὸς -κός (v.l. -κόν) Id.*Metaph.*1039^{b}32; ἀποδείξεις Id.*APo.*75^{a}30; συλλογισμός ib.71^{b}18; αἴσθησις Phld.*Mus.*p.11 K.; λόγοι Gal.*UP*12. 6; ἐπίγνωσις *Theol.Ar.*17; οὐκ ἦν εὔλογον οὐδ' ἐ. ib.58: Sup. -ώτατον, ἔργον [ὁ κόσμος] Ph.2.217. Adv. -κῶς Arist.*Top.*114^{b}10, Ph.2.417.

ἐπίστημ-ος, ον, = ἐπιστήμων, *knowing*, c. gen. rei, Hp.*Epid.*6.8.10. Adv. -μως *skilfully*, *IGRom.*3.208 (Ancyra). -οσύνη, ἡ, *skill*, περὶ ἐ., title of work by Xenocr. (D.L.4.13). -όω, *make wise*, Aq.*Ps.* 2.10 (Pass.), al. II. *make scientific*, Eustr. *in EN*1.5. -ων, ον, gen. ονος, (ἐπίσταμαι) *knowing, wise, prudent*, ἐ. βουλῇ τε νόῳ τε Od. 16.374; ἄρχοντες X.*Oec.*21.5; ἐπιστήμων γὰρ εἶ, = ἐπίστασαι γάρ, E. *Supp.*843. 2. *acquainted with* a thing, *skilled* or *versed in*, c. gen., κακῶν S.*Fr.*589; τῆς θαλάσσης, τοῦ ναυτικοῦ, Th.1.142, 8.45; τῆς τέχνης Pl.*Grg.*448b; τῶν τόπων *POxy.*1469.12 (iii A.D.); also περί τινος or τι, Pl.*R.*599b, *Sis.*389e: with neut. Adj., τὰ προσήκοντα ἐπιστήμων X.*Cyr.*3.3.9, cf. *Oec.*2.16 (Sup.). 3. c. inf., *knowing how*, λέγειν τε καὶ σιγᾶν Pl.*Phdr.*276a, cf. X.*Oec.*19.16: Comp. -ονέστερος Pl.*Chrm.*174a. Adv. Comp. -ονέστερον X.*Oec.*3.14: Sup. -ονέστατα Pl.*R.*534d. II. *possessed of perfect knowledge*, Id.*Plt.*301b, etc.; opp. δοξαστής, τινός Id.*Tht.*208e; in Arist., *scientifically versed in* a thing, *APo.*74^{b}28, *Cat.*11^{a}33. Adv. -ονως, ἔχειν πρός τι Pl.*Sph.*233c: λέγειν *with science, with art*, Id.*Tht.*207b; εἰπεῖν use *technical* or *scientific* terminology, Aristid.*Or.*26(14).97.

ἐπιστηρ-ιγμα, ατος, τό, *support*, Lxx *2Ki.*22.19. -ίζω, *cause to rest on*, ἐπιστηριῶ ἐπὶ σὲ τοὺς ὀφθαλμούς μου ib.*Ps.*31(32).8; *make to lean on*, τί τινι Opp.*C.*4.256; *set over*, Δεῖμον κεραυνῷ Nonn.*D.*2. 417; *confirm*, τινά *Act.Ap.*15.32:—Pass., *to be supported*, ἐν τῷ ὕδατι Arist.*Pr.*933^{a}10; τινί Luc.*Ind.*6; ἐπιστηριχθήσομαι and ἐπεστηρίχθη ἐπὶ [τοὺς κίονας], Lxx *Jd.*16.26, 29, cf. Aq.*Ex.*17.12.

ἐπιστής, ῆτος, perh. *prop*, *Inscr.Délos* 340.11 (ii B.C.). (Gender undetermined.)

ἐπιστητ-έον, *one must know*, Sch.D.T.p.316 H., *An.Ox.*3.207. -ός, ή, όν, (ἐπίσταμαι) *that can be scientifically known, matter of science*, Pl.*Tht.*201d, etc.; τὸ ἐ. Arist.*EN*1139^{b}23, al.: Dor. ἐπιστᾱτός Ps.-Archyt.ap.Iamb.*Comm.Math.*8.

ἐπιστιγμή, ἡ, *point* or *dot upon* a thing, Aen.Tact.31.2.

ἐπιστίζω, *mark with spots on the surface, speckle*, Nic.*Th.*332; νῶτον ἱμάσθλῃ Nonn.*D.*37.410 (s.v.l.):—Pass., *to be spotted* or *speckled*, Thphr.*HP*3.7.5; τῷ νώτῳ οἱ σημεῖα ἐπέστικται Ael.*NA*11. 24; *to be marked with a dot*, ὁ ἐπεστιγμένος Aen.Tact.31.29.—In Moer. and Hsch., ἐπιστίζω, -στιγμα, are for ἐπι-σίζω, -σιγμα.

ἐπιστίλβω, *glisten on the surface*, Plu.*Lys.*28, Luc.*Am.*26; ἐπὶ παντὶ τῷ νοητῷ ἐ. Plot.6.7.36.

ἐπίστιον, τό, *slip* or *shed* for a ship, νῆες.. εἰρύαται· πᾶσιν γὰρ ἐπίστιόν ἐστιν ἑκάστῳ Od.6.265. (Expld. by Aristarch.(ap.Sch.*Il.*2.125 ἐπ' ἱστιόν.. ὡσεὶ κατάλυμα παρὰ τῇ νηΐ) as Ion. for ἐφέστιον, cf. sq.; but elsewh. Hom. always uses the form ἐφέστιος; Sch. has ἐποίκιον, νεώριον.., παρὰ τὸ ἱστίον.)

ἐπίστιος, ον, Ion. for ἐφέστιος (q.v.). II. ἐπίστιος, ἡ, = ἀνίσωμα, πίνουσα τὴν ἐ. Anacr.90.4.

ἐπίστῐχος, ον, *in a row*, *EM*634.40, Sch.D *Il.*11.68, Sch.Opp.*H.* 1.625.

ἐπιστοβέω, *scoff at*, A.R.3.663, 4.1725.

ἐπιστοιβ-άζω, *pile up*, ξύλα ἐπὶ τὸ πῦρ Lxx *Le.*1.7, *Si.*8.3. -ασις, εως, ἡ, *piling up*, metaph., τῶν παρίσων Eust.774.5.

ἐπιστοιχειόω, *furnish the elements* of a compound, Maria ap.Zos. Alch.p.200 B.

ἐπιστολαγραφεῖον, v. ἐπιστολογραφεῖον.

ἐπιστολᾰγράφος [γρᾰ], ὁ, *royal secretary*, *BCH*32.431 (Delos, Ptolemaic period), Plb.30.25.16 cod., *OGI*259 (v. *BCH* l.c.); cf. ἐπιστολογράφος.

ἐπιστολάδην [ᾰ], Adv. *girt up*, of dress, like ἀνεσταλμένως, Hes. *Sc.*287.

ἐπιστολαφόρος, v. ἐπιστοληφόρος.

ἐπιστολ-εύς, έως, ὁ, (ἐπιστολή) *secretary*, τοῦ Αὐτοκράτορος *IG*14. 1085; also in Persia, Suid. s.v. ἐπιστέλλει. II. among the Spartans, *admiral second in command, vice-admiral*, X.*HG*2.1.7, 4.8.11, Plu.*Lys.*7; he carries dispatches, X.*HG*1.1.23. -ή, ἡ, (ἐπιστέλλω) *anything sent by a messenger, message, order, commission*, whether verbal or in writing, Hdt.4.10, Th.8.45, etc.; ἐξ ἐπιστολῆς by *command*, Hdt.6.50: used by Trag. always in pl., A.*Pr.*3, *Pers.*783, *Supp.*1012, S.*Aj.*781, *OC*1601, etc.; Πενθέως ἐπιστολαῖς *by his commands*, E.*Ba.*442; τέκνων ἐπιστολὰς ἔγραψεν *commands about* her children, Id.*Hipp.*858. 2. *letter*, ἐ. διαπέμπειν, ἀποδοῦναι, Th.1. 129, 7.10; λύειν Id.1.132; ἐ. ἔδωκεν ἀποδοῦναι Lys.20.27; πέμπειν τινί E.*IT*589 (pl.): in pl. of one letter, like γράμματα, Lat. *litterae*, Id.*IA*111, 314, Th.1.132, etc.; ὁ ἐπὶ τῶν ἐπιστολῶν.. τοῦ Ὄθωνος, Lat. *ab epistulis Othoni*, his *secretary*, Plu.*Oth.*9; νομογραφικὴ ἐ. *BGU*1135.7 (i B.C.). -ηφόρος, ὁ, *letter-carrier*, Zoroaster in *Cat. Cod.Astr.*2.193.38:—in form **ἐπιστολᾱφόρος**, *PRyl.*78.24 (ii A.D.), *PLond.ined.*2172 (ii/iii A.D.), *PPetersb.*1 (iii A.D.).

ἐπιστολιαφόρος, ὁ, *bearer of dispatches* (v. ἐπιστολεύς II), X.*HG*6. 2.25.

ἐπιστολίδιον, τό, = ἐπιστόλιον, *POxy.*1069.14 (iii A.D.), etc.

ἐπιστολ-ικός, ή, όν, *suited to a letter*, Arist.*Fr.*670; *in the style of letters*, λόγοι D.H.*Lys.*1.3; as book-title, Gal.8.150, D.L.10.25, prob. cj. in Sor.2.53; χαρακτήρ Demetr.*Eloc.*223, Ap.Ty.*Ep.*19. Adv. -κῶς

Demetr.*Eloc.*233. —**ῐμαῖος**, ον, *in* or *of letters*, συνουσίαι Philostr. *VA*4.46; ξυμβουλίαι ib.7.8; γράμματα Ph.2.533; δυνάμεις ἐ. forces *promised by letter* and decreed, but never sent, *paper*-armies, D.4.19.

ἐπιστόλιον, τό, Dim. of ἐπιστολή, Epicur.*Fr.*143, *UPZ*69.3,5 (ii B.C.), Plb.31.16.3, Plu.*Ages.*13, M.Ant.1.7, *POxy.*1481.3 (ii A.D.), etc.

ἐπιστολογρᾰφ-εῖον, τό, *registry*, prob. in *UPZ*14.133 (ii B.C.):—also in form **ἐπιστολαγραφεῖον** *PCornell*1.155 (-γράφιον ib. 150). —**ικός**, ή, όν, *used in writing letters*, Porph.*VP*12. —**ος**, ὁ, *letter-writer, secretary*, *OGI*139.14 (Ptol.), 194.24 (i B.C.), *PTeb.*112.87 (ii B.C.), *UPZ*108.34 (i B.C.), *PPar.*70; cf. ἐπιστολαγράφος.

ἐπιστομ-ᾰτίζω, = ἐπιστομίζω, Ph.1.85 codd. —**ία**, ἡ, read by Zenod. for ἐπεσβολία, Od.4.159. —**ίζω**, Att. fut. -ιῶ D.7.33: (στόμα):—*bridle, curb*, ἵππον cj. in Ph.1.85; [δελφῖνας] Philostr. *Im.*2.18: metaph., *curb, bridle*, τοὺς ἐχθρούς Ar.*Eq.*845, cf. D.7.33, Aeschin.2.110, *Ep.Tit.*1.11; τὴν Ἰουδαίων νεωτεροποιίαν J.*AJ*17.10.1; *silence* a speaker, Philostr.*VS*2.30, cf. Ph.2.191; οἷον ἐ. καὶ χαλινοῦντες τὸ φιλόφωνον Plu.2.967b:—Pass., ἐπεστομίσθη Pl.*Grg.*482e. II. of flute-players, ἐ. ἑαυτὸν φορβειᾷ καὶ αὐλοῖς *put on the mouthpiece* and flutes, Plu.2.713d; but ὁ αὐλὸς ἐ. Id.*Alc.*2: hence, *gag*, Luc.*Merc. Cond.*7. III. *throw on his face*, τινά Id.*Pr.Im.*10, *Cal.*12. —**ίς**, ίδος, ἡ, = φορβειά II, Hsch. s.v. ἐπίχαλκον. —**ισμα**, ατος, τό, metaph., *curb, restraint*, J.*AJ*19.3.3, 18.9.8. —**όω**, *stop up, close*, Hero *Spir.*1.19:—Pass., ib.33.

ἐπιστονᾰχ-έω, = ἐπιστένω, of the waves, Il.24.79. —**ίζω**, = foreg., Nonn.*D.*2.87; v.l. for -στεναχ-, Hes.*Th.*843.

ἐπιστορέννῡμι or (Hsch. s.v. ψιάθια) -**στόρνῡμι**: fut. -στρώσω: aor. 1 -εστόρεσα or -έστρωσα: aor. Med. -εστορέσαντο Nonn.*D.*24.334:—*strew* or *spread upon*, ἐστόρεσεν δ' ἐπὶ δέρμα *upon* the bed, Od.14.50; ἱμάτιον ἐπὶ τὸ ξύλον Hp.*Art.*75; a barbarous fut., ἐπιστρωννύσω τῇ γῇ νιφετόν, only in Ps.-Luc.*Philopatr.*24. 2. *saddle*, ἐπιστρῶσαι τὸν ὄνον J.*AJ*8.9.1; [ἡ κάμηλος] ἁλουργίδι ἐπέστρωτο Luc.*Prom.Es*4.

ἐπίστρατα· ἀποπίπτοντα τῶν πεμμάτων· καὶ ἕρματα, Hsch.

ἐπιστρᾰτ-άομαι, = ἐπιστρατεύω, Nonn.*D.*1.267, 48.32, in Ep. 3 pl. impf. ἐπεστρατόωντο. —**εία**, Ion. -ηΐη, ἡ, *march* or *expedition against*, Hdt.9.3; τῶν Πλαταιῶν *against* Plataea, Th.2.79; σὺν Κύρῳ X.*An.*2.4.1. —**ευσις**, εως, ἡ, = foreg., Hdt.3.4. —**εύω**, *march against, make war upon*, τινί E.*Ba.*784, Ar.*Av.*1522, Th.3.54, etc.; ἐπί τινα Arist.*Oec.*1351^{b}20; ἐπὶ τοὺς Ἕλληνας *IG*2^2.680.9; ἐπὶ τὴν Ἑλλάδα And.1.107, cf. Pl.*Mx.*239b; εἰς Θετταλίαν Aeschin.3.83: in Poets c. acc. loci, ἐ. πατρίδα τὴν ταύτης S.*Tr.*362; Εὐβοΐδα χώραν ib.75, cf. E.*Tr.*22; so ἐ. τινά Id.*IA*1154, Th.4.60,92: abs., πολλά A.*Pers.*780; στρατῷ ξύμπαντι S.*Aj.*1056; πεζῷ καὶ ναυσί Plu.*Nic.*7:—Med., with pf. Pass., ἐπιστρατεύεσθαι ἐπ' Αἴγυπτον Hdt.3.107, cf. 6.132: c. dat., E.*Med.*1185, Ar.*V.*11, etc.: c. acc. loci, E.*Ph.*605. —**ηγέω**, *hold office of* ἐπιστράτηγος, *OGI*708.16, etc. —**ηγία**, ἡ, *district in Egypt under an* ἐπιστράτηγος, Dessau *ILS*1409, al. —**ηγος**, ὁ, *viceroy* of one of the three provinces of Egypt formed by Ptolemy V, *OGI*103.4 (ii B.C.), *PGiss.*36.1 (ii B.C.); also under the Romans, Str.17.1.13, *IGRom.*1.1141, al.

ἐπιστρᾰτοπεδ-εία, ἡ, *encamping over against*, Plb.1.77.7; ἡ τῶν πολεμίων ἐ. *the fact that* the enemy *was encamped near*, Id.5.76.9. —**εύω**, *encamp over against*, τοῖς Ῥωμαίοις Id.1.19.5; ἐπὶ τὸ ὄρος Id.5.30.4, etc.

ἐπιστρᾰφής, ές, = ἐπιστρεφής, Ammon.*Diff.*p.54 V., Ptol.Asc. p.395 H.

ἐπί-στρεμμα, ατος, τό, *turn* or *return* of a boundary line, *IG*14.352 i 28 (Halaesa). —**στρεπτέον**, *one must turn back*, πάλιν, in a speech, Aristid.1.99 J.; εἰς ὑγιεινὴν δίαιταν Sor.1.98. II. c. gen., *account must be taken of*, Phld.*Mort.*32. —**στρεπτικός**, ή, όν, *reflexive, capable of returning* to its source, δύναμις Procl.*in Prm.* p.607 S.; ἐ. πρὸς ἑαυτό Id.*Inst.*15; κλητικὸν εἰς ἑαυτὸ καὶ ἐ. Herm. *in Phdr.*p.65 A.: Comp., Dam.*Pr.*77. Adv. -κῶς ib.221:—also as gloss on ἐπιστροφάδην, Eust.1956.49. —**στρεπτος** or -**τός**, όν, *to be turned outwards, looked at and admired*, αἰών A.*Ch.*350 (lyr.); ὤραν.. ἐ. βροτοῖς Id.*Supp.*997. II. *that can be turned round, reversible*, Hero *Aut.*15.3, *Spir.*1.28. III. Adv. -τως *diligently*, *Inscr.Perg.*163 A 12. —**στρέφεια**, ἡ, *strictness, severity*, *POxy.*1121.5 (iii A.D.), etc. —**στρεφής**, ές, *turning one's eyes* or *mind* to a thing, *attentive*, ῥήτωρ X.*HG*6.3.7; θεός Plu.2.276a; ἐπιστρεφεῖς πρὸς τὴν θεραπείαν Phld.*Ir.*p.21 W. 2. *exact, strict, severe*, καταγραφαί D.H.10.33 (Comp.); ἀρχή Hdn.7.8.7; δίαιτα Id.5.2.5. Adv. -φῶς, Ion. -φέως, *earnestly, vehemently*, εἴρετο ἐ. Hdt.1.30; ἐ. καὶ ῥητορικῶς φήσουσι Aeschin.1.71; ἐ. πάνυ καὶ θρασέως D.H.7.34: Comp. -έστερον *UPZ* 24.24 (ii B.C.), Phleg.*Olymp.Fr.*1, etc.; cf. ἐπιστρέφω II. 5:—ἐπιστρεφῶς is v.l. for ἐπιστρόφως in Eub.150.7 = Ephipp.3.10. II. *flexible, supple*, ἰσχίον Philostr.*Gym.*35: metaph., *modulated, varied*, φωνὴ ἐ., of the nightingale, Arist.*HA*632^{b}24. 2. = ἐπιστρεπτικός, μερισμός Dam.*Pr.*272; νοῦς ib.304. —**στρεφομένως** (-νος cod.), gloss on ἐπιστροφάδην, Hsch. —**στρέφω**, pf. ἐπέστροφα Diog. (v. infr. I. 2a):—*turn about, turn round*, νῶτον Orac.ap.Hdt.7.141; δεῦρ' ἐ. κάρα E.*Heracl.*942, cf. X.*Cyn.*10.12; στροφεῖς Hero *Aut.* 23.3; ἐ. τὰς ναῦς *tack* (cf. ἐπιστροφή II. 1), Th.2.90; also, *put* an enemy *to flight*, X.*HG*6.4.9; *wheel about*, τοὺς ἱππεῖς Plu.*Sull.*19; *wheel through a right angle*, Ascl.*Tact.*10.5 (Act. and Pass.), etc.; intr., ib.12.11, etc. b. intr., *turn about, turn round*, ἕλκε δ' ἐπιστρέψας Il.3.370; here only in Hom., and perh. trans., *whirl*, but v. Hdt.2.103, S.*Tr.*566; ἀλλὰ πᾶς ἐπίστρεφε δεῦρο Ar.*V.*422; of ships, *put about*, Plb.1.47.8, 50.5; of a wild boar, *turn upon* the hunter, ἐπί τινα X.*Cyn.*10.15; *return*, ἀπὸ τῆς στρατείας Epist. Philipp. in *IG*9(2).517.37 (Larissa), cf. *Ev.Matt.*12.44, etc.; of an illness, *recur*, f.l. for ὑπο-, Hp.*Coac.*124: as Hebraism, c. inf., as periphrasis of πάλιν, ἐπιστρέψει.. εὐφρανθῆναι Lxx *De.*30.9, cf. 2*Es.*9.14, al.; so with καί and finite Verb, ἐπέστρεψεν καὶ ᾠκοδόμησεν ib.2*Ch.*33.3, cf. *Ma.*1.4, al. 2. *turn towards*, νόημα Thgn.1083; ἦθος κατά τινα Id.213; ἐ. τινά *turn* his *attention towards* one, Luc. *Tim.*11; τινὰ πρός τι, εἰς ἑαυτόν, Plu.2.21c, 69f, cf. Hdn.5.3.8; οἱ τὴν Ἑλλάδα ἐπεστροφότες ἐπὶ σοφίαν Diog.*Ep.*34.1; ἐ. πίστιν *press* a pledge *upon* one, S.*Tr.*1182; ἐ. τὴν φάλαγγα *bring* it *into action*, Plu. *Ant.*42: hence, b. intr., *turn* (oneself) *towards*, X.*Eq.*8.12, etc.; ἐ. εἰς or πρὸς ἑαυτόν, of νοῦς, *reflect*, Plot.5.3.1, Procl.*Inst.*15; τὸ ἐπιστρέφον βαθρικόν the steps *leading to* the sarcophagus, Judeich *Altertümer von Hierapolis* 152. 3. *turn* or *convert* from an error, *correct, cause to repent*, Luc.*Hist.Conscr.*5, Plu.*Alc.*16; πλημμελοῦντας Id.*Cat. Mi.*14; *warn*, Philostr.*VS*1.7.1; *coerce*, *Cod.Just.*4.20.15.1. b. Pass., *to be converted, return*, ἐπὶ Κύριον Lxx *De.*30.2; intr., *repent*, ib.*Ju.*5.19, al., *Ev.Matt.*13.15, *Ev.Luc.*22.32, etc. c. Philos., *cause to return* to the source of Being, τινὰς εἰς τὰ ἐναντία καὶ τὰ πρῶτα Plot. 5.1.1; τι πρὸς τἀγαθόν Procl.*Inst.*144:—Pass., Plot.1.2.4, 5.2.1; τὸ προϊὸν ἀπό τινος -στρέφεται πρὸς ἐκεῖνο ἀφ' οὗ πρόεισιν Procl.*Inst.*31; πρὸς τὸ ἕν Dam.*Pr.*27:—also intr. in Act., ἐ. εἰς ἑαυτόν Plot.5.3.6; τὸ γεννηθὲν φύσει πρὸς τὸ γεννῆσαν ἐ. Porph.*Sent.*13; οὐδὲν τῶν σωμάτων πρὸς ἑαυτὸ πέφυκεν ἐ. Procl.*Inst.*15. 4. *curve, twist*, ὀδύνη σε περὶ τὰ σπλάγχν' ἔοικ' ἐπιστρέφειν v.l. in Ar.*Pl.*1131; ἐ. ἐπισκύνιον *AP*11.376.8 (Agath.):—Pass., *to be distorted*, ἢν τράχηλος ἐπιστραφῇ Hp. *Aph.*4.35; of hair, *curl*, οἷς ἐπέστραπται τὸ τρίχιον Arist.*Pr.*963^{b}10; ἐπεστραμμένος, of a tree, *crooked*, Thphr.*HP*3.8.4; of fir-needles, *bent*, ib.3.9.6. II. Med. and Pass., esp. in aor. 2 Pass. ἐπεστράφην [ᾰ], also ἐπεστρέφθην Opp.*C.*4.179: Dor. 3 sg. fut. Pass. -στραφησεῖται *GDI*3089.27 (Callatis):—*turn oneself round, turn about*, ἤϊε ἐπιστρεφόμενος *constantly turning*, as if to look behind one, Hdt. 3.156: and with acc., πολλὰ θάλαμον ἐξιοῦσ' ἐπεστράφη *turned to gaze on* it, E.*Alc.*187; so of a lion retreating, Arist.*HA*629^{b}15; δι' οὗ πάσας ἐπιστρέφεσθαι τὰς περιφοράς by which all the revolving spheres *are turned*, Pl.*R.*616c; δόξα τῇδ' ἐπεστράφη thus *turned about, changed*, S.*Ant.*1111. 2. *go back- and forwards*, πάντη *h.Hom.*27.10; κατ' ἄλσος A.*Supp.*508: c. acc., γαῖαν ἐπιστρέφεται *wanders over* the earth, with collat. sense of *observing, studying* it, Hes.*Th.*753, Thgn.648; so ἐ. ὀρέων κορυφάς Anacr.2.4: also c. acc. loci, *turn to* a place, πόθεν γῆς τῆσδ' ἐπεστράφης πέδον; E.*Hel.*83, cf. 89,768, *Ion*352 (also εἰς χώρας X.*Oec.*4.13): c. acc. cogn., [διεξόδους] ἐπιστρέφεσθαι *walk in*.., Pl.*Phdr.*247a; of the sun, *revolve*, D.P.584. 3. *turn the mind towards, pay attention to, regard* (cf. ἐπιστροφή II. 3), τινός Anacr.96, S. *Ph.*599, Phld.*Lib.*p.15 O., *AP*5.47 (Rufin.); τῶν ἰδίων οὐδὲν ἐ. Thgn. 440; εἴς τι Alex.Aphr.*in Sens.*57.18: abs., *return to oneself, pay attention*, ἐπιστραφείς Hdt.1.88; οὐκ ἦλθες,..οὐδ' ἐπεστράφης E.*Rh.* 400; οὐκ ἐπεστράφη, = οὐκ ἐφρόντισε (just above), D.23.136, cf. 10.9, *AP*11.319 (Autom.). b. *conduct oneself, behave*, ἀξίως τᾶς τιμᾶς *SIG*539 A 22 (Decr. Amphict., iii B.C.). 4. c. acc., θεοῦ νιν κέλευσμ' ἐπεστράφη *turned against* her, E.*Andr.*101 (lyr.). 5. pf.part. Pass. ἐπεστραμμένος, = ἐπιστρεφής, *earnest, vehement*, λέγειν ἐπεστραμμένα Hdt.8.62; ἀφέλεια -στραμμένη Philostr.*VS*1.7.1. —**στρεψις**, εως, ἡ, *turning, twisting*, ἀγκῶνος Hp.*Art.*18.

ἐπιστρογγύλλομαι, Pass., *to be rounded*, Nic.*Th.*514.

ἐπιστρόγγῠλος, ον, *rounded, roundish*, f.l. in Arist.*HA*555^{a}29.

ἐπιστροφ-άδην [ᾰ], Adv. *turning this way and that way*, κτεῖνε δ' ἐπιστροφάδην Il.10.483; τύπτε δ' ἐ. 21.20, cf. Od.22.308, 24.184 (or perh., = ἐπιστρεφῶς, *earnestly, vehemently*, cf. Hsch.); ἐ. βαδίζειν wander *back- and forwards*, *h.Merc.*210; *on all sides*, Opp.*C.*1.79: Poet. and late Prose, ἐ. κτείνειν, ἀναιρεῖν, Ph.2.33,320. —**εύς**, έως, ὁ, *turning on a pivot*, a name for *the first of the neck-vertebrae*, Poll.2.131. II. *one who causes to return* to its source, τοῦ γενομένου κόσμου Dam.*Pr.*270. —**ή**, ἡ, *turning about*, τῆς τοῦ ἀτράκτου δίνης Pl.*R.*620e; *twisting*, Thphr.*HP*3.13.3; of strands, Ph.*Bel.*58.15; τῶν σχοινίων Plu.*Alex.*25 (pl.); ἡ εἴσω ἐ. τῶν δακτύλων Philostr.*Im.*1.23. 2. *bending* of a bow, Str.2.5.22. 3. *curve, winding* of a bay, ib.33; of a river, Ptol.*Alm.*8.1. II. intr., *turning* or *wheeling about*, δαΐων ἀνδρῶν ἐπιστροφαί, i.e. hostile men *turning to bay*, S.*OC*1045 (lyr.); *tossing*, of a restless patient, Hp.*Epid.*7.83 (pl.); μυρίων ἐπιστροφαὶ κακῶν *renewed assaults* of ills unnumbered, S.*OC*537 (lyr.), cf. Arr. *An.*7.17.5; esp. in military evolutions, Plb.10.23.3, Plu.*Phil.*7; *wheeling through a right angle*, Ascl.*Tact.*10.4, etc. (but, as a general term, αἱ ἐ. τῶν ἵππων ib.7.2, cf. Arr.*Tact.*16.7); of ships, *putting about, tacking*, Th.2.90,91; ἐξ ἐπιστροφῆς *by a sudden wheel*, Plb.1.76.5, Plu.*Tim.*27; but ἐξ ἐπιστροφῆς παθεῖν to have *a relapse*, Hp. *Coac.*251. 2. *turn* of affairs, *reaction, counter-revolution*, μή τις ἐ. γένηται Th.3.71; *result, end*, Plb.21.32.15 (dub.l.). 3. *attention paid to* a person or thing (ἐπιστρέφω II. 3), ξενοτίμους δωμάτων ἐ. *respect* for guests, A.*Eu.*548; πρὸ τοῦ θανόντος τήνδ' ἔθεσθ' ἐ. S.*OT*134; ὧν ἐ. τις ἦν to whom any *regard* was due, E.*IT*671; so ἐπιστροφῆς ἄξιον X.*HG*5.2.9; παραμυθέεσθαι μετ' ἐπιστροφῆς καὶ ὑποδέξιος Hp. *Decent.*16; ἐ. ποιεῖσθαι Philipp.ap.D.12.1, cf. 19.306, etc.; ἐ. ἔχειν τινός Men.836; περί τινος Chrysipp.*Stoic.*3.187, etc.; ἐπιστροφῆς τυγχάνειν Plb.4.4.4, etc. b. Philos., *turning towards*, πρὸς τὰ τῇδε Plot.4.3.4; ψυχὴ καταδεῖται πρὸς τὸ σῶμα τῇ ἐ. τῇ πρὸς τὰ πάθη τὰ ἀπ' αὐτοῦ Porph.*Sent.*7. 4. *moving up and down in* a place, mostly in pl., πατρῴων δωμάτων ἐπιστροφαί *the range* of them, A.*Th.*648; οἷσιν οὐκ ἐπιστροφαί men who have no *business here*, E.*Hel.*440; βούνομοι ἐ. *haunts* of the grazing herds, A.*Fr.*249; so Κίλιξ δὲ χώρα καὶ Σύρων ἐπιστροφαί (cj. for Σηρῶν ἐνστροφαί) ib.271. 5. *intentness, vehemence,* ἐπιστροφὴν εἶχεν ὁ λόγος καὶ ἔρρωτο Philostr.*VS*1.21.5; θρασυτέρᾳ τῇ ἐ. χρήσασθαι ib.2.5.2. b. *gravity* of deportment, ἡ ἐ. τοῦ εἴδους Id.*Im.* 2.16. 6. *correction, reproof,* Plu.2.55b. 7. *conversion, Act.Ap.*15.3; ἡ πρὸς θεὸν ἐ. Hierocl.*in CA*24p.473 M. 8. in Philos., *return* to the source of Being, Plot.1.2.4; ἡ ἐ. πρὸς αὑτόν Id.5.3.6, cf. Procl. *Inst.*31; [ἡ ἐ.] τοῦ προελθόντος ἐπάνοδος εἰς τὸ γεννῆσαν Dam.*Pr.*75; ἡ ἐ. τῆς ἐκστάσεώς ἐστιν ἐπανόρθωσις ib.61. 9. in Logic, *conversion* of a proposition, ἡ σὺν ἀντιθέσει ἐ. *the contraposition,* Suppl. ad Procl. *in Prm.*p.1004 S. **-ία**, ἡ, title of Aphrodite, *Verticordia,* Paus.1.40.5. **-ίς** (A), ίδος, ἡ, *dislocation,* Hsch. 2. in pl., *curls,* Eust.1561.38. **-ίς** (B), ίδος, ἡ, = Lat. *anaticula* (part of a door), *Gloss.* **-ος**, ον, *having dealings with, conversant,* ἐ. ἦν ἀνθρώπων Od.1.177; read by Ar.Byz. for ἐπίσκοπος, 8.163; ἐ. τινος *concerned with* or *in* it, A.*Ag.*397 (lyr.). 2. = ἐπιστρεφής, *curved, winding,* A.R.2.979; ὅρμος D.P.75. 3. Adv. -φως *diligently, exactly,* Ephipp.3.10, Memn.7.3.

ἐπιστρώννῡμι or **-ύω**, v. ἐπιστορέννυμι.

ἐπιστρωφ-άω, Frequentat. of ἐπιστρέφω, only intr., c. acc., *visit* or *frequent* a place, θεοὶ .. ἐπιστρωφῶσι πόληας Od.17.486; ἀνέρος, ὅν τε θαμιναὶ ἐπιστρωφῶσι μέριμναι *haunt* him, *h.Merc.*44; γαῖαν Orph.*A.*830; εἰς γῆν Phryn.Trag.5:—Med., *go in and out of, frequent, haunt,* δῶμ' ἐπιστρωφωμένου A.*Ag.*972; also, *come to,* πόθεν γῆς τῆσδ' ἐ. πέδον; E.*Med.*666. **-ησις**, εως, ἡ, *going to and fro,* κατὰ τὸν σύμπαντα κόσμον Onat.ap.Stob.1.1.39 (pl., -ώσιες codd.).

ἐπιστύλ-ιον [ῠ], τό, (στῦλος) *architrave, IG*1².372, *Tab.Heracl.*1.6, *CIG*2751 (Aphrodisias), Plu.*Per.*13, Ph.*Bel.*62.6, Callix.2, Vitr.3.5.8, etc.: also as Adj., ἐπιστύλια ξύλα *IG*1².313.106. 2. *shelf* with pigeon-holes, Arist.*Ath.*47.5 (pl.). **-ίς**, ίδος, ἡ, = foreg. 1, Ph.1.666. **-ον**, τό, = foreg., *Gp.*14.6.6.

ἐπιστύφω [ῡ], *draw up,* of the effect of astringents, Nic.*Al.*79,278; τὰ ἐπιστύφοντα .. βρώματα Heraclid.Tarent.ap.Ath.3.120c; τὸν στόμαχον prob. in Plu.2.687d: metaph., of the ears, D.H.*Dem.*38; *reprove,* τὴν ἀπόνοιαν τῶν πλεόντων Alciphr.1.3, cf. Hierocl.*in CA*19 p.461 M. 2. *apply a second mordant,* as preparation for dyeing, *PHolm.*16.28.

ἐπίστυψις, εως, ἡ, *use of astringent remedies,* Plot.4.4.45 (pl.).

ἐπισυγ-κάμπτω, *bend together besides,* Hp.*Art.*58. **-κροτέω**, *weld together, combine* in one body, J.*BJ*1.1.6. **-κρούω**, *meet with a check* or *reverse,* D.C.*Fr.*50.2. **-χέω**, in Pass., *to be in confusion,* τὰς περὶ θεοῦ δόξας .. ἐπισυγκεχύσθαι Ph.1.320 codd. **-χωννύω**, *cover up with earth, Gp.*5.26.2.

ἐπισυ-ζεύγνῡμι, *join,* Gal.18(1).741, Sch.Il.2.278. **-ζῠγία**, ἡ, *squadron of* 8 *war-chariots,* = 2 συζυγίαι, Ascl.*Tact.*8, Ael.*Tact.*22.2.

ἐπισῡκοφαντέω, *harass yet more with frivolous accusations,* Hyp.*Fr.*243, Plu.*Ant.*21.

ἐπισυλ-λαμβάνω, = ἐπικυΐσκομαι, Orib.22.7.2, Sor.1.23. **-λέγω**, *collect besides* or *after,* Hp.*Off.*11 (Pass.); πᾶσαν τὴν δύναμιν J.*BJ*1.6.3:—Pass., τὸν -λεγέντα ὀπόν v.l. in Dsc.4.153, cf. Gal.18(1).781. **-ληψις**, εως, ἡ, *second conception, Placit.*5.10.3, Orib.22.7.2. **-λογίζομαι**, *draw a subsequent inference,* A.D.*Conj.*252.5: c. acc. et inf., Iamb.*VP*3.16.

ἐπισυμ-βαίνω, *happen besides, supervene,* Arist.*Rh.Al.*1426ᵃ6, *APr.*64ᵇ30; ἐπισυνέβη, c. acc. et inf., J.*AJ*15.7.10; τὰ -οντα ἀρρωστήματα Jul.*Ep.*75b, cf. Herod.Med.ap.Orib.5.30.15. II. *come into existence afterwards,* S.E.*M.*9.371, 11.130. 2. c. dat., ὃ ἂν γενομένῃ τῇ οὐσίᾳ ἐπισυμβῇ Plot.6.3.8. **-βάλλομαι**, f.l. for ἐπὶ νοῦν β., Phylarch.24 J. **-μᾰχία**, ἡ, *alliance against a common enemy,* Philipp.ap.D.12.7 codd. (leg. ἐπιμαχία). **-μειγνῡμι**, *add,* Vett.Val.215.6. **-μύω**, *close up,* Thphr.*CP*1.6.3. **-πάρειμι**, Astrol., of planets, *to be present as well,* Nech.ap.Vett.Val.280.5. **-πίπτω**, *collapse, decay,* Ph.2.221, Anon.Lond.27.31; *spring together again,* Str.6.1.12; *contract,* of the heart in systole, Ruf.*Syn.Puls.*3. II. *happen besides* or *in addition to,* τοῖς γεγονόσιν J.*AJ*15.10.3; -πίπτουσαι διαστροφαὶ *casual* distortions, Ptol.*Tetr.*108. **-πλέκω**, *add* a drug to a mixture, Paul.Aeg.4.4:—Pass., *to be combined,* τὸ -όμενον πτωτικόν A.D.*Synt.*124.27. **-πτωσις**, εως, ἡ, *falling together,* Anon.Lond.27.29; *incidence,* ἡ ἔξωθεν ἐ. τῶν πραγμάτων Andronic. Rhod.p.570 M. **-φέρω**, *contribute, Theol.Ar.*32. **-φορος**, ον, *contributing their influence, Cat.Cod.Astr.*5(1).180.16.

ἐπισυν-άγω [ᾰ], *collect and bring to* a place, Plb.1.75.2 (Pass.), 5.97.3, Wilcken *Chr.*11 *A* 5 (ii B.C.); *gather together,* Lxx *Ge.*6.16, al., *Ev.Matt.*23.37, etc.:—Pass., *OGI*90.23 (Rosetta, ii B.C.), *Placit.*3.4.1, Ph.1.338; οἱ -συνηγμένοι ἐν Ξόει Βοιωτοί *Supp.Epigr.*2.871 (Egypt, ii B.C.); *to be combined,* τὰ ἐκ τῶν πληθυντικῶν εἰς τὰ ἑνικὰ -όμενα Longin.24.1; ἐπισυναχθέντες τόκοι *accumulated* interest, *PGrenf.*2.72.8 (iii/iv A.D.), cf. *PFlor.*1.46.14 (ii A.D.); ἐπισυναγόμενος ἀριθμός *counted up,* Ptol.*Tetr.*43. II. *bring in,* in a discussion, περιττὸν -ειν καὶ ταύτας Phld.*Acad.Ind.*28. 2. Astrol., = ἐπισυμφέρω, Vett.Val.288.29. III. *conclude, infer,* συλλογιζόμενοι τὸν μεταξὺ χρόνον ἐπισυνάγουσιν ὅτι .. Procl.*Hyp.*5.54. **-ᾰγωγή**, ἡ, *gathering* or *being gathered together,* Lxx 2*Ma.*2.7, 2*Ep.Thess.*2.1, etc. b. *collection* of a sum of money, *IG*12(3).1270.11 (Syme, ii/i B.C.). 2. *collective view, table,* ὁρίων Ptol.*Tetr.*44. 3. pl., *successive additions,* Id.*Alm.*2.7. 4. Astrol., *aggregation* of planets in contact, Porph.*in Ptol.*188. **-αθροίζω**, *collect besides,* Hsch. s.v. ἐπαγείρειν. **-αινέω**, *give one's adhesion to,* τινί J.*AJ*5.1.16. **-ακτέον**, *one must connect, link,* τί τινι Dam.*Pr.*83 bis. **-ᾰλοιφή**, ἡ, *elision at the close of a verse,* Choerob.*in Heph.*p.226 C. II. *coalescence of two syllables in one,* Isid.*Etym.*1.35.5. **-αντάω**, *meet at one point,* Theo Sm. p.184 H. **-απτέον**, *one must subjoin,* S.E.*M.*10.20. **-απτικός**, ή, όν, *apt to cause a combination,* κακῶν, of the moon, *Cat.Cod.Astr.*7.115.8. **-άπτω**, *join on, subjoin, attach,* τί τινι Hp.*Art.*71, Plb.3.2.8, Phld.*Vit.*p.43 J., cf. D.H.1.87, etc.; *add,* περί τινος S.E.*M.*1.120:—Pass., [λέξεις] A.D.*Synt.*6.28. 2. = συνάπτειν, μάχην τινί D.S.14.94. 3. c. dat., *assist, promote,* τῷ τάχει Ph.*Bel.*69.8. II. Med., *link oneself with,* τινί Eustr.*in EN*6.18. **-άρχομαι**, *begin together with,* τινί Hippodam.ap.Stob.4.39.26. **-ᾰφή**, ἡ, in Music, *combination of three tetrachords by* συναφή (q.v.), Bacch.*Intr.*84. II. Rhet., *subjoining,* Anon.*Fig.*p.146 S. **-δεσις**, εως, ἡ, *concatenation,* αἰτιῶν *Placit.*1.28.4, cf. Chrysipp.*Stoic.*2.274; πάντων τῶν ἐν τῷ κόσμῳ M.Ant.6.38. **-δεσμέω**, *act as astringent, Hippiatr.*8,10,34 (v.l. **-δεσμεύω**). **-δέω**, *bind on top,* Aen.Tact.37.9: metaph., τὴν ἀπορίαν ἐ. μᾶλλον 'tie the knot tighter', Thphr.*CP*2.17.7. 2. *connect,* as words in a sentence, A.D.*Adv.*133.26:—Med., ἐπισυνδέοιτο ⟨ἂν⟩ τὰ τῆς κοινωνίας Hierocl.p.62 A. II. *make firm* or *compact,* τὰ σώματα Agathin.ap.Orib.10.7.14. **-δίδωμι**, *rush in together,* of streams, Plu.*Aem.*14. **-ειμι**, (εἶμι *ibo*) *come together again,* ἐκ τῆς φυγῆς D.H.1.63. **-είρω**, *join together besides,* S.E.*M.*1.142. **-έμπτωσις**, εως, ἡ, *succession of words with like terminations and containing the same vowels* (cf. Il.23.116), Eust.1291.43. **-εργέω**, *contribute,* πρός τι Euryph.ap.Stob.4.39.27, cf. Ocell.4.1, Ptol.*Tetr.*142. II. *restrict still further,* τροφῆς πλῆθος Sor.1.56 (-εργεῖν cod.: -έργειν vel -είργειν edd.). **-έχω** γυναῖκα *take to oneself* a wife, Lxx 1*Es.*9.17. **-ήθης**, ες, = συνήθης, Sch.Il.1.35. **-θεσις**, εως, ἡ, *addition,* Vett.Val.280.13, Herm.*in Phdr.*p.107 A.; *combination,* S.E.*M.*1.22; τῶν μελῶν Longin.40.1; *complexity,* Marcellin.*Puls.*464. **-θετικός**, ή, όν, *combining*: hence, *eclectic,* of the school founded by Agathinus, Gal.19.353; Leonidas ὁ ἐ. Cael.Aur.*CP*2.1. Adv. -κῶς, = κατ' ἐπισύνθεσιν, S.E.*M.*3.40. **-θετος**, ον, *compound*: hence -σύνθετον (sc. μέτρον), τό, *metre composed of* κῶλα *of different* γένη, Heph.15.10. **-θήκη**, ἡ, *additional article to a treaty, Schwyzer* 631.4 (Milet. (decree of Methymna), ii B.C.): pl., Plb.3.27.7. **-ίστημι** (also **-ιστάω** J.*AJ*14.1.3), *cause to coagulate afterwards,* γάλα Sch.Nic.*Al.*373. 2. *band together,* τινὰς κατά τινος J. l.c.; ἡ φθορὰ ἐ. πλείους τισί Id.*BJ*2.3.4; simply, *incite to conspiracy against,* τινὶ τὸν υἱόν Str.13.4.2. II. Pass. with fut. -στήσομαι S.E.*M.*11.119, and aor. 2 and pf. Act.:—*to be collected, gather upon,* c. dat., *Placit.*3.5.10, cf. Procl.*in Prm.*p.645 S. 2. *to be classed along with,* τὸ ποιητικὸν τῆς ἀλγηδόνος ἐπισυστήσεται τῇ ἀλγηδόνι S.E. l.c. 3. *come into being afterwards,* ib.3.85: c. dat., μεθέξεσιν Dam.*Pr.*349; *to be made up of,* ἐκ προτέρων τινῶν Iamb.*Comm.Math.*10. 4. *conspire against, attack* or *resist jointly,* τινί Satyr.*Vit.Eur.Fr.*39 x 23, *SIG*663.23 (Delos, iii/ii B.C.), Parth.35.2, Socr.*Ep.*15.1, cf. Str.7 *Fr.*18: abs., Plu.2.227a; πρὸς τὴν τιμωρίαν τινός D.C.60.21. b. *combine to oppose,* εἰ δ' ἄν τις -συνίσταιτο ταῖς ἐσδόσεσι τῶν ἔργων *IG*5(2).6.15 (Tegea, iv B.C.). **-νέω**, *pile up, lay together,* D.C.40.2. **-οικίζω**, *bring in new colonists,* Str.5.1.6:—Pass., of a place, *to be colonized anew,* Paus.6.22.5. **-τάσσω**, *contrive against,* διαβολάς τινι J.*BJ*1.28.1. II. *bring in as well,* ἑτέραν γυναῖκα ἢ παλλακίδα *PMasp.*6 ii 36 (vi A.D.). **-τείνω**, *intensify effort,* Poll.3.121:—Pass., *have a feeling of tightness,* Hp.*Acut.*(*Sp.*)44. **-τελέω**, *finish completely, PMagd.*2.4 (iii B.C.). **-τέμνω**, *abbreviate,* Sch.Il.2.156. **-τήκω**, *liquefy besides,* Gal.18(2).906:—Pass., of patients, *waste away,* ἐπιξυντακέντες ὤλοντο Aret.*SD*1.14. **-τίθημι**, *add successively,* Archim.*Sph.Cyl.*1.2, Vett.Val.31.25, al., S.E.*P.*2.207, Nicom.*Ar.*1.16:—Pass., Dam.*Pr.*87. II. ἐ. τὰ χείλη *close* the edges of a wound, Orib.46.25.6. III. Med., ἐπισυντέθειμαι I *have made an* ἐπισυνθήκη, Oikonomos Ἐπιγραφαὶ τῆς Μακεδονίας p.2. **-τρέχω**, *run together* to a place, *Ev.Marc.*9.25. **-ωθέω**, = συνωθέω, Epicur.*Ep.*2 p.47 U. (Pass.).

ἐπισῡρ-ιγμός, ὁ, *wheezing,* Herod.Med. in *Rh.Mus.*58.86. **-ίζω**, = sq., Nonn.*D.*1.71,170. **-ίττω**, *hiss* or *whistle at* a thing, *make a signal by screaming,* Arist.*HA*614ᵇ22.

ἐπί-συρμα, ατος, τό, (ἐπισύρω) *anything trailed after* one: *trail* of a snake, Hp.*Ep.*15; *trail* or *track made by dragging* a thing, X.*Cyn.*9.18. **-συρμός**, ὁ, *laziness, negligence,* εἰς ἐ. καὶ λήθην ἄγειν Plb.4.49.1, cf. 38.15.10. II. *mockery,* Stoic.ap.Stob.2.7.11ᵐ.

ἐπισυρ-ρέω, *flow together,* Str.5.3.13, Dsc.4.153; of a crowd, Ph.2.365: c. dat., D.H.4.55, *Placit.*3.7.3. **-ροια**, ἡ, *conflux,* Ael.*NA*12.20.

ἐπισύρω [ῡ], *drag* or *trail after* one, τὼ πόδε D.L.1.81; χλαμύδα λαμπράν Posidon.36 J.:—Med., ποδήρεις χιτῶνας Luc.*VH*2.46; φελλούς ib.45; φόρτον Porph.*VP*25; γυναῖκας J.*BJ*4.1.10:—Pass., *crawl* or *creep along,* ἐπὶ τῆς γῆς X.*Cyn.*5.13, cf. Ael.*NA*2.23; *to be drawn over, rub against,* μήνιγγι Heliod.ap.Orib.46.19.2; *to be trailed on the ground,* Ph.2.148; *to be protracted,* Just.*Nov.*42.1.2. 2. *draw gently,* τὸ πνεῦμα Alciphr.3.12. 3. Med., *draw over oneself,* δέρμα αἰγός Longus 3.24. b. *draw up by friction,* Steph.*in Gal.*1.326 D. 4. Pass., *to be impeded* in movements, Aret.*SD*1.7. II. c. acc., *do in a slovenly, careless way, slur over, evade intentionally,* τὰ πράγματα Lys.26.3; τὰς πράξεις Plb.29.12.6; γραφήν D.H.1.7 (v.l. ὑπο-); βίον Jul.*Gal.*43b (Pass.): abs., ἐπισύροντες ἐροῦσι D.20.131; ἐπισύρων γέγραφα Jul.*Ep.*4; ἐ. ἐν ταῖς πράξεσι *to be negligent,* M.Ant.8.51; καταφρονεῖν ὧν οὐκ οἶδεν καὶ ἐπισύρειν Porph.*Abst.*2.53: in this sense freq. in pf. part. Pass., *slurred over, neglected,* Plb.16.20.3; τὸ -μένον [τῶν λέξεων] Phld.*Rh.*1.49 S.; γράμματα ἐπισεσυρμένα *slovenly, hastily written,* Luc.*DMeretr.*10.3; φθέγγεσθαι ἐ. τι καὶ συνεχὲς καὶ ἐπίτροχον Id.*Nav.*2; χρέμπτεσθαι ἐ. Ps.-Luc.*Philopatr.*20; ἐ. καὶ ῥυπαρός *slovenly* and dirty, of a man, D.L.1.81; ἐ. ἤθη *lax* morals, Procl.*in Prm.*p.553 S. Adv. ἐπισεσυρμένως *carelessly*, Epict.*Ench.*31, Sch.Ar.*Ra.*1545.

ἐπισύ-στᾰσις, εως, ἡ, *gathering, riotous meeting*, τοῦ ὄχλου *Act. Ap.*24.12 (nisi leg. ἐπίστασις); αἱ τῶν κρατούντων τῆς χώρας βαρβάρων ἐ. *SIG*708.27 (Istropolis, ii B.C.); *insurrection*, Beros.ap.J.*Ap.*1.20, Lxx *Nu.*16.40(17.5): c. gen., *rising against*, τοῦ Κυρίου ib.26.9. 2. *collection*, κακῶν S.E.*M.*11.127; ὑδατίδων Sor.1.58. 3. v.l. for ἐπίστασις, 2*Ep.Cor.*11.28. **-στέλλομαι**, Pass., *to be drawn together, contracted*, of a wasp's waist, Sch.Ar.*Pl.*301: metaph., of style, *to be lowered in tone*, Arist.*Rh.*1404b17. **-στρέφω**, *collect together*, Lxx *Nu.*16.42(17.7):—Pass., J.*AJ*13.13.3. II. *compress into unity*, Longin.24.1. III. *brace up, restore*, στόμαχον ὑπτιωμένον Sor.1.50 (-στροφ[εῖ] cod.). **-σχεσις**, εως, ἡ, *reception*, 1*Enoch* 22.4.

ἐπίσυχνος, ον, neut. as Adv., *generally*, Hp.*Prorrh.*1.140 (v.l. ἐπὶ συχνόν). Adv. -νως Malch.(?)ap.Suid. s. v. Λογγῖνος (ἐπιδείπνως cod. opt., ἐπὶ δείπνῳ Bernh.).

ἐπισφᾰγίς, ίδος, ἡ, (σφαγή) *nape of the neck* where the axe strikes the bull, Poll.2.134.

ἐπισφάζω, later **-σφάττω**, *slaughter over* or *upon*, esp. of sacrifices at a tomb, κἄμ' ἐπισφάξαι τάφῳ E.*Hec.*505; πρόβατά τινι ἐ. *sacrifice* them *to* the dead, X.*Cyr.*7.3.7 (Pass.). 2. αἷμα μηλείου φόνου ἐ. *shed* the blood of slaughtered sheep *over*, E.*El.*92, cf. 281; αἷμ' ἐπισφάξας νέον Id.*Sthen.*p.44 A.:—Pass., αἷμα ἀρτίως ἐπεσφαγμένον Arist. *Col.*796a15. II. *kill upon* or *besides*, τρίτον θῦμ' ὡς ἐπισφάξων δυοῖν E.*HF*995, cf. X.*An.*1.8.29 (also ἑαυτὸν ἐπισφάξασθαι ibid.); Ἀντώνιον ἐ. Καίσαρι Plu.*Brut.*18:—Pass., ἐπεσφάγη τοῖς παισίν J.*BJ*5.13.1, cf. Philostr.*VA*4.16. 2. *kill over again*, νεκρούς D.L.2.135. III. *dispatch, strike the death-blow*, Thphr.ap.Porph.*Abst.* 2.30, Plu.*Ant.*76: metaph., *talk* one *to death*, Luc.*JTr.*43.

ἐπίσφαιρα, ων, τά, *boxing-gloves* used in the σφαιρομαχία, to deaden the blows, Plu.2.825e; so μάχαιραι μετ' ἐπισφαιρῶν swords *tipped with buttons*, like foils, Plb.10.20.3.

ἐπισφαίριον, τό, *tip* of the nose, Gal.18(1).805.

ἐπισφᾰκελ-ίζω, *become gangrenous, sphacelate*, Hp.*Art.*14, Aret. *SD*2.9. **-ισις**, εως, ἡ, *necrosis, caries*, τῶν ὀστέων Hp.*Art.*49.

ἐπισφάλ-εια [ᾰ], ἡ, *precariousness*, τῆς τύχης Plb.38.21.3. **-ής**, ές, (σφάλλομαι) *prone to fall, unstable, precarious*, τὰ μεγάλα πάντα ἐπισφαλῆ Pl.*R.*497d; -εστέρα δύναμις D.2.15, cf. Arist.*EN*1155a10; ἐπισφαλές [ἐστι] Id.*Pol.*1264b6; ἐ. φύσει βίος Men.*Epit.*126. II. (σφάλλω) *making to fall, misleading*, εἰς βλάβην Plu.2.653d, etc. 2. *dangerous*, νόσημα Hp.*VM*9; νόσοι Ph.2.413; καιροί Plb.1.66.12: Sup. -εστάτη, χώρα Id.2.29.2; τοῦ ἀγχιβαθοῦς τῶν ἑλῶν Ῥωμαίοις -σφαλοῦς ἐσομένου Hdn.7.2.5; ἐπισφαλές [ἐστι] παρακοῦσαι Epicur. *Fr.*200. Adv. -λῶς, ἔχειν, διακεῖσθαι, to be *in danger*, Plb.6.25.4, Plu.*Sol.*13; ἐ. βεβηκώς Lxx *Wi.*4.4: Sup. -έστατα, περᾶσαι Plu.*Cat. Mi.*15. 3. *dubious*, Adv. Comp. -έστερον Aristeas 314.

ἐπισφάλλω, *trip up, make to fall*, J.*BJ*3.7.29, Onos.42.6.

ἐπίσφατον· ἐπιμωμητόν, ἢ συνομιλητόν, ἢ ἐπὶ κακῷ ὠνομασμένον, Hsch.; = ἐπιβόητος, Poet.ap.Ammon.*Diff.*p.43 V., *Et.Gud.d.* s. v. διαβόητος; = ἐπιρρητός, *EM*365.11; Eust.1728.12 derives it fr. πεφάσθαι and translates it ὀλέθριος; but cf. περίσφατος.

ἐπισφάττω, later form of ἐπισφάζω.

ἐπισφελίτης [ῑ], ου, ὁ, (σφέλας) = θρανίτης, Paus.Gr.*Fr.*175.

ἐπισφετερίζομαι, *appropriate*, τἀλλότρια Harp. s. v. Σθένελος.

ἐπισφήκ-ιον, τό, dub. sens. in *Inscr.Délos* 370.32 (iii B.C.). **-όω**, *bind on* or *to*, Nonn.*D.*9.123:—Med., ib.2.111.

ἐπίσφην-ος, ον, *wedge-shaped*, *IG*7.3073.153 (Lebad.). **-όω**, *plug, stop*, Gal.19.654 (Pass.), Sor.2.60 (Pass.). **-ωσις**, εως, ἡ, *stoppage* in difficult labour, Paul.Aeg.3.76.

ἐπισφίγγω, *bind tight, tighten*, κημούς Ph.1.698; νάρθηκας (splints) Gal.18(2).398; πέδιλα ἐ. τοὺς πόδας Luc.*Am.*41; ἐ. τινὰ πήχεσι in the arms, *AP*5.242 (Maced.); ἐ. τοὺς ἀναγωγέας *tie* the shoe-strings *tight*, Ath.12.543f; μοσχεύματα *Gp.*10.12.3: metaph., *shut up tightly*, [θησαυροὺς] κακῶν Ph.1.108; ἐ. τὴν ἀμφισβήτησιν *complicate* it, opp. λύειν, S.E.*M.*2.96; also ἐ. τὴν νήτην *screw* it *tighter*, *tune* the instrument, Ael.*VH*9.36: metaph., '*screw up*', *intensify*, ὀδύνας (ὠδίνας cod.) Ph.1.680.

ἐπισφοδρύνω, *make rigid, intensify*, Plu.*Cleom.*10; *corroborate, confirm*, Phld.*Sign.*28.

ἐπισφρᾱγ-ίζω, Ep. **-σφρηγ-**, *put a seal on*, *PRyl.*237.1,2 (Pass., iii A.D.). 2. *confirm, ratify*, θανόντι *APl.*5.366, cf. Vett.Val.354.19:—Med., ἐ. διὰ τῆς συγκλήτου τὴν αὑτοῦ παρανομίαν *get* it *sanctioned*, Plb. 32.6.3; *give one's sanction to*, δόγμα Hierocl.*in CA*10p.437 M. II. Med., *confirm, ratify*, Pl.*Lg.*855e, 957b, Ph.2.71, etc.; ἐ. τινί τι *give* it him *as a solemn gift*, *GDI*2517.16 (Delph.). 2. *put as a seal upon, impress upon*, [τῇ πολιτικῇ] μίαν ἰδέαν Pl.*Plt.*258c; οἷς -όμεθα τὸ "αὐτὸ ὅ ἐστι" prob. cj. in Id.*Phd.*75d; ἁγνείαν ψυχαῖς Ph.2.381; σιγὴν χείλεσι ἐ. Nonn.*D.*47.218 (but in Hld.6.15 σιγῇ ἐ. τι, and so [ἀριθμῷ] γένη ζῴων -ίζεται *marks with..*, Ph.2.353; -ιζομένην (sc. τέχνην) βεβαιότητι τὰ παθῶν μέτρα Max.Tyr.33.9):—Pass., *to be impressed upon*, τὸ γεγονὸς ἐν ταῖς γνώμαις -ίσθη Plb.15.25.8; *to be marked*, φελλοῖς, of nets, *AP*6.90 (Phil.). **-ισις**, εως, ἡ, = sq., Greg.Cor.*in Hermog.* in Rh.7.1319 W. 2. *cadence* of a verse, Sch.Heph.p.118 C. **-ισμός**, ὁ, *confirmation*, Sch.Hermog. in Rh.7.425 W. **-ιστής**, οῦ, ὁ, *one who seals* or *signs*, Luc.*Alex.*23.

ἐπισφύζω, *continue to throb*, Gal.4.733.

ἐπισφύρ-ια [ῠ], τά, *leg-guards*; in Hom., always of silver, Il.3. 331, al. 2. the part *above the ankle-joint, ankle*, *AP*6.206.8 (Antip. Sid.), Opp.*C.*4.438; cf. sq. **-ιος**, ον, (σφυρόν) *on the ankle*, γέρας ἐ., of the *lunula* on the Senators' shoes at Rome, *IG*14.1389 i 31, Philostr.*VS*2.1.8. **-ος**, ον, = foreg., ποδίστρας *AP*6.107 (Phil.).

ἐπισχάζω, v. ἐπισκάζω.

ἐπισχεδί-α, ἡ, dub. sens. in *PSI*7.858 (iii B.C.). **-άζω**, *say* or *do offhand*, τῷ καιρῷ *make a* suitable *impromptu*, Philostr.*VS*1.2:—Pass., -ασμένα πάντα τῷ καιρῷ Id.*Gym.*54.

ἐπισχεδόν, Adv. *near at hand, hard by*, ἐ. ἐρχομένοιο *h.Ap.*3, cf. A.R.2.490: as Prep. c. dat. vel gen., ib.604, 4.948.

ἐπισχεθεῖν, poet. aor. 2 of ἐπέχω, *hold in, check*, A.*Th.*453 (lyr.): aor. 1 Pass. ἐπισχεθῆναι Posidon.36 J.

ἐπισχερώ, Ep. Adv., (σχερός) *in a row, one after another*, εἰσανέβαινον ἐ. Il.18.68, cf. 11.668, 23.125; ἐ. ἀλλήλοισι A.R.1.528: c. gen., τὸ γὰρ ἧμιν ἐ. ἦεν ἀοιδῆς *the next thing in..*, Id.4.451. II. of Time, τρὶς ἐ. thrice *successively*, Simon.155.5; *by degrees*, Theoc.14.69.

ἐπι-σχεσία, ἡ, *thing held out, pretext*, μύθου ποιήσασθαι ἐπισχεσίην Od.21.71. **-σχεσις**, εως, ἡ, (ἐπέχω) *checking, stoppage*, ἐξ ἐπισχέσιος after an *abatement* of fever, Hp.*Epid.*1.7; ἐπισχέσεις γενέσεως Pl.*Lg.*740d; πνεύματος Arist.*Pr.*962a1; ἀναπνοῆς Gal.7. 175; τῆς φωνῆς Plu.*Demetr.*38; πολέμου Id.*Alc.*18; τῶν ἀδικούντων Arr.*Epict.*2.20.23. 2. *delay, reluctance*, ἐπεὶ οὔ τις ἐπίσχεσις οὐδ' ἐλεητύς Od.17.451; ἡ ἐν τῇ Οἰνόῃ ἐ. *delay* or *lingering* there, Th.2.18, cf. *PCair.Zen.*283.5 (iii B.C.). **-σχετέον**, (ἐπέχω) *one must refrain*, Pl.*Phdr.*272a. II. *one must check*, ἱδρῶτας ῥυπισμοῖς (leg. ῥιπ.) Herod.Med.in *Rh.Mus.*58.100. **-σχετικός**, ή, όν, *checking, stopping*, τῆς κοιλίας Erasistr.ap.Ath.15.666a; γαστρός Gal. 6.523; ἐπισχετικὸν ὁ πταρμός Hsch. s. v. ἐπιπτάρνυμαι.

ἐπισχετλιάζω, *lament over*, Sch.Il.16.686.

ἐπισχημᾰτίζω, *make up*, τὸ πρόσωπον εἰς λύπην J.*BJ*2.2.5.

ἐπι-σχίζω, *cleave at top*, ἄρουραν A.R.2.662; τὸν φλοιόν Str.16.2. 41; *split* the end of a bandage, Sor.*Fasc.*12.514 C., cf. 510 C.:—Pass., Dsc.3.147. **-σχισμα**, ατος, τό, *torn piece, rag*, *EM*555.38 (pl.).

ἐπισχύω, (ἰσχύς) *make strong* or *powerful*, τὴν πόλιν X.*Oec.*11. 13. II. intr., *to be* or *grow strong*, Thphr.*CP*2.1.4; *prevail*, D.S. 5.59, Corn.*ND*7; *to be urgent*, ἐπίσχυον λέγοντες *Ev.Luc.*23.5; ὁ λόγος -ύσει πρὸς συμβουλίαν ἢ διδαχήν Vett.Val.48.6.

ἐπίσχω, redupl. pres. of ἐπέχω, *hold* or *direct towards*, ἐπίσχειν ὠκέας ἵππους Il.17.465; νῶϊν against us, Hes.*Sc.*350; [σελάννα] φάος ἐπίσχει θάλασσαν ἐπ' ἀλμύραν Sapph.*Supp.*25.9. II. *restrain, keep in check*, ἔπισχε μένος Hes.*Sc.*446; τόδε γε [τὸ δέος] οὐδὲν ἐπίσχει Th.3.45, cf. Pl.*Lg.*932e, *Phlb.*45d; τὸ ἐπίσχον *obstruction*, Arist.*Cael.* 311a9: c. gen., ἐπίσχετε θυμὸν ἐνιπῆς καὶ χειρῶν Od.20.266; τινὰ τοῦ θράσους Pl.*Hp.Ma.*298a:—Med., ἐπισχόμεναι ἑανῶν πτύχας *girding up*, *h.Cer.*176; ἐπίσχετ' ὀργῇ χεῖρας Euphro 8.3 (dub.):—Pass., *to be stopped*, ἐπίσχεται τὸ τῆς κοιλίας Thphr.*Sud.*20. III. intr., *leave off, stop, wait*, ἔπισχε *hold!* E.*El.*758. 2. c. gen., *cease from*, τοῦ γράφειν Pl.*Phdr.*257c, cf. *Prm.*152b.

ἐπισωμᾰτ-όομαι, Pass., *to be condensed into a mass*, Dsc.5. 74. **-ος**, ον, = ἐπίσωμος, in Comp., Id.2.146. **-ωσις**, εως, ἡ, *condensation into a mass*, Zos.Alch.p.107 B.

ἐπίσωμος, ον, (σῶμα) *bulky, fat*, *Hippiatr.*9.

ἐπισωρ-εία, ἡ, *heaping up*, Nicom.*Ar.*2.15. **-ευμα**, ατος, τό, *heap*, *Gramm.Lat.*4.581 K., *Gloss.* **-ευσις**, εως, ἡ, = ἐπισωρεία, Gal. 17(2).413, Sch.Opp.*H.*1.116. **-εύω**, *heap upon*, τινί τι Ath.3. 123e; *heap up, accumulate*, διδασκάλους 2*Ep.Ti.*4.3; ἓν ἐξ ἑνός Arr. *Epict.*1.10.5; ἀμηχανίας Plu.2.830a:—Pass., Id. *in Hes.*34, Vett.Val. 344.12.

ἐπίσωτρον, Poll.1.144, Hsch., Ep. **ἐπίσσωτρον** (as always in Hom.), τό, *metal hoop upon the felloe* (σῶτρον), *tire* of a wheel, Il.23. 519: mostly in pl., 5.725, 11.537, al.:—ὀπίσσωτρον is v.l. in Hom. and Hsch.

ἐπι-τᾰγή, ἡ, (ἐπιτάσσω) = -ταγμα, Plb.13.4.3, Lxx 1*Es.*1.18; νόμων ἐπιταγαί D.S.1.70; τὰς ἐ. δυσχερῶς φέροντες Plb.21.6.1; *imposition* of taxes, αἱ ἐ. τῶν εἰσφορῶν D.H.4.19. 2. esp. of oracles or divine commands, κατ' ἐπιταγήν *SIG*1153 (Athens); κατ' ἐ. τοῦ θεοῦ *JHS*26.28, etc.; κατ' ἐ. τοῦ αἰωνίου θεοῦ *Ep.Rom.*16.26, cf. 1*Ep. Cor.*7.6. **-τᾰγίδιον**, τό, *little commission*, *POxy.*2156.16 (iv/v A.D.). **-ταγμα**, ατος, τό, *injunction, command*, *SIG*22.6 (pl., Epist. Darei), etc.; τὸ ὑπὸ τοῦ νόμου ἐ. Pl.*R.*359a; ἐ. ἐπιτάξαι Aeschin.1.3; ἐξ ἐπιταγμάτων And.3.11; ἐξ ἐπιτάγματος D.19.185; κατ' ἐπίταγμα, = κατ' ἐπιταγήν (cf. ἐπιταγή 2), *IG*3.163, 209; τυραννικὸν ἐ. Pl.*Lg.* 722e, cf. Hyp.*Dem.Fr.*5, Arist.*Pol.*1292a20; τὰ ἐ. the *orders* or *demands* of a courtesan, D.59.29. 2. *condition of a treaty*, Plb. 1.31.5. 3. Math., ποιεῖν τὸ ἐ. satisfy the *required conditions*, Archim.*Sph.Cyl.*1.2, al. b. *problem*, τά τε θεωρήματα καὶ τὰ ἐ. χρείαν ἔχοντα εἰς.. Id.*Con.Sph.Praef.*; *subdivision of a problem*, Papp.644.9, etc. 4. *tribute*, Lyd.*Mens.*3.23 (pl.). II. *reserve* or *subsidiary force*, Plb.5.53.5, Plu.*Pomp.*69. 2. *detachment of* 8,192 ψιλοί, = *two* στίφη, Ascl.*Tact.*6.3, etc. b. *detachment of* 4,096 *cavalry*, = *two* τέλη, ib.7.11, etc., cf. *PGrenf.*1.18.6 (ii B.C.). **-ταγματικός**, ή, όν, *subsidiary*, of the pronoun αὐτός, A.D.*Pron.*45.12, *Synt.* 194.8, cf. Arc.144.7.

ἐπιτάδε, sts. in Mss. for ἐπὶ τάδε, opp. ἐπέκεινα, as Epicur.*Ep.*1 p.17 U.

ἐπιτᾱδεοτρώκτας, α, ὁ, (Dor. for ἐπιτηδ–) *one who eats only what is necessary*, Cerc.4.15.

ἐπί-τᾱδες, Dor. for ἐπίτηδες. **-τάδιος**· ἐραστής, Hsch. **-τάδουμα**, v. ἐπιτήδευμα.

ἐπιταινίδιος, ον, *belonging to a ταινία*, in neut. pl., $SIG^2$588.188 (Delos, ii B. C.).

ἐπιτακ-τέον, *one must enjoin*, Procl. *in Ti.*1.35 D. **–τήρ**, ῆρος, ὁ, = sq., X.*Cyr.*2.3.4. **–της**, ου, ὁ, *commander*, *Gp.*17.2.4: used to transl. Lat. *Imperiosus*, the surname of Manlius Torquatus, Plu. 2.308e. **–τικός**, ή, όν, *commanding, authoritative*, Arist.*EN*1143^{a}8; ἡ ἐ. τέχνη the art or faculty *of command*, Pl.*Plt.*260c sq.; so τὸ ἐ. μέρος ib.b. Adv. –κῶς D.S.15.40. **–τος**, ον, *enjoined, prescribed*, μέτρον Pi.*P.*4.236; of the labours of Heracles, Call.*Fr.*7.38 P. 2. ἐπίτακτα, τά, *injunctions, orders*, *IG*5(1).1432 (Messene, i B.C./i A.D.). II. *drawn up behind*, οἱ ἐ. *the reserve* of an army, Th.6. 67; ἐ. σπεῖραι Plu.*Sull.*17. **–τωρ**, ορος, ὁ, gloss on σημάντωρ, Hsch., Suid.

ἐπιτᾰλαιπωρέω, *suffer* or *labour at*, Th.1.123; πρὸς πολιτικοῖς Pl. *R.*540b; ἔργοις J.*AJ*17.13.3. 2. *labour yet further*, D.H.9.35.

ἐπιτᾰλάριος [ᾰρ], ον, *with a basket*, Ἀφροδίτη Plu.2.323a.

ἐπίταλον· πολυχρόνιον, Hsch.

ἐπίτᾰμα, ατος, τό, (ἐπιτείνω) *extension*, Plu.2.457c.

ἐπιτάμνω, Ion. for ἐπιτέμνω.

ἐπιτανύω, = ἐπιτείνω, *stretch*, Hp.*Art.*14; *spread over*, Ζεὺς ἐπὶ νύκτ' ὀλοὴν τάνυσε.. ὑσμίνῃ Il.16.567. 2. *stretch tight*, οὔτοι πόλλ' ἐπὶ τόξα τανύσσεται (fut. Med. in pass. sense) Archil.3; *push home* [a bolt], ἐπὶ δὲ κληῗδ' ἐτάνυσσεν ἱμάντι Od.1.442.

ἐπιτάξ, Adv., (ἐπιτάσσω) *in a row*, Arat.380. II. = συντόμως, *Com.Adesp.*1296; *forthwith, straightway*, cj. in E.*Fr.*292.2. III. *by command* or *pre-arrangement*, Call.*Aet.*1.1.9, dub. in *Iamb.*1.239. (Cf. ἐπιπάξ.)

ἐπιταξίδια (–ίδις cod.)· σιδηραῖ τινες, ὡς ἄγκυραι, Hsch.

ἐπίταξις, εως, ἡ, *injunction*, ἡ ἐ. τοῦ φόρου *the assessment* of the tribute, Hdt.3.89: pl., *assessments*, ib.97: *a command, order*, Pl.*Lg.* 834d (pl.); κατὰ τὴν τῆς αὑτοῦ ψυχῆς ἐ. ib.687c; κατὰ τὰν ἐ. τῶ Ἀπόλλωνος *Abh.Berl.Akad.*1925(5).21 (Cyrene). 2. *command*, ἄρχοντος ἔργον ἐ. Arist.*Pol.*1326^{b}14, cf. 1325^{a}26; κατ' ἐπίταξιν *imperatively*, Id.*Po.*1457^{a}22. 3. in Tactics, *station on the flanks*, opp. πρόταξις, ὑπόταξις, Ascl.*Tact.*10.1, cf. Ael.*Tact.*24.3.

ἐπιτάπεινος [ᾰ], ον, f.l. in Antyll.ap.Orib.9.14.2.

ἐπιτάρ-αξις [τᾰ], εως, ἡ, *bewilderment, confusion*, Pl.*R.*518a (pl.). **–άσσω**, Att. –ττω, *trouble* or *disquiet yet more*, Hdt.2.139; ἡ κοιλίη ἐπεταράχθη Hp.*Epid.*1.15; πάθει τοὺς λογισμοὺς ἐπιταραττόμενος Plu. 2.788e; ᾄδων ἐ. τὰς οἰμωγάς Luc.*DMort.*2.1:—Pass., *to be disarranged*, Sor.1.38. **–ᾰχος**, ον, *liable to disturbance, easily alarmed*, Vett.Val.38.21.

ἐπιτάρροθος, ὁ, Ep. for ἐπίρροθος, *helper, defender*, in Hom. always of the gods that help in fight, τινί Il.11.366, Od.24.182; μάχης ἐ. *in* fight, Il.17.339; Δαναοῖσι μάχης ἐπιτάρροθοι 12.180; γράμμα δίκης ἐπιτάρροθον Maiist.59: as fem., τοίη οἱ ἐγὼν ἐπιτάρροθος ἦα Il.5.808, cf. 828; Δίκα.. καλῶν ἐ. ἔργων Terp.6. 2. *master, lord*, Τεγέης Orac.ap.Hdt.1.67; cf. τάρροθος.

ἐπίταρχον· ἐπιτάφιον, Hsch.

ἐπίτᾰσις, εως, ἡ, (ἐπιτείνω) *stretching*, [νεύρων] Hp.*Art.*8 (pl.); δέρματος Thphr.*Fr.*172.2; ἐ. καὶ ἄνεσις τῶν χορδῶν *tightening* and slackening, Pl.*R.*349e, cf. Plu.2.99c. 2. *discharge, fire* of artillery, Ph.*Bel.*79.26 (pl.); ἐ. τῶν καταπελτῶν App.*Pun.*93 (pl.). 3. *increase in intensity* or *force*, opp. ἄνεσις, Arist.*Cael.*288^{a}19, al.; ἐπιτάσιες πυρετῶν, opp. ἀνέσιες, Hp.*Acut.*(*Sp.*)54; χειμῶνος Thphr.*Sign.* 43; ὄμβρων Plb.4.39.9 (pl.); πόνων Thphr.*Sud.*11, cf. Plu.2.732c sq.; ἐ. εἴς τι λαμβάνειν Porph.*Sent.*32; of style, *intensity*, opp. ἄνεσις, Phld.*Rh.*1.198 S., D.H.*Isoc.*13; *exaggeration*, Longin.38.6; *emphasis*, Hdn.*Fig.*p.91 S.; in Gramm., ἐπιρρήματα ἐπιτάσεως, e.g. λίαν, σφόδρα, D.T.642.13, cf. A.D.*Conj.*223.4. 4. *presence of pitch accent*, opp. ἄνεσις, Phld.*Po.*2.18, *Po.*IVa.4(p.274 H.). 5. *vehemence, asperity*, opp. ἠπιότης, Id.*Hom.*p.33 O.; διαβολῆς Id.*Vit.*p.42 J. 6. = ἐπέκτασις (quod fort. leg.), *Theol.Ar.*55.

ἐπιτάσσω, Att. –ττω, *put upon* one *as a duty, enjoin*, τι Hdt.5.111, S.*OC*839, etc.; τί τινι, as ἐ. ἄεθλόν τινι Hdt.4.43, cf. 1.155; ἐπέταξε πόνους ἄλλοισιν ἄλλους B.*Fr.*9; ἐπιτάξαντος τᾷ πόλει Γαλλίου σῖτον καὶ Ἀνχαρίου ἱμάτια *SIG*748.25 (i B. C.): c. dat. pers. et inf., *order* one *to* do, ἐ. τοῖσι μὲν πεζὸν στρατὸν.. παρέχειν Hdt.4.83, cf. 3.159, Ar.*V.* 69, And.3.11, etc.: rarely c. acc. et inf., *enjoin* or *order that*.., X.*Lac.* 5.8; with the case omitted, ἐ. ἀποφορὴν ἐπιτελέειν Hdt.2.109, cf. 137: abs., *impose commands*, Th.1.140, al.; τινί on one, S.*Ant.*664:— Pass., *accept orders, submit to commands*, εἰ 'πιταξόμεσθα δή E.*Supp.* 521; ἐπιταττόμενος Ar.*V.*686: c. inf., οἱ ἐπιταττόμενοι γαμεῖν Pl.*Lg.* 925e: c. acc. rei, ἄλλο τι ἐπιταχθήσεσθε Th.1.140; of things, *to be ordered*, ὁ στρατὸς ὁ –θεὶς ἑκάστοισι Hdt.6.95; so Λακεδαιμονίοις.. ναῦς ἐπετάχθησαν ποιεῖσθαι Th.2.7 s.v.l.; τὰ ἐπιτασσόμενα ἐπετέλεον *orders given*, Hdt.1.115; τἀπιταχθέντα Pl.*Ti.*20b, al.; κατὰ νόμον τὸν ἐπιταχθησόμενον Id.*Lg.*740c; δικαίωσις τοῖς πέλας –ομένη *dictated*, Th.1. 141: Math., τὸ ἐπιταχθέν what was *prescribed*, Euc.4.1, al.; πλευρὰς ἔχον ὅσας ἄν τις ἐπιτάξῃ with as many sides as you *please*, Papp.290. 26. 2. *use the imperative mood*, εὔχεσθαι οἰόμενος ἐπιτάττει εἰπὼν "μῆνιν ἄειδε θεά".. τὸ γὰρ κελεῦσαι, φησί,.. ἐπίταξίς ἐστιν Arist.*Po.* 1456^{b}16; opp. κελεύειν, $IG1^2$.76.33. II. *place next* or *beside*, [Σαγάρτιοι] ἐπετετάχατο ἐς τοὺς Πέρσας Hdt.7.85; ἐπέτακτο Ἀριστοκράτει Περικλῆς X.*HG*1.6.29:—Med., τοὺς ἱππέας ἐπετάξαντο ἐπὶ τῷ δεξιῷ they *had* the cavalry *placed next*, Th.6.67. 2. *place behind*, ὄπισθεν τοῦ πεζοῦ τὴν ἵππον Hdt.1.80, cf. Pl.*R.*471d (Pass.):—Med., ἐπιτάξασθαι τῇ φάλαγγι λόχους X.*An.*6.5.9:—Pass., τοῖσι μυρίοισι ἐπετέτακτο ἵππος Περσέων μυρίη Hdt.7.41, cf. Plu.*Luc.*31, Ael.*Tact.* 29.8, Arr.*Tact.*25.10; Ἀράβιοι ἔσχατοι ἐπετετάχατο Hdt.7.87. b. Gramm., *place after*, in Pass., "αὐτὸς" πάσῃ ἀντωνυμίᾳ –τάσσεται A.D.*Pron.*34.10, cf. *Synt.*138.23. 3. *set in command over*, τινί Arr.*An.*1.24.1:—Pass., οἱ ἐπιτεταγμένοι *set as guards over* the wagons, Th.5.72; ταῖς βασιλικαῖς ἐπιστολαῖς –ταχθείς Philostr.*VS*2. 24.1, cf. Jul.*Or.*2.63d.

ἐπιτᾰτικός, ή, όν, (ἐπιτείνω) *intensive*, τὸ "δα–" ἐ. Sch.Theoc.2.14; of μᾶλλον, A.D.*Conj.*223.4. Adv. –κῶς Sch.S.*OC*632: Comp. –ώτερον Vett.Val.117.36.

ἐπίταυρον· ἰσχυρόν, Hsch. (Prob. ἐπίγαυρον, q. v.)

ἐπιτᾰφ-έω, *to be present at a funeral*, *SIG*1109.161. **–ιος**, ον, (τάφος) *over* or *at a tomb*, ἀγὼν ἐ. *funeral* games, Arist.*Ath.*58.1, D.S.17.117; ἐπιτάφιον (sc. ἀγῶνα) ἀγωνίσασθαι *IG*5(1).660, Plu. *Pyrrh.*31, Luc.*Eun.*4; esp. ἐ. λόγος a *funeral* oration, such as was spoken at Athens over the citizens who had fallen in battle, Pl.*Mx.* 236b, D.20.141 (pl.); also ὁ ἐ. (sc. λόγος) Arist.*Rh.*1365^{a}31; title of work by Gorgias; applied to Pl.*Mx.* by D.H.*Comp.*9; ἐ. ἔπαινος Plu.2.218a; ἐ. σοφιστής, of one *who makes such speeches*, Ach.Tat.3. 25. II. ἐπιτάφια, τά, = ἐπιτάφιος ἀγών, $IG2^2$.1006.22, 12(5).946. 16 (Tenos).

ἐπιτᾰχ-ύνω, *hasten on, urge forward*, τινὰ τῆς ὁδοῦ Th.4.47; τὸν πόλεμον, τὴν ὁδόν, Plu.*Per.*29, Hdn.2.11.1; τὴν φράσιν *making* it *rapid*, Plu.2.1011e; τὴν σύνθεσιν D.H.*Comp.*20; τῇ Ἑλλάδι τὴν πεπρωμένην Paus.8.51.4:—Pass., ὑπὸ μαστίγων –όμενος Plu.*Ant.* 68. **–υσις**, εως, ἡ, *hurrying on*, Diotog.ap.Stob.4.7.62.

ἐπιτέγγω, *pour liquid upon, moisten*, τί τινι Hp.*Fract.*29, cf. Gal. *UP*14.11, al.; τοὺς ὀφθαλμοὺς δακρύοις Philostr.*VS*2.5.3; ἐ. καὶ μαλάττει Gal.6.122; = ἐπιστάζω, νέκταρ *Anacreont.*53.41.

ἐπιτέγειος, ον, *on the roof*, Eust.878.37.

ἐπιτέγιος, ον, as pr. name, Ἥρως Ἐ. $IG1^2$.310.82, 3.290.

ἐπίτεγκτος, ον, of applications, *capable of being kept moist*, Hp. *Art.*67, Gal.18(1).712.

ἐπίτεγξις, εως, ἡ, *fomentation, embrocation*, Hp.*Fract.*29. II. *moistening*, Id.*Loc.Hom.*17, Gal.10.442; *moisture, humidity*, interpol. in Sor.2.84 (= Aët.16.71).

ἐπιτεθειασμένως, Adv. pf. Pass., *enthusiastically*, Poll.1.16.

ἐπιτείνω, Ion. iterat. ἐπιτείνεσκον Hdt.1.186: pf. –τέτακα *PTeb.* 19.6 (ii B.C.):—*stretch upon* or *over*, ξύλα ἐπὶ τὴν γέφυραν Hdt. l. c.; ὑπὲρ [τάφρης] Id.4.201:—Hom. only in Pass., ἐπὶ νὺξ ὀλοὴ τέταται δειλοῖσι βροτοῖσι Od.11.19; ἐπὶ πτόλεμος τέτατό σφιν Il.17.736. 2. *stretch as on a frame, tighten, screw up*, esp. of musical strings, ἐ. τὰς χορδάς Pl.*Ly.*209b; ὥσπερ λύραν ἐ. ἕως ἂν ἁρμόσῃ Macho 2.9:— Pass., χορδαὶ –όμεναι Arist.*Pr.*920^{b}3, cf. *GA*787^{b}13, Pl.*Phd.*98c. b. of sounds, *raise* them *to a higher pitch*, ἐ. τὸν φθόγγον καὶ ὀξὺ φθέγγεσθαι Arist.*Phgn.*807^{a}15, cf. 806^{b}27 (Pass.); of pitch accent, Phld.*Po.* 2.18 (Pass.). c. metaph., *increase in intensity, augment, heighten*, ἡδονάς Pl.*Lg.*645d; τὰ τιμήματα ἐ. ἢ ἀνιέναι Arist.*Pol.*1308^{b}4; τὰ [τῆς ψυχῆς] γυμνάσια Pl.*R.*498b; ἐ. [τὴν πολιτείαν] Arist.*Pol.*1309^b 33, cf. 1301^{b}17 (Pass.), *Rh.*1360^{a}25 (Pass.); ἐ. τὴν κρᾶσιν *make* it *stronger*, Plu.2.677f; *heighten* by contrast, τὰ φωτεινὰ καὶ λαμπρὰ τοῖς σκιεροῖς καὶ σκοτεινοῖς ἐ., of painters, ib.57c; τῇ γλυκύτητι τοῦ νουθετοῦντος ἐ. τὸ πικρὸν.. τῆς νουθεσίας ib.67b: abs., *exert oneself greatly*, D.56.13, Arist.*EN*1138^{b}23; *strain matters to an extreme*, Id. *Pol.*1293^{a}26:—Pass., εἰ ἐπιτείνοιντο δυσκατάποτοι if their difficulty in swallowing *increases*, Archig.ap.Gal.12.976; so in pf. part. Pass., *intensified*, ταραχή Epicur.*Ep.*1 p.30 U.; ἐπιτίμησις Phld.*Ir.*p.72 W.: impers., ἐπιτείνεται *increase arises*, Arist.*Cael.*289^{a}3. d. intr., *increase*, of fevers, Hp.*Coac.*114; ἐπέτεινε ὁ λιμός Plu.*Cam.*28; of motion, Arist.*Ph.*238^{a}5. e. intr., *rise*, of price, *PTeb.*8.17 (iii B.C.). 3. *urge on, incite*, τινὰ ποιεῖν τι X.*Eq.Mag.*1.13; τινὰ ἵνα.. *PFay.*112.5 (i A.D.); ἐ. ἑαυτόν *exert* himself, Plu.*Alex.*40. 4. *expedite*, τὰ πράγματα *PTeb.*19.6 (ii B.C.). II. Pass., *suffer more intensely*, τῷ πυρετῷ Hp.*Epid.*5.50; simply, *to be tormented, racked*, ὑπὸ νόσων Pl.*Phd.*86c: then generally, *to be tortured*, ζηλοτυπῶν Luc. *DMeretr.*9.4. 2. *to be on the stretch, screwed up to the uttermost*, αἱ τιμαὶ ἐπετέταντο prices *were* '*screwed up*', D.56.24, cf. Men.Eph. ap.J.*AJ*9.14.2; πολλαπλασίως ταῖς εὐνοίαις ἐπιταθέντες Plb.18.16. 3. 3. ἐ. τινί *to be passionately devoted to*, Parth.23.1; also of things, ἐ. [βιβλίοις] Luc.*Ind.*27; εἴς τι D.S.1.37. 4. *hold out, last, endure*, ἐπιταθῆναι πλείω χρόνον, of men, X.*Lac.*2.5, cf. Thphr. *HP*7.10.3.

ἐπιτειχ-ίζω, *build a fort* or *stronghold on the frontier* of the enemy's country to serve as the basis of operations *against* him, abs., Th.1. 142, 7.47; ἐ. [Δεκέλειαν] τῇ πατρίδι And.1.101, cf. Lys.14.30, Plu.*Alc.* 23; ἐ. [ἐν add. codd.] τῷ Φλιοῦντι τὸ.. Τρικάρανον X.*HG*7.2.1, cf. 5.1.2; and in Pass., Δεκελείας ἐπιτετειχισμένης Aeschin.2.76: metaph., ἐ. τυράννους ἐν χώρᾳ *plant* them *like such forts* in a country, D.10.8, cf. 8.36; so τῷ πλούτῳ τὴν ὑπεροψίαν ἐ. Luc.*Nigr.*23; ἐ. [τινὰ] τῇ συνωμοσίᾳ.. πολέμιον Plu.*Brut.*20. **–ισις**, εως, ἡ, *building a fort on the enemy's frontier*, Th.1.142; ἐ. Δεκελείας Id.6.93. **–ισμα**, ατος, τό, *fort* or *stronghold placed on the enemy's frontier*, v.l. in Id.8.95, cf. X.*HG*5.1.2; τινί or ἐπί τινα *against* one, κατασκευάζειν ὑμῖν ἐ. τὴν Εὔβοιαν D.8.66; ἐπὶ τὴν Ἀττικήν Id.18.71; κατὰ τῆς πόλεως D.H.3. 43: c. gen., ἔχουσι τοσαῦτ' ἐ. τῆς αὑτοῦ χώρας holding so many *fortresses which command* his country, D.4.5. 2. metaph., τῆς αὐτῆς ἀρχῆς ἐ. πρὸς τὸ μηδ' ὁτιοῦν παρακινεῖν *a barrier* or *obstacle to*.., Id.15.12; ὥσπερ ἐ. τοῖς υἱοῖς κατάγει τὸν Ἀντίπατρον J.*BJ*1.23.1; τὴν φιλοσοφίαν ἐ. τῶν νόμων *a barrier against*, or *a bulwark in defence of*, the laws, Alcid.ap.Arist.*Rh.*1406^{b}11; ἐ. τῶν ἀνθρωπίνων παθῶν ἡ ποιητικὴ καθέστηκεν S.E.*M*.1.298. **-ισμός**, ὁ, = -ισις, Th.7.18, X.*HG*5.1.2; τῇ χώρᾳ *against* it, Th.1.122: metaph., ἕτερον κατὰ τῆς πόλεως ἐ. ἐζήτει D.18.87. **-ος**, εος, τό, *wall upon a wall*, Eust.969.5.

ἐπιτεκμαίρομαι, *detect* a star *by means of*, ζώνῃ Arat.229; so κείνων (v.l. κείνους) ἧχι κέονται Id.457; *predict*, c. gen., νιφετοῦ Id. 1038, cf. 1129(tm.); *infer, conjecture*, ἐ. οἷος.. Id.142.

ἐπίτεκν-ος, ον, *capable of bearing children, fruitful*, Hp.*Aph*.5.62. **-όω**, *beget afterwards*, J.*AJ*6.5.6.

ἐπιτεκτ-αίνομαι, *devise against*, δόλον Opp.*C*.3.405. **-αντῆρες**· οἱ παρασκευασταί, Hsch.

ἐπιτέλ-εια, ἡ, *oversight, command*, prob. f.l. for -μέλεια, Polyaen. 6.9.3(pl.). II. *fulfilment*, ἐπιτέλειαν ὁ θεὸς ποιήσει τῶν ἀξιουμένων Aristeas 18; καλῶν ἔργων Id.272. **-ειος**, α, ον, *bringing to fulfilment*, epith. of Aphrodite, *BCH*49.79 (Delph.); of Zeus, *SIG*961 note 2 (iv B.C.). **-ειόω**, *complete*, esp. a sacrifice, Lycurg.*Fr*.36 (-λεοῦν codd.); τὴν θυσίαν Plu.*Mar*.22; cf. ἐπιτελέωμα. **-είωσις**, εως, ἡ, *after-offering*, esp. in thanksgiving for the birth of a child, Pl.*Lg*.784d. II. *accomplishment, completion*, τῆς εὐχῆς Plu.*Num*. 14, cf. 2.961c; ἐ. τῆς πολιτείας, of the Censorship at Rome, Id.*Cat.Ma*.16, *Flam*.18. **-εσις**, εως, ἡ, *completion*, τοῦ σώματος Arist.*Pr*.894^{a}35; θεωριῶν M.Ant.1.16. **-εσμα**, ατος, τό, *that which is completed*, Poll.6.181. **-εστέον**, *one must accomplish*, Isoc.12.37. **-εστής**, οῦ, ὁ, *accomplisher*, Sch.Lyc.305. **-εστικός**, ή, όν, *capable of effecting one's purpose*, Arist.*Phgn*.813^{b}21, cf. Chrysipp.*Stoic*.3.123; *for fulfilment*, ἐ. τῶν εὐχῶν θυσία Hsch. s.v. τελήεσσας: Sup., Sch.Il.8.247. II. *capable of celebrating*, μυστηρίων Ptol.*Tetr*.72. **-ευτή**, ἡ, *death*, *Princeton Exp.Inscr*.787[10]. **-έω**, fut. -τελῶ *SIG*229.17 (Erythrae, iv B.C.), Dor. 3 pl. fut. -τελεσσεῦντι *Annuario* 4/5.225.27 (Rhodes, ii B.C.), 3 pl. pf. -τετελέκαντι *SIG*1158.3 (Delph., iii B.C.):—*complete, finish, accomplish*, ἐ. τὰ ἐπιτασσόμενα Hdt.1.115, cf. 51, 90; τὰς ἐντολάς ib.157; τὸν προκείμενον ἄεθλον ib. 126; ἀποδείξιας Archyt.4; ἐ. ἔργῳ ἃ ἂν γνῶσιν Th.1.70; ταῦτα τοῖς ἔργοις ἐ. Isoc.2.38; πόλεμον Plb.1.65.2; esp. of *the fulfilment* of oracles, visions, etc., Hdt.1.13 (Pass.), al.; εὐχήν ib.86; ἃ ὑπέσχετο Th.1.138:—Med., τὴν κρίσιν ἐπιτελέσασθαι *get* it *completed*, Pl.*Phlb*.27c; καλὴν καὶ σεμνὴν πρᾶξιν -τετελεσμένος Plb.15.22.1:—Pass., ὅπως ἂν ἡ εἰρήνη ἐπιτελεσθῇ that it *may be brought to pass*, Decr.ap.D.18.29; of movements, Hero *Aut*.19.5; [παθήματα] τῇ ἀδελφότητι ἐ. 1*Ep.Pet*.5.9. 2. *bring to perfection*, τὴν γένεσιν Arist.*GA*741^{b}5, cf. *HA*539^{a}33:—Pass., Id.*GA*758^{b}26. 3. Pass. in Logic, of a syllogism, *to be made perfect*, by reduction to the first figure, Id.*APr*.28^{a}5, 41^{b}4. II. *discharge* a religious duty, θυσίας Hdt.2.63, Thphr. ap.Porph.*Abst*.2.16, *Inscr.Prien*.108.27 (ii B.C.); τὰ νομιζόμενα τοῖς θεοῖς *PAmh*.2.35.50 (ii B.C.); νηστείας καὶ ὁρτάς Hdt.4.186; λατρείας *Ep.Hebr*.9.6 (so in Med., εὐωχίαν ἐπετελέσατο *Inscr.Prien*.113.61 (i B.C.)): abs., *sacrifice*, τινί Ael.*VH*12.61. 2. *celebrate*, τὴν τοῦ Κυνὸς ἐ. ἐπιτολήν Olymp.*in Mete*.113.14. III. *pay in full*, ἀποφορήν Hdt. 2.109; πεντακόσια τάλαντα βασιλέϊ τὸν ἐπέτειον φόρον Id.5.49, cf. 82, 84; ἐπιμήνια Id.8.41: metaph. in Med., ἐπιτελεῖσθαι τὰ τοῦ γήρως *to have to pay, be subject to*, the burdens of old age, X.*Mem*.4.8.8; ἐ. θάνατον *have to pay the debt of* death, Id.*Ap*.33:—Pass., ἡ δίκη.. τοῦ φόνου..ἐκ Μαρδονίου ἐπετελέετο *was paid in full* by.., Hdt.9.64. IV. *impose upon*, ἀσεβείας δίκην τινί Pl.*Lg*.910d. **-έωμα**, ατος, τό, *something offered besides the usual sacrifice*, Lycurg.*Fr*.36. **-ής**, ές, (τέλος) *brought to an end, completed, accomplished*, ποιεῖν τι ἐπιτελές, = ἐπιτελεῖν, Hdt.1.117, 3.141, Hp.*Jusj*., etc.; ἐπιτελῆ ποιῆσαι ἐντολάν τινος *Test.Epict*.1.18; ἐ. ἐγίνετό τι Hdt.1.124, Th.1.141; εὐχαὶ ἐ. γενόμεναι Pl.*Lg*.931e, cf. *SIG*581.5 (ii B.C.); κρίσιν λαμβάνει ὁ πόλεμος ἐπιτελῆ D.H.10.46; of persons, *adult*, Hsch. Ion. Adv. -έως *at last*, Aret.*SA*2.8. II. Act., *effective*, Ant.Lib. 19.3. III. *subject to taxation*, ἔλαιον ἐ. τελῶν *Milet*.3.149.19 (ii B.C.). **-ίζω**, = ἐπιτελέω, in Pass., -ισμένας ἑορτάς *IGRom*.4.1272 (Thyatira).

ἐπιτέλλω (A), aor. ἐπέτειλα:—Med., aor. ἐπετειλάμην A.R.3.264:—Pass., 3 sg. plpf. ἐπὶ.. ἐτέταλτο Il.2.643:—*enjoin, prescribe, command*, Hom., etc.—Constr.: c. dat. pers. et acc. rei, ἀλόχῳ δ' ἐπὶ μῦθον ἔτελλεν *spake* a speech of *command* to her, Od.23.349: c. acc. rei only, κρατερὸν δ' ἐπὶ μῦθον ἔτελλε Il.1.25, etc.; μῦθον.. ὃν Νέστωρ ἐπέτελλε 11.840; ἐλήθετο συνθεσιάων ἃς ἐπέτελλε.. Διομήδης which he *enjoined, prescribed*, 5.320; ἐφετμέων ἃς ἐπέτειλας ib.818; [ἀέθλους] Hes.*Th*.995; so θάνατον ἐπιτέλλειν Pi.*N*.10.77; ἐ. μόχθων τέρματα *fix* them, A.*Pr*.100 (where others take it intr. *arise, appear*): c. dat. pers. only, *give orders to*, ἐπὴν εὖ τοῖς ἐπιτείλω Il.10.63, 13.753, etc.: and so abs., ὁ δὲ σημαίνων ἐπέτελλεν 21.445: c. dat. pers. et inf., *order* him to do, 12.84, 21.230; so πέμπων μ' ὧδ' ἐπέτελλε (sc. ποιεῖν) 24.780, cf. 11.765, Od.17.9:—Med., just like Act., ἄλλοισιν δὴ ταῦτ' ἐπιτέλλεο Il.1.295; [νόστον Ἀχαιῶν] ἐπετείλατο Παλλὰς Od.1.327; ὅ δέ μοι χαλεποὺς ἐπετέλλετ' ἀέθλους 11.622; κραδίῃ ἀνίας A.R. 3.264: c. dat. pers. et inf., Od.21.240: abs., 17.21; ἁγητὴρ υἱῷ ἐπιτελλόμενος Pi.*P*.1.70:—Pass., τῷ δ' ἐπὶ πάντ' ἐτέταλτο ἀνασσέμεν Αἰτωλοῖσι Il.2.643, cf. Od.11.524.—Poet. and later Prose, *BGU*886.2 (Med., ii A.D.), *PThead*.18.4 (iii/iv A.D.).

ἐπιτέλλω (B), Pass., *rise*, of stars, Πληϊάδων.. ἐπιτελλομενάων Hes.*Op*.383; Ἀρκτοῦρος.. ἐπιτέλλεται ib.567; ἠελίοιο νέον -ομένοιο *h.Merc*.371: so intr. in Act., Hp.*Int*.39, Democr.14, Arist.*Mete*.345^{b}23, Plb. 9.15.9, etc.: the aor. part. ἐπιπλόμενος belongs as much to this verb as to ἐπιπέλομαι (q.v.). 2. metaph. of love, ὡραῖος καὶ Ἔρως ἐπιτέλλεται Thgn.1275. (Hence ἐπιπολή and (later) ἐπιτολή.)

ἐπιτελουμένως, Adv. *decisively*, *PMag.Par*.1.2638 (s.v.l.).

ἐπιτέμνω, Ion. -τάμνω, fut. -τεμῶ Antyll. (v. infr.): aor. ἐπέτᾰμον:—*cut upon the surface, make an incision into, gash*, τὸ ἔσω τῶν χειρῶν Hdt.3.8, cf. 4.70; κατὰ μῆκος τὰς σάρκας Id.6.75; φλέβα Hp.*Aër*.22; ἐ. τὴν σαυτοῦ κεφαλήν Aeschin.2.93:—Med., ἐπεὰν ἐπιτάμωνται τοὺς βραχίονας ἐς τὴν ὁμοχροίην Hdt.1.74; κατά τι in a place, Thphr.*HP*1.8.4. 2. *make a further incision*, opp. τέμνειν, Antyll.ap.Orib. 44.23.2. II. *cut short*, τὰ λοιπὰ τῶν ἐπιχειρημάτων Arist.*SE*174^{b}29; λέγοντα ἐ. τινά Plb.28.23.3; τὰς προφάσεις Id.35.4.6, cf. 5.58.3; *prune*, Thphr.*HP*6.6.6. 2. *abridge, shorten, epitomize* a book, Plu.*Art*.11:—Med., Luc.*Pr.Im*.16:—Pass., κεφαλαιωδέστατα -τετμημένα Epicur.*Ep*.1 p.31 U., cf. Phld.*D*.3.14. 3. *cut off* the view, Man.2.115:—Pass., *to be cut short*, τὰ αὐτοσχέδια ἐ. Ph.2.582.

ἐπίτεξ, εκος, ἡ, (τεκεῖν) *at the birth, about to bring forth*, γυνὴ ἐ. ἐοῦσα Hdt.1.111, cf. Hp.*Mul*.1.34, Luc.*Merc.Cond*.34; ὄϊς *GDI*4963 (Gortyn); ἐπίτεξ, οὐκ ἐπίτοκος Thom.Mag.p.124 R.; cf. ἐπίτοκος.

ἐπιτέον, *one must traverse*, Str.2.5.34 (s.v.l.).

ἐπίτερα· ἐκπιάσματα ἐλαιῶν, Hsch.

ἐπιτερᾰτεύομαι, *heighten a marvellous story*, Paus.8.2.7.

ἐπιτέρεναι· εἶδος ἄρτων, Hsch.

ἐπιτερμᾰτίζω, in Pass., gloss on ἐπικραίνω, Sch.Pi.*O*.6.137.

ἐπι-τέρμιος, ον, (τέρμα) *at the limits*, Hsch.; esp. as epith. of Hermes, Id. **-τερμος**, ον, *adjacent*, *BGU*473.10 (ii/iii A.D.).

ἐπιτερπ-ής, ές, *pleasing, delightful*, χῶρος *h.Ap*.413; ἃ καὶ λόγῳ.. ἀκούειν οὐκ ἐπιτερπές Pl.*Phdr*.240e; ἰδεῖν Plu.*Rom*.16; τῶν πεπραγμένων ἐ. αἱ μνῆμαι Arist.*EN*1166^{a}25: Sup., τὰ -έστατα Democr.233. Adv. -πῶς, διατίθεσθαι Phld.*Mus*.p.84 K., cf. Plu.*Num*.13. II. *devoted to pleasure* (unless = *pleasant companion*), Id.*Alc*.23. **-νος**, ον, = foreg. 1, in Comp., Thgn.1066. **-ομαι**, Ep. Verb (also in later Prose, Agath.3.21), *rejoice* or *delight in*, ἄλλος ἄλλοισιν ἀνὴρ ἐπιτέρπεται ἔργοις Od.14.228, cf. Hes.*Th*.158; ἵπποις Pi.*O*.5.22; ἀγαθοῖς Thgn.1218; ἐπιτέρπεσθαι θυμόν *h.Ap*.204; Δήλῳ ἐ. ἦτορ ib. 146: c. inf., *AP*9.766 (Agath.).

ἐπιτεσσαρακοστόπεμπτος λόγος ratio *of* 46:45, Ptol.*Harm*.1.15.

ἐπιτεσσαρεσκαιδέκατος λόγος ratio *of* 15:14, Ptol.*Harm*.1.13.

ἐπιτεσσερασκαιδεκάτους τόκους (acc. pl.) interest *at* $7\frac{1}{7}$%, *SIG*364.90 (Ephesus, iii B.C.).

ἐπιτετᾰμένως, Adv., (ἐπιτείνω) *intensely*, ἐ. λευκός Dsc.5.152; θερμαίνειν Id.1.77; *vehemently*, λαλεῖν Phld.*Ir*.p.74 W.; προπίνειν Ath. 2.45d, etc.

ἐπιτέταρτος λόγος ratio *of* 4:3, Theo Sm.p.109 H., Ptol.*Harm*.1.13, Nicom.*Ar*.1.22.

ἐπιτετευγμένως, Adv., (ἐπιτυγχάνω) *successfully*, D.L.2.42, Ach. Tat.*Intr.Arat*.p.79 M.

ἐπιτετηδευμένως, Adv., (ἐπιτηδεύω) *deliberately*, D.H.*Comp*.25; κινεῖσθαι Adam.2.38.

ἐπιτετμημένως, Adv., (ἐπιτέμνω) *briefly*, '*for short*', ὀνομάζεσθαι Str.4.6.2; *succinctly*, Corn.*ND*35, Ptol.*Tetr*.107, Hld.2.32.

ἐπιτετρᾰ-έβδομος, ον, *containing one plus four-sevenths*, v.l. for τετρακισεφέβδομος, Nicom.*Ar*.1.23. **-μερής**, ές, *containing one plus four-fifths*, ib.20, al. **-πεμπτος**, ον, = foreg., ib.21.

ἐπιτετράφαται, v. ἐπιτρέπω I. 6.

ἐπιτετυχημένως, = εὐτυχῶς, Sch.rec.S.*El*.944.

ἐπί-τευγμα, ατος, τό, (ἐπιτυγχάνω) *a hit*, opp. ἀπότευγμα, Phld.*Rh*.1.67 S., al.; *success*, D.S.1.27; '*coup*', Cic.*Att*.13.27.1: pl., ποιητῶν ἀγαθῶν ἐ. D.S.15.6; τὰ περὶ ποιητικὴν ἐ. D.L.8.57; τὰ ἀπὸ τύχης ἐ. J.*BJ*3.5.6; of successful medical diagnoses, Harp.Astr. in *Cat.Cod.Astr*.8(3).137.10. 2. *natural advantage*, τὸ τῆς χώρας ἐ. Agatharch. 89; τὰ τῶν τόπων ἐ. D.S.33.28^d.3. **-τευκτικός**, ή, όν, *able to attain* or *achieve*, ἕξις ἐ. τῶν βελτίστων Arist.*MM*1199^{a}8, cf. Phld.*Vit*.p.24 J.; σύνεσις ἐ. τοῦ μετρίου D.H.*Pomp*.5, cf. Arr.*Epict*.3.12.5. Adv. -κῶς Phld.*Rh*.1.74 S. 2. abs., *successful, effective*, φάρμακον Paul.Aeg. 3.78; ζῆλος Plb.10.22.7. b. Subst. -κόν, τό, *spell, charm for securing success*, *PMag.Leid.W*.8.28 (pl.). II. *advantageous, favourable*, χώρα Plb.2.29.3 (Sup.). **-τευξις**, εως, ἡ, *hitting the mark, attainment*, εὐκαιρία χρόνου ἐ. Pl.*Def*.413c, cf. Arist.*MM*1207^{b}16, Phld.*Rh*.1.204 S. (pl.). 2. *success*, App.*Pun*.105. II. *conversation*, f.l. for ἔντευξις in Thphr.*Char*.12.1.

ἐπιτεύχω, *make* or *build for*, Ἰλίῳ μέλλοντες ἐπὶ στέφανον τεῦξαι Pi.*O*.8.32.

ἐπιτεχν-άζω, *scheme against*, τῇ βουλῇ App.*BC*3.39. II. Med., = sq., Opp.*H*.3.194. **-άομαι**, *contrive for* a purpose or *to meet* an emergency, *invent*, βουλήν Hdt.1.63; τοιόνδε ib.123, 2.2, cf. 119, 121.δ'; πάσας πείρας D.H.4.55. 2. *contrive against*, ἄλλους ἐπ' ἄλλοις πολέμους Id.6.20, cf. Luc.*Bis Acc*.1. **-ημα**, ατος, τό, *contrivance*, Ael.*NA*12.16: pl., *devices*, Ptol.*Alm*.13.2, Jul.*Or*.2.91c. **-ησις**, εως, ἡ, *contrivance for* a purpose, *invention*, Th.1.71, Arist.*Mu*.398^{b}10, Ph.1.296; τολμήματα καὶ -ήσεις παρασχέσθαι εἴς τινα Paus.1.6.6; *artifice*, in speaking, D.H.*Is*.3; *artificial preparation*, ψυχρῶν ὑδάτων Ath.3.124e, cf. Antyll.ap.Orib.10.2.2; αἱ δι' -ήσεως κομμώσεις Ath.13.568a. **-ητός**, όν (ή, όν Philum. (v. infr.)), *artificially made*, Luc.*Prom*.18, *Salt*.27; πυρίαι Philum.ap.Orib.45.29.40.

ἐπιτεχνολογέω, *add to the rules of an art*, Alex.Aphr.*in Top*.[518.4].

ἐπιτηγᾰνίζω, *fry*, μέλιτι Dsc.*Eup*.2.51.

ἐπιτηδ-ειόομαι, *to be made fit* or *capable*, Iamb.*VP*32.228. **-ειος**, α, ον: Ion. -εος, έη, εον Hdt.4.158, al. (cf. ἐπιταδεοτρώκτας): Dor. -τάδειος [ᾱ] *SIG*524.36 (Praesus, iii B.C.): regul. Comp. and Sup. -ειότερος, -ειότατος, Th.4.54, 7.86, etc.; -έστερος, -έστατος, Anon. ap.Suid. s.v., Democr.121: Ion. -εότερος, -εότατος, Hdt.9.2, 1.110, al.: (ἐπιτηδές):—*made for an end* or *purpose, fit* or *adapted for* it, *suitable, convenient*, νομαί ibid., etc.:—Constr.: ἐ. ἔς τι ib.115 (Sup.), etc.; πρός τι Pl.*R.*390b: c. inf., χωρίον -ότατον ἐνιππεῦσαι *most fit* to ride in, Hdt.6.102, cf. 9.2 (Comp.), Th.2.20, Ar. *Pax* 1228, E.*Ba.*508; ἄνδρα -ότατον.. δέξαι Hdt.3.134, cf. Ar.*Ec.* 79; so ἐ. τῷ σώματι κινδυνεύειν Antipho 5.63; ἐ. ὑπεξαιρεθῆναι *convenient* to be put out of the way, Th.8.70; τεθνάναι μᾶλλον ἢ σῴζεσθαι And.4.25, cf. Lys.30.24; ἐ. ξυνεῖναι a *fit* person to live with, E.*Andr.*206; also ἐ. ὀστρακισθῆναι *deserving* to be ostracized, And. 4.36; ἐ. πάσχειν D.22.57; ἐκλεγόμενος τὸν ἐ. ἔπαισεν ἂν struck *him who deserved it*, X.*An.*2.3.11; but ἐ. ἐς ὀλιγαρχίαν ἐλθεῖν *likely* or *inclined* to come, Th.8.63; also ὑμῖν ἐπιτήδεόν [ἐστι] οἰκέειν Hdt.4.158, etc. **II.** *useful, serviceable, necessary,* **1.** of things, ὀλιγαρχία ἐ. τοῖς Λακεδαιμονίοις *fit* or *serviceable for*.., Th.5.81; ἐ. τῷ δήμῳ πράττειν Lys.13.51; καταστήσειν ἐς τὸ ἐ. to their *advantage*, Th.4.76; οὐδὲν ηὕροντο ἐ. no *advantage*, Id.1.58; οὐκ ἐ. καταγνῶναί τινος Hdt. 6.97; ἱερὰ οὐκ ἐ., opp. καλά, Id.9.37: esp. as Subst., τὰ ἐ. things *requisite, necessaries*, esp. of *provisions*, Id.2.174, Th.2.23, X.*HG* 2.2.2, etc.: also in sg., *what is requisite, needful*, Id.*Vect.*4.38. **2.** of persons, *serviceable, friendly*, Hdt.4.72 (Sup.), Th.3.40; τινί to one, Id.4.78, Lys.12.14; ἐ. ποιεῖν τινα And.4.41; ἐ. τῷ πατρί *conformable to* his *will*, Hdt.3.52; ἐ. τοῖς πρασσομένοις *favourable* to.., Th. 8.54: also as Subst., *a close friend*, οἱ ἐ. one's *friends*, Id.5.64; Ἀθηναίων ἐ. Id.7.73; μοι ἐ. καὶ φίλος Lys.1.22. **3.** c. gen., = ἄξιος, *SIG*1073.19 (Olympia, ii A.D.). **III.** Adv. -είως, Ion. -έως, *studiously, carefully*, ὑπηρετέεσθαι Hdt.1.108, 4.139. **2.** *suitably, conveniently, fitly*, ποιέειν ἐ. Id.9.7.β'; ἐ. σφίσιν αὐτοῖς πολιτεύειν Th.1. 19; ἐ. ἔχειν Id.5.82: Comp. -ότερον Id.4.54; -οτέρως, διαιτᾶσθαι Hp.*Mul.*1.32. **3.** ἐ. ἔχειν τινί to be *on friendly terms* with.., Paus. 3.9.3. **-ειότης,** ητος, ἡ, *fitness, suitableness, convenience* for a purpose, Hp.*Fract.*27; πρός τι Pl.*Lg.*778a, cf. Epicur.*Ep.*1 p.9 U. (pl.): *tendency, liability*, Theon Gymn.ap.Gal.6.208. **2.** ἐ. πρὸς πόλεμον all *material*, etc., for carrying on war, Plb.2.23.11. **3.** *requirement*, ἵνα πρὸς ἑκάστην ἐ. τὸ προσῆκον γένηται Ael.*Tact.*35.1. **II.** *friendliness, kindness*, πρὸς ἅπαντας Aristid.1.112 J. **-ές,** Adv. *of set purpose, advisedly*, twice in Hom., ἐρέτας ἐ. ἀγείρομεν Il.1.142; μνηστήρων σ' ἐ. ἀριστῆες λοχόωσιν Od.15.28:—later proparox., **ἐπίτηδες,** Hdt.3.130, al., Hp.*VC*11, Ar.*Eq.*893, al., Th.3.112, Pl.*Cri.* 43b, etc.: Dor. **ἐπίταδες** Theoc.7.42: hence, *cunningly, deceitfully*, E.*IA*476; εἰς καιρὸν καὶ ὥσπερ ἐ. *fittingly, as best may be*, Plu.2.577e; cf. ἐξεπίτηδες. **-ευμα,** Cret. **ἐπιτάδουμα** (*SIG*721.12 (Delos (decree of Cnossus), ii B.C.)), ατος, τό, *pursuit, business, custom*, τὰ ἐ. τῆς χώρας Th.1.138, cf. 6.15; μάθημα ἢ ἐ. Pl.*La.*180a; πρὸς τίνα τέχνην ἢ τί ἐ.; Id.*R.*455a, cf. *Euthd.*275b; ἀρετὴ κάλλιστον τῶν ἐ. Isoc.10.54; τὰ καθ' ἡμέραν ἐ. everyday *habits*, Th.2.37, cf. Antipho 3.2.10, etc.; ἐ. πρὸς ὑμᾶς ἄλογον καὶ ἐς τὰ ἡμέτερα ἀξύμφορον Th.1.32; ἐπιτηδεύματα ἀρετῆς, καπηλείας, *practice* of.., Pl.*Lg.*711b, 918a. **2.** *habit of life*, Hp.*Epid.*1.23: pl., *ways of living*, Pl.*Phdr.*233d, *Lg.* 793d. **-ευματικῶς,** Adv. *studiedly*, opp. ἀνεπιτηδεύτως, Phld. *Rh.*1.156 S. **-ευσις,** εως, ἡ, *devotion* or *attention to* a pursuit or business, Th.2.36, Pl.*Ax.*369b, etc.; *cultivation of a habit* or *character*, ἐς ἀρετήν Th.7.86; ἀρετῆς Pl.*Lg.*853b; βιότου ἀτρεκεῖς ἐ. scrupulous *refinements*, E.*Hipp.*261 (anap.); τὸ ἐξ -εύσεως, of a *studied* style, D.H. *Lys.*8; of baths, ἐξ ἐ., opp. αὐτοφυῆ, Antyll.ap.Orib.10.2.1; κατ' ἐπιτήδευσιν *as a special study*, opp. κατὰ περίπτωσιν, Gal.2.289; χωρὶς τινος ἐ. Sor.1.59; opp. κρίσις, D.C.60.5. **-ευτέον,** *one must pursue*, Pl.*Lg.* 858d. Adj. -τέος, α, ον, *to be pursued*, Plu.2.10b. **-ευτής,** ὁ, οῦ, *one who practises*, ἀπράγμονος βίου J.*AJ*19.1.5, cf. Ptol.*Tetr.*163. **-ευτικός,** ή, όν, *apt to practise*, ἔργων Andronic.Rhod.p.575 M. **-ευτός,** ή, όν, *artificial, counterfeit*, Sch.Il.5.831. **-εύω,** impf. ἐπετήδευον Pl.*Phd.*64a: aor. ἐπετήδευσα Th.1.37: pf. ἐπιτετήδευκα, Pass. -ευμαι, Pl.*Hp.Ma.*304b, Lys.13.65: (as if a compd. of ἐπί, *τηδεύω, but it is formed directly from ἐπιτηδές):—*pursue* or *practise* a thing, *make it one's business*, c. acc., εὐπαθείας Hdt.1.135, etc.; ἐν τοῖς κακοῖς.. ἀνάγκη κἀπιτηδεύειν κακά S.*El.*309; λαλιάν Ar.*Ra.*1069; εὐσέβειαν Antipho 2.3.11; τὸ δ' ἐπὶ κακουργίᾳ καὶ οὐκ ἀρετῇ ἐπετήδευσαν Th.1.37; τέχνην, μουσικήν, Pl.*Tht.*149a, X.*Ath.*1.13, etc.; ἐ. τι πρός τι *invent* with a view to.., Hdt.6.125:—Pass., *to be practised*, ὅσα κακὰ καὶ αἰσχρά τινι ἐπιτετήδευται Lys.13.65; also, *to be made* so and so *by art*, opp. to being so by nature, Hdt.1.98; of dogs, *to be carefully trained*, πρός τι X.*Cyr.*1.6.40. **2.** c. inf., *take care* to do, *use* to do, Hdt.3.18, 4.170, Pl.*Grg.*524c, Jul.*Or.*1.3d, etc.; also ἐ. ὅπως.. Hdt.3.102. **3.** abs. in part., οὐδὲν αὐτοὶ ἐπιτηδεύοντες without any *deliberate purpose* on our part, Speus.ap.*Theol.Ar.*61; ἐπιτηδεύσας *on purpose*, Hld.5. 31. **-έως,** Adv. of ἐπιτήδεος, Ion. for ἐπιτηδείως (q.v.).

ἐπιτήθη or **-τηθή,** ἡ, *great-grandmother*, Theopomp.Com.42. **2.** *great-great-grandmother*, Poll.3.18.

ἐπί-τηκτος, ον, *overlaid with gold*, στέφανον χρυσοῦν, οὐ γὰρ ἐπίτηκτόν τινα Alex.96. **2.** *with gold* or *gilded ornaments laid on*, κρατὴρ ὑπάργυρος ἐ. *IG*2².1386.16; στλεγγίδιον ἐ. ib.1544.13. **II.** metaph., *counterfeit*, ἐπίτηκτα φιλεῖν *AP*5.186 (Mel.); '*veneer*', Cic.*Att.*7.1. 5. **-τήκω,** *melt upon, pour when melted over* a thing, κηρὸν ἐπὶ γράμματα Hdt.7.239; κηρὸν τῷ νεκρῷ Plu.*Ages.*40.

ἐπιτηλίς, ίδος, ἡ, *horned poppy, Glaucium flavum*, Nic.*Th.*852.

ἐπιτηρ-έω, *look out* or *watch for*, νύκτα *h.Cer.*244; σιτία Ar.*Ach.* 197; Βορέαν ib.922; καιρόν Plu.*Publ.*17; ἐπετήρουν ἀπιόντας αὐτούς Th.5.37; τὴν θεράπαιναν Lys.1.8; ἐ. τὸ βλάβος *watch to detect* it, Ar. *Ra.*1151; ἐ. ὅταν.., ὁπόταν.., Id.*Ec.*633, *Eq.*1031; ὁπότε.. X.*HG* 2.2.16; τί παρ' ὑμῖν ἐψήφισται, τοῦτ' ἐπετήρουν D.19.288: c. inf., ἰδεῖν τι Gal.15.661:—Med., Hld.5.20. **II.** *keep an eye on*, τινά App.*BC*4.39:—Pass., *to be kept under surveillance*, *POxy.*1413.10 (iii A.D.). **2.** *supervise*, *PAmh.*2.77.8 (ii A.D.):—Pass., *PFlor.*1.16 (ii A.D.), etc. **-ησις,** εως, ἡ, *observation*, οὐρανίων Porph.*Abst.*4. 8. **2.** *guardianship*, Sch.rec.S.*Ant.*1135. **3.** *office of* ἐπιτηρητής 2, *BGU*478.9 (ii A.D.). **-ητέον,** *one must watch for*, τὸν καιρόν τινος Ph.2.305, cf. Heph.Astr.3.1. **-ητής,** οῦ, ὁ, *watcher, scout*, Sch. rec.A.*Th.*36. **2.** *superintendent* of taxes, ἐ. ἱερᾶς πύλης (at Elephantine in Egypt) *Ostr.*144 (ii A.D.), cf. 1020, al.; νομῶν *BGU* 478.4 (ii A.D.), *Arch.Pap.*4.143 (ii A.D.); πλοίων *POxy.*2116.1 (iii A.D.). **-ητικός,** ή, όν, *watching for an opportunity*, esp. *to do ill*, Andronic.Rhod.p.572 M., D.L.7.114: c. gen., Plu.2.538d. **-ία,** ἡ, *care*, *Schwyzer*686.4 (Pamphylia).

ἐπιτίθημι, Pass. mostly furnished by ἐπίκειμαι: **A.** Act., *lay, put* or *place upon*, of offerings *laid on* the altar, ἐπὶ μηρία θέντες Ἀπόλλωνι Od.21.267, cf. 3.179; λιβανωτόν Ar.*Nu.*426, *V.*96, Antipho 1.18; *set* meats *on* the table, εἴδατα πόλλ' ἐπιθεῖσα Od.1.140, cf. 10.355; πάντ' ἐπιθεῖτε *on* the car, Il.24.264; [νέκυας] ἐπὶ νηυσὶ τιθέντες Od.24.419; τινὶ κύρτον καὶ κώπαν, as a grave-monument, *AP*7.505 (= Sapph.120): Constr. mostly ἐ. τινί τι, τῷ ἰσχυροτέρῳ πλέον βάρος X.*Oec.*17.9, etc.: but also c. gen., ἐ. λεχέων τινά Il.24. 589; ἐ. τι ἐπί τινος Hdt.2.121.δ'; κεφαλὴν ἐπὶ στέρνα τινός X.*Cyr.*7. 3.14: c. acc. only, *put upon, set up*, ἐ. φάρμακα *apply* salves, Il.4.190; δέελον δ' ἐπὶ σῆμά τ' ἔθηκε 10.466; στήλην λίθου Hdt.7.183; φάκελον ξύλων E.*Cyc.*243; ἐ. μνημεῖά τινι to him, Id.*IT*702, cf. *IG*14.446 (Tauromenium), 1².1068. **2.** *set upon, turn towards*, Ἑκτορέοις ἐπὶ φρένα θῆχ' ἱεροῖσιν Il.10.46; but τῇ δ' ἄρ' ἐπὶ φρεσὶ θῆκε c. inf., *put* it *into* her mind to.., Od.21.1. **II.** *put on* a covering or lid, ὡς εἴ τε φαρέτρῃ πῶμ' ἐπιθείη 9.314; κεφαλῇ ἐπέθηκε (as v. l. for ἐφύπερθε) καλύπτρην 5.232; λίθον δ' ἐπέθηκε θύρῃσι, i. e. *put* a stone *as a door* to the cave, *put* it *before* the door, 13.370; also, *put* a door *to*, κολλητὰς ἐπέθηκα θύρας 23.194; θύρας ἐπέθηκε φαεινάς 21.45; θυρεὸν μέγαν 9.240 (v. infr. B. II). **2.** *set* a seal *on*, *BGU*361 iii 22 (ii A.D.); *apply* a pessary, Hp.*Steril.*214 (Pass.); a cupping instrument, Sor.2.11 (Pass.). **III.** *put to, add, grant* or *give besides*, ὅσσα τε νῦν ὔμμ' ἐστὶ καὶ εἴ ποθεν ἄλλ' ἐπιθεῖτε Od.22.62, cf. Il.7.364, etc.; κράτος, κῦδός τινι, 1.509 (tm.), 23.400 (tm.), 406 (tm.); ἡμιτάλαντον χρυσοῦ ib.796. **2.** of Time, *add, bring on*, ἕβδομον ἦμαρ ἐπὶ Ζεὺς θῆκε Od.12.399; μάλα πολλὰ [ἔτεα] Hes.*Op.*697. **IV.** *put on* as a finish, χρυσέην ἐπέθηκε κορώνην Il.4.111; περόνην Od. 19.256: metaph., οὐδὲ τέλος μύθῳ ἐπιθήσεις *add* fulfilment, Il.19.107, cf. 20.369; so later ἐ. κεφάλαι' ἐφ' ἅπασι D.21.18; κολοφῶνα ἐ. τῇ σοφίᾳ Pl.*Euthd.*301e; τέλος ἐπιτεθήκατον ib.272a; πέρας ἐ. τῇ γενέσει Arist.*GA*776ᵃ4; πίστιν ἐ. D.12.22, 49.42; ὁ δὲ μισθωσάμενος πίστιν ἐπιθήσει πρὸς τοὺς νεωποίας *SIG*963.34 (Arcesine, iv B.C.); πέρας ἐ. τῷ πράγματι *PGiss.*25.7 (ii A.D.), etc.; ὅρον ἐ. τῷ πράγματι Mitteis *Chr.*87.2 (ii A.D.). **V.** *impose, inflict* a penalty, σοὶ δέ, γέρον, θωὴν ἐπιθήσομεν Od.2.192; δίκην, ζημίην, ἄποινα ἐ. τινί, Hdt.1. 120, 144, 9.120, etc.; θάνατον δίκην ἐ. τινί Pl.*Lg.*838c; δίκην τὴν πρέπουσαν Id.*Criti.*106b; ἔργων ἀντ' ἀδίκων χαλεπὴν ἐ. ἀμοιβήν Hes.*Op.* 334; τιμωρίαν ὑπέρ τινος D.60.11 (cf. infr. B. IV): so of burdens, grievances, etc., θήσειν.. ἐπ' ἄλγεα Τρωσί Il.2.39; οἷσιν ἐπὶ Ζεὺς θῆκε κακὸν μόρον 6.357; [ἄτην] οἱ ἐπὶ φρεσὶ θῆκε.. Ἐρινύς Od.15.234; ἀνάγκην ἐ. c. inf., X.*Lac.*10.7; ἐ... μὴ τυγχάνειν *imposing as a penalty* not to.., ib.3.3 (v. infr. B. IV). **VI.** *dispatch* a letter, ἐ. τι ἐς Αἴγυπτον, ἐς Μυτιλήνην, Hdt.3.42, 5.95; ἐ. [ἐπιστολάς] D.34.28. **VII.** *give* a name, Hdt.5.68, Pl.*Smp.*205b, etc. **VIII.** *contribute* (capital) *to* a venture, ἐς πεῖραν *Leg.Gort.*9.44.

B. Med., with pf. Pass. ἐπιτέθειμαι Plu.2.975d, also aor. Pass., *Inscr.Prien.* (v. infr.), etc.:—*put on oneself* or *for oneself*, ἐπὶ στεφάνην κεφαλῆφιν.. θήκατο *placed* a helmet *on his* head, Il.10.30; κρατὶ δ' ἐπὶ.. κυνέην θέτο 5.743, cf. E.*Ba.*702 (tm.), etc.; χεῖρας ἐπ' ἀνδροφόνους θέμενος στήθεσσι *laying one's* hands *upon*.., Il.18.317; κτύπημα χειρὸς κάρᾳ *on one's* head, E.*Andr.*1210 (lyr.). **II.** *put on* or *to*, as a door, πύλας τοῖς ὠσὶν ἐπίθεσθε Pl.*Smp.*218b; θύρας Orph.*Fr.* 245, al., etc. (v. supr. A. II). **III.** *apply oneself to, employ oneself on* or *in*, c. dat., ναυτιλίῃσι μακρῇσι Hdt.1.1; τῇ πείρᾳ, τοῖς ἔργοις, Th.7.42, X.*Mem.*2.8.3, etc.; τοῖς πολιτικοῖς Pl.*Grg.*527d: c. inf., *attempt to*.., φιλοσοφεῖν ἐπέθετο Alex.36.3; γράφειν Isoc.5.1, cf. Pl. *Sph.*242b:—Pass., ἐπετέθη πρὸς τὸν πόλεμον *Inscr.Prien.*17.38 (iii B.C.). **2.** *make an attempt upon, attack*, τῇ Εὐβοίῃ Hdt.5.31; Ἐφεσίοισι Id.1.26, cf. 102, 8.27; τῷ δήμῳ Th.6.61; τῇ δημοκρατίᾳ X.*Ath.* 3.12; ἐ. τῇ τοῦ δήμου καταλύσει *attempt* it, Aeschin.3.235; τυραννίδι Lycurg.125; ἀρχῇ Plu.2.772d; ἐ. ταῖς ἁμαρτίαις or τοῖς ἀτυχήμασί τινος *take advantage of* them, Isoc.2.3, D.23.70: abs., *make an attack*, κατ' ἀμφότερα Th.7.42, cf. Arist.*Pol.*1302ᵇ25. **3.** abs., δικαιοσύνην ἐπιθέμενος ἤσκεε he practised justice *with assiduity*, Hdt.1.96, cf. 6. 60. **IV.** *bring on oneself*, ἐπέθου θύος δημοθρόους τ' ἀρὰς A.*Ag.* 1409. **2.** *cause* a penalty *to be imposed*, θάνατον ζημίαν ἐπιθέσθαι Th.2.24; φόβον τινὶ X.*Cyr.*4.5.41. **V.** *lay commands on*, τί τινι Hdt.1.111, cf. *OGI*669.61 (Egypt, i A.D.): also c. inf., Hdt.3.63, v.l. in Ath.11.465d. **VI.** *give* a name, τινί Od.8.554 (tm.), cf. Arist. *Po.*1451ᵇ10. **VII.** *contribute*, πολλοὶ ἐπέθεντο τὰς ἐπιδόσεις εἰς τὴν παρασκευὴν τοῦ πολέμου prob. in *SIG*346.29 (iv B.C.).

ἐπιτίκτω, *bring forth after*, Hp.*Superf.*1; τῷ πρώτῳ ἕτερον ἐ. Sor.(?) ap.Orib.22.7.2, cf. Plu.*Phil.*1.

ἐπιτίμ-αιος [τῐ], ὁ, (ἐπιτιμάω II. 2) *fault-finder*, nickname of the historian Timaeus, Ister ap.Ath.6.272b, D.S.5.1. **-άω,** Ion. and Delph. -τιμέω, Hdt.6.39, *Schwyzer*346.11 (ii B.C.):—*lay a value upon*: hence, **1.** *show honour to*, τινά Hdt. l.c. **2.** *raise in* *price*, οἶνον ἐ. πολύ Diph.32.27: abs., Ael.NA10.50; τὴν αἴτησιν ἐ. *raise* the demand, Anon.ap.Suid.:—Pass., *rise in price*, of corn, D.34.39, 50.6, PSI4.356.7 (iii A.D.). II. of judges, *lay a penalty on* a person, τοῖς ἐξάρνοις ἐ. ταλάντου ἑκάστῳ v.l. in Aeschin.1.113; ἐ. ἀργύριον Hermes17.4 (Delos); but ἐ. τὴν ἀρχαίην δίκην *make* the original trial *the ground of punishment*, Hdt.4.43. 2. *object to* one *as blameable*, τινί τι Pl.Phdr.237c, Isoc.1.17, etc.:—Pass., Arist.Po.1455a26. b. c. acc. rei only, *censure*, οὐ τοῦτ' ἐπιτιμῶ D.20.148, cf. Anaxandr.49:—Pass., τὸ.. ὑπὸ τῶν πολλῶν ἐπιτιμώμενον X.Mem.1.2.31, cf. Arist.EN1114a29. c. c. dat. only, *rebuke, censure*, of persons, Lys.24.17; of things, τοῖς ψηφισθεῖσιν Isoc.8.52; τοῖς πεπραγμένοις D.18.64; τοῖς ἀνέμοις Ev.Matt.8.26; τινὶ περί τι Plb.8.9.1; τινὶ ὡς.. D.12.7; τῷ λόγῳ, ὅτι.. Pl.Tht.169d:—Pass., ἐπιτετιμημένος ἐπί τινι Plb.7.12.9. d. abs., λόγῳ καλῶς ἐ. by word, Th.3.38, cf. 4.28; τὸ μὲν ἐπιτιμᾶν.. φήσαι τις ἂν ῥᾴδιον εἶναι D.1.16, cf. Arist.Pol.1284a27. **-ή**, Dor. **-ά**, ἡ, = ἐπιτιμία I, SIG 254A11, 257.10 (Delph., iv B.C.), 417.12 (ibid., iii B.C.), etc. II. = ἐπιτιμία II, PPetr.3pp.41,48 (pl., iii B.C.). **-ημα**, ατος, τό, *legal penalty*, IG1^2.75, 11(2).199A65 (Delos, iii B.C.), etc. 2. *censure, criticism*, Arist.Po.1461b22 (pl.), Plu.2.1110e (pl.). **-ησις**, εως, ἡ, *castigation, censure, criticism*, Th.7.48, Antiph.258, Arist.Rh.1355a24; ἐπιτίμησιν ἐπιτιμᾶν Id.Pol.1340b40: pl., D.S.5.1. II. *enhancement in price*, σίτου App.BC4.117. 2. Rhet., *heightening*, by use of a stronger term, Alex.Fig.2.28. **-ητέον**, *one must censure*, τινί Arist.Top.118a24, Plb.8.35.2, Ph.2.437, al. II. Adj. -ητέος, α, ον, *censurable*, Arist.MM1202b22. **-ητήρ**, ῆρος, ὁ, = sq. II, Opp. H.1.682. **-ητής**, οῦ, ὁ, *estimator, valuer*, Antipho 5.32, IG1^2.75, 2^2.1176, 11(2).287A87 (iii B.C.), al.; ἔργων *appraiser, overseer* (i.e. Zeus), A.Pr.77. II. *punisher, chastiser*, κολασταὶ κἀπ. κακῶν S. Fr.533; τούτων κολαστὴν κἀπιτιμητὴν E.Supp.255; διακωλυταὶ καὶ ἐ. τῆς.. ὁμιλίας Pl.Phdr.240a. **-ητικός**, ή, όν, *censorious, critical*, Luc. JTr.23; λόγος ἐ. Pl.Def.416 fin.; σχῆμα D.H.Th.44; ἐμειδίασεν -τικόν Aristaenet.1.4; προσβλέψας ἡμῖν -κόν τι Gal.8.655. **-ητός**, όν, *liable to penalties*, dub. in BGU747 ii 7 (ii A.D.). **-ήτωρ**, ορος, ὁ, *avenger*, Ζεὺς ἐ. ἱκετάων τε ξείνων τε, i.e. Zeus ξένιος, Od.9.270. **-ία**, ἡ, *the condition of an* ἐπίτιμος, *enjoyment of all civil rights and privileges*, opp. ἀτιμία, Aeschin.2.88, D.21.106; τὸ συνειλεγμένον εἰς τὴν ἐ. money collected for the *recovery of the franchise*, Id.18.312; ἡ ἐ. σου οὐδὲν βλαβήσεται POxy.1405.10 (iii A.D.), cf. Schwyzer328.11 (Delph., iii B.C.). II. *punishment, penalty*, Lxx Wi.3.10, OGI 669.43 (Egypt, i A.D.). III. *dignity, respect*, ἀξιώματος Artem.1.45; *good name*, πάντα ποιεῖν ὑπὲρ τῆς ἰδίας ἐ. Ph.2.312. **-ιον**, τό, mostly in pl., ἐπιτίμια, τά, *value, price*, or *estimate of* a thing, i.e., 1. *the honours paid to* a person, ἔστ' Ὀρέστου ταῦτα τἀπ. S.El.915 (nisi leg. τἀπιτύμβια). 2. *assessment of damages, penalty* or *penalties*, ἐ. διδόναι τινί inflict..., Hdt.4.80, cf. E.Hec.1086, etc.; τῶνδε τἀπ. *for* these things, A.Pers.823; τοῖς ἐ. ἔνοχοι τοῦ φόνου Antipho4.1.4; τὰ ἐκ τῶν νόμων ἐ. Lycurg.4; ἐ. δυσσεβείας *the wages* of ungodliness, S. El.1382, cf. X.Mem.3.12.3; κρίσεις.. μεγάλ' ἔχουσαι τἀπιτίμια D.18.14: in sg., τοὐπιτίμιον λαβεῖν exact *the penalty*, A.Th.1026; ἐ. ἔπεστί τινι Is.3.47; θάνατον ἔταξε τὸ ἐ. Arist.Oec.1349b30; ἐ. ὁρίζειν τινί IG2^2.1104; τριπλάσια τὰ ἐ. ἀποτεισάτω PHal.1.208 (iii B.C.), cf. Foed.Delph. Pell.2A21. **-ιος**, α, ον, *honourable*, πόλις IG12(8).528 (Thasos). **-ος**, ον, of a citizen, *in possession of his rights and franchises* (τιμαί), opp. ἄτιμος (q.v.), Ar.Ra.702, And.1.73, Th.5.34, X.HG2.2.11, etc.; χρήματα ἐ. property *not confiscated*, though the owner was in exile, Lex ap.D.23.44. II. *valuable*, Agath.1.8. 2. *subject to penalty*: hence, *contraband*, ἐλαϊκόν PTeb.39.10 (ii B.C.). 3. Subst. ἐπίτιμον, τό, = ἐπιτίμιον 2, SIG685.81 (pl., Crete, ii B.C.), PRev. Laws43.8 (iii B.C.), Test.Epict.6.31, PGen.1.20.15 (ii B.C.), etc.

ἐπιτίνω, *punish*, dub. in SIG1208.9 (Thespiae, ii B.C.).

ἐπιτίτθιος, ον, *at the breast*, παῖς AP11.243 (Nicarch.): Subst., ὁ, *a suckling*, Theoc.24.54.

ἐπιτιτράω, aor. 1 inf. ἐπιτρῆσαι, *pierce, cut holes in* stones, IG11(2).161A55 (Delos, iii B.C.); *trepan*, Heliod.ap.Orib.46.15.3.

***ἐπιτλάω**, only aor. 2 ἐπέτλην, *bear patiently, be patient*, τῶ τοι ἐπιτλήτω κραδίη Il.23.591; τῶ τοι ἐπιτλήτω κραδίη μύθοισιν ἐμοῖσιν *let it listen patiently to* them, 19.220; μυρί' ἐπιτλάς Nic.Al.241.

ἐπιτμήγω, Ep. for ἐπιτέμνω, A.R.4.707.

ἐπιτμητέον, *one must summarize*, Nicom.Ar.2.28.

ἐπιτοκ-ία, ἡ, *compound interest*, Ph.2.285 (pl.); dub. cj. in Thphr. Char.10.2. **-ίζω**, *make liable to a higher rate of interest*, SIG364.48 (Ephesus, iii B.C.):—Pass., ib.50. **-ιον**, τό, = ἐπιτοκία, BGU223.7 (ii A.D.), v.l. in Aesop.177b (p.257 Chambry) (pl.). **-ος**, ον, (τόκος I) *near childbirth*, Hp.Superf.17, Antiph.306 (condemned by Phryn. 310), Arist.HA573a2, etc.: heterocl. acc. sg. ἐπίτοκα IG5(1).1390.33 (Andania). 2. *fruitful, having borne children*, Hp.Epid.6.8.32. II. (τόκος II) *bearing interest upon interest*, τόκοι ἐ. *compound* interest, Pl. Lg.842d.

ἐπιτολή, ἡ, (ἐπιτέλλω (B)) *the rising of a star*, ἄστρων E.Ph.1116 (pl.), cf. Archyt.1, Ptol.Alm.8.4: hence, *the season of a star's appearance in the heavens*, Hp.Aër.2, Thphr.CP2.19.4, etc.; Ἀρκτούρου Th. 2.78 (pl.); Κυνός Arist.HA602a26; τῆς Πλειάδος Plb.4.37.2; later of the sun or moon, App.BC5.90, Philostr.VA6.4 (pl.), Artem.1.3 (pl.):—as explained by Gem.13.3, ἐ. = *rising* (ἀνατολή) of a star *as the sun rises or sets* (ἐ. ἀληθινή, ἑῴα ἢ ἑσπερία), or *just before sunrise or after sunset* (ἐ. φαινομένη). 2. *rising* of the wind, Palaeph.17 (pl., s.v.l.); *rise* or *source* of a river, or perh. = ἐπιπολή I. 1, dub.l. in GDI 5075.52 (Latos).

ἐπιτολμ-άω, *submit* or *endure* to do, σοὶ ἐπιτολμάτω κραδίη καὶ θυμὸς ἀκούειν Od.1.353, cf. Thgn.445: abs., ἐπετόλμησε he *stood firm*, Od. 17.238. 2. *dare, venture*, abs., Ph.1.594: c. inf., ib.671, al., Gal. 12.710: c. dat., *venture upon*, τῇ διαβάσει, ἔργῳ, Plu.Phil.10, Ant.69; τῷ δίφρῳ *mount* it, Philostr.Im.1.11; ἐ. τινί Ruf.Ren.Ves.2.36, Ael. NA7.19, Anon.ap.Suid. s.v. ἀστάθμητον. **-ητέον**, *one must venture*, c. inf., Ph.1.2, v.l. in Max.Tyr.24.4: c. dat., Gal.UP14.6, Orib. Fr.138. **-ητός**, όν, *to be ventured*, Max.Tyr.24.4 (v.l. -ητέον).

ἐπιτομ-ή, ἡ, (ἐπιτέμνω) *cutting on the surface, incision*, τῆς κεφαλῆς Aeschin.3.51, cf. Ph.Bel.64.1. II. *epitome, abridgement*, φυσικῶν Arist.Pr.891a7; ἐ. καὶ στοιχείωσις Epicur.Ep.1p.4U.; title of works by Chrysippus, etc., Stoic.2.5, etc.; ἐ. κεφαλαιώδεις D.H.1.5, cf. Lxx 2Ma.2.28; ἐν ἐπιτομῇ *briefly*, Cic.Att.5.20.1; ἐ. τῆς οἰκουμένης, of Rome, Ath.1.20b. III. *right of cutting*, εἰ δέ κα ἀμπέλους, ἐπιτομὰ ἔστω Supp.Epigr.2.293.11 (Delph., iii/ii B.C.). **-ικός**, ή, όν, *compendious*, πραγματεία Gal.9.479 (-ατικ- codd.). Adv. -κῶς Phld.Lib.p.47O., Theo Sm.p.116H., Suid. s.v. Εὐτρόπιος. **-ος**, ον, *cut off*, ἐ. ξύλα timber *cut in short lengths* for the joiner, Thphr.HP 5.1.12, cf. 3.13.1 (of bark). 2. *short, compendious*, ὁδός D.H.1. 68, Ph.2.25; τὰ ἐ. τῆς χώρας Paus.10.31.7; ἐπίτομον δείξας ἢ λεωφόρον D.Chr.18.4; περαιώσεις Hld.10.4. 3. *abridged*, Max.Tyr.31. 2, Suid. s.v. Διογενειανός. Adv. -ως Phld.Sign.28: Comp. -ώτερον A.D.Pron.3.8, Synt.215.9.

ἐπιτόν-αιον, τό, Archit., perh. *tie-beam*, IG2^2.1682.23 (Eleusis, iii B.C.). **-ιον**, τό, *peg* or *key* by which the strings of an instrument are tuned, ἐ. ψαλτηρίου (-ήριον cod.) prob. in Ath.10.456d: metaph., ἡ συντροφία ὥσπερ ἐ. ἐστι τῆς εὐνοίας Plu.2.3d. 2. *pitch-pipe* for giving the note to a choir, Et.Gud.d. s.v. ἀπότομον. II. any *peg* shaped like ἐ. 1, Orib.49.4.26, al.; *handle* of a tap, *turn-cock*, Hero Aut.13.5, Varro RR3.5.16, Vitr.9.8.11, Ulp.ap.Dig.19.1.17.8; *handle* of a syringe, Hero Spir.2.18. 2. *valve* or *stop* in an organ-pipe, Vitr.10.8.5. 3. pl., *sockets* in which a roller was set, Bito 49. 10. **-ος**, ον, *on the stretch, strained, intense*, D.S.10.17; of sound, Philostr.VS1.25.7. II. ἐπίτονος (sc. ἱμάς), ὁ, *a rope for stretching* or *tightening, back-stay* of a mast (opp. πρότονος), ἐπ' αὐτῷ [ἱστῷ] ἐπίτονος βέβλητο, βοὸς ῥινοῖο τετευχώς Od.12.423 (a στίχος ἀκέφαλος). 2. ἐπίτονοι, οἱ, the *great sinews of the shoulder and arm*, Pl.Ti.84e, Arist.HA515b9 (sg.); νεύρων ἐπίτονοι Pl.Lg.945c. **-όω**, *brace, 'tune up'*, Sor.1.25; τὰς ἕξεις ὁ ψυχρὸς οἶνος ἐ. Gal.15.195.

ἐπιτοξ-άζομαι, *shoot at*, τῷ δ' ἐπετοξάζοντο Il.3.79; also in late Prose, Luc.Cal.12, D.C.74.6: abs., Agath.3.22. **-εύω**, = foreg., τινί D.C.68.31; ταῖς τῶν ὀμμάτων βολαῖς Aristaenet.1.1: abs., Agath. 5.19. **-ίς**, ίδος, ἡ, dub. sens. in IG2^2.1357 (iv B.C.). 2. = sq., Vitr.10.10.4 codd. **-ῖτις**, ιδος, ἡ, *groove* or *slot* for the arrow in a catapult, Ph.Bel.73.51, 75.2, Hero Bel.77.10, cj. in Vitr.10.10.4.

ἐπιτοπ-ίζω, = κατοικίζω, Suid. **-ιος**, ον, *on the spot*, Sch.Opp. H.1.596.

ἐπιτόπως, Adv. *suitably*, κείμενοι ἐ., χρηματίζοντες ἐ., of stars, Vett.Val.5.3,7, al.

ἐπιτόσσαις, Aeol. part. of ἐπέτοσσε (q.v.).

ἐπιτρᾰγημᾰτίζω, *serve up as dessert*, Arist.(Fr.105)ap.Jul.Ep.180 (Pass.).

ἐπιτρᾰγ-ία, ἡ, epith. of Aphrodite, from a she-goat, which was changed into a he-goat (τράγος), Plu.Thes.18, IG3.335. **-ίας**, ου, ὁ, *a kind of fish*, which is barren and so grows fat (cf. sq.), Arist.HA 538a14. **-οι**, οἱ, (τραγάω) *the over-luxuriant shoots* of a vine, D.H.19.1, Poll.7.152; gloss on ἐπιφυλλίδες, EM367.20. **-ῳδέω**, *make a tragic story of* a thing, *exaggerate*, Thphr.HP9.8.5, D.H.Th. 28, Plu.Art.18 (Pass.), Luc.Tox.12; οὐδὲν ἐ. πρὸς σεμνότερον ὄγκον Ph.2.105; *descant solemnly upon*, τινί Plu.Per.28, Demetr.Eloc.122; *lament tragically*, Hld.1.3; *add to a tragedy*, καινὸν ἐπεισόδιον Id.7.6, cf. 2.29.

ἐπιτρᾰπεζ-ίδιος· ὁ παράσιτος, Hsch. **-ιος**, ον, *on* or *at table*, ὕδωρ Luc.Herm.68; λέξις Eust.1561.58; *seated on a table*, Ἡρακλῆς, of a statuette, Stat.Silv.4.6 tit. II. = foreg., Hsch. s.v. τραπεζῆες. **-ος**, ον, = foreg. 1, τὰ ἐ. σκεύη Thphr.Lap.42. **-ωμα**, ατος, τό, *a dish set on table*, Pl.Com.74, cf. Ath.4.170e.

ἐπιτρᾰπέουσι, Ep. 3 pl. pres. for ἐπιτρέπουσι, Il.10.421.

ἐπιτρᾰχήλιος, ον, (τράχηλος) *on the neck*, κόσμος Suid.

ἐπιτρεπ-τέον, *one must commit, permit*, c. dat., X.Hier.8.9, Pl. Smp.213e; τινὶ περί τινος Men.Epit.2; τινὶ c. inf., Jul.Or.2.85d: also pl., ἐκείνοισι.. οὐκ ἐπιτρεπτέα ἐστὶ Hdt.9.58. **-τικός**, ή, όν, *hortatory*, Aristid.2.310J.; *encouraging*, γυμνάσιον νεύρων καταλλάξεως ἐπιτρεπτικόν Antyll.ap.Orib.6.35.1. **-ω**, Ion. **-τράπω** [ᾰ] Hdt.3.81: fut. -τρέψω; Dor. 3 pl. -τρέψοντι Pi.O.6.21; Cret. inf. -τραψῆν GDI 5039.21, 5024.12: aor. 1 -έτρεψα Il.10.116, etc.: aor. 2 -έτραπον ib. 59: pf. -τέτρᾰφα Plb.30.6.6:—**Med.**, fut. -τρέψομαι (v.l. -τράψ-) Hdt.3.155: aor. 2 -ετρᾰπόμην Od.9.12:—**Pass.**, fut. -τετράψομαι Pisistr.ap.D.L.1.54: aor. 1 -ετρέφθην Antipho 4.3.5; Ion. -ετράφθην, part. -τραφθείς Hdt.1.7: aor. 2 -ετράπην [ᾰ] Th.5.31: pf. (v. infr. 1.6):—prop. *to turn to* or *towards*, used by Hom. in aor. 2 Med., σοὶ.. θυμὸς ἐπετράπετο εἴρεσθαι thy mind *inclined itself* to ask, Od.9.12. b. *to overturn upon*, τινί τι Luc.Lex.8. 2. *turn over to, transfer, bequeath*, παισὶν ἐπιτρέψειεν ἕκαστος κτήματ' ἐνὶ μεγάροισι Od.7.149. 3. *commit, entrust to* another as trustee, guardian, or vicegerent, οἱ.. ἐπέτρεπεν οἶκον ἅπαντα 2.226; ἐπιτρέψειας ἕκαστα δμῳάων [ἐκείνῃ] ἥ τις.. ἀρίστη 15.24, cf. Il.17.509; θεοῖσι μῦθον ἐπιτρέψαι *leave* it to them, Od.22.289, cf. 19.502; so κάκοισι θῦμον ἐπιτρέπην (Aeol. inf.) Alc.35. 1; σμικραῖς ἑαυτοὺς ἐ. ἐλπίσιν E.Fr.921; freq. in Prose, ἐ. τινί τὰ πρήγματα Hdt.6.26; τὴν πόλιν Id.4.202; Νάξον Λυγδάμι Id.1.64; τὰ πάντα Th.2.65; πλεῖστα τῷ ἀλογίστῳ Id.5.99; τὴν ἀρχήν X.*An*.6.1.31, etc.; also a son for education, Pl.*La*.200d: c. dat. et inf., τινά τινι γεροντᾰγωγεῖν Ar.*Eq*.1098: freq. in Att., *refer* a legal issue to any one, τινὶ δίαιταν D.59.45; διάγνωσις –τετράφθω τῷ ἐπιμελητῇ Pl.*Lg*.936a; οἷς (attracted for ἃ) ἂν ἐπιτρέψωσιν οἱ δὲ τάξωσι, τούτοις ἐμμένειν, i.e. acquiesce in the court and abide by its decision, ib.784c (for the constr. cf. And.3.34 fin.). **4.** c. dat. only, *rely upon, leave to*, τοῖσιν γὰρ ἐπετράπομέν γε μάλιστα Il.10.59; ἐπιτρέψαι δὲ θεοῖσιν Od.21.279; ἐ. τῇ ὀλιγαρχίῃ Hdt.3.81; ὥς οἱ (sc. ἰατρῷ) ἐπέτρεψε ib.130: c. dat. et inf., σοὶ ἐπέτρεψεν πονέεσθαι he *left* it to you to work, Il.10.116, cf. 421, Hdt.9.10: freq. in Att., *refer the matter* to a person, *leave it to his arbitration*, Ar.*Ach*.1115, *V*.521, *Ra*.811; τινὶ δικαστῇ to one as a judge, Th.4.83; τῷ ἐν Δελφοῖς μαντείῳ Id.1.28; ἐ. τῷ θεῷ περί τινος Pl.*Grg*.512e, cf. *Alc*.1.117e; ὑμῖν ἐπιτρέπω καὶ τῷ θεῷ κρῖναι Id.*Ap*.35d; Ἀθηναίοις ἐ. περὶ σφῶν αὐτῶν πλὴν θανάτου *to leave* their case to the A. save as to the penalty of death, Th.4.54; περὶ ὧν διαφερόμεθα τοῖς οἰκείοις ἐ. D.27.1:—Pass., δίκης Λακεδαιμονίοις ἐπιτραπείσης Th.5.31. **5.** Med., *entrust oneself, leave one's case to*, τινί Hdt.1.96; διαιτητῇ Id.5.95, cf. X.*An*.1.5.8; also, *to entrust what is one's own to* another, Hdt.3.155,157. **6.** Pass., *to be entrusted*, ᾧ λαοί τ' ἐπιτετράφαται (3 pl. pf. for ἐπιτετραμμένοι εἰσί) Il.2.25; τῇς (sc. Ὥραις) ἐπιτέτραπται μέγας οὐρανός heaven's gate *is committed to* them (to open and to shut), 5.750, cf. Hdt.3.142; ὑπό τινων ἐπιτρεφθῆναι (sc. ἰατρῷ), of a patient, Antipho 4.3.5: c. acc. rei, ἐπιτρέπομαί τι I *am entrusted with* a thing, ἐπιτραφθέντες τὴν ἀρχήν Hdt.1.7; ἐπιτετραμμένοι τὴν φυλακήν Th.1.126. **II.** *give up, yield*, Ποσειδάωνι δὲ νίκην πᾶσαν ἐπέτρεψας Il.21.473; later ἐ. τινί c. inf., *permit, suffer*, Ar.*Pl*.1078, Pl.*Chrm*.171e, etc.: c. acc. et inf., X.*An*.7.7.8; also ἐ. Θηβαίοις αὐτονόμους εἶναι Id.*HG*6.3.9; οὐδενὶ ἐ. κακῷ εἶναι Id.*An*.3.2.31; ἐ. ἀδικέοντι τῷ ἀδελφεῷ Hdt.2.120; μὴ ἐ. τῷ ἀσεβοῦντι Pl.*Euthphr*.5e: abs., *give way*, Pi.*O*.6.21, Ar.*Nu*.799, *Pl*.915, Th.1.71, Pl.*Ap*.35b:—Pass., ἄνευ τοῦ ἐπιτραπῆναι without *leave*, *POxy*.474.40 (ii A.D.). **2.** intr., *give way*, οὐ μὲν ἐπέτρεπε γήραϊ λυγρῷ Il.10.79; *indulge*, μὴ πάντα ἡλικίῃ καὶ θυμῷ ἐπίτρεπε Hdt.3.36; ταις ἡδοναῖς καὶ ἐπιθυμίαις Pl.*Lg*.802c; τῇ ὀργῇ D.H.7.45. **III.** *command*, τὴν μὲν [τάξιν] ἐπὶ τῷ δεξιῷ ἐπέτρεψεν ἐφέπεσθαι X.*An*.6.5.11: elsewh. c. dat., *PLond*.3.1173.3 (ii A.D.), etc.:—Pass., ἐπετράπην ὑπὸ σοῦ *POxy*.51.5 (ii A.D.).

ἐπιτρέφω, fut. –θρέψω Hdt.8.142: pf. –τέτροφα *AP*7.536 (Alc.):—Pass. (v. infr. II, III):—*grow*, in act. sense, κόμην J.*AJ*14.9.4. **2.** *rear upon*, ἐπιτέτροφε τύμβῳ βότρυν *AP* l.c. **3.** generally, *support, maintain*, Hdt.8.142,144; κακὸν τῇ πόλει D.H.10.6; τοῦ ὀμβρίου ὕδατος –ομένου ἀεὶ νέου a fresh *supply* being always *maintained*, Hp.*Aër*.7. **II.** Med., *cause to grow upon*, λασίην βροτοῖς ἐπεθρέψατο χαίτην Man.3.291:—Pass., *form upon*, –όμενος τοῖς σώμασι ῥύπος Gal.10.176; ὅταν σὰρξ ἐπιτραφῇ Id.18(2).780. **III.** Pass., *grow up after*, as posterity, ἐκ τουτέων σφι ἐπετράφη νεότης Hdt.4.3; οἱ ὕστερον ἐπιτραφέντες βασιλέες Id.2.121.α': generally, *grow up as a rival* or *successor*, Id.1.123, D.H.7.9 codd.

ἐπιτρέχω, fut. –δρᾰμοῦμαι X.*Cyn*.9.6, D.17.19: aor. 2 –έδρᾰμον Il.4.524, al. (rarely aor. 1 –έθρεξα 13.409): pf. –δεδράμηκα X.*Oec*.15.6; poet. –δέδρομα Od., etc. (v. infr. II. 2):—Pass., pf. –δεδράμημαι X.*Oec*.15.1:—*run upon* or *at*, mostly for the purpose of attack, abs., ὁ δ' ἐπέδραμεν Il.4.524, cf. 18.527; of dogs, οἱ μὲν κεκλήγοντες ἐπέδραμον Od.14.30; *make an assault upon*, τινί Th.4.32, X.*Cyn*.9.6; ἐπί τινα Id.*HG*5.4.51. **b.** *approach*, εἰς ἃς (sc. μοίρας) ἐπιτρέχει ἡ Σελήνη, τούτοις συνάπτει Serapio in *Cat.Cod.Astr*.8(4).228. **2.** *run after, be eager* or *greedy*, οὔτι ἐπιδραμὼν πάντα τὰ διδόμενα ἐδέκετο Hdt.3.135; συγχωρεῖν ἐπιδραμών *in haste*, Pl.*Lg*.799c; οὐκ ἂν ἡγεῖσθε αὐτὸν κἂν ἐπιδραμεῖν ὥστε γενέσθαι D.27.56: c. dat., *to be greedy for*, App.*Pun*.94. **II.** *run over* a space, τόσσον ἐπεδραμέτην, of horses, Il.23.433, cf. 418,447; *run over* or *graze the surface*, ἀσπὶς ἐπιθρέξαντος ἄϋσεν ἔγχεος 13.409: c. dat., ἀσταχύεσσιν Call.*Aet*.3.1.46. **2.** *to be spread over*, λευκὴ δ' ἐπιδέδρομεν αἴγλη Od.6.45; κακὴ δ' ἐπιδέδρομεν ἀχλύς 20.357: c. dat., τῷ.. ἐπιδέδρομεν ὀδμή Hermipp.82.3 (hex.); ἐπιδέδρομε νυκτὶ φέγγος A.R.2.670; οἱ ἔρευθος ἐπιτρέχει Arat.834, cf. Opp.*C*.3.94; ἐξανθήματα ἐ. τοῖς σώμασιν Plu.2.671a; ὄρεσι.. ἀφ' ἡλίου μορφαὶ ἐ. ib.934f; σημείων τῷ νεκρῷ μοχθηρῶν ἐπιδραμ. Id.*TG*13, etc.: c. acc., οἶδμα ὅταν ἔρεβος ὕφαλον ἐπιδράμῃ when the billow *runs over* the darkness of the deep, S.*Ant*.588 (lyr.); τὴν χώραν, of lava, Arist.*Mir*.840^{a}5; ψυχὴν ἐπιδέδρομε λήθη A.R.1.645; Ῥώμην ἐπέδραμε λόγος c. acc. et inf., Plu.*Aem*.25. **3.** of a musician, *run over, play upon*, ἐ. καλάμους χείλεσι Longus 1.24; τὴν σύριγγα τῇ γλώττῃ Alciphr.3.12; τῷ πλήκτρῳ τὰς χορδάς Ath.4.139e. **4.** *overrun*, as an army does a country, ἐ. πεδίον πᾶν Hdt.1.161; τὰς κώμας πάσας Id.8.23; τὴν χώρην πᾶσαν ib.32; τὰ ἔξω Th.4.104. **5.** *run over, treat lightly* or *summarily of*, X.*Oec*.25.1 (Pass.); τῷ λόγῳ ib.6; εὐπόρως ἐ. περί τινος Isoc.*Ep*.9.6; μικρὰ περὶ αὐτῶν D.17.19; τὰς ἀπορίας ἐ. Arist.*Pol*.1286^{a}7; Ἡροδότου.. ἡ λέξις.. ῥᾳδίως ἐπιτρέχουσα τοῖς πράγμασιν Plu.2.854e; ἐ. διὰ βραχυτάτων ib.119e; τὸ ἐπιτρέχον σχῆμα Hermog.*Id*.1.11. **6.** of a country, *spread, extend*, ἐπὶ.. D.P.809; μέσην ἐ. νῆσον ib.1092. **7.** τῷ τῆς κώμης –οντι *inspector*, *PFay*.107.7 (ii A.D.): pl., –οντες *POxy*.2121.22 (iii A.D.). **III.** *run close after*, ἅρματα.. ἵπποις ὠκυπόδεσσιν ἐπέδραμον Il.23.504; ἐ. τὰ ἴχνη, of hounds, X.*Cyn*.3.6: c. dat., *follow*, Arat.316; ἐ. τοῖς θήλεσιν, of the male, Plu.2.965e.

ἐπίτρησις, εως, ἡ, *trepanning*, Heliod.ap.Orib.46.14.2.

ἐπιτρῐᾱκοστὸς λόγος ratio *of* 31:30, Ptol.*Harm*.2.14: so **ἐπιτρῐᾱκοστό-μονος**, 32:31, ibid.: **–δεύτερος, –τριτος, –τέταρτος**, 33:32, 34:33, 35:34, Aristid.Quint.3.1: **–πεμπτος, –όγδοος, –ένατος**, 36:35, 39:38, 40:39, Ptol. l.c., cf. 1.13.

ἐπιτρῐβή, ἡ, *irritation, provocation*, Baillet *Inscr. des tombeaux des rois* 1405 (dub. sens.). **II.** *destruction, damnation*, Sch.rec.S.*Aj*.103.

ἐπιτρίβω [τρῑ], fut. –ψω Hsch.: pf. –τετρῐφα Ar.*Lys*.952: aor. 2 Pass. ἐπετρίβην [ῐ] Id.*Th*.557, al.: fut. Med. in pass. sense, Luc.*Icar*.33 (v.l. ἐπιτετρίψονται, as in Ar.*Pax* 246):—*rub on the surface, crush*, κᾄπνιγε κἀπέτριβεν v.l. in Id.*Nu*.1376, cf. *Ra*.571:—Pass., τυπτόμενον ἐπιτριβῆναι Id.*Nu*.1408; ἐπιτριβόμενος τὸν ὦμον *galled* by the weight, Id.*Ra*.88. **2.** metaph., *afflict, destroy*, [ἥλιος] καίων ἐ. τούς τε ἀνθρώπους καὶ τὴν χώρην Hdt.4.184; γάμον ὅς μ' ἐπέτριψεν Ar.*Nu*.438, cf. 243; ταῦτά με ἐ. πόθῳ Id.*Lys*.888; ὀδύναις τινὰ ἐ. X.*Mem*.1.3.12; ἐ. τοὺς ἀπόρους D.18.104; opp. σῴζειν, Men.*Epit*.550; of an actor, *murder* a part, D.18.180; ἐ. Μένανδρον Plu.2.531b:—Pass., *to be utterly destroyed* or *undone*, Sol.33.7, Ar.*Ach*.1022, *Pax* 246, 369; ἐπιτριβείης *damn you!* Id.*Av*.1530, *Th*.557; ἐπιτριβείην εἴ τι ἐψευσάμην Luc.*DMeretr*.2.3; *to be worried*, Phld.*Ir*.p.27 W.; *to be burdened*, *POxy*.1252^{v}32 (iii A.D.), etc. **3.** c. dat., *waste time over*, στοχαστικοῖς Gal.15.172. **II.** Med., *rub paint on one's cheeks*, of women, Phryn.*PS* p.71 B. (cod.), cf. Sch.Ar.*Th*.396 (Act.). **III.** *inflame* by friction, ἐ. τὴν νόσον *aggravate* it, App.*BC*5.59, cf. Gal.19.680; *irritate, excite*, τινά Plb.4.84.8; τινὰ ἐς πόλεμον App.*Mac*.11.7, cf. *PSI*5.452.15 (iv A.D.).

ἐπιτρῐηραρχ-έω, *to be trierarch beyond the legal time*, D.50.24,54: –τετριηράρχηκα τέτταρας μῆνας ib.36:—Pass., ἐπιτετριηραρχημένων ἤδη μοι δυοῖν μηνοῖν two months *beyond* my *term of office having elapsed*, and my successor not having relieved me, ib.20. **–ημα**, ατος, τό, *burden of a trierarchy continued beyond the legal term*, ib.50.1, 54. **–ος**, ὁ, *trierarch subject to this burden*, *IG*2^{2}.1612.136.

ἐπιτρῐμερής, ές, *containing* $1+\frac{3}{4}$, Nicom.*Ar*.1.20.

ἐπι-τριμμός, ὁ, (ἐπιτρίβω) *crushing*, Aq.*De*.23.1(2). **–τριπτικός**, ή, όν, (ἐπιτρίβω III) *irritating, exciting*, λόγοι Antyll.ap.Orib.6.6.5. **–τριπτος**, ον, of persons to whom one says ἐπιτριβείης (= ἄξιος τοῦ ἐπιτριβῆναι, *EM*367.1), *accursed, damned*, τοὐπίτριπτον κίναδος the *damned* fox, S.*Aj*.103 (= τὸ ἐξῶλες θηρίον, Sch.), cf. And.1.99; ἐ. ψωμοκόλακες Sannyr.10; οὑπίτριπτος the *rogue*, Ar.*Pl*.275, Alex.105, cf. Ar.*Pl*.619; ὦπίτριπτε Ar.*Ach*.557; *rascally*, ῥήτορες Luc.*Tim*.37: Sup., *Com.Adesp*.1348. **2.** ἡ νῦν ἐ. καὶ κατεαγυῖα μουσική the *disreputable* and effeminate music of to-day, S.E.*M*.6.14. (For this sense of a participial formation, cf. οὐλόμενος and ὀνήμενος.)

ἐπίτρῐτος, ον (η, ον, v. infr. 4), *containing an integer and one-third* ($1+\frac{1}{3}$), i.e. *in the* ratio *of* 4:3, ἐ. πυθμήν Pl.*R*.546c; ἀριθμοί Ph.2.183; λόγος Id.1.10, al., cf. *PTeb*.72.388 (ii B.C.), etc. Adv. –τως Nicom.*Ar*.2.20. **2.** in Music, ἐ. διαστάσεις, of the interval of the *fourth*, Pl.*Ti*.36a, cf. Plu.2.1138f, Aristid.Quint.3.1; ἐ. ἁρμονία Ph.1.23; ἁ δὲ συλλαβὰ ἐπίτριτον Philol.6. **3.** πούς ἐ., or ἐ., ὁ, a *metrical foot*, of three longs and one short, in which the ratio of θέσις and ἄρσις is 4:3, Sch.Heph.p.112 C.; ἐ. πρῶτος, δεύτερος, τρίτος, τέταρτος, ⏑ – – –, – ⏑ – –, – – ⏑ –, – – – ⏑, Heph.3.3. **4.** in usury, ἐπίτριτον (sc. δάνεισμα), τό, *a loan of which* $\frac{1}{3}$ *is annually paid as interest*, i.e. $33\frac{1}{3}$ *per cent.*, X.*Vect*.3.9; τόκοι ἐ. Arist.*Rh*.1411^{a}17; ἑξακόσιαι δραχμαὶ ἐπίτριται 600 drachmae *at* $33\frac{1}{3}$ *per cent.*, Is.*Fr*.79 S. **5.** ἐπίτριτον, τό, tax in Egypt, *PSI*8.902.9 (i A.D.).

ἐπιτρῐτόω, *repeat for the third time*, Anaxil.1.

ἐπίτριψις, εως, ἡ, *wearing away*, of the action of waves, Lxx *Ps*.92(93).3 (pl.). **II.** *ruin*, ἀνθρώπων prob. in *OGI*669.63 (Egypt, i A.D.).

ἐπιτρομέω, *to be in fear of*, τι Q.S.2.474.

ἐπίτρομος, ον, (τρέμω) *in fear, alarmed*, Sch.rec.A.*Th*.78.

ἐπιτροπ-άδην [ᾰ], Adv., = ἐπιθέτως, *insincerely*, Hsch. **–αῖος**, α, ον, *entrusted to one, delegated*, ἐ. λαβεῖν τὴν ἀρχήν Hdt.3.142; ἐ. ἔχειν τὴν βασιληΐην Id.4.147. **–εία**, ἡ, *charge, guardianship*, τινός *over* one, Pl.*Phdr*.239e, Arist.*Pol*.1271^{b}25, Plb.15.25^{a}.27, cf. Lys.*Fr*.43; τὴν ἐ. τινὸς λαβεῖν D.H.4.33, etc. **II.** *office of a Roman procurator*, τοῖς κατ' ἐπιτροπείας παρ' ἐμοῦ ἀπεσταλμένοις *PFay*.20.17 (Imperial edict, iii/iv A.D.); τῶν ἐθνῶν Them.*Or*.8.117a (pl.). **–εύσιμος**, ον, *subject to wardship*, *BCH*4.453 (cod. Sinait.). **–ευσις**, εως, ἡ, = –εία I, Pl.*R*.554c. **–ευτικός**, ή, όν, *fitted for the office of steward*, X.*Oec*.12.3. **–εύω**, *to be an administrator, guardian*, etc. **1.** abs., Hdt.1.134, X.*Oec*.12.8, 13.1, *IG*3.392, etc.; τινί *for* one, Pl.*Lg*.849b. **2.** c. gen., Λεωβώτεω Hdt.1.65; Αἰγύπτου ἐ. Id.3.15; τοῦ πλήθεος ib.82; Βαβυλῶνος Id.7.62; τινός *PSI*4.281.30 (ii A.D.); χώρας J.*AJ*11.4.6 (Med., v.l. Act.). **3.** c. acc., *govern, manage*, τὴν πατρίδα Hdt.3.36; πόλιν Id.8.127, Pl.*R*.519c; τὸν δῆμον Ar.*Eq*.212, al.; τὴν κτῆσιν Pl.*Lg*.877c:—Pass., *to be managed by bailiffs*, Arist.*Oec*.1345^{a}8. **b.** c. acc. pers., ἐ. τινά *to be guardian and regent for* him, Th.1.132, Lys.10.5:—Pass., *to be under guardians*, Is.1.10; ὑπό τινων *SIG*364.58 (Ephesus, iii B.C.), etc.; κακῶς.. ἐπιτροπευθῆναι *to be* ill-*treated by one's guardians*, Pl.*Lg*.928c, cf. D.27.5; αἰσχρῶς –τετροπευμένους ὑπὸ τοῦ πάππου Lys.32.3: metaph., ὁ σοφὸς –εύεται ὑπὸ θεοῦ Porph.*Marc*.16. **4.** in Roman Law, *to be procurator*, *IG*14.911, Plu.2.471a, etc.; τῆς Ἰουδαίας v.l. in *Ev.Luc*.3.1. **b.** *act as agent, represent* a person's interest, Mitteis *Chr*.372 ii 2 (ii A.D.). **II.** = ἐπιτρέπω, *grant, allow*, δίαιταν Is.5.31 codd. **–έω**, = foreg., dub. in Pl.Com.265. **–ή**, ἡ, *reference*, esp. to an arbiter in decision of a law-suit, ἠξίουν δίκης ἐπιτροπὴν σφίσι γενέσθαι ἢ ἐς πόλιν τινὰ ἢ ἰδιώτην Th.5.41; ἡ ἐ.

τούτῳ πρὸς Παρμένοντα γέγονε D.33.23; εἰς ἐ. ἔρχεσθαι ib.14; ἡ ἐ. ἐγένετό μοι ib.16; τὴν ἐ. λῦσαι ibid.; ἀνέντες τὴν ἐ. having declined it, Th. 5.31. 2. generally, *power to decide*, ἐ. διδόναι τινὶ περί τινος Hp. *Decent.*17, cf. *Schwyzer*195.10 (Crete (from Delos), ii B.C.); διδόναι τῇ συγκλήτῳ τὴν ἐ. Plb.18.39.5; διδόναι ἑαυτοὺς εἰς ἐ., or τὴν ἐ. διδόναι περὶ σφῶν αὐτῶν, Lat. *dedere se in fidem*, to surrender absolutely, Id.2.11.8, 15.8.14, etc.; ἐ. λαβεῖν εἰς τὸ διαλῦσαι to receive *full powers* to treat, Id.3.15.7, cf. D.H.2.45, D.S.17.47; μετ' ἐξουσίας καὶ ἐ. *Act. Ap.*26.12. II. *guardianship*, Pl.*Lg.*924b, etc.; ἐπιτροπῆς κατάστασις, διαδικασία, Arist.*Ath.*56.6; ἀποχὴ τῆς ἐ. *POxy.*898.24 (ii A.D.); ἐπιτροπῆς δικάζεσθαι, of an action brought by a ward against a guardian, Lys.*Fr.*27; καταγιγνώσκειν τὴν ἐ. D.29.58; ἐπιτροπῆς κρίνειν τινά Plu.2.844c. 2. *office of a Roman procurator*, ἡ τοῦ ἰδίου λόγου ἐ. *BGU*16.8 (ii A.D.): generally, *stewardship*, *PLond.*2.454.10 (iv A.D.). **-ία**, ἡ, metaph., *protection*, dub. in Arist.*EE*1247^{a}30. **-ιάζω** (corrupt acc. to Phryn.65) and **-ιασμός**, *relapse*, *Gloss.*; cf. ὑπο- and ἐπανα-τροπιάζω. **-ικός**, ή, όν, *of* or *for a trustee* or *guardian*, ἐ. νόμοι the laws *of guardianship*, Pl.*Lg.*927e; ἐ. λόγος D.H.*Lys.*20, cf. Hyp.*Or.*65 tit., *BGU*300.24 (ii A.D.), *Cod.Just.*3.10.1.2. 2. of character, εὐεργετικοὺς ἐπιτροπικοὺς χρηστοήθεις *protective*, *fit to be a guardian* or *trustee*, Ptol.*Tetr.*163. II. *having held the office of procurator*, *Ephes.*3 No.49. **-ος**, ον, (ἐπιτρέπω) *one to whom the charge of anything is entrusted*, *steward*, *trustee*, *administrator*, c. gen. rei, τῶν ἑωυτοῦ Hdt.1.108; τῶν οἰκίων Id.3.63: abs., X.*Oec.*12.3, D.21.78, 27.19, *Ev.Luc.*8.3, etc.; *steward*, *messman*, X.*Cyr.*4.2.35: metaph., τῶν [τοῦ Πρωταγόρου] ἐ. Pl.*Tht.*165a. 2. = Lat. *procurator*, Καίσαρος ἐ. Str.3.4.20, Plu.2.813e, etc.; ἐ. Σεβαστοῦ, -τῶν, *OGI*502.10 (Aezani, ii A.D.), 501.2 (Tralles, ii A.D.); ἐ. τῆς Ἠπείρου Arr.*Epict.*3.4.1; τῶν μετάλλων *OGI*678.5 (Egypt, ii A.D.), etc. 3. *governor*, *viceroy*, οἱ ἐ. τῆς Μέμφιος, Μιλήτου ἐ., Hdt.3.27, 5.30, cf. 106. 4. *executor*, *PPetr.*3 p.9, al. (iii B.C.). II. c. gen. pers., *trustee*, *guardian*, Hdt.4.76, Th.2.80, etc.; ἐ. τινι παίδων Hyp.*Epit.*42: abs., Pl.*Lg.*924b, etc.; ὑπὸ ἐπιτρόπους εἶναι *Ep. Gal.*4.2; καθιστάναι ἐ. *PRyl.*153.18 (ii A.D.): metaph., *guardian*, *protector*, θεὸς ἐ. ἐών Pi.*O.*1.106.

ἐπιτροφή, ἡ, (ἐπιτρέφω) *sustenance*, *BCH*35.69 (pl., Delos), J.*AJ* 18.9.1.

ἐπιτροχ-άδην [ᾰ], Adv. *trippingly*, *fluently*, *glibly*: in Hom. only in phrase ἐ. ἀγορεύειν Il.3.213, Od.18.26. II. *cursorily*, D.H. *Amm.*2.2, Man.1.11. **-άζω**, *run lightly over*: hence, *treat briefly*, ῥαθύμως ἐπιτετροχασμένα D.H.*Th.*16. 2. *trot gently*, *Hippiatr.*33 (p.171.14 O.; ἐντρ- Grynaeus, and so codd. p.164.16 O., al.). **-ᾰλος**, ον, *quickly passing*, '*tripping*', χρόνοι D.H.*Comp.*18: metaph., *glib*, *flowing*, ῥύσις τῆς λέξεως Id.*Dem.*40. **-ασμός**, ὁ, *rapid succession of statements*, as a figure of speech, Phld.*Herc.*862.14 (pl.), Alex. *Fig.*1.17, Phoeb.*Fig.*2.1. **-αστέον**, verb. Adj. *one must run over*, Nicom.*Harm.*3. **-άω**, = ἐπιτροχάζω, c. dat., ὕδωρ ἐ. ψαμάθοισι A.R.4.1266: c. acc., σάρκα..-τροχόωσαι σμώδιγγες Nic.*Al.*544: c. gen., κύματος *AP*9.306 (Antiphil.): abs., λοξαὶ ἐπιτροχάουσι κέλευθοι D.P.148; εἶθαρ -τροχάων A.R.4.1606; ῥαθάμιγγες ἐπιτροχόωσ' ὑετοῖο Arat.889. **-ίζω**, *turbino*, *Gloss.* **-ος**, ον, *running easily*, *easily inclined*, ἐπιτροχώτερον ῥέψαι Hp.*Art.*14; περίπατοι ἐ. οἱ μέσοι walks *which break into a run*, Aret.*CD*1.3; βλέφαρον οὐκ ἐ. not very *mobile*, Id.*SD*1.7: metaph., *tripping*, μέλη Hld.4.17; ῥυθμοί Aristid. Quint.2.15; *voluble*, *glib*, στωμύλα καὶ ἐ. λαλεῖν Luc.*DDeor.*7.3; ἐ. καὶ ἀσαφὲς φθέγγεσθαι Id.*Nec.*7. Adv. -ως, φθέγγεσθαι Ael.*NA*7.7.

ἐπιτρύζω, *squeak beside* or *over*, πέμφιγες -τρύζουσι θανόντα Euph. 134; τό μοι τελχῖνες -τρύζουσιν *mutter*, Call.*Aet.Oxy.*2079 *Fr.*1.1, cf. Hsch.; μῦς -τρύξας τινί Babr.112.8: abs., [τέττιξ] ἁβρὸν ἐ. *chirps*, *AP*6.54 (Paul. Sil.). (In part perh. f.l. for -τρίζω.)

ἐπιτρῡπάω, *bore*, *pierce*, Philostr.*Im.*1.20 (Pass.).

ἐπιτρύσσειν· ἐπίμεινον (Lacon.), Hsch.

ἐπιτρῡφάω, *luxuriate*, *revel in*, δόγμασιν v.l. for ἐντρ- in Ph.2.392.

ἐπιτρώγω, *eat with* or *after*, Luc.*Sat.*21, 28: c. gen. partit., *eat afterwards of..*, χελώνη -τραγοῦσα (aor. 2 part.) ὀριγάνου Ael.*NA*3.5. II. generally, *eat*, *POxy.*1185.11 (ii/iii A.D.).

ἐπιτρωπάω, poet. for ἐπιτρέπω, *allow*, τινί τι or c. inf., Opp.*H.*2.223, 5.188. 2. *entrust*, κῦδός τινι μέλεσθαι A.R.1.351.

ἐπιτυγχάνω, fut. -τεύξομαι Pl.*R.*431c: aor. 2 ἐπέτῠχον: pf. -τετύχηκα Arist.*Oec.*1352^{b}5:—prop. *hit the mark*, τοῦ σκοποῦ, opp. ἀποτυγχάνω, Id.*EN*1106^{b}33; οἱ πολλὰ βάλλοντες ἐπιτυγχάνουσι πολλάκις Plu.2.438a: hence, II. *light* or *fall upon*, *meet with*, 1. c. dat. pers., Ar.*Nu.*195, 535, Th.3.75; ἐ. γυναικὶ βιαζομένῃ Pl.*Lg.*874c: also c. dat. rei, ἐ. σορῷ Hdt.1.68; ναυσί Th.8.34; βιβλίῳ Luc.*Dem.Enc.*27; ἐ. [ταῖς θύραις] ἀνεῳγμέναις *to find* them open, Pl.*Smp.*223b. 2. c. gen. pers., μετρίου ἀνδρός Ar.*Pl.*245, cf. Plu.*Art.*12: c. gen. rei, ἐ. ὁλκάδος ἀναγομένης Th.3.3; εὐώνων ἐ. a low market, Arist.*Oec.* l.c. 3. rarely c. acc., τὰς ἁπλᾶς [ἐπιθυμίας] ἐν ὀλίγοις ἐπιτεύξῃ Pl. *R.*431c; ἅττ' ἂν ἐπιτύχῃς Eub.123.5. 4. abs., Ar.*Ra.*570, Th.6.38; mostly ὁ ἐπιτυχών *the first person one meets*, *any chance person*, esp. in pl., Hdt.2.2, Antipho 2.1.1: with neg., οὐδὲ φαύλων ἀνδρῶν οὐδὲ τῶν ἐ. Pl.*Cra.*390d; οὐ γὰρ οἶμαι τοῦ ἐ. εἶναι.. Id.*Euthphr.*4a; οὐ περὶ τοῦ ἐ. on *no common matter*, Id.*R.*352d: without the Art., ἐπιτυχόντος ἀνθρώπου λόγος E.*HF*1248, cf. Phot.p.140 R. (= gloss on Eup. 25 D.). III. *attain to*, *reach*, *gain* one's end, c. gen. rei, X.*Mem.* 4.2.28, D.48.3; εὐχωλᾶς *Inscr.Cypr.*134 H. (iv B.C.); πολιτείας *BGU* 113.3 (ii A.D.), etc.; τοῦ καλῶς [μειγνύναι] Pl.*Phlb.*61d; ἐ. τοῦ ἀγῶνος *gain* one's suit, D.48.30; *profit by*, *benefit by*, φιλανθρωπίας *BGU* 522.8 (ii A.D.): abs., οὐ δύνασθε ἐπιτυχεῖν *Ep.Jac.*4.2. 2. c. part., *succeed in* doing, Hdt.8.101, 103 (but ζητέων ἐπιτυγχάνειν *find*, *light upon* by searching, Hp.*VM*24): so c. inf., Luc.*Nec.*6; γαμβροῦ ὁ ἐπιτυχὼν εὗρεν υἱόν he who *is lucky in* his son-in-law, Democr.272. 3. c. dat. modi, *to be lucky*, *successful in* a thing, μάχῃ Aeschin.3.165: abs., *to be successful*, Pl.*Men.*97c, Th.3.42, Arist.*Rh.*1354^{a}9; ἂν ἐπιτύχῃ if she *succeeds*, Men.*Epit.*346; τἆλλα ἐ. X.*HG*4.5.19: also impers., αὐτῷ οὐδὲν ἐπετύγχανε Ant.Lib.41.6. 4. Pass., *turn out well*, αἱ ἐπιτετευγμέναι πράξεις *successful*, Plb.6.53.2, cf. Hipparch.ap. Stob.4.44.81, D.S.1.1, Plu.2.674a; φάρμακον -τετευγμένον *proved* remedy, Heraclid.Tarent.ap.Gal.12.403. IV. c. dat. pers., *converse*, *talk with* one, Pl.*Lg.*758c.

ἐπιτῠλίσσω, Att. -ττω, *roll up*, τι ἐν φύλλοισιν Hp.*Steril.*216. II. *turn over* or *open a book*, D.L.9.114.

ἐπιτυμβ-ίδιος, α, ον, (τύμβος) *at* or *over a tomb*, θρῆνοι A.*Ch.*342 (lyr.); τὴν δ' ἐ. τούτῳ θῆκεν χάριν *IG*14.1409.5. II. ἐπιτυμβίδιοι κορυδαλλίδες *frequenting tombs*, or *with tomb-like crests*, or *with tombs in their heads* (v. Ar.*Av.*475), Theoc.7.23, cf. Sch. ad loc. **-ιος**, ον (also α, ον Plu. (v. infr.)), = foreg. 1, αἶνος, θρῆνος, A.*Ag.*1547 (lyr.), *Ch.*335 (lyr.); εὖχος *APl.*5.368; χοαί S.*Ant.*901; σῆμα *Epigr.Gr.*339.1 (Cyzicus); κρηπὶς *AP*7.657.11 (Leon.), cf. Hld.4.8; Ἀφροδίτη ἐπιτυμβία, = Lat. *Venus Libitina*, Plu.2.269b; θεοὶ ἐ. *Tab.Defix.*99.9. II. of an old woman 'with one foot in the grave', Alciphr.3.62.

ἐπιτῠραννέω, *rule*, ὥσπερ ἐπ' ἀκροπόλει τῆς γενέσεως Porph.*in Ptol.* 192.

ἐπίτῡρον, τό, *confection of olives*, Lat. *epityrum*, Cato *RR*119, Plaut. *Mil.*24; commonest in Sicily, Varro *LL*7.86; cf. ἐπίτερα. II. ἐπιτυρά, dub. l. in Hsch. s. v. κάρκαρα (= Semon.33).

ἐπιτυφλόω, *stop* the pores, Arist.*Pr.*890^{b}39 (Pass.); ἐ. τὰ φλεβία Thphr.*Sens.*66. II. *blind*, τὸν νοῦν Phld.*Rh.*1.178 S.

ἐπιτύφομαι [ῡ], Pass., aor. 2 -ετύφην [ῠ] Ar.*Lys.*221:—*to be burnt up*, esp. by lightning, Philostr.*VS*1.21.2, cf. *Im.*2.29: metaph., *to be inflamed* by love, τινος *for* one, Ar. l. c.; ἐπιτεθυμμένος *furious*, Pl. *Phdr.*230a.

ἐπιτῡφῶσαι· ἐπιπυριάσασα, Hsch.: ἐπιτετυφωμένον ἢ ἐπικεκαυμένον, = Att. ἐπιτεθυμμένον, Moer.p.150 P.

ἐπιτύχ-ημα [ῠ], ατος, τό, = ἐπίτευγμα, *EM*548.45. **-ής**, ές, (ἐπιτυγχάνω) *hitting the mark*, *successful* (opp. ἀποτυχής, Pl.*Sis.*391c (Comp.)), κότος A.*Supp.*744 Turneb. (lyr.); ἔν τινι Arist.*Div.Somn.* 463^{b}19, D.S.4.83; κατά τι Plb.5.102.1; ἐς πάντα App.*BC*2.149 (Sup.): c. gen., ἐ. τῶν καιρῶν δόξα *that always hits* the right nail on the head, Isoc.12.30. Adv. -χῶς, εἰπεῖν Pl.*Phlb.*38d; διειλέχθαι Isoc.12.230, cf. Plu.*Mar.*17, Aët.9.28. II. Pass., *easy to hit*, εὔβλητοι καὶ ἐ. App.*Syr.*35. **-ία**, ἡ, *luck*, *chance*, ὁκόσα -τυχίῃ ποιέουσιν οἱ ἰητροί Hp.*Morb.*1.1. 2. *success*, opp. ἀποτυχίη, Democr.275; ἐν ταῖς μάχαις Plb.1.6.4; τῶν μαντευμάτων D.H.3.70; ἔργων *OGI*678.2 (Egypt, ii A.D.): pl., Phld.*Po.*2.33; *advantage*, Ph.2.326. b. κατ' ἐπιτυχίαν *casually*, *by a fortunate coincidence*, Plot.2.3.7. 3. *undertaking*, ματαία ἐ. *BGU*1060.3 (i B.C.).

ἐπιτωθ-άζω, *mock*, *jest*, Pl.*Ax.*364c, Hp.*Ep.*17; *mock at*, *jeer*, τινα, τινι, App.*BC*2.67, 5.125, cf. Hieronym.Hist.7; τοῖς γινομένοις Men. Rh.p.420 S. **-ασμός**, ὁ, *mockery*, *raillery*, Plb.3.80.4, Hld.10.25.

ἐπίϋδρος, ον, *capable of irrigation*, κτῆμα *PSI*3.188.7 (vi A.D.).

ἐπιφᾰγεῖν, aor. 2 inf. of ἐπεσθίω (q. v.).

ἐπιφαιδρύνω, *make bright* or *clean*, κάρη A.R.4.663:—Pass., Hld. 8.9.

ἐπιφαίνω, aor. 1 (late) -έφᾱνα Lxx *De.*33.2, *Ev.Luc.*1.79:—*show forth*, *display*, abs., μηδὲ λίην ἐπίφαινε Thgn.359 (s. v. l.); ἐ. προστασίαν ἀξιωματικήν Plb.10.18.8; μηδὲν τεχνικόν D.H.*Amm.*1.10; τὸ ἀγέρωχον, τὴν προαίρεσιν, Plu.*Marc.*1, 2.139d; ἀνθρωποπόμορφόν τι Luc.*Alex.* 12; τὸν μισοπόνηρον *play* the μ., Phld.*Ir.*p.74 W.:—Pass., *come into view*, ἠέλιος δ' ἐπέλαμψε, μάχη δ' ἐπὶ πᾶσα φαάνθη Il.17.650; of an enemy, Hdt.2.152, 4.122, Th.8.42, etc.; διὰ τὸ ἐπιφανέντα με κωλῦσαι Test.ap.D.21.22; ἐ. ἐς τὴν Νάξον Hdt.5.30, cf. X.*An.*3.4.13; ἐπιφανῆναι ἐπὶ τὸ ἔργον Id.*Oec.*21.10; ἐπὶ τὰ Δρέπανα Plb.1.49.7; ἐ. τινὶ ἐς οἶκον *to present oneself*, Hdt.4.97; ἐ. τινί *show oneself*, *appear* to one, Id.1.24, al.; freq. of dreams and visions, Id.2.91, 3.27; ἐν τῷ ὕπνῳ Id.7.16; of a divine manifestation, ἐπιφαινομένης αὐτοῖς Ἀρτέμιδος *SIG* 557.5 (Magn. Mae., iii B.C.), cf. *IG*4.951.26 (Epid., iii B.C.); so ἡ χρηστότης ἐπεφάνη τοῦ θεοῦ *Ep.Tit.*3.4; of an Emperor, δήμοις ἑορτάζουσιν ἐπιφανείς Hdn.1.7.2; also ἵνα σφι τιμωρίη.. ἐπιφανήσεται Hdt. 8.49; τὰ ἐπιφαινόμενα *symptoms which make their appearance*, Hp. *Aph.*1.12, cf. Sor.1.17, al. 2. c. acc. et inf., *make it manifest that..*, Plu.2.1044d. 3. Pass., lit. *appear upon the surface*, Ti.Locr.101d; ἐ. ταῖς εἰκόσιν ἰδέα Plu.*Arat.*3: metaph., τὸ ἦθος ὡς χρῶμα ταῖς πράξεσιν ἐ. ib.48, cf. *Galb.*23. II. seemingly intr., in Act., *show light*, *dawn*, ἡμέρας ἐπιφαινούσης Plb.5.6.6 (so ἀνατολῆς ἐπιφαινομένης Id.3.113.1); ἐπιφᾶναι τοῖς ἐν σκότει καθημένοις *to shine upon..*, *Ev.Luc.* 1.79, cf. Lxx *De.*33.2.

ἐπίφαλλος, ὁ, *flute-tune for dancing to*, Trypho ap.Ath.14.618c, cf. Eust.1236.56.

ἐπιφάν-εια [ᾰ], ἡ, *appearance*, *coming into light* or *view*, τῆς ἡμέρας *day-break*, *dawn*, Plb.3.94.3; in war, *sudden appearance* of an enemy, Aen.Tact.31.8, Plb.1.54.2, Ascl.*Tact.*12.10 (pl.), Onos.22.3 (pl.). 2. esp. of deities appearing to a worshipper, *manifestation*, D.H.2.68, Plu.*Them.*30; *advent*, D.S.2.47; τὰς ὑπ' αὐτῆς (sc. Ἀρτέμιδος) γενομένας ἐναργεῖς ἐ. *SIG*867.35 (Ephesus, ii A.D.); *a manifestation* of divine power, τὰς ἐ. τᾶς Παρθένου *Klio*16.204 (Chersonesus, iii B.C.), cf. Lxx 2*Ma.*15.27, D.S.1.25. 3. *the first coming* of Christ, 2*Ep. Ti.*1.10; *the second*, 1*Ep.Ti.*6.14, al. 4. of the *accession* of Caligula,

Inscr.Cos 391. 5. *appearance, aspect,* οἰκετικὴ ἐ. Myro 2 J.; κατὰ τὴν ἐ., distd. fr. κατὰ τὴν ἐπίφασιν, Plb. 25.3.6. II. *visible surface* of a body, *superficies,* Democr. 155 (pl.), Arist.*Cat.* 5ᵃ2, *Metaph.* 1002ᵃ 4, *Ph.* 209ᵃ8, *Sens.* 439ᵃ31, Euc.*El.* 1 *Deff.*, Ph.*Bel.* 70.27, Damian.*Opt.* 11; ἡ κατὰ πρόσωπον ἐ. the *front,* Plb. 1.22.10; κατὰ τὰς ἐ. μάχεσθαι to fight in *front,* Id. 3.116.10; ἐ. ἡ ἐκ δεξιῶν Arr.*Tact.* 21.3; αἱ τρεῖς ἐ. τῆς πόλεως its three *visible sides,* Plb. 4.70.9; the *surface* or *skin* of the body, D.S. 3.29, Pap. in *AJP* 24.327, Gal. 16.530, etc.; μυδῶντα τὴν ἐ. Luc.*Philops.* 11; τῆς ἔνδον ἐ. τῶν ἐντέρων Gal. 18(1).2. 2. *outward show, fame, distinction,* esp. arising from something unexpected, Pl. *Alc.* 1.124c; ἐ. ποιεῖν to create a *sensation,* Is. 7.13: in pl., Isoc. 6. 104, D.S. 19.1; τὰ πρὸς ἐπιφάνειαν καὶ δόξαν ἀνήκοντα *OGI* 763.19 (Milet., ii B.C.), cf. Arr.*Epict.* 3.22.29. **-εια** (sc. ἱερά), τά, *sacrifices in celebration of an* ἐπιφάνεια, Δημήτριος τὰ ἐ. τοῦ ἀδελφοῦ θύων Caryst. 10. **-ής**, ές, *coming to light, coming suddenly into view, appearing,* of gods, Hdt. 3.27, etc.: hence, *present to aid,* θεοὶ -έστατοι D.S. 1.17. 2. of places and things, *in full view,* πόλις ἐ. ἔξωθεν, of a place *commanded by another,* Th. 5.10, cf. 6.96, 7.19; τινι *to* one, ib. 3; ἔχειν ἐπιφανεῖς θηλὰς *visible,* Arist.*HA* 504ᵇ23; φλέβες *prominent,* Gal. 17(2).209. 3. *manifest, evident,* ὄνειδος Democr. 218 (Comp.); ἐκ τῶν ἐπιφανεστάτων σημείων Th. 1.21; διὰ τὸ μὴ ἐ. εἶναι Arist.*EN* 1126ᵃ23. II. of men, *conspicuous, notable, distinguished* by rank, Hdt. 2.89, al.; οἰκίη οὐκ ἐ. ib. 172; *notable,* either for good or ill, X. *Mem.* 3.1.10, Lys. 14.12 (Sup.); ἀνδρείᾳ *for* courage, Th. 6.72; πρὸς τὸν πόλεμον Pl.*Lg.* 629e; *famous, renowned,* Pi.*P.* 7.6 (Comp.), etc.; ἀνδρῶν ἐ. πᾶσα γῆ τάφος Th. 2.43; of things, places, etc., χώρα *OGI* 90. 46 (Rosetta, ii B.C.); -εστέρα τιμή *IPE* 1².34.22 (Olbia, i B.C.); -έσταται τιμαί *IG* 9(2).1109.10 (Magn. Thess.). 2. of things, *remarkable,* οὗτοί σφεων οἱ -έστατοι νόμοι εἰσί Hdt. 5.6; -εστάτη χρεία Plb. 1.78. 11; -εστάτη μάχη Anon.Hist.*Oxy.* 12 ii 31. 3. as a title of divinities, τῶν -εστάτων θεῶν *IG* 5(1).1179 (Sparta); also of Eastern Kings, e.g. Ptolemy V, *OGI* 90.5 (Rosetta, ii B.C.); Antiochus of Syria, Plb. 26.1ᵃ.1, etc. III. Adv. -νῶς *openly, conspicuously,* Th. 1.91, 5.105 (Sup.). 2. *with distinction,* λαμπρῶς καὶ ἐ. *IGRom.* 4.844 (Phrygia), cf. J.*BJ* 7.3.1: Comp. -έστερον, ζῆν *with greater distinction,* Men. 223.19. **-τος**, ον, *in the light, alive,* S.*Ant.* 841 (lyr.); *visible, manifest,* Διοσκούρων ἐ. prob. in Poet.ap.Stob. 1.1.31ᵃ.

ἐπιφαρμάσσω, *apply medicine again to,* ἐ. τὰ σπλάγχνα ἤδη πεφαρμαγμένα Ach.Tat. 4.16.

ἐπίφᾰσις, εως, ἡ, *becoming visible,* f.l. in Thphr.*Sens.* 27 codd. (ἔμφασις Schneider); *outward appearance,* ἐ. βασιλική Plb. 4.77.3; κατὰ τὴν ἐ. καταπλαγῆναι by his *outward appearance,* Id. 11.27.8; opp. κατ' ἀλήθειαν, Id. 14.2.9; but distd. from κατὰ τὴν ἐπιφάνειαν, Id. 25. 3.6. II. *indication, display,* ἑτοιμότητος, ἀκριβείας, εὐδαιμονίας, Id. 4.11.4, 12.10.4, 31.25.7; ἠθῶν dub. in Phld.*Mus.* p.64 K. (pl.).

ἐπιφάσκω, *pretend, profess,* c. inf., εἰδέναι σαφῶς Ph. 1.457; ἰᾶσθαι Id.ap.Eus.*PE* 8.14; *act* a part, ἐ. τὸν [σεμνόν] Phld.*Vit.* p.36 J.; τὸν πλούσιον Ph. 2.536.

ἐπιφατνίδιος, α, ον, (φάτνη) *at the manger,* φορβειά X.*Eq.* 5.1.

ἐπιφάτνιος· ὁ ἑωσφόρος ἀστήρ, Hsch.

ἐπίφᾰτος, ον, *notorious,* S.*Fr.* 1048 (codd. Eust., sed leg. ἐπίσφατος). II. (*φένω) = ὀλέθριος, Eust. 1728.14 (-φατος codd.).

ἐπιφαυλίζω, *make of small account,* v.l. for -φυλλ- in Lxx *La.* 1.22, 2.20.

ἐπιφαύσκω, fut. -φαύσω (v. infr.):—*shine out,* of the sun or moon, Lxx *Jb.* 25.5, 31.26: also in pass. form, ib. 41.9(10); ἐπιφαύσει σοι ὁ Χριστός *will shine out* for thee, *Ep.Eph.* 5.14.

ἐπιφέρβομαι, *feed on,* ὁπόσοι γῆν -όμεθα Phanocl. 2.2.

ἐπιφερής, ές, *prone,* Hsch. s.v. πρωλύθιον.

ἐπιφέρνια, τά, *dowry,* Sch.Il. 9.147, Eust. 1417.14.

ἐπιφέρω, fut. ἐποίσω: aor. 1 ἐπήνεγκα: aor. 2 ἐπήνεγκον: Arc. aor. 1 subj. 3 sg. ἐποίσῃ *Schwyzer* 654.21:—**Pass.,** fut. ἐποισθήσεται· ἐπενεχθήσεται, Hsch.:—*bring, put* or *lay upon,* σοὶ ... βαρείας χεῖρας ἐποίσει *will lay* heavy hands *upon* thee, Il. 1.89; χεῖρας ἐποίσει Od. 16.438; ἐπ' ἀλλήλοισι φέρον πολύδακρυν Ἄρηα Il. 3.132, cf. 8.516; ἐπ' ἰχθύσι κῆρα φέρουσα 24.82; so ἐ. δόρυ A.*Eu.* 766, cf. E.*Supp.* 1192, Ar.*Av.* 344 (lyr.); and in Prose, ἐ. τινὶ πόλεμον *make* war *upon* him, Hdt. 5.81, cf. Th. 1.141; ὅπλα Id. 4.16, 7.18, D. 37.36; ἐ. τὸ διάφορόν τισι *to bring* discord *upon* them, Th. 7.55; ἐ. δίκην, τιμωρίαν τινί, Pl.*Lg.* 943d; ἀμοιβήν τινι Plb. 1.84.10: abs., εἰ γὰρ ὧδ' ἐποίσεις if you *shall pursue your attack* thus, Ar.*Eq.* 837. b. *inflict,* πληγήν, πληγάς τινι, J.*AJ* 2.14.2, *PTeb.* 331.10 (ii A.D.); *vent,* ὀργήν *Ep.Rom.* 3.5. 2. *place upon,* esp. of placing offerings on the grave, ἐ. ἀπαρχάς Th. 3.58, cf. 2.34; τῷ νεκρῷ στέφανον Plu.*Per.* 36; ταφὴν εἴς τινα App.*BC* 1.73; τὰ ἐπιφερόμενα the *offerings,* Isoc. 9.1; *lay on, apply,* φάρμακον Pl.*Ep.* 354b; ἐ. τὰ στοιχεῖα ἐπὶ τὰ πράγματα Id.*Cra.* 424e. 3. *bring* as a charge *against,* ἐ. τινὶ αἰτίην Hdt. 1.68, cf. 26, Antipho 5.38, Pl.*Phd.* 98a; ἔγκλημα E.*Or.* 766 (troch.); μέμψιν Ar.*Ra.* 1253 (lyr.); ψόγον Th. 1.70; ἐ. μωρίην, μανίην τινί, *impute* it *to* him, Hdt. 1.131, 6.112; ἀδικίας -ομένης Th. 3.42; τὴν Κλεοπάτραν αὐτῷ *cast* Cl. *in his teeth,* D.C. 50.1; τι ἐπί τινα Arist.*EN* 1143ᵃ27. 4. *bring,* i.e. *confer, impose, upon,* in good or bad sense, ἐ. τιμὰν θνατοῖς Pi.*O.* 1. 31; ἐλευθερίαν Th. 4.85; δουλείαν Id. 3.56. 5. *add to, increase,* ἐ. τὴν ὑπερβολήν ib. 82; ὀργὰς ἐπιφέρειν τινί *minister* to his passions, *gratify* him, Cratin. 230, Th. 8.83 (cf. Sch.); for ἐπὶ ἦρα φέρειν, v. ἦρα. 6. *give* a name *to,* ὄνομα ἐ. τινί Pl.*Plt.* 307b, *R.* 596a, al., Arist.*Rh.* 1408ᵃ7, al.; *assign* an attribute to a substantive, τῷ ἀνθρώπῳ χρώματα καὶ σχήματα καὶ κακίας καὶ ἀρετὰς Pl.*Sph.* 251a. 7. ἐ. ψῆφον *to give* a vote, D.H. 2.14. 8. *subjoin, add,* A.D.*Synt.* 60. 26, al., Demetr.*Eloc.* 34, al., Alex.Aphr. *in Sens.* 5.9. 9. *adduce, cite,* Εὐριπίδεια D.H.*Comp.* 4; παροιμίαν Demetr.*Eloc.* 122 (prob.); *produce* proofs, documents, etc., ἀποδείξεις *POxy.* 257.19 (i A.D.); κυρία ἡ συγγραφή, ὅπου ἂν -φέρηται *PEleph.* 2.16 (iii B.C.). 10. in Logic, *assert as a conclusion* or *inference,* τὸ λῆγον, τὸ λοιπόν, Chrysipp.*Stoic.* 2.80; τὸ μὴ ἀκολουθοῦν Str. 2.1.21; ὅτι... ib. 27; ὅσα ἐπιφέρουσιν ἄτοπα οἱ Ζήνωνος λόγοι Procl. *in Prm.* p.535 S.:—Pass., τὸ τοῖς ἐξ ὑποθέσεως ληφθεῖσιν ἐπιφερόμενον the conclusion which *follows from* the premises, Chrysipp.*Stoic.* 2.89, cf. Arr.*Epict.* 1.7.16. 11. ἐπιφέρων, ὁ, a throw at dice, Eub. 57.6. II. Med., *bring with* or *upon oneself, bring as a dowry,* τι Lys. 19.14, D. 40.19; of soldiers, σιτία Plu.*Sert.* 13; ὕδωρ Str. 3.1.4. 2. *consume* (*eat*) *in addition,* οἱ μὲν πίνουσι μόνον, οἱ δὲ σιτίον -ονται Hp.*Prorrh.* 2.3:—Pass., -ομένη τροφή Sor. 1.52. 3. *wear* or *carry on one's person,* Hld. 8.11. III. Pass., *rush upon* or *after, attack, assault,* ὅς τις... ἐπὶ νηυσὶ φέροιτο Il. 15.743; τισι Th. 3.23: abs., X.*Cyr.* 2.4.19, etc.; of a ship, *bear down upon* another, Hdt. 8.90; θάλαττα μεγάλη ἐπιφέρεται a great sea *strikes the ship,* X.*An.* 5.8.20; *inveigh against,* Hdt. 8.61: c. inf., *to be eager to* do, Plb. 29.24.5. b. of humours etc. in the body, τὸ -όμενον the *accumulation* of milk, Sor. 1.77; διαφορεῖν τὸ ἐπενεχθέν disperse the *abscess,* Gal. 1.137; cf. ἐπιφορά 1.5a. 2. *to be borne onwards,* of a raft, Hdt. 2.96; ἐ. ἐπί τι *to be led to* an opinion, Arist. *Sens.* 443ᵃ22 (s.v.l.). 3. *impend, threaten,* ἐ. κίνδυνος Plb. 2.23.7; mostly in part., προδεικνύειν τὰ ἐπιφερόμενα *coming events,* Hdt. 1.209, cf. 3.16; ἐ. κακά Antipho 2.1.7; ὑπεκστῆναι τὸν λόγον ἐπιφερόμενον Pl.*Phlb.* 43a; τὰ ἐ. *the following* (in speaking or writing), Plb. 3.6. 8. 4. of phrases, *to be applied,* ἡ λέξις -φέρεται τοῖς πράγμασιν Plu. 2.41c; but οἱ διὰ μακροῦ -φερόμενοι λόγοι sustained *outbursts,* Demetr. *Eloc.* 196. 5. Gramm., *follow,* of letters in a word, D.T. 633.2, Heph. 1.4, al., etc.

ἐπίφευκτος, ον, *to be avoided,* Asp. *in EN* 186.28.

ἐπιφημητῆρες· οἱ ἐπευφημοῦντες, κτλ., Hsch. (-τέρ- cod.).

ἐπίφημι, *agree, assent,* νόμῳ Emp. 9.5: Aeol. aor. inf. Act. ἐπιφάμεναι, = συγκαταθέσθαι, Hsch.

ἐπιφημ-ίζω, *utter words ominous of the event,* ἰόντος αὐτοῦ ἐπὶ τὴν πεντηκόντερον ἐπεφημίζετο (Med.) Hdt. 3.124; ἐ. τινὶ πολλὰ καὶ ἄτοπα D.C. 39.39. 2. *promise, pledge,* κείνῳ παῖδ' ἐπεφήμισα... ἐκδώσειν cj. in E.*IA* 130 (anap.); ἡ ἐκ παιδὸς ἐπιφημισθεῖσα τῷ ἀνδρὶ ἑβδόμη ὑπατεία (of Marius) App.*BC* 1.61. II. *apply the name of* A (acc.) *to* B (dat.), where A is usu. a god, *ascribe* or *assign* B *to* A, ἑκάστῃ μοίρᾳ θεόν Pl.*Lg.* 771d; ὅσα τις πράττει τοὺς θεοὺς ἐπιφημίζων *in the name of* the gods, D. 20.126; ἅπασι τοῖς μεγάλοις ἐ. τὸ δαιμόνιον Plu. *Publ.* 23. 2. later the constr. is reversed, τοῖς θεοῖς τι J.*Ap.* 2.37; τὴν ἐλαίας γένεσιν... τῇ Ἀθηνᾷ Max.Tyr. 30.5:—Pass., θεοῖς... παῖδες ἐπεφημίσθησαν D.C. 44.37; ὅσα θεῖα Ἐλευσῖνι ἐπιφημίζεται τῇ χώρᾳ Aristid. 1.445 J.; μέρη τῆς γῆς Ποσειδῶνι ἐπιπεφήμισται Id.*Or.* 46(3). 16. III. *call, name,* c. dupl. acc., τὸ ἀγαθὸν ἐ. λυσιτελοῦν Pl.*Cra.* 417c, cf. *Ti.* 73d; ἀέρα ἐ. σκότος Ph. 1.6, cf. 2.43, al., Porph.*Abst.* 1.7; Ἥλιον -ίζοντας Αἰήτην υἱέα Jul.*Or.* 2.82d. 2. with epexegetic inf., τὴν ἔξω φορὰν ἐπεφήμισεν εἶναι τῆς ταὐτοῦ φύσεως the outer revolution he *called* the revolution of the Same, *ordained* that it should be..., Pl.*Ti.* 36c: hence, b. c. acc. et inf., *allege, declare,* αὐτὸν Ἀσκληπιοῦ θεράποντα εἶναι Ael.*NA* 8.12; πολλὰ ἐ. αὐτῷ δηλοῦν [τὴν ἔλαφον] Plu. *Sert.* 11. 3. *bestow* a name *on,* ὀνόματά τισι Ph. 1.304, al., D.C. 54. 33; πομπῇ ἐπεφήμισαν οὔνομα νηῶν *named* [the fish πομπίλος] *after*..., Opp.*H.* 1.187. IV. in later Prose, *dedicate, devote* to a god, Luc.*Sacr.* 10; Διὶ ἀγάλματα Max.Tyr. 8.8; τοὺς γενομένους τότε παῖδας Ἄρεως ἐ. Str. 5.4.12:—Pass., Id. 6.2.9, Ph. 2.565, Plu.*Cam.* 7, etc. **-ισμα,** ατος, τό, *word of ominous import*: of ill omen, Th. 7.75; of good omen, J.*AJ* 17.5.1 (pl.). **-ισμός,** ὁ, *dedication,* Str. 6.2.9. **-ιστέον,** *one must assign, ascribe,* δουλείαν τινί Ph. 2.452, cf. 477.

ἐπιφθάνω [ᾰ], *reach first,* aor. 2 part. ἐπιφθάς Batr. 213: generally, *reach, attain,* ἡλικίαν, Suid. s.v. ἄνηβος; ἐπέφθη τυραννίδι *PLond.* 5. 1676.43 (vi A.D.); *arrive,* ὁ Μουκιανὸς οὔπω ἐπεφθάκει D.C. 65.18:—Med., *see before* others, ἐπιτέλλουσαν [Αἶγα] Anon.ap.Suid.

ἐπι-φθέγγομαι, *utter after* or *in accordance,* A.*Ch.* 457 (lyr.); *utter during* or *in connexion with,* φωνὰς ἐπὶ τῇ καθιερώσει Plu.*Publ.* 14; μικρὰ ταῖς σπονδαῖς Id. 2.150d. 2. *attach* a name to, *predicate* a quality of, μίαν ἐπ' αὐτοῖς τέχνην ἐπεφθέγξατο Pl.*Phlb.* 18d, cf. Plu. 2.1110e. b. *name, call,* ἃ κρίνα, λείρια δ' ἄλλοι -ονται Nic.*Fr.* 74. 27. 3. *quote,* τὸ ῥῆμα, ὅτι... Ph.*Fr.* 12 H.; τοῦτο τὸ κοινὸν πᾶσι πράγμασι Plu. 2.436d. 4. simply, *utter, pronounce,* Pl.*Cra.* 383a:—Pass., Id.*Sph.* 257c. II. *respond,* ὁ μὲν ἡγεῖτο λέγων "ἔξω Χριστιανούς", τὸ δὲ πλῆθος -ετο "ἔξω Ἐπικουρείους" Luc.*Alex.* 38. **-φθεγμα,** ατος, τό, *refrain,* παιανικὸν ἐ., of the refrain ἰὴ Παιάν, Ath. 15. 696f. II. *interjection,* A.D.*Synt.* 52.26. **-φθεγματικός,** ή, όν, *containing a refrain,* [σύστημα] Heph.*Poëm.* 7.3. **-φθεγξις,** εως, ἡ, *charm, invocation,* Philagr.ap.Aët. 12.51; *cry addressed* to dogs, Sch. Ar.*V.* 702.

ἐπιφθίνω, *perish upon,* λείρια στήλῃσιν ἐ. Nic.*Fr.* 74.70.

ἐπιφθον-έω, *grudge* any one's doing a thing, ᾧδέ κ' ἐπιφθονέοις (sc. ἆσσον ἴμεν) Od. 11.149. II. *bear hate* or *a grudge against,* τινι Hdt. 9.79, *PMasp.* 154.9 (vi A.D.):—Pass., *to be regarded with jealous hate,* D.H. 9.43. **-ος,** ον, *liable to envy* or *jealousy, looked on with jealousy, odious,* αἱ λίην ἰσχυραὶ τιμωρίαι πρὸς θεῶν ἐ. γίνονται Hdt. 4.205; γνώμη πρὸς ἀνθρώπων ἐ. Id. 7.139; μηδ'... ἐ. πόρον τίθει A.*Ag.* 921; τινι by one, E.*Med.* 303, *Supp.* 893; εἴ τῳ θεῶν ἐ. ἐστρατεύσαμεν Th. 7.77; [πενία] ἥκιστα ἐ. X.*Smp.* 3.9; -ώτεραι (sc. αἱ ἐμαὶ διατριβαί) Pl.*Ap.*

37d, cf. *R.*502d; ἐπίφθονόν ἐστι c. inf., it is *invidious, hateful* to.., Ar.*Eq.*1274; εἴ τῳ "μακαρίως" -ώτερον εἰπεῖν Arist.*EE*1215ᵃ10; τὸ ἐ. *envy*, ἐπὶ μεγίστοις τὸ ἐ. λαμβάνειν Th.2.64. 2. Act., *bearing a grudge against*, τινι A.*Ag.*133 (lyr.): abs., *malignant, hostile*, Id.*Eu.* 376 (lyr.), *Sammelb.*3924.35 (i A.D.); τὸ δαιμόνιον.. ἐ. App.*Pun.*59; ἐ. βλέμμα Hld.4.5. II. Adv. ἐπιφθόνως, διακεῖσθαί τινι to be *liable to* his *hatred*, Th.1.75; ἐ. διαπράξασθαί τι *in an invidious manner*, Id. 3.82; ἥκιστα ἐ. *with least invidiousness*, X.*Cyr.*7.5.37. 2. ἐ. ἔχειν πρός τινα to be *at enmity* with him, ib.3.3.10, 8.2.28.

ἐπίφθορος, ον, (φθορά) *deadly*, φάρμακον Poll.5.132.

ἐπιφθύζω, Dor. **ἐπιφθύσδω**, = ἐπιπτύω, *spit at*, so as to avert a spell of witchcraft, Theoc.7.127, 2.62.

ἐπιφῐλο-πονέομαι, Dep., *labour willingly and earnestly at*, τινι X. *Oec.*5.5. **-τῑμέομαι**, *bestow*, κοινὰς δωρεὰς ἐ. [ὁ νομοθέτης] Lib.*Decl.* 43.29. **-τῑμία**, ἡ, *endowment*, prob. in *IG*2².1369 (ii A.D., pl.).

ἐπίφλεβος, ον, (φλέψ) *with prominent veins*, Hp.*Epid.*6.4.19, Arist. *HA*493ᵃ3, etc.

ἐπιφλεβοτομέω, *bleed again*, Antyll.ap.Orib.7.7.11.

ἐπιφλεγ-έθω, = ἐπιφλέγω, Nic.*Al.*282. **-ής**, ές, (φλέγω) *fiery*, χρῶμα Arist.*Phgn.*812ᵃ25. **-μα**, ατος, τό, *inflammation on the surface*, Iamb.*Protr.*21.κϛ'. **-μαίνω**, *suffer from supervening inflammation*, Hp.*Fract.*38, Aret.*SA*1.9, etc.

ἐπι-φλέγω, *burn up*, πῦρ.. ἐπιφλέγει ἄσπετον ὕλην Il.2.455; ὄφρ' ἤτοι τοῦτον μὲν [νεκρὸν] ἐπιφλέγῃ.. πῦρ 23.52; of an enemy, πάντα ἐπέφλεγον καὶ ἔκειρον Hdt.8.32; ἐ. τὴν πόλιν *set fire to* it, Th.2.77:— Pass., Nic.*Th.*188. 2. *heat, inflame*, τὴν ἐπιφάνειαν Aët.15.20: metaph., *inflame, excite*, σάλπιγξ ἀϋτῇ πάντ' ἐκεῖν' ἐπέφλεγεν A.*Pers.* 395; ἐ. τινὰ αἴθοπι μώμῳ Tim.*Pers.*222; Ἀννίβας εὐτυχῶν ἐ. τὴν Ἰταλίαν Plu.*Cat.Ma.*1; with love, Λαΐς ἐ. πόθῳ τὴν Ἑλλάδα Id.2.767f: —Pass., Arist.*Phgn.*812ᵃ27, Ael.*NA*15.9. 3. *illumine*, ἠέλιος.. ἐ. ἀκτίνεσσιν D.P.1110: metaph., *make illustrious*, ἐ. πόλιν ἀοιδαῖς Pi. *O.*9.22. II. intr., *to be scorching hot*, of the sun, Luc.*Anach.*25, D.C.59.7: metaph., *to be brilliant*, εὐφροσύνα τε καὶ δόξ' ἐ. Pi.*P.*11. 45. **-φλεξις**, εως, ἡ, *application of heat*, καῦσις κατ' ἐ., opp. caustics, Paul.Aeg.4.5.

ἐπιφλεύω, *scorch*, χεῖρα *IG*4.955 (Epid.).

ἐπιφλόγ-ισμα, ατος, τό, *superficial inflammation*, Hp.*Aph.*5.23 (pl.), Erot. s.v. φῷδες (pl.). **-ώδης**, ες, *looking as if inflamed*, dub. l. in Hp.*Coac.*456.

ἐπιφλυγμός, ὁ, *flooding*, v.l. for -βλυσμός, Aq.*Ge.*2.6.

ἐπιφλυκταινόομαι, Pass., *have pustules on the top*, Hp.*Epid.*4.20.

ἐπιφλύω [ῡ], *sputter at*, τινι A.R.1.481.

ἐπίφοβος, ον, *frightful, terrible*, A.*Ag.*1152 (lyr.); *alarming*, γειτνίασις Plu.*Pyrrh.*7; τινι J.*AJ*12.7.5. Adv. -βως, τινι App.*Syr.*35. II. Pass., *in fear, timid*, Gal.19.707. Adv. -βως, διάγειν Vett.Val.42. 9. 2. *risky*, θεραπεία Steph. *in Hp.*1.211 D.

ἐπιφοινῑκίζω, *get a purple tinge*, Arist.*Col.*796ᵃ2.

ἐπιφοινίσσω, *make red on the surface*, Luc.*Am.*41. II. intr., *incline to be red, be reddish*, Arist.*Phgn.*812ᵃ33; -φοινίσσον σημεῖον Thphr.*Sign.*10:—Pass., -ίσσεται τὸ πρόσωπον Arist.*Phgn.*812ᵃ32; -ίσσονται τοὺς ὀφθαλμοὺς ib.37.

ἐπιφοιτ-άω, Ion. -έω, *come habitually* or *in addition*, πλεῦνος αἰεὶ γινομένου τοῦ ἐπιφοιτέοντος Hdt.1.97; οἱ ἐπιφοιτῶντές τε καὶ οἱ ἀρχὴν ἐλθόντες the *subsequent arrivals*, Id.9.28; ὁ ἐπιφοιτῶν κέραμος every *new* wine-jar *imported*, Id.3.6; ἐ. ἐς.. *to go about* to different places, Th.1.135; τὴν γῆν δῃοῦν ἐπιφοιτῶντες *visiting, invading* it, ib.81; τὰς πόλεις Jul.*Or.*7.221b: c. dat., τοῖς θεάτροις Ael.*VH*2.13. 2. c. dat. pers., σπάνιος ἐ. σφι *visits* them rarely, of the Phoenix, Hdt.2.73, cf. Ph.1.265, Palaeph.37, Luc.*Am.*9, etc. 3. c. acc. pers., of visions, *haunt*, Hdt.7.16.γ', cf. 15; of a disease, *recur*, Hp.*Coac.*316; *spread*, ἅπασι [τοῖσι νεύροισι], of rheumatic pains, Aret.*SD*2.12; ἐπεφοίτα πανταχόσε he *went round* to every ship, Plu.*Ant.*65. 4. in mal. part., ταῖς θυγατράσι τινός Hdn.5.3.10. **-εύω**, = foreg. 3, ἡ νοῦσος ἐ. ἐς τὸν ἄνθρωπον Aret.*CD*1.4. **-ησις**, εως, ἡ, *a coming upon* one, τῶν στρατιωτῶν J.*AJ*19.3.2; of a god, *intervention, manifestation*, ib. 17.2.4, Jul.*Or.*7.221c, Steph. *in Hp.*1.74 D. 2. *frequenting*, ἐπὶ τὴν αὐτῷ ποέπουσαν κοινωνίαν Procl. *in Prm.*p.519 S. **-ος**, ον, *coming upon*, τινι Man.4.83.

ἐπιφονεύω, *slay*, *Sammelb.*4309.15 (iii B.C.).

ἐπιφορ-ά, ἡ, (ἐπιφέρω) *bringing to* or *upon*: hence, 1. *donative, extra pay*, in pl., Th.6.31, D.S.17.94; so ἡ ἔξωθεν ἐ. τῆς εὐδαιμονίας Plb.5.90.4. 2. *application*, ὀνομάτων Pl.*Lg.*944b, cf. *Cra.*430d. 3. *second course* [at dinner], Damox.2.58 (pl.). 4. *fine* paid by contractor for failure to keep time, *BCH*35.44 (Delos), cf. *Hermes*17.5 (ibid.); = καταδίκη, Hsch. (pl.). 5. *application*, τὴν τῆς αἰσθήσεως ἐ. ποιεῖσθαι to *concentrate* attention, Plu.2.1144b. b. *infliction*, πληγῶν *POxy.* 283.15 (i A.D.). 6. *additional payment of* φόρος, *IG*1².205, al. II. (from Pass.) *offering made at the grave*, Plu.*Num.*22. 2. *impact*, Epicur.*Nat.*15.26, al.; *sudden attack*, Plb.6.55.2, etc.; ἐπιφορὰς πρός τινα ποιῆσαι, in controversy, Phld.*Lib.*p.35 O.; ἐ. ὄμβρων *sudden burst* of rain, Plb.4.41.7; of wind, Thphr.*CP*5.12.11; ἡ τοῦ κωρύκου ἐ. Philostr.*Gym.*57; *attack* of an orator, opp. ἀπολογία, Id. *VS*1.25.10 (pl.). 3. *vehemence* in oratory, Hermog.*Id.*1.11, al., Philostr.*VS*1.17.1, al. 4. *growth* by assimilation of nourishment, *Stoic.*2.229. 5. Medic., *epiphora, persistent flow* of tears, as a disease, Dsc.*Eup.*1.35, Gal.14.749,768 (but non-technically, *floods* of tears, Plb.15.26.3); *deflux* of morbid humours, Meno *Iatr.*5.30, Plu.2.102a (pl.); τοῦ γάλακτος Sor.1.76; ὀχθώδεις ἐ. tuberous *eruption*, Ruf.ap.Orib.8.24.35. b. *attack*, πυρετῶν, etc., Vett.Val.3.4 (pl.), al. 6. *propensity*, -φορὰς ἔχειν πρός τι Men.Rh.p.342 S. III. Rhet., *second clause* in a sentence, opp. ἀρχή, D.H.*Dem.* 20. 2. *repetition*, συνδέσμου Demetr.*Eloc.*196. 3. *succession of clauses ending in the same word*, opp. ἐπιβολή, Rut.Lup.1.8. IV. in Stoic Logic, *the conclusion* of a syllogism, Chrysipp.*Stoic.*2.80, Crinis ib.3.269, Procl. *in Prm.*p.534 S. 2. *question at issue*, τῆς ἐ. ἀπερρυηκέναι Phld.*Mus.*p.96 K. V. in Gramm., ἔχειν ἐν ἐπιφορᾷ τὸ λλ to have λλ *immediately following*, Hdn.Gr.2.932. **-έω**, *put, pile upon*, ἐπιπολῆς τῶν ξύλων χοῦν γῆς ἐ. Hdt.4.201, cf. 8.28; ἐπὶ τὸν ἄλα γῆν ἐ. Id.4.183; ὕλην Id.7.36; τῆς γῆς πολλήν Ar.*Pax*167, cf. X.*An.*3.5.10; [λίθους] ἄνωθεν Ar.*Pax*225. 2. *bring, offer*, Ph.1. 259. **-ημα**, ατος, τό, in pl., *dishes served up besides* or *after, dessert*, Hdt.1.133, Ar.*Fr.*774, Archipp.9, etc.: in sg., Eudox.Com. 2, Luc.*Lex.*8. 2. *offering at the grave*, Iamb.*VP*27.122. **-ικός**, ή, όν, (ἐπιφορά II. 3) *impetuous*, of style, τὸ ἐ. καὶ σφοδρόν Hermog.*Id.* 2.6; ἐ. σχήματα Aristid.*Rh.*1p.494 S.; ἐ. λόγος (viz. D.21) Longin. *Fr.*18. II. *inferential, illative*, [σύνδεσμος] A.D.*Conj.*227.25, al. Adv. -κῶς Sch.D.T.p.65 H. III. (ἐπιφορά III) *forming the second* or *subsequent clause*, [ἔκ]φρασις Lesb.Gramm.12. **-ος**, ον, (ἐπιφέρω) *carrying towards*, εἰ ἄνεμος ἐπεγένετο τῇ φλογὶ ἐπίφορος ἐς [τὴν πόλιν] Th.3.74, cf. 2.77; *favourable*, of winds, Paus.8.28.4; ἐπιφορώτατος [Ἑρμῆς] A.*Ch.*813 (lyr.). II. *leaning* or *prone to* a thing, ἐ. κάτω ῥέψαι gloss in Hp.*Art.*14 (Comp.); πρὸς δεισιδαιμονίαν Plu.2.703d; *well-suited*, εἴς τι Longin.5, Plu.2.623d. Adv. -ρως, ἔχειν πρός τι Str.12.3.26. b. of documents, *applicable, relating* to the matter in hand (cf. ἐπιφέρω I. 9), *POxy.*266.14, 1282.33 (i A.D.). 2. of ground, *sloping*, Hp.*Ep.*17. III. *pregnant*, Id. *Prorrh.*1.103; *near the time of bringing forth*, X.*Cyn.*7.2; of plants, Thphr.*CP*3.2.8.

ἐπιφορτ-ίζω, *load heavily, overload*, J.*Ap.*2.9; ἄμπελον *Gp.*9.14.6: metaph., τί τινι Phld.*Po.*5.2; τὴν τέχνην τισί Gal.8.785; ἐ. πλεῖον τῷ πάσχοντι *lay* a heavier *burden upon*, Aët.7.91:—Med., X.Eph.5.2: metaph., *levy blackmail on*, τινι Sch.Ar.*Pl.*379:—Pass., *have excessive burdens laid on one*, *PSI*4.317.6 (i A.D.). **-ισμός**, ὁ, *lading*, *Gloss.*

ἐπίφραγμα, ατος, τό, (ἐπιφράσσω) *covering, lid*, Hero *Spir.*1.5; ἐπιφράγματα· τὰ ὑπὸ τὸ στόμα, Hsch.

ἐπιφρᾰδ-έως, Adv., (ἐπιφράζομαι) *circumspectly, wisely*, Parm.1. 16, A.R.1.1336; *carefully*, Id.2.1134, 3.83: Comp. -έστερον Hsch. **-μων**· ψευδολόγος, Id.

ἐπιφράζω, *say besides*, Hdt.1.179 (Bekk. ἔτι φράσαι; for ἐπέφραδε v. sub φράζω); ἐπέφρασεν is prob. f.l. for ἐπεφράσατ' in Orph.*Fr.* 257. II. elsewh. only in Med., mostly aor. 1, and (in same sense) Pass. aor. 1 ἐπεφράσθην: 1. c. inf., *think of* doing, *take into one's head to* do, οἷον δὴ τὸν μῦθον ἐπεφράσθης ἀγορεῦσαι Od.5.183; τὸ μὲν οὔ τις ἐπεφράσατ'.., ἐξερύσαι δόρυ Il.5.665. 2. c. acc., *devise, contrive*, ὑμῖν δ' ἐπιφράσσετ' ὄλεθρον Od.15.444; κακὴν ἐπεφράσσατο τέχνην Hes.*Th.*160 (s.v.l.); ἐπιφράζεται τοιάδε Hdt.6.61; ἀμήχανον ἐξευρεῖν καὶ -φράσασθαι Id.1.48; [γάμον] Theoc.22.166: abs., ὧδε ἐπιφρασθεὶς *having come to* this *conclusion*, Hdt.4.200; ἐπιφρασθεῖσα αὐτὴ *by* her own *mother wit*, Id.7.239. 3. *notice, observe*, Ἀλκίνοος δέ μιν οἶος ἐπεφράσατ' ἠδ' ἐνόησεν Od.8.94; ἐ. τινὰ ποιέοντα Heraclit.5: c. acc., Arr.*An.*4.8.2, etc.; ὅσσον.. Il.21.410; ὅτι.. Arr.*Ind.*27.8; ἐ. κατὰ θυμόν h.*Ap.*402; *recognize*, ἵνα μή μιν ἐπιφρασσαίατ' Ἀχαιοί Od. 18.94; *acquaint oneself with, take cognisance of*, ὡς.. ἐπιφρασσαίατο βουλὴν Il.2.282, cf. 13.741; ἐ. ὅκως.. *imagine* how.., Hdt.5.9.

ἐπί-φραξις, εως, ἡ, (ἐπιφράσσω) *obstruction* of the earth, in eclipses, Plu.2.891f, Anaximand.11. **-φρᾰσις**, εως, ἡ, Rhet., *specific mention* of an individual, a form of pleonasm, Phoeb.*Fig.*1.3.

ἐπι-φράσσω, Att. -ττω, *block up*, ὕλῃ [τὴν δίοδον] Thphr.*HP*9.3.2; πόρους Nic.*Al.*285: metaph., Ph.1.299, al.:—Med., κηρῷ ἐ. τὰ ὦτα *stop one's* ears, Luc.*Im.*14:—Pass., *to be obstructed*, *Placit.*2.29.1; τὰ τοῦ μέλλοντος ἀκούειν ὦτα ἐπεφράχθη Ph.2.165. **-φραστικῶς**, Adv. *descriptively, vividly*, Sch.Opp.*H.*2.331.

ἐπίφρενα· ὑποχόνδρια, Hsch.

ἐπί-φρικτος, η, ον, *bristling on the surface*, φολίδεσσι Nic.*Th.* 157. **-φρίξ**· ἡ ἐπανάστασις τῶν κυμάτων, *EM*800.28. **-φρίσσω**, Att. -ττω, *to be rough* or *bristling on the surface*, χαῖται νώτοις ἐπιπεφρίκασιν Emp.83.2; φολίδεσσι D.P.443; Σειληνοὺς πολιῇσιν -φρίσσοντας ἐθείραις cj. in Nonn.*D.*35.55; esp. of water, νέποδες.. ἐπιφρίσσουσι γαλήνῃ *make a ripple* on the calm sea, Opp.*C.*1.384, cf. Orph. *A.*1149, Poll.1.106.

ἐπι-φρονέω, *to be shrewd, prudent*, only in part. fem. ἐπιφρονέουσα, = ἐπίφρων, Od.19.385 (exc. that Pl.*R.*424b substitutes it for the Verb in the Hom. phrase ἀοιδὴν μᾶλλον ἐπικλείουσ' ἄνθρωποι). **-φροσύνη**, ἡ, *thoughtfulness, wisdom*, εἰ μὴ ἐπιφροσύνην δῶκε..' Ἀθήνη Od.5.437: in pl., ἐπιφροσύνας ἀνελέσθαι 19.22, cf. Hes.*Th.*658, A.R.4.1115; *observation*, Arat.762; *prudent reserve*, A.R.3.659: also in late Prose, θεία ἐ. Ph.1.203, al.; κατ' ἐπιφροσύνην J.*AJ*15.11.3; κατὰ τὴν Σεβαστοῦ Καίσαρος ἐ. Onos.*Praef.*1.

ἐπίφρουρος, ον, *keeping watch over*, metaph., ξίφος ἐ. δέρῃ E.*Or.* 1575.

ἐπίφρων, ον, gen. ονος, (φρήν) *thoughtful*, οἵ τε δύνανται ἄφρονα ποιῆσαι.. ἐπίφρονα to make *the thoughtful* thoughtless, Od.23.12; αἰχμητὴν.. καὶ ἐπίφρονα βουλὴν *sage* in counsel, 16.242; ἐ. Αὐγείαο Theoc.25.29; also ἐ. βουλή Od.3.128, Hes.*Th.*122; ἐ. μῆτις Od.19. 326, B.15.25.—Ep. and Lyr., never in Il.

ἐπι-φύλαξ [ῠ], ἄκος, ὁ, *watchman*, Longus 1.21. **-φῠλάσσω**, *watch for*, πλοῦν Pl.*Lg.*866d.

ἐπιφύλιος [ῠ], ον, (φυλή) *distributed to the tribes*, χθών E.*Ion* 1577.

ἐπιφυλλ-ίζω, *glean grapes in a vineyard*: metaph., *deal hardly with*, Lxx *La.*1.22, 2.20; cf. ἐπιφαυλίζω. **-ίς**, ίδος, ἡ, (φύλλον) *small grapes left for gleaners*, *AP*6.191 (Corn. Long.), Lxx *La.*2.20; interpol. in Dsc.4.142: metaph., of poetasters, Ar.*Ra.*92, cf. Sch. ad loc., D.H.*Rh.*10.18.

ἐπιφυλλόκαρπος, ον, *with fruit upon the leaves*, Thphr.*HP*1.10.8, 3.17.4.

ἐπί-φυσις, εως, ἡ, *ongrowth, excrescence*, ἐ. βλεφάρων, = σῦκον II, Hp.*Epid.*3.7 (pl.); ἐ. σαρκός, of flesh covering the bone, Id.*Fract.*4; χονδρίων -φύσιες Id.*Art.*45; ἡ ἐ. τοῦ δέρματος, such as fishes' scales, Mnesith.ap.Ath.8.357c. 2. Anat., *epiphysis*, Hp.*Art.*27, *Fract.* 12; opp. ἀπόφυσις (q. v.), Gal.2.733. 3. *growth*, -φυσιν λαμβάνειν Thphr.*HP*1.1.2: metaph., *accretion*, Ph.1.667; λογικῆς φύσεως ib. 636 (pl.). **-φῠτεύω**, *plant over* or *upon* a thing, Ar.*Pax* 168 (anap.): metaph., in Pass., Lxx 4*Ma.*15.6. **-φύω**, *make to grow, produce on* or *besides*, Thphr.*HP*1.9.3. II. Pass., with aor. 2 and pf. Act., ἐπέφῠν, ἐπιπέφυκα:—*grow upon*, [τῷ σήματι] ἐπιπέφυκε ἐλαίη Hdt.4.34; esp. as an excrescence, Arist.*HA*605^{a}3; ταῖς ψυχαῖς ἐ. μελανίαι Plb.1.81.7; ὁ ἐπιπεφυκώς, with or without ὑμήν, *the conjunctiva*, Gal.7.101, Steph. *in Hp.*1.88 D.: hence, *adhere, cling closely to* (cf. ἐμφύω), ἀμφοῖν τοῖν χεροῖν with both hands, Plb.12.10.6, cf. D.S.36.15; esp. of dogs, ἐ. τοῖς θηρίοις *stick close to* them, *run* them *hard*, Plu.*Luc.*1: metaph., τοῖς πλείστοις..οἷον κῆρες ἐπιπεφύκασιν Pl.*Lg.*937d, cf. Ph.1.345; *cleave to*, ἀγαθοῖς interpol. in Plu.2.6c; *attack*, τινι Id.*Pomp.*51; δόγματι, opp. ὑπερδικεῖν, Id.2.694e, cf. Jul. *Or.*2.86b; ἐπιφύντα νέον ἄνδρα an upstart *interloper*, Plu.*Cleom.*16.

ἐπιφων-έω, *mention by name, tell of*, ἐπιφωνεῖν..ἱερὰν θήκην S.*OC* 1762 (anap.), cf. Aristaenet.1.14:—Med., Il.Parv.*Fr.*2. b. *add a title*, Ph.1.337. 2. *say with respect to*, τινὶ ἐπιφώνημα Plu.*Alex.* 3; εἴς τι Id.*Luc.*39; ἐπί τινος Apollon.Cit.3; *apply* a phrase *to*, τινι Ath.5.178e: freq. of quoted sayings, ἐ. τὸ τραγικόν κτλ. Ph.1.127, cf. Plu.*Alc.*23, al. 3. *call out, proclaim, exclaim*, ἐ. ὡς "εὖ ἡμῖν βεβίωται" Epicur.*Sent.Vat.*47; ἐπεφώνουν λέγοντες κτλ. *Ev.Luc.*23. 21, cf. *PRyl.*77.33 (ii A.D.); ἐ. τινὶ καλῶς λέγειν Aristeas 196, cf. Phld.*Herc.*1251.17, al., *IG*14.830 (Puteoli, ii A.D.); τῷ παρὰ δεῖπνον ἀκράτῳ προσδιδομένῳ τὸν Ἀγαθὸν ἐπιφωνοῦσι Δαίμονα Philonid.Med.ap. Ath.15.675b:—Pass., τὸ τοῖς γαμοῦσιν -φωνούμενον "Ταλασίῳ" Plu. *Pomp.*4. 4. *respond*, in ritual, Lxx 2*Ma.*1.23. 5. *subjoin, add as a finishing touch*, Demetr.*Eloc.*107:—Pass., ib.110, Hermog.*Inv.*4. 9. **-ημα**, ατος, τό, *a witty saying*, Plu.*Alex.*3. 2. Rhet., *phrase added by way of ornament* or *as a finishing touch*, Phld.*Rh.*1.173 S. (dub.), D.H.*Rh.*10.18, Demetr.*Eloc.*106, 109, Quint.8.5.11, Hermog. *Inv.*4.9, S.E.*M.*2.57. 3. Gramm., *interjection*, *AB*100, Hsch. s. v. κόγξ; σίττα· ἐ. αἰξίν, Id. **-ηματικός**, ή, όν, *of the nature of an* ἐπιφώνημα 2, Hermog.*Inv.*4.9, Eust.1038.38. Adv. -κῶς Demetr.*Eloc.*109, Hermog.*Inv.*1.5 (Comp.). **-ημάτιον**, τό, Dim. of ἐπιφώνημα 2, Arr. *Epict.*3.23.31. **-ησις**, εως, ἡ, *acclamation, cry*, Plu.*Pomp.*4. II. *added remark*, Ps.-Plu.*Vit.Hom.*65. III. *uttering* of a spell, Herm.ap.Stob.1.49.44 (pl.). IV. *address*, Phld.*Lib.*p.14 O.; πρὸς τοὺς ἀνθρώπους Sch.Opp.*H.*2.217. **-ητής**, οῦ, ὁ, gloss on λιγύς, Hsch. **-ητικός**, ή, όν: hence -κόν, τό, *an added word*, Sch.Opp. *H.*1.204.

ἐπιφώσκω, = ἐπιφαύσκω, *grow towards daylight, dawn*, *Ev.Matt.* 28.1, *Ev.Luc.*23.54, *PLond.*1.130.39 (i A.D.). II. trans., *let shine forth*, φέγγος Poet. *de herb.*24.

ἐπιφωτ-ίζω, *illuminate*, *POxy.*2146.4 (iii A.D.):—Pass., Plot.4.3. 10, *Corp.Herm.*13.21. **-ισμός**, ὁ, *illuminating light*, Plu.2.936b.

ἐπιχαίνω, *gape at*, τινι Luc.*Tim.*18, *Sacr.*9, al. 2. *desire greedily*, ἐπικέχηνε πᾶσι τοῖς ἐκτός Ph.1.211, cf. 2.202. II. = ἐγχαίνω, *mock at*, Anon.ap.Suid.

ἐπιχαιράγᾰθος [ᾰγ], ον, *taking delight in what is good*, formed as an opp. to ἐπιχαιρέκακος, Eratosth.ap.Str.1.3.22.

ἐπιχαιρεκᾰκ-έω, *rejoice at another's misfortune*, ἀλλήλοις Phld.*D.* 1.11, cf. Ph.1.314. **-ία**, ἡ, *joy over one's neighbour's misfortune, spite, malignity*, Arist.*EN*1107^{a}10, Ph.2.394, Plu.2.91b, etc. **-ος**, ον, *rejoicing over one's neighbour's misfortune*, Anaxandr.59, Alex.51, Arist.*EN*1108^{b}5, Ph.2.269, Gal.4.817.

ἐπιχαίρω, *rejoice over, exult over*, mostly of malignant joy, c. dat. rei, κακοῖς τοῖς τοῦδε S.*Aj.*961; ἀτυχίαις τῶν πέλας Men.673, cf. Arist. *Rh.*1379^{b}17: c. dat. pers., D.21.134; τινὶ τεθνηκότι Plu.*Eum.*2; ἐπί τινι Phld.*Mort.*20: abs., Ar.*Pax* 1015 (anap.), D.9.61: also in aor. 1 Med., ἐπεχήρατο A.R.4.55:—Pass., Phld.*Mort.*20. 2. rarely in good sense, ἐπιχαρῆναι (aor. 2 Pass.) *rejoice in* another's *joy*, Ar.*Th.* 314 (lyr.): c. acc., σὲ μὲν εὖ πράσσοντ' ἐπιχαίρω S.*Aj.*136 (anap.). 3. *take pleasure in*, c. dat., Hld.6.14.

ἐπιχαλᾶ· τὴν τὸ κανοῦν φέρουσαν εἰς τὰς θυσίας θεράπαιναν (-νας cod.), Hsch.

ἐπιχᾰλαζάω, *shower hail upon*, τινά Luc.*Tim.*58.

ἐπιχᾰλᾰρός, ά, όν, *somewhat loose*, Hp.*Art.*50 (Comp.).

ἐπιχᾰλάω, fut. -άσω [ᾰ], *loosen, slacken*, τὸ καλῴδιον Plb.34.3.5; δεσμόν Luc.*Herc.*3; ἄκρατος ἐ. τόνους ψυχῆς Ph.2.227. 2. *drop in*, ἔριον εἰς τὴν ἔξέρασιν *PHolm.*15.39. II. intr., *give way*, δύαισιν οὐδὲν ἐπιχαλᾷς A.*Pr.*181 (lyr.); ἐπιθυμίαις Ph.2.298.

ἐπιχᾰλεπαίνω, *to be angry at*, Hsch. and Apollon.*Lex.* s. v. ἐπαλαστήσασα.

ἐπιχαλκ-εύω, *forge upon* an anvil, μύδρους A.*Fr.*307; ἐπιχαλκεύειν παρέχοιμ' ἄν, i.e. you can use me as an anvil (I am so hard), Ar.*Nu.*422; '*drive home*' a point, Arist.*Rh.*1419^{b}15 (dub. sens.). II. Pass., *to be wrought upon*, λεπίδες [τοῖς κίοσιν] -κεχαλκευμέναι J.*AJ*3.6.3. **-ῖται**, οἱ, = ὁπλῖται, Hsch. **-ος**, ον, *covered with copper* or brass, *brazen*, ἀσπίς Hdt.4.200, Ar.*V.*18; στόμα, of a flute-player, Alc.Com.20; ἐπίχαλκος (sc. ἀσπίς), ἡ, Amips. 17. **-όω**, = -χαλκεύω II, in Pass., J.*AJ*3.6.2 (s.v.l.).

ἐπιχάραγμα [χᾰ], ατος, τό, *impression* on a coin, Hsch. s. v. γλαῦκες Λαυριωτικαί.

ἐπιχᾰράσσω, Att. -ττω, *cut into*, φύλλον ἐπικεχαραγμένον a *notched* or *serrated* leaf, Thphr.*HP*6.2.5. 2. *slash through*, κατὰ μίαν ἐπιβολὴν ὅλα τὰ σώματα Heliod.ap.Orib.47.14.3. II. *impress upon*, βοῦν νομίσμασιν Plu.*Publ.*11:—Pass., *to be branded*, [ἵπποις] ἐπικεχαράχθαι πρόσωπον Sch.Il.*Oxy.*1086.30. 2. *impress subsequently*, Ph.1.64.

ἐπιχάρ-εια [χᾰ], ἡ, *charm, attractiveness*, *PMag.Leid.V.*12 (prob. cj.). **-ής**, ές, *gratifying, agreeable*, τίς ὧδε τλησικάρδιος.., ὅτῳ τάδ' ἐπιχαρῆ; A.*Pr.*161 (lyr.); πόρνη καλὴ καὶ ἐ. Lxx *Na.*3.4. II. of a person, *rejoiced at*, πτώματι ἐχθρῶν Lxx *Jb.*31.29. **-ιεντίζομαι**, *quote as a good joke*, Luc.*Symp.*12. **-ιεντισμός**, ὁ, *ornamental epithet*, Sch.Opp.*H.*1.661. **-ίζομαι**, *make a present of*, τινά τινι X.*Eq.* 6.12. 2. intr., ἐπιχάριτται (Boeot. for ἐπιχάρισαι) τῷ ξένῳ *be civil to* him, Ar.*Ach.*884. **-ις**, ὁ, ἡ, neut. ἐπίχαρι, *pleasing, charming*, οὐδ' ἐ. Ἄρης A.*Th.*910 (lyr.), etc.; ἐ. ἐν ταῖς συνουσίαις X.*Cyr.*1.4.4; χάρις οὐκ ἐ. Pl.*Lg.*853d; σιμός, ἐ. κληθεὶς Id.*R.*474d; θηρίον ἐ., of the hare, X.*Cyn.*5.33; τὸ ἐ. *pleasantness of manner*, Id.*An.*2.6.12; *elegance*, of mathematical study, Pl.*R.*528d: Comp. and Sup. ἐπιχαριτώτερος, -τατος (as if from **ἐπιχάριτος** which is found later, Alciphr. 2.4, Ptol.*Tetr.*166, prob. in 164), X.*Smp.*7.5, *Oec.*7.37. Adv. -τως Id.*Ap.*4, Isoc.15.8; Boeot. ἐπιχαρίτως dub. l. in Ar.*Ach.*867.

ἐπίχαρμα, ατος, τό, *object of malignant joy*, E.*HF*459, Theoc.2.20, Posidipp.42: condemned by Poll.3.101. II. *malignant joy*, E. *Ph.*1555 (pl., anap.).

ἐπιχάροψ, οπος, ὁ, ἡ, *bluish-eyed*, *Arch.Pap.*4.142 (ii A.D.).

ἐπιχάρ-της, ου, ὁ, *one who rejoices malignantly*, Philonid.11: condemned by Poll.3.101. **-τικός**, ή, όν, *expressive of joy*, ἐπιφώνημα *AB*100. **-τος**, ον, *wherein one feels joy*, ἔργον S.*Tr.*1262 (anap.); γεραροῖς ἐπίχαρτον A.*Ag.*722 (lyr.). 2. more freq., *wherein one feels malignant joy*, ἐχθροῖς ἐπίχαρτα πέπονθα Id.*Pr.*159 (anap.); οἱ δικαίως τι πάσχοντες ἐ. Th.3.67, cf. D.45.85; βαρβάροις ἐ. γενόμενος Pl.*Ep.*356b.

ἐπιχαρωπός, όν, *bluish*, dub. l. in *Stad.*307 (leg. ἐπιχάροπος vel ἐστὶ χ.).

ἐπιχασμάομαι, *yawn at* a thing, Hld.4.5.

ἐπιχαταί (χατέω)· ἐνδεεῖς, Hsch.

ἐπιχαυνόω, *relax*, τὰς χορδάς Phlp. *in Ph.*201.30:—Pass., metaph., *to be elated at*, εὐτυχίαις Iamb.*Protr.*21.κϛʹ.

ἐπιχέζω, fut. -χεσοῦμαι, *ease oneself upon*, Ar.*Lys.*440, *Ec.*640: pf., ἐπικέχοδα Id.*Av.*68.

ἐπιχειλής, ές, (χεῖλος) *on* or *at the lips*, γλῶσσα ἐ. a *ready, chattering* tongue, Poll.6.120. II. *full up to the rim* (i.e. not quite full, as the rim was deep), of Themistocles, ἐποίησεν τὴν πόλιν ἡμῶν μεστήν, εὑρὼν ἐπιχειλῆ Ar.*Eq.*814. 2. later, *brim-full*, πίθος ἐ. τῶν ἀγαθῶν Them.*Or.*13.174d, cf. 8.115a: metaph., πλήρεις καὶ ἐ. ἁμαρτίαι Ph.1.517. III. *with the lips drawn in*, like old people, Alciphr. 3.55.

ἐπιχειμ-άζω, *pass the winter at* a place or *in* an enterprise, Th.1. 89. II. impers., *it is stormy at the same time*, c. dat., Gem.*Calend.* 5:—Pass., -άζεται ὑετῷ ibid. III. trans., *distress*, σεαυτόν Men. 970. **-έριος**, ον, *exposed to stormy weather*, Thphr.*Vent.*14.

ἐπιχειρ-έω, (χείρ) *put one's hand to*, οἱ μὲν δείπνῳ ἐπεχείρεον Od. 24.386, cf. 395; πηδαλίοις Ar.*Eq.*542. 2. *put one's hand to* a work, *set to work at, attempt*, τῇ διώρυχι Hdt.2.158; δρησμῷ ἐ. *attempt* an escape, Id.6.70; τῇ ὁδῷ Id.7.43, cf. E.*Ba.*819; τοῖσι βασιληΐοισι Hdt.3.61; τυραννίδι Id.5.46; ἔργῳ τοσούτῳ Id.9.27; λόγοις, τέχνῃ, Pl.*Phdr.*279a, *Grg.*521d, etc.; τοῖς ἀδυνάτοις X.*Mem.*2.3.5, cf. Isoc. 5.41, etc. 3. less freq. c. acc., μεγάλα ἔργα Thgn.75; δίκαιον πρᾶγμα Pl.*Cri.*45c, *Phlb.*57b:—Pass., *to be attempted*, Th.4.55, 6.31, X.*Cyr.*6.1.41, etc.; τὸ ἐπιχειρούμενον *the thing attempted*, Pl.*Lg.* 746b. 4. c. inf., *endeavour, attempt* to do, Hdt.3.38, 65, 9.42, Ar. *Ra.*81, Th.2.40, etc.: c. fut. inf., J.*BJ*6.7.3:—Pass., ἃ τὸ πρῶτον ἐπεχειρήθη πραχθῆναι Pl.*Ep.*337d, cf. Id.*Ti.*53a, al. 5. ἐπεχειρήθη c. dat., *an operation was performed*, τῇσιν αἱμορροΐσι Hp.*Epid.*5. 20. II. *make an attempt on, attack*, τινι Hdt.1.11, 26, 190, Th.3. 94, Ar.*V.*1030, etc.; πρός τινα Th.7.21; ἐπί τινα Pl.*Mx.*241d (but ἐπὶ τὴν τοῦ σώματος διαφθοράν with a view to.., Arist.*Pol.*1315^{a}24); εἰς τὰς σατραπείας D.S.14.80: abs., Hdt.5.72, 8.108, etc.; κτείνων ἢ ἐπιχειρῶν Lex ap. And.1.98:—Pass., Th.2.11. b. sens. obsc., ἐ. μειρακίοις Jul.*Mis.*359d. III. *attempt to prove, argue dialectically*, Pl.*Tht.*205a, Hermog.*Inv.*3.4; περί τινος Arist.*Top.*101^{a}30; ἔκ τινος from a topic, ib.115^{a}26; ἔς τι D.L.4.28; ἐ. ὅτι.. Arist.*Top.*128^{b}26: abs., Id.*APr.*66^{a}34; λογικώτερον ἔστιν ἐπιχειρεῖν ὧδε Id.*Cael.*275^b 12. **-ημα**, ατος, τό, *undertaking, attempt*, esp. of a military *enterprise*, Th.7.47, X.*HG*1.2.6, Isoc.2.8, etc.; μανικὸν ἐ. ἐπιχειρεῖν Pl. *Alc.*1.113c; πολλὴ μωρία καὶ τοῦ ἐ. Id.*Prt.*317a. 2. *base of operations against*, κατὰ Κύπρου App.*Syr.*52. II. in the Logic of Arist., *attempted*, i.e. *dialectical proof*, opp. a demonstrative syllogism (φιλόσοφημα), *Top.*162^{a}16, etc.: so in Rhet., [Cic.] *ad Herenn.*2.2.2, D.H. *Din.*6, *Is.*16, Demetr.Lac.1055.18 F., Hermog.*Inv.*3.4, Gal.5.221, etc.; περὶ -ημάτων, title of work by Minucianus. **-ηματικός**, ή, όν, *tentative*, λόγοι Arist.*Mem.*451^{a}19. Adv. -κῶς Aristid.*Rh.*2 p.540 S.,

Syrian. *in Metaph.* 32.3. **-ησις**, εως, ἡ, *an attempt upon, attack*, Hdt.1.11, Th.2.11 (pl.), 4.130; ἡ ἐ. τινος ἐπί τινας *Act.Ap.* 12.1 cod. D; τὴν ἐ. μὴ συντάχυνε the *attempt*, Hdt.3.71; ἐκφέρειν τὴν ἐ. Id.8.132; ἐ. ποιεῖσθαί τινος *attempt* a thing, Th.1.70; ἡ ὑμετέρα ἐ. the *attempt* upon you, ib.33; ἡ ἐ. τοῦ σῶσαι Pl.*Alc.* 1.115b, cf. *Lg.* 631a. II. *dialectical reasoning* (cf. ἐπιχείρημα II), Arist.*Top.* 111b16, al.; τὴν ἐ. ποιεῖσθαι κατὰ τὸν εἰκότα λόγον Plb.12.7.4, cf. Phld.*Sign.* 29 (pl.), D.H.*Amm.* 1.8, Plu.2.698a, S.E.*P.* 2.192 (pl.); τὰ ἐφ' ἑκάτερα τὴν ἐ. δεχόμενα things capable of proof or disproof, Hermog.*Prog.* 5. **-ητέον** or **-έα**, *one must attempt*, Pl.*Ap.* 19a; μείζοσι Isoc.*Ep.* 9.18. 2. ἐπιχειρητέα *one must attack*, Th.1.118, 2.3. 3. *one must argue dialectically*, πρός τι to a conclusion, Arist.*Top.* 120b 8. II. **-ητέος**, α, ον, *to be attempted*, ὅμως δὲ καὶ τοῦτο ἐ. Antipho 2.2.4. **-ητής**, οῦ, ὁ, *an enterprising person*, opp. ἄτολμος, Th.8.96, cf. D.C.59.17: c. gen., *ready to attempt*, παντός Pl.*Ti.* 69d. **-ητικός**, ή, όν, *in* or *for attack*, δεινότης Plu.2.978b. II. ἡ -κὴ δύναμις the faculty *of argumentation*, Arr.*Epict.* 1.8.7. 2. *attempting to prove*, Ascl. *in Metaph.* 224.6, Alex.Aphr. *in Metaph.* 176.35. **-ίζω**, *set upon, attack*, Hsch. s. v. ἀλληλίζεσθαι (s.v.l.). II. ἐν ᾗ ἦν ἐπικεχειρισμένος βασιλικῇ γραμματείᾳ while *at his post of* basilicogrammateus, *POxy.* 1274.7 (iii A. D.), cf. *Sammelb.* 4472.

ἐπιχειρογρᾰφέω, *add an attestation to*, σύνταξιν *PSI* 5.509.18 (iii B.C.), cf. 515.8 (iii B.C.).

ἐπίχειρον, τό, (χείρ) *arm*, Lxx *Je.* 31(48).25. II. in pl., **ἐπίχειρα**, τά, prop. *wages of manual labour*: hence, *wages, pay*, 1. of *reward*, Ar.*V.* 581, *Trag.Adesp.* 116, Theoc.*Ep.* 18.8; ἀρετῆς ἐ. Pl.*R.* 608c; ironically in D.*Ep.* 3.38, Plb.8.12.5, etc.: rarely in sg., Id. 38.3.2. 2. more freq. of *punishment*, τοιαῦτα τῆς ὑψηγόρου γλώσσης.. τἀπίχειρα γίγνεται A.*Pr.* 321, cf. Antipho 1.20, Arr.*Epict.* 3.24.24, Ph.1.512, etc.; τῆς προπετείας πικρὰ κομίζονται τὰ. Phld.*Ir.* p.32 W.; ξιφέων ἐ. λαχοῦσα *the wages* of the sword, i. e. slaughter by it, S.*Ant.* 820 (lyr.). (Sts. written ἐπιχείρια in codd., vulg. in Hp. *Praec.* 1.)

ἐπιχειρο-νομέω, *gesticulate*, Ph.1.298, 2.485: metaph., *grasp at*, ταῖς πλεονεξίαις ib.371 (s.v.l.); οἱ ἐπιχειρονομοῦντες, = οἱ ταῖς χερσὶν ὡς νόμοις χρώμενοι, Hsch. **-τονέω**, *sanction* or *confirm by vote*, of the Assembly, ἐπειδὰν ἐπιχειροτονῆτε τὰς γνώμας D.4.30; ἡ εἰρήνη ἡ ἐπιχειροτονηθεῖσα Decr.ap.eund.18.29; incorrectly, ἐπεχειροτόνησεν ἡ βουλὴ καὶ ὁ δῆμος Decr.ib.105. 2. *confirm in office*, τὰς ἀρχάς Arist.*Ath.* 43.4, cf. 37.1; τοὺς προέδρους -τονεῖν the π. shall *confirm* the appointment, Lex ap.D.24.39: hence, of a Roman Tribune, ἐπεχειροτόνησε τῷ Μαρίῳ τὴν στρατηγίαν *got* the Praetorship for him, Plu.*Mar.* 35. **-τονία**, ἡ, *voting by show of hands*, Pl.*Lg.* 755e; -τονίαν διδόναι, εἰ δοκεῖ.. ἢ μή Arist.*Ath.* 43.5. 2. *confirmation* of the powers of magistrates, D.58.27 (pl.), Arist.*Ath.* 55.4; ἐ. αὐτῶν ἐστι.. εἰ δοκοῦσιν καλῶς ἄρχειν ib.61.2. b. ἐ. νόμων *confirmation* of the existing laws, Lex ap.D.24.20.

ἐπιχερρονησιάζω, *approach a peninsular form*, dub. in Str.6.3.1 (ἐστὶ δέ τι χερρονησιάζουσα Coraes).

ἐπιχέω, fut. -χέω, 2 sg. ἐπιχεῖς Ar.*Pax* 169: aor. 1 ἐπέχεα; Ep. aor. 1 ἐπέχευα, inf. ἐπιχεῦαι (v. infr.):—*pour over*, χέρνιβα δ' ἀμφίπολος προχόῳ ἐπέχευε.. νίψασθαι Od.1.136, etc.; in full, χερσὶν ὕδωρ ἐπιχεῦαι Il.24.303; χερσὶ δ' ἐφ' ὕδωρ χευάντων Od.4.213, etc.; also οἴνῳ ἐπιχεῖν ὕδωρ X.*Oec.* 17.9. 2. metaph., τοῖσι δ' ἐφ' ὕπνον ἔχευε Il.24.445; Τρῶες δ' ἐπὶ δούρατ' ἔχευαν 5.618; ἀνέμων ἐπ' ἀϋτμένα χεῦε Od.3.289; θρῆνον *pour* a lament *over* one, Pi.*I.* 8(7).64 (tm.); ὀδμήν A.R.2.191 (tm.); βλασφημιῶν ἐ. (gen. partit.) Luc.*JTr.* 35. 3. of solids, *heap up*, θανόντι χυτὴν ἐπὶ γαῖαν ἔχευαν Od.3.258, cf. Il.23.256; ἐπὶ σῆμ' ἔχεεν 6.419:—Med., ὕπερθ' ἐπὶ σῆμα χέεσθαι A.R.3.205. II. *pour in*, ἀπαντλοῦντα καὶ ἐ. Pl.*R.* 407d; ἓν ἀγαθὸν ἐπιχέασα, τρί' ἐπαντλεῖ κακά Diph.107 codd. Stob.; *fill* a cup, Νανvοῦς καὶ Λύδης ἐπίχει δύο *AP* 12.168 (Posidipp.).

B. Med., *pour* or *throw over oneself*, χύσιν δ' ἐπεχεύατο φύλλων Od.5.487; κατακλιθεὶς ἐπιχείσθω τὴν πέριξ ἄμμον Antyll.ap.Orib.10.8.4; ἐπεχεύατο πήχεε παιδί she *threw her* arms *round* the boy, A.R.1.268; but πολλὴν ἐπεχεύατο ὕλην *for himself*, Od.5.257. 2. *pour itself over*, Q.S.14.604. 3. *anoint oneself*, ἀπὸ δείπνου *Test.Epict.* 4.22. II. *have poured out for one to drink*, ἐ. ἄκρατόν τινος *drink* it to any one's health or honour, esp. of lovers' toasts, Theoc.14.18, cf. Antiph.81.2 codd. Ath.; ἔρωτος ἀκράτω (gen. partit.) ἐπεχεῖτο Theoc.2.152; also simply ἐπιχεῖσθαί τινος Phylarch.31 J.

C. Pass., *to be poured over*, ἰλύος ἐπιχυθείσης X.*Oec.* 17.12: metaph., τοῖς Ἑλληνικοῖς ὀνόμασι τῶν Ἰταλικῶν ἐπικεχυμένων Plu.*Rom.* 15. 2. metaph., of a crowd, *stream on* or *in pursuit*, ἐπέχυντο (Ep. aor. 2 Pass.) Il.15.654; ἀνὰ νῆας 16.295; so, *come like a stream over*, τοῖσι ἐναντίοισι ἐπιχυθέντας.. μῦς ἀρουραίους Hdt.2.141; τοσούτων μοι πραγμάτων ἐπικεχυμένων Theopomp.Hist.217c. 3. *to be poured in as an addition*, τοῦ νῦν ἐπικεχυμένου λόγου, of the discussion, *that has now been started*, Pl.*Plt.* 302c; ὁ νυνδὴ λόγος ἡμῖν ἐπιχυθεὶς Id.*Lg.* 793b. II. *to be drowned in*, ἰχθῦς νάπυϊ ἐπικεχυμένους Luc.*Asin.* 47.

ἐπιχηρεύω, *remain in widowhood*, μετά τινος τελευτήν J.*AJ* 20.7.3.

ἐπιχητία(ς)· ἐνδεής, Hsch.

ἐπιχθόνιος, ον, Ep. Adj., (χθών) *upon the earth, earthly*, freq. in Hom., as epith. of ἄνθρωποι, ἄνδρες, βροτοί, Od.8.479, Il.1.266, 272: abs., ἐπιχθόνιοι *earthly ones, men on earth* (cf. χαμαί), opp. ἐπουράνιοι θεοί, 24.220, cf. Pi.*O.* 6.50, B.4.15, etc.; so ἐ. γένος ἀνδρῶν Pi.*Fr.* 213.3; ἐ. δαίμονες *who haunt the earth*, Hes.*Op.* 123. 2. in pl., *natives* of a country, D.P.459, 1093. 3. *terrestrial*, opp. marine, ἑρπετόν Opp.*H.* 2.425.

ἐπιχιλάδιον· τὸ χιλιοστόν, Hsch. **ἐπιχιλές**· τὸ ἐλλιπές, Id. **ἐπιχιλοῦντες**· πληροῦντες, Id.; cf. χιλός.

ἐπιχλευάζω, *jeer*, abs., Ph.1.193, 426, al.: c. acc., *make a mock of*, τι Plu.*Num.* 22; τινα App.*Syr.* 53; *mock at*, τινὶ ὅτι.. Plu.2.93b; *say scornfully*, κερδῶ δ' ἐπεχλεύαζεν ὡς.. Babr.82.4, cf. Ph.2.436.

ἐπιχλιαίνω, *warm on the surface* or *slightly*, Luc.*Alex.* 21:—Pass., *grow warm*, Hp.*Coac.* 611.

ἐπίχλοος, ον, (χλόα) *with a green surface*, πέτραι ποιῇσιν ἐ. Opp.*H.* 1.131.

ἐπιχνοάω, *to be downy on the surface*, ἐθείραις A.R.1.672.

ἐπίχνοος, contr. -χνους, ὁ, *a wool-like covering* on the eyes, Hp.*Prorrh.* 1.17.

ἐπι-χόα· κατάχυσις, Hsch. **-χοάζω**, *pour libations upon*, τοῖς τελευτήσασι Lyd.*Mens.* 4.31.

ἐπιχοή, ἡ, *alluvial soil*, Str.15.1.16.

ἐπιχολ-όομαι, (χολή) *turn into bile*, Gal.15.599. **-ος**, ον, *full of bile, bilious*, πυρετοί Hp.*Fract.* 35; *splenetic, ill-tempered*, Philostr.*VS* 2.8.2; ταῖς ὀργαῖς Plu.2.129c. II. Act., *producing bile*, ποίη -ωτάτη Hdt.4.58.

ἐπιχορδίς, ίδος, ἡ, (χορδή) earlier name for μεσεντέριον (q. v.), Aret.*SA* 2.6.

ἐπιχορεύω, *dance to* or *in honour of* a thing, Ar.*Pax* 1317; *come dancing on*, X.*Smp.* 9.4; comically of dishes brought to table, ἄριστον ἐπεχόρευσεν Diph.44.1; εἰς τὸ μέσον ἐ. σαπέρδης Id.64.4. II. *add a chorus* or *choral song*, τοιοῦτό τι Philostr.*VA* 5.14.

ἐπιχορηγ-έω, *supply, furnish*, Hero *Dioptr.* 31; σπέρμα τῷ σπείροντι 2*Ep.Cor.* 9.10; ὑμῖν τὸ πνεῦμα *Ep.Gal.* 3.5; τὸ ἐοικέναι τοῖς νοητοῖς εἴδεσιν Dam.*Pr.* 341; esp. of a husband, *provide for* a wife, ἐ. τῇ γαμουμένῃ τὰ δέοντα *POxy.* 905.10 (ii A. D.), cf. 282.6 (i A. D.); conversely, ἐὰν [γυνὴ] ἐ. τῷ ἀνδρὶ αὐτῆς Lxx *Si.* 25.22(30):—Pass., τὰ ἀπὸ Λιμυρικῆς -ούμενα *Peripl.M.Rubr.* 60; τοῖς παρ' ἑτέρων -ηθεῖσι πλούτοις D.H.1.42; πᾶν τὸ σῶμα διὰ τῶν ἁφῶν.. ἐπιχορηγούμενον καὶ συμβιβαζόμενον *Ep.Col.* 2.19. **-ημα**, ατος, τό, *an additional supply*, Ath.4.140c (pl.). **-ητέον**, *one must supply*, Sor.1.87. **-ία**, ἡ, *supply, provision*, τῆς ἐ. γενομένης ἐκ τῶν ἱερῶν προσόδων *SIG* 818.9 (Ephesus, i A. D.); πᾶν τὸ σῶμα.. συμβιβαζόμενον διὰ πάσης ἁφῆς τῆς ἐπιχορηγίας, = διὰ πασῶν τῶν ἐπιχορηγουσῶν ἁφῶν (cf. ἐπιχορηγέω fin.), *Ep.Eph.* 4.16; διὰ τῆς ἐ. τοῦ πνεύματος *Ep.Phil.* 1.19.

ἐπιχορῐαμβικὸν μέτρον, metre in which choriambs and trochees are combined, Heph.14.2, Aristid.Quint.1.28, Sch.metr.Pi.*O.* 8, etc.

ἐπιχορτάζω, *supply with provender*, Sosith.2.13.

ἐπιχραίνω, *colour on the surface*, τὸ σῶμα Luc.*Bis Acc.* 6; ἐπικεχράνθαι (vulg. -κεχρῶσθαι) Id.*JTr.* 8.

ἐπίχρᾱσις, εως, ἡ, apptly. for ἐπίχρησις, *use*, *BCH* 6.23 (Delos, ii B.C.).

ἐπιχράω (A), (χράω A) *touch on the surface, graze*, c. gen., τάων (sc. Ἁρπυιῶν) ἀκροτάτῃσιν ἐπέχραον.. χερσί A.R.2.283: c. acc., τυτθὸν ἐπέχραε δέρμα Q.S.11.480.

ἐπιχράω (B), (χράω B), poet. word, only aor. 2 or impf. ἐπέχρᾰον, *attack, assault*, c. dat., ὡς δὲ λύκοι ἄρνεσσιν ἐπέχραον.. ὣς Δαναοὶ Τρώεσσιν ἐπέχραον, Il.16.352, 356; μητέρι μοι μνηστῆρες ἐπέχραον *beset* her, Od.2.50. 2. abs., *to be violent, rage*, of the winds, A.R.2.498. 3. c. inf., *to be urgent* or *eager* to do, Id.4.508: c. acc. et inf., [ἀνάγκη] με.. νεῖσθαι ἐπέχραε *was urgent* that I should come, Id.3.431.

***ἐπιχράω** (C), *lend besides*, cf. ἐπικίχρημι. II. **ἐπιχράομαι**, *make use of besides*, ἐ. χθονί *to have the use of* it besides, E.*Rh.* 942; *make use of also*, Ruf.ap.Orib.8.39.2. 2. c. dat. pers., *have dealings with* one, Th.1.41; αἱ ἐπιχρεώμεναι [αὐτῇ] μάλιστα γυναῖκες her most *intimate* friends, Hdt.3.99, cf. Pl.*Lg.* 953a.

ἐπι-χρεία, ἡ, *use, need*, *PFlor.* 207 (iii A. D.); *equipment, stores*, of a ship, *PLond.* 3.948.12 (iii A. D.). **-χρειον**, τό, *what is necessary*, τὸ τῆς διατροφῆς ἐ. ib.5.1708.223 (vi A. D.).

ἐπιχρεμέθω, *neigh, whinny to*, A.R.3.1260, Q.S.11.328.

ἐπιχρέμπτομαι, *punctuate with spitting*, τοῖς λεγομένοις Luc.*Rh.Pr.* 19.

ἐπιχρηματ-ίζω, *enact a subsequent measure*, *SIG* 704 *H* 24 (Epist. Amphict., ii B.C.). **-ισμός**, ὁ, dub. sens. in *IGRom.* 4.503 (Pergam.).

ἐπιχρησῐμεύω, *make more effective*, Paul.Al.*O.* 4.

ἐπιχρησμῳδέω, *make an oracular pronouncement upon*, τῷ ἑαυτοῦ βίῳ Philostr.*VS* 1.8.2: c. acc., ἑαυτοῦ λόγον Id.*VA* 5.14.

ἐπιχρίμπτω, *bring upon*, νέφος ἐπὶ γαῖαν B.*Fr.* 20.3. 2. *attack*, τινα Opp.*C.* 2.171. II. Pass., *lean over* or *towards*, A.R.1.1235.

ἐπί-χρισις, εως, ἡ, *smearing over*, βελῶν Str.4.4.6 (pl.), cf. Sever.ap.Aët.7.96. **-χρισμα**, ατος, τό, *unguent*, Dsc.1.70.3, cf. Gal.19.382. **-χριστέον**, *one must smear over*, *Gp.* 16.18.1, Aët.7.51. **-χριστος**, ον, *smeared on*, φύκη Luc.*Am.* 41; φάρμακα Str.11.8.7, cf. Porph.*Abst.* 1.27. 2. *rouged, painted*, ἑταίρας ἄνθος Max.Tyr.37.4: metaph., Id.31.6; εὐμορφία Luc.*Tim.* 28. **-χρίω** [ῑ], *anoint, besmear*, ἐπιχρίοντες ἀλοιφῇ (sc. τὸ τόξον) Od.21.179; χρῶτ' ἀπονιψαμένη καὶ ἐπιχρίσασα παρειάς 18.172:—Med., χρῶτ' ἀπονίπτεσθαι καὶ ἐπιχρίεσθαι ἀλοιφῇ ib.179. 2. *plaster over*, τινι with a thing, Luc.*Hist.Conscr.* 62. II. *lay on* ointment, μετὰ τὸ -χρισθῆναι Zopyr.ap.Orib.14.58.1; κροτάφοις -χριόμενα v.l. in Dsc.3.22; πηλὸν ἐπὶ τοὺς ὀφθαλμούς *Ev.Jo.* 9.6, cf. *IG* 14.966 (Rome, ii A. D.). 2. abs., *use for anointing*, Call.*Iamb.* 1.270. **-χροά**, ἡ, *tinge*, Thphr.*Fr.* 159 (pl.).

ἐπιχρόϊσις, εως, ἡ, perh. *stains* on clothes, Thphr.*CP*2.5.4 codd. (pl.); cf. ἐπίχρωσις.

ἐπιχρον-ίζω, *last long*, Thphr.*Ign*.61; ὅταν [τὸ θερμὸν] -χρονίσῃ Arist.*Pr*.936^{a}20; ἐπικεχρονικός *inveterate, chronic*, Gal.11.103:—Pass., ἀὴρ -όμενος ψυχθεὶς when cooled *in course of time*, Arist.*Pr*.942^{a}33. **-ιος**, α, ον, *lasting for a time, long*, Cic.*Att*.6.9.3. **-ος**· ἐπίχαρτος, Hsch.

ἐπίχροος, ον, *coloured*, *Gloss*.

ἐπίχρῡσ-ος, ον, *overlaid* or *plated with gold*, Hdt.1.50, al., *IG*1^{2}.280, X.*Mem*.3.10.14, Longus 1.5, etc.; ὑπάργυρα ἐ. *IG*1^{2}.386.7. **II.** *rich*, prob. for ὑπό–, Hld.2.8. **-όω**, *overlay with gold*, *Gloss*.:—Pass., γρῦπες -κεχρυσωμένοι· *BCH*35.260 (Delos, ii B.C.), cf. *Edict. Diocl.Geronthr*.9.22.

ἐπιχρῴζω, = ἐπιχρώννυμι, *tinge*, Arist.*Col*.791^{a}9; λίτρῳ χαλινά Nic.*Al*.337:—Pass., D.S.2.52.

ἐπιχρωματίζω, *render colour*, χρώματα τῶν τεχνῶν τοῖς ὀνόμασι καὶ ῥήμασι with words, Pl.*R*.601a.

ἐπιχρωματικός, ή, όν, *partly chromatic*, Ptol.*Harm*.2.1.

ἐπιχρωνῆν, dub. l. in Thphr.*Char*.16.2.

ἐπι-χρώννῡμι and -ύω, fut. -χρώσω: pf. -κέχρωκα Plu. (v. infr.):—*rub* or *smear over, colour on the surface, tinge*, τι Ruf.*Anat*.30, Plu.2.395e, cf. Plot.4.5.7; τινι with a thing, Luc.*Dom*.8; οὐκ ἄχρι τοῦ ἐπικεχρῶσθαι μόνον, ἀλλ' ἐς βάθος.. φαρμάκοις.. καταβαφεῖσα Id.*Im*.16: metaph., ψυχὴ ἐπακτὸν νοῦν ἔχει -χρωννύντα αὐτήν Plot.5.6.4:—Pass., δόξαις ἐπικεχρωσμένοι *merely tinged* with.., Pl.*Ep*.340d. **-χρωσις**, εως, ἡ, *surface-stain*, Plu.2.382c (pl.), Gal.*Phil.Hist*.27 (= Zeno *Stoic*.1.26); cf. ἐπιχροΐσις.

ἐπί-χῠμα, ατος, τό, (ἐπιχέω) an eye-disease, = ὑπόχυμα, Sch.rec.A.*Pr*.499, Phlp.*in de An*.350.33. **II.** *extra amount* of oil, *PRyl*.97.5 (ii A.D.). **-χύνω**, late form for ἐπιχέω, Herm.ap.Stob.1.49.69, *JHS*19.73 (Galatia), etc. **-χῠσις**, εως, ἡ, (ἐπιχέω) *pouring upon* or *in, influx*, Pl.*Ti*.77d, Arist.*Mete*.356^{a}6; ποταμῶν ἐπιχύσεις Ath.8.331d; τῶν ὄμβρων D.C.41.45: metaph., ἐ. πολιτῶν Pl.*Lg*.740e; τῆς τῶν ἡδονῶν ῥύμης ib.841a. **2.** = ὑπόχυσις, Phlp.*in de An*.291.32. **3.** = κονίασις, Hsch. **II.** *toast*, Plb.16.21.12 (pl.); ἐπιχύσεις τινὸς λαμβάνειν, ποιεῖσθαι (cf. ἐπιχέω II), Plu.*Demetr*.25, *Brut*.24. **2.** *anointing*, ἐν ταῖς ἐπιχύσεσι *IG*12(1).155.121 (Rhodes). **III.** *beaker* or *wine-jug*, Men.503, Phylarch.44J., Plaut.*Rud*.1319; ἐ. τοῦ χαλκίου Ar.*Fr*.214. **-χῠτέον**, *one must pour in* or *over*, Dsc.2.76.5; *one must pour in more*, Herod.Med.ap.Orib.10.37.12. **-χῠτήρ**, ῆρος, ὁ, = ἐπίχυσις III, Sm.*Za*.4.2. **-χῠτήριον**, *perfusorium*, *Gloss*. **-χύτης** [ῠ], ου, Dor. **-χύτας**, ὁ, = -χυτήρ, *IG*11(2).161*B*26 (Delos, iii B.C.), *BCH*33.172 (Argos). **-χῠτος**, ον, (ἐπιχέω) *poured over*: as Subst., ἐπίχυτος (sc. πλακοῦς), ὁ, *cake made in a mould* (cf. ἔγχυτος), Nicopho 15. **2.** ἐπίχυτον, τό, *coin* or *cast* of silver or lead, Hsch.

ἐπιχωνεύω, *remould*, κεράμια *PSI*4.441.7 (iii B.C.); *cast*, *PLeid*.*X*.21, 84; *cast upon, on top*, Ph.Byz.*Mir*.4.3.

ἐπιχώνια· κάρυα, Hsch.

ἐπιχώννῡμι and -ύω, *heap up*, Ἀρχ.Ἐφ.1923.39 (Oropus, iv B.C.); τὰ περιμήκιστα τῶν ὀρῶν Ph.1.405; νεκρῷ θῖνα γῆς Plu.*Art*.18; τούτοις γῆν ἐπιχώσας *IG*14.1746.13:—Pass., ἐ. τὸ ἔδαφος ἐπὶ τὴν λίμνην Arist. *Mir*.837^{b}11; βωμὸς ἐπικεχωσμένος Arg.S.*Ph*. **II.** *fill up*, τὴν δίοδον Thphr.*HP*9.3.2; τάφρον X.Eph.4.6; τοὺς λιμένας D.S.13.107 codd.

ἐπιχώομαι, Dep. *to be angry at*, ἐπεχώσατο μύθοις A.R.3.367.

ἐπιχωρ-έω, *yield, give way*, τοῖς ἀπιστοῦσι S.*Ant*.219, cf. Plb.4.17.8; ἐ. τινὶ πρός τι, of things, *permit* one to do.., Plu.*Dem*.2; ἐ. τῷ ἐπιγράμματι *to be in accordance with*.., Arist.*Mir*.844^{a}1; ἐπί τινος ἐπιχωρεῖ πᾶς καιρός any time *will suit*, Ruf.ap.Orib.8.24.59. **2.** ἐ. τινί τι *surrender, concede*, τινὶ ἀρούρας *PStrassb*.114.1, cf. Arr.*An*.1.27.5, Plu.2.422a: c. inf., ἐπικεχώρηταί τινι ποιεῖν τι *IG*2^{2}.1012.24: abs., *give one's consent*, *SIG*546*B*3 (iii B.C.), *BCH*6.26 (Delos, ii B.C.). **3.** *forgive*, [ἁμαρτήματα] Plu.*Alex*.45, cf. 2.482a. **II.** *come towards, join* one *as an ally*, Th.4.107; πρός τινα X.*HG*2.4.34. **2.** *to go against, attack*, Id.*An*.1.2.17. **3.** *follow after*, προεμβάλλει τοὺς πόδας, καὶ αὐτὸς ἐπιχωρεῖ Paus.9.39.11. **4.** *take possession of* an inheritance, *Leg.Gort*.11.6. **-ησις**, εως, ἡ, *concession, permission*, Lxx 2*Es*.3.7, J.*AJ*19.3.3, Arr.*An*.6.25.2; εἰ οὖν τιν' ἐ. ποιεῖ ἔντυχε ἐκείνῳ *PHib*.1.151 (iii B.C.). **-ιάζω**, **1.** of persons, *to be in the habit of visiting*, ἐ. Ἀθήναζε Pl.*Phd*.57a; ἐ. τινί *live much with*, Luc.*Pseudol*.19; τοῖς ἄνω πράγμασι *to be occupied with*, Id.*Cont*.1. **2.** of things, *to be customary, be the fashion in* a place, περὶ Ἀθήνας Arist.*Pol*.1341^{a}34; μαθήματα τοῖς Ἕλλησιν -άζοντα Stesimbr.4J.; παρά τισι Plb.6.46.3; τῇ νήσῳ Str.10.5.9:—Pass., *to be the custom* or *fashion*, v.l. in Arist.*Pol*.1335^{a}16 (nisi leg. -άζει), cf. Nymphis 9. **3.** of vegetables, *acquire the local character*, Diph. Siph.ap.Ath.9.369f. **4.** of the sea, *make an inroad*, Polem.*Call*.25. **II.** Act., *call in the language of the country*, Βροῦτον τὸν μῶρον Lyd.*Mag*.1.31; also καλεῖν -άζοντες Olymp.*in Mete*.200.20.

ἐπιχώριος, α, ον, also ος, ον Pi.*P*.4.80, Ar.*Nu*.601, E.*Ion* 1111, etc.: (χώρα):—*in* or *of the country*, **1.** of persons, οἱ ἐ. *the people of the country, natives*, Hdt.1.78, 181, al.; οὑπιχώριοι χθονὸς S.*OT*939, cf. E.*Ion* l.c.; also of birds, ἐ. ὄρνιθες A.*Supp*.800, cf. 661 (lyr.); οὐ πολλαχοῦ ἐ. Arist.*HA*615^{a}14. **2.** of things, *of* or *used in the country*, ὑποδήματα Hdt.1.195; κράνεα Id.7.91, cf. Pi.*P*.4.80; τὸν ἐ. τρόπον Ar.*Pl*.47; freq. in neut., τὸ ἐ., τοὐπιχώριον *the custom of the country, fashion*, Id.*Nu*.1173, Th.6.27, etc.; τὰ ἐν Πέρσαις ἐ. X.*Cyr*.1.4.25, cf. Hp.*Aër*.1: c. dat., *usual*, οἷόν τ' ἐπιχώριον ἀνδράσι γυῖον Emp.62.8; ἐπιχώριον ὂν ἡμῖν c. inf., as it *is the custom of* our country, Th.4.17: c. gen., τῆς ἡμετέρας μούσης ἐ. Pl.*Smp*.189b; ἐπιχωρίου ὄντος τοῖς Πέρσαις φιλεῖν it being their *custom* to.., X.*Ages*.5.4; ἐπιχώρια *common things*, Pi.*P*.3.22, cf. Ar.*Pl*.342; καλὰ ἐ. honours *of the country*, Pi.*I*.7(6).2; ἐ. ἁμαρτήματα *against fellow-countrymen*, Pl.*Lg*.730a; ἐπιχώριαι ἐνενήκοντα (sc. δραχμαί) *Michel* 838 (Didyma). Adv. -ίως Ar.*V*.859; *in the language of the country*, D.C.38.13, Lyd. *Mag*.1.7; *in the local dialect*, Gal.14.303.

ἐπίχωσις, εως, ἡ, (ἐπιχώννυμι) *a heaping up*, esp. *the choking of a channel*, Plb.4.41.9 (pl.): metaph., *exaggeration*, *Gloss*.

ἐπιχωστέον, *one must heap upon*, *Gp*.5.9.7.

ἐπιψαίρω, *skim the surface of* a thing, Opp.*H*.4.512.

ἐπιψᾰκάζω, old Att. for ἐπιψεκάζω (q.v.).

ἐπι-ψάλλω, *play the lyre*, S.*Fr*.60, Poll.4.58 (Pass.); μέλεσι καὶ ῥυθμοῖς Plu.2.713b; *sing*, τοὺς ὕμνους Lxx 2*Ma*.1.30:—Pass., Ph.1.626. **-ψαλμός**, ὁ, *accompaniment* on a stringed instrument, Ptol.*Harm*.2.12.

ἐπιψαμμίζω, *cover with sand*, Hero *Geom*.23.68.

ἐπι-ψαύδην, Adv. *grazing*, gloss on ἐπιλίγδην, Sch.Il.17.599, cf. Suid. **-ψαυσις**, εως, ἡ, *touching lightly*, Plu.2.395e (pl.), Ael. *NA*8.7, Ptol.*Harm*.2.1 (pl.). **-ψαύω**, Dor. fut. -ψαυσῶ Archim. *Con.Sph*.30:—*touch on the surface, touch lightly*, c. gen., Hes.*Sc*.217, Hdt.3.87, etc.; *attain*, abs., κατὰ πᾶν τέλος Pi.*I*.4(3).11; ἐ. φιλοτάτων *to aspire to* loves, Id.*P*.4.92; ἐ. τινὸς οὐδὲ κατὰ μικρόν Phan.Hist.19; γῆς ἐ., of shipwrecked persons, S.*Fr*.636.2: generally, *handle*, κώπης Id.*Ph*.1255; *meddle with*, τάφου Id.*Aj*.1394: metaph., also, *touch lightly upon*, Hdt.2.65. **b.** Geom., ἡ -ψαύουσα (sc. γραμμή) *tangent*, Archim.*Sph.Cyl*.1.12, etc. **2.** c. dat., Q.S.2.456. **3.** c. acc., Id.12.551. **II.** once in Hom., intr. and metaph., ὅς τ' ὀλίγον περ ἐπιψαύῃ πραπίδεσσιν who *can reach* ever so little way by his wits, Od.8.547.

ἐπιψᾱφίδδω, Boeot. for ἐπιψηφίζω, *IG*7.504 (Tanagra), al.

ἐπιψάω, *stroke*, τὴν κόμην *An.Ox*.3.206.

ἐπιψέγω, = ἐπικηδεύω (*bury*), Hsch. s. v. ψέγος.

ἐπιψεκάζω, old Att. **-ψᾰκάζω**, *keep dropping*, ἂν.. οἱ παῖδες ἡμῖν.. μικραῖς κύλιξι πυκνὰ ἐπιψακάζωσιν, jocosely for ἐπιπίνωσιν, X.*Smp*.2.26; ἐ. ὀλίγα τινὶ τῶν χαρίτων Luc.*Merc.Cond*.27: abs., ὁ θεὸς ἐπιψακάζει, of small rain, Ar.*Pax* 1141: metaph., θεὸς ἐ. σοφίαν διανοίαις Ph.1.501, cf. 2.383. **2.** *sprinkle*, [σπίνον] Thphr.*Lap*.13; πυρκαϊάν Hld.6.14.

ἐπίψεκτος, f.l. for εὐεπίψογος, Heph.Astr.1.1 (= *Cat.Cod.Astr*.8 (2).42).

ἐπιψέλιον, τό, *curb-chain*, *AP*6.233.4 (Maec.).

ἐπιψελλίζω, *lisp*, Arr.*Epict*.3.24.88.

ἐπιψεύδομαι, *lie still more*, X.*Hier*.2.16. **II.** *attribute falsely*, τι θεοῖσιν A.R.3.381, cf. Ph.2.319, Plu.*Mar*.16, Luc.*Tox*.42. **III.** *falsify* a number, Plu.*Flam*.9; ὄνομα *call by a wrong* name, Ph.2.398; *feign*, συμφοράν J.*AJ*18.6.8. **IV.** *deceive*, τινα Herod.6.46.

ἐπίψηγμα (better -ψημα), ατος, τό, *scrapings*, ἁλός Dsc.5.110.

ἐπιψηλᾰφάω, *feel by passing the hand over the surface*, τι Pl.*R*.360a; ἐ. τινός *feel for* it, Id.*Prt*.310c.

ἐπιψηφ-ίζω, *put to the vote*, in Senate or Assembly, ἐ. τὰς γνώμας Antipho 6.45, etc.; ταῦτα D.22.9: c. inf., *put it to the vote that*.., Th.2.24; of the President in the Amphict. Council, ἐ. τὰς γνώμας Aeschin.3.124. **2.** abs., *put the question*, Th.6.14, etc.; οὐκ ἠθέλησεν ἐπιψηφίσαι, of Socrates, X.*Mem*.1.1.18; in the preface to decrees, τῶν προέδρων ἐπεψήφιζε ὁ δεῖνα *IG*2^{2}.44, al., cf. Decr.ap.And.1.77; ἐ. ἐς τὴν ἐκκλησίαν (at Sparta) Th.1.87; ἐ. τῇ ἐκκλησίᾳ Luc. *Tim*.44. **3.** ἐ. τινί *to put the question for* or *at the instance of* any one, Hdt.8.61. **4.** ἐ. τοὺς παρόντας *to put the question to* them, *take* their *votes*, Pl.*Grg*.474a, cf. 476a. **II.** Pass., *to be put to the vote*, Aeschin.2.67, 3.126, *Michel* 163.40 (Delos); of an office, *to be voted upon*, Arist.*Pol*.1301^{b}25. **III.** later in Med., of the Assembly itself, or generally of voters, *vote, approve*, τὰ ῥηθέντα D.S.19.61, cf. D.H.6.71, 84, Plu.*Cic*.33 (also in Act., D.H.7.38, Luc.*Charid*.12). **2.** ἐ. χρόνον τινί *vote an extension of* command, Plu.*Flam*.7; also στρατιὰν ἄλλην ἐ. πέμπειν v.l. in Th.7.16. **3.** Med. in act. sense, *IG* 12(7).239 (Amorgos), 12(9).4 (Carystus), Just.*Nov*.15.6 *Ep*. **IV.** *confirm*, εὐσέβειαν *IGRom*.3.209.17 (Ancyra, ii A.D.). **V.** *calculate*, Vett.Val.352.22. **-ισις**, εως, ἡ, *calculation, accurate measurement*, Hero *Stereom*.2.69.5. **-ισμός**, ὁ, *confirmatory vote*, τῆς πατρίδος *Arch.Anz*.29.422 (Augusta Traiana). **-ιστής**, οῦ, ὁ, *magistrate who puts a question to the vote*, *BGU*362 xii 2 (iii A.D.).

ἐπιψῐθῠρίζω, *whisper in*, οὐασί τινος Nonn.*D*.22.89, cf. Procop. *Arc*.25.

ἐπιψίσει (-ψίσῃ cod.)· ἐπιψιεῖ, ἐπιψωμιεῖ, Hsch.

ἐπίψογος, ον, *exposed to blame, blameworthy*, X.*Lac*.14.7, Plu. *Comp.Cim.Luc*.1; τὸ ἐ. Max.Tyr.18.9: neut. pl. -ψογα, as Adv., Man.4.506. Adv. -γως *with blame*, λέγεσθαι Plu.*Comp.Dem.Cic*.3. **II.** Act., *blaming, censorious*, φάτις A.*Ag*.611.

ἐπιψοφ-έω, *rattle at* or *with*, Call.*Dian*.247; *applaud*, Oenom.ap. Eus.*PE*5.33. **-ησις**, εως, ἡ, *increpatio*, *Gloss*.

ἐπί-ψῡξις, εως, ἡ, *cooling*, Philagr.ap.Orib.5.19.3. **-ψύχω** [ῡ], *cool*, A.R.2.525, Ph.2.345, Plu.*Sert*.8. **II.** Pass., *take a chill afterwards*, Hp.*Mul*.1.54; but ἐπιψυγῆναι *to be cooled still more*, Gal.11.567.

ἐπιψωμίζω, fut. -ιῶ, gloss on ἐπιψίω, Hsch.

ἐπιωγαί, ῶν, αἱ (ἰωγή), *places of shelter* for ships, *roadsteads*, Od.5.404, Opp.*H*.1.602: after Hom. in sg., A.R.4.1640.

ἐπῐωνικὸν μέτρον, metre in which Ionics are combined with iambi, Heph.14.3, 5, Aristid.Quint.1.28.

ἐπιώψατο, v. ἐπιόψομαι.

ἔπλε, for ἔπελε, impf. Act. of πέλω: **ἔπλεο, ἔπλευ, ἔπλετο**, aor. Med. of πέλω. **ἔπληντο**, 3 pl. Ep. aor. 2 Pass. of πελάζω, Il.4.449, 8.63.

ἐπόγδοος, ον, $1\frac{1}{8}$, Pl.*Ti*.36a,b; ἐ. λόγος the ratio *of* 9:8, Plu.2.367f; ἐ. [τόκος] interest *at the rate of* $\frac{1}{8}$ *of the principal*, i.e. $12\frac{1}{2}$%, D.50.17: neut. as Subst., *whole tone* in Music, Philol.6, Hsch.

ἐπόγκιαι· αἱ τοῦ πλοίου παραθῆκαι, Hsch.

ἔπογκ-ος, ον, *pregnant*, Iambl.*VP*31.194. **-όω**, *stuff*, δορὰν βοὸς χόρτῳ Porph.*Abst*.2.30.

ἐπογμ-εύω, (ὄγμος) *trace a furrow*: hence, metaph. of dancing, ἐ. κύκλον ὀρχηθμοῖο Tryph.354. **-ιος**, ον, *presiding over the furrows*, Δαμάτηρ *AP*6.258 (Adaeus).

ἐπόδια, ἐποδιάζω, Ion. for ἐφοδ–.

ἐποδύρομαι [ῡ], *bewail*, *AP*7.10.7.

ἐπόζω, *become stinking*, fut. –οζέσω Lxx *Ex*.7.18, cf. Gal.19.100.

ἐποίγνυμι or **ἐποίγω**, v. ἐπῴχατο: but **ἐποίγω**, Aeol. for ἐπείγω, Hdn.Gr.2.436.

ἐποιδ-αίνω, *swell up*, Nic.*Al*.477. **-αλέος**, α, ον, *swollen*, Hp.*Int*.23. **-έω**, = ἐποιδαίνω, Id.*Prorrh*.1.71, Thphr.*HP*3.5.5, 6.4.2. **-ησις**, εως, ἡ, *swelling*, ib.3.5.5. **-ίσκομαι**, Pass., = ἐποιδαίνω, Hp.*Epid*.5.21, Gal.19.429.

ἐποίζω, impf. –ῴζον, *lament over*, τοῖς τεθνηκόσι prob. in A.*Fr*.157.

ἐποικ-έω, *go as settler* or *colonist to* a place, *settle in* a place, c. acc., Κυκλάδας E.*Ion* 1583; Βοιωτίαν Str.9.2.25; also ἐν τῇ Ἀσίᾳ X.*Cyr*.6.2.10: abs., Pl.*Lg*.752e. II. *to be settled near* or *with hostile views against*, ὑμῖν Th.6.86:—Pass., ἡ Δεκέλεια τῇ χώρᾳ ἐπῳκεῖτο Decelea *was occupied as the seat of offensive operations against* their country, Id.7.27. **-ία**, ἡ, = ἀποικία, *IG*9(1).334.1 (in Locr. form ἐπιϝοικία); but f.l. for ἀποικία, App.*BC*2.135. II. = ἐποίκιον 1, *Gp*.10.1.1 (pl., s.v.l.). **-ίδιος**, α, ον, *presiding over the house*, of Demeter at Corinth, Hsch. 2. gloss on ὑπωρόφιος, Sch.Pi.*P*.1.188. **-ίζω**, *settle in a colony*, τινὰς πόλεσι App.*BC*1.96, etc.:—Pass., *to be built near*, τεῖχος ἐπὶ τῇ Σαλώνῃ –ισμένον D.C.56.12. II. = ἐπιτειχίζω, τινί Paus.4.26.6:—Pass., ib.28.1. III. *bring into cultivation*, ἔδωκεν.. γῆν ψιλὴν ἀγρὸν ἐποικίσαι *SIG*302 (Gambreum, iv B.C.). **-ιον**, τό, *outhouse, farmstead*, etc., *IG*9(1).47 (Stiris), *Tab.Heracl*.1.146, *PPetr*.2 p.83, 3 p.225, al. (iii B.C.), Str.11.3.1, J.*AJ*14.10.6, etc. II. *village*, Lxx 1*Ch*.27.25, *PTeb*.382.6 (i B.C./i A.D.), *POxy*.2137.12, 2142.3 (iii A.D.). **-ισις**, εως, ἡ, *settlement of a colony*, App.*BC*5.137. **-ισμός**, ὁ, *settlement*, *Gloss*.

ἐποικοδομ-έω, *build up*, –ήσαντας αὐτὸ (sc. τὸ τεῖχος) ὑψηλότερον Th.7.4, cf. X.*HG*6.5.12, D.55.25: metaph., *pile up, use a climax*, Arist.*Rh*.1365^{a}16, *Rh.Al*.1426^{b}3. 2. *build upon*, ἐπὶ κρηπῖδι X.*An*.3.4.11; ἐπὶ κρηπῖδος Pl.*Lg*.736e; ἐπὶ τοὺς τοίχους *OGI*483.117 (Pergam., ii B.C.): metaph., Pl.*Lg*.793c (Pass.); φύσει μαθήματα Ph.1.610; τινὶ εὐτονίαν, ἀσφάλειαν, Arr.*Epict*.2.15.8 (Pass.); ἐπὶ θεμέλιον or θεμελίῳ, 1*Ep.Cor*.3.12, *Ep.Eph*.2.20; θεμελίοις Sor.1.47 (Pass.); τοῖς ἀληθέσιν ἐψευσμένα Paus.8.2.6, cf. Dam.*Pr*.87 (Pass.). b. *edify*, ἑαυτοὺς τῇ πίστει *Ep.Jud*.20:—Pass., –ούμενοι ἐν Χριστῷ *Ep.Col*.2.7. II. = ἐπιτειχίζω, Plb.2.46.5:—Med., στρατόπεδα πέντε –ησάμενος Arr.*An*.2.1.2. **-ή**, Dor. **ἐπιοικοδομά**, ἡ, *superstructure*, *Tab.Heracl*.1.150. **-ησις**, εως, ἡ, *building up*: metaph., *piling up* of expressions, *climax*, Arist.*GA*724^{a}29; ἡ τῶν λέξεων ἐ. Longin.39.3. **-ία**, ἡ, = foreg., Haussoullier *Cinquantenaire de l'école des hautes études* p.89 (Didyma, ii B.C.), *SIG*799 ii 4 (Cyzicus, i A.D.), prob. in J.*AJ*19.1.15 (pl.).

ἐποικονομ-έομαι, Pass., *to be administered*, Arist.*Oec*.1346^{a}14 (s.v.l.). **-ητέον**, *one must treat*, Herod.Med.ap.Aët.9.13. **-ία**, ἡ, *apportionment*, ἔργων ἢ παθῶν ἐ. *rhetorical arrangement* of them, Longin.11.2 (nisi leg. ἐποικοδομία).

ἔποικος, ὁ, *settler, sojourner*, Pi.*O*.9.69. 2. *stranger, alien*, S.*El*.189 (lyr., as fem.), cf. Pl.*Lg*.742a, *GDI*5048 (Crete). 3. more freq., *colonist*, Ar.*Av*.1307, *IG*9(1).334.5 (in Locr. form ἐπίϝοικος), ib.1^2.397; ἐποίκους πέμπειν, ἀποστέλλειν, Th.2.27, Isoc.5.6; esp. of *additional settlers*, ἐ. δέχεσθαι, ἐπάγεσθαι, Arist.*Pol*.1303^{a}28,37; λαὸν ἔποικον ἄγοις Call.*Aet.Oxy*.2080.69, cf. Ant.Lib.4.4, al. II. *neighbouring*, ἔ. Ἀσίας ἁγνᾶς ἕδος A.*Pr*.411 (lyr.). 2. Subst. *neighbour*, S.*OC*506.

ἐποικουρέω, f.l. for ὑπ–, Ph.2.202 (Pass.).

ἐποικτ-είρω or –ίρω, *have compassion on*, τινα Xenoph.7.3, S.*Aj*.121, *OT*671, etc.: abs., A.*Ag*.1069. (Written –ειρ– Isyll.72; v. οἰκτείρω.) **-ίζω**, *compassionate*, c. acc., S.*OT*1296:—Med., *bewail, lament*, J.*BJ*1.27.3. **-ιστος**, ον, *pitiable*, A.*Ag*.1221. **-ος**, ον, = *piteous*, φόνος ib.1614.

ἐποιμώζω, *to lament over*, πάθει A.*Ch*.547.

ἐποίνιος, ον, (οἶνος) *bacchanalian*, Nonn.*D*.11.301; cf. ἐπιοίνιος.

ἐποιστ-έον, *one must charge against*, τινὶ οὐκ ἐ. ἀτοπίαν Plb.12.22.5. **-ικός**, ή, όν, *capable of conferring*, εἶδος ἄδεκτον ἁπασῶν ἐνεργειῶν ὧν ἐποιστικὸν ἄλλῳ Plot.1.1.2. 2. *productive*, συμπτωμάτων *Stoic*.3.49; συμφορῶν Phld.*Ir*.p.30 W., cf. Simp.*in Cat*.224.23.

ἐποιχνέω, *ply, practise*, μαντοσύναν Aristonous 1.11. 2. *visit*, *AP*12.131 (Posidipp.), cf. *PBodl.ined*.32471, prob. l. in B.9.1.

ἐποίχομαι, *go towards, approach*, μνηστῆρας ἐπῴχετο Od.1.324; αἰτίζειν.. ἐποιχόμενον μνηστῆρας 17.346, cf. 6.282; ἐ. δόμον ἄλλον Thgn.353; [θεοὺς] τραπέζαις ἐ. *draw near to* the gods with sacrificial feasts, Pi.*O*.3.40; εὐεργέταν Id.*P*.2.24. 2. *approach with hostile purpose, attack*, c. acc., Κύπριν ἐπῴχετο νηλέϊ χαλκῷ Il.5.330, cf. 10.487. II. *go over, traverse*, νηῶν ἴκρια 15.676. 2. *go round, visit in succession*, of one who hands round wine, αὐτοῖσιν θάμ' ἐπῴχετο οἰνοχοεύων Od.1.143; of a general, *pass along* troops, στίχας ἀνδρῶν Il.15.279, cf. 16.155; *inspect*, [φώκας] Od.4.451: abs., *go his rounds*, Il.10.171, 17.215; πάντοσ' ἐποιχόμενος 5.508; πάντῃ ἐ. 6.81, 10.167, etc. 3. of arrows *visiting* persons with death, τὰ δ' ἐπῴχετο κῆλα θεοῖο πάντῃ ἀνὰ στρατόν 1.383, cf. 50; οἷς ἀγανοῖσι βέλεσσιν ἐποιχόμενος (or –νη) κατέπεφνεν, 24.759, Od.3.280, 5.124, etc. 4. *go over* or *ply* one's task, ἔργον ἐ. Il.6.492, Od.1.358, 17.227, etc.; δόρπον ἐ. *set about preparing* it, 13.34; freq. of women, ἱστὸν ἐ. *ply* the loom, Il.1.31, Od.5.62, al., cf. Ephor.5 J.; ἔργον φυλόπιδος ἐ. Mimn.14.10; φύλοπιν Hes.*Sc*.200 (tm.); [γύας καὶ ἀλωὰς] ἔργοισιν ἐ. *with* labour, Theoc.25.32: c. dat., ἔργῳ ἐ. Q.S.12.343 codd.: abs. in part., with another Verb, *busily*, ἡ μὲν ἐποιχομένη... ἔντυεν ἵππους Il.5.720.

ἐποιωνίζομαι, *forebode*, Hsch. s.v. ἐπιγλωσσῶ.

ἐποκέλλω, = ἐπικέλλω, *run ashore*, νέας, τὴν νέα, Hdt.6.16, 7.182; πλοῖα Th.4.26. 2. of the ship, *run aground, be wrecked*, Id.8.102, Plb.1.20.15; *put in*, Arr.*An*.2.23.3; of tunnies, Arist.*Mir*.844^{a}30.

ἐποκλάζω, *cower with bent knees upon*, τῇ γῇ Hld.4.17.

ἐποκρῑ-άω, *to be rough in* or *upon*, χηλαὶ ἐποκριόωσι παγούροις Nic.*Th*.790. **-όεις**, εσσα, εν, *uneven, projecting*, στέρνα, of a skeleton, *AP*7.401 (Crin.).

ἐποκτᾰμερής, ές, *in the ratio of* $1\frac{8}{9}$:1, Nicom.*Ar*.1.23.

ἐποκτωκαιδέκατος λόγος ratio *of* 19:18, Theo Sm.p.87 H.

ἐπολβ-ίζω, *call happy*, τὸν θανόντα Dionys.Trag.3, cf. Nonn.*D*.46.325. **-ος**, ον, *prosperous*, Man.3.112, al.

ἐπόλιος, ὁ, a night-bird, perh. = αἰγωλιός, Suid.

ἐπολισθάνω, *slip* or *glide upon*, [σανίσιν] J.*BJ*3.7.29; κυλίνδροις ἐς βυθόν *AP*10.15.3 (Paul. Sil.): metaph., ἐ. ἀμπλακίαις ib.5.277 (Agath.).

ἔπολμις, = ἔνολμις (v. ἔνολμος), Hsch.

ἐπολολύζω, *shout for joy, triumph at*, abs., A.*Ag*.1236 (Med.), Ar.*Eq*.616 (lyr.); τινι *at* or *to* one, A.*Th*.825 (lyr.); τι *over* or *at* a thing, Id.*Ch*.942 (lyr.).

ἐπολοφύρομαι [ῡ], *lament over*, τινι J.*BJPraef*.4; πολλὰ ἔργῳ ib.6.4.8.

ἕπομαι, v. ἕπω (B).

ἐπομβρ-έω, *pour rain upon*:—Pass., *AP*11.365.7 (Agath.). 2. *pour like rain upon*, τί τινι Ph.1.48,296. II. intr., *gush out over, abound as rain*, τὰ –οῦντα Id.1.441. **-ησις**, εως, ἡ, *watering with rain*, Suid. **-ία**, ἡ, *heavy rain, abundance of rain*, Hp.*Aph*.3.15 (pl.), D.55.11, etc.: generally, *abundance of wet*, πνευμάτων A.*Fr*.300: opp. αὐχμός, Hp.*Aër*.23, Ar.*Nu*.1120: pl., Arist.*Mete*.360^{b}6, Thphr.*HP*3.1.5, Str.11.3.4, etc.: metaph., *shower*, χερμάδων Lyc.333; *deluge*, δέλτων Lib.*Ep*.333.5. 2. *the Deluge*, J.*AJ*1.2.3, al. II. *humidity*, of the body, Aret.*SA*2.4, *SD*2.1. **-ίζω**, *water with rain*, Hld.9.9. **-ιος**, ον, = sq., Arist.*HA*601^{b}10, Thphr.*CP*3.11.5. **-ος**, ον, *very rainy*, ἔαρ, ἔτος, Hp.*Aph*.3.11, *Epid*.3.2; ἔαρ, θέρος, φθινόπωρον, Arist.*HA*601^{b}26 (v.l. –ιον); χῶραι Thphr.*HP*8.7.6.

ἐπομένως, Adv. pres. part. of ἕπομαι, *in a secondary manner*, opp. πρώτως, Arist.*Metaph*.1030^{a}22, cf. Plu.2.569e: opp. προηγουμένως, Hierocl.*in CA* 3p.424 M. II. *in accordance with*, τῷ νόμῳ Pl.*Lg*.844e, cf. Arist.*de An*.405^{a}3; τῷ τῆς ἀκολουθίας εἱρμῷ Ph.2.194. III. *next* in order, Arist.*GA*736^{b}13, Plb.4.1.7, Ph.1.560.

ἐπόμιλλος, Aeol. for ἐφόμιλος, *Et.Gud*.561.5.

ἐπομμάδιος, v. ἐπωμάδιος.

ἐπόμμᾰσις, εως, ἡ, Astrol., *aspect*, Gal.19.560.

ἐπόμνυμι or –ύω (v. infr. 3), fut. ἐπομοῦμαι Ar.*Lys*.211: aor. ἐπώμοσα:—*swear after, swear in accordance* (with an order given), οἱ δ' ἄρα πάντες ἐπώμνυον Od.15.437, cf. Th.2.5. 2. c. acc. cogn., ἐπίορκον ἐπώμοσε Il.10.332; ὅς κεν τὴν ἐπίορκον.. ἐπομόσσῃ whosoever *swear* a false oath *by* it [the Styx], Hes.*Th*.793, cf. Emp.115.4; also ἐ. ὅρκον τινί *swear* an oath *at* his *dictation*, Plu.*Cic*.23:—Med., ἐ. ὅρκον *Stud.Pal*.20.122.16 (v A.D.), etc. 3. c. acc. pers., ἐ. ἥλιον *to swear by*.., Hdt.1.212; ἐ. τινὰ θεῶν E.*IT*747, cf. Ar.*Nu*.1227, *Schwyzer* 721.5 (iv B.C.), etc.; ἐ. θεοὺς ὡς.. E.*Ph*.433; ἐπομνύω σοι τὴν ἐμὴν καὶ σὴν φιλίαν X.*Cyr*.6.4.6; ἐ. τὴν σὴν (sc. Καίσαρος) τύχην J.*AJ*16.10.8: c. dupl. acc., μή τι θεοὺς ἐπίορκον ἐπόμνυθι Thgn.1195:—Med., ἐπόμνυμαι Δία f.l. in Jusj.ap.D.24.151; ἐπόμνυσθαι κατά τινος Luc.*Icar*.9, *Cal*.18. 4. c. acc. rei, *swear to* a thing, Ar.*Lys*.211: abs., Pl.*Lg*.917b. 5. c. inf., *swear that*, ἐ. θεοὺς μὴ πρότερον ἐκδύσεσθαι.. Hdt.5.106, cf. E.*IT*974, Pl.*Criti*.120a:—Med., ἐπωμόσατο.. εἰδέναι Αἰσχίνην Test.ap.D.18.137; ἐπομνύειν ἢ μήν c. pres. inf., Plu.*Alex*.47; Ep., ἦ μέν.. c. fut. inf., A.R.2.715, etc.; ἐ. ὅτι.. Plu.*Per*.30. 6. abs. in aor. part., with another Verb, ἐπομόσας εἶπε he said *with an oath*, Hdt.8.5, X.*An*.7.8.2. II. Med., = ὑπόμνυσθαι (nisi hoc leg.), Ar.*Pl*.725.

ἐπομφάλιος [ᾰ], ον, (ὀμφαλός) *on the navel* or *central point*, βάλεν δεινὸν σάκος.. μέσσον ἐ. *in the centre, on the boss* of the shield, Il.7.267; σῦκον ἐ. a fig *with a navel-like stalk*, *AP*6.22 (Zon.). II. Subst. ἐπομφάλιον, τό, *the umbilical region*, Parth.35.4, Poll.2.169. 2. *plaster applied to the navel*, ἐ. καθαρτικά Aët.3.135, cf. Philum.ib.9.25.

ἐπονείδιστος, ον, *to be reproached, disgraceful, shameful*, E.*IT*689; ἐ. εἰρήνη Isoc.12.106 (Comp.), cf. D.19.336; ἀμαθία Pl.*Ap*.29b, etc.; τινι to one, X.*Smp*.8.34; ἐπονείδιστόν ἐστι παρά τισι is *matter of reproach*, D.26.19; ὄνομα τοὐπονείδιστον βροτοῖς the name *of reproach* among men, E.*Fr*.922: Comp., Arist.*EN*1119^{a}25: Sup., X.*Smp*.8.19. Adv. –τως *shamefully*, Pl.*Lg*.633e, Isoc.4.60; also in act. sense, *so as to shame*, ψέγειν Plb.1.14.5.

ἐπονήμενοι, dub. sens. in Alc.*Oxy.*1788 *Fr.*15 ii 25, 1789 *Fr.*1 i 5 (v. l. -νάμ-).

ἐπόνησις, Aeol. **-ᾱσις**, εως, ἡ, *enjoyment*, συμποσίας v.l. in Alc.46.

ἐπονομ-άζω, *apply* a word (accus.) *as a name* to a thing (dat.), ᾧ γένει κέραμον ἐπωνομάκαμεν to which sort we *have given the name* pottery, Pl.*Ti.*60d; ᾧ τὸ "ἔστιν" ἐπονομάζεις Id.*Tht.*185c; πᾶσι ταὐτὸν ἐ. ὄνομα Id.*Plt.*263c (reversely, τίς Ἀλεξάνδρῳ τὸν ἑαυτοῦ βίον ἐπονομάζει καθάπερ Πλάτωνι; who *dedicates* his life to A., *calls* himself an Alexandrist? Them.*Or.*31.354b):—Pass., τῇ ἀρχῇ ὕβρις ἐπωνομάσθη *the name* insolence *was given to* this rule, Pl.*Phdr.*238a, cf. *Cra.*404b. 2. *call by* a name, ἀπὸ τοῦ θεῖν θεοὺς αὐτοὺς ἐπονομάσαι [φαίνονται] ib.397d; τὰς Μούσας ἀπὸ τοῦ μῶσθαι τὸ ὄνομα τοῦτο ἐ. *called* the Muses *by* this name (viz. Muses), ib.406a; ἐ. αὐτὰ τῇ ἐκείνων ἐπωνυμίᾳ Id.*Phd.*103b; with εἶναι pleon., Id.*Prm.*133d:—Pass., *to be named*, ἀπό τινος after one, Th.6.2, etc.; also τινος, *to be named* the temple *of*.., E.*HF*1329, Pl.*Lg.*738b (but in 626d the gen. depends on ἄξιος); πατρόθεν ἐ. Id.*Ly.*204e; πατρὸς.. δαῖτ' ἐπωνομασμένην, i.e. *called after* Agamemnon (cf. ἐπώνυμος), S.*El.*284; esp. *to be surnamed*, Th.2.29; Ἰουδαῖος ἐπονομάζῃ *Ep.Rom.*2.17. 3. generally, *name, call* so and so, ἀφνειὸν ἐ. τὸ χωρίον Th.1.13; σοφιστὴν ἐ. σεαυτόν Pl.*Prt.*349a, cf. *Phd.*113b, al.; παρακαταθήκην ἐ. D. 28.15. 4. *pronounce* a name, ἐ. τὰ οὐνόματα ἐν τῷ ὕμνῳ Hdt.4.35, cf. 7.117; ἐπονομάζων τινά *uttering* his *name* as he throws the cottabus, Cratin.273, cf. Clearch.Com.1. **-αστέον**, *one must call by a name*, ὅσους θεοὺς οὐρανίους ἐ. Pl.*Lg.*828c. **-αστικῶς**, gloss on ἐπικλήδην Sch.Opp.*H.*1.776.

ἐποξ-ίζω, *turn acid*, Erot. and Suid. s. v. ὀξυρεγμίη. **-ύνω** [ῡ], *hasten*, τὴν πορείαν Lxx 2*Ma.*9.7. 2. *stimulate, excite*, τὸ ἐπιθυμητικὸν πρὸς τὸ ἀκόλαστον Hierocl.*in CA*8 p.431 M. **-υς**, υ, *sharpish in taste*, v.l. for ὕπ-, Hp.*Acut.*59.

ἐποπάζω, *bestow besides*, θεὸς δ' ἐπὶ ὄλβον ὀ. Rhian.1.9; ἐπὶ κλέος ὤπασε Μοῖρα *AP*9.521.

ἐποπίζομαι, only pres. and impf., *regard with awe, reverence*, Διὸς δ' ἐποπίζεο μῆνιν Od.5.146, cf. *h.Ven.*290, Thgn.1297.

ἐπόπισθεν, Adv. *coming after* (better divisim, ἐπ' ὄπ.), Hes.*Fr.* 166.

ἐποποῖ, a cry to mimic that of the hoopoe (ἔποψ), Ar.*Av.*58.

ἐποποι-ία, Ep. -ίη, ἡ, *epic poetry* or *an epic poem*, Hdt.2.116, Arist. *Po.*1459^{b}8, etc. II. *divination by means of Homeric verses*, *PMag. Berol.*1.328. **-ικός**, ή, όν, *of epic poetry*, σύστημα Arist.*Po.*1456^{a}11; μίμησις ib.1461^{b}26. **-ός**, ὁ, *epic poet*, Hdt.2.120, Arist.*Po.* 1447^{b}14, Neanth.26 J.: generally, *verse-maker*, Luc.*JTr.*6.

ἔποπος, etym. of πόποι, *An.Ox.*4.410.

ἐποπτάω, *roast besides* or *after*, Od.12.363, Diph.Siph.ap.Ath.3. 121c; ἐφθὸν ἐποπτᾶν οὔ φασι δεῖν Philoch.171. 2. Pass., *to be burnt*, Paul.Aeg.3.67. II. (as a pun) = ἐπωπάω, *Com.Adesp.*1325.

ἐποπτ-εία, ἡ, *highest grade of initiation at the Eleusinian mysteries*, Plu.*Demetr.*26, Sch.Ar.*Ra.*757; ἐ. τινός *initiation into*.., Mich.*in EN* 603.34; ἡ διαλεκτικὴ τῶν ὄντων ἐ. Hierocl.*in CA*26 p.481 M. **-ειρα**, ἡ, fem. of ἐπόπτης I, cj. for ἐποπτετῆρα in Herm.ap.Stob.1.49.44. **-εύω**, (ἐπόπτης) *overlook, watch*, of an overseer, ἔργα τ' ἐποπτεύεσκε Od.16. 140, cf. Hes.*Op.*767; Ἑρμῆ.. πατρῷ' ἐποπτεύων κράτη A.*Ch.*1; ἐ. μάχην ib.489; ὁ πάντ' ἐ. τάδε ἥλιος ib.993(985); δίκας Id.*Eu.*224; ἄλλοτε δ' ἄλλον ἐποπτεύει Χάρις φόρμιγγι Pi.*O.*7.11; αἰῶνας -εύουσα χελιδών *IGRom.*4.235(hex.). 2. *visit, punish*, κότῳ A.*Eu.*220. 3. abs., *keep watch*, οἱ περὶ τοὺς νόμους ἐποπτεύοντες Pl.*Lg.*951d. II. *become an* ἐπόπτης, *be admitted to the highest grade at the mysteries*, Id. *Ep.*333e, Plu.*Demetr.*26: c. acc., *view as an* ἐπόπτης, Pl.*Phdr.*250c: prov., of *attaining to the highest earthly happiness*, ἐποπτεύειν δοκῶ Ar. *Ra.*745. III. *study, meditate on*, c. dat., καθαρῇσιν ἐ. μελέτῃσιν Emp. 110.2. (Cf. ἐπιοπτεύω.) **-ήρ**, ῆρος, ὁ, = sq., of tutelary gods, λιτῶν A.*Th.*640; also ἐ. φρυκτωριῶν Arist.*Mu.*398^{a}31. **-ης**, ου, ὁ, (ἐπόψομαι) *overseer, watcher*, esp. of a god, Πυθῶνος Pi.*N.*9.5, cf. Epich.266; ὁ πάντων ἐ. θεός Lxx *Es.*5.1; title of Poseidon, Paus.8.30.1; of the Sun, *OGI*666.25 (Egypt, i A. D.); δαίμονες ἐ. τῶν ἀνθρωπίνων Ti.Locr. 105a; ὥσπερ ἐπόπτας τῶν στρατηγουμένων D.4.25; ἐ. γῆς καὶ θαλάσσης, of Pompey, *JHS*27.64 (Cyzicus); of Augustus, *IGRom.*4.309 (Pergam.); ἐ. εἰρήνης, of a police *magistrate*, *POxy.*991 (iv A. D.). 2. simply, *spectator*, πόνων A.*Pr.*301. 3. *inspector*, *Cod.Just.*10.16.13 *Intr.* II. *one admitted to the highest grade of the mysteries*, *IG*1^2.6. 51, Plu.*Alc.*22, etc., cf. ἐφόπται *IG*12(8).205.3 (Samothrace): c. gen., μυστηρίων ἐ. *Michel* 1141 (ibid.); τινος *PMag.Lond.*121.572: metaph., ἐ. τῆς ἐκείνου μεγαλειότητος 2*Ep.Pet.*1.16. **-ικός**, ή, όν, *of* or *for an* ἐπόπτης, τὰ τέλεα καὶ ἐ. *the highest mysteries*, Pl.*Smp.*210a, cf. Philoch. 148, Plu.*Demetr.*26; *esoteric*, διδασκαλίαι Id.*Alex.*7; μέρος φιλοσοφίας Id.2.382d; οἱ -ώτεροι the *more deeply initiated*, Hld.9.9. **-ις**, ιδος, ἡ, fem. of ἐπόπτης, v.l. in Corn.*ND*34; αἱ Ἐπόπτιδες, title of a book by Soranus, Plin.*HN Praef.*33. **-ος**, ον, *visible*, Str.5.3.12.

ἐποράω, Ion. for ἐφοράω. **ἐπορβεῖται**· φθονεῖ, Hsch.

ἐποργάω, in form ἐποργῶσαι· μηνιῶσαι, Suid.

ἐποργιάζω, *revel in* or *among*, πόλεσσι *Anacreont.*13.23.

ἐποργίζομαι, *to be wroth at*, τινι Lxx *Da.*11.40: abs., ib.2*Ma.*7.33.

ἐπορέγω, *hold out to, give yet more*, εἴ περ ἄν.. Ζεὺς ἐπὶ Τυδεΐδῃ Διομήδεϊ κῦδος ὀρέξῃ Il.5.225:—Med., τιμῆς οὔτ' ἀφελὼν οὔτ' ἐπορεξάμενος Sol.5.2. 2. metaph., [τὸ θεῖον] τισιν ἐ. τὰς μεταδόσεις τῆς ὑπερπλήρους ἀγαθότητος Procl.*Inst.*131. II. Med., *stretch oneself towards*, once in Hom., ἐπορεξάμενος *reaching forward* to strike, Il.5.335; χειρί τινος ἐ. *reach at* a thing, A.R.1.1313; οὗ παλάμη ἐπορέχθην Matro *Conv.*70; also χεῖράς τινι ἐ. A.R.2.1212; ἐ. πρός τι Hp. *Epid.*7.11: abs., ib.7.5. 2. ἐ. τινός *yearn for* it, ἀλλοίων ἐ. Emp. 110.6, cf. Pl.*R.*437c, *Tht.*186a. 3. *rise in one's demands*, Hdt. 9.34. **-όρεκτος**, ον, *eager*, πρός τι Sch.Nic.*Th.*75.

ἐπορέομαι, = ἐπόρνυμαι, prob. in Emp.137.2.

ἐπορθιάζω, *set upright*, ἐ. τὰ ὦτα *prick* the ears, v.l. in Ph.2.4: but mostly of the voice, *lift up at* or *over*, ὀλολυγμὸν τῇδε λαμπάδι A.*Ag.* 29; Ἐρινὺν τήνδε δώμασιν ib.1120: abs., ἐ. γόοις *lift up the voice* in wailing, Id.*Pers.*1050 (lyr.).

ἐπορθρ-εύω, *rise early*, Hsch., *EM*368.1:—Med., D.Chr.12.3, Luc. *Gall.*1, Poll.1.71. **-ισμός**, ὁ, *rising early*, τελωνικῶν κεκραγμῶν -ισμοί *morning cries* of noisy tax-gatherers, Plu.2.654f.

ἐποριγνάομαι, = ἐπορέγομαι, τινος Them.*Or.*2.33a.

ἐπορίνω [ῑ], *urge on*, v.l. in Nic.*Th.*671, Man.6.597.

ἐπορκιστής, οῦ, ὁ, = ἐξ- (which is used in Ptol.*Tetr.*182), Procl. *Par.Ptol.*253 (s. v. l.).

ἐπορμάω, ἐπορμέω, Ion. for ἐφ-.

ἐπόρνῡμι and -ύω, aor. 1 -ῶρσα, poet. Verb, *stir up, arouse, excite*, ὅς μοι ἐπῶρσε μένος who *called up* my might, Il.20.93. 2. *rouse and send against*, ἄγρει μάν οἱ ἔπορσον Ἀθηναίην 5.765, cf. Od.21.100, E.*Cyc.*12: c. inf., οἷον ἐπόρσειαν πολεμίζειν Ἕκτορι Il.7.42; also of things, τὴν [ὀϊζύν] μοι ἐπῶρσε Ποσειδάων Od.7.271; οἱ ἐπώρνυε μόρσιμον ἦμαρ Il.15.613; ἥ σφιν ἐπῶρσ' ἄνεμον Od.5.109; τῇ τις θεὸς ὕπνον ἐπῶρσε *sent* sleep *upon* her, Od.22.429, cf. Il.12.252 (tm.); λαίλαπας Cerc.5.9. II. Pass., **ἐπόρνῠμαι**, with pf. ἐπόρωρα, later 3 sg. ἐπώρορε Pancr.*Oxy.*1085.15: 3 sg. Ep. aor. 2 Pass. ἐπῶρτο:—*rise against, fly upon* one, c. dat., ἦ καὶ ἐπῶρτ' Ἀχιλῆϊ Il.21.324: abs., ἐπὶ δ' ὄρνυντο δῖος Ἐπειός 23.689, cf. 759, Euph.23: c. acc. cogn., τόνδ' ἐπόρνυνται στόλον A.*Supp.*187; of things, c. inf., ὦρτο δ' ἐπὶ.. οὖρος ἀήμεναι Od.3.176; ἐπὶ δίψος ὄρωρεν Nic.*Th.*774.

ἐπορούω, Ep. Verb, *spring at*, in hostile sense, τῷ δὲ Μέγης ἐπόρουσεν Il.15.520: abs., ἐπόρουσε κύων ὥς ib.579. 2. Τυδεΐδῃ δ' ἐπόρουσε θεά *sprang to* his side, 5.793; ὅτε οἱ γλυκὺς ὕπνος λυσιμελὴς ἐπόρουσε *came suddenly upon* him, Od.23.343. 3. *spring upon*, c. acc., ἅρμ' ἐπορούσας Il.17.481.

ἐποροφόω, *to put on as a roof* or *cover*, τὸν οὐρανόν Heraclit.*All.*48.

ἐπ-όρυξις, εως, ἡ, *digging up*, δαπέδου *IG*4.823.51 (Troezen). **-ορύττω**, *dig into*, τὸ τραῦμα Ach.Tat.3.8.

ἐπορχέομαι, *dance over* or *at*, ἐπορχούμενος ὑῆς ἄττης *dancing to the tune of*.., D.18.260: abs., *dance*, Ph.2.485: metaph., *triumph over*, τινι App.*Pun.*66.

ἔπος, older ϝέπος *SIG*9 (v. infr.), etc., εος, τό (Skt. *vácas* 'word', 'hymn', cf. εἶπον): I. *word*, παύρῳ ἔπει in short *utterance*, Pi.*O.* 13.98; ἐπέων κόσμος Parm.8.52, Democr.21; ἔπους σμικροῦ χάριν S. *OC*443; λόγοι ἔπεσι κοσμηθέντες Th.3.67: generally, *that which is uttered in words, speech, tale*, ἔπος ἐρέειν Il.3.83, etc.; φάσθαι Xenoph. 7.3, Parm.1.23, etc.; joined with μῦθος, Od.4.597, 11.561.—Special uses, 1. *song* or *lay accompanied by music*, 8.91, 17.519. 2. *pledged word, promise*, Il.8.8; τελέσαι ἔπος fulfil, keep *one's word*, 14.44, cf. A.*Pr.*1033. 3. *word in season, counsel*, Il.1.216, 2.807, Od.18.166, etc.; freq. in Trag., E.*Hel.*513, etc. 4. *word of a deity, oracle*, Od.12.266, Hdt.1.13, etc. 5. *saying, proverb*, τὸ παλαιὸν ἔπος Id.7.51, cf. Ar.*Av.*507. 6. *word*, opp. *deed*, ἔπε' ἀκράαντα *words* of none effect, opp. ἔτυμα, Od.19.565, cf. E.*HF*111 (lyr.); opp. ἔργον, Il.15.234, Od.2.272, etc., cf. II. 1; αἴτε ϝέπος αἴτε ϝάργον *SIG*9 (Elis, vi B.C.); opp. βίη, Il.15.106; opp. χεῖρες, 1.77 (pl.). 7. *subject of a speech, message*, 11.652, 17.701, S.*OT* 1144, etc. II. later usages, 1. joined with ἔργον or πρᾶγμα Heraclit.1, A.*Pers.*174 (troch.), Ar.*Eq.*39, etc.; ἔργῳ τε καὶ ἔπει Pl. *Lg.*879c; ἅμα ἔπος τε καὶ ἔργον ἐποίεε Hdt.3.134; χρηστὰ ἔργα καὶ ἔπεα ποιέειν Id.1.90. 2. κατ' ἔπος *word by word*, κατ' ἔ. βασανιεῖν φησι τὰς τραγῳδίας Ar.*Ra.*802. 3. πρὸς ἔπος at *the first word*, Luc. *Ep.Sat.*37. b. *word* in exchange for *word*, ἀμείβεσθαι, ἀποκρίνεσθαι, of an oracle, Id.*Alex.*19, *Philops.*38; also ἐ. δ' ἀμείβου πρὸς ἔ. A.*Eu.* 586, cf. Ar.*Nu.*1375, Pl.*Sph.*217d. c. οὐδὲν πρὸς ἔ. *to no purpose*, Ar.*Ec.*751; also, nothing to *the purpose*, ἐὰν μηδὲν πρὸς ἔ. ἀποκρίνωμαι Pl.*Euthd.*295c, cf. Luc.*Herm.*36; τί πρὸς ἔπος; Pl.*Phlb.*18d. 4. ὡς ἔπος εἰπεῖν *almost, practically*, qualifying a too absolute expression, esp. with πᾶς and οὐδείς (not with metaphors), Pl.*Ap.*17a, *Phd.* 78e, *Grg.*456a, al., Arist.*Metaph.*1009^{b}16, *Pol.*1252^{b}29, D.9.47, etc.; opp. ὄντως or ἀκριβεῖ λόγῳ, Pl.*Lg.*656e, *R.*341b; later ὡς ἔ. ἐστὶν εἰπεῖν *POxy.*67.14 (iv A. D.); in Trag., ὡς εἰπεῖν ἔ. A.*Pers.*714 (troch.), E.*Heracl.*167, *Hipp.*1162, once in Pl., *Lg.*967b (s. v. l.). 5. ἐνὶ ἔπει in one *word, briefly*, ἐνὶ ἔπεϊ πάντα συλλαβόντα λέγειν Hdt.3.82. III. of single *words*, esp. with ref. to etymology or usage, Id.2.30, Ar. *Nu.*638, Pl.*Prt.*339a, etc.; ὀρθότης ἐπῶν, = ὀρθοέπεια (q. v.), Ar.*Ra.* 1181; ἄριστ' ἐπῶν ἔχον ib.1161. IV. in pl., *epic poetry*, opp. μέλη (lyric poetry), ἰαμβεῖα, διθύραμβοι, etc., ῥαπτῶν ἐπέων ἀοιδοί Pi.*N.*2. 2; τὰ Κύπρια ἔπεα Hdt.2.117, cf. Th.1.3, X.*Mem.*1.4.3, Pl.*R.*379a, etc.; ἔπεά τε ποιεῖν πρὸς λύραν τ' ἀείδειν Theoc.*Ep.*21.6; νικήσας ἔπος *IG*3.1020; ποητὴς ἐπῶν ib.7.3197.9 (Orchom. Boeot.), cf. *OGI*51.37 (Egypt, iii B.C.). b. generally, *poetry*, even lyrics, Alcm.25 (prob.), Pi.*O.*3.8, etc. c. *lines, verses*, esp. of spoken *lines* in the drama, Ar.*Ra.*862, 956, etc.: sg., *verse, line* of poetry, Hdt.4.29, Pl.*Min.* 319d; *group of verses*, Id.*R.*386c, Hdt.7.143. d. *lines* of writing, μυρίων ἐπῶν μῆκος Isoc.12.136; ἐν ὅλοις ἑπτὰ ἔπεσι παραδραμεῖν, of a historian, Luc.*Hist.Conscr.*28.

ἐποστρᾰκ-ίζω, *send potsherds skimming over the water, play at ducks and drakes*, *EM*368.3: hence, -ισμός, ὁ, Poll.9.119.

ἐπόσχιον, τό, *offshoot* of a vine, Gal.19.100.

ἐποτοτύζω, *cry out, utter lamentably*, ἄλλος ἄλλ' ἐπωτότυζε E.*Ph.* 1038 (lyr.).

ἐποτρύνω, *stir up, excite, urge on*, abs., θυμὸς ἐποτρύνει καὶ ἀνώγει Il. 6.439, al.: c. acc. pers., Hdt.7.170, al.; ἐς τὸ πρόσω ἐ. ib.223; ἐπὶ τὰ δεινά Th.1.84 (v.l.); τινὰς ἐς μάχην Plu.*Crass.*23; μαχομένους Id. *Aem.*33: c. inf., ἐ. τινὰ μαχέσασθαι Il.20.171, cf. Hp.*Fract.*22; στείχειν Pi.*N.*9.20; μολεῖν S.*El.*1264 (lyr.); ἔρδειν ὅττι κε κεῖνος ἐποτρύνῃ καὶ ἀνώγῃ [ἔρδειν] Il.15.148: c. dat. et inf., ἑτάροισιν ἐποτρῦναι καὶ ἀνῶξαι.. κατακῆαι *to urge* and order them.. to burn, Od.10.531; ἵππεῦσιν ἐπότρυνον.. ἐλαυνέμεν Il.15.258, cf. 16.525, Q.S.8.337; ἑτάροισιν ἐποτρύνας ἐκέλευσεν Od.2.422, cf. 9.488. 2. c. acc. rei, νῶϊν ἐποτρύνει πόλεμον *stirs up* war *against* us, 22.152; also πόλεμόν.. ἐ. γίγνεσθαι Th.7.25; ἀγγελίας.. ἐ. Κεφαλλήνων πολίεσσι *send urgent* messages to the cities of the C., Od.24.355; σαλπιγκταὶ ξύνοδον ἐπώτρυνον τοῖς ὁπλίταις *gave the signal for* engagement to the men-at-arms, Th.6.69:—Med., ἐποτρυνώμεθα πομπήν *let us urge on our* escort, Od.8.31:—Pass., *press on, hasten*, A.*Th.*698 (lyr.).

ἐπουδαῖος, ον, (οὖδας) *terrestrial*, Hsch.

ἐπουλ-ίς, ίδος, ἡ, (οὖλον) *growth on the gum*, Dsc.5.79, Aët.8. 27. **-ος**, ον (proparox.), *frilled, puckered*, of leaves, Thphr.*HP*3. 10.5. **-όω**, *scar over*, Gal.13.449:—Pass., Hp.*Art.*11, Gal.11. 440. **-ωσις**, εως, ἡ, *cicatrization*, Id.18(1).723. **-ωτικός**, ή, όν, *promoting cicatrization*, Id.11.756.

ἐπουραῖος, α, ον, (οὐρά) *on the tail*, δῆγμα *AP*9.252.4.

ἐπουράνιος [ᾰ], ον, Ep. η, ον Arat. (v. infr.), Q.S.2.429:—*heavenly*, in Hom. only of the gods, ἐ. θεός, θεοί, Od.17.484, Il.6.129, al.; εὐσεβέων ἐ. ψυχαί Pi.*Fr.*132.3; πατήρ *Ev.Matt.*18.35; ἡ ἐ. πορεία f.l. in Pl.*Phdr.*256d. 2. pl., as Subst., οἱ ἐ., = θεοί, Theoc.25.5, Mosch. 2.21; opp. ἐπίγειοι, *Ep.Phil.*2.11; so ἤδη ἐ. εἶ Luc.*DDeor.*4.3; τὰ ἐ., = τὰ μετέωρα, v.l. in Pl.*Ap.*19b (ἐ. σώματα 1*Ep.Cor.*15.40). 3. *up to heaven*, ἔπτατ' ἐπουρανίη v.l. in Arat.134.

ἐπουρέω, *make water upon*, Pythag.ap.D.L.8.17, Arist.*PA*679^{a}29.

ἐπουρ-ιάζω, (οὖρος) of a fair wind, *waft onwards*, τὰ ἀκάτια Luc. *Hist.Conscr.*45; *swell*, τὴν ὀθόνην Id.*Dom.*12. II. metaph., τὰ ὦτα ἐπουριάσας ἕνεκα πολυπράγμονος περιεργίας *spreading out* his ears to catch gossip, v.l. in Ph.2.4. **-ίζω**, = foreg., of the sea, *waft onwards*, Str.3.2.4: metaph., ὥσπερ ἂν λαμπρότερον ἐπουρίσῃ τὸ τῆς τύχης the more freshly the breeze of fortune *blows*, Pl.*Alc.*2.147a (dub. l.); ἀλλ' οὔτι ταύτῃ σὸν φρόνημ' ἐπούρισας *hast turned* thy mind to it, E.*Andr.*610: c. acc. cogn., πνεῦμα αἱματηρὸν ἐ. τινί (of the Erinyes) *send after* him *the gale* of gory breath, A.*Eu.*137. II. intr., *sail with a fair wind*, τρέχε κατὰ τοὺς κόρακας ἐπουρίσας Ar.*Th.* 1226, cf. Epicr.10. **-ος**, ον, *blowing favourably*, αὔρα S.*Tr.*954 (lyr.). II. a kind of *fish*, Hsch. **-όω**, *have a fair wind*, Plb.2. 10.6. **-ωσις**, εως, ἡ, dub. in Licymn.ap.Arist.*Rh.*1414^{b}17, prob. *a speeding onward, as by a gale*: v.l. ἐπόρουσις ap.Sch. ad loc.

ἐπουσι-α, ἡ, *surplus*, Gem.18.15, Vett.Val.353.16, etc. **-αστικός**, ή, όν, *denoting material*, of Adjs. in -ειος, *An.Ox.*1.58. **-ώδης**, ες, *added to the essence, non-essential*, Phlp. *in Ph.*38.26; f.l. for ἐπεισοδιώδης, Porph.*Intr.*21.14. II. *symptomatic*, of fever, Alex.Aphr. *Febr.*31, Pall.*Febr.*3.

ἐπουτίς· οὐσία (Rhod.), Hsch.

ἐποφείλω, *owe still*, φόρους Th.8.5, cf. D.C.51.21:—Pass., τόκος ἐποφειλόμενός τισι Id.42.51.

ἐποφθαλμ-έω, = sq., c. dat., Charito 1.7, *PThead.*19.9 (iv A.D.). **-ιάω**, *cast longing glances at, ogle*, τινι Ael.*NA*3.44, cf. *Fr.*81; ἐ. χρήμασι Plu.*Caes.*2; πρὸς τὸν πλοῦτον Id.*Dem.*25; *eye jealously*, τοῖς ἔργοις τινός *POxy.*1630.6 (iii A.D.); v.l. in Hyp.*Fr.*258. **-ίζω**, = foreg., c. dat., Pherecyd.34J., Plu.*Aem.*30.

ἐποφλισκάνω, *owe still more*, τί τινι Them.*Or.*6.83a, cf. Men.Prot. p.34 D.:—Pass., aor. part. -οφληθείς *PMasp.*168.63 (vi A.D.).

ἐποφρύδιον, τό, gloss on ἐπισκύνιον, *Et.Gud.*202.36; cf. ἐποφρύδιον· μέτωπον, Hsch. (-φρυδῶν cod.).

ἐποχέομαι, Pass. with fut. (and in Nonn.*D.*45.322, aor.) Med., *be carried upon, ride upon*, οὐ μὰν ὑμῖν γε (the horses of Achilles) καὶ ἅρμασι δαιδαλέοισιν Ἕκτωρ.. ἐποχήσεται Il.17.449, cf. Arr.*Tact.*17.1; ἐφ' ἵππῳ Paus.6.20.16: abs., κάμηλον ὥστε ἐποχεῖσθαι a camel *to ride on*, X.*Cyr.*7.1.49; of a fractured bone, *rest* or *ride on* the adjoining one, Hp.*Art.*15; com., ἐμβάταις ὑψηλοῖς ἐ. *to be mounted on* high shoes, Luc.*Salt.*27; ἡ κωμῳδία ἀναπαίστοις ἐ. Id.*Prom.Es*6. 2. *float upon*, [ἡ γῆ] ἐ. τῷ ἀέρι *Placit.*3.15.8; *float on the surface*, Gal.7. 604, Aët.5.137. 3. metaph., of a higher power, *transcend* the lower, [θεὸν] -ούμενον τῇ νοητῇ φύσει Plot.1.1.8; θεοὶ τοῖς δαίμοσιν ἄνωθεν -ούμενοι Procl. *in Alc.*p.69 C.; θεία ἀρετὴ ἐπὶ ἀνθρωπίνην ἐ. Hierocl. *in CA* 20 p.463 M. b. *to be borne upon, employ as a vehicle* or *medium*, Plot.4.5.6; τῇ οὐσίᾳ Dam.*Pr.*89, cf. 5. c. *hover over, brood over, play about*, Plot.2.2.3, 2.5.5, 4.3.7.

ἐποχετ-εία, ἡ, *watering by sluices*, Str.16.1.10 (pl.). **-ευσις**, εως, ἡ, = foreg., metaph., ἀγαθῶν Procl. *in Alc.*p.2 C. (pl.). **-εύω**, *carry* water *by sluices* or *courses*, Pl.*Grg.*493e; τὸ ἀπορρέον.. δι' ὀχετῶν ἐ. Id.*Criti.*117b; τροφὴν τοῖς φυτευθεῖσι Ph.1.398; ἐ. ἄνθεσιν ὕδωρ Longus 4.4: metaph., ὑφηγήσεις ἐ. ἀκοαῖς Ph.2.359; λόγος οἴνῳ τὸ φιλάνθρωπον ἐπὶ τὴν ψυχὴν.. ἐ. Plu.2.660c, cf. Jul.*Or.*4.137d, Dam. *Pr.*35, etc.:—Pass., *to be so brought*, [αἷμα] ἐκ τῆς καρδίας ἐποχετεύεται καὶ εἰς τὰς φλέβας Arist.*PA*666^{a}6; [αἱ φλέβες] ἐς ἀλλήλας ἐποχετεύονται *are conducted* one into another, Hp.*Oss.*15; ὕδωρ τὸ Ἰούλιον.. εἰς τὴν πόλιν ἐπωχετεύθη D.C.48.32, cf. 49.42: metaph., ἐλλάμψις ἐκ τῶν πρώτων δυνάμεων ταῖς δευτέραις -εύεται Herm. *in Phdr.*p.145 A.:—Med., *to have* water *brought upon them, to be irrigated*, ἐποχετεύεται τοῖς κοχλίαις τὰ λίαν ἔξαλα Str.17.1.52: metaph., ἐ. ἵμερον *bring the waters of* desire *over oneself, bathe in* them, Pl.*Phdr.*251e.

ἐποχεύς, έως, ὁ, (ἐπέχω) *brake*, prob. for ἐποχλεύς (q.v.).

ἐποχεύω, of the male animal, *spring upon, cover*, Arist.*GA*741^{a} 31:—Med., *couple with*, θερμὸν δ' ἐποχεύετο θερμῷ Emp.90 (dub. l.).

ἐποχή, ἡ, (ἐπέχω) *check, cessation*, ἡ κατὰ τὸν πόλεμον ἐ. Plb.38.11.2; μετ' ἐποχῆς with *a check*, Id.10.23.4; ἐποχὰς ποιεῖν.. τῆς προκοπῆς to *check* advance, Plu.2.76d, cf. Plot.6.2.13. 2. *retention*, σπέρματος Gal.8.420; οὔρων Philum.*Ven.*25.2; σκυβάλων Sor.2.20; ἀναπνοῆς (in hysteria) ib.26; γαστρός Gal.6.315; but ἐ. ἐμμήνων *suppression* (not *retention*) of the menses, Sor.2.6, al. II. Philos., *suspension of judgement*, Metrod.*Herc.*831.6, Chrysipp.*Stoic.*2.39, Cic.*Acad.Pr.* 2.18.59, Arr.*Epict.*1.4.11, S.E.*P.*1.10, Gal.1.40, etc. 2. *suspense* of payment, etc., τὰ ἐν ἐποχῇ ἕως ὁρισμοῦ καρπῶν *BGU*599.3 (ii A.D.), cf. *PRyl.*214.34 (ii A.D.), etc. III. *stoppage, pause*, of light during an eclipse, Plu.2.923b. 2. Astron., *position* as referred to celestial or terrestrial latitude and longitude, Ptol.*Alm.*7.4, 12.8; πόλεων ib.2.13 (pl.); ἀστέρων ἐποχαί *positions* (longitudes) of stars in a horoscope, Plu.*Rom.*12; αἱ φαινόμεναι τῆς σελήνης ἐ., opp. αἱ οὖσαι, Procl.*Hyp.*4.49. b. *fixed point in time* in reference to which positions are defined and from which their changes are computed, *epoch*, Ptol.*Alm.*3.9; perh. also *position at such a fixed point* (also called *epoch*), ib.3.7. 3. in Musical theory, *period* of vibration, Nicom.*Harm.*3 (pl.).

ἐποχθίδιος, α, ον, (ὄχθη) *on* or *of the river-banks*, Νύμφαι *AP*9.556 (Zon.).

ἐποχθίζω, *groan* or *grieve for*, ὀδύνῃσι Opp.*H.*5.170.

ἐποχλεύς, έως, ὁ, *brake, sprag*, = τροχοπέδη, prob. f.l. for ἐποχεύς, Simarist.ap.Ath.3.99c.

ἐποχλίζομαι, *to be bolted*, of doors, Apollon.*Lex.* s. v. ἐπώχατο.

ἐποχμάζω, = ἐποχεύω, c. dat., Opp.*C.*1.389.

ἔποχον, τό, *saddle-cloth, housing*, X.*Eq.*12.9.

ἔποχος, ον, (ἐπί, Ϝέχω, cf. Lat. *veho*) *mounted upon*, esp. on horses, chariots, and ships, c. gen. vel dat., ναῶν, ἅρμασιν, A.*Pers.*54, 45 (anap.), cf. S.*Ichn.*181 (lyr.); τῷ ἐ. τοῦ οὐρανοῦ καὶ ἡνιόχῳ Ph.1.486, cf. Lib.*Or.*59.110: metaph., λόγος μανίας ἔ. words borne on madness, i. e. frantic words, E.*Hipp.*214 (anap.). 2. abs., *having a good seat* on horseback, X.*Cyr.*1.4.4; ἐπόχους ἡ θήρα ἀποδεικνύει ib. 8.1.35; ἔ. εἶναι to *have a good seat*, Id.*Eq.*8.10, cf. Ar.*Lys.*677; also ἱππασίαις ἔ. *practised in*.., Plu.*Mar.*34. Adv. -χως, ἐγκαθῆσθαι to sit *fast*, Poll.1.209. II. Pass., ποταμὸς ναυσὶ ἔ. *navigable* by ships, Plu.*Mar.*15.

ἔποψ, οπος, ὁ, *hoopoe*, *Upupa epops*, so called from its cry, Epich. 166, Ar.*Av.*226, Arist.*HA*615^{a}16, Ant.Lib.11.10, etc.; ἐπόπτην ἔποπα τῶν αὐτοῦ κακῶν A.*Fr.*304.

ἐποψ-άομαι, (ὄψον) *eat as* ὄψον, ζωμόν Plu.*Lyc.*12. **-ειασμός**, ὁ, sine expl., Suid., *Et.Gud.d.* **-ημα**, ατος, τό, *that which is eaten with bread*, *IG*7.2712.81 (Acraephia). **-ησις**, εως, ἡ, *eating as* ὄψον, Ath.5.186d.

ἐποψία, ἡ, *inspection*, Them.*Or.*1.2c, *Cod.Just.*10.16.13 *Intr.*

ἐποψίδιος, ον, *for eating with bread*, χόνδρος *AP*7.736.8 (Leon.).

ἐπόψ-ιμος, ον, (ἐπόψομαι) *that can be looked on*, δεινόν, οὐδ' ἀκουστόν, οὐδ' ἐ. S.*OT*1312. **-ιος**, ον, also α, ον Arat.258: (ὄψις):—*full in view, conspicuous*, τόπος S.*Ant.*1110, v.l. in Id.*OC*1600: metaph., *conspicuous, famous*, βωμός *h.Ap.*496: also read by Ar.Byz. for ὑπόψιος, Il.3.42. II. Act., *overlooking all things*, epith. of gods, S. *Ph.*1040; esp. of Zeus, *SIG*1264 (Itanus, iv B.C.), A.R.2.1123, 1133, Call.*Jov.*82, Ant.Lib.6.2. **-ις**, εως, ἡ, *view over*, ἐπ' ὅσον ἔ. τοῦ ἱροῦ εἶχε so far as *the view from* the temple reached, Hdt.1.64; ἐκτὸς τῆς ἡμετέρας ἐ. beyond our *range of vision*, Pl.*R.*499d; ἀνώμαλον τὴν ἔποψιν τῆς ναυμαχίας ἐκ τῆς γῆς ἠναγκάζοντο ἔχειν *to view* the sea-fight, Th.7.71; ἔποψίν τινος παρέχειν Plu.*Pomp.*32; καταστὰς εἰς ἔ. τῶν πολεμίων Id.*Luc.*8; ἐν ἐπόψει ἀλλήλοις within *view*, Str.14.5. 16. II. *oversight, superintendence*, ἔ. θεία περὶ τὸν κόσμον Hippod. ap.Stob.4.39.26.

ἐπόψομαι, fut. of ἐφοράω. II. v. ἐπιόψομαι. **ἔππᾱσις**, v. ἔμπᾱσις. **ἐπράθην** [ᾱ], aor. 1 Pass. of πιπράσκω. **ἔπραθον**, aor. 2 of πέρθω. **ἔπρεσε**, Ep. for ἔπρησε, aor. 1 of πρήθω, Hes.*Th.* 856. **ἐπρήθην**, Ion. aor. 1 Pass. of πιπράσκω. **ἔπρηξα**, Ion. for ἔπραξα, aor. 1 of πράσσω. **ἔπρησα**, aor. 1 of πρήθω.

ἑπτά, οἱ, αἱ, τά, indecl. *seven*, Il.6.421, etc.; as a mystical number, Arist.*Metaph.*1093^{a}13, etc.; αἱ ἑ. νῆσοι the *seven* largest islands, Alex.268, cf. Arist.*Mir.*837^{a}31; τὰ ἑ. θεάματα the *Seven* Wonders, Str.17.1.33, cf. D.S.2.11, etc.; οἱ ἑ. σοφισταί the *Seven* Sages, Isoc. 15.109, Aristid.2.311 J.; οἱ ἑ. σοφοί Stob.3.1.172; οἱ ἑ. alone, D.L. 1.40, Lib.*Ep.*286.3. 2. οἱ ἑ., board of magistrates at Olbia, *SIG* 495.2 (iii B.C.); οἱ ἑ. ἄνδρες, = Lat. *septemviri epulones*, D.C.48.32. (I.-E. *septḿ*, cf. Skt. *saptá*, Lat. *septem* (fancifully connected with σέβομαι, Ph.1.30, *Theol.Ar.*43): Hsch. has τεπτά, i. e. ϝεπτά.)

ἑπτᾰ-βόειος, ον, *of seven bulls'-hides*, σάκος Il.7.220, 222, etc.; comically, θυμοὶ ἑ. Ar.*Ra.*1017. **-βοιος**, ον, = foreg., ἑ. ἄρρηκτον σάκος S.*Aj.*576. **-βυρσος**, ον, gloss on ἑπταβόειος, Apollon.*Lex.*, Hsch. **-γλωσσος**, ον, *seven-toned*, φόρμιγξ Pi.*N.*5.24. **-γράμμᾰτος**, ον, *of seven letters*, Hsch. (glossed by τὸ "ὀργίλον", ἢ "σκληρόν", καὶ "Σάραπιν"). **-γωνικός**, ή, όν, = sq., ἀριθμός Iamb. *in Nic.* p.60 P. **-γωνος**, ον, *heptagonal*, ἀριθμός Nicom.*Ar.*2.7, 11. II. ἑπτάγωνα, τά, certain *musical instruments*, Arist.*Pol.*1341^{a}41.

ἑπτᾰδεύω, *to be a member of a board of seven* (cf. ἑπτά 2), *SIG*1039. 1 (Olbia, iii B.C.).

ἑπτά-δουλος [ᾰ], ὁ, *sevenfold-slave*, Hippon.113B, Herod.5.75. **-δραχμος**, ον, *worth seven drachmae*, Theoc.15.19. **-δρομος**, ον, *having seven laps*, δόλιχος Tz.*H*.6.704.

ἑπτάδῠμος [ᾰ], ον, in pl., *seven at a birth*, Arist.ap.Str.15.1.22.

ἑπτά-ειδος [ᾰ], ον, *containing seven ingredients*, ἀντίδοτος Paul.Aeg. 3.78.22; cf. ἑξάειδος. **-εικοσαπλᾰσίων**, ον, gen. ονος, *twenty-seven times as great*, Hipparch.ap.Theon.Sm.p.197H. **-ενος**, ον, = ἑπταετής, Hsch. **-εξ**, *six or seven*, Tz.*H*.11.342. **-ετής**, ές, = ἑπτέτης, *seven years old*, v.l. in Hp.*Prog*.19, v.l. for ἑπτέτης in Pl.*Grg*.471c: as fem., *IG*14.1935, Arr.*Ind*.9.1: regul. fem. -έτις, ιδος, ἡ, Amyntas Epigr.*Oxy*.662.30: as Adj., ἑ. ἡλικία Ph.1.393. II. parox. -έτης, ες, *of seven years*: neut. ἑπτάετες, as Adv., *for seven years*, Od. 3.304, 7.259. **-ετία**, ἡ, *age of seven years*, εἰς ἑπταετίαν ἀφικέσθαι Pl.*Ax*.366d. 2. *period of seven years*, Ph.1.25, J.*AJ*1.19.6, Plu. *Demetr*.44. **-ζωνος**, ον, *seven-zoned*, of the planetary system, Vett. Val.144.14, Paul.Al.*I*.3, Nonn.*D*.1.241; ἡ ἑ. (sc. σφαῖρα) *PMag.Leid. W*.6.5. **-ήμερος**, ον, *lasting seven days*, D.C.76.1. **-θεος**, ον, *having seven gods*, gloss on the name Ἀρδάβδα, *Peripl.M.Eux*.p.415M.

ἑπταῖος, α, ον, f.l. for ἑπτάκις in Hp.*Nat.Puer*.13.

ἑπτᾰκαίδεκα, οἱ, αἱ, τά, indecl. *seventeen*, Hdt.1.50, al.; in Hom., ἑπτὰ δὲ καὶ δέκα Od.5.278, al.

ἑπτᾰκαιδεκᾰετής, ές, *of seventeen years*, χρόνος D.S.2.2. 2. (parox.) *seventeen years old*, Plb.4.24.1, Poll.1.55: -δεκέτης D.L.5.6.

ἑπτᾰκαιδεκάκις, Adv. *seventeen times*, Ptol.*Tetr*.138.

ἑπτᾰκαιδεκά-μετρος, ον, *containing seventeen measures*, περίοδος Sch.Ar.*Pax*1320. **-πηχυς**, υ, *seventeen cubits long*, Antig.*Mir*. 91. **-πους**, ὁ, ἡ, neut. -πουν, *seventeen feet long*, Pl.*Tht*.147d.

ἑπτᾰκαιδεκᾰταῖος, α, ον, *on the seventeenth day*, Hp.*Aph*.4.36.

ἑπτᾰκαιδέκᾰτος, η, ον, *seventeenth*, Hp.*Aph*.2.24, Th.7.28, etc.; δημαρχικῆς ἐξουσίας τὸ ἑ. *Notiz.Arch*.4.20.

ἑπτᾰκαιδεκέτης, ες, v. ἑπτακαιδεκαέτης.

ἑπτᾰκαιεικοσα-έτης, ες, *twenty-seven years old*, D.H.4.7, etc. **-πλάσιος** [πλᾰ], ον, *twenty-seven fold*, Pl.*Ti*.35c (v.l. -σιπλ-), *Theol. Ar*.4.41 (v.l. -σιπλ-):—also **-πλασίων**, ονος, ὁ, ἡ, *Placit*.2.21.1.

ἑπτᾰκαιεικοσέτης, ες, *twenty-seven years old*, *IG*9(1).873 (Corc., iii B.C.).

ἑπτᾰκαιεικοσι-μόριος, ον, *containing a twenty-seventh part*, *Theol. Ar*.4. **-πλάσιος**, ον, v. ἑπτακαιεικοσαπλάσιος.

ἑπτᾰκάτιοι [κᾰ], αι, α, Dor. for ἑπτακόσιοι, *Tab.Heracl*.1.47.

ἑπτά-καυλος [ᾰ], ον, *seven-stemmed*, *Theol.Ar*.48. **-κέφᾰλος**, ον, *seven-headed*, δράκοντες Dam.*Isid*.67, cf. *Pr*.265.

ἑπτάκις [ᾰ], Adv. *seven times*, Pi.*O*.13.40, Ar.*Lys*.698, etc.:— poet. **ἑπτάκι** Simon.156, A.R.3.861, etc.: also in later Prose, *SIG* 1068.8 (Patmos, iii/ii B.C.), Iamb.*in Nic*.p.17P.:—Lacon. **ἑπτάκιν** *IG*5(1).213.16 (v B.C.).

ἑπτᾰκισ-μύριοι [ῡ], αι, α, *seventy thousand*, Hdt.4.86, Plu.*Demetr*. 28. **-χίλιοι** [χῑ], αι, α, *seven thousand*, Hdt.2.43, etc.; ἑπτασχίλιαι (sic) *PSI*3.250 (iii/iv A.D.).

ἑπτά-κλῑνος, ον, *with seven couches* or *beds*, οἶκος Phryn.Com.66, X.*Smp*.2.18; κοιτών Callix.1; and without οἶκος, Tim.Com.1; θὲς ἑπτάκλινον place *seven seats*, Eub.121; τὸ δέρμα κατέχει εἰς ἑ. ἀποταθέν provides sitting-room for *seven*, Arist.*HA*630^{a}22: hence, as a measure of area, Ph.*Bel*.80.48.

ἑπτᾰκόσιοι, αι, α, *seven hundred*, Hdt.2.140, etc.

ἑπτᾰκοσιοστός, ή, όν, *seven-hundredth*, Archim.*Aren*.1.10, Cleom. 2.1, D.L.1.24.

ἑπτᾰκότῠλος, ον, *holding seven cotylae*, λήκυθος Ar.*Fr*.472.

ἑπτᾰκτῖς, ῖνος, ὁ, ἡ, *with seven rays*, of the sun, Jul.*Or*.5.172d, Procl.*in Ti*.1.34D.

ἑπτά-κτῠπος, ον, *seven-toned*, φόρμιγξ Pi.*P*.2.70. **-κωλος**, ον, *of seven members*, περίοδος Sch.Ar.*Ra*.221. **-λοβος**, ον, *with seven lobes*, Ar.Byz.*Epit*.90.16. **-λογχος**, ον, *of seven lances*, i.e. *seven bodies of spearmen*, στόλος S.*OC*1305. **-λόφιον**, = Lat. *septimontium*, *Gloss*. **-λοφος**, ον, *seven-hilled*, ἄστυ, of Rome, Cic.*Att*. 6.5.2, *AP*14.121 (Metrod.), cf. Plu.2.280d. **-μελής**, ές, *having seven members*, Procl.*in Ti*.2.209D. **-μερής**, ές, *having seven parts*, ψυχῆς τὸ ἄλογον ἑ. Ph.1.45, cf. Procl.*in Ti*.2.209D. **-μέριον**, τό, dub. sens. in *PMag.Berol*.1.201. **-μήκης** κύκλος, dub. sens. in Call.*Iamb*.1.126 (cf. D.S.10.6); perh. referring to the Pythagorean harmony of the planetary spheres. **-μηνιαῖος**, α, ον, *born in the seventh month*, Cic.*Att*.10.18.1, J.*AJ*5.11.4, *Placit*. 5.18.5:—also **-μήνιος**, ον, *Theol.Ar*.48. **-μηνος**, ον, παιδίον, βρέφος, τέκνον, *a seven months' child*, Hp.*Septim*.passim; τίκτειν τινὰ ἑπτάμηνον, τίκτειν ἑπτάμηνα [τέκνα], Hdt.6.69, cf. Arist.*HA*584^a 36. II. ἑπτάμηνος, ἡ, *a space of seven months*, *Placit*.5.18.1, cf. *IG*12(1).53 (Rhodes). **-μήτωρ**, ορος, ἡ, *mother of seven children*, Lxx 4*Ma*.16.24. **-μῐτος**, ον, *seven-stringed*, Luc.*Astr*.10; κιθάρη *AP*9.250 (Honest.). **-μναῖος**, α, ον, *weighing seven minae*, Hsch. s.v. μολβίς. **-μοιρία**, ἡ, *arc of seven degrees*, Paul.Al.*H*.1. **-μόριον**, τό, = Lat. *Septempagi*, Plu.*Rom*.25. **-μυξος**, ον, *with seven wicks*, λύχνος *PMag.Lond*.121.593: Subst. -μυξος (sc. λύχνος), ὁ, *seven-branched candlestick*, *JHS*28.195 (Side). **-μῠχος**, ον, *with seven recesses*, σπέος Call.*Del*.65: title of work by Pherecyd.Syr. **-νευρον**, τό, prob. f.l. for ἑπτάπλευρον II, Paul.Aeg.7.17, Apul.*Herb*.1. **-όριον**, τό, = Lat. *septimontium*, *Gloss*. **-ούγκιον**, τό, = Lat. *septunx*, ib. **-πάλαιστος** [πᾰ], ον, *seven palms long*, S.E.*M*.9.321:—early Att. **-πάλαστος** *IG*1^2.373.237. **-πεκτος**· ἡ βαθείας τρίχας ἔχουσα, Hsch. (-ιος cod.), cf. Suid.; ἡ δυναμένη ἑπτάκις τμηθῆναι, *EM*368. 11. **-πέλεθρος**, ον, *seven plethra large*, Ἄρης Nonn.*D*.36.14. **-πηχυς**, υ, *seven cubits long*, Hdt.1.68, Pl.*Ep*.363a, etc.; *seven cubits tall*, ἀνήρ J.*AJ*18.4.5. **-πλᾰνής**, ές, *with seven revolutions*, v.l. in Secund.*Sent*.1. **-πλᾰσιάζω**, *multiply seven times*, Dam.*Pr*.98, Hero *Geom*.17.7: hence, **-πλᾰσιασμός**, ὁ, ib.33: **-πλᾰσιέφεκτος** λόγος ratio *of* $7\frac{1}{8}:1$, Procl.*Hyp*.4.109. **-πλάσιος** [πλᾰ], α, ον, *sevenfold*, -πλασίῳ φαυλότερος Pl.*Ep*.332a, cf. Iamb.*in Nic*.p.102P. Adv. -ίως Lxx *Ps*.11(12).6, al. **-πλᾰσίων**, ον, gen. ονος, = foreg., Orib.*Fr*.90, Suid. **-πλευρος**, ον, *having seven ribs*, Arist.*HA* 493^{b}15. II. **-πλευρον**, τό, = ἀρνόγλωσσον, Dsc.2.126. **-πλόος**, ον, contr. **-πλοῦς**, οῦν, *sevenfold*, ἑπταπλᾶ ἀνταποδώσει σοι Lxx *Si*.32 (35).13. **-πόδης**, ου, ὁ, *seven feet long*, θρῆνυς Il.15.729; ἄξων Hes. *Op*.424. **-πολις**, ὁ, ἡ, *containing seven cities*: ἑ. μεσάτη ἤπειρος, of Egypt, D.P.251. **-πορος**, ον, *with seven tracks* or *paths*, τείρεα, of the planets, *h.Hom*.8.7; Πλειάς or Πελειάς, E.*IA*7, *Or*.1005 (both anap.); Πληιὰς ἑ. *Epigr.Gr*.223.4 (Milet.); *seven-mouthed*, of the Nile, Mosch.2.51, D.P.264. **-πους**, ὁ, ἡ, *seven feet long*, σκιά Ar.*Fr*.675, cf. *IG*1^2.372.19, Anon.*in Tht*.34.25. 2. *having seven feet*, πολύπους Ael. *Fr*.143. **-πτῠχος**, ον, gloss on ἑπταβόειος, Sch.D Il.7.220. **-πῠλος**, ον, *with seven gates*, epith. of Boeotian Thebes (cf. ἑκατόμπυλος), Il.4.406, Od.11.263, B.18.47, Anaxandr.41.21, cf. A.*Th*.165 (lyr.), S.*Ant*.119 (lyr.). II. ἑ. κλῖμαξ stairway symbolizing the ascent of the soul through the seven planetary spheres, Cels.ap.Orig.*Cels*.6. 22 (prob. for ὑψί-). **-πυργος**, ον, *seven-towered*, of Boeotian Thebes, E.*Ph*.245 (lyr.), etc.: metaph., εὐλογιστία Lxx 4*Ma*.13.7. **-πῠρος**, ον, *with seven flames* or *wicks*, λύχνος *SIG*1106.119 (Cos, iv/iii B.C.).

ἑπτᾰρουρ-ικὸς κλῆρος allotment *of seven* ἄρουραι (q.v.), *PTeb*.13 *Intr*. (ii B.C.), cf. 128 (ii B.C.): **-ος**, ὁ, *holder of seven* ἄρουραι, ib.60.30 (ii B.C.), etc.: **-ον**, τό, *plot of seven* ἄρουραι, *PFay*.118.25 (ii A.D.).

ἑπτάρροος, ον, contr. **-ρους**, ουν, (ῥόος) *with seven channels*, Νεῖλος ἑπτάρους A.*Fr*.300.

ἑπτάς, άδος, ἡ, *period of seven days*, Arist.*HA*553^{a}3 (pl.). II. *period of seven years*, *Syria*5.338, etc. III. *the number seven*, *Theol.Ar*.43, Nicom.*Ar*.1.16.

ἑπτά-σημος [ᾰ], ον, *of seven times*, in metre, συζυγίαι Heph.11.5, cf. 12.1, Aristid.Quint.1.14. **-στάδιος** [στᾰ], ον, *seven stades long*, διῶρυξ Scymn.649; πορθμός Str.2.5.19; χῶμα J.*AJ*12.2.13: Subst., τὸ ἑ. *space of seven stades*, Str.2.5.22.

ἑπτάστερος, ον, *of seven stars*, Eratosth.*Cat*.14, Gal.9.935.

ἑπτά-στομος, ον, *seven-mouthed*, πύλαι ἑ., of Boeotian Thebes, E. *Supp*.401; ἑ. πύργωμα, πόλισμα, Id.*Ph*.287, *Ba*.919; πύλαι S.*Fr*.773; of rivers, Str.4.1.8, 7.3.15. **-τάλαντος** [τᾰλ], ον, *weighing seven talents*, λίθος Them.*Or*.23.284b. **-τειχεῖς** ἔξοδοι the *seven* outlets *of the walls* of Thebes, A.*Th*.285. **-τευχος** (sc. βίβλος), ἡ, *book in seven volumes*, Sidon.Apoll.*Ep*.5.15. **-τονος**, ον, *seven-toned*, φόρμιγξ Terp.5; γᾶρυς B.*Scol.Oxy*.1361 *Fr*.1.2; λύρα Ion Eleg.3.3; χέλυς E.*Alc*.446 (lyr.). **-φᾰής**, ές, *sevenfold shining*, Orph.*H*.7. 8. **-φάρμᾰκον**, τό, *drug compounded of seven ingredients*, Aët. 15.26. **-φεγγής**, ές, *with seven luminaries*, σφαῖρα Ph.1. 504. **-φθογγος**, ον, *seven-toned*, κιθάρα E.*Ion*881 (lyr.); συμφωνία Nicom.*Exc*.6. **-φυλλος**, ον, *seven-leaved*, κράμβη Hippon. 37. **-φωνος**, ον, *seven-voiced*, στοά, of a colonnade *with a sevenfold echo* at Olympia, Plu.2.502d, Luc.*Peregr*.40, Plin.*HN*36.100.

ἕπτᾰχᾰ, Adv. *in seven parts*, Od.14.434:—so **ἑπταχῆ** D.C.55.26: **ἑπταχῶς** Gal.19.280.

ἑπτά-χορδος, ον, *seven-stringed*, ἁρμονίαι Arist.*Pr*.919^{b}21, al., cf. Nicom.*Harm*.3. **-χους**, ουν, *holding seven* χόες, Arist.*Ath*.67. 2. **-χρονος**, ον, *of seven times*, πούς Heph.3.3. **-ωρος**, ον, *lasting seven days*, σεληνιακαὶ φάσεις *Theol.Ar*.45.

ἑπτ-ετηρίς, ίδος, ἡ, *festival celebrated every seven years*, Arist.*Ath*. 54.7. **-έτης**, = ἑπταετής, *seven years old*, Chionid.3, Ar.*Ra*.422: nom. pl. ἑπτέτεις Pl.*Alc*.1.121e:—fem. **-έτις**, ιδος, Ar.*Th*.480, Luc. *Tox*.61. **-ῆμαρ**, *for a space of seven days*, Orph.*Fr*.47. **-ήμερος**, ον, Ion. for ἑπταήμ-, αἰών *going by 'sevens'*, Hp.*Carn*.19. **-ήρης**, ες, *with seven banks of oars* (sc. ναῦς), Plb.1.23.4, D.S.20.50, Ath.5. 203d. **-ορόγυιος**, ον, (ὄργυια) *seven fathoms long*, πόδες Sapph. 98. **-υσχλος**, ὁ, *sandal laced with seven straps*, Hermipp.67 (pl.), cf. ὕσχλος, ἐννήυσκλοι, πτύσχλοι. **-ώροφος**, ον, *seven stories high*, D.S.14.30 (codd. opt. -όροφος).

ἔπυδρος, ον, Ion. for ἔφυδρος, Hdt.4.198.

ἐπύλλιον, τό, Dim. of ἔπος, *versicle, scrap of poetry*, Ar.*Ach*.398, *Pax*532, *Ra*.942. II. *short epic poem*, Ath.2.65a.

ἔπω, *say, call, name*, ἣν Πέρσειον ἔπουσιν Nic.*Al*.429, cf. 490, *Th*. 508. (Prob. invented by Nic., as pres. of εἶπον.)

ἕπω (A), *to be about, busy oneself with*, τὸν δ' εὗρ' ἐν θαλάμῳ περικαλλέα τεύχε' ἕποντα Il.6.321: elsewh. with Preps., in tmesi, cf. ἀμφέπω, διέπω, ἐφέπω, μεθέπω, περιέπω. (Cf. Skt. *sapati* 'worship', 'tend', *saparyati* 'worship', 'honour', Lat. *sepelio* 'give funeral honours'; not related to ἕπομαι.)

***ἕπω** (B), only in Med., **ἕπομαι**, impf. εἱπόμην Il.4.274, al., Hdt.1. 45, Th.3.10, etc., Ep. also ἑπόμην Od.2.413, al.: fut. ἕψομαι Il.10.108, etc.: aor. 2 ἑσπόμην 12.398, al., in moods without ἑ- (v. infr.), imper. σπεῖο 10.285, συνεπί-σπεο *Lyr.Alex.Adesp*.20, inf. σπέσθαι Il.5.423, Od.22.324, part. σπόμενος Call.*Hec*.1.4.7; in Prose in compds., ἐπισπέσθαι Pl.*Phdr*.248c, ἐπι-σπόμενος Th.3.43, etc. (Cf. Skt. *sacate* 'accompany', 'follow', Lat. *sequor*, Lith. *sèkti* 'follow'; ἑσπόμην (Ἀρίσταρχος δασύνει Sch.Il.10.246) fr. ἐ-σπ-όμην, ἐ- (augm.) becoming ἑ- under the influence of ἕπομαι: ἑσπ- does not certainly occur in the moods in Hom.; when found (usu. with v.l. σπ-), it is preceded by an elided vowel, so that σπ- can be read (cf. Ptol.Asc.ap.Sch.Il. l.c.);

Pi.*O*.8.11, 9.83, 10(11).78, *I*.5(4).36 are indecisive (ἑσπ– only cj. in *P*.10.17, *I*.6(5).17); but ἑσποίμην occurs A.R.3.35, ἑσπόμενος 1.103, 470, 3.615, 4.434, Mosch.2.147, pres. indic. ἕσπεται A.R.4.1607, D.P.436, 1140, v.l. for ἔρχεται in Od.4.826: pres. part. ἐφεσπόμενος Maiist.46: Skt. has a redupl. pres. stem *saśc(a)–*):—*to be* or *come after, follow*, I. of Persons, whether *after* or *in company with*, abs., ὁ μὲν ἦρχ', ὁ δ' ἅμ' ἕσπετο Il.11.472; ἡγήσατο, τοὶ δ' ἅμ' ἕποντο Od.2.413:—Constr.: c. dat., υἱέϊ σῷ Il.3.174, cf. 9.428, 10.108, etc.: c. acc., Pi.*N*.10.37 (s.v.l.), Luc.*Asin*.51; ἕ. ἅμα τινί Il.2.534, etc.; σοὶ γὰρ ἑψόμεσθ' ἅμα S.*El*.253; with ἅμα doubled, οἵ τοι ἅμ' αὐτῷ Ἴλιον εἰς ἅμ' ἕποντο Od.11.372, cf. 15.541; abs., v. infr. II. 2; less freq. ἐπί τινος Apollod.Ath.ap.Ath.7.281f (v. infr. II. 1); ἐπί τινι E.*Alc*.1032, X.*Cyr*.5.2.1, etc.; ἐπὶ βασιλέα against the king, Id. *An*.1.4.14; μετά τινι Il.18.234; μετά τινα 13.492; μετά τινος Ar.*Pl*. 823; σύν τινι Od.7.304, etc.; ὄπισθε Hdt.1.45, etc. 2. *follow*, as attendants, οὐκ οἴη, ἅμα τῇ γε καὶ ἀμφίπολοι δύ' ἕποντο Od.1. 331, cf. 8.46, etc.; also, *escort, attend*, by way of honour, θεοὶ δ' ἅμα πάντες ἕποντο Il.1.424; νέῳ ὧδε θεοὶ πομπῆες ἕπονται Od.3. 376. 3. in hostile sense, *pursue*, Il.11.154, etc.; ἀμφὶ δ' ἄρ' αὐτὸν ἕποντο they *pressed* upon him, ib.474 (never in Od.); οἱ πελτασταὶ εἵποντο διώκοντες X.*An*.5.4.24. 4. *keep pace with*, ὃς καὶ θνητὸς ἐὼν ἕπεθ' ἵπποις ἀθανάτοισι Il.16.154, cf. Od.6.319: metaph. of a man's limbs or strength, γούναθ' ἕποιτο, δύναμις καὶ χεῖρες ἕπονται, they *do his bidding*, Il.4.314, Od.20.237; ἕπεσθαι τοῖς καιροῖς τοῦ πολέμου Plu.*Pomp*.17. 5. *follow* the motions of another, ὁ δ' ἑσπόμενος (better δὲ σπ.) πέσε δουρί, of one from whose body a spear is drawn, Il.12.395; τρυφάλεια ἅμ' ἕσπετο χειρί the helm *went with* his hand, i.e. *came off* in his hand, 3.376; [ἔπαλξις] ἕσπετο, i.e. the battlement *came down*, 12.398. 6. *follow on the track of*, τῷ στίβῳ τῶν ἵππων X.*An*.7.3.43: abs., ἕπεσθε, ὦ κύνες Id.*Cyn*.6.19. 7. *follow, obey*, νόμῳ Hdt.5.18, Th.2.35; τῷ ξυνῷ Heraclit.2; μηνυτῆρος φραδαῖς A.*Eu*.245: abs., Id.*Ag*.1053, Hdt.9.16; *accept an invitation*, X.*Smp*.1.7; ἕ. κακοῖς *submit* to them, S.*Tr*.1074. 8. simply, *come near, approach*, in imper., ἕπεο προτέρω *come on* nearer, Il.18. 387, Od.5.91. 9. *follow up*, esp. *in mind, understand*, ἆρ' ἕπομαί σου τῷ λόγῳ; Pl.*Prt*.319a; οὐχ ἕσπου τοῖς λεχθεῖσιν Id.*Plt*.280b; οὐχ ἕπομαι τοῖς λεγομένοις Id.*Euthphr*.12a. 10. of Time, παραδοῦναι τοῖς ἑπομένοις *to succeeding generations*, Id.*Phlb*.17d. 11. impers., ἕπεται διελθεῖν *it follows* to.., Arist.*EN*1111^{b}5. 12. ἑπόμενα, τά, opp. προηγούμενα, *backward* points, i.e. those lying on the opposite side of the radius vector of a spiral from the direction of its motion, Archim.*Spir*.11*Def*.6. b. Astron., positions *following* in the daily movement of the heavens, *eastward* positions, Hipparch.1.11.5, etc. II. of Things, as of bridal presents, ὅσσα ἔοικε φίλης ἐπὶ παιδὸς ἕπεσθαι *go with* her from the parent's house, Od.1.278, 2.197 (v. supr. 4 and 5). 2. of honour, glory, etc., τούτῳ.. κῦδος ἅμ' ἕψεται Il.4.415; so ἄτη, τιμὴ ἕπεταί τινι, 9.512, 513, ἕπεται παλαιὸς ὄλβος Pi.*P*.5.55; πειθὼ δ' ἕποιτο καὶ τύχη A.*Supp*.523, etc.; ἦ οὐ γιγνώσκεις ὅ τοι ἐκ Διὸς οὐχ ἕπετ' ἀλκή; that no defence *attendeth* thee from Zeus, Il.8.140, cf. Pi.*N*.11.43, A.*Ag*.854. 3. *follow upon* (i.e. *result from*), τῇ ἀχαριστίᾳ ἡ ἀναισχυντία ἕ. X.*Cyr*. 1.2.7, etc.; τὰ ἑπόμενα τῆς τοιαύτης κατακοσμήσεως its *consequences*, Pl.*Plt*.271e, cf. *R*.504b; ἑπόμενος, opp. προηγούμενος, *consequent* (opp. antecedent), Dam.*Pr*.115; τὰ ἑ. [μεγέθη] the *consequents* in a proportion, opp. ἡγούμενα, Euc.5*Def*.11, etc. 4. *follow suit, agree with*, ἕπεται ὁ λόγος.. Κάδμοιο κούραις Pi.*O*.2.22; ἕπεται ἐν ἑκάστῳ μέτρον ib.13.47; ἑπόμενα σωφροσύνῃ things *agreeing with*.., Pl.*Lg*. 632c; ἔργα –όμενα τῇ γραφῇ ib.934c; τὰ τούτοις ἑ. the *like* to these, Id.*R*.406d; ἀναγκαῖα καὶ ἑ. ἀλλήλοις *interdependent*, ib.486e; τὸ πρέπον καὶ ἑπόμενον πάσῃ τῇ πολιτείᾳ Id.*Lg*.835c; of Nymphs, οὔτε θνητοῖς οὔτ' ἀθανάτοισιν ἕπονται they *belong to*.., *h.Ven*.259.

ἐπῳ-άδιος [ᾰ], ον, (ᾠόν) *upon the egg, hatched*, Opp.*H*.1.752 (vulg. ὑπῳάδιος). **–άζω**, *sit* or *brood upon eggs*, mostly of birds, Arist. *GA*752^{b}16, al.; also of tortoises, Id.*HA*558^{a}7; bees, ib.554^{a}18; spiders, ib.555^{a}30; crustacea, ib.550^{b}1. II. trans., *hatch, incubate young birds* by artificial heat, D.S.1.74. **–ᾰσις**, εως, ἡ, *sitting on eggs, incubation*, Arist.*HA*563^{a}29. **–ασμός**, ὁ, = foreg., ib.558^{b} 15, 564^{b}9. **–αστικός**, ή, όν, *fond of sitting*, of birds, ib.560^{a}3 (Comp.).

ἐπωβελία, ἡ, (ὀβελός) *fine of an obol in the drachma*, i.e. *one-sixth of the sum* at which the damages were laid, paid as compensation to the defendant by the plaintiff in case the latter failed to gain one-fifth of the votes, τὴν ἐ. ὀφλεῖν, τῆς ἐ. κινδυνεύειν, D.27.67, 31.14. 2. *added payment of one-sixth* per mensem, as a penalty for failure to discharge debts, Pl.*Lg*.921d. 3. dub. sens. in *PCair.Zen*.15^{r}.44 (iii B.C.).

ἐπῳδή, Ion. and poet. **ἐπᾱοιδή**, ἡ, *song sung to* or *over*: hence, *enchantment, spell*, ἐπαοιδῇ δ' αἷμα.. ἔσχεθον Od.19.457, cf. Pi.*P*.4. 217; οὐ πρὸς ἰατροῦ σοφοῦ θρηνεῖν ἐπῳδὰς πρὸς τομῶντι πήματι S.*Aj*. 582; of the Magi, Hdt.1.132; μελιγλώσσοις πειθοῦς ἐπαοιδαῖσιν A.*Pr*. 174, cf. S.*OC*1194; ἐπῳδὰς ἐπάδειν X.*Mem*.2.6.10 sq.; ἐπῳδαῖς ἁλίσκεσθαι Anaxandr.33.13; οὔτε φάρμακα.. οὐδ' αὖ ἐπῳδαί Pl.*R*.426b; θυσίαι καὶ ἐ. ib.364b; τὰς θυσίας καὶ τελετὰς καὶ τὰς ἐ. Id.*Smp*.202e, etc.: c. gen. obj., *charm for* or *against*.., τούτων ἐπῳδὰς οὐκ ἐποίησεν πατήρ A.*Eu*.649. II. apptly., = ἐπῳδός II, Poet.*Oxy*.661.21 (pl.).

ἐπώδης, ες, (ἐπόζω) *rank-smelling*, Hp.ap.Gal.19.100.

ἐπῳδικός, ή, όν, *of* or *for an* ἐπῳδός II, *epodic*, τὰ –κά Heph.*Poëm*.4. 1, al. Adv. –κῶς, γεγράφθαι Id.p.62 C.

ἐπωδίνω [ῑ], *suffer birth-pangs*, metaph., ἐπωδίνουσι μέριμναι Archyt.Amph.4.

ἐπῴδ-ιον, τό, Dim. of ἐπῳδός II, Hsch. s.v. ἐπιρρήματα. **–ός**, όν, (ἐπᾴδω) *singing to* or *over, using songs* or *charms* to heal wounds, ἐπῳδοὶ μῦθοι Pl.*Lg*.903b. b. Subst., *enchanter*, ἐ. καὶ γόης E.*Hipp*. 1038 (but γόης ἐ. *Ba*.234): c. gen., *a charm for* or *against*, ἔθυσεν αὐτοῦ παῖδα ἐπῳδὸν Θρῃκίων ἀημάτων A.*Ag*.1418; ἐ. τῶν τοιούτων *one to charm away* such fears, Pl.*Phd*.78a. c. c. dat., *assisting, profitable*, ἐ. γίγνεσθαι νέοις πρὸς ἀρετήν Id.*Lg*.671a; δυσπραξίᾳ ληφθεὶς ἐ. ἐστι τῷ πειρωμένῳ *Trag.Adesp*.364.4. 2. Pass., *sung to music*, φωναί Plu.2.622d; *fit for singing*, ποιητικὴν ἐ. παρέχειν S.E.*M*.6. 16. b. *sung* or *said after*, μορφῆς ἐπῳδόν *called after* this form, E. *Hec*.1272. II. in Metre, as Subst., 1. ἐπῳδός, ἡ, Sch.metr. Pi.*O*.4 (ὁ, Gal.*UP*17.3, dub. in D.H.*Comp*.19), *epode, part of a lyric ode sung after the strophe and antistrophe*, ib.26, Gal. l. c., Sch.metr. Pi. l. c., etc. 2. ἐπῳδός, ὁ, *verse* or *passage returning* at intervals, in Alcaics and Sapphics, D.H.*Comp*.19; *chorus, burden, refrain*, Ph. 1.312: metaph., ὁ κοινὸς ἁπάσης ἀδολεσχίας ἐ. the 'old story', Plu.2. 507e. b. *shorter verse of a couplet*, as in the metres invented by Archilochus, Hermog.*Inv*.4.4: hence of short poems written in such metres, ἐπῳδοί Heph.*Poëm*.7.2; ἐπῳδά Plu.2.1141a.

ἐπωδῠν-ία, ἡ, *pain, anguish*, Str.15.1.45. **–ος**, ον, (ὀδύνη) *painful*, Hp.*VM*22, *Prog*.7; τραύματα Ar.*Ach*.1205 (lyr.); ζωή Ph.2.579; δάκρυα Plu.2.114c: irreg. Comp. –νέστερος Hp.*Art*.49. Adv. –νως Id.*Epid*.1.26.γ', Ph.1.136.

ἐπῴζω, = ἐπῳάζω, Epich.172, Cratin.108; *cluck*, like a laying hen, Ar.*Av*.266.

ἐπωθ-έω, *push on, impel*, ἐπὶ ῥίον ὦσεν ἄναξ *h.Ap*.382, cf. Arist.*Mete*. 370^{b}23, *Pr*.915^{a}2, Arr.*Tact*.16.13; ἐ. ὁρμήν Agatharch.14; παχὺν ἐ. τῷ σιδήρῳ τὸν κοντόν dub. l. in Plu.*Crass*.27. 2. Pass., of tumours, *to be brought to a head*, v.l. in Hp.*Epid*.7.105. **–ίζω**, = foreg., ζέφυρος κύμασι Ps.-Luc.*Philopatr*.3.

ἐπωκ-ής, ές, *somewhat sharp* or *acid*, in Comp., φακῇ ἑφθῇ –εστέρῃ τῷ ὄξει Hp.*Int*.21 (v.l.), cf. 22. **–ύνω**, *sharpen, quicken*, τὴν ἐνέργειαν Gal.6.187.

ἐπώλεθρος, ον, (ὄλεθρος) *destructive*, Hdn.*Epim*.203.

ἐπωλένιος, ον, *upon the arm*, –ένιον κιθαρίζειν *h.Merc*.433, 510; φορέειν A.R.1.557.

ἐπωμ-άδιος [ᾰ], ον, (ὦμος) *on the shoulders*, πτέρυγας Theoc. 29.29 (v.l. ἐπ' ὀμμασίαις, fort. leg. ἐπομμαδίαις), cf. *APl*.4.108 (Jul.). **–ᾰδόν**, Adv. *on the shoulder*, A.R.1.738, Q.S.13.541, *APl*.4.279. **–ίδιος**, α, ον, *on the shoulder*, φλέψ Hp.*Oss*. 12. II. Subst. –ίδιον, τό, Dim. of ἐπωμίς, *horse's trappings*, App. *Mith*.115. **–ίζομαι**, Med., *put on one's shoulder*, Ps.-Luc.*Philopatr*.4. **–ιος**, ον, = ἐπωμάδιος, E.*Hyps.Fr*.32(58).9, Luc.*Am*.44; ἐ. τι ἀνελέσθαι Alciphr.1.1. **–ίς**, ίδος, ἡ, (ὦμος) *the point of the shoulder*, where it joins the collar-bone, Hp.*Art*.1, al., X.*Mem*.3.10. 13, Gal.2.273, etc.; the adjacent part of the collar-bone, Poll.2.133; acc. to Arist.*HA*493^{a}9, *back part of the neck*: pl., Id.*Phgn*.810^{b} 35. 2. Poet., *shoulder*, Achae.4, Call.*Del*.143, *AP*9.588 (Alc. Mess.). 3. part of a ship, Archimel.ap.Ath.5.209d (s.v.l.). 4. in pl., *leaves of a folding-door*, Lxx*Ez*.41.2. II. *part of the women's tunic that was fastened on the shoulder by brooches, shoulder-strap*, E. *Hec*.558, Chaerem.14.2, Apollod.Car.4, *IG*11(2).287 *A*87 (iii B.C.); *tunic* of a rower, E.*IT*1404; the high-priest's *ephod*, Lxx*Ex*.28.6, Ph.2.151, al.

ἐπωμ-οσία, ἡ, (ἐπόμνυμι) = ὑπωμοσία, Sch.Ar.*Pl*.725. **–οσις**, εως, ἡ, *swearing to* a thing, Eust.809.32. **–ότης**, ου, ὁ, *additional juror*, *IG*9(1).333.10 (Locr., v B.C.). **–οτικόν**, τό, *oath* (= ὁμοτικόν), Stoic.ap.Rh.2.662, 7.4 W. **–οτος**, ον, *on oath, sworn*, ἐ. λέγων S.*Tr*.427; cf. ἐνώμοτος. II. Pass., *witness of oaths*, like ὅρκιος, Ζῆν' ἔχων ἐπώμοτον ib.1188.

ἐπώνια, τά, (ὠνή) *duty on goods sold*, *IG*1^{2}.329.5, Is.*Fr*.43, *PCair. Zen*.206.20, al. (iii B.C.), Poll.7.15: also in sg., ἐπώνιον, τό, *SIG*1014. 5 (Erythrae, iii B.C.), etc. II. *something given into the bargain in a sale*, Phryn.*PS* p.70 B.

ἐπωνῠμ-ία, Ion. –ίη, ἡ, (ἐπώνυμος) *derived* or *significant name*, as Ἔπαφος, A.*Supp*.45 (lyr.); Πολυνείκης, Id.*Th*.829 (lyr.); ἐ. ποιεῖσθαι ἀπό or ἐπί τινος, Hdt.2.42, 1.94; ὅθεν ἔθεντο τὰς ἐ. Id.4.45; ἔχειν ἐ. ἐπί τινος ibid.; καλεῖσθαι ἐ. ἐπί τινος Id.1.14; κατὰ τὴν ἐ. τινὸς κληθῆναι Id.1.173; ἐ. ἔχειν or σχεῖν τινός, Id.4.15, Pl.*Criti*.114a; ἐ. ἀπό τινος ἔχειν, ἐγκαταλιπεῖν, λαβεῖν, Hdt.7.121, Th.2.102, Pl.*Phdr*.238c; τῆς θεοῦ ἐπωνυμίας ἄξιος the *name derived* from her, Id.*Lg*.626d; τὴν τῇδε ἐ. αὐτοῦ its *namesake* here, Id.*Phdr*.250e; ἐ. ἀφ' ἑαυτῶν παρέχεσθαι Th.1.3; but ἐ. σχεῖν χώρας to have *the naming* of it, i.e. have it *named after* one, ib.9; ἐ. τινὶ Μαργίτην τίθεσθαι *as a nickname*, Aeschin.3.160; προσείληφε τὴν ἐ... συκοφάντης Id.2.99; ἔχουσα τὴν ἐ. τὴν τοῦ ὃ ἔστιν Pl.*Phd*.92d: folld. by inf., ἐ. ἔχει σμικρός τε καὶ μέγας εἶναι he has *the name of* being, ib.102c; ἀποβαλεῖν τὴν ἐ. τὸ.. καλὸς κἀγαθὸς κεκλῆσθαι X.*Oec*.12.2; ἐ. ἔχοντος Θασίου εἶναι Hdt.2. 44: acc. as Adv., Ὀλυμπίῳ ἐπωνυμίην θύειν *by surname*, ibid.; ἀπὸ τῆς κυψέλης ἐ. Κύψελος οὔνομα ἐτέθη Id.5.92.ε'. 2. generally, *name, title*, θεῶν –ίαι Id.2.4, cf. Pl.*R*.394a, *PHal*.1.251 (iii B.C.), etc.; συγγραμμάτων Sor.*Vit.Hippocr*.13. **–ιον**, τό, *surname*, Plu. 2.560e; ἐ. παιδικόν Id.*Pyrrh*.1; = Lat. *cognomen*, D.H.5.19. **–ιος**, α, ον, poet. for sq. I. 3, *called after* or *by the name of*, τινος Pi.*P*.1.30, v.l. in Hdt.2.112; ἐπωνυμίαν χάριν νίκας Pi.*O*.10(11).78. **–ος**, ον (for the form cf. ἀν-ώνυμος), *given as a significant name*, τῷ δ' Ὀδυσεὺς ὄνομ' ἔστω ἐπώνυμον Od.19.409 (cf. ὀδυσσάμενος τόδ' ἱκάνω ib.407); Ἀλκυόνην καλέεσκον ἐπώνυμον, οὕνεκ'.. Il.9.562, cf. *h.Ap*. 373; Κύκλωπες δ' ὄνομ' ἦσαν ἐπώνυμοι, οὕνεκα.. Hes.*Th*.144; τῷ μὲν ἐπώνυμον ἦεν [Χρυσάωρ], ὅτ'.. ib.282; when the reason is omitted, the name is itself significant, Ἀρήτη δ' ὄνομ' ἐστὶν ἐπώνυμον ('the Desired') Od.7.54; κάρτα δ' ὢν ἐ., πομπαῖος ἴσθι, of Hermes, A.*Eu.* 90; Ζεὺς ἀλεξητήριος ἐ. γένοιτο may he become a defender *according to his name*, Id.*Th.*9, cf. 405; ἐπωνύμῳ δὲ κάρτα Πολυνείκει λέγω ib.658; ὦ Πολύνεικες ἔφυς ἄρ' ἐ. *rightly* wert thou *named*.., E.*Ph.* 1494 (anap.). 2. *surnamed*, Ἀθηναίη ἐ. Κραθίη Hdt.5.45; πολλῶν ὀνομάτων ἐ., of Aphrodite, S.*Fr.*941.2; τόδ' ἐπώνυμον this is her *proper name* (sc. Αἴγλα), Isyll.47. 3. freq. c. gen., *named after* a person or thing, ἐμοῦ δ'.. ἐπώνυμον γένος Πελασγῶν A.*Supp.*252, cf. *Pr.*850, S.*OC*65; ἐ. ὄρνιχος *called after* it, Pi.*I.*6(5).53, cf. Hdt. 7.11, S.*Fr.*323, Euph.34.3; τῇ Ἀρτέμιδι, ἧς ἐστιν ἐ. ἡ φρατρία *Rev. Epigr.*1.239 (Naples, ii A.D.); ἔνθεν ἔστ' ἐ. A.*Eu.*689; ἐ. δεῖπνα Θυέστου E.*Or.*1008 (anap.); πόλεις ἐ. βασιλέων Plu.*Comp.Thes.Rom.*4; ἐ. τοῦ θανάτου τινὸς γενέσθαι Id.*Flam.*21; ἐ. ἐπί τινος Hdt.4.184; ἔκ τινος D.P.779; ἀπό τινος Scymn.547: c. dat., Ὀδυσσεύς εἰμ' ἐ. κακοῖς S.*Fr.*965 (s. v. l.); πόλιν ποιεῖν ἐ. τινι Pl.*Lg.*969a; φυλὴν ἐ. ἐποίησαν Ἀττάλῳ Plb.16.25.9; ἐ. ἑαυτῷ D.H.1.9; χῶραι ἐ. *local names* of places, Plb.5.21.7; = Lat. *cognomen*, D.H.5.25 codd.; τῆς πράξεως ἐ., of Mummius, i.e. *Achaïcus*, Plu.*Mar.*1; *title*, D.C.72.22. Adv. -μως *by being named after*, ἔκ τινος Ath.3.121a; ἐ. τῇ γεννώσῃ χώρᾳ Dsc.3.23. II. Act., *giving one's name to* a thing or person, αὐτό μοι σύ, παῖ, λαβὼν ἐ. (sc. τὸ σάκος) *which gives* thee *thy name* (of Eurysaces), S.*Aj.*574; τοῦ ἐ. τῆς πόλεως Διονύσου *SIG*762.13 (Dionysopolis, i B.C.). 2. at Athens, οἱ ἐ. (sc. ἥρωες) the heroes *who gave their names to the Attic* φυλαί, Decr.ap.And.1.83, Isoc.18.61, D.21.103, etc. b. ἄρχων ἐ. the first Archon, *who gave his name to the current year*, *IG*3. 81, al., Poll.8.89; also of the Spartan Ephors, Paus.3.11.2; of the Roman *consules ordinarii*, *IG*14.1389 i 34, Hdn.1.16.3; οἱ τὰ ἐ. ἄρξαντες App.*Syr.*51; ἄρξαντα τὴν ἐ. ἀρχήν *SIG*872.6 (Eleusis, ii A.D.).

ἔπωπα· ἀλεκτρυόνα (-ωνα cod.) ἄγριον, Hsch. (leg. ἔποπα).

ἐπωπ-άζω, = sq., Hsch. **-άω**, (ὠπάομαι) = ἐφοράω, *observe, regard*, πολλὰ A.*Ch.*693; πάντα φρενί Id.*Eu.*275 (lyr.); *guide, direct*, γλῶσσαν καὶ στόμ' ἐπωπᾷ [Πειθώ] ib.971. **-ετής**, οῦ, ὁ, epith. of Zeus at Athens, Hsch. **-εύς**, έως, ὁ, *inspector*, dub. in Agatharch. 26 (κοπεῦσι Müller). II. a divinity (perh. Zeus), *Schwyzer*720. 24 (Theb.ad Mycalen, iv B.C.). **-ή**, ἡ, *look-out place, observation-post*, A.*Supp.*539 (pl., lyr.). **-ίς**, ίδος, ἡ, *watcher* (Lacon.), Hsch. II. epith. of Demeter at Sicyon, Id.

ἐπωπίς, ίδος, ἡ, (ἕπομαι) *attendant, companion*, Lyc.1176 (v.l. ἐπ- = foreg., cf. *EM*368.32).

ἐπωρεύει· ὡραῖα συντελεῖ, Hsch. **ἐπωριάζω**, (ὥρα) *to be concerned about* a thing, Id. (Cf. εὐωριάζω.)

ἐπωροφ-ία, ἡ, *roof*, *IG*1².372.81, 373.243. **-ίς**, ίδος, ἡ, = foreg., ib.11(2).287 *A* 62 (Delos, iii B.C.), *Inscr.Délos* 290.171 (iii B.C.).

ἐπωρυδόν· ἐπιρρεόντως, Hsch. (fort. ἐγὼ ῥυδόν, cf. Od.15.426).

ἐπωρύω [ῡ], *howl at*, *AP*9.311 (Phil.):—in Med., Lxx *Za.*11.8.

ἔπωσις, εως, ἡ, *pushing* or '*spooning*' *stroke*, opp. ἄπωσις, Arist. *Ph.*243ᵃ18.

ἐπωστρίδες· αἱ κατὰ Σάμον ταῖς γυναιξὶ τὴν δεξιὰν χεῖρα ἐπέχουσαι κατὰ τὴν ὀσφύν, Hsch.

ἐπωτειλόομαι, Pass., *to be scarred over*, Aret.*SD*2.4.

ἐπωτίδες, αἱ, (οὖς) *beams projecting like ears on each side of a ship's bows*, whence the anchors were let down, *cat-heads*, used also as an armament, E.*IT*1350, Th.7.34,36, Str.3.1.4, D.S.17.115: later in sg., App.*BC*5.107.

ἐπωφέλ-εια, ἡ, *help, advantage*, Democr.278. **-έω**, *aid, succour*, τινα S.*El.*578, *Ph.*905; τινὰ οὐδέν Id.*El.*1005, E.*Or.*955, cf. Ar.*Nu.* 1442; τινι S.*OC*441, E.*Andr.*677: abs., Pl.*Lg.*843c; ἐν πολέμῳ Seleuc.ap.Ath.15.697d:—Pass., *receive aid*, Phalar.*Ep.*137.—In S. *OC*541 (lyr.), ἐδεξάμην δῶρον, ὃ μήποτ'.. ἐπωφέλησα πόλεος ἐξελέσθαι, the Sch. takes ἐπωφέλησα as, = ὤφελον, *would that* I never had received: -ήσας cj. Jebb. **-ημα**, ατος, τό, *help, store*, βορᾶς S.*Ph.* 275. **-ής**, ές, *helpful, useful*, Sever.*Clyst.*p.17 D., Poll.5.136, *Cod. Just.*1.2.17.1; ἡμῖν Hierocl.*in CA*11 p.441 M. Adv. -λῶς Poll.5.135, Vett.Val.165.18, Them.*Or.*21.252a, 22.278c. **-ία**, ἡ, = ἐπωφέλεια, *AP*6.33 (Maec.). **-ιμος**, ον, = ἐπωφελής, ἔργα *Carm.Aur.*6.

ἐπῴχατο, Ep. 3 pl. plpf. Pass., πᾶσαι γὰρ [πύλαι] ἐπῴχατο all *were shut to*, Il.12.340 (= ἐπικεκλιμέναι ἦσαν, ἐπέκειντο, Aristarch., who derived it from ἐποίγω, prob. rightly, cf. προσοίγνυμι; = ἐπωχλισμέναι ἦσαν *were bolted*, Apollon.*Lex.*, reading ἐπώχατο; πάσας γὰρ ἐπῴχετο Zenod., vulg.).

ἔπωχρος, ον, *yellowish*, of a bone, Hp.*VC*19: of the complexion, *sallow*, Aret.*SD*2.5.

ἔρα, ἡ, *earth*, Erot.s.v. ἔρπει, Sch.Il.*Oxy.*221 x 28, *EM*369.24. Hsch. (also expld. as, = κοιλία), cf. Str.16.4.27:—Adv. **ἔραζε**, Dor. **ἔρασδε**, *to earth*, κατὰ δὲ πτερὰ χεῦεν ἔραζε Od.15.527; ἀπὸ δ' εἴδατα χεῦεν ἔ. 22.85, cf. Hes.*Op.*421,473; so νιφάδες δ' ὡς πῖπτον ἔ. Il.12.156; οὐμὸς δὲ πότμος.. κυρῶν ἄνω ἔ. πίπτει A.*Fr.*159; ὄρπακες βραβύλοισι καταβρίθοντες ἔρασδε Theoc.7.146; *on the ground*, θάλλειν Mosch.2.66.

ἔραδος· παρὰ τὸ ἐρίζειν· παιδίονα, νεῖκος, συνδρομή, λοιδορία, ἀνεξικακία, Hsch.

ἔρᾰμαι, 2 sg. Ep. ἔρασσαι or ἔρᾱσαι Theoc.1.78, 3 sg. ἔρᾱται Id.2. 149 (with unexpld. ᾱ); 2 pl. ἐράασθε Il.16.208; 3 sg. subj. Aeol. and Dor. ἔρᾱται Sapph.*Supp.*5.4, Pi.*P.*4.92; opt. ἐραίμαν ib.11.50; impf. ἠράμην [ᾰ] Sapph.33, Thgn.1346, etc.: fut. ἐρασθήσομαι A.*Eu.*852: aor. ἠράσθην Alcm.33, Hdt.1.8,96, E.*Med.*700, *IG*1².920.2, poet. ἐράσθην Phoen.1.19; poet. aor. Med. ἠρασάμην Il.16.182, Hermesian. 7.49,96 (Ep. and Lyr. ἠράσσατο Il.20.223, Archil.26, Nicaen.1.5; ἐράσσατο Hes.*Th.*915, Pi.*P.*2.27): pf. ἤρασμαι Parth.2.3: **ἐράω** (q.v.) supplies the pres. and impf. in Prose. I. *love*, c. gen. pers., prop. of the sexual passion, as always in Hom.; mostly of the man, ὥς σεο νῦν ἔραμαι Il.3.446, cf. 16.182, 20.223, etc.; λέχους E.*Med.*491; τῆς ἑωυτοῦ γυναικός Hdt.1.8; but of the woman, ἣ.. ἠράσσατ' Ἐνιπῆος Od.11.238: c. acc. cogn., ἐ. μέγαν γ' ἔρωτα E.*Med.*697. II. of things, *desire passionately, lust after*, ὃς πολέμου ἔραται ἐπιδημίου Il. 9.64; φυλόπιδος.. ἧς τὸ πρίν γ' ἐράασθε 16.208; ἐρασθεὶς τυραννίδος Hdt.1.96; τῶν ἀπεόντων Pi.*P.*3.20; καλῶν ib.11.50; γῆς τῆσδε A. *Eu.*852; κείνων ἔραμαι E.*Alc.*866 (anap.); θανάτου ἔρανται Aret.*CA* 2.5. 2. c. inf., *desire eagerly*, οὐκ ἔραμαι πλουτεῖν Thgn.1155; ἤρατο ἐπιψαύειν Pi.*P.*4.92; ἔραται γλῶσσα μέλιτος ἄωτον [προχέειν] Id.*Pae.*6.58; ἔραμαι πυθέσθαι S.*OC*511 (lyr.); λαβεῖν τι E.*Med.*700; φαγεῖν Ar.*Fr.*51 (lyr.).

ἔρανα· ἐκ συνεισφορᾶς δῶρα κτλ., Hsch. **ἐράναι**· βωμοί, Id.

ἐρᾰν-άρχης, ου, ὁ, *president of an* ἔρανος, *collector of contributions to it*, *BGU*1133.5 (i B.C.), D.L.6.63, Artem.1.35 (pl.), Harp. s.v. πληρωτής:—hence **-αρχέω**, *hold this office*, *IG*11(4).1223 (Delos). **-έμπορος**, ὁ, *trader on borrowed capital*, Hsch., Phot., Suid. **-εστάς**, ὁ, = ἐρανιστής, *Schwyzer*427.3 (Dyme). **-ησις**, v. ἐράνισις. **-ίζω**, *lay under contribution*, c. acc. pers., τοὺς φίλους D.*Ep.*3.38, cf. D.L. 6.63 (pun on ἐναρίζω). 2. *collect by way of contribution*, στεφάνους Aeschin.3.45; ἐ. φίλον παρὰ φίλοις Pl.*Lg.*915e: abs., Thphr.*Char.* 1.5; τισι for their benefit, *IG*7.411.7 (Oropus): metaph., *bring together, combine*, εἰς ὅλον *AP*9.13ᵇ (Antiphil.), cf. 11 (Phil.), Ael.*VH*12. 1; ἠράνισαι (2 sg. pf. Pass.) νεφέλαις *art swollen up* with.., *AP*9. 277 (Antiphil.):—Med., *collect for oneself, borrow*, τροφὴν παρ' ἑτέρων Plu.2.1058d, cf. Poll.4.43; πανταχόθεν ἡδονὴν ἐρανίζεσθαι Luc.*Vit. Auct.*12, cf. *Salt.*49; λόγους εἰς εὐωχίαν Hld.5.16, cf. Men.Rh.p.433 S.: abs., D.L.9.50; *beg one's bread*, *BCH*48.517 (Palestine). II. *assist by contributions*, πολλοῖς (πολλούς codd.) Antipho 2.2.12; τούτους (v.l. -οις) Ph.1.635:—Pass., *to be so assisted*, ἐρανισθεὶς πρὸς τῶν φίλων D.L.8.87. 2. metaph., of '*log-rolling*', ἐφ' οἷς -ίζει τοῖς περὶ αὐτόν D.39.18. **-ικός**, ή, όν, *of* or *for an* ἔρανος, ἐ. δίκη an action *arising out of the matters of an* ἔρανος, Arist.*Ath.*52.2, cf. Poll.8.37; ἐ. συγγραφή *BGU*1165.30 (i A.D.); νόμος ἐ. ibid.; ἐ. λόγος a speech (of Dinarchus) *on these matters*, D.H.*Din.*12; ἀκροάσεις ἐ. lectures *paid for by fees*, Posidon.36 J. **-ιον**, τό, Dim. of ἔρανος, Hsch. **-ῐσις**, εως, ἡ, *collecting of contributions, contributing*, Pl.*Lg.*915e. II. (written ἐράνησις) *feeding, maintenance*, προβάτων *PMasp.*141ᵛ *b* 11 (vi A.D.). **-ισμός**, ὁ, = foreg. 1, D.H.6.96. **-ιστής**, οῦ, ὁ, *member of* or *contributor to an* ἔρανος I, Pherecyd.11 J. (pl.); ἑστιᾶν ἐρανιστάς to give a club-dinner, Ar.*Fr.*408, Arist.*EN*1123ᵃ22; *member of an* ἔρανος III, *IG*2².1265 (pl.), 11(4).1223 (Delos, pl.), etc.

ἐραννός, ή, όν, (ἔραμαι) *lovely*, in Hom. only of places, Il.9.531, Od. 7.18, al., Ar.*Lys.*1297 (lyr.), Theoc.28.21, Mosch.3.89: after Hom., generally, ἐ. Ἀοῦς φάος B.16.42; ὕδωρ Simon.45; φιλότης D.P.777; φηγός, ἄλσος, Orph.*A.*991,987; seldom of persons, Ἑκάτη Id.*H.*1. 1 codd. (ἐρεμνήν Wiel); τὸ ἐ., in Neo-Platonic Philos., the *Beatific Vision*, Anon.*in Prm.*2.30.

ἔρᾰνος, ὁ, *meal to which each contributed his share, picnic*, εἰλαπίνη ἠὲ γάμος; ἐπεὶ οὐκ ἔρανος τάδε γ' ἐστίν Od.1.226, cf. 11.415: metaph., Pl.*Smp.*177c. 2. generally, *feast, festival*, Pi.*O.*1.38; πολύθυτος ἔ. Id.*P.*5.77; *wedding-banquet*, ib.12.14, Pherecyd.11 J.; ἔρανον εἰς θεοὺς.. ἐποίεις E.*Hel.*388. II. *loan* raised by contributions for the benefit of an individual, bearing no interest, but recoverable at law, in instalments, παρὰ τῶν φίλων ἔ. συλλέξαι Antipho 2.2.9, cf. Thphr.*Char.*22.9; κομισόμενος τὸν ἔ. recover the *loan*, Arist.*Ph.*196ᵇ 34; ἔ. εἰσενεγκεῖν τινι Thphr.*Char.*15.7, Philem.213.14; ἔ. τινι εἰς τὰ λύτρα εἰσφέρειν D.53.8; ἔ. εἰς ἐλευθερίαν Id.59.31, cf. *GDI*2317 (Delph.), al.; ἔ. ἀναλαμβάνειν *BGU*1165.16 (i B.C., with mention of interest); ἔ. εἰκοσίμνως Lys.*Fr.*19; πεντακοσιόδραχμος *SIG*1215.5 (Myconos); διτάλαντον εἶχες ἔ. [δωρεὰν] παρά τινων D.18.312: in pl., *debts* thus contracted, Ar.*Ach.*615 (prob.), Hyp.*Ath.*9; τοὺς ἐ. διενεγκεῖν pay off such *debts*, Lycurg.22; ἐράνους λέλοιπε he has left *repayment-instalments* unpaid, D.27.25; ἔ. συνεφήβοις ἀπενεγκεῖν (cf. infr. III) Luc.*DMeretr.*7.1. 2. metaph., τοὐράνου γάρ μοι μέτεστι· καὶ γὰρ ἄνδρας εἰσφέρω (spoken by Lysistrata), Ar.*Lys.*651; δεῖ τοῖς γονεῦσι τὸν ὡρισμένον ἐξ ἀμφοτέρων ἔ. καὶ παρὰ τῆς φύσεως καὶ παρὰ τοῦ νόμου δικαίως φέρειν D.10.40, cf. 21.101, Isoc.10.20, Pl.*Lg.*927c; κάλλιστον ἔ. [τῇ πόλει] προϊέμενοι Th.2.43, cf. X.*Cyr.*7.1.12, Ph.2. 553, etc.: generally, *favour, service*, esp. one which brings a return, κάλλιστον ἔ., δοὺς γὰρ ἀντιλάζυται E.*Supp.*363; ἔ. ἀντιλαμβάνειν Arist.*Pol.*1332ᵇ40; ἀποδοῦναι Alex.280; ironically, τὸν αὐτὸν ἔ. ἀποδοῦναι 'pay him back in his own coin', D.59.8. III. *a permanent association* apparently religious in character (cf. ἐρανιστής), *IG*12(1). 155.12 (Rhodes, ii B.C.), 2².1369 (Athens, ii A.D.); ἔ. συνάγειν Μηνὶ Τυράννῳ ib.3.74; καλεῖται ὁ αὐτὸς καὶ ἔ. καὶ θίασος Ath.8.362e; functioning as a *friendly society*, Plin.*Ep.Trai.*92; it could apparently lend to a non-member, ὅρος χωρίων ὑποκειμένων τῷ ἐ. καὶ τῷ ἀρχεράνῳ *SIG*1198 (Amorgos, iii B.C.), cf. *BGU*1133-6 (i B.C.).

ἐραπίδα· ὃ ἡμεῖς ἐλαπέδα, Hsch. **ἔρασδε**, Dor. for ἔραζε (q.v.).

ἐρᾰσί-μολπος [ῐ], ον, *delighting in song*, of Thalia, Pi.*O.*14.15. **-πλόκᾰμος**, ον, *decked with love-locks*, Ibyc.9, Pi.*P.*4.136. **-πτερος**, ον, *of amorous wing*, Nonn.*D.*10.256.

ἔρᾰσις, εως, ἡ, (ἔραμαι) *love*, as etym. of ἥρως, *EM*437.38, etc.

ἐρᾰσιχρήμᾰτος, ον, *loving money*, X.*Mem.*1.2.5, Philostr.*VS*2.29.

ἐράσμιος, ον, also η, ον Anacr.20:—*lovely, pleasant*, Semon.7.52; τὴν ψυχὴν ἐ. X.*Smp.*8.36: Comp., Them.*Or.*17.216a: Sup. -ώτατον, ψυχῆς ἦθος X.*Mem*.3.10.3; τὸ ἐ. Plot.1.3.2; *beloved, desired*, πόλει A.*Ag*.605; ταῖς ἀγέλαισιν Mosch.3.20; ἐ. ἄγειν τινά treat *affectionately*, J.*AJ*19.6.1: neut. as Adv., ἐράσμιον ἀνθήσασα *AP*7.219 (Pomp. Jun.).

ἐραστ-εύω, = ἐράω (A), ἐραστεῦσαι γάμων A.*Pr*.893 (lyr.). **-ής**, οῦ, ὁ, (ἔραμαι) *lover*, prop. c. gen. pers., Ar.*Eq*.732, etc. b. *admirer*, Pl.*Men*.70b, *Ly*.222a, *Prt*.317c. 2. metaph., c. gen. rei, τυραννίδος Hdt.3.53; τῆσδε τῆς γνώμης *an adherent* of.., S.*OT*601; πολέμων E.*Heracl*.377 (lyr.); παίδων *eager for* children, Id.*Supp*.1088; πραγμάτων, = πολυπράγμων, Ar.*Pax* 191, *Nu*.1459; τοῦ πονεῖν *fond* of work, Id.*Pl*.254; λόγων, νοῦ καὶ ἐπιστήμης, Pl.*Phdr*.228c, *Ti*.46d; ἐπαίνου X.*Cyr*.1.5.12, cf. Plu.*Cam*.25, etc.; also ἐ. περὶ τὸ καλὸν καὶ τῆς Ἀφροδίτης καλῆς οὔσης Pl.*Smp*.203c: as fem., ἐρασταὶ αὐτοῦ πολλαὶ πόλεις Philostr.*VS*1.25.1; ἐ. γυνή Luc.*Philops*.15. **-ικός**, ή, όν, *loving*, καλῶν *Cat.Cod.Astr*.2.176. **-ός**, ή, όν, = ἐρατός, *beloved, lovely*, in Prose the usual form, Pl.*Smp*.204c, *Phdr*.250d; also in [Simon.]178.1; τόνδε δρόμον ποίησεν ἐραστόν *IG*1².817: Comp., *AP*12.197 (Strat.). **-ρια**, ἡ, fem. of ἐραστής, *lover*, Eup.414; ἀλλοτρίων λεχέων Perict.ap.Stob.4.28.19, cf. Ael.*NA*3.40. **-ριάω**, *to be amorous*, Phot.

ἔρᾶται, 3 sg. subj. (also ind. in Theoc.) of ἔραμαι; but **ἐρᾶται**, ind. Pass. of ἐράω.

ἐρατεινεύειν (-τειχεύειν Phot.)· στρατεύεσθαι, ἢ δυσφορεῖν, Hsch.

ἐρᾰτεινός, ή, όν, *lovely*, in Hom. mostly of places, Il.2.532, 5.210, al.; also of things, ἠνορέη, φιλότης, 6.156, Od.23.300; ὕδωρ Pi.*O*.6.85; εὐναί Id.*Fr*.122.7: rarely of persons, and then mostly of women, ἐγείνατο παῖδ' ἐρατεινήν Od.4.13, cf. *h.Cer*.423, Hes.*Th*.136, 909; ὁμηλικίη ἐ. her *lovely* companions, Il.3.175; of Polyphemus, οὐδ' ἄρ' ἔμελλ' ἑτάροισι φανεὶς ἐ. ἔσεσθαι a *welcome, glad* sight to my comrades, Od.9.230.—Ep. and Lyr. word: epith. of ὕδατα, Hp.*Aër*.5.

ἐρᾰτίζω, Ep. form of ἔραμαι, used by Hom. always in phrase, κρειῶν ἐρατίζων *greedy after* it, Il.11.551, 17.660, *h.Merc*.64, 287. II. *love*, Ζεὺς ἐράτιζε τριηκοσίους ἐνιαυτούς Call.*Fr*.20.

ἐρᾰτο-γλέφᾰρος, ον, *with lovely eyes*, Λατοῦς ἔρνος Limen.26 (prob.). **-πλόκᾰμος**, ον, = ἐρασιπλόκαμος, Orph.*H*.44.2.

ἐρᾰτός, ή, όν, (ἔραμαι) *lovely*, of places and things, δῶρ' ἐρατὰ.. χρυσέης Ἀφροδίτης Il.3.64; ἔργ' ἀνθρώπων Hes.*Th*.879; φιλότης ib.970; χέλυς, φωνή, πόλις, *h.Merc*.153, 426, *h.Ap*.477; βᾶμα *beloved* footfall, Sapph.*Supp*.5.17; χῶρος Archil.21.4; ἔπεα Alcm.45; ὄψ B.16.129; νίκα Corinn.*Supp*.1.24; αἰδώς, κῶμοι, Pi.*P*.9.12, *I*.2.31; ὠδίς Id.*O*.6.43: Sup., παίδων -ώτατον ἄνθος *AP*12.151: used by Trag. in Lyr., στήθεα A.*Th*.864 (anap.); λέχος E.*Heracl*.915; μολπαί Id.*El*.718 (s.v.l.); ὕμνοι Ar.*Th*.993; of persons, φυὴν ἐρατή Hes.*Th*.259, 355; νέοι ἄνδρες ἐ. Thgn.242; παῖς Pi.*O*.10(11).99: neut. as Adv., ἐρατὸν κιθαρίζειν *h.Merc*.423, 455. 2. *beloved*, ἀνδράσι μὲν θνητὸς ἰδεῖν ἐ. δὲ γυναιξί Tyrt.10.29.—Ep. and Lyr. word.

ἐρᾰτό-στομος, ον, *lovely-mouthed*, *Lyr.Adesp*. in *Philol*.80.333. **-χροος**, ον, *fair of complexion*, *AP*5.75 (Rufin.).

ἐρᾱτύω, Dor. for ἐρητύω, B.16.12, S.*OC*164; ἐράτοθεν· ἀνεπαύσαντο, Hsch. (prob. Cypr. for ἐρήτυθεν Il.2.99).

Ἐρᾰτώ, οῦς, ἡ, *Erato, the Lovely*, one of the nine Muses, Hes.*Th*.78, etc.: Pythag. name for *two*, *Theol.Ar*.11. 2. one of the Oceanides, Hes.*Th*.246.

ἐρᾰτ-ώνῠμος, ον, *of gracious fame*, κόρα B.16.31; ἀοιδά cj. in Stes. 44. **-ῶπις**, ιδος, ἡ, *of lovely look*, *IG*14.1356.8, v.l. in Hom.*Epigr*. 1.2.

ἔραυνα, later form for ἔρευνα, *POxy*.67.18 (iv A.D.), Ph.1.485 (Pap.):—also **ἐραυν-άω** Lxx 1*Ch*.19.3 (v.l.), 1*Ep.Cor*.2.10, al., *POxy*.294.9 (i A.D., Pass.), Ph.1.484 (Pap.): **-ησις**, *PMasp*.166.21 (vi A.D.): **-ητής**, *PFay*.104 (iii A.D.), *POxy*.1651.18 (iii A.D.): **-ητικόν**, τό, *examination-dues*, ib.1650.6, al. (i/ii A.D.).

ἐραχάται, οἱ, *binders of sheaves*, and **ἔραχος**, τό, *sheaf* (Boeot.), Hsch. (Perh. cf. ἔρχατος.)

ἐράω (A), used in Act. only in pres. and impf. (which in Poetry are ἔραμαι, ἠράμην), Ion. ἐρέω Archil.25.3: impf. ἤρων Hdt.9.108, E.*Fr*.161, Ar.*Ach*.146:—**Pass.**, ἀντ-ερᾶται X.*Smp*.8.3; opt. ἐρῷο Id.*Hier*.11.11; inf. ἐρᾶσθαι Plu.*Brut*.29, etc.; part. ἐρώμενος (v. infr.):—also **ἐράομαι**, 3 sg. ἐρᾶται Plu.2.753b, Philostr.*Gym*.48 (ἐράασθε v. sub ἔραμαι): all other tenses will be found under ἔραμαι:—*love*, c. gen. pers., prop. of the sexual passion, *to be in love with* (οὐκ ἐρᾷ ἀδελφὸς ἀδελφῆς.. οὐδὲ πατὴρ θυγατρός X.*Cyr*.5.1.10), ἤρα τῆς.. γυναικός Hdt.9.108, etc.: c. acc. cogn., ἐρᾶν ἔρωτα E.*Hipp*.32, Pl.*Smp*.181b: abs., ἐρῶν *a lover*, v.l. in Pi.*O*.1.80 (pl.), S.*Fr*.149.8 (pl.); opp. ἡ ἐρωμένη *the beloved one*, Hdt.3.31, S.E.*P*.3.196; [ὁ] ἐρώμενος X.*Smp*.8.36, Pl.*Phdr*.239a, cf. Ar.*Eq*.737 (pl.); τὸν ἐρώμενον αὐτοῦ, Lat. *delicias ejus*, Arist.*Pol*.1303ᵇ23. 2. without sexual reference, *love warmly*, opp. φιλέω, οὐδ' ἤρα οὐδ' ἐφίλει Pl.*Ly*.222a:—and in Pass., ὥστε οὐ μόνον φιλοῖο ἂν ἀλλὰ καὶ ἐρῷο X.*Hier*.11.11, cf. Plu.*Brut*.29; κινεῖ [τὸ οὗ ἕνεκα] ὡς ἐρώμενον Arist.*Metaph*.1072ᵇ3. II. c. gen. rei, *love* or *desire passionately*, τυραννίδος Archil.25.3; τερπνότατον τοῦ τις ἐρᾷ τὸ τυχεῖν Thgn.256; μάχης ἐρῶν A.*Th*.392; μόνος θεῶν γὰρ Θάνατος οὐ δώρων ἐρᾷ Id.*Fr*.161; ἀμηχάνων ἐρᾷς S.*Ant*.90; πατρίδος ἐρᾶν E.*Ph*.359; οὗ ἐπιθυμεῖ τε καὶ ἐρᾷ Pl.*Smp*.200a: and c. inf., *desire* to do, A.*Fr*.44.1; θανεῖν ἐρᾷ S.*Ant*.220; ἀποθανεῖν ἐρῶντες Hp.*de Arte* 7; φαγεῖν Ar.*Ach*.146; πληροῦσθαι Pl.*Phlb*.35a.

ἐράω (B), *pour forth, vomit*, ἐρᾶσαι· κενῶσαι, Hsch.: usu. in compds., ἀπὸ σφαγὴν ἐρῶν A.*Ag*.1599, cf. ἀπ-, ἐξ-, κατ-, κατεξ-, μετ-, συν-εράω.

ἔρβως (i.e. ἔρϝως)· εὐρώς, Hsch.

ἐργάδεις, f.l. for Ἀργαδεῖς in Plu.*Sol*.23 codd. (corr. Cobet).

ἐργάζομαι, Il.18.469, etc., Cret. ϝεργάδδομαι *Schwyzer* 181 v 5: fut. -άσομαι Thgn.1116, etc., Dor. ἐργαξοῦμαι Theoc.10.23, ἐργῶμαι *PCair.Zen*.107.4 (iii B.C.), Lxx *Ge*.29.27, al., *IG*7.3073.12 (Lebad., ii B.C.) (but Hsch. ἐργᾷ· ἐργάζει): aor. εἰργασάμην, Ion. ἐργ- Hdt.2.115, A.*Th*.845 (lyr.), etc., 3 pl. opt. ἐργασαίατο Ar.*Av*.1147, *Lys*.42; Dor. ἠργάξαντο *SIG*248 *M* (Delph., iv B.C.): pf. εἴργασμαι, Ion. ἔργ- Hdt.2.121.ε', A.*Fr*.311, etc.—These tenses are used both in Med. and Pass. signfs.: for other Pass. tenses, v. infr. III:—Att. Inscrr. of cent. iv have ἠργαζόμην, ἠργασάμην, (ἐξ-) *IG*2².1585.11, 1669.10, al., but εἴργασμαι ib.1666 *A* 27; so also ἠργάσατο ib.7.424 (Oropus, iv B.C.), εἰργασμένος ib.3073.51 (Lebad., ii B.C.), ἐξήργασατο *UPZ*19.8 (ii B.C.), εἴργασμαι *PCair.Zen*.146.3 (iii B.C.); but this rule is often broken in later Pap., Inscrr., and codd.:—*work, labour*, esp. of husbandry, Hes.*Op*.299, 309, Th.2.72, etc.; but also of all manual labour, of slaves, ἐ. ἀνάγκῃ Od.14.272; of quarrymen, Hdt.2.124, etc.; τὴν οὐσίαν οὐ δικαζόμενον ἀλλ' ἐργαζόμενον κεκτημένον Antipho 2.2.12; ἐ. ἐν τοῖς ἔργοις in the mines, D.42.31: c. dat. instr., χαλκῷ with brass, Hes.*Op*.151; also of animals, βοῦς ἐργάτης ἐργάζεται S.*Fr*.563; of birds *working* to get food, Arist.*HA*616ᵇ35; of bees, ib. 625ᵇ22; of Hephaestus' self-acting bellows, Il.18.469; τὸ χρῆμ' ἐργάζεται the matter *works*, i.e. *goes on*, Ar.*Ec*.148; ὁ ἀὴρ ἐργάζεται *produces an effect*, Thphr.*CP*5.12.7; οὐχ ὁμοίως ἐργάσεται τὸ θερμόν ib.6.18.11. II. trans., *work at, make*, ἔργα κλυτά, of Athena, Od.20.72, cf. 22.422; ἀγάλματα, ὕμνους, Pi.*N*.5.1, *I*.2.46; τρίποδα, Νίκην, *SIG*34 (Delph., v B.C.); ἁμαξίδας Ar.*Nu*.880; οἰκοδόμημα Th.2.76; εἰκόνας, ἀνδριάντας, καλὰ ἔργα, Pl.*Cra*.431c, X.*Mem*.2.6.6, Pl.*Men*.91d; κηρόν, σχαδόνας, of bees, Arist.*HA*627ᵃ6, 30; μέλι Sor.*Vit.Hippocr*.11; *make* so and so, ξηρὸν ἐ. τινά Luc.*DMar*.11.2; μέγαν Ael.*VH*3.1. 2. *do, perform*, ἔργα ἀεικέα Il.24.733; ἔργον ἐπ' ἔργῳ ἐ., of husbandmen, Hes.*Op*.382, cf. 397; ἐργασίας ἐ. Arist.*EN*1121ᵇ33, cf. X.*Oec*.7.20; ἐναίσιμα, φίλα ἐ., Od.17.321, 24.210; θαυμαστά Pl.*Smp*.213d; περὶ θεοὺς ἄδικον μηδὲν Id.*Grg*.522d; ἐ. πρᾶγμα, opp. βουλεύειν, S.*Ant*.267, cf. *OT*347; τὸ ἔργον Κυρίου 1*Ep.Cor*.16.10: c. dupl. acc., *do* something *to*.., τά περ νῦν ἐ. [ὁ ἥλιος] τὸν Νεῖλον Hdt.2.26, etc.; chiefly in bad sense, *do* one ill, *do* one a shrewd turn, κακὰ ἐργάζεσθαί τινα S.*Ph*.786, Th.1.137, etc.; so οἷά μ' εἰργάσω, τί μ' ἐργάσει; S.*Ph*.928, 1172 (lyr.), etc.; μὴ δῆτα τοῦτό μ' ἐργάσῃ Id.*El*.1206; αἴσχιστα ἐ. τινά Ar.*V*.787; less freq., ἀγαθὰ ἐ. τινά Hdt.8.79, cf. Th.3.52, Pl.*Cri*.53a; πολλὰ καὶ καλὰ τὴν Ἑλλάδα Id.*Phdr*.244b; seldom τινί τι Ar.*V*.1350; οἷν ἐμοὶ δυοῖν ἔργ' ἐστὶ κρείσσον' ἀγχόνης εἰργασμένα S.*OT*1374. b. *perform* rites, τὰ ἱερὰ ἐ. 1*Ep.Cor*.9.13. c. in Law, ζημίαν ἐ. *do* damage, Is.6.20, cf. Hyp.*Ath*.22. 3. *work* a material, ὅπλα.. οἷσίν τε χρυσὸν εἰργάζετο Od.3.435; ἐ. γῆν *till* the land, Hdt.1.17, etc.; ἐ. [ἀγροὺς] ἐργάταις X.*Cyr*.1.6.11; γῆν καὶ ξύλα καὶ λίθους Id.*HG*3.3.7; [ἀργυρῖτιν] Docum.ap.D.37.28; ἐ. θάλασσαν, of traders, D.H.3.46; γλαυκὴν ἐ., of fishers, Hes.*Th*.440. 4. *earn by working*, χρήματα Hdt.1.24, Ar.*Eq*.840, etc.; καινὸν βίον ἐκ τοῦ δικαίου And.1.144, cf. Hes.*Op*.43; ἀργύριον ἀπὸ σοφίας Pl.*Hp.Ma*.282d; μισθοῦ τὰ ἐπιτήδεια X.*Mem*.2.8.2. 5. *work at, practise*, μουσικήν, τέχνας, etc., Pl.*Phd*.60e, *R*.374a, etc.; ἐπιστήμας X.*Oec*.1.7; ἀρετὴν καὶ σωφροσύνην v.l. in Isoc.13.6; δικαιοσύνην, ἀνομίαν, *Act.Ap*.10.35, *Ev.Matt*.7.23. 6. abs., *work at a trade* or *business, traffic, trade*, ἐν [γναφείῳ] Lys.23.2; ἐν ἐμπορίῳ καὶ χρήμασιν D.36.44; ἐν τῇ ἀγορᾷ Id.57.31 (also οἱ τὴν τετράγωνον (sc. ἀγοράν) ἐργαζόμενοι those who *trade in* the square, *BCH*8.126 (cf. *Glotta*14.73)); κατὰ θάλατταν D.56.48; τούτοις.. ναυτικοῖς ἐ. *trade* with this money on bottomry, Id.33.4; δὶς ἢ τρὶς ἐ. τῷ αὐτῷ ἀργυρίῳ Id.56.30; ταῦτα ἐ. thus he *trades*, Id.25.82; οἱ ἐργαζόμενοι *traders*, Id.34.51; οἱ ἐν Δήλῳ ἐ., = Lat. *qui Deli negotiantur*, *CIG*2285b; esp. of courtesans, σώματι ἐ., Lat. *quaestum corpore facere*, D.59.20; ἐπὶ τέγους ἀπὸ τοῦ σώματος Plb.12.13.2; ἀπὸ τῆς ὥρας Alexis Sam.ap. Ath.13.572f, Plu.*Tim*.14. 7. *cause*, κολακείην Democr.268; πημονάς S.*Ant*.326; πόθον τινί D.61.11; σύριγγας ἀνιάτους Paul.Aeg. 6.44. III. Pass., rarely in pres. and impf., D.H.8.87 (ἐξ-), Hyp.*Eux*.35: fut. ἐργασθήσομαι S.*Tr*.1218, (ἐξ-) Isoc.*Ep*.6.8: pf. εἴργασμαι (v. infr.): aor. 1 εἰργάσθην Pl.*R*.353a, Thphr.*HP*6.3.2, etc. 1. *to be made* or *built*, ἔργαστο τὸ τεῖχος Hdt.1.179; ἐκ πέτρας εἰργασμένος A.*Pr*.244; οἰκοδόμημα διὰ ταχέων εἰργ. Th.4.8; λίθοι εἰργ. *wrought* stones, Id.1.93; γῆ εἰργ. X.*Oec*.19.8; θώρακας εὖ εἰργ. Id.*Mem*.3.10.9. 2. *to be done*, A.*Ag*.354, 1346, E.*Hec*.1085; εἰργασμένα *things done, deeds*, Hdt.7.53 (ἐργ-), E.*Ion*1281, cf. S.*OT*1369.

ἐργᾰθεῖν, Ep. **ἐεργᾰθεῖν**, Att. **εἰργᾰθεῖν**, poet. aor. 2 inf. of εἴργω, *sever, cut off*, ἀπὸ δ' αὐχένος ὦμον ἐέργαθεν Il.5.147; ἀπὸ πλευρῶν χρόα ἔργαθεν 11.437. II. *hold back, check*, S.*El*.1271, E.*Ph*.1175, A.R.3.1171.

Ἐργαῖος· ἀέριος Ζεύς, Hsch.

ἐργᾰλ-εῖον, Ion. -ήϊον, Cret. ϝεργαλεῖον *Schwyzer* 180, τό, (ἔργον) *tool, instrument*, Hdt.3.131, Th.6.44, Pl.*Plt*.281c, etc. **-ίδιον**, τό, Dim. of foreg., *PMasp*.1.24, 273 (vi A.D.).

ἐργᾰλοθήκη (leg. ἐργαλειο-), ἡ, *case for instruments*, gloss on συγλάριον, Hsch.

ἔργανα, τά (also γέργανα, i.e. ϝέργ-), = ἐργαλεῖα, Hsch. **ἐργανεῖον** (-λεῖον cod., extra ordinem), τό, = ἐργαστήριον (Tarent.), Id.

ἐργάνη [ᾰ], ἡ, *worker*, epith. of Athena, τὴν Διὸς γοργῶπιν Ἐ. S.*Fr*.844.2, cf. *IG*1².561, 2.1434, al., 4.990 (Epid.), Ael.*VH*1.2, Paus. 1.24.3, prob. l. for ἐργάτις in *APr*.461: Delph. ϝαργάνα *Schwyzer* 319(1) (vi/v B.C.); cf. ὀργάνη. II. = ἐργασία, *PPetr*.2 p.60 (iii B.C.), Hsch.

ἐργᾰσ-είω, Desiderat. of ἐργάζομαι, *long to do, be about to do*, ὡς ἐργασείων οὐδέν S.*Tr.*1232; τί δ' ἐργασείεις; Id.*Ph.*1001. **-ία**, Ion. **-ίη**, Cret. **ϝεργασία** *Leg.Gort.*8.44, ἡ, (ἐργάτης) *work, business,* ἐργασίην φεύγουσα *h.Merc.*486, etc.; opp. ἀργία, X.*Mem.*2.7.7; ἐ. ἀγαθή productive *labour,* Id.*Vect.*4.29; ἐργασίᾳ ἐγχειρεῖν, of bees, Arist. *HA*625b24; ἡ περὶ τὴν θάλατταν ἐ., of seamen, Pl.*R.*371b; μὴ γενομένης ἐργασίας if no *work* was done, D.27.20; δὸς ἐργασίαν, c. inf., Lat. *da operam ut..*, *Ev.Luc.*12.58, cf. *OGI*441.109 (*SC. de Stratonicensibus,* i B.C.): pl., τὰς ἐν ὑπαίθρῳ ἐ. ἐργάζεσθαι X.*Oec.*7.20; ἐ. ἀνελεύθεροι Arist.*EN*1121b33, cf. Epicur.*Fr.*196 (dub.). 2. *function,* ἥπατος Aret.*SD*1.15. II. *working at, making, manufacture,* ἱματίων, ὑποδημάτων, etc., Pl.*Grg.*449d, *Tht.*146d, etc.; ἡ τῆς ἐσθῆτος ἐκ τῶν ἐρίων ἐ. X.*Oec.*7.21; *making up* of a prescription, Hp.*Ulc.*14: metaph., Πέργαμος ἀμφὶ τεαῖς χερὸς ἐργασίαις ἁλίσκεται Troy is (i.e. is doomed to be) taken in the part *wrought by* thy *hands,* Pi.*O.*8.42; ἐ. ἡδονῆς *production* of pleasure, Pl.*Prt.*353d; ἐ. χρημάτων money-*making,* Arist.*EN*1160a16 (but *administration* of property, *Leg.Gort.* l. c.). 2. *working* of a material, ἡ ἐ. τοῦ σιδήρου Hdt.1.68; χαλκοῦ, ἐρίων, ξύλων, Pl.*Chrm.*173e; τῶν χρυσείων μετάλλων Th.4.105, cf. Hyp.*Eux.*36; πίττης Thphr.*HP*9.2.6: most commonly, *tillage* of the ground, ἐ. γῆς, χώρας, Ar.*Ra.*1034 (pl.), Isoc.7.30, etc.; ἐ. κήπων Pl. *Min.*316b; ἐ. περὶ τὴν τροφὴν *preparation* (i.e. mastication and digestion) of food, Arist.*Juv.*469a3; *treatment* of silphium, Thphr.*HP*6.3.2. 3. generally, *trade, business,* X.*Mem.*3.10.1; ἐπὶ τῆς ἐργασίας ὢν τῆς κατὰ θάλατταν engaged in *trade* by sea, D.33.4; ἡ ἐ. τῆς τραπέζης the banking *business,* Id.36.6; ἐ. χρυσοχοϊκή, ἀρωματική, *PLond.*3.906.6 (ii A.D.), *PFay.*93.7 (ii A.D.); βαφεῖς τὴν ἐ. dyers by *trade,* *PTeb.*287.3 (ii A.D.); esp. of *a courtesan's trade,* Hdt.2.135, D.18.129; of sexual *intercourse,* Arist.*Pr.*876a39. b. ἐὰν ἐργασίαν εὕρῃ ὁ οἰκέτης if a slave brings in *earnings,* Hyp.*Ath.*22. 4. *practising, exercising,* τῶν τεχνῶν Pl.*Grg.*450c; Κύπριδος *AP*5.218 (Paul. Sil.); ἀκαθαρσίας *Ep.Eph.*4.19. 5. *work of art, production,* τετράγωνος ἐ., of the Hermae, Th.6.27 (non legit Sch.); τῶν τειχῶν αἱ ἐργασίαι the fortification *works,* Id.7.6. 6. literary *execution,* ἐ. ποιητική Phld. *Po.*5.11; *elaboration* of a topic, Sch.Pi.*P.*2.24. 7. *production* of a play, Arg.Men.*Oxy.*1235.108. III. *guild* or *company* of workmen, ἡ ἐ. τῶν βαφέων Judeich *Altertümer von Hierapolis* 50; ἐριοπλυτῶν ib. 40; ἐ. θρεμματική dub. sens., ib.227. **-ίμη**, ἡ, *poor kind of myrrh,* Dsc.1.64.2. **-ιμος**, ον, *to be worked, that can be worked,* Alc.ap. Sch.Gen.Il.21.319, Plu.2.701c; ξύλα, opp. καύσιμα, Poll.7.109; σκεῦος ἐ. δέρματος Lxx *Le.*13.49; mostly of land, ἐ. χωρία *tillable* land, Pl.*Lg.*639a, 958d, Arist.*Pr.*924a1 (sg. in *PHal.*1.103 (iii B.C.)); τὰ ἐ. X.*Cyr.*1.4.16, etc.; τὰ τεμένη, ὅσα.. θεμιτόν ἐστιν ἐ. ποιεῖν to bring *into cultivation,* *IG*2.1059.17 (iv B.C.); ἡ ἐ. (sc. γῆ) Thphr.*HP* 6.3.5. 2. ἐ. ἡμέρα a *work*-day, Lxx 1 *Ki.*20.19. 3. ἐ., τό, *cost of manufacture,* ἄρτων *UPZ*149.25, cf. 20 (ii B.C.). II. Act., *working for a livelihood,* τὸ ἐ. the *working people,* App.*BC*3.72; esp. of courtesans, Artem.1.78. 2. *active,* θρασύτης Orph.*H.*60.7. **-ις**, εως, ἡ, *perpetration,* φόνου Sch.E.*Med.*864. **-τέον**, *one must till the land,* X.*Eq.Mag.*8.8. II. τοὔργον ἔστ' ἐ. *it must be done* or *one must do* it, A.*Ch.*298, cf. E.*Med.*791, X.*Oec.*7.35; τὰ ἔργα..ὡς ἔστιν ἐργαστέα ib.13.3; ὅτ' ἦν ἐ. when it was *necessary to act,* S.*Tr.* 688. **-τήρ**, ῆρος, ὁ, *workman,* esp. *in husbandry,* X.*Oec.*5.15; of a smith, Orph.*H.*66.4. **-τηριακός**, ή, όν, *practising a handicraft,* ἄνθρωποι Plb.38.12.5: -κοί, οἱ, *work-people,* D.S.31.25. **-τηριάρχης**, ου, ὁ, *foreman of a workshop,* *CIG*4968 (Egypt), *Anatolian Studies* 30 (Ephesus). **-τηρίδιον**, τό, Dim. of ἐργαστήριον, *BGU* 1127.9 (i B.C.). **-τήριον**, τό, *any place in which work is done*: *workshop, manufactory,* Hdt.4.14, Lys.12.8, *IG*2².1013.9; attached to a mine, ib.1582.58, al., D.37.4, Is.3.22; butcher's *shop,* Ar.*Eq.*744; perfumer's *shop,* Hyp.*Ath.*6; barber's *shop,* Plu.2.973b; μισθώσασθαι ἐ. πρὸς ἄνοιξιν καπηλείου *POxy.*2109.31 (iii A.D.); euphem. for *a brothel,* D.59.67, Alciphr.*Fr.*5.1. 2. metaph., τὴν πόλιν ὄντως εἶναι πολέμου ἐ. X.*HG*3.4.17; λόγων ἐ. Lib.*Or.*55.34. b. of persons, *gang,* συκοφαντῶν ἐ. D.39.2, 40.9; πειρατικὸν ἐ. Hld.5.20. c. as Adj., φάρμακον ἐ. τινός Sch.S.*Tr.*846. **-τής**, οῦ, ὁ, = ἐργάτης, A.D. *Adv.*135.4, *IGRom.*4.1209 (Thyatira); = Lat. *negotiator,* *SIG*1229.1 (Hierapolis); v.l. in J.*AJ*18.1.1, Gal.*Thras.*33. **-τικός**, ή, όν, *able to work, working, industrious,* Hp.*Prorrh.*2.4 (Comp.), Pl.*Men.* 81e (v.l.), X.*Mem.*3.1.6; οἱ ἐ. the *working men,* Plb.10.16.1: Comp., Phld.*Oec.*p.32 J. 2. *skilled in producing,* c. gen., φωνῆς Epicur. *Sent.Vat.*45: generally, *productive,* σωφροσύνης Phld.*Mus.*p.24 K.; ὑγιείας *Gp.*11.2.6; ἡ ἐ. (sc. τέχνη) the *art of manufacturing,* c. gen., ἐρεοῦ προβλήματος, στήμονος καὶ κρόκης, Pl.*Plt.*280e, 281a; τὸ τῆς τροφῆς ἐ. the organ *that prepares* food, the mouth, Arist.*Pol.*1290b 27. II. *of a workman,* ἱμάτια *Lex.Mess.* in *Rh.Mus.*47.412 (nisi ἐργατ- legend.). **-τῖναι**· αἱ τὸν πέπλον ὑφαίνουσαι, Hsch. (cf. *IG*2².1034, *EM*149.21, Suid. s. v. Χαλκεῖα). **-τρα**, τά, *reward of labour, wage-cost,* χλαμύδος *PEdgar* 65.89 (iii B.C.). II. name of an object belonging to an οἰνοχόη, φιάλη, etc., *IG*2².839.85, 1640.16, *BCH*32.6 (Delos, iv B.C.). **-τρίς**, ίδος, ἡ, = ἐργάτις, Hsch. s. v. καιρωστρίδες.

ἐργᾰτ-εία, ἡ, *labour, work, handicraft,* in pl., Lxx *Wi.*7.16, *BGU* 1159.9 (i B.C.). 2. *gang of workmen,* ibid., *POxy.*1450.6 (iii A.D.). II. Ἐργάτ(ε)ια, τά, festival of Heracles in Laconia, Hsch. **-εύομαι**, *work hard, labour,* Lxx *To.*5.5, D.S.20.92:—Act., -εύω *UPZ*110.102 (ii B.C.). **-ης**, ου, ὁ, *workman,* *Hermes* 17.5 (Delos), *Ev.Matt.*10.10, etc.; esp. *one who works the soil, husbandman,* γῆς ἐ. Hdt.4.109, 5.6; οἱ ἐ. οἱ περὶ γεωργίαν D.35.32: abs., S.*OT*859, E.*El.*75, etc.: also with Subst., ἐ. ἀνήρ Theoc.10.9, D. 59.50; οὐργάτης λεώς the *country*-folk, Ar.*Pax* 632; of animals, βοῦς ἐ. a *working* ox, Archil.39, S.*Fr.*563; ἐ. σφῆκες Arist.*HA*627b32; also ἐ. θαλάττης, of a fisher, Alciphr.1.11; ἐ. λίθων a stone-*mason,* Luc.*Somn.*2. b. in the religious sense, 2*Ep.Ti.*2.15, 2*Ep.Cor.*11.13 (pl.). 2. Adj. *hard-working, strenuous,* ἐ. στρατηγός X.*Cyr.*1.6.18; σώφρων κἀ. Ar.*Ach.*611; opp. ἀργός, Pl.*Euthd.*281c; φειδωλὸς καὶ ἐ. Id.*R.*554a. II. *one who practises* an art, τῶν ἐν πολέμῳ X.*Cyr.*4.1.4; ἐ. δίκης, of a judge, Lyc.128: abs., *practitioner* in some special branch of surgery, e.g. lithotomy, ἐ. ἄνδρες Hp.*Jusj.* III. *doer,* ἄσημος οὐργ. τις ἦν S.*Ant.*252; τῶν καλῶν X.*Mem.*2.1.27; ἀνομίας Lxx 1 *Ma.*3.6; τῆς ἀδικίας *Ev.Luc.*13.27. IV. *producer,* τῶν ἐν τῷ κόσμῳ γινομένων Heraclit.75; [Αἰὼν] θείας φύσεως ἐ. *SIG*1125.12 (Eleusis). V. a sort of *capstan* or *windlass,* Bito 58.12, Vitr.10.2.7, al., Orib.49.4.1. **-ήσιος**, α, ον, = ἐργάσιμος, χώρα dub. in Plu. *Cat.Ma.*21 (v.l. ἔργα πίσσια). **-ικός**, ή, όν, = ἐργαστικός, opp. ἐργατῶν ἄρχων, Pl.*Plt.*259e; *like a workman,* γυνὴ ἐ. Luc.*Somn.*6; *hard-working,* Pl.*Men.*81e (with v.l.); δοῦλοι Plu.*Cat.Ma.*4; ἐ. καὶ γεωργικός D.H.*Rh.*11.6; ἐ. κτήνη, ὄνος, *PFay.*111.6 (i A.D.), *PSI* 1.38.5 (ii A.D.); τὸ ἐ. Hp.*Aër.*24: Comp. -ώτερος, Sup. -ώτατος, of bees, Arist.*HA*624b29, 622b19; ποταμὸς ἐ., of the Nile, Hdt.2.11. Adv. -κῶς, πρός τι *advantageously* for.., Plu.*Cam.*16. **-ίνης** [ῑ], ου, ὁ, = ἐργάτης, esp. *husbandman,* Theoc.10.1, A.R.2.376 (pl.); ἐ. ἄνδρες Theoc.21.3, *AP*11.58 (Maced.); βοῦς ἐ. A.R.2.663 (pl.), *AP* 6.228 (Adaeus). II. c. gen., *making* a thing or *practising* an art, μέλιτος ὁ χρυσὸς ἐ. *AP*5.239 (Maced.); Κύπριδος ib.274 (Paul. Sil.). **-ις** (parox.), ιδος, fem. of ἐργάτης, *workwoman*; of the *worker* bees, Arist.*HA*627a12, *Lyr.Alex.Adesp.*7.12; μάθε ὡς ἐ. ἐστὶν [ἡ μέλισσα] Lxx *Pr.*6.8a; ἐ. βοῦς *AP*9.741. 2. Adj. *laborious, industrious,* γυναῖκες οὕτω ἐ. Hdt.5.13; γλῶσσαν μὲν ἀργὸν χεῖρα δ' εἶχεν ἐργάτιν S.*Ph.*97; βιοτά *APl.*1.15.6. 3. *working for hire,* Μοῖσ' οὐ πω ἐ. ἦν Pi.*I.*2.6; of a courtesan, Archil.184. II. c. gen., *working at* or *producing,* μνήμην ἁπάντων μουσομήτορ' ἐργάτιν A.*Pr.* 461 (ἐργάνην Stob.); νέκταρος ἐ., of bees, *AP*9.404.8 (Antiphil.); νήματος ἠλακάτα ib.6.174 (Antip. ⟨Sid.⟩); σελίδων, of poetesses, ib.9.26.8 (Antip. Thess.); Κύπριδος, of courtesans, ib.5.244.8 (Maced.); rare in Prose, πόλις ἐ. τῶν ἀγαθῶν D.H.2.76.

ἐργᾰτοκῡλίνδριος τόπος place *for a windlass* (cf. ἐργάτης v), Bito 55.5.

ἐργατώδης, f.l. for ἐργώδης, Marcellin.*Puls.*150.

ἐργατῶνες, Att. **ἐρχατῶνες**, *shelters* for slaves in country districts, Hsch.: but **ἐργάτωνες**, in Crete, *undertakers,* Id.

ἐργεπείκτης, ου, ὁ, (ἐπείγω) *taskmaster,* Eust.588.16.

ἐργεπιστᾰσία, ἡ, *superintendence of works,* *CIG*2779 (Aphrodisias, pl.), *IGRom.*4.861 (Laodicea ad Lycum, pl.), Keil-Premerstein *Erster Bericht* 16.

ἐργεπιστᾰτ-έω, *to be superintendent of works,* *OGI*510.12 (Ephesus), *IGRom.*4.1352 (Lydia), 818 (Hierapolis), Sch.Ar.*Pax* 605. **-ης**, ου, ὁ, *superintendent of works,* Epich.212, Artem.4.31, *IG*3.486 (ii A.D.), 12(5).253 (Paros).

ἐργέτην· ἐργασίαν, Hsch. **ἔργετος**· φραγμός, Id.

ἐργμα (**ἔργμα** Pi.*N.*4.6), ατος, τό, poet. for ἔργον, *work, deed, business,* *h.Hom.*27.20, 32.19, Thgn.29, Archil.70, Sol.4.11, Pi.*N.* l. c., A.*Th.*556, *Eu.*501 (lyr.); ἔργμασιν ἐν πολέμου Epigr. (= *IG*1².394) ap.Hdt.5.77: rare in Prose, as Democr.43, Perict.ap.Stob.4.28.19, Procl. *in Prm.*p.590 S.

ἔργμα, ατος, τό, (εἴργω) *fence, guard,* Arist.*PA*658b18; τάφου S. *Ant.*848 (lyr.); *obstacle,* Hp.*Steril.*213; *means of hindering,* δυνάμεως Hierocl. *in CA* 24 p.473 M.

ἐργνύω, = εἴργω, *enclose,* Hsch.; cf. καθείργνυμι.

ἐργοδιώκτ-έω, *to be a taskmaster,* Lxx 2*Ch.*8.10. **-ης**, ου, ὁ, *taskmaster,* *PPetr.*2 p.6 (iii B.C.), Lxx *Ex.*3.7, Ph.2.86.

ἐργοδοσία, ἡ, *letting out work,* *Arch.Anz.*1904.8 (Milet.).

ἐργοδοτ-έω, *let out work,* opp. ἐργολαβέω, Apollod.Com.20, *CIG* 2826.5 (Aphrodisias). **-ης**, ου, ὁ, *one who farms out work,* X.*Cyr.* 8.2.5, *CIG*3467.22 (Sardes); un-Attic, acc. to Phryn.326; incorrectly used of *workmen,* Aret.*SD*1.6.

ἐργολάβ-εια [ᾰ], ἡ, = ἐργολαβία II, τῶν μειρακίων *making profit out of* them, Alciphr.1.34. **-έω**, *contract for the execution of work,* opp. ἐργοδοτέω, *CIG*3467.24 (Sardes) (also in Med., Polyaen.6.51): c. acc., ἐ. ἀνδριάντας X.*Mem.*3.1.2, cf. Philoch.97; τὸ ἱερὸν ἢ δαμόσιον ἔργον *SIG*²940.7 (Cos, i B.C.); τὸ ἰατρικὸν ἔργον *BCH*25.235 (Amphissa); τὸ μακρὸν τεῖχος Plu.*Per.*13: c. inf., *SIG*²588.220 (Delos, ii B.C.), *IG*12(8).640.6 (Peparethus, ii B.C.). II. *make profit out of,* τὰ ἰατρικά Phld.*Rh.*1.329 S.; so of Sophists, ἐ. τὰ μειράκια Alciphr.3.55: so abs., freq. in Oratt., σοφιστὴς ἐργολαβῶν Aeschin.2.112, cf. D.22.49; ἔν τινι in a matter, Aeschin.3.33; τινι for one, D.25.47; ἐπί τινα or κατά τινος against one, Aeschin.1.173, D.*Ep.*3.34. **-ία**, ἡ, *contract for the execution of work,* πρὸς ἐργολαβίαν γεγράφθαι [λόγους] Isoc.5.25: pl., *Ath.Mitt.*51.29 (Samos), Plu.*Cat.Ma.*19. II. *profit-making,* ἐργολαβίας ἕνεκεν παραμένειν ἐν τῷ μαθήματι D.S.2.29, cf. Lib.*Decl.*23.20. **-ος**, ὁ, *contractor,* Pl.*R.*373b, *IG*9(1).694.32 (Corc.); τοῦ ἀγάλματος *for making* it, Plu.*Per.*31; ἐ. δικῶν brief-mongers, i.e. advocates, Them.*Or.*21.260b; but, *collusive plaintiff,* Paul.Al.O.2. II. Adj. *for gain, gainful,* v.l. in Plb.20.12.1.

ἐργο-λήπτης, ου, ὁ, = foreg., Teleclid.56. **-μίσης** [ῑ], ου, ὁ, *one who hates work,* Hdn.Gr.2.685. **-μωκεύω**, *flatter, wheedle,* *Gloss.*:—Med., = *assentior, ancillor,* prob. in Dosith.p.430 K. (= p.95 T.):—hence **-μωκία, -μωκος**, *Gloss.*; **-μωκέω**, = ἐμπαίζω, Hsch.

ἔργον, Dor. **ϝέργον** *IG*4.800 (vi B.C.), Elean **ϝάργον** *SIG*9 (vi B.C.), τό: (ἔρδω, OE. weorc (neut.) 'work', Avest. *varəza-*):—

work, Il.2.436, etc.; ἔ. οὐδὲν ὄνειδος, ἀεργίη δέ τ' ὄνειδος Hes.*Op.*311; πλεόνων δέ τε ἔ. ἄμεινον Il.12.412; ἔ. ἐποίχεσθαι 6.492; νῦν ἔπλετο ἔ. ἅπασι 12.271; esp. in pl., ἄλλος ἄλλοισιν.. ἐπιτέρπεται ἔργοις Od. 14.228; ἐπὶ ἔργα τράποντο Il.3.422; ἔργων παύσασθαι Od.4.683; τὰ σ' αὐτῆς ἔργα κόμιζε see to thine own *tasks*, Il.6.490: esp. in the following relations, 1. in Il. mostly of *works* or *deeds* of war, πολεμήϊα ἔ. Il.2.338, al., Od.12.116; ἔργον μάχης Il.6.522; alone, ἀτελευτήτῳ ἐπὶ ἔργῳ 4.175, cf. 539; ὑπέσχετο δὲ μέγα ἔργον 13.366; ἐπ' αὐτῷ δ' ἔργον ἐτύχθη ἀργαλέον 4.470; later, ἔργον.. Ἄρης κρινεῖ A.*Th.*414; ἐν τῷ ἔ. during the *action*, Th.2.89, cf. 7.71; τὸ ἐν Πλαταιαῖς ἔ. Pl.*Mx.* 241c; τῶν πρότερον ἔ. μέγιστον ἐπράχθη τὸ Μηδικόν Th.1.23; ἔργου ἔχεσθαι to engage in *battle*, ib.49. 2. of peaceful *contests*, κρατεῖν ἔ. Pi.*O.*9.85; ἔργου ἔχεσθαι Id.*P.*4.233; also ἔργα θῆκε κάλλιστ' ἀμφὶ κόμαις placed [the reward of] noble *deeds* about his hair, Id.*O.*13. 38. 3. of *works of industry*, a. of *tillage*, *tilled lands*, ἀνδρῶν πίονα ἔ. Il.12.283, etc.; ἔργ' ἀνθρώπων 16.392, Od.6.259; βροτῶν 10.147; οὔτε βοῶν οὔτ' ἀνδρῶν φαίνετο ἔργα ib.98; ἔργα alone, 16.140, etc.; Ἔργα καὶ Ἡμέραι—the title of Hesiod's work; πατρώϊα ἔ. their father's *lands*, Od.2.22; οὔτ' ἐπὶ ἔργα.. ἴμεν will neither go to our *farms*, ib. 127, cf. 252; Ἰθάκης.. ἔργα *the tilled lands* of Ithaca, 14.344; ἀμφὶ.. Τιταρησσὸν ἔργ' ἐνέμοντο inhabited *lands*, Il.2.751; τὰ τῶν Μυσῶν ἔ. Hdt.1.36; so later, *PBaden* 40.5 (ii A.D.): generally, *property*, *wealth*, *possessions*, θεὸς δ' ἐπὶ ἔργον ἀέξῃ Od.14.65, cf. 15.372. b. of women's *work*, weaving, Il.9.390, etc.; ἀμύμονα ἔ. ἰδυίας ib.128; ἔργα ἐργάζεσθαι Od.22.422, 20.72. c. of other *occupations*, θαλάσσια ἔ. fishing, 5.67; a seaman's life, Il.2.614: periphr., δαιτὸς.. ἔργα *works* of feasting, 9.228; φιλοτήσια ἔ. Od.11.246; ἔργα γάμοιο Il.5. 429; ἔργα Κυπρογενοῦς Sol.26; Ἀφροδίτης *h.Ven.*1; also τέκνων ἐς ἔ. A.*Ag.*1207: abs., ἔργον Luc.*DDeor.*17.1, *AP*12.209 (pl., Strat., s.v.l.); also ἔργα ἰσχύος καὶ τάχους X.*Cyr.*1.2.12; φίλα ἔργα μελίσσαις, of flowers, Theoc.22.42; of *mines*, etc., ἔ. ἀργυρεῖα X.*Vect.*4.5, D.21.167, etc.; ἔργα πίσσια dub. l. in Plu.*Cat.Ma.*21. 4. *deed*, *action*, ἔργ' ἀνδρῶν τε θεῶν τε Od.1.338; θέσκελα ἔ. Τρώων Il.3.130; ἀήσυλα ἔ. 5.876; καρτερά, ἀεικέα ἔ., ib.872, 22.395; παλίντιτα, ἄντιτα ἔ., Od.1.379, 17.51; ἔργα ἀποδέκνυσθαι Hdt.1.16, cf. Pl.*Alc.*1.119e, D.C.37.52; opp. ἔπος, *deed*, not word (v. ἔπος II.1); opp. μῦθος, Il. 9.443, 19.242, A.*Pr.*1080 (anap.), etc.; opp. λόγος, S.*El.*358, E.*Alc.* 339; ἔργῳ, opp. λόγῳ, freq. in Att., etc., Th.2.65, etc.: so in pl., λόγῳ μὲν.. τοῖσι δ' ἔργοισιν S.*OC*782, cf. E.*Fr.*360.13; λόγοισιν εἴτ' ἔργοισιν S.*OT*517; opp. ῥήματα, Id.*OC*873; opp. ὄνομα, E.*IA*128 (anap.), Th.8.78, 89; in many phrases, πέπρακται τοὔργον A.*Pr.*75, cf. *Ag.*1346; χωρῶ πρὸς ἔργον S.*Aj.*116; τὸ μὲν ἐνθύμημα χαρίεν.., τὸ δὲ ἔ. ἀδύνατον its *execution*, X.*An.*3.5.12; ἐν ἔργῳ χέρνιβες ξίφος τε ready for *action*, E.*IT*1190; ἡ κατάρα ὑπὸ τοῦ δαίμονος εἰς ἔ. ἤγετο Jul.*Or.*7.228b. II. *thing*, *matter*, πᾶν ἔ... ὑπείξομαι in every *point*, Il.1.294; ἃ Ζεὺς μήδετο ἔ. 2.38, etc.; τάρος τάδε ἔ. γενέσθαι 6.348, etc.; ὅπως ἔσται τάδε ἔ. 2.252, Od.17.78, etc.; μέμνημαι τόδε ἔ. Il.9. 527; ἄκουε τοὔργον S.*Tr.*1157, cf. *OT*847, *Aj.*466; in bad sense, *mischief*, *trouble*, of disease, αἰτίη τοῦ ἔ. Aret.*SA*1.9; μέγα ἔ. a serious *matter*, Od.4.663, Th.3.3. 2. μέγα ἔ., like μέγα χρῆμα, χερμάδιον λάβε χειρὶ Τυδεΐδης, μέγα ἔ. a monstrous *thing*, Il.5.303, cf. 20.286; φυλόπιδος μέγα ἔ. a *mighty* call to arms, 16.208. III. Pass., *that which is wrought* or *made*, *work*, οἷ' ἐπιεικὲς ἔργ' ἔμεν ἀθανάτων, of the arms of Achilles, Il.19.22; ἔ. Ἡφαίστοιο metal-*work*, Od.4.617; πέπλοι.., ἔργα γυναικῶν Il.6.289, Od.7.97, cf. 10.223; ὕφασμα, σῆς ἔ. χερὸς A.*Ch.*231; κολεόν.. λώτινον ἔ. Theoc.24.45; of a wall, Ar.*Av.*1125; of a statue, X.*Mem.*3.10.7: in pl., of siege-*works*, ἔ. καὶ μηχαναί Plb.5.3.6; of a *machine*, Apollod.*Poliorc.*157. 4, al., Ath.Mech.15.2, al.; of public *buildings*, *Mon.Anc.Gr.*18.20; of an author's *works*, D.H.*Comp.*25; τὸ περὶ ψυχῆς ἔργον Ἀριστοτέλους *AP*11.354.8 (Agath.). 2. *result of work*, *profit* or *interest*, ἔργον [χρημάτων] *interest* or *profit* on money, Is.11.42, cf. D.27.10. IV. special phrases: 1. ἔργον ἐστί, a. c. gen. pers., it is his *business*, his *proper work*, ἀνδρῶν τόδ' ἐστὶν ἔ. A.*Ch.*673; ὅπερ ἐστὶν ἔ. ἀγαθοῦ πολίτου Pl.*Grg.*517c; of things, φραδέος νόου ἔργα τέτυκται it is *a matter* (which calls) for a wary mind, Il.24.354; *function*, ἅπερ νεῶν ἄμεινον πλεουσῶν ἔργα ἐστίν Th.2.89; οὐ θερμότητος ἔργον ψύχειν Pl.*R.*335d; τοῦτο ἑκάστου ἔ. ὃ ἂν ἢ μόνον τι ἢ κάλλιστα τῶν ἄλλων ἀπεργάζηται ib.353a; ἔργα τοῦ ἐγκεφάλου *functions*, Gal.16.518: c. dat. pers., οἷς τοῦτο ἔ. ἦν X.*Cyr.*4.5.36, cf. 6.3.27: with the possessive Pron., σὸν ἔ. [ἐστί] c. inf., A.*Pr.*635; ἐμὸν τόδ' ἔ. κρῖναι Id.*Eu.* 734; σὸν ἔ., θῦε θεοῖς Ar.*Av.*862; ὑμέτερον ἐντεῦθεν ἔ. Id.*Pax*426: with Art., νῦν ἡμέτερον τὸ ἔ. Hdt.5.1. b. c. gen. rei, *there is need* of.., τί δῆτα τόξων ἔ.; E.*Alc.*39; πολλῆς φυλακῆς ἔ. [ἐστί] Pl.*R.* 537d: esp. with neg., οὐδὲν.. ὀδόντων ἔ. ἐστ' Ar.*Pax*1310; οὐ δόλου νῦν ἔ. Id.*Pl.*1158, cf. E.*Hipp.*911: c. dat. pers., ἐπέδρης μὴ εἶναι ἔ. τῇ στρατιῇ Hdt.1.17: with Art., οὐκ ἂν μακρῶν λόγων ἡμῖν τόδ' εἴη τοὔργον S.*El.*1373: with a part. added, οὐδὲν ἦν ἔ. αὐτοῦ κατατεινόντος Plu.*Publ.*13: also c. inf., οὐδὲν ἔ. ἑστάναι there is no *use in* standing still, Ar.*Lys.*424, cf. *Av.*1308; οὐδὲν ἔ. ταῦτα θρηνεῖσθαι S. *Aj.*852, cf. 12. c. c. inf., *it is hard work*, *difficult* to do, πολὺ ἔ. ἂν εἴη διεξελθεῖν X.*Mem.*4.6.1; πολὺ ἔ. ἦν τῷ νομοθέτῃ πάντα γράφειν Lys.10.7; ἔ. ἐστὶν εἰ ἐροῦμεν D.24.51; ἔ. εὑρεῖν πρόφασιν Men.76; also μέγα ἔ. ταῖς.. ἐπιθυμίαις καλῶς χρῆσθαι Pl.*Smp.*187e; χαλεπὸν ἔ. διαιρεῖν Ar.*Ra.*1100 (lyr.): also in gen., πλείονος ἔ. ἐστὶ.. μαθεῖν Pl. *Euthphr.*14b: rarely with a part., οὐδὲν ἔ. μαχομένῳ Philippid.15.3; ἔ. [ἐστί] c. acc. et inf., *it can scarcely happen* that.., ἔ. ἅμα πάντας ὀργισθῆναι καὶ ἁμαρτεῖν Arist.*Pol.*1286ᵃ35. 2. ἔργον παρασχεῖν τινί give one *trouble*, Ar.*Nu.*523, cf. *AP*9.161 (Marc. Arg., punning on Hesiod's Ἔργα); ἔργον ἔχειν take *trouble*, c. part., X.*Cyr.*8.4.6; c. inf., Id.*Mem.*2.10.6. 3. ἔ. γίγνεσθαι τῆς νόσου to be its *victim*, Anon.ap.Suid. s.v. ἄτολμοι; κτεινόμενος ὑμέτερον ἔ. εἰμί Plu.*Eum.* 17; τῆς ὑμετέρας γέγονεν ἔ. ὀλιγωρίας Luc.*Dem.Enc.*29. 4. ἔ. ποιεῖσθαί τι to make a matter *one's business*, *attend to* it, Pl.*Phdr.* 232a, X.*Hier.*9.10; so ἐν ἔργῳ τίθεσθαι Ael.*VH*4.15. V. = ἐργασία III, τὸ ἔ. βαφέων *CIG*3498 (Thyatira).

ἐργο-ποιΐα, ἡ, *method*, *proceeding*, Ath.Mech.38.2. II. *manufacture*, *Gloss.* **-πονέομαι**, *work hard*, Artem.3.6. **-πόνος**, ὁ, *husbandman*, *AP*11.9 (Leon.); *hunter*, Opp.*C.*1.148; *fisher*, Nic. *Th.*831; ἐ. ἐλέφαντος *a worker in*.., Man.1.298: as Adj., *laborious*, Coluth.195 (fem.); in bad sense (cf. πόνηρος, πανοῦργος), Rhetor. in *Cat.Cod.Astr.*7.198. **-στόλος**, ον, = ἐργεπιστάτης, Charito 4.2, *CIG*3700 (Cyzicus). **-τεχνίτης** [ῐ], ου, ὁ, *skilled craftsman*, *expert*, Orph.*Fr.*180, Iamb.*Myst.*9.2 (pl.).

ἐργότρυς, ὁ, (ὀτρύνω) = ἐργεπείκτης, Hsch.

ἐργο-φόρος, ον, *worker* bee, Ael.*NA*5.42. **-χειρον**, τό, *manual labour*, *PMasp.*23.20 (vi A.D.), *PLond.*4.1708.56 (vi A.D.), etc.

ἐργύλον· στάτην (Ion.), Hsch.

ἔργω, Ep. and Ion., and **ἐέργω**, Ep. for Att. **εἴργω** (or **εἵργω**, v. infr.), which occurs once in Hom., τῆλέ με εἴργουσι ψυχαί Il.23.72 (s.v.l.): impf. εἶργον Th.1.106, (ἐξ-) Hdt.5.22: fut. ἔρξω (ξυν-) S. *Aj.*593, εἴρξω or εἵρξω Id.*Ph.*1407, E.*El.*1255, Th.4.9: aor. 1 ἔρξα Od. 14.411, v.l. for εἶρξα in Hdt.3.136, εἶρξα E.*Ba.*443, Philipp.ap.D.12. 2, etc.: aor. 2 εἰργάθον (v. ἐργαθεῖν):—Med. and Pass., pres., Il.17. 571, Hdt.5.57, etc.: fut. ἔρξομαι S.*OT*890 (lyr.), εἴρξομαι X.*An.*6.6.16, Aeschin.3.122: aor. 1 ἔρχθην Il.21.282, Hp.*Mul.*1.4, εἴρχθην Lycurg. 112, D.59.66: pf. ἔργμαι *h.Merc.*123, Ep. 3 pl. ἔρχαται Od.10.283; εἶργμαι Ar.*Av.*1085, εἷργμαι X.*HG*5.2.31; Ep. part. ἐεργμένος Il.5. 89: plpf., Ep. 3 pl. ἔρχατο 17.354, ἐέρχατο Od.10.241. (εἵργω, = *shut in*, εἴργω, = *shut out*, acc. to Eust.1387.3; cf. the compds. ἀπείργω, καθείργω, but ἄφ-ερκτος occurs A.*Ch.*446 (lyr.); the aspirate was always used in Att. acc. to Tz. in *An.Ox.*3.352, but v. κατείργω: at Heraclea it occurs in ἀφ-, ἐφ-, and συν-hέργω (qq.v.): ϝεργ-, cf. Skt. *vrajás* 'enclosure', and perh. Lat. *urgeo*; ἐ- is prothetic in Ep. ἐ-ϝέργω):—*bar one's way* either *by shutting in* or *shutting out*: I. *shut in*, *shut up*, ἐρχθέντ' ἐν ποταμῷ Il.21.282; *pen*, ἐνὶ Κίρκης ἔρχαται ὥς τε σύες Od.10.283; [ἄρνες] διακεκριμέναι ἕκασται ἔρχατο 9.221; τὰς μὲν ἄρα ἔρξαν κατὰ ἤθεα κοιμηθῆναι 14.411; ὅσσους Ἑλλήσποντος ἐντὸς ἐέργει *encloses*, Il.2.845 (so ἔνδον εἵρξας Ar.*Ach.*330); ἂψ ἐπὶ νῆας ἔεργε [φάλαγγας] *drove* them to the ships *and shut* them *up* there, Il. 16.395, cf. 12.219, Th.1.106; *shut up*, θανόντων ψυχάς Thgn.710; esp. in prison, Hdt.3.136, Philipp.ap.D.12.2, Lycurg.112 (Pass.), D.59. 66, etc.; of things, θύραι δόμον ἐντὸς ἔεργον Od.7.88; σύμπαντα ἐντὸς μιᾶς ὁμοιότητος ἔρξας *having included*.., Pl.*Plt.*285b:—Pass., σάκεσσι γὰρ ἔρχατο πάντῃ *were fenced in*, *secured*, Il.17.354; γέφυραι ἐεργμέναι *well-secured*, *strong-built*, *compact*, 5.89: Medic., of discharges, *to be retained*, Hp.*Mul.*1.4, 8; ἐὰν ἡ τοῦ βλεφάρου θρὶξ εἱρχθῇ if the eyelash *is caught* (in the loop), Paul.Aeg.6.13 (fort. εἰρθῇ, vel ἐρθῇ, cf. ἐρτός). II. *shut out*, Il.23.72, Th.4.9, etc.; ἀμφὶς ἐέργει Il.13.706 (v. ἀμφίς A.II); κλῄθροις ἂν εἰργοίμεσθα E.*Hel.*288. 2. c. gen., *shut out* or *keep away from*, ὡς ὅτε μήτηρ παιδὸς ἐέργῃ μυῖαν Il.4.131, cf. Od.12.219; τῶν μὲν πάμπαν ἔεργε.. θυμὸν Hes.*Op.*335, cf. Parm.1.33; ἔργειν τινὰ σιτίων Hdt.3.48:—freq. in Pass., [μυῖα] ἐργομένη χροός Il. 17.571; εἴργεσθαι ἱερῶν, νομίμων, ἀγορᾶς, *to be excluded from participation in*.., Isoc.4.157, Antipho 6.36, Lys.6.24; but εἰργόμενον θανάτου καὶ τοῦ ἀνάπηρον ποιῆσαι *short of*, *excluding* death and maiming, Aeschin.1.183: with Preps., ἔ. [βέλος] ἀπὸ χροὸς Il.4.130; τινα ἀπὸ τιμῆς Od.11.503; [ἀηδὼν] ἀπὸ χλωρῶν πετάλων ἐργομένα A.*Supp.*63 (lyr.); ἐκ τῶν Ἑλληνίδων πόλεων X.*An.*6.6.16, etc.: rarely c. dat. pers., εἴργειν.. μητρὶ πολέμιον δόρυ *to keep* it *off* from her, A.*Th.*416:—Med., *keep oneself*, *abstain*, *withdraw from*, c. gen., πόλιος Hdt.4.164; τῶν ἀσέπτων ἔρξεται S.*OT*890 (lyr.); γελώτων Pl.*Lg.*732c, etc.; ἔργετο [τοῦ ἄλσεος] he *kept away from* it, i.e. *spared* it, Hdt.7.197. 3. *hinder*, *prevent from* doing, abs., Thgn.686, Pl.*Lg.*784c: c. dupl. acc., ἀλλ' ἡμᾶς τουτό γε μηδὲν.. εἴρξῃ Id.*Sph.*242a, cf. Ar.*V.*334 (lyr.):— Pass., οὐδὲν εἴργεται nothing *is barred*, i.e. all things are permitted, S.*Tr.*344; εἴργου *stop! cease!* Id.*OC*836. b. c. inf., mostly with μή or μὴ οὐ added, οὐ νὺξ ἔργει μὴ οὐ κατανύσαι Hdt.8.98; εἴργει τόνδε μὴ θνήσκειν νόμος E.*Heracl.*963, cf. A.*Ag.*1027 (lyr.): c. inf. only, κακὸν δὲ ποῖον εἶργε τοῦτ' ἐξειδέναι; S.*OT*129; εἴρξω πελάζειν Id.*Ph.*1407 (troch.); οὐδὲν εἴργει.. τελειοῦσθαι τάδε Id.*Tr.*1257: with the Art., εἰργαθεῖν τὸ μὴ οὐχ ἑλεῖν E.*Ph.*1175; also εἴργ. ὥστε.. or ὥστε μή.., c. inf., X.*HG*7.2.13, *An.*3.3.

***ἔργω**, *do work*, v. ἔρδω.

ἐργώδης, ες, *difficult*, *troublesome*, ἐ. φαρμακεύεσθαι *hard* to purge, Hp.*Aph.*2.37, cf. X.*Mem.*2.6.9; ἐ. αἱ φαρμακεῖαι Hp.*Aph.*4.5; of persons, Thphr.*Char.*6.10; θυγάτηρ κτῆμ' ἐστὶν ἐργῶδες πατρί Men. 60; πολέμιος Plu.*Marc.*30; ἐργῶδές [ἐστιν] c. inf., Arist.*EN*1171ᵃ5, Philippid.9.9, cf. Sosip.1.24: Comp. -έστερον Arist.*EN*1102ᵃ25, Luc.*Halc.*4: Sup. -έστατος X.*Mem.*1.3.6. Adv. -δῶς *with difficulty*, ὑγιάζεται Hp.*Aph.*6.6, cf. Thphr.*HP*9.16.5, Ph.*Bel.*84.12.

ἐργων-έω, *contract for a work*, *Hermes* 17.4 (Delos), *IG*11(2).150*A* 14 (ibid., iii B.C.), 7.3073.92 (Lebad., ii B.C.). **-ης**, ου, ὁ, (ὠνέομαι) *a contractor*, *Hermes* 17.4 (Delos), *IG*11(2).150*A* 9 (ibid., iii B.C.), 7.3073.4 (Lebad., ii B.C.), *SIG*495.135 (Olbia, iii B.C.): Dor. -ας *IG* 4.1508 (Epid., iii B.C.). **-ία**, ἡ, = ἐργολαβία, Plb.6.17.5, *IG*5(2).6. 42 (Tegea, iv B.C.), 7.3073.25 (Lebad., ii B.C.).

ἔρδω, impf. ἔρδον Il.11.707, Ion. ἔρδεσκον 9.540, Hdt.7.33: fut.

ἔρξω Od.11.80, Hes.*Op.*327, A.*Pers.*1059(lyr.), S.*Ph.*1406(troch.): aor. ἔρξα Od.8.490, Hdt.5.65; and so in A.*Th.*923 (but ἦρξεν *Ag.*1529 codd.): pf. ἔοργα Il.5.175, etc.; 3 pl. ἔοργαν Batr.179: plpf. ἐώργειν, 3 sg. ἐώργει Od.4.693, 14.289, ἐόργεε Hdt.1.127: pf. part. Pass. ἐργμένος B.12.207: aor. 1 part. Pass. ἐρχθείς ib.65. (Aspirated acc. to Sch.Ar.*Ach.*329, and so freq. in codd. of Hom., cf. Thgn.690, Epic. ap.Pl.*Euthphr.*12a: fr. Ϝέργ-yω (through Ϝέρζδω), cf. ἔργον: impf. ἔερδον Sol.ap.Arist.*Ath.*12.3: aor. 1 ἐϜέρξα *Inscr.Cypr.*146 H.; written βέρδηι in *Schwyzer* 183 (Crete, iii/ii B.C.), cf. Ϝηρόντων (imper.) *GDI*5013 ii 10, Ϝήροντι ib.4987 *a* 2):—poet. and Ion. Verb, *do*, ὅσσ' ἔρξαν τ' ἔπαθόν τε Od.8.490; ἔρξον ὅπως ἐθέλεις Il.4.37; ἔρξον ὅπῃ.. νόος ἔπλετο 22.185; εἰ δέ κεν ὣς ἔρξῃς 2.364; εὖ ἔρξαντα 5.650, cf. *Inscr.Cypr.* l.c.; οὔτε εὖ ἔρδων οὔτε κακῶς Thgn.368; αἴ τις τούτων τι Ϝέρκσαι *Leg.Gort.*10.30; opp. πάσχω, ἔρξαι τε καὶ παθεῖν Pi.*P.*8.6; παθεῖν ἔρξαντες prob. in A.*Ag.*1658 (troch.): freq. c. acc., ἔ. ἔργα βίαια, μέγα ἔργον, Od.2.236, 19.92; ἔ. φίλα, ἐσθλά, πολλά, etc., 15.360, Il.2.272, 9.320, etc.: sts. c. dat. pers., ὃς δὴ πολλὰ κάκ' ἀνθρώποισιν ἐώργει Od.14.289; μὴ Νυκτὶ.. ἀποθύμια ἔρδοι Il.14.261, cf. Mosch.4.93 codd.: more freq. c. dupl. acc., ὅ με πρότερος κάκ' ἔοργε Il.3.351; κακὰ πολλὰ ἔοργε Τρῶας 5.175, cf. 9.540, A.*Pers.*236 (troch.), etc.; ἀνήκεστον πάθος ἔ. τινά Hdt.1.137; also εὖ ἔ. τινά Thgn.105,955, Semon.7.80, etc.; κακῶς Hdt.6.88, E.*Med.*1302: without an Adv., ἔ. τινά *to do* one *harm*, S.*Ph.*683 (lyr.): less freq. with Subst. alone as object, ἔ. πήματα A.*Pers.*786; προσωφέλησιν S.*Ph.* 1406 (troch.); ἔρδοι τις ἣν ἕκαστος εἰδείη τέχνην *let him practise*.., Ar.*V.*1431; also φάρμακα ταῦτ' ἔρδοισα χερείονα μήτε τι Κίρκας Theoc.2.15:—Pass., τὸ καλῶς ἐργμένον B.12.207; εὖ ἐρχθέντος ib.65. 2. *offer* a sacrifice (cf. ῥέζω), not in pf. and plpf.; ἔρδομεν ἀθανάτοισι τεληέσσας ἑκατόμβας Il.2.306; ἔ. ἱερὰ καλά Hes.*Th.*417; σφάγια θεοῖσιν ἔρδειν A.*Th.*231; Διὶ θυσίας Hdt.1.131:—Pass., θυσίη ἐρδομένη ὧδε Id.4.60; θανόντεσσιν ἐρδόμενον μέρος Pi.*O.*8.78: abs., *offer sacrifice*, ἔρδειν.. ἱεροῖς ἐπὶ βωμοῖς Hes.*Op.*136, cf. Porph.*Abst.*2.59.—Found in late Ion. Prose, Aret.*CA*2.3. (ῥέζω is another form of this verb.)

ἐρέα, ἡ, *wool*, = ἔριον, Callix.2, Str.4.4.3, Isig.ap.Sotion.p.183 W.; but ἐρεῶν *PHib.*1.115.20 (iii B.C.), *PCair.Zen.*176.322 (iii B.C.) may be gen. pl. of ἐρεοῦς.

ἐρέας, v. *ἐρής.

ἐρεβεννός, ή, όν, Ep. Adj., (Ἔρεβος) *dark, gloomy*, νύξ Il.8.488, Hes.*Op.*17, etc.; ἀήρ Il.5.864; νέφεα 22.309. (Never in Od.; cf. ἐρεμνός.)

Ἐρέβεσφιν, Ἐρέβευσφιν, v. Ἔρεβος.

ἐρεβίνθ-ειος, ον, *of the* ἐρέβινθος *kind*, Διόνυσος ἐ., proverb of any *worthless* article, Zen.3.83. **-η**, ἡ, = ἐρέβινθος, *EM*569.14. **-ιαῖος**, α, ον, *of the size of an* ἐρέβινθος, Dsc.5.137,152. **-ινος**, η, ον, = ἐρεβίνθειος, Hsch., Phot., Suid. **-ιον**, τό, Dim. of ἐρέβινθος, *POxy.*1837.15 (pl., vi A.D.), *Stud.Pal.*20.75. **-οπώλης**, *cicerarius*, Gloss. **-ος** (proparox.), ὁ, *chick-pea, Cicer arietinum*, κύαμοι ἢ ἐ. Il.13.589, cf. Pl.*R.*372c; eaten as dessert, Xenoph.22.3, Ar.*Pax* 1136, Crobyl.9, etc.; χρύσειοι ἐ. Sapph.30; κριὸς ἐ., of a special variety, Sophil.8, cf. Thphr.*HP*8.5.1. II. metaph., of the *membrum virile*, Ar.*Ach.*801, *Ra.*545 (lyr.); cf. κριθή IV. (Cf. ὄροβος, Lat. *ervum*.) **-οφόρος**, ον, *bearing chick-pea*, [γῆ] *PLond.ined.*2361 (iii B.C.). **-ώδης**, ες, *like chick-peas*, φύλλον Thphr.*HP*6.5.3.

ἐρεβοδῖφάω, *grope about in Erebos*, ὑπὸ τὸν Τάρταρον Ar.*Nu.*192.

ἐρεβόθεν, *from nether gloom*, E.*Or.*178.

Ἔρεβος, τό: Att. gen. Ἐρέβους Ar.*Av.*694, Ion. Ἐρέβευς Il.8.368, Od.11.37, Ἐρέβεσφιν or Ἐρέβευσφιν, Hes.*Th.*669, *h.Cer.*349, ἐξ Ἐρεβ- Il.9.572: no dat. or pl. occurs:—*Erebos*, a place of nether darkness, forming a passage from Earth to Hades, Il.16.327, Od.10.528, al., Hes.*Th.*515, etc.; rare in Prose, Pl.*Ax.*371e, Plu.2.953a, 1130d: metaph., ἔ. ὕφαλον *the darkness* of the deep, S.*Ant.*589 (lyr.); of a riddle, ἀξυνέτοις ἔ. *AP*7.429 (Alc.). II. personified, Hes.*Th.*125. (Skt. *rájas*, Goth. *riqis*, ONorse *røkkr* 'darkness'.)

Ἐρεβόσδε, Adv. *to* or *into Erebos*, Od.20.356.

Ἐρεβοφοῖτις, ἡ, *she that walks in Erebos*, Sch.Il.19.87.

ἐρεβ-ώδης, ες, *dark as Erebos*, θάλασσα *Lyr.Adesp.*132 (= *Trag. Adesp.*377), cf. Apollod.1.1.2, Ph.Bybl.ap.Eus.*PE*1.10. **-ῶπις**, ιδος, ἡ, *gloomy-looking*, Orph.*L.*544.

ἐρεγ-μα, ατος, τό, *bruised corn*, Thphr.*CP*4.12.12 (pl.); φακῶν ἐρέγματα Erot. **-μῖνος**, η, ον, *made of bruised beans*, ἄλευρον Dsc.3.80.3, Orib.4.8.7. **-μός**, ὁ, = ἔρεγμα, Gal.6.533, Archig.ap.eund.12.812, *PTeb.*9.10 (ii B.C.), *PHolm.*23.37,39; = ὁ δίχα διῃρημένος κύαμος, Erot. II. = ἐρυγμός, *Mim.Oxy.*413.19, Moer.p.158 P., *EM*371.20.

ἐρεείνω, (ἐρέω A) *ask, inquire*: c. acc. pers., *ask of* one, *question* him, Od.7.31, 5.85, *h.Merc.*487, etc.: c. acc. rei, *ask about* a thing, Il.6.145, etc.: c. dupl. acc., ἐ. τινά τι Od.1.220, 4.137; ἐ. ἀμφὶ ξείνῳ *ask* about one, 24.262:—Med., ἐρεείνετο μύθῳ 17.305; *search after*, ἐρεείνειν τινά Batr.52. 2. *visit* a place, D.P.713. 3. *ask for*, τι *h.Merc.*533. II. *say, speak*, ib.313.—Ep. word, used in hex. by Theopomp.Com.30; ἐὰν μὴ μεῖζον ἅτερος θατέρου ἐρεείνῃ, Spartan saying in Plu.2.228e codd. (ἐρατέημεν Id.*Lyc.*19 codd.: leg. μέσδων.. ἐρᾶτε ἦμεν.)

Ἐρεθειμιάζω, v. Ἐρεθίμιος.

ἐρεθίζω, Ep. inf. -ιζέμεν Il.4.5: impf. ἠρέθιζον S.*Ant.*965 (lyr.), Ep. ἐρ- Il.5.419: fut. -ίσω Gal.1.385, -ιῶ Hp.*Mochl.*2, Plb.13.4.2: aor. 1 ἠρέθισα D.H.3.72; poet. ἐρ- A.*Pr.*183 (lyr.), inf. ἐρεθίξαι *AP*12.37 (Diosc.): pf. ἠρέθικα Aeschin.2.37:—Pass., aor. 1 ἠρεθίσθην, part. ἐρεθισθείς Hdt.6.40, D.H.4.57: pf. ἠρέθισμαι Hp. (v. infr.), etc.: (ἐρέθω):—*rouse to anger, rouse to fight*, Il.1.32; κερτομίοις ἐπέεσσι 5.419; κύνας τ' ἄνδρας τε, of a lion, 17.658; ἐ. τοὺς Πέρσας Hdt.3.146; φιλαύλους τ' ἠρ. Μούσας S.*Ant.*965 (lyr.); ὥσπερ σφηκιὰν ἐ. τινά Ar.*Lys.*475; χεῖρον.. ἐρεθίσαι γραῦν ἢ κύνα Men.802; πὺξ ἐ. *challenge to* a boxing-match, Theoc.22.2; *provoke to curiosity*, μητέρα σήν Od.19.45: generally, *excite, chafe*, φρένας ἐ. φόβος A.*Pr.*183 (lyr.); of physical *irritation*, Hp.*Mochl.*2; βῆχες βραχέα -ουσαι *causing* brief *irritation*, Id.*Aph.*4.54: metaph., ἐ. πλανάτας χοροῖσιν E.*Ba.*148 (lyr.); ἐ. μάγαδιν *to touch* it, Telest.4; φλόγα Hld.8.9; τὸ φονικὸν καὶ θηριῶδες Plu.2.822c; *incite* to rivalry, 2*Ep.Cor.*9.2:—Pass., *to be provoked, excited*, ὑπό τινος Hdt.6.40, cf. Ar.*V.*1104; ἠρεθισμένος *under provocation*, Men.574; ὀργῇ χεῖρας -ισμένας Euphro 8.3; of love, τοῖς νέοισιν -ισμένος Timocl.30; of fire, φέψαλος.. -όμενος.. ῥιπίδι Ar.*Ach.*669 (lyr.); αἰθὴρ -έσθω βροντῇ A.*Pr.*1045 (anap.); πνεῦμα ἠρεθισμένον, of one who has run till he is out of breath, E.*Med.*1119; ἕλκος ἠρεθισμένον *irritated*, Hp.*Fract.*27, cf. 31, Plb.1.81.6; ὀσμῇ -ισμένη Eub.75.9; ἐπὶ τὴν ὕβριν ἠρεθίσθαι Luc.*Am.*22. II. abs., *to be quarrelsome* or *perverse*, Ph.1.359.

Ἐρεθίμιος, ὁ, epith. of Apollo in Rhodes, *SIG*724 (i B.C.):—hence **Ἐρεθίμια**, τά, his festival, prob. in *IG*12(1).735: **Ἐρεθειμιάζω**, *belong to a guild of worshippers of* Ἀ.Ἐ., Inscrr. in *Hermes* 61.477; cf. Ἐρεθύμιος, Ἐρυθίβιος, Ἐριδίμιος.

ἐρέθ-ισμα, ατος, τό, *provocation*, App.*Sam.*3; χορῶν ἐ. Ar.*Nu.*312 (pl.); συμποσίων ἐ., of Anacreon, Critias 1 D.; φύσας ἄγειν κάτω -ίσμασι, i.e. by purging, Aret.*CA*2.5. **-ισμός**, ὁ, *irritation*, Hp.*Acut.*43; ἐ. κνησμώδης Thphr.*Sud.*16; ῥῖγος καὶ ἐ. Lxx *De.*28.22, *IG*12(9).1179: in pl., *stimulating treatment*, Hp.*Aph.*1.20; -ισμοὶ πρὸς ἀφροδίσια Porph.*Abst.*1.47. II. *provocation*, Phld.*Ir.*p.54 W. (pl.), D.H.10.33. 2. *rebelliousness*, Lxx *De.*31.27; *perverseness*, Ph.1.359. **-ιστέον**, *one must irritate*, Pl.*Ti.*89b; *one must stimulate* bowel-action, Gal.6.413, Aët.4.20, Paul.Aeg.1.34. **-ιστής**, οῦ, ὁ, *rebellious* or *perverse person*, Lxx *De.*21.18, Ph.1.359, Hsch. s.v. ἔριθος. **-ιστικός**, ή, όν, *of* or *for irritation*, σημεῖον Hp.*Acut.*48: c. gen., *provocative*, ὀρέξεως Diph.Siph.ap.Ath.3.120e. Adv. -κῶς Sch.Il.16.36. **-ιστός**, ή, όν, *easily provoked, 'touchy'*, Phld.*Lib.*p.42 O.

Ἐρεθύμιος, epith. of Apollo in Lycia: also **Ἐρεθύμια**, τά, festival in his honour, Hsch.; cf. Ἐρεθίμιος.

ἐρέθω, impf. ἤρεθον Mosch.3.84, Theoc. (v. infr.), Ep. ἐρέθεσκον A.R.3.618, 1103:—poet. form of ἐρεθίζω, in Il. *stir to anger, provoke*, μή μ' ἔρεθε, σχετλίη 3.414; ὅτ' ἄν μ' ἐρέθῃσιν ὀνειδείοις ἐπέεσσιν 1.519; in Od. of all sources of *disquiet*, ὀδυνάων.., αἵ μ' ἐρέθουσι 4.813; μελεδῶναι 19.517: c. inf., *h.Hom.*8.14: c. acc. rei, ἤρεθον ᾠδάν they *raised* a song, Theoc.21.21 codd.; ἐ. ἐρωμανίην *increase* it, *AP*5.255 (Paul. Sil.). II. *explore, search*, ἰλυούς v.l. for ἐρέοντες in Nic.*Th.*143.

ἐρειγμός, ὁ, v.l. for ἐρεγμός in Gal.6.533.

ἐρείδω, Ep. impf. ἔρειδον Il.13.131: fut. ἐρείσω Call.*Del.*234, Aristid.*Or.*17(15).10 codd.: aor. 1 ἤρεισα S.*Ant.*1236, Pl.*Phdr.*254e, *Ti.*91e; Boeot. 3 sg. εἴρισε Corinn.*Supp.*1.32; Ep. ἔρεισα (ἐπ-) Il.7.269: pf. ἤρεικα (συν-) Hp.*Morb.Sacr.*7, (προσ-) Plb.5.60.8; but ἐρήρεικα Dsc.*Eup.*1.84, (προσ-) Plu.*Aem.*19:—Med., fut. ἐρείσομαι (ἀπ-) Arist.*Pr.*885b29, Plb.15.25.25: aor. 1 ἠρεισάμην Hes.*Sc.*362, (ἀπ-) Pl.*R.*508d; Ep. ἐρ- Il.5.309:—Pass., 3 fut. ἐρηρείσεται Hp.*Mul.*2.133: Ep. aor. 1 ἐρείσθην Il.7.145: pf. ἐρήρεισμαι Hdt.4.152, Hp.*Art.*78 (but 2 sg. ἠρήρεισθα Archil.94 is from ἀραρίσκω); also ἤρεισμαι Ti.Locr.98e (ἐρήρ- ib.97e), D.S.4.12, Paus.6.25.5; Ion. 3 pl. pf. ἐρηρέδαται Il.23.284, 329, Ep. ἐρήρειντα A.R.2.320: plpf. ἠρήρειστο Il.4.136; 3 pl. ἐρηρέδατο Od.7.95, ἠρήρειντο A.R.3.1398:—Hom. uses the augm. only in ἠρήρειστο, Hes.*Sc.*362 in ἠρείσατο.—Ep., Ion., and poet. Verb, also found in Pl. and later Prose:—*cause to lean, prop*, δόρυ.. πρὸς τεῖχος ἐρείσας Il.22.112; θρόνον πρὸς κίονα μακρὸν ἐρείσας Od.8.66; πύργῳ ἔπι προὔχοντι.. ἀσπίδ' ἐρείσας Il.22.97; [νέκυας] ἀλλήλοισιν ἐ. *piling* them *against* each other, Od.22.450; ἐρείσατε.. πλευρὸν ἀμφιδέξιον S.*OC*1112; πρὸς στέρν' ἐρείσας (sc. τοὺς παῖδας) E.*HF*1362, cf. *Ba.*684; τὰ ἰσχία πρὸς τὴν γῆν Pl.*Phdr.*254e; ἐ. τινὰ εἰς ἕδραν E.*Heracl.*603; τὰς κεφαλὰς εἰς γῆν Pl.*Ti.*91e; ἐς χεῖρας ἐ. τι Theoc.7.104; ἐ. τὴν κεφαλὴν ἐπὶ γῆς Pl.*Ti.*43e; τὸ γόνυ κατὰ τοῦ ἰσχίου Plu.*Flam.*20; ῥόῳ ἔνι κάλπιν A.R.1.1234: generally, *fix firmly, plant*, ἄγκυραν χθονί Pi.*P.*10.51; εἰς γῆν ἐ. ὄμμα E.*IA*1123, cf. Aristid.*Or.*17(15).10; ἐπὶ χθονὸς ὄμματ' A.R.1.784; ἐ. πόδας ἐς βένθος *plant* the foot *firm*, ib.1010: metaph., ἐ. τὰν γνώμαν *fix* one's mind *firmly* on a thing, Theoc.21.61. 2. *prop up, support, stay*, ἀσπὶς ἄρ' ἀσπίδ' ἔρειδε, κόρυς κόρυν, ἀνέρα δ' ἀνήρ, of close ranks of men-at-arms, Il.13.131; ἐπ' ἀσπίδος ἀσπίδ' ἔρεισον Tyrt.11.31; πέλτην ἐρεῖσαι E.*Rh.*487; κίον' οὐρανοῦ τε καὶ χθονὸς ὤμοιν ἐ. A.*Pr.*352. 3. *press hard, attack*, τινα Pi.*O.*9.32: sens. obsc., ἐ. γυναῖκα Ar.*Ec.*616, *Fr.*74. 4. *push, thrust*, ὅπῃ κέ τις.. ἐρείδῃ Emp.12.3; ἔπη.. ἤρειδε κατὰ τῶν ἱππέων *hurled forth*.., Ar.*Eq.*627; ὁ χορὸς ἤρειδεν ὁρμαθοὺς μελῶν τέτταρας Id.*Ra.*914:—Med., ἔπος πρὸς ἔπος ἠρειδόμεσθ' Id.*Nu.*1375. 5. *infix, plant in*, πλευραῖς ἔγχος S.*Ant.*1236; ἀνταίαν πληγήν *inflict* it, E.*Andr.*844 (lyr.):—Pass., ἄλγημα ἐρηρεισμένον *fixed* pain, Gal.8.385. 6. *press down, depress*, πλάστιγγα τοῦ βίου S.*Fr.*576.5. 7. of wagers or matches, *match, set* one pledge *against* another, Theoc.5.24. II. intr., *press hard*, ἀμφ' αὐτῷ πελεμίξαι ἐρείδοντες βελέεσσιν Il.16.108; εἴς τινα Ar.*Nu.*558; νέφος ἐ. ἐπὶ γῆν Plu.*Num.*2; πνεῦμα κατὰ τῆς σχεδίας Id.*Crass.*19; of an illness or pain, *settle upon* a particular part, νόσος ὁμότοιχος ἐ. A.*Ag.*1004 (lyr.), cf. Ruf.ap.Orib.45.30.27, Gal.11.61; *exert pressure*: hence, *rest*, ἐπὶ τὸ ἔδαφος Hero *Aut.*2.7. 2. *set to work, fall to*, esp. of eating, ἔρειδε Ar.*Pax* 31, cf. 25 (where, acc. to Sch., it is metaph. from rowers); ἐρείδετον Id.*Fr.*493. 3. *become fixed*, πρῷρα ἐρείσασα *Act.Ap.*27.

41. III. Med. and Pass., *prop oneself, lean upon*, τῷ ὅ γ' ἐρεισάμενος (sc. σκήπτρῳ) Il.2.109; ἔγχει ἐ. 14.38; ἐπὶ μελίης.. ἐρεισθεὶς 22.225: c. gen., ἐρείσατο χειρὶ παχείῃ γαίης *leant* with his hand *against* the earth, 5.309: abs., ἐρεισάμενος βάλε *having planted himself firm, taken a firm stand*, 12.457, cf. 16.736; of one fallen, ὁ δ' ὕπτιος οὔδει ἐρείσθη 7.145, 11.144; οὔδεϊ.. σφι χαῖται ἐρηρέδαται their hair *rests on* the ground, 23.284; γόνατος κονίαισιν ἐρειδομένου *set, planted* in.., A.*Ag.*64 (anap.); τοῖσι γούνασι ἐρηρεισμένοι Hdt.4.152; ταῖς χερσὶν ἐπὶ δόρατι ἠρεισμένος Paus.6.25.5, cf. Corn.*ND*9; *press closely, be tight*, of bandages, Hp.*Off.*8; τοὺς ὀδόντας ἐρήρεισται *has* her teeth *clenched*, Hp.ap.Erot. (ξυνερήρ. codd. Hp.). 2. *to be fixed firm, planted*, ἔγχος διὰ θώρηκος ἠρήρειστο *had been fixed*, Il.3.358, etc.; λᾶε ἐρηρέδαται *stand firmly fixed*, 23.329; θρόνοι περὶ τοῖχον ἐρηρέδατ' Od.7.95; ἁ γᾶ ἐρήρεισται ἐπὶ τᾶς αὐτᾶς ῥοπᾶς Ti.Locr.97e: abs., δίκας ἐρείδεται πυθμήν *is set firm*, A.*Ch.*646 (lyr.); opp. πλανᾶσθαι, Arist.*GA*720^{a}12; ἐρηρεικός, of a bone *stuck* in the throat, Dsc.*Eup.*1.84. 3. ἐρείδεσθαι ναυαγίαις *to be driven ashore* in shipwreck, Pi.*I.*1.36. IV. Med., 1. in recipr. sense, *struggle* one with another, Il.23.735 (v.l. ἐρίζεσθον). 2. c. acc., *support* or *set firmly for oneself*, πλησίον ἠρείσαντο καρήατα Simon.172; βάκτρῳ δ' ἐρείδου.. στίβον E.*Ion* 743; ἐπὶ γαῖαν ἴχνος *AP*12.84 (Mel.); ἐπὶ τοίχῳ λίθον Theoc.23.49; ἐπὶ χειρὶ παρειήν A.R.3.1160; χεῖρας σκηπανίῳ *AP*6.83 (Maced.); ἐπὶ σκίπωνος τὸ γῆρας ib.7.457 (Aristo); ἐς πόλον ἐκ γαίης μῆτιν ἐ. *to raise one's* thoughts.., ib.9.782 (Paul. Sil.).

ἐρεικ-αῖον (sc. μέλι), τό, *heather honey*, Plin.*HN*11.41. **-η**, ἡ, *heath, Erica arborea*, A.*Ag.*295, Eup.14.4, Theoc.5.64, Thphr.*HP*1.14.2, Dsc.1.88.—The Inscr. quoted s.v. ἐρεικόεις proves that ἐρείκη is correct; ἐρίκη [ῐ] is the later spelling, v. ἐρείκινος. **-ηρὸν κολλούριον** eye-salve *made with* ἐρείκη, Sever.ap.Aët.7.103. **-ινος**, η, ον, *of* ἐρείκη, ξύλα, φυτά, *BGU*731 ii 8 (ii A.D.), *PStrassb.*29.11 (iii A.D.): written ἐρικ-. **-ιον**, τό, *crumbly pastry*, = ἴτριον, Gal.19.100. II. ἐρίκια, τά, *heath-plants*, *PLond.*3.905 (ii A.D.). **-ίς**, ίδος, ἡ, (ἐρείκω) *pounded barley, groats*, mostly in pl., written ἐρικ-, Gal.19.100:—Cret. **-άς**, ἡ, Hsch. **-ίτας** [ῑ] ἄρτος bread *of groats*, Seleuc.ap.Ath.3.114b (ἐρικ-). **-όεις**, εσσα, εν, *heathery*, pr. n. Ἐρεικοῦς λόφος *Schwyzer*720 (Theb. ad Mycalen, iv B.C.): Ἐρεικοῦσσα, one of the Aeolian Isles (N. of Sicily), Str.6.2.11, St.Byz. s.v., Sch.Ar.*Pl.*586: Ἐρεικώδης Sch.A.R.3.41. **-της**, v. ἐρέκτης. **-τός**, ή, όν, *bruised, pounded*, πυρός (ὥστε δύο ἐξ ἑνὸς γεγονέναι) Paus.Gr.*Fr.*177: also ἐρικτά, τά, *barley-broth*, Hp.*Mul.*2.118, Hsch., Suid. **-ω**, A.*Pers.*1060: aor. 1 imper. ἔρειξον Ar.*Fr.*22, part. ἐρείξας Hp.*Morb.*2.67, *Nat.Mul.*32 (ἐρίξας *Mul.*2.113 codd.): aor. 2 ἤρικον Il.17.295, (δι-) Alex.Aet.3.21 (tm.):—Med., aor. 1 ἐρειξάμην Porph.*Abst.*2.6:—**Pass.**, pf. ἐρήριγμαι (v. infr.):—*rend*, ἤρεικον χθόνα *rent* it with the ploughshare, Hes.*Sc.*287; πέπλον ἐ. A.*Pers.*1060 (lyr.): in this sense Hom. has only Pass., ἐρεικόμενος περὶ δουρί Il.13.441. 2. *bruise, pound*, of pulse, Ar.*Fr.*22, cf. Dieuch.ap.Orib.4.6.4; κάχρυς, ζειάς, Hp.*Morb.*2.67, *Mul.*2.113, *Superf.*34; κριθαὶ ἐρηριγμέναι Id.*Nat.Mul.*103; κύαμοι ἐρηρ. Arist.*HA*595^{b}7; ἐρειχθείσης τῆς κνήκου Diocl.*Fr.*140; ναῦς πρὸς ἀλλήλαισι πνοαὶ ἤρεικον *shattered* them, A.*Ag.*655; of pain, ὀδύναι μιν ἤρικον S.*Fr.*152 (lyr.). II. intr., aor. 2 ἤρῐκον *to be rent* or *shattered*, ἤρικε.. κόρυς περὶ δουρὸς ἀκωκῇ Il.17.295.

ἐρεινοῦς, ῆ, οῦν, *woollen*, *PGrenf.*2.111.13 (v/vi A.D.).

ἔρειξις, εως, ἡ, (ἐρείκω) *pounding, grinding*, Suid. II. = ἐσχισμένη γῆ, *EM*372.17.

ἐρειοί, οἱ, dub. l. in Theoc.15.50.

ἐρειοῦς, v. ἐρεοῦς.

ἐρείπ-ιον, τό, (ἐρείπω) *fallen ruin, wreck*, Arist.*Rh.*1413^{a}6, Aristid.*Or.*49(25).42, Opp.*H.*5.324: generally in pl., ναυτικὰ ἐ. *wreckage*, A.*Ag.*660, *Fr.*274, E.*Hel.*1080; θραύμασίν τ' ἐρειπίων A.*Pers.*425; *ruins*, οἰκημάτων, [τειχέων], Hdt.2.154, 4.124; δόμων E.*Ba.*7; ἐρείπια alone, ἐν τοῖς Κιμωνίοις ἐ. Cratin.151; ἐ. χλανιδίων *fragments* of garments, *Trag.Adesp.*7; πέπλων E.*Tr.*1025; νεκρῶν ἐ. *dead carcasses*, S.*Aj.*308, E.*Fr.*266.—Poet. and later Prose (exc. Arist. and Hdt. ll. cc.), D.H.1.14, *CIG*2700*e* (Mylasa), Paus.10.38.13, Aristid. l.c., etc. **-ιος**, ον, *falling, ruinous*, οἰκία Ph.1.197, cf. 2.436; ἐρείπιος γῆ· ἡ χέρσος, Suid. **-ιώδης**, ες, *ruinous*, *Gloss.* **-ιών**, ῶνος, ὁ, *heap of ruins*, dub. in *CIG*2554.113 (Crete), dub. in Lyd.*Mag.*3.71. **-οτόπιον**, τό, *heap of ruins*, Sch.Opp.*H.*1.54. **-ω**, Ep. impf. ἔρειπον Il.12.258 (v. sub fin.): fut. ἐρείψω S.*OC*1373, X.*Cyr.*7.4.1: aor. 1 ἤρειψα Hdt.1.164, (ἐξ-) Pi.*P.*4.264: intr. in aor. 2 ἤρῐπον (v. infr. II), and pf. ἐρήρῖπα (κατ-) Il.14.55:—**Med.**, aor. 1 ἠρειψάμην (ἀν-) only f.l., v. *ἀνερείπομαι: aor. 2 ἠριπόμην (in pass. sense) *AP*9.152 (Agath.):—**Pass.**, aor. 1 part. ἐρειφθείς S.*Aj.*309; ind. ἠρίφθην Arr.*An.*1.21.4 codd., (κατ-) ib.2.22.7: aor. 2 ἠρίπην [ῐ] (v. infr.): pf. ἐρήριμμαι ib.1.21.6; ἤρειμμαι (κατ-) *IG*12(3).326.20 (Thera, ii A.D.): plpf. ἐρήριπτο (κατ-) Arr.*An.*1.19.2; cj. for ἠρείπετο in Plu.*Brut.*42; Ep. ἐρέριπτο Il.14.15; late Prose ἠρήριπτο Agath.1.10.—Poet. Verb (also in Hdt., X., Plb. and later Prose):—*throw* or *dash down, tear down*, ἔρειπον ἐπάλξεις Il.12.258; ἔρειπε δὲ τεῖχος Ἀχαιῶν 15.361; ὄχθας καπέτοιο.. ποσσὶν ἐρείπων ib.356; προμαχεῶνα ἕνα τοῦ τείχεος ἐ. Hdt.1.164 (v. sub fin.); πόλιν.. ἐρείψεις S.*OC*1373: metaph., λαοὺς διχοστασίαις ἤρειπον B.10.68; [Λαβδακίδας] ἐρείπει θεῶν τις some god *casts* them *down*, S.*Ant.*596 (lyr.):—Pass., *to be thrown down, fall in ruins*, ἐρέριπτο δὲ τεῖχος Ἀχαιῶν Il.14.15; τῆς μὲν ἐρειπομένης (sc. γαίης) Hes.*Th.*704; τῶν πύργων ἐρειπομένων Plb.1.42.10; ἐν δ' ἐρειπίοις νεκρῶν ἐρειφθεὶς ἕζετο S.*Aj.*309 (v.l. ἐρεισθείς); ἐρείπεται κτύπος.. Διόβολος the thunder *comes crashing down*, Id.*OC*1462 (lyr.); ἐρείπεσθαι εἴς τινα *to fall* upon.., Plu.*Alex.*33: aor. 2 part. Pass. ἐριπέντι *fallen*, Pi.*O.*2.43 (v.l. -όντι, cf. A.D.*Synt.*280.21). II. intr., aor. 2 ἤρῐπον, Ep. ἔρῐπον, *fall down*, ἤριπε δ' ἐξ ὀχέων Il.5.47, etc.; γνὺξ δ' ἔριπε *fell* on his knee, ib.68; ἐν κονίῃ, ἐν κονίῃσι, ib.75, 11.743; of trees, ἡ δ' ἐκ ῥιζέων ἐριποῦσα 21.243: hence, of a warrior, ἤριπε δ' ὡς ὅτε τις δρῦς ἤριπεν 13.389; ἀπ' οὐρανοῦ ἤριπεν ἀστὴρ ἐν πόντῳ Theoc.13.50: metaph., δείματι ἤριπεν her heart *sank* with terror, Simon.37.3; where this tense is apptly. trans., as in Hdt.9.70, Paus.10.32.6, ἤρειπον may be restored.

ἔρ-εισις, εως, ἡ, *propping up, shoring up*, οἰκίας *BCH*35.243 (Delos, ii B.C.). 2. *resting, supporting*, ἡ ἐπ' ἐδάφους ἔ. τοῦ ποδός Aristeas 69. 3. *pushing against, thrusting*, τοῦ πέτρου D.H.*Comp.*20; τοῦ χείλους Ath.11.488e. 4. *leverage*, Menesth.ap.Erot. s.v. ἄμβην. **-εισμα**, ατος, τό, *prop, stay, support*, σκῆπτρα, χειρὸς ἐρείσματα E.*HF*254; ἀμφὶ βάκτροις ἔρεισμα θέμενος, = ἐρεισάμενος, ib.108: in pl., *stays* of a house, Pl.*Lg.*793c; *props* to keep a boat on shore upright (cf. ἕρμα), Theoc.21.12; ἁμμάτων ἐ. *strong* knots, E.*HF*1036 (lyr.); of the legs *which support* the body, Arist.*PA*689^{b}19, *IA*708^{b}15; of the framework of the body, Id.*PA*655^{a}25, cf. *HA*532^{b}3; of food, ἀμβροσία γαστρὸς ἔ. λεπτῆς *Arch.Pap.*8.256. 2. metaph., of a person, Θήρων' ἔ. Ἀκράγαντος *pillar* of Agrigentum, Pi.*O.*2.6; Ἑλλάδος ἔ. κλειναὶ Ἀθᾶναι Id.*Fr.*76, cf. Luc.*Dem.Enc.*10, *Tim.*50; ἔ. Ἀθηνῶν, of the (future) tomb of Oedipus, S.*OC*58. b. of good fortune, εἰς ἀπροσδόκητον ἔ. καταντῶσιν Vett.Val.333.30. II. *contusion*, Hp.*Fract.*11. **-εισμός**, ὁ, = foreg. 1, Aq.*Is.*3.1. **-ειστικός**, ή, όν, *pushing, thrusting*, κινήσεις Ruf.*Anat.*68; δένδρον Hdn.Gr.ap.Orion.61.24.

ἐρείψιμος, ον, *thrown down, in ruins*, στέγος E.*IT*48.

ἐρειψῐπύλας [ῠ], α, ὁ, *overthrowing gates*, B.5.56.

ἔρειψις, εως, ἡ, *throwing down, ruin*, *IG*2^{2}.463.104.

ἐρειψίτοιχος [ῐ], ον, *overthrowing walls*, δωμάτων A.*Th.*883 (lyr.): perh. to be read in B.12.167.

ἐρέκτης, ου, ὁ, *one who splits* beans, Orion 54.8 (fort. leg. ἐρείκτης).

ἐρεμν-αῖος, η, ον, = sq., Q.S.2.510. **-ός**, ή, όν, (*ἐρεβ-νός, cf. Ἔρεβος) *murky, black, dark*, ἐρεμνὴν γαῖαν ἔδυντε Od.24.106, cf. *h.Merc.*427; ἐρεμνῇ νυκτὶ ἐοικώς Od.11.606, cf. Sapph.*Supp.*1.18; ἐρεμνῇ λαίλαπι ἶσοι Il.12.375; ἐ. αἰγίς 4.167, Hes.*Sc.*444; ἕσπερος A.R.4.1289; ἐρεμνῇ ψακάδι φοινίας δρόσου, of bloodshed, A.*Ag.*1390; ἐ. αἷμα S.*Aj.*376 (lyr.); Ἅιδου μυχοί prob. in E.*Heracl.*218: metaph., ἐ. φάτις a *dark, obscure* rumour, S.*Ant.*700; ἔρος ἐ. Ibyc.1.

ἐρεό-ξυλον, τό, *cotton*, *PLond.*3.928.1 (ii A.D.); cf. ἐριόξυλον. **-πώλης**, ου, ὁ, *wool-seller*, *POxy.*1669.5 (iii A.D.); cf. ἐριοπώλης.

ἐρεοῦς, ᾶ, οῦν, (ἐρέα) contr. from ἐρέεος, *of wool, woollen*, *IG*1^{2}.386.18, Pl.*Plt.*280e, al., *PCair.Zen.*54.37 (iii B.C.), *PPetr.*2p.108 (ii B.C.); τὰ ἐρεᾶ *PCair.Zen.*295 (iii B.C.); τελαμῶνες Sor.1.83; v.l. for ἐριοῦς, Dsc.1.19:—also written **ἐρειοῦς**, ᾶ, οῦν, ἐσθής *IG*11(2).161*B*62 (Delos, iii B.C.); cf. χιθῶνα ἐριοῦν *BGU*816.18 (iii A.D.). (Cf. ἐρέα fin.)

ἐρέπτομαι, *feed on*, c. acc., only in pres. part., mostly of granivorous animals, λωτὸν, κρῖ λευκόν, πυρὸν ἐρεπτόμενοι, Il.2.776, 5.196, Od.19.553, al.; of men, λωτὸν ἐ. 9.97, *AP*9.618; βότρυν ib.7.20; of fish, δημὸν ἐ. *feeding on* the fat of a carcase, Il.21.204.—Ep. Verb, used burlesquely by Ar.*Eq.*1295, ἐρεπτόμενον τὰ τῶν ἐχόντων:—Act., ἐρέπτω *eat*, Nonn.*D.*40.306; also causal, = τρέφω, Hsch.

ἐρέπτω, = ἐρέφω, *crown*, στεφάνοισι ποίας Pi.*P.*4.240, cf. B.4.16, Opp.*C.*4.262, etc.: metaph., λαῶν γενεὰν ἐ. ἄνθεσιν εὐνομίας Pi.*Pae.*1.9:—Med., κεφαλὴν ἀνθέμοις ἐρέπτομαι Cratin.98. II. *pluck*, ἄνθος cj. in Nonn.*D.*47.466.

ἐρέριπτο, v. ἐρείπω. **ἔρερον**, = εἴρερον, Hsch. s. v. εἰς ἔρερον. **ἐρέσθαι** and **ἔρεσθαι**, v. ἔρομαι. **ἐρεσία**, ἡ, = εἰρεσία, *Gloss.* **ἐρεσιμήτρην**· τὴν γεωμετρίαν, Hsch. **ἐρεσκίη**· θρησκ(ε)ία, Id. **ἐρεσμεῖ**· καταπνεῖ (fort. -πλεῖ), Id. **ἐρεσμεί**· κώπη, Id. **ἐρεσμίονες**· αἱ χεῖρες, Id.

ἐρέσσω, Plu.2.1128c, *Pomp.*73, *Cic.*47, rarely **-ττω**, Luc.*Cont.*1, al. (earlier ἐλαύνω): Ep. impf. ἔρεσσον Od.11.78: aor. ἤρεσα A.R.1.1110, (δι-) Od.12.444, ἤρεσσα (δι-) 14.351: (ἐρέτης):—*row*, ἄνδρας ἐρεσσέμεναι μεμαῶτας Il.9.361; οἱ δὲ προπεσόντες ἔρεσσον Od.9.490, 12.194; ἐρετμόν, τῷ καὶ ζωὸς ἔρεσσον 11.78; πομπίμοις κώπαις ἐ. S.*Tr.*561; ἤρεσαν ἐς λιμένα A.R.1.1110; of birds flying, πτεροῖς ἐ. E.*IT*289: abs., Id.*Ion*161 (lyr.); [ναυτίλος] οὖλος ἐρέσσων ποσσίν Call.*Ep.*6.5. II. trans., *speed by rowing*: metaph., γόων.. ἐρέσσετ'.. πόμπιμον χεροῖν πίτυλον *ply* with your hands *the measured* stroke of lamentation, A.*Th.*855 (cf. ἔρεσσ' ἔρεσσε καὶ στέναζ' Id.*Pers.*1046):—Pass., ναῦς ἠρέσσετο ib.422, cf. *Supp.*723, A.R.1.633; of birds, πτερύγων ἐρετμοῖσιν ἐρεσσόμενοι A.*Ag.*52. 2. generally, *put in quick motion, ply*, τὸν πόδα E.*IA*138 (anap.), *AP*10.22 (Bianor); γεωτόμον ὅπλον ib.101 (Id.): metaph., τοίας ἐρέσσουσιν ἀπειλὰς.. καθ' ἡμῶν S.*Aj.*251 (lyr.); ἐ. μῆτιν Id.*Ant.*158 (anap.):—Pass., of a bow, *to be plied, handled*, Id.*Ph.*1135 (lyr.); of Io, οἴστρῳ ἐρεσσομένα *driven onward*, A.*Supp.*541 (lyr.). III. *row through, traverse*, in Pass., νήεσσιν ἐρέσσεται.. ὕδωρ *AP*4.3^{b}.30 (Agath.).

ἐρεσ-χελία, ἡ, = φλυαρία, *EM*371.1, Suid. s. v. Ἀδάμ; = *decudia* (?), *Gloss.*; *quarrel*, *PMonac.*1.23 (vi A.D., -χειλία Pap.). **-χηλέω** (freq. with v.l. -χελέω), used only in pres., *talk lightly, to be jocular*, παίζειν καὶ ἐ. Pl.*R.*545e, cf. *Lg.*885c, Luc.*DMort.*16.3, etc.: c. inf., *discuss jocularly whether*.., Philostr.*VA*2.14. II. trans., *quiz, banter*, τινα Pl.*Phdr.*236b; τι Ath.6.223e, etc.; *tease, worry*, Ael.*NA*3.37, 15.22, Luc.*Musc.Enc.*10: c. dat. pers., ὁ λόγος ἐ. νῷν Pl.*Phlb.*53e. 2. c. acc. cogn., προφάσεις, πολέμου ἀφορμὰς ἐ., *find trifling* excuses or occasions, App.*Pun.*74, *Mith.*64; cf. ἐρίσχηλος.

ἐρετ-αίνω, = ἐρέσσω, Hsch. **-άνης**· ναύτης, Id. **-ή**· ἐπιθυμητή, Id. **-ης**, ου, ὁ, mostly in pl., *rowers*, Od.1.280, al., A.*Pers.* 39 (anap.), Hdt.6.12, Th.1.31, etc.: sg., Ar.*Eq.*542: metaph., κυλίκων ἐρέται, of tipplers, Dionys.Eleg.5.2. II. in pl., also, *oars*, *AP*6.4.6 (Leon.). (Root *erə-*, cf. Skt. *aritár-* 'rower', ἁλι-ήρης, τρι-ήρης, etc.) **-ικός**, ή, όν, *of* or *for rowers* or *rowing*: ἡ -κή (sc. τέχνη) the *art of rowing*, Pl.*Lg.*707a; ἐ. πληρώματα crews *of rowers*, Plu. *Pomp.*25; ἐρετικόν, τό, *crews*, App.*Hann.*54 (but, *service as a rower*, *PGnom.*143); ἐ. αὐλήματα Poll.4.56. **-μίον**, τό, Dim. of sq., cj. in *Com.Adesp.*607. **-μόν**, τό, *oar*, poet. for κώπη, πῆξαί τ' ἐπὶ τύμβῳ ἐρετμόν Od.11.77, cf. 23.276, Pi.*P.*4.18, E.*El.*433 (lyr.), etc.; εὐῆρες ἐ. Od.11.121,129, etc.: pl., εὐήρε' ἐ. ib.125; ἐρετμοῖσι φρύξουσι Orac. ap.Hdt.8.96, cf. E.*IA*1388 (troch.), *IT*1485: metaph., πτερύγων ἐ. A.*Ag.*52 (anap.). II. = τὸ ἀνδρεῖον αἰδοῖον, Hsch. (A fem. form ἐρετμαῖς = κώπαις is found in Hsch.) **-μός**, ὁ, *rowing*, Hdn.*Epim.* 36. **-μόω**, *furnish with oars, set to row*, χέρας E.*Med.*4; but χεῖρας ἐ. *lay* their hands *to the oar*, Orph.*A.*358; *use* their hands *as oars*, *swim*, Nonn.*D.*7.185. 2. ἐ. πορείην *pursue* a course, ib.33.191, al. 3. *traverse* as if with oars, ib.14.4:—Pass., ἀὴρ ἐρετμώθη πτερύγεσσιν ib.6.388.

ἔρετο· ὡρμήθη, Hsch.

Ἐρέτρια, Ep. (metri gr.) **Εἰρέτρια**, ἡ, Il.2.537:—*Eretria*, *IG*1^2. 304.17, Th.8.60, Hdt.6.43, etc.:—hence **Ἐρετριεύς**, έως, ὁ, *an Eretrian*, Hdt.5.99, al., etc.: pl. Ἐρετριῆς *IG*2^2.43.85 (iv B.C.); Ἐρετριεῖς ib.12(9).207.5 (iii B.C.), etc.; acc. Ἐρετριᾶς ib.188; gen. Ἐρετριῶν ib.1^2.49.12, al., Ἐρετριέων ib.12(9).187.13, etc.; written Ἐρετριείων ib.201.7 (acc. sg. contr. Ἐρετρῆ prob. in CratesTheb.2):—Adj. **Ἐρετρικός**, ή, όν, *Eretrian*, Hdt.6.101, etc.; οἱ Ἐ. the disciples of the *Eretrian* Menedemus, Str.9.1.8 (v.l. **Ἐρετριακοί**, as in D.L.1.18, etc.): **Ἐρετριάς** (sc. γῆ), άδος, ἡ, *a kind of clay*, Hp.*Morb.* 3.16, Dsc.5.152.

ἐρετριάζει· σκώπτει, παίζει, Hsch.

ἐρευγ-μᾰτώδης, ες, *causing eructation*, κρέα Hp.*Acut.*(*Sp.*).49. **-μός**, ὁ, *eructation*, Id.*Coac.*138 (pl.), Arist.*Pr.*895^{b}15. **-μώδης**, ες, v.l. for ἐρευγματώδης, Hp.*Vict.*2.42.

ἐρεύγομαι (A), also **ἐρυγγάνω** (q.v.), fut. ἐρεύξομαι Hp.*Mul.*1.41: aor. 1 ἠρευξάμην Procop.*Goth.*2.4: aor. 2 ἤρῠγον Arist.*Pr.*895^{b}22, Nic. *Al.*111:—*belch out, disgorge*, c. acc., ἐρευγόμενοι φόνον αἵματος Il.16. 162; ἰόν Nic.*Th.*232: abs., *belch*, ἐρεύγετο οἰνοβαρείων Od.9.374, cf. Hp. *Morb.*2.69, Arist.*Pr.*895^{b}12. 2. metaph., of volcanoes, ἐρεύγονται πυρὸς παγαί Pi.*P.*1.21, cf. Procop.*Goth.*4.35; of a river, *discharge itself*, ἐς τὴν θάλασσαν App.*Mith.*103, cf. Alc.*Supp.*11.3: c. acc. cogn., ἐρεύγονται σκότον.. νυκτὸς ποταμοί, of the rivers of hell, Pi.*Fr.* 130.8; κόλπος ἀφρὸν ἐρευγόμενος D.P.539, cf. Lxx *Le.*11.10; ἵππος ἐρεύγεται ἄνδρα, as the description of a Centaur, *APl.*4.115. 3. *blurt out* (cf. ἐξερυγγάνω), *belch forth, utter*, ἡμέρα τῇ ἡμέρᾳ ἐρεύγεται ῥῆμα Lxx *Ps.*18(19).2; ἐρεύξομαι κεκρυμμένα *Ev.Matt.*13.35. (Cf. Lat. *ērūgĕre*, Lith. *riáugėti* 'belch'.)

ἐρεύγομαι (B), aor. 2 Act. ἤρῠγον, *bellow, roar*, ἤρυγεν, ὡς ὅτε ταῦρος ἤρυγεν Il.20.403; τόν γ' ἐρυγόντα λίπε.. θυμός ib.406; ὅσον βαθὺς ἤρυγε λαιμός *roared* to the full depth of his throat or voice, Theoc.13. 58; of the sea, ἀμφὶ δέ τ' ἄκραι ἠϊόνες βοόωσιν ἐρευγομένης ἁλὸς ἔξω the headlands echo to the *roar* of the sea, Il.17.265; κῦμα.. δεινὸν ἐρευγόμενον Od.5.403; ἐρεύγεται ἠπειρόνδε ib.438 (cf. βοάω I. 2):—so in later Gr., λέων ἐρεύξεται Lxx *Ho.*11.10, *Am.*3.8; σκύμνος ἐρευγόμενος ib.1*Ma.*3.4; with v.l. ὠρύομαι, ib.*Ez.*22.25; cf. προσερεύγομαι. (Cf. Lat. *rūgio* 'roar'.)

ἐρευθ-ᾰλέος, η, ον, (ἔρευθος) *ruddy*, Nonn.*D.*12.329,359. **-έδᾰνον**, τό, *madder*, *Rubia tinctorum*, Hdt.4.189; of the wild form, *Rubia tinctorum*, Thphr.*HP*9.13.6, Dsc.3.143 (ἐρευθέδανος ῥίζα Ps.-Dsc. ibid.): hence, *dye* made therefrom, *PHolm.*26.36. **-έω**, *to be red*, Luc.*Ner.*7; *to be flushed*, *BGU*928.14 (iii A.D.). **-ήεις**, εσσα, εν, *red*, A.R.1.727, Nic.*Th.*899 (v.l. -ιόεις). **-ημα**, ατος, τό, *redness*, Gal.19.433. **-ής**, ές, = ἐρευθήεις, ὕδωρ Str.16.4.20; σελήνη Arat.784, cf. Opp.*C.*3.94. **-ιάω**, *become red*, Hp.*Mul.*2. 112, Opp.*H.*3.25. **-ιόεις**, v. ἐρευθήεις. **-ος**, εος, τό, *redness, flush*, Hp.*Epid.*1.26.ε', Plu.2.48c; of dye, A.R.1.726; [ἡδονὴ] ἔρευθος εἰργασμένη with *painted* cheeks, Ph.2.266. **-ω**, aor. 1 inf. ἐρεῦσαι Il. (v. infr.):—*make red, stain with red*, αἵματι γαῖαν 11.394; γαῖαν ἐρεῦσαι αὐτοῦ ἐνὶ Τροίῃ 18.329; βωμὸν φόνοισι Pythag.ap.S.E. *M.*9.128:—Pass., *to be* or *become red*, Sapph.93, Hp.*Epid.*2.3.1, *Morb. Sacr.*15, Theoc.17.127; [ἀστὴρ] καλὸν -όμενος A.R.1.778. II. intr. in Act., ἐρ]ευθε φώτων [αἷμα]τι γαῖα B.12.152; τὸ πρόσωπον ἐ. Hp. *Morb.*4.38. (ONorse *rjóða*, OE. *rēodan* 'redden', OE. *rēad* 'red'; v. ἐρυθρός.)

ἐρευκτικός, ή, όν, (ἐρεύγομαι A) *promoting eructation*, Dsc.1.70.3.

ἔρευν-α, ης, ἡ, *inquiry, search*, ἔ. τινός *search* for.., S.*OT*566, cf. *Ichn.*92; οὐδ' ἧξας εἰς ἔ. ἐξευρεῖν γονάς; E.*Ion*328; ἔ. ποιεῖσθαι τῶν οἰκιῶν Arist.*Oec.*1351^{b}34, cf. *PTeb.*38.19 (ii B.C.); v. ἔραυνα. II. *exploratory operation*, Herod.Med.ap.Orib.50.46.2. **-άς**, άδος, ὁ, = Lat. *quaestor*, Lyd.*Mag.*1.25 (pl.); = Lat. *quaesitor*, ib.2.29. **-άω**, also -ίω *GDI*5075.35 (Crete), and **ἐραυνάω** (q.v.):—*seek* or *search for, search after, track*, ἴχνι' ἐρευνῶντες κύνες ἤϊσαν Od.19.436; μετ' ἀνέρος ἴχνι' ἐρευνῶν Il.18.321; τεύχε' ἐ. Od.22.180; τὴν σοφὴν εὐβουλίαν A. *Pr.*1038; θεῶν βουλεύματ' Pi.*Fr.*61; νεκροὺς E.*Med.*1318; κακούργους X.*Cyr.*1.2.12; ἄν τινα οἴωμαι σοφὸν εἶναι Pl.*Ap.*23b, cf. 41b; τὸ γραμματεῖον D.25.61; ὧν.. ἂν θεὸς χρείαν ἐρευνᾷ the things whereof he *seeks after* the use, i.e. whatever things he finds serviceable, S.*OT*725. 2. *search, explore* a place, Hdt.5.92.δ', Sor.*Vit.Hippocr.*3; τεναγέων ῥοάς Pi.*N.*3.24; ὄρος Theoc.25.221; τοὺς ὑπόπτους τῶν τόπων Ael. *Tact.*17: abs., εὑρήσεις ἐρευνῶν thou wilt find *by searching*, Pi.*O.*13. 113, cf. S.*Ant.*268; εἰσβάντες εἰς τὸ πλοῖον ἠρεύνων Antipho 5.29. 3. *inquire after*, φάτιν E.*Hel.*662 (lyr.); παίδων ἐρευνῶν σπέρμ' ὅπως γένοιτό μοι Id.*Med.*669; *examine into* a question, ib.1084 (anap.), cf. Pl.*Tht.*200e, al.:—also in Med., διάνοια πᾶσαν φύσιν -ωμένη ib.174a; οἰκημάτιον X.Eph.2.10. 4. c. inf., *seek* to do, Theoc.7.45. **-ητέον**, *one must inquire*, ποῖα.. X.*Smp.*8.39; εἰ.. Ph.2.27. **-ητήρ**, ῆρος, ὁ, = sq., Nonn.*D.*2.25. **-ητής**, οῦ, ὁ, *searcher, inquirer*, Clearch. 25, Parth.1.1: c. gen., τῶν ἐλέγχων, τῶν ἀδήλων, J.*AJ*17.5.5, *BJ* 1.30.7; διόπται καὶ ἐ. *spies*, D.C.78.14; *inspector, customs-officer*, *UPZ*149.15 (iii/ii B.C.); cf. ἐραυνητ-ής, -ικόν. **-ήτρια**, ἡ, fem. of foreg., Corn.*ND*10.

ἔρευξις, εως, ἡ, (ἐρεύγομαι A) *eructation*, Hp.*Epid.*1.23 (pl.), Aret. *SA*2.3 (pl.).

ἐρευνάω, = ἐρευνάω, Eust.670.65, Hsch.:—hence **ἐρευτής**, οῦ, ὁ, = ἐρευνητής, *exactor, collector of state-debts*, *SIG*527.132 (Dreros, iii B.C.), *GDI*5073.18 (Cnossus, ii B.C.). (Cf. ἐρέω (A).)

ἐρεφύλλινον ἄνθος, dub. sens. in *PMag.Leid.W.*1.23.

ἐρέφω, impf. ἤρεφον Ar.*Fr.*73, poet. ἔρ- Pi.*O.*1.68, also **ἐρέπτω** (q.v.): fut. ἐρέψω Ar.*Av.*1110: aor. 1 ἤρεψα D.19.265 (nowhere else in Att. Prose), Ep. and Lyr. ἔρεψα Hom., Pi.*O.*13.32:—**Med.**, fut. ἐρέψομαι E.*Ba.*323: aor. 1 ἠρεψάμην A.R.2.159, etc., (κατ-) Ar.*V.* 1294:—**Pass.**, Corn.*ND*17: pf. ἤρεπται Philostr.*VA*1.25: (cf. ὄροφος, ἐρέπτω):—*cover with a roof*, καθύπερθεν ἔρεψαν.. ὄροφον λειμωνόθεν ἀμήσαντες, i.e. they *thatched* [the hut] with reeds Il.24.450, cf. Od.23.193; τὰς.. οἰκίας ἐρέψομεν πρὸς αἰετόν Ar.*Av.*1110, cf. *Fr.*73; ἤρεψε τὴν οἰκίαν ξύλοις D. l.c.:—Pass., τὰ βασίλεια χαλκῷ ἤρεπται Philostr. l.c. 2. *cover with a crown, crown*, δύο δ' αὐτὸν ἔρεψαν πλόκοι σελίνων Pi.*O.*13.32; [κρατῆρων] κρᾶτ' ἔρεψον καὶ λαβὰς S.*OC* 473:—Med., *crown oneself*, κισσῷ E.*Ba.*323; στεφάνῳ κόμαν B.8.24; δάφνῃ μέτωπα *one's* forehead, A.R.2.159:—Pass., στεφάνοισι χαίταν ἐρεφθείς B.12.70. 3. *wreathe as with garlands*, ναὸν κρανίοις Pi.*I.* 4(3).54: generally, *cover*, λάχναι νιν μέλαν γένειον ἔρεφον Id.*O.*1.68.

Ἐρεχθεύς, έως, Ep. ῆος, ὁ, an ancient hero of Attica, first in Il. 2.547, Od.7.81:—hence **Ἐρέχθειον**, τό, *Temple of Erechtheus* at Athens, Paus.1.26.5, Plu.2.843e: **Ἐρεχθεῖδαι**, οἱ, *members of the Erechtheid tribe*, *SIG*911.17: hence, a name of the Athenians, Pi.*I.* 2.19, E.*Med.*824 (-εῖδαι, lyr.), etc.: sg. in Ar.*Eq.*1015,1030:—**Ἐρεχθηΐς**, ΐδος, contr. **-ῃς**, ῇδος, fem. Adj. *of Erechtheus*, θάλασσα Ἐ. a fountain at Athens *sacred to him*, Apollod.3.14.1: also a name of one of the Attic Tribes, *IG*1^2.929, D.21.68, etc. II. name of Poseidon at Athens, Plu.2.843b, Lyc.158,431; Ποσειδῶνι Ἐρεχθεῖ *IG*1^2.580.

ἐρεχθῖτις, ιδος, ἡ, = ἀριστολοχεία στρογγύλη, Ps.-Dsc.3.4; = ἠριγέρων, ib.4.96.

ἐρέχθω, *rend, break*, δάκρυσι καὶ στοναχῇσι καὶ ἄλγεσι θυμὸν ἐρέχθων Od.5.83:—Pass., ἐρεχθομένην ἀνέμοισι, of a ship, *buffeted* by the winds, Il.23.317: metaph., ὀδύνῃσιν ἐρεχθομένη *h.Ap.*358; πρήξεσιν οὐχ ὁσίαις ἐ. Procl.*H.*7.38.

ἐρεχμός, ὁ, Aeol. for ἐρεγμός, *EM*371.19.

ἐρέψιμος, ον, *of* or *for roofing*, δένδρα ἐ. Pl.*Criti.*111c; ὕλη Thphr. *HP*4.2.8.

ἔρεψις, εως, ἡ, *roofing*, Thphr.*HP*5.6.1, *Supp.Epigr.*3.147 (iii B.C.); *style of roof*, Plu.*Per.*13, *Ant.*45, etc.

ἐρέω (A), Ep. Verb, = ἐρεείνω, ἔρομαι, ἐρωτάω, *ask, inquire*, c. acc. rei, *about* a thing, ἐρέων γενεήν τε τόκον τε Il.7.128, cf. Od.21.31; *seek for*, Ὕλαν A.R.1.1354. 2. c. acc. pers., *question*, μάντιν ἐρείομεν (v.infr.) ἢ ἱερῆα Il.1.62; ἀλλήλους ἐρέοιμεν Od.4.192; ὅπως ἐρέοιμι ἑκάστην 11.229. 3. c. acc. rei, *search, explore*, ἰλυούς Nic.*Th.*143 (v.l. ἐρέθοντες). (Prob. ἐρε(ϝ)-, cf. ἐρευτής: ἐρείομεν perh. metri gr. for ἐρέ(ϝ)-ο-μεν, pres. subj. of non-thematic stem.)

ἐρέω (B), Ion. for ἐρῶ, I *will say*; v. ἐρῶ.

ἐρέω (C), Ion. for ἐράω (A).

ἐρημ-άζω, (ἔρημος) *to be left lonely, go alone*, ἐρημάζεσκον (Iterat.) Theoc.22.35, cf. *AP*7.315 (Zenod. or Rhian.):—also in Med., Satyr. *Vit.Eur.Fr.*39 xxi 8. **-αῖος**, η, ον, poet. for ἐρῆμος, *desolate, solitary*, Mosch.3.21, A.R.2.672, etc.; *silent*, νύξ Emp.49; *deserted*, νεοσσοί A.R.4.1298: c. gen., *reft of*, *AP*9.439 (Crin.). **-άς**, άδος, ἡ, pecul. fem. of ἐρῆμος, Man.6.67. **-η** (sc. δίκη), ἡ, v. ἐρῆμος III.

Ἐρημήσιος, ὁ, epith. of Zeus at Lesbos, Hsch.

ἐρημ-ία, ἡ, I. of places, *a solitude, desert, wilderness*, Hdt.3.98, A.*Pr.*2, etc.; ἡ Σκυθῶν ἐ. Ar.*Ach.*704; ἀφίκετ' εἰς ἐ. Id.*Lys.*787; ἕρπει εἰς τὰς ἐρημίας to *solitary places*, Arist.*HA*610^{b}24, etc. II. as a state or condition, *solitude, loneliness*, ἐρημίαν ἄγειν, to keep *alone*, E.*Med.*50; μονάδ' ἔχουσ' ἐ. Id.*Ba.*609 (troch.); ἐρημίας τυχὼν Id. *El.*510; ἐν ἐρημίᾳ ἐλοιδοροῦντο Antipho 2.1.4; of persons, *isolation, destitution*, S.*OC*957, Lys.18.25; πολλὴν ἡμῶν ἐ. καταγνόντες Is.1.2; δι' ἐρημίαν from *being left alone*, Th.1.71, cf. 3.67; ἐρημίας ἐπειλημμένοι D.3.27; εὑρετικὸν εἶναί φασι τὴν ἐ. Men.39. b. of places, *desolation*, ἐρημία δοῦναί τι E.*Tr.*97; ἐρημία.. πόλιν ὅταν λάβῃ ib.26; ἀτριβὴς ὑπ' ἐρημίας Th.4.8. 2. c. gen., *want of, absence*, φίλων X.*Mem.* 2.2.14; ἀρσένων, βροτῶν, ἀνδρῶν, E.*Hec.*1017, *Ba.*875 (lyr., pl.), Th. 6.102; λύχνων Ar.*Av.*1484 (lyr.), etc.; δι' ἐρημίας πολεμίων πορευόμενος *without finding* any enemy, X.*HG*3.4.21; τὴν ἐ. τῶν κωλυσόντων ὁρῶν seeing that there would be *none* to hinder him, D.4.49; ἐ. σώματος, = κενόν, Zeno *Stoic.*1.26; even ἐ. κακῶν *freedom from* evil, E. *HF*1157. **-ικός**, ή, όν, *of* or *for solitude, living in a desert*, Lxx *Ps.*101(102).7. **-ίτης** [ῑ], ου, ὁ, *of the desert*, ὄνος ib.*Jb.*11.12.

ἐρημο-βάτης [ᾰ], ου, ὁ, *traveller in deserts*, *Cat.Cod.Astr.*8(4).151.

-βόας, *bubo, Gloss.* **-δίκιον** [ῐκ], τό, = δίκη ἐρήμη, *Cod.Just.*3.1.13.3, *Gloss.* **-θωκος·** ἐρημολόγος, Hsch. **-κόμης,** gen. ου, *void of hair,* κρατός *AP*6.294 (Phan.); κόρση ib.7.383 (Phil.). **-λάλος** [ᾰ], ον, *chattering in the desert,* μοῦσα (of the τέττιξ) ib.196 (Mel.). **-λόγος,** gloss on ἐρημόθωκος, Hsch. **-νόμος,** ον, *haunting the wilds,* θεαί A.R.4.1333; θῆρες *AP*6.184 (Zos.); also in late Prose, ζῷα ἐ. Agath.2.24. II. ἐρημόνομος, ον, *desolate,* λόχμη, πόντος, Nonn.*D.*37.12, 47.510. **-πλάνος** [ᾰ], ον, *wandering alone,* Orph.*H.*39.4 (ἐρημοπλάνα codd.); noted as διθυραμβῶδες by Demetr. *Eloc.*116. **-ποιός,** όν, *making desolate,* gloss on ἐρημωτής, Suid., cf. *PMag.Leid.V.*15.23. **-πολέω,** *play the hermit,* Eustr. *in EN* 7.10. **-πολις,** ι, gen. ιδος, *reft of one's city,* E.*Tr.*603 (lyr.).

ἐρῆμος, ον, fem. ἐρήμη Od.3.270, S.*OC*1719 (lyr.), *Ant.*739, *Tr.*530 (lyr.), and in the phrase δίκη ἐρήμη (v. infr. III): Att. **ἔρημος,** ον, acc. to Hdn.Gr.2.938: Comp. -ότερος Th.3.11, Lys.29.1, etc.: Sup. -ότατος Hdt.9.118:—*desolate, lonely, solitary,* 1. of places, ἐς νῆσον ἐρήμην Od.3.270; χῶρος Il.10.520; τὰ ἐ. τῆς Λιβύης the *desert parts..,* Hdt.2.32, cf. Th.2.17; ἡ ἐρῆμος (sc. χώρα) Hdt.4.18; ἡ ἐρήμη Ael.*NA* 7.48: pl., ib.3.26; *empty,* πνύξ Ar.*Ach.*20. 2. of persons or animals, τὰ δ' ἐρῆμα φοβεῖται (i.e. the sheep), Il.5.140; Ξέρξην ἐ. μολεῖν A. *Pers.*734 (troch.); ἧσθαι δόμοις ἐ. Id.*Ag.*862; πόρτις ἐρήμα S.*Tr.*530 (lyr.); ἐ. κᾴφιλος Id.*Ph.*228; τὸν θεὸν ἐ. ἀπολιπόντε Ar.*Pl.*447; freq. of poor, friendless persons, And.4.15, etc.; ἐρημότεροι, opp. δυνατώτεροι, Th.3.11; οὐκ ὢν οὔτε τῶν ἐρημοτάτων οὔτε τῶν ἀπόρων κομιδῇ D. 21.111; εἰς ὀρφανὰ καὶ ἐ. ὑβρίζειν Pl.*Lg.*927c; ὄρνιθες *solitary, not gregarious,* Plu.*Caes.*63: neut. as Adv., ἔρημα κλαίω I weep *in solitude,* E.*Supp.*775; ἔρημον ἐμβλέπειν to look *vacantly,* Ar.*Fr.*456. 3. of conditions, πλάνος S.*OC*1114. II. c. gen., *reft of, void* or *destitute of,* [χώρη] ἐ. πάντων Hdt.2.32; ἀνθρώπων Id.4.17, cf. 18; ἀνδρῶν Id.6.23, S.*OT*57; Ἀθηναίων Hdt.8.65; στέγαι φίλων ἔ. S.*El.* 1405; Πειραιᾶ ἔ. ὄντα νεῶν Th.8.96; τῇ ἦν ἐρημότατον τῶν πολεμίων (sc. τὸ τεῖχος) Hdt.9.118; [τὰ γεγραμμένα] ἀπόντος τοῦ γράψαντος ἔρημα τοῦ βοηθήσοντός ἐστιν Isoc.*Ep.*1.3; θεῶν ἔρημα εἶναι πάντα Pl.*Lg.* 908c. 2. of persons, *bereft of,* συμμάχων Hdt.7.160; πατρός S. *OC*1719 (lyr.); πατρὸς ἢ μητρός Pl.*Lg.*927d; πρὸς φίλων S.*Ant.*919; so ἔ. οἶκος a house *without heirs,* Is.7.31. 3. with no bad sense, *wanting, without,* ἐσθὴς ἐρῆμος ὅπλων Hdt.9.63; *free from,* ἀνδρῶν κακῶν ἔρημος πόλις Pl.*Lg.*862e. III. ἐρήμη, rarely ἔρημος (with or more commonly without γραφή, δίκη, δίαιτα), ἡ, an *undefended* action, *in which one party does not appear,* and judgement goes against him *by default,* ἤλπιζε..τὴν γραφὴν..ἐρήμην ἔσεσθαι would be *undefended,* Antipho 2.1.7; ἐρήμη δίκη θάνατον καταγιγνώσκειν τινός Th.6.61; δίκην εἷλον ἐρήμην I got *judgement by default,* D.21.81; ἐρήμην αὐτὸν λαβόντες..εἷλον Lys.20.18; τὴν ἔρημον δεδωκότα having given *it by default* in one's favour, D.21.85; ἔρημον ὦφλε δίκην he let it go *by default,* ib.87, cf. Antipho 5.13; ἐρήμην τινὸς καταγνῶναι τὴν δίαιταν D.33.33; ἐρήμην καταδιαιτῆσαί τινος Id.40.17; γενομένης ἐρήμου κατὰ Μειδίου Test.ap.eund.21.93; ἐρήμην κατηγορεῖν to accuse *in a case where there was no defence,* Pl.*Ap.*18c, cf. D.21.87; ἐρήμην or ἐξ ἐρήμης κρατεῖν, Luc.*Anach.*40, *JTr.*25; ἁλῶναι Id.*Tox.*11, etc. 2. *unclaimed, vacant,* Arist.*Ath.*43.4, *EN*1125ᵇ17, Is.3.61. 3. for ἐρήμας τρυγᾶν v. sub τρυγάω.

ἐρημο-σκόπος, ὁ, *one who keeps watch negligently,* Anon.ap.Suid. **-σύνη,** ἡ, *solitude, AP*9.4 (Cyllen.), 665 (Agath.). **-τελωνία,** ἡ, *tax for maintenance of desert-police, PLond.*2.88 (ii A.D.), etc. **-φίλης** [ῐ], ου, ὁ, *loving solitude, AP*9.396 (Paul. Sil.), *APl.*4.256. **-φύλαξ** [ῠ], ακος, ὁ, *desert-policeman, PCair.Zen.*172.25 (iii B.C.), etc.:—hence **-φῠλακία,** ἡ, *maintenance of this force, PFay.*68 (ii A.D.), etc.

ἐρημ-όω, *strip bare, desolate, lay waste,* ἱερὰ θεῶν Th.3.58; τὴν χώραν And.3.21; πλοῦτον Lxx *Si.*21.4; ὁ κτίζων καὶ ἐρημῶν θεός *POsl.* 1.105:—Pass., ἐρημωθείσης Κρήτης Hdt.7.171; πόλεις ἠρημώθησαν Th.1.23; μιᾷ ὥρᾳ ἠρημώθη ὁ τοσοῦτος πλοῦτος *Apoc.*18.17. II. *bereave* one *of* a thing, c. dupl. acc., ἐ. τινὰ εὐφροσύνας μέρος Pi.*P.*3.97: c. acc. et gen., ἀνδρῶν ἐ. ἑστίαν Id.*I.*4(3).17; ἐ. ναυβατῶν ἐρετμά *to leave* the oars *without* men, E.*Hel.*1609; ἑαυτὸν ἐρημοῖ (sc. φίλων) Pl.*Alex.*39:—Pass., *to be bereft of,* ἀνδρῶν Hdt.1.164; συμμάχων Id. 7.174; Μίλητος Μιλησίων ἠρήμωτο Id.6.22; ἄρσενος θρόνου A.*Ag.* 260; πατρός E.*Andr.*805; τὰ ἐρημούμενα φυλακῆς *left without,* X.*Eq. Mag.*4.18. 2. *set free, deliver from,* Διὸς ἄλσος ἠρήμωσε λέοντος E. *HF*360 (lyr.); Ἀσίαν Περσικῶν ὅπλων Plu.*Cim.*12:—Pass., πνεῦμα ὀσμῶν ἐρημωθέν *being free from..,* Pl.*Ti.*66e. III. *abandon, desert,* ἑὸν χῶρον Pi.*P.*4.269; τάξιν ἠρήμου θανών A.*Pers.*298, cf. E.*Andr.*314, Pl.*Lg.*865e; ἐ. Συρακούσας *to evacuate* it, Th.5.4; τόνδ' ἐρημώσασ' ὄχον *having left* it *empty,* by stepping out of it, A.*Ag.*1070:—Pass., [πόλιν] ἐρημοῦσθαι ὑπὸ τῶν πατρικίων D.H.11.9. IV. *leave alone, keep isolated,* A.*Supp.*516, E.*Med.*90:—Pass., ὄνοι ἐρημωθέντες τοῦ ὁμίλου *being isolated from..,* Hdt.4.135. **-ωσις,** εως, ἡ, *making desolate,* Lxx *Le.*26.34, al., Heph.Astr.1.21; χωρίου Arr.*An.*1.9.7; βδέλυγμα τῶν ἐ. Lxx *Da.*9.27, cf. *Ev.Matt.*24.15. **-ωτής,** οῦ, ὁ, *desolator,* θῆρα Μακηδονίας *AP*6.115 (Antip.).

ἐρηρέδαται, -ατο, v. ἐρείδω. **ἐρήριμμαι,** v. ἐρείπω. **ἐρήρισται,** v. ἐρίζω.

***ἐρής** (nom. not found), *son, child,* gen. pl. ἐρέων, dat. pl. ἔρεσσι Puchstein *Epigr.Gr.*p.76; acc. pl. ἐρέας, dat. pl. ἐρέεσφι, = τέκνα, τέκνοις (Thess.), Hsch.

ἐρητύω, Dor. **ἐρᾱτύω,** impf. ἐρήτυον (without augm.) Il.18.503, Ion. -ύεσκον A.R.1.1301, Q.S.11.341: fut. -ύσω A.R.1.296, (κατ-) S.*Ph.*1416 (anap.): aor. 1 opt. ἐρητύσειε Il.1.192, imper. ἐρήτυσον E. *Ph.*1260, Iterat. ἐρητύσασκε Il.2.189, 11.567, Theoc.25.75:—Pass. (v. infr.). [ῠ before a vowel, unless it be a long syll., as ἐρητῡοντο μένοντες Il.8.345 (exc. ἐρατύει [ῠ] S.*OC*164 (lyr.)); long before σ, and in 3 pl. aor. 1 Pass. ἐρήτῡθεν.]:—Ep. Verb (used twice in Trag.), *restrain, check,* κήρυκες δ' ἄρα λαὸν ἐρήτυον Il.18.503; ἐρητύσασκε φάλαγγας 11.567; ἐπέεσσιν ἐρήτυε φῶτα ἕκαστον 2.164, cf. Od.9.493; ἐρητύσειέ τε θυμόν Il.1.192; πολλὰ κέλευθος ἐρατύει a long road *parts* us, S.*OC*l.c. (ἐρατύοι Musgr.):—Med., ἐρητύοντό τε λαόν Il.15.723:—Pass., παρὰ νηυσὶν ἐρητύοντο μένοντες 8.345; ἐρητύετ' ἐν φρεσὶ θυμός 9.462; ἐρήτυθεν (3 pl.) δὲ καθ' ἕδρας 2.99, 211. 2. later c. gen., *to keep away from,* τέκνα δεινῆς ἁμίλλης E.*Ph.*1260; [κύνας] ὑλαγμοῦ Theoc.25.75; τινὰ κακότητος A.R.1.296:—Pass., c. inf., ναυτιλίης ..ἐρητύοντο μέλεσθαι Id.2.835. 3. c. inf., *prevent,* ἐ. τινὰ μίμνειν Nonn.*D.*14.63.

ἔρι, τό, indecl. form of ἔριον, *wool,* Philet.19.

ἐρῐ-, insepar. Particle, like ἀρι-, used as a prefix to strengthen the sense of a word, *very, much*; mostly Ep. and Lyr.

ἐρι-αύχην, ενος, ὁ, ἡ, *with arched neck,* opp. βυσαύχην, ἐριαύχενες ἵπποι Il.10.305, al., never in Od. **-αχθής,** ές, (ἔριον, ἄχθος) *laden with wool, woolly,* or (ἐρι-, ἄχθος) *heavy-laden,* ποίμνη Max.520. **-βόας,** ου, ὁ, *loud-shouting,* of Bacchus, Pi.*Fr.*75.10; of Hermes, *AP*15. 27.5 (Besant.).

ἐρίβοια· νύξ· καὶ μεγάλως τιμωμένη, Hsch.

ἐρί-βομβος, ον, *loud-buzzing,* μέλισσαι Orph.*Fr.*154, 189. **-βους,** etym. of Ἠερίβοια, Eust.562.40. **-βρεμέθων,** οντος, = sq., prob. in *Hymn.Is.*166. **-βρεμέτης,** ου, Ep. εω, ὁ, *loud-thundering,* Ζεύς Il.13.624; of Aeschylus, Ar.*Ra.*814 (hex.); Διόνυσος D.P.578, etc.; *loud-roaring,* λέοντες Pi.*I.*4(3).46; *loud-sounding,* αὐλός *AP*6.195 (Arch.). **-βρεμής,** ές, = ἐρίβρομος, τρίπους ib.344. **-βρῑθής,** ές, *very heavy,* Opp.*H.*5.636. **-βρομος,** ον, *loud-shouting,* of Bacchus, *h.Bacch.*56, Anacr.11, Panyas.13.2; *loud-roaring,* λέοντες Pi.*O.*11(10).21; χθών, νεφέλα, Id.*P.*6.3, 11. **-βρύχης** [ῡ], ου, Ep. εω, ὁ, = sq., ταῦρος Hes.*Th.*832; σῦς B.5.116; πόντος, λέων, Opp.*H.*1.476, 709. **-βρῡχος,** ον, *loud-bellowing,* λέων Q.S.3.171; *loud-braying,* of the trumpet, *AP*6.159 (Antip. Sid.). **-βῶλαξ,** ἄκος, ὁ, ἡ, *with large clods,* of rich, loamy soil: hence, *very fertile,* once in Od., ἐριβώλακος ἠπείροιο 13.235; freq. in Il., ἐν Φθίῃ ἐριβώλακι 1. 155, etc.; γαῖα Orph.*L.*655; πόλεως ἐ. Cratin.56. **-βωλος,** ον, = foreg., Od.5.34, Il.21.154, al.; ἄρουραι *h.Cer.*471. **-βωτος** (-βωλος cod.), = μεγαλόψοφος (i.e. ἐριβόητος), Hsch. **-γάστωρ,** ορος, ὁ, ἡ, *pot-bellied,* μόσχοι Nic.*Al.*344. **-γδουπέω,** *rattle loud,* coined by Sch. Il.6.507. **-γδουπος,** ον, = ἐρίδουπος (q.v.), *loud-sounding, thundering,* in Hom. epith. of Zeus, Διὸς υἱὸν ἐριγδούποιο Il.5.672; ἐ. πόσις Ἥρης Od.15.112; exc. in Il.11.152 ἐ. πόδες ἵππων; so after Hom., Ναΐδων ἐ. στοναχαί Pi.*Dith.Oxy.*2.12; καλαῦροψ *APl.*4.74; βοείη Nonn.*D.*18.105. **-γηθής,** ές, *very joyful,* Orph.*L.Prooem.* 24. **-γηρυς,** ὁ, ἡ, *loud-speaking,* Hsch. **-γληνος,** ον, *with large eye-balls, full-eyed,* Opp.*C.*1.310.

ἔριγμα, ατος, τό, (ἐρείκω) *bruised beans,* φακῶν ἢ ἐρεβίνθων Hp. *Coac.*621 (pl.):—also **ἐρίγμη,** ἡ, Sch.Ar.*Ra.*508.

ἐρῐδ-αίνω, impf. ἠρίδαινον Babr.68.3: Ep. aor. 1 ἐρίδηνα A.R.1.89:—Med., Q.S.5.105: Ep. aor. 1 inf. ἐρῑδήσασθαι Il.23.792 (with vv. ll., dub.); elsewh. Hom. uses only pres.: (ἐρίζω):—*wrangle, quarrel,* μετ' ἀνδράσι Od.21.310; αὔτως γάρ ῥ' ἐπέεσσ' ἐριδαίνομεν Il.2.342; νῦν δὲ περὶ πτωχῶν ἐ. Od.18.403; εἰ δὴ σφὼ ἕνεκα θνητῶν ἐ. Il.1.574; εἵνεκα τῆς ἀρετῆς ἐ. we *strive* (as for a prize) for her excellence, Od.2.206: c. dat., Εὖρός τε Νότος τ' ἐριδαίνετον ἀλλήλοιιν..πελεμιζέμεν Il.16.765, cf. A.R.1.89; also ἀντία πάντων..ἐριδαινέμεν οἷος Od.1.79; τι in a thing, Call.*Dian.*262; of war, first in A.R.2.986, etc.:—Med., ποσσὶν ἐριδήσασθαι *compete in* the foot-race, Il.23.792.—Ep. word: also c. acc., τεθυμωμένον ἄνδρα μὴ ἐριδαίνειν (fort. -δμαίνειν) Demetr.Byz. ap.Ath.10.452d; Luc.*Pisc.*6 may be a reminiscence of A.R.1. 89. **-άντης,** ου, ὁ, *wrangler,* Timo 28.2: Ion. gen. pl. ἐριδαντέων Democr.150: Dor. **Ἐριδάντας,** epith. of Heracles at Tarentum, Hsch.

ἐρί-δηλος, ον, = ἀρίδηλος, Hdn.*Epim.*185.

ἐριδίαν· ἅμαξα, Hsch.; cf. ἐρωδία.

Ἐριδίμιος, ὁ, epith. of Zeus at Rhodes, Hsch. (Cf. Ἐρεθίμιος.)

ἐριδῑνής, ές, (δῖνος) *whirling, eddying swiftly,* Tryph.231 (v.l. περιδ-).

ἐρίδιον, τό [-ῐδ- Luc.*Ocyp.*89], Dim. of ἔριον, Heliod.ap.Orib.46. 19.4, Sor.1.82, Luc. l. c., Arr.*Epict.*3.22.71, *PMeyer* 20.36 (iii A.D.).

ἐριδμαίνω, = ἐρεθίζω, *to provoke to strife, irritate,* σφήκεσσιν ἐοικότες..οὓς παῖδες ἐριδμαίνωσιν Il.16.260. II. intr., = ἐριδαίνω, *contend,* A.R.3.94; of friendly rivalry, Mosch.2.69; διάτι *APl.*4.297; ἐριδμαίνεσκε χροιῆς ὕπερ Nic.*Al.*407; περὶ νίκης Nonn.*D.*37.490: c. inf., φιλήματος ἄκρα φέρεσθαι Theoc.12.31. 2. c. dat., *contend against,* Nonn.*D.*7.355, al.

ἐρί-δμᾱτος, ον, (δέμω) *strongly-built,* i.e. *immovable, unconquerable,* ἔρις ἐ. A.*Ag.*1461 (lyr.). **-δουπος,** ον, = ἐρίγδουπος, in Hom. always of things and places, ἀκταί, ποταμοί, Il.20.50, Od.10.515; αἴθουσα Il.24.323, Od.20.176; *resounding,* ἀκοή Emp.4.11. **-δωρος,** ον, *rich in gifts, abundant,* ὀπώρη Opp.*C.*3.504. **-έμπορος,** ὁ, *wool-merchant, PTeb.*103.26 (i B.C.), *Sammelb.*3965.

ἐρίζω, Dor. 3 pl. ἐρίζοντι Pi.*N.*5.39; Ep. inf. ἐριζέμεναι, -έμεν, Il. 1.277, 23.404: impf. ἤριζον D.9.11, Dor. ἔρισδον Theoc.6.5, Ep. ἔριζον Il.2.555, Ion. ἐρίζεσκον Od.8.225, Crates Theb.1.3: fut. ἐρίσω *Ev.Matt.*12.19, (δι-) App.*BC*5.127 codd., Dor. ἐρίξω Pi.*Fr.*11: aor. 1 ἤρισα Hes.*Th.*928, Lys.2.42, poet. ἔρισα Pi.*I.*8(7).30, ἔριξα Id.*Pae.* 6.87; Ep. opt. ἐρίσσειε Il.3.223; Dor. part. ἐρίξαντες *Tab.Heracl.*2. 26: pf. ἤρῐκα Plb.3.91.7:—**Med.,** Ep. impf. ἐρίζετο Hes.*Th.*534: aor.

subj. ἐρίσσεται Od.4.80:—Pass., Ep. pf. ἐρήρισμαι (in act. sense), v. infr.: (ἔρις):—*strive, wrangle, quarrel*, διαστήτην ἐρίσαντε Il.1.6, etc.; τὸ δίκαιον οὐκ ἔχει λόγον δυοῖν ἐρίζειν S.*El*.467: c. dat., Hes.*Th*.928, Pi.*Pae*.l.c., etc.; ἀλλήλοις Od.18.277; ἀντιβίην τινί Il.1.277; ἀντία τοῖς ἀγαθοῖς Pi.*P*.4.285; πρὸς θεόν ib.2.88; πρός τινα περί τινος Plu.*Tim*.14; ὅς ποτ' Ἀθαναίαν ἔριν ἤρισε Theoc.5.23; πρὸς πᾶν τὸ λεγόμενον Hdt.7.50; περί τινος about a thing, Il.12.423, al.; περὶ μικρῶν ἀκριβῶς ἐ. Isoc.2.39: folld. by a relat., ἐ. ὅστις ἀρείων Theoc.5.67; ὁπότερος γενναιότερος Pl.*Ly*.207c: c. inf., *contend* that.., ἤριζον οἱ πολλοὶ οὐ λυσιτελήσειν τὴν πάροδον D.9.11: abs., of *sophistical disputations*, opp. διαλέγεσθαι, ἀμφισβητεῖν, Pl.*R*.454a, *Prt*.337b, cf. Crates Theb.1.3; of political *discord*, c. dat., Foed.ap.Th.5.79. 2. *rival, vie with, challenge*, οὐκ ἂν ἔπειτ' Ὀδυσῆΐ γ' ἐρίσσειε βροτὸς ἄλλος Il.3.223; ἐπεὶ σφισιν οὔ τις ἔριζεν Od.8.371: c. acc. rei, *rival* or *contend with* one in a thing, οὐδ' εἰ.. Ἀφροδίτῃ κάλλος ἐρίζοι Il.9.389, cf. Od.5.213, Hes.*Sc*.5: c. dat. rei, δρηστοσύνῃ οὐκ ἄν μοι ἐρίσσειε βροτὸς ἄλλος in service, Od.15.321; ποσί Il.13.325; γνώμῃ καὶ πλήθει καὶ ἀρετῇ ἐ. τινί Lys.2.42; ἐρίσσειαν περὶ μύθων Il.15.284; ἀθανάτοισιν ἐρίζεσκον περὶ τόξων Od.8.225; τῷ Διὶ πλούτου πέρι Hdt.5.49: c. inf., ἐρίζετον ἀλλήλοιιν χερσὶ μαχέσσασθαι Od.18.38; ἶσα δὲ πίνειν οὔτις οἱ ἀνθρώπων ἤρισεν Phalaec.ap.Ath.10.440e; πρὸς θεούς Pl.*R*.395d; Νέστωρ οἶος ἔριζε N. alone *rivalled* (him), Il.2.555, cf. X.*Cyn*.1.12. II. Med., like Act., ᾧ [τόξῳ] οὔ τίς τοι ἐρίζεται Il.5.172; μοι ἐρίσσεται.. κτήμασιν Od.4.80; ἐρίζετο βουλὰς Κρονίωνι Hes.*Th*.534, cf. Pi.*I*.4(3).29: also in pf. Pass., τῷ οὔ τις ἐρήρισται κράτος Hes.*Fr*.195. 2. Pass., ταχυτὰς ποδῶν ἐρίζεται *there are contests in* fleetness of foot, Pi.*O*.1.95.

ἐρί-ζωος, ον, = πάνυ ζῶν, Hsch. **-ήκοος**, ον, (ἀκοή) *sharp of hearing*, λεπτῆς ἀϋτῆς Orph.*L*.468. **-ηρά**, ἡ, (ἔριον) *tax on wool*, *Arch.Pap*.1.552. **-ηρος**, ον, as epith. of ἑταῖρος, perh. *faithful, trusty* (μεγάλως τιμώμενοι κτλ., Hsch.), ἐ. ἑταῖρος, in sg., only in Il.4.266: elsewh. always in heterocl. pl. ἐρίηρες ἑταῖροι, acc. ἐρίηρας ἑταίρους or ἑτάρους ἐρίηρας, Od.9.100, Il.3.47, etc.; parodied by Cratin.143; ἐρίηρος ἀοιδός *loyal* to his master's house, Od.1.346, al. **-ηχής**, ές, (ἠχέω) *loud-sounding*, Opp.*H*.3.213.

ἐριθάκη, ἡ, *bee-bread*, Arist.*HA*554^{a}17, 627^{a}22, Varr.*RR*3.16, Plin.*HN*11.17. 2. *soft parts* of crustaceans, *entrails* of pigs, Hsch.

ἐρῑθακίς, ίδος, ἡ, = ἔριθος (ἡ), *a female day-labourer*, Theoc.3.35.

ἐρίθακος, ὁ, *robin-redbreast, Erithacus rubecula*, Arist.*HA*592^{b}22, *Gp*.15.1.22, etc.; cf. ἐριθεύς, ἐρίθυλος:—the bird described as imitative by Porph.*Abst*.3.4 must be different.

ἐρῑθακώδης, ες, *full of* ἐριθάκη 2, γραῖαι Epich.61.

ἐρι-θᾱλής, ές, (θάλλω) = ἐριθηλής, Limen.6, Hsch. II. Subst. **ἐριθαλές**, τό, *stone-crop, Sedum altissimum*, Plin.*HN*25.160; cf. ἐριθαλίς· εἶδος δένδρου, Hsch.; dub. l. in Ps.-Dsc.4.88. **-θαλλος**, ον, *growing luxuriantly, flourishing*, of plants and trees, Simon.54 (s.v.l.).

Ἐριθάσεος, ὁ, title of Apollo in Attica, *IG*2^{2}.1362 (iv B.C.): written Ἐρισαθεύς in cod. Hsch. (post ἐριθαλεῖς).

ἐρῑθ-εία, ἡ, *labour for wages*, Hsch. (pl.), Suid. II. *canvassing for public office, intriguing*, Arist.*Pol*.1302^{b}4, 1303^{a}14 (pl.). 2. *selfish* or *factious ambition*, ζῆλος καὶ ἐ. *Ep.Jac*.3.14; οἱ ἐξ -είας *Ep.Phil*.1.17; pl., *intrigues, party squabbles*, *Ep.Gal*.5.20. **-εύομαι**, Dep., (ἔριθος) *serve, work for hire*, Lxx *To*.2.11:—so in Act., Hld.1.5. II. of public officers or characters, *canvass, intrigue for office*, οἱ ἐριθευόμενοι Arist.*Pol*.1303^{a}16; cf. ἐξεριθεύομαι. 2. later Act., generally, *compete with*, τινι Sch.S.*Aj*.833: abs., *indulge in petty intrigue*, Eust.1162.23. **-εύς**, έως, ὁ, = ἐρίθακος, Thphr.*Sign*.39, Arat.1025. **-ευτός**, Cret. -εοτός, ή, όν, *corrupt*, δίκα *SIG*526.26 (Itanos, iii B.C.).

ἐρίθεχνα, τά, *for wool-work* (?), ἔρια κηρίθεκνα ϝεργαλεῖα dub. in *Schwyzer*180 (Crete): more prob. χηρίτεχνα, = χειρίτεχνα.

ἐρῑθηλής, ές, (θάλλω) *very flourishing, luxuriant*, of plants, μυρίκης τ' ἐριθηλέας ὄζους Il.10.467; ἔρνος.. ἐριθηλὲς ἐλαίης 17.53; δάφνης ἐριθηλέος ὄζον Hes.*Th*.30; of gardens, ἀλωάων ἐριθηλέων Il.5.90; γαῖα A.R.2.723: metaph., εὐνομία *APl*.4.72.5, cf. Orph.*Fr*.142, 206.

Ἐρίθιος, ὁ, epith. of Apollo in Cyprus, Ptol.Heph.ap.Phot.*Bibl*.p.153 B.

ἔρῑθος, ὁ, ἡ, *day-labourer, hired servant*; of *mowers* or *reapers*, Il.18.550, 560; later ἔριθοι, αἱ, *spinsters* and *weavers, workers in wool* (prob. because popularly derived from ἔριον), D.57.45, Theoc.15.80; ἐρίων ἔριθοι *PHib*.1.121.34 (iii B.C.); of spiders, πάντα δ' ἐρίθων ἀραχνᾶν βρίθει S.*Fr*.286, cf. Philostr.*Im*.2.28. II. metaph., *servant, minister*, τλήμων γαστρὸς ἔριθος, = *crepitus ventris*, *h.Merc*.296; Ἔρις .. Νίκης κασιγνήτη καὶ ἔ. Timo 21.2; ὕπνον νυκτὸς ἔ. Epic.Anon. in *BKT*5(1)p.70.

ἐρίθυλος, ὁ, = ἐρίθακος, Sch.Ar.*V*.922.

ἐρί-θῡμος, ον, *high-spirited*, Q.S.1.742, Orph.*Fr*.270. **-θυρίς**, Aeol. ἔρθυρις· ἡ μεγάλη θυρίς, *EM*377.35.

ἐρικάνην· φραγμόν, Hsch.:—also **ἐρικέα**· φράγματα, and **ἐρίκεος**· φραγμοῦ, Id. (Perh. to be connected with ἐρικάνη, ἔρκος.)

ἐρῑκεῖν, v. ἐρείκω. **ἐρικευθές**· πυθμήν, Hsch.

ἐρίκ-η, -ηρόν, etc., later spellings of ἐρείκ-η, -ηρόν, etc.

ἐρι-κλάγκτης, ου, ὁ, (κλάζω) *loud-sounding*, γόος Pi.*P*.12.21. **-κλαυτος**, ον, *much-weeping*, γονεῖς *AP*7.560 (Paul. Sil.); πένθος *Epigr.Gr*.406.8 (Iconium). II. Pass., *much-wept, bewailed*, Opp.*H*.2.668 (-κλαυστ-), Epic.Anon. in *BKT*5(1)p.85. **-κλῡτός**, όν, *much-renowned*, cj. for ἀγακλυτός, Orph.*A*.1030.

ἐρῑκόεις, later spelling of ἐρεικόεις.

ἐρικός, ή, όν, *woollen*, *PRev.Laws*103.2 (iii B.C.).

ἐρικτέᾰνος, ον, *wealthy*, Opp.*C*.1.312.

ἐρικτός, ή, όν, v. ἐρεικτός.

ἐρί-κτῠπος, ον, *loud-sounding*, of Poseidon, Hes.*Th*.456, 930. **-κῡδής**, ές, *very famous, glorious*, of gods and their descendants, Il.14.327, Od.11.576, 631; of their gifts, θεῶν ἐ. δῶρα Il.3.65, 20.265; ἥβη ἐ. 11.225, Hes.*Th*.988; νίκα B.12.190: generally, ἐ. δαίς *a splendid* banquet, Il.24.802, Od.3.66, al.; of places and men, ἄστυ Orac.ap.Hdt.7.220; θεῶν ἐ. οἶκοι Theoc.17.108; φῶτες Orph.*L*.302: Sup. -έστατος, Ἰάμβλιχος Eun.*VS* p.461 B. **-κύμων** [ῡ], ον, (κύω) *big with young*, ἐ. φέρματι γέννας A.*Ag*.119 codd. recc. (ἐρικύματα cod. Med.). **-λαμπέτις**, ἡ, pecul. fem. of sq., Max.103. **-λαμπής**, ές, *bright-shining*, σοφίη Procl.*H*.4.13.

ἐρίμη· ἔξοδος, Hsch. (Cf. ἐξίθμη, ἑρμή.)

ἐρι-μύκης [ῡ], ου, ὁ, = sq., ταῦρος Call.*Fr*.13^{b} (dub. l.). **-μῡκος**, ον, (μυκάομαι, μέμυκα) *loud-bellowing*, βοῶν ὑπὸ πόσσ' ἐριμύκων Il.20.497, cf. 23.775, Od.15.235, Hes.*Op*.790; ὀλολυγά *AP*6.219.17 (Antip.).

ἐρῑν-άζω, aor. 1 inf. ἐρινάξαι and ἐρινάσαι, Hsch.:—*hang fruiting branches of the wild fig* (ἐρινεός) *near the cultivated fig* (συκῇ) in order that the gall-insect (ψήν) which lives in the wild fruit may carry pollen to the σῦκον, Thphr.*CP*2.9.5:—Pass., τὸ ἐρινασμένον *the fig subjected to caprification*, Id.*HP*2.8.3. II. *gather wild figs*, Poll.7.143. **-άς**, άδος, ἡ, = ἐρινεός, Nic.*Th*.854. II. = ὄλυνθος, Amer.ap.Ath.3.76e (ἐρίνακας codd.), Hsch. **-άς**· νέας βοῦς, Id. **-ασμός**, ὁ, *caprification*, Thphr.*CP*2.9.5, *HP*2.8.1. **-αστός**, ή, όν, *subjected to caprification*, Id.*CP*2.9.12. **-εόν**, τό, *fruit of the* ἐρινεός, Hp.*Loc.Hom*.47: pl., ἐρινεά *PCair.Zen*.33.12 (iii B.C.), v.l. in Arist.*HA*557^{b}28. **-εός**, ὁ, *wild fig-tree, Ficus Caprificus*, Il.6.433, al., Hes.*Fr*.160, Arist.*HA*557^{b}25, Thphr.*HP*2.2.4; Att. **ἐρινεώς** Lync.ap.Ath.3.75d; ἐρινεὼν ἕνα χαλκωτόν *BCH*35.16 (Delos). 2. = ἐρινεόν, Arist.*HA*557^{b}25, Dsc.1.128. 3. = ἔρινος, v.l. in Diocl.*Fr*.149 (= Sch.Nic.*Th*.647). II. Adj. **ἐρινεός**, ά, όν, contr. **-οῦς**, ῆ, οῦν, *of the wild fig-tree*, ἐρινεὸν σῦκον, = ἐρινεός, Arist.*HA*554^{a}15; ἐρινῶν σύκων Ath.3.76c (quoting ἐρινοῖς fr. Epich.128); κράδαις ἐριναῖς E.*Fr*.679.

ἐρίνεος [ῐ], α, ον, Ion. also **εἰρίνεος**, η, ον, *woollen*, κιθών, εἵματα, πῖλοι εἰρ., Hdt.1.195, 2.81, 4.73; τρυχία, προσκεφάλαιον, Hp.*Art*.78, *Fract*.16 (ἐρ- codd., but εἰρ- *Acut*.21); cf. Att. ἐρεοῦς.

ἐρῑν-εώδης, ες, *full of wild fig-trees*, Str.13.1.35. **-εώς**, εώ, ὁ, v. ἐρινεός I.1. **-όν**, τό, *wild fig*, ἐρίν' ἀπέδοτο, σῦκα πωλεῖν ὀμνύων Alex.128.8, cf. Thphr.*HP*2.8.2, v.l. in Arist.*HA*557^{b}28; read by Aristarch. in Od.5.281. **-ός**, ὁ, = ἐρινεός, *wild fig-tree*, Stratt.42, Theoc.25.250, Lyc.741, *IG*11(2).287*A*153 (Delos, iii B.C.), *Inscr.Délos*353*A*37 (iii B.C.), v.l. in Arist.*HA*557^{b}31. 2. = ἐρινόν, *a wild fig*, πέπων ἐ. S.*Fr*.181; ὀπόεντας ἐ. Nic.*Al*.319.

ἔρινος, ὁ, a plant like *basil*, Nic.*Th*.647, cf. Diocl.*Fr*.149. 2. = ἐπιμήδιον, Ps.-Dsc.4.19, v.l. for ἐχῖνος, Dsc.4.141, cf. Paul.Aeg.7.3.

Ἐρῑνύς (so, not Ἐριννύς, in best codd. and Inscrr., cf. *Tab.Defix*.108 (iii/ii B.C.), *IG*12(3).367 (Thera); later Ἐρεινύας ib.12(9).1179.34 (Euboea, ii A.D.)), gen. ύος, ἡ: pl. Ἐρινύες, acc. Ἐρινῦς Od.2.135, etc.; gen. pl. Ἐρινύων trisyll., E.*IT*931, 970. [ῡ in trisyll. cases (nom. sg. -ῦς E.*Med*.1389 (anap.), but acc. sg. -ῦν ib.1260 (lyr., s.v.l.)), ῠ in quadrisyll.]:—*the Erinys*, an avenging deity, ἠεροφοῖτις Ἐ. Il.9.571, 19.87; δασπλῆτις Ἐ. Od.15.234: more freq. in pl., μήτηρ στυγερὰς ἀρήσετ' Ἐρινῦς 2.135, etc.; Γαῖα.. γείνατ' Ἐρινῦς Hes.*Th*.185; later three in number, μίαν τριῶν Ἐ. E.*Tr*.457 (troch.), cf. Apollod.1.1.4, etc.; avengers of perjury, homicide, unfilial conduct, etc., Il.19.259, 9.454; upholders of the natural and moral order, ἥλιος οὐχ ὑπερβήσεται μέτρα· εἰ δὲ μή, Ἐρινύες μιν Δίκης ἐπίκουροι ἐξευρήσουσιν Heraclit.94; Ἐρινύες ἔσχεθον αὐδήν (sc. of the horse of Achilles, as rebuking presumption), Il.19.418: com., Ἐρινύων ἀπορρώξ, of Timon, Ar.*Lys*.811 (lyr.). II. in less personal sense, *guilt, punishment invoked* upon the guilty, freq. c. gen., μητρὸς Ἐρινύες *curses from* one's mother, Il.21.412, Od.11.280; τείσαιτο ἐρινῦς πατρὸς παίδων τε Hes.*Th*.472; ἱδρύσαντο Ἐρινύων τῶν Λαΐου τε καὶ Οἰδιπόδεω ἱρόν Hdt.4.149; Ἀρά τ' Ἐρινὺς πατρὸς ἡ μεγασθενής A.*Th*.70, cf. S.*OC*1434, etc.; later in Prose, ξενικαὶ Ἐ. Pl.*Ep*.357a; ἐρινῦς καὶ ποινὰς τῶν δι' ἐκεῖνον ἠτυχηκότων Plb.23.10.2; of persons in whom such powers are embodied, νυμφόκλαυτος Ἐ. A.*Ag*.749 (lyr.); ἔτεκε νύμφα δόμοις Ἐ. S.*Tr*.895 (lyr.), cf. E.*Med*.1260 (lyr.), etc.; φρενῶν Ἐρινὺς *frenzy* of the soul, S.*Ant*.603 (lyr.); Ἐρινὺν ἐπορθιάζειν raise a *Fury-song*, A.*Ag*.1119. III. epith. of Demeter in Arcadia, Antim.28, Call.*Fr*.207, Paus.8.25.6. IV. = Ἀφροδίτης εἴδωλον, Hsch. (Derived from Arc. ἐρινύειν, = θυμῷ χρῆσθαι, by Paus. l.c.)

ἐρῑνύω, v. foreg. ad fin.

Ἐρῑνῡώδης, ες, *like the* Ἐρινύες, Plu.2.458c; συκοφαντίαι ib.602e.

ἐρίξας, v. ἐρείκω. **ἐριοῖ**· ἐργάζεται, Hsch.

ἐριο-κάρτης, ου, ὁ, (κείρω) *shearer*, *PFlor*.71.438, al. (iv A.D.); perh. cf. ἐριωκαίτης, ἐριωκέδης, *PTeb*.401.1, 16 (i A.D.). **-κόμος**, ὁ, = ἐριουργός, Hdn.*Philet*.p.449 P.; cf. εἰροκόμος.

ἔριον, τό, Ion. εἴριον *GDI* iv p.876 (Chios, iv B.C., also written ἔρια ibid.), Hdt., Hp., and always in Hom. (indicating ἐρϝ-) exc. gen. ἐρίοιο in Od.4.124:—*wool*, Il.12.434, Od.l.c., Pl.*Smp*.175d; ἐρίῳ στέψαντες, i.e. with woollen fillets, Id.*R*.398a, etc.: freq. in pl., Il.3.388, Od.18.316; εἴρια ῥυπαρά, ἔρια οἰσυπηρά, greasy wool, Hp.*Fract*.21, Dsc.2.74; ἔρια καθαρά *PCair.Zen*.12.62 (iii B.C.); τἄρια, crasis for τὰ ἔ., Ar.*Ra*.1387; οὖλα ἔρια ib.1067; ἔ. πεπταμένα outspread *flocks of wool*, Id.*Nu*.343; ἐρίων τάλαντον Id.*V*.1147; τὰ Μιλήσια ἔ. Eub.90.3, cf. Amphis 27.1; εἴρια ἀπὸ ξύλου *cotton*, Hdt.3.

47, cf. 106; τὸ ἔ. [τῆς ἀράχνης] a spider's *web*, Philostr.*Im.*2.28; τὰ ἐκ τῆς θαλάττης ἔ., of the *byssus* of the pinna, Alciphr.1.2. (ἔρια *Schwyzer* 180 (Crete) without initial ϝ-; Lat. *vervex* perh. not cogn.)

ἐριό-ξῦλον, τό, *cotton*, Ulp.ap.*Dig.*32.70.9; cf. ἐρεόξ-. **-πλύτης** [ῠ], ου, ὁ, (πλύνω) *wool-cleaner, fuller*, Dsc.2.163, *BGU* 118 iii 7 (ii A.D.); ἡ ἐργασία τῶν ἐ. *IGRom.*4.821 (Hierapolis). **-πωλέω**, *sell* or *deal in wool*, Poll.7.28. **-πώλης**, ου, ὁ, *a dealer in wool*, Critias 70 D., Poll.7.28, *PLips.*14.6 (iv A.D.); cf. ἐρεοπώλης. **-πωλικῶς**, Adv. *like a wool-dealer, roguishly*, Ar.*Ra.*1386. **-πώλιον**, τό, *woolshop*, in pl., Zeno *Stoic.*1.58, J.*BJ* 5.8.1. **-ραβδιστής**, οῦ, ὁ, *wool-beater*, *Stud.Pal.*4 p.70 (i A.D.). **-στεπτος**, ον, (στέφω) *wreathed in wool*, κλάδοι A.*Supp.*22 (anap., Auratus for ἱεροστ-).

ἐριούνης, ὁ, v. sq.

ἐριούνιος and **ἐριούνης**, ὁ, Ep. epith. of Hermes, of uncertain meaning, σῶκος ἐριούνιος Ἑρμῆς Il.20.72; Ἑρμείας ἐριούνιος 24.457, 679; ἐριούνης Ἑρμείας 20.34, Od.8.322; Διὸς ἐριούνιος υἱός *h.Merc.* 28; θεῶν ἐριούνιε δαῖμον ib.551: abs., ἐριούνιος, i.e. Hermes, Il.24.360, 440; Ἑρμῆς ἐ., opp. δόλιος, Ar.*Ra.*1144, cf. *EM* 374.24; also in later Prose, θεοί Ant.Lib.25.2. II. as Adj., ἐ. νόος Orph.*L.*199.

ἐριουργ-εῖον, τό, *wool-factory*, Poll.7.28. **-έω**, *work in wool*, X.*HG* 5.4.7, *Lac.*1.3, etc. **-ία**, ἡ, *wool-working*, Poll.7.28, Sor.1.4 (pl.). **-ικός**, ή, όν, *for wool-work*, [σφόνδυλος] ib.110. **-ός**, όν, *working in wool*, D.C.79.7: as Subst., *wool-worker*, Gal.10.11, *PRyl.*94.14 (i A.D.), Ath.14.618e; ἡ ἱερὰ φυλὴ τῶν ἐ., at Philadelphia, *IGRom.*4.1632.28.

ἐριοῦς, v. ἐρεοῦς.

ἐριο-ῠφάντης, ου, ὁ, *weaver of wool*, *PTeb.*5.239 (ii B.C.). **-φόρος**, ον, *wool-bearing*, δένδρον *cotton*-tree, *Gossypium arboreum*, Thphr. *HP* 4.7.7 (pl.); ἐ. βολβός, *Pancratium maritimum*, ib.7.13.8.

ἐριπεῖν, v. ἐρείπω. **ἔριπες**· δαλοί, Hsch. **ἐρίπεσθαι**· φθίνειν (φθονεῖν cod.), Id.

ἐρίπλευρος, ον, *with sturdy sides, stout*, φυά Pi.*P.*4.235.

ἐρίπνη, ἡ, (ἐρείπω) *broken cliff, crag*, in pl., E.*El.*210 (lyr.), A.R.1.581, 2.1247, etc.: sg., Nic.*Th.*22; any *sheer ascent*, ἐπάλξεων ἐρίπναι E.*Ph.*1168.

ἐρίπνοος, ον, *blowing strongly*, Lyr. in *Philol.*80.338.

ἐριπόω, = ἐρείπω, *EM* 374.32.

ἐριπτοίητος, ον, *much scared*, Nonn.*D.*28.13.

ἐρίπτω, = ἐρείπω, *EM* 374.34, Sch.Il.14.15.

ἔρις (A), ιδος, ἡ, acc. ἔριν Od.3.136, etc.; also ἔριδα, usu. in Ep.: pl. ἔριδες, later ἔρεις *Ep.Tit.*3.9, etc.:—*strife, quarrel, contention*: I. in Il., mostly of *battle-strife*, αἰεὶ γάρ τοι ἔ. τε φίλη πόλεμοί τε μάχαι τε 1.177; μεμαυῖ' ἔριδος καὶ ἀϋτῆς 5.732, cf. 13.358; κακὴ ἔ. 3.7; ἔ. πτολέμοιο 14.389, al.; reversely, ἔριδος νεῖκος 17.384; ἔριδα ξυνάγοντες Ἄρηος 5.861; ἔριδι or ἐξ ἔριδος μάχεσθαι, 1.8, 7.111; ἔριδι ξυνιέναι 20.66, 21.390; later, τὰν Ἀδράστου τάν τε Καδμείων ἔριν Pi.*N.*8.51; ἔρις ἐνόπλιος Gorg.*Fr.*6 D. II. generally, *quarrel, strife*, ἔρις θυμοβόρος Il.20.253, etc.: less freq. in pl., ἔριδας καὶ νείκεα ib.251: freq. of political or domestic *discord*, φόνοι, στάσεις, ἔρις, μάχαι S.*OC* 1234 (lyr.); ἔριδες, νείκη, στάσις, . . πόλεμος Ar.*Th.*788; ἔριδος ἀγών S.*Aj.* 1163 (anap.); ὅταν φίλοι φίλοισι συμβάλωσ' ἔριν E.*Med.*521; ἔριν περί τινος ἐκφυγεῖν Pl.*Lg.*736c; λύειν, καταοβέσαι, E.*Ph.*81, S.*OC* 422; γενέσθαι ἔριν πρὸς σφᾶς αὐτούς Th.6.31: with Preps., ἐς ἔριν ἐλθεῖν τινι Hdt.9.33, cf. Ar.*Ra.*877 (hex.); ἀφῖχθαι, ἐμπεσεῖν, E.*IA* 319 (troch.), 377; ἐν πολλῇ ἔριδι εἶναι Th.2.21; ἐν ἔριδι εἶναι πρὸς ἀλλήλους Id.6.35; ὑπὲρ τοῦ μέλλοντος δι' ἐρίδων ἦν Plu.*Caes.*33: c. inf., εἰσῆλθε τοῖν τρὶς ἀθλίοιν ἔρις . . ἀρχῆς λαβέσθαι S.*OC* 372. 2. *wordy wrangling, disputation*, ἐκ τῆς ἔριδος . . ἐμάχοντο Hdt.1.82; κοινῶν λόγων δώσοντες ἀλλήλοις ἔριν E.*Ba.*715; ἐγένετο ἔρις τοῖς ἀνθρώποις μὴ λοιμὸν ὠνομάσθαι ἀλλὰ λιμόν Th.2.54; ἦν ἔρις καὶ ἄγνοια εἴτε . . Id.3.111; μεστὸς ἐρίδων καὶ δοξοσοφίας Pl.*Phlb.*49a, cf. *Ti.*88a; ἡ περὶ τὰς ἔριδας φιλοσοφία Isoc.10.6; ἔριδος ἕνεκα Pl.*Sph.*237b; cf. ἐριστικός. III. Personified, *Eris*, a goddess who excites to war, Ἔ. κρατερή Il.20.48; ἐν δ' Ἔ. ἐν δὲ Κυδοιμὸς ὁμίλεον, ἐν δ' ὀλοὴ Κήρ 18.535; Νὺξ . . Ἔριν τέκε καρτερόθυμον Hes.*Th.*225: hence, as goddess of *Discord*, at the marriage of Peleus and Thetis, Coluth.39, al. 2. as a principle of nature, πάντα κατ' ἔριν γίνεσθαι Heraclit.8: pl., Emp.124.2. IV. *contention, rivalry*, freq. in Od., ἔργοιο in work, 18.366; ὅς τις ἔριδα προφέρηται ἀέθλων for prizes, 8.210; ἔρις χερσὶ γένηται 18.13; ἔριδα προφέρουσαι in eager *rivalry*, 6.92; ἔριν στήσαντες ἐν ὑμῖν 16.292: in later Poets, *contest*, καλλονᾶς, μελῳδίας, E.*IA* 1308, *Rh.*923; ὅπλων ἔριν ἔθηκε συμμάχοις Id.*Hel.*100; ἔριν ἔχειν ἀμφὶ μουσικῇ Hdt.6.129; Ἥρα Παλλάδι τ' ἔριν μορφᾶς ἁ Κύπρις ἔσχεν E.*IA* 183; ἔριν ἐμβάλλειν τισὶ πρὸς ἀλλήλους ὅπως . . X.*Cyr.*6.2.4; εἰς ἔριν ὁρμᾶσθαι ταύτης τῆς μάχης πρὸς τοὺς πεπαιδευμένους ib.2.3.15; εἰς ἔριν συμβάλλειν τινὰς περὶ ἀρετῆς Id.*Lac.*4.2; κατ' ἔριν τὴν Ἀθηναίων out of *rivalry with* . ., Hdt.5.88, cf. Pl.*Criti.*109b; ἔβα Πινδάροιο (leg. -οι) ποτ' ἔριν Corinn. 21; Διὸς βρονταῖσιν εἰς ἔριν κτυπῶν in *rivalry with* . ., E.*Cyc.*328; in good sense, ἔρις ἀγαθῶν A.*Eu.*975 (lyr.), cf. Hes.*Op.*24.

ἔρις (B), = ἶρις, Att., acc. to Hsch. s. v. ἔριδας.

ἐρίς, ἡ, perh. *wool-worker*, *PLond.ined.*2172 (ii A.D.).

Ἐρισαθεύς, v. Ἐριθάσεος.

ἐρῐσάλπιγξ, ιγγος, ὁ, ἡ, *loud-trumpeting*, name of a bird in Sch. Ar.*Av.*884: in Hsch. **ἠρισάλπιγξ**.

ἐρισθενής, ές, *very mighty*, epith. of Zeus, Il.13.54, Od.8.289, Hes. *Th.*4, etc.; also of Poseidon, Id.*Cat.Oxy.*1358 *Fr.*2.27; of men, A.R.1.41, etc.; of the Furies, Orph.*H.*69.7; ἐ. ἕρμα πόληος *Epigr. Gr.*452.11 (Syria); ἐ. θέμεθλα *AP* 9.808.6 (Cyrus).

ἐρισία, ἡ, = ἔρις, Theognost.*Can.*87.

ἐρίσκηπτον, τό, (ἔρις (B), σκήπτω) = ἐρυσίσκηπτρον, Hsch., prob. cj. in Plu.2.664f; *erisceptron* is v.l. in Dsc.1.4, *aerisceptron* in 1.20.

ἔρισμα, ατος, τό, (ἐρίζω) *cause of quarrel*, Il.4.38. II. ἐρίσμασιν· εἰρεσίαις, Hsch.

ἐρισμάρᾰγος [μᾰ], ον, *loud-thundering*, epith. of Zeus, Hes.*Th.*815, *IGRom.*4.360.13 (Pergam.), etc.; θάλασσα Musae.318; ἀστραπή Luc. *Tim.*1.

ἐρισμός, ὁ, = ἔρις, Timo 28.3.

ἐρί-σπορος, ον, *well-sown*, αἶα Opp.*C.*2.119. **-στάφῠλος** [ᾰ], ον, of wine, *made of fine grapes*, Od.9.111, 358. II. *rich in grapes*, of Lesbos, Archestr.*Fr.*56.9; of Bacchus, *AP* 9.580.6, Nonn.*D.*12.251. **-στέφᾰνος**, ον, *eminently crowned*, epith. of Rhea, *Rev.Ét. Gr.*19.268 (Aphrodisias).

ἐριστήρ· μαρσίππιον (-ίππιος cod.), σάκκος, ἢ ἔρκτης καὶ πράκτης, Hsch. (leg. ἐρκτήρ).

ἐριστ-ής, οῦ, ὁ, (ἐρίζω) *wrangler*, Lxx *Ps.*138(139).20 (pl., v.l.). **-ικός**, ή, όν, *eager for strife* or *battle*, Sch.E.*IA* 588. 2. *involving a contest* (or perh. *debate*), παιδιαί Arist.*Rh.*1371ᵃ1. II. esp. *fond of wrangling* or *arguing, captious*, Pl.*Ly.*211b, etc.; ὁ ἐ. ἐστί πως οὕτως ἔχων πρὸς τὸν διαλεκτικὸν ὡς ὁ ψευδογράφος πρὸς τὸν γεωμετρικόν Arist.*SE* 171ᵇ35; οἱ Ἀκαδημιακοὶ τῶν ἄλλων ἐριστικώτεροι Luc.*Pisc.* 43: Sup. -ώτατος D.L.2.134; Ἐριστικοί, οἱ, nickname of the Megarian school, ib.106; ἡ -κὴ τέχνη *sophistry*, Pl.*Sph.*231e, al.; τὸ -κόν, defined as τὸ ἔντεχνον καὶ περὶ δικαίων . . καὶ ἀδίκων ἀμφισβητοῦν ib.225c; τὰ ἐ. Arist.*Rh.*1402ᵃ3; ἐ. συλλογισμός, λόγος, *sophism, fallacy*, Id.*Top.*100ᵇ23, *Metaph.*1012ᵃ19 (pl.); τέχνη ἐριστικῶν, a work of Protagoras, D.L.9.55. Adv. -κῶς Pl.*R.*454b, Arist. *Ph.*186ᵃ6. **-ός**, ή, όν, *that may be contested*, τὰ δὲ τοῖς δυνατοῖς οὐκ ἐριστὰ πλάθειν such *contests* cannot *be waged* with the powerful, so as to engage with them, S.*El.*220 (lyr.).

ἐρισύβη, ἡ, = ἐρυσίβη, Lxx *De.*28.42, Hsch.

ἐρι-σφάρᾰγος [φᾰ], ον, *loud-roaring*, of Poseidon, *h.Merc.*187; of Zeus, Pi.*Fr.*15, B.5.20; *loud-voiced*, of men, Plu.2.698e. **-σφηλος**, ον, *overthrowing much*, of Heracles, Stesich.82.

ἐρίσχηλος, ον, = λοίδορος, ἐρισχήλοις κορυνήταις Parth.*Fr.*18; cf. ἐρεσχηλέω.

ἐρι-ταρβής, ές, *very timid*, Hsch. **-τῑμος**, ον, *highly-prized, precious*, of gold, Il.9.126; of the Aegis, 2.447; τρίποδες *h.Ap.*443, Ar.*Eq.*1016; of persons, Man.3.324; Μοῖραι dub. cj. in *Epigr.Gr.* 248.9; in later Prose, φιλοσοφία Them.*Or.*2.54d; iron., δουλείη *IG* 14.1363. II. as Subst., a fish, prob. a kind of *sardine*, Dorio and Epaenet.ap.Ath.7.328f, Diph.Siph.ib.355f, *PLips.*92.3 [*Arch. Pap.*4.482] (ii/iii A.D.). **-τμητος**, ον, *well-cut*, ἱμάντες Opp.*C.* 4.106.

ἐριφέας· χίμαρος, Hsch.

ἐριφεγγής, ές, *very brilliant*, Procl.*H.*3.13(7), Man.6.22.

ἐρίφειος, ον, (ἔριφος) *of a kid*, Pherecr.130.9, Antiph.222.7, X.*An.* 4.5.31; ζωμός Dieuch.ap.Orib.4.6.1: **Ἐρίφιος**, epith. of Dionysus at Metapontum, Apollod.ap.St.Byz. s. v. Ἀκρώρεια, cf. Hsch.

ἐριφιήματα· ἔριφοι (Lacon.), Hsch.

ἐρίφιον, τό, Dim. of ἔριφος, Athenio 1.30, *Ev.Matt.*25.33, Gal.8.443, *PLond.*1.113.4, etc. II. = *rubus agrestis*, *Gloss.*

ἐρι-φλεγής, ές, *much-flaming*, Nonn.*D.*26.33. **-φλοιος**, ον, *with thick bark*, δρύες, Pergamene wood, Agathocl.ap.Eust.994.42.

ἔρῐφος, ὁ (ἡ, Alc.*Supp.*24.1, *GDI* 5029 (Crete)), *kid*, ἀρνεσσιν . . ἠ ἐρίφοισι Il.16.352, cf. 24.262, Od.9.226, Alc. l.c., Orph.*Fr.*32c, etc. II. Ἔριφοι, οἱ, the constellation *Haedi*, Democr.14, Theoc. 7.53 (cf. Sch. ad loc.), Arat.158, Eratosth.*Cat.*13, Chio *Ep.*4.1, Ptol. *Alm.*7.5, etc.

ἐρῐφοστάσιον [ᾰ], τό, *fold, pen for kids*, *Gloss.*

Ἐριφύλλιος, ὁ, epith. of Apollo and Hermes, Hsch.

ἐρίφυλλος, ον, *with many* or *large leaves*, Hsch.

Ἐριχθόνιος, ὁ, an Attic hero, A.*Fr.*368, E.*Ion* 21, Arist.*Fr.*637, etc.: **Ἐριχθονίδαι**, = Ἐρεχθεῖδαι, *IG* 3.771.

ἐρίχρῡσος, ον, *rich in gold, wealthy*, βασιλῆες *AP* 9.785.

ἔριψ· σωμάτιον, Hsch.

ἐριώδης, ες, Ion. εἰρι-, *like wool, woolly*, Hp.*Art.*49, Arist.*HA* 630ᵃ 30, Thphr.*HP* 3.7.4; κιρσοί Orib.45.18.28.

ἐριωδία· ἅμαξα, Hsch.; cf. ἐριδίαν, ἐρωδία.

ἐριώδῠνος, ον, (ὀδύνη) *very painful*, Max.161, Hsch.

ἐριώδων, οντος, ὁ, ἡ, (ὀδούς) *with large teeth*, Hsch.

ἐριώλη (on the accent, v. Hdn.Gr.1.324), ἡ, *whirlwind, hurricane*, A.R.1.1132 (prob. cj.), 4.1778; applied to Cleon, Ar.*Eq.*511, with pun on ἔριον, ὀλλύναι, *V.*1148, cf. Dionys.Trag.12.

ἐριώπης, ου, ὁ, fem. -ῶπις, ιδος, (ὤψ) *large-eyed, full-eyed*, in fem., Hom.*Epigr.*1.2: fem. acc. ἐριώπεα Max.545 (s. v. l.); ἐρίωπα Id.32.

ἐρκάζειν· σκώπτειν, Hsch.

ἐρκάνη, ἡ, (ἕρκος) *fence, enclosure*, Ael.Dion.*Fr.*179; *stall, pen*, Them.*Or.*23.292a.

ἐρκατή· φυλακή, Hsch. **ἔρκατος**· φραγμός, Id.

ἑρκ-εῖος (freq. written ἕρκειος in codd.), ον, also α, ον A.*Ch.*653:—*of* or *in the* ἕρκος or *front court*, Ζεὺς Ἑ., as the household god, Od.22.335, Hdt.6.68, S.*Ant.*487, E.*Tr.*17, Cratin.Jun.9, Pl.*Euthd.*302d, Arist.*Mu.*401ᵃ20: abs., Ἑρκεῖος, ὁ, Paus.4.17.4; also βωμὸς ἑ. Pi. *Pae.*6.114. 2. Ἑρκεῖοι, οἱ, = Lat. *Penates*, D.H.1.67. 3. πύλαι, θύρα ἑ., the gates, door *of the court*, A.*Ch.*561, 571, 653; πρὸς κίον' ἑρκείου στέγης S.*Aj.*108; ἐφ' ἑρκείῳ πυρᾷ E.*Tr.*483. **-ίον**, τό, *fence, enclosure*, αὐλῆς Il.9.476, Od.18.102; ἐξ ἑρκίων καὶ ἐξ οἰκίας ἐκπετόμενος Thphr.*Sign.*53; later, *dwelling*, A.R.2.1073. **-ίτης**

[ῐ], ου, ὁ, name for a *farm-slave*, Amer.ap.Ath.6.267c. (Written ἑρκῆται in Hsch.)

ἑρκο-θηρικός, ή, όν, (θήρα) *of* or *for netting* or *fishing with nets*, Pl.*Sph.*220c: **-θηρευτικός**, Poll.7.139: Subst. **-ρευτής**, οῦ, ὁ, ib. 137. **-πεζα**, ἡ, *thorn-hedge*, Hsch., Phot. (Cf. ἅρπεζα.)

ἕρκος, εος, τό, *fence, enclosure* (πᾶν ὅσον ἂν ἕνεκα κωλύσεως εἴργῃ τι περιέχον Pl.*Sph.*220b) round gardens and vineyards, Od.7.113, Il. 5.90, 18.564; esp. round the court-yards of houses, Od.21.238 (pl.), al.; ὑπὲρ ἕρκος ὑπερθορεῖν Sol.4.29, Hdt.6.134: pl., S.*Aj.*1274; also, *the place enclosed, court-yard*, στὰς μέσῳ ἕρκεϊ Il.16.231, cf. Od.8.57 (pl.), etc.; Κίσσιον ἕρκος, i.e. Susa, A.*Pers.*17 (anap.); ποῖον γαίας ἕ.; what city? E.*Heracl.*441; ἕ. ἱερόν sacred *enclosure*, S.*Tr.*607; shell of the pinna, Plu.2.980b. 2. *wall for defence*, ἕρκεϊ χαλκείῳ Il.15.567; ἕρκος.. ἐκ ναυηγίων περιεβάλοντο Hdt.7.191, cf. 9.99. 3. periphr., ἕ. ὀδόντων the *fence* (consisting) of the teeth, mostly in phrase, ποῖόν σε ἔπος φύγεν ἕ. ὀδόντων; Il.4.350, cf. Sol.27.1; ἀμείψεται ἕ. ὀδόντων Il.9.409, Od.10.328; κάρχαρον ἕ., without ὀδόντων, Opp.*H.*1. 506; ἀγγέων ἕρκεσι, = ἄγγεσι, Pi.*N.*10.36; μέλαν ἕ. ἅλμας, i.e. the sea, Id.*Dith.Oxy.*1.16, cf. *P.*2.80 (= ἐπιφάνεια, Sch.); σφραγῖδος ἕ., i.e. a seal, S.*Tr.*615. 4. metaph., *defence*, ἕ. ἀκόντων, of a shield, *a defence against* javelins, Il.15.646; ἕ. βελέων 5.316; ἕ. ἰωχμοῖο, of the lion's skin, Theoc.25.279; ἕρκεσιν εἴργειν κῦμα θαλάσσας A. *Pers.*89 (lyr.). b. of persons, ἕ. Ἀχαιῶν, of Ajax, Il.3.229; of Achilles, Pi.*Pae.*6.85; of soldiers, ἕρκος πολέμοιο *a defence against* war, Il.4.299; of Achilles, ἕ. Ἀχαιοῖσιν.. πολέμοιο 1.284; of Clytaemnestra, γαίας μονόφρουρον ἕ. A.*Ag.*257 (lyr.): abs., Pi.*P.*5.113, etc. 5. *a net, toils*, for birds, Od.22.469: mostly in pl., σπίζ' ὅπως ἐν ἕρκεσιν S.*Fr.*431, cf. Ar.*Av.*528 (anap.), Pherecr.209, Arist. *HA*617^{b}24; for deer, Pi.*N.*3.51; *coils* of a lasso, Hdt.7.85: metaph., τῆς Δίκης ἐν ἕρκεσιν A.*Ag.*1611, cf. S.*Aj.*60, E.*Med.*986 (lyr.); λέκτρων ἔχεσθαι φιλτάτοις ἐν ἕρκεσι Id.*Ba.*958, cf.*Hymn.Is.*158; χρυσοδέτοις ἕρκεσιν.. γυναικῶν, of Eriphyle's necklace, S.*El.*838 (lyr.).

ἑρκοῦρος, ον, *watching an enclosure*, *AP*12.257 (Mel., ὀρκοῦρος cod.).

ἑρκτή, ἡ, Ion. for εἱρκτή. **ἑρκτήρ**, v. ἐριστήρ.

ἑρκτός, ή, όν, = ῥεκτός, *feasible*, Arr.*Ind.*20 (fort. leg. ἐπικτόν).

ἕρκτωρ, ορος, ὁ, (ἔρδω) *a doer*, κακῶν Antim.*Eleg.*5.

Ἕρκῡνα or **-υννα**, ἡ, title of Demeter at Lebadea, Lyc.153:— hence **Ἑρκύνια** (-κήνια cod.), τά, festival of Demeter, Hsch.

ἕρμα, ατος, τό, *prop, support*: in pl., of the *props* used to keep ships upright when hauled ashore, νῆα.. ἐπ' ἠπείροιο ἔρυσσαν ὑψοῦ ἐπὶ ψαμάθοις, ὑπὸ δ' ἕρματα μακρὰ τάνυσσαν Il.1.486, cf. 2.154: metaph., of men, ἕ. πόληος *prop* or *stay* of the city, 16.549, Od.23.121, *Epigr.Gr.* 452.11 (Syria); τοῦτο.. οἷον ἕ. πόλεως κείσθω as *a foundation* for the city, Pl.*Lg.*737b; ὥσπερ ἕ. τῆς πολιτείας βέβαιον Plu.2.814c; ἕ. ἐχέγγυον [ἑταιρίας] D.C.*Fr.*40.15; ὥσπερ ἕρματος ἀεὶ δεόμενοι τῆς τροφῆς Gal.19.208. 2. *sunken rock, reef*, Alc.*Supp.*26.6, Hdt.7.183, Th. 7.25, E.*Hel.*854; ἄσημα ἕ. Anacr.38; ἄφαντον ἕ. A.*Ag.*1007 (lyr.), cf. *Eu.*564 (lyr.); ἕ. ὕφαλα D.H.1.52; ἕ. γῆς ἁπαλόν a soft *bank* of mud, App.*BC*5.101. 3. *cairn, barrow*, πρὸς ἕρμα τυμβόχωστον... τάφου S.*Ant.*848 (lyr., nisi leg. ἔργμα); Ἑρμᾶν ἀφετήριον ἕρμα starting-*post*, *AP*9.319 (Philox.); ἕρματα τῶν θεμελίων *ruins* of the foundations, D.S.5.70. 4. *that which keeps a ship steady, ballast*, Plu.2. 782b; of *stones* with which cranes and bees were supposed to steady themselves in their flight, Arist.*HA*597^{b}1, 626^{b}25; μετὰ τῶν γεράνων ἀναχωρῶ πάλιν, ἀνθ' ἕρματος πολλὰς καταπεπωκὼς δίκας Ar.*Av.*1429: metaph., τῆς ψυχῆς ἐχούσης ἕ. Chrysipp.*Stoic.*2.299; τὸ ἀπὸ τῆς φρονήσεως ἕ. Socr.ap.Stob.3.3.61; οἷον ἕ. τὴν τῶν γερόντων ἀρχὴν θεμένη Plu.*Lyc.*5; οὔτε τι ἕ. ἐν τῇ ψυχῇ ἔχει D.C.46.3; also λαβοῦσα ἕ. Δῖον having *conceived* by Zeus, A.*Supp.*580 (lyr.); so perh. μελαινέων ἕρμ' ὀδυνάων *freight* of dark pains, Il.4.117 (athetized by Aristarch.). II. (εἴρω A) in pl., ἕρματα *ear-rings*, 14.182, Od.18.297; *band, noose*, Ael. *NA*17.35; a serpent's *coils*, ib.37.

ἑρμᾰγέλη, ἡ, *a herd of Hermae*, *AP*11.353.6 (Pall.).

Ἑρμάδιον, τό, Dim. of Ἑρμῆς I. 2, Keil-Premerstein *Dritter Bericht* 117, Suid. II. Dim. of Ἑρμῆς I. 1, Luc.*Cont.*1.

ἑρμάζω, (ἕρμα) *steady, support*, Hp.*Art.*44. II. ἑρμάσαι· ἐλαφρῶς περιελίξαι, Hsch.

Ἑρμ-ᾰθήνη, ἡ, *terminal bust* (cf. Ἑρμῆς I. 2) *with head of Athena*, Cic.*Att.*1.1.5, 1.4.3; so of busts with heads of other divinities, of Eros, **-έρως**, Plin.*HN*36.33 (pl.); of Heracles, **-ηρακλῆς**, Cic.*Att.*1. 10.3, *Milet.*1(7) No.305; of Pan, cf. Ἑρμόπαν. (Cic.*Att.*1.4.3 appears to explain *Hermathena* as a Janus-like bust of Hermes and Athena; this is perh. a pun, but cf. Ἑρμῆς I. 2.)

Ἑρμᾰΐζομαι, *imitate Hermes*, Eust.10.25.

Ἑρμᾰϊκός, ή, όν, *of Hermes*, σειρά Marin.*Procl.*28; *of the planet Mercury*, σφαῖρα Procl.*in Alc.*p.113C.; so in Astrol., Ἑ. ἔργα *Cat. Cod.Astr.*2.203; Ἑ. πράξεις ib.8(4).238, cf. Sch.Ptol.*Tetr.*77; also of certain ζῴδια, Jul.Laod. in *Cat.Cod.Astr.*5(1).187. Adv. **-κῶς** Eust. 808.19. II. pl., = sq. I. 1, *Cat.Cod.Astr.*1.150.

ἕρμ-αιον, τό, prop. *gift of Hermes*, i.e. *unexpected piece of luck, godsend, wind-fall, treasure-trove* (cf. Ἑρμῆς II), S.*Ant.*397; ἕ. ἂν ἦν τινι c. inf., Pl.*Phd.*107c, *R.*368d; ἕ. ἂν εἴη ἡμῖν, εἰ.. Id.*Smp.*176c; ἑρμαίῳ ἐντετυχηκέναι Id.*Grg.*486e; ἕ. ἡγήσασθαι, ποιεῖσθαί τι, Id.*Smp.* 217a, *Grg.*489c; νομίζειν D.38.6. 2. = ἕρμαξ, Sch.Od.16.471. 3. *barrow, tomb*, *Papers of Amer. School* 3 Nos.501, 585 (Tymandos). 4. = ἠρύγγη, Ps.-Dsc.3.21; = ἀλόη, ib.22. II. Ἕρμαια (sc. ἱερά), τά, *festival of Hermes*, Pl.*Ly.*206d, Aeschin.1.10, *IG*2^2.1227 (ii B.C.), Durrbach *Choix d' inscr. de Délos* 117 (ii B.C.). 2. Ἕρμαιον, τό, *temple of Hermes*, *SIG*546*B*6 (Melitaea, iii B.C.), *Schwyzer* 709 (Ephesus, iii B.C.), al. (Prop. neut. of Ἑρμαῖος, but as Subst. proparox., Hdn.Gr.1.369.) **-αῖος**, α, ον, *called after Hermes*, Ἑ. λόφος, in Ithaca, Od.16.471 (expl. as = ἕρμαξ by Sch. ad loc.); Ἑ. λέπας Λήμνου A.*Ag.*283, cf. S.*Ph.*1459 (anap.). 2. *of Hermes*, Λύρη, the constellation *Lyra*, Arat.674; Ἑρμαῖος, ὁ (sc. μήν), month at Argos, etc., Polyaen.8.33; in Boeotia, *IG*7.289, al.; in the Aetolian league, *GDI*1745, al.; cf. Ἑρμαιών. 3. *gainful*, δαιμόνων δόσις A. *Eu.*947. 4. fem. **Ἑρμαΐς**, ίδος, ἡ, κρήνη Hp.*Ep.*17. **-αϊσταί**, οἱ, *worshippers of Hermes*, *IG*12(1).162 (Rhodes), *Inscr.Cos* 156; = Lat. *Mercuriales*, *SIG*726.1 (Delos, i B.C.). (Written Ἑρμαιισταί, *Exploration archéologique de Délos* 7(1).118.) **-αιών**, ῶνος, ὁ, name of a month at Halicarnassus, *SIG*45.4 (v B.C.); in Ceos, *IG*2^2.1128.

ἕρμακον· ὄρνεον, Hsch.

ἑρμάν, f.l. for ἕρμα, Phot., Harp. **Ἑρμάν**, v. Ἑρμῆς.

Ἑρμάνουβις or **-ης** [ᾰ], ιδος, ὁ, Graecized form of Anubis, Plu.2. 375e, Porph.ap.Eus.*PE*3.11, *AP*11.360.

ἕρμαξ, ᾰκος, ἡ, (ἕρμα) *heap of stones, cairn*, Nic.*Th.*150; λίθακές τε καὶ ἕρμακες Epic. in *Arch.Pap.*7.10. II. = ἕρμα I. 2, Hsch.

Ἑρμάριον, τό, Dim. of Ἑρμῆς, etym. of ἁρμάριον, *EM*146.56.

ἑρμ-ᾰσις, εως, ἡ, (ἑρμάζω) *supporting*, Erot. s.v. ἥρμοσται: Dor. **ἕρμασσις**, αὐλῶν *IG*4.823.41 (Troezen). **-ασμα**, ατος, τό, *prop, support*, Hp.*Off.*25. **-ασμός**, ὁ, *supporting*, Id.*Fract.*29.

ἑρμᾰτ-ίζω, = ἑρμάζω, *support by means of a sling*, τῆς κνήμης ἡρματισμένης Hp.*Fract.*23. II. (ἕρμα I. 4) *steady as by ballast*, ἑ. ἑαυτοὺς λιθιδίοις Plu.2.967b:—Med., *ballast themselves*, λιθιδίοις ib.979b: —Pass., τοῖς ἀξιολόγοις ἀγαθοῖς ἡρματίσθαι Phld.*Mort.*18. 2. trans. in Med., νύμφας ἐς οἴκους ἑρματίζονται *they take* brides into *their* houses *as ballast*, E.*Fr.*402.8, cf. Lyc.1319. **-ικός**, ή, όν, *on a firm base*, κράβ(β)ατος *PGen.*68.10 (iv A.D.). **-ίτης** [ῑ], ου, ὁ, *serving as ballast*, πέτρος Lyc.618.

Ἑρμ-αφρόδῑτος, ὁ, *Hermaphrodite*, or *person partaking of the attributes of both sexes*, so called from Hermaphroditus, son of Hermes and Aphrodite, D.S.4.6, Luc.*DDeor.*23.1, Ptol.*Tetr.*124, Gal.4. 619. 2. as Adj., ἑ. πάθος Leonid.ap.Paul.Aeg.6.69.

Ἑρμάων, Ἑρμέας, Ἑρμείας, v. Ἑρμῆς.

Ἑρμεῖον, τό, *shrine of Hermes*, or perh. = ἕρμαξ I, Str.8.3.12 (pl.).

Ἑρμέρως, ωτος, ὁ, v. Ἑρμαθήνη.

ἑρμή· ἔξοδος, Hsch. (Cf. ἐξίθμη, ἐρίμη.)

Ἑρμήδιον, τό, Dim. of Ἑρμῆς, Ar.*Pax*924: as term of endearment, ὡρμήδιον ib.382. (-ίδιον codd. Ar.)

ἑρμην-εία, ἡ, (ἑρμηνεύω) *interpretation, explanation*, Pl.*R.*524b (pl.), *Tht.*209a, Epicur.*Nat.*28.1; esp. of thoughts by words, *expression*, Diog.Apoll.1, X.*Mem.*4.3.12; χρῆσθαι τῇ γλώσσῃ πρὸς ἑρμηνείαν Arist.*PA*660^{a}35, cf. *de An.*420^{b}19, *Resp.*476^{a}19, Hermog.*Inv.*1.1, etc.; *mediation*, Pl.*Epin.*984e; *style*, D.H.*Comp.*1, al., Demetr.*Eloc.* 1, etc.; *an expression*, ἡ ἀκόλουθος ἑ. Sch.Pi.*O.*3.1: also in pl., αἱ Πλατωνικαὶ ἑ. Plato's *gifts of style*, D.H.*Pomp.*1.2. 2. in Music, *expression*, Plu.2.1138a, 1144d. 3. *translation*, Aristeas 3, Ph.2. 141; ἑ. τῶν Ῥωμαϊκῶν *POxy.*1201.12 (iii A.D.); ἑ. ἔχειν to *mean when translated*, Ph.1.232, Porph.*Plot.*17. **-ευμα**, ατος, τό, *interpretation, explanation*, in pl., E.*Ph.*470, *HF*1137, Ph.2.300. 2. *symbol, monument*, Νηρῇδος γάμων E.*Andr.*46. **-ευματικὰ** βιβλία *glossaries*, Gloss. **-εύς**, έως, ὁ, *interpreter*, esp. of foreign tongues, *dragoman*, Hdt.2.125, 154, al., X.*An.*1.2.17, *PCair.Zen.*65 (iii B.C.), *PTheb.Bank* 9.1 (ii B.C.), etc. b. *court interpreter*, *POxy.*237 vii 37 (ii A.D.), etc. 2. *matrimonial agent, go-between*, Ptol.*Tetr.* 181. 3. *broker, commissionaire*, *POxy.*1517.6 (iii A.D.), etc. II. *interpreter, expounder*, Pi.*O.*2.85, A.*Ag.*616, 1062, etc.; ἑρμηνῆς τῶν θεῶν, of poets, Pl.*Ion* 534e; λόγος τῶν νόμων ἑ. Id.*Lg.*907d; σιωπῇ δ' ἄπορος ἑ. λόγων E.*Fr.*126. 2. applied to planets, D.S.2. 30. **-ευσις**, εως, ἡ, *style, expression*, Longin.*Rh.*p.187 H. 2. *interpretation*, D.C.66.1. **-ευτέον**, *one must express*: ἑ. προσφόρως *one must use* the appropriate *style*, Demetr.*Eloc.*120. 2. *one must interpret*, Sch.rec.A.*Pr.*226. **-ευτής**, οῦ, ὁ, = ἑρμηνεύς, Pl. *Plt.*290c, Lxx *Ge.*42.23, Poll.5.154. **-ευτικός**, ή, όν, *of* or *for interpreting*: ἡ -κή (sc. τέχνη) Pl.*Plt.*260d; διάλεκτος ἑ. τινός Id.*Def.* 414d; λόγος Ph.1.58; ἑ. δύναμις power *of expression*, gift *of style*, Luc.*Hist.Conscr.*34, Theod.(?)ap.Nicol.*Prog.*p.2 F. **-εύτρια**, ἡ, fem. of ἑρμηνευτής, Sch.E.*Hipp.*589. **-εύω**, Dor. **ἑρμᾱνεύω** *SIG*1168.88 (Epid.), *interpret* foreign tongues, X.*An.*5.4.4; *translate*, D.H.*Th.*49, etc.; ἀπὸ Ῥωμαϊκῶν *PRyl.*62.30 (iii A.D.):—Pass., Ἑλληνιστί D.H.2.12, cf. Lxx *Jb.*42.17, etc. II. *explain, expound*, S.*OC*398, E.*Fr.*636.5, etc.; ὑμῖν ταῦτα Antipho 3.2.1; ὅ τι λέγει Philyll.11; τὰ τῶν ποιητῶν Pl.*Ion* 535a:—Med., Id.*Epin.*985b:— Pass., Arist.*SE*166^{b}11. 2. *put into words, express*, Th.2.60, Pl. *Lg.*966b, etc.; τι διά τινος Hermog.*Id.*2.5; τι πεζῶς Id.*Meth.*30:— Pass., D.H.*Comp.*25. 3. *describe, write about*, τὸν Νεῖλον Demetr. *Eloc.*121. III. abs., *speak clearly, articulate*, Hp.*Epid.*5.74.

Ἑρμηρακλῆς, έους, ὁ, v. Ἑρμαθήνη.

Ἑρμῆς, οῦ, ὁ, nom. Ἑρμῆς Od.5.54, etc.: acc. Ἑρμῆν 8.334, etc., Ion. Ἑρμέην Hdt.5.7, late Ἑρμῆ *CIG*5094 (Nubia): dat. Ἑρμῇ Od.14. 435, Ἑρμέᾳ Il.5.390: voc. Ἑρμῆ *h.Hom.*18.12, A.*Pers.*629, *Eu.*90: Ep. gen. Ἑρμέω *h.Merc.*413, *h.Ven.*148, Hdt.5.7, etc.; lengthd. Ἑρμείω Il.15.214:—Ep. nom. **Ἑρμείας**, Od.1.42, al., *IG*5(2).558 (Arc.), acc. -αν Od.1.38, 5.28, al.; later **Ἑρμείης**, Call.*Dian.*69, etc.; gen. Ἑρμείαο Od.12.390, 15.319, Ἑρμεία *AP*7.480 (Leon.); dat. Ἑρμείᾳ *IG*1^2.631 (vi B.C.); voc. Ἑρμεία Od.5.29, al.:—Boeot. and Dor. nom. **Ἑρμᾶς**, gen. ᾶ, Corinn.*Supp.*2.57, Pi.*P.*2.10, etc., voc. Ἑρμᾶ A.*Fr.*384, acc. Ἑρμᾶν ib.273: also **Ἑρμάων** [ᾱ], Hes.*Fr.*23, Bion *Fr.*7.

8, *AP*4.3b.64 (Agath.):—contr. Ἑρμάν (not -ᾶν), ᾶνος, Call.*Fr.*32 P., *IG*5(2).360, al. (Arc.), ib.5(1).1390.33 (Andania, i B.C.), *Supp.Epigr.* 2.165 (Laconia): Thess. dat. Ἑρμαίου *IG*9(2).716 (dub.), Ἑρμάου ib. 715, al., Ἑρμάο ib.471, Ἑρμᾶ ib.356: Cret. acc. Ἑρμᾶον *Schwyzer* 179a:—*Hermes*, son of Zeus and Maia, Od.5.28, 14.435, Hes.*Th.* 938, etc. **2.** *pillar surmounted by bust*, at Athens and elsewhere, And.1.37, Th.6.27, etc.; τῶν ἱερῶν Ἑρμῶν *IG*12(8).188.14 (Samothrace); as a decorative piece, with two faces, Keil-Premerstein *Dritter Bericht* 117: Ἑ. τρικέφαλος, τετρακέφαλος, Hsch. **3.** ὁ τοῦ Ἑρμοῦ ἀστήρ the planet *Mercury*, Pl.*Ti.*38d, *Epin.*987b, Arist.*Mete.* 342b33, *Metaph.*1073b32, Thphr.*Sign.*46, etc.: later Ἑρμῆς, ὁ, in same sense, *Placit.*2.32.1, Plu.2.1028b, Cleom.2.7: hence, Ἑρμοῦ ἡμέρα D.C.37.19. **4.** Ἑρμαῖ· παραφυάδια δένδρων ἄχρηστα, Hsch. **5.** *cake* in the shape of a κηρυκεῖον, *Schwyzer* 694 (Chios, iv B.C.), Hsch. **II.** prov. and phrases: **1.** Ἑρμῆν ἕλκειν to *make a last effort*, from the parting cup at a feast being drunk *to Hermes*, Stratt.22. **2.** κοινὸς Ἑρμῆς *shares in your luck!* Arist. *Rh.*1401a21, Thphr.*Char.*30.9, Men.*Epit.*67, etc. **3.** ἐν τῷ λίθῳ Ἑρμῆς, of the actual potentially in the material, Arist.*Metaph.*1002a 22, 1017b7. **4.** Ἑρμῆς ἐπεισελήλυθε '*Hermes* is come in', a saying used when conversation suddenly ceased, Plu.2.502f. **5.** τὸ Ἑρμοῦ ῥαβδίον, like 'Fortunatus' cap', Arr.*Epict.*3.20.12. **6.** Ἑρμοῦ βοτάνιον, Ἑρμοῦ πόα, = λινόζωστις, Dsc.4.189, Plin.*HN*25.38.

ἑρμητής, οῦ, ὁ, = Ἑρμῆς 1.5, *GDI* iv p.883 (Erythrae).

Ἑρμίδιον, v. Ἑρμήδιον.

ἑρμίν (Hdn.Gr.2.431) or **ἑρμίς** (Philem.226), ῖνος, ὁ, = ἕρμα, *bedpost*, Od.8.278, 23.198, Herod.3.16.

ἑρμογλῠφ-εῖον, τό, *statuary's shop*, Pl.*Smp.*215b. **-εύς**, έως, ὁ, *carver of Hermae*: generally, *statuary*, Luc.*Somn.*2, Plu.2. 580e. **-ικός**, ή, όν, *of* or *for a statuary*: ἡ -κὴ τέχνη *the art of a statuary*, Luc.*Somn.*7. **-ος**, ὁ, = ἑρμογλυφεύς, ib.2, Porph. *Hist.Phil.Fr.*11, Iamb.*VP*34.245.

Ἑρμο-δάκτῠλον, τό, a plant, in two varieties, *Colchicum luteum* and *autumnale*, [Gal.]14.760, Alex.Trall.11. **-κοπίδης**, ου, ὁ, (κόπτω) *a Hermes-mutilator*, in pl., Ar.*Lys.*1094, Plu.*Alc.*20. **-λογέω**, *build with loose stones*, τάφον *AP*7.554 (Phil.). **-μᾰχέω**, *fight with* Ἑρμαῖ 1.4, as a game, Hsch. s. v. Ἑρμαῖ.

Ἑρμόπᾱν, ᾶνος, ὁ, a deity partaking of the attributes of Hermes and Pan, Hdn.Gr.1.13, Porph.ap.Eus.*PE*3.11: a Hermes-Heracles-Pan statue is described (but not named) in *APl.*4.234 (Phld.).

ἔρνατις· ἀναδενδράς, Hsch.

ἐρνεσίπεπλος [ῐ], ον, *wrapt in foliage*, Orph.*H.*30.5.

ἐρνίον, τό, Dim. of ἔρνος II, *Lyr.Alex.Adesp.*4.17.

ἐρνοκόμος, ον, *tending young plants*, Hsch.

ἐρνόομαι, Pass., *shoot up*, Ph.2.402.

ἔρνος, εος, τό, *young sprout, shoot*, ὁ δ' ἀνέδραμεν ἔρνεϊ ἶσος shot up like *a young plant*, Il.18.56, cf. Od.14.175; οἷον δὲ τρέφει ἔ. ἀνὴρ ἐριθηλὲς ἐλαίης Il.17.53, cf. Od.6.163; σκιεροῖσιν ὑφ' ἔρνεσιν (sic codd. Ath.) οἰναρέοις Ibyc.1.5; ἔ. δάφνης, δόνακος, ὕλας, E.*Med.*1213, *Hel.* 183 (lyr.), *Ba.*876 (lyr.). **2.** in pl., *wreaths* worn by victors in games, Pi.*N.*11.29, *I.*1.29. **II.** metaph., *scion, offspring*, Id.*N.*6. 37 (pl.), B.5.87, A.*Ag.*1525 (lyr.), *Eu.*661, 666, S.*OC*1108 (pl.), *Sammelb.*4229.10; Ἡρακλέος ἱερὸν ἔ. Theoc.2.121; ἔ. τῆς νηδύος E.*Ba.* 1306; [κεράων] ἔ., periphr. for κέραα, Opp.*C.*2.210; of Delos, as *having sprung out of the sea*, Pi.*Fr.*87.2. **2.** *fruit*, of the apple of Discord, Coluth.60, al.

ἐρνύγας (acc. pl.), poet. coined word for κέρατα, Arist.*Po.*1457b 35: perh. cf. sq.

ἔρνυτας· ἔρνη, βλαστήματα, κλάδοι, Hsch.

ἐρνώδης, ες, *like a young sprout*, Dsc.1 *Praef.*8, *Gp.*10.22.5 (Sup.).

Ἐρξείης or **Ἐρξίης**, ὁ, Greek equivalent of Darius, either *doer* (cf. ἐρξίας, ὁ πρακτικός *EM*376.52) or *restrainer* (εἴργω), Hdt.6.98.

ἔρξω, ἔρξα, v. ἔρδω.

ἐρόδανα· ἔργον ἐρινάζει, Hsch.

ἐρόεις, εσσα, εν, (ἔρος) poet., *lovely, charming*, Ἀλίη Hes.*Th.*245, cf. *h.Ven.*263, *h.Merc.*31; βῶμος Sapph.54, cf. Ar.*Av.*246 (lyr.); Νημερτής Emp.122.4; Ἑλένης τύπος *APl.*4.149 (Arab.).

ἔρομαι (not found in pres. ind. (exc. 2 sg. ἔρεαι Orac. in Certamen *Prooem.*), its place being taken by ἐρέω (A), ἐρωτάω): Ion. and Ep. **εἴρομαι** Il.1.553, Od.1.284, al.: impf. (= aor.) εἰρόμην Il.1.513, Pi.*O.*6. 49, Hdt.2.44, etc.: fut. ἐρήσομαι S.*OT*1166, Ar.*Nu.*1409, Pl.*Prt.*355c; Ion. εἰρήσομαι Od.4.61, 7.237, Hdt.1.67 (ἐπ-): aor. 2 ἠρόμην Sapph. 1.15, E.*Ion*541, Th.3.113, etc.; imper. ἐροῦ S.*El.*563, E.*Or.*763 (troch.), etc., Ep. ἔρειο Il.11.611; subj. ἔρωμαι Od.8.133, Pl.*R.*538d, etc.; εἴρωμαι Od.16.402, Hdt.4.76; opt. ἐροίμην Od.1.135, 3.77, etc.; inf. ἐρέσθαι in Hom. always in the phrase μεταλλῆσαι καὶ ἐρέσθαι 3.69, al. (exc. in 1.405) (ἔρεσθαι is freq. in codd., as Lys.12.24, E.*El.*548, cf. Hdn.Gr.1.466); part. ἐρόμενος Ar.*Eq.*574, Th.4.40:—Ep. and Ion. also **ἐρέομαι** in subj. ἐρέωμαι Od.17.509, inf. ἐρέεσθαι 6.298, 23.106, Hp.*Prorrh.*2.41, impf. ἐρέοντο Il.1.332, 8.445; ἐπ-ειρεόμενος is v.l. in Hdt.3.64:—*ask, inquire*, mostly folld. by indirect question, εἴροντο.. ὅττι ἑ κήδοι Od.9.402, etc.; ἤρετο ὅτι θαυμάζοι Th.3.113; τὸν ξεῖνον ἐρώμεθα εἴ τιν' ἄεθλον οἶδε Od.8.133, etc.; ἠρόμην ὅπου.. Pl.*R.*327b; διὰ τί.. Id.*Prt.*355c, etc.: folld. by a direct question, ἤρετο Ξενοφῶντα, εἰπέ μοι, ἔφη, ὦ Ξενοφῶν, οὐ σὺ ἐνόμιζες..; X.*Mem.*1.3.8; ἐρομένου δὲ τοῦ Ἀγησιλάου, ἆρ' ἂν ἐν καιρῷ γένοιτο, εἰ..; Id.*HG*4.3.2, cf. *Cyr.*1.4.19. **2.** c. acc. objecti, *learn by inquiry*, ἐρέεσθαι δώματα πατρός Od.6.298; *ask after* or *for*, εἰρόμεναι παῖδας Il.6.239; εἴρεαι Ἕκτορα δῖον 24.390; θεῶν εἰρώμεθα βουλάς Od.16.402. **3.** c. acc. pers., *question*, Il.1.332, etc., Hdt.1.32, Lys.12.24; εἴρετο δ' ἡμέας, ὦ ξεῖνοι, τίνες ἐστέ; Od.9.251; ἀλλήλους εἴροντο τίς εἴη καὶ πόθεν ἔλθοι 17. 368, cf. E.*Or.*763 (troch.), etc.; in later Prose, Jul.*Or.*7.229b. **4.** c. acc. pers., *petition*, Ar.*Eq.*574. **5.** c. dupl. acc., *to ask* one *about* a thing, τὸ μέν σε πρῶτον.. εἰρήσομαι.., τίς πόθεν εἰς ἀνδρῶν; Od.7. 237, cf. 19.509; ἐρήσομαί σε τουτί· παῖδά μ' ὄντ' ἔτυπτες; Ar.*Nu.* 1409. **6.** freq. τινὰ περί τινος, as ἵνα μιν περὶ πατρὸς.. ἔροιτο Od.1. 135, 3.77, cf. Hdt.4.76, al., E.*El.*548; also οἱ δέ μιν ἀμφὶ δίκας εἴροντο Od.11.570; ἀμφὶ πόσει εἴρεσθαι 19.95. (Ion. εἰρ- Att. ἐρ- from ἐρϝ- (aor. stem), cf. ἐρέ(ϝ)ω, ἐρευτής: pres. ἐρέ(ϝ)ομαι: ἐροίμην and similar forms in Hom. are variously expld. or emended.)

ἐρόντι· μάλα, λίαν, πάνυ, Hsch.; perh. cf. ἐρρεντί.

ἔρος (A), ὁ, acc. ἔρον, dat. ἔρῳ: poet. form of ἔρως:—*love, desire*, οὐ.. θεᾶς ἔρος οὐδὲ γυναικὸς Il.14.315, cf. Od.18.212; freq. in phrase αὐτὰρ ἐπεὶ πόσιος καὶ ἐδητύος ἐξ ἔρον ἕντο Il.1.469, al.; ἱμερτῶν ἔργων ἐξ ἔρον ἱέμενον Thgn.1064; ἔρος λυσιμελής Hes.*Th.*910, cf. Ibyc.1.6, etc.: used by Trag. in lyrics, S.*El.*197, E.*Med.*152, and by E. in dialogue, *Hipp.*337, *El.*297, al.; also in late Prose, ἔρῳ φέρεσθαι Luc. *Asin.*33. **II.** as pr. n., *Eros*, the god of love, Hes.*Th.*120, Alcm. 36, Sapph.74, Theoc.29.22.

ἔρος (B), τό, *wool*, only in Ion. form εἶρος (q. v.), but cf. ἔπερος, εὔερος.

ἐροτή, ἡ, = ἑορτή, *POxy.*2084.26 (iii A.D.); Cypr. acc. to Hsch.: **ἔροτις** Aeol. (acc. to Eust.1908.57), E.*El.*625: also in Dor. Inscrr., *IG*4.583.6 (Argos), *SIG*1009.5 (Chalcedon); θεοῖς ὧνπερ ἔην ἔ. *IG*11 (4).1150 (Delos).

ἔρουα· πορεύου, ἀναπαύου (Cypr.), Hsch. (cf. ἐρωέω).

ἔροψ, a bird, Hsch.

ἐρπάκανθα [ᾰκ], ἡ, = ἄκανθος, Ps.-Dsc.3.17.

ἐρπεδό⟨ε⟩σσα· ἐπίπεδος, Hsch. (Cf. ἀρπεδόεις.)

ἑρπετό-δηκτος, ον, *bitten by a reptile*, Dsc.3.68, Crateuas *Fr.*5. **-εις**, εσσα, εν, *of reptiles*, γένος Opp.*C.*2.274.

ἑρπετόν, Aeol. perh. ὄρπετον (q. v.), τό, (ἕρπω) *beast* or *animal which goes on all fours*, Od.4.418; πᾶν ἑ. πληγῇ νέμεται Heraclit.11; ἑρπετὰ ὅσσα τρέφει μέλαινα γαῖα Alcm.60.3; ὄφις καὶ σαύρας καὶ τὰ τοιαῦτα τῶν ἑρπετῶν Hdt.4.183; τοῖς μὲν ἄλλοις ἑρπετοῖς πόδας ἔδωκεν.., ἀνθρώπῳ δὲ καὶ χεῖρας X.*Mem.*1.4.11; ἑρπετά, opp. πετεινά, Hdt.1.140, cf. Theoc.15.118, A.R.4.1240: generally, ἑ. οὐδὲ γυνή Call.*Jov.*13; πυκινώτατον ἑ., of a hound, Pi.*Fr.*106; of insects, Semon.13, Nic.*Fr.* 74.46. **II.** *creeping thing, reptile*, esp. *snake*, E.*Andr.*269, Theoc. 24.57; περὶ κιναδέων τε καὶ ἑ. Democr.259; ἑρπετά τε καὶ δάκετα ⟨πάντα⟩ Ar.*Av.*1069; of the monster Typhoeus, with a *snake's* body, Pi.*P.*1.25. **2.** as Adj., *creeping*, κακὸν ἑ. πρᾶγμα *POxy.*1060.7 (vi A.D.); τὰ ἑ. θηρία Philum.*Ven.*10.1.

Ἑρπετοσῖται, οἱ, name of a tribe of *snake-eaters*, Porph.*Chr.*69.

ἑρπετώδης, ες, *snake-like*, προβολή, of the elephant's trunk, Aret. *SD*2.13.

ἑρπηδών, όνος, ἡ, *a crawling*, Nic.*Al.*418, ubi Sch. male ἑρπυδόνα.

ἕρπηλα, a kind of *shell-fish*, Numen.ap.Ath.7.306c (v.l. ἕρπιλαν); ἑρπήλας δολιχήποδας Id.ap.eund.7.305a (v.l. ἕρπηνας).

ἑρπηνώδης, ες, *of the nature of* ἕρπης, Ph.2.205, Antyll.ap.Orib.10. 34.6.

ἕρπης, ητος, ὁ, (ἕρπω) *shingles*, Hp.*Prorrh.*2.11 (pl.); ἕ. ἐσθιόμενοι Id.*Aph.*5.22:—also **ἑρπήν**, ῆνος, ὁ, Ph.2.64; **ἑρπήνη**, ἡ, *EM*377. 7. **II.** ἕρπης, ητος, ὁ, name of an animal (snake?), Plin.*HN*30. 116, prob. in Philum.*Ven.*19.1 (ὅπητες cod.).

ἑρπηστ-ήρ, ῆρος, ὁ, v.l. for ἑρπυστήρ, Orph.*L.*49, Opp.*C.*3.110, 411. **-ής**, οῦ, ὁ, = ἑρπετόν, Nic.*Th.*9, etc.; of a mouse, *AP*9.86 (Antiphil.). **b.** *guinea-worm*, *Hippiatr.*58. **2.** Adj. *creeping*, ἑρπηστὴν πόδα, κισσέ, χορεύσας *AP*11.33 (Phil.). **-ικός**, f.l. for ἑρπυστικός (q. v.).

ἕρπιλα, v. ἕρπηλα.

ἕρπις, ὁ, Egypt. word for *wine*, Hippon.51.2, f.l. for ὄλπιν in Sapph.51, cf. Tz. ad Lyc.579.

ἕρπνουν, etym. of τερπνόν coined by Pl.*Cra.*419d.

ἑρπτόν, τό, = ἑρπετόν, Arist.ap.Eust.481.36.

ἑρπύζω, impf. εἵρπυζον Q.S.13.93: pres. only in Hom.: aor. 1 ἑρπύσαι in Att. (v. ἕρπω):—*creep, crawl*, in Hom. always of persons weighed down by age or deep distress, ἑρπύζοντ' ἀνὰ γουνὸν Od.1. 193; ἑρπύζων παρὰ θῖνα 13.220, cf. Il.23.225, A.R.4.1289; of quadrupeds and children, Nic.*Al.*542; χρόνος ἑρπύζων *AP*6.19 (Jul.); of ivy, ib.7.22 (Simm. Theb.).

ἑρπυλλ-άριον, τό, Dim. of ἕρπυλλος, Damocr.ap.Gal.14.192. **-ῐνος**, η, ον, *made of tufted thyme*, στέφανος Eub.99; μύρον Antiph. 106.7, cf. Gal.12.512. **-ιον**, τό, = ἕρπυλλος, Aret.*CD*1.3 (ἕρπυλλον Hude, and so *Hippiatr.*54). **-ίς**, ίδος, ἡ, *grasshopper*, Hsch. **-ος**, ὁ, poet. also ἡ, Theoc.*Ep.*1, *AP*4.1.54 (Mel.), Pancr.ap.Ath.15. 677f:—*tufted thyme, Thymus Sibthorpii*, Cratin.98, Ar.*Pax*168, Thphr.*HP*1.9.4, al., *CP*2.18.2, Dsc.3.38.

ἑρπ-ύσιμος, *reptabundus*, *Gloss.* **-υσις**, εως, ἡ, (ἑρπύζω) *creeping*, Sch.D.P.121. **-υσμός**, ὁ, = foreg., Suid.; also, = ἡ φωνὴ τῶν χοίρων, Hsch. **-υστάζω**, = ἑρπύζω, Apollon.*Lex.* s. v. ἀταλλε. **-υστήρ**, ῆρος, ὁ, = ἑρπηστής, *a reptile*, Opp.*C.*3.110 (v.l.). **2.** Adj. *creeping*, ὄφεις ἑ. ib.411 (v.l.), Orph.*L.*49 (v.l.). **-υστής**, οῦ, ὁ, *a crawling child*, *AP*9.302 (Antip.). **-υστικός**, ή, όν, *creeping*, ζῷα ἑ. *serpents*, Arist.*HA*487b21; of squirrels, etc., Id.*PA*688a9: Medic., ἑρπυστικά (sc. ἕλκη), τά, *spreading ulcers*, Hp.*Ulc.*3, *Coac.*618, etc. (Freq. written ἑρπηστ-, cf. Max.Tyr.13.7, etc.)

ἕρπω, impf. εἷρπον Od.12.395 codd., E.*Cyc.*423, etc., ἧρπον *IG*4. 951.86 (Epid.): Dor. fut. ἑρψῶ Theoc.5.45, 18.40, Att. only in compd.

ἐφέρψω, later ἑρπύσω (διεξ–) Arist.*Mu*.398^{b}33: aor. ἧρψα (ἐξ–) Lxx *Ps*.104(105).30; Att. εἵρπῦσα Ar.*V*.272: (cf. Lat. *serpo*):—*move slowly, walk*, ἥμενος ἢ ἕρπων Od.17.158; ὅσσα τε γαῖαν ἔπι πνείει τε καὶ ἕρπει Il.17.447; ἔργα ζωοῖσιν ἑρπόντεσσί θ' ὁμοῖα Pi.*O*.7.52; ἕρπον (εἷρπον codd.) ῥινοί *began to move*, Od.12.395; of infants, A.*Th*.17; of a lame man, S.*Ph*.207 (lyr.); ἕ. ἐξ εὐνῆς Ar.*V*.552; ἕρπον τοῖς ὀδοῦσι θηρίον an animal that *walks* on its teeth, *Carm.Pop*.35. 2. simply, *go, come*, in Dor. dialects, where the aor. is ἔμολον, ἦνθον, etc., εἰς τὸ ἱερόν *IG*4.951.86 (Epid.), cf. *GDI*5040.39 (Crete), *BMus. Inscr*.968*A* 6 (Cos), etc., cf. καθέρπω: also freq. in Trag., A.*Pr*.810, etc.; ἕρπεθ' ὡς τάχιστα S.*OC*1643; Θησεὺς ὅδ' ἕρπει E.*HF*1154; ἕρπειν ἐς μῦθον, πρὸς ᾠδάς, Id.*Hel*.316, *Cyc*.423; ἕρπε δεῦρο *come* hither, Id.*Andr*.722: and c. acc. cogn., ἐξόδους ἕ. κενάς S.*Aj*.287; κέλευθον Id.*Ph*.1223; εὐθεῖαν ἕρπε τήνδε A.*Fr*.195. b. of things, events, etc., ἕρπει ἄντα τῶ σιδάρω τὸ καλῶς κιθαρίσδην Alcm.35; βότρυς ἐπ' ἦμαρ ἕρπει S.*Fr*.255; ἥβη ἕρπουσα πρόσω Id.*Tr*.547; of a tear *stealing* from the eye, Id.*El*.1231; πρὸς τὸν ἔχονθ' ὁ φθόνος ἕρπει Id.*Aj*.157; τὸ ἐς αὔριον αἰεὶ τυφλὸν ἕρπει Id.*Fr*.593; τοῦτο γὰρ ἀθάνατον φωνᾶεν ἕρπει this (word) *goeth forth* undying, Pi.*I*.4(3).40; ὁ πόλεμος ἑρπέτω *let* it *take its course*, Ar.*Eq*.673, *Lys*.129; of *coming* events, εἰ δὲ δαίμων γενέθλιος ἕρποι Pi.*O*.13.105, cf. *N*.4.43, 7.68; of calamities, *come suddenly* on one, S.*Ant*.585, 618 (both lyr.), *Aj*.1087.

ἐρρ–, see also ἐνρ–.

ἔρρα· ζιζάνια, Hsch. (leg. αἶρα).

ἐρραγέως· ταχέως, Hsch. (Fort. ἐμμαπέως.) **ἐρράδᾶται**, v. ῥαίνω.

ἔρραος, ὁ, *ram*, Lyc.1316. 2. *wild boar*, Call.*Fr*.335: **ἐρράς**, Hsch.

ἐρραστωνευμένως, Adv. *carelessly*, Thom.Mag.p.325 R.

ἐρράπτω, = ἐνράπτω, D.S.5.52, Ael.*NA*2.22 (Pass.):—Med., Aristid.*Or*.41(4).3. **ἐρρέθην**, v. ἐρῶ.

ἔρρειθρος, ον, *canalized*, Hero *Geom*.23.68.

ἐρρεντί, Adv. (said to be formed from a part. ἐρρείς, as if from ἐρρῶ (*ἔρρημι), = ἔρρω), of unknown meaning, Alc.130; perh. cf. ἐρόντι.

ἐρρετός· φθόρος, Hsch.; cf. ἔρρω. **ἐρρηγεῖα**, v. ῥήγνυμι. **ἐρ-ρήεις**, = ἐρσήεις, Hsch.

ἐρρήθην, v. ἐρῶ, εἰπεῖν.

ἐρρηνοβοσκός, όν, = προβατοβοσκός, S.*Fr*.655.

ἐρρη-φορέω, = ἀρρηφορέω, *IG*3.916, al. **–φόρος**, = ἀρρηφόρος, ib.902. (Cf. ἐρση-φορία, –φόρος.)

ἔρρῑγα, pf. of ῥιγέω.

ἔρρῑνον, τό, (ἐν, ῥίς) *sternutatory medicine*, Antyll.ap.Orib.8.13.1. II. as Adj., ἕ. ἄλευρον Archig.ap.Aët.6.28; ἕ. φάρμακα Gal.11.769, 12.30, al.:—written **ἔνρινον**, Paus.Gr.*Fr*.166.

ἔρριψις, εως, ἡ, *prostration*, Hp.*Hum*.4, *Epid*.6.1.15: also expld. as *restlessness* or *morbid fears*, cf. Gal.7.592, Diocl.*Fr*.192: v.l. ἔριψις; cf. ἔρειψις.

Ἔρρος· ὁ Ζεύς, Hsch. (Perh. cf. Ἔρσος.)

ἔρρους, ουν, (ἐν, ῥόος) *irrigated*, Hero *Geom*.23.68.

ἐρρυθμισμένως, Adv. pf. part. Pass., (ῥυθμίζω) *gracefully*, ἀναθορεῖν D.C.79.16.

ἔρρυθμος, ον, = ἔνρυθμος (q.v.).

ἔρρυσος, ον, *somewhat wrinkled, subrugose*, Dsc.3.105.

ἔρρω (A), Locr. ϝέρρω (v. infr.), fut. ἐρρήσω *h.Merc*.259, Ar. (v. infr.): aor. 1 ἤρρησα Id.*Ra*.1192: pf. ἤρρηκα (εἰσ–) Id.*Th*.1075:—*go slowly*: ἔρρων *limping*, of Hephaestus, Il.18.421; ἥ μ' οἴῳ ἔρροντι συνήντετο met me *wandering* alone, Od.4.367. II. *go* or *come to one's own harm*, ἐνθάδε ἔρρων Il.8.239, 9.364; ὑπὸ γαίη ἐρρήσεις *h.Merc*.l.c.; ἄτιμος ἔρρειν A.*Eu*.884; ὡς Πόλυβον ἤρρησεν he *went with a murrain* to Polybus, Ar.*Ra*.1192, cf. *Lys*.336 (lyr.). 2. mostly in imper., ἔρρε *away! begone!* Il.8.164, Thgn.601; ἔρρ' οὕτως Il.22.498: pl., ἔρρετε 24.239, A.R.3.562: 3 sg., ἐρρέτω *away with him, let him go to ruin*, Il.20.349, Od.5.139; ἀσπὶς ἐκείνη ἐρρέτω Archil.6.4; in a legal formula, αὐτὸς μὲν ϝερρέτω *Berl.Sitzb*.1927.8 (Locr., v B.C.), cf. *Schwyzer*415 (Elis, v B.C.); ϝάρρην ib.409; ἐρρέτω Ἴλιον *perish* Troy! S.*Ph*.1200 (anap.): with a Prep., ἔρρ' ἐκ νήσου θᾶσσον Od.10.72; ἔρρ' ἀπ' ἐμεῦ Theoc.20.2; ἔρρ' ἐκ προσώπου Herod.8.59; in Att. strengthd., ἔρρ' ἐς κόρακας *go hang!* Ar.*Pl*.604 (anap.), Pherecr.70.5, etc.; ἐς κόρακας ἔρρειν φασὶν ἐκ τῆς Ἀττικῆς Alex.94.5; ἔρρε εἰς ὄλεθρόν τε καὶ Ἄβυδον Lys.*Fr*.5a: opt. ἔρροις *AP*5.2 (Antip. Thess.): part., ἔρρων νυν αὐτὸς χὴ ξυνοικήσασά σοι.. γηράσκετ' E.*Alc*.734: fut., οὐκ ἐρρήσετε; οὐκ ἐς κόρακας ἐρρήσετε; Ar.*Lys*.1240, *Pax* 500; εἰ μὴ 'ρρήσεθ' Id.*V*.1329 (lyr.). 3. of persons and things, *to be clean gone, perish, disappear*, ἔρρων ἐκ ναός A.*Pers*.964 (lyr.); ἔρρει πανώλης ib.732 (troch.); ἄφαντος ἔρρει S.*OT*560, cf. Pl.*Lg*.677c; ἔρρει ταῦτα ἐκ τῆς αὐτῶν χώρας Id.*Phlb*.24d; ἔρρειν ἐκ τῆς τοῦ εἶναι ἕδρας Plot.3.7.4; ἔρρει τὰ κᾶλα the ships *are lost*, Hippocr.ap.X.*HG*1.1.23 (prob.); ἔρρει πᾶσ' Ἀφροδίτα A.*Ag*.419 (lyr.); ἔρρει τὰ θεῖα the honour due to the gods *is gone*, S.*OT*910 (lyr.); ἔρρει δέμας φλογιστόν Id.*El*.57; ἔρρεις μάτην E.*Hel*.1220; θανόντας ἔρρειν Id.*Supp*.1113; ἐξ οἵων καλῶν ἔρρεις from what fortunes *hast* thou *fallen*, Id.*IT*379; ἔρρει τὰ ἐμὰ πράγματα X.*Smp*.1.15, cf. *Cyr*.6.1.3.

ἔρρω (B), Aeol. for εἴρω, *EM*90.12.

ἔρρωγα, pf. of ῥήγνυμι.

ἐρρωμένος, η, ον, pf. part. Pass. of ῥώννυμι: generally used as Adj., *in good health*, D.2.21, etc.; ἐρρωμένος ὤν, opp. ἀσθενέστερος, Lys.24.7; *powerful, influential, formidable*, ἐρρωμένη τέχνης δύναμις Pl.*Phdr*.268a; μηχαναί Hero *Aut*.21.2 (sed leg. αἰρομένας): irreg. Comp., τειχομαχίη ἐρρωμενεστέρη Hdt.9.70; οἱ –έστεροι τῶν ἀνθρώπων Pl.*Grg*.483c; ἐρρωμενεστέραις ταῖς γνώμαις X.*Cyr*.3.3.31; τὸ φύσει –έστερον Pl.*Smp*.181c: Sup. –έστατος And.4.37, Pl.*R*.477d. Adv. ἐρρωμένως *stoutly, manfully, vigorously*, A.*Pr*.65, 76, Ar.*V*.230; ἐσθίειν Critias *Fr*.32 D.; χωρεῖν X.*Ages*.2.11: Comp. –έστερον Pl. *Hp.Ma*.287a, –εστέρως Isoc.4.163: Sup. –έστατα Pl.*R*.401d.

ἐρρώμην, v. ῥώννυμι. **ἐρρώοντο, ἐρρώσαντο**, v. ῥώομαι. **ἔρρωσο**, v. sub ῥώννυμι. **ἐρσαῖος**, α, ον, = ἐρσήεις, Hsch.

ἐρσενικός, ή, όν, = ἀρρενικός, *PPetr*.3 pp.14, 173 (iii B.C.).

ἔρσεο· διεγείρου, and **ἔρση·** ὁρμήση, Hsch.

ἔρση, ἡ: Ep. **ἐέρση**, later **ἀέρση** *PLit.Lond*.60 (Posidipp.): Aeol., Dor. **ἐέρσᾱ** Sapph.*Supp*.25.12 (αδερσα (= ἀ δ' ἐέρσα) Pap.), **ἔερσᾰ** Pi. *N*.3.78, cf. Hdn.Gr.2.90: Cret. **ἄερσα** Hsch.: **ἔρσα** Alcm.48, **ἔρσα** Theoc.20.16:—*dew*, Il.23.598, etc.; τεθαλυῖά τ' ἐέρση (v.l. θ' ἐέρση) abundant *dew*, Od.13.245; θῆλυς ἐ. 5.467, Hes.*Sc*.395: pl., *raindrops*, κατὰ δ' ὑψόθεν ἧκεν ἐέρσας αἵματι μυδαλέας Il.11.53; στιλπναὶ δ' ἀπέπιπτον ἕ. (sc. τῆς νεφέλης) 14.351, cf. Theoc.2.107; χλωραῖς ἐ. Pi.*N*.8.40: generally, of any *liquid*, ἄνθεμον ποντίας ὑφελοῖσ' ἐέρσας from the *water* of the sea, ib.7.79; *foam*, ib.3.78; γλυκερὴ ἐέρση, of *honey*, Hes.*Th*.83. II. metaph., of *young and tender animals*, χωρὶς δ' αὖθ' ἔρσαι (this form only here in Hom.) Od.9.222, cf. Hsch.; esp. of *kids born in winter*, Id. (Cf. Skt. *varṣám* 'rain'.)

ἐρσήεις, Ep. **ἐερσ–** (Dor. **ἐρσάεις** *Hymn.Is*.167), εσσα, εν, *dewy*, λωτόν θ' ἑρσήεντα Il.14.348; λειμών *AP*9.668.3 (Marian.): metaph., of a corpse, οἷον ἐερσήεις κεῖται *fresh*, Il.24.419; νῦν δέ μοι ἑρσήεις καὶ πρόσφατος.. κεῖσαι ib.757.

ἔρσην, ενος, ὁ, Aeol., Dor., Ion., for ἄρσην, *IG*12(2).73.3 (Mytil.), 4.952.132 (Epid.), *BMus.Inscr*.968*B* 13 (Cos), *Leg.Gort*.10.49, Hdt.1.109, 192, etc.; also *PHib*.1.32.11, al. (iii B.C.): Comp. ἐρσεναίτερος *Schwyzer*424.2 (Elis, iv B.C.).

ἐρσηφορία, –φόρος, = ἀρρηφορία, –φόρος, Sch.Ar.*Lys*.643 (written ἐρσε–), *IG*3.318, 319; cf. ἐρρηφορέω, ἐρσοφόρος.

ἔρσις, εως, ἡ, (εἴρω A) *a binding, band*, Suid., etc., v.l. in Th.1.6.

Ἔρσος, ὁ, epith. of Apollo in Attica, *IG*1².783; perh. cf. Ἔρρος.

ἐρσοφόρος, = ἀρρηφόρος, τῶν ἁγιωτάτων μυσταρίων prob. in *IG*12(2).255 (Mytil.); cf. ἐρρηφορέω, ἐρσηφορία.

ἐρσόω, (ἔρση) *bedew, moisten*, like ἄρδω, Nic.*Th*.62, 631 (both Pass.).

ἐρσώδης, ες, = ἐρσήεις, ἀήρ Thphr.*CP*3.2.6.

ἔρτις· κρημνός, Hsch.

ἐρτός, ή, όν, (εἴρω A) *threaded, passed through*, βρόχος Heracl.ap. Orib.48.1.1.

ἐρῠγ-άζομαι, = sq., Sor.1.108 (ῥυγιάζεσθαι cod.). **–άω**, *belch*, *Gp*.17.17.1.

ἐρυγγάνω, Prose and Att. form of ἐρεύγομαι (A), *belch*, Hp.*Vict*.3.76, Cratin.58: c. acc., [Βάκχιον] ἐ. E.*Cyc*.523, cf. Eup.198; σκοροδάλμην Luc.*Alex*.39: metaph., δάνει' ἐρυγγάνων Diph.43.21:—also in Med., c. acc., Hp.*Vict*.3.75.

ἐρῠγ-ή, ἡ, *belching*, Sch.Ar.*Pax*528, Aret.*SD*1.5, Gal.1.629. II. *bellowing*, Hsch. **–ήτωρ**, ορος, ὁ, *bellower*, Id. **–μα**, ατος, τό, = ἐρυγή I, Hp.*Morb*.2.66. **–μαίνω**, *bellow*, Hsch. **–μᾰτώδης**, ες, *causing eructation*, νοῦσος Hp.*Morb*.2.69. **–μηλος**, η, ον, (ἐρύγειν) *loud-bellowing*, ταῦρος Il.18.580. II. ἐρυγμήλη, ἐπίθετον ῥαφανίου, ἴσως ἀπὸ τῆς ἐρυγῆς, *EM*379.27, cf. Hsch. (ἐρυγηλή cod.). **–μός**, ὁ, = ἐρυγή I, Arist.*Pr*.908^{a}3 (pl.), al., Thphr.*Od*.59 (pl.).

ἐρῠθ-αίνω, aor. ἐρύθηνα A.R.1.791, Lxx *Wi*.13.14:—Pass., Hom. (v. infr.), etc.:—poet. and later Prose word for ἐρυθραίνω, ἐρεύθω, *dye red*, αἷμα πέπλον ἐρύθηνεν A.R.4.474; φύκει –ήνας χρόαν Lxx l.c.; *make to blush*, A.R.1.791:—Pass., *to be dyed red*, ἐρυθαίνετο αἵματι γαῖα Il.10.484, cf. 21.21: c. gen., Nonn.*D*.11.92 (s.v.l.); *blush scarlet*, *AP*12.8 (Strat.):—Pass., also in later Prose, Arr.ap.Stob.1.31.8, Poll.2.87. **–ημα**, ατος, τό, *redness* or *flush upon the skin*, Hp.*Aph*.7.49, Th.2.49 (pl.); ἐ. προσώπου *blush*, E.*Ph*.1488 (lyr.), Hp.*Acut*.(*Sp*.)6 (pl.); ἐ. ῥόδων φέρειν Aristaenet.1.10: abs., *redness*, X.*Cyn*.5.18; *blush*, Chaerem.1.4. II. concrete, ἐρύθημα ἱματίων *scarlet* garments, Lxx *Is*.63.1.

ἐρυθίβη, –ιος, said to be Rhodian for ἐρυσίβ-η, –ιος (q.v.).

ἐρῠθῖνος, ὁ, = ἐρυθρῖνος, Henioch.3.3, D.L.8.19, Opp.*H*.1.97.

ἐρῠθράδιον, τό, = ἐρυθρόδανον, Sch.Nic.*Th*.74.

Ἐρυθραί, αἱ, *Erythrae* in Ionia, Hdt.1.142, etc.; locat. Ἐρυθρᾶσι *IG*1².10.14:—hence **Ἐρυθραϊκὸν** σατύριον, *Serapias cordigera*, Dsc.3.128, Plin.*HN*26.97:—but **Ἐρυθριὰς γῆ** is f.l. for Ἐρετριάς, Heras ap.Gal.13.545.

Ἐρυθραϊκός, ή, όν, *of the Red Sea*, κυβερνήτης *OGI*674.10 (i A.D.).

ἐρυθρ-αίνω, *paint red, rouge*, πρόσωπον Perict.ap.Stob.4.28.19; παρειάς Hdn.5.6.10:—Pass., *become red*, Thphr.*HP*3.12.5, Sor.1.108; *blush*, X.*Cyr*.1.4.4, Arist.*EN*1128^{b}13. II. intr., *to be red*, Id.*Pr*.890^{a}8; ἡ τέρμινθος.. χλοερὸν ἐνέγκασα [καρπὸν] μετὰ ταῦτα ἐρυθραίνει Thphr.*HP*3.15.3. **–αῖος**, α, ον, = ἐρυθρός, πόντος, θάλασσα, D.P.597, 958, etc.; κάλαμος Id.1127. II. *of* or *from Erythrae*, Hdt.1.18, etc. **–ᾰνός**, όν, κισσὸς *red-berried* ivy, Plin. *HN*24.82. **–ημα**, ατος, τό, = ἐρύθημα (perh. f.l.), Poll.6.180, v.l. in Lxx *Is*.63.1. **–ίας**, ου, ὁ, *of ruddy complexion*, opp. ὠχρίας, Arist.*Cat*.9^{b}31, *PPetr*.3 p.30 (iii B.C.). **–ίᾶσις**, Ion. –ησις, εως, ἡ, *ruddiness, blushing*, Hp.*Decent*.5, Hsch. s.v. λατραπία. **–ιάω**, Ep. part. –ιόων Musae.161: impf. ἠρυθρίων Luc.*Laps*.1, etc.: aor. 1 ἠρυθρίᾱσα Pl.*Ly*.204c, etc.: pf. ἠρυθρίᾱκα *PTeb*.37.10 (i B.C.) (v. ἀπηρυθριακότως):—*blush, colour up*, Pl.*Prt*.312a, D.18.128; ἀστεῖόν γε.. ὅτι ἐρυθριᾷς Pl.*Ly*.204c: c. part., *blush at* doing, Dromo 1; ὅστις δ' ἐρυθριᾷ.. πρὸς τοὺς ἑαυτοῦ γονέας, οὐκ ἔστιν κακός Antiph.261, cf. Men.782, Diph.135; also ἐ. τινά *to blush before* one, Aristaenet.1.13, Lyd.*Mag*.3.38; τὴν ἀρχήν ib.50: c. inf., Ph.2.310, Chor. in Lib.4.775 Reiske. 2. *to be inflamed*, Aret.*SA*1.8.

ἐρυθρῖνος, also **ἐρυθῖνος** (q.v.), ὁ, a hermaphrodite fish, prob. *Serranus anthias*, Arist.*HA*538a20. 2. a sea-fish, prob. *Pagellus erythrinus*, Speus.ap.Ath.7.300e, Hierocl. *in CA*26 p.480 M., etc.

ἐρυθρίς, = foreg., *Gloss.*

ἐρυθρο-βαφής, ές, *red-dyed*, Eust.6.8. **-βωλος**, ον, *with red earth*, Sch.D.P.183. **-γραμμος**, ον, *with red lines*, Arist.*Fr.*294, cf. Ath.7.321e. **-δάκτῠλος**, ον, *red-fingered*, criticized as unpoet., Arist.*Rh.*1405b21.

ἐρυθρόδᾰν-ον, τό, = ἐρευθέδανον, Dsc.3.143: **ἐρυθρόδανος**, ἡ, Plin. *HN*24.94 (v.l.); cf. ἐρυθρύδανον. **-όω**, *dye with madder, dye red*, Lxx *Ex.*25.5, 26.14. **-ωσις**, εως, ἡ, *dyeing scarlet*, Zos.Alch.p.220 B.

ἐρυθρο-ειδής, f.l. for ἐλυτρο- (q.v.). **-κάρδιος**, ον, *with red pith*, Thphr.*HP*3.12.3. **-κομίς**, ίδος, ἡ, *with red down*, a kind of pomegranate, Plin.*HN*13.113. **-λευκος**, ον, *reddish-white*, Gal.17(1).835, Hsch. s.v. φλογόλευκον. **-μέλας**, αινα, αν, *blackish-red*, Philem.Lex.ap.Ath.14.652f.

ἐρυθρόνιον, τό, = σατύριον, Ps.-Dsc.3.128.

ἐρυθρό-ξανθος, ον, *reddish-yellow*, Aët.12.13. **-ποίκῐλος**, ον, *spotted with red*, συνόδοντες Epich.69. **-πους**, ὁ, ἡ, neut. πουν, *red-footed*, πελειάς Arist.*HA*544b4. II. a bird, prob. *the redshank, Totanus calidris*, Ar.*Av.*303. **-πρόσωπος**, ον, *of a ruddy look*, Anon.ap.Suid. s.v. Ἁρμάτος.

ἐρυθρός, ά, όν, [ῠ by nature, Ar.*Ach.*787, al.: hence the later Comp. and Sup. are perh. -ώτερος, -ώτατος, as in Pl.*Ti.*83b, *Epin.* 987c; but the metre requires -ότερος in Anaxandr.22, Dromo 1, cf. Choerob.*in Theod.*2.76]:—*red*, νέκταρ ἐ. Il.19.38, Od.5.93; χαλκός Il. 9.365; χρυσὸν ἐ. ἰδεῖν Thgn.450; κῆρυξ ἐ., a ship painted with vermilion, Orac.ap.Hdt.3.57; -ότερον κόκκου Dromo l.c.; ἐ. πέλανος, of blood, A.*Eu.*265 (lyr.); ἐρυθρά, τά, *red pimples, eruption*, Hp.*Liqu.*6; but ἐ. διελθόντα *red* motions, Id.*Coac.*178. 2. ἐρυθρά, ἡ, = μελισσόφυλλον, Ps.-Dsc.3.104; ἐρυθρός, ὁ (sc. ῥοῦς), fruit of the ῥοῦς βυρσοδεψική, Dsc.1.108. 3. ἐρυθρόν, τό, ᾠοῦ *yolk*, Sor.1.124, Orib.*Syn.*5. 13. II. Ἐρυθρὴ θάλασσα in Hdt. *the Indian Ocean*, in which the Red Sea (Ἀράβιος κόλπος) is sts. included (of the existence of the Persian Gulf he was ignorant), 1.180, 2.11,158, 4.42, al.; πόντος Ἐ. Pi.*P.*4.251—later the *Red Sea* only, *OGI*69,186,190, al.: also of the *Persian Gulf*, X.*Cyr.*8.6.20, D.S.2.11; *Peripl.M.Rubr.* prob. mentions Zanzibar and China; used of remote and unknown places, μόνον οὐκ ἐπὶ τὴν Ἐ. θάλατταν πρεσβείας πέμπειν D.19.304: really ἡ Ἐρύθρα θάλασσα sea *of Erythras*, acc. to Agatharch.5. (Lat. *rubro-* fr. **rudhro-*, cf. Skt. *rudhirá-*; v. ἐρεύθω.)

ἐρυθρότης, ητος, ἡ, *redness, ruddiness*, τῆς χρόας Gal.1.582, cf. Phlp. *in Cat.*148.5.

ἐρυθρό-χλωρος, ον, *pale-red*, Hp.*Epid.*6.3.13 (vulg. -χολος: al. -χροος, acc. to Gal.17(2).66). **-χροος**, ον, contr. **-χρους**, ουν, *red-coloured*, ὑπόδεσις D.C.43.43. **-χρως**, ωτος, ὁ, ἡ, = foreg., Cratin.221.

ἐρυθρύδανον, τό, = ἐρυθρόδανον, *PSI*5.489 (iii B.C.).

ἐρυθρώδης, ες, = ἐρυθροειδής, Ath.3.76b.

ἐρύθω, = ἐρεύθω, *Hymn.Is.*147.

ἐρῠκᾰνάω, poet. for ἐρύκω, *restrain, withhold*, κεῖνον ἐρυκανόωσ' ἀέκοντα Od.1.199: c. inf., *from* doing, Q.S.12.205: also Ep. impf. ἐρύκανε (from **ἐρῠκάνω**) Od.10.429, cf. Orph.*A.*647.

ἐρυκτῆρες, οἱ, *a class of freedmen* at Sparta, Myro 1 J.

ἐρύκω [ῡ], Il.24.658, Hdt.4.125, S.*Tr.*121 (lyr.), etc., rare in Prose, X.*An.*3.1.25, Plb.*Fr.*45; Ep. inf. ἐρῡκέμεν Il.11.48: fut. ἐρύξω Od.7. 315, al. (not later): aor. 1 ἤρυξα A.*Th.*1081 (anap.), (ἀπ-) X.*An.*5.8. 25; Ep. ἔρυξα Il.3.113, Od.17.515, etc.: Ep. aor. 2 ἠρύκᾰκον Il.5.321, 20.458, ἐρύκᾰκον 11.352, etc., inf. ἐρῡκᾰκέειν 5.262, Od.11.105:—Med., Il.12.285:—Pass., v. infr. II: cf. ἐρυκάνω, -ανάω: (perh. akin to ἐρύω B):—*keep in, curb, restrain*, ἵππους Il.11.48, etc.; λαὸν ἐρυκάκετε *keep* them *back* (from flight or fighting), 6.80, cf. 24.658; but λαὸν ἔρυκε *kept* them *in their place*, 23.258; αἰθὴρ ὄμβρον ἐρύκει *forces* it *back*, Emp. 100.18; θυμὸν ἐρυκακέειν *to curb* desire, Od.11.105; πολύστονον ἐρύκεν (inf.) ὕβριν B.16.41; ἕτερος δέ με θυμὸς ἔρυκεν another mind *checked* me (opp. ἀνῆκεν), Od.9.302; ἐρυκέμεν εὐρύοπα Ζῆν *to restrain* him, Il.8.206; γυίων πίστιν ἐ., i.e. to mistrust, Emp.4.13; ἔρυκέ μιν ἔνδοθεν αἰδώς A.R.3.652: c. gen., μηδέ μ' ἔρυκε μάχης *keep* me *not from* fight, Il.18. 126; ἀλλά τις θεῶν. . Ἅιδα σφε δόμων ἐρύκει S.*Tr.*121; μηδέ σ' Ἔρις ἀπ' ἔργου θυμὸν ἐρύκοι Hes.*Op.*28: c. inf. praes., *hinder from* doing, Pi.*N.* 4.33; aor., E.*HF*317; fut., ἄλλον ἀναστήσεσθαι ἐρύξω A.R.1.346: c. acc. et inf., ἤρυξε πόλιν μὴ 'νατραπῆναι A.*Th.*1081; ἐ. τἄλλα ἰχθύδια μὴ διαρπάσωσι. . Arist.*HA*621a24. 2. abs., *hinder*, ἐρύκακε γὰρ τρυφάλεια Il.11.352; ἐρυκέμεν *to stay* [their flight], 21.7. 3. *hold in check, keep off* the enemy, εἴ κεν ἐρύξομεν ἀντιάσαντες Il.15.297, cf. Od.22.138; so τὰ δ' οὐ μένος ἀμὸν ἐρύξει Il.8.178; ἐ. τοὺς ἐπιόντας Hdt.4.125, cf. 5.15, etc. 4. *detain* a guest, ξείνισσ' ἐνὶ μεγάροισιν ἐείκοσιν ἤματ' ἐρύξας Il.6.217, cf. Od.17.408, al.; also, *detain* by force, *confine*, [πόντος] πολέας ἀέκοντας ἐρύκει Il.21.59, cf. Od.1.14, 7.315, etc.; ἔρυξον ἐνὶ μεγάροισι γυναῖκας *keep* them *close*, 19.16; of the dead, ἥ μιν ἐρύξει γῆ φυσίζοος ἤ τε κατὰ κρατερόν περ ἐρύκει Il.21.62; σφωε δόλος καὶ δεσμὸς ἐρύξει Od.8.317; ὅσσ' ἔτι Νεῖκος ἔρυκε Emp.35.9:—Med., κῦμα δέ μιν (sc. χιόνα). . ἐρύκεται Il.12.285. 5. *ward off*, θεοῦ δ' ἠρύκακε δῶρα (sc. ἄκοντα) 21.594; ἅ κέν τοι λιμὸν ἐρύκοι Od.5. 166; κακόν, τό οἱ οὔ τις ἐρύκακεν Il.15.450; ἐ. ψευδέων ἐνιπάν Pi.*O.* 10(11).5; τὰ μὴ καλὰ νόσφιν ἐ. Theoc.7.127; ἀπ' ἐμαυτοῦ τὰ κακὰ X. *An.*3.1.25; τὸν πόλεμον ἀπὸ τῆς Μακεδονίας Plb.*Fr.*45. 6. *keep away*, ὀλίγος δ' ἔτι χῶρος ἐρύκει Il.10.161. II. Pass., *to be held back, detained*, δηθ' ἐνὶ νήσῳ ἐρύκεαι Od.4.373, cf. 17.17. 2. abs., *hold back, keep back*, μή μοι ἐρύκεσθον, says the driver to his horses, Il. 23.443. 3. *to be kept away*, τοῦ Ἀσωποῦ (v.l. ἀπὸ τοῦ Ἀ.) Hdt.9. 49. 4. ἀνέδην ὅδε χῶρος ἐρύκεται this place *is* remissly *guarded*, i.e. *is free* or *open* to all, S.*Ph.*1153 (lyr., dub. l.).

ἔρῠμα, ατος, τό, (ἐρύω B) *fence, guard*, ἔ. χροός, of defensive armour, Il.4.137; of a cloak, Hes.*Op.*536; θώρακας, ἐρύματα σωμάτων X.*Cyr.*4.3.9; ἔ. νιφετοῦ *a defence against*. ., Call.*Fr.*142; τὸ ἔ. τοῦ τείχεος the *defence given by* it, Hdt.7.223,225; περιβαλέσθαι ἕρκος, ἔ. τῶν νεῶν Id.9.96, cf. Th.8.40; ἔ. Τρώων *the wall* of Troy, S.*Aj.*467; ἔ. λίθοις ὤρθωσαν *a breast-work*, Th.6.66; ἔ. τειχίζεσθαι, τειχίζειν, Id. 1.11, X.*HG*2.3.46; also of a river or trench used as a military *defence*, Id.*An.*2.4.22. 2. *safeguard* or *defence*, ἔ. χώρας, of the Areopagus, A.*Eu.*701; παῖδας ἔ. δώμασι E.*Med.*597; ἔ. πολεμίας χερός *against*. ., ib.1322; ἔ. χθονὸς ὄφρα βάλοιτο Call.*Hec.*1.2.8.

ἐρῠμάτιον, τό, Dim. of foreg., Luc.*DMeretr.*9.5.

ἐρυμνάομαι, Pass., *to be defended*, Anon.ap.Suid.

ἐρυμνόνωτος, ον, *with fenced back*, of a crab, f.l. for τερεμνό-, *AP* 6.196 (Stat. Flacc.).

ἐρυμν-ός, ή, όν, Comp. -ότερος, Sup. -ότατος, *AP*7.138 (Acerat.), 599 (Jul.): (ἐρύω B):—*fenced, fortified, strong*, by art or nature, Γλήχωνά τ' ἐρυμνήν Hes.*Fr.*38, cf. Th.5.65, Plb.1.30.8, Plu.*Cam.*9, etc.; ἐ. δώματα E.*Hel.*68; κεῖναι μὲν πύργοισι. . ἐρυμναί, Δῆλος δ' Ἀπόλλωνι Call.*Del.*23; τὰ ἐρυμνά *strong positions*, X.*An.*5.7.31, etc.; τόποι οἱ ἐ. Arist.*Pol.*1330b18; τὸ ἐ. Onos.42.15; of hills, *steep, sheer*, Ὄθρυς A.R.2.514, etc. Adv. Comp. -οτέρως Arist.*Pol.*1331a30. **-ότης**, ητος, ἡ, *strength* or *security* of a place, X.*Cyr.*6.1.23; τῶν τειχῶν Arist.*Pol.*1330b37; αἱ ἐ. τῶν Ἄλπεων *the difficulties of passing* them, Plb.3.47.9, etc. **-όω**, *fortify, make strong*, Agath.2.4, *EM*378. 31:—Pass., μερόπεσσιν -ώθησαν ἀγυιαί Nonn.*D.*6.386 (s.v.l.).

ἐρυμνῶδις (sic)· λύπην καὶ φλεγμονὴν παρέχων, ἢ ὑπερήφανον, Hsch. (cf. Lat. *aerumnosus*). **Ἐρυμός**· Ζεύς, καὶ ζυγός, καὶ ζεύγλη, Id. (cf. ῥυμός). **ἐρύμυλον**· τὸν μεγάλως μυκώμενον ταῦρον (leg. ἐρύγμηλον), Id. **ἐρυνόν**· σκοτεινόν, ἠσφαλισμένον, Id. (confusion of ἐρεμνόν and ἐρυμνόν).

ἔρυξις, εως, ἡ, = ἔρευξις, Hp.*Epid.*6.8.8.

ἐρύσαιθρον, *apiastrum*, *Gloss.*; cf. *olusatrum*.

ἐρῠσάρμᾰτες, acc. -ᾰτας, nom. and acc. pl., with no sg. in use, *chariot-drawing*, ἵπποι Il.15.354, 16.370, Hes.*Sc.*369.

ἐρῠσῖβ-άω, *suffer from rust*, Thphr.*CP*4.14.2. **-η** [ῑ Orph.*L.* 600], ἡ, *rust*, in corn, Pl.*R.*609a; αὐχμοὶ καὶ ἐ. Arist.*HA*553b20: pl., Pl.*Smp.*188b, X.*Oec.*5.18, Thphr.*CP*3.22.1, etc. II. title of Demeter in Lydia, *Et.Gud.*210.25. **-ῖος**, ὁ, *averting rust*, epith. of Apollo at Rhodes, Str.13.1.64 (in alleged Rhod. form ἐρυθίβιος, from ἐρυθίβη: v.l. ἐρεθίβιος, etc., cf. Ἐρεθίμιος). **-όω**, *affect with rust*, Thphr.*CP*3.24 fin.:—Pass., = ἐρυσιβάω, ib.22.2, Ath.Med.ap.Orib.1. 2.12, etc. **-ώδης**, ες, *affected with rust*, ἄνθη, ὕλη, Arist.*HA*605b 18, 626b23; *liable to mildew*, Thphr.*HP*8.3.2; χῶραι Id.*CP*3.24.4.

ἐρῠσίθριξ ἵππων ψήκτρη comb *for drawing through the hair, curry-comb*, *AP*6.246 (Phld. or Marc. Arg.).

ἐρύσῖμον [ῠ], τό, *hedge-mustard, Sisymbrium polyceratium*, Thphr. *HP*8.3.1, Dsc.2.158: **εἰρύσιμον** in Nic.*Th.*894, Orph.*A.*917; cf. ῥύσιμον. 2. as Adj., ἐρύσιμον· ἑλκύσιμον, Phot.

ἐρῠσί-νηΐς, ΐδος, ἡ, either *preserving ships* or *checking ships* (cf. ἰσχάς), ἄγκυρα *AP*6.90 (Phil.). **-πελας**, πέλατος, τό, *erysipelas*, Hp.*VM*19 (pl.), *Prog.*23, *Aph.*5.23, Gal.10.949, Orib.45.1.3 (pl.), *Gp.* 12.23.5 (pl.), etc. **-πελᾰτώδης**, ες, *of the nature of* ἐρυσίπελας, οἴδημα Hp.*VC*20; φλεγμοναί Dsc.1.26; διάθεσις Ruf.ap.Orib.8.24.16. Adv. -δῶς, ἔχειν Gal.18(1).448. **-πτολις**, ὁ, ἡ, (ἐρύω B) *protecting the city*, epith. of Athena, Il.6.305 codd. (ῥυσ- Sch.), *h.Hom.*11.1, 28.3.

ἔρῠσις, εως, ἡ, (ἐρύω A) *a drawing*, νεῶν Max.Tyr.19.4 (pl.).

ἐρυσί-σκηπτρον, τό, a plant, = ἀσπάλαθος, Thphr.*Od.*57, Dsc.1. 20; = κύπερος, ib.4; also, = ἄκανθα λευκή, Ps.-Dsc.3.12; = ἱερὰ βοτάνη ib.4.60; cf. ἐρίσκηπτον. **-χαιος**, ον, expl. as, = *carrying a shepherd's staff*, Alcm.24.4; but prob. = *inhabitant of* Ἐρυσίχη in Acarnania, cf. Hdn.Gr.ap.Bgk.ad loc. **-χθονίδαι**, οἱ, name of an Athenian γένος, *SIG*728 D[1] (i B.C.). **-χθων**, ὁ, ἡ, gen. χθονος, *tearing up the earth*, of an ox ploughing, Strato Com.1.19.

ἐρυσμός, ὁ, *safeguard* against witchcraft, *h.Cer.*230. II. a vegetable, the seed of which was eaten by women in childbirth, Paus. Gr.*Fr.*182.

ἔρυσος, ὁ, *basket*, Hsch.

ἐρυστός, ή, όν, *drawn*, κολεῶν ἐρυστὰ. . ξίφη S.*Aj.*730.

ἐρῠτήρ, ῆρος, ὁ, *that which draws up*, ἐ. φάρυγγος, of a strip of papyrus used to induce vomiting, Nic.*Al.*363.

ἐρύφαζε· κατεπάτησεν, ἐτόξευσεν, Hsch.

ἐρύω (A), Il.4.467, al., Ion. **εἰρύω**, Dor. **ϝερύω** (v. infr.): Ep. inf. εἰρύμεναι [ῠ] Hes.*Op.*818: impf. εἴρυον Mosch.2.14, ἔρυον Il.12.258, ἐρύεσκον Nonn.*D.*43.50: fut. ἐρύω Il.11.454, al., ἐρύσω Opp.*H.*5.375; Ep. ἐρύσσω Orph.*L.*35, Nonn.*D.*17.183: aor. εἴρῠσα Od.2.389, Hdt. 2.136 (in Hdt. εἴρυσα takes the place of εἵλκυσα), ἔρυσα Il.5.573; εἴρυσσα 3.373, Od.8.85; lengthd. ἐρύσασκε (ἐξ-) Il.10.490; imper. εἴρυσον S.*Tr.*1033 (hex.), Dor. ϝερυσάτω (dub. sens.) *BCH*50.15 (Delphi, iv B.C.); subj. ἐρύσω Il.17.230, εἰρύσω Hp.*Morb.*2.8, etc.; 2 sg. ἐρύσσῃς Il.5.110; Ep. 1 pl. ἐρύσσομεν (for -ωμεν) 14.76, 17.635; opt. ἐρύσαιμι 8. 21, εἰρύσαιμι Timo 59; inf. ἐρύσαι, ἐρύσσαι, Il.17.419, 8.23, εἰρύσαι Hp. *Morb.*1.29, (δι-, ἐξ-) Hdt.7.24, 1.141; part. ἐρύσας Il.23.21, ἐρύσαις Pi. *N.*7.67, εἰρύσας Hdt.4.10, ἐρύσσας A.R.3.913.—Ion., Dor., and poet. Verb:—*drag, draw*, implying force or violence, νῆα. . εἰς ἅλα, ἅλαδε, ἤπειρόνδε, Il.1.141, Od.2.389, 10.423; ἐπ' ἠπείροιο on land, 16.325,359; [δόρυ] ἐ. ἐπ' ἄκρης, of the Trojan horse, 8.508; freq. of the dead, νεκρόν, νεκροὺς ἐ., of the friends, *drag* them *away, rescue* them, Il.5.573, 16.781; of the enemy, *drag* them *off for plunder, ransom*, etc., 4.467, al.; τρὶς ἐρύσας περὶ σῆμα (sc. Ἕκτορα) 24.16; of dogs and birds of prey, *drag and tear*, οἰωνοὶ ὠμησταὶ ἐρύουσι 11.454, etc.; *drag away, carry off violently*, Od.9.99: c. gen. partit., διὰ δώματ' ἐ.. ἢ ποδὸς ἢ καὶ χειρός 17.479; ἐ. τινὰ κουρίξ by the hair, 22.187; also, *pull down, tear away*, κρόσσας μὲν πύργων ἔρυον Il.12.258, cf. 14.35. 2. simply, *draw, pull*, δόρυ ἐξ ὠτειλῆς 16.863; φάρμακον ἐκ γαίης Od.10.303; ἐξ οὐρανόθεν πεδίονδε Ζῆν' Il.8.21; κίον' ἂν' ὑψηλὴν ἐρύσαι Od.22.176; φᾶρος.. κὰκ κεφαλῆς εἴρυσσε *drew* it *over* his head, 8.85; ἄλλον μὲν χλαίνης ἐρύων, ἄλλον δὲ χιτῶνος *pulling* or *plucking* him by.., Il.22.493; νευρὴν ἐπὶ τῷ ἐ. *drawing* the bowstring at him, 15.464; ἐ. τόξον Hdt.3.30, 4.10; εἴρυσον ἔγχος *draw* thy sword, S.*Tr.*1033 (hex.); *attract, absorb*, [ὑγρόν] Hp.*Loc.Hom.*14: c. gen. partit., τῆς χολῆς Id.*Morb.*1.29; ἐπί τινι κλῆρον ἐ. *draw* lots for.., Call.*Jov.*62; ἐκ ποδὸς ἐ. *to put* aside, Pi.*N.*7.67; ὅππῃ ἐμὸν νόον εἰρύσαιμι Timo l. c.; also πλίνθους εἰρύσαι *make* bricks, Hdt.2.136.

B. Med. **ἐρύομαι**, Ion. **εἰρύομαι** [ῠ], fut. inf. ἐρύεσθαι Il.14.422, al., ἐρύσσεσθαι v.l. in Od.21.125, Il.21.176: aor. 1 εἰρύσσατο 22.306, ἐρύσαντο 1.466, etc.; subj. ἐρύσωμαι A.R.1.1204; opt. ἐρύσαιο, -αίατο, Il.5.456, 298; inf. ἐρύσσασθαι 22.351; part. ἐρυσσάμενος 1.190, εἰρυσάμενος (ἐπ-) Hdt.4.8:—*draw for oneself*, ἐρυσαίμεθα νῆας *launch us* ships, Il.14.79; [ἵππον] ἐς ἀκρόπολιν ἐ. Od.8.504; ξίφος, ἄορ, μάχαιραν ἐρύεσθαι, *draw one's* sword, Il.4.530, 21.173, 3.271; ἄορ ἐκ κολεοῖο Theoc.22.191; δόρυ ἐξ ὠτειλῆς εἰρυσάμην Od.10.165; of meat on the spit, ἐρύσαντό τε πάντα they *drew* all *off*, Il.1.466, etc.; ἐρύσσασθαι μενεαίνων in his anxiety *to draw* [the bow], Od.21.125; βύρσαν θηρὸς ἀπὸ μελέων Theoc.25.273; simply, *wrench*, ὅταν ἱστὸν ἀνέμοιο καταΐξ.. ὑπὲκ προτόνων ἐρύσηται A.R.1.1204. 2. of captives, χρυσῷ ἐρύσασθαι *weigh* against gold (cf. ἕλκω): hence, *ransom*, Il.22.351 (cf. ἀντερύομαι). 3. *draw towards oneself*, ἔθεν ἆσσον ἐρύσσατο Od.19.481. b. *assimilate, retain*, γονήν, τροφήν, Hp.*Mul.*2.166, 171. II. *draw out of* the press, ἐρύσασθαί τινα μάχης Il.5.456; esp. of friends *dragging away* the body of a slain hero, οὐδέ κε.. ἐκ βελέων ἐρύσαντο νέκυν 18.152; of enemies, 14.422, 17.161: c. dat., *in spite of, from*, 5.298, 17.104.

C. Pass., pf. εἴρῡμαι, plpf. 3 pl. εἰρύατο [ῡ Il.14.30, al., ῠ 4.248], εἴρυντο (v. infr.): aor. ἐρύσθην or εἰρ-, Hp.*Epid.*5.47, *Mul.*1.36:—*to be drawn ashore, drawn up in line*, of ships, εἴρυντο νέες ταχὺν ἀμφ' Ἀχιλῆα Il.18.69; εἰρύατο νῆες θῖν' ἐφ' ἁλὸς πολιῆς 14.30, cf. 4.248. 2. *to be drawn, attracted*, of moisture, Hp. l. c.; *to be contracted*, ἐς τοὔπισθεν ἐρυσθείς, of tetanic convulsions, Id.*Epid.*5.47; τὴν γνάθον ἐρυσθεῖσα ib.4.36. (Ϝερῠ-, Ϝρῡ-, cf. ῥῡ-τήρ (βρύτηρ), ῥῦ-μα, ῥῡ-μός.)

ἐρύω (B), only in Med. **ἐρύομαι**, redupl. non-thematic pres. 3 pl. εἰρύαται [ῠ] Il.1.239, *h.Cer.*152, [ῡ] Od.16.463; inf. εἴρυσθαι 3.268, 23.151 (from *se-srū-*, v. infr.); impf. εἴρῡτο Il.16.542, 24.499, Od.23.229, Hes.*Sc.*138, εἴρυντο Il.12.454, εἰρύατο [ῠ] 22.303: from unredupl. stem ῥῡ- (*srū-*), non-thematic 3 pl. impf. ῥύατ' [ῡ] 18.515, Od.17.201, inf. ῥῦσθαι Il.15.141, iterat. ῥύσκευ 24.730: thematic pres. **ῥύομαι** [ῡ] Od.14.107, 15.35, Il.9.396, 10.259, 417, Hes.*Sc.*105; with ῠ, ῥύομ' Il.15.257, ῥύοιτο 12.8, ῥύοισθε 17.224; impf. ῥύετ' [ῠ] 16.799: ῡ in Trag. (E.*HF*197, al., also A.*Eleg.*3), but ῠ in Id.*Th.*303 (lyr.), 824 (anap.): thematic impf. ἐρύετο [ῠ] Il.6.403; non-thematic ἔρῡτο 4.138, 5.23, al., ἔρῡσο 22.507 (ἔρῡτο as aor. 2 S.*OT*1351 (lyr.)): pres. inf. ἔρυσθαι Od.5.484, 9.194, al.; later pres. ind. ἔρῡται A.R.2.1208: fut. ἐρύσσεται Il.10.44, ἐρύεσθαι [ῠ] 20.195, ῥύσομαι [ῡ] Hes.*Th.*662, Hdt.1.86, A.*Th.*91 (lyr.); 3 pl. ῥυσεῦνται Call.*Lav.Pall.*112: aor. 1 εἰρῡσάμην (from *e-serū-*) Il.4.186, 20.93, 21.230; opt. ἐρύσαιτο [ῡ] 24.584; ind. also ἐρρύσατο [ῡ] Od.1.6, al., ἐρύσατο [ῡ] Il.5.344, al., once with ῥῠ, ῥῠσάμην 15.29: from the redupl. pres. εἴρῡμαι are formed fut. ind. 3 pl. εἰρύσσονται 18.276, 1 pl. εἰρῠόμεσθα 21.588: aor. 1 inf. εἰρύσσασθαι 1.216; opt. εἰρυσσαίμην 8.143, 17.327, Od.16.459:—later Pass., aor. ἐρρύσθην *Ev.Luc.*1.74, 2*Ep.Ti.*4.17, Hld.10.7: for ἔρῡτο and ἐρυσσάμενοι as Pass., v. infr. 4:—*protect, guard*, of armour, [πήληξ] κάρη ῥύετ' Ἀχιλλῆος Il.16.799; [κυνέη] εἴρυτο κάρη Hes.*Sc.*138; ῥύεται δὲ κάρη Il.10.259, etc.; μίτρης.. ἥ οἱ πλεῖστον ἔρυτο 4.138, cf. 23.819; ἄστυ δὲ πύργοι ὑψηλαί τε πύλαι σανίδες τ'.. εἰρύσσονται 18.276, cf. 12.454; ἀμφὶ δὲ τάφρον ἤλασαν, ὄφρα σφιν νῆας.. ῥύοιτο ib.8; οἶος ἐρύετο Ἴλιον Ἕκτωρ 6.403, cf. 22.507, 24.499; οἵ με πάρος γε εἰρύατο 22.303; ὅς σε πάρος περ ῥύομ' 15.257, cf. A.*Th.*91 (lyr.), etc.; καὶ πῶς βέβηλον ἄλσος ἂν ῥύοιτό με; Id.*Supp.*509; Λυκίην εἴρυτο δίκῃσί τε καὶ σθένεϊ ᾧ Il.16.542; ἀριστήων οἵ τε πτολίεθρα ῥύονται 9.396; [ἔλαφον] ὕλη εἰρύσατο 15.274; of warders or watchmen, 10.417; σῦς τάσδε φυλάσσω τε ῥύομαί τε Od.14.107; νῆα, νῆας ἔρυσθαι, 9.194, 10.444, 14.260, 17.429; εἴρυσθαι μέγα δῶμα 23.151; ἡ νῶϊν εἴρυτο θύρας, of a female slave, ib.229; ἐπέτελλεν.. εἴρυσθαι ἄκοιτιν 3.268; αὖλιν ἔρυντο, of dogs, Theoc.25.76; ἔτι μ' αὐτ' εἰρύαται οἴκαδ' ἰόντα *lie in wait for* me, Od.16.463; χαλεπόν σε θεῶν.. δήνεα εἴρυσθαι *to discover* them, 23.82 (here perh. a difft. word, cogn. with ἐρευνάω, cf. Pi.*Fr.*61); φρεσὶν εἰρύσσαιτο *keep* in his heart, *conceal*, Od.16.459; οἵ τε θέμιστας πρὸς Διὸς εἰρύαται *maintain* them, Il.1.239: hence, *support, hold in honour*, with notion of obedience, οὐ σύ γε βουλὰς εἰρύσαο Κρονίωνος 21.230; ἔπος εἰρύσσασθαι 1.216. 2. without any notion of defence, merely *cover*, ὡς ῥύσαιτο περὶ χροῒ μήδεα φωτός Od.6.129; φύλλων χύσις ἤλιθα πολλή ὅσσον τ' ἠὲ δύω ἠὲ τρεῖς ἄνδρας ἔρυσθαι 5.484. 3. c. acc. rei, *keep off, ward off*, ἀλλ' οὐκ οἰωνοῖσιν ἐρύσσατο κῆρα μέλαιναν by no augury *could* he *ward off* black death, Il.2.859; ἡ δ' (sc. ἀσπὶς) οὐκ ἔγχος ἔρυτο 5.538, 17.518, Od.24.524; ἀλλὰ πάροιθεν εἰρύσατο ζωστήρ Il.4.186. 4. *thwart, check, curb*, much like ἐρύκω, Διὸς νόον εἰρύσσαιτο 8.143; μὴ ὁ μὲν κραδίῃ χόλον οὐκ ἐρύσαιτο 24.584; Ἠῶ ῥύσατ' ἐπ' Ὠκεανῷ Od.23.244; νῆά τ' ἔρυσθαι A.R.3.607; so prob. in Τρωΐας ἶνας ἐκταμὼν δορί, ταί νιν ῥύοντό ποτε (*thwarted* him) μάχας.. ἔργον.. κορύσσοντα Pi.*I.*8(7).57; νόστον ἐρυσσάμενοι *having been balked of* their return (Med. in pass. sense, cf. ἐστεφανώσατο, κατασχόμενος), Id.*N.*9.23 (v.l. ἐρεισ-):—Pass., ἡ δ' ἔρῡτ' εἶν Ἀρίμοισι Hes.*Th.*304. 5. *rescue, save, deliver* (not in Att. Prose exc. Th.5.63); μετὰ χερσὶν ἐρύσατο Φοῖβος Ἀπόλλων Il.5.344, cf. 11.363; πῶς ἂν.. εἰρύσσαισθε Ἴλιον; 17.327; Ποσειδάων.. Νέστορος υἱὸν ἔρυτο 13.555; βουλῆς.. ἥ τις κεν ἐρύσσεται ἠδὲ σαώσει Ἀργείους 10.44; ἀλλ' Ἥφαιστος ἔρυτο σάωσε δὲ 5.23; ὁ δ' ἐρύσατο καί μ' ἐλέησεν Od.14.279; ἐρρύσατο καὶ ἐσάωσεν Il.15.290; ἀρήξω τὸν ἱκέτην τε ῥύσομαι A.*Eu.*232; πατρίδα ῥυομένους Id.*Eleg.*3; ῥύου με κἀκφύλασσε S.*OC*285, cf. Hdt.7.217, 8.114: freq. folld. by a Prep., οὐ γάρ κεν ῥύσαιτό σ' ὑπὲκ κακοῦ Od.12.107; Ζεῦ πάτερ, ἀλλὰ σὺ ῥῦσαι ὑπ' ἠέρος υἷας Ἀχαιῶν Il.17.645, cf. 224; ἐκ.. πόνων ἐρρύσατο Pi.*P.*12.19; ῥύσασθαί μιν ἐκ τοῦ παρεόντος κακοῦ Hdt.1.87; ὡς ἂν ἀλλὰ παῖδ' ἐμὴν ῥυσώμεθ' ἀνδρῶν ἐκ χερῶν μιαιφόνων E.*Or.*1563: ἀπὸ φόνου S.*OT*1351 (lyr.); ἀπὸ τοῦ πονηροῦ *Ev.Matt.*6.13: c. gen., ῥ. τινὰ τοῦ μὴ κατακαυθῆναι Hdt.1.86; κακῶν μυρίων E.*Alc.*770; τόξων Id.*Ion* 165 (lyr.); πολέμου καὶ μανιῶν ῥ. Ἑλλάδα Ar.*Lys.*342: c. inf., ῥ. τινὰ θανεῖν E.*Alc.*11; τινα μὴ κατθανεῖν Id.*HF*197, cf. *Or.*599, Hdt.7.11; also, *save from an illness, cure*, Id.4.187: generally, Id.3.132. 6. *set free, redeem*, τὸν ἔνθεν ῥυσάμην I *set him free* from thence, Il.15.29; ἐκ δουλοσύνης Hdt.5.49, 9.90; δουλοσύνης ib.76; μάντιν Ἠλεῖον.. ἀπημελημένον ἐν τοῖσι ἀνδραπόδοισι ἐρρύσατο Id.3.132; but χρυσῷ ἐρύσασθαι Il.22.351 seems to come from (Ϝ)ερύω (v. ἐρύω (A) B. I. 2). b. metaph., *redeem, compensate for*.., ἔργῳ γὰρ ἀγαθῷ ῥύσεσθαι τὰς αἰτίας (v.l. λύσεσθαι) Th.5.63; ταῦτα πάντα κατθανοῦσα ῥύσομαι my death *will redeem* (*purchase*) all this, E.*IA* 1383 (troch.); ῥ. καμάτους *Epigr.Gr.*853.6:—double sense in S.*OT* 312, 313 ῥῦσαι σεαυτὸν καὶ πόλιν, ῥῦσαι δ' ἐμέ, ῥῦσαι δὲ πᾶν μίασμα τοῦ τεθνηκότος *redeem* (*deliver*) thyself and the state and me, and *redeem* the pollution from the dead (the μίασμα being thought of as an unpaid debt). (ἐρῡ- ῥῡ- from *serū- srū-*, cogn. with Lat. *servare*, v. οὖρος 'guard', ἔρυμα, ἐρυμνός.)

ἔρφος, εος, τό, *a skin*, = στέρφος, τέρφος, Nic.*Al.*248, *Th.*376.

ἐρχανήεις, εσσα, εν, *like a fence*, πυλών Hsch.; cf. ἐρκάνη, ἔρχατος.

ἔρχᾰται, ἔρχᾰτο, Ion. pf. and plpf. Pass. of ἔργω.

***ἐρχᾰτάομαι**, Pass., *to be kept* or *shut up*, ἐν δὲ ἑκάστῳ [συφεῷ] πεντήκοντα σύες.. ἐρχατόωντο Od.14.15. (Lengthd. fr. ἔρχατο.)

ἔρχᾰτος, ὁ, *fence, enclosure, hedge*, Hsch.; cf. ἔρκατος.

ἔρχομαι Il.13.256, etc. (Act. ἔρχω as barbarism, Tim.*Pers.*167): impf. ἠρχόμην Hp.*Epid.*7.59, Arat.102, (δι-) Pi.*O.*9.93; freq. in later Prose, Lxx *Ge.*48.7, *Ev.Marc.*1.45, Luc.*Jud.Voc.*4, Paus.5.8.5, etc.; in Att. rare even in compds., ἐπ-ηρχόμην Th.4.120 (perh. fr. ἐπάρχομαι), προσ- ib.121 (perh. fr. προσάρχομαι), περι- Ar.*Th.*504 cod.: from ἐλυθ- (cf. ἐλεύθω) come fut. ἐλεύσομαι, Hom., Ion., Trag. (A.*Pr.*854, *Supp.*522, S.*OC*1206, *Tr.*595), in Att. Prose only in Lys.22.11, freq. later, D.H.3.15, etc.: aor., Ep. and Lyr. ἤλῠθον Il.1.152, Pi.*P.*3.99, etc., used by E. (not A. or S.) in dialogue (*Rh.*660, *El.*598, *Tr.*374, cf. Neophr.1.1); but ἦλθον is more freq. even in Hom., and is the only form used in obl. moods, ἐλθέ, ἔλθω, ἔλθοιμι, ἐλθεῖν, ἐλθών; Ep. inf. ἐλθέμεναι, -έμεν, Il.1.151, 15.146 (indic. never ἐλυθ- unaugmented unless ἐξ-ελύθη Il.5.293 has replaced ἐξ-έλυθε); Dor. ἦνθον Epich.180, Sophr.144, Theoc.2.118; imper. ἐνθέ Aristonous 1.9; part. ἐνθών *IG*9(1).867 (Corc., vi B.C.), (κατ-) *Schwyzer* 657.4 (Arc., iv B.C.); subj. ἔνθῃ *Berl.Sitzb.*1927.164 (Cyrene); Lacon. ἔλσῃ, ἔλσοιμι, ἐλσών, Ar.*Lys.*105, 118, 1081; later ἦλθα Lxx 2*Ki.*24.7, *Ev.Matt.*25.36, *BGU*530.11 (i A.D.), *IG*14.1320, etc.; 3 pl. ἤλθοσαν Lxx *Jo.*2.22, al., *PTeb.*179 (ii B.C.), etc.; ἤλυθα *IG*14.1971, Nonn.*D.*37.424, (ἐπ-) *AP*14.44: pf. ἐλήλυθα (not in Hom.) A.*Pr.*943, etc.; sync. pl. ἐλήλῠμεν, -υτε, Cratin.235, Achae.24, 43; Ep. εἰλήλουθα, whence 1 pl. εἰλήλουθμεν Il.9.49, Od.3.81, part. εἰληλουθώς 19.28, 20.360; once ἐληλουθώς Il.15.81, part. κατ-εληλευθυῖα *Berl.Sitzb.*1927.166 (Cyrene); Cret. pf. inf. ἀμφ-εληλεύθεν, v. ἀμφέρχομαι: Boeot. pf. διεσσ-είλθεικε *Schwyzer* 485.2 (Thesp., iii B.C.), part. κατηνθηκότι ib.657.39 (Arc., iv B.C.): plpf. ἐληλύθειν Ar.*Eq.*1306; Ion. ἐληλύθεε Hdt.5.98; Ep. εἰληλούθει Il.4.520, εἰληλούθειν Call.*Fr.*532.—In Att. the obl. moods of pres., as well as the impf. and fut. were replaced by forms of εἶμι *ibo* (q.v.): in Lxx and Hellenistic Greek the place of the compounds, esp. ἐξ-, εἰσ-έρχομαι, is commonly taken by ἐκ-, εἰσ-πορεύομαι, etc., the fut., aor., and pf. being supplied as before by ἐλυθ- (ἐλθ-): I. *start, set out*, ἧ μέν μοι μάλα πολλὰ.. Λυκάων ἐρχομένῳ ἐπέτελλε when I *was setting out*, Il.5.198, cf. 150; τύχησε γὰρ ἐρχομένη νηῦς a ship *was* just *starting*, Od.14.334; ἐς πλόον ἐρχομένοις (v.l. ἀρχ-) Pi.*P.*1.34. 2. *walk*, = περιπατέω, χαμαὶ ἐρχομένων ἀνθρώπων Il.5.442; σὲ δ' ἐρχόμενον ἐν δίκᾳ πολὺς ὄλβος ἀμφινέμεται *walking* in justice, Pi.*P.*5.14: the two foreg. rare signfs. belong only to the pres. ἔρχομαι. II. (much more freq.) *come* or *go* (the latter esp. in Ep. and Lyr.), ἦλθες thou *art come*, Od.16.461, etc.; χαίροισ' ἔρχεο *go* and fare thee well, Sapph.*Supp.*23.7, cf. Il.9.43, Od.10.320, 1.281; ἀγγελίην στρατοῦ.. ἐρχομένοιο 2.30, cf. 10.267; πάλιν ἐλθέμεν, αὖτε εἰλήλουθα, 19.533, 549; οἶκον ἐλεύσεται ib.313; οἴκαδε 5.220; ἐς οἴκους A.*Pers.*833: as a hortatory exclamation, ἀλλ' ἔρχευ, λέκτρονδ' ἴομεν Od.23.254, cf. 17.529. III. c. acc. cogn., ὁδὸν ἐλθέμεναι *to go* a journey, Il.1.151; ἄλλην ὁδόν, ἄλλα κέλευθα ἤλθομεν Od.9.262; τηϋσίην ὁδὸν ἔλθῃς 3.316: freq. in Trag., A.*Pr.*962, *Th.*714 (also κατὰ τὴν αὐτὴν ὁδὸν Pl.*Lg.*707d); νόστιμον ἐλθεῖν πόδα (v.l. δόμον) E.*Alc.*1153; ἀγγελίην, ἐξεσίην ἐλθεῖν, *go* on an embassy, Il.11.140, Od.21.20. 2. c. acc. loci, *come to, arrive at*, rare in Hom., Ἀΐδαο δόμους ἔρχεαι Il. 22.483; ἔρχεσθον κλισίην 1.322: freq. in later Poets, Pi.*P.*4.52, S. *Tr.*259, etc.; *traverse*, ὁ ἥλιος ἔρχεται τῆς Λιβύης τὰ ἄνω Hdt.2.24: c. acc. pers., αἴ κέν τι νέκυς (acc. pl.) ᾐσχυμμένος ἔλθῃ Il.18.180; σὲ δ', ὦ τέκνον, τόδ' ἐλήλυθεν πᾶν κράτος S.*Ph.*141 (lyr.). 3. c. gen. loci, ἔρχονται πεδίοιο *through* or *across* the plain, Il.2.801; but also, *from* a place, γῆς τινος S.*OC*572. 4. c. dat. pers., *come to*, i.e. *come to aid* or *relieve* one, rare in Hom., Od.16.453; freq. later, Pi.*O.*1.100, Th.1.13, etc.; ἀποροῦντι αὐτῷ ἔρχεται Προμηθεὺς ἐπισκεψόμενος τὴν νομήν Pl.*Prt.*321c; also in hostile sense, ἔρχομαί σοι *Apoc.*2.5. IV. c. fut. part., to denote the object, ἔρχομαι ἔγχος οἰσόμενος I *go to* fetch.., Il.13.256; ἔρχομαι ὀψομένη 14.301: freq. in Trag., μαρτυρήσων ἦλθον A.*Eu.*576; ἐκσώσων E.*Med.*1303. 2. in Hdt. like an auxiliary Verb, ἔρχομαι ἐρέων, φράσων, I *am going to* tell, 1.5, 3.6, al.; σημανέων 4.99; μηκυνέων 2.35: rare in Att., ἔ. κατηγορήσων, ἀποθανούμενος, Pl.*Euthphr.*2c, *Thg.*129a; ἔρχομαι ἐπιχειρῶν σοι ἐπιδείξασθαι, for ἔ. σοι ἐπιδειξόμενος, Id.*Phd.*100b; οὐ τοῦτο λέξων ἔρχομαι, ὡς.. X.*Ages.*2.7. 3. c. part. pres., aor., or pf., in Hom., to show the manner of moving, ἄγγελος ἦλθε θέουσα she *came* running, Il.11.715, al.; μὴ πεφοβημένος ἔλθῃς lest thou *come thither* in full flight, 10.510; ἦλθε φθάμενος he *came* first, 23.779; κεχαρισμένος ἔλθοι Od.2.54. 4. aor. part. ἐλθών added to Verbs, οὐ δύναμαι.. μάχεσθαι ἐλθών *go and* fight, Il.16.521; κάθηρον ἐλθών *come and* cleanse, ib.668; λέγοιμ' ἂν ἐλθών A.*Supp.*928; δρᾶ νυν τάδ' ἐλθών S.*Ant.*1107. V. of any kind of motion, ἐξ ἁλὸς ἐλθεῖν *to rise* out of the sea, Od.4.448, al.; ἐπὶ πόντον *to go* over it, 2.265; with qualifying phrase, πόδεσσιν ἔ. *to go* on foot, 6.40 (but πεζὸς εἰλήλουθα *have come* as a foot-soldier, Il. 5.204); of birds, 17.755, etc.; of ships, 15.549, Od.14.334; of spears or javelins, freq. in Il.; of natural phenomena, as rivers, 5.91; wind and storm, 9.6, Od.12.288; clouds, Il.4.276, 16.364; stars, *rise*, Od. 13.94; time, εἰς ὅ κεν ἔλθῃ νύξ Il.14.77, cf. 24.351; ἐπὴν ἔλθῃσι θέρος Od.11.192; ἔτος ἦλθε 1.16; of events and conditions, εἰς ὅ κε γῆρας ἔλθῃ καὶ θάνατος 13.59, cf. 11.135; of feelings, *go*, ἦ κέ μοι αἰνὸν ἀπὸ πραπίδων ἄχος ἔλθοι Il.22.43; ἀπὸ πραπίδων ἦλθ' ἵμερος 24.514; of sounds, etc., τὸν.. περὶ φρένας ἤλυθ' ἰωή 10.139; Κύκλωπα περὶ φρένας ἤλυθεν οἶνος Od.9.362; without φρένας, περὶ δέ σφεας ἤλυθ' ἰωή 17.261, cf. 16.6; of battle, ὁμόσ' ἦλθε μάχη Il.13.337; of things sent or taken, ὄφρα κε δῶρα ἐκ κλισίης ἔλθῃσι 19.191, cf. 1.120; so later, esp. of danger or evil, c. dat., εἰ πάλιν ἔλθοι τῇ Ἑλλάδι κίνδυνος ὑπὸ βαρβάρων X.*HG*6.5.43; ἦλθεν αὐτῷ Ζηνὸς βέλος A.*Pr.*360; μηδ' ὑπ' ἀνάγκας γάμος ἔλθοι Id.*Supp.*1032 (lyr.), cf. *Pers.*436; of reports, commands, etc., Id.*Pr.*663, Th.8.19; τοῖς Ἀθηναίοις ὡς ἦλθε τὰ γεγενημένα *came to* their *ears*, ib.96; τὰ ἐρχόμενα ἐπ' αὐτόν that which *was about to happen* to him, *Ev.Jo.*18.4; of property, which *comes* or *passes* to a person by bequest, conveyance, gift, etc., τὰ ἐληλυθότα εἴς με ἀπὸ κληρονομίας *BGU*919.7 (ii A.D.); ἔ. εἴς τινα ἀπὸ παραχωρήσεως, κατὰ δωρεάν, *PLond.*3.1164e6 (iii A.D.), *PMasp.*96.22 (vi A.D.):—Geom., *pass, fall*, ἔ. ἐπὶ τὸ αὐτὸ σαμεῖον *pass* through the same point, Archim.*Aequil.*1.15; ὅπου ἂν ἔρχηται τὸ ἕτερον σαμεῖον wherever the other point *falls*, ib.2.10.

B. Post-Homeric phrases: 1. ἐς λόγους ἔρχεσθαί τινι *come to* speech with, Hdt.6.86.α', S.*OC*1164 codd.; so ἐς ὄψιν τινὶ ἐλθεῖν Hdt. 3.42. 2. εἰς χεῖρας ἐλθεῖν τινι (v. χείρ); so ἐς μάχην ἐλθεῖν τινι Id. 7.9.γ'; εἰς ὀργάς τισιν Pl.*R.*572a. 3. ἐπὶ μεῖζον ἔ. increase, S.*Ph.* 259; ἐπὶ μηδέν Id.*Fr.*871.8, *El.*1000; ἐπὶ πᾶν ἐλθεῖν try everything, X.*An.*3.1.18. 4. ἐς τὸ δεινόν, ἐς τὰ ἀλγεινὰ ἐλθεῖν, *come* into danger, etc., Th.3.45, 2.39; εἰς τοσοῦτον αἰσχύνης ἐληλύθατον ὥστε.. Pl.*Grg.*487b, etc.; εἰς τὸ ἔσχατον ἀδικίας Id.*R.*361d; ἐπ' ἔσχατον ἐλθεῖν ἀηδίας Id *Phdr.*240d; ὅσοι ἐνταῦθα ἦλθον ἡλικίας *arrived* at that time of life, Id.*R.*329b; ἐς ἀσθενὲς ἔ. *come* to an impotent conclusion, Hdt.1.120; ἐς ἀριθμὸν ἐλθεῖν to be numbered, Th.2.72; εἰς ἔρωτά τινος ἐλθεῖν Anaxil.21.6; εἰς ἔλεγχον Philem.93.3, etc.; εἰς ἑαυτὸν ἐλθεῖν *come* to oneself, *Ev.Luc.*15.17, Arr.*Epict.*3.1.15. 5. παρὰ μικρὸν ἐλθεῖν c. inf., *come within a little of, be near* a thing, E. *Heracl.*296 (anap.); παρ' ὀλίγον ἐλθεῖν Plu.*Pyrrh.*10; παρὰ τοσοῦτον ἡ Μυτιλήνη ἦλθε κινδύνου so narrow was her escape, Th.3.49; παρ' οὐδὲν ἐλθόντες τοῦ ἀποβαλεῖν Plb.1.45.14; παρ' οὐδὲν ἐλθ. ἀπολέσθαι Plu. *Cam.*8. 6. with διά and gen., periphr. for a Verb, e.g. διὰ μάχης τινὶ ἐλθεῖν for μάχεσθαί τινι Hdt.6.9, E.*Hel.*978, Th.4.92; διὰ πυρὸς ἐλθεῖν τινι rage furiously against.., E.*Andr.*488 (lyr.); but οἱ διὰ πάντων τῶν καλῶν ἐληλυθότες *who have gone* through the whole circle of duties, have fulfilled them all, X.*Cyr.*1.2.15; διὰ πολλῶν κινδύνων ἐλθόντες Pl.*Alc.*2.142a. 7. ἔ. παρὰ τὴν γυναῖκα, παρὰ Ἀρίστωνα, of sexual intercourse, *go in to* her, *to* him, Hdt.2.115, 6.68; πρός τινα, of marriage, X.*Oec.*7.5. 8. ἔ. ἐπὶ πόλιν *attack*, Th.2.11. 9. ἔ. ἐς *depend* upon or *be concerned* with, τό γ' εἰς ἀνθρώπους ἐλθόν Aristid. 1.149 J.; τοῖς λογισμοῖς εἰς ἑαυτοὺς ἐρχόμενοι D.S.13.95; ὅσα εἰς ἀρετὴν ἔρχεται Lib.*Or.*22.18; τῶν πραττομένων οὐκ ὀλίγον εἰς ἐκεῖνον ἤρχετο ib.14.31.

Ἐρχομενός, ὁ or ἡ, = Ὀρχομενός, Hes.*Fr.*38, *IG*7.3171, etc.

ἔρψις, εως, ἡ, (ἕρπω) *creeping*, Pl.*Cra.*419d, Arist.*PA*639b3.

ἐρῶ, Att. fut. of εἴρω (B), Th.6.9, A.*Eu.*45, Ar.*Ra.*61, etc., Ion. and Ep. **ἐρέω** (later as pres., Nic.*Th.*484, Ath.9.400a, Gal.15.878, al.); opt. ἐροίην X.*Cyr.*3.1.14, Lib.*Or.*1.87: impf. ἤρεον (v.l. εἴρεον) Hp.*Epid.*2.2.9: pf. Act. εἴρηκα A.*Pr.*821, Ar.*Ra.*558, etc.: plpf. εἰρήκειν Plu.2.184d:—**Pass.**, pf. εἴρημαι Il.4.363, Ar.*Lys.*13, etc.; Ion. 3 pl. εἰρέαται Hdt.7.81, contr. εἴρηται *Schwyzer*811.17 (Oropus, iv B.C.); part. εἰρημένος, Cret. ϝερημένος *Supp.Epigr.*2.509, Arg. ϝεϝρημένος *Schwyzer* 98 (Mycenae): plpf. εἴρητο Il.10.540, Hdt.8.27, etc.: aor. 1 Pass. ἐρρήθην Pl.*Lg.*664d, later ἐρρέθην Arist.*Cat.* 11b12, al.; Ion. εἰρέθην Hdt.4.77, 156: fut. ῥηθήσομαι Th.1.73, Pl. *R.*473e, Isoc.8.73, D.27.53: more freq. εἰρήσομαι, mostly in 3 sg. -ήσεται Il.23.795, Pi.*I.*6(5).59, S.*Ph.*1276, etc.; part. -όμενος Hp. *Art.*53.—Hom. uses only fut. ἐρέω, 3 sg. pf. and plpf. Pass., with part. εἰρημένος, aor. part. ῥηθείς in the phrase ἐπὶ ῥηθέντι δικαίῳ (v. infr.), and fut. Pass.—The place of the pres. εἴρω (q.v.) is supplied by φημί, λέγω or ἀγορεύω; εἶπον serves as aor. (ϝερε-: ϝρη-, cf. ῥήτρα, ῥητός, Lat. *verbum*, Engl. *word*.) I. I *will say* or *speak*, c. acc. rei et dat. pers., Il.1.297: abs., οὐδὲ πάλιν ἐρέει he *will say* nothing against it, 9.56; ἐν δ' ὑμῖν ἐρέω among you, ib.528, cf. Od. 16.378: freq. in Att., ἐρεῖν τι πρός τινα Pl.*R.*520a (Act.), 595b, *Tht.* 179a (both Pass.); τι περί τινος Id.*Phlb.*29d, etc.: c. acc. pers., *speak of*, κακῶς ἐρεῖν τινα Thgn.796, E.*Alc.*705: and c. dupl. acc., ἐρεῖ δέ μ'.. τάδε ib.954, cf. Pl.*Cri.*48a:—Pass., μῦθος.. εἰρημένος ἔστω Il.8. 524; εἰρημένα μυθολογεύειν Od.12.453; λίαν εἰρημένος too *true*, A.*Pr.* 1031; ἐπὶ ῥηθέντι δικαίῳ after justice *has been pronounced*, Od.18. 414; ἐπὶ τοσοῦτον εἰρήσθω περί τινος *let* this *suffice*, Arist.*EN*1117b 21. II. I *will tell, proclaim*, ἔπος Il.1.419, etc.; Ἠὼς.. Ζηνὶ φόως ἐρέουσα *announce* it, 2.49; ἐρέω τιν' ὑμῖν αἶνον Archil.89.1. 2. *tell, order*, c. dat. pers. et inf., X.*HG*3.2.6, etc.: c. acc. et inf., Id.*Cyr.*8. 3.6:—Pass., εἴρητο συλλέγεσθαι τὸν στρατόν *orders had been given*.., Hdt.7.26, etc. III. Pass., *to be mentioned*, οὗτοι μὲν οἱ παραθαλάσσιοι.. εἰρέαται Id.4.181, cf. Arist.*Mu.*393b27. 2. *to be specified, agreed, promised*, εἰρημένος μισθός Hes.*Op.*370, Hdt.6.23; εἰρημένον, abs., *when it had been agreed*, Th.1.140; κὰ(τ) τὰ ϝεϝρημένα *Schwyzer* l.c.

ἐρωγάς, = sq., Hsch.

ἐρωδία· ἅμαξα, Hsch.; cf. ἐριδίαν, ἐριωδία.

ἐρῳδιός, ὁ, *heron*, Il.10.274, Epich.46, Semon.9, Ar.*Av.*886, Call. *Aet.Oxy.*2080.64, Clitarch.22 J., Ant.Lib.7.7, etc.:—also **ῥῳδιός**, Hippon.63, and **ἀρῳδιός** (q.v.):—Aristotle mentions three kinds: ὁ πέλλος, prob. *common heron, Ardea cinerea*; ὁ λευκός, *egret, A. alba, gazetta*; ὁ ἀστερίας, *bittern, A. stellaris*, *HA*609b21: the ἐρῳδιός in Il. l.c. (cf. Ael.*NA*1.1) was prob. a *shearwater*. (ἐρωδιός freq. in codd., even in Pap. of Call. l.c. (ii A.D.), but ἐρῳδιός (with ωι and oxyt.) Hdn.Gr.2.924 and codd. Hom.)

ἔρωες, οἱ, coined as etym. of ἥρωες by Hierocl. *in CA*3 p.424 M.

ἐρω-έω, (ἐρωή) Ep.Verb, *rush, rush forth*, αἷμα κελαινὸν ἐρωήσει περὶ δουρί Il.1.303, Od.16.441; ἠρώησαν ὀπίσσω, of horses, they *started back*, Il.23.433; *escape harm*, Nic.*Th.*117. 2. c. gen. rei, *draw back* or *rest from*, ἐρωῆσαι πολέμοιο Il.13.776, cf. 17.422; ἐρωήσουσι δὲ χάρμης 14.101; ἐρώησαν καμάτοιο *h.Cer.*301; οἴνου Epic. in *Arch.Pap.* 7.4; [νεφέλη] οὔ ποτ' ἐρωεῖ (sc. σκοπέλου) the cloud never *fails from* it, never *leaves* it, Od.12.75; ἴθι νῦν κατὰ λαὸν Ἀχαιῶν, μηδ' ἔτ' ἐρώει (sc. τοῦ ἰέναι) Il.2.179: c. acc., *leave, quit*, Theoc.13.74, 24.101. II. trans., *drive* or *force back*, once in Hom., τῶ κε καὶ ἐσσύμενόν περ ἐρωήσαιτ' ἀπὸ νηῶν Il.13.57; χεῖρας ὑσμίνης Theoc.22.174; ῥόον Call. *Del.*133; θηρὸς ὁλοὸν κέρας Id.*Fr.*249; δρόμον ἐλεφάντων cj. in Nonn. *D.*36.188: c. acc. et inf., Ἀχαιοὺς ἐ. κορέσασθαι Q.S.3.520.—Dub. in late Prose, Ant.Lib.7.3. -ή, ἡ, Ep. Noun (Hom. only in Il.), *quick motion, rush, force*, ἀνδρὸς ἐ. Il.3.62, cf. 14.488; mostly of things, δουρὸς ἐ. 15.358; βελέων ἐ. 4.542; λείπετο δουρὸς ἐ. a spear's *throw* behind, 23.529, cf. 21.251; λικμητῆρος ἐ. *the force* or *swing* of the winnower's (shovel), 13.590; ἐκτὸς ἐρωῆς πετράων A.R.4.1657; πυρὸς *AP*9.490 (Heliod.). 2. *impulse, desire*, περὶ Κύπριν ἐ. ib.10. 112, cf. Procl.*H.*3.10; γαστρὸς ἐ. Opp.*C.*3.175. II. c. gen. rei, *drawing back from, rest from*, πολέμου δ' οὐ γίγνετ' ἐ. Il.16.302, 17. 761; μάχης Theoc.22.192; δακρύων Mosch.4.40: abs., *escape*, D.P.601.

ἐρωμᾰν-έω, *to be mad for love*, Opp.*C.*3.368, Nonn.*D.*1.136, al., *AP*5.266.10 (Agath.). -ής, ές, *maddened by love*, διάθεσις πρὸς μειράκιον D.S.30.22, cf. Nonn.*D.*16.10, al. 2. *exciting mad love*, φίλτρα Orph.*H.*55.14 (ἐρωτομ- codd.). -ία, Ep. -ίη, ἡ, *mad love*, *AP*5.46 (Rufin.), 219 (Agath.), 254 (Paul. Sil.).

ἐρωμένιον, τό, *a little love, darling*, *AP*11.168 (Antiphan.).

ἔρως, ωτος, ὁ, acc. ἔρων for ἔρωτα Alex.Aet.3.12, *AP*9.39 (Musicius): in Ep. and Lyr. usu. **ἔρος** (q.v.): (ἔραμαι, ἐράω A):—*love*, mostly of the sexual passion, θηλυκρατὴς ἔ. A.*Ch.*600 (lyr.); ἐρῶσ' ἔρωτ' ἔκδημον E.*Hipp.*32; ἔ. τινός *love for* one, S.*Tr.*433; παίδων E. *Ion*67: generally, *love of* a thing, *desire for* it, πατρῴας γῆς A.*Ag.*540; δεινὸς εὐκλείας ἔ. Id.*Eu.*865, etc.; ἔχειν ἔμφυτον ἔρωτα περί τι Pl.*Lg.* 782e; πρὸς τοὺς λόγους Luc.*Nigr.Praef.*; ἔρωτα σχὼν τῆς Ἑλλάδος τύραννος γενέσθαι Hdt.5.32; ἔ. ἔχει με c. inf., A.*Supp.*521; θανόντι κείνῳ συνθανεῖν ἔρως μ' ἔχει S.*Fr.*953; αὐτοῖς ἦν ἔρως θρόνους ἐᾶσθαι Id.*OC*367; ἔ. ἐμπίπτει μοι c. inf., A.*Ag.*341, cf. Th.6.24; εἰς ἔρωτά τινος ἀφικέσθαι, ἐλθεῖν, Antiph.212.3, Anaxil.21.5: pl., *loves, amours*, ἀλλοτρίων Pi.*N.*3.30; οὐχ ὅσιοι ἔ. E.*Hipp.*765 (lyr.); ἔρωτες ἐμᾶς πόλεως Ar.*Av.*1316 (lyr.), etc.; of dolphins, πρὸς παῖδας Arist.*HA*631a 10: generally, *desires*, S.*Ant.*617 (lyr.). 2. *object of love* or *desire*, ἀπρόσικτοι ἔρωτες Pi.*N.*11.48, cf. Luc.*Tim.*14. 3. *passionate joy*, S.*Aj.*693 (lyr.). II. pr. n., *the god of love*, Anacr.65, Parm.13, E.*Hipp.*525 (lyr.), etc.; Ἔ. ἀνίκατε μάχαν S.*Ant.*781 (lyr.): in pl., Simon.184.3, etc. III. at Nicaea, a *funeral wreath*, *EM*379. 54. IV. name of the κλῆρος Ἀφροδίτης, *Cat.Cod.Astr.*1.168; = third κλῆρος, Paul.Al.*K.*3; one of the τόποι, Vett.Val.69.16.

Ἐρωτάριον, τό, Dim. of ἔρως II, *a little Cupid*, *BCH*29.543 (Delos), *AP*11.174 (Lucill.).

ἐρωτ-άω, Ep. and Ion. **εἰρωτάω**, contr. in Hom. and best codd. of Hdt., as 3.119, 4.145, al.: impf. ἠρώτων Hp.*Epid.*7.3, (ἐπ-) Th.7.10, etc.; εἰρώταOd.15.423; Ion. εἰρώτευν Hdt.1.158, part. -τεῦντας v. l. in 3.62 (elsewh. εἰρώτων 3.140): fut. -ήσω Hp.*VM*15, Pl.*R*.350e, etc.: aor. 1 ἠρώτησα X.*Cyr*.4.5.21, S.*Tr*.403, etc.: pf. ἠρώτηκα Pl.*Phlb*. 18a:—used in Att. to supply the defective tenses of ἔρομαι:—*ask*, τινά τι something *of* one, ἅ μ' εἰρωτᾷς Od.4.347; εἰρωτᾷς μ' ὄνομα κλυτόν 9.364; ὅσ' ἂν σ' ἐρωτῶ S.*OT*1122; οὐ τοῦτ' ἐρωτῶ σ' Ar.*Nu*.641:—Pass., *to be asked*, τι Pl.*Lg*.895e, X.*Cyr*.1.4.3. 2. ἐ. τι *ask about* a thing, A.*Pr*.228, Pl.*R*.508a; τι περί τινος Id.*Tht*.185c; ἐ. ἐρώτημα *to ask* a question, Id.*R*.487e; τὰς πύστεις ἐρωτῶντες εἰ.. *putting* the question, whether.., Th.1.5:—Pass., τὸ ἐρωτηθέν, τὸ ἐρωτώμενον ἀποκρίνασθαι, to answer the *question*, Th.3.61, X.*Mem*.4.2.23, etc.; τὰ ἔμπροσθεν ἠρωτημένα Pl.*Lg*.662e:—Pass., also with person as subject, ἐρωτηθεὶς τὸ καλόν *asked about* beauty, Id.*Hp.Ma*.289c. 3. folld. by indirect question, εἰρώτα.. τίς εἴη καὶ πόθεν ἔλθοι Od.15.423; ἐ. εἰ.. or ἤν.. *to ask* whether.., Hp.*Steril*.230, cf. Th.8.53; ἐ. ἦ.. A.*Th*.181; αἰτίαν καθ' ἥντινα Id.*Pr*.228; πότεροι.. Ar.*Ach*.648; τοῦτο πρῶτον ἠρώτα, πότερον.. X.*An*.3.1.7; ἐ. πῶς δεῖ ποιεῖν Id.*Mem*.1.3.1. II. *question* a person, εἰρωτᾷς μ' ἐλθόντα θεὰ θεόν Od.5.97; ἐ. καὶ ἐλέγχειν Antipho 6.23; τινα ἀμφί τινος E.*Ion* 236 (lyr.):—Pass., *to be questioned*, ἐρωτᾶσθαι θέλω Id.*IA*1130. b. of sentries, *challenge*, Aen.Tact.22.12; τὸ ἐρωτώμενον the *password*, Id.26.9. 2. in Dialectic, opp. demonstration, *question* an opponent *in order to refute him from his answers*, Arist.*APr*.24ᵃ24; τι ib.42ᵃ39; hence later, *submit, set forth, propound* an argument, λόγον Gal.5.257:—Pass., ὁ λόγος.. ἠρωτῆσθαι φαίνεται Arr.*Epict*.2.19.1; ἐρωτηθέντος τοῦ σοφίσματος S.E.*P*.2.237. III. later, = αἰτέω, *beg, entreat*, ἐ. τινὰ τὰ εἰς εἰρήνην Lxx 1*Ki*.30.21, al.; ἐρωτᾶτε τὰ εἰς εἰρήνην τὴν Ἱερουσαλήμ ib.*Ps*.121(122).6; ἅ σε ἐρωτῶ *PMag.Par*.1.272; ἐ. τινὰ ποιεῖν τι *POxy*.292.7 (i A.D.), *Ev.Luc*.8.37, etc.; ἐ. τινὰ ἵνα.. ib.7.36; ὅπως.. ib.7.3, al., *PMag.Leid.W*.16.13; ἐ. τὸν πατέρα περὶ ὑμῶν *Ev.Jo*.16.26. (Perh. from ἐρ(ϝ)ωτάω, cogn. with ἐρ(ϝ)έσθαι (v. ἔρομαι).) -ημα, ατος, τό, *that which is asked, question*, Th.3.54, etc.; ἡ πρὸς τὸ ἐ. ἀπόκρισις ib.60; τὰ ἐ. τοῦ ξυνθήματος *asking for* the password, Id.7.44; ἐ. περί τινος Pl.*Prt*.336d; ἐ. ἐρέσθαι, Id.*Phlb*.42e; διπλᾶ ἔστρεφε τὰ -ήματα Id.*Euthd*.276d. 2. in Stoic terminology, a question requiring the answer 'Yes' or 'No', opp. πύσμα, Chrysipp.*Stoic*.2.61. II. in Dialectic, *question inviting an answer which may help to refute an opponent*, Arist.*APr*.64ᵃ36 (pl.), *APo*.77ᵃ36, al. -ηματίζω, = ἐρωτάω II. 2, Id.*Top*.155ᵇ4. -ηματικός, ή, όν, *interrogative*, ὄνομα D.T.636.11; χρεῖαι Hermog.*Prog*.3. Adv. -κῶς Theo *Prog*.4, Sch.Ar.*Nu*.1225, etc. -ησις, εως, ἡ, *questioning, interrogation*, Hp.*Steril*.213, Pl.*Prt*.312d, al., X.*Cyr*.8.4.13, al.; ἐ. ποιήσασθαι Isoc.8.58; τινος *about* a thing, Pl.*Tht*.147c; ἐρωτήσεως [ἐπιρρήματα] *interrogative* adverbs, D.T.642.12. II. ἐ. ἀντιφάσεως ('Is A B or is it not B?') Arist.*APr*.24ᵃ25, ᵇ10; v. ἐρώτημα II. III. *proposition, matter submitted*, δηλοῖ τὴν ἐ. φόβον ἔχειν *Cat.Cod.Astr*.1.103. -ητέον, verb. Adj. *one must ask*, ἐρώτημα Arist.*APo*.77ᵇ7. -ητικός, ή, όν, *skilled in questioning*, Pl.*Cra*.398e. II. ἡ -κή (sc. τέχνη) *the art of putting questions*, Arist.*SE*172ᵃ16; ἐ. λόγοι ib.183ᵇ38; v. ἐρωτάω II. 2.

ἐρωτ-ιάς, άδος, ἡ, pecul. fem. of ἐρωτικός, Νύμφαι *AP*9.627 (Marian.). **-ιάω**, *to be lovesick*, Hp.*Ep*.19 (*Hermes* 53.69), Ach.Tat.6.20, Aen.Gaz.*Thphr*.p.24 B. **-ιδεύς**, έως, ὁ, *a young Eros*: pl., ἐρωτιδεῖς *Anacreont*.25.13. **-ίδια** (sc. ἱερά), τά, *festival of Eros* at Thespiae, Ath.13.561e, Sch.Pi.*O*.7.154: also **-ίδαια** *IG*5(1).656, **-ίδεια** ib.659,7.48, etc.

ἐρωτίζω, = ἐρωτάω, Hsch. s. v. ἠρώτιζον.

ἐρωτ-ικός, ή, όν, *of* or *caused by love*, ὀργή, λύπη, Th.6.57,59; ἐ. ξυντυχία a *love*-affair, ib.54; ἐ. λόγος a discourse *on love*, Pl.*Phdr*.227c; ἐ. μέλος a *love* song, Bion 2.2; περὶ ἐ. αἰτίαν Arist.*Pol*.1303ᵇ22; ἐ. ἀρετή Phld.*D*.3*Fr*.76; ἐ. δυνάμεις Ph.2.481; δεινὸς περὶ τὰ ἐ. Pl.*Smp*.193e, al.; τοῖς περὶ τὰς γυναῖκας ἐρωτικοῖς ἔνοχος Plu.*Cim*.4; also, = Ἐρωτίδια, Plu.2.748f; ἡ -κή (sc. φιλία), Arist.*EN*1164ᵃ3. II. of persons, *amorous*, Pl.*R*.474d, Arist.*EN*1156ᵇ1, Theoc.14.61, etc.; περὶ τὰ εὐμορφότατα Luc.*Dom*.2: Comp. -ώτερος X.*Smp*.4.62: generally, *fond of* a thing, πρὸς χρυσίον Plu.*Dem*.25; τὰ τοῦ σώματος -ικὰ πρὸς πλησμονὴν καὶ κένωσιν the *cravings* of the body, Pl.*Smp*.186c. Adv. -κῶς, περιαλγήσας Th.6.54; ἐ. μεταχειρίζεσθαί τινα Lys.*Fr*.1.5; ἐ. διατίθεσθαι Pl.*Smp*.207b; ἐ. ἔχειν τοῦ Σωκράτους ib.222c; τοῦ ποιεῖν τι X.*Cyr*.3.3.12: Sup. -ώτατα, ἔχειν τοῦ ἔργου Id.*Hier*.1.21. **-ιον**, τό, = Ἐρωτάριον, *IG*11(2).161*B*118 (Delos, iii B.C.), Luc.*Philops*.14. II. *charming, sweet child*, Aristaenet.1.19. 2. = ἐρώμενον (Tarent.), Hsch. **-ίς**, ίδος, ἡ, *loved one, darling*, Theoc.4.59. II. as Adj., ἐρωτίδες νῆσοι islands *of love*, *AP*7.628 (Crin.). **-ίσκος**, ὁ, = ἐρωτάριον, *Schwyzer*462*B*54 (Tanagra, iii B.C.), *Gloss*.

ἐρωτο-γράφος [ᾰ], ον, *for writing of love*, μέτρον *AP*7.421.10 (Mel.). **-διδάσκαλος**, ὁ, ἡ, *teacher of the art of love*, Ath.5.219d. **-εις**, εσσα, εν, *loving*, Hdn.*Epim*.206. **-ληπτος**, ον, *love-smitten*, Procop.*Arc*.1; ἔς τινα ib.4. **-μανέω**, = ἐρωμανέω, Stoic.ap.Stob.2.7.5ᵇ⁹ (dub.), Poll.3.68. **-μανής**, ές, = ἐρωμανής, cj. in Stoic.ap.Stob.2.7.5ᵇ⁹, Orph.*H*.55.14 codd., Ath.13.599e, Aristaenet.1.27, etc. Adv. -ῶς Zonar. **-μανία**, ἡ, = ἐρωμανία, *raving love*, Plu.2.451f. **-παίγνιον**, τό, in pl., title of *amatory poems* by Laevius, Gell.2.24.8. **-πλάνος** [ᾰ], ον, *beguiling love*, φθόγγος *AP*7.195 (Mel.). **-πλοέω**, *sail on love's ocean*, ib.5.155 (Id.). **-τόκος**, ον, *producing love*, μῦθοι Musae.159; πρόσωπον Nonn.*D*.4.129; Κυθερείη Procl.*H*.2.13:—fem. **-τόκεια**, ἡ, Ἀφροδίτη *PMag.Par*.1.2557. **-τρόφος**, ον, *the nurse* or *mother of love*, i. e. Aphrodite, Orph.*A*.478, cf. 868.

ἐρωτύλος, ὁ, Dor. word, *a darling, sweetheart*, Theoc.3.7. II. as Adj., ἐρωτύλα ἀείδειν sing *love-songs*, Bion *Fr*.7.10, cf. 13: dub. as epith. of Ἔρος, *PMag.Lond*.121.471 (-τυλλ- Pap.). III. name of a very small star, *AP*9.614 (Leont.). IV. name of a gem, Ps.-Democr.ap.Plin.*HN*37.160.

ἐς, Ion., old Att., Dor. form of εἰς: all compounds must be sought under εἰσ-, except a few words which appear only in the form ἐσ-. II. Arc., = ἐκ, *IG*5(2).6.49 (Tegea, iv B.C.), al.; also Delph., *BCH*23.611, and Arg., *IG*4.492 (Mycenae, vi B.C.); v. ἐκ init.

ἐσαπλῶς, perh. = ἁπλῶς, dub. in Diogenian.Epicur.2.50.

ἐσάχρι, Adv., (εἰς ἄχρι) *as far as*, c. gen., A.R.1.604, *APl*.4.307 (Leon.); ἐ. τούτων τῶν χρόνων Ezek.*Exag*.5.

ἐσαώρας· εἰς καιρούς, Hsch.

ἔσβηνες· εἶδος ποτηρίου (Tarent.), Hsch. **ἔσγονος**, v. ἔκγ-. **ἐσδέλλω**, v. ἐκβάλλω. **ἐσδοκά**, v. ἐκδοχή. **ἔσδοσις, -δοτήρ**, v. ἔκδ-. **ἐσδραμύλιξον**· εἴσδραμε, Id. **ἐσδύομαι**, v. ἐκδύω I. 3.

ἐσεργνύναι, Ion. for εἰσείργειν, *shut in, enclose*, Hdt.2.86.

ἐσηλυσίη, ἡ, = εἰσέλευσις, *AP*9.625 (Maced.).

ἕσθαι, aor. 2 inf. Med. of ἵημι, and pf. Pass. of ἕννυμι.

ἐσθ-έω, (ἐσθής) *clothe*: only pf. and plpf. Pass., mostly in part. ἠσθημένος, Ion. ἐσθημένος, *clothed* or *clad*, τι *in* a thing, ἐσθῆτα ἐσθημένος Hdt.6.112: c. dat., ῥάκεσι ἐσθημένος Id.3.129; ἠσθημένοι πέπλοισι E.*Hel*.1539; Πελοποννησιακῶς ἠσθημένος Pythaen.6: 3 pl. pf. ἤσθηνται Ael.*Fr*.121: 3 sg. plpf. ἤσθητο Id.*VH*12.32; ἠσθῆσθαι Id.*NA*16.34. **-ημα**, ατος, τό, *garment*, always in pl. in Trag., *clothes, raiment*, as A.*Pers*.836, *Ag*.562, S.*El*.268, cf. Th.3.58, etc.: later in sg., Ael.*VH*1.2, Jul.*Or*.2.85a.

ἔσθην, 3 dual plpf. Pass. of ἕννυμι, Il.18.517.

ἐσθής, ῆτος, Dor. **ἐσθάς**, ᾶτος, Pi.*P*.4.79,253, ἡ, acc. ἐσθήν *SIG*1215.7 (Myconos, iii/ii B.C.): (ἕννυμι):—*clothing, raiment*, χαλκόν τε χρυσόν τε ἅλις ἐσθῆτά τε δόντες Od.5.38; χρηστηρία ἐ. *the dress* of prophetesses, A.*Ag*.1270; Ἀργολὶς ἐ. Id.*Supp*.237; μετρίᾳ ἐσθῆτι χρήσασθαι to *dress* simply, Th.1.6: καθαρὰ ἐ., = Lat. *toga pura*, Nic.Dam.*Fr*.127 J.; τὴν ἐσθῆτα μεταβαλεῖν, = Lat. *mutare vestem*, put on mourning, D.C.37.33 (but τὰς ἐσθῆτας μεταβαλέσθαι Plu.*Pomp*.59): in pl., of *the clothes of several* persons, A.*Th*.872 (anap.); *of one*, E.*Hel*.421: abstract pl., πλούτους καὶ τρυφὰς καὶ ἐσθῆτας Pl.*Alc*.1.122c, cf. cj. in Arist.*Rh*.1386ᵃ32, dub. in Pl.*Grg*.465b. II. collectively, *clothes*, ἐσθῆτα ἔσφερον εἴσω, i. e. *the clothes* just washed, Od.7.6; ἔντυνον εὐνὴν ἐσθῆτος μαλακῆς 23.290; τὰ ἐσθῆτος ἐχόμενα εἶχον κατηρείκοντο Hdt.3.66, cf. X.*An*.3.1.19: rarely in later Gr., Plu.*CG*2, *PThead*.49.4 (iv A.D.), *POxy*.2110.5 (iv A.D.). III. metaph., ἐ. τῆς πόλεως, of walls, Demad.*Fr*.4.

ἔσθησις, εως, ἡ, (ἐσθέω) *clothing, raiment*, dub. l. in Arist.*Rh*.1386ᵃ32, cf. Poll.10.51: pl., Ath.1.18e, *Act.Ap*.1.10: dat. pl., ἐσθήσεσι Ph.2.158, Str.3.3.7, v.l. in *Ev.Luc*.24.4.

ἔσθι, = ἴσθι, v. εἰμί A.

ἐσθίω (cf. ἔσθω, ἔδω, the latter of which is the radic. form, and supplies fut. and pf. of ἐσθίω), impf. ἤσθιον Hes.*Op*.147: fut. ἔδομαι (old pres. subj. of non-thematic stem) Il.4.237, Ar.*Pax* 1357 (lyr.), etc.; ἐδοῦμαι late, (προκατ-) Luc.*Hes*.7, etc.: pf. ἐδήδοκα Ar.*Eq*.362, X.*An*.4.8.20; opt. ἐδηδοκοίη Cratin.320; Ep. part. ἐδηδώς, -υῖα, Il.17.542, *h.Merc*.560: plpf. ἐδηδόκειν Luc.*Gall*.4 (v. l.):—Med., aor. 1 ἠδεσάμην (κατ-) Gal.5.752:—**Pass.**, ἐσθίομαι Od.4.318, Thphr.*HP*1.12.4, Luc.*Cyn*.11, etc.: aor. 1 ἠδέσθην v. l. in Hp.*Vict*.2.54, Arist.*Pr*.908ᵃ29, (ἀπ-, κατ-) Pl.Com.138,35: pf. ἐδήδεσμαι (κατ-) Pl.*Phd*.110e, ἐδήδεμαι (ἀπ-) Arist.*HA*591ᵃ5 (v. l.); Ep. 3 sg. ἐδήδοται Od.22.56.—The aor. 2 and later also the fut. are supplied by φαγ- (v. φαγεῖν); in Ion. and Hellenistic Greek the pf. is βέβρωκα βέβρωμαι, aor. Pass. ἐβρώθην; in late Greek the pres. is τρώγω:—*eat*, ἐσθιέμεν καὶ πινέμεν Od.2.305, 21.69; τὰ ἐσθίοντα ἐν στρατιᾷ the *ration-strength*, X.*Cyr*.1.6.17: usu. c. acc., κρέα ἤσθιον Od.20.348, cf. S.*Fr*.671 (from a satyric drama), E.*Cyc*.233: c. gen., ἐ. τινὸς *eat of*.., X.*HG*3.3.6, etc.; of animals, *devour*, ἤσθιε δ' ὥς τε λέων ὀρεσίτροφος Od.9.292; χρόα γῦπες ἔδονται Il.4.237, cf. Hes.*Th*.524,773, Semon.9, etc.; *consume*, βίοτον καὶ κτήματ' ἔδονται Od.2.123:—Pass., ἐσθίεταί μοι οἶκος my house *is eaten up*, I am *eaten* out of house and home, 4.318; ὅσσα τοι ἐκπέποται καὶ ἐδήδοται 22.56. 2. metaph., πάντας πῦρ ἐσθίει the fire *devours* all, Il.23.182; of an *eating* sore, A.*Fr*.253:—Pass., ὀδόντες ἐσθιόμενοι *decayed* teeth, Thphr.*Char*.19.3; ἐσθιόμενα *eroded* parts of the bowel, Hp.*Epid*.4.20. 3. *fret, vex*, ἐ. ἑαυτόν Ar.*V*.287 (lyr.); ἐ. τὴν χελύνην ὑπ' ὀργῆς *to bite* the lip, ib.1083; ἐ. καρδίαν Pythag.ap.Plu.2.12e. 4. *take in one's mouth*, γλῶτταν αὐλοῦ Philostr.*Im*.1.20.

ἐσθλαί· ξύλινα παίγνια,.. (Cypr.), Hsch.

ἐσθλοδότης, ου, ὁ, *giver of good*, Man.2.142.

ἐσθλός, ή, όν, Aeol. **ἔσλος** Sapph.28, Alc.96: Dor. **ἐσλός**, ά, όν, Pi.*P*.8.73, etc. (never in B.); Arc. **ἐσλός** *Inscr.Olymp*.266 (v B.C.): Comp. and Sup. -ότερος, -ότατος, *AP*9.156 (Antiphil.), 6.240 (Phil.):—poet. Adj., = ἀγαθός, *good* of his kind, ἐ. ἐν σταδίῃ Il.15.283: later c. inf., A.R.1.106, etc.: hence I. of persons, *brave, stout*, ἐσθλὸν ἐνὶ προμάχοισι Il.4.458, etc.; opp. δειλός, Hes.*Op*.214; *noble*, opp. κακός, οὔ τινα γὰρ τίεσκον.. οὐ κακὸν οὐδὲ μὲν ἐ. Od.22.415; πένιχρος οὐδεὶς πέλετ' ἔσλος οὐδὲ τίμιος Alc.49; τόκηες Id.*Supp*.25.12; εἴτ' εὐγενὴς πέφυκας εἴτ' ἐσθλῶν κακή S.*Ant*.38; ἐσθλοῦ πατρὸς παῖς Id.*Ph*.96; ἀπ' ἐσθλῶν δωμάτων E.*Andr*.772 (lyr.), etc.; of horses, *well-bred*, Il.23.348. 2. morally *good, faithful*, φίλος S.*OT*611; εἰς ἡμᾶς γεγώς Id.*El*.24; τινι Naumach.ap.Stob.4.23.7; κύνα ἐσθλὴν ἐκείνῳ, πολεμίαν τοῖς δύσφροσιν A.*Ag*.608. 3. like ἐΰς and φίλος, weakened almost to a possess. pron., ἐσθλὸν ἀνεψιὸν ἐξεναρίξας Il.16.

573, cf. 5.469, Od.3.379. **II.** of things, *good* of their kind, φάρμακα, κτήματα, κειμήλια, Il.11.831, Od.2.312, Il.9.330, etc. **2.** of mind, qualities, etc., νόος Od.7.73; βουλή Il.9.76; ἔπος 1.108; κλέος 5.3, Pi.*P.*4.175: freq. in neut. pl., μυρί'.. ἐσθλὰ ἔοργε Il.2.272; ἔσθλ' ἀγορεύοντες, κακὰ δὲ φρεσὶ βυσσοδόμευον Od.17.66; ἔσλων ἢ κάλων Sapph.28, cf. *Supp.*2.4. **3.** *fortunate, lucky*, ὄρνιθες Od. 24.311; ὕπαρ 19.547; χάρματα Pi.*O.*2.19; γάμοι E.*IA*609; τύχη S.*OC*1506; ἀράσαντο πάμπαν ἔσλα τῷ γάμβρῳ Sapph.51.4; ἐσθλόν, τό, *good luck, prosperity*, opp. κακόν, Il.24.530; παρὰ καὶ κακῷ ἐσθλὸν ἔθηκεν Od.15.488; ἐσλὸν βαθὺ Pi.*O.*12.12. **4.** Subst. ἐσθλά, τά, *goods*, πυρὴν ἐμπλησέμεν ἐσθλῶν Od.10.523; εἴ τις ἐσλὰ πέπαται Pi. *P.*8.73. **5.** ἐσθλόν [ἐστι] c. inf., *it is good, expedient to..*, Il.24. 301: also pl., οὐ γὰρ ἐσθλὰ.. κερτομέειν Archil.64.—Poet. word, used by X.*Cyr.*1.5.9, Chrysipp.*Stoic.*3.60, Luc.*Syr.D.*19 (Ion.), etc.

ἐσθλότης, ητος, ἡ, *goodness*, Chrysipp.*Stoic.*3.60 (pl.).

ἔσθος, εος, τό, rare form for ἔσθημα, Il.24.94, Ar.*Av.*943 (lyr.); τὸ ἔ. (with hiatus, i.e. ϝέσθος) in the mouth of a Laconian, Id.*Lys.* 1096; cf. βέστον *EM*195.45, γεστία Hsch.

ἔσθω, Ep. inf. ἐσθέμεναι Od.7.220: impf. ἦσθον 6.249, Matro *Conv.* 115:—poet. form of ἐσθίω, *eat*, ἔσθειν καὶ πίνειν Od.5.197, cf. 7.220; ἐσθέμεναι κειμήλιά τε πρόβασίν τε, i.e. *eat up* chattel and cattle, i.e. all one has, 2.75; of worms or animals, *feed on, devour*, Il.24.415, Od.13.409: also in Trag., Com., and later Poets, A.*Ag.*1597, Archipp.20, Philippid.9.5, Python 1.13, Call.*Iamb.*1.270, Matro l.c.: sts. in later Prose, Lxx *Le.*17.10, 19.26, Plu.2.101d codd.; in Cos, *Arch.f.Religionswiss.*10.402 (iii B.C.):—Pass., Lxx *Le.*17.13.

ἐσία, ἡ, v.l. for ἐσσία in Pl.*Cra.*401c.

ἐσία, ἡ, (ἵημι) *a mission, embassy*, Suid., etc.; cf. ἐξ-εσίη.

ἐσιάλλοντι· ἐκτείνουσιν, ἐκπέμπουσιν, Hsch.; cf. ἰάλλω.

ἐσιέμεναι, fem. pres. part. Med. of εἰσίημι, Od.22.470.

Ἐσιῆς, = Egyptian *ḥsy, praised*, used of the dead, *Jahrb.*32.201 (Memphis), *PMag.Lond.*46.259, 262, *PMag.Par.*2.1.

ἐσικνέομαι, ἐσίπταμαι, v. sub εἰσ-.

ἔσις, εως, ἡ, (ἵημι) *a sending forth*, *EM*469.49. **2.** (ἵεμαι) *an aiming at*, coined by Pl.*Cra.*411d, 420a: but the compd. ἔφεσις is found. **II.** (ἕζω) *a sitting*, Hellad.ap.Phot.*Bibl.*p.535 B.

ἐσιώθην· ἐσώθη, Hsch.

ἐσκάλισις, εως, ἡ, prob. *packing in a wooden crate* (cf. κᾶλον), *IG*4. 1485.85 (Epid.); cf. παρκάλισις and perh. διακάλισις, unless all three words belong to καλινδέω (καλίω).

ἐσκατάμιζεν· ἐσκάριζεν, Hsch. **ἔσκε**, v. ἔστε.

ἐσκεθῆν, Arc. aor. inf., perh. = ἐκ-σχεθεῖν, fr. ἐξέχω, *keep out, exclude*, *Schwyzer*665 C^{1}4 (iv B.C.).

ἐσκεμμένως, Adv. pf. part. Pass., *deliberately*, D.24.157, Lib.*Ep.* 61.7.

ἐσκιχρέμεν, Dor. pres. inf. of ἐσκίχρημι, *lend out*, [ἀργύριον] *Schwyzer*617 (Dodona, iii B.C.).

ἔσκληκα, intr. pf. of σκέλλω.

ἔσκλητος, ἡ, Dor., = ἔκκλητος, *an assembly of Notables* at Syracuse, Hsch., cf. *IG*14.612 (Rhegium).

ἔσκον, Ep. and Ion. impf. of εἰμί *sum* (q.v.).

ἐσλιήνω, Boeot., = ἐκλειαίνω, *cancel* a debt, aor. 1 imper. ἐσλιανάτω *IG*7.3172.73 (Orchom., iii B.C.), *Supp.Epigr.*3.342.28 (Thisbe, iii B.C.); ἐσλιήνει (3 sg. pres. subj.) τὰν οὐπεραμερίαν ib.30.

ἐσλός, Dor. for ἐσθλός (q.v.).

ἔσμα, ατος, τό, = μίσχος, *stalk, pedicle*, Arist.*Fr.*271.

ἔσμιον· νόστιμον, Hsch.

ἐσμονῶ· ἐξελεύσομαι, Hsch. (fort. ἐσμολίω, Boeot.(?) fut. of ἐκμολεῖν).

ἑσμός, ὁ, (ἕζομαι) *that which settles*, esp. *a swarm of bees*, Hdt.5.114, Pl.*Lg.*708b, X.*HG*3.2.28; ἑ. λαμβάνειν Plu.*Dio*24; of wasps, καθ' ἑσμοὺς in *swarms*, Ar.*V.*1107. **2.** *any swarm* or *flock*, ἑ. ὑβριστής, of men, A.*Supp.*30 (anap.); ἑ. ὡς πελειάδων ἵζεσθε ib.223; γυναικῶν Ar.*Lys.*353, etc.; [τεχνιτ]ῶν *Pae.Delph.*14; στρατιᾶς *Epigr.Gr.*985 (Philae). **3.** (ἵημι) of things, ἑσμοὶ γάλακτος *streams* of milk, E.*Ba.* 710; ἑ. μελίσσης γλυκύς, i.e. honey, Epin.1.7; ἑ. νούσων A.*Supp.* 684 (lyr.); λόγων Pl.*R.*450b; πληγῶν Ph.2.95; παθῶν Porph.*Abst.* 1.34. **4.** = ὁδός, Hsch.; πατρίδος καλῆς τὸν ἐπάξιον ἑ. ἐλέσθαι *Arch. Pap.*1.220 (ii B.C.). (ἐ- freq. in codd., but cf. Ar.*V.* l.c., Eust.178.16.)

ἑσμοτόκος, ον, *producing swarms of bees*, *AP*6.239 (Apollonid.).

ἑσμοφύλαξ [ῠ], ἄκος, ὁ, *watcher of a swarm of bees*, *Gp.*15.2.9.

ἐσόβδην, Adv., v. sub ὄβδη. **ἔσοπτρον**, v. εἴσ-. **ἔσοπτρος**, ὁ, = foreg., Orph.*Fr.*3130. **ἐσοῦ**, late form of σοῦ, v. σύ. **ἐσοῦμαι**, Dor. for ἔσομαι, fut. of εἰμί *sum*.

ἐσπαρμένως, Adv., (σπείρω) gloss on σποράδην, Hsch.

ἑσπέρα, Ion. -έρη, ἡ, prop. fem. of ἕσπερος: **I.** (sc. ὥρα), *evening*, ἑσπέρας *at eve*, Pi.*P.*4.40, Eup.322, Pl.*Phd.*59e, al.; τῆς ἑσπέρας Alex.125.7; also ἑσπέρην Hp.*Mul.*2.121; ἀπὸ ἑσπέρας εὐθύς just at *nightfall*, Th.3.112; ἄκρᾳ σὺν ἑσπέρᾳ Pi.*P.*11.10; πρὸς ἑσπέραν towards *evening*, Ar.*V.*1085, X.*HG*1.1.30, *Ev.Luc.*24.29; εἰς ἑσπέραν Pl.*Smp.*223d; ἐπειδὴ ἑσπέρα ἦν ib.220c; ἐπεὶ πρὸς ἑσπέραν ἦν X.*HG*4.3.22; ἑσπέρας γιγνομένης Pl.*R.*621a; περὶ ἑσπέραν βαθεῖαν late in *the evening*, Plu.2.179e: metaph., ὁ βίος ἑσπέραν ἄγει life is wearing to its *eve*, Alex.228; ἑ. βίου Anon.ap.Arist.*Po.*1457^{b}24: pl., διχομήνιδες ἑσπέραι *evenings* when the moon is full, Pi.*I.*8(7).47. **2.** *night*, μίαν ἑ. αὐλισάμενος J.*BJ*5.2.1. **II.** (sc. χώρα) *the west*, πρὸς ἑσπέραν φέρει E.*Or.*1260; ἡ πρὸς ἑσπέρην [χώρη] Hdt.1.82, cf. 3. 115; τὸ πρὸς ἑσπέρης Id.8.130, 132, 4.38; τὰ πρὸς ἑσπέραν Th.6.2; τὴν ἀνατολὴν ποιεῖσθαι ἀφ' ἑσπέρας Arist.*Mete.*345^{a}3, cf. 344^{b}34; τὰ πνεύματα πνεῖ τῆς δείλης ἀπὸ τῆς ἑ. Thphr.*Vent.*47: metaph. in political sense, τὰ προφαινόμενα ἀπὸ τῆς ἑ. νέφη Plb.5.104.9, cf. 9.37.10: Ἑ., ἡ, the *Western Empire*, Agath.4.29, 5.16.

ἐσπεράσαι, v. ἐκπεράω.

Ἑσπερ-ία (sc. χθών), ἡ, *the Western land*, of Italy, Agathyll.ap. D.H.1.49; of Spain, Suid. s.v. Ἰβηρία. **-ικός**, ή, όν, = sq.: Ἑ. μῆλον, = κίτριον, Juba 24. **-ῐνός**, ή, όν, = -ιος, X.*Lac.*12.6, *AP*5. 201 (Asclep. or Posidipp.), Ptol.*Alm.*8.4, D.C.69.18; θυσία Lxx 4*Ki.* 16.15, al.: Ἑσπέρινος, ὁ (sc. μήν), name of month in Doris, *GDI*2172 (Erineos). **-ιον**, *citreum*, *Gloss.* **-ιος**, α, ον, and ος, ον E.*HF* 395 (lyr.): (ἕσπερος): **I.** of Time, *towards evening*, Hom., esp. in Od., usu. with Verbs, ἑ. δ' εἰς ἄστυ.. κάτειμι Od.15.505; ἑσπερίους ἀγέρεσθαι ἀνώγει 2.385; ἀπονέεσθαι ἑ. 9.452; ἑ. φλέγεν Pi.*N.*6.38; ἑσπερίῃσι (sc. ὥραις) *at eventide*, Opp.*C.*1.138, cf. Man.2.422; ἄχρι ἑσπερίου (sc. χρόνου) Arist.*HA*619^{b}21 (v. ἀκρέσπερος); ἑ. ἀοιδαί songs sung *at even*, Pi.*P.*3.19: in late Prose, ἑσπέριος [γένεσις] Vett.Val. 72.21. **II.** of Place, *western*, ἠὲ πρὸς ἠοίων ἢ ἑ. ἀνθρώπων Od.8.29, cf. E. l.c.; ἔριφοι Theoc.7.53; ἅλς Arat.407, cf. Call.*Fr.*443; τὰ ἑ. *the western parts*, Th.6.2, Plu.*Ant.*30; ἀφ' ἑσπερίης (sc. χώρης) from *the west*, *IG*14.1020. **III.** Ἑσπέριος, ὁ, = Ἕσπερος, the star, Gal. 17(1).16. (ϝεσπ-, cf. ϝεσπάριοι, of the *Western* Locrians, *IG*9(1).334 (v B.C.), Lat. *vesper.*) **-ίς**, ίδος, pecul. fem. of ἑσπέριος, *western*, ἅλμη Nonn.*D.*6.219. **II.** as Subst., *night-scented stock, Matthiola tristis*, Thphr.*CP*6.17.3, Plin.*HN*21.39; = *citreum*, *Gloss.* **2.** as pr. n., Ἑσπερίδες, αἱ, *the Hesperides, daughters of Night*, who dwelt in an island, *on the western verge of the world*, and guarded a garden with golden apples, Hes.*Th.*215, E.*Hipp.*742 (lyr.), D.S.4.27, etc.: hence Ἑσπερίδων μῆλα *quinces*, Pamphil.ap.Ath.2.82d. **3.** Ἑ. νῆσοι, = Κασσιτερίδες, D.P.563. **-ισμα**, ατος, τό, (*ἑσπερίζω) *supper*, Philem.Lex.ap.Ath.1.11d. **-ίτης** [ῑ], ου, ὁ, fem. **-ῖτις**, ιδος, *western*, χώρα D.L.4.27; λίμνη Suid. **-όθεν**, Adv. *from the west*, Arat.891.

ἑσπερόμορφος, ον, *dark, shadowy*, Tz.*H.*11.224.

ἕσπερος, ον (v. sub fin.), *of* or *at evening*, [ἀστήρ] ἕ. the *evening*-star, Il.22.318; opp. ἑῷος ἀστήρ, *AP*7.670 (Pl.); prov., οὐθ' ἕσπερος οὐθ' ἑῷος οὕτω θαυμαστός Arist.*EN*1129^{b}28: as Subst., without ἀστήρ, E.*Ion* 1149, Bion *Fr.*8.1; ἕσπερε πάντα φέρων ὅσα φαίνολις ἐσκέδασ' αὔως Sapph.95; esp. of the planet Venus, Eratosth.*Cat.*43, Cic.*ND*2.20. 53; also ἕ. σελάνας φάος Pi.*O.*10(11).73; ἕ. θεός the god *of darkness*, i.e. Hades or death, S.*OT*178 (lyr.); like ἑσπέριος, joined with a Verb, *h.Hom.*19.14; ἕ. γίγνεται, of the planet Venus, Ti.Locr.96e. **2.** as Subst., *evening*, μέλας ἐπὶ ἕσπερος ἦλθε Od.1.423; μένον δ' ἐπὶ ἕσπερον ἐλθεῖν waited the coming on of *evening*, 4.786; ποτὶ ἕσπερον at *eventide*, Hes.*Op.*552: also heterocl. pl., ποτὶ ἕσπερα Od.17.191; ὑφ' ἕσπερα *AP*5.304: fem., ἐρεμνὴ ἕσπερος A.R.4.1290: metaph. of age, τί δ' ἕσπερός ἐστι γυναικῶν; *AP*5.232 (Maced.). **II.** *western*, τόποι A.*Pr.*350; ἀγκῶνες S.*Aj.*805; ὠκεανός D.P.63; ἕ. (sc. γῆ) *the west country*, ἀφ' ἑσπέρου Call.*Del.*174; πρὸς ἑσπέρου D.P.335; ἑσπέρου κέρας, promontory in Africa, Ptol.*Geog.*4.6.2: as Adj., ὁ Ἥλιος..-ον κύκλον διανύων Nech.ap.Vett.Val.154.29. (ϝέσπ-, cf. Ἑσπέριος fin.)

ἐσπευσμένως, Adv., (σπεύδω) *with eager haste*, D.H.*Dem.*54, J.*AJ* 5.6.3, Arr.*Epict.*1.20.12.

ἐσπίφρημι, in inf. -πιφράναι, *insert*, Arist.*HA*541^{b}11.

ἕσπομαι, later Ep. form of ἕπομαι (q.v.).

ἑσπόμην, inf. σπέσθαι, aor. 2 of ἕπομαι.

ἔσπον, aor. 2 of ἐνέπω: only in 2 pl. in the formula ἔσπετε νῦν μοι, Μοῦσαι *tell* me now, ye Muses, Il.2.484, al.; later ἔσπετε νῦν μοι ὅσοι πολυπράγμονές ἐστε σοφισταί Timo 1. (Prob. fr. ἐν-σπ-ετε (v.l. in Il. l.c.); σπ- (cf. ἐνι-σπ-εῖν) is the weak form of seq^{u}, cf. Lith. *sekù* 'say', Lat. *in-sece.*)

ἐσπουδασμένως, Adv. pf. part. Pass., *seriously, in earnest*, Pl.*Sis.* 390c; *zealously*, Str.10.3.5, J.*AJ*16.7.1; *hastily*, Hld.1.27.

ἐσπρεμμίττεν, Cret., = ἐκπρεμνίζειν, *GDI*5027 (Gortyn).

ἔσρος, (ἐσ-ρέω) coined as etym. of ἔρως by Pl.*Cra.*420b.

ἕσσα, Ep. aor. 1 Act. of ἕννυμι, inf. **ἕσσαι**: part. aor. 1 Med. **ἑσσάμενος**. **II. ἕσσαι**, = ἕσαι, aor. 1 inf. of ἵζω. **ἔσσα**, Aeol. and Dor. fem. part. of εἰμί *sum*.

ἔσσᾱμον, τό, = ἐνσημον, *standard*, *Inscr.Magn.*26.23.

ἐσσεδάριος, ὁ, = Lat. *essedarius, gladiator who fought in a car*, *Rev. Ét.Anc.*29.46 (Smyrna), *CIG*2889 (Miletus), *IG*12(8).547 (Thasos).

ἐσσεῖται, Ep. and Dor. 3 sg. fut. of εἰμί *sum*. **ἔσσευα**, Ep. aor. 1 Act. of σεύω.

ἐσσῆαι· ἐκχέαι, Hsch.

ἐσσήν (A), ῆνος, ὁ, *priest of Artemis* of Ephesus, in pl., *SIG*352.6 (iv B.C.), 363.10 (iii B.C.), Paus.8.13.1. **II.** *king*, θεῶν ἐ. Call.*Jov.* 66; Μυρμιδόνων ἐ. Id.*Aet.*1.1.23 (expld. as, = οἰκιστής by Hdn.Gr.2. 923): prop. *king bee* (i.e. *queen bee*), acc. to *EM*383.31. (ἐσσήν in Call.*Aet.*1.1.23 (Pap.), perh. because of supposed connexion with ἑσμός, ἕσσαι, or ἠσσάω.)

ἐσσήν (B), ῆνος, ὁ, transliteration of Hebr. *ḥōšen*, worn by Jewish priests, J.*AJ*3.7.5, 3.8.9, where it is said to mean λόγιον, by which word it is rendered in Lxx *Ex.*28.15.

ἐσσηνεύω, *hold office of* ἐσσήν (A), *BMus.Inscr.*578c7 (Ephesus); cf. ἐσσίνευσεν.

ἐσσηνία, ἡ, *term of office as* ἐσσήν (A), Ἀρχ.Δελτ.7.258 (Ephesus, ii A.D.).

ἐσσήτιοι· μάντεις, Hsch. **ἐσσί**, Ep. and Dor. 2 sg. of εἰμί *sum*.

ἐσσία, ἡ, Pythag. Dor. for οὐσία, Pl.*Cra.*401c. **ἔσσιμος**, v. ἔνσιμος.

ἐσσίνευσεν· ἐσίμηνεν, Hsch. (fort. ἐσσήν-· ἐσήμ-).

ἐσσίταλα· πρόσοδος, ἐμπολή, Hsch. (cf. ἐξίταλα).

ἕσσο, 2 sg. plpf. Pass. of ἕννυμι, Il.3.57, Od.16.199. **ἔσσομαι**, Ep. and Aeol. fut. of εἰμί *sum*. **ἐσσόν**· ἱμάτιον, Hsch. **ἐσσόομαι**, Ion. for ἡσσάομαι.

ἐσσόριον, τό, = ἐνσόριον, *CIG*3270 (Smyrna).

ἔσσῠμαι, pf. Pass. of σεύω.

ἐσσύμενος [ῠ], η, ον, Ep. and Lyr. part. Pass. of σεύω (in sense and accent pres., but redupl. as if pf.), *hurrying, eager, impetuous*, Il.6.518, Pi.*P*.4.135; *eager, yearning for*, c. gen., πολέμου, ὁδοῖο, Il.24.404, Od.4.733: also c. inf., πολεμίζειν, ἀλύξαι, Il.11.717, Od.4.416, cf. 15.73; ἐλαύνειν Pi.*Fr*.107.5. II. Adv. ἐσσυμένως *furiously, eagerly*, ἐμάχοντο, δόρπον ἕλοντο, Il.15.698, Od.14.347, cf. Pi.*Fr*.166, *APl*.4.43.

ἔσσῠο, ἔσσῠτο, 2, 3 sg. plpf., or Ep. aor. 2 Pass. of σεύω. **ἐσσυρευτόν**· βλοσυρόν, δοκερόν, Hsch. **ἐσσύτερον**· ἰσχυρότερον, Id. **ἔσσωμαι**, pf. Pass. of ἐσσόομαι, v. ἡσσάομαι. **ἔσσων**, ον, Ion. for ἥσσων. **ἔστα**· ἐνδύματα, Id.; cf. ἔστη. **ἔστᾰκα**, trans. pf. of ἵστημι (q.v.); but **ἕστᾰκα**, Dor. for ἕστηκα. **ἐστάλᾰτο**, Ion. 3 pl. plpf. Pass. of στέλλω, Hes.*Sc*.288. **ἑστάμεν, -άμεναι** [ᾰ], Ep. pf. inf. of ἵστημι: but II. **ἕστᾰμεν**, 1 pl. ind. **ἕσταν, ἑστᾰότες**, v. ἵστημι. **ἑστᾰότως**, Adv. *standing still, quietly*, v.l. for ἑσταότος, Il.19.79. **ἕστᾰσαν**, 3 pl. plpf. of ἵστημι, *they stood*, Hom.: but **ἔστᾰσαν**, for ἔστησαν, 3 pl. aor. 1, *they set* or *placed*, Il.12.56 (Aristarch., codd. aliq.), 2.525, Od.3.182, al. (but the v.l. ἵστασαν is to be preferred). **ἑστᾶσι, ἑστᾰτε, ἑστᾰτον**, v. ἵστημι.

ἔστε, Dor. **ἔστε** *EM*382.8, v.l. in Theoc.5.22, al., cf. Eust.161 fin. (written **εστε** in *IG*14.352 ii 60 (Halaesa)); Locr. **ἕντε** ib.9(1).334.15; Delph. **ἕντε** *Schwyzer*323*B*44 (also εἴστε, v. infr.); Boeot. **ἔττε** *IG*7.3054.7 (Lebad.): from ἐνς (= εἰς) with suffix -τε as in ὅ-τε, and so **εἴστε** *SIG*241.69 (Delph., iv B.C.). (ἔσκε Archil.14, *AP*7.727 (Theaet.) may be f.l.).—Found in post-Homeric Ep., Ion., Trag., X., *POxy*.2120.7 (iii A.D.), etc. (it is f.l. in Pl.*Smp*.211c). I. Conjunction, = ἕως: 1. *up to the time that, until*, a. with aor. ind., of actual occurrence in past time, ἄτερ γνώμης τὸ πᾶν ἔπρασσον ἔ. δή σφιν ἀντολὰς ἐγὼ ἄστρων ἔδειξα A.*Pr*.457, cf. S.*Ant*.415, *Aj*.1031, *El*.753; ἔ. περ A.R.2.85; παίουσι τὸν Σωτηρίδαν ἔστε ἠνάγκασαν πορεύεσθαι X.*An*.3.4.49, cf. 2.5.30. b. with aor. subj. and ἄν, of future time, after primary tenses, ἐγὼ δὲ τὴν παροῦσαν ἀντλήσω τύχην ἔστ' ἂν Διὸς φρόνημα λωφήσῃ χόλου A.*Pr*.378, cf. 697, *Eu*.449; τῇδε μενέομεν ἔστ' ἂν καὶ τελευτήσωμεν Hdt.7.141, cf. 158; περιμένετε ἔστ' ἂν ἐγὼ ἔλθω X.*An*.5.1.4; ἕντε, ἕντε κ' ἀποτείσῃ, *IG*9(1).334.15, *Schwyzer*323*B*44 (v/iv B.C.); ἔστε κε indef., *until such time as*.., Theoc.5.22; χιμάρῳ δὲ καλὸν κρέας ἔστε κ' ἀμέλξῃς Id.1.6, cf. 6.32; also after historical tenses, ἐδέοντο Εὐρυβιάδεω προσμεῖναι ἔστ' ἂν αὐτοὶ τέκνα τε καὶ τοὺς οἰκέτας ὑπεκθέωνται Hdt.8.4, cf. X.*HG*3.1.15, *An*.4.5.28: retained in orat. obliq., αὐτὸς ἔφη παραμενεῖν ἔστ' ἂν τοὺς βότρυς ποιήσωσι γλεῦκος Longus 4.5: ἄν omitted, ἀρήγετ' ἔστ' ἐγὼ μόλω S.*Aj*.1183; cf. ἄν (A) B.1.2. c. with aor. opt. after historical tenses (representing ἔστ' ἄν with subj.), ἐπιμεῖναι ἐκέλευσαν ἔστε βουλεύσαιντο X.*An*.5.5.2; ἀνέμενεν αὐτοὺς ἔστ' ἐμφάγοιέν τι he always waited *until*.., Id.*Cyr*.8.1.44; in orat. obliq., ὅτι..δέοιτο ἂν αὐτοῦ μένειν ἔστε σὺ ἀπέλθοις ib.5.3.13. d. with aor. inf., in orat. obliq. and the like for opt., ἔστε αὐτὴν νέμεσθαι Κρῆτας, = ἔστε αὐτὴν νέμοιντο Κρῆτες, Hdt.7.171; freq. in later writers, ἔστε Δαρεῖον γνῶναι, = ἔστε Δαρεῖος γνοίη, Arr.*An*.2.1.3; ἔστε παρελθεῖν ib.4.7.1, cf. Ael.*HA*2.11; for ἔστ' ἄν with subj., Arr.*Cyn*.2.4, 25.2, 31.5. e. with impf. ind., ἔστ' ἀφίκανεν A.R.4.849. 2. *so long as, while*, a. with impf. ind. of actual occurrence in past time, ἔστε μὲν..ἔπινον, ἡδὺ τέως ἐδόκει Thgn.959; ἔστε μὲν αἱ σπονδαὶ ἦσαν, οὔποτε ἐπαυόμην X.*An*.3.1.19, cf. *Mem*.1.2.18, Arr.*An*.2.11.6. b. with pres. subj. and ἄν, of future time, ἔστ' ἂν ἀοιδάων ᾖ γένος Ἑλλαδικῶν Xenoph.6.4; οὐ μὲν δὴ λήξω ἔστ' ἄν..λεύσσω..τόδ' ἦμαρ S.*El*.105 (anap.), cf. E.*Alc*.337; ἔστ' ἄν περ ἐπιδεικνύηται X.*Eq*.11.9; ἔστ' ἂν ἔκδημος (sc. ᾖ) χθονὸς Θησεύς, ἄπειμι E.*Hipp*.659: so with pf. subj., = pres., ὑμῖν Λακεδαιμόνιοι ἐπαγγέλλονται γυναῖκας ἐπιθρέψειν, ἔστ' ἂν ὁ πόλεμος ὅδε συνεστήκῃ Hdt.8.142; of present time, Emp.42.2. c. with pres. opt. after historical tenses (representing ἔστ' ἄν with subj.), ἐδόκει τοῖς στρατηγοῖς βέλτιον εἶναι τὸν πόλεμον ἀκήρυκτον εἶναι, ἔστ' ἐν τῇ πολεμίᾳ εἶεν X.*An*.3.3.5; τοσοῦτον χρόνον ζῆν ἔστε νικῴη.. ib.1.9.11. d. with aor. subj. and ἄν, ἔστ' ἂν πολεμίους δείσωσι κελευόμενα πάντα ποιοῦσι Id.*Mem*.3.5.6. II. Adv. *even to*, a. of Space, *up to*, βόθροι ἐγίγνοντο μεγάλοι ἔστε ἐπὶ τὸ δάπεδον Id.*An*.4.5.6, cf. 4.8.8, Arr.*An*.1.28.3; ἔστ' ἐπὶ πᾶχυν Theoc.7.67. b. of Time, ἔστε ἐπὶ κνέφας Arr.*An*.7.25.2; ἔστε ἐς.., κατὰ.., *IG*14.352 ii 60, i 65 (Halaesa); εἴστε εἰς Θεύχαριν ἄρχοντα *SIG*241.69 (Delph., iv B.C.); ἔστε πρὸς τὸ ἐφηβικόν Luc.*Nav*.3. III. Preposition, c. acc., a. of Space, *up to*, ἔστε τὸν ὅρον, ἔστε καὶ τὰν φάραγγα, *Schwyzer*289.166, 169 (ii B.C.); παρατείνει ἔστε τὴν θάλασσαν Arr.*Ind*.2.2 (⟨ἐπὶ⟩ Hercher). b. of Time, *until, up to*, ἔ. καὶ τὸν νῦν χρόνον *Schwyzer*289.113; ἔ. καὶ τὰν τριακάδα τοῦ Ἀλσείου *SIG*1023.25 (Cos, iii/ii B.C.).

ἔστεισις, Arc., = ἔκτεισις (q.v.).

ἐστεκνόομαι, Cret., = ἐκτ-, *bring forth issue*, *Leg.Gort*.8.24.

ἐστενωμένως, Adv., (στενόω) *in brief compass*, Eustr.*in APo*.199.2.

ἔστη· στολή (Cypr.), Hsch.; cf. ἐσθής.

ἕστηκα, ἑστήξω and **-ομαι, ἔστησα, ἔστην, ἑστηώς**, v. ἵστημι.

ἑστηκότως, Adv. *firmly*, ἑ. καὶ βεβαίως Phld.*Rh*.1.70S.

ἑστήκω, v. sub στήκω.

ἑστηριγμένως, Adv. *firmly*, Sch.Opp.*H*.2.395. **ἑστηῶσι**, v. ἵστημι.

ἑστία, ἡ, Ion. **ἱστίη** (as always in Hom. (exc. in ἀνέστιος, ἐφέστιος) and Hdt., cf. *Schwyzer*687.1 (Chios, vii/vi B.C.), *IG*12(5).554 (Ceos), and v. ἐφέστιος; ἑστίη is f.l. in Hes.*Op*.734); Boeot. **ἱστία** (Ἰ.) *IG*7.556 (Tanagra); also Coan, *SIG*1025.29, and Arc., ib.559.55; Locr. **ἱστία** *IG*9(1).334.7; both forms in Cretan, **Ἑστία** *SIG*527.15 (iii B.C.), **Ἱστία** *GDI*5079.7, al.:—*hearth of a house*, in Hom. only in solemn appeals, ἴστω νῦν Ζεὺς πρῶτα θεῶν..ἱστίη τ' Ὀδυσῆος Od.14.159, al., cf. Hdt.4.68, S.*El*.881; καθῆσθαι παρ' ἑστίᾳ, of suppliants, Pi.*Fr*.81; ἐπὶ τὴν ἑστίαν καθίζεσθαι Th.1.136; ἡ δορύξενος ἑ. S.*OC* 633; ἑ. μεσόμφαλος A.*Ag*.1056; ἐν στέγῃ τις ἥμενος παρ' ἑστίᾳ Id.*Fr*.362.3. 2. *the house itself, home*, Pi.*O*.1.11, *P*.11.13: freq. in Trag., as A.*Ch*.264, etc.; διξὰς ἱστίας οἴκεε Hdt.5.40; καταλείποντα ἐν τᾷ ἱστίᾳ παῖδα ἡβάταν, of a colonist, *IG*9(1).334 (Locr., v B.C.): metaph., of *the last home, the grave*, τὰν χθόνιον ἑ. ἰδεῖν S.*OC*1726 (lyr.). 3. *household, family*, οἱ πολλοί, πλὴν ὀγδώκοντα ἱστιέων κτλ., Hdt.1.176; ἱστίη οὐδεμία νομιζομένη εἶναι Γλαύκου Id.6.86.δ'. 4. *altar*, like ἐσχάρα, A.*Th*.275, *Eu*.282; βούθυτος ἑ. S.*OC*1495 (lyr.); γᾶς μεσσόμφαλος ἑ., of the Delphic shrine, E.*Ion*462 (lyr.); Πυθόμαντις ἑ. S.*OT*965; βωμός, ἑ. χθονός (as a sanctuary) A.*Supp*.372 (lyr.); ἡ κοινὴ ἑ. the public *altar*, serving as a sanctuary to refugees, *IG*2[2].1029, Arist.*Pol*.1322[b]28; πολιτικὴ ἑ. App.*Pun*.84:—ἡ κοινὴ ἑ. also of *the public table*, ἐδέξαντο τοὺς πρεσβευτὰς ἐπὶ τὴν κοινὴν ἑ. Plb.29.5.6, cf. *IG*5(1).961 (Cotyrta), 7.21 (Orchomenus in Boeotia), Poll.9.40; μυηθεὶς ἀφ' ἑστίας, of a class of public initiates at Eleusis, Is.*Fr*.84, cf. *IG*2.1355, al.; so ὁ ἀφ' ἑ. παῖς Porph.*Abst*.4.5; simply ὁ ἀφ' ἑ., ἡ ἀφ' ἑ., Ἐφ.Ἀρχ.1894.176, 1885.146. 5. metaph., of places which are to a country as the hearth to a house, as a metropolis, Plb.5.58.4; ἑ. καὶ μητρόπολις D.S.4.19; of Delos, ἱστίη ὦ νήσων Call.*Del*.325:—Pythag., of the *central fire* of the universe, Philol.7, etc., cf. Alex.Aphr.*in Metaph*.38.23; of the earth, E.*Fr*.944; of the heart in the body, Arist.*PA*670[a]25; μίαν, ἰδίαν ἑ. ἤθους οὐκ ἔχειν, Plu.2.52a, 97a; of the liver as *focus* of a fever, Gal.15.742. II. as pr. n. **Ἑστία**, Ion. **Ἱστίη, Ἑστίη**, *h.Hom*.24.1, v.l. in Hes.*Th*.454:—*the hearth-goddess*, *h.Ven*.22, Hes.*Th*. l.c., Pi.*N*.11.1, etc., cf. *h.Hom*.24, 29, Orph.*H*.84, D.S.5.68; Ἑ. βουλαία *IG*12(5).732 (Andros), Aeschin.2.45, App.*Mith*.23; Ἑ. πρυτανεία *IG*12(5).659 (Syros); worshipped as ἡ κοινὴ Ἑ. by the Getae, D.S.1.94, cf. Hdt.4.127: prov., ἀφ' Ἑστίας ἄρχεσθαι to begin from *the beginning*, Ar.*V*.846, Pl.*Euthphr*.3a; ἀπ' ἄλλης Ἑ. καὶ ἀρχῆς τὰς πράξεις προχειρίζεσθαι Str.1.1.16 (also ἐξ ἑ. ἄρχεσθαι Hsch.); ἡ Ἑ. γελᾷ, of the *fire* crackling, Arist.*Mete*.369[a]32. 2. = Lat. *Vesta*, Str.5.2.3, Plu.*Rom*.2, etc. 3. title of a priestess, *IG*9(1).486 (Acarnania); ἑ. πόλεως, as an honorary title, ib.5(1).583 (Sparta). [ῑ in Od. in the appellat. 14.159, ῐ in *h.Hom*. in pr. n.; in Hes. the reverse: ῐ always in Com. and Trag.] (Etymological connexion with Vesta is doubtful; the dialects never have ϝ-, exc. in the pr. n. ϝιστίαυ (gen. sg. masc.) *IG*5(2).271.18 (Mantinea); cf. γιστία.)

Ἑστιαῖον, τό, *temple of Vesta*, D.C.*Fr*.6.2, al. II. Ion. **Ἱστιήϊα**, τά, *funds of the temple of* Ἱστίη, *SIG*57.40 (Miletus, v B.C.).

Ἑστιαῖος, ὁ (sc. μήν), name of month in Cyprus, *Hemerolog.Flor*. (-έος).

ἑστί-ᾱμα, ατος, τό, (ἑστιάω) *banquet*, τὰ Ταντάλου θεοῖσιν ἑ. E.*IT* 387: metaph., ἐμπιπλὰς ὀργὴν κακῶν ἑστιαμάτων Pl.*Lg*.935a. **-αρχέω**, *to be* ἑστιάρχης, Luc.*Am*.10. **-άρχης**, ου, ὁ, *the master of a feast*, Plu.2.643d, prob. in *CIG*2052.4 (Apollonia in Thrace).

Ἑστιάς, only pl. **Ἑστιάδες**, αἱ, *Vestal virgins*, D.H.2.64, Plu.*Ant*.21; Ἑ. παρθένοι Id.*Num*.13.

ἑστίᾱσις, εως, ἡ, *feasting, banqueting, entertainment*, Th.6.46 (pl.), Pl.*R*.612a (pl.), D.19.234; λόγων ἑ. a *banquet* of speeches, Pl.*Ti*.27b; ἑ. συμφορητός, = ἔρανος, Arist.*Pol*.1286[a]29. II. *public dinner given by a citizen to his fellow-citizens*, as a λειτουργία, ib.1321[a]37.

Ἑστιασταί, οἱ, association of *worshippers of Hestia* at Rhodes, *IG*12(1).162.8.

ἑστιατήρ· ὁ δοκιμαζόμενος, Hsch.

ἑστιᾱτ-ήριον, τό, *banqueting-hall*, *Rev.Épigr*.1.239 (Naples, ii A.D.), Philostr.*VS*2.23. **-ικός**, ή, όν, *convivial*, ἐπιπλοκαί Antip.*Stoic*.3.254. II. Subst. **-ικόν**, τό, *fund for public banquets* at Delos, *Inscr.Délos* 320*B*77 (iii B.C.). **-ορία**, ἡ, *allowance of food*, Lxx 4*Ki*.25.30. 2. *feast*, ib.*Da*.5.23; ἑ. γερδίων *PTeb*.584 (ii A.D.). **-όριον**, later **-ειον**, τό, = ἑστιατήριον, *IG*11(2).144*A*68 (Delos, iv B.C.), Theopomp.Hist.32, *Bull.Soc.Arch*.5.126 (iii B.C.), *Sammelb*.6596 (ii B.C.), D.H.2.23, *SIG*1109.141 (Athens, ii A.D., -είου): Ion. **ἱστιητόριον** Hdt.4.35: Rhod. **ἱστιατόριον** *IG*12(1).677 (iii B.C.). **-ορίς**, ἡ, *Areca nut* (kernel of the palm *Areca Catechu*), Plin.*HN*24.165 (v.l.). **-ωρ**, ορος, ὁ, *one who gives a banquet, host*, Pl.*R*.421b, *Ti*.17a, Charond.ap.Stob.4.2.24, Ph.2.70, Them.*Or*.24.301a. 2. at Athens, *the citizen on whom the liturgy of* ἑστίασις (q.v.) *fell*, D.20.21, 39.7. b. at Delphi, *manager of the commissariat* at the Pythais, *SIG*711 *D*[2] 17, al. (ii B.C.). 3. metaph., ἑ. τοῦ λόγου Philostr.*VA*6.10. II. *guest*, Posidon.9J. III. **ἱστιάτορες**, οἱ, *office-bearers of a religious association* (ὀργεῶνες), *IG*2[2].1259 (iv B.C.); = ἐσσῆνες (A) 1, at Ephesus, Paus.8.13.1.

ἑστιᾶχος· οἰκουρός κτλ., Hsch. (cf. ἑστιοῦχος).

ἑστιάω, Ion. and Dor. **ἱστιάω**, impf. εἱστίων Lys.19.27, Ion. 3 sg. ἱστία Hdt.7.135: fut. ἑστιάσω [ᾱ] Antiph.68.1: aor. 1 εἱστίασα X.*Cyr*.1.3.10, Is.8.18, inf. ἑστιᾶσαι Ar.*Nu*.1212 (later ἡστίασεν *SIG*1104.26 (Athens, i B.C.), ἱσστίασεν ib.714.31 (Eretria, ii B.C.)): pf. εἱστίακα D.21.156:—**Med.** and **Pass.**, v. infr.: (ἑστία) :—*receive at one's hearth* or *in one's house*, ξένους Lys.12.8; *entertain, feast*, τινα Hdt. l.c., Ar.*Nu*.1212; ἐν δόμοισιν ξένον E.*Alc*.765; ἑ. τινὰ ἰχθύσι on fish, Pl.*R*.404b; at Athens, ἑ. τὴν φυλήν (cf. ἑστίασις) D.21.156; τὴν πόλιν Arist.*EN*1122[b]23; of the dining-room, ὁ ἀνδρὼν ὁ..

ἑστιῶν αὐτούς Ael.*VH*8.7. 2. abs., *give a feast*, ἑ. μεγαλοπρεπῶς ib.12.51; οἱ ἑστιῶντες *entertainers*, Pl.*Grg.*518d; τὸν ἱστιῶντ' ἐπαινέω Epich.35.4. 3. c. acc. cogn., Ζεὺς.. Πέλοπι ἔρανον ἱστιῶν Id. 87; γάμους ἑ. *give a* marriage *feast*, E.*HF*483, Ar.*Av.*132; ἑ. νικητήρια X.*Cyr.*8.4.1; ἐπινίκια D.59.33; δεκάτην ὑπέρ τινος Id.40.28; γενέθλια Luc.*Herm.*11: and c. dupl. acc., ἅμα θύσαντα τὰ ἱερὰ ἑστιᾶσαι ἐκεῖνον Antipho 1.16; θεσμοφόρια ἑ. τὰς γυναῖκας Is.3.80; τὴν γενέθλιον ἑ. τινά Luc.*Dem.Enc.*26, cf. *Symp.*2: c. dat., Eup.59. 4. metaph., ἑ. τινὰ λόγων καλῶν Pl.*R.*571d, cf. Luc.*Philops.*39; ἑ. τὰς ἀκοάς, τὴν ὄψιν, Ael.*VH*3.1, *NA*17.23, etc. II. Pass., with fut. Med. ἑστιάσομαι Pl.*R.*345c, *Tht.*178d; later ἑστιαθήσομαι Sch.Ar. *Ach.*977: aor. 1 εἱστιάθην Pl.*Phdr.*247e, (συν-) D.19.190; later ἑστιάσασθαι S.E.*M.*8.186: pf. εἱστίαμαι Pl.*R.*354a, Ion. inf. ἱστιῆσθαι Hdt. 5.20:—*to be a guest, be feasted*, Id. l. c., Pl.*R.*372c; ἑ. παρὰ ἀνδρὶ φίλῳ Antipho 1.26: c. acc. rei, *feast on..*, ἑ. ἐνύπνιον *have a* visionary *feast*, 'feast with the Barmecide', Ar.*V.*1218; ἑ. γῆν, τὰ ὄντα, Pl.*R.*612a, *Phdr.*247e: c. dat., εὐωδίᾳ X.*Smp.*2.3; λόγοις Ath.7.275b: metaph., ταῦτά σοι εἱστιάσθω ἐν τοῖς Βενδιδείοις Pl.*R.*354a.

ἔστιοι, = νεκροί, at Clitor in Arcadia, *AB*1096.

ἑστιόομαι, Pass., (ἑστία) δῶμ' ἑστιοῦται the house *is founded* or *established* (by children), E.*Ion* 1464 (lyr.).

ἑστιοπάμων [ᾰ], ονος, ὁ, *householder*, Dor. and Aeol., Poll.1.74, 10.20.

ἔστιος, α, ον, *of the* ἑστία, θεοί, ἐσχάρα, Hld.1.30, 4.18. II. Ἔστιος, ὁ (sc. μήν), name of month in Magnesia, *IG*9(2).1117.11.

ἑστιουχ-έω, (ἔχω) *preside over the home* or *state*, ἄρχοντες ἑ. πόλεως καὶ πολιτῶν σωτηρίας Charond.ap.Stob.4.2.24. **-ος**, ον, *guarding the house*, Δήμητερ ἑστιοῦχ' Ἐλευσῖνος χθονὸς *guardian of..*, E.*Supp.* 1, cf. Ar.*Av.*866, Pl.*Lg.*878a. 2. *having an altar* or *hearth*, γαῖα, πόλις, αὐλά, A.*Pers.*511, S.*Ant.*1083, E.*Andr.*283 (lyr.). 3. *on the hearth* or *altar*, ἑ. ψόλος A.*Fr.*281.2 (prob.); πῦρ Plu.2. 158c. II. *entertainer, feaster, host*, Ar.*Fr.*776, Ph.1.389.

ἑστιῶτις, ιδος, ἡ, *of* or *from the house*, αὔρα S.*Tr.*954 (lyr.).

ἕστο, v. ἕννυμι.

ἐστοχασμένως, Adv. pf. part. Pass., *hitting the mark*: c. gen., ἐ. τοῦ σκοποῦ Hld.7.5: abs., Ptol.*Tetr.*9.

ἐστραμμένως, Adv., (στρέφω) *in a varied manner*, Thom.Mag. p.294 R.

ἐστρίς, Adv. *until three times, thrice*, Pi.*O.*2.68, *Pae.Erythr.*tit. p.140 P.: better written divisim.

ἐστυμμένως, Adv., (στύφω) *tightly*, Eust.155.19.

Ἐστρῆνες· Σειρῆνες, Hsch.

ἐστώ, οῦς, ἡ, Dor. for οὐσία (*substance*), opp. μορφή, Archyt.ap. Stob.1.40.2, Philol.6. II. Pythag., *dyad*, Phot.*Bibl.*p.143 B.

ἕστωρ, ορος, ὁ, *peg at the end of the pole*, passing through the yoke and having a ring (κρίκος) affixed, prob. for passing the inside reins through, Il.24.272 (v.l. ἕκτορι), Aristobul.7 J.

ἐσύνηκεν, aor. 1 with double augm. of συνίημι.

ἐσύστερον, Adv. for εἰς ὕστερον, *hereafter*, Od.12.126, Hdt.5.41: better written divisim.

ἔσφᾱλα, Dor. for ἔσφηλα, aor. 1 of σφάλλω.

ἐσφαλμένως, Adv., (σφάλλω) *erringly, amiss*, *AP*15.38 (Cometas), Sch.Th.1.140.

ἐσφέρω, ἐσφορά, v. εἰσ-.

ἐσφιγμένως, Adv., (σφίγγω) *tightly*, Dosith.p.412 K.

ἐσ-φλᾰσις, εως, ἡ, *contused fracture* of the skull *with depression*, Hp.*VC*6: **-φλάω**, in Pass., *to be so fractured*, ibid.

ἐσχάζοσαν, Alexandr. for ἔσχαζον, Lyc.21, cf. Choerob.*in Theod.* 2.64.

ἐσχάρ-α, Ion. **-άρη** [ᾰ], ἡ, Ep. gen. and dat. ἐσχαρόφιν (ἀπ' ἐσχ- Od.7.169, ἐπ' ἐσχ- 5.59, 19.389):—*hearth, fire-place*, like ἑστία, Hom. (esp. in Od.), ἡ μὲν ἐπ' ἐσχάρῃ ἧστο Od.6.52; ἧσται ἐπ' ἐσχάρῃ ἐν πυρὸς αὐγῇ ib.305; of suppliants, ἕζετ' ἐπ' ἐσχάρῃ ἐν κονίῃσι 7. 153. 2. *pan of coals, brazier*, Ar.*Ach.*888, *V.*938, cf. Poll.10.94, 95. 3. Τρώων πυρὸς ἐσχάραι *watch-fires* of the camp, Il.10.418. II. *sacrificial hearth* (hollowed out in the ground and so dist. from βωμός, structural altar, St.Byz. s. v. βωμοί, Phot.; used esp. in hero-worship, Neanth.7 J.), Od.14.420, S.*Ant.*1016: but freq. used generally, *altar of burnt-offering*, πρὸς ἐσχάραν Φοίβου A.*Pers.*205; ἐπ' ἐσχάρᾳ πυρός Id.*Eu.*108; ἡμένας ἐπ' ἐσχάραις ib.806; Πυθικὴ E.*Andr.* 1240; at Eleusis, D.59.116, cf. Lycurg.*Fr.*37; Ἡρακλειδῶν ἐ. *IG*2. 1658 (iv B.C.); so βώμιοι ἐσχάραι structured *altars*, E.*Ph.*274; sometimes movable, X.*Cyr.*8.3.12, Callix.2, *PCair.Zen.*13 (iii B.C.). III. *fire-stick* (bored with the τρύπανον, q. v.), Thphr.*HP*5.9.7, *Ign.* 64. IV. *platform, stand, basis*, Ph.*Bel.*92.13, Ath.Mech.32.10, Vitr.10.11.9. 2. *grating*, Lxx *Ex.*27.4, al. V. Medic., *scab, eschar* on a wound caused by burning or otherwise, τὰς ἐκπτώσιας τῶν ἐ. Hp.*Art.*11, cf. Pl.Com.184.4, Arist.*Pr.*863ᵃ12, Dsc.1.56, Gal.10. 315, etc. VI. in pl., = τὰ χείλη τῶν γυναικείων αἰδοίων, Ar.*Eq.* 1286. **-άδιν**, *landica*, Gloss. **-εῖον**, τό, *platform, scaffolding*, *IG*2².1672.308. **-εύς**, έως, ὁ, *a ship's cook*, Poll.1.95, Them. *Or.*15.195b. **-εών**, ῶνος, ὁ, = ἐσχάρα I, Theoc.24.48, *AP*7.648 (Leon.). 2. *forge*, Nonn.*D.*14.22, al. **-ίδιον**, τό, Dim. of ἐσχαρίς, *IG*11(2).164 B17 (Delos, iii B.C.). **-ινθον**, τό, a dance at Sparta, Poll.4.104. **-ιον**, τό, Dim. of ἐσχάρα: 1. *pan of coals*, Ar.*Fr.*516 (pl.). 2. *stand, platform*, Plb.9.41.4 (pl.), D.S. 20.91. 3. *cradle for launching ships*, Callix.1. 4. *eschar*, Archig.ap.Orib.51.42.3. **-ιος**, ον, *of* or *on the hearth*, πῦρ *AP*7.210 (Antip.). **-ίς**, ίδος, ἡ, *brazier*, Alex.250, Plu.*Crass.*16, etc.; ἐ. χρυσῆ *CIG*2859 (Branchidae); ἐ. ἀργυρᾶ *IG*12(8).51.22 (Imbros, ii B.C.); used in fishing by night, Ael.*NA*2.8. **-ίτης** [ῑ] (sc. ἄρτος), ὁ, *bread baked over the fire*, Antidot.3, Crobyl.2, Lxx 2*Ki.*6.19, J.*AJ*7.4.2.

ἐσχᾰρόπεπτος, ον, *grilled*, Hp.*Epid.*4.41.

ἔσχαρος, ὁ, *a fish*, = κόρις, perh. a kind of *sole*, Archipp.24 (prob. l.), Mnesim.4.44, Dorio ap.Ath.7.330a (written ἐσχαρός in Hsch.).

ἐσχᾰρόφιν, Ep. gen. and dat. sg. of ἐσχάρα.

ἐσχᾰρ-όω, (ἐσχάρα V) *form an eschar*, of ointments, Orib.50.8.2:—Pass., *come to an eschar*, ἠσχαρωμένα ἕλκη Dsc.4.171. II. *ulcerate*, τὴν ὑστέραν Sor.2.12: abs., *to be caustic*, Dsc.5.75. **-ώδης**, ες, *scab-like*, Poll.4.204, Gal.19.434. **-ωμα**, ατος, τό, *scab, eschar*, *Hippiatr.*81. **-ών**, ῶνος, ὁ, (ἐσχάρα I) *place for a hearth*, *IG*11(2).144 A61 (Delos, iv B.C.), Roussel *Cultes Égyptiens* 222. **-ωσις**, εως, ἡ, *formation of an eschar*, Arist.*Pr.*863ᵃ14, Heliod.ap.Orib.45.19.1, Sor. 2.41. **-ωτικός**, ή, όν, *tending to form an eschar*, Dsc.2.73; φάρμακα *caustics*, Lycus ap.Orib.8.25.24, Gal.10.324.

ἐσχᾰτ-άω, (ἔσχατος) *to be at the edge*, Hom. (only in Il.) always in Ep. part., εἴ τινά που δηΐων ἕλοι ἐσχατόωντα *straying about the edge* of the camp, Il.10.206; Ἀνθηδών, Μύρσινος ἐσχατόωσα, *lying on the border*, 2.508, 616; ἕσπερος ἐ. the *extreme* west, Call.*Del.*174, cf. Theoc.7.77; κάρηνον ἐ. *sinciput*, Arat.207: with a Verb, τεχθήσεται ἐσχατόωσα *at last*, Man.4.459. **-εύω**, *to be at the end*, τὰ ἐσχατεύοντα τῶν δένδρων the parts *farthest off*, i.e. the branches, Thphr. *CP*5.1.3, cf. Plu.2.366b; -εύοντες τόποι Arist.*Cael.*298ᵃ14; *to be at the extremity*, τῆς Ἀρκαδίας Plb.4.77.8. II. *to be the lowest* or *meanest*, τῶν διδασκόντων Phld.*Rh.*2.54 S. **-ιά**, Ion. **-ιή**, ἡ, *farthest part, edge, border*, esp. of a place, Ep., Ion., Lyr., and sts. in Trag. (lyr.); νήσου ἐπ' ἐσχατιῆς Od.5.238; ἀγροῦ ἐπ' ἐσχατιήν (v.l. -ῇς) on *the edge* of the land, 4.517, cf. 5.489 (v.l. -ῇς, -ῇ); simply ἐπ' ἐσχατιῇ, -ῆς, on *the edge* or *shore*, 9.182, 280; ἐπ' ἐσχατιῇ λιμένος at *the mouth* of the harbour, 2.391; ἐσχατιῇ πολέμοιο on *the skirts* of battle (i.e. *farthest parts* of the field), Il.11.524, cf. 20.328; ἐσχατιῇ *round the edge* [of the funeral pile], 23.242; ἐσχατιαῖς, for ἐν ἐ., *on the outskirts*, S.*Ph.*144 (anap.); also, of parts of the body, καρδίης ἡ ἐ. Hp.*Cord.*4; γέννος Arat.57: metaph., *the extremity, highest point*, ὄλβου πρὸς ἐσχατιαῖς (v.l. -ιάς) Pi.*I.*6(5).12; πρὸς ἐσχατιὰν ἀρεταῖσιν ἱκάνων Id.*O.*3.43; τὸ μηδαμῶς ὂν ἐ. τῆς πρώτης αἰτίας Dam.*Pr.*441; μέχρι τῶν ἐ. Ph.1.685. 2. *border* of a country, ἐσχατιῇ Γόρτυνος Od.3.294; ναῖον δ' ἐσχατιὴν Φθίης Il.9.484; ἐσχατιῇ alone, Od.14.104; ἀν' ἐσχατιήν Archil.89.4: pl., αἱ ἐ. τῆς οἰκεομένης *the extremities* of the world, Hdt.3.106; also, *borders, frontier-land*, τῆς Αἰτωλίδος Id.6.127; abs., Id.3.115, 116, X.*HG*2.4.4, etc.: in Attica, *a boundary estate*, i.e. one at the sea-side or the foot of the mountains (cf. *AB*256), Aeschin.1.97, D.42.5, *IG*2².1594 (iv B.C.), Alciphr.3.34, cf. *IG*12(5).872.82 (Tenos): pl., ib.88. 3. of Time, ἀν' ἐσχατιάν *at last*, Pi.*P.*11.56: so dat., ἐσχατιῇ Nic.*Th.*437. 4. in pl., = δύσεις, Arat.574. **-ίζω**, *to be last, to come too late*, Lxx 1*Ma.*5.53: c. inf., ἐ. παραγενέσθαι ib.*Jd.*5.28 cod. A. **-ιος**, α, ον, poet. for ἔσχατος, Nic.*Th.*746, *AP*7.555 (Joann. Poet.), Opp.*C.*1. 124. **-ιώτης**, ου, ὁ, fem. **-ῶτις**, ιδος, *on the frontier*, as pr. n. of one from Ἐσχατιά (in Tenos), *IG*12(5).872, al.

ἐσχᾰτό-γηρως, ων, *in extreme old age*, D.S.15.76, Str.14.1.48, M. Ant.9.33: gen. sg. -γηρως Mitteis *Chr.*31 vii 29 (ii B.C.), v.l. in Lxx *Si.* 42.8: as fem., Poll.2.18: **-γηρος**, ον, Lxx *Si.* l. c., Ruf.*Fr.*64:—later **-γέρων**, οντος, ὁ, Procop.*Arc.*9.

ἐσχᾰτόεις, in acc. ἐσχατόεντα, f.l. for ἐσχατόωντα, D.P.65.

ἐσχᾰτοκόλλιον, τό, *end* of a papyrus roll, Mart.2.6.3; cf. πρωτόκολλον.

ἔσχᾰτος, η, ον, also ος, ον Arat.625 (prob. fr. ἐκ, ἐξ, perh. *eghz-κατος (cf. ἐχθός) like ἔγ-κατα): I. of Space, as always in Hom., *farthest, uttermost, extreme*, θάλαμος ἐ. the *hindmost* chamber, Od.21. 9; ἔσχατοι ἄλλων *at the end of the lines*, Il.10.434, cf. 8.225; ἔσχατοι ἀνδρῶν, of the Aethiopians, Od.1.23; οἰκέομεν.. ἔσχατοι 6.205; ἐσχάτη τῶν οἰκεομένων ἡ Ἰνδική Hdt.3.106, cf. Th.2.96, etc.; τὸ ἐ. τῆς ἀγορᾶς X.*HG*3.3.5; ὑπ'.. ἐσχάτην στήλην S.*El.*720; τάξις ἐ. the *farthest part* of the army, Id.*Aj.*4: pl., ἔσχατα γαίης Hes.*Th.*731; τὰ ἐ. τῶν στρατοπέδων Th.4.96; ἐπ' ἔσχατα χθονός S.*Fr.*956; αἱ ἐπ' ἔσχατα τοῦ ἄστεως οἰκίαι Th.8.95; ἐξ ἐσχάτων ἐς ἔσχατα ἀπικέσθαι from *end* to *end*, Hdt.7.100, cf. X.*Vect.*1.6; παρ' ἔσχατα λίμνης Pl.*Phd.*113b, cf. Th.3. 106:—in various senses, *uppermost*, ἐ. πυρά S.*El.*900; *lowest, deepest*, ἅλς *AP*13.27 (Phal.); *innermost*, σάρκες S.*Tr.* 1053; *last, hindmost*, ἤλαυνε δ' ἐ. Id.*El.*734; ἐπ' ἐσχάτῳ at the *close* of a document, *PTeb.*68.54 (ii B.C.), etc. 2. of Degree, *uttermost, highest*, τὸ ἐ. κορυφοῦται βασιλεῦσι Pi.*O.*1.113; ἀνορέαι ἐ. Id.*I.*4(3). 11; σοφία Lib.*Or.*59.88; of misfortunes, sufferings, etc., *utmost, last, worst*, πόνος, ἀδικία, κίνδυνοι, Pl.*Phdr.*247b, *R.*361a, *Grg.*511d; ὀδύναι αἱ ἐ. Id.*Prt.*354b; δῆμος ἐ. *extreme* democracy, Arist.*Pol.*1296ᵃ2. b. Subst., τὸ ἐ., τὰ ἐ., *the utmost*, ἐς τὸ ἐ. κακοῦ ἀπιγμένοι Hdt.8.52; τετρῦσθαι ἐς τὸ ἐ. κακοῦ Id.1.22; without Art., ἐπ' ἔσχατα βαίνεις S. *OC*217 (lyr.); προβᾶσ' ἐπ' ἔσχατον θράσους Id.*Ant.*853 (lyr.); ἐπ' ἐ. ἐλθεῖν ἀηδίας Pl.*Phdr.*240d, cf. *R.*361d, etc.; ὃ πάντων κακῶν ἔσχατόν ἐστι, τοῦτο πάσχει Id.*Phd.*83c; οἱ τὰ ἐ. πεποιηκότες X.*Cyr.*8.8.2; ζημιοῦσθαι πᾶσι τοῖς ἐ., Lat. *extremis suppliciis*, Pl.*Plt.*297e; ἔσχατ' ἐσχάτων κακά *worst of possible* evils, S.*Ph.*65, cf. Philem.178; εἰς τὰ ἐ. ἐληλυθώς *UPZ*60.12 (ii B.C.): Comp. οὔτε γὰρ τοῦ ἐσχάτου -ώτερον εἴη ἄν τι Arist.*Metaph.*1055ᵃ20: Sup. -ώτατος f.l. in X.*HG*2.3.49, cf. Phryn.51; τὰ -ώτατα Phld.*Hom.*p.32 O. 3. of Persons, *lowest, meanest*, D.S.8.18, D.C.42.5, Alciphr.3.43: prov., οὐδείς, οὐδ' ὁ Μυσῶν ἔ., i.e. *the meanest* of mankind, Magnes 5, cf. Philem.77; in

Pl.*Tht.*209b it seems to mean the *remotest* of mankind, cf. πρὸς ἐσχάτην Μυσῶν v.l. in *App.Prov.*2.85 (παρὰ τοῖς ἐ. τῆς Μυσίας Apostol.8. 1); similarly οὐδὲ τὸν ἔσχατον Καρῶν Plu.2.871b. 4. of Time, *last*, ἐς τὸ ἔ. to the *end*, Hdt.7.107, Th.3.46; ἔ. πλόος, ναυτιλίαι, *the end of* it, Pi.*P.*10.28, *N.*3.22; ἐσχάτας ὑπὲρ ῥίζας over *the last* scion of the race, S.*Ant.*599 (lyr.); ἔ. Ἑλλήνων, Ῥωμαίων, Plu.*Phil.*1, *Brut.*44: neut. ἔσχατον, as Adv., *for the last time*, S.*OC*1550; *finally, best of all*, 1*Ep.Cor.*15.8; *at the latest*, ἔ. ἐν τρισὶ μησίν *SIG*1219.11 (Gambreion, iii B.C.), cf. *Inscr.Prien.*4.45 (iv B.C.); εἰς τὴν ἐσχάτην at the *last*, Lxx*Ec.*1.11; ἐπ' ἐσχάτῳ ib.2*Ki.*24.25, al.: Subst. ἐσχάτη, ἡ, *end*, οὐχ ἕξεις ἐ. καλήν Astramps.*Orac.*21.4, cf. 40.3. 5. in the Logic of Arist., τὰ ἔ. are the *last* or *lowest species*, *Metaph.*1059^{b}26, or *individuals*, ib.998^{b}16, cf. *APo.*96^{b}12, al.; τὸ ἔ. ἄτομον *Metaph.*1058^b 10. b. ὁ ἔ. ὅρος the *minor* term of a syllogism, *EN*1147^{b}14. c. *last step* in geom. analysis or *ultimate condition* of action, τὸ ἔ. ἀρχὴ τῆς πράξεως *de An.*433^{a}16. II. Adv. -τως *to the uttermost, exceedingly*, πῦρ ἐ. καίει Hp.*de Arte*8; ἐ. διαμάχεσθαι Arist.*HA*613^{a}11; ἐ. φιλοπόλεμος X.*An.*2.6.1; φοβοῦμαί σ' ἐ. Men.912, cf. Epicur.*Ep.* 1 p.31 U. b. -τως διακεῖσθαι to be *at the last extremity*, Plb.1.24.2, D.S.18.48; ἔχειν *Ev.Marc.*5.23; ἀπορεῖν Phld.*Oec.*p.72 J. 2. so ἐς τὸ ἔ., = ἐσχάτως, Hdt.7.229; εἰς τὰ ἔ. X.*HG*5.4.33; εἰς τὰ ἔ. μάλα Id.*Lac.*1.2; τὸ ἔ. *finally, in the end*, Pl.*Grg.*473c; but, τὸ ἔ. *what is worst of all*, ib.508d.

ἔσχεθον, v. sub ἔχω.

ἐσχηματισμένως, Adv. pf. part. Pass., *by the possession of form*, Syrian. *in Metaph.*113.29. II. *figuratively*, Aps.p.331 H., Sch. Ar.*Pl.*23; *artificially, disingenuously*, of argument, Herm. *in Phdr.* p.84 A.; *fraudulently*, Just.*Nov.*6.5.

ἔσχων, impf. of *σχάω, = σχάζω (q.v.).

ἔσω, Adv. related to ἐς as εἰς to εἴσω (qq.v.): Comp., ἐσωτέρω τῆς Ἑλλάδος Hdt.8.66: Sup., ὡς ἐσωτάτω τῆς μασχάλης Hp.*Art.*7; τὰ ἔ. Id.*Oss.*9, cf. Corn.*ND*28.

ἔσωθεν (εἴσωθεν only in Hp.*Art.*46 codd.), rarely **ἔσωθε** E.*Heracl.* 42: Adv.:—*from within*, Hdt.7.36, 8.37, Aen.Tact.32.7, etc. 2. *within, inside*, Hdt.1.181, 2.36, A.*Ag.*991 (lyr.), S.*Tr.*601: c. gen., ἔσωθεν ἄντρων E.*Cyc.*516 (lyr.); ἔσωθε ναοῦ Id.*Heracl.* l. c.

ἐσωπή, ἡ, (ὤψ) *appearance, look*, Opp.*H.*4.358.

ἐσωρῆ(σ)αι· ὑπουργῆσαι τοὺς αὐτούς, Hsch.

ἐσώτατος, η, ον, Sup. of ἔσω, *innermost*, opp. ἐξώτατος, Ph.2.147, *Fr.*67 H., Sch.Pi.*N.*1.61: Comp. **ἐσώτερος**, α, ον, *Act.Ap.*16.24; εἰς -ώτερον *PMagd.*29.10 (iii B.C.); cf. ἔσω.

ἐσωτεριαῖος, α, ον, *inner*, λίθοι for an *inner* wall, *POxy.*498.14 (ii A.D.).

ἐσωτερικός, ή, όν, *inner, esoteric*: ἐσωτερικά, τά, of certain Stoic doctrines, Gal.5.313; ἐ. μαθήματα Iamb.*Comm.Math.*18; of persons, -κοί, οἱ, the disciples of Pythagoras, Id.*VP*17.72; μέμνησο τὸν μὲν ἐ., τὸν δὲ ἐξ. καλεῖν (of Aristotle), Luc.*Vit.Auct.*26. (Prob. coined to correspond with ἐξωτερικός (q.v.).)

ἐσωτέρω, Comp. of ἔσω (q.v.).

ἐσωτικός, ή, όν, *internal*: -κόν, τό, *household, family*, *Rev.Arch.* 20(1912).258 (Thrace).

ἐσώφωτον, τό, *hollow, interior space*, Hero *Stereom.*1.41.2.

ἐτάζω, aor. 1 ἤτασα (v. infr.), *examine, test*, mostly in compd. ἐξετάζω (for which it is v.l. in Hdt.3.62, ap.*AB*96), cf. παρετάζω; τοὺς ἀδικέοντας Democr.266; ἐτάζει (etym. of ἔτος) Pl.*Cra.*410d; freq. in Lxx, ὁ ἐτάζων καρδίας 1*Ch.*29.17; ἐτάζουσι Polusap.Stob.3.9.51: aor. 1 inf. ἐτάσαι Aristid.1.460 J. (prob. l.): c. dupl. acc., ἥν με Μουσάων ἐτάσης χάριν *AP*7.17 (Tull. Laur.); *reveal, unmask*, τινα ib.12. 135 (Asclep.):—Pass., Lxx*Wi.*6.7, al. 2. *visit, try, afflict*, τινα μεγάλοις ἐτασμοῖς ib.*Ge.*12.17. (Fr. ἐτός (B) as δοκιμάζω fr. δόκιμος.)

ἑταίρ-α, Ion. -η, ἡ, v. sub ἑταῖρος II. **-εία**, ἡ, also **ἑταιρία**, E. *Or.*1072, 1079, Th.3.82, Pl.*R.*365d, D.19.259, Arist.*Pol.*1272^{b}34, al.; Ion. **-ηΐη**: (ἑταῖρος):—*association, brotherhood*, τῶν ἡλικιωτέων Hdt. 5.71; ἑ. ποιεῖσθαι Isoc.3.54 (pl.); μαρτύρων συνεστῶσ' ἑ. D.21.139; αἱ βόες νέμονται καθ' ἑταιρείας Arist.*HA*611^{a}7; of a *social group* in Crete, *Leg.Gort.*10.38. 2. at Athens and elsewhere, *political club* or *union for party purposes*, Eup.8.6 D., *Com.Adesp.*23.31 D., Th.3. 82, Lys.12.55, Isoc.4.79 (pl.); -ίας συνάξομεν Pl.*R.*365d; σπουδαὶ ἑταιριῶν ἐπ' ἀρχὰς Id.*Tht.*173d; at Carthage, τὰ συσσίτια τῶν ἑ., compared to the φιδίτια at Sparta, Arist.*Pol.*1272^{b}34, cf. 1305^{b}32. 3. = Lat. *collegium*, ἑταιρία Ἰουλιανή, = *collegium Lupercorum Juliorum*, D.C.44.6. II. generally, *friendly connexion, friendship, comradeship*, Simon.118, S.*Aj.*683, E.*Or.*1072, *AP*7.51 (Adaeus); opp. ἔχθρα, D.29.23. III. = ἑταίρησις, And.1.100, v.l. in D.S.2. 18: Anaxil.21.3 combines signfs. II and III. **-εῖος**, α, ον, Ion. **-ήϊος**, η, ον, (ἑταίρειος Hdn.Gr.1.137):—*of* or *belonging to companions*: Ζεὺς ἑ. *presiding over fellowship*, Hdt.1.44, Diph.20, D.Chr. 1.39, etc.; so, of God, Ph.2.452; φόνος ἑ. the murder *of a comrade*, *AP*9.519 (Alc. Mess.). II. *amorous*, ἑ. φιλότης *h.Merc.*58; στόλος *AP*9.415 (Antiphil.). III. ἑταιρεῖον, τό, *house of a* ἑταίρα, Sch. Ar.*Eq.*873. **-ειώτης**, ου, ὁ, *member of a* ἑταιρεία, Hdn.*Epim.* 37. **-εύομαι**, Pass., *prostitute oneself*, D.S.12.21, Theopomp. Hist.217^c. **-έω**, *keep company with*, Aeschin.1.13, Phoenicid.4. 2; τινι *with* a man, And.1.100, etc.; φιλία ἑταιροῦσα *meretricious* friendship, Plu.2.62d; οἱ πολλοὶ αὐτῶν ἡταιρήκασιν Lys.14.41; οὐκέτι φαίνεται μόνον ἡταιρηκώς, ἀλλὰ καὶ πεπορνευμένος Aeschin.1.52. II. Med., = ἑταιρεύομαι, of men, Theopomp.Hist.217^b; of women, Plu. *Ant.*18. **-ηΐη**, **ἑταιρήϊος**, η, ον, Ion. for ἑταιρεία, ἑταιρεῖος, α, ον. **-ησις**, εως, ἡ, *unchastity*, Aeschin.1.13, D.22.21, Ph.2.381, etc. **-ία**, ἡ, v. ἑταιρεία. **-ίδεια** (sc. ἱερά), τά, *the festival of* Ζεὺς ἑταιρεῖος at Magnesia, Hegesand.25. **-ίδιον**, Dim. of ἑταίρα, Ph.ap. Eus.*PE*8.14 (pl.), Plu.2.808e, Hld.7.10. **-ίζω**, *to be* ἑταῖρος or *comrade* to any one, c. dat., ἀνδρὶ ἑταιρίσσαι Il.24.335; of the Graces, *h.Ven.*96. 2. trans. in Med., *associate with oneself, choose for one's comrade*, ἤ τινά που Τρώων ἑταρίσσαιτο Il.13.456, cf. Call.*Dian.* 206, Naumach.ap.Stob.4.23.7. b. *win over*, App.*Hann.*32, *BC*3. 21. II. = ἑταιρεύομαι, *to be a courtesan*, in Act., Luc.*DMeretr.*7.3; of a man, Sch.Ar.*Th.*261:—Med., Ath.13.593b, *Cat.Cod.Astr.*8(4). 169. 2. *associate with* ἑταῖραι, *Com.Adesp.*1012. **-ικός**, ή, όν, *of* or *befitting a companion*: ἡ ἑταιρική *companionship*, Arist.*EN*1157^b 23; in full, ἑ. φιλία ib.1161^{b}12. Adv. -κῶς, προσφέρεσθαι Id.*EE*1243^a 5. 2. τὸ ἑταιρικόν, = ἑταιρεία I. 2, Th.8.48; ἑ. συνάγειν Hyp.*Eux.*8; τὰ ἑταιρικά *factions, clubs*, Plu.*Lys.*5, D.C.37.57; = Lat. *collegia*, Id. 38.13. b. *ties of party*, opp. τὸ ξυγγενές, Th.3.82. 3. ἵππος -κή horse-*guards* of the Macedonian kings, Plb.16.18.7, D.S.17.37, Arr.*An.*3.16.11. II. *of* or *like a* ἑταίρα, *meretricious*, γυνή Plu. 2.140c, etc.; τὸ ἑ. the *custom of* ἑταῖραι, Alciphr.2.1; *concerning* ἑταῖραι, λόγοι D.H.*Lys.*3: so Adv. -κῶς *meretriciously*, κεκοσμημένοι Zeno *Stoic.*1.58, Luc.*Bis Acc.*20, Plu.*Pomp.*2. 2. ἑ. (sc. τέλος), τό, *tax on courtesans*, *Ostr.*83 (ii B.C.); τελώνης ἑταιρεικοῦ (sic) Ἀφροδίτη *Arch.Pap.*6.219 (Elephantine, ii B.C.). **-ίς**, ίδος, ἡ, = ἑταίρα, v.l. in X.*HG*5.4.6, cf. Ph.1.40, *AP*6.208 (Antip. Thess.); περὶ τῶν Ἀθήνησι Ἑ., title of several works, Ath.13.567a:—not good Att., acc. to Thom.Mag.p.129 R. **-ισμα**, ατος, τό, = ἑταιρικὸν τέλος, *PGrenf.* 2.41 (i A.D., pl.). **-ισμός**, ὁ, (ἑταιρίζω II) *harlotry*, Clearch.6, *OGI*674.17 (Egypt, i A.D.). **-ιστής**, οῦ, ὁ, *lewd man*, Poll.6.188:—fem. -ίστρια, = τριβάς, Pl.*Smp.*191e, Luc.*DMeretr.*5.2, Tim.*Lex.*

ἑταιροποιέομαι, *make friends*, Sch.Il.12.310.

ἑταῖρ-ος, Ep. and Dor. also **ἕταρος**, Cleobul.ap.D.L.1.93, A.*Pers.* 988 (lyr.), ὁ:—*comrade, companion*, in Hom. esp. of the followers of a chief, *comrades-in-arms*, Il.1.179, al.; *messmate*, 17.577; *fellow-slave*, Od.14.407, al.: joined with ἀνήρ, 8.584, Hdt.5.95, Antipho 1. 18; later, as a term of address, φίλ' ἑταῖρε Thgn.753, cf. Pl.*Grg.* 482a; ὦταῖρε Scol.ap.Ar.*V.*1238, cf. *Ev.Matt.*20.13, al.: c. gen., δαιτὸς ἑταῖρε *partner* of my feast, *h.Merc.*436; νυκτὸς ἑ. ib.290; πόσιος καὶ βρώσιος ἑταῖροι messmates, Thgn.115; ἑ. ἐν πρήγματι Id.116. 2. metaph., of things, ἐσθλὸς ἑταῖρος, of a fair wind, Od.11.7, 12.149; φθόνος κενεοφρόνων ἑ. Pi.*Fr.*212; γέλως ἑ. ὕβρεων Plu.2.622b: c. dat., βίον. . τὸν σοφοῖς ἕταρον *AP*7.470 (Mel.). 3. *pupil, disciple*, e.g. of Socrates, X.*Mem.*2.8.1, al., cf. Arist.*Pol.*1274^{a}28; Λεύκιππος καὶ ὁ ἑ. αὐτοῦ Δημόκριτος Id.*Metaph.*985^{b}4: pl., *fellow-pupils*, Poll.4. 45. 4. of political *partisans* (cf. ἑταιρεία I. 2), Lys.12.43, Th.8.48; οἱ περὶ αὐτὸν ἑ. his *club-mates*, D.21.20. 5. *members of a religious guild*, *OGI*573.1 (Cilicia, Jewish). 6. rarely of *lovers*, Semon.7. 49, Ar.*Ec.*912 (lyr.). 7. ἑταῖροι, οἱ, the *guards*, i.e. the *cavalry* of the Macedonian kings, Theopomp.Hist.217, Anaximen.Lamps. ap.Harp. s.v. πεζέταιροι, Arr.*An.*3.16.11, etc.; to be distinguished from the king's immediate *retinue* (cf. supr. 1), Theopomp. l.c., Arr. *An.*2.12.6, al.; of the *Comites* of the Roman Emperor, Βαρβίλλῳ τῷ ἐμῷ ἑτέρῳ (sic) *PLond.*1912.105 (Epist. Claudii), cf. *SIG*798.6 (Cyzicus, i A.D., pl.). 8. as Adj., *associate of*, τὸ ἐπιθυμητικὸν ἡδονῶν ἑ. Pl.*R.*439d: Sup., τοῖς σεαυτοῦ ἑταιροτάτοις your *closest companions*, Id.*Grg.*487d, cf. *Phd.*89e, D.Chr.1.44; σαργῶν γένος πέτρῃσιν ἑ. *constant to* the rocks, Opp.*H.*4.267: abs., of animals, *gregarious*, Id.*C.*2.325. II. **ἑταίρα**, Ion. **ἑταίρη**, Ep. **ἑτάρη** [ᾰ], ἡ, *companion*, Ἔρις. . Ἄρεος. . κασιγνήτη ἑτάρη τε Il.4.441; Λάτω καὶ Νιόβα μάλα μὲν φίλαι ἦσαν ἑ. Sapph.31, cf. 11; φύζα, φόβου κρυόεντος ἑ. Il.9.2; φόρμιγξ. . ἣν ἄρα δαιτὶ θεοὶ ποίησαν ἑ. Od.17.271, cf. *h.Merc.*478; Νίκην, ἣ χορικῶν ἐστιν ἑ. Ar.*Eq.*589; μιμητικὴ. . τῷ ἐν ἡμῖν ἑ. καὶ φίλη ἐστί Pl.*R.*603b; Ποσειδάωνος ἑ., of a submerged city, Call.*Del.*101. 2. *courtesan*, Hdt.2.134, Ar.*Pl.*149, Ath.13.567a, 571d, etc.; opp. πόρνη (a common *prostitute*), Anaxil.22.1; opp. γαμετή, Philetaer.5; Ἀφροδίτη ἑ. Apollod.Hist.17. **-οσύνη**, ἡ, = ἑταιρεία, Paul.Al.*D.* 3. **-όσυνος**, η, ον, *friendly, a friend*, *AP*12.247 (Strat.). **-ότης**, *contubernium*, *Gloss.* **-οτρόφος**, ον, *keeping mistresses*, Man.4. 313, Jul.*Gal.*238e.

ἔταλον, τό, (ἔτος) *yearling*, *Schwyzer*644.18 (Aegae, iv/iii B.C.); also **ἔτελον**, ib.252.11 (Cos, iii B.C.).

ἐτάλασσας, v. sub *τλάω.

ἐτανόν· ἀληθῶς, σφόδρα, Hsch.; cf. ἐτεός. 2. ἐτανός *yearly*, coined by Tz. ad Hes.*Op.*31.

ἕταρος, ἑτάρη, v. ἑταῖρος I and II. **ἔτας**, v. ἔτης.

ἔτ-ασις, εως, ἡ, (ἐτάζω) *trial, affliction*, Lxx*Jb.*10.17. **-ασμός**, ὁ, = foreg., ib.*Ge.*12.17 (pl.). **-αστής**, οῦ, ὁ, = ἐξεταστής, *CIG* (add.)3641 *b* 42 (Lampsacus), Suid. s.v. δοκιμαστῆρες.

ἐταυτῶς· ἀληθῶς, Hsch. **ἐτέα**, ἡ, prob., = ἰτέα, Theognost. *Can.*7. **ἐτεῇ**, v. ἐτεός.

ἔτειος, α, ον (ος, ον E.*Fr.*330 (s.v.l.)), (ἔτος) *yearly, annual*, ἄεθλα Pi.*I.*4(3).67; δασμός E.*Rh.*435; *of the year*, ὧραι Thphr.*Od.* 68; μεταλλαγαί E.*Fr.*330 (prob.); ἐτεία, ἡ, *yearly board of officials* or *the term of such a board*, *SIG*559.45 (Magn. Mae., iii B.C., but Arc.): neut. pl. ἔτεια, as Adv., Lyc.721. 2. *lasting a year*, φρουρά A.*Ag.*2. II. *of one year, yearling*, X.*Cyn.*5.14; βρέφος Poll.2.8.

ἔτελις, ὁ, a fish, Arist.*HA*567^{a}20. **ἔτελον**, v. ἔταλον.

ἔτεμεν· ἠμελγεν, Hsch.; cf. τέμνοντα.

Ἐτεοβουτάδης, ου, ὁ, *a genuine son of Butes*, one of the family which supplied the hereditary priests of Athena Polias, Alex.201, D.21.182, cf. Harp.

ἐτεοδμώς, ῶος, ὁ, *honest slave*: καί κ' ἐτεοδμώων read by Ptol. Ascal. for καί κέ τεο δμώων in Od.16.305.

Ἐτεόκρητες, οἱ, *true Cretans*, Od.19.176, *POxy.*1241 v 27.

ἐτεόκριθος (sc. κριθή), ἡ, *genuine, good barley*, Thphr.*CP*3.22.2.

ἐτεός, ά, όν (not found in masc.), *true, genuine*, πόλλ' ἐτεά Il.20.255; ἢ ἐτεὸν Κάλχας μαντεύεται 2.300; εἰ ἐτεόν περ whether it be *true* indeed, 14.125; εἰ δή ῥ' ἐ. γε καὶ ἀτρεκέως ἀγορεύεις 15.53. II. ἐτεόν, as Adv., *in truth, verily*, εἰπέ μοι εἰ ἐ. γε φίλην ἐς πατρίδ' ἱκάνω Od.13.328, cf. Il.8.423; εἰ ἐ... μιμνήσκομαι *rightly*, Theoc.25.173. 2. in Ar. (not in other Com.) interrog., *really, indeed*, οὐκ ἀκούσεσθ' ἐ...; *Ach.*322, cf. 609; ἐ. ἡγεῖ γὰρ θεούς; *Eq.*32, cf. 733; in asking for information, τί οὖν τοῦτ' ἐστὶν ἐ.; *Nu.*93, cf. *V.*8; τί δὲ τοῦτ' ἐγέλασας ἐ.; *Nu.*820; cf. ἐτός (B). 3. fem., ἐτεή, ἡ, *reality*, [ἄνθρωπος] ἐτεῇς ἀπήλλακται Democr.6; dat. ἐτεῇ, as Adv., *in reality*, νόμῳ γλυκύ, νόμῳ πικρόν, ἐτεῇ δ' ἄτομα καὶ κενόν Id.125; ἐ. οὐδὲν ἴσμεν Id.7.

ἑτεράλκ-εια, ἡ, *varying fortune of battle*, coined by Eust.662.46. **-έομαι**, *to be conquered*, Sch.Il.15.738. **-ής**, ές, *giving strength to the other side*, μάχης ἑτεραλκέα νίκην victory in battle *inclining to the other side*, Il.16.362; σῆμα τιθεὶς Τρώεσσι, μ. ἑ. ν. a sign that victory *was changing sides*, 8.171; ἵνα δὴ Δαναοῖσι μ. ἑ. ν. δῷς *inclining to their side*, 7.26; without μάχης, δίδου ἑτεραλκέα νίκην 17.627, Od.22.236; Ἄρης ἑ. A.*Pers.*952 (lyr.): in late Prose, ἑ. νίκη Ps.-Luc.*Philopatr.*8, Ael.*Fr.*135. 2. Act., ἑ. δῆμος a body of men *which decides the victory*, Il.15.738; λύσις ἑ. κήδευς Nic.*Th.*2; ποδῶν ἑ. ταρσῷ, of a lame man, Nonn.*D.*9.230. II. *inclining first to one side then to the other, doubtful*, μάχη Hdt.9.103; μόθου ἑ. κλωγμῷ Orac.ap.Luc.*JTr.*31. Ion. Adv. -αλκέως, ἀγωνίζεσθαι *with varying fortune*, Hdt.8.11.

ἑτερ-άριθμος [ᾰ], ον, *of different number*: τὸ ἑ. *change of number*, as a figure of speech, Phoeb.*Fig.*1.5. **-αχθέω**, = ἑτεροκλινέω, Phryn.*PS*p.68 B. **-εγκεφᾰλάω** or **-έω**, *to suffer in half the brain, to be half-mad, crazy*, Ar.*Fr.*778. **-ειδής**, ές, = ἑτεροειδής, *illusory*, ἄλην ἑ. λεύσσων Nic.*Al.*84. **-ήμερος**, ον, *on alternate days, day and day about*, ζώουσ' ἑτερήμεροι, of the Dioscuri, Od.11.303, cf. Ph.2.189, Jul.*Or.*4.147a; ἑ. ὁ βίος τῶν ἀσκητῶν Ph.1.643; of an intermittent fever, Orph.*L.*633. **-ήρης**, ες, (*ἄρω) = ἀμφήρης, Max.165.

ἑτέρηφι, Ep. dat. fem. of ἕτερος.

ἑτερο-βάρεια [βᾰ], ἡ, *weighing down to one side*, Hsch., Suid. s. v. κατὰ πρόσκλισιν. **-βαρής**, ές, *weighing down one side*, Eust.1316.26. **-γᾰμία**, ἡ, *second marriage*, Tz. ad Lyc.1317. **-γάστριος**, ον, *by another mother*, opp. ὁμογάστριος, Tz. ad Hes.*Op.*374. **-γενέω**, *differ in kind*, Nicom.*Ar.*1.10. **-γενής**, ές, *of different kinds*, τὰ ἑ. Arist.*Cat.*1^{b}16; of animals, Id.*HA*601^{a}25; ἑ. ζῷα Ph.2.370; ᾠά *Gp.*14.7.28; ἐξ ἑτερογενῶν σωμάτων ὑπάρξαι, of Centaurs, D.S.4.8; μόρια, i.e. not paired, Gal.*UP*16.14. 2. *of different kind* or *race*, Demetr.Lac.1012.36 F., D.T.635.7; [ἑτερότης] ἑ. καὶ ἀλλόφυλος πρὸς αὐτήν Dam.*Pr.*308; simply, *different*, πράξεις D.S.1.9. Adv. -νῶς, διαφέρειν ἀλλήλων S.E.*M.*7.361, cf. Nicom.*Ar.*1.10. 3. *of diverse materials*, of a garment, Sm.*De.*22.11: generally, *complex*, opp. ὁμογενής, Demetr.Lac.1429.2 F. II. Gramm., *of different gender*, A.D.*Conj.*243.1 (s. v. l.); -γενές, τό, *change of gender* in a *constructio ad sensum*, Phoeb.*Fig.*1.5. **-γλαυκος**, ον, *with one eye grey*, Arist.*GA*779^{b}4. **-γλωσσος**, Att. **-ττος**, ον, *of other* (i.e. *foreign*) *tongue*, Plb.23.13.2, Str.8.1.2; ἐν ἑτερογλώσσοις λαλεῖν *by men of foreign tongue*, 1*Ep.Cor.*14.21, cf. Onos.26.2, Aq.*Is.*33.19. 2. *of diverse tongues*, ζῷα Ph.1.406. **-γνᾰθος**, ον, *with one side of the mouth harder than the other*, [ἵπποι] X.*Eq.*1.9, al.; glossed by ἀπειθής, ἢ ἀπλήστος, Phot. **-γνης**, ητος, ὁ, = ἑτερογενής, Hdn.Gr.1.83. **-γνωμοσύνη**, ἡ, *difference of opinion*, J.*AJ*10.11.7, Hsch. s. v. διχόνοια. **-γνώμων**, ον, gen. ονος, = ἀλλογνώμων, τόποι Vett.Val.79.18; τὰ ἐς θεὸν -γνώμονες Agath.4.2, cf. 3.12. **-γονος**, ον, = ἑτερογενής, *Hippiatr.*11, Hsch. s. v. ἀμφίσγονοι. **-δίδακτος** [ῐ], ον, *taught by another*, opp. αὐτοφυής, Olymp.*in Alc.*p.11 C. **-δῐδασκᾰλέω**, *teach differently, teach false doctrine*, 1*Ep.Ti.*1.3. **-δοξέω**, *hold an erroneous opinion*, Pl.*Tht.*190e; *differ in opinion*, περί τινος Ph.1.508. **-δοξία**, ἡ, *a taking one thing for another, error of opinion*, Pl.*Tht.*193d. 2. *difference of opinion*, Ph.*Fr.*72 H. (pl.). **-δοξος**, ον, *differing in opinion*, Luc.*Eun.*2. 2. *holding opinions other than the right, heterodox*, Ph.1.403, al., Arr.*Epict.*2.9.19, J.*BJ*2.8.5; [ἰατρός] Sor.1.52, cf. Gal.9.670. Adv. -ξως *in heterodox manner*, τῆς μουσικῆς ἀκροᾶσθαι Philostr.*VS*2.1.11. **-δῠνᾰμία**, ἡ, *shifting of strength*, Sch.Il.7.26. **-δύνᾰμος** [ῠ], ον, *of different power* or *faculty*, Porph.*Sent.*33 (prob. l.). 2. **-εθνής**, ές, *of another tribe, foreign*, Str.8.1.2, Ph.2.400. **-είδεια**, ἡ, *numerical diversity*, *Theol.Ar.*8. **-ειδής**, ές, *of another kind*, Arist.*HA*508^{b}11, f.l. in *Placit.*2.30.5; *of diverse kinds*, Ph.*Fr.*29 H. 2. *having the form of diversity*, Dam.*Pr.*303; opp. ταυτοειδής, ib.340. Adv. -δῶς ib.55. **-ζηλος**, ον, *zealous for one side*. Adv. -λως *unfairly*, Hes.*Th.*544. II. *zealous in another pursuit*, *AP*11.216 (Lucill.). 2. *of different tastes*, S.E.*M.*7.56. **-ζῠγέω**, *draw unequally*, Apollon.*Lex.* s. v. ἰσοφόροι: c. dat., ἑ. ἀπίστοις *to be yoked in unequal partnership* with unbelievers, 2*Ep.Cor.*6.14. **-ζῠγία**, ἡ, *inclination to one side*, of the balance, Sch.Luc.*Lex.*3. **-ζῠγος**, ον, *unevenly yoked*, of *animals of diverse kind*, Lxx *Le.*19.19, cf. Ph.2.369; of vases, *not pairs*, *PCair.Zen.*38.12 (iii B.C.). 2. of the balance, *leaning to one side*, Ps.-Phoc.15. II. *yoked with another*, i.e. *double*, Nonn.*D.*10.348. III. Gramm., *differently formed*, A.D.*Adv.*171.17. Adv. -γως *in a different declension*, Hdn.Gr.ap. Eust.113.35; also τὰ ἑ. λεγόμενα (e.g. σπουδαῖος, as Adj. of ἀρετή) Procl.*in Cra.*p.40 P. **-ζυξ**, ῠγος, ὁ, ἡ, *yoked singly, without its yokefellow*, metaph., μήτε τὴν πόλιν ἑτερόζυγα περιδεῖν γεγενημένην Cimon ap.Plu.*Cim.*16. II. = foreg. II, Nonn.*D.*5.148. **-θάλής**, ές, *flourishing on one side*: of children of the same father, but different mothers, *Cat.Cod.Astr.*8(3).110, Eust.1283.2, Tz. ad Hes.*Op.*374. **-θρησκος**, ον, *practising a false religion*, interpol. in Suid. s. v. θρῆσκος. **-θροος**, ον, *speaking different tongues*, Nonn.*D.*36.426, al. 2. *sounding different from before*, ib.9.256, al. 3. *of twofold sounds*, ἠχώ ib.42.255.

ἑτεροῖ-ος, α, ον, Ep. **-οῖιος**, η, ον, D.P.1180:—*of a different kind, diverse*, Hdt.1.99, al.; τὰ ἑ. οὐκ ἀλλοῖα; Pl.*Prm.*161a, al.; τί φαίνεται ἑτεροῖον διανοηθεὶς ὁ ἰητρὸς ἤ..; Hp.*VM*7; ἑ. τινός ib.9; *unusual, strange*, Id.*Acut.*6; φωναί Phld.*Po.*994 *Fr.*10. Adv. -οίως, διαιτηθῆναι Hp.*Acut.*39, cf. Gal.2.219. II. *diversified, differentiated*, κόσμος, ἀριθμός, Dam.*Pr.*194, 204. III. *different from what should be, untoward*, ἤν τι ἑ. ἀποβαίνῃ Luc.*JTr.*32. **-ότης**, ητος, ἡ, *difference in kind*, Pl.*Prm.*160d, Ph.1.5; ἡ ἑτερότης ἄρα ἑτεροιότης Dam.*Pr.*440. **-όω**, *make of different kind, alter*, Hp.*Acut.*37, Plu.2.559c; ἐς τοιήνδε ἕξιν τὸν ἄνθρωπον Aret.*SD*2.1:—Pass., Hdt.2.142, 7.225, Hp.*VM*14, *Fract.*15, Ph.2.93; τὸ -ούμενον τῆς πτώσεως A.D.*Synt.*96.4. II. Pass., *to be differentiated*, Dam.*Pr.*220. **-ωσις**, εως, ἡ, *alteration*, Diog.Apoll.5 (pl.); opp. φορά, Arist.*Ph.*217^{b}26, cf. *Mu.*400^{a}24 (pl.); ἀέρος Epicur.*Ep.*2 p.43 U. (pl.); (sc. ψυχῆς) of sensation, Chrysipp.*Stoic.*2.23; τῆς οὐσίας, τοῦ τέλους, τοῦ περιέχοντος, Plu.2.430c, A.D.*Pron.*18.15, M.Ant.4.39: Ἑτεροιούμενα, τά, *mythological transformations*, title of work by Nicander, Ant.Lib.1, etc. **-ωτικός**, ή, όν, *alterative*, ἡ τερατολογουμένη -ωτική, of Chrysippus' theory of sensation (cf. ἑτεροίωσις), *Stoic.*1.108.

ἑτερό-καρπος, ον, *bearing different fruit*, of grafts, Hp.*Nat.Puer.*26. **-κῑνησία**, ἡ, *motion externally caused*, Procl.*in Alc.*p.225 C. **-κίνητος** [ῑ], ον, *moved by external force, incapable of self-motion*, opp. αὐτοκίνητος, Id.*Inst.*14, Simp.*in Epict.*p.10 D., Dam.*Pr.*18, al., Syrian.*in Metaph.*23.21. Adv. -τως Simp.*in Epict.*p.4 D. **-κλῐνέω**, *lean on one side*, Anon.*Intr.Arat.*p.98 M., Sm.*Ps.*16(17).11, Phryn.*PS*p.68 B.; cf. -κλονέω. **-κλινής**, ές, *leaning to one side, uneven*, Hp.*Art.*24; of a building, D.C.57.21; τὰ ἑ. τῶν χωρίων *sloping* ground, X.*Cyn.*2.7. Adv. -νῶς *one-sidedly*, Sor.2.62; ἑ. ἔχειν πρὸς ἡδονήν to have *a propensity* to it, Arr.*Epict.*3.12.7. **-κλῐτος**, ον, (κλίνω) *irregularly inflected*, of nouns, as γυνή, γυναικός, A.D.*Synt.*102.12, etc.; of Verbs, as ἔσθω, ἔφαγον, Id.*Pron.*13.2. Adv. -τως Eust.113.41. **-κλονέω**, *shake to one side*, Opp.*C.*4.204 (v. l. -κλινέω). **-κοπία**, ἡ, *exercise in which two parties are engaged*, Cael.Aur.*TP*5.11.133 (*hatero-* codd.). **-κρᾶνία**, ἡ, *pain on one side of the head* (cf. ἡμικρανία), Archig.ap.Gal.8.94, Aret.*CD*1.2, etc. (also **-κράνιον**, τό, Gal.14.400). Adj. **-κρᾱνικός**, ή, όν, *liable to such pain*, Antyll.ap.Orib.10.19.1. **-κτῠπος**, ον, *repeating sound*, Ἠχώ Nonn.*D.*39.347. **-κωφέω**, *to be deaf of one ear*, Lxx *Si.*19.27 (nisi leg. ἐθελο-). **-κωφος**, ον, *deaf on one side*, Cyrill.ap.Valck.*Ammon.*p.65. **-λογία**, ἡ, *different*, i.e. *false, speech*, Sm.*Ps.*138(139).4. **-μαλλος**, ον, *woolly, shaggy on one side*, Str.5.1.12: also **-μαλλής**, ές, Hsch. s. v. καυνάκαι. **-μάσχᾰλος** χιτών, ὁ, a frock *with* only *one hole for the arm*, i.e. *only coming over one shoulder*, worn by slaves, opp. ἀμφιμάσχαλος, Poll.7.47, Sch.Ar.*Eq.*878. **-μεγεθέω**, *increase on one side*, Artem.1.31. **-μέρεια**, ἡ, *inclination to one side*, Suid., Phot. s. v. κατὰ πρόσκλισιν. **-μερής**, ές, *leaning to one side, one-sided*, βίος Crito ap.Stob.3.3.64. Adv. -ρῶς *one-sidedly* (i.e. not in equal proportions), Speus.ap.*Theol.Ar.*61 (nisi leg. -ρεῖς). 2. τὸ ἑ. *separation*, Porph.ap.Stob.1.49.25^a. **-μετρία**, ἡ, *difference of metre*: **-μετρος**, ον, *of different metre*, both in Heph.*Poëm.*p.74 C. **-μήκης**, ες, *with sides of uneven length*, i.e. *oblong*, X.*Eq.*7.14; ἑτερόμηκες, τό, *oblong rectangle*, Arist.*Cat.*11^{a}10, *de An.*413^{a}17, Euc.1 *Def.*22. 2. of numbers, *not square*, i.e. produced by the multiplication of two *unequal* factors, as 6 = 3 × 2, Pl.*Tht.*148a, Plu.2.367f; opp. ἰσόπλευρος (both of line and number), Arist.*APo.*73^{b}1. **-μηκικὸς** λόγος the ratio *of the sides of a rectangle*, Iamb.*in Nic.*pp.72, 94 P. **-μήτριος**, ον, *born of another mother*, Sch.Lyc.19 (ed. Bachm.). **-μήτωρ**, ορος, ὁ, ἡ, = foreg., Sch.A.R.4.223.

ἑτερομοιότης, ητος, ἡ, *identity in diversity*, Procl.*Theol.Plat.*1.21.

ἑτερο-μόλιος δίκη, (μολεῖν) a trial *in which only one of the two parties appears*, Zen.3.88, Eust.999.63, Hsch. (-μυνος cod.). (Perh. rather to be connected with *μωλέω, as in Cret. ἀμφιμωλέω etc.) **-μορφος**, ον, *of different* or *diverse form*, Ael.*NA*12.16, Ph.1.655; opp. ἀνθρωποειδής, Ptol.*Tetr.*145; so of monstrosities, Alex.Aphr.*Pr.*2.47: hence **-μορφία**, ἡ, *monstrosity*, of the Minotaur, Isid.*Etym.*11.3.9. **-ούσιος**, ον, *differing in substance*, Porph.*Sent.*35. Adv. -ίως ib.37:—also in form **ἑτερούσιος**, ψυχὴν ἐν ἀλλοτρίῳ πράγματι καὶ ἑτερουσίῳ συνδεδεμένην ib.32, cf. Iamb.*Myst.*1.19. **-πάθεια** [πᾰ], ἡ, (παθεῖν) *counter-irritation*, Dsc.2.154. **-πᾰχής**, ές, *of unequal thickness*, ξύλα Apollod.*Poliorc.*164.8. **-πλᾰνής**, ές, *wandering hither and thither*, ὄθμα Nic.*Al.*243. **-πλᾰτής**, ές, *with unequal sides*, of beams, Apollod.*Poliorc.*161.12: **-πλᾰτέω**, *vary in breadth*, Hero *Mens.*59. **-πλευρος**, ον, *with two visible faces*, λίθοι *SIG*247 ii 70 (Delph., iv B.C.); cf. ἀτερόπλευρος. II. *with unequal sides*, Scymn.267. **-πλοκος**, ον, *irregularly combined*, Diom.p.481 K. **-πλοος**, ον, contr. **-πλους**, ουν, *lent on bottomry with the risk of the outward*, but not of the homeward, *voyage*, ἀργύριον D.34.30; δανείσαντες ἑ. τἀργύριον εἰς Ἀθήνας Id.56.29; τὰ ἑ. (sc. ἀργύρια) Id.34.8. **-πνοοι** αὐλοί, οἱ, *uneven, double* flutes, *Anacreont.*2 B.4 (dub. l.). **-ποδέω**, (ἑτερόπους) *go lame of one foot*, *Hippiatr.*109. **-ποιός**, όν, *making different*, Iamb.*Myst.*1.18; *creating difference*, Dam.*Pr.*192, al.; δυναμις, opp. ταυτοποιός, Procl.*in Cra.*p.20 P.; ἡ κίνησις ἐκστατική ἐστι καὶ ἑ. Simp.*in Epict.*p.99 D. **-πορπος**, ον, (πόρπη) *clasped on one side*, of a woman's dress, Call.*Fr.*225. **-πους**, ὁ, ἡ, gen. ποδος, *with uneven feet, halting*, Alciphr.3.27, Philostr.*VS*1.21.1, *Hippiatr.* 13. **-πρόσωπος**, ον, *of another person*: σχῆμα ἑ. when a statement is made *in the words of another*, Phoeb.*Fig.*1.5, cf. Choerob.Rh. p.256 S. Adv. -πως, ἀνατίθησι *Proll.Hermog.* in Rh.7.7 W. **-πτολις**, ὁ, ἡ, *of another city*, Erinn.5; *of various cities*, λαός Nonn.*D.*26.41. **-πτωτος**, ον, *having cases formed from different stems*, e.g. μέγας, μεγάλου, A.D.*Pron.*11.4. II. -πτωτον, τό, *change of case*, as a figure of speech, Phoeb.*Fig.*1.5. **-ρρέπεια**, ἡ, *leaning to one side*, Poll.8.14. **-ρρεπέω**, *lean on one side*, Plu.2.1026e. **-ρρεπής**, ές, Act., *making now one side and now another preponderate*, Ζεύς A. *Supp.*403 (lyr.). II. *inclining to one side or the other*, of patients in the crisis of a disease, Hp.*Acut.*(*Sp.*)21. 2. *one-sided*, ἑ. ζήτημα where the *weight* of evidence *preponderates*, Hermog.*Stat.* 1. III. Adv. -πῶς v.l. in Poll.8.13. **-ρροπία**, ἡ, = ἑτερορρέπεια, Id.4.172. **-ρροπος**, ον, *inclined to one side*, ἡ κλῖμαξ ἑ. ἐπὶ γῆν ἀφίξεται will come down *on one corner, unevenly*, Hp.*Art.*43; ἑ. ἐπάρματα swellings *on one side*, Id.*Epid.*1.1; φλεγμοναί ibid.; τὰ ἑ., of crippled limbs, Id.*Off.*23. 2. *inclining to one side or the other*, θεῶν ἑ. δῶρα gifts *that may prove either good or evil*, Rhian.1.2. II. Adv. -πως Poll.4.172, Gal.8.430, Aspasia ap.Aët.16.72. **-ρρυθμος** (Ion. **-ρρυσμος** Hsch.), ον, *of different rhythm*: hence, of the pulse, *having a false rhythm*, i.e. unsuitable to the patient's age, Gal.8.516, al.

ἕτερος, α, ον, only Att.-Ion. with ἕ-, Dor. **ἅτερος** [ᾰ] *IG*4.914.9 (Epid.), etc. (and Att. in crasis, v. infr.), Aeol. **ἄτερος** Alc.41.5, etc.:—but **ἅτερος** [ᾱ], Att. crasis for ὁ ἅτερος, *Com.Adesp.*14.23 D., al., Ion. **οὕτερος** (fr. ὁ ἕτ-) Hdt.1.34, etc., Dor. **ὥτερος** Theoc.7.36; neut. θάτερον A.*Ag.*344, And.2.7, etc., Ion. τοὔτερον Hdt.1.32: pl. ἅτεροι, for οἱ ἅτεροι, Arist.*Pol.*1255ᵃ20; θἄτερα S.*El.*345, Th.1.87, etc.; gen. θατέρου S.*Ph.*597, etc., Ion. τοὐτέρου Semon.7.113, Dor. θατέρω Ti.Locr.94a, θωτέρω Epich.71 (dub. l.); dat. θατέρῳ A.*Pr.*778; fem. nom. ἡτέρα *IG*2².1498.76, 1615.14,87 (iv B.C.), S.*OC*497, Ar.*Lys.*85, 90 codd., Paus.Gr.*Fr.*82; dat. θητέρᾳ S.*OT*782, *Tr.*272, E.*Hipp.* 894, Ar.*Av.*1365, etc., cf. Paus.Gr. l.c. (in Mss. sts. θατέρᾳ), Ion. τητέρῃ Phoen.5.2.—Later masc. and fem. θάτερος, θατέρα, even with the Art., Men.846, Chrysipp.ap.Paus.Gr.*Fr.*82, Lyc.590, Polem. *Cyn.*4, Luc.*DMort.*26.1 (condemned in *Pseudol.*29), *Gp.*14.20.2, etc.; τῶν θατέρων Iamb.*in Nic.*p.83 P.; θάτερον acc. sg. masc., E. *Ion*[849]. I. *one* or *the other of two*, usu. c. Art. exc. in Poets; freq. of natural pairs, σκαιῇ (sc. χειρὶ) ἔγχος ἔχων, ἑτέρηφι δὲ λάζετο πέτρον Il.16.734; τῇ ἑτέρῃ μὲν.. τῇ δ' ἑτέρῃ.. 14.272, cf. X.*Cyn.*10.11; χειρὶ ἑτέρῃ with *one* hand, Il.12.452, Od.10.171 (but χεὶρ ἑτέρη commonly of the *left* hand, v. infr. IV. 1); ἑτέροιο διὰ κροτάφοιο Il.4.502; χωλὸς δ' ἕτερον πόδα 2.217, cf. Ar.*Ec.*162, Din.1.82; ἀμφότεραι αἱ γνάθοι, ἢ ἡ ἑτέρα X.*Eq.*1.9; ἐκκοπεὶς τὸν ἑ. τῶν ὀφθαλμῶν D.H.5.23; εἰς γόνυ θάτερον Philostr.*Im.*2.20; of pairs in general, Il.5.258, etc.; τὴν ἑ. πύλην *one of the* two gates, Hdt.3.156; ὁ ἑ. τῶν στρατηγῶν Th.4.43; τὸ ἑ. τοῖν δυοῖν τειχοῖν Id.7.24: freq. of alternatives presented, τῶνδε τὰ ἑ. ποιέειν Hdt.4.126; ἑλοῦ γε θάτερ', ἢ.. ἢ.. S.*El.*345; τοῖνδ' ἑλοῦ δυοῖν πότμοιν τὸν ἕ. E.*Ph.*952; δυοῖν ἀγαθοῖν τοῦ ἑτέρου τεύξεσθαι Th.4.28; δυοῖν θάτερα, ἢ.. ἤ.. Pl. *Tht.*187c; ὅταν δυοῖν καλοῖν θάτερον κάλλιον ᾖ, ἢ τῷ ἑτέρῳ τούτοιν ἢ ἀμφοτέροις ὑπερβάλλον κάλλιόν ἐστιν Id.*Grg.*475a: in pl., *one of two parties* or *sets*, Od.11.258; τῶν ἕτεροί γε παῖδα κλαύσονται *one set* of parents, either mine or thine, Il.20.210; δώῃ δ' ἑτέροισί γε νίκην 7.292; ἑτέροισι δὲ κῦδος ἔδωκαν 13.303: freq. with neg., οὐδ' ἕτεροι 11.71. 2. in double clauses ἕτερος (in Prose always ὁ ἕτερος) is generally repeated; ἑ. μὲν δουρὶ.., τῷ δ' ἑ. 21.164; τὸν ἕ., ἕ. δὲ.. Od. 5.266; ἕ. λευκόν, ἑτέρην δὲ μέλαιναν Il.3.103, etc.: but sts. omitted in one clause, [ἕτερος μὲν] κακῶν, ἕ. δὲ ἑάων 24.528, cf. 7.420, *IG*2². 1388.46 (prob.), etc.; ἡ μὲν.., ἡ δ' ἑτέρη Il.22.149, *IG*1².76.50; ἕ..., ὁ δὲ.. Od.8.374; answered by ἄλλος, ἕτερον μὲν κεύθῃ ἐνὶ φρεσίν, ἄλλο δὲ εἴπῃ Il.9.313, cf. Od.7.123; reversely ἄλλῳ ὀρχηστύν, ἑτέρῳ κίθαριν [ἔδωκε] Il.13.731, cf. Pl.*R.*439b, *Tht.*184e; τότε μὲν ἕτερα.., τότε δὲ ἄλλα.. Pl.*Alc.*1.116e; ὁ ἕτερος.., ὁ λοιπός.. X.*An.*4.1.23; ἕτερα.., τὰ δὲ.. S.*OC*1454 (lyr.); later μίαν μὲν... ἑτέραν δέ A.D. *Synt.*172.5; τὴν μίαν.. τὴν δ' ἑτέρην *AP*9.680. 3. repeated in the same clause, ἐξ ἑτέρων ἕτερ' ἐστίν *one* building follows on *another*, Od.17.266; (ἁ) δ' ἀτέρα τὰν ἀτέραν κύλιξ ὠθήτω let *one* cup push on *the other*, Alc.41.5; ἢ θάτερον δεῖ δυστυχεῖν ἢ θάτερον *one party* or *the other*, E.*Ion*[849]; ἕτεροι ἑτέρων ἠξίωσαν ἄρχειν Th.2.64; ἕτερος ἀφ' ἑτέρου θεραπείας ἀναπιμπλάμενοι ἔθνῃσκον ib.51; εἴ τίς τι ἕτερος ἑτέρου προφέρει Id.7.64; ξυμμειγνυμένων ἑτέρων ἑτέροις Ar.*Av.*701; συμφορὰ ἑτέρα ἑτέρους πιέζει *one* calamity oppresses *one, another others*, E.*Alc.* 893 (lyr.); ἑτέρᾳ δ' ἕτερος ἕτερον ὄλβῳ καὶ δυνάμει παρῆλθεν Id.*Ba.*905, cf. S.*OC*231 (anap.); ἄλλη δ' εἰς ἑτέρην ὀλοφύρετο A.R.1.250. 4. = δεύτερος, *second*, ἡ μὲν.., ἡ δ' ἑτέρη.., ἡ δὲ τρίτη.. Od.10.352 sq., cf. Il.16.179, al., X.*Cyr.*3.3.22; ἡ ἑ. πρότασις the *minor* premiss, Arist. *EN*1143ᵇ3: without Art., ἕ. τέρας Hdt.7.57; προσαγορεύεις αὐτὰ ἑτέρῳ ὀνόματι you call them further by a *new* name, Pl.*Phlb.*13a; cf. IV. 1 b. b. with Pronouns of quantity, ordinals, etc., τόσσοι δ' αὖθ' ἕτεροι ποταμοὶ as many *more*, Hes.*Th.*367; ἕτερον τοσοῦτον as much *again*, Hdt.2.149; ἑτέρου τοσούτου χρόνου for as long *again*, Isoc. 4.153; ἕ. τοιαῦτα *other things* of like kind, Hdt.1.120,191; ἑτέρων τοιῶνδε (sc. ἀνθρώπων) ἄρχεις ib.207; τῷ αὐτῷ τρόπῳ.. τῷ ἑτέρῳ in the same way *over again*, Id.2.127; ἄλλα τε τοιαῦθ' ἕτερα μυρία Ar.*Fr.*333.4; χιλίας ἑτέρας [δραχμάς] D.58.6; δεύτερον, τρίτον ἕ. δικαστήριον, Id.23.71,74; ἕ. ἐγώ, of a friend, Pythag.ap.Iamb.*in Nic.* p.35 P.; ἕτεροι αὐτοί *second* selves, Arist.*EN*1161ᵇ28; εὕρηκε τὸν ἕ., τὸν σέ Men.474. II. without Art., *another*, of many, with a sense of *difference*, Il.4.306, Od.7.123, Ar.*Ach.*422, *Lys.*66, etc.; ἕ. αὖ τις Id. *Eq.*949; ἕ. αὖ Id.*Pax* 295, etc.; ἕτερα ἄττα Pl.*Tht.*188b; repeated ἑτέραν χἀτέραν τρικυμίαν Men.536.8: with neg., οἷα οὐχ ἕτερα [ἐγένετο] such as none *like them* had happened, Th.1.23; ναυμαχία.. οἵα οὐχ ἑτέρα τῶν προτέρων Id.7.70; οὐδεμιᾶς ἧσσων μᾶλλον ἑτέρας ib. 29 (s.v.l.); οὐχ ἕτερον ἀλλά.. *none other than*, Plu.2.671b, cf. *UPZ* 71.9 (ii B.C.). b. οἱ ἕ. *the rest*, Hdt.4.169. c. ὁ ἕ. '*one's neighbour*', ἀγαπᾶν τὸν ἕ. *Ep.Rom.*13.6, cf. *Ep.Gal.*6.4. III. *of another kind, different*, ἕ. δέ με θυμὸς ἔρυκεν Od.9.302; τὸ μὲν ἕ., τὸ δὲ ἕ., i.e. they are *different*, Pl.*Men.*97d, cf. *R.*346a; ἕ. τε καὶ ἀνόμοιον Id.*Smp.* 186b; τὸ δὲ ταὐτὸν ἕ. ἀποφαίνειν καὶ τὸ θάτερον ταὐτόν Id.*Sph.*259d; ἑ. ἤδη ἦν καὶ οὐχ ὁ αὐτός D.34.12; ἑτέραν ἔδωκεν παντὶ τῷ κόσμῳ ὄψιν *OGI*458.7 (i B.C.); ἑ. εὐαγγέλιον *Ep.Gal.*1.6: coupled with ἄλλος, χἀτέρους ἄλλους πόνους and other *different* toils, E.*Supp.*573 (s.v.l.), cf. *Or.*345 (dub. l.); 'Ρόδον καὶ ἄλλας ἑτέρας πόλεις D.15.27; ἕτερον τό τ' ἀλγεῖν καὶ θεωρεῖν ἔστ' ἴσως Philem.75.7; ἕτερα φρονῶν καὶ δημηγορῶν Din.1.17: c. gen., *other than, different from*, φίλους.. ἑτέρους τῶν νῦν ὄντων Th.1.28, cf. Pl.*Prt.*333a, D.10.44, etc.; ἕτερον, ἕτερα ἢ.., E.*Or.*345, X.*Cyr.*1.6.2; παρὰ ταῦτα πάντα ἕτερόν τι Pl.*Phd.*74a; ἕτερα πολιτείας εἴδη παρὰ μοναρχίαν Arist.*Pol.*1294ᵃ25, cf. 1286ᵇ 21. 2. *other than should be*, euphem. for κακός, παθεῖν μὲν εὖ, παθεῖν δὲ θάτερα S.*Ph.*503; ἀγάθ' ἢ θάτερα, ἵνα μηδὲν εἴπω φλαῦρον D. 22.12: abs., δαίμων ἕ. Pi.*P.*3.34; λέκτρα, συμφοραί, E.*Med.*639 (lyr.), *HF*1238; ἐὰν τὰ ἕ. ψηφίσωνται οἱ δικασταί D.48.30; πλέον θάτερον ἐποίησαν did more *harm* (than good), Isoc.19.25, cf. Pl.*Phd.*114e, *Euthd.*280e, Aristid.2.117 J. IV. Special Phrases: 1. elliptical, mostly in dat. fem., a. τῇ ἑτέρᾳ (sc. χειρί), Ep. ἑτέρῃ or ἑτέρηφι, *with one hand* (v. sub init.); *with the left hand*, Od.3.441, Il.22.80, Theoc.24.45: hence prov., οὐ τῇ ἑτέρᾳ ληπτός not to be caught with *one* hand, Pl.*Sph.*226a; ἐκ δ' ἑτέρης A.R.1.1115, *AP* 9.650 (Leont.). b. θατέρᾳ (sc. ἡμέρᾳ) *on the morrow*, S.*OT*782, E.*Rh.*449; τῆς ἑτέρας Pl.*Cri.*44a; but τῇ ἑτέρᾳ *on the following* (i.e. *the third*) day, X.*Cyr.*4.6.10. c. (sc. ὁδῷ) *in another* or *a different way*, καὶ τῇδε φῦναι χἀτέρᾳ S.*OC*1444; *another way*, τρέπεσθαι Ar.*Nu.*812; ἑτέρᾳ πῃ Id.*Eq.*35; τότ' ἄλλοσ'.., θατέρᾳ δὲ.. S.*Tr.* 272; θατέρᾳ.., θατέρᾳ.. *in one way.., in the other..*, Henioch.5.16; ἑτέρηφι Hes.*Op.*216: acc. ἑτέραν ἐκτρέπεσθαι Luc.*Tim.*5. 2. adverb. with Preps.: a. ἐπὶ θάτερα *to the one* or *the other side, one* or *the other way*, ἐπὶ μὲν θάτερα.., ἐπὶ θ. δὲ.. Hp.*Art.*7; τότε μὲν ἐπὶ θάτερα, τότε δ' ἐπὶ θ. Pl.*Sph.*259c: also with another Prep., ἐς τὰ ἐπὶ θάτερα *to* or *on the other side*, Th.1.87; ἐκ τοῦ ἐπὶ θάτερα *from the other side*, Id.7.37; ἐκ μὲν τοῦ ἐπὶ θ., ἐκ δὲ τοῦ ἐπὶ θ. Pl.*Prt.*314e: c. gen., ἐς τὰ ἐπὶ θ. τοῦ ποταμοῦ Th.7.84; εἰς τἀπὶ θ. τῆς πόλεως X.*HG*6.2.7; τὸ ἐπὶ θάτερον τῆς ῥινός Hp.*Art.*35. b. κατὰ θάτερα *on the one* or *other side*, κατὰ θ. ἀστός D.57.30; ψόφου κατὰ θ. προσπεσόντος Plu.*Brut.*51, etc.; but καθ' ἕτερα *at other points*, Th.7.42. V. Adv. **ἑτέρως** *in one* or *the other way*, opp. ἀμφοτέρως, Pl.*Tht.*181e; ἑ. τε καὶ ἑ., = ἀμφοτέρως, Id.*Phdr.*235a; τοῦ σκέλους ἑ. ἔχειν, = ἑτεροσκελὴς εἶναι, Philostr.*VA*3.39. 2. *differently*, rarely in Poetry, οὐχ ἑ. τις ἐρεῖ Theoc.*Ep.*10.3; ἑ. ἔχειν to be *different*, Ar.*Pl.*371: freq. in Prose, ὡς ἑ. *in the other way* (cf. ὡς), ἢν ἡ ἑτέρη γνάθος ἐκστῇ ὡς ἑ. χρὴ τὴν ἐπίδεσιν ἄγειν Hp.*Art.*34, cf. Pl.*Sph.*266a, etc.; ἐάν τε καλῶς, ἐάν θ' ὡς ἑ. D.18.85, cf. 212: c. gen., *differently from*, ἑ. πως τῶν εἰωθότων Pl.*Plt.*295d; ἑ. ἤπερ.. Ael.*NA*12.28. 3. *otherwise than should be, badly, wrongly*, once in Hom., ἑ. ἐβόλοντο Od.1.234; εἰ καὶ ἑ. τοῦτο ἀπέβη *SIG*851.10 (Marc. Aur.); εἴ τι ἑ. φρονεῖτε *Ep.Phil.* 3.15.

ἑτερο-σήμαντος, ον, *of different signification*, Eust.1411.43. Adv. -τως Sch.Hes.*Sc.*354. **-σκελής**, ές, *with uneven legs*, *Hippiatr.*13; of a triangle, *scalene*, Poll.4.161. **-σκιος**, ον, (σκιά) *throwing a shadow only one way* (at noon), of those who live north and south of the tropics, Posidon.ap.Str.2.5.43, Cleom.1.7. **-σσυτος**, ον, *darting from the other side*, Nonn.*D.*38.244. **-στοιχος**, ον, *belonging to the other series*, Hsch., Phot. **-στομος**, ον, *one-edged*, πέλεκυς Poll.1.137. II. ἑ. φάλαγξ a marching formation in which the λοχαγοί of the leading κέρας are on the r., those of the rear κέρας on the l., or vice versa, Ascl.*Tact.*10.22, etc. Adv. -μως ib.11.4. **-στροφος**, ον, *consisting of two different strophes*, Heph.*Poëm.* 5.3, Sch.Ar.*Nu.*263. **-σφυκτος**, ον, *having one wrist-pulse different from the other*, Marcellin.*Puls.*147:—hence **-σφυξία**, ἡ, Gal. 18(2).301. **-σχημάτιστος**, ον, *differently formed*: τὸ ἑ. *change of grammatical form*, as a figure of speech, Phoeb.*Fig.*1.5. **-σχήμων**, ον, *of varying shape*, φύλλα Thphr.*HP*1.10.1; *altered in shape, distorted*, Luc.*Hist.Conscr.*51. Adv. -μόνως Vett.Val.333.20:—later **-σχημος**, ον, *irregular*, διαλείμματα Heliod.ap.Orib.48.20.15. **-ταγής**, ές, *belonging to a different series* or *order*, opp. ὁμοταγής, Procl.*Inst.*21, Dam.*Pr.*38.

ἑτερότης, ητος, ἡ, *otherness, difference*, λέγω γένους διαφορὰν -τητα Arist.*Metaph.*1058ᵃ8, cf. *Ph.*201ᵇ20, Epicur.*Nat.*49 G., etc.; opp. ταυτότης, Plu.2.1013a, etc.: pl., Phld.*Rh.*1.8 S. 2. *civil discord*, ἑ. καὶ διαφορά Plu.*Num.*17.

ἑτερο-τράχηλος [ᾰ], ον, *with neck turned to one side*, of Alexander, Tz.*H.*11 No.368 tit. **-τροπος**, ον, *of different sort* or *fashion*, κακόν Ar.*Th.*724; γαλεῶν ἑ. φῦλα Opp.*H.*1.379; *various*, τύχης ἑ. ὁρμή *AP*9.768 (Agath.), cf. Nonn.*D.*2.669, 7.7.

ἑτερ-ούας, ὁ, ἡ, τό, *one-eared, one-handled*, *An.Ox.*2.7, Eust. 870.2. **-ουΐς**, ΐδος, ἡ, *vessel with one handle*, Hsch.

ἑτερούσιος, v. ἑτεροούσιος.

ἑτεροφᾰνής, ές, *diverse in appearance*, Gal.18(1).777.

ἑτεροφθαλμ-ία, ἡ, *difference of the two eyes*, *Hippiatr.*13, Dem. Ophth.ap.Simon.Jan. s. v. ethereoftalmia. **-ος**, ον, *one-eyed*, D. 24.141, Arist.*Metaph.*1023ᵃ5; ἑ. γενομένη ἡ Ἑλλάς, metaph., of the proposed destruction of Athens, Leptines ap. Arist.*Rh.*1411ᵃ5, cf. Demad.65 B., Plu.2.803a. **II.** *with different-coloured eyes*, *Gp.* 16.2.1.

ἑτερο-φορέομαι, Pass., = ἑτερορρεπέω, Tim.*Lex.* s. v. ταλαντοῦσθαι. **-φρονέω**, *to be distraught*, Epicur.*Sent.Vat.*17. **-φροσύνη**, ἡ, *difference of opinion, discord*, Iamb.*VP*7.34. **-φρων**, ον, gen. ονος, *thinking strangely, raving*, Tryph.439; λύσσα *AP*1.19 (Claudian.), cf. Nonn.*D.*9.49. **-φυής**, ές, *of different nature*, Anon. *in Cat.* 61.8. **-φῦλος**, ον, *of another race* or *breed*, Ael.*NA*16.27, Scymn. 101; opp. πολίτης, Iamb.*VP*16.69: generally, *differing in kind*, πρός τι Dam.*Pr.*74; *of different kinds*, Simp. *in Ph.*890.16. **-φῦτον** δένδρον, τό, *a grafted* tree, Jul.*Ep.*180. **-φωνέομαι**, *to be different in sound*, Eust.1626.3. **-φωνία**, ἡ, *diversity of note*, ἑ. καὶ ποικιλία τῆς λύρας Pl.*Lg.*812d; περὶ ἑτεροφωνίας τῶν ὁμογενῶν, title of work, Thphr.*Fr.*181. **-φωνος**, ον, *of different voice*: hence, *foreign*, A.*Th.* 170 (lyr.). **II.** *discrepant*, opp. σύμφωνος, Porph.*Chr.*15. **-χηλος**, ον, *with unequal hoofs*, *Hippiatr.*109. **-χροέω**, *to be of different colour*, *AB*386; *to be discoloured*, of bones, Orib.46.11.7. **-χροια**, ἡ, *difference of colour*, Hierocl.p.21 A., Xenocr.28, Gal.14. 325. **-χροιος**, ον, = ἑτερόχρους, Polem.*Phgn.*9. **-χροιότης**, ητος, ἡ, *difference of colour*, Pyrrho ap.D.L.9.86. **-χρονος**, ον, *of different times*: τὸ ἑ. *a change of tense*, as a figure of speech, Phoeb.*Fig.* 1.5. **-χροος**, ον, contr. **-χρους**, ουν, *of different colour*, Thphr.*CP* 5.3.2; *of varied colours*, χορὸς ὀρνίθων Nonn.*D.*5.186: heterocl. dat. and acc. ἑτερόχροϊ, -χροα, ib.12.305, 5.58. **II.** *piebald*, βοῦς Porph. *Abst.*4.7. **-χρωμᾰτέω**, = ἑτεροχροέω, *Gp.*2.6.37. **-χρωμος**, ον, = ἑτερόχροος, *Hippiatr.*14. **-χρως**, ωτος, ὁ, ἡ, = ἑτερόχροος, Poll.9.98. **II.** ἑτερόχρωτες ὕπνοι sleep *with one of different sex*, Luc.*Am.*42.

ἑτέρσετο, v. τερσαίνω.

ἑτέρ-ωθεν (or -θε Hes.*Sc.*281, cf. A.D.*Adv.*194.4), Adv. *from the other side*, Il.1.247, al.; ἐκ δ' ἑτέρωθεν v.l. in Theoc.22.91. **2.** in pregnant sense with Verbs of rest, *on the other side, opposite*, ἕστηκ' Il.3.230, cf. 6.247. **II.** *from another quarter, from outside*, Lys. 17.4, Pl.*Lg.*702c, Arist.*EN*1121ᵃ34, Bato 5.9. **-ωθι**, Adv. *on the other side*, ἔνθεν.., ἑ. δὲ.. Od.12.235: in later Prose, Ph.1.301, Jul.*Or.*2.69a. **II.** = ἄλλοθι, *elsewhere*, Il.5.351, 15.348, Od.4.531, Pl.*Prm.*146c, etc.; οὐδαμόθι ἑ. nowhere *else*, Hdt.3.113; ἑ. πανταχοῦ anywhere *else*, Antipho 6.39; λέγει ἑ. ὅτι *in another passage*, Ph.1.372, cf. Hdt.9.58: c. gen., ἑ. τοῦ λόγου *in another part* of my story, Id.6.19; ἑ. που τοῦ σώματος Arist.*PA*663ᵇ3. **III.** *at another time*, τότε μὲν.., ἑ. δὲ.. Hdt.3.35. **-ώνιος**, ον, *another's property*, Eust.1214.27, cf. Hsch. **-ωνῠμέω**, Math., *to have a different denominator*, Nicom.*Ar.*1.17. **-ώνῠμος**, ον, *with different designation*, Simp. *in Cat.*38, Procl. *in Prm.*p.955 S. **II.** *with different denominator*, Nicom.*Ar.*1.13, al. **-ωνῠμία**, ἡ, *difference of name*, Eust.304.24. **-ωσε**, Adv. *to the other side*, Il.4.492, Od.16. 179; ἔνθεν μὲν.., ἑ. δὲ.. Pl.*Sph.*224a; *on one side*, ἑ. κάρη βάλεν Il. 8.306, cf. Od.22.17. **2.** in pregnant sense with certain Verbs, *on the other side*, οἱ δ' ἑ. καθῖζον Il.20.151; κἂν ἑ. πατάξῃ τις D.4.40. **II.** = ἄλλοσε, *elsewhither, aside*, ἑ. λιασθεὶς Il.23.231; κύνες ἑ. φόβηθεν Od.16.163, etc.; ἑ. τρέχων Ar.*Ach.*828; also εἰς ἑ. A.R.4.1315. **2.** *elsewhere*, Luc.*Charid.*22.

ἑτέρωτα, Aeol. for ἑτέρωθι, Sapph.1.5, cf. A.D.*Adv.*194.5.

ἔτετμε, v. τέτμον.

ἐτέτυμον· ἀληθές, ἢ ἀληθῶς, Hsch. **ἐτεωνέω**· ἀληθεύω, and **ἐτεώνια**· ἀληθῆ, Id.; cf. ἐτεός.

ἐτήρ, ῆρος, ὁ, *one year old*, ἐτῆρας ἀμνοὺς θεοῖς ἔρεξ' ἐπακτίοις S.*Fr.* 751 (v.l. εὐείρας).

ἐτηρίς, ίδος, ἡ, *term of years*, Hierocl.*Facet.*62.

ἔτης, ὁ, Elean ϝέτας (v. infr.), in Hom. always in pl. **ἔται**, οἱ:— *clansmen*, i.e. *kinsmen and dependents of a great house*, ἀμύνων σοῖσιν ἔτησι Il.6.262; δαινύντα γάμον πολλοῖσι ἔτησιν Od.4.3; παῖδάς τε κασιγνήτους τε ἔτας τε Il.6.239, cf. Od.15.273; ἔται καὶ ἀνεψιοί Il.9. 464; ἔτας καὶ ἑταίρους 7.295; γείτονες ἠδὲ ἔται Od.4.16. **II.** later, *citizen*, ἔταις ἀμαχανίαν ἀλέξων τεοῖσιν Pi.*Pae.*6.10, cf. Epic. in *Arch. Pap.*7.4; τὼς ἔτας καττὰ πάτρια δικάζεσθαι Foed.Lac. in Th.5.79: in sg., *a private citizen*, opp. those who hold office, πρός σε.. ὡς ἔτην λέγω A.*Supp.*247; οὔτε δῆμος οὔτ' ἔτης ἀνήρ Id.*Fr.*377; ἀρχῷ, φωτὶ δ' οὐκ ἔτῃ πρέπων E.*Fr.*1014; αἴτε ϝέτας αἴτε τελεστά *SIG*9.8 (Olympia, vi B.C.), cf. 141.12 (Corc. nigra, iv B.C.), *Mus.Belg.*16.70 (Athens, ii A.D.), *IG*5(2).20 (Tegea). (On the breathing, see Hdn.Gr.2.55.)

ἐτησ-ίαι, οἱ, gen. ἐτησίων Hdn.Gr.1.425: (ἔτος):—with or without ἄνεμοι, *periodic winds*, esp. those blowing from north-west during the summer, Hdt.2.20, 6.140, cf. Hp.*Aër.*10, D.4.31, Arist.*Mete.*361ᵇ35; of the *southerly monsoon* in the Indian Ocean, Arr.*An.*6.21.1; Εὖροι ἐ. Posidon.ap.Str.3.2.5. **II.** sg., as nickname of Antipater, who reigned for forty-five days, *King of the Dog-days*, *PCair.Zen.*19.6 (iii B.C.), Porph.*Fr.Hist.*4.6. **-ιάς**, άδος, poet. fem. of sq., epith. of αὔρη, Nonn.*D.*12.286. **-ιος**, ον, and in Hp. η, ον: (ἔτος):— *lasting a year*, πένθος οὐκ ἐ. E.*Alc.*336; προστασία f.l. in Th.2.80; ἐτησίους ἄρχειν to govern *for a year*, D.C.60.24. **2.** *annual*, ὧραι Plu.2.993e; θυσίαι Th.5.11, etc., cf. *SIG*1024.24 (Myconus); φόρος *IG*7.2227 (Thisbe); ἐτήσιοι πρόσιτ' ἀεί Cratin.23; βορέαι ἐ., = ἐτησίαι, Arist.*Pr.*940ᵃ35; ἐ. πνεύματα Arr.*Ind.*21.1. Adv. -ίως Sch.Lyc. 107: neut. as Adv., τρυγόωσιν ἐτήσιον *AP*5.226 (Maced.).

ἐτητῠμ-ία, poet. -ίη, ἡ, *truth*, Call.*Aet.*3.1.76, *AP*9.771 (Jul.), Max.462, Orph.*Fr.*280.7. **-ος**, ον, poet. redupl. for ἔτυμος, *true*, οὐκ ἔσθ' ὅδε μῦθος ἐ. Od.23.62; ἐ. ἄγγελος ἔλθῶν Il.22.438; ἐτήτυμα μυθησαίμην Hes.*Op.*10; τοῦτ' ἀγόρευσον ἐτήτυμον tell me this *true*, Od.1.174; τοῦτ' ἐ.; c. inf., is this *true*, that..? A.*Pers.*737 (troch.); εἰ λέγεις ἐτήτυμα S.*Ph.*1290; τὸ δ' ἐ. but *the truth* is.., Ar.*Pax* 119. **2.** of persons, *truthful*, οὐ ψευδόμαντις.., ἀλλ' ἐ. E.*Or.*1667; ἐ. στόμα Id.*IT*1085. **3.** *genuine, real*, κείνῳ δ' οὐκέτι νόστος ἐ. for him there remains no *true, real* return, Od.3.241; ἀλάθεια, κλέος, Pi.*O.*10(11). 54, *N.*7.63; ἐ. Διὸς κόρα A.*Ch.*948; παῖς ἐ. γεγώς S.*Tr.*1064; χρυσός Theoc.12.37: in late Prose, Them.*Or.*22.279d. **II.** as Adv., in neut. ἐτήτυμον, *truly, really*, Od.4.157, Il.13.111, 18.128, Archil.62: regul. Adv. -μως A.*Ag.*167 (lyr.), 682 (lyr.); ὡς ἐ. S.*El.*1452.

ἔτι [ῐ], Adv.: **I.** of Time, **1.** of the Present, *yet, still*, ἔ. μοι μένος ἔμπεδον Il.5.254; ἔ. τυτθὸν ἐόντα 6.222; εἰ Ζεὺς ἔ. Ζεύς S.*OC*623; ἔτ' ἐκ βρέφεος *ever* since babyhood, *AP*9.567 (Antip.); ἔ. καὶ νῦν Il. 1.455; ἔ. καὶ ἐκ παρόντων v.l. in Th.7.77; ἔτ' ἂν ἐκ τῶνδε θεὸς χρῄζων θείη A.*Ch.*340; ἔ. καὶ νυνί Pl.*Smp.*215d; νῦν ἔ. ζεῖ A.*Th.*708 (lyr.), cf. *Ag.*818. **2.** of the Past, mostly with impf., ἀήθεσσον γὰρ ἔτ' αὐτῶν Il.10.493, cf. Hdt.9.102, Th.5.111, etc.: with aor., Pl.*Prt.*310c, etc.; ἔ. πρότερον, πρόσθεν, Th.8.45, Pl.*Sph.*242d: with the sense, *already*, γεγονέναι ἔ. οὐχ ἧττον ἢ εἶναι Id.*Men.*93a. **3.** of the Future, *yet, longer*, ἄλγε' ἔδωκεν.. ἠδ' ἔ. δώσει Il.1.96, cf. 5.465: c. opt., ἔ... φιλέοι Od.15.305: c. imper., μή τις ἔ... ἔστω 2.230; *hereafter*, A.*Pr.*907, S.*El.*66, Ar.*V.*758 (anap.), etc. **4.** with a neg., no *longer*, οὐδὲ.. ἔ. παρέμειναν D.H.5.46; v. οὐκέτι, μηκέτι. **II.** of Degree, *still, besides*, ἐς δεκάτην γενεὴν ἕτερόν γ' ἔ. βόσκοι *another* (and another and so on), Od.14.325; ἔτ' ἄλλο Hes.*Op.*157, cf. Il.6.411, Od.11.623, S.*Ant.*218, etc.; τίν' οὖν ἔτ' ἄλλον..; A.*Ch.*114; πρὸς τοῖσδ' ἔ., πρὸς τούτοις ἔ. (cf. προσέτι), S.*Ph.*1339, Ar.*Nu.*720 (anap.); ἔ. τε and *besides, nay more*, Pl.*Phdr.*279a; ἔ. τοσόνδε this *further* point, Id.*Tht.* 184b; ἔ. δὲ καί Th.1.80, etc.; πρῶτον μὲν.., ἔπειτα δὲ.., ἔ. δὲ.. X.*An.*6.6.13; ἔ. καί alone, τά τε εἴδωλα, ἔ. καὶ τὰ γεγραμμένα Pl. *Sph.*239d; ἔτι καὶ ἔ. ἀεί *Theol.Ar.*30. **2.** freq. to strengthen a Comp., ἔ. μᾶλλον *yet* more, Il.14.97, 362; μᾶλλον ἔ. Od.18.22; ἔ. καὶ μ. Pi.*P.*10.57; καὶ ἔ. καὶ μᾶλλον Ael.*NA*16.24; ἔ. πλέον Hdt.7.6; πλέον ἔ. Th.1.80; παῖς τε κἄτι τοῦδ' ἀνούστερος A.*Pr.*987; πότμῳ τῷ νῦν.. κἄτι τοῦδ' ἐχθίονι S.*OT*272, cf. *El.*559, 1189. **3.** with the Posit., ἔ. ἄνω *yet* higher up, X.*An.*7.5.9; ἔ. μάλα Ar.*Pax* 53, 462, *Ra.* 864. (Skt. *áti* 'beyond', Lat. *et*, Goth. *iþ* 'but', 'however'.)

ἔτλην, ης, η, aor. 2 of *τλάω.

ἐτν-ηρός, ά, όν, (ἔτνος) *like soup*, ἕψημα Phaenias ap.Ath.9.406c. **-ήρῠσις**, εως, ἡ, (ἀρύω A) *soup-ladle*, Ar.*Ach.*245, *Fr.*779. **-ίτης**, Dor. -ίτας [ῑ], ἄρτος, ὁ, = λεκιθίτης, Eucrat.ap.Ath.3.111b, Seleuc. ib.114b.

ἐτνοδόνος, ον, *soup-stirring*, τορύνα *AP*6.305 (Leon.), 306 (Aristo).

ἔτνος, εος, τό, *thick soup* made with pease or beans, Ar.*Ach.*246, *Ra.*62, 506, Pl.*Hp.Ma.*290d; ἔ. πίσινον Ar.*Eq.*1171; φάκινον Hp. *Acut.*(*Sp.*)53; κυάμινον Gal.*Vict.Att.*53; as poultice, τὸ ἔτνος τὸ ἐκ τῶν κυάμων Lycus ap.Orib.9.35.1. (ἔτνος from a false deriv. from ἕω, *EM*387.9, etc.)

ἑτοιμ-άζω, pf. ἡτοίμακα Plb.3.72.6: pf. Pass. ἡτοίμασμαι both in med. and pass. sense (v. infr.): (ἕτοιμος):—*get ready, prepare*, ἐμοὶ γέρας αὐτίχ' ἑτοιμάσατ' Il.1.118; [νέας] Hdt.6.95; στρατιώτας *Act. Ap.*23.23; ὁδὸν Lxx *Is.*40.3, al.; ἔγκλημα μικρὸν αἰτίαν τε S.*Tr.*361; δῶμα E.*Alc.*364; βουλήν Id.*Heracl.*472; δάκρυα δ' ἑτοιμάζουσι *to those furnishing* them, Id.*Supp.*454; ἀργύριον ῥητὸν Th.2.7, etc.; ἑαυτὸν ἵνα.. *Apoc.*8.6. **II.** Med., *cause to be prepared*, ὄφρ' ἱρὸν ἑτοιμασσαίατ' Ἀθήνῃ Il.10.571; ἑτοιμάσσαντο δὲ ταύρους Od.13.184, cf. Hdt. 8.24; ἑτοιμασάμενος ἃ δεῖ *Inscr.Prien.*55.34 (ii B.C.). **2.** with pf. Pass. ἡτοίμασμαι, *prepare for oneself*, τἄλλα ἡτοιμάζετο *made his* other *arrangements*, Th.4.77; ὅπως ἑτοιμάσαιντο τιμωρίαν Id.1.58; πλείονα ἡτοιμασμένος X.*Cyr.*3.3.5; τροφὴν ἡτοιμασμένοι D.23.209; τὰ πρὸς τὸν βίον Epicur.*Sent.Vat.*30, cf. Metrod.*Fr.*53. **3.** *prepare oneself, make oneself ready*, c. inf., X.*Ap.*8; πρὸς τὴν χειμασίαν Plb. 3.105.11. **III.** Pass., *to be prepared*, ἔλεγε ἡτοιμάσθαι *that preparations had been made*, Th.6.64, cf. 7.62, etc.; ἑ. τι *to be prepared with..*, Plb.8.30.7. **-ᾰσία**, ἡ, *readiness*, πρὸς τὰς ὑπουργίας Hp. *Decent.*12; εἰς ἑ. ὑμῶν παρέχειν to place at your *disposal*, J.*AJ*10.1. 2. **II.** *preparation*, ἀρμένων Aen.Tact.21.1, cf. Lxx *Ps.*9.38(10. 17); τροφῆς ib.*Wi.*13.12; *equipment*, ἐν -ασίᾳ εὐαγγελίου *Ep.Eph.* 6.15.

ἑτοιμό-δακρυς, υ, gen. υος, *easily moved to tears*, Eust.115.30. **-εγρήγορος** ὕπνος *light* sleep, Steph. *in Hp.*1.146 D. **-θάνᾰτος** [θᾰ], ον, *ready for death*, Str.15.1.59. **-κόλλιξ**, ῑκος, ὁ, *one who gives rolls freely*, Com.Adesp.1094. **-κοπία**, ἡ, *officiousness*, Hp.*Praec.* 12 (s.v.l.). **-λόγος**, ον, *talkative*, Phot. s.v. εὐρεσίλογος. **-μεμφής**, ές, *ready to censure*, Eust.873.3. **-πειθής**, ές, *ready to obey*, Hdn.*Epim.*38. **-πτωτος**, ον, *inclined to fall*, gloss on ἀκροσφαλής, *AB*367. **-πωλεῖον**, τό, *cook-shop where dressed meats are sold*, *BGU* 1647.6 (ii A.D.). **-πώλης**, ου, ὁ, *one who keeps such a shop*, Demetr. Astrol. in *Cat.Cod.Astr.*1.106. **-πωλις**, ιδος, ἡ, = -πωλεῖον, *Gloss.*

ἑτοῖμος, ον, also fem. ἑτοίμη Il.9.425, Hp.*Art.*66, -μᾱ S.*El.*1079 (lyr.), etc.:—in v B.C. and later **ἕτοιμος**, η, ον, or ος, ον, cf. Hdn.Gr. 2.938:—*at hand, ready, prepared*, ὀνείαθ' ἑτοῖμα προκείμενα Od.14.453, etc.; τὶν δ' αἶνος ἑτοῖμος Pi.*O.*6.12; [τὰ κρέα] εἶχε ἕτοιμα Hdt.1.119, cf. 3.123; ἑτοιμοτάταν ἐπὶ δαῖτα Theoc.13.63, cf. E.*Cyc.*357 (lyr.); ἕ. χρήματα money *in hand*, Hdt.5.31; ἐξ ἑ. *in ready money*, *POxy.*2106.23 (iv A.D.); ἕ. ἀεὶ παρακείμενον ἐκμαγεῖον Pl.*Ti.*72c; ἕ. ποιήσασθαι to make *ready*, Hdt.1.11; ὡς ἑτοῖμα ἦν Th.2.3; ἐπειδὴ αὐτῷ ἑ. ἦν ib.98; ἐξ ἑτοίμου *at once and without hesitation, immediately, offhand*, ἐξ ἑ. λαμβάνειν Isoc.5.96; ἐξ ἑ. ὑπακούειν X.*Oec.*14.3; ἐξ ἑτοιμοτάτου διώκειν Id.*Cyr.*5.3.57; ἐξ ἑ. φίλον εἶναι Id.*Mem.*2.6.16; γίνεται ταῦτα ἐξ -οτάτου are *most likely to attack*, Hp.*Prog.*24; ἐν ἑτοίμῳ ἐστί Epicur.*Ep.*3 p.62 U., cf. Theoc.22.61; ἐν ἑ. ἔχειν Plb.2.34.2, *2Ep.Cor.*10.6, etc.; ἑτοιμότερα γέλωτος λίβη tears *that came more readily than*.., A.*Ch.*448; τὰ ἑ. *that which is ready to hand*, ἐπὶ τὰ ἑ. μᾶλλον τρέπονται Th.1.20; τὰ ἑ. βλάψαι ib.70; τοῖς ἑ. περὶ τῶν ἀφανῶν.. κινδυνεύειν Id.6.9. 2. of the future, *sure to come, certain*, αὐτίκα γάρ τοι ἔπειτα μεθ' Ἕκτορα πότμος ἑ. Il.18.96; χώλωσις ἑτοίμη τοῖσι περιγινομένοισι Hp.*Art.*66; also, *easy to be done, feasible*, ἐπεὶ οὔ σφισιν ἥδε γ' ἑτοίμη (sc. μῆτις) Il.9.425; ἕ. [ἐστι] τὸ διαφθαρῆναι *imminent*, Plu.2.706c: c. inf., ἕ. μᾶλλόν [ἐστι] ἀπεχθάνεσθαι Pl.*R.*567a, cf. E.*HF*86; οὐ γάρ τι ἕ. μεταπεῖσαι it is not *easy*.., Paus.2.23.6. 3. of the past, *carried into effect, realized*, ταῦτα ἑ. τετεύχαται Il.14.53; ἤδ' ἄρ' ἑτοῖμα τέτυκτο and this promise has been *made good*, Od.8.384. II. of persons, *ready, active, zealous*, ἕ. ἦν ἐμοὶ σειραφόρος A.*Ag.*842; τινι *in* or *for* a thing, Pi.*O.*4.16; ἐς τι for a thing, Hdt.8.96; πρός τι X.*Mem.*4.5.12: c. dat. pers., *ready to assist* or *go with* him, etc., Pi.*N.*4.74, Hdt.1.70: c. inf., *ready to* do, ib.42,113, al.; ἐπιστενάχειν πᾶς τις ἕ. A.*Ag.*791; χωρεῖν ἑ. S.*Aj.*813, cf. *Ant.*264, Antipho 6.23, Ar.*V.*341 (lyr.); ὑπακούειν ἑτοιμότεροι *too ready*.., Th.4.61; θηρία ἕ. διαμάχεσθαι Pl.*Smp.*207b: c. Art., τὸ μὴ βλέπειν ἑτοίμα S.*El.*1079 (lyr.); ἦν ἕτοιμος, abs., he was *ready*, Hdt.1.10; ἑ. ἔχειν τινάς Id.3.45; ἑ. ποιέεσθαί τινας Id.5.86. 2. of the mind, *ready, bold*, λῆμα Ar.*Nu.*458 (lyr.); ἡ γνώμη Th.4.123; τὸ ἕ. *readiness, resolution*, E.*Or.*1106; τὸ ἕ. τῆς γνώμης Philostr.*Her.*8.1; τὰ θερμά τε καὶ ἕ. τῶν θηρίων Id.*VA* 7.14. III. Adv. -μως *readily, willingly*, Th.1.80; ἑ. ἔχω τελευτᾶν I am *ready* to die, Demad.4, cf. D.18.161, *PAmh.*2.32.6 (ii B.C.), *Act.Ap.*21.13; ἑ. ἥκειν X.*An.*2.5.2; διδόναι *IG*2².956.24; ἑ. παρορᾷς *evidently*, Pl.*Hp.Ma.*300c: Comp. ἑτοιμότερον Is.4.14, -οτέρως Alex.Trall.12: Sup. -ότατα Pl.*Plt.*290a.

ἑτοιμότης, ητος, ἡ, *readiness*, πρὸς τὸ ποιεῖν ὁτιοῦν D.54.36; λόγων ἑ. *power* of speaking *offhand*, Plu.2.6e, cf. *Cam.*32: pl., M.Ant.4.12; of things, ἑ. κτήσεως Phld.*Oec.*p.46 J.; *aptitude*, Ph.1.392. II. *predisposition*, Plot.6.1.8; in Medic. sense, Gal.7.291.

ἑτοιμο-τόμος, ον, *ready to cut*, χεῖρες *AP*9.282 (Antip. Thess.). **-φθαρτος**, ον, *easily decomposed*, Steph. *in Hp.*1.102 D.

ἔτος, εος, τό, irreg. dat. ἔτῃ *IG*2.1059.18:—*year*, τῶν προτέρων ἐτέων in bygone *years*, Il.11.691; τόδ' ἐεικοστὸν ἔ. ἐστὶν ἐξ οὗ.. 24.765, cf. Od.2.89, 19.222; ὅτε.. ὀγδόον μοι ἐπιπλόμενον ἔ. ἦλθε 7.261; ἔ. ἐνιαυτῶν, v. ἐνιαυτός; ἑκάστου ἔτους Pl.*Phd.*58b; ἀν' ἕκαστον ἔ. Thphr.*HP*4.4.4; ἀνὰ πᾶν ἔ. *AP*9.430 (Crin.); ἀνὰ πάντα ἔτεα Hdt. 8.65; δι' ἔτους πέμπτου every fifth *year*, Ar.*Pl.*584; κατὰ ἔ. every *year*, Th.4.53, D.S.3.2, *Ev.Luc.*2.41, etc. (freq. καθ' ἔ., as *PPetr.*3 p.34 (iii B.C.) and later); ἔ. εἰς ἔ. *year* after *year*, S.*Ant.*340 (lyr.); δι' ἔτους *annually*, Ph.1.19,378; εἰς ἔ. Theoc.*Ep.*13.4; εἰς ἔ. ἐξ ἔτεος Id.18.15; ἔ. ἐξ ἔτους Lxx *Le.*25.50; παρὰ ἔ. every other *year*, Paus.9.32.3 (but πὰρ ϝέτος *yearly*, *Tab.Heracl.*1.101); πάλαι πολλὰ ἤδη ἔτη Pl.*Ap.*18b; τρίτῳ ἔτει Th.1.101; τρίτῳ ἔτεϊ πρότερον Hdt.6.40; τρίτῳ ἔτεϊ τούτων in the third *year* after this, ibid., etc.; freq. in acc., ἔ. τόδ' ἤδη δέκατον.. βόσκων now for these ten *years*, S.*Ph.*312; τύραννος ἐγεγόνει ἤδη χιλιοστὸν ἔτος Pl.*R.*615c, cf. D.3.4, 33.23; of a person's age, γεγονὼς ἔτη τρία ἀπολείποντα τῶν ἑκατόν Isoc.12.270; οἱ ὑπὲρ τὰ στρατεύσιμα ἔτη γεγονότες X.*Cyr.*1.2.4, cf. 13, etc.; without γεγονώς, τοὺς ὑπὲρ τετταράκοντα ἔτη Id.*An.*5.3.1; οἱ μέχρι τετταράκοντα ἐτῶν ib.6.4.25, etc.: in gen., ἐπειδὰν ἐτῶν ᾖ τις τριάκοντα Pl.*Lg.*721b; μυρίων ἐτῶν *within a period of* 10,000 *years*, Id.*Phdr.*248e; ὥρα ἔτους, v. ὥρα I. 2. *regnal year*, τὸ πέμπτον ἔ. Δομιτιανοῦ *POxy.*477.8 (ii A.D.). (ϝέτος *SIG*9.2 (Olympia, vi B.C.), *Berl.Sitzb.*1927.8 (Locr., v B.C.), *Inscr.Cypr.*135.1 H., *Tab.Heracl.* l.c.; cf. Lat. *vetus.*)

ἐτός (A), Adv. *without reason, in vain*, only with neg., οὐκ ἐτὸς *no wonder*, Ar.*Ach.*411, al., Philetaer.5, Anaxil.30, Pl.*R.*414e, 568a; οὐκ ἐτὸς ἄρ' ἦσθα δεινὴ καὶ σοφή Ar.*Ec.*245, cf. *Pl.*404.

ἐτός (B), ή, όν, = ἐτεός, *true*, Hsch., perh. to be read in Crates Com.8: neut. pl. ἐτά *truly*, Call.*Fr.anon.*283.

ἑτός, ή, όν, verb. Adj. of ἵημι, *sent*, only in compds., as ἀν-ετός, ἀφ-ετός. **ἔτρᾰγον**, aor. 2 of τρώγω. **ἔτταικαν**· ἔστησαν, Hsch. **ἔττε**, v. sub ἔστε.

ἐττημένος, η, ον, perf. part. Pass. of *ττάω (cf. δια-ττάω), *sifted*, Pherecr.211; ἐττησμένα Hsch.

ἐτῠμ-ηγορέω, *derive*, ἀπὸ αἰτίας ὄνομα Procl. *in Cra.*p.43 P. **-ηγορία**, ἡ, = ἐτυμολογία, ib.p.45 P. (pl.). **-ηγόρος**, ον, (ἀγορεύω) *speaking truth*, Orph.*A.*4,1178.

ἐτῠμόδρῡς, υος, ἡ, *true oak, Quercus Robur*, Thphr.*HP*3.8.2,7.

ἐτῠμολογ-έω, *argue from etymology*, Diogenian.Epicur.2.18, Gal.5.214. II. *analyse a word and find its origin*, Πλάτων -λογῶν τὸν οἶνον Ath.2.35b, cf. Corn.*ND*32; ἐ. τι ἀπό τινος ib.1, Str.1.2.34; ἔκ τινος *An.Ox.*3.220; παρά τι *EM*220.37; πρός τι Phlp. *in de An.*92.4:—Pass., -εῖσθαι ταῖς Ἑλληνικαῖς φωναῖς Str.13.1.52. **-ία**, ἡ, *etymology*, Id.16.4.29, D.H.*Comp.*16, A.D.*Adv.*153.13, Ph.1.354, etc. **-ικός**, ή, όν, *belonging to* ἐτυμολογία, Eust.1799.25; -κά, τά, title of work by Chrysipp. (*Stoic.*2.9, al.); ἡ -κή *the science of etymology*, Varro *LL*7.109; τὸ -κόν *an etymological dictionary*, *EM*212.13 (pl.), Sch.Il.13.130 (pl.), etc. Adv. -κῶς Eust.396.15. **-ος**, ον, *studying etymology*: as Subst., ἐ., ὁ, *etymologist*, *EM*199.24, Varro *LL*6.39.

ἔτῠμος, ον, also η, ον S.*Ph.*205 (lyr.) (only in neut. in Hom.):—poet. Adj. *true*, ψεύσομαι, ἢ ἔτυμον ἐρέω; Il.10.534; φάμ' ἔτυμον S.*Ant.*1320 (lyr.), cf. Call.*Fr.*1.39 P.; ψεύδεα πολλὰ λέγων ἐτύμοισιν ὁμοῖα Od.19.203, cf. Hes.*Th.*27, Thgn.713; οἵ ῥ' ἔτυμα κραίνουσι those [dreams] have *true* issues, Od.19.567; γνώσει τάδ' ὡς ἔ. A.*Pr.*295 (anap.); ἔ. λόγος Stesich.32, Pi.*P.*1.68; ἔ. ἄγγελος, φήμη, φάτις, A.*Th.*82 (lyr.), E.*El.*818, Ar.*Pax* 114 (anap.); βάλλει μ' ἐτύμα φθογγά S.*Ph.*205 (lyr.); πάθεα A.*Eu.*496; τέχνη Dor.ap.Pl.*Phdr.*260e; ὡς ἔτυμ' ἑστάκαντι how *natural*.., Theoc.15.82. 2. neut. ἔτυμον, as Adv., ἀλλ' ἔτυμόν τοι ἦλθ' Ὀδυσεὺς Od.23.26; οὔ σ' ἔτυμόν γε φάμεν πεπνῦσθαι Il.23.440; ὡς ἔτυμον *AP*7.352: regul. Adv. -μως Xenoph. 8.4, Pi.*O.*6.77, A.*Th.*918 (lyr.), B.12.228, etc.; ὡς ἐτύμως A.*Eu.*534 (lyr.). II. ἔτυμον, τό, as Subst., *the true sense* of a word *according to its origin*, its *etymology*, D.S.1.11, Plu.2.278c, Ath.13.571d. Adv. -μως *etymologically*, Arist.*Mu.*400ᵃ6, Str.9.2.17, Ph.1.30: Comp. -ώτερον *EM*526.2: Sup. -ώτατα Nicom.*Ar.*2.27.—Never in Att. Prose; in later writers only in signf. II, exc. in Pl.*Ax.*366b.

ἐτῠμότης, ητος, ἡ, *true meaning* of a word, Str.5.4.10, 8.3.19, Plu.2.638e.

ἐτῠμώνιον· ἀληθές, Hsch.

ἐτωσιοεργός, όν, *working in vain* or *sluggishly*, Hes.*Op.*411.

ἐτώσιος, ον, (ἐτός A) Ep. Adj. *to no purpose, fruitless*, βέλος ὠκὺ ἐ. ἔκφυγε χειρός Il.14.407; ἐτώσια πίπτει ἔραζε [βέλεα] 17.633; τὰ δὲ πάντα ἐ. θῆκεν Ἀθήνη made them *fruitless*, Od.22.256; δῶρα δ' ἐ. ταῦτα χαρίζεο 24.283; *useless, unprofitable*, ἐ. ἄχθος ἀρούρης Il.18.104; ἐ. πόλλ' ἀγορεύειν Hes.*Op.*402; ἔργον ἐ. λιπεῖν to leave it *undone*, ib. 440; ἐτώσια χερσὶ προδεικνύς, i.e. making *mere* feints, not real blows, Theoc.22.102: masc., first in Id.25.236 (ὀϊστός): fem., Orph.*L.*539: neut. ἐτώσιον, as Adv., Id.*A.*700; pl., ἐτώσια γηράσκοντας A.R. 2.893, cf. Theoc.1.38: regul. Adv. -ίως Sch.Ar.*Ec.*246.

εὖ, Ep. also **ἐΰ** Od.1.302, etc., cf. A.D.*Adv.*200.20: Adv. (prop. neut. of ἐΰς):—*well*, opp. κακῶς (as in Th.4.63), Hom., etc. I. of knowledge or action, *well, thoroughly, competently*, εὖ μέν τις δόρυ θηξάσθω, εὖ δ' ἀσπίδα θέσθω Il.2.382; εὖ καὶ ἐπισταμένως κέασαν ξύλα Od. 20.161; τὴν πόλιν κοσμέων καλῶς τε καὶ εὖ Hdt.1.59; τὸ πρᾶγμα βασανίσας καλῶς τε καὶ εὖ Pl.*Euthd.*307b, etc.; τόξων εὖ εἰδώς *cunning* with the bow, Il.2.718, etc.; εὖ τόδ' ἴσθι A.*Pers.*173 (troch.); εὖ γὰρ σαφῶς τόδ' ἴστε ib.784; εὖ οἶδ' ὅτι parenthetic in colloquial speech, σὺ γὰρ εὖ οἶδ' ὅτι οὐ πράγματ' ᾄσει Ar.*Pax* 1296, cf. D.14.2, etc.; εὖ οἶδα, in answers, Dioxipp.4; εὖ μήδεο consider *well*, Il.2.360; εὖ λέγεις *well* spoken! Pl.*Ap.*24e, cf. D.5.2, etc.: with λέγω omitted, οὐδὲ τοῦτ' εὖ Ἐρατοσθένης Str.1.3.1. 2. *morally well, kindly*, εὖ ἔρδειν, = εὐεργετεῖν, Il.5.650; εὖ εἰπεῖν τινα to speak *well* of him, Od.1.302; εὖ δρᾶν εὖ παθών S.*Ph.*672, etc. 3. with passive or intransitive Verbs, *fortunately, happily, in good case*, εὖ ζώουσι Od.19.79; εὖ οἴκαδ' ἱκέσθαι *safely*, Il.1.19, cf. Od.3.188; τοῦ βίου εὖ ἥκειν Hdt.1.30; εὖ φρονῶν in one's *right* mind, A.*Pr.*387, etc. (but εὖ φρονεῖν εἴς τινας, τὰ σά, to be *well-disposed* towards, And.2.4, S.*Aj.*491); standing last for emphasis, ἄνδρες γεγονότες εὖ Hdt.7.134; νόμους μὴ λύειν ἔχοντας εὖ Id.3.82; τελευτήσει τὸν βίον εὖ Id.1.32, cf. Th.1.71, Arist.*EN*1124ᵇ13, etc.: separated from its Verb, εὖ πρᾶγμα συντεθὲν D.18.144. II. coupled with other Adverbs, esp. when qualifying nouns, adjectives, and adverbs, εὖ μάλα Od.4.96, etc.; ἡ ἀορτὴ εὖ μάλα κοίλη Arist.*HA*514ᵇ22; εὖ μάλα πᾶσαι *h.Ap.*171; εὖ μάλα πολλά Heraclit.35; εὖ μάλα πρεσβύτης Pl.*Euthphr.*4a; μάλα εὖ καὶ κομψῶς Id.*Sph.*236d; εὖ καὶ μάλα Id.*Smp.*194a (sed cf. *CQ*15.4); κάρτα εὖ Hdt.3.150; εὖ.. πάνυ or πάνυ εὖ, Ar.*Pl.*198, Pl.*Men.*80b; εὖ σφόδρα Nicostr.8, Philem.75.4; εὖ κἀνδρικῶς, εὖ κἀνδρείως, Ar.*Eq.*379 (lyr.), *Th.*656; καλῶς τε καὶ εὖ (v. supr. I.1); εὖ τε καὶ καλῶς Pl.*R.*503d. III. as Subst., τὸ εὖ the *right*, the *good cause*, τὸ δ' εὖ νικάτω A.*Ag.*121; τὸ γὰρ εὖ μετ' ἐμοῦ Ar.*Ach.*661; the *Good*, final cause, τὸ εὖ τεκταινόμενος ἐν πᾶσιν τοῖς γιγνομένοις Pl.*Ti.*68e; τοῦ εὖ ἕνεκα Arist.*Sens.*437ᵃ1, cf. eund.*Metaph.*1092ᵇ26: in Art, *perfection, the ideal*, τὸ εὖ διὰ πολλῶν ἀριθμῶν γίνεται Polyclit.2. IV. as the Predicate of a propos., τί τῶνδ' εὖ; A.*Ch.*338 (lyr.), cf. 116; εὖ εἴη may it be *well*, Id.*Ag.*216 (lyr.); εὐορκεῦντι μέμ μοι εὖ εἶμεν or εἴη, *SIG*953.9 (Calymna, ii B.C.), *PEleph.*23.19 (iii B.C.); εὖ σοι γένοιτο *well* be with thee, E.*Alc.*627, cf. *Fr.*707. V. Interjection, *well done!* to cheer on dogs, εὖ κύνες X.*Cyn.*9.20; *ahoy! ho! Lyr.Alex.Adesp.*20.11; cf. εὖγε. VI. in Compds., implying *abundance* (εὔανδρία), *prosperity* (εὐδαίμων, opp. κακοδαίμων), *ease* (εὔβατος, opp. δύσβατος): compounded only with Nouns and Adjs. (hence εὖ πάσχω, εὖ ποιέω are better written divisim, but εὐποιητικός implies εὐποιέω: v. ἀντευποιέω); εὐδοκέω is exceptional. (Replaced by καλῶς in later Gr., exc. in set phrases.)

εὗ, enclit. εὑ, Ion. and Ep. for οὗ (οὑ), gen. of reflex. Pron. of 3rd pers., Il.20.464; for αὐτοῦ, Hdt.3.135. II. for αὐτοῦ, Il.14.427, 24.293. III. apptly. for ἑῷ, *Trans.Am.Phil.Ass.*57.202 (Laodicea Combusta).

εὖα· ἐπιφημισμὸς ληναϊκὸς καὶ μυστικός, Hsch. II. for acc. sg. εὖαν, v. εὖας. III. εὐά· τράγου φωνῆς μίμημα Anon.ap.Suid.

εὐαγγελ-έω, = εὐαγγελίζομαι, Pl.ap.Phryn.235 (prob. referring to *R.*432d, *Tht.*144b, where codd. and edd. have εὖ ἀγγέλλω). **-ία**, ἡ, *good tidings*, Lxx *4Ki.*7.9, J.*AJ*18.6.10. **-ίζομαι**, impf., Paus. 4.19.5: fut. part. -ιούμενος J.*AJ*6.4.2, 18.6.10, Luc.*Icar.*34: aor. (v. infr.):—Act., only in later Gr., Lxx *1Ki.*31.9, *Apoc.*10.7, *PGiss.*27.6 (ii A.D.): plpf. εὐηγγελίκειν dub. in D.C.61.13: (εὐάγγελος):—

bring good news, announce them, λόγους ἀγαθοὺς φέρων εὐαγγελίσασθαί τινι Ar.*Eq.*643, cf. Phryn.Com.44, D.18.323; τὴν εὐτοκίαν Sor. 1.70; εὐτυχίας τῇ πατρίδι Lycurg.18; πρός σε ταῦτα Men.*Georg.* 83; also τινά τι J.*AJ*18.6.10, Alciphr.3.12, Hld.2.10; εὐ. ὅτι... Thphr.*Char.*17.7; τινι ὅτι.. Luc.*Philops.*31: c. acc. et inf., Plu. *Mar.*22:—Act., εὐ. τὰ τῆς νίκης *PGiss.* l. c.; τισιν ὡς.. Polyaen.5. 7:—Pass., *receive good tidings*, ἐν ᾗ -ίσθη ἡ πόλις ἡμέρᾳ *AJA*18. 323 (Sardes, i B.C.). II. *preach* or *proclaim as glad tidings*, τὴν βασιλείαν τοῦ Θεοῦ *Ev.Luc.*4.43, etc.; εἰρήνην ὑμῖν *Ep.Eph.*2.17, etc. 2. abs., *proclaim glad tidings*, πτωχοῖς Lxx*Is.*61.1, cf. *Ev. Luc.*4.18, etc.: c. acc., *preach the glad tidings of the gospel to*, τὸν λαόν ib.3.18; κώμας τῶν Σαμαρειτῶν *Act.Ap.*8.25:—so in Act., *Apoc.* 10.7; τινι Lxx 1*Ki.*31.9:—Pass., *have the gospel preached to* one, *Ev. Matt.*11.5, *Ep.Hebr.*4.2,6; also of the gospel, *to be preached*, *Ev.Luc.* 16.16, *Ep.Gal.*1.11. **-ιον**, τό, *reward of good tidings*, given to the messenger, εὐαγγέλιον δέ μοι ἔστω Od.14.152; οὐ..εὐ. τόδε τείσω ib.166; ἀπολήψῃ τὸ εὐ. Plu.*Demetr.*17: in Att. always in pl., εὐαγγέλια θύειν to make a thank-offering for *good-tidings*, Isoc.7.10, Men. *Pk.*415; εὐ. θύειν ἑκατὸν βοῦς τῇ θεῷ Ar.*Eq.*656; ἐβουθύτει ὡς εὐ. X. *HG*4.3.14; εὐαγγελίων θυσίαι Aeschin.3.160; εὐ. στεφανοῦν, ἀναδῆσαί τινα, to crown one for *good news brought*, Ar.*Eq.*647, *Pl.*765; ἐστεφανωμένη ἐπ' εὐαγγελίοις Plu.*Sert.*11, cf. *Supp.Epigr.*1.362.7 (Samos, iv B.C.). II. *good tidings, good news*, in pl., Lxx 2*Ki.*4. 10, Cic.*Att.*2.3.1, 13.40.1, *Inscr.Prien.*105.40 (i B.C.): sg., J.*BJ*2. 17.4, Luc.*Asin.*26, App.*BC*3.93, *Sammelb.*421 (iii A.D.). 2. in Christian sense, *the gospel*, *Ep.Gal.*1.11, etc.

Εὐαγγέλιος, ὁ, *giver of glad tidings*, epith. of Zeus, Aristid.*Or.*53 (55).3. II. (sc. μήν) month in an Asiatic calendar, *Hemerolog.Flor.*

εὐαγγελ-ιστής, οῦ, ὁ, *bringer of good tidings*: hence, *evangelist, preacher of the gospel*, *Act.Ap.*21.8. II. *proclaimer of oracular messages*, *IG*12(1).675 (Rhodes). **-ος**, ον, (ἀγγέλλω) *bringing good news*, πῦρ A.*Ag.*21; ἐλπίδες ib.262, etc.; σωτηρίων πραγμάτων εὐ. ib.646; Φήμη εὐ. *IG*14.1120; ῥινός Opp.*H.*5.237; title of Hermes, Hsch.

εὐάγ-εια [ᾰ], ἡ, (εὐαγής) *brightness, clearness, alertness*, [τῆς ψυχῆς] Iamb.*VP*24.107: pl., ἀγχίνοιαί τε καὶ ψυχῆς εὐάγειαι ib.17. 74: prob. cj. ib.3.13. **-έω** [ᾰ], (εὐαγής A) *to be pure, holy*, E. *Ba.*1008 (lyr.); αὐτὸς δ' εὐαγέοιμι καὶ εὐαγέεσσιν ἅδοιμι Theoc.26.30, cf. Orph.*Fr.*222; εὐαγέων καὶ εὐαγέεσσι μελοίμην Call.*Del.*98. II. in Pass., *to be purified*, *IG*12(1).677 (Rhodes).

εὐαγής (A), ές, (ἄγος A) *free from pollution, pure*: 1. of persons, *guiltless*, ὁ δὲ ἀποκτείνας τὸν ταῦτα ποιήσαντα... ὅσιος ἔστω καὶ εὐ. Lex ap.And.1.96, cf. Porph.*VP*15; εὐαγεστάτων ἱππέων, v.l. for εὐγενεστάτων, D.H.10.13; of bees, *chaste* (cf. Virg.*G.*4.198), *AP*9. 404.7 (Antiphil.). 2. of actions, *holy, lawful*, τίς οἶδεν εἰ κάτωθεν εὐαγῆ τάδε; S.*Ant.*521; εὐαγές ἐστι τὸ ἀποκτεῖναι D.9.44, cf. Arist.*Fr.*538, App.*BC*2.148; τοῦτο δ' οὐκ εὐαγές μοι ἀπέβη *well-omened, favourable*, Pl.*Ep.*312a. Adv. εὐαγέως, ἔρδειν *h.Cer.*274,369, cf. A.R.2.699, *POxy.*1203.5 (i A.D.), etc.; οὐκ εὐαγῶς Ph.2.472: Sup. -έστατα Jul.*Or.*7.230d. 3. of offerings or services, *undefiled*: hence, *lawful*, ἐλέφας... οὐκ εὐ. ἀνάθημα Pl.*Lg.*956a; θυηλαί A.R.1. 1140, etc.; ὕμνοι *AP*7.34 (Antip. Sid.); λύσις a solution *free from defilement*, S.*OT*921; οὐκ εὐ. ἀπολογίαι Porph.*Abst.*2.10. (Εὐηάγης as pr. n., *IG*12(9).56.118 (Styra, v B.C.).)

εὐᾱγής (B), ές, (ἄγνυμι) = καλῶς κεκλασμένος, Suid., cf. *EM*266.3.

εὐᾱγής, ές, (v. fin.) *bright, clear*, εὐᾱγέος ἠελίοιο (cf. ἀγής II) Parm. 10.2; καθαρὰ καὶ εὐαγέα, of the sun and heavenly bodies, Hp. *Insomn.*89, cf. Democr.ap.Thphr.*Sens.*73,78; λευκῆς χιόνος... εὐαγεῖς βολαί E.*Ba.*662; εὐαγέστερον γίγνεσθαι, opp. σκοτωδέστερα φαίνεσθαι καὶ ἀσαφῆ, Pl.*Lg.*952a; εὐαγέστατος, opp. θολερώτατος, of air, Id. *Ti.*58d; χεύων ὁλκὰν εὐαγῆ *Lyr.Alex.Adesp.*35.19; σὺν... εὐαγεῖ (also εὐαγεῖ, εὐαυγεῖ) Ὑγιείᾳ *Pae.Erythr.*15, al.; ὀφθαλμοί Aret.*SA*2.4, Adam.1.13. 2. metaph., *alert*, ἄνθρωποι Hp.*Vict.*2.62 (v.l. γίνεται εὐαγής (sc. ἥ τε ὄψις καὶ ἡ ἀκοή), cf. εὐαγέα (v.l. εὐπαγέα) καὶ εὐήκοα ibid.). II. *far-seen* or *conspicuous*, πέτρα Pi.*Pae.Fr.*19.25; ἕδραν παντὸς εὐαγῆ στρατοῦ a seat *in full view* of the army, A.*Pers.*466; ἔστην θεατὴς πύργον εὐαγῆ λαβών E.*Supp.*652. (ᾱ Parm. l. c., *Lyr. Alex.* l. c., *AP*6.204 (Leon., s. v. l.).—Perh. fr. εὐ-αυγής (αὐγή lengthd., cf. εὐᾱγορέω, εὐᾱής, etc.), as ἑᾱτοῦ fr. ἑαυτοῦ: εὐαυγ- is a correction in Pi. l. c., v.l. in *Pae.Erythr.* l. c., and may be the original spelling; cf. εὐαυγής.)

εὐάγητος, ον, = εὐᾱγής, *bright*, φύσιν εὐ., of clouds, Ar.*Nu.*276 (lyr.). (ᾱ, which prohibits the other expl. given by Sch., = εὐκίνητος.—The sense *ductile*, from ἡγέομαι, is very dub.)

εὐάγκᾰλος, ον, (ἀγκάλη) *easy to bear in the arms*, ἄχθος οὐκ εὐάγκαλον A.*Pr.*352; τόξον E.*Fr.*785 (Nauck ἄγκυλον); φόρτος, of Anchises, Ael.*Fr.*148, cf. Porph.*Abst.*1.45: metaph., λόγοι Them.*Or.* 18.219d; *pleasant to embrace*, Luc.*Am.*25.

εὐάγκεια, poet. fem. of sq., Πίνδον ἀν' εὐάγκειαν Call.*Cer.*83. (Formed like Κυπρογένεια.)

εὐαγκής, ές, (ἄγκος) *with sweet glades*, Pi.*N.*5.46.

εὔαγλις, ἡ, *consisting of many* or *fine cloves* (ἄγλιθες), of a head of garlic, Nic.*Al.*432 (cod. opt., melius εὐάγλις).

εὐᾰγόραστος, ον, *easily bought, cheap*, Hsch. s. v. εὔωνον.

εὐᾱγορέω, εὐᾱγορία, Dor. for εὐηγ-.

εὐάγρ-ευτος, ον, = εὔαγρος, Sch.Opp.*H.*4.587. **-έω**, *to have good sport*, *AP*6.304.8 (Phan.), Antig.Car.ap.Ath.7.297f: c. acc., εὐαγρεῖν ἠέρα γαῖαν ὕδωρ *AP*6.12 (Jul.). **-ής**, ές, = εὔαγρος, Opp. *H.*3.49, 4.157. **-ία**, poet. **-ίη**, ἡ, *good sport*, Plb.8.29.6, *AP*6. 187 (Alph.), 9.268 (Antip. Thess.). **-ος**, ον, (ἄγρα) *lucky in the chase*, S.*OC*1088 (lyr.), *AP*6.34 (Rhian.); *affording good sport*, ib.9. 555 (Crin.); epith. of Pan, *Sammelb.*4031, 4053; of Ares, *BMus. Inscr.*1064 (Egypt).

εὐάγωγ-ία, ἡ, *good education*, ἡ Ἐπικράτους εὐ. τοῦ ἀδελφοῦ Aeschin. 2.151, cf. Simp. *in Epict.*p.19 D., al. II. *easiness of being led*, ψυχῆς πρὸς λόγους Pl.*Def.*413b, cf. Them.*Or.*13.175c: abs., *docility*, Arist. *VV*1250ᵇ32; κουφότης καὶ εὐ. Philostr.*VA*6.13. **-ος**, ον, *easily led, ductile*, ἐπί τι, εἴς τι, τινι πρός τι, Pl.*R.*486d, X.*Oec.*12.15, Arist.*Pol.* 1327ᵇ38; πρὸς πᾶν Plb.11.29.9; εἰς ἀκολασίαν S.E.*M.*6.34; τινι *by* a master, Pl.*Lg.*671b; πόλις -οτέρα ὑπὸ τῶν τυχόντων Isoc.*Ep.*2.15; εὐάγωγόν ἐστι πᾶς ἀνὴρ ἐρῶν Men.352. 2. *easily purged*, -ότατος χυμός Gal.15.78. II. metaph., *easily managed*, of the Nile, Isoc. 11.13; of horses, *docile*, Poll.1.195; of the voice, *easily trained*, Id. 2.117; δακτύλων τὸ εὐ., of a statue, Luc.*Im.*6; of land, *easily cultivated*, Str.5.3.12; *commodious*, ἐνδιαιτήσεις Ph.1.334. III. Adv. -γως *in an accommodating spirit*, Cic.*Att.*13.23.3.

εὐάγων [ᾰ], ωνος, ὁ, ἡ, *of successful contests*, τιμά Pi.*N.*10.38.

εὐαδές· εὔπνουν, and **εὐαδής**· εὐήνεμος, οἱ δὲ εὐαής, Hsch. (cf. S.*Ph.* 828 (lyr.)). II. **εὐαδέα** (accus.?) dub. l. in Hp.*Decent.*4 codd.

εὐᾰδίκητος [ῐ], ον, (ἀδικέω) *liable to wrong*, And.4.15, Luc.*Tim.* 32, Hipparch.ap.Stob.4.4.4. II. Medic., *easily injured*, Sor.1.47, 106, Ath.Med.ap.Orib.*inc.*21.16, Gal.10.542.

εὔαδον, v. ἁνδάνω.

εὐᾱερ-ία, ἡ, *freshness of air*, prob. in Callix.1, cf. Ptol.*Tetr.*86; *fineness of weather*, Plu.2.787e, Eust.1505.19: Ion. **εὐηερίη**, v. εὐήρεια. **-ος**, ον, *with fresh, good air*, τὸ εὐ. Str.3.2.13, cf. Herod.Med. in *Rh.Mus.*58.73, Orib.9.20.1.

εὐάζω, *cry* εὐαί, in honour of Bacchus, S.*Ant.*1134 (lyr.), E.*Ba.* 1034 (lyr.); Διονύσῳ *AP*9.363.11 (Mel.), cf. D.S.4.3, Callistr.*Stat.*2: c. acc. cogn., μελῳδὸν εὐ. χορόν Sopat.10:—Med., Βάκχιον -ομένα E. *Ba.*68 (lyr.).

εὐᾱής, ές, (ἄημι) *well ventilated, fresh, airy*, χώρῳ ἐν εὐαεῖ Hes.*Op.* 599 (εὐᾶεϊ codd., Rzach). II. Act., of a wind, *favourably blowing, fair*, opp. δυσαής, Hdt.2.117, E.*Hel.*1504 (lyr.); ἀνέμων εὐαέσσιν ῥοθίοις prob. in E.*Fr.*773.36 (lyr.): metaph., *favourable*, Ὕπνε.., εὐαὲς ἡμῖν ἔλθοις [with ᾰ] S.*Ph.*828 (lyr., s. v. l.).

εὔαθλος, ον, *successful in contests*, Pi.*I.*6(5).3. II. *happily won*, γέρα *APl.*5.363.

εὐαί (εὔαἵ Hdn.Gr.1.503), a cry of joy like εὐοῖ, Ar.*Lys.*1294 (lyr.), etc.; εὐαὶ σαβαῖ Eup.84.

εὐαιμ-ία, ἡ, (αἷμα) *goodness of blood*, Gal.7.564. **-ορράγητος** [ρᾰ], ον, *easily bleeding*, Id.19.457, Leonid.ap.Aët.15.5, Paul.Aeg.6. 30. **-ος**, ον, *full-blooded*, in Comp., μόριον Gal.17(2).423, cf. 11.290.

εὐαίν-ετος, ον, (αἰνέω) *much-extolled*, μέριμνα B.18.11; ἵππος Antim.25. **-ητος**, ον, = foreg., Ὀρφεύς Pi.*P.*4.177.

εὐαίρετος, ον, (αἱρέω) *easy to be taken*, χώρη Hdt.7.130; λαγώς Poll. 5.50, cf. X.*Mem.*3.1.10.

εὐαισθ-ησία, ἡ, *quick sensibility, vigorous capacity of sensation*, Pl. *Ti.*76d, Arist.*PA*656ᵃ16, *Stoic.*3.32, Aristeas 259, Ph.1.104, al., Gal. *UP*8.6, Iamb.*Protr.*2. **-ητέω**, *have keen perceptions*, Tz.*H.*4. 451. **-ητικός**, ή, όν, = sq., Gal.16.360; δύναμις *sensory* faculty, Steph. *in Gal.*1.234 D. **-ητος**, ον, (αἰσθάνομαι) *with quick senses* or *keen perceptions*, περί τι Pl.*Lg.*812b; ἐλέφας εὐ. ζῷον Arist.*HA* 630ᵇ21: Comp. -ότερος Pl.*Ti.*75c; τῆς καρδίας τὴν ὑπεροχὴν -οτέραν ἔχειν Plu.2.14d: Sup. ὁ ἄνθρωπος -ότατος τῶν ἄλλων ζῴων Arist.*PA* 660ᵃ20; τὸ εὐ., = εὐαισθησία, Gal.10.387. Adv. -τως, ἔχειν τινός have *keen perceptions* of..., Pl.*Lg.*670b, cf. 661b: Comp. -οτέρως, ἔχειν περὶ ὥρας καὶ μηνῶν καὶ ἐνιαυτῶν Id.*R.*527d. II. of things, *easy to perceive*, Arist.*Cael.*289ᵃ7 (Comp.), Plu.2.956f.

εὐαίων, ωνος, ὁ, ἡ, *happy in life*, of persons, E.*Ion* 126 (lyr.), Call. *Del.*292, etc.; *happy, fortunate*, βίοτος A.*Pers.*711, S.*Tr.*81; πλοῦτος S.*Fr.*592.3 (lyr.); [Ὕπνος] Id.*Ph.*829 (lyr.); πότμος E.*IA*550 (lyr.).

εὐάκεστος [ᾰ], ον, (ἀκέομαι) *easy to remedy*, ἁμαρτάδες εὐακεστότεραι Hp.*Acut.*39.

εὐᾰκής, ές, = foreg., -έστερόν [ἐστι] Ruf.(?)ap.Orib.*inc.*4.54. Ion. Adv. -ακέως *by an easy process of healing*, Aret.*CA*2.2.

εὐᾰκοέω, εὐάκοος, ον, v. εὐηκ-.

εὐᾰκόνητος, ον, *well-whetted*, gloss on εὐήκης, Sch.Nic.*Al.*411.

εὐάκουστος [ᾰ], ον, = εὐήκοος I. 3, Ἡρακλῆς *IG*14.904.

εὐάκτῑν, ῖνος, ὁ, ἡ, *with beautiful rays*, Hdn.Gr.1.18.

εὐᾰλαζόνευτος, ον, *easy to pretend about*, Arist.*Rh.*1390ᵇ21.

εὐᾰλάκᾰτος [ᾰκ], ον, Aeol. for εὐηλ-, Theoc.28.22.

εὐαλδής, ές, (ἀλδαίνω) *well-grown, luxuriant*, φῦκος, χιλός, *AP*9. 325, *IG*14.1389 ii 24. Ion. Adv. -έως Hp.*Lex* 2. II. Act., *fertilizing*, Ἱπποκρήνη Arat.217, cf. Plu.2.664c: Comp. -έστερα [ὕδατα] ib. 912f.

εὐαλθής, ές, (ἀλθαίνω) *easily healed*, Hp.*Art.*39: Comp., ib.68: Sup., Antyll.ap.Orib.45.16.4. II. Act., *healing*, Nic.*Al.*326,622.

εὐάλιος, ον, Dor. for εὐήλιος.

εὐαλλοίωτος, ον, (ἀλλοιόω) *easily changed*, Gal.*UP*8.6, al., Paul. Aeg.1.50.

εὐαλσής, ές, (ἄλσος) *with beautiful groves*, prob. in Str.3.3.1.

εὐάλφῐτος, ον, *of good meal*, *AP*7.736 (Leon.).

Εὐαλῶς· εὐχερῶς θηρώμενος, Hsch. (leg. -άλωτος vel -αλής).

Εὐᾰλωσία, ἡ, (ἅλως) *filling the threshing-floor*, of Demeter, Hsch.

εὐάλωτος [ᾰ], ον, *easy to be taken* or *caught*, X.*Cyn.*9.9, Pl.*Phdr.* 240a, Demetr.Com.Vet.4; ὑπὸ πάντων διὰ κολακείας εὐ. Plu.*Crass.*6; οὔτε ὑφ' ἡδονῆς οὔτε ὑπὸ δέους εὐ. Id.*Sert.*10; εὐ. εἰς δεισιδαιμονίαν, πρὸς ἡδονάς, *easily led away* to..., ib.11, Id.2.256e; εὐ. εἰς τὸ μιμεῖσθαι *easily led* to imitate, ib.334d: Comp. -ωτότερος Ph.2.132, Luc. *Abd.*28 (εὐαλούστερος is corrupt in Alciphr.2.1): Sup. -ότατος Ph.1.458, D.C.60.2. Adv. -τως Ph.1.129. II. Medic., *easily affected*, Sor.1.47; παλμῷ Gal.7.599; but also, *easily cured*, ὑπὸ τῆς τέχνης Alex.Trall.1.11.

εὐᾱμερία, -άμερος, Dor. for εὐημ-.

εὐάμπελος, ον, *with fine vines*, E.*Fr.*530.3, Str.3.3.1, al.: epith. of Dionysus, *AP*9.524.6.

εὐάμπυξ, ῠκος, *with fair fillet*, Μοῖσαι Pi.*Dith.Oxy.*1.13.

εὐάν [ᾰ] (εὔαν D.T.642.18, Hdn.Gr.1.503, 2.12), *euhan*, a cry of the Bacchanals, cf. εὐοῖ, E.*Tr.*326, Luc.*Trag.*38.—Acc. to Hsch., an Indian name for *ivy*, which was sacred to Bacchus.

εὐανά-βλαστος, ον, *shooting up freely*, θαλλοί Sch.Opp.*H.*2.491. **-γνωστος,** ον, *easy to read aloud*, Arist.*Rh.*1407^{b}11, Phld.*Rh.*1.199 S.

εὐανάγωγος [ᾰγ], ον, *easy to expectorate*, Dsc.3.36, Gal.14.271.

εὐανα-διδάκτως, Adv., gloss on εὐανακλήτως, Suid., Zonar.926. **-δοτος,** ον, *easy to digest*, Ath.1.26a, Diph.Siph.ap.eund.8.356b (v.l. εὐαπόδοτον), Dsc.2.85, Iamb.*VP*3.13. **-κλητος,** ον, *easy to call out*, of the names of dogs, X.*Cyn.*7.5. II. *easy to recall*, πρὸς τὸ κοινὸν συμφέρον Plu.*Cim.*17; εὐ. ἑαυτὸν παρέχειν Id.*TG*2. Adv. εὐανακλήτως, διακεῖσθαι πρός τινα M.Ant.1.7. 2. *easily cured*, Aret.*SD*1.7. **-κόμιστος,** ον, *easy to bring back*, Plu.2.458e; *easily restored*, of health, Gal.6.297. **-ληπτος,** ον, *easy to recover*, Str.1.2.16; *easily reparable*, Hp.*Epid.*6.4.7; *easily, comfortably suspended*, of fractured limbs in a sling, Id.*Fract.*47 (Sup.). Adv. -τως Id.*Off.*9. II. Act., *easily taking in, of good capacity for*, ἀρετῆς Stob.2.7.11^{m}. **-λῠτος,** ον, *easily analysed*, Simp.*in Cat.*217.18. Adv. -τως ib.212.16. **-λωτος,** ον, dub. l. in Antyll.ap.Orib.10.2.2 (εὐανάδοτος Daremb.). **-μνηστος,** ον, *easily remembering*, Hierocl.*in CA*8 p.432 M. **-πειστος,** *credulus*, Gloss. **-πνευστος,** ον, *easy to repeat in a breath*, ἡ ἐν κώλοις λέξις Arist.*Rh.*1409^{b}14. **-σειστος,** ον, *easily excited*, πρὸς τοῦ πάθους Phld.*Ir.*p.38 W.

Εὐάνασσα, ἡ, epith. of Demeter, Hsch.

εὐανά-στροφος, ον, *ready to turn back, cautious*, Ptol.*Tetr.*159. **-σφαλτος,** ον, *quickly recovering*, Hp.*Alim.*28; ὕπνοι *from which one wakes easily*, Ruf.(?)ap.Orib.*inc.*4.55. **-τμητος,** ον, *easy to dissect*, Gal.2.454. **-τρεπτος,** ον, *easy to upset, actiones* Cic.*Att.*2.14.1, cf. Heph.Astr.*Praef.*; *easily refuted*, Iamb.*Protr.*21.κʹ. 2. Medic., '*shaky*', Gal.18(1).605; but τὸ τῆς σαρκὸς εὐ. *mobility*, Id.*UP*1.7. **-τροφος,** ον, *well-fed*, Sch.Lyc.307.

εὐανδρ-έω, *abound in men*, Aristeas 108, Str.1.2.40, Ph.1.641; εὐ. πολλῇ ἡλικίᾳ Plu.*Cat.Ma.*26:—Med., Scymn.252, Ocell.4.4. II. *to be in full vigour*, πλήρωμα, φάλαγξ εὐ., Plu.*Cam.*8, App.*Syr.*37. **-ία,** ἡ, *abundance of men*, esp. *of good men and true*, οὐδὲ εὐ. ἐν ἄλλῃ πόλει ὁμοία X.*Mem.*3.3.12, cf. D.H.1.16, Str.16.2.13, Plu.*Per.*19. II. *physical fitness*, as a subject of a contest, Din.*Fr.*16.2, *IG*2^{2}.956.48, al.; εὐανδρίᾳ νικᾶν And.4.42: so in pl., ἐν ταῖς εὐανδρίαις Ath.13.565f; πληρωμάτων εὐανδρίαις *by* the crews *being able-bodied men*, Plu.*Pomp.*24. 2. *manliness*, E.*El.*367; ἡ δ' εὐανδρία διδακτός Id.*Supp.*913; παρασκευάζειν πρὸς εὐανδρίαν to train to *manly spirit*, Antig.Rex ap.D.L.7.7. **-ος,** ον, (ἀνήρ) *abounding in good men and true*, Σπάρτα Tyrt.15.1; χώρα, γᾶ, Pi.*P.*1.40, E.*Tr.*229 (lyr.), Ar.*Nu.*300 (lyr.), etc.; εὐανδροτάτη πόλις Plu.2.209e. II. *prosperous to men*, συμφοραί A.*Eu.*1031.

εὐάνεμος [ᾱ], Dor. for εὐήνεμος.

εὐάνετος, ον, (ἀνίημι) *easy to dissolve*, Dsc.5.134.

εὐάνθ-εμον, τό, *a plant like camomile*, Hp.*Mul.*1.78 (v.l. βοάνθεμον). **-εμος,** ον, *flowery, blooming*, φυά Pi.*O.*1.67; ἥβη *AP*7.602 (Agath.); ἶρις ib.4.1.9 (Mel.). **-έω,** *to be flowery* or *blooming*, Luc.*VH*2.6 (dub.): metaph., *to be overgrown, hypertrophied*, Hp.*Nat.Mul.*8 (ἐκθέωσι Littré fr. Erot.), v.l. in *Mul.*2.135; but later, *to be flourishing, prosperous*, *BGU*1080.24 (iii A.D.). **-ής,** ές, *blooming, downy*, πυκάσαι τε γένυς εὐανθεῖ λάχνῃ Od.11.320. II. *rich in flowers, flowery*, ἀγροί Thgn.1200; κόλποι λειμώνων Ar.*Ra.*373 (lyr.); τόπος Pl.*Smp.*196b; *decked with flowers*, στόλος Pi.*P.*2.62, cf. Sapph.78; *freely flowering*, Thphr.*HP*6.2.3. 2. *flowered, gay-coloured, gay, bright*, χρῶμα Pl.*Phd.*110d, cf. Arist.*Col.*792^{a}15, 794^{b}5 (Comp.); θρόμβοι αἵματος Hp.*Coac.*621, cf. 575; στρωμναί Ph.1.639 (Sup.); ἐσθής Luc.*Rh.Pr.*15; βαφαί Ael.*NA*16.41; πορφύρη *AP*6.250 (Antiphil.); λίθος Jul.*Or.*2.51a; τὸ εὐ. τοῦ ὄρνιθος its *bright colours*, Ath.9.399a; *pink, flushed*, σῶμα Sor.1.100. III. metaph., *blooming, fresh, goodly*, ὄλβος Pi.*I.*5(4).12; of persons, ἁλικία ib.7(6).34, cf. *O.*6.84, Ar.*Nu.*1002; εὐ. ὀργά a *goodly, noble* temper, Pi.*P.*1.89: ἐν ἅλμῃ.. εὐανθεστέρᾳ in *fresher* brine, Sotad.Com.1.21: Sup. -εστάτη ἡλικία Plu.2.120a.

εὐάνιος [ᾰ], ον, (ἀνία) *taking trouble easily*, Hsch. (also glossed by πειθήνιος, i.e. εὐάνιος [ᾱ], Dor. for εὐήνιος).

εὐᾱνορία, ἡ, Dor. for εὐηνορία.

εὐαντ-έω, *meet graciously*, c. dat., Call.*Dian.*268. **-ης** (or -ής), ες, = sq., opp. δυσάντης, A.R.4.148. **-ητος,** ον, (ἀντάω) *accessible, gracious*, θεός *BMus.Inscr.*1012 (Chalcedon, i B.C.); Μήτηρ θεῶν *IG* 3.134, *Bull.Soc.Arch.*4.188 (ii B.C.). II. *acceptable*, ἄγρη Opp.*C.*2.488, cf. *H.*2.149.

εὐαντόλως, *correpte*, Gloss. (dub. l.).

εὐάντυξ, ῠγος, ὁ, ἡ, of a chariot, *with beautiful rail*, Suid., Phot. (but cf. εὐάξων).

εὐάνωρ [ᾱ], ορος, ὁ, ἡ, Dor. for εὐήνωρ. **εὐαξής,** v. εὐαυξής.

εὐάξιος, ον, *valuable, considerable*, *PFlor.*37.7 (v/vi A.D.).

εὐάξων, *with beautiful axles*, gloss on εὐάντυξ, Suid., Phot.

εὐαπάλλακτος, ον, *easy to get rid of*, ἵππος (i.e. *finding a ready sale*) X.*Eq.*3.1; -ότερον πάθος Arist.*Pr.*883^{a}18, cf. Ruf.ap.Orib.6.38.19, Max.Tyr.13.3. Adv. -τως, ἔχειν to be *easy to evacuate*, of a position, Aen.Tact.16.18.

εὐαπαντ-ησία, ἡ, *affability*, Chrysipp.*Stoic.*3.60 (pl.). **-ητος,** ον, *affable, courteous*, τινι *IG*4.1.26 (Aegina, ii B.C.); φιλανθρωπία Lxx 2*Ma.*14.9.

εὐαπάρτιστος, ον, *well-finished, perfect*, Sch.E.*Hipp.*362.

εὐᾰπάτητος [πᾰ], ον, *easy to cheat*, Pl.*Phdr.*263b (Comp.); οἱ ἀγαθοὶ εὐ. Bias ap.Stob.3.37.36, cf. Arist.*Insomn.*460^{b}9, al. II. Act., *cheating readily*, τὸ θῆλυ -ότερον Id.*HA*608^{b}12.

εὐαπήγητος, ον, Ion. for εὐαφήγητος.

εὐαπό-βᾰτος, ον, *easy to disembark on*, νῆσος -ωτέρα Th.4.30. **-βλητος,** ον, *easily lost*, Alex.Aphr.*Quaest.*122.8, Simp.*in Epict.* p.52 D., *in Ph.*274.29. **-δεικτος,** ον, *easily demonstrated*, Ph.*Bel.*62.27. **-δεκτος,** ον, *acceptable*, Ptol.*Tetr.*44, Sch.Il.2.235. **-δοτος,** ον, *easy of digestion*, f.l. for εὐανάδοτος (q.v.). 2. *easy of solution* or *explanation*, πράγματα Str.2.4.5, cf. S.E.*M.*8.85. **-κρῐτικός,** ή, όν, *ready at answering questions*, Chrysipp.*Stoic.*2.42. **-κρῐτος,** ον, *easy to expound by answers*, Sor.1.1 (s.v.l.). II. Act., in Adv. -τως, ἔχειν πρός τινας to have *an easy answer...*, Artem.4.63. **-κύλιστος** [ῠ], ον, *easy to roll off*, Gal.*UP*7.15, 10.6. **-λόγητος,** ον, *easy to excuse*, Str.10.3.1, Plu.*Agis* 17, Hierocl.*in CA*19 p.461 M. **-λῠτος,** ον, *easy to be separated from*, ὀστέων Hp.*Mochl.*1; ἀπό τινος Id.*Art.*14: abs., Arist.*HA*530^{a}6; *easily uprooted*, Thphr.*HP*1.3.1. II. *easily solved*, of a question, Phld.*Sign.*11, Demetr.Lac.1055.23 F., A.D.*Pron.*30.13. **-νιπτος,** ον, *easy to wash off*, Sch.D.T.p.204 H. **-πνοος,** ον, *easily evaporating*, Thphr.*Od.*42. **-πτωτος,** ον, *easily falling off*, Id.*CP*2.9.3. **-ρρῠτος,** ον, *easily flowing away*, Hp.*Fract.*28; *too fluid*, Gal.12.389. II. *easily slipping off*, of bandages, Id.18(2).765. **-σβεστος,** ον, *easy to extinguish*, Artem.1.74. **-σείστως,** Adv. *so as to be easily shaken off*: hence, *insecurely*, καταλαμβάνειν Chrysipp.*Stoic.*2.90. **-σπαστος,** ον, *easy to be torn from*, ἀλλήλων [τὰ ᾠά] Arist.*HA*550^{a}12. **-τείχιστος,** ον, *easy to wall off, blockade*, Th.6.75, X.*HG*2.4.31. **-φυκτος,** ον, *easily escaping, slippery*, τὸ ἐν τοῖς λόγοις εὐ. Sch.Ar.*Ra.*848.

εὐαρδής, ές, *well-watered*, γῆ Agath.5.12.

εὔαρ, etym. of ἔαρ, coined by Hellad.ap.Phot.*Bibl.*p.535 B.

εὐάρεσκος, v. sub εὐάρεστος.

εὐάρεστ-έω, *to be well pleasing*, τῷ Κοινῷ τῶν Δελφῶν *SIG*611.19 (ii B.C.), cf. Lxx *Ge.*5.22, al., D.S.14.4: abs., Ph.1.102; εὐαρέστησεν *it seemed good, it was resolved*, *IG*14.757.8 (Naples, i A.D.): —Pass., *to be well pleased, satisfied*, τινι *with* a thing, Ph.*Bel.*55.23; τῇ νήσῳ, τῇ ἡγεμονίᾳ, D.S.3.55, 20.79; θυσίαις *Ep.Hebr.*13.16. 2. Medic., in Pass., *to be benefited, get relief*, of patients, Herod.Med. in *Rh.Mus.*58.72, 79. II. intr., = Pass., Lysipp. 7, Apollon.Perg.*Con.*1 *Praef.*, D.H.11.60, Hierocl.*in CA*11 p.442 M. **-ημα,** ατος, τό, *individual taste, preference*, Herod.Med.ap. Orib.5.27.6. **-ήριος,** ον, *propitiatory*, θυσίαι v.l. for ἀρεστ-, D.H.1.67. **-ησις,** εως, ἡ, *being well pleased*, πρὸς τὴν κοινὴν εὐ. *to please* the public, D.H.10.57, cf. Hierocl.p.52 A.; ἢ διὰ φόβον ἢ δι' εὐ. from fear or *favour*, J.*AJ*12.6.2: pl., Ph.1.290. II. *satisfaction*, Aq., Sm., Thd.*Ex.*29.18. III. Medic., *relief, benefit*, Herod.Med. in *Rh.Mus.*58.71, Sor.1.32, Philum.ap.Orib.8.45.7. **-ητέον,** *one must be content with*, τοῖς ἐν τῷ κόσμῳ πραττομένοις Ph.2.413. **-ία,** ἡ, = εὐαρέστησις, Hierocl.*in CA*11 p.442 M.: in pl., *individual tastes, predilections*, Phld.*Rh.*1.152 S. **-ικός,** ή, όν, *easily contented*, διάθεσις εὐ. πρὸς πᾶν τὸ συμβαῖνον M.Ant.9.6. **-ος,** ον, (ἀρέσκω) *well-pleasing, acceptable*, τὸ ἀγαθὸν εὐ. Cleanth.3.6; τινι Lxx *Wi.*4.10, Ph.2.69, 2*Ep.Cor.*5.9, etc.; τισι *Ath.Mitt.*15.134 (Nisyrus); παρά τινι Lxx *Wi.*9.10; ἐν τοῖς ἀναλώμασι *Inscr.Prien.*114.15 (i B.C.): abs., ἀποδημία εὐ. Ph.2.77; θέλημα τοῦ θεοῦ *Ep.Rom.*12.2; χρῆσις *pleasant*, Herod.Med.ap.Orib.5.27.20; σύμμαχοι prob. in *PHib.*1.15.26 (Comp., iii B.C.); τὸ εὐ. Ph.1.585. Adv. -τως, ἔργον συνετέλεσεν *IG*12(8).640.10 (Peparethus, ii B.C.): Comp. -οτέρως, διακεῖσθαί τινι X.*Mem.*3.5.5 (εὐαρεσκοτέρως codd.); -τως ἱερησάμενος *SIG*708.20 (Istropolis, ii B.C.), cf. *IPE*1^{2}.94 (Olbia); λατρεύειν τῷ θεῷ *Ep.Hebr.*12.28. II. *choice*, οἶνος, πυρός, *PStrassb.*1.9 (vi A.D.), *PFlor.*30.30 (iv A.D.). III. *according to taste*, λαχανόσπερμον λαμβάνειν εὐ. *PFay.*90.17 (iii A.D.).

εὐάρητος ὄνειρος· εὔτακτος, Hsch.

εὐᾰρίθμητος, ον, *easy to count*, i.e. *few in number*, Hp.*Acut.*3, Pl.*Ap.*40d, *Smp.*179c; τὸ πλῆθος οὐκ εὐ. ἦν J.*AJ*2.15.1; ὀλίγα καὶ εὐ. Jul.*Or.*3.102c.

εὐαρίστως, Adv., later spelling of εὐαρέστως, *IPE*1^{2}.107 (Olbia).

εὔαρκτος, ον, (ἄρχω) *easy to govern, manageable*, of a horse's mouth, A.*Pers.*193.

εὐάρμᾰτος, ον, (ἅρμα) *with beauteous car*, Θήβα S.*Ant.*845 (lyr.). 2. *victorious in the chariot-race*, Pi.*P.*2.5, *I.*2.17.

εὐαρμοστ-έω, *to be well tempered* or *composed*, Hp.*Praec.*9; *to be of convenient size*, Ph.*Bel.*53.29; *suit, agree with*, c. dat., Dieuch.ap. Orib.4.7.25. **-ία,** ἡ, *happy adaptation, suitableness*, μὴ μόνοις τοῖς λεγομένοις, ἀλλὰ καὶ ταῖς τούτων εὐ. συμπείθειν Isoc.15.189; εὐ. ψυχῆς πρὸς τὰς ἡδονάς Pl.*Def.*411e, cf. Ph.2.79, etc. II. of men's dispositions and tempers (with metaphor from music), Pl.*R.*400d, *Prt.*326b, etc.; εὐ. τρόπων D.61.19; εὐ. πρὸς ἔντευξιν Pl.*Pomp.*1; of political *concord*, κοινὸν ἀγαθὸν εὐ. τις Ecphant.ap.Stob.4.7.64. **-ος,** ον, (ἁρμόζω) *well-joined, harmonious*, κάλαμοι E.*El.*702 (lyr.); μέλος, ὄνομα, Pl.*Lg.*655a,*Cra.*405a. II. of men, *well-tempered*, Hp.*Epid.* 2.6.1; *accommodating, harmonious*, πρὸς ἅπαντα τὴν ἕξιν τῆς ψυχῆς εὐ. ἔχειν Isoc.12.32; εὐ. ἑαυτὸν ἐν πᾶσι παρέχων Pl.*R.*413e: Comp. and Sup., Id.*Prt.*326b, *R.*412a; τὸ εὐ., = εὐαρμοστία, Ph.1.5. Adv. -τως, ἔχειν πρός τι Isoc.11.12, cf. Ruf.ap.Orib.7.26.135; ἀπηκριβῶσθαι Ph.1.33.

εὔαρνος, ον, *rich in sheep*, *AP*6.108 (Myrin.); *in lambs*, ὄϊς ib.7.657.9 (Leon.).

εὐάροτος [ᾰ], ον, (ἀρόω) *well-ploughed* or *easy to be ploughed*, A.R.2.810; ὀργάς *AP*6.41 (Agath.); αὖλαξ ib.9.347 (Leon.):—also **-αροτρίαστος**, ον, *EM*141.2.

εὐάρτῦτος, ον, (ἀρτύω) *well-seasoned*, χοιρίον Ath.4.165b; ἅλες Orib.*Fr.*80; ὀσμή Archig.ap.Gal.13.175.

εὐαρχ-ία, ἡ, *good government*, *PMasp.*2iii9 (vi A.D.), *EM*390.38; gloss on εὐηγεσία, Sch.Od.19.114. **-ίζω**, in fut. -ιῶ, = ἄρξομαι, Hsch.: also aor. 1 Med. -ίσασθαι· ἀπάρξασθαι, Id. **-ισμός**, ὁ, *good discipline*, Lyd.*Mens.*4.4. II. = Lat. *strena*, *Gloss.* **-ος**, ον, *governing well*, Lyc.233. 2. *easily governed*, Arist.*Oec.*1344b 14. II. *beginning well*, λόγος Luc.*Lex.*1; *making a good beginning*, of one's first customer in the market, *AP*6.304 (Phan., s.v.l.).

εὐας, = Lat. *ovatio*, Plu.*Marc.*22; cf. εὐαστής II.

εὐάς, άδος, ἡ, *one who cries* εὐαί, i.e. *a Bacchanal*, κούρη Orph.*H.*49.1: as Subst., Philostr.*Im.*1.19. 2. as Adj., ὁ, ἡ, *Bacchic*, φωνή Nonn.*D.*19.110. II. Εὔας, ὁ, a name of Bacchus, Hsch.

εὐάσκεται· εὐωδεῖται, Hsch.

εὔ-ασμα, ατος, τό, *a Bacchanalian shout*, in pl., E.*Ba.*129, 151 (both lyr.). **-ασμός**, ὁ, *the cry of* εὐαί, Hermesian.7.18, Str.4.4.6, Plu.*Marc.*22, *Ant.*75 (pl.).

εὐάστ-ειρα, ἡ, fem. of εὐαστήρ, Orph.*H.*51.8, 69.1. **-ερος**, ον, (ἀστήρ) *rich in stars*, Arat.237. II. *fair star*, of the moon, Orph.*H.*9.3.

εὐαστήρ, ῆρος, ὁ, = sq., Orph.*H.*30.1, Epic. *in Arch.Pap.*7.4; Βάκχος *AP*9.246 (Marc. Arg.). **-ής**, οῦ, or parox. **εὐάστης**, ου, ὁ, (εὐάζω) *one who cries* εὐαί, *a Bacchanal*, Orph.*H.*54.5, *APl.*1.15, etc. 2. εὐ. θεός, = Βάκχος, *Ath.Mitt.*27.94 (Pergam., ii B.C.). II. ὁ εὐ. θρίαμβος, = Lat. *ovatio*, D.H.5.47 (nisi leg. οὐαστής). **-ικός**, ή, όν, *Bacchanalian*, ἐπίρρημα, ἀναφώνημα, A.D.*Adv.*121.21, Hsch. s. v. εὔσαμα.

εὐάτριος [ᾱ], ον, Dor. for εὐήτριος.

εὐαυγής, ές, *bright, shining*, v.l. in Pi.*Pae.Fr.*19.25, v.l. in *Pae. Erythr.*15, al.: Sup. -έστατος v.l. in Arist.*Mu.*397a16; cf. εὐαγής.

εὐαυγία, ἡ, *illumination*, Iamb.*Protr.*21.κδ'; cf. εὐάγεια.

εὐαυξής, ές, *easily elongated, elastic*, Arist.*HA*493a30; *increased in growth*, in Comp. -έστερος Id.*PA*673b34; *quick-growing*, Thphr.*CP* 1.8.4: Comp., *Gp.*10.57.9 (v.l. -ότερον); *tall*, Suid. s. v. βλωθρή: Sup., Gal.*UP*11.14. (εὐαξ- Suid., Hsch. s. v. εὐαλδῆ, v.l. in Arist. *PA* l.c., Thphr. l. c. (codd. Urb., Med.), *Gp.* l. c., εὐαυξ- v.l. ib.10.13.3: prob. εὐᾱξ- from εὐάυξ-, cf. εὐαγής.)

εὐαφαίρετος, ον, *easy to disperse*, Thphr.*Od.*42.

εὐάφεια [ᾰφ], ἡ, *softness to the touch*, Heraclid.Cum.5; -είας χάριν Heliod.ap.Orib.49.8.3, cf. Antyll.ib.45.2.1, Gal.12.844.

εὐαφήγητος, Ion. **εὐαπ-**, ον, *easy to describe*, Hdt.7.63, D.C.42.26.

εὐαφήδισεν· ἄφρων τις ἐν αὐταῖς ἰσχυρόν, Hsch.

εὐαφής, ές, (ἁφή) *soft*, of seeds ready to germinate, Thphr.*CP*2.17.10; σπλήν Aret.*SD*1.14; of tumours, = εὐείκτος, Paul.Aeg.6.3: metaph., *susceptible*, νοῦς Plu.2.588e. Adv. Sup. -εστάτως, σκευαζομένη ἔμπλαστρος Aët.16.47. II. Act., *having a gentle, delicate touch*, ἀνήρ Aret.*CA*2.9; τὸ εὐαφὲς τῶν δακτύλων Luc.*Im.*14; σπόγγοι Paul.Aeg.4.21: Sup. τὸ -έστατον Ph.*Fr.*14 H.: metaph., εὐ. μετάβασις an *easy, unforced* transition, Luc.*Hist.Conscr.*55. Adv. -ῶς, Ion. -έως, *gently*, Id.*Harm.*1, Aret.*CA*1.6: metaph., δεικνύναι point out *gently*, M.Ant.11.18.4.

εὐάφίη, ἡ, Ion. for εὐάφεια, *AP*5.34 (Rufin.), 293.16 (Agath.).

εὐάφιον, τό, *mild ointment*, Asclep.ap.Gal.13.314.

εὐαφόρμως, Adv. *opportunely*, Sch.S.*OC*111, Ulp. ad D.21.143, 19.188.

εὐαφρόδῑτος, prob. f. l. for ἐπαφρ-, *Cat.Cod.Astr.*7.221.

εὐᾱχής, εὐάχητος, Dor. for εὐηχ-.

εὐβαλκής, ές, dub. sens., of a form of ἀγών, *IG*5(1).267, al. (Sparta). (Perh. for εὐϝαλκής (ἀλκή) with secondary ϝ.)

εὐβάστακτος, ον, *easy to carry* or *move*, μηχανή Hdt.2.125, cf. Arist.*Rh.*1373a32, *Pol.*1257a34; ἐλαφροὶ καὶ εὐ. Corn.*ND*30; τοῖς ὠταρίοις by the ears (handles), Demoph.*Sim.*3. II. *well-supported*, Hp.*Fract.*30 (dub. sens.).

εὔβᾰτος, ον, (βαίνω) *accessible, passable*, οὐ γὰρ εὔ. περᾶν A.*Pr.*718; ποιεῖν τι εὔ. τινί Pl.*Lg.*761a: Comp. -ώτερος X.*HG*4.6.9. II. of dwarf fig-trees, in Comp., *more accessible* or *manageable*, Thphr.*HP* 2.6.12.

εὐβαφής, ές, *well steeped* or *dyed*, Herm.ap.Stob.1.49.44 (dub. l.); *vivid*, of the colours of plants, Sabin.ap.Orib.9.17.2. II. Adv. -βαφῶς prob. f.l. for εὐαφῶς in Herod.Med. in *Rh.Mus.*58.72:—so εὐβαφία, ἡ, f.l. for εὐάφεια, ib.87; εὐβαφῶν (σπόγγων) f.l. for εὐαφῶν, Paul.Aeg.4.21.

εὔβῐος, ον, = sq. I, Arist.*HA*620a21 (Sup.). II. = sq. II, *Supp. Epigr.*2.530.1 (Puteoli, ii/iii A.D.).

εὐβίοτος [ῐ], ον, *easily finding their food*, of certain animals, Arist. *HA*609b19, 615a18. II. *leading an honest life, respectable*, D.C. 52.39, prob. in Antioch.Astr. in *Cat.Cod.Astr.*1.110: written -βίωτος in *IG*5(2).491 (Megalopolis, ii/iii A.D.).

εὔβλαπτος, ον, *easily hurt*, Arist.*GA*719a34, *Gp.*9.9.10.

εὐβλαστ-έω, *grow vigorously*, Thphr.*CP*1.20.5; *germinate well*, of seeds, ib.4.7.2, cf. 4.3.3; *strike readily*, of cuttings, ib.3.7.11. **-ής**, ές, *growing vigorously*, ib.1.8.1. II. Act., *making to grow luxuriantly*, ib.2.3.3. **-ία**, ἡ, *vigorous growth*, ib.1.20.5, al. (Sts. written -βλάστεια.) **-ος**, ον, = εὐβλαστής I, Ph.2.56, al.

εὐβλέφᾰρος, ον, *with beautiful eyelids*, Δίκη *AP*14.122.

εὔβλητος, ον, *easily hit, exposed to blows*, App.*BC*2.79; τοῖς πολεμίοις Id.*Syr.*35.

εὐβοήθητος, ον, *easily assisted* or *defended*, χώρα Arist.*Pol.*1327a3, cf. 21. 2. of diseases, *easily cured*, Hp.*Acut.*(*Sp.*)8 (Comp.), Arist.*Pr.*862b6.

εὐβόητος, ον, = εὔφημος, Hsch. s.v. ἐν εὐφήμῳ.

Εὔβοια, gen. ας, Ion. ης, ἡ, *Euboea*, Il.2.535, etc.: **Εὐβοίηθεν**, poet. -θε, *from Euboea*, Call.*Del.*197: **Εὐβοεύς** (not Εὐβοιεύς *EM*389.10, and so gen. pl. Εὐβοέων *SIG*419.4 (Delphi, iii B.C.), al., but Εὐβοιέων ib.417.4 (ibid., iii B.C.), al., where οι may be short as in βοιηθέω), έως, ὁ, acc. Εὐβοᾶ, pl. -οᾶς (in codd. often -οέας, cf. Th.4.92) A.D. *Pron.*99.22:—*a Euboean*, Hdt.8.4, etc.:—Adj. **Εὐβοϊκός**, ή, όν, *Euboean*, Id.3.89 (v.l. -εικός), etc. (perh. trisyll. in A.*Fr.*356, E. *Hel.*767); -βοϊκή, ἡ, = ἀκτῆ, Ps.-Dsc.4.173; -κόν, τό, *sweet chestnut*, Thphr.*HP*1.11.3, 4.5.4: masc. **Εὐβοΐτης**, ου, ὁ, Str.10.1.14; fem. **Εὐβοΐς**, gen. Εὐβοΐδος, Hdt.3.89, D.S.12.11; Εὐβοΐς, ἡ, = Εὐβοϊκόν, D.Chr.7.74; contr. forms Εὐβοῖδα, etc., S.*Tr.*74, E.*Heracl.*83 (lyr.), *El.*442 (lyr.), A.*Fr.*30, Ion Trag.18; lengthd. **Εὐβοιΐς** S.*Tr.*237, 401, *Fr.*255.

εὐβολ-έω, *make a good throw* with the dice, Luc.*Am.*16. **-ος**, ον, *throwing luckily* (with the dice), Μίδας ἐν κύβοισιν εὐβολώτατος Eub.58, cf. Poll.9.94, Suid. s. v. Μίδας: generally, *lucky*, ἄγρη Opp. *H.*3.71, Hld.5.18. Adv., ἦν γὰρ -λως ἔχων he was *in luck*, cj. Pors. for εὐβούλως, A.*Ch.*696: Comp., πεσσοὶ -ώτερον πίπτοντες Aristaenet. 1.23.

εὐβοσία, ἡ, *good pasture*, ἡ χώρα ἔχει πολλὴν εὐ. Arist.*HA*522b22, cf. 575b32; *good culture*, Thphr.*HP*1.11.4. 2. *good living*, Arist. *GA*726a6. 3. *good condition*, τοῦ σώματος ib.774b25. 4. *abundance, plenty*, ἐν εὐ. ὑπάρχειν *Inscr.Prien.*108.48 (ii B.C.); ἔθυον -βοσίαν γενέσθαι St.Byz. s. v. Ἀζανοί; ἵνα ὁ δῆμος ἐν εὐβοσίᾳ διαγένηται *Supp.Epigr.*1.366.49 (Samos, iii B.C.); ἐξ ἁλός *AP*11.199 (Leon.). II. divinity worshipped in Asia Minor, *Zeitschr.f. Numism.*7.223 (coin of Hierapolis); Σεβαστὴ Εὐ., of a deified Empress, *IGRom.*4.654 (Acmonia): also spelt Εὐποσία (q. v.):—hence **Εὐβοσιάρχης**, ου, ὁ, official title (like Εὐθηνιάρχης), *Papers of Amer. School* 3 No.317; cf. Εὐποσιάρχης.

εὐβόστρῠχος, ον, *of beautiful locks*, αἴγλη *AP*5.250 (Iren.), cf. Poll. 2.27.

εὐβοτ-έομαι, *furnish good pasture*, Str.11.3.2. **-ος**, ον, (βόσκω) *abounding in pasture*, Od.15.406 (or, *with fine oxen*, cf. βοτόν (Addenda)); τοῖς ζῴοις πᾶσιν εὔβοτον Pl.*Criti.*111a, cf. Ph.1.669, Plu. *Cam.*16: Sup., Scymn.607, prob. in E.*Fr.*1083.6. II. *well-fed, thriving*, ἀμνός Theoc.5.24.

εὔβοτρυς, υ, gen. υος, *rich in grapes*, S.*Ph.*548, *AP*9.668.9 (Marian.): **εὐβότρυος**, ον, f.l. in *Anacreont.*4.17.

εὐβουλ-εύς, έως, ὁ, like εὔβουλος, *he of good counsel*, epith. of Zeus, D.S.5.72; of Dionysus, Orph.*H.*30.6: acc. εὐβουλῆ Plu.2.714c: Εὐ. alone, = Πλούτων, Nic.*Al.*14, Orph.*Fr.*237, Hsch. **-ία**, ἡ, *good counsel, soundness of judgement, prudence*, A.*Pr.*1035, 1038, S. *Ant.*1050, Th.1.78, Isoc.9.46, Arist.*EN*1142b6, etc.; περί τινος Pl. *Prt.*318e: pl., αἱ τῶν προγόνων εὐ. Aeschin.2.75. II. Pythag. name for *three*, *Theol.Ar.*14. **-ος**, ον, *well-advised, prudent*, Thgn.329, Hdt.8.110, Pi.*O.*13.8, B.14.37, Th.1.84, Pl.*R.*428b, Arist. *EN*1141b13: Comp., Ar.*Pax*689: Sup., And.1.140. Adv. -λως (v. εὔβολος): Comp. -ότερον D.C.43.16: Sup. -ότατα *Gp.*5.16.1.

εὐβρᾰχής, or **-βρεχής**, ές, *well steeped* or *soaked*, Nic.*Al.*298.

εὐβρῑθής, ές, *laden with fine* yarn, σπάθαι *AP*6.288.7 (Leon.).

εὔβροχος, ον, *well-noosed, well-knit*, ἅμμα *AP*6.179 (Arch.).

εὔβρωτος, ον, *good to eat*, Str.17.1.51; πρὸς ξηροφαγίαν Ath.3. 113b.

εὐβύριος, ον, = εὔοικος, Euph.128; said to be from a Messapian word, *EM*389.24.

εὔβυρσος, ον, *with beautiful hide* or *skin*, Sch.A.R.3.1299.

εὔβωλος, ον, (βῶλον) *fertile* (v. sub εὔπωλος).

εὐβωλοστρόφητος, ον, *easy to plough*, Eust.385.36, 1431.53.

εὐγᾱθής, εὐγάθητος, Dor. for. εὐγηθ-.

εὔγαιος, ον, freq. v.l. for εὔγειος.

εὐγάλακτος [γᾰ], ον, *yielding much* or *good milk*, αἴξ Alciphr.3.21; τροφός Orib.*Eup.*1.1 (Sup.); νομή Gal.19.121: heterocl. nom. pl. εὐγάλακτες, = εὔτροφοι, Hsch. II. εὐγάλακτον, τό, a plant, = γλαύξ, Plin.*HN*27.82.

εὐγάληνος [ᾰ], ον, *very calm*, Lyc.20. Adv. -νως Sch.A.R.4.1776.

εὐγᾰμ-έω, *marry happily*, Heph.Astr.1.1. **-ία**, ἡ, *happy marriage*, ib.1.20, Paul.Al.*M.*3, Poll.9.160. **-ος**, ον, *happily married*, of persons, Heph.Astr.1.1, Paul.Al.*N.*4, Nonn.*D.*1.27; also εὐνή, ὕδωρ, Id.13.352, 20.144.

εὖγε or **εὖ γε**, Adv. *well, rightly*, in replies confirming or approving what has been said: as σοὶ γὰρ χαρίζομαι. Answ. εὖγε σὺ ποιῶν Pl. *R.*351c; εὖγ', εὖγε ποιήσαντες Ar.*Pax*285; εὖγε, εὖγε, ὦ κύνες, ἕπεσθε X.*Cyn.*6.19: iron., εὖ γοῦν θίγοις ἂν χερνίβων E.*Or.*1602; εὖγε μέντἂν διετέθην Ar.*Av.*1692. 2. without a Verb, *good! well said! well done!* Pl.*Grg.*494c, al.; doubled εὖγ', εὖγε Ar.*Eq.*470; εὖγ', εὖγε, νὴ Δί', εὖγε Id.*Ec.*213; εὖγ', ὅτι ἐπείσθης Id.*Nu.*866: c. gen., εὖγε τῆς προαιρέσεως Luc.*Vit.Auct.*8.

εὔγειος, ον, (γῆ) *of* or *with good soil*, Thphr.*HP*4.11.1, D.S.5.40, Dsc.1.64; εὐγειος (sc. γῆ or χώρα), ἡ, *fertile land*, Thphr.*CP*5.13.2 (pl.), *Gp.*2.21.1; cf. εὔγεως. II. metaph., ψυχή Ph.1.651.

εὐγένεια, poet. **εὐγενία** (q.v.), ἡ, *nobility of birth*, A.*Pers.*442, E.*Fr.*53, al., Isoc.3.42, Arist.*Rh.*1390b16, etc.; ἐμῶν εὐ. παίδων, = ἐμοὶ εὐγενεῖς παῖδες, E.*Tr.*583 (lyr.): pl., Pl.*Euthd.*279b, *R.*618d; *pure breeding*, of animals, Onos.1.21. 2. = γενναιότης, *nobleness* of mind, Plu.*Dem.*24, *Ant.*86, Ael.*VH*12.1, D.Chr.52.16, etc. 3. bodily *excellence*, ἡ ἐν τοῖς σώμασιν εὐ. Plu.*Rom.*6, cf. Gal.*UP*10.6; of materials, χαλκοῦ Philostr.*VA*3.54: generally, *excellence*, Lib.*Or.*49.27. 4. of style, *elevation, nobility*, Longin.34.2; ποιημάτων D.H.*Comp.*18. 5. as a title, ἡ εὐ. σου *PGen.*1.50.14 (iv A.D.).

εὐγένειος, Ep. **ἠϋγέν-**, ον, (γένειον) of a lion, *well-maned*, λέων.. ἠϋγένειος Od.4.456; λίς Il.15.275; of Pan, *well-bearded*, *h.Hom.*19.39; of men, Pl.*Euthphr.*2b, Luc.*Icar.*10.

εὐγεν-έτης, ου, Dor. **-τας**, ὁ, = sq., used by E. in lyr., *Ion* 1060, al., cf. Tim.*Pers.*219, *AP*12.195 (Strat.):—fem. **-έτειρα**, ib.9.788, *IG*14.192 (Syracuse); also **-έτις**, prob. in *IG*5(1).259 (Sparta). **-ής**, ές, in Hom. **εὐηγενής** (q.v.), and in *h.Ven.*94 **ἠϋγενής**: (γένος):—*well-born*, A.*Pers.*704 (troch.), S.*OC*728, etc.; εὐ. δόμος E.*Ion* 1540; τὸ μὲν ἐστίχθαι εὐγενὲς κέκριται being tattooed is esteemed *a mark of nobility*, Hdt.5.6. 2. in Trag. etc. with the connotation *noble-minded, generous* (more prop. γενναῖος, cf. Arist.*Rh.*1390b22), S.*Ant.*38, *Ph.*874, etc.; διαφέρει φύσις γενναίου σκύλακος.. νεανίσκου εὐ. Pl.*R.*375a. 3. of animals, *high-bred*, ἵππος Thgn.184, S.*El.*25; λέων A.*Ag.*1259; ὄρνιθες Plb.1.58.7; of plants, *of a good sort*, Ael.*VH*2.14; ῥόαι Eriph.2.11; πυροί Gal.11.120; βλαστοί *Gp.*5.37.2: so in Comp., Eub.44; φλέβες καὶ ἶνες Thphr.*HP*5.1.7 (s.v.l., cf. εὐτενής); χαλκός S.*Fr.*864 (v.l.): metaph., of a wife, ὥσπερ εὐγενῆ χώραν ἐντεκνώσασθαι παρασχεῖν Plu.*Cat.Mi.*25. 4. of outward form, *noble*, δέρη, πρόσωπον, E.*Hel.*136, *Med.*1072; of style, τὸ εὐ. τῆς λέξεως Ael.*NA Epil.*; εὐ. ῥυθμοί D.H.*Comp.*18. II. Adv. **-ῶς** *nobly, bravely*, κατθανούμεν E.*Cyc.*201, cf. *Tr.*727; εὐτυχεῖν Plu.2.7f. **-ία**, ἡ, = εὐγένεια, E.*HF*696 (lyr.), *AP*7.337.6; *eugenia*, a kind of vine, Plin.*HN*14.25. **-ίζω**, *ennoble*, πόλιν Philem.180, cf. Lib.*Eth.*17.4. **-ιος**· εὐγενής, καὶ εἶδος ἀμπέλου, Hsch. II. **-ιον**, τό, name of a kind of *laurel*, *Gp.*11.3.4. **-ίς**, ίδος, fem. of εὐγενής, J.*AJ*7.3.3, *CIG*3200 (Smyrna), *Cat.Cod.Astr.*8(4).159; = Lat. *Matrona*, Lyd.*Mens.*3.22, cf. Hdn.Gr.1.95.

εὐγεφύρωτος [ῡ], ον, *easy to bridge over*, τόπος Plb.3.66.5.

εὐγεώργ-ητος, ον, *easy to cultivate*, Sch.S.*Ant.*569:—also **-ος**, ον, Scyl.24.

εὔγεως, ων, = εὔγειος, Str.7.4.6, Plu.*Sull.*16, Ael.*NA*5.56, App.*BC*4.102 codd.

εὐγηθ-ής, Dor. **εὐγᾱθ-**, ές, *joyous, cheerful*, E.*HF*793 (lyr.). **-ητος**, Dor. **εὐγάθ-**, ον, = foreg., Id.*IT*212 (lyr.).

εὐγηρ-έω, *grow old happily*, *Stoic.*3.156. **-ία**, ἡ, *green old age*, Arist.*Rh.*1361b26, *Stoic.*3.24, Plu.2.111b, *Cat.Cod.Astr.*8(4).167; χλόης Ph.2.163.

εὔγηρυς, υ, *sweet-sounding*, ἀοιδά Ar.*Ra.*213 (lyr.), cf. Opp.*H.*5.617.

εὐγήρως, ων, *enjoying a green old age*, Arist.*Rh.*1361b28, Call.*Ep.*41.6, *Epigr.Gr.*223.2 (Milet.), Ph.1.515, al.: nom. pl. εὐγηροι Hp.*Vict.*1.32, Arist.*HA*615a33: neut. εὐγηρα Hp.*Art.*58.

εὐγλάγ-ετος [ᾰ], ον, = sq., Luc.*Trag.*110. **-ής**, ές, Nic.*Th.*617; and **εὔγλᾰγος**, ον, Lyc.307:—*abounding in milk*: metapl. dat. εὐγλαγι *AP*9.744 (Leon.).

εὔγληνος, Ep. also **ἐΰ-**, ον, *bright-eyed*, of wild beasts or fish, Lyc.597, Opp.*C.*3.97, Marc.Sid.59.

εὔγλυπτος, ον, *well-carved*, μέταλλον *AP*7.363:—also **εὐγλύφᾰνος** [ῠ], ον, Nonn.*D.*34.228; **εὐγλῠφής**, ές, κάλαμοι *AP*6.63.4 (Damoch.).

εὐγλωσσ-ία, Att. **-ττία**, ἡ, *glibness of tongue, fluency of speech*, E.*Fr.*206.4, Ar.*Eq.*837, Ps.-Ptol.*Centil.*38, Iamb.*Protr.*20. II. *sweetness of song*, Ael.*NA*17.23. **-ος**, Att. **-ττος**, ον, Cret. **-γλωθος** *GDI*5112 (Phaestos, iii/ii B.C.):—*good of tongue, eloquent*, A.*Supp.*775: τὸ Νεστόρειον εὔ. μέλος E.*Fr.*899.1; *glib of tongue, voluble*, Ar.*Nu.*445 (anap.). 2. *sweet-sounding*, of the Attic dialect, *AP*9.188, cf. Gal.8.586; τὸ εὔ. *that which is pleasant to the ear*, D.H.*Comp.*1. 3. = εὔφημος, *GDI* l.c. II. Act., *loosing the tongue, making eloquent*, οἶνος *AP*9.403 (Maec.).

εὐγλωττ-έω, gloss on εὐστομέω, Thom.Mag.p.160 R. **-ίζω**, *make sweet-voiced*, ὁπόσα -ίζοι τοὺς χαραδριούς Philostr.*VA*6.36.

εὐγλώχῑν, ῖνος, ὁ, ἡ, *keen-pointed*, Opp.*H.*5.439, Q.S.8.406.

εὖγμα, ατος, τό, (εὔχομαι) *boast, boasting*, κενὰ εὔγματα εἰπών Od.22.249. II. in pl., *prayers, wishes*, A.*Pr.*584 (lyr.), *Th.*267, *Ch.*463 (lyr.), S.*Ant.*1185, Ar.*Th.*354 (lyr.), Call.*Lav.Pall.*139.

εὐγμᾰλέος, α, ον, *to be prayed for*, prob. in Hsch., Phot.

εὔγναμπτος, Ep. **ἐΰγν-**, ον, *well-bent, well-twisted*, κληῖσιν ἐϋγνάμπτοις Od.18.294; χαλινοί Opp.*H.*5.498; περόναι A.R.3.833; ἄγκυρα Orph.*A.*498, etc. **εὐγναπτοις**· καλῶς κατεσκευασμένοις, Hsch. (v.l. in Od.18.294).

εὔγνητος, ον, = εὐγενής, Philox.1.

εὐγνωμ-ονέω, *have good sense* or *feeling, show a reasonable* or *conciliatory spirit*, Arist.*Rh.Al.*1420a16, Epicur.*Sent.Vat.*62, Plu.*Num.*12, etc.; opp. κακοδαιμονᾶν, Id.*Luc.*4; πρὸς τοὺς ἐχθροὺς D.S.13.22. II. *reward, repay*, τοὺς ἱερέας Lib.*Decl.*34.26, cf. *PAmh.*2.142.17 (iv A.D.); εὐ. τὴν ἀντίδοσιν *make* a return gift *in token of gratitude*, Him.*Or.*8.7. **-ονία**, ἡ, = sq., *PLond.*2.1000.6 (vi A.D.). **-οσύνη**, ἡ, *considerateness, courtesy*, Aeschin.3.170, Procl.*in Prm.*p.551 S.; *a reasonable spirit*, Arist.*MM*1198b34, Anon.Hist.Alex.Magn.p.825 J., v.l. in Luc.*JConf.*7. 2. *prudence*, Plu.*Them.*7, etc. **-ων**, ον, gen. ονος, (γνώμη) *of good feeling, considerate, reasonable*, And.2.6 (Comp.), X.*Mem.*2.8.6; φιλάνθρωπος καὶ εὐ. ψυχή Aeschin.1.137; τὸ μὲν κρῖναι τοῦ εὐγνώμονος, τὸ δὲ δὴ πράττειν κατὰ τὴν κρίσιν τοῦ ἐπιεικοῦς Arist.*MM*1199a2; πολέμιοι -έστεροι Plb.2.57.8; ψεῦδος -έστερον Luc.*VH*1.4: metaph., of a game, εὐ. εἰς τὰς ἄλλας πράξεις *not interfering with* them, Gal.*Parv.Pil.*2; παθεῖν εὐγνώμονα to be *indulgently* treated, D.S.13.23: Sup., ὡς -εστάτων τυγχάνειν D.*Ep.*3.45. 2. *sensible, prudent*, Aeschin.3.170, etc.; εὐ. ὁ μὴ λυπεόμενος ἐφ' οἷσιν οὐκ ἔχει, ἀλλὰ χαίρων ἐφ' οἷσιν ἔχει Democr.231; τὸ λέγειν πρὸς μὴ παρόντας οὐκ εὐ. φαίνεται Plu.2.420f. 3. εὔγνωμον τὸ πόνημα is an offering *of gratitude*, *APl.*4.41 (Agath.). II. Adv. **-νως** *considerately, kindly*, τοῖς πλήθεσι προσφέρεσθαι D.S.19.9, cf. Plu.*Ant.*63; *reasonably*, *BGU*1011.16 (ii B.C.), Luc.*Tox.*5. 2. *gratefully*, Plu.*Sull.*10, Ael.*NA*2.8. 3. *prudently*, χρῆσθαι ἑαυτῷ X.*Ages.*2.25.

εὔγνωστος, ον, *well-known, familiar*, E.*Or.*[1394], Lys.17.4, Pl.*Sph.*218e; opp. ἄγνωστος, Epicur.*Nat.*28.5. 2. *easy to discern*, S.*Aj.*704 (lyr., with v.l. -γνωτος); τὰ εὐ. καὶ εὐμαθῆ X.*Oec.*20.14: Sup., Arr.*Tact.*2.1; εὐγνωστον.. πότερος ἡμῶν ἐσθ' ὁ πονηρός D.29.1; ὅτι.. Lys.17.4. Adv. -τως, κρίνειν TheoSm.p.65 H.

εὔγομφος, ον, *well-nailed, well-fastened*, πύλαι E.*IT*1286:—also **εὐγόμφωτος**, ον, Opp.*H.*1.58.

εὐγον-έω, *to be fruitful*, of flocks, Thphr.*CP*1.14.1. **-ία**, ἡ, *fruitfulness*, Pl.*R.*546a, X.*Lac.*1.6, Ph.2.390, etc.; opp. ἀγονία, Iamb.*Comm.Math.*15. **-ος**, ον, *productive*, v.l. in E.*Hec.*581 (Sup.); τὸ εὔγονον *productive power*, J.*BJ*4.8.3 codd. (sed leg. εὔτονον).

εὐγραμμᾰτία, ἡ, *calligraphy*, Gal.14.587.

εὐγράμμᾰτος, ὁ, *a good writer*, Heph.Astr.1.1.

εὐγραμμ-ία, ἡ, *good design*, of figures in tapestry, Callix.2. **-ος**, ον, *well-designed*, γραφαί D.H.*Is.*4; *well-drawn*, Luc.*JTr.*33; *of graceful contour*, εὔ. τῇ συστάσει, of a person, Str.4.5.2; ὀφρύων τὸ εὔ. their *fine lines*, Luc.*Im.*6. Adv. -γράμμως, of architecture, Lyd.*Mag.*3.70. II. *well-defined*, περίοδοι D.H.*Dem.*40; so τὸ εὔ. Id.*Comp.*23. III. masc., *a good writer*, Man.5.245.

εὐγρᾰφής, ές, (γράφω) *well-painted*, *AP*6.221 (Leon.). II. Act., *writing well*, κάλαμος ib.6.66.6 (Paul. Sil.), cf. 65.10 (Id.).

εὐγρᾰφία, poet. **-γρᾰφίη**, ἡ, *skill in painting*, *Epigr.Gr.*841 (Thrace, ii A.D.).

εὐγύᾰλος [ῠ], ον, *well arched* or *rounded*, Tryph.537, Nonn.*D.*13.68 codd. (εὐρυάλω Ludwich).

εὔγυιος, ον, *with fine limbs, stalwart*, νέοι B.10.10.

εὔγῡρος, ον, *tortuous* (= γυρός, q.v.), πάλη *APl.*3.25 (Phil.).

εὐγων-ία, ἡ, *regularity of angles*, prob. cj. in E.*Ion* 1137. **-ιος**, ον, *with regular angles*, X.*Oec.*4.21, Arist.*Pr.*912b15; *with perfect angles, four square*, of blocks, *IG*2².1666 *A* 64, etc.; *right-angled*, Gal.18(2).856.

εὐδαίδᾰλος, ον, *beautifully wrought*, νᾶα B.16.88; ναόν Id.*Fr.*11.3.

εὐδαιμον-έω, pf. εὐδαιμόνηκα Arist.*Metaph.*1048b26: (εὐδαίμων):—*to be prosperous, well off*, Hdt.1.170, Th.8.24, etc.; τι in respect to..., Hdt.2.177, S.*Ant.*506, etc.; οὔτις ἀνδρῶν εἰς ἅπαντ' εὐ. E.*Fr.*45; ἔν τινι Luc.*DMort.*24.3; εὐδαιμονοίης E.*El.*231, *Ph.*1086: dual, εὐδαιμονοῖτον Id.*Med.*1073; parodied by Ar.*Ach.*446, 457. II. *to be truly happy*, εὐδαιμονοῦσιν ἄνθρωποι ὀρθοσύνῃ καὶ πολυφροσύνῃ Democr.40, cf. Arist.*Pol.*1339b19, Diog.Oen.25, etc. **-ημα**, ατος, τό, *piece of good luck*, Luc.*Im.*22, *Stoic.*3.136 (pl.). **-ησις**, εως, ἡ, *possession of* εὐδαιμονία, Eustr.*in EN*91.27. **-ία**, Ion. **-ίη**, ἡ, *prosperity, good fortune, opulence*, *h.Hom.*11.5, Pi.*N.*7.56, Hdt.1.5,32, Hp.*Ep.*11 (v.l.), etc.; χρημάτων προσόδῳ καὶ τῇ ἄλλῃ εὐ. Th.2.97; of countries, Hdt.5.28, 7.220, etc.; μοῖρ' εὐδαιμονίας Pi.*P.*3.84: pl., E.*IA*591 (anap.), Pl.*Phd.*115d. 2. *true, full happiness*, εὐ. οὐκ ἐν βοσκήμασιν οἰκεῖ οὐδ' ἐν χρυσῷ Democr.171; εὐ. ψυχῆς, opp. κακοδαιμονίη, Id.170, cf. Pl.*Def.*412d, Arist.*EN*1095a18, Zeno *Stoic.*1.46, etc. b. personified as a divinity, *SIG*985.8 (Philadelphia). **-ίζω**, *call* or *account happy*, εὐδαιμόνιζε παῖδα σήν E.*Tr.*268, cf. X.*Mem.*2.7.7, Arist.*EN*1096a2, etc.; τὴν πόλιν Isoc.8.83: c. gen. rei, οὐ.. μοίρας εὐδαιμονίσαι πρώτης for his eminent fortune, S.*OC*144, cf. Pl.*R.*516c, al.; αὐτὸν εὐδαιμονιεῖ τῆς περιουσίας D.21.109, cf. 19.67; εὐ. τινὰ ὑπέρ τινος X.*An.*1.7.3 (s.v.l.); ἐπί τινι D.18.260; διά τι Luc.*Nigr.*23:—Pass., διά τι Pl.*R.*465d, al. **-ικός**, ή, όν, *tending* or *conducive to happiness*, Arist.*EN*1176b16, *Rh.*1367b13; τὰ εὐ. *the constituents thereof*, X.*Mem.*4.2.34; τελετὴ καλή τε καὶ εὐ. Pl.*Phdr.*253c. 2. of persons, *likely to be happy*, Ar.*Ec.*1134, Arist.*EN*1099b3; οἱ εὐ. philosophers *who make happiness the chief good*, D.L.1.17; esp. of Anaxarchus, Clearch.14; so also εὐ. αἵρεσις Gal.*Phil.Hist.*4. Adv. -κῶς, πράττειν, διάγειν, Ar.*Pax* 856 (lyr.), X.*HG*3.2.9. **-ισμα**, ατος, τό, *that which is thought to be a happiness*, Pl.*Ep.*354c. II. *congratulation*, App.*BC*4.16. **-ισμός**, ὁ, *thinking* or *calling happy, predication of happiness*, Arist.*Rh.*1367b34, *EN*1127b18, Plu.*Pel.*34, etc.: pl., ὕμνοι καὶ εὐ. Ph.1.312, al. **-ιστέον**, *one must pronounce happy*, Arist.*EN*1100a10. 2. -έος, α, ον, *to be called happy*, Arr.*An.*1.12.2.

εὐδαιμ-οσύνη, ἡ, = εὐδαιμονία, Archyt.ap.Stob.3.1.112,114, Perict. ib.4.28.19, X.Eph.1.16. **-ων**, ον, gen. ονος, *blessed with a good genius*: hence, *fortunate*, τάων εὐδαίμων τε καὶ ὄλβιος *happy in respect to* them (the days), Hes.*Op.*826; εὐ. καὶ ὄλβιος Thgn.1013; εὐ. καὶ ὑμνητός Pi.*P.*10.22: freq. in Trag., A.*Pr.*647, *Pers.*768, S.*Ant.*582, etc.: c. gen. rei, *happy in* or *on account of*.., Hes. l.c.; εὐ. τοῦ τρόπου Pl.Phd.58e; ironically, εὐ. εἶ, ὅτι οἴει.. Id.R.422e; τὸ εὔδαιμον, = εὐδαιμονία, Th.2.43. Adv. -μόνως E.Or.601, Ar.Pl.802, Arist.Pol. 1281a2, etc.: Comp. -έστερον, διάγοντες X.An.3.1.43: Sup., πόλις -έστατα διάξει Pl.Lg.710b. 2. of outward prosperity, wealthy, οἱ εὐδαίμονες αὐτῶν Hdt.1.133, cf. 196, 5.8, Th.1.6, etc.; ἐν πολλοῖς χρήμασιν εὐδαίμονες ὄντες Lys.32.17; οἱ πλούσιοι καὶ εὐ. Pl.R.406c; οἰκία μεγάλη τε καὶ εὐ. Id.Prt.316b; αἱ Ἀθῆναι μεγάλαι τε καὶ εὐδαίμονες Hdt.8.111; Εὐβοίῃ, νήσῳ μεγάλῃ τε καὶ εὐ. Id.5.31; Κυράνα Pi. P.4.276, etc.; πόλις εὐ. Gorg.Fr.10 D.; Ἀραβία εὐ. Peripl.MRubr.26; γῆ ἀρόσαι οὐκ εὐ. Philostr.Im.2.24; opp. εὐτυχής, ὄλβου δ' ἐπιρρυέντος εὐτυχέστερος ἄλλου γένοιτ' ἂν ἄλλος, εὐδαίμων δ' ἂν οὔ E.Med. 1230. 3. truly happy, βίος Pl.Phlb.11d; ὁ εὖ ζῶν μακάριός τε καὶ εὐ. Id.R.354a, cf. 580b (Sup.), Arist.EN1098b21, etc.

εὐδάκρῡτος, ον, (δακρύω) tearful, lamentable, A.Ch.181.

εὐδάκτῠλος, ον, with beautiful fingers, Alciphr.3.67.

Εὐδαλαγῖνες· αἱ Χάριτες, Hsch. **εὐδάμνας**· εὐδάμαστος, easily subdued, Id.

Εὐδάνεμος [ᾰ], ὁ, Storm-stiller, a hero worshipped at Eleusis, Arr.An.3.16.8; = ἄγγελος, Hsch.: also in pl., Εὐδανέμων βωμός, at Athens, Arr. l. c., cf. D.H.Din.11. (Εὐδ. codd. Arr.)

εὐδάνει, prob. f.l. for ἐνδαύει, Lyc.1354.

εὔδαος, ον, dub. sens. in Sammelb.5199.2.

εὐδάπᾰνος [δᾰ], ον, (δαπάνη) lavish of expense, liberal, ἐλευθεριότης εὐ. εἰς τὰ καλά Arist.VV1250a13; τὸ εὐ. Plu.Sol.3: Sup., D.C.44. 39. II. of moderate expense, cheap, D.H.2.23, D.C.52.30, Porph. Abst.2.14.

εὐδαρκής· εὐόφθαλμος, Hsch. (prob. f.l. for εὐδρακής or εὐδερκής).

εὐδείελος, ον, clear, distinct, Hom. (only in Od.), usu. of Ithaca, 2.167, 9.21, etc.: generally, ἤ πού τις νήσων εὐδείελος 13.234; far-seen, Κρόνιον Pi.O.1.111; ἄστυ Orac.ap.Eus.PE6.7. II. open to the sun, sunny, χθὼν Ἰαολκοῦ Pi.P.4.76; Κρίση h.Ap.438; ὅσσα φύει εὐ. αἶα Euph.50. (In signf. 1 perh. fr. δέελος (dub. l.), δῆλος (*δεάλος?): the alternative expl. from δείλη (cf. supr. II) given by ancient Gramm., e. g. Apollon.Lex. and Str.9.2.41, does not suit signf. 1, but suits the forms.)

εὐδεινός, ή, όν, later contr. of εὐδιεινός, Orph.H.22.5 codd.: Comp. -ότερος An.Ox.2.207; also εὐδινή (v.l. -διεινή) Str.6.3.9, cf. OGI 194.22 (Egypt, i B.C.), Hsch.

εὐδειπν-ία, ἡ, feast offered to departed souls, Harmod.1; cf. sq. II. **-ος**, ον, with goodly feasts, δαῖτες εὐ. well-appointed, sumptuous feasts, E.Med.200 (anap.). II. epith. of departed souls to whom offerings were made (cf. foreg.), παρ' εὐδείπνοις ἔσῃ ἄτιμος ἐμπύροισι κνισωτοῖς χθονός A.Ch.484; taken by some Gramm. as applied to the festival itself, Hsch., Phot., EM42.3.

εὔδεκτος, ον, capacious, σῶμα IG11(4).1247 (Delos, iii/ii B.C.).

εὔδενδρος, ον, well-wooded, abounding in fair trees, ἄλσος Pi.O.8.9; μάτηρ (sc. Γαῖα) Id.P.4.74; τέμενος Simon.13; χόρτοι E.IT134 (lyr.), etc.: also in Prose, Hp.Aër.12 (Sup.), Str.2.3.4, Ph.2.117.

εὐδερκής, ές, seeing brightly, bright-eyed, Max.151, 263.

εὐδέρμᾰτος, ον, (δέρμα) with good, stout hide, Sch.A.R.2.125.

εὐδές (post εὐετηρία)· εὔυπνον, εὐήνεμον, Hsch. (fort. εὐαές).

εὐδέψητος, ον, (δεψέω) well-tanned, δέρματα Hp.Art.30 (Sup.), cf. Gal.18(1).436.

εὔδηλος, ον, quite clear, abundantly manifest, A.Pers.1009 (lyr.), etc.; εὔ. [ἐστὶ] κελεύων may be seen bidding..., Ar.Ach.1130 (sed cod. R ἔνδηλος); ῥυθμός easily distinguishable, Arist.Pr.882b9; εὔ. γράμματα plainly legible, POxy.1100.3 (iii A.D.); εὔδηλόν [ἐστιν] ὅτι.. Pl.Plt.308d; φιλόσοφός τις εἶ—εὔδηλον Alex.135.11; ἐν εὐδήλῳ [ἐστί] Hp. de Arte9. Adv. -λως Plu.Thes.3.

εὐδία, Ion. -ίη, ἡ, fair weather, εὐδία ἐκ χειμῶνος Pi.I.7(6).38, cf. Antipho 2.2.1, Hp.Insomn.89; ἐν εὐδίᾳ χειμῶνα ποιεῖν X.HG2.4.14; ὅταν εὐ. γένηται Arist.HA551a3; εὐδίας (gen.) in fine weather, ib.597b 13: pl., ἔν γε χειμῶσιν καὶ ἐν εὐδίαις Pl.Lg.961e; εὐδιῶν οὐσῶν Arist. HA626a4. 2. metaph., tranquillity, peace, Pi.O.1.98, P.5.10, A. Th.795, X.An.5.8.20; τὴν Αἴγυπτον εἰς εὐδίαν ἀγαγεῖν OGI90.11 (Rosetta, ii B.C.), cf. Herod.1.28; εὐ. καὶ διαγωγὴ ἄλυπος Polystr. p.17 W.; of the mind, Protag.9; σαρκὸς εὐ. good condition of.., Plu. 2.126c; εἰς ἔμ' εὐδίαν ἔχων being at ease so far as I am concerned, S.Ichn.346. [On the prosody, v. εὔδιος.]

εὐδιά-βᾰτος, ον, easy to cross, ποταμός X.HG4.2.11, Colot.ap.Plu. 2.1117d, cf. Polyaen.2.2.1. **-βλητος**, ον, = εὐδιάβολος, Arist.EE 1237b23, Chrysipp.Stoic.3.77, S.E.M.3.160, Ptol.Tetr.2: Sup., Eus. Mynd.47. **-βόητος**, ον, readily talked about, Ptol.Tetr.172. **-βολος**, ον, easy to misrepresent, Pl.Lg.944b; εὐδιάβολα τὰ τοιαῦτα πρὸς τοὺς πολλούς Id.Euthphr.3b. Adv. -λως, ἔχειν D.61.17. **-γνωστος**, ον, easy to distinguish, Gal.14.63 (Sup.), Nicom.Harm.2.

εὐδιάγωγος [ᾰ], ον, cheerful, Dsc.4.60 (Comp.); pleasant, ἀνάπαυλαι Ph.1.52, etc.

εὐδιάζω, calm, still, χειμῶνας Ph.2.567 (metaph.):—in Med., = εὐδιάω, βίος ἀσαλεύτῳ ἡσυχίᾳ εὐδιαζόμενος Pl.Ax.370d. II. intr. in Act., to be calm, εὐδιαζούσας ἡμέρας Antig.Mir.150.

εὐδιά-θετος, ον, well-arranged. Adv. -τως J.BJ3.5.2. 2. easily affected, ὑπὸ τῶν ἔξωθεν A.D.Synt.291.15. II. well-disposed, of persons. Adv. -τως, = εὐγνωμόνως, Hsch. III. easy to dispose of (in marriage), Id. s. v. οὐκ εὐ.; also of arguments or objections, Them. in APo.62.33. **-θρυπτος**, ον, easily crushed, Phlp. in de An.360.15.

εὐδίαιος or **-ιαῖος**, ὁ, hole in a ship, for letting off the bilge-water, Plu.2.699f, Poll.1.92, Hsch., Suid. II. **εὐδίαιον**, τό, the end of a clyster-pipe, Paul. ex Fest.p.69 L.; εὔδιον Poll.4.181. 2. = γυναικεῖον μόριον, Hsch. 3. = πρωκτός, Id. III. as Adj., εὐδιαῖος, α, ον, caught in fair weather, τριγόλας Sophr.67.

εὐδιαίρετος, ον, easy to divide, Arist.Ph.215b11 (Comp.); easy to tear, destroy, Thphr.HP7.13.1, Arist.PA654a30, etc.; easy to take to pieces, of a machine, Ph.Bel.56.35.

εὐδιαίτερος, α, ον, irreg. Comp. of εὔδιος (q.v.).

εὐδῐαίτητος, ον, easy to decide, Str.8.1.1, Gal.2.881.

εὐδίαιτος [ῐ], ον, living temperately, opp. πολυδάπανος, X.Ap.19, cf. Poll.6.27, etc.

εὐδιακόμιστος, ον, easy to convey through or across, Hsch. s.v. ἀγχίπους.

εὐδιάκονος [ᾱ], serving well, Hsch. s. v. ἀκόμης.

εὐδιά-κοπος, **-κοπτος**, ον, easy to cut through, Plb.3.46.4, 55. 1. **-κόσμητος**, ον, easy to arrange, Id.8.34.9. **-κρῐτος**, ον, easy to distinguish, A.D.Adv.164.12, Gal.1.317. 2. easy to explain, clear, σαφῆ καὶ εὐ. Just.Nov.166Pr., cf. Sch.Il.24.23. **-λειπτος**, ον, intermittent, πῦρ Ps.-Plu.Vit.Hom.105 (s.v.l.).

εὐδιάλλακτος, ον, easy to reconcile, placable, D.H.4.38, Plu.2.332d. Adv. -τως Id.Caes.54, M.Ant.1.7 (v.l. εὐαναδιδάκτως codd. Suid.).

εὐδιά-λογος, = εὐόμιλος, Suid., Zonar. **-λῠτος**, ον, easy to undo or open, of traps, Str.6.2.6. 2. easy to dissolve or break up, gloss on ὑποψάθυρος, Gal.16.762: metaph., φιλίαι Arist.EN1156a19, cf. Ph.1.379; Ἑλλάς Plu.Phil.8. 3. easy to solve or refute, D.H. Rh.9.5, Hermog.Meth.22. 4. easy to dissolve, and so to digest, Hices.ap.Ath.3.87e. II. easy to reconcile, Plb.29.11.5.

εὐδῐάναξ [ᾰν], ακτος, ὁ, ruler of the calm, Luc.VH1.15.

εὐδιανέμητος, ον, divisible, Gloss.

εὐδιανόητος, ον, of good understanding, Sm.1Ki.25.3.

εὐδιᾱνός, ή, όν, = εὔδιος, ψυχρᾶν εὐδιανὸν φάρμακον αὐρᾶν a warm remedy for chill airs, i.e. a warm cloak, Pi.O.9.97, cj. in P.5.10.

εὐδιά-πλαστος, ον, easily moulded, plastic, of water, Olymp.Alch. p.82 B. **-πνευστος**, ον, = sq., Thphr.Od.39, Ath.1.26e, Ath. Med.ap.Orib.1.2.2. II. Act., perspiring freely, ib.9.5.3, Gal.6. 407. **-πνοος**, ον, contr. **-πνους**, ουν, easily transpiring, τὸ ὑγρόν Arist.PA671a32. **-πτωτος**, ον, prone to error, ὁρμή Porph.Marc.22.

εὐδιάρθρωτος, ον, well-articulated, of style, Eust.106.12, al.

εὐδιά-σειστος, ον, easily shaken, ἀνέμῳ EM104.5, cf. Hsch. s. v. ῥαδινόν, etc. II. easy to disprove, A.D.Pron.4.23. **-σκέδαστος**, ον, easily spread, of a plaster, Orib.9.37.7. II. easily dispersed, ἡδονή Eus.Mynd.63. **-σπαστος**, ον, easily torn asunder, χάραξ Plb. 18.18.9. **-φθαρτος**, ον, easily spoiled, Pl.Lg.845d. **-φθορος**, ον, easily destroyed, ὀλιγαρχία Arist.Pol.1306a10; [ἔντομα] Id.PA682b 16; of papyrus rolls, Arch.Pap.6.101 (i A.D.). II. easily corrupted, Arist.Ath.41.2 (Comp.); easily going bad, of food, Xenocr.ap.Orib. 2.58.145, Dsc.1.105.

εὐδιαφορ-έω, = εὐφορέω, κατὰ τὴν γέννησιν Gp.19.6.12. **-ησία**, ἡ, freedom of perspiration, Sor.1.29. **-ητος**, ον, easily carried off by perspiration or secretion, Dsc.ap.Ath.1.10c, Phlp. in de An.443. 27. 2. easily distributed or digested, of foods, Gal.6.661, Xenocr. 2, PGoodsp.Cair.2 ii 1 (ii A.D.). 3. easily evaporated, ὕδωρ Olymp. in Mete.299.8. II. Act., easily perspiring, Gal.15.583.

εὐδιά-χῠτος, ον, easily dissolved, φάρμακα ὑπὸ τῶν κοιλιῶν Arist. Pr.864a29; γῆ Thphr.CP3.2.6. 2. easily diffused, ἀήρ Placit.4. 13.11. 3. flexible, Sch.Pi.P.1.17. II. easily relieved, τὴν ὄρεξιν εὐ. ἔχειν Epicur.Sent.26. **-χώρητος**, ον, of food, easy to digest and pass, Xenocr.31, cf. Ruf.Interrog.40: Comp., Arist.Pr.927b22.

εὐδῐάω, Ep. part. εὐδιόων, (εὔδιος) to be fair or calm, of sea and weather, κόλπος A.R.2.371; [ἄνεμος] Opp.H.3.58; πάντη Διὸς -όωντος Arat.899; of persons, to enjoy such weather, A.R.2.903.

εὐδίδακτος [ῐ], ον, docile, D.S.2.29.

εὐδιεινός, ή, όν, = εὔδιος, χειμών Hp.Aph.3.12 (v.l.), Plu. in Arat.7 (Comp.); γαλήνη Pl.Lg.919a; τροπαί Arist.HA542b5; ὁ ζέφυρος Id. Pr.943b21, etc.; ἐν εὐδιεινοῖς in sheltered spots, X.Cyn.5.9, Arist.HA 548b21, cf. Mete.347a23 (Comp.), Thphr.HP3.2.5. Adv. -νῶς calmly, gently, ἱλαρῶς καὶ εὐ. παρακελεύειν Hp.Decent.16; later contr. εὐδεινός (q.v.).

εὐδιέξοδος, ον, easily going out, Hp.Flat.8; εὐ. κοιλίη an easy evacuation, Id.Salubr.5.

εὐδίετος, ον, (διΐημι) easily melting, Dsc.1.19.

εὐδιήγητος, ον, easy to tell, Isoc.19.28, Procop.Aed.4.1, etc.

εὐδῐκ-ία, Ion. -ίη, ἡ, (δίκη) righteous dealing, righteousness, εὐδικίας ἀνέχῃσι Od.19.111; εὐδικίῃ righteously, A.R.4.343; σύντροφος εὐδικίης IG3.1151; ὃς εὐδικίης ἀγανῇσι σῶσε...πόλιας Epigr.Gr.915, cf. BCH50.444 (Thespiae, iv A.D.): also in late Prose, Phld.Hom.p.43 O., Ph.1.664, Plu.2.781f. **-ος**, ον, righteous, BCH23.302 (Termessus): as pr. n., IG1².393 (vi B.C.), etc.

εὐδῑν-ής, ές, = sq., χοροῦ κύκλος Orac.ap.Porph.Plot.22 (acc. -δίνεα codd.). **-ητος**, ον, easily turning, τρύπανα AP6.205.7 (Leon.). II. well-rounded, Nonn.D.6.109.

εὐδινός, ή, όν, v. εὐδεινός.

εὐδιόδ-ευτος, ον, = sq., Plu. in Hes.13. **-ος**, ον, easy to go through, permeable, χώρα Thphr.HP1.7.1; permeable by the breezes, ἕξις τῆς σαρκός Arist.Pr.887b24. II. easily passing through, πρὸς τοὺς πόρους Thphr.Od.60; τροφή Aret.CA2.6.

εὐδιοίκητος, ον, easy to assimilate or digest, Herod.(?)Med. in Rh.Mus.58.112, Ath.Med.ap.Orib.1.9.2, Xenocr.33, Alex.Aphr. in Top.153.6, Gal.14.736. II. well-ordered, ἁρμονία (of structure and function) Antyll.ap.Orib.6.10.4. III. as a complimentary term of address, POxy.1413.32 (iii A.D.).

εὔδιον, τό, v. εὐδίαιος II.

εὐδιοποιέω, *clear the sky, Gloss.*

εὐδί-οπτος, ον, *easy to see through*, Arist.*PA*658^{a}5, *Pr.*932^{b}8 (Comp.), cf. Thphr.*Sens.*80; τὸ εὐ. τῆς θαλάσσης Arist.*GA*779^{b}31. **-όρθωτος**, ον, *easy to restore* or *correct*, νοῦσοι Hp. *de Arte* 13; συμφορά D.H.10.42. II. *easily repaired*, Apollod.*Poliorc.*139.7. **-όριστος**, ον, *easy to define*, Arist. *de An.*421^{a}7; *easy to distinguish*, Gal.7.778.

εὔδιος, ον, *calm, fine, clear*, of air, weather, sea, ἄνεμος X.*HG*1.6.38 (Comp.); εὔδια πάντα Theoc.22.22; ἁλὸς ἄκραι A.R.1.521, etc.; *warm, mild*, χειμών Hp.*Aër.*10; *peaceful*, εὐ. καὶ γαληνὸς βίος Ph.1.411; of persons, *mild, gracious*, εὐδίja *the Gracious one*, Inscr. Cypr. in *Berl.Sitzb.*1911.639, cf. Opp.*H.*4.29; τὸ εὔδιον τοῦ προσώπου M.Ant.6.30: neut. εὔδιον, εὔδια, as Adv., Opp.*C.*1.44, *AP*10.14.1 (Agath.): Comp. -αίτερος X.l.c.: Sup. -εστάτη [χώρη] Hp.*Aër.*12. II. *in fine weather*, κέπφοι εὔδιοι ποτέονται Arat.916; *bringing fine weather*, Orph.*H.*38.24. (For εὐδιϝος, cf. Ζεύς.) [ῐ in εὐδία, εὔδιος, exc. metri gr., Orph. l. c., Arat. l. c.]

εὐδίπλωτος, ον, *easily folded*, Eust.1056.65.

εὔδιφρος, ον, *with beautiful chariots*, of Elis, Nonn.*D.*37.139.

εὔδμητος, Dor. **-δμᾱτος**, ον, *well-built*, βωμός Il.1.448; πύργοι Hes.*Sc.*242; κολώνα Pi.*P.*12.3; ἀγυιαί A.R.1.317. (Always in Ep. form ἐΰδμ-, exc. in Od.20.302 ὁ δ' εὔδμητον βάλε τοῖχον.)

εὐδοκ-έω, *to be well pleased* or *content*, Plb.2.49.2, al.; ἐάν... Id.29.12.8: c. part., Id.15.36.6: c. dat., *to be content with, find pleasure in* a person or thing, Id.18.52.5, D.S.17.47, D.H.8.74; τῇ ἀδικίᾳ 2*Ep. Thess.*2.12; ἔν τινι Lxx*Is.*62.4, al., 2*Ep.Cor.*12.10, al.; εἴς τινα 2*Ep. Pet.*1.17; ἐπί τινι Lxx*Ju.*15.10: also c. acc., τινα ib.*Ge.*33.10; [ἐγγύους] *SIG*672.27 (Delph., ii B. C.); ἡ γῆ -ήσει τὰ σάββατα Lxx*Le.*26.34. 2. *consent, approve*, c. dat., τοῖς γεγραμμένοις *PLond.*3.1168.15 (i A. D.), al.; τῇ δημοσιώσει *POxy.*1273.40 (iii A. D.); also ἐπί τινι *PTeb.*317.33 (ii A. D.), al.: freq. abs. in legal documents, *PRyl.*120.24 (ii A. D.), etc. 3. c. inf., *consent, agree to do*, Plb.1.78.8, al. (and c. acc. et inf., *consent* that.., Id.1.8.4, Lxx 2*Ma.*14.35); *to be ready, willing*, *PGrenf.*1.1.17 (ii B. C.), 1*Ep.Thess.*2.8. b. *determine, resolve*, *Ev.Luc.*12.32, etc. 4. *to be content, happy*, Phld.*D.*1.1:—also in Med., τῆς εὐδοκουμένης ζωῆς Id.*Mort.*36. 5. Med., = Act. in signf. 1, ἐπί τινι Plb.1.8.4; τινι Id.3.31.6, D.S.15.16 codd.; περί τινος Phld.*Rh.Supp.*p.44 S. II. Pass., *to be favoured*, i. e. *prosper*, Lxx 1*Ch.*29.23: c. dat., *find approval with*, τισι Plb.1.88.4, al. 2. *to be approved*, ὑπό τινων *BGU*1157.12 (i B. C.). III. of persons or things, *to be well-pleasing* or *acceptable, find favour with*, τινι Plb.20.5.10, Max.Tyr.32.5; τὰ -οῦντα ἑαυτῷ Phld.*Rh.Supp.*p.54 S. IV. c. acc. et gen., *deem worthy of*, τινα τιμῆς *PLond.*1.3.6 (ii B. C.). **-ησις**, εως, ἡ, *satisfaction, approval*, Plb.16.20.4, D.S.15.6, D.H.3.13, S.E.*M.*7.200; *consent, concurrence*, *POxy.*1273.39 (iii A. D.); ἔλαβον -ησιν *SIG*685.108 (Crete, ii B. C.). **-ητός**, ή, όν, *well-pleasing, acceptable*, Sm.*Ps.*67(68).31, D.L.2.87. Adv. -τῶς *with good repute*, *Vit.Philonid.*p.9 C. **-ία**, ἡ, = εὐδόκησις, esp. of God, Lxx 1*Ch.*16.10, al., *Ev.Luc.*2.14, al.; *good will*, *Ep.Phil.*1.15; *contentment*, Phld.*Piet.*25. 2. *object of desire*, Lxx*Ps.*144.16, *Si.*18.31. 3. v.l. for εὐδοκιμίη in Hp.*Praec.*6.

εὐδοκίμ-άζω, *choose, select*, *PThead.*19.17 (iv A. D.). (Incorrect form.) **-έω**, impf. ηὐδοκίμουν Pl.*Grg.*515e: aor. ηὐδοκίμησα X.*Cyr.*7.1.46, D.7.20: pf. ηὐδοκίμηκα Ar.*Nu.*1031: the augm. is omitted in Ion., Hdt.3.131, 7.227, and freq. in codd. of Att., etc., as Ar. l. c., X.*HG*6.1.2, etc.:—*to be of good repute, highly esteemed, popular*, Thgn.587, E.*Fr.*546 (lyr.), Ar. l. c., Pl.*Grg.* l. c., etc.; εὐ. ἐνθυμήματι *gain credit by*.., X.*HG*4.5.4; εὐ. ἔν τινι *to be distinguished* in a thing, Hdt.1.59, Th.2.37; ἐπὶ σοφίᾳ ἐν πᾶσι τοῖς Ἕλλησιν Pl.*Hp.Ma.*291a, cf. Isoc.3.30; ἐπὶ τῶν λόγων D.*Prooem.*9; τὰ ἄλλα D.C.60.8; περί τι Pl.*R.*368a, etc.; παρὰ τοῖς ἀνθρώποις ἔκ τινος Isoc.11.28, cf. Plu.*Dio* 34; ἀπό τινων Eus.Mynd.55; ἀπ' ἀρετῆς ἐκ γένους ἀλλ' οὐκ ἐκ τοῦ προστυχόντος εὐ. D.C.*Fr.*57.48; ἐς φήμην Id.*Fr.*54.7; εὐ. μάλιστα τῶν Πρωταγόρου μαθητῶν Pl.*Prt.*315a; διὰ πάντων τῶν βασιλέων Hdt.6.63; εὐ. παρὰ βασιλεῖ *to have influence* with him, Id.8.87, cf. Lys.25.24, etc.:—later in Med., *Com.Adesp.*110.4. 2. of wine, meats, etc., *to be highly esteemed, popular*, εὐ. σφόδρα Alex.282, cf. Philem.122; σκῶπες σφόδρα εὐ., i. e. their flesh, Arist.*HA*618^{a}3; so of things generally, θεάματα κατὰ τὰς τέχνας -οῦντα Isoc.4.45, cf. 9.11; παρὰ τοῖς Ἕλλησι -δοκιμῶν νόμος D.21.50, cf. Arist.*EN*1181^{a}16; of popular arguments, Id.*Rh.*1400^{b}25; of physicians and medical treatments, Gal.10.390, Herod.Med. in *Rh.Mus.*58.112; ἐκ τούτων ἡ νῦν εὐ. σοφία *AP*11.157 (Ammian.):—also in Pass., ἀκρόαμα -ούμενον Plu.*Galb.*16; *to be recognized, approved*, *PTeb.*25.16 (ii B. C.). 3. of money, *to be genuine*, Lxx*Ge.*43.23. II. in Med., *hold in honour*, D.S.4.24 codd. **-ησις**, εως, ἡ, *good repute, reputation, credit*, mostly in pl., Pl.*R.*358a, 363a, Luc.*Pisc.*25: sg., Them.*Or.*29.347c. **-ία**, ἡ, = foreg., Pl.*Phlb.*58d (pl.); v.l. in Hp.*Praec.*6. **-ίζω**, *nobilito*, *Gloss.* **-ος**, ον, *in good repute, honoured, famous, glorious*, στρατιά A.*Pers.*858 (lyr.); θανάτου μέρος E.*Heracl.*621 (lyr.); εὐ. εἴς τι, πρός τι, in Sup., Pl.*Ap.*29d, *Lg.*878a; ἐπί τινι Plu.*Lys.*22; ἐν πᾶσιν Pl.*Lg.*631b; τὴν πατρίδα ἐν τῇ Ἑλλάδι -ωτέραν ποιεῖν X.*Mem.*3.7.1.

εὐδοκουμένως, Adv. pres. part. Med. of εὐδοκέω, *satisfactorily*, c. dat., Plb.18.51.10, D.S.28.11.

εὐδόμητος, ον, formed to expl. εὔδμητος, Eust.782.24.

εὔδομος, Boeot. for ἕβδομος, *BCH*21.558 (Thespiae).

εὐδοξ-έω, *to be in good repute, to be honoured, famous*, E.*Rh.*496, X.*Mem.*3.6.16, D.20.142, Ph.2.61, etc.; τὰ πολλὰ X.*HG*1.1.31. **-ία**, ἡ, *good repute, honour*, Simon.4.6, Pi.*P.*5.8, E.*Tr.*643, Isoc.11.29, etc., cf. Arist.*Rh.*1361^{a}25; *virtue, excellence*, Pi.*N.*3.40: in pl., D.18.322. 2. *approval*, μετ' εὐδοξίας πλήθους ἀριστοκρατία Pl.*Mx.*238d. II. *good judgement*, opp. ἐπιστήμη, Id.*Men.*99b. **-ος**, ον, (δόξα) *of good repute, honoured*, Thgn.195, Pi.*P.*12.5, Th.1.84 (Sup.), etc.; Νίκη Simon.145, cf. Pi.*P.*6.17; εὐ. παρά τισι Pl.*Lg.*773a; νέες εὐδοξόταται '*crack*' ships, Hdt.7.99. Adv. -ξως *remarkably*, '*famously*', Pl.*Hp.Ma.*287e; *with distinction*, στεφανῶσαί τινα Man.1.102.

εὔδουλος, ον, *good to one's slaves*, Achae.32, Pherecr.212.

εὐδρᾰκής, ές, (δέρκομαι) *sharp-sighted*, S.*Ph.*847 (lyr.).

εὐδρᾰν-εια [δρᾰ], ἡ, (δραίνω) *bodily strength and health*, Lxx *Wi.*13.19, Hsch. **-ής**, ές, *vigorous*, Phot.

εὐδρομ-έω, *to be fleet of foot*, Men.681, Plu.*Phil.*18: metaph., *go off well*, Philostr.*Im.*1.30; *to be successful*, S.E.*M.*10.36. **-ία**, Ion. -ίη, ἡ, *swiftness*, πλόου Hp.*Ep.*14. **-ίας**, poet. -ίης, ου, ὁ, *rapid swimmer*, of a fish, Eratosth.12 codd. **-ος**, ον, *running well, swift*, κλωστήρ *AP*6.160 (Antip. Sid.); Ἄρτεμις Orph.*H.*36.6; of pulleys, Gal.18(1).521: metaph. in Sup. -ώτατος, πρὸς ἀρετήν Max.Tyr.16.8. 2. *easily traversed*, ὄρη Id.26.2 (Sup.), cf. Poll.1.186. II. in Medic. sense, *lively*, σῶμα Plu.2.715e; = εὐδιαχώρητος, τροφαί Aret.*CA*2.6.

εὔδροσος, ον, *with plenteous dew, abounding in water*, παγαί E.*IA* 1517 (lyr.); τόποι Ar.*Av.*245 (lyr.); νασμοί Aristonous 1.42.

εὐδυκήμερος· εὔστοχος, Hsch.

εὐδύνᾰμος [ῠ], ον, *mighty*, Sch.Pi.*O.*1.165.

εὐδύνᾰτος [ῠ], ον, = foreg., Orph.*H.*29.20, al.

εὐδυσώπητος, ον, *soon put out of countenance*: *easily worked upon by entreaty*, Plu.2.528e, dub. in *PMed.Lond.*155 iii 33.

εὕδω, impf. ηὗδον Pl.*Smp.*203b, E.*Rh.*763, 779, εὗδον Il.2.2, Theoc.2.126; Ep. iter. εὕδεσκε Il.22.503: fut. εὑδήσω A.*Ag.*337: aor. εὕδησα (καθ–) Hp.*Int.*12:—*sleep*, Il.2.19, Hdt.1.34, etc.: c. acc. cogn., ὁππότ' ἂν αὖτε εὕδησθα γλυκὺν ὕπνον Od.8.445; ὕπνον οὐκ εὐδαίμονα E.*HF*1013; γλυκερὸν καὶ ἐγέρσιμον ὕπνον Theoc.24.7; μακρὸν ἀτέρμονα νήγρετον ὕπνον Mosch.3.104; ὕπνῳ γ' εὕδοντα *slumbering* in sleep, S.*OT*65; εὕδειν... παρὰ χρυσέῃ Ἀφροδίτῃ Od.8.337, cf. 342; ξὺν ὁμήλικι εὕδειν Thgn.1063; ὅλην διατελεῖν νύκτα εὕδοντα Pl.*Lg.*807e; of the *sleep of death*, Πρόμαχος δεδμημένος εὕδει ἔγχει ἐμῷ Il.14.482; οὑμὸς εὕδων... νέκυς S.*OC*621. II. metaph., *rest, be still*, ὄφρ' εὕδησι μένος Βορέαο Il.5.524; εὑδέτω πόντος εὑδέτω δ' ἄμοτον κακόν Simon.37.15, cf. A.*Ag.*566; πόλεμον εὕδοντ' ἐπεγείρει Sol.4.19; εὕδουσιν ὀρέων κορυφαί Alcm.60.1; οὔπω κακὸν τόδ' εὕδει E.*Supp.*1147 (lyr.); εὕδει χάρις *sleeps, ceases*, Pi.*I.*7(6).17; οὔποθ' εὕδει λυπρά σου κηρύγματα E.*Hec.*662; of the mind or heart, *to be at ease*, πυκνῆς ἀκοῦσαι ψακάδος εὑδούσῃ φρενί S.*Fr.*636, cf. Theoc.2.126; of persons, *take one's ease, be inactive*, κεῖ βραδὺς εὕδει S.*OC*307; Γοργίαν ἐάσομεν εὕδειν we will let him *rest*, Pl.*Phdr.*267a. (καθεύδω is generally used in Att. and later Prose, exc. Pl. ll.c., X.*Cyn.*5.11.)

εὐδώρητος, ον, *abundantly given*, Opp.*H.*4.359.

εὔδωρος, poet. **ἐΰδ–**, ον, *generous*, Opp.*H.*2.39.

Εὐδωσώ, ἡ, title of Aphrodite at Syracuse, Hsch.

εὐέᾱνος, ον, *richly robed*, Mosch.4.75, Max.477, 562: pr. n. Εὐ]εάνο[ν], = Εὐηνόν (acc.), dub. in B.*Scol.Oxy.*2081(*e*).

εὐέγρετος, ον, (ἔγρομαι, ἐγείρω) *easily aroused, stimulated*, πρὸς διδασκαλίαν v.l. in Hierocl. in *CA*8 p.432 M.

εὐεγχής, ές, *with mighty spear*, Ἄρης B.12.147.

εὔεδνα· ἀγλαΐα, Hsch.

εὔεδρος, ον, (ἕδρα) *on stately throne*, of gods, A.*Th.*96, 319 (both lyr.). 2. εὐ. καθέδρα *a firm* seat on horseback, etc., Anon.ap. Suid.; τὸ εὐ. Ph.1.21; *well-poised*, Apollod.*Poliorc.*157.3. Adv. -ρως, = βεβαίως, Hsch., Phot. 3. of ships, = εὐσσελμος, Theoc.13.21. 4. *well-fitting*, of building materials, D.H.*Comp.*6. Adv. -ρως, = εὐθέτως, Hsch. II. Pass., *easy to sit*, ἵππος X.*Eq.*1.12 (Comp.). III. *in a right* or *lucky place*, εὔεδρος ὄρνις a bird of augury *appearing in a lucky quarter*, Ael.*NA*16.16.

εὐέθειρα, fem. Adj. *beautiful-haired*, κούρα Anacr.76; Ἶσις *Sammelb.*4127.21.

εὐέθωκεν (i. e. ἐϝέθωκεν)· εἴωθεν, Hsch.

εὐειδ-εια or -ία, ἡ, *good looks*, Lesb.Rh.2.7, Corn.*ND*15 (v.l. εὐήδεια). **-ής**, ές, *well-shaped, comely*, γυνή Il.3.48; prop. of female beauty (v. Eust. adloc.), cf. Hes.*Th.*250, Thgn.1002, Pi.*I.*8(7).31, B.12.102, Hdt.1.196 (Sup.), al., Pl.*Cri.*44a, X.*Mem.*3.11.4; of males, Hdt.1.112, 6.32 (Sup.), A.*Pers.*324, E.*Hel.*1540, X.*HG*5.3.9: generally, *beautiful*, χρωτὸς εὐειδὴς φύσις E.*Alc.*174; τὸ εὐ. *beauty of face*, Cret. usage mentioned by Arist.*Po.*1461^{a}14.

εὐείκαστος, ον, *easy to conjecture*, Hsch. II. *good at guessing*, Ptol.*Tetr.*155.

εὔεικτος, ον, *pliant, tractable*, D.C.69.20 (Zonar., εὔοικτος (q. v.) codd.); *soft, yielding*, τὰ εὐ. Alex.Aphr.*Pr.*2.23, cf. Heraclit.*All.*51 (εὔθικτος codd.); of abscesses, Paul.Aeg.4.18: Comp. -ότερος, gloss on λειότερος, Sch.Orib.49.3.5. Adv. -τως (-τῶς cod.) f.l. for εὐεκτικῶς, Hsch.

εὐείλατος, v. εὐίλατος.

εὐείλητος, ον, *well rolled up, tight*, gloss on οὖλος, Eust.1056.65.

εὔειλος, ον, (εἵλη) *sunny, warm*, Ar.*Fr.*780; χωρία Arist.*HA*597^{b}7, Thphr.*HP*4.1.1, al.

εὐειμᾰτέω, *to be well-dressed*, Antiph.54, Arist.*Rh.Al.*1420^{a}17, Gerhard *Phoinix* p.6, Sotad.9.3 (v.l. **εὐειμονῆς**).

εὐείμων, ον, gen. ονος, *well-dressed*, A.*Pers.*181: Sup. -ειμονώτατος Max.Tyr.3.10.

εὔειρος, ον, (εἶρος, ἔριον) *with* or *of good wool, fleecy*, Hp.*Mul.*2.187

(Sup.), *AP*7.657 (Leon.):—Att. **εὔερος** (cf. Phryn.122) S.*Tr*.675 (Lob. for εὐείρῳ); εὔερόν τ' ἄγραν (Schneidew. for εὐκερών τ') Id.*Aj.* 297; εἴ τινα πόλιν φράσειας ἡμῖν εὔερον Ar.*Av*.121; γλῶσσαν εὐέρων βοτῶν Cratin.175: heterocl. acc. pl. εὐείρας v.l. for ἐτῆρας, S.*Fr*.751.

εὐείσβολος, ον, *easily invaded*, Aen.Tact.16.16. 2. *easy of entrance*, στόμα λιμένος Str.17.1.6.

εὐέκ-βᾰτος, ον, *easy to get out of*, πύαλος Hp.*Acut*.65. **-κάθαρτος** [κᾰ], ον, *easily cleared up*, prob. in Phld.*Herc*.1251.4. **-καρτέρητος**, ον, *easy to endure*, Id.*D*.1.12: written for εὐεγκ. **-καυστος**, ον, = sq., Corn.*ND*32. **-καυτος**, ον, *easily flaring up*, Gal.11.405. **-κρῐτος**, ον, of food, *easy to excrete*, Hp.*Acut*.10, Diph.Siph.ap.Ath.2.62f, Dsc.2.9, Xenocr.33, Gal.6.503. **-νιπτος**, ον, *easy to wash out*, of a colour, Poll.1.44. **-πλήρωτος**, ον, *easily fulfilled* or *realized*, Phld. *D*.1.13. **-πλῠτος**, ον, = εὐέκνιπτος, Poll.1.44. II. Act., *purging, relaxing*, v.l. for εὐέκκριτος in Hp.*Acut*.10. **-ποίητος**, ον, *easy to turn to account*, i.e. *assimilate*, of food, Ath.Med.ap.Orib.1.2. 2. **-πόρθητος**, ον, *easily sacked*, in Comp., Apollon.*Lex.* s.v. ἀλαπαδνότεροι. **-πτωτος**, ον, *prone to failure*, Ptol.*Tetr*.161. **-πύρωτος** [ῠ], ον, *easily heated*, Str.12.8.17, Eust.346.25. **-ρυπτος**, ον, *easy to wash out*, Poll.1.44.

εὐεκτ-έω, *to be in good condition*, τῷ σώματι Ceb.16, cf. Ph.1.611, Gal.*UP*1.21, Aesop.185, etc.; ὅταν ἢ ζῷον ἢ δένδρον εὐεκτῇ Plu.2.919c. **-ης**, ου, ὁ, (ἔχω) *of a good habit of body*, opp. καχέκτης, Plb. 3.88.2, D.L.2.22: as Adj., ἀθληταί Ph.1.583. **-ία**, ἡ, = εὐεξία, Archyt.ap.Stob.3.1.110, 112. **-ικός**, ή, όν, *in good case, healthy*, σώματα Pl.*Lg*.684c, cf. Ph.2.84, Gal.6.662; of persons, Arist.*EN* 1176ᵃ15. 2. *conducive to* εὐεξία, *wholesome*, Id.*Top*.105ᵃ31, *EN* 1129ᵃ20. Adv. -κῶς Gal.8.106, Hierocl.*in CA*16 p.456 M.; also glossed by σχετικῶς, Suid. **-ός**, όν, = εὐέκτης, Sch.E.*Hipp*.109 (Comp.). Adv. -τῶς, gloss on λίπα, Sch.D Il.10.577, Zonar., prob. for εὐκτεῶς, = ὑγιῶς, Hsch. (cf. εὐεστότερος).

εὐέκ-φορος, ον, *bringing forth timely births*, γυναῖκες Arist.*HA*584ᵇ 7. II. *easy to pronounce*, Phld.*Po*.1676.8:—hence **-φορία**, ἡ, ibid. **-χόλωτος**, ον, *easily made bilious*, Philagr.ap.Paul.Aeg.7.6.

εὐέλαιος, ον, *rich in olive-trees* or *oil*, Str.5.4.3.

εὐέλᾰτος, ον, gloss on εὐήλατος, Hsch.

εὐέλεγκτος, ον, *easy to refute* or *detect*, of persons or arguments, Pl. *Tht*.157b, Arist.*Rh*.1418ᵇ19. 2. *easy to test*, Pl.*Ap*.33c.

εὐελίδης· αὐθάδης, Hsch.; also epith. of Zeus in Cyprus, Id. **εὐελιέστερα**· εὐάγωγος, Id.

εὐέλικτος, ον, *easily rolling*, Eust.229.36, Poll.2.117.

εὐέλιον· ἐλλιπὲς ἐν ἱερείῳ, Hsch.

εὐελκής, ές, *easily healing, favourable for healing*, of the constitution, opp. δυσελκής, Hp.*Acut*.46, Gal.10.386.

εὐέλκτος, ον, *easy to draw*, Gal.11.402.

εὔελον· εὐήλιον, Hsch. (Fort. εὔε(ι)λον, sed cf. ἕλα.)

εὔελπ-ις, ὁ, ἡ, neut. εὔελπι, gen. ῐδος, *hopeful, cheerful*, Th.4.10, 62, X.*An*.2.1.18, etc.; ἐν τοῖς δεινοῖς Th.1.70; περὶ τῆς ψυχῆς Pl. *Hp.Mi*.364a; πρὸς τὸν θάνατον Id.*Ap*.41c, cf. Luc.*Demon*.6, D.C.57. 19; τοῦ κρατήσειν D.S.30.16. 2. c. acc. et fut. inf., εὔελπίς εἰμί σ' ἰσχύσειν A.*Pr*.509; εὔελπις σωθήσεσθαι *in good hope* to be saved, Th. 6.24: c. acc. et pres. inf., Pl.*Phd*.63c; τὸ εὔελπι *hopefulness*, Plu.2. 1101d, D.C.42.1, etc.; εὔ. λαλιά *cheerful* talk, Plb.1.32.6. II. Pass., *well hoped of, the subject of hope*, Lxx*Pr*.19.15(18): Medic., of a patient, Aret.*SD*1.13. **-ιστία**, ἡ, *hopefulness, sanguine temper, confidence*, περὶ τοῦ μέλλοντος Epicur.*Sent.Vat*.39, cf. Plb.11. 3.6, Phld.*Oec*.p.73 J., Cic.*Att*.2.17.2; τινος Ph.1.502, Perict.ap.Stob. 4.28.19; θάρρος καὶ εὐ. Procl.*in Cra*.p.88 P.

εὐέμ-βᾰτος, ον, *easy to get into*, πύαλος Hp.*Acut*.65; ψυχὴ οὐδενὶ τῶν τοιούτων βουλευμάτων εὐ. Chio*Ep*.16.2; τινι εὐ. ἀπολιπεῖν τὴν ἀκρόπολιν ib.15.3. **-βλητος**, ον, *easy to put in*, of dislocated joints, Hp.*Art*.71. **-βολος**, ον, *exposed to invasion*, χώρα Arist. *Pol*.1331ᵃ4. II. = foreg., Hp.*Fract*.42.

εὐέμετος or **εὐήμετος**, ον, (ἔμετος) *vomiting readily*, Hp.*Art*.40 (εὐημετης, εὐήμετος codd.):—also **-εμής** or **-ημής**, ές, Id.*Mul*.2.125, *Aph*.4.6, Dsc.2.169 (Comp.); ὅπως εὐεμὲς ᾖ (cod. Urb.) that *vomiting may be easy*, Thphr.*HP*9.10.2.

εὐέμ-πρηστος, ον, *easily set on fire*, dub. in Diog.Oen.8. **-πτωσία**, ἡ, *liability, proneness to* a thing: hence, *evil proclivity*, *Stoic*.3.102: in Medic., *an illness to which people are commonly liable*, such as colds, Posidon.ap.Gal.5.434, *Stoic*.3.103 (pl.). **-πτωτος**, ον, *easily falling into*: hence, *prone, liable*, εἴς τι Posidon.ap.Gal.5.434; εἰς ὀργὴν *Stoic*.3.110: Comp., εἰς τὰς ὀργάς Phld.*Ir*.p.97 W.; ἐπί τι Id. *Rh.Supp*.p.26 S.: abs., Ptol.*Tetr*.164. Adv. -τως Gal.5.448, Dsc. *Ther.Praef.*; εὐ. ἔχειν πρός τι Phlp.*in de An*.53.15. **-φρακτος**, ον, *easily obstructed*, Gal.6.497.

εὐέν, an exclamation like εὐάν, εὐοῖ, Hdn.Gr.1.503 (nisi leg. εὐαί).

εὐέν-δοτος, ον, *easily yielding*, γῆ Str.16.1.9; βύρσα *Hippiatr.* 8. 2. *morally weak*, Ph.2.269, al.; τὸ εὐ. Id.1.153. **-τευκτος**, ον, *affable*, Id.2.187, Poll.5.138. Adv. -τως ib.139. **-τρεπτος**, ον, *reverend*, σεμνοὶ καὶ εὐ. Ptol.*Tetr*.159. **-τροπος**, *reverens*, *Gloss.*

εὐεξ-άγωγος [ᾰ], ον, *easy of export*, Str.5.2.5. **-άλειπτος** [ᾰ], ον, *easy to wipe out*, X.*HG*2.3.53 (Comp.), Sch.D.T.p.505 H. **-ανάλωτος** [νᾰ], ον, *easy of digestion*, Hp.*Alim*.49. **-ᾰπάτητος** [πᾱ], ον, *easily deceived*, ὑπό τινος Pl.*R*.409a, cf. X.*Eq.Mag*.7.15, Corn.*ND* 25. **-απτος**, ον, *easily kindled* or *lighted*, M.Ant.9.9, Gal.7.342, al. **-άρτῡτος**, ον, *easy to get ready*, Ph.*Bel*.56.34. **-έλεγκτος**, ον, *easy to refute*, Pl.*Hp.Ma*.293d. **-έλικτος**, ον, *skilful in manœuvre*, Str.3.3.6. **-έλκυστος**, ον, *easily extracted*, Heraclid.Tar.ap.Gal.12. 692. **-έταστος**, ον, *easy to criticize*, Arist.*de An*.408ᵃ10. **-ής**, f.l. for εὐαξής, Phot. s.v. εὐαλδεῖ (cf. Hsch.): Comp. -έστερος f.l. for εὐαξέστερος, Aët.6.58; v. εὐαυξής.

εὐεξία, ἡ, (εὐέκτης) *good habit of body, good health*, Hp.*Aph*.1.3 (pl.); σαρκός E.*Fr*.201; εὐ. τῶν σωμάτων καὶ καχεξία Pl.*Grg*.450a, cf. Arist.*EN*1129ᵃ19, *Top*.105ᵃ31; εὐ. πολιτική *bodily vigour* required of a citizen, Id.*Pol*.1335ᵇ6; ὑγίεια καὶ εὐ. Pl.*R*.559a: pl., εὐεξίαι τῶν σωμάτων Id.*Prt*.354b, cf. Aeschin.1.189, Plb.1.57.1, v.l. in Isoc.4.1; περὶ εὐεξίας (opp. ὑγίεια, as temporary *high condition* to permanent *health*), title of work by Gal.4.750, 1.408, *Thras*.12; νικᾶν εὐεξίαν, εὐεξίᾳ, *SIG*1060 (iv/iii B.C.), 1061 (ii B.C.). II. generally, *vigour, good condition*, ὑγίεια καὶ κάλλος καὶ εὐ. ψυχῆς Pl.*R*.444d; τῆς πολιτείας Plb.20.4.1; φωνῆς Plu.2.804b, etc. 2. *skill, ability*, περὶ τὸ ἐπιτάδουμα *SIG*721.12 (Delos, ii B.C.); εὐ. ἐν τοῖς πολεμικοῖς Plb.3.6.12.

εὐεξίλαστος [ῐ], ον, *placable*, Sch.A.R.4.148.

εὐέξοδος, ον, *easy to get out of* or *escape from*, ἔστι δ' οὐκ εὐέξοδον A. *Pers*.688; εὐ. χώρα, opp. δυσέμβολος, Arist.*Pol*.1326ᵇ41, cf. 1330ᵇ 2. II. Act., *easily escaping*, ὕδωρ Id.*Pr*.874ᵃ32.

εὔεξος· εὐφυής, Hsch.

εὐεπ-άγωγος [ᾰ], ον, *easy to lead on*, πρός τι Plb.31.8.5. **-αίσθητος**, ον, *easily feeling, sensitive*, Hp.*Mul*.1.38. **-ᾰκολούθητος**, ον, *easy to follow*, of a train of argument, Arist.*Rh*.1357ᵃ11. **-ανόρθωτος**, ον, *easy to correct*, σώματα Hp.*de Arte*11.

εὐέπεια, Ion. and poet. **εὐεπίη** (q.v.), ἡ, (εὐεπής) *beauty of language, eloquence*, Pl.*Phdr*.267c; ἐν ταῖς ὁμιλίαις Ph.2.79; εὐέπειαι λόγων Pl.*Ax*.369d; esp. with ref. to sound, *euphony*, D.H.*Comp*.23, al.: coupled with καλλιλογία, Id.*Dem*.25. II. *welcome words*, S.*OT*932 (cf. εὐεπής II).

εὐεπ-έκτᾰτος, ον, *naturally lengthened*, cj. in A.D.*Pron*.99.2. **-έραστος**, ον, v. εὐεπηρέαστος. **-ήβολος**, ον, cf. εὐεπίβολος. **-ήκοος**, ον, *responsive*, ὕλη Steph.*in Hp*.1.173 D. **-ηρέαστος**, ον, *exposed to harm*, Arr.*Epict*.4.1.111 (Sup.), Vett.Val.49.4; ὑπό τινος Gal.6. 124; πρὸς τὰς νόσους Sor.1.109; *liable to wanton damage*, κώμη prob. in *SIG*888.16 (Thrace, iii A.D., εὐεπεράστῳ lapis).

εὐεπής, ές, (ἔπος) *melodious*, φωνή X.*Cyn*.13.16; *euphonious*, λέξις D.H.*Comp*.22; ἁρμονία -εστέρα ibid. Adv. -πῶς, κῶλα εὐ. συγκείμενα ibid.: Sup., ποίησις -έστατα ἔχουσα D.Chr.52.15. 2. *eloquent*, εὐ. ἐν τῷ λέγειν Hsch. s.v. λιγύς. 3. *making eloquent, inspiring*, ὕδωρ, of Helicon, *AP*11.24 (Antip.). II. Pass., *well-spoken, acceptable*, λόγος Hdt.5.50.

εὐεπί-βᾰτος, ον, *easy to ascend*, λόφος Str.5.3.7; τεῖχος Polyaen. 6.5; καταρράκται App.*BC*5.82 (Comp.). II. *easy of attack*, τόποι Ph.*Bel*.94.40: metaph., Id.1.459, Luc.*Cal*.19. **-βλεπτος**, ον, *easily seen, manifest*, Poll.1.172, dub. in Epicur.*Nat*.2.6, Phld.*D*.3 *Fr*.36. **-βλητος**, ον, *easily grasped*, Simp.*in de An*.259.28. **-βολος**, ον, *hitting the mark*: hence, *shrewd, intelligent*, Vett.Val.38.1, al., Ptol.*Tetr*.57, v.l. in S.E.*M*.7.322: also spelt εὐεπήβ-. Adv. -λως Sch.Ptol.*Tetr*.99, Simp.*in Ph*.738.4. **-βούλευτος**, ον, *exposed to treachery* or *stratagem*, χώρα Str.2.3.4, cf. Ph.2.552, Vett.Val.236.27: Comp., X.*Cyr*.8.4.3, Onos.36.6, D.C.38.31. **-βουλος**, ον, *fond of plotting* or *intriguing*, Ptol.*Tetr*.162. **-γνωστος** or **-γνωτος**, ον, *easy to recognize* or *understand*, Sor.1.58, Artem.4.84, *Cat.Cod.Astr*.1. 114; αἰτίαι Corn.*ND*9: Comp., *a more skilled recognizer*, cj. in Hp.*Ep.* 22. **-δεκτος**, ον, *easily receiving*, τινος Sch.A.R.1.1005. **-δοτος**, ον, = εὐένδοτος, Antyll.ap.Orib.45.15.5. **-δρομος**, ον, *easily scaled*, γεώλοφον Agath.2.2; *assailable*, χωρία τοῖς βαρβάροις Id.5.14: metaph., φιλοσοφία εὐ. σοφισταῖς Them.*Or*.20.235d.

εὐεπίη, ἡ, Ion. for εὐέπεια, Hp.*Decent*.3, *AP*6.322 (Leon.), *IG*14. 1089, 2012 *C*b4.

εὐεπί-θετος, ον, *easy to set upon* or *attack*, τινι Th.6.34, D.C.50.32 (Comp.); τόποι Plb.4.19.12; εὐεπίθετον ἦν ... τοῖς πολεμίοις was *easy* for them *to make an attack*, X.*An*.3.4.20 (but εὐ. τοῖς ἐχθροῖς *exposed to assault* by ..., Antip.*Stoic*.3.255); εὐ. ὁ μεθύων Arist.*Pol*.1314ᵇ34; εὐ. τοῖς ... ἀμφισβητητικοῖς Pl.*Plt*.306a. Adv. εὐεπιθέτως, ἔχειν to be *exposed*, Aen.Tact.23.4. **-κλειστος**, ον, gloss on εὐκλῄς, Sch.Il. 24.318. **-ληπτος**, ον, *open to censure*, Plb.29.5.1. **-λόγιστος**, ον, *easily inferred*, S.E.*M*.1.297, Gal.18(2).27. **-μεικτος**, ον, *accessible*, χώρα πᾶσα εὐ. Str.11.2.2; of men, τὸ εὐ. πρὸς ἀλλήλους Id.11.4. 6, cf. Poll.5.138. Adv. -τως ib.139. **-νόητος**, ον, *fertile in devices, 'sharp' in business*, Vett.Val.44.22. **-πόλαστος**, ον, *tending to return* or *be vomited*, Sor.1.109. **-σημος**, ον, *easily distinguished*, Sch. D Il.23.240. **-στρεπτος**, ον, *easily turned*, ἐπὶ τὸ χεῖρον App.*Pun.* 50. **-στροφος**, ον, *easily twisted*, *EM*616.7. II. *beautifully curved*, of a dome, Agath.5.9. **-τακτος**, ον, *submissive*, εἴς τι *AP* 11.73 (Nicarch.). **-τευκτος**, ον, *easily hitting the mark, successful*, περί, πρός, εἴς τι, Vett.Val.39.20, 40.36, 45.10; ἐν μάχαις Malch. p.391 D.; *opportune*, βοήθημα Sever.*Clyst*.p.34 D. **-τήδευμα**, ατος, τό, *act embodying good conduct*, cj. in Stoic.ap.Stob.2.7.11ᵉ (pl.). **-φορία**, ἡ, *'embarras de richesse'*, in respect of plurality of causes, S.E.*P*.1.181. **-φορος**, ον, *inclined, prone*, πρός τι Corn. *ND*35; εἴς τι Sch.Ar.*Pl*.990: Comp., Phld.*Lib*.p.43 O.; esp. of authors who are fond of particular phrases, freq. in Gramm., ἐπί... Sch.S.*Aj*.693: c. inf., Sch.E.*Ph*.4. Adv. -ρως v.l. in Sch.Pi.*P*.4. 207; εὐ. ἔχειν πρός τι Str.1.2.20. II. *leading easily*, ὁδὸς ἐπί τινα D.H.10.46. **-χείρητος**, ον, *easy to be attacked*, Str.5.3.7, Poll.1. 172. Adv. -τως Hierocl.*in CA*10 p.436 M. 2. *easy to be attempted* or *proven*, πρόβλημα Arist.*APr*.42ᵇ29, cf. *Top*.111ᵃ11 (Comp.). 3. *insidious*, Ph.2.107 (Comp.). II. *readily attempting*, D.L.4. 30. **-ψογος**, ον, *open to censure*, διὰ γυναῖκα Heph.Astr.1.1.

εὐέργ-εια, Ion. -είη, ἡ, = sq. I, *AP*15.34 (Arethas). 2. *ease* of a surgical operation, Orib.45.18.14. **-εσία**, Ion. -εσίη, ἡ, *well-doing*, opp. κακοεργίη, Od.22.374; opp. κακότης, Thgn.548, etc. II. *a good deed, kindness*, εὐεργεσίας ἀποτίνειν Od.22.235, cf. Hes.*Th*.503 (pl.); ἡ ἐξ Ἱστιαίου εὐ. done by him, Hdt.5.11; ἐκτίνειν Id.3.47 (pl.); εὐεργεσίας ἀποδέξασθαι ἔς τινας ib.67; καταθέσθαι ἔς τινα Th.1.128; εὐ. πεποιημέναι ἔς τινα Hdt.4.165; προέσθαι X.*An*.7.7.47; προσφέρειν Pl.*Grg*.513e; opp. εὐ. ἀπολαβεῖν Isoc.14.57; εὐ. ὀφείλεταί μοι Th.1.137, cf. 32; ἀντ' εὐεργεσίης for *service done*, Simon.97.6, Theoc.17.116, cf. B.1.47 (pl.), *IG*1^2.108; ἀπ' εὐεργεσίας καθίστασαν τοὺς βασιλεῖς Arist.*Pol*.1286^{b}10: c. gen., εὐ. τῆς πόλεως *good service done* the state, Pl.*Lg*.850b: pl., *public services*, τὰς τῶν προγόνων εὐεργεσίας Lys.14.24, etc. 2. ψηφίζεσθαί [τινι] εὐεργεσίαν to vote him *the title of* εὐεργέτης (q.v.), D.20.60, cf. *IG*2^2.29, etc.; κείσεταί σοι εὐ. ἐν τῷ ἡμετέρῳ οἴκῳ ἐς αἰεὶ ἀνάγραπτος Th.1.129, cf. X.*HG*1.1.26, etc. III. Εὐεργεσία, personified, = Lat. *Liberalitas*, D.C.71.34. 2. epith. of Hera at Argos, Hsch.

Εὐεργέσια, τά, festival of Ptolemy Euergetes at Delos, *SIG*^{2}588.54 (ii B.C.).

εὐεργέτ-εια, ἡ, = εὐεργέτις, *UPZ*81 ii9,10 (iv B.C.). **-έω**, the augm. εὐηργ- is sts. found, esp. in codd., as impf. εὐηργέτουν X.*Ap*.26: aor. εὐηργέτησα Ar.*Pl*.835, v.l. in Din.1.16, but ηὐεργέτησα Lys.9.14: pf. εὐηργέτηκα v.l. in Lycurg.140: pf. Pass. εὐηργέτημαι X.*Mem*.2.2.3, *SIG*798.5 (Cyzicus, i A.D.), but Inscrr. and Pap. have εὐεργέτηκα *IG*2^2.573 (iv B.C.), εὐεργέτημαι *PLond*.2.169.26 (i A.D.), εὐεργετήθην *IG*7.2808 (Hyettus, iii A.D.), ηὐεργετημένοι *PTeb*.326.16 (iii A.D.):—*to be a benefactor*, S.*Ph*.670, *IG*2^2.786, etc.; [Ἰησοῦς] διῆλθεν -τῶν *Act.Ap*.10.38. 2. *to be proclaimed as* εὐεργέτης I. 2, *JHS*10.76 (Patara, i A.D.). II. c. acc. pers., *do good services* or *show kindness to* one, τοὺς θανόντας εἰ θέλεις εὐεργετεῖν A.*Fr*.266.1, cf. *Eu*.725, E.*Ion*1540, Lys. l.c., etc.; ὁ νόμος βούλεται -τεῖν βίον ἀνθρώπων Democr.248; εὐ. τὸν δῆμον *IG*2^2.791.25, etc.; τὸν θεὸν εὐεργετηκότες *SIG*417.13 (Delph., iii B.C.): c. acc. cogn., εὐ. τινὰ τὴν μεγίστην εὐεργεσίαν Pl.*Ap*.36c, cf. *R*.615b; ὅ τι ἂν ἡμᾶς εὐεργετήσῃς ib.345a; μεγάλως or μεγάλα εὐ., X.*Cyr*.8.2.10,12: c. dat. rei, χρήμασιν εὐ. ib.2:—Pass., *have a kindness done one*, εὐεργεσίαν εὐεργετηθεὶς Pl.*Grg*.520c; μείζω εὐηργετημένοι X.*Mem*.2.2.3; καί τι εὐεργέτηται ὑπ' ἐμοῦ Pl.*Cri*.43a; ἀντὶ πολλῶν καὶ μεγάλων ὧν εὐεργετήθη παρὰ τοῦ θεοῦ *IG*7.2808 (Hyettus, iii A.D.); εὐεργετούμενος εἰς χρήματα Pl.*Smp*.184b. **-ημα**, ατος, τό, *service done, kindness*, πρός τινα X.*Cyr*.8.2.2, cf. Hp.*Ep*.25 (pl.), etc.: pl., X.*Cyr*.5.5.34, Isoc.4.34, Arist.*EN*1161^{a}16, *IG*2^2.808, etc. **-ης** (Thess. εὐϝεργέτας *IG*9(2).257.5 (v B.C.)), ου, ὁ, *benefactor*, Pi.*P*.2.24, S.*Ant*.284; τινι to one, Hdt.6.30, E.*HF*1252: more commonly c. gen., τῆς γῆς Id.*Rh*.151, cf. Pl.*Cra*.403e, etc. 2. as an honorary title, εὐ. βασιλέος ἀνεγράφη was registered as the King's *benefactor*, Hdt.8.85, cf. 3.140; πρόξεινος καὶ εὐ. Id.8.136, cf. *IG*1^2.82, X.*HG*6.1.4, etc.; μέγιστος εὐ. παρ' ἐμοὶ ἀναγεγράφῃ Pl.*Grg*.506c, cf. Lys.20.19, etc.; οἱ ἐξουσιασταὶ αὐτῶν εὐ. καλοῦνται *Ev.Luc*.22.25: conferred on kings and emperors, as Antigonus, *Inscr.Prien*.2.6 (iv B.C.); ὁ παντὸς κόσμου σωτὴρ καὶ εὐ., of Trajan, *IG*12(1).978 (Carpathos); σὺ ὁ εὐ., mode of address to a superior, *POxy*.38.13 (i A.D.), 486.27 (ii A.D.), etc. II. as Adj., *beneficent, bountiful*, ἀνήρ Pi.*O*.2.94, cf. *P*.4.30. **-ητέον**, *one must show kindness to*, τοὺς φίλους X.*Mem*.2.1.28. **-ητικός**, ή, όν, *beneficent*, v.l. in Arist.*EN*1171^{b}16, cf. *Gloss*. **-ία**, ἡ, = εὐεργεσία II, *Philol*.71.39 (Delph., iii B.C.). **-ικός**, ή, όν, *productive of benefit, beneficent*, ὠφέλιμα καὶ εὐ. Arist.*Rh*.1388^{b}12, cf. Phld.*Piet*.11, etc.; δόξα εὐ. a reputation *for beneficence*, Arist.*Rh*.1361^{a}28; ἀρετὴ δύναμις εὐ. πολλῶν καὶ μεγάλων ib.1366^{a}38: c. gen. pers., φιλανθρωπία ἕξις εὐ. ἀνθρώπων Pl.*Def*.412e; τὸ εὐ. *beneficence*, D.S.1.25: Comp., τὸ -ώτερον Hdn.6.9.8; of persons, *beneficent, bountiful*, εὐεργετικὸν (v.l. -τητικὸν) εἶναι καλόν Arist.*EN*1171^{b}16, etc.; εὐ. χρηστὸς φιλάνθρωπος Muson.*Fr*.8 p.39 H.: Sup. -ώτατος, εἰς τοὺς Ἕλληνας Plb.7.8.6. Adv. -κῶς, διακείμενος *OGI*90.11 (Rosetta, Ptol. V), cf. *IG*5(2).266.13 (Mantinea, i B.C.). **-ις**, ιδος, (parox.) fem. of εὐεργέτης, E.*Alc*.1058: as Adj., εὐ. ψυχή Pl.*Lg*.896e; ἀρετή Ph.2.164:—also -ισσα, ἡ, Demitsas Μακεδ. No.421 (Thessalonica, ii A.D.).

εὐεργ-έω, *cultivate land well*, *BGU*1118.27, al. (i B.C.). **-ημα**, ατος, τό, late form, = εὐεργέτημα, *JHS*22.366 (dub. l.). **-ής**, ές, (ἔργον) *well-wrought, well-made*, of chariots, εὐεργέος ἔκπεσε δίφρου Il.5.585; of ships, μία δ' ἤγαγε νηῦς εὐ. 24.396, and freq. in Od., cf. *IG*1^2.74.27; πηδάλιον Hes.*Op*.629; of garments, ἀμφ' ὤμοισιν ἔχουσ' εὐεργέα λώπην Od.13.224; of gold, *wrought*, χρυσοῦ... εὐεργέος ἑπτὰ τάλαντα 24.274. 2. *well-done*: hence in pl., εὐεργέα, = the Prose εὐεργεσίαι, *benefits, services*, οὐκ ἔστι χάρις μετόπισθ' εὐεργέων 22.319, cf. 4.695; also ἀθάνατοι χαίρουσι βροτῶν εὐεργέσι τιμαῖς *Milet*.1(7).205*b* (ii A.D.). 3. = εὐεργός II. 2, τῷ ψυχρῷ Olymp. *in Mete*.313.9. 4. *easy*, of a surgical operation, Antyll.ap.Orib.45.2.6. 5. *effective*, τὴν εὐώνυμον χεῖρα -εστέραν Sor.2.61. **-ία**· τορύνη, εὐπιστία, Hsch. (cf. ἐόργη and εὐοργία). **-ός**, όν, *doing good* or *well, upright*, of women, Hom., only in Od., in phrase καὶ ἥ κ' εὐεργὸς ἔῃσιν 11.434, al. 2. *serviceable*, πρὸς τὴν χρῆσιν Arist.*PA*660^{a}10, cf. Zeno *Stoic*.1.28; χάρτη εὐ. εἰς ἀπογραφήν (of τὸ ἡγεμονικόν) *Stoic*.2.28. Adv. -γῶς, ἔχειν πρός τι Arist.*Mete*.377^{b}25. 3. Astrol., = ἀγαθοποιός, Man.3.63, al. II. Pass., *well-wrought, well-tilled*, γῆ *Gp*.2.46.2. 2. *easy to work*, [ὕαλος] Hdt.3.24; ὕλη Arist.*Ph*.194^{a}34; ξύλον Thphr.*HP*3.9.6 (Comp.); ἔρια Luc.*Fug*.12; *easily reaped*, λᾷον Theoc.10.43.

εὐερέθιστος, ον, *easily excited, irritable*, Str.14.2.24; μέρη Ruf.ap. Orib.8.39.1; διαθέσεις Antyll.ap.eund.10.13.6; *easily provoked*, εἰς ὀργάς Plot.1.8.14.

εὐερία, ἡ, *fineness of wool, fleeciness*, Pl.Com.169.

εὐέριος, ον, = εὔερος, Phot. s. v. εὔειρον: condemned by Phryn.122.

εὐέρκ-εια, ἡ, *security*, Pl.*Lg*.778c, 779b. **-ής** (Cret. οὐερκής *Hymn.Curet*.10), ές, (ἕρκος) *well-fenced, well-walled*, αὐλή Il.9.472, Od.21.389; οἶκος Pi.*Pae*.4.45; ἄλσος Id.*O*.13.109; πόλις A.*Supp*.955; ἀκρόπολις J.*AJ*15.11.4; χώρα εὐ. πρὸς τοὺς πολεμίους Pl.*Lg*.760e; ὑποδοχή ib.848e: Sup., -έσταται πράξεις ὡσανεὶ πόλεις Ph.1.681; *secure*, θύραι δ' εὐερκέες εἰσί Od.17.267 (v.l. εὐεργέες). Adv. -κῶς Plu.2.503c. 2. *girding in, surrounding*, of nets, Opp.*H*.4.655.

εὐέρκτης, ου, ὁ, poet. for εὐεργέτης, *AP*9.92 (Antip. Thess.), *BCH* 23.302 (Termessus): pl., as a title of rank, *Arch.Pap*.1.220 (ii B.C.).

εὐερμ-έω, *to be favoured by Hermes, to be fortunate*, Poll.5.135 (Phot. wrongly εὐερνῶ). **-ής**, ές, (Ἑρμῆς) *fortunate*, Vett.Val.14.24, Hsch. **-ία**, ἡ, *good luck*, Ael.*NA*5.39, Poll.5.135.

εὐερνής, ές, (ἔρνος) *sprouting well, flourishing*, δάφνα E.*IT*1100 (lyr.); of a kind of Cassia, Dsc.1.13; δένδρον -έστατον Ph.1.629; of men and animals, *well-grown*, Posidon.*Fr*.28 J. (Comp.), Str.11.4.3, *Epigr.Gr*.314.10 (Smyrna): Comp. -έστερα, νήπια Gal.17(1).826; of countries, *rich in plants*, εὔβοτος καὶ εὐ. Str.16.1.24.

εὔερος, ον, Att. form of εὔειρος (q.v.).

εὐερωτητικός, ή, όν, *good at questioning*, Chrysipp.*Stoic*.2.42.

εὐέστιος, ον, (εὐεστώ) *prosperous*, of Delos, Call.*Del*.325; γῆρας Id.*Epigr*. in *Berl.Sitzb*.1912.548.

εὐεστότερος, ον, Comp. (no Posit.), *in better case, healthier*, Aët.5.53; cf. sq. (Fort. εὐεκτότερος.)

εὐεστώ, οῦς, ἡ, (εὖ, ἑστώ, v. sub εὖ) *well-being*, title of work by Democr. (of Happiness as the Supreme Good), *prosperity*, ἐν τῇ παρελθούσῃ εὐεστοῖ Hdt.1.85; ἐν εὐ. φίλῃ A.*Th*.187, *Ag*.929; χαίρουσαν εὐεστοῖ πόλιν ib.647, cf. Call.*Aet*.4.1.7.

εὐετηρία, ἡ, (ἔτος) *a good season* (for the fruits of the earth), X.*HG*5.2.4, etc.: in pl., ἐν ταῖς εὐ. Arist.*GA*760^{b}3. 2. *thriving*, Pl.*Smp*.188a; of cattle, Arist.*HA*574^{a}14, al. 3. generally, *prosperity, plenty*, ἡ ἐκτὸς εὐ. Id.*EN*1098^{b}26, cf. 1155^{a}8, *Pol*.1306^{b}11, *SIG*799.16 (Cyzicus, i A.D.), etc.: personified, Εὐ. *IG*12(2).262 (Mytil.), *Ath.Mitt*.37.288 (Pergam., ii A.D.), etc.; as name of a trireme, *IG*2^2.1607.6.

εὐετία, poet. -ίη, ἡ, = foreg., *AP*14.121.4 (Metrod.).

εὐεύρετος, ον, (εὑρίσκω) *easy to find*, χώρα εὐεύρετος ἑκάστοις a place *in which it will be easy to find* everything, X.*Oec*.8.17, cf. *Mem*.3.1.10.

εὐέφικτος, ον, *easy to find in use, current*, ἡ τοῦ ἄρθρου παράθεσις, ἡ εἰς τὸ πληθυντικὸν μετάθεσις, A.D.*Synt*.44.26, 185.21, prob. in Phld.*Rh*.2.254, cf. 1.63 S.

εὐεφόδευτος, ον, *easily approached* or *comprehended*, λόγος Iamb. *in Nic*.p.95 P.

εὐέφοδος, ον, *easy to come at* or *attack, assailable, accessible*, of places, X.*Cyr*.2.4.13, Plb.1.26.2, etc. II. *easily conducted*, ζήτησις S.E.*M*.7.25.

εὐέψητος, ον, *readily cooked*, Thphr.*CP*4.12.12, Dsc.1.128, *Gp*.2.25.1 (Comp.).

εὐζηλ-ία, ἡ, *good, correct style* (cf. ζῆλος), ἡ ἐν τοῖς λόγοις εὐ. καὶ καθαριότης Plu.*Lyc*.21. **-ος**, ον, *in good style* (cf. ζῆλος), οὐκ εὔ. ἀναχρονισμός Eust.361.24. Adv. -λως, μελετᾶν *AP*11.144 (Cereal.). II. *enviable*, Nic.*Al*.9.

εὐζήτητος, ον, *readily ascertained*, Gal.10.590.

εὔζῠγος, Ep. ἐΰζ-, ον, (ζυγόν III) of ships, *well-benched*, Od.13.116, 17.288, A.R.1.4; ἅρμα θαλάσσης Opp.*H*.1.190; εὐσδύγων prob. in Alc.*Oxy*.1233 *Fr*.4.9.

εὔζῡμος, ον, *well-leavened*, Gal.14.46.

εὔζυξ, ῠγος, ὁ, ἡ, *well-matched*, μαζοί *AP*5.55 (Diosc.).

εὐζω-έω, *live well*, M.Ant.3.12. **-ΐα**, ἡ, *well-living*, Arist.*EN*1098^{b}21, Hierocl. *in CA Praef*.p.416 M., al.; *civil well-being*, *PMasp*.19.28, al. (vi A.D.); also, *means of subsistence*, *PLond*.5.1708.20 (vi A.D.): trisyll., metri gr., ἱερὸν εὐζῴας ἄωτον Pi.*P*.4.131: pl. -ζωΐαι, opp. κακοζωΐαι, Herm. *in Phdr*.p.179 A. **-ΐτου**· καλῆς ζωῆς, Suid., Phot.

εὔζωμον, τό, *rocket, Eruca sativa*, Thphr.*HP*1.6.6, al., *CP*2.5.3, *PCair.Zen*.292.15 (iii B.C.), Dsc.2.140, *POxy*.1088.15 (i A.D.), Ael.*NA*6.46, Gal.1.681. (Prop. neut. of **εὔζωμος**, ον, *making good broth*.)

εὐζων-ία, ἡ, *marauding by light-armed men*, used for Heb. *Gad* (Phoen. deity, = Τύχη) by Aq.*Ge*.30.11, with ref. to the play on *gādh* (quasi 'marauding band') ib.49.19:—hence -ίζω, ibid.

εὔζωνος, Ep. ἐΰζ-, ον, (ζώνη) *well-girdled*, Hom. (only in Il. and *h.Cer*.), as epith. of women, Il.1.429, *h.Cer*.255, al. 2. later, of men, *girt up for exercise, active*, μῆκος δ' ὁδοῦ εὐζώνῳ ἀνδρὶ πέντε ἡμέραι ἀναισιμοῦνται Hdt.1.72; τριήκοντα ἡμερέων εὐζώνῳ ὁδὸς ib.104, cf. 2.34, Th.2.97; of light troops, X.*An*.5.4.23, Plb.3.35.7, Plu.*Demetr*.9; of ὁπλῖται without their heavy shields, X.*An*.7.3.46: generally, *well-equipped*, Lxx *Jo*.4.13; also εὔ. τῇ κεφαλῇ πυκτεύειν Philostr.*Im*.2.19; later, of ships, Max.Tyr.1.3. Adv. -νως Alciphr.3.55. 3. of a garment, *well-girded*, dub. in S.*Fr*.342. 4. metaph., *unencumbered*, πενία Plu.*Pel*.3; εὔ. καὶ ἐλεύθερος βίος D.C.56.6. 5. in Lit. Crit., *work-a-day, unpretending*; in depreciatory sense, *cheap*, τὸ εὔ. καὶ οἷον εὐτελὲς εἶδος τοῦ λόγου Hermog.*Id*.2.10; τὸ εὔ. χωρὶς εὐτελείας ib.1.11; ἐκπίπτειν τὸν λόγον εἰς τὸ -ότερον ib.1.5.

εὔζωος, ον, (ζωή) *living long, tenacious of life*, Thphr.*CP*4.4.10 (Comp.), 5.4.3.

εὔζωρος, ον, *quite pure, unmixed*, of wine, Hp.*Morb*.3.14, E.*Alc*.

757, Ar.*Ec.*227 : Comp. -ότερος, εὐζωρότερον.., ὦ παῖ, δός Diph.58, cf. Cratin.412, Eup.382 ; also κέρασον εὐζωρέστερον Antiph.139 ; πίνειν.. κύλικας εὐζωρεστέρας Eub.150.8 (= Ephipp.3.11), cf. *Lyr. Adesp.*p.681 Bgk.

εὔζωστος, ον, (ζώννυμαι) *easily girt, convenient for girding*, ἡ εὐζωστότατος αὐτὸς ἑωυτοῦ ἐστι Hp.*Art.*14; gloss on εὔζωνος, Sch.D Il.1.429.

εὐηγενής, ές, Ep. for εὐγενής, *h.Ven.*229, Theoc.27.43, *IG*14.1389 i 29 (cf. εὐηφενής).

εὐηγεσία, ἡ, (ἡγέομαι) *good leadership*, ἐξ εὐηγεσίης Od.19.114.

εὐηγής, ές, = εὐαγής, dub. l. in Aret.*CD*1.13.

εὐηγορ-έω, Dor. **εὐᾱγ-**, *speak well of, praise*, Pi.*I.*1.51 (Pass.). **-ία**, ἡ, *good words, praise*, Call.*Lav.Pall.*139. **-ος**, ον, (ἀγορεύω) *speaking well* or *auspiciously*, Eub.71 codd. Ath.

εὐήδεια, ἡ, prob. f.l. for εὐείδεια, Corn.*ND*15.

εὐήδονος, ον, *attractive*, ὀφθαλμός Heph.*Astr.*1.1.

εὐήδυντος, ον, *palatable*, Orib.*inc.*13.34. **εὐηερίη**, v. εὐαερία.

εὐήθ-εια, poet. also **εὐηθία**, Ion. -ίη, ἡ, *goodness of heart, guilelessness*, generally in ironical sense, πάνυ γενναίαν εὐ. Pl.*R.*348c, cf. D. 24.52, *Com.Adesp.*773; δι' εὐηθίην by his *good nature*, Hdt.3.139. 2. in bad sense, *simplicity, silliness*, ἐς τοσοῦτο εὐηθίης ἀνήκει τοῦτο Id.7. 16.γ', cf. 1.60; κουφόνους εὐηθίᾳ A.*Pr.*385; ἀνωφελὴς εὐηθίᾳ.. γυνή E.*Hipp.*639; πολλῆς -είας, ὅστις οἴεται Th.3.45; -ειάν τινος καταγιγνώσκειν Lys.26.2. **-ης**, ες, (ἦθος) *good-hearted, simple-minded, guileless*, Pl.*R.*349b; of swans, Arist.*HA*615^{a}33; -έστεροι, opp. πανουργότατοι, Lys.3.44; τὸ εὔηθες, = εὐήθεια, Th.3.83. b. of a courtesan, *of easy virtue*, Archil.19. 2. in bad sense, *simple, silly*, πρῆγμα εὐηθέστατον Hdt.1.60; μῦθος, λόγος, Id.2.45, Pl.*Lg.*818b (Sup.); ἥψατο πρῶτον τοῦ -εστάτου attacked the *silliest* argument first, Arist.*Rh.*1418^{b}23; κακοήθης δ' ὢν τοῦτο παντελῶς εὔηθες φήθης D.18. 11; τὸ τῶν προβάτων ἦθος εὐ. Arist.*HA*610^{b}23 : as Subst., *simpleton*, X.*HG*2.3.16; εὔηθές [ἐστι] c. inf., it is *simple, foolish, absurd*, Arist. *Metaph.*1062^{b}34, cf. Democr.67; λίαν εὐ. Arist.*APo.*88^{b}17. 3. metaph., of wounds or illnesses, *mild, easily treated*, opp. κακοήθης (malignant), Hp.*VM*8 : Comp., Id.*Prorrh.*1.98 : Sup., Id.*Prog.* 20. b. [τρώματα] ἐν χωρίοισι εἶναι εὐήθεσι.. φαινόμενα *innocent* (not dangerous), Id.*Prorrh.*2.12; cf. εὐχερής III. 2. II. Adv. -θως, ἔχω Pl.*Phd.*100d, cf. Arist.*Metaph.*1024^{b}32 : Comp. -έστερα, τοῦ δέοντος Pl.*Plt.*276e : Sup. -έστατα E.*Andr.*625 (εὐήθης and -εια discussed by Gal.18(2).236–8). **-ία**, Ion. **-ίη**, = foreg. (q.v.). **-ίζομαι**, Med., *to act like an* εὐήθης, *play the fool*, πρὸς ἀλλήλους Pl.*R.*336c; *to be merry, jest*, Philostr.*VA*8.7. **-ικός**, ή, όν, *like an* εὐήθης, *good-natured*, ironically, Pl.*R.*343c, *Chrm.*175c. 2. *simple, foolish*, εὐηθικώτερόν ἐστι ἢ ὥστε.. Arist.*Ph.*218^{b}8, cf. Iamb.*Myst.*3.17. Adv. -κῶς Ar.*Nu.*1258, Arist.*GA*757^{a}2; εὐ. ἔχειν Pl.*Hp.Ma.*301d.

Εὐήιος, = Εὔιος, Ph.2.559.

εὐήκης, ες, (ἀκή A) *well-pointed*, αἰχμῆς.. εὐήκεος Il.22.319; *keen-edged*, φάσγανα A.R.2.101, Phanocl.1.8; ξυρόν Nic.*Al.*411.

εὐηκής, ές, (ἄκος) *healing*, βάξις Emp.112.11.

εὐηκο-έω, *to be* εὐήκοος, *listen and obey willingly*, c. gen., τῶν κρινόντων Jusj.ap.Stob.4.1.48. **-ΐα**, ἡ, *ready obedience*, D.S.17.55. II. *readiness to hear prayer*, Eun.*VS*p.458 B., Procl.*in Cra.*p.72 P., Marin.*Procl.*1, 34 (pl.). **-ος**, Dor. **εὐᾱκ-** [ᾱ], ον, (ἀκοή) *hearing well* or *easily*, Hp.*Aph.*3.17 (Comp.). 2. *hearing willingly, obedient*, Arist.*EN*1102^{b}27 (Comp.). 3. *inclined to give ear*, of the gods, θνατοῖς *AP*9.316.5 (Leon.), cf. *IG*12(2).101,105 (Mytil.); written εὐήκουος, *Sammelb.*4607.5 : generally, *inclined*, πρὸς μεταβολήν Thphr.*CP* 2.14.5 (Sup.). Adv. -όως, διακεῖσθαι πρός τι Plb.27.7.7. II. Pass., *easily heard, audible*, Arist.*Top.*107^{b}2; -οώτερα τὰ τῆς νυκτός Id.*Pr.* 899^{a}19. 2. *pleasant to the ear, agreeable*, τὸ εὐ. Demetr.*Eloc.*48, al.

εὐηλάκᾰτος [ᾰκ], Aeol. **εὐᾱλ-**, ον, *possessing a fine distaff*, of women, Theoc.28.22.

εὐήλᾰτος, ον, (ἐλαύνω) *easy to drive* or *ride over*, πεδία *fit for cavalry operations*, X.*Cyr.*1.4.16, cf. *HG*5.4.54; ἡ τῆς ἀρετῆς [ὁδὸς] τὰ πρῶτα οὐκ εὐήλατά κως παρέχειν δοκέει Eus.Mynd.63. II. *well-ground*, ἄλφι Antim.64; *well-hammered*, ἄκμων Euph.51.10.

εὐῆλιξ, ῐκος, ὁ, ἡ, (ἡλικία) *of good stature*, Polem.*Phgn.*5; Στάτιος (στάτης cod.) ὁ εὐῆλιξ εἴρηται Lyd.*Mag.*1.23.

εὐήλιος, Dor. **εὐᾱλ-** [ᾱ], ον, *sunny, genial*, χώρη Hp.*Aff.*60, cf. E. *Hipp.*129 (lyr.), X.*Oec.*9.4; ἁμέραι Ar.*Ra.*242 (lyr.); εὐάλιον πῦρ *the sun's heat*, E.*IT*1138 (lyr.); εὐ. οἰκία Arist.*Oec.*1345^{a}32; ἐν εὐηλίῳ in *a sunny spot*, Id.*HA*616^{b}14; τὸ μετόπωρον εὐ. Philostr.*VA*4.17. Adv. -ίως *in sunlight*, A.*Eu.*906. II. of persons, *fond of the sun, fond of basking*, Philostr.*VA*6.4.

εὐημερ-έω, (εὐήμερος) *spend one's days cheerfully*, S.*El.*653; ταῖσι Θήβαις εἰ.. εὐημερεῖ καλῶς τὰ πρὸς σέ though your relations with Thebes *are all fair weather*, Id.*OC*616; τὸ εὐημεροῦν τῆς πόλεως the *prosperous* class, Arist.*Pol.*1308^{b}24; πόλεις εὐημεροῦσαι ib.1322^{b}38; εὐ. καὶ τροφὴν ἄφθονον ἔχειν *thrive*, Id.*HA*573^{b}22; opp. χαλεπῶς ἔχειν, ib.597^{b}10; εὐ. τοῖς σώμασι Id.*GA*775^{b}16. 2. *to be successful in* a thing, τὴν ἐκκλησίαν -ήσας ψῆφον φέρων Aeschin.2.63; καθ' ὑπερβολὴν εὐ. Thphr.*Char.*21.11; τῆς Λεαίνης παρὰ τῷ Δημητρίῳ -ούσης Macho ap.Ath.13.577d; of physicians, *to be successful* with a remedy, Gal.12.749 : c. acc., τοὺς Ἐπιγόνους εὐημερήκει, of a dramatist, Ath.13.584d; of an actor, εὐ. ἐπὶ τραγῳδίας Suid. s. v. σαυτὴν ἐπαινεῖς; ἀκρόαμα εὐημεροῦν Plu.2.521f : generally, *have good luck*, ἐν ἅπασιν Philem.79.3, cf. *Com.Adesp.*110.8. **-ημα**, ατος, τό, *a success*, usu. in the military sense, Plb.3.72.2, *OGI*299.7 (Pergam., pl.), Cic. *Att.*5.21.2, D.S.13.13, Ph.2.120 : pl., *successes*, *Inscr.Prien.*109.90 (ii B.C.), 111.130 (i B.C.) : generally, *strokes of good fortune*, Epicur. *Fr.*488; σωματικὰ εὐ. bodily *excellencies*, Vett.Val.161.16. **-ία**, Dor. **εὐᾱμ-**, ἡ, *fine weather*, εὐημερίας οὔσης X.*HG*2.4.2; γενομένης Arist.*HA*569^{b}10 : pl., ib.542^{b}28. II. *prosperity, health and wealth*, E.*El.*197 (lyr.); ἡ ἐκτὸς εὐ. Arist.*EN*1178^{b}33; *happiness*, Pherecr.213; *joy of living*, ἐνούσης τινὸς εὐ. ἐν [τῷ ζῆν] Arist.*Pol.* 1278^{b}29; personified, Εὐ. Alex.161, *Schwyzer*462 *A* 6 (Tanagra, iii B.C.); -ίας ἡμέραν ἐπιτελεῖν to keep a day of *rejoicing*, Alciphr.1. 21; *good living*, Phld.*Acad.Ind.*p.59 M., al. : pl., ἁδραὶ εὐ. *PRyl.* 233.16 (ii A.D.). 2. *thriving condition, healthiness*, τοῦ σώματος Arist.*HA*543^{b}26; πρὸς εὐ. καὶ πρὸς ὑγίειαν with a view to.., Id. *Oec.*1345^{a}26. 3. *honour and glory*, Pi.*I.*1.40; *piece of good luck*, Cic.*Att.*9.13.1, Plu.2.498c; *military success*, Plb.7.9.10; εὐ. ἐμπορικαὶ success in trade, Hippod.ap.Stob.4.1.94; of virtuosi, ἡ παρὰ τοῖς θεάτροις εὐ. Ath.14.631f. **-ος**, Dor. **εὐάμ-** [ᾱ], ον, (ἡμέρα) *of a fine* or *prosperous day*, εὐ. φάος a *happy* day, S.*Aj.*708 (lyr.). 2. *bright, happy*, εὐάμεροι μολπαί E.*Fr.*773.47 (lyr., nisi leg. -αμερίαι); χρόνῳ δ' ἐξέλαμψεν εὐ. Id.*Hyps.Fr.*41(64).62 (lyr.); πρόσωπον Ar.*Av.* 1322 (lyr.); μοῖρα Pl.*Ti.*71d (perh. with play on ἥμερος); τὸ εὐ. *a prosperous life*, Ph.1.515.

εὐήμετος, εὐημής, v. sub εὐέμετος, εὐεμής.

εὐημονία, ἡ, (ἥμων) *skill in throwing* or *hitting*, glossed by ἐμπειρία, Hsch.

εὐηνεμ-ία, ἡ, *fair wind*, Luc.*Lex.*15. **-ος**, Dor. **εὐάν-** [ᾱ, exc. in *AP*9.555 (Crin.)], ον, *well as to the winds*, i. e., I. *serene, calm*, πόντου χεῦμα E.*Fr.*316; πλόος εὐ. a *fair* voyage, Theoc.28.5. b. epith. of Zeus at Sparta, Paus.3.13.8. 2. *sheltered from the wind*, λιμένες E.*Andr.*749 (and perh. also λίμνα S.*Fr.*371 (lyr.)); χώρα Luc.*Abd.*27. II. *open to the wind*, [ὡς πῦρ] ἐν εὐανέμοις βάσσαις (cf. εὔπνοος II) S.*Aj.*197 (lyr.), cf. Orib.9.20.1.

εὐήνιος, ον, (ἡνία) *obedient to the rein*, ἅρμα Emp.4.5; ὀχήματα Pl. *Phdr.*247b; ἵπποι -ώτατοι Id.*R.*467e; of persons, *tractable, docile*, Id.*Lg.*730b; τὸ ἀγαθὸν εὐ. ὄν Porph.*Abst.*2.39; of a disease, *easily yielding*, Hp.*Virg.*1; cf. εὐάνιος. Adv. -ίως *patiently, tractably*, Pl. *Sph.*217d, Plu.2.9b; ζῆν Arr.*Epict.*4.7.12.

εὐηνορία, Dor. **-ᾱνορία**, ἡ, (εὐήνωρ) *manliness*, E.*HF*407 (lyr.) : pl., Pi.*O.*5.20.

εὐήνῠτος, ον, (ἀνύω) *easy to achieve*, Hsch.: **εὐήνυστος**, Zonar.

εὐήνωρ, Dor. **εὐάνωρ** [ᾱ], ορος, ὁ, ἡ, Hom. (only in Od.), prob. '*the joy of men*', φέρον δ' εὐήνορα οἶνον 4.622; φέρον δ' εὐήνορα χαλκόν 13. 19. II. later, of communities, etc., *well-manned, abounding in brave men*, Pi.*O.*1.24, 6.80, etc.; λαός Id.*N.*10.36; ἵππος, of the Trojan horse, Tryph.468.

εὐηπελ-ής, ές, *prosperous*, Hsch. (glossed by πρᾶοι, wh. however belongs to εὐήνιοι; perh. fr. *ἄπελος 'strength', cf. ONorse *afl* 'strength'; v. ἀναπελάσας, ἀνηπελίη, κακηπελίη, νηπελέω, ὀλιγηπελέω). **-ία**, ἡ, *prosperity*, Call.*Cer.*136, Hsch.

εὐήρᾰτος, ον, (ἔραμαι) *lovely*, σταθμοί Pi.*O.*5.9; φιλοφροσύναι ib. 6.98; κάλλος Telest.1.6.

εὐήρεια· εὔπλοια, εὐχέρεια, Hsch., cf. *EM*390.50. (Leg. εὐηερίη (= εὐαερία), cf. the corrupt gloss εὐηχερία· εὐηρία, εὔπλοια, Hsch.)

εὐήρετμος, ον, (ἐρετμόν) *well fitted to the oar*, σκαλμός A.*Pers.* 376. 2. *well-rowed*, πλάτα S.*OC*716 (lyr.); ναῦς E.*Ion* 1160.

εὐηρημένοι· τετορυνημένοι, Hsch.

εὐήρης, ες, (ἀραρίσκω) *well-fitted*, Hom. (only in Od.) always of the oar, *well-poised, easy to handle*, λαβὼν εὐ. ἐρετμόν 11.121; οὐδ' εὐήρε' ἐρετμά ib.125, al.; νεὼς εὐ. πίτυλος the plash *of the well-poised oars*, E.*IT*1050; σκάφη Plu.*Ant.*65; *well-knit*, γυῖα Nic.*Th.*81 : generally, ὄργανα εὐ. πρὸς τὴν χρείαν *well-fitted for*.., Hp.*Medic.*2; εὐ. τεύχη Orac.ap.Paus.4.12.4; εὐήρεας ἵππους, = εὐαγώγους, Hsch.: fem. εὐῆρις, pr. n. in Paus.1.27.4 (s.v.l.).

εὐήροτος, ον, (ἀρόω) *easy to cultivate*, πεδίον Str.9.4.5 (s.v.l.), cf. Poll.1.227 : irreg. Sup. εὐηρότατον Hsch. (glossed by εὔδιον), Suid.

εὐήρῠτος, ον, (ἀρύω A) *good to draw*, ὕδωρ *h.Cer.*106.

εὐήτριος (A), Dor. **εὐᾱτρ-**, ον, (ἥτριον) *with good* or *fine thread, well-woven*, A.*Fr.*47; ὕφασμα Pl.*Plt.*310e; ὕφη (v. l. ὑφαί) D.H.*Comp.*23; ἱμάτιον Luc.*Lex.*9; αἱ εὐ. σινδόνες, of cotton, Str.15.1.20. II. Act., *well-weaving*, τὰν πέπλων εὐάτριον ἐργάτιν.. κερκίδα *AP*6.289 (Leon.).

εὐήτριος (B), ον, (ἦτρον), = εὐκοίλιος, Hsch.

εὐηφεν-έω, *to be wealthy, prosperous*, Epic.*Oxy.*1794.13. **-ής**, ές, (ἄφενος) *wealthy*, Il.11.427, 23.81 (vulg. εὐηγ-) : as pr. n., *IG*12 (8).376.14 (Thasos).

εὐήχ-εια, ἡ, *euphony*, Phld.*Po.*994.24. **-έομαι**, *to be euphonious*, ib.18. **-ής**, Dor. **εὐᾱχ-**, ές, *well-sounding, tuneful*, ὕμνος Pi.*P.*2. 14; ὑμέναιος Call.*Del.*296; ὄργανον Plu.2.437d; *euphonious*, Phld. *Po.*2.3. **-ητος**, Dor. **εὐάχ-** [ᾱ], ον, = foreg., ὕμνοι E.*Ion* 884 (lyr.); *loud-sounding*, πόντος Id.*Hipp.*1272 (lyr.). **-ος**, ον, = εὐηχής, *euphonious*, Phld.*Po.*994.24, v.l. in D.H.*Comp.*14, cf. Longin.24.2; *melodious*, of the voice, Ath.3.80d; εὐ. φωνητήρια ὄργανα Ph.1.511; ἀρτηρίαν εὐ. παρασκευάζειν Dsc.2.27; κύμβαλα Lxx*Ps.*150.5 : neut. pl. εὔηχα as Adv., κελαδεῖν Ps.-Luc.*Philopatr.*3 : regul. Adv. -ήχως Thom.Mag.p.223 R.

εὐθάλᾰμος [θᾰ], ον, *blessing wedlock*, Ἀφροδίτη Nonn.*D.*2.324.

εὐθάλασσος [θᾰ], ον, *lying well by the sea*, Philostr.*VS*2.1.3. 2. δῶρον εὐ. the gift *of sea-power*, S.*OC*711 (lyr., with allusion to θάλασσα 3). II. *a 'good sailor'*, Alciphr.2.4.

εὐθάλ-εια [θᾰ], ἡ, *bloom, flower* of a thing, εὐδαιμοσύνας Archyt.ap. Stob.3.1.107 : **εὐθαλία** τῶν καρπῶν *EM*442.13. **-έω**, *bloom, thrive*, Nic.*Fr.*74.16, Plu.2.28e, *POxy.*729.22 (ii A.D.), Q.S.4.423 : metaph., Them.*Or.*27.339c. **-ής**, ές, *blooming, flourishing, thriving*,

Αἴγυπτος A.Fr.300.5; γῆρας Men.Mon.388; ἄνηθον Mosch.3.100, cf. AP9.3 (Antip.), Orph.A.912; Χάριτες AP7.600 (Jul.): later in Prose, δένδρον SIG889.9 (Arcesine, iii A.D.); εὐθαλέστερα παιδία Sabin.ap.Orib.9.17.3; ζῷα εὐθαλῆ POxy.902.15 (v A.D.): metaph., τὸ εὐ. [τῆς ψυχῆς] Ph.1.512; πτερὰ εὐ. τῆς ψυχῆς Them.Or.21.251b.

εὐθᾱλής, ές, Dor. Adj. *flourishing, thriving*, τύχα Pi.P.9.72; πέδον B.8.5; εὐκάρπεια E.Tr.217 (lyr.); καρποί Ar.Av.1062 (lyr.); φύλλα AP9.313 (Anyte); εὐθηλής is cj. ib.247 (Phil.), h.Mart.9:—also **-θᾰλος**, ον, *thriving well*, v.l. in EM197.34.

εὐθαλπής, ές, *warming well, genial*, θέρος Q.S.4.441.

εὐθᾰνᾰσία, ἡ, *easy, happy death*, Posidipp.18, August.ap.Suet. Oct.99, Ph.1.182. 2. *noble death*, Cic.Att.16.7.3.

εὐθᾰνᾰτ-έω, *die a noble death*, Stoic.3.156, Plb.5.38.9, J.AJ9.4.5. **-ος**, ον, *dying easily* or *happily*: εὐ. θάνατος, = εὐθανασία, Men.23, cf. Paul.Al.M.3. Adv. -τως Cratin.413, Men.481.16.

εὐθάρσ-εια, ἡ, *good courage*, App.BC3.91: -ία, Pl.Def.412a. **-έω**, *to be of good courage*, And.2.16: prob. to be written divisim in A.Th.34, Supp.1015. **-ής**, ές, *of good courage*, h.Mart.9 (v.l.), A.Ag.930, Supp.249, E.El.526; ἐν τοῖς δεινοῖς X.Ages.11.10; πρὸς κίνδυνον D.S.11.35; τὸ εὐθαρσὴ εἶναι Andronic.Rhod.p.575 M.: Comp. -έστερος Diph.111, Plu.2.69a; of *bolder* interpreters, Ph.1.606: Sup. -έστατος X.HG7.1.9. Adv. -σῶς, ἔχειν πρός τι Arist.EN1115a21. 2. *safe, secure*, τὰ δεινὰ καὶ τὰ εὐ. X.Eq.Mag.4.11.

εὐθέᾱτος, ον, (θεάομαι) *easy to be seen*, Poll.5.150.

εὐθεῖ· ἤρει, Hsch. **εὐθεῖα**, ἡ, v. εὐθύς A. 3.

εὐθεῖν· ἐλθεῖν (Cret.), Hsch. **εὐθεῖος**, = εὐόμιλος, Zonar.

εὐθέμῐτος, ον, *just, righteous*, σαδράπαι Ἀρχ.Ἐφ.1927.27 (Aranda).

εὐθένεια, ἡ, *supply, provisioning*, ὀμνύω... ἔχειν παρ' ἐμαυτῷ χοίρους... εἰς τὴν εὐθένιαν (or -ίαν) τῆς... πόλεως BGU649.16 (ii A.D.); εἰς εὐθένειαν τῶν.. στρατιωτῶν.. οἴνου ξέστας ib.974.6 (iv A.D.), cf. PGoodsp.Cair.11.5 (iv A.D.), POxy.1412.6 (iii A.D.), 1261.7 (iv A.D.), PLond.3.1245.5 (iv A.D.); πᾶσαν εὐθένειαν *supplies* of all kinds, POxy.1252v.14 (iii A.D., but εὐθηνιαρχικός ib.17); [ᾧα] πρὸς διάπρασιν καὶ εὐθένιαν (or -ίαν) τῆς... πόλεως ib.83.11 (iv A.D.), cf. PSI 4.309 (iv A.D.); ἐραυνηταῖς εὐθε[ίας] PFay.104.18 (iii A.D.); ἐπὶ τῶν μερισμῶν τῶν σπερμάτων καὶ τῆς εὐθενίας PTeb.397.19 (ii A.D., but κοσμητεύσας εὐθηνίας ib.15,28); εὐθενίας ἔπαρχος, = Lat. *praefectus annonae*, IG14.1072 (Rome, ii A.D.); εὐθενείας ἔ. ib.917 (iii A.D.). II. *welfare, prosperity, abundance*, Poll.9.160; gloss on εὔσοια, Sch.S.OC390, v.l. in Arist.Rh.1360b16, HA602a15, al.; *good* physical *condition*, τοῦ σκήνεος εὐθένεια cj. for εὐσθ- in Democr.57.

εὐθενέω, *thrive, flourish*, of animals and plants, μῆλα... εὐθενοῦντα A.Eu.944 (lyr.); καρπόν τε γαίας καὶ βοτῶν.. ἀστοῖσιν εὐθενοῦντα ib.908, cf. Thphr.CP2.4.5, 5.11.3; μή τιν' οἶκον εὐθενεῖν A.Eu.895 (Scalig. for εὐσθ-); εὐθενούντων τῶν πραγμάτων D.18.286; also of men, τοὺς στρατιώτας... εὐθενεῖν Id.8.20; ἡ Λοκρὶς εὐθηνεῖ (leg. εὐθενεῖ) τῷ ζεφύρῳ Thphr.Vent.44, cf. Plu.Publ.11, Ael.NA5.13. II. Pass. in same sense, [οἱ Λακεδαιμόνιοι] εὐθενήθησαν Hdt.1.66 codd. (elswh. εὐθηνέω in codd. Hdt.); τὴν πόλιν εὐθενεῖσθαι D.19.231 (s.v.l.). (εὐθηνέω (q.v.) is freq. v.l.; εὐθενέω (Att. acc. to Zonar.) is required by metre in A.Eu.895 (cj.), Cratin.327, and is found in best codd. of D., Arist. (v.l. in PA680a28, HA601b9, Mete.352a6, al., εὐσθεν- v.l. in EN1100a6, GA775a29, etc.), cod. Urb. of Thphr. CP5.11.3, al., Aristid.Or.46(3).42, v.l. in Ael.VH13.1, etc.)

εὐθενής· εὐπαθοῦσα· ἰσχυρά, Hsch.: Sup. -έστατος, οἶκος PIand.62.9 (vi A.D.).

εὐθενία, ἡ, = εὐθένεια II (q.v.), from which it cannot be distd. after ii B.C.: Ion. **εὐθενίη** (–⏑⏑–) Epigr. in Rev.Phil.19.178 (i B.C.), Epigr.Gr.1036.19 (Nicomedia); εὐθενία is v.l. in Arist.Rh.1360b16, HA602a15 (v.l. εὐσθένεια, εὐθένεια), Porph.Gaur.16.2.—From ii A.D. εὐθένεια and εὐθενία begin to be confused with εὐθηνία.

εὐθενιᾰκός, ή, όν, *for food-supply*, εἴδη -κά *provisions*, Stud.Pal. 20.84.3 (iii A.D.).

εὐθενιαρχέω, = εὐθηνιαρχέω, PSI6.705 (iii A.D.).

εὐθερᾰπ-ευσία, ἡ, *ease of treatment*, Heliod.ap.Orib.46.22.11. **-ευτος**, ον, *easy to cure*, Hp.Coac.501 (Comp.), Thphr.HP9.16.6, etc.: Comp., Phld.D.1.24. 2. *easy to help* or *remedy*, D.C.38.24. II. *easily won by kindness* or *attention*, X.Cyr.2.2.10.

εὐθέριστος, ον, *easily harvested*: εὐθέριστον, τό, *a kind of balsam*, Plin.HN12.114, prob. in Dsc.1.19.

εὐθέρμαντος, ον, *easy to warm*, Thphr.CP4.7.3 (Comp.).

εὔθερμος, ον, *very warm*, Hp.Nat.Puer.24 (Comp., nisi leg. ἔνθ-).

εὔθερος, ον, *pleasant in summer, sunny*, Poll.5.108 codd. (fort. εὐάερος).

εὐθεσία, ἡ, *good condition, habit of body*, Hp.ap.Gal.19.101; ἐνιαυτὸς εὐθεσίης a year *of plenty*, ibid.

εὐθέσμως, Adv. *lawfully*, ἄλοχον λάβε AP9.444 (Eratosth.).

εὐθετ-έω, *to be suitable, convenient*, εὐθετεῖ πᾶσι χρῆσθαι for all to use, Thphr.HP5.7.4; εὐ. εἴς τι D.S.2.41,48; *to be timely, opportune*, Orph.Fr.272; of an epithet, *to be suitable*, Sch.Il.Oxy.1086.110; so of food, Diocl.Fr.141; of bandages, Gal.18(1).789, al.; λιμένας... ταῖς μακραῖς ναυσὶν εὐθετοῦντας D.S.5.12: f.l. in Thphr.HP1.1.3 codd. II. trans., *set in order*, ἕκαστα Luc.DDeor.24.1 (v.l. for εὐθετίσαντα), cf. SIG1240 (ii A.D.); [τὰς τρίχας] Ar.Fr.782; *adorn*, εὐ. ἑαυτήν D.C.51.13; *lay out* a corpse, Id.40.49, cf. Phryn.PS p.71 B. **-ησις**, εως, ἡ, *prosperity*, Eust.1383.13. **-ίζω**, *set in order, arrange orderly*, Hes.Th.541; χελιδὼν... καλιὴν ηὐθέτιζεν Babr.118.2; τὰς κόμας Luc.Ind.29, etc.:—Med., ὀστέον εὐθετισάμενος Hp.Fract.8, cf. 16. II. in Pass., *to be suitably employed*, εἴς τι A.D.Adv.140.11, Synt.169.19. **-ισμός**, ὁ, *convenience, propriety*, Id.Adv.144.19, Synt.309.12; *orderly arrangement*, Simp.in Ph.487.29, in Cat.336.38. **-ος**, ον, (τίθημι) *well-arranged, conveniently placed*, ὀστέα Hp.Off.15: Comp. -ώτερος Id.Fract.4; ἐν εὐ. τόπῳ in a *suitable* place, Ἀρχ.Δελτ.7.200 (Ephesus). b. of the ashes of a corpse, *easily stowed*, A.Ag.444 (lyr.); so of the corpse, *laid out* for burial (cf. εὐθετέω), Supp.Epigr.1.449 (Phrygia, iii A.D.); εὐ. σάκος, ἀρβύλαι, *well-fitting, ready for use*, A.Th.642 (Sch., εὔκυκλον cod. Med.), Fr.259; εὐ. εἴς τι D.S.2.57; πρός τι Id.5.37; εὔθετόν ἐστι c. inf., it is *convenient*..., Id.21.21; καιρὸς εὐ. Lxx Ps.31(32).6, D.S.5.57. 2. of persons, *well-adapted*, εἰς τοὺς τραγῳδοὺς εὐ., οὐκ εἰς τὸν βίον Philem.105.5; εἰς, πρὸς φιλίαν, Phld.Ir.p.46 W., Lib.p.45 O.; εἰς τὴν βασιλείαν τοῦ θεοῦ Ev.Luc.9.62; πράγματι for a business, Nicol.ap.Stob.3.1.40; πρός τι Plb.25.3.6, etc.; *quick, able*, κατὰ τὰς ἐντεύξεις τοῖς ὄχλοις εὐ. D.S.33.22: abs., εὔθετοι *fit and proper persons*, PTeb.27.44 (ii B.C.), etc. Adv. -τως, ἔχειν Hp.Fract.23; πρός τι D.S.33.4.

εὐθεώρητος, ον, *easily seen* or *observed*, Arist.HA578a20, Thphr.HP1.1.1 (Comp.); τινι D.S.19.37. 2. *easy to perceive*, Arist.Rh.1376b31; εὐθεώρητόν ἐστι περί τινος *it is easy to conduct an inquiry about...*, Id.GA724a17; οὐκ ἔστιν εὐ. ποτέρως.. Id.SE180b3; τίνες εἰσὶ καὶ πόσαι.. Iamb.Comm.Math.24: c. acc. et inf., Phld.Herc.1251.7.

εὐθέως, Adv. of εὐθύς (q.v.).

εὐθηγής, ές, *sharpening well*, AP6.63 (Damoch.).

εὔθηκτος, ον, *well-sharpened, keen*, Lyc.1105, Nonn.D.17.121.

εὐθηλ-έομαι, Pass., (εὐθηλής) *to be well-suckled, fatted up*, χοῖρος A.Fr.309.1:—also in Act., [παιδία] εὐθηλέοντα, = εὐθαλῆ, Democr.276. **-ήμων**, ον, gen. ονος, = sq., μόσχος AP6.263 (Leon.). **-ής**, ές, v. εὐθαλής. **-ία**, ἡ, gloss on εὐθηνία, Suid. **-ος**, ον, (θηλή) *with distended udder*, E.IA579 (lyr.), Ba.737, AP9.224 (Crin.); εὐ. μαστὸς θεᾶς Lyc.1328.

εὐθήμελκτος, ον, = νεήμελκτος, Aët.9.42; cf. εὐθυμελγής.

εὐθημ-ονέομαι, Dep. *keep in order, manage*, Pl.Lg.758b:—Act., intr., *to be in good order*, Simp.in Ph.1067.24; trans. in Tz.H.1.367. **-οσύνη**, ἡ, *habit of good management, tidiness*, Hes.Op.471, X.Cyr.8.5.7, Ael.NA9.17, Dam.Isid.231. II. *good order*, of the course of nature, Plot.4.4.6, 6.8.17. III. personified, Orph.Fr.336. **-ων**, ον, gen. ονος, (τίθημι) *tidy in habits*, of animals, Arist.HA616b23, 618b30. 2. *harmonious*, ἀοιδή A.R.1.569. II. Act., *setting in order*, c. gen., δμωαὶ... δωμάτων εὐ. A.Ch.84.

εὐθηνέω, *thrive, flourish*, εὐθηνέειν Αἴγυπτον Hdt.2.91,124 codd., cf. X.Ath.2.6 codd.; κτήνεσιν εὐθηνεῖ (sc. ὁ ὄλβιος) h.Hom.30.10; πρόβατα εὐθηνεῖν may their sheep *thrive*, SIG526.42 (Crete, iii B.C.); τὰ κτήνεα εὐθηνεῖν εἰκός prob. in Hp.Aër.12 (εὐθύνειν codd.), cf. Epid.6.4.20 (εὐθυνεῖ vulg., εὐθενεῖ Gal.); freq. in Lxx (Jb.21.9, al.), cf. BGU1118.30 (i B.C.), al., Ph.1.211, 2.429:—Pass., Αἴγυπτος καρποῖς ἀφθόνοις εὐθηνεῖτο POxy.1381.238 (ii A.D.). (εὐθηνέω—Ion. acc. to Zonar.—is freq. v.l. for εὐθενέω (q.v.) and is required by metre in h.Hom. l.c.)

εὐθήνησις, εως, ἡ, = sq., Phld.Lib.p.11 O. (s.v.l.).

εὐθηνία, ἡ, *prosperity, plenty*, Lxx Ge.41.29, al., Ph.2.1, al.; ὅπως οἱ ἄλλοι ἐν εὐθηνίᾳ ὦσι OGI90.13 (Rosetta, ii B.C.); ὑπηρετεῖν τῇ τε εὐθηνίᾳ καὶ τῇ εὐδαιμονίᾳ ib.669.4 (Egypt, i A.D.); τῶν τὰς καλὰς ἀγόντων ἡμέρας εὐθηνία, description of Isis, POxy.1380.135 (ii A.D.); πάντα τὰ πρὸς εὐθηνίαν τῆς χώρας Peripl.M.Rubr.48; σώματος *good condition*, Andronic.Rhod.p.573 M. 2. personified as a goddess, *Abundance, Plenty*, IG4.676 (Thyreatis), J. of P.11.144 (Anazarba), prob. in CIL10.1624 (Puteoli). 3. generally, *abundance*, φρονήσεως Ph.1.618; τῶν ἀναγκαίων Id.Fr.109 H.; v.l. in Arist.Rh.1360b16, al. II. like Lat. *annona, corn-supply*, εἰς εὐθηνίαν σιτωνίας SIG783.16 (Mantinea, i B.C.); ἡ ἀπὸ σιτίων φερομένη εὐθηνία Plu.2.307d; εὐθηνίας ἐπιμελητής IG4.795 (ii A.D.); γεναμένῳ ἀγορανόμῳ καὶ ἐπὶ τῆς εὐθηνίας Mitteis Chr.227.9 (ii A.D.), cf. PFlor. 382.76 (iii A.D.), OGI705 (Alexandria, ii A.D., εὐθυνίας lapis); κοσμητεύσας εὐθηνίας (v. εὐθένεια). 2. *a largess of corn*, εὐθηνία ἔτους τρίτου, personified on coins of Alexandria, B.Mus.Cat. No.1164: so in pl., χρήματα πολιτικὰ ἐς εὐθηνίας ἢ νομὰς ἀθροιζόμενα Hdn.7.2.5.

εὐθηνιάρχ-ης, ου, ὁ, *commissioner of food-* (esp. *corn-*) *supply*, BGU556 ii 12, POxy.1412.1 (both iii A.D.):—hence **-έω**, ib.908.19 (ii A.D.), 2108.3 (iii A.D.), BCH12.84 (Zeus Panamaros). **-ία**, ἡ, CPHerm.7 i 6 (iii A.D.). **-ικός**, ή, όν, στέφανος POxy.1252v.17 (iii A.D.).

εὐθηνός, όν, *thriving, flourishing*, καρποί Lyd.Ost.38, cf. Hdn.Epim. 175; εὔθυνος, v.l. in EM197.34, should perh. be εὐθηνός (εὔθηνος?).

εὐθήξ, ῆγος, ὁ, ἡ, (θήγω) = εὔθηκτος, Theognost.Can.40:—hence **εὐθηξία**, ἡ, EM256.18.

εὐθήρ-ᾱτος, ον, *easy to catch* or *win*, Διὸς ἵμερος οὐκ εὐ. ἐτύχθη A.Supp.87; ἔτ' εὐ. AP12.105 (Asclep.), cf. Corn.ND28; στέφανος Plb.31.25.3; εὐ. ὑπὸ τῶν τοιούτων Arist.EN1110b14:—Ion. **εὐθήρητος**, v.l. **-ευτος**, Opp.H.5.426. **-ία**, ἡ, *success in sport*, Ael.NA10.48 (pl.), Poll.1.108. II. metaph., of the 'battue' of Persians at Marathon, Agath.2.10. **-ος**, ον, (θήρα) *lucky* or *successful in hunting*, E.Ba.1253; εὔθηρος ὀρνέων ἴρηξ Babr.72.21 (cj.); of Pan, AP6.185 (Zos.); εὔθηροι, οἱ, club of *sportsmen* at Pergamum, Ath.Mitt.33.409; εὐ. ἄγρη *successful sport*, AP6.27 (Theaet.), cf. 253 (Crin.); τὸ εὐ. *good sport*, Ph.2.114; εὐ. κάλαμοι *successful* fishing-rods, AP6.89 (Maec.); *successful as bait*, Ael.NA12.42. II. (θήρ) *abounding in game, good for hunting*, ὄρος Str.14.1.12; ῥίον AP6.268 (Mnasalc.); εὐ. καὶ εὔϊχθυς Aristid.Or.44(17).16.

εὐθής, ές, only in later Lxx translators for εὐθύς A, Lxx 1*Ki.*29.6, *Ps.* 118(119).137; βιβλίον τοῦ εὐθοῦς the Book of the *Righteous* (*Jashar*), ib.2*Ki.*1.18: neut. pl. εὐθεῖα ib.2*Es.*19.13, cf. interpol. in Thom. Mag. p.165 R., Suid. s. v. εὐθυγενής.

εὐθήσαυρος, ον, *well-stored, precious*, ἔλαιον *AP*6.300 (Leon.).

εὐθικός, ή, όν, (εὐθύς) *straight*, κίνησις S.E.*M.*10.51.

εὐθικτ-έω, *find the range*, of artillery, Apollod.*Poliorc.*144.11. **-ος**, ον, (θιγεῖν) *touching the point, clever, quick*, εὔ. τὴν διάνοιαν Arist.*HA* 616b22; εὔ. πρὸς τὰς ἀποκρίσεις *quick* in repartee, Ath.13.583f; εὔ. νοῦς, γνώμη, προσβολή, Ph.1.54,240,286; *witty*, Plb.18.4.4, *AP*6.322 (Leon.): f.l. for εὔεικτος, Heraclit.*All.*51 codd. Adv. -τως Lxx 2*Ma.* 15.38, Hdn.4.7.2.

εὐθιξία, ἡ, *cleverness, tact*, Ph.1.54,157,593, Anon.ap.Suid.

εὔθλαστος, ον, (θλάω) *easily indented* or *bruised*, Arist.*Mete.*386a26, Hero *Spir.*1 *Praef.*, *Gp.*9.17.3.

εὐθλίζοντι (dat. sg.), prob. f.l. for ὑελίζοντι, Hermes Trism. in *Rev. Phil.*32.264.

εὐθνήσιμος, ον, *in* or *with easy death*, A.*Ag.*1293.

εὔθοινος, ον, *eating hugely*, of Hercules, Plu.2.267f. II. εὔ. γέρας *a sumptuous* offering, A.*Ch.*257.

εὐθορύβητος [ῠ], ον, *easily confounded*, πρός τινα before.., Plu.*Nic.*2.

εὔθραυστος, ον, (θραύω) *easily injured* or *broken*, Arist.*GA*775a9 (v.l. εὔφθαρτον), Plu.2.174d, Apollod.*Poliorc.*185.15.

εὔθρεπτος, ον, *well-reared*, *EM*28.41 (Comp.).

εὔθριγκος, ον, *well-coped*, of high walls, E.*Hel.*70.

εὔθριξ, Ep. **ἐΰθρ-**, τρῐχος, ὁ, ἡ, *with beautiful hair*, Eub.104 (lyr.); in Il. always of horses, *with flowing mane*, ἵππους 23.13,301; of dogs, X.*Cyn.*4.6; of birds, *well-plumed*, Theoc.18.57. 2. *fleecy, thick*, λῆνος Nic.*Al.*452. II. *attached to a stout line*, of a fish-hook, *AP* 9.52 (Carph.).

εὔθρονος, Ep. **ἐΰθρ-**, ον, *with beautiful seat* or *throne*, ἐΰθρονος Ἠώς Il.8.565, Od.6.48, al.; Ἀφροδίτα Pi.*I.*2.5; Ὧραι Id.*P.*9.60, cf. B.15. 3, etc.

εὔθροος, Ep. **ἐΰθρ-**, ον, *loud-sounding*, Opp.*C.*3.285, *AP*6.39 (Arch.).

εὐθρῠβής, ές, = εὔθρυπτος I, Dsc.1.70, 5.124.

εὐθρύλλητος, ον, = πολυθρυλ(λ)ητος (in bad sense), Vett.Val.187. 4, 199.2.

εὔθρυπτος, ον, (θρύπτω) *easily broken*, αὐχήν Arist.*PA*694b29; *easily dispersed*, ἀήρ Id.*de An.*420a8, cf. Democr.ap.Thphr.*Sens.*73; of earth, *crumbling*, Str.12.8.17, Plu.*Sert.*17; of the fleshy parts of fish, Id.2.916b. II. metaph., *enervated*, Gal.1.186, Sor.1.25.

εὐθύ, neut. of εὐθύς, used as Adv.; v. εὐθύς B.

Εὐθυαῖος, ὁ (sc. μήν), name of a month in the Aetolian Calendar, *IG*9(1).379 (Naupactus), *GDI*1950 (Delph.), etc.

εὐθῠβολ-έω, *throw forward*, τὸν γόνον *Placit.*5.9.2:—Pass., S.E. *M.*5.58. II. intr., *dart* or *go right forward*, τοῦ σπέρματος -οῦντος εἰς [τὴν μήτραν] *Placit.*5.14.2. 2. metaph., *hit the mark*, ἔχων τὸν νοῦν εὐθιξίᾳ πρὸς τὴν θεραπείαν -οῦντα Anon.ap.Suid. s. v. εὐθιξία, cf. Ph.2. 176. **-ία**, ἡ, *direct throw*, Plu.*Nic.*25. **-ος**, ον, (βάλλω) *throwing straight*: hence, *hitting the mark, accurate, exact*, prob. for εὐθύβουλος in Aristox.ap.Stob.1.7.18; ἀπόκρισις, στοχασμοί, Ph.1.617, 2.126; ὄνομα εὐ. the *exact* name, Id.1.73 (Sup.), al.: Comp., Id.1.618: Sup., Id.1.300; τὸ εὐ., = foreg., Id.2.465. Adv. -λως Id.1.99, al., Procl. *in Prm.*p.872 S.: in the lit. sense, *in a direct course*, εὐ. περαιωθῆναι τὸ πέλαγος Hld.5.22.

εὐθῠ-γένειος, ον, *with straight beard*, Polem.*Phgn.*67. **-γενής**, prob. f.l. for -τενής in Suid., Phot. **-γλωσσος**, Att. **-ττος**, ον, *straightforward, plain-spoken*, Pi.*P.*2.86, Dam.*Isid.*23, Procop.*Arc.* 29. **-γνωμίας**, ου, ὁ, *witness who gives direct evidence*, Phot. **-γνωμος**, ον, *straightforward*, Democr.181. **-γραμμᾰτίζω**, *reduce to a rectilinear figure*, ὁ κύκλος -ίζεται Phlp.*in APr.*477.2. **-γραμμικός**, ή, όν, *rectilinear*, ἀριθμός Iamb.*in Nic.*p.56 P. Adv. -κῶς, στίχος εὐ. ἐκκείμενος ib.p.96 P. **-γραμμος**, ον, = foreg., Arist.*Cael.*286b13, al.; γωνία Oenopides ap.Procl.*in Euc.*p.333 F., cf. Euc.1.44; τὸ εὐ. (with or without σχῆμα) *rectilinear figure*, Arist.*APr.*69a31, *Pr.*913b 18, Thphr.*HP*1.12.1.

εὐθυδήμονα (leg. εὐθύδημον)· ἁπλοῦν πολίτην, E.*Fr.*227.

εὐθῠ-δίκαι [ῐ], in pl., = εὐθύδικοι, of the Eumenides, A.*Eu.*312 (lyr., s. v. l., -δίκαιοι Herm.; cf. ὀρθοδίκαιος). **-δῐκία**, ἡ, *direct trial*, on the merits of the case, without exceptions or technical pleas, εὐθυδικίας ἀποδέχεσθαι Is.7.3; εἰσιέναι D.34.4; also εὐθυδικίᾳ εἰσιέναι, εἰσελθεῖν, Id.45.6, Is.6.43; τὸν ἐξ εὐθυδικίας λόγον συνίστασθαι Mitteis *Chr.* 31 vi 13 (ii B.C.). **-δῐκος**, ον, *righteous-judging*, B.5.6, A.*Ag.*761 (lyr.), *AP*6.346 (Anacr.). II. εὐθύδικον, τό, = εὐθυδικία, *IG*5(2). 357.25 (Stymphalus, iii B.C.). **-δρομέω**, of ships, *run a straight course*, Ph.1.131,327, *Act.Ap.*16.11: metaph., of persons, Agath.2. 21. **-δρόμος**, ον, *running a straight course*, ἄνεμοι Plb.34.4.5; νῆες Orph.*H.*22.10. **-έντερος**, ον, *with straight intestines*, Arist.*HA*507b 34. **-έπεια**, ἡ, *straight speaking*, Adam.1.11, Hsch. (pl.). **-επής**, ές, (ἔπος) *plain-spoken*, Adam.1.16. **-εργής**, ές, *accurately wrought*, Luc. *Hist.Conscr.*27 (nisi leg. εὐεργής). **-ζωμον**, τό, *extemporized broth*, coined by Eust.1191.14. **-θάνᾰτος** [θᾰ], ον, *quick-killing, mortal*, πληγή Plu.*Ant.*76. **-θριξ**, τρῐχος, ὁ, ἡ, *with straight hair*, Arist.*GA* 782b34, Poll.2.22. **-καινα**· ἡ σχοῖνος, διὰ τὸ εὐθέως κτείνειν, καὶ δύναται εἶναι **εὐθυκταίνα**, Hsch.; cf. καίνω. **-καυλος**, ον, *with a straight stalk*, Thphr.*HP*6.4.5 (Comp.). **-κρέων**· παχύς, Hsch. **-κτέανον**· ἰθὺ πεφυκυῖαν, εἰς ὀρθόν, Id. (-κτέσαν cod., cf. ἰθυκτέανον, εὐκτέανος.) **-ληπτος**, ον, *easy to get at, to procure*, Anon.ap.Suid. **-λογία**, ἡ, = εὐθυέπεια, Polem.*Phgn.*15. **-λόγος**, ον, gloss on εὐθυρρήμων, Suid.

εὐθῠμᾰχ-έω, *fight fairly*, Hsch. s. v. Θετταλὸν σόφισμα. **-ης**, ου, Dor. **-χᾱς**, ὁ, *fighting openly*, Pi.*O.*7.15. **-ία**, ἡ, *fair fight*, Plu. *Sert.*10. **-ος** [ᾰ], ον, = εὐθυμάχης, Simon.137.

εὐθῠμελγής, ές, = νεημέλκτος, Aët.3.38.

εὐθῠμετρ-ία, ἡ, *survey*, κώμης *PTeb.*12.6 (ii B. C.), etc. **-ικός**, ή, όν, *linear, 'running'*, opp. στερεός, πόδες *Supp.Epigr.*2.568.12 (Didyma, ii B.C.), cf. Hero *Geom.*3.19. II. *linear*, of number, [ἀριθμός] Theo Sm.p.95 H., cf. Iamb.*in Nic.*p.57 P.; ἑβδομάς *Theol. Ar.*44.

εὐθῡμ-έω, *to be of good cheer*, E.*Cyc.*530, *AP*5.100, *Ep.Jac.*5.13: fem. dat. pl. pres. part. εὐθυμεύσαις Theoc.15.143; περὶ τῆς κριθῆς εὐθύμει *do not be anxious* about.., *PAmh.*2.133.4 (ii A. D.). II. trans., *cheer, delight*, τινα A.*Fr.*350.4, cf. Democr.279:—Pass., *to be cheerful*, Id.3, X.*HG*7.4.36; ἐπί τινι Id.*Cyr.*4.1.19; ἐν ταῖς ἀτυχίαις Arist.*Rh.*1379b 18; πάντα -εῖσθαι χρή Aret.*CA*1.1. **-ητέον**, *one must be cheerful*, X.*Ap.*27. **-ία**, ἡ, *cheerfulness, contentment*, Pi.*I.*1.63, *Pae.*1.2, B.16.125, X.*Cyr.*4.5.7, Philem.96.4, Men.231, etc.: in pl., Pi.*O.*2. 34, X.*Cyr.*1.3.12, Arist.*Pr.*954a25; περὶ εὐθυμίης, title of works by Democritus and Hipparchus Pythagoreus. II. Εὐ. personified, Pi.*Fr.*155, Memn.4.2, *LW*45 (Erythrae). **-ος**, ον, *kind, generous*, ἄναξ Od.14.63. II. *cheerful*, Democr.174, X.*Cyr.*6.4.13 (Comp.), Pl.*Lg.*792b; συμπόσια εὐ. Ion Eleg.1.14; φέρειν γῆρας εὐ. εἰς τελευτάν Pi.*O.*5.22; of horses, *spirited*, X.*Eq.*11.12 (Sup.); τὸ εὐ., = εὐθυμία, Plu.2.1106c, D.C.42.1. Adv. -μως *cheerfully*, Batr.159, A.*Ag.* 1592: Comp. -ότερον X.*Cyr.*2.2.27: Sup. -ότατα ib.3.3.12.

εὐθῦνα (v. infr.), ἡ, gen. εὐθύνης, acc. εὔθυναν, nom. pl. εὔθυναι: (εὐθύνω):—*setting straight, correction, chastisement*, Pl.*Prt.*326e (pl.); *calling to account*, *POxy.*1203.9 (i A. D.), etc. II. esp. at Athens, *public examination of the conduct of officials*, held on the expiration of their term of office (dist. fr. λόγος 'rendering of accounts', οὔτε χρήματα διαχειρίσας τῆς πόλεως δίδωμι λόγον αὐτῶν, οὔτε ἀρχὴν ἄρξας οὐδεμίαν εὐθύνας ὑπέχω αὐτῆς Lys.24.26; λόγον διδόντων τῶν χρημάτων ..καὶ εὐθύνας διδόντων *IG*1².91.27), used in sg. by Ar.*V.*571, Lys.10. 27, al.; ἡ εὐ. βλάβη τις δικαία ἐστίν Arist.*Rh.*1411b20: more freq. in pl., *IG*l.c., Ar.*Eq.*825 (anap.), etc.; πρεσβείας εὔθυναι *an account* of one's embassage, D.19.82; [τῆς στρατηγίας] ἔμ' ἀπαιτεῖς εὐθύνας Id. 18.245; opp. εὐθύνας διδόναι Ar.*Pax* 1187, And.1.90; ὑποσχεῖν Lys.30. 3; κατηγορεῖν [τινος] εἰς τὰς εὐ. Antipho 6.43; τὰς εὐ. κατηγορεῖν, ἐπὶ τὰς εὐθύνας ἐλθεῖν, D.19.81,2; εὔθυνάν τινι ἐμβαλέσθαι Arist.*Ath.*48.4, cf. Decr.ib.39.6; εὐθύνας or εὔθυναν ὀφλεῖν to be convicted, or accused, of malversation, And.1.73, Lys.10.27; κλοπῆς ἕνεκα Aeschin.3.10; εὐθύνας ἀποφυγεῖν, διαφυγεῖν, to be acquitted thereof, Pl.*Lg.*946d, 947e; τῆς εὐθύνης ἀπολύειν τινά Ar.*V.*571: metaph., τὰς εὐ. τὰς τοῦ βίου *the accounts rendered* of your life, Alex.262.8, cf. Ph.2.214, al. (On the accent see Hdn.Gr.1.257.37: the later form εὐθύνη, nom. pl. εὐθῦναι is sts. found in codd. of early writers, as Lys.10.27, Pl.*Prt.* 326e, but shd. prob. be corrected.)

εὐθυνία, freq. f.l. for εὐθηνία, as Aët.5.94: so perh. **εὔθυνος** in *EM* 197.34 for εὔθηνος.

εὐθύνομος [ῠ], ον, = εὐθύδικος, Simon.93.

εὔθῡν-ος, ὁ, *corrector, chastiser, judge*, A.*Pers.*828, *Eu.*273 (lyr.). II. at Athens and elsewhere, *public examiner* (cf. εὔθυνα), *IG*1².188, Decr.ap.And.1.78, Pl.*Lg.*945a sq., Arist.*Pol.*1322b11, *Ath.*48.4, *SIG* 38.3 (Teos, v B.C.); official of a guild, *Supp.Epigr.*2.458 (Moesia, ii/iii A. D.), etc. **-σις**, εως, ἡ, (εὐθύνω) *straightening*, opp. κάμψις, Arist. *Mete.*386a7, *IA*708b24; τῆς ῥινός Gal.18(1).481. **-τέον**, *one must correct*, τοὺς Εὐκλείδου ὅρους Iamb.*in Nic.*p.26 P. **-τήρ**, ῆρος, ὁ, *corrector, chastiser*, ὕβριος Thgn.40. 2. *one who levels* or *straightens*, θριγκῶν Man.4.293. 3. as Adj., εὐθυντὴρ οἴαξ the *guiding* rudder, A. *Supp.*717. **-τηριαῖος**, α, ον, *belonging to the* εὐθυντηρία (cf. sq. II. 1 b), *Milet.*7.59 (Didyma). **-τήριος**, α, ον, *making straight: directing, ruling*, σκῆπτρον A.*Pers.*764. II. Subst. εὐθυντηρία, ἡ, *the part of a ship wherein the rudder was fixed*, E.*IT*1356. b. *base, plinth, socle* of a wall, *IG*2².1668.16, *BCH*26.43 (Delph.), *IGRom.*4.293a i 38 (Pergam., ii B.C.); εὐ.· τὸ ἐν τῷ ἐδάφει σύμμαγμα ὑπὸ τῶν ἀρχιτεκτόνων, Hsch. 2. -τήριον, τό, *rule, norm*, γνώμων καὶ εὐ. *Theol.Ar.*59. **-τής**, οῦ, ὁ, = εὔθυνος, Pl.*Lg.*945b,c; δῆμος εὐθυντὴς χθονός cj. Markl. for αὐθέντης, E.*Supp.*442. **-τικός**, ή, όν, *of* or *for the conduct of* εὔθυνα (q. v.), εἶδος δικαστηρίων Arist.*Pol.*1300b19; λόγος εὐ. D.H.*Din.* 11. **-τός**, ή, όν, *capable of being straightened*, Arist.*Mete.*385b27. **-ω**, (εὐθύς) = the Homeric ἰθύνω (which is a freq. v.l., as in A.*Pers.*773): —*guide straight, direct*, οἰωνὸν γνώμῃ στομίων ἄτερ εὐθύνων Id.*Pr.*289; εὐ. ἡνίας Ar.*Av.*1739 (lyr.); [ἅρματα] Isoc.1.32; εὐ. δόρυ *steer* the bark *straight*, E.*Cyc.*15; εὐ. πλάτην Id.*Hec.*39; ὁ εὐθύνων *the helmsman*, *Ep.Jac.*3.4; εὐ. ἀγέλας *lead* or *drive* them, X.*Cyr.*1.1.2; εὐ. χερσί *manage, guide* him, S.*Aj.*542; εὐ. πόδα E.*Heracl.*728, etc. 2. metaph., *direct, govern*, Κύρου δὲ παῖς... ηὔθυνε στρατόν A.*Pers.*773; πᾶσαν εὐθύνων πόλιν S.*Ant.*178, cf. 1164, E.*Hec.*9, Pl.*Min.*320d. 3. *make straight, straighten*, opp. κάμπτειν, πτέρυγας Arist.*IA*709b10:— Pass., Id.*Mete.*385b32. II. *make* or *put straight*, εὐ. δίκας σκολιάς *make* crooked judgements *straight*, Sol.4.37; εὐ. λαοῖς δίκας Pi.*P.*4. 153; εὐ. οὖρον *send a straight* fair wind, Id.*O.*13.28; εὐ. ὄλβον Id.*P.* 1.46; ὥσπερ ξύλον διαστρεφόμενον..εὐ. ἀπειλαῖς καὶ πληγαῖς Pl.*Prt.* 325d, cf. 326e. III. *examine the conduct of* an official, Id.*Plt.* 299a; εὐ. τὰς ἀρχάς Arist.*Pol.*1271a6, 1274a17, al.:—Pass., c. gen., -όμενος τῆς ἐφορείας Id.*Rh.*1419a31. 2. c. gen. criminis, *call to account for*.., τινα κλοπῆς Plu.*Cic.*9:—Pass., τῶν ἀδικημάτων ηὐθύνθη

Th.1.95; οἱ -όμενοι *the culprits*, Mitteis *Chr.*31 iii 10 (ii B.C.), cf. *Notiz. Arch.*4.21 (Cyrene, i B.C.): c. dat., εὐ. φόνῳ *PTeb.*14.4 (ii B.C.); *to be mulcted, punished,* ἐπί τινι D.C.*Fr.*90, al.: abs., *IG*1^{2}.41.6; ἑκατὸν δραχμῇσι ib.4.15, al. 3. generally, *refute* or *censure*, τοὺς λόγους τινός Phld.*Piet.*67; τὴν Φιλίστου διάλεκτον Plu.*Nic.*1:—Pass., *to be refuted*, δι' αὐτῶν τῶν φαινομένων Phld.*Sign.*30, cf. Plot.3.6.13; but also, *to be critically examined*, Id.4.6.13. 4. *examine by torture*, Procop.*Goth.*3.32 (Pass.). IV. intr., *serve as* εὔθυνος, Pl.*Lg.*946d.

εὐθῡ-ονειρία, ἡ, *vivid dream*, Arist.*Div.Somn.*463^{a}25, *Gp.*2.35.4 (pl.). **-όνειρος**, ον, *dreaming vividly*, Arist.*Div.Somn.*463^{b}16, cf. Plu.2.437f. **-ορϝία**, v. εὐθυωρία. **-ορον·** τόπος ἐπ' εὐθείας ἔχων τὸν ὅρον, *EM*391.48, Phot. **-πλοέω**, *sail straight*, ἐπί τι Str.11.2.3, cf. Arr.*Cyn.*25.8: metaph., Cerc.5.16. **-πλοια**, ἡ, *straight voyage*, in dat. -πλοίᾳ Str.3.3.1, prob. l. in Id.6.3.7. **-πλοκία**, ἡ, (πλοκή) *straight weaving, evenness of texture*, Pl.*Plt.*283a, 311b. **-πλοος**, ον, contr. **-πλους**, ουν, *sailing straight*, Str.6.3.7 (dub. l.). **-πνοος**, ον, contr. **-πνους**, ουν, *straight-blowing*, Pi.*N.*7.29; ἄνεμοι Arist.*Mu.*394^{b}35. II. *breathing freely*, Hp.*Epid.*6.2.19. **-πομπός**, όν, *guiding straight*, αἰών Pi.*N.*2.7.

εὐθυπορ-έω, *go straight forward*, πότμος εὐθυπορῶν (metaph. from a ship) *unswerving* destiny, A.*Ag.*1005 (lyr.); of motion, Arist.*IA* 710^{a}7; opp. ἀνακάμπτειν, of ἀποδείξεις, Id.*deAn.*407^{a}29: c. acc. cogn., εὐ. ὁδόν, δρόμον, *hold a straight* course, Pi.*O.*7.91, *I.*5(4).60. II. *have a straight grain*, of trees, Thphr.*CP*1.8.4. **-ία**, ἡ, *straightness of course*, Pl.*Lg.*747a, Arist.*Aud.*802^{a}30. II. *straightness of grain* in wood, Thphr.*HP*5.6.2. **-ικός**, ή, όν, *moving in a straight line*: -κά, τά, Phlp. *in Mete.*12.33. **-ος**, ον, *going straight*, of colour, Democr.ap.Thphr.*Sens.*73; τάσις, opp. μεταληπτική, Gal.10.443: metaph., *straightforward*, ἦθος Pl.*Lg.*775d. II. *with a straight passage*, κέρας Arist.*Aud.*802^{b}11; *with straight grain*, of wood, Thphr.*CP*5.17.3 (Sup.).

εὐθύρῑνος, ον, = εὐθύρριν, *PLips.*2.6 (i A.D.), 5 ii 7 (iii A.D.), in gen. sg. -ρίνου.

εὐθυρρημ-ονέω, *speak in a straightforward manner*, '*call a spade a spade*', ὁ σοφὸς -ήσει Zeno *Stoic.*1.22; *utter off-hand*, Plu.*Demetr.*14. **-οσύνη**, ἡ, *plainness of speech*, Phld.*Rh.*2.281 S., M.Ant.11.6, S.E.*M.*2.22. **-ων**, ον, gen. ονος, (ῥῆμα) *plain-spoken*, Cic.*Fam.*12.16.3 (Comp.), Poll.5.119. Adv. -μόνως Id.4.24. II. gloss on εὐθύγλωσσος, Sch.Pi.*P.*2.157.

εὐθύ-ρριζος, ον, *straight-rooted*, Thphr.*HP*1.7.2. **-ρρῑν** (or **εὐθύριν**), ῖνος, ὁ, ἡ, *straight-nosed*, *PAmh.*2.51.23 (i B.C.), *BGU*993 ii 11 (ii B.C.), al.; nom. -ρρις (v.l. -ριν) Poll.2.73.

εὔθυρσος, ον, *with beautiful shaft*, νάρθηξ E.*Ba.*1158 (lyr.).

εὐθύς, εῖα, ύ, Ion. and Ep. **ἰθύς** (q.v.: so always in Hom. and Hdt.), *straight, direct*, whether vertically or horizontally, opp. σκολιός, καμπύλος, Pl.*Tht.*194b, *R.*602c, etc.; κατὰ τὸ εὐθὺ ἑστάναι stands still with reference to *the vertical*, of a spinning top, ib.436e; εὐ. πλόος, ὁδοί, Pi.*O.*6.103, *N.*1.25, etc.; εὐθυτέρα ὁδὸς X.*Cyr.*1.3.4; ὁδοὺς εὐθείας ἔτεμε Th.2.100; ῥόμβος ἀκόντων Pi.*O.*13.93; εὐθεῖα (sc. ὁδῷ) *by the straight road*, Pl.*Lg.*716a; εὐθεῖαν ἕρπε A.*Fr.*195; τὴν εὐ. E.*Med.*384; ἐπ' εὐθείας D.S.19.38, Ascl.*Tact.*2.6, Plot.2.1.8; so also εἰς τὸ εὐ. βλέπειν X.*Eq.*7.17, etc.; πλήρης τοῦ εὐθέος tired *of going straight forward*, ib.14; ἡ ἐς τὸ εὐ. τῆς ῥητορικῆς ὁδὸς the *direct* road to . ., Luc.*Rh.Pr.*10; κατ' εὐθὺ on *level ground*, Lxx 3*Ki.*21.23; but ἡ κατ' εὐ. τάσις *in the direct line*, Apollon.Cit.2; *on the same side*, Gal.8.62; also, εἰς τὸ ἐντός, Plot.6.7.14. 2. in moral sense, *straightforward, frank*, of persons, εὐθὺν χρὴ τὸν ἑταῖρον ἔμμεν καὶ μὴ σκολιὰ φρονεῖν *Scol.*16; κοινᾶνι παρ' εὐθυτάτῳ Pi.*P.*3.28; ῥῆτραι Tyrt.4.6; τόλμα Pi.*O.*13.12; δίκα Id.*N.*10.12; κρῖνε δ' εὐθεῖαν δίκην A.*Eu.*433, cf. Ἀρχ.Ἐφ.1911.134 (Gonni); ὁ εὐθὺς λόγος E.*Hipp.*492; τὸ εὐ. τε καὶ τὸ ἐλεύθερον Pl.*Tht.*173a; ἀπὸ τοῦ εὐθέος λέγειν to speak *straight out*, Th.3.43; ἐκ τοῦ εὐ. ὑπουργεῖν *outright, openly, without reserve*, Id.1.34; ἐκ τοῦ εὐ., opp. δι' αἰνιγμάτων, Paus.8.8.3: in fem., τὴν εὐθεῖάν τινι συνειπεῖν Plu.*Cic.*7; ἁπλῶς καὶ δι' εὐθείας Id.2.408e; ἀπ' εὐθείας ib.57a, *Fab.*3; κατ' εὐθεῖαν *by direct reasoning*, Dam.*Pr.*432; μηδὲν ἐξ εὐθείας παρέχει (an amulet) does no good *directly*, Sor.2.42. 3. εὐθεῖα, ἡ, as Subst., a. (sc. γραμμή) *straight line*, Arist.*APr.*49^{b}35, al., Euc. 1 *Def.*7, al.; ἐπ' εὐθείας εἶναι lie in a *straight line*, Archim.*Con.Sph.*7, al.; ἐπὶ τὴν αὐτὴν εὐ., ἐπὶ τῆς αὐτῆς εὐ. ἐκτείνειν, in the same *line*, Plb.3.113.2,3; ἐπὶ μίαν εὐ. ib.8: Comp., εὐθυτέρα ἡ γραμμὴ γίνεται Arist.*Mech.*855^{a}24. b. (sc. πτῶσις) *nominative case*, D.T.636.5, A.D.*Pron.*6.11, etc.; κατ' εὐθὺ in *the nominative*, Arist.*SE*182^{a}3.

B. as Adv., **εὐθύς** and **εὐθύ**, the former prop. of Time, the latter of Place, Phryn.119, etc. I. **εὐθύ**, of Place, *straight*, usu. of motion or direction, εὐθὺ Πύλονδε *straight to* . ., *h.Merc.*342; εὐθὺ πρὸς τὰ νυμφικὰ λέχη S.*OT*1242; εὐ. [τὴν ἐπὶ] Βαβυλῶνος *straight towards* . ., X.*Cyr.*5.2.37: and so c. gen., εὐ. τῶν κυρηβίων, εὐθὺ Πελλήνης, Ar.*Eq.*254, *Av.*1421; εὐ. τοῦ Διός Id.*Pax*68; εὐ. τοὐρόφου Eup.47; εὐ. τῆς σωτηρίας Ar.*Pax*301, cf. Th.8.88, etc.; ἀποθανούμενος ἤει εὐ. τοῦ δαιμονίου *in opposition to* . ., Pl.*Thg.*129a (s.v.l.); cf. ἰθύς. b. νῆσον οἰκεῖ εὐθὺ Ἴστρου *opposite* . ., Max.Tyr.15.7. 2. = ἁπλῶς, *simply*, καλεῖν Thphr.*HP*3.8.2, cf. 9.13.2. 3. rarely of Time, Philoch.144, Arist.*Rh.*1414^{b}25, *UPZ*77.27 (ii B.C.), *PGrenf.*1.1.24 (ii B.C.), Aristeas 24, Luc.*Nav.*22. II. **εὐθύς**, 1. of Time, *straightway, forthwith*, Pi.*O.*8.41; ὁ δ' εὐ. ὡς ἤκουσε A.*Pers.*361; ὁ δ' εὐ. ἐξῴμωξεν S.*Aj.*317; τὸ μὲν εὐ. τὸ δὲ καὶ διανοούμενον Th.1.1, cf. 5.3, 7.77; joined with other adverbial words, τάχα δ' εὐ. ἰών Pi.*P.*4.83; εὐ. κατὰ τάχος Th.6.101; εὐ. παραχρῆμα (v. sub παραχρῆμα); εὐ. ἀπ' ἀρχῆς Ar.*Pax*84 (anap.); εὐ. ἐξ ἀρχῆς X.*Cyr.*7.2.16; ἐξ ἀρχῆς εὐ. Arist.*Pol.*1287^{b}10; εὐ. κατ' ἀρχάς Pl.*Ti.*24b; ἀφ' ἑσπέρας εὐ. ἤδη Luc.*Gall.*1; εὐ. ἐκ νέου, ἐκ παιδός, *even* from one's youth, Pl.*R.*485d, 519a; εὐ. ἐκ παιδίου X.*Cyr.*1.6.20: with a part., εὐ. νέοι ὄντες Th.2.39; εὐ. ἥκων X.*An.*4.7.2; εὐ. ἀπεκτονώς D.23.127; τοῦ θέρους εὐ. ἀρχομένου *just* at the beginning of summer, Th.2.47; ἀρξάμενος εὐ. καθισταμένου [τοῦ πολέμου] from the *very* beginning of the war, Id.1.1; εὐ. ἀποβεβηκότι *immediately* on disembarking, Id.4.43; εὐ. γενομένοις at *the moment of* birth, Pl.*Tht.*186b: metaph., *at once, naturally*, ὑπάρχει εὐθὺς γένη ἔχον τὸ ὂν Being falls *at once* into genera, Arist.*Metaph.*1004^{a}5, cf. *Po.*1452^{a}14: with Subst., ἡ τῶν Ἰταλιωτῶν εὐθὺς φυγή Hdn.8.1.5. 2. less freq. in a local relation, ὑπὲρ τῆς πόλεως εὐ. *just* above the city, Th.6.96; παρ' αὐτὴν εὐ. ὁ ἔσπλους ἐστίν *directly* past it (the mole), Id.8.90; ἐγγύτατα τούτου εὐ. ἐχομένη *immediately* adjoining this, ibid., cf. Theoc.25.23; εὐ. ἐπὶ τὴν γέφυραν Foed.ap.Th.4.118, cf. X.*Cyr.*7.2.1,2, 2.4.24, *Ages.*1.29; τὴν εὐ. Ἄργους κἀπιδαυρίας ὁδόν the road *leading straight to* Argos, E.*Hipp.*1197 (condemned by Phot.); εὐ. Λυκείου Pherecr.110, cf. Arist.*HA*498^{a}32, etc. 3. of Manner, *directly, simply*, v.l. in Pl.*Men.*100a. 4. like αὐτίκα II: *for instance, to take the first example that occurs*, ὥσπερ ζῷον εὐθύς Arist.*Pol.*1277^{a}6, cf. *Cael.*284^{b}10, etc.; οἷον εὐθύς Cleom.1.1, D.Chr.11.145.

C. regul. Adv. **εὐθέως**, used just as εὐθύς, S.*Aj.*31, *OC*994, E.*Fr.*31, Pl.*Phd.*63a, etc.; αἰσθόμενος εὐθέως *as soon as* he perceived, Lys.3.11; ἐπεὶ εὐθέως ᾔσθοντο X.*HG*3.2.4; εὐθέως παραχρῆμα Antipho 1.20, D.52.6. 2. = εὐθύς B. II. 4, οἷον εὐθέως as *for example*, Plb.6.52.1, 12.5.6 (dub. sens. in Hp.*Art.*55); so εὐ. alone, Ph.2.589. (εὐθέως is the commoner form in later Greek, *PCair.Zen.*34.17 (iii B.C.), etc.)

εὐθύσᾰνος [ῠ], ον, *well-fringed*, ζώνη *AP*6.202 (Leon.).

εὐθῡσία, ἡ, *auspicious sacrifice*, Phld.*Oec.*p.33 J. (pl.).

εὐθυ-σκόλιος, ον, *slightly curved*, Orib.45.18.33. **-σκοπέω**, *look straight at*, Plu.2.737a. **-σκόπος**, ον, *seeing straight*, Hsch. s.v. οὐκ εὐθυσκόπου.

εὐθυσμός, ὁ, (εὐθύνω) *straightness*, trans. of Hebr. *Shur*, Ph.1.576.

εὐθύ-στομος, ον, *talking plainly*, *EM*191.33, Sch.Luc.*JTr.*27; f.l. for εὔστομος, Poll.5.60. **-τενής**, ές, (τείνω) *straight*, ὁδός Ph.1.456, cf. Dion.Byz.3; πλοῦς Iamb.*VP*3.16; εὐ. τὴν τρίχα Ael.*NA*4.34: Medic., τομή Antyll.ap.Orib.44.8.1. Adv. -νῶς ib.9, Ph.1.338, Gal.18(1).797.

εὐθύτης [ῠ], ητος, ἡ, (εὐθύς) *straightness*, opp. καμπυλότης, Arist.*Cat.*10^{a}12; opp. περιφέρεια, Id.*Mete.*385^{b}30; εὐ. τριχῶν, opp. οὐλότης, Id.*GA*782^{a}3; ἡ εὐ. τῆς τάσεως the *direction* . ., Gal.6.193. II. *righteousness*, Lxx *Jo.*24.14, al.

εὐθῡ-τοκία, ἡ, *simple interest*, *IG*12(5).860.25 (Tenos), 5(1).1146.37 (Gythium). **-τομέω**, *make a straight incision*, Antyll.ap.Orib.44.8.23:—hence **-τομία**, ἡ, ib.4, al. **-τομος**, ον, *cut straight, straight*, ὁδός Pi.*P.*5.90. **-τονος**, ον, opp. παλίντονος, term applied to the lighter torsion-engines, τὰ εὐ. ὄργανα Hero *Bel.*74.5, 104.4; καταπάλται Ath.Mech.14.6. **-τράχηλος** [ᾰ], ον, *with a straight neck*, of the bladder, Sor.1.18. **-τρεχής**, ές, *running in a straight line*, *IG*2^{2}.463.73. **-τρητος**, ον, *bored straight through*, [ὀστᾶ] Gal.*UP*8.7, cf. Ruf.ap.Orib.8.24.62, Antyll.ib.8.13.1. **-τρῐχος**, ον, = εὐθύθριξ, Arist.*HA*629^{b}35, Polem.*Phgn.*57. **-τρῡπος**, ον, = εὐθύτρητος, Democr.ap.Thphr.*Sens.*73. **-φερής**, ές, *running in a straight line*, Pl.*Lg.*815b. **-φλοιος**, ον, *straight-barked*, name of a kind of *oak*, Thphr.*HP*3.8.2. **-φορέομαι**, Pass., *to move in a straight line*, Procl. *in Prm.*p.906 S. **-φορία**, ἡ, *motion in a straight line*, Arist.*Ph.*227^{b}18. **-φρων**, ον, gen. ονος, (φρήν) *whole-hearted, sincere*, A.*Eu.*1040, f.l. ib.1034 (both lyr.). **-φυής**, ές, *straight-grown*, opp. παρεστραμμένος, cj. Scalig. in Thphr.*HP*4.2.6. **-χαλκος**, ον, *payable on demand in cash* (copper), *POxy.*1482.15 (ii A.D.). **-ώνυξ**, υχος, ὁ, ἡ, or **-ώνῠχος**, ον, *with straight nails* or *talons*, Arist.*HA*517^{a}33, 600^{a}19, 633^{b}2. **-ωρέω**, *go straight forward*, v.l. for εὐθυπορέω, Id.*Pr.*905^{b}6. **-ωρία**, ἡ, *straight course* or *direction*, Pl.*R.*436e, *Ti.*45c, Arist.*deAn.*406^{b}31; κατ' εὐθυωρίαν *longitudinally*, Id.*PA*654^{a}17; also ἀντικρούσαι κατ' εὐ. to oppose *directly*, Id.*Rh.*1379^{a}11; κατ' εὐ. νοῆσθαι, opp. κατ' ἀναλογίαν, Ti.Locr.94b; ἄπειρα εἰς εὐ. *in an infinite series*, Arist.*Metaph.*994^{a}2; εὐθυωρίᾳ ἐπὶ θάλασσαν *SIG*685.65 (Itanos, ii B.C.), cf. ib.421.48 (Thermon, iii B.C.); ἂν εὐθυωρείαν (sic) *Tab.Heracl.*1.65; also Arc. εὐθυορϝίαν *BCH*39.55 (Orchom. Arc., iv B.C.); cf. ἰθυωρίη. **-ωρος**, ον, *in a straight direction*: mostly in neut. εὐθύωρον as Adv., = εὐθύς, εὐ. ἄγειν X.*An.*2.2.16, Ael.*NA*11.16; ὁρᾶν ib.7.5: as Adj., εὐθύωρον τὴν ἀναχώρησιν ἐποιήσαντο Anon.ap.*EM*391.42, cf. Procop.*Aed.*2.2.

εὐθώρηξ, ηκος, ὁ, ἡ, *well-mailed*, *AP*9.389 (Trajan), Nonn.*D.*15.156; μύες Marcell.Sid.30.

εὔια· δέδια, Hsch.

εὐιάζω, = εὐάζω, S.*Ichn.*221, E.*Cyc.*495 (lyr.).

εὐιακός, ή, όν, *Bacchic*, θίασοι *APl.*4.289:—fem. **εὐιάς**, άδος, *AP*9.603 (Antip.); οἴνη *IG*3.779.

εὐίᾱτος, Ion. -ητος, ον, (ἰάομαι) *easy to heal* or *remedy*, Arist.*EN*1121^{a}20, Thphr.*HP*5.4.5, Porph.*Abst.*1.56, freq. in Comp., Hp.*Art.*14, X.*Eq.*4.2, etc.

εὔιδε (i.e. ἔϝιδε), Aeol., = εἶδε, v. *εἴδω A.

εὐίδρως, ωτος, ὁ, ἡ, *easily perspiring*, Thphr.*Sud.*20: but neut. **εὔιδρον**, ib.19:—also **εὐίδρωτος**, ον, Gal.6.222: pl. εὐίδρωτα Arist.*Pr.*867^{b}35.

εὐιερία, ἡ, *sanctity, sacredness*, *Sammelb.*1007 (i A.D.).

εὐίερος [ῐ], ον, *fit for sacrifice*, πέλανοι *Pae.Oxy.*675.14; θύματα *IG*

5(1).1390.70 (Andania, i B.C.); θυηπολίαι *AP*6.231 (Phil.): generally, *holy*, θυμέλαι *Ath.Mitt.*17.272 (iii A.D.); βοαί Orac. in *Milet.*7.64 (ii/iii A.D.).

εὐϊκέτευτος, ον, *open to entreaty*, gloss on εὐάντητος, *EM*388.40.

εὐιλασία· εὐπειστία, prob. in Hsch., cf. *Gloss.*

εὐϊλάσιμος, ον, = sq., prob. l. in *Sammelb.*4116.5.

εὐΐλᾰτ-ος [ῑ], ον, (ἵλημι) *very merciful*, of deities, *PCair.Zen.*34.19 (iii B.C.), *IG*3.73, *GDI*3543 (Cnidus), etc.; εὐ. ἐγένου αὐτοῖς Lxx *Ps.*98(99).8; also τυχεῖν εὐιλάτου τοῦ βασιλέος *PPetr.*2 p.45 (iii B.C.); later written εὐειλ- *GDI*3536 (Cnidus), *UPZ*109.6 (i B.C.):—hence **-εύω**, *to be merciful*, Lxx *De.*29.20(19), al.

εὔϊνος, ον, (ἴς) *with stout fibres*, ξύλον Thphr.*HP*3.10.1, *Ign.*72.

Εὔιος (**Εὐΐος** *EM*391.15, cf. Lat. *Euhius*), ὁ, name of Bacchus, from the cry εὐαΐ, εὐοῖ, in lyr. passages, S.*OT*211, E.*Ba.*157, Ecphantid.3, etc.; Εὔιος, = Βάκχος, E.*Ba.*566,579. **II.** εὔιος, ον, as Adj., *Bacchic*, πῦρ S.*Ant.*964; τελεταί E.*Ba.*238; ἀγάλματα Id.*Tro.*451 (troch.).

εὔϊππος, Ep. **ἐΰιππ-**, ον, of persons, *delighting in horses*, *h.Ap.*210, Hes.*Cat.Oxy.*1358.21, Pi.*O.*3.39: Sup., X.*HG*4.2.5, etc. **2.** of places, *famed for horses*, Pi.*P.*4.2, S.*OC*668 (lyr.).

εὔϊστος πόθος, ὁ, desire *of knowledge*, Epigr.ap.Plu.2.14c (leg. εὐκταῖον).

εὐίσχιος, ον, *with beautiful hips*, γυνή *Inscr.Prien.*317, cf. *AP*5.115 (Marc. Arg.); of a horse, *with fine quarters*, *Hippiatr.*115; βόες Hsch. s. v. κάμινοι.

εὔιχθυς, υ, *abounding in fish*, θάλασσα D.S.11.57, cf. Ath.8.360e, Aristid.*Or.*44(17).16, Philostr.*VA*3.55.

εὐϊώτης, ου, ὁ, (εὔιος) *Bacchic*, χοροί *Lyr.Alex.Adesp.*22:—fem. **εὐϊῶτις**, ιδος, οἴνη Moschio Trag.6.11.

εὐκᾱής, ές, (καίω) *easily burnt*, Dsc.4.150, Sch.A.R.1.434 (Sup.).

εὐκαθ-αίρετος, ον, *easy to conquer*, Th.7.18 (Comp.); *easily exhausted*, δυνάμεις Herod.Med.ap.Orib.5.30.11; *unstable*, τύχη, πρᾶγμα, Vett.Val.175.30, 212.21. **-εδρος**, ον, gloss on εὔσσελμος, Hsch., Sch.Od.2.390, etc.; on ἐΰζυγος, Sch.A.R.1.4. **-εκτος**, ον, *easy to keep under* or *restrain*, X.*Cyr.*7.5.69 (Sup.). **-οσίωτος**, ον, *consecrated*, *IG*14.455 (Catana, v A.D.).

εὐκαιρ-έω (late, acc. to Phryn.103), *have opportunity, leisure* or *time*, *PSI*4.342.2 (iii B.C.), Plb.20.9.4, 1*Ep.Cor.*16.12, etc.: c. inf., οὐδὲ φαγεῖν ηὐκαίρουν *Ev.Marc.*6.31, cf. Plu.2.223d, Luc.*Am.*33; τοῦ διαβῆναι *PEleph.*29.7 (iii B.C.). **II.** τινι or εἴς τι, *devote one's leisure* to a thing, εὐ. τοῖς ἀθανάτοις ἑαυτοῦ Chio *Ep.*16.6; εὐ. εἰς οὐδὲν ἕτερον ἤ.. *Act.Ap.*17.21. **III.** *enjoy good times, prosper*, Plb.4.60.10; τοῖς βίοις Id.32.5.12: in this sense also εὐκαιρέομαι, Posidon.59J. **2.** *to be timely*, Phld.*Rh.*2.64S., Epicur.(?)*Oxy.*215 ii 2. **-ή**, ἡ, *favourable opportunity*, dub. in *POxy.*123.3 (iii/iv A.D.). **-ημα**, ατος, τό, *seasonable, opportune act*, *Stoic.*3.136 (pl.). **-ία**, Ion. **-ίη**, ἡ, *good season, opportunity*, τὴν εὐ. διαφυλάττειν Isoc.12.34; ἀπολαύειν τῆς εὐ. Phld.*D.*3 *Fr.*89; εὐκαιρίαν ζητεῖν ἵνα.. *Ev.Matt.*26.16; εὐ. τοῦ ἐλθεῖν *PMich.* in *Class.Phil.*22.250 (ii A.D.); *leisure*, Hp.*Ep.*17, 23; κατὰ πολλὴν εὐ. καὶ σχολήν D.H.*Comp.*23—a usage condemned by Phot. and Suid. s. v. σχολή. **II.** *appropriateness*, opp. ἀκαιρία, Pl.*Phdr.*272a; μεταφορᾶς, στίχων, Plu.2.16b, 736f. **2.** *convenient situation*, τῶν πόλεων Plb.16.29.3, cf. 4.44.11, Ph.1.4. **3.** *opportune supply*, ὑδάτων, of rainfall or irrigation, Thphr.*CP*3.23.4 (pl.), D.S.1.52. **III.** *wealth, prosperity*, αἱ τῶν βίων εὐ. Plb.1.59.7, cf. 13.9.2 (cj.), etc.; εὐ. οὐκ ἔχει he has no *property*, *BGU*665 ii 4 (i A.D.). **-ος**, ον, *well-timed, seasonable*, λόγος Philem.113; θάνατος *Com.Adesp.*116; ὕδατα (rainfall) Thphr.*HP*8.7.6; *nihil -ότερον epistula tua*, Cic.*Att.*4.7.1: c. inf., χὤ τι σοι λέγειν εὔκαιρόν ἐστι S.*OC*32, cf. Epicur.*Nat.*28.4; -ότερον ἔσται διελθεῖν J.*AJ*12.9.7; τὸ εὔκαιρον, = εὐκαιρία, D.H.*Din.*7; τὸ μέτριον καὶ τὸ εὔ. ἐν ἡδοναῖς Aristo *Stoic.*1.86; εὔκαιρον ἀείσας *in season*, Pl.*Epigr.*5.5. **II.** of places, *convenient, well situated*, τόποι *PPetr.*2 p.28 (iii B.C., Sup.), cf. Plb.4.38.1 (Sup.), D.S.1.63, etc. **III.** *rich, wealthy*, dub. l. in St.Byz. s. v. Χαττηνία. **IV.** Adv. -ρως *seasonably, opportunely*, Hp.*Medic.*3, Nico 1, *PCair.Zen.*38.28 (iii B.C.), al., etc.; εὐ. χρῆσθαί τινι Isoc.5.143; εὐ. ἔχειν πρός τι Id.11.12, Arist.*HA*582ᵃ28; *favourably, propitiously*, *PCair.Zen.*46 (iii B.C.), *POxy.*2086ʳ.6 (ii A.D., εὐκερως Pap.): Comp. -ότερον Pl.*Phd.*78a: Sup. -ότατα Plb.5.63.13. **2.** οὐκ -ρως ἔχειν to have no *leisure*, Id.5.26.10.

εὐκάκωτος [ᾰ], ον, *easily affected* by disease, Aët.12.19; to be read for εὐπαθής in Gal.19.208.

εὐκαλλώπιστος, ον, *beautifully adorned*, Hsch. s. v. κοσμιωτάτη, Phot. s. v. κεκομψευμένος.

εὔκᾱλος, εὐκᾱλία, Dor. for εὔκηλ-.

εὐκάμᾰτος [κᾰ], ον, *of easy labour, easy*, κάματος E.*Ba.*66 (lyr.). **2.** εὐ. στέφανοι crowns *won by noble toils*, *APl.*4.335. **3.** *easily enduring fatigue*, Philostr.*Gym.*42. **4.** *laborious*, ἄγρη Nonn.*D.*5.483; *caused by toil*, ἱδρῶτες Id.25.28.

εὐκᾱμία· ἡσυχία, ἤτοι εὐφημία (Dor.), *EM*392.5 (i.e. εὐκᾱλία, = ἡσυχία, and εὐκᾱμία (fr. κημός), = εὐφιμία, cf. Hsch. s. v. εὐκαλεία, εὐκληρία).

εὐκάμπ-εια, ἡ, *flexibility*, of the body, Antyll.ap.Orib.6.35.1. **-ής**, ές, (κάμπτω) *well-bent* or *curved*, δρέπανον Od.18.368; κληῗδ' εὐκαμπέα 21.6; χαλάσασ' εὐκαμπέα τόξα *h.Hom.*27.12; ἄροτρον, ἅρπη, Max.458, A.R.3.1388; εὐκαμπὴς τὰ κέρατα Luc.*DMar.*15.2; τὸ εὐ. τῶν μελῶν Id.*Im.*14. **II.** *flexible*, φλοιός Thphr.*HP*3.10.4; κλάδοι Str.15.1.20; κατασκευάζειν τὸ κέρας εὐ. Plu.*Sull.*17; of timber, Orib.9.19.2 (Comp.); πῦον *slippery*, Aret.*SD*1.10. (εὐκαμπὲς ἄγκιστρον *AP*6.4 (Leon.) is corrupt: εὐκἄπές (κάπτω) *easily swallowed*, Salm.) **-ος**, ον, = sq., Hp.*Art.*60 (v.l. -πτοι). **-τος**, ον, *flexible*, Sapph.*Supp.*5.13, Arist.*PA*692ᵃ2.

εὐκαμψία, ἡ, *flexibility*, of the voice, Arist.*GA*786ᵇ10.

εὐκᾰπής, v. εὐκαμπής.

εὐκάρδιος, ον, (καρδία) *stout-hearted*, S.*Aj.*364 (lyr.), *Ph.*535, Chrysipp.*Stoic.*2.247, etc.; of a horse, *spirited*, X.*Eq.*6.14. Adv. -ίως *with stout heart*, E.*Hec.*549, D.H.5.8, J.*AJ*12.9.4, *BJ*7.8.7. **II.** *good for the stomach*, Diocl.*Fr.*120 (Comp.), Ruf.ap.Orib.5.11.3 (Sup.), Xenocr.8. **2.** *good for the heart, restorative, cordial*, Hp.*Aff.*41, 54, Alex.Trall.*Febr.*4.

εὐκάρπ-εια, ἡ, = εὐκαρπία, in dat. -είᾳ (-ίᾳ codd.), E.*Tr.*217 (lyr.); cf. παγκάρπεια. **-έω**, *bear good fruit* or *crops*, Hp.*Ep.*10, Thphr.*CP*1.20.5, *HP*2.7.7, Str.5.2.7, *BGU*1040.5 (ii A.D.). **-ησις**, εως, ἡ, f.l. for ἐκκάρπησις, Gal.6.665. **-ία**, ἡ, *fruitfulness*, *IG*1².76.45, Arist.*Fr.*252, Thphr.*CP*2.1.2; cf. εὐκάρπεια. **-ος**, ον, *fruitful*, of women, *h.Hom.*30.5; of trees, corn, land, Pi.*P.*1.30, *N.*1.14, *Pae.*2.26, etc.; of sheep, Palaeph.18; φυτά, ζῷα, Ocell.4.9; [χώρη] -οτάτη Hp.*Aër.*12; εὔ. θέρος S.*Aj.*671: metaph., -οτάτη ἀρετή Ph.1.647. **II.** Act., *fruitful, fertilizing*, ἀήρ Thphr.*CP*2.3.3; epith. of Aphrodite, S.*Fr.*847; of Dionysus, *AP*6.31; of Demeter, ib.7.394 (Phil.).

εὐκάρφωτος, ον, gloss on εὐγόμφωτος, Sch.Opp.*H.*1.58.

εὐκατά-βλητος, ον, *easily overthrown*, Eust.1055.51. **-γέλαστος**, ον, *exposed to ridicule*, Alex.Aphr.*Pr.*1.80. **-γνωστος**, ον, *blameworthy*, Mitteis *Chr.*31 viii 11 (ii B.C.), *EM*400.6.

εὐκατ-άγωγος [ᾰγ], ον, *easy to wind up*, of a torsion-engine (cf. καταγωγίς), Ph.*Bel.*53.33. **2.** *good for landing in*, λιμήν Eust. ad D.P.195. **-αγώνιστος**, ον, *easily conquered*, Plb.9.4.8, Luc.*Tyr.*22.

εὐκατά-καυστος, ον, *easily burnt*, gloss on εὐκατάπρηστος, Suid., Phot. **-κλαστος**, ον, gloss on εὐκέατος, Sch.Od.5.60. **-κόμιστος**, ον, *easy to be transported*, ὕλη Str.12.3.12. **-κράτητος** [κρᾰ], ον, *easy to hold* or *defend*, Plb.4.56.9.

εὐκάτακτος, ον, (ἄγνυμι) *easily broken, fragile*, τὸ εὐ. Ph.2.309, Artem.1.66 (-έακτον codd.).

εὐκατά-ληκτος, ον, *with a good termination*, Eust.1613.33. **-ληπτος**, ον, *easy to apprehend* or *recognize*, Erot.*Praef.*, Heliod.ap.Orib.46.28.3, Artem.1.1ᵃ, etc. **II.** Adv. -τως, ἔχειν to be *easily bandaged* by κατάληψις (q. v.), Hp.*Off.*9. **III.** *easy to capture*, of cities, Hsch. s. v. διατειχίζειν.

εὐκατάλλακτος, ον, *easily appeased, placable*, opp. μνησίκακος, Arist.*Rh.*1381ᵇ5, cf. *Vit.Philonid.*p.3C., Lxx 3*Ma.*5.13. Adv. -τως, ἔχειν πρός τινας Sch.S.*Aj.*1345.

εὐκατά-λῠτος, ον, *easy to overthrow*, X.*HG*3.5.15 (Comp.). **-μάθητος** [μᾰ], ον, *easy to understand*, Hp.*Acut.*28, Gal.7.463. **-μάχητος** [μᾰ], ον, *easily conquered*, Sch.Th.6.17. **-μικτος**, *affabilis*, *Gloss.* **-νόητος**, ον, *easy to observe* or *understand*, Plb.18.30.11, Ptol.*Tetr.*30. **-πάλαιστος** [πᾰ], ον, *easy to throw in wrestling*, *EM*400.5. **-παυστος**, ον, *easily pacified*, Gal.1.334, Paul.Aeg.1.66. **-πληκτος**, ον, *easily scared*, Lib.*Arg.D.Prooem.*11. **-ποτος**, ον, *easily swallowed*, Philum.ap.Aët.9.19. **-πρακτος**, ον, *easily accomplished*, Poll.9.161. **-πρᾰΰντος** [πρᾱ], ον, *placable*, *Gloss.* **-πρηστος**, ον, *easily kindled* or *set on fire*, ὕλη Ph.*Fr.*103 H., Suid.

εὐκατᾰρίθμητος, ον, *easily counted*, Gal.7.463.

εὐκατά-σειστος, ον, *easily shaken* or *thrown down*, Eust.969.61. **-σκεπτος**, ον, *convenient for inspection*, Hp.*Fract.*30, Gal.2.700. **-σκεύαστος**, ον, *easily constructed*, Ph.*Bel.*60.51: Comp., ib.61.6. **2.** *well-made*, ἅρμα Sch.E.*Hipp.*1226. **-στᾰτος**, ον, *well-fixed, firmly established*, διάθεσις Alex.Aphr.*Pr.*1.87, cf. Asp. *in EN*106.11; τὰ τοῦ τόνου εὐ. γίνεται A.D.*Adv.*157.16. **-στροφος**, ον, *brought to a good conclusion, well-turned*, of a period: only in Adv. -φως, ἀπηρτίσθαι Demetr.*Eloc.*10. **-σχετος**, ον, *easily held fast*, Hp.*Fract.*22 (Comp.). **-τακτος**, ον, *easy to set in order*, Ptol.*Geog.*1.1. **-τρόχαστος**, ον, *easily overrun* or *attacked*, Str.14.5.6; of writers, *open to attack, incorrect*, Id.1.2.2:—also **-τροχος**, Hsch. **-φερής**, ές, = εὐκατάφορος, Id. s. v. ὑγρός. **-φθορος**, *corruptibilis*, *Gloss.* **-φορία**, ἡ, *propensity, proclivity*, *Stoic.*3.25 (pl.). **-φορος**, ον, *prone towards*, πρός τι Arist.*EN*1109ᵃ15, Plu.2.503c. **-φρόνητος**, ον, *easy to be despised, contemptible*, ὑπό τινος X.*HG*6.4.1, cf. *Cyr.*8.3.1, D.4.18, Men.*Sam.*297, Arist.*Pol.*1312ᵇ24, etc.; *negligible*, πᾶσα ἀλγηδὼν εὐ. Epicur.*Sent.Vat.*4, cf. Phld.*D.*1.25, al.; esp. in Lit. Crit., D.H.*Comp.*3, Longin.3.1, Demetr.*Eloc.*4, etc. Adv. -τως Plu.*Demetr.*16. **-φρόντιστος**, ον, *well-considered*, dub. l. in Ph.1.664. **-ψευστος**, ον, *safe to tell lies about*, Str.1.2.19.

εὐκατ-έργαστος, ον, *easy to work*, χώρα Thphr.*CP*4.7.3 (Comp.); ἔρια Gal.18(2).525; of food, *easy of digestion*, X.*Mem.*4.3.6 (Comp.), Diph.Siph.ap.Ath.2.91e, Dsc.2.90, Sor.1.49. **2.** *easy of accomplishment*, D.*Ep.*1.6 (Comp.), Arist.*Rh.*1363ᵃ31; εὐκατεργαστότερόν ἐστι c. inf., X.*HG*6.1.12. **3.** *easy to subdue* or *conquer*, D.H.3.20; πᾶσιν Plu.*Pyrrh.*19. **-ηγόρητος**, ον, *easy to blame, open to accusation*, Antipho Soph.51, Th.6.77, Plb.4.29.3. **-οίκητος**, ον, *convenient for dwelling in*, gloss on εὔκτιτος, Sch.E.*Or.*1621. **-οπτος**, ον, *easily seen, conspicuous*, χῶρος Aen.Tact.27.2: c. dat., τοῖς ἀθανάτοις εὐ. Satyr.*Vit.Eur.Fr.*39 ii 22. **-όρθωτος**, ον, *easily effected*, πολιορκία D.S.34/5.2.45; χειρουργία Heliod.ap.Orib.44.23.23. Adv. -τως Sch.A.R.1.246.

εὔκαυστος, ον, *easily burning*, Thphr.*Ign.*72 (Comp.), Sch.Ar.*Pax* 1134 (Sup., εὐκαστοτα cod.): **-καυτος**, Phot. s. v. πισσοκωνήτῳ πυρί.

εὐκέαστος, ον, (κεάζω) *easily cleft* or *split*, Eust.1241.48.

εὐκέᾰτος, ον, poet. for foreg., κέδρου τ' εὐκεάτοιο Od.5.60; ἐρινεοῦ εὐ. Theoc.25.248.

εὐκέλᾰδος, ον, *well-sounding, melodious*, λωτός E.*Ba.*160 (lyr.); χοροί Ar.*Nu.*312 (lyr.); μολπά *AP*7.194 (Mnasalc.); κιθάρης γῆρυς *Not.Scav.*1912.459 (Ostia), cf. Epic. in *Arch.Pap.*7.8.

εὔκεντρος, ον, *pointed*, βέλος *AP*9.339 (Arch.).

εὐκένωτος, ον, *easily evacuated*, Gal.10.626.

εὐκεραΐστος [ᾰ], ον, *easily disabled*, δύναμις, to be read in Gal.19.207.

εὐκέρᾰος, ον, *with beautiful horns*, Mosch.2.52; Διόνυσος *AP*9.827 (Ammon.).

εὐκερᾰσία, ἡ, = εὐκρασία, *well-tempered constitution*, *PMag.Leid.W.*17.35.

εὐκέραστος, ον, *well-mixed, well-tempered*, ἀήρ Plu.2.922e; ἦχος D.H.*Comp.*22.

εὐκερδής, ές, *gainful*, Opp.*C.*1.37.

εὐκερμᾰτέω, (κέρμα) *to be rich in money*, Eub.144; condemned by Phryn.339.

εὔκερως, ων, contr. for εὐκέραος, ἄγρα S.*Aj.*64; [τράγος] Herod. 8.17: neut. pl., τὰ εὔκερω Max.Tyr.35.7: acc. pl. εὐκέρωτας *Gp.*18.1.3:—poet. **ἠΰκερος**, Μήνη Doroth.ap.Heph.Astr.3.30.

εὐκέφᾰλος, ον, *with a good head*, Arr.*Cyn.*4.4 (del. Hercher), Poll. 2.43, *Hippiatr.*115.

εὐκηλήτειρα, ἡ, (κηλέω) *she that lulls* or *soothes*, παίδων εὐ. Hes. *Op.*464.

εὐκηλία, Dor. **-κᾱλία**, ἡ, *quiet*, Hsch.

εὔκηλος (A), ον (cf. Hdn.Gr.1.161), Dor. **εὔκᾱλος**, (v. ἕκηλος) *free from care, at one's ease*, εὔκηλος τὰ φράζεαι ἅσσ' ἐθέλησθα Il.1.554; εὗδον δ' εὔκηλοι Od.14.479, cf. S.*El.*241 (lyr.); ἡμεῖς μὲν.. πολέας τελέοντες ἀέθλους.., ὁ δ' εὔκηλος.. Od.3.263; εὔκηλοι πολέμιζον Il. 17.371; εὔκηλος τότε νῆα θοὴν.. ἑλκέμεν ἐς πόντον, i.e. *without fear*, Hes.*Op.*671, cf. *h.Merc.*480; εὔ. τέρπου φρένα Pherecr.152. 2. in Alexandr. and later Ep. of things, νὺξ εὔ. *still, silent*, Theoc.2.166; πτέρυγες εὔ. *steady, even*, A.R.2.935; αὖραι εὔ. Opp.*H.*4.415. Adv. -λως A.R.2.861.

εὔκηλος (B), ον, (καίω) *easily burning*, or (cf. εὐκέατος) *easily split*, Ion Trag.28.

εὐκήπευτος, ον, *easy to cultivate*, Thphr.*HP*7.7.2 (cod. Urb.).

εὐκῑν-ησία, ἡ, *ease of motion, mobility*, Antyll.ap.Stob.4.37.16; μελῶν Herod.Med.ap.Orib.5.27.20; τροχιλιῶν Orib.49.4.34; πυρός Simp.*in Cael.*662.20; βάσεως Artemo 12; *mobility* of troops, Plb.8.26.3, D.S.3.49 (pl.): generally, Dam.*Pr.*287. 2. *mobility* of mind, τῆς ψυχῆς αἱ εὐ. Epicur.*Ep.*1 p.20 U., cf. Phld.*Ir.*p.72 W., Ath.Mech. 32.1. **-ητος**, ον, *easily moved, agile*, Hp.*Aph.*3.17, Pl.*Ti.*58e; -ότατον εἶδος ib.56a; -ότερον ψυχὴ σώματος Arist.*MM*1199ᵇ32; -ότατον τὸ σφαιροειδές Id.*de An.*405ᵃ12, al.; of persons, Id.*HA*491ᵇ13; *mobile*, of troops, Plb.1.40.7. 2. *easily moved, changeable*, Arist.*Cat.*8ᵇ35; τὸ εὐ. *fickleness*, Hdn.7.7.1. Adv. -τως D.S.20.95. 3. *easily moved, inclinable*, πρὸς ἀρετήν, πρὸς ὀργήν, Arist.*Cat.*13ᵃ27 (Comp.), *Rh.*1379ᵃ26; πρὸς ἀδικίαν Zaleuc.ap.Stob.4.2.19. 4. = εὐέλεγκτος, Arist.*Metaph.*991ᵃ16. 5. of language, *flowing, graceful*, Phld. *Po.*994.35.

εὔκισσος, ον, *ivied*, Ἑλικών *AP*7.407 (Diosc.).

εὐκίων [ῐ], ον, gen. ονος, *with beautiful pillars*, αὐλαί E.*Ion* 185 (lyr.), cf. *AP*7.648.7 (Leon.).

εὔκλᾰδος, ον, *with fine boughs*, Quint.*Ps.*47(48).3; gloss on εὐκνημος, Sch.Nic.*Th.*648; on εὔπτορθον, Suid.

εὔκλαστος, ον, (κλάω) *easily broken*, Dsc.4.146, Ath.Mech.18.1; gloss on εὐκέατος, Sch.Od.5.60.

εὐκλεής, ές, acc. sg. *εὐκλεέα, contr. εὐκλεᾶ Pi.*P.*12.24 (-έα codd.), shortened εὐκλέᾰ Id.*N.*6.29, S.*OT*161 (lyr., s.v.l.), disyll., B.5.196; dat. *εὐκλεέϊ, shortened εὐκλέϊ Pi.*N.*2.24: acc. pl. *εὐκλεέας, contr. ἐϋκλεῖας Il.10.281, Od.21.331, shortened εὐκλέᾰς Id.*O.*2.90, Simon. 95.1; later poet. εὐκλειής *Epigr.Gr.*946 (Tralles), ἐϋκλειής A.R.1.73; gen. εὐκλειοῦς *Arch.Pap.*1.220 (ii B.C.): (κλέος):—*of good report, famous*, freq. of persons, Od. l.c., etc.; also of things, οὐ μὰν ἧμιν ἐϋκλεὲς ἀπονέεσθαι Il.17.415; οἰστοί Pi.*O.*2.90, cf. *N.*6.29, etc.; εὐκλέα γλῶσσαν a song *that tells of his glory*, B. l.c.; γόος εὐκλεὴς.. Ἀτρείδαις A.*Ch.*321 (lyr.); βίου πονηροῦ θάνατος -έστερος Id.*Fr.*90; -έστατος βίος E.*Alc.*623, etc.: in Prose, of persons, X. *Vect.*6.1 (Comp.), *HG*7.2.20 (Sup.), Pl.*Mx.*247d; δόξα εὐ. Id.*Smp.* 208d; later πόσῳ εὐκλέεστερον..; c. inf., Muson.*Fr.*19 p.109 H.; εὐ. θάνατος Ph.2.574 (Sup.). Adv. -εῶς, Ep. -ειῶς, ὀλέσθαι ἐϋκλειῶς πρὸ πόληος Il.22.110, cf. *AP*6.332.8 (Hadr.); εὐκλεῶς ἀπολέσθαι, κατθανεῖν, A.*Pers.*328, *Ag.*1304: Sup. εὐκλεέστατα X.*Eq.Mag.*1.1. II. Εὐκλῆς, Orphic title of Hades, *IG*14.641 (Thurii).

εὔκλειᾰ, ἡ, -κλεία metri gr., A.*Th.*685: Ep. **ἐϋκλείη** Il.8.285, Od. 14.402; **εὐκλείη** *IG*14.1663:—*good repute, glory*, τὸν.. ἐϋκλείης ἐπίβησον Il. l.c., cf. Antipho Soph.49, Th.2.44, X.*An.*7.6.33, Pl.*Mx.* 247a, *Ep.*354b, A.R.1.141, etc.; λιπὼν.. εὔκλειαν ἐν δόμοισι A.*Ch.*348 (lyr.); στέφανος εὐκλείας S.*Aj.*465, E.*Supp.*315; ἄγαλμα εὐκλείας S.*Ant.*703. II. Εὔ. personified, B.12.183, *IG*3.277. 2. title of Artemis in Boeotia, etc., Plu.*Arist.*20, Paus.9.17.1,2:—hence **Εὔκλεια**, τά, festival at Delphi, *Schwyzer* 323 *D* 7 (Delph., v/iv B.C.): **Εὔκλειος**, ὁ, epith. of Zeus, B.1.6; (sc. μήν) name of month, e.g. at Corcyra, *IG*9(1).694.51, al.; at Tauromenium, ib.14.430 ii 9.

εὐκλεΐζω, *bring honour to*, Sapph.118.6; *praise*, Tyrt.12.24: Dor. aor. 1 εὐκλέϊξα Pi.*P.*9.91, B.6.16; πατέρα εὐκλείζων (trisyll.) ἐνὶ δήμῳ *IG*1².1085.

ἐϋκλειής, Adv. **ἐϋκλειῶς**, Ep. for εὐκλεής, εὐκλεῶς.

εὔκλεινος, ον, *much-famed*, Arist.*Fr.*640(40).

εὔκλειστος, ον, (κλείω) *well-shut*, Eust.1937.61, Hdn.*Epim.*178.

ἐϋκληΐς [ῑ], ῖδος, ἡ, Ep. for foreg., *well-closed, close-shut*, θύρη.. ἐϋκληῒς, ἀραρυῖα Il.24.318 Aristarch. (ἐϋ κληῖσ' (dat. pl.) Trypho).

εὐκλημᾰτέω, *grow luxuriantly*, of vines, Lxx *Ho.*10.1, Ph.1.681, Phlp.*in GA*43.26.

εὐκληρ-έω, *to be fortunate*, Teles p.60 H.: c. acc. cogn., [κλῆρον] *AP*11.128 (Pollian.). **-ημα**, ατος, τό, *a piece of good fortune*, Antiph.317, Teles p.26 H., D.S.18.13, Str.5.3.7. (εὐκλήρωμα is f.l. in *AB*77.) **-ία**, ἡ, *good luck in drawing lots*, Lib.*Decl.*16.30. 2. generally, *good fortune*, φύσεως D.H.3.14, cf. Ael.*NA*1.54. **-ος**, Dor. **-κλᾱρος**, ον, *fortunate*, Lxx *De.*4.20, *APl.*4.296 (Antip.), Ael. *Fr.*288: euphem. of the dead, *BGU*1209.5 (i B.C.).

εὔκλωνος, ον, *with fine twigs*, πενταπέτηλον Androm.ap.Gal.14.40.

ἐΰκλωστος, ον, *well-spun*, χιτών *h.Ap.*203; λίνον, νῆμα, *AP*6.33 (Maec.), 284.

εὔκμητος· εὐπαγής, Hsch.

ἐϋκνήμῑς, ῖδος, ὁ, ἡ, *well-greaved*, freq. in nom. and acc. pl. ἐϋκνήμιδες, ἐϋκνήμιδας, in Il. always epith. of Ἀχαιοί 1.17, al.; in Od. also of ἑταῖροι, 2.402, 9.550: gen. sg. as fem., -κνήμιδος Ἰτώνης Poet.ap. *EM*519.1. II. *with goodly spokes*, ἀπήνη Nonn.*D.*7.140.

εὔκνημος, ον, *with beautiful ankle*, πούς *AP*5.202 (Asclep.); *with handsome legs*, of a statue, Plin.*HN*34.82; of men, Herm.ap.Stob. 1.49.45; *with strong calves*, *UPZ*121.6 (ii B.C.). II. as Subst., a plant in Nic.*Th.*648, *Al.*372.

εὔκνιστος, ον, (κνίζω) *ticklish, irritable*, Man.5.337.

εὐκοίλιος, ον, *easing the bowels*, Diocl.*Fr.*126, Plu.2.137a, Dsc.2.120, Diph.Siph.ap.Ath.9.371b (Comp.):—hence Subst. **-κοιλιότης**, ητος, ἡ, Paul.Aeg.3.77.

εὐκοινόμητις, ὁ, ἡ, *deliberating for the public weal*, ἀρχά A.*Supp.* 700 (lyr.).

εὐκοινων-ησία, ἡ, *good fellowship*, *Stoic.*3.64, M.Ant.11.20. **-ητος**, ον, *easy to deal with*, εἰς χρήματα Arist.*EN*1121ᵃ4, cf. Them.*Or.*22. 269c.

εὐκολία, ἡ, (εὔκολος) prop. *contentedness with one's food*, Plu.2. 461c; ἡ περὶ τὴν δίαιταν εὐ. Id.*Caes.*17: but, in earlier authors, 2. of the mind, *contentedness, good temper*, Pl.*Alc.*1.122c, etc.; ὀλιγόδεια καὶ εὐ. Ph.2.457. 3. of the body, *ease and lightness in moving*, εὐ. καὶ εὐχέρεια Pl.*Lg.*942d: metaph., εὐ. πρὸς τὴν ποίησιν *facility* in verse-making, Plu.*Cic.*40; εὐ. πρήξιος *AP*7.694 (Adaeus).

εὐκολίδες· [εὖ] τῆς εὐκολίας ποιητικαί, Hsch.

Εὐκολίνη, ἡ, epith. of Hecate, Call.*Fr.*17 P.

εὐκόλλ-ητος, ον, *well soldered*, *POxy.*1449.24 (iii A.D.). **-ος**, ον, (κόλλα) *gluing well, sticky*, ἰκμάς *AP*6.109 (Antip.).

εὔκολος, ον, (κόλον): I. of persons, *easily satisfied, contented with one's food*, Ἑρμείας *AP*9.72 (Antip.); εὔ. τῇ διαίτῃ Plu.*Lyc.*16; τὸ εὔκολον τῆς διαίτης Id.*Galb.*3: but, in earlier authors, 2. of the mind, opp. δύσκολος, *easily satisfied, contented, good-natured*, ὁ δ' εὔ. μὲν ἐνθάδ', εὔ. δ' ἐκεῖ, of Sophocles, Ar.*Ra.*82, cf. Arist.*Rh.*1381ᵃ31: Sup., Max.Tyr.26.2: c. dat., εὔ. πολίταις *at peace with* them, Ar.*Ra.* 359; εὔ. ἑαυτῷ Pl.*R.*330a; εὔ. πρὸς τοὺς συνήθεις Plu.*Fab.*1: c. inf., εὔ. φέρειν ἧτταν Id.2.629a. Adv. -λως *calmly*, εὐχερῶς καὶ εὐ. ἐξέπιεν Pl.*Phd.*117c, cf. Isoc.9.3 (v.l. -κλεῶς); εὐ. φέρειν τι Arist.*EN*1100ᵇ31, cf. Anaxandr.53.4; εὔ. ἔχειν Lys.4.9; εὐθύμως καὶ εὐ. ζῆν X.*Mem.*4. 8.2; *carelessly*, διειλέχθαι Pl.*Sph.*242c: Comp. -ώτερον, ἀποθανούμεθα Plu.2.235c; -ωτέρως Steph. *in Gal.*1.294 D.; also -ώτερον κρατῆσαι *more easily*, Polyaen.5.13.2. 3. *ready, agile*, *AP*5.205.2 (Leon.); of soldiers, ἐλαφροί, εὔ., εὐχερεῖς Poll.1.130; τὴν ἀναπνοὴν οὐκ εὔ. Aret. *SD*1.15. 4. rarely in bad sense, *easily led, prone*, πρὸς ἀδικίαν Luc.*Merc.Cond.*40; -ώτεροι ταῖς ὀργαῖς Plu.2.463d; τὰ ἀνόητα καὶ εὔ. Philostr.*VA*3.28. II. of things, *easy*, οὐ γὰρ εὐκόλῳ ἔοικεν Pl.*R.* 453d, cf. *Prm.*131e: Sup. -ώτατοι Id.*Lg.*779e; *easy to understand*, Lxx 2*Ki.*15.3. Adv. Comp. -ώτερον *more easily*, Ph.2.211. 2. *lithe*, εὔ., ὑγρομελής, of the pyrrhich, Poll.4.96. III. epith. of Hermes at Metapontum, Hsch.; of Asclepius at Epidaurus, *IG*4.1260.

εὔκολπος, ον, *with beautiful bays*, Archestr.*Fr.*9.3. 2. *in goodly folds*, of a net, *AP*6.28 (Jul.).

εὐκόλυμβος, ον, *diving well*, Heph.Astr.2.2, Sch.Lyc.387.

εὐκόμης, ου, ὁ, (κόμη) = εὔκομος, Poll.2.24, 5.83, Max.Tyr.3.8.

εὐκομῐδής, ές, (κομιδή) *well cared for*, νομαί Hdt.4.53 (Sup.), cf. Hsch.

εὐκόμιστος, ον, (κομίζω) = foreg., Poll.9.161, Eust.1560.6. 2. *easily extracted*, Sor.2.62; *easily carried off*, App.*Mith.*90.

εὔκομος, ον, (κόμη) *lovely-haired*, of goddesses and noble ladies, Ep. and Lyr. form **ἠΰκομος**, Il.1.36, Hes.*Th.*241, Pi.*O.*6.91, *P.*5.45; Σελήνη Epimenid.2: in Prose, Philostr.*Ep.*29; *well-fleeced*, εὔκομα μῆλα *AP*9.363.20 (Mel.); *with goodly foliage*, δένδρεσιν ἠϋκόμοισιν Emp.127.2, cf. Alex.Aphr.*Pr.*2.51.

εὔκομπος, ον, *loud-sounding*, εὔκομποι πληγαὶ ποδός, in dancing, E.*Tr.*152 (lyr.).

εὔκονος (sc. ἄρτος), ὁ, *bread made with bran*, Amerias and Timachidas ap.Ath.3.114e.

εὐκοπ-έω, *enjoy an easy life*, διὰ ὅλου βίου *PSI*4.286.38 (iii/iv A.D.). **-ία**, ἡ, *ease, facility*, D.S.1.36, 3.17, Lxx 2*Ma.*2.25; ἐν πάσῃ εὐ. *PMag.Par.*1.159. **-ος**, ον, *easy*, Plb.18.18.2: mostly in Comp., -ωτέρα σκευασία Dsc.1.39; -ώτερόν [ἐστι] c. inf., *Ev.Matt.*9.5, 19.24, etc. Adv. -πως Hp.*Epid.*2.6.31, Ar.*Fr.*783, D.S.3.24, Ph.*Bel.*56.16: Comp. -ώτερον Antip.*Stoic.*3.256.

εὐκόρῠθος, ον, (κόρυς) *with beautiful helmet*, Opp.*C.*1.363.

εὐκόρῠφος, ον, (κορυφή) *with handsome head*, Herm.ap.Stob.1.49.45: metaph., of sentences, *well wound up, ending well*, D.H.*Dem.* 40, 43.

εὐκοσμ-έω, *behave orderly*, Lxx 1*Ma.*8.15. **-ητος**, ον, *well-adorned*, *h.Merc.*384. **-ία**, ἡ, *orderly behaviour, good conduct, decency*, E.*Ba.*693, X.*Cyr.*1.2.3, Arist.*Pol.*1299^{b}16, etc.; τῆς εὐ. τῆς περὶ τὸ θέατρον *IG*2^2.354.16 (iv B.C.); εὐ. τοῦ θεάτρου ib.2^2.223*B*8; εὐ. ἡ κατὰ τὸ ἱερόν *SIG*1007.24 (Pergam., ii B.C.); εὐκοσμία τῶν παίδων Pl.*Prt.*325d; ὁ ἐπὶ τῆς εὐκοσμίας καὶ τῶν παρθένων *CIG*3185.19 (Smyrna); ὁ ἐπὶ τῆς εὐ. ἄρχων *IGRom.*4.582 (Aezani). **-ίως**, Adv. *decently*, περιστέλλεσθαι Anon.Hist.*Oxy.*218 ii 9. **-ος**, ον, *behaving well, orderly, decorous*, Sol.4.33, Th.6.42 (Comp.); οὐκ εὔκοσμον αἴρονται φυγήν A.*Pers.*481; τὸ εὐ., = εὐκοσμία, Th.1.84; ὁ εὐ., official title at Pergamum, *IGRom.*4.353^{b}3 (ii A.D.); at Athens, *SIG*1109.94, 136 (ii A.D.). 2. *well-adorned*, τοῖχοι γραφῇσιν εὔκοσμοι Aret.*CA*1.1. II. Adv. -μως *in good order*, Od.21.123, Hes. *Op.*628: Sup. -ότατα X.*Cyr.*2.4.1. 2. *ornamentally, gracefully*, ξεῖν A.R.1.1120; διαλέγεσθαι Plu.*Dem.*11.

εὔκουρος, ον, (κείρω) *well-shorn*, Hegem.ap.Ath.15.698e.

εὐκράδαντος [κρᾰ], ον, (κρᾰδαίνω) *well-poised*, gloss on ῥαδαλός, *EM*701.53.

εὐκρᾰδής, ές, (κράδη) εὐκραδέος.. συκέης *a fine fig-tree*, Nic.*Al.*347 (v.l. εὐκραδέης, εὐκραδίης).

εὐκρᾰδίως, = εὐκαρδίως, *App.Anth.*3.292.

εὐκρᾱής, Ep. ἐϋκρ-, ές, = εὔκρᾱτος (v.l. for ἀκραής in Od.14.299, Hes.*Op.*594); of winds, *gentle*, A.R.2.1228, 4.891; ἀὴρ Thphr.*CP*1.11.6, 2.3.3 (nisi leg. εὐκράς); *temperate*, neither too dry nor too wet, τόποι Arist.*Mete.*352^{a}7; of love, Opp.*H.*4.33. II. = εὐκράς (A) 2, Poll.6.23 (interpol.). III. Adv. -αῶς prob. cj. for εὐκραής in Aristaenet.1.3.

εὐκραίρης, ητος, ὁ, ἡ, = sq., Max.84.

εὔκραιρος, Ep. ἐΰκρ-, ον, also η, ον, (κραῖρα) *with fine horns*, esp. of oxen, βουσὶν ἐϋκραίρῃσιν *h.Merc.*209; εὐκραίρῳ βοΐ A.*Supp.*300. 2. of ships, *with beautiful beak*, Opp.*H.*2.516, Tryph.213.

εὐκράς (A), ᾶτος, ὁ, ἡ, = εὔκρατος, *temperate, of even temperature*, κρήνη εὐκρὰς πρὸς χειμῶνα καὶ θέρος Pl.*Criti.*112d; of climate, Thphr. *HP*7.1.4: metaph., ἔστιν οἷς βίος ὁ μικρὸς εὐκρὰς ἐγένεθ' E.*Fr.*504; ἡδονή ib.197. 2. *mixed for drinking*, οἶνος Poll.6.23. 3. of persons, *mixing readily with*, οὐ πολλοῖς εὐ. *AP*12.105 (Asclep.). (εὔκρας E.*Fr.*197, Poll.)

εὐκράς (B), κρᾶτος, ὁ, ἡ, = εὐκέφαλος, Hsch.

εὐκρᾱσία (late -κρᾱσίη Man.5.59), ἡ, *good temperature, mildness*, τῶν ὡρῶν Pl.*Ti.*24c; τοῦ ἀέρος Plb.34.8.4: abs., Arist.*Pr.*860^{b}12; ἐν ταῖς εὐκρασίαις *in good climates*, Thphr.*CP*3.21.1. 2. of persons, εὐ. τοῦ σώματος *good temperament*, Arist.*PA*673^{b}25, cf. *GA*744^{a}30, Zeno *Stoic.*1.37, Gal.6.31, etc.

εὐκρᾱτό-μελι, ιτος, τό, *honey-wine*, Ruf.*Fr.*117, Choerob. *in Theod.* 1.344. **-ποσία**, ἡ, *drinking of* εὔκρατον, Alex.Trall.5.5.

εὔκρᾱτος, Ion. εὔκρητος, ον, (κεράννυμι) *well-tempered, temperate*, E.*Fr.*772; ἐγκέφαλος Democr.ap.Thphr.*Sens.*56; ἀήρ Pl.*Ax.*371d; ὥρα Arist.*GA*752^{b}30; εὔκρατον ποιεῖ τὴν θερμότητα Id.*PA*652^{b}26; of countries, D.S.1.10; τόποι Ath.Med.ap.Orib.9.12.5 (Sup.); οἰκήσεις Plb.34.1.8 (Comp.); οἶκος Aret.*CA*1.1; of the *temperate* zone, *Stoic.*2.195, etc.; μεῖξις Chrysipp.ib.219; of liquids, *tempered, lukewarm*, ὕδωρ *IG*5(1).1390.108 (Andania), cf. Gal.6.101, etc.; of wine, *mixed for drinking*, Arist.*Pr.*874^{a}28. 2. metaph., *temperate, mild*, ὀλιγαρχία Id.*Pol.*1320^{b}21; τὸ εὐ. τοῦ ἤθους M.Ant.1.15; Κύπρις *AP* 6.208 (Antip.Thess.): in Astrol., of beneficent planetary influences, Gal.9.911. 3. in Lit. Crit., εὐ. ἁρμονία, ἑρμηνεία, *mixed* style, D.H. *Comp.*21 (v.l. κοινή), *Dem.*3; συνθήκη ὀνομάτων Luc.*Hist.Conscr.* 46. II. of persons, εὔκρητοι πρὸς ἅπαντας (cf. εὐκράς (A) 3) Hp. *Decent.*3. III. Adv. -τως *temperately*, ἀνδρείως καὶ εὐ. Phld.*Herc.* 1251.14; *temperately*, Gal.1.342. 2. εὐ. ἔχειν to be *temperate*, of climate, Cleom.1.2; to be *lukewarm*, Artem.1.64.

εὐκρᾱτόω, *temper*, in Pass., Sch.Hes.*Th.*p.461 G., Sch.Lyc.177 (-τυνθῆναι codd., Scheer).

εὐκρᾰτῶς, Adv. (Adj. -κρατής is not found) *firmly, fast*, ἔχειν τι Arist.*Pr.*875^{a}22; cf. δυσκρατής.

εὔκρεκτος, ον, (κρέκω) *well-struck, well-sounding*, of stringed instruments, φόρμιγξ A.R.4.1194. 2. *well-woven*, of the threads of the warp, μίτοι *AP*6.174 (Antip. (Sid.)).

ἐϋκρήδεμνος, ον, *with beauteous fillet*, Nonn.*D.*26.338.

ἐΰκρημνος, ον, *with fair cliffs*, Opp.*C.*3.251.

εὔκρηνος, Ep. also ἐΰκρ-, ον, (κρήνη) *well-watered*, πέτρη *APl.*4.230 (Leon.); *with fair fountains*, πτολίεθρον Call.*Aet.*3.1.72.

ἐϋκρήπῑς, ῖδος, ὁ, ἡ, *well-based*, Nonn.*D.*40.258.

εὔκρητος, ον, Ion. for εὔκρατος.

εὔκρῑθος, ον, (κριθή) *rich in barley*, ἀλωά Theoc.7.34; ἄρουρα *AP*6.258.6 (Adaeus).

εὐκρῑν-εια [ῐ], ἡ, (εὐκρινής) *clear-sightedness*, Pl.*Def.*414a. 2. *distinctness of outline*, Diocl.*Fr.*141. 3. *limpidity* of style, εὐ. καὶ καθαρότης Hermog.*Id.*1.2, cf. 4. 4. *clear distinction*, προσώπων καὶ πραγμάτων Procl. *in R.*1.15 K. **-έω**, *keep distinct, keep in good order*, τοὺς στρατευσομένους δεῖ εὐκρινεῖν X.*HG*4.2.6 (nisi leg. διευκρ-); τὰ εὐκρινοῦντα τὴν σύγχυσιν Hermog.*Id.*1.4, cf. 11. II. *judge fit, decide*, *PCair.Zen.*150.22 (iii B.C.). **-ής**, ές, (κρίνω) *well-separated*, X.*Eq.Mag.*3.3; *well-opened*, στόματα (sc. τῆς μήτρας) Hp.*Mul.*1.17 (s. v.l., cf. III). II. *distinct, clear*, τῆμος δ' εὐκρινέες τ' αὖραι καὶ πόντος ἀπήμων then the winds are *regular, steady*, Hes.*Op.*670; ἡ διάγνωσις εὐ. γενήσεται Is.10.2; οὐκ εὐκρινές ἐστι πρὸς τὴν ἀκοήν there is no *clear discernment*, Arist.*Pr.*903^{a}17. Adv. -νῶς, ἔχειν Pl. *Sph.*242c; εὐκρινέστερον ἰδεῖν Id.*R.*564c; οὐκ εὐκρινῶς εἴτε.. εἴτε.. without *distinction*, Str.16.4.20, cf. 6.1.11. 2. of literary style, *pellucid*, opp. ἀμφίβολον, Phld.*Po.*1676.8; τὸ καθαρὸν καὶ εὐ. Hermog.*Id.*1.1; of authors, such as Critias and Xenophon, ib.2.11, 12. III. *well-arranged, in good order*, Hp.*Mul.*1.17 (if σώματα be read); πάντα... εὐκρινέα ποιέεσθαι Hdt.9.42. Adv. -νῶς, κεῖσθαι X. *Oec.*8.19. 2. of bandages, *simple, not creased*, Hp.*Off.*10, cf. Gal. 18(2).776. Adv. -νῶς ib.725; Ion. -νέως Hp.*Off.*3. IV. *having had a favourable crisis, convalescent*, σωμάτιον Isoc.*Ep.*4.11, cf. Hsch.; but, *indicating a good crisis, favourable*, of symptoms, Hp.*Coac.*604, Antyll.ap.Orib.9.4.2: metaph., Men.*Pk.*163. 2. of illnesses, *easily brought to a crisis*, Hp.*Aph.*3.8, *Epid.*2.1.5 (Sup.). 3. = νεκρός, Hsch.: Att. use, acc. to *EM*392.32. **-ητος**, ον, *highly sensitive*, prob. f.l. for εὐκίνητος, Aret.*SD*1.6.

εὔκρῐτος, ον, (κρίνω) *easy to decide*, οὐκ εὐ. τὸ κρῖμα A.*Supp.*397; εὐ. [ἐστιν] ὅτι.. it is *easily discerned, manifest*, Pl.*Plt.*272c, cf. d; εὔκριτ' ἐστί Men.*Epit.*136; ἴχνη *distinct*, Poll.5.66. 2. Medic., *having a good crisis*, νόσημα Hp.*Aph.*1.12; κρίσιες -ώτεραι Id.*Acut.* 14. Adv. -τως, opp. ἀνακρίτως, Pall. *in Hp.*2.181 D.

ἐϋκρόκᾰλος, ον, *pebbly*, Nonn.*D.*15.95.

εὐκρότᾰλος, Ep. ἐϋκρ-, ον, *accompanied by castanets*, χορεῖαι *AP* 9.139 (Claudian.); *lively, rattling*, πλατάγη ib.6.309 (Leon.).

εὐκρότητος, ον, *well-hammered, well-wrought*, πρόχους S.*Ant.*430; Δωρίς E.*El.*819.

εὔκροτος, ον, *well-sounding*, ἀνάπαιστα Alciphr.3.43. Adv. -τως Sopat. in Rh.8.14 W. II. Adv. -τως, = εὐκροτήτως, applied to the elements in the body, Meno *Iatr.*19.27.

εὔκρυπτος, ον, *easy to hide*, Hp.*Fract.*18 (Comp.), A.*Ag.*623.

εὐκρῠφής, ές, = foreg., Arist.*HA*623^{a}28.

εὐκτάζομαι, Frequentat. of εὔχομαι, Hsch., Phot.

εὐκταῖος, α, ον, (εὔχομαι) Att. Adj. (used chiefly by Trag., cf. ἀραῖος): 1. *of* or *for prayer, votive*, Ἅιδου.. εὐκταίαν χάριν A.*Ag.* 1387; τρίτην Διὸς σωτῆρος εὐκταίαν λίβα Id.*Fr.*55; εὐχαί Ar.*Av.* 1060; ἐπῳδαί Pl.*Lg.*906b; εὐ. [νύμφα] *devoted*, E.*IT*213 (lyr.); πανηγύρεις εὐ., Lat. *ludi votivi*, D.C.58.12: εὐκταῖα, τά, *votive offerings, vows, prayers*, A.*Supp.*631 (lyr.), S.*Tr.*239. 2. epith. of gods, *invoked in* or *by special prayer*, πατρὸς εὐκταίαν Ἐρινύν, πατρόθεν εὐκταία φάτις, of the curse *invoked by* Oedipus, A.*Th.*723, 841 (both lyr.); Θέμις εὐκταία E.*Med.*169 (anap.); τοῖσι δυστυχοῦσιν εὐκταία θεός Id. *Or.*214. 3. generally, *prayed for, desired*, ἠώς, λιμένες, *AP*6.242 (Crin.), 9.41 (Theon); γάμος γάρ.. εὐκταῖον κακόν Men.*Mon.*102, cf. Epicur.*Sent.Vat.*35; *desirable*, f.l. for εὐκτέον in Pl.*Lg.*687e: Sup., τήβεννος (of the *latus clavus*), *AJA*18.323 (Sardes, i B.C.); ἴασις Gal. 7.738, cf. Luc.*Tyr.*17. Adv. -αίως, ἔχειν Sch.Pi.*P.*5.159; δέχεσθαί τινα J.*BJ*7.2.1.

εὐκτέᾰνος (A), ον, (κτέανον) *wealthy*, A.*Pers.*897 (lyr.), *AP*9.442 (Agath.).

εὐκτέᾰνος (B), ον, = εὐκτήδων, Thphr.*HP*3.9.3 (Comp.); δρῦς Plu. *Marc.*8.

εὐκτέον, (εὔχομαι) *one must pray for* or *desire*, Pl.*Lg.*687e, Heraclit.*Ep.*7.8; θεῷ τὰ ἄξια θεοῦ prob. cj. in Porph.*Marc.*12: abs., Max. Tyr.11.4.

εὐκτήδων, ον, gen. ονος, *straight-grained*, of wood, Thphr.*HP*5.1.11.

εὐκτημοσύνη, ἡ, *wealth*, Poll.6.196.

ἐϋκτήμων, ον, gen. ονος, (κτῆμα) *wealthy*, Pi.*N.*7.92; εὐκτ- Paul. Al.*M.*2.

εὐκτήριος, α, ον, *of* or *for prayer*, οἶκος *Cod.Just.*1.2.15 *Intr.* II. Subst. εὐκτήριον, τό, *oratory*, Just.*Nov.*131.7 *Intr.*, *Rev.Bibl.*1911.287 (Jericho, vi A.D.).

εὔκτητος, ον, *honestly acquired*, πλοῦτος Crates Theb.10.9, cf. Paul. Al.*N.*4; τἀγαθὸν εὐ. Phld.*Sto.*339.4.

εὐκτικός, ή, όν, (εὐκτός) *expressing a wish*, in Gramm., ἐπίρρημα A.D.*Synt.*248.6, cf. Ph.1.541: -κή, ἡ (with or without ἔγκλισις), the *optative* mood, A.D.*Synt.*245.27, D.T.638.7, etc. Adv. -κῶς *in the optative*, Suid. s. v. ἀγαπῴην. 2. *expressing a prayer* or *vow*: -κόν, τό, *utterance in the form of a prayer* or *wish*, *Stoic.*2.61 (pl.); εὐ. ὕμνοι Men.Rh.p.333 S.: so -κά, τά, Procl.*Chr.*ap.Phot.*Bibl.*p.320 B.; but, *liturgy*, Philostr.*VA*6.40, S.E.*M.*8.72. Adv. -κῶς *in the form of a prayer*, Theon *Prog.*5.

ἐϋκτίμενος [ῐ], η, ον, (κτίζω) = εὖ ναιόμενος, *good to dwell in*, epith. of cities, ἐϋ. πτολίεθρον Il.2.501, etc.; πόλις B.5.149; of anything on which man's labour has been bestowed, νῆσον ἐϋκτιμένην ἐκάμοντο wrought it *so as to be good to dwell in*, Od.9.130; ἐϋ. ἐν ἀλωῇ on a *well-made* threshing-floor, Il.20.496, 21.77; the same phrase, of a garden, *well-wrought*, Od.24.226. (εὐκτ- in *h.Ap.*36, B. l.c.)

εὔκτιστος, ον, poet. ἐΰκτ-, (κτίζω) = foreg., Sch.Hes.*Sc.*270.

ἐΰκτῐτος, ον, = ἐϋκτίμενος, of places, Il.2.592, = *h.Ap.*423, cf. D.P. 552; πόλις Hes.*Fr.*81.5; μέγαρα B.3.46. (Glossed by εὐκατοίκητος (q. v.).)

εὐκτός, ή, όν, (εὔχομαι) *wished for, desired*, ὄφρ' ἔτι μᾶλλον Τρωσὶ μὲν εὐκτὰ γένηται that *what they wish for* may happen, Il.14.98; τὰ δ' εὐκτὰ παρὰ θεῶν ᾐτησάμην S.*Fr.*843. 2. *to be wished for*, εὐκτὸν ἀνθρώποισι E.*Ion*642, cf. Isoc.12.243, Men.*Georg.*82; εὐ. ὁ τῷ βατράχῳ βίος Theoc.10.52; εὐκτότατος γάμος Eup.383: εὐκτόν ἐστι c.inf., E.*Heracl.*458, X.*Mem.*1.5.5. II. *vowed, dedicated*, ἴουλος *AP*10.19 (Apollonid.).

εὐκτῠπέων, ουσα, ον, (κτυπέω) *clattering*, Q.S.5.21.

εὐκύβέω, (κύβος) *to be lucky with the dice*, Amphis 11.

εὐκυκλής, ές, = sq., Ἀληθείη Parm.1.29.

εὔκυκλος, ον, *well-rounded, round*, in Il. always of ἀσπίς, 5.453, 797, al., A.*Th.*590; εὐ. ἕδρα Pi.*N.*4.66; σφαίρη Parm.8.43; στεφάναι X.*Cyn.*9.12; εὔκυκλον ποιεῖν Pl.*Ti.*40a; ὀφθαλμοὶ σελήνης -ότεροι Alciphr.*Fr.*5. 2. in Od. as epith. of ἀπήνη, *well-wheeled*, 6.58,70; ὄχοι A.*Pr.*710; ἀντίπηξ E.*Ion* 1391. 3. of bandages, *in horizontal circles, orbicular*, Heliod.ap.Orib.48.61 tit., Gal.18(1).786. II. *moving in a circle, circling*, χορεία Ar.*Th.*968 (lyr.). Adv. -λως Orph. *L.*135.

εὐκύκλωτος, ον, *well-rounded*, Eub.56.4, Aristopho 14.

εὐκύλῐκος [ῠ], η, ον, (κύλιξ) *suited to the wine-cup*, λαλιή *AP*7.440.8 (Leon.).

εὐκύλιστος [ῠ], ον, *easily rolled*, Hero *Aut.*2.4, Phlp.*in Ph.*647.2. Adv. -τως Hero *Aut.*11.11.

εὐκύμαντος [ῡ], ον, *easily made to undulate*, ἐποχαί Nicom.*Harm.* 3 (Comp.). II. metaph., *strong-surging*, εἰς θυμόν Eust.1392.49.

εὔκωπος, ον, *well-equipt with oars*, Opp.*H.*5.242; gloss on εὔσελμος, Hsch.

εὐλάβ-εια [λᾰ], ἡ, Ion. -ίη Thgn.118, Agatho in *PLG* ii p.268 B.:— *discretion, caution*, Thgn. l.c., Agatho l.c., etc.; ἐσῴζετ' ἂν τὴν -ειαν S.*El.*994; personified in E.*Ph.*782; ἡ εὐ. σῴζει πάντα Ar.*Av.*376; εὐλάβειαν ἔχειν μή.., = εὐλαβεῖσθαι μή.., Pl.*Prt.*321a; so εὐ. αὕτη.. τὸ μὴ νέους.. γεύεσθαι *caution to prevent* their tasting, Id.*R.*539b; εὐλαβείας οὐ μικρᾶς δεῖται, εὐ. ἐστὶ πολλῆς, D.19.262, Arist.*Pol.*1269^{a}14; εὐ. ποιητέον περί τινας ib.1315^{a}17; δι' εὐλαβείας ἔχειν ἀλλήλους D.H. 5.38; ἐπ' εὐλαβείᾳ..προείρηται by way of *caution*, Pl.*R.*539d; ἐπ' εὐ. in A.*Ag.*1024 is f.l. for ἐπ' ἀβλ., cf. Sch. ad loc. 2. c. gen., *caution* or *discretion in* a thing, πολλὴ εὐ. τούτων ποιητέα Antipho 3.3. 11; εὐλάβειαι πληγῶν *avoidance of..*, Pl.*Lg.*815a; τῶν αἰσχρῶν Arist.*EN*1121^{b}24; ηὐλάβεια τῶν ποιουμένων S.*OC*116; εὐλάβειαν τῶνδε προυθέμην Id.*El.*1334; ἡ τῶν περιεχόντων εὐ. *careful employment of..*, Phld.*D.*3*Fr.*32. 3. *reverence, piety*, πρὸς or περὶ τὸ θεῖον, D.S.13.12, Plu.*Num.*22 (but also πρός τινα Ph.2.581): abs., *godly fear*, *Ep.Hebr.*5.7, 12.28; *religious scruple*, οὐδεμίαν εὐ. προορωμένων *UPZ*42.21 (ii B.C.). b. as title, ἡ σὴ εὐ. your *reverence*, *PFlor.* 73.7 (vi A.D.). 4. in bad sense, *over-caution, timidity*, Plu.*Fab.*1, 2. 432e; εὐλαβίη γὰρ ἀπειρίη Aret.*CA*1.2. **-έομαι,** impf. ηὐλαβούμην v.l. in E.*Or.*748 (troch.), 1059, εὐλ- Aeschin.1.25: fut. -ήσομαι Pl. *R.*410a, Arist.*EN*1127^{b}6; also -ηθήσομαι Lxx *De.*2.4, al., D.L.7.116, Gal.5.249: aor. ηὐλαβήθην (or εὐλ-) Pl.*Phd.*89c:—*to be discreet, cautious, beware*, folld. by μή or ὅπως μή with subj., εὐ. μὴ φανῇς κακὸς γεγώς S.*Tr.*1129, cf. E.*Hipp.*100, Ar.*Eq.*253, Pl.*Phd.*89c, etc.: by fut. ind., ὅπως μή..οἰχήσομαι ib.91c (om. cod. B): c. inf., εὐλαβουμένῳ πεσεῖν S.*OT*616; εὐ. λέγειν Pl.*Phd.*101c: with μή inserted, εὐ. μὴ σῴζειν φίλους E.*Or.*1059, cf. Ar.*Lys.*1277, Cydias 1. 2. *take care*, ὅπως κατοίσεις Ar.*Ach.*955; εὐ. περί τι Pl.*Lg.*927c, *Ion* 537a; περί τινος Id.*Lg.*691b; ἀμφί τινι Luc.*Gall.*21: abs., εὐλαβήθηθ' S.*OT*47; εὐλαβούμενος ἠρόμην Pl.*Prt.*333e, cf. 316d; εἰ μηδὲν εὐλαβηθέντα τἀληθὲς εἰπεῖν δέοι *without reserve*, D.18.159; *take precautions*, Arist. *Pol.*1303^{b}27. 3. *incur risk*, εὐλαβήθη περὶ καθαιρέσεως δόξης Vett. Val.231.19, cf. 209.11. II. c. acc., *have a care of, beware of*, εὐλαβοῦ στρόμβον..μή σ' ἀναρπάσῃ A.*Fr.*195; εὐ. τὴν κύνα *'ware* the dog, Ar.*Lys.*1215; εὐ. πενίαν Pl.*R.*372c; τὸν φθόνον D.18.305; τὸ ψεῦδος Arist.*EN*1127^{b}6; τοὺς ὑβρίζεσθαι νομίζοντας Id.*Pol.*1315^{a}27; τὰς μυίας Id.*HA*611^{b}11. 2. *reverence, pay honour to*, τὸν θεόν Pl. *Lg.*879e; τὸν δῆμον Plu.*Per.*7; in Lxx, *fear* God, *Na.*1.7; εὐ. ἀπὸ τοῦ ὀνόματος Κυρίου *Ze.*3.12; μηδὲν -ούμενον, ὡς οἱ πολλοὶ λέγουσιν, ὅτι ..δεῖ.. Sor.1.49. 3. *watch for, await quietly*, καιρόν E.*Or.*699. 4. *put out of harm's way*, τὰ κοῖλα γαστρός Id.*Ph.*1411. III. later in Act., εὐλαβεῖν τινα *beware of*, *BGU*665.4 (i A.D.); cf. εὐλάβησον, -ῆσαι, Phot. **-ής,** ές, (λαβεῖν) *taking hold well, holding fast, clinging*, metaph., πενία Luc.*Tim.*29: lit. in Adv. εὐλαβῶς, κατέχειν Ael.*NA*3.13, 6.55 (Sup.): but mostly, II. metaph., *undertaking prudently, discreet, cautious*, Democr.91, Pl.*Plt.*311a, al.; τὸ εὐλαβές, = εὐλάβεια, ib. b; εὐλαβὴς περί τι Plu.*CG*3; τὸ πρὸς τὰ μεγάλα τῶν τετολμημένων εὐ. Hdn.2.8.2; εὐ. ἀπό τινος *keeping* from..., Lxx *Le.* 15.31. Adv. -βῶς Pl.*Sph.*246b; εὐ. διακείμενος D.S.13.12, etc.: Comp. -εστέρως E.*IT*1375; -έστερον διακεῖσθαι πρός τι Plb.1.18. 1. 2. *reverent, pious*, Lxx *Mi.*7.2 (v.l. εὐσεβής), *Ev.Luc.*2.25, *Act. Ap.*2.5, etc.: Sup. -έστατος, as title, Dionys.*Ep.*71, Procop.Gaz.*Ep.* 126. III. Pass., *easy to get hold of*, κέρκος Luc.*Lex.*7. 2. *cautiously undertaken* or *effected*, μετάβασις Pl.*Lg.*736d; ἡδοναί Plu.*Per.* 15 (ἀβλ- Reiske). **-ητέον,** *one must beware of*, c. acc., Pl.*R.*608a, *Grg.*527b, cf. 480e, Epicur.*Fr.*465, Dsc.*Eup.*2.160, etc. **-ητέος,** *verecundus, Gloss.* **-ητικός,** ή, όν, c. gen., *careful to avoid*, Pl.*Def.* 412a; ὀρθοῦ ψόγου Stoic.ap.Stob.2.7.5^{b2}. **-ίη,** Ion. for εὐλάβεια.

εὐλάζω, (εὐλή) = σκωληκιάω, Hsch.

εὐλᾶϊγξ, ὁ, ἡ, gen. ιγγος, poet. for εὔλιθος, τράπεζα *AP*9.767 (Agath.); σορός ib.7.605 (Jul.), cf. Coluth.46, Nonn.*D.*5.134.

εὐλάκα, ἡ, Dor. word, ἀργυρέᾳ εὐλάκᾳ **εὐλαξεῖν** (Lacon. fut. inf.), *should plough* with silver *ploughshare*, intimating that there would be a dearth, corn being worth its weight in silver, Orac.ap.Th.5.16 (v.l. εὐλάχα, Phot.).—Neither Verb nor Noun occurs elsewh. (Cf. αὖλαχα, αὖλαξ.)

εὔλᾰλος, ον, *sweetly-speaking*, Lxx *Si.*6.5; epith. of Apollo, *AP*9. 525.6; of the Argo, Orph.*A.*244: metaph., of a wine-jar, *AP*9. 229 (Marc. Arg.). II. = εὔγλωσσος II, Lxx *Jb.*11.2.

εὐλαμπής, ές, *bright-shining*, Max.582, Max.Tyr.17.10 (Sup.); ὀφθαλμοί Adam.1.8; τὸ εὐ. ib.19:—also **εὔλαμπρος,** ον, v.l. for εὔχαλκος in Antiph.208.2.

εὐλάχᾰνος [λᾰ], ον, *fruitful in herbs*, *AP*7.321.6; τόποι *Gp.*12. 3.3.

εὐλεί-αντος and **εὐλέαντος,** ον, (λεαίνω) *easily triturated*, Xenocr.42; τροφή Arist.*PA*674^{b}33: Comp., Antyll.ap.Orib.10.13.12: **-ωτος,** ον, *easily powdered*, Gal.12.189, Asclep.ap.eund.13.678.

εὔλειμος, ον, = sq., E.*Ba.*1084 codd. (prob. ὕλιμος).

εὐλείμων (ἐῠ-), ον, gen. ονος, *with goodly meadows*, οὐ γάρ τις νήσων ἱππήλατος οὐδ' εὐ. Od.4.607, cf. *h.Ap.*529, Hes.*Fr.*134.

εὔλεκτρος, ον, *bringing wedded happiness*, of Aphrodite, S.*Tr.*515 (lyr.), *AP*5.244 (Maced.). 2. *a beauteous bride*, S.*Ant.*796 (lyr.).

εὔλεξις, ι, ὁ, ἡ, *with good choice of words*, ridiculed by Luc.*Lex.*1, *Rh.Pr.*17.

εὐλέπιστος, ον, *easily peeled* or *shelled*, βάλανος Dsc.4.157.

εὐλεχής, ές, = εὔλεκτρος, θάλαμος *AP*7.649 (Anyte); Κύπρις *APl.* 4.182 (Leon.).

εὐλή, ἡ, *worm, maggot*, the larva of the fly (rarely in sg., *AP*7. 472.10 (Leon.)), different fr. ἕλμινς; Hom. only in Il., of worms bred in flesh, 19.26, 24.414, al.; ὑπ' εὐλέων καταβρωθῆναι Hdt.3.16, cf. 4.205, Hp.*Mul.*1.75, Pl.*Ax.*365c, Arist.*HA*506^{a}30:—of common worms, Orph.*L.*600.

εὔληκτος, ον, *soon ceasing*, Luc.*Trag.*324.

εὐλημᾰτέω, (λῆμα) *to be of good spirit*, A.*Fr.*106.

εὐληνής, ές, *fleecy*, *EM*393.6, Hsch.

εὔληπτος, ον, *easily taken hold of*, οὐδ' εὔληπτον εἶναι τὸ ὕδωρ J.*AJ* 1.16.2, cf. Gal.*UP*11.5 (Sup.). Adv., τὸ ἔκπωμα εὐληπτότατα ἐνδιδόναι to give it *so that one can most easily take hold of it*, X.*Cyr.*1.3.8: metaph., εὔ. τὰ τῆς διατριβῆς Iamb.*VP*7.33. 2. *easy to be taken* or *reduced*, νησιῶται Th.6.85; ἧττον εὔ. πόλις D.H.3.43; εὔ. ὀργῇ, κόλαξι, Ph.2.590, Plu.2.66b; *easy to gain* or *obtain*, Luc.*Merc.Cond.*10; *easy to apprehend*, τοῖς ἀκούουσι Iamb.*Protr.*4.

εὔληρα, ων, τά, *reins*, Il.23.481, Q.S.4.508, 9.156; Dor. **αὔληρα** Epich.178 (for ἀϝληρα, cf. ἀβληρά Hsch.):—hence **εὐληρωσίων** (εὐληροσιῶν cod.)· πληγῶν, Id. (Cf. ταυληρόντα.)

εὔλητο· ἐπέφυρτο, ἐτετάρακτο, Hsch. (Perh. for ἐόλητο.)

εὐλίβᾰνος [ῐ], ον, *rich in frankincense*, Aristonous 1.23, Orph.*H.* 55.17.

εὔλῐθος, ον, *of goodly stone*, ἄντρον Orph.*H.*59.4; *made of fair stones*, J.*BJ*5.5.6.

εὐλίμεν-ος [ῐ], ον, (λιμήν) *with good harbours*, ἀκταί E.*Hel.*1463; [πόλις] εὐλιμενωτέρα Pl.*Lg.*705a, cf. 704b,d; εὐ. ἁλὸς οἶκοι Archestr. *Fr.*26: c. gen., ἱερὸν παντὸς κύματος εὐλίμενον *App.Anth.*3.81 (Posidipp.):—also **-λῐμήν, -ένος,** πορθμοί Procop.*Aed.*1.5. **-ότης,** ητος, ἡ, *good harbourage*, Men.Rh.p.352S.

εὔλιμνος, ον, (λίμνη) *abounding in lakes*, Arist.*HA*601^{b}22.

εὔλῖνος, ον, *spinning well*, epith. of Ilithyia, Olen ap.Paus.8.21.3.

εὐλῖπής, ές, (λίπος) *very fat*, Lyc.874. 2. *rich in resin*, πεύκη Epigr.ap.Philostr.*Her.*19.17.

εὐλῐτάνευτος [ᾰ], ον, (λιτανεύω) *easily entreated*, Sch.A.R.1.1141.

εὐλογ-έω, impf. εὐλόγουν or ηὐλ- Ar.*Ec.*454, Isoc.12.206: fut. -ήσω E.*Hec.*465 (lyr.): aor. εὐλόγησα or ηὐλ- Lxx *Ge.*1.22, al.: inf. εὐλογῆσαι Ar.*Eq.*565: pf. εὐλόγηκα Lxx *Nu.*23.11:—Pass., with fut. Med. εὐλογήσομαι (v.l. -ηθήσομαι, as always in Lxx, 2*Ki.*7.29, al.) Isoc.9.5: aor. εὐλογήθην Phalar.*Ep.*119.3 (opt.): pf. εὐλόγημαι Lxx *Ru.*2.19:—*speak well of, praise*, πόλιν A.*Ag.*580; πατέρα τὸν ἀμόν S.*Ph.*1314, cf. Ar.*Eq.* l.c., E.*Hec.* l.c., al., Isoc. ll. cc.; *deliver a panegyric upon*, Arist.*Rh.Al.*1426^{a}3: with neut. Adj., εὐ. καὶ δίκαια κἄδικα Ar.*Ach.*372, cf. *Ec.*454; θεοὶ εὐλογοῦσί τινα *honour* him, E. *Supp.*927:—Pass., ἐπαίνοις εὐλογούμενον πέδον S.*OC*720; τὸν ἐν Δωδῶνι δαίμον' εὐλογούμενον Id.*Fr.*461. II. of God or men, Lxx *Ge.*35.9, al., *Act.Ap.*3.26, al.: freq. in pf. part. Pass. εὐλογημένος, as Lxx *De.*28.3, *Ev.Luc.*1.28. 2. *bless, praise* a god, *OGI*73 (Egypt), cf. εὐ. τὴν Εἶσιν (sic) *CIG*4705c (ibid.); σου τὰς δυνάμεις Buresch *Aus Lydien* 113; so in Lxx and NT, *Jo.*22.23, al., *Ep.Jac.*3.9. 3. also, apptly. by a Hebr. euphemism, *curse*, Lxx 3*Ki.*20(21).10, cf. *Jb.*2.5. **-ητός,** ή, όν, *blessed*, ib.*Ge.*9.26, al., Ph.1.453, *Ev.Luc.* 1.68, *Ep.Rom.*1.25, etc. **-ία,** ἡ, *good* or *fine language*, Pl.*R.*400d, Luc.*Lex.*1. 2. *plausibility*, ἔχει τινὰ εὐλογίαν Thphr.*CP*6.31.1; *habet* εὐλογίαν Cic.*Att.*13.22.4, cf. *Ep.Rom.*16.18; ἡ τοῦ δόγματος εὐ. prob. in Phld.*Sign.*27; ἡ εὐ. τῶν πραγμάτων Id.*Herc.*1251. 8. II. *praise, eulogy*, Pi.*N.*4.5, Th.2.42; ὑμνῆσαι δι' εὐλογίας E. *HF*356 (lyr.); ἄξιος εὐλογίας Ar.*Pax*738: pl., Pi.*I.*3.3, 6(5).21, Pl. *Ax.*365a; *good fame, glory*, ἀγήραντος εὐ. Simon.100, cf. Pi.*O.*5.24; εὐλογίαν φέρει *Lyr.Alex.Adesp.*21.10; ἔχειν εὐ. τινὰ πρός τινα *POxy.* 65.4 (iii/iv A.D.). 2. esp. *praise* to God, Lxx *Si.*50.20(22), *Apoc.* 7.12, *OGI*74 (Egypt). III. *act of blessing*, opp. κατάρα, Lxx *Ge.* 27.12, *Ep.Jac.*3.10. 2. *blessing called down* or *bestowed*, Lxx *Pr.* 10.22, 1*Ep.Pet.*3.9. 3. *gift, bounty*, Lxx *Jo.*15.19, 4*Ki.*5.15, 2*Ep. Cor.*9.5; ὁ σπείρων ἐπ' εὐλογίαις ἐπ' εὐλογίαις καὶ θερίσει *bountifully*, ib. 6, cf. Ph.1.129. **-ίζω,** = εὐλογέω, v.l. in Lxx *To.*4.12:—Pass., v.l. in Ph.1.395. **-ιμος,** *benedictus, Gloss.* **-ιστέω,** *act rationally, prudently*, Diog.Bab.*Stoic.*3.219, Antip.ib.253, Ph.1.395; ἔν τινι D.L.7.88, Arr.*Epict.*2.23.35; πρός τι Plu.*Oth.*13, etc. II. = εὐλογέω II, *bless*, Ph.1.125,130, al. **-ιστία,** ἡ, *circumspection, prudence*, Pl.*Def.*412e, *Stoic.*3.64, Antip.ib.253, Phld.*D.*3*Fr.*81, Plu.2.103a, M.Ant.4.26, Phalar.*Ep.*119.4. II. = εὐλογία III, *blessing*, Ph.1.597, al. **-ιστος,** ον, *easily computed*, hence of ratios, *simple*, Arist.*Sens.*439^{b}32; opp. περιττός, Id.*Metaph.*1092^{b}27; πλῆθυς D.H.4.15. 2. *well-weighed*, αἰτίαι Id.1.4; *well-calculated, reasonable*, ὁδός Id.5.55; *rational*, ἐκλογή Antip.*Stoic.*3.253, Chrysipp.ib. 46; λόγος Phld.*Rh.*2.160 S.; τῶν ἀλγεινῶν ὑπομονή Hierocl. *in CA* 11 p.441 M. 3. *probable*, Phld.*Lib.*p.27 O. 4. *blessed*, Ph.1.46, al. II. Act., *calculating well* or *rightly*: hence, *prudent, circumspect*, ἀνδρὸς τὸ κρατέειν (sc. θυμοῦ) εὐλογίστου Democr.236, cf. Arist. *Rh.*1385^{b}27, Plb.10.2.7, Phld.*Ir.*p.81 W., etc.: Sup., Ph.1.644; τὸ εὐ., = εὐλογιστία, Arr.*Epict.*1.11.17, Ps.-Dsc.1.103. Adv. -τως *rationally*, opp. ἀλογίστως, Epicur.*Ep.*3 p.66 U.; *prudently, wisely*, κεχρῆσθαι τοῖς καιροῖς Plb.18.33.7 (Sup.); εὐ. φέρειν D.H.4.21, cf. Arr.*Epict.* 3.2.2, M.Ant.8.32.

εὐλογοποιέω, *excuse*, Sch.E.*Hec.*1187, Eust.1233.54.

εὔλογος, ον, *reasonable, sensible*, νουθετήματα A.*Pers.*830; οὐκ εὐλόγῳ ἔοικεν Pl.*R.*605e; εὔ. ὀργή Phld.*Ir.*p.45 W.; εὔλογόν [ἐστι] c. inf., *it is reasonable that..*, Pl.*Cra.*396b, Arist.*Pol.*1286^{b}15, etc.; -ώτερόν [ἐστι] Id.*EN*1102^{b}2: Sup., Id.*Cael.*286^{b}34. 2. *reasonable, fair*, πρόφασις Th.3.82, D.18.152, etc.; τὸ εὔ. *a fair reason*, Th. 4.87. 3. *probable*, c. dat. et inf., Hp.*de Arte* 7 (Comp.), cf. Sphaer. *Stoic.*1.141, Cic.*Att.*14.22.2; διὰ σημείων εὐ. Phld.*Lib.*p.30 O.; ἐκ τῶν εὐ. *in all probability*, Plb.10.44.6, cf. Plu.*Them.*13; ἐκτὸς τῶν εὐ. πίπτειν to be beyond *all probability*, Arist.*Metaph.*1060^{a}18: Comp., Pl.*Ep.*352a: Sup., Cic.*Att.*13.6.4. Adv. -γως Phld.*Lib.*p.33 O. 4. *suitable, conformable*, c. dat., Plot.6.5.10. 5. *creditable*, κατορθώσασι εὔ. [ἐστί] Ar.*Ra.*736. 6. *eloquent*, v.l. for ἱκανός, Lxx *Ex.* 4.10, whence Ezek.*Exag.*113, Ph.2.93, 1.166 (interpr. as *reasonable*). II. Adv. -γως *with good reason, reasonably*, A.*Th.*508, *Supp.*47 (lyr.), *Fr.*6, Ar.*V.*771, Lys.12.7; εὐ. ἄπρακτοι ἀπίασιν Th. 4.61; εὐ. φέρειν (Abresch εὐλόφως, q.v.) E.*Fr.*175; εὐ. ἔχειν Pl. *Phd.*62d; εὐ. φθονεῖν τινι Alex.219.1; τοῖς εὐ. καὶ τοῖς κακῶς ἔχουσι Men.48; freq. like εἰκότως, at the close of a sentence, implying assent, Arist.*EN*1153^{b}15, 1162^{b}6: Comp. -ωτέρως Isoc.6.28; -ώτερον Plb.7.7.7. 2. εὐ. τινὰ ἐπιδέξασθαι (v.l. ἐνδόξως) *honourably*, Lxx 1*Ma.*12.43.

εὐλογοφανής, ές, *seeming probable*, Doxop.in Rh.2.316 W., Sch. S.*OC*761.

εὐλογχ-έω, *to be lucky*, prob. in Hsch. for εὐλογεῖν· εὐμοιρεῖν. **-ος**, ον, (λέλογχα) *fortunate, propitious*, Democr.166.

εὐλοιδόρητος, ον, *open to reproach*, Men.439, Plu.2.757a.

εὐλοκοπέομαι, *to be eaten of worms*, Artem.5.81.

εὔλοφος, ον, *well-plumed*, κυνῆ S.*Aj.*1286, cf. *Fr.*341; κράνος Hld. 7.5. II. *taking the yoke well, strong, patient*, opp. δύσλοφος, νῶτον Lyc.776; αὐχήν Dam.*Isid.*89. Adv. -φως, ὑποφέρειν τι Phld.*Mort.* 35; φέρειν Dam.*Isid.*190, Eust.1653.6; ἀγωνίζεσθαι Anon.ap.Suid.

εὐλοχία, ἡ, *glorious progeny*, *Hymn.Is.*156.

εὔλοχος, ον, *helping in childbirth*, of Artemis, E.*Hipp.*166 (lyr.); Εἰλήθυια Call.*Ep.*54.

εὐλύγιστος, ον, (λυγίζω) *flexible*, *EM*530.56, Eust.73.19.

εὐλύρ-ας [ῠ], α, ὁ, = εὔλυρος, epith. of Apollo, Sapph.*Supp.*20c.5, B.*Scol.Oxy.*1361 *Fr.*12, E.*Alc.*570 (lyr.), Ar.*Th.*969 (lyr.), Limen. 4. **-ία**, ἡ, dub.l. in *PMag.Leid.V.*8.8 (fort. εὐμυρία, = -μοιρία). **-ος**, ον, (λύρα) *skilled in the lyre*, of Apollo, E.*Fr.*477; of the Muses, Ar. *Ra.*229 (lyr.); of a harper, *IG*14.1663.

εὐλῠσία, ἡ, *suppleness, ease of movement*, D.L.6.70, Muson.*Fr.*19 p.107 H.; εὐ. κοιλίας *a healthy motion* of the bowels, Cic.*Fam.*16. 18.1. II. *release, redemption*, opp. στένωσις, *PFlor.*296.21 (vi A.D.).

εὐλῦτ-έω, *discharge* a debt, prob. in Hsch. s.v. καταθεῖναι τὴν τιμήν. **-ησις**, εως, ἡ, *discharge of a debt*, *BMus.Inscr.*4.481*.307 (Ephesus). **-ος**, ον, (λύω) *easy to untie* or *loose*, X.*Cyn.*6.12; ὑποδέσεις D.S.15.44; *loose*, θύραι στροφὰς ἔχουσαι εὐ. Id.3.22. 2. *easy to relax, relaxed*, διαχωρήσιες Hp.*Prog.*18, cf. Arist.*Pr.*876^{b}31. 3. *loosely knit, supple*, of joints, Id.*Phgn.*809^{b}26 (Comp.), 811^{a}1; *loose*, of a machine, Hero *Aut.*26.3. 4. *soluble, easily dissolved*, Dsc.5.159; σπλήν *friable*, Aret.*SD*1.14; *soft, yielding*, of the *os uteri*, Hp.*Mul.* 2.115: hence metaph., *easily dissolved* or *broken*, στέργηθρα E.*Hipp.* 256 (anap.); of engagements, X.*HG*5.2.19; of health, Gal.5.443; of problems, *easy to solve*, Arist.*GA*755^{b}23, Just.*Nov.*97.6 *Intr.* 5. *easily released*, of the foetus, εὐ. πρὸς τὸν τόκον Hp.*Septim.*4 (Comp.): so metaph., στόμα εὔ. πρὸς λοιδορίαν Thphr.*Char.*6.10. b. *free from burdens, at ease*, Jul.*Caes.*315b. II. Adv. -τως *easily, freely*, οὖρα οὐκ εὐ. ἰόντα Hp.*Coac.*446; εὐ. στρέφεσθαι Hero *Aut.*18.1; εὐ. [πέλτην] μεταφέρειν D.S.5.34; *loosely*, ἐναγκυλίζεσθαι Plb.27.11.5. **-όω**, aor. 1 imper. εὐλύτωσον· ἀπάλλαξον, Hsch.

εὔλωστοι (-λαστ- cod.)· εὐφεῖς, Hsch.; cf. λωστός, λῶμα.

εὐμάθ-εια [μᾰ], ἡ, *readiness in learning, docility*, Pl.*R.*490c, Arist. *Rh.*1362^{b}24, Call.*Fr.*32 P., etc.: pl., Ph.1.326: also in poet. form **εὐμαθία**, Pl.*Chrm.*159e, *Men.*88a: Ion. -ίη *AP*6.325 (Leon. Alex.), al. **-ής**, ές, (μαθεῖν) *ready* or *quick at learning*, opp. δυσμαθής, Pl. *R.*486c, al.; τινος Id.*Ep.*344a; πρός τι D.24.17 (Comp.). Adv. -θῶς, παρακολουθεῖν Aeschin.1.116: Comp. -έστερον Pl.*Lg.*723a. II. Pass., *easy to learn* or *know, intelligible*, A.*Eu.*442, Arist.*Rh.*1409^{b}4; εὐ. φώνημα *well-known*, S.*Aj.*15; εὔγνωστα καὶ εὐ. X.*Oec.*20.14, cf. S.*Tr.*614: Comp., διήγησις Plb.14.12.5. **-ία, -ίη**, v. εὐμάθεια.

εὐμάκης [ᾱ], ες, v. εὐμήκης.

εὐμάλακτος [μᾰ], ον, *easily moulded*, Dsc.1.97; gloss on εὔστρεπτος, Eust.1453.3. II. Gramm., *liquid*, of consonants, *EM*700.24.

εὔμαλλος, ον, *of fine wool*, μίτρα Pi.*I.*5(4).62.

εὔμᾱλος, Dor. for εὔμηλος.

εὐμάρᾰθος [μᾰ], ον, *abounding in fennel*, *AP*9.318 (Leon.).

εὐμάραντος [μᾰ], ον, *soon withering*, Artem.1.77.

εὐμάρ-εια [ᾰ], ἡ, (Ion. dat. -έῃ is found in Hdt.2.35 codd., cited by Greg.Cor.p.521 S., Suid.), also -ία Pl.*Ly.*204d, but Ion. acc. -ίην only as v.l. for -είην in Hdt.4.113:—*easiness, ease, opportunity*, τινι *for doing* a thing, E.*Fr.*181; but more commonly τινος, S.*Ph.*284, 704 (lyr.); εὐ. φυγῆς Anon.ap.Suid.; τῆς ζητήσεως Arist.*Pol.*1276^a 24. 2. *ease of movement, dexterity*, χεροῖν E.*Ba.*1128, cf. Arist. *Mu.*398^{b}35. 3. of internal condition, *ease, comfort*, εὐμαρείᾳ χρώμενος πολλῇ S.*Tr.*193; but also εὐμαρείῃ (-έῃ codd.) χρᾶσθαι euphem. for *alvum exonerare, to ease oneself*, Hdt.2.35, cf. 4.113; εὐ. παρασκευάζειν to provide *easy* or *ready means*, Pl.*Lg.*738d; πρὸς τὰς ἐκ Διὸς ὥρας εὐ. μηχανᾶσθαι *provision for, protection against*, Id.*Prt.* 321a; εὐ. ἐστί c. inf., it is *easy* to.., Id.*Ly.* l.c., X.*Oec.*5.9; δι' εὐμαρείας *easily*, Luc.*Am.*13; κατὰ πολλὴν εὐ., μετὰ πάσης εὐ., Ph.2. 428, 1.670; πρὸς εὐμάρειάν τινος for his *convenience*, Luc.*Hipp.*5; ἐν πάσῃ εὐ. εὐθὺς γίνεται M.Ant.4.3. **-έω**, *have abundance*, πάντων B.1.65. **-ής**, ές, *easy, convenient*, most commonly of things, εὐμάρεα προλέξαις Alc.*Supp.*22.7; εὐ. χείρωμα an *easy* prey, A.*Ag.* 1326; δυστυχούντων γ' εὐμαρὴς ἀπαλλαγή Id.*Supp.*339; ἔνθεσις Pherecr.108.6: Comp., Ph.1.19, Ascl.*Tact.*7.3; εὐμαρές [ἐστι] c. inf., *'tis easy*, Sapph.*Supp.*5.5, Thgn.845, Simon.125.5, Pi.*P.*3.115, *N.*3.21, E.*Alc.*492; so ἐν εὐμαρεῖ [ἐστι] Id.*IA*969, *Hel.*1227, *Fr.* 382.10; [Ἡράκλειαν] ἐξ εὐμαροῦς ἔλαβεν Phleg.*Mir.*3. b. *easy to obtain, abundant, cheap*, σῖτος *IG*12(5).714.15 (Andros, iv B.C., Comp.). 2. rarely of persons, *bringing ease*, χρόνος γὰρ εὐ. θεός S.*El.*179 (lyr.); *gentle*, Aret.*SD*1.6: Comp. -έστερος *more 'in touch'*, Hp.*Decent.*13. II. Adv. -ρῶς, poet. -ρέως, *easily, readily*, πείθομαι B.5.195, cf. A.*Fr.*366, Pl.*Criti.*113e, *Lg.*706b, Luc.*Am.*53, Sor.1.33, etc.; τλήσεται εὐ. *AP*5.245 (Paul. Sil.): Comp. -έστερον *Trag.Adesp.*383, Hdn.8.7.6: Sup. -έστατα Ph.2.419; εὐμαρέως τοι χρῆμα θεοὶ δόσαν οὔτε τι δειλὸν οὔτ' ἀγαθόν Thgn.463. (From μάρη = χείρ (cf. εὐχερής) Sch.Il.15.137.) [ᾰ, for καταφαγῆμεν εὐμᾰρέα shd. be read in Epich.42.] **-ίη**, ἡ, v. εὐμάρεια.

εὔμᾱρις [later ᾰ (v. infr.)], ιδος, ἡ, acc. εὔμαριν A.*Pers.*660 (lyr.); but acc. pl. εὐμαρίδας (sic) Lyc.855 (on the accent, v. Hdn.Gr.1.99):—*an Asiatic shoe* or *slipper* (made of deerskin, Poll.7.90), βαρβάροις ἐν εὐμάρισι E.*Or.*1370 (lyr.); κροκόβαπτον..εὔμαριν ἀείρων A. l.c.; βαθύπελμος εὔμᾰρις *AP*7.413 (Antip.), cf. Lyc. l.c. (Prob. a foreign word.)

εὐμᾰρότης, ητος, ἡ, = εὐμάρεια, Callistr.*Stat.*3.

εὐμάχᾰνος [μᾱ], ον, Dor. for εὐμήχανος.

εὔμᾰχος, ον, *easy to fight against, assailable*, Max.Tyr.26.2 (Sup.).

εὐμεγέθης, ες, *of good size, large*, Ar.*Pl.*543, Eub.110; ἀστράγαλος Aen.Tact.31.17; ποταμὸς μάλα εὐ. X.*HG*5.2.4; *tall*, γυνή *AP*5.37 (Nicarch.), cf. *PLips.*1.3 (ii B.C.), etc. 2. *considerable, weighty, important*, μαρτυρία D.23.16; πρᾶγμα Ph.2.196.

εὐμέζεος (-μάξεως cod.)· εὐφυής (ἐφυεὶς cod.) τοῖς αἰδοίοις, Hsch.

εὐμεθόδευτος, ον, = sq. II, Ptol.*Alm.*1.10; *having a good method*, ἰατρός Steph. *in Hp.*2.317 D.

εὐμέθοδος, ον, *easily compassed* or *discovered*, Archim.*Spir.Praef.*; *well-arranged*, τὸ εὐ. Lyd.*Mag.*3.53, Olymp. *in Alc.*p.131 C., Alex. Trall.*Praef.* Adv. -δως Id.1.11, Aristaenet.1.13, Hierocl. *in CA Praef.*p.416 M. II. of persons, *scientific*, ἰατρός Alex.Trall.1.12.

εὐμέθυστος, ον, *easily made drunk*, Gp.7.34.2.

εὐμειδής, ές, *smiling, propitious*, A.R.4.715, Call.*Dian.*129.

εὐμείλικτος, ον, *easily appeased*, Corn.*ND*12:—also **εὐμειλής**, ές, and **εὐμ⟨ε⟩ίλῐχος**, ον, Hsch.

εὐμέλαθρος, ον, *with fair halls*, *Trag.Adesp.* in *Gött.Nachr.*1922. 25.

εὐμέλᾰνος, ον, *well-blackened, inky*, βροχίς *AP*6.295.4 (Phan.).

εὐμέλ-εια, ἡ, *melody*, D.S.4.84, Plu.2.456b, etc. 2. *melodious language*, Longin.28.2; v.l. for ἐμμ-, D.H.*Comp.*18; εὐ. φωνῆς Phld.*Rh.*1.196 S. **-ής**, ές, *melodious*, μουσική Arist.*Pol.*1341^{b}26, Sopat.10; opp. ἐμμελής (metrical), D.H.*Comp.*11, etc.: generally, *agreeable*, συμπόσια Pl.*Ax.*371d. Adv. -λῶς *gracefully*, Macho ap. Ath.13.577d. II. *with stout limbs*, Ael.*Fr.*110.

εὐμελῐτέω, *to have a good stock of honey*, Arist.*HA*625^{a}24, Thphr. *HP*6.2.3.

εὐμένεια, ἡ, poet. -ία Pi.*P.*12.4:—*goodwill, favour*, ἡμῖν..παρὰ τῶν θεῶν..εὐ. εἴη Hdt.2.45, cf. S.*OC*631, E.*Hel.*313, X.*Ap.*7, Pl. *Smp.*197d, etc.; ἡ πρὸς τὸ θεῖον εὐ. the *favour* of the gods (v. πρός) Th.5.105; ἡ συναντωμένη τισὶν εὐ. παρὰ τοῦ δαιμονίου *SIG*601.14 (Teos, ii B.C.); ἐπ' εὐμενείᾳ to gain *favour*, Luc.*Tox.*1; σὺν εὐμενίᾳ *kindly*, Pi. l.c. II. of smell, *pleasantness*, Thphr.*CP*6.14.12.

Εὐμέν-ειος, α, ον, Adj. of Εὐμένης, pr. n. of two kings of Pergamum, στρατιῶται Polyaen.4.6.13. II. **-εια**, τά, festival in honour of Eumenes II of Pergamum, at Pergamum, *OGI*267.34; at Aegina, ib.329.40; at Sardes, ib.305.9. **-ειος**, ὁ (sc. -μήν), name of month at Pergamum, ib.338.2. **-έτης**, ου, ὁ, poet. for εὐμενής, *well-wisher*, χάρματα δ' εὐμενέτῃσι Od.6.185, *IG*12(8).23 (Lemnos, ii A.D.):—fem. **-έτειρα**, Hsch. **-έω**, *to be gracious*, Ps.-Phoc.142, Opp.*C.*1.9, etc.; τινι to one, A.R.2.260, Theoc.17.62. II. c. acc., *deal kindly with*, ἀνεψιόν Pi.*P.*4.127 (s.v.l.); but also, 2. Pass., of benefits *graciously bestowed*, *IPE*1^2.362.12 (Cherson.). **-ής**, ές, (μένος) *well-disposed, kindly*, τινι *to* one, epith. of gods, *h.Hom.* 22.7 (not in Il. or Od.), Pi.*P.*2.25, A.*Supp.*686 (lyr.), cf. X.*HG*6.4. 2; ἵλεως καὶ εὐ. Id.*Cyr.*1.6.2, Theoc.5.18; Ἑρμῆς *IGRom.*1.1228 (Egypt, ii A.D.); τὸ τῶν θεῶν εὐ. D.4.45. 2. of men, A.*Pers.*175

(troch.), *Supp.*488 (Comp.); πόλει S.*Ant.*212, etc.; εὐ. πρός τι *well-disposed* for it, Plu.*Luc.*42; τὸ εὐ., = εὐμένεια, Pl.*Lg.*792e; ξεῖνος δὲ ξείνῳ..-έστατον πάντων Hdt.7.237: in Dor. Prose, *Schwyzer* 84 (Argos, v B.C.). **3.** of actions, etc., εὐμενεῖ τύχᾳ, νόῳ, Pi.*O.*14.15, *P.*8.18; εὐ. ὀλολυγμός *signifying goodwill, friendly*, A.*Th.*268. **4.** of places and things, γῆ εὐ. ἐναγωνίσασθαι *favourable* to fight in, Th.2.74; εὐμενεῖ ποτῷ (of a river) *kindly, bounteous*, A.*Pers.*487; of the air, *mild, soft*, Thphr.*CP*2.1.6; so of medicines, *beneficial*, ὑποχονδρίῳ καὶ σπλάγχνοισιν Hp.*Acut.*59, cf. Aret.*CA*1.3; but also, *agreeable*, [κόμμι] -έστερον κόλλης Hp.*Art.*33; of a road, *easy*, X.*An.*4.6.12 (Comp.). **II.** Adv. -νῶς, Ion. -έως, A.*Ag.*952, Pl.*Phd.*89a, A.R.2.1275, etc.: Comp. -έστερον E.*Hel.*1298, Pl.*Lg.*718d; also -εστέρως Isoc.4.43, D.H.*Rh.*5. **-ία**, ἡ, v. εὐμένεια. **-ίδες** (sc. θεαί), αἱ, strictly *the gracious goddesses*, euphem. of *the* Ἐρινύες or Furies, name of play by A.; ὥς σφας καλοῦμεν Εὐμενίδας, ἐξ εὐμενῶν στέρνων δέχεσθαι τὸν ἱκέτην S.*OC*486; ὀνομάζειν γὰρ αἰδοῦμαι θεὰς Εὐμενίδας E.*Or.*38; distd. from the σεμναὶ θεαί by Philem.217. **-ίζομαι**, *propitiate*, ἥρωας X.*Cyr.*3.3.22, cf. Ael.*NA*7.44; τινα διά τινος App.*BC*4.54. **-ικός**, ἡ, όν, *like the* εὐμενής, of persons, Arist.*VV* 1251^{b}32; διόρθωσις Plb.12.7.6. **-ισταί**, οἱ, *guild of worshippers of Eumenes*, *Ath.Mitt.*27.172.

εὐμερδής· εὔρωστος, Hsch.; cf. εὐσμερδής.

εὐμέριστος, ον, (μερίζω) *easily divided*, Thphr.*CP*6.10.8. **2.** *easily calculated*, Hp.*Septim.*3.

εὐμετα-βλησία, ἡ, *changeableness*, Sch.Th.3.37. **-βλητος**, ον, (μεταβάλλω) *easily changed, changeable*, Arist.*Rh.*1373^{a}30, M.Ant.5.33, etc.; of food, *easy of digestion*, Hp.*Alim.*49; τὸ εὐ., = foreg., Aesop.367, Iamb.*Protr.*21.κϛʹ. Adv. -τως Sch.Th.3.37. **-βολος**, ον, = foreg., *changeable*, of things and persons, Gorg.*Hel.*13, Pl.*R.*503c, X.*HG*2.3.32, Arist.*EN*1100^{b}3, etc.; εὐ. ἐστὶν..βίος Diph.118; ἀνὴρ εὐ. γλώσσῃ LXX *Pr.*17.20; τὸ εὐ., = εὐμεταβλησία, M.Ant.4.3; τὸ εὐ. τῆς τύχης Diogenian.Epicur.2.60. **-γνωτος**, ον, *fickle*, Vett.Val.304.28 (nisi leg. -γνωστος).

εὐμετάγωγος [ᾰ], ον, *easy to put aside, get rid of*, Gal.19.558; *easily moved*, Antyll.ap.Orib.45.2.2.

εὐμετά-δοτος, ον, *readily imparting, generous*, 1*Ep.Ti.*6.18, Vett.Val.46.24, al., Herm.*in Phdr.*p.94 A.; τὸ εὐ. *generosity*, M.Ant.1.14. **II.** Pass., *easily imparted*, μυστήρια Sch.Ar.*Pl.*1014; of leprosy, *contagious*, Paul.Aeg.4.1. Adv. -τως Hsch. s.v. εὐσυναλλάκτως. **-θετος**, ον, *easily changing*, πρὸς ἔλεον Plu.2.799c; *changeable, fickle*, Id.*Dio*53, Vett.Val.243.30, App.*Mac.*16. **II.** *portable*, Gal.11.215. **-κίνητος** [ῑ], ον, *easily moved* or *changed*, ἐπὶ τὸ χεῖρον Arist.*Metaph.*1019^{a}28; τὸ εὐ. *caprice*, M.Ant.1.16. **-κόμιστος**, ον, *ready to migrate*, Sch.Th.1.2. **2.** *portable*, Aët.1.39. **-κύλιστος** [ῠ], ον, *easy to roll over*, τὸ τῆς βάσεως (sc. τῆς τύχης) εὐ. Gal.*Protr.*2. **-νόητος**, ον, *inconstant, fickle*, Vett.Val.11.17, al. **-πειστος**, *easy to persuade*, Arist.*EN*1151^{b}6, Them.*Or.*7.98b. **-ποίητος**, ον, *easily altered*, ὑπὸ φύσιος καὶ ὑπὸ τύχης Hp.*Decent.*13. **-πτωτος**, ον, *unstable*, παιδία Thphr.*Sens.*45; τὸ τῆς τύχης εὐ. D.S.9.10, cf. Secund.*Sent.*9. Adv. -τως v.l. in Arr.*Epict.*2.22.8. **-ρρευστος**, ον, *easily diverted from its course*, χυμός Aët.5.57 (-ρυστός ed.). **-στᾰτος**, ον, *unsteady, changeable*, Plu.2.5d. **-τρεπτος**, ον, *revocable*, gloss on παλινάγρετον, Sch.Il.1.526, cf. Suid. s.v. ἀβέβαιος. **2.** τὸ εὐ. *easy convertibility*, Gal.6.825. **-φορος**, ον, *easily moved*: *moving quickly*, ὀφθαλμοί *EM*255.52; gloss on θοός, Sch.A.R.1.741. **-χείριστος**, ον, *manageable*, of persons, Isoc.*Ep.*2.20, Pl.*Phdr.*240a, X.*An.*2.6.20; of things, Onos.6.5; λόγος -ότερος Isoc.*Ep.*9.2; σώματα εὐ. τῇ τέχνῃ Max.Tyr.10.3; χρεία εὐ. πρὸς τὸ ζῆν Arist.*Pol.*1257^{a}37. **2.** *easy to cope with*, ἰσχύς Th.6.85, cf. X.*HG*5.2.15; of persons, D.H.8.6 (Comp.). **II.** in Act. signf., Adv. -τως *handily, adroitly*, τῇ ἀσπίδι χρῆσθαι Philostr.*Gym.*19, cf. Eustr.*in EN*343.32.

εὐμετρ-ία, ἡ, *good measure* or *proportion*, Aret.*CA*2.3; θεία εὐ. Hierocl.*in CA*23 p.468 M., cf. Longin.*Proll.Heph.*5. **2.** *excellence of metre*, Eust.1414.9. **-ος**, ον, *well-measured, well-calculated*, σφενδόνα A.*Ag.*1010 (lyr.); *well-proportioned*, v.l. for ἔμμητρον, Theoc.25.209. **2.** *of moderate size* or *proportions*, οἶκος Aret.*CA*1.1. Adv. -ως ib.1.6, Sor.1.86. **3.** *excellent in metre*, [λέξις] εὔ. καὶ εὔρυθμος D.H.*Comp.*25; opp. κακόμετρος, Phld.*Po.*1676.8.

εὐμήκης, Dor. **εὐμάκης** [ᾱ], ες, (μῆκος) *tall*, Pl.*Prm.*127b, Thphr.*HP*3.9.2, Theoc.14.25; *long*, ξυστοί Jul.*Or.*2.60a: Comp. -έστερος Arist.*PA*696^{a}17: Sup. -έστατος *PPetr.*2 p.14 (iii B.C.), Str.5.2.5. **2.** *considerable, great*, τύχαι E.*IA*595 (anap.). **3.** εὔμηκες, τό, kind of *balsam*, Plin.*HN*12.114.

εὔμηλος, Dor. **εὔμᾱλος**, ον, *rich in sheep*, Od.15.406, *h.Ap.*54, Pi.*O.*6.100, Simon.103, Theoc.22.157, etc.

εὔμηρος, ον, *with beautiful thighs*, Poll.2.187, 9.162.

εὐμήρῡτος, ον, (μηρύω) *easy to spin out*, Luc.*Fug.*12.

εὔμητις, ιδος, ὁ, ἡ, *wise, prudent*, Opp.*H.*5.97, *AP*9.59.8 (Antip. ⟨Thess.⟩), prob. in Phld.*Rh.*2.14 S.

εὐμηχάν-ημα [χᾰ], ατος, τό, *ingenious contrivance*, dub. in Chrysipp.ap.*EM*701.25 (cf. *Stoic.*2.318). **-ία**, Dor. **εὐμᾱχ-**, ἡ, *skill in devising means*, c. inf., Pi.*I.*4(3).2, *Pae.*7 *Fr.*16.11; = εὐπορία, *Stoic.*3.64, Plu.*Tim.*16; *inventive skill*, Andronic.Rhod.p.578 M., Luc.*Phal.*1.12. **-ος**, Dor. **εὐμάχ-** [μᾱ], ον, **I.** of persons, *skilful in contriving, inventive*, opp. ἀμήχανος, A.*Eu.*381 (lyr.), Pl.*Prt.*344d, etc.: c. gen., εὐμήχανος λόγου Id.*Cra.*408b; ἁλίων εὐ. ἔργων Opp.*H.*4.593: with a Prep., εὐ. πρὸς τὸν βίον, of birds, *full of devices* for supporting life, Arist.*HA*614^{b}34, cf. 616^{b}34: Sup., of the bee, *Gp.*15.3.1; ἔν τινι D.S.20.92: τὸ εὐ., = foreg., Plu.2.830c. Adv. -νως Ph.1.170, Plu.*Per.*31, Aristaenet.2.15, etc. **II.** Pass., of things, *skilfully contrived, ingenious*, ἐκ τῶν ἀμηχάνων πόρους εὐμηχάνους πορίζων Ar.*Eq.*759 (-ος πορίζειν Bentl.); ἐπίνοιαι Pl.*R.*600a.

εὔμικτος, ον, *social*, Them.*Or.*22.270d. **2.** of a road, *frequented*, v.l. for εὐεπίμικτος, Poll.3.96.

εὐμίμητος [ῑ], ον, *easily imitated*, Pl.*R.*605a.

εὐμιξία, ἡ, *happy union*, *Sammelb.*5656.7 (vi A.D.).

εὐμίσητος [ι], ον, *well-hated*, in Sup., X.*Cyr.*3.1.9, Longin.*Rh.*p.198 H.

εὔμῐτος, ον, *with fine threads*, εὐμίτοις πλοκαῖς, i.e. τὸν μίτον εὖ πλέκουσα, E.*IT*817.

εὔμιτρος, ον, *with beautiful* μίτρα (q.v.), Mosch.4.98.

ἐϋμμελίης, ὁ, (εὖ, μελία) *armed with good ashen spear*, ἐϋμμελίω (Ion. gen.) Πριάμοιο Il.4.47, al.; Πάνθου υἱὸς ἐϋμμελίης 17.9, cf. Od.3.400, Hes.*Sc.*368, etc.: Dor. gen. ἐϋμμελία *APl.*1.6.

εὔμναστος, ον, Dor. for εὔμνηστος.

εὐμνημόνευτος, ον, *easy to remember*, Pl.*Ti.*18c, d, D.56.45, Aen.Tact.24.14, Ath.7.277c, etc.: Comp. -ότερος Arist.*Rh.*1367^{a}26: Sup., ib.1409^{b}6. **II.** *at one's fingers' ends*, ἔστω σοι εὐ. φάρμακα Hp.*Decent.*9.

εὐμνήμων, ον, gen. ονος, in Adv. Comp. -εστέρως, ἔχειν to be *easier to remember*, X.*Ages.*11.1.

εὔμνηστος, Dor. **-μναστος**, ον, *well-remembering, mindful*, τινος S.*Tr.*108 (lyr.); χρηστήριον Boeo 1.

εὐμογία, poet. **-ίη**, ἡ, *industry*, Aglaïas 4.

εὐμοιρ-ᾱτέω, = sq., Ti.Locr.99e. **-έω**, *to be well off for*, c. gen., Hp.*Ep.*27, Phalar.*Ep.*53 (v.l. for εὐπορεῖν), Anon.*Fig.*p.156 S.; εὐμοίρει, in Epitaphs, *IG*14.2387, etc. **-ία**, ἡ, *happy possession* of a thing, σώματος, φωνῆς, Luc.*Eun.*8, *Salt.*72; εὐ. τῆς αἱρέσεως *excelling*, Id.*Rh.Pr.*8; φύσεως εὐ. Ph.1.238, al.: abs., D.H.*Rh.*5.3; *good fortune*, Plu.2.14c, etc. **-ίτης** [ῑ], ου, ὁ, = μακαρίτης, of the dead, *IG*14.555 (Catana), 2300 (Comum, v A.D.). **-ος**, ον, *well-endowed by fortune*, B.5.1; opp. ἄμοιρος, Pl.*Smp.*197d, cf. Ph.1.282, Call.*Del.*295, *AP*6.278 (Rhian.), Luc.*JConf.*19. Adv. -ρως, ἀποθανεῖν J.*AJ*8.12.6; βιώσασα *IG*12(5).319 (Paros): Comp. -ότερον, ἀποθνῄσκειν App.*Hann.*29.

εὐμολπ-έω, *sing well*, *h.Merc.*478. **-ία**, ἡ, *sweet song*, Hsch.: title of poem by Musaeus, Paus.10.5.6. **-ος**, ον, *sweetly singing*, *AP*9.396 (Paul. Sil.): as pr. n. in *h.Cer.*154, etc.

εὐμορφία, ἡ, *beauty of form*, Democr.294, E.*Tr.*936, Pl.*Smp.*218e; σώματος Id.*Lg.*716a; λόγων εὐμορφίαι E.*Cyc.*317, cf. *AP*9.400 (Pall.); εὐμορφίαι τῶν ὄψεων J.*AJ*10.10.1; χολῆς λοβοῦ τε...εὐ. *symmetry* in the σπλάγχνα, A.*Pr.*495; αἱ ἐκ τῶν διδασκαλείων εὐ. *elegances* of the School (in Rhet.), Epicur.*Fr.*50.

εὐμορφολογέω, gloss on ἀστειορρημονέω, Zonar.

εὔμορφ-ος, ον, *fair of form, comely, goodly*, Sapph.76 (Comp.), Hdt.1.196, A.*Ag.*416, 454 (both lyr.); σῶμα...εὔ. ἰδεῖν S.*Fr.*88.10: γαμεταί, ἀνδράποδα, D.H.11.2, Ph.2.478 (Sup.): metaph., εὔ. κράτος A.*Ch.*490. **-ότης**, ητος, ἡ, *comeliness*, Sch.Opp.*H.*1.505. **-όω**, *become beautiful*, dub. l. in Vett.Val.344.9.

εὐμουσ-ία, ἡ, *sense for beauty and art*, πραγμάτων εὐ. E.*Fr.*188, cf. Ps.-Plu.*Vit.Hom.*92; *skill in music*, Men.Rh.p.443 S. **II.** *good music*, κινεῖ ἡμᾶς ἡ εὐ., ἐνοχλεῖ δ' ἡ ἀμουσία *Placit.*4.20.2; *sweetness of song*, Arg.Theoc.5. **-ος**, ον, *skilled in the arts*, esp. *in poetry, music, and dancing*, Man.4.60, 5.269; but usu., **2.** *musical, melodious*, μολπά E.*IT*145 (lyr.); τιμαί Ar.*Th.*112 (lyr.); παιδιά Luc.*Am.*53; χεύματα *AP*9.661 (Jul.). Adv. -σως *gracefully*, Corn.*ND* 14, Plu.2.1119d.

εὔμοχθος, ον, *laborious*, γυμνάς (= γυμνάσιον) *Epigr.Gr.*239, cf. *IG*3.758*a*.

εὔμῡθος, ον, *eloquent*, *AP*4.3b.61 (Agath.).

εὔμῡκος, ον, *loud-bellowing*, *AP*6.255 (Eryc., dub. l.); βουκόλια ib.9.104 (Alph.).

εὔμωλος, ον, (μῶλος) = ἀγαθὸς πολεμιστής, εὔοπλος, Hsch. (-μολ- cod.): Sup. -ότατον, = ἁπαλόν, νεώτατον, Id.

εὐνάεις, εσσα, εν, v. εὐνάων.

εὐνάζω, fut. -άσω [ᾰ] Od.4.408, X.*Cyn.*9.3; Dor. εὐνάξω Pi. (v. infr.): aor. ηὔνᾰσα E.*Rh.*762, εὔνασα Simon.184.10, A.R.3.1000:—Med., v. infr.:—Pass., Od.5.65: aor. 1 ηὐνάσθην or εὐν-, Pi.*P.*3.25, E.*Ion*17, 1484, (ξυν-) S.*OT*982; Ep. 3 pl. εὔνασθεν (κατ-) Il.3.448: pf. ηὔνασμαι (κατ-) E.*Rh.*611: (εὐνή):—mostly poet., cf. εὐνάω: **1.** *lay* or *place in ambush*, ἔνθα σ' ἐγὼν..εὐνάσω ἑξείης Od.4.408. **2.** *put to bed, put to sleep*, οὔ σε παιηόνων ἄδορπον εὐνάξομεν Pi.*Pae.*6.128, cf. A.R.4.1060, etc.; of animals, *lay* their young *in a form*, X.*Cyn.*9.3: metaph., of death, *lay asleep*, S.*OT*961, cf. *Tr.*1042 (lyr.), E.*Rh.*762; so βάρβιτον οὐδὲ θανὼν εὔνασεν εἰν Ἀΐδῃ Simon. l.c.; *calm, soothe*, εὐνάζειν...βλεφάρων πόθον S.*Tr.*106 (lyr.); χόλον A.R.3.1000:—Pass., *go to bed, sleep*, Hom., only in Od., ἐν προδόμῳ εὐνάζετο δῖος Ὀδυσσεύς 20.1; εὐνάζοντο κατὰ μέγαρα 23.299, cf. Hes.*Op.*339, etc.; σκληρῶς εὐ. X.*Cyn.*12.2; also ἔνθα δέ τ' ὄρνιθες..εὐνάζοντο there they *used to roost*, Od.5.65; of sexual intercourse, παρ' ἀνδράσιν εὐνάζεσθαι ib.119; so θεαῖς εὐνάζεται *h.Ven.*190; θεῷ E.*Ion*17; εὐνάσθη ξένου λέκτροισιν Pi.*P.*3.25; εὐνάσθην ὑπὸ σπαργάνοις Id.*Fr.*193; γάμοις..βασιλικοῖς εὐνάζεται E.*Med.*18; Φοίβῳ κρυπτόμενον λέχος ηὐνάσθην Id.*Ion*1484 (lyr.); of animals, Arist.*HA*609^{b}23:—so in Med., κούρῳ παρθένος εὐνάσατο Call.*Aet.*3.1.1. **3.** *give in marriage*, τέκνα E.*Fr.*17. **4.** of pain, *lull, deaden*, τὴν ταλαιπωρίην Aret.*CA*2.1:—Pass., σὺ γάρ μ' ἀπ' εὐνασθέντος ἐκκινεῖς κακοῦ S.*Tr.*1242.

εὐνᾰής, ές, *fair-flowing*, B.8.42, 1.75 (p.439 J.).

εὐναῖος, α, ον, (εὐνή) *in one's bed* or *couch*, εὐ. [λαγώς] a hare *in its form*, X.*Cyn*.5.9; εὐ. [ἴχνη] traces *of the form*, ib.7, cf. S.*Fr*.174, *Ichn*. 226, Stratt.3 (dub. l.). 2. mostly of the marriage-bed, εὐ. δάμαρ, γαμέτας, A.*Fr*.383, E.*Supp*.1028 (lyr.); Κύπρις Id.*Andr*.179; εὐ. γάμοι A.*Supp*.332; ἄτα εὐ., of Helen, E.*Andr*.104 (eleg.); λέχος Critias 2.6 D.; θάλαμοι *BCH*29.412 (Callatis). 3. *keeping one's bed*, λύπᾳ εὐναίᾳ δέδεται ψυχά E.*Hipp*.160 (lyr.); εὐ. πτέρυγες *brooding*, of a bird on the nest, *AP*9.95 (Alph.). 4. εὐναία, ἡ, *a nest* (v. sub καρφηρός); but εὐναῖα, τά, *bed*, is f.l. in Orph.*L*.223. 5. personified, Εὐναίη, ἡ, *the Spirit of Repose*, Emp.123.1. II. (εὐνή II) *of* or *for anchorage*: hence, generally, *steadying, guiding a ship*, πηδάλια E.*IT*432 (lyr.). 2. as Subst., εὐναία, = εὐνή II, *an anchor*, λίθος εὐναίης A.R.1.955: in pl., ib.1277.

εὐνάν, ᾶνος, ὁ (masc. acc. to Lupercus, sine expl., fem. acc. to others, = γυνή), Pi.*Fr*.303.

εὐν-άσιμος, ον, *good for sleeping in*: εὐνάσιμα, τά, *convenient sleeping-places*, X.*Cyn*.8.4. **-αστήρ**, ῆρος, ὁ, (εὐνάζω) = εὐνητήρ, Lyc. 144:—fem. **εὐνάστειρα**, metaph., Androm.ap.Gal.14.36. II. *serving as an anchor*, λίθος Opp.*H*.3.373. **-ᾱτήρ, -άτειρα, -άτρια, -άτωρ**, v. εὐνητ-. **-ᾱτήριον**, τό, *bed-chamber*, A.*Pers*.160 (troch.), S.*Tr*.918 (pl.); *marriage-chamber*, E.*Or*.590. (**εὐναστήριον** is a later form found in codd. of S. and E. ll. cc.) **-άω**, fut. -ήσω *AP*10.12: aor. 1 εὔνησα Od.4.440:—**Pass.**, aor. 1 εὐνήθην v. infr., etc.: pf. εὔνημαι *AP*7.397 (Eryc.): (εὐνή):—poet. Verb, = εὐνάζω, rare in Trag.: 1. *lay* or *place in ambush*, ἑξείης δ' εὔνησε [ἡμᾶς] Od. l. c. 2. *lay asleep, lull to sleep*, φρουρὸν ὄφιν A.R.4.87: metaph., τῆς δ' εὔνησε γόον Od. 4.758; κάματον, ἐλπίδας, χόλον, *AP*10.12, 4.3b.41 (Agath.), Nonn.*D*. 13.276:—Pass., *make one's couch*, prob. in S.*Aj*.604 (lyr.); *lie asleep*, esp. of death, εὐνήθης ὕπνον ὀφειλόμενον *AP*7.78 (Dionys. Cyz.), cf. 397 (Eryc.); πόλλ' ἐν κακοῖσι θυμὸς εὐνηθεὶς ὁρᾷ S.*Fr*.661; of a dog, *to lie kennelled*, Id.*OC*1571 (lyr.):—Hom. only in aor. Pass., of the winds, παύσασθαι δ' ἐκέλευσε καὶ εὐνηθῆναι Od.5.384; elsewh. of sexual intercourse, 10.296, al.; φιλότητι or ἐν φιλότητι εὐνηθέντε, Il. 3.441, 14.314, cf. 331, al.: c. dat. pers., *to be bedded with*.., θεὰ βροτῷ εὐνηθεῖσα, γυνὴ θεῷ εὐνηθεῖσα, 2.821, 16.176; παρ' ἀνδράσιν εὐνηθεῖσαι Hes.*Th*.967. II. Med., *stupefy* with narcotics, Aret.*CA*2.5.

εὐνάων, ουσα, ον, (νάω) *fair-flowing, liquid*, ἀπ' εὐνάοντος οὐρανοῦ dub. l. in A.*Fr*.44 (v.l. εὐνάεντος).

εὐνεικής, ές, *easy to decide*, of a suit: hence, *easy to interpret*, of an oracle, Antim.75.

εὐνέτης, ου, ὁ, (εὐνή) = εὐναστήρ, E.*Or*.1392 (lyr.), *AP*9.241 (Antip. ⟨Thess.⟩):—fem. **εὐνέτις**, ιδος, Hp.*Epid*.7.42, A.R.4.96, etc.

εὔνεως, ων, (ναῦς) *well furnished with ships*, Max.Tyr.5.5, 31.7.

εὐν-ή, ἡ, Ep. gen. sg. and pl. εὐνῆφι, -φιν Od.2.2, al.:—*bed*, εὐνῇ ἐνὶ μαλακῇ Il.9.618, etc.; ἔβη εἰς εὐνήν Od.1.427, etc.; ὤρνυτ' ἄρ' ἐξ εὐνῆφιν Od.2.2, al.: in Cret. Prose, εὐνά *Schwyzer* 180. 2. *bedding*, dist. fr. λέχος (the bedstead), λέχος πόρσυνε καὶ εὐνήν Od.3.403; ἐκθεῖσαι πυκινὸν λέχος ἐμβάλετ' εὐνήν 23.179; cf. ἐνεύναιος. b. esp. of soldiers in the field, Th.3.112, 4.32, 6.67, Pl.*R*.415e, A.*Ag*.559, E. *Rh*.1 (anap.). 3. εὐναὶ νυμφάων their *abode*, Il.24.615; of animals, συφεοὺς δυοκαίδεκα ποίει.. εὐνὰς συσί Od.14.14; *lair* of a deer, 4.338, Il.11.115; [νεβρὸν] ἐξ εὐνῆφι θορόντα 15.580; *form* of a hare, X.*Cyn*. 6.16; *nest*, S.*Ant*.425; κριοῦ εὐναί, a place in Colchis where the ram of Phrixus rested, A.R.4.116. 4. *marriage-bed*, μεμνημένος οὔτε τι σίτου οὔτ' εὐνῆς Il.24.130; εὐνῆς ἐπιβήμεναι 9.133; ἐξ εὐνῆς ἀνστᾶσα 14.336; usu. with some word added to denote this, ἔτλην ἀνέρος εὐνήν 18.433; ἀνδρὸς ἐν εὐνῇ ἤθελον εὐνηθῆναι Od.4.333; ἀπανήνασθαι θεοῦ εὐνήν 10.297; ἐμίγην φιλότητι καὶ εὐνῇ Il.3.445, etc.; ζαλωτὸν ὁμόφρονος εὐνᾶς Pi.*O*.7.6; εὐναῖς ἀνανδρώτοισι S.*Tr*.109 (lyr.); εὐναὶ γαμήλιοι, νυμφίδιοι, κρύφιαι, E.*Med*.1027, *Alc*.886 (anap.), *El*.720 (lyr.); without such a word, Διὸς εὐναί Pi.*P*.2.27; ἄλλην τιν' εὐνὴν ἀντὶ σοῦ στέργει πόσις; E.*Andr*.907, cf. *Hipp*.1011; of Pyrrha and Deucalion, ἄτερ εὐνᾶς κτισσάσθαν λίθινον γόνον Pi.*O*.9.44; ὅσιος ἀπ' εὐνᾶς E.*Ion* 150 (lyr.). 5. *one's last bed, the grave*, ἔνθα σ' ἔχουσιν εὐναί A. *Ch*.318 (lyr.); εἰς εὐνὴν πατρός S.*El*.436; Ἄϊδος εὐνάς *Epigr.Gr*.431 (Antioch.) (so some take Τυφωέος εὐναί in Il.2.783). II. pl. εὐναί, *stones thrown out from the prow and used as anchors*, ἐκ δ' εὐνὰς ἔβαλον, κατὰ δὲ πρυμνήσι' ἔδησαν Il.1.436, = Od.15.498; ὕψι δ' ἐπ' εὐνάων ὁρμίσσομεν we will let the ships ride *at anchor* in deep water, Il.14.77; εὐνὰς δ' ἔνθ' ἔβαλον κατὰ βένθεος Q.S.12.346; even of iron anchors, Sch.Il.1.436.—Rare in early Prose, X.*Mem*.3.11.8: in pl., Th.ll. cc., Pl.*Prt*.321a, *R*.415e, *Plt*.272a. **-ῆθεν**, Adv. *from, out of bed*, Od. 20.124, A.R.2.197. **-ημα**, ατος, τό, (εὐνάω) *marriage*, E.*Ion* 304 (pl.).

εὔνησος, ον, *with beautiful islands*, πόλις Nonn.*D*.41.15.

εὐν-ητήρ, Dor. **-ᾱτήρ**, ῆρος, ὁ, (εὐνάω) *a bedfellow, husband*, A.*Pers*. 137 (lyr.); of fish, Opp.*H*.4.383:—fem. **-ήτειρα** (Dor. form used by Trag.), θεοῦ μὲν εὐ. *partner of his bed*, A.*Pers*.157 (troch.); εὐ. Διὸς λεχέων Id.*Pr*.895 (lyr.), cf. Theoc.*Syrinx* 1: metaph., εὐνήτειρα νὺξ ἔργων *that makes* works *cease*, A.R.4.1058. II. χιτὼν εὐνητήρ a *night*-shirt, *Com.Adesp*.920. **-ήτης**, ου, Dor. **-άτας**, ὁ, = εὐνητήρ, E.*Med*.159 (lyr.), cf. Hsch.:—fem. **-ήτρια**, S.*Tr*.922 codd. (leg. -άτρια). **-ήτωρ**, Dor. **-άτωρ**, ορος, ὁ, = εὐνητήρ, A.*Supp*.665 (lyr.), E.*Ion* 912 (lyr.), *HF*27, 97.

εὔνια, ων, τά, *beds*, ἐξ εὐνίων ἀναπηδᾶν App.*BC*5.117, Anon.ap. Suid.

εὐνίκητος [ῑ], Dor. **-ᾱτος**, ον, *easily overcome*, Gal.1.338 (Sup.); ταῖς πρὸς ἄνδρα κοίταις Myia *Ep*.1.

εὖνις (A), ὁ, ἡ, acc. εὖνιν, gen. εὔνιδος and εὔνιος Hdn.Gr.2.641, nom. pl. εὔνιδες and εὔνιες (v. infr.):—*reft of, bereaved of*, c. gen., ὅς μ' υἱῶν .. εὖνιν ἔθηκε Il.22.44; ψυχῆς τε καὶ αἰῶνός σε.. εὖνιν ποιήσας Od.9. 524; βραχίονες εὔνιδες ὤμων *lacking*.., Emp.57.2; εὔνιες ἀνδρείων ἀχέων *free from*..., Id.147.2; γέενναν εὖνιν πατρός A.*Ch*.247, cf. 794 (lyr.); εὖνιν ἔθηκ' ἀρετῆς *IG*14.2100: abs., *bereaved of children*, πολλὰς Περσίδων.. ἔκτισσαν εὔνιδας ἠδ' ἀνάνδρους A.*Pers*.289 (lyr.).

εὖνις (B), ιδος, ἡ, (on the accent cf. Hdn.Gr.1.95), = εὐνέτις, *bedfellow, wife*, S.*Tr*.563, E.*Or*.929, *IA*397 (troch.), 807, *AP*9.355 (Leon. Alex.).—Masc. in *EM*393.38.

ἐΰννητος, ον, Ep. for εὔνητος (νέω), *well spun* or *woven*, οἱ δὲ χιτῶνας εἵατ' ἐϋννήτους Il.18.596, cf. 24.580; πέπλοι λεπτοὶ ἐΰννητοι Od.7.97.

εὐνο-έω, *to be well-inclined* or *favourable*, c. dat., τοῖσι ἐμοῖσι πρήγμασι Hdt.7.237; τινι S.*Aj*.689, Lys.13.13, Ar.*Nu*.1411, X.*Oec*.12.5, etc.; ὀμνύω.. εὐνοήσειν Καίσαρι *OGI*532.9 (Galatia, Aug.); τῷ ἀντιδίκῳ *be at peace with*, *Ev.Matt*.5.25: abs., Hdt.9.79; ὁ εὐνοῶν one's *well-wisher*, Arist.*EE*1241ᵃ11:—Med., Phalar.*Ep*.119:—Pass., *to be kindly* or *affectionately treated*, dub. l. in Men.1087; ὑπὸ γυναικός Vett. Val.68.3; *to be liked*, ὑπὸ θεῶν καὶ ὑπὸ γυναικῶν Heph.Astr.1.1. **-ημα**, f.l. for εὐνόμημα (q. v.). **-ησις**, εως, ἡ, f.l. in Artem.2.12. **-ητικός**, ή, όν, *kindly disposed*, πρὸς ἑαυτό Hierocl.p.41 A. Adv. *benevolently*, διακεῖσθαι πρὸς ἀλλήλους Stoic.ap.Stob.2.7.11ⁱ. **-ητος**, ον, *easily understood*, Iamb.*Protr*.21. II. *intelligent*, οἰκονόμος Vett.Val.45. 28. 2. *well-disposed*, τινι Anon.*in Rh*.88.29.

εὐνόθευτος, ον, *easily adulterated*, ἔλαιον Corn.*ND*20.

εὔνοιᾰ, ἡ, Ion. **εὐνοίη** (εὔνοιαν is f.l. in Hdt.3.36), poet. **εὐνοΐη** *IG*14.815: (εὔνους):—*goodwill, favour* (dist. fr. φιλία, Arist.*EN*1155ᵇ 33, 1166ᵇ30), κατὰ εὐνοίην Hdt.6.108; δι' εὐνοίας Th.2.40; δι' εὔνοιαν Pl.*Prt*.337b; εὐνοίας ἕνεκα Docum.ap.D.18.54, etc.; εὐνοίας ἕνεκα τῆς εἰς τὸν δῆμον *IG*2².212.32, etc.; κατ' εὔνοιαν κρίνειν *partially*, Antipho 3.4.1; κατ' εὔνοιαν φρενῶν A.*Supp*.940; μετ' εὐνοίας And.1.9, Pl.*Phdr*.241c, D.18.276, *Ep.Eph*.6.7; ὑπ' εὐνοίας D.2.9; εὐνοίῃ τι ποιῆσαι Hdt.7.239; εὐνοίᾳ λέγειν S.*Ph*.1322; εὐνοίᾳ μᾶλλον ἢ ἐλέγχῳ τὰ γιγνόμενα δοκιμάζειν Lys.31.22; εὐνοίᾳ τῇ σῇ *for the love of* you, Pl.*Grg*.486a: with objective gen., ἐπ' εὐνοίᾳ χθονὸς *for love of* fatherland, A.*Th*.1012; εὐνοίᾳ τῇ ἑαυτοῦ Pl.*Grg*.485a; ἕνεκα τῆς τῶν Ἑλλήνων εὐνοίας *goodwill towards* them, X.*An*.4.7.20; [εὔνοιαν] ἔχειν εἴς τινα Docum.ap.D.18.54; πρός τινα Pl.*R*.470a; πρὸς τὸν δῆμον *IPE*1². 32.7 (Olbia), etc.; εὐ. παρὰ τῶν θεῶν D.2.1; εὔνοιαν ἔκ τινων κτᾶσθαι X.*Cyr*.8.2.22; εὔνοιαν παρασχεῖν to show *favour*, S.*Tr*.708; ἔργῳ δεικνύναι Antipho 5.76; εὔνοιαν ἔχειν to *wish heartily* that.., Th.2.11; ὡς ἑκατέρων τις εὐνοίας... ἔχοι Id.1.22; ἡ εὐ. παρὰ πολὺ ἐποίει τῶν ἀνθρώπων μᾶλλον ἐς τοὺς Λακεδαιμονίους Id.2.8: in pl., *impulses of kindness, favours*, τοῖς ἥσσοσιν γὰρ πᾶς τις εὐνοίας φέρει A.*Supp*.489; Ἀρτέμιδος εὐνοίαισι Id.*Th*.450; ταῖς εὐ. μεθ' ὑμῶν ἦσαν Isoc.14.15; but, *acts of kindness, favours*, D.S.15.9. II. *gift* or *present in token of goodwill*, D.19.282: pl., *benevolences*, Id.8.25. [εὔνοια as dactyl, *Arch.Pap*.1.220 (twice, ii B. C.).]

εὐνο-ΐζομαι, = εὐνοέω, Arist.*EE*1241ᵃ8. **-ϊκός**, ή, όν, *well-disposed, kindly, favourable*, εὐνοϊκωτέρους ὑπάρχειν τινί D.57.1, cf. Amphis 1: Sup. -ώτατος, περὶ τοὺς οἰκείους Lib.*Decl*.49.16. Adv. εὐνοϊκῶς, ἔχειν τινί X.*HG*4.4.15; πρός τινα Id.*Mem*.2.6.34, Arist. *Rh.Al*.1436ᵇ18; εὐ. διακεῖσθαι πρός τινα Isoc.12.237; πρὸς τὴν πόλιν *SIG*810.25 (Nero); εὐ. ἀκοῦσαι Hyp.*Lyc*.19; εὐ. προσδέχεσθαι D.18. 7: Comp. -ωτέρως Id.51.2; -ώτερον Lib.*Decl*.49.31: Sup. -ώτατα X.*Cyr*.8.4.1.

εὔνοιος, ον, = foreg., φίλοι καὶ εὐ. *SIG*559.52 (Magn. Mae., iii B. C.), cf. *IGRom*.4.247.34 (Assos). Adv. -οίως *Sammelb*.5294.9 (iii A. D.).

εὐνομ-έομαι, fut. -ήσομαι Hdt.1.97, Pl.*R*.380b: aor. 1 εὐνομήθην Hdt.1.66, ηὐν- Th.1.18: pf. εὐνόμημαι Epimenid.ap.D.L.1.113:—*have good laws, be well-ordered*, Hdt.ll. cc., Th.1.18, etc.; [πόλις] μέλλει εὐνομήσεσθαι Pl. l. c.; πόλις -ουμένη D.24.139, cf. Arist.*Rh*.1354ᵃ20, *Pol*.1294ᵃ3; οἰκία οὐκ εὐ. Aeschin.1.171; ἰσχύσετε, ὅταν εὐνομῆσθε when you *observe the laws*, ib.5. (Act. only in pres. part. εὐνομοῦσα Pl.*Lg*.927b.) **-ημα**, ατος, τό, *law-abiding, virtuous action*, Chrysipp.*Stoic*.3.73: pl., *Stoic*.3.136. **-ία**, Ep. and Ion. -ίη, ἡ, *good order*, ἀνθρώπων ὕβριν τε καὶ εὐνομίην ἐφορῶντες Od.17.487; ἐν εὐ. εἶναι Xenoph.2.19; μετέβαλον ὧδε ἐς εὐ. Hdt.1.65, cf. 2.124: pl., εὐνομίῃσι πόλιν κάτα... κοιρανέουσ' *h.Hom*.30.11, cf. Pl.*Sph*.216b; ἀπόλεμος εὐ. Pi.*P*.5.67, cf. *AP*6.195 (Arch.); Καίσαρος εὐ. ib.236 (Phil.); εὐνομίαν διὰ τῆς μουσικῆς εἰσδέχεσθαι Pl.*R*.425a; οὐκ ἔστι εὐνομία τὸ εὖ κεῖσθαι τοὺς νόμους, μὴ πείθεσθαι δέ Arist.*Pol*.1294ᵃ3, cf. 1280ᵇ6, Pl. *Def*.413e; οἱ ἐπὶ τῆς εὐνομίας, title of officials in Crete, *GDI*5075.35 (Latos). 2. *loyalty to divine law*, εὐνομίᾳ σέβων μεγίστᾳ S.*Aj*.713 (lyr.). 3. personified as daughter of Themis, Hes.*Th*.902, cf. Pi.*O*.9.16, 13.6, B.12.186, D.25.11, *Lyr.Adesp*.140.6, *IG*2.1598; title of a poem by Tyrtaeus, cf. Arist.*Pol*.1307ᵃ1, Str.8.4.10. 4. *observance of the laws of art*, εὐ. μουσική Longus 2.35. II. (εὔνομος II) *diligence in foraging*: metaph., of bees, Philostr.*Im*.2.2; *regularity in pasturing*, of sheep, Longus 1.5. **-ος**, ον, (νόμος) *under good laws, well-ordered*, πόλις Pi.*I*.5(4).22, Pl.*Ti*.20a (Sup.); Σκύθαι A.*Fr*.198; ἄνδρες Pl.*Lg*.815b; πολιτεία Zeno *Stoic*.1.27 (Sup.). 2. of things, ἔρανος -ώτατος Pi.*O*.1.37; μοῖρα εὐ., = εὐνομία, Id.*N*.9. 29. II. (νομή) of places, *good for pasture*, Longus 4.4 (Sup.).

εὔνοος, ον, Att. contr. **εὔνους**, ουν, dat. εὔνῳ Th.4.87: pl. εὖνοι, also heterocl. εὔνους (contr. from εὔνοες) Lys.8.19, Philem.222, *IG*2². 505.10, al.: gen. pl. εὐνόων Th.6.64 codd., εὔνων edd.:—*well-disposed, kindly, friendly*, ἀνὴρ φίλος καὶ εὐ. Hdt.5.24; ἐνυπνίων κριτὴς A.*Pers*. 226 (troch.); τινι to one, Hdt.7.173, al., S.*Ph*.1351, etc.; τῷ δήμῳ And.4.16, *IG*2².808.10, etc.; τῇ πόλει *SIG*572.5 (Nisyros, iii B. C.), etc.; οἱ ἐμοὶ εὖνοι my *well-wishers*, X.*Ap.*27; τὸ εὔνουν, = εὔνοια, S.*El.* 1203, Th.4.87, al.; opp. δυσμενής, X.*Cyr.*8.3.5; dist. fr. φίλος, Arist. *EN*1156^{a}2: Comp. εὐνούστερος Lys.27.13, etc.; Ion. εὐνοέστερος Hdt. 5.24, Herod.6.72; also εὐνοώτερος Philox.Gramm.ap.*EM*394.13: Sup. εὐνούστατος S.*Aj.*822, Ar.*Eq.*874, etc.; εὐνοέστατος *EM*394.5. 2. of things, τὴν πάροδον ἵν' ἔχῃς.. εὐνουστέραν *more favourable*, Dionys. Com.3.17. Adv. εὐνόως *IG*7.1 (Megara, iv/iii B.C.), etc.; ἔχειν πρός τινα Plu.*Galb.*8, cf. Aristeas 242; διακείμενος Phld.*Lib.*p.38 O.; contr. εὔνως, χρῆσθαί τινι M.Ant.3.11: Comp. -νούστερον, ἔχειν τινί Arr. *Epict.*4.6.7: Sup. -νούστατα, διακεῖσθαι πρός τινα D.S.19.6.

εὔνοστος, ἡ, *Good Yield, tutelary genius of corn-mills*, Eust.214.18, 1383.42, Hsch., Suid. s.v. προμυλαία, *EM*394.3. II. εὐνόστου λιμήν, a harbour of Alexandria, harbour *of happy return*, Str.17.1. 6, 10.

εὐνουχ-εῖον, τό, a kind of *lettuce*, = ἀστυτίς, Plin.*HN*19.127. **-ίας**, ου, ὁ, *like a eunuch, impotent*, Hp.*Aër.*22, Arist.*GA*746^{b}24. II. metaph., of *a melon without seeds*, opp. σπερματίας, Pl.Com.64.4; εὐ. κάλαμοι reeds *without inflorescence*, Thphr.*HP*4.11.4. **-ίζω**, *castrate*, τινα *Ev.Matt.*19.12 (Act. and Pass.), Luc.*Sat.*12, etc.; γυναῖκας Xanth.19: metaph., γῆν Philostr.*VA*6.42; φάρμακον Archig. ap.Orib.8.2.8:—Pass., Gal.4.570, D.C.68.2. **-ισμός**, ὁ, *castration*, Gal.4.576: **-ιστής**, οῦ, ὁ, *castrator*, *Gloss.* **-ιστέον**, *one must defertilize*, τοὺς μόσχους *Gp.*17.8.2.

εὐνουχοειδής, ές, *like a eunuch*, Hp.*Aër.*22 (Sup.):—also **εὐνουχώδης**, ες, Philostr.*VS*1.25.9, Aët.16.26, Suid. s.v. ἄρρεν.

εὐνοῦχος, ὁ, (εὐνή, ἔχω) *castrated person, eunuch*, employed to take charge of the women and act as *chamberlain* (whence the name, ὁ τὴν εὐνὴν ἔχων), Hdt.3.130, al., Ar.*Ach.*117, X.*Cyr.*7.5.60, etc. 2. of animals, Philostr.*Her.*1.3, Sch.Par.A.R.1.585. 3. of dates, *without stones*, Arist.*Fr.*267:—Pythag. name for θρίδαξ, Lycus ap. Ath.2.69e. II. as Adj., *watching the bed, sleepless*, λαμπάδες εὐνούχοισιν ὄμμασιν S.*Fr.*789.

εὖντα, Dor. for ἐόντα, neut. pl. of part. ὤν, Theoc.2.3.

εὔνυμφος, ον, *of a fair bride*, λέχος *Cat.Cod.Astr.*2.175.

εὐνώμας, α, ὁ, (νωμάω) = εὐκίνητος, *mobile*, αἰὲν εὐνώμᾳ χρόνῳ by the *ceaseless* march of time, S.*Aj.*604 (lyr., s.v.l., cf. εὐνάω I. 2).

εὔνωτος, ον, *stout-backed*, Arist.*Phgn.*809^{b}28.

εὔξαντος, ον, (ξαίνω) *well-carded*, of wool, *AP*6.282 (Theod.).

εὔξενος, Ion. **εὔξεινος**, ον, *kind to strangers, hospitable*, ἀνδρῶνας εὐ. δόμων *the guest-*chambers, A.*Ch.*712; λιμὴν εὐξεινότατος ναύταις E. *Hipp.*157 (lyr.). Ep. Adv. εὐξείνως A.R.1.963, 1179. II. πόντος εὔ. *the Euxine*, now *the Black Sea*, Hdt.1.6, al., E.*IT*125 (lyr., codd., sed leg. Ἀξείνου); and so εὔ. (leg. ἄξ-) οἶδμα Id.*HF*410 (lyr.); εὔ. πέλαγος Pi.*N.*4.49; ὁ Εὔξεινος alone, Str.11.1.5; cf. ἄξενος: εὔξεινος is a euphemism, like Εὐμενίδες.

εὔξεστος, Ep. **ἐΰξεστος**, η, ον, but ος, ον Od.15.333: (ξέω):—*well-planed, well-polished*, of carpenters' work, ῥυμός, ἀπήνη, φάτνη, Il.24. 271, 275, 280; χηλός Od.13.10; ἄκοντες 14.225; τράπεζαι 15.333; τὸ εὔξεστον Luc.*Hist.Conscr.*27.

εὐξήραντος, ον, *easily drying* or *evaporating*, Arist.*GA*782^{b}4, *Long.* 466^{a}26.

εὐξόᾰνος, ον, *skilled in sculpture*, Man.4.569.

εὔξοος, Ep. **ἐΰξοος**, ον, gen. ἐΰξου Il.10.373:—= εὔξεστος, ἅρμα, δίφρος, Il.2.390, Od.4.590; δόρυ Il.10.373; σκέπαρνον ἐΰ. an axe *of polished metal* or *haft*, Od.5.237. II. *easy to polish*, εὐξοώτερα Thphr.*HP*5.6.4.

εὐξῠλεία, ἡ, *abundance of timber*, name of a field, *IG*9(1).61.26 (Daulis).

εὐξυλῆ, prob. f.l. for εὔχυλα or εὐαυξῆ, Thphr.*CP*1.20.3.

εὐξῠλοεργός, όν, *skilled in carpentry*, πελεκήτορες Man.4.324.

εὔξῠλος, ον, *furnishing handsome timber*, Thphr.*HP*4.4.6; *abounding in timber*, App.*Hann.*58.

εὐξύμβλητος, εὐξύμβολος, εὐξυνεσία, εὐξύνετος, Att. for εὐσ–.

εὔξυστος, ον, (ξύω) *easily scraped* or *rasped*, Hp.*VC*19.

εὐογκ-ία, Ion. **-ίη**, ἡ, *being moderate in bulk*, εὐ. ἀσφαλέστερον μεγαλογκίης Democr.3. **-ος**, ον, *of good size, bulky, massive*, Hp. *Art.*23; κοιλίη Id.*Prog.*11; οὐδ' ἄγαν εὔ. E.*Fr.*688.3; εὔ. εἶναι γαστρὶ μὴ πληρουμένη *Trag.Adesp.*546.5; εὔ. φωνή *a full, rich* voice, opp. ψιλή, Philoch.66: Comp., -ότεραι ἀπὸ τῶν ἰσχίων Sor.2.53: metaph., *weighty, important*, opp. εὐτελής, Arist.*Rh.*1408^{a}12: Comp., Phld.*Po.* 2.38. II. *of moderate* or *convenient bulk, compact*, Aen.Tact.29.6 (Comp.), 31.23 (Sup.), Arist.*Mete.*380^{a}5 (Comp.), *GA*766^{b}20, Mnesith.ap.Ath.7.357f, etc.; *portable*, Thphr.*HP*9.16.8; τὰ εὐ. τῶν ἀναθημάτων Plu.2.969e; στρατόπεδον *of manageable size*, Polyaen.5.16.1: metaph., τῆς λέξεως τὸ εὐ. *compact, concise*, of γνῶθι σεαυτόν, Plu.2.511b. Adv. -κως, διάγειν *preserve a moderate embonpoint*, Diocl.*Fr.*141.

εὐοδ-έω, *have a free course* or *passage*, of running water, D.55.10; of bodily secretions, Arist.*GA*725^{a}35, etc.; of trees, *have root-room*, Thphr.*HP*1.6.4:—impers. in Pass., εὐοδεῖται *there is a free passage*, Arist.*GA*739^{a}35. 2. metaph., *fare well, prosper*, εὐοδῶν πορεύομαι Theopomp.Com.74, cf. Ph.1.430, Procl.*Hyp.*4.31; κατὰ τὸν βίον Herm.*in Phdr.*p.155 A.; τέχναι, ψυχὴ εὐ., Ph.1.687, 240; εὐώδει σοι τὰ πράγματα ib.145; ἀπόδειξις -οῦσα πρὸς τὰ συμπεράσματα Dam.*Pr.* 376; [ἡ ἀρετὴ].. προϊοῦσα εὐοδεῖ M.Ant.6.17; εὐόδει, on a gravestone, *IG*12(7).449. **-ία**, ἡ, *a good journey*, καὶ σοὶ δ' εὐοδίης τρίβον ὄλβιον εὔχομαι εἶναι *Arch.Pap.*1.221 (ii B.C.): hence εὐοδίαν ἀπὸ στόματος χέειν *good wishes for one's success*, A.*Fr.*36; personified, *OGI*77 (Alexandria, iii B.C.): metaph., κατ' εὐοδίαν Phld.*Rh.*2. 27 S.: c. gen., εὐ. τοῦ ἐλθεῖν *a good opportunity* of coming, *PMich.* in *Class.Phil.*22.250 (ii A.D.). II. *success*, Demetr.Lac.1012.47 F., 1429.2 F. III. *permeability*, τῶν πόρων Sor.1.86. **-ιάζω**, *pass, insert in the right way*, [καθετῆρα] Paul.Aeg.6.59:—Subst. **-ιασμός**, ὁ, ibid. **-ιος**, ον, *boni itineris*, *Gloss.*

εὐοδμία, εὔοδμος, v. εὐοσμία, εὔοσμος.

εὔοδ-ος, ον, *easy to pass*, of mountains, X.*An.*4.8.10; of a road, *easy to travel*, ὁδὸς.. εὐοδωτάτη τοῖς ὑποζυγίοις ib.4.2.9; οὐκ εὔοδα ἔσται ὑμῖν Lxx *Nu.*14.41. Adv. -όδως, πορεύεσθαι ib.*Pr.*24.64 (30. 29). 2. metaph., *free from difficulty, simple*, Epicur.*Fr.*18, Ptol. *Alm.*1.2 (Comp.). Adv. *simply, readily*, νοεῖσθαι Phld.*D.*3.11: Sup. -ώτατα, τῷ τῆς ἀνδρείας ὀνόματι προσαγορεύεσθαι ib.*Fr.*81. 3. *favourable*, πρός τι Mnesith.ap.Ath.3.92c; ὁ εὔοδος θεός, of Pan, *CIG* 4705*b*, cf. *OGI*38 (Egypt, iii B.C.), al., *Epigr.Gr.*826, etc. **-όω**, *help on the way*, c. dat. pers., σφῷν δ' εὐοδοίη Ζεύς S.*OC*1435 (nisi leg. σφώ): c. acc. pers., Lxx *Ge.*24.27, *PSI*4.299.14: abs., τὸ εὐοδοῦν Thphr.*CP*5.6.7. 2. Pass., *have a prosperous journey*, Lxx *Da.*8.11, al., *Ep.Rom.*1.10; of things, *prosper, be successful*, ὡς Κλεομένεϊ εὐωδώθη τὸ πρῆγμα v.l. in Hdt.6.73; θησαυρίζων ὅ τι ἂν εὐοδῶται, = εὐπορῇ, 1*Ep.Cor.*16.2, cf. *Act.Ap.*11.29. **-ωσις**, εως, ἡ, *successful progress*, Protag.Astrol. in *Cat.Cod.Astr.*8(2).119, Asp.*in EN*386.25.

εὐοῖ (εὔοι A.D.*Synt.*320.1, cf. Lat. *euhoe*), exclamation used in the cult of Dionysus, Ar.*Lys.*1294 (lyr.), etc.; cf. εὐαί, εὐάν: εὐοῖ σαβοῖ D.18.260: as an interjection, ἀναταράσσει—εὐοῖ—μ' ὁ κισσός S.*Tr.*219 (lyr.).

εὐοίκ-ητος, ον, *favourably placed*, τόπος Philoch.76: gloss on εὔπωλος, Eust.1431.54. 2. *comfortable*, of a house, Alex.Aphr. *in Top.*269.16. **-ονόμητος**, ον, *well arranged*, only in Adv. -τως Sch. E.*Or.*470. 2. *easy to digest*, Diph.Siph.ap.Ath.2.54d: Comp., Id.ib.3.80c, Eust.866.21. **-ος**, ον, *with good houses*, gloss on εὔβύριον, *EM*389.24. 2. *convenient to inhabit, comfortable*, κύρτος Opp.*H.*3.370. II. *good economist*, D.C.44.39 (Sup.). 2. *kind to servants* (οἰκέται), Achae.32.

εὔοικτος, ον, *compassionate*, αὐτοκράτωρ D.C.69.20 (-εικτος Zonar.; fort. εὔθικτος).

εὐοιν-έω, *abound in good wine*, Str.11.10.1, Max.Tyr.30.4. **-ία**, ἡ, *abundance of good wine*, Str.2.1.14, Horap.2.92, St.Byz. s.v. Λάμψακος (cj.), Eun.*VS*p.467 B. (cj.). **-ιστος**, ον, *of good wine*, ἐπιλοιβαί dub.l. in Orph.*A.*603. **-ος**, ον, *abounding in wine*, Λέσβος Hermesian.7.55, cf. Str.5.4.2; σταφυλή *AP*6.300.5 (Leon.): Sup., Max.Tyr.3.10.

εὐοιώνιστος, ον, *of good omen*, D.S.33.28^a, Sch.Luc.*JTr.*47, prob. in Phryn.*PS*p.71 B.

εὔολβος, ον, *wealthy, prosperous*, βασιλεῖς E.*IT*189 (lyr.); πάτρα *IG*7.530 (Tanagra); βίος, οἶκοι, Orph.*H.*29.19, Man.3.46.

εὐολίσθ-ητος, ον, *easily slipping, unsteady*, Iamb.*Protr.*21.κ'. **-ος**, ον, *slippery*, *Placit.*1.4.2; κόπρος Alex.Aphr.*Pr.*1.90; πηλαμύς Xenocr. ap.Orib.2.58.142, cf. Apollod.*Poliorc.*149.3, Hierocl. *in CA*16 p.456 M. II. metaph., *unsteady*, ἡλικία Ph.2.463.

εὐόλκιμος, ον, (ὁλκή) *easily drawn, ductile, sticky*, Hp.*Art.*36.

εὐόμᾰλος, ον, *level*, πεδία Agath.3.19.

εὐομβρ-ία, ἡ, *abundance of rain*, Lyd.*Ost.*38. **-ος**, ον, *abounding in rain*: *well-watered*, Str.4.1.7.

εὐομίλ-ητος [ῐ], ον, *affable*, πρὸς πᾶσαν ἀπάντησιν *SIG*708.16 (Istropolis, ii B.C.). **-ία**, ἡ, *charm of conversation, wit*, Charis.pp.33. 12, 549.10 K. **-ος**, ον, *sociable*, *Com.Adesp.*1015, Vett.Val.40.4, M.Ant.1.16, Hld.3.10, Dam.*Isid.*49, Agath.1.13.

εὐόμμᾰτος, ον, *keen-sighted*, *EM*284.8.

εὐομολόγητος, ον, *easy to concede, indisputable*, Pl.*R.*527b.

εὔομφος, ον, Arc. for εὔοσμος, Timachidas ap.Ath.15.683c (εὐόμφαλον codd.). II. εὔομφα· ὀνόματα, Hsch.

εὐόνειρος, ον, *having auspicious dreams*, Str.16.2.35; *bringing such dreams*, νύξ Hld.3.5; εὐ. καὶ ἄλυπα, opp. φοβερόν, Plu.2.83d.

εὐόνυξ, ὕχος, ὁ, ἡ, *with strong claws*, Marc.Sid.34.

εὐοπλ-έω, *to be well-equipped*, *AP*12.120 (Posidipp.), Ph.1.20, Hld.8.16, Arr.*Tact.*5.3. **-ία**, ἡ, *a good state of arms and equipments*, X.*Hier.*9.6; as a subject of competition, *IG*2^2.956.58. **-ος**, ον, (ὅπλον) *well-armed, well-equipped*, Ar.*Ach.*592; λόχος, πόλις, X. *HG*4.2.5 (Sup.), *Hier.*11.3; τῶν ζῴων τὰ ἄρρενα -ότερα Arist.*HA*538^b 4. II. (ὁπλή) *with good hoofs*, Poll.1.194.

εὔοπτος, ον, (ὁράω, ὄψομαι) *open to view*, οὐκ ἐν εὐόπτῳ οἰκέουσιν αἱ νοῦσοι Hp. *de Arte*11; *conspicuous*, Lxx *Ep.Je.*60, Longus 4.3. 2. *attractive, good-looking*, Muson.*Fr.*21 p.116 H. (Sup.), *EM*276.36, *Cat.Cod.Astr.*8(2).59. II. (ὀπτάω) *well-cooked*, τροφή Ath.Med. ap.Orib.*inc.*23.3.

εὐόρᾱτος, ον, (ὁράω) = foreg. I, Eust.86.42.

εὐοργ-ησία, ἡ, *gentleness of temper*, E.*Hipp.*1039, *Ba.*641 (troch.). **-ητος**, ον, *good-tempered*, ἦθεα Hp.*Aër.*12 (Comp.); εὐ. πρὸς τὸ πρέπον Gorg.*Fr.*6 D.; τοῖς κόλαξι.. εὐόργητος Eub.25; τὸ εὐ. καὶ πρᾶον Arist.*MM*1186^{a}23, cf. Plu.2.413c. Adv. -τως, προσομιλεῖν τῷ πολέμῳ *with good temper*, opp. ὀργισθείς, Th.1.122. **-ία**· ἀπιστία (sic), Hsch. (cf. εὐεργία). **-ος**, ον, (ὀργή) = εὐόργητος, Id. (perh. from Archil., cf. *PLG*2 p.439 B.).

εὐόρεκτος, ον, *appetizing*, τὸ ἥδιον εὐορεκτότερον Plu.2.663f, cf. Dsc.5.13. II. *with a better appetite*, Gal.18(2).299.

εὐόριστος, ον, *easily bounded* or *limited*, Arist.*Mete.*360^{a}23; τὸ εὐ., opp. τὸ δυσόριστον, ib.378^{b}24, *GC*329^{b}31; μέτρον ἀριθμῷ οὐκ εὐ. Herod. Med.ap.Orib.6.25.4.

εὐορκ-έω, *swear truly, take a true oath*, opp. ἐπιορκέω, Gorg.*Fr.* 15 D., Isoc.1.23, Iamb.*VP*28.144, etc.; *keep one's oath* when taken,

Lex.ap.And.1.98; τινι to one, Th.5.30; [τὴν ψυχήν] *by* one's soul, E.*Or.*1517 (troch.); εὐορκοῦντες κρίνειν X.*HG*1.7.25. II. Act., *keep one's oath by*, τινας Sch.A.R.2.259:—Pass., ἡ θεὸς εὐορκεῖτο Call.*Aet.*3.1.42. **-ησία,** ἡ, *fidelity to one's oath*, Alexand.Com. 2. **-ία,** ἡ, = foreg., Pi.*O.*2.66 (pl.), App.*Pun.*63, Hierocl. *in CA*2 p.422 M. II. in pl., *oaths taken with a good conscience*, Lib.*Or.*59. 122. **-ος,** ον, *keeping one's oath, faithful to one's oath*, ἀνδρὸς δ' εὐόρκου γενεὴ μετόπισθεν ἀμείνων Hes.*Op.*285, cf. 190, Orac.ap.Hdt. 6.86.γ', Ar.*Pl.*61, X.*HG*2.4.42, etc.; εἴς τινα E.*Med.*495. II. of oaths, εὔορκα ἀντομωμοκώς Antipho 1.8; [διομόσασθαι] εὐορκότερα Id. 6.16; ψηφίσασθαι Is.2.47; γνῶναι D.18.249; εὐορκοτέραν θήσεσθε τὴν ψῆφον Id.29.4, cf. 21.24; εὐορκοτάτην ⟨τὴν⟩ ψῆφον ἐνεγκεῖν Lycurg. 13: Sup., Lys.19.11; *in accordance with* one's *oath, no breach of oath*, εὔορκόν [ἐστι] Foed.ap.Th.5.18, cf. 23, 29; εὔορκα ταῦθ' ὑμῖν ἐστι D. 21.34 (v.l. ἔνορκα): so in Adv., τάδ' εὐόρκως ἔχει A.*Ch.*979; εὐ. θέσθαι τὴν ψῆφον Arist.*Rh.Al.*1433^{a}1. **-ωμα,** ατος, τό, *faithful oath*, A.*Ch.*901 (pl.). **-ωτος,** ον, = εὔορκος, Poll.1.39.

εὐόρμ-ητος, ον, gloss on sq., Sch.A.R.4.900. **-ος,** ον, *with good mooring-places*, ἐν δὲ λιμὴν εὔορμος Od.4.358, 9.136, Hes.*Sc.*207, cf. Il.21.23; γῆ S.*Ph.*221; εὐορμόταται λιμένες Ph.2.567. 2. *well-moored*, εὐόρμων.. πρυμνήσια νηῶν *AP*10.4 (Marc. Arg.).

εὐορν-ῑθία, ἡ, *good augury*, S.*Fr.*1049. **-ις,** ῑθος, ὁ, ἡ, *of good augury*, τύχη *Trag.Adesp.*343; οἰωνοί D.H.2.73. II. *abounding in birds*, epith. of Tanagra in *AP*7.424 (Antip. Sid.).

εὐόροφος, ον, *well-roofed*, *AP*9.59.5 (Antip. ⟨Thess.⟩).

εὐόρπηξ, ηκος, ὁ, ἡ, *with fine branches*, Nonn.*D.*21.298.

εὐοσμέω, *smell well, be fragrant*, Thphr.*CP*6.16.1, cj. in E.*Ba.*235.

εὐοσμία, ἡ, *fragrance, perfume*, S.*Fr.*370 (pl.), Thphr.*CP*6.14.4:—but **εὐοδμία,** Id.*Od.*51, Antipho Soph.8; this form is stated to be poet., Ion., and Aeol. by Poll.2.75.

εὔοσμος or **εὔοδμος,** ον, (ὀδμή, ὀσμή) *sweet-smelling, fragrant*, εὔοδμον ἔαρ Pi.*Fr.*75.15; εὐόδμοισι προσθετοῖσι Hp.*Loc.Hom.*47; εὔοσμον μύρον Achae.17, cf. E.*Ba.*235; εὐόδμοισι σελίνοις, νέκταρος εὐόδμοιο, Theoc.3.23, 17.29; v.l. for εὐώδης in D.P.937; εὔοδμος τῇ ὀσφρήσει Thphr.*HP*9.13.3: Comp. and Sup., Id.*CP*6.16.1.

εὐοσφρ-αντικωτάτη, gloss on εὐρινοτάτη, Hsch. **-ητος,** ον, *keen-scented*, gloss on εὔρινος, *EM*765.53.

εὐόφθαλμος, ον, *with beautiful eyes*, X.*Cyr.*8.1.41 (Comp.), *BGU* 316.14 (iv A. D.). 2. *keen-eyed*, X.*Smp.*5.5 (Sup.). II. *pleasing to the eye*, Aristox.*Fr.Hist.*15, *Cat.Cod.Astr.*8(4).240: metaph., *fair only to the eye, specious*, εὐόφθαλμον ἀκοῦσαι μόνον Arist.*Pol.*1268^{b}24. Adv. -μως Antipho *Fr.*59.

εὔοφρυς, υ, *with fine eyebrows*, Philostr.*Her.*19.9, *AP*5.75 (Rufin.).

εὐοχέω, *guide well*, in Pass., of an elephant, Suid.; of horses, f. l. for εὐωχέομαι, X.*Eq.Mag.*8.4.

εὐοχθ-έω, *to be in plenty, to be in good case*, Hes.*Op.*477, Rhian.1. 9. **-ος,** ον, *with goodly banks, fertile, rich*, γῆ Hom.*Epigr.*7.2; also εὔοχθοι δαῖτες B.*Fr.*18.4; βορά E.*Ion* 1169.

εὔοχος, ον, (ἔχω) *holding firmly*, δεσμός Hp.*Art.*43. II. *easy to maintain*, σχῆμα Id.*Fract.*47 (Sup.).

εὐοψ-έω, *abound in fish*, Str.4.1.8, 14.2.21. **-ία** (A), ἡ, (ὄψον) *abundance of* ὄψα (q. v.), i. e. fish in Alciphr.3.3, but pork in Plu.*Fr. inc.*145. **-ία** (B), ἡ, (ὄψις) *good looks*, Alex.38. **-ος,** ον, *abounding in* ὄψα, esp. fish, ἀγορά Anaxandr.33.10, Timocl.11.1; χωρίον Archestr.*Fr.*50 B., cf. Str.10.2.21; ἡ θάλασσα τῆς γῆς -οτέρα Plu.2. 667c, etc. **-ωνία,** ἡ, = εὐοψία (A), Alex.316.

εὐπᾰγής, ές, (πήγνυμι) of the body or limbs, *compact, firm*, Pl.*Lg.* 775c, X.*Cyn.*4.1, 5.30, Philostr.*Gym.*34; παιδάριον Plu.*Lyc.*16; of things, σχαλίδες X.*Cyn.*2.7; βάκτρον Theoc.25.208; of blood, *readily coagulating*, Aret.*SD*2.4: Comp., Ph.1.418; *firm in texture, well-woven*, *BGU*1564.10 (ii A. D.): metaph., *sound, solid*, of style, Phld. *Po.*994.34, 35. Adv. -γέως Opp.*H.*3.401.

εὐπάθ-εια [πᾰ], Ion. -είη, ἡ, (εὐπαθής) *comfort, ease*, X.*Ages.*9.3; οὐ καρτερίαν τὴν ἀρετὴν ἀλλ' εὐ. νομίζειν ib.11.9, cf. Plu.2.132c: esp. in pl., *enjoyments, luxuries*, ἐν εὐπαθείῃσι εἶναι *enjoy oneself, make merry*, Hdt.1.22, 191, 8.99; εὐπαθείας ἐπιτηδεύειν Id.1.135; also, *delicacies, dainties*, εὐπαθείας ἐκ τῆς ἀγορᾶς πολυτελεῖς πορίζεσθαι X.*Ap.*18, cf. Pl.*R.*404d. 2. pl. in Stoic Philos., *innocent emotions*, opp. πάθη, *Stoic.*3.105, al. 3. = τὸ εὖ πάσχειν, *receipt of benefits*, Arist.*EN* 1159^{a}21. 4. *sensitiveness* to impressions, Alex.Aphr.*Pr.*2.53; to disease, Gal.8.205, al.; *passivity*, Plu.2.589. **-έω,** *enjoy oneself, make merry*, πίνειν καὶ εὐπαθέειν Hdt.2.133, 174; *indulge oneself, live comfortably*, Pl.*R.*347c; of the soul, τρέφεται καὶ εὐπαθεῖ Id.*Phdr.* 247d; opp. δυστυχέω, D.C.56.45. 2. *receive benefits*, ὑπό τινος from one, Plu.2.176b (better divisim). **-ής,** ές, (πάθος) *enjoying good things, easy, luxurious*, βίος Crates Com.16. II. *easily affected*, ὑπὸ τοῦ ἀέρος Arist.*Pr.*887^{b}23 (Sup.); εἰς τὸ πάσχειν Thphr. *CP*5.14.7 (Comp.); τὸ εὐ. τῆς φύσεως Alex.Aphr.*Pr.*2.53; εὐ. τῷ ἀέρι Plu.2.949e (Comp.); πρὸς τὸ πῦρ Id.*Alex.*35; τροφῆς -έστατον ὑπὸ πέψεως Id.2.661c; -έστερος οἶνος *Gp.*5.45.1; *susceptible* to disease, Aret.*SD*1.11; of persons, *susceptible*, πρὸς τὸ φαινόμενον αἰσχρόν Plu. 2.528d; [τάξεις] -έστεραι πρὸς τὰς τῶν πολεμίων ἐπιφανείας Onos. 6.3. **-ητικός,** ή, όν, *easily contracted*, νοσήματα *Cat.Cod.Astr.*8(4). 174. **-ητος,** ον, = εὐπαθής II, *Corp.Herm.*10.10.

εὐπαιδ-ευσία, ἡ, *goodness of education*, E.*Fr.*1100, Men.*Mon.*653, Aret.*SD*1.6; *culture, scholarship*, ἐπιστολαὶ -ευσίας μεσταί Philostr. *VS*1.18.4. **-ευτος,** ον, *well-educated, well-trained*, Hp.*Art.*43, cf. E.*Or.*410; τῶν ἄλλων -ότατοι Phld.*Piet.*65; *docile*, of an elephant, Philostr.*VA*2.11; εὐπαίδευτόν ἐστι it is *a thing easily learnt*, c. inf., Hp.*Art.*1; εὐ. ἐπιστολή a *scholarly* letter, D.H.*Pomp.*1.1. Adv. -τως Aret.*CD*1.3: Comp. -ότερον Athenocles ap.Ath.5.177e.

εὐπαιδία, ἡ, *a goodly race of children*, A.*Fr.*350 (pl.); τέρπεται δ' εὐπαιδίᾳ E.*Supp.*490; εὐπαιδίαν ἔχοντ' *blest* in his *children*, Id.*Ion*678 (dochm.); ὦ μακάριε τῆς εὐπαιδίας Ar.*V.*1512; τῆς.. ἡμετέρας εὐ. Isoc.11.41, cf. 9.72; τὰ τῆς εὐ. δίκαια, = Lat. *jus trium liberorum*, *POxy.*1264.18 (iii A. D.).

εὔπαις, παιδος, ὁ, ἡ, *blest with children*, i. e. *with many* or *with good, fine children*, *h.Hom.*30.5, Hdt.1.32, E.*Hec.*810; Ἀσκληπιός Ar.*Pl.* 639 (lyr.); βιοτά E.*Ion* 491 (lyr.); Ἀθῆναι *AP*6.330 (Aeschin.); but Λατοῦς γόνος εὔπαις her *noble son*, E.*HF*689, *IT*1234 (both lyr.).

εὔπακτος, Dor. for εὔπηκτος, B.16.82, etc.

εὐπάλαιστος [πᾰ], ον, *easy to overcome in wrestling*, [Epich.]254.

εὐπάλαιστρος [πᾰ], ον, *skilful in contest*, metaph., τὸ κατὰ τὰς εἰρωνείας εὐ. Longin.34.2.

εὐπάλᾰμος [πᾰ], ον, *handy, skilful, ingenious*, of persons, Phoronis *Fr.*2, Nonn.*D.*5.216, al.: more freq. in the abstract, *inventive*, μέριμνα A.*Ag.*1531 (lyr.); Ἔρως Orph.*H.*58.4; σοφίη *IG*14.967. 2. *skilfully wrought*, ὕμνοι Cratin.70, cf. Nonn.*D.*17.146, al. b. *easily manipulated*, Ph.*Bel.*60.47.

εὐπᾰλής, ές, (πάλη) *easy to wrestle with*: hence, *easy of accomplishment*, ἄεθλοι A.R.2.618. Adv. εὐπαλέως Id.4.193. II. (πάλλω) *easily handled*, θύρσος S.*Ichn.*220.

εὐπάξ, ᾶγος, ὁ, ἡ, Dor. for εὐπηγής, εὐπᾶγι κύκλῳ cj. for εὐπαγεῖ, E. *Or.*1428 (lyr.).

εὐπαράγωγος [ᾰγ], ον, *easy to bring into place*, ὀστέα Hp.*Fract.*6; *flexible*, αὐχήν Aret.*SD*1.8. II. *easy to lead by the nose, easy to lead astray*, Ar.*Eq.*1115 (lyr.); ἐλπίς Pl.*Ti.*69d; *credulous*, νόσος Philostr.*VA*7.39. 2. Act., *seductive, alluring*, λόγος, πλάσματα, Ph.1.268, 2.481.

εὐπαράδεκτος, ον, *easily received, acceptable*, ἐπίνοιαι Plb.10.2.11 (Comp.), cf. Phld.*D.*1.24 (Comp.): in Gramm., *admissible*, A.D. *Pron.*89.7, al.; opp. ἀπόβλητος, Id.*Synt.*164.25; *easy to admit*, σαφὲς καὶ εὐ. Plot.6.4.1. II. *receiving readily*, [λάκκοι] εὐ. ὕδατος Ph.1. 572: metaph., [εὐφυία] εὐ. σπερμάτων ἀρετῆς ib.136; εὐ. πρὸς τὰ θεωρήματα ib.572.

εὐπαραίτητος, ον, *placable*, Plu.*Phoc.*29, *Dio*47; ἐπί τινι γενέσθαι D.C.42.18 (ἀπ- codd.). 2. *easily disposed of*, τρόπος S.E.*P.*2. 204. 3. *furnishing a good ground of excuse*, D.L.3.78 (s. v. l.).

εὐπαράκλητος, ον, *easily influenced*, πρός τι Pl.*Ep.*328a, cf. Aristaenet.2.1.

εὐπαρᾰκολούθ-ητος, ον, *easy to follow*, of a narrative, argument, etc., Plb.4.28.6, Hero *Bel.*73.12, D.H.*Pomp.*6.2; τοῦ εὐ. ἕνεκα Arist. *EN*1108^{a}19. Adv. -τως D.H.*Th.*37. II. Act., *quick to follow*, Hsch. **-ος,** ον, = foreg. II, *Et.Gud.*220.3.

εὐπαρα-κόμιστος, ον, *easy to steer*, πρὸς τὴν γῆν Plu.*Luc.*13; εὐ. ὁ πλοῦς ἐπὶ τὰ στενά Plb.4.44.6: metaph., *easy to bring over*, λογισμὸ πρὸς τὸ συμφέρον εὐ. Plu.2.597b. II. [πόλις] εὐ. πρὸς τὰς παραπομπὰς τῆς ὕλης *conveniently situated for the supply* of wood, Arist.*Pol.*1327^a 10. **-κρουστος,** ον, *easy to set aside, refute*, συνηγορία A.D.*Pron.* 6.20. **-ληπτος,** ον, *readily applicable*, Eust.746.44.

εὐπαράλλακτος, ον, *subject to change, unstable*, κάλλος εὐ. κτῆμα Secund.*Sent.*14.

εὐπαρα-λόγιστος, ον, *easily cheated* or *misled*, εὐ. πᾶς ὄχλος Plb. 11.29.9, cf. Phld.*Ir.*p.38 W., J.*AJ*4.6.11, Hierocl. *in CA*13 p.448 M.: Sup., Plb.5.75.2. **-μύθητος** [ῡ], ον, *easily appeased*, θύμασιν καὶ εὐχαῖς Pl.*Lg.*888c. 2. *admitting of easy consolation*, θάνατος Plu. 2.110e, Onos.42.21, cf. Vett.Val.286.16; εὐ. τὸ δεινόν Luc.*DDeor.*11. 2 (dub. l.), cf. Hld.4.5. 3. *easily proved*, S.E.*M.*10.212.

εὐπαράος (so, without iota, codd.), ον, Dor. for εὐπάρειος, Pi.*P.* 12.16.

εὐπαρά-πειστος, ον, *easily persuaded*, φίλοις X.*Ages.*11.12 (Sup.). **-πλους,** ουν, *easy to coast along*, Str.17.3.22. **-τήρητος,** ον, *noticeable*, σολοικισμός [Hdn.Gr.] post *Lex.Vind.*p.307 N. **-τρεπτος,** ον, *easy to turn from his opinion*, Poll.8.12. **-τύπωτος** [ῠ], ον, *easily misled by false impressions*, αἰσθητήρια M.Ant.5.33. **-φορος,** ον, *easily distracted*, Hsch. **-χώρητος,** ον, *readily admissible*, Archim. *Quadr.Praef.*

εὐπάρεδρος, ον, *constantly attending*, τὸ εὐ. τῷ Κυρίῳ *constant waiting* on the Lord, 1*Ep.Cor.*7.35 (v. l. εὐπρόσ-), cf. Hsch., Suid.

εὐπάρειος [ᾰ], ον, *with fair cheeks*, Poll.2.87, 9.162: Dor. **-αος** (q. v.).

εὐπαρ-είσδῠτος, ον, *easily accessible*, Hp.*Art.*30 codd.: sed leg. **-έκδυτος,** *slipping out of place easily*. II. *easily inserted*, Paul.Aeg.6. 114. **-ηγόρητος,** ον, *easily alleviated*, πάθη Ptol.*Tetr.*153; *easily consoled*, εὐ. τὴν ψυχήν Vett.Val.166.8. Adv. -τως dub. l. in Phalar.*Ep.*10.

εὐπάρθενος, ον, *famed for fair maidens*, Tryph.51, Nonn.*D.*39. 188. II. εὐ. Δίρκα Dirce, *happy maid!* E.*Ba.*520 (lyr.), cf. *AP*6. 287 (Antip.), Nonn.*D.*16.311; cf. εὔπαις.

εὐπαρ-όδευτος, ον, *easy to pass by, ignore*, κάλλος οὐκ εὐ. *striking* beauty, Malch.p.393 D. **-οδος,** ον, *easy of access*, Str.3.2.11 (Comp.). 2. *easy of introduction*, Sever.*Clyst.*p.37 D. **-οιστοι·** εὐπαράγωγοι, Hsch. **-όξυντος,** ον, *easily provoked, irritated*, ὑπὸ κακῶν Plu.*Ant.*73. **-όρμητος,** ον, *easily excited*, πρός τινας Arist. *Rh.*1379^{a}17. **-οχος,** ον, *submissive*, of a mare, *Hippiatr.*14.

εὐπαρρησίαστος, ον, *speaking with bold freedom*, Heph.Astr.1.1; *a fit subject for free speech*, Vett.Val.241.12.

εὐπάρῠφος, ον, *with a fine purple border*, περίζωμα Plu.*Aem.*33: as Subst., εὐπάρυφος, ἡ, *a fine garment*, Nicostr.Com.9, Hdn.1.16.3: neut.

pl. εὐπάρυφα, τά, LXX *Ez.*23.12. 2. of persons, *wearing such a garment*, εὐ. τις *a grandee*, Ph.2.346 (pl.), Plu.2.57a, cf. Luc.*Somn.*16, *Demon.*15, Alciphr.3.42. 3. metaph., *pompous*, διηγήματα Plu.2.547e; but εὐ. λόγοι *equivocal, lascivious* stories, Ath.10.453a.

εὐπάτειρα [ᾰ], ἡ, = sq., Men.616 (with v.l. εὐπατέρεια), Choerob. in *An.Ox.*2.196, Theognost.*Can.*99, Gramm. in Reitzenstein *Gesch.d. Gr.Etym.*p.306, *Et.Gud.*, *EM*318.55; cf. ἀπάτειρα.

εὐπᾰτέρεια, ἡ, (πατήρ) *daughter of a noble sire*, epith. of Helen, Il.6.292, Od.22.227; of Tyro, 11.235; ἑταῖραι Mosch.2.29, cf. A.R.1.570, *AP*9.688. 2. of places, *belonging to a noble father*, αὐλά E.*Hipp.*68 (lyr.).

εὐπᾰτόριον, τό (v.l. -ος, ὁ), *Agrimonia Eupatorium* (so called from Mithridates *Eupator*), *agrimony*, Dsc.4.41. 2. = πράσιον, Ps.-Dsc. 3.105.

εὐπᾰτρίδης, ου, Dor. **-δας**, α, ὁ, (πατήρ) *of good* or *noble sire, of noble family*, of persons, used by Trag. in lyr., S.*El.*162, E.*Alc.*920 (anap.), *Hipp.*152, etc.; εὐ. οἶκοι Id.*Ion* 1073: also in later Prose, Muson.*Fr.*13ᴮ p.69 H. II. Εὐ., οἱ, at Athens, the *old aristocracy*, opp. ἀγροῖκοι (or γεωμόροι Plu.*Thes.*25) and δημιουργοί, Arist.*Ath.*13.2, cf. *Scol.*14, Isoc.16.25, X.*Smp.*8.40; πένητας Εὐπατρίδας οὐδεὶς ὁρᾷ Alex.90.3; but τὰ τῶν Εὐ. πάτρια sacred traditions of the *Eup.*, Ath.9.410a and ἐξηγητὴς ἐξ Εὐ. *IG*3.267, 1335, refer to a particular family of that name. 2. at Rome, *Patricians*, Plu.*Publ.*18, *Fab.*16, etc.

εὐπᾰτρις, ιδος, ἡ, fem. of foreg., *born of a noble sire*, E.*IA*1077 (lyr.); τίς ἂν εὔ. ὧδε βλάστοι; S.*El.*1081 (lyr.); ἐλπίδων.. εὐπατρίδων of hopes *derived from those of noble birth*, dub. cj. ib.858 (-ιδᾶν vel -ιδῶν codd.). 2. at Rome, αἱ εὐπάτριδες ἀρχαί *magistratus patricii*, D.C.46.45: γυνὴ εὐ., = Lat. *patricia*, Id.72.5 (here acc. sg. -ίδα, but cf. κακόπατρις, ὁμόπατρις).

εὐπάτωρ [ᾰ], ορος, ὁ, ἡ, = foreg., A.*Pers.*970, Ael.*Fr.*292. II. *a good father*, dub. in Man.4.86.

εὐπέδῐλος, ον, *well-sandalled*, Ἶρις Alc.13 B (-πέδιλλ- Ahrens).

εὐπέδιος, ον, *with level* or *good soil*, Q.S.11.125, perh. f.l. for εὐρυπέδοιο:—fem. **εὐπεδιάς**, άδος, Sch.Ar.*Lys.*88.

εὔπεζος, ον, (πέζα) *with beautiful feet*, Poll.2.192.

εὐπείθ-εια, ἡ, *ready obedience*, Zeno *Stoic.*1.56, Ti.Locr.104b, Str.7.4.8, LXX 4*Ma.*5.16, Plu.*Dio*4, etc.; also εὐπειθία or εὐπείθια *IG*5(1).548 (Sparta, ii A.D.); Ion. **-πειθείη** Eus.Mynd.ap.Stob.4.5.29 (v.l. -πειθίη). **-έω**, *to be disposed to obey*, Charond.ap.Stob.4.2.24. II. *comply* with an order, *OGI*665.5 (Egypt, i A.D.). III. v.l. for εὐπιθέω (q.v.). **-ής**, ές, (cf. εὐπιθής) *ready to obey, obedient*, τινι Pl.*Phdr.*254a; τοῖς νόμοις -έστατος Id.*Lg.*715c, cf. 890c: c. gen., τῶν νόμων ib.632b; -έστατοι πρὸς ἀρετήν ib.718c; εἴς τι Id.*Phdr.*271d; *compliant*, εὐ. γεγονέναι *BGU*1104.23 (i B.C.), LXX 4*Ma.*12.6, etc.; of things, as of the voice, *under control*, Arist.*Aud.*802ᵃ6; ὕλη (material) εἰς ἅπαν εὐ. Gal.6.3; of food, Plu.2.669b. Adv. -θῶς ib. 981a. II. Act., *persuasive*, of a rein, ἐϋπειθεῖ δεσμῷ Opp.*C.*1.313; dub. l. in A. (v. εὐπιθής).

εὔπειστος, ον, (πείθομαι) of persons, *easily persuaded*, Arist.*EN* 1151ᵇ10. 2. *easy to demonstrate*, Id.*LI*969ᵇ22; *easy to convince people of*, S.*Aj.*151 (anap., v.l. εὔπιστ-).

εὔπεκτος, ον, = εὔποκος, Hsch.

εὐπελᾰγής, ές, *lying fairly by the sea*, Orph.*A.*167.

εὐπελέκητος, ον, *easy to work with the axe*, Thphr.*HP*5.6.4 (Comp.).

εὐπελής, ές, (πέλω) *easy*, dub. in Orac.ap.Eus.*PE*5.23.

εὐπέμπελος, ον, only in A.*Eu.*476 ἔχουσι μοῖραν οὐκ εὐπέμπελον (sc. Εὐμενίδες), acc. to Sch. *placable, gentle*, opp. δυσπέμφελος; perh. *easily sent away, dismissed* (πέμπω).

εὔπεμπτος, *missilis*, Gloss.

εὐπένθερος, ον, *with a good father-in-law*, Theoc.18.49

εὐπέπαντος, ον, *well-ripened*: *mellow*, of scents, Thphr.*Od.*39.

εὔπεπλος, Ep. **ἐΰ-**, ον, *with beautiful peplos, beautifully robed*, of women, Il.5.424, Od.6.49, Hes.*Th.*273; οὐρανοῦ θυγάτηρ Pi.*Pae.Fr.*16.10, cf. B.8.61. II. εὔπεπλον, τό, = δαφνοειδές, Ps.-Dsc.4.146.

εὐπεπτ-έω, *have a good digestion*, Hp.*Dent.*4, Gal.12.288. **-ος**, ον, *easy of digestion*, opp. δύσπεπτος, Hp.*Acut.*15 (Sup.), Arist.*EN* 1141ᵇ18, Gal.6.577 (Comp.):—Act., *having a good digestion*, Ruf.ap. Orib.8.47.7, Ath.Med.ap.Orib.9.5.6 (Comp.). 2. *easy of coction*, of a humour, Gal.1.280 (Sup.).

εὐπέραντος, ον, *well-finished, distinctly outlined*, Eust.1613.35:—also **-περάτωτος** [ᾰ], ον, ib.36.

εὐπέρᾱτος, ον, *easy to pass*, ποταμός Str.15.1.26 (Comp.), cf. Eust. 892.28.

εὐπερι-άγωγος [ᾰ], ον, *easily turned round*, Luc.*Musc.Enc.*3. **-αίρετος**, ον, *easily stripped off*, φλοιός Thphr.*HP*5.1.1. **-βλεπτος**, *conspicuus, perspicuus*, Gloss. **-βλητος**, ον, *well-dressed*, Simp. in *Cat.*270.24, Anon. in *Cat.*51.2. **-βολος**, ον, gloss on εὐερκής, Hsch. **-γραπτος**, ον, = sq. 2, Luc.*JTr.*33; σάρξ Theon Gymn. ap.Gal.6.91. **-γρᾰφος**, ον, *easy to trace* or *sketch out*, Str.2.1.22, 5.1.2. 2. *with a good outline* or *contour*, Luc.*Am.*14, Ael.*NA*10.13; τοῦ ποδὸς τὸ μὴ εὐ. Luc.*Dom.*7. 3. Adv. -φως *by easy definition*, ὅρῳ ὑποπεσεῖν Iamb.*VP*29.159. 4. *concise*, διαλογισμός Epicur.*Ep.*2 p.35 U. **-θραυστος**, ον, *easy to break*, τὸ θυμικόν Plu.2.458e. **-κάλυπτος** [ᾰ], ον, *easy to conceal*, δυσπραξία *Trag. Adesp.*547.10. **-κοπτος**, ον, *suffering importunity readily*, εὐ. τὰς ἐντεύξεις *waiving ceremony* in his address, Plb.11.10.3. **-κτητος**, ον, *easily acquiring possessions*, Paul.Al.*M.*3, *N.*4. **-ληπτος**, ον, *easily embraced*, Hippiatr.14. 2. metaph., *limited*, ὑποθέσεις Plb.7.7.6. II. *easy to comprehend*, ἀνθρώπῳ Porph.*Abst.*3.4. **-νόητος**, ον, *well-considered*, στίχος *Epigr.Gr.*1096.9 (Stratonicea). **-οπτος**, ον, *easily slighted, despicable*, ἀρχή Plb.*Fr.*157. **-όριστος**, ον, *well-defined*, Str.2.1.30; gloss on εὐδείελος, Apollon.*Lex.* **-πᾰτος**, ον, *allowing one to walk easily*, Luc.*Trag.*324. **-σπαστος**, ον, *easy to pull away*, X.*Cyn.*2.7. **-σταλτος**, ον, *lightly clad* for exercise, Eust.198.43. **-στᾰτος**, ον, *easily besetting*, ἁμαρτία *Ep. Hebr.*12.1; perh. *leading to distress*, cf. περίστασις; εὐπερίστατον, = εὔκολον, εὐχερῆ, Hsch. **-στολος**, ον, *circumspect, wary*, Ptol. *Tetr.*164. **-στρεπτος**, ον, *easily turned* or *wheeled about*, *EM*728.42, Sch.Opp.*H.*4.294. **-στροφος**, ον, = foreg., Ascl. in *Metaph.* 5.8. 2. *wriggling*, τὸ τοῦ δράκοντος εὐ. Eust.229.37, cf. Hsch. s.v. ἀγχίστροφος. **-τρεπτος**, ον, *easy to turn over*, λίθος Seleuc. ap.Ath.4.155e; *supple*, κάμψις Gal.*UP*2.4. II. *easily refuted* or *reversible*, Luc.*JTr.*50. **-φρόνητος**, ον, *contemptible*, Suid. s.v. ἐκ παντὸς ξύλου. **-φωρος**, ον, *easily detected*, τοῖς πολεμίοις Plu. 2.238f. **-χῠτος**, ον, *easily diffused*, ib.954d, Herm.ap.Stob.1.49.44. **-ψογος**, ον, *open to blame*, διὰ γυναῖκα Heph.Astr.1.1. **-ψυκτος**, ον, *easily cooled*, Sor.1.99, Philum.ap.Aët.9.21, Cass. *Pr.*2.

εὐπέτᾰλος, ον, *with beautiful leaves, leafy*, δάφνα Pi.*Parth.*2.69; κισσός Ar.*Th.*1000 (lyr.); λεύκη *AP*4.1.19 (Mel.). II. as Subst., **εὐπέταλον**, τό, = δαφνοειδές, Dsc.4.146, cf. Ruf.ap.Orib.7.26.39. 2. **εὐπέταλος**, ὁ, a precious stone, Orph.*L.*230, Plin.*HN*37.161.

εὐπέταστον· πλατύ, εὐρίπιστον, Hsch.

εὐπέτ-εια, Ion. **-είη**, ἡ, *ease*, δι' εὐπετείας *easily*, E.*Ph.*262; μετ' εὐπετείας γίγνεσθαι Pl.*Ti.*64d; κατὰ πολλὴν εὐπέτειαν D.H.6.52: pl., εὐπετείας διδόναι give *facilities*, grant *indulgences*, κακίας πέρι Pl.*R.*364c. 2. *easiness of getting* or *having*, γυναικῶν Hdt.5.20; τροφῆς X.*Oec.*5.5; τῶν προθυμουμένων Pl.*Lg.*718d; ἀγορᾶς Plu.*Nic.*20. 3. *easy decline, degeneration*, Hp.*Nat.Hom.*12. **-ής**, ές, (πίπτω) prop. of dice, *falling well*: metaph., *favourable, fortunate*, A.*Supp.*1011: Gramm., τὸ εὐ. *good cadence*, v.l. for εὐεπές, D.H.*Comp.*22: generally, *easy, without trouble*, ὁδός, πρόσοδος, Pl.*Sph.*218d (Comp.), X. *Cyr.*5.2.3 (Sup.), etc.; πάντα δ' εὐπετῆ θεοῖς E.*Ph.*689 (lyr.); οὐδὲν εὐ. τῶν μεγάλων Pl.*R.*365c: c. inf., εὐπετὴς χειρωθῆναι Hdt.3.120, 145; ὀφθῆναι, εἰσακοῦσαι, Pl.*Sph.*254a, *R.*494d; also εὐπετές [ἐστι] *it is easy* to..., πολλοὺς εὐπετέστερον διαβάλλειν ἢ ἕνα Hdt.5.97, cf. A. *Supp.*995, X.*Cyr.*4.3.13. 2. Adv. -τῶς, Ion. -τέως, *favourably, fortunately*, εὐπετῶς ἔχειν A.*Ag.*552; οὐ χαλεπῶς, ἀλλ' εὐ. *easily*, Hdt.3.69, cf. 1.189, al.; εὐ. φυλάξασθαι Antipho 3.4.7; ἔχειν τι X. *An.*2.5.23; with numerals, ἑξακοσίους ἀμφορέας εὐ. χωρέει it *easily* holds 600 amphoreis, i.e. *full* 600, Hdt.4.81; τὸ πλάτος γίνεται τεσσέρων εὐ. δακτύλων comes to *full* four fingers, Id.1.193: Comp. -εστέρως Id.3.143; also -έστερον, φέρειν τὸ νόσημα Hp.*Prog.*6. II. of garments and arms, *easy to wear, light*, σάγοι, θυρεοί, Plb.2.28.7, Plu.*Phil.*9. 2. of wine, *easily affected*, Arist.*Pr.*907ᵇ16 (Comp.). III. of persons, *contented, accommodating*, E.*Cyc.*526; *accommodating*, εὐ. ἦθος D.H.*Pomp.*4.2. Adv. -τῶς, φέρειν S.*Fr.* 585; *readily*, Id.*Ichn.*242 (lyr.).

εὐπέτης, ες, (πέτομαι) *flying well*, Eust.899.55.

εὔπετρος, ον, *of good hard stone*, *AP*6.306.8 (Aristo).

εὐπεψία, ἡ, *digestibility*, Arist.*PA*650ᵃ11, 677ᵇ31, Gal.16.245, etc.

εὐπηγής, ές, = sq., once in Hom., ξεῖνος μέγας ἠδ' εὐπηγής *well-built, stout*, Od.21.334; μῆτραι Hp.*Mul.*1.47; δικλίδες A.R.3.236: Dor. perh. **εὐπᾱγής**, v. εὐπάξ.

εὔπηκτος, ον, (πήγνυμι) *well put together, well-built*, ἐνὶ μεγάρῳ εὐ. Il.2.661; μυχῷ κλισίης εὐ. 9.663; μυχῷ θαλάμων εὐ. Od.23.41; σύριγγα ἐκ καρῶ εὐπάκτοιο of *well-moulded, compact*, wax, Theoc.1.128 (s.v.l.); *firm*, of bandaging, Gal.18(2).904. II. of fluids, *easily congealed* or *frozen*, Arist.*Long.*466ᵃ31, 467ᵃ8. 2. Act., εὐ. ἀήρ Thphr.*CP*5.14.3 (Comp.).

εὐπήληξ, ηκος, ὁ, ἡ, *with beautiful helmet*, *AP*6.120 (Leon.). 2. *with fine crest*, ταὧς Babr.65.1a.

εὔπηνος, ον, (πήνη) *of fine texture*, ὑφαί E.*IT*312, 814.

εὐπηξία, ἡ, (εὔπηκτος) *compactness*, [τραχήλου] Adam.2.21.

εὔπηχυς, υ, *with beautiful arms*, χεῖρες E.*Hipp.*200 (anap.); epith. of Athena, Rhian.1.14.

εὐπῖδαξ, ἄκος, ὁ, ἡ, *abounding in fountains*, *AP*6.253.1 (Crin.).

εὐπῐθ-έω, = εὐπειθέω, of an instrument, v.l. in Hp.*Mul.*2.133. **-ής**, ές, = εὐπειθής I, οὐ πείσεις νιν, οὐ γὰρ εὐπιθής A.*Pr.*335: here and in *Ag.*274, *Ch.*259, *Eu.*829, *Supp.*623 cod. Med. has -πειθ-, but -πῐθ- is required by the metre in *Pr.* l.c. and is possible elsewh. (but in *Ag.*982 (-πιθ- codd.) the metre perh. favours -πειθ-); the sense is sts. Act., ὀνείρων φάσματ' εὐπ(ε)ιθῆ σέβεις; *Ag.*274; σῆμα τ' εὐπ(ε)ιθῆ βροτοῖς *Ch.*259; perh. also θάρσος εὐπ(ε)ιθές *Ag.*982 (lyr.); δημηγόρους.. εὐπ(ε)ιθεῖς στροφάς *Supp.*623 (s.v.l.); sts. Pass., σὺ δ' εὐπ(ε)ιθὴς ἐμοί *Eu.*829, cf. *Pr.* l.c.

εὐπίλητος [ῑ], ον, *well-compressed, dense*, dub. l. in Arist.*Sens.* 438ᵃ15 (Comp.).

εὐπίν-εια [ῐ], ἡ, perh. *elegance* of style, Longin.30.1; cf. sq. II. 2. εὐπινείας χάριν for *embellishment*, Heliod.ap.Orib.49.4.42. **-ής**, ές, (πίνος) *neat, tidy*, οὐδ' ἐρημίᾳ γυναικὸς οἶκος εὐπινὴς οὐδ' ὄλβιος E. *Melanipp.Capt.Fr.*6.11 (s.v.l.); so perh. Cratin.414. II. *bright, decorative*, τὸν χαλκὸν.. ἔφασαν.. λειότερον, εὐπινέστερον, δυσιωτότερόν τε εἶναι τοῦ σιδήρου (therefore preferable in machine-construction) Heliod.ap.Orib.49.3.5 (Comp.), cf. 7: hence metaph., of the style of ancient writers, *elegant, simple, quaint*, Caesar mihi irridere visus est 'quaeso' illud tuum, quod erat εὐπινὲς et urbanum, Cic.*Att.* 12.6.3 (Adv. -νῶς ib.15.17.2); as v.l. for ἀπηνής, ἁρμονία D.H.*Comp.*

22. (εὐπινής· εὐειδής, πίνος γὰρ τὸ εἶδος, *Et.Gud.d*, *EM*395.4: εὐπινές· τὸ ἀφελὲς καὶ μὴ λίαν τετημελημένον, ἀλλὰ μέτριον πίνον ἔχον, Phot.)

εὔπιστ-ία, ἡ, *pious belief*, prob. cj. in Jul.*Or*.4.153a. **-ος**, ον, (πίστις) *trustworthy, trusty*, of persons, X.*Cyr*.1.2.12 (Sup.); δῆμος *BCH*37.124 (Abdera, ii B.C.); εὔπιστα *things easy to believe*, S.*Aj*.151 (anap., v.l. εὔπειστα). II. Act., *easily believing, credulous*, Men. 380, Arist.*Rh*.1389^{a}18. Adv. εὐπίστως, ἔχειν Ar.*Th*.105. III. *readily obeying*, Euc.ap.Stob.3.6.63 (sed leg. εὔπειστος).

εὐπίων [ῑ], ον, gen. ονος, *very fat*: *very rich*, φόρτος *AP*7.654 (Leon.).

εὐπλᾰδής, ές, *pliant, ductile*, ὕλη Iamb.*Comm.Math*.4; cf. πλαδαρός.

εὐπλᾰνής, ές, *successfully tracking* Opp.*C*.4.365.

εὐπλαστ-ία, ἡ, *credibility in fiction*, Eust.990.42. **-ος**, ον, *easy to mould* or *put into shape*, of a broken nose, Hp.*Art*.39 (Sup.); φύσει ποὺς εὔ. Aristaenet.1.12. 2. *easy to mould, ductile*, εὐπλαστότερον κηροῦ Pl.*R*.588d, cf. Ael.*NA*17.9, Dsc.4.75; φύσις (of sea-water) Arist.*GA*761^{a}34 (Comp.); ἦθος Pl.*Lg*.666c (Comp.); of men, *impressionable*, Arist.*Po*.1455^{a}33.

εὐπλᾰτής, ές, *of a good breadth*, λόγχη X.*Cyn*.10.3.

ἐΰπλειος, η, ον, *well filled*, κὰδ δ' ἄρα πήρην θῆκεν ἐϋπλείην Od.17.467.

εὐπλεκής, Ep. **ἐϋπλ-**, ές, = sq., θύσανοι.. πάντες ἐϋπλεκέες Il.2.449; δίφροι (cf. sq.) 23.436, Hes.*Sc*.306; σπυρίδες *AP*6.28 (Jul.); of cords, Opp.*H*.5.379: metaph., ἀοιδαί Pi.*Pae*.3.12.

εὔπλεκτος, Ep. **ἐΰπλ-**, ον, also η, ον Nonn.*D*.13.200 (cj. for ἀπλ-): (πλέκω):—*well-plaited, well-twisted*, σειρὰς τ' εὐπλέκτους Il.23.115; ἐϋπλέκτῳ ἐνὶ δίφρῳ a chariot *with sides of wicker* or *basket-work*, ib. 335; of nets, E.*Ba*.870 (lyr.); of hair, *AP*5.286.6 (Agath.).

εὔπλευρος, ον, *with strong lungs*, Arist.*HA*587^{a}3, *Phgn*.810^{b}12.

εὐπληθής, ές, *luxuriant*, Thphr.*HP*4.11.4 (Comp.).

εὔπληκτος, ον, *easily struck*, so as to sound, Plu.2.721f.

εὐπλήρωτος, ον, *easily filled*: *full*, Gal.1.329, al., Alex.Trall.1.11.

εὐ-πλοέω, *have a good voyage*, Ps.-Hdt.*Vit.Hom*.18, Telesp.25 H., Euryph.ap.Stob.4.39.27, D.Chr.63.2, Heph.Astr.3.30; εὐπλοεῖτε, as a wish, *IG*14.933; εὐπλόι (= -όει) ib.2409, cf. 2472 (Arelate). 2. *prosper, receive promotion*, μέχρι τῶν Σεβαστείων χαρακτήρων *SIG* 783.24 (Mantinea, i B.C.). **-πλοια**, poet. **-οΐη**, ἡ, *a fair voyage*, εἰ δέ κεν εὐπλοίην δώῃ... ἐννοσίγαιος Il.9.362; εὔπλοιαν ἔπραξαν A.*Supp*. 1045 (lyr.); εὐπλοίας τυχὼν S.*OT*423, etc. (εὐπλοΐη is required by the metre in *AP*9.9 (Polyaen.), 107 (Leon. or Antip. Thess.), *BMus. Inscr*.1012 (Chalcedon); **εὐπλωΐα** *Cat.Cod.Astr*.2.169.) II. Εὔπλοια, a name of Aphrodite, *IGRom*.3.921 (Cilicia), *IPE*1.94 (Olbia), Paus.1.1.3; on a lamp dedicated to Helioserapis, *IG*14.2405.48 (Puteoli). III. dub. sens. in *PCair.Zen*.15^r.40 (iii B.C.).

ἐϋπλοκᾰμ-ίς, ῖδος, Ep. fem. of sq., ἐϋπλοκαμῖδες Ἀχαιαί Od.2.119, 19.542. **-ος**, Ep. **ἐϋπλ-**, ον, *with goodly locks, fair-haired*, epith. of goddesses and women, in Hom., etc., esp. of Eos and Artemis, Od.5.390, 20.80, cf. B.3.34, etc.; later also of boys and men, Mosch. 1.12, Orph.*L*.439; εὐ. κόμαι *goodly* tresses, E.*IA*790 (lyr.): metaph., ἐϋπλοκάμου πολιῆς ἁλὸς Archil.11, cf. Opp.*C*.2.131; of the tentacles of polypi, ib.3.182.

ἐΰπλοκος, ον, (πλέκω) = εὔπλεκτος, Opp.*H*.3.75, *AP*6.174 (Antip. (Sid.)).

εὔπλοος, ον, contr. **-πλους**, ουν, (πλέω) *good for sailing, fair*, εὔ. πλόος, = εὔπλοια, Erinn.1. II. of a person, *having a fair voyage*, εὔπλοος ὅρμον ἵκοιτο Theoc.7.62 (-πλοον codd.), cf. *BGU*665 ii 7 (i A.D.).

εὔπλουτον· κανοῦν· εὖ ἔχον πλούτου, διὰ τὰς ἐπ' αὐτῷ ὁλάς· πλοῦτον γὰρ ἔλεγον τὴν ἐκ τῶν κριθῶν καὶ τῶν πυρῶν περιουσίαν, Hsch.

ἐϋπλῡνής, ές, (πλύνω) *well-washed, well-cleansed*, φᾶρος Od.8.392, 425, 13.67, 16.173.

εὔπλωτος, ον, *favourable to sailing*, κῦμα *AP*10.25 (Antip.).

εὐ-πνοέω, = εὔπνοός εἰμι, Arist.*Pr*.896^{a}32. II. *respire freely*, ὅταν εὐπνοῇ ὅλον τὸ σῶμα Philistion *Fr*.4. **-πνοια**, ἡ, *easiness of breathing*, Hp.*Prog*.5, Arist.*Pr*.960^{b}24, al.; ἡ τῆς ζωῆς εὐ. Chrysipp. *Stoic*.2.238. II. *free blowing*, ἀνέμων D.S.2.40. 2. *airy situation*, Arist.*Pr*.909^{b}5; ἐν εὐπνοίᾳ Thphr.*CP*6.16.5; εὔπνοιαι εὐήλιοι dub. l. in Dsc.3.119. III. *fragrance*, *AP*12.7 (Strat., in poet. form εὐπνοΐη). **-πνοος**, ον, contr. **-πνους**, ουν, Ep. **ἐΰπνοος**, (πνέω) *breathing well* or *freely*, Hp.*Prog*.15, *Epid*.4.26 (Comp.), Max.Tyr. 30.6 (v.l. ἄϋπνος). 2. causal, *making one breathe freely, relieving oppression of the breath*, λουτρόν Hp.*Acut*.66. 3. *sweet-smelling*, λείρια Mosch.2.32; ῥόδον *IG*14.2040.3. II. *affording a free passage to the air*, μυκτῆρες X.*Eq*.1.10 (Comp.); ὁ [περὶ τὴν κεφαλὴν] τόπος εὔ. Arist.*PA*653^{b}2, cf. 673^{b}23 (Sup.); κάλαμοι Longus 2.35; νεφέλαι εὔ. αὔραις Orph.*H*.21.6. 2. *open to the winds, airy*, οἰκία εὔπνους μὲν τοῦ θέρους, εὐήλιος δὲ τοῦ χειμῶνος Arist.*Oec*.1345^{a}31; τόποι Id.*Pr*.869^{a}34 (Comp.); δένδρα Thphr.*CP*1.15.4; τὸ εὔ. τοῦ τόπου Pl.*Phdr*.230c. III. *good to breathe, fresh and pure*, of the air, Thphr.*CP*1.13.8, Str.3.2.13: Comp. εὐπνοώτερος X. l. c., Hp. *Epid*.4.26; also εὐπνούστερος ib.7.39, Arist.*Pr*.960^{b}22, Gal.5.911: Sup. -ούστατος Arist.*PA*673^{b}23.

εὐποδία, ἡ, (εὔπους) *goodness of foot*, X.*Eq*.1.3, Poll.1.194.

εὐποιέω, freq. written in codd. for εὖ ποιέω, as Hp.*Loc.Hom*.46, etc.

εὐποίημα, ατος, τό, *benefaction*, *PLond*.5.1729.21 (pl., vi A.D.).

εὐποιητικός, ή, όν, *disposed to do good, beneficent*, εἰς or περὶ χρήματα, Arist.*Rh*.1381^{a}20, 1366^{b}16; τινος towards one, ib.1379^{b}32, Porph.*Abst*.3.26; τὸ εὐ. *beneficence*, Arist.*Rh*.1371^{b}3, Antip.*Stoic*.3. 249. 2. Astrol., *beneficent*, of planetary influences, opp. κακοποιητικός, ἰδιοτροπία Ptol.*Tetr*.210.

εὐποίητος, ον (v. infr.), *well-made, well-wrought*, ἔν τε θρόνοις εὐ. Od.20.150; εὐποιητόν τε πυράγρην 3.434; ἅρμα B.5.177, cf. Hes.*Sc*. 64, A.R.3.871, etc.: fem. -τῇσι, -τάων, Il.5.466, 16.636 (nisi scrib. divisim, cf. Sch.Il. ll. cc.).

εὐποιΐα, ἡ, *beneficence*, *Ep.Hebr*.13.16, *Inscr.Perg*.333, Luc.*Abd*. 25, D.L.10.10, Procl. *in Alc*.p.121 C.; τῆς εἴς τινας εὐ. *IG*3.1054:—in form **εὐποΐα**, εἰς πλῆθος *Inscr.Prien*.112.19 (i B.C.): in pl., ib.113. 76 (i B.C.), Ph.1.582, Hierocl.p.59 A.

εὐποίκῐλος, ον, *variegated*, ἄνθος *AP*6.154 (Leon. or Gaet.).

εὐποιός, όν, (ποιέω) = εὐποιητικός, Hsch.

εὔποκος, ον, *fleecy*, νομεύματα A.*Ag*.1416, cf. *Hymn.Curet*.48.

εὐπολέμ-ητος, ον, *easy to be conquered*, Poll.1.158. **-ος**, ον, *good at war, successful in war*, Νίκη *h.Mart*.4; πόλις X.*Vect*.4.51 (Comp.), *Oec*.4.3; of warriors, *APl*.4.331 (Agath.). Adv. -μως *skilfully*, of an officer, D.C.78.38.

Εὐπολίδειος, ον, *in the style of Eupolis*, D.H.*Rh*.11.10; -ειον (sc. μέτρον), τό, *metre invented by him*, Heph.16.5.

εὔπολις, ιδος, ὁ, ἡ, *abounding in cities*, Poll.9.27.

εὔπομπος, ον, *well-conducting, conducting to a happy issue*, S.*OT* 697 (lyr.); εὐπόμπῳ τύχῃ (in allusion to Hermes πομπαῖος) A.*Eu*.93.

εὔπονος, ον, *toilsome*, φυλακαί Aristonous 1.38.

εὐπόρευτος, ον, *easy to travel*, ὁδός Ceb.16. II. *easily passing*, Sch.Lyc.686.

εὐπορ-έω, fut. -ήσω: aor. εὐπόρησα: pf. εὐπόρηκα Diph.43.19, etc., ηὐπ- Pl.*Hp.Ma*.297e, Plu.2.403f:—*prosper, thrive*, εὐποροῦσι γὰρ οἱ ὀλίγοι *are wealthy*, Arist.*Pol*.1280^{a}4, cf. *SIG*344.116 (Teos, iv B.C.); εὐ. ἀπὸ τῶν πονηροτάτων X.*Mem*.2.7.4; οἱ εὐποροῦντες Amphis 15.6; of things, ὅθεν ὁ πόλεμος εὐπορεῖ from which sources war *is successfully maintained*, Th.6.34. b. c. gen. rei, *have plenty of, abound in*, χρημάτων Lys.19.25, Antiph.228.2; σίτων X.*HG*1.6.19; ῥημάτων, ὀνομάτων, λόγων, Pl.*Ion*536c, *Sph*.267d, *Smp*.209b; ἐφοδίων Plu.*Them*. 10; εὐ. ἵππων *gain possession of*.., X.*HG*1.1.10; εὐ. τῆς ἀληθείας *attain* it, Arist.*Metaph*.996^{a}16; also εὐ. ἔν τινι Antipho 5.66; τοῖς ἀναγκαίοις Plb.1.17.2. 2. *find a way, find means*, abs., ὡς ἕκαστοι ηὐπόρησαν Th.6.44, cf. Pl.*Grg*.478a: c. inf., *to be able* to do, ἐπιχειρεῖν Arist. *Top*.102^{a}13 (also τοῦ πολλὰ λέγειν Pl.*Phdr*.235a); also εὐπορῶ ὅ τι λέγω I *have plenty* to say, Id.*Ion*532c: c. part., Id.*Lg*.634b; τοῦτο εὐ. *to be provided with an answer* on this point, Id.*Euthd*.279a; οὐκ εὐ. ὅπῃ.. not *to know how* to do, Id.*Smp*.219e; μᾶλλον εὐ. πρὸς τὴν γνῶσιν Arist.*PA*644^{b}28. II. c. acc. rei, *supply* or *furnish*, τἀργύριον Is.7.8; δέκα μνᾶς τινι D.33.7; *procure*, ἄλλοθεν χρήματα Id.40.36; ὅθεν σιτοπομπίας εὐπόρησε τοῖς στρατιώταις Id.23.155; *bring forward*, ἀποδείξεις D.S.2.31; *find available*, μὴ -ήσας πλοῖον (leg. πλοίων) *POxy*. 1068.3 (iii A.D.):—hence in Pass., = intr. Act., *have plenty of, abound in*, τινος Arist.*Oec*.1347^{b}4; μαθητῶν *Act.Ap*.11.29; τινι Plb.5.43.8; *obtain the use of*, πλοίου *PFlor*.367.8 (iii A.D.): abs., οἱ εὐπορούμενοι *SIG*495.66 (Olbia, iii B.C.), cf. Luc.*BisAcc*.27, *PMag.Par*.1.3125:—εὐπορηθέν in strict pass. sense, *being furnished*, Ps.-Plu.*Vit.Hom*. 210. III. as Philos. term, opp. ἀπορέω, *have one's doubts resolved, gain clear knowledge*, Pl.*Men*.80c, Arist.*Metaph*.995^{a}27; εὐ. περί τινος Id.*de An*.403^{b}21. **-ημα**, ατος, τό, *advantage, help*, Alcid.*Soph*.26 (pl.). **-ησις**, εως, ἡ, in pl., *facilities*, Phld.*Rh*.2.217 S. **-ητέον**, *one must have plenty*, καθαρσίων Ph.5 p.147 C. **-ητος**· ὁ καλῶς διοικῶν, Hsch. **-ία**, ἡ, (εὔπορος) *ease, facility*, of doing a thing, c. inf., Emp.100.5; ναῦς εὐ. ἦν ποιεῖσθαι Th.4.52: abs., ὅτε πολλὴ ὑμῖν εὐ. φαίνεται X.*An*.7.6.37: c. gen. rei, *easy means of providing*, τοῦ βίου Pl.*Prt*.321e; τοῦ καθ' ἡμέραν Th.3.82; also εὐ. ἐν τῇ τέχνῃ, ἐκ τῆς τέχνης, Lys.24.5; εὐ. τῆς τύχης Th.3.45; εὐπορίαν τῇ βδελυρίᾳ τῇ ἑαυτοῦ τοὺς συμμάχους ποιεῖσθαι to make them *a means of satisfying* his brutal passions, Aeschin.1.107; ἡ παρ' ἀλλήλων εὐ. mutual *assistance*, Isoc.6.67. 2. *plenty, abundance*, opp. πενίη, Democr. 101; χρημάτων X.*HG*4.8.28; ἀγαθῶν Arist.*Metaph*.1091^{b}26; ἡ περὶ τὸν βίον εὐ. Isoc.12.7; ἡ περὶ τὴν οὐσίαν εὐ. Arist.*Pol*.1326^{b}34: abs., *welfare*, X.*Cyr*.3.3.7; opp. ἀπορία, Arist.*Pol*.1279^{b}27: in pl., *advantages*, Isoc.15.253, D.5.8; εὐπορίαι προσόδων Arist.*Pol*.1293^{a}3; ἀρουραίη εὐ. rustic *wealth*, *AP*9.373.6; μιῆς οἶος καὶ βοὸς εὐ. *consisting of* one sheep or ox, ib.149 (Antip.); ἡ Εὐ. θεά *SIG*1111 (Piraeus, iii A.D.). II. opp. ἀπορία, *solution of doubts* or *difficulties*, Pl.*Phlb*. 15c; opp. ἀμηχανία, X.*Oec*.9.1; ἡ ὕστερον εὐ. λύσις τῶν πρότερον ἀπορουμένων Arist.*Metaph*.995^{a}29; *resourcefulness*, Hp.*Off*.7. **-ίζω**, *supply, provide means for*, ἐνεργείαις Gal.18(2).722 (dub. l.). **-ιστία**, ἡ, *ease of procuring* a thing, Epicur.*Fr*.470. **-ιστος**, ον, (πορίζω) *easy to procure* or *secure*, Id.*Ep*.3 p.63 U., *Sent*.21, *Fr*.469, Dsc.*Eup. Praef*.: Sup., ἀμπεχόνη, οἰκία, Ph.2.424, cf. Phld.*D*.1.15; *feasible*, Cic.*Att*.7.1.7; εὐπόριστα (sc. φάρμακα), τά, *common, family medicines*: title of work by Dsc., Orib.*Eup.Praef*. (called περὶ ἁπλῶν φαρμάκων in codd. of Dsc.*Eup*.); also, *ordinary food*, opp. *game out of season*, Plu.*Luc*.40, *Pomp*.2. II. Act., *providing one's subsistence with ease*, Ptol.*Tetr*.155. **-ος**, ον, *easy to pass* or *travel through*, ἄτης.. πέλαγος οὐ μάλ' εὔ. A.*Supp*.470; ὁδός Pl.*R*.328e; τὰ εὔ. *open ground*, X.*Eq.Mag*.4.4; εὔπορον ἦν διιέναι Th.4.78, cf. X.*An*.3.5.17; εὔ. ποιεῖν τὰ ὦτα to *open* one's ears, Luc.*Lex*.1; μήτρα *lax*, Sor.1.34. 2. *easily got, easily done, easy*, τὰ μέγιστα.. σφι εὔπορά ἐστι Hdt.4.59; πολλά τοι θεὸς κακ τῶν ἀέλπτων εὔπορ' ἀνθρώποις τελεῖ E.*Fr*.100; παρ' ἐμοὶ δ' ἔστιν ταῦτα εὔ. Ar.*Pl*.532, cf. Pl. *R*.404c; φιλία... εὔ. εἴη Ar.*Lys*.1266; τὴν κατὰ θάλασσαν ἔφοδον -ωτέραν Th.1.93; πλεῖστον... μέλι καὶ -ώτατον Pl.*R*.564e; τὸ εὔ., = εὐπορία, εὑρίσκειν τὸ εὔ. Hp.*Art*.78; διὰ τὸ εὔ. τῆς ἐλπίδος Th.8. 48; εὔπορόν ἐστι it is *easy*, c. inf., X.*An*.3.5.17, D.3.18, etc.; ἐν εὐπόρῳ κεῖται c. inf., Str.10.3.8: Comp. -ώτερον Pl.*R*.404c. II. *ready, glib*, γλῶττα Ar.*Eq*.637. 2. of persons, *full of resources* or *devices, ingenious, inventive*, opp. ἄπορος, E.*Fr*.430 (Sup.); εἰ οὖν τις ..-ώτερος ἐμοῦ Pl.*Phd*.86d; εὐ. ἐν τοῖς ἀπόροις Alex.234.5; -ώτεροι πρὸς ἅπαν ἔργον Pl.*Prt*.348d: c. inf., χρήματα πορίζειν -ώτατον γυνή Ar.*Ec*.236; ἐς τὴν δίαιταν -ώτατοι Id.*V*.1112. III. *well-provided with, rich in*, πόλιν τοῖς πᾶσιν -ωτάτην Th.2.64; τὰ περὶ τὸν βίον -ώτεροι Isoc.8.19; τίς -ώτερος χρημάτων; D.Chr.3.132: abs., *fertile*, γῆ Poll.1.186; *well-furnished*, πράγματ' -ώτερα D.19.89; *well off, wealthy*, οἱ εὔ. Id.1.28, etc.; opp. οἱ ἄποροι, Arist.*Pol*.1279^{b}8, etc.; *persons of substance*, capable of bearing taxation, *SIG*344.115 (Sup., Teos, iv B.C.); εὔ. καὶ ἐπιτήδειος *POxy*.1187.11 (iii A.D.), etc. IV. Adv. -ρως *easily*, X.*Cyr*.1.6.9, etc.: Comp. -ώτερον Pl.*Smp*.204e. 2. *in abundance*, εὐ. ἔχειν πάντα Th.8.36; οὐκ εὐ. ἔχω I don't feel *well*, Luc.*Lex*.2 codd. (εὐφ– Cobet). 3. *resourcefully*, Hp.*Off*.7.

εὐπόρφῠρος, ον, *of bright purple colour*, v.l. in Lxx*Ez*.23.12.

εὐποσία, ἡ, *abundance*, *IPE*1^{2}.140,141 (Olbia); θεὰ Εὐ. Judeich *Altertümer von Hierapolis* 26.

εὐποσιάρχης, ου, ὁ, = εὐβοσιάρχης (q.v.), *CIG*3385.2 (Smyrna), *IG*12(8).526 (Thasos), *Supp.Epigr*.1.332 (Tomi):—hence **-αρχέω**, *LW*53 (Erythrae).

εὐπότιστος, *riguus*, *Gloss*.

εὐποτμ-έω, *to be lucky, fortunate*, Plu.*Aem*.26. **-ία**, ἡ, *good fortune*, Xanth.10, Plu.*Arist*.24, Luc.*DDeor*.15.1, Ael.*NA*11.40. **-ος**, ον, *happy, prosperous*, αἰών A.*Ag*.246 (lyr.); δύνασις -οτάτα μελέων S.*Fr*.568, cf. Plu.2.58d (Comp.); of trees, *flourishing*, Sever.ap.Orib.9.17.2 (Comp.). Adv. -μως Epist.Anaximen.ap.D.L.2.4, Muson.*Fr*.17 p.93 H.

εὔποτος, ον, (πίνω) *easy to drink, pleasant to the taste*, ῥέος A.*Pr*.676, 812; ὕδωρ Ath.Med.ap.Orib.*inc*.23.15; of milk, A.*Pers*.611. II. *good to drink from*, ἐκπώματα Eratosth.ap.Ath.11.482b (Sup.). III. *accustomed to drink*, Aret.*CA*2.3.

εὔπους, ὁ, ἡ, πουν, τό, gen. ποδος, *with good feet*, of horses and dogs, X.*Eq*.1.3, *Cyn*.3.2; of a bird, εὔπους καὶ κακόπτερος Arist.*HA*617^{b}4; *fleet of foot*, Δηωΐνη Call.*Fr*.48. II. *with good feet, flowing*, ἁρμονία *AP*6.54 (Paul. Sil.).

εὐπρᾱγ-έω, = εὖ πράσσω, *do well, be well off, flourish*, Th.2.60, 6.16, X.*Ap*.27, etc. **-ημα**, ατος, τό, *a success*, in war, in pl., App.*Pun*.4, *BC*1.51: generally, Sch.Pi.*I*.3.1. **-ία**, Ion. **εὐπρηγίη**, ἡ, Eus.Mynd.59:—*welfare, success*, Pi.*O*.8.14, *P*.7.16, Antipho 2.4.9, Th.5.46, etc.: pl., Id.1.84, 4.17, Pl.*Lg*.732c, Isoc.9.42. II. *well doing*, opp. mere success, Pl.*Alc*.1.116b, *Euthd*.281b; περὶ αὐλημάτων εὐ. ib.279e, cf. *Prt*.345a; *good deeds, services*, Arist.*Rh*.1367^{a}4 (pl.); cf. εὐπραξία.

εὐπρακτ-έω, *prosper*, Vett.Val.198.28. **-ος**, Ep. **-πρηκτος**, ον, *easy to be done*, X.*An*.2.3.20 (Comp.); οὐκ εὔπρηκτα κέλευθα Opp.*H*.5.63. II. *well-to-do, prosperous*, Vett.Val.72.11, Man.1.352.

εὐπραξία, Ion. **εὐπρηξίη**, ἡ, = εὐπραγία, Hdt.7.49, 8.54, A.*Th*.224, S.*OC*1554, etc.: pl., E.*Ion* 566; also in codd. of Th.1.33, 3.39 (–πραγία Phot.): both forms in Arist., –πραγία *Pol*.1325^{a}22, –πραξία *EN*1098^{b}22. 2. epith. of Artemis at Tyndaris, *IG*14.375. II. *good conduct*, X.*Mem*.3.9.14, Arist.*EN*1140^{b}7.

εὔπραξις, εως, ἡ, poet. for εὐπραξία, A.*Ag*.255 (lyr., sed scrib. divisim).

εὔπρᾱτος, ον, gloss on εὔωνος, Hsch.

εὔπρεμνος, ον, *with good stem*, δρῦς *AP*6.221.10 (Leon.); εὐπρέμνοις· εὐστελεχέσιν, Hsch.

εὐπρέπ-εια, ἡ, *goodly appearance, comeliness*, εὐπρεπείᾳ προέχειν Th.6.31; opp. ἀπρέπεια, Pl.*Phdr*.274b, al.; *majesty*, εὐ. τῆς δόξης Lxx*Je*.23.9, cf. *Ep.Jac*.1.11; *dignity*, *SIG*880.19 (Pizus, iii A.D.); ἐστεφάνωσε ἁ πόλις..-είας καὶ εὐνοίας ἕνεκα τᾶς ἐς τὰν πόλιν *IG*4.1418 (Epid., iv B.C.). II. *speciousness, plausibility*, εὐπρεπείᾳ λόγου Th.3.11, 82; ἔχει..εὐπρέπειαν μᾶλλον ἢ ἀλήθειαν Pl.*Euthd*.305e; *pretext*, c. inf., Plu.*Pyrrh*.23. **-έω**, *to be seemly, acceptable*, Aq.*Pr*.2.10. **-ής**, ές, (πρέπω) *well-looking, comely*, of outward appearance, σχῆμα -έστατον Hdt.1.60, cf. 2.37; [κόσμος] εὐ. A.*Pers*.833; εὐ. ἰδεῖν *fair* to look on, Ar.*Th*.192, X.*Mem*.2.1.22; εἶδος -εστάτη E.*Hec*.269 (v.l. ἐκπρ–); τὴν ὄψιν D.40.27; κοσμοῦντες..οἰκοδομήμασιν -έστερα Pl.*Lg*.761c. 2. *decent, seemly*, ἄνδρα δ' -έστερον (sc. ἐξελθεῖν ἐστι) A.*Ch*.664, etc.; οὐ γὰρ εὐ. λέγειν E.*Or*.1145; λόγος ἐμοὶ οὐκ -έστερος λέγεσθαι Hdt.2.47; νόσημα ῥηθῆναι οὐκ εὐ. Isoc.12.267; τελευτὴ -εστάτη a *most glorious* end, Th.2.44. 3. *specious, plausible*, opp. ἀληθής, E.*Tr*.951; σκῆψις -εστάτη Hdt.3.72; εὐ. αἰτία Th.6.76; εὐ. δειλία cowardice *veiled under a fine name*, Id.3.82; μετ' ὀνόματος εὐ. ibid.; ἀπάτη εὐπρεπεῖ Id.4.86; ἐκ τοῦ εὐ. *in pretence*, Id.7.57; τὸ εὐ. τοῦ λόγου, = εὐπρέπεια II, Id.3.38, 44; εὐ. ἦν πρὸς τοὺς πλείους Id.8.66. II. Adv. -πῶς, Ion. -πέως, οὐκ ἔχειν -έως ἐκλιπεῖν τὴν τάξιν Hdt.7.220, cf. A.*Ag*.616, etc.; *with a good pretext*, Th.6.6: Comp. -πέστερον E.*Rh*.841; -πεστέρως *Gloss*.: Sup. -πέστατα Th.8.109. **-ίζω**, in Pass., *to be acceptable*, Aq.*Ps*.140(141).6.

εὔπρεπτος, ον, *conspicuous*, A.*Supp*.722.

εὐπρηγίη, v. εὐπραγία. **εὐπρηξίη**, Ion. for εὐπραξία.

εὔπρηστος, ον, (πρήθω) *well-blowing, strong-blowing*, εὔπρηστον ἀϋτμὴν ἐξανιεῖσαι, of bellows, Il.18.471.

εὐπριστία, ἡ, *the being skilfully sawn*, ξύλων Sch.Il.8.93.

εὔπριστος, ον, *easily sawn*, Thphr.*HP*5.6.3, f.l. for καπυρόν in Hp.*VC*19.

εὐπρο-αίρετος, ον, *having a good moral purpose*, Ptol.*Tetr*.158, Vett.Val.82.11, al. Adv. -τως, ζῶντες Artem.2.37. **-ιρον**, (πρωρ– cod. extra ordinem)· εὐπρόσωπον, εὐκέφαλον, Hsch.; cf. προίρης. **-ορᾱτος**, ον, *easily foreseen*, *Gloss*.

εὐπροσ-αγκάλιστος, gloss on εὐάγκαλος, Hsch. **-δεκτος**, ον, *acceptable*, *Ep.Rom*.15.16, 31; τοῖς πολλοῖς Plu.2.801c; εὐχή, θυσία, Porph.*Marc*.24, Sch.Ar.*Pax* 1054; ὥσπερ οὐκ εὐ. (sc. ὄν) c. inf., Phld.*Rh.Supp*.p.7S. **-δόκητος**, ον, *well-expected*, Iamb.*Protr*.20. **-εδρος**, ον, v.l. for εὐπάρεδρος (q.v.). **-ηγορία**, ἡ, *affability*, Isoc.1.20. **-ήγορος**, ον, *easy of address*, i.e. *affable, courteous*, ἐν -οισίν ἐστί τις χάρις; E.*Hipp*.95; εὐ. φρήν Id.*Alc*.775; γῆρας *Trag.Adesp*.552, cf. Trag. in *Gött.Nachr*.1922.31; τῷ λόγῳ εὐ. Isoc.1.20; οὐκ εὐ. ἆται miseries that forbid *my being spoken to*, E.*HF*1284: Sup. -ώτατος J.*AJ*19.1.13. Adv. -ρως D.H.*Rh*.5.4. **-θετος**, ον, *easily assimilated*, τροφή Hp.*Alim*.49; of medicines, Gal.14.267. **-ῐτος**, ον, *easy of access*, of places, Str.12.3.11, Luc.*VH*2.44. 2. of persons, *accessible, affable, agreeable*, Gal.*Anim.Pass*.8, Alex.Aphr.*inTop*.531.21, Man.5.288, *Gp*.2.44.2. Adv. -τως Poll.5.139.

εὐπρόσκοπος, ον, *far-seeing, cautious*, τὸ τῶν ἠθῶν εὐκινητότερον καὶ πολυτροπώτερον καὶ -πώτερον Ptol.*Tetr*.173; cf. ἀπρόσκοπος (B). II. *easily taking offence*, ἀθύμῳ καὶ ἀσθενικῷ καὶ εὐπροσκόπῳ καὶ πρὸς πάντας δυσαρέστῳ ib.207; cf. ἀπρόσκοπος (A).

εὐπροσ-όδευτος, ον, *income-producing*, of flowers, *Gp*.10.1.3. **-οδος**, ον, of persons, *accessible*, πᾶσιν Th.6.57, X.*Ages*.9.2, Plu.*Publ*.4. 2. of places, *easily accessible*, in Sup., X.*HG*6.5.24, *An*.5.4.30; ἔνθα ᾤετο εἶναι -ώτατον ὅσα δεῖ προσκομίζεσθαι *the readiest way of approach* for..., Id.*Cyr*.6.1.23, cf. Aen.Tact.22.15. II. Act., *approaching easily, manageable*, νῆες Ph.*Bel*.104.16. **-οιστος**, ον, *easy of approach*: generally, *easy*, ἔκβασις E.*Med*.279. **-όμῑλος**, ον, *pleasant, nice to deal with*, dist. fr. εὐόμιλος, Phryn.*PS*p.68 B. (= *Com.Adesp*.1015): Sup. -ότατος Suid. **-όρμιστος**, ον, *easy to land on*, νῆσος D.S.5.13, cf. Poll.1.100. **-ρητος**, ον, = εὐπροσήγορος, condemned by Id.5.138. **-φθέγκτοις**· εὐήχοις, Hsch. **-φορος**, ον, *easily uttering, fluent*, ἐν τῇ Ῥωμαίων φωνῇ Hdn.8.3.7. II. *easily assimilated, nutritious*, of food, Xenocr.9. **-φῠτος**, ον, *easily growing to*, τῷ ὁμοίῳ τὸ ὅμοιον Thphr.*CP*1.6.2.

εὐπροσωπ-έω, *make a good show*, *PTeb*.19.12 (ii B.C.), *Ep.Gal*.6.12. **-ία**, ἡ, *fair appearance*, D.H.3.11. **-ίζομαι**, Pass., = εὐπροσωπέω, Al.*Ps*.140(141).6.

εὐπροσωποκοίτης, ὁ, *lying so as to present a fair face*, τύχαι εὐ. (metaph. from the dice), A.*Ch*.969 Franz (lyr.).

εὐπρόσωπος, ον, *fair of face*, Cratin.304, Anaxandr.9.5; μειράκιον Ar.*Pl*.976, cf. *Ra*.412 (lyr.), X.*Mem*.1.3.10 (Sup.); *with glad countenance*, S.*Aj*.1009; comice, λοπάς Eub.44.1. 2. metaph., *fair in outward show, specious*, ὑπεκρίναντο..εὐπρόσωπα Hdt.7.168; οὐκ εὐ. φροιμίοις E.*Ph*.1336; λόγους εὐ. καὶ μύθους D.18.149; εὐ. ἡ τοιαύτη νομοθεσία Arist.*Pol*.1263^{b}15: Comp., Aristid.1.429 J. Adv. -πως Philostr.*VS*1.18.4, Aristaenet.1.9, Jul.*Or*.7.224b. 3. perh. *possessing legal personality*, Antig.ap.Plu.2.458f (with pun on signf. 1).

εὐπροφάσιστος [ᾰ], ον, *with good pretext, plausible*, αἰτία Th.6.105; ἀφορμαί Ptol.*Tetr*.2; -ιστον (sc. ἐστί) c. inf., App.*BC*3.76; εὐπροφάσιστα ἀδικεῖν Ph.2.496. Adv. -τως Ptol.*Tetr*.6, Vett.Val.286.14. 2. *easily admitting of pretexts*, App.*Pun*.64.

εὐπρόφορος, ον, *easy to pronounce*, D.H.*Comp*.12. Adv. -ρως, dub. sens., *PMag.Leid.V*.8.26.

εὐπροχώρητος, ον, *progressing easily*, Ptol.*Tetr*.157.

εὐπρυμν-ής, ές, *well-steering, well-governing*, εὐπρυμνῇ φρενὸς χάριν A.*Supp*.989 (s.v.l.). **-ος**, ον, *with goodly stern* or *poop*, νῆες Il.4.248, B.12.150, cf. Hp.*Ep*.14, E.*IT*1000, 1357; πλᾶται Id.*IA*723.

εὔπρῳρος, ον, *with goodly prow* or *head*, πλάτα E.*IA*765 (lyr.); cf. εὔπροιρον.

εὔπταιστος, ον, *easily stumbling*: metaph., *unreliable*, of words as compared with facts, Hp.*Praec*.2.

εὔπτερος, ον, *well-winged, well-plumed*, of birds, S.*OT*175 (lyr.); αὐχένες, δέμας, E.*Ion*1200, 1203; φαρέτρα v.l. in Bion 1.82 (Tricl.): metaph., εὔ. γυναῖκες *high-plumed* dames, Ar.*Nu*.800. II. εὔπτερον, τό, = ἀδίαντον, Ps.-Dsc.4.134; = τριχομανές, ib.135.

εὐπτέρῠγος, ον, = foreg. 1, Opp.*C*.3.125; of ships, *AP*10.6 (Satyr., dub. l.).

εὐπτησία, ἡ, *expertness in flying*, Artem.5.69, Max.Tyr.31.2.

εὐπτόητος, ον, *easily scared*, πρὸς ἅπαν Plu.2.642a, cf. Sch.A.*Th*.78.

εὐπτόλεμος, ον, poet. for εὐπόλεμος, *AP*4.3b.22 (Agath.); Ep. ἐΰπτ– Q.S.5.320.

εὔπτορθος, ον, *finely branching*, of horns, *APl*.4.96.4.

εὐπῡγία, ἡ, *fine shape in the hinder parts*, Alex.98.11.

εὐπυγμέω, *to be in vigorous health*, *PLond*.3.1244.7 (iv A.D.).

εὔπῡγος, ον, (πυγή) *well-shaped in the hinder parts*, Herm.ap.Stob.1.49.45 (Comp.), Poll.2.184.

εὐπυνδάκωτος [ᾰ], ον, *well-bottomed*, of a cup, Luc.*Lex*.13.

εὔπυργος, ον, *well-towered*, of fortified towns, Τροίην εὔ. Il.7.71, cf. Hes.*Sc*.270, B.5.184, *AP*9.62 (Even.): poet. **ἠΰπυργος** prob. in Pi.*N*.4.12.

εὔπῡρος, ον, *fertile in corn*, Poll.9.162.

εὐπῡροφόρος, = foreg., Str.5.4.2 (s.v.l.).

εὐπύρωτος, ον, (πυρόω) *easily set fire to*, Thphr.*CP*1.22.5.

εὐπώγων, ωνος, ὁ, *well-bearded*, Arist.*Phgn*.808^{a}23, *AP*9.99 (Leon.), 744 (Id.).

εὔπωλος, ον, *abounding in foals* or *horses*, in Hom. as epith. of Troy, Ἴλιον εἰς εὔ. Il.5.551, al.; αὔχημα εὔιππον, εὔπωλον the glory of noble steeds and *their offspring*, S.*OC*711 (lyr.).

εὔπωνος ὄμβρος· εὔποτος, Hsch.; cf. πώνω, γακουπώνης.

εὑραί, *αἱ*, f. l. for θύραι, Poll.1.146. II. **εὖραι**· αὖραι, Hsch.

εὑρακύλων, *ωνος*, *ὁ*, name of a north-east wind, = Lat. (Vulg.) *euroaquilo*, ἄνεμος τυφωνικὸς ὁ καλούμενος εὐ. *Act.Ap.*27.14, with many vv.ll., including εὑροκλύδων.

εὑράξ, Adv. *on one side, sideways*, στῆ δ' εὐ. σὺν δουρί Il.11.251, 15.541, cf. Lyc.920. II. εὐ. πατάξ, an exclamation in Ar.*Av.*1258, to frighten away birds.

εὔραπτος, *ον*, *well-sewn*, *Gloss.*: gloss on ἐϋρραφής, Sch.Od.2.354.

εὐράχαντες· ἥκοντες· ῥαχίας γὰρ ἐκάλουν τοὺς τραχεῖς καὶ παρήκοντας τόπους, *EM*395.21, Phot.

εὔρειθρος, *ον*, = ἐϋρρεής, Man.1.141.

εὐρέϊος, *α*, *ον*, (Εὖρος) *easterly*, A.*Supp.*871 (lyr.) cod. Med.

εὐρείτης, v. ἐϋρρείτης.

εὐρέκτης, *ου*, *ὁ*, (ῥέζω) *beneficent*, *IGRom.*4.854 (Laodicea ad Lycum).

εὕρεμα, *ατος*, *τό*, later form of εὕρημα, v.l. in Hp.*Vict.*1.2, *SIG* 1012.11 (Cos, ii/i B.C.), *PMag.Leid.W.*7.34, Str.16.2.24, *AP*7.411 (Diosc.), Babr.*Prooem.* ii 2.

εὑρεσι-έπεια, v. εὑρησι-. **-κᾰκος**, *ον*, *inventive of evil*, Sch.E. *Med.*407. **-λογέω, -λογία, -λογος**, v. εὑρησιλογέω, etc.

εὑρέσιος Ζεύς, *ὁ*, = *Juppiter Inventor*, D.H.1.39.

εὕρεσις, *εως*, *ἡ*, *a finding, discovery*, Pl.*R.*336e, *Cra.*436a; οὐχ εὕ. τοῦτ' ἔστιν, ἀλλ' ἀφαίρεσις Men.*Epit.*102. II. of writings, *invention, conception*, παρασκευήν, ἣν οἱ παλαιοὶ καλοῦσιν εὕρεσιν, opp. χρῆσις, D.H.*Dem.*51, cf. *Stoic.*2.96.

εὑρεσίτεχνος [ῐ], *ον*, *inventor of arts*, Orph.*H.*32.14.

εὑρέσφι· γυναιξίν, Hsch. (cf. ἔορ, ἔορες).

εὑρετ-έος, *α*, *ον*, *to be discovered, found out*, Th.3.45. **-ής**, *οῦ*, *ὁ*, *an inventor, discoverer*, Pl.*La.*186e, Isoc.2.17, *SIG*728*K*3 (Delph., i B.C.), etc.; cf. εὑρέτις. **-ικός**, *ή*, *όν*, *inventive, ingenious*, Pl.*Smp.* 209a: Comp. in Id.*Plt.*286e, 287a; ἰατρός Gal.7.212: Comp., Procl. *in Alc.*p.177 C.; εὑρετικὸν εἶναί φασι τὴν ἐρημίαν Men.39: c. gen., λόγων D.H.*Lys.*15; also, *able to make discoveries from...*, οὗ ἔμαθεν Pl.*R.*455b, cf. Andronic.Rhod.p.578 M. II. *concerned with inquiry* or *discovery*, λόγος, opp. ἀποδεικτικός, Gal.4.650. **-ις** (parox.), *ιδος*, fem. of εὑρετής, S.*Fr.*101 (v.l. εὑρετής), Secund.*Sent.* 10 (v.l. εὑρετής); acc. εὑρέτιν D.S.1.25 (this form determines the accent; for the acc. of εὑρετίς would be εὑρετίδα). **-ός**, *ή*, *όν*, *discoverable*, Hp.*Vict.*1.2; τὰ μὲν διδακτὰ μανθάνω, τὰ δ' εὑρετὰ ζητῶ S.*Fr.*843; εὑρετὰ ἀνθρώποις X.*Mem.*4.7.6.

εὕρετρα, *τά*, *reward given to finder* of lost property, Ulp. in *Dig.* 47.2.43.

εὑρέτρια, *ἡ*, = εὑρέτις, D.S.5.67, *POxy.*1380.185 (ii A.D.).

εὔρηκτος, *ον*, *easy to break*, Aret.*CD*1.13, Orib.49.3.8.

εὕρημα, *ατος*, *τό*, later εὕρεμα (q.v.), (εὑρίσκω) *invention, discovery, thing discovered not by chance but by thought*, Hp.*VM*4; ἀριθμῶν καὶ μέτρων εὑρήματα S.*Fr.*432; πολλῶν λόγων εὑρήμαθ' E.*Hec.* 250, cf. Ar.*Nu.*561, Pl.*Tht.*150d, al.; τύμπανα, Ῥέας... εὑ. E.*Ba.*59, cf. *HF*188; τὰ τῶν ἰατρῶν εὑ. D.26.26; opp. ὑπηρέτημα, Antipho 1.15. 2. c. gen., *invention for* or *against* a thing, *remedy*, τῆσδε συμφορᾶς E.*Hipp.*716. 3. *excuse*, εἰς συκοφαντίαν *POxy.*472.33 (ii A.D.). II. *that which is found unexpectedly*, i.e. much like Ἕρμαιον (q.v.), *piece of good luck, windfall*, Hdt.7.155; εὑ. εὕρηκε ib.10.δ', 8.109; εὑ.... κάλλιστον εὕρηκ' E.*Heracl.*533; εὑ... οἷον ηὕρηκας τόδε Id.*Med.*716, cf. 553; εὑρήμασι πλούσιος ἐγένετο Hdt.7.190; εὑ. γίγνεται τόδε E.*El.*606; ἐκείνοις δὲ δυστυχοῦσι εὑ. εἶναι διακινδυνεῦσαι Th.5.46; εὑ. ἐδόκει εἶναι X.*An.*7.3.13, cf. Is.9.26, Herod.6.30, etc. 2. of a child, *foundling*, εὑ. δέξατ' ἐκ Νυμφᾶν S.*OT*1106 (lyr.), cf. E.*Ion* 1349. III. (in form εὕρεμα) *sum realized* by a sale, *SIG*1012.11 (Cos, ii/i B.C.); cf. ἀφ-, ὑπερεύρεμα.

εὑρημοσύνη, *ἡ*, *fluency, eloquence*, Poll.2.128.

εὑρήμων, *ον*, gen. *ονος*, (ῥῆμα) *fluent, eloquent*, Poll.2.128, Hsch.

εὑρήσει· λοιδορήσει, Hsch.; cf. εὑρητοῖς.

εὑρησῐ-επής, *ές*, *inventive of* ἔπη, *creative in poetry*, Pi.*O.*9.80; in bad sense, *coiner of phrases*, Ar.*Nu.*447 (anap.):—later **εὑρεσιέπεια**, glossed by εὑρεσιλογία, Suid.: pl., Hsch. **-λογέω**, *invent ingenious arguments, explanations*, or *pretexts*, Plb.26.1.2, al., Phld.*Rh.*1.207 S., Str.13.1.69, Ph.1.314, al., Plu.2.31e, Porph.*Antr.*36; ταῦτα Plu.2.625c. **-λογία**, *ἡ*, *skill in finding arguments*, esp. *perverse* or *sophistical ingenuity*, Plb.18.46.3, D.S.1.37, Ph.1.628, 698, Plu.2.1033b, Arr.*Epict.*2.20.35: pl., Plb.12.26^{c}.4, 29.1.2: **-ίαν** ἔχειν, of a phenomenon, admit of *an ingenious explanation*, Str.17.1.34. **-λογος**, *ον*, *ingenious in argument, sophistical*, Corn.*ND*31: Sup., D.L.4.37.—εὑρησι- is freq. in Pap. in this group of words, e.g. *PRein.*14.23, 15.21 (ii B.C.), Phld.*Rh.*1.207 S., etc.; εὑρεσι- first in Pap. of iv A.D., *POxy.*71 i 9 (corr. fr. εὑρησι-), *PMasp.*153.32 (vi A.D.), etc., f.l. in Plb.18.46.3, Ph. ll. cc. (εὑρησ- v.l. 1.628), etc.

εὕρησις, *εως*, *ἡ*, worse form of εὕρεσις, Apollod.3.3.1.

εὑρητοῖς· τοῖς ἀτιμήμασιν, Hsch.; cf. εὑρήσει.

εὔρητος, *ον*, (ῥηθῆναι) *easy to tell*, Ael.*NA*17.23.

εὑρήτωρ, *ορος*, *ὁ*, = εὑρετής, v.l. for εἰδήμονα, *AP*9.505.4.

εὔριζος, Ep. **ἐΰρρ-**, *ον*, *well-rooted*, Nic.*Fr.*74.17 codd. Ath. (dub. l.), cf. Lxx *Ps.*47(48).3.

εὖριν, late form of εὖρις (q.v.).

εὔρῑνος (A), Ep. **ἐΰρρ-**, *ον*, (ῥίς) = εὖρις, Babr.43.8, Opp.*C.*2.456, Ael.*NA*2.15, Heph.Astr.1.1 (admitted by *EM*765.53, Suid., in S.*Aj.* 8): Sup. in Hsch.

εὔρῑνος (B), Ep. **ἐΰρρ-**, *ον*, *of good leather*, A.R.3.1299, *AP*14.55.9.

εὐρῑπῐδ-ἀριστοφᾰνίζω, *write in the style of Euripides and Aristophanes*, Cratin.307. **-ειος**, *α*, *ον*, *of* or *like Euripides*, Εὐ. τι συμβήσεται Pl.*Tht.*154d; τὸ Εὐ. *the saying of Euripides*, Plu.*Pyrrh.* 14. II. τὸ Εὐ. (sc. μέτρον) an asynartete verse so called, Heph. 15.16. **-ης**, *ου*, *ὁ*, *Euripides*, n. pr. II. nickname given to the *cast 40* of the dice, from one Euripides who held office with the Forty at Athens, Diph.73.3, cf. Ath.6.247a, Poll.9.101. **-ικῶς**, Adv. *like Euripides*, Sch.Ar.*Eq.*18. **-ιον**, *τό*, *little Euripides*, term of endearment, Ar.*Ach.*404, 475.

Εὐρῑπική σχοῖνος, name of a kind of reed, Dsc.4.52, *Eup.*1.26, Plin.*HN*21.119.

εὐρίπιστος [ρι], *ον*, (ῥιπίζω) *easily fanned into flame*, Cic.*Att.*14.5.2. II. *unstable*, Alex.Aphr. *in Sens.*26.21, Hsch. s.v. γάγγαλος.

εὔρῑπος, *ὁ*, *any strait* or *narrow sea, where the flux and reflux is violent*, X.*HG*1.6.22, Arist.*HA*544^{a}21, 548^{a}9, *Mu.*396^{a}25; esp. *the strait which separates Euboea from Boeotia*, *h.Ap.*222, Hdt.5.77, etc., cf. Str.9.2.8: prov. of *an unstable, weak-minded* person (cf. Poll.6.121), πλείους τραπόμενος τροπὰς τοῦ Εὐρίπου Aeschin.3.90; μεταρρεῖ ὥσπερ Εὔριπος Arist.*EN*1167^{b}7; ἄστατα καὶ ἀβέβαια Εὐρίπου τρόπον Hipparch.ap.Stob.4.44.81; Εὔριποι γενόμενοι Lib.*Ep.*907. II. generally, *canal, ditch*, etc., *SIG*799.7 (Cyzicus, i A.D.), Babr.120.2, *AP*14.135.2 (Metrod.), D.H.3.68. 2. the *Spina* in the Circus, Lyd.*Mens.*1.12. III. *ventilator, fan*, ἐξ εὐρίπου τινὸς αὔραν εἰσπνεῖν ἐπιτεχνώμενον Gal.10.649. (εὖ, ῥιπή, ῥιπίζω.)

εὐρῑπώδης, *ες*, *like a Euripus*, τόποι Arist.*GA*763^{b}2. II. *living in such a place*, Id.*HA*621^{b}23.

εὖρῑς, *ινος*, *ὁ*, *ἡ*, *with a good nose*, i.e. *keen-scented*, κυνὸς... ὥς τις εὔρινος βάσις S.*Aj.*8 (v. εὔρινος), cf. Nic.*Fr.*98; of Cassandra, εὖρις.., κυνὸς δίκην A.*Ag.*1093; late Ep. dat. pl. ἐΰρρίνεσσι Opp.*C.*4.357.

εὑρίσκω, impf. ηὕρισκον or εὕρ- S.*OT*68, etc.: fut. εὑρήσω *h.Merc.* 302, Th.7.67, etc.: aor. 2 εὗρον Il.1.498, etc., later ηὗρον or εὗρον E.*Med.*553, etc.; 3 pl. εὕροσαν Lxx *De.*31.17, *BGU*1201.16 (i A.D.); imper. εὑρέ Hdn.Gr.2.23; Ep. inf. εὑρέμεναι Od.12.393: later aor. 1 εὕρησα Man.5.137; εὕρα v.l. in *Ev.Luc.*8.35, *Act.Ap.*5.10, (ἐν-) *PGen.*3.19 (ii A.D.): pf. εὕρηκα S.*OT*546, etc., pf. imper. 2 sg. εὕρηκε Nausicr.1 D.:—**Med.**, fut. εὑρήσομαι Hdt.9.6, Lys.13.9, etc.: aor. 2 εὑρόμην Hom., Att. ηὑρ- or εὑρ- A.*Pr.*269, Th.1.58, etc.: aor. 1 εὑράμην Hes.*Fr.*116.3 (testes omnes), Str.12.34.4, Iamb.*VP*35.255, *AP*9.29 (Antiphil.), Epigr.ap.Paus.6.20.14, *Ep.Hebr.*9.12, *IG*3.900 (ii A.D.):—**Pass.**, fut. εὑρεθήσομαι S.*OT*108, E.*IA*1105, Isoc.9.41: aor. 1 ηὑρέθην or εὑρέθην S.*Aj.*1135, etc.: pf. ηὕρημαι or εὕρ- A.*Pers.*743 (troch.), etc.—Hom. has only aor. Act. and Med., exc. ἔθ' εὑρίσκω (v.l. ἐφευρίσκω) Od.19.158. (Earlier Att. Inscrr. have ηὑρέθην, ηὕρημαι, as *IG*2^{2}.1636.32, al., *Epigr.Gr.*35 (iv B.C.): εὑρέθην *SIG*679.80 (Magn. Mae., ii B.C.): the augm. is seldom found in Papyri, ηὕρισκεν *PPetr.* 3 p.101 (iii B.C.); never in those of Men. or Phld.):—*find*, εὗρεν δ' εὐρύοπα Κρονίδην ἄτερ ἥμενον ἄλλων Il.1.498, etc.; εὕρημα εὑ., v. εὕρημα. 2. c. part., *find that..*, εὕρισκε Λακεδαιμονίους.. προέχοντας Hdt.1.56, cf. 1.5:—and in Pass., ἣν εὑρεθῇς μὴ δίκαιος ὤν S.*Tr.*411, cf. *OT*839, *OC*946: with part. omitted, ὅταν τοὺς θεοὺς εὕρω κακούς (sc. ὄντας) Id.*Ph.*452; εὑρήσει τοσαῦτα ἔτη (sc. ὄντα) Th.5.26; θῆλυς εὕρημαι (sc. ὤν) S.*Tr.*1075; ἄνους ηὑρέθη Id.*Aj.*763. 3. c. inf., εὕρισκε πρῆγμά οἱ εἶναι.. *found* that the thing for him was ..., Hdt.1.79:—Med., εὑρίσκεται (sed leg. εὑρίσκέ τε) ταῦτα καιριώτατα εἶναι ib.125:—Act., also, *find means, be able*, οὐχ εὑρίσκει χρήσασθαι Arr.*Epict.*2.12.2. 4. εὑ. ὅπως.. *to find* by what means.., Th.7.67:—Med., c. inf., *find out* or *discover how to..*, ηὕρετο.. παύειν E.*Med.*196 (anap.). 5. Pass., εὑρέθη ὅτι... *it was found that..*, Lxx 1*Es.*2.22(26). 6. *befall*, of evils, τινα ib.*Ge.*44.34, *De.*31.17. II. *find out, discover*, οὐδέ τι μῆχος εὑρέμεναι δυνάμεσθα Od.12.393; οὐδέ τι τέκμωρ εὑρέμεναι δύνασαι 4.374, cf. Il.7.31; εὑ. ὁδόν Pi.*P.*10.29; ἐξ ἀμηχάνων πόρον A.*Pr.*59; μηχανὴν σωτηρίας Id.*Th.* 209; πημάτων ἄρηξιν S.*El.*875; τινα ἐμοῦ βελτίονα Ar.*Pl.*104, etc.: abs., εὕρηκα Archim.ap.Plu.2.1094c:—Med., εὕρετο τέκμωρ Il.16.472; ὄνομ' εὕρεο *think of* a name to give him, Od.19.403; εἴ τιν' ἑταίροισιν θανάτου λύσιν... εὑροίμην 9.422. 2. c. inf., *get a chance of, be able*, ἵνα εὕρωμεν ἐπιστολὴν γράψαι *BGU*822.28 (ii/iii A.D.), cf. 17, 20, *PGrenf.*1.64.3 (vi A.D.), etc. III. *devise, invent*, ὀχήματα A.*Pr.* 468, etc.; πρόφασιν Antipho 5.65:—Med., τὰ δ' ἔργα τοὺς λόγους εὑρίσκεται deeds *make themselves* words, S.*El.*625. IV. *get, gain*, ἀρετάν, δόξαν, Pi.*O.*7.89, *P.*2.64; τὰ χρήματ' ἀνθρώποισιν εὑρίσκει φίλους S.*Fr.*88; ἐξ ὀλβίων ἄζηλον εὑροῦσαι βίον Id.*Tr.*284, cf. E.*Med.* 1107 (anap.); δεινὰ δ' εὑροῦσαν πρὸς αὐθαίμων πάθη S.*OC*1078 (lyr.); ἀφ' ὧν ὄνασιν εὕρωσι Id.*El.*1061; μέγ' εὑρεῖν κέρδος ib.1305; εὑ. σωτηρίαν τῷ ἀνθρώπῳ Pl.*Prt.*321c; εὑ. μητρὶ φόνον *bring about* murder, E.*El.*650: abs., *acquire wealth*, Lxx *Le.*25.47:—Med., *find* or *get for oneself, bring on oneself*, οἷ.. αὐτῷ πρώτῳ κακὸν εὕρετο Od.21.304 (so in Act., μή πού τις ἐπίσπαστον κακὸν εὕρῃ 24.462); αὐτὸς ηὑρόμην πόνους A.*Pr.*269; μοῖραν ηὕρετ' ἀσφαλῆ Id.*Ag.*1588, cf. *Th.*880 (lyr.): so in pf. Pass., μέγα πένθος ηὕρηται S.*Aj.*615 (lyr.); εὑρήσεται τιμωρίην *will get for himself, obtain*, Hdt.3.148, cf. 9.26; ἀλεωρήν Id.9.6; κλέος Pi.*P.*3.111; ἄδειαν εὑρόμενος And.1.15; ἀτέλειαν D.20.1; εὑρίσκεσθαι ὠφελίαν ἀπό τινος Th.1.31; τι παρά τινος *IG*1^{2}.108.47, Lys.13.9; εὑ. παρά τινος c. inf., *procure* from him that.., Hdt.9.28; δεηθέντες οὐκ ἐδύναντο εὑρέσθαι Lys.14.20. V. esp. of merchandise, etc., *fetch, earn* money, εὑροῦσα πολλὸν χρυσίον *having fetched* a large sum, Hdt. 1.196; ηὗρε πλέον ἢ ἐνενήκοντα τάλαντα X.*HG*3.4.24, cf. *Vect.*4.40; οἰκία εὑρίσκουσα δισχιλίας (sc. δραχμάς) Is.8.35; ἐγδίδομεν... τοὺς θριγκοὺς.. ὅτι ἂν εὕρωσιν for what they *will fetch*, *IG*7.3073.7 (Lebad.); ἐρωτᾶν τί εὑρίσκει what it *will fetch*, Thphr.*Char.*15.4. 2.

of the sum or bid which *secures* an article or contract, οἰκέτην .. ἀποδίδοται τοῦ εὑρόντος sells *for what he will fetch*, X.*Mem.*2.5.5; τοῦ ἤδη εὑρίσκοντος ἀπεδίδοτο Aeschin.1.96, cf. *SIG*966.37 (Attica, iv B.C.), 581.99 (Rhodes-Hierapytna, ii B.C.); ἐκτιθέτωσαν τὸ εὑρίσκον ἐφ' ἡμέρας δέκα the *highest* or *winning* bid, *PRev.Laws*48.16 (iii B.C.), cf. *UPZ*112vi9 (iii B.C.); προσέβαλον αὐτῷ τοῦ εὑρίσκοντος ἀνὰ [x] ἱερεῖα [x] I have placed at his disposal [x] pigs at the *current price* of [x], *PCair.Zen.*161.5 (iii B.C.), cf. *UPZ*114(1).24 (ii B.C.).

εὐροέω, (εὔροος) *flow well* or *abundantly*, Thphr.*CP*5.6.4. **II.** metaph., *go on well*, *be favourable*, ὅταν δ' ὁ δαίμων εὐροῇ A.*Pers.*601; τῶν πραγμάτων αὐτῷ εὐροούντων Plb.4.48.11; τῆς τύχης εὐροούσης D.S.2.45; of men, *to be prosperous*, Arr.*Epict.*1.1.22, 3.10.10. **III.** *to be fluent*, *speak successfully*, Plu.*Alex.*53.

εὐροή, ἡ, = εὔροια I, αἵματος Aret.*CA*2.3.

εὐρόθιος, ον, *rushing rapidly*, κεραυνοί Orph.*H.*19.7 (s.v.l.).

εὔροια, ἡ, *good flow*, *free passage*, ὑδάτων Pl.*Lg.*779c; τῶν φλεβῶν Arist.*Somn.*457ᵃ26. **II.** *flow of words*, *fluency*, εὔροιά σε εἴληφεν Pl.*Phdr.*238c; σὺν εὐροίᾳ σχεδιάσαι Philostr.*VS*1.8.4. **III.** *prosperous course*, Pl.*Lg.*784b; πραγμάτων Plb.2.44.2, etc.; *abundance*, τῶν πάντων Clearch.8. **2.** εὔροια βίου *happy life*, Zeno *Stoic.* 1.46, Cleanth.ib.126, Chrysipp.ib.3.4, al.

εὐροίζητος, ον, *loud-whizzing*, of an arrow, *APl.*4.104 (Phil.).

εὐρο-κλύδων, v. εὐρακύλων. **-νοτος**, ὁ and ἡ, *a wind between* Εὖρος *and* Νότος, *SSE.*, Arist.*Mete.*363ᵇ22 (pl.), *Mu.*394ᵇ33, Agathem.2.7, *IG*14.1308, Gal.16.400.

εὔροος, Ep. **ἐΰρροος**, ον, contr. **εὔρους**, ουν, *fair-flowing*, Σκάμανδρος Il.7.329; ποταμός 21.130; Σπερχειός S.*Ph.*491; Εὐρώτας E.*Hec.* 650 (lyr.); in Prose, *flowing well*, *IG*7.4255.17 (Oropus, iv B.C.), Pl. *Ti.*77d. **II.** Medic., of the body, *with the pores and passages open*, Hp.*Aph.*2.9; σῶμα Arist.*HA*581ᵇ19; τὰ ὑγρά, αἷμα, Aret.*SA*1.10, Gal.15.843: Comp. εὐροώτερος Hp.*Mul.*1.1; εὐρούστερος Gal.16.360. Adv. -ρόως, ῥυῆναι Aret.*CA*1.7. **III.** of words, etc., *fluent*, *glib*, στόματα v.l. in E.*Fr.*439; λέξις D.H.*Comp.*23; ποικιλία -ροωτέρα v.l. ib.19. **IV.** *prosperous*, *successful*, οἷς ἂν εὔ. ᾖ γένεσις Pl.*Lg.*740d; βίος Archyt.ap.Stob.2.31.120, M.Ant.2.5: Sup. -ροώτατος Max.Tyr. 27.8. Adv. -ρόως, βιώσεσθαι, διεξάγειν, Arr.*Epict.*1.4.27, 3.22.45; βιοῦν S.E.*M.*11.110; contr. εὔρως Poll.4.23.

εὔροπος, ον, (ῥοπή) *easily inclining*, εὔ. ἅμμα an *easy-sliding* noose, *AP*9.543 (Phil.). Adv., οὐκ εὐρόπως εἶχεν it was not *easy* ..., Antipho 5.76.

Εὖρος, ὁ, *the East wind* (later, as dist. fr. ἀπηλιώτης, *ESE.*), Il.2.145, Arist.*Mete.*363ᵇ21, *Mu.*394ᵇ20, *IG*14.1308, etc. (Connected with ἠώς by Gell.2.22.7, with αὔρα by Vitr.1.6.11. Possibly from εὕω, because *parching*.)

εὖρος, εος, τό, *breadth*, *width*, mostly abs., εὖρος *in breadth*, opp. μῆκος or ὕψος, Od.11.312, Hdt.1.93,178, al.; ποταμὸς εὖρος πλέθρου X.*An.*1.4.4 (τὸ εὖρος πλέθρου ib.1.4.9); εἰς εὖρος E.*Cyc.*390; ἐν εὔρει A.*Th.*763 (lyr.).

ἐΰρρᾰπις, ιδος, ὁ, ἡ, *with beautiful staff*, Nonn.*D.*4.1.

ἐΰρρᾰφής, ές, (ῥάπτω) *well-stitched*, ἐϋρραφέεσσι δοροῖσι Od.2.354, 380; ἐϋρραφέος παρὰ μηροῦ D.P.940; γενύων σφίγκτωρ *AP*6.233 (Maec.).

ἐΰρρεής, ές, (ῥέω) *fair-flowing*, Hom. (only in Il.) always in Ep. gen. ἐϋρρεῖος (for -ρεέος) ποταμοῖο, Il.6.508, al.; εὐρεῖος Πείροιο Hes. *Fr.*74 (v.l. εὐρῆος codd. Str.).

ἐΰρρείτης, ου, ὁ, (ῥέω) = foreg., Σατνιόεντος ἐϋρρείταο Il.6.34; Αἴγυπτον ἐϋρρείτην Od.14.257; Σιμόεντι ἐπ' εὐρείτᾳ E.*Tr.*810 (lyr.); εὐρείτας οἶνος Philox.16: **ἐΰρρειτος**, η, ον, prob. in Orac.ap.Paus.5.7.3.

ἐΰρρην, Ep. for *εὔρην, *abounding in sheep*, A.R.1.49.

ἐΰρρηνος, ον, = foreg., A.R.3.1086. **2.** *of a good sheep*, κόρση Orac. in *AP*14.149.

ἐΰρρηχος, ον, (ῥηχός) *very prickly*, παλίουρος Nic.*Th.*868.

ἐΰρρῑν, **ἐΰρροος**, Ep. for εὔριν, εὔροος.

εὐρῠ-άγυιᾰ [ᾰγ], fem. Adj. used only in nom. and acc., *with wide streets*, Τροίη Il.2.141, al.; Ἀθήνη Od.7.80; Μυκήνη Il.4.52; πτόλις εὐ. Od.15.384; χθὼν εὐρυάγυια, = εὐρυόδεια (q.v.), *h.Cer.*16; εὐ. δίκα, i.e. *public*, Terp.6. **-αίχμας**, Dor. gen. α, ὁ, *far-stretching with the spear*, *far-conquering*, στρατός Pi.*Fr.*173. **-ᾰλος**, ον, (ἅλως) *with wide threshing-floor*, *broad*, χῶρος Opp.*H.*1.62; νέφεα dub. in *AP*7.748 (Antip. Sid.):—in Nonn.*D.*4.409, etc. (cj. in 13.68), also **εὐρυάλως**, ωος. **II. Εὐρύαλος**· ὁ Ἀπόλλων, Hsch. **-ᾰναξ**, ακτος, ὁ, *wide-ruling*, Ζεύς B.5.19:—fem. **-άνασσα**, ἡ, Call.*Cer.*122. **-βάλινδος**, epith. of Dionysus, Hsch. **-βᾰτος**, ον, *wide-stepping*, Ζεύς Ar.*Fr.*184, with a play on II. **2.** *spacious*, Q.S.2.283 (v.l. for ἠλίβ-), Nonn.*D.*28.79. **II.** pr. n. (later -της Alciphr.3.20, v.l. in Harp.), a proverbial cheat, Pl.*Prt.*327d, D.18.24, Aeschin.3.137; the betrayer of Croesus, Ephor.58 J., D.S.9.32:—hence **-βᾰτεύομαι**, *cheat like Eurybatus*, Diogenian.4.76, Suid. **-βίας**, Ion. and Ep. **-βίης** (Dor. gen. -βία prob. in B.10.52), ὁ, = εὐρυσθενής, Hes.*Th.*931, *h. Cer.*294, Pi.*O.*6.58, *Pae.*6.103, al., B.10.52, A.R.4.1552; φθόνος εὐ. B.15.31; εὐ. ταῦρος *Supp.Epigr.*2.518 (Rome, iv A.D.). **-βόας**, ου, ὁ, *far-shouting*, *loud-shouting*, Lib.*Decl.*43.74. **-γάστωρ**, ορος, ὁ, ἡ, *big-bellied*: metaph., of the sea, Orac.ap.Apollod.2.8.2. **-γένειος**, ον, *broad-chinned*, Opp.*C.*2.104; *broad-bearded*, Nonn.*D.*18.345. **-δαμηνός**, epith. of Zeus, *JHS*18.96. **-δίκεια**, τά, *festival of Eurydice* at Cassandrea, Polyaen.6.7.2. **-δίνης** [ῑ], Dor. **-νᾶς**, ὁ, *wide-eddying*, Ἀλφεός B.3.7, 5.38. **-εδής**, ές, *broad-seated*, *spacious*, -έδους .. χθονός Simon.5.17 (v.l. -όδου); cf. εὐρυόδεια, εὐρώδης. **-ζῠγος**, ον, *broad-throned*, *wide-ruling* (cf. ὑψίζυγος), Ζεύς Pi.*Fr.*14. **-θέμειλος**, ον, *with broad foundations*, of Ἅιδης, *IG*14.1015 (-μιλος lapis); also (with v.l. -θέμεθλον) βρέτας Call.*Dian.*248.

εὔρυθμ-ία, ἡ, *rhythmical order* or *movement*, κατὰ ῥυθμὸν εὐρυθμίαν παραδιδόναι Pl.*R.*522a, cf. *Prt.*326b; αἱ περὶ τὴν λέξιν εὐ. *the measured cadences* of language, Isoc.5.27; ἡ κυκλικὴ εὐ. τῶν περιόδων D.H. *Pomp.*6.10. **2.** *harmony* between the orator and his hearers, Plu.2.45e. **3.** of persons, *gracefulness*, Pl.*R.*400d; ἡ δ' εὐ. τό τ' ἦθος Damox.3.7; εὐ. τῶν σωμάτων *graceful movement*, Plu.2.8c, cf. Quint.1.10.26, Luc.*Salt.*8. **4.** εὐ. χειρέων *delicacy* of touch, in a surgeon, etc., Hp.*Decent.*8, cf. Plu.2.67e. **-ίζω**, *shape* (by massage), κρανίον Sor.1.102. **-ιστος**, ον, *easily shaped*, Gal.7.677. **-ος**, ον, Ep. **ἐΰρρ-** Man.1.60:—*rhythmical*, μουσικὴ εὔ., distd. fr. εὐμελής, Arist.*Pol.*1341ᵇ26; λέξις Id.*Rh.*1409ᵃ21; opp. ἔρρυθμος, D.H.*Comp.* 11,25; εὔ. κρούματα Ar.*Th.*121 (lyr.); εὔ. πούς *moving in time*, *keeping time*, ib.985 (lyr.); προβήματα Id.*Pl.*759; μέλος Pl.*Lg.*655a; κίνησις ib.795e; σφυγμὸς εὔ. a *regular* pulse, Gal.19.409. Adv. -μως, καὶ μουσικῶς εἰπεῖν Isoc.13.16; φέρεσθαι Plu.2.45e. **2.** of persons, *orderly*, *graceful*, Pl.*Prt.*326b (Comp.), *R.*413e, etc.; εὔ. βακτηρία '*the nice conduct of* a cane', Antiph.33.4. Adv. -μως *gracefully*, E. *Cyc.*563; πέμπειν εὐ. τὸν κότταβον Pl.Com.47. **3.** *well-proportioned*, *well-fitted*, both of the armour and the body, X.*Mem.*3.10.10 (Comp.), 11; τὸν πόδα -ότερον τοῦ ὑποδήματος Thphr.*Char.*2.7; εὔ. ὀρνίθιον Arist.*HA*592ᵇ24; φύλλα Thphr.*HP*3.18.7 (Comp.), cf. 12.9. **4.** of surgical operations, in Adv., *neatly*, Hp.*Off.*4.

εὐρυθμο-κάρηνος [ᾰ], ον, *broad-headed*, σιγύνη Opp.*C.*1.152; Πίθος Nonn.*D.*20.127. **-κερως**, ωτος, ὁ, ἡ, *with spreading horns*, of deer and oxen, Opp.*C.*2.293, v.l. in Mosch.2.153.

Εὐρυκλῆς, έους, ὁ, name of a famous ventriloquist: hence as appellat., *ventriloquist*, Ar.*V.*1019, Pl.*Sph.*252c (cf. Sch. ad loc.), Plu.2.414e.

Εὐρυκλύδων, ωνος, ὁ, = Τυφῶν, *EM*772.31; cf. Εὐρακύλων.

εὐρυκόας· μεγαλόνους, μέγα ἰσχύων, εὐήκοος, κτλ., Hsch.

εὐρῠ-κοίλιος, ον, *hollow*, of the right ventricle of the heart, Hp. *Cord.*4; *with wide cavity*, of the caecum, Ruf.ap.Orib.7.26.25. **-κολπος**, ον, = εὐρύστερνος, χθών Pi.*N.*7.33. **-κόωσα**, (κοάω, = κοέω) epith. of night, variously expld. by Hsch. (-κόωσα perh. = -μέδουσα). **2.** of the sea-goddess Ceto, Euph.112. **-κρείων**, οντος, ὁ, *wide-ruling*, Il.1.102, al., shd. be written divisim. **-λείμων**, ον, gen. ωνος, *with broad meadows*, Λιβύα Pi.*P.*9.55. **-μέδων**, οντος, ὁ, = εὐρυκρείων, of αἰθήρ, Emp.135.1; Ποσειδάν Pi.*O.*8.31; γόνον εὐ. Κρόνου, i.e. Chiron, Id.*P.*3.4:—in Hom. only as pr. n.; so also fem. **Εὐρυμέδουσα**. **-μενής**, ές, *broad and strong*, τεῖχος, Φᾶσις, Orph. *A.*987, 1052. **-μέτωπος**, ον, *broad-fronted*, of oxen, Il.10.292, al., Hes.*Th.*291, Strato Com.1.20.

εὐρυμνάσαι· ἐρευνῆσαι, Hsch., *EM*397.11.

εὐρῠ-νεφής, ές, *lord of spreading clouds*, Ζεύς B.15.17. **-νοος**, ον, *broad-minded*, ῥήτρη Diosc. in *PLit.Lond.*98 ii 1.

εὐρυντέον, *one must dilate*, τοὺς πόρους Antyll.ap.Orib.6.10.12.

εὐρύνω, (εὐρύς) *make wide* or *broad*, εὔρυναν ἀγῶνα *cleared* the arena (for dancing), Od.8.260; τὸ μέσον εὐ. *leave a wide space* in the middle, Hdt.4.52; εὐ. τοὺς μυκτῆρας *dilate* them, X.*Eq.*1.10; αὔλακας εὐ. Theoc.13.31; *widen* a wound, ὄνυξι App.*BC*2.99; στήθεα Opp.*C.* 3.442:—Pass., *to be widened*, *become wider*, Ph.2.112, D.P.92, Luc. *Electr.*6; γῆς -ομένης ὑπὸ πνευμάτων καὶ ὑδάτων, of the formation of valleys, Ocell.3.4. **2.** metaph., *extend*, ξενίου δαίμονος ἐργασίην *AP*7.698 (Christod.).

εὐρύ-νωτος [ῠ], ον, *broad-backed*, φῶτες S.*Aj.*1251. **-όδειά**, ἡ, (ὁδός) fem. Adj. used only in gen., *with broad ways*, in Hom. always of the earth (as εὐρύπορος of the sea), χθονὸς εὐρυοδείης Il.16.635, Od.3.453, etc. **II.** epith. of Demeter at Scarpheia, Hsch. (Derived fr. ἕδος by *EM*396.24; cf. εὐρυεδής.)

εὐρυοδίνης, f.l. for ἀργυροδίνης in Orac.ap.Str.1.3.8, 12.2.4.

εὐρύοδος, ον, v. εὐρυεδής.

εὐρύοπᾰ, ὁ, Ep. epith. of Zeus, used as nom. in fifth foot, Od. 14.235, al., cf. Pi.*Pae.*6.134, 8.24; as voc. (only once in Hom.), εὐρύοπα Ζεῦ Il.16.241; εὐρύοπα Κρονίδης Orac.ap.Hdt.8.77, cf. *h.Hom.* 23.4; also as acc. (as if from nom. εὐρύοψ), εὐρύοπα Ζῆν Il.8.206, al.; εὗρεν δ' εὐρύοπα Κρονίδην 1.498, cf. 24.98; Ζῆνα ... εὐρύοπα κρείοντα *h. Hom.*23.2; later, of a mortal, κῆρυξ εὐ. *BMus.Inscr.*902 (Halic., iii B.C.). [ᾰ by nature, freq. ᾱ by position.] (Derived by the Greeks from ὀπ-, ὄψομαι, *wide-eyed* (cf. ἥλιος εὐ. Orph.*L.*701) or from ὀπ- 'voice' (cf. ϝέπος, ὄψ (A), *vox*), *far-sounding*, i.e. *thundering* (cf. χορὸς εὐρύοπα κέλαδον φθεγγόμενος *Lyr.Adesp.*93, cf. Sch.Il.1.498): prob. cogn. with Skt. *urūcī* 'wide', epith. of Heaven-and-Earth, etc., fem. of *uru-vyác-* or **uru-ác-*.)

εὐρῠ-πέδῑλος, ον, *broad-sandalled*: *broad*, ὁπλή Opp.*C.*1.288. **-πεδος**, ον, *with broad surface*, *spacious*, γαῖα *Lyr.Adesp.*138.3, *AP*7.748 (Antip. Sid.). **-πορος**, ον, *with broad ways*, in Hom. always of the sea (as εὐρυόδεια of the earth), *where all may roam at will*, μέγα κῦμα θαλάσσης εὐρυπόροιο Il.15.381, cf. Od.4.432, 12.2, A. *Pers.*108. **-πρωκτία**, ἡ, *the character of a* εὐρύπρωκτος, Ar.*Ach.* 843, *V.*1070 (both lyr.), al. **-πρωκτος**, ον, *wide-breeched*, i.e. *pathicus*, Id.*Ach.*716, *Nu.*1090: Comp., Eub.120.7.

εὔρυπτος, ον, (ῥύπτω) *easy to wash out*, Poll.1.44.

εὐρῠ-πῠλής, ές, *with broad gates*, ἂν' εὐρυπυλὲς Ἄϊδος δῶ Il.23.74, cf. Od.11.571. **-ρέεθρος**, ον, *with broad channel*, *broad-flowing*, Il.21.141; cf. sq. **-ρέων**, ουσα, ον, *broad-flowing*, shd. be written divisim, Il.2.849, etc.

εὐρύς, εὐρεῖα, εὐρύ, Ion. fem. εὐρέα (not εὐρέη) Hdt.1.178, cf. Theoc.

7.78; Aeol. fem. εὔρηα Alc.*Supp*.12.5: gen. εὐρέος, είας, έος: acc. sg. εὐρύν, (in Hom.) sts. εὐρέα (v. infr.): gen. εὐρέος as fem., Asius 13, Opp.*C*.3.323: so nom. pl. εὐρέες *AP*9.413 (Antiphil.):—*wide, broad*, οὐρανὸν εὐρύν Il.3.364, al.; εὐρεῖα χθών 4.182, al.; εὐρέα πόντον 6.291; εὐρέα κόλπον 18.140, al.; εὐ. σχεδίη Od.5.163; ὦμοι Il.3.210, Od.18.68, al. (Comp. εὐρύτερος δ' ὤμοισιν ἰδὲ στέρνοισιν ἰδέσθαι Il.3.194); μετάφρενον 10.29; σάκος 11.527; τεῖχος 12.5; ὁδὸς εὐρυτέρη 23.427; εὐρὺν ἀγῶνα (v. ἀγών); κατά, ἀνά, μετὰ στρατὸν εὐρὺν Ἀχαιῶν, 1.229, 384, 478: freq. in Ep. and Lyr., rare in Trag. (exc. in lyr.); in iambic trimeters, E.*Fr*.921; ποιεῖν τὸν δῆμον εὐρὺν καὶ στενόν Ar.*Eq*.720; not common in Prose (never in Papyri), εὐ. τάφρος Hdt.1.178; κόθορνοι εὐρύτατοι *loose* boots, Id.6.125; οἰκίαι X.*An*.4.5.25; οὔτ' εὐρεῖα οὔτε στενὴ διαφυγή Pl.*Lg*.737a; φλέβες εὐρύτεραι, opp. λεπτότεραι, Diog.Apoll.6, cf. Pl.*Ti*.66d; πόροι Thphr.*CP*3.11.2; κατὰ στενότερα καὶ εὐρύτερα Pl.*Phd*.111d. 2. *far-reaching, far-spread*, κλέος εὐρύ Od.23.137; κληδών Simon.84.6; εὐ. ἐλπίδες Pl.*Epigr*.7. II. as Adv.: the neut. εὐρύ is used as positive, Pi.*O*.13.24; cf. εὐρυκρείων, εὐρυρέων: Comp. εὐρυτέρως, ἔχειν Ar.*Lys*.419. (Skt. *urú-* 'wide', Comp. *várīyān*.)

εὐρύ-σάκης [ᾰ], ες, *with broad shield*: only as name of Ajax' son, S.*Aj*.575, Plu.*Sol*.10:—hence **Εὐρυσάκειον**, τό, his shrine, *IG*2².1232.22, Hyp.*Fr*.35. **-σθενής**, ές, *of far-extended might, mighty*, in Hom. always of Poseidon, Il.7.455, 8.201, Od.13.140; of Zeus, B.18.17; Apollo, Pi.*I*.2.18; Telamon, Id.*N*.3.36; Himera, Id.*O*.12.2; ἀρεταί, πλοῦτος, ib.4.12, *P*.5.1.

εὐρυσμᾰτώδης, ες, *like a dilatation*, βρογχοκήλη Paul.Aeg.6.38.

εὐρύ-σορος [ῠ], ον, *with wide bier* or *tomb*, σῆμα *AP*7.528 (Theodorid.). **-στερνος**, ον, *broad-breasted*, Γαῖ' εὐ. Hes.*Th*.117; οὐρανός *APl*.4.303, Orph.*L*.645; Ἀθάνα Theoc.18.36: later in Prose, Gal.4.629; of Poseidon, Corn.*ND*22. **-στήθης**, ες, = foreg., Arist.*HA*632^{b}11. **-στιχαιός**, f.l. for Ἐρυσίχαιος, *EM*180.27. **-στομία**, ἡ, *broadness of pronunciation*, Eust.11.43. **-στομος**, ον, *wide-mouthed*, μῆτραι Hp.*Mul*.1.48, cf. X.*Eq*.10.10, Ath.10.453a. **-τενής**, ές, *wide-extended*, Nonn.*D*.21.328.

εὐρύτης [ῠ], ητος, ἡ, (εὐρύς) *width* or *breadth*, Hp.*Acut*.(*Sp*.)9. II. *broadness* of sound, Sch.Th.1.72.

εὐρύτῑμος [ῠ], ον, *honoured far and wide*, Ζεύς Pi.*O*.1.42.

εὔρῠτος, ον, (ῥέω) *full-flowing*, κρήνη E.*IA*420.

εὐρύ-τρητος, ον, *with wide holes*, ἠθμός Dsc.1.66. **-τρῦπος**, ον, (τρυπάω) = foreg., f.l. for εὐθυ- in Democr.ap.Thphr.*Sens*.73.

Εὐρῠφάεσσα [φᾰ], ης, ἡ, *Far-shining*, wife of Hyperion and mother of Helios, *h.Hom*.31.2, 4.

εὐρῠ-φάρέτρης, Dor. **-τρᾱς**, ὁ, *with wide quiver*, of Apollo, Pi.*P*.9.26: acc. sg. -φάρετρᾱν Id.*Pae*.6.111; εὐρυφάρετρ' Ἄπολλον Id.*Fr*.148. **-φλεβος**, ον, *with wide veins*, Gal.6.30. **-φυής**, ές, *broad-growing, broad-eared*, in reference to the manner in which the grains of barley (κρῖ) are set on the stalk, Od.4.604. **-φωνία**, ἡ, *broadness of sound*, Eust.39.42. **-φωνος**, ον, gloss on Τηλεβόαι, Id.1396.3. **-χᾰδής**, ές, (χανδάνω) *wide-gaping, wide-mouthed*, of cups, *AP*6.305 (Leon.), Luc.*Lex*.7. **-χαίτης**, Dor. **-τᾱς**, ὁ, *with wide-streaming hair*, of Dionysus, Pi.*I*.7(6).4. **-χανδής**, ές, = εὐρυχαδής, Eust.870.55. **-χᾰνής**, ές, = foreg., γαστήρ Opp.*H*.3.344; of a wounded man, Nonn.*D*.22.242. **-χορος**, ον, *with broad places, spacious*, Μυκαλησσός, Λακεδαίμων, Il.2.498, Od.15.1, etc.; Ἑλλάς Il.9.478; πτόλις, of Troy, Sapph.*Supp*.20a.12; Ἀσία, Λιβύα, Pi.*O*.7.18, *P*.4.43; Ἄργος B.9.31; ἀγυιαί Pi.*P*.8.55, E.*Ba*.87 (lyr.), Orac.ap.D.21.52; οἶκος *AP*6.319 (Nicod.). (Prop. *with broad dancing-places*, cf. χορός; then a conventional epithet, perh. connected by poets with χῶρος.)

εὐρῠχωρ-έω, *enlarge*, Sm.*Ps*.17(18).37. **-ής**, ές, = εὐρύχωρος, Hp.*VM*22 (dub. l.), Paus.3.19.1: Comp. -έστερος Arist.*HA*508^{a}28: Sup. -έστατος Id.*PA*668^{b}16. **-ία**, Ion. **-ίη**, ἡ, *open space, free room*, ἐν τῇ λοιπῇ εὐ. τῆς θήκης Hdt.4.71; πολλὴν εὐ. ἔχειν D.19.272; εὐ. ποιεῖτε τῷ θεῷ *Carm.Pop*.7; -ίας σε δεῖ *Com.Adesp*.46 D.; ἡ ἄνω εὐ., of a dislocated joint, Hp.*Art*.11 (in later Medic., of bodily *orifices*, Sor.1.58 (pl.); ἡ ἀκουστικὴ εὐ., *meatus auditorius*, ib.10); ἐν εὐ. εἶναι to have *plenty of room*, Pl.*Tht*.194d: prov., ἔκητι Συλοσῶντος εὐρυχωρίη Heraclid.*Pol*.34, Zen.3.90: pl., Pl.*Lg*.804c (εὐρυχώρια, τά, codd.), Aen.Tact.1.9, 2.1. 2. *an open field* for battle, X.*Cyr*.4.1.18, *HG*7.4.24; ἐν εὐρυχωρίῃ ναυμαχέειν to fight *with plenty of sea-room*, Hdt.8.60.β', cf. Th.2.83, al. 3. metaph., *free space, room for doing* a thing, τῆς ἀποδείξεως Pl.*Min*.315d; εὐ. τινὸς διδόναι, παρέχειν, Plu.2.48f, 828d. **-ος**, ον, *roomy, wide*, Arist.*PA*675^{b}27; πεδίον D.S.19.84; ναῦς Max.Tyr.1.3; τὰ εὐ. *wide spaces*, Aen.Tact.2.2, Ph.*Bel*.92.47.

εὐρώγης, ες, (ῥώξ) *of fine grapes*, πεντάς *AP*6.190 (Gaet.).

εὐρώδης, ες, poet. for εὐρύς, S.*Aj*.1190 (lyr., s. v. l.; εὐρυεδῆ cj. Musgr.).

εὐρωεία, ἡ, perh. = εὐρωΐα (q. v.), *Sammelb*.4324.7.

εὐρώεις, εσσα, εν, (εὐρώς) *mouldy, dank*, οἰκία... εὐρώεντα, of the nether world, Il.20.65; εἰς Ἀΐδεω δόμον εὐρώεντα Od.10.512, 23.322, cf. Hes.*Op*.153; πείρατα, of Tartarus, Id.*Th*.739; εὐρώεντα κέλευθα Od.24.10; ὑπὸ ζόφῳ εὐρώεντι *h.Cer*.482; τάφον εὐρώεντα S.*Aj*.1167 (anap.); later, *dank, slimy*, ἰλύς, πηλός, Opp.*H*.1.781, 2.89. (Expld. as = εὐρέα or πλατέα, ἀναπεπταμένα (cf. εὐρύς) by Apollon.*Lex*., Hsch., *EM* 397.57, and possibly so used in late Poets, κόλπος θαλάσσης Opp.*H*.5.3, βέρεθρον Nonn.*D*.26.107; of a monster's throat, ib.25.476.)

εὐρωΐαν· εὐεξίαν, ὑγίειαν, Hsch.; cf. εὐρωεία.

Εὐρωπαῖος, α, ον, *European*, ἔθνη D.H.1.2; Ion. **Εὐρωπήϊος**, η, ον, Hdt.7.73:—later **Εὐρώπειος**, η, ον, γαίη D.P.152:—fem. **Εὐρωπίς**, ίδος, St.Byz.

Εὐρώπη, ἡ, *Europa, Europe*, as a geog. name, first in *h.Ap*.251, Pi.*N*.4.70, A.*Fr*.191, Hdt.1.4, al. II. fem. pr. n. in Hes.*Th*.357, Hdt.1.2, etc.:—also **Εὐρώπεια**, ἡ, Mosch.2.15.

Εὐρωπία, ἡ, = Εὐρώπη 1, S.*Fr*.39, E.*Fr*.381. II. *broad surface*, Ἀχελῴου κρανᾶν Pi.*Fr*.249^{b} Schroeder.

εὐρῶπις· ἡ πατρίς, Hsch.

εὐρωπός, ή, όν, = εὐρύς, E.*IT*626, Opp.*H*.3.20, 4.526.

εὐρώς, ῶτος, ὁ, *mould, dank decay*, Thgn.452, Simon.4.4, B.*Fr*.3.8, E.*Ion*1393, Pl.*Ti*.84b, Arist.*GA*784^{b}10, Theoc.4.28, Call.*Fr*.313, Ph.2.461; εὐρὼς ψυχῆς Plu.2.48c; εὐρῶτι γήρως τὰς τρίχας βεβαμμένος *Com.Adesp*.53 D.

εὐρωστ-έω, *to be robust*, Poll.3.121, *POxy*.1493.8 (iii/iv A.D.), prob. in Gal.13.194; ἐὰν εὐρωστῇ σοι τὰ πράγματα Ph.2.403. II. *display moral strength*, πρὸς τὰς ἀλγηδόνας Phld.*Piet*.33^{b}. **-ία**, ἡ, *stoutness, strength*, Arist.*Mir*.830^{a}9, D.S.17.88, *PRyl*.235.8 (ii A.D.); τῆς ψυχῆς Plu.*Cat.Mi*.44; personified, Εὐ. *Ath.Mitt*.32.308 (Pergam.). **-ος**, ον, (ῥώννυμι) *stout, strong*, ἱππεῖς X.*HG*4.3.6, cf. Aen.Tact.1.7, *PCair.Zen*.56.1 (iii B.C.), etc.; στόμα Arist.*HA*617^{b}3; εὔρωστος τὸ σῶμα X.*HG*6.1.6; τῷ σώματι Isoc.15.116 (Sup.); τὰς ψυχάς Arist.*Phgn*.810^{a}25. Adv. **-τως** X.*Ages*.2.24; εὐ. τὸν βίον διάξετε Antiph.1 D.

εὐρωστόψῡχος, ον, *stout-hearted*, *Et.Gud*. s. v. Αἰθίοψ: perh. corrupted to εὐροστουχε (voc.) in *PMag.Par*.1.2231.

Εὐρώτας, α, ὁ, *Eurotas*, the chief river of Laconia. II. *pudenda muliebria*, with allusion to εὐρύς, *AP*5.59 (Rufin.).

εὐρωτιάω, (εὐρώς) *to be* or *become mouldy, decay*, Thphr.*CP*1.6.8, Luc.*Nec*.15, etc.; βίος εὐρωτιῶν the life *of 'the great unwashed'*, Ar.*Nu*.44.

ἐΰς, ὁ (v. εὖ), *good, brave, noble*, Ep. word freq. in nom., ἐΰς πάϊς Ἀγχίσαο Il.2.819, etc.; once in acc. ἐΰν 8.303; neut. always ἠΰ (v. ἠΰς) (εὖ only as Adv.): irreg. gen. sg. ἑῆος, παιδὸς ἑῆος 1.393; υἷος ἑῆος 15.138, 24.422, 550; ἀνδρὸς ἑῆος 19.342; φιλότητι καὶ αἰδοῖ φωτὸς ἑῆος Od.14.505; always at end of verse (exc. in Od.15.450): freq. with v.l. ἑοῖο, as Il.18.71: irreg. gen. pl. ἐάων *good things, good fortune*, 24.528; θεοὶ δωτῆρες ἐάων Od.8.325; δῶτορ ἐάων ib.335, *h.Hom*.18.12, 29.8, cf. Hes.*Th*.46, 111. ((1) ἑῆος: for this form Zenod. read ἑοῖο; but ἑῆος (= ἀγαθοῦ, Sch.Il.15.138) became, like ἐσθλός (v. ἐσθλός 1.3) and φίλος, almost a possess. Pron. of 1st, 2nd, and 3rd pers., and may be retained. Some Gramm. wrongly took εηος to be a form of ἑός ('his') and conversely gave to ἑός ('his') the signf. 'good' (Anon.ap.A.D.*Synt*.156.1, *EM*307.33, 318.1): hence the erroneous forms ἑῆος, ἑάων (but ἐΰς rightly), *Lex. de Spir*.pp.194, 196, 198, freq. in codd. The reading ἑῆος (ἑῆος) is well attested only where a substituted ἑοῖο would have had to mean *my* or *thy*: where the reference is to the 3rd pers. we find υἷος ἑοῖο, πατρὸς ἑοῖο, παιδὸς ἑοῖο almost without v. l., Il.13.522, al. (v.l. ἑῆος Il.14.9, 18.71, 138). (2) The origin of the forms ἑῆος ἐάων and the variation ἐϋ-: ἠϋ- are obscure: ἐάων perh. had ϝ-, Il.24.528.)

εὖσα, Dor. fem. part. of εἰμί (*sum*), Theoc.2.76, (παρ-) 5.26; but **εὖσα**, aor. 1 of εὕω.

εὐσᾰβέω, = εὐσεβέω, *Schwyzer*418.15 (Elis).

εὐσάλευτος [ᾰ], ον, (σαλεύω) *easily shaken*, πράξεις Ph.1.96.

εὔσᾰλος, ον, *with a good roadstead*, ἐμπόριον *Peripl.M.Rubr*.24.

εὔσαμα· ἀναφώνημα βακχικόν, κτλ., Hsch. (fort. εὔασμα).

εὔσανα, τά, = ἐγκαύματα, Poll.6.91, Hsch.; also, = εὔστραι, Id.

εὐσᾰνίδωτος [ῐ], ον, (σανίς) gloss on εὔσελμος, Hsch. (-όπου cod.).

εὐσαρκ-έω, *to be fleshy*, Sch.Ar.*Pl*.561. **-ία**, ἡ, *fullness of flesh, good condition*, Hp.*Art*.53, Arist.*HA*493^{b}22, Ph.1.666; coupled with κάλλος, Phld.*Mort*.29: pl., Antyll.ap.Stob.4.37.16; of fruit, Thphr.*CP*1.9.2. **-ος**, ον, (σάρξ) *fleshy, in good condition*, Hp.*Aph*.4.7, X.*Lac*.5.8, Arist.*HA*583^{a}9, Phld.*Mort*.30, etc.; of meat, Amphis 16; opp. σαρκώδης on the one hand, and ἄσαρκος on the other, Gal.6.30. **-όω**, *make* εὔσαρκος, Id.10.998. **-ωσις**, εως, ἡ, = εὐσαρκία, Hp.*Acut*.(*Sp*.)29.

εὔσβεστος, ον, *easily quenched*, θερμασία ἔμφυτος Gal.17(2).548; ὑπεκκαύματα ἡδονῶν Ph.2.63.

εὐσέβεια, ἡ (cf. εὐσεβία), *reverence towards the gods* or *parents, piety* or *filial respect*, εὐ. εἰς θεοὺς καὶ γονέας Pl.*R*.615c, etc.; μιαίνων εὐσέβειαν Ἄρης A.*Th*.344 (lyr.); εὐ. Ζηνός *towards* him, S.*El*.1097 (lyr.); πρὸς εὐσέβειαν, = εὐσεβῶς, ib.464; εὐ. πρός, περὶ τοὺς θεούς, Pl.*Smp*.193d, Isoc.12.124, cf. 10.58; πρὸς ἀδελφόν D.C.48.5; ἡ πρὸς τὸ θεῖον εὐ. *Inscr.Prien*.117.63 (i B.C.), etc.; τὴν εὐ. τῶν πραχθέντων Antipho 3.2.12: pl., *acts of piety*, Arist.*Rh.Al*.1423^{b}28. 2. *loyalty*, ἡ ὑμετέρα πρός με εὐ. *PLond*.3.1178.14 (Claudius); ἡ εἴς με εὔνοια καὶ εὐ. *SIG*814.2 (Nero). 3. = Lat. *Pietas*, App.*BC*2.104, Mitteis *Chr*.71.12 (v A.D.), Orph.*Fr*.159, etc. 4. *credit* or *character for piety*, εὐσέβειαν οἴσῃ S.*El*.968.

Εὐσέβεια, τά, games in honour of Antoninus Pius, at Puteoli, *IG* 3.129, 14.737.8, 7.49.23:—also **Εὐσέβειος** ἀγών *Annuario*6/7.447: **Εὐσέβειος**, ὁ (sc. μήν), month named after Antoninus Pius, *BGU* 741.51 (ii A.D.): **Εὐσεβείωνες**, οἱ (sc. θεοί), *patrons of* εὐσέβεια, *Supp.Epigr*.3.545.

εὐσεβ-έω, *live* or *act piously* or *reverently*, abs., Thgn.145, *Berl.Sitzb*.1927.8 (Locr., v B.C.), S.*Aj*.1350, etc.; εἴς τινα towards one, Id.*Ant*.731; περί τινα E.*Alc*.1148; περὶ θεούς Pl.*Smp*.193a; πρὸς τὸν θεόν Men.*Mon*.567; πρὸς θεούς *AP*10.107 (E.); εὐ. τὰ πρὸς θεοὺς S.*Ph*.1441; τὰ περὶ τοὺς θεοὺς Isoc.3.2; of outward acts of service, θύουσα καὶ εὐσεβοῦσα τοῖς θεοῖς *PRyl*.112(a).4 (iii A.D.); εὐ. θεούς *to reverence* them, A.*Ag*.338 (nisi leg. εὖ σέβειν); εὐσεβήσασαν τὴν θεόν *BCH*44.77 (Lagina):—Pass., εὐσεβεῖσθαι *to be reverenced*, Antipho

3.3.11, Ph.2.201; of a duty, *to be reverently discharged*, Pl.*Ax.* 364c. **-ημα**, ατος, τό, *deed of piety*, Demetr.*Eloc.*281. **-ής**, ές (dat. pl. -σεβέοις *IG*5(1).1390.5 (Andania)), (σέβω) *pious, religious*, opp. δυσσεβής (q.v.), Thgn.1141, Hdt.2.141, Pi.*O.*3.41; τρόπος Ar.*Ra.* 457 (lyr.): not common in early Prose, Gorg.*Fr.*6D., Pl.*Phlb.*39e; *dutiful*, esp. *discharging sacred duties*, πρός or ἔς τινα, A.*Supp.*340, E. *El.*253; ἀνὴρ εὐ. (v.l. εὐλαβὴς) κατὰ τὸν νόμον *Act.Ap.*22.12; εὐ. καὶ φοβούμενος τὸν θεόν ib.10.2: c. acc. modi, -εστέρα χεῖρα *more righteous* in act, A.*Ch.*141; εὐσεβεῖς κἀξ εὐσεβῶν βλαστόντας S.*El.*589; ὁ τῶν εὐσεβῶν χῶρος, of a place in the nether world, Pl.*Ax.*371c; ἐν εὐσεβέων (sc. χώρῳ) Call.*Ep.*12, cf. *Sammelb.*2048 (ii B.C.). b. Astrol., αἱ τῶν εὐσεβῶν μοῖραι *Cat.Cod.Astr.*8(4).227. 2. as epith. of Emperors, = *Pius*, *IGRom.*3.91 (iii A.D.), al., *PGrenf.*1.49.28 (iii A.D.), *PHamb.*1.13.2 (iii A.D.), etc.; esp. of Antoninus Pius, *IGRom.*3.1293, al. b. of taxes, etc., due to the Emperor, *BGU*917.15 (iv A.D.), etc. 3. metaph., of a piece of land, *dutiful*, i.e. *productive*, ἀγρὸν -έστερον γεωργεῖν οὐδ' ἕνα οἶμαι Men.*Georg.*35. II. of acts, things, etc., *holy, sacred*, ταὐτὰ μοὐστὶν εὐσεβῆ θεῶν πάρα A.*Ch.*122; εὐ. χρηστήριον E.*El.*1272; ἐν εὐσεβεῖ [ἐστι] c. inf., Id.*Hel.*1277; τὸ εὐ., = εὐσέβεια, S.*OC*1125, E.*Tr.*43; τὸ ὑμέτερον εὐ. Antipho 5.96; τοὐμὸν εὐ. E.*Hipp.*656; τι τῶν ἐν ἀνθρώποις εὐσεβῶν παραβαίνειν Philipp.ap. D.18.157. III. Adv. εὐσεβέως, Att. -βῶς, Pi.*O.*6.79, etc.; εὐσεβῶς ἔχει, for εὐσεβές ἐστι, S.*OT*1431, D.19.212: Comp. -έστερον X.*Mem.* 4.3.16: Sup. -έστατα Isoc.4.33. **-ία**, Ion. -ίη, ἡ, poet. for εὐσέβεια, Thgn.1142 codd., Pi.*O.*8.8, S.*Ant.*943 (lyr.), *OC*189 (lyr.); personified, Emp.4.5, Critias 6.22, *Epigr.Gr.*1055 (Syria), etc.

εὔσειστος, ον, *liable to earthquakes*, Str.10.1.9.

εὐσέλᾶος, ον, *bright-shining*, or **εὐσέλᾱνος** (Dor. for -σέληνος), ον, *moon-lit*, εὐσέλανον δῖον οἶκον *Lyr.Adesp.*79 C (εὐσέλαον Διὸς οἶκον cj. Salm.): **εὐσέληνος**, ον, *of the bright moon*, φέγγος E.*Rh.* (spurious prologue).

εὔσελμος, Ep. **ἐΰσσελμος**, ον, (σέλμα) *well-benched* or *-decked*, Hom. always in Ep. form, νηός, νῆες, Il.2.170, Od.2.390, al., cf. Stes.32, E. *Rh.*97; cj. in Id.*IT*1383.

εὔσεπτος, ον, (σέβω) *reverent*, S.*OT*864 (lyr.).

εὐσήκωτος, ον, *well-poised*, κανών Bito 65.10.

εὐσήμ-αντος, ον, *easily remarked* or *observed*, Ptol.*Alm.*5.12 (Comp.). II. *easily designated*, *PMeyer* 20.46 (iii A.D.). **-είωτον**, *bene clavatum*, *Gloss.* **-ία**, ἡ, *good prognostic*, Hp.*Epid.*6.2.17 (-είη Gal. ad loc.). 2. *favourable omen*, Arist.*Ath.*44.4. 3. generally, *favourable sign*, *PMasp.*9 ii 28 (vi A.D.). **-ος**, Dor. **-σᾱμος**, ον, *of good signs* or *omens*, φάσμα ναυβάταις E.*IA*252 (lyr.), cf. Plu.*Caes.*43; ἱερά Philostr.*VA*8.7.12; [πῦρ] ib.1.31. II. *easily known by signs, conspicuous*, εὔσημον γὰρ οὐ με λανθάνει [τὸ πλοῖον] A.*Supp.*714; καπνῷ δ' ἁλοῦσα... εὐ. πόλις Id.*Ag.*818; σημεῖα Hp.*Mochl.*16; τόπος *Annuario* 4/5.225 (Rhodes, ii B.C.); ἴχνη Thphr.*CP*6.19.5 (Comp.); οὐκ εὔσημον, ὅθεν... *not easy to distinguish*, ib.3.8.2; *legible, clear*, ὅπως -σαμοτέρα ὑπάρχῃ ἁ ἀναγραφά *SIG*1023.96 (Cos, iii/ii B.C.); εὐ. γράμματα *OGI*665.12 (Egypt, i A.D.); εὐ. προσαγόρευσις Men.381; of sound, *distinct*, βοαί S.*Ant.*1021; ἦχοι Phld.*Po.*2.16 (Sup.); *well-marked*, βραχίων Philostr.*Gym.*35; οὐλὴ εὔσημος *PPetr.*1 p.54 (iii B.C.). 2. *clear, intelligible*, λόγον εὐ. δοῦναι 1*Ep.Cor.*14.9; διδασκαλία Erot.*Prooem.*, Heliod.ap.Orib.48.20.7. 3. *evident*, τινι Phld.*Ir.* p.91 W., cf. Porph.*Abst.*3.5. 4. εὔσημα, τά, = Lat. *insignia*, f.l. for σύσσημα, D.S.36.2. 5. of garments, *with fine edging*, *BGU*1564.11 (ii A.D.). II. Adv. -μως *clearly, distinctly*, ἔχειν Arist.*Mete.* 363ᵃ27; μεμνῆσθαι Str.10.2.23; προσανένεγκε *POxy.*1188.5 (i A.D.): Sup. -ότατα Plu.2.1022a. **-ων**, dub. in Heph.Astr.1.1.

εὔσηπτος, ον, (σήπω) *easily putrefying* or *decaying*, Arist.*GA*785ᵃ2, *Pr.*861ᵃ38, Dsc.2.160: Comp., Plu.2.912c.

εὐσηψία, ἡ, *readiness to decay*, Thphr.*HP*8.9.1.

εὐσθέν-εια, ἡ, *strength, firmness*, Democr.57 codd. (εὐθ- Dind.), Thphr.*CP*3.1.6, 2.1 (v.l. εὐθ-), Ph.2.548 (v.l. εὐθηνία); ἡ πρὸς τὴν πύρωσιν εὐ., of scents, Thphr.*Od.*19. **-έω**, *to be strong, healthy*, Hp.*Morb.Sacr.*10 (prob. l.), E.*Cyc.*2, Arist.*Pr.*862ᵃ11, 925ᵃ3 (v.l. εὐθενέω); f.l. for εὐθενεῖν, A.*Eu.*895; so prob. in D.C.53.8. **-ής**, Ep. ἐϋσθ-, ές, (σθένος) *stout*, εἶδος Il.Pers.6, cf. Ph.*Bel.*56.31, Q.S.14.633; *strong, firm*, σίδηρος *APl.*4.323 (Mesom.): irreg. Sup. -ώτατος Ps.-Luc.*Philopatr.*28. Adv. -νῶς Gal.17(2).185, f.l. in Ph.1.264.

εὐσίδηρος [ῐ], ον, *well-ironed*, i.e. *bound with iron*, Sch.Hes.*Sc.*270.

εὐσίπυος [ῐ], ον, (σιπύα) *with full bread-basket*, *AP*6.288.10 (Leon.).

εὐσῑτ-έω, *to have a good appetite*, Hp.*Aph.*2.31; f.l. for συσσ-, Pyrgio 1; *to be well fed*, f.l. in Thphr.*HP*4.8.13. **-ία**, ἡ, *hearty appetite*, Aret.*SD*1.16. **-ος**, ον, *with good appetite*, Hp.*Coac.*124; εὔ. πολλῶν σιτίων Aret.*SD*1.16. 2. *easy to feed*, ζῷον Philostr.*VA* 1.41. 3. *well-provided with food*, κῶμαι ib.1.21. II. *producing a hearty appetite*, εὔσιτον οἱ πόνοι Ruf.ap.Orib.*inc.*6.33: Comp. and Sup., Id.ib.7.26.77, 5.11.3. III. = εὔκριθος (q.v.), Sch.Theoc.7.34.

εὔσκαλμος, ον, *well-tholed*, ναῦς prob. in *AP*7.215 (Anyte).

εὐσκάνδιξ, ῑκος, ὁ, ἡ, *abounding in chervil*, πρηών *AP*9.318 (Leon.).

εὔσκαρθμος, Ep. **ἐΰσκ-**, ον, (σκαίρω) *swift-springing, bounding*, ἵπποι Il.13.31; νῆες Q.S.14.10; Πάν *AP*6.32 (Agath.).

εὐσκάριστος [ᾰ], ον, (σκαρίζω) gloss on foreg., Sch.Il.13.31, *EM* 398.23.

εὔσκᾰφος, ον, (σκάπτω) *easy to dig*, Hsch. s.v. λάχεια.

εὐσκέδαστος, ον, (σκεδάζω) *easy to disperse*, Gal.10.842, al.

εὐσκέπαστος, ον, *well-covered, well-protected*, Th.5.71 (Sup.); τὸ εὐ. *good shelter*, D.C.49.30.

εὐσκεπής, ές, (σκέπας) = foreg., τῶν ἔξω πνευμάτων *from...*, Thphr. *Vent.*24; τοὺς εὐ. καὶ εὐηλίους [τόπους] *sheltered* and sunny, Id.*HP*4.1.1, cf. *CP*1.13.11.

εὔσκεπτος, ον, *easy to examine*, σκέψις Pl.*Phlb.*65d.

εὐσκευέω, *to be well equipped*, S.*Aj.*823.

εὔσκευος, ον, *well-wrought*, δέμας, of a statue, dub. in *App.Anth.* 1.193 (Egypt).

εὐσκί-αστος [ῐ], ον, *well-shaded, shadowy*, S.*OC*1707 (lyr.). **-ος**, ον, (σκιά) = foreg., Ἀχέροντος ἀκτά Pi.*P.*11.21; ἐν εὐσκίοις δρόμοισιν Ἀκαδήμου θεοῦ Eup.32; οἰκία X.*Oec.*9.4; ἄλσος Theoc.7.8.

εὐσκόπελος, ον, *rocky*, Pisand.ap.St.Byz. s.v. Νιφάτης.

εὔσκοπος, Ep. **ἐΰσκ-**, ον, (σκοπέω) *keen-sighted, watchful*, ἐΰσκοπος Ἀργεϊφόντης Il.24.24, Od.7.137; of Artemis, 11.198 (cf. II); of Heracles, Theoc.25.143; of Pan, Orph.*H.*11.9; of men, *AP*11.112 (Nicarch.). 2. *far-seen*, of stars and light, Ar.*Ec.*2 (v.l.), A.R.4.1716; of places, *commanding a wide view*, τὰ -ώτατα X.*Cyr.*6.3.2, cf. Arist.*HA*628ᵃ11 (nisi leg. εὐσκεπῆ), Plu.*Cat.Ma.*13. II. (σκοπός) *shooting well, of unerring aim* (as some explain Od.11.198), of Apollo, Orac.ap.Hdt.5.61; Βριτόμαρτις Call.*Dian.*190; τόξοις πρόσωθεν εὐσκόποις χειρουμένη A.*Ch.*694; εὐσκοπώτερα βάλλειν Hld.9.5. Adv. -πως, βάλλειν Ph.2.355: metaph., ἐξομοιοῦν Id.1.681; εὐ. ἔχειν τῶν ἀποκρίσεων Philostr.*VS*2.1.9.

εὔσκυλτος, *agilis, mobilis*, *Gloss.*

εὐσκωμμοσύνη, ἡ, *quickness in jesting* or *repartee*, Poll.5.161.

εὐσκώμμων, ον, gen. ονος, (σκῶμμα) *of ready wit*, esp. in *bantering* or *repartee*, Poll.5.161, Lib.*Decl.*15.25. Adv. -μόνως Poll.5.161.

εὔσμαλον· εὔχαρι, Hsch. **εὐσμερδής**· εὔρωστος, Id.; cf. σμερδαλέος.

ἐΰσμηκτος, ον, *well-cleaned*, σίδηρος Max.285.

ἐΰσμηνος, ον, *forming fine swarms*, μέλισσα Nonn.*D.*7.332.

ἐϋσμῆριγξ, ιγγος, ὁ, ἡ, *with beautiful tresses*, Ἠώς Nonn.*D.*11.388.

εὐσμίλευτος [ῑ], ον, *well-chiselled*, Hsch. (εὐσμήλωτα cod.).

εὐσοΐα, ἡ, *happiness, prosperity*, S.*OC*390 (Sch.), *Fr.*122.

εὔσοος, ον, *safe and well, happy*, εὔσοα τέκνα Theoc.24.8: **εὔσως**, Bato 5.10 is corrupt; cf. εὔσους· ὁ διευτυχῶν, καὶ ἥρως ἐγχώριος, καὶ εὐκίνητος, εὔφορος (cf. σεύω), Hsch.

εὐσότρου· εὐδρόμου, Hsch. (leg. ἐϋσσώτρου).

εὐσπάθητος [ᾰ], ον, *closely woven*, Hsch. s.v. τρίμιτον: prob. l. for εὐσπάρτεος, Id. **εὐσπαλές** (-εύς cod.)· εὐτελές, Id. **εὐσπάρτεος** ἱστός· οὗ μήτε ἀραιὸς μήτε πυκνὸς ὁ στήμων τυγχάνει, Id.

εὐσπειρής, ές, *well-coiled*, δράκων *AP*6.206 (Antip. Sid.):—also **εὔσπειρος**, ον, *well-wreathed*, κόρυμβοι ib.219.3 (Antip.).

εὐσπλαγχν-ία, ἡ, *good heart, firmness*, E.*Rh.*192, *PMasp.*97 *D*69 (vi A.D.). **-ος**, ον, *with healthy bowels*, Hp.*Prorrh.*2.6. II. *compassionate*, Lxx *Prec.Man.*7, *Ep.Eph.*4.32, 1*Ep.Pet.*3.8, *PMag. Leid.V.*9.3, *PMasp.*20.11 (vi A.D.).

εὔσπολον· εὐείμονα, εὐσταλέα, Hsch.

εὔσπορος, Ep. **ἐΰσπ-**, ον, *well-sown*, γύαι Ar.*Av.*230 (lyr.); Αἴγυπτος *APl.*4.295. 2. *rich in seed*, ἀνθέμιον cj. in *AP*4.1.36 (Mel.). II. *favourable to seed*, of Hermes, dub. cj. in Herm.ap.Stob.1.5.14.

ἐΰσσελμος, ἐΰσσωτρος, Ep. for εὔσελμος, εὔσωτρος.

εὐστάθ-εια [ᾰ] (also -ία *IPE*1².91.11 (Olbia, ii/iii A.D.), poet. -ίη *AP*12.199 (Strat.)), ἡ, *stability, tranquillity*, coupled with εὐνομία, Ph. 1.248; κατὰ τὰς πόλεις ib.680; ὑπὲρ εὐσταθείας τῆς πόλεως *IPE*1².94.11 (Olbia); τὴν Αἴγυπτον ἐν εὐ. διάγουσαν *OGI*669.4 (Egypt, i A.D.); εὐστάθειαν τῷ Βακχείῳ *SIG*1109.15 (ii A.D.). 2. esp. of *bodily health*, εὐ. σαρκός Epicur.*Fr.*8, 424, Olympic.ap.Gal.10.56. 3. of persons, εὐσταθίη ἡ ἐν ἑωυτῷ *self-possession*, Hp.*Decent.*12; *stedfastness, tranquillity*, Phld.*Mus.*p.33 K., Ph.1.231, al.; ἐν βουλαῖς Plu.2.342f, al.; τῆς ψυχῆς Ath.Med.ap.Orib.*inc.*21.20, cf. Ptol.*Tetr.*11; *steadiness*, ὁρμῶν *Stoic.*3.65. **-έω**, *to be steady, stable*, ὅταν πολίταις εὐσταθῶσι δαίμονες *are favourable*, E.*Rh.*317; εὐ. ταῖς διανοίαις D.H.6.51; εὐστάθει *rest in peace!* in an epitaph, *IG*14.1464; *to be calm, tranquil*, of the sea, Luc.*VH*1.30; οὐκ εὐ. οἱ ὄρνιθες Plu.2.281b. 2. *enjoy sound, stable health*, εὐ. καὶ ὑγιαίνειν Epicur.*Fr.*68, cf. 413, Sor.1.87, Herod. Med.ap.Orib.7.8.1. 3. of cities or countries, *enjoy tranquillity*, εὐσταθοῦσα βασιλεία *OGI*56.19 (Canopus, Ptol. III); τὴν πόλιν εὐ. *SIG* 708.37 (Istropolis, ii B.C.), cf. App.*Hisp.*9. **-ής**, ές, Ep. **ἐΰστ-**, as always in Hom., (ἵσταμαι) *well-based, well-built*, περὶ τοῖχον ἐϋσταθέος μεγάροιο Il.18.374, al.; ἐντὸς ἐϋσταθέος μεγάρου, ἐκτὸς ἐϋ. θαλάμου, Od. 20.258, 23.178. II. metaph., *steadfast, tranquil*, ψυχαί Democr. 191; ἀνήρ Plu.2.44a; οἱ -έστεροι Hdn.2.6.5; γνώμη Aret.*SA*1.10; -έστεροι γνώμῃ ib.2.3; περὶ τῆς εὐσταθοῦς τῶν θεῶν διαγωγῆς dub. in Phld.*D.*3 tit. 2. of the body, *sound, healthy*, σαρκὸς εὐσταθὲς κατάστημα Epicur.*Fr.*68, Metrod.*Fr.*5; of persons, *healthy, sound*, Ath. Med.ap.Orib.*inc.*7.1. 3. εὐ. νοῦσοι *easily cured, not serious*, Hp.*Aph.* 3.8; καῦσοι Id.*Epid.*1.1. 4. of weather, *steady, settled, calm*, θέρος ib. 3.15; Ζέφυρος A.R.4.821. 5. generally, *steady, quiet*, βίος Hierocl. p.53 A.; ἁρμονία D.H.*Dem.*36; in political sense, *firmly established*, μοναρχία Phld.*Hom.*p.31 O. III. Adv. -θῶς, ἔχειν Sor.1.40, cf. D.L.7.182, Asp.*in EN*115.3; στρατοπεδεῦσαι App.*Hisp.*25, al.: Sup. -έστατα Id.*BC*2.115; Aeol. -θέως *IG*12(2).243 (Mytilene).

εὐσταθμ-ία, ἡ, f.l. for εὐστομία, Orib.45.29.22. **-ος**, ον, *accurately measured*, dub. in *PTeb.*5.85 (ii B.C.), v.l. in Lxx *Si.*26.18(23); *of full weight*, νομίσματα *Cod.Just.*10.27.2.6. Adv. -μως, ἴσον *precisely* equal *in weight*, Hp.*Mul.*1.1: Comp. -ότερον *BKT*3 p.15.

εὐστάλ-εια [ᾰ], Ion. -ίη, ἡ, *simple arrangement*, Hp.*Art.*82. 2. *orderliness*, ἐπιθυμιῶν καὶ φόβων Phld.*Oec.*p.65 J. 3. of troops, *light equipment*, Plu.*Sert.*12. **-ής**, ές, (στέλλω) *well-equipped*, στόλος A. *Pers.*795; of troops, *light-armed*, εὐσταλεῖς τῇ ὁπλίσει Th.3.22; ἱππεὺς

-έστατος X.*Eq.*7.8, etc.; ὁπλισμὸς -έστερος D.H.7.59; τὸ εὐσταλὲς πρὸς πόλεμον, = εὐστάλεια, Hdn.3.8.5. 2. *convenient, neat,* Hp.*Fract.* 37 (Comp.), prob. in Id.*Mochl.*1; *convenient to handle, manageable,* σωμάτιον Id.*Superf.*7 (Comp.); πλοῦς οὔριός τε κεὐσταλής a fair and *easy* voyage, S.*Ph.*780. 3. *compact,* εὐ. τὸν ὄγκον Plu.*Mar.*34; σώματα Id.2.353a; εὐ. δίαιτα *light* diet, Philum.ap.Orib.45.29.8. 4. *correct in habit and manners, well-behaved,* κόσμιος καὶ εὐ. ἀνήρ Pl.*Men.* 90a, cf. Diod.Com.2.17; *orderly,* ἱερουργίαι Plu.*Sol.*12; in dress, *neat, trim,* Luc.*Tim.*54. II. Adv. -λῶς, Ion. -λέως, of dress, *well girt up,* Hp.*Off.*3, Opp.*C.*1.97; of light-armed troops, κούφως καὶ εὐ. ἐκτρέχειν Hdn.4.15.1. 2. of bandaging, *compactly,* Hp.*Off.*9 (Sup.), *Mochl.*1 codd. 3. *decently, in order,* ταφῆναι Phld.*Mort.*31.

εὐστάφῠλος [ᾰ], Ep. **ἐΰστ-**, ον, *rich in grapes,* epith. of Dionysus, *IG*7.3098 (Lebad.); ἐϋ. ἐνὶ Νάξῳ *PSI*7.845.16 (v/vi A.D.).

εὔστᾰχυς, υ, *rich in corn,* *AP*6.36 (Phil.): Ep. **ἐΰστ-** Orac.ap. Hld.2.26; σπόρος, γῆ, Ph.2.14,21: metaph., *blooming, fruitful,* ἡλικίη *AP*7.589 (Agath.); τεκέων εὐ. ἀνθοσύνην ib.5.275 (Id.). 2. νάρδος εὐ. *with a fine spike,* Nic.*Th.*604.

εὐστεγής, ές, *well-covered,* Sch.Lyc.350.

εὐστείλ(ε)ος, ον, *with a good haft* or *handle,* Hsch.

ἐϋστείρη, fem. Adj. *with good keel,* ἐϋστείρης . . νηός A.R.1.401.

εὔστεκτος, ον, *guarded, self-controlled,* Call.*Iamb.*1.300.

εὐστελέχης, ες, quoted as compound of στέλεχος, Hdn.Gr.2.687.

εὔστερνος, ον, *broad-chested,* Man.4.96; δαμάλεις *Gp.*17.2.1: metaph., χοάνοισι, of the earth, Emp.96.1.

εὐστέφᾰνος, Ep. **ἐΰστ-**, ον, epith. of Artemis, Il.21.511; of Aphrodite, Od.8.267, al., Hes.*Th.*196, al.; of Demeter, *h.Cer.*224, Hes. *Op.*300; of a Nereid, Id.*Th.*255 (expld. by Sch. as *well-girdled,* = εὔζωνος). 2. εὐ. θεῶν θυσίαι *graced with beauteous garlands,* Ar. *Nu.*309 (lyr.); θυμέλαι *IG*5(1).734 (Sparta); λειμῶνες εὐ. *crowned with flowers,* Opp.*C.*1.462. II. of cities, *crowned, circled with walls and towers,* of Thebes, Il.19.99, Hes.*Sc.*80, *Th.*978; Mycenae, Od.2.120; εὐ. ἀγυιαί Pi.*P.*2.58; Κρότων D.P.369.

εὐστεφής, ές, (στέφος) = foreg., Orac.ap.Amm.Marc.31.1.5, Max. 529.

εὐστήρικτος, ον, *firm, fixed,* Sch.rec.A.*Th.*312.

εὐστῐβής, ές, (στείβω) *well-trodden,* αἰθυίαις λέπας *AP*6.23.

ἐΰστικτος, ον, *variegated,* Opp.*C.*1.336.

εὔστιπτος, Ep. **ἐΰστ-**, ον, *closely-woven* or *well-fulled,* φᾶρος A.R. 2.30.

εὐστῐχία, poet. -ίη, ἡ, in poetry, *good ordering of lines,* σχεδίου *IG*14.2012*Cb*6.

εὔστολος, ον, = εὐσταλής 1.1, ναῦς S.*Ph.*516 (lyr.); ὁλκάς A.R.1. 603. 2. = εὐσταλής 1.4, Πλάτων Luc.*Epigr.*45 (acc. to Planudes).

εὐστομᾰχ-έω, *have a good appetite,* Phld.*Sign.*38. -ία, ἡ, *wholesomeness* of food, Hices.ap.Ath.7.298b, Aët.9.30, Paul.Aeg.2. 49; f.l. for εὐστομία, Dsc.2.16. -ος, ον, *equable, tranquil.* Adv. εὐστομάχως, *ferre* Cic.*Att.*9.5.2; ἀπορέγχειν *AP*11.4 (Parmen.). II. *good for the stomach, wholesome,* Diocl.*Fr.*125, Dsc.1.117, Sor.1.94, Hices.ap.Ath.15.689c, Gal.6.593: Sup., lemma ad Ath.7.310a.

εὐστομ-έω, *to be* εὔστομος, *sing sweetly,* of the nightingale, S.*OC* 18, cf. Ael.*NA*1.20, Philostr.*VS*2.10.5; *speak finely,* Luc.*Trag.*181; *employ euphonious words,* Dam.*Pr.*81. 2. generally, = εὐφημέω, A.*Ch.*983(997), Ar.*Nu.*833. -ία, poet. -ίη, ἡ, *goodness of sound, euphony,* Pl.*Cra.*404d, D.H.*Comp.*7, etc.; *sweet singing,* Ael.*NA*17. 23; *beauty of language,* D.H.*Lys.*12, *Dem.*13, etc.; δάκρυσον νεότητα καὶ εὐ. *Syria* 5.337 (Sidon). II. *pleasantness to the mouth, goodness of taste,* Thphr.*CP*6.16.2, Dsc.2.16: pl., Plu.2.687d; f.l. for εὐστομαχία, Hices.ap.Ath.7.310f. III. *skill with the mouth,* of a flute-player, Philostr.*VA*5.21. -ος, ον, (στόμα) *with mouth of good size,* of dogs, X.*Cyn.*4.2; of horses, εὐ. τῷ χαλινῷ *well-bitted,* opp. ἄστομος, Plu.2.39a. 2. *with large mouth,* of cups, Luc.*Lex.* 7; of a harbour, Poll.1.100. 3. *easy to keep open,* of a vein, Aret. *CA*2.2. II. *speaking well, eloquent,* *AP*14.10.8 (Comp.), Ptol. *Tetr.*166; *making eloquent,* λάγυνος *AP*9.229 (Marc. Arg.). Adv. -μως *with clear utterance,* Ael.*NA*4.42: Sup. -ώτατα ib.13.18; *melodiously,* ib.1.43; ᾖδον Aristaenet.2.19. 2. like εὔφημος, *avoiding words of ill omen,* and so, *keeping silence,* περὶ μὲν τούτων . . μοι . . εὔστομα κείσθω on these things... let me keep *a religious silence,* Hdt. 2.171, cf. Ael.*NA*14.28, Porph.*Abst.*2.36; εὔστομ' ἔχε *peace, be still!* S.*Ph.*201 (lyr.). III. *pleasant to the mouth, palatable,* Thphr.*HP* 2.6.10 (Comp.), 4.3.4, Sor.1.94, Dsc.1.110 (Comp.).

εὐστοργος, ον, *contented:* Sup. -ότατος Suid. s. v. ἀπαθέστατα (misquoting M.Ant.1.9).

εὐστόρθυγξ, Ep. **ἐΰστ-**, υγγος, ὁ, ἡ, *consisting of a fine branch,* κορύνα *AP*6.35 (Leon.); Πρίαπος ib.232 (Crin.).

εὐστόν or **εὗστόν,** τό, (εὕω) *victim whose skin is singed,* *SIG*1037.5 (Milet., iv/iii B.C.).

εὐστοχ-έω, pf. inf. εὐστοχηκέναι D.S.2.31:—*hit the mark, succeed,* opp. ἁμαρτάνω, Plb.1.14.7, etc.: c. gen., εὐ. πάσης περιστάσεως, τῶν καιρῶν, τῆς ἐλπίδος, *to hit* them *exactly,* Id.2.45.5, 28.3.6, 32.3.10; τῆς εἰσβολῆς τοῦ λιμένος Str.17.1.6; περί τι Id.5.3.8: c. acc., θηρίον Apollod.1.7.4: abs., Plb.9.12.1; ἐν ἅπασιν J.*BJ*1.15.1; *guess aright,* Plu.2.617d:—Pass., impers., Antyll.ap.Orib.44.23.44; εὐστοχηθεῖσα χάρις blessing *seasonably granted,* J.*AJ*15.9.2. -ημα, ατος, τό, *lucky hit,* D.L.5.34. -ία, Ep. -ίη, ἡ, *skill in shooting at a mark, good aim,* ἐπὶ τόξων εὐστοχίᾳ γάνυται E.*IT*1239 (lyr.), cf. Call. *Dian.*217, Pancrat.*Oxy.*1085.8; χερὸς εὐ., periphr. for *a bow,* E.*Tr.* 812 (lyr.): in later Prose, D.S.5.18: pl., Id.3.25: metaph., εὐ. καιροῦ Plu.2.74d. II. metaph., *sagacity, shrewdness,* Arist.*EN*1142b2, Plb.18.33.7; χειρῶν εὐ., of artists, D.H.*Comp.*25, cf. *APl.*4.310 (Damocharis), etc.; εὐ. μνήμης Ph.*Fr.*11 H. -ος, ον, *well-aimed,* τῷδ' ἂν εὐστόχῳ πτερῷ (Elmsl. for πέτρῳ) E.*Hel.*76; ἀκόντιον X.*Eq.*12.13 (Sup.); πληγή Plb.6.25.9. II. *aiming well,* ὅσοι δὲ τόξοις χεῖρ' ἔχουσιν εὐ. E.*HF*195; λόγχαις . . . -ώτατοι Id.*Ph.*140, cf. *Fr.*321 (Comp.); εὐ. τὴν τοξικήν Luc.*Nav.*33. Adv. -χως, βάλλειν X.*Cyr.*1.4.8; εὔστοχα βάλλειν, τοξεύειν, Parth.15.1, Luc.*Nigr.*36: Sup. -ώτατα D.C. 67.14. 2. metaph., *making good shots,* i.e. *guessing well, hitting the right nail on the head,* Arist.*Div.Somn.*464a33; *shrewd,* Id.*Rh.* 1412a12, Ephipp.14.1, cj. in Luc.*Epigr.*45; βουλευτήριον *Com.Adesp.* 201; εὔστοχόν τι ἔνεστι τοῖς κακοῖς Pl.*Lg.*950b; εὐ. ἐν ἀπαντήσεσιν *ready* at repartee, D.L.6.74. Adv. -χως Pl.*Lg.*792d, Arist.*PA*639a5, Phld.*Rh.*2.108 S. 3. *successful,* ἄγρη Opp.*H.*3.280; εὐχαί *AP*9. 158.8.

εὕστρα or **εὔστρα** (*EM*398.31), ἡ: (εὕω):—*place for singeing slaughtered swine,* Ar.*Eq.*1236 (pl.). II. *roasted barley,* from which ἄλφιτα were made, Paus.Gr.*Fr.*184, cf. *EM*90.31. 2. a kind of *pulse,* *PTeb.*9.14, 11.9 (ii B.C.).

εὐστρᾰφής, ές, (στρέφω) = sq., Ammon.*Diff.*p.54 V., Sch.Il.*Oxy.* 1086.111.

εὔστρεπτος, Ep. **ἐΰστρ-**, ον, *well-twisted,* of leathern ropes, ἐϋστρέπτοισι βοεῦσι Od.2.426. II. *well-plied, nimble,* πόδες *AP*9. 533; πρόσωπον *turning hither and thither,* Nonn.*D.*3.180.

ἐϋστρεφής, ές, (στρέφω) *well-twisted,* of a bow-string, ἐϋστρεφέα νευρήν Il.15.463; of a lyre-string, ἐϋστρεφὲς ἔντερον οἰός Od.21.408; πεῖσμα ἐϋ. 10.167; ὅπλῳ ἐϋστρεφεῖ 14.346; ἐϋστρεφέεσσι λύγοισι 9.427; v. εὔστροφος. II. *shapely,* ὦμοι Simm.1.10 (s. v. l.).

εὐστροφάλιγξ [ᾰ], ιγγος, ὁ, ἡ, *curly,* of hair, *AP*6.219.18 (Antip.).

εὐστροφία, ἡ, *suppleness, versatility,* ἔν τινι Chrysipp.*Stoic.*3.178, cf. Porph.*Abst.*3.23; τὸ μετ' εὐστροφίας ὀξὺ πρὸς τὰς ἀπαντήσεις Plu. 2.510f, cf. 975a, Lxx *Pr.*14.35.

εὔστροφος, Ep. **ἐΰστρ-**, ον, *well-twisted,* ἐϋστρόφῳ οἰὸς ἀώτῳ with *well-twisted* wool (i. e. a sling), Il.13.599, 716 (ἐϋστρεφεῖ Aristarch.). II. *easily turned, manageable,* νῆες E.*IA*293 (Sup., lyr.); *turning easily on a pivot,* Hero *Aut.*26.2: metaph., ζῷον, of man, Pl. *Criti.*109c; πρὸς τὰς ἀπαντήσεις εὐ. λόγος Plu.2.803f; τὸ εὐ. τοῦ φθέγματος Philostr.*VS*2.10.5. Adv. -φως, τέθριππον ἕλκων *APl.*4.385, cf. Alex.Trall.1.16.

εὔστρωτος, Ep. **ἐΰστρ-**, ον, (στρώννυμι) *well spread with clothes,* λέχος *h.Ven.*157, cf. *h.Cer.*285, Nonn.*D.*18.164.

εὔστῡλος, ον, *with goodly pillars,* ναοί E.*IT*128 (lyr.). II. *with columns at the best distances,* Vitr.3.3.1.

εὐσύγ-κρῐτος, ον, either *well-compounded, well-constituted,* or *discriminating,* Diog.Oen.1, 2. -κρυπτος, ον, *well-covered,* Hp.*Fract.* 4, Aret.*SD*1.8. -χώρητος, gloss on ἐπιεικτός, Sch.D Il.8.32.

εὐσύϊνος, = οἰσύ-, *IG*5(1).1390.23 (Andania, i B.C.).

εὐσῡκοφάντητος, ον, *exposed to calumny,* Plu.2.707f.

εὐσύλληπτος, ον, *easily taken* or *caught,* Horap.1.54 (Comp.). II. Act., *receptive,* τοῦ σπέρματος *Gp.*17.1 (Comp.): abs., *conceiving easily,* Gal.19.153, S.E.*M.*5.60, Ptol.*Tetr.*72; τὸ εὐ., of the earth, Corn. *ND*28.

εὐσυλλόγιστος, ον, *well-concluded, conclusive,* εὐσυλλογιστότερα . . . τἀληθῆ Arist.*Rh.*1355a38. 2. *easily inferred,* ἔκ τινων πόσον . . . Plb. 12.18.8, cf. 8.37.1.

εὐσυμ-βίβαστος [ῐ], ον, *probable, consistent,* Eust.247.29. -βίωτος [ῐ], ον, *easy to live with,* Vett.Val.42.19. -βλητος, old Att. **εὐξ-**, ον, = sq. 1, τέρας Hdt.7.57; ἧδ' οὐκέτ' εὐξύμβλητος ἡ χρησμῳδία A.*Pr.*775. -βολος, old Att. **εὐξ-**, ον, *easy to divine* or *understand,* εὐξ. τόδ' ἐστὶ παντὶ δοξάσαι A.*Ch.*170, cf. D.C.40.17. II. *easy to deal with, honest, upright,* X.*Mem.*2.6.5; εὐξ. δίκαι suits *which afford easy arbitration,* A.*Supp.*701 (lyr.). Adv. εὐξυμβόλως Poll.5.139. 2. *readily contributing one's* συμβολή, Antipho Soph.74. III. *affording a good omen, auspicious,* πρός τι Plu.*Demetr.*12, cf. Ael.*NA*3.9, Hld.9.25. Adv. -λως Sch.Pi.*I.*6(5).67. -βουλος, ον, *giving good counsel,* Hdn.Gr.2.791, Tz.*H.*6.839. -μέτρως, Adv. *in suitable proportions,* Archig.ap.Orib.8.2.32. -περίφορος, ον, *easy to live with, accommodating,* D.L.7.13. -πλήρωτος, ον, *easily filled up, attained,* πέρας Epicur.*Ep.*3 p.65 U. -πτωτος, ον, *collapsing easily,* Anon.Lond.27.26. -φῠτος, ον, *easily growing together,* Thphr.*CP*3.7.10.

εὐσυν-άγωγος [ᾰγ], ον, *easily collected together,* τόπος τοῖς πεμπομένοις εὐ. a place *convenient for collecting* imports, Arist.*Pol.*1331b 2. -άλλακτος, ον, *easy to deal with,* πρὸς ἀκρόασιν Plu.2.42f, cf. Ptol.*Tetr.*165, Vett.Val.116.32. Adv. -τως Lxx *Pr.*25.10. -αλλαξία, ἡ, *fair dealing,* *Stoic.*3.64, 67. -άντητος, ον, gloss on εὐάντητος, Sch.Opp.*H.*2.149. -άρμοστος, ον, *easily fitted together,* Arist.*GA*718a29. -δεξίαστος [ῐ], ον, *loyal to pledges given,* Ptol. *Tetr.*165. -δετος, ον, *readily combining,* τὰ φῶτα *Cat.Cod.Astr.*8 (4).119. -ειδησία, ἡ, *conscientiousness, integrity,* *PSI*5.452.26 (iv A.D.). -ειδητος, ον, *with a good conscience,* M.Ant.6.30. II. *honest,* πρᾶγμα *Sammelb.*4426.12 (iii A.D.).

εὐσυνεσία, old Att. **εὐξ-**, ἡ, *shrewdness,* Critias *Fr.*73 D., Arist. *EN*1143a10.

εὐσύνετος, old Att. **εὐξ-**, ον, *quick of apprehension,* Arist.*EN*1143a 11; -ώτεροι εἰς ταῦτα ib.1181b11: c. gen., γνώμης θείας Porph. ad Il. p.324 S. Adv. -τως Suid. s. v. ἀστικῶς: Comp. -ώτερον Th.4. 18. II. *easily understood,* ξυνετοῖς E.*IT*1092 (lyr.); διανόημα Phld.*Po.*2.40; κέντροις εὐσυνέτοις Epigr.Astrol.*Oxy.*464.42 (iii A.D.).

εὐσυν-ήγορος, ον, *skilled in advocacy*, Hdn.Gr.2.791, al. **-θεσία**, ἡ, *good arrangement* of words, Eust.85.34. II. *observance of treaties*, Ph.2.267. **-θετέω**, *keep faith*, opp. ἀσυνθετέω, Chrysipp. *Stoic.*2.63, Plu.*Rom.*5; ἐν πᾶσι Plb.21.42.5, cf. *PTeb.*61(*a*).32 (ii B.C.); πρός τινα Procop.*Vand.*2.2. II. *grant*, τί τισι *PPetr.*2 p.22 (iii B.C.). **-θετος**, ον, *easy to compound into a word*, λόγος Arist.*Rh.* 1406^{a}36. Adv. -τως *suitably*, ἐκλέγεσθαι Eust.2.22; prob. in *PLit. Lond.*170 (i A.D.). 2. *easy to put together* or *construct*, Ph.*Bel.*56. 34, Apollod.*Poliorc.*155.16. II. of persons, in act. sense, *constructive, inventive*, εἰς τὸ νοῆσαι Man.5.272. 2. *easy to deal with*, Ptol.*Tetr.*165. **-θεώρητος**, ον, *easy to observe*, Epicur.*Nat.*28. 9. **-οπτος**, ον, *easily taken in at a glance, seen at once*, Isoc.15. 172, Aeschin.3.118, Thphr.*HP*1.9.5; μέγεθος Arist.*Po.*1451^{a}4; πλῆθος, χώρα, Id.*Pol.*1327^{a}1; τάφοι ἀλλήλοις εὐ. *within easy sight of* each other, ib.1274^{a}37; δύναμις εὐ. τοῖς ἐκ τῆς πόλεως Plb.5.24.6. II. metaph., *easily taken in by the mind*, of a poem, Arist.*Po.*1459^{a}33; λέγω δὲ περίοδον λέξιν ἔχουσαν... μέγεθος εὐ. Id.*Rh.*1409^{b}1; of the facts of a case, ib.1414^{a}12, cf. *Pol.*1323^{b}7; of a falsity or error, *easily seen* or *detected*, Id.*Sens.*441^{a}10. Adv. -τως Id.*Mir.*838^{b}10. **-τακτος**, ον, *well-arranged*, τάξις Arr.*Tact.*16.10. 2. *with good syntax, easy*, ἑρμηνεία Eust.66.36. Adv. -τως Id.336.4. **-τέλεστος**, ον, *easily brought to a conclusion*, Vett.Val.212.17. **-τριπτος**, ον, *easily broken*, Plb.9.19.7.

εὐσύστᾰτος, ον, *of proper consistency*, Crito ap.Gal.13.884; ἔμβρυα εὐ. Antyll.ap.Orib.6.31.5 codd. (nisi leg. ἀσύστ-). II. *easy to make friends with*, Vett.Val.39.14.

εὐσύστροφος, ον, *alert*, opp. ἀσύστροφος, Olymp.*in Grg.*p.258 J.

εὔσφαιρος, ον, *fair and round*, of pearls, Tz.*H.*11.490; ζῷα ib.7. 726.

εὔσφυκτος, ον, (σφύζω) *with a good pulse*, Gal.9.802 (Comp.), Aret. *CA*2.4.

εὐσφυξία, ἡ, *goodness, healthiness of pulse*, Aret.*CA*1.4.

εὔσφῡρος, Ep. ἐΰσφ-, ον, *with beautiful ankles*, of women, Hes. *Sc.*16, *Th.*254, Theoc.28.13, etc.; πούς E.*Hel.*1570.

εὔσχετος, ον, (σχεῖν) *easily kept in its place*, Hp.*Off.*15.

εὐσχημάτιστος [ᾰ], ον, *well-formed*, Eust.1570.47.

εὐσχημον-έω, *to behave with decorum*, Pl.*Lg.*732c, Men.*Mon.*646, Phld.*Rh.*2.281 S., *PSI*5.541.5. **-ημα**, ατος, τό, *decorous act*, *Stoic.* 3.136. **-ίζω**, *train, educate*, *GDI*1708.14 (Delph.).

εὔσχημ-ος, ον, = εὐσχήμων, *EM*398.19; ῥυθμοί v.l. in D.H.*Comp.* 17. Adv. -μως v.l. in E.*Hec.*569. **-οσύνη**, ἡ, *gracefulness, elegance*, Pl.*Smp.*196a, X.*Cyr.*5.1.5; *decorum*, Arist.*EN*1128^{a}25; *refinement*, Id.*Pol.*1329^{b}28; βίου, ῥημάτων, Pl.*R.*588a, *Lg.*627d (but also κίβδηλος εὐ. a spurious *respectability*, Id.*R.*366b). 2. of the body, 1*Ep.Cor.*12.23; ἡ τοῦ σώματος εὐ. *IGRom.*4.1029.35 (Astypalaea, i B.C.). II. *proper treatment, adequate maintenance*, *IG*9(1).189 (Tithora). **-ων**, ον, gen. ονος, (σχῆμα) *elegant in figure, mien and bearing, graceful*, opp. ἀσχήμων, Pl.*R.*413e, al.; ἀλεκτρυών Cratin. 108; τὰ εὐ. ἡμῶν (sc. μόρια) 1*Ep.Cor.*12.24: Comp. -έστερος *more respectable*, Pl.*R.*554e: Sup. -έστατοι, πονεῖν ἵπποι X.*Eq.*11.12. 2. in bad sense, *with an outside show of goodness, specious in behaviour*, εἴς τινα E.*Med.*584. II. of things, *decent, becoming*, λόγοι Id.*Hipp.* 490, D.60.9; πρᾶγμα οὐδαμῶς εὔσχημον λέγειν Aeschin.3.162; λέγειν εὐσχήμονα Arist.*EN*1128^{a}7; τὸ εὔσχημον *decorum*, Pl.*R.*401c, *Lg.* 797b. Adv. -μόνως *with grace and dignity, like a gentleman*, Ar.*V.* 1210, X.*Cyr.*1.3.8, Arist.*EN*1101^{a}1; ζῆν Phld.*Herc.*1251.18: Comp -έστερον, ἔχειν Pl.*Epin.*981a; τι φέρειν D.60.35: Sup. -έστατα *IG* 2^{2}.1034.11. 2. later also, *noble, honourable*, in rank (condemned by Phryn.309), *Ev.Marc.*15.43, *Act.Ap.*13.50, J.*Vit.*9, Vett.Val.66. 7, al.; ἡ εὐ. *the noble lady*, *PFlor.*16.20 (iii A.D.). b. title of a village magistrate, in pl., εὐ. κώμης *BGU*147 (ii/iii A.D.): sg., ἡ οἰκία τοῦ εὐ. *PRyl.*236.15 (iii A.D.).

εὐσχῐδής, Ep. ἐΰσχ-, ές, = sq., Opp.*C.*2.211; κάλαμοι *AP*6.68 (Jul. Aegypt.).

εὔσχιστος, ον, *easy to split*, Thphr.*HP*5.6.3, Dsc.5.127. 2. *well-split*, of a pen, *AP*6.227 (Crin.).

εὐσχολ-έω, *to have abundant leisure*, Phld.*Rh.*1.377 S., D.S. 10.7, M.Ant.11.18: c. inf., J.*AJ*5.2.5; εἴς τι Id.*BJ*3.7.29; τινος *for* a thing, Luc.*Am.*33: εἰ -εῖτε ἐπαινέσαι με Muson.*Fr.*48 p.130 H. **-ία**, ἡ, *leisure*, Aq., Thd.3*Ki.*6.17, Longus 3.13. **-ος**, ον, *unoccupied*, esp. *by war*, Plb.4.32.6; *leisured, leisurely*, ἀναχώρησις Phld.*Oec.*p.64 J.; εὐ. τὴν ψυχήν Hierocl.ap.Stob.4.22.24 (corr. Gaisf.): Comp. -ώτερος Teles p.47 H., M.Ant.4.24.

εὐσωμᾰτ-έω, *to be well-grown, to be strong and lusty*, E.*Andr.*765, Ar.*Nu.*799; ἀλεκτορίδες τὸν χειμῶνα οὐ πάνυ εὐσωματοῦσι Orib.1.3.5; of trees, εὐ. τοῖς μεγέθεσι Plu.2.641a. **-ία**, ἡ, *strength* or *good habit of body*, Poll.2.235. **-ος**, ον, *well-grown*, ibid. **-ώδης**, ες, = sq., Arist.*Pr.*869^{b}14 (Comp.).

εὔσωμος, ον, *sound in body*, *EM*105.46. **εὐσωπία**· ἡσυχία, Hsch.

εὔσως, ων, = εὔσοος (q.v.).

εὔσωτρος, Ep. ἐΰσσ-, ον, *with good felloes*, i.e. *with good wheels*, ἀπήνη Hes.*Sc.*273 (v.l. Il.24.578).

εὐτᾱκής, ές, (τήκω) *easy to soften by heat*, Luc.*Herm.*61.

εὐτακτ-έω, *to be orderly, behave well*, Th.8.1, X.*Mem.*4.4.1, etc.; of soldiers, *obey discipline*, ib.3.5.21; εὐ. πρὸς ἀρχήν *to be obedient* towards.., Plu.*Cam.*18; *to be continent*, Epict.*Ench.*29.2, D.L.4.42, *AP*5.39.7 (Nicarch.). II. Act., *pay regularly*, τοὺς φόρους *PHib.* 1.35.6 (iii B.C.), cf. *POxy.*1471.16 (i A.D.); τὰ ὀψώνια *PSI*4.350.2 (iii B.C.), etc.:—Pass., ὅπως οἱ μισθοὶ τοῖς παιδευταῖς εὐτακτέωνται *SIG* 672.10 (Delph., ii B.C.), cf. *BGU*1107.11. III. Pass., *to be reduced to order*, ὑπὸ τοῦ διανοητικοῦ ὡς ὑπό τινος ἰσότητος Nicom.*Ar.*1.23; -ουμένη ἀπόβασις, def. of εἱμαρμένη, *Theol.Ar.*60: c. acc. cogn., τὸν τοῦ νοῦ λόγον -ούμενος Iamb.*VP*15.66. **-ημα**, ατος, τό, *act of orderly behaviour*, *Stoic.*3.136. **-ος**, ον, (τάσσω) *well-ordered, orderly*, πόλις Ar.*Av.*829; σιωπή Posidon.24 J.; βίος Men.*Mon.*298; εὐ. τὸν βίον, τὴν δίαιταν, Plu.2.749d, D.L.2.25; περὶ τὸν βίον Hp. *Medic.*1. 2. esp. of soldiers, etc., *orderly, well-disciplined*, Ar.*V.* 424, Th.2.89, *IG*7.1.7 (Megara, iv B.C.), etc.; πορεία Th.7.77: Comp., X.*An.*3.2.30; *well-behaved*, Epicur.*Fr.*217; name of a category of ἔφηβοι, *IGRom.*4.482 (Pergam., i B.C.); κατὰ χρόνους εὐτάκτους at *regular* intervals, Sor.1.19. II. Adv. -τως *in an orderly manner*, Hp.*Epid.*1.6, Epicur.*Fr.*127, etc.; *in order*, A.*Pers.*399, Ar.*Nu.*964; *regularly*, of payments, *PTeb.*5.55 (ii B.C.), *BGU*1147.12 (i B.C.): Comp. -ότερον D.45.77; -τέρως X.*Eq.Mag.*2.7.

εὐτᾰμίευτος, ον, *easily regulated* or *graduated*, Arist.*GA*787^{b}5, Hp. *Art.*33,38. 2. *easily stored*, i.e. *lasting*, of perfumes, Thphr.*Od.*13.

εὐταξία, ἡ, *good arrangement*, τῶν φλεβῶν, of a gem, *AP*9.695 (pl.); τῶν τῆς ψυχῆς μερῶν πρὸς ἄλληλα Pl.*Def.*411d; ψυχῆς πρὸς ἡδονάς ibid.e; *good condition*, ὅπλων καὶ ἵππων X.*Mem.*3.3.14. 2. *good order, discipline*, Th.6.72; *orderly behaviour*, Pl.*Alc.*1.122c, etc.; as a subject of competition, *SIG*1061.4 (Samos, ii B.C.), cf. *IG*2^{2}.417; in a state, *orderliness, order*, ἡ εὐνομία εὐταξία Arist.*Pol.*1326^{a}30, cf. 1321^{a}4; ὁ αἱρεθεὶς ἐπὶ τὴν εὐ. *IG*7.4254. 3. *moderation in diet*, Erasistr.ap.*Placit.*5.30.3. 4. *continence*, Gal.8.451. II. Stoic term, *practical judgement, tact*, *Stoic.*3.64, al.

εὐτάρακτος [τᾰρ], ον, *easily disturbed*, Plu.*Arat.*10.

εὔταρσος, ον, *delicate winged*, ἰξύς (of the grasshopper) *AP*7.213 (Arch.). 2. *of delicate ankles*, ἀστράγαλοι ib.6.254 (Myrin.).

εὖτε, Ep., Ion., and poet. Adv. (rare in Trag., never in Com. or Att. Prose): I. of Time, *when*, 1. with ind., of a definite occurrence in past time, εὖτέ μιν προὔπεμψεν *when* he sent him, Il.8. 367, cf. 11.735, 23.85, E.*Ion*888 (lyr.): with impf., ἤκουσας... εὖτε ὁρμῶμεν Hdt.7.209, prob. in B.3.25: freq. with a corresp. Particle in apodosi, τῆμος δή Od.13.93; δὴ τότε γε 22.182; καὶ τότε δή ῥα 24. 147; τόφρα δέ 20.73; δέ Il.23.62, Od.17.359; δ' ἄρα 20.56: the clause with εὖτε may stand last, Il.5.396, 6.515, Pi.*O.*3.28. 2. with subj., εὖτ' ἄν (like ὅταν), a. referring to future time, οὔ τι δυνήσεαι χραισμεῖν, εὖτ' ἂν πολλοὶ πίπτωσι *when* many shall be falling, Il.1.242, cf. 2.34, A.*Pers.*230 (troch.). b. with pres. in apod., *whenever, so often as*, ἥμισυ ἀρετῆς ἀποαίνυται, εὖτ' ἄν μιν κατὰ δούλιον ἦμαρ ἕλῃσιν *whenever* it comes upon him, Od.17.323, cf. 320, Hdt.6. 27, A.*Ag.*12: in orat. obl. (for opt. after past tense), Pi.*O.*6.67: ἄν is sts. omitted, εὖτ' ἔρδωμεν *whenever* we offer, Od.7.202, cf. Hes.*Th.* 28, B.1.73, A.*Th.*338 (lyr.), A.R.2.801, *AP*14.45. 3. with opt., *whenever, as often as*, with impf. in apodosi, εὖτε μάχοιτο *whenever* he fought, Hes.*Sc.*164, cf. *h.Hom.*18.8, B.12.118, A.*Ag.*565, A.R.2. 471. II. causal, *since*, with aor. ind., S.*Aj.*716 (lyr.), *OC*84, *Ph.* 1098 (lyr.). III. Adv. of Comparison, for ἠΰτε, *as*, twice in Il., εὖτ' ὄρεος κορυφῇσι κτλ. 3.10; τῷ δ' εὖτε πτερὰ γίγνετ' 19.386 (so Aristarch., but with vv.ll. ὥστε, αὖτε): freq. in Q.S., 1.549, al.

εὐτείχ-εος, ον, (τεῖχος) *well-walled*, Τροίη Il.1.129, etc. **-ής**, ές, Pi.*O.*6.1, *N.*7.46, E.*Andr.*1009 (lyr.); prop. oxytone, cf. Hdn. Gr.2.37,687; but acc. εὐτείχεα (Id.2.99) Il.16.57. **-ητος**, ον, (τεῖχος) = εὐτείχεος, Φρυγίη *h.Ven.*112. **-ιστος**, ον, *well-fortified*, f.l. for ἀτ-, Plb.3.90.8. **-ος**, ον, = εὐτείχεος, Max.Tyr.27.3 (Sup.), A.D.*Synt.*187.11, al.

εὐτέκμαρτος· καλῶς τυπούμενος, Hsch.

εὐτεκν-έω, *to be happy in children*, E.*Fr.*520, *Stoic.*3.156, Plu.2. 278b. **-ία**, poet. -ίη, ἡ, *blessing of children*, εὐτεκνίας κύρσαι E.*Ion* 470 (lyr.); εὐτεκνίᾳ δυστυχίαν... καθελεῖν Id.*Supp.*66 (lyr.), cf. Arist. *Rh.*1361^{a}1, *EN*1099^{b}3, *Stoic.*3.24, *IG*9(1).979; εὐ. παίδων Epigr.ap. Plu.*Fr.*22.7; *fruitfulness*, *IG*14.1615. II. personified, Εὐτεκνεία (sic) *Syria*6.295 (Philippopolis). [-τἔκ- in ll. cc. poet., and Theoc. 18.51.] **-ος**, ον, *blest with children*, Sup. -ωτάτη E.*Hec.*581, etc.; of Priam, ib.620 (Sup.); εὔ. βοῦς (i.e. Io) A.*Supp.*275; πατρὶς E. *HF*1405; εὔ. χρησμοί oracles *that give promise of fair children*, Id.*Ion* 423; εὔ. ξυνωρίς a pair *of fair children*, Id.*Ph.*1618: Comp. -ότερος D.S.4.74: Sup. -ώτατος ll.cc. II. of animals, *kind to their young*, Arist.*HA*563^{b}6, 614^{b}33. **-όω**, *make people happy in their children*, εἰς τέκνα *Cat.Cod.Astr.*7.217.

εὐτέλ-εια, Ion. εὐτελείη or εὐτελίη (v. infr. II. 2), ἡ, *having little to pay, cheapness*, πρὸς εὐτελείην τῶν σιτίων to procure *cheapness* of ..., Hdt.2.92; εἰς εὐτέλειαν *cheaply*, i.e. *vilely*, εἰς εὐ. χηνὶ συγγεγραμμένῳ Ar.*Av.*805; κρέα δὲ τίνος ἥδιστ' ἂν ἐσθίοις; Answ. εἰς εὐτέλειαν *the cheapest*, Antiph.20; μᾶζα πρὸς εὐτέλειαν ἐξωπλισμένη Id.226. 2. 2. *meanness, shabbiness*, εὐσέβειαν καὶ οὐκ εὐ. ὑμῖν ἀνέγραψε Lys.30.21; εὐ. οἴκου καὶ ἀμορφία Luc.*Dom.*14. II. *thrift, economy*, ἐπ' εὐτελείᾳ *economically*, Ar.*Ra.*406 (lyr.); φιλοκαλοῦμεν μετ' εὐτελείας *without extravagance*, Th.2.40; ἐς εὐ. ξυντετμῆσθαι to be cut down to *an economical standard*, Id.8.86; ἐς εὐ. σωφρονίσαι ib.1: in pl., *economies*, ταῖς εὐτελείαις οἱ θεοὶ χαίρουσι Antiph.164.1. 2. Εὐτελίη personified, Εὐ., κλεινῆς ἔκγονε Σωφροσύνης Crates Theb. 12. **-ής**, ές, (τέλος) *easily paid for, cheap*, Hdt.2.86 (Comp. and Sup.), Pl.*Cri.*45a, etc.; *slight, easy*, Id.*Lg.*649d; τὰ εὐ. ἐν χειρουργίᾳ *simple* methods of treatment, *BKT*3 p.24; εὐτελέστερα δὲ τὰ δεινά the danger would be *more cheaply met*, Th.8.46 codd. (dub.). Adv. -λῶς *at a cheap rate*, X.*Smp.*4.49; ἀγόρασον εὐ. Ephipp.15.1: Comp. -έστερον X.*Cyr.*8.3.46; -εστέρως *Gloss.*: Sup. -έστατα, σκευάσαι *IG*1^2.44.9; f. l. for εὐσταλέστατα, Hdn.2.11.1. 2. *mean, paltry, worthless*, of persons, σηματουργὸς δ' οὔ τις εὐ. ἄρ' ἦν A.*Th*.491; of character, Arist.*Pol*.1272^{b}41; opp. σεμνότερος, Id.*Po*.1448^{b}26 (Comp.); ὅστις -έστατος Eup.189; παιδισκάριον Men.338; ἀνόητος, εὐ. ὑπερβολῇ Id.615; so of things, εὐ. βίος *shabby*, Pl.*Lg*.806a; of land, *depreciated in value*, *PTeb*.61(*b*).30 (ii B.C.); -εστέρα ἄσκησις *paltry, requiring no exertion*, X.*Eq.Mag*.1.16; τἆλλα δὲ..-έστατα Pl.Com. 174.11, cf. Epin.1.4. II. *thrifty, frugal*, δίαιτα X.*Mem*.1.3.5; δεῖπνον Plu.2.150c (Comp.). -ίζω, *disparage*, ib.1073c, Luc. *Pr.Im*.13, *Anacreont*.27A.10; *make disreputable*, *Cat.Cod.Astr*.8(4). 205. -ισμός, ὁ, *disparagement*, Longin.11.2 (pl.). -ιστής, οῦ, ὁ, *disparager*, Phld.*Vit*.p.42 J.

εὐτενής, ές, = εὔτονος, cj. for εὐγενής in Thphr.*HP*5.1.7 and Plu. *Fr*.12.2. II. of stones, *squared*, *IG*2^2.1666*A* 29, al., 7.4255.20.

Εὐτέρπη, ἡ, *the Well-pleasing*, name of a Muse, Hes.*Th*.77, etc.: Pythag. name for *eight*, *Theol.Ar*.55.

εὐτερπής, ές, *delightful, charming*, ἄνθος, φωνή, Pi.*O*.6.105, *AP*9. 364 (Nestor).

εὔτευκτος, ον, = εὔτυκτος, τάφος *Epigr.Gr*.238 (Smyrna).

εὐτέχν-ητος, ον, *skilfully wrought*, *AP*6.260 (Gemin.). -ία, ἡ, *skill in art*, Str.1.2.33, D.H.*Dem*.35, Luc.*Herm*.20, *APl*.4.142. 6. -ος, ον, *skilfully wrought*, ναυτικόν Hp.*Ep*.14. 2. *skilful*, of persons, σκυτοτόμοι *AP*6.206 (Antip. Sid.), cf. *Epigr.Gr*.979 (Philae, i B.C.). 3. Adv. -νως, = ἐπισταμένως, Sch.Opp.*H*.3.536.

εὔτηκτος, ον, *easily melted* or *dissolved*, Arist.*Pr*.865^{b}1 (Comp.), *de An*.422^{a}19, Lxx *Wi*.19.21, Man.6.524: hence **εὐτηξία**, ἡ, *fusibility*, Arist.*Mir*.834^{a}7.

εὐτιθάσευτος [ᾰ], ον, *easily tamed*, Str.15.1.43.

εὐτιμώρητος, ον, *easily punished*, Ptol.*Tetr*.157.

εὐτίνακτος [ῐ], ον, *easily shaken*, Hsch. s. v. κροτητά.

εὐτλήμων, Dor. -τλάμων [ᾱ], ον, gen. ονος, *much-enduring, steadfast*, εὐτλήμονι δόξῃ A.*Pers*.28 (anap.).

εὔτμητος, Ep. ἔϋτμ-, ον, (τέμνω) *well-cut*, ἱμάντες Il.10.567, Theoc. 25.102; τελαμών Il.7.304. 2. *easily cut*, σώματα Aret.*CD*1.2.

εὔτοιχος, ον, *with good walls*, Man.4.151.

εὐτοκ-έω, *bring forth easily*, Hp.*Superf*.2, Cic.*Att*.10.18.1. 2. *to be prolific*, of trees or animals, Thphr.*CP*1.14.1, Ph.1.249, al.: metaph., ib.520:—Pass., *to be brought forth easily*, Corn.*ND*34. -ία, ἡ, *easy delivery*, Call.*Ep*.54, *AP*9.268 (Antip. Thess.), Sor.1.70, Plu. *Rom*.21; τρισσὴ εὐ. *three children happily born*, *AP*9.349 (Leon.). 2. *fertility*, γυναικῶν Ph.1.183; of crops, ib.301. -ιος, ον, *aiding in childbirth*, φάρμακον Aët.1.115. -ος, ον, *bringing forth easily*, Arist. *HA*576^{a}22 (Comp.), 573^{a}9 (Sup.), Chrysipp.*Stoic*.2.212 (Sup.). 2. = εὔτεκνος 1 (which is v.l.), Ph.1.274; *fertile*, Hp.*Nat.Mul*.16.

εὐτολμ-έω, *to be daring enough*, ἀδικεῖν D.C.55.16. -ία, ἡ, *courage, boldness*, E.*Med*.469, Arist.*Rh.Al*.1423^{b}3, *VV*1250^{b}5: pl., D.S.17.10, Ph.2.382. -ος, ον, *brave-spirited, courageous*, εὐ. ψυχῆς λῆμα Simon.140; ἀπ' εὐ. φρενός A.*Ag*.1302; of men, v.l. in X.*An*.1.7.4, etc.: Comp., Ph.2.122: Sup., ib.68, D.H.6.14, etc.: usu. in good sense, εὔ. εἶναι κρῖνε, τολμηρὸς δὲ μή Men.*Mon*.153, but iron., εὔ. ἰατρός Gal.15.913; κύνες Opp.*C*.3.383; εὔ. ἄκεα *heroic* remedies, Aret.*CD*1.2; so εὔτολμόν ἐστι c. inf., Id.*CA*2.1; τὸ εὔ. πρὸς τοὺς κινδύνους Andronic.Rhod.p.576 M. Adv. -μως Tyrt.15, A. *Ag*.1298, D.S.17.34: Comp. -ότερον Plu.*Sol*.14, Aret.*CA*1.1: Sup. -ότατα Ph.2.461. II. in bad sense, *daring, audacious*, *Anatolian Studies* 204 (Termessus).

εὔτομος, ον, *well-divided, regular*, of a city, Arist.*Pol*.1330^{b}23. II. *well-cut*, of a gem, *POxy*.1449.14 (iii A.D.).

εὐτον-έω, *have power* or *faculties*, Hp.*Ep*.16, 17; *have power* or *means* to do, εἰπεῖν τι Plu.2.531b, cf. 533e; παρέχειν τι *IG*14.830.10 (Puteoli, ii A.D.), cf. Wilcken *Chr*.176.18 (i A.D.); τοῦ μηδὲν αὐτῶν λυθῆναι *SIG*1109.30, cf. 49 (ii A.D.). -ία, ἡ, *tension, vigour*, D.S.5.39; σκελῶν ib.34: esp. in Stoic philos. (cf. τόνος), Chrysipp.*Stoic*.2.146, etc.; ὁ ἐν τῇ ψυχῇ τόνος λέγεται ὡς εὐ. καὶ ἀτονία ib. 3.123, cf. Phld.*Ir*.p.69 W.; εὐ. ψυχῆς, of courage, *Stoic*.3.66, cf. 73: generally, *vigour* of character, Plu.*Phoc*.3, 2.456f, *BGU*786ii 1 (ii A.D.); also, *vigour* of style, D.H.*Vett.Cens*.2.3, Hermog.*Id*.1.11, Aps.p.282 H. b. Medic., *tension*, Ruf.*Sat.Gon*.46 (pl.); also μαλθακὴ εὐ. gentle *force*, Hp.*Ep*.15. c. *elasticity*, Ph.*Bel*.71.33. -ος, ον, (τείνω) *well-strung, vigorous*, of men's bodies or limbs, Hp.*Aph*.3. 17, Arist.*IA*710^{a}31, Luc.*Anach*.24, *AP*12.216 (Strat.): Comp., Men. 693; of men, -ώτεροι τοῖς σώμασι D.S.4.3; τὸ εὔ., = εὐτονία, Pl.*Lg*. 815a, etc.: esp. in Stoic philos. (cf. τόνος), Chrysipp.*Stoic*.3.121, 123; of engines, Plb.8.5.2 (Comp.); of the wind, D.S.1.41; of wine, Arist.*Mir*.832^{a}11; τὸ εὔ., name of an eyesalve, Aët.7.115; εὔ. πληγή Hero *Bel*.74.12. b. *distended*, εὐτόνῳ φλεβί (sens. obsc.) Neophr.(?) *Medea* in *PLit.Lond*.77 *Fr*.2.7. c. *elastic, yielding*, -ώτερος χαλκοῦ χρυσός Porph. ad Il.20.259. 2. *active, energetic*, πρόνοια *POxy*. 1468.7 (iii A.D.); προσοχή Iamb.*Protr*.21.κα' (Sup.); of persons, -ώτατος εἶναι c. part., *OGI*315.52 (Pessinus, ii B.C.). 3. of an orator, *forcible*, εὐ. τῇ φράσει D.H.*Vett.Cens*.5.4; τῆς λέξεως τὸ εὔ. ib.3.2, cf. Phld.*Po*.5.5. 4. Adv. -νως *with might and main, vigorously*, Ar. *Pl*.1095, X.*Hier*.9.6, Arist.*Pr*.885^{a}6, Ph.1.311, *Ev.Luc*.23.10: Comp. -ώτερον, τοῦ δέοντος ἀφιᾶσι Luc.*Nigr*.36. 5. *strenuously*, Phld. *Herc*.1251.23, *Po*.2 p.274 H. 6. *peremptorily*, -ώτερον ἐπιστεῖλαι, γράψαι, *PLille* 1.3 i 14 (iii B.C.), *PPetr*.2 p.22, 3 p.132 (cf. p. x) (iii B.C.). II. of the voice, *well-pitched*, Arist.*GA*786^{b}8. (Sts. as v.l. in codd. for ἔντονος, Plb.l.c.; εὔτονος is perh. f.l. for ἔντονον in S. *Fr*.966.) -όω, '*tone up*', *brace*, τὴν δύναμιν Gal.14.252.

εὐτοξ-ία, ἡ, *skill in archery*, Hdn.1.15.2 codd. (dub. l.). -ος, ον, *with good arrows*, φαρέτρη *APl*.4.214 (Secund.).

εὐτόρν-ευτος, ον, = sq. 1, *AP*5.134. -ος, ον, *well-turned, rounded, circular*, E.*Tr*.1197, Lyc.664. 2. *easy to turn*, of wood, Thphr. *HP*5.6.4 (Comp.), 5.6.2 (Sup.).

εὐτράπεζος, ον, *with good table, hospitable*, ἀνδρῶνες A.*Ag*.244 (lyr.); of persons, Plu.*CG*19. 2. *luxurious*, βίος E.*Fr*.670.2; of men, Eriph.6; *dainty, sumptuous*, ἀγορά Plu.2.667c.

εὐτρᾰπελ-εύομαι, *to be witty, ready*, Plb.12.16.14, D.S.38/9.7; cj. Dind. for εὐτραπεζευόμενοι, Eust.1053.18. -ία, ἡ, *ready wit, liveliness*, Hp.*Decent*.7, Pl.*R*.563a, Posidipp.28.5, Cic.*Fam*.7.32.1, D.S.15.6: pl., *pleasantries*, Demetr.*Eloc*.177; defined by Arist. as πεπαιδευμένη ὕβρις, *Rh*.1389^{b}11, cf. *EN*1108^{a}24; ἡ περὶ τὰς παιδιὰς καὶ τὰς ὁμιλίας εὐ. Plu.*Ant*.43. 2. rarely in bad sense, = βωμολοχία, *Ep.Eph*.5.4. -ίζομαι, = Lat. *jocor*, Dosith.p.431 K.:—hence -ισμός, ὁ, *Et.Gud*.505.55. -ος, ον, (τρέπω) *easily turning* or *changing*, of the Athenians, Ael.*VH*5.13; *nimble*, of apes, Id.*NA*5. 26; in earlier Gr. always metaph., λόγος εὐ. *a dexterous, ready* plea, Ar.*V*.469 (lyr.). Adv. -λως *dexterously, readily, without awkwardness*, Th.2.41. 2. of persons, *ready with an answer* or *repartee, witty*, Arist.*EN*1108^{a}24, 1128^{a}10; εὐ. παρὰ τὰς συνουσίας Plb.23.5.7; τίτθη εὐ. Jul.*Or*.7.227a: Sup., Plb.9.23.3. b. in bad sense, *jesting, ribald*, Isoc.7.49; εὐτράπελόν ἐστι c. acc. et inf., it is *ludicrous* that.., Plu.2.1062b. 3. *tricky, dishonest*, v.l. in Pi.*P*.4.105; εὐ. κέρδη *time-serving* arts, of flatterers, ib.1.92.

εὐτρᾰφ-έω, *to be well-nourished, thrive*, Thphr.*CP*4.10.1 (nisi leg. -τροφεῖ). -ής, ές, (τρέφω) *well-fed, thriving, fat*, Hp.*Aër*.12, E. *Med*.920, *IT*304, Arist.*HA*546^{a}15, etc.; *large, well-grown*, of peppercorns, Gal.6.270 (Sup.); *luxuriant*, of hair-growth, Id.1.326 (Sup.); τὸ εὐτραφές, = εὐτροφία, Polyaen.7.36. Adv. -φῶς, Ion. -φέως, ἔχειν to be *fat*, Hp.*Septim*.8, cf. Philostr.*VS*2.1.7. II. Act., *nourishing*, ὕδωρ A.*Th*.308 (Sup., lyr.); γάλα Id.*Ch*.898, Philostr.*VA*3.9; v.l. in Thphr.*CP*1.18.1. -ητος, ὁ, *epicure*, *EM*122.31. -ία, Ion. -ίη, ἡ, *good husbandry*, *Epigr.Gr*.1036 (Nicomedia).

εὐτράχηλος [ᾰ], ον, *with fine neck*, Tim.Gaz.ap.Ar.Byz.*Epit*.81.8, *Hippiatr*.115.

εὐτρεπ-ής, ές, (τρέπω) *readily turning*: hence generally, *prepared, ready*, εὐτρεπὲς ποιεῖσθαί τι E.*Ba*.440; τοὐμὸν εὐ. πάρα ib.844; εὐτρεπῆ.. τὸν κοντὸν ποιοῦ Epicr.10.4; δεῖπνον εὐ. Antiph.80.12; ἄριστον Men.*Pk*.117; τούτων -πῶν γενομένων Plb.6.26.10; also of persons, εἰδὼς εὐτρεπεῖς ὑμᾶς D.4.18; συνήγοροι.. καθ' ἡμῶν εὐ. Id.21.112, cf. *Com.Adesp*.15.19 D.; εὐ. πρός τι D.H.2.3, Ph.1.174. Adv. εὐτρεπῶς, ἔχειν to be *in a state of preparation*, D.1.21. -ίζω, Att. fut. -ιῶ: pf. εὐτρέπικα *AP*9.316.8 (Leon.):—*make ready*, ξίφος A.*Ag*.1651; ἃ χρή E.*IT*470; πάντα D.1.13, cf. 3.13, 4.16, Men.*Sam*.6; τὰ τείχη *to restore* them, X.*HG*2.2.4; τὴν σύριγγα *lubricates* the windpipe, Hp.*Cord*.2:—Med., *get ready for oneself*, or something *of one's own*, Th.4.123, 2.18, Ph.1.619:—Pass., *to be prepared, made ready*, E. *IA*1111, Ar.*Pl*.626; [ναῦς] ἱστίοις -ομένη Arist.*Fr*.11; σφαγαῖσιν ηὐτρεπισμένος *ready for*.., Lyc.614, cf. Aen.Tact.18.1, Jul.*Mis*.362b; *to be performed, executed*, Phld.*Po*.5.21. 2. Medic., *treat*, Hp. *Loc.Hom*.1, al.; dub. in Thphr.*Char*.13.9. II. *win over, conciliate*, τινά τινι X.*HG*4.8.12:—so in Med., ib.6: pf. Pass., in med. sense, ἅπαντας ηὐτρέπισται D.18.175. -ισμός, ὁ, *preparation*, Simp.*in Ph*.793.7, Suid. -ιστέον, *one must treat*, of a doctor, Hp. *Loc.Hom*.30; *one must prepare*, Hld.4.15. 2. Adj. -ιστέος, α, ον, Poll.10.76. -ιστής, οῦ, ὁ, *one who gets ready*, Sch.rec.S.*El*.72.

εὔτρεπτος, ον, *easily changing*, Arist.*Mu*.400^{a}23, Plu.*Mar*.21; ζωή Man.4.532; ὕδατα Plu.2.912b. 2. Medic., of diseases, *mild*, Gal.15.590; but εὔ. ἐς συγκοπήν *easily turning* to.., Aret.*CA* 1.1. b. of the skin, *sensitive*, Menemach.ap.Orib.10.15.3. 3. *ready, inclined*, τὸ εὔ. πρὸς μεταβολάς Plu.2.978f. 4. *versatile*, Poll.6.121, cj. in Man.4.86. 5. Adv. -τως v.l. for εὐτρεπῶς, J. *Vit*.61.

εὐτρεφής, Ep. ἐϋτρ-, ές, (τρέφω) *well-fed*, ὄϊες ἐϋ. Od.9.425; αἰγὸς ἐϋ. 14.530; σαρκὸς εὐτρεφέστατον πάχος E.*Cyc*.380 (prob. l.), cf. Pl. *Lg*.835d. II. *nourishing*, Thphr.*CP*1.18.1 (v. l. εὐτραφοῦς).

εὐτρήρων, ωνος, ὁ, ἡ, *abounding in doves*, Nonn.*D*.13.62.

εὐτρήσιος, prob. = *muliebria passus, pathicus*, Eup.56.

εὔτρητος, Ep. ἐΰτρ-, ον, (τετραίνω) *well-pierced*, λοβοί Il.14.182; χόανα Hes.*Th*.863; δόνακες *APl*.1.8 (Alc.); *with many orifices*, φλέβια Thphr.*Sens*.56; *porous*, σπόγγος Q.S.9.429; πέδον *AP*6.21.5.

εὐτρίαινα [ῐ], ὁ, acc. -τρίαιναν, *with goodly trident*, epith. of Poseidon, Pi.*O*.1.73.

εὐτρῐβής, ές, *well-rubbed, powdered fine*, Dsc.5.121, as v.l. for εὐθρυβής, cf. Nic.*Al*.328, 405: heterocl. dat. εὔτριβι (as from εὔτριψ), ib.44.

εὔτριπτος, ον, (τρίβω) *easy to pound*, Democr.ap.Gal.14.130; *friable*, Dsc.2.24, Gal.13.124.

εὔτρῐχος, ον, = εὔθριξ, γενειάς E.*HF*934 (s. v.l.).

εὐτριψία, ἡ, *sensitiveness to friction*, Cass.*Pr*.68.

εὐτροπ-έομαι, Pass., *to be easily dealt with*, ὑπό τινος Apollod. *Poliorc*.138.5. -ία, ἡ, (εὔτροπος) *versatility*, ἡ περὶ τὸ ἦθος εὐ. Plu. 2.500d. II. *good disposition*, ἤθεος Democr.57; πρὸς τὰς ὑφηγήσεις Ph.2.399. III. in reading aloud, *expression*, Aët.16.67.

εὔτροπις, ιδος, ὁ, ἡ, *with good keel*, gloss on ἐϋστείρης, Sch.A.R.1. 401.

εὔτροπος, ον, (τρέπω) *versatile*, etym. of εὐτράπελος, Arist.*EN*1128^a 10. II. (τρόπος) *morally good*, Sch.Od.1.1; of diseases, *mild*,

Hp.*Hum.*13; εὔτροπος ἀνθρώποισι δαίμων dub. sens. in *PHib.*1.2.6 (cf. Epich.258). Adv. –πως, gloss on εὐοργήτως, Sch.Th.1.122.

εὐτρόσσεσθαι· ἐπιστρέφεσθαι (Paphian), Hsch.

εὐτροφ-έω, *thrive, flourish*, Arist.*GA*765b26, Thphr.*HP*8.8.4, etc.:—also Med. or Pass., Id.*CP*4.1.4. **–ής, ές**, = εὐτραφής, Hp.*Dent.* 29 (s.v.l.). **–ία, ἡ**, *good nurture, thriving condition*, τῶν σωμάτων, τῶν ψυχῶν, Pl.*Prt.*351a,b, cf. Arist.*HA*542a28, Thphr.*HP*5.2.2, Orph.*Fr.*49 vi 89: pl., Ph.2.1, Antyll.ap.Stob.4.37.16. **–ιάω**, gloss on μυσιάω, Hsch. **–ος, ον**, *nourishing, healthy*, χώρα Thphr.*CP*1.14.1; ἔαρ Opp.*C.*3.180. **II.** Pass., *well-nourished, thriving*, of trees, D.S.17.89; of children, Hp.*Dent.*1, Orph.*Fr.*49 vi 88: Comp., Hp.*Dent.*13, Ath.Med.ap.Orib.9.5.6: metaph., of diseases, Luc. *Abd.*27.

εὐτρόχᾰλος, Ep. **ἐΰτρ–**, ον, (τρέχω) *running well, quick-moving*, ποταμός Opp.*C.*2.131; μέλισσα *APl.*4.36 (Agath.); ἀοιδή A.R.4.907; γλῶσσα *IG*5(1).264 (Sparta, Aug.). **II.** *well-rounded*, σφαῖρα, κύκλος, A.R.3.135, Man.2.130; λίνον Nic.*Al.*134; ἐϋτροχάλῳ ἐν ἀλωῇ on the *rounded* threshing-floor, Hes.*Op.*599, 806.

εὔτροχος, Ep. and Lyr. **ἐΰτρ–**, ον, poet. metapl. acc. ἐΰτροχα *An. Ox.*1.271: (τροχός):—*well-wheeled*, ἐΰτροχον ἅρμα καὶ ἵππους Il.8.438, Hes.*Sc.*463; ἅμαξαν ἐΰ. Od.6.72, Il.24.150, etc.; σατίναι ἐΰ. Sapph.*Supp.*20a.13; εὔ. κύκλος E.*Ion* 19. **II.** (τρέχω) *smoothly-running*, Pl.*Ti.*37c; *running easily*, of a cord put through loops, X.*Cyn.*2.4; εὔ. γλῶσσα a *ready, glib* tongue, E.*Ba.*268; γλῶσσα εὔ. ἐν τῷ διαλέγεσθαι Plu.*Per.*7; of style, D.H.*Comp.*20; τὸ τῆς φύσεως, τῆς διανοίας εὔ., Ph.1.240, Dam.*Isid.*80, cf. 32; τὸ σφαιροειδὲς ἡμῶν οὐκ εὔ. Plot.2.2.2. Adv. –χως, ἀναγινώσκειν to read *fluently*, Ph.1.303. **III.** *well-rounded, round*, τεῖχος *IG*14.1389 ii 13.

εὐτρύγητος [ῠ], ον, *convenient for the vintage*, of low vines, Thphr. *CP*3.7.4 (Comp.).

εὐτρύπητος [ῡ], ον, *easily pierced*, Sch.Orib.4 p.531 D. (Comp.).

εὐτρῡφάλειος [ᾰ], gloss on εὐκόρυφος, Sch.Opp.*C.*1.362.

εὔτρωτος, ον, *easily wounded*, Gal.*UP*1.2.

εὐτῠκ-άζομαι, *make ready*: εὐτυκάζου (εὐτύκαζον cod.)· εὔτυκτον ἔχε, ἕτοιμον, Hsch.: hence restored by Dind. for . . τυκάζου in A. *Th.*149 (lyr.). **–ής, ές**, *easily worked*, and Adv. **–ῶς**· ῥᾳδίως, Hsch. **–ίζω**, = εὐτυκάζομαι, Id., *EM*399.17. **–ος, ον**, rare form for sq., *well-built*, εὐτύκους δόμους A.*Supp.*959 (Porson). **II.** *ready*, γλῶσσα ib.994: c. inf., πᾶς τις ἐπειπεῖν ψόγον . . . εὔτυκος ib.974 (anap.); ὑμνεῖν B.8.4; ἐς χορόν Pratin.Lyr.2; πῦρ εὔ. ἔστω Theoc. 24.88; ἁ θεὸς εὔ. ἕρπει (fort. ἕρπειν) Call.*Lav.Pall.*3; [κρέα] v.l. in Hdt.1.119.

εὔτυκτος, ον, (τεύχω) *well-made, well-wrought*, κυνέη Il.3.336, etc.; ἱμάσθλη 8.44, etc.; κλισίη 10.566, Od.4.123; κυνέα B.17.50; κρέα εὔ. ποιήσασθαι to get meat *ready for eating*, v.l. in Hdt.1.119.

εὐτύπωτος [ῠ], ον, *easily taking an impression*, κηρός Gal.*UP*6.13, cf. Id.1.322, Phlp.*in de An.*605.16, Eust.633.23, prob. in Plu.2.660c.

εὐτύχ-εια [ῠ], ἡ, poet. for εὐτυχία, S.*Fr.*1050. **II.** Εὐτύχεια, τά, festival in honour of Eutyches, *SIG*[2]588.55 (ii B.C.): sg., Εὐτύχειον, τό, fund devoted to its maintenance, *Inscr.Délos* 370.44 (iii B.C.). **–ευδοξέω**, *enjoy fame and fortune*, *PTeb.*418.19 (iii A.D.). **–έω**, impf. ηὐτύχουν or εὐτ– S.*Fr.*107.10, etc.: fut. –ήσω E.*Or.*1212: aor. 1 ηὐτύχησα or εὐτ– ib.542, etc.: pf. ηὐτύχηκα or εὐτ– Pl.*Lg.*811c, etc.: 3 pl. plpf. ηὐτυχήκεσαν D.18.18:—**Pass.**, aor. 1 εὐτυχήθην Hdn.2.8.3, 2.9.3: pf. εὐτύχημαι Th.7.77, etc.:—*to be prosperous, fortunate*, Pi.*O.*7.81, *I.*3.1, etc.; οἱ εὐτυχοῦντες *people in prosperity*, Antipho 2.4.9; εὐ. τινός *to be well off for* a thing, Luc. *Charid.*23; εἰ μνήμης εὐτυχῶ if I remember rightly, Ath.2.58c: c. dat., τῷ πολέμῳ Hdt.1.171, cf. S.*El.*68; τῷ βίῳ Men.655: more freq. c. acc. rei, τοὺς ἄλλους πολέμους Hdt.1.65; τὰ πάντα Id.3.40, cf. S.*OT*88; ἐς τέκνα E.*Or.*542, *Ion* 567; ἔν τινι X.*HG*7.1.5: c. part., *to succeed in* doing, E.*Or.*1212, cf. X.*HG*7.1.11: later c. inf., Plu.2.333e, Vett.Val.241.11, Longus 4.19, D.L.9.100: c. acc. cogn., εὐ. εὐτύχημα X.*An.*6.3.6; εὐτύχει at the close of letters, Pl.*Ep.*321c; εὐτυχεῖτε Ep.Philipp.ap.D.18.78, Septimius Severus in *IG*12(7).243.30; εὐτύχει on gravestones, *CIG*4346 (Side), 4837 (Egypt); ἀλλ' εὐτυχοίης *fare thee well!* A.*Ch.*1063, S.*OT*1478, E. *Med.*688. **2.** of things, *turn out well, prosper*, βρότεια πράγματ' εὐτυχοῦντα A.*Ag.*1327; πόνου τοι χωρὶς οὐδὲν εὐτυχεῖ S.*El.*945; τὰ εὐτυχοῦντα Id.*Fr.*681; τὰ πολλὰ . . . εὐτυχοῦντα *if they succeed*, Th. 3.39, cf. 4.79:—also in Pass., ἱκανὰ τοῖς πολεμίοις ηὐτύχηται Id.7.77; τὰ τῆς μάχης εὐτυχεῖτο Plu.*Num.*12: ταῦτα αὐτοῖς ἐς κάλλος εὐτύχηται Gal.*Protr.*12; ἄπιστον τὸ –ούμενον Alciphr.2.3; of a person, εὐτυχηθείς Iamb.*VP*2.9. **II.** Act., *obtain, attain to*, παρὰ τῶν Σεβαστῶν στέφανον *Ephes.*3 No.70, cf. Sch.Pi.*P.*9.173, *PMasp.*23.23 (vi A.D.). **–ημα, ατος, τό**, *piece of good luck, success*, E.*Ph.*1356, Pl.*Smp.*217a, Men.5.3 D., etc.; εὐτυχεῖν εὐ. X.*An.*6.3.6. **–ής, ές**, *successful, fortunate*, of persons and events, Hdt.1.32, etc.: Comp., S.*Aj.*550: Sup., Pl.*Lg.*877e; opp. ὄλβιος, Hdt. l.c.; opp. εὐδαίμων, E.*Med.*1229 (Comp.); εὐτυχεῖ πότμῳ A.*Pers.*709 (troch.); εὐτυχῆ κλύουσα πρᾶξιν S.*Tr.*293: c. dat., εὐ. ἱκέσθαι τινί to come *with blessings* to him, Id.*OC*308; δαίμων δὲ τοῖς μὲν εὐτυχὴς καθ' ἡμέραν Id.*El.*999; τὸ εὐτυχές, οἳ ἂν . . . Th.2.44. **II.** Adv. –χῶς Pi.*N.*7.90, A.*Pers.*325, etc.; Ion. –χέως Hdt.3.39: Comp. –έστερον E.*Heracl.*247 (v.l. –ρος); πράττειν Pl.*Euthd.*280a: Sup. –έστατα Men.*Sam.*44:—εὐτυχῶς Ἀμμαίῳ at close of letter, D.H.*Amm.*2 fin. **–ησις, εως, ἡ**, in pl., *lucky strokes of fortune*, Phld.*Rh.*2.217 S. **–ία**, Ion. **–ίη, ἡ**, *good luck, success*, Pi.*O.*6.81, Hdt.1.32, Th.7.77, etc.; τὴν ἀτυχίαν εἰς εὐ. αἰτοῦμαι μεταστῆναι Antipho 2.4.4; defined, Arist.*Rh.*1361b39; ἐπ' εὐτυχίᾳ, –ίαισιν, E.*IT*1490 (anap.), Ar.*Ec.*573 (lyr.); πολλῇ εὐ. χρῆσθαι Pl.*Men.*72a; κατά τινα θείαν εὐ. Id.*Lg.*798b; ἡ κατὰ πόλεμον εὐ. Th.1.120: pl., *pieces of good luck, successes*, Id.2.44.

εὐῠ́ᾰλος, ον, *of good glass*, φιάλαι *AP*11.55, acc. to Planudes (Pall.).

εὔυγρος, ον, *very moist*, Vett.Val.9.24.

εὐυδρ-έω, *to abound in water*, Str.8.6.8. **–ία, ἡ**, *abundance of water*, Id.5.1.12. **–ος, ον**, (ὕδωρ) *well-watered, abounding in water*, ἄστυ Simon.96; ἀκτά Pi.*P.*1.79; Μαραθών Call.*Hec.*1.1.8; νάπη Nic.*Al.*622; γῆ ποιώδης καὶ εὔ. Hdt.4.47; χῶρος –ότερος Id.9.25; [ὄρη] –ότερα *Gp.*2.6.5 (v.l. ἐν–). **2.** of a river or spring, *with beautiful water*, Κάσας B.10.119; Εὐρώτας E.*IT*399 (lyr.); Κασταλίς *Pae.Delph.*5; so prob. εὔυδρον ποτόν (vulg. ἔνυδρον τόπον) Polyzel.2.

εὐυμν-ία, ἡ, gloss on εὐμολπία, Hsch. (ἐν– cod.). **–ος, ον**, *celebrated in many hymns*, *h.Ap.*19, Call.*Ap.*31, etc.: Sup., Id.*Fr.*36. **II.** *used in beautiful hymns*, ῥήματα Id.*Epigr.* in *Berl.Sitzb.* 1912.548. [The penult. short in Epich.91.]

εὐυπάντητος, ον, *easily approached*, Dumont-Homolle *Mélanges d'Archéologie* 459 (Apollonia in Thrace).

εὐυπέρ-βᾰτος, ον, *easily stepped over*: of a socket, *out of which the end of a bone easily slips*, Hp.*Art.*8. **II.** *easy of access*, *PFay.*110.9 (i A.D.), *POxy.*1272.16 (ii A.D.). **–βλητος**, ον, *easily surpassed*, Arist.*EN*1123a17.

εὔυπνος, ον, *sleeping well* or *soundly*, Hp.*Dent.*15, cj. in Max.Tyr. 30.6: Comp., Gal.18(2).299, etc. **II.** Act., *granting good sleep*, of Zeus at Delphi, Hsch.

εὐυπό-δητος, ον, of a sandal, *easy to bind under the foot*, Tz. ad Lyc. 853. **–κρῐτος**, ον, *playing one's part well*, Vett.Val.48.1; also εὐ. συμβίωσις, of marriage, Id.119.33. **–ληπτος**, ον, *easy to take up, light*, Heph.Astr.2.2. **II.** in Comp., *more easily enclosed*, v.l. in Arist.*Sens.*438a15, cf. Alex.Aphr. *in Sens.*26.20, 36.1. **III.** *enjoying a good reputation*, *Cod.Just.*1.4.26 *Intr.*, Just.*Nov.*128.18.

εὐύποπτα σώματα persons *believed to be dangerously ill*, Aët.5.78.

εὐυποχώρητος, ον, *easily yielding*, σώματα Herm.ap.Stob.1.49.69.

εὐύφ-αντος [ῠ], ον, (ὑφαίνω) = sq., Suid. **–ής, ές**, (ὑφή) *well-woven*, στολή Tim.*Pers.*180; λαίφεα *AP*10.2 (Antip. Sid.); ἱμάτιον Herm. *in Phdr.*p.192 A., *BGU*1564.10; πέπλος v.l. in S.*Tr.*602.

εὐφαής, ές, (φάος) *very bright*, Nonn.*D.*8.111.

εὐφάλαρα· λαμπρά, Hsch., *EM*399.32.

εὐφᾱμέω, εὔφᾱμος, Dor. for εὐφημ–.

εὐφαντ-ᾰσίωτος, ον, *gifted with a vivid imagination*, Vett.Val.47.1, Quint.6.2.30; πρᾶξις *Cat.Cod.Astr.*8(4).209; also in bad sense, *fantastic, fanciful*, Vett.Val.150.12. **–αστος**, ον, *imaginative*, Phlp. *in de An.*155.30, Platon.*Diff.Com.*15. **II.** *easily imagined*, Procl. *in Prm.*p.518 S.

εὔφαπτον· ὑπὸ θεοῦ κατεχόμενον, Hsch.

εὐφᾰρέτρης, ου, Dor. **–ας, α, ὁ**, *with beautiful quiver*, Ἀπόλλων S. *Tr.*208 (lyr.), Maced.*Pae.*1.

εὐφάρμᾰκος, ον, *abounding in drugs*, ὄρος Thphr.*HP*9.10.3.

εὐφέγγ-εια, ἡ, *brilliancy*, Iamb.*Protr.*21.ιϛ'. **–ής, ές**, *bright, brilliant*, ἡμέρα . . . εὐ. ἰδεῖν A.*Pers.*387, cf. B.18.26; Ἄρκτος A.R.3.1195; σελάνα B.8.29, cf. Plu.2.161e; πεύκη, of a torch, *AP*7.407.5 (Diosc.); τὸ εὐ. Luc.*Hipp.*8. **2.** *shiny*, τοῖχοι Suid. s.v. δύο τοίχους.

εὐφεροσύνη, etym. of εὐφροσύνη, coined by Pl.*Cra.*419d.

εὔφηβος, written for ἔφηβος, *IG*3.1104 (ii A.D.).

εὐφημ-έω, Dor. **εὐφᾱμέω**, (εὔφημος) *use words of good omen*, opp. δυσφημέω: **I.** *avoid all unlucky words*, during sacred rites: hence, as the surest mode of avoiding them, *keep a religious silence*, φέρτε δὲ χερσὶν ὕδωρ εὐφημῆσαί τε κέλεσθε Il.9.171, cf. Call.*Ap.*17, 18, etc.; mostly imper., εὐφήμει, εὐφημεῖτε, *hush! be still!* Ar.*Nu.*297, *Ach.*241, al.; οἱ δὲ ἀμβώσαντες μέγα εὐφημέειν μιν ἐκέλευον Hdt.3.38; εὐφημεῖν χρὴ τὸν πρεσβύτην Ar.*Nu.*263; εὐφήμει τοῦτό γε, ἦν δ' ἐγώ Pl. *Euthd.*301a, cf. *R.*329c; οὐκ εὐφημήσεις; Id.*Smp.*214d:—Pass., εὔφημον εἴη τοὔπος εὐφημουμένη *since* you *have been spoken fair*, A.*Supp.*512. **II.** *shout in triumph*, Id.*Ag.*596, *Eu.*1035 (lyr.), Ar.*Pl.*758, D.S.5.49. **2.** c. acc., *honour by praise, speak well of*, θεούς Pl.*Epin.*992d, cf. X.*Smp.*4.49:—Pass., *to be called by a mild name*, πολιτεία . . . εὐφημούμενος λῆρος D.S.37.17; also, *to be honoured*, Hp.*Ep.*27, *CIG*4389 (Isauria); *to be applauded*, Ph.2.589; πρὸς πάντων –ηθείς Hdn.2.3.11; ὑπὸ ὄχλων Vett.Val.38.25. **III.** *sound triumphantly*, κέλαδος Ἑλλήνων πάρα . . ηὐφήμησεν A.*Pers.*389; ὀλολυγμὸς εὐφημῶν Id.*Ag.*28. **–ητέον**, *one must use words of good omen*, ἐπί τισι Ph.2.257. **–ητικός, ή, όν**, *of happy significance*, ἀντίφρασις Eust. 763.37. **–ία, ἡ**, *use of words of good omen*, opp. δυσφημία: **I.** *abstinence from inauspicious language, religious silence*, εὐφημίαν ἴσχε, = εὐφήμει, S.*Tr.*178; εὐ. ἐσχηκέναι πρός τινα Pl.*Lg.*717c; εὐφημία 'στω, εὐφημία 'στω, as a proclamation of *silence* before a prayer, Ar. *Th.*295, cf. *Av.*959; so εὐφημίαν . . κηρύξας ἔχω S.*Fr.*893; Ταλθύβιος . . . εὐφημίαν ἀνεῖπε καὶ σιγὴν στρατῷ E.*IA*1564; μετ' εὐ. διδάσκειν Pl. *Lg.*949b; ἐν εὐ. χρὴ τελευτᾶν Id.*Phd.*117e; πρὸς εὐφημίαν τρεπέσθω Luc.*Laps.*17. **II.** in positive sense, *auspiciousness*, λόγων εὐ. E.*IA*608, Aeschin.1.169; πᾶσαν εὐ. παρειχόμην D.*Ep.*2.19; esp. *a fair* or *honourable name* for a bad thing, *euphemism* (as Εὐμενίδες, εὐφρόνη, etc.), δι' εὐφημίας Pl.*Lg.*736a; εὐφημίας ἕνεκα Aeschin.3.92, cf. Plu.2.449a. **2.** f.l. for εὐφωνία, Demetr.*Eloc.*175. **III.** *prayer and praise, worship*, offered to the gods, E.*IA*1469; = εὐχή, Pl.*Alc.*2.149b; εὐξάμενον μετ' εὐφημίας Din.2.14: pl., Pi.*P.*10.35. **2.** *honour, good repute* enjoyed by men, Phld.*Ind.Sto.*16, 20; ἀθάνατος εὐ. D.S1.2; opp. δυσφημία, 2*Ep.Cor.*6.8; ἀδιάλειπτος Plu.2.121e; ἡ ὕστερον εὐ. D.Chr.31.20; τὴν παρὰ πᾶσιν ἀγαθὴν εὐ. good *repute*, *IG*12(5).860.39 (Tenos, i B.C.); ἡ ἐκ τῶν ξένων εὐ. *OGI* 339.30 (Sestos, ii B.C.); *panegyric*, Jul.*Or*.3.106a, Lib.*Or*.62.3; ἡ εὐ. σου, as a form of address, *PLond*.3.891.9 (iv A.D.); αἱ εὐ. *plaudits, acclamations* in a local senate, *POxy*.2110.2 (iv A.D.). **-ίζομαι**, *use words of good omen*, A.D.*Pron*.10.22, Hsch. s.v. εὐοίαιον, *EM* 388.43. **-ισμός**, ὁ, *use of an auspicious word for an inauspicious one*, e.g. Εὐμενίδες for Ἐρινύες, εὐφρόνη for νύξ, etc., Eust.1398.52, Demetr.*Eloc*.281; κατ' εὐφημισμόν Corn.*ND*21, Hermog.*Prog*. 7, Palaeph.51, Olymp.*in Mete*.105.19; ἀπ' εὐφημισμοῦ Phld.*Piet*. 111. **-ος**, Dor. **εὔφᾱμος**, ον, (φήμη) *uttering sounds of good omen*, ἀετός Arist.*HA*$618^{b}31$: usu. in derived senses, I. *abstaining from inauspicious words*, i.e. *religiously silent*, εὔφημον .. κοίμησον στόμα A.*Ag*.1247; γλῶσσαν εὔ. φέρειν Id.*Ch*.581; so perh. εὔ. γόοι Id.*Fr*.40; εὐφάμου στόμα φροντίδος ἱέντες moving the lips of *reverent* thought, i.e. keeping a holy silence, S.*OC*132 (lyr.); so ὑπ' εὐφήμου βοῆς, i.e. in silence, Id.*El*.630; εὔφημα φώνει, = εὐφήμει, Id.*Aj*.362, 591, E.*IT*687; εὔφημος ἴσθι S.*Fr*.478; εὔ. πᾶς ἔστω λαός Ar.*Th*.39 (anap.). 2. *mild, softening* (cf. εὐφημία II. 1, εὐφημισμός), ἐν-οτάτοις ὀνόμασι. . κατονομάζειν Pl.*Alc*.2.140c; πρὸς τὸ -ότατον, Lat. *in meliorem partem*, Luc.*Prom.Es* 3. Adv. Comp. -ότερον Eust.1398.49. 3. *fair-spoken*, εἰς τὸ δαιμόνιον Phld.*Piet*.18. II. in positive sense, *fair-sounding, auspicious*, μῦθοι Xenoph.1.14; ἦμαρ A.*Ag*.636; ἔπος Id.*Supp*.512; εὔφημοι κέλαδοι E.*Tr*.1072 (lyr.); εὔφαμον δ' ἐπὶ βωμοῖς μοῦσαν θεῖατ' ἀοιδοί A.*Supp*.694 (lyr.); Μούσης ἀνοίγειν.. εὔφημον στόμα Ar.*Av*.1719; εὔ. πόνοι *pious, holy*, E.*Ion*134 (lyr.); δόμοι Id.*Andr*.1144; ᾠδῆς γένος, ἐρωτήματα, Pl.*Lg*.800e, *Hp.Ma*.293a, cf. *Ep.Phil*.4.8; πλοῦς Iamb.*VP*3.16 (Sup.). Adv. -μως *with* or *in words of good omen*, *h.Ap*.171 (dub. l.), A.*Eu*.287, *IG*1^{2}.108.55, Pl.*Phdr*. 265c: Comp. -ότερον Aristaenet.2.9. III. *laudatory*, λόγοι εὔ. *panegyrics*, Plb.31.3.4. (Also f.l. for εὔχυμος Aët.5.58, for εὔφιμος Nic.*Al*.275.)

εὔφθαρτος, ον, *easily destroyed, perishable*, Arist.*Cael*.$280^{b}25$, $305^{a}6$ (Comp.), Plb.2.35.6, M.Ant.2.12. 2. *easily corrupted*, Gal.8. 34. II. *easy of digestion*, Diph.Siph.ap.Ath.2.68f.

εὐφθογγ-έω, gloss on εὐστομέω, Sch.S.*OC*18. **-ος**, ον, *well-sounding, cheerful*, λύρη Thgn.534; κελάδους -οτέρους A.*Ch*.341 (anap.); σύριγγες E.*Tr*.127 (lyr.); *sweet-voiced*, of birds, Str.15.1. 69: Sup., Id.6.1.9.

εὐφῐλ-ής, ές, *well-loved*, χείρ A.*Ag*.34. II. Act., *loving well*, ποίμνης τοιαύτης οὔτις εὐ. θεῶν Id.*Eu*.197. **-ητος**, η, ον, *well-beloved*, only in Id.*Th*.107 (lyr.).

εὐφῐλό-παις, παιδος, ὁ, ἡ, *the children's darling*, of a lion's whelp, A.*Ag*.721 (lyr.). **-τίμητος** [τῐ], ον, *properly made an object of ambition*, δαπανήματα Arist.*EN*$1122^{b}22$.

εὔφῑμος, ον, *well-bitted, well-bridled*, Hdn.*Epim*.178 (hence **εὐφῑμία**, v. εὐκαμία). II. *astringent, styptic*, Nic.*Al*.275.

εὔφλαστος, ον, *easily crushed*, Sch.Lyc.26.

εὐφλεβής, ές, = εὔτονος I. 1b, κέρας Neophr.(?) *Medea* in *PLit.Lond.* 77 *Fr*.2.19.

εὔφλεκτος, ον, *easily set on fire*, X.*Cyr*.7.5.22, Arr.*An*.2.19.1.

εὐφορβ-ία, ἡ, *high feeding*, σφαδάζεις πῶλος ὣς εὐφορβίᾳ S.*Fr*. 848. **-ιον**, τό, *spurge, Euphorbia resinifera*, Dsc.3.82, Gal.13. 270; freq. also, *its resinous juice*, S.E.*P*.1.93, *Edict.Diocl*.32. 70. **-ος**, ον, (φέρβω) *well-fed*, Orph.*Fr*.285.65.

εὐφορ-έω, *bear well, be productive*, Hp.*Ep*.10, *Ev.Luc*.12.16, Ph.2. 64, al.: metaph., λόγος εὐ. πλημμύραις ῥημάτων καὶ ὀνομάτων Id.1. 690 (ἐμφ- cod.): c. acc., εὐ. σταφυλάς Gal.1.547. II. of ships, *have a prosperous voyage*, Luc.*Lex*.15. **-ητος**, ον, *endurable*, τινι A.*Ch*.353 (lyr.). **-ία**, ἡ, *power of enduring easily*, Hp.*Fract*.35; *contentment*, Phld.*Lib*.p.17 O. 2. *sense of well-being* in disease, τοῦ νοσοῦντος Herod.Med. in *Rh.Mus*.58.106, cf. Gal.11.10, 14.615, Orib.*Syn*.6.6. II. *fertility*, Ph.2.57, al.: in pl., γαστέρων εὐφορίαι Hp.*Epid*.6.7.2; *periods of productivity*, Chrysipp.*Stoic*.2.337; ψυχῶν εὐφορίαι ibid.; *abundant produce*, καρπῶν, οἴνου, Xenag.3, Alciphr. 1.24; ἐλαίου *IG*2^{2}.1100.59; σίτου Ἀρχ.Ἐφ.1913.7 (Nisyros, iii B.C.). III. *grace of movement*, in dancing, Poll.4.97.

εὐφόρμιγξ, ιγγος, ὁ, ἡ, *with beautiful lyre*: *playing beautifully on it*, Λύκειος *AP*7.10. II. Pass., of lyrical music, *beautifully played* or *accompanied*, Opp.*H*.5.618.

εὔφορος, ον, (φέρω) *well* or *patiently borne*, πόνοι Pi.*N*.10.24. 2. *easy to bear* or *wear, manageable, light*, ὅπλα X.*Cyr*.2.3.14 (Sup.); δόρυ Id.*Eq*.7.8 (Sup.); ἔκπωμα Critias *Fr*.34 D. (Sup.); σφενδόνη Luc. *Dom*.7; *ductile*, of clay, Ph.1.418 (Sup.); of wines, -ώτατοι κεφαλῇ καὶ πέψεσιν Ruf.ap.Orib.6.38.15. 3. *easily borne, spreading rapidly*, of diseases, Luc.*Abd*.27; of persons, εὔ. πρὸς ἡδονὰς λόγων Longin.44.1. II. of the body, *active, vigorous, healthy*, Phoc.3.4; εὔ. ἔχειν τὸ σῶμα Arist.*HA*$575^{a}33$; but, *capable of graceful movement*, in dancing, -ώτερον τὸ σῶμα ἕξειν X.*Smp*.2.16. 2. *able to endure, patient*: in Adv. -ρως, τλῆναι S.*Ph*.872; ὀχεῖν Democr.173: Comp. -ώτερον, φέρειν Hp.*Fract*.18: Sup. -ώτατα, φέρειν *Aph*.1.13; τὰ κρύη καὶ τοὺς χειμῶνας εὔ. ἔχειν Plu.2.651c. 3. of animals and plants, *productive, fertile*, Arist.*HA*$538^{a}1$, Thphr.*CP*1.17.10; χώρα Ph.2.297 (Sup.); ἀγρός Plu.2.59a: c. gen., ὀπώρας Hdn.1.6.1; πυρετῶν Gal.7.334: metaph., εὔ. γνῶσις Phld.*Hom*.p.62 O. (dub.); πόλις εὔ. πρὸς ἀνδρῶν ἀρετήν *rich* in manly virtue, D.H.*Rh*.3.3. 4. *easily able* to do, c. inf., Aret.*SD*1.2. 5. Adv. -ρως *easily*, εὐ. καὶ μετὰ ῥαστώνης ἐνεργεῖν Ph.2.283; ἐς τὸ πάθος ἐκφερόμενος App.*BC*2.146 (Sup.); εὐφόρως ἔχειν τῆς γλώττης to have a *ready* tongue, Philostr. *VS*1.25.5; εὐφόρως ἔχειν to feel *well*, Gal.11.28: with no Verb expressed, κοιλίαι τοῖσι πλείστοισι πάνυ εὐφόρως Hp.*Epid*.1.3, cf. Gal. 17(1).209: Comp. -ωτέρως, περιγίνεσθαι Hp.*Art*.69.—An irreg. Comp. εὐφορέστερος in Aret.*CA*1.4.

εὔφορτος, ον, *well-freighted, well-ballasted*, νᾶες *AP*12.53 (Mel.): metaph., *agreeable, gracious*, opp. βαρὺς ἐπὶ ταῖς εὐπραγίαις, [στρατηγός] Onos.42.24; μέλη Opp.*C*.1.85, cf. 4.447.

εὐφράδ-εια [ᾰ], ἡ, *correctness of language*, Phld.*Rh*.1.165 S., S.E. *M*.1.98. **-ής**, ές, (φράζω) *expressing oneself correctly* or *accurately*, Simp.*in Ph*.968.30, Suid. Ep. Adv. -έως *eloquently*, πεπνυμένα πάντ' ἀγορεύειν Od.19.352. 2. Pass., *well-expressed*, λόγος Lyd.*Mens*.4. 64, cf. Sch.Il.14.382 (Comp.), etc. **-ίη**, ἡ, Ion. and poet. for εὐφράδεια, *IG*14.1294.

εὐφραίνω, Ep. ἐϋφρ-, fut. Att. εὐφρᾰνῶ A.*Ch*.742, etc., Ion. and Ep. εὐφρανέω Il.5.688, 7.297: aor. 1 εὔφρᾱνα or ηὔφρ- Simon. 155.12, Pi.*I*.7(6).3, E.*Or*.217, etc.; Ep. εὔφρηνα Il.24.102, subj. εὐφρήνῃς 7.294:—**Pass.**, with fut. Med. εὐφρᾰνοῦμαι X.*Smp*.7.5; Ion. 2 sg. εὐφρανέαι (v.l. -έεαι) Hdt.4.9; also Pass. εὐφρανθήσομαι Ar.*Lys*. 165, Aeschin.1.191, Men.*Pk*.68: aor. 1 εὐφράνθην or ηὐ- Pi.*O*.9.62, Ar. *Ach*.5: (εὔφρων):—*cheer, gladden*, εὐφρανέειν ἄλοχον Il.5.688; ἐϋφραίνοιτε γυναῖκας Od.13.44; ἀνδρὸς ἐϋφραίνοιμι νόημα 20.82; εὐ. θυμόν τινος Pi.*I*.7(6).3; νόον, φρένα, A.*Ch*.742, *Supp*.515; [τινὰ] ἐπέεσσι Il. 24.102; τινὰ δι' ἀρετήν Pl.*Mx*.237a; τινά τι Agatho 12; πλεῖστα X. *Mem*.2.4.6. II. Pass., *make merry, enjoy oneself*, εὐφραίνεσθαι ἕκηλον Od.2.311, cf. Hdt.4.9, *Ev.Luc*.16.19, etc.; τινι *at* or *in* a thing, Pi.*P*.9.16, Ar.*Nu*.561, Pl.*Lg*.796b; ἐπί τινι Ar.*Ach*.5, X.*Smp*.7.5, Aeschin.1.191; ἔν τινι X.*Hier*.1.16; διά τινος ib.8; ἀπό τινος ib.4.6: c. part., εὐφράνθη ἰδών *was rejoiced at* seeing, Pi.*O*.9.62, cf. Men.*Pk*. 68; εἰ πεπαυμένος μηδέν τι μᾶλλον ἢ νοσῶν εὐφραίνεται S.*Aj*.280, cf. E.*Med*.36; τὰ ἐμὰ εὐ. *enjoy a pleasure* in my stead, Luc.*DMar*.13.2.

εὐφράν-της, ου, ὁ, *one who cheers*, *EM*436.3. **-τικός**, ή, όν, *cheering*, ὀφθαλμῶν Ath.13.608a. 2. of persons, *cheery*, Vett.Val. 9.3, al.: Comp. -ώτερος *more cheered* by good fortune, *Cat.Cod.Astr*. 8(4).238. **-τοποιός**, όν, = foreg. 1, Sch.Ar.*Pax*519. **-τός**, ή, όν, *pleasant*, dub. in Gal.5.88: Εὐφραντά, τά, title of work by Timocrates, D.L.10.6, cf. Sch.E.*Hec*.100, al. 2. *cheered, delighted*, Sch. rec.A.*Pr*.536.

εὐφρᾱσία, ἡ, *good cheer*, ἡ ἐν τῇ ψυχῇ εὐ. Epict.*Gnom*.19, cf. Melamp.p.24 D., al., *PFlor*.391.1, al. (iii A.D.), *PRyl*.28.47, al. (iv A.D.), Hsch. s.v. δαῖτος.

εὔφραστος, ον, (φράζω) *easy to make intelligible*, Arist.*Rh*.$1407^{b}12$; *distinct*, ὀπωπή D.P.171.

εὐφρονέων, Ep. ἐϋφρ-, *with kind* (or *prudent*) *mind*, ὅ (or ὅς) σφιν ἐϋφρονέων ἀγορήσατο καὶ μετέειπεν Il.1.73, al.; fem. -έουσα A.R.3. 998: pl. -έοντες Man.1.233. (The Verb -φρονέω is not found; perh. better divisim.)

εὐφρόνη, ἡ, (εὔφρων) *the kindly time*, euphem. for νύξ, *night*, chiefly poet., Hes.*Op*.560, Pi.*N*.7.3, etc.: also in Ion. and late Prose, Heraclit.26, 57, Hdt.7.12, 56, al., Hp.*Mul*.1.1, Jul.*Or*.2.85b; ἄστρων εὐ., = ἀστερόεσσα εὐ., S.*El*.19; εὐφρόνης, = νυκτός, *by night*, Epist.Anaximen. ap.D.L.2.4; κατ' εὐφρόνην A.*Pers*.221 (troch.), S.*El*.259. II. = εὐφροσύνη, Hsch., cf. E.*Hel*.1470 codd. (lyr., sed leg. εὐφροσύναν).

εὐφρονίδης, ου, ὁ, *son of Night*, *Epigr.Gr*.1029.6 (Cius).

εὐφροσύνη, Ep. ἐϋφρ-, ἡ, (εὔφρων) *mirth, merriment*, γέλω τε καὶ εὐφροσύνην παρέχουσαι Od.20.8, cf. 10.465, etc.; esp. of a banquet, *good cheer, festivity*, οὐ. . τί φημι χαριέστερον εἶναι ἢ ὅτ' ἐϋφροσύνη μὲν ἔχῃ κατὰ δῆμον ἅπαντα κτλ. 9.6, cf. *h.Merc*.449, 482, etc.; κρατὴρ μεστὸς ἐϋφροσύνης Xenoph.1.4: pl., σφισι θυμὸς αἰὲν ἐϋφροσύνῃσιν ἰαίνεται is cheered *with glad thoughts*, Od.6.156; *festivities*, A.*Pr*. 539, E.*Ba*.377 (both lyr.), etc.: chiefly poet., used by X.*Cyr*.8.1.32, *Ages*.9.4 (pl.): in sg., Id.*Cyr*.3.3.7, Pl.*Ti*.80b; ἡ χαρὰ καὶ ἡ εὐ. Epicur.*Fr*.2: also in later Prose, Lxx *Ge*.31.27, al., *Act.Ap*.2.28, Diogenian.Epicur.4.50, *PLips*.119 ii 1 (iii A.D.), etc.; εὐ. ψυχῆς οἶνος πινόμενος Lxx *Si*.34.28(31.36). II. pr. n., *Euphrosyne*, one of the Graces, Hes.*Th*.909, etc.

εὐφρόσῠνος, η, ον, also ος, ον dub. in *AP*5.39.6 (Nicarch.), *IGRom*. 4.416 (Pergam.):—poet. and later Prose for εὔφρων, *cheery, merry*, Ptol.*Tetr*.166, Vett.Val.15.5, *Sammelb*.411 (iii/iv A.D.). Adv. -νως *in good cheer*, Thgn.766. II. Act., *cheering, making cheerful*, Dsc.4.127; νύξ Orph.*H*.3.5, etc. 2. εὐφρόσυνον, τό, = βούγλωσσον, Plin.*HN*25.81.

εὔφρουρος, ον, (φρουρά) *watchful*, κομιδή Opp.*H*.5.621.

εὔφρων, Ep. ἐΰφρ-, ον, both in Hom.: (φρήν):—*cheerful, merry*, of persons, εἴ πέρ τις. . δαίνυται εὔφρων Il.15.99, etc.; θυμός Od.17.531; ἶλαι Pi.*N*.5.38. Adv. -νως *with good cheer*, Id.*P*.10.40, etc. 2. Act., *cheering, making glad* or *merry*, οἶνος Il.3.246; οἶμος Pi.*Pae*. 6.115; εὔφρων πόνος εὖ τελέσασι A.*Ag*.806 codd.; ὦ φέγγος εὖφρον ib.1577; ῥοαὶ εὔφρονες Ἀργείοις S.*Aj*.420 (lyr.): neut. pl., εὔφροσιν δεδεγμένη, = εὐφροσύναις, A.*Eu*.632 (s.v.l.). II. *kindly, gracious*, θεὸς εὔ. εἴη εὐχαῖς Pi.*O*.4.14, cf. A.*Pers*.772, S.*Aj*.705 (lyr.), A.R.4. 1411, etc.; γαῖαν ἀνθρώποισι καὶ εὔφρονα μήλοις Pi.*O*.7.63; εὔ. ἥδ' ὁμιλία A.*Eu*.1030; ψῆφον δ' εὔφρον' ἔθεντο Id.*Supp*.640 (lyr.); v.l. for ἐπίφρονος in Theoc.25.29. Adv. -νως A.*Ag*.351, al. 2. *of sound mind, reasonable*, ἄνδρες Xenoph.1.13. III. = εὔφημος, πῶς εὔφρον' εἴπω; A.*Ch*.88; οὐδ' αὖ τόδ' εὔφρον Id.*Supp*.378.

εὐφῠ-ής, ές, (φυή) *well-grown, shapely*, μηροί Il.4.147; πτελέη 21. 243; κλάδος, of ivy, E.*Fr*.88; πρόσωπον Id.*Med*.1198; ὀδόντες Alex. 98.20; μαζοί *AP*5.55 (Diosc.); *suitably formed*, πόδες Arist.*PA*$691^{b}15$; χορείας εὐφυὴς βάσις *well-ordered, graceful*, Ar.*Th*.968 (lyr.). II.

of good natural disposition, X.*Mem*.1.6.13, al., Arist.*EN*1114b8, Thphr.*Char*.29.4; of horses and dogs, X.*Mem*.4.1.3 (Sup.), Jul. *Or*.2.87a. 2. *naturally suited* or *adapted*, πρός τι Pl.*R*.455b; πρὸς τὰς τέχνας Isoc.4.33 (Sup.); εἴς τι Pl.*Prt*.327b(Sup.); οὐκ εὐ. λέγειν Aeschin.1.181; εὐ. τὰ σώματα καὶ τὰς ψυχάς Pl.*R*.409e; -έστατος τὴν γνώμην Isoc.9.41: rarely in bad sense, εὐ. πρὸς ἀγονίαν Arist.*GA* 748b8. Adv., εὐφυῶς ἔχει c. inf., Id.*Pol*.1321a9; εὐ. ἔχειν πρὸς.. ib. 1303b8: Comp. -έστερον, ἔχειν D.61.42; also -εστέρως Hierocl. p.27 A. 3. of place, *well situated*, Arist.*PA*666a14 (Sup.); of time, καιρὸς εὐ. πρὸς σωτηρίαν Plb.1.19.12. Adv. -ῶς, κεῖσθαι πρὸς.., Arist. *Pol*.1327a33. III. *naturally clever*, like εὐτράπελος, euphem. for βωμολόχος, Isoc.7.49,15.284; σοφιστὴς εὐ. Alex.36.4, cf. 135.13; εὐφυής *a man of genius*, Arist.*Po*.1455a32, cf. *Rh*.1390b28; opp. γεγυμνασμένος, ib.1410b8; of hounds, Id.*HA*608a27 (Comp.). Adv. εὐφυῶς *cleverly, skilfully*, Pl.*R*.401c; κολακεύειν Antiph.144.2; ὀψοποιεῖν Alex.24.1. -ΐα, ἡ, *natural goodness of growth* or *shape, shapeliness*, δακτύλων Hp.*Off*.4, cf. *Art*.82; εὐ. καὶ ὥρα Plu.*Sol*.1; ἡ τῶν ζῴων εὐ. Porph.*Abst*.3.24. II. *good natural parts*, and morally, *goodness of disposition*, freq. in both senses at once, Arist.*EN*1114b 12, *Rh*.1362b24, etc.; defined as τάχος μαθήσεως, Pl.*Def*.413d. 2. of places, *fertility, favourable situation*, etc., εὐ. πρός τι Thphr.*CP*1. 2.3; ἡ τῶν τόπων εὐ. Plb.2.68.5.—εὐφύεια is cited from Alex.317, and is found in Pap., as Anon. *in Tht*.4.43, al.

εὐφύλακτος [ῠ], ον, *easy to keep* or *guard*, A.*Supp*.998; εὐ. ἡ καρδία *well-guarded*, Arist.*PA*670a26; εὐφυλακτότερον τὸ ὕδωρ τοῦ ἀέρος *more easily confined*, Id.*Sens*.438a15, cf. *PA*656b2 (Sup.); ἐν εὐφυλάκτῳ εἶναι to be *on one's guard*, E.*HF*201; -ότερα αὐτοῖς ἐγίγνετο it was *easier* for them *to keep a look-out*, Th.8.55; ὅπως εὐφύλακτα αὐτοῖς εἴη Id.3.92, cf. Plu.*Rom*.18. II. (φυλάττομαι) *easy to guard against*, Arist.*SE*174b35 (Comp.), D.C.57.1.

εὔφυλλος, ον, *leafy*, Νεμέα Pi.*I*.6(5).61; δάφνα E.*IT*1246 (lyr.).

εὐφύσητος [ῡ], ον, gloss on εὔπρηστος, Sch.Il.18.471; *easily blown away*, *EM*273.35.

εὔφῦτος, ον, (φυτόν) *well-planted*, Poll.1.228.

εὐφων-έω, *have a good voice*, Phld.*Rh*.1.367 S. -ία, ἡ, *goodness of voice*, X.*Mem*.3.3.13, Arist.*Pr*.903b27; τόλμα καὶ εὐ., of an orator, Plu.2.838e. 2. *excellence of tone*, of horns, Arist.*Aud*.802b2. II. *euphony*, D.H.*Comp*.25, Quint.1.5.4, Demetr.*Eloc*.68. -ος, ον, *sweet-voiced, musical*, Πιερίδες Pi.*I*.1.64; χορός A.*Ag*.1187; *sweet-toned*, λύρα Arist.*Metaph*.1019b15; τὸ βαρὺ ἀπὸ τοῦ ὀξέος -ότερον Id. *Pr*.920a23; εὐ. θαλίαι *accompanied with sweet songs*, Pi.*P*.1.38. 2. *loud-voiced*, of a herald, Ar.*Ec*.713, X.*HG*2.4.20, cf. D.19.126; οἱ -ότατοι Hdn.2.6.4. 3. *euphonious*, Democr.18b, D.H.*Comp*.12, Demetr.*Eloc*.70; -ότατον τὸ ᾱ D.H.*Comp*.14. 4. Adv. -νως Poll. 2.113: Comp. -οτέρως Demetr.*Eloc*.255; -ότερον Plu.2.1132b: Sup. -ότατα, ᾄδειν Philostr.*VA*4.42.

εὐφώρᾱτος, ον, *easy to detect*, Gal.13.333; διαφορά Plu.2.63c; συκοφαντία Lib.*Decl*.49.79: Comp., Gal.6.95: **Εὐφωρατ[.]** dub. in *Lyr Alex.Adesp*.19 tit.

εὐχαίτης, ου, ὁ, *with beautiful hair*, Γανυμήδης Call.*Ep*.53; epith. of Hades, *Ath.Mitt*.24.257(Thrace); of horses, *with beautiful mane*, Poll. 5.83; of plants, *with beautiful leaves*, λωτός *AP*4.1.51 (Mel.); κισσός ib.9.669 (Marian.): also **εὔχαιτος**, ον, σώματα Herm.ap.Stob.1.49.60.

εὐχαιτίας, ου, ὁ, v.l. for foreg., D.S.20.54.

εὐχάλῑν-ος [ᾰ], ον, *well-bridled*, S.E.*M*.1.169. -ωτος, ον, (χαλινόω) = foreg., Hdn.*Epim*.178.

εὔχαλκος, ον, *wrought of fine brass* or *well-wrought in* (or *pointed with*) *brass*, στεφάνη Il.7.12; ἀξίνη 13.612; μελίη 20.322; τρίποδες Od.15.84; κράνος A.*Th*.459; ὅπλα Id.*Pers*.456.

εὐχάλκωτος, ον, (χαλκόω) = foreg., κρεάγρα *AP*6.305.5 (Leon.).

εὐχανδής, ές, *spacious*, Man.6.463; νηδύς Nic.*Al*.63.

εὐχᾰράκτ-ηρος, *bene figuratus, formosus*, *Gloss*. -ος, ον, *clearly stamped*, νομισμάτια *PLips*.13.10 (iv A.D.).

εὐχάρ-εια [χᾰ], ἡ, *grace, charm*, Simp. *in Epict*.p.119 D.; cf. εὐχαρίη II. -ής, ές, = εὔχαρις, Men.Rh.p.406 S.; v.l. for εὔχαρις, Lxx *Wi*.14.20. -ίζω, *render thanks*, τόπῳ *Sammelb*.4563. -ίη, ἡ, = εὐχαριστία, Ἀθήναιον 7.210 (Patrae). II. = εὐχάρεια, *urbanity*, Hp. *Praec*.10 (v.l. εὐχαριστίη). -ις, neut. εὔχαρι, gen. ιτος, *charming, gracious*, esp. in society, Democr.104, Pl.*R*.486d, 487a, X.*Cyr*.7. 4.1; ἀστεῖοι καὶ εὐ. ib.2.2.12; εὐ. κατὰ τὰς ἐντεύξεις, ἐν ταῖς ὁμιλίαις, Plb.22.21.3, 23.5.7; τὸ εὐ. *urbanity*, X.*Ages*.8.1, 11.11, M.Ant.1.16. 5; of Aphrodite, *gracious*, E.*Heracl*.894 (lyr.), *Med*.631 (lyr.); of animals, Arist.*HA*592b24: Comp. -τώτερος Plot.3.6.6: Sup. -τώτατος, ἐς τὸν δῆμον App.*BC*2.26. II. of places, *pleasant*, Arist.*Pol*. 1331a36. -ισμα, *corollarium*, *Gloss*.

εὐχᾰριστ-έω, *bestow a favour on, oblige*, τῷ δήμῳ τῷ Δηλίων *IG*11 (4).665 (Delos, iii B.C.); τινι *PPetr*.2 p.4 (iii B.C.), *PHib*.1.66.5 (iii B.C.). 2. *to be thankful, return thanks*, Decr.ap.D.18.92, *IPE*1². 352.14 (Chersonesus, ii B.C.); τοῖς Ἀθηναίοις Posidon.36 J., cf. Phld. *Ir*.p.92 W., al.; ἐπί τινι or περί τινος *for* a thing, Plb.4.72.7, D.S.16. 11, etc.; esp. to the gods, ἐπὶ τῷ ἐρρῶσθαί σε τοῖς θεοῖς εὐ. *UPZ*59.10 (ii B.C.), cf. Lxx *Ju*.8.25, 1*Ep.Cor*.1.4, etc.:—Pass., *to be thanked*, ηὐχαρίστηται κεραυνοῖς Hp.*Ep*.17; *to be received with thanks*, 2*Ep. Cor*.1.11. 3. *pray*, τῷ θεῷ περί τινος *PLond*.2.413,418 (iv A.D.). -ήριος, ον, *expressive of gratitude*, ὁλοκαύτωμα εὐ. τινός Ph. 2.157; εὐχαί *PMasp*.6.6 (vi A.D.): as Subst., εὐχαριστήρια (sc. ἱερά), τά, *thank-offering*, τοῖς θεοῖς θύειν εὐ. Plb.5.14.8, cf. Sch.Pi.*P*.7.9; *mission of thanks* to the Senate, D.S.29.11: sg., Ἀσκληπιῷ καὶ Ὑγείᾳ .. εὐχαριστήριον (sc. ἀνέθηκεν) *IG*12(3).1086 (Melos), cf. 3.132*l*, *IPE* 1².162.2, *OGI*699 (Egypt), Lxx 2*Ma*.12.45. -ητέον, *one must give thanks*, τινι Ph.1.273; ὑπέρ τινος ib.533. -ητικός, ή, όν, = -ιστικός, λόγος, ὕμνος, ib.177, 371. Adv. -κῶς ib.273 (v.l. -ιστικῶς). -ία, ἡ, *thankfulness, gratitude*, Decr.ap.D.18.91, *Stoic*.3.67, Phld.*Ir*.p.93 W.; τοῦ δήμου *OGI*227.6 (Didyma, iii B.C.); πρός τινα D.S.17.59, *PLond*.3.1178.25 (ii A.D.); πρὸς τὸν θεόν Plb.1.36.1; ἀπόντι μᾶλλον εὐ. ποίει Men.693. 2. *giving of thanks*, εἰς εὐ. θεοῦ *SIG*798.5 (Cyzicus, i A.D.), cf. Ph.1.60, Lxx *Wi*.16.28, *Corp.Herm*.1.29, etc.: pl., ποιεῖσθαι -ίας 1*Ep.Ti*.2.1. -ικός, ή, όν, *of gratitude*, ὕμνοι Ph. 2.109; εὐχή *JHS*37.101 (Lydia, ii A.D.). Adv. -κῶς Ph.1.59. -ος, ον, *agreeable*, τινι τέχνῃ X.*Oec*.5.10 (Comp.); λόγοι Id.*Cyr*.2.2.1 (Sup.); -ότατα καὶ πιθανώτατα εἴρηκε Plb.12.28.11; εὐχάριστα *acceptable gifts*, *AJA*30.249 (Cypr.). Adv. -τως, τελευτᾶν τὸν βίον to die *happily*, Hdt.1.32. II. *grateful, thankful*, X.*Cyr*.8.3.49 (Sup.), *Inscr. Prien*.103.8 (ii/i B.C.), *Ep.Col*.3.15, etc. Adv. -τως, διακεῖσθαι πρός τινα D.S.1.90; ἀποδιδόναι Ph.1.520; τῶν γεγονότων μνημονεύειν Plu.2. 477f. III. *beneficent*, θεοί *UPZ*41.13 (ii B.C.); title of Ptolemy V, *OGI*90.5 (Rosetta); τὸ τῆς ψυχῆς εὐ. D.S.18.28; βεβαιωτής (-ότης codd.) εὐχάριστος, of God, Ph.1.128 codd. (ἰσχυρότατος cj. Cohn).

εὐχάρῑτος, ον, freq. v.l. for foreg., as in Arist.*HA*592b24.

εὐχάροπος [ᾰ], ον, strengthd. for χάροπος, *Gp*.14.16.2.

εὐχατῆσαι· ἐπικαυχήσασθαι, Hsch. **εὐχατότερον**· πλουσιώτερον, Id.

εὐχείμερος, ον, (χεῖμα) *healthy* or *convenient to winter in*, πόλεις Arist.*Pol*.1330a41. II. Act., *bearing the winter* or *the cold well*, ὄϊες Id.*HA*596b4 (Comp.).

εὐχείμων, prob. f.l. for λευχ-, Suid.

εὐχεῖον, τό, *house of prayer, synagogue*, *PLond*.3.1177.60 (iii A.D.).

εὔχειρ, χειρος, ὁ, ἡ, *quick* or *ready of hand, handy, dexterous*, Pi.*O*. 9.111; σὺν νόῳ εὔχειρες Hp.*Art*.33, cf. S.*OC*472.

εὐχειρία, Ion. -ίη, ἡ, *manual dexterity, skill*, ἀνόητος εὐ. Hp.*Art*. 35, cf. Ruf.ap.Orib.*inc*.20.1; in flute-playing, Poll.4.72; in battle, Plb.11.13.3, 16.19.1, *Fr*.158 (pl.), Hdn.1.17.12, etc. (Sts. confused in codd. with εὐχέρεια.)

εὐχείρωτος, ον, (χειρόω) *easy to master* or *overcome*, A.*Pers*.452, X.*HG*5.3.4, etc.; *easy to train*, τῷ νομοθέτῃ Arist.*Pol*.1332b9; simply, *easy*, Porph.*Abst*.3.4. (Comp. εὐχειρότερος D.C.37.7, and Sup. εὐχειρότατος X.*Cyr*.1.6.36, *Oec*.8.4, Thphr.*HP*4.14.7, are ff.ll. for -ωτότερος, -ωτότατος.)

εὐχέρ-εια, ἡ, *tolerance of* or *indifference to* evil, μὴ ἡμῖν πολλὴν εὐχέρειαν ἐντίκτωσι τοῖς νέοις πονηρίας Pl.*R*.392a; *licentiousness*, A. *Eu*.494 (lyr.); ἡ τῆς πράξεως εὐ. Aeschin.1.124; *unscrupulous conduct*, ἡ πρὸς τὸν δῆμον εὐ. Plu.*Demetr*.11; *looseness*, περὶ τὰς γυναῖκας, περὶ τοὺς ὅρκους, Id.*Lyc*.15, *Lys*.8; *recklessness*, πρὸς τὸν ὅρκον εὐ. καὶ ταχύτης Id.2.271c; *hastiness*, Ph.2.276; πρὸς ὀργήν Luc.*Prom*.9; of a historian, *irresponsibility*, εὐ. καὶ τόλμα καὶ ῥᾳδιουργία Plb.12. 25e.2, cf. 16.18.3; εἰκαιότης καὶ εὐ. Ph.1.193; of an artist, *uncritical facility*, ἐν τῷ ποιεῖν εὐ. καὶ ταχύτης Plu.*Per*.13. II. *indifference to danger* or *hardship*: hence, *coolness, fortitude*, ἀνδρεία καὶ εὐ. (ironical) Pl.*R*.426d; εὐκολία καὶ εὐ. Id.*Lg*.942d, cf. *Alc*.1.122c; περὶ τὰς κυνηγίας εὐ. καὶ τόλμα Plb.22.3.8; cf. εὐχειρία. III. *ease, agreeableness*, κατὰ τὴν προφοράν Phld.*Po*.994.8; *comfort*, ὁδὸς πρὸς εὐχέρειαν ὡδοποιημένη *OGI*175.9 (Egypt, ii B.C.); περὶ τὰς δυστοκίας τῶν γυναικῶν τῇ εὐχερείᾳ.. βοηθεῖν to minister to the *comfort* (or promote the *fortitude*) of women.., Arist.*HA*587a11 (cf. εὐχερής II). IV. *dexterity, skill*, εὐ. Πραξιτέλους Luc.*Am*.11 (nisi leg. εὐχειρία). -ής, ές, *tolerant of* or *indifferent to evil, unpleasantness* or *inaccuracy, not squeamish*, ἡ ὗς -έστατον πρὸς πᾶσαν τροφὴν ζῴων ἐστίν Arist. *HA*595a18; οὐδενὸς γὰρ πώποτε ἀπέβαλεν ὀσπρίου λέπος· οὕτως ἐκεῖνός ἐστιν εὐ. ἀνήρ Alex.266.8, cf. Aristopho12.5, S.*Ph*.519,875; of lizard-eaters, λίαν εὐχερεῖς Menesth.ap.Orib.2.68.13; εὐ. βίος of the swine-herd, Pl.*Plt*.266d; τὸ εὐ. τῶν ὀνομάτων the *loose* use of names, Id. *Tht*.184c. Adv. -ρῶς, φέρειν τὴν ὠχρότητα, i.e. gloss it over, Id.*R*. 474e, cf. *Tht*.154b; εὐ. ἔχειν πρὸς τὴν ἀνθρωποφαγίαν Arist.*Pol*.1338b 21; -ρῶς ὥσπερ θηρίον ὕειον ἐν ἀμαθίᾳ μολύνηται Pl.*R*.535e: Comp. -έστερον, πρὸς πᾶν βρῶμα ἔχειν X.*Lac*.2.5; ἄλλο μικρῷ μεῖζον -έστερον κινοῦσιν *more readily, with fewer qualms*, Arist.*Pol*.1307b5, cf. Din. 1.55. 2. *unscrupulous, reckless*, D.21.103, Arist.*Metaph*.1025a2. Adv. -ρῶς *heedlessly, recklessly*, ᾧ λέγων εὐχερῶς ὅτι ἂν βουληθῇς D.18. 70, cf. 264. II. *indifferent to danger* or *suffering, cool, unconcerned, unflinching*, τῆς πολεμικῆς χρείας τῆς κατ' ἄνδρα.. εὐχερεῖς καὶ πρακτικοί *cool* and efficient in individual fighting, Plb.4.8.9; εἰς εὐχερῆ τῆς ἀποτέξεως ὑπομονήν Sor.1.46 (cf. εὐχέρεια II). Adv. -ρῶς καὶ εὐκόλως ἐξέπιεν drank the hemlock *coolly* and good-humouredly, Pl.*Phd*.117c. III. *easy*, εὐχερές ἐστι c. inf., Batr.62; τὰ λαχανευόμενα μεταφυτεύεται πρὸς εὐχερῆ τελείωσιν Sor.1.87: Comp., ib.108. Adv. -ρῶς, νόσου γινομένης εὐχερῶς ἀποξύνεται τὸ γάλα Id.1.115, cf. *PLond*.2.401.24 (ii B.C.): Sup. -έστατα, τρέπονται (sc. εἰς φυγήν) D.S.31.38. 2. σπασμοὶ εὐχερέες, i.e. *not dangerous*, Hp.*Prorrh*.1. 119 (cf. Gal.16.773); cf. εὐήθης I.3. 3. c. dat., *suitable, adapted*, θάλασσα.. μεγάλαις ναυσὶν οὐκ εὐ. App.*BC*2.84.

εὐχετάομαι, Ep. for εὔχομαι, only in pres. and impf. (without augm.):—*pray*, θεοῖσι.. μεγάλ' εὐχετόωντο ἕκαστος Il.8.347, 15.369; Κρονίωνι.. εὐχετάασθαι 6.268; πάντες δ' εὐχετόωντο θεῶν Διῒ Νέστορί τ' ἀνδρῶν 11.761, cf. Od.8.467. II. *boast, profess*, c. inf., τίνες ἔμμεναι εὐχετόωντο; Od.1.172, etc.; with inf. omitted, A.R.1.189, Orph.*A*.289; *brag*, ἵνα μή τις.. εὐχετόωτ' ἐπέεσσι Il.12.391; οὐ μὲν καλὸν ὑπέρβιον εὐχετάασθαι 17.19; μὰψ αὔτως εὐχετάασθαι 20.348; κταμένοισιν ἐπ' ἀνδράσιν εὐχετάασθαι *to glory* over them, Od.22.412.

εὐχέτης, ου, ὁ, *one who prays*, Eust.1725.57, Zonar.

εὐχετίαζον· ηὔχοντο, Hsch.

εὐχή, ἡ, (εὔχομαι) *prayer* or *vow*, once in Hom. (cf. εὖχος, εὐχωλή), ἐπὴν εὐχῇσι λίσῃ Od.10.526, cf. Hes.*Th.*419, Thgn.341, Hdt.1.31, etc.; θεὸς εὔφρων εἴη.. εὐχαῖς Pi.*O.*4.15; εὐχὰς ἀνασχεῖν τινι S.*El.*636; εὐχὴν ἐπιτελέσαι, Lat. *vota persolvere*, Hdt.1.86; εὐχὰς ἀποδιδόναι X.*Mem.*2.2.10; εὐχὴν ἀνέστησεν *SIG*1142 (Phrygia, i/ii A.D.); εὐχῇ χρῆσθαι, Lat. *votis potiri*, Pl.*Lg.*688b; κατὰ χιλίων.. εὐχὴν ποιήσασθαι χιμάρων to make *a vow* of a thousand goats, Ar.*Eq.*661; ἐν θεῶν εὐχαῖσι S.*OT*239, etc.; εὐχαὶ πρὸς θεούς Pl.*Lg.*700b; εὐχὰς εὔχεσθαι τοῖς θεοῖς D.19.130; εὐχὰς εὔξεται ὑπὲρ τῆς πόλεως *Inscr.Prien.*174.18 (ii B.C.); εὐχὰς ποιεῖσθαι Th.6.32, Arist.*Mu.*400a17; εὐχὴν ἀποθύειν Diph.43.10; κατ' εὐχήν, ἐξ εὐχῆς, Lat. *ex voto*, Call.*Ep.*48, *AP*6.357 (Theaet.); ἔχειν εὐχήν to be under *a vow*, *Act.Ap.*18.18. 2. *wish* or *aspiration*, opp. reality, εὐχαῖς ὅμοια λέγειν to build '*castles in the air*', Pl.*R.*499c, cf. 540d; μὴ εὐ. δοκῇ εἶναι ὁ λόγος ib.450d; κατὰ τὴν τῶν παίδων εὐ. like a boy's *wish*, Id.*Sph.*249d; εὐχῆς ἄξια things *to be wished*, but not expected, Isoc.4.182; πολιτεία ἡ κατ' εὐχὴν γινομένη the *ideal* state, Arist.*Pol.*1295a29, cf. 1288b23; ζῆν κατ' εὐχήν ib.1260b29. 3. *prayer for evil*, i.e. *curse*, *imprecation*, πατρὸς κατ' εὐχάς A.*Th.*820, cf. E.*Ph.*70.

εὐχήμων, ον, gen. ονος, *to be wished for*, Hsch.

εὔχῑλος, ον, *rich in fodder*, κάπη Lyc.95. II. of a horse, *feeding well*, X.*Eq.*1.12 (Comp.), cf. Arist.*PA*675b15 (Comp.).

εὐχίμᾰρος [ῐ], ον, *rich in goats*, *AP*6.108 (Myrin.).

εὐχίον, τό, Dim. of εὐχή, dub. in *IG*14.622 (Rhegium).

εὔχλοος, ον, contr. **-χλους**, ουν, (χλόη) *fresh and green*, epith. of Demeter, S.*OC*1600, cf. Nonn.*D.*41.15.

εὔχλωρος, f.l. for ἔγχλωρος (Coraes), Thphr.*HP*3.5.2.

εὔχομαι, impf. εὐχόμην (Att. ηὐ-) Il.3.275, etc.: fut. εὔξομαι Ar.*Av.*622 (anap.), etc.: aor. 1 εὐξάμην (Att. ηὐ-) Il.8.254, etc.: 2 sg. subj. εὔξεαι Od.3.45: (augm. ηὐ- only Att. acc. to Hdn.Gr.2.789, Moer.175):—*pray*, θεοῖς Il.3.296, Hdt.8.64, Th.3.58, etc.; ἀγάλμασι Heraclit.5; ἀνέμοισι Hdt.7.178; Ἀργείοισι A.*Supp.*980: c. acc. cogn., εὐχὰς εὔ. τοῖς θεοῖς D.19.130; εὐχὰς ὑπέρ τινος πρὸς τοὺς θεοὺς εὔ. Aeschin.3.18; εὔ. ἔπος *to utter* it *in prayer*, Simon.37.19, Pi.*P.*3.2, A.*Supp.*1059 (lyr.); μεγάλα, μέγα εὔ., *pray* aloud, Il.3.275, Od.17.239; πολλὰ Ποσειδάωνι 3.54: later, c. acc., Ἄρτεμιν εὔ. *AP*9.268 (Antip. Thess.): abs., Il.7.298, A.*Ch.*465 (lyr.), Ar.*Fr.*39 D. (lyr.), etc. 2. c. acc. et inf., *pray that*, Od.15.353, 21.211, Hdt.1.31; of an unrealizable wish (cf. εὐχή 2), Arist.*EN*1118a32, cf. Macho ap.Ath.8.341d: c. inf. alone, εὔ. θάνατον φυγεῖν Il.2.401; τί δοκέεις εὔχεσθαι ἄλλο ἢ ..λαβεῖν; Hdt.1.27; οἶκον ἰδεῖν Pi.*P.*4.293, etc.; τοῖς θεοῖς c. acc. et inf., Pl.*Phd.*117c; also εὔ. τοὺς θεοὺς δοῦναί μοι *pray* that the gods may give, Ar.*Th.*351, X.*An.*6.1.26; πρὸς τοὺς θεοὺς διδόναι Id.*Mem.*1.3.2; ταῖς Μούσαις εἰπεῖν Pl.*R.*545d, etc.; later εὔ. ἵνα Aristeas 45, D.H.9.53, Arr.*Epict.*2.6.12; ὅπως *Wien.Stud.*44.159. 3. c. acc. obj., *pray for*, *long* or *wish for*, χρυσόν Pi.*N.*8.37, etc.; εὐχόμενος ἄν τις ταῦτα εὔξαιτο Antipho 6.1; εὔ. τινί τι *pray for* something *for* a person, S.*Ph.*1019; κακόν τινι Lys.21.21; also, *pray for* a thing *from*.., τοῖς θεοῖς πολλὰ ἀγαθὰ ὑπέρ τινος X.*Mem.*2.2.10; τοῖς θεοῖς πολυκαρπίαν ib.3.14.3; δεινὸν κατά τινος Luc.*Abd.*32. II. *vow* or *promise to* do.., c. fut. inf., εὔχομαι ἐξελάαν κύνας Il.8.526; θεοῖσι.. ἑκατόμβας ῥέξειν Od.17.50, cf. Il.4.101, Pl.*Phd.*58b, *IG*1².108.55, 2².112.6 (iv B.C.): c. aor. inf., εὔχετο πάντ' ἀποδοῦναι *claimed* (the right) to pay in full, Il.18.499 (unless in signf. III. 3): c. pres. inf., ηὔξω θεοῖς.. ἂν ὧδ' ἔρδειν τάδε; A.*Ag.*933, cf. S.*Ph.*1032 codd. 2. c. acc. rei, *vow* a thing, πολλῶν πατησμὸν εἱμάτων A.*Ag.*963; ἱερεῖον Ar.*Av.*1619; [λύχνον] περὶ παιδός Call.*Ep.*56.3. 3. εὔ. κατά τινος of the thing vowed (as though on the altar), εὔ. τοῖς θεοῖς κατὰ ἑκατόμβης Plu.*Mar.*26, cf. 2.294b; κατὰ νικητηρίων D.*Ep.*1.16. III. *profess loudly*, *boast*, *vaunt*, οὕτω φησὶ καὶ εὔχεται, οὕνεκ' Ἀχιλλεὺς νηυσὶν ἔπι γλαφυρῇσι μένει Il.14.366; εὑρεῖν Emp.2.6: mostly, not of empty boasting, but of something of which one has a right to be proud, ταύτης τοι γενεῆς τε καὶ αἵματος εὔχομαι εἶναι Il.6.211, cf. 8.190; πατρὸς δ' ἐξ ἀγαθοῦ καὶ ἐγὼ γένος εὔχομαι εἶναι 14.113, cf. Pl.*Grg.*449a: rarely without inf., ἐκ Κρητάων γένος εὔχομαι (sc. εἶναι) Od.14.199; τὸ πατρόθεν ἐκ Διὸς εὔχονται Pi.*O.*7.23, cf. *P.*4.97; πόρτις εὔχεται βοός (sc. εἶναι) A.*Supp.*314; ἔνθεν εὔχομαι γένος E.*Fr.*696; but also, 2. *boast vainly*, *brag*, εὔχεαι αὔτως Il.11.388: c. inf., εὔ. δῃώσειν S.*OC*1318. 3. simply, *profess* or *declare*, ἱκέτης δέ τοι εὔ. εἶναι Od.5.450; οὔτ' ὢν ἀκοῦσαι οὔτ' ἰδεῖν εὔχοντο Pi.*O.*6.53; τίς χθὼν εὔχεται ἥδε [εἶναι]; A.R.4.1251; cf. supr. II. 1. IV. Pass., ἐμοὶ μετρίως ηὖκται I *have prayed* sufficiently, Pl.*Phdr.*279c: pf. inf., ταῦτα μὲν ηὖχθαι *IG*2².112.12 (iv B.C.); ἡ πανήγυρις ἡ.. εὐχθεῖσα *vowed*, D.C.48.32: but plpf. (or non-thematic preterite) ηὔγμην in act. sense, S.*Tr.*610; so εὖκτο Thebaïs *Fr.*3. (Cf. Skt. *óhate* 'to (be able to) boast that one is', 'to brag', Avest. *aog-* 'declare solemnly'.)

εὔχορδος, ον, *well-strung*, λύρα Pi.*N.*10.21.

εὔχορος, v. ἠΰχ-.

εὔχορτος, ον, of pasture, *fattening*, τοῦτο (sc. τὸ χωρίον) Arist.*HA*595b26; εὔχορτα πεδία Poetae ap.Poll.7.184: neut. pl. -χορτα *pastures*, *IGRom.*4.1349 (Lydia).

εὖχος, εος, τό, (εὔχομαι) poet. Noun: I. *thing prayed for*, *object of prayer*, εὖχος δοῦναι, ὀρέξαι, πορεῖν τινι, Il.5.285, 22.130, Od.22.7, S.*Ph.*1203; εὖχος ἀρέσθαι to obtain *it*, Il.7.203; ἑλεῖν Tyrt.12.36, Pi.*P.*5.21; Τεῦκρον.. εὖχος ἀπηύρα took *it* away from him, Il.15.462. II. *boast*, *vaunt*, μέλεον δέ οἱ εὖχος ἔδωκας 21.473; εὖχος ἔργῳ καθελών Pi.*O.*10(11).63, al.; of persons, Ἀνάκρεον, εὐ. Ἰώνων *AP*7.27 (Antip. Sid.). III. later, *vow*, *votive offering*, Pl.*Epigr.*5.3.

εὔχρεως, ων, f.l. for χρυσέῳ, Antim.*Eleg.*4.

εὐχρημᾰτ-έω, *to be wealthy*, Poll.3.109, 6.196. **-ία**, ἡ, *wealth*, ibid. **-ιστος**, ον, *good man of business*, Vett.Val.38.35, Ptol.*Tetr.*163. 2. *richly endowed*, ὑπὸ θεῶν Heph.Astr.1.1. **-ος**, ον, *wealthy*, Poll.3.109.

εὐχρημονέω, = εὐχρηματέω, Pl.Com.ap.Poll.6.196.

εὐχρηστ-έω, *to be serviceable*, τινι for a thing, Plb.12.18.3; εἴς τι Dsc.1.7; ἐπί τινι Ruf.ap.Orib.8.39.5, etc.; τινι to a person, *SIG*618.13 (Heraclea ad Latm., ii B.C.): abs., Chrysipp.*Stoic.*3.184, Diog.Bab.ib.3.233, *Michel* 163.22 (Delos). 2. *lend*, *advance*, *UPZ*123.26, *Inscr.Prien.*108.109 (ii B.C.). II. Pass., εὐχρηστεῖσθαι διά τινα *to receive assistance* through his means, D.S.5.12; ὑπό τινος Plu.2.185e. 2. *to be in common use*, of words, Eust.964.21, etc. **-ημα**, ατος, τό, *advantage received*, *Stoic.*3.23. **-ία**, ἡ, *ready use*, σκευῶν Arist.*Oec.*1345b1, cf. Ph.*Bel.*72.7; *utility*, *serviceableness*, Chrysipp.*Stoic.*3.168; πρός τι Plb.9.7.5. 2. *service rendered*, πλείστην εὐ. τῇ ἐπαρχείᾳ παρέξεσθαι *Inscr.Prien.*105.25 (i B.C.). II. *credit*, D.S.1.79. **-ος**, ον, also -η, ον Orph.*Fr.*272: (χράομαι):—*useful*, *serviceable*, ἔν τινι Hp.*Fract.*16 (Sup.); πρός τι Pl.*Lg.*777b, X.*Mem.*3.8.5, etc.; εἴς τι D.S.5.40 (Sup.); of persons, c. dat., *PPetr.*3p.153 (iii B.C.); τῷ δήμῳ *Inscr.Prien.*102.5 (ii/i B.C.); σκεῦος εὔ. τῷ δεσπότῃ 2*Ep.Ti.*2.21; εὔχρησται ἡμέραι, in astrology, Orph.*Fr.*272. Adv. -τως Chrysipp.*Stoic.*2.334; εὐ. ἔχειν πρός τι Plb.3.73.5, Ael.*Tact.*3.2. II. *easy to execute*, διίππευσις ib.18.4. **-ότης**, ητος, ἡ, *serviceableness*, Simp.*in Ph.*373.26 (pl.).

εὐχρηστόψῡχος, ον, *having useful moral qualities*, *Cat.Cod.Astr.*8(3).188.

εὐχρόαστος, ον, f.l. for εὔχρηστος in X.*Eq.*1.17.

εὐ-χροέω, *to be of a good*, *healthy look*, Hp.*Morb.*2.1, Ar.*Lys.*80, Gal.17(2).215. **-χροής**, ές, rare poet. form for εὔχροος, δέρμα βόειον εὐχροές Od.14.24. **-χροια**, Ion. -οίη, ἡ, *goodness of complexion*, *fresh and healthy look*, Hp.*Coac.*67, Arist.*HA*584a14, Thphr.*Sud.*39, Dsc.*Eup.*1.105, Aret.*SA*2.4. **-χροος**, ον, contr. **-χρους**, ουν, Ion. **-χροιος**, ον, (χρόα) *well-coloured*, *of good* or *healthy complexion*, Hp.*Aph.*3.17, X.*Lac.*5.8, etc.; κριὸν εὔχρουν *IG*5(1).1390.67 (Andania, i B.C.): Comp. -οώτερος X.*Cyr.*8.1.41; -ούστερος Arist.*Pr.*863b1: Sup. -ούστατος ib.960b5. 2. in Music, εὔχροα χρώματα Philoch.66.

εὔχρῡσος, ον, *rich in gold*, of the Pactolus, S.*Ph.*394 (lyr.); Σάρδεις Max.Tyr.27.3 (Sup.).

εὔχρωμος, ον, = εὔχρως, *Gloss.* Adv. -μως '*safe and sound*', *PRyl.*237.8 (iii A.D.); also in an epitaph, ζήσας εὐχρώμως *Rendic.d.Pontif.Accad.Rom.Ser.*iii vol.3.192.

εὔχρως, ων, = εὔχροος, Ar.*Eq.*1171, *Th.*644, Theopomp.Com.24, X.*Oec.*10.5: pl., εὔχρω Arist.*PA*677a23; *ruddy*, Thphr.*HP.*3.9.7; *bright-coloured*, ib.7.3.1. 2. of music, = εὔχροος, condemned by Pl.*Lg.*655a. (Only used in nom. and acc.)

εὐχρωτέω, imper. -χρώτ(ε)ι, in an epitaph, = ὑγίαινε, χαῖρε, etc., *IG*14.2305.

εὐχῡλ-ία, ἡ, *goodness of flavour*, Hices.ap.Ath.3.87c, Xenocr.ap.Orib.2.58.57; *wholesomeness of juice*, Sor.1.53. **-ος**, ον, *juicy*, *succulent*, Thphr.*CP*6.11.15 (Comp.), Archig.ap.Gal.12.460, etc.; of meat, Alex.189, Diph.Siph.ap.Ath.2.62c, Hices.ib.7.282d: metaph., Phld.*Po.*1676 *Fr.*11. Adv. -λως Hp.*Mul.*1.17.

εὐχῡμ-ία, ἡ, = εὐχυλία, Hp.*Loc.Hom.*10 (dub. l.), Thphr.*CP*6.11.4. II. Medic., *healthy state of the humours*, Gal.11.491, al. 2. of food, *faculty of producing such a state*, Id.6.749. **-ος**, ον, *well-flavoured*, Posidon.3 J.; πρὸς τὴν ἐδωδὴν εὔ. Arist.*GA*763b7: Comp., Plu.2.690a. II. *productive of healthy humours*, *wholesome*, Hp.*Aff.*55, Gal.17(2).876. III. *plump*, *in good condition*, Ptol.*Tetr.*144.

εὔχῠτος, ον, *easily dissolved*, Dsc.5.153; ἔς τι Aret.*CD*1.3; gloss on ἑανοῦ, Sch.D Il.18.612.

εὐχωλ-ή, ἡ, (εὔχομαι) Ep. form of εὐχή, *prayer*, *vow*, οὔτ' ἄρ' ὅ γ' εὐχωλῆς ἐπιμέμφεται οὔθ' ἑκατόμβης Il.1.93, cf. 65; θυέεσσι καὶ εὐχωλῇς ἀγανῇσι 9.499, cf. Od.13.357; εὐχωλέων οὐκ ἔκλυε Φοῖβος Hes.*Sc.*68; also in *Inscr.Cypr.*94 H. and Ion. Prose, Hdt.2.63, Protag.A 1 Diels, Luc.*Syr.D.*28, 29. 2. *votive offering*, *Sammelb.*1719, al. II. *boast*, *vaunt*, πῇ ἔβαν εὐχωλαί, ὅτε δὴ φάμεν εἶναι ἄριστοι Il.8.229; *shout of triumph*, ἔνθα δ' ἅμ' οἰμωγή τε καὶ εὐχωλὴ πέλεν ἀνδρῶν 4.450. 2. *object of boasting*, *glory*, κὰδ δέ κεν εὐχωλὴν Πριάμῳ καὶ Τρωσὶ λίποιεν Ἀργείην Ἑλένην 2.160, cf. 4.173; ὅ μοι.. εὐ. κατὰ ἄστυ πελέσκεο 22.433. **-ῐμαῖος**, α, ον, *bound by a vow*, *under a vow*, Hdt.2.63; used as translation of Celtic *soldurii*, Nic.Dam.*Fr.*80 J. 2. εὐ. θέαι, = Lat. *ludi votivi*, D.C.79.9. II. = εὐκταῖος, *yearned*, *longed for*, Poll.5.130.

εὐχώρητος, ον, *giving free passage*, φλέβες, ἀρτηρίαι, Steph.*in Hp.*2.373 D. II. *easily accommodated*, *EM*285.16.

εὐχώριστος, ον, (χωρίζω) *easy to separate*, Thphr.*CP*4.6.8, Nicom.*Harm.*2.

εὐψάμαθος [ψᾰ], ον, *sandy*, *AP*6.223 (Antip.).

εὐψηλάφητος [ᾰ], ον, gloss on εὐαφής, Suid.; on εὔθικτος, *EM*391.30. Adv. -τως, gloss on εὐθίκτως, Hsch.

εὔψηφις, ιδος, ὁ, ἡ, *with many pebbles*, *shingly*, Nonn.*D.*10.163.

εὔψοφος, ον, *well-sounding*, cj. in D.Chr.12.36.

εὔψυκτος, ον, *easy to cool* or *chill*, Arist.*Sens.*444a12, *Pr.*887b31 (Comp.), Gal.1.329.

εὐψυχ-έω, *to be of good courage*, *Ep.Phil.*2.19, J.*AJ*11.6.9, *BGU*1097.15 (i A.D.), Poll.3.135. II. εὐψύχει *farewell!* a common inscr.

on tombs, *IG*12(2).393 (Mytilene), etc. 2. εὐψυχεῖν, = χαίρειν, in a letter of condolence, *POxy.*115.1 (ii A.D.). -ής, ές, (ψῦχος) *agreeably cool*, τὸ τῆς πόλεως εὐ. Hdn.6.6.4: Comp., Id.1.12.2, Antyll.ap. Orib.9.13.1: written -ψυγής, Aët.5.74. -ία, ἡ, *good courage, high spirit*, A.*Pers.*326, E.*Med.*403, Th.1.121, etc.; *goodness of soul*, opp. κακοψυχία, Pl.*Lg.*791c. -ος, ον, (ψυχή) *of good courage, stout of heart*, θράσος A.*Pers.*394; ἀνήρ E.*Rh.*510, etc.: Comp., Philostr. *VA*6.20; τὸ.. ἐς τὰ ἔργα εὔψυχον Th.2.39, cf. 43, 4.126; -ότατοι πρὸς τὸ ἐπιέναι Id.2.11. Adv. -χως X.*Eq.Mag.*8.21. II. (ψύχω) *cooling*, Thphr.*CP*5.14.1 (Comp.).

εὕω, aor. 1 εὖσα (v. infr.), *singe*, esp. of singeing off the bristles of swine before they are cooked, εὗσέ τε μίστυλλέν τε καὶ ἀμφ' ὀβελοῖσιν ἔπειρεν Od.14.75, cf. 426, 2.300; σύες εὑόμενοι τανύοντο διὰ φλογός Il.9.468; so of the Cyclops, πάντα δέ οἱ βλέφαρ' ἀμφὶ καὶ ὀφρύας εὗσεν ἀϋτμή Od.9.389: metaph., of a shrewish wife, ἄνδρα.. εὕει ἄτερ δαλοῦ Hes.*Op.*705 (αὔει codd. Stob.). (Sts. εὔω in codd., v.l. Il.9.468 (cf. *EM*401.24), Od.2.300 (cf. *EM*398.34), Hes. l.c.: but v. ἀφ-εύω, ἐφ-εύω; cf. Lat. *uro* fr. **eus-ō*.)

εὐωδ-έω, *to be fragrant*, Hdn.*Epim.*250. -ης, ες, (ὄδωδα) *sweet-smelling, fragrant*, ἐν θαλάμῳ εὐώδεϊ Il.3.382; ἔλαιον Od.2.339; κυπάρισσος 5.64: Comp. -έστερος Pl.*Hp.Ma.*290e, Arist.*Pr.*877^b25: Sup. -έστατος Hdt.3.112; ἄδυτον Pi.*O.*7.32, cf. B.13.40, etc.; ὀδόντες Hp.*Mul.*2.185; opp. δυσώδης, Arist.*de An.*421^b23; εὐῶδες ὄζειν Id. *Pr.*906^b14; of wines, *having a bouquet*, *PTeb.*120.62 (i B.C.), etc. -ία, Ion. -ίη, ἡ, *sweet smell*, Hdt.4.75, X.*Smp.*2.3, etc.; esp. of sacrifices, ὀσμὴ -ίας LXX *Ge.*8.21: metaph. in *Ep.Eph.*5.2: in pl., Pl.*Ti.* 65a: in pl., also, *fragrant substances*, D.S.1.84. -ιάζω, *have a sweet savour*, '*bouquet*', οἶνος -άζων LXX *Za.*9.17: c. acc. cogn., ὀσμὴν εὐ. *emit a sweet* savour, ib.*Si.*39.14:—Pass., *to be fragrant*, Str.15. 2.3, Dsc.2.76.8. -ίζομαι, *perceive a sweet smell*, S.E.*M.*7.293; ὑπό τινος ib.11.227.

εὐώδῑν, ῑνος, ὁ, ἡ, *happy as a parent, fruitful*, Opp.*C.*3.19; νηδύς *AP*6.201 (Marc. Arg.); epith. of Demeter, Max.529; εὐ. ἐς ζῴων γένεσιν Ael.*NA*13.5; of women, *easily delivered*, ib.4.29. II. Pass., *happily born*, Coluth.281, Nonn.*D.*14.148.

εὐώλενος, ον, *fair-armed*, Pi.*P.*9.17 codd.; δεξιά E.*Hipp.*605.

εὐωμοσία, ἡ, *observance of an oath*, Hdn.*Epim.*205.

εὐώμοτος, ον, (ὄμνυμι) *observing oaths*, Poll.1.39.

εὐων-έω, *buy cheaply*, *PGiss.*79 iii 15 (ii A.D.). -ητος, ον, *well-bought, cheap*, τὸ εὐ. Str.5.1.12. -ία, ἡ, *cheapness*, Plb.2.15.4, *PGiss.*79 iii 14 (ii A.D.). -ίζω, *hold cheap*, Aq.*Ps.*11(12).9 (Pass.).

Εὐώνιος, ὁ (sc. μήν), name of a month at Halos, *GDI*1461.

εὔωνος, ον, *of fair price, cheap*, Hp.*Nat.Mul.*59 (Sup.), Epich.42. 10, Pl.*Euthd.*304b (Sup.), D.18.89 (Comp.), *PCair.Zen.*48.5 (iii B.C.), etc.; ἀείσιτος Epich.34; φίλοι X.*Mem.*2.10.4 (Sup.); θάνατος *AP*11. 169 (Nicarch.); of persons, εὐ. εἰς ὅ τι μισθοῖντο App.*BC*2.120: irreg. Comp. -νέστερος Epich.121. Adv. -νως, Sup. -ότατα *IG*12(3).169 (Astypalaea). [εὐ- short in Hippon.22 B.]

εὐωνύμ-ιος [ῠ], α, ον, dub. cj. in Corinn.19. -ος (A), ον, (ὄνομα) *of good name, honoured*, Hes.*Th.*409, Pi.*O.*2.7, etc.; εὐ. χάρις the honour *of a good name*, Id.*P.*11.58; δίκη.. μὴ εὐ. not *creditable*, Pl.*Lg.* 754e. 2. *expressed in well-chosen terms*, λόγος Luc.*Lex.*1. II. *having an auspicious name* or *sound*, ἀριστοκρατία Pl.*Plt.*302d; πρόσρημα D.C.52.4. 2. *prosperous, fortunate*, δίκα, πόδες, Pi.*N.* 7.48, 8.47, cf. Eust.895.37. 3. epith. of Artemis, 'Αρχ. 'Εφ. 1914.20 (Gonni, iv/iii B.C.). III. euphem. (like ἀριστερός) for *left, on the left hand* (because *bad omens came from the left*), ὠλένη εὐ. S.*Tr.*926; ἐξ εὐωνύμου χειρός Hdt.7.109; ἐξ εὐωνύμου (sc. χειρός) Id.1.72; κατὰ τὰ εὐ. X.*Lac.*11.10; εἰς τὰ εὐ. παρεκκλίνειν Arist.*PA* 666^b7; ἐπὶ τὰ εὐ. ἀνακλίνεσθαι Id.*HA*498^a11; ἐξ -ωνύμων *Ev.Matt.* 20.21; as military term, τὸ εὐ. κέρας Hdt.6.111, Th.5.67, etc.; τὸ εὐ. (without κέρας) Th.4.96. 2. euphem. of *bad* omens, opp. οἱ δεξιοί φύσιν, A.*Pr.*490, cf. *SIG*1167.3 (Ephesus, vi/v B.C.). 3. Astron., *southerly*, Cleom.1.1. -ος (B), ἡ, *spindle-tree, Euonymus europaeus*, Plin.*HN*13.118; τὸ εὐ. δένδρον Thphr.*HP*3.18.13.

εὐώπιον, = πυρὰ παρθενική, at Troezen, Hsch.

εὐῶπις, ιδος, ἡ, (ὤψ) *fair-eyed*, or *fair to look on*, εὐώπιδα κούρην Od. 6.113, 142, *h.Cer.*333, cf. S.*Tr.*523 (lyr.), *Pae.Erythr.*13, Call.*Dian.* 204; εὐ. Σελάνα Pi.*O.*10(11).74: in later Prose, of Hera, Max.Tyr. 14.6.

εὐωπός (A), όν, = εὐώψ, E.*Or.*918, D.P.1075, Babr.124.9; εὐ. πύλαι *friendly* gates, E.*Ion* 1611 (troch.): in later Prose, Max.Tyr.8.3. II. *seeing well*, Arist.*GA*780^b36; εὐ. ὄμμα, of a snake, Ael.*NA*8.12.

εὐωπός (B), ὁ, a *sea-fish*, Opp.*H.*1.256.

εὐωρέω, (εὔωρος I) *to be negligent*, Hsch.

εὐωρία, ἡ, (ὥρα) *fineness of the season*, Longus 1.9. II. (ὥρα) *freedom from care*, *Sammelb.*4324.7.

εὐωριάζω, = εὐωρέω, S.*Fr.*561, prob. for ἐξωρ- in A.*Pr.*17 (cf. Hsch. and Phot.).

εὔωρος, ον, (ὥρα) *careless, neglectful*, οὐδέ τοι εὔωροι θυέων Euph. 129. II. (ὥρα) εὔωρος γῆ *fruitful* land, Hsch.; εὔωρος γάμος, Lat. *maturae nuptiae*, S.*Fr.*200.

εὐωχ-έω, fut. -ήσω Thphr.*Char.*8.3: aor. 1 -ησα Metag.14, etc.:—Med. and Pass., Aeol. part. εὐωχήμενος Alc.*Supp.*23.5: fut. Med. -ήσομαι Ar.*Ec.*717, Pl.*R.*372b: aor. 1 εὐωχησάμην Luc.*Sat.*11: but fut. Pass. εὐωχηθήσομαι *IG*12(5).946.8 (Tenos): aor. 1 εὐωχήθην (v. infr.): pf. εὐώχημαι Hp.*Steril.*220, Ar.*Lys.*1224:—the augm. is never found (it is cj. in Pl.*Grg.*522a): (εὖ, ἔχω, cf. Ath.8.363b):—*entertain sumptuously*, c. acc. pers., Hdt.1.126, 4.73, 95, E.*Cyc.*346, Ar.*V.*341, etc.; of animals, *to feed well*, θηρίον Pl.*R.*588e; τὰς ὗς Arist.*HA*595^a24:—Med. and Pass., *fare sumptuously, feast*, εὐωχήμενος Alc. l.c.; εὐωχέονται Hdt.5.8; ὡς ἔθυσαν καὶ εὐωχήθησαν Id.1.31; εὐωχημένοι, εὐωχηθέντες, *after dinner*, Ar.*Lys.*1224, *Ec.*664: c. acc. cogn., *feast upon, enjoy*, κρέα εὐωχοῦ X.*Cyr.*1.3.6, cf. Hp.*Steril.* l.c., Plb.8.24.13; εὐωχεῖσθαι ἐπινίκια *to hold a feast* of triumph, Luc. *Nav.*39; εὐ. γάμους, ἑορτήν, Hld.7.26, 8.7; of animals, *eat their fill*, X.*An.*5.3.11, *Eq.Mag.*8.4; καχρύων ὀνίδιον εὐωχημένον *having eaten its fill of* barley, Ar.*V.*1306. II. metaph., of other luxuries, εὐωχοῦντες [αὐτοὺς] ὧν ἐπεθύμουν Pl.*Grg.*518e; πολλὰ καὶ ἡδέα.. ηὐώχουν ὑμᾶς ib.522a (εὐ- codd.); so εὐωχεῖν τινα καινῶν λόγων *to entertain* him *with* them, Thphr.*Char.*8.3:—Med., *relish, enjoy*, c. gen., εὐωχοῦ τοῦ λόγου Pl.*R.*352b. III. Act. in med. sense, And.*Fr.*1. -ητέον, *one must feast*, λόγοις τὰς ἀγαθὰς ψυχάς Max.Tyr.28.5. -ητήριον, τό, *banqueting-house*, Greg.Cor.p.527 S. -ητής, οῦ, ὁ, *a reveller, guest*, Sch.rec.A.*Pr.*1022. -ητικός, ή, όν, *festive*, *Gloss.* -ία, ἡ, *good cheer, feasting*, Ar.*Ach.*1009 (lyr.), *Ra.*85, Hp.*Aff.*27, etc.; ποιεῖν τὴν εὐ. to hold the *wake*, *CIG*3028 (Ephesus): in pl., *festivities*, Ar.*Fr.*216, Pl.*R.*329a, al. 2. generally, *supply of provisions* for an army, Plb.3.92.9; *plenty*, σίτου Ruf.ap.Orib.6.38.10. II. metaph., λόγων εὐωχίαι *feasts* of reason, *AP*4.3.6 (Agath.). -ιάζω, = εὐωχέω, v.l. in Lib.*Descr.*9.5. -ιαστικός, ὁ, translation of Lat. *Cibullius*, Lyd.*Mens.*4.1.

εὐώψ, ῶπος, ὁ, ἡ, (ὤψ) *fair-eyed* or *fair to look on*, παρειά S.*Ant.*530 (anap.); εὐῶπα πέμψον ἀλκάν send *goodly* aid, Id.*OT*189 (lyr.).

ἔφα, Dor. for ἔφη, v. φημί. **ἐφαάνθη**, Ep. for ἐφάνθη, v. φαίνω. **ἔφᾱβος, ἐφᾱβικός**, Dor. for ἐφηβ-.

ἐφαγιστεύω, ἐφαγνίζω, v. ἀφ-.

ἐφαιμάσσω, *make bloody*, Orib.46.24.3, Cleopatra ap. Gal.12. 404:—Pass., Cass.*Pr.*57.

ἐφαιμορρᾱγέω, *have secondary haemorrhage*, Heliod.ap.Orib.50. 52.1:—also -**αιμορροέω**, Id.ib.50.51.1.

ἐφαιρέω, *take hold on, overspread*, ἐπὶ χλόος εἷλε παρειάς A.R.2. 1216. II. Med. -**αιρέομαι**, aor. 2 -ειλόμην, *choose as successor*, D.C.49.43:—Pass., *to be chosen* or *appointed to succeed* another, ἄρχειν Th.4.38, cf. *IG*9(1).694.93 (Corc.). 2. ὅσσουν ἐφάγγρενθείν κινες Thess. for ὅσων ἐφαιροῦνται (= κατηγοροῦσι) τινες whomsoever any persons *accuse*, ib.9(2).517.41 (Larissa, iii B.C.).

ἐφᾰκέομαι, v. ἐπακέομαι.

ἐφάλιος [ᾰ], ον, (ἅλς B) = ἔφαλος, Phot., Suid.

ἐφάλλομαι, fut. -αλοῦμαι LXX 1*Ki.*10.6: Ep. aor. 2 ἐπᾶλτο, part. ἐπάλμενος, ἐπιάλμενος (v. infr.): regul. aor. 2 inf. -αλέσθαι *IG*4.951. 27 (Epid., iv B.C.):—*spring upon*, so as to *attack*, c. dat., 'Αστεροπαίῳ ἐπᾶλτο Il.21.140, cf. 13.643; Τρώεσσιν ἐπάλμενος 11.489, etc.; ἐπάλμενος ὀξέϊ δουρί ib.421, cf. Od.14.220: without hostile sense, c. gen., ἵππων ἐπιάλμενος *having leaped upon* the chariot, Il.7.15; κύσσε.. μιν .. ἐπιάλμενος Od.24.320; of fame, ἐς Αἰθίοπας ἐπᾶλτο Pi.*N.*6.50: rare in Prose, ἐπὶ τὸν οὐδὸν ἐ. (a Homeric reminiscence) Pl.*Ion* 535b; ἐπὶ τὰν χήρα *IG* l.c.; ἐπί τινας *Act.Ap.*19.16; ἵπποις Plu.2.139b; θαλάττης Alciphr.1.10; ζῴῳ, in hostile sense, Philum.*Ven.*33.3; εἰς τοὐπίσω ἐ., of an exercise, Gal.6.145: metaph., of the spirit of prophecy, LXX l.c.

ἔφαλμος, ον, *steeped in brine, salted*, βρώματα Plu.2.687d: **ἔφαλμα**, ατος, τό, in Thphr.*CP*5.9.6, is prob. corrupt.

ἔφᾰλος, ον, (ἅλς B) *on the sea*, of seaports, Κηρινθόν τ' ἔφαλον Il.2. 538, cf. 584, S.*Aj.*190 (lyr.); οἰκία Philostr.*Im.*1.12; ἡ ἔ. (sc. γῆ) *the coast*, Luc.*Am.*7.

ἐφᾱλόω, Dor. for ἐφηλ-, Hsch.

ἔφαλσις, εως, ἡ, *bouncing on* to a surface, Arist.*Pr.*913^b30 (s.v.l.).

ἐφάμᾱν [φᾰ], Dor. for ἐφάμην, v. φημί.

ἐφᾰμαρτάνω, causal, *seduce to sin*, LXX *Je.*39(32).35. II. abs., *miss one's aim*, Tryph.*Trop.*p.194 S.

ἐφᾰμαρτέω, = ἐφομαρτέω, Herod.5.43; read by Aristarch. in Il. 12.412, al.

ἐφάμαρτος [ᾰμ], ον, *sinful*, Eust.1365.40. **ἐφαμάω**, v. ἐπαμάομαι.

ἐφάμερος, ἐφᾱμέριος, Dor. for ἐφημ-.

ἐφάμιλλος [ᾰ], ον, (ἅμιλλα) *a match for, equal to, rivalling*, ἐ. γίγνεσθαί τινι X.*Mem.*3.3.12, Isoc.1.12 codd.; ἀρχὴ ἐ. ταῖς μεγίσταις Plb. 32.8.3; τὸ ἐ. *equality, evenness*, Plu.2.153f. Adv. -λως, ἀγωνίσασθαι Id.*Cleom.*39, cf. Aristaenet.1.2. II. Pass., *regarded as an object of rivalry* or *contention*, ἐφαμίλλου τῆς εἰς τὴν πατρίδα εὐνοίας ἐν κοινῷ πᾶσι κειμένης D.18.320; ἐφάμιλλον ποιεῖν τι Id.20.102; νίκην ἐ. ποιεῖν Plu. 2.214d; ὅπως ἐφάμιλλον ᾖ πᾶσι.. φιλοδοξεῖν *IG*2².1227.20, cf. 1292.18.

'Εφάμιος, epith. of Zeus, Hsch.

ἔφαμμ-α, ατος, τό, = ἐφαπτίς, Plb.2.28.8. -ᾰτίζω, *bind upon* or *together*, Orib.49.22.23, cj. in Sor.*Fasc.*48. -ίζω, in Pass., *become covered with sand*, *PTeb.*60.42 (ii B.C.). -ος, ον, *sandy*, Thphr. *CP*2.4.4, etc. (nisi leg. ὕφαμμος).

ἔφᾰν, Ep. for ἔφασαν, v. φημί.

ἐφανδάνω, Ep. **ἐπιανδάνω**, *please, be grateful to*, c. dat., ἐμοὶ δ' ἐπιανδάνει οὕτως Il.7.407; βουλήν, ἥ ῥα θεοῖσιν ἐφήνδανε ib.45; τοῖσιν δ' ἐπήνδανε μῦθος Od.16.406: aor. ἐπεύαδεν Musae.180: c. inf., A.R. 3.950, Orph.*A.*773.

ἐφάπᾰλος [ᾰπ], ον, *somewhat tender*, φυτόν *Gp.*10.78.3.

ἐφάπαξ [ᾰπ], Adv. *once for all*, Eup.175, *Ep.Rom.*6.10, *Ep.Hebr.* 7.27, etc. II. *at once*, 1*Ep.Cor.*15.6.

ἐφαπλ-όω, *spread* or *unfold over*, ἄωτον Orph.*A.*1336: c. gen., λέων .. γυῖα γῆς ἐφαπλώσας Babr.95.2; στῆθος ἐφαπλώσας.. ὄχθης Nonn. *D.*15.9: c. dat., δίκτυα νεπόδεσσιν ἐ. ib.20.385; ἐρετμοῖς χεῖρας Orph.

A.457: metaph., ἐ. τὸ ἀγαθὸν διὰ τοῦ κόσμου Hierocl.*in CA*21 p.467 M.:—Pass., τοὺς ἐμπροσθίους πόδας ἐφηπλῶσθαι ταῖς χερσί *to have* the skin of the front feet *spread over* the hands, Longus 1.20; σκότος ἐφήπλωται v.l. in Plu.2.167a. **-ωμα**, ατος, τό, *anything spread over, rug, cloak*, Eust.1347.40. **-ωτέον**, *one must spread over*, κατά τινων ὀθόνιον Sor.2.11.

ἐφαπτίς, ίδος, ἡ, *soldier's upper garment*, *PMagd*.13.6 (iii B.C.), Plb.30.25.10, Callix.2, Anon.ap.Suid.: Astron., the *cloak* of the figure Sagittarius, Ptol.*Tetr*.25 (pl.), Heph.Astr.1.3 (pl.). 2. *ephod*, J.*AJ*3.7.7. II. *woman's garment*, Str.7.2.3.

ἐφάπτ-ω, Ion. **ἐπάπτω**, *bind on* or *to*, πότμον ἐφάψαις ὀρφανόν *having fixed* it as his doom, Pi.*O*.9.60; τί δ'.. ἐγὼ λύουσ' ἂν ἢ 'φάπτουσα προσθείμην πλέον; what should I gain by undoing or *by making fast* [Creon's command]? v.l. in S.*Ant*.40; ἔγνω..τοὔργον κατ' ὀργὴν ὡς ἐφάψειεν τόδε he knew that she *had made fast* (i.e. perpetrated) the deed, Id.*Tr*.933:—Pass., 3 sg. pf. and plpf. ἐφῆπται, -το, *is* or *was hung over* one, *fixed as* one's *fate* or *doom*, c. dat. pers., Τρώεσσι κήδε' ἐφῆπται Il.2.15, cf. 6.241; Τρώεσσιν ὀλέθρου πείρατ' ἐφῆπται 7.402, cf. Od.22.41; ἐφῆπτο ib.33; ἀθανάτοισιν ἔρις καὶ νεῖκος ἐφῆπται Il.21.513. II. Med., aor. 1 ἐφηψάμην, 3 sg. ἐφάψατο Pi.*P*.8.63; *lay hold of*, once in Hom., ἐπὴν χείρεσσιν ἐφάψεαι ἠπείροιο Od.5.348, cf. Thgn.6, A.*Supp*.412, etc.; ἱκέτης ἔφαψαι πατρός S.*Aj*.1172, etc.; ξίφους E.*El*.1225 (lyr.); *partake of* food, Iamb.*VP*3.17; *treat*, ἰατρῶν δίκην ἐ. Philostr.*VA*8.7; ἐπεί γε τοῦδ' ἐφάπτομαι τόπου *reach* it, E.*Hel*.556; σκοπιᾶς ἐφάψασθαι ποδοῖν Pi.*N*.9.47. b. Geom., *touch*, Euc.3 *Def*.3, etc.; in Arist., of a circle, *pass through* angular points, *Mete*.376ᵇ9; of a point, *lie on* a circle as locus, ib.376ᵃ6. c. as law-term, c. gen., *claim as one's property*, S.*OC*859, Pl.*Lg*.915c, *GDI*1883.17 (Delph.), *Milet*.3 No.140.29: c. dat., *GDI*1780.8 (Delph.). d. generally, *lay violent hands upon*, τοίχου, ἱματίου, Pl.*R*.574d. 2. *lay hold of* or *reach* with the mind, *attain to*, τοῦ ἀληθοῦς Id.*Smp*.212a; ἐ. τινὸς μνήμῃ, αἰσθήσει, Id.*Phdr*.253a, *Phd*.65d; ἐ. ἀμφοῖν τῇ ψυχῇ Id.*Tht*.190c (c. acc., dub. in *Lg*.664e); ἐ. λόγων *touch upon, meddle with*, Pi.*O*.9.12; ζητημάτων Pl.*Lg*.891c; *apply oneself to*, ἐξηγήσεως Gal.16.558. 3. c. dat. rei, *apply oneself to*, ἔπεσι, τέχναις, κελεύθοις ζωᾶς, Pi.*O*.1.86, *P*.8.63, *N*.8.36. 4. c. gen. rei, εἴδεος ἐπαμμένος *possessing* a certain degree of beauty, Hdt.1.199, 8.105; τὰ ἐν τῷ μέσῳ ἁπάσης ταύτης τῆς ἕξεως ἐφαπτόμενα [σώματα] bodies *possessing* all these qualities in moderation, Pl.*Lg*.728e; θηριώδους καὶ ἀλόγου μᾶλλον ἢ λογικῆς ἐφάπτεσθαι δοκεῖ φωνῆς, of the sibilant *s*, D.H.*Comp*.14. 5. *follow, come next*, f.l. for ἐφεψάσθω, Theoc.9.2. III. Pass., *to be kindled*: hence, *blush*, Id.14.23. **-ώδης**, ες, *like an* ἐφαπτίς, Phot. s. v. σπολάς. **-ωρ**, ορος, ὁ, also ἡ, *laying hold of, seizing*, ῥυσίων A.*Supp*.728. II. *one who strokes* or *caresses*, ib.312, 535 (lyr.) (with ref. to the name Ἔπαφος).

ἐφαρδμόν· ἀρδευτὸν πεδίον, Hsch. **ἐφαρίξαντο**· ἐψήσαντο, Id. (fort. ἐψαφίξαντο· ἐψηφίσαντο).

ἐφαρμ-ογή, ἡ, *adjustment*, πρός τι Plu.2.780b: Geom., of figures, *coincidence*, Cleom.2.5, Simp.*in Cael*.184.21; *adjustment of claims*, Hero *Metr*.3 *Praef*. II. *agreement*, τῶν προλήψεων ταῖς οὐσίαις Arr.*Epict*.1.22.2. III. *union*, Plot.6.9.11. **-όζω**, Att. **-όττω**, Dor. **-όσδω** Theoc.1.53. I. intr., *fit on* or *to*, πειρήθη δ' ἕο αὐτοῦ ἐν ἔντεσι ..εἰ οἷ ἐφαρμόσσειε Il.19.385 (unless trans.). 2. *to be adapted* or *capable of adaptation to*, τινι Arist.*APo*.88ᵃ33, *Pol*.1276ᵇ25, al.; ἐπί τινος Id.*Ph*.201ᵇ14, al.; ἐπί τι ib.228ᵇ25, al.; ὁ..μάλιστ' ἂν ἐφαρμόσας πολίτης ἐπὶ πάντας τοὺς..πολίτας Id.*Pol*.1275ᵃ33: abs., ὁ λόγος οὐκ ἐ. Id.*Cael*.308ᵇ2, etc.; *tally*, Id.*Resp*.474ᵃ10: Geom., *coincide*, ἐπί τι Euc.1.4, Archim.*Con.Sph*.18: c. dat., ibid., Papp.244.9:—Pass., c. dat., Plot.4.4.23. 3. *befit, suit*, [οἴνῳ] ἐφαρμόζουσιν ἀοιδαί Panyas.14.2; *to be applicable*, of a test, ἐπί τινος Arist.*Pol*.1275ᵇ32. II. trans., *fit* one thing *on to* another, οἱ χροῒ κόσμον Hes.*Op*.76; τοὔνομ'..ἐλεγείῳ Critias 4 D.; σχοίνῳ [τοὺς ἀνθέρικας] Theoc.1.53:—Med., ζεύγλαν ἐφηρμόσατο *AP*9.19 (Arch.). b. Geom., in Pass., of a figure, *to be applied to* another figure, ἐπί τι Euc.1.4, Archim.*Aequil.Prooem*.; γραμμὴ γραμμῇ Plot.2.7.1. 2. *suit, accommodate*, τὰς δαπάνας ταῖς προσόδοις X.*Ages*.8.8; τοὺς λόγους τοῖς προσώποις D.H.*Lys*.13; λόγῳ μέλη καὶ μέτρα καὶ ῥυθμούς, Plu.2.769c, cf. Orph.*A*.1001; *apply*, τι ἐπί τι Arist.*APo*.75ᵇ4; *refer*, τι ἔς τινα Luc.*Pisc*.38; λόγων τε πίστιν ..ἐφαρμόσαι *to add fitting* assurance, S.*Tr*.623:—Med., χάρματι καὶ λύπῃ μέτρον ἐφηρμόσατο *AP*9.768 (Agath.), cf. 10.26 (Luc.):—Pass., *adapt oneself to*, τινι Epic.ap.Clearch.47, cf. Antig.*Mir*.25. **-οσις**, εως, ἡ, = ἐφαρμογή, τόπων καὶ τάξιος Ti.Locr.95c, cf. Procl.*Hyp*.3.13. **-οστέον**, *one must adapt*, τινί τι Plb.1.14.8, Plu.2.34f, Luc.*Hist.Conscr*.6.

ἐφάρξαντο, Att. for ἐφράξαντο.

ἐφαρπάζω, perh. by mistake for ἀφαρπ–, *Sammelb*.4315.4.

ἐφαύριον, = ἐπαύριον, *PHamb*.27.4 (iii B.C.), *PTeb*.119.17 (ii B.C.).

ἔφαψις, εως, ἡ, *touching, caressing*, A.*Supp*.45 (lyr.), Sch.A.R.1.842. 2. *knot*, Paul.Aeg.6.51.

ἐφέασθεν· ἐγέλασαν, διεχύθησαν, Hsch.

ἐφεβδομᾰτικός, ή, όν, *presiding over the week*, θεοί *PLeid.W*.1.34, 2.10.

ἐφέβδομος, ον, *containing* $1+\frac{1}{7}$, Theo Sm.p.77 H., Iamb.*in Nic*.p.84 P., Hero *Stereom*.1.20.2, al.; cf. ἐπιέβδομος.

ἐφεγρήσσων· ὁ ἀγρυπνῶν, Hsch. **ἐφεδές**· ἐπίπεδον, ταπεινόν, χαμαί, Id. **ἐφεδέτα(ι)**, title of officials at Samos, Id.

ἐφέδρ-α, Ion. **ἐπέδρη**, ἡ, *sitting by* or *before* a place: hence, *siege, blockade*, Hdt.1.17; ἐπέδρην ποιήσασθαι Id.5.65; *observation* of a besieged place, Ath.Mech.18.14 (pl.). 2. *sitting upon*, Pl.*Plt*.288a. II. *stable*, Phleg.*Mir*.3. 2. *base*, Hero *Spir*.1.30. 3. *surface* of a threshold, *Rev.Phil*.44.249 (Didyma, ii B.C.). III. a plant, = ἵππουρις, Hsch., Plin.*HN*26.36, Ps.-Dsc.4.46. **-άζω**, pf. part. ἐφηδρακώς, *set* or *rest upon*, τί τινι S.E.*P*.2.211, Hld.1.2. II. *support*, τὴν βάσιν τοῦ πρεσβύτου Id.7.8:—Pass., Sor.1.70. **-ᾰνον**, τό, *that on which one sits*, οἷον ἐ. γλουτός Arist.*HA*493ᵃ23: pl., Ruf.*Onom*.116, Poll.2.184. 2. *seat*, Phryn.Trag.7 (s. v. l.). 3. ἐφέδρανον ὄργανον apparatus *for persons under operation to sit on*, Orib.49.2.1, 49.4.68. II. = ἐφέδρα III, Ps.-Dsc.4.46. **-εία**, ἡ, *a sitting upon*, ἐπὶ δένδρεσι Arist.*HA*614ᵇ6; ἡ ἐπὶ τοῖς ᾠοῖς ἐ. Id.*IA*713ᵃ21. II. *sitting by, waiting for one's turn*, of pugilists, etc., *drawing 'byes'*, Pl.*Lg*.819b. 2. in war, *reserve*, Plb.1.9.2, D.S.17.12, D.H.9.57 (pl.): but in pl., *observation-posts*, Ath.Mech.16.4. III. *lying near, protection*, ἡ τῶν πολεμίων ἐ. Plb.23.16.2; *station, post*, τῷ φυγόντι ἐξ ἐ. Id.1.17.11; *lying in wait*, Plu.*Flam*.8, Onos.14.1. IV. *watchfulness* against symptoms of disease, περὶ ἐ., title of work by Antonius the Epicurean, Gal.5.1. (Sts. written -ρία.) **-εύω**, (ἔφεδρος) *sit upon, rest upon*, ἄγγος ἐφεδρεῦον κάρᾳ E.*El*.55; *sit on* eggs, Arist.*HA*564ᵃ11. 2. *occupy* land, *PStrassb*.114.3. II. *lie by* or *near, lie in wait*, of an enemy watching for an opportunity of attack, Th.4.71, 8.92; ὅταν εἰδῶσιν ἐφεδρεύουσαν τὴν δύναμιν Isoc.8.137; ἐ. τινί *keep watch over*, as a prisoner, E.*Or*.1627: generally, *watch for*, τοῖς..ἀγαθοῖς ἐφεδρεύων ἕτερος καθεδεῖται D.5.15; τοῖς καιροῖς τινος Id.8.42, cf. *PBaden* 39 iii 7 (ii A.D.), Him.*Or*.2.26; τοῖς ἀτυχήμασί [τινος] Arist.*Pol*.1269ᵃ38; τοῖς ἐσομένοις Hld.4.17: metaph., of disease, *lie in wait*, Hp.*Ep*.19 (*Hermes* 53.64); but, *to be associated with* other diseases, Id.*Flat*.6. 2. of a third combatant, *draw a 'bye'*, Luc.*Herm*.40. 3. in war, *form the reserve*, Plb.18.32.2. 4. *watch over, protect*, τῇ τοῦ σίτου κομιδῇ Id.5.95.5. III. *halt*, Plu.*Pyrrh*.32, etc. **-ευσις**, εως, ἡ, *lying in wait*, v.l. in Aq.*Jb*.37.3 (pl.). **-ήσσω**, poet. for ἐφεδράζω, *sit upon*, ἕδρης Coluth.256; ἅρμασι Nonn.*D*.20.36. 2. *sit by*, τινι *AP*7.161 (Antip. Sid.): abs., Coluth.69:—also **-ιάω**, Id.15. **-ίζω**, *sit* or *ride upon*, in a game wherein the loser carried the winner on his back, Ἐφεδρίζοντες, title of play by Philemon. **-ισμός** or **-ιασμός**, ὁ, *the game itself*, Poll.9.118, Hsch. **-ιστήρ**, ῆρος, ὁ, *one who plays the game*, Id.:—also **-ίτης** [ῑ], ου, ὁ, Phot. s. v. παλαιστή. **-ος**, ον, (ἕδρα) *sitting* or *seated upon*, c. gen., λεόντων ἔφεδρε, of Cybele, S.*Ph*.401 (lyr.); ἵππου ἐ. E.*Ion* 202 (lyr.); γῆς ἐ. στρατός Id.*Rh*.954. 2. ἔφεδρον, τό, *firm seat, bench*, Hp.*Fract*.8. 3. ἔφεδρον, τό, = ἵππουρις, prob. in Dsc.4.46, Plin.*HN*26.133. II. *sitting by, at*, or *near*, τῶν πηδαλίων, of a helmsman, Pl.*Plt*.273e: also c. dat., σκηναῖς E.*Tr*.139 (anap.): abs., ξύνεστιν ἔφεδρος lies *close at hand*, S.*Aj*.610 (lyr.). 2. *posted in support* or *reserve*, ἐφέδρους ἱππότας..ἱππόταις ἔταξε posted horsemen *to support* horsemen, E.*Ph*.1095, cf. Plb.8.31.6, Onos.21.6, al. 3. *lying by and watching, waiting on*, τῶν καιρῶν, τοῖς καιροῖς, Plb.3.12.6, *Fr*.160, cf. Call.*Del*.125; ἐ. βίου *waiting upon* his life, i.e. *for* his death, Men.663; χαλεπώτατοι ἐ., of debtors in a city, Aen.Tact.14.1. 4. the third competitor in contests, *who sits by to fight the conqueror*, Pi.*N*.4.96, E.*Rh*.119, Ar.*Ra*.792, cf. Luc.*Herm*.41 sq.; πρὸς βασιλέα τὸν μέγιστον ἔφεδρον ἀγωνιζόμεθα X.*An*.2.5.10; καθάπερ ἐ. ἀθλητῇ Plu.*Sull*.29; Κράσσος, ὃς ἐ. ἦν ἀμφοῖν Id.*Caes*.28; ἐ. τοῦ ἀγῶνος Id.*Pomp*.53; μόνος ὢν ἔφεδρος δισσοῖς, i.e. one *against* two, with no one to take his place if beaten, A.*Ch*.866 (anap.). 5. generally, *one who waits to take another's place, a successor*, ἐ. βασιλεύς Hdt.5.41; ἐ. τινός Luc.*Gall*.9.

ἐφέζομαι, chiefly used in part. and 3 sg. impf.; inf. ἐφέζεσθαι Od.4.717; imper. ἐφέζεο *AP*15.13 (Const. Sic.):—*sit upon*, c. dat., δενδρέῳ ἐφεζόμενοι Il.3.152; πατρὸς ἐφέζετο γούνασι 21.506; δίφρῳ ἐφέζεσθαι Od.4.717, cf. 509; ἔνθα δ' ἄρ' αὐτὸς ἐφέζετο 17.334; ὄχῳ Ar.*Av*.774 (lyr.): also c. gen., Pi.*N*.4.67, A.R.3.1001; ἐπὶ νώτοις Mosch.2.125; εἰς αὖλιν *AP*5.236.10 (Agath.): also c. acc., Εὐρώταν ἐφεζόμεναι E.*Hel*.1492 (lyr.); τύχη..ναῦν θέλουσ' ἐ. A.*Ag*.664. 2. *sit by* or near, c. acc., οὐδ' ἔχων μύσος..τὸ σὸν ἐφεζόμην βρέτας prob. for ἐφεζομένη, Id.*Eu*.446. Cf. ἐφίζω.

ἐφέηκα, Ep. for ἐφῆκα, v. ἐφίημι.

ἐφεικοστα, τά, *additional tax of* $\frac{1}{20}$, *PRev.Laws* 34.3 (iii B.C.).

ἐφείω, Ep. aor. 2 subj. 1 sg. of ἐφίημι.

ἐφεκᾰτέρωθεν, *on either side*, Ph.*Bel*.95.10 (s. v. l.).

ἐφεκκαιδέκᾰτος, ον, *containing the ratio* 17 : 16, Theo Sm.p.69 H., Aristid.Quint.3.1; cf. ἐφεξκαιδέκατος.

ἐφεκ-τέον, (ἐπέχω) *one must suspend judgement*, περί τινος S.E.*P*.2.94, *M*.8.160, cf. D.L.9.81. **-τικός**, ή, όν, *able to check* or *stop*, κοιλίας Diph.Siph.ap.Ath.8.355e, Mnesith.ap.eund.2.57d; ἱδρώτων Dsc.1.30; ἀφροδισίων *Gp*.12.27.3 (Comp.); σηπεδόνων Dsc.5.109. II. *practising suspense of judgement*, of the Sceptics, *Stoic*.2.37, Gell.11.5.6, Philostr.*VS*1.8.4, D.L.*Prooem*.16, Syrian.*in Metaph*.73.16. Adv. -κῶς Arr.*Epict*.1.14.7. III. Geom., ἐ. τόπος *immobile* locus, opp. διεξοδικός (q. v.), Apollon.Perg.*Fr*.22. **-τός**, ή, όν, *to be held back*: τὰ ἐφεκτά subjects *on which to suspend the judgement*, S.E.*P*.3.55.

ἔφεκτος, ον, *containing* $1+\frac{1}{6}$, Vitr.3.1.6; τόκος ἐ. *when* $\frac{1}{6}$ *of the principal was paid as interest*, $= 16\frac{2}{3}\%$, D.34.23: ἔφεκτον, τό, *charge of* $\frac{1}{6}$ on payments for grain-transport, *PLond.ined*.2093 (iii B.C.).

ἐφέλης· ἐπίαλτος, Hsch.; Aeol. acc. ἐφέλην Id. s. v. ἐπιάλης.

ἐφελίσσω (only in form ἐπε(ι)λ–; aor. 1 part. ἐπειλίξας dub. in D.23.161 (iii p.lxxxviii Blass), but found in Gal.18(2).7):—*roll up*, τὸ μεταξὺ τοῦ βιβλίου, i.e. *skip*.., Gal. l. c.:—Med., *wriggle behind one*, οὐρήν Nic.*Th*.220:—Pass., *to be rolled up*, ἐπείλικτο ὥσπερ τὰ βιβλία Paus.4.26.8.

ἐφελκ-ίς, ίδος, ἡ, *scab of a sore* or *wound*, Aret.*SD*2.3, Gal.8.6, al., Archig.ap.eund.12.679. **-όομαι**, Pass., *break out into sores*, Hp. *Epid*.6.8.21.

ἐφελκ-τικός, ή, όν, *attractive*, Eust.1765.9; φάρμακον *Hippiatr*.20; τὸ ἤλεκτρον ἐ. τῶν ἀχύρων Phld.*Sign*.1. **-υσις**, εως, ἡ, *attraction*, Asp. *in EN*160.5. **-υσμός**, ὁ, = foreg., Eust.52.24; *suction*, Sor.1.118; opp. διωσμός, Paul.Aeg.6.88. **-υστής**, οῦ, ὁ, = βοηθός, Phot., Suid. **-υστικός**, ή, όν, *drawing on*, *attractive*, τᾶς ψυχᾶς Hippod.ap.Stob.4.1.94; τὸ ε̄ .. γίνεται ἐ. τοῦ ν̄ Choerob.*in Theod*.2.38, cf. *EM*431.22, Eust.52.22. Adv. -κῶς Sch.Luc.*VH* 2.25. II. in later Gramm., Pass., *attracted*, *suffixed*, τὸ ν̄ ἐφελκυστικὸν γίνεται *EM*438.50, cf. Sch.D.T.p.465 H. **-ω**, Ion. ἐπ-, fut. ἐφέλξω E.*HF*632: aor. 1 inf. -ελκύσαι Thphr.*Char*.30. 10:—Med., fut. -ελκύσομαι A.D.*Synt*.50.21: aor. 1 part. -ελκυσάμενος Thphr.*CP*5.1.10: (Hom. only in Med. and Pass., v. infr. II, III):—*drag* or *trail after* one, ἐ. τὰς [οὐράς], of long-tailed sheep, Hdt.3.113; ἵππον ἐκ τοῦ βραχίονος ἐ. *to lead* a horse by a rein upon the arm, Id.5.12; ναῦς ὣς ἐφέλξω *will take in tow*, E. l.c., cf. Th.4.26; ἐ. ξύλον, of a log tied to the leg, Polyzel.3; τὰ ὀπίσθια σκέλη ἐφέλκουσιν ἐπὶ τὰ ἐμπρόσθια *drag forward*, in the disease of horses called εἰλεός, Arist.*HA*604^{b}1; τὰς ὁπλὰς καὶ τὰ ἰσχία ἐ. *draw* them *up*, ib.18, cf. *Hippiatr*.121. 2. *bring on*, *bring in its train* (v. infr. III. 4), πολλὰς ἐφέλκων ξυμφοράς E.*Med*.552, cf. *Ion* 1149, *HF* 776 (lyr.); ἄλλην αἴσθησιν μετὰ τοῦ λογισμοῦ Pl.*Phd*.65e:—Med., *AP*10.37 (Luc.). 3. *draw* or *drink off*, E.*Cyc*.151. 4. ἐ. πλείους ἡμέρας *delay* for several days, Thphr.*Char*. l. c.:—Pass., τὰ ἐφελκόμενα *arrears* of payment, *PPetr*.3p.151 (iii B.C.), cf. *PSI*4. 350.4 (iii B.C.), *UPZ*50.33 (ii B.C.); ἐφέλκεται τῷ Φιλίππῳ he *is in arrears* of tax-payments to P. (the tax-collector), *PPetr*.2p.108 (iii B.C.). II. Pass., ἐφελκομένοισι πόδεσσιν with feet *trailing after* him, of one who is dragged lifeless away, Il.23.696; τὸ δ' ἐφέλκετο μείλινον ἔγχος 13.597; ὁ λίθος ὄπισθε ἐπελκόμενος *dragging behind* (the boat), Hdt.2.96; of camels, Id.3.105; also οἱ ἐπελκόμενοι *the stragglers* of an army, Id.4.203; -ομένη προθυμία *lagging*, *tardy*, Plb.9.40.2. 2. *to be attracted*, ῥείθροισιν *h.Hom*.19.9; μηδὲ .. τούτῳ ἐφέλκεσθαι be not *led away* by this argument, Th.1.42. III. Med. like Act., *drag after one*, χωλαίνει καὶ ἐφέλκεται (sc. τὸν πόδα) Pl.*Lg*.795b, cf. Antip.*Stoic*.3.256; τἆλλα Pl.*R*.544e. 2. *draw to oneself*, *attract*, αὐτὸς γὰρ ἐφέλκεται ἄνδρα σίδηρος the very sight of iron (i.e. arms) *draws* men *on*, i.e. *tempts* them *to use them*, Od. 16.294, 19.13; ὕδωρ ἐπ' ἑωυτὸν ὁ ἥλιος ἐ. Hdt.4.50; ἐ. τινὰ πρός τι Plb.9.1.3; of flowers, ἠϊθέας -όμεναι χροιῇσι Nic.*Fr*.74.65; κάλλεϊ.. πάντας ἐ. *APl*.4.288 (Leont.). 3. *draw* or *pull to*, τὴν θύραν ἐφελκύσασθαι Luc.*Am*.16; προστίθησι τὴν θύραν καὶ τὴν κλεῖν ἐφέλκεται Lys.1.13; ἐ. ὀφρῦν to frown, *AP*7.440 (Leon.); ἐ. κατὰ τῆς κεφαλῆς τὸ ἱμάτιον Plu.*Caes*.66, cf. *Pomp*.79. 4. *bring on* consequences, πόλλ' ἐφέλκεται φυγὴ κακά E.*Med*.462; ὃ καὶ σίδηρον ἀγχόνας τ' ἐ. Id.*Fr*.362.26, cf. Hp.*Decent*.1; κινδύνους Isoc.*Ep*.4.6; τοὔμπαλιν οὗ βούλονται ἐ. X.*Cyr*.8.4.32. 5. *claim for oneself*, *assume*, ἀλλότριον κάλλος Pl.*Grg*.465b; Μοῦσαν ὀθνείην *AP*9.434 (Theoc., = p.xvi W.). 6. *drag behind one as inferior*, i.e. *surpass*, τινὰ κάρτεϊ A.R.1.1162. 7. Gramm., *attract to the close of a word*, τὸ νῦ δι' εὐφωνίαν Demetr.*Eloc*.175, cf. Eust.52.19. 8. ἐ. ἄσθμα *draw* a *deep* breath, Philostr.*Im*.2.22.

ἐφέλκωσις, εως, ἡ, (ἐφελκόομαι) *ulceration*, Hp.*Epid*.6.7.2 (pl.), Gal. 18(2).789.

ἔφελξις, εως, ἡ, *a dragging after* one, τοῦ πεπηρωμένου μορίου Arist. *IA*708^{b}10.

ἐφέμεν, Ep. for ἐφεῖναι, aor. 2 inf. of ἐφίημι. **ἐφενάπται**· ἐπακολουθῆσαι (Lacon.), Hsch. (fort. ἐφέψασθαι). **ἐφέννῡμι**, v. ἐπιέννυμι.

ἐφεξῆς, Ion. **ἐπεξῆς**, poet. **ἐφεξείης** Orph.*A*.327, 357:—Adv. *in order*, *in a row*, *one after another*, ἵζεσθαι Hdt.5.18; χωρεῖν E.*Hel*. 1390; ἑστάναι Ar.*Ec*.842, etc.; ἵστασθ' ἐ. πάντες all *in a row*, Id.*Fr*. 66; ἐ. ἐπὶ κέρως τεταγμέναι Eub.67.4, Xenarch.4.6; φάλαγγα βάθος ἐ. X.*HG*7.5.23; τὰ ἐ. λεγόμενα Pl.*Sph*.261d; ἵν' ἐ. ἡμῖν ὁ λόγος ἴῃ Id. *Plt*.281d; τὰς πράξεις ἐ. διελθεῖν Isoc.4.26; ἐ. ἀποκρίνεσθαι *in a connected manner*, Ruf.*Interrog*.2: c. Art., ᾗ τὰ ἐ. [πολιτείας] ἐρῶν Pl. *R*.449a, cf. *Lg*.696e; ἡ ἐ. γωνία the *adjacent* angle, Euc.1.14; αἱ ἐ. τομαί *adjacent* sections, of branches of a hyperbola and its conjugate, Apollon.Perg.*Con*.2.19; γραμμαὶ ἐ. κείμεναι a *series* of straight lines, Archim.*Spir*.10; ἡ ἐ. [οἰκία] *next door*, Men.*Inc*.2.31; τὸ ἐ. ῥητέον Pl.*Phdr*.239d, cf. Arist.*Cael*.281^{a}28, etc. 2. c. dat., *next to*, Pl. *Prm*.149a, al.; τὸ ἐ. τούτοις Id.*Phlb*.34d; ἐ. τοῖς εἰρημένοις Arist. *Pol*.1294^{a}32: rarely c. gen., [γωνίας] Pl.*Ti*.55a. II. *successively*, *continuously*, esp. with πᾶς, ἐ. πάντας X.*Oec*.12.10; δῃοῦν πᾶσαν τὴν γῆν ἐ. Id.*HG*4.6.4; τὴν Ἑλλάδα πᾶσαν ἐ. ἁρπάζειν D.8.55; μὴ τοῖς αἰτίοις, ἀλλὰ πᾶσιν ἐ. ὀργίζεσθαι Id.*Prooem*.38.2. 2. less freq. of Time, τρεῖς ἡμέρας ἐπεξῆς Hdt.2.77, cf. Lys.19.52; ἐ. τέτταρες Ar. *Ra*.915; δὶς ἐ. Call.*Ep*.37. 3. *thereupon*, *immediately afterwards*, εὐθὺς ἐ. D.18.31; εἰσελθὼν οἴκαδε καὶ ἐ. οὑτωσὶ καθεζόμενος Id.21. 119.

ἔφεξις, εως, ἡ, (ἐπέχω) = ἐπισχεσία, *excuse*, *pretext*, τοῦ δ' ἔφεξιν; = τίνος χάριν; Ar.*V*.338 (troch.), cf. E.*Fr*.599 (tragic use, acc. to Sch. Ar. l.c.). II. *checking*, *stopping*, *IG*12(9).207.10 (Eretria).

ἐφεξκαιδέκατος, ον, = ἑκκαιδέκατος, λόγος Plu.2.1021e.

ἐφεπτακαιδέκατος, ον, *containing* $1+\frac{1}{17}$, λόγος Plu.2.1021d, Aristid. Quint.3.1.

ἐφέπω, Ep. impf. ἔφεπον, iterat. ἐφέπεσκον, Il.16.732, Od.12.330: fut. ἐφέψω Il.21.588: aor. 2 ἐπέσπον A.*Pers*.552 (lyr.) (the only place in Trag.), inf. ἐπισπεῖν, part. ἐπισπών (v. infr. III):—*ply*, *wield*, ἔγχος Pi.*P*.6.33. 2. c. dat. pers., *apply*, *direct towards* or *against*, Πατρόκλῳ ἔφεπε κρατερώνυχας ἵππους Il.16.732, cf. 724. 3. *ply*, *belabour*, *lay on to*, [ἵππους] μάστιγι 24.326; of warriors, *belabour*, *harass* the enemy, 11.177, 22.188; σφεδανὸν ἔφεπ' ἔγχεϊ 21.542: c. acc. loci, ὣς ἔφεπε κλονέων πεδίον 11.496; of hunters, *beat*, *drive*, κορυφὰς ὀρέων Od.9.121 (but ἄγρην ἐφέπεσκον, .. ἰχθῦς ὄρνιθάς τε *plied* (ἐνήργουν Sch.) the chase, (hunting) fish and birds, 12.330): abs. metaph., *punish*, παραιβασίας Hes.*Th*.220. II. *ply* or *practise* a pursuit, ἄλλοι δ' ἐπὶ ἔργον ἔποιεν Od.14.195; πόλεμον ἐ. Simon.142.2 (codd. *AP*); τερπωλὰς καὶ θαλίας Archil.13; συμποσίας Pi.*P*.4.294; ὅσια καὶ νόμιμα Ar.*Th*.675; πολλὰ ἐπέπουσι (v.l. ἐφ-) Hdt.7.8.α'; τὰν Φιλοκτήταο δίκαν ἐ. *practising* his way, Pi.*P*.1.50. 2. *govern*, *administer*, Θήβας A.*Pers*.38 (anap.), cf. 552; πόλιας θνητῶν v.l. in Simon.142.2; Ζεὺς ὥρην ἐφέπων Man.3.32; *face* (*ply*, *cope with*) a task, οὐδὲ κ' Ἀθήνη τοσσῆσδ' ὑσμίνης ἐφέποι στόμα Il.20.359; τοσσούσδ' ἀνθρώπους ἐφέπειν καὶ πᾶσι μάχεσθαι ib.357; μαιμώων ἔφεπ' ἔγχεϊ *faced* (*plied*) them with his spear, 15.742. 3. c. acc. loci, *haunt*, *frequent*, of gods, nymphs, etc., γαῖαν καὶ βένθεα λίμνης Hes. *Th*.366, cf. Pi.*P*.1.30, *Pae.Delph*.7; of birds, A.R.2.384; γῆν καὶ θάλασσαν Luc.*Trag*.267; *visit*, σῴζων ἐφέποις ἡμᾶς Aristonous 1. 47. 4. *molest*, *follow* a woman, Herod.2.47; cf. ἐφέπειν (-έπτειν cod.)· ἐπακολουθεῖν, Hsch. III. *come upon*, *encounter*, *face*, πότμον ἐπίσπῃς, etc. Il.6.412, etc.; θάνατον καὶ πότμον ἐ. Od.24.31; θανεῖν καὶ πότμον ἐ. Il.7.52, Od.4.562, etc.; κακὸν οἶτον ἐ. 3.134; ὀλέθριον ἦμαρ ἐ. Il.19.294; ἐ. αἴσιμον ἦμαρ 21.100; reversely, αἰὼν ἔφεπε μόρσιμος Pi.*O*.2.10.—The Act. is rare in Att. (v. supr.).

B. Med., ἐφέπομαι (in later Poets ἐφέσπομαι Maiist.46, Naumach. ap.Stob.4.23.7, Nonn.*D*.16.401, ἐπιέσπομαι Opp.*C*.3.272): impf. ἐφειπόμην: fut. ἐφέψομαι S.*Ant*.636, ἐπιέψομαι A.R.2.18: aor. 2 ἐφεσπόμην (but 3 pl. ἐπέσποντ(ο) Pi.*P*.4.133), imper. ἐπίσπου, inf. ἐπισπέσθαι: also aor. 1 imper. ἐφεψάσθω (v.l. ἐφαψ-) Theoc.9.2:—*follow*, *pursue*, once in Hom. in hostile sense, λῃϊστῆρσιν ἐπισπόμενος Ταφίοισιν Od.16.426, cf. Hdt.1.103, 3.54, Th.4.96, etc. II. *follow*, *attend*, λαῶν ἔθνος ἐπισπόμενον ἑοῖ αὐτῷ Il.13.495; ἐπισπέσθαι ποσίν *attend* on foot, i. e. keep up with, 14.521, cf. Hdt.3.14, 31, al.; εἰ μὴ οἱ τύχη ἐπίσποιτο if fortune *attend* him not, Id.1.32, etc.; ᾧ χάρις ἐφέσπετο Ar.*V*.1278: abs., opp. ἡγεῖσθαι, Th.3.45. 2. *obey*, *attend to*, ἐπισπόμενοι θεοῦ ὀμφῇ Od.3.215; ἐπισπόμενοι μένεϊ σφῷ *giving the reins to* their passion, 14.262; τῇ γνώμῃ τινὸς ἐ. Hdt.7.10.γ'; βουλῇ.. ἐπισπέσθαι πατρὸς A.*Eu*.620; [γνώμαις], βουλεύμασι, τῷ δικαίῳ, S.*Ant*. 636, *El*.967, 1037: abs., ὁ ἐπισπόμενος, opp. ὁ πείσας, Th.3.43; also, *agree*, *approve*, εἰ δὲ .. ἐπὶ δ' ἕσπωνται θεοὶ ἄλλοι Od.12.349, cf. Pi.*P*. 4.133. 3. *follow* an argument, μόγις πως ἐ. Pl.*Lg*.644d, cf. *Tht*. 192e, etc.

ἐφέργω, *confine*, ὕδωρ *Tab.Heracl*.1.131.

ἐφερμήν-ευσις, εως, ἡ, *explanation*, Procl. *in Prm*.p.494 S. **-ευτέον**, *one must explain*, ib.p.670 S. **-ευτικός**, ή, όν, *explanatory*, Phlp. *in APo*.359.31, Eust.777.57, Sch.rec.Theoc.2.48. **-εύω**, *interpret*, τί τινι Philostr.*VA*3.25: abs., τοῦ -οντος δεῖσθαι Philostr. Jun.*Im*.8, cf. Phlp. *in APo*.435.30.

ἐφερπύζω, later pres. for sq., Nic.*Fr*.74.41, *AP*9.231 (Antip. [Sid.]), Orph.*L*.707, etc.

ἐφέρπω, fut. -ψω A.*Eu*.500 (lyr.): aor. 1 ἐφείρπῡσα Ar.*Pl*.675 (ἐφερπύσας is f. l. for -ποίσας in Theoc.22.15):—*creep upon*, ἐπὶ [χύτραν] Ar. l. c. II. poet., *come on* or *over*, *come gradually* or *stealthily upon*, τινα A.*Eu*.314 (anap.); ἐπ' ὄσσοισι νὺξ ἐφέρπει E.*Alc*.269 (lyr.): abs., μηδ' ἐφερπέτω νόσος A.*Eu*.943 (lyr.). 2. abs., *go forth*, *proceed*, ib.500 (lyr.); esp. in part., *coming on*, *future*, χρόνος ἐφέρπων Pi.*O*. 6.97; ἐφέρποισα κρίσις Id.*Fr*.131.5; τᾶς -ούσας νυκτός during the *following* night, *IG*4.952.15 (Epid.).

ἐφεσίαν· ἀντιποίησιν, ἐπιθυμίαν, Hsch.

ἐφέσιμος δίκη, ἡ, suit *in which there was the right of* ἔφεσις or *appeal* to another court, Poll.8.62, Gal.10.19, Luc.*Pr.Im*.15; γνῶσις ἐ. D. 7.9; κρίσις Arist.*Ath*.45.2; τὰ ἐ. D.C.52.33. II. (ἐφίεμαι) *accessible*, μὴ πᾶσιν ἀλλ' ἑνὶ τὴν ἀρχὴν ἐ. εἶναι J.*AJ*19.4.3.

ἔφεσις, εως, ἡ, (ἐφίημι) *throwing* or *hurling at*, *shooting*, ἡ τοῖς βέλεσιν ἔ. Pl.*Lg*.717a. 2. (ἐφίημι A. IV) as law-term, *appeal to a judicial tribunal* from a lower tribunal, *IG*1².39.74; from an administrative decision, ἡ εἰς τὸ δικαστήριον ἔ. Arist.*Ath*.9.1, cf. 45.2, 55.2; from the vote of a δῆμος, D.57.6; also of appeals to a popular assembly, ἀπὸ βουλῆς ἐπὶ δῆμον Poll.8.62; ἐπὶ τὸν δῆμον ἀπὸ τῶν πατρικίων D.H.6.58; πρὸς τὸν Ἐρχιέων δῆμον Id.*Is*.14. 3. *permission*, *licence*, *Sammelb*.6236.39 (Theadelphia, i B.C.). II. (ἐφίεμαι) *aiming at a thing*, *appetite*, *desire*, τινος Archyt.ap.Stob.2.31.120, Pl.*Lg*.864b, Arist.*EN*1114^{b}6, Gal.*Nat.Fac*.3.6, Plot.5.5.12, etc.: abs., Pl.*Def*. 413c; ἐφέσεις καὶ διώξεις Plu.2.468c. 2. *attempt upon*, c. gen., ἔ. τῆς ἀρχῆς ποιήσασθαι D.C.71.23, cf. 43.38.

Ἔφεσος, ἡ, *Ephesus*, Hdt.1.142, etc.:—Adj. **Ἐφέσιος**, α, ον, γράμματα a *magic* formula, Plu.2.706e, Eust.1864.16 (also **Ἐφεσήϊα**, γρ. Anaxil.18.7 (anap.)): **Ἐφεσία**, ἡ, = ἀριστολόχεια στρογγύλη, Ps.-Dsc. 3.4; = ἀρτεμισία, ib.113: **Ἐφέσια**, τά, festival of Artemis at Ephesus, Th.3.104 (also Ἐφέσεια, τά, *OGI*10.10): **Ἐφεσηονίκης** [ῑ], ὁ, victor in these games, *Ephes*.2.72 (iii A.D.): **Ἐφεσίς**, ίδος, ἡ, in pl., title of poem by Aeschrio, Sch.Lyc.688.

ἐφεσπερ-εία, ἡ, *keeping awake in the evening*, Suid. **-εύω**, *keep awake in the evening*, Poll.1.71. **-ος**, ον, (ἑσπέρα) *western*, νομὸς prob. in S.*OC*1059 (lyr.).

ἐφέσσαι, ἔφεσσαι, ἐφέσσεσθαι, v. ἐφίζω. **ἐφέστα·** τὸ ἑσπερινὸν δίκτυον, Hsch.

ἐφεστι-άζομαι, *feast, make merry,* Hsch., Phot., Suid. **-ος,** Ion. **ἐπίστιος,** ον, Hdt. (v. infr.), **ἐφ[ίστιος]** prob. in *SIG*1218.17 (Iulis, v B.C.): (ἑστία):—*at one's own fireside, at home,* ἀπολέσθαι ἐ. Od.3.234; Τρῶες, ἐ. ὅσσοι ἔασιν as many as are in *their own homes,* opp. ἐπίκουροι, Il.2.125: with Verbs of motion, ἀλλ' ἐμὲ.. ἐφέστιον ἤγαγε δαίμων (i.e. ἐπὶ τὴν ἑστίαν) Od.7.248; ἦλθε.. ἐ. 23.55, cf. E.*Rh.*201; ἐφέστιον πῆξαι.. σκῆπτρον (i.e. ἐπὶ τῇ ἑστίᾳ) S.*El.*419; of suppliants who claim protection by *sitting by the fireside,* ἐπίστιος ἐμοὶ ἐγένεο Hdt.1.35; ἱκέτης καὶ δόμων ἐ. *inmate* of the temple, A.*Eu.*577, cf. 669; κάθησθε δωμάτων ἐ. Id.*Supp.*365; τόνδ' ἐ. θεῶν ib.503, cf. S.*OT*32; *guest,* ἐλθόντ' ἐς δόμους ἐφέστιον Id.*Tr.*262; freq. in A.R., ἐ. ἐν μεγάροισιν 1.909, 3.1117, etc.: c. dat. pers., ἐ. ἀθανάτοισιν *dwelling with* them, 3.116, cf. 4.518: c. dat. loci, πηγῇσιν ἐ. Ἀσωποῖο 1.117. II. generally, *of* or *in the house* or *family,* πόνοι.. δόμων ἐφέστιοι A.*Th.*853 (lyr.); θύματα Id.*Ag.*1310; μίασμα Id.*Eu.*169 (lyr.); ἀλαλαγαί S.*Tr.*206 (lyr.); περιστερὰ οἰκέτις ἐ. τε Id.*Fr.*866; εὐναί E.*El.*216; ἐ. δόμοι the chambers *of the house,* A.*Th.*73: Ion. ἐπίστιον, τό, *household, family,* Hdt.5.72,73; later ἐφέστιον, τό, D.H.1.24, *POxy.*2106.18 (iv A.D.). III. θεοὶ ἐ. *the household* gods, to whom the hearth was dedicated, Hierocl.p.54 A.; Ζεὺς ἐπίστιος or ἐφέστιος as *presiding over hospitality,* Hdt.1.44, S.*Aj.*492; ἐ. ἵδρυμα ἐν οἰκίᾳ ἔχων, a living image *by the hearth,* Pl.*Lg.*931a. IV. ἐπίστιος, ἡ, v. ἐπίστιος II.

ἐφεστρίδιον, τό, Dim. of sq., Luc.*Merc.Cond.*37, *DMort.*10.4, al.

ἐφεστρίς, ίδος, ἡ, (ἐφέννυμι) *upper garment, wrapper,* X.*Smp.*4.38; a philosopher's *mantle,* Ath.3.98a; soldier's *cloak,* Plu.*Luc.*28; πᾶσα ἡ σύγκλητος μελαίναις ἐ. χρώμενοι Hdn.4.2.3, cf. 7.11.2,3; also a woman's *robe,* *AP*9.153 (Agath.), etc. 2. χλαμὺς ἐ. Ath.5.215c. II. *coverlet,* Poll.6.10, 10.42, Hsch.

ἐφέτειος, ον, = ἐπέτειος, *of one year's standing,* ἐφηβεύσαντες *BCH* 11.86 (Apollonis); of animals, *yearling, Arch.Pap.*5.394 (ii A.D.).

ἐφετ-έον, (ἐφίημι) *one must allow,* τινι c. inf., Cic.*Att.*9.4.2, cf. J.*AJ* 4.8.23. **-ηρία,** ἡ, dub. sens., *IG*1².313.122, 314.136 (pl.). **-ης,** ου, ὁ, *commander,* in pl., A.*Pers.*79 (lyr.). II. **ἐφέται,** οἱ, at Athens, *the Ephetae,* a court which tried cases of homicide under the ἄρχων βασιλεύς, *IG*1².115, Decr.ap.And.1.78, prob. in Arist.*Ath.*57.4, Lex ap.D.23.37, Harp. III. *judge of appeals,* Just.*Nov.*49 *Pr.* 2. **-ικός,** ή, όν, (ἐφίεμαι) *actuated by desire,* Thphr.*Metaph.*9. 2. Gramm., *expressive of desire,* ῥήματα Choerob. *in Theod.*2.212, al. II. ἐ. χρόνοι periods *within which appeals may be lodged,* Just.*Nov.*49.1 *Intr.* **-ίνδα** παίζειν, Adv., play at *catch-ball* (with play on ἔφεσις I. 2), Cratin.415.

ἐφετινός, ή, όν, *yearling,* of animals, *PMasp.*141 vi 9, al. (vi A.D.). II. *of the present year,* χόρτος *POxy.*1482.12 (ii A.D.).

ἐφετ-μή, ἡ, (ἐφίημι) poet. word, *command, behest,* Il.14.249; θεῶν ὤτρυνεν ἐφετμή 21.299: freq. in pl., *behests,* esp. of the gods or one's parents, 5.508, Pi.*O.*3.11, etc.; Θέτις δ' οὐ λήθετ' ἐφετμέων παιδὸς ἑοῦ Il.1.495, cf. Pi.*P.*2.21, A.*Ch.*300, E.*IA*634; *demands, prayers,* Pi.*I.*6(5).18. **-ός,** ή, όν, (ἐφίεμαι) *desirable,* θεῖόν τι καὶ ἐ. Arist.*Ph.*192ª17, cf. Plu.2.374d; ἐφετόν, τό, *object,* τὸ γνωστὸν ἐ. ἐστι τοῦ γνωστικοῦ Dam.*Pr.*27; οἰκεῖον ἐ. ib.12. II. ἐφετο[ς] perh. for ἐφ' ἔτος, = ἐπ' ἔτος, *this year's,* *IG*5(2).433.7 (Megalop., ii B.C.); [τῷ πρὸ τοῦ ἐ]φ' ἔτος ἐνιαυτῷ *SIG*742.56 (Ephesus, i B.C.).

ἐφευάζω, = ἐπευάζω, Plu.*Marc.*22.

ἐφεύρ-εμα, ατος, τό, *discovery, invention,* in pl., Sch.E.*Hec.*627; *artifices, tricks,* *IG*2².1119.4 (iii A.D.). **-εσις,** εως, ἡ, *discovering, discovery,* Sch.D.T.p.31 H., Just.*Nov.*84.1.1 (pl.), David *Proll.*44.8. **-ετής,** οῦ, ὁ, *inventor, contriver, Anacreont.*36.3; κακῶν *Ep.Rom.*1.30:—fem. **-έτρια,** Sch.Opp.*H.*1.354. **-ετικός,** ή, όν, *inventive,* Sch.Od.1.349. **-ημα,** ατος, τό, = ἐφεύρεμα, Sch.D.T.p.108 H. (pl.), Sch.E.*Hec.*626 (pl.). **-ησις,** εως, ἡ, = ἐφεύρεσις, Sch.Ar.*Pl.*1160 (pl.). **-ίσκω,** Ion. ἐπ-, fut. ἐφευρήσω: aor. 2 ἐφηῦρον or ἐφεῦ-; Aeol. ἐπεύρ[οι] Sapph.*Supp.*4.9: pf. ἐφηύρηκα S.*El.*1093 (lyr.), Euphro 1.17, etc.:—*find* or *discover, find anywhere,* εἴ που ἐφεύροι ἠϊόνας λιμένας τε Od.5.439, cf. 417, Pl.*Phdr.*266a: usu. c. part., ὃν δ' αὖ.. βοῶντα ἐφεύροι Il.2.198; δαινυμένους δ' εὖ πάντας ἐφεύρομεν Od.10.452; τήν γ' ἀλλύουσαν ἐφεύρομεν ἀγλαὸν ἱστόν we *discovered* her undoing it, 24.145, cf. S.*El.*1093 (lyr.), Pl.*Plt.*307c; Κύπρι.. σε πικροτάταν ἐπεύροι prob. in Sapph. l.c.:—Pass., μὴ ἐπευρεθῇ πρήσσων Hdt.9.109; κλέπτων ὅταν τις.. ἐφευρεθῇ S.*Fr.*930; δρῶν ἐφευρίσκῃ (2 sg.) Id.*OC*938; ἐφηύρημαι κακός (sc. ὤν) Id.*OT*1421, cf. *Ant.*281; δειλὸς ὢν ἐφηυρέθης E.*Supp.*319. 2. *discover besides,* v. l. for ἕθ' εὑρ. in Od.19.158; ταῖς ἀρχαίαις τέσσαρας χορδὰς Paus.3.12.10. 3. *bring in besides,* ὅσα δ' ἂν ἐφευρίσκῃ [τὰ τέλη] X.*Vect.*4.40. II. *find out, invent,* of arts, [τέχναν] Pi.*P.*12.7 (Med. μῆτιν -ευρομένοις ib.4.262); σοφῶς ἐφεῦρες ὥστε μὴ θανεῖν E.*Alc.*699. 2. *find out, discover,* ἐφεῦρε δ' ἄστρων μέτρα καὶ περιστροφάς S.*Fr.*432.8; χρόνου διατριβάς ib.479, cf. Cratin.140; ἴδιόν τι Euphro 1.17; ὁσίαν ἐπίνοιαν *SIG*799.5 (Cyzicus, i A.D.).

ἐφεύω, *cook together with,* Nic.*Fr.*79.

ἐφεψῐάομαι, *mock* or *scoff at,* τεθνεῶτί γ' ἐφεψιόωνται ἅπαντες Od.19.331, cf. 370.

ἐφέψω, *boil over again,* Philoch.171:—Pass., -εψομένου ὕδατος *boiling over,* Pall.*Febr.*12.

ἐφήβαιον, τό, *pubes,* Dsc.1.3, Gal.8.4; *hair of the pubes,* Suid. s.v. βλήχων: more freq. in pl., -βαια γυναικεῖα Heraclid.Syrac.ap.Ath.14.647a, etc.

ἐφήβ-αρχος, ὁ, (ἔφηβος, ἄρχω) *overseer of the youth,* a magistrate in several Greek cities, *OGI*339.42 (Sestos), *IG*12(2).134 (Mytilene, in form ἐφάβ-), 12(3).524 (Thera), *SIG*798.23 (Cyzicus), etc., cf. Arr.*Epict.*3.1.34, 7.19: **-αρχέω,** *hold this office,* *CIG*1957g (Beroea), *OGI*583.10 (Cyprus), *Not.Arch.*4.189 (Cyrene, iii A.D.). **-άω,** Ion. ἐπ-, *come to man's estate, grow up to manhood,* Hdt.6.83, A.*Th.*665, E.*Fr.*559, X.*Cyr.*6.1.12. **-εία,** ἡ, *youth, adolescence,* περὶ Ἐπικούρου -είας D.L.10.4. 2. *ephebic training,* *IG*2².1028.42, *SIG*1109.130, etc. 3. *body of* ἔφηβοι, prob. in Str.5.4.7. **-εῖον,** τό, *principal court* in the παλαίστρα, Vitr.5.11.2. **-ειος,** α, ον, *youthful,* ἁλικία *AP*7.427.12 (Antip. Sid.); ἀκμαί *Epigr.Gr.*231 (Cnios). **-εύω,** *to be an* ἔφηβος, *arrive at man's estate,* Str.14.1.18, Paus.7.27.5, Artem.1.54; οἱ ἐφηβεύσαντες *those who have undergone the ephebic training,* *IG*2².665, etc., cf. Hp.*Ep.*25; τὸ ἐφηβεῦον, = οἱ ἔφηβοι, Hld.7.8. **-ία,** ἡ, = ἐφηβεία 1, Artem.1.54 codd. II. = ἐφηβεία 3, Lxx 2*Ma.*4.9. **-ικός,** ή, όν, Dor. **ἐφᾱβ-,** ά, όν, *of* or *for an* ἔφηβος, ἆθλα Theoc.23.56. II. τὸ ἐφηβικόν, 1. = ἐφηβεία 1, Luc.*Nav.*3. 2. *part of the theatre assigned to the youths,* Poll.4.122; -κὸς τόπος Sch.Ar.*Av.*795. **-ιος,** α, ον, = foreg. 1, τὴν πρωτότμητον τρίχα τὴν -ίην κείρας *IG*12(5).173 iv (Paros). 2. **ἐφήβια,** τά, *celebration on reaching adolescence,* *EM*532.2. II. *pubic, ossa* Cael.Aur.*CP*3.140. **-ος,** hyperdor. **ἔφᾱβος,** ὁ, (ἥβη) *one arrived at adolescence* (i.e. the age of 18 years, Poll.8.105, Harp. s.v. ἐπιδιετές; in Persia 16 or 17 years, X.*Cyr.*1.2.8), Lycurg.76, Arist.*Ath.*42.2, *IG*2².1156, al., *SIG*959.12 (Chios), etc.; εἰς τοὺς ἐφήβους ἐγγραφῆναι Pl.*Ax.*366e; ἐξ ἐφήβων ἐστὶ καὶ ἤδη εἴκοσι ἐτῶν Teles p.50 H.: generally, *boy,* καλός ἐστιν ἔ. ὁ σός *PLit.Lond.*52. 2. *young girl,* Hsch. II. *kind of cup,* Steph.Com.1.5, Philem.Lex.ap.Ath.11.469a. III. *throw of the dice,* *AP*7.427.5 (Antip. Sid.). IV. a woman's *shoe,* Herod.7.61. **-οσύνη,** ἡ, *age of an* ἔφηβος, *adolescence,* *AP*6.282.6 (Theod.). **-οτης,** *pubertas, Gloss.*

ἐφηβοφύλαξ [ῠ], ἄκος, ὁ, title of official at Pergamum, *IGRom.*4.396.

ἐφηγ-έομαι, *lead to* a place: c. dat. pers., esp. as Att. law-term, *lead the magistrate to a place where a criminal lay concealed,* whom the informer durst not seize himself, D.22.26, cf. 26.9, Poll.8.50. **-ησις,** εως, ἡ, *action against one who harboured a criminal,* or *concealed public property,* *AB*187, Phot., *EM*403.23, Suid., Zonar.

ἐφήδομαι, *exult over,* τινι X.*HG*5.3.20, D.Chr.11.64, etc.; Θηβαίοις.. ἐφησθῆναι παθοῦσιν D.18.18; ἐπ' ἐχθρῷ D.C.*Fr.*109.16: abs., X.*Ages.*7.5; οὐκ ἐπιτήδειος ὁ καιρὸς -ησθῆναι D.15.21: rarely in good sense, Aristaenet.1.12.

ἐφηδύνω, *sweeten, give a relish to, season,* τὴν τροφήν Plu.2.668d; οἶνον κινναμώμοις ib.693c; τὸ ἀτερπές Ruf.ap.Orib.7.26.118: metaph., λόγοις τὴν διατριβὴν ἐ. Plu.2.514f; ὁ Εὐριπίδης τὸ αὐτὸ ἑτέρως -ύνας Longin.15.6, cf. 34.2 (Pass.), Pythag.ap.Porph.*Abst.*3.26. 2. *soothe, win over,* τινὰ πειθοῖ Ph.1.566, cf. 2.268.

ἐφήκω, fut. -ξω S.*El.*304:—*to have arrived,* Id.*Aj.*34, *Ant.*1257 (anap.), etc.; ἐπειδὴ ἡ ἡμέρα ἐφῆκε Th.8.67. 2. ὅσον ἂν ἡ μόρα ἐφήκῃ so far as it *reaches,* so much space as it *occupies,* X.*Lac.*12.5.

ἐφῆλιξ, Dor. -ᾶλιξ, ῐκος, ὁ, ἡ, *adolescent,* νεότας *AP*7.427.5 (Antip. Sid.).

ἐφῆλις, Ion. ἐπ- (q.v.), ιδος, also **ἐφηλίς,** ίδος, ἡ: (ἧλος):—*rivet, burr* or *clinch* to secure a nail, Ph.*Bel.*63.50, *IG*11(2).165.13 (Delos, iii B.C.). II. in pl., *rough spots which stud the face* (from ἧλος), or, acc. to others, *freckles* (from ἥλιος), Hp.*Prorrh.*2.23, *Alim.*20, *Mul.*2.215, Thphr.*HP*9.20.3, Sor.1.44 (sg.), etc.: acc. pl. ἐφήλεις Dsc.1.123. 2. in sg., = λέπρα, ἐ. ἀργινόεσσα, λευκή, Nic.*Th.*333, 858.

ἔφηλος, ον, (ἧλος) *nailed on* or *to,* Suid. II. *with a white speck on it,* ὀφθαλμός Ael.*NA*15.18; ὀφθαλμοῖσιν ἔφηλος Call.*Fr.anon.*106; of persons suffering from the complaint, Lxx *Le.*21.20.

ἐφηλότης, ητος, ἡ, *white speck on the eye,* S.E.*M.*7.233.

ἐφηλ-όω, *nail on,* in Pass., Apollod.*Poliorc.*158.8, Ath.Mech.25.3: metaph., τῶνδ' ἐφήλωται τορῶς γόμφος διαμπάξ the bolt is *driven home,* i.e. it *is irrevocably fixed,* A.*Supp.*944; cf. ἐφαλόω. **-ώδης,** ες, gloss on φολλικώδεα, Erot. **-ωτός,** ή, όν, *nailed on,* Hero *Aut.*2.2.

ἔφημαι, pf. Pass. used as a pres., (cf. ἧμαι) *to be seated on, sit on,* κληῗδεσσιν ἐφήμενοι Od.12.215; [θρόνῳ] 6.309; πύλῃσιν Nic.*Al.*507: c. gen., πόντου θινὸς ἐφήμενος S.*Ph.*1124, cf. Lyc.367; *to be seated at* or *in,* δόμοις, τάφῳ, A.*Ag.*1217, *Ch.*501: c. acc., βρέτας ἐφήμενος Id.*Eu.*409; τάφον Id.*Fr.*157 (ἐφιμένη cod. Hsch.): βωμία ἐφημένη, = βωμῷ ἐ., E.*Supp.*93. II. *act as assessor* (cf. ἔφεδρος), Παλλὰς οἵ τ' ἐφήμενοι A.*Eu.*629. III. ἐπήμενοι dub. sens. (or from ἐφίημι?) in Alc.*Supp.*4.14.

ἐφημερ-ευτήριον, τό, *guard-room, lock-up,* *PPetr.*2 p.26 (iii B.C.). **-ευτής,** οῦ, ὁ, in pl., title of those who *took their turn of serving* their equals at a Jewish festival, Ph.2.481. **-εύω,** *keep guard by day,* Plb.21.27.6, *IGRom.*1.817 (Callipolis); ἐπὶ τῶν πυλῶν *SIG*731.14 (Tomi, i B.C.): c. dat., τοῖς κινδύνοις D.S.11.8 codd. II. τῶν νυνὶ ἐφημερευόντων those cleaners *who are now taking their turn of service* in the temple, *UPZ*7.6 (ii B.C.); cf. ἐφημερία. **-έω,** *to be president for the day,* prob. in *IG*14.830.20 (Puteoli, ii A.D.). **-ία,** ἡ, *division* of the priests *for the daily service of the temple,* Lxx 1*Ch.*23.6, *Ne.*23.30, *Ev.Luc.*1.5. 2. the *service* itself, Lxx 1*Es.*1.16. **-ινός,** ή, όν, = sq., Alex.262.9, Ph.2.395, *POxy.*924.2 (ἐπιημ-, iv A.D.). **-ιος,** Dor. **ἐφᾱμ-,** ον, also α, ον Pi.*N.*6.6: (ἡμέρα):—*on, for* or *during the day,* οὔ κεν ἐφημέριός γε βάλοι κατὰ δάκρυ παρειῶν Od.4.223; *by day,* opp. μετὰ νύκτας, στάθμα Pi. l.c. 2. *for a day only,* ἐφημέρια φρονέοντες taking no thought for the morrow, Od.21.

85; κῆδος ἐ. *short-lived*, Thgn.656; of men, ἐφημέριοι *creatures of a day*, A.*Pr.*547 (lyr.), Ar.*Av.*687; θνατά τε καὶ ἐφαμ. ζῷα Ti.Locr. 99d. 3. *for the day, daily*, ἀμβροσία Plu.2.938b; λάτρις ἐ. *hired by the day*, Thgn.486; μισθὸς *AP*7.634 (Antiphil.). **-ίς**, ίδος, ἡ, *diary, journal*, esp. *a military record*, as kept by Alexander's staff, Ath.10.434b, Plu.*Alex.*23, Arr.*An.*7.25.1; of Caesar's *commentarii*, Plu. *Caes.*22; of office *registers*, *BGU*1168.10 (i B.C.). 2. *day-book, account-book*, *PCornell* 1.2 (iii B.C.), *PCair.Zen.*176.357 (pl., iii B.C.), Plu.2.829c, D.L.6.86; εἰς τὰς ἐ. φιλοσοφεῖν to profess philosophy for the *ledger*, Plu.2.999a. II. = ἐφημερία, J.*Vit.*1: pl., Id.*AJ*7.14.7, 12.6.1. **-όβῐος**, ον, *living for the day, from hand to mouth*, χειροτέχνης Ph.2.389, cf. Ptol.*Tetr.*160. **-ον**, τό, *short-lived insect, the may-fly*, *Ephemera longicauda*, Arist.*HA*490ᵃ34, 552ᵇ23. II. *a poisonous plant, Colchicum autumnale*, Thphr.*HP*9.16.6, Nic.*Al.* 250; = κολχικόν, Dsc.4.83. 2. *Polygonatum multiflorum*, ib. 84. **-ος**, ον, Dor. **ἐπάμ-** Pi.*P.*8.95, *Fr.*182 (**ἐφαμ-** *I.*7(6).40, *Fr.*157): (ἡμέρα):—more common form of ἐφημέριος, esp. in Prose, *living but a day*: hence, *short-lived*, τερπνόν Id.*I.* l. c.; τύχαι E.*Heracl.*866, Diph.45; ὄλβος οὐ βέβαιος, ἀλλ' ἐ. E.*Ph.*[558]; ἐ. σώματα καὶ χρήματα ἡγεῖσθαι Th.2.53; χρῆσις Arist.*Pol.*1252ᵇ16; ἐ. καὶ προπετῆ βίον Men.382; τὸ ἐ. Arist.*EN*1096ᵇ5; ἐ. πᾶν τὸ τῶν πολλῶν ἀγαθόν Epicur. *Fr.*489. 2. of men, ἐφήμεροι *creatures of a day*, Pi.*P.*8.95, Semon. 1.3, A.*Pr.*83; ὦ τάλας ἐφάμερε Pi.*Fr.*157; ὦφήμερε Ar.*Nu.*223; ὦ φίλοι καὶ ἀτεχνῶς ἐ. Pl.*Lg.*923a. II. *for the day, daily*, πυρετός Hp.*Aph.*4.55; τροφή D.H.8.41, *Ep.Jac.*2.15, Vett.Val.62.17, cf. D.S.3.32 (pl.); γυμνασία Ascl.*Tact.*1.4; πράξεις Luc. *Pseudol.*17; δαπάνη Plu.*Per.*16, etc.: neut. pl. as Adv., *once a day*, Orib.*Eup.*1.9. III. φάρμακον ἐ. *killing on the same day*, Plu.*Them.*31. **-ούσιος**, ον, = ἐφημερόβιος, Procl.*Par.Ptol.*225.

ἐφημίαι· ἀγροί, καὶ βελτίονα φήμης, Hsch.

ἐφημῐόλιος, ον, less correct form of ἡμιόλιος, v. l. in Theo Sm.p.77 H., Bacch.Sen.p.106 Bellermann.

ἐφήμῑσυς, υ, *half as much again*, *POxy.*1668.10 (iii A.D.).

ἐφημοσύνη, ἡ, (ἐφίημι) *command, behest*, οὐδ' ὡς Μενελάου ἐφημοσύνης ἀμέλησε Il.17.697, cf. Od.12.226, Pi.*P.*6.20, S.*Ph.*1144 (lyr.): pl., A.R.1.33. **ἔφησθα**, = ἔφης, v. φημί.

ἐφησῠχάζω, *remain quiet*, Plb.2.64.5 (v.l. ἀφ-), Ph.2.65 (v. l. for ἡσ-); ὀλίγον χρόνον Hld.4.11; μικρὸν -ησυχάσας τοῖς εἰρημένοις Id. 6.7; ἀπὸ τῆς αἰώρης Aret.*CD*1.8. 2. *acquiesce in*, τῇ δικαιολογίᾳ *PLond.*5.1708.261 (vi A.D.); τοῖς κρινομένοις Just.*Nov.*123.21 *Intr.* II. Act., *pass over in silence, omit*, τὰ πλήθη τῶν ἄλλων Ph. 2.3 (v.l. for ἀφ-).

ἐφθᾰλέος, α, ον, (ἕψω) *cooked*, Hsch., Phot., Suid.

ἐφθαρμένως, Adv. pf. Pass., (φθείρω) *corruptly*, *Theol.Ar.*43.

ἐφθέος, α, ον, (ἕψω) *to be boiled*, opp. ὠμός, Nic.*Al.*392.

ἐφθήμερος, ον, *lasting seven days*, ἀνοχαί Plu.2.223a.

ἐφθημῐμερής, ές, *containing seven halves*, i.e. $3\frac{1}{2}$: esp. in metre, -μερές, τό, *a measure of three feet and a half*, such as the first $3\frac{1}{2}$ feet of a Hexameter or Iambic Trimeter, Heph.7.3, Sch.Ar.*Pl.*302 (pl.), etc.; ἐ. τομή a caesura after such a phrase, Aristid.Quint.1.25.

ἐφθίατο, v. φθίνω.

ἐφθονημένως, Adv. pf. Pass., (φθονέω) *grudgingly*, Vett.Val.301.6.

ἐφθοπώλιον, τό, *place where dressed meat is sold, cook-shop*, Posidipp.21.

ἐφθός, ή, όν, verb. Adj. of ἕψω, *boiled*, of meat or fish, Hdt. 2.77, Hp.*VM*13, E.*Cyc.*246, Ar.*Pax*717, Ecphantid.1, Pl.*R.*404c, etc.; of vegetables, Antiph.6; of water, Arist.*Mete.*380ᵇ10; of a hot bath, ἐφθόν [με]..πεποίηκεν Antiph.245. 2. ἐφθὸς χρυσὸς *refined* gold, Simon.64. II. metaph., *languid, unnerved*, Hp.*Epid.*4.16.

ἐφθότης, ητος, ἡ, *languor*, Hp.*Acut.*49.

ἐφθόω, *roast, boil*, Suid. **ἐφιάλλω**, v. φιάλλω.

ἐφῐαλτ-εία, ἡ, a herb (= ἐφιαλτία) used as a *preventive of nightmare*, Poet. *de herb.*162 (ἐφιάλτιον cod.). **-ης**, ου, ὁ, Aeol. **ἐπιάλτης** Alc.129, also **ἐπίαλος** ibid.:—*nightmare*, conceived as a throttling demon, Phryn.Com.1, Dsc.3.140 (pl.), Artem.2.37, Ruf.ap.Orib. 7.26.177, Str.1.2.8; pr. n. of one of the Aloidae, Il.5.385, Od.11.308, Pi.*P.*4.89 (Ἐπ- acc. to Sch.Od. l. c., cf. A.D.*Synt.*179.22), and Att. pr. n., cf. Ael.Dion.*Fr.*381, *IG*1².950.92, etc. (Identified with ἠπιόλης by A.D.*Fr.*8.12 (or Apollodorus, v. Sophr.68 note); ἐπιάλτης is expld. as ῥιγοπύρετον by Suid.; popularly connected with ἐφάλλομαι, Sch.B Il.5.385, or ἐφιάλλω, *EM*403.32; cf. *incubo*.) **-ία**, ἡ, = γλυκυσίδη, Aët.1.84; = ἐφιαλτεία (q. v.). **-ικός**, ή, όν, *suffering from nightmare*, Orib.*Syn.*8.2, Paul.Aeg.3.15. **-ιον**, τό, = δρακοντία μικρά, Ps.-Dsc.2.167.

ἐφιδρόω, Ion. **ἐπιδρ-**, *perspire in addition to* or *after*, πυρετῷ Hp. *Epid.*1.3 (as v.l. for ὑφ-); *perspire slightly over the whole body* or *on the upper part only*, Id.*Prorrh.*1.4, al., Gal.16.513:—Pass., *perspire consecutively*, Antyll.ap.Orib.9.23.6.

ἐφίδρ-ῡσις, εως, ἡ, *planting firmly*, in pl., of the feet, Ph.1.125. **-ύω**, *place* or *set upon*, φύσις ἐ. πάντα γαστρί ib.116:—Med. with pf. Pass., *place oneself upon, mount*, ib.21, al.: metaph., λόγος ἐ. θυμῷ ib.114.

ἐφίδρωσις, εως, ἡ, *superficial perspiration*, Plu.*Brut.*25 (pl.), Gal. 16.601.

ἐφιδύειν· ὀκνεῖν, Hsch. **ἐφιδύη**· ὄκνος, Theognost.*Can.*7.30.

ἐφιελίς, ίδος, ἡ, = κάλυξ, part of a priest's crown, J.*AJ*3.7.6 (fort. φιελίς).

ἐφιέρ-εια· τὰ ἐπὶ τοῖς ἱερείοις ἀποθυόμενα, Hsch. **-ον**, τό, *sacrificial cake*, *IG*3.74 (pl.):—also **-ος**, ὁ, Poll.6.76. II. v. ἐπίαρον.

ἐφιζάνω, Aeol. impf. ἐπίσδανον Alc.*Supp.*28.7:—Hom. only in Il., always in impf., *sit at* or *in*, δείπνῳ, αἰθούσῃσιν, 10.578, v.l. in 20.11; *sit upon*, ὕπνος ἐπὶ βλεφάροισιν ἐφίζανεν 10.26; νώτοισιν ἐφίζανε Mosch.2.108: c. acc., θῶκον A.R.1.667: later also in pres., χείλεσι ἀφρὸς ἐ. Aret.*SA*2.12; ἐ. τις ὥρα καὶ ῥυτίδι πρώτῃ Philostr.*Im.*2.1, cf. Porph.*Antr.*19· abs., *form a deposit*, Dsc.5.75.

ἐφίζω, Dor. **ἐφίσδω** Theoc.5.97: I. causal, in Ep. aor. ἐφέσσαι, ἐφέσσασθαι:—*set upon*, once in Hom. in Act., τούς μ' ἐκέλευσα Πύλονδε καταστῆσαι καὶ ἐφέσσαι *set* me *ashore*, Od.13.274:—more freq. in Med., γούνασιν οἷσιν ἐφεσσάμενος *having set* [me] *on* his knees, 16.443: fut. ἐφέσσεσθαι Il.9.455: imper., με νηὸς ἔφεσσαι Od.15.277; ἐς Λιβύην μ' ἐπὶ νηὸς ἐφέσσατο 14.295 (Rhianus: ἐέσσατο codd.):—Med. also, *reduce* a dislocation, Hp.*Mochl.*25. II. intr., *sit at* or *by*, abs., *sit*, Hom. only in Od., always in impf., ἐφῖζε Od.3.411, 19.55; ἔνθα.. ἐφίζεσκε 17.331: later in pres., βαρὺς δ' ἐφίζει A.*Supp.* 651 (lyr.); ὥρα ἐφίζοισα γλεφάροις *sitting upon*, Pi.*N.*8.2; ὕπνος.. βλεφάροισιν ἐφίζων Mosch.2.3; πρὸς ὄμμ' ἀχλὺς ἐφίζει Critias 6.11 D.; ἀμφὶ μήλοις Nic.*Al.*478; τηνεὶ γὰρ ἐφίσδει (Dor.) Theoc.5.97.

ἐφίημι, Ion. **ἐπ-**, Dor. 3 sg. ἐφίητι Pi.*I.*2.9, Ion. 3 pl. ἐπιεῖσι Hdt.4.30: fut. ἐφήσω Od.13.376: aor. 1 ind. ἐφῆκα, Ep. ἐφέηκα 9.38, Ion. ἐπῆκα Hdt.5.63; in other moods aor. 2 forms were used, imper. ἔφες Il.5.174; Ep. subj. ἐφείω 1.567, 2 sg. ἐφῇς S.*El.*554, opt. ἐφείην Il.18.124; Ion. inf. ἐπεῖναι Hdt.2.100; part. ἐφείς S.*Aj.*495 (v.l.), etc.:—Med., pres. inf. ἐφίεσθαι Antipho 5.79; part. ἐφιέμενος Od.13.7: fut. ἐφήσομαι Il.23.82: aor. 2 ἐφεῖτο S.*Ph.*619:—Pass., pf. ἐφέωται and ἐφεῖται Hsch.: [ἐφῑημι Ep., ἐφῐημι Att.; yet Hom. always uses ἐφιείς, ἐφίει, ἐφιέμενος with ῐ, exc. ἐφῑει Od.24.180]:—*send to* one, Πριάμῳ.. Ἶριν ἐφήσω Il.24.117; μ' ἐφέηκε.. καλέειν *sent* me to call, A.R.1.712. 2. in Hom., c. inf., *set on, incite* to do, ἠλεός, ὅς τ' ἐφέηκε πολύφρονά περ μάλ' ἀεῖσαι Od.14.464; so ἐ. τινὰ ἐχθοδοπῆσαι, χαλεπῆναι, στοναχῆσαι, Il.1.518, 18.108,124. 3. of things, *throw* or *launch at* one, ὅς τοι πρῶτος ἐφῆκε βέλος 16.812; ἄλλοις ἐφίει βέλεα Od.24.180, etc.; [ἔγχος], μελίην, Il.20.346, 21.170; οἰστὸν ἐπί τινι E.*Med.*632 (lyr.); ἐ. χεῖράς τινι *to lay* hands *on* him, μνηστῆρσιν ἀναιδέσι χεῖρας ἐφήσω Od.20.39, cf. Il.1.567, etc. 4. of events, destinies, etc., *send upon* one, τοῖσιν ἀεικέα πότμον ἐφῆκε 4.396, etc.; Ἀργείοισι πολύστονα κήδε' ἐφῆκεν 1.445, cf. 21.524; μνηστήρεσσιν ἄεθλον τοῦτον ἐφήσω Od. 19.576; νόστον.., ὅν μοι Ζεὺς ἐφέηκε which he *hath laid upon* me, 9.38; so πάντ' ἐφήσω μόρον A.*Eu.*502 (lyr.); τέκνοις ἀρὰς ἐ. Id.*Th.*786 (lyr.). 5. *send against*, in hostile sense, τῷ στρατοπέδῳ τὴν ἵππον Hdt.5.63; τὴν ἵππον ἐπὶ τοὺς Ἕλληνας Id.9.49; ἡνίοχοι ἐφίεσαν ὠκέας ἵππους Hes.*Sc.*307; στρατὸν ἐς πεδία E.*Heracl.*393. 6. *let in*, freq. of water, ἐπεῖναι τὸν ποταμὸν ἐπὶ τὴν χώρην Hdt.7.130, cf. 2.100; τὸ ὕδωρ ἐπὶ τὴν ἔσοδον Id.7.176; also ἐ. ἀκτῖνα Θήβαισι E.*Ph.*5; ἀγέλας ἐπὶ τὰ χωρία X.*Cyr.*1.1.2; ἄγαν ἐφῆκας γλῶσσαν *did'st let loose*, E. *Andr.*954; ὀργῇ τινι ἐ. Pl.*Lg.*731d. 7. *throw into*, ἐς λέβητ' ἐφῆκεν ἕψεσθαι μέλη E.*Cyc.*404. II. *let go, loosen*, esp. the rein, ἐ. καὶ χαλάσαι τὰς ἡνίας τοῖς λόγοις Pl.*Prt.*338a; οὐρίᾳ ἐφέντα (abs.) ibid.; πᾶσαν ἐφεὶς ὀθόνην [τῷ ἀνέμῳ] *AP*10.1 (Leon.), cf. A.R.2.934. b. *give up, yield*, τινὶ τὴν ἡγεμονίαν Th.1.95; πάντ' ἐφέντες ἡδονῇ E.*Fr.* 564; *allow*, τἆλλα τοῖς δούλοις Arist.*Pol.*1264ᵃ21. c. c. inf., *permit, allow*, τινὶ ὀνειδίσαι Hdt.1.90, cf. 3.113; σοί γ' ἐφῆκα πᾶν λέγειν S.*El.* 631; ἢν ἐφῇς μοι (sc. λέγειν) ib.554, cf. 556,649: c. acc. et inf., τοὺς νεωτέρους ἐ. διώκειν X.*Cyr.*4.2.24 (v.l. for ἀφ-):—Pass., ἐφεθήσεταί τινι c. inf., Luc.*Pr.Im.*24. d. *command*, Pi.*I.*2.9 (v.infr. B). 2. *give up, leave as a prey*, ἐφῆκεν ἐλλοῖς ἰχθύσιν διαφθοράν S.*Aj.*1297, cf. 495 (v.l.); τὴν ἀποσκευὴν ἐ. τοῖς στρατιώταις διαρπάσαι D.S.14.75; intr. (sc. ἑαυτόν), *give oneself up to*, ἰσχυρῷ γέλωτι Pl.*R.*388e; [παιδιᾷ] Id.*Ti.*59c. III. *put* the male *to* the female, ἐπῆκε ὀχεῦσαι τὸν ἵππον Hdt.3.85, cf. 4.30, Arist.*HA*630ᵇ33. IV. as law-term, *leave* to another to decide, *refer*, δίκας ἐ. εἴς τινας D.40.31; εἰς δικαστήριον ibid.; ἐ. τινὰ εἰς τὸ δικαστήριον *refer* him to.., Id.34.21; (sc. ἑαυτόν) *appeal*, εἰς τοὺς δικαστάς Id.29.59; ἐπί τινα Luc.*Bis Acc.*4; εἰς ἕτερον δικαστήριον Id.*Herm.*30; ἀπό τινος D.C.64.2: abs., Id.37.27.

B. Med., *lay one's command* or *behest upon*, ὑμέων δ' ἀνδρὶ ἑκάστῳ ἐφιέμενος τάδε εἴρω Od.13.7, cf. Il.23.82, 24.300; ἐπιστολὰς ἅς σοι πατὴρ ἐφεῖτο A.*Pr.*4; πρός τι τοῦτ' ἐφίεσαι; S.*OT*766: c. inf., ἐ. τινὶ ἀγγεῖλαι Id.*El.*1111, cf. Ar.*V.*242; χαίρειν τἆλλ' ἐγώ σ' ἐ. I *bid* thee have thy will, S.*Aj.*112, cf. A.*Ch.*1039: abs., ὡς ἐφίεσαι Id.*Pers.*228 (troch.), cf. E.*IT*1483; ἐ. ἐς Λακεδαίμονα *send orders to*.., Th.4.108. 2. *allow* or *permit* one to do, κάρα τέμνειν ἐφεῖτο τῷ θέλοντι S.*Ph.*619; f.l. for ὑφ- in X.*An.*6.6.31, etc. II. c. gen., *aim at*, καλῶν Isoc.2.25; ἀγαθοῦ τινος Arist.*EN*1094ᵃ2, etc.; in fighting, τῶν προσώπων, τῶν ὄψεων, Plu.*Pomp.*71, *Caes.*45. 2. *long for, desire*, τί μοι τῶν δυσφόρων ἐφίῃ; S.*El.*143 (lyr.); τί.. ἐφίεσαι φιλοτιμίας; E.*Ph.*531; τῶν ἀλλοτρίων Antipho 5.79; τῶν κερδῶν, ἀρχῆς, Th.1.8,128; τῶν ἐν Σικελίᾳ ἀγαθῶν Id.4.61; ἰσότητος Arist.*Pol.*1302ᵃ25: c. gen. pers., X.*Mem.*4.1.2: c. inf., ὧν..σου τυχεῖν ἐφίεμαι ἄκουσον S.*Ph.*1315; ἐ. ἄρξειν Th.6.6 codd. (leg. ἄρξαι): c. acc. et inf., S.*OT*1055.

ἐφῑκάνω [ᾰ], = sq., χαλεπὸν δ' ἐπὶ γῆρας ἱκάνει Od.11.196; ὅσον τ' ἐπὶ θυμὸς ἱκάνοι Parm.1.1.

ἐφικνέομαι, Ion. **ἐπ-**, fut. ἐφίξομαι Xenoph.6.3: aor. 2 ἐφῑκόμην, Ep. -ῐκόμην Il.13.613: pf. ἐφῖγμαι D.25.101: I. *reach at, aim at*, c. gen., of two combatants, ἅμα δ' ἀλλήλων ἐφίκοντο Il.13.613; simply, *reach* or *hit* with a stick, εὖ μάλα μου ἐφικέσθαι πειράσεται Pl.*Hp.Ma.*292a; ὅσων ἂν ἐφικέσθαι δυνηθῶσιν Isoc.12.227; ἐφίκται πάντων ἡ τούτου κακοπραγμοσύνη D.25.101, cf. Plu.2.267c, etc.; σφενδόνῃ οὐκ ἂν ἐφικοίμην αὐτόσε Antiph.55.20; τὰ βέλη ἐ. ἄχρι πρὸς τὸν σκοπόν Luc.*Nigr.*36. 2. *reach, extend*, ὅσον ὁ ἥλιος ἐ. Thphr.*HP*1.

7.1, etc.; ἐφ' ὅσον ἀνθρώπων μνήμη ἐ. X.*Cyr.*5.5.8; ἐ. ἐπὶ τοσαύτην γῆν τῷ ἀφ' ἑαυτοῦ φόβῳ *to reach* by the terror of his name over.., ib.1.1.5; ἐ. ἐς τὸ λεπτότατον *to reach* to the smallest matter, Luc.*JConf.*19; ὅπου μὴ ἐ. ἡ λεοντῆ, προσραπτέον..τὴν ἀλωπεκῆν Plu.2.190e; c. part., ἐ. φθεγγόμενον Id.*TG*18; ἐ. βλέποντα μέχρι τινός D.Chr.62.1. 3. metaph., *hit, touch the right points*, ἐ. ἐξαριθμούμενος Plb.1.57.3; τὰ ἄλλα λέγων ἐπίκεο ἀληθέστατα Hdt.7.9. 4. *reach, attain to*, τῆς ἀρετῆς Isoc.1.5; ἀνδραγαθίας Aeschin.3.189; τοῦ τριηραρχεῖν D.20.28, cf. 122; τῷ λόγῳ τῶν ἐκεῖ κακῶν Id.19.65: c. inf., ἐ. τῷ λόγῳ διελθεῖν *to be able to*.., Plu.2.338c, cf. Plb.1.4.11, *Inscr.Prien.*105.47 (i B.C.): abs., *succeed in one's projects*, App.*Mith.*102; of a poison, *reach* a vital part, *take effect*, ib.111. II. c. acc., *to come upon*, like ἐφικάνω, εἴ σε μοῖρ' ἐφίκοιτο Pi.*I.*5(4).15: c. dupl. acc., ἐπικέσθαι μάστιγι πληγὰς τὸν Ἑλλήσποντον *to visit* it *with* blows, Hdt.7.35. III. c. acc., *befit, be suitable to* (cf. ἱκνέομαι III), Hp.*Fract.*17.

ἐφικτός, ή, όν, *easy to reach, accessible, attainable*, v.l. for ἀνυστόν in Parm.4.7; οὐκ..ἐν ὀφθαλμοῖσιν ἐφικτόν Emp.133.1; οὔτε τέχνη οὔτε σοφίη ἐφικτόν, ἢν μὴ μάθῃ τις Democr.59; ἐλπίδες ἐφικταί Id.58, cf. Plb.12.25¹.9, Phld.*Herc.*1457.11; τὸ μέσον ἐπίπαν ἐ. Arist.*PA*666a15; ἐφικτὸς εἰκότι λόγῳ Plu.*Thes.*1. II. ἐφικτόν ἐστι it is *possible*, c. inf., Plb.9.24.5; καθόσον ἐφικτόν to the best of one's *power*, Arist.*Mu.*391b3; ὡς οὐκ ἦν ἐφικτὰ αὐτοῖς Ael.*NA*5.7; οἱ ἐν ἐφικτῷ τόποι *within reach*, Thphr.*Lap.*25, cf. *Ign.*70; ἐν ἐφικτῷ τῆς ἐλπίδος, τοῦ φιλῆσαι, Plu.2.494e, 496c; εἰς ἐφικτὸν προελθοῦσα coming *within reach*, D.H.2.38. III. Act., *attacking*, Ποιναί *Trag.Adesp.*256.

ἐφῑμείρω, strengthd. for ἱμείρω, c. acc., Nic.*Fr.*74.42: c. gen., *AP*5.268 (Agath.), Nonn.*D.*14.355: c. inf., ἐ. θεὸς εἶναι Musae.80:—Med., in tmesi, ἐφ' αἵματος ἱμείρονται Arat.975.

ἐφίμερος [ῑ], ον, *desired, delightful*, φιλότης Hes.*Sc.*15, *Th.*132; χῶρος Archil.21; ὕμνος Thgn.993, Theoc.1.61; φάτις A.*Ch.*840; ἡ τέκνων ὄψις ἐ. προσλεύσσειν ἐμοί S.*OT*1375; τὴν ἐ. κόμην Anaxil.38; ἐ. ἀνδράσιν ἄγρη Opp.*H.*4.110.

ἔφιξις, εως, ἡ, *reaching the mark*, τὴν ἔ. ποιεῖσθαι, of projectiles, Ph.*Bel.*81.33.

ἐφι-ορκέω, = ἐπιορκέω, *IG*2².1126 (Decr. Amphict.), 5(1).1390.6 (Andania, i B.C.), *PTeb.*78.17 (ii B.C.), etc. **-ορκία**, = ἐπιορκία, Lxx *Wi.*14.25.

ἐφιππ-άζομαι, *ride a tilt at*, λόγοις Cratin.358. 2. *ride upon*, ἐπὶ δελφῖνος Luc.*DMar.*6.2; sens. obsc., Artem.1.79. 3. abs., *ride*, Palaeph.52, Jul.*Or.*2.60a. **-αρχία**, ἡ, *double* ἱππαρχία, consisting of 1024 horse, Ascl.*Tact.*7.11, Arr.*Tact.*18.4, Suid. s. v. ἐφίππων. **-αστήρ**, ῆρος, ὁ, = ἐπιβήτωρ, Apollon.*Lex.* s. v. ἐπιβώτορι. **-εύω**, *ride against, attack with cavalry*, τινι D.S.17.19. II. *ride upon*, Babr.76.15. b. *cover* the female, Opp.*C.*1.390. **-ιος**, ον, *for putting on a horse*, κασᾶς X.*Cyr.*8.3.6, *PLond.*2.402 ii 5 (ii B.C.); πῖλος Plu.*Art.*11; ἐ., τό, *saddle-cloth*, Antiph.109, X.*Eq.*7.5, Epict.*Fr.*18 (pl.); *saddle*, Luc.*Nav.*30, *Hist.Conscr.*45: pl., Hor.*Epist.*1.14.43. II. ἐφίππιος (sc. δρόμος), ὁ, *horse-course*, a course of a certain length so called, Pl.*Lg.*833b. (-ειος codd. Plu.*Art.* l. c., Epict. l. c., etc., but -ῖος Antiph. l. c., Hor. l. c.) **-ίς**, ίδος, ἡ, prob. = ἐφίππιον, gloss on ἰπνή (Sicel word), Hsch. **-ος**, ον, *on horseback, riding*, Eup.27; ἔ. εἰς τὸν τόπον ἠνέχθη Plu.2.306f; ἔ. ὄντες, opp. ὁπλιτεύοντες, Lys.14.10 (as v.l.); ἀνδριὰς ἔ. *an equestrian* statue, Plu.*Publ.*19; ἔ. εἰκὼν χαλκῆ Id.*Fab.*22 (so, with εἰκών omitted, *PSI* 3.204.6 (ii A.D.)); βίος Philostr.*Her.*19.19. 2. κλύδων ἔ. a rushing wave *of horses*, S.*El.*733.

ἐφίπταμαι, late pres. of ἐπιπέτομαι, Mosch.1.16, Arist.*Mir.*841b31, J.*AJ*1.10.3, 3.1.5, Plu.*Cleom.*39, Porph.*Abst.*1.25.

ἐφίσδω, Dor. for ἐφίζω. **ἐφίσης**, = ἐπ' ἴσης, v. ἴσος.

ἐφιστάνω, late form for ἐφίστημι, *set over*, τινά τινι Plu.2.233e. II. *stop, check*, v.l. in Dsc.4.16. 2. *attend to* a thing, c. dat., Plb.5.35.6; *consider carefully*, πῶς.. Id.11.2.5; εἰ.., ὅτι.., Arr.*Epict.*1.26.16, 2.18.31; *note*, of a commentator, Ammon. *in APr.*68.10. 3. *attack*, c. dat., Simp. *in Ph.*795.17.

ἐφίστασις, εως, ἡ, incorrect form for ἐπίστασις II. 5, in pl., Erot. s. v. ἐπαναιώρημα.

ἐφιστάω, = ἐφιστάνω II. 1, Dsc.2.32.

ἐφίστημι, Ion. ἐπ-: A. causal in pres., impf., fut., and aor. 1 (also in the later pf. and plpf. ἐφέστᾰκα, ἐφεστάκειν [ᾰ], v. infr. II. 1, VI. 2): I. *set, place upon*, τεῖχος τείχει Th.2.75; τι ἐπί τινος Pl.*Criti.*116a; τι ἐπί τινι X.*HG*3.1.7; ὅρους ἐπὶ οἰκίαν D.41.6: metaph., ἐ. τὴν ἐκεῖ μοῖραν βίῳ Pl.*R.*498c; ἀνάγκην τινί D.H.1.16. II. *set over*, μ' Ἀπόλλων τῷδ' ἐπέστησεν τέλει A.*Ag.*1202; φύλακ' ἐπέστησεν βοΐ Id.*Supp.*303; ἐ. τινὰ ὕπαρχόν τισι Hdt.5.27; τινὰ παιδαγωγόν τινι Pl.*Alc.*1.122b, cf. X.*Lac.*2.1; τινὰ πεντηκοντόρῳ Id.*An.*5.1.15; τινὰ τοῖς πράγμασι Isoc.2.27; τὸν νόμον Arist.*Pol.*1292b28; ἐπὶ [συμμάχων] τινά Plb.2.65.9; ἐφεστάκει τινὰς πρὸς χρείαν Id.10.20.5; κύνα ἐπὶ ποίμνην D.26.22; τινὰ ἐπὶ τὰς εὐθύνας Id.18.112: c. inf., βουλὴν ἐπιμελεῖσθαι τῆς εὐκοσμίας Isoc.7.37:—Pass., *to be appointed, instituted*, *PTeb.*61(b).358 (ii B.C.), etc. 2. *bring in*, ἡ τύχη ἐπιστήσασα Ῥωμαίους Plb.15.20.6; Φίλιππον ἐ. τοῖς πράγμασι *to let* him *have a hand in* the business, D.19.34. 3. *bring in, cause, occasion*, κατάπληξίν τισι D.S.14.62; κίνδυνον, ἀγῶνά τινι, App.*Hann.*55, *Syr.*10; ἡ τύχη λοιμικὴν διάθεσιν ἐπέστησε Γαλάταις Plb.2.20.7. III. *set up, establish*, ἀγῶνα Hdt.1.167, 6.38: c. acc. et inf., *ordain, prescribe*, ὁ νόμος ἐφίστησι τὰ λοιπὰ κρίνειν τοὺς ἄρχοντας Arist.*Pol.*1287a26; ἐπιστήσατε quid facere debeamus, Plin.*Ep.*6.31.12. IV. *set by* or *near to*, ἐπιστήσαντες κύκλῳ τὸ σῆμα ἱππέας Hdt.4.72; esp. *place in rear*, of troops, τὴν φάλαγγα τούτοις κατόπιν ἐ. Plb.1.33.6, cf. 1.26.14. V. *stop, cause to halt*, ἐπιστῆσαι τὸ στράτευμα X.*Cyr.*4.2.18; τὴν ὁδόν, τὴν πορείαν, D.S.17.112, Plu.*Cim.*1; τοὺς ἱππέας τοῦ πρόσω Arr.*An.*5.16.1; ἐ. τὴν ὁρμήν *check* it, Plb.16.34.2; τὴν διήγησιν *interrupt* it, Id.7.11.1; *check*, ἔμμηνα Dsc.1.125, cf. *POxy.*1088.20 (i A.D.): abs., ἐπιστήσας (sc. ἑαυτόν) *having halted*, X.*An.*1.8.15:—Pass., *to be checked, stopped*, *PPetr.*2 p.62 (iii B.C.); ἐὰν ἐφίστηται ἡ κοιλία Sor.1.122. VI. ἐφίστημι τὴν διάνοιαν κατά τι, περί τινος, *fix one's mind upon it, attend* to it, Isoc.9.69, Arist.*Metaph.*987b3, Thphr.*Char.Prooem.*, etc.; τὴν σκέψιν περί τινος Arist.*Metaph.*1090a2; τὸν λόγον Id.*Juv.*470b5; τὸν νοῦν τινι D.S.12.1; αὐτὸν ἐπιστήσας ἐπί τι Arist.*Top.*135a26: ἐπιστῆσαι abs., *give attention*, τούτοις ἐπιστήσαντες Id.*Mu.*391a26; περί τινος Id.*GC*315b18; περί τι Id.*HA*487a13; ἐπί τι Plb.1.65.5, etc.; ἐπιστήσασι μᾶλλον λεκτέον one must speak *with* more *care and accuracy*, Arist.*Pol.*1335b3, cf. *EN*1144a22; πότερον..ἢ Jul. *ad Them.*265b; ὅτι.. Sor.1.97 (hence ἐπίσταμαι, ἐπιστήμη, qq.v.). 2. c. acc. pers., *arrest the attention of*, Plu.*TG*17, cf. 2.17e, Gal.18(2).105; ἐπιστῆσαί τινα ἐπί τι *call* his *attention* to, Plb.2.61.11, cf. 4.34.9; τοῦ καιροῦ τοῦ κατὰ τὴν διήγησιν ἐφεστακότος ἡμᾶς ἐπί τι *having led* us to.., Id.10.21.2, cf. 31.23.1: hence, *object*, Plot.1.4.5.

B. intr. in Med. and Pass., ἐφίσταμαι, aor. 1 ἐπεστάθην [S.]*Fr.*[1127.5], E.*Hipp.*819, *IT*1375, etc., with pf., plpf. (Aeol. plpf. 3 sg. ἐπήστᾱκε *Schwyzer*646.16 (Cyme, ii B.C.): Dor. plpf. 3 pl. ἐφεστάκεον [ᾰ] *SIG*241.146 (Delph., iv B.C.)), and aor. 2 Act.: (the causal tenses are not found in Hom., the Med. or Pass. only in impf. ἐφίστατο Il.11.644; elsewh. always aor. 2 or pf. Act. with Ep. inf. ἐφεστάμεναι Od.24.380):—*stand upon*, τεῖχος..ῥύατ' ἐφεσταότες Il.18.515; πύργῳ ἐφεστήκει 6.373; δίφρῳ ἐφεσταότος 17.609, etc.; ἐπέστη βηλῷ ἔπι λιθέῳ 23.201; ἡ..ἐπισταθεῖσα ὀρθή Arist.*Metaph.*1051a28; ἐπὶ τὰς..σχεδίας Plb.3.46.8. 2. *to be imposed upon*, μόχθων τῶν ἐφεστώτων ἐμοί S.*Tr.*1170. 3. *stand on the top* or *surface*, τὸ ἐπιστάμενον [τοῦ γάλακτος], i. e. *cream*, Hdt.4.2; λιπαρότητες ἄνω ἐφιστάμεναι Hp.*Prog.*12; ἐ. καθάπερ ὀρρὸς [γάλακτι] Dsc.1.72; of vapour, *form*, Arist.*Juv.*469b31. II. *to be set over*, ἐφίσταται πύλαις A.*Th.*538; οἷός τε πολλοῖς προβατίοις ἐφεστάναι Ar.*V.*955; οἷοι νῷν ἐφεστᾶσι σκοποί S.*Aj.*945; ἄρχοντες ἐφ' ἑκάστῳ μέρει ἐ. X.*Hier.*9.5; ἐπί τινος Pl.*R.*460b; ἐπὶ τῆς πολιτείας D.19.298: rarely c. gen., τὸν ἐπεστεῶτα τῆς διώρυχος Hdt.7.117; ὅσοι θεοῦ χρημάτων ἐφέστασαν E.*Andr.*1098: abs. in part., ὁ ἐφεστηκώς the *person in authority*, the *officer in command*, X.*Oec.*21.9; οἱ ἐφεστῶτες, Ion. οἱ ἐπεστεῶτες, Hdt.2.148, S.*Aj.*1072, X.*Mem.*3.5.19. III. *stand by* or *near*, ὡς πυκνοὶ ἐφέστασαν ἀλλήλοισιν Il.13.133; ἐπ' ἄκρῳ χείλει ἐφεσταότες, ἐ. παρὰ τάφρῳ, 12.52,199; θύρῃσιν ἐφίστατο 11.644; ἐπὶ τὰς πύλας, ἐπὶ τὰς θύρας, Hdt.3.77, Pl.*Smp.*212d; ἐπὶ τοῖς προθύροις Id.*Phlb.*64c; esp. of dreams or visions, *appear to*, εὕδοντι ἐπέστη ὄνειρος Hdt.1.34, cf. 7.14; ὄναρ κεφαλῆφιν ἐπέστη Il.10.496; ἐπιστᾶσα τῆς νυκτός Isoc.10.65; ἄγγελος ἐπέστη αὐτοῖς *Ev.Luc.*2.9: abs., *stand by*, Hdt.3.78; πολλῶν ἐφεστώτων App.*Syr.*10; ἤμην ἐφεστὼς *Act.Ap.*22.20; οἱ λέβητες ἐπεστεῶτες Hdt.1.59; ὁ ἀντίδικος ἐφέστηκε Pl.*Tht.*172e, cf. Aeschin.3.79; without hostile sense, ἐπέστης S.*OC*558, cf. *Ev.Luc.*2.38, etc.; of troops, *to be posted after* or *behind*, κατόπιν ἐ. τοῖς θηρίοις Plb.16.18.7. 2. in hostile sense, *stand against*, τὰ φρονέοντες ἐφέστασαν ἀλλήλοισιν Il.15.703, cf. 5.624; ἔνθα μένος πνείοντες ἐφέστασαν Od.22.203, cf. 24.380; *appear before*, of an army, ἐπὶ τῇ πόλι Hdt.4.203; ἐπὶ τὸ βασίλειον Isoc.9.58; *come upon suddenly* or *by surprise*, Th.8.69; ἐξαίφνης ἐπιστὰς τοῖς γιγνομένοις Isoc.8.41, cf. D.6.5, Luc.*DDeor.*17.1; εἰς τοὺς ὄχλους Isoc.18.9; so of events, etc., αἰφνίδιος αὐτοῖς ἐ. ὄλεθρος 1*Ep.Thess.*5.3, cf. *Ev.Luc.*21.34; διὰ τὸν ἐφεστῶτα ζόφον Plb.18.20.7; διὰ τὸν ὑετὸν τὸν ἐφεστῶτα *Act.Ap.*28.2. 3. metaph., of events, *spring upon* one, *occur*, πρίν μοι τύχη τοιάδ' ἐπέστη S.*OT*777, cf. Th.3.82; in pf., *impend, be at hand*, τὸν ἐφεστηκότα κίνδυνον τῇ πόλει D.18.176; ὁ καιρὸς..ἐφέστηκε 2*Ep.Ti.*4.6; περὶ τοῦ βασιλέως..ὁ λόγος ἐφέστηκε νῦν Arist.*Pol.*1287a2, cf. *Metaph.*999a25; of a more remote future, *to be in store, lie in wait for*, κῆρες ἐφεστᾶσιν θανάτοιο Il.12.326. IV. *halt, stop*, as in a march, ἄλλοτε καὶ ἄλλοτε ἐφιστάμενος X.*An.*2.4.26 (cf. A.V); ἐπιστὰς περιέμεινα Pl.*Smp.*172a: c. gen., ἐ. τοῦ πλοῦ Th.2.91. V. *fix one's mind on, give one's attention to*, σφαγῇ E.*Andr.*547; τῇ τρύγῃ *PFlor.*236.4 (iii A.D.); ἐπί τι Isoc.10.29, D.18.60; τοῖς πράγμασιν..ἐπιστάντες Id.4.12; ἐπιστάς abs. (sc. τοῖς πράγμασι), Id.18.233; διὰ ταῦτ' ἐγρήγορεν, ἐφέστηκεν Id.6.19.

C. aor. 1 Med. in causal sense, *set up*, τὰς θύρας X.*Ages.*8.7; *set, post*, φρουροὺς ἐπεστησάμην Id.*Cyr.*8.2.19; τέλος ἐπιστήσασθαι, Lat. *finem imponere*, Pl.*Lg.*802a: pres. is once so used, τοῦ με τὴνδ' ἐφίστασαι βάσιν; why dost thou *cause* me *to halt*? S.*Tr.*339. 2. ἐπιστησάμενος, intr., *having been* ἐπιστάτης, *IGRom.*4.1265 (Thyatira).

ἐφίστιος, v. ἐφέστιος.

ἐφιστορέω, *inquire* or *search further*, Hsch.

ἔφλᾰδον, v. φλάζω.

ἐφοδ-εία, ἡ, (ἐφοδεύω) *going the rounds, visiting sentries*, Plb.6.35.8: pl., Ph.*Bel.*93.5, Polyaen.7.14.2:—written -ία, D.S.20.16. 2. *making a round of visits*, *SIG*656.26 (Abdera, ii B.C.). II. *inspectorate*, *PTeb.*96.2 (i B.C.). **-ευτέον**, *one must examine*, τὰ καθ' ἕκαστα Str.14.1.4, cf. S.E.*P.*2.198; περί τινος Iamb. *in Nic.*p.58 P. **-ευτής**, οῦ, ὁ, *one who goes the rounds*: *spy*, Aq.*Ge.*42.9. **-ευτικῶς**, Adv. *by tracing an argument, advancing to a conclusion*, S.E.*M.*8.308, *P.*2.142. **-εύω**, *go the rounds*, X.*HG*2.4.24, 5.3.22, Ph.*Bel.*80.38; κώδωνι Plu.*Arat.*7: c. acc., *visit, inspect*, ἔ. φυλακάς Plb.

6.35.11; τὰ ἔργα PTeb.13.3 (ii B.C.); τὴν πόλιν SIG731.16 (Tomi, i B.C.); τὰ ὅπλα καὶ τὰ τείχη Plu.2.781d; make a tour of, τὰ μαγειρεῖα Thphr.Char.6.9: generally, make a tour of inspection, X.Cyr.8.6.16; of the γυναικονόμος, Timocl.32.2:—Pass., ἐφοδεύεται the rounds are made, Ar.Av.1160. 2. rarely c. dat., superintend, watch over, ἀγῶσιν A.Ch.728 (anap.). 3. visit as a spy, spy out, Lxx De.1.22, al.: metaph., of a geographer, explore, Str.8.6.4, 17.1.1:—Pass., περιγεγραμμένων τῶν μεταρσίων ἐφοδευθήσεται καὶ τὰ πρόσγεια Placit.3.8.2. 4. metaph., of reasoning, carry on methodically, λόγον Sor.2.25, cf. S.E.M.8.222, Ptol.Tetr.103, Max.Tyr.16.8. **–ηγέω**, act as guide, Suid. **–ια**, τά, v. ἐφόδιον. **–ιάζω**, Ion. **ἐποδ–**, furnish with supplies for a journey, ἀποπέμπουσι ἐποδιάσαντες ἐς Ἀθήνας Hdt.9.99; τινα Plu.Cat.Mi.65: c. dupl. acc., ἐφόδιον –ιάσεις αὐτόν Lxx De.15.14: metaph., of Philosophy, ἐ. τινὰ πρὸς τὴν στρατείαν Plu.2.327e:—Med., supply oneself, ἐκ τῆς πόλεως Plb.18.20.2:—Pass., to be supplied with, τι Lxx Jo.9.12; λαμπρῶς –ασθείς J.BJ2.7.1: metaph., Ph.1.535; διὰ τὸ μὴ ἐφωδιάσθαι ἀπὸ φυσιολογίας Theo Sm. p.188 H. 2. generally, supply or furnish with a thing, αὐτοὺς ἀλκῇ καὶ ὅπλοις D.S.5.34; also ταῦτά σοι ἐφωδίασα Apollod.Poliorc.138.1. 3. reduce to system, Ptol.Tetr.9. 4. = impetum facio, irruo, Gloss. II. Med., c. acc. rei, πενταδραχμίαν ἑκάστῳ ἐφοδιασάμενος having seen that five drachmae were paid to each, X.HG1.6.12. 2. metaph., maintain, promote, ἀργίαν Plu.Sol.23; τὴν ἀπείθειαν Id. Cor.16. **–ιασμός**, ὁ, gloss on ἐπισιτισμός, Hsch. **–ιαστής**, οῦ, ὁ, Dor. **–τάς**, ᾶ, traveller (?), IG9(2).1358 (Lamia); = invasor, Gloss. **–ικός**, ή, όν, appertaining to method, [λόγος], title of work by Archimedes, Hero Metr.1.32. Adv. –κῶς systematically, Ptol. Tetr.106. 2. of an inspector, λειτουργίαι PTeb.32.4 (ii B.C.), etc.; μέτρῳ ἐφοδικῷ dub. in ib.208 (i B.C.). **–ιον**, τό, mostly in pl. **ἐφόδια**, Ion. **ἐπόδια**, τά (v. infr.), supplies for travelling, money and provisions, esp. of an army, ἐπόδια δοῦναι, λαβεῖν, Hdt.4.203, 6.70; δι' ἀπορίαν ἐφοδίων τοῖς στρατευομένοις D.3.20; of an ambassador's travelling-allowance, ἐφόδι' οὐκ ἔχω Ar.Ach.53, cf. Men.Pk.160; ἐφόδι' ἀναλίσκειν D.19.311, cf. BCH6.25 (Delos, ii B.C.): sg. in PSI 4.363.17 (iii B.C.): generally, ways and means, maintenance, ἐφόδια τῷ γήρᾳ ἱκανά D.49.67, cf. Ar.Pl.1024; τὰ τῆς φυγῆς ἐ. Aeschin.1.172, Plu.Arat.6; τὰ ἐ. τοῦ πολέμου the sinews of war, Arist.Rh.1411ᵃ12; ἐφόδια τοῖς ἵπποις And.4.30; of public money, οὐδὲ μιᾶς ἡμέρας ἐφόδι' ἐστὶν ἐν τῷ κοινῷ D.23.209; in phys. sense, τὰ ἐν σώματι ὑπάρχοντα ἐ. Arist.Pr.871ᵇ24. 2. less freq. in sg., εὐσεβὴς βίος μέγιστον ἐ. Epich.[261]; ἀργύριόν τι ῥητὸν ἔχοντας ἐ. Th.2.70; οὐκ ἔχων.. εἰ μὴ παῖδα καὶ ὅσον ἐ. X.An.7.3.20; χιλίας λαβόντες δραχμὰς ἐφόδιον παρ' ὑμῶν D.19.158, cf. SIG390.58 (iii B.C.): metaph., εἰς τὴν εὔνοιαν Hyp. Epit.27; ἡ χρηστότης.. θαυμαστὸν ἐ. βίῳ Men.472, cf. 360, 792; πρὸς εὔνοιαν Phld.Lib.p.18 O.; τὴν Ἰλιάδα τῆς πολεμικῆς ἀρετῆς ἐ. νομίζων Plu.Alex.8; τὴν σωφροσύνην ἐ. εἰς τὸ γῆρας ἀποτίθεσθαι Id.2.8c; ἐ. παιδείας ὁ πλοῦτος Artem.4.67. 3. metaph., = ἀφορμή, D.34.35, Hyp.Eux.19; εἰς τὸ ἐπιβουλεύειν Sor.1.3. **–ιος**, ον, for a journey, εὐχαί EM348.43. II. on the road, accessible, BGU1116.8 (i B.C.). **–ος** (A), ον, accessible, f.l. for εὐεφ–, Th.6.66 (in Sup. –ώτατος), Polyaen.1.49. **–ος** (B), ὁ, one who goes the rounds, X. Cyr.8.6.16, Plb.6.36.6. 2. inspector, PTeb.30.27 (ii B.C.). **–ος** (C), ἡ, approach, Th.4.129, 6.99 (pl.); αὐτόθεν ἐπὶ τοὺς πολεμίους X. An.4.2.6; εἰς τὸν λόφον ib.3.4.41; entrance to a holy place, Jahresh. 18 Beibl.23 (Cilicia, ii A.D.); ἔφοδον θύειν sacrifice on arrival, GDI 2501.34 (Delph.). b. ἔφοδοι θαλάττης advance of the tides, Thphr. Metaph.29. c. in argument, method of reasoning, ἡ ἀπὸ τῶν καθ' ἕκαστον ἐπὶ τὰ καθόλου ἔ. Arist.Top.105ᵃ14; τὰ ἀκόλουθα, τὰ ἑξῆς τῆς ἐ., Ph.1.572, 598; ἐξ ἐναργέος ἐφόδου, i.e. from the clear teaching of experience, Hp.Praec.1. d. Archit., course of masonry, IG2².244.98 (iv B.C.), 5(2).33 (Tegea, iii B.C.). 2. means of approach, Plb.1.13.9; right of access, δίδοσθαί τινι τὴν ἔ. ἐπὶ τοὺς πολλοὺς Id.4.34.5; ἐπὶ τὰς ἀρχὰς καὶ τὸν δῆμον SIG278.12 (Priene, iv B.C.), cf. IG11(4).547 (Delos, iii B.C.); access for traffic and intercourse, communication, ἔφοδοι παρ' ἀλλήλους Th.1.6; πρὸς ἀλλ. Id.5.35; right of importation, τῶν ἐπιτηδείων X.HG2.4.3. b. pl., natural passages, e.g. nostrils, Hp.Epid.6.2.16. 3. attempt, plan, method, ib.6.5.1, Arist.EE1230ᵃ35, Thphr.Sens.60; ἔ. τῆς ἐξηγήσεως Plb.3.1.11; method of procedure, Vett.Val.24.12; σοφιστικοῖς λόγοις καὶ ἐφόδοις χρησάμενοι Id.334.9. II. attack, onslaught, A.Eu.375 (lyr., pl.), Th.1.93, etc.; τοῦ στρατεύματος X.An.2.2.18; ἔφοδον ποιεῖσθαι Th.2.95; δέξασθαι Id.4.126, Pl.Phd.95b; γνώμης μᾶλλον ἐφόδῳ ἢ ἰσχύος Th.3.11; ἐξ ἐφόδου τρέψασθαι at the first assault, Plb.1.36.11, cf. OGI 654.4 (Egypt, i B.C.), etc.; τῇ πρώτῃ ἐφόδῳ ἁλῶναι D.H.4.51; αὐτῇ ἐ. τρεψόμενοι τοὺς πολεμίους Id.3.4; of ships, εἰς τὴν ὁδὸν καὶ εἰς τὴν ἔφοδον dub. l. in Plb.3.25.4 codd. (leg. ἀφ–); νυκτιπόλοι ἔφοδοι of the haunting powers of darkness, as subject to Persephone, E.Ion 1049 (lyr.). 2. attack or access of fever, Hp.Prog.20; afflux of heat or cold, Id.Vict.1.32 (pl.). 3. Rhet., artful exordium, D.H.Is.3 (pl.), Lys.15; = insinuatio, [Cic.] ad Herenn.1.4.6, cf. Aphth.Prog. 13, etc. III. proceedings in a law-court, suit, PHib.1.96.10 (iii B.C.), etc.

ἐφοίτη, Dor. 3 sg. impf. of φοιτάω.

ἐφόλκ-αιον, τό, (ἐφέλκω) prob. lading-plank, ξεστὸν ἐ. Od.14.350. **–ή**, ἡ, tension, pull, Sor.2.62. **–ιον**, τό, small boat towed after a ship, Moschio ap.Ath.5.208f, Plu.Pomp.73, Philostr.VA4.32: pl., Str.2.3.4. 2. generally, appendage, AP7.67 (Leon.), Plu.Pomp.40; of a verse or phrase, Aristid.2.23 J., 330 J.; = sq. 2, Men.Pk.380. 3. rudder, Hsch. **–ίς**, ίδος, ἡ, = foreg. 1, Ach.Tat.3.3, Philostr.VA 4.9. 2. = foreg. 2, burdensome appendage, τινι E.Andr.200, cf. HF631, 1424 (pl.), Ael.Fr.110. **–ός**, όν, drawing on, enticing, ἐφολκὰ λέγειν Th.4.108: c. gen., παιδὸς ἐφολκόν Call.Fr.291; ἐ. εἰς παρρησίαν Ael.VH8.12; ὅσα κυνὶ ὀρέγεται ἐ. εἰς τὴν ἑαυτοῦ φιλίαν Id. NA7.10. II. requiring to be drawn on, laggard, Ar.V.268; μὴ πρόλεσχος μηδ' ἐ. ἐν λόγῳ not eager to begin, nor yet lagging, tedious in reply, A.Supp.200.

ἐφομαρτέω, accompany, come on (with), abs., Il.8.191, 12.412, 23.414 (ἐφαμ- Aristarch.), Nic.Al.479: c. dat., A.R.1.201: rare in Prose, as Arr.An.1.19.2.

ἐφομῑλέω, live with or among, c. acc., dub. in Hermesian.7.51: c. dat., Nonn.D.5.410.

ἐφόνιον, τό, saddle for an ass, PCair.Zen.355.86 (iii B.C.).

ἐφοπλίζω, get ready, of meals, δόρπον, δεῖπνον ἐ., Il.23.55, Od.19.419; δαῖτα γέρουσιν ἐφοπλίζωμεν Il.4.344:—Med., δόρπα τ' ἐφοπλισόμεσθα we will get ready our suppers, 8.503, 9.66. 2. fit out, equip, make ready, ἡμιόνους καὶ ἅμαξαν ἐφοπλίσαι Od.6.37, cf. 57, 69, Il.24.263; [νῆα] ἐφοπλίσσαντες Od.2.295: c. inf., A.R.4.1720. 3. arm against, τινά τινι Opp.C.3.244:—Med., Ἔρων ὔμμιν ἐφοπλίσομαι AP9.39 (Music.), cf. APl.4.151.9. II. Med. in prop. sense, arm oneself, ἐς ἀγῶνα Opp.H.5.617; get ready to attack, λαγωοῖς Id.C. 3.86.

ἐφόρ-ᾱσις, εως, ἡ, observation, ἡ τῶν θεῶν ἐ. Porph.Marc.21. **–ᾱτέον**, one must observe, Heph.Astr.3.4. **–ᾱτικός**, ή, όν, fit for overlooking, ἔργων X.Oec.12.19. **–άω**, Ion. 3 sg. ἐπορᾷ, inf. ἐπορᾶν, Hdt.1.10, 3.53: Aeol. pres. part. ἐπόρεις (ἐφορεῖς cod.) Lyr.Adesp. 61: impf. ἐφεώρων, Ion. 3 sg. ἐπώρα Hdt.1.48: fut. ἐπόψομαι Od.19.260, A.Ag.1642, etc.: aor. 1 ἐπόψατο Pi.Fr.88.6 (but ἐπεῖδον (q.v.) generally used as aor. 1):—Pass., Dor. aor. 1 inf. ἐποφθῆμεν Diotog. ap.Stob.4.1.96: (ἐπιόψομαι (q.v.), ἐπιώψατο are from a diff t. root):—oversee, observe, of the sun, πάντ' ἐφορᾷς καὶ πάντ' ἐπακούεις Il.3.277, cf. Od.11.109, S.El.824 (lyr.); ὁπόσας ἐφορᾷ φέγγος ἀελίου E.Hipp. 849 (lyr., codd.); of the gods, watch over, visit, Ζεὺς.. ὅς τε καὶ ἄλλους ἀνθρώπους ἐφορᾷ Od.13.214; θεοὶ.. ἀνθρώπων ὕβριν τε καὶ εὐνομίην ἐφορῶντες 17.487; Ζεὺς πάντων ἐφορᾷ τέλος Sol.13.17; σὲ γὰρ θεοὶ ἐπορῶσι Hdt.1.124; Ζεὺς ὃς ἐφορᾷ πάντα S.El.175 (lyr.); Δίκην πάντα τὰ τῶν ἀνθρώπων ἐφορᾶν D.25.11 (later c. gen., χώρα ἧς ὁ Ἥλιος ἐφορᾷ UPZ14.30 (ii B.C.), etc.); λιμὸς μαλθακόν σφ' ἐπόψεται A.Ag.1642; of men, τὰ πρήγματα ἐπορᾶν τε καὶ διέπειν Hdt.3.53; [τὰς πόλεις] Eup. 290; πάντ' ἐφορῶν καὶ διοικῶν D.3.34; οὐ ῥᾴδιον ἐφορᾶν πολλὰ τὸν ἕνα Arist.Pol.1287ᵇ8; ἀρχὴ ἐφορῶσα περὶ τὰ συμβόλαια ib.1321ᵇ13; of a general going his rounds, Th.6.67, X.Cyr.5.3.59; visit the wounded, αὐτόπτης ἐ. ib.5.4.18; δαῖτα ἐποψόμενος attend it, Pi.O.8.52 (s.v.l.):—Pass., of insane persons, δοκοῦσιν ὑπό τινων μειζόνων ἐφορᾶσθαι δυνάμεων Paul.Aeg.3.14. 2. look upon, behold, ἐποψόμενος Τιτυόν Od.7.324; ἕκαστα τῶν συγγραμμάτων inspect them, Hdt.1.48: freq. c. part., ἐπόψεαι.. φεύγοντας Il.14.145; κτεινομένους μνηστῆρας Od.20.233; ἐπορᾷ μιν ἐξιόντα Hdt.1.10; ἐ. τοὺς φίλους εὐδαίμονας γενομένους X. Cyr.8.7.7, etc.; cf. ἐπεῖδον: esp. of evils, ἐποψόμενος Κακοΐλιον Od. 19.260, al.; Ἀγαμέμνονός σέ φημ' ἐπόψεσθαι μόρον A.Ag.1246; τὰ μέλλοντ' οὐδεὶς ἐ. S.Tr.1270 (anap.), cf. Ar.Th.1048 (lyr.):—Pass., ὅσον ἐφεωρᾶτο τῆς νήσου as much of it as was in view, Th.3.104. 3. Astrol., = ἐπιβλέπω III, Cat.Cod.Astr.1.126.

ἐφορ-εία, ἡ, (ἐφορεύω II) office of ephor, X.Lac.8.3, Lys.Fr.315 S.; with v.l. **ἐφορία**, Arist.Pol.1270ᵇ7, Rh.1419ᵃ31. II. (ὅρος) frontier, Hecat.217 J. **–εῖον**, τό, office or court of the ephors, X.Ages. 1.36, Plu.2.232f. **–εύω**, = ἐφοράω, c. acc., A.Supp.627 (anap.), 677 (lyr.), Eu.531 (lyr.); χώρας Id.Pers.7 (anap.); περί τινος Luc. Charid.10. II. to be ephor, Th.8.6, X.HG1.3.1, Abh.Berl.Akad. 1925(5).8 (Cyrene), Tab.Heracl.1.122. **–ικός**, ή, όν, of or for the ephors, δίφροι X.Lac.15.6.

ἐφόριος, α, ον, (ὅρος) bordering on, Ῥωμαίων App.BC5.9; on the border or frontier, ἀγορὰ ἐ., where the people of adjacent states met for market and other purposes, IG1².115.27 (= D.23.37); ἐ. πόλεις Aristid.Or.26(14).81; στήλη Poll.9.8; δένδρα prob. in Ostr.Strassb. 772 (ii A.D.). II. ἐφόρια, τά, boundaries, PFay.23(a).5 (ii A.D.).

ἐφορμ-αίνω, rush on, δρόμῳ A.Pers.208, cf. Orph.H.33.5, 74.7; τινι upon or against one, Opp.C.3.367. **–άω**, Ion. **ἐπ–**, stir up, rouse against one, οἵ μοι ἐφώρμησαν πόλεμον Il.3.165; ὅς μοι ἐφορμήσας ἀνέμους Od.7.272; ἐπορμῆσαι τοὺς λύκους set them on, Hdt.9.93; ᾧ καὶ Ζεὺς ἐφορμήσῃ κακά S.Fr.680; σὺν Ant.Lib.2.2: c. dupl. acc., ναύτας ἐφορμήσαντα.. τὸ πλεῖν having urged them on to sail, S.Aj. 1143: c. acc. et inf., Orph.L.26. II. intr., rush upon, attack, τινι E.Hipp.1275 (lyr.), Plu.Pomp.19, etc.; ἐπί τινα D.C.36.24: abs., Plb.8.6.1: c. inf., desire, Opp.H.2.94, Orph.L.34; f.l. for ἀφορμ– in X.HG1.6.21.—This use is more freq. in Pass. (v. infr.). III. Pass. and Med., to be stirred up: c. inf., to be eager or desire to do, θυμὸς ἐφορμᾶται πολεμίζειν ἠδὲ μάχεσθαι Il.13.74, cf. Od.1.275, 21.399, etc.: abs., rush furiously on, ἔγχει ἐφορμᾶσθαι Il.17.465: mostly in aor. part. Pass., ἐφορμηθείς 6.410, etc.; ἄκοντι ἐφορμαθείς Pi.N.10.69; ἐφορμηθέντες ἐξ ἑνὸς ῥόθου A.Pers.462: without hostile sense, spring forward, τρὶς μὲν ἐφωρμήθην Od.11.206, cf. Hes.Op.459: c. acc., rush upon, make a dash at, ὥς τ' ὀρνίθων.. αἰετὸς αἴθων ἔθνος ἐφορμᾶται Il.15.691, cf. 20.461; so ἐφορμήσεσθαι ἀέθλους Hes.Sc.127: rarely (if ever) found in Prose, dub. l. in Th.6.49. **–έω**, Ion. **ἐπ–**, lie moored at or over against a place, blockade it, λαθὼν τοὺς ἐπορμέοντας having escaped the blockading fleet, Hdt.8.81, cf. Th.8.75, X.An.7.6.25; πεζῇ τε καὶ ναυσὶν ἐ. Th.4.24: c. dat., ἐ. τῷ λιμένι Id.7.3, cf. 3.31; ἐπὶ τῇ Μιλήτῳ Id.8.30; ἐπὶ τῷ λιμένι X.HG6.2.7; ἐπὶ τοῦ στόματος Plb.

1.46.5: c. acc., ἐ. ναυσὶ τὴν ἀκτὴν App.*BC*5.72: generally, *lie by and watch*, S.*OC*812; ἐ. τοῖς καιροῖς D.3.7; *rely on*, εἰκόσι καὶ πιθανοῖς Ph. 2.413, al.:—Pass., *to be blockaded*, Th.1.142, 8.20. **-ή**, ἡ, *way of attack*, μία δ' οἴη γίγνετ' ἐφορμή only *room* for one *to attack*, Od.22. 130, cf. A.R.4.148, Opp.*H*.4.623; *assault, attack*, πόλεις ἐφορμαῖς λαβεῖν Th.6.90; *enterprise*, A.R.4.204. **-ησις** (A), εως, ἡ, (ἐφορμέω) *lying at anchor so as to watch* an enemy, *blockading*, Th.2.89, 8.15; *means of so doing*, Id.6.48; ἐ. παρασχεῖν Id.3.33. **-ησις** (B), εως, ἡ, (ἐφορμάω) *onset, attack*, ἐχθρῶν Ph.2.174; κατ' ἐχθρῶν ib.296: pl., App.*BC*5.106. 2. *approach*, Hld.8.9. **-ητικός**, ή, όν, *capable of urging on*, Max.Tyr.7.8, v.l. for ἐξορμ- in Poll.4.86. **-ίζω**, (ὅρμος) *bring* a ship *to her moorings, bring to shore*, in Med., ἀμφὶ ταύτην θῖνα *AP*7.636 (Crin.):—Med. and Pass., *come to anchor*, ἐς [λιμένα] Th.4.8:—in Med. also, = ἐφορμέω, -ορμιούμενος τοῖς πολεμίοις App.*BC*5.108. II. intr. in Act., *seek refuge in*, [ἔλαφοι] ποταμοῖσιν ἐφώρμισαν *AP*9.244 (Apollonid.), cf. 254 (Phil.). **-ος** (A), ον, *at anchor*, αἱ νῆες.. ἔφορμοι οὖσαι Th.3.76 (s. v. l.); τὸ πλοῖον ἔφορμον ποιήσω *Mim.Oxy*.413.194 (ii A.D.). **-ος** (B), ὁ, = ἐφόρμησις, τοὺς ἐ. ποιεῖσθαι Th.3.6, cf. 4.27; ἐς ἔ. πλεῖν ib.32.

ἔφορος, ὁ, (cf. ἐπίουρος) *overseer, guardian, ruler*, στρατιᾶς A.*Pers.* 25 (anap.); χώρας S.*OC*145 (lyr.); σφαγίων E.*Rh*.30 (lyr.); τῶν παίδων Pl.*Phdr*.265c; καρπῶν, οἰάκων, Aristid.*Or*.41(4).10, 42(6).4; ὁ τῆς γενέσεως ἔ. θεός Procl.*in Ti*.1.53 D., al.: as fem., Ael.*Fr*.160: later in neut. pl., ἔφορα Iamb.*Myst*.4.1. II. at Sparta, ἔφοροι, οἱ, *the ephors*, Hdt.1.65, 6.82, 9.76, Pl.*Lg*.692a, Arist.*Pol*.1265b39, 1272a5; also, title of magistrates at Heraclea, *Tab.Heracl*.1. 1, al.; at Thera, *Test.Epict*.4.1; in the Eleuthero-Laconian cities, *IG*5(1).1110, al.; also of officials of corporations, ib.209.8 (sg.), 26.4 (pl.).

ἐφοστρίδες· εἶδος ἱματίου, Hsch. (nisi leg. ἐφεστρ-).

ἐφυβρ-ίζω, *insult over* one, ἐφυβρίζων ἔλετο Il.9.368: c. dat., S. *Aj*.1385: c. acc., τὴν ἀμαθίαν ὑμῶν Plu.2.579c, cf. *APl*.1.4 (also Med., μὴ 'φυβρίζεσθαι νεκρούς E.*Ph*.1663): with neut. Adj., πολλὰ ἐ. τινά Id.*Heracl*.947; τὰ δεινὰ πόλει Id.*Ph*.179; εἰς ἀδελφὸν οἷ' ἐφύβρισας Id.*Andr*.624; ἐφύβριζον ἄλλα τε καὶ εἰ.. they *gave vent to insulting language*, asking especially whether.., Th.6.63. II. *exult maliciously*, S.*Aj*.955 (lyr.). **-ιστήρ**, ῆρος, ὁ, *insulting*, ἴαμβοι v.l. in *AP*7.352. **-ιστής**, οῦ, ὁ, *insolent person*, Ptol.*Tetr*.165. **-ιστος**, ον, *wanton, insolent*, Vett.Val.71.18; τυραννίς Hdn.2.4.2, 6.1.2; ἐφύβριστα πάσχειν Id.2.7.3: c. dat., ἐ. ἀναστροφῇ *revelling in*.., Man.4. 312. Adv. -τως Plu.*Art*.30, Hdn.2.13.11. II. Pass., *contemptible*, Lxx *Wi*.17.7. Adv. -τως, κατέστρεψε τὸν βίον Posidon.7 J.

ἐφυγρ-αίνομαι, Pass., *become moist*: of the bowels, *to be relaxed*, Hp.*Epid*.1.10. **-ος**, ον, *moist on the surface*, Arist.*Pr*.935a28; ὀμφαλοί ib.896a17: Comp., τὰ -ότερα Thphr.*CP*2.4.7.

ἐφυδάτιος [ᾰ], η, ον, *in* or *of the water*, Νύμφη ἐφυδατίη A.R.1. 1229.

ἐφυδρ-εύω, *water*, τι Thphr.*HP*2.7.1. **-ιάς**, άδος, ἡ, *of the water*, Νύμφαι Alex.Aet.3.22, *AP*9.327 (Hermocr.), 329 (Leon.). **-ίς**, *water-spider*, *Gloss*.; ἐφυδρίδες is prob. f.l. in Artem.2.38 marg. **-ος**, Ion. ἔπ-, ον, (ὕδωρ) *moist, rainy*, of the west wind, Od.14.458; ἡμέρα Aristid.*Or*.48(24).50. 2. *abounding in water*, [γῆ] ἔπυδρος πίδαξι Hdt.4.198, cf. Hp.*Aër*.1, Arist.*Mete*.347a31, Dsc.1.15. 3. *living on the water*, νῆτται Philostr.*Im*.1.9 (cf. ἐπίυδρος).

ἐφ' ὕδωρ (not ἐφύδωρ), ὁ, *keeper of the water-clock* (κλεψύδρα) in the Athen. law-courts, Poll.8.113 (but ἐφ' ὕδωρ *under water, submerged*, *CPR*32.11 (iii A.D.)).

ἐφῠλακτέω, *bark at*, τινι Plu.2.551c.

ἐφυμν-έω, *sing* or *chant at* or *after*, οὐ γὰρ ὡς φυγῇ παιᾶν' ἐφύμνουν A.*Pers*.393; *chant* or *utter over*, τί οὖν μ' ἄνωγας τῇδ' ἐφυμνῆσαι χθονί; Id.*Eu*.902, cf. *Ch*.386 (lyr.); κακὰς πράξεις ἐφυμνήσασα τῷ παιδοκτόνῳ S.*Ant*.1305; τὸ πάτριον μέλος ἐ. Pl.*Lg*.947c, cf. *Smp*.197e; later of orations, etc., ἐ. τῇ θεῷ Philostr.*VS*1.25.3; τίνι μύθων φῆμαι θαυμαστότερα ἐφύμνησαν; Aristid.*Or*.22(19).2:—Pass., Pl.*Lg*.799a; [ἐπῳδὸν] ἐφυμνεῖσθαι καλόν Ph.1.312. 2. of music, *sound in accord*, ἐφυμνεῖ πηκτίδος συγχορδία S.*Fr*.412. II. *sing a dirge* or *mournful strain*, Id.*OT*1275. III. *sing of, descant on*, Δία Id.*Ant*. 658. **-ιάζω**, *sing as the refrain*, Eratosth.ap.Sch.Pi.*O*.9.1 (Pass.). **-ιον**, τό, *burden, refrain*, of a hymn, A.R.2.713, Call. *Ap*.98, *Sos*.8.4, Ph.1.535, Ath.15.701c, Sch.Pi.*O*.9.1.

ἐφύπερα [ῠ], τά, *upper floor*, *BGU*1247.11 (ii B.C.).

ἐφύπερθε [ῠ], before a vowel -θεν, Adv. *above, atop*, στορέσαι ἐ. Il. 24.645, cf. 9.213; κεφαλή τ' ἐ. τε χαῖται Od.4.150, cf. Il.14.184; *from above*, Od.9.383, Theoc.23.59: c. gen., Simon.183.7: Geog., *above*, c. gen., A.R.2.393.

ἐφυπν-όω, *sleep meantime*, Hsch. **-ώττω**, *go to sleep over*, τοῖς Ὁμήρου ποιήμασιν Jul.*Ep*.190.

Ἐφύρα [ῠ], Ion. -ρη, ἡ, *Ephyra*, old name of Corinth, Il.6.152; also perh. of other cities in Elis and Thesprotia, Sch.Od.1.259, 2. 328:—hence **Ἐφύρ-ηθεν**, A.R.4.1212: **-ηνδε**, Call.*Del*.42.

ἐφυστερ-έω, *to be late, in arrear*, ὅσα ἐφυστερήκει τοῖς καιροῖς J. *AJ*19.1.5, cf. 18.9.3; *to be deferred*, Sor.1.21, Gal.7.471: c. gen., *to be left behind by*, τοῦ ἡλίου Alex.Aphr.*in Mete*.31.28. **-ητικός**, ή, όν, '*postponing*', of increasingly rare attacks of fever, Gal.19. 201. **-ίζω**, *come later, come after*, τὰ ἐφυστερίζοντα, = αἱ ὑστεροῦσαι πόλεις, Th.3.82, cf. D.H.*Th*.29; *to be deferred, overdue*, Gal.7.471.

ἐφῠφαίνω, *weave in* or *upon*, ἐπὶ μῆτιν ὑφαίνων Opp.*C*.3.415.

ἐφῠφή, ἡ, *woof*, opp. στήμων, Pl.*Lg*.734e.

ἐφύω [ῡ], *rain upon*: impers. ἐφύει, c. dat., Thphr.*HP*4.14.8, etc.: abs., *it rains after*, Id.*CP*6.17.7:—pf. part. Pass. ἐφυσμένος *exposed to rain*, X.*Cyn*.9.5.

ἐφ' ᾧ, ἐφ' ᾧτε, i.e. ἐπὶ τούτῳ ὥστε, v. ἐπί B. III. 3.

ἐφώδει· ἐπέληγε (Lacon.), Hsch. **ἐφώσια**· τὰ νομιζόμενα, Id.

ἐφώριος, ον, (ὥρα) *mature*, *AP*9.563 (Leon.).

ἔχᾰδον, v. χανδάνω.

ἐχέβοιον, τό, = μεσάβοιον, Poll.1.252.

ἐχέβωμον, τό, *altar-base* or *chapel containing an altar*, *IG*12(5).595 *B*24, *Mus.Belg*.25.108 (Iulis).

ἐχέγγῠος, ον, *having given* or *able to give security, trustworthy, secure*, δόμοι E.*Med*.387; λόγος Id.*Andr*.192; ποιεῖν δόσιν ἐ. Id.*Ph*. 759; ζημία ἐ. a penalty *to be relied on* (for the prevention of crime), Th.3.46; φρουρά D.H.2.37: Comp. -ώτερος Them.*Or*.26.321d: Sup. -ώτατος, μάρτυς Ath.9.398f; τὸ τῆς φρουρᾶς ἐ. *security*, Hdn.2.13.8; ἐ. πρὸς ἀσφάλειαν, εἰς σωτηρίαν, Plu.2.595f, 1055b: c. gen., σωφροσύνης τρόπος οὗτος ἐ. *AP*10.56.11 (Pall.); ἀπορρήτων ἐ. *safe to be entrusted with* secrets, Plu.*Publ*.4; ἀξίωμα ἐ. πρὸς ἡγεμονίαν *equal* to command, Id.*Per*.37, cf. Hdn.3.13.4: c. inf., *sufficiently strong* to.., Plu.*Aem*. 8, 2.923c; οὐκ ἐ. πρὸς τὸ ἀριθμεῖν not *sufficient justification* for counting.., Longin.ap.Porph.*Plot*.20. II. Pass., *having received a pledge, secured against danger*, ἱκέτης S.*OC*284.

ἐχε-γλωττία, ἡ, *tongue-truce*, '*linguistice*', coined by Luc.*Lex*.9, after ἐκεχειρία (*armistice*). **-γνάθον**, τό, *bit*, dub. in *PStrassb*.37.9 (ii A.D.). **-δερμία**, ἡ, *being hide-bound*, of horses, *Hippiatr*.26; = Lat. *coriago*, Veget.*Mulom*.2.118. **-δημία**, ἡ, = *Academia* (after Echemos, king of Arcadia), coined by Dicaearch.ap.Plu.*Thes*.32. **-θῡμος**, ον, *a master of one's passions, under self-control*, Od.8.320:—Subst. **-θῡμία** is v. l. for -μυθία in Ph.2.267.

ἐχείδιον, τό, Dim. of ἔχις, *little adder*, Suid. s. v. ἔχις; cf. ἐχίδιον.

ἐχε-κήλης, (κήλη) *ruptured*, Hsch. **-κολλος**, ον, *glutinous, sticky*, Hp.*Art*.33 (Comp.); πηλὸς Plu.2.966d; τὸ ἐχέκολλον ib.735f; ἐχέκολλον μάλιστα ἡ πεύκη *takes glue* best, Thphr.*HP*5.6.2. Adv. -λως Dsc.5.153. **-κτέᾰνος**, ον, *with great possessions*, Rhian.1.7, Nonn.*D*.11.37. **-μῡθέω**, *to hold one's peace*, Ph.1.309, al., J.*BJ* 1.24.1, Luc.*DDeor*.21.2; τὰ ἀπόρρητα καὶ ἐχεμυθούμενα *things unspoken*, Iambl.*Protr*.21; a Pythagorean word, εἰ δύνανται ἐ. Id.*VP* 20.94. **-μῡθία**, ἡ, *silence, reserve*, ἡ Πυθαγόρειος ἐ. Plu.*Num*.8, cf. 2.728d, Ph.2.267 (v. l. -θυμία), Alciphr.3.55, Ath.7.308d, Iamb.*VP* 6.32, etc. **-μῡθος**, ον, *taciturn*, in Sup., Suid. **-νηΐς**, ΐδος, contr. **-νῆς**, ῆδος, ἡ, (ναῦς) *ship-detaining*, ἄπλοιαι A.*Ag*.149 (lyr.); ἄγκυρα *AP*6.27.5 (Theaet.); γαλήνη Nonn.*D*.13.114. II. a small fish, supposed to have the power of *holding ships back*, Arist.*HA*505b19, Opp.*H*.1.212, Plin.*HN*9.79; in form **ἐχεναΐς**, = Lat. *remora*, Donat. ad Ter.*Andr*.739, *Eun*.302. **-νίκειον** [νῑ], τό, *endowment created by Echenice*, *Inscr.Délos* 370.42:—hence **-εια**, τά, *festival maintained thereby*, ib.366*A* 133 (iii B.C.).

ἐχεόδηκτος, ον, *bitten by a viper*, Str.13.1.14 codd., Dsc.2.120, Philum.*Ven*.17.11.

ἐχε-πάμων [ᾱ], ον, gen. ονος, *holding property*: hence, *heir* or *representative*, *IG*9(1).334.16 (Locr.). **-πευκής**, ές, (πευκ-, cf. *pungo*) *sharp, piercing*, βέλος Il.1.51, 4.129: expld. by Eust., etc., as *bitter*, and so later σμύρνη Nic.*Th*.600; σικύοιο ῥίζα ib.866, cf. Orph.*L*.475. **-πικρος**, ον, = foreg., Eust.42.33. **-πωλος**, ον, *having horses*, Hsch., Suid. **-ρρημοσύνη**, ἡ, (ῥῆμα) = ἐχεμυθία, Iamb.*VP*34.246. **-σᾱμία**· ὅτε θέρους ὄντος ψεκάσῃ ἢ βροντήσῃ, Hsch. (i.e. a sign which causes public business to be suspended, cf. διοσημία). **-σαρκος**, ον *clinging close to the body*, χιτών Ath.13. 590f.

ἔχεσκον, v. ἔχω.

ἐχέστονος, ον, *bringing sorrows*, ἰός Theoc.25.213.

ἐχέτης, ου, ὁ, = ὁ ἔχων, *man of substance*, Pi.*Fr*.304.

ἐχέτλ-η, ἡ, (ἔχω) *plough-handle*, Hes.*Op*.467, A.R.3.1325, *AP* 7.650 (Phalaec.), D.S.9.7, Alciphr.3.19, Luc.*JTr*.31:—hence **-εύω**, *plough*, Hsch. **-ήεις**, εσσα, εν, *of an* ἐχέτλη, γόμφος *AP*6.41 (Agath.). **-ιον**, τό, *hold* of a ship, Nic.*Th*.825.

ἐχετογνώμονες, οἱ, *sluices* or *penstocks to hold up the water at a certain height*, Abyd.8.

ἐχέτρωσις, εως, ἡ, *Bryonia cretica*, Hp.*Nat.Mul*.33, Gal.19.101, cj. in Dsc.4.182.

ἔχευα, ας, ε, Ep. aor. 1 of χέω, Hom.:—Med., ἐχεύατο Il.5.314.

ἐχε-φρονέω, *to be prudent*, *APl*.4.332.6 (Agath.). **-φροσύνη**, ἡ, *prudence, good sense*, *AP*9.767 (Agath.). **-φρων**, ον, gen. ονος, (φρήν) *sensible, prudent*, ἀνὴρ ἀγαθὸς καὶ ἐ. Il.9.341, cf. Od.13.332; freq. as epith. of Penelope, 4.111, etc.; later of animals, σκύλακες Nonn.*D*.16.226: late in Prose, Syn.Alch.p.65B. Adv. -νως D.S. 15.33.

ἐχήνια, τά, *part of a bridle* or *bit*, *IG*2^{2}.1388.74, 1464.13.

ἔχης, ητος, ὁ, = ἐχέτης, Hdn.*Epim*.38, *EM*404.23.

ἔχησις, εως, ἡ, *having*, Alex.Aphr.*in Metaph*.417.27.

ἐχθ-αίρω, Dor. 3 pl. -οντι Theoc.24.29: impf. ἤχθαιρον E.*Supp*. 879: aor. 1 ἤχθηρα Il.20.306, A.*Pers*.772, etc.; Dor. ἤχθᾱρα Timocr. 1.4:—Med., Ep. aor. 1 ἠχθήρατο in act. sense, Nic.*Al*.618, cf. ἀπεχθαίρω:—Pass., S.*Aj*.458: fut. Med. ἐχθαροῦμαι in pass. sense, Id.*Ant*.93: (ἔχθος):—*hate, detest*, ἵν' ἐχθήρειε γέροντα Il.9.452, cf. Od.4.692; ὄφρα σε Λιμὸς ἐχθαίρῃ, φιλέῃ δέ.. Δημήτηρ Hes.*Op*.300 (cf. *Certam*.317); Θεμιστοκλῆ' ἤχθαρε Λατώ Timocr.l.c., cf. Ion Trag. 44, parodied by Ar.*Ra*.1425: c. acc. cogn., ἔχθος ἐχθαίρω μέγα S. *Ph*.59: with acc. pers. added, οὐδ' αὖ τοσοῦτον ἔχθος ἐχθαίρω σε I *do* not *bear* thee so great *hatred*, Id.*El*.1034:—Pass., *to be hateful*, θεοῖσι A.*Supp.*754, cf. S.*Aj.*458 : abs., A.*Ch.*241 : fut. Med., ἐχθαρῇ μὲν ἐξ ἐμοῦ S.*Ant.*93 :—Med. in act. sense, Nic.*Al.*618.—Poet. word, used by Hp.*Ep.*17, Arist.*EN*1126ᵇ24, 1180ᵃ22, and late Prose, Parth. 36.2, Str.17.2.3, Ph.2.543,555 (c. inf., ἅ τις παθεῖν ἐχθαίρει (v.l. ἐχθραίνῃ) Id.ap.Eus.*PE*8.7), Plu.*Rom.*17, D.C.37.38, etc. (ἐχθραίνω is f.l. in E.*Med.*555, etc.) **-αρτέος**, α, ον, *to be hated*, S.*Aj.* 679.

ἔχθαρ, τό, = ἔχθος, Theognost.*Can.*79.

ἐχθέγιον, τό, dub. sens. in *BGU*950.4 (Byz.).

ἐχθές, Adv. = χθές, *yesterday*, Ar.*Nu.*175, *Th.*616, etc.; ἀπ' ἐ. *AP* 11.35 (Phld.); μέσφα τό γ' ἐ. Theoc.2.144; οὐ γάρ τι νῦν γε κἀ. to-day or *yesterday*, S.*Ant.*456; οὐκ ἐ. οὐδὲ πρῴην Antipho *Fr.*58; ἐ. καὶ τρίτης [ἡμέρας] Lxx *Ru.*2.11, cf. M.Ant.10.7. (ἐχθές is commoner than χθές in Com. and Lxx, is the only form used in *NT*, and freq. in papyri of all periods, *PSI*4.442.21 (iii B. C.), etc.; cf. χθές.)

ἐχθεσῐνός, ή, όν, = χθεσινός, *yesterday's*, διαγωγή *AP*10.79 (Pall.), cf. Dosith.p.397 K.

ἐχθέω, v. ἔχθω (A).

ἔχθημα, ατος, τό, = μίσημα, S.*Fr.*651.

ἐχθιζινός, ή, όν, = ἐχθεσινός, Men.303.

ἐχθ-ίζομαι, *incur odium*, Phot. **-ιστος**, η, ον, Sup. of ἐχθρός, *most hateful*, Ἀχιλῆϊ Il.2.220; ἔ. δέ μοί ἐσσι θεῶν 5.890, etc.; τὸν θεοῖς ἔ. θεόν A.*Pr.*37; ἔ. ὁρᾶν S.*Aj.*818; ἔ. γεγώς E.*Med.*467. 2. *most hostile*, τῶν ἡμῖν ἐχθίστων Th.2.71; ὡς δὲ ἐχθροὶ καὶ ἔ., πάντες ἴστε Id.7.68: c. gen., οἱ ἐκείνου ἔ. his *bitterest enemies*, X.*An.*3.2.5: Luc. has also ἐχθίστατος *Trag.*246. **-ίων**, ον, gen. ονος, Comp. of ἐχθρός, *more hateful*, A.*Pers.*438, S.*OT*272, E.*El.*222, Ar.*Av.*370, Th.4.86, Pl.*Ly.*214c. Adv. ἐχθιόνως, ἔχειν X.*Smp.*4.3.

ἐχθο-δᾰπός, όν, *foreign, hostile*, φῶτες *IGRom.*4.360.38 (Pergam., ii A. D.): perh. formed fr. ἐχθός, cf. ἀλλοδαπός, ἡμεδαπός, etc. **-δοπέω**, *show enmity towards, engage in hostility with*, ὅ τέ μ' ἐχθοδοπῆσαι ἐφήσεις Ἥρῃ Il.1.518. **-δοπός**, όν, *hateful*, φώς S.*Ph.*1137 (lyr.); πόλεμος Ar.*Ach.*226 (lyr.); τοῖα.. ἀνεστέναζες.. ἐχθοδόπ' Ἀτρείδαις S.*Aj.*931 (lyr.); τῆς ὁδοῦ ἐχθοδοποῦ γεγονυίας πολλοῖς, ἴσως δὲ.. ἑτέροις προσφιλοῦς Pl.*Lg.*810d; of a drug, Pl.Com. 196; ἐ. ὄμματα A.R.4.1669. (Perh. by assimilation fr. ἐχθοδαπός 'foreign', 'hostile' (q. v.).)

ἔχθοι, Adv. *outside*, *IG*4.1484.66 (Epid.).

ἔχθος, εος, τό, *hate*, Διὸς ἔχθος ἀλευάμενος Od.9.277: and in pl., ἔχθεα λυγρά Il.3.416, cf. Pi.*P.*2.55; ἴδια, κοινὰ ἔχθεα, Hdt.3.82; κατὰ ἔχθος τινὸς *hatred for* one, Id.9.15, cf. Th.1.103, 7.57; ἔχθει c. gen., A.*Supp.*332, Th.1.95; ἐς ἔχθεα ἀπικνέεσθαί τινι to incur his *enmity*, Hdt.3.82; εἰς ἔχθος ἐλθεῖν τινι E.*Ph.*879; ὑπ' ἔχθους Plu.*Publ.*9. II. ὦ πλεῖστον ἔ. *object of* direst *hate*, A.*Pers.*284.—In Prose ἔχθρα is more freq.

ἐχθός, Adv. = ἐκτός, *outside*, τᾶς ϝοικίας *Schwyzer* 323*C*35 (Delph., iv B. C.). 2. *except*, προξένω ib.363.11 (Locr., v B. C.).

ἐχθόσδῐκος δίκα suit *with a foreigner*, *IG*5(2).357.26 (Stymphalus, iii B. C.).

ἔχθρ-α, Ion. **ἔχθρη**, ἡ, *hatred, enmity*, Hdt.5.81, Pi.*P.*4.145, etc.: in philos. sense, = νεῖκος 1.5, Plot.3.2.2; ἔ. τινός *hatred for, enmity to* one, Antipho 2.4.1, Th.3.10; κατ' ἔχθραν τινός Ar.*Pax*133; ἔ. ἔς τινα Hdt.1.5, Th.2.68; εἰς θεόν *Ep.Rom.*8.7; πρός τινα A.*Pr.*491 (pl.), Th.2.68; δι' ἔχθρας μολεῖν, ἀφῖχθαί τινι, to be *at feud* with one, E.*Ph.* 479, *Hipp.*1164; δι' ἔχθρας οὐδετέρῳ γενήσομαι Ar.*Ra.*1412; εἰς ἔ. βάλλειν τινά A.*Pr.*390; εἰς ἔ. ἐλθεῖν D.21.62; καταστῆσαί τινας εἰς ἔχθραν τῷ δήμῳ X.*HG*3.5.9; πολλὴν εἰς ἔχθραν ἀλλήλοις καὶ πολλῶν πέρι καθίστανται Pl.*Plt.*307d, cf. Isoc.9.67; πρὸς ἔχθραν from *personal enmity*, D.18.141; ἔ. συμβάλλειν, συνάπτειν τινί, to engage in *hostility* with.., E.*Med.*45, *Heracl.*459; ἔ. τισὶν ἄρασθαι D.21.132; καταλλάσσεσθαι τὰς ἔ. Hdt.7.145; λύσασαν ἔ. τὴν πάρος E.*Tr.*50; τὰς μεγάλας ἔ. διαλύεσθαι Th.4.19; πρὸς ἀλλήλους ἔ. ἀνείλοντο Is.1.9; διαλλαχθῆναι τῆς ἔ. And.2.26: prov., Ἐμπεδοκλέους ἔ., of undying *hatred*, Lys. *Fr.*261 S. **-αίνω**, impf. ἤχθραινον X.*Ages.*11.5: aor. 1 ἤχθρηνα Max.67, -ᾶνα Ph.2.394; later form of ἐχθαίρω (q. v.): (ἐχθρός):—*hate*, τινα X. l. c.; τι Ph.2.297; οἱ ἐχθράναντες *one's enemies*, ib.394:—Pass., ὑπό τινων Phld.*Mort.*20; also ἐ. τινί *to be at enmity with*, Lxx *Nu.*25.18, al., Ael.*NA*5.2. II. *make hateful* or *hostile*, τινά τινι Max. l. c. **-ασμα**, ατος, τό, = ἔχθρα, Hsch. **-εύω**, *to be at enmity with*, τινι Lxx *Ex.*23.22, al., Phld.*Rh.*2.134 S., Tz.*H.*1. 671. **-ία**, ἡ, late form of ἔχθρα, Lxx *Ge.*26.21. **-ικός**, ή, όν, *hostile*, interpol. in Hermog.*Id.*1.8, cf. Astramps.*Onir.*1.

ἐχθρο-δαίμων, ον, gen. ονος, *hated of the gods*, S.*OT*816. **-ειδῶς**, Adv. = ὑπόπτως, Hsch. **-λέων**, οντος, ὁ, *opponent-lion*, *IG*2.2836 (εἰχθρ- lapis). **-ξενος**, ον, *hostile to strangers, inhospitable*, ναύταισι A.*Pr.*727, cf. *Th.*606,621; δόμοι E.*Alc.*558. **-ποιέω**, *make hostile*, App.*BC*5.60, cf. Hsch.:—Pass., Ptol.*Tetr.*191. **-ποιός**, όν, *causing enmity*, δαίμονες Charond.ap.Stob.4.2.24, cf. App.*BC*1.54.

ἐχθρός, ά, όν, (ἔχθος) *hated, hateful*, of persons and things, freq. from Hom. downwds. (Hom. has it only in this pass. sense); ἐ. γάρ μοι κεῖνος ὁμῶς Ἀΐδαο πύλῃσι Od.14.156, Il.9.312; ἐχθρὸν δέ μοί ἐστιν c. inf., 'tis *hateful* to me to.., Od.12.452; θεοῖσιν ἐ. Hes.*Th.* 766, Thgn.601, Ar.*Eq.*34; ὁ θεοῖσιν ἐ. Pl.Com.74, etc.; cf. θεοισεχθρός. II. Act., *hating, hostile*, first in Hes. and Pi. (v. infr. III), τινι D.10.11, X.*Ages.*6.1, etc.: c. gen., ὕβριος ἐχθρὰν ὁδὸν *averse from* insolence, Pi.*O.*7.90: abs., ἐ. γλῶσσα A.*Ch.*309 (anap.); ὀργαί Id.*Eu.*937 (anap.), etc.; ἀστέρες Vett.Val.143.5. III. as Subst., ἐχθρός, ὁ, *enemy*, where the act. and pass. senses freq. coincide, Hes.*Op.*342, Pi.*P.*2.84, etc.; ἀνὴρ ἐ. Hdt.1.92; ὁ Διὸς ἐ. A.*Pr.*120 (anap.); ἐχθροῖς ἐχθρὰ πορσύνων Id.*Ag.*1374; εἴ.. τινα ἴδοι ἐχθρὸν ἑαυτοῦ Th.4.47; οἱ ἐμοὶ ἐ. Id.6.89, etc.—Acc. to Ammon.*Diff.*p.63 V., ἐχθρός is *one who has been* φίλος, *but is alienated*; πολέμιος *one who is at war*; δυσμενής *one who has long been alienated and refuses to be reconciled.* IV. regul. Comp. ἐχθρότερος D.*Prooem.*40.3, *AP*5. 160 (Hedyl. or Asclep.); Sup. -ότατος Pi.*N.*1.65, S.*OT*1346 (lyr.), D.19.300: but more freq. irreg. ἐχθίων, ἔχθιστος (qq. v.). V. Adv. ἐχθρῶς, μισοῦντες Pl.*Lg.*697d, etc.: Comp. -οτέρως D.5.18: Sup. -ότατα Id.23.149.

ἐχθρόφρων, ον, gen. ονος, *hostile in disposition*, *EM*245.23.

ἐχθρωδ-έω, *to be hostile*, πρός τινας Suid. s. v. Ἐμπεδοκλέους ἔχθρα. **-ης**, ες, *hostile*, Sch.Opp.*H.*1.685: Comp. -έστερος Sch. E.*Hec.*745, *Or.*614. Adv. -δῶς, διαθεῖναί τινα πρός τινας J.*BJ*1.24.2; ἐ. ἔχειν τινί D.C.43.10, cf. Nic.Dam.57 J., Sch.E.*Med.*290.

ἐχθῦσαι· ἐξεμέσαι, and **ἐχθύσῃ**· ἐκφυσήσῃ, Hsch.

ἐχθῡσία, v. ἐκθυσία.

ἔχθω (A), *hate*, οὐ δικαίως θάνατον ἔχθουσιν βροτοί A.*Fr.*353; ἔχθεις S.*Ph.*510 (lyr.), E.*Med.*117 (anap.); ἔχθει S.*Aj.*459: c. dupl. acc., ταῦτά τοί σ' ἔχθει πόσις E.*Andr.*212:—Hom. only in Pass., καὶ ἐχθομένη περ Ἀθήνῃ Od.4.502; οὐ γὰρ οἴω πάγχυ θεοῖς..[αὐτὸν] ἔχθεσθαι ib. 756; ἤ τοι ἐμοὶ ῥήγεα σιγαλόεντα ἤχθεθ' 19.338; ἤχθετο πᾶσι θεοῖσι 14. 366; κολοσσῶν ἔχθεται χάρις ἀνδρί A.*Ag.*417 (lyr.); σωφρονοῦντι δ' ἤχθετο E.*Hipp.*1402.—Only pres. and impf., exc. pf. part. Pass. ἠχθημένος Lyc.827: the forms ἔχθει (imper.) Thgn.1032, ἤχθεε Hermesian.7.39 are corrupt.

ἔχθω (B), = ἔξω, *except*, c. gen., *Schwyzer* 323*C*43 (Delph., iv B. C.).

ἐχίδιον, τό, *young viper*, Arist.*HA*558ᵃ29 (v. l. ἐχίδνιον); cf. ἐχείδιον.

ἔχιδν-α, ἡ, (ἔχις) *viper*, Hdt.3.108, S.*Tr.*771, Pl.*Smp.*218a, etc.; prob. of a *constrictor snake*, *Act.Ap.*28.3: metaph., of a treacherous wife or friend, A.*Ch.*249, S.*Ant.*531; ἱματισμένη ἔ., of woman, Secund.*Sent.*8; γεννήματα ἐχιδνῶν brood *of vipers*, term of reproach, in *Ev.Matt.*3.7. II. pr. n. of a monster, Hes.*Th.*297, S.*Tr.* 1099. **-αῖος**, α, ον, *of* or *like a viper*, χόλος *AP*7.71 (Gaet.). 2. *snaky*, κόρυμβος Nonn.*D.*14.216. II. pr. Adj. Ἐχιδναῖος, α, ον, *born of Echidna*, δάκετον Call.*Fr.*161. **-ήεις**, εσσα, εν, = foreg., Nic.*Th.*209; δίφρος ἐ. *drawn by vipers*, Nonn.*D.*13.191.

ἐχιδνο-ειδής, ές, *snake-like*, *Gloss.* **-κέφᾰλος**, ον, *snake-headed*, Sch.E.*Ph.*1136. **-κομος**, ον, *snaky-haired*, Nonn.*D.*1. 173. **-λογέω**, *collect vipers*, Eust. ad D.P.376. **-τοκος**, ον, *born of a viper*, Anon.*Prog.*9 in Rh.1.626 W. **-φᾰγία**, ἡ, *eating of vipers*, Dsc.*Eup.*1.227.

ἐχιδνώδης, ες, = ἐχιδνοειδής, Sch.E.*Ph.*1136.

ἐχίειον [ῐ], τό, = ἔχιον II, Nic.*Th.*65, 637. II. Adj. -ειος, α, ον, = ἐχιδναῖος, Tz.*H.*12.840.

ἐχῑεύς, έως, ὁ, *a young viper*, pl. ἐχιῆες Nic.*Th.*133.

Ἐχῖναι, ῶν, αἱ, *islands in the Ionian sea*, Il.2.625, E.*IA*286 (lyr.), etc.:—commonly called **Ἐχινάδες**, αἱ, Hdt.2.10, Th.2.102, etc.

ἐχιναῖος, ον, = ἐχιδναῖος, dub. in Nic.*Th.*230.

ἐχῖνᾰλώπηξ, εκος, ὁ, *hedgehog-fox*, St.Byz. s. v. Ἀζανοί.

ἐχινέα, ἡ, a kind of *vase*, *BCH*35.286 (Delos, ii B. C.), *Ath.Mitt.* 33.377 (Pergam.), *Chron.Lind.*B.101; contr. **ἐχινῆ** (q. v.).

ἐχινέες, οἱ, *kind of mouse with rough bristling hair*, in Libya, Hdt. 4.192 (v. l. ἐχῖνες): acc. pl. ἐχίνας Arist.*Mir.*832ᵇ3.

ἐχινῆ (sc. δορά), ἡ, *hedgehog's skin*, Hdn.Gr.1.334. II. ἐ. στρατιωτική, prob. = ἐχινέα, *IG*11(2).161*B*125 (Delos, iii B. C.).

ἐχίνιον, τό, = ἱπποφαές, Ps.-Dsc.4.159.

ἐχῖνίς, ίδος, ἡ, = ἐχῖνος II. 1, Hp.*Nat.Mul.*32.

ἐχῖνίσκος, ὁ, Dim. of ἐχῖνος, *hollow of the ear*, Poll.2.86. II. Dim. of ἐχῖνος II, Id.10.95.

ἐχῖνο-μήτρα, ἡ, *the largest kind of sea-urchin*, *Echinus melo*, Arist. *HA*530ᵇ6. **-πους**, ποδος, ὁ, *kind of prickly-plant*, *Genista acanthoclada*, perh. the same as ἔχιον, Eleg.ap.Plu.2.44e (pl.), cf. Hsch. s. v. λυκόφανον, *EM*405.12.

ἐχῖνος, ὁ (on the accent, v. Hdn.Gr.1.183), *hedgehog* (prop. ἐ. χερσαῖος, as in Thphr.*Sign.*30), *Erinaceus europaeus*, Archil.118, Emp. 83, Ar.*Pax*1086, Ion Trag.38, S.*Ichn.*121, etc. 2. *sea-urchin*, Epich.53, Archipp.24; ἐ. θαλάττιος Pl.*Euthd.*298d. II. *large wide-mouthed jar*, Hp.*Mul.*2.172, *Steril.*230, Ar.*V.*1436, Eup.415, Men.*Epit.Fr.*10, Erot., Hsch., Poll.6.91. 2. *vase* in which the notes of evidence were sealed up by the διαιτηταί, in cases of appeal from their decision, D.45.17, 48.48, Arist.*Ath.*53.2, Thphr.*Char.*6. 8. III. hard *case* of beech-mast, chestnuts, etc., Id.*HP*3.10. 1, Xenocr.43, Hsch. 2. *neck-vertebra* of the κεστρεύς, Dorio ap. Ath.7.306f. IV. *third stomach of ruminating animals*, Arist.*PA* 676ᵃ11, 674ᵇ15, *HA*507ᵇ6, Antig.*Mir.*17; βοῶν ἐ. Call.*Fr.*250; also, *gizzard* of graminivorous birds, Ael.*NA*14.7. V. pl., *sharp points* at each end of a bit, X.*Eq.*10.6, Poll.1.148; but = τῶν ὑποστομίων τὰ κοῖλα, ib.184. VI. Archit., *cushion of the Doric and Tuscan capital* (prob. from its form), Vitr.4.3.4, 4.7.3. 2. = οἱ τῶν τειχῶν ἀγκῶνες, Hsch. VII. a kind of *cake*, Lync.ap.Ath.14.647a, Hsch. VIII. a plant, v. l. ἔρινος (q. v.), Dsc.4.141, Gal.11.880, Paul.Aeg.7.3. (Cf. OHG. *igil*, Slav. *ježĭ*, Lith. *ežỹs*.)

ἐχῖνώδης, ες, *prickly, like a hedgehog*, Arist.*Mir.*832ᵇ3, cf. Ar.Byz. *Epit.*109.9: generally, *rugged*, Str.12.3.11.

ἐχῐόδηκτος, ον, = ἐχιδνόδηκτος, Dsc.1.13, al., *Gp.*12.30.1; v. l. for ἐχεό-, Str.13.1.14.

ἔχιον, τό, (ἔχις) a plant, *Echium plantagineum*, Dsc.4.27 (*echios* Plin.*HN*25.104). II. = ὠκιμοειδές, Dsc.4.28, Sch.Nic.*Th.*637.

ἔχῐς [Nic.*Th*.223, -ῑς metri gr. *IG*2.1660], εως, ὁ (ἡ Opp.*C*.3.439), gen. pl. ἔχεων Pl.*Euthd*.290a: gen. sg. ἔχιος Nic.*Th*.130: pl., dat. ἐχίεσσι ib.826; gen. ἐχίων ib.653; acc. ἔχιας ib.9, but ἔχεις Thphr. *Char*.1.7:—*viper*, Pl.*Smp*.217e, Arist.*HA*511ᵃ16, etc.: metaph., συκοφάντης καὶ ἔ. τὴν φύσιν D.25.96; ὥσπερ ἔ. ἢ σκορπίος ἠρκὼς τὸ κέντρον ib.52; cf. ἔχιδνα. II. = ἔχιον II, Nic.*Th*.541, 636, Plin. *HN*22.50.

ἐχίτης [ῑ], ου, ὁ, a kind of *stone*, Plin.*HN*37.187, *Gloss*.

ἔχμα, ατος, τό, (ἔχω) *that which holds*; and so, I. *hindrance, impediment*, Il.21.259 (pl.). 2. c. gen., *bulwark, defence against*, ἐπηλυσίης *h.Merc*.37; βολάων A.R.4.201. II. *holdfast, stay*, ἔχματα πέτρης *the grip* of the rock (viz. the river-bed), Il.13.139; ἔχματα πύργων *buttresses* of the fortifications, 12.260; ἔχματα νηῶν *props* or *cradles* for the ships, 14.410; ἔχματα γαίης, of the earth which *holds fast* the roots of a tree, A.R.1.1200; ἔχματα γούνων, of muscles, Nic.*Th*.724:—also **ἐχμός**, ὁ, Eust.1411.24.

ἐχμάζω, *hold fast, hinder*, Eust.904.4, Sch.E.*Or*.265, Hsch.; cf. ὀχμάζω.

ἐχομένιον, τό, *coriander*, *POxy*.729.31 (ii A.D.), 1279.17 (ii A.D.).

ἐχομένως, Adv. pres. part. of ἔχομαι, = ἐφεξῆς, prob. in Epicur. *Ep*.2 p.40 U., cf. Apollod.3.1.1, Ph.1.84, A.D.*Pron*.101.6, Bito 57.1, Petos.ap.Vett.Val.332.32, etc.; ἐ. τινός *next after* him, D.L.4.23.

ἐχόντως, Adv. pres. part. of ἔχω, in phrase ἐ. νοῦν, = νουνεχόντως (q.v.), Pl.*Lg*.686e; ἐχόντως ἑαυτὸν τὸν νοῦν Id.*Phlb*.64a.

ἐχυρῆσαι· τῷ διὰ χειρὸς ὅρκῳ συνθέσθαι, καὶ κρατηθῆναι, Hsch.

ἐχῡρ-ός, ά, όν, (ἔχω) = ὀχυρός, *strong, secure*, λιμήν, χωρία, Th.4.8, X.*Cyr*.2.4.13; ἀπὸ ἐχυροῦ ποθέν Th.1.90; ἐν τῷ ἐχυρῷ εἶναι to be in *safety*, Id.7.77; ἐν -ωτάτῳ ποιεῖσθαί τι X.*Cyr*.1.6.26. 2. of arguments, etc., *strong*, λόγος Th.3.83; ἐλπίς Id.7.41; ἐχυρὰ παρέχεσθαι to give *good reasons*, Id.1.32; τὴν τόλμαν..-ωτέραν παρέχεσθαι Id.2.62; -ωτέρα δύναμις Id.1.42; τοῦτο ὁ φόβος ἐχυρὸν παρεῖχε Id.3.12; ἀποδείξεις -ώταται Ph.1.420. 3. of persons, ἐ. πρὸς τοὺς καλούς *proof* against, Plu.*Sol*.1. II. Adv. -ρῶς Th.5.26: Comp. -ώτερον Id.8.24. (ὀχυρός is v.l. in A.*Pers*.78, 89 (lyr.), and is the usual form in Plb., exc. 2.30.6; but ἐχυρός is usual in Ph., as 1.257, al.) **-ότης**, ητος, ἡ, *strength*, ἐν οἰκοδομίαις Ph.2.116, cf. 120, 1.478 (ἐχ- Pap.), 688, J.*AJ*15.11.4. (ὀχυρότης is a v.l. and shd. be preferred in Plb.1.57.6, but for καὶ ὀχ- (v.l. καὶ ἰσχ-) in Ph.1.644 καὶ ἐχ- shd. be restored.) **-όφρων**, ον, gen. ονος, (φρήν) *strong-minded*, Hsch. **-όω**, *make secure, fortify*, Phot., Suid.; ἐχυρῶσαι is v.l. for ὁρίσαι, Isoc.5.122.

ἔχω (A), 2 sg. ἔχεισθα cj. in Thgn.1316 (ἔχοισθα cod.), ἔχησθα cj. in Sapph.21 (ἔχεισθα cod.); 2 sg. subj. ἔχησθα Il.19.180: impf. εἶχον, Ep. ἔχον Od.2.22, al., Ion. and poet. ἔχεσκον Il.13.257, Hdt.6.12, *Epigr.Gr*.988.6 (Balbilla): fut. ἕξω, Ep. inf. ἑξέμεναι Call.*Aet*.3.1.27 (of duration) or σχήσω (of momentary action, esp. in sense *check*, v. infr. A. II. 9, not found in Att. Inscrr. or *NT*); 2 sg. σχήσησθα *h.Cer*.366 codd.: aor. 1 ἔσχησα f.l. in Nonn.*D*.17.177, also ἔσχα *IG*3.1363.6, 14.1728, 3 pl. μετ-έσχαν ib.12(7).271.12 (Amorgos, iii A.D.): aor. 2 ἔσχον, imper. σχές S.*El*.1013, E.*Hipp*.1353 (anap.) (σχέ only in Orac.ap. Sch.E.*Ph*.638 (dub.l.), sts. in compds. in codd., as πάρασχε E.*Hec*. 842, κάτασχε Id.*HF*1210); subj. σχῶ Il.21.309, etc.; opt. σχοίην Isoc. 1.45, in compds. σχοῖμι (as μετάσχοιμι S.*OC*1484 (lyr.), κατάσχοιμεν Th.6.11); 3 pl. σχοίησαν Hyp.*Eux*.32, σχοῖεν Th.6.33; inf. σχεῖν Il. 16.520, etc., Ep. σχέμεν 8.254 (in Alexandr. Gr. 3 pl. impf. and aor. 2 εἴχοσαν *AP*5.208 (Posidipp. or Asclep.), v.l. in *Ev.Jo*.15.22, ἔσχοσαν Scymn.695): for the poet. form ἔσχεθον, v. *σχέθω: pf. ἔσχηκα Pl.*Lg*.765a, εἴσχηκα in Inscrr. of iii/i B.C., *SIG*679.54, etc.; Ep. ὄχωκα is dub., v. συνόχωκα:—Med., impf. εἰχόμην Pi.*P*.4.244, etc.: fut. ἕξομαι Il.9.102, etc.; σχήσομαι ib.235, Ar.*Av*.1335, more freq. in compds. (ἀνα-) A.*Th*.252, (παρα-) Lys.9.8, etc.: pf. Pass. παρ-έσχημαι in med. sense, X.*An*.7.6.11, etc.: aor. 2 ἐσχόμην Hom., Hdt.6. 85, rare in Att. exc. in compds.; imper. σχέο Il.21.379, σχέσθε 22. 416, later σχοῦ in compds. (ἀνά-) E.*Ion*947, etc.; inf. σχέσθαι Od.4. 422, Hes.*Fr*.79:—Pass., fut. Med. ἐν-έξομαι in pass. sense, E.*Or*. 516, D.51.11, later σχεθήσομαι Gal.*UP*15.3, freq. in compds. (συ-) Phld.*Ir*.p.83 W., (ἐν-) Plu.2.980f, (ἐπι-) S.E.*P*.1.186: aor. 1 ἐσχέθην Arr.*An*.5.7.4, 6.11.2, Aret.*SA*2.5, (κατ-, συν-) Plu.*Sol*.21, Hp.*Int*. 45 vulg.: fut. Med. σχήσομαι in pass. sense, Il.9.235 (dub.), 655, 13. 630: aor. 2 Med. in pass. sense, ἐσχόμην Il.17.696, al., Hdt.1.31 (σχέτο Il.7.248, 21.345), part. σχόμενος Od.11.279, prob. in Isoc.19. 11, (κατα-) Pi.*P*.1.10, Pl.*Phdr*.244e, Parth.33.2 (s.v.l.): pf. ἔσχημαι Paus.4.21.2; also in compds., freq. written -ίσχημαι, -ήσχημαι in codd. of late authors. (I.-E. *segh-* (cf. Skt. *sáhate* 'overpower', Goth. *sigis* 'victory', Gr. ἔχ- dissim. fr. ἕχ-), reduced form *sgh-* (σχ-), whence redupl. ἴσχω (= *si-sgh-o*) (q.v.): cf. ἕκ-τωρ, ἕξω, ἕξις; but ἡέχ- *IG*1².374.161, al., is a mere error (ἔχ- ib.1².116.4, 16).)

A. Trans., *have, hold*: I. *possess*, of property, the most common usage, Od.2.336, 16.386, etc.; οἵ τι ἔχοντες the *propertied class*, Hdt.6.22; ὁ ἔχων a *wealthy man*, S.*Aj*.157 (anap.); οἱ ἔχοντες E.*Alc*.57, Ar.*Eq*.1295, *Pl*.596; οἱ οὐκ ἔχοντες the *poor*, E.*Supp*.240; κακὸν τὸ μὴ 'χειν Id.*Ph*.405; ἔχειν χρέα *to have* debts *due to one*, D. 36.41, cf. 37.12; *to have received*, θεῶν ἄπο κάλλος ἔ. *h.Ven*.77; τι ἔκ τινος S.*OC*1618; παρά τινος Id.*Aj*.663; πρός τινος X.*An*.7.6.33, etc.; ὑπὸ..θεοῖσι *h.Ap*.191; πλέον, ἔλασσον ἔ. (v. h. vv.): in aor., *acquire, get*, ὄνομα E.*Ion*997: also fut. σχήσω, δύναμιν Th.6.6; λέχος E.*Hel*.30, cf. Pi.*P*.9.116:—Pass., *to be possessed*, ἔντεα..μετὰ Τρώεσσιν ἔχονται Il.18.130, cf. 197. 2. *keep, have charge of*, ἔχον πατρώϊα ἔργα Od. 2.22; κῆπον 4.737; Εἰλείθυιαι..ὠδῖνας ἔχουσαι Il.11.271; πύλαι.., ἃς ἔχον Ὧραι 5.749, 8.393; τὰς ἀγέλας X.*Cyr*.7.3.7; διαιτητῶν ἐχόντων τὰς δίκας *having control of*, D.47.45; *to be engaged in*, φυλακὰς ἔχον *kept* watch, Il.9.1, 471; σκοπιὴν ἔχεν Od.8.302; ἀλαοσκοπιὴν εἶχε Il. 10.515, 13.10; σκοπιὴν ἔ. τινός *for* a thing, Hdt.5.13; δυσμενῶν θήραν ἔχων S.*Aj*.564, etc.; ἐν χερσὶν ἔ. τι (v. χείρ). b. metaph., of a patient, οὐκ ἔχει ἑωυτόν *is* not *himself*, Hp.*Int*.49. 3. c. acc. loci, *inhabit*, οὐρανόν Il.21.267; Ὄλυμπον 5.890; *haunt*, [Νύμφαι] ἔχουσ' ὀρέων αἰπεινὰ κάρηνα Od.6.123; Βρόμιος ἔχει τὸν χῶρον A.*Eu*.24; esp. of tutelary gods and heroes, Th.2.74, X.*Cyr*.8.3.24; of men, πόλιν καὶ γαῖαν Od.6.177, 195, etc.; Θήβας ἔσχον (ἔσχεν codd.) *ruled* it, E.*HF*4; ἔχεις γὰρ χῶρον *occupiest* it, S.*OC*37, cf. Od.23.46; in military sense, ἔ. τὸ δεξιόν (with or without κέρας) Th.3.107, X.*An*.2.1.15; of beasts, τὰ ὄρη ἔ. Id.*Cyn*.5.12. 4. *have to wife* or *as husband* (usu. without γυναῖκα, ἄνδρα), οὕνεκ' ἔχεις Ἑλένην καί σφιν γαμβρὸς Διός ἐσσι Od. 4.569, cf. 7.313, Il.3.53, etc.; ἔσχε ἄλλην ἀδελφεήν Hdt.3.31, cf. Th.2. 29; νυμφίον Call.*Aet*.3.1.27; also of a lover, Th.6.54, *AP*5.185 (Posidipp.), etc.; ἔχω Λαΐδα, ἀλλ' οὐκ ἔχομαι Aristipp.ap.D.L.2.75, cf. Ath. 12.544d:—in Pass., τοῦ περ θυγάτηρ ἔχεθ' Ἕκτορι Il.6.398. 5. *have in one's house, entertain*, Od.17.515, 20.377, *h.Ven*.231, 273. 6. pres. part. with Verbs, almost, = *with*, ἤϊε ἔχων ταῦτα Hdt.3.128, cf. 2.115; ὃς ἂν ἥκῃ ἔχων στρατόν Id.7.8.δ', cf. X.*Cyr*.1.6.10.—Prose use. 7. of Place, ἐπ' ἀριστερὰ ἔ. τι *keep* it on one's left, i.e. to keep to the right of it, Od.3.171; ἐπ' ἀριστερὰ χειρὸς ἔ. 5.277; ἐν δεξιᾷ, ἐν ἀριστερᾷ ἔ., Th.3.106; τοὺς οἰκέτας ὑστάτους ἔ. X.*Cyr*.4.2.2: but in aor., *get*, περιπλώοντες τὴν Λιβύην τὸν ἥλιον ἔσχον ἐς τὰ δεξιά Hdt.4.42. 8. of Habits, States, or Conditions, bodily or mental, γῆρας λυγρὸν ἔ. Od.24.250; ἀνεκτὸν ἔχει κακόν 20.83; ἕλκος Il.16.517; λύσσαν 9.305; μάχην ἔ. 14.57; ἀρετῆς πέρι δῆριν ἔ. Od.24.515; ὕβριν ἔ. *indulge in*.., 1.368, etc.; [Ἀφροδίτην] 22.445; [φρένας] ἔ. Il.13.394, etc.; βουλήν 2.344; τλήμονα θυμὸν 5.670; τόνδε νόον καὶ θυμὸν ἐνὶ στήθεσσιν ἔχοντες 4.309, cf. Od.14.490 (for later senses of νοῦν ἔχειν, v. νοῦς); ἄλγεα Il.5.895, etc.; ἄχεα θυμῷ 3.412; πένθος μετὰ φρεσὶν 24. 105; πένθος φρεσίν Od.7.219; πόνον..καὶ ὀϊζὺν Il.13.2, Od.8.529; οὐδὲν βίαιον Hdt.3.15; πρήγματα ἔ. Id.7.147, cf. Pl.*Tht*.174b, etc.: in periphrastic phrases, ποθὴν ἔ. τινός, = ποθεῖν, Il.6.362; ἐπιδευὲς ἔ. τινός, = ἐπιδεύεσθαι, 19.180; ἔ. τέλος, = τελεῖσθαι, 18.378; κότον ἔ. τινί, = κοτεῖσθαι, 13.517; ἐπιθυμίαν τινός E.*Andr*.1281; φροντίδα τινός Id.*Med*.1301; ἡσυχίην ἔ. *keep* quiet, Hdt.2.45, etc. (fut. ἡσυχίαν ἕξειν D.47.29, but οὐκ ἔσθ' ὅπως..ἡ. σχήσει *will* not *keep* still *for a moment*, Id.1.14); αἰτίαν ἔ. *to be* accused, X.*An*.7.1.8; ὑπό τινος A.*Eu*.99 (but μομφὴν ἔ., = μέμφεσθαι, E.*Or*.1069, A.*Pr*.445): in aor., of entering upon a state, ἔσχεν χόλον *conceived* anger, B. 5.104; ἔχειν τι κατά τινος *have* something against somebody, *Ev. Matt*.5.23, *Ev.Marc*.11.25, *Apoc*.2.4; ἔχω τι πρός τινα *Act.Ap*.24. 19; ἔχειν πρός τινα *2Ep.Cor*.5.12; ἕξει πρὸς τὸν Θεόν *JRS*14.85 (Laodicea):—these phrases are freq. inverted, οὓς ἔχε γῆρας Il.18.515; οὐδὲ Ποσειδάωνα γέλως ἔχε Od.8.344; ἀμηχανίη δ' ἔχε θυμόν 9.295; θάμβος δ' ἔχεν εἰσορόωντας Il.4.79; σ' αὔτως κλέος ἐσθλὸν ἔχει 17.143; Διὸς αἴσῃ, ἥ μ' ἕξει παρὰ νηυσί 9.609 (unless the antecedent is τιμῆς in l.608); ὥς σφεας ἡσυχίη τῆς πολιορκίης ἔσχε Hdt.6.135; ὄφρα με βίος ἔχῃ S.*El*.225 (lyr.): c. dupl. acc., φόβος μ' ἔχει φρένας A.*Supp*.379; also of external objects, αἴθρη ἔχει κορυφήν Od.12.76; μιν ἔχεν μένος ἠελίοιο 10.160; σε οἶνος ἔχει φρένας 18.331; ἔχῃ βέλος ὀξὺ γυναῖκα, of a woman in travail, Il.11.269; λόγος ἔχει τινά c. inf., the story *goes, that*.., S.*OC*1573 (lyr.); and so in later Gr., Plu.*Dem*.28, Ph. 1.331, Ael.*VH*3.14, *NA*5.42, Ath.13.592e; ὡς ἡ φάτις μιν ἔχει Hdt. 7.3, cf. 5.26, 9.78 (but also ἔχει φάτιν Διονυσοφάνης θάψαι Μαρδόνιον Id.9.84; [Κλεισθένης] λόγον ἔχει τὴν Πυθίην ἀναπεῖσαι Id.5.66); ὡς ἂν λόγος ἔχῃ πρὸς ἀνθρώπους, ὅτι.. Plu.*Alex*.38:—Pass., ἔχεσθαι κακότητι καὶ ἄλγεσι Od.8.182; κωκυτῷ καὶ οἰμωγῇ Il.22.409; ὀργῇ Hdt.1.141; νούσῳ Hp.*Epid*.5.6; ἀγρυπνίῃσι Hdt.3.129; ὑπὸ πυρετοῦ Hp.*Aph*.4.34; ὑπὸ τοῦ ὕδρωπος Id.*Prorrh*.2.6, ἐν ἀπόρῳ Th.1. 25; ἐν συμφοραῖς Pl.*R*.395e. 9. *possess mentally, understand*, ἵππων δμῆσιν Il.17.476; τέχνην Hes.*Th*.770; πάντ' ἔχεις λόγον A. *Ag*.582, cf. E.*Alc*.51; ἔχετε τὸ πρᾶγμα S.*Ph*.789; ἔχεις τι; *do you understand?* Ar.*Nu*.733: imper. ἔχε *attend! listen!* Pl.*Alc*.1.109b; ἔ. οὖν ib.129b: with imper., ἔχ', ἀποκάθαιρε Ar.*Pax*1193; ἔ. νυν, ἄλειψον Id.*Eq*.490; ἔχεις τοῦτο ἰσχυρῶς; Pl.*Tht*.154a; *know of* a thing, μαντικῆς ὁδόν S.*OT*311; τινὰ σωτηρίαν; E.*Or*.778 (troch.). 10. *keep up, maintain*, καναχὴν ἔχε *made* a rattling noise, Il.16.105, 794; βοὴν ἔχον, of flutes and lyres, 18.495. 11. *involve, admit of*, τά γ' αἰσχρὰ κἀνθάδ' αἰσχύνην ἔχει E.*Andr*.244, cf. Th.1.5; βάσανον Lys.12.31; ταῦτ' ἀπιστίαν, ταῦτ' ὀργὴν ἔχει D.10.44; ἀγανάκτησιν, κατάμεμψιν, Th.2.41; τὰ ἀόρατα νοσήματα δυσχερεστέραν ἔχει τὴν θεραπείαν Onos. 1.15. 12. of Measure or Value, τὸ Δαμαρέτειον..εἶχε Ἀττικὰς δραχμὰς δέκα D.S.11.26; ἔχει τὸ Εὐβοϊκὸν τάλαντον Ἀλεξανδρείους δραχμὰς ἑπτακισχιλίας App.*Sic*.2.2; χοῖρος ἔχων τὸ ὕψος δύο καὶ ἡμίσους πήχεων Ptol.Euerg.9. b. Geom., ἡ ἔχουσα τὰ κέντρα the (straight line) *containing* the centres, Archim.*Aequil*.1.6; ὁ κύκλος ἔχων τὸ πολύγωνον the circle *containing* (*circumscribing*) the polygon, Id.*Sph.Cyl*.1.23. 13. c. dupl. acc., Ὀρφέα ἄνακτ' ἔχειν E.*Hipp*.953; Ζῆν' ἔχειν ἐπώμοτον S.*Tr*.1188; παιδιὰν ἔ. τὸν ἐκείνου θάνατον Seleuc. Alex.ap.Ath.4.155e. II. *hold*: 1. *hold*, ἔ. χερσίν, ἐν χερσίν, μετὰ χερσίν, etc., v. χείρ; μετὰ γαμφηλῇσιν ἔ. Il.13.200; πρόσθεν ἔ. ἀσπίδα ib.157; ὑψοῦ, πασάων ὕπερ, ὕπιθεν κάρη ἔ., 6.509, Od.6.107, Il. 23.136; ἔ. τινί τι *to hold* it for him, as his helper, 9.209, 13.600; *uphold*, οὐρανὸν..κεφαλῇ τε καὶ ἀκαμάτῃσι χέρεσσι Hes.*Th*.517, 746; ἔχει δέ τε κίονας, of Atlas, Od.1.53; ἐπ' ὤμων πατέρα S.*Fr*.

373. 2. *hold fast*, χειρὸς ἔχων Μενέλαον *holding* him *by* the hand, Il.4.154, cf. 16.763, 11.488 (v. infr. C.I); ἔ. τινὰ μέσον *grip* one by the middle, of wrestlers, Ar.*Nu.*1047; ἔχομαι μέσος Id.*Ach.*571, cf. *Eq.*388, *Ra.*469: metaph., ἔ. φρεσί *keep* in one's mind, Il.2.33; νῷ ἔ. τινά Pl.*Euthphr.*2b, cf. *R.*490a. 3. of arms and clothes, *bear, wear*, εἶμα δ' ἔχ' ἀμφ' ὤμοισι Il.18.538, cf. 595; παρδαλέην ὤμοισιν ἔ. 3.17; σάκος ὤμῳ 14.376; κυνέην κεφαλῇ Od.24.231; τάδε εἵματ' ἔχω 17.24, cf. 573, etc.; στολὴν ἀμφὶ σῶμα E.*Hel.*554, cf. X.*Cyr.*1.4.26, etc.; πολιὰς ἔχω I am grey-haired, Aeschin.1.49: abs., as a category, Arist.*Cat.*2^a3. 4. of a woman, *to be pregnant*, Hdt.5.41, Hp.*Epid.*4.21, Arist.*Pol.*1335^b18; in full ἐν γαστρὶ ἔ. Hdt.3.32; also πρὸς ἑωυτῇ ἔχειν Hp.*Epid.*1.26.ιγ'. b. παῖδα ἔσχεν she *had*, i.e. *bore*, a child, Nic.Dam.11 J. 5. *support, sustain*, esp. an attack, c. acc. pers., Il.13.51, 20.27; cf. B.I.1, C.III. 6. *hold fast, keep close*, ὀχῆες εἶχον [πύλας] 12.456; θύρην ἔχε μοῦνος ἐπιβλής 24.453. 7. *enclose*, φρένες ἧπαρ ἔχουσι Od.9.301; σάρκας τε καὶ ὀστέα ἶνες ἔ. 11.219; τοὺς δ' ἄκραντος ἔχει νύξ A.*Ch.*65 (lyr.); of places, *contain*, θηρῶν οὓς ὅδ' ἔχει χῶρος S.*Ph.*1147 (lyr.), cf. X.*Cyn.*5.4; [τεῖχος] νῆας ἐντὸς ἔχον Il.12.8; ὅσσους Κρήτη ἐντὸς ἔχει *h.Ap.*30. 8. *hold* or *keep in a certain direction*, ὀϊστὸν ἔχε *aimed* it, Il.23.871; more fully χεῖράς τε καὶ ἔγχεα.. ἀντίον ἀλλήλων 5.569; of horses or ships, *guide, drive, steer*, πεδίονδ' ἔχον ὠκέας ἵππους 3.263, cf. 11.760; φόβονδε 8.139; τῇ ῥα.. ἔχον ἵππους 5.752, etc.; παρὲξ ἔχε δίφρον Hes.*Sc.*352; ὅπῃ ἔσχες.. εὐεργέα νῆα Od.9.279; παρὰ τὴν ἤπειρον ἔ. νέας Hdt.6.95, etc.: abs., τῇ ῥ' ἔχε that way he *held his course*, Il.16.378, cf. 23.422; Πύλονδ' ἔχον I *held on* to Pylos, Od.3.182, cf. S.*El.*720: metaph., ἐπὶ ῥητορείαν ἔσχε Hsch.Mil.(?)ap.Sch.Pl.*R.*600c; also (esp. in fut. σχήσω, aor. 2 ἔσχον), *put in, land*, νέες ἔσχον ἐς τὴν Ἀργολίδα χώρην Hdt.6.92; σχεῖν πρὸς τὴν Σαλαμῖνα Id.8.40; ἐς Φειάν, τῷ Δήλῳ, κατὰ τὸ Ποσειδώνιον, Th.2.25, 3.29, 4.129; τάχ' οὖν τις ἄκων ἔσχε S.*Ph.*305; ποῖ σχήσειν δοκεῖς; Ar.*Ra.*188; ἔχε.. ἀρὰν ἐπ' ἄλλοις *point* it against others, S.*Ph.*1119 (lyr.); ὄμμ' ἔ. *to turn* or *keep* one's eye *fixed*, Id.*Aj.*191 (lyr.); ἐπὶ ἔργῳ θυμὸν ἔ. Hes.*Op.*445; ἄλλοσ' ὄμμα θητέρᾳ δὲ νοῦν ἔ. S.*Tr.*272; τὸν δὲ νοῦν ἐκεῖσ' ἔχει E.*Ph.*360; δεῦρο νοῦν ἔχε *attend to* this, Id.*Or.*1181; πρός τινα or πρός τι τὸν νοῦν ἔ., Th.3.22, 7.19; so πρός τινα τὴν γνώμην ἔ. Id.3.25. 9. *hold in, stay, keep back*, ἵππους Il.4.302, 16.712; *check, stop*, [τινα] 23.720, etc. (σχήσω is usu. fut. in this sense, τὸ πεπρωμένον οὐ σιδάρεον σχήσει τεῖχος Pi.*Fr.*232, cf. Il.11.820, Ar.*Lys.*284, D.19.272, but ἕξω Il.13.51); χεῖρας ἔχων Ἀχιλῆος *holding* his hands, 18.33; but οὐ σχήσει χεῖρας *will* not *stay* his hands, Od.22.70; ἔ. [δάκρυον] 16.191; ἔ. ὀδύνας *allay, assuage* them, Il.11.848; ἔσχε κῦμα Od.5.451; σιγῇ μῦθον 19.502 (so εἶχε σιγῇ καὶ ἔφραζε οὐδενί Hdt.9.93); ἐν φρεσὶ μῦθον Od.15.445; στόμα σῖγα, ἐν ἡσυχίᾳ, E.*Hipp.*660, *Fr.*773.61 (lyr.); πόδα Id.*IT*1159; πόδα ἔξω or ἐκτός τινος ἔχειν, v. πούς:—Pass., οὖρα σχεθέντα Aret.*SA* 2.5. 10. *keep away from*, c. gen. rei, τινὰ ἀγοράων, νεῶν, Il.2.275, 13.687; γόων S.*El.*375; φόνου E.*HF*1005: c. inf., ἦ τινα.. σχήσω ἀμυνέμεναι Il.17.182; *stop, hinder from* doing, τοῦ μὴ καταδῦναι X.*An.*3.5.11, cf. *HG*4.8.5; ἔσχον μὴ κτανεῖν E.*Andr.*686, cf. Hdt.1.158, etc.; μὴ οὐ τάδ' ἐξειπεῖν E.*Hipp.*658; ὥστε μή.. X.*An.*3.5.11; τὸ μὴ ἀδικεῖν A.*Eu.*691, cf. Hdt.5.101: also c. part., ἔ. τινὰ βουθυτοῦντα S.*OC*888 (troch.); μαργῶντα E.*Ph.*1156. 11. *keep back, withhold* a thing, ὅς οἱ χρήματα εἶχε βίῃ Od.15.231, cf. D.30.14; Ἕκτορ' ἔχει.. οὐδ' ἀπέλυσεν Il.24.115, cf. 136; αὐτὸς ἔχε *pray keep* it, a civil form of declining, E.*Cyc.*270. 12. *hold in guard, keep safe*, Il.24.730; of armour, *protect*, 22.322. 13. with predicate, *keep* in a condition or place, εἶχον ἀτρέμας σφέας αὐτούς Hdt.9.54, cf. 53, Ar.*Th.*230; ἔ. ἑωυτοὺς κατ' οἴκους Hdt.3.79; σαυτὸν ἐκποδὼν A.*Pr.*346, cf. X.*Cyr.*6.1.37; σῖγα νάπη φύλλ' εἶχε E.*Ba.*1085; τοὺς στρατιώτας πολὺν χρόνον πειθομένους ἔ. X.*Cyr.*7.2.11. 14. *hold, consider*, τινὰ θέᾳ ἰκέλαν Sapph.*Supp.*25.3 (dub.), cf. E.*Supp.*164; τινὰ ὡς προφήτην *Ev.Matt.*14.5; τινὰ ὅτι προφήτης ἦν *Ev.Marc.*11.32; ἔχε με παρῃτημένον *Ev.Luc.*14.18, cf. *POxy.*292.6 (i A.D.). III. c. inf., *have means* or *power* to do, *to be able*, c. aor. inf., Il.7.217, 16.110, etc.: c. pres. inf., Od.18.364, etc.; πόλλ' ἂν λέγειν ἔχοιμι S.*Ph.*1047: sts. with inf. omitted or supplied from context, ἀλλ' οὔ πως ἔτι εἶχε he *could* not, Il.17.354; οἷά κ' ἔχωμεν so far as we *be able*, Od.15.281; ἐξ οἵων ἔχω S.*El.*1379; ὅσον εἶχες E.*IA*1452; ὡς ἔχω Id.*Hec.*614. b. *have to face, be obliged*, παθεῖν Porph.*Chr.*63; εἰ ἕξω βλαβῆναι Astramps.*Orac.*p.5 H.; βάπτισμα ἔχω βαπτισθῆναι *Ev.Luc.*12.50. 2. after Hom., οὐκ ἔχω, folld. by a dependent clause, I *know* not.., οὐκ εἶχον τίς ἂν γενοίμαν A.*Pr.*905, cf. Isoc.12.130; οὐδ' ἔχω πῶς με χρὴ.. ἀφανίσαι S.*OC*1710; οὐκ ἔχων ὅ τι χρὴ λέγειν X.*Cyr.*1.4.24; οὐκ ἔχω ποῖ πέσω S.*Tr.*705; ὅπως μολούμεθ' οὐκ ἔχω Id.*OC*1743; the two constructions combined, οὐ γὰρ εἴχομεν οὔτ' ἀντιφωνεῖν οὔθ' ὅπως.. πράξαιμεν Id.*Ant.*270. IV. impers. c. acc., *there is*.. (as in Mod. Gr.), ἔχει δὲ φυλακτήριον πρὸς τὸ μή σε καταπεσεῖν *PMag.Par.*1.2505, cf. 1262, 1840.

B. intrans., *hold oneself*, i.e. *keep*, so and so, ἔχον [οὕτως], ὥς τε τάλαντα γυνή (sc. ἔχει) *kept balanced*, like the scales which.., Il.12.433; ἕξω δ' ὡς ὅτε τις στερεὴ λίθος I *will keep unmoved*, as a stone.., Od.19.494, cf. Il.13.679, 24.27; νωλεμέως ἐχέμεν 5.492; ἔγχος ἔχ' ἀτρέμας it *kept* still, 13.557; σχὲς οὗπερ εἶ *keep* where thou art, S.*OC*1169; ἕξειν κατὰ χώραν Ar.*Ra.*793, cf. Hdt.6.42, X.*Oec.*10.10; διὰ φυλακῆς ἔχοντες *to keep* on their guard, Th.2.81; ἔχε ἠρέμα *keep* still, Pl.*Cra.*399e, etc.; ἔχε δή *stay now*, Id.*Prt.*349e, *Grg.*460a, etc.; ἔχ' αὐτοῦ D.45.26. 2. *hold fast*, οὐδέ οἱ ἔσχεν ὀστέον Il.16.740; cf. A.II.6. 3. c. gen., *keep from*, πολέμου Th.1.112 (cf. C.IV). 4. with Preps., *to be engaged* or *busy*, ἀμφί τι A.*Th.*102 (lyr.), X.*An.*5.2.26, etc.; περί τινας Id.*HG*7.4.28. II. simply, *be*, ἑκὰς εἶχον Od.12.435; ἔ. κατ' οἴκους Hdt.6.39; περὶ πολλῶν ἔ. πρηγμάτων Id.3.128; ἀγῶνα διὰ πάσης ἀγωνίης ἔχοντα *consisting* in.., Id.2.91; ἔ. ἐν ἀνάγκαισι E.*Ba.*88 (lyr.); ὅπου συμφορᾶς ἔχεις Id.*El.*238; ἐκποδὼν ἔχειν Id.*IT*1226, etc. 2. freq. with Advbs. of manner, εὖ ἔχει Od.24.245, etc.; καλῶς ἔχει, κακῶς ἔχει, *it is, is going on* well or ill, v. καλός, κακός (but fut. σχήσειν καλῶς *will turn out* well, D.1.9, cf. 18.45; εὖ σχήσει S.*Aj.*684); οὕτως.. σχεῖν *to turn out, happen* thus, Pl.*Ap.*39b; οὕτως ἔχει so *the case stands*, Ar.*Pl.*110; οὕτως ἐχόντων, Lat. *cum res ita se habeant*, X.*An.*3.2.10; ὡς ὧδ' ἐχόντων S.*Aj.*981; οὕτω χρὴ διὰ στέρνων ἔχειν Id.*Ant.*639; οὕτως ἔ. περί τινος X.*Mem.*4.8.7, cf. Hdt.6.16; πρός τι D.9.45; τῇδ' ἔ. S.*Ph.*1336; κοσμίως ἔ. Ar.*Th.*854; ἥδιον ἔ. πρός τινας D.9.63; ὡς εἶχε just as he *was*, Hdt.1.114; ὥσπερ εἶχε Th.1.134, X.*HG*4.1.30; ὡς ἔχω how I *am*, Ar.*Lys.*610; ὥσπερ ἔχομεν Th.3.30; τἀναντία εἶχεν D.9.41; ἀσφαλέως, ἀναγκαίως ἔχει, = ἀσφαλές, ἀναγκαῖόν ἐστι, Hdt.1.86, 9.27; καλῶς ἔχει *no, I thank you*, v. καλός. b. c. gen. modi, εὖ ἔ. τινός *to be well off for* a thing, *abound in* it; καλῶς ἔ. μέθης *to be* well off for drink, i.e. *to be* pretty well drunk, Hdt.5.20; σπόρου ἀνακῶς ἐ. *to be* busy with sowing, Id.8.109; εὖ ἐ. φρενῶν, σώματος, E.*Hipp.*462, Pl.*R.*404d; εὖ ὥρας ἔχον χωρίον Poll.5.108; cf. ἥκω; so ὡς ποδῶν εἶχον as fast as they could go, Hdt.6.116, 9.59; ὡς τάχεος εἶχε ἕκαστος Id.8.107; ὡς.. τις εὐνοίας ἢ μνήμης ἔχοι Th.1.22; ὡς ὀργῆς ἔχω S.*OT*345, cf. E.*Hel.*313, 857, etc.; πῶς ἔχεις δόξης; Pl.*R.*456d; οὕτω τρόπου ἔχεις X.*Cyr.*7.5.56; μετρίως ἔ. βίου Hdt.1.32; ὑγιεινῶς ἔ. αὐτὸς αὑτοῦ καὶ σωφρόνως Pl.*R.*571d; οὐκ εὖ σεαυτοῦ τυγχάνεις ἔχων Philem.4.11: also c. acc., εὖ ἔ. τὸ σῶμα καὶ τὴν ψυχήν Pl.*Grg.*464a, cf. X.*Oec.*21.7: c. dat., οὕτως ἐχόντων τούτων τῇ φύσει D.18.315; πῶς ἔχετε ταῖς διανοίαις Lycurg.75; τῇ λέξει κακῶς ἔ. Isoc.9.10. III. of direction, *hold* or *turn* towards, v. supr. A.II.8. 2. *stand up, jut out*, κίονες ὑψόσ' ἔχοντες Od.19.38; δι' ὤμου ἔγχος ἔσχεν Il.13.520. 3. *lead towards*, ὁδοὶ ἐπὶ τὸν ποταμὸν ἔ. Hdt.1.180, cf. 191, 2.17; ἔ. εἴς τι *to be directed, point* towards, ἔχθρης ἐχούσης ἐς Ἀθηναίους Id.5.81; τὸ ἐς τοὺς Ἀργείους ἔχον *what concerns* them, Id.6.19; ταῦτα ἐς τὴν ἀπόστασιν ἔχοντα ib.2, etc.; of Place, *extend, reach to*, ἐπ' ὅσον ἔποψις τοῦ ἱροῦ εἶχε Id.1.64. 4. ἐπί τινι ἔ. *have* hostile *feelings* towards.., Id.6.49, S.*Ant.*987 (lyr.). IV. after Hom., ἔχω as auxiliary, c. aor. part. giving a perfect sense, κρύψαντες ἔχουσι Hes.*Op.*42; ἀποκληΐσας ἔχεις Hdt.1.37; ἐγκλῄσασ' ἔχει Ar.*Ec.*355, cf. *Th.*706; freq. in S., θαυμάσας ἔχω *OC*1140, cf. *Ant.*22, al.: also in late Prose, ἀναλώσας ἔχεις Aristid.*Or.*18(20).1; ὅς σφε νῦν ἀτιμάσας ἔχει E.*Med.*33: less freq. c. pf. part., S.*OT*701, *Ph.*600, X.*An.*1.3.14, 4.7.1: rarely c. pres. part., πατρίδα καταστένουσ' ἔχεις E.*Tr.*318 (lyr.), cf. X.*Cyn.*10.11. 2. part. ἔχων, with pres., adds a notion of duration to that of present action, τί κυπτάζεις ἔ.; why do you *keep* poking about there? Ar.*Nu.*509; τί δῆτα διατρίβεις ἔ.; why then *keep* wasting time? Id.*Ec.*1151; τί γὰρ ἕστηκ' ἔ.; ib.853, cf. *Th.*473, 852: without interrog., φλυαρεῖς ἔ., ἔ. φλυαρεῖς, you *keep* chattering, Pl.*Grg.*490e, *Euthd.*295c; κακοῦν ἔχοντ' αὐτὸν ἀποκτιννύναι D.23.35 (and so possibly ἐνεργεῖ ἔ. Arist.*Metaph.*1072^b23); παίσδεις ἔ. Theoc.14.8: so in later Prose, παίζεις ἔ. Luc.*Icar.*24; but ῥιπτεῖς ἔ.; do you throw away the prize *when it is in your grasp?* Aristid.1.443 J.

C. Med., *hold oneself fast, cling closely*, τῷ προσφὺς ἐχόμην Od.12.433, cf. Il.1.513, etc.; πρὸς ἀλλήλῃσιν Od.5.329: mostly c. gen., *hold on by, cling to*, [πέτρης] ib.429; χερσὶν ἀώτου 9.435; βρετέων A.*Th.*98 (lyr.); ἐξόμεσθά σου Ar.*Pl.*101; τῆς πληγῆς ἔχεται *claps his hand on* the place struck, D.4.40. 2. metaph., *cleave, cling to*, ἔργου Hdt.8.11, X.*HG*7.2.19; γεωργίας *BGU*7.6 (iii A.D.); τῶν πραγμάτων Jul.*Or.*1.19a; βιοτᾶς, ἐλπίδος, E.*Ion*491, *Fr.*409; τῆς αὐτῆς γνώμης Th.1.140; *lay hold on, take advantage of*, τῶν ἀγαθῶν ἔχεο Thgn.32; προφάσιος ἔχεσθαι Hdt.6.94; *fasten upon, attack*, D.18.79; *lay claim to*, ἀμφοτέρων τῶν ἐπωνυμιέων Hdt.2.17; *to be zealous for*, [μάχης] S.*OC*424; ἀληθείας Pl.*Lg.*709c; κοινῇ τῆς σωτηρίας X.*An.*6.3.17, etc. 3. *come next to, follow closely*, ib.1.8.4; ἕπεσθαι ἐχομένους ὅτι μάλιστα τῶν ἁρμάτων Id.*Cyr.*7.1.9; of peoples or places, *to be close, border on*, c. gen., Hdt.4.169, Th.2.96, etc.; freq. in part., τὴν ἐχομένην [τῶν νεωρίων] στοάν Aen.Tact.11.3; οἱ ἐ. the *neighbouring* people, Hdt.1.134; ὁ ἐχόμενος the *next* man, Aen.Tact.22.27; of Time, τὸ ἐχόμενον ἔτος the *next* year, Th.6.3; ὁ ἐ. διαλογισμός *PRev.Laws*16.15 (iii B.C.); τὰ ἐχόμενα τούτοις *what follows*, Pl.*Grg.*494e (without τούτοις Isoc.6.29). 4. *depend*, ἔκ τινος Od.6.197, 11.346: c. gen., σέο δ' ἕξεται Il.9.102. b. *to be connected with* by etymology, τὸ θύειν τοῦ θυμιᾶν εἴχετο Porph.*Abst.*2.59. 5. *pertain to*, ὅσα ἔχεται τῶν αἰσθήσεων Pl.*Lg.*661b; ἃ διδασκάλων εἴχετο Id.*Prt.*319e; ὅσα τέχνης ἔχεται Id.*Men.*94b, etc.: esp. in Hdt. in periphrases, τὰ τῶν ὀνειράτων, καρπῶν ἐχόμενα, 1.120, 193; ὀρνίθων ἢ ἰχθύων 2.77; σιτίων, ἐσθῆτος, 3.25, 66. II. *bear* or *hold for oneself*, κρήδεμνα ἄντα παρειάων σχομένη before her cheeks, Od.1.334; ἀσπίδα πρόσθ' ἔσχετο *his* shield, Il.12.294, cf. 298, 20.262. III. *maintain oneself, hold one's ground*, 12.126; ἔχεο κρατερῶς 16.501. 2. c. acc., *keep off from oneself, repel*, 17.639 (unless σχήσεσθαι is Pass., cf. 9.235). IV. *keep oneself back, abstain* or *refrain from*, ἀϋτῆς, μάχης, 2.98, 3.84; βίης Od.4.422; ἐχώμεθα δηϊοτῆτος ἐκ βελέων Il.14.129; τῆς ἀγωγῆς Hdt.6.85; τῆς τιμωρίης Id.7.169; τῶν ἀθίκτων S.*OT*891 (lyr., s.v.l.): c. inf., A.R.1.328; οὐκ ἂν ἐσχόμην τὸ μὴ ἀποκλῇσαι S.*OT*1387; κακῶν ἄπο χεῖρας ἔχεσθαι *to keep one's* hands from ill, Od.22.316; Μενέλεω σχέσθαι χέρα E.*Rh.*174: abs., σχέο, σχέσθε, *hold! cease!* Il.21.379, 22.416. V. Pass. of ἔχω B.I, ἐπὶ ξυροῦ ἀκμῆς ἔχεται ἡμῖν τὰ πρήγματα *are balanced* on.., Hdt.6.11.

ἔχω (B), *bear, carry, bring*, imper. ϝεχέτω *Schwyzer*686.24 (Pamphyl., iv B.C.): 3 sg. aor. 1 ἔϝεξε *brought as an offering*, *Inscr.Cypr.* 66 H. (Cf. Skt. *váhati*, Lat. *veho*, Γαιάϝοχος.)

ἐψάλᾰται, Ion. 3 pl. pf. Pass. of ψάλλω.

ἑψ-ᾰλέος, η, ον, (ἕψω) *boiled*, *fit for boiling*, Nic.*Al.*552. **-άνδρα**, ἡ, (ἀνήρ) *cooking up men*, epith. of Medea, from her renewing old Aeson, *AP*15.26.5 (Dosiad.). **-άνη**, ἡ, (ἕψω) = ἑψητήριον, Hsch. **-ᾰνός**, ή, όν, *boiled*, Hp.*Mul.*2.117, Arist.*Pr.*923a17, Dsc. 2.107; ῥαφανῖδες Polyaen.4.3.32; ἑψανά, τά, = ἑψήματα, Diocl.*Fr.* 120: sg., *BGU*1120.14 (i B.C.).

ἑψεῖνα, τά, dub. sens. in *PLond.*3.1177.217 (ii A.D.).

ἕψεμα, ατος, τό, late form of ἕψημα, Lxx 4*Ki.*4.38,39.

ἐψευσμένως, Adv. pf. part. Pass., (ψεύδομαι) *falsely*, *wrongly*, Pl. *Lg.*897a, Str.1.2.30, etc.

ἑψέω, ἑψάω, v. ἕψω.

ἕψ-ημα, ατος, τό, *anything boiled*: in pl., *vegetables fit for kitchen use*, Pl.*R.*372c,455c, Diocl.*Frr.*119,141, D.S.1.80, etc. 2. *mash*, Thphr.*HP*4.4.10. II. *must boiled down to one third part*, Hp. *Vict.*2.52, Pl.Com.149, *PPetr.*3p.310 (iii B.C.), Dsc.5.6. **-ηματώδης**, ες, *like* ἕψημα, ὀσμή Id.1.26. **-ησις**, εως, ἡ, *boiling*, Hp.*VM* 5; ἡ ἕ. τῶν κρεῶν Hdt.4.61, cf. *SIG*57.34 (Milet., v B.C.); λινῶν *PTeb.*406.22 (iii A.D.); *smelting* of ore, Thphr.*HP*5.9.1; *concoction*, *softening*, Gal.13.415, Aret.*SA*2.6: pl., Pl.*Plt.*303e. **-ητεῖς**· τὰ μικρὰ ἰχθύδια, Hsch. **-ητέον**, *one must boil*, Dsc.2.76, Sor.1.51, *Gp.*18.16.1. **-ητήρ**, ῆρος, ὁ, *dish* or *pan for boiling*, *AP*6.305 (Leon.). **-ητήριον**, τό, = foreg., Hsch. **-ητής**, οῦ, ὁ, *one who smelts* ore, Agatharch.28. **-ητικός**, ή, όν, *of* or *for boiling*, *Gloss.* **-ητός**, ή, όν, *boiled*, ὄξος X.*An.*2.3.14; ὕδατα Nic.*Al.*111; ἑψητός (sc. οἶνος), ὁ, *must*, *Gp.*7.12.23, al. II. ἑψητοί, ῶν, οἱ, *small fish boiled for eating*, Ar.*V.*679, Nicopho 18, Arist.*HA*569a20: sg., Archipp.16, Eub.93, Posidipp.3, *PCair.Zen.*83.3 (iii B.C.), cf. Gal. 19.102; cf. ἑψητεῖς.

ἑψί-α [ῐ], Ion. -ίη, ἡ, *amusement*, S.*Fr.*3; *plaything*, Nic.*Th.*880: pl., ἕψια, τά, *EM*406.8; **ἕψεια**, Hsch. (Etym. uncertain: derived by Hsch. from ἕπομαι, by *EM* from ἔπος. The connexion with Lat. *jocus* is doubtful.) **-άομαι**, (ἑψία) Ep. Verb, *amuse oneself*, θύρῃσι καθήμενοι ἑψιαάσθων Od.17.530; ἑψιάασθαι μολπῇ καὶ φόρμιγγι 21. 429; ἀμφ' ἀστραγάλοισι.. ἑψιόωντο A.R.3.118, cf. 1.459, Call.*Dian.* 3, *Cer.*39, Nonn.*D.*10.326 (ἐψιόωντο, as if from ἔπος, Philon.(?)ap. Sch.A.R.3.118; but cf. ἀφεψιάομαι). **-άτιμον**· γυμναστικόν, παιγνιῶδες, Hsch.

ἑψιέω, f.l. in A.*Fr.*51; v. ἐμψίω.

ἑψικός, ή, όν, *for boiling*, dub. in *PLond.*2.429.13 (iv A.D.).

ἐψῑλωμένως, Adv. pf. part. Pass., (ψιλόω) *in an expressionless tone*, ἐκφέρειν, of reciters or rhapsodes, Phld.*Rh.*1.200S.

ἐψιμῡθισμένως, Adv. pf. part. Pass., (ψιμυθίζω) *with paint* or *cosmetics*, Sch.Ar.*Pl.*1064.

ἑψόπωλις, *popina*, *Gloss.*; cf. ὀψοπώλιον.

ἕψω, impf. ἧψον Ar.*Ra.*505, al.: fut. ἑψήσω Nicoch.15, Men.260: aor. ἥψησα Hdt.1.119 (v.l. ἕψ-), Ar.*Fr.*4, Pl.*Euthd.*301d, etc.; cf. συν-έψω: pf. ἥψηκα Ph.2.245:—**Med.**, imper. ἕψου A.*Fr.*310: fut. ἑψήσομαι Pl.*R.*372c:—**Pass.**, ἕψεται Antiph.217.4, part. ἑψόμενος Pi. *N.*4.82, Hp.*Int.*44: fut. ἑψηθήσομαι Gal.13.398: aor. ἡψήθην Hdt.4. 61, Plu.2.690c, etc., part. ἑψηθείς Dsc.5.85, *Eup.*1.139 (v.l. ἐφθέντες): pf. ἡψημένος D.S.2.9, ἑψ- Arist.*Pr.*884b14, Hp.*Mul.*1.78.—**ἕψω** is Att. acc. to Hdn.Gr.1.456: **ἑψέω** is dub., imper. ἕψεε v.l. in Hp.*Acut.* (*Sp.*)63, impf. ἧψεε v.l. ἕψεε Hdt.1.48; elsewh. in Hdt. and Hp. the uncontracted forms are found: **ἑψάω** is a late form, Olymp.*in Mete.*315.8, al.:—*boil*, *seethe*, of meat and the like (never in Hom., where meat is roasted, v. ὀπτάω), Hdt.1.48, al., Hp.*VM*3, Pl.*Euthd.* 301c, etc.; ἕ. χύτραν '*to keep* the pot *boiling*', Ar.*Ec.*845, Pl.*Hp.Ma.* 290d; prov. of useless labour, λίθον ἕψεις Ar.*V.*280 (lyr.), Pl.*Erx.* 405b: c. gen. partit., ἥψομεν τοῦ κορκόρου we *boiled some* pimpernel, Ar.*V.*239:—Med., ἕψου μηδὲ λυπηθῇς πυρί A.*Fr.*310:—Pass., *to be boiled*, of meat, Hdt.4.61, etc.; of liquids, *boil*, Arist.*Mete.*379b28, Plu.2.690c. 2. *digest*, τὰ σιτία Hp.*Acut.*28. 3. of metals, *smelt*, *refine*, ἑψόμενος χρυσός Pi.*N.*4.82. 4. Med., ἑψήσασθαι κόμην *dye* it, Poll.2.35:—also in Act., Phot., Hsch. (ἐψεῖν cod.). 5. metaph., γῆρας ἀνώνυμον ἕψειν *cherish* an inglorious old age, Pi.*O.*1.83.

ἕω, Ion. subj. pres. of εἰμί (*sum*). **ἕω**, Ion. subj. aor. 2 of ἵημι. 2. gen. and acc. of ἕως (A), *the dawn*. **ἑώα**· ἡ τοῖς προβάτοις περιτιθεμένη διφθέρα, Hsch.; cf. ὄα, ὤα, also ὑποδίφθερος. **ἔωγα, ἔωγμαι**, v. οἴγνυμι. **ἔωθα, ἐώθεα**, v. ἔθω.

ἕωθεν, Ep. ἠῶθεν (q.v.), Adv., (ἕως (A)) *from morn*, i.e. *at earliest dawn*, Pl.*Phd.*59d, etc.; ἕ. εὐθύς Ar.*Pl.*1121, Eub.119.8. 2. αὔριον ἕ. to-morrow *early*, X.*Cyr.*4.2.6, Pl.*La.*201c; so ἕωθεν alone, Ar.*Ach.*278, etc.; τό γ' ἕωθεν Arist.*HA*546a22.

ἑωθῐνός, ή, όν, (ἕως (A)) *in the morning*, *early*, ὁ ἥλιος ὁ ἑ. Hdt.3.104; ἑωθινὸς εἶδον στρατόν S.*Fr.*502; οὔσης.. ἐκκλησίας ἑ. Ar.*Ach.*20; πότοι Bato 5.3; τὸ ἑ., as Adv., *early in the morning*, Hdt. l.c., Hp. *Aër.*6; ἐξ ἑωθινοῦ, = ἕωθεν, Ar.*Th.*2, Pl.*Phdr.*228b, etc.; ἐξ ἑ. μέχρι δείλης X.*HG*1.1.5; εὐθὺς ἐξ ἑ. Alex.257.4; περὶ τὴν ἑ. φυλακήν about the *morning* watch, Plb.3.67.2; ὑπὸ τὴν ἑ. (alone) ib.43.1, cf. Lxx 1*Ma.*5.30; ἑ. φυλακῆς Plu.*Pomp.*68; προσειπεῖν τὸ ἑ. to wish one *good morning*, Luc.*Laps.*1, cf. Machoap.Ath.13.580d (dub. l.); ἑ. δίκαι, prov. for *business soon transacted*, *AB*258. 2. *eastern*, ἔθνος D.P.697: Comp. -ώτερος Str.11.2.2: Sup. -ώτατος Id.4.5.1.

ἑώϊος, ον, also α, ον, poet. for ἑῷος, epith. of Apollo, A.R.2.686, 700. 2. *eastern*, ἄκρη D.P.111.

ἐῴκει, v. ἔοικα.

ἑωλ-ίζω, (ἕωλος) *keep till next day*, τὰ κρέα Gal.16.761, cf. Ruf.ap. Orib.4.2.8. II. Pass., *to be* or *become stale*, of grain, Gal.6. 518. 2. in good sense, *to be capable of being kept till next day*, ib. 713. **-ισμός**, ὁ, *keeping till next day*, of food, Ruf.ap.Orib.4.2. 7 (pl.).

ἑωλο-κρᾰσία, ἡ, (κρᾶσις) *mixture of dregs*, *heel-taps*, etc., with which the drunken were dosed at the end of a revel by their stronger-headed companions: metaph., ἑωλοκρασίαν τινά μου τῆς πονηρίας κατασκεδάσας having discharged *the stale dregs* of his rascality over me, D.18.50, cf. Harp., Luc.*Symp.*3; also, = κραιπάλη, ἐμμένει τὸ.. δυσάρεστον, ὥσπερ ἑ. τις ὕβρεως ἢ ὀργῆς Plu.2.148a. **-νεκρός**, ὁ (cf. sq. I)· ὁ πρὸ πολλοῦ τεθνηκώς, Suid.

ἕωλος, ον (prob. from ἕως (A), ἠώς), *a day old*, *kept till the morrow*, *stale*, of bread, Hp.*Aff.*52, Antyll.ap.Orib.4.11.2; of meat and fish, ἕωλοι κείμενοι δύ' ἡμέρας ἢ τρεῖς Antiph.161.6; αὔριον ἕωλον τοῦτ' ἔχων [τὸ τέμαχος] Axionic.6.15; πρόσφατον καὶ νέον ὕδωρ τὸ ὑόμενον, ἕ. δὲ καὶ παλαιὸν τὸ λιμναῖον Arist.*Fr.*215; ἕ. νεκρός Luc.*Cat.*18; ἕ. ἡμέρα the day *after a feast*, esp. after a wedding, when the scraps were eaten, Axionic.8.6; ἕ. θρυαλλίς a *stinking* wick (after the lamp has been blown out), Luc.*Tim.*2. 2. of actions, etc., *stale*, *out of date*, τἀδικήμαθ' ἕ. ... ὡς ὑμᾶς καὶ ψύχρ' ἀφικνεῖται D.21.112; ῥαψῳδίαι, πράγματα, Plu.2.514c,674f; ἕωλόν ἐστι τὸ λέγειν ib.777b, cf. Luc.*Pseudol.*5; δόξα J.*BJ*4.6.2 (Comp.); σοφισμάτια Porph.*Abst.*1.3; *old-fashioned*, φιλοτιμία prob. in Phld.*D.*1.1; later, of legal instruments, *out-of-date*, *expired*, γράμμα *PSI*5.452.22 (iv A.D.), cf. *PLond.*1.77.60 (vi A.D.); of payments, *in arrear*, *Sammelb.*1093.3, 1090.5 (ii A.D.). 3. of money, *lying without use*, *hoarded*, Philetaer.7.7. 4. of persons, *coming a day too late*, Plu.*Nic.*21; of things, *belated*, προθυμία Procop.*Goth.*4.23. 5. *on the day after a debauch*, i.e. *suffering from its effects*, Plu.2.128d; ἕ. ταῖς μνήμαις ib.611f.

ἐώλπει, v. ἔλπομαι.

ἕωμεν (v.l. ἕομεν), subj. form for ἧομεν (cf. ἄω c), ἐπεί χ' ἕ. πολέμοιο when we *have had our fill* of war, Il.19.402.

ἐών, Ep. and Ion. part. of εἰμί (*sum*). **ἐώνημαι, ἐωνήμην**, v. ὠνέομαι. **ἑῳνοχόει**, v. οἰνοχοέω. **ἔωξα**, v. οἴγνυμι.

ἑῷος, α, ον, A.*Pr.*25, etc.; also ος, ον E.*Ph.*169 (lyr.), D.H.1.12, dub. in Gem.*Calend.*p.220 M.: poet. **ἑώϊος**, Ion. and in Hom. **ἠοῖος** (qq.v.): (ἕως (A)):—*in* or *of the morning*, πάχνην ἑ. ἥλιος σκεδᾷ the *morning* rime, A. l.c.; ἑ. φθέγματ' ὀρνίθων S.*El.*18, etc.; ἑ. ἀστήρ, = Ἑωσφόρος, E.*Fr.*929, cf. Pl.*Epigr.*15; οὔθ' ἕσπερος οὔθ' ἑ. οὕτω θαυμαστός Arist.*EN*1129b28; ἑ. ἐξαναστῆναι to get up *early*, E.*El.*786. 2. *eastern*, τεῖχος X.*HG*4.4.9; τὰ ἑ. *eastern parts*, Luc.*Cont.*5; ἐξ ἑῴας (sc. χώρας) Arist.*Pr.*946b14; κατὰ τὰς ἑῴας Id.*Mu.*394a11 (perh. *in the morning*). b. ἑῴα, ἡ, = *Oriens*, the *Eastern provinces* of the Roman Empire, ὁ τὴν ἑῴαν ἐπιτροπεύων Philostr.*VS*2.1.13; ἀρχὸς ἑῴας, = Lat. *magister militum per Orientem*, *IG*14.1073; ὕπαρχος ἑῴας, = Lat. *praefectus praetorio Orientis*, *AP*9.690 (v A.D.).

ἑώρα, v. αἰώρα, cf. Ael.Dion.*Fr.*23: pl., of a festival in honour of Erigone, Arist.*Fr.*515 (αἰ- codd.). **ἑωρέω**, = αἰωρέω, prob. in S. *OC*1084 (lyr.), cf. Hsch., Dosith.p.431 K. **ἑώρημα**, = αἰώρημα, Sch.Ar.*Pax*77. **ἑωρίζεται**· μετεωρίζεται, ἀναπατεῖ, Hsch.

ἔωρτο, v. ἀείρω. **ἕως** (A) ἡ, Att. form of the Ion. ἠώς (q.v.).

ἕως (B), Ep. **εἵως, ἧος** (v. sub fin.), Dor. **ἇς**, Aeol. **ἆς** (qq.v.), Boeot. **ἇς** *IG*7.3303, al., and **ἄως** ib.2228,3315. A. Relat. Particle, expressing the point of Time up to which an action goes, with reference to the end of the action, *until*, *till*; or to its continuance, *while*: I. *until*, *till*, 1. with Ind., of a fact in past time, θῦνε διὰ προμάχων, ἧος φίλον ὤλεσε θυμόν Il.11.342, cf. Od.5.123; ἕ. ἀπώλεσέν τε καὐτὸς ἐξαπώλετο S.*Fr.*236, cf. A.*Pers.*428, Pl.*Chrm.*155c, etc.; for πρίν, μὴ πρότερον ἀπελθεῖν ἕως ἀποκατέστησε τὰ πράγματα D.S.27.4: with impf. with ἄν in apodosi, of an unaccomplished action, ἡδέως ἂν Καλλικλεῖ διελεγόμην, ἕ. ἀπέδωκα I would have gone on conversing *till* I had.., Pl.*Grg.*506b, cf. *Cra.*396c. 2. ἕ. ἄν or κε with Subj. (mostly of aor.), of an event at an uncertain future time, μαχήσομαι.. ἧός κε τέλος πολέμοιο κιχείω *till* I find, Il.3.291, cf. 24.183, A.*Pr.*810, etc.: ἄν is sts. omitted in Trag., ἕ. μάθης S.*Aj.*555; ἕ. κληθῇ Id.*Tr.*148; ἕ. ἀνῇ τὸ πῆμα Id.*Ph.*764: so freq. in later Gr., *UPZ*18.10 (ii B.C.), *PGrenf.* 2.38.16 (i B.C.), *Ev.Marc.*14.32, Vett.Val.68.18, etc.; ἕ. οὐ γένηται Gem.8.32. 3. ἕ. with Opt. (mostly of aor.), relating to an event future in relation to past time, ὦρσε.. Βορέην, ἧος ὁ Φαιήκεσσι.. μιγείη caused it to blow, *till* he should reach.., Od.5.386, cf. 9.376, Ar.*Ra.*766, Pl.*Phd.*59d; ἕως δέοι βοηθεῖν Th.3.102, cf. Lys.13.25: ἄν or κε is added to the Opt. (not to ἕως), if the event is represented as conditional, ἕ. κ' ἀπὸ πάντα δοθείη *till* (if possible) all things should be given back, Od.2.78; οὐκ [ἂν] ἀποκρίναιο, ἕ. ἂν σκέψαιο Pl.*Phd.*101d, cf. S.*Tr.*687 codd., Isoc.17.15, *IG*2².1328 (ii B.C.). b. in orat. obliq., ἔδωκεν.. ἕ. ἀνὴρ εἶναι δοκιμασθείην D.27.5. c. by assimilation to an opt. with ἄν, [λόγον] ἂν διδοίης ἕ. ἔλθοις Pl.*Phd.*101d. 4. c. subj. or opt., expressing purpose, *in order that*, Od.4.800, 6.80, 19.367; πορεύου εἰς Διονυσιάδα.. ἕως τὸν ἐκεῖ ἐλαιῶνα ποτίσῃς *PFay.*118.12 (ii A.D.); σπούδασον ἕως οὗ ἀγοράσῃ κτλ. *POxy.*113.25 (ii A.D.); χρυσίον ἐδανισάμην ἕως ὅτε δυνηθῶ ἀγοράσαι ib.130.13 (vi A.D.). 5. with Inf. in orat. obliq., ἐντειλάμενος διεκπλέειν ἕ... ἀπικνέεσθαι Hdt.4.42: otherwise only in later Gr., ἕ. ἐλθεῖν ἐς.. Lxx *Ge.*10.19, cf. *PLond.*1. 131r251 (i A.D.), D.H.9.4 (v.l.), Anon.ap.Suid. s.v. ἰλυσπώμενον. 6. with Advbs. of Time and Place, ἕ. ὅτε *till the time when*, c. ind., v.l. for ἔστε in X.*Cyr.*5.1.25; ἕ. οὗ, f.l. for ἐς οὗ, Hdt.2.143: freq. in later Gr., Gem. l.c., *Ev.Matt.*1.25, etc.; ἕ. ὅτου ib.5.25, etc.; ἕ. πότε; *how long?* ib.17.17, *Ev.Jo.*10.24; ἕ. τότε Lxx *Ne.*2.16; ἕ. ὀψέ *till* late, f.l. for ἐς ὀψέ, Th.3.108; ἕ. ἄρτι 1*Ep.Jo.*2.9; ἕ. ὧδε *as far as* this place, *Ev.Luc.*23.5. b. with Preps., of Time, ἕ. πρὸς καλὸν ἑῷον ἀστέρα *AP*5.200; of Place, ἕ. εἰς τὸν χάρακα Plb.1.11.14; ἕ. πρὸς τὸν Καύκασον D.S.2.43; ἕ. ἐπὶ τὴν θάλασσαν *Act.Ap.*17.14. II. as Prep., 1. of Time, c. gen., *until*, ἕως τοῦ ἀποτεῖσαι *until* he has made payment, Lex ap.Aeschin.1.42, cf. Lxx *Ge.*3.19, etc.; ἕ. τελειώσεως Epicur.*Ep.* 2 p.38 U.; ἕ. ὡρισμένων χρόνων Phld.*D.*1.7; ἕ. τινός *for* a time, Parth. 9.2, etc.; ἕ. τοῦ νῦν *Ev.Matt.*24.21; ἕ. Ἰωάννου ib.11.13. b. of Place, ἕ. τοῦ γενέσθαι.. *up to the point where*.. Arist.*PA*668^{b}2, cf. *HA*630^{b}27, Plb.9.36.1; *as far as*, ἕ. Σάρδεων *Ath.Mitt.*44.25 (Samos, iii B.C.); ἕ. τοῦ Ἀρσινοΐτου νομοῦ *PTeb.*33.5 (ii B.C.); ἕ. Φοινίκης *Act. Ap.*11.19: so c. gen. pers., ἦλθον ἕ. αὐτοῦ *Ev.Luc.*4.42, cf. Lxx 4*Ki.* 4.22. c. of Number or Degree, ἕ. τριῶν πλοίων Docum.ap.D.18.106; διδόναι ἕ. ταλάντων ἑκατόν Lxx 1*Es.*8.19(21); οὐκ ἔστιν ἕ. ἑνός ib.*Ps.* 13.3; οὐκ ἔχομεν ἕ. τῆς τροφῆς τῶν κτηνῶν *PTeb.*56.7 (ii B.C.); ἐᾶτε ἕ. τούτου *Ev.Luc.*22.51; μαχοῦμαι ἕ. ζωῆς καὶ θανάτου *OGI*266.29 (Pergam., iii B.C.); ἕ. μέθης Corn.*ND*30. 2. rarely c. acc., ἕ. πρωΐ Lxx *Jd.*19.25; ἕ. μεσημβρίαν *PLond.*1.131^{r}346,515 (i A.D.); ἕ. τὸ "βωμῷ" *down to* the word "βωμῷ", Sch.Pi.*O.*6.111. III. *while, so long as*, c. ind., ἧος ἐνὶ Τροίῃ πολεμίζομεν Od.13.315, cf. 17.358,390; ἕ. δ' ἔτ' ἔμφρων εἰμί A.*Ch.*1026, cf. *Pers.*710 (troch.); ἕ. ἔτι ἐλπὶς [ἦν] Th.8.40; ἕ. ἔτι νέος εἶ Pl.*Prm.*135d: in this sense answered in apodosi by τῆος, Od.4.90, Il.20.41; by τόφρα, Od.12.327, Il.18.15; by τόφρα δέ, 10.507; by δέ alone, 1.193, Od.4.120 codd. b. ἕ. ἄν c. subj., when the whole action is future, οὔ μοι.. ἐλπίς, ἕ. ἂν αἴθῃ πῦρ A.*Ag.* 1435; λέγειν τε χρὴ καὶ ἐρωτᾶν, ἕως ἂν ἐῶσιν Pl.*Phd.*85b; οὐδὲν ἔστ' αὐτῷ βεβαίως ἔχειν ἕ. ἂν ὑμεῖς δημοκρατῆσθε D.10.13. c. ἕως c. opt. in a Conditional relative clause, φήσομεν μηδὲν ἂν μεῖζον μηδὲ ἔλαττον γενέσθαι ἕ. ἴσον εἴη αὐτὸ ἑαυτῷ Pl.*Tht.*155a.

B. in Hom. sts. Demonstr., = τέως, *for a time*, ἧος μὲν.. ὄρνυον· αὐτὰρ ἐπεὶ.. Il.12.141; ἧος μὲν ἀπείλει..· ἀλλ' ὅτε δὴ.. 13.143, cf. 17. 727,730, Od.2.148; ἧος μὲν.. ἕποντο.. αὐτὰρ ἐπεὶ.. Il.15.277; *all that time*, Od.3.126, cf. Hdt.8.74. (ἕως, as iambus, only once in Hom., Od.2.78; as a monosyll., Il.17.727, dub.l. in Od.2.148; when the first syllable is to be long codd. Hom. have εἵως or ἕως (never εἶος or ἧος, Ludwich *WkP*1890.512, exc. ειος v.l. (*PFay.*160) in Il.20.41), 3.291, 11.342, al.; εἵως (or ἕως) is found even when the metre requires a trochee, 1.193, al.; comparison of Dor. ἇς (from *ἆος) with Att.-Ion. ἕως points to early Ion. *ἧος (cf. Skt. *yāvat* 'as great as, as long as, until') and this should prob. be restored in Hom.; cf. τέως.)

ἔωσα, v. ὠθέω. **ἕωσι**, Ion. for ὦσι, 3 pl. pres. subj. of εἰμί (*sum*).

ἕωσπερ, strengthd. for ἕως, Th.7.19, Pl.*Phdr.*243e, v.l. in D.25. 70, etc.

Ἑωσφόρος, Dor. **Ἀωσφόρος**, ὁ, *Bringer of morn, the Morning-star*, Il.23.226, Hes.*Th.*381, Pi.*I.*4(3).24; = ἕσπερος and Ἀφροδίτης ἀστήρ, Ibyc.42, Pl.*Ti.*38d, Eudox.*Ars* 5.2, *Placit.*2.15.4. (Trisyll. in Hom. and Pi., quadrisyll. in Hes. (s.v.l.): Ἀεσφόρος (cf. ἑασφόρος) is cj. in Pi. l.c.)

ἑωυτοῦ, ἑωυτέων. Ion. for ἑαυτοῦ, etc.

F

F (Ϝ), also ⊏, sixth letter of the oldest Gr. alphabets, pronounced like Engl. *w*, *IG*9(1).334 (Locr., v B.C.), 4.333, 14.2420, Alcm. 23.6, Sapph.*Supp.*1.6, Corinn.ib.1.29, etc.; it was written in many dialects until ii B.C. (and pronounced even later); in others (incl. Ion. and Att.) it died out (with the sound) before the date of the earliest Inscrr., surviving only as a numeral, = 6, in the form ⊏, *SIG* 46.106 (Halic., v B.C.), *IG*1^{2}.760 (Athens, v B.C.), *PCair.Zen.*13.4 (iii B.C.), *BMus.Cat.Coins*, Egypt Pl.XVI 4 (200/199 B.C.), later in the form ϛ, ib.Egypt Pl.XXX 5 (47 B.C.), *PMag.Lond.*121.770 (iii A.D., Pl.61) and medieval Mss. Its name was Ϝαῦ (cf. Semitic *wāw*) acc. to Varro and Didymus (v.Varro *LL* p.209 G.-S.), later δίγαμμα (q.v.). (Words with initial Ϝ will be found under the second letter.)

Z

ζ, ζῆτα (q.v.), τό, indecl., seventh (later sixth) letter of Gr. alphabet (cf. *IG*14.2420): as numeral ζ' = ἑπτά and ἕβδομος (ϛ', i.e. Ϝ, Ϝαῦ, the digamma, being retained to represent ἕξ, ἕκτος), but ͵ζ = 7,000.

Zeta, being a double consonant (pronounced either as *zd* or as *dz* acc. to dialect and date), made a short vowel at the end of the foregoing syllable long by position; exc. before pr. names, which could not otherwise come into the hexam., ἄστῠ Ζελείης Il.4.103, 121; ὑλήεσσᾰ Ζάκυνθος *h.Ap.*429, etc.: afterwds. pronounced as Engl. *z*, cf. ζμῆνος *PCair.Zen.*151.4 (iii B.C.), ζμύρνης ib.9 (iii B.C.), ἀμφιζβήτησιν Mitteis *Chr.*31 viii 6 (ii B.C.), cf. Ael.Dion.*Fr.*187; sts. σζ was written, ἐνδέσζμους *IG*2^{2}.1672.308 (iv B.C.), θυσιάσζειν *IG* 3.73.

ζά [ᾰ], Aeol. for διά, rarely as Prep., ζὰ τὰν σὰν ἰδέαν Theoc.29.6, cf. *IG*12(2).484.3 (Mytil.); ζὰ νυκτός ap.Jo.Gramm.*Comp.*3.3; ζὰ χῶρις ἔχην Sapph.*Oxy.*1787 *Fr.*3 ii 18; ζαβάλλω, ζάημι, etc. 2. as Prefix (cf. διά), *very*, in Ep. Adjs., ζαής, ζάθεος, ζάκοτος, etc.; cf. ζαμενέω, ζάπλουτος, ζάφελος.

ζᾶ, = γῆ, *Inscr.Cypr.*135.8 H.; but ζαν, dub. sens. in the phrase ὐϜαις ζαν, ib.10 (fort. = διὰ βίου).

ζαβάλλω, Aeol. for διαβάλλω, = ἐξαπατῶ, Hsch., *EM*406.42.

ζάβατος, ον, Aeol. for διαβατός, Sapph.158. 2. = πίναξ ἰχθυηρός (Paph.), Hsch. (cf. γαβαθόν, καβάθα).

ζαβλεμένως· μεγάλως πεποιθώς, Hsch.; cf. βλεμεαίνω, ἀβλεμέως.

ζάβοτος, ον, (βόσκω) = πολύφορβος, πολύκτηνος, Hsch.

ζαβρός, όν, for ζάβορος (?), = πολυφάγος, Hsch., Phot., Suid.

ζάγκλη, ἡ, = sq., Nic.*Al.*180. II. an ancient name of Sicilian Messene, from the shape of the natural mole which forms the harbour, Th.6.4, etc.

ζάγκλον, τό, *reaping-hook, sickle*, Sicilian for δρέπανον, Th.6.4, cf. Call.*Aet.Oxy.*2080.73. (ζάγκλιον, = σκολιόν, acc. to Str.6.2.3.)

ζάγρα, ἡ, and Dim. **ζάγριον**, τό, a term of abuse, Timostr.4.

Ζαγραῖος, ὁ, epith. of Dionysus, Orph.*Fr.*210.

Ζαγρεύς, έως, ὁ, son of Zeus and Persephone, slain by the Titans and resuscitated as Dionysus, πότνια γῆ, Ζαγρεῦ τε θεῶν πανυπέρτατε πάντων Alcmaeonis *Fr.*3 (*EGF* p.77), cf. E.*Fr.*472.11 (anap.), Call.*Fr.* 171, Nonn.*D.*10.294; identified with Ἅιδης by A.*Fr.*228. (Glossed by μεγάλως ἀγρεύων *Et.Gud.*227.37.)

ζάγρη· βόθρος, λάπαθον, Hsch. **ζάγρος**, α, ον, *barefoot*, Zonar., interpol. in Suid.

ζάδηλος, ον, for διάδηλος, of a sail *with holes in it*, Alc.18.7.

ζαελεξάμαν, = διελεξάμην, I *discoursed with*, τινι Sapph.87 (with vv.ll.; ζὰ δ' ἐλ. cj. Ahrens).

ζαζαῖος· εἶδος ἰχθύος, Opp.ap.Cyr. in *An.Par.*4.182; ζάζεος Cyr. ap.Schmidt Hsch. s.v. ζαιός.

ζάημι, = διάημι, part. ζαέντες, Hsch.: 3 sg. ζάει Id.: but **ζάει**· βινεῖ, Id. is connected with βία (q.v.).

ζᾱής, ές, (ζα-, ἄημι) Ep. Adj. *strong-blowing, stormy*, ἄνεμος ζαής Il.12.157, Od.5.368, prob. cj. in Hes.*Th.*253; ὦρσεν ἔπι ζαῆν ἄνεμον Od.12.313 (cf. Hdn.Gr.2.154,923); ζαοῦς Νότου *AP*9.290 (Phil.).

ζάθεος [ᾰ], α, ον, also ος, ον E.*Tr.*256 (lyr.), 1075 (lyr.); poet. Adj. (used by Trag. only in lyrics):—*very divine, sacred*, of places favoured by the gods, Il.1.38, al. (not in Od.), *h.Ap.*223; ζ. Πύλος, Ἰσθμός, Pi.*P.*5.70, *I.*1.32, cf. B.2.7; νᾶσος Id.5.10; Πέλοπος δάπεδα Id.10.24; ἔναυλοι E.*Ba.*121 (lyr.), etc.; Ὤλενος A.*Fr.*284; of things, ἄνεμοι Hes.*Th.*253; χρόνος Pi.*Pae.*6.5; κλῆδες, σελᾶναι, E. *Tr.* ll. cc.; ποταμοί Ar.*Nu.*283 (lyr.); μολπαί Id.*Ra.*385; τιμαί Castorio 1; later of persons, Ἀπόλλων *AP*9.525.7. Adv. -έως Hdn.Gr.1.514.

ζᾰθερής, ές, (θέρος) *scorching*, καῦμα *AP*6.120 (Leon.).

ζαιός· εἶδος ἰχθύος, Hsch., cf. Plin.*HN*9.68 (v. ζαζαῖος).

ζᾰκαλλής, ές, (κάλλος) *very beautiful*, Hsch. **ζακελτίδες**, v. ζεκ-.

ζᾰκορ-εύω, *to be a* ζάκορος, *IG*3.162.12, *CIG*2298 (Delos). **-ίσου** (gen. sg.), name of a kind of balsam, scanned as four long syllables, Aglaïas 23 (ζακορύτιον Polydorus ap.Sch.). **-ος**, ὁ and ἡ, *attendant in a temple* (more honourable than νεωκόρος acc. to Philem.Lex. (cf. *Philol.*57.353 sqq.) in Reitzenstein *Gesch.d.Gr.Etym.*p.394), ζ. Ἀφροδίτης Hyp.*Fr.*178; θεῶν Plu.*Cam.*30; Δηοῦς *IG*3.713.1: abs., Anon.*Oxy.*218 ii 14; τὰς ἱερείας καὶ τὰς ζ. *IG*1^{2}.4.14 (v B.C.), cf. ib.7. 1883 (Thespiae), Men.126,311, *IG*12(2).484.21 (Mytil., late), Plu. *Sull.*7, etc.

ζάκοτος [ᾰ], ον, *exceeding wroth*, Il.3.220, Theoc.25.83; of things, ἔγχος Pi.*N.*6.53; ὕδωρ Id.*Pae.*9.18.

ζακρῠόεις, εσσα, εν, (κρυόεις) *very numbing, freezing*, θάνατος Alc. *Supp.*12.8.

ζάκτι· κρίμνου ἐν ἔτνει (-νοῦ ἐν ἔθνει cod.) ἑφθῷ, Hsch.

ζᾰκυνθίδες, αἱ, = κολοκύνται, *from Zacynthus*, Hsch., cf. *AB* 261. **ζάλ**· μέγα, ἰσχυρόν, πολύ, Hsch. **ζάλα**· θόρυβος, Id. **ζαλαγεῦσα**, f.l. for λαλ- or σαλ-, *AP*9.412 (Phld.). **ζᾰλαίνω**, = μωραίνω, Hsch., *EM*406.43. **ζάλακες**· ἐχῖνοι, Hsch. **ζαλαύδα**· κινοῦ, Id.

ζᾰλάω, in Ep. part. ζαλόωσα.. χάλαζα *driving* hail, Nic.*Th.*252.

ζαλέγομαι, v. διαλέγομαι, ζαελεξάμαν.

ζαλεία, ἡ, = δάφνη Ἀλεξανδρεία, Dsc.4.145.

ζάλευκος [ᾱ], ον, *very white*, f.l. in Orac.ap.Zos.2.6 (πάνλευκος ap. Phleg.*Macr.*4).

ζᾱλέω, v. ζηλέω.

ζάλη [ᾰ], ἡ, *squall, storm, driving rain*, A.*Ag.*656, S.*Aj.*352 (lyr.), etc.; κονιορτοῦ καὶ ζάλης ὑπὸ πνεύματος φερομένου Pl.*R.*496d; ζάλῃ πνευμάτων by a *storm* of winds, Id.*Ti.*43c; χειμὼν καὶ ζ. Hp.*Insomn.* 89; ζ. ἀνέμων Plu.2.993e; βέλεσι πυρπνόου ζάλης, of the fiery rain from Aetna, A.*Pr.*373: metaph., ζάλαι *storms, distresses*, Pi.*O.*12. 12; ἡ τοῦ βίου ζ. Procop.Gaz.*Ep.*47; λογισμῶν ζάλαι *Cat.Cod.Astr.* 2.211; οἴκου ζ., of women, Secund.*Sent.*8.

ζαλλεύω, Aeol. imper. 3 pl. ζαλλευόντον dub. sens. in Alc.*Oxy.* 1789 *Fr.*1 i marg. (= *Fr.*12 Lobel).

ζαλμός, ὁ, Thracian word for a *skin*, Porph.*VP*14.

ζάλος [ᾰ], ὁ, *mud*, ζ. ἰλυόεις, = βορβορῶδες κῦμα, Nic.*Th.*568; ζάλον (ζαλόν cod.)· πηλόν, Hsch.: metaph., Lib.*Ep.*1144.

ζᾶλος, ζᾱλόω, ζᾱλωτός, Dor. for ζῆλος, etc.

ζάματος, = ζάβατος 2, Hsch.: **ζαμάτιον**, τό, = τρύβλιον, Id. **ζαμελής**· μέγα μέλος ἔχων, Id.

ζᾰμεν-έω, *to put forth all one's fury*, Hes.*Th.*928. **-ής**, ές, (μένος) poet. Adj. *very strong, mighty, raging*, *h.Merc.*307 (in Sup. ζαμενέστατε); Κένταυρος, ἅλιος, Pi.*P.*9.38, *N.*4.13, cf. *Sammelb.*

5829.8: once in Trag., ζ. λόγος word *of violence* or *enmity*, S.*Aj.*137 (anap.); also in late Ep., ζ. χόλος Opp.*C.*3.448: neut. as Adv., ἐπὶ ζαμενὲς κοτέουσα Nic.*Th.*181:—in form **ζᾰμενός**, ή, όν, Orac.ap. Porph.*Plot.*22 codd., Hsch.

ζαμερίτας, α, ὁ, Dor. word for μακαρίτης, Phot.

ζαμῆται· μεγαλουργοί, Hsch. **ζαμίλαμπις**, a kind of *stone*, Orph.*L.*263 (s. v.l.).

ζᾱμία, ζᾱμιόω, etc., Aeol., etc., for ζημ-.

ζᾱμιοργία, Elean for δημιουργία, *Schwyzer* 409.6 (vi B.C.).

Ζάν, Ζανός, ὁ, Dor. and Ion. for Ζήν, Ζηνός, v. Ζεύς.

ζᾰνεκέως or **ζᾰνεκῶς**, Adv., Aeol. for διανεκῶς, cj. in Corinn.9; cf. αἰζηνεκές· διηνεκές, αἰώνιον, Hsch. **ζανίδες**· ἡγεμονίδες, Id.

ζάπεδον [ᾰ], τό, = δάπεδον, Xenoph.1.1, *IG*12(5).215 (Paros).

ζᾰπίμελος [ῑ], ον, *very fat*, Hsch.

ζαπληθής ές, (πλήθω) *very full*, ζ. γενειάς *a thick, full* beard, A. *Pers.*316; ζ. στόμα Μούσης *full-sounding*, *AP*7.75 (Antip.).

ζάπλουτος, ον, *very rich*, Hdt.1.32, E.*Andr.*1282, Lib.*Decl.*30.12, Jul.*Ep.*89b.

ζᾰπότης, ου, ὁ, *toper*, Hsch.

ζάπῡρος [ᾰ], ον, (πῦρ) *very fiery*, ἕλικες στεροπῆς A.*Pr.*1084 (anap.); πωτήματα Orac.ap.Porph.ap.Eus.*PE*6.3.

ζαργάνη, = ταινία, Sch.Opp.*H.*1.100.

ζάρηκες (-ικές cod. extra ordinem)· ἐπίθετον πελαγῶν (-αργῶν Mus.), Hsch.

ζάρος, ὁ, a bird of prey, Sch.E.*Ph.*45.

ζαροῦν· καθεύδειν, Hsch. **ζαρτός**· ζωμὸς τριπτός, Id. **ζᾰτεύω, ζατρεῖον**, Dor. for ζητ-. **ζατήσασθαι**· αἰσθέσθαι, Id.; cf. ζατόω. **ζατός**, v. ζητός.

ζατόω, = φράζω, *EM*408.11, cf. Hsch.:—Med. with aor. Pass., = αἰσθάνομαι, Id. s. v. ἐζατώθη, ἐζατωσάμην. **ζατράπης**, v. σατράπης.

ζατρεφής, ές, (τρέφω) Ep. Adj. *well-fed, fat, goodly*, ταύρων ζατρεφέων Il.7.223; φώκας ζατρεφέας Od.4.451.

ζατρίκιον, τό, *the game of chess*, Sch.Theoc.6.18. (From Skt. *catur-aṅga-* 'four members', through Pers. and Arab.)

ζαυκίτροφος, ον, (σαυκρός) *tenderly reared*, Hsch. (ζακκί- cod.).

ζᾰφεγγής, ές, *very bright*, Id. **ζᾰφελής**, ές, *violent*, with Adv. -λῶς, Id.; cf. ἐπιζαφελῶς; = πάνυ ἀφελής, Suid.:—also **ζάφελος**, ον, Nic. *Al.*556, *EM*408.17.

ζαφλεγής, ές, Ep. Adj. *full of fire*, of men at their prime, ἄλλοτε μέν τε ζαφλεγέες τελέθουσιν.. ἄλλοτε δὲ φθινύθουσιν ἀκήριοι Il.21.465; of *fiery* horses, *h.Hom.*8.8. II. *shining, bright*, ἄστρα Orac.ap. Eus.*PE*3.15; σέλας Nonn.*D.*2.26.

ζαφοίταισα, v. διαφοιτάω.

ζαφόρος, ον, = πολυφόρος, Hsch.:—hence **ζαφορέω**, *to be fertile*, prob. l. Id. **ζάχμα** (ζαγμά cod.)· ἡνία, Id.

ζάχολος [ᾰ], ον, (χολή) = ζάκοτος, *AP*9.524.7.

ζαχρᾱής, ές, prob. = ζαχρηής, Epic.in *Arch.Pap.*7 p.6.

ζαχρειής, v.l. for ζαχρηής. Adv. ζαχρειές *violently*, Nic.*Th.*290.

ζαχρεῖος, ον, (χρεία) *very needy*: c. gen., ζ. ὁδοῦ *one who wants to know* the way, *asks eagerly after* it, Theoc.25.6.

ζαχρηής, ές, used only in pl., *attacking violently, furious, raging*, μένος Βορέαο καὶ ἄλλων ζαχρηῶν ἀνέμων Il.5.525 (-χρει- most codd.); of warriors, ζαχρηεῖς.. κατὰ κρατερὰς ὑσμίνας 12.347, cf. 13.684; cf. ζαχραής, ζαχρειής. (From ζᾰ- and χράω (B); cf. ἐπιχράω (B).)

ζάχρῡσος, ον, *rich in gold*, Θρῃκία, ἐμπολά, E.*Alc.*498, *IT*1111 (lyr.): in late Prose, Lib.*Or.*11.140.

ζάχῡτος [ᾰ], ον, = διάχυτος, Nonn.*D.*19.347.

ζάψ, ἡ, *surf*, καρίδας ἣ ζ. ἐκφέρει κἰχθύδια Cratin.Jun.13, cf. Euph. 3, Simm.11; πόντου.. περιστείνει ἁλυκὴ ζ. Dionys.Iamb.ap.Clem.Al. *Strom.*5.8.47 (who says some took ζ. = πῦρ).

ζάω, v. ζῶ.

Ζβελσοῦρδος, ὁ, divinity worshipped in Thrace, *Rev.Ét.Gr.*26. 247:—also in forms Ζβερθοῦρδος, Ζβελθι- or Ζβερθι-οῦρδος, etc.

ζβίχ (ζαβίχ cod.)· λευκόν, Hsch. (hence κνὰξ ζβὶχ λευκόν cj. Salm. in Thespis 4; cf. κναξζβί).

-ζε, inseparable Suffix, denoting *motion towards*:—prop. representing -σδε, as in Ἀθήναζε, Θήβαζε, θύραζε for Ἀθήνασδε, Θήβασδε, θύρασδε: but sts. found with sg. Nouns, as ἔραζε, χαμᾶζε, Ὀλυμπίαζε, Μουνυχίαζε, cf. A.D.*Adv.*194.18.

ζέα, ἡ, = ζειά, D.H.2.25, Dsc.2.89 (v.l. ζειά): nom. sg. **ζέη** *PPetr.* 2 p.69 (iii B.C.). 2. = λιβανωτὶς κάρπιμος, Dsc.3.74. II. *the roof of a horse's mouth*, *Hippiatr.*1,8. (With ζέα I, cf. Skt. *yávas* (masc.), Lith. *javaĩ* (masc. pl.) 'corn'.)

ζεγέριες, οἱ, a Libyan word, = βουνοί, but used as a name for a kind of *mouse*, Hdt.4.192; **ζεγερίαι**, Hsch.

ζειά, ἡ, usu. in pl. ζειαί (sg., v. infr.), *one-seeded wheat, Triticum monococcum*, used as fodder for horses, Hom. only in Od.; πὰρ δ' ἔβαλον ζειάς, ἀνὰ δὲ κρῖ λευκὸν ἔμειξαν 4.41, cf. 604; in Il. ὄλυραι, e.g. ἵπποι.. κρῖ λευκὸν ἐρεπτόμενοι καὶ ὀλύρας 5.196, 8.564; ἀπὸ ὀλυρέων ποιεῦνται σιτία (sc. οἱ Αἰγύπτιοι), τὰς ζειὰς μετεξέτεροι καλέουσι Hdt. 2.36, cf. Eup.14D., X.*An.*5.4.27, Str.15.1.18, Asclep.ap.Gal.13.257: in sg., ζειὰ ἁπλῆ Dsc.2.89 (v.l. ζέα), = Gal.6.517. 2. *rice-wheat*, in sg., Thphr.*HP*8.9.2, al. (where ὄλυρα is a cultural variety); ζ. δίκοκκος, *Triticum dicoccum*, Dsc. l.c. (v.l. ζέα), Gal. l.c.

ζειγάρη· τέττιξ παρὰ Σιδήταις, Hsch.

ζείδωρος, ον, *zea-giving* (Plin.*HN*18.82, *EM*410.6), as epith. of the earth, ζείδωρος ἄρουρα Il.2.548, Od.3.3, Hes.*Op.*173; ζ. ἀρδμός Nonn.*D.*26.185: c. gen., ζ. ὀπώρης ἀχράς *AP*9.4 (Cyllen.): also in late Prose, Hld.9.22 (ζε(Ϝ)έ-δωρος, cf. ζέα). II. some authors derived it from ζάω, = βιόδωρος (so expld. by Hsch.), *life-giving*, Ἀφροδίτη Emp.151; Ἥλιος Nonn.*D.*12.23, cf. 22.276. **ζείζιν**, *mamma*, Gloss.

ζειλίαυρος, = ἀναγαλλὶς κυανῆ, Ps.-Dsc.2.178. **ζεῖνος**, v. ζῆνος.

ζείνυμεν (-αμεν cod.)· σβέννυμεν, Hsch. **ζειπῖτις**· ὁ περιχύτης, Id. (ζειποίτης Gramm. in Reitzenstein *Ind.Lect.Rost.*1892/3 p.10).

ζειρά, ἡ, *a wide upper garment*, girded about the loins and falling over the feet, worn by Arabians, Hdt.7.69; by Thracians, ib.75, X.*An.*7.4.4: ζιραί Hsch.; but ζειρά is prescribed by Gramm. in Reitzenstein *Ind.Lect.Rost.*1892/3 p.10.

ζειρατείς· ἱμάτιόν τι Σύρων, Hsch. **ζειρεῖν**· ἀρωματοποιεῖν, Id. **ζειρόν**· ποικίλον, Id. **ζεῖρος**, a kind of *grape*, Id.

ζειροφόρος, ον, *wearing a* ζειρά, Ἀΐδης Antim.88. II. ζειροφόρους· ζωνοφόρους, Hsch. (χων- cod.).

ζείω, late Ep. for ζέω, A.R.1.734, Call.*Dian.*60.

ζεκαμναία, ᾱ, Elean for δεκα-, *sum of ten minae*, *Schwyzer* 409.7 (vi B.C.).

ζεκελτίδες (v.l. ζακ- as in Hsch.), αἱ, Boeot. for γογγυλίδες or κολοκύνται, Nic. etc. ap.Ath.9.369a.

ζελᾶς, ὁ, gen. and dat. ζελᾶ, Thracian word, = οἶνος, Choerob. *in Theod.*1.145: but dat. τῷ ζῆλα Eup.(*Fr.*355) ibid., cf. Hsch. s.v. ζίλαι, Phot. s. v. ζειλα (sic).

ζέλκια· λάχανα (Phryg.), Hsch. (ζέλμια poscit ordo): ζέλκεια· λάχανα παρὰ Φρυξὶ τὰ παρ' ἡμῖν λεγόμενα Φρύγια Gramm. in Reitzenstein *Ind.Lect.Rost.*1892/3 p.9.

ζέλλω, aor. 2 ἔζελον, Arc. for βάλλω, Hsch., *EM*408.42.

ζέμα, ατος, τό, (ζέω) *fermentation*, Heras ap.Gal.13.1044: metaph., *lewdness*, Lxx *Jd.*20.6. II. *boiling*, ἐνδοὺς ζέμα bringing it to *the boil*, Heras ap.Gal.13.548; δὸς ζέμα keep it on *the boil*, Orib.*Fr.*113; ὄρνις ἀπὸ ζέματος a *boiled* fowl, Alex.Trall.*Febr.*1. 2. *that which is boiled, decoction*, Dsc.*Alex.*7, *Gp.*8.37.3:—also **ζέμμα**, Lxx *Ez.*24.13.

ζέμελεν· βάρβαρον ἀνδράποδον (Phryg.), Hsch.

ζέννῡμι, = ζέω, Philagr.ap.Orib.5.17.7, *PHolm.*15.22 (Pass.), al.:—Pass., Dsc.2.70, Alex.Aphr.*Pr.*1.104.

ζεο-ποίιον, τό, *mill for grinding* ζέα, prob. in *AB*261. **-πῡρον**, τό, (ζέα, πυρός) a variety of *Triticum monococcum*, Gal.6.515.

ζέρεθρον, τό, Arc. for βέρεθρον, βάραθρον, Str.8.8.4.

ζέρνα, ἡ, = κύπειρος, *Gp.*2.6.23.

ζεσελαιοπᾰγής, ές, *cooked in boiling oil*, Philox.3.18.

ζέσις, εως, ἡ, (ζέω) *seething, effervescence, boiling*, Pl.*Ti.*66b, Ocell. 2.9, etc.; χολῆς Gal.16.577; οὔρων ib.661; ὅταν ἑψηθῇ μέχρι ζέσεως up to *boiling heat*, Plu.2.690c: metaph., ζ. τῆς ψυχῆς Pl.*Cra.*419e; [ὀργὴ] ζ. τοῦ περὶ καρδίαν αἵματος Arist.*de An.*403ᵃ31.

ζεστάκρατα, τά, (ζεστός, ἄκρατον) *hot wine*, Pall.*in Hp.*2.162 D.

ζεστολουσία, ἡ, *washing in hot water*, Theon ap.Gal.6.208, 212.

ζεστός, ή, όν, (ζέω) *seethed, boiled*, κρέα ζ. καὶ ὀπτά App.*Hisp.* 85. II. *hot*, ὕδωρ Nic.*Fr.*70.11, Dsc.1.33, Sor.1.50; ὕδατα ζ., of hot springs, Str.12.8.17; opp. χλιαρός, S.E.*P.*1.101; ψάμμος D.L.6. 23; λίθος Ps.-Plu.*Fluv.*1.2; εἰ δὲ -οτέρας κράσεως δέοιντο if they want the oil-bath *hotter*, Herod.Med.ap.Orib.10.37.12: metaph., χλιαρὸς εἶ καὶ οὔτε ζ. οὔτε ψυχρός *Apoc.*3.15.

ζεστότης, ητος, ἡ, *heat*, Paus.10.11.4.

ζετραία, ἡ, Thracian for χύτρα, Poll.10.95.

ζευγάριον [ᾰ], τό, Dim. of ζεῦγος, *a puny pair* or *team*, esp. of oxen, Ar.*Av.*582; ζ. βοεικόν Id.*Fr.*109; βοοῖν ib.387, cf. *PCair.Zen.*251.7 (iii B.C.).

ζεύγελα· διάβροχα ξύλα· καὶ τῶν βοῶν ἢ ἡμιόνων ζευκτά· καὶ τέμαχος ἐκ πλευρᾶς ἡλισμένης, Hsch.

ζευγελάτης [ᾰ], ου, ὁ, = ζευγηλάτης, Hsch.

ζευγηλ-ᾰσία, ἡ, *the driving a yoke of oxen*, Eust.361.13. **-ᾰτέω**, *drive a yoke of oxen*, X.*An.*6.1.9, *Dialex.*7.2. **-άτης** [ᾰ], ου, ὁ, *the driver of a yoke of oxen, teamster*, S.*Fr.*616, X.*An.*6.1.8, *PFay.*112.6 (i A.D.), *Dialex.*7.2: pl., D.S.31.24:—a fem. **-ᾰτρίς**, ίδος, S.*Fr.*878.

ζευγίζω, *yoke in pairs, unite*, in Pass., *PGrenf.*1.1.1 (ii B.C.), Lxx 1*Ma.*1.15, Aq.*Nu.*25.3.

ζευγίον, τό, = ζυγόν III. 2, *IG*11(2).287*A* 51 (iii B.C.), 12(5).872.37 (iii B.C.).

ζευγίππης, ου, ὁ, in pl., dub. l. in D.S.19.106 (leg. ζευγίτας).

ζευγίς, ίδος, ἡ, *rope*, *BGU*544.5 (ii A.D.).

ζευγίσιον, τό, *rating of the* ζευγῖται, ζ. τελεῖν Arist.*Ath.*7.4, cf. Poll.8.130.

ζευγίτης [ῑ], ου, ὁ, fem. **ζευγῖτις**, ιδος, (ζεῦγος) *yoked in pairs*, ζευγίτιδες ἵπποι Call.*Ap.*48; ἡμίονοι ζευγῖται D.S.17.71; of soldiers, *in the same rank*, Plu.*Pel.*23; κάλαμος ζ. a reed *of which were made the mouthpieces of the double flutes* (ζεύγη), Thphr.*HP*4.11.3. II. ζευγῖται, οἱ, the third of Solon's four classes of Athenian citizens, so called from *their being able to keep a team* (ζεῦγος) *of oxen*, Arist.*Pol.* 1274ᵃ20, *Ath.*4.3, Lex ap.D.43.54, *IG*1².45.40, etc.

ζεῦγλᾰ, ἡ, poet. for sq., ἄτης E.*Fr.*285.10, cf. *Lyr.Alex.Adesp.*11. 8, *AP*9.19 (Arch.), Choerob. *in Theod.*1.304.

ζεύγλ-η, ἡ, *loop attached to the yoke* (ζυγόν), through which the beasts' heads were put, χαίτη ζεύγλης ἐξεριποῦσα παρὰ ζυγόν Il.17. 440; ἔζευξα.. ἐν ζυγοῖσι κνώδαλα ζεύγλαισι δουλεύοντα A.*Pr.*463; ὑποδύντες ὑπὸ τὴν ζ. Hdt.1.31; βόας ζεύγλᾳ πέλασσεν Pi.*P.*4.227; ὑπάγειν τοὺς ἵππους τῇ ζ. Luc.*DMar.*6.2. 2. = ζεῦγος I. 1, *BGU*1507 (iii B.C.).—Not found in good Att. Prose. II. *cross-bar* of the double rudder, E.*Hel.*1536. **-ηθεν**, Adv., for ἐκ τῆς ζεύγλης, A.R.3.1319. **-ηφι**, Ep. gen. or dat. of ζεύγλη, Call.*Dian.*162.

ζευγλόδεσμον, τό, = ζυγόδεσμον, Hsch.

ζεῦγμα, ατος, τό, (ζεύγνυμι) *that which is used for joining, band, bond*, τὸ ζ. τοῦ λιμένος the *barrier* of ships moored across the mouth of the harbour, Th.7.69, cf. 70, D.S.13.14:—written **ζεογμα**, *Rev. Phil.*50.70 (Didyma, ii B.C.). 2. *bridge of boats*, *AP*9.147 (Antag.); τὰ ζ. τῶν ποταμῶν D.H.9.31, cf. Plu.2.174e, etc.; *pier* or *platform formed by lashing several vessels together*, Plb.3.46.2, Plu.*Marc.*14, 15. 3. *canal-lock*, *PPetr.*2 p.123, 3 p.210 (iii B.C.): metaph., ζεύγματ' ἀνάγκης *the bonds* of necessity, E.*IA*443. II. Gramm., *zeugma*, a figure of speech, wherein two subjects are used jointly with the same predicate, which strictly belongs only to one, Alex. *Fig.*2.17.

ζευγματικόν, τό, *lock-toll*, *PLond.*3.1157.6, al. (iii A.D.), *POxy.* 2129.4, al. (iii A.D.).

ζεύγνῡμι, ζευγνῦσι A.*Pers.*191, (ὑπο–) Pl.*Plt.*309a; 2 pl. imper. ζεύγνυτε E.*Rh.*33 (lyr.); inf. –ύναι (μετα–) X.*Cyr.*6.3.21, Ep. ζευγνῦμεν Il.16.145; part. ζευγνύς Hdt.1.206, 4.89; impf. 3 pl. ἐζεύγνῡσαν Id.7.33, Ep. ζεύγν– Il.24.783: also **ζευγνύω** Hdt.1.205, Plb.5. 52.4, etc.: impf. ἐζεύγνυον Hdt.4.89 (Ep. ζεύγν– v.l. Il.19.393): fut. ζεύξω Pi.*I.*1.6, etc.: aor. 1 ἔζευξα Od.3.478, etc.: late pf. ἔζευχα (ἐπ–) Philostr.*VA*2.14:—Med., Ep. impf. 3 dual ζευγνύσθην Il.24.281, 3 pl. ἐζεύγνυντο Od.3.492: fut. ζεύξομαι E.*Hec.*469 (lyr.), etc.: aor. 1 ἐζευξάμην Hdt.3.102, E.*Ion*901 (lyr.):—Pass., fut. ζευχθήσομαι (δια–) Gal.9.938: aor. 1 ἐζεύχθην Pi.*O.*3.6, Hdt.7.6, A.*Ag.*842, Pl.*Plt.*302e: more commonly aor. 2 ἐζύγην [ῠ] Pi.*N.*7.6, E.*Supp.*822 (lyr.), (συ–) Pl.*R.*546c: pf. ἔζευγμαι Il.18.276: plpf. ἔζευκτο Hdt.4.85.—Usu. in aor. Act. in Hom.: the simple Verb is rare in Att. Prose:—*yoke, put to*, ὑπ' ὄχεσφιν ἵππους Il.23.130; ὑφ' ἅρμασιν ἵππους 24.14; ὑπ' ἀμάξῃσιν βόας ἡμιόνους τε ib.783; κἄζευξα πρῶτος ἐν ζυγοῖσι κνώδαλα A.*Pr.*462:—Med. (esp. in Od.), ἵππους ζεύγνυσθαι *put to one's* horses, Od.3.492, al.: abs., ζευγνύσθην Il.24.281; ζεύξομαι ἄρα πώλους E.*Hec.* 469 (lyr.); καμήλους Hdt.3.102; of riding horses, *harness, saddle and bridle*, ζεῦξαι Πάγασον Pi.*O.*13.64, cf. Ar.*Pax*128, 135; of chariots, *put to, get ready*, ζ. ἅρμα, ὄχους, Pi.*P.*10.65, E.*Andr.*1020 (lyr.):—Med., τέθριππα Id.*Alc.*428. 2. *bind fast*, ἀσκοὺς δεσμοῖς X.*An.*3.5.10: —Pass., φάρη.. ἐζευγμέναι πόρπαισιν *having* them *fastened*.., E.*El.* 317. 3. metaph., πότμῳ ζυγείς *in the yoke of* fate, Pi.*N.*7.6; ζυγεὶς ἐν ἅρμασι πημάτων A.*Ch.*795 (lyr.); ἀνάγκῃ ζυγείς S.*Ph.*1025; ζεύχθη *was tamed*, Id.*Ant.*955 (lyr.); θεσφάτοις.. ζυγείς E.*Supp.*220; ὁρκίοισι ζ. Id.*Med.*735; μοναρχία ζευχθεῖσα ἐν γράμμασιν ἀγαθοῖς Pl.*Plt.*302e: —Med., τόνδ' ἐν ὅρκοις ζεύξομαι E.*Supp.*1229. II. *join together*, σανίδες.. μακραὶ ἐΰξεστοι ἐζευγμέναι *well-joined*, Il.18.276 (elsewh. in Hom. only in signf. 1); ζεῦξαι ὀδόντας, in setting a fractured jaw, Hp.*Art.* 32; τὼ πόδε ζευγνύντες, of sculptors who made their statues with *joined* feet, Hld.3.13. 2. *join in wedlock*, ἐπειδὰν εὐφρόνη ζεύξῃ μία *yokes* her *in wedlock*, S.*Fr.*583.11; of the parents or authors of the marriage, τίς ταύτην ἔζευξε; E.*IA*698; ζ. τὴν θυγατέρα τινί App. *BC*2.14, cf. Ath.12.554d:—in Med., of the husband, *wed*, ἄκοιτιν ζεύξασθαι E.*Alc.*994 (lyr.); παρθένειον ἐζεύξω λέχος Id.*Tr.*676 (so in Act., γάμοις ἔζευξ' Ἀδράστου παῖδα I *married* his daughter, Id.*Ph.* 1366; ὁ Σεμέλην ζεύξας γάμοις Id.*Ba.*468):—Pass., *to be married*, ἐζευγμένη, opp. κόρη, S.*Tr.*536; γάμοις ζευχθῆναι or ζυγῆναι, Id.*OT* 826, E.*IA*907, etc.; ἐν γάμοις Id.*El.*99; ἐς ἀνδρὸς εὐνάν Id.*Supp.*822 (lyr.): metaph., ζ. μέλος ἔργμασι Pi.*N.*1.7, cf. *I.*1.6. 3. *join* opposite banks *by bridges*, ποταμὸν ζεῦξαι Hdt.1.206; τὸν Ἑλλήσποντον Id.7.33, Lys.2.29; μηχαναῖς ἔζευξεν Ἕλλης πορθμόν A.*Pers.*722 (troch.):—also in Med., ζεύγνυσθαι τὸν Βόσπορον Hdt.4.83 (v.l. –ύναι):—Pass., Id.7.6,34; διῶρυξ ἐζευγμένη πλοίοις X.*An.*1.2.5; but also, b. γεφύρας ζεῦξαι Hdt.1.205, cf. 4.85,118, al. 4. *furnish* ships *with cross-benches* (ζυγόν III), Hes.*Fr.*76.6; but ζεύξαντες τὰς παλαιὰς [ναῦς] ὥστε πλωΐμους εἶναι *having strengthened* them *with thwarts*, Th.1.29, cf. Sch. ad loc. 5. *pair* or *match* gladiators, Arr.*Epict.*1.29.37. 6. *join* issue at law, in Pass., [δίκαι] ὑπέρ τινος ἐζευγμέναι *SIG*742.44 (Ephesus, i B.C.). (Cf. Skt. *yunákti*, pl. *yuñjánti* 'yoke', Lat. *jungo, jugum.*)

ζευγοποιία, ἡ, *the making of mouthpieces for double flutes*, Thphr. *HP*4.11.6.

ζεῦγος, εος, τό, (ζεύγνυμι) *yoke of beasts, pair* or *team of mules, oxen* or *horses*, Il.18.543, *IG*5(2).3.1 (Arc., iv B.C.), etc.; ζ. ἵππων And. 4.26. 2. *carriage drawn by a yoke of beasts, a chariot*, ζεύγεϊ κομίζεσθαι Hdt.1.31; ἐπὶ ζευγέων ἐλάσασαι ib.199; ἐπὶ ζεύγους ἄγειν And. 1.45; τῷ ζεύγει δ' ἦγεν τὴν γυναῖκα Hyp.*Lyc.*5; *wagons*, ζεύγεσι τοὺς λίθους ἄγουσι *SIG*124 (iv B.C.); βοεικά Th.4.128; *racing-car*, = τέθριππον, Id.5.50; ζ. τέθριππον A.*Fr.*346; ἢ συνωρίδι ἢ ζεύγει νενίκηκεν Pl.*Ap.*36d (but = συνωρίς, Plu.2.146d); ζ. μίσθιον a hired *chariot*, Id. *Ant.*6; λευκὸν ζ. *with* white *horses*, D.21.158. II. *pair* or *couple* of any things, ἰρήκων, αἰγυπιῶν, Hdt.3.76; πεδέων ib.130; Ἀτρειδᾶν A. *Ag.*44 (anap.); ἐμβάδων Ar.*Eq.*872, cf. Herod.7.51; ἐνωτίων *BGU* 1050.9 (Aug.), etc.; κεράμου *IG*1².313.23, al.; [κεράμων] *SIG*245 *G*i 36 (Delph., iv B.C.); θυρῶν *IG*1².313.110; ταῶν Antiph.205; καλλιπύγων Cerc.14: abs., *married couple*, τὸ ζ., ὃ καλεῖται θῆλυ καὶ ἄρρεν X.*Oec.* 7.18; τὸ ἐρωτικὸν ζ. Luc.*Am.*11; κατὰ ζεῦγος *in pairs*, Plu.2.93d; ἐς ζεύγεα Luc.*Syr.D.*12. 2. *mouthpiece of a double flute*, Thphr.*HP* 4.11.4,6. 3. ζ. ἱματίων *suit* of clothes, *BGU*814.9 (iii A.D.). III. incorrectly also of *more than two things* or *persons joined together*, ζ. τριπάρθενον three maiden sisters, of the Graces, E.*Fr.*357; so ζ. τρίδουλον Ar.*Fr.*576; ζ. νεκρῶν, where parents and children are spoken of, E.*HF*454. IV. = Lat. *jugerum*, *Cod.Just.*10.27.2.8.

ζευγοτροφ-έω, *keep a yoke of beasts*, Poll.8.132. **–ος**, ον, *keeping a yoke of beasts*, *IG*2².1576.73 (iv B.C.), Plu.*Per.*12.

ζευγοφορέομαι, Pass., *to be drawn by a yoke of oxen*, cj. in Ph. Bybl.ap.Eus.*PE*1.10 (ζυγ– codd.).

ζευγῶχος, ὁ, (ἔχω) *owner of a* ζεῦγος, *IG*4.742.8 (Hermione).

ζεύκ-τειρα, ἡ, fem. from sq., of Aphrodite, Orph.*H.*55.3. **–τήρ**, ῆρος, ὁ, *one who yokes* or *joins*: hence Adj. ζ. ἱμάντες the straps *of the yoke*, J.*AJ*12.4.6, cf. Hsch. s.v. ζεύγλας. **–τήριος**, α, ον, *fit for joining* or *yoking*, γέφυρα γαῖν δυοῖν ζ. A.*Pers.*736 (troch.); πάτερ.. Μαινάδων ζευκτήριε Id.*Fr.*382. II. as Subst., ζευκτήριον, τό, = ζυγόν, *yoke*, Id.*Ag.*529, *POxy.*934.5 (iii A.D.); ζευκτηρία, ἡ, = ζεύγλη II, *Act.Ap.*27.40. **–τὴς** λαοῦ, gloss on ζευξίλεως, Hsch. (prob. for ζευκτὸς λαός cod.); = *junctor*, *Gloss.* **–τικός**, ή, όν, = εὐναῖος, of Aphrodite, Sch.Opp.*H.*4.156; = ζευκτήριος, ἡνίαι *Gloss.*

ζευκτός, ή, όν, (ζεύγνυμι) *yoked, harnessed*, Plu.2.278b, etc.; *joined in pairs*, κάλαμοι Pl.*Epigr.*24.4; στίχος ἡρῴῳ ζ. ποδί, of the pentameter, *AP*7.9 (Damag.). 2. *joined*, πορθμὸς γεφύρᾳ ζευκτός Str. 10.2.8. II. ζευκτόν, τό, = ζεῦγος I.2, Sor.1.49, prob. in Aët.9.30.

ζεῦμαν· τὴν πηγήν (Phryg.), Hsch.

ζευξίγᾰμος [ῐ], ἡ, *she that yokes in marriage*, epith. of the planet Venus, *Cat.Cod.Astr.*1.173.

Ζευξιδία, epith. of Hera at Argos, *EM*409.28.

ζευξίλεως [ῐ], ω, ὁ, *subjugator of men*, of a king, S.*Fr.*133.

ζεύξιππος, *desultor, junctor*, *Gloss.*

ζεῦξις, εως, ἡ, (ζεύγνυμι) *yoking* or *manner of yoking* oxen, ζεύξι τοιαύτῃ χρεώμενοι Hdt.3.104. II. *bridging*, τοῦ Βοσπόρου Id.4.88; τοῦ Ἑλλησπόντου Id.7.35.

Ζεύς, ὁ, nom. Il.1.175, al., once written Ζηύς *IG*12(3).1313 (Thera), but Ζεύς ib.1316, al.; Boeot. Δεύς (q.v.); voc. Ζεῦ Il.1.503, etc.; gen. Διϝός *BMus.Inscr.*952 (Cephallenia, vi B.C.), Διός Il.1.63, etc.; dat. Διϝί *Schwyzer* 80 (Argive, from Olympia, v B.C.), Διί Il.1.578, al., *IG*1².80.12 (v B.C.), etc., contr. Δί [ῑ] Pi.*O.*13.106, *SIG*9, 35 (Elis, vi B.C., Syrac., v B.C., from Olympia); late Δεΐ *JHS*32.167 (Pisidia), etc.; acc. Δία, rarer than Διός, Διί in Hom. (Il.1.394, al.), freq. later (cf. Skt. *dyaúṣ*, gen. *divás*, loc. *diví* 'sky', 'heaven', 'day', loc. also *dyávi*, = Lat. *Jove*, acc. *dyā́m*, = Lat. *diem*, = Gr. Ζῆν (v. infr.)): also nom. **Ζήν** prob. in A.*Supp.*162 (lyr.); gen. dat. acc. Ζηνός, Ζηνί, Ζῆνα, Il.4.408, 2.49, 14.157, al., freq. in Trag. (Com. only in Trag. phrases); Coan Ζηνί *SIG*1025.24 (iv/iii B.C.); acc. Ζῆν (Ζῆν' Aristarch.) Il.8.206, 14.265, 24.331, Hes.*Th.*884, at end of verse, before vowel in next verse (stem Ζην– prob. originated in acc. sg.); Cret. Τηνός, Τηνί, *GDI*5024.23,77, Τῆνα, Τηνί, ib.5039.11, 5145.12, Δῆνα *SIG*527.17 (iii B.C.); nom. Δήν Hdn.Gr.2.911:—Dor. and Att.-Ion. forms with α (of doubtful origin), nom. **Ζάν** Pythag.ap.Porph.*VP*17, Ar.*Av.*570; gen. Ζανός *Schwyzer* 696 (Chios, iv B.C.), Cerc.1.7, Philox.3.10, *IG*5(1).407 (Sparta, ii A.D.); Ζανός and Ζανί, *Lyr.Adesp.* 82 A, B (Ionic); acc. Ζᾶνα Call.*Fr.*10.6 P., cf. Euhem.24 J. (*FGrH* 63); nom. **Ζάς** Pherecyd.Syr.1, 2 (Ζής ap.Hdn.Gr. l.c.), Ζάς Ζαντός Choerob. *in Theod.*1.116; **Δάν** (q.v.); **Τάν** Head *Hist.Num.*²469 (Crete); nom. **Δίς** Rhinth.14, Hdn.Gr. l.c.:—obl. cases Ζεός, Ζεΐ, Ζέα, cited by S.E.*M.*1.177,195; Ζεῦν f.l. for Ζῆν' Aeschrio 8.5: the pl. Δίες, Δίας, Διῶν, Διοί, Ael.Dion.*Fr.*127; τοὺς κτησίους Δίας Ath. 11.473b; Δίες καὶ Ζῆνες *Stoic.*2.191; Elean Ζᾶνες Paus.5.21.2:— *Zeus*, the sky-god, ὕει μὲν ὁ Ζ. Alc.34, cf. *SIG*93.34 (v B.C.), Thphr. *Char.*14.12, etc.; Ζεῦ ἄλλοι τε θεοί Il.6.476; ὦ Ζεῦ καὶ πάντες θεοί, ὦ Ζεῦ καὶ θεοί, X.*Cyr.*2.2.10, Ar.*Pl.*1, etc.; Ζεῦ Ζεῦ A.*Ch.*246, Ar.*V.*323 (lyr., prob. l.); ὦ Ζεῦ βασιλεῦ, τῆς λεπτότητος τῶν φρενῶν Id.*Nu.*153; in oaths, οὐ μὰ Ζῆνα, twice in Hom., Il.23.43, Od.20.339: freq. in Com. and Prose, οὐ μὰ Δία Ar.*V.*193, Pl.*R.*426b (c. Art., μὰ τὸν Δί', οὐ Ar.*V.*169, al.); ναὶ μὰ Δία Id.*Ach.*88, X.*Mem.*2.7.14; νὴ τὸν Δία or νὴ Δία, Ar.*V.*217, *Eq.*319, etc.; cf. νηδί; πρὸς τοῦ Διός Id.*Av.*130; πρὸς Διός X.*An.*5.7.32; οὐ τὸν Δία alone, Ar.*Lys.*986: prov. of enormous wealth, τῷ Διὶ πλούτου πέρι ἐρίζειν Hdt.5.49. II. of other deities, Ζ. καταχθόνιος, = Πλούτων, Il.9.457; Ζ. χθόνιος S.*OC*1606, *SIG*1024. 25 (Myconos, iii/ii B.C.); of non-Greek divinities, Ζ. Ἄμμων Pi.*P.* 4.16, etc.; freq. of Semitic Baalim, Ζ. Βεελβώσωρος, etc., *OGI*620 (Gerasa, i A.D.)), etc.; Ζ. Ὠρομάσδης, = Pers. *Ahuramazda*, ib.383.41 (Nemrud Dagh, i B.C.). III. of persons, ὁ σχινοκέφαλος Ζ., iron. of Pericles, Cratin.71; in flattery of kings, Hdt.7.56 (of Xerxes); Ξέρξης ὁ τῶν Περσῶν Ζ. Gorg.*Fr.*5a D.; [ἱερεὺς] Σελεύκου Διὸς Νικάτορος *OGI*245.10 (ii B.C.); of the Roman emperors, Opp.*C.*1.3; Νέρων Ζ. Ἐλευθέριος *IG*7.2713.41 (Acraephiae), etc.; Ζῆνα τὸν Αἰνεάδην *AP*9.307 (Phil.). IV. Διὸς ἀστήρ the *planet Jupiter*, Pl.*Epin.* 987c, Arist.*Mete.*343ᵇ30, etc.; so Ζεύς *Placit.*2.32.1, Cleom.2.7; Διὸς ἡμέρα a day of the week, D.C.37.19. V. Pythag. name for the *monad*, *Theol.Ar.*12.

ζεύσασθαι· γεύσασθαι, Hsch.

ζεφῠρ-ήϊος, ον, = ζεφύριος, Nonn.*D.*48.517. **–ηΐς**, ΐδος, pecul. fem. of ζεφύριος, ἀκτή Posidipp.ap.Ath.7.318d codd. (–ῖτιδος Valck.). 2. *of the god Zephyros*, γενέθλη Nonn.*D.*37.335, cf. 47.341. **–ίη** (sc. πνοή), ἡ, = Ζέφυρος, *the west wind*, Od.7.119. [Ζεφ– long metri gr.] **–ικός**, ή, όν, = sq., Arist.*Mete.*364ᵃ20, Thphr.*HP*8.7.7. **–ιος**, ον, sts. also α, ον (cf. Ζεφυρίη), *of the West* or *west wind, westerly*, Id.*CP*2.3.1; τοῖς ζ. (sc. ἀνέμοις) *at the period of west winds*, Arist.*HA*618ᵃ7; *western*, τοῖχος *Inscr.Délos* 290.166 (iii B.C.), cf. *IG*12(5).126 (Paros, ii B.C.). II. ᾠὸν ζ. *wind-egg*, also ἀνεμιαῖον, ὑπηνέμιον, Arist.*HA*560ᵃ6, *GA*749ᵇ 1. III. Ζ. ἄκρα or Ζεφύριον, τό, name of a cape in Cyprus, Str.14. 6.3, Ath.7.318d: Ζεφύριον, τό, cape in S. Italy, Str.6.1.7. **–ίτης** [ῑ], ου, ὁ, = foreg. I, epith. of the month of March, Lyd.*Mens.*4.152: fem. **–ῖτις**, ιδος, ἡ, = foreg. I, αὖραι Orph.*H.*81.1; = foreg. III, epith. of Aphrodite, as worshipped in Cyprus, Call.*Ep.*6; cf. ζεφυρηΐς I.

Ζέφῠρος, ὁ, any *westerly wind*, Βορέης καὶ Ζ., τώ τε Θρῄκηθεν ἄητον Il.9.5: coupled with Νότος, 21.334; opp. Εὖρος, Od.5.332, 19.206; Ζ. δυσαής, ἔφυδρος, 5.295, 14.458; ψυχρός Arist.*Pr.*946ᵃ17; but εὐδιεινὸς καὶ ἥδιστος ib.943ᵇ21; ὁπότε νέφεα Ζ. στυφελίξῃ Il.11.305; ἅμα πνοιῇ Ζεφύροιο θέοιμεν, of horses, 19.415; later, *the due West wind*, opp. ἀπηλιώτης, Arist.*Mete.*363ᵇ12, cf. *Mu.*394ᵇ26; but rather *north-west* in Id.*Pol.*1290ᵃ19. (Prob. cogn. with ζόφος, cf. ζοφόπνοια.)

ζέω, contr. 3 sg. ζεῖ even in Il.21.362; later Ep. **ζείω** Call.*Dian.* 60, subj. ζείησι Epic. in *Arch.Pap.*7 p.7; in late Prose **ζέννυμι** (q.v.): impf. ζέε Il.21.365, ἔζεε Hes.*Th.*695, ἔζει S.*OC*434: fut. ζέσω (ἐξανα–) A.*Pr.*372: aor. ἔζεσα Hdt.7.188, cf. ἐπιζέω; Ep. ζέσσα Il.18. 349:—Pass., aor. ἐζέσθην (ἀπ–) Dsc.1.3, (ἐν–) Aret.*CA*1.2: pf. ἔζεσμαι *Gp.*10.54.3:—*boil, seethe*, of water, ἐπεὶ δὴ ζέσσεν ὕδωρ ἐνὶ ἤνοπι χαλκῷ Il.18.349, Od.10.360; ὡς δὲ λέβης ζεῖ ἔνδον as the kettle *boils*, Il.21.362, cf. E.*Cyc.*343; rarely of solids, *to be fiery hot*, χθὼν ἔζεε Hes.*Th.*695, 847; χαλκός Call. l. c. 2. *ferment*, Hp.*VM*11; γλεύκους ζέοντος Dsc.5.8. 3. metaph., *boil* or *bubble up*, τῆς θαλάσσης ζεσάσης Hdt.7.188; αἷμα διὰ χρωτὸς ζέσσ' *AP*7.208 (Anyte); οἶνος ζεῖ Pl.*Lg.*773d. b. of passion, ὁπηνίκ' ἔζει θυμός S.*OC*434, cf. Pl.*R.*440c, etc.; τὸ ζέον τῆς μάχης Hld.1.33. 4. c. gen., *boil up* or *over with* a thing, λίμνη ζέουσα ὕδατος καὶ πηλοῦ Pl.*Phd.*113a; πίθος ζ. [οἴνου] Thphr.*HP*9.17.3; πεδία ζέιοντ' Ἀγαρηνῶν *boiling, teeming with..*, *APl.*4.39 (Arab.); of persons, ζ. σκωλήκων Luc.*Alex.*59: c. dat., ζ. φθειρί Id.*Sat.*26; ζ. φλογμῷ Lyc.690; θάλαττα αἵματι καὶ ῥοθίῳ ζέουσα Aristid.1.142 J. II. causal, *make to boil, boil*, τοὶ δὲ λοετρὰ πυρὶ ζέον A.R.3.273; θυμὸν ἐπὶ Τροίῃ πόσον ἔζεσας; *AP*7.385 (Phil.). 2. *exhale*, ἀϋτμήν (v.l. –μῇ) A.R.1.734. (ζέ(σ)-ω, cf. ζεσ-τός, Skt. *yásati* 'boil', OHG. *jësan* 'ferment', 'foam', Engl. *yeast.*)

ζῆ, ζῆθι, imper. of ζῶ (q.v.). **ζηβήνη**, v. ζιβύνη.

ζηλ-αῖος, α, ον, (ζῆλος) *jealous*, *AP*9.524.7. **–άς**, *paelex*, *Gloss.* **–ευτής**, οῦ, ὁ, = ζηλωτής in vulgar language, Eust.1527. 34. **–εύω**, = ζηλόω, Democr.55 (v.l.), Simp.*in Epict.*p.56 D. **–έω**, = ζηλοτυπέω, etym. of ζηλήμων, Eust.70.30:—in Dor. form **ζᾱλέω**, *to be zealous for*, τᾶς αὐτοσαυτοῦ πατρίδος *SIG*734.7 (Delph., i B.C.). **–η**, ἡ, *female rival*, X.Eph.2.11, Aristaenet.1.25 codd.

ζηλημ-οσύνη, ἡ, poet. for ζῆλος, Q.S.13.388 (pl.). **–ων**, ον, gen. ονος, (ζηλέω) *jealous*, σχέτλιοί ἐστε, θεοί, ζηλήμονες ἔξοχον ἄλλων Od.5.118; and late Ep., as Call.*Dian.*30, Opp.*C.*3.191, Musae.36, 37; μῆνις *AP*3.7 (Inscr. Cyzic.).

ζηλο-δοτήρ, ῆρος, ὁ, *giver of bliss*, *AP*9.524.7. **–μανής**, ές, *mad with jealousy*, κόλασμα ib.5.217 (Agath.), cf. Nonn.*D.*41.211.

ζῆλος, ου, ὁ, later εος, τό, *Ep.Phil.*3.6 codd. opt.; Dor. **ζᾶλος** *IG*12(5).891, etc.:—*jealousy* (= φθόνος), Hes.*Op.*195, S.*OT*1526: coupled with φθόνος by Democr.191, Lys.2.48, Pl.*Phlb.*47e, 50c, *Lg.* 679c (pl.); εἰς ζῆλον ἰέναι Id.*R.*550e: more usu. in good sense, *eager rivalry, emulation*, Id.*Mx.*242a, Arist.*Rh.*1388ᵃ30. 2. c. gen. pers., *zeal for* one, ξυναίμων S.*OC*943; κατὰ ζῆλον Ἡρακλέους in *emulation* of him, Plu.*Thes.*25; ζ. πρός τινα Luc.*Dem.*57: abs., *passion*, *PGrenf.*1.1.13 (ii B.C.). 3. c. gen. rei, ζῆλον.. γάμων ἔχουσα causing *rivalry* for my hand, E.*Hec.*352; ζ. ἀζήλων καὶ φόβον ἀφόβων Phld.*Oec.*p.66 J.; ζ. τῶν ἀρίστων *emulous desire* for..., opp. φυγὴ τῶν χειρόνων, Luc.*Ind.*17; ἀνδραγαθίας Plu.*Cor.*4; so ζ. πρός τι Phld.*Rh.*2.53 S., Plu.*Per.*2; ζ. περὶ τὰ στρατιωτικά Str.14.2.27: pl., *ambitions*, Phld.*Rh.*2.54 S. 4. *fervour, zeal*, Lxx 4*Ki.*19.31, al., 1*Ep.Cor.*14.1, al.; *indignation*, ζ. πυρός *Ep.Hebr.*10.27. 5. personified as son of Styx, brother of Βία, Κράτος, Νίκη, Hes.*Th.* 384. II. *pride, honour, glory*, S.*Aj.*503; ζ. καὶ χαρά D.18.217; τὸν αὐτὸν ἔχει ζῆλον ὁ στέφανος, ib.120; ζῆλον καὶ τιμὴν φέρει τῇ πόλει Id.23.64, cf. 18.273, 60.33. III. *spirit*, τῆς πολιτείας Plb.4.27.8: pl., *tastes, interests*, τοῖς ἀπὸ διαφόρων ἐπιτηδευμάτων, βίων, ζήλων, ἡλικιῶν, Longin.7.4. 2. esp. in Lit. Crit., *style*, τοῦ Ἀσιανοῦ λεγομένου ζήλου Str.14.1.41, cf. Plu.*Ant.*2.

ζηλοσύνη, ἡ, poet. for ζῆλος, *h.Ap.*100.

ζηλοτυπ-έω, *to be jealous of*, c. acc., ζηλοτυπῶν με καὶ φθονῶν Pl. *Smp.*213d; τὴν αὑτοῦ γυναῖκα Ath.12.532a, cf. *POxy.*472.11 (ii A.D.); ζ. δούλην ἐπὶ τῷ ἀνδρί in regard to her husband, Plu.2.267d: c. dat., *emulate*, ζ. τινὶ ἐπαινουμένῳ Demetr.*Eloc.*292:—Pass., ἡ –ουμένη μεμοιχεῦσθαι Ph.1.141. 2. *envy*, Cic.*Att.*13.18.2 (Pass., ib.13.1); ζ. τινά τινος Jul.*Or.*5.167c. II. c. acc. rei, *regard with jealous anger*, τὰ γιγνόμενα Aeschin.1.58. 2. *pretend to, affect*, κάθαρμα ζηλοτυποῦν ἀρετήν Id.3.211; *imitate, follow*, τὴν Θάλητος δόξαν Suid. s. v. Φερεκύδης:—Pass., ἡ ζηλοτυπουμένη τυραννίς Plu.*Arat.*25. **–ία**, ἡ, *jealousy, rivalry, envy*, Aeschin.3.81, *Com.Adesp.*16.20 D.; ζ. καὶ φθόνος τῆς δόξης Plu.*Per.*10; ἡ κατὰ τὴν τέχνην ζ. Luc.*Cal.*2; ζ. πρός τινα Plu.2.276b; θυσία ζηλοτυπίας Lxx *Nu.*5.15: pl., Phld.*Rh.*2. 139 S. **–ος**, ον, (τύπτω) *jealous*, Ar.*Pl.*1016, Men.*Pk.*409, J.*AJ* 5.8.2, etc.; title of mime by Herodas; ζ. ὀδύναι *AP*5.151 (Mel.); τὸ ζ. Phld.*Hom.*p.41 O. Adv. –πως Str.14.1.20; ζ. ἔχειν διὰ τὸν ἔρωτα J.*BJ*1.22.3; πρός τινα Aeschin.Socr.*Oxy.*1608.83: Sup. –ώτατα, διατεθῆναι πρός τινα Ael.*VH*12.16. 2. *eager*, πρὸς τὴν τῶν ἀρρένων συνουσίαν Ptol.*Tetr.*62.

ζηλ-όω, (ζῆλος): I. c. acc. pers., *vie with, emulate*, τινα Th.2. 37, Pl.*R.*553a, *Michel* 1007.29 (Teos, ii B.C.):—Pass., Phld.*Rh.*1. 125 S., etc.: c. acc. rei, Th.2.64; in bad sense, *to be jealous of, envy*, ζηλοῖ δέ τε γείτονα γείτων Hes.*Op.*23, cf. *h.Cer.*168, 223, Theoc.6.27; τὴν αὐτοῦ γυναῖκα Lxx *Si.*9.1: abs., *to be jealous*, 1*Ep.Cor.*13.4; ζηλώσαντες *through jealousy*, *Act.Ap.*7.9. b. c. acc. pers., *to be jealous for*, Lxx *Nu.*11.29. 2. *esteem* or *pronounce happy, admire, praise*, τινά τινος one for a thing, S.*El.*1027, Isoc.4.91; ζηλῶ σε τῆς εὐβουλίας Ar.*Ach.*1008 (lyr.); τῆς εὐγλωττίας Id.*Eq.*837; τῆς εὐτυχίας τὸν πρέσβυν Id.*V.*1450 (lyr.); τοῦ πλούτου X.*Smp.*4.45; τινὰ ἐπί τισι *IG* 12(5).860.47 (Tenos, i B.C.): more rarely, ζ. τινά τι S.*Aj.*552; ζ. σε ὁθούνεκα.. A.*Pr.*332; τὴν πόλιν, ὅτι.. X.*HG*6.5.45; πολλά σε ζηλῶ βίου, μάλιστα δ' εἰ.. S.*Fr.*584: c. part., σε ζ. θανόντα πρὶν κακῶν ἰδεῖν βάθος A.*Pers.*712 (troch.), cf. E.*Or.*521: iron., ζηλῶ σε happy in your ignorance! Id.*Med.*60; ὑμῶν οὐ ζηλοῦμεν τὸ ἄφρον Th.5.105:—Pass., *to be deemed fortunate*, ὑπό τινων Pl.*Phdr.*232a. II. c. acc. rei, *desire emulously, strive after, affect*, ὁ μὲν δόξης ἐπιθυμεῖ καὶ τοῦτ' ἐζήλωκε D.2.15; ἀρετήν Id.20.141; ἀστρολογίαν Epicur.*Ep.*2 p.53 U.; μάθησιν *PSI*1.94.9 (ii A.D.); πίστιν *Cod.Just.*1.1.3.2:—Pass., ἡ ἀρετὴ ὑπὸ πάντων τῶν ἀνθρώπων ζηλοῦται Lys.2.26; τὰ ζηλούμενα Arist.*Rh.* 1360ᵇ34. III. also of persons, *pay zealous court to*, *Ep.Gal.*4. 17:—Pass., ib.18. **–ωμα**, ατος, τό, *that which is emulated*: *object of envy* or *ambition*, Phld.*Rh.*2.27 S.: in pl., *high fortune*, E.*IT*379; ζ. τυραννικά D.H.7.55. II. in pl. also, *emulous efforts, rivalries*, νέων ζ. Aeschin.1.191, *AP*7.219 (Pomp. Jun.), cf. D.19.260. 2. *emulation*, ζήλωμα τῆς τῶν Ῥωμαίων ἀρετῆς App.*BC*5.113: pl., Lyc. 355, Max.Tyr.7.7. **–ωσις**, εως, ἡ, *emulation, imitation*, τῶν βαρβάρων Th.1.132; μεγάλων συγγραφέων μίμησις καὶ ζ. Longin.13.2, cf. Max.Tyr.7.9. II. *zealous pursuit*, αἱ πολύτροποι τοῦ βίου ζ. Ph. 1.362; *custom, fashion*, ἀρχαιότροποι ζ. ib.468. III. *jealousy*, Lxx *Nu.*5.14. **–ωτέος**, α, ον, *to be emulated*, D.L.5.74. II. ζηλωτέον *one must emulate* or *copy*, Plb.4.27.8, Plu.2.12a; νέοις ζ. τοὺς γέροντας Id.*Fr.inc.*2. 2. *one must strive after*, πραότητι Ath. Med.ap.Orib.*inc.*21.18. **–ωτής**, οῦ, ὁ, *emulator, zealous admirer* or *follower*, μιμητὴς καὶ ζ. τῆς πατρῴας ἀρετῆς Isoc.1.11; ζ. καὶ ἐρασταὶ τῆς Λακεδαιμονίων παιδείας Pl.*Prt.*343a; τῆς ἡλικίας τοῦ μειρακίου Aeschin.2.166; τῶν καλῶν βουλευμάτων ib.171; τῆς αὐτῆς αἱρέσεως *SIG*675.27 (Oropus, ii B.C.); μαθήσεως Phld.*Rh.*2.262 S.; πνευμάτων 1*Ep.Cor.*14.12; τῶν ἀγαθῶν τῶν εἰς τὴν πόλιν μαρτυρουμένων *IG*7.2712. 99 (Acraephiae): c. gen. pers., τοῦ Διός Muson.*Fr.*8 p.37 H.; τῷ πράτω θεῶ Sthenid.ap.Stob.4.7.63 (nom. sg. ζηλωτάς codd.); Θουκυδίδου, Ἀντισθένους, Luc.*Hist.Conscr.*15, *Herm.*14; perh. *champion*, Epicur.*Nat.*70 G. 2. *jealous*, θεὸς ζ. Lxx *Ex.*20.5. II. *zealot*, used to translate Καναανίτης or Καναναῖος, *Ev.Luc.*6.15, *Act.Ap.*1. 13, J.*BJ*4.3.9; τῶν πατρίων ἐθῶν Id.*AJ*12.6.2; τῶν νόμων Lxx 2*Ma.* 4.2. **–ωτικός**, ή, όν, *emulous*, Arist.*Rh.*1388ᵃ36, Ptol.*Tetr.*167; περί τι Arist.*Rh.*1388ᵇ9; λόγος Ph.1.135. **–ωτός**, ή, όν, also ός, όν E.*Andr.*5, *Med.*1035; Dor. **ζᾱλ–** Simon., Pi. (v. infr.):—*enviable*, of things, σοφία Pl.*Hp.Mi.*368b; καλὰ καὶ ζ. ἐπιγράμματα D.22.72: Comp., Isoc.6.95; ζηλωτὸν ὁ πλοῦτος Lycurg.*Fr.*97. 2. *to be deemed happy, to be envied*, of persons, Thgn.455, S.*Ant.*1161; τινι by one, A. *Pers.*710 (troch.), E.*Med.*1035, Pl.*Smp.*197d, etc.; ὑπό τινος Isoc.5. 69: c. gen. rei, θῆκέ μιν ζαλωτὸν ὁμόφρονος εὐνᾶς Pi.*O.*7.6; ζ. τῆς εὐνοίας Plu.*Pomp.*61: c. dat., Id.*Luc.*38. 3. of conditions, *enviable, blessed*, αἰών Simon.71, E.*Med.*243; πότμος Arist.*Fr.*675; ζηλωτότατος βίος Ar.*Nu.*464 (lyr.); γάμος Plu.2.289b, etc.

ζημία, Dor. **ζᾱμία** (*SIG*239 *D* iii 5 (Delph., iv B.C.), etc., later **σαμία** *Delph.*3(1).342 (ii B.C.), cf. ταμία, ἀττάμιος), ἡ, *loss, damage*, Epich. 148; opp. κέρδος, Lys.7.12, Pl.*Lg.*835b, Arist.*EN*1132ᵇ12; ζημίαν or –ίας λαβεῖν to sustain *loss*, S.*Fr.*807, D.11.11; ζ. ποιεῖν Ar.*Pl.*1124; ζ. ἐργάζεσθαι Is.6.20 (unless in signf. I.2); ζ. φέρειν τῇ πόλει Pl.*Lg.* l.c.; ζ. εἶναι νομίζειν consider *as loss*, Isoc.3.50, Is.7.23; ζ. πλείονα ὑπομένειν τῆς τιμῆς *PFlor.*142.8 (iii A.D.). 2. ζ. ἐργάζεσθαι, of a slave, be guilty of a *delict*, Is.6.20 (v. supr.), Hyp.*Ath.*22. II. *penalty* in money, *fine*, ζημίην ἀποτίνειν Hdt.2.65, cf. *PHal.*1.195 (iii B.C.); ἐκτίνειν Pl. *Lg.*774e; ἱρὴν ζ. ὀφείλειν Hdt.3.52; ζ. καταβάλλειν D.24.83, cf. *SIG* l.c.; μετὰ.. χρημάτων ζημίας Pl.*Lg.*862d; ζ. ἐπέκειτο στατήρ Th.3.70; ζημίαν ὀφείλειν τάλαντον Plu.*Lys.*27; τῆς ζ. ἀφεθῆναι Id.*Arist.*4. 2. generally, *penalty*, ζ. ἐπιτιθέναι τινί Hdt.1.144; ζ. ἔπεστί τινι Id. 2.136; πρόσκειταί τινι X.*Vect.*4.21; γλώσσῃ ζ. προστρίβεται A.*Pr.* 331, cf. 384; with the penalty added, θάνατον ζ. ἐπιθέσθαι, προθεῖναι, τάξαι, to make death *the penalty*, Th.2.24, 3.44, D.20.135; θάνατος ἡ ζ. ἐπίκειται Hdt.2.38, cf. 65; but ἐφ' οἷς.. θάνατος ἡ ζ. Pl.*Prt.*325b: in pl., θανάτου ζημίαι πρόκεινται Th.3.45 (v.l.): c. gen. criminis, ζ. ἀδικίας *penalty for..*, Pl.*Tht.*176d, cf. *Lg.*860e (pl.). b. simply, *expense*, *SIG*717.81 (ii/i B.C.), *PLond.*5.1660.10, 1674.23 (pl., vi A.D.). III. of what is bought too dearly, a *bad bargain*, a *dead loss*, X.*Mem.*2.3.2: usu. with Adj., φανερὰ ζᾱμία Ar.*Ach.*737; καθαρὰ ζ., λαμπρὰ ζ., Alciphr.3.21, 38, cf. Alex.56.6.

ζημιάζω, *damno*, *Gloss.*

ζημιο-πρακτέω, *exact punishment from*, τινὰ τὰ μὴ καθήκοντα *PTaur.*7.7 (ii B.C.). **–ψῡχος**, *damnatissimus*, *Gloss.*

ζημι-όω, fut. –ώσω Lys.1.48: aor. 1 ἐζημίωσα E.*Or.*578, Th.2.65, etc.: pf. ἐζημίωκα D.21.49:—**Pass.**, fut. ζημιωθήσομαι Lys.29.4, Is.10. 16, X.*Mem.*3.9.12; more freq. Med. ζημιώσομαι in pass. sense, Hdt. 7.39, And.1.72, Th.3.40, Isoc.18.37, D.1.27, Arist.*Pol.*1320ᵃ10: aor. ἐζημιώθην Pl.*Lg.*855b, Isoc.15.160: pf. ἐζημίωμαι Din.3.16, Arist.*Rh.* 1372ᵇ8:—*cause loss* or *do damage to, penalize*, πόλιν Lys.30.25; τοσαύτας ἡμέρας ζημιοῦν τινα *to cause* one *the loss of..*, Ael.*VH*3.23: c. Adj. neut., μηδὲν μηδένα Pl.*Lg.*846a; οὐδὲν ζ. τὸ κοινόν Isoc.6.5; πλείω ζ. σαυτὸν ἤ.. X.*Cyr.*3.1.30:—Pass., μεγάλα ζημιώσεται *will suffer* great *losses*, Th.3.40; πολλά Pl.*Lg.*916e: abs., Id.*Grg.* 490c. II. *fine, mulct in* a sum of money, c. dat. rei, ζ. τινὰ χιλίῃσι δραχμῇσι Hdt.6.21, cf. 136; χρήμασιν Th.2.65; μναῖς τρισί Pl.*Lg.* 936a; also ζ. τινὰ ἕως τριάκοντα μνᾶς Lycurg.*Fr.*40 (dub. l.); τινά τινος *deprive* of.., Lyd.*Mag.*2.19:—Pass., *to be fined* or *amerced in* a thing, c. dat. rei, χρήμασι Antipho 2.4.7; δραχμῇ τῆς ἡμέρας Pl.*Lg.*

766d; μέχρι τοσούτου ib.855b: also, c. acc. rei, ταῦτα ib.774b; ζ. τριάκοντα λίτρας Arist.*Fr.*476; *suffer financial loss*, *PFlor.*142.8 (iii A.D.): hence metaph., τοῦ ἑνὸς τοῦ περιέχεαι μάλιστα τῇ ψυχῇ ζημιώσεαι *wilt lose*, Hdt.7.39; τὴν ψυχὴν αὐτοῦ *Ev.Matt.*16.26; ἑαυτόν *Ev.Luc.* 9.25; τὰ κέρατα Ael.*NA*10.1. 2. generally, *punish*, τὴν θάλασσαν Hdt.7.35; σφέας Id.9.77; τινὰ θανάτῳ Id.3.27; τινὰ φυγῇ, πληγαῖς, Th.4.65, 8.74:—Pass., ζημιοῦσθαι ζημίαις ἐσχάταις Lys.31.26; θανάτῳ Antipho 3.3.9, *PTeb.*5.92 (ii B.C.); θανάτῳ καὶ πᾶσι τοῖς ἐσχάτοις Pl.*Plt.*297e; χρήμασιν καὶ ἀτιμίᾳ Id.*Lg.*721b. **-ώδης**, ες, *causing loss*, *ruinous*, Id.*Cra.*417d, *Lg.*650a, X.*Mem.*3.4.11. Adv. -δῶς, censured by Poll.8.147. **-ωμα**, ατος, τό, (ζημιόω) *penalty*, *fine*, Luc.*Prom.*13, *Sammelb.*5174.13 (vi A.D.), etc.; τῆς ἀταξίας for their disorder, X.*HG*3.1.9; -ώματα ἔστω ἀστυνόμοις let them have *the right of imposing penalties*, Pl.*Lg.*764c. 2. *loss*, opp. λῆμμα, *BGU*419.13 (iii A.D.); *injury*, *damage*, ζ. προστρίβεσθαί τινι D.C.52.33. **-ωσις**, εως, ἡ, *infliction of penalties*, Arist.*Pol.*1300^{b}22 (pl.). **-ωτής**, οῦ, ὁ, *one who punishes*, Sch.rec.A.*Pr.*77; *executioner*, Eust.1833.53. **-ωτικός**, ή, όν, *likely to suffer loss*, Vett.Val.67.19, al.

Ζήν, v. Ζεύς. **Ζήνιον** ὕδωρ (cf. foreg.), *rain*-water, *PMag.Par.*1.225.

Ζηνοδότειος, α, ον, *of the School of Zenodotus*, D.L.2.15.

Ζηνοδοτήρ, ῆρος, ὁ, *giver of Zeus*, i.e. of his counsel, *AP*9.525.7.

Ζηνοποσειδῶν, ὁ, *Zeus-Poseidon*, a divinity worshipped in Caria, Macho ap.Ath.8.337c, cf. 2.42a, *CIG*2700 add. (Mylasa); Dor. **Ζᾱνοποτειδάν** *GDI*5163*b*12 (ibid.).

ζῆνος, η, ον, perh. = ζεῖνος, *made of spelt* (ζέα), *UPZ*94.1, al. (ii B.C.).

Ζηνόφρων, ον, gen. ονος, (Ζήν, φρήν) *knowing the mind of Zeus*, epith. of Apollo as revealing Zeus' will in oracles, *AP*9.525.7.

Ζηνώνειος, ον, *of Zeno*, αἵρεσις D.L.1.19; τὸ Ζ. Ph.2.460; Ζ., ὁ, *Stoic philosopher*, D.L.7.5:—also **Ζηνωνικός**, Dor. **Ζᾱν-**, ή, όν, ἔρως Cerc.9.16.

ζῆσις, εως, ἡ, *vitalization*, Dam.*Pr.*83 bis.

ζῆτα, τό, indecl., *the letter* ζ, Pl.*Cra.*419b, etc.; of the *sixth* book of the Iliad, *POxy.*930.15 (ii/iii A.D.), *Epigr.Gr.*1095. (Semitic *zayin*, influenced by the names of the following letters, Gr. ἦτα, θῆτα.)

ζητᾰρετησιάδης, ου, ὁ, *virtue-seeker*, Epigr.ap.Hegesand.2.

ζητ-εύω, poet. for sq., Hes.*Op.*400, *h.Ap.*215, *h.Merc.*392: Dor. **ζᾱτεύω** Alcm.33.8. **-έω**, Dor. part. **ζάτεισα** Theoc.1.85: impf. ἐζήτουν, Ep. 3 sg. ζήτει Il.14.258 (nowh. else in Hom.): aor. 1 ἐζήτησα Isoc.16.14: pf. ἐζήτηκα Din.2.19:—Med., aor. 1 ἐζητησάμην (ἀν-) Longus *Prooem.*2:—Pass., fut. ζητηθήσομαι S.E.*P.*1.60, *M.*8.16; but ζητήσομαι in pass. sense, ib.1.28, Gal.1.649:—*seek*, *seek for*, ἐμὲ δ' ἔξοχα πάντων ζήτει Il. l.c.; ζ. πημάτων ἀπαλλαγάς A.*Pr.*318, cf. 264; εὑρήσεις ζητῶν Ar.*Pl.*105; μὴ ζητῶν without *seeking*, X.*Ages.* 8.1; τὸ ζητούμενον ἁλωτόν *what is sought for* may be found, S.*OT* 110. 2. *inquire for*, τὰ πινάκια καὶ τὰ γραμματεῖα *IG*1^2.91.11; τοὺς ἄρχοντας X.*An.*2.3.2: with relat. clause, ὅτου δέοιτο ὁ Κῦρος Id.*Cyr.* 8.5.13. 3. *search after*, *search out*, τὸν αὐτόχειρα S.*OT*266; μεγάλοις μηνύτροις ἐζητοῦντο οἱ δράσαντες Th.6.27; of huntsmen, ζ. τὸν λαγώ X.*Cyn.*6.25. 4. *search* or *inquire into*, *investigate*, *examine*, of philosophical investigation, ζ. τὰ θεῖα X.*Mem.*1.1.15; ζ. καὶ ἐρευνῶ κατὰ τὸν θεόν Pl.*Ap.*23b; ζητουμένης ἀρετῆς ὅ τι ἐστίν Id.*Men.*79d; τὸ ζητούμενον the *matter of inquiry*, the *question*, Id.*Tht.*201a, Arist. *Top.*110^{a}7, Str.2.1.18, A.D.*Adv.*188.13; also of judicial *inquiry*, ζ. περὶ ἀδικημάτων Din.1.8; ζήτησιν τὴν ὑπέρ τινος ζ. ib.10; ἔνοχος εἶναι τοῖς ζητουμένοις ib.55: generally, ζ. πότερον.. ἤ Pl.*Phlb.*27c; ζ. πρὸς ἐμαυτόν Luc.*Lex.*17. 5. *require*, *demand*, τῶν πράξεων παρὰ τοῦ στρατηγοῦ τὸν λόγον ζητοῦντες D.4.33: metaph., ὁ περικράνιος ὑμὴν.. τὴν ἐπιδιαίρεσιν ζ. *requires* the opening up of the wound, Heliod.ap.Orib.46.7.3. II. *seek after*, *desire*, ἀμήχανα E.*Alc.*203; ἐμοὶ ζητῶν ὄλεθρον S.*OT*659; of natural tendencies, ὁ θερμὸς ὕφαμμον χώραν ζητεῖ Thphr.*HP*8.11.8:—Pass., ζητούμενος *sought after*, *in great demand*, *PMag.Par.*1.3086, 3114. 2. c. inf., *seek to* do, ἐκμαθεῖν τι ζ. Hdt.3.137, A.*Pr.*776; μεταλαβεῖν Ar.*Pl.*370, cf. Pl.*Prt.* 322b, *Men.*90e, *SIG*372.7 (Samothrace, iii B.C.): c. fut. inf., ζητεῖς ἀναπείσειν Ar.*Pl.*573 codd. (sed leg. -πείθειν): c. acc. et inf., *seek* or *desire that*, Pl.*R.*443b, *Chrm.*172c. III. *have to seek*, *feel the want of*, ἵνα μὴ ζητέοιεν σιτία Hdt.1.94; Νέρωνα Plu.*Galb.*8:—Pass., ζητούμενος οἷς ἀπέλειπες *Epigr.Gr.*215.3 (Rhenea). **-ημα**, ατος, τό, *that which is sought*, Hp.*VM*3; οὐ ῥᾴδιον ζ. *a thing* not easy *to find*, of Pentheus' mutilated limbs, E.*Ba.*1139; δυσνοούμενον ζ., of God, Secund.*Sent.*3. II. *inquiry*, *question*, S.*OT*278, *Act.Ap.*15.2, al.; esp. of a philosophic nature, τὸ περὶ νόμους ζ. Pl.*Lg.*631a; τὰ περὶ φύσεως ζ. ib.891c; ποιητικῶν ζ. λύσεις Metrod.*Herc.*831.13; also τοῦτ'.. οὗ τυγχάνει ζ. Pl.*Cra.*421a; ἐκεῖνό γ' ἦν τὸ ζ. πρῶτον, πότερον.. Id.*Sph.*221c; *search*, σῶμα μυρίοις ζητήμασιν εὑρών E.*Ba.*1218; μητρὸς *after* her, Id.*Ion*1352. 2. *official* or *judicial inquiry*, *POxy.*97.14 (ii A.D.). III. in pl., *claims*, *PRyl.*117.14 (iii A.D.); *subjects of dispute*, *SIG*785.8 (i A.D.), *Act.Ap.*25.19. **-ημάτιον**, τό, Dim. of foreg. II, Arr.*Epict.*2.16.20, Lib.*Decl.*46 *Pr.*2. **-ηματικός**, ή, όν, = ζητητικός 2, Sch.Pl.p.212 H.

Ζητήρ, epith. of Zeus in Cyprus, Hsch.

ζητ-ήσιμος, ον, *to be searched*, τὰ ζ. *places to be beaten* for game, X.*Cyn.*6.6. **-ησις**, εως, ἡ, *seeking*, *search for*, κατ' Εὐρώπης ζήτησιν ἐκπλῶσαι Hdt.2.44; κατὰ βίου τε καὶ γῆς ζ. Id.1.94, cf. 2.54; ἀνδρὸς κατὰ ζήτησιν in *quest* of him, S.*Tr.*55; ἡ ζ. τῶν δρασάντων Th.8.66; ζ. ἐπιστήμης Pl.*Tht.*196d, etc.; τῆς τροφῆς Th.8.57; τῆς ἀληθείας Id. 1.20. 2. *searching*, *examining*, ζήτησιν ἐποιέετο τῶν νεῶν *searched* the ships, Hdt.6.118, cf. Lys.12.30, Aeschin.1.43. 3. *inquiry*, *investigation*, esp. of a philosophic nature, Pl.*Cra.*406a, *Ap.*29c, al.; περὶ τῆς τοῦ παντὸς φύσεως Id.*Ti.*47a; ζ. τοῦ μέλλοντος διὰ ὀρνίθων ποιεῖσθαι *inquire into* the future by augury, Id.*Phdr.*244c: in pl., Id.*Phd.*66d, Phld.*Rh.*1.276 S., 2.185 S. 4. *judicial inquiry*, Din.1.10, *POxy.*237 vi 7 (ii A.D.), etc.: pl., *suits*, *controversies*, *OGI*629.9 (Palmyra, ii A.D.). **-ητέος**, α, ον, *to be sought*, S.*Aj.*470, Ar.*Th.* 604, etc. II. ζητητέον, *one must seek*, Id.*Nu.*761, Sannyr.8; ἤ τινα ἑτέραν [δύναμιν]..ἡμῖν ζ. Pl.*Phlb.*58d. **-ητήριον**, τό, = βασανιστήριον, Anon.ap.Suid. **-ητής**, οῦ, ὁ, *seeker*, *inquirer*, τινος Pl.*R.* 618c; φαῦλος ζ. Id.*Chrm.*175e. II. ζητηταί, οἱ, at Athens, *commissioners to inquire into extraordinary offences* or *to recover moneys owing to the State*, And.1.14 (sg.), Lys.21.16, D.24.11, Pl.Com.125 (sg.). **-ητικός**, ή, όν, *disposed to search* or *inquire*, Pl.*Men.*81e, Ptol.*Tetr.*6; τινος *into* a thing, Pl.*Ax.*366b; περί τι Id.*R.*528c. 2. οἱ ζ. διάλογοι Plato's dialogues *of search* or *investigation*, opp. οἱ ὑφηγητικοί, Thrasyll.ap.D.L.3.49; τὸ ζ. ἔχουσι πάντες οἱ τοῦ Σωκράτους λόγοι are *devoted to search* or *inquiry*, Arist.*Pol.*1265^{a}12. Adv. -κῶς Procl. *in Prm.*p.515 S. 3. οἱ ζητητικοί, a name given to *the Sceptics*, D.L.9.69; ἡ ζητητική *their philosophy*, ib.70; ἡ ζ. ἀγωγή S.E. *P.*1.7. **-ητός**, ή, όν, *sought for*, τινι S.*OC*389.

ζητός, Arc. **ζατός**, = ζητητός, *IG*5(2).4.22 (Tegea, iv B.C.).

ζήτρ-ειον or **-εῖον**, τό, *a place of punishment for slaves* at Chios, Eup.19 D., Theopomp.Com.63, cf. *EM*411.33, Eust.837.44: **-ιον**, prob. in Herod.5.32, cf. Choerob.ap.*EM* l.c.: metaph. in dat. pl. -ίοις, 'treadmills', dub. in Phld.*Oec.*p.44 J.:—the forms **ζώστειον**, Ar.*Fr.*93; **ζώντειον** or **-εῖον**, Poll.3.78, Zonar.; **ζώτειον**, *EM*414.40 are incorrect. **-εύω**, in Dor. form **ζατρ-**, = ἐν μυλῶνι βασανίζω, *EM*408.12. **-ός**, ὁ, *executioner*, Hsch.

ζήτωρ, ορος, ὁ, = ζητητής, Hsch., Phot.

ζιβύνη, ἡ, = σιβύνη, Lxx *Is.*2.4, Ph.*Bel.*92.44, Porph.ap.Eus.*PE* 3.12: **ζηβήνη**, Hsch.:—Dim. **ζιβύννιον**, τό, Id.

ζιγγίβερις, εως, *Edict.Diocl.*32.68 (*Delph.*, *Clit.*), ὁ, ἡ (both in *Edict. Diocl.* l.c.); or **ζιγγίβερι**, τό, Dsc. (codd. opt.) and Gal. ll. cc.:—an Arabian spice-plant, the root of which was used in medicine, prob. *ginger*, Dsc.2.160, Gal.6.572, 11.880. (Perh. fr. Malay *inchi-ver* (*inchi* = root) through Skt. *śr̥ṅgaveram* and a Prakrit *singaber*.)

ζίγγος, ὁ, *humming* of bees, etc., Hsch.

ζιγγόω, *drink* (Cilician word), Nicostr.Com.38.

ζίγλας· κῶλα, Hsch.

ζιγνίς, ίδος, ἡ, a kind of *lizard*, Arist.*HA*604^{b}24 (v.ll. δειμνύς, ζιγνύς, διγνύς, ζίγνης).

ζιγνῶσαι· σκυθρωπάσαι, *EM*411.52, Hsch. (ζικν- cod.).

ζιζάνιον, τό, a weed that grows in wheat, = αἶρα II, prob. *darnel*, *Lolium temulentum*, *Gp.*2.43, *EM*411.46: pl., *Ev.Matt.*13.25, *Gp.* 10.87.1. (Cf. Sumer. *zizân* 'wheat'.)

ζιζουλά, τό, *jujube*, Alex.Trall.6.5; cf. sq. and Ital. *giuggiola*, *zizzola*.

ζίζῠφον, τό, a tree, the fruit of which is *the jujube*, *Zizyphus vulgaris*, *Gp.*10.3.4; *ziziphus*, Colum.9.4.3: gen. pl. *zizuforum*, *Edict. Diocl.*6.56.

ζίκαιος, Elean for δίκαιος, *Schwyzer*409 (vi B.C.):—also perh. written **ζικέα**, epith. of Nemesis, *BMus.Inscr.*1079 (Egypt (?)).

ζίλαι, v. ζελᾶς. **ζινίχιον**, τό, *shoe-latchet*, Suid. **ζιτᾶνα**· καταπύγονα, Hsch. **ζίφυιος**, Elean for δίφ-. **ζίω**, = ζητέω, *EM*411.51: ζίεται· ζητεῖται, ibid., Hsch. **ζμαράγδινος**, v. σμαρ-. **ζμάω**, v. σμάω. **ζμῆμα**, v. σμῆμα. **ζμιρριεῖα**, τά, *emery*, *IG*12(8).51.20 (Imbros, ii B.C.); cf. σμύρις. **ζμύρνη, ζμύρνινος**, etc., v. σμύρν-. **ζόα, ζόη, ζοΐα**, v. ζωή. **ζόασον**· σβέσον, Hsch. **ζοός**, v. ζωός. **ζορκάς**, άδος, and ζόρξ, ζορκός, ἡ, v. δορκάς. **ζούγωνερ**, Lacon. for ζύγωνες, *ploughing oxen*, Id. **ζουΐον ἢ ζοῦον**· θηρίον, ἢ ἐρυσίπελας, Id. (Prob. Thess. for ζῷον.) **ζούσθω**· ζωννύσθω, Id. (Prob. Thess.)

ζόφ-εος, α, ον, v.l. for sq., νύξ Nic.*Al.*501. **-ερός**, ά, όν, (ζόφος) *dusky*, *gloomy*, Χάος Hes.*Th.*814; οἴκημα Hp.*Acut.*(*Sp.*)18, cf. Hierocl.p.33 A.; opp. λαμπρός, of the air, *misty*, Chrysipp.*Stoic.* 2.140, cf. Luc.*Nigr.*4; τὴν θάλασσαν ζοφερὰν διαφαίνεσθαι Arist.*Mir.* 843^{a}25; τὸ ζοφερόν Hp.*Virg.*1, Arist.*de An.*426^{b}2. 2. metaph., ζ. φροντίδες *AP*5.296.8 (Agath.). **-ιος**, ον, = ζόφεος, ζοφερός, ib. 7.377 (Eryc.).

ζοφο-δορπίδας, α, ὁ, *supping in the dark* or *in secret*, of Pittacus, Alc. 37 B, cf. Plu.2.726a: **-δορπίας** in Theognost.*Can.*20, Zonar.; **-δερκίας**, Hsch., Suid. **-είδελος**, ον, *dusky*, *gloomy*, Nic.*Th.* 657. **-ειδής**, ές, *dark-coloured*, Hp.*Mul.*1.11; of the colour of an elephant, Aret.*SD*2.13. **-εις**, εσσα, εν, = foreg., Nic.*Th.*775, *Al.* 474, Orph.*H.*78.4. **-μηνία**, ἡ, (μήνη) = σκοτομηνία, Hsch., Gramm. in Reitzenstein *Ind.Lect.Rost.*1892/3 p.10. **-πνοια**, ἡ, = ἡ ἀπὸ δύσεως πνοή, Sch.Il.21.334.

ζόφος, ὁ, *nether darkness*, ἱεμένων Ἔρεβόσδε ὑπὸ ζόφον Od.20.356, cf. 11.155, Il.21.56, *Ep.Jud.*6; Ἀΐδης δ' ἔλαχε ζόφον ἠερόεντα obtained *the realms of gloom* for his share, Il.15.191, cf. Od.11.57, *h.Cer.* 402, 446, etc.; γῆς ὑπὸ ζόφον A.*Pers.*839. 2. generally, *gloom*, *darkness*, Hes.*Sc.*227, Plb.18.20.7, Arist.*Mu.*400^{a}8, *Ep.Hebr.*12.18, Plu.*Alc.*28, Luc.*DMort.*15.2; χειμέριος ζ. *the gloom* of winter, Pi.*I.* 4(3).18: metaph., τῆς ψυχῆς.. ζ. Plu.2.48c. II. *the dark quarter*, i.e. *the West*, ἤδη γὰρ φάος οἴχεθ' ὑπὸ ζόφον Od.3.335; οὐ γὰρ ἴδμεν ὅπη ζ. οὐδ' ὅπη ἠώς 10.190; ποτὶ ζόφον, opp. πρὸς ἠῶ τ' ἠέλιόν τε, Il.12. 240, Od.13.241, 9.26 (*the North* acc. to Str.10.2.12); Γαδείρων τὸ πρὸς ζόφον *to the west of*..., Pi.*N.*4.69.—Poet. and later Prose. (Prob. cogn. with ζέφυρος.)

ζοφ-όω, *darken*, Hld.2.15:—Pass., *to be* or *become dark*, γῆρα κανθὸν ἐζοφωμένος *AP*6.92 (Phil.); τὴν ὄψιν ἐζοφωμένος Ps.-Luc.*Philopatr.*

4. **-ώδης**, ες, = ζοφοειδής, οὖρον Hp.*Coac.*570; θάλαττα Arist.*Pr.* 944^{b}22; ἀήρ ib.946^{a}34 (Sup.), cf. Vett.Val.312.32; [σελήνη] Thphr. *Sign.*12; Βόσπορος Str.1.2.9; Εὖρος App.*Hann.*20; *opaque*, Cleom. 1.4. **-ωσις**, εως, ἡ, *a darkening*, ἀέρος Sch.E.*Ph.*1534.

ζόω, v. ζῶ.

ζῠγάδην [ᾰ], Adv., (ζυγόν) *jointly, in pairs*, Ph.1.237, al., Phot., Suid.

ζῠγάδιον, τό, a kind of *shoe*, prob. in Suid. s.v. ξυρίδες.

ζύγαινα [ῠ], ης, ἡ, *the hammer-headed shark*, Epich.59, Arist.*HA* 506^{b}10, Philotim.ap.Gal.6.727, Ael.*NA*9.49, Opp.*H.*1.367.

ζῠγάρχ-ης, ου, ὁ, *leader of a line of horsemen*, Ascl.*Tact.*7.9, Ael. *Tact.*19.8:—hence **-έω**, Ascl. l.c. **-ία**, ἡ, *detachment of two chariots*, ib.8, Ael.*Tact.*22.2.

ζῠγάστριον, τό, Dim. of sq., Poll.7.79, 10.138.

ζύγαστρον [ῠ], τό, *chest, box* (κιβωτός, κυρίως δὲ ξυλίνη σορός, παρὰ τὸ ἐζυγῶσθαι, Phot.), S.*Tr.*692, E.ap.Phot., X.*Cyr.*7.3.1. 2. at Delphi, = γραμματοφυλάκιον, *SIG*241.49,146 (iv B.C.), *Delph.*3(2). 205 (iii B.C.), Phot. 3. in pl., *fastenings*, λάρνακος Sch.Theoc. 7.78.

ζυγαστροφέω, doubtful word in Sophr.90.

ζῠγ-έω, *march in line*, opp. στοιχεῖν (in file), Ascl.*Tact.*2.6, al. 2. *form a line*, of contingents, Plb.3.113.8. **-ή**, ἡ, *pair*, *PSI*3.225.4 (vi A.D.); *faggot*, ib.5.481.4 (v/vi A.D.). **-ηδόν**, Adv. *in pairs*, Hld.10.27.

ζῠγηφόρος, ον, poet. for ζυγοφόρος (q.v.), A.*Fr.*326, E.*Rh.*303.

ζῠγία, ἡ, *maple, Acer campestre*, Thphr.*HP*3.3.1, 5.3.3, Dicaearch. 2.2, Plin.*HN*16.67.

ζῠγ-ιατής, *jumentarius*, *Gloss.* **-ίζω**, = ζευγ-, Suid. **-ικός**, ή, όν, (ζυγός) *of* or *for a balance*, τὰ -κά Nicom.*Harm.*2. **-ιμος**, ον, = ζύγιος I, βοῦς Plb.34.8.9. **-ινος**, η, ον, *of the tree* ζυγία, Thphr. *HP*5.3.3. **-ιον**, τό, = ζυγόν III. 1, ὑπὸ τὰ ζ. Callix.1, cf. Aq., Sm. *Pr.*11.1. **-ιος**, α, ον, also ος, ον E. (v. infr.), *IG*2^2.1604.71 (iv B.C.): (ζῠγόν):—*of* or *for the yoke*, esp. (sc. ἵππος) *draught-horse*, opp. σειραφόρος, E.*IA*221 (lyr.), Ar.*Nu.*122: c. gen., θηρῶν ζυγίους ζεύξασα σατίνας having yoked cars to *teams* of beasts, E.*Hel.*1310: as Subst., κατασκευάσαι.. ὁδὸν ζυγίοις πορευτήν *Milet.*3 No.149.45 (ii B.C.). II. epith. of Hera as patroness of marriage, A.R.4.96, Musae.275; also of other divinities, as Aphrodite, *IG*3.171, cf. *AP* 7.555 (Joann.), Hsch. III. ζύγιος, ὁ, = ζυγίτης, Poll.1.87,120; κώπη ζ. *IG*2^2. l.c., Polyaen.5.22.4 (pl.). IV. *of full weight*, νομίσματα *Stud.Pal.*20.121.18 (v A.D.). **-ίς**, ίδος, ἡ, = ἕρπυλλος, Dsc. 3.38, Philin.ap.Ath.15.681f. **-ίσκον**, τό, Dim. of ζύγιον, *IG*2^2. 1549.9. **-ίτης** [ῑ], ου, ὁ, *the rower who sat on the mid-most of the three banks*, like μεσόνεος, Sch.Ar.*Ra.*1106.

ζῠγῖτις, ιδος, fem. of ζύγιος II, Nicom.ap.Phot.*Bibl.*p.144 B.

ζυγκλεῖ· μύει, ὁρμᾷ, σκυθρωπάζει, Hsch.

ζῠγο-δέσμιον, τό, Dim. of sq., *PLond.*1821.113. **-δεσμον**, τό, (ζυγόν I) *yoke-band*, i.e. a band for fastening the yoke to the pole, ζ. ἅμα ζυγῷ ἐννεάπηχυ Il.24.270, cf. *PFay.*121.5 (i/ii A.D.); of the Gordian knot, Plu.*Alex.*18, etc.: pl., ζυγόδεσμα Procl.*H.*1.31, *AP* 9.155 (Agath.), 741, etc.:—also **-δεσμος**, ὁ, Artem.2.24, Them.*Or.* 2.30b. **-δέτης**, ου, ὁ, (δέω A) = foreg., Hsch. **-ειδής**, ές, *like a yoke*, ὀστᾶ Gal.14.721. **-εις**· βούτυρος, Cyr. (ζυγοήσεις· βότρυς Hsch.). **-κέφᾰλον**, τό, *tax on land at so much a jugum*, *CIG*2712. 5 (Mylasa, v A.D.), Just.*Nov.*17.8. **-κρούστης**, ου, ὁ, *one who uses a false balance*, Artem.4.57. **-λωρον**, τό, = ζυγόδεσμος, Sch.rec.A. *Pers.*188. **-μᾰχέω**, *struggle with one's yoke-fellow*, ἵππου ἐν ἅρματι ζ. App.*Syr.*33. 2. generally, *struggle, quarrel*, τινι *Com.Adesp.* 207, cf. Hyp.*Fr.*245, Procop.Gaz.p.141 B.; πορνοβοσκοῖς.. διὰ βίου ζ. Phld.*Herc.*223.8; περί τινος D.39.6; πρὸς τὴν τύχην Men.673; πρὸς οἰκέτην Plu.*Cat.Ma.*21, cf. Chor. in *Hermes* 17.235; ὑπὲρ ὀνόματος Gal. 10.963. **-μᾰχία**, ἡ, *quarrelling, strife*, Aristaenet.1.2.

ζῠγόν, τό, also **ζυγός**, ὁ (in various senses), *h.Cer.*217, Pl.*Ti.*63b, Theoc.30.29, Lxx*Ge.*27.40, al., Plb.4.82.2, *Ev.Matt.*11.29, Jul.*Or.*5. 173a, etc.: rarely in pl., ζυγοί Lxx*Pr.*11.1, Sch.Th.1.29: Delph. **δυγός** (q.v.). I. *yoke* of a plough or carriage, ζ. ἵππειον Il.5.799, 23.392; ὑπὸ ζυγὸν ἤγαγεν ἵππους 5.731, cf. Od.3.383; ἐπὶ ζυγὸν αὐχένι θεῖναι βουσί Hes.*Op.*815, cf. 581; ὑπὸ ζυγόφιν (i.e. ζυγοῦ) λύον ἵππους Il.24.576: prov., τὸν αὐτὸν ἕλκειν ζ. 'to be in the same boat', Aristaenet.2.7, Zen.3.43; ταὔτ' ἐμοὶ ζ. τρίβεις Herod.6.12. 2. metaph., ἐπὶ ζυγὸς αὐχένι κεῖται *h.Cer.*217; ἐχθροῖσιν ὑπὸ ζυγὸν αὐχένα θήσω Thgn.1023; ἐπαυχένιον λαβεῖν ζ. Pi.*P.*2.93; δούλιον ζ. *the yoke* of slavery, Hdt.7.8.γ', A.*Th.*75 (pl.), 471, etc.; δουλείας, ἀνάγκης ζ., S.*Aj.*944, E.*Or.*1330; ὑπὸ ζυγῷ λόφον δικαίως εἶχον S.*Ant.*291; ἐπιτιθέναι τινὶ ζυγὰ τοῦ μή.. so as to prevent.., X.*Cyr.*3.1.27; ζυγῷ ζυγῆναι Pl.*R.*508a; ἄγειν ὑπὸ τὸν ζ. τινάς Plb.4.82.2, cf. D.H.3.22; ὑπὸ τὸν ζ. ὑπαγαγεῖν D.C.*Fr.*36.10; ζυγὸν ὑποστῆναι D.H.10.20. II. *cross-bar* of the φόρμιγξ, Il.9.187. 2. ζυγὸς ἡ τῆς ἀμπέλου πρὸς τὴν χάρακα συζυγία *Gp.*5.29.6. III. in pl., *thwarts* or *benches joining* the opposite sides of a ship, Od.9.99, 13.21, Hdt.2.96: rarely in sg., θοὸν εἰρεσίας ζυγόν S.*Aj.*249 (lyr.): metaph., of the seat of authority compared to the helmsman's seat, ἐς τὸ πρῶτον πόλεος ζ. E.*Ion* 595; ἐπεὶ δ' ἐπὶ ζυγοῖς καθέζετ' ἀρχῆς Id.*Ph.*74; σὺ ταῦτα φωνεῖς νερτέρᾳ προσήμενος κώπῃ, κρατούντων τῶν ἐπὶ ζυγῷ δορός; while on the *main thwart* sits authority, A.*Ag.*1618; also of a coachman's *seat, box*, *PMasp.*303.15 (vi A.D.). 2. in pl., *panels* of a door, *IG*1^2.372. 199, 2^2.1457.14, 1672.155; cf. ζευγίον. IV *beam of the balance*, ζυγὸν ταλάντου A.*Supp.*822 (lyr.), cf. Arist.*Mech.*850^{a}4: hence, *the balance itself* (cf. πῆχυς IV), αἴρειν τὸν ζυγόν Pl.*Ti.*63b; ἐν πλάστιγγι ζυγοῦ κεῖσθαι Id.*R.*550e; ζυγῷ or ἐν τῷ ζ. ἱστάναι, Lys.10.18, Pl. *Prt.*356b; ζυγὸν ἱστάναι D.*Prooem.*55: in pl., Id.25.46, *SIG*975.39 (Delos, iii B.C.): prov., ζ. μὴ ὑπερβαίνειν Pythag.ap.D.L.8.18. b. the constellation *Libra*, Hipparch.3.1.5, Ph.1.28, Man.2.137, etc.; ζ. Ἀφροδίτης Porph.*Antr.*22. V. καρχασίου the *yard-arm* at the mast-head, Pi.*N.*5.51, cf. Ach.Tat.5.16. VI. *cross-strap* of a sandal, Ar.*Lys.*417, Poll.7.81; ζυγός, ὁ, Phot. VII. *pair*, κλεινὸν ζυγόν, of persons, E.*Hel.*392; κατὰ ζυγά *in pairs*, Arist.*HA* 544^{a}5, Theoc.13.32. VIII. *rank* or *line* of soldiers, opp. *file* (στοῖχος), ἐν τῷ πρώτῳ ζ. ἐμάχοντο τέσσαρες Th.5.68; ὁ ζυγός Polyaen.4.4.3 (τὰ ζυγά 2.10.4); κατὰ ζυγὸν *line with line*, Plb.1.45.9; κατ' ἄνδρα καὶ ζ. Id.3.81.2; esp. *front rank*, Ael.*Tact.*7.1, Arr.*Tact.*8.1; also of the Chorus, Poll.4.108. IX. ζυγὰ ἢ ἄζυγα *even* or odd, a game, Sch.Ar.*Pl.*817. X. measure of land, *SIG*963.13 (Amorgos, iv B.C.).

ζῠγοποι-έω, *make yokes*, wrongly cited by Poll.7.115 fr. Ar.*Pl.* 513. **-ός**, ὁ, *maker of yokes*, Pherecr.130.

ζῠγός, ὁ, v. sub ζυγόν.

ζῠγοσταθμ-έω, = ζυγοστατέω, Tz.ad Lyc.270, 275 (both Pass.). **-ος**, ὁ, *balance*, Plu.2.928b.

ζῠγοστᾰσ-ία, ἡ, *weighing*, *PGrenf.*2.46^{a}8 (ii A.D.). **-ιον**, τό, *weigh-house*, *CIG*3705 (Apollonia ad Rhyndacum), *JRS*2.87 (Antioch in Pisidia): pl., *IGRom.*4.657 (Acmonia); -στασίου [τέλος] *weighing*-toll, *BGU*337.20 (ii/iii A.D.). 2. *zygostasii munus*, office of ζυγοστάτης, *Cod.Just.*11.28.1.

ζῠγοστᾰτ-έω, *weigh by the balance, weigh*, ὥσπερ ἐν τρυτάνῃ Luc. *Hist.Conscr.*49; τινὰς πρὸς τὸν Τιμάρχου βραχίονα Alciphr.2.2. b. *act as libripens*, Mitteis *Chr.*316 ii 4 (ii A.D.). II. Pass., *to be in equilibrium*, Plb.6.10.7; ἐζυγοστατεῖτο αὐτοῖς ὁ πόλεμος Id.1.20. 5. **-ημα**, ατος, τό, *balance*, Eust.665.29. **-ης**, ου, Dor. **-ᾱς**, ὁ, *public weigher*, *Cod.Just.*10.73.2 (iv A.D.), Artem.2.37: metaph., ὀρθὸς ὢν ζ., of Zeus, Cerc.4.33.

ζῠγό-ταυρον, τό, *yoke, pair of oxen*, *PFlor.*167.3, 256.3 (iii A.D.). **-τράχηλον** [ᾰ], τό, *neck-piece of yoke*, *PLond.*3.1177.190 (ii A.D.). **-τρῠτάνη** [ᾰ], ἡ, *balance*, Phot. s.v. ζυγός.

ζῠγουλκός, όν, *drawing the yoke*, βόες Moschio Trag.6.26.

ζῠγόφιν, Ep. gen. of ζυγόν, Il.24.576; ὑπὸ ζ. Poet.ap.D.Chr.32.85.

ζῠγοφορ-έω, *weigh*, in Pass., Hsch. II. v. ζευγοφορέομαι. **-ος**, ον, *bearing the yoke*, πῶλος E.*HF*121 (lyr., -ηφόρος codd.); ἵπποι Plu. 2.524a: elsewh. in poet. form **ζυγηφόρος** (q.v.).

ζῠγόω, (ζυγόν) *yoke, join together*, [σκέλη] Sor.1.84; ζ. κιθάραν *put the cross-bar to* the lyre, Luc.*DDeor.*7.4, *DMar.*1.4; κανόνες ἐζυγωμένοι δύο Agatho 4.2, cf. Lxx*Ez.*41.26. 2. *close*, χείλη ῥαφαῖς Paul.Aeg.6.67 (prob.); *shut off*, Hp.*Cord.*12 (Pass.). 3. metaph., *bring under the yoke, subdue*, A.*Fr.*115.

ζύγρα, ἡ, dialectic form for διύγρα (sc. χώρα), *marsh-land*, Eust. 295.28.

ζυγωγόν, glossed ἧπαρ, dub. l. in *PLond.*1821.50 (prob. ζυγωτόν = συκωτόν).

ζῠγ-ώδης, ες, f.l. for ζυγάδην (wh. is restored fr. Lyd.*Mens.*2.12), Ph.1.22. **-ωθρίζω**, *weigh, examine*, Ar.*Nu.*745, acc. to Sch.: but acc. to Poll.10.26 from **ζύγωθρον** (*the bar of a door*), *lock up*. **-ωμα**, ατος, τό, *bolt, bar*, Plb.7.16.5. b. *cross-rod*, Apollod.*Poliorc.*177. 8. II. = ζυγόν III. 1, Sch.Th.1.29. III. *arcus zygomaticus*, which connects the cranial with the facial bones, Gal.2.437, 746, Poll.2.85; cf. ζυγοειδής. IV. = ζυγόν II, Ptol.*Alm.*7.5. V. *canal-lock*, *PFlor.*273.20 (iii A.D.). **-ωσις**, εως, ἡ, (cf. ζυγόν IV) *a balancing*, κατὰ τὴν ζύγωσιν, of heavy oars, Callix.1. **-ωτός**, ή, όν, (ζυγόω) *yoked*, ἅρματα ζ. S.*El.*702.

ζύθιον, τό, Dim. of ζῦθος, = ἀλφίτου πόσις, Hsch. (ἡ ἐξ ἀ. π. Gramm. in Reitzenstein *Ind.Lect.Rost.*1892/3 p.12.)

ζῡθοπώλης, ου, ὁ, *beer-seller*, *POxy.*85 iv 4 (iv A.D.):—fem. only in form **ζυτόπωλις** (q.v.).

ζῦθος, ου, ὁ (also -εος, τό, Thphr. (v. infr.), D.S. (v. infr.)), an Egyptian kind of *beer*, brewed with barley, Thphr.*CP*6.11.2, Dsc.2. 87, Str.17.1.14, D.S.1.34, etc.; cf. ζῦτος. 2. *beer* of northern nations, Posidon.15 J., Str.3.3.7, D.S.5.26. (The word was used in Egypt acc. to Thphr. l.c., etc.: written ζυτο- (q.v.) in the older Pap.: freq. accented ζύθος in codd., but ζῦθος Phot., ζῡ- in verse, Poet.ap.D.Chr.32.82, Colum.10.116.)

ζύμ-η [ῡ], ἡ, *leaven*, Arist.*GA*755^{a}18, Lxx*Ex.*12.15; *beer-yeast*, *PTeb.*375.27 (ii A.D.), etc.: metaph., of *corruption, falsehood*, *Ev. Matt.*16.6, etc. (ζῡ-μᾱ or ζῡσ-μᾱ, cf. Skt. *yauti* 'mix', Skt. *yūs*, Lat. *jūs* 'soup', Lett. *jaut* 'stir dough', *javs* 'dough'.) **-ήεις**, εσσα, εν, *leavened*, ἄρτος Hsch. **-ίζω**, *to be like leaven*, τὴν ὀσμὴν Dsc.2. 80. **-ίτης ἄρτος** [ῑ], ὁ, *leavened* bread, Cratin.99 (prob. l.), Hp. *Vict.*2.42, 3.75, X.*An.*7.3.21, Lxx*Le.*7.3(13), Sor.1.94, Philostr.*Im.* 2.26. **-ίωσις**, εως, ἡ, = ζύμωσις, subject of lost work by Zos. Alch.p.216 B.

ζῡμοειδής, ές, = ζυμώδης, Sch.Orib.4 p.526 D.

ζῡμ-ουργός, ὁ, *maker of leaven*, *PAmh.*2.128.29 (ii A.D.), *PFay.* 333 (ii A.D.). **-όω**, (ζύμη) *leaven*, μικρὰ ζύμη ὅλον τὸ φύραμα ζ. 1 *Ep. Cor.*5.6:—Pass., *to be leavened, ferment*, Lxx*Ex.*12.34,39, Plu.2. 659b, etc.; of digestion, τὰ μέλανα -οῦται Hp.*Acut.*61; [κοιλίη] ἐζυμωμένη *in a ferment*, Id.*VM*11. 2. *cause to effervesce*, γῆν Gal.10. 964, Aët.1 *Praef.*:—Pass., ζυμουμένη [χύτρα] Alex.124.8. **-ώδης**, ες, *like leaven*, Arist.*GA*755^{a}23. **-ωμα**, ατος, τό, *fermented mixture*, Pl.*Ti.*74d; ζύμωμα χθονός, of a fungus, Nic.*Al.*521, cf. 525 cum Sch. ad loc. **-ωσις**, εως, ἡ, *fermentation*, Pl.*Ti.*66b, Plu.2.659b, Gal.16.

661; ἥπατος ζύμωσις *a swelling* of the liver, Hp.*Epid*.4.8. **-ωτικός**, ή, όν, *causing to ferment*, τινος Diocl.*Fr*.118. **-ωτός**, ή, όν, *fermented, leavened*, Lxx *Ex*.13.7, al.

ζῡτᾶς, ᾶ, ὁ, *brewer*, *BGU*1087 ii 2 (iii A. D.).

ζῡτηρά, ἡ, *tax on brewing*, *PCair.Zen*.176.30 (iii B. C.), *PTeb*.40.4 (ii B. C.).

ζῡτο-ποιέω, *brew beer*, *PCair.Zen*.199.9 (iii B. C.). **-ποιΐα**, ἡ, *brewing*, *Ostr.Fay*.10.4 (i A. D.). **-ποιός**, ὁ, *brewer*, *PPetr*.3 p.85 (iii B. C.), al., *PTeb*.5.173 (ii B. C.), etc. **-πώλιον**, τό, *beer-shop*, *PCair.Zen*.189.6 (iii B. C.), al., *PRyl*.127.12 (i A. D.). **-πωλις**, ιδος, ἡ, *woman who sells beer*, *BGU*38.18 (ii/iii A. D.).

ζῦτος, ὁ, = ζῦθος, *PCair.Zen*.176.4 (iii B. C.), al., *PPetr*.3 p.327 (iii B. C.), *UPZ*149.14 (iii/ii B. C.), *PMag.Par*.1.908, *OGI*200.16 (Axum, iv A. D.):—also **ζῦτος**, εος, τό, *PHib*.1.113.6 (iii B. C.), Glauc.ap. *POxy*.1802.42.

ζῡτουργεῖον, τό, *brewery*, *PPetr.ined*. iii No. 124 (iii B. C.), v. indicem.

ζῶ (contr. fr. ζάω: ζάω only in Gramm., *EM*410.38), ζῇς (Choerob. *in Theod*.2.28), ζῇ, ζῆτε (but ζῇς, ζῇ acc. to Anon.ap.*EM*410.48, Sophronius ap.Choerob. *in Theod*.2.416); imper. ζῆ S.*Fr*.167, E.*IT* 699, ζῆθι (as if from ζῆμι, cf. *EM* l.c.) Pherecr.11 D., Men.*Mon*. 191, *AP*10.43, σύ-ζηθι Philem.ap.*Et.Gen*. s. v. ζῆ; opt. ζῴην; inf. ζῆν: impf. ἔζων S.*El*.323, Ar.*Ra*.1072; ἔζην in most codd. of D.24.7 is a form suggested by ἔζης, ἔζη; 3 pl. ἔζων Ar.*V*.709, Pl.*Lg*.679c: fut. ζήσω Ar.*Pl*.263, Pl.*R*.465d, Men.*Mon*.186, [Epich.]267, ζήσομαι Hp.*Nat.Puer*.30, D.25.82, Arist.*Pol*.1327^{b}5: aor. 1 ἔζησα Hp. *Prog*.1, *AP*7.470 (Mel.), Plu.2.786a, etc.: pf. ἔζηκα Arist.*Metaph*. 1048^{b}25, D.H.5.68, etc.: but in Att. aor. and pf. are mostly supplied from βιόω.—Exc. part. ζῶντος, Il.1.88, Hom. always uses the Ep. Ion. Lyr. pres. **ζώω** (also in Pi.*O*.2.25, Hdt.7.46, al., Diog.Apoll.4, Herod.2.29, *IG*12(8).600.9 (Thasos), and Trag. (in lyr.), S.*El*.157, *OC*1213, cf. *BCH*47.95 (Cavalla), *Bull.Soc.Arch.Bulg*.7.13 (Macedonia); subj. ζώῃ *IG*12(8).262.12 (Thasos, v B. C.), cf. *Schwyzer*339, al. (Delph.), contr. ζῷ *Berl.Sitzb*.1927.161 (Cyrene); Cret. **δώω** *Leg. Gort*.4.21, al.); inf. ζωέμεναι, -έμεν, Od.7.149, 24.436: impf. ἔζωον 22.245, Hes.*Op*.112, Hdt.4.112; Ion. ζώεσκον Hes.*Op*.90, Bion 1.30: aor. 1 ἔζωσα (ἐπ-) Hdt.1.120; inf. ζῶσαι *IG*11(4).1299 (Delos): pf. part. ἐζωκότα *BMus.Inscr*.1009 (Cyzicus); inf. ζόειν Semon.1.17: impf. ζόεν *AP*13.21 (Theodorid.). (Root *g^{w}iē-, g^{w}iō-* also in βίος and ὑγιής (q. v.).)

I. prop. of animal life, *live*, Hom. (v. infr.), etc.; also of plants, τὸ ζῆν κοινὸν εἶναι φαίνεται καὶ τοῖς φυτοῖς Arist.*EN*1097^{b}33; ἐλέγχιστε ζωόντων vilest *of living men*, Od.10.72; ζώειν καὶ ὁρᾶν φάος ἠελίοιο Il. 24.558; ζῶντος καὶ ἐπὶ χθονὶ δερκομένοιο 1.88, cf. Od.16.439; ζῶν καὶ βλέπων A.*Ag*.677; ζώει τε καὶ ἔστιν Od.24.263; ζώντων καὶ ὄντων D. 18.72; τοῦ εἶναί τε καὶ ζῆν ἕνεκα Pl.*R*.369d; ζῶσα πόλις καὶ ἐγρηγορυῖα Id.*Lg*.809d; ζῶν καὶ ἔμψυχος Id.*Phdr*.276a; ῥεῖα ζώοντες *living* at ease, of the gods, Il.6.138, al.; ζῶν κατακαυθῆναι to be burnt *alive*, Hdt.1.86: c. acc. temp., ζ. ἤματα πάντα *h.Ven*.221, etc.; ὀλίγα ἔτεα Hdt.3.22: c. dat. modi, δμῶες.. ἄλλα τε πολλὰ οἷσίν τ' εὖ ζώουσι whereby men *live* in comfort, Od.17.423, cf. D.60.5; κοράκων πονηρίᾳ Ar.*Th*.868; ἐπὶ τοῖς αἰσχίστοις ἔργοις, ἐπὶ τοῖς παροῦσιν ἀγαθοῖς, And.1.100, Isoc.10.18; also ζῆν ἀπό τινος *to live on* a thing, Thgn. 1156, Hdt.1.216, 2.36, 4.22, Ar.*Pax*850, etc.; ἔκ τινος Id.*Ec*.591, D. 57.36, 1*Ep.Cor*.9.14: c. part., ζῆν συκοφαντῶν And.1.99; ἐργαζόμενοι Arist.*Pol*.1292^{b}27: c. dat. commodi, ζῆν ἑαυτῷ *for* oneself, dub. l. in E.*Ion*646, cf. Ar.*Pl*.470, Men.507; τὸ ζῆν, = ζωή, A.*Pr*.681, Pl. *Phd*.77d (without Art. εἰς ἕτερον ζ. Id.*Ax*.365d); διὰ παντὸς τοῦ ζῆν *Ep.Hebr*.2.15; also, *a living*, τὸ ζ. οὐκ ἔχομεν *OGI*515.57 (Mylasa, iii A. D.); ζήτω ὁ βασιλεύς *long live* the king, Lxx 1*Ki*.10.24; βασιλεῦ, εἰς τὸν αἰῶνα ζῆθι ib.*Da*.3.9; asseverations, ζῶ ἐγώ, καὶ ζῶν τὸ ὄνομά μου, καί.. ib.*Nu*.14.21; ζῇ κύριος, εἰ.., ὅτι.., ib.1*Ki*.19.6, 29.6; ζῇ ἡ ψυχή σου, εἰ οἶδα ib.17.55. **2.** = βιόω, *live, pass one's life*, c. acc. cogn., ζώεις δ' ἀγαθὸν βίον Od.15.491; ζ. βίον μοχθηρόν S.*El*.599, cf. E.*Med*.249, Ar.*V*.506, etc.; ζόην τὴν αὐτήν Hdt.4.112, cf. Pl.*R*.344e; τὸν βίον ἀσφαλῶς Philem.213.5; ἥδιστον ἀνθρώπων βίον S.*Fr*.583.4; νυμφίων βίον Ar.*Av*.161; also ζ. ἀβλαβεῖ βίῳ S.*El*.650, cf. *Tr*.168; εὖ ζῆν Id.*Ph*.505; κακῶς Id.*OC*799; ζ. δοῦλος Id.*OT*410; ἐκ τῶν ἄλλων ὧν ἔζης from the other *acts of your life*, D.21.134; ποιεῖσθαι φθόνον ἐξ ὧν ζῇς ib.196. **3.** aor. 1 ἔζησα, causal, *quicken*, ἐν τῇ ὁδῷ σου ζῆσόν με Lxx *Ps*.118(119).37, al. **II.** *live* in the fullest sense, δι' ὧν ζῆν ἐπιστάμεθα X.*Mem*.3.3.11, etc.; βιοὺς μὲν ἔτη τόσα, ζήσας δὲ ἔτη ἑπτά D.C.69.19; in religious or mystical sense, *Ep.Rom*.7.9, al., cf. Ramsay *Cities and Bishoprics* 2 p.565 (Phryg.); θεὸς ζῶν Lxx *De*.5. 26(23), etc.: freq. metaph. of things, *to be in full vigour*, ὄλβος ζώει μάσσων Pi.*I*.3.5; ἄτης θύελλαι ζῶσι A.*Ag*.819; ζῶντι χρώμενος ποδί S.*Fr*.790; [μαντεῖα] αἰεὶ ζῶντα περιποτᾶται Id.*OT*482; ἀεὶ ζῇ ταῦτα [νόμιμα] Id.*Ant*.457; τὰς ξυμφορὰς τῶν βουλευμάτων ζώσας μάλιστα *have* most *living power*, Id.*OT*45; λόγια ζῶντα *Act.Ap*.7.38; χρόνῳ τῷ ζῶντι καὶ παρόντι S.*Tr*.1169; ζῶσα φλόξ *living* fire, E.*Ba*.8; ὕδωρ ζῶν *spring* water, Lxx *Nu*.5.17 (and metaph., *Ev.Jo*.4.10); ζώσης φωνῆς Cic.*Att*.2.12.2.

ζωαγρία, ἡ, = ζωγρεῖον, Ael.*NA*13.10.

ζωάγρια, ων, τά, (ζωός, ἀγρέω, orig. *ransom paid for a prisoner taken alive*) *reward for life saved*, ζωάγρι' ὀφέλλεις Od.8.462; δῶρα λάμψονται ζωάγρια Κροίσου Hdt.3.36; Θέτι.. ζωάγρια τίνειν Il.18.407, cf. Call.*Fr*.162, *AP*6.220.15 (Diosc.); rare in Prose, Demetr.Lac. *Herc*.1014.49; also, *offerings* to Aesculapius and other gods *for recovery from illness*, *IG*14.967*a*5: c. gen., νούσων ibid.; ζ. ἀποθύειν Ael.*NA*11.31: sg. in Orac.ap.Plu.*Arat*.53:—a form **ζώγρια**, τά, Suid.:—Adj. **ζωάγριος**, ον, ζ. μοι χάριτας ὀφλήσεις you will owe me thanks *for a life saved*, Babr.50.15.

ζωαλκής, ές, *life-preserving*, χείρ, of Παιάν, *IG*14.1015.

ζῳάριον, τό, Dim. of ζῷον, *Sammelb*.5224.57, Sch.A.R.1.1265, 3.276.

ζωάρκεια, ἡ, *means of subsistence*, Sch.E.*Hec*.362: **ζωαρκία**, Anon. *Prog*. in Rh.1.599 W.: **ζωαρκέω**, *support life*, Gramm. in Reitzenstein *Ind.Lect.Rost*.1892/3 p.10.

ζωαρκής, ές, *life-supporting*, αὐγή *Milet*.6.18 (ii A. D.), cf. Procl.*H*. 1.2, Nonn.*D*.25.178; χρεία *PLond*.5.1729.17, al. (vi A. D.); τὰ ζ. *the necessaries of life*, Phot.

ζῴαρχος, ον, *commander of one elephant*, Ascl.*Tact*.9.1, Ael.*Tact*. 23.1.

ζωγάνης, ὁ, *slave-king* at festival in Babylon, Beros.3.

ζώγη, a kind of *plant*, Hsch.

ζωγλύφος [ῠ], = ζῳογλ-, Mitteis *Chr*.129.15 (ii B. C.); recommended by Philem.Lex. (cf. *Philol*.57.353 sqq.) in Reitzenstein *Gesch.d.Gr. Etym*.p.394.

ζωγονέω, = ζῳογονέω, of a *living* tree, *POxy*.1188.4 (i A. D.):—Pass., S.E.*M*.1.264 (s. v. l.).

ζωγορίτης· ὁ ὀπὸς τοῦ ὀποβαλσάμου, Hsch.

ζωγρᾰφ-εῖον, τό, *painter's studio*, Plu.2.471f. **-έω**, *paint from life, paint*, τινα Pl.*R*.598b, etc.:—Pass., Id.*Cra*.434b: metaph., ἡδοναὶ.. ἐζωγραφημέναι Id.*Phlb*.40b; ὀνείρους ζ. Porph.*Chr*.23. **II.** *adorn with paint*, τὰς ληκύθους Ar.*Ec*.996; τὰς ὀφρῦς ἀσβόλῳ Alex. 98.16, cf. Nicostr.ap.Stob.4.23.62. **III.** generally, *adorn*, κῆπον σὺν τοῖς φυτοῖς *Arch.Pap*.2.449. **-ημα**, ατος, τό, *a picture*, Pl.*Phlb*. 39d, *Cra*.430b sq. **-ητός**, ή, όν, *painted, parti-coloured*, Hsch. s. v. ποικίλον. **-ία**, ἡ, *art of painting*, Democr.28^a, Pl.*Phdr*.275d, X.*Mem*.1.4.3: metaph., φυσικὴ ζ. Secund.*Sent*.14. **II.** *painting*, τῶν παρειῶν v.l. in Philostr.*Ep*.22 (cod. Barocc.50); τοῦ στύλου *IGRom*.1.1272 (Egypt, ii A. D.). **2.** metaph., ἐπὶ σκιᾷ (sc. οὐσίᾳ) ζωγραφία καὶ τὸ φαίνεσθαι Plot.6.3.8. **-ίδες**, *picturae*, *Gloss*. **-ικός**, ή, όν, *skilled in painting*, Pl.*Tht*.145a, X.*Smp*.4. 21: ἡ -κή (sc. τέχνη) *the art of painting*, D.S.14.46; *connected with painting, used by painters*, γένη *BGU*10.11 (ii A. D.); ἀσβολή Dsc.5. 162. Adv. -κῶς S.E.*M*.11.255. **-ος**, ὁ, (ζωός or ζωή, γράφω) *one who paints from life* or *from nature*, Hdt.2.46, Pl.*Grg*.448c, 453c, *Lg*.656e, etc.: metaph., πολιτειῶν ζ. Id.*R*.501c: generally, *painter*, Luc.*Herod*.4, *Epigr*.41. (ζωγρ- without iota, *PSI*4.346, 407 (iii B. C.), *SIG*682.3 (ii B. C.), Pap. in *Abh.Berl.Akad*.1904(2).6 (ii B. C.), *EM* 412.53: so ζωγραφία *SIG*960.13 (ii B. C.), Phld.*Rh*.2.166 S.)

ζωγρ-εία, v. ζωγρία. **-εῖον** (sts. written **ζώγριον** as in Porph. *Gaur*.14.4), τό, *place for keeping animals, a menagerie*, Str.12.3.30 (pl.), Epict.*Gnom*.62 (pl.), Porph.*Sent*.28; *cage*, Aq.*Je*.5.27; *trap*, Onos.11.3; *fish-pond*, Plu.2.89a, Ael.*NA*11.34, Xenocr.34. **II.** pl., ζωγρεῖα, τά, = ζωάγρια, Hld.8.17. **-εύς**, έως, ὁ, dub. l. (for ζῷον?) in Gal.4.497 (*BpW*36.799). **-εύω**, = ζωγρέω, Polyaen.4. 3.27 (Pass.). **-έω**, (ζωός, ἀγρέω) *take, save alive, take captive* instead of killing, ζώγρει, Ἀτρέος υἱέ, σὺ δ' ἄξια δέξαι ἄποινα Il.6.46, cf. 10.378, Hdt.1.86, etc.; εἷλε.. καὶ ἐζώγρησε Id.3.52; τοὺς μὲν ἀπέκτειναν, τινὰς δὲ καὶ ἐζώγρησαν Th.2.92; πλὴν ὅσον ἐκ τριῶν νεῶν οὓς ἐζώγρησαν Id.7.23; πλὴν μηδαμῇ μηδαμῶς ζωγροῦντας provided that they do not *spare* him *alive*, Pl.*Lg*.868c; opp. διαφθείρειν, ἀποκτεῖναι, Plb.3.84.10, Lxx *Nu*.31.18: metaph., ἀνθρώπους ἔσῃ ζωγρῶν *Ev.Luc*. 5.10; of ships, ἃς ἐζώγρησεν αὐτάνδρους Charito 7.6:—Pass., Hdt.1. 66, 5.77. **II.** *restore to life and strength, revive*, περὶ δὲ πνοιὴ Βορέαο ζώγρει ἐπιπνείουσα Il.5.698 (quoted by Aret.*CA*2.3); *preserve alive*, ζώγρει, δέσποτ' ἄναξ, τὸν σὸν ναετῆρα *Epigr.Gr*.841.7 (Thrace, ii A. D.). **-ία**, Ion. **-ίη**, ἡ, *taking alive*, ζωγρίῃ λαβεῖν or αἱρέειν, = ζωγρεῖν, Hdt.6.28, 37; συλλαβεῖν *SIG*700.30 (Macedonia, ii B. C.) ζωγρίᾳ ἐγκρατὴς or κύριος γενέσθαι τινός, Plb.1.9.8, 1.79.4; ζωγρίᾳ ἀνάγεσθαι or εἰσανάγεσθαι, Str.11.11.6, Plb.1.82.2; ζ. ἀποβαλεῖν τινα to lose him *by his being captured*, ib.15.2, Str.8.4.2; ζ. ἁλῶναι Plb.5. 86.5. **-ια**, τά, v. ζωάγρια. **-ιον**, τό, v. ζωγρεῖον. **-ίας**, ου, ὁ, *one taken alive*, ζωγρίαν συλλαμβάνειν, ἑλεῖν τινα, Ctes.*Fr*.29.3, 9, Zos.1. 51; οὐ κατελίπομεν ζωγρίαν Lxx *De*.2.34; ζωγρίας ἐλήφθη D.S.25.10; ζωγρίας ἔλαβε δισχιλίους ibid.; ζωγρίαι ἑάλωσαν Memn.56.3.

ζῶγρος, ὁ, late form for ζωγρεῖον, *cage*, Phlp. *in de An*.106.12, Sch. Nic.*Th*.825. **II. ζῶγρον**· ἐγρήγορον, Hsch.

ζωγύς, v. ζωτύς.

ζῳδαρίδιον, τό, Dim. of ζῷον, *tiny figure*, Hero *Spir*.2.34 (p.312. 10 S.), *Wiener Denkschr*.47(4).59.

ζῳδάριον, τό, = foreg., Dim. of ζῷον, *animalcule*, as *a grub*, Alex. 140, Arist.*HA*557^{b}1, etc. **II.** = ζῴδιον I, *IG*2^2.1491.4, *Inscr.Délos* 298*A*31 (iii B. C.), *SIG*^{2}588.31 (Delos, ii B. C.), Hero *Spir*.2.34, *PMag. Leid.V*.10.1.

ζῳδι-ᾰκός, ή, όν, (ζῴδιον) *of* or *for* ζῴδια, ζῳδιακός (with or without κύκλος), ὁ, *the Zodiac*, Eudem.ap.Theon.Sm.p.198 H., Phld.*Mus*.p.100 K., Cleom.1.4, al., D.S.2.31, etc.; also ἡ ζῳδιακή (sc. ὁδός) Man.4. 168. Adv. -κῶς Ptol.*Tetr*.198, Vett.Val.22.12, *PMich*. in *Class.Phil*. 22.13. **-άρχης**, ου, ὁ, = ζῳδιοκράτωρ, Dam.*Pr*.132.

ζῳδιο-γλύφος [ῠ], ον, (γλύφω) = ζῳογλύφος, Plu.2.712e. **-κράτωρ** [ᾰ], ορος, ὁ, *divinity presiding over the zodiac*, Dam.*Pr*.131, 351.

ζῴδι-ον, τό, Dim. of ζῷον II, *small figure, painted* or *carved*, Hdt. 1.70, *IG*1^2.374.288, 11(2).161*B*74 (Delos, iii B. C.), Plu.2.673f; *statuette*, *OGI*717.6 (Egypt, iii A. D.); of large figures, ζ. πηχῶν ἑκκαίδεκα D.S.1.47. **II.** Astron., *sign of the Zodiac*, διὰ μέσων τῶν ζ. Arist.*Metaph*.1073^{b}20; ὁ κύκλος ὁ τῶν ζ. Id.*Mete*.343^{a}24, cf. Plb.9.15.

7, Zeno *Stoic.*1.34, Hipparch.2.1.3, al., Gem.1.3, Autol.1.10, etc.:—also **ζωΐδιον**, τό, Arat.544, Man.1.309, al. **-οποιός**, *signarius*, *Gloss.* **-οφόρος**, *signifer*, ib. **-ωτός**, ή, όν, (ζῴδιον) = ζῳωτός, Poll.7.55, Hsch.

ζώζω, late spelling of σῴζω, *UPZ*81 ii 19, *Sammelb.*1060, etc.

ζῴειος, α, ον, *animal*, opp. ἀνθρώπειος, ἵππειος, Dam.*Pr.*85.

ζωή (**ζωιή** (prob. an error) *SIG*577.34 (Milet., iii/ii B.C.)), Dor. **ζωά**: Ion. and poet. **ζόη**, Hdt.1.32, Herod.10.4, S.*Fr.*556, etc. (v. infr.), cf. *IG*9(1).86 (Hyampolis), Dor. **ζόα**: Aeol. **ζοΐα** Theoc. 29.5: ἡ:—*living*, i.e. one's *substance, property*, ἦ γάρ οἱ ζ. γ' ἦν ἄσπετος Od.14.96; τοὶ δὲ ζωὴν ἐδάσαντο ib.208; κατὰ ζωὴν φαγέειν 16.429; τὴν ζόην ποιέεσθαι or καταστήσασθαι ἀπὸ or ἐκ.. to get one's *living* by.., Hdt.8.105, cf. 2.36, Arist.*HA*608^{b}21; ἐξ ἁλός Theoc.*Beren.* 2. 2. after Hom., *life, existence*, opp. death, Tyrt.15.5, Pi.*N.*8.36, etc.; θανάτου πέρι καὶ ζωᾶς ib.9.29; οὐδὲν γὰρ ἄλγος οἷον ἡ πολλὴ ζόη S.*Fr.*556; ζόας (ζωᾶς codd.) βιοτά E.*HF*664 (lyr.); τοῦ βίου ζωή Pl. *Ti.*44c; ὁ τῆς ζ. χρόνος *SIG*1210 (Calymna), etc.: as a term of affection, ζωή *my life!* Juv.6.195: pl., ζόαι A.*Fr.*99.13; ζωαί Lxx*Ps.*62(63). 3(4); μετὰ τὴν μίαν ζ. πολλαί ζ. Dam.*Pr.*100; αἱ τῆς ψυχῆς ζ. καὶ δυνάμεις Iamb.*Comm.Math.*3. 3. *way of life*, ζόην ἔζωον τὴν αὐτήν Hdt. 4.112, cf. 114. II. ζωή, = γραῦς II, *the scum on milk*, Eust.906.52; ζόη· τὸ ἐπάνω τοῦ μέλιτος, Hsch. [The form ζόη (paroxyt.) is required by the metre in trimeters in S.*Fr.*556, E.*Hec.*1108, and in lyrics S. *Fr.*592, E.*Med.*976, al., ζωή never: ζόη in other Poets, Call.*Fr.*114, Theoc.*Ep.*18.9, Herod.10.4.] (For the root, cf. ζῶ: fancifully connected with ζέω and ζητέω, Dam.*Pr.*81: in signf. II ζόη prob. fr. ζέω.)

ζωηδόν, Adv., (ζῷον) *in the manner of beasts*, Plb.6.5.9.

ζωηρός, ά, όν, (ζωή) *living* and *giving life*, Suid.

ζωητός, ή, όν, *capable of being vitalized*, Dam.*Pr.*83 bis.

ζωηφόρος, ον, *life-bringing*, Them.*Or.*19.228d, Sch.Il.8.70; ζ. γραμμὴ [χειρός] line *of life*, in palmistry, *Cat.Cod.Astr.*7.238.

ζωθάλμιος, ον, (ζωή, θάλλω) *giving the bloom and freshness of life*, Pi.*O.*7.11.

ζωθαλπής, ές, (θάλπω) *warming* or *cheering life*, Nonn.*D.*1.454:—fem. **ζώθαλπις**, ιδος, ib.16.397 (v.l. -πέες).

ζωθήκη, ἡ, *small room wherein to rest by day*, opp. *dormitorium* (the bedroom), Plin.*Ep.*2.17.21; *zothecula*, ib.5.6.38. II. *niche* in a wall, prob. in Apollod.*Poliorc.*145.1 (pl.); used as a *chapel*, *Supp.Epigr.*2.849 (Alexandria); Lat. *zotheca*, Dessau *ILS*5449, al.

ζωΐδιον, τό, v. ζῴδιον ad fin.

ζωϊκός, ή, όν, (ζῷον) *of* or *proper to animals*, ἡ ζ. φύσις Arist.*PA* 645^{a}6, cf. 681^{b}4; ἡ ζ. ἱστορία a history *of animals*, ib.668^{b}30: περὶ ζωϊκῶν, title of lost work by Aristotle, Ath.7.328f. 2. *animal*, ψυχή, σῶμα, Porph.*Gaur.*1.2, 13.4; ζ. ἄνθρωπος Dam.*Pr.*200.

ζώϊον, τό, poet. for ζῷον, Semon.13.

ζωϊτός or **-τόν**, or **ζωτ-**, dub. sens. in *BCH*8.307 (Delos, iv B.C.).

ζωκτήρ, ῆρος, ὁ, dub. l. in *PLond.*2.236.8 (iii A.D., fort. ζωστήρ).

ζῶμα, ατος, τό, (ζώννυμι) *loin-cloth, drawers*, worn next the body in a boxing contest, ζ. δέ οἱ πρῶτον παρακάββαλεν Il.23.683; in war, 4.216; ἑπόμην σάκος οἷον ἔχων καὶ ζ. φαεινόν Od.14.482; ζώματα καὶ κυπάσσιδες Alc.15.6. 2. = ἔνδυμα, πεζοφόροις ζ. A.*Fr.*246. 3. *band* used in surgery, Hp.*Art.*14. II. = ζώνη, *woman's girdle*, ἔλυσε ζ. παρθένῳ Alc.*Supp.*8.10, cf. S.*El.*452, *IG*2^2.1514.15, Ar.*Fr.* 320.7, Men.432, *AP*6.272 (Pers.).—A non-Att. form **ζῶσμα** (v. Thom.Mag.p.165 R.) in Str.7.2.3, Sor.*Fasc.*45, al., Ach.Tat.1.1, 3. 21, Hld.3.1.

ζωμάλμη· ζωμὸς ἅλμης Θασίας, Sch.Suid. s.v. Θασίαν.

ζωμ-άριον, τό, Dim. of ζωμός, Damocr.ap.Gal.14.94. **-άρυστρον** [ᾰ], τό, = ζωμήρυσις, Sch.Ar.*Ach.*244 (v.l. -ος, ἡ); spelt **-ιστρον**, *POxy.*1289.3 (v A.D.). **-ευμα**, ατος, τό, *soup*, ζωμεύματα put by way of joke for ὑποζώματα νεώς (v. ὑπόζωμα fin.), Ar.*Eq.*279. **-εύω**, (ζωμός) *boil into soup*, κρεάδια ἐζωμευμένα Id.*Fr.*591, cf. Phryn.*PS* p.68 B.:—Pass., Hp.*Int.*35, Dsc.*Eup.*2.122: **-ευτός**, ή, όν, Orib.*Fr.* 119 (-ιστούς in Paul.Aeg.5.13 codd.). **-ήρυσις**, εως, ἡ, (ἀρύω A) *soup-ladle*, Antiph.249, Philem.Jun.1.6, Anaxipp.6.1, *IG*2^2.1416 (iv B.C.), Ath.3.126d, *AP*6.101 (Phil.). **-ίδιον**, τό, Dim. of ζωμός, *a little sauce*, Ar.*Nu.*389.

ζωμίλη, ἡ, = ἄνηθον, Hsch., Phot.

ζωμ-ίον, τό, Dim. of ζωμός, *PTeb.*112.75 (ii B.C.). **-ιστός**, v. ζωμευτός.

ζωμοποι-έω, *make into soup* or *sauce*, Xenocr.54 (Pass.). **-ός**, όν, *making sauce*, Plu.2.218c. II. *serving to flavour soup*, of mushrooms, Dsc.4.82.

ζωμός, Dor. **δωμός** (q.v.), ὁ, *soup* or *sauce* to eat with meat, fish, etc., Ar.*Eq.*1174, *Pax*716, al.; οἱ ζ. οἱ τῶν πιόνων *soups* made from animals with soft fat (πιμελή), Arist.*HA*520^{a}8, cf. *PA*651^{a}29; ζ. μέλας black *broth* of the Spartans, Matro *Conv.*94, cf. Plu.*Lyc.*12: metaph., *bloodshed*, Thphr.*Char.*8.7. 2. Com. name for *fat, greasy fellow*, λιπαρὸς περιπατεῖ Δημοκλῆς, ζ. κατωνόμασται Anaxandr.34.5, cf. Aristopho 4.3. 3. in Alchemy, *wash*, Ps.-Democr.Alch.p.48 B., Zos.Alch.p.169 B.

ζωμοτάριχος [ᾰ], ὁ, *stewed salt-fish*, as a nickname, Alex.42.

ζων-αῖοι, οἱ, an order of divine beings (cf. ζώνη IV), Dam.*Pr.*130; ζ. κόσμος the world over which they preside, ib.206. Adv. -ως ib. 131. **-άριον**, τό, Dim. of sq., Anon.*in Rh.*114.19, Hdn.*Epim.* 41. **-η**, ἡ, (ζώννυμι) *belt, girdle*: I. prop. *the lower girdle worn by women* just *above the hips*, περὶ δὲ ζώνην βάλετ' ἰξυῖ Od.5.231, 10. 544, cf. Il.14.181, Hdt.1.51, etc.—Phrases: 1. λῦσε δὲ παρθενίην ζ. unloosed her maiden *girdle*, of the bridegroom, Od.11.245, cf. *Lyr. Alex.Adesp.*11.18, Plu.*Lyc.*15:—Med., of the bride, μούνῳ ἐνὶ ζώναν ἀνέρι λυσαμένα *AP*7.324 (hence ζώνη, abs., of *marriage*, E.*IT*204 (lyr.); of *sexual intercourse*, Philostr.*VA*7.6): but also, b. ζ. λῦσαι to loose *the girdle* for childbirth, Hyp.*Fr.*67; later λύσασθαι or ἀπολύσασθαι, Call.*Del.*209, Opp.*C.*3.56; so ζώναν καταθέσθαι Pi.*O.*6. 39. c. of men on a march, ζ. λύσασθαι to slacken one's *belt*, i.e. rest oneself, Hdt.8.120; ζ. ἀναλύεσθαι Call.*Del.*237. 2. of pregnant women, τέκνων ἤνεγχ' ὑπὸ ζώνην βάρος A.*Ch.*1000; πῶς γάρ σ' ἔθρεψεν ἐντὸς.. ζώνης; Id.*Eu.*608; τοῦτον.. ἔφερον ζώνης ὕπο E.*Hec.* 762; also ὑπὸ ζώνη θέσθαι to *conceive*, *h.Ven.*255. 3. prov., εἰς ζώνην δεδόσθαι to be given *for girdle-money* (as we should say, *pin-money*), of Oriental queens who had cities given them for their small expenses, X.*An.*1.4.9; ἣν [χώραν] καλεῖν.. ζ. τῆς βασιλέως γυναικός Pl.*Alc.*1.123b. II. man's *belt* (more freq. ζωστήρ), ἡ ζ. τοῦ Ὠρίωνος the three stars that form the *belt* of Orion, Arist.*Mete.* 343^{b}24; the *belt* of barbarians, in which they wore the dagger, X.*An.*1.6.10, 4.7.16, Theopomp.Hist.39a, Luc.*Anach.*33, Pl.*Hp.Mi.* 368c. b. belt used as a *purse*, *PRyl.*127.32 (i A.D.), *Ev.Matt.*10. 9, Plu.2.665b; ζ. χρυσίου Luc.*Fug.*31. 2. *part round which the girdle passed, waist*, Ἄρεϊ ζώνην ἴκελος Il.2.479 (misunderstood by Paus.9.17.3), cf. Il.11.234, Orph.*Fr.*168.28, Hp.ap.Erot. (also expld. as = ὀσφύς). 3. = Lat. *cingulum*, *belt* worn by Roman civil and military officers, [Demod.]5; = ἀξίωμα, Suid.; οἱ ὑπὸ ζώνην *soldiers*, Anon.ap.eund. s.v. αὐθεντήσαντα, cf. *Cod.Just.*1.5.12.6, 11, Just.*Edict.* 13.26, *PLond.*5.1680.21 (vi A.D.). III. *anything that goes round like a belt*, Plu.2.935a, Luc.*Musc.Enc.*3; of the *girdle* of ocean, Porph. *Chr.*69. 2. *one of the zones of the terrestrial sphere*, *Stoic.*2.195, Posidon.ap.Str.2.2.2, *Placit.*2.12.1 (pl.), etc.; ζ. διακεκαυμένη, εὔκρατος, Str.1.2.24, 1.4.6. b. *one of the planetary spheres*, οἱ μὲν [τῶν πλανητῶν] ὑψηλὴν ζ. φέρονται οἱ δὲ ταπεινήν Diog.Oen.8, cf. Vett.Val.26.18, *Corp.Herm.*1.25. c. Astrol., = ζῴδιον, Porph. *in Ptol.*186. 3. in Archit., = διάζωμα, *frieze*, Paus.5.10.5. 4. Lat. *zona*, in Medic., *shingles*, Scrib.Larg.63, 247; cf. ζωστήρ III. 3. 5. *stripes* on fish, Ael.*NA*3.28, al. IV. pl., an order of divine beings presiding over, or *engirdled with* cosmic *zones*, opp. ἄζωνοι, Dam.*Pr.*96, Procl.*in Prm.*p.494 S. **-ιαῖος**, α, ον, *as thick as a girdle*, πάχος Ath.Mech.38.3. **-ιον**, τό, Dim. of ζώνη, Ar. *Lys.*72, Arist.*Mir.*832^{b}23, *AP*5.157 (Asclep.), Plu.2.154b.

ζωνιοπλόκος, ον, *plaiting* or *embroidering girdles*, Thom.Mag. p.168 R.

ζωνῖτις, ιδος, ἡ, *in belts* or *seams*, καδμεία Dsc.5.74; cf. ζώννυμι III. 2.

ζώννῡμι (ὑπο-ζωνύναι *IG*1^2.73.9), (παρα-) Pl.*R.*553c; **ζωννύω** Hp. *Mul.*1.68: impf. ἐζώννυον *Ev.Jo.*21.18: fut. ζώσω Lxx*Ex.*29.9, *Ev. Jo.* l.c.: aor. 1 ἔζωσα Od.18.76, Hp.*Art.*14: pf. ἔζωκα Paus.8.40.2, (δι-) D.H.2.5:—Med. (v. infr. II):—Pass., aor. 1 ἐζώσθην (δι-) Thphr.*Sign.*22: pf. ἔζωμαι (δι-) Th.1.6 ap.Phot., Suid. s.v. σέσωται, 3 sg. ἔζωται (δι-) *IG*2^2.1491.36, (ὑπ-) ib.1621.68, ἔζωσται Hp.*Art.* l.c.; also in med. sense (v. infr.): rare in Att., even in compds.:—*gird*, esp. *gird round the loins* for a pugilistic conflict (v. infr.), ἄγον ζώσαντες ἀνάγκῃ Od.18.76 (here only Act. in Hom.); ζῶσέ [μιν]... Ἀθήνη Hes.*Op.*72; ζ. τινά *hug* him in wrestling, Paus.8.40.2; ζ. γαῖαν, of Ocean, *AP*9.778 (Phil.); ζ. νῆα ὅπλῳ, = ὑποζώννυμι II, A.R.1.368: c. dupl. acc., ζ. τινὰ ζώνην Lxx*Le.*8.7, cf. 1*Ki.*17.39. II. Med., **ζώννῠμαι**, *gird oneself*, esp. of athletes, γυμνός, ζωννυμένων τῶν πρὶν ἐν σταδίῳ *IG*7.52.6 (Megara, iv B.C.); τὼ δὲ ζωσαμένω βήτην ἐς μέσσον ἀγῶνα Il.23.685, cf. 710; ζώννυνταί τε νέοι καὶ ἐπεντύνονται ἄεθλα Od.24.89; Ὀδυσσεὺς ζώσατο μὲν ῥάκεσιν περὶ μήδεα 18.67, cf. Parth. 10.2. 2. generally, *gird up one's loins* for battle, ζώννυσθαι ἄνωγεν Ἀργείους Il.11.15; ζώννυσθαι [ζωστῆρι] 10.78: c. acc., ὅθι ζωννύσκετο μίτρην 5.857 (vulg.); ζώσατο δὲ ζώνην 14.181 (vulg.); χαλκὸν ζώννυσθαι 23.130; ἐς γόνυ μέχρι χιτῶνα ζώννυσθαι Call.*Dian.*12; χιτῶνα εἰς μηρὸν ἔζωστο Plu.*Ant.*4; for labour, Hes.*Op.*345; ἐπὶ βουσίν A.R.1.426, etc.; ζώννυσθαι τὰς κοιλίας ζώναις Theopomp.Hist. 39a. III. Pass., *to be fixed by means of girths*, Lxx 1*Ma.*6.37. 2. *to be formed in belts* or *seams*, καδμεία ἐζωσμένη (ἐζωσμ- codd.) prob. in Ps.-Democr.Alch.p.45 B. (cf. ζωνῖτις). (ζω(σ)- from I.-E. *yōs-*, cf. Lith. *júosti* 'to gird', *júostas*, Avest. *yāsta-*, = ζωστός 'girt'.)

ζωνο-γάστορες (-γάστριαι cod.)· οἱ τὰς γαστέρας ζωννύμενοι, Hsch.: ζωνογάστωρ· ὁ τὴν γαστέρα ζωννύμενος, Gramm. in Reitzenstein *Ind. Lect.Rost.*1892/3 p.11, cf. Hsch. s.v. μεσογάστορα. **-δρακοντις** [ᾰ], *girdled with snakes*, epith. of the moon, *PMag.Par.*1.2864. **-ειδής**, ές, *like a belt* or *girdle*, Apollon.*Lex.* s.v. ἴρεσσιν ἐοικότες, Eust. 1068.24. Adv. -δῶς *in belts*, Olymp.*in Mete.*191.21.

ζωνός, f.l. for εὔζωνος, Arist.*Phgn.*810^{b}4.

ζωνοφόρος, ον, *wearing a belt*, *PRain.* in *Wiener Denkschr.*42(2).4.

ζώντειον or **ζωντεῖον**, v. ζητρεῖον.

ζώντως, *vivide*, *Gloss.*

ζῳο-γενής, ές, *of animate kind, mortal*, opp. ἀειγενής, Pl.*Plt.*309c. **-γλύφος** [ῠ], ὁ, *sculptor*, *AP*12.56 (Mel.), 57 (Id.); cf. ζωγλύφος.

ζῳογον-έω, *propagate* or *engender living creatures*, of inanimate substances, ἡ φύσις ζ. Thphr.*CP*3.22.3, cf. *HP*8.11.2 (so in Med., Id.*CP*3.24.3), Arist.*Mir.*835^{b}26; of animals, *breed*, like ζῳοτοκέω, D.S.1.88, Plu.2.494c:—Pass., Arist.*Mir.*832^{a}14: generally, *engender* [στοιχεῖον] ἕκαστον ἀπὸ ἑτέρου -εῖται Vett.Val.162.17. II. *to be viviparous*, Thphr.*HP*7.14.3; *produce alive*, Luc.*Am.*19; ζ. παρθένον, of Zeus, *producing* Pallas *alive* from his head, Id.*DDeor.*8, cf. D.S.1.23. 2. *make alive, quicken*, τι Thphr.*CP*4.15.2:—Pass., Arist.*Fr.*311, Isid.ap.Ath.2.93f: metaph., σωφροσύνη ζ. τὸ φρονοῦν Ph.2.378, cf. 435. 3. = ζωγρέω, *preserve alive*, Lxx*Ex.*1.17, 1*Ki.*

27.9; κύριος θανατοῖ καὶ ζ. ib.2.6, cf. Ev.Luc.17.33:—Pass., Act.Ap. 7.19. **-ησις**, εως, ἡ, *creation of life*, Theol.Ar.46. **-ητικός**, ή, όν, *capable of generation*, ib.49; σύλληψις Aët.1.142. **-ία**, ἡ, *production of animals*, Pl.Epin.980c, Ph.1.14; *of living things*, Dam.Pr.284; *breeding of worms*, Thphr.CP5.9.3; *generation*, Sor. 1.2. **-ικός**, ή, όν, = ζωογονητικός, Ph.2.148, Procl.Inst.155; νοῦς Dam.Pr.272. Adv. -κῶς Procl.in Alc.p.52 C. **-ος**, ον, *producing animals, generative*, Aret.SD2.5, Orph.H.38.3; name of Apollo, AP 9.525.7; *producing life*, Procl.Inst.155; θεός Jul.Or.5.175c, Dam.Pr. 267; ῥοίζημα ib.282; ῥαθάμιγγες Procl.H.1.10.

ζωο-γράφος [ᾰ], ον, poet. for ζωγρ-, Theoc.15.81 (v.l. ζῳο-). **-δοτήρ**, ῆρος, ὁ, *giver of life*, Orph.Fr.65:—fem. **-δότειρα**, Hsch. **-δότης**, ου, ὁ, = foreg., Vett.Val.124.31, Them.Or.15. 198b. **-δότιον**, τό, = μελίλωτον, Ps.-Dsc.3.40. **-ειδής**, ές, (ζῳο-) *like an animal*, Gp.10.9.4. **-θετέω**, (τίθημι) *make alive*, -οῦσα φύσις Archel.ap.Antig.Mir.19. **-θηρία**, ἡ, (ζῳο-) *chasing living creatures*, Pl.Sph.223b. **-θηρικός**, ή, όν, (ζῳο-) *of* or *for* ζῳοθηρία, ib.221b: ἡ -κή (sc. τέχνη) = ζῳοθηρία, ib.220a, 222a. **-θῠτέω**, *sacrifice live victims*, Thphr.(?) ap.Porph.Abst.2.26. **-κέφᾰλος**, ον, (ζῳο-) *animal-headed*, Anon. post Max.p.111 L. **-μορφος**, ον, (ζῳο-) *in the shape of an animal*, Plu.Num.8.

ζῷον, τό, *living being, animal*, Hdt.5.10 (of bees), Ar.V.551, Pl. 443, etc.; πᾶν ὅ τι περ ἂν μετάσχῃ τοῦ ζῆν ζῷον ἂν λέγοιτο Pl.Ti.77b; ζῷα, opp. φυτά, Id.Phd.70d, 110e, etc.; ζ. θαλάττιον, χερσαῖον, Phld. Rh.1.98 S.; contemptuously, ὅπως ἡ χώρα τοῦ τοιούτου ζῴου καθαρὰ γίγνηται *may be free from this kind of animal* (i.e. beggars), Pl.Lg. 936c; ζ. πονηρόν, of women, Secund.Sent.8. II. in art, *figure, image*, not necessarily of animals (cf. ζῴδιον), ζῷον δέ οἱ ἐνῆν, ἀνὴρ ἱππεύς Hdt.3.88: mostly in pl., ζῷα ἐς τὴν ἐσθῆτα ἐγγράφειν Id.1.203, cf. 2.4,124,148, Pl.R.515a, etc.; ζῷα γράψασθαι τὴν ζεῦξιν τοῦ Βοσπόρου *to have pictures* of the bridging of the Bosporus painted, Hdt.4. 88; cf. ζωγραφέω: ζῷα ποιεῖν Plu.Per.13. III. *sign* of the Zodiac, Man.2.166.—The word is post-Hom., no generic word used for *animal* being found till after the middle of the fifth cent. B.C. (ζώϊον Semon.13, whence Att. ζῷον by contraction: ι is found in IG1².372. 42, al., 11(2).161 B76 (Delos, iii B.C.), Phld.Rh.2.166 S., and in codd. opt. in the Noun; the Adj. ζωός (q.v.) had no ι: for the compds. (exc. ζωγλύφος, ζωγράφος) decisive evidence is lacking: ζῳάγρια with ι was read by Aristarch. in Il.18.407.)

ζωόνῠχον, τό, a name of the plant λεοντοπόδιον, Ps.-Dsc.4.133.

ζωοπλαστ-έω, *mould to the life, make into statues*, analogous to ζωγραφέω, Lyc.844 (ζῳο- codd.). II. *work into life-shape*, ζ. θνητὰ γένη Ph.1.13. **-ης**, ου, ὁ, *the Creator*, ib.184. II. *a moulder of creatures, sculptor*, etc., Id.2.211. **-ία**, ἡ, *artistic representation*, Eust.1157.25.

ζωοποι-έω, = ζωογονέω I, Arist.HA555^{b}9; = ζωογονέω II. 2, Id.GA 730^{a}2, Thphr.CP3.22.4: metaph., D.S.2.52. II. *make alive*, θανατῶσα καὶ ζ. Lxx 4Ki.5.7, cf. Ev.Jo.5.21; *bring to life*, νεκρά Luc. VH1.22, cf. Sch.E.Alc.122; *endow with life*, ἑαυτό Dam.Pr.78, al., cf. Procl.Inst.25:—Pass., ib.209. 2. *preserve alive*, Lxx Jd.21. 14. **-ησις**, εως, ἡ, *making alive*, ib.2Es.9.8. **-ητικός**, ή, όν, *generative*, Theol.Ar.31; τὸ ζ. Diocl.Fr.172; *vitalizing*, θερμότης Steph.in Hp.1.132 D. **-ία**, ἡ, = ζωογόνησις, Thphr.CP5.18.2, Dam. Pr.100. **-ός**, όν, *creative of life*, Thphr.CP2.9.6, Procl.Inst.145, Porph.ap.Eus.PE3.11, Dam.Pr.80, al.: c. gen., ζ. τῆς ὅλης γενέσεως ib.283; ζ. τὸ ὕδωρ καὶ γόνιμον Sch.E.Ph.347.

ζωο-πώλης, ου, ὁ, *selling animals*, esp. for sacrifice, Hsch. **-πωλις** (sc. ἀγορά), ἡ, *beast-market*, Id. (nisi leg. -πώλιον).

ζωός (without ι, cf. Schwyzer436.2 (Crimisa, v/iv B.C.), Cret. **δωός** Leg.Gort.3.41, Cypr. pr. n. ΖωϜόθεμις Schwyzer684 (v B.C.)), ή, όν, (ζῶ) *alive, living*, Pi.P.4.209, Hdt.2.70, etc.; οὐ.. ζωοῦ οὐδὲ θανόντος Od.17.115; ζωὸν ἑλεῖν τινα *to take prisoner*, Il.6.38; ζωὸν λαβεῖν X. HG1.2.5; cf. ζωγρέω: metaph., ζωὸν δὲ φθιμένων.. κλέος A.Eleg.3. —Also **ζώς** Il.5.887, 16.445, Hdt.1.194, JRS15.145,148 (Cotiaeum) (ζῶς Ptol.Ascal., ζώς Hdn.Gr.2.53; on the other cases, ib.712); **ζοός** Archil.63, Epich.189, Berl.Sitzb.1927.161 (Cyrene), Theoc.2.5 (ζόος in Epich. l. c., Hdn.Gr.2.947).

ζωοστάσιον [ᾰ], τό, (ἵστημι) *stall* or *stable*, Eust.531.17 (pl.).

ζωοτάμον, f.l. in Orph.A.315 codd. (ζωὰ ταμών Lobeck).

ζωότης, ητος, ἡ, *animal nature*, Demetr.Lac.Herc.1055.15, Plu.2. 1001b, A.D.Pron.6.24, Gal.19.163, Porph.Gaur.16.5; *vitality*, Dam. Pr.58.

ζωοτοκ-έω, *to be viviparous*, opp. ᾠοτοκέω, Arist.Pol.1256^{b}13; τὰ -οῦντα *viviparous* animals, Id.GA732^{b}8: generally ζωοτοκεῖ ἀήρ Ph. 1.263:—Pass., *to be born alive*, Arist.PA693^{b}23. **-ία**, ἡ, Id.GA 754^{b}29. **-ος**, ον, opp. ᾠοτόκος, Id.HA489^{a}34, al., Ph.1.502; [βόες] *bringing forth live* calves, Theoc.25.125. 2. *life-giving*, Nonn.D. 26.191, al.

ζωοτροφ-εῖον, τό, *place for keeping animals*, Gloss. **-έω**, *breed* or *have parasitic animals*, Thphr.CP2.17.8: generally ἀὴρ ζ. μᾶλλον γῆς Ph.1.641. II. *keep animals*, Id.2.233. **-ία**, ἡ, *feeding of animals*, Pl.Plt.261e. **-ικός**, ή, όν, *connected with the feeding of animals*, ib.263e: ἡ -κή (sc. τέχνη), = ζῳοτροφία, ib.267b. **-ος**, ον, *nourishing animals*, Max.Tyr.39.4, 41.5.

ζωοτύπος [ῠ], ον, *modelling animals from life*, Nonn.D.5.527, Man. 4.343: generally, *modelling to the life*, of a sculptor, AP15.1.

ζωοφᾰγ-έω, *live on animal food*, Arist.HA590^{b}1. **-ία**, ἡ, *a living on animal food*, ib.628^{b}13, Porph.Abst.2.27, 4.21. **-ος**, ον, *carnivorous*, opp. καρποφάγος, Arist.Pol.1256^{a}25, cf. PA696^{b}29.

ζωόφθαλμον, τό, = ἀείζωον τὸ μέγα, Dsc.4.88. 2. = *leaf-rosette*, Plin.HN25.160.

ζωοφορ-έω, of animals, *bring forth alive*, Arist.HA638^{a}31; of plants, *bear fruit*, Gp.5.13.1. **-ος**, ον, *life-giving*, IG3.171; ἄνεμοι AP9.765 (Paul. Sil.). II. **ζῳοφόρος**, ον, *bearing animals*: and so, 1. *bearing the figures of animals, sculptured*, πίνακες D.S.18. 26; Lat. *zophorus*, as Subst., *frieze*, Vitr.3.5.10. 2. ὁ ζ. κύκλος, = ὁ ζῳδιακός, Arist.Mu.392^{a}11, Corp.Herm.13.12, etc.; without κύκλος, Ph.2.153, AP14.124; σφαῖρα ἡ ζ. (ζωηφ- cod.) Ph.2.294.

ζωοφῠτ-έω, *put forth live shoots, flourish*, PCair.Zen.72.4 (iii B.C.), Apollod.Hist.ap.Ath.15.682d, PMasp.104.6 (vi A.D.). II. *produce alive* or *endow with life*, Ph.2.372: with v.l. **ζωοφυεῖν**, ib.294. **-ος**, ον, = ζώφυτος II, μέρη Plu.2.701c. II. **ζωόφῠτον**, τό, *zoöphyte*, S.E.P.1.41 codd. 2. = ἀείζωον τὸ μέγα Ps.-Dsc.4.88.

ζῳόω, *fashion into an animal*, pf. inf. Pass. ἐζῳῶσθαι Alex.Aphr. in Top.137.26.

ζωόω, *impregnate*, ζωοῦσα θορή Aret.SD2.5:—Pass., Porph.Gaur. 1.1, 3.1. 2. *quicken, make alive*, Lxx Ps.79(80).18; *endow with life*, ἑαυτὸ οὐσιοῖ καὶ ζωοῖ Dam.Pr.80, Phlp.in GC200.6:—Pass., Hp. Alim.38, Gal.19.174,180, Phlp.in GC151.5, Id.in de An.64.7, al.; θηρίον ζωωθὲν τὸ σῶμα Plot.1.1.10, cf. 4.4.28; [γῆ] ἐζωωμένη Id.6. 7.12. II. Pass., of putrescent plants, *breed worms*, Thphr.CP5. 18.2 (nisi leg. ζῳο-).

ζώπισσα, ἡ, *pitch and wax from old ships*, or *pine-resin*, Dsc.1.72.

ζωπονέω, *represent alive*, AP9.742 (Phil.).

ζωπύρα, ἡ, a plant, = κλινοπόδιον, Hsch.; *zopyrontion*, Plin.HN 24.137.

ζωπύρειος, ἡ, medicine named after the physician Zopyrus, Orib. Fr.125, cf. Gal.14.205, Paul.Aeg.7.11.

ζωπῠρ-έω, (ζώπυρον) *kindle into flame, cause to blaze up*, ζ. τοὺς ἄνθρακας Men.71; τὸ πνεῦμα ζ. Thphr.Ign.27:—in Pass., *to be quickened by fire*, of the foetus, Hp.Vict.1.9. 2. metaph., μέριμναι ζωπυροῦσι τάρβος A.Th.290 (lyr.); ζωπυρουμένας φρενός Id.Ag.1034 (lyr.); τῆς φύσεως τὸ ζωπυροῦν Arist.PA670^{a}25, cf. Plu.2.940c; ζ. τινά *to provoke* him, Ar.Lys.682 (lyr.); ζ. τρυφήν *increase* it, Plu.Lyc.9; in Magic, *quicken, fill with power*, PMag.Leid.V.10.7 (Pass.). II. intr., *burst into flame*, ἣν ἡ θέρμη ζωπυρῇ Aret.SD1.8. **-ημα**, ατος, τό, = ζώπυρον I, gloss on φεψάλυξ, Sch.Ar.Lys.107. **-ητέον**, *one must kindle*, Ph.1.187. **-ιον**, τό, = κλινοπόδιον, prob. in Dsc.3.95 (from the name of the physician Zopyrus). II. **ζωπύρια**, τά, *bellows*, Phot., Suid. (nisi leg. ζωπυρεῖα). **-ίς**, ίδος, ἡ, *kindling up, reviving*, Jul. Or.5.172b. **-ον**, τό, *spark* or *hot coal*, used to kindle *a fire*: hence metaph., σμικρὰ ζ. τοῦ τῶν ἀνθρώπων διασεσωσμένα γένους (of the survivors of the flood), Pl.Lg.677b, cf. Luc.Tim.3; so [τὸ βαρὺ καὶ κοῦφον] οἷον ζ. ἄττα κινήσεως Arist.Cael.308^{a}2; βραχέα τινὰ ζ. τῆς Λυκούργου νομοθεσίας Plu.2.240a; ζ. τι πρὸς σωτηρίαν βίου Max.Tyr. 2.4; ζώπυρα τῆς ἰδίας σωτηρίας Ph.2.519; ζ. φιλανθρωπίας *flashes* of humanity, Nic.Dam.Fr.127 J. II. Act., *pair of bellows*, Ephor. 42 J. **-ος**, ον, *glowing*, of desire, θερμὸν καὶ ζ. Philostr.VA1. 34. 2. *restorative*, ἔχει τι ζ. ὁ τοῦ προσώπου περισπογγισμός Sor. 2.28. **-ωσις**, εως, ἡ, *kindling*, Max.Tyr.9.7.

ζωροποτ-έω, *drink neat wine*, Call.Fr.109, AP11.25 (Apollonid.). **-ης**, ου, ὁ, *drinking neat wine*, Hedyl.ap.Ath.11.497d; οἴνου Man.4. 300; ὀφθαλμοὶ.. κάλλεος ἀκρήτου ζωροπόται AP5.225 (Paul. Sil.).

ζωρός, όν, *pure, sheer*, prop. of wine without water, like ἄκρατος, ζ. μέθυ A.R.1.477; πόμα AP12.50 (Asclep.); πότος Hippoloch.ap. Ath.4.129d: abs., ζωρός (sc. οἶνος) AP6.105 (Apollonid.), etc.: Comp., ζωρότερον δὲ κέραιε mix the wine *more pure*, i.e. add less water, Il.9.203, cf. Arist.Po.1461^{a}14; κεράσας ζωρότερον Ὁμηρικῶς Ephipp.10; so later -ότερον πίνειν Hdt.6.84; and in the sense drink *hard*, ζ. πιεῖν Thphr.Char.4.6, cf. Ael.VH13.4, Luc.Tim.54, etc.; πίνειν -οτέρῳ χρώμενον οἰνοχόῳ Antiph.149; ζωρὸν δέπας a cup *of sheer wine*, AP11.28 (Marc. Arg.); ζωρὸν πέλαγος a sea *of wine*, ib.7.457.6 (Aristo); ζωρότερον κισσύβιον ib.5.288.4 (Agath.); of drugs, Luc. DMort.7.1, Nav.45; διδόναι τι ζωρότερον ἐσθίειν Hp.Nat.Mul.69; -ότερον γάλα Ruf.Fr.118: metaph., ζωροτάτη μανίη AP7.30 (Antip. Sid.). (In Philum.Ven.2.3, 4.2 ζωρός is opp. ἄκρατος, and so perh. in Emp.35.15, but the reading is doubtful.)

ζωρύα, ἡ, perh. = *pipe for running water*, (ζωός, ῥέω) IG4.823.46 (Troezen); cf. ὑδρορύα.

ζῶρυξ, = διῶρυξ, PMeyer20.18 (iii A.D.), Stud.Pal.20.70.25 (iii A.D.).

ζώς, rarer form for ζωός (q.v.).

ζώσιμος, ον, (ζῶ) *viable*, Alex.Aphr.Pr.2.47; *likely to survive*, Aët. 13.22, Horap.1.38. II. *pertaining to this life*, τὰ ζ. prob. in Phld. Herc.1251.9.

ζῶσις, εως, ἡ, (ζώννυμι) *girding on, cincture*, σάκκων Lxx Is.22.12.

ζῶσμα, v. ζῶμα. **ζώστειον**, v. ζήτρειον.

ζωστήρ, ῆρος, ὁ, (ζώννυμι) in Il. always *a warrior's belt*, prob. of leather covered with metal plates, ὅθι ζωστῆρος ὀχῆες χρύσειοι σύνεχον 4.132; δαιδάλεος, παναίολος, ib.135,186; φοίνικι φαεινός 7.305, cf. Hdt.9.74, S.Aj.1030; of an Amazon, Pi.Fr.172: in Od., a swineherd's *belt*, 14.72, cf. Theoc.7.18, 26.17. II. later, = ζώνη, *a woman's girdle*, Paus.1.31.1: metaph., of the encircling sea, νῆσοι.., ἃς.. ζ. Αἰγαίου κύματος ἐντὸς ἔχει AP9.421 (Antip. Thess.); ὠκεανὸς ἀτλαντικὸς ζ. Secund.Sent.2. III. *anything that goes round like a girdle*: 1. *stripe marking certain height in the ship*, Hld.1.1. 2. *grass-wrack, Posidonia oceanica*, Thphr.HP4.6.2, Plin.HN13.135. 3. = ζώνη III.4, ib.26.121. IV. name of a cape on the west coast of Attica, Hdt.8.107, Hyp.*Fr.*67, etc. 2. epith. of Apollo at Zoster, *AB*261 (sed leg. Ζωστήριος). V. ζωστῆρες Ἐνυοῦς, of warriors, Call.*Ap.*85. VI. name of a πηγή in the Chaldaean system, Dam.*Pr.*96.

Ζωστήριος, α, ον, *of* Ζωστήρ (a place on the west coast of Attica), Ζωστήριος Ἀπόλλων *IG*1[2].324.70, Euph.95b, Paus.1.31.1, cf. foreg. IV. 2; Ζωστηρία, epith. of Athena, *Schwyzer* 319 (Delph., vi/v B.C.), *IG* 1[2].324.97 (v B.C.), Paus.9.17.2, St.Byz. s. v. Ζωστήρ, Hsch. (-στειρα cod.); Ἀθηνᾶ ζωστῆρα (sic) *AB*261. 2. ζωστήριον, τό, = ζωστήρ, dub. in *PLond.*2.402.8 (ii B.C.), cf. *Gloss.*

ζωστηροκλέπτης, ου, ὁ, *one who steals belts*, Lyc.1329.

ζώστ-ης, ου, ὁ, *one who girds*, *Gloss.* **-ός**, ή, όν, *girded*, ὑπένδυμα Plu.*Alex.*32, cf. X.Eph.1.2, Hsch. s. v. ζῶστρα. **-ρα**, ἡ, *head-band, fillet*, Theoc.2.122 (pl.). **-ρίς**, *cingulum*, *Gloss.* **-ρον**, τό, *belt, girdle*, Od.6.38 (pl.).

Ζωτεάτας, epith. of Apollo at Argos, Hsch.: **Ζωτελιστής**, epith. of Apollo at Corinth, Id.

ζώτειον, τό, v. ζήτρειον.

ζωτικός, ή, όν, (ζῶ) *fit for giving* or *maintaining life*, ἐπιθυμία Pl. *Ti.*91b; δυνάμεις Ti.Locr.100d, cf. D.S.2.51 (Sup.), Gal.15.506; πνεῦμα LXX *Wi.*15.11; ἰκμάς Corn.*ND*2; φῶς Porph.*Marc.*13; τὸ ὑγρὸν -ώτερον τοῦ ξηροῦ Arist.*GA*761[a]27, cf. 733[a]11; [ἔαρ] -ωτάτη ὥρα Thphr.*CP*1.13.4. II. *full of life, alive*, Pl.*R.*610e, Thphr. *HP*1.14.2, Porph.*Gaur.*16.3,5; τὰ τήθυα ζωτικώτερα τῶν σπόγγων *more like animals*, Arist.*PA*681[a]10; τὰ -ώτατα μέρη (of the body) Plu.2.130b. Adv. -κῶς, ἔχειν to be *fond of life*, Id.*Cat.Mi.*70. 2. *characteristic of life, vital*, τὸ αὐτὰ ὑφ' αὑτῶν κινεῖσθαι ζωτικόν Arist. *Ph.*255[a]6; τόνος, πνεῦμα, φύσις, *Stoic.*2.235, 241, 272; κίνησις Herm. ap.Stob.1.41.7, cf. Plot.6.7.5 (Comp.), Porph.*Sent.*37; κατὰ τὸ ζ. Procl.*Inst.*189. Adv. -κῶς ib.39, Dam.*Pr.*79, Herm.ap.Stob.l.c. 3. ζ. χρόνος duration *of life*, Vett.Val.132.4; of works of Art, *true to life*, τὸ ζ. φαίνεσθαι πῶς ἐνεργάζῃ τοῖς ἀνδριᾶσιν; X.*Mem.*3.10.6; -ώτατα ἐξεργάσασθαι Plu.2.668d.

ζωτύς (or **ζωγύς**)· θώραξ, Hsch.

ζωύλλιον, τό, = sq., Tz.*H.*9.957.

ζωΰφιον [ῠ], τό, Dim. of ζῷον, ζῴδιον, Ath.5.210c, Gal.6.666, Hsch., cj. for ζωόφυτα in S.E.*P.*1.41.

ζωφορ-ία, Ion. -ίη, ἡ, *the sun's progress through the zodiac*, Man. 4.510. **-ος**, ον, (φέρω) = ζωοφόρος (q. v.).

ζωφύτ-έω, *thrive, flourish*, of trees or plants, *POxy.*1188.3 (i A.D.), cf. *PLond.*2.214 (iii A.D.); ζωφυτοῦν ἄλσος *BCH*44.79 (Lagina). **-ος**, ον, (φύω) *giving life to plants, fertilizing*, αἷμα A.*Supp.*857; γῆ Plu. *Rom.*20. II. Pass., *spring from the earth*, τὰ ζ. *plants*, Diusap. Stob.4.21.16.

ζώω, Ep. and Ion. for ζῶ.

ζω-ώδης, ες, *like an animal, animal*, κάλλος Democr.105; δαίμων Posidon.ap.Gal.5.469; βίος Plu.2.8a, Aret.*SD*1.5; αἰσθήσεις Ph.2. 22 (Sup.), cf. M.Ant.7.55; ἐνέργειαι Dam.*Pr.*102; ἡδονή Marin.*Procl.* 4; of persons, *brutish*, Aret.*SD*1.7; but ἐς χροιὴν ζ. *like a living person* (of one dead), Id.*SA*2.11. **-ωδία**, ἡ, *animal nature*, Iamb. *Protr.*21.ιε'.

ζώωσις, εως, ἡ, (ζωόω) *making alive*, [Gal.]19.174.

ζωωτός (with ι, Inscrr., v. infr.), ή, όν, also ός, όν Chares ap.Ath. 12.538d: (ζῷον):—*adorned with figures*, φαρέτρα *IG*11(2).161*B*100 (Delos, iii B.C.); χιτών Callix.2; ἐφαπτίς Plb.30.25.10; σκύφος *OGI* 214.54 (iii B.C.); αὐλαῖαι Chares l.c.

H

Η η, ἦτα (q.v.), τό, indecl., eighth (later seventh) letter of the Gr. alphabet; as numeral η' = ὀκτώ and ὄγδοος, but ͵η, = 8,000. In most local alphabets of v B.C. and earlier it represents *h*, in others (incl. the Ion. = later general Gr. alphabet) one of the long *ē* sounds (cf. βῆ βῆ). Described by E.*Fr.*382.5, Agatho 4.2.

ἤ (A), Ep. also ἠέ (in signf. A. II ἤ (or ἠέ) folld. by ἦ (or ἦε), v. infr.), Conj. with two chief senses, Disj. (*or*) and Comp. (*than*).

A. DISJUNCTIVE, *or*, ἐγὼ.. ἢ ἄλλος Ἀχαιῶν Il.2.231, cf. 397, 800, 4.142, 7.236, al.; θεόσυτος ἢ βρότειος ἢ κεκραμένη A.*Pr.*116. 2. ἤ.. ἤ *either.. or*, ἢ νῦν δηθύνοντ' ἢ ὕστερον αὖτις ἰόντα Il.1.27, cf. 151, 5.484, etc.; so ἤ.. ἤτοι.. Pi.*N.*6.4, *Fr.*138; ἤτοι.. ἤ.. A.*Ag.*662, S. *Ant.*1182, Th.2.40, etc. (in Classical Gr. the alternative introduced by ἤτοι is emphasized, later no distn. is implied, *Ep.Rom.*6.16; ἤτοι.. ἤ.. ἤ.. *PTeb.*5.59 (ii B.C.)); ἤ repeated any number of times, ἐγὼ δέ κεν αὐτὸς ἕλωμαι ἢ τεὸν ἢ Αἴαντος ἰὼν γέρας ἢ Ὀδυσῆος Il.1.138, cf. Od.15.84, S.*Ant.*707; ἤ is prob. wrongly accented in codd. of Il.2.289, Od.3.348, 19.109, v. ἦ Adv. I. 3: ἢ πόλις βροτός θ' ὁμοίως A.*Eu.*524 (lyr.) is exceptional. 3. *or else, otherwise*, εἰδέναι δεῖ περὶ οὗ ἂν ᾖ ἡ βουλή, ἢ παντὸς ἁμαρτάνειν ἀνάγκη Pl.*Phdr.*237c; μή με λυπεῖτε, ἢ φεύξομ' ἐκ τῆς οἰκίης Herod.5.74; ζῶντα κακῶς λέγειν ἐκώλυσε.., ἢ τρεῖς δραχμὰς ἀποτίνειν ἔταξε Lex Sol.ap.Plu.*Sol.*21, cf. 24, *IG*1[2].94.10, Them.*Or.*21.260a. II. in Questions or Deliberations in Disj. form (the accentuation is ἤ (ἠέ) folld. by ἦ (ἦε), Hdn. Gr.2.24, al., A.D.*Conj.*224.28): 1. Direct questions, a. introduced by ἤ (ἠέ), ἢ δολιχὴ νοῦσος ἦ Ἄρτεμις ἰοχέαιρα.. κατέπεφνεν; Od.11.172; ἤ τι κατὰ πρῆξιν ἦ μαψιδίως ἀλάλησθε..; 3.72, cf. 1.408, 16.462, Il.6.378, 15.735, 16.12, etc. b. without an introductory Particle, θεός νύ τις ἦ βροτός ἐσσι; art thou a goddess *or* a mortal? Od.6.149, cf. 1.226, 4.314, 372, 643, 20.130, 21.194, Il.10.63, 425, 534, 15.203: accented ἦ, Hdn.Gr.2.145, al., but ἤ freq. in codd. of Hom. and always in codd. of later writers: ἤκουσας ἢ οὐκ ἤκουσας ἢ κωφῇ λέγω; A.*Th.*202; ἄρτι δὲ ἥκεις ἢ πάλαι; Pl.*Cri.*43a; κακουργεῖν δεῖ ἢ οὔ; ib.49c; preceded by πότερον, πότερον δοκεῖ σοι κάκιον εἶναι, τὸ ἀδικεῖν ἢ τὸ ἀδικεῖσθαι; Id.*Grg.*474c, etc. 2. Indirect questions, freq. epexegetic of a preceding question and identical in form with direct questions. a. εἴπ' ἄγε, .. ἤ ῥ' ἐθέλει.., ἦ ἀπέειπε.. Il.9.674; ὄφρα δαῶμεν ἢ ἐτεὸν Κάλχας μαντεύεται ἦε καὶ οὐκί 2.300; διάνδιχα μερμήριξεν ἢ ὅ γε.. ἐναρίζοι ἦε χόλον παύσειεν 1.190; later with εἰ.. ἤ A.*Ch.*890, *Ag.*478, S.*OC*80, etc.; πότερον or πότερα.. ἤ.. Id.*Pers.*148, 352, *Ag.*630, etc.; sts. εἴτε.. ἤ E.*El.*897; ἤ.. εἴτε S.*Aj.* 177. b. without introductory Particle, οὐδέ τι οἶδα ζώει ὅ γ' ἦ τέθνηκε Od.11.464, cf. Il.10.546, Od.24.238.

B. COMPARATIVE, *than, as*, after a Comp., Il.11.162, etc.: after positive Adjs. which imply comparison, ἄλλος, ἕτερος ἤ.., S.*OT*595, *Tr.*835 (lyr.); ἐναντίος ἤ Pl.*Grg.*481c; ἴδιόν τι πάσχειν πάθος ἢ οἱ ἄλλοι ibid.: after Advbs. or adverbial phrases, πλήν, πρίν, πρόσθεν, χωρίς (qq. v.), ἀλλά (v. ἀλλ' ἤ); τῇ ὑστεραίᾳ ἤ.. Id.*Cri.*44a (f.l. in *Smp.*173a); ἐν τῷ πέμπτῳ καὶ δεκάτῳ ϝέτει ἀπὸ τῶ ποτεχεῖ ϝέτεος ἢ Ἀριστίων ἐφορεύει *Tab.Heracl.*1.121; παρὰ δόξαν ἢ ὡς αὐτὸς κατεδόκεε Hdt.1.79, cf. 8.4; διαφερόντως ἤ.. Pl.*Phd.*85b; οὐδ' ὅσον ἤ.. not so much *as*.., not more *than*.., Theoc.9.21: after Verbs implying comparison, βούλεσθαι ἤ.. to wish *rather than*.., v. βούλομαι IV, αἱρέω B. II. 1b; so φθάνειν ἤ.. to come sooner *than*.., Il.23.445, Od.11.58; ἐπιθυμεῖν ἤ.. X.*Cyr.*1.4.3; δέχεσθαι ἤ.. Lys.10.21: less freq. after a word not implying comparison, δίκαιον ἡμέας ἔχειν.. (sc. μᾶλλον) ἤ περ Ἀθηναίους Hdt.9.26; ἐμοὶ πικρὸς.. ἢ κείνοις γλυκύς S.*Aj.*966 (s. v. l.); δεδικαιωμένος ἢ ἐκεῖνος *Ev.Luc.*18.14. 2. joining two Comparatives which refer to the same subject, πάντες κ' ἀρησαίατ' ἐλαφρότεροι πόδας εἶναι ἢ ἀφνειότεροι Od.1.165; ταχύτερα ἢ σοφώτερα Hdt.3.65; μανικώτεροι ἢ ἀνδρειότεροι Pl.*Tht.*144b, cf. Ar.*Ach.*1078. 3. rarely after a Sup., πλεῖστα θωμάσια ἔχει Αἴγυπτος ἢ ἄλλη πᾶσα χώρη Hdt.2.35 (s. v. l.); πίθοιτό κεν ὔμμι μάλιστα ἢ ἐμοί A.R.3.91. 4. ἢ οὐ is used when a neg. precedes, οὐδέν τι μᾶλλον ἐπ' ἡμέας ἢ οὐ καὶ ἐπ' ὑμέας Hdt.4.118, cf. 5.94, Th.2.62, etc.: after an implied neg., ὠμὸν.. πόλιν ὅλην διαφθεῖραι μᾶλλον ἢ οὐ τοὺς αἰτίους Id.3.36. 5. freq. omitted with numerals after πλείων, ἐλάττων, μείων, ἔτη.. πλείω ἑβδομήκοντα v.l. in Pl.*Ap.*17d; οὐ μεῖον πεντακοσίους X.*An.*6.4.24: sts. with an inf. or conditional clause, τί γὰρ ἀνδρὶ κακὸν μεῖζον ἁμαρτεῖν E.*Alc.* 879; τίς εὐπραξία σπανιωτέρα.., εἰ [δύναμις] πάρεστιν (for ἢ δύναμιν παρεῖναι); Th.1.33. 6. pleon. with a gen., τίς ἂν αἰσχίων εἴη ταύτης δόξα, ἢ δοκεῖν.. Pl.*Cri.*44c, cf. Lys.10.28. 7. the Disj. and Comp. uses are found together in Il.15.511 βέλτερον, ἢ ἀπολέσθαι ἕνα χρόνον ἠὲ βιῶναι, ἢ δηθὰ στρεύγεσθαι ἐν αἰνῇ δηϊοτῆτι better, *either* to die once for all *or* win life, *than* long to toil in battle. [ἢ οὐ, ἢ οὐκ combine by Synizesis into one syll. in Trag. and Com., A.*Pr.*330, S.*Aj.*334, Ar.*Lys.*128; so usually in Ep., Od.1.298, al.; ἢ αὐτός Hes.*Fr.*194; ἢ εἰ Alex.201.]

ἦ (B), an exclamation expressing disapproval, ἦ ἦ σιώπα Ar.*Nu.* 105; ἦ ἦ· τί δρᾷς; E.*HF*906 (lyr.), cf. Suid. 2. to call attention, ποῦ Ξανθίας; ἦ Ξανθία where 's Xanthias? *hi*, Xanthias! Ar.*Ra.*271.

ἤ (or **ἦ**) (C), Cypr. for *if*, *Inscr.Cypr.*135.6 H. 2. Cret. for *when, after*, ἤ κ' ἀποστᾷ μωλῆν *after* retiring, he shall take proceedings, *Leg.Gort.*1.52; ἐν ταῖς τριάκοντα ἤ κα ϝείποντι within 30 days *from the time of* their proclamation, ib.8.18.

ἦ, Adv., never in the form ἦε (ἠέ):

I. TO CONFIRM an assertion, *in truth, of a surety*, ἦ ὀλίγον οἷ παῖδα ἐοικότα γείνατο Τυδεύς Il.5.800, etc.; ironically, 1.229, al.; with concessive force, *it is true that*..: hence, *although*.., ἦ καὶ γένει ὕστερος ἦεν 3.215: freq. strengthd. by the addition of one or two other Particles, as ἦ ἄρα Od.24.193; ἦ ἄρα δή Il.13.446; ἦ ῥα 4.82; ἦ ῥά νυ 6.215; ἦ γάρ 1.78; ἦ γάρ τοι Od.16.199; ἦ δή Il.2.272; ἦ δή που 21.583; ἦ δῆτα S.*OT*429; ἦ θην Il.20.452; ἦ κάρτα S. *El.*1279; ἦ μάλα Il.3.204; ἦ μάλα δή 5.422; ἦ μήν and ἦ μέν (v. infr.); ἦ νυ Il.22.11; ἦ τάχα Od.18.73; ἦ τε 13.211: and to express doubt, ἦ που, v. ἦ που and πού: esp. ἦ μήν used in oaths and asseverations, Il.2.291, 7.393, A.*Pr.*73, 168, etc.; also ἦ μάν Il.2.370, 13.354, Sapph.*Supp.*23.5; ἦ μέν Od.10.65 (later εἶ μήν, v. εἶ): c. inf. in orat. obliq., after Verbs of swearing, etc., σὺ δὲ σύνθεο, καί μοι ὄμοσσον, ἦ μέν μοι πρόφρων ἔπεσιν καὶ χερσὶν ἀρήξειν Il.1.77; ἦ μέν also in Ion. historical Prose, Hdt.4.154, 5.93, al.; ἐγγυᾶσθαι, ἦ μὴν παραμενεῖν Pl. *Phd.*115d; ἐγγυητὰς καταστῆσαι ἦ μὴν ἐκτείσειν Lex ap.D.24.39: with other Particles, ἦ μὲν δή Il.2.798, Od.18.257, al.; ἦ δὴ μάν Il.17. 538. 2. in the combinations ἐπεὶ ἦ, ὅτι ἦ and τί ἦ; A.D.*Conj.*255. 5, *Synt.*307.19 (cf. Hdn.Gr.1.520), recognizes an 'expletive' ἦ (παραπληρωματικὸς σύνδεσμος) perispom. after ἐπεί, barytone after ὅτι or τί. It is prob. the same as the affirmative ἦ (cf. A.D.*Conj.* l. c.), and occurs in the same combinations, ἐπεὶ ἦ πολύ.. Il.1.169, al.; ἐπεὶ ἦ μάλα ib.156, Od.10.465; ἐπεὶ ἦ καί.. Il.20.437, Od.16.442. Trypho took τίη as one word, and this can be supported by τί ἦ δὲ σύ.. Il.6.55, but A.D.(*Conj.* l. c.) infers from the accent of ὅτι ἦ that τί ἦ was two words. The Attic accentuation is said by Eust.45 init., 118.39, 907.14 to be τιή, ὁτιή (qq. v.). 3. this ἦ (or ἤ) is prob. to be recognized in ὥς τε γὰρ ἦ Il.2.289, ὥς τέ τευ ἦ Od.3.348, 19.109, where codd. have ἤ (in Od.3.348 ἠδέ (cj. Bekker) shd. perh. be read for ἠέ).

II. in Questions not involving alternatives: 1. Direct

questions, a. epexegetic of a preceding question, suggesting the answer to it, τίπτ' εἰλήλουθας; ἦ ἵνα ὕβριν ἴδῃ Ἀγαμέμνονος; why hast thou come? *is it* that thou mayst see..? Il.1.203, cf. 5.466, 7.26, Od.4.710, 13.418, 17.376, B.17.5; τί δῆτα χρῄζεις; ἦ με γῆς ἔξω βαλεῖν; S.*OT*622, cf. E.*Or.*1425 (ἤ codd.); τίς σοι διηγεῖτο; ἦ αὐτὸς Σωκράτης; Pl.*Smp.*173a (perispom., cod. B): on the accent, Hdn. Gr.2.112. b. not epexegetic of a preceding question, ἦ σύ γ' Ὀδυσσεύς ἐσσι πολύτροπος; art thou the wily Odysseus? Od.10.330, cf. Il.11.666, 15.504; ἦ οὐκ ὀτρύνοντος ἀκούετε.. Ἕκτορος; do you not hear..? ib.506, cf. Od.16.424; ἦ τὸ πλοῖον ἀφῖκται; Pl.*Cri.*43c; ἦ οὐ δοκεῖ καὶ σοὶ οὕτω; don't you think so too? Id.*Grg.*479b (perispom., cod. T); ἦ βούλει συλλογισώμεθα αὐτά; shall we work them (the consequences) out? ib.479c (perispom., cod. T); ἦ τορῶς λέγω; A.*Ag.*269; ἦ κἀν δόμοισι τυγχάνει τανῦν παρών; S.*OT*757: freq. with other Particles, ἦ ἄρ..; Od.20.166, Il.19.56; mostly ἦ ῥα..; 5.421, 762, Od.4.632; also in Trag. (in lyr.), A.*Pers.*633, S.*Aj.*172, 955: esp. to mark the first of several questions, Pi.*I.*7(6).3 sqq.; ἦ ἄρα δή..; Il.13.446; ἦ ῥά νυ..; 4.93; ἦ νυ..; 15.128; ἦ ταῦτα δή..; S.*Ph.*565, *El.*385; ἦ ταῦτα δῆτα..; Id.*OT*429; ἦ γάρ..; A.*Pr.*745, 757, S.*OT*1000: in Att. Prose, ἦ γάρ; standing alone, *is it not so?* Pl.*Tht.*160e, *Grg.*449d, 468d; ἦ καί..; A.*Ag.*1207, 1362:—ἦ usu. begins the sentence, except that the vocative may precede, as in Il.5.421, 762, Od.4.632, S.*OC*863, 1102, or ἀλλά, as in A.*Ag.*276, *Ch.*774:—by Crasis ἦ combines with ἄρα in Att. and the κοινή to ἆρα (q.v.), in all other dialects (cf. A.D.*Conj.*223.24) to ἦρα (q.v.), but ἆρα is found in Pi.*P.*4.78 (ἄρα codd.), al., Archil.86, 89. 2. Indirect questions, οἴχετο πευσόμενος μετὰ σὸν κλέος ἤ που ἔτ' εἴης Od.13.415 (v.l. εἰ, which alone has Ms. authority in Il.1.83, Od.19.325); ὄφρα καὶ Ἕκτωρ εἴσεται ἤ καὶ ἐμὸν δόρυ μαίνεται ἐν παλάμῃσιν Il.8.111 (v.l. εἰ); ἀλλ' ἄγε μοι τόδε εἰπὲ..ἤ καὶ Λαέρτῃ αὐτὴν ὁδὸν ἄγγελος ἔλθω; Od.16.138 (v.l. εἰ); ἀμφίστασθαι ἤ κα πεφυτεύκωντι πάντα κὰτ τὰν συνθήκαν they shall investigate *whether*.. *Tab.Heracl.*1.125; μαντεύσασθαί οἱ..ἤ λῷόν οἵ κα εἴη Isyll.34; διαψαφίξασθαι ἤ δοκεῖ αὐτὸν στεφανῶσαι *IG*12(3).170.12 (Astypalaea): accented ἤ in codd. Hom., but it shd. perh. be perispom.

ἦ, for ἔφη, 3 sg. impf. or aor. 2 of ἠμί (q.v.). **ἦ**, for ἦν, Att. contr. from Ion. ἔα, impf. of εἰμί (*sum*).

ᾗ, Adv. of Place, *where*, *Berl.Sitzb.*1927.170 (Cyrene), *Leg.Gort.* 6.31.

ᾗ, dat. sg. fem. of relat. Pron. ὅς, ἥ, ὅ, in adverb. sense, 1. of Place, *which way, where, whither*, relat. to τῇ, Il.13.53, 15.46; also in Trag. and Att., S.*El.*1435; τῇδε..ᾗ A.*Ch.*308; ἐκείνῃ..ᾗ Pl.*Phd.* 82d; Dor. ᾇ *SIG*56.28 (Argos, v B.C.). II. of Manner, *how, as*, ᾗ καὶ Λοξίας ἐφήμισεν A.*Ch.*558; ᾗ νομίζεται S.*OC*1603; ᾗ βούλονται Th.8.71, etc.:—not in Hom., unless we read ᾗ θέμις ἐστί for ἣ θέμις, v. θέμις. 2. *wherefore*, Th.1.25, 2.2, al. 3. *in so far as*, διαφέρειν τὰ ἑκούσια τῶν ἀκουσίων ᾗ ὁ μὲν..τῷ δέ.. X.*Mem.*2.1.18, cf. Pl. *Men.*72b; ῥήτορες ᾗ ῥήτορες Phld.*Rh.*2.265 S.; ᾗ ἄνθρωπος *qua* man, Arist.*EN*1096^{b}2. III. with Sup., ᾗ ἐδύνατο τάχιστα *as* quickly *as* he could, X.*An.*1.2.4, etc.; ᾗ δυνατὸν μάλιστα ib.1.3.15; ᾗ ἄριστον Id.*Cyr.*2.4.32, etc.; ᾗ ῥᾷστά τε καὶ ἥδιστα Id.*Mem.*2.1.9; ᾗ ἂν δύνωμαι τάχιστα Id.*Cyr.*7.1.9.

ἦα, ἤεν, 1 and 3 sg. Ep. impf. of εἰμί (*sum*). **ᾖα**, contr. for ἤϊα, Ion. impf. of εἶμι (*ibo*). **ᾖα**, τά, contr. from ἤϊα (q.v.).

ἠᾰρινός, v. ἐαρινός.

Ἤατος, ὁ (sc. μήν), name of month at Heraclea Trachinia, *GDI*1895.

ἠβαιός, ά, όν, Ion. (Cypr. acc. to *AB*1095) for βαιός, *small*, usu. with neg. οὐδέ, οὔ οἱ ἔνι φρένες, οὐδ' ἠβαιαί no sense is in him, no not *the least*, Il.14.141, cf. Od.21.288; οὔ οἱ ἔνι τρίχες, οὐδ' ἠβαιαί no not even *a few*, 18.355; also ἠβαιὴν οὔτι κατὰ πρόφασιν Call.*Fr.*540: rarely without neg., [πηλαμύδες] καὶ ἠβαιαί περ ἐοῦσαι Opp.*H.*4.514. II. often in neut. as Adv., οὐδ' ἠβαιόν not *in the least*, not *at all*, Il.2.380, Od.3.14, etc., cf. Phylarch.(?)84J.: rarely without a neg., ἠβαιὸν ἀπὸ σπείους *a little* from the cave, Od.9.462.

ἡβ-άσκω, Incept. of ἡβάω, *come to puberty*, Hp.*Aph.*3.28, X.*An.* 4.6.1; παῖς ἡβάσκων ἄρτι ib.7.4.7; of women, *become marriageable*, Ruf.ap.Orib.*inc.*2.2. 2. metaph., νῦν ἔθ' ἡβάσκει κακόν (read by Gal. for ἡβᾷ σοι) E.*Alc.*1085; ἡμῖν ἡβάσκει πενίη *AP*6.30 (Maced.); ποιητικὴ οὔπω ἡβάσκουσα Philostr.*Her.Praef.* 3. *reach*, or *show the outward signs of, manhood*, Aristaenet.1.11, Philostr.*Im.*2.7. **-άω**, Cret. **ἡβίω** *Leg.Gort.*7.41, al., Aeol.(?) **ἀβάω** Hdn.Gr.2.16, Alc.*Supp.*7.11 (dub.); Ep. opt. ἡβώοιμι, part. ἡβώων (v. infr.): impf. ἥβων Ar.*V.*357: fut. -ήσω (ἐφ-) X.*Cyr.*6.1.12, Dor. ἡβάσω [ᾱ] *AP*7.482: aor. 1 ἥβησα Od.1.41, Hes.*Op.*132, Pl.*Ap.*41e: pf. ἥβηκα (παρ-) Hdt.3.53, etc.: (ἥβη):—*attain* or *have attained puberty*, ὅταν ἡβῆσαί τε καὶ ἥβης μέτρον ἵκοιτο Hes.*Op.*132; ἡβῶσιν ὀψὲ Hp.*Aër.*4; ἐπειδὰν ἡβήσωσι Pl.*Ap.*l.c.; of women, γυνὴ τέτορ' ἡβώοι (sc. ἔτη) four years *past puberty*, Hes.*Op.*698; ἡβάσεις ἥβαν *AP*l.c.; ἡβᾶν ἐπὶ διετές, v. sub διετής; ὀμόσαι Χαλκιδέων τοὺς ἡβῶντας ἅπαντας all the *adults*, *IG*1^{2}.39.32, cf. Ar.*Ra.*1055, Th.4.132. 2. *to be in the prime of youth*, εἴθ' ὣς ἡβώοιμι, βίη τέ μοι ἔμπεδος εἴη Od.14.468, al.; ἀνὴρ οὐδὲ μάλ' ἡβῶν not even *in the prime of life*, Il.12.382, cf. Od. 23.187, A.*Ch.*879; γέροντα τὸν νοῦν, σάρκα δ' ἡβῶσαν φέρει Id.*Th.* 622; ἡβᾶν σθένος *to be young* and strong, E.*HF*436 (lyr.); ἥβων I *was young*, Ar.*V.*357; ἡ. τὰς αἰσθήσεις, of an old man, Philostr.*VS*1.9.3; of plants, ἡμερὶς ἡβώωσα *a young, luxuriant* vine, Od.5.69, cf. Simon.183.3, Longus 4.5; ἡβῶντ' ἀρτίως οἰνίσκον (παρὰ προσδοκίαν for νεανίσκον) Cratin.183. 3. metaph., *to be fresh, vigorous*, ἡβώοις, φίλε θυμέ Thgn.877 (dub. l.); ἀεὶ γὰρ ἡβᾷ τοῖς γέρουσιν εὖ μαθεῖν 'tis always *youth* for old men to learn, i.e. 'tis never too late to learn, A.*Ag.*584 (nisi leg. ἥβη); ἡβᾷ δῆμος εἰς ὀργὴν πεσών the people *rages like a passionate youth*, E.*Or.*696, cf. νεανικός; ἄγγελον..γέρονθ', ἡβῶντα δ' εὐγλώσσῳ φρενί *exulting*, A.*Supp.*775; also of things, γάμοι, ἔαρ ἡ., Opp.*H.*1.474, 2.252. 4. *to have the outward signs of puberty*, Arist.*GA*746^{b}23; γένυς ἡβᾷ *AP*12.31 (Phan.). **-η**, Dor. **ἥβα**, Aeol. **ἄβα** Alc.101, ἡ: (v. sub fin.):—*youthful prime, youth*, νεηνίῃ ἀνδρὶ ἐοικώς, πρῶτον ὑπηνήτῃ, τοῦ περ χαριέστατος ἥβη Od.10.279, cf. Il.24.348; καὶ δ' ἔχει ἥβης ἄνθος ὅ τε κράτος ἐστὶ μέγιστον 13.484, cf. Hes.*Th.*988; ἐρικυδής Il.11.225, Hes.l.c.; πολυήρατος Od.15.366, etc.; ἥβης μέτρον ἱκέσθαι or ἱκάνειν, = ἡβάσκειν, 11.317, 18.217, etc.; ἥβην πολυήρατον ἱκόμεθ' 15.366, cf. Il.24.728; ἥβης ἀπόνασθαι, ταρπῆναι, 17.25, Od.23.212; ἐφ' ἥβης Ar.*Eq.*524; θρέψασθαί τινα πρὸς ἥβην until *manhood*, Pl.*Mx.*238b; μέχρι ἥβης Th.2.46. b. *strength and vigour of youth*, [δίσκον] ἀφῆκεν..πειρώμενος ἥβης Il.23.432; ἥβῃ τε πεποίθεα χερσί τ' ἐμῇσι Od.8.181, cf. 16.174; ἥβης ἀκμή S.*OT* 741: in pl., καρποτρόφοι νεάνιδες ἧβαι E.*Ion* 477 (lyr.). c. as a legal term, ἥβη was *the time before manhood*, at Athens sixteen years of age, *AB*255.15; fourteen acc. to *EM*359.17, Harp. s. v. ἐπιδιετές; at Sparta eighteen, τὰ δέκα ἀφ' ἥβης (sc. ἔτη), i.e. men of twenty-eight, X.*HG*2.4.32, 3.4.23; τὰ τετταράκοντα ἀφ' ἡ. ib.6.4.17; of women, ἐπεὶ δ' ἐς ἥβην ἦλθεν ὡραίαν γάμων E.*Hel.*12. d. of oxen, ἥβης μέτρον ἔχοντε Hes.*Op.*438; of the *fresh* skin of a snake, Nic.*Th.* 138. 2. metaph., *cheer, merriment*, Pi.*P.*4.295; δαιτὸς ἥβη E.*Cyc.* 504 (lyr.); also, *youthful fire, spirit*, Pi.*P.*6.48. 3. *body of youth*, A.*Pers.*512, 733, *Ag.*109 (lyr.), etc. 4. *the pubes*, Hp.*Epid.*3.4, Ar. *Nu.*976, Theopomp.Com.37, Arist.*HA*493^{b}3, al. II. a kind of *vine*, Hsch.; Dor. ἆβαι (pl.) v.l. in Theoc.5.109. III. pr.n., Ἥβη *Hebe*, Il.4.2, Od.11.603, Hes.*Th.*950; later allegorized as *goddess of youth*. (Cf. Lith. *jëgà* 'power'.) **-ηδόν**, Adv. *from the youth upwards*, ἅπαντες ἡβηδόν Hdt.1.172, cf. 6.21, Luc.*Vit.Auct.*14, al.; ἄξιον Ἐφεσίοις ἡ. ἀπάγξασθαι Heraclit.121; τοὺς ἄνδρας ἡ. ἀποσφάξαι D.S.3.54, cf. D.H.2.16, al. **-ησις**, εως, ἡ, *pubescence*, περὶ τὸ ἦτρον Sor.1.24. **-ητήρ**, ῆρος, ὁ, = ἡβητής, *AP*5.276 (Eratosth.), 6.76 (Agath.), Coluth.71. **-ητηρία**, ἡ, *the age of* ἥβη, *IG*12(9).916.22 (Chalcis). **-ητήριον**, τό, *a place where young people meet*, for exercise and amusement, Plu.*Pomp.*40, 53, Ath.10.425e, D.C.61.17, Hsch. **-ητής**, οῦ, ὁ, Dor. **ἡβᾱτάς** *IG*9(1).334 (Locr., v B.C.), *Berl.Sitzb.*1927.160 (Cyrene), **ἀβᾱτάς** only in Call. (v. infr.); Thess. **εἰβᾱτάς** (q.v.): (ἡβάω):—*in one's prime, adult*, κοῦροι ἡβηταί *h.Merc.*56, cf. Call.*Lav.Pall.*109; βραχιόνων ἡβητὴν τύπον E.*Heracl.* 858. **-ητικός**, ή, όν, *youthful*, λόγοι X.*HG*5.3.20; ἡλικία Id.*Lac.* 4.7, Gal.17(2).791. **-ήτωρ**, ορος, ὁ, = ἡβητήρ, κίχλαι Matro *Conv.* 78. **-ικός**, ή, όν, = ἡβητικός, ἡλικία Gal.16.655 (with v.ll.), Steph.*in Hp.*2.373 D.

ἠβολεῖν· ἀργεῖν, Hsch.

ἤβολον ἦμαρ· καθὸ ἀπα(ν)τῶσιν εἰς ταὐτόν, ἢ εὔκαιρον, ἱερόν, Hsch. (= Call.*Fr.anon.*170).

ἡβυλλιάω, Comic Dim. of ἡβάω, *to be in the bloom of youth*, Ar.*Ra.* 516, Pherecr.108.29.

ἠγάθεος [ᾰ], η, ον, Dor. **ἀγάθ-**, *most holy*, of places immediately under divine protection, Πύλος, Λῆμνος, Il.1.252, 2.722; Πυθώ Hes. *Th.*499, Pi.*P.*9.71; χῶρος, ἄντρον, A.R.3.981, 4.1131. (ἀγα-, θεός with Epic metrical lengthening.)

ἠγᾰλέος, α, ον, (ἄγνυμι) *broken in pieces*, Call.*Fr.anon.*91.

ἠγάνεα· πέμματα τὰ ἀπὸ τηγάνου, Hsch.; cf. ἤγανον. **ἠγανές·** καθαρόν, νέον, and **ἠγάν(ε)ος·** νεανίσκος, Id.

ἤγᾰνον, τό, Ion. for τήγανον, Anacr.26.

ἡγέμαχος· πολέμαρχος, Hsch., cf. *EM*299.43.

ἡγεμόν-εια, ἡ, fem. of ἡγεμονεύς, = ἡγεμόνη, Orph.*A.*909. **-ευμα**, ατος, τό, *leading*: but in E.*Ph.*1492 ἁγεμόνευμα νεκροῖσι, = ἡγεμὼν νεκρῶν, cf. Sch. ad loc. **-εύς**, έως, ὁ, Dor. **ἁγ-** *IG*5(1).540 (iii A.D.), Ep. for ἡγεμών, acc. ἡγεμονῆα, -ῆας, Opp.*C.*1.224, *AP*14.72.11, Man. 1.36, etc.; of a Roman *governor*, *IG*14.1437, *Supp.Epigr.*1.405 *A* 2 (Samos). **-εύω**, Dor. **ἁγ-**, *lead the way*, προτὶ Ἴλιον Il.16.92; πρὸς δώματα, ἀγορήνδε, λέχοσδε, δεῦρο, Od.3.386, 8.4, 23.293, 17.372; πρόσθ' ἡγεμόνευεν 22.400, 24.155; αὖλιν ἐφ' ἡμετέρην Theoc. 25.60; ἐπιθυμίας καὶ ἔρωτος ἡγεμονεύσαντος Pl.*Smp.*197a: c. dat. pers., Od.3.386, 8.4, Hes.*Th.*387, etc.; τῇ ἴμεν, ᾗ κεν δὴ σὺ..ἡγεμονεύῃς Il.15.46; ὁδὸν ἡ. *to lead* the way, ἐγὼ δ' ὁδὸν ἡγεμονεύσω Od.6.261, cf. Parm.1.5: twice in Hom., c. dat. et acc., τοῖσι γέρων ὁδὸν ἡγεμόνευε Od.24.225; ὕδατι ῥόον ἡ. *make* a course for the water, Il.21.258. II. *lead* in war, *rule, command*, once in Hom., c. dat., Τρωσὶ μὲν ἡγεμόνευε..Ἕκτωρ 2.816: elsewh., c. gen., Λοκρῶν δ' ἡ. Αἴας ib.527, cf. 552, Hdt.7.99, 160, etc.; ἡγεμόνων ἡ. X. *Ages.*1.3, etc.; ἡ. τῆς σκέψεως *to take the lead* in it, Pl.*Prt.*351e: abs., *to have* or *take the command*, Hdt.8.2; ἡ. ἐν πόλει Pl.*R.*474c:—Pass., *to be ruled*, ὑπό τινος Th.3.61.—Signf. II never occurs in Od., and signf. I rarely in Il. III. *to be governor*, τῆς Συρίας *Ev. Luc.*2.2: abs., *PTeb.*302.7 (i A.D.), *IGRom.*3.162 (Ancyra, ii A.D.), etc. **-έω**, *have authority*, ἔν τινι Pl.*Ti.*41c, 70c; *have the primacy*, Id.*Lg.*631c. **-η**, Dor. **ἁγ-** *JHS*13.353 (Aetol.), fem. of ἡγεμών:—*queen*, epith. of Artemis, Call.*Dian.*227, Ant.Lib.4.5; Ἄρτεμις Ὀρθωσία Ἡ. *IG*2.1663c; of Aphrodite, Hsch.; at Athens, one of the Charites, Paus.9.35.2; *flagship*, Hsch. **-ηΐς**, ΐδος, ἡ, poet. for ἡγεμονίς, Man.4.98. **-ία**, ἡ, *leading the way, going first*, Hdt.2.93; τῇ τῶν δυναστευόντων ἡ. by their *example*, Pl.*Lg.*711c. II. *authority, rule*, of dynasties or nations, Hdt.1.7, 3.65, etc.; of a general or officer, Th.4.91; ἐν ἡγεμονίαις Id.7.15; ἡ ἡ. τῶν Ἰώνων τοῦ πολέμου Hdt.6.2; ἡ κατὰ πόλεμον ἡ., τῶν πολεμικῶν ἡ ἡ., Arist.*Pol.* 1285^{b}9,18; αἱ ἡ. τῶν στρατοπέδων Pl.*Euthd.*273c; τῶν ὀπισθοφυλάκων X.*An.*4.7.8; ἡ. δικαστηρίου *presidency* in a court, Aeschin.3.14; *headship* of a philosophical school, Phld.*Acad.Ind.*p.59 M. 2. *political supremacy*, ἡ ἡ. τῆς Ἑλλάδος X.*HG*7.1.33; παρ' ἑκόντων τῶν Ἑλλήνων τὴν ἡ. ἐλάβομεν Isoc.8.30; ἡ. ἡ κατὰ θάλατταν Id.12.67, cf. Arist. *Ath.*23.2; ἡ ἐν Ἀρείῳ πάγῳ βουλὴ οὐδενὶ δόγματι λαβοῦσα τὴν ἡ. ib.1, cf. *Pol.*1304^{a}23; *political leadership* of an individual, ib.1296^{a}39; γένος ὑπερέχον πρὸς ἡ. πολιτικήν ib.1288^{a}9. b. = Lat. *imperium*, Plu. *Mar.*36, D.C.60.17, etc.; Αἴγυπτον δήμου Ῥωμαίων ἡγεμονίᾳ προσέθηκα *Mon.Anc.Gr.*15.1; τοῖς καλοῖς τῆς ἡ. νόμοις Ath.Mech.39.7; τριῶν τῶν μεγίστων ἡ. Plu.*Luc.*30; *reign of an Emperor*, *Ev.Luc.*3.1; *office of prefect*, *POxy.*237 v6 (ii A.D.), al. III. *military unit, regiment*, *IG*2^2.657 (pl.), *PRein.*9.13 (ii B.C.), Plu.*Cam.*23 (pl.); but αἱ μείζονες ἡ. the higher *commands*, Ael.*Tact.*10.4. IV. *chief thing, principal part*, ἡ. τῆς τέχνης Diph.17.5. V. *a principality*, Lxx *Ge.*36.30; *a Roman governorship*, ἡ Ἰλλυρίδος ἡ. Hdn.6.7.2, cf. 7.5.2; *tenure of office of a governor*, *PRyl.*77.36 (ii A.D.); ἡ Ἡ. the *Government*, *PGrenf.*2.73.11 (iii A.D.). -ίδης, ου, ὁ, = ἡγεμών, Lxx 2*Ma.* 13.24. -ικός, ή, όν, *of* or *for a leader, ready to lead* or *guide*, πρός τι X.*Mem.*2.3.14 (Comp.); πρὸς τὰ πονηρὰ Id.*Cyr.*2.2.25; κλῆμα -ώτατον τῆς ἀμπέλου *Gp.*4.13.4; ἡ. τόπος *vital* spot, Vett.Val.38.13. II. *capable of command, authoritative*, ψυχὴ ἐν τοῖς ἥλιξι ἡ. X.*Smp.*8.16; ἡ. φύσις Philol.11; ἡ. τὴν φύσιν Pl.*Phdr.*252e; ἡ. τέχναι Id.*Phlb.*55d; οἱ κατ' ἀρετὴν ἡ. πρὸς πολιτικὴν ἀρχὴν Arist.*Pol.*1288^{a}12; τὸ ἄρρεν.. τοῦ θήλεος -ώτερον ib.1259^{b}2; -ωτάτη [ἐπιστήμη] Id.*Metaph.*996^{b}10; ἡ. καὶ πολιτικὸς βίος (sc. τῆς πόλεως) Id.*Pol.*1327^{b}5; ζῴδια, viz. Aries, Leo, Sagittarius, *Cat.Cod.Astr.*1.165, Ptol.*Tetr.*34; ἡγεμονικόν, *authoritative*, of knowledge, Pl.*Prt.*352b; τὸ ἡγεμονικόν *the authoritative part of the soul* (reason), esp. in Stoic philosophy, Zeno *Stoic.*1.39, etc.; but also, *the governing part* of the universe, of the aether or sun, Chrysipp.*Stoic.*2.186,192, Cleanth.ib.1.112. Adv. -κῶς *like a leader*, opp. δεσποτικῶς, Arist.*Fr.*658; ἡ. καὶ βασιλικῶς Plb.2.64.6, cf. Procl.*in Alc.*p.52 C.: Comp. -ώτερον *more like an Emperor*, J.*AJ*19.4.2. 2. = Lat. *consularis*, Plu.*Pomp.*26. 3. *of* or *belonging to the prefect of Egypt*, ὑπηρέτης *CPR*18.35 (ii A.D.); πλοῖα *POxy.*2116.1 (iii A.D.). 4. -κά, τά, *payment to a* ἡγεμών, ἐδίδοτο Κλέωνι ἐν Ἀλεξανδρείᾳ ἡ...καὶ σῖτος ἀκόλουθος *PLond.ined.* 2089 (iii B.C.). -ιος, ον, *guiding*, epith. of Hermes, as *the guide* of departed souls, cf. ψυχοπομπός, Ar.*Pl.*1159, *IG*2^2.1496.85, Corn. *ND*16. -ίς, ίδος, ἡ, fem. of ἡγεμών, *imperial*, πόλεις Str.8.6.10, cf. *CIG*2721 (Stratonicea); γῆ App.*BC*2.65: metaph., δικαιοσύνη ἡ ἐν ἀρεταῖς ἡ. Ph.2.5; αἰσθήσεων ἡ. ὅρασις Id.2.24.

ἡγεμόσῠνα (sc. ἱερά), τά, *thank-offerings for safe-conduct*, X.*An.* 4.8.25.

ἡγεμών, Dor. **ἁγ-**, Aeol. **ἀγίμων** *IG*12(2).164 (Mytil.), al., όνος, ὁ; also ἡ, Pi.*I.*8(7).22, A.*Supp.*722, Aeschin.1.171, X.*Oec.* (infr. II):— *one who leads*; and so, I. in Od., *guide*, 10.505, 15.310, Hdt.5.14, S.*Ant.*1014, Pl.*Men.*97b; ἡγεμόνες γενέσθαι τινὶ τῆς ὁδοῦ Hdt.8.31, cf. E.*Hec.*281, X.*Mem.*1.3.4; ἡ. ποδὸς τυφλοῦ E.*Ph.*1616; ἡγεμόνες τοῦ πλοῦ Th.7.50; of a charioteer, S.*OT*804. 2. *one who does a thing first, shows the way* to others, τοῖς νεωτέροις ἡ. ἠθῶν χρηστῶν γίγνεσθαι Pl.*Lg.*670e; πατέρες τῆς σοφίας καὶ ἡ. Id.*Ly.*214a; πόνους τοῦ ζῆν ἡδέως ἡγεμόνας νομίζετε X.*Cyr.*1.5.12; τῆς εἰρήνης ἡ. D.18.24; [ἀχαριστία] ἐπὶ πάντα τὰ αἰσχρὰ ἡ. X.*Cyr.*1.2.7: abs., of choir-*leaders*, *Mnemos.*47.253 (Argos, ii/i B.C.). II. in Il., *leader, commander, chief*, opp. λαοί, πληθύς, 2.365, 11.304: c. gen., ἡγεμόνες Δαναῶν, φυλάκων, etc., 2.487, 9.85, cf. Hdt.6.43, 7.62, al.; στρατηγὸς καὶ ἡ. τῶν Ἑλλήνων πρὸς τὸν βάρβαρον ib.158; ἡ. τῶν πολεμίων Id.9.33; ἔχοντες ἡγεμόνας τῶν πάντων [στρατηγῶν] Th.8.89; = λοχαγός, Arr.*Tact.* 5.6; ἡ. τῶν ἐν προχειρισμῷ *PAmh.*2.39 (ii B.C.); *chief, sovereign*, Pi.*I.* 8(7).22, etc.; ἡ. γῆς τῆσδε S.*OT*103, cf. *OC*289; πάντων..καὶ αὐτοῦ βασιλέως ἡ. X.*HG*3.5.14; ἡ. συμμορίας D.21.157; of the *queen*-bee and *queen*-wasp, regarded by Arist. as males, Arist.*HA*553^{a}25, 629^{a}3 (but ἡ τῶν μελισσῶν ἡ. X.*Oec.*7.32, cf. 38); ὁ ἡ. τῶν προβάτων, of the bell-wether, Arist.*HA*573^{b}24; τῶν βοῶν ib.575^{b}1; νέμειν τὰ κρέα τοῦ ἡγεμόνος βοὸς *SIG*144.36 (Piraeus, iv B.C.), cf. X.*HG*6.4. 29. b. ἡ. χοροῦ *leader* of a chorus, Poll.4.106; παῖδες ἡ. *IG*7.3196 (Orchom. Boeot.); *president* of a gymnasium, ib.3.1086, al. c. *a Roman Emperor*, Str.4.3.2, Plu.*Cic.*2, al.; as translation of *princeps*, *Mon.Anc.Gr.*7.9; ἡ. νεότητος, = Lat. *princeps juventutis*, ib.18; *a provincial governor*, Str.17.3.25, *Ev.Matt.*27.2, *Act.Ap.*23.24: freq. of the *praefectus Aegypti*, *PRyl.*119.4 (i A.D.), etc.; ἡ. ἀμφοτέρων, i.e. of Upper and Lower Egypt, *POxy.*39.6 (i A.D.); ἡ. Κύπρου *Tab. Defix.Aud.*25.13 (iii A.D.). 2. as Adj., ἀνὴρ Pl.*Criti.*119a; [ναῦς], of the flagship, A.*Supp.*722; ἡ. τῆς φυλῆς κορυφαῖος D.21.60 (s.v.l.); ἡ. πόδες Arist.*HA*490^{b}5, *IA*713^{b}32: as neut., ἡγεμόσι μέρεσι Pl.*Ti.* 91e. III. in Prosody, = πυρρίχιος, D.H.*Comp.*17, *Dem.*47. IV. ἡγεμόνες, Dor. ἁγ-, αἱ, in Architecture, *coping-tiles* of the roof, *IG*2^2. 463.70, 1627.303, 4.1484.100 (Epid.). V. a kind of fish, = ἡγητήρ 2, Plu.2.980f.

ἡγέομαι, Dor. **ἁγ-** (irreg. pres. part. ἀγώμενος *Hymn.Curet.*4), impf. ἡγούμην Il.12.28, etc., Ion. -εύμην Hdt.2.115, ἡγέοντο Id.9.15: fut. ἡγήσομαι Il.14.374, etc.: aor. 1 ἡγησάμην Od.14.48, etc.: aor. 1 ἡγήθην in pass. sense, *PGiss.*48.20 (iii A.D.) (cf. περιηγ-): pf. ἥγημαι Hdt.1.126, 2.115, ἄγημαι Pi.*P.*4.248:—*go before, lead the way*, ὣς εἰπὼν ἡγεῖθ', ἡ δ' ἕσπετο Παλλὰς Ἀθήνη Od.1.125; ἂν παῖς ἡγήσαιτο νήπιος 6.300, etc.; πρόσθεν δὲ..Ἶρις ἡγεῖτ' Il.24.96; ἡγοῦ πάροιθε E. *Ph.*834; ἡ. ἐπὶ νῆα Od.13.65; ἐς τεῖχος Il.20.144; κλισίηνδε Od.14. 48, cf. Hdt.2.93, etc.; ἡγησόμενος οὐδεὶς ἔσται X.*An.*2.4.5: Astron., *precede* in the daily movement, Autol.2.3, al. b. c. dat. pers., Τρωσὶ ποτὶ πτόλιν ἡγήσασθαι Il.22.101; ἐκ Δουλιχίου..ἡγεῖτο μνηστῆρσι Od.16.397; οἱ γὰρ βλέποντες τοῖς τυφλοῖς ἡγούμεθα Ar.*Pl.*15; ἡ. τοῖς πολίταις πρὸς ἀρετήν X.*Ages.*10.2. c. with ὁδόν added, ὁδὸν ἡγήσασθαι *to go before* on the way, Od.10.263; ἡ. τινὶ τὴν ὁδόν Hdt.9.15. d. c. acc. loci, ἥ οἱ..πόλιν ἡγήσαιτο who *might guide* him to the city, Od.6.114, cf. 7.22, 15.82; ἡ. βωμοὺς ἀστικούς A.*Supp.*501. e. ἅρματα ἡ. *drive* chariots, Philostr.*Im.*2.23. f. of logical priority, *to be antecedent*, opp. ἕπεσθαι, *Stoic.*2.71,88, S.E. *M.*8.110, al., Dam.*Pr.*241, Phlp.*in GC*195.13, *in Ph.*496.14. g. ἡγούμενον, τό, the *leading principle*, the *main thing*, Ph.*Bel.*63.14, cf. Sosip.1.47. 2. c. dat. pers. et gen. rei, *to be* one's *leader in a* thing, θεῖος ἀοιδὸς..ἡμῖν ἡγείσθω..ὀρχηθμοῖο Od.23.134; ἡ. τινὶ σοφίας, ᾠδῆς, Pi.*P.* l.c., Pl.*Alc.*1.125d; ἀλήθεια δὴ πάντων μὲν ἀγαθῶν θεοῖς ἡγεῖται πάντων δὲ ἀνθρώποις Id.*Lg.*730c; ἡ. τοῦ χοροῦ Πέρσαις X.*Cyr.*8.7.1, cf. Call.*Del.*313: c. gen. rei, ἁ. νόμων *to lead* the song, Pi.*N.*5.25; φρόνησις ἡ. τοῦ ὀρθῶς πράττειν Pl.*Men.*97c; ἡ. παντὸς καὶ λόγου καὶ ἔργου X.*Mem.*2.3.15: also, τὸ ὀρθῶς τοῖς τοιούτοις χρῆσθαι ἐπιστήμη ἦν ἡγουμένη Pl.*Euthd.*281a. 3. c. dat. rei, *to be leader in..*, κερδοσύνῃ, νηπιέῃσι ἡ. τινί, Il.22.247, Od.24.469. 4. c. acc. rei, *lead, conduct*, ἡ. τὰς πομπάς D.21.174; τὴν ἀποδημίαν (v.l. for ἡτήσατο) Dinon 7; τὰς τύχας E.*Supp.*226: with adverbial acc., ἡ γλῶσσα πάνθ' ἡγουμένη S.*Ph.*99. 5. part. ἡγούμενος, η, ον, as Adj., σκέλη ἡγούμενα, opp. ἑπόμενα, the *front* legs, Arist.*IA*713^{b}6; ὁ ἡ. πούς the *advanced* foot, Id.*Fr.*74. II. *lead, command* in war, c. dat., νῆες θοαί, ᾗσιν Ἀχιλλεὺς ἐς Τροίην ἡγεῖτο Il.16.169, cf. Od.14.238; οὐ γὰρ ἔην ὅς τίς σφιν ἐπὶ στίχας ἡγήσαιτο *might lead* them to their ranks, Il.2.687; ἡ. Τρώεσσιν ἐς Ἴλιον 5.211; ἡ. Μῄοσιν 2.864; λόγχαισιν E.*Ba.*1360; ἑτέροις Lys. 31.17, cf. X.*An.*5.2.6; ἐν ταῖς στρατείαις, αἷς ἡγεῖται βασιλεὺς Isoc. 12.180: also generally, πόλει E.*Fr.*282.24; but usu. c. gen., Σαρπηδὼν δ' ἡγήσατ'..ἐπικούρων Il.12.101; ἡγήσατο λαῶν 15.311, cf. 2.567, al.; ἡ. τῆς ἐξόδου Th.2.10; ἡγούμενος τῶν ἡδονῶν ἀλλ' οὐκ ἀγόμενος ὑπ' αὐτῶν Isoc.9.45: abs., *to be in command*, Id.16.21, etc. 2. *rule, have dominion*, c. gen., τῆς Ἀσίης, τῆς συμμαχίης, Hdt.1.95, 7.148; οἱ Θεσσαλίης ἡγεόμενοι Id.9.1: abs., οἱ ἡγούμενοι *the rulers*, S. *Ph.*386, cf. A.*Ag.*1363; ἡ. ἐν τοῖς ἀδελφοῖς *leading men*, *Act.Ap.* 15.22; ἡ. σχολῆς *to be the head* of a philosophical school, Phld.*Acad. Ind.*p.107 M., al. 3. as official title, ἡγούμενος, ὁ, *president*, συνόδου *PGrenf.*2.67.3 (iii A.D.); γερδίων ib.43.9 (i A.D.); ἱερέων *PLond.* 2.281.2 (i A.D.): abs., *PFay.*110.26 (i A.D.). b. of Roman governors, ἡ. ἔθνους, = Lat. *praeses provinciae*, *POxy.*1020.5 (ii/iii A.D.); ἡ. τῆς Γαλατίας Luc.*Alex.*44. c. of subordinate *officials*, ἡ. τοῦ στρατηγοῦ *POxy.*294.19 (i A.D.); κώμης *PRyl.*125.3 (i A.D.). d. *abbot*, Just.*Nov.*7.1, al.: fem. -μένη *abbess*, ibid. 4. ἡγούμενος as Adj., *principal*, πυλών *PFlor.*382.15 (iii A.D.), *POxy.*55.9 (iii A.D.). III. post-Hom., *believe, hold*, Hdt. (usu. in pf. ἥγημαι, 3 pl. ἡγέαται), etc.; ἡ. τι εἶναι Id.1.126, al.; ἡγεῖσθε δὲ [θεοὺς] βλέπειν... πρὸς τὸν εὐσεβῆ βροτῶν S.*OC*278, cf. Th.2.89, Ar.*Nu.*1020 (lyr.), etc. 2. with an attributive word added, ἡ. τινὰ βασιλέα *hold* or *regard* as king, Hdt.6.52; μηδ' αὐθαδίαν εὐβουλίας ἀμείνον' ἡγήσῃ ποτέ A.*Pr.*1035; ἅπαντας ἐχθροὺς τῶν θεῶν ἡγοῦ πλέον Id.*Ch.*902, cf. 905; ἡ.τἆλλα πάντα δεύτερα *to hold* everything else secondary, S.*Ph.*1442; οὐκ αἰσχρὸν ἡγῇ..τὰ ψευδῆ λέγειν; ib.108, cf. *Ant.*1167; τὰς τούτων ἀπορίας ἀντιπάλους ἡ. τῷ ἡμετέρῳ πλήθει Th.4.10; περὶ πολλοῦ ἥγημαι μὴ ξεινοκτονέειν Hdt.2.115; περὶ πλείονος Isoc.19.10; περὶ πλείστου Th.2.89; περὶ οὐδενός Lys.7.26; παρ' οὐδέν Decr.ap.D.18.164: c. part., πᾶν κέρδος ἡγοῦ ζημιουμένη φυγῇ E.*Med.*454. 3. esp. of belief in gods, τὴν μεγίστην δαίμονα ἥγηνται εἶναι Hdt.2.40, cf. 3.8; ἡ. θεοὺς *to believe in* gods, Ar.*Eq.*32, E.*Hec.*800, *Ba.*1326; δαίμονας ἡ. Pl.*Ap.*27d. 4. ἡγοῦμαι δεῖν *think* fit, *deem* necessary, c. inf., And.1.23, D.1.20: without δεῖν, παθεῖν μᾶλλον ἡγησάμενοι ἤ.. Th.2. 42 (s.v.l.); ἡγησάμην διατάγματι αὐτοὺς σωφρονίσαι *Inscr.Magn.*114 (ii A.D.); ἡγήσατο ἐπαινέσαι Pl.*Prt.*346b. IV. pf. in pass. sense, τὰ ἀγημένα, = τὰ νομιζόμενα, Orac.ap.D.43.66; ἡγεόμενον *being led*, Hdt.3.14 (ἀγόμενον Dind.): hence act. form ἡγέω, Hdn.Gr.2.950. (*săg-*, cf. Lat. *praesagio*.)

ἠγερέθομαι, Ep. form of ἀγείρομαι (Pass.) *gather together, assemble*, only 3 pl. pres. and impf., and inf., ἀμφὶ δέ μιν..ἀγοὶ ἠγερέθονται Il. 3.231, cf. *h.Ap.*147; ἀμφ' Ἀτρεΐωνα ἀολλέες ἠγερέθοντο Il.23.233; περὶ δ' ἔσθλοὶ ἑταῖροι ἀθρόοι ἠγερέθοντο Od.2.392; ἀμφ' αἷμα..ἀολλέες ἠγερέθοντο 11.228; σφιν ἐπέφραδον ἠγερέθεσθαι Il.10.127 Aristarch. (ἠγερέεσθαι codd.): subj. ἠγερέθωνται Opp.*H.*3.360.

ἤγερθεν, Ep. 3 pl. aor. 1 Pass. of ἀγείρω.

ἡγεσία, ἡ, (ἡγέομαι) = ἥγησις, Hsch. (ἡγεσκίης· ὁδηγησίας cod.).

ἡγεσίλαος, ἡγησίλεως [ῐ], v. ἀγησίλαος.

ἡγέτης, ου, ὁ, Dor. **ἁγ-** (**ἀγ-**), (ἡγέομαι) *leader*, voc. ἡγέτα ὁδοῖο *Epigr.Gr.*1035.13 (Pergam.); ἀγέτα κώμων Orph.*H.*52.7 codd.; ἁ. θηροσύνας *AP*6.167 (Agath.):—fem. **ἀγέτις**, ιδος, ib.7.425 (Antip.Sid.).

ἡγηλάζω, Ep. collat. form of ἡγέομαι, *guide, lead*, κακὸς κακὸν ἡγηλάζει Od.17.217; but κακὸν μόρον ἡ. *lead* a wretched life, 11. 618; βίοτον βαρὺν ib. A.R.1.272; ἱερὸν γόον Orac.ap.Zos.1.57: for Arat.893, v. ὑφηνηλάζω.

ἡγηλᾰτέω, prob. f.l. for ἀγ-, Them.*Or.*4.56c.

ἥγ-ημα, ατος, τό, *that which guides*, *Inscr.Perg.*246.27. II. (ἡγέομαι III) *thought, purpose*, Lxx *Ez.*17.3. -ησίπολις [σῐ], εως, ὁ, *leader of the state*, D.L.2.131. -ησις, εως, ἡ, *command*, Lxx *Jd.*5.15 (v.l.), 1*Ma.*9.31. -ήτειρα, ἡ, fem. of ἡγητήρ, Pl.*Epigr.*5.7, Opp.

*C.*1.253. **-ητέον,** *one must lead*, X.*HG*4.7.2, *Eq.Mag.*4.3. II. *one must hold, consider*, Pl.*R.*361a, Plb.1.35.9, Hierocl.p.63A., etc. **-ητήρ,** Dor. **ἁγ-,** ῆρος, ὁ, = ἡγητής, *a guide*, S.*OC*1521; σοφίης ἑὸν ἡγητῆρα his *guide* to philosophy, *IG*3.947. 2. the *pilot-fish*, Opp.*H.*5.70. 3. = ἡγήτωρ, *a leader*, ἁ. ἀνήρ Pi.*P.*1.69. **-ητηρία** (sc. παλάθη), ἡ, *mass of dried figs, borne in procession at the Attic* Πλυντήρια, in memory of the discovery of this food, *which was considered the first step in civilized life*, Ath.3.74d, Porph.*Abst.*2.7, Hsch., Phot.: **-ητορία,** *EM*418.49: **-ήτρια,** Eust. 1399.29. **-ητής,** οῦ, ὁ, = ἡγητήρ, *a guide*, νόσφιν ἡγητῶν A.*Supp.*239. **-ητικός,** Dor. **ἁγ-,** ή, όν, = ἡγεμονικός, *authoritative, leading*, τοὔνομ' οὐχ ἁ. *Com.Adesp.*in *Gött.Nachr.*1922.28; opp. ἀπορητικός, Procl.*in Prm.*p.483S.; dub. sens. in Vett.Val.15.16. **-ήτωρ** (Dor. **ἁγ-** Ibyc.*Oxy.*2081(*f*)*Fr.*4), ορος, ὁ, *leader, commander, chief*, Τρώων, φυλάκων, Il.3.153, 10.181; ἡγήτορες ἠδὲ μέδοντες *chiefs in war* and leaders in council, 2.79, etc.; ἡ. ὀνείρων, of Hermes, *h.Merc.*14. II. title of chief priest of Aphrodite in Cyprus, *BMus.Inscr.*975.10 (Amathus), cf. Hsch. s.v. ἀγήτωρ.

ἡγιασμένως, Adv. pf. Pass., (ἁγιάζω) *in holy manner*, Al.*Ps.*133 (134).2.

ἡγμένως, Adv. pf. Pass., (ἄγω) *reasonably*, Suid. (prob. l.).

ἡγνευμένως, Adv. pf. Pass., (ἁγνεύω) *purely*, Poll.1.32.

ἡγόν (ἦγον cod.)· κατεαγός, Hsch.; cf. ἠγαλέος.

ἠγορόωντο, Ep. and Ion. lengthd. for ἠγορῶντο, v. ἀγοράομαι.

ἡγός, ὁ, = ἡγεμών, *EM*390.36; = εὐδαίμων (Ionic), ib.37.

ἡγούμενος, ὁ, v. ἡγέομαι II. 3.

ἤγουν, Conj., (ἤ γε οὖν) *that is to say, or rather*, to define a word more correctly, freq. in glosses, cf. Eust.50.15, Lyd.*Mens.*4.23, etc.: sts. introduced into the text, κακὰ πάντα [ἤγουν τήν τε ἀπεψίην] καί.. Hp.*Acut.*(*Sp.*)49 (ii 491 L.); διὰ ξηρότητα [ἤγουν χαυνότητα] τῆς γῆς X.*Oec.*19.11: in late Prose, *or at any rate*, *PMasp.*328 i 20 (vi A.D.), al.: generally, *or*, *POxy.*941.5 (vi A.D.).

ἡδᾰνός, ή, όν, = ἡδύς, etym. of ἑδανός, Eust.974.53.

ἠδέ, *and*, prop. correlative to ἠμέν: ἠμὲν.., ἠδὲ.., *both.., and..*, Il.7.302, etc. II. without ἠμέν, *and*, ἡγήτορες ἠδὲ μέδοντες 2.79, cf. 1.41,96,251, etc.: sts. with τε before it, σκῆπτρόν τ' ἠδὲ θέμιστας 9.99; Ἕκτορ τ' ἠδ' ἄλλοι 12.61; Ἥρη τ' ἠδὲ Ποσειδάων καὶ Παλλὰς Ἀθήνη 1.400; αὐτός τ' ἀναχάζομαι ἠδὲ.. 5.822, cf. Pi.*O.*13.44; also μὲν.., ἠδὲ.. Od.1.240, 12.381, etc.; μέν τε.., ἠδὲ.. Orph.*H.*14.9; παίδων ἠδ' ἀλόχων καὶ κτήσιος ἠδὲ τοκήων Il.15.663; ἠ. καί *and* also, 1.334, Od.2.209, 4.235, 1.240; ἠδ' ἔτι καί Il.1.455, 2.118; ἠδέ τε *AP*9.788.9.—The Trag. use ἠ. in anapaestics and lyrics, A.*Pers.*16, 289, etc.; and (less freq.) in iamb., as Id.*Ch.*1025, *Eu.*414, S.*Fr.*386, 549, E.*Hec.*323, *HF*30: twice found in Com., Eup.14 (anap.), Alex.133.6 (trim., s.v.l.). Not in Att. Prose; used by Hp. (= ἔτι δέ) acc. to Gal.19.102, cf. Aret.*CD*2.7; ἀτὰρ ἠδέ ib.1.3.

ᾔδεα, ᾔδειν, v. *εἴδω.

ἠδελφισμένως, Adv. pf. Pass., prop. *with brotherly likeness*: metaph., ἠ. ἐν γαστρὶ ἐχούσῃ *just as if..*, Hp.*Mul.*1.3: abs., *in like manner*, ib.2.205.

ἡδέως, Adv. of ἡδύς, v. ἡδύς III.

ἤδη, Adv.: 1. *already, by this time*, νὺξ ἤ. τελέθει 'tis *already* night, Il.7.282; ἤ. Τρώεσσιν ὀλέθρου πείρατ' ἐφῆπται ib.402: with numerals, ἤ. γὰρ τρίτον ἐστὶν ἔτος Od.2.89; τρίτην ἤ. ἡμέραν Pl.*Prt.*309d; ἔτος τόδ' ἤ. δέκατον S.*Ph.*312; ἦν δ' ἦμαρ ἤ. δεύτερον ib.354; τελοῦντες ἕκτον ἕβδομόν τ' ἤ. δρόμον Id.*El.*726; ἤ. γὰρ πολὺς ἐκτέταται χρόνος Id.*Aj.*1402. 2. *forthwith, immediately*, φρονέω δὲ διακρινθήμεναι ἤ. Ἀργείους καὶ Τρῶας Il.3.98; λέξον νῦν με τάχιστα, ὄφρα καὶ ἤδη.. ταρπώμεθα κοιμηθέντες Il.24.635, cf. Od.4.294; ἤ. νῦν.. μεγάλ' εὔχεο Il.16.844; στείχοις ἂν ἤ. S.*Tr.*624; ἤδη.. στέλλεσθε; Id.*Ph.*466; μετὰ τοῦτ' ἤ. Ar.*Th.*655; ἤ. ποτέ *now at length*, Mitteis *Chr.*87.8 (ii A.D.); on the verso of a letter, *urgent, immediate*, *PCair.Zen.*154 (iii B.C.); ἤ. ἤ. ταχὺ ταχύ *PMag.Osl.*1.319. 3. opp. to the future or past, *actually, now*, οὐκ ὄναρ, ἀλλ' ὕπαρ ἤ. Od.20.90; τοῖς μὲν γὰρ ἤ., τοῖς δ' ἐν ὑστέρῳ χρόνῳ S.*OC*614; οἱ μὲν τάχ', οἱ δ' ἐσαῦθις, οἱ δ' ἤ. E.*Supp.*551; οὐ τάχ', ἀλλ' ἤ. Ar.*Ra.*527; ἡ ἤ. χάρις *present* favour, D.23.134; τὸ ἤ. κολάζειν X.*An.*7.7.24. 4. of logical proximity, ἤ. γὰρ ἂν προστίθεσθαι Pl.*Tht.*201e; τὰ ἐκ τούτων ἤ. συγκείμενα ib.202b; πᾶς ἤ. ἂν εὕροι Id.*R.*398c; ἂν σὺ ὁμολογήσῃς, ταῦτ' ἤ. ἐστὶν αὐτὰ τἀληθῆ Id.*Grg.*486e; τοῦτο τοὔπος δεινὸν ἤ. Ar.*Ach.*315; τὰ πάντα τὰ πράγματα διαφθείραντα ταῦτ' ἐστὶν ἤ. D.19.19. b. καὶ ἤ. and *further, as well*, ἐμέ τε καὶ σὲ καὶ τἆλλ' ἤ. Pl.*Tht.*159b, cf. S.E.*P.*1.53,219, etc. c. *for instance*, Aen.Tact.4.1, 10.25. d. *only then, then and not before*, τότ' ἤδη A.*Pr.*911, Isoc.12.25, *Ep.*6.9; ἐνταῦθ' ἤ. Aeschin.3.140; κακοπαθοῦντες ἤ. τῶν λόγων ἅπτονται Th.1.78. 5. with Sup., ὦ πάντων ἀνδρῶν ἤ. μάλιστα.. κτησάμενε *up to this time*, Hdt.8.106; μέγιστος ἤ. διάπλους Th.6.31: with Comp., ἤδη.. λόγου μέζων Hdt.2.148. II. joined with other words of time, ἤ. νῦν *now already*, Il.1.456, A.*Ag.*1578; νῦν ἤ. Od.23.54, S.*Ant.*801 (anap.); ἤ. ποτέ Il.1.260, S.*Aj.*1142, Ar.*Nu.*346; ποτ' ἤ. A.*Eu.*50; ἤ. πώποτε Eup.214, Pl.*R.*493d; πάλαι ἤ. S.*OC*510 (lyr.); ἤ. τότε *even then*, Pl.*R.*417b; ἐπεὶ ἤ. Od.4.260; εἰ ἤ. Il.22.52; τὸ τηνίκ' ἤ. S.*OC*440; τὸ λοιπὸν ἤ. Id.*Ph.*454; ἄλλοτε ἤ. πολλάκις Pl.*R.*507a; ἤ. γε even *now*, D.19.52. III. of place, ἀπὸ ταύτης ἤ. Αἴγυπτος after this Egypt begins, Hdt.3.5, cf. 2.15, 4.99, E.*Hipp.*1200; Φωκεῦσιν ἤ. ὅμορος ἡ Βοιωτία ἐστίν Th.3.95. (In general, cf. Arist.*Ph.*$222^{b}7$.)

ᾔδη, ᾔδης, ᾔδησθα, v. *εἴδω. **ἥδιστος, ἡδίων,** Sup. and Comp. of ἡδύς.

ἥδομαι, Boeot. **ϝᾱδ-** [ᾱ] Corinn. in *BKT*5(2).34, Dor. **ἅδ-** [ᾱ], Aeol. **ἄδ-** [ᾱ] Sapph.*Supp.*24.10: fut. ἡσθήσομαι S.*OT*453, Pl.*Phdr.*233e, etc.: aor. 1 ἥσθην (post-Homeric, v. infr.), also ἡδέσθην (sic) Hsch., Med. ἡσάμην Od.9.353: (*swād-*, cf. ἁνδάνω, ἡδύς):—*enjoy oneself, take one's pleasure*, once in Hom., Od. l. c.; freq. in Hdt. and Att.:—Constr.: 1. with part., ἥσατο πίνων Od. l. c.; ἥσθη ἀκούσας he *was glad* to have heard, Hdt.3.34; ἥδοι' ἂν.. ἰδοῦσα A.*Pr.*758, cf. S.*Ph.*882; δρῶντες ἂν ἡδώμεθα (sc. δρῶντες) Id.*Aj.*1085; οἶ' ἂν.. ἡσθείη λαβών Id.*El.*1325; ἡ. θωπευομένους Ar.*Ach.*635, etc. 2. c. dat., ἥδεσθαί τινι *to delight in* or *at* a thing or person, Hdt.1.69, al., Th.1.120, etc.; ἅπαντες ἡδόμεσθά σοι Ar.*Eq.*623 (lyr.): in aor., ironically, ἥσθην ἀπειλαῖς I *am amused* at your threats, ib.696, cf. *Nu.*174: once c. gen., πώματος ἥσθη he *enjoyed* the draught, S.*Ph.*715 (lyr.). 3. c. acc. and part., ἥσθην πατέρα τὸν ἀμὸν εὐλογοῦντά σε I *am pleased to hear* you praising him, ib.1314; δόμους ἥδεται πληρουμένους E.*Fr.*328.1. 4. with neut. Adj., ἕτερον ἥσθην Ar.*Ach.*13; τοῦθ' ἥδομαι Id.*Ra.*748 (cod. R); ἥσθην βαιά Id.*Ach.*2; βραχέα ἡσθεῖσα Th.3.40: c. acc. cogn., ἡδονὰς ἥδεσθαι Pl.*Phlb.*63a, etc. 5. folld. by a Prep., ἥδεσθαι ἐπί τινι X.*Cyr.*8.4.11, Pl.*Phlb.*48b, etc.; ὑπέρ τινος Lys.2.26; but πρὸς ὀλίγον ἡσθεὶς ναυτιᾷ for a little time, Arr.*Epict.*4.9.4. 6. ἥδομαι ὅτι... Ar.*Nu.*773. 7. abs., ὡς ἥδομαι καὶ χαίρομαι κεὐφραίνομαι Ar.*Pax* 291, cf. Plu.2.449a, etc.; esp. in part., as Adj., *glad, delighted* ἡδομένᾳ ψυχᾷ, φωνᾷ, E.*Fr.*754 (lyr.), Ar.*Av.*236 (lyr.); τὸ ἡδόμενον Plu.2.1025e, 1101f: freq. in dat., ἡδομένοισι ἦν τὸ γινόμενον they were *pleased at..*, Hdt.8.10, cf. 9.46; ἐὰν ὑμῖν ἡδομένοις (sc. ᾖ) Antipho 6.8, cf. Pl.*Phd.*78b, *La.*187c; τὸ ἡδόμενον κατὰ σάρκα Epicur.*Sent.*4. II. Act., ἥδω *please, delight*, c. acc. pers., aor., ἧσε Anacr.148: so later pres., ἥδει Muson.*Fr.*18B p.103 H.; ἥδομεν Men.*Mon.*38: aor. 1 ἧσα Ephipp.6.5 (s.v.l.), Ael.*NA*10.48, Hld.10.32, *AP*7 lemma (λαλῆσαι f.l. for ἀλλ' ἧσαι); τὰ ἥδοντα *joys, pleasures*, opp. τὰ λυποῦντα, Antipho Soph.*Oxy.*1364.116, cf. Pl.*Ax.*366a, Diog.Oen.29; τὸ ἧδον S.E.*M.*7.203.

ἡδομένως, Adv. of foreg., *with joy, gladly*. πράττειν τι X.*Cyr.*8.4.9.

ἡδονή, Dor. **ἁδονά** (or in Trag. chorus **ἡδονά** S.*OT*1339), ἡ, (ἥδομαι) *enjoyment, pleasure*, first in Simon.71, S. l. c., Hdt.1.24, al.; prop. of sensual pleasures, αἱ τοῦ σώματος or περὶ τὸ σῶμα ἡ., X.*HG*4.8.22, 6.1.4; αἱ κατὰ τὸ σῶμα ἡ. Pl.*R.*328d; σωματικαὶ ἡ. Arist.*EN*$1151^{a}13$; αἱ περὶ πότους καὶ περὶ ἐδωδὰς ἡ. Pl.*R.*389e; but also ἀκοῆς ἡ. Th.3.38; ἡ ἀπὸ τοῦ εἰδέναι ἡ. Pl.*R.*582b; of *malicious pleasure*, ἡ ἐπὶ τοῖς τῶν φίλων κακοῖς, ἐπὶ ταῖς λοιδορίαις ἡ., Id.*Phlb.*50a, D.18.138; ἡδονῇ ἡσσᾶσθαι, ἡδοναῖς χαρίζεσθαι, to give way *to pleasure*, Th. l.c., Pl.*Lg.*727c; κότερα ἀληθείῃ χρήσομαι ἢ ἡδονῇ; shall I speak truly or *so as to humour you?* Hdt.7.101; εἰ ὑμῖν ἡδονὴ τοῦ ἡγεμονεύειν ib.160; ἡ. εἰσέρχεταί τινι εἰ.. one feels *pleasure* at the thought that.., Id.1.24; ἡδονὴν ἔχειν τινός to be *satisfied with..*, S.*OC*1604; ἡδονὴν ἔχει, φέρει, Pherecr.145.2, Alex.263.6; ἡδονὴ ἰδέσθαι (like θαῦμα ἰδέσθαι), of a temple, Hdt.2.137: with Preps. in Adv. sense, δαίμοσιν πρὸς ἡδονήν A.*Pr.*494; ὃ μέν ἐστι πρὸς ἡ. D.18.4; πρὸς ἡ. λέγειν to speak so *as to please another*, S.*El.*921, Th.2.65; δημηγορεῖν D.4.38; οὐ πρὸς ἡ. οἱ ἦν τὰ ἀγγελλόμενα Hdt.3.126; πάντα πρὸς ἡ. ἀκούοντας D.8.34; later πρὸς ἡδονῆς εἶναί τινι Parth.8.8, Lib.*Or.*12.1; καθ' ἡδονὴν κλύειν S.*Tr.*197; καθ' ἡδονήν [ἐστί] μοι c. inf., A.*Pr.*263; καθ' ἡ. τι δρᾶν, ποιεῖν, Th.2.37,53; καθ' ἡδονὰς τῷ δήμῳ τὰ πράγματα ἐνδιδόναι ib.65; ἐν ἡδονῇ ἐστί τινι it is *a pleasure* or *delight* to another, Hdt.4.139; folld. by inf., E.*IT*494; by acc. et inf., Hdt.7.15; ἐν ἡδονῇ ἔχειν τινάς to take *pleasure* in them, Th.3.9; ἐν ἡδονῇ ἄρχοντες, opp. οἱ λυπηροί, Id.1.99; μεθ' ἡδονῆς Id.4.19; ὑφ' ἡδονῆς S.*Ant.*648, etc.; ὑπὸ τῆς ἡ. Alex.24, 110.23: as dat. modi, ἡδονᾷ *with pleasure*, S.*OT*1339 (lyr.), cf. Hdt.2.137 (f.l.). 2. concrete, *a pleasure*, S.*El.*873 (pl.), Ar.*Nu.*1072 (pl.); ἡδοναὶ τραγημάτων *sweetmeats*, Sopat.17. 3. pl., *desires after pleasure, pleasant lusts*, X.*Mem.*1.2.23, *Ep.Tit.*3.3, al. II. in Ion. Philosophers, *taste, flavour*, usu. joined with χροιή, Diog.Apoll.5, Anaxag.4 (pl.), cf. Arist.*PA*$660^{b}9$, Thphr.*HP*4.4.7, Lxx *Nu.*11.8, Eudem.ap.Ath.9.369f, Mnesith.ap.eund.8.357f.

ἡδονικός, ή, όν, *of* or *for* ἡδονή, *pleasurable*, Chrysipp.Tyan.ap.Ath.14.647d; βίος ἡ. Arist.ap.D.L.5.31. II. οἱ ἡ. the *voluptuaries*, of the Cyrenaic school of philosophers, Ceb.13, Ath.13.588a; ἡ ἡ. αἵρεσις Gal.*Libr.Propr.*16; ἐπὶ σωφροσύνης οὐχὶ ἡ. λέγεται ὁ ὑπερβάλλων ἀλλ' ἀκόλαστος Asp.*in EN*53.19. Adv. **-κῶς** Procl.*in Prm.*p.521S.

ἡδονο-κρᾰσία, ἡ, *rule of pleasure*, Aristeas 278. **-πληκτος,** Dor. **ἁδονόπλακτος,** ον, *pleasure-struck*, Cerc.6.10:—also **-πλήξ,** ῆγος, ὁ, ἡ, φύσις Timo 58.4.

ἧδος, εος, τό (Aeolic, acc. to Hdn.Gr.2.904), *delight, pleasure*, οὐδέ τι δαιτὸς ἐσθλῆς ἔσσεται ἦ. Il.1.576; ἀλλὰ μίνυνθα ἡμέων ἔσσεται ἦ. 11.318; ἀλλὰ τί μοι τῶν ἦ.; what *delight* have I therefrom? 18.80; αὐτὰρ ἐμοὶ τί τόδ' ἦ.; Od.24.95, cf. Theoc.16.40, A.R.3.314.—In this sense almost confined to Ep. and nom. sg.; in late Prose, πρὸς τὸ ἦ. Alex.Aphr.*Pr.*1.20. II. = ὄξος, *vinegar*, used as a flavouring, τοῦτο μόνον Ἀττικοὶ τῶν ἡδυσμάτων ἦ. καλοῦσι Ath.2.67c, cf. Poll.6.65, Eust.1417.19, prob. l. in Antiph.134.4:—Dor. form **ἆδος** (in both senses), *EM*18.12, Hsch. s.v. γᾶδος.

ἦ δ' ὅς, for ἔφη ἐκεῖνος, v. ἠμί.

ἡδοσύνη, ἡ, = ἡδονή, Dor. **ἁδοσύνᾱ,** Hsch.

ἡδύ-βῐος [ῠ], ον, *sweetening life*: τὰ ἡ. a name of certain *cakes*, Chrysipp.Tyan.ap.Ath.14.647c. II. *living pleasantly*, Ptol.*Tetr.*162, Vett.Val.18.29, Sch.Ar.*V.*504. **-βόης,** Dor. **ἁδῠβόας,** ου, ὁ, *sweet-sounding*, ἁδυβόᾳ.. αὐλῶν πνεύματι E.*Ba.*127; ἡ. κόσσυφος *AP*9.396 (Paul. Sil.); δόναξ *APl.*4.231 (Anyte). **-γαιον,** τό, = σίκυον, Heraclid.Tarent.ap.Ath.2.74b(ἡδυνέον isf. l. in Hsch.). -γἄμος, ον, *sweetening marriage*, κέρδος *AP*5.242 (Maced.). -γελως, ωτος, ὁ, ἡ, *sweetly laughing*, *h.Hom.*19.37, *AP*5.134. -γλωσσία, ἡ, *sweetness of tongue*, *PMag.Leid.V.*20. -γλωσσος, Dor. ἁδ-, ον, *sweet-tongued*, βοά Pi.*O*.13.100. -γνώμων, ον, gen. ονος, (γνώμη) *of pleasant mind*, opp. ἡδυσώματος, X.*Smp*.8.30. -δειπνος, ον, *dainty-supping*, name of a parasite, Alciphr.3.68 tit. -επής, Dor. ἁδ-, ές, *sweet-speaking*, Il.1.248; Ὅμηρος Pi.*N*.7.21, cf. *AP*9.525.8, etc.; *sweet-sounding*, λύρα Pi.*O*.10(11).93; ὕμνος Id.*N*.1.4: voc., ὦ Διὸς ἁδυεπὲς φάτι S.*OT*151: poet. fem. pl., ἡδυέπειαι Μοῦσαι Ὀλυμπιάδες Hes.*Th*.965, 1021: sg., -έπεια σῦριγξ Nonn.*D*.10.390. -θροος, ον, contr. -θρους, ουν, *sweet-strained*, Μοῦσα E.*El*.703 (lyr.); Διόνυσος *AP*9.524.8: Dor. ἁδ-, κίθαρις *Pae.Delph*.13. -καρπος, ον, *with sweet fruit*, Pherecyd.178 J.; δένδρον Thphr.*HP*4.4.5. -κρεως, ων, gen. ω, *of sweet flesh*, Arist.*HA*564^{a}3, al.: Comp. -κρεώτερος Id. *GA*786^{a}15. -κωμος, ὁ, name of a kind of αὔλησις, Trypho ap. Ath.14.618c; of a dance, Poll.4.100. -λάλος [ἄ], ον, = ἡδυλόγος, φθόγγοι *IG*12(7).95.4 (Amorgos).

Ἡδύλειος [ῡ], α, ον, *of* or *connected with Hedylus*, κύλιξ *IG*11(2).154 *B*50 (Delos, iii B.C.).

ἡδῠλ-ίζω, (ἥδυλος) *flatter, wheedle*, Men.28. -ισμός, ὁ, *flattering*, Eust.1417.21, Phot.

ἡδῠλογ-έω, *speak sweet things*, τινι Phryn.Com.3.4. -ία, ἡ, *jesting*, in pl., Ath.4.164e. -ος, Dor. ἁδ-, Aeol. ἀδ-, ον, *sweet-speaking, sweet-voiced*, Sapph.*Oxy*.1787 *Fr*.11.4; σοφία Cratin.238, Timo 67.4; λύραι μολπαί τε Pi.*O*.6.96; Χάρις *AP*5.136 (Mel.); γλῶσσα ib.7.159 (Nicarch.). 2. of persons, *flattering, fawning*, E.*Hec*.132 (anap.): as Subst., *jester*, Ath.4.165b. (In signf. 1 proparox., in 2 parox.)

ἥδῠλος [ῠ], η, ον, Dim. of ἡδύς, only as pr. n. (exc. A.D.*Adv*.172.1, *EM*742.52).

ἡδῠ-λύρης [ῠ], ου, ὁ, *singing sweetly to the lyre*, Πίνδαρος *AP*11.370 (Maced.): Dor. ἁδυλύρας, epith. of Apollo, *Philol*.71.6 (Argos, iv B.C.). -μᾰνής, ές, *full of sweet frenzy*, Nonn.*D*.7.269. -μέλεια, ἡ, *sweetness of melody*, Vett.Val.3.20 (pl.). -μελής, Dor. ἁδ-, Aeol. ἀδ-, ές, *sweet-singing*, χελιδοῖ Anacr.67, cf. Sapph.122 (Comp.), Pi.*N*.2.25; *sweet-sounding*, ξόανα S.*Fr*.238, etc.: poet. fem., ἡδυμέλεια σῦριγξ Nonn.*D*.29.287. -μελι, = μελισσόφυλλον, prob. in Ps.-Dsc.3.104. -μελίφθογγος, ον, *of honey-sweet voice*, Σιμωνίδης *AP*9.571 (acc. to Planudes). -μῑγής, Dor. ἁδ-, ές, *sweetly-mixed*, χόνδρος ib.7.736 (Leon.).

ἥδῠμος, Dor. ἅδ- ον, poet. for ἡδύς, *sweet, pleasant*, usu. epith. of sleep (v. νήδυμος, for which it is v.l. in Il.2.2, Od.4.793, 12.311, cf. Hsch. s.v. νήδυμος), *h.Merc*.241, 449, Antim.74, Simon.79, A.R.2.407; λόγοι Epich.179; οἶνος Orph.*Fr*.261: irreg. Sup. -έστατος Alcm.137.

ἡδυν-τέον, *one must season*, Alex.186.4. -τήρ, ῆρος, ὁ, *seasoning*, ἅλες Eratosth.ap.Hsch., Poll.6.71. -τήριος, α, ον, *sweetening, soothing*, Sch.E.*Hec*.535. -τικός, ή, όν, *fit for seasoning*, Arist.*Pr*.923^{a}29. II. -κή τέχνη *an art of seasoning*, Pl.*Sph*.223a. -τός, ή, όν, *seasoned*, πίσσα, στέαρ, Hp.*Mul*.1.88, 2.205. -ω, aor. 1 ἥδυνα Pl.*Tht*.175e, Diph.24:—Pass., aor. 1 ἡδύνθην Antiph.90: pf. ἥδυσμαι Pl. (v. infr.), inf. ἡδύνθαι Phot.: (ἡδύς):—*season* a dish, c. acc., [κόκκυγας] Epich.164; ὄψον Pl.*Tht*. l. c.; κρόμμυον . . οὐ μόνον σῖτον ἀλλὰ καὶ ποτὸν ἡδύνει X.*Smp*.4.8; *make pleasant*, γεῦσιν, οἴνους, Thphr.*Od*.9,10; even of salt (cf. ἡδονή II), Arist.*Mete*.359^{a}34. II. metaph., ἡ. θῶπας λόγους Pl.*Tht*. l. c.; ὁ ποιητὴς ἡ. τὸ ἄτοπον Arist.*Po*.1460^{b}2:—Pass., τὴν ἡδυσμένην μοῦσαν παραδέξῃ ἐν μέλεσιν Pl.*R*.607a, cf. Arist.*Po*.1449^{b}28, *Pol*.1340^{b}17, D.H.*Comp*.25; τοὺς λόγους ἡδύνεσθαι ἄν τι ὑπὸ τῶν φθόγγων X.*Smp*.6.4. 2. *delight, coax, gratify*, κόλαξ ἡδυνέ τινα λόγῳ Diph.24; ἡ. τὴν ἀκοήν D.H.*Comp*.14:—Pass., Timo 17.

ἡδῠ-οδμος [ῠ], Dor. ἁδ-, ον, = ἡδύοσμος, οἶνος Hp.*Mul*.1.34; ἔαρ Simon.74. -οινία, ἡ, *sweetness of wine*, Hp.*Morb*.4.34, *Gp*.5.2.19. -οινος, Dor. ἁδ-, ον, *producing sweet wine*, ἄμπελοι X.*An*.6.4.6; -ότερος καρπός Thphr.*CP*3.15.1. 2. *containing sweet wine*, λεπαστά Apolloph.6. II. ἡδύοινοι, οἱ, *dealers in sweet wine*, X.*Vect*.5.3. -όνειρος, ον, *causing sweet dreams*, ἰσχάδες Hermipp.63.16. -οσμος, ον, *sweet-smelling, fragrant*, στρώματα Ar.*Fr*.695. II. **ἡδύοσμον**, τό, = μίνθη, *green mint*, *Mentha viridis*, Thphr.*HP*7.7.1, Str.8.3.14; ἡ. ἄγριον *wild mint*, *M. longifolia*, Dsc.3.34. [As trisyll., *AP*11.413 (Ammian.).] -όφθαλμος, ον, *sweet-eyed*, Hsch. s. v. μελίγληνος.

ἡδῠπάθ-εια [πᾰ], ἡ, *pleasant living, luxury*, X.*Cyr*.7.5.74, Hp.*Ep*.17, Plu.2.6b, al., Sor.1.34, Luc.*DMort*.10.8: in pl., Ath.4.165e, Just.*Nov*.105.1; title of work by Archestratus, Ath.1.4e. -έω, *live pleasantly, enjoy oneself*, X.*Cyr*.1.5.1, Jul.*Mis*.342b; ἡ. ἀπό τινος X.*Oec*.5.2. -ημα, ατος, τό, *enjoyment*, σαρκός *AP*9.496 ((Ath.)). -ής, ές, (παθεῖν) *living pleasantly, enjoying oneself, luxurious*, Antiph.91, Aristox.*Fr.Hist*.15.

ἡδῠ-πνευστος, ον, = ἡδύπνοος, *AP*5.117 (Marc. Arg.). -πνοΐς, ΐδος, ἡ, *ox-tongue*, *Helminthia echioides*, Plin.*HN*20.75; to be restored in Hsch. for **ἡδυπνοΐδης**. -πνοος, Dor. ἁδ-, ον, contr. -πνους, ουν, *sweet-breathing*, αὖραι E.*Med*.840 (lyr.); of musical sound, Pi.*O*.13.22, *I*.2.25; of auspicious dreams, S.*El*.480 (lyr.). 2. *sweet-smelling, fragrant*, λεπαστή Telecl.24 (lyr.); χῶρος *AP*9.564 (Nic.); κρόκος *IG*14.607e (Carales); ὅρμος (necklace) Dsc.1.99. 3. v. ἡδύχρους II. -πολις, Dor. ἁδ-, ὁ, ἡ, *dear to the people*, S.*OT*510 (lyr.). -πορφύρα [ῠ], ἡ, a kind of πορφύρα, Arist.*Fr*.304. -πότης, ου, *fond of drinking*, epith. of Dionysus, *AP*9.524.8, cf. Hedyl. ap.Ath.4.176d, Man.4.493. II. *furnishing sweet drink*, ἄμπελος Nonn.*D*.12.249. -πότις, ιδος, ἡ, *something that makes drink taste pleasant*, name of a cup, Epig.5, *IG*11(2).110.26 (Delos, iii B.C.), *SIG*[2] 588.7 (ib., ii B.C.), Semus ap.Ath.11.469c:—Dim. -ποτίδιον, *IG*7.303 (Oropus, iii B.C.), 11(2).203*B*29 (Delos, iii B.C.):—also -πότιον, Cratin.Jun.14 (s. v. l.), *IG*2[2].1534.220 (iii B.C.), al. -ποτος, ον, *sweet to drink*, οἶνος Od.2.340, 3.391, etc.; also of a cup, ἡ. κύλιξ *Philol*.72.547 (Olbia, v B.C.). -πρόσωπος, ον, *of sweet countenance*, χόνδρος Matro *Conv*.102. -ραβδον, τό, = κιννάμωμον, Hsch.

ἡδύς, ἡδεῖα, ἡδύ, ἡδὺς ἀϋτμή (as fem.) once in Hom., Od.12.369: Dor. ἁδύς [ᾱ], Boeot. neut. ϝαδού (written γάδου) cj. in Corinn.17 (cf. pr. n. ϝαδιούλογος *IG*7.2788.3), Elean βαδύς (q. v.): irreg. acc. ἁδέα for ἡδύν Theoc.20.44, for ἡδεῖαν ib.[8], Mosch.3.82: Ion. fem. ἡδέα, Dor. ἁδέα: Comp. ἡδίων [ῑ], Sup. ἥδιστος Od.13.80, etc.; also ἡδύτερος Thphr.*HP*3.2.1, Ps.-Phoc.195, *AP*9.247 (Phil.); ἡδύτατος ib.11.298.7, Plu.2.98e. I. *pleasant* to the taste, δεῖπνον Od.20.391; of wine, 3.51, 9.197, etc.; to the smell, ἀμβροσίην . . ἡδὺ μάλα πνείουσαν 4.446; ὀδμὴ δ' ἡδεῖα ἀπὸ κρητῆρος ὀδώδει 9.210; to the hearing, δίδου δ' ἡδεῖαν ἀοιδήν 8.64; αὐδή Hes.*Th*.40; feelings or states, ἡ. ὕπνος Il.4.131, Od.1.364, al.; κοῖτος 19.510; ἡδὺ μάλα κνώσσουσα 4.809; ἡδὺς μῦθος, opp. ἀλγεινός, S.*Ant*.12: c. inf., φέγγος ἥδιον δρακεῖν A.*Ag*.602; ἡδὺς ἀκοῦσαι [λόγος] Pl.*Men*.81d, cf. Ar.*V*.503; later ἡ. ἀκουσθῆναι D.H.*Comp*.9; εἰ . . τόδε πᾶσι φίλον καὶ ἡδὺ γένοιτο Il.4.17, cf. 7.387: c. inf., οὐκ ἂν ἐμοί γε μετὰ φρεσὶν ἡδὺ γένοιτο ζωέμεν Od.24.435; ἁδύ τι θαρσαλέαις τὸν μακρὸν τείνειν βίον ἐλπίσι A.*Pr*.536, etc.; so οὔ μοι ἡδιόν ἐστι λέγειν I had *rather* not . ., Hdt.2.46: neut. as Subst., τὸ δι' ἀκοῆς τε καὶ δι' ὄψεως ἡδύ Pl.*Hp.Ma*.298a; μεμιγμένον τῷ σεμνῷ τὸ ἡ. D.H.*Comp*.1; τὰ ἡ. *pleasures*, Th.5.105, Pl.*Grg*.495a, etc.: neut. as Adv., ἐπ' αὐτῷ ἡδὺ γέλασσαν *merrily*, Il.2.270, etc.; ἁδὺ δὲ καὶ τὺ συρίσδες *sweetly*, Theoc.1.2. II. after Hom., of persons, *welcome*, S.*OT*82, *Ph*.530 (Sup.), *El*.929; ironically, ἥδιστος . . δεσμώτης ἔσω θακεῖ Id.*Aj*.105; like εὐήθης, *innocent, simple*, ὡς ἡ. εἶ Pl.*Grg*.491e, Plu.*Art*.17, etc.: Sup., ὦ ἥδιστε *my good friend* (iron.), Pl.*R*.348c, al. 2. *well-pleased, glad*, ἡδίους ἔσεσθ' ἀκούσαντες D.23.64; ἡδίους ταῖς ἐλπίσιν Plu.*Cam*.32; τὴν γνώμην ἡδίω πρὸς τὸ μέλλον ποιεῖν to open *a pleasanter* view of the future, Id.*Fab*.5. III. Adv. ἡδέως *pleasantly, with pleasure*, καθεύδειν Pl.*Cri*.43b; εὕδειν S.*Tr*.175; δρᾶν Id.*Ant*.70; ὁρᾶν τινα E.*IA*1122; βίοτον ἄγειν Id.*Cyc*.453; λαβεῖν, δέχεσθαι, Ar.*Eq*.440, X.*Mem*.1.2.4; ἡ. ἂν ἐροίμην I would *gladly* ask, should *like to* ask, D.18.64; ἡ. ἔχειν τι to be *pleased* or *content* with, E.*Ion*647 (but ἵν' ἡ δόκησις Ξούθον ἡ. ἔχῃ ib.1602); οὐδὲ πότων ἡ. εἶχον had no *inclination* to drink, Hp.*Epid*.3.13; τινος, of a person, Macho ap.Ath.13.577e; ἡ. ἔχειν πρὸς ἅπαντας to be *suave, courteous* towards . ., Isoc.1.20; τινι D.5.15; ἡ. ἔχειν, of things, to be *pleasant*, E.*IA*483; ἡ. ἔμοιγε κἀλγεινῶς ἅμα S.*Ant*.436; iron., ἡ. γε '*prettily* said', Pl.*Hp.Ma*.300c: Comp. ἥδιον Lys.7.40, Pherecr.67, etc.: Sup., ἥδιστα μεντἂν ἤκουσα Pl.*Tht*.183d, etc. 2. in Hom. neut. ἡδύ as Adv. (v. supr.), cf. ἥδομαι. [ἥδῐον E.*Supp*.1101 (s. v. l.), Ar. *V*.298 (lyr.), Alex.25.6, but ἡδίον(α) [ῑ] E.*Cyc*.251, etc.] (Skt. *svādús*, Lat. *suāvis*.)

ἡδύσᾰρον, τό, *axe-weed*, *Bonaveria Securidaca*, Dsc.3.130.

ἥδυσμα, ατος, τό, (ἡδύνω) *relish, seasoning, sauce*, Ar.*Eq*.678, *V*.496, Pl.*R*.332d, X.*Mem*.3.14.5, Thphr.*CP*6.4.6, etc.; of vinegar, Ath.2.67c: metaph., οὐ . . ἡδύσματι χρῆται ἀλλ' ὡς ἐδέσματι τοῖς ἐπιθέτοις Arist.*Rh*.1406^{a}19; ἡ μελοποιΐα μέγιστον τῶν ἡ. Id.*Po*.1450^{b}16, cf. Jul.*Or*.7.207b: in pl., *spices, aromatics*, Hp.*Mul*.2.202, Dsc.1.61, Plu.2.995c.

ἡδυσμάτιον, τό, Dim. of foreg., Telecl.1.11.

ἡδυσματο-θήκη, ἡ, *spice-box*, Poll.10.93. -ληρος, ον, *absurdly dainty*, ὀψάρια Archestr.*Fr*.45.18.

ἡδυσμός, ὁ, (ἡδύνω) *a sweet savour, sweetness*, Lxx *Ex*.30.34.

ἡδύστομος, *jocosus*, Gloss.

ἡδῠσώμᾰτος [ῠ], ον, *of sweet form*, opp. ἡδυγνώμων, X.*Smp*.8.30.

ἡδύτεραι· αἱ τρυγόνες, Hsch.

ἡδύτης [ῠ], ητος, ἡ, (ἡδύς) *sweetness*, Sch.Ar.*Av*.222.

ἡδῠ-τόκος, ον, *producing sweets*, Nonn.*D*.3.150. -φἄής, Dor. ἁδ-, ές, *sweet-shining*, ἤλεκτρος D.P.317; πλινθίς *AP*6.295 (Phan.). -φάρυγξ [ᾰ], υγγος, ὁ, ἡ, *sweet to the throat*, prob. in Philox.2.18. -φθογγος, ον, *sweet-voiced*, τέττιγες Hsch. s. v. ἠχηταί. -φρων, ονος, ὁ, ἡ, *sweet-minded*, *AP*9.525.8. -φωνία, ἡ, *sweetness of sound*, Babr.9.3, Alciphr.3.12, etc. -φωνος, Dor. ἁδ-, Aeol. ἀδ-, ον, *sweet-voiced*, Sapph.61; ὄρτυξ Pratin.Lyr.4, cf. Aristaenet.1.10. -χἄρής, ές, *sweetly joyous*, *AP*3.18 (Inscr. Cyzic.). -χροος, ον, contr. -χρους, ουν, *of sweet complexion*, πρόσωπα *IG*14.2040.7; ἡδύχρουν μύρον a *fragrant* perfume, Dsc.1.58; τὸ ἡ. Androm.ap.Gal.14.52, Alex.Trall.7.3; *hedychrum*, Cic.*Tusc*.3.19.46. II. ἡδύχρους, also ἡδύπνους, ὁ, a lamb not yet weaned, Phot.

ἥδω, v. ἥδομαι II. **ἠδώ**· ἶρις, ἤγουν τόξον, Hsch. **ἠέ**, v. ἤ, *or, whether*. **ἠέ**, exclam. *ah!* A.*Th*.966, 980, *Supp*.831 (all lyr.). **ἦε**, **ἤει**, v. εἶμι (*ibo*). **ἠείδης**, **ἠείδη**, v. εἴδω. **ἠέλιος**, ὁ, v. ἥλιος. **ἠελιῶτις**, v. ἡλιώτης.

ἠερέθομαι, Ep. for ἀείρομαι, only in 3 pl. pres. and impf., *hang floating* or *waving in the air*, αἰγίδα . . τῆς ἑκατὸν θύσανοι . . ἠερέθονται Il.2.448; of a flight of locusts, 21.12; of flying-fish, Opp.*H*.1.435; ἐξ χεῖρες ἑκάστῳ -ονται A.R.1.944: metaph., ὁπλοτέρων ἀνδρῶν φρένες ἠερέθονται young men's minds *turn with every wind*, Il.3.108.—The form ἀερέθονται in Hsch., cf. *EM*421.6.

ἠέριος, η, ον, (ἦρι) *early, at* or *with early morn*, ἠερίη δ' ἀνέβη μέγαν οὐρανόν Il.1.497, cf. 557, 3.7 (Sch. ἐαριναί), Od.9.52, A.R.3.417. II.

later, (ἠήρ) *misty, dimly seen,* Arat.349, A.R.1.580, 4.1239. 2. *high in air,* ἠ. Γεράνεια Simon.114; of birds, Opp.*C*.1.380, *H*.3.203; of flying-fish, ib.1.430; ἄγραι *AP*6.180 (Arch.), cf. Nonn.*D*.7.315, al. 3. *airy, air-like,* πῦρ Hp.*Vict*.1.10.

ἠερο-δίνης [ῑ], εω, ὁ, *wheeling in mid air,* αἰετός *AP*9.223 (Bianor). **-ειδής**, ές, Ion. and Ep. for ἀερ-, which is not found, *misty, cloudy, dark* (esp. in Od.), ἐπ' ἠεροειδέα πόντον Od.2.263, etc.; σπέος ἠ. 12.80, cf. 13.103; πέτρη, of Scylla's cave, 12.233: neut. as Adv., *in the far distance, dimly,* ὅσσον δ' ἠεροειδὲς ἀνὴρ ἴδεν Il.5.770; ἠ. νεφέλη Hes. *Th*.757; πνοιαί Orph.*H*.38.22.—Ep. word, ἠ. αὐγαί Arist.*Col*.792b8: Comp., ὕδωρ πάντων -έστερον Arr.*Ind*.6.3. **-εις**, εσσα, εν, Ion. and Ep. for ἀερόεις (q.v., cf. cj. in Telest.1.12) *cloudy, murky,* Τάρταρος Il.8.13, al., cf. Hes.*Th*.119; ζόφος Il.15.191, etc.; ἠερόεντα κέλευθα *the murky* road (i.e. death), Od.20.64; later ἠ. ἴασπις D.P. 724; μόλυβδος Man.6.391; *livid,* χροιή Nic.*Th*.257. II. epith. of ὄναγρος, = ταχύς, acc. to Sch., Opp.*C*.3.183. **-θεν**, Ion. and Ep. for ἀερ-, *from air,* *APl*.4.107 (Jul.). **-μήκης**, ες, Ep. for ἀερ-, *high as heaven,* Orph.*A*.924. **-μικτος**, ον, (μείγνυμι) *mingling with air,* φωναί Id.*Fr*.297b2 (in form ἀερό-). **-μορφος**, ον, (μορφή) *air-formed,* αὖραι Id.*H*.81.6, cf. 16.1. **-πλαγκτος**, ον, *wandering in mid air,* ib.7.8, Man.4.509. **-ποιταν**· ἐπιτιμῶσαν, and **-πομπα**· κατὰ τὸν ἀέρα φαινόμενα, Hsch.

ἠέροπος, ὁ, Ion. for ἀέροψ, Ant.Lib.18.3.

ἠερο-φεγγής, ές, *shining in the air,* Ζεύς Orph.*H*.20.2. **-φοίτης**, ου, ὁ, = ἠερόφοιτος, Ion Lyr.10, Orph.*L*.45, Nonn.*D*.24.79, al. **-φοῖτις**, ιδος, ἡ, *walking in darkness, coming unseen,* Ἐρινύς Il.9.571, 19.87. II. *air-traversing,* of the moon, Orph.*H*.9.2; μέλισσα Ps.-Phoc.171. **-φοιτος**, ον, (φοιτάω) *air-wandering,* φύσις, of birds, ib.125; οἶστρος Orph.*A*.47; of cuttle-fish, Opp.*H*.3.166 (cf. ἠέρα τέμνουσι 1.427); of the moon, Max.485, etc. **-φωνος**, ον, *sounding through air, loud-voiced,* κήρυκες Il.18.505 (s.v.l., ἱεροφώνων cj. Ahrens); γέρανοι Opp.*H*.1.621.

ἠερτίζω, = ἀερτάζω, Hsch. **ἠήν**, exclam., = ἢ ἤ, Men.*Per*. 15. **ἠήρ**, v. ἀήρ.

ἠθάδιος [ᾰ], ον, poet. for ἠθάς, Opp.*C*.1.448.

ἠθαῖος, α, ον, Dor. for ἠθεῖος, Pi.*I*.2.48.

ἠθᾰλέος, η, ον, (ἦθος) *accustomed,* εὐναί Opp.*C*.2.307; [ταῦροι] ib. 88, cf. *Epigr.Gr*.1035.23 (Pergam.).

ἠθάνιον, τό, Dim. of ἠθμός, Hellanic.53 J.; cf. ἠθήνιον.

ἠθάς, ἄδος, ὁ, ἡ, (ἦθος II) *accustomed to* a thing, *acquainted with* it, c. gen., ἠ. εἰμί πως τῶν τῆσδε μύθων S.*El*.372; θήρης Opp.*H*.4.122; τῶν χωρίων Ael.*NA*7.6: c. dat., πέτραις ib.9.36. 2. abs., *inured, accustomed,* Hp.*Mul*.1.1; τῶν γὰρ ἠθάδων φίλων νέοι.. εὐπιθέστεροι E. *Andr*.818; of animals, *tame,* [ὄρνιθες] ἠ. *domestic* fowls, Ar.*Av*.271; of decoy-birds, Plu.*Sull*.28; ἠ. σκόμβροι Ael.*NA*14.1. II. of things, *usual, customary,* νίκη *APl*.5.354; πάγαι *AP*9.264 (Apollonid. or Phil.): as neut., τὰ καινά γ' ἐκ τῶν ἠθάδων ἥδιόν ἐστι E.*Cyc*.250; τοῖς ἠθάσι λίαν τοῖς τ' ἀρχαίοις ἐνδιατρίβειν Ar.*Ec*.584, cf. 151.

ἠθεῖος, also **ἠθαῖος**, α, ον, *trusty, honoured,* term of address used to express respect, ἠθεῖε Il.6.518, al., Hes.*Sc*.103: periphr., ἠθείη κεφαλή Il.23.94; ἀλλά μιν ἠθεῖον καλέω Od.14.147; ξεῖνον ἐμὸν ἠθαῖον Pi.*I*.2.48; ἠθαῖοι *trusty friends,* Antim.22. (Cf. ἦθος.)

ἤθεος, ὁ, ἡ, Att. for ἠίθεος (q.v.).

ἠθ-έω, aor. 1 ἤθησα (ἤθισα codd.), gloss on ἧσα, v. ἤθω:—Med., aor. 1 ἠθησάμην Nic.*Al*.324: (ἤθω):—*sift, strain,* Nic. l.c.:—Pass., *to be strained,* τὸ ἠθούμενον Pl.*Cra*.402d; [οἶνος] ἠθημένος Epil.6; χρυσὸς ἠθημένος διὰ πέτρας *filtered through,* Pl.*Ti*.59b: metaph., ἐκ τετρημένης [τὴν ῥῆσιν] ἠθεῖ *lets it trickle out,* Herod.3.33. **-ημα**, ατος, τό, *that which is sifted* or *strained,* Dieuch.ap.Orib.4.7.26. **-ήνιον**· ἠθάνιον, Hsch. **-ησις**, εως, ἡ, *riddling,* λίθων *IG*4.1485.124 (Epid.); prob. l. for ἤθισις, Arist.*Pr*.870b18. **-ητήρ**, ῆρος, ὁ, = ἠθμός, Marc.Sid.76. **-ητήριον**, τό, = ἠθμός, Str.3.2.9. **-ητικός**, ή, όν, *capable of being strained,* of wines, Thphr.*CP*6.16.6.

ἠθῐκ-εύομαι, *speak ethically,* Phoeb.*Fig*.1.1, Sch.Il.7.408. **-ός**, ή, όν, (ἦθος II) *moral,* opp. διανοητικός, Arist.*EN*1103a5, al.; τὰ ἠθικά *a treatise on morals,* Id.*Pol*.1295a36, cf. Democr.4a; οἱ ἠ. λόγοι Phld. *Herc*.1251.13; τὸ ἠ. φιλοσοφίας, opp. φυσικόν, διαλεκτικόν, D.L. *Prooem*.18; ἡ ἠ. φιλοσοφία Str.1.1.18; ἡ ἠ. alone, Ph.1.370. II. *showing moral character, expressive thereof,* λέξις Arist.*Rh*.1408a11; πῶς..τοὺς λόγους ἠ. ποιητέον ib.1391b22, cf. 1395b13; ἠ. τραγῳδία Id. *Po*.1456a1; ἡ Ἰλιὰς παθητικόν, ἡ δὲ Ὀδύσσεια ἠ. ib.1459b15; ἠ. μέλη, ἁρμονίαι, Id.*Pol*.1341b34, 1342a3 (Sup.); οὐκ ἔστιν ὁ αὐλὸς ἠθικόν, ἀλλὰ..ὀργιαστικόν ib.1341a21; ἠ. γραφεύς, ἀγαλματοποιός, ib.1340a38; ἠθικὴ ἡ ἐν ὀφθαλμοῖς *the expression of character* by the eyes, Philostr. *Gym*.25. Adv. -κῶς, λεκτέον (opp. ἀποδεικτικῶς) Arist.*Rh*.1418a39; ἠ. μειδιάσας laughing *expressively,* Plu.*Brut*.51; ἐπικροτεῖν τὸ μετακάρπιον Aristaenet.1.27; *in character,* Demetr.*Eloc*.216; *naturally,* ib.297. 2. *tactful,* Plu.2.73f (Comp.). Adv. -κῶς Id.*Alex*.52.

ἤθῐσις, v. ἤθησις. **ἠθμάριον**, τό, Dim. of ἠθμός, Hsch.

ἠθμοειδής, ές, *like a strainer, perforated,* Hero *Spir*.1.8, Plu.2.699a; κοιλίαι Aret.*SD*2.3. II. τὸ ἠ. ὀστοῦν the *ethmoid* or *perforated* bone at the root of the nose, Gal.*UP*11.12: more freq. in pl., τὰ -ειδῆ, with or without ὀστᾶ, ib.8.7; ἠ. δεξαμεναί, of the kidneys, prob. in Ph.2.244 (αἱμο-, ἰσθμο- codd., cf. Gal.*Nat.Fac*.1.15). Adv. -δῶς Ruf.*Anat*.52.

ἠθμός, *SIG*2 (Sigeum, vi B.C.), Hdn.Gr.1.543, in codd. usu. (but perh. wrongly) **ἡθμός**, ὁ, (ἤθω) *strainer, colander,* *SIG* l.c., E.*Fr*. 374, *IG*2².1416.11, 4.39.20, Gal.*Nat.Fac*.1.15; esp. *wine-strainer,* Pherecr.41; part of an eel-trap, Arist.*HA*534a22; of the eyelashes, X.*Mem*.1.4.6; prov., τῷ ἠθμῷ ἀντλεῖν, of fruitless toil, Arist.*Oec*. 1344b25. II. ἠ. σχοίνινος, = κημός III, Cratin.132, cf. *AP*9.482.23 (Agath.). III. *sluice* or *weir* (?), *IG*11(2).287 *A* 75 (Delos, iii B.C.).

ἠθμώδης, ες, = ἠθμοειδής, Sch.Ar.*V*.99.

ἠθογρᾰφ-έω, *paint* or *describe character,* Marcellin.*Vit.Thuc*.50. **-ος**, ὁ, *painter of character,* Arist.*Po*.1450a28.

ἠθολογ-έω, *express characteristically,* γονέων πάθη Lxx 4*Ma*.15.4:—Pass., κωμῳδία -ουμένη comedy *of manners,* Longin.9.15. **-ία**, ἡ, *painting of character,* esp. by mimic gestures (cf. χαρακτηρισμός), Posidon.ap.Sen.*Ep*.95.65, Quint.1.9.3, Suet.*Gramm*.4 (pl.). **-ος**, ον, *painting character* by mimic gestures (cf. βιολόγος), of dramatic and mimic performers, D.S.20.63, Cic.*Orat*.2.59.242, Ath.1.20a; of Socrates, Timo 62.

ἠθονόη, coined as etym. of Ἀθηνᾶ, Pl.*Cra*.407b.

ἠθοποι-έω, *mould the character of* a person, τὸν θεατήν Plu.*Per*.2; τὴν ψυχήν S.E.*M*.6.30. II. *express* or *delineate character,* D.H. *Lys*.19: c. acc., τὸ σχῆμα τῆς γυναικός Aps.p.322 H. **-ητικός**, ή, όν, *expressive of character.* Adv. -κῶς Eust.1955.54. **-ία**, ἡ, *formation of character,* Str.2.5.26 (pl.), Gal.15.97. II. *delineation of character,* Phld.*Po*.5.9 (pl.), Str.14.1.41, D.H.*Lys*.8, *Isoc*.11 (pl.), Hermog.*Prog*.9, Aphth.*Prog*.11, etc. **-ός**, όν, *forming character,* ἠ. τὸ θερμόν Arist.*Pr*.955a32; μέλη S.E.*M*.6.36; παιδεύσεις Plu.*Them*. 2; τὸ ἠ., = foreg. 1, Id.2.660c.

ἦθος, εος, τό (cf. ἔθος), *an accustomed place*: hence, in pl., *haunts* or *abodes* of animals, μετά τ' ἤθεα καὶ νομὸν ἵππων Il.6.511; [σύας] ἔρξαν κατὰ ἤθεα κοιμηθῆναι Od.14.411; of lions, Hdt.7.125; of fish, Opp.*H*.1.93; of *the abodes of men,* Hes.*Op*.167, 525, Hdt.1.15, 157, A.*Supp*.64 (lyr.), E.*Hel*.274, Pl.*Lg*.865e, Arist.*Mu*.398b33; ἔλεγον ἐξ ἠθέων τὸν ἥλιον ἀνατεῖλαι away from his *accustomed place,* Hdt. 2.142; of plants, Callistr.*Stat*.7: metaph., with play on signf. II, Pl.*Phdr*.277a. II. *custom, usage*: in pl., *manners, customs,* Hes.*Op*.137, *Th*.66, Hdt.2.30, 35, 4.106, Th.2.61; τρόποι καὶ ἤθη Pl. *Lg*.896c; ἐθρέψω Ξέρξην ἐν τοῖς αὐτοῖς ἤ. ib.695e; φθείρουσιν ἤθη χρήσθ' ὁμιλίαι κακαί *PHib*.1.7.94 (E.*Fr*.1024 = Men.218); τοῖς ἤθεσιν ἁπλοῦς D.S.5.21. 2. *disposition, character,* ἐπίκλοπον ἦθος Hes.*Op*. 67, 78; ἠ. ἐμφυές Pi.*O*.11(10).21; ἀκίχητα ἤ., of Zeus, A.*Pr*.187; τοὐμὸν ἤ. παιδεύειν S.*Aj*.595; ὦ μιαρὸν ἤ. Id.*Ant*.746; τὸ τῆς πόλεως ἤ. Isoc.2.31; βελτίων τῆς πόλεως τὸ ἤ. D.20.14; esp. *moral character,* opp. διάνοια, Arist.*EN*1139a1; as the result of habit, τὸ πᾶν ἤ. διὰ ἔθος Pl.*Lg*.792e, cf. Arist.*EE*1220a39; ἤ. ἀνθρώπῳ δαίμων Heraclit.119; ἤ. πηγὴ βίου Stoic.ap.Stob.2.7.1; τῆς ψυχῆς, τῆς γνώμης, Pl.*R*.400d, D.61.16: freq. opp. πάθος, Arist.*Rh*.1356a23 (pl.), etc.; ἠθῶν τε καὶ παθῶν μίμησις D.H.*Pomp*.3; τὸ ἤ. πρᾶος Pl.*Phdr*.243c: less freq. in dat., ἀγοραῖος τῷ ἤ. Thphr.*Char*.6.2, cf. *Inscr.Magn*.164.3 (i/ii A.D.): pl., *traits, characteristics,* Pl.*R*.402d, Arist.*EN*1144b4 (in sg., τὸ τῆς ἀνδρείας ἤ. Pl.*Lg*.836d): seldom in pl., of an individual, στερρὸν τὰ ἤθεα Hp.*Ep*.11; ἱερὸς κατὰ τὰ ἤθη Ath.1.1e. b. of outward *bearing,* ὡς ἱλαρὸν τὸ ἤ. X.*Smp*.8.3; ὑγρότης ἤθους Lycurg.33; ὑψηλὸς τῷ ἤ. Plu.*Dio* 4: in pl., of facial expression, ὀφθαλμῶν ἤθη Philostr.*Gym*. 25. c. in Rhet., *delineation of character,* ἤ. ἔχουσιν οἱ λόγοι ἐν ὅσοις δήλη ἡ προαίρεσις Arist.*Rh*.1395b13; ἤ. ἐμφαίνειν Phld.*Rh*.1.200 S.; esp. opp. πάθος, Longin.9.15, etc.; κατ' ἤ. λέγεσθαι, opp. κατὰ πάθος, D.H.*Comp*.22, cf. *Lys*.19: in pl., πραγμάτων καὶ ἠθῶν Phld.*Po*.5.5; ἐν πάθεσι καὶ ἤθεσιν Demetr.*Eloc*.28, etc.; so of works of art, ἡ Ζεύξιδος γραφὴ οὐδὲν ἔχει ἤ. Arist.*Po*.1450a29; πάθος καὶ ἤ. καὶ σχημάτων χρῆσις Ael.*VH*4.3; πολλὰ ἤθη ἐπιφαίνει Philostr.*Her*.2.10; also of Music, S.E.*M*.6.49. d. *dramatis persona,* εἰσάγει ἄνδρα ἢ γυναῖκα ἢ ἄλλο τι ἤ. Arist.*Po*.1460a11, al. 3. also of animals, ἤ. τὸ πρὸς τοκέων (prob. l. for ἔθος) A.*Ag*.727, cf. E.*Hipp*.1219, Pl.*R*.375e, Arist. *HA*487a12 (pl.); τὸ ἤ. ἀσθενής, of a bird, ib.615a18; of things, *nature, kind,* παρὰ δ' ἤ. ἑκάστῳ (to each of the four elements) Emp. 17.28; τοῦ πυρετοῦ Gal.7.353. 4. ἐν ἤθει *tactfully* (cf. ἠθικός II.2), προσφέρεσθαι τοῖς ἁμαρτάνουσιν Plu.2.73e, cf. Herm. *in Phdr*.p.195 A.; διὰ μέτρου ἦθος, of the expression δοκεῖ μοι, Steph. *in Hp*.1.59 D.

ἠθροισμένως, Adv. pf. part. Pass. of ἀθροίζω, gloss on ἀγεληδόν, Hsch.

ἤθω, collat. form of ἠθέω (q.v.), aor. 1 ἦσα, Hp.ap.Gal.19.103.

ἠΐ, Boeot. for αἰεί (= ἀεί), *Schwyzer* 462 *A* 25 (Tanagra, iii B.C.), Hdn.Gr.1.497.

ἤϊα (A), contr. **ᾖα**, τά, *provisions for a journey,* Ep. word, Hom. mostly in Od., δεῦτε, φίλοι, ἤϊα φερώμεθα 2.410, cf. 289; καί νύ κεν ἤϊα πάντα κατέφθιτο 4.363; ἐξέφθιτο ἤϊα πάντα 12.329; ἐν δὲ καὶ ᾖα κωρύκῳ [ἔθηκε] 5.266, cf. 9.212: generally, [ἔλαφοι] παρδαλίων τε λύκων τ' ἤϊα πέλονται *food* for wolves, Il.13.103; ἤϊα κριθάων, = ἄλευρα, Nic.*Al*.412. II. ὡς δ' ἄνεμος..ἠΐων θημῶνα τινάξῃ καρφαλέων, i.e. a heap of *husks* or *chaff* (= ὀσπρίων καλάμαι acc. to Eratosth.ap.Eust.1445.42), Od.5. 368; τὴν γαστέρ' ᾔων κἀχύρων σεσαγμένος Pherecr.161. (Etym. uncertain: not related to the sg. ἤϊον which is glossed by παρειάν, γνάθον, Hsch.; cf. εἰαί, εἰοι.) [ῐ, but ῑ Od.2.289, 410, Il.13.103.]

ἤϊα (B), Ion. for ᾔειν, impf. of εἶμι (*ibo*).

ἠίθεος [ῐ], contr. **ἤθεος** (v. infr.), Dor. **ἀΐθεος** Cerc.9.11, but Aeol. (?) **ἤϊθεος** Sapph. (v. infr.): ὁ:—*unmarried youth* (ἠίθεον ἢ καὶ γεγαμηκότα ἄπαιδα Pl.*Lg*.877e), Sapph.*Supp*.20a.18 (pl.); παρθένος ἠ. τε joined, Il.22.127, al.; χοροὺς παρθένων τε καὶ ἠιθέων Hdt.3.48, cf. Plu. *Thes*.15; including παρθένοι, B.16 tit., cf. 43, al.; of the θεωροί sent to Delos, Arist.*Ath*.56.3; οὐ γάρ ἐστιν ἤθεος E.*Ph*.945; of animals, *unmated,* Pl.*Lg*.840d: later as Adj., παῖδες ἠίθεοι Plu.*Thes*.17; ἠϊθέοισιν ἐφήβοισιν *IG*3.1151. 2. ἠίθεοι, οἱ, *ghosts of those who die unmarried,* *Tab.Defix.Aud*.52.7. II. rare as fem., ἠϊθέη, = παρθένος,

Nic.*Fr.*74.64, *AP*9.241 (Antip. ⟨Thess.⟩); κόρη ἤθεος Eup.332. III. metaph. as Adj., νοῦς Porph.*Marc.*33. (ἠιθ– shd. be read as ἠθ– in Prose.)

ἡικανός· ὁ ἀλεκτρυών, Hsch. **ἤϊκτο**, v. ἔοικα. **ἤϊξε**, v. ἀΐσσω.

ἠιόεις, εσσα, εν, (ἠϊα A) Ep. word of doubtful meaning, ἐπ' ἠϊόεντι Σκαμάνδρῳ Il.5.36; perh. connected by later poets with ἠϊών, hence ἠ. Πάνορμος Q.S.1.283; κόλλουρος *haunting the shore*, Marc.Sid.22: but perh. also with ἤϊα (A), χήνεσιν ἠϊόεν πεδίον κάτα βοσκομένοισιν Q.S.5.299; derived from ἴον by *EM*423.14.

ἤϊον, Ep. for ᾖεσαν, 3 pl. impf. of εἶμι (*ibo*); also 1 sg., Luc.*Syr.D.* 24. II. Ion. impf. of ἀΐω, read by Zenod. for ἔκλυον, Od.2. 42. III. v. ἤϊα (A) fin.

ἤϊος, ὁ, epith. of Phoebus, ἤϊε Φοῖβε Il.15.365, 20.152, *h.Ap.*120. (Prob. from the cry ἤ, ἤ, cf. ἰήϊος.)

ἠϊόω, (ἤϊα A) *provide with food*, in Pass., Hsch.

ἠϊών, Trag. ᾐών E.*Or.*994, Dor. ἀϊών Pi.*I.*1.33, A.*Ag.*1158 (lyr.), ᾀών Mosch.3.37 (cj.): όνος, ἡ:—*shore, beach*, ὅθι κύματ' ἐπ' ἠϊόνος κλύζεσκον Il.23.61; ἀμφὶ δέ τ' ἄκραι ἠϊόνες βοόωσιν 17.265; ἂμ πέτρῃσι καὶ ἠϊόνεσσι καθίζων (Ep. dat.) Od.5.156, cf. Hdt.2.113, 8.96, E.*Tr.* 827 (lyr.), X.*HG*1.1.5, Sotion p.191 W., D.C.59.25. 2. after Hom., in pl., of other *banks*, as of a lake, Pi.*I.*1.33; of a river, A.*Ag.*l.c., A.R.2.659, 4.130, D.H.4.27. 3. metaph., of the *lower part of the face*, over which the tears flow, Hsch. (pl.): sg., = πᾶσα ἡ τῶν ὀφθαλμῶν περιγραφή, Poll.2.71.

ἦκα, Adv.: I. of Place or Motion, *slightly, a little*, ἦκ' ἐπ' ἀριστερὰ *a little* to the left, Il.23.336; ἠ. παρακλίνας κεφαλήν Od.20.301: hence, generally, *softly, gently*, ἠ. ἐλάσαι 18.94, cf. 92; ἀπώσατο ἠ. γέροντα Il.24.508; ἠ. μάλα ψύξασα 20.440; ἠ. κιόντας Od.17.254; ἠ. βιησάμενος Nic.*Al.*226. II. of Sound, *softly, low*, ἠ. πρὸς ἀλλήλους ἀγόρευον Il.3.155; ἠ. μύρεσθαι, μάλ' ὀμαδῆσαι, A.R.3.463, 565. III. of Sight, *softly, smoothly*, ἠ. στίλβοντας ἐλαίῳ with oil *soft*-shining, Il.18.596; ἦκ' ἐπιμειδήσας *soft*-smiling, Hes.*Th.*547; ἠ. μέλαν *slightly* black, Opp.*C.*3.39. IV. of Time, *by little and little*, *AP*5.278 (Paul. Sil.), Opp.*H.*2.67. (Perh. connected with Lat. *sēg-nis* (for *sēc-nis*): but Hsch. has γάκα (i.e. ϝᾶκα)· ἡδέως; cf. ἥσσων, ἥκιστος, ἥκιστος, ἠκαῖον, ἤκαλος, ἠκαλέον.)

ἧκα, aor. 1 of ἵημι.

ἠκάδα· ἠνδρωμένην γυναῖκα, Hsch. **ἠκαῖον**· ἀσθενές, Id. **ἤκαλος**, ον, = ἀκαλός, Call.*Fr.*27 P.:—also **ἠκαλέον** γελόωσα· πράως, οὐκ ἐσκυθρωπακυῖα, Hsch. **ἤκαχε**, v. ἀχεύω, ἀχέω (A) II. 1.

ἤκεστος, η, ον, (Ep. for *ἄκεστος, from κεντέω) *untouched by the goad*, of young heifers reserved for sacrifices, βοῦς.. ἤνις ἠκέστας Il. 6.94, 275, 309:—also **ἠκέστης**· ἀδάμαστος, Suid.

ἠκή, ἡ, Ion. for ἀκή (A), ἀκωκή, Hsch.: hence, *edge, meeting-point*, κύματός τε κἀνέμου Archil.43.

ἠκής, ές, *sharp*, Hsch.

ἥκιστος, η, ον, Sup. Adj. of Adv. ἦκα, ἥκιστος ἐλαυνέμεν *the gentlest* or *slowest* in driving, Il.23.531 (ἡκ– Eust.1314.27, *EM*424.27; cf. sq.).

ἥκιστος, η, ον, prob., like foreg., Sup. of ἦκα, *least*, ὁ δ' ἥκιστ' ἔχων μακάρτατος S.*Fr.*410. 2. c. inf., *worst* at.., ἠ. θηρᾶν, κρυμῷ ὁμιλεῖν, Ael.*NA*9.1, 4.31 (cf. foreg.). II. mostly as Adv., ἥκιστα *least*, Hp.*Acut.*68, S.*Ph.*427, etc.; οὐκ ἠ. ἀλλὰ μάλιστα Hdt.4.170; ὡς ἠ. *as little as possible*, Th.1.91. 2. in reply to a question, *not at all*, S.*OT*623, E.*HF*299, etc.; ἥκιστά γε S.*OT*1386, Pl.*Phdr.*276c; ἠ. πάντων Ar.*Pl.*440. 3. οὐχ ἠ., freq. in litotes, *above all, more than all*, A.*Ch.*116; οἵ τε ἄλλοι καὶ οὐχ ἠ. Ἀθηναῖοι Pl.*Prt.*324c, cf. *Tht.* 177c, *Smp.*178a, al.; ἐπὶ πολλῶν μέν.., οὐχ ἠ. δὲ ἐν τοῖς παροῦσι πράγμασι D.2.1, cf. Th.7.44, etc.: c. gen., οὐχ ἠ. Ἀθηναίων σέ, ἀλλ' ἐν τοῖς μάλιστα Pl.*Cri.*52a.

ἠκρῑβωμένως, Adv. pf. part. Pass. of ἀκριβόω, *exactly*, Aristeas 310, Eust.1406.29 (ed. Rom.).

ἥκω, Il.5.478: impf. ἧκον (v. infr.): fut. ἥξω (v. infr.); Dor. ἡξῶ Theoc.4.47, Call.*Fr.*1.65 P. (in Dor. and Hom. more commonly ἵκω): all other tenses late; aor. 1 part. ἥξας Paus.2.11.5, Gal.6.56, 10.609: pf. ἧκα Philostr.*VA*3.24, Scymn.62, 1 pl. ἥκαμεν *UPZ* 72. 9 (ii B.C.), *CIG*4762 (Egypt, i A.D.), Dor. ἥκαμες f.l. in Plu.2.225b, 2 pl. ἥκατε *PGrenf.*2.36.18 (i B.C.), 3 pl. ἧκασι Lxx 4*Ki.*20.14, *Ev. Marc.*8.3; inf. ἡκέναι *UPZ*6.30 (ii B.C.): plpf. ἥκεσαν J.*AJ*19.1.14: —Med., pres. subj. ἥκηται Aret.*SD*2.1: fut. ἥξομαι v.l. in M.Ant. 2.4:—*to have come, be present*, prop. in a pf. sense, with impf. ἧκον as plpf., I *had come*, and fut. ἥξω as fut. pf., I *shall have come*, μάλα τηλόθεν ἥκω Il.5.478, cf. Od.13.325, Pi.*O.*4.12 (ἵκω codd. vett.): impf. ἧκον A.*Pr.*661, Th.1.91, al., Pl.*R.*327c, Hdt.8.50, etc.: fut. ἥξω A.*Pr.* 103, al., E.*Andr.*738, Ar.*Pax*265, Orac.ap.Th.2.54, etc.; ἧκε imper., S.*Aj.*1116, Ar.*Pax*275, X.*Cyr.*4.5.25; ἡκέτω E.*Rh.*337:—Constr. mostly with εἰς, Hdt.8.50, A.*Ch.*3, etc.; παρά τινα Hdt.7.157, Th.1. 137; πρός τινα A.*Ch.*659; πρὸς δαίμονα S.*Fr.*770; esp. in worship, ἥκω πρὸς τὴν κυρίαν Ἶσιν *OGI*186.6 (Egypt, i B.C.), cf. *Ev.Jo.*6.37; πρὸς πόλιν S.*OC*734; ἐπί τινα *to set upon, attack*, Pl.*R.*336b, Aeschin. 2.178; but ἠ. ἐπὶ τὸ στράτευμα *to have come to fetch* the army, X. *An.*7.6.2; οἱ ἐπὶ ταῦθ' ἥκοντες D.18.28; ἐπ' ὀλέθρῳ E.*IA*886 (troch.); περὶ σπονδῶν X.*An.*2.3.4: c. acc., ἥξεις ποταμόν A.*Pr.*717, cf. 724, 730; ἠ. δῆμον τὸν Λυκείου S.*Fr.*271.6, cf. E.*Ba.*1; ἥκουσιν αὐτῷ ἄγγελοι X.*Cyr.*5.3.26; ἐς ταὐτὸν ἠ. *to have come* to the same point, to agree, E.*Hec.*748, *Hipp.*273: with Adv. of motion, ἠ. ἐνθάδε, δεῦρο, S.*Ph.*377, D.19.58; βῆναι κεῖθεν ὅθενπερ ἥκει S.*OC*1227: c. neut. Pron., αὐτὰ ταῦτα ἥκω παρά σε Pl.*Prt.*310e; ἐρωτώμενοι ὅ τι ἥκοιεν for what they *had come*, X.*HG*4.5.9: c. acc. cogn., ὁδὸν μακρὰν ἥκειν Id.*Cyr.*5.5.42: c. inf., μανθάνειν γὰρ ἥκομεν we *are here* to learn, S. *OC*12. 2. *to have reached a point*, ἐς τοσήνδ' ὕβριν ib.1030; εἰς τοῦτο ἀμαθίας E.*Andr.*170; εἰς τοσοῦτον ἀμαθίας Pl.*Ap.*25e; εἰς ὅσον ἡλικίας Id.*Chrm.*157d, etc.; πρὸς γάμων ἀκμάς S.*OT*1492; ὁρᾷς ἵν' ἥκεις; ib.687, etc.; Geom., *pass* through a point, διὰ τῶν πόλων Autol.*Sph.*10, cf. Archim.*Con.Sph.*9. b. διὰ μάχης, δι' ὀργῆς ἥκειν, A.*Supp.*475, S.*OC*905; cf. διά A. IV. c. with an Adv. folld. by gen., οὕτω πόρρω σοφίας ἥκεις Pl.*Euthd.*294e; εὖ ἥκειν τινός *to be* well *off for* a thing, *have plenty of* it, τοῦ βίου, χρημάτων, Hdt.1.30, 5.62; ἑωυτῶν Id.1.102; θεῶν χρηστῶν Id.8.111; πιθανότητος Demetr.Magn. ap.D.H.*Din.*1; οὐκ ὁμοίως ἠ. τινός not *to be* equally *well off* in respect of.., Hdt.1.149; πῶς ἀγῶνος ἥκομεν; how *have* we *sped* in the contest? E.*El.*751; ὧδε γένους ἠ. τινί *to be* this *degree* of kin to him, Id.*Heracl.*213; ὡς δυνάμεως ἥκεις Paus.4.21.10; ἐς μῆκος εὖ ἥκων Ael.*NA*4.34: abs., εὖ ἥκειν *to be flourishing*, Hdt.1.30: rarely c. gen. only, σὺ δὲ δυνάμιος ἥκεις μεγάλης thou *art in* great power, Id.7.157 (nisi leg. μεγάλως). 3. *to have come back, returned*, D.20.73; from exile, And.2.13; αὐτίκα ἥξω I *shall be back* in a moment, X.*An.*2.1.9; ἧκέ νυν ταχύ *come back* soon, Ar.*Pax*275; ἄψορρον ἥξεις A.*Pr.* 1021; ἄψορρον ἡξόμεν πάλιν S.*El.*53. 4. c. part., ἥκω φέρων I *have come* bringing (i.e. with), Id.*OC*579, cf. 357, Ar.*Pax*265, Eup.22 D., Pl.*Grg.*518d; ἧκεν ἄγων Id.*Phd.*117a; ἕτερόν τι ἥκεις ἔχων Id.*Grg.* 491c, etc.: c. fut. part., like ἔρχομαι, ἥκω φράσων, ἀγγελῶν, etc., I *am going*, I *intend* to say, E.*Ph.*706, 1075, etc. 5. *to have come to be*, θεοῖς ἔχθιστος ἥκω S.*OT*1519 (troch.), cf. *Aj.*636 (lyr.), *El.*1201, etc.; *take one's origin*, ἀπὸ πολιτειῶν τοιούτων ἥκετε, ἐν αἷς.. Th.4.126. II. of things, in various uses: of meats, *to have come to table*, Alex.132; ὡς τὰ περιφερόμενα ἧκε πρὸς ἡμᾶς X.*Cyr.*2.2.3; of reports, ἐμοὶ ἀγγελίη ἥκει παρὰ βασιλέος Hdt.8.140.α', cf. S.*OC*1177; of events, πῆμα ἥκει τινί A.*Pr.*103, cf. Ar.*Ra.*606, etc.; ἐπ' ἀνδρὶ ἥκει βίου τελευτή S. *OC*1472; ἵν' ἥκει τὰ μαντεύματα what they *have come to*, Id.*OT*953; ὡς αὐτὸν ἥξοι μοῖρα ib.713 codd.; ἥξει πόλεμος Orac.ap.Th.2.54; ἐς αὐτὸν ἥξει τὸ δεινόν Id.6.77; of Time, ἥκει ἦμαρ, νύξ, A.*Ag.*1301, E.*IT*42; ἥκει ὑμῖν ὁ καιρός Lys.12.79; τὸ μέλλον ἥξει A.*Ag.*1240. 2. *concern, relate to*, ποῖ λόγος ἥκει; to what *do* the words *relate?* E.*Tr.*154 (lyr.); εἰς ἔμ' ἥκει.. τὰ πράγματα Ar.*Pl.*919; εἰς ἐμὲ τὸ ἐλλεῖπον ἥξει *will fall* upon me, X.*Cyr.*1.5.13: freq. in part., τὰ εἰς τοὺς κινδύνους ἥκοντα Antipho 5.81; τὰ εἰς πλοῦτον ἠ. Pl.*Erx.*392d; τὰ πρὸς ἔπαινον, εἰς φιλανθρωπίαν ἠ., Plb.12.15.9, 28.17.2, etc. 3. *depend upon*, ὅσα τῆς Φωκέων σωτηρίας ἐπὶ τὴν πρεσβείαν ἧκε D.19.30; τό γε ἐπ' αὐτοὺς ἧκον μέρος Ph.2.21; ὅσα γ' εἰς βούλησιν ἥκειν τὴν ἐμήν Hld.4.7. 4. c. inf., ἧκέ μοι γένει.. πενθεῖν *it has come* to me by birth.., my birth lays it on me.., S.*OC*738, cf. *Ichn.*356; καλῶς αὐτοῖς κατθανεῖν ἧκον βίου *it being well for them at their age to die*, E.*Alc.*291. 5. c. part., ὃ καὶ νῦν ἥκει γινόμενον which *commonly* happens even now, Plb.24. 9.11 codd. (v.l. γενόμενον). (Prob. from same root as ἵκω.)

ἦλ, ἦλι, apoc. for ἧλος, or for ἥλιος, Euph.153a, b.

ἠλαιθερής, ές, = ἠλιοθερής, *EM*425.9: Comp., prob. in Hsch.

ἠλαίνω, Ep. for ἀλαίνω, *wander, stray, flit about*, ἠλαίνοντι Theoc. 7.23 (ἠλαίνονται codd., but cf. Gal.12.361): metaph., *wander in mind*, Call.*Dian.*251.

ἠλάκατα [ᾰκ], ων, τά, only in pl., *wool on the distaff*, ἠλάκατα στρωφῶσ' ἁλιπόρφυρα Od.6.53, 306, cf. 7.105; ἠ. στροφαλίζετε 18.315; ἠ. ἀνελισσομένης Alex.Aet.3.4.

Ἠλακάτεια, τά, festival at Sparta, Sosib.18 (–ατοία cod. Hsch.).

ἠλακάτη [κᾰ], ἡ (so in Att. Inscr., *IG*2².1517.209, but **ἠλεκ**– *SIG*² 588.17 (Delos, ii B.C.), *AJA*17.162 (Cyrene), *Sammelb.*5873, cf. Hsch.; v. ἠλεκάτιον), Dor. **ἠλᾰκάτᾱ** E.*Or.*1431 (lyr.), Aeol. **ἀλᾰκάτᾱ** Theoc.28.1 (ἀλ– also in χρυσαλάκατος, εὐαλάκατος, Dor. ἠλ– is dub.):—*distaff*, Od.4.135, 1.357, Il.6.491, E. l.c., etc.; ἡ ἠ. [τοῦ ἀτράκτου] *the stalk* of the spindle, Pl.*R.*616c: metaph., γηραιῇσι.. ἠλακάτῃσι with *the fate* of old age, *IG*14.1389 i 18. II. of *distaff-shaped* objects: 1. *one joint of a reed* or *cane*, Thphr.*HP*2.2.1; *a reed*, = δόναξ, Hsch.; ὥσπερ ἠ., of the pistil of the citron-flower, Thphr.*HP*1.13.4, cf. 4.4.3. 2. in Compds. (e.g. χρυσηλάκατος), *arrow*, Hsch. 3. *the upper part of the mast*, which was made to turn round, A.R.1.565 (v. Sch.), Ath.11.475a. 4. *windlass*, Sch.Th.7.25 (v.l. ἠλεκ–). 5. the constellation *Coma Berenices*, Sch.Arat.146.

ἠλᾰκᾰτῆνες, ων, οἱ, large sea-fish, prob. of the *tunny* kind, Men. *Kol.Fr.*7, Mnesim.4.35, Mnaseas 33. (Sg. only in Hdn.Gr.2.923.)

ἠλάμην, ἥλατο, v. ἅλλομαι.

ἠλαξός and **ἠλαξόος**, sine expl., *EM*425.5 (perh. ἡ λαξός, misunderstood).

ἡλάριον, τό, Dim. of ἧλος, *small nail*, *POxy.*1658.11 (iv A.D.), Suid. s.v. ἧλος.

ἤλᾰσα, v. ἐλαύνω.

ἠλασκάζω, lengthd. form of ἠλάσκω, ὑπὸ πτόλιν ἠλασκάζων Il.18. 281: c. acc. loci, *h.Ap.*142 codd. II. *shun, flee from*, c. acc., ἐμὸν μένος ἠλασκάζει Od.9.457 (v.l. ἠλυσκάζει).

ἠλάσκω, Ep. form of ἀλαίνω (cf. ἠλαίνω), *wander, stray, roam*, [ἔλαφοι] αὔτως ἠλάσκουσαι ἀνάλκιδες Il.13.104; [μυῖαι] κατὰ σταθμὸν ποιμνήϊον ἠλάσκουσιν 2.470; of persons, Emp.121.4, D.P.675.

Ἠλειακός or **Ἠλιακός**, ή, όν, (Ἦλις) *of* or *from Elis*: τὰ Ἠλιακά *the Antiquities of Elis*, Paus.5 tit.; οἱ Ἠλειακοί *philosophers of the school of Elis*, disciples of Phaedo, Str.9.1.8, D.L.*Prooem.*17, 2.105, 126.

ἠλεκάτιον [ᾰ], τό, Dim. of ἠλεκάτη (v. ἠλακ–), *BCH*35.286 (Delos, ii B.C.).

ἠλέκτρῐνος, η, ον, Dor. ἀλ–, *made of* ἤλεκτρον, Luc.*VH*1.20, Hld. 3.3. II. *shining like it*, ὕδωρ Call.*Cer.*29.

ἠλεκτρίς, ίδος, ἡ, fem. of ἠλέκτωρ, epith. of the Moon, Orph.*H*.9.6. II. Ἠλεκτρίδες νῆσοι *amber* islands, at the mouth of the Po, Str.5.1.9, cf. Plin.*HN*4.103.

ἤλεκτρον, τό, and **ἤλεκτρος**, ὁ or ἡ (gender indeterminate in Hom., Hes., and Pl., neut. in Hdt.3.115, Thphr.*HP*9.18.2, Ti.Locr.102a, masc. in S.*Ant*.1038 codd., Eust. ad D.P.293, fem. in Ar.*Eq*.532, Alex. Aphr.*Pr.Praef*.), *amber* (cf. Ἠλεκτρίδες), [ὅρμος] μετὰ..ἠλέκτροισιν (i.e. *pieces of amber*) ἔερτο Od.15.460, cf. 18.296, Hdt.3.115, Pl.*Ti*.80c, Phld.*Sign*.1, D.L.1.24, etc.; ἠλέκτρου λιβάδες A.R.4.606. II. *an alloy of gold and silver*, χρυσοῦ τ' ἠλέκτρου τε καὶ ἀργύρου ἠδ' ἐλέφαντος Od.4.73, cf. Hes.*Sc*.142, Hom.*Epigr*.15.10, Pytheas ap.Ath.11.465d; τἀπὸ Σάρδεων ἤ. S.*Ant*.1038 (cj.): in pl., of the pegs of a lyre, ἐκπιπτουσῶν τῶν ἠλέκτρων Ar.*Eq*.532. (The two senses are difficult to distinguish in early Poetry; cf. Paus.5.12.7, Plin.*HN*33.80, 37.31. The word is connected with ἠλέκτωρ.)

ἠλεκτρό-ομαι, Pass., *become electrum*, Zos.Alch.p.180 B. **-φαής**, ές, *amber-gleaming*, αὐγαί, of the tears of the Phaethontiades, E.*Hipp*.741 (lyr.). **-φόρος**, ον, *amber-bearing*, δένδρα, δάκρυον, Tz.*H*.4.381, 690.

ἠλεκτρώδης, ες, *amber-like*, κοιλίης ταραχή Hp.*Epid*.4.38; βάλανοι Philostr.*VA*1.21.

ἠλέκτωρ, ορος, ὁ, *the beaming sun*, τεύχεσι παμφαίνων ὥς τ' ἠλέκτωρ Il.6.513; ὥς τ' ἠλέκτωρ Ὑπερίων 19.398; *fire* as an element, ἠ. τε χθών τε καὶ οὐρανὸς ἠδὲ θάλασσα Emp.22.2: gen. ἠλέκτωρος Choerob. *in Theod*.1.301 H.: dat. ἠλέκτωρι Epic. in *Arch.Pap*.7.4: hence acc. ἠλέκτωρα has been restored in Euph.110.

ἠλέμᾰτος, Dor. and Aeol. **ἀλέματος**, ον, *idle, vain*, Sapph.*Supp*.15.5, Alc.*Supp*.23.4; ὦ τᾶς ἀλεμάτω ψυχᾶς prob. l. in Theoc.15.4 (ἀδεμ-, ἀδαμ- codd.); of a person, Timo 34.3, cf. 66.4 (cj.); βροντή Sotad.2; χειρὸς ἐκηβολίη *AP*6.75 (Paul. Sil.); φαντασίη ib.11.350 (Agath.). Adv. -τως *idly*, A.R.4.1206; *in vain*, Call.*Cer*.91: so neut. pl. ἠλέματα Opp.*H*.4.590.

ἠλεός, ή, όν, *distraught, crazed*, φρένας ἠλεέ Od.2.243; in shorter form φρένας ἠλέ (perh. replacing Aeol. ἄλλε, written αλε), Il.15.128; ἠλεὰ ῥέξας Call.*Fr*.174, cf. 173: neut. pl., as Adv., *foolishly*, *AP*7.639 (Antip.), Call.*Aet*.3.1.66: Aeol. **ἄλλος** prob. in Sapph.35, 110, dub. in ἀλλοφρονέω, ἀλλοφάσσω; cf. ἀλοσύνα (s.v. ἠλοσύνη). 2. Act., *distracting, crazing*, οἶνος Od.14.464. II. **ἀλεός** [ᾰ], is cited from A. (*Fr*.410) by Hsch. (ἀλαιός cod.), cf. Hdn.Gr.2.909, *EM*59.45; cf. **ἀλεόφρων**· ὁ παράφρων ibid.: **ἀλ(ε)ώσσειν**· μωραίνειν, Hsch.

ἠλέσθην, v. ἀλέω (A). **ἠλεύατο**, 3 sg. 1 aor. of ἀλέομαι.

ἠλήλατο, **ἠλήλαντο**, v. ἐλαύνω. **ἦλημα**, v. βήλημα.

Ἡλιάδης, ου, ὁ, *child of the Sun*, Luc.*Am*.2; οἱ Ἡλιάδαι, an ancient family in Rhodes, Str.14.2.8, D.S.5.56.

ἡλιάζομαι, fut. -άσομαι (v. infr.): aor. 1 inf. -άσασθαι Ar.*Eq*.798:—*sit in the court* Ἡλιαία, *be a Heliast*, Id.*Lys*.380 (-άξεις, -άζεις codd., -άζει Cobet), *V*.772 (with a play on the word, ἡλιάσει πρὸς ἥλιον), Lex ap.D.24.50.

ἡλιάζω, *bake in the sun*, [μάζας] Str.16.4.13, cf. Dieuch.ap.Orib.4.8.1:—Pass., *bask in the sun*, Arist.*HA*611ᵇ14; *ferment*, -άζεται ἡ β ληνός *BGU*1551.1,10 (iii B.C.); πολλάκις ὁ οἶνος -αζόμενος τελειοῦται τῇ κράσει καὶ τῇ δυνάμει Anon.*Incred*.17. II. Pass., = ἐξηλιάζομαι, Lxx 2*Ki*.21.14.

ἡλιαία, ἡ, at Athens, *public place* or *hall*, in which the chief law-court was held, ἐν ἡλιαίᾳ Ar.*Eq*.897; ἀναβὰς εἰς τὴν ἡ. τὴν τῶν θεσμοθετῶν prob. in Antipho 6.21, cf. *IG*1².39.75, 63.14. 2. *supreme court* at Athens, Lex Solonis ap.Lys.10.16, Lex ap.D.21.47, Paus.1.28.8, etc. II. = ἁλία (A) (q.v.). III. ἡλιαίη, = ἀλέα (B), Hsch.

Ἡλιαῖα, τά, *festival of Helios*, Jul.*Or*.4.156c.

ἡλιᾰκός, Dor. **ἁλιακός**, ή, όν, *of the sun, solar*, Zeno *Stoic*.1.34; φάντασμα, εἴδωλον, Demetr.Lac.*Herc*.1013.17; κύκλος ἡ. *the sun's orbit, the ecliptic* (v. ἐκλειπτικός), D.S.1.98; ἡ. (sc. κύκλος), ὁ, Cleom.1.4, etc.; φῶς ἡ. Ph.2.254, al.; ἔκλειψις ἡ. D.L.1.23; ἐνιαυτός Gem.8.47, *Placit*.2.32.3; ἔτος, στέφανος ἁ., at Rhodes, *Com.Adesp*.336.4,6; κάνθαρος ἡ. *dung*-beetle (v. ἡλιοκάνθαρος), *PMag.Par*.1.751; τροχίσκος ἡ. (magical remedy), Nech.ap.Harp.Astr. in *Cat.Cod.Astr*.8(3).135; ἡλιακή (sc. περίοδος), ἡ, *solar year*, Plu.*Caes*.59. Adv. -κῶς Procl. *in Prm*.p.631 S.

ἡλιανθές, τό, *laudanum-plant*, *Cistus laurifolius*, Ps.-Democr.ap.Plin.*HN*24.165.

ἡλιάς, άδος, ἡ, fem. of ἡλιακός, ἀκτίς Orac.ap.Luc.*Alex*.34; Ῥόδος Id.*Am*.7. II. Ἡλιάδες, αἱ, *daughters of the Sun*, who were changed into poplars and wept amber, Parm.1.9, A.R.4.604, Str.5.1.9; ἡ Ἡλιὰς αἴγειρος Philostr.*VA*5.5. III. ἡλιάδες· αἱ κατάχρυσοι κλῖναι, Hsch.

ἡλίᾰσις (A), εως, ἡ, = ἡλίωσις, *exposure to the sun*, Gal.4.807 (pl.), D.C.59.7, *Gp*.7.1.3.

ἡλίᾰσις (B), εως, ἡ, *sitting in the* Ἡλιαία, Jusj.ap.D.24.150.

ἡλιαστ-ήριον, τό, *place for sunning oneself*, Str.17.1.44, Gal.18(1).518; *place for drying fruit*, etc., *PRyl*.206.48 (iii A.D.), *POxy*.1631.17 (iii A.D.), etc. **-ής**, οῦ, ὁ, (ἡλιαία 2) *Heliast*, Ar.*V*.206, 891, *Eq*.255, *IG*1².63.14, etc. II. *fuller*, = Lat. *lutor*, *Gloss*. **-ικός**, ή, όν, *of, for*, or *like a Heliast*, γέρων Ar.*V*.195; ὀβολός Id.*Nu*.863; ὅρκος Lex ap.D.24.21, Hyp.*Eux*.40.

ἡλι-αυγής, ές, (αὐγή) *gleaming like the sun*, *EM*425.24. **-άω**, *to be like the sun*, κόμαι ἡλιῶσαι *Anacreont*.16.5, cf. Hld.3.4, Philostr.*VA*7.42. II. Act., *expose to the sun*, τὰς σταφυλάς Arist.*Pr*.926ᵇ38.

ἡλῐβᾰτᾶς [βᾰ], ὁ, *haunting the heights*, τράγος Antiph.133.3, cf. Anaxil.12 (-βάτους codd.):—hence **-βᾰτέω**, *haunt the heights*, Sch.Il.15.273.

ἠλίβᾰτος [ῐ], Dor. **ἀλ-**, ον, *high, steep*, always in Hom. as epith. of πέτρη or πέτραι, Il.15.273, al., cf. Hes.*Th*.675, 786, Thgn.176, Pi.*O*.6.64, A.*Supp*.352 (lyr.), E.*Supp*.80 (lyr.), Theoc.26.10, etc.; ὄρος, ἄκρη, ἐρίπναι, A.R.2.169, 361, 1248; of the Olympian throne of Zeus, Ar.*Av*.1732; of trees, *h.Ven*.267 (so prob. in Hes.*Sc*.422).—Also in X. and later Prose, πέτραι ἠ. *An*.1.4.4; τόποι Plb.4.41.9; πέτρος Str.17.1.50; δένδρα Agatharch.97; πῦρ Hanno *Peripl*.16; σταυρός Epigr.ap.Plu.*Flam*.9. II. *deep, abysmal*, ἄντρῳ ἐν ἠ. Hes.*Th*.483; Τάρταρος ἠ. Stes.83; ἠ. ὑπὸ κευθμῶσι E.*Hipp*.732 (lyr.); πελάγεσσιν ἐν ἠ. Opp.*H*.3.171: metaph., κακὸν ἠ. Damox.2.22; εὐήθεια Porph.*Abst*.1.12. III. in later Poets (perh. from a misunderstanding of [Κύκλωψ] ἠ. πέτρην ἐπέθηκε θύρῃσιν Od.9.243), *huge, enormous*, μέλεα Opp.*H*.5.66; σχεδίη Q.S.11.312; so in Prose, κῦμα, σκιαί, Plu.2.163c, 935f. (Etym. dub., cf. ἄλιψ· πέτρα, Hsch.)

Ἡλίεια, only in Rhod. form **Ἁλίεια**, τά, *festival of the Sun*, *SIG* 724 (Rhodes, ii/i B.C.), al.; written Ἅλεια in Ath.13.561e, Ἁλίων (gen.) in Aristid.*Or*.25(43).32, ἀλιειτα (for Ἁλίεια τά..) in *Com.Adesp*.336.

ἠλῖθα, Adv. *very much, exceedingly*, ληΐδα..συνελάσσαμεν ἠ. πολλήν Il.11.677, cf. Od.5.483; ἄστρα ἠ. μυρία Man.2.3; καθαρὴν γλάγεος πόσιν ἠ. πίνειν Nic.*Al*.423, cf. A.R.3.342 (expl. by Sch. as, = ἀθρόως), 4.177, 1265. II. *in vain, to no purpose*, Call.*Lav.Pall*.124, A.R.2.283; ἔβρασεν ἠ. νηδὺς πνεύματα Nic.*Al*.25, cf. 140. (Prob. connected with ἠλεός in both uses.)

ἠλῐθι-άζω, *speak* or *act idly, foolishly*, Ar.*Eq*.1124. **-ος**, Dor. **ἀλ-**, α, ον, also ος, ον Hdt.1.60: (ἠλίθα II):—*idle, vain*, χόλος Pi.*P*.3.11; βέλος A.*Ag*.366 (anap.); ὁδός Theoc.16.9. II. *foolish, silly*, εὐηθίη Hdt.1.60; ἠλίθιον θάρρος θαρρεῖν Pl.*Phd*.95c; νόμος *PThead*.25.7 (iv A.D.); freq. of persons, E.*Cyc*.537, Ar.*Ach*.443, etc.: Comp. -ώτερος X.*Smp*.3.6: Sup. -ώτατος Ar.*Ec*.765; ἠλίθιόν [ἐστι] c. inf., Arist.*Pol*.1286ᵃ12, prob. in Antiph.58; also ἠλιθίων ἐστί is the mark *of a fool*, Phld.*Po*.5.32. Adv. -ίως, διακεῖσθαι Lys.1.10; οἰόμενοι Pl.*Tht*.180d, cf. Theoc.10.40: Comp. -ώτερον Jul.*Gal*.89a: neut. ἠλίθιον as Adv., Ar.*Nu*.872. 2. *without sense*, of the dead, *Tab.Defix.Aud*.43.7. **-ότης**, ητος, ἡ, *folly, silliness*, Cratin.188, Pl.*R*.560d, al., Phld.*Rh*.1.249 S., etc.; γνώμης Them.*Or*.1.11d. **-όω**, *make foolish, distract*, φρένας A.*Pr*.1061 (anap.). **-ώδης**, ες, *like a fool*, Philostr.*VS*2.1.10. **-ώνη**, ἡ, *one who makes foolish* or *distracts*, epith. of the Ἐρινύες, *Tab.Defix*.108.

ἠλῐθοποιός, όν, gloss on ἠλεός, Sch.Od.14.464.

ἡλῐκί-α, Ion. **-ίη**, Dor. **ἁλικία**, ἡ, (ἧλιξ) *time of life, age*, ἥν πως ἡλικίην αἰδέσσεται ἠδ' ἐλεήσῃ γῆρας Il.22.419; γηραιὸν μέρος ἁλικίας Pi.*P*.4.157; παρὰ τὸν ἁλικίας ἐοικότα χρόνον Id.*O*.4.29; τήνδ' ἡ. ἀστῶν, i.e. their old *age*, A.*Pers*.914: acc. used adverbially, *in age*, νέος ἡλικίην Hdt.3.134; ἐτέων ἐὼν ἡλικίην πέντε καὶ τριήκοντα Id.1.26, cf. X.*Cyn*.2.3: so in dat., ἡλικίᾳ ἔτι τότε ὢν νέος Th.5.43; προεληλυθότες ταῖς ἡ. X.*HG*6.1.4; also ὑπὸ τῆς ἡ. from our *age*, Pl.*La*.180d; αἱ δι' ἡλικίαν ἄτοκοι Id.*Tht*.149c; οἱ ἐν τῇ αὐτῇ ἡ. Th.1.80; τὸ ἀχρεῖον τῆς ἡ. Id.2.44; ὅταν..τοῦ γεννᾶν ἐκβῶσι τὴν ἡ. Pl.*R*.461b; πόρρω τῆς ἡ. to an advanced *age*, Id.*Grg*.484c; προήκων ἐς βαθὺ τῆς ἡ. Ar.*Nu*.514; προϊούσης τῆς ἡ. Pl.*Phdr*.279a; ὁ παρ' ἡλικίαν νοῦς beyond *one's age*, Men.*Mon*.690: in pl., ἐν ἁπάσαις ταῖς ἡ. Pl.*R*.412e, cf. *Lg*.625b, al. 2. *prime of life, manhood*, ἐν ἁλικίᾳ πρώτᾳ Pi.*N*.9.42; αὐτὴ ἡ ἡ. τῶν νέων κατέκρινε Antipho 4.4.2; ἡλικίαν ἔχειν, εἰς ἡ. ἐλθεῖν, ἀφικέσθαι, Pl.*Euthd*.306d, *Tht*.142d, *Men*.89b; ἡλικίην ἔχειν c. inf., to be *of fit age* for doing, Hdt.1.209, cf. Pl.*Tht*.146b; ἡλικίας μετέχειν Th.7.60; οἱ ἐν τῇ ἡλικίᾳ men *of military age*, Id.8.75; ἐν ἡλικίᾳ στρατεύεσθαι D.4.7; ἐστρατευμένος ἁπάσας τὰς ἐν ἡλικίᾳ στρατείας Id.21.95; οἱ τῆς ἡ. ἐντὸς γεγονότες Lys.2.50; ἡ καθεστηκυῖα ἡ. maturity, Th.2.36, cf. *IG*12(7).239.21 (Amorgos); of women, *womanhood, marriageable age*, Hp.*Prorrh*.2.30, D.59.22; αἱ ἐν ἡ. γυναῖκες Pl.*R*.461b; τὴν ἡλικίαν τὴν ἑαυτοῦ καταμεμψάμενος Is.7.14: in pl., οἱ ταῖς ἡ. οὐ καλῶς κεχρημένοι Aeschin.1.194. 3. *youthful passion*, ἡλικίῃ καὶ θυμῷ ἐπιτρέπειν Hdt.3.36; εἴκειν Id.7.18. 4. *maidenhood*, τὴν ἡ. οὐ καλῶς διαφυλάξασαν Aeschin.1.182. II. as collective Noun, = οἱ ἥλικες, *those of the same age, comrades*, ὃς ἡλικίην ἐκέκαστο ἔγχεϊ Il.16.808, cf. Pi.*P*.1.74; esp. *those of military age*, τῆς ἡ. ἀπούσης ἐν ταῖς ναυσί Lys.2.49, cf. Th.3.67, 8.1, etc.; also, *men of any age*, παίδων τε καὶ ἀνδρῶν καὶ πάσης ἡ. Pl.*Lg*.959e. III. *time*, ταῦτα ἡλικίην ἂν εἴη κατὰ Λάϊον about the *time* of Laius, Hdt.5.59, cf. 60, 71; ἡ. τετρακοσίοισι ἔτεσι..πρεσβυτέρους Id.2.53. IV. *age, generation*, ἐπὶ τῆς νῦν ἡ. Isoc.4.167; πρὸ τῆς ἡμετέρας ἡ. Din.1.38; εἰς τὴν νῦν ζῶσαν ἡ. D.60.11; πολλαῖς ἔμπροσθεν ἡ. Plu.*Per*.27, cf. D.L.5.37. V. of the body, *stature*, as a sign of age, Hdt.3.16, Pl.*Euthd*.271b, D.40.56; τῇ ἡ. μικρός *Ev.Luc*.19.3 (but προσθεῖναι ἐπὶ τὴν ἡ. πῆχυν ἕνα add a cubit to one's *age* (cf. πήχυιος), *Ev.Matt*.6.27); ἄνδρας ἡμισταδιαίους τὰς ἡ. Luc.*VH*1.40; *height* of a pillar, Id.*Syr.D*.28. **-άζομαι**, Pass., *assume this* or *that quality*, dub. in Herm.ap.Stob.1.49.69. **-ώτης**, ου, ὁ, Cret. **ϝαλικιώτας** (written βαλικιώτης), Hsch.:—*equal in age, comrade*, Hdt.5.71, Ar.*Nu*.1006, And.1.48; ἡ. τινί Lys.20.36; ἐμὸς ἡ. Pl.*Ap*.33d; ἡ. καὶ ἑταῖροι Id.*Smp*.183c, al.: c. gen., ἡ. τῶν λόγων Him.*Or*.12.4:—fem. **-ῶτις**, ιδος, Plu.2.554a, Luc.*DMar*.15.2; ἡ. ἱστορία *contemporary* history, Plu.*Per*.13; πράξεις ἡ. D.S.1.58: c. dat., *contemporaneous with*, ib.9: c. gen., Max.Tyr.3.2, Them.*Or*.4.58b.

ἥλικος [ῐ], η, ον, *as big as*, πόσος τις; μικρός, ἥλικος Μόλων Ar.*Ra*.55; τί τοσοῦτον ὕβρισεν, ἥλικον..; D.21.147; τηλικοῦτος, ἡ. οὐδεὶς πω βασιλεὺς Id.1.9. 2. of age, *as old as*, ἄνδρα..ἥλικον Θουκυδίδην Ar.*Ach*.703; τοῖσιν ἡλίκοισι νῷν, = τηλίκοις ἡλίκοι νώ, Id.*Ec*.465; οἱ ἡλίκοι ἐγώ, = τηλίκοι ἡλίκοι ἐγώ, Pl.La.180d: rare in Trag., ὁρᾷς μὲν ἡμᾶς, ἡλίκοι.. of what various ages.., S.OT15. 3. in indirect questions, how big, how great, Thphr.Char.23.2, Crates Theb.18, etc.; ὁρῶν ἡ. ἐστὶ Φίλιππος D.6.6, cf. Pl.Chrm.154b; freq. in expressions of wonder, θαυμάσι' ἡλίκα extraordinarily great, D.19.24; θαυμαστὸν ἡλίκον Id.24.122; μέγιστα ἡλίκα Luc.Merc.Cond.13; also, how small, ἰδοὺ ἡλίκον πῦρ ἡλίκην ὕλην ἀνάπτει Ep.Jac.3.5; ἂν ἴδω γὰρ ἡλίκον ἰχθὺν ὅσου τιμῶσι Antiph.166.6, cf. Luc.Herm.5. 4. in exclamations, ἡλίκον λαλεῖς Men.Sam.40. (Compd. of yo-, relat. Pron. stem (cf. ὅς), and -āli- (cf. ἧλιξ), with suffix -κο-; cf. πηλίκος, τηλίκος.)

ἡλῐκοσοῦν, strengthd. for ἡλίκος, however so great, Plot.1.4.7.

ἧλιξ, Dor. **ἆλιξ**, Aeol. **ἆλιξ** Sapph.119, ἴκος, ὁ, ἡ:—of the same age, καταίθουσα παιδὸς.. δαλὸν ἧλικ', of Meleager's torch, A.Ch.608; δρῦς A.R.2.479; Πηλῆος.. ἡ. χαίτην Tryph.637: mostly in pl., βόες.. ἥλικες ἰσοφόροι Od.18.373; ἅλικες οἷα παρθένοι Pi.P.3.17; ἄνδρες ἡ. Ar.V.245; ὑφ' ἡλίκων νεανίδων Id.Th.1030(lyr.); ἐν ἅλικι χρόνῳ in equal time, B.7.45. 2. Subst., fellow, comrade, οἱ ἥλικες Hdt.1.34, 2.32; ἥλικές θ' ἥβης ἐμῆς A.Pers.681; τὸν ἥλικα τόνδε Ar.Ach.336 codd. (sed leg. ὁμήλικα); μετὰ τῶν ἡ. Antipho 3.2.3; prov., ἧλιξ ἥλικα τέρπει Pl.Phdr.240c, cf. Arist.EN1161^{b}34. (Fr. ϝᾶλιξ, cf. βαλικιώτης: compd. of swo- 'one's own' (cf. ϝός, Lat. suus) and -āli- 'size', 'growth' (cf. Lat. alo, aequ-āli-s, Gr. ὁμ-ᾶλι-ξ), with suffix -κ-.)

ἡλιό-βᾰτος, ον, coined as etym. of ἠλίβατος, EM427.45. **-βλητος**, ον, = ἡλιόβολος, πλάκες E.Ba.14; of a tree, sun-scorched, Ael.NA8.26. **-βολέομαι**, Pass., to be sun-struck, Zen.5.53. **-βολος**, ον, exposed to the sun, sunny, of places, Thphr.CP4.12.3. **-δρόμος**, ὁ, sun's messenger, ἡ. Διός Ramsay Cities and Bishoprics 2 p.566 (Acmonia); title of a grade of initiates in Mithras-worship, Cumont Mystères de Mithra 1.317. **-δύσιον** [ῠ], τό, sunset, Vett.Val.362.34. **-ειδής**, ές, like the sun, bright and beaming, Pl.R.509a, Gal.5.635, Plot.1.6.9; ἀήρ Arist.Fr.42; [σῶμα] Porph.Sent.29: Sup. -ειδέστατος Pl.R.508b, Gal.UP3.10. **-θαλπής**, ές, warmed by the sun, gloss on ἑλαθερής, Hsch. **-θερέω**, to sun oneself, Gal.6.137. **-θερής**, ές, (θέρω) warmed in the sun, EM58.1. **-κάης**, ές, (κάω, καίω) sunburnt, Luc.Lex.2; ὄστρακον v.l. in Dsc.2.2: -καές, τό, name of a powder, Orib.Fr.115. **-κᾰΐα**, ἡ, sun-burning, exposure to the sun, D.L.7.1 (pl.), Paul.Aeg.3.6 (pl.), Phlp.in Ph.60.13, in GC148.14. **-καλλίς**, ίδος, ἡ, = ἡλιανθές, Plin.HN24.165. **-κάμῑνος** [ᾰ], ὁ, a room exposed to the sun, for winter use, Plin.Ep.2.17.20, IGRom.4.1431.43 (Smyrna). **-κάνθᾰρος**, ον, the dung-beetle or scarab, Alex.Trall.Febr.7. **-καυστος**, Dor. ἀλ-, ον, (καίω) = ἡλιοκαής, Theoc.10.27, Dsc.2.2. **-καυτέω**, to be sunburnt, Alex.Aphr.ap.Simp.in Ph.968.25. **-κεντρίς**, ίδος, ἡ, a kind of fly, Gloss. **-κόμας**, ου, ὁ, with hair like the sun, Eust.976.53. **-κτῠπος**, ον, sunburnt, A.Supp.155(lyr.) (ἡδιόκτυπον cod. Med.). **-μᾰνής**, ές, sun-mad, mad for love of the sun, epith. of the cicada, Ar.Av.1096 (lyr.). **-μαντεία**, ἡ, magical invocation of the sun, PMag.Leid.W.4. **-μορφος**, ον, sun-shaped, Castorio 1.

ἡλιόομαι, Pass., live in the sun, be exposed to the sun, ἡλιωμένος, opp. ἐσκιατροφηκώς, Pl.R.556d; of Places, ὅπως ἡ γῆ ἡλιωθῇ Thphr.CP3.4.1, cf. HP1.10.3; τὰ ἡλιούμενα parts exposed to the sun, X.Oec.19.18; -ούμενος ἀήρ Ath.Med.ap.Orib.9.5.1. 2. to be sun-struck, ἡλιοῦσθαι τὴν κεφαλήν Hp.Aër.3; or sunburnt, Muson.Fr.19 p.107 H. 3. to be illuminated by the sunlight, Arist.de An.419^{b}31, Pr.913^{a}22:—late in Act. **ἡλιόω**, place in the sun, Aët.1.102,112, al.

ἡλιοπάλιος or -ον, name of a plant or stone, PMag.Berol.2.18 (perh. sun-opal, cf. ὀπάλλιος).

ἡλιό-πεπτος, ον, ripened in the sun, σταφίς Hippiatr.58. **-πλήξ**, πλῆγος, ὁ, ἡ, sunburnt, Call.Iamb.1.219. **-πους**, ποδος, ὁ, = ἡλιοτρόπιον, Ps.-Dsc.4.190.

ἥλιος, ὁ, Ep. **ἠέλιος**, as always in Hom. (exc. in the late passage Od.8.271) and Hes., cf. Hp.Alim.42: Dor. **ἀέλιος** [ᾱ] Pi.P.4.144, Call.Cer.92, Lav.Pall.89, and lyr. in Trag., S.Ant.809, E.Ph.175, al., but **ἅλιος** [ᾱ], S.Tr.96, E.Alc.395 (ἀέλιος S.Tr.835): Cret. **ἀβέλιος** (i.e. ἀϝ-), Hsch.: Aeol. **ἀέλιος** Sapph.79 (= Oxy.1787 Fr.1.25), Supp.25.7; **ἄλιος** Sapph.69 (s.v.l.): Arc. **ἀέλιος** (or ἀ-) IG5(2).4.12 (Tegea, iv B.C.):—sun, Il.7.421, etc.; ὁρᾶν φάος ἠελίοιο to see the light of life, live, 18.61, etc.; ὑπ' ἠελίῳ τε καὶ οὐρανῷ ἀστερόεντι ναιετάουσι 4.44; γυνή.. ἀρίστη τῶν ὑφ' ἡλίῳ E.Alc.151; οὐκέτ' ἔστιν ὑφ' ἁλίῳ ib.395; also ὑπὸ ἡλίου ἑωρᾶσθαι Th.2.102; οἱ ὑπὸ τοῦτον τὸν ἥλιον ἄνθρωποι D.18.270; τριῶν τῶν ὑπὸ τὸν ἡ. μεγίστων ἡγεμονιῶν Plu.Luc.30: prov., οὐδ' ὁ ἡ. εἴσεται Hld.7.21; ὥσπερ σελήνη γ' ἡλίῳ (sc. ὅμοιος) a pale reflection, Com.Adesp.5.15 D. 2. to determine the cardinal points, πρὸς ἠῶ τ' ἠέλιόν τε towards the East, opp. πρὸς ζόφον: εἴτ' ἐπὶ δεξί' ἴωσι πρὸς ἠῶ τ' ἠέλιόν τε, εἴτ' ἐπ' ἀριστερὰ τοί γε ποτὶ ζόφον ἠερόεντα Il.12.239, cf. Od.9.26; ὅσοι ναίουσι πρὸς ἠῶ τ' ἠέλιόν τε, ἠδ' ὅσσοι μετόπισθε ποτὶ ζόφον 13.240; πρὸς ἠῶ τε καὶ ἡλίου ἀνατολάς, opp. πρὸς ἑσπέρην, Hdt.7.58; τὰ πρὸς ἠῶ τε καὶ ἥλιον ἀνατέλλοντα Id.4.40; οἱ ἀπὸ ἡλίου ἀνατολέων Αἰθίοπες the eastern.., Id.7.70. 3. day, S.El.424; a day, Pi.O.13.37, Hp.Alim.42, E.Hel.652 (pl.), Ps.-Luc.Philopatr.4,26, etc.; later, year, Herod.10.1. 4. sunshine, sun's heat, ἐπὶ τοῖς ὄρεσιν Pl.Phd.116e; ἡ. πολὺς Luc.Nav.35, cf. Herm.25; πολὺν τὸν ἡ. ἐμφαίνειν, of a sunburnt person, Id.Ind.3, cf. Rh.Pr.9: pl., sunbeams, Thphr.Sign.22, Ael.NA16.17; hot sunny days, Th.7.87. 5. metaph., sunshine, brightness, ψυχῆς Plu.2.994e, cf. Artem.2.36, etc.; of a person, Ἑλλάνων δόξης δεύτερον Ἀέλιον IG14.1188; of Ptol. VI, UPZ15.33; νέος Ἥ., of Nero and Caligula, SIG814.34, 798.3. II. as pr. n., Helios, the sun-god, Od.8.271, etc.; νὴ τὸν Ἥ. Men.Sam.108; ὑπὸ Δία Γῆν Ἥλιον, in manumission-formula, POxy.48.6, 49.8 (i A.D.), IG9(1).412 (Aetolia), IPE2.54.10 (iii A.D.); [Ἥλιος] δούλους ἐλευθέρους ποιεῖ Artem.2.36; identified with Apollo, Carm.Pop.12, E.Fr.781.11; with Dionysus, D.Chr.31.11, etc. 2. Ἡλίου ἀστήρ, of the planet Saturn, v.l. in Pl.Epin.987c, cf. D.S.2.30, Theo Sm. p.130 H. (I.-E. sāwelios, cf. Cret. ἀβέλιος, Lith. sáulė, Lat. sōl.)

ἡλιοσέληνος, ὁ, sunstone, imitatur quodammodo congressum solis et lunae, figuratque colore, Procl. de sacrificio et magia 101 (Kroll Analecta Gr., Greifsw. 1901 p.8).

Ἡλιο-σέρᾱπις, ιδος, ὁ, an Egyptian divinity, IG14.2405.48 (Puteoli). **-σκόπιος**, ον, looking to the sun: ἡ. τιθύμαλλος sun-spurge, Euphorbia helioscopia, Dsc.4.164, cf. Ruf.ap.Orib.7.26.39 (v.l. -σκοπος), Plin.HN26.69. **-σκόπος**, ὁ, a Hermetic plant, Cat.Cod.Astr.8(2).163. **-στᾰσία**, ἡ, solstice, Gloss. **-στερής**, ές, depriving of sun, i.e. shading from the sun, epith. of the Thessalian hat, S.OC313. **-στῐβής**, ές, sun-trodden, ἀντολαί A.Pr.791. **-τρόπιον**, τό, heliotrope, Thphr.HP7.3.1, Gal.19.732; ἡ. τὸ μέγα, Heliotropium villosum, Dsc.4.190; ἡ. τὸ μικρόν, H. supinum, ib.191. 2. = Croton tinctorius, PHolm.8.3, al. II. sun-dial, Moschio ap.Ath.5.207f, IG11(2).287 A117 (Delos, iii B.C.), Plu.Dio 29, Sch.Ar.Av.998, etc. III. green stone streaked with red, blood-stone, Plin.HN37.165, Herm.Trism. in Rev.Phil.32.258. **-τρόπιος**, ον, belonging to foreg. 1, ξύλον Theb.Ostr.144.1 (i A.D.). II. v. Ἁλιοτρόπιος. **-τροπος**, ὁ, = ἡλιοτρόπιον 1, Ps.-Dsc.4.190.

ἡλιοῦχος, ον, possessing sun, PMag.Par.1.3228 (s.v.l.).

ἡλιο-φεγγής, Dor. ἁλ-, ές, shining like the sun, Philod.Scarph.136. **-φῠές**, τό, = κλύμενον, Ps.-Dsc.4.13. **-φῠτον**, τό, = μῖλαξ τραχεῖα, ib.4.142.

ἡλιόω, v. ἡλιόομαι.

ἡλίσκος, ὁ, Dim. of ἧλος, little nail, Ar.Fr.314.

ἤλῑτε, v. ἀλιταίνω.

ἠλῐτενής, ές, lofty, πέτρα Suid.; cf. ἠλίβατος.

ἡλίτης [ῑ], ου, ὁ, (ἥλιος) = ἡλιοειδής, λίθος Dam.Isid.233; helitis (leg. -es) lapis, Procl. de sacrificio et magia 91 (Kroll Analecta Gr., Greifsw. 1901 p.8).

ἡλῖτις, ιδος, ἡ, (ἧλος) of or like nails, ἡ. λεπίς iron that scales off from nails, Dsc.5.78, Aët.2.58.

ἠλῐτο-εργός, όν, missing the work, failing in one's aim, AP7.210 (Antip.), dub. l. in Alc.Oxy.1360 Fr.6. **-μηνις**· ὁ μάτην ἐγκαλῶν, Hsch.: acc. sg. -μηνιν Epic. in Arch.Pap.7.5. **-μηνος**, ον, missing the right month, i.e. untimely born, Il.19.118, Tryph.556, Plu.2.358e, AP12.228 (Strat.).

ἡλιφάρμᾰκος, ἡ, a plant useful to staunch blood, Timag.ap.Stob.4.36.19. **ἠλίφατος**, variant for ἠλίβατος, Hsch.

ἧλιψ, ῖπος, ὁ, a Dorian shoe (cf. ἀνήλιπος), Sch.Theoc.4.56.

ἡλῐ-ώδης, ες, = ἡλιοειδής, εἴδωλον Chaerem.14.14; μῆλα Philostr.Im.1.6; κόμη Anon.ap.Eust.432.26. **-ών**, ῶνος, ὁ, month at Termessus, Lanckoroński Städte Pamphyliens und Pisidiens 2.34. **-ωπός**, όν, lit by the sun's eye, οὐρανός Ζεὺς S.Fr.26 (= E.Fr.p.531 N.), 470. **-ωσις**, εως, ἡ, (ἡλιόομαι) exposure to the sun, Hp.Epid.7.82, Thphr.CP6.16.5, Sor.2.38, S.E.P.3.16. **-ωτέος**, α, ον, needing exposure to the sun, Philostr.Gym.58. **-ώτης**, ου, ὁ, fem. **-ῶτις**, poet. **ἠελιῶτις**, ιδος, (ἥλιος) of the sun, ἀκτῖν' ἐς ἡλιῶτιν S.Tr.697; ἠελιῶτις αἴγλη AP7.601 (Jul.Aeg.); αὐγαί Paul.Al.M.3; οἱ ἡλιῶται the inhabitants of the sun, Luc.VH1.17. II. ἡλιῶτις, ἡ, Ion. name for the dawn, EM440.55.

ἤλκησε, v. ἑλκέω.

ἡλληγορημένως, Adv. pf. part. Pass., (ἀλληγορέω) allegorically, Tz. ad Hes.Op.56.

ἡλό-κεντρον, τό, spur, Gloss. **-κοπέω**, = Lat. clavo, Dosith. p.435 K., Gloss.; ὑποδήματα -κεκοπημένα hob-nailed shoes, Gal.13.326. **-κοπική** τέχνη nail-smith's trade, BGU1124.11 (i B.C.). **-κόπον**, τό, = Lat. forma clavaris, Gloss. **-κόπος**, ὁ, (κόπτω) nail-smith, BGU1028.19 (ii A.D.), Judeich Altertümer von Hierapolis 133; = Lat. clavarius, clavifixor, clavorum faber, Gloss.

ἧλον, τό, = βράβιλον or κοκκύμηλον, Seleuc.ap.Ath.2.50a.

ἡλο-πᾰγής, ές, (πήγνυμι) fixed with nails, Man.1.149. **-πληκτος**, ον, hurt by a nail, Hippiatr.34. **-ποιός**, ὁ, nail-smith, Lat. clavarius, Gloss.

ἧλος, Dor. **ἆλος**, IG4.1484.62 (Epid.), SIG245 i 69 (Delph., iv B.C.), Pi. (v. infr.), Aeol.(?) ϝάλλοι (pl.) written γάλλοι, Hsch.: ὁ:—nail-head, stud, as an ornament, σκῆπτρον χρυσείοις ἥλοισι πεπαρμένον Il.1.246, cf. 11.633; ἐν δέ οἱ [τῷ ξίφει] ἧλοι χρύσειοι πάμφαινον ib.29, cf. Ath.11.488b,c: hence, of the stars, Placit.2.14.3. 2. after Hom., nail, Pi.P.4.71; ἧλοι σιδηροῖ καὶ ξύλινοι X.Cyn.9.12, etc.; of shoe-nails, Thphr.Char.4.13: prov., ἥλῳ ἐκκρούειν τὸν ἧλον Luc.Laps.7; ἥλῳ ὁ ἧλος (sc. ἐκκρούεται) Arist.Pol.1314^{a}5, etc. 3. = Lat. acutus (= spur), Gloss. II. wart, callus, Thphr.Ign.37, Nic.Th.272; ἧλοι καὶ τύλοι Dsc.1.104, cf. Asclep.ap.Gal.13.647; also on plants, esp. the olive, Thphr.HP4.14.3.

ἦλος, ὁ, barren spot, Hsch.

ἠλός, supposed nom. of the voc. ἠλέ, v. sub ἠλεός.

ἠλοσύνη, ἡ, = ἠλιθιότης, Nic.Al.420: Aeol. **ἀλοσύνα** Theoc.30.12; cf. ἀλλος (s.v. ἠλεός).

ἡλόω, sharpen, ἡλοῦσιν αὐτὸ (sc. τὸ κοντάριον) ξυλοπυρίας (sic) Anon. in Rh.236.18. II. Pass., become callous, ἡλωμένοι ἐξοχαί Gal.17(1).902.

ἥλπετο, v. ἔλπομαι.

ἠλσάμην, = ἠλασάμην, (ἐλαύνω) Ibyc.55; διηλσάμην is prob. l. in Semon.17.

ἠλῠγ-άζω, (ἠλυξ) *overshadow*, only in compd. ἐπηλ- (q.v.). **-αῖος,** α, ον, *shadowy, dark*, Suid. **-η** [ῠ], ἡ, *shadow*, Erot. s. v. ἐπηλυγάζονται, Hsch. s. v. ἠλυγισμένος: metaph., δίκης ἠ. *the 'fog'* of a lawsuit, Ar.*Ach*.684; cf. ἦλυξ. **-ίζω,** = ἠλυγάζω, in pf. part. Pass. ἠλυγισμένος, Hsch.

ἤλῠθον, v. ἔρχομαι. **ἦλυξ,** ὕγος, ὁ, = ἠλύγη, Choerob. *in Theod*. 2. 400; ἠλύγων ὀρέων· ἐν σκότῳ κατεχομένων, Hsch. (leg. -αίων). **ἤλυξα,** v. ἀλύσκω. **ἠλῠσίη,** ἡ, = ἤλυσις, ὁδός, Id., cf. *EM*497.9.

Ἠλύσιον [ῠ] πεδίον, τό, *the Elysian* fields, Od.4.563, A.R.4.811, Str.1.1.4, Plu.*Sert*.8, etc.: in pl., *IG*14.1973; χῶρος Ἠλύσιος ib.2012 *Ca*8; λειμών Luc.*JConf*.17; ἐν Ἠλυσίῳ alone, *IG*14.1750. II. **ἠλύσια,** τά, = ἐνηλύσια (q.v.), Polem.Hist.93.

Ἠλύσιος, α, ον, *Elysian*, αὖραι *IG*14.1389i 22; χοροστασίαι ib.58.

ἤλῠσις, εως, ἡ, = ἔλευσις, *step, gait*, βραδύπουν ἤ. προτιθεῖσα E.*Hec*. 67; πυκνὴν βαίνων ἤ. Id.*Ph*.844; πικρὰν διώκων ἤ. Id.*HF*1041.

ἠλυσκάζω, v. ἠλασκάζω. **ἦλφον,** v. ἀλφάνω. **ἤλω,** v. ἁλίσκομαι. **ἠλώμην,** v. ἀλάομαι.

ἡλωτός, ή, όν, (ἡλόω) *nailed, nail-shaped*, Paul.Aeg.6.66.

ἧμα, ατος, τό, (ἵημι) *that which is thrown, dart, javelin*, ἥμασιν ἔπλευ ἄριστος best *at darting*, Il.23.891: hence ἥμων (q.v.). II. ϝῆμα, v. εἶμα.

ἠμᾰθόεις, εσσα, εν (or -όεις, εν if Πύλος (q. v.) be fem.), Ep. for ἀμ-, (ἄμαθος) *sandy*, epith. of the Elean Pylos, Πύλον ἠμαθόεντα Od.1. 93, al., Hes.*Sc*.360: generally ἠμαθόεσσα ἠϊών A.R.1.932. (Deriv. from the name of a river by Str.8.3.14.)

ἧμαι, ἧσαι, ἧσται E.*Alc*. (v. infr.) (but κάθ-ηται, v. κάθημαι), ἧσθον *h.Ap*.456, ἥμεθα, ἧσθε, ἧνται Call.*Fr*.122, Ep. εἵαται Il.10.100, ἕαται 3.134 (κατέαται Hdt.1.199); imper. ἧσο Hom., ἥσθω (καθ-) A.*Pr*.916; subj. and opt. only in compd. καθ-; inf. ἧσθαι; part. ἥμενος: impf. ἥμην, ἧσο, ἧστο (but ἐκάθητο, καθ-ῆτο, v. κάθημαι), dual ἥσθην (ἑήσθην Orph.*A*.815), pl. ἥμεθα (ἥμεσθα E.*IA*88), ἧσθε Cratin.142, ἧντο, Ep. εἵατο Il.7.61, ἕατο ib.414, ἐκατέατο Hdt.8.73 (v.l. ἐκαθ-): (I.-E. *ēs*-, cf. Skt. *āste* (= ἧσται) 'sits'; aspirate borrowed from ἵζω, ἕζομαι; Ep. εἵαται εἵατο fr. ἥαται ἥατο (which shd. perh. be restored) through ἕαται ἕατο):—*to be seated, sit*, Il.1.498, etc.: freq. with collat. sense, *sit still, sit idle*, 2.255, 18.104, etc.; ἧσθαι ἐν εἰρήνῃ Callin.1.4; κατ' οἴκους ἐκτὸς ἥμενῳ πόνων E.*Fr*.10; of an army, *encamp*, Il.15.740, 24. 542; πόλιν ἀμφὶ 18.509; πρόσθε τειχέων E.*Supp*.664; of a spy, *lurk*, Il.18.523: metaph., πρὸς ἐμᾷ ψυχᾷ θάρσος ἧσται c. acc. et inf., E.*Alc*. 604 (lyr.); *lie hid*, ἥατ' ἐνὶ Τρώων ἀγορῇ κεκαλυμμένοι ἵππῳ, i. e. in the wooden horse, Od.8.503, cf. 512; of magistrates, ἐν ἀρχαῖς ἥμενοι E. *Andr*.699; δαιμόνων σέλμα σεμνὸν ἡμένων A.*Ag*.183 (lyr.); later, of things, *lie*, ἱρὸν ἧσται Hdt.9.57; ἐπὶ στέγος ἱερὸν ἧνται κάλπιδες Call. *Fr*.122, cf. Luc.*Syr.D*.31; ἡμένῳ ἐν χώρῳ (or χόρτῳ) in *a low* place, Theoc.13.40:—Constr.: mostly with Preps., ἐνὶ δίφρῳ Il.16.403, cf. A.*Pr*.368, etc.; ἐπὶ κορυφῆς Il.14.158; ἐπ' ἐσχάραις A.*Eu*.806; παρὰ κλισίῃ Il.1.330, etc.; ἀνὰ Γαργάρῳ 15.153: c. dat., Ὀλύμπῳ 13.524, cf. 21.389, etc.; ἐρετμοῖς at the oar, E.*Cyc*.16; ἀνορόφοις πέτραις Id.*Ba*. 38: rarely c. acc., A.*Ag*.183 (v. supr.); Σιμόεντος κοίτας E.*Rh*.547: c. part., τίη..ἧσ' ὀλιγηπελέων; Il.15.245; ὀδυρόμενος, ἀλλοφρονέων, Od.14.41, 10.374; πεφυλαγμένος ἧσο Orac.ap.Hdt.7.148; ἐκπεπληγμένη S.*Tr*.24.

ἡμαιθον, τό, *half-obol*, or *two-obol piece* at Cyzicus, Herod.3.45, Phoen.2.3, cf. Hsch.

ἦμαρ, Dor. and Arc. **ἆμαρ,** ατος, τό, = ἡμέρα, *day*, the prevailing form in Hom., νύκτες τε καὶ ἤματα Od.11.183; νύκτας τε καὶ ἦμαρ by night and *day*, Il.5.490, Od.24.63 (where sg. ἦμαρ is used as pl., as in ποσσῆμαρ, ἐννῆμαρ, ἐξῆμαρ); ἅμαρ ἢ νύκτες Pi.*P*.4.256; ἦμαρ alone, *by day*, Hes.*Op*.176 (but τὸ ἦ. *on that day*, *JHS*12.234 (Cilicia)); μέσον ἦ. midday, Il.21.111, cf. Pi.*P*.9.113, etc.; δείελον ἦ. evening, Od.17.606; ἤματι χειμερίῳ on a winter's *day*, Il.12.279, cf. 16. 385. 2. used in Ep. with Adjs., of a state or condition, αἴσιμον, ὀλέθριον, μόρσιμον, νηλεὲς ἦ., *the day* of destiny, of death, Il.8.72, 19. 294, Od.10.175, Il.11.484; ἐλεύθερον, δούλιον, ἀναγκαῖον ἦ., *the day* of freedom, of slavery, 6.455, 463, 16.836; νόστιμον ἦ. Od.1.9, al.; ἦ. ὀρφανικόν Il.22.490. II. with Preps., ἐπ' ἤματι *day by day, daily*, Od.12.105, 14.105 (αἰὲν ἐπ' ἤματι S.*OC*688); *in a day, within a day's space*, Il.10.48, 19.229, Od.2.284; ἐπ' ἄματι *at the close of day*, Theoc.24.139; ἐπ' ἆ. *by day*, S.*OT*199; ἐπ' ἦ. *for a day*, Id.*Fr*.255.3, E.*Ph*.401; ἐπ' ἆμαρ ἕκαστον, ἆμαρ ἐπ' ἆμαρ, Theoc.17.96, 11.69; ἦ. ἐπ' ἦ. ἀεί *AP*9.499; κατ' ἦ. *day by day*, S.*Ph*.798, E.*Hec*.628; κατ' ἦ. αἰεί S.*OC*682 (lyr.); ἀεὶ κατ' ἦ. E.*Tr*.392; ἀεὶ τὸ κατ' ἦ. Id.*El*.145 (lyr.); τὸ κατ' ἆμαρ *the needs of the day, one's daily bread*, S.*Ph*.1089, *Fr*.593 (lyr.); but κατ' ἆ. also, *this day, to-day*, Id.*OC*1079, cf. *Aj*.753; τὸ μὲν παρ' ἆ., τὸ δὲ *on one day, and on the next*.., Pi.*P*.11.63; παρ' ἦ. *on the morrow*, S.*OC*1455 (lyr.); παρ' ἦ. ἡμέρα day *after day*, Id.*Aj*.475; ἰν ἄματα πάντα *in perpetuity*, *IG*5(2).5 (Tegea); without ἰν, ib.262.22 (Mantinea).

ἡμαρτημένως, Adv. pf. part. Pass. of ἁμαρτάνω, *faultily*, ἡγεῖσθαι Pl.*Men*.88e; ἠ. ἔχειν Id.*Lg*.670c, Iamb.*VP*33.233.

ἠμάτιος [ᾰ], η, ον, (ἦμαρ) poet. for ἡμερήσιος, *by day*, ἠματίη μὲν ὑφαίνεσκεν μέγαν ἱστόν, νύκτας δ' ἀλλύεσκεν Od.2.104, cf. 19.149; ἠμάτιαι σπεύδουσι [μέλισσαι] Hes.*Th*.597; ἠ. φέγγος, i. e. the sun, *AP*9.651 (Paul. Sil.). 2. *day by day, daily*, Il.9.72.

ἤμβροτον, Ep. aor. 2 of ἁμαρτάνω.

ἡμεδᾰπός, ή, όν, (ἡμεῖς) *of our land* or *country, native*, opp. ἀλλοδαπός, χαρακτήρ Ar.*Pax*220; νόμισμα ἡ. *IG*1².91.4; στρατιή Call.*Fr*. 152: of a person, Pl.*Thg*.124d, Luc.*Phal*.1.11; ἡ ἡμεδαπή (sc. γῆ) *IG*1².115.30; of the Roman empire, opp. to barbarian lands, Hdn. 1.1.4. (ἡμεδ- = Skt. *asmad*-, stem of 1st pers. pl. pron.; for the termin. -απος, cf. ἀλλοδαπός.)

ἡμέδιμνον, τό, = ἡμιμέδιμνον, in pl., *IG*2².1675.265, *SIG*1027.11 (Cos); also **ἡμέδιμνος,** ὁ, *IG*14.423 i 34 (Tauromenium), Did. in *Gramm.Lat*.3.412 K.; **ἡμίδιμμνον,** τό, *SIG*998.8 (Epid., v B. C.).

ἡμεῖς, v. ἐγώ. **ἡμεκτέω,** v. περιημεκτέω.

ἠμελημένως, Adv. pf. part. Pass. of ἀμελέω, *in a state of neglect*, διάγειν Isoc.*Ep*.8.10; ἠ. ἔχειν X.*Mem*.3.11.4; ἐς προῦπτον κίνδυνον ἐκπέμπεσθαι Arr.*Ind*.20.3; *with studied neglect*, ἑαυτὴν ἠ. πως κοσμήσασα D.C.51.12; *carelessly*, Max.Tyr.28.5.

ἤμελλον, v. μέλλω.

ἠμέν, Ep. Conj., correl. to ἠδέ (from ἦ and μέν, δέ), *both*..and.., ἠ. νέοι ἠδὲ γέροντες Il.2.789, etc.; ἠ. ἀνακλῖναι πυκινὸν νέφος ἠδ' ἐπιθεῖναι 5.751; sts. καί is added to ἠδέ, ἠ. θεὸν ἠδὲ καὶ ἄνδρα 5.128; ἠ. δέμας ἠδὲ καὶ αὐδήν Od.2.268; ἠ. δή ποτ' ἐμεῦ πάρος ἔκλυες..ἠδ' ἔτι καὶ νῦν μοι.. ἐπικρήηνον ἐέλδωρ Il.1.453: rarely folld. by δέ or τε, ἠ...πολλοὶ δέ.. 12.428; ἠ. ὅσοι χαλεποί..οἵ τε φιλόξεινοι Od.8.575: more freq. by καί, Il.15.664, 670, Hes.*Op*.339.

ἡμέρα, Ep. and Ion. **ἡμέρη** *IG*12(5).1 (Ios), Dor. **ἁμέρα** ib.5(1).213. 43, al., 1390.109, 1432.25, *Test.Epict*.4.12, *Michel*995*A* 32, etc., Locr. **ἀμάρα** *IG*9(1).334.42 (aspirated perh. only in Att. and West Ion., cf. ἐπάμερος Pi., etc., αὐθημερόν *IG*7.235.18 (Oropus), etc.; usu. unaspirated in early Att. Inscrr., *IG*1².49.6, al.; aspirated in codd. even in dialects: original ἀμέρα prob. took aspirate from ἑσπέρα): ἡ:—*day*, less freq. than ἦμαρ in Hom., ἡ. ἥδε κακὸν φέρει Il.8.541, 13.828; τίς νύ μοι ἡ. ἥδε; Od.24.514; νύκτες τε καὶ ἡ. 14.93; μῆνές τε καὶ ἡ. ib.293; νοῦσοι ἐφ' ἡμέρῃ αἱ δ' ἐπὶ νυκτί Hes.*Op*.102; ἡ σήμερον ἡ., v. σήμερον: ἅμα ἡμέρᾳ or ἅμα τῇ ἡμέρᾳ *at daybreak*, X.*An*.6.3.6, Aeschin.3.76; ἅμ' ἡμέρῃ διαφωσκούσῃ Hdt.3.86; ἡ. διέλαμψεν, ἐξέλαμψεν, ὑπέφαινε, Ar.*Pl*.744, *Pax*304, X.*Cyr*.4.5.14; τῆς ἡ. ὀψέ late *in the day*, Id.*HG*2. 1.23. 2. sts. like Ep. ἦμαρ, with Adjs. to describe *a state* or *time of life*, ἐπίπονος ἁ. *a life* of misery, S.*Tr*.654 (lyr.); λυπρὰν ἄγειν ἡ. E. *Hec*.364; ἐχθρὰ ἡ. Id.*Ph*.540; παλαιὰ ἁ. old *age*, S.*Aj*.623 (but θεία ἡ. Id.*Fr*.950 is dub. l.); τερμία ἁ. Id.*Ant*.1330 (lyr.); αἱ μακραὶ ἁμέραι length of *days*, Id.*OC*1216 (lyr.); νέα ἁ. youth, E.*Ion*720 (lyr.); so τῇ πρώτῃ ἡ. Arist.*Rh*.1389ᵃ24; ἐπὶ τῇ τελευταίᾳ ἡ. at the close of *life*, ib.1389ᵇ33, cf. S.*OT*1529; ζοὴν βλέπουσιν ἡ. look *life*-like, Herod.4. 68. 3. poet. for *time*, ἡ. κλίνει τε κἀνάγει πάλιν ἅπαντα τἀνθρώπεια S.*Aj*.131; ἐς τόδ' ἡμέρας Id.*OC*1138: pl., ἐν ἡμέραις τινός *in the days* of.., Lxx 1*Ch*.4.41, etc.; ἡ. ἀρχαῖαι ib.*Ps*.142(143).5. 4. *birth-day*, D.L.4.41. 5. *a fixed day*, τακτῇ ἡ. *Act.Ap*.12.21; ῥητὴ ἡ. Luc.*Alex*.19; ἡ. ἔστησαν ἀρχαιρεσιῶν D.H.6.48, cf. *Act.Ap*.17.31; ἡ. Κυρίου Lxx *Jl*.2.1, cf. 2*Ep.Pet*.3.12, etc.; ἡ. κρίσεως *Ev.Matt*.10. 15: so abs., ὑπὸ ἀνθρωπίνης ἡμέρας a human *tribunal*, 1*Ep.Cor*.4.3; ἡμέραι καὶ ἀγῶνες *Jahresh*.23 *Beibl*.93 (Pamphyl.). 6. in pl., *age*, προβεβηκὼς ἐν ταῖς ἡ. *Ev.Luc*.1.7, cf. Lxx *Ge*.47.8, etc. II. abs. usages, 1. gen., τριῶν ἡμερέων *within* three *days*, Hdt.2.115, cf. Th.7.3; ἡμερῶν ὀλίγων *within* a few *days*, Id.4.26, etc.; ἄλλης ἡ. another *day*, S.*El*.698; τῆς αὐτῆς ἡ. Isoc.4.87; μιᾶς ἁμέρας *IG*5(1). 213.43 (Sparta, v B. C.); ἡμέρας *by day*, opp. νυκτός, S.*Fr*.65; οὐθ' ἡμέρας οὔτε νυκτός Pl.*Phdr*.240c; τοὺς..τῆς ἡ. ἄρτους δ *daily*, *UPZ* 47.21 (ii B. C.); δὶς τῆς ἡμέρης ἑκάστης twice every *day*, Hdt.2.37; δὶς τῆς ἡ. Pl.Com.207; πεντάκις τῆς ἡ. Men.326; κατεσθίω..τῆς ἡ. πένθ' ἡμιμέδιμνα five *every day*, Pherecr.1. 2. dat., τῇδε θἠμέρᾳ, = σήμερον, S.*OT*1283; τῇ τόθ' ἡ. Id.*El*.1134. 3. acc., πᾶσαν ἡ. any *day*, i. e. soon, Hdt.1.111, 7.203; τὴν μὲν αὐτίχ' ἡ. S.*OC*433; ὅλην τὴν ἡ. Eup.233; τρίτην ἡ. ἥκων two *days* after one's arrival, Th.8.23; οὐδεμίαν ἡ. ὑπεύθυνος εἶναί φημι D.18.112; πέντε ἡμέρας during five *days*, Th.8.103; τὰς ἡ. in the *daytime*, X.*Cyr*.1.3.12; τὴν ἡ. *daily*, Lxx *Ex*. 29.38. III. with Preps., μίαν ἀν' ἁμέραν on one *day*, Pi.*O*.9.85; ἀνὰ πᾶσαν ἡ. every *day*, Hdt.7.198; ἀφ' ἡμέρας τῆς νῦν from this *day*, S.*OT*351; but ἀφ' ἡμέρας γίνεσθαι ἐν τῷ Μουσείῳ *from early in the day*, Plb.8.25.11: διʼ ἡμέρης, Att. -ρας, the whole *day* long, Hdt.1.97, 2. 173, Pherecr.64, Ar.*Ra*.260 (lyr.); διὰ τρίτης ἡ. every other *day*, Hdt. 2.37; διὰ πολλῶν ἡ. at a distance of many *days*, Th.2.29; δι' ἡμερῶν τινων Thphr.*HP*4.3.6; εἰς ἡμέραν *yearly*, Lxx *Jd*.17.10; ἐν ἡμέρῃ *in a single day*, Hdt.1.126, cf. Men.*Pk*.377; ἐν ἡ. μιᾷ S.*OT*615; τῇδ' ἐν ἡ. Id.*OC*1612; ἐν ἐκείνῃ τῇ ἡ. *Ev.Jo*.14.20; ἐν ὑστεραίσιν ἡ. A.*Ag*.1666; ἐν ὀκτὼ ἡ. Lys.20.10; but ἐν τρισὶν ἡ. *within* three *days*, *Ev.Jo*.2.19; ἐξ ἡμέρας by *day*, οὔτε νυκτὸς οὔτ' ἐξ ἡ. S.*El*.780; ἡμέραν ἐξ ἡμέρας *day* after *day*, Henioch.5.13, Lxx *Ge*.39.10, 2*Ep.Pet*.2.8 (but ἐξ ἡμερῶν εἰς ἡμέρας Lxx 2*Ch*.21.15); ἐπ' ἡμέρην ἔχειν, ἐφ' -ραν χρῆσθαι, *sufficient for the day*, Hdt.1.32, Th.4.69; τὸ γὰρ βρότειον σπέρμ' ἐφ' ἡ. φρονεῖ A. *Fr*.399; τῆς ἐφ' ἡ. βορᾶς E.*El*.429; but τοὐφ' ἡμέραν *day by day*, Id.*Cyc*. 336: c. dat., ἐπ' ἡμέρῃ ἑκάστῃ (v. l. -ρης -της) every *day*, Hdt.5.117; ὁ ἥλιος νέος ἐφ' ἡμέρῃ Heraclit.6; καθ' ἡμέραν *by day*, A.*Ch*.818 (lyr.); καθ' ἡ. τὴν νῦν *to-day*, S.*OC*3, *Aj*.801; but καθ' ἡ. commonly means *day by day*, *IG*1².84.40, etc.; καθ' ἡ. ἀεί [S.]*Fr*.1120.4: with Art., τὸν καθ' ἡ. βίον Id.*OC*1364; ἡ καθ' ἡ. ἀναγκαία τροφή Th.1.2; τὰ καθ' ἡ. ἐπιτηδεύματα Id.2.37; τὸ καθ' ἡ. ἀδεές Id.3.37, etc.; τὸ καθ' ἡ. *every day*, Ar.*Eq*.1126 (lyr.), etc.; also τὰ καθ' ἑκάστην τὴν ἡ. ἐπιτηδεύματα Isoc.4.78; μετ' ἡμέρην *in broad daylight*, opp. νυκτός, Hdt.2.150, cf. Ar.*Pl*.930; opp. νύκτωρ, Aeschin.3.77; μεθ' ἡμέρας *some days* after, Lxx *Jd*.15.1; ἡμέρα παρ' ἡμέραν γιγνομένη day following on day, Antipho 5.72; but παρ' ἡμέραν *every other day*, Dsc.3.137, Luc.*DDeor*.24. 2; παρ' ἡ. ἄρχειν Plu.*Fab*.15; καθ' ἡμέραν εἰώθειν ὀργίζεσθαι, νῦν παρ' ἡμέραν, εἶτα παρὰ δύο, εἶτα παρὰ τρεῖς Arr.*Epict*.2.18.13; πρὸ ἡμέρας before *day-break*, Diph.22; but πρὸ ἁμερᾶν δέκα ἢ κα μέλλωντι ἀναγινώσκεν *GDI*5040.42 (Crete); πρὸ ἡμερῶν ἑπτὰ εἰδυῶν Ὀκτωμβρίων *SIG*646.2 (Thisbe, ii B.C.); γίγνεται, ἔστι πρὸς ἡμέραν, towards *day*, near *day*, X.*HG*2.4.6, Lys.1.14; also, *for the day, daily*, Charito 4.2. IV. as pr. n., *the goddess of day*, Hes.*Th.*124. 2. v. ἥμερος II.

ἡμεραῖος, α, ον, *of the daytime*, ἡμεραίας (sc. ὥρας) *PLips.*40 iii 5 (iv A.D.). II. *a day long*, πλοῦς Scyl.69.

ἡμεράλωψ [ᾰ], ὁ, ἡ, the contrary of νυκτάλωψ (q.v.), Gal.14.768 (from Dem.Ophth., cf. Simon.Jan. s.v. *nictilopa*).

Ἡμερασία, ἡ, (ἥμερος) epith. of Artemis in Arcadia, Paus.8.18.8: **-άσια**, τά, her festival, *IG*5(1).1387.5 (Thuria, iii B.C.); Ἡ. τὰ ἐν Λούσοις *Ath.Mitt.*49.118 (Aegium in Achaea).

ἡμέρ-ευσις, εως, ἡ, *spending of the day*, Aq.*Ps.*1.2. **-εύω**, *spend the day*, ἐν τόπῳ ἐρήμῳ X.*HG*5.4.3; ἐν τῇ ἀγορᾷ D.44.4; πρὸς πῦρ X.*Oec.*4.2; ἐν πόνοισιν E.*Fr.*525 codd.: abs., *to travel the whole day*, A.*Ch.*710. 2. *pass one's days*, ἔκηλα ἡ. S.*El.*787:—Med., δίαιταν ἥντιν' ἡμερεύεται dub. l. in E.*Fr.*812.6. 3. *work by day*, *PLond.*3.1177.78 (ii A.D.). **-ήσιος**, Dor. ἁμ-, α, ον, also ος, ον Plb.9.13.6, Str.7.1.5, Gem.18.4: (ἡμέρα):—*of the day*, τὰ ἡ. Hp.*Mul.*1.11; ὕπνοι Democr.212; ἡ. φάος light *as of the day*, A.*Ag.*22; θεοί *PMag.Leid.W.*2.10. II. *a day long*, ἡ. ὁδός a day's journey, Hdt.4.101, Pl.*R.*616b; ἡ. λόγος a speech *lasting a whole day*, Isoc.15.320; ἁ. χρόνος Ti.Locr.97c, etc.; ζωή Plu.2.111c. III. *of* or *for a day*, ἀνωμαλία Gem. l. c.; μισθός *PFay.*91.23 (i A.D.); τὸ ἡ. (sc. μίσθωμα) *a day's wages*, Suid.; πεντακοσίους γράφει στίχους ἡμερησίους 500 lines *every day*, D.L.7.181. Adv. -ίως *daily*, *POxy.*83.12 (iv A.D.), prob. in *PGrenf.*2.67.11 (iii A.D.). 2. ἡ. μνημόσυνον *calendar*, *Epigr.Gr.*1096.1 (Stratonicea). 3. ἡμερησία, ἡ, *day-book*, *BGU*12.32, 870.3 (ii A.D.). **-ία**, Dor. ἁμ- (sc. ὥρα), ἡ, = ἡμέρα, S.*Aj.*208 (s.v.l.).

ἡμερίδης, ου, ὁ, (ἥμερος) of wine, *mild, mellow*, Plu.2.663d, 692e. 2. epith. of Dionysus, as patron of the *cultivated* vine (ἡμερίς), ib.451c, 994a.

ἡμερ-ίδιον, τό, Dim. of ἡμέρα, *Gloss.* **-ινός**, ή, όν, *of day*, φῶς Pl.*R.*508c; *by day*, opp. νυκτερινός, πυρετός Hp.*Epid.*1.5; ἄγγελος ἡ. *day*-messenger, X.*Cyr.*8.6.18; cf. ἡμεροδρόμος; ἡ. θεωρίαι Plb.9.14.6; βοηλάται *PLond.*3.1177.153 (ii A.D.). II. ἡ. σῖτα, in Ar.*Pax* 163 (anap.), is expl. by Sch., θνητά, ἐπίγεια (v.l. ἡμερίων); ἰχθὺς ἡ. is dub. in Ephipp.5.2 (anap.). **-ιος**, Dor. ἁμ-, ον, used by Trag. in lyr., *lasting but a day*, γέννα, αἷμα, E.*Ph.*130, 1512; οὔτε θεῶν γένος οὔθ' ἁμερίων .. ἀνθρώπων S.*Aj.*398, cf. *Ant.*789; κάματος *Hymn.Is.*87: abs., ἡμέριοι *mortals*, Orac.ap.D.S.7.12, Opp.*H.*2.669, *AP*7.372 (Loll. Bass.); ἡ. μισθός *PMasp.*164.6 (vi A.D.). II. *daily*, κύκλος Ph.1.92 (nisi leg. ἡμερ⟨ήσ⟩ιος).—Poet. Adj., for in X.*Oec.*21.3 ἡμερινός should be read.

ἡμερίς, ίδος, fem. of ἥμερος: as Subst., ἡμερίς (sc. ἄμπελος), ἡ, *the cultivated vine*, opp. ἀγριάς, Od.5.69, Simon.183, Opp.*C.*3.458, Jul. *Or.*7.221b, etc.; distd. from ἀμπελίς, Ar.*Ach.*997: metaph., ἡ ποιητικὴ ἡ. τῶν Μουσῶν Plu.2.15e. 2. = ἡμερόδρυς, Thphr.*HP*3.8.2.

ἡμερό-βιος, ον, *living for a day*: τὸ ἡ., = τὸ ἐφήμερον, *an insect*, esp. *may-fly*, Thphr.*Metaph.*29, Plin.*HN*11.120; of Diogenes, *living from hand to mouth*, Satyr.ap.Porph.*Abst.*p.270 N. **-γράφος** [ᾰ], ὁ, *one who keeps a diary*, Marin.*Procl.*37. **-δᾰνειστής**, οῦ, ὁ, *one who lends on daily interest*, D.L.6.99, 100. **-δοτος**, ον, *bestowed for a day*, Theognost.*Can.*136 (but Ἡρόδοτος ib.84). **-δρομέω**, *to be a* ἡμεροδρόμος, Str.5.4.13, Luc.*DDeor.*24.1. **-δρόμης**, Dor. (?) **-ας**, ου, ὁ, *long-distance runner, courier*, Hdt.6.105, *SIG*303 (Olympia, iv B.C.). **-δρόμιον**, τό, *astrological calendar*, title of work by Pappus, *Cat.Cod.Astr.*1.69. **-δρόμος**, ον, *taking a day to traverse*, χώρα Tim.*Pers.*41. 2. -δρόμος, ὁ, = ἡμεροδρόμης, Hdt.9.12, Pl.*Prt.* 335e, Arist.*Mu.*398ᵃ30, D.S.15.82: metaph., of the *sun*, prob. in *PMag.Par.*2.190, cf. Hsch. **-δρῦς**, υος, ἡ, *nut-gall oak, Quercus infectoria*, Id. **-ειδής**, ές, *of the form of day*, φάντασμα Epicur.*Fr.* 294 (p.353 U.); τὸ τῆς φιλοσοφίας ἡ. Iamb.*Protr.*21.κθ'. **-θαλλής**, ές, (θάλλω) *gently-sprouting*, *AP*9.374 (nisi leg. -θηλέσι). **-θηρικός**, ή, όν, *of* or *for the hunting of tame beasts*: ἡ -κή (sc. τέχνη) *the art of hunting them*, Pl.*Sph.*222c. **-καλλές**, οῦς, τό, *Martagon lily, Lilium Martagon*, Cratin.98.5, Thphr.*HP*6.1.1, 6.6.11, Dsc.3.122:—also **ἡμεροκατάλλακτον**, τό, ibid. **-κλέπτης**, ου, ὁ, *one who robs by day*, *Gloss.* **-κοίτης**, ου, ὁ, a fish, = ἀνωδόρκας, Opp.*H.*2.199, 224. **-κοιτος**, Dor. ἁμ-, ον, *sleeping by day*, epith. of a thief, Hes. *Op.*605, Opp.*H.*2.408; ἁμερόκοιτοι βλαχαὶ τεκέων, for ἁμεροκοίτων, E. *Cyc.*58. **-λεγδόν**, Adv., (λέγω) *by count of days*, A.*Pers.*63 (anap.); λογεῦσαι *PRev.Laws*4.1 (iii B.C.); *in the form of a diary*, ἡ. *perscripta omnia*, Cic.*Att.*4.15.3. 2. *to the very day*, Arist.*HA*575ᵃ27. **-λογέω**, *to count by days*, τὸν χρόνον Hdt.1.47. **-λόγιον**, τό, *calendar*, Plu. *Caes.*59 (v.l. -λογεῖον):—also **-λογικά**, τά, Ptol.*Phas.*p.11 H. II. -λόγιον, τό, = μέρος τι τῶν περὶ τὴν κύστιν, Hsch. **-μαντεία**, ἡ, *divination by day*, *PMag.Lond.*121.155. **-μᾰχία**, ἡ, *battle by day*, Aristid.2.314 J. (s.v.l.). **-νύκτιον**, τό, = νυχθήμερον, Vett.Val.314.21, Phlp.ap.Simp.*in Ph.*1179.17, Phlp.*in Ph.*711.12, al., *Cat.Cod. Astr.*8(3).113, *EM*540.21. **-πῐτυς**, υος, ἡ, *cultivated pine*, Hsch. s.v. μήκωνες. **-ποιέω**, = ἡμερόω, Id. s.v. ἐξημερῶσαι: **-ποιός**, όν, *Gloss.* **-πόσιον**, τό, *day's portion of wine*, *BMus.Inscr.*1006 (Cyzic., i A.D.).

ἥμερος, Dor. ἅμ-, in codd. of Pi. (v. infr.) and A. (v. infr.), but ἡμ- *Tab.Heracl.*1.172, ον, also α, ον Hdt.5.82, Pi.*N.*9.44, etc. (v. infr. II). 1. *tame*, of animals, χῆνα φέρων .. ἥμερον ἐξ αὐλῆς Od.15.162; ἡ. ζῷα Pl.*Phdr.*260b; κρέα θήρεια καὶ τῶν ἡ. X.*Cyr.*1.3.6. 2. of plants and trees, *cultivated*, ἐλαίη Hdt.5.82; δένδρεα Id.4.21, 8.115; καρπός Pl.*Criti.*115a, cf. *Ti.*77b; τροφή, of corn, Corn.*ND* 2. 3. of countries, *cultivated, reclaimed*, ἡμερωτέρη χώρη Hp.*Aër.* 12; so ἡμερώταται ὁδοί *smooth, easy* roads, Pl.*Lg.*761a. 4. of men, *civilized, gentle*, Hdt.2.30 (Comp.), Pi.*P.*1.71, 3.6; ἄνδρες οὕτως ἡ. καὶ φιλάνθρωποι D.21.49, cf. Phld.*Ir.*p.88 W. (Sup.); ἁμέροις χερσίν, αἰὼν ἁ., Pi.*N.*8.3, 9.44; οἶκος ἁ. ἀστοῖς Id.*O.*13.2; so of a lion, ἐν βιότου προτελείοις ἅμερον A.*Ag.*721; κρατηθεὶς -ώτερος φανεῖ ib.1632, cf. Pl.*Prt.*326b, Isoc.9.67. Adv. -ρως Plb.5.54.9: Comp. -ωτέρως Pl.*Lg.*867d: Sup. -ώτατα D.C.57.18. 5. Medic., of tumours, *benign*, opp. κακοήθης, Leonid.ap.Aët.15.5. II. Ἡμέρα, ἡ, title of Artemis in Arcadia, B.10.39, Call.*Dian.*236, *IG*5(2).398 (Lusi).

ἡμεροσκοπ-εῖον, τό, *place for watching by day*, Aen.Tact.6.6, Str. 3.4.6. **-έω**, *keep day-watch*, Aen.Tact.6.1. **-ία**, ἡ, *watching by day*, [Id.]6.tit. **-ος**, ον, *watching by day*, φύλαξ Ar.*Av.*1174: as Subst., *day-watcher*, Hdt.7.183, 192, S.*Ant.*253, X.*HG*1.1.2, Aen. Tact.6.1, al.: metaph., πιστὸν ἡ. ὀφθαλμὸν ἔξω A.*Th.*66.

ἡμερότης, ητος, ἡ, (ἥμερος) *cultivation*, of a country, Hp.*Aër.* 12. 2. of men, *gentleness*, Pl.*R.*410d, Ephor.31(b) J., Epicur. *Sent.Vat.*36, Phld.*Hom.*p.32 O., D.S.32.27, etc.; of animals, Arist. *HA*588ᵃ21. II. as a title, *Clemency*, ἡ ἡμετέρα ἡ. Just.*Nov.*115 *Pr.*

ἡμεροτοκέω, *produce eatable fruits*, Ph.1.402: metaph., ib.455.

ἡμεροτροφίς, ίδος, ἡ, *feeding for the day*: = χοῖνιξ, Heraclid.Lemb.5.

ἡμερούσιος, α, ον, *daily*, *Gloss.* Adv. -σίως *PSI*4.287.12 (iv A.D.), etc.

ἡμερο-φᾰής, ές, *shining by day*, ἄστρον Theano *Ep.*10:—also **-φᾰνής**, ές, Pl.*Def.*411b, Arist.*Top.*142ᵇ1. **-φαντος**, ον, *appearing by day*, ὄναρ A.*Ag.*82 (lyr.). **-φῠλᾰκέω**, *to be a day-watcher*, App. *BC*4.62. **-φύλαξ** [ῠ], ᾰκος, ὁ, = ἡμεροσκόπος, X.*HG*7.2.6, Ph.2.236, *Ostr.Strassb.*534.1 (ii A.D.). **-φυλλος**, ον, = ἥμερος, ἐλαία Isyll. 20 (Dor. with ἡμ-). **-φωνος**, ον, *heralding the day*, epith. of the cock, v.l. for ἱμερό-, Simon.80 B.

ἡμερ-όω, (ἥμερος) *tame, make tame*, 1. prop. of wild beasts, Arist.*HA*488ᵃ29 (Pass.), *Gp.*16.21.2; but simply, *to be pacified*, Pl. *R.*493b (Pass.); δώροις Id.*Lg.*906d. 2. of plants and trees, *reclaim, cultivate*, ἡ. ἐξ ἀγρίων Hp.*Aër.*12, cf. Thphr.*CP*2.14.1, 5.15.6; also of land, Crates Com.55. 3. of countries, *clear* them of robbers and wild beasts, as Hercules and Theseus did, ναυτιλίαισι πορθμὸν ἁμερώσαις Pi.*I.*4(3).57; χθόνα ἀνήμερον τιθέντες ἡμερωμένην A.*Eu.*14; or *to cultivate* them, Thphr.*CP*5.15.6, al. 4. of men also, *civilize, humanize*, λόγῳ Pl.*R.*554d; ἁρμονίᾳ τε καὶ ῥυθμῷ ib.442a; δίκη πάντα ἡμέρωκεν τὰ ἀνθρώπινα Id.*Lg.*937e; τὸ θυμούμενον Eus.Mynd.1:—Pass., ὑπὸ παιδείας Pl.*Lg.*935a. b. *tame by conquest, subdue*, ἡμερώσας δὲ Αἴγυπτον ἐξυβρίσασαν Hdt.7.5:—Med., πᾶν ἔθνος ἡμερούμενος βασιλέϊ Id.5.2, cf. 4.118:—Pass., πόθεν σου ὁ ὀφθαλμὸς ἡμέρωται; whence that *crest-fallen* look? *Mim.Oxy.*413.153. **-ωλίας**· τοὺς ἐν αὐλῇ διακόνους, Hsch. **-ωμα**, ατος, τό, *cultivated plant*, Thphr.*CP*5.6.8 (pl.), prob. in *HP*1.7.1 (pl.). **-ωρέω**, = ἡμεροφυλακέω, Hsch., Phot.:—Subst. **-ωρία**, ἡ (-ῴα cod.), Id. **-ωσις**, εως, ἡ, *a taming, reclaiming*, τῆς χώρας (by clearing it of wild beasts), D.S.1.24; *cultivation*, of lands, Thphr.*CP*2.4.3; of men, *civilizing*, Plu.*Num.*6 (pl.), Scymn.187. **-ωτής**, οῦ, ὁ, *tamer, civilizer*, of Hercules, Max.Tyr.3.7.

ἧμες, Dor. for ἦμεν, 1 pl. impf. of εἰμί (*sum*).

ἡμετέρειος, ον, = ἡμεδαπός, Anacr.71, Anaxandr.9.

ἡμέτερος, Dor. ἁμέτ-, Aeol. ἀμμέτ-, α, ον, (ἡμεῖς) *our*, Il.2.374, etc.; εἰς ἡμέτερον (sc. δῶμα) Od.2.55, 17.534; so ἡμέτερόνδε 8.39, 15.513; ἐφ' ἡμέτερ' ib.88, Il.9.619; ἐν ἡμετέρου Hdt.1.35, 7.8.δ'; ἡ ἡ. (sc. χώρα) Th.6.21, etc.; τὸ ἡ. *our case*, Pl.*Ti.*27d; τὸ ἡ. γέλωτ' ἂν πάμπολυν ὄφλοι Id.*Lg.*778e, etc.; τὰ ἡ. φρονεῖν to take *our part*, X. *HG*6.3.14, etc.; ἄνδρες ἡ. they are *in our power*, Pl.*R.*556d, cf. X. *Cyr.*2.3.2; ἡ. κέρδη τῶν σοφῶν, = ἡμῶν τῶν σοφῶν, Ar.*Nu.*1202; ἡμέτερον αὐτῶν [οἰκοδόμημα], = ἡμῶν αὐτῶν, Pl.*Grg.*514b; representing an objective gen., τὸ ἡ. δέος fear *of us*, Th.1.77; εἰς τὴν ἡ. διδασκαλίαν *Ep.Rom.*15.4. II. sts. for ἐμός, Od.11.562, al., Theoc.2.31, etc.; τὰ ἡ. *my* property, *PRyl.*114.18 (iii A.D.); so in Imperial titles, as ἡ ἡ. ἡμερότης Just.*Nov.*115 *Pr.*

ἠμί (v. sub fin.), *I say*, the 1st pers. of pres. being used in Att. dialogue in emphatic repetitions, παῖ ἠμί, παῖ boy *I say*, boy! Ar.*Nu.*1145, *Ra.*37; otherwise only in 3 sg. ἠσί Hermipp.1, Aeol. ἦσι Sappha.97, Dor. ἠτί Alcm.139. II. impf. ἦν, 3 sg. ἦ (the only part used by Hom., chiefly in Il., always at the end of a speech), ἦ, καὶ ἐπ' ἀργυρέῃ κώπῃ σχέθε χεῖρα he *spake* and .., Il.1.219, etc.; ἦ ῥα, καὶ ἀμπεπαλὼν προΐει .. ἔγχος 3.355, etc.; rarely with the subject expressed, ἦ ῥα γυνὴ ταμίη 6.390, cf. Theoc.22.75: freq. in Att. in the phrases ἦν δ' ἐγώ *said I*, Pl.*R.*327c, etc.; ἦ δ' ὅς *said he*, Cratin.192, etc.; ἦ δ' ὃς λέγων Ar.*V.*795; ἦ δ' ἥ Pl.*Smp.*205c; with the subject repeated, ἦ δ' ὃς ὁ Γλαύκων Id.*R.*327b, etc.; later without ὅς, ἦ δ' ὁ Νεῖλος Philostr.*VA*6.16. (Cf. Lat. *aio, ad-agium*: ἦ fr. *ἦκτ, hence ἠμί etc. on analogy of φη: φημί, etc.)

ἡμῐ-, insep. Prefix, used in compos., *half-*. (Cf. Skt. *sāmi-*, Lat. *sēmi-*.)

ἡμι-άγρυπνος, ον, *half-awake*, Agath.4.19. **-αλφα**, τό, *half-alpha*, a musical note, ⅄, ⊬, Alyp.4, al.

ἡμιαμβεῖον, τό, *half-iambic line*, i.e. catalectic dimeters, in pl., Cleanth.*Stoic.*1.129, *Anacreont.*tit.

ἡμιαμβικός, ὁ, *writer of such verses*, dub. in Sch.Nic.*Th.*377.

ἡμι-αμφόριον, τό, *half*-ἀμφορεύς, *IG*11(2).161 *A* 121 (Delos, iii B.C.), J.*BJ*2.21.2. **-ανδρος**, ὁ, *half-man, eunuch*, Hippon.114, Luc. *DDeor.*23.1. **-άνθρωπος**, ὁ, = foreg., Id.*Deor.Conc.*4. **-άρου-**

ριον, τό, *half an aroura*, *BGU*417 (ii/iii A. D.); as a measure, *produce of half an aroura*, χόρτου ἡ. *PSI*4.368 (iii B. C.). **-άρρην**, ενος, ὁ, = ἡμιάνθρωπος, v.l. in Ctes.*Fr.*29.5, Theopomp.Hist.101. **-αρτάβιον** [ᾰβ], τό, *half an* ἀρτάβη, *PRyl.*167.17 (i A. D.), *POxy.*708.6 (ii A. D.). **-άρτᾰβος**, ον, *of half an* ἀρτάβη, μέτρον ib.1031.22 (iii A. D.). **-άρτιον**, τό, *half-loaf*, Epich.52, Sophr.27, 28. **-ασσάριον**, τό, *half-as*, Lat. *semissis*, Plb.2.15.6, Head *Hist.Num.*[2] 601. **-άστᾰτον**, τό, *the half-indefinite*, a figure of speech expressing certainty as to the genus but doubt as to the species (e.g. Virg.*Aen.*8.352), Sacerd.p.469 K. **-αστρᾰγάλιον** [ᾰλ], τό, *creature with only one* ἀστράγαλος, Arist.*HA*499^{b}25 (v.l. **-αστράγαλος**). **-βάρβᾰρος**, ον, *half-barbarous*, Str.13.1.58, Philostr. *VS*2.1.13. **-βᾰφής**, ές, *half-dipped*, *half-dyed*, Nonn.*D.*1.358. **-βῐος**, ον, *half-alive*, Man.2.358. **-βρᾰχής** or **-βρεχής**, ές, *half-watered*, γῆ Thphr.*CP*3.23.1; *sodden*, θέρμοι *AP*11.413 (Ammian.). **-βρᾰχυς**, εια, υ, in prosody, *half of a short*, ἡμιβράχεια (sc. προσῳδία) Sch.D.T.p.207 H.: pl., ἡμιβράχεα, τά, ib.p.208 H. **-βροτος**, ον, *half-man*, ἵππος ἡ. a centaur, Opp.*C.*2.7. **-βροχος**, ον, = ἡμιβρεχής, Thphr.*HP*3.1.6, 8.6.1. **-βρώς**, ῶτος, ὁ, ἡ, = sq., Antiph.89, *AP*6.57 (Paul. Sil.). **-βρωτος**, ον, *half-eaten*, X.*An.*1.9.26, Axionic.8.2, Nic.*Th.*919, etc. **-γᾰμος**, ον, *half-married*, i.e. *a concubine*, Philostr.*VS*1.21.4. **-γένειος**, ον, *but half-bearded*, of a youth, Theoc.6.3. **-γενής**, ές, *intermediate*, *equivocal*, Pl.*Ti.*66d; of fruits, *half-formed*, Thphr.*HP*1.14.1. **-γραμμον**, τό, (γράμμα II.5) *half a scruple*, Hippiatr.22. **-γρᾰφος**, ον, *half-written*, Men.1014. **-γυμνος**, ον, *half-naked*, Luc.*DMar.*14.3, Arr.*Ind.*24.8. **-γύναιξ** [ῠ], αικος, ὁ, ἡ, *half-woman*, Simon.179.9, Suid. s.v. ἄρρεν:—also **-γύναιος** [ῠ], ον, Id. s.v. Πολύευκτος. **-δᾰής**, ές, (δαίω A) *half-burnt*, νηῦς Il.16.294; Φαέθων A.R.4.598. II. (δατέομαι) *half-divided*, *half-mangled*, σκύβαλον *AP*9.375; χειρὸς βάρος Nic.*Al.*55 (cf. ἡμιδεής). **-δάϊκτος** [ᾰ], ον, (δαΐζω) *half-slain*, Opp.*C.*2.281, *H.*5.669. **-δακτῠλιαῖος**, α, ον, *half a finger long*, S.E.*M.*10.137. **-δακτύλιον** [ῠ], τό, *half-finger's breadth*, *IG*2[2].1013.25, 5(1).1390.16 (Andania, i B. C.), Plb.6.23.11, Ph.*Bel.*65.3, Plu.2.935d. **-δᾰμής**, ές, *half-slain*, Opp.*H.*1.716 (v.ll. ἡμιθανής, ἡμιδαής). **-δᾰνάκη** [νᾰ], ἡ, *half-*δανάκη, prob.l. in Theon *Prog.*13:—Dim. **-ιον**, τό, Hsch. **-δᾰπής**, ές, expld. by ἡμιτελής, Phot., Suid. **-δᾰρεικόν**, τό, *half-daric*, X.*An.*1.3.21, prob. in *SIG*276.13 (Delphi, iv B. C.). **-δεής**, ές, (δέω B) *wanting half*, *half-full*, X.*An.*1.9.25, *AP*5.182 (Posidipp.), *PSI*4.428.24, cj. for -δαής in Nic.*Al.*55; ἐξ ἡμιδεοῦς γέμοντα ἤδη *from being only half-full*.., Them.*Or.*18.222b. **-δελτα**, τό, *half-delta*, a musical note, ᐱ, Alyp.4, al. **-δέξιον**, τό, *dactylic trimeter*, Sacerd.pp.514, 544 K. **-δίμνον**, v. ἡμέδιμνον. **-διπλοΐδιον**, τό, *a woman's dress folded at the top so as to fall half-way down the figure*, Ar.*Ec.*318, cf. *EM*430.46. **-δουλεία**, ἡ, *half-slavery*, Chrysipp.*Stoic.*2.284. **-δουλος**, ον, *half-slave*, E.*Andr.*942, Chrysipp.*Stoic.*2.284. **-δραχμον**, τό, *half-drachma*, Poll.6.160; τέταρτον ἡ. *IG*1[2].373.18: as an apothecaries' weight, Gal.13.674, al. **-δωδέκατον**, τό, = ἡμίχουν, Hsch. **-ειλος**, ον, (εἵλη) *half-exposed to the sun*, Thphr.*HP*3.23.1. **-εκταΐδιον**, τό, Dim. of sq., dub. in *IG*9(2).1222. **-έκτεων**, gen. -εω, τό, *half-*ἑκτεύς, acc. sg. -εων (written -εον) ib.1[2].76.7; gen. -εω ib.2[2].1356; but -έου Ar.*Nu.*643; nom. -έον ib.645, *Mémoires présentés à l'Acad. des Inscr.*1923.2 (iv B. C.); written -ειον ibid.; pl. -εια *IG*2[2].1672.15, 268, al.; -έα prob. cj. in Pl.Com.174.12: Ion. pl. -εκτῆ *Milet.*7.27. (Accent doubtful, parox. in codd.; -ειον, -εια may have short ει as in εἰάν, etc.) **-εκτον**, τό, *half-*ἑκτεύς, D.34.37, Thphr.*HP*2.6.2, *IG*3.98, etc.; *a vessel containing thus much*, Hp.*Steril.*230 (-εκτέον ap. Erot.). II. ἡ. χρυσοῦ, = 8 obols, Crates Com.20, cf. *SIG*45.26 (Halic., v B. C.), *IG*1[2].310.118 (cf. p.303). **-εκφᾰνής**, ές, *half-brilliant*, of stars of the lesser magnitudes, Ptol.*Alm.*7.1. **-έλλην**, ηνος, ὁ, ἡ, *half-Greek*, Luc.*Salt.*64. **-επές**, τό, *half-hexameter*, Mar. Vict.p.73 K., Sacerd.p.544 K. **-έργαστος**, ον, *half-wrought*, *half-completed*, ὕλη Gal.5.538:—also **-εργής**, ές, Luc.*Astr.*5, and **-εργος**, ον, ἔμβρυον Hp.*Mul.*1.78; [αἷμα] Gal.5.535; of buildings, *IG*1[2].372.5; τεῖχος ἡ. μετῆκε Hdt.4.124, cf. Th.7.2, J.*AJ*14.16.2, Plu.2.841d. **-ετης**, ες, (ἔτος) *of half a year*, ἡμιέτες, καὶ ἡ. χρόνος Poll.1.54. **-εφθος**, ον, (ἕψω) *half-boiled*, Hp.*Art.*63, Lxx *Is.*51.20, Dsc.*Eup.*1.84, Gal.6.725: generally, *half-cooked*, even by roasting or frying, of Empedocles in Luc.*DMort.*20.4; v.l. for ἡμίοπτος, Id.*Gall.*2. **-ζύγιος** [ῠ], ον, *forming half a pair of scales*, Arist.*Mech.*853^{b}26. **-ζωνον** (-ζώνιον cod.), *semicinctum*, *Gloss.* **-ζως**, *half-alive*, Hdn.*Epim.*239. **-θᾰλής**, ές, (θάλλω) *half-green*, στέφανοι *AP*7.465 (Heraclit.). **-θᾰνής**, ές, *half-dead*, Str.2.3.4, Lxx 4*Ma.*4.11, *Ev.Luc.*10.30, *AP*11.392 (Lucill.), *PAmh.*2.141.13 (iv A. D.). **-θέα**, Ep. **-θέη**, ἡ, *demigoddess*, Call.*Aet.*3.1.71: gen. pl. -θεάων *IG*14.1389 i 57. **-θέαινα**, ἡ, *demigoddess*, Opp.*C.*3.245. **-θεος**, Aeol. **αἰμί-** Alc.*Supp.*8.13, Dor. **ἁμί-** Theoc.18.18 codd., **ἡμίσῐος** Alcm.23.7: ὁ:—*demigod*, ἀνδρῶν ἡρώων θεῖον γένος, οἳ καλέονται ἡμίθεοι Hes.*Op.*160, cf. *h.Hom.*31.19, 32.19, Pi.*P.*4.184, Pl.*Ap.*28c, Isoc.9.70, etc.; once in Hom. (if genuine), ἡμιθέων γένος ἀνδρῶν Il.12.23. II. Pythag. name for *five*, *Theol.Ar.*32. **-θηλυς**, υ, *half-woman*, Ἄττις *Anacreont.*11.2. **-θηρ**, ηρος, ὁ, ἡ, *half-beast*, Apollod.1.6.3, Philostr.Jun.*Im.*4. **-θῆτα**, τό, *half-theta*, a musical note, ⊓, Alyp.13. **-θνής**, ῆτος, ὁ, ἡ, = ἡμιθανής, Ar.*Nu.*504, Th.2.52, Plb.14.5.7, Gal.10.1021; of fear, Aeschin.3.159; ὕπνος βαθὺς καὶ ἡ. Philostr.*VA*2.36. **-θνητος**, ον, *half-mortal*, of the Dioscuri, Lyc.511, cf. Gal.17(1).235. 2. *half-dead*, Lxx *Wi.*18.18. **-θραυστος**, ον, *half-broken*, E.*HF*1096, Lyc.378, *AP*9.568.5 (Diosc.). **-θωράκιον** [ᾰ], τό, *front plate of the* θώραξ, *SIG*421.40 (Aetolia, iii B. C.), Plu.2.596d. **-ϊουδαῖος**, ὁ, *half-Jew*, J.*AJ*14.15.2. **-ιππος**, ὁ, coined on analogy of ἡμίονος, Sch.D.T.p.167 H. **-κάδιον** [ᾰ], τό, *half-*κάδος, Philoch.155a, *IG*14.422 iii 81 (Tauromenium), *BGU*1095.16 (i A. D.). **-κᾰκος**, ον, *half a villain*, S.*Fr.*1051, Alex.10, Oenom.ap.Eus.*PE*5.24. Adv. **-κως**, ἐβοσκόμην Ar.*Th.*449. **-κᾰλάθιον** [λᾰ], τό, *half a basket*, ἀνθράκων *IG*11(2).161 *A* 109 (Delos, iii B. C.); ἰσχάδων *Inscr.Magn.*116.38. **-καυστος** (so Thphr.*Lap.*53, Charito 1.3) or **-καυτος**, ον, *half-burnt*, Ael.*VH*13.2, D.C.50.35, Jul.*Or.*1.27d. **-κενος**, ον, *half-empty*, S.E.*M.*5.77, Poll.5.133. **-κεντρος**, ον, *half-way between cardinal points*, prob. in Jul.Laod. in *Cat.Cod.Astr.*5(1).190. **-κερᾰμία** and **-κέρᾰμον**, *urna*, *Gloss.* **-κεραύνιος**, ὁ, name of a *bandage*, Gal.12.496 Chart. **-κεφάλαιον** [ᾰ], τό, less Att. form for ἡμίκρανον (i.e. ἡμίκραιρα), acc. to Phryn.303: **-κεφάλιον** and **-λον**, *Gloss.*; = *sinciput*, Dosith.p.389 K. **-κίριον**, τό, *cloth* or *sackcloth of half size*, *PCair.Zen.*69.10 (iii B. C.). **-κλάδευτος** [ᾰ], ον, *half-pruned*, *Gloss.* **-κλαστος**, ον, (κλάω) *half-broken*, Plu.2.306b, 317d. **-κλειστος**, ον, *half-shut*, prob. l. for ἡμικλεῖς in Anon.ap.Suid. **-κλήριον**, τό, (κλῆρος A) *half the inheritance*, Is.7.6, D.48.20; pleon., τοῦ κλήρου τὸ ἡ. Is.11.24. II. *half a* κλῆρος, *PPetr.*3 p.245 (iii B. C.), *PMagd.*1.6 (iii B. C.), *Schwyzer* 734.4 (Zelea). **-κλῖβᾰνος** [ῑ], ὁ, *half-share in a bakehouse*, *PLond.*5.1724.33 (vi A. D.). **-κλῖνον**, τό, *half-sized couch*, *IG*11(2).147 *B* 14 (Delos, iv B. C.). **-κόγγιον**, τό, *half-congius*, Dsc.ap.Gal.19.776. **-κόλλιον**, v. -κόριον. **-κοπος**, ον, *half-mangled*, gloss on ἡμιδαής, Sch.Opp.*H.*1.716; expld. by ἡμίπλευρος, Hsch. II. **-κοπον**, τό, *half-carcase*, *Sammelb.*4630.16 (ii A. D.), *PSI*6.683.33 (ii A. D.). **-κόριον**, τό, *half-*κόρος, a dry measure, Hsch. (-κόλλιον cod.):—also **-κορος**, ὁ, Aq., Sm., Thd.*Hos.*3.2. **-κόσμιον**, τό, *half the universe*, Cleom.1.9, 11. **-κοτύλη** [ῠ], ἡ, *half-*κοτύλη, *POxy.*1142.2 (iii A. D.), v.l. in Hp.*Nat.Mul.*107, Hero *Spir.*2.30. **-κοτῠλίειος**, α, ον, *holding half a* κοτύλη, *PCair.Zen.*89.6 (iii B. C.), al. **-κοτύλιον** [ῠ], τό, *half-*κοτύλη, Hp.*Nat.Mul.*47, 107, Arist.*HA*573^{a}7, Dieuch. ap.Orib.4.7.37, etc., dub. in *IG*1[2].842 *A* 2. **-κουρος**, ον, *half-sheared*, *PHib.*1.32 (iii B. C.). **-κραιρα**, ἡ, *half the head* or *face*, Ar.*Th.*227, Amips.7, Crobyl.6; ἡμίκραιραν χορδῆς *IG*2[2].1356. 2. = sq., Gal.12.591, al. **-κρᾱνία**, ἡ, (κρανίον) *pain on one side of the head* or *face*, ib.592:—also **-κράνιον**, τό, *PMag.Lond.*121.199, *Arch.f. Religionswiss.*24.176 (Carnuntum). **-κρᾱνικός**, ή, όν, *of* or *like* ἡμικρανία, ἀλγήματα Gal.12.594; πάθος Aët.6.49; οἱ ἡ. *persons suffering therefrom*, Gal.8.206, Paul.Aeg.3.5; φάρμακα *remedies for* ἡ., Gal.12.592. **-κρᾱνον**, τό, = ἡμίκραιρα I, Alex.Trall.1.12. **-κρής**, ῆτος, ὁ, *half a Cretan*, Lyc.150. **-κύᾰθος** [ῠ], ὁ, *half-*κύαθος, Thessal. in *Cat.Cod.Astr.*8(3).149, Aret.*CA*2.2, Gal.19.770. **-κυκλικός**, ή, όν, = sq., Sch.Pl.*Alc.*1.129c. **-κύκλιος**, ον, (κύκλος) *semicircular*, Sch. A.R.4.1613:—also **-κυκλος**, ον, στοά Philostr.*Im.*1.12, cf. Hld.8.14. II. as Subst., **-κύκλιον**, τό, *semicircle*, Arist.*APo.*41^{b}17, *Ph.*264^{b}24; *hemisphere*, Ach.Tat.*Intr.Arat.*27, Heph.Astr.2.11; of a tactical formation, κατὰ τὸ ἡ. Onos.21.5. 2. *a place for public entertainment* or *meeting*, Plu.*Alc.*17, *Nic.*12; *place of assembly* at Samos, Porph.*VP*9. 3. *semicircular seat*, *armchair*, Cic.*Lael.*1.2, Poll.6.9. 4. *semicircular dial*, Vitr.9.8.1. 5. *semicircular statue-base*, *IG*11(2).287 *B* 73 (Delos, iii B. C.), *BCH*29.543 (ibid.); *drum of a half-column*, *Rev.Phil.*43.182 (Didym.). 6. *barrel-vault*, Ph.*Bel.*87.12. 7. *theatrical machine*, described by Poll.4.127, 131. **-κυκλιώδης**, ες, *semicircular*, γραμμή Str.13.1.34:—also **-κυκλώδης**, Hsch. s.v. ἡμίαρτον: **-κυκλοειδής**, ές, Heliod.(?)ap.Orib.46.11.34. Adv. **-κυκλοειδῶς** Tz. ad Hes.*Op.*450. **-κυκλος**, ον, v. ἡμικύκλιος. **-κύλινδρος** [ῠ], ὁ, *half-cylinder*, D.L.8.83:—Dim. **-κυλίνδριον**, τό, Porph.*Abst.*4.7, Eutoc. ad Archim.*Sph.Cyl.*2. 2. as Adj., *semicylindrical*, πύργοι Ph.*Bel.*84.25 (s.v.l.). **-κῠνες**, οἱ, *half-dogs*, name of a fabulous nation, elsewh. κυνοκέφαλοι, Hes.*Fr.*62, Simm.1.9. **-κυπρον**, τό, (κύπρος II.2) *a measure*, Hippon.24; said to = ½ μέδιμνος, Hsch. **-κώνιον**, τό, *half-cone*, Euc.*Opt.*30. **-κῳον**, τό, *half a* κῷον, *Sammelb.*4425 vii 12 (ii A. D.). **-λᾰγος**, ὁ, *half-hare*, i.e. *rabbit*, *Edict.Diocl.*4.33. **-λάμιον**· μέρος Μεσσαπίων, Hsch. **-λαμπρος**, ον, *at half brilliancy*, φῶς Sch.Arat.733. **-λάσταυρος**, ὁ, *half a rogue*, Men.1014. **-λέπιστος**, ον, *half-peeled* or *shelled*, Str.17.1.34. **-λεπτος**, ον, *half-hatched*, *Anacreont.*25.10. **-λευκος**, ον, *half-white*, Luc.*Prom.Es*4. **-λιτριαῖος**, α, ον, *weighing half a pound*, βῶλοι Str.3.2.8. **-λίτριον**, τό, *half-pound*, Epich.9, *POxy.*1051.12 (iii A. D.), Archig.ap.Orib.8.1.27. **-λιτρον**, τό, in Sicily, *half-obol*, Arist.*Fr.*510. 2. *half-pound*, Asclep.ap.Gal.13.445, al. **-λουτος**, ον, *half-washed*, Cratin.416. **-λοχία**, ἡ, *half-*λόχος, Suid. s.v. διμοιρίτης:—also **-λόχιον**, τό, Ascl.*Tact.*2.2, Ael.*Tact.*5.2. **-λοχίτης** [ῑ], ου, ὁ, *leader of a* ἡμιλοχία, Ascl.*Tact.*2.2, Ael.*Tact.*5.2, Suid. l.c. **-μᾰθής**, ές, *half-learned*, Philostr. *VS*2.5.4, Poll.6.160. **-μᾰνής**, ές, *half-mad*, Aeschin.1.171, Luc.*Deor.Conc.*4. **-μάραντος** [μᾰ], ον, *half-withered*, Id.*Tox.*13, Alciphr.3.62. **-μάσητος** [μᾰ], ον, *half-chewed*, Crates Com.49. **-μέγιστον**, τό, *half-mina*, Hsch. **-μέδιμνον**, τό, *half-*μέδιμνος, Pherecr.1, D.55.24, Dicaearch.Hist.23:—also **-μέδιμνος**, ὁ, *SIG*945.3 (Assos, iv B. C.), Poll.4.168; cf. ἡμέδιμνον. **-μεθής**, ές, *half-drunk*, *AP*6.251 (Phil.). **-μέθῠσος**, ον, (μεθύω) = foreg., Poll.6.160. **-μείλιον**, τό, *half a mile*, *BCH*37.149 (Trajanopolis, ii/iii A. D.). **-μέριστος**, ον, *divided in half*, gloss on ἡμιδάϊκτος, Sch. Opp.*H.*2.287. **-μεστος**, ον, *half-full*, Poll.5.133. **-μετρον**, τό, gloss on ἡμικάδιον, Suid. **-μηδος**, ὁ, *half a Mede*, Oenom.ap.Eus. *PE*5.21. **-μηνιαῖος**, α, ον, (μήν) and **-μήνιος**, ον, *half-monthly*,

Gloss. **-μιτρον**, τό, *half-mitra* (v. μίτρα), Poll.10.191, Hsch. **-μναῖον**, τό, *half-mina*, *IG*1².371.7, X.*Mem.*2.5.2, Pl.*Lg.* 774d, etc.:—the form **-μνεα** (pl.) is found in Plu.*Lyc.*12 codd., Porph.*Abst.*4.4 codd.: sg. **-μνοῦν** Asclep.ap.Gal.13.746. **-μόδιον**, τό, *half a modius*, *Gp.*7.24.2. **-μοιραῖος**, α, ον, *equal to half a degree*, μέγεθος Cleom.2.2. **-μοίριον**, τό, *half a part*, Hp.*Ulc.* 12. II. *half a degree*, Cleom.2.1, Ptol.*Alm.*1.10, al. **-μόριον**, τό, sine expl., Poll.6.160 (v.l. -μοίριον). **-μόχθηρος**, ον, *half-evil, half a villain*, Pl.*R.*352c, Ph.2.346; *half-bad*, of things, Gal.6.56. **-μυ**, *half-μυ*, ⊣, a musical note, Alyp.4, al.

ἡμίνα, ἡ, (ἥμισυς) *half*, *Leg.Gort.*2.49, *SIG*525.13 (Gortyn, iii B.C.), prob. in Hsch. s.v. ἰνιμίνα. II. a Sicil. measure, = κοτύλη, Epich. [290], Sophr.105; ἡ. βασιλική, = ἡμικοτύλιον, Aristid.*Or.*49(25).32, cf. *IG*7.2712.66 (Acraeph.). (Hence Lat. *hemīna*; Italic and properisp. acc. to Theognost.*Can.*101, but prob. orig. Greek.)

ἡμί-ναυλον, τό, *half-freight*, *PGoodsp.Cair.*30 xli 19 (ii A.D.), *PFay.* 104.7 (iii A.D.). **-ναυον**, τό, prob. an Egyptian measure of length, *PCair.Zen.*383 (iii B.C.). **-νεοτελής**, ές, gloss on νεοτελής, Herm.*in Phdr.*p.159 A. (s. v. l.). **-νηρος**, ον, contr. for ἡμινέαρος, *half-fresh*, and so of fish, *half-salted*, Xenocr.77, Ath.3.118f. **-ξεστον**, τό, *half-ξέστης* (Alexandrian, acc. to Diph.Siph.ap.Ath.3. 121b), Dsc.1.25, *Hippiatr.*100, Sch.Ar.*Pl.*436. **-ξηρος**, ον, *half-dry*, *PFlor.*118.3 (iii A.D.), *AP*9.137 tit., Suid. s.v. λαιψηρόν. **-ξύρητος** [ῠ], ον, (ξυράω) *half-shorn*, D.L.6.33. **-όγδοον**, τό, = *two* χόες, Hsch. **-οβόλιον**, τό, *half-obol weight*, Paul.Aeg. 3.29; in form **-οβελιν**, on coins of Aegium, Head *Hist.Num.*² 413. **-όδελος**, ὁ, = ἡμιωβέλιον, dub. in *GDI*2562.26 (Delph., iv B.C.). **-όδιον**, *semita*, *Gloss.* **-όδιος**, ον, prob. f.l. in Arist. *Oec.*1352ᵇ26.

ἡμιολ-ιασμός, ὁ, *multiplying by one and a half*, Antipho Soph. 75. **-ίζω**, *increase by one half*, χρέος *Schwyzer* 418.8 (Elis). **-ιος**, α, ον, hyperdor. ἁμ-, ον, (ὅλος) *containing one and a half, half as much or as large again*, Pl.*Tht.*154c; περίμετρος Plb.6.32.7; ηὔξησε τὰ δόρατα ἡμιολίῳ μεγέθει D.S.15.44: c. gen., τὰς περόνας ἡμιολίας.. τοῦ τότε κατεστεῶτος μέτρου *half as large again as..*, Hdt.5.88; [γωνία] ἁμιόλιος τᾶς μέσας Ti.Locr.98a; [ὁ γνήσιος ἀετὸς] ἡ. τῶν ἀετῶν Arist.*HA* 619ᵃ13; neut., *half as much again*, ἡμιόλιον οὗ πρότερον ἔφερον X.*An.*1. 3.21; ἡμιόλιον ὀφλέτω ὅ τι συλάσαι let him be fined *half as much again* as the amount he seized, *IG*9(1).333.5 (Locr., v B.C.); of numbers, *half as many again*, ποιήσας ἡμιολίους τοὺς ναύτας ἢ πρόσθεν Plb.10. 17.12. II. *in the ratio of one and a half to one* (3 : 2), as in musical sounds, ἡμιολίαι διαστάσεις Pl.*Ti.*36a; τὸ δι' ὀξειᾶν ἡ. Philol.6; ἡ ἡμιολία *this ratio*, τὴν ἡ. τοῦ τιμήματος Pl.*Lg.*956d; ἀποτίνειν τὴν φέρνην σὺν τῇ ἡ. Mitteis *Chr.*280.15 (ii B.C.). Adv. -ίως Nicom.*Ar.*2.20, Procl.*in Ti.*2.223 D. III. ἡμιολία ναῦς *a light vessel with one and a half banks of oars*, D.S.19.65; also ἡμιολία alone, Thphr.*Char.*25.2, D.S.16.61, *Mus.Belg.*14.20 (but -ίους Plb.5.101.2, -ιον Hsch.), etc.; used by pirates, Thphr.*Char.* l. c.; ἡ. λῃστρικαί Arr.*An.*3.2.5, etc.; expld. by δίκροτος (q. v.) ναῦς, Hsch. IV. τροχαϊκὸς ἡ. (sc. στίχος) trochaic verse *consisting of a metre and a half*, Heph.15.2. **-ίς**, ίδος, ἡ, = ἡμιολία ναῦς, Poll.1.82.

ἡμιόλκιον, τό, (ὁλκή) *half-drachm*, Archig.ap.Orib.8.46.16.

ἡμιον-άγριον, τό, *mule* (produce of ὄναγρος), *PEdgar*13.3 (iii B.C.). **-ειος**, α, ον, Ion. -εος Hdt.1.188:—*of, belonging to a mule*, ἅμαξα ἡ. *drawn by mules*, Od.6.72, Il.24.189; ζυγὸν ἡ. ib.268; κόπρος ἡμιονείη, = ἡμιονίς, Pampho ap. Philostr.*Her.*2.19, cf. Suid. s. v. II. ἡμιόνειος πόα, = ἡμιόνιον I, Dsc.*Eup.*2.100. **-ηγός** (-ᾱγός *Gloss.*), ὁ, *muleteer*, *PLond.ined.*2358 (iii B.C.), *Rev.Phil.*50.67 (Didyma, ii B.C.), Str.14.2.24. **-ικός**, ή, όν, = ἡμιόνειος, ζεῦγος X.*An.*7.5.2; ὁδὸς ἡ. a road *only fit for mules*, Str.6.3.7; ἡ. ἅρμα *drawn by mules*, *BGU*814.6 (iii A.D.). **-ιον**, τό, *milt-wort, Asplenium Ceterach*, Thphr.*HP*9.18.7, Plin.*HN*27.34; = ἄσπληνος, Dsc.3.134. II. Dim. of ἡμίονος, Str.5.3.6 (s.v.l.). III. a kind of *bird*, Hsch. **-ίς**, ίδος, ἡ, *mule-dung*, Hp.*Nat.Mul.*90. **-ίτης** [ῑ], ου, ὁ, *muleteer*, *PCair.Zen.*4.69 (iii B.C.). **-ῖτις**, ιδος, ἡ, *of* or *for a mule*, ἵππος ἡμιονῖτις a mare *in foal of a mule*, Str.5.1.4. II. ἡμιονῖτις, ιδος, ἡ, *mule-fern, Scolopendrium Hemionitis*, Dsc.3.135. **-όκουρος**, ὁ, *mule-clipper*, *Gloss.* **-ος**, ἡ, Il.2.852, Pi.*O.*6.22, *Rev.Phil.* 50.67 (Didyma, ii B.C.), etc.; ὁ, Il.17.742, Pl.*Ap.*27e, etc.: Aeol. **αἰμί-** Sapph.*Supp.*20a.14:—*half-ass*, i.e. *mule*, Il.10.352, al., Arist. *HA*576ᵇ11, etc.; ταλαεργός Il.23.654: prov., γνοίης ὅσσον ὄνων κρέσσονες ἡμίονοι Thgn.996; ἐφ' ἡμιόνων on a car drawn by mules, Il.24. 702; εἰς ἡμιόνους ποιεῖν to write an ode on *a team of racing-mules*, Arist.*Rh.*1405ᵇ26: prov., ἐπεὰν ἡμίονοι τέκωσι, i.e. never, Hdt.3. 153: metaph., ἡ. βασιλεύς, i.e. half-Mede, half-Persian, Orac.ap.Hdt. 1.55. 2. ἡ. ἀγροτέρα *wild ass, onager*, Il.2.852; αἱ ἐν Συρίᾳ καλούμεναι ἡ. Arist.*HA*491ᵃ2, cf. 580ᵇ1, al. II. as Adj., βρέφος ἡμίονον *a mule*-foal, Il.23.266.

ἡμί-οπλος, ον, *half-armed*, *Gloss.* **-οπος**, ον, (ὀπή) *with half its holes*, ἡ. αὐλοί flutes *with only three holes*, Anacr.20; ἡ. (without αὐλός), ὁ, used metaph. of *something small*, A.*Fr.*91. II. ἡμίοπον· ἥμισυ, Gal.19.102. **-οπτος**, ον, *half-roasted*, Alex.175, Luc.*Gall.*2 (v.l.), Hld.2.19. **-ουγκιαῖος**, α, ον, = Lat. *semuncialis*, *Gloss.* **-ούγκιον**, τό, *half* οὐγκία or *ounce*, Lat. *semuncia*, Epich.8:—written **-ούγγιον** in Gal.13.558. **-πᾱγής**, ές, *half-congealed, half-hardened*, Pl.*Ti.*59e, 60d; δρόσος Arist.*Mu.*394ᵃ26; ᾠὰ ἡ. *half-hard, medium-boiled* eggs, Hp.*Acut.*(*Sp.*)53: metaph., ἡ. σοφία Ph.1.322. **-πᾰθής**, ές, *half-suffering*, μέρεα Aret.*SD*1. 7. **-πᾰχής**, f.l. for κνημοπαχής, Thphr.*CP*3.4.3. **-πέλεκκον**, τό, *half-axe*, i.e. *one-edged axe* (the πέλεκυς being double-edged), Il.23.851, 858, 883. **-πέ(πε)ιρος**, ον, *half-ripe*, Hsch. s. v. βλήσσα. **-πεπτος**, ον, *half-ripened*, Plu.*Caes.*69; *half-digested*, τροφή Gal.11.666, al. **-πέπων**, ον, gen. ονος, *half-ripe*, Herod.Med.ap. Orib.5.31.6. **-πέρσης**, ου, ὁ, *half a Persian*, Oenom.ap.Eus.*PE* 5.21. **-πήχειον**, τό, *half-cubit*, S.E.*M.*7.105:—also **-πήχιον**, τό, Hipparch.3.5.6, Theo Sm.p.53 H. **-πηχῠαῖος**, α, ον, *half a cubit long*, Dsc.3.129, *Gp.*10.4.1. **-πηχυς**, υ, *of half a cubit*, διάστημα S.E.*M.*10.132: as Subst., δύο -πήχεα ib.127; *half a cubit high*, ἄνθρωπος Phld.*Sign.*2. **-πλεθρον**, τό, *half-πλέθρον*, Hdt.7. 176, X.*An.*4.7.6. **-πλεκτος**, ον, *half-plaited*, Philyll.31. **-πλευρος**, v. ἡμίκοπος. **-πλεως**, ων, *half-full*, Poll.5.133. **-πληγής**, ές, *half-struck*, Olymp.*in Mete.*200.15. **-πληγία**, ἡ, *paralysis*, Paul.Aeg.3.16. **-πλήξ**, ῆγος, ὁ, ἡ, *half-felled*, of a tree, *cleft*, [πεύκη] A.R.4.1683. **-πλήρης**, ες, *half-full*, κύστιες Aret.*CA*1. 6. **-πλήρωτος**, ον, *half-manned*, [πλοῖα] Poll.1.121; *half-full*, Id.5.133. **-πλίνθιον**, τό, (πλίνθος) *half-plinth, brick* (two of which formed a plinth), ἡμιπλίνθια χρυσοῦ *ingots* of gold, Hdt.1.50, cf. *IG*1².314.82:—also **-πλινθος**, ὁ, *Gloss.* **-πνικτος**, ον, (πνίγω) *half-choked*, *Gloss.* **-πνοος**, ον, contr. -πνους, ουν, *half-breathing, half-alive*, Batr.252, Gal.*UP*6.3. **-ποδιαῖος**, α, ον, *half a foot broad* or *high*, Apollod.*Poliorc.*146.7, Bito 45.4. **-πόδιον**, τό, *half-foot*, *IG*1².372.49, 163, al., Thphr.*HP*7.2.7, Plb.6.23.2, *Hermes* 17.4 (Delos): **-πόδιος**, v.l. in *Gp.*4.12.2. **-ποίητος**, ον, *half-made*, Poll.6.160. **-πολον**, τό, *half the sphere*, Hsch. **-πόνηρος**, ον, *half-evil*, Arist.*EN*1152ᵃ17, *Pol.*1315ᵇ10. **-πους**, ποδος, ὁ, *half-foot*, Apollod.*Poliorc.*178.3. **-πτωτος**, ον, (πίπτω) *half-fallen*, Suid. s. v. ἐρείπιον. **-πύργιον**, τό, *half-tower*, Philostr.*VS*2.1. 11. **-πῦρος**, ον, (πῦρ) *half of fire*, Arist.*Mu.*395ᵃ23, Cleom.2.4, Plu.2.928e. **-πύρωτος** [ῠ], ον, *half-burnt*, *AP*7.401.5 (Crin.).

ἡμιρόδιον, τό, *half a* ῥοδία (q.v.), Roussel *Cultes Égyptiens* 236 (Delos, ii B.C.).

ἡμι-ρρᾰγής, ές, *half-broken*, πίνακες Aristid.*Or.*25(43).32. **-ρρήνιον**, τό, *half-grown sheep*, *Michel* 995 *D* 33:—fem. **-ρρηνιαία**, ἡ, ib. 35 (Delph.). **-ρρομβιαῖος**, α, ον, *like a* ἡμιρρόμβιον, Gal.18(1). 788. **-ρρόμβιον**, τό, = ἡμίτομος II. 2b, Heliod.ap.Orib.48.20.13, Gal. 18(1).797, 838. **-ρρόπως**, Adv. *half turning the scale*, i.e. *lightly, gently*, opp. ἀθρόως, Hp.*Epid.*2.1.7. **-ρρῠπος**, ον, *half-dirty*, εἴριον Id.*Mul.*2.205. **-σάκιον**, τό, (σάκος or σάκκος) *half-sack*, σησάμων Poll.10.169.

ἡμῐσάκις, Adv. *half a time*, Iamb.*in Nic.*p.14 P., al.; δὶς καὶ ἡ. two and *a half times*, Papp.556.16.

ἡμι-σάλευτος [ᾰ], ον, (σαλεύω) *half-shaken*, Hsch. **-σᾰπής**, ές, (σήπομαι) *half-putrid*, Hp.*Morb.*1.31, Gal.7.301, al.

ἡμίσεια, ἡ, **ἡμίσεον**, τό, **ἡμίσεος**, **ἥμισος**, v. ἥμισυς.

ἡμισελήνιον, τό, *half the apparent breadth of the moon*, Ptol.*Alm.* 9.10.

ἡμῐσεύελπις, ιδος, ὁ, ἡ, *half-hopeful*, f.l. in Luc.*Cal.*10.

ἡμίσ-ευμα [ῐ], ατος, τό, *a half*, Lxx *Nu.*31.36; παραλληλογράμμου *Theol.Ar.*39; name of a tax on vines, *PSI*4.434.4 (sg., iii B.C.), *Raccolta Lumbroso* 123 (pl., iii B.C.). **-ευτής**, οῦ, ὁ, gloss on ἡμιτιεύς, Hsch. **-εύω**, (ἥμισυς) *halve*, Lxx *Ps.*54(55).24, Aq.*Ge.* 33.1. 2. *boil down to one half*, *Hippiatr.*2.

ἡμῐσιάζω, *halve*, Asclep.*Tact.*12.11: **-σειάζω**, Hero *Geom.*7.4 (Pass.), al.

ἡμί-σικλον, τό, *half-σίκλος*, J.*AJ*7.13.1: **-σίκλιον**, Hsch. **-σιος**, v. ἡμίθεος. **-σκουτον**, τό, *half-σκοῦτα*, Hero *Mens.*14. **-σοφος**, ον, *half-wise*, Luc.*Herm.*15, *Bis Acc.*8. **-σπάθιον** [ᾰ], τό, *half-spatula*, Heliod.ap.Orib.44.14.4, 23.66, Leonid.ap.Paul.Aeg.6. 78. **-σπαστος**, ον, *half pulled down*, Str.17.3.12; *half torn away*, *AP*10.21 (Phld.). **-σπῐθᾰμιαῖος**, α, ον, *of half a span*, σπλῆνες πλάτος -ιαῖοι Hp.*Fract.*29. **-σπίθᾰμος** [πῐ], ον, = foreg., Ph.*Bel.* 56.4. **-σπονδος**, ον, *half bound by treaty*, Poll.6.30. **-στᾰδιαῖος**, α, ον, *of half a stadium*, Luc.*VH*1.40, etc. **-στάδιον** [ᾰ], τό, *half-stadium*, Plb.3.54.7, Str.17.1.48, Ath.Mech.8.8. **-στατήρ**, ῆρος, ὁ, = sq., prob. in *IG*12(3).1638 (Thera). **-στάτηρον** [ᾰ], τό, *half-στατήρ*, *IG*1².917 (prob.), *SIG*218.25 (Olbia, iv B.C.), *Schwyzer* 701 (Erythrae, v B.C.), Arist.*Fr.*529, cf. Hsch. s. v. ἡμίχα. **-στίχιον** [τῐ], τό, *half-line, half-verse*, D.H.*Comp.*26, Hipparch.1.4.9, S.E.*M.* 1.165, Iamb.*VP*29.162. **-στρᾰτιώτης**, ου, ὁ, *half-soldier*, Luc. *Bacch.*3 codd. (dub.l.). **-στρόγγῠλος**, ον, *half-round*, Id.*Ocyp.* 97. **-στρόφιον**, τό, f.l. for στροφεῖον, Poll.4.127.

ἡμισύ-δουλος [ῠ], ὁ, *half a slave*, Man.4.600. **-θλαστος**, ον, *half-crushed*, Hsch.

ἡμισύνθεσις, εως, ἡ, *half-set*, *POxy.*741.15 (pl., ii A.D.).

ἥμῐσυς, εια, υ, gen. ἡμίσεος Hdt.2.126, Th.2.78, 4.83, X.*Oec.*18.8, Pl.*Smp.*205e, *IG*2².1612.267, D.23.213, etc. (ἡμίσεως is sts. a v.l., as in Th. ll.cc., and is found in later writers, as Dsc.2.70); also as fem., Th.4.104; later contr. ἡμίσους D.H.4.17, Plu.*Mar.*34, etc. (as fem., Lxx 3*Ki.*16.9): nom. and acc. pl. masc., Ion. ἡμίσεες, -εας, Il. 21.7, Hdt.9.51, Att. ἡμίσεις Th.3.20, Pl.*Tht.*154c (ἡμίσεας is preferred by Phryn.*PS*p.73 B.): neut. pl. ἡμίσεα Th.4.16, Pl.*R.*438c, later ἡμίση D.36.36 (cod. S), al., *IG*2².1678.23, Thphr.*Char.*30.16, *IG*12 (5).872.107 (Tenos), *SIG*²588.4 (Delos, ii B.C.), etc.: Ion. fem. ἡμίσεᾰ Hdt.5.111 (hyperion. -σέη Luc.*Syr.D.*14), acc. pl. -έας Hdt.8.27, also acc. sg. ἡμισέαν *IG*2.1055.16, 1059.14, gen. ἡμισέας Pl.*Men.*83c: **ἥμυσυς** (assim.), *Rev.Phil.*54.192 (Erythrae, v B.C.), *IG*2².43 *A* 45 (iv B.C.), *PEleph.*20.40 (iv B.C.), *IG*11(2).161 *A* 23 (Delos, iii B.C.), *UPZ* 54.6 (ii B.C.), etc.: neut. **ἥμισον**, τό, *Berl.Sitzb.*1927.8 (Locr., v B.C.),

*SIG*1011.7 (Chalcedon, iii/ii B.C.), ib.671 *A* 13 (Delph., ii B.C.), *BGU* 183.41 (i A.D.): pl. ἥμισα *SIG*56.7 (Argos, v B.C.); also **ἥμισσον,** τό, ib.306.14 (Arc., iv B.C.), 1009.20 (Ephesus, iii/ii B.C.): pl. ἥμισσα ib. 240 *P* (Delph., iv B.C.): acc. pl. τοὺς ἡμίσους *Not.Arch.*4.20 (Cyrene, Aug.):—*half,* I. as Adj., ἡμίσεες λαοὶ *half* the people, ἡ. δ' ἄρα λαοὶ ἐρητύοντο.. ἡ. δ' ἀναβάντες ἐλαύνομεν Od.3.155 sq., cf. Il.21.7 (elsewh. Hom. uses only neut. ἥμισυ as Subst. (v. infr. II)); τοὺς ἡμίσεας ἀποστέλλειν Hdt.9.51, cf. Th.3.20, X.*Cyr.*2.1.6, etc.; ἥμισυς λόγος *half* the tale, A.*Eu.*428 (λόγου cod. Med.); τὸ ἥμισυ τεῖχος Th.2.78; ὁ ἡ. ἀριθμός Pl.*Lg.*946a: c. gen., like a Comp., τὸ ὕψος ἥμισυ ἐτελέσθη οὗ διενοεῖτο *half of* what he intended, Th.1.93: metaph., οὐδ' ἂν ἥμισυς ἑαυτοῦ γένοιτο πρὸς ἀρετήν Pl.*Lg.*647d (οὐ δι' ἥμισυν stands for οὐ δίημ. '*half-and-half*', ib.806c). 2. in Prose also with the Subst. in gen. and giving its gender and number to ἥμισυς, τῶν νήσων τὰς ἡμισέας Hdt.2.10; τῶν ἀνδραπόδων τὰ ἡμίσεα Id.6.23; αἱ ἡμίσειαι τῶν νεῶν *half of* the ships, Th.8.8; οἱ ἡμίσεις τῶν ἄρτων X.*Cyr.*4.5.4; ὁ ἥμισυς τοῦ ἀριθμοῦ Pl.*Phd.*104a; τοῦ χρόνου D.20.8: abs., οἱ ἡ. *half* of them, Th.3. 20. II. as Subst. in neut., ἡ. τιμῆς, ἐνάρων, ἀρετῆς, Il.9.616, 17.231, Od.17.322; τὸ μὲν.., τὸ δ' ἡ. Il.13.565; πλέον ἡ. παντός Hes.*Op.*40, Pl.*R.*466c; ὑπὲρ ἡ. πάντων X.*Cyr.*3.3.47; ἡ. οὗ δεῖ Pl.*Phd.*77c, etc.; ἐν ἡμίσει τῆς νυκτός at *mid*night, Lxx *Jd.*16.3: usu. c. Art., τὸ ἡ. τοῦ στρατοῦ Th.4.83, etc.; also τὤμισυ Hes.*Op.*559, *Schwyzer*701 (Erythrae, v B.C.); θἤμισυ Ar.*Lys.*116: indecl., ἀπὸ τοῦ ἡ. Lxx *Ex.*30.15; τῷ ἡ. φυλῆς ib.*Nu.*32.33: pl., τῆς χορείας τὰ ἡμίσεα Pl.*Lg.*672e; ἄρτων ἡμίσεα X.*An.*1.9.26; ῥαφανίδων τὰ ἡ. Thphr. l. c.: after Numerals, ἐν δυοῖν καὶ ἡμίσει ἡμέρας *IG*2².1673.73; δεκατεττάρων καὶ ἡμίσους Str.2.5.39; μνῶν.. δώδεκα καὶ ἡμίσους D.H.4.17; τετραποδίαν μίαν καὶ ἥμισυ *IG* 1².373.28; without καί, μυριάδων ἑπτὰ ἡμίσους Plu.*Mar.*34: indecl., τριῶν ἥμισυ σταδίων Str.8.6.21, cf. *PTeb.*110.5 (i B.C.), Plu.*Cat.Mi.* 44, etc.: as Adv., ἡ. μὲν νύμφην.., ἡ. δ' αὖτε ὄφιν Hes.*Th.*298, cf. Pi.*N.*10.87: so in pl., τὰ μὲν ἡμίσεα φιλόπονος, τὰ δὲ ἡ. ἄπονος Pl.*R.* 535d: with Preps., οὐδ' εἰς ἡ. not *half,* Ar.*Th.*452: regul. Adv. ἡμισέως *half-done,* Pl.*R.*601c. b. ἥμισυ, τό, = ἡμίεκτον, Hsch. 2. fem., ἡ ἡμίσεια (sc. μοῖρα), τῇ ἡμισείᾳ τῆς γῆς Th.5.31; ἡ ἡ. τοῦ τιμήματος Pl.*Lg.*956d; οὐ γὰρ ἐφ' ἡμισείᾳ χρηστὸν εἶναι δεῖ *by halves,* D. 19.277; ἐξ ἡμισείας Luc.*Cat.*1, Artem.1.26, S.E.*M.*10.145. (ἡμισυ- fr. ἡμιτυ-, ἡμισσο- fr. ἡμιτϝο-, cf. ἡμίτεια, ἡμιτύεκτον; enlarged fr. ἡμι-.)

ἡμῐσύ-τρῐτον, τό, *a third half,* i.e. *one and a half,* Archil.167. **-χοῖνιξ,** ικος, ἡ, = ἡμιχοῖνιξ, Hdn.Gr.2.261. **-χοιρος,** sine expl., ibid.

ἡμι-σφᾰγής, ές, *half-slain, Gloss.* **-σφαίριον,** τό, *hemisphere,* Alex.261.7, Pl.*Ax.*371b, Hero *Spir.*1.8, Porph.*Antr.*24, etc.: dual in Ph.2.155. **-σφήκιον,** τό, dub. sens. in *BCH*35.243 (Delos, ii B.C.). **-σχετος,** ον, *half-related* (cf. ἄσχετος 3), σχέσις Olymp. *in Phd.*p.19 N.; τὸ ἡ. τῆς προνοίας Dam.*Pr.*131. Adv. -τως ibid. **-σχοινον,** τό, *half a schoenus, Tab.Heracl.*1.29, al., *AB* 263. **-ταινίδιον,** τό, *half a* ταινία, *PSI*7.858.9 (iii B.C.). **-τᾰλαντιαῖος,** α, ον, *in which the prize is half a talent,* ἀγών *CIG*2810.19 (Aphrod.), *IGRom.*4.161 (Cyzicus). **-τάλαντον** [τᾰ], τό, *a half-talent,* as a weight, χρυσοῦ Il.23.751, cf. *IG*1².371.6; πέντ' ἡμιτάλαντα Is.7.44; τρίτον ἡμιτάλαντον *two talents and a half,* ἕνατον ἡ., = $8\frac{1}{2}$, Hdt.1.50, 51, cf. Poll.9.54, *EM*744.25. **-τάρῑχος** [ᾰ], ον, *half-salted,* = ἡμίνηρος, Archestr.*Fr.*38.7, Ael.*NA*13.2.

ἡμίτεια, ἡ, prob. = ἡμίεκτον, *SIG*998.9 (Epid., v B.C.), *IG*11(2). 147 *A* 8 (Delos, iv/iii B.C.).

ἡμιτέλ-εια, ἡ, (τέλος) *remission of half the tribute,* ἡ. τῶν κακῶν ἐδέδοτο Luc.*Nec.*14. **-εστος,** ον, (τελέω) *half-finished,* Th.3.3, dub. in D.H.1.59, etc.; of a lady's hair, *half-done,* Aeschin.Socr.18; of a child, Nonn.*D.*1.5. **-έω,** *complete one-half of,* χρόνον *Ath.Mitt.* 25.412 (Pergam.). **-ής,** ές, (τέλος) *half-finished,* δόμος ἡ. a house *but half complete,* i.e. childless, Il.2.701; βίος Str.7.3.3, cf. Luc. *DMort.*19.1; 'Ολύμπιον Dicaearch.1.1; ἡ. θάλαμος *AP*7.627 (Diod.); ἡ. νίκη D.H.2.42; φωναί Id.*Comp.*14; ἐνέργειαι Aret.*SD*1.7; of a child, Luc.*Sacr.*5; οὐδὲν ἡμιτελὲς καταλείπειν X.*Cyr.*8.1.3; ἡ. ἀφιέναι D.H.*Th.*9; ἡ. ἀνήρ, opp. τελείως ἀγαθός, X.*Cyr.*3.3.38; ἡ. περὶ λόγους D.H.*Dem.*23; ἡ. τὴν ἀρετήν Ph.2.199. Adv. -λῶς Longin. ap.Porph.*Plot.*19.

ἡμι-τεσσέριον, τό, a liquid measure, οἴνου *Inscr.Prien.*362.16 (iv B.C.). **-τέταρτον,** τό, a weight, = $\frac{1}{8}$ μνᾶ, *Ann.dell' Inst.*37.201. 2. = $\frac{3}{4}$, ἡ. ὕδρευμα *PFlor.*50.99. **-τετράγωνος** [ᾰ], hyperdor. **ἁμ-,** ον, *forming half a square,* of the isosceles right-angled triangle, Speus. ap.*Theol.Ar.*63, Ti.Locr.98a,b, Simp. *in Cael.*638.3. **-τέχνιον,** τό, *half* (i.e. *trivial*) *art,* Sch.D.T.p.110 H.

ἡμιτιεύς· ἡμισευτής, Hsch.: **ἡμίτιον·** τετράχουν, Id.

ἡμι-τμής, ῆτος, ὁ, ἡ, = ἡμίτομος I, Man.4.6. **-τμητος,** ον, (τέμνω) gloss on ἡμιδάϊκτος, Sch.Opp.*H.*2.287. **-τομίας,** ου, ὁ, (τομή) *half an eunuch,* Sch.Theoc.3.4. **-τομος,** ον, (τέμνω) *cut in two,* ξύλα *IG*1².313.98; ἄντυξ Mosch.2.88. 2. of the moon, *half-full, Theol. Ar.*12. II. as Subst., **-τομος,** ὁ, a kind of *cup,* Pamphil.ap.Ath.11. 470d. 2. **-τομον,** τό, *half,* Hdt.7.39, 9.37, *Inscr.Délos* 298 *A* 182 (iii B.C.), *AP*9.137; κύκλου Ael.*NA*15.4; ἡμίτομα ᾠῶν Alex.261.10: —also **-τόμιον,** τό, *flat side of a half-bean,* Dsc.2.105, v.l. in Luc. *VH*2.38. b. *lozenge-shaped bandage,* = ἡμιρρόμβιον, Hp.*Off.*7, Gal. 18(2).732. **-τονιαῖος,** α, ον, *consisting of a semitone,* Aristox.*Harm.* p.52 M., Theo Sm.p.53 H.; ὑπεροχή Ptol.*Harm.*2.9. **-τόνιον,** τό, *semitone,* Philol.6, Aristox.*Harm.*p.21 M., al., D.H.*Comp.*11, Arr. *Epict.*2.11.2, etc. II. *half the skein* or *bundle of gut* in a torsion-engine, Ph.*Bel.*68.46, Hero *Aut.*2.6. 2. *one of the two frames containing the* τόνος in such an engine, Id.*Bel.*90.4. **-τρής,** ῆτος, ὁ, ἡ, *half-bored,* Choerob. *in Theod.*1.185. **-τρῖβής,** ές, (τρίβω) *half worn out,* χλαμύς *PCair.Zen.*92.5 (iii B.C.), cf. *CPR*27.8 (ii A.D.), Sch.Ar.*Pl.*729. II. *blunt,* ξοῖς *BCH*35.43 (Delos); λείστριον ib. 8.323 (ibid.). **-τρίγωνος** [ῐ], hyperdor. **ἁμ-,** ον, *forming half a triangle,* τρίγωνον, of the triangles made by drawing a perpendicular from an angle of an equilateral triangle, Speus.ap.*Theol.Ar.*63; neut. as Subst., Ti.Locr.98a, Simp. *in Cael.*561.13. **-τρῐταῖος,** α, ον, *half every three days,* τρόπος ἡ., of *a semi-tertian* fever, Hp.*Epid.*1. 2, Gal.17(1).233: **-τριταϊκός,** ή, όν, Ptol.*Tetr.*199. **-τρῖτον,** τό, *the sixth part* (of a mina), Inscr. on a weight, *CIG*8535. **-τριψις,** εως, ἡ, *half-massage,* Gal.18(2).873.

ἡμίτρωτος, ον, gloss on ἡμιδαής, Sch.Opp.*H.*1.716.

ἡμιτύβιον [ῠ], τό, *linen cloth, towel, napkin,* Sapph.116, Hp.*Art.* 37, Ar.*Pl.*729; of a kind of material, *Michel*832.23 (Samos, iv B.C.). (Egypt. acc. to Poll.7.71:—in codd. sts. **ἡμιτύμβιον,** as in Aret.*CD* 1.3, v.l. in Lib.*Decl.*26.42, which is interpr. by Suid., *a half* (i.e. *small*) *grave*; but prob. this form is due to the copyists, who wished to find a meaning in the word.)

ἡμιτύεκτον, τό, = ἡμιέκτεων, *GDI*4957 *a* 4 (Crete).

ἡμι-τύλιον [ῠ], τό, *half a* τύλη, *BGU*40.12 (pl., iii A.D.). **-τυμπάνιστος** [ᾰ], ον, sine expl. (cf. ἀποτυμπανίζω), Poll.6.160; = ἡμιθανής, Hsch. (-στής cod.). **-ϋπνος,** ον, *half-asleep, Gloss.* **-ΰφαντος** [ῠ], ον, *half-woven,* Aen.Tact.29.6. **-υφής,** ές, = foreg., *IG*2².1522. 26, 1524.213, etc. **-φᾰής,** ές, *half-shining,* = ἡμιφανής, λάρναξ *AP* 7.478 (Leon., sed leg. ἡμιχανεῖ). **-φάλακρος** [φᾰ], ον, *half-bald,* ib.11.132 (Lucill.). **-φᾰνής,** ές, (φαίνομαι) *half-visible,* Str.17.1. 32. **-φάριον** [ᾱ], τό, (φᾶρος) *half-robe,* Aristaenet.1.4, Suid., Hsch. **-φᾰτος,** ον, *half* (cf. δίφατος), Id. **-φαυλος,** ον, *half-knavish,* Luc.*Bis Acc.*8. **-φαυστος,** ον, *half-lit,* Poll.6.160. **-φι,** τό, *half-*φῖ, ϸ, a musical note, Gaud.*Harm.*21, 22. **-φλεκτος,** ον, *half-burnt,* App.*BC*5.88, Luc.*DDeor.*13.2; by love, Theoc.2.133; *half-cooked,* Hp.*Epid.*2.6.29. **-φόριον,** τό, *half-subscription, SIG* 1109.40 (Athens, ii A.D.). **-φόρμιον,** τό, *half a* φορμός, Demioprat. ap.Poll.10.169. **-φρακτος,** ον, *half-fenced,* Id.6.160. **-φυής,** ές, (φυή) *half-grown,* Men.1014. **-φωνος,** ον, *half-pronounced,* λέξις Aristaenet.1.10. 2. Subst. ἡμίφωνον, τό, *a semi-vowel,* as ρ σ, Arist.*Po.*1456ᵇ27, Phld.*Po.*2.16, D.H.*Comp.*14, D.T.631.16, etc. II. *half able to speak,* Gal.*UP*6.3; *half-vocal,* of certain signs of the Zodiac, *Cat.Cod.Astr.*1.166, Vett.Val.5.24:—hence **-φωνία,** ἡ, Steph. *in Hp.*1.184 D. **-φωσώνιον,** τό, a kind of *garment,* Ar.*Fr.*784; cf. φώσσων.

ἡμίχα· ἡμιστάτηρα, Hsch. **ἡμιχανής,** ές, *half-open,* v. ἡμιφαής.

ἡμί-χῖον, τό, a measure, *half a* χῖον, *PCair.Zen.*12.17 (iii B.C.), etc. **-χλωρος,** ον, *half-green, Gloss.* **-χοαῖος,** α, ον, *holding a half-*χόος, Thphr.*HP*9.6.4. **-χοεῖος,** α, ον, = foreg., *PCair.Zen.* 353.16 (iii B.C.). **-χοινίκιον** [ῐκ], τό, *half-*χοῖνιξ, Hp.*Nat.Mul.*50, *IG*2².1013.21, Dieuch.ap.Orib.4.7.18. **-χοίνῑκος,** ον, *holding a half-*χοῖνιξ: τὸ ἡ. *a half-*χοῖνιξ, Thphr.*HP*8.4.5, Dsc.5.72. **-χοῖνιξ,** ῑκος, ἡ, *half-*χοῖνιξ, v.l. in Hp.*Nat.Mul.*50, *Morb.*3.17. **-χοιρον,** τό, = ἡμισύχοιρος, Hsch. s.v. δέλιχρα. **-χολώδης,** ες, *half-bilious,* dub. l. in Hp.*Epid.*7.29. **-χοον,** τό, *half-*χόος, Id.*Int.*42 (in pl. ἡμίχοα, as *SIG*1027.15 (Cos), Arist.*HA*627ᵇ3); also ἡμίχα *IG*11(2). 199 *B* 80 (Delos, iii B.C.); -χόεα Hp.*Morb.*3.17: contr. **-χουν** Arist. *Ath.*69.2, *IG*1².188.22, *PAmh.*2.93.12 (ii A.D.). **-χόριον,** τό, *half-chorus, semi-chorus,* Poll.4.107, Sch.Ar.*Eq.*586. **-χρηστος,** ον, *half-good,* Arist.*Pol.*1315ᵇ9. **-χρύσους** [ῡ], ὁ, *half-stater,* Anaxandr.5: **-χρῡσος** *CIG*2855.31 (Milet., ii B.C.), *Annuario*6/7.407. **-χώνη,** ἡ, *half-*χώνη, Kretschmer *Gr.Vaseninschr.*p.143. **-χώριον,** τό, *half of an office* or *liturgy jointly undertaken, POxy.*1413.1 (iii A.D.). **-χωστος,** ον, (χώννυμι) = Lat. *semirutus, Gloss.* **-ψίλιον** [ψῐ], τό, ψιλή *of half size, PSI*7.858.3 (iii B.C.), *PLond.ined.*2095 (iii B.C.). **-ψυκτος,** ον, *half-dried,* Str.15.1.18:—also **-ψῡγής,** ές, κόνυζα *Gp.*2.27.9; *half-cooled,* κλίβανα Dsc.3.86, cf. Paul.Aeg.3. 54. **-ψῡχος,** *semianimis, Gloss.* **-ωβελιαῖος,** α, ον, *costing* or *worth half an obol, PCair.Zen.*19.5 (iii B.C.):—less correctly written **-ωβολιαῖος,** κρέα Ar.*Ra.*554; *as large as a half-obol,* X.*Mem.*1.3.12. (-βελιαῖος shd. prob. be restored.) **-ωβέλιον,** τό, *half-obol, IG*1². 6.90, Eup.154, Aeschin.Socr.41, Arist.*Rh.*1374ᵇ26, *IG*11.(2).287 *A* 40 (Delos, iii B.C.), etc.:—less correctly **-ωβόλιον,** X.*An.*1.5.6 codd., Arist.*Fr.*589 codd. Poll., Thphr.*Char.*6.9, Dsc.4.175: **-ώβολον** Thphr. *Lap.*46 (-ος cod.), Sor.1.63 (v.l.), Hdn.*Epim.*204: Dor. **-ωδέλιον,** τό, *GDI*2562.26 (Delph.), *IG*14.2406.77: Boeot. **ἐμνιωβέλιον,** τό, *Supp. Epigr.*3.356.5, 7 (Acraeph., iii B.C.). **-ωρία,** ἡ, (ὥρα) *half-hour,* Dam.*Pr.*389. **-ωριαῖος,** α, ον, *lasting half an hour*: neut. as Subst., Phlp. *in Ph.*802.15. **-ώριον,** τό, = ἡμιωρία, Men.1015, Str.2. 5.36, Hipparch.2.4.2, Cleom.1.6, *Apoc.*8.1 (v.l. ἡμίωρον), Dsc.1.33.

ἧμμαι, v. ἅπτω.

ἥμορος, ον, = ἄμοιρος, Hsch., Phot.:—fem. **ἡμορίς,** ίδος, A.*Fr.* 165: **ἡμόριξεν·** ἄμοιρον ἐποίησεν, Hsch. (ἥμορος Ion. form = Aeol. ἄμμορος (q. v.).)

ἦμος, Dor. **ἆμος,** Adv. of Time, correl. to τῆμος, *at which time, when,* in Hom., freq. in protasi with τῆμος, τῆμος ἄρα.., τῆμος δή.., etc., in apodosi (v. τῆμος); ἆμος.., τᾶμος.. Theoc.13.25; ἦ.., δὴ τότε Il.1.475, al.: folld. by δὴ τότ' ἔπειτα Od.17.1; by καὶ τότε δὴ Il.8.68; by καὶ τότ' ἔπειτα 1.477; by καὶ τότε δή ῥα 16.779; by ἄρα or ῥά alone, Od.2.1, 19.428, cf. S.*Aj.*935 (lyr.); by τηνικαῦτα Hdt.4. 28; by τότε S.*Tr.*155: rarely without some particle in apodosi, as Od. 3.491, E.*Hec.*915 (lyr.); ἡ. ὅτε A.R.4.267, 452, 1310, Orph.*A.*120, *IG* 14.1389 i 25, etc.: rarely with Subj., without ἄν, ἦ. δ' ἠέλιος.. οὐρανὸν ἀμφιβεβήκῃ Od.4.400; ἡ. ἥλιος δύνῃ Hp.*Mul.*1.23, cf. *Prorrh.*2.

4 (v.l.). 2. with pres., *while, so long as*, S.*Tr.*531: or impf., Id. *OT*1134.

ἡμοσύνη, ἡ, (ἥμων) *skill in throwing* or *shooting*, Hsch.

ἡμῠόεις, εσσα, εν, *drooping*, v.l. in Nic.*Th.*626.

ἡμύω, aor. ἤμυσα (v. infr.): pf. part. ἠμυκώς Sch.Nic.*Th.*626; cf. ὑπ-εμνήμυκε:—Ep. Verb, *bow down, sink*, Hom., only in Il., ἑτέρωσ' ἤμυσε κάρη πήληκι βαρυνθέν 8.308; ἤμυσε καρήατι, of a horse, 19.405; of a corn-field, ἐπί τ' ἠμύει ἀσταχύεσσιν 2.148: metaph., of cities, *totter, fall*, τῷ κε τάχ' ἠμύσειε πόλις Πριάμοιο ἄνακτος ib.373; rare in Trag., χρόνῳ δ'.. ἤμυσε στέγος S.*Fr.*864; later, simply, *fall, perish*, οὔνομα δ' οὐκ ἤμυσε Λεωνίδου *AP*7.715 (Leon.). II. trans., *cause to fall, ruin*, πόλιν Musae.*Fr.*22. (In Hom. ῠ in pres., ῡ in aor. 1; but ῡ in pres. κατ-ημύουσιν A.R.3.1400, cf. Opp.*H.*1.228, Nic.*Al.*453; ῠ in aor., *AP*9.262 (Phil.), but ῡ ib.7.715 (v. supr.); cf. ἀμύω, ἐπημύω.)

ἠμφισβητημένως, Adv. pf. part. Pass., (ἀμφισβητέω) *in a questionable manner*, [διαλέκτους] προσφέρεσθαι dub. in Phld.*Rh.Supp.*p.56 S.

ἡμωδίαν· αἱμωδίαν and **ἡμωδίασαν**· ἐνάρκησαν (ἠνάρχ- cod.), αἱμωδίασαν, Hsch.; Att. acc. to Moer.

ἧμων, v. ἀμάω (A).

ἥμων, ονος, ὁ, (ἵημι) *thrower, darter*, ἥ. ἄνδρες Il.23.886.

ἤν (A), contr. fr. εἰ ἄν and ἐάν (q.v.).

ἤν (B), Interject. *see there!* ἤν, οὐχ ἡδύ; Ar.*Eq.*26; ἤν, μεθίεμεν Id. *Pl.*75; ἀλλ' ἤν χιτών σοι Men.148; ἤν, τότε βακχίαζε.. χθών Philod. Scarph.14; also ἤν ἰδού Pratin.Lyr.1.15, Ar.*Ra.*1390, Herod.1.4, Luc.*DMort.*10.10, Anach.1, Alciphr.*Fr.*6.6, cf. Theoc.8.26; folld. by καὶ δή, E.*HF*867, Ar.*Pax*327:—also **ἠνίδε** (i.e. ἤν ἴδε) Pl.*Epigr.* 20, Theoc.2.38, Call.*Del.*132; with τοι, Theoc.1.149, 3.10.

ἦν, v. φημί, εἰμί (*sum*). **ἦνα**, inf. ἦναι, v. αἴνω.

ἠναγκασμένως, Adv. pf. part. Pass., (ἀναγκάζω) *perforce*, D.H. *Pomp.*3 (dub. l.).

ἠναντιωμένως, Adv. pf. part. Pass., (ἐναντιόομαι) *in opposite ways*, διακεῖσθαι Phld.*Mus.*p.103 K.

ἤνεγκα, ἤνεγκον, ἤνεικα, v. φέρω. ἤνεκα, v. αἰνέω.

ἠνεκής, ές, *bearing onwards*, i.e. *far-stretching*, ἠνεκέεσσι τρίβοις Nic.*Al.*592. Adv. -κέως *continuously, without break*, τὸ πάντων νόμιμον.. ἠ. τέταται Emp.135.2: neut. ἠνεκές as Adv., Arat.445, Call. *Aet.*1.2.8; of Time, ἠνεκὲς αἰέν Emp.17.35, cf. Nic.*Al.*517, etc. (Found in early Ep. only in compds., such as διηνεκής.)

ἠνέμιον, τό, = ἀνεμώνη, v.l. for ἠρέμιον in Dsc.2.176.

ἠνεμ⟨ο⟩ειδές· ἠχῶδες, Hsch.

ἠνεμό-εις, Dor. **ἀνεμόεις** [ᾱ], εσσα, εν, (ἄνεμος) *windy, airy*, δι' ἄκριας ἠνεμοέσσας Od.9.400; προτὶ Ἴλιον ἠνεμόεσσαν Il.3.305, etc.; πτύχας ἠνεμοέσσας Od.19.432, cf. Tyrt.2.3, Pi.*O.*4.8, E.*Heracl.*781 (lyr.); of Places, Call.*Del.*11, D.P.472; οὔρεα ἠ. Id.1129. 2. of motion, *rapid, rushing*, αἰγίδες A.*Ch.*592 codd. (lyr.); αὔρα S.*Tr.*953 (lyr.); λαγωός Nic.*Th.*453; πέτευρον Man.6.444; ἀνεμόεν φρόνημα *high-soaring, airy* thought, S.*Ant.*354 (lyr.). 3. *stirred, waved by the wind*, ἐρινεός Il.22.145; *filled by the wind*, ἱστίον Pi.*P.*1.92. **-φοιτος**, ον, *walking on the wind*, βροντή Nonn.*D.*2.24; ψυχή ib.37.85.

ἤνετο, v. ἄνω (A), = ἀνύω. **ἦνθον**, ες, ε, Dor. for ἦλθον, v. ἔρχομαι.

ἡνία (A), Dor. **ἀνία**, ίων, τά (v. sub fin.), *reins*, Il.5.226, Od.3.483, Hes.*Sc.*95, Pi.*P.*4.18, *I.*1.15: rare exc. in Poets, ἐφ' ἡνία, = ἐφ' ἡνίαν (v. sq.), Ael.*Tact.*19.12. II. sg., **ἡνίον**, τό, *bit*, Poll.1.148. (I.-E. *ŋsiyo-*, cf. Skt. *nāsyam* 'nose-rein', Ir. *éssi* 'reins'.)

ἡνία (B), Dor. **ἀνία**, ἡ, post-Hom., = foreg., *bridle, reins*, in pl., Pi. *P.*5.32, A.*Pers.*193, etc.; πρὸς ἡνίας μάχεσθαι Id.*Pr.*1010; εἰς τοὐπίσω ἑλκύσαι τὰς ἡ. Pl.*Phdr.*254c: less freq. in sg., Ἥλιε.. ἐπισχὼν χρυσόνωτον ἡ. S.*Aj.*847; ἡ. χαλᾶν E.*Fr.*409: the sg. for *one rein*, ἔπειτα λύων ἡ. ἀριστεράν S.*El.*743. 2. metaph., Ἔρως.. ἡνίας ηὔθυνε παλιντόνους Ar.*Av.*1739; δυοῖν γυναικοῖν ἄνδρ' ἕν' ἡνίας ἔχειν E.*Andr.*178; ἐφεῖναι καὶ χαλάσαι τὰς ἡ. τοῖς λόγοις Pl.*Prt.*338a; παραλαβοῦσαι τῆς πόλεως τὰς ἡ. Ar.*Ec.*466; τούτῳ παραδώσω τῆς πυκνὸς τὰς ἡ. Id.*Eq.* 1109; γαστρὸς πᾶσαν ἡ. κρατεῖν Men.*Mon.*81; τῷ δήμῳ τὰς ἡ. ἀνείς Plu.*Per.*11; ἐνδιδόναι τοῖς βουλήμασι τὰς ἡ. D.H.7.35; παρὰ τὴν ἡ. πράττειν Philostr.*Im.*2.18; πρὸς ταῖς ἡ., of high officials, *BCH*32.431 (Delos); ἐπὶ τῶν ἡ. Lxx 1*Ma.*6.28. 3. as a military term, ἐφ' ἡνίαν *wheeling to the left* (*the left being the bridle hand*), Plb.10.23.2, Ascl. *Tact.*10.2, Polyaen.4.3.21; [τὸν ἵππον] περισπάσας ἐφ' ἡνίαν τῷ χαλινῷ Plu.*Marc.*6; ἐξ ἡνίας, opp. ἐκ δόρατος, Plb.11.23.6. II. *any leather thong*, esp. *sandal-thong*, ἡνίαι Λακωνικαί Ar.*Ec.*508.

ἥνια, τά, gen. pl. ἡνίων, = τῶν κεκομμένων, Hp.ap.Gal.19.103; cf. ἦνα.

ἠνιγμένως, Adv. pf. part. Pass., (αἰνίσσομαι) *as in a riddle, obscurely*, Plot.6.2.22.

ἠνίδε, v. ἤν (B).

ἡνίκᾰ [ῐ], Dor. **ἁνίκα** Pi.*P.*4.24, al., Theoc.5.41; Aeol. **ἄνικα** Id. 29.33:—Adv. of Time, relat. to τηνίκα, *at the time when*, usu. with past tenses of ind., Od.22.198 (nowhere else in Hom.), Pi. l.c., S. *Aj.*1144, al., Th.7.73, Ar.*Nu.*607, Lys.19.4, Pl.*Grg.*509e, D.21.78, etc.; ἡνίκ' ἐχρῆν δύνειν, νῦν ἄρχεται ἡδύνεσθαι Timo 17: with pres. ind., ἡνίκαπερ X.*Cyr.*8.8.9; μετὰ τὴν ζωὴν.. ἡνίκ' οὐκ εἰσίν Phld.*Mort.* 36; rarely *while*, ἡ. ἦν ἔτ' ἐν φάει E.*Ion* 726. 2. ἡνίκ' ἄν, like ὅταν, with Subj., of fut. time, *whenever*, S.*Ph.*880, *OT*1492: to denote repeated occurrence in pres. time, Id.*Ph.*310, Ar.*Pax*1179, X.*Cyr.*1. 2.4, etc.; ἄν shd. be restored in A.*Fr.*304.7; ἄν goes with Verb in ἡνίκ' ἂν ὠφέλει *when* it would have been to his advantage, D.29.16; but ἡνίκ' ἂν ἀνέβη ἡ νεφέλη, of repeated occurrence, Lxx *Ex.*40.36(30). 3. with opt. in orat. obliq., or to denote an uncertain or repeated occurrence in past time, *whenever*, S.*Ph.*705 (lyr.): also in orat. obliq., of future time, ἡνίκα.. ἀπείη *when* he should have been absent, Id.*Tr.*164; but ἡνίκ' ἂν ἡμεῖς μὴ δυναίμεθα, with implied protasis, D.4.31; and so ἡνίκ' ⟨ἂν⟩ καταλαμβάνοιμι, εἰ τυγχάνοιμι X.*Oec.*11.14. 4. c. gen., ἡ. τοῦ χρόνου *at which point* of time, Ael.*NA*12.35. 5. ἡ. χρὴ φλεβοτομεῖν *in which case*.., Orib.*Syn.*6.13. 6. after Verbs of knowing or remembering, οὐ μνημονεύεις.. ἡνίκα..; S.*Aj.*1273; οἶδ' ἡνίκ' Αἴας εἷλκε Κασάνδραν E.*Tr.*70, cf. Ar.*Ec.*815.

ἡνίον, τό, v. ἡνία, τά.

ἡνιο-ποιεῖον, τό, *saddler's shop*, X.*Mem.*4.2.8. **-ρράφος** [ᾰ], ὁ, *saddler*, Gloss.

ἡνιοστροφ-έω, *guide by reins, drive*, ἅρμα E.*Ph.*172. **-ος** (parox.), ὁ, *charioteer*, S.*El.*731. II. ἡνιόστροφος, ον, Pass., *guided by reins*, ἡνιοστρόφου δρόμου A.*Ch.*1022 (sed leg. ἡνιοστροφῶ).

ἡνιοχαράτης, ὁ, *riding-master* (Lacon.), Hsch.

ἡνιοχ-εία (-ία v.l. in Pl.*Thg.*123d), ἡ, *chariot-driving*, Id.*Grg.* 516e, al.: pl., Id.*Lg.*795a; ἡ. ἁρμάτων Hdn.1.13.8: generally, *conduct, management*, τῆς μηχανῆς Plu.2.966f. **-εύς**, έως, Ep. ῆος, ὁ, poet. for ἡνίοχος, ὑπὸ δ' ἔστρεφον ἡνιοχῆες Il.5.505; θρασὺν Ἕκτορος ἡνιοχῆα 8. 312, cf. *APl.*5.337; *the constellation Auriga*, Nonn.*D.*1.178, al. **-ευτικός**, ή, όν, = ἡνιοχικός, ἀρετή Sch.Pi.*O.*10(11).83. Adv. -κῶς *Et.Gud.* 672.29. **-εύω**, Dor. **ἀν-**, poet. form of ἡνιοχέω, *act as charioteer*, ὁ μὲν νόθος ἡνιόχευεν Il.11.103, cf. 23.641, Od.6.319: metaph., *direct, guide*, πηδαλίῳ... ἀνιόχευεν Alex.Aet.2: c. gen., τῆς ἐμῆς ψυχῆς ἡ. Anacr.4: c. acc., χορὸν ἡ. *IG*3.82a. **-έω**, Lacon. **ἀνιοχίω** (v. ἀνιοχίων), prose form of ἡνιοχεύω, *hold the reins*, ἀνωτέρω,.. κατωτέρω ταῖς χερσίν higher up or lower down, i.e. longer or shorter, X.*Eq.*7.10: c. acc., *drive*, ἅρματα Hdt.4.193; λέοντας Luc.*DDeor.*12.2: metaph., Μουσῶν στόμαθ' ἡνιοχήσας Ar.*V.*1022; τὴν διάνοιαν Luc.*Am.*37; ἔθνεα.. φρεσὶν ἡ. *Epigr.Gr.*922 (Emesa); τῆς ἱερᾶς κεφαλῆς τῆς πάντα -ούσης Lib.*Ep.*987.5; βασιλεύει καὶ ἡ. Plu.2.155a: rarely c. gen., συνωρίδος Pl.*Phdr.*246b:—Pass., *to be guided*, ib.253d, X.*Cyr.*6.1. 29: metaph., of the months, *AP*7.482. **-η**, ἡ, fem. of ἡνίοχος, a name of Hera, Paus.9.39.5. **-ησις**, εως, ἡ, = ἡνιοχεία, Pl.*Phdr.* 246b, D.Chr.36.42; νεφέλης ὀπισθοφυλακούσης Ph.2.174. **-ητικός**, ή, όν, = sq., Procl.*in Prm.*p.520 S. (v.l. -οχικός). **-ικός**, ή, όν, *of* or *for driving*, εἶδος Pl.*Phdr.*253c sq.; χιτὼν ἡ. a *driver's* coat, Callix.2; στολή Jul.*Or.*3.122c: ἡ -κή (sc. τέχνη) *the art of driving*, Pl.*Ion* 538b. Adv. -κῶς Eust.1303.35. **-ος**, Dor. and Aeol. **ἀν-** Pi.*P.*5.50 (v.l. ἀν- as in *N.*6.66, but cf. ἀνιοχίω), Sapph.*Supp.*20a.19, ὁ: (ἡνία, ἔχω):—*one who holds the reins, driver, charioteer*, Il.8.89, etc.: sts. opp. παραιβάτης, 23.132; ἡ. θεράπων 5.580, 8.119; παρεβεβήκεε δέ οἱ ἡ. Hdt.7.40. 2. generally, *chariot-driver*, as in the games, etc., Pi. *P.*5.50, Ar.*Pax* 905 (pl.), X.*HG*3.2.21, Pl.*Phdr.*254b, *PPetr.*3p.180 (pl., iii B.C.), etc.; ὑποπτέρων ἵππων ἡ. Pl.*Criti.*116e. b. *rider*, Thgn. 260. 3. ὁ ἡ. τῆς νεὼς *the helmsman*, Poll.1.98. 4. metaph., *one who guides, governs*, χειρῶν καὶ ἰσχύος ἀ. Pi.*N.*6.66; παλαισμοσύνας δεξιὸς ἡ. Simon.149; ἡ. τέχνης τραγικῆς *IG*2.2263 (iv B.C.); παντοίης ἀρετῆς ib.7.2539.2 (Thebes); ἡ. κιθάρας, of a harper, Epigr.ap.St. Byz. s.v. Μίλητος: fem., αἰγίδος ἡ., of Athena, Ar.*Nu.*602; in Prose with οἷον prefixed, Pl.*Plt.*266e, etc.; of love, Plu.2.759d, Hermesian.7.84. 5. as Adj., *guiding*, γνώμη *Carm.Aur.*69; ἄνεμοι Man.5.153. II. ἡνίοχοι, οἱ, at Athens, a class of rich citizens *who had to furnish chariots* for public service, Ael.Dion.*Fr.*196, Phot. III. in pl., also, = ἔκφοροι (ἔκφορος III), Id. IV. *the constellation Auriga*, Arat.156, Eudox.ap.Hipparch.1.2.10, etc.

ἠνίπαπε, v. ἐνίπτω.

***ἤνις**, ἡ, epith. of cows, of uncertain meaning (*yearling*, fr. ἔνος (C), acc. to *EM*432.2, Hsch.), used by Hom. only in acc. sg. and pl.: gen. ἤνιος A.R.4.174:—βοῦς... ἤνις ἠκέστας Il.6.94, 275, 309; βοῦν ἦνιν εὐρυμέτωπον ἀδμήτην 10.292, Od.3.382. (ἦνιν codd. and Ptol. Oroandae ap.Hdn.Gr.2.71; ἤνιν Tyrannio ibid.: perh. a stem in ῑ.)

ἡνίσκος, ὁ, Dim. of ἡνία (B) II, *small thong* or *strap*, cj. in Herod. 7.22.

ἦνον, v. ἄνω (A), = ἀνύω.

ἠνορέη, Dor. **ἀνορέα**, ἡ, (ἀνήρ) poet. word for ἀνδρεία, *manhood, prowess*, ἠνορέῃ πίσυνοι καὶ κάρτεϊ χειρῶν Il.8.226; κάρτεΐ τε σθένεΐ τε πεποιθότας ἠνορέῃ τε 17.329; ἱπποσύνῃ τε καὶ ἠνορέηφι πεποιθώς 4.303; ἀλκῇ τ' ἠνορέῃ τε κεκάσμεθα Od.24.509; ἀνορέας οὐκ ἀμπλακών Pi.*O.* 8.67; *manly beauty*, ἡ. ἐρατεινήν Il.6.156; ὕδατος ἡ. its *strength*, Epigr.ap.Ael.*NA*10.40; *force*, πολλάκι τοι ῥέα μῦθος, ὃ κεν μόλις ἐξανύσειεν ἠνορέη, τόδ' ἔρεξε A.R.3.189: in pl., *triumphs of manhood*, Pi.*N.*3.20. (Perh. fr. *ἀνορία with Aeol. -ρε- fr. -ρι-.)

ἦνοψ, οπος, ὁ, ἡ, perh. *gleaming*, ἤνοπι χαλκῷ Il.16.408, 18.349, Od.10.360; οὐρανός Call.*Fr.anon.*24; πυρός ib.28. (Expld. as, = ἄν-οψ, *not to be looked at, dazzling*, by Scholl. in Lexx., but ϝῆνοψ is prob. in Hom.)

ἤνπερ, related to εἴπερ, as ἤν (ἐάν) to εἰ, X.*An.*3.2.21.

ἤνσει, Lacon. 3 sg. impf. of ἀνθέω, Ar.*Lys.*1258.

ἤνυστρον, τό, *fourth stomach of ruminating animals*, Arist.*PA* 674ᵇ15, *HA*507ᵇ9 (not the *first stomach*, as Poll.2.204, Hsch.); as a dish, Ar.*Eq.*356, 1179, Alex.273: pl., Diox.1:—written **ἔνυστρον** in Lxx *De.*18.3, *Ma.*2.3, ἐν- condemned by Phryn.140.

ἠνώγεα, ἠνώγει, v. ἄνωγα.

ἡνωμένως, Adv. pf. part. Pass., (ἑνόω) *in one word* (e.g. καλὸς κἀγαθός), Procl.*in Prm.*p.525 S.; *in a unity*, Id.*in Euc.*p.138 F., Dam.*Pr.* 1; *together*, Hero *Geom.*12.53.

ἠνώχλουν, v. ἐνοχλέω. **ἦξα**, v. ἀΐσσω, ᾄσσω:—but **ἦξα**, v. ἄγνυμι.

ἧξις, εως, ἡ, (ἥκω) *coming*, v.l. for ἴξις in E.*Tr.*396 ap.*AB*99.

Ἠοῖαι, αἱ, title of a poem of Hesiod, of which each section began ἢ οἵη, Paus.9.31.5, Ath.10.428b.

ἠοῖος, α, ον, Ion. **ἠοῖος**, Dor. **ἀοῖος**, = ἑῷος, *of the morning*, ἀστήρ Ion Lyr.*Fr.*10; ἠοῖαι σαίρεσκον Euph.53.2; ἡ ἠοίη (sc. ὥρα) *the morning*, πᾶσαν δ' ἠοίην.. Od.4.447, cf. Hsch. 2. *toward the dawn, eastern*, ἠὲ πρὸς ἠοίων ἢ ἑσπερίων ἀνθρώπων Od.8.29; πρὸς θαλάσσης ἠοίης Hdt.4.100; πρὸς τοὺς ἠ. τῶν Λιβύων ib.160; πρὸς ἠοίην (sc. γῆν) towards *the East*, Call.*Del.*280. (Cf. ἠῷος.)

ἤομεν, 1 pl. impf. of εἶμι (*ibo*).

ἠονή, coined (fr. ὄνησις) as etym. of ἡδονή, Pl.*Cra.*419c.

ἠόνιος, η, ον, contr. from ἠϊόνιος, *on the shore*, σῶμα *AP*7.383 (Phil.); ψάμμος ib.365 (Zonas or Diod.).

ἠπᾰνάω and -έω, *to be in want*, Hsch.: **ἠπᾰνία**, ἡ, *want*, Id., *EM* 433.17, prob. l. in *AP*5.238 (Paul. Sil.).

ἠπ-άομαι, *mend, repair* (rare word for the common ἀκέομαι), τὰ ῥαγέντα τῶν ἱματίων Gal.*Thras.*25: abs., Id.*UP*3.1:—Med., aor. 1 inf. ἠπήσασθαι Hes.*Fr.*172; κόσκινον Ar.*Fr.*227; ῥαγὲν ἱμάτιον Gal.*Thras.* 5: pf. part. Pass., ἱμάτια ἠπημένα Aristid.2.307 J., cf. *BCH*51.326.

ἧπαρ, ᾰτος, τό, (v. sub fin.) *liver*, Od.9.301, Gal.2.575, etc.; of various animals, as a favourite dish, κάπρου Ar.*Fr.*318.5; καπρίσκου Crobyl.7; [ἐρίφου] Euphro 1.23; εἰ μὴ σὺ χηνὸς ἧπαρ ἔχεις Eub.101, cf. Ath.3.106fsq., Poll.6.49; φασγάνῳ οὖτα καθ' ἧπαρ Il.20.469; παῖσαι ὑφ' ἧπαρ or πρὸς ἧπαρ, S.*Ant.*1315, E.*Or.*1063; ὑφ' ἧπαρ πεπληγμένη S.*Tr.*931; ὑφ' ἥπατος φέρειν, of *pregnant* women, E.*Supp.*919 (lyr.): as the seat of the passions, anger, fear, etc., A.*Ag.*432 (lyr.), 792 (anap.), *Eu.*135, E.*Supp.*599 (lyr.); χολὴν οὐκ ἔχεις ἐφ' ἥπατι Archil.131; χωρεῖ πρὸς ἧπαρ.. δύη S.*Aj.*938; τήκειν ἧ. Call.*Aet.Oxy.* 2079.8, cf. *Fr.*222; of love, χαλεπὸς γὰρ ἔσω θεὸς ἧπαρ ἀμύσσει Theoc. 13.71; τὸ μὲν θυμοειδὲς περὶ τὰν καρδίαν, τὸ δ' ἐπιθυματικὸν περὶ τὸ ἧπαρ Ti.Locr.100a, cf. Plu.2.450f. II. *fruitful land*, Agroetas ap. Sch.A.R.2.1248. III. = ἥπατος, Plin.*HN*32.149. (I.-E. *yeq^{w}r̥t*, cf. Lat. *jecur*, Skt. *yákr̥t*.)

ἡπᾰτ-ηρός, ά, όν, = ἡπατικός, δυσεντερία Steph. *in Hp.*1.130 D., Paul.Aeg.3.42. **-ιαῖος**, α, ον, = ἡπατικός 1, λοβός Hp.*Oss.* 18. **-ίας**, ου, ὁ, = ἡπατικός 1, λοβοί Poll.2.215. **-ίζω**, *to be liver-coloured*, Dsc.3.22, Aët.16.104(94). 2. *suffer from hepatic dropsy*, Diocl.*Fr.*46 (prob. l.). **-ικός**, ή, όν, *of the liver*, πάθος Plu.2. 733c; τὸ ἡπατικόν *divination from the liver*, Sch.rec.A.*Pr.*484. II. *suffering from liver-complaint*, Dsc.2.70, Philagr.ap.Orib.5.19.7, *POxy.*1088.48; διάθεσις Dsc.1.109. 2. *for liver-complaint*, φάρμακον Gal.11.749. **-ιον**, τό, Dim. of ἧπαρ, a common dish at Athens, Ar.*Fr.*506, Alc.Com.25, Alex.110.16, *PLond.*3.1259.36 (iv A.D.), etc. **-ῖτις**, ιδος, ἡ, *of* or *in the liver*, δυσεντερία Gal.18(1). 145; ἡ ἡ. (sc. φλέψ) the *vena cava ascendens*, Hp.*Oss.*10, Diog.Apoll. 6, Arist.*HA*512^{a}6. 2. *liver-coloured*, ἀλόη *Gp.*6.6.2, Alex.Trall. 7.6; *hepatitis* [*gemma*], Plin.*HN*37.186. II. as Subst., *liver-wort*, = εὐπατώριον, Ps.-Dsc.4.41.

ἡπᾰτοειδής, ές, *liver-like*, τῷ χρώματι Dsc.5.85.

ἥπᾰτος, ὁ, a fish of uncertain kind, Eub.61, Arist.*HA*508^{b}19, Speus.ap.Ath.7.300e, Philotim.ap.Gal.6.720.

ἡπᾰτοσκοπ-έω, *inspect the liver for soothsaying*, Lxx *Ez.*21.21 (26). **-ία**, ἡ, *inspecting of the liver*, Hdn.8.3.7. **-ικός**, ή, όν, *connected with soothsaying*, τέχνη Phleg.*Macr.*4, cf. Jul.*Gal.*298b. **-ος**, ον, *inspecting the liver, soothsaying*, Artem.2.69; ἡ. ἱερά, Hsch. s.v. ῥυτά.

ἡπᾰτουργός, όν, *liver-destroying*, epith. of Perseus, who killed the sea-monster by leaping down its throat sword in hand, Lyc.839.

ἡπᾰτοφᾰγέομαι, Pass., *to have one's liver eaten*, ὑπὸ γυπῶν S.E.*M.* 1.286. **ἤπᾰφε**, v. ἀπαφίσκω.

ἠπεδᾰνός, ή, όν, *weakly*, Il.8.104; *halting*, of Hephaistos, Od.8. 311; ἄνδρες, χέρες, A.R.2.800, 3.82; λέων Babr.*Fab.Hex.*9; νόος Man.2.160; in Ion. Prose, ἠ. πῦρ *a slight, trifling* fever, Hp.*Mul.*1.4; of a child, *weakly*, ib.27; τὰ ἠ. ib.78; ἠ. ὕπνος *light, slight*, dub. in Ion Trag.4; of ghosts, prob. cj. in Euph.134. 2. c. gen., *void of*, φάμας ἔσσεαι ἠπεδανά *AP*9.521. II. Act., *weakening*, δεῖμα Orph. *L.*382, cf. *Fr.*142. (Derived by Gramm. fr. ἀ- priv., πέδον, cf. *EM* 433.26, and v. νηπεδανός: better fr. ἀ- and πούς, Hsch.; for the termination perh. cf. οὐτιδ-ανός.)

ἠπειγμένως, Adv. pf. part. Pass., (ἐπείγω) *hurriedly*, Hsch.

ἠπειρογενής, ές, (γενέσθαι) *born* or *living in the mainland*, ἔθνος, of the Lydians and Ionians, A.*Pers.*42.

ἠπειρόθεν, Adv. *from the mainland*, Arat.1094.

ἤπειρ-ος, Dor. **ἄπ-** [ᾰ], ἡ, *terra firma, land*, opp. *the sea*, Od.3.90, 10.56, Il.1.485, Hes.*Op.*624, etc.; κατ' ἤπειρον by *land*, Hdt.4.97, 8. 66; μήτ' ἐν θαλάττῃ μήτ' ἐν ἠπείρῳ Ar.*Ach.*534, cf. Timocr.8: hence, even of an island, ἤπειρόνδε Od.5.56; but, II. esp. *the mainland of Western Greece*, opp. the neighbouring islands, Od.14.97, al.; ἤπειρόνδε 18.84, cf. Th.3.114 (so as pr. n., Pi.*N.*4.51, X.*HG*6.1.7, etc.): generally, *mainland*, opp. islands, Hdt.1.148,171, al., Th.1.5, Philostr.*VA*1.20, etc. III. later, *a continent*, esp. of Asia, Hdt.1.96, 4.91, A.*Pers.*718 (troch.), X.*HG*3.1.5, D.60.11, etc.; ῥεῖθρον ἠπείροιν (-ων codd.) ὅρον, of the Tanais or Phasis, A.*Pr.*790; so δισσαὶ ἄπειροι, i.e. Europe and Asia, S.*Tr.*101 (lyr.); τὼ δύ' ἠπείρω Id.*Fr.*881; ἐφ' ἑκατέρας τῆς ἠ. Isoc.4.35; ἠ. δοιαί, δίδυμαι, ἀμφότεραι, Mosch. 2.8, *AP*7.18 (Antip. Thess.), 240 (Adaeus), Lib.*Ep.*783.3; ῥίζαν ἀπείρου τρίταν, of Libya, Pi.*P.*9.8. IV. *plain*, opp. mountain, ἤπειρόνδε A.R.2.734,976. V. in Egypt, *land above inundation-level*, *PGiss.*48.8 (iii A.D.); more freq., γῆ ἠ. *PLond.*3.1201.2 (ii B.C.), etc. (Fr. ἄπερ-yos, cf. Germ. *Ufer*.) **-όω**, *to make into mainland*, opp. θαλαττόω, Arist.*Mu.*400^{a}28; βυθόν *AP*9.670:—Pass., *to become so*, Th.2.102, Ph.2.511. **-ώτης**, ου, ὁ, fem. **-ῶτις**, ιδος, *landsman*, Luc.*Ind.*19; ἄγειν ἀπειρώταν [ἰχθύν] to treat it *as a landsman*, Theoc.21.58 (prob. l.); ἵπποι Philostr.*Im.*1.30. II. Subst. -ώτης, ὁ, *dweller on the mainland*, opp. νησιώτης, Hdt.6.49, cf. 1.171, Isoc.4.132: fem. Adj., αἱ ἠπειρώτιδες Αἰολίδες πόλιες, opp. to those in islands, Hdt.1.151, cf. 7.109, Th.1.5, al.; also ἠ. ξυμμαχία alliance *with a military power*, opp. ναυτική, ib.35, cf. 4.12; πόλεις τῇ παρασκευῇ ἠπειρώτιδας Id.6.86. III. *Asiatic*, ψυχή E.*Andr.*159: Subst. fem., ib.652. 2. Ἠπειρώτης, ου, ὁ, *an Epirote*, Arist.*Fr.*494. **-ωτικός**, ή, όν, *continental*, ἔθνη X.*HG*6.1.12, Arist.*Pol.*1338^{b}22. 2. *of a landsman*, βίος Max.Tyr.19.7, cf. 8.9, al. II. *of Epirus*, πᾶν τὸ Ἠπειρωτικόν Th.3.102; Ἠ. [μῆλα] Dsc.1.115.

ἤπερ, poet. **ἠέπερ**, (ἤ) *than at all, than even*, after a Comp., v. ἤ (A).

ᾗπερ, *in the same way as*, v. ὅσπερ II. 4.

ἠπερόπ-ευμα, ατος, τό, *cozener*, γυναικῶν Critias 1.3 D. **-εύς**, έως, Ep. ῆος, ὁ, = ἠπεροπευτής, ἠπεροπῆά τ' ἔμεν καὶ ἐπίκλοπον Od.11. 364; of Bacchus, *AP*9.524.8; of dreams, A.R.3.617. **-ευτής**, οῦ, ὁ, *a cheat, deceiver*, of Paris (cf. sq.), γυναιμανές, ἠπεροπευτά (Ep. voc.) Il.3.39, cf. *h.Merc.*282, etc. **-εύω**, Ep. Verb, used only in pres. and impf., *cheat, cajole*: c. acc. pers., esp. of *seduction*, γυναῖκας ἀνάλκιδας ἠπεροπεύεις Il.5.349; τά τε φρένας ἠπεροπεύει θηλυτέρῃσι γυναιξί Od.15.421; so of Aphrodite, τί με ταῦτα λιλαίεαι ἠπεροπεύειν; Il.3.399: generally, 23.605, Od.14.400, 15.419; ἐμὰς φρένας 13.327, Hes.*Op.*55. **-ηΐς**, ΐδος, ἡ, pecul. fem. of ἠπεροπεύς, ἠ. τέχνη *cheating* arts, [Hom.] ap.Str.1.2.4, etc.

ἤπ-ησις, εως, ἡ, *mending*, Eust.1647.60: **-ητής**, οῦ, ὁ, *repairer, mender*, Batr.184, *POxy.*2149.21 (ii/iii A.D.), v.l. in X.*Cyr.*1.6.16; condemned by Phryn.73; προστάτης τῶν ἠ. *Sammelb.*3939, cf. 3962: —fem. **-ήτρια**, ἡ, *needlewoman*, *UPZ*91.16 (ii B.C.), *POxy.*1679.5 (iii A.D.), Hsch. (-πίτ- cod.) (Dor. **ἀπήτρια** Id.): **-ητήριον**, τό, *needle*, Ael.Dion.*Fr.*29, *Gloss.* **-ητρον**, τό, in pl., *mender's wages*, *POxy.* 736.10 (i B.C./i A.D.), *PTeb.*120 *Intr.* (i B.C.).

ἠπιαίνω, (ἤπιος) *mitigate*, prob. in Arist.*Mu.*397^{b}1.

ἠπῐᾰλ-έω, *have a fever* or *ague*, Ar.*Ach.*1165 (lyr.), Arist.*Pr.*947^b 21. **-ης**, ητος, ὁ, = ἐφιάλτης, *nightmare*, personified in Sophr.68: acc. Ἠπιάλητα Id.70: -όλης Hdn.Gr.2.518; cf. sq. **-ος**, ὁ, *ague*, Thgn.174, Gal.7.347; ἠ. πυρετός Hp.*Superf.*34, Dsc.4.68; ἠ. πυρετοῦ πρόδρομος Ar.*Fr.*332: in pl., ἠ. καὶ πυρετοί Hp.*Aër.*3: metaph., ἀηδόνων ἠ. *ague* to nightingales, Com. name of a bad poet, Phryn. Com.69. II. = foreg., *nightmare*, Ar.*V.*1038, as expld. by Did. ap.Sch. (but coupled with πυρετοί). **-ώδης**, ες, *like the* ἠπίαλος, *aguish*, πυρετοί Hp.*Epid.*4.20.

ἠπιάργυρον· τὸ βάλσαμον, Hsch.

ἠπιάω, aor. 1 Pass. ἠπιήθη, = ἐταπεινώθη, Hsch. (s.v.l.).

ἠπιο-δίνητος [δῑ], ον, *softly-rolling*, βλέφαρα *AP*5.249 (Paul. Sil.). **-δωρος**, ον, *soothing by gifts, bountiful, fond*, μήτηρ Il.6.251; Κύπρις Stesich.26; Μοῦσαι Opp.*H.*4.7, etc. **-δώτης**, ου, ὁ, *giver of* ἤπια (φάρμακα), of Asclepius, Orph.Εὐχὴ 37. **-θῡμος**, ον, *gentle of mood*, *APl.*4.65, Orph.*H.*59.15.

ἠπιόλης and **ἠπ-**, ου, ὁ, v. ἠπιάλης and ἠπίολος.

ἠπιόλιον, τό, Dim. of ἠπίαλος, Hsch.

ἠπίολος, ὁ, *moth*, Arist.*HA*605^{b}14 (v.l. ἠπιόλης).

ἠπιό-μοιρος, ον, *of kindly fate*, Castorio 1 codd. Ath. (sed leg. ἠλιόμορφος, q.v.). **-μῦθος**, ον, *soft-speaking*, Max.68.

ἤπιος, α, ον, also ος, ον Hes.*Th.*407, E.*Tr.*53, etc. 1. of persons, *gentle, kind*, πατὴρ ὣς ἤπιος αἰεί Il.24.770, cf. Od.2.47,234; of a monarch, ἀγανὸς καὶ ἠ. ib.230, 5.8, cf. 14.139; ἡνίοχος Il.23.281: c. dat. pers., ἐθέλω δέ τοι ἤπιος εἶναι 8.40, cf. Od.10.337, etc.; ἠ. ἀνθρώποισι καὶ ἀθανάτοισι θεοῖσι Hes.*Th.*407; ἠπιώτερος τοῦ πατρός Hdt. 5.92.ζ'; of the gods, σωτῆρας..ἠπίους θ' ἡμῖν μολεῖν S.*Ph.*738; θεὸς ἀνθρώποισιν -ώτατος E.*Ba.*861, cf. Ar.*V.*879 (lyr.); ἐχίδνης οὐδὲν -ωτέρα E.*Alc.*310; οὐδέ πω ἤπιος *appeased*, Id.*Med.*133: later in Prose, 1*Ep.Thess.*2.7, 2*Ep.Ti.*2.24. 2. of feelings, words, etc., εἴ μοι κρείων Ἀγαμέμνων ἤπια εἰδείη had *kindly feeling* towards me, Il.16.73; ὁμῶς δέ τοι ἤπια οἶδε Od.13.405, cf. 15.557; ἠ. δήνεα οἶδε Il.4.361; μῦθος ἠ. Od.20.327; ὀργαί, φρένες, E.*Tr.*53, *Fr.*362.6; πρὸς τὸ -ώτερον καταστῆσαί τινα Th.2.59. 3. of heat and cold, *mild, less intense*, τὸ πνῖγος -ώτερον γέγονεν Pl.*Phdr.*279b, cf. *Ti.*85a (Comp.); ἠπιώτεραι αἱ θέρμαι, of a fever, Hp.*Epid.*7.1; τὰ τοῦ πυρετοῦ ἤπια ib.5.73; αἰθέριον πῦρ ἠ. ὄν Parm.8.57; of river-currents, -ώτερα ῥεύματα Meno *Iatr.*16.26. II. Act., *soothing, assuaging*, φάρμακα Il.4.218, 11. 515; opp. ἰσχυρά, Hdt.3.130, cf. 7.142 (Comp.); ἀκέσματα A.*Pr.*482; φύλλα S.*Ph.*698 (lyr.); ποτήματα *soft* drinks, opp. φαρμακώδη καὶ δριμέα, Sor.2.44: Sup., Phld.*Ir.*p.44 W. 2. ἤπιον ἦμαρ c. inf., a day *favourable* for beginning a thing, Hes.*Op.*787. III. Adv. -ίως Hdt.7.105,143, S.*El.*1439 (lyr.); ἠ. ἀμείψασθαι Hdt.8.60; χρήσετ' αὐτῇ σοι τότ' ἠ. Men.*Epit.*495: Comp. -ωτέρως, ἔχειν πρός τινα D.56. 44; -ώτερον καὶ κηδεμονικώτερον Phld.*Piet.*65: Sup. -ωτάτως Hsch.

ἠπιότης, ητος, ἡ, *gentleness*, Epicur.*Fr.*462, Hecat.Abd.ap.J.*Ap.* 1.22, Lxx *Es.*3.13(13.2), Phld.*Hom.*p.33 O., Ph.2.267.

ἠπιό-φρων, ονος, ὁ, ἡ, *gentle-minded*, ἠ. φιλότητος... ὁρμή Emp.35. 13; Αἴγινα B.12.78; Ἀσκληπιός *IG*3.171. **-χειρ**, χειρος, ὁ, ἡ, *with soothing hand*, *AP*9.525.8, prob. in Orph.*H.*23.8, 84.8.

ἠπιόω, intr., *feel easier*, ἠπίωσε τῷ σώματι Hp.*Epid.*5.20 (nisi leg. ἠπίως ⟨εἶχ⟩ε):—Pass., *to be softened*, ἠπιοῦσθαι ὑπὸ τῆς μουσικῆς Phld. *Mus.*p.33 K.: aor. ἠπιώθην Sch.Il.1.146.

ἠπίταδες· ἐπίτηδες, Hsch.

ἠπλωμένως, Adv. pf. part. Pass., (ἁπλόω) gloss on ἐκτεταμένως, prob. in Hsch.

ἧπου or **ἦ που**, *I ween*, ἦ που σοφὸς ἦν ὅστις ἔφασκεν.. Ar.*V.*725; ἦ που νέος γ' ὢν ἦσθ' ὑβριστής Id.*Th.*63, cf. Il.3.43, 16.830; ironical,

S.*Aj.*1008, E.*Med.*1308; χαλεπὸν πόλιν κατασκευάσασθαι, ἦ που δὴ .. *much more*.., Th.1.142; so ἦ που alone, Lys.30.17, Pl.*Phd.*84d; ἦ πού γε Isoc.1.49; also ἦ που δή.. *much less*, prob. in Th.8.27; also ἦ πού γε δή Id.6.37: and with a neg., ἦ που..γε..οὐ δεῖ χρήσασθαι And.1.86. II. to make a hesitating suggestion, *surely*..? Od. 13.234, A.*Pr.*521, Ar.*Pl.*970.

ἠπύη· φωνή Hsch. (fort. ἠπύει· φωνεῖ).

ἠπύτᾰ [ῠ], ὁ, Ep. for ἠπύτης (which is not found), (ἠπύω) *calling, crying*, ἠπύτα κῆρυξ the *loud-voiced* herald, Il.7.384; ἠ. σύριγξ the *shrill* pipe, Q.S.6.170; πόντος Opp.*C.*2.136.

ἠπύω, Dor. and Arc. **ἀπύω** [ᾱ], *IG*5(2).6.3 (Tegea, iv B.C.), and Trag. (who use the Verb only in lyr., exc. aor. 1 ἤπῡσα E.*Rh.*776): [ῠ in pres., exc. in Mosch. (v. infr.); ῡ in fut. and aor.]:—*call to*, c. acc., ὅθι ποιμένα ποιμὴν ἠπύει Od.10.83, cf. 9.399; ἀλλά με Πυθὼ.. ἀπύει Pi.*P.*10.4; *invoke*, ἄπυεν Εὐτρίαιναν Id.*O.*1.72, cf. *P.*5.104; ἰαλέμῳ τοὺς θανόντας ἀπύεις E.*Tr.*1304: c. dupl. acc., τί με τόδε χρέος ἀπύεις; why *callest* thou *on* me for this? Id.*Or.*1253: c. dat. pers., ἤπυσα δ' αὐτοῖς μὴ πελάζεσθαι *called to* them not.., Id.*Rh.*776. 2. abs., of the wind, *roar*, οὔτ' ἄνεμος τόσσον περὶ δρυσὶν ὑψικόμοισι ἠπύει Il.14.399; of the lyre, *sound*, ἐν δέ τε φόρμιγξ ἠπύει Od.17.271; *sing*, Λυδίοις ἀπύων ἐν αὐλοῖς Pi.*O.*5.19: c. acc. cogn., μέλος ἠπύοντες Mosch. 2.124. 3. *utter, speak*, πατρὸς ὄνομ' ἀπύεις A.*Pr.*593; τί ποτ' ἀπύσω; E.*Hec.*154; ἀπύσατ' ἀντίφων' ἐμῶν στεναγμάτων Id.*Supp.*800; πρὸ σοῦ γὰρ ἀπύω (Com. for ὑλακτῶ) Ar.*Eq.*1023. 4. folld. by an interrog., τίς ἂν ἀπύοι εἰ..; *would tell* whether..? S.*Aj.*887; ἀπύσει τίς ὅδε..; E.*Ba.*984 (nisi leg. ἀπύσει· τίς..;). II. Med., *summon, prosecute*, ἀπυέσθω ὁ ἀδικήμενος τὸν ἀδικέντα *IG* l. c.

ἦρ, contr. for ἔαρ. **ἦρ**, v. ἦρα (B).

ἦρᾰ, 3 sg. impf. of ἐράω. II. Boeot. for ἦρω, 2 sg. aor. 1 Med. of αἴρω, Ar.*Ach.*913 (v.l. ἦρω).

ἦρᾰ (A), 1 sg. aor. 1 of αἴρω:—but ἦρα', i.e. ἤραο, Ep. for ἤρω, 2 sg. aor. 1 Med. of αἴρω, Od.24.33. II. contr. fr. ἦ ἄρα in dialects other than Att., as Sapph.102, Alc.94, Alcm.61, Pi.*P.*9.37, B.5. 165, Sophr.1 D., Hp.*Prorrh.*1.117,120,121 (ἆρα ibid.), Herod.4.21, 5.14, Call.*Fr.*1.51 P., cf. A.D.*Conj.*223.25.

ἦρα (B), acc. sg., = χάριν, *service, gratification*, θυμῷ ἦ. φέροντες Il. 14.132; μητρὶ φίλῃ ἐπὶ ἦ. φέρων 1.572, cf. 578; ἐπ' Ἀτρεΐδῃ Ἀγαμέμνονι ἦ. φέροντες Od.3.164; λαοί.. ἐφ' ἡμῖν ἦ. φέρουσιν 16.375; ἐπ' Ἴρῳ ἦ. φέρων 18.56; ἦ. κομίζειν Orph.*L.*761. II. later c. gen., = χάριν, *for the sake of, on account of, for*, ἦ. πάλας B.10.21; ἦ. φιλοξενίης Call.*Fr.*41, cf. Dosiad.*Ara* 18; τίνος ἦ.; *wherefore? APl.*4.299. (Hdn.Gr.1.398 rightly makes it acc. of a Subst. ἤρ; Aristarch. took ἐπίηρα as one word, Sch.Il.1.572, Apollon.*Lex.*, but there is no ἐπί in Il.14.132, and ἐπίηρα (q.v.) in later poets proves nothing for Hom.:—prob. (ϝ)ῆρα, perh. cogn. with ONorse *værr* 'snug', 'comfortable', OHG. *alawâri* 'friendly' (Germ. *albern*), Goth. *unwērjan* (= ἀγανακτεῖν), Gr. ἐρίηρος, βρίηρον.)

Ἥρα, Ion. **Ἥρη**, ἡ, *Hera*, Il.16.432, etc.; νὴ τὴν Ἥραν, an oath of Athen. women, X.*Mem.*1.5.5. 2. applied to the Empresses of Rome, as Ζεύς to the Emperors, *IG*9(2).333 (Thess.), *CIG*3956[b] (add.). 3. Pythag. name for *nine, Theol.Ar.*58. 4. the planet Venus, Arist.*Mu.*392[a]28, Ti.Locr.96e. (Perh. connected with ἥρως and Lat. *servo*, cf. Ἡρϝαῶοι, = *inhabitants of Heraea*.)

ἠραινεῖ (sic)· ληρεῖ, Hsch.; cf. ἤρης.

Ἡραῖος, α, ον, *of Hera*, Ἥραιον or Ἡραῖον (sc. ἱερόν), τό, *temple of Hera*, Hdt.1.70, Th.3.68, Duris 60 J., etc.: Ἡραῖα (sc. ἱερά), τά, *her festival*, Ἡ. τὰ ἐν Ἄργει *SIG*1064.9 (Halic.), cf. Paus.2.24.2; epith. of Zeus, Διὶ Ἡραίῳ χοῖρος *IG*1².840.21. II. Ἡραῖος, ὁ (sc. μήν), a month at Delphi, *GDI*1693, al.; at Olus, ib.5075: Aeol. Ἥραος *OGI*265.15 (Temnos, from Pergam.):—also **Ἡραιών**, ῶνος, at Tenos, *IG*12(5).875.23; and Magnesia, *SIG*589.13.

ἠραιωμένως, Adv. pf. part. Pass., (ἀραιόομαι) gloss on ἀποκριδόν, Sch.Opp.*H.*1.547.

ἤρακεν· ἠνίασεν, Hsch.

Ἡρακλέης, contr. **-κλῆς**, ὁ, the former in Ep., Pi., Hdt., and E. *Heracl.*210, *Ion* 1144, *HF*924; the latter also in E., S., and Att. Prose: the orig. forms of the obl. cases Ἡρακλέεος, -κλέεϊ, -κλέεα nowhere appear in use; but in Att. the contracted forms Ἡρακλέους Ar. *Nu.*1050, Ἡρακλέει E.*Heracl.*8,988, Ar.*Av.*567, Ἡρακλέᾱ Id.*V.*757 (anap.) (also in *h.Hom.*15.1, Hes.*Sc.*448, Theoc.24.1); in Ion. and Ep., Ἡρακλῆος, -κλῆϊ, -κλῆα (-κλῆϊ Pi.*I.*5(4).37, -κλῆος dub. in E. *Heracl.*541):—these forms are still further shortd., Ἡρακλέος Hdt.2. 42 (v.l. -έους), Pi.*O.*3.44 (scanned ⏑⏑ – *P.*10.3), E.*HF*806 (lyr.), Ἡρακλέϊ Hdt.2.145, Theoc.25.71; Ἡρακλέᾱ Hdt.2.42 sq., Pi.*O.*10(11). 16, *AP*9.391 (Diotim. or Call.) (scanned – ⏑ – S.*Tr.*233, Ar.*Th.*26); again contr. Ἡρᾰκλῆ S.*Tr.*476 cod. A, interpol. in Pl.*Phd.*89c, Ael. *VH*1.24; Ἡρακλεῖ B.8.9, Th.7.73: irreg. acc. Ἡρακλέην A.R.2.767, dub. l. in Theoc.13.73; contr. Ἡρακλῆν v.l. in Paus.8.31.3 and Epigr. ap.Alcid.*Od.*24, *BGU*166.12 (ii A.D.): voc. Ἡράκλεες Archil.119, Pi. *N.*7.86, E.*HF*175; Att. Ἡράκλεις Pl.*Euthd.*303a, etc., later Ἥρακλες Orph.*H.*12.1 [ᾰ], *AP*9.468 [ᾰ], Gramm.ap.Lib.*Ep.*255: pl. Ἡρακλέες Pl.*Tht.*169b (but Ἡρακλεῖς Hdn.Gr.1.424), acc. -έας Ar.*Pax* 741: dual Ἡρακλέε Philostr.*VA*5.5: (Ἥρα, κλέος):—*Heracles*, Il.14. 266, etc.; Ἡρακλέος στᾶλαι (v. Ἡράκλειος), prov. of going to the farthest point, Pi.*O.*3.44; Ἡρακλέους ὀργήν τιν' ἔχων a temper *like Heracles*, Ar.*V.*1030, *Pax* 752; prov. of close friendship, ἄλλος Ἡρακλῆς, ἄλλος αὐτός (Mss. οὗτος) Arist.*EE*1245[a]30; but ἄλλος οὗτος Ἡρακλῆς 'a second *Heracles*', Id.*MM*1213[a]13, Varr.*Sat.Men.*tit.: voc. Ἡράκλεις as an exclamation of surprise, anger, or disgust, Ar.*Ach.*284, *Nu.*184. 2. the planet Mars, Arist.*Mu.*392[a]25, Ach. Tat.*Intr.Arat.*17. [ᾰ, long by position in Ep. and E., as *Heracl.* 123.]

Ἡρακλεῖδαι, οἱ, *the Heraclidae* or *descendants of Heracles*, Hdt.1.7, etc.; title of play by Euripides.

Ἡράκλειος, α, ον, also ος, ον S.*Tr.*51; Ep. **-ήειος**, in Ion. Prose **-ήϊος**, η, ον:—*of Heracles*, βίη Ἡρακληείη, i.e. *Heracles himself*, Il. 11.690, al., Theoc.25.154, etc.; Ἡ. στῆλαι the opposite headlands of Gibraltar and Apes' Hill near Tangier, Hdt.2.33, 4.8 (where -κλέων is the best reading); στᾶλαι Ἡ. Pi.*I.*4(3).12. Adv. -είως *like Heracles*, Luc.*Peregr.*33. II. Ἡράκλειον or -εῖον, Ion. -ήϊον (sc. ἱερόν), τό, *temple of Heracles*, Hdt.2.44, al.; also, *a huge drinking-cup*, such as Heracles used, Ath.11.469c. 2. Ἡράκλεια (sc. ἱερά), τά, *his festival*, Ar.*Ra.*651, *IG*3.129; Ἡ. θύειν D.19.86, etc. 3. Ἡρακλεία, ἡ, *frothy poppy, Silene viscosa*, Thphr.*HP*9.12.5, 9.15.5, Dsc.4.66. b. title of poem by Rhianus. III. νοῦσος Ἡρακλείη *epilepsy*, Hp.*Mul.* 1.7, cf. Gal.17(2).341; but Ἡ. πάθος *elephantiasis*, Aret.*SD*2.13. IV. Ἡράκλεια λουτρά *hot* baths, Ar.*Nu.*1051, ubi v. Sch. (also Ἡρακλέους κοῖται soft bedding, Megaclid.ap.Ath.12.512f). V. λίθος Ἡρακλεία or Ἡράκλεια, ἡ, *the magnet*, Pl.*Ti.*80c, *Ion* 533d, Epicur.*Fr.*293; from Heraclea in Lydia, acc. to Hsch. 2. πάνακες Ἡράκλειον *opopanax*, Zopyr.ap.Orib.14.62.1. VI. Ἡράκλειος, ὁ (sc. μήν), a month at Delphi, *GDI*1685, al.; at Halicarnassus, *SIG*1015.1.

Ἡρακλείτ-ειος, α, ον, *of Heraclitus*, ἥλιος Pl.*R.*498b; Ἡ., οἱ, *his disciples*, Id.*Tht.*179e, D.L.9.6. **-ίζω**, *to be a follower of Heraclitus*, Arist.*Metaph.*1010[a]11. **-ιστής**, οῦ, ὁ, *follower of Heraclitus*, D.L. 9.15.

Ἡρακλεών, ῶνος, ὁ, name of month at Stratonicea, *BCH*11.226; at Lagina, ib.44.70.

Ἡρακλεώτης, ου, ὁ, *a man of Heraclea*, Arist.*Pol.*1327[b]14, *IG*2². 1271 (-ειώτης ib.1².145):—Adj. **Ἡρακλεωτικός**, ή, όν, *of Heraclea*, Arist.*HA*525[b]5; ἅμμα Heracl.ap.Orib.48.8.1; [καρύα] Thphr.*HP* 1.10.6, 3.6.5, cf. Zopyr.ap.Orib.14.50.2; ἀμύγδαλα Diocl.*Fr.*126; ὀρίγανος -κή Philum.*Ven.*16.9; but σκύφος Ἡρακλεωτικός is said to derive its name directly from *Heracles*, Ath.11.500a:—fem. also **-ῶτις** Thphr.*HP*3.3.8, al.

Ἡρακληΐς, ΐδος, ἡ, *Heracleid*, a poem *on Heracles*, Arist.*Po.*1451[a] 20; cf. καρύα.

Ἡρακλῆς, ὁ, contr. from Ἡρακλέης (q.v.).

Ἡρακλίσκος, ὁ, Dim. of Ἡρακλῆς, title of Theoc.24:—a form **Ἡρακλεΐσκος** mentioned as dub. by Choerob. in *An.Ox.*2.268.

ἠράνθεμον, τό, = ἀνθεμίς, Dsc.3.137.

ἤρᾰνος, ὁ, *keeper*, μήλων A.R.2.513; Ἡσίοδος πάσης ἤ. ἱστορίης Hermesian.7.22; Μουσαῖος Χαρίτων ἤ. ib.16; ἤραν' ἁλίων μυχῶν Simm.13; glossed by βασιλεὺς ἢ βοηθός, *EM*436.28, cf. Hsch.: **ἠρανέων·** βοηθῶν, χαριζόμενος, Id. (Cf. ἐπιήρανος II.)

Ἥραος, v. Ἡραῖος II.

ἤρᾰρε, v. ἀραρίσκω. **ἠρασάμην**, v. ἔραμαι. **Ἡράσιος**, ὁ (sc. μήν), name of month at Sparta, Hsch. **ἤρᾰτο**, 3 sg. aor. of ἄρνυμαι, Hom. II. 3 sg. impf. of ἔραμαι, Thgn.1346, Pi.*P.*3. 20. **ἠρᾶτο**, v. ἀράομαι. **ἠρᾶτον·** τὸν ἠρέα στράτιον, Hsch.

ἠρέμᾰ (ἠρέμας before a vowel in A.R.3.170), Adv. *gently, softly*, ἥσυχος, ἠ., said as to a horse, Ar.*Pax* 82 (anap.); ψήχειν ἠ. τὸν βουκέφαλον Id.*Fr.*42; ἠ. ἐπιγελάσαι Pl.*Phd.*62a; ἔχε ἠ. keep *still*, Id.*Cra.* 399e; ἠ. πρόμην Id.*Prt.*333e. b. on the stage, *aside*, in *a stage-whisper*, Sch.E.*Hec.*1023, *Or.*671, Sch.A.*Ch.*46. 2. *slightly*, ἠ. ῥιγοῦν Pl.*Tht.*152b; ἀγανακτεῖν Id.*Phlb.*47a; δάκτυλοι.. ἠ. διηρθρωμένοι Arist.*HA*517[a]32: sts. with an Adj., ἐν ἠ. προσάντει Pl.*Phdr.* 230c; ἠ. λευκός Arist.*Mete.*375[a]21; ἠ. θερμός Id.*GC*326[a]12; ἠ. παθητικός ib.328[b]7; ἠ. ὁμοῖος Id.*Top.*117[b]23; ἠ. ψεκτός Id.*EN*1126[b]8; ἠ. καὶ γελοῖον *rather* ludicrous, dub. in Luc.*Merc.Cond.*28 codd. 3. *slowly*, περιφέρεσθαι Pl.*R.*617a.

ἠρεμ-άζω, *to be still, silent*, esp. from grief, Lxx 2*Es.*9.3. **-αῖος**, α, ον, *quiet, gentle*, λῦπαι, ἡδοναί, Pl.*Lg.*734a; γένεσις Id.*Plt.*307a; πῦρ ἠ. a *slight* fever, Hp.*Mul.*1.38; σμικρὰ καὶ ἠ., opp. μεγάλα καὶ σφοδρά, Pl.*Lg.*733c: Comp., πόλιν -οτέραν ποιεῖν Plu.*Sol.*31: irreg., ἠρεμέστερος X.*Cyr.*7.5.63, Thphr.*Vent.*29. Adv. -αίως, = ἠρέμα, X. *Eq.*9.5, *Gp.*12.14.1: Comp. -αίτερον (v.l. -αιότερον) Arist.*Mete.*368[a] 12; -εστέρως ἔχειν X.*Cyr.*3.1.30. **-αιότης**, ητος, ἡ, *tranquillity*, Hp.*Praec.*2. **-εί**, v. ἠρεμί.

ἠρεμ-έω, hyperdor. ἀρεμ- Ti.Locr.95d:—*to be still, keep quiet, be at rest*, opp. κινέομαι, Hp.*Fract.*6, Arist.*Ph.*238[b]23, al., Aristox.*Harm.* p.12 M.; τὸ ἠρεμοῦν, opp. τὸ κινούμενον, Pythag.ap.Arist.*Metaph.* 986[a]24; of the object of knowledge, Pl.*Phd.*96b, Arist.*APo.*100[a]6; ἐν τοῖς νόμοις ἠρεμοῦντες διαμένειν X.*Ages.*7.3; *acquiesce* in a verdict, Pl.*Lg.*956d; ἠ. τῇ διανοίᾳ Arr.*Epict.*2.21.22: acc. to Stoics, only of animate beings, *Stoic.*2.161. 2. *to be unmoved, remain fixed*, μόνος οὗτος ἠ. ὁ λόγος Pl.*Grg.*527b, cf. *Lg.*891a. 3. c. inf., *refrain from* doing.., Luc.*Jud.Voc.*4 (s.v.l.). **-ητέον**, *one must keep quiet*, Ph.1.89, Archig.ap.Gal.13.168. **-ησις**, hyperdor. ἀρέμ-, εως, ἡ, Ti.Locr.104b:—*rest*, opp. κίνησις, Arist.*Ph.*251[a]26, al.; ἡ νόησις ἔοικεν -ήσει μᾶλλον ἢ κινήσει Id.*de An.*407[a]32; ἐν ἀρεμήσει, of ἐπιθυμία, Ti.Locr. l. c. **-ί** [ῐ], Adv. for ἠρέμα, Ar.*Ra.* 315, v.l. in Aristaenet.1.22 (-μεί Theognost.*Can.*165). **-ία**, ἡ, *rest*, opp. κίνησις, Arist.*Ph.*202[a]4; ἐν ἠ. εἶναι Id.*Metaph.*988[b]4, cf. Aristox.*Harm.*p.12 M., Sor.1.46. 2. of the mind, *quietude*, ἠ. ψυχῆς περὶ τὰ δεινά Pl.*Def.*412a, cf. Arist.*de An.*406[a]27 (pl.); ἐπὶ πολλῆς ἠ. ὑμῶν leaving you entirely *at rest*, v.l. for ἐρημίας, D.13.8 (ἠρεμίη κοίτης is perh. a mistake for ἐρημίη, *Epigr.Gr.*321.11). **-ίζω**, bring to rest, stop, ἵππον X.Eq.7.18; ὁρμήν Arist.EE1224^{b}8:—Pass., Id.APo.87^{b}9, Ph.238^{b}25, al.; καθίσταται καὶ -ίζεται is calmed and brought to rest, ib.248^{a}2. II. intr., = ἠρεμέω, X.Lac.1.3. **-ιος,** α, ον, = ἠρεμαῖος, Procl. in Prm.p.803 S. II. -ιον, τό, = ἀνεμώνη, Dsc.2.176 (v.l. ἠνέμιον). **-ισις,** εως, ἡ, tranquillizing, πράϋνσις ἠ. ὀργῆς Arist.Rh.1380^{a}8 (-ησις codd.). **-ισμα,** ατος, τό, point of rest, Simp. in Ph.1311.32. **-ος,** ον, later form for ἠρεμαῖος, quiet, ἠ. καὶ ἡσύχιος βίος 1Ep.Ti.2.2, cf. OGI519.10 (iii A.D.), Procl. in Prm.p.536 S.; ἠ. πούς Luc.Trag.207; ἤρεμον ἑαυτὸν παρέχειν IPE1².40.24 (Olbia, ii/iii A.D.); -ώτερος ἐπισπασμός gentler traction, Sor.1.73. 2. τὸ ἠ. smoothness, of pigments, Thphr.Lap.62. 3. Adv. -μως quietly, Asp. in EN120.13. (Cf. Lith. rìmti 'grow still', Goth. rimis (= ἡσυχία), Skt. ramnāti 'set at rest'.) **-ότης,** ητος, ἡ, = ἠρεμία, ψυχῆς Cleonid.Harm.13.

ἠρεσίδες, αἱ, priestesses of Hera at Argos, EM436.49 (which derives the word from Ἥρα or ἀρύω).

ἤρευν, Ion. impf. of αἱρέω, Hes.Sc.302. **ἠρήρει,** v. ἀραρίσκω. **ἠρήρειντο, ἠρήρειστο,** v. ἐρείδω. **ἤρης·** ἄφρων, Hsch.

-ήρης, an Adj. termin., 1. from ἀραρ-εῖν, ἀραρ-ίσκω, as in θυμαρής, φρενήρης, χαλκήρης, εὐήρης. 2. from ἐρε- (ἐρέ-της), as in ἀμφήρης, ἁλιήρης, τριήρης, etc. 3. prob. from (ϝ)ηρ- (cf. ἦρα B) in pr. n. Περιήρης, Διώρης (fr. Διοήρης).

ἦρι, Ep. Adv. (Boeot. acc. to AB1095) early, ἦ. μάλ' Il.9.360; μάλ' ἦ. Od.20.156; ἠῶθεν δὲ μάλ' ἦ. 19.320; in the morning, μαντεύεσθαι Schwyzer789 (Cumae). (ᾱ(y)ερι, cf. ἠέριος, ἄριστον.)

ἠρῐ-γένεια, ἡ, (ἦρι, γενέσθαι) early-born, child of morn, epith. of Ἠώς, Od.4.195, etc.: also abs., = Ἠώς, 22.197, 23.347; καθαρᾶς ἅπερ ἠριγενείας as at clear morn, Theoc.24.39; γενέθλιον ἠριγένειαν a birthday morning, AP9.353 (Leon. Alex.); later, epith. of the Moon, Hymn. Mag.5.3. 2. in later Ep., a day, Nonn.D.38.271, Q.S.10.478. II. (ἔαρ) bearing in spring, λέαινα A.Fr.426 (nisi leg. ἠυγ-). **-γένειον,** τό, = περιστερεὼν ὕπτιος, Ps.-Dsc.4.60; = ἠρύγγιον, Hsch. **-γενής,** ές, = ἠριγένεια, epith. of Ἠώς, A.R.3.1224: abs., = Ἠώς, Id.2.450; a day, Orph.Fr.275. **-γέρων,** οντος, ὁ, early-old, name of groundsel, from its hoary down, Senecio vulgaris, Thphr.HP7.7.1, Dsc.4.96.

Ἠρῐδᾰνός, ὁ, Eridanus, a legendary river, Hes.Th.338, Hdt.3.115; later identified with the Po, E.Hipp.737 (lyr.), etc. II. a river in Attica, Call.Fr.100e, Paus.1.19.5.

ἠρι-εργής, ὁ, (ἠρίον) grave-digger, Hsch. **-εύς,** έως, ὁ, a corpse, Id.

Ἠρικᾰπαῖος or **Ἠρικεπ-,** ὁ, a bi-sexual Orphic divinity, Ἠ. πρωτόγονος Orph.Fr.167a.1, cf. H.6.4, Fr.60, al.; epith. of Dionysus, Hsch.

ἤρῐκε, v. ἐρείκω.

ἠρινό-θερμον· τὸ ἄνθεμον, Hsch. **-λόγος,** ον, talking in spring, τέττιξ, Id.

ἠρῐνός, ή, όν, (ἦρ) = ἐαρινός, ἄνεμος Sol.13.19; φύλλα Pi.P.9.46; κάλυκες Cratin.98; λειμών E.Supp.448; φθέγματα Ar.Av.683 (lyr.); χρόνος X.HG3.2.10: neut. as Adv., in spring, γῆ τ' ἠρινὸν θάλλουσα E.Fr.316.3; ὅταν ἠρινὰ.. χελιδὼν κελαδῇ Ar.Pax800.

ἠρίον, τό, mound, barrow, tomb, ἔνθ' ἄρ' Ἀχιλλεὺς φράσσατο Πατρόκλῳ μέγα ἠ. Il.23.126, cf. SIG11 (Delph.), IG12(1).168 (Rhodes), A.R.1.1165, etc.; ἠρία νεκύων, Κορύθοιο, Theoc.2.13, Nic.Fr.108; εἴσατο βωμόν..., ἠ. ὄφρα γένοιτο Epigr.Gr.411 (Patara); κατὰ χθονὸς ἠρία τεῦχον AP7.180 (Apollonid.), cf. Epigr.Gr.214.1 (Rhenea); in Prose, Arist.Ath.55.3, D.57.67, prob. in Din.2.17, cf. Lycurg.109, Plu.TG9, etc.: metaph., ἠρία τῶν ψυχῶν τὰς βίβλους Them.Or.4.59d. (Derived from ἔρα by Harp., etc.: ϝηρίον prob. in Hom.)

ἠρι-πόλη, ἡ, (πολέω) early-walking: hence, dawn, AP5.227 (Paul. Sil.), 253 (Id.). **-σάλπιγξ,** v. ἐρι-.

ἠρίσκος, ὁ, perh. Dim. of ἦρος, IG11(2).199B35 (Delos, iii B.C.).

ἠρίστριον, τό, spring-garment, formed like θερίστριον, Hsch.

ἠρίφακον· θαμνίσκον (Lacon.), Hsch.

ἠρμένως, Adv. pf. part. Pass., (αἴρω) loftily, Poll.9.147.

ἡρμοσμένως, Adv. pf. part. Pass., (ἁρμόζω) fitly, D.S.17.19.

ἠροάνθια, τά, a feast of the Peloponnesian women at which they wore spring flowers, Phot.: **ἠροσάνθεια,** Hsch.

ἠροικάκαι· κοιλώματα τῆς γῆς, Hsch.

ἡροϊκός, ή, όν, in late Poets for ἡρωϊκός, Man.1.13, IG12(7).125 (Amorgos).

ἦρος, ὁ, dub. sens. in IG11(2).144A72 (Delos, iv B.C.); ἦρον ὠνουμένων ἔδωκεν.., τὸν ἦρον ἐνδήσαντι..., τέλος ἐν Πάρῳ τοῦ ἦρου, ib.203A 39,40 (iii B.C.); cf. ἠρίσκος.

Ἡροφάνεια, τά, festival at Megara, IG7.48 (ii B.C.).

ἠρόχια· τὰ Θεοδαίσια· οἱ δὲ ἑορτήν, οἱ δὲ ἱερά, Hsch.

ἡρπαγμένως, raptim, Gloss. **ἦρσα,** v. ἀραρίσκω.

ἠρύγγ-ιον, τό, v. ἤρυγγος. **-ίς,** ίδος, ἡ, of or belonging to the ἤρυγγος, ῥίζαι Nic.Al.564. **-ος,** ἡ, eryngo, Eryngium creticum, Id.Th. 645, 849: more freq. as Dim., **ἠρύγγιον,** τό, E. campestre, Thphr. HP6.1.3, Plu.2.700d, 776f (both forms in Dsc.3.21, ἠρύγγιον also = ἀλόη, Ps.-Dsc.3.22):—also **ἠρύγγη,** ἡ, Plin.HN22.18, Phot.; = πόλιον, Hp.ap.Erot. (perh. to be read in Ulc.11); **ἠρυγγίτης** [ῑ], ου, ὁ, Plu.2.558e, Suid. II. **ἤρυγγος,** ὁ, goat's beard, Arist.HA610^b 29 (s.v.l.).

ἤρῡγε, v. ἐρεύγομαι. **ἠρύκᾰκε,** v. ἐρύκω.

ἤρυς or **ἠρῦς,** ἡ, fem. of ἥρως, Glotta15.306 (Lilybaeum, ii B.C.).

ἥρῳ, poet. dat. sg. of ἥρως: **ἥρω,** gen. and acc. of same.

ἡρώασσα, ἡ, Cret., = ἡρωΐνη, GDI4952 (Dreros).

ἡρώειον, τό, = ἡρῷον (q.v.).

ἡρω-ίαμβος [ῐ], ὁ, poem consisting of hexameters and iambics, Tz. H.4.868. **-ΐζω,** write heroic verse or an epic poem, Eust.4.1: **-ισμός,** ὁ, worship of heroes, IG12(2).29 (Mytil., spelt -οισμός):—hence **-οϊσταί,** οἱ, IG2².1339 (i B.C.); **-ωεισταί** Annuario4/5.482; **-ωιασταί** BCH50.15 (Delph., iv B.C.), 22.255 (Acraephia): later **ἡρωστής** (q.v.). **-ικός,** ή, όν, of the heroes, κατὰ τοὺς ἡ. χρόνους (cf. ἥρως I.1) Arist.Pol.1285^{b}4; ἡ χλαῖνα ἡ. φόρημα Ammon.Diff. p.140V. 2. of or for a hero, heroic, φῦλον Pl.Cra.398e; ἡ. σώματα of heroic stature, Phld.Po.2.43; ἀρετή Arist.EN1145^{a}20; ἡρωϊκὰ φρονεῖν Luc.Am.20. Adv. -κῶς like a hero, τελευτῆσαι τὸν βίον D.S. 2.45; cf. ἡροϊκός. II. in Metre, ἡ. στίχος heroic verse, hexameter, Pl.Lg.958e; μέτρον Arist.Po.1459^{b}32; εἰς τὴν ἡ. τάξιν ἐπανῆχθαι to be brought into an Epic poem, D.60.9. Adv. -κῶς, τὴν τραγῳδίαν ἀναγνῶναι D.T.629.18. **-ίνη** [ῑ], ἡ, fem. of ἥρως, heroine, Theoc. 13.20, 26.36, Call.Del.161, D.P.1022, Luc.Nec.15, D.C.48.50: contr. **ἡρῴνη,** Ar.Nu.315, IG14.1389 i 55, 2².1358.8, al.; **ἡροῖνα** ib.12(2). 228 (Mytil.). II. a deceased woman (cf. ἥρως II), CIG2259 (Samos), IG3.889; of a deified Empress, Jul.Caes.334b. **-ιος,** α, ον, = ἡρωικός, ἀρεταί Pi.O.13.51; πομπαί Id.N.7.46 [ᾰ]. **-ίς,** ίδος, ἡ, = ἡρωίνη I, Id.P.11.7, Call.Fr.126. 2. = ἡρωίνη II, IG12(7).51 (Amorgos), Rev.Phil.36.55 (Iconium), AJP48.33 (Apamea). II. as fem. of ἡρωικός, τιμαί A.R.1.1048; ἀοιδή Epic, AP9.504. 2. (sc. ἐννεετηρίς) nine-yearly festival at Delphi, Plu.2.293c. **-ΐσσα,** contr. **ἡρῷσσα,** = ἡρωίνη, A.R.4.1309, 1358, IG5(1).610 (Sparta), al., 12(5).325 (Paros), AP6.225 (Nicaen.). **-ϊστής,** v. -ίζω.

Ἥρων, ωνος, ὁ, name of a god, BCH24.374 (Bithynia), Annales du Service20.238 (Theadelphia), etc.; also **Ἥρως,** ωος, ὁ, Epigr.Gr.841 (Thrace), Call.Ep.26.

ἡρώνα, ἁ, perh. service, office, ἐπιτελέσσαντα ταῖς ἡρώναις παίσαις (acc. pl.) dub. in IG12(2).242 (Mytil.).

ἡρωο-γονία, ἡ, a poem of Hesiod, Procl.Vit.Hes.p.8 G. **-λογέω,** (λέγω) tell of heroes, Str.11.6.3. **-λογία,** ἡ, tale of heroes, title of work by Anaximander, Ath.11.498b.

ἡρῷον, Ion. **-ώϊον,** τό, 1. (sc. ἱερόν or ἕδος) shrine of a hero, Hdt. 5.47, 67, Th.2.17, etc.; θὡρῷον, i.e. τὸ ἡρῷον, Ar.V.819. 2. tomb, IG12(7).478 (Amorgos), IGRom.4.799 (Apamea, iii A.D.), etc.:—in form **ἡρώειον,** CIG4418 (Cilicia), etc. 3. (sc. μέτρον) hexameter, Plu.Num.4, etc. 4. ἡρῷα (sc. ἱερά), τά, festival of a hero, δειπνεῖν Id.2.811d, cf. IG2².974.

ἡρῷος, α, ον, contr. for ἡρώϊος (q.v.); ὁ ἡ. (sc. ῥυθμός) the heroic measure, hexameter, Pl.R.400b, cf. Arist.Rh.1408^{b}32; ἡ. [μέτρον] Id. Po.1460^{a}3; πούς ἡ. dactyl, AP7.9 (Damag.), etc.

ἠρώπτει· σκώπτει, Hsch.; cf. **ἠρόπτω·** σκώπτω (v.l. κόπτω), EM 437.27.

ἥρως, ὁ (also ἡ in signf. III), gen. ἥρωος (ἥρως codd. in Od.6.303, fort. leg. ἥρῶος), IG2².1641.6 (iv B.C.), etc.; also ἥρω D.19.249, IG2. 1191 (iii B.C.), Paus.10.4.10: dat. ἥρωϊ, mostly in form ἥρῳ Il.7.453, Od.8.483, Pl.Com.174.18, Orac.ap.D.43.66: acc. ἥρωα Pl.Lg.738d, IG3.810 (ἥρῳα Epigr.Gr.774 (Priene)); usu. in form ἥρω IG2.1058.25 (iv B.C.), Pl.R.391d, A.R.2.766, etc., also ἥρων Hdt.1.167:—Plur., nom. ἥρωες (ῶ Pi.P.4.58), rarely contr. ἥρως, as in Ar.Fr.304: dat. ἥρωσιν A.Fr.55, Ar.Av.1485; ἡρώνεσσι Sophr.154: acc. ἥρωας (ῶ Pi.P.1.53), rarely ἥρως, as in A.Ag.516, Luc.Dem.Enc.4:—hero, ἥρωες Δαναοί, Ἀχαιοί, Il.2.110, 19.34; στίχας ἀνδρῶν ἡρώων Od.1. 101; ἡρώων ἀγοράς, of the Phaeacians, 7.44; ἥρῳ Δημοδόκῳ 8.483; οἱ ἡγεμόνες τῶν ἀρχαίων μόνοι ἦσαν ἥρωες, οἱ δὲ λαοὶ ἄνθρωποι Arist.Pr. 922^{b}18, but cf. ll. cc. 2. the Fourth Age of men, between δαίμονες and ἄνθρωποι, Hes.Op.172, cf. Pl.Cra.398c. 3. heroes, as objects of worship, ἡ. ἀντίθεοι Pi.P.1.53, 4.58; ἥ. θεός, of Heracles, Id.N.3.22; but [Ἡρακλέϊ] τῷ μὲν ὡς Ὀλυμπίῳ θύουσι, τῷ δὲ ἑτέρῳ ὡς ἥρωι ἐναγίζουσι Hdt.2.44; Σίσυφος ἥ. Thgn.711; twice in A., Ag.516, Fr.55; once in E., Fr.446 (lyr.); οὔτε θεοὺς οὔθ' ἥρωας αἰσχυνθεῖσα Antipho 1.27; esp. of local deities, founders of cities, patrons of tribes, etc., Hdt.1.168, Th.4.87, Pl.Lg. l. c., Arist.Pol.1332^{b}18, etc.; at Athens, ἥ. ἐπώνυμοι heroes after whom the φυλαί were named, Paus.1.5.1, 2, cf. Hdt.5.66; of historical persons to whom divine honours were paid, as Brasidas at Amphipolis, Th.5.11, cf. Hdt.5.114, 7.117: hence, = Lat. divus, ἥρωα ἀπεδείξατε [τὸν Αὔγουστον] D.C.56.41; also, = Lares, D.H.4.14; ὁ κατ' οἰκίαν ἥ., = Lar familiaris, ib.2. II. later, = μακαρίτης, deceased, Alciphr.3.37, Hld.7.13: pl., PMag.Par.1.1390: freq. in Inscrr., ἥρως χρηστέ, χαῖρε IG9(2).806, cf. 14.223, etc.; even of women, ib.9(2).961 (Larissa), al.; θεοῖς ἥρωσι, = Dis Manibus, ib.14. 1795 (Rome), etc.; ὑβρίσαντας τοὺς ἥρωας τῶν τέκνων ἡμῶν SIG1243. 23 (Acraeph.). III. ἡ. ποικίλος, = στιγματίας, Hsch., Phot. IV. βοῦς ἥ., = ἡγεμών, IG2².1126.32. V. v. Ἥρων.

ἡρῷσσα, v. ἡρωΐσσα. **ἡρωστής,** = ἡρωϊστής, Keil-Premerstein Dritter Bericht117 (Tire).

ἡρωφόρος, ον, bearing heroes, EM230.40.

ἧς, Dor. and Aeol. 3 sg. impf. of εἰμί (sum). **ἧς,** gen. sg. fem. of ὅς. II. Dor. for εἷς, one. **ἧσα,** aor. 1 of ᾄδω; but, II. **ἧσα,** aor. 1 of ἥδω. **ᾔσαν,** Att. for ᾔδεσαν, 3 pl. plpf. (used as impf.) of οἶδα. II. Att. for ᾔεσαν, 3 pl. impf. of εἶμι (ibo). **ἥσατο,** v. ἥδομαι.

ἥσθημα, ατος, τό, (ἥδομαι) = ἡδονή, Eup.131.

ἡσῐεπής, (ἵημι) throwing words, i.e. babbler, EM669.7.

Ἡσίοδος, ὁ, Hesiod, Pi.I.6(5).67, etc.; Aeol. **Αἰσ-** EM452.37:—Adj. **Ἡσιόδειος,** α, ον, Pl.Lg.658d, Plu.2.657d.

ἧσις, εως, ἡ, (ἥδομαι) = τέρψις, Suid.; but ησει, = ἦσαν (3 pl. impf. of εἰμί), PLond.3.1170^{v}387, al. (iii A.D.); ησιν, = ἦσαν, Bell Jews and Christians in Egypt1914.16 (iv A.D.); also ησει, perh. = ἦσαν (3 pl. impf. of εἰμί), Sammelb.7194^{r}14 (ii A.D.).

ἥσιχερ· δαψιλής, Hsch.; cf. ἀσιχήρ.

ἠσκημένως, Adv. pf. part. Pass., (ἀσκέω) *in a practised manner*, Poll.1.157.

ἧσμεν, Att. for ᾔδειμεν, v. *εἴδω. **ἧσο,** v. ἧμαι.

ἧσσα, Att. **ἧττα,** ης, ἡ, *defeat, discomfiture*, Th.5.12, 7.72, Pl.*Lg.* 638b; πολέμου in war, Id.*La.*196a; ἧττα.. πολέμου καὶ δικῶν καὶ ἀγορῶν Aeschin.3.111, cf. Plu.2.840c; μὴ δι' ἧτταν, ἀλλὰ διὰ προαίρεσιν Arist.*EN*1150ᵃ24; ἧτταν προσίεσθαι to let oneself be *conquered*, X.*Cyr.*3.3.45: c. gen. rei, *yielding* or *giving way to* a thing, ἡδονῶν, ἐπιθυμιῶν, Pl.*Lg.*869e (pl.); ἡ ἐν τοῖς τοιούτοις ἧ. καλή D.*Ep.*3.45; ἡ ὑπὸ τῶν λιπαρούντων ἧ. Plu.*Brut.*6.

ἡσσ-άομαι, Att. **ἡττ-,** S.*Fr.*936, Th.3.57: fut. ἡσσηθήσομαι E.*Hipp.* 727, 976, ἡττ- Lys.20.32, X.*Cyr.*3.3.42: fut. Med. ἡττήσομαι in pass. sense, Lys.28.9, X.*An.*2.3.23: aor. ἡσσήθην E.*Andr.*917, etc.: pf. ἥσσημαι S.*Aj.*1242, E.*Alc.*697: plpf. ἥττητο D.19.160: Ion. **ἑσσόομαι,** part. ἑσσούμενος Hdt.1.82: impf. ἑσσοῦτο (without augm.) Id.7.166, 8.75: aor. ἑσσώθην Id.2.169, etc.: pf. ἕσσωμαι Id.8.130 (and v.l. in 7.9.β'), Herod.8.19: (ἥσσων):—*to be less* or *weaker than, inferior to*, c. gen. pers., E.*Alc.*697: c. gen. pers. et part., ἡττᾶσθαί τινος εὖ ποιοῦντος X.*An.*3.2.23, cf. *Cyr.*5.4.32; ἡττᾶσθαί τινός τινι ib.8.2.13; ἔν τινι in a thing, ib.3.3.42, etc.: c. gen. rei, τὸ μὴ δίκαιον τῆς δίκης -ώμενον E.*Ion* 1117: c. neut. Adj. in acc., ὃ ἡττῷτο wherein he *had proved inferior*, X.*Cyr.*1.4.5. 2. as a real Pass., *to be defeated, discomfited*, ὑπό τινος Hdt.3.106, And.4.28, Th.2.39; ὑπ' ἔρωτος, ὑπ' ἔχθρας, Pl.*Phdr.*233c, *Plt.*305c, etc.; πρὸς τἀφροδίσια Id. *Lg.*650a: c. gen. pers., E.*Hec.*1252, Ar.*Av.*70, Th.3.57, etc.: c. gen. rei, τοῦ κόπου γὰρ ἕσσωμαι Herod. l. c.: c. dat. modi, ἑσσωθῆναι μάχῃ ὑπό τινων Hdt.5.46, etc.; τοῖς ὅλοις D.9.64, etc.; also c. acc., μάχην Isoc.5.47, D.19.320; ἀγῶνα D.C.63.9: c. dat., τῷ θυμῷ *to be broken* in spirit, Hdt.8.130; ἑσσωθέντες τῇ γνώμῃ πρὸς Κύρου Id.9.122; ἡ. περί τι Pl.*Sph.*239b: abs., οἱ ἡσσώμενοι, opp. οἱ κρατοῦντες, A.*Th.* 516, cf. Hdt.7.9.β'; τὴν γνώμην αὐτῶν οὐχ ἡσσῆσθαι Th.6.72. 3. as law-term, *to be cast in a suit*, S.*Aj.*1242, Ar.*Pl.*482, etc.; ἡττ. ἐν τοῖς δικαστηρίοις X.*Mem.*4.4.17; δίκην, παραγραφήν, Pl.*Lg.*880c, D.45. 51. 4. *give way, yield*, c. gen. pers., οἱ φύσαντες ἡσσῶνται τέκνων S.*Fr.*936; εἰ παθών γε σοῦ τάδ' ἡσσηθήσομαι E.*Hipp.*976; *give way, be a slave to* passion and the like, νηδύος ἡσσημένος Id.*Fr.*282.5; τοῦ παρόντος δεινοῦ Th.4.37; τῶν φόβων Pl.*Lg.*635d; ἡδονῆς X.*Ages.*5.1; ὕπνου Id.*Cyr.*1.5.11; [χρημάτων] Lys.28.9; τῆς τούτων παρασκευῆς ib. 11; θνητοῦ κάλλους Isoc.10.60; πικροῦ ἔρωτος E.*Hipp.*727: c. gen. pers., *to be in love with*.., Plu.2.771f; of other things, ἡττ. τοῦ ὕδατος X.*HG*5.2.5; τοῦ δικαίου ib.5.4.31; τῆς ἀληθείας D.18.273; τὸ δίκαιον ἡττ. τοῦ φθόνου D.25.75. 5. c. dat., *to be overcome by*.., ἀκοῆς ἡδονῇ ἡσσώμενοι Th.3.38, cf. 7.25; ὕπνῳ Ael.*NA*13.22; τοῖς δικαίοις Plu. *Cat.Mi.*16. II. later in Act. **ἡττάω,** *overcome*, τινα Corn.*ND*9, Arr.*Epict.*2.22.6, al.: aor. 1 ἥττησα, τὰς ψυχὰς τῶν ὑπεναντίων Plb.1. 75.3; ταῖς ψυχαῖς τοὺς ὑπεναντίους Id.3.18.5, cf. Heraclit.*Incred.*16; *defeat*, τοὺς Λακεδαιμονίους ἀπὸ κράτους ἡττηκότες D.S.15.87. **-ητέος,** α, ον, neut. pl. ἡσσητέα *one must be beaten*, γυναικός *by* a woman, S. *Ant.*678, cf. Ar.*Lys.*450.

ἡσσόνως, Adv. of sq., J.*AJ*17.5.5, 18.2.4, 19.1.15, prob. in Hp. *Art.*69.

ἥσσων, ἧσσον, gen. ονος; Att. **ἥττων,** Ion. **ἥσσων** (not ἕσσων) Hdt. (v. infr.), Democr.50, Hp.*VC*2: formed from ἧκα (prop. ἡσσ-, cf. ἥκιστος), but in sense Comp. of κακός, μικρός: I. c. gen. pers., *inferior*; esp. in force, *weaker*, αἴθ' ὅσον ἡ. εἰμὶ τόσον σέο φέρτερος εἴην Il.16.722; of horses, 23.322, al.; ῥώμῃ ἥσσονες τῶν Περσέων Hdt.8 113, cf. 9.62; γυναικῶν ἥσσονες S.*Ant.*680; Κύπριδος E.*Andr.*631; ἔς τι in a thing, Hdt.3.102: c. inf. modi, ἡσσ. τινὸς θέειν *not so good* at running, ib.105; οὐδενὸς ἡσσ. γνῶναι *second* to none in judging, Th.2.60; ἱππεύειν ἡττ. τῶν ἡλίκων *inferior* to them in riding, X.*Cyr.* 1.3.15. 2. abs., οἱ ἡσσ. *the weaker party*, A.*Supp.*203, 489; οὐχ ἥσσους γενέσθαι to have the best of it, Th.4.72; τὸ λαμβάνειν τὰ τῶν ἡττ. X.*An.*5.6.32: c. dat. modi, ἥσσονες ναυμαχίῃ Hdt.5.86: c. acc. modi, τὸν νοῦν ἡσσ. S.*El.*1023, cf. X.*Cyr.*1.4.4; of things, τὸν ἥττω λόγον κρείττω ποιεῖν 'to make *the worse* appear the better cause', Pl.*Ap.*18b, cf. Ar.*Nu.*114: pl., οἱ ἥττους λόγοι ib.1042, Isoc.15.15; τὸ ἡσσ. ἀδικίᾳ νέμεις E.*Supp.*379 (lyr.). b. *less, fewer*, ἵνα πλείω μὲν ἀκούωμεν, ἥττονα δὲ λέγωμεν Zeno *Stoic.*1.68. II. c. gen. rei, *giving way* or *yielding to* a thing, *a slave to*.., τοῦ τῆσδ' ἔρωτος εἰς ἅπανθ' ἡσσ. S.*Tr.*489; τῶν αἰσχρῶν Id.*Ant.*747; ὀργῆς Id.*Fr.*929; γάμων E.*IA*1354; κέρδους Ar.*Pl.*363; ἡδονῶν Pl.*Prt.*353c; γαστρὸς ἢ οἴνου ἢ ἀφροδισίων ἢ πόνου ἢ ὕπνου X.*Mem.*1.5.1; χρημάτων Democr. l. c., Theopomp.Hist.121: generally, *unable to resist*, τοῦ πεπρωμένου E.*Hel.*1660; νόσων καὶ γήρως Lys.2.78; οἱ ἥττους τῶν πόνων [ἵπποι] X.*Eq.Mag.*1.3, 2.78. III. neut. ἧσσον, ἧττον, as Adv., *less*, ὀλίγον δέ τί μ' ἡσσ. ἐτίμα Od.15.365, cf. E.*Hipp.*264 (anap.); ἡσσόν τι Th. 3.75; ἡσσ. ἑτέρων Id.1.84; ὁμοίως τε τρωθεὶς καὶ ἡσσ. Hp. l. c.: mostly with Verbs, but also with Adjs., ἀριστοκρατίαι ... αἱ μὲν ἡττ., αἱ δὲ μᾶλλον μόνιμοι Arist.*Pol.*1307ᵃ14, cf. *Mete.*340ᵇ8: with a Comp., ἡττ. ἀκριβέστερον Id.*Pr.*957ᵇ8; ἡττ. εὐληπτοτέραν D.H.3.43 codd.: with neg., οὐχ ἡσσ., οὐδ' ἡσσ., not a whit *less, just as much*, A.*Ch.*181, 708, Th.1.8; οὐδὲν ἡσσ., μηδὲν ἡσσ., S.*Aj.*276, 1329; for τὸ μᾶλλον καὶ ἡττ., v. μάλα.

ἡστ-ικός, ή, όν, (ἥδομαι) *pleasing, agreeable*, πάθος S.E.*M.*6.33. Adv. -κῶς, opp. ἀλγεινῶς, ib.10.225. **-ός,** ή, όν, = foreg., Simp. *in de An.*266.25, al., Hsch., Suid.

ἡσῠχ-άζω, fut. -άσω Th.2.84, *AP*5.132 (Maec.), -άσομαι Luc. *Gall.*1: aor. ἡσύχᾰσα Th.1.12: (ἥσυχος):—*keep quiet, be at rest*, σὺ δ' ἡσύχαζε A.*Pr.*329, cf. 346; ἡ ἀπορία τοῦ μὴ ἡσυχάζειν the difficulty of *finding rest*, Th.2.49; οἱ πολέμιοι ἡσύχαζον X.*An.*5.4.16; ἀνάγκη τὸ ἡσυχάζον ἑστάναι Pl.*Prm.*162e; τοὺς [νόμους] οὐκ ἐῶν ἡσυχάζειν ἐν τιμωρίαις Luc.*Abd.*19; ἡ. πρὸς μίαν θύρην, of a lover, *AP*5.166 (Asclep.); ὁ διαλεκτικὸς ἡσυχάσει S.E.*P.*2.239: freq. in part., ἡσυχάζων προσμενῶ S.*OT*620, cf. E.*Or.*134; ὥστε μὴ ἡσυχάσασα αὐξηθῆναι *by resting from war*, Th.1.12; ἡσυχαζουσῶν τῶν νεῶν ib.49; μόλις ἡσυχάσαντες Id.8.86; ἡσυχάζουσαν ἔχων τὴν διάνοιαν Isoc.5.24; τὸ ἡσυχάζον τῆς νυκτὸς *the dead* of night, Th.7.83; ἡ. ἀπό τινος *keep away* from.., *AP*5.132 (Maec.): c. dat., *suspend work on*, *PFay.*117.23 (ii A.D.); ἀλλ' ἡσύχαζε only *be tranquil, calm thyself*, E.*HF*98, *IA* 973. b. ὁ -άζων, with or without λόγος, a fallacy, Chrysipp.*Stoic.* 2.8 (pl.), Gell.1.2.4 (pl.). II. trans., *bring to rest*, ἡσυχάσας τὼ δύο εἴδη, τὸ τρίτον δὲ κινήσας Pl.*R.*572a. b. abs., *impose silence*, D.C.69.6. 2. *leave unspoken*, ἃ χρὴ λέγειν Ph.1.254, cf. 2.268; τὰς ἀπειλὰς J.*AJ*7.7.3. III. Pass. in impers. sense, ἡσυχάζεται ἐπὶ τῆς γῆς *there is quiet*, Lxx *Jb.*37.17. **-αῖος,** Dor. **ἁσῠχ-,** α, ον, = ἥσυχος, βάσις S.*OC*197 (lyr.); ἐλάσεις X.*Eq.*9.6; *gentle*, Pl.*Plt.*307a; of persons, E.*Med.*808; *at rest*, of the embryo, Pl.*Lg.*775c; τὸ ἡ. *peace, tranquillity*, S.*Fr.*941.6; τὸ ἡ. ἀργόν E.*Fr.*552.4: neut. as Adv., ἡσυχαῖον κράζειν, ᾄδειν, Thphr.*Sign.*52, 53; λύχνος καιόμενος -αῖον prob. in ib.54. **-αίτερος, -τατος,** irreg. Comp. and Sup. of ἥσυχος (q.v.). **-αστέον,** *one must keep quiet*, Ph.1.2. 2. ἡσυχαστέος, α, ον, *to be kept secret, unsaid*, Id.2.5. **-αστής,** οῦ, ὁ, *hermit*, Just. *Nov.*5.3. **-αστικός,** ή, όν, *soothing*, τρόπος, of music, Aristid. Quint.1.19; ἦθος μελοποιίας Cleonid.*Harm.*13. **-άστρια,** ἡ, *she who soothes*, gloss on εὐκηλήτειρα, Hsch., Suid., cf. *EM*59.35. **-άω,** Ep. part. ἡσυχόωσα, gloss on γαληνιόωσα, Sch.Opp.*C.*1.115. **-ῇ** (with ι *PHib.*1.73.6 (iii B.C.), *PCair.Zen.* (v. infr.)), Dor. **-ᾷ,** Adv. *stilly, quietly, softly, gently*, Pi.*P.*11.55, etc.; ἡ. κατακεῖσθαι Ar.*Pl.*692; μετέρχεσθαί τινα E.*Hipp.*444; ἔχ' ἡ. keep *quiet!* Pl.*Hp.Ma.*298c; ἡ. ἔχειν τὴν οὐράν to keep it *still*, X.*Cyn.*3.4; ἡ. γελάσαι Pl.*Phd.*115c; κοσμίως πάντα πράττειν καὶ ἡ. Id.*Chrm.*159b, etc.; ἡ. ἀναμιμνήσκεσθαι to recollect *quietly, at one's ease*, Aeschin.2.35; εὐσεβεῖν E.*Fr.* 286.9. 2. *by stealth, secretly*, Plu.*Alc.*24, Th.8.69, Plot.2.9. 18. 3. *to some extent*, Men.*Her.*20; *slightly*, φύλλον περικεχαραγμένον ἡ. Thphr.*HP*3.14.1; βηχίον ἡ. ξηρόν Hp.*Epid.*4.27; ὀξύς Theoc. 14.10 (prob. l.); ὑπόσιμος *PCair.Zen.*76.11 (iii B.C.); μακροπρόσωπος *PStrassb.*87.11 (ii B.C.); ἐνερευθές Dsc.3.131; τοῦ αὐχένος εἰς εὐώνυμον ἡ. κεκλιμένου Plu.*Alex.*4; γρυπὸς Ael.*NA*3.28. **-ία,** Ion. **-ίη,** Dor. **ἁσ-** (?), ἡ, *rest, quiet*, Od.18.22, etc.; personified in Pi.*P.*8.1, Ar. *Av.*1321 (lyr.); ἁ. φιλεῖ συμπόσιον Pi.*N.*9.48: c. gen. obj., ἡ. τῆς πολιορκίης *rest from*.., Hdt.6.135; τῆς ἡδονῆς Pl.*R.*583e; τοῦ λυπεῖσθαι ibid; περί τι ib.c; ἡ ἀπὸ τῆς εἰρήνης ἡ. D.5.25: in pl., αἱ ἡ. σήπουσι Pl. *Tht.*153c. 2. *silence, stillness*, E.*Alc.*77 (anap.); esp. of the Pythagoreans, Luc.*Vit.Auct.*3. 3. with Preps., δι' ἡσυχίης εἶναι keep *quiet*, Hdt.1.206; ἐν τῇ ἡσυχίᾳ, opp. ἐν τῷ πολέμῳ, Th.3.12; ἐν ἡ. ἔχειν τι to keep it *quiet*, not speak of it, Hdt.5.92.γ'; ἐν ἡ. ἔχειν σφέας αὐτοὺς ib.93; ἐν ἡ. διατρίβειν Hdn.2.5.2; ἐφ' ἡσυχίας Ar.*V.*1517; μένειν ἐπὶ ἡσυχίᾳ Hdn.1.13.2; κατ' ἡσυχίην πολλήν quite at one's *ease*, Hdt.1.9, cf. 7.208, D.8.12; καθ' ἡσυχίαν at *leisure*, Ar.*Lys.*1224, Th. 3.48, etc.; opp. διὰ σπουδῆς, X.*HG*6.2.28; μετὰ.. ἡσυχίας *quietly*, E. *Hipp.*205 (anap.). 4. with Verbs, a. ἡσυχίαν ἄγειν keep *quiet*, be *at peace* or *at rest*, Hdt.1.66, Pl.*Ap.*38a, Isoc.6.2, D.4.1, etc.; περὶ μὲν τῶν ἄλλων ἡ. ἦγον, ὑπὲρ δὲ.. Isoc.10.49; κινήσεων *from* movements, Pl.*Ti.*89e; keep *silent*, Hdt.5.92, E.*Andr.*143 (lyr.), Ar. *Ra.*321: pl., τὰς ἡ. ἄγειν or ἔχειν, Ath.3.114a, 11.493f. b. ἡσυχίαν ἔχειν, = ἡ. ἄγειν, but generally implying less continuance, Hdt.2.45, 7.150, X.*Cyr.*1.4.18, *HG*3.2.27; ἡ. ἔχειν πρός τινα Lys.28.7; keep *silent*, τὰ δεινὰ ἡ. ἐκτέον *about* them, D.58.60. II. *solitude, a sequestered place*, *h.Merc.*356, X.*Mem.*2.1.21.

Ἡσῠχίδες, αἱ, priestesses of the Eumenides, Call.*Fr.*123.

ἡσῠχ-ικός, ή, όν, *peaceable*, in Sup., prob. in Plot.3.8.6. **-ιμος,** Dor. **ἁσ-** (v.l. **ἡσ-**), ον, = ἥσυχος, ἁμέρα Pi.*O.*2.32. **-ιος,** Dor. **ἁσ-** (v.l. **ἡσ-**), ον, = ἥσυχος, *still, quiet, at rest*, ἡσύχιον δ' ἄρα μιν πολέμου ἔκπεμπε Il.21.598; εἰρήνα Pi.*P.*9.22; also in Prose, τρόπου ἡ. of a *quiet* disposition, Hdt.1.107; οὐδ' ἡ. ὁ σώφρων βίος Pl.*Chrm.*160b; αἱ ἡ. πράξεις ib.c; τὸ ἡ. ἦθος Id.*R.*604e; οἱ ἡ. Antipho 3.2.1; τὸ ἡ. τῆς εἰρήνης (v.l. ἥσυχον) Th.1.120: Comp. -ώτερος *more reposeful*, Phld.*Rh.* 2.260S. Adv. -ίως *h.Merc.*438, Pl.*Tht.*179e. **-ιότης,** ητος, ἡ, = ἡσυχία, Id.*Chrm.*159b, d; ἡ. τινός his *quiet disposition*, Lys.26.5. **-όομαι,** Pass., *keep quiet, be at rest*, Aq.*Am.*6.10. **-οποιός,** *silentiarius*, *Gloss.* **-ος,** Dor. **ἅσ-** (v. fin.), ον, *quiet*, ἡ. ἀνστρέφεται Hes.*Th.* 763; ἥσυχοι ἔργ' ἐνέμοντο Id.*Op.*119; ἡ... ὁδὸν ἔρχεο go thy way *in peace*, Thgn.331; ἡ. καθεύδειν Anacr.88; ἡ. θακεῖν, θάσσειν, S.*Aj.* 325, E.*Hec.*35; ἥσυχοι ἔστε Hdt.7.13, cf. 1.88; ἔχ' ἥσυχος keep *quiet*, keep *still*, Id.8.65, E.*Med.*550; μέν' ἡ. Ar.*Av.*1199, *Th.*925; γίγνεσθε E.*Cyc.*94, cf. *Ba.*1362; κατεθεᾶτο X.*Cyr.*5.3.55; ἡσύχῳ ποδὶ χωρεῖν E.*Or.*[136]; ἡσύχῳ φρενῶν βάσει, i. e. in thought, A.*Ch.*452; ἐν ἡσύχῳ *quietly*, S.*OC*82; ἡ. δορὶ *inactive* with it, E.*Fr.*998; τὸ ἡ. τῆς εἰρήνης, v.l. for ἡσύχιον, Th.1.120; νοῦς ἡ. τῶν πράξεων *at rest from*.., *free from*.., Plot.6.8.5. 2. *quiet, gentle*, of character, in Comp. -αιτέρα, A.*Eu.*223, cf. E.*Supp.*952, etc.; οἱ δ' ἀφ' ἡσύχου ποδὸς δύσκλειαν ἐκτήσαντο Id.*Med.*217; ὄμματος παρ' ἡ. A.*Supp.*199; γλῶσσα -ωτέρα S.*Ant.*1089; ὀργῇ ὑπόθες ἥσυχον πόδα *moderate* thy wrath, E. *Ba.*647; τὸ ξύνηθες ἡ. their accustomed *quietness*, Th.6.34; ἡσυχαίτερα *less severe*, Id.3.82. 3. *cautious*, πρόνοια E.*Or.*1407 (lyr.); of persons, Id.*Supp.*509. 4. of the voice, *gentle*, φωνὴ -αιτέρα X. *Cyr.*1.4.4. 5. *implicit*, Plot.6.2.20. II. Comp. and Sup. -αίτερος,

-αίτατος, A.*Eu.* l. c., Th.3.82, Pl.*Phlb.*24c, X.*Cyr.*1.4.4, 6.2.12; -ώτερος, -ώτατος, S.*Ant.*1089, Pl.*Chrm.*160a (nisi leg. -ιώτατος); -έστατος Sch.Lyc.3. III. Adv. -χως A.*Supp.*724; κάρτ' ἂν εἶχον ἡ. E.*Supp.* 305; ἡ. ναίειν Id.*Heracl.*7; *gently, cautiously,* Id.*Or.*698; *slowly,* πορεύεσθαι X.*Cyr.*5.3.53, etc.: Ion. Comp. ἡσυχέστερον Hp.*Salubr.*3, 5: Sup., ὡς ἡσυχαίτατα Pl.*Chrm.*160a: neut. ἥσυχον, Dor. ἅσυχον, as Adv., v.l. in Theoc.14.27: pl., ἅσυχα Id.2.11, 100, 6.12, *Hymn.Is.*103. (Dor. ἁσ- is dub., ἥσυχος, ἡσυχῇ, ἡσυχία codd. Pi., ἡσύχ-ιμος, -ιος, as v.l.)

ᾐσχυμμένος, v. αἰσχύνω.

ἦτα, τό, *the letter η,* Hp.*VC* 1, Pl.*Cra.*418c, *Epigr.Gr.*1095, *AP*9.385 (Steph.Gramm., v.l. ἧ): **ἧτα,** Sch.D.T.p.486 H. (Hebr. *hêth.*)

ἤτε or ἤ τε, *or also,* Il.19.148; later simply, *or,* Ascl.*Tact.*2. 7. 2. ἤ τε..ἤ τε *both..and,* Il.9.276; *either..or,* ib.11.410, 17. 42. II. *than,* Od.16.216.

ἦ τε, *surely, doubtless*; v. ἦ 1. 1. **ἦτε, ἤτην,** Att. 2 pl. and 3 dual of εἰμί (*ibo*).

ἤτοι: I. = ἦ τοι, Il.18.446, Pi.*O.*2.3, etc. II. = ἤ τοι, v. ἤ (A).

ἦτορ, τό, Ep. and Lyr. word, always in nom. or acc.; exc. dat. ἤτορι Simon.37.6 codd. Ath.:—*heart,* ἐν ἐμοὶ αὐτῇ στήθεσι πάλλεται ἦ. ἀνὰ στόμα *my heart* beats up to my throat, Il.22.452; *the seat of life, life,* φίλον ἦ. ὀλέσσαι 5.250, etc.; λῦτο γούνατα καὶ φίλον ἦ. 21.114, etc.; ἀνέψυχον φίλον ἦ. 13.84; τὰς δ' ἐσσυμένως λίπεν ἦ. Q.S.1.257 (v.l.): most freq., as *the seat of feeling, passion, desire,* etc., ἐγέλασσε δέ οἱ φίλον ἦ. Il.21.389; κατεπλήγη φίλον ἦ. 3.31; ἄχεϊ βεβολημένος ἦ. 9.9; μινύθει δέ μοι ἔνδοθεν ἦ. Od.4.467; ἐν δέ οἱ ἦ. χαίρει A.R.4.169; βοᾷ ⟨μοι⟩ μελέων ἔντοσθεν ἦ. A.*Pers.*991 (lyr.); ποτῆτος ἄασασθαι φίλον ἦ. Il. 19.307; ποθέουσα φίλον κατατήκομαι ἦ. Od.19.136; εἰ δ' ἄεθλα γαρύεν ἔλδεαι, φίλον ἦ. Pi.*O.*1.4; Κύκλωπας ὑπέρβιον ἦ. ἔχοντας Hes.*Th.*139; ἦ. ἄλκιμον Pi.*N.*8.24 (so ἐν δέ τέ οἱ κραδίῃ στένει ἄλκιμον ἦ. Il.20.169); *of the reasoning powers,* ἐν δέ οἱ ἦ. στήθεσσιν..διάνδιχα μερμήριξεν Il. 1.188, cf. 15.252; Ζηνὸς ἦ. λιταῖς ἔπεισε Pi.*O.*2.79. (Cf. OHG. *ādara,* OE. *ǣdre* 'vein', pl. 'kidneys'.)

ἠτριαῖος, α, ον, (ἦτρον) *of the stomach,* τεμάχη *Com.Adesp.*863; τὸ ἠ. *stomach, paunch,* Ar.*Fr.*318.6:—also **ἠτριαία,** ἡ, ib.506.5, Luc. *Lex.*6, Ath.1.4c.

ἤτριον, Dor. **ἄτριον,** τό, *warp* (the woof being κρόκη), Pl.*Phdr.* 268a, Theoc.18.33, *AP*6.288 (Leon., pl.): in pl., *a thin, fine cloth,* such that one could see between the threads, ἤτρια πέπλων E.*Ion* 1421; ἤτρια βύβλων *leaves made of strips of* papyrus, prob. cj. in *AP* 9.350 (Leon. Alex.); τὸ διὰ ἠτρίου ἠθημένον Gal.19.98.

ἦτρον, τό, *abdomen,* esp. the *lower part of* it, Hp.*Aph.*2.35, Pl.*Phd.* 118a, X.*An.*4.7.15, D.54.11, Arist.*HA*493ᵃ19, Sor.1.24: metaph., *belly* of a pot, Ar.*Th.*509. II. *pith* of a reed, Nic.*Th.*595.

ἧττα, ἡττάομαι, ἡττάω, ἥττων, Att. for ἡσσ-.

ἥττημα, ατος, τό, *discomfiture,* Lxx *Is.*31.8; *loss,* 1*Ep.Cor.*6.7: **ἥττησις,** εως, ἡ, = foreg., Suid. s. v. ἧττα.

ἥττων, v. ἥσσων.

ἤτω, late form for ἔστω, 3 sg. imper. of εἰμί (*sum*), *IG*3.3509, *BGU* 419.13 (iii A. D.), etc.

ἠΰ, = ἠΰτε, Anon. *in Rh.*178.4 (s. v.l., cf. Uhlig ad D.T.642.7).

ἠΰ-γένειος, -γενής, -δενδρος, -κάρηνος, -κομος, -πυργος, etc., Ep. and Lyr. for εὐ-.

ηὐξημένως, Adv. pf. part. Pass., (αὐξάνω) gloss on ζαφελῶς, Eust. 769.23.

ἠΰς, neut. ἠΰ, Ep. for ἐΰς (q. v.), *good, brave*: only masc. nom. and acc. ἠΰς, ἠΰν, neut. nom. and acc. ἠΰ (neut. pl. ἠέα prob. in Emp. 128.10); ἠ. τε μέγας τε Il.2.653, etc.; ἠ. θεράπων 16.464, 653; μένος ἠΰ 17.456, etc.

ἠΰτε, Ep. Particle, *as, like as,* ἠ. κούρη Il.2.872, etc.; ἠ. νεβρός B. 12.87; freq. in similes, Il.1.359, 2.87, etc.: after a Comp., τῷ δέ τ' ἄνευθεν ἐόντι μελάντερον ἠ. πίσσα φαίνεται [the cloud] appears to him while afar off very black, *even as* pitch, 4.277, v. Sch.; ἔχετο κλαίουσ' ἀδινώτερον, ἠΰτε κούρη with sobs coming quicker and quicker, *like* a girl, A.R.1.269; but it may = *than* in these passages; cf. εὖτε. (ἠ + I.-E. *ute* (cf. Skt. *uta*) 'also', 'even'.)

ηὐτομᾰτισμένως, Adv. pf. part. Pass., (αὐτοματίζω) *arbitrarily,* Procl. *in Prm.*p.650 S.

Ἡφαιστεῖον (on the accent v. Hdn.Gr.1.375), τό (sc. ἱερόν), *temple of Hephaestus,* Hdt.2.110, al., D.33.18; at Rome, = Lat. *Volcanal,* D.H.7.17; at Perusia, App.*BC*5.49:—also **Ἡφαιστιεῖον,** *temple of Ptah* at Memphis, *UPZ*109.13 (i B. C.).

Ἡφαίστια, τά, *festival of Hephaestus, IG*2².1158 (v/iv B. C.), And. 1.132, X.*Ath.*3.4; = Lat. *Volcanalia,* D.C.78.25.

Ἡφαιστιάς, άδος, ἡ, name of a *plaster,* Gal.12.234.

Ἡφαίστιος, ὁ (sc. μήν), a month (perh. at Lesbos), *CIG*6850.

Ἡφαιστιών, ῶνος, ὁ (sc. μήν), a month in Magnesia (Thess.), dub. in *IG*9(2).1118.

Ἡφαιστῖτις (sc. λίθος), ἡ, a precious stone, Plin.*HN*37.166.

Ἡφαιστό-δαπτα· πυρίκαυτα, Hsch. **-πονος,** ον, *wrought by Hephaestus,* ὅπλα E.*IA*1072 (lyr.).

Ἥφαιστος (Aeol. and Dor. Ἄφ- (Ἄφ-) Sapph.66, Pi.*O.*7.35, etc.), ὁ, *Hephaestus,* Il.18.391, etc.; ἔργον Ἡφαίστοιο, of a bowl, Od.4.617; κνημῖδας ὀρειχάλκοιο..Ἡφαίστου κλυτὰ δῶρα Hes.*Sc.*123; φλογὶ Ἡφαίστοιο Il.17.88, cf. Antim.44; μὰ τὸν Ἥ. *Com.Adesp.*17.35 D. 2. = Lat. *Volcanus,* D.H.2.54, Plu.2.276b, App.*BC*5.49, etc. 3. = Egypt. *Ptah, OGI*90.2 (Rosetta, ii B. C.). 4. Pythag. name for *nine, Theol.Ar.*58. II. meton. for πῦρ, *fire,* Il.2.426, Hom.*Fr.*18, S.*Ant.*123 (lyr.), 1007, cf. Chrysipp.*Stoic.*2.315, al., D.S.5.74, etc.

Ἡφαιστό-τευκτος, ον, *wrought by Hephaestus,* σέλας S.*Ph.*987, cf. Simon.202 A, D.L.1.32:—also **-τευχής,** ές, δέπας A.*Fr.*69 (lyr., leg. Ἡφαιστοτῠκές). **-χειρος,** sine expl., Choerob.*Orth.* in *AB*1380.

ἦφι, Ep. for ᾗ, Il.22.107.

ἠχάνω, = πτωχεύω, Suid. (i.e. ἰχάνω): **ἤχανεν·** εἶπεν, Hsch.

ἠχέεις, εσσα, εν, poet. for ἠχήεις, restored for ἠχήεντα in Archil. 74.8, cf. Hdn.Gr.2.925.

ἠχεῖον, τό, (ἦχος) *drum, gong,* Plu.*Crass.*23, Apollod.ap.Sch. Theoc.2.36, Procop.Gaz.*Ecphr.*p.153 B.; *tambourine,* as head-dress, Herm.Trism. in *Rev.Phil.*32.254; used for stage-thunder, Sch.Ar. *Nu.*292; as sounding-boards in the theatre, Vitr.5.5.2. II. in the lyre, = χάλκωμα, apptly. *a metallic sounding-plate,* Hsch.; so of the palate, Gal.*UP*7.5. 2. Adj. ἠχεῖον ὄργανον *sounding* instrument, Ph.1.588, cj. ib.444, 510.

ἠχέτης, ου, ὁ, Ep. **ἠχέτᾰ,** Dor. **ἀχέτας, ἀχέτᾰ,** (ἠχέω) *clear-sounding, musical, shrill,* δόναξ ἀχέτας A.*Pr.*575 (lyr.); κύκνος E.*El.*151 (lyr.); epith. of the cicada, *chirping,* ἠχέτα τέττιξ Hes.*Op.*582, *AP* 7.201 (Pamphil.); ἀχέτα τ. ib.213 (Arch.): abs., ἀχέτας, ὁ, *the chirper,* i. e. *the male cicada,* Anan.5.6, Ar.*Pax*1159 (lyr.), *Av.*1095 (lyr.), cf. Arist.*HA*532ᵇ16, 556ᵃ20: Orph.*A.*1250 has Ep. acc. ἠχέτα πορθμόν the *sounding* strait.

ἠχ-έω, Aeol. and Dor. **ἀχέω** [ᾱ]: I. intr., *sound, ring, peal,* ἠχεῖ δὲ κάρη..Ὀλύμπου Hes.*Th.*42; ὅταν ἀχήσῃ πολιὸς βυθός Mosch.*Fr.*1.4; ἀχοῦσι προσπόλων χέρες E.*Supp.*72 (lyr.); of metal, ἠχέεσκε ὁ χαλκὸς τῆς ἀσπίδος Hdt.4.200; τὰ χαλκία πληγέντα μακρὸν ἠχεῖ Pl.*Prt.*329a, cf. Men.66.4; of the grasshopper, *chirp,* Alc.39, Theoc.16.96; of the ears, *tingle,* ἠχήσει τὰ ὦτα Lxx 1*Ki.*3.11; διὰ τί ἠχεῖ ἢ διὰ τί ἐμφαίνεται; impers., of *an echo,* Arist.*APo.*98ᵃ27. 2. *suffer from noises in the ears,* Herod.Med.ap.Orib.10.40.3. II. c. acc. cogn., ἀχεῖν (ἰαχεῖν codd.) ὕμνον *to let* it *sound,* A.*Th.*869 (lyr.); κωκυτόν S.*Tr.*866; γόους Id.*Fr.*523; ὕμνους E.*Ion*883 (lyr.); χαλκέον ἄχει *sound* the cymbal! Theoc.2.36; ἐφεξῆς ἠχοῦντα αὐτά (sc. τὰ φωνήεντα) Demetr.*Eloc.*71:—Med., ἀχεῖσθαί τινα *to sound* his praises, dub. in Pi.*Fr.*75.19:—Pass., ἠχεῖται κτύπος a sound *is made,* S.*OC*1500. (Cf. sq.) **-ή,** Dor. **ἀχά,** ἡ, *sound, noise,* ἠ. ἀμφοτέρων (sc. Ἀργείων καὶ Τρώων) ἵκετ' αἰθέρα Il.13.837: freq. in dat., ἠχῇ, ὡς ὅτε κῦμα..βρέμεται 2.209; of trees, πρὸς ἀλλήλας δὲ βάλον τανυήκεας ὄζους ἠχῇ θεσπεσίῃ 16.769; πέτρη ..ἡ δέ τε ἠχῇ ἔρχεται ἐμμεμαυῖα Hes.*Sc.*438; in Trag., *cry* of sorrow, *wail,* E.*Med.*149 (lyr.), *Hipp.*585 (lyr.), cf. Nic.*Al.*304; but also σάλπιγγος ἠ. E.*Ph.*1378; ἐν ἐμοὶ ἡ ἠ. τῶν λόγων βομβεῖ Pl.*Cri.*54d, cf. *Ti.* 37b; of the grasshopper, Longus 1.23: rarely of articulate sounds, E.*Ph.*1148, Opp.*C.*1.23; *rumour, talk,* Plu.*Cat.Ma.*22. (Perh. fr. *swāgh-,* cf. ἰαχέω, OE. *swógan* 'resound', Engl. *sough.*) **-ήεις,** Dor. **ἀχ-,** εσσα, εν, *sounding, ringing, roaring,* θάλασσα Il.1.157; δώματα ἠχήεντα *high, echoing* rooms or halls, Od.4.72; δόμοι ἠχήεντες Hes.*Th.*767; χαλκός A.R.1.1236; *id.* prob. l. in A.*Th.*915 (lyr.); θρόος αὐλῶν Epic.ap.Plu.2.654f; τέττιξ *AP*7.196 (Mel.): of the ears, ἠ. ἀκουή Parm.1.35; cf. ἠχέεις. **-ημα,** Dor. **ἄχ-,** ατος, τό, *sound,* f.l. in Ph.1.444; μελῳδοῖς ἀχήμασι prob. l. for ἰαχ-, E.*IA*1045 (lyr.).

ἠχῆνες, οἱ, = πτωχοί, Hsch.; cf. ἀχήν.

ἠχ-ητής, οῦ, ὁ, = ἠχέτης, Hsch. **-ητικός,** ή, όν, *sounding, ringing,* Diom.p.497 K., Simp. *in de An.*142.17, al., Eust.918.19; gloss on βύκτης, *EM*216.50. Adv. -κῶς Hsch. s. v. καναχηδά.

ἤχθετο, impf. of ἄχθομαι. 2. impf. Pass. of ἔχθω.

ἦχι (not ἠχι), Ep. for ᾗ, Adv. *where,* Il.1.607, Call.*Ap.*91, etc.; ἦχί περ, D.P.176, 258; ἦχί τε Id.67.

ἠχικός, ή, όν, (ἦχος) = ἠχητικός, of Alcaeus, ἠ. Αἰολίδης, i. e. *singing* in Aeolic, Epigr.ap.Sch.Pi.*O.*p.10 D.

ἠχοῖ, Adv., = ἦχι, *IG*7.235.16 (Oropus, iv B. C.).

ἠχόπους, ὁ, ἡ, πουν, τό, gen. ποδος, = Lat. *sonipes,* of horses, Eust. 918.20.

ἦχος, ὁ, later form of ἠχή, Arist.*Aud.*804ᵃ30, Theoc.27.57, *Ep. Hebr.*12.19, Ael.*Tact.*35.3, etc.; τεττίγων λιγὺν ἦ. Call.*Aet.Oxy.* 2079.29 (ἦχον Pap.); παγᾶς Mosch.*Fr.*1.12; αὐλοῦ Id.2.98; οἱ τῶν πριόνων ἦχοι A.D.*Synt.*290.24; of the *sound* of words, opp. sense, Phld.*Rh.*2.258 S.; ἦχοι καὶ ψόφοι ib.1.150 S.; τῆς φωνῆς ὁ ἦ. ἐν ταῖς ἀκοαῖς παρεμένει Luc.*Nigr.*7; γραμμάτων Demetr.*Eloc.*71; ἦ. ἐν ὠσί, or abs., ἦχοι, ἦχος, *ringing in the ears,* Hp.*Coac.*189, 190, *Prorrh.*1.18, Thphr.*Sens.*19; ἦχοι ὤτων Aret.*SA*1.5. 2. *echo,* Arist.*Pr.*899ᵇ 30. 3. Gramm., *breathing,* ἦχοι ὁ μὲν δασύς, ὁ δὲ ψιλός Demetr. *Eloc.*73. 4. *voice,* τὸν ἦ. εὔτονον καὶ λαμπρὸν ἀποτελεῖ Dsc.5.17. (**ἦχος,** τό, is found in Lxx *Je.*28(51).16, dub. in *Ev.Luc.*21.25.)

ἠχοῦ, Adv., = ἦχι, prob. cj. in *h.Merc.*400.

ἠχώ, Dor. **ἀχώ,** ἡ, gen. ἠχοῦς, Dor. ἀχῶς Mosch.*Fr.*2.1: acc. ἠχώ, Dor. ἀχώ ib.3:—*echo, h.Hom.*19.21, Hes.*Sc.*279, 348, A.*Pers.*391, etc.: personified in Ar.*Th.*1059, Paus.2.35.10, Mosch.*Fr.*2, Orph. *H.*11.9. 2. generally, *ringing sound,* κτύπου γὰρ ἀχὼ χάλυβος διῇξεν ἄντρων μυχόν A.*Pr.*133 (lyr.); ἠχὼ προφωνεῖν to utter loud *cries,* S.*El.*109 (anap.); ἠ. χθόνιος E.*Hipp.*1201; ἠ. βαρεῖα προσπόλων ib.791; ὀρθία σάλπιγγος ἠ. Id.*Tr.*1267; ἅπασαν τὴν Βοιωτίην κατεῖχε ἠ. all Boeotia *rang with the noise* of mourning, Hdt.9.24; voc. Ἀχοῖ *Rumour,* Pi.*O.*14.21.

ἠχώδης, ες, *sonorous,* of the hexameter, Demetr.*Eloc.*42. 2. neut. pl. as Subst., *ringing in the ears,* Hp.*Coac.*163. 3. *full of sounds,* τῆς ἡμέρας -εστέρα ἡ νύξ Plu.2.720c; τὸ τῆς νυκτὸς ἠ. Id.*Arat.*22.

ἠῶα· ἡ κέδρος, ἐθνικῶς, Hsch. **ἠωήματι·** μιᾷ ἡμέρᾳ, Id. (leg. ἰῷ ἤματι).

ἠῶθεν, Dor. **ἀῶθεν,** Adv., (ἠώς) *from morn,* i. e. *at dawn, at break of day,* Il.11.555, 18.136, Od.1.372, etc.; ἠῶθεν μάλ' ἦρι 19.320; ἀῶθεν ἅμα δρόσῳ Theoc.15.132. 2. *to-morrow morning*, Od.15.506; *in the morning*, A.R.4.1224.

ἠῶθι, old Ep. loc. of ἠώς (q.v.).

ἠώκοιτος ὕπνος, ὁ, *morning*-sleep, Hsch., Suid.

ἠών, όνος, ἡ, contr. from ἠϊών (q.v.).

ἠῷος, ῴα, ῷον, = ἠοῖος, *at break of day*, with Verbs, ἠ. γεγονώς *h. Merc.*17; [τέττιξ] ἠ. χέει αὐδήν Hes.*Sc.*396, cf. *Op.*548; ἠῷοι ἔμελλον .. θυμὸν ἀμύξειν Call.*Aet.*3.1.10; ἠ. ἀλέκτωρ κηρύσσων *AP*5.2 (Antip. Thess.): without Verbs, ἠ. ὕπνος ib.7.726 (Leon.); ἀστήρ A.R.1.1274. 2. *eastern*, Πέρσης ἀνὴρ ἐπάγων .. τὸν ἠῷον στρατόν Hdt.7.157; εἰς ἅλα .. ἠῴην A.R.2.745.

ἠώς, ἡ, gen. ἠοῦς: dat. ἠοῖ: acc. (ἠόα A.D.*Pron.*88.5) ἠῶ, also ἠοῦν Hedyl.ap.Ath.11.473a, *AP*7.472 (Leon.); Ep. loc. ἠῶθι: never used (exc. by Gramm.) in the uncontr. forms, unless Ἀόος be read in Pi.*N.*6.52:—Att. **ἕως**, gen. and acc. ἕω: Dor. **ἀώς, ἀβώρ** (qq.v.): Aeol. **αὔως** Sapph.18, gen. αὔως *Epigr.Gr.*992 (Balbilla), acc. αὔων Sapph. *Oxy.*1787 *Fr.*1 + 2.18: Boeot. **ἄας**· ἐς αὔριον, Hsch.:—*dawn*, ἦμος δ' ἠριγένεια φάνη ῥοδοδάκτυλος Ἠώς Od.2.1; *light of day*, ὅσον τ' ἐπικίδναται ἠ. Il.7.451, etc.; esp. *morning* as a time of day, opp. μέσον ἦμαρ, δείλη, 21.111, etc.: gen. ἠοῦς *at morn, early*, 8.470, 525: acc. ἠῶ *the morning long*, Od.2.434; στάντα πρὸς πρώτην ἕω S.*OC*477; ἐξ ἠοῦς μέχρι δείλης ὀψίης Hdt.7.167; ἐξ ἠοῦς εἰς ἠοῦν Hedyl. l. c.; ἠοῦν ἐξ ἠοῦς *AP* l. c.; ἅμα ἠοῖ with, i.e. at, *daybreak*, Hdt.7.219; Att. ἅμα ἕῳ or ἅμα τῇ ἕῳ, Th.2.90, 4.72; πρὸ τῆς ἕω ib.31; Ep. ἠῶθι πρό Il.11.50, Od.5.469, 6.36; ἐπὶ τὴν ἕω Th.2.84; εἰς τὴν ἐπιοῦσαν ἕω X.*An.*1.7.1; ἐς ἀῶ *to-morrow*, Theoc.18.14. 2. *day*, Il.1.493, al., Od.19.192, Theoc.12.1, Call.*Aet.*1.1.1; ἠ. δέ μοί ἐστιν ἥδε δυωδεκάτη, ὅτε .. Il.21.80; κατήϊεν ἐς δύσιν ἠ. Musae.110; μεσάτη ἠ. Orph.*A.*649. 3. *life*, Q.S.10.431; φῶς λίπες ἠοῦς *IG*14.1853. 4. *the East*, πρὸς ἠῶ τ' ἠέλιόν τε Il.12.239 (*South* acc. to Str.10.2.12); ἀπὸ ἠοῦς πρὸς ἑσπέρην Hdt.2.8; τὰ πρὸς τὴν ἠῶ ibid.; τὰ πρὸς ἠῶ τε καὶ ἥλιον ἀνατέλλοντα Id.4.40, cf. Pl.*Lg.*760d, etc.; πρὸς ἕω τῆς πόλεως, τοῦ ποταμοῦ, *to the East* of .., X.*HG*5.4.49, Plu.*Luc.*27; πρὸ ἠοῦς τοῦ βωμοῦ *IG* 7.235.45 (Oropus, iv B.C.). II. pr. n., Ἠώς *the goddess of dawn*, Il.11.1, Hes.*Th.*372, 378, etc. (Cf. Skt. *uṣā́s* 'dawn', Lat. *aurora*, etc.)

Θ θ, **θῆτα**, τό, indecl., ninth (later eighth) letter of the Gr. alphabet: as numeral θ' = ἐννέα, ἔνατος, but ͵θ = 9,000: abbreviation for θάνατος (or ἀπέθανε, τέθνηκε, θανατωτέον) found in certain Ptolemaic Mss. of Hp., acc. to Gal.17(1).612, cf. Pers.4.13, Mart.7.37, Wessely *Schrifttaf. zur ält. lat. Paläogr.* No.8 (ii A.D.), *PFay.*105 iii 26 (ii A.D.), Dessau *Inscr.Lat.Sel.*5140, etc.; v. θῆτα.

-θα, insep. affix in adverbial forms, e.g. ἔνθα.

θαάσσω, Ep. form of θάσσω, used only in pres. and impf., *sit*, λιπὼν ἕδος ἔνθα θαάσσεν Il.9.194, cf. 15.124; οὐδὲ ἔοικε .. ἐν δαιτὶ θαασσέμεν Od.3.336, cf. *h.Merc.*172; μετ' ἀθανάτοισι θαάσσεις ib.468.

θαβακόν (i.e. θάϝακον)· θακὸν ἢ ὁμορόν (fort. θᾶκον ἢ θρόνον), Hsch.

θάεο [ᾱ], imper. of *θάομαι.

θαέομαι, Dor. for θηέομαι (Ion. form of θεάομαι), Pi.*P.*8.45: aor. 1 θαήσατο *Lyr.Adesp.*40; imper. θάησαι Epigr.ap.Phan.Hist.12; cf. *θάομαι.

θαζός, ή, όν, *seated*, Cyr.: **θάζω**, *to be seated*, Id.

θάημα [θᾱ], ατος, τό, Dor. for θέαμα (θήημα), αἰπολικὸν θάημα Theoc.1.56, cf. Aus.*Ep.*10.33.

θαητός, ή, όν, Dor. for θηητός (q.v.).

θαιραῖος, α, ον, *for axles*, ξύλα Poll.1.253.

θαιροδύτης [ῠ], ου, ὁ, pl., *rings through which the reins pass*, Hsch.

θαιρός, ὁ, *pivot of a door* or *gate*, ῥῆξε δ' ἀπ' ἀμφοτέρους θαιρούς Il.12.459, cf. Q.S.3.27, Agath.1.10. II. *axle* of a chariot, S.*Fr.*596. (Perh. for θϝᾰρ-yos, cf. θύρα.)

θαΐς, ΐδος, ἡ, a kind of *bandage*, Gal.18(1).792.

θᾱκαθαλπάς, άδος, ἡ, *sitting hen*, *Lyr.Alex.Adesp.*4.22 (fort. θακοθ–).

θᾱκ-εῖον, τό, *seat*, *IG*2².1672.145 (iv B.C.). **-εύω**, = ἀποπατῶ, Plu.*Lyc.*20, Artem.1.2. **-έω**, Ion. and Dor. **θωκέω**, impf. ἐθάκει Cratin.239: Dor. fut. θωκησῶ Epich.99.1:—*sit*, ἐν θρόνῳ θωκέων Hdt.2.173; θωκεῖτε Sophr.60; ἀνωτέρω θακῶν .. Ζεύς A.*Pr.*315; ἥσυχος θακεῖ S.*Aj.*325; κόραι θάκουν (impf.) .. ἤνουν τε (Herm. θάκους .. ἤνουν, om. τε) E.*Hec.*1153: c. acc. cogn., θακοῦντι παγκρατεῖς ἕδρας *sitting on* imperial throne, A.*Pr.*391; of suppliants, S.*OT*20, *Aj.*1173; βώμιος θακεῖς E.*Heracl.*239. **-ημα**, ατος, τό, *sitting*, esp. as a suppliant, S.*OC*1160, 1179. 2. *seat*, Πανὸς -ήματα E.*Ion*492 (lyr.). **-ησις**, εως, ἡ, *means of sitting, seat*, prob. in S.*OC*9.

θᾶκος, Ion. and Ep. **θῶκος**, Ep. also **θόωκος**, ὁ, *seat, chair*, Νυμφέων καλοὶ χοροὶ ἠδὲ θόωκοι Od.12.318; θεῶν δ' ἐξίκετο θώκους Il.8.439; θῶκοι ἀμπαυστήριοι *seats* for resting, Hdt.1.181, cf. 9.94; κραιπνόσυτος θᾶκος, of the winged car of the Oceanids, A.*Pr.*282 (anap.); θᾶκος Διός, of Dodona, ib.831; σεμνοὶ θ., of the palace, Id.*Ag.*519; εἰς παλαιὸν θᾶκον ὀρνιθοσκόπον ἵζων, of Teiresias, S.*Ant.*999; νεκροῖσι γείτονας θάκους ἔχων E.*HF*1097; θάκους θάσσειν Id.*Tr.*138 (anap.); τῶν θ. τοῖς πρεσβυτέροις ὑπανίστασθαι Ar.*Nu.*993; ἐκαθήμεθα ἐπὶ τῶν θ. Aeschin.Socr.2. 2. *chair of office*, τὸν θᾶκον τὸν ἐμὸν παράδος Σοφοκλεῖ τηρεῖν Ar.*Ra.*1515. 3. *privy*, Hp.*Epid.*7.47, 84 (in form θῶκος), Thphr.*Char.*14.5, Mnesith.ap.Orib.8.38.11. II. in Hom., *sitting in council, a council*, like βουλή, οὔτε .. ἀγορὴ γένετ' οὔτε θόωκος Od.2.26; ἐς θῶκον πρόμολον δήμοιό τε φῆμιν 15.468; θῶκόνδε καθίζανον 5.3; ἐν θώκῳ κατήμενος sitting in *council*, Hdt.6.63. (Cf. θάβακος, θάσσω.)

θᾰλᾰμ-αῖος, ον, *shut up, kept at home*, γυνή Ph.2.297. **-αξ**, ᾶκος, ὁ, = θαλαμίτης, Ar.*Ra.*1074. **-ευμα**, ατος, τό, = θαλάμη, θάλαμος II, Κουρήτων E.*Ba.*120 (lyr.), *Supp.Epigr.*2.461 (pl., i B.C.). **-ευτός**, ή, όν, *hidden in a* θάλαμος, θησαυρὸς Μουσᾶν Tim.*Pers.*245. **-εύτρια**, ἡ, = νυμφεύτρια, *bridesmaid*, Poll.3.41. **-εύω**, *lead into the* θάλαμος, i.e. *take to wife*, Hld.4.6:—Pass., of women, *to be shut up, kept at home*, Aristaenet.2.5; *to be taken to wife*, Ph.1.323. **-η**, ἡ, *lurking-place, den, lair*, πουλύποδος θαλάμης ἐξελκομένοιο Od.5.432, cf. Arist.*HA* 599ᵇ15, Numen.ap.Ath.7.315b; of the σωλήν and polypus, Arist.*HA* 535ᵃ17, 549ᵇ32; of the *nest* of the fish φωλίς, ib.621ᵇ9; of the Theban dragon's *den*, E.*Ph.*931 (pl.); of the *cave* of Trophonius, Id.*Ion* 394 (pl.); of the *grave*, Id.*Supp.*980 (anap., pl.); of the *hive* or *nest* of bees, in pl., *AP*6.239 (Apollonid.), 9.404 (Antiphil.); cj. in E.*Ba.*561 (v. θάλαμος II). 2. of *cavities* in the body, Hp. *de Arte* 10 (pl.); *ventricle* of the heart, Arist.*Somn.Vig.*458ᵃ17; of *the pores* of sponges, Id.*HA* 548ᵃ28; *the nostrils*, Poll.2.79; αὕτη τῶν κοιλιῶν ἡ οἷον θ. of the (Galenic) optic *thalamus*, Gal.*UP*16.3; of *recesses* in the cranial bones, ib.11.3; of the eye-*socket*, Steph. *in Hp.*1.93D. II. = θάλαμος III, Luc. *Nav.*2. **-ηγός**, όν, (ἄγω) *carrying* θάλαμοι: as Subst., θ., ὁ, *Egyptian house-boat* or *barge*, Str.17.1.15 (also πλοῖον θ. *POxy.*1650.20 (i/ii A.D.); and θαλαμηγός (sc. ναῦς), ἡ, ib.1738.2 (iii A.D.)); *state-barge*, Callix.1, D.S.1.85; θαλαμηγόν, τό, App.*Prooem.*10. **-ηϊάδης**, ου, ὁ, *son of the* θαλάμη or *hole*, comic patron. of the tunny, Matro *Conv.*53. **-ήϊος**, η, ον (-ος, ον, A.R.4.1130), *of* or *belonging to a* θάλαμος, *fit for building one*, δοῦρα Hes.*Op.*807. II. *bridal*, εὐνή A.R. l. c.; ὕμνος Epigr.ap.Luc.*Symp.*41.

θᾰλᾰμηπολ-έω, *to be a* θαλαμηπόλος, Sch.Lyc.132. 2. *put to the stud*, of animals, Opp.*C.*1.393. **-ος**, ἡ, (parox.) *attendant in a lady's chamber, waiting-maid*, Od.7.8, 23.293; but, = ταμίη (cf. θάλαμος I.2 b), A.*Th.*359 (lyr.). 2. θ., ὁ, in later Gr., *eunuch of the bed-chamber*, Plu.*Alex.*30, Agath.1.7; of the Galli or *eunuch-priests of Cybele*, *AP*6.220 (Diosc.); but also ἡ, *a priestess of Cybele*, Rhian.67.1. II. rarely, *bridegroom*, S.*OT*1210 (lyr.). III. Adj., *bridal*, ὄρφνη Musae.231; epith. of Aphrodite, *APl.*4.177 (Phil.).

θᾰλᾰμ-ίας, ου, ὁ, = θαλαμίτης, App.*BC*5.107, Them.*Or.*15.195b. **-ιός**, ά, όν (oxyt., Arc.40.13), *of* or *belonging to the* θάλαμος: as Subst., I. θαλαμιός, ὁ, = θαλαμίτης, Th.4.32 (gen. pl., perh. fr. θαλαμίας), S.*Fr.*1052 (dub.). II. θαλαμιά, Ion. -ιή (sc. κώπη), ἡ, *the oar of the* θαλαμίτης, Ar.*Ach.*553 (pl.): pl., *IG*2².1604.55. 2. (sc. ὀπή) *the hole in the ship's side, through which this oar worked*, διὰ θαλαμιῆς διελεῖν τινα to place a man so that his upper half projected through *this hole*, Hdt.5.33: metaph., Ar.*Pax* 1232. **-ίς**, ίδος, ἡ, = θαλαμηπόλος, *An.Ox.*2.376. **-ίτης** [ῑ], ου, ὁ, (θάλαμος III) *one of the rowers on the lowest bench* of a trireme, who had the shortest oars and the least pay, Sch.Ar.*Ra.*1106. **-όνδε**, Adv. *to the bed-chamber*, Od.21.8, 22.109, 161.

θᾰλᾰμοποιός, όν, *preparing the bed-chamber*: Θαλαμοποιοί, name of a play of Aeschylus, Poll.7.122.

θάλᾰμος [θᾰ], ὁ, *an inner room* or *chamber, surrounded by other buildings*: freq. in Hom., 1. generally, *women's apartment, inner part of the house*, like μυχός, Il.3.142, 174, Od.4.121, etc.: in pl., Il.18.492; ἐκ τῶν ἀνδρεώνων .. ἐς τοὺς θ. Hdt.1.34. 2. *a special chamber in this part of the house*, a. *bedroom*, esp. of the lady of the house, Il.3.423, al., Hdt.1.12, 3.78, Plu.*Alc.*23; esp. *bride-chamber*, Il.11.227, Pi.*P.*2.33 (pl.), S.*Tr.*913, E.*Hipp.*540 (lyr., pl.); also, *bedroom of an unmarried son*, Od.1.425, 19.48. b. *store-room*, esp. for valuables, Il.24.191, Od.21.8, X.*Oec.*9.3, etc.; ὄλβου διοίγων θάλαμον E.*Fr.*285.8. c. generally, *chamber, room*, Od.23.192, *POxy.*1144.2 (i/ii A.D.). 3. *house, mansion* (not in Hom.), Pi.*O.*5.13 (pl.), 6.1; βασιλικοὶ θ. E.*Ion* 486 (lyr.). II. metaph., ὁ παγκοίτας θ., of *the grave*, S.*Ant.*804 (anap.); τυμβήρης θ., of the prison of Danae, ib.947 (lyr.); θάλαμοι ὑπὸ γῆς the *realms* below, A.*Pers.*624; γᾶς θάλαμοι E.*HF*807 (lyr.); θ. Περσεφονείας Id.*Supp.*1022 (lyr.); θ. Ἀμφιτρίτας, of the sea, S.*OT*195 (lyr.); πολυδένδρεσσιν Ὀλύμπου θαλάμοις E.*Ba.*561 (lyr., θαλάμαις cj. Barnes); ἀρνῶν θ. *folds* or *pens*, Id.*Cyc.*57 (lyr.). III. *the lowest, darkest part of the ship, the hold*, Timae.114, Poll.1.87; cf. θαλάμη II. IV. used of *certain mystic shrines* or *chapels*, sacred to Apis, Ael.*NA*11.10, cf. Plin.*HN*8.185; *the innermost shrine*, Luc.*Syr.D.*31.

θάλασσα [θᾰ], Att. **-ττα** *IG*1².57 (but θάλασσα 2².236 (338/7 B.C.)), ἡ:—*sea*, Il.2.294, etc.: freq. of the Mediterranean *sea*, ἥδε ἡ θ. Hdt.1.1, 185, 4.39, etc.; ἡ παρ' ἡμῖν θ. Pl.*Phd.*113a; ἡ θ. ἡ καθ' ἡμᾶς Plb.1.3.9; ἡ ἐντὸς καὶ κ. ἡ. λεγομένη θ. Str.2.5.18; ἡ ἔσω θ. Arist.*Mu.*393ᵇ29; ἡ ἔξω θ., of the Ocean, Id.*Mete.*350ᵃ22; ἡ Ἀτλαντικὴ θ. Id.*Mu.*392ᵇ22; ἡ μεγάλη θ. Plu.*Alex.*73; of a *salt lake*, Arist.*Mete.*351ᵃ9; ἐς θάλασσαν τὴν τοῦ Εὐξείνου πόντου Hdt.2.33; πέλαγος θαλάσσης A.R.2.608; κατὰ θάλασσαν by *sea*, opp. πεζῇ, Hdt.5.63; opp. κατὰ γῆς, Th.7.28 codd.; κατά τε γῆν καὶ κατὰ θ. Pl.*Mx.*241a; χέρσον καὶ θ. ἐκπερῶν A.*Eu.*240; τῆς θ. ἀνθεκτέα ἐστί one must engage in *maritime affairs*, Th.1.93; οἱ περὶ τὴν θ. *sea*-faring men, Arist.*HA* 598ᵇ24, cf. *Pol.*1291ᵇ20; θ. καὶ πῦρ καὶ γυνή—τρίτον κακόν Men.*Mon.*231, cf. 264: metaph., κακῶν θ. *a sea* of troubles, A.*Th.*758 (lyr.); ὁ Κρὴς τὴν θ. (sc. ἀγνοεῖ), of pretended ignorance, Suid. 2. *sea-water*, ἔστω ἐν χαλκῷ ἡ θ. Hp.*Coac.*427, cf. Diph.Siph.ap.Ath.3.121d, Moschio ib.5.208a, Plb.16.5.4, Dsc.2.83. 3. *well of salt water*, said to be produced by a stroke of

Poseidon's trident, in the Acropolis at Athens, Hdt.8.55; θ. Ἐρεχθηΐς Apollod.3.14.1. 4. *channel*, Lxx3*Ki*.18.32. 5. χαλκῆ θ. *laver*, ib.2*Ki*.8.8. 6. θ. κοίλη wooden *theatre*, Paus.Gr.*Fr*.208 (= *Com.Adesp*.864).—For the Lacon. form σάλασσα, v. θαλασσομέδων.

θᾰλασσ-αίγλη, ἡ, *bhang*, *Cannabis sativa*, Plin.*HN*24.164. **-αῖος**, α, ον, = θαλάσσιος, δῖναι Simon.57.4, cf. Pi.*P*.2.50: **θαλάσσειος**, θεά *Trag.* or *Com.Adesp.* in *PLit.Lond*.84.16; dub. in Orib.14.62.1. 2. *dyed purple*, Tryph.345. **-ερός**, ὁ, a kind of *eyesalve*, Gal.12.781, etc. **-εύς**, έως, ὁ, *fisherman*, Hsch. **-εύω**, *to be at sea*, νῆες τοσοῦτον χρόνον ἤδη θαλασσεύουσαι Th.7.12, cf. App.*BC*1.62; τὰ θαλαττεύοντα τῆς νεὼς μέρη the parts *under water*, Plu.*Luc*.3. 2. *use nautical expressions*, Heraclit.*All*.5. **-ία**, ἡ, = ἀνδρόσακες, Ps.-Dsc.3.133.

θᾰλασσίγονος [ῐ], ον, *sea-born*, Nonn.*D*.13.458 (v.l. θαλασσο-).

θᾰλασσ-ίδιος, α, ον, = θαλάσσιος, χῶροι Hdt.4.199. **-ίζω**, *resemble sea-water*, Diph.Siph. ap. Ath.3.92a, Dem.Ophth. ap. Aët.7.53; τὴν γεῦσιν Xenocr.60. 2. *wash in sea-water*, *PHolm*.17.2. **-ιος**, later Att. **-ττιος**, α, ον, also ος, ον E.*IT*236: (θάλασσα):—*of*, *in*, *on*, or *from the sea*, οὔ σφι θ. ἔργα μεμήλει Il.2.614; κορῶναι εἰνάλιαι, τῇσίν τε θ. ἔργα μέμηλεν Od.5.67; θ. βίος Archil.51; χέλυς Alc.51; θ. ἀνέμων ῥιπαί, κλύδων, Pi.*N*.3.59, E.*Med*.28; Χάριτες *Lyr.Adesp*.85.11; ὁ θ. [Ποσειδῶν] Ar.*Pl*.396; of animals, opp. χερσαῖα, Hdt.2.123, cf. Pl. *Euthd*.298d, Arist.*HA*487^{a}26; πεζοί τε καὶ θ. landsmen and *seamen*, A.*Pers*.558 (lyr.); θ. ἐκρίψαί τινα to throw one *into the sea*, S.*OT*1411; θ. νεκρός, of one drowned, Thgn.1229; πλοῖον θ. *sea-going* vessel, *POxy*.1288.6 (iv A. D.). 2. *skilled in the sea*, *nautical*, Hdt.7.144; γεωργοὶ καὶ οὐ θ. Th.1.142. 3. *like the sea*, in colour, τῇ χρόᾳ Plu.2.395b; = ἁλουργής, στρώματα D.S.34/5.2.35. II. θαλάσσιαι, αἱ, name of certain priestesses at Cyzicus, *CIG*3657.4. **-ίτης** [ῑ] οἶνος, ὁ, wine *sunk in the sea*, to ripen it, Plin.*HN*14.78.

θᾰλασσο-βᾰφέω, *dye purple*, Ph.Byz.*Mir*.2.4 (Pass.). **-βαφής**, ές, gloss on ἁλιπόρφυρος, Sch.Od.6.53. **-βίωτος** [ῐ], ον, *living on* or *by the sea*, App.*Pun*.89:—also **-βῐος**, ον, Sch.Opp.*H*.2.1. **-βρᾰχής**, ές, *soaked in brine*, Antyll.ap.Orib.8.12.3. **-γενής**, ές, (γενέσθαι) *sea-born*, κήρυκες Archestr.*Fr*.56.7. **-γράφος** [γρᾰ], ον, *describing the sea*, Tz.*H*.1.843.

θᾰλασσ-οδο-μέτρης, ου, ὁ, *ship's log*, Tz.*H*.12.977.

θᾰλασσο-ειδής, ές, *like the sea*, *sea-green*, Hp.*Vid.Ac*.1, Democr. Eph.1, Str.17.1.35; χρῶμα Hero *Aut*.30.6. **-κλυστος**, ον, *dashed by the sea*, Sch.Barocc.S.*Aj*.696 (= 704 ed. T. Johnson, Oxon. 1705). **-κοπέω**, (κόπτω) *strike the sea with the oar*, *make a splash*, metaph. in Ar.*Eq*.830, Lib.*Decl*.26.18. **-κράμβη**, ἡ, *sea-kale*, *Gp*.12.1.1, Gal.6.354. **-κρᾰτέω**, *to be master of the sea*, Hdt.3.122, Th.7.48, Plb.1.7.6, Phylarch.1J.:—Pass., *to be beaten at sea*, Demetr.Com. Vet.2. **-κρᾰτία**, ἡ, *empire of the sea*, ἡ Μίνω θ. Str.1.3.2. **-κράτωρ** [κρᾰ], ορος, ὁ, ἡ, *master of the sea*, Hdt.5.83, Th.8.63, X.*HG*1.6.2. **-μᾰχέω**, *fight by sea*, Vett.Val.354.26. **-μάχος** [μᾰ], ον, *fighting by sea*, A.D.*Adv*.188.26, Vett.Val.18.35. **-μέδων**, οντος, ὁ, *lord of the sea*, Nonn.*D*.21.95: Lacon. fem. **σαλασσομέδοισα** Alcm. 84. **-μελι**, ιτος, τό, *drink of brine and honey*, Dsc.5.12. **-μῐγής**, ές, *mixed with sea-water*, Hsch. s.v. ἁλικίαves. **-μοθος**, ον, *fighting with the sea*, Nonn.*D*.39.370. **-νόμος**, ον, *dwelling in the sea*, Emp. 76.1, Nonn.*D*.37.265. **-παις**, παιδος, ὁ, ἡ, *child of the sea*, Lyc. 892. **-πλαγκτος**, ον, (πλάζω) *made to wander o'er the sea*, *sea-tost*, of ships, A.*Pr*.467; of a corpse, E.*Hec*.782:—also **-πλάνητος** [πλᾰ], ον, Sch.Opp.*H*.4.582. **-πληκτος**, ον, (πλήσσω) *sea-beaten*, νῆσος A.*Pers*.307. **-πλοος**, ον, contr. **-πλους**, ουν, gloss on ποντοπόρος, Hsch. **-ποιός**, όν, *sea-making*, [δύναμις] Porph.ap.Eus. *PE*3.11. **-πορέω**, *traverse the sea*, Call.*Ep*.59. **-πόρος**, ον, *sea-faring*, *AP*6.27.7 (Theaet.), 9.376; ὑμέναιοι Musae.2. **-πόρφῠρος**, ον, = ἁλιπόρφυρος, Suid. s.v. ἁλουργά, *AB*379. **-πρᾰσον**, τό, *sea-weed*, Ath.Mech.18.5. **-σημος**, ον, = θαλασσοπόρφυρος, *Tab. Defix.Aud*.41 *A* 1 (Megara, i A. D.). **-τείχιστος**, ον, gloss on ἁλιερκής, Sch.Pi.*O*.8.34. **-τοκος**, ον, *sea-born*, Nonn.*D*.39.341.

θᾰλασσουργ-έω, *to be busy with the sea*, Plb.6.52.1, Str.6.1.1, Max. Tyr.22.3, etc. **-ία**, ἡ, *business on the sea*, *fishing*, etc., Hp.*Vict*. 3.68 (pl.), Them.*Or*.24.305d. **-ός**, ὁ, *one who works on the sea*, *a fisherman* or *sailor*, Charon 10, X.*Oec*.16.7, Plb.10.8.5: as Adj., θ. ἔθνος Philostr.*VA*4.32.

θᾰλασσ-όω, Att. **-ττόω**, *make* or *change into sea*, ἠπείρους Arist.*Mu*. 400^{a}27; Νεῖλος θ. τὴν Αἴγυπτον Hld.2.28. 2. *purify with sea-water*, Hsch. (Pass.). II. Pass., ναῦς θαλαττοῦται she *leaks*, Plb.16.15.2. 2. of wine, *to be mixed with sea-water*, Thphr.*CP*6.7.6; οἶνοι τεθαλασσωμένοι Ath.1.32d, cf. Gal.13.247 (sg.), *POxy*.468 (iii A. D.). III. Med., *to be a sea-faring man*, Luc.*Ner*.1. **-ώδης**, ες, = θαλασσοειδής, λίμνη Hanno *Peripl*.14; gloss on οἰδματόεις, Sch. Opp.*H*.5.273. **-ωσις**, εως, ἡ, *inundation*, *submergence*, Thphr.*Fr*. 30.3, Ph.2.174.

θάλαττα, -ττεύω, -ττιος, etc., Att. for θάλασσα, etc.

θάλεα [ᾰ], Lacon. **σάλ-** (v. infr.), τά, *good cheer*, *happy thoughts*, of the sleeping Astyanax, θαλέων ἐμπλησάμενος κῆρ Il.22.504; ἐν σάλεσσι πολλοῖς ἥμενος Alcm.10; θαλέεσσιν ἀνατρέφειν τινά Call.*Fr*. *anon*.31.—In form and accent pl. of θάλος, in meaning closer to θάλεια, θαλία.

θᾰλέθω, poet. for θάλλω (cf. θαλέω), *bloom*, *thrive*, used by Hom. only in part., θάμνος ἐλαίης.. θαλέθων Od.23.191, cf. Ibyc.1.6, A.R. 2.843; βίου θαλέθοντος Emp.20.3; of men, ἠΐθεοι θαλέθοντες Od.6.63; θαλέθοντα τόκον *IG*14.1363; θαλέθεσκες ἐν εἴαρι *AP*11.374 (Maced.); αἰεὶ θαλέθοντι βίῳ *Lyr.Adesp*.98 (= *Trag.Adesp*.373); σύες θαλέθοντες ἀλοιφῇ *swelling*, *wantoning* in fat, Il.9.467, cf. 23.32: c. acc., ποίην λειμῶνες θαλέθουσιν Theoc.25.16.

θάλεια [θᾰ], ἡ, *rich*, *plentiful*, : in Ep. always of banquets, θεῶν ἐν δαιτὶ θαλείῃ Od.8.76, Hes.*Op*.742; θεοῦ ἐς δαῖτα θάλειαν Od. 3.420, cf. 8.99, Il.7.475; so later, Pherecr.152; πίνειν ἐν δαιτὶ θ. Hermipp.82.11; θ. ἑορτὴν ἀγάγωμεν Anacr.54; Δαὶς θ., πρεσβίστη θεῶν S.*Fr*.605; μοῖραν θάλειαν *a goodly* portion, Pi.*N*.10.53; θ. ἥβα *bloom of youth*, B.3.89; without δαίς, dub. cj. for θαλάσσης in Alex. Aet.3.15: in form and accent (cf. ἐλάχεια, λίγεια and Eust.742.36) a fem. Adj., as if from θαλύς: masc. θαλείοις στέφεσιν Emp.112.6. II. as Subst., = θαλία I, in pl., Pl.*R*.573d (nisi hoc legend.). 2. v. θαλλία II. III. as pr. n., Θάλεια, ἡ, one of the Muses, Hes.*Th*.77; later, the Muse of Comedy, Θαλίη *AP*9.505, cf. Plu.2.744f, 746c. 2. one of the Graces, *patroness of festive meetings*, ib.778d; Θαλίη in Hes.*Th*.909. IV. Pythag. name for *six*, *Theol.Ar*.38.

θᾰλερόμμᾰτος, ον, *bright-eyed*, αἰθήρ Orph.*H*.80.5.

θᾰλεροποιός, όν, *making full of bloom*, Sch.Hes.*Th*.138.

θᾰλερός, ά, όν, (θάλλω, θαλεῖν) *stout*, *sturdy*, *buxom*, in Hom. of persons, θ. αἰζηοί, πόσις, παρακοίτης, Il.3.26, 8.190, 6.430, cf. Pi.*N*. 1.71; γόνος *h.Ven*.104; τοκεύς Hes.*Th*.138. 2. *blooming*, *fresh*, θ. γάμος the marriage *of a youthful pair*, Od.6.66, 20.74; Ὀϊκλῆος θ. λέχος εἰσαναβᾶσα Hes.*Cat.Oxy*.2075.25; θαλερὸς ἥβης χρόνος E.*El*. 20; πρωθήβης ἔαρος θαλερώτερος Alex.Aet.3.7; of plants, ἀμάρακος Chaerem.14.16; ἄνθεον *IG*12(7).410.17 (Amorgos). II. of parts of the body, *stout*, *sturdy*, μηρώ Il.15.113; χαίτη *luxuriant* mane, 17.439; θ. ἀλοιφή *rich* fat, Od.8.476: hence generally, θ. κατὰ δάκρυ χέουσα shedding *big* tears, Il.6.496, cf. 24.9, 794, etc.; θ. δέ οἱ ἔκπεσε δάκρυ 2.266; θαλερώτερα δάκρυα Mosch.4.56 (so θαλερώτερον ἔκλαεν Theoc.14.32); θ. γόος the *thick and frequent* sob, Od.10.457; θ. φωνή *strong* voice, Il.17.696, al.; μῦθοι *impassioned*, *torrential*, A.R.4.1072; θαλερώτερον πνεῦμα *a more genial* wind, dub. in A.*Th*.707 (lyr.); θαλερὸν πνεῦμα *thick*, i. e. *laboured* or *rapid*, breathing, v.l. for θολερὸν πν. in Hp.*Prorrh*.1.39, cf. Gal.16.596; θ. ὕπνος *deep* sleep, E.*Ba*. 692. 2. later θ. πρόσωπον, glossed by εὐεκτικὸν καὶ εὔχρουν, Gal. 16.596; τὸ σῶμα τοῦ ζῴου, μέχρι μὲν ἔμπνουν ἐστὶ καὶ θ. Plu.2.955c, cf. E.*Supp*.62 (lyr.).

θᾰλερῶπις, ιδος, ἡ, (ὤψ) = θαλερόμματος, Ἠριγένεια *AP*7.204 (Agath.).

θᾰλέω, Dor. for θηλέω (q.v.).

θᾰλέω, = θαλέθω, Q.S.11.96 codd., Nonn.*D*.16.78; θαλέων Hp. *Insomn*.90; θαλέεσκε v.l. for θαλέθεσκε in Mosch.2.67.

Θαλῆς, ὁ, gen. Θάλεω, dat. Θαλῇ, acc. Θαλῆν; gen. also Θαλοῦ Str. 1.1.11; and in Poets Θάλητος, acc. Θάλητα, Call.*Fr*.94, 96, Epigr.ap. D.L.1.34, 39:—*Thales* of Miletus, Hdt.1.74, etc.

θᾰλία, Ion. **-ίη**, ἡ, (θάλλω) *abundance*, *good cheer*, τρέφεται θαλίῃ ἐνὶ πολλῇ Il.9.143, 285: in pl., *festivities*, μετ' ἀθανάτοισι θεοῖσι τέρπεται ἐν θαλίῃς Od.11.603, cf. *h.Merc*.56, Hes.*Op*.115, Archil.9, Xenoph. 1.12 (sg.), Pi.*O*.7.94, *Trag.Adesp*.397 (anap.), Ar.*Nu*.309, *Pax* 780 (both lyr.), *Av*.733 (anap.); εἶναι ἐν θαλίῃσι Hdt.3.27; θ. κισσοφόροι E.*Ba*.384 (lyr.); of a *funeral-feast*, ἀμφ' ὁσίῃ θαλίῃ.. ἄνακτος Orac. ap.Plu.*Arat*.53. II. v. θαλλία II. III. as pr. n., v. θάλεια III.

θᾰλιάζω, *enjoy oneself*, *make merry*, Plu.2.746f, al. (θαλειάζω ib. 357e); ἑορτὴν θ. Polyaen.4.15.

θάλικτρον, τό, prob. *Thalictrum minus*, *meadow-rue*, Dsc.4.97 (sed fort. θαλίητρον: **θαλίηκτρον** Gal.11.884).

θαλιοποιοί, οἱ, *leather-covered-box-makers*, Hsch. (Cf. σαλία, θολία.)

θαλλία, ἡ, = κάππαρις, Dsc.2.173. II. *foliage*, *leaf-buds* or *twigs*, esp. of the olive, Thphr.*CP*5.1.3 (cod. Urb.), Ath.11.459, Dsc. 5.75 (v.l. in 2.70), Antyll.ap.Orib.10.23.20, Aët.6.29: pl., Thphr. *CP*1.20.3 (θαλλίας cod. Urb., θαλείας vulg. as in 3.5.1 (sg.), Porph. *Antr*.33); in codd. sts. θαλία, as Thphr.*HP*2.2.12, 2.3.3, v.l. in *CP* 5.1.3; βάτου θαλία Sor.2.41.

θάλλῐνος, η, ον, (θαλλός) *of* or *for young shoots*, στέφανος *IG*12(1). 162.3 (Rhodes); ἀγγεῖα Sch.Ar.*Av*.799: **θαλλῑνώδης**, ες, *covered with shoots*, of the Wooden Horse, Cyr.

θαλλίον, τό, in pl., *presents* (cf. θαλλός III), *POxy*.1481.7 (ii A. D.): pl. written θάλεια, Wilcken *Chr*.323.20 (ii A. D.).

θαλλός, ὁ, (θάλλω) *young shoot*, *young branch*, Od.17.224, S.*El*. 422, Theoc.4.45, etc.: generally, *branch*, *Gp*.11.10.3; esp. of the olive (cf. Tim.*Lex*. s.v. θαλλός), ἐστεφανῶσθαι ἐλαίης θαλλῷ Hdt.7.19; ἐλαίας θ. E.*IT*1101 (lyr.); and freq. without ἐλαίας, A.*Ch*.1035, S. *OC*474, etc.; ἱκτὴρ θ. E.*Supp*.10, cf. A.*Ch*.1035; θ. χρυσοῦς *IG*1^2.287. 200; στεφανῶσαι θαλλοῦ στεφάνῳ as a mark of distinction, Aeschin. 3.187, cf. *IG*2^2.207, 229, Phld.*Ind.Sto*.68, etc.; στέφανος θαλλοῦ χρυσοῦς *IG*2^2.1388.33; στέφανος τὸ νικητήριον θαλλοῦ Pl.*Lg*.943c; prov., θαλλὸν προσείοντες ἄγουσι they entice, as one does cattle, by holding out *a green bough*, Id.*Phdr*.230d; θαλλῷ προδειχθέντι ἀκολουθεῖν Luc. *Herm*.68, cf. Lib.*Ep*.212.3. II. θαλλοί, οἱ, *palm-leaves*, which were plaited into baskets, *Gp*.10.6.2. III. *gift* (prob. at first a branch, later in other forms) given to a landlord by one whose bid for a lease was accepted, *UPZ*112 iii 15 (ii B. C.); repeated annually, θαλλῶν κατ' ἔτος ἄρτων ἡμιαρταβίου καὶ ἀλέκτορος *PRyl*.167.16 (i A. D.), etc.; esp. at festivals, *PAmh*.2.93.11 (ii A. D.); *gratuity* additional to wages, *PCair.Preis*.31.21 (ii A. D.); any *gift* given annually at a festival, Ps.-Callisth.1.32.

θαλλο-φᾰγέω, *eat young olive-shoots*, Ath.11.587a. **-φορέω**, *carry olive-shoots*, Cratin.31, Pherecr.57, Dicaearch.Hist.46. **-φόρος**, ον, *carrying young olive-shoots*, as the old men did at the Panathenaea, Ar.V.544 (lyr.), X.Smp.4.17; as a name of Heracles, IG 14.904.

θάλλω, Hes.Op.173, h.Cer.402, etc.: aor. 1 ἔθηλα (ἀν-) Ael.NA2.25, 9.21: aor. 2 θάλε h.Hom.19.33; ἀν-έθαλον Lxx Wi.4.4, Ep.Phil.4.10: pf. τέθηλα, in Hom. only part. in pres. sense τεθηλώς, Ep. fem. τεθαλυῖα, and 3 sg. plpf. τεθήλει Od.5.69; 3 sg. ind. τέθηλε Hes.Op.227, Emp.77, S.Ph.259; Aeol. and Dor. τέθαλα Sapph.Supp.25.12, Pi.Fr.129.5, B.9.40, IG3.171; subj. τεθήλῃ Epigr.ap.Pl.Phdr.264d; inf. τεθηλέναι Id.Cra.414a; part. τεθαλώς prob. in A.Supp.107 (lyr.):—Pass., fut. θαλήσομαι (ἀνα-) AP7.281 (Heraclid.): (cf. θηλέω):—*sprout, grow, thrive*, esp. of fruit-trees, ἐρινεὸς.. φύλλοισι τεθηλώς Od.12.103; τεθήλει δὲ σταφυλῇσι, of a vine, 5.69; ἄνθεσι γαῖα θάλλει h.Cer. l.c.; ⟨δένδρεα⟩ τέθηλε καρπῶν ἀφθονίῃσι Emp.77; ὦ χρυσέᾳ κόμᾳ θάλλων Λοξία Pi.I.7(6).49; πώγωνι θάλλων S.Ichn.358: abs., καρπὸν τρὶς ἔτεος θάλλοντα Hes.Op.173; θάλλει κατ' ἦμαρ αἰεὶ νάρκισσος S.OC681 (lyr.), etc.: freq. in pf. part., as Adj., *luxuriant*, τεθαλυῖά τ' ὀπώρη Od.11.192; τεθαλυῖά τ' ἀλωή 6.293: also, c. acc. cogn., οὐ δένδρε' ἔθαλλεν χῶρος the place *grew* no trees, Pi.O.3.23, cf. AP9.78 (s. v. l., Leon.); ἐν φύλλοισι θαλλούσης βίον ξανθῆς ἐλαίας (Dind. ἴσον) A.Pers.616; simply, *bloom*, Thphr.HP1.1.2; but of σίκυοι, etc., ἡ ἀπὸ τοῦ ὕδατος ἀτμὶς οἷον θάλλοντας παρέχει Id.CP5.6.5. b. of other natural objects, τεθαλυῖά τ' ἐέρση *copious* dew, Od.13.245; ῥάχιν τεθαλυῖαν ἀλοιφῇ *rich* with fat, Il.9.208, cf. Od.13.410; εἰλαπίνῃ τεθαλυίῃ at a *sumptuous* feast, 11.415. 2. of persons, states or conditions, *bloom*, θ. ἁπαλὸν χρόα Archil.100; *thrive, flourish*, Εἰρήνη τεθαλυῖα Hes.Th.902; θάλλοισα εὐδαιμονία, ἀρετά, Pi.P.7.19, I.5(4).17; πατρὸς θάλλοντος S.Ant.703, cf. Ph.420, etc.; ζῶν καὶ θάλλων alive and *prosperous*, Id.Tr.235; ζῇ καὶ θάλλει [ἡ παίδευσις] Antipho Soph.60; θάλε πόθος h.Hom.19.33; Ἔρως ἐπὶ Χαλκιδέων θάλλει πόλεσιν Carm.Pop.44; Ἔρως τότε μὲν θ. τε καὶ ζῇ, ὅταν εὐπορήσῃ, τότε δὲ ἀποθνήσκει Pl.Smp.203e; θ. καὶ εὐδαιμονεῖ χώρα καὶ πόλις Id.Lg.945d: c. dat. modi, θάλλουσιν δ' ἀγαθοῖσι Hes.Op.236; ἀγλαΐῃ τεθαλυῖαι [δμωαί] Id.Sc.276; τοῖσι (sc. ἀνδράσι) τέθηλε πόλις Id.Op.227; πόλις ἐλευθερίᾳ τεθαλυῖα Simon.102; θ. ἀρεταῖς Pi.O.9.16; ἐλπίδι B.9.40; εὐγενεῖ τέκνων σπορᾷ S.Ant.1164; παρρησίᾳ E.Hipp.422; δαίμων ἀφθίτῳ θ. βίῳ Critias 25.17 D.; θ. ἐπὶ γυμνάδος ἔργοις Epigr.Gr.233 (Chios). 3. of disease and the like, in bad sense, *to be fresh, active*, ἡ δ' ἐμὴ νόσος ἀεὶ τέθηλε S.Ph.259; πήματα... ἀεὶ θάλλοντα μᾶλλον ἢ καταφθίνοντα *waxing*, Id.El.260; ἔρις θάλλει E.Ph.812 (lyr.): c. dat., ἀφροσύναις θάλλουσ' Ὕβρις B.14.58. b. τοῖσι αὐτοῖσιν ὅ τε σπλὴν θάλλει καὶ τὸ σῶμα φθίνει the spleen *becomes swollen*, Hp.Loc.Hom.24; also τεθηλός (in neutral sense) of the liver, Id.VM22.

Θαλλώ, οῦς, ἡ, one of the Ὧραι, a divinity of increase, Jusj.ap.Lycurg.77, Paus.9.35.2.

θάλος [ᾰ], εος, τό, prop. = **θαλλός**, but only nom. and acc. in metaph. sense of *scion, child*, φίλον θ. Il.22.87; λευσσόντων τοιόνδε θ. Od.6.157; γλυκερόν, νέον θ., h.Cer.66, 187; σεμνὸν θ. Ἀλκαϊδᾶν Pi.O.6.68, cf. 2.45, E.El.15, etc.—For the pl., v. θάλεα, τά.

θαλπ-εινός, ή, όν, = θαλπνός, but as gloss on ἰσχνόν, EM479.22. **-είω**, Ep. for θάλπω, ib.620.46. **-ιάω**, (θάλπω) *to be* or *become warm*, εὖ θαλπιόων right *warm and comfortable*, Od.19.319, cf. Arat.1073. **-νός**, ή, όν, *warming, fostering*, θαλπνότερον ἄστρον Pi.O.1.6. **-ος**, εος, τό, *warmth, heat*, esp. *summer-heat*, opp. χειμών, A.Ag.565, 969; ἐν μεσημβρίας θ. Id.Supp.747; θ. θεοῦ the sun's *heat*, S.Tr.145, etc.; μεσημβρινοῖσι θάλπεσιν A.Th.431, 446; in Prose, θάλπος, opp. ψῦχος, Hp.Aph.3.4: pl., ῥίγη καὶ θάλπη, ψύχη καὶ θ., X.Oec.7.23, Cyr.1.2.10. 2. metaph., *sting, smart*, [τοξευμάτων] S.Ant.1086; of love, AP6.207 (Arch.). **-τέον**, *one must warm*, Aët.5.68, Hippiatr.1. **-τήριον**, *fomentum, fomes*, Gloss. **-τήριος**, ον, *warming*, σάνδαλα... ποδῶν θ. AP6.206.1 (Antip. Sid.). **-ω**, fut. -ψω Orph.Fr.258, Alciphr.2.4: fut. Med. in pass. sense θάλψομαι Id.3.42:—*heat, soften by heat*, Od.21.179, al.:—Pass., ἐτήκετο κασσίτερος ὡς ... θαλφθεὶς Hes.Th.864, cf. S.Tr.697: metaph., *to be softened, deceived*, αἴ κε μὴ θαλφθῇ λόγοις Ar.Eq.210. II. *heat, warm*, without any notion of *softening*, καῦμ' ἔθαλπε (sc. ἡμᾶς) S.Ant.417; θερμὴ ἡμᾶς ἀκτὶς θ. Ar.Av.1092; *keep warm*, χλανιδίων ἐρειπίοις θάλπουσα καὶ ψύχουσα Trag.Adesp.7: prov., θ. τὸν δίφρον, of an idle life, Herod.1.37; θ. τὰς κοχώνας Id.7.48; τὴν βαίτην θάλπουσαν εὖ ib.129:—Pass., Hp.Aff.4; θάλπεσθαι τοῦ θέρους *to be warm* in summer, X.Cyr.5.1.11; τῷ πυρὶ θάλψομαι Alciphr.3.42: metaph., ἔτι ἁλίῳ θάλπεσθαι *to be alive*, Pi.N.4.14. 2. *warm at the fire, dry*, θάλπεται ῥάκη S.Ph.38, cf. E.Hel.183 (lyr.). 3. *hatch*, ᾠά Gp.14.1.4: so abs., *sit*, ib.3; θ. ἐπὶ τῶν νοσσῶν, ἐπὶ τῶν ᾠῶν, Lxx De.22.6. III. metaph., of passion, *heat, inflame*, ἢ Διὸς θάλπει κέαρ ἔρωτι A.Pr.590, cf. S.Fr.474 (Pass.); ἔθαλψεν ἄτης σπασμὸς Id.Tr.1082:—Pass., ἱμέρου βέλει τεθάλφθαι πρός τινος A.Pr.650; θάλπῃ (2 sg.) ἀνηκέστῳ πυρί S.El.888; εἴ σευ θάλπεταί τι τῶν ἔνδον Herod.2.81. 2. *comfort*, ὕπνος.. θάλπει κέαρ B.Fr.3.11, cf. Fr.16.2, Com.Adesp.5.16 D.; *cherish, foster*, ἄλλον θάλπε φίλον Theoc.14.38; ὡς ἐὰν τροφὸς θάλπῃ τὰ ἑαυτῆς τέκνα 1Ep.Thess.2.7; τὴν ἑαυτοῦ σάρκα Ep.Eph.5.29; τὸ ἀσθενοῦν Alciphr.2.4; θ. καὶ τρέφειν PMasp.6B132 (vi A. D.); τὴν πόλιν θ. *tend* it *with fostering care*, OGI194.5 (Egypt, i B. C.). 3. ἐμὲ οὐδὲν θ. ἡ δόξα *I care* nothing for glory, Alciphr.2.2; ἐμὲ οὐδὲν θ. κέρδος Aristaenet.1.24. IV. intr., *to be full of heat, vigorous*, Arist.Pr.879a33; θάλψαι τρεῖς ποίας *to live* three summers, AP7.731 (Leon.). **-ωρή**, ἡ, *warming*: metaph., *comfort, consolation*, οὐ γὰρ ἔτ' ἄλλη θαλπωρὴ Il.6.412, cf. Od.1.167; ἀντὶ δὲ θαλπωρᾶν [θῆκα γονεῦσι γόους] IG4.623 (Argos): pl., Tryph.128.—In late Prose, Jul.Or.8.243c.

θαλυκρός, ά, όν, *hot, glowing*, ἀπάντῃ πάντα θ. ἐγώ Call.Fr.anon.69; θ. κέντρον ἐρωμανίης AP5.219 (Agath.):—hence **θαλυκρέομαι**, = ψεύδομαι, Hsch.

θαλ-ύνω, = θάλλειν ποιῶ, Hsch. **-ύπτω**, = θάλπω, aor. 1 inf. θαλύψαι, Id.; cf. ἀκροθάλυπτος.

θαλύσια [ῠ], τά, (θάλος) *offerings of first-fruits*, made to Artemis, Il.9.534; later to Demeter, Theoc.7.3; to Demeter and Dionysus, Men.Rh.p.391 S. 2. θαλύσιος [ἄρτος] bread *made from the first-fruits*, Ath.3.114a.

θαλῡσιάς, άδος, fem. Adj., κούρη θ. a priestess of Demeter (cf. foreg.), Nonn.D.12.103; θ. ὁδός a journey *to the* θαλύσια, Theoc.7.31.

θαλύσσω, = θάλπω, Hsch. (Pass.):—also **θαλύεσθαι** (dub. l.), Id.

θάλψις, εως, ἡ, (θάλπω) *warming, fomenting*, Hp.Acut.21, S.E.M.7.354, Ruf.Sat.Gon.47. 2. opp. ψῦξις, of seasons, Hp.Aph.3.1; *heat, heating property*, Gal.18(1).228. II. *cherishing*, PLond.5.1727.10 (vi A. D.).

θαμά (oxyt., A.D.Adv.153.5, Hdn.Gr.2.141), Adv. *often*, Il.16.207, Od.16.27, Pi.O.1.17, B.12.193, S.El.524, Ar.Eq.990 (lyr.), Pl.1166, Pl.Phd.72e, X.Mem.2.1.22; θ. τῆς ἡμέρας POxy.1158.4 (iii A. D.). (Orig. 'thickly', cf. θαμέες, θάμνος.)

θαμάκης· σύμβιος, Cyr.

θαμάκις, Adv. = θαμά, Pi.I.1.28, N.10.38.

θαματροχεῖ· οὐχ ἡσυχάζει, Hsch.

θαμβ-αίνω, = θαμβέω, *to be astonished at*, Pi.O.3.32, v. l. for θαυμαίνω in h.Ven.84. **-ᾰλέος**, α, ον, *astonished*, Nonn.D.1.126. II. = θαυμαστός, φοβερός, Hsch. **-ευτής**, οῦ, ὁ, *terrifying* person, Aq.Ze.3.4. **-εύω**, *terrify*, Id.Ge.49.4. **-έω**, *to be astounded*, οἱ δὲ ἰδόντες θάμβησαν Il.8.77, cf. B.5.84; οἱ δ' ἀνὰ θυμὸν ἐθάμβεον Od.4.638, etc.; καὐτὸς τεθάμβηκ' S.Ant.1246; ἐθάμβησεν δὲ πᾶς.. ὅμιλος E.Ion 1205. 2. c. acc., *to be astonished at*, θάμβησαν δ' ὄρνιθας Od.2.155, cf. 16.178; τὸν ἐθάμβεον Ἄρτεμίς τε καὶ Ἀθάνα Pi.N.3.50; τέρας δ' ἐθάμβουν A.Supp.570 (lyr.): in late Prose, Plu.Aem.34. II. later also causal, *alarm*, Lxx 2Ki.22.5; τοὺς ὀφθαλμούς τινος PMag.Par.1.237:—Pass., *to be astounded*, Ev.Marc.1.27, POxy.654.7, PMag.Leid.W.11.39; τεθαμβημένος *astounded*, Plu.Brut.20; διά τινος Id.Caes.[45]. **-ημα**, ατος, τό, *alarm, terror*, Man.4.559. **-ησις**, εως, ἡ, = foreg., Aq.Ps.30(31).23, Man.4.365. II. *haste*, Aq.De.16.3, Is.52.12. **-ήτειρα**, ἡ, *the fearful one*, of the Furies, Orph.A.973 (pl.). **-ητός**, ή, όν, *astonishing*, Lyc.552, Maiist.1. **-όομαι**, *to be terrified*, pf. part. τεθαμβωμένος, Aët.16.66 (s. v. l.). **-ος**, εος, τό, also ὁ Simon.237, Lxx Ec.12.5 (pl.): (τέθηπα):—*amazement*, θ. δ' ἔχεν εἰσορόωντας Il.4.79; θ. δ' ἕλε πάντας ἰδόντας Od.3.372; θάμβει δυσφόρῳ τερπνῷ τε μιχθεὶς Pi.N.1.55; θάμβει ἐκπλαγέντες E.Rh.291, cf. Ar.Av.781 (lyr.), Th.6.31, Pl.Phdr.254c: pl., Onos.41.2. 2. in objective sense, θάμβοι *terrors* in the way, Lxx l.c.; *object of wonder*, Epigr.Gr.1068 (Gerasa). **-ός**, ή, όν, *astonished*, Eust.906.53.

θᾰμ-έες, οἱ, gen. θαμέω[ν] dub. in Sapph.Supp.15.1; dat. θαμέσι, acc. θαμέας (nom. sg. masc. θαμύς A.D.Adv.153.4): fem. nom. and acc. θαμειαί, -άς (oxyt., Aristarch.ap.Hdn.Gr.2.22):—poet. Adj. used only in pl., *crowded, close-set*, ὀδόντες.. ὑὸς θαμέες ἔχον Il.10.264; ὀδόντες πυκνοὶ καὶ θ. Od.12.92; θαμέες γὰρ ἄκοντες... ἀΐσσουσι Il.11.552, 17.661; ἴκρια.. ἀραρὼν θαμέσι σταμίνεσσι Od.5.252; πυραί, λίθοι θ., Il.1.52, 12.287; *frequent*, λυγμοί Nic.Th.434, Al.581 (in Comp. θαμειότερος): Comp. θαμύντερος Hsch. Adv. θαμέως, = θαμά, Alc.Supp.25.5 (dub.), Hp.Superf.25, Max.600. **-ίζω**, (θαμά) *come often*, πάρος γε μὲν οὔ τι θαμίζεις Il.18.386, al.; ἅμα νηῒ πολυκληῗδι θαμίζων *plying*, Od.8.161; θ. εἰς τούσδε τοὺς τόπους Pl.Hp.Ma.281b; ἐφ' ἡμᾶς X.Cyr.7.3.2; κεῖσε A.R.2.451; ἐν δονάκεσσι θ. *to haunt* them, Nic.Al.578; ἐν ταῖς πομπαῖς Corn.ND30; τοῖς μαχομένοις Chor. in Hermes 17.227; σοφίης ἐπ' ἄκροισι θαμίζειν v. l. for θοάζειν in Emp.4.8. 2. *to be accustomed*: c. part., οὔ τι κομιζόμενός γε θάμιζεν he *was* not *wont* to be so cared for, Od.8.451; οὐ δὲ θαμίζεις ἡμῖν καταβαίνων we do not *often see* you coming down, Pl.R.328c; μινύρεται θαμίζουσα μάλιστ' ἀηδών mourns *constantly*, S.OC672 (lyr.): abs., διὰ τὸ θαμίζειν by dint of *repetition*, Pl.Lg.843b. II. Med., = Act., τῇδε (τῷδε codd.) S.Fr.503.

θᾰμῑνάκις, Adv. = θαμάκις, θαμά, Hp.Mul.2.203.

θᾰμῑνός and **θαμῖνός** (h.Merc.44, Call.Aet.3.1.36, Nic.Th.239 (v. l.); **θαμεινός** Choerob. in An.Ox.2.180), ή, όν, *crowded, close-set*, Call.Cer.65, Lyr.Alex.Adesp.7.14: usu. neut. pl. θαμινά, as Adv. = θαμά, Pi.O.1.53, Pae.6.16, Ar.Pl.292 (lyr.), X.Mem.3.11.15, An.4.1.16 (v. l. θαμεινά): sg., θαμινόν A.R.3.1266: Sup. -ώτατος Suid. Adv. -νῶς Hsch.: Comp. -ώτερον Parth.Fr.29.

θάμιξ· ἀλώπηξ, Hsch.

θάμνα, ἡ, *wine from pressed grapes*, a local term, Gp.6.13.2; so prob. τὴν προκυκλίην θάμνην Herod.6.90.

θαμν-άς, άδος, ἡ, (θάμνος) = ῥίζα, EM442.23. **-ίσκος**, ὁ, Dim. of θάμνος, Dsc.4.108, Herod.Med.ap.Orib.8.4.6, Gal.2.355.

θάμνισον· ἀποκάλυψον, Hsch.

θαμνῖτις, ιδος, ἡ, *shrubby*, ῥάμνος Nic.Th.883.

θαμνο-ειδής, ές, *shrubby*, Thphr.HP3.17.3, Crateuas ap.Dsc.2.127. **-μήκης** ῥάβδος *a long stick cut from a bush*, Ion Trag.40.

θάμνος, ὁ, also ἡ D.S.2.49: (cf. θαμέες):—*bush, shrub*, καταπτήξας ὑπὸ θάμνῳ Il.22.191; θάμνῳ ὕπ' ἀμφικόμῳ 17.677; θάμνοις ἐν πυκινοῖσι in the thick *copse*, Od.5.471; θ. δρυός Pi.Pae.4.52; θ. ἐλαίης a *bushy* olive, Od.23.190, cf. Archil.6.1, A.Ag.1316, E.Ba.722, S.El.55, Ar.Pax 1298 (hex.), Pl.R.432b, etc.; θ. τὸ ἀπὸ ῥίζης πολύκλαδον Thphr.HP1.3.1.

θαμνοφάγος [ᾰ], ον, *eating shrubs*, S.E.P.1.56.

θαμνώδης, ες, = θαμνοειδής, Thphr.HP3.12.1 (Comp.), CP5.12.5.

θᾰμῠρίζω, *assemble*, Hsch.; *take part in a meeting*, θαμυριδδόντων [τῶν δεῖνα] *BCH*50.401 (Thespiae); **θάμῠρις**, ἡ, *assembly*, Hsch.

Θάμῠρις [ᾰ], ὁ, dat. Θαμύριδι Paus.10.30.8, Θαμύρι v.l. in Poll.4.75; acc. Θάμυριν Il.2.595, E.*Rh.*925:—*Thamyris*, a Thracian bard, ll. cc., Str.7 *Fr.*35:—Att. **Θαμύρας** (cf. Cyr.) S.*Fr.*245 (lyr.), Pl.*R.*620a, etc.

θᾰμῠρός, ά, όν, *frequented*, ὁδός Hsch.

θαμύς, v. θαμέες.

θᾰνάσῐμος [νᾰ], ον, (θάνατος) *deadly, fatal*, Hp.*Aph.*2.1, Pl.*R.*610e, etc.; τύχαι A.*Ag.*1276; πέσημα S.*Aj.*1033; χείρωμα Id.*OT*560; πέπλος Id.*Tr.*758; φάρμακα E.*Ion*616, Ph.*Bel.*103.31, cf. Metrod.53, etc.; θηρία θ., *of poisonous* reptiles, Plb.1.56.4: θανάσιμα, τά, *poisons*, *Ev.Marc.*16.18, Dsc.4.108, Gal.14.154. Adv. -μως, τύπτειν to strike *with deadly blow*, Antipho 4.3.4: neut. pl. as Adv., ἀσπίδες -μα δάκνουσαι D.S.1.87. 2. *belonging to death*, θ. αἷμα the *life*-blood, A. *Ag.*1019 (lyr.); μέλψασα θ. γόον having sung her *death*-song, ib.1445; θ. ἐκπνοαί E.*Hipp.*1438. II. of persons, *near death*, S.*Ph.*819; θ. ἤδη ὄντα Pl.*R.*408b; *liable to the death-penalty*, *Abh.Berl.Akad.* 1925(5).21 (Cyrene). 2. *dead*, S.*Aj.*517; θ. βεβηκότα Id.*OT*959.

θᾰνᾰτ-άω, Desiderat. of θανεῖν, *desire to die*, Pl.*Phd.*64b, *Ax.*366c, Alex.211, J.*BJ*3.7.18, Gal.8.190, Max.Tyr.26.9, Philostr.*VA*7.31. II. *to be moribund*, Ph.2.505, Lyd.*Mag.*3.40, v.l. in 45. **-ηγός**, όν, *death-bringing*, epith. of Hecate, *PMag.Par.*1.2865; f.l. for θάργηλος, Timocl.7. **-ήριος**, ον, v. θανατήσιος. **-ήσιμος**, v. sq. **-ήσιος**, ον, = θανάσιμος, rejected by Poll.5.132 (cod. C; -ήσιμος cett.), but found in Afric.*Cest.*14,16,17 (*Math.Vett.*p.294 Thévenot); cf. θανατήσιον, οὐ θανάσιμον λέγουσιν, Phot.; **θανατήριον** ἀξιοῦσιν οὐ θανάσιμον λέγειν *AB*99 (quoting Pl.*R.*Bk.ii, E.*Med.*). **-ηρός**, ά, όν, *poisonous*, βοτάνη Eust.1336.20; γῆ Sch.rec.S.*OT*181.

θᾰνᾰτηφορ-ία, ἡ, *a causing of death*, *AP*5.113 (Maec.). **-ος**, ον, *death-bringing*, αἶσα A.*Ch.*369 (lyr.); περίοδος θ. cycle *of mortality*, Pl.*R.*617d; of hurts or accidents, Hp.*Art.*48; of a surgical operation, Antyll.ap.Orib.45.17.6; ῥίζα ἐν Αἰθιοπίᾳ, of arrow-poison, *Acokanthera Schimperi*, Thphr.*HP*9.15.2; ὀδύναι Arist.*PA*672ª36; γένεθλα .. θ. κεῖται *causing death by contagion*, S.*OT*181 (lyr.); πᾶσαι μεταβολαὶ πολιτειῶν θ. X.*HG*2.3.32; ἁμαρτία Lxx *Nu.*18.22; δίκαι *capital* trials, *Not.Arch.*4.19 (Cyrene, Aug.); ἐπιστολή Hdn.4.12.8; περιστάσεις Vett.Val.225.7. Adv. -ρως, νοσεῖν Phld.*Rh.*2.148 S.: neut. sg. as Adv., ἐπλήγη οὐχὶ -φόρον Aen.Tact.27.9; but -φόρον ᾄδειν to sing *a death song*, *AP*11.186 (Nicarch.).

θᾰνᾰτ-ιάω, = θανατάω II, Luc.*Peregr.*32, S.E.*M.*9.153. **-ικός**, ή, όν, *deadly*, θ. ἐγκλήματα *capital* charges, D.S.37.5; νόμοι, ζημία, J.*BJ*3.5.7, *AJ*15.11.5; δίκη θ. trial *on a capital charge*, Plu.*Per.*10, *Alex.*42; of planetary influences, Vett.Val.129.4. 2. Medic., *fatal*, συνδρομή Gal.16.545. 3. Adv. -κῶς, λέγεσθαι, as expl. of δυσηλεγής, Eust.321.40. **-όεις**, εσσα, εν, *deadly*, ἁμαρτήματα S. *Ant.*1262 (lyr.); μόρος E.*IA*1288 (lyr.).

θᾰνᾰτοποιός, όν, *causing death*, Sch.S.*Tr.*858.

θᾰνᾰτος [θᾰ], ὁ, (θνήσκω) *death*, whether natural or violent, Hom., etc.; τῶν ὑπαλευάμενος θάνατον *the death threatened* by them, Od.15.275; ὡς θάνον οἰκτίστῳ θανάτῳ 11.412; θάνατόνδε *to death*, Il.16.693, 22.297; θανάτου τέλος, μοῖρα, A.*Th.*906 (lyr.), *Pers.*917 (anap.), etc.; θανάτου πέρι καὶ ζωᾶς for life and *death*, Pi.*N.*9.29; θ. ἢ βίον φέρει S. *Aj.*802; θάνατος μὲν τάδ' ἀκούειν Id.*OC*529; θανάτῳ ἴσον πάθος Id.*Aj.*215; ἐν ἀγχόναις θάνατον λαβεῖν E.*Hel.*201; πόλεώς ἐστι θ., ἀνάστατον γενέσθαι it is its *death*, Lycurg.61; γῆρας ζῶν θ. Secund.*Sent.*12; θάνατον ἀποθνήσκειν, τελευτᾶν, Plu.*Crass.*25, D.H.4.76. 2. in Law, *death-penalty*, θάνατον καταγνῶναί τινος to pass *sentence of death* on one, Th.3.81; θανάτου δίκῃ κρίνεσθαι ib.57; θανάτου κρίνειν X.*Cyr.*1.2.14, Plb.6.14.6; περὶ θανάτου διώκειν X.*HG*7.3.6; πρὸς τοὺς ἐχθροὺς .. ἀγωνίσασθαι περὶ θ. D.4.47; θ. τῆς ζημίας ἐπικειμένης the penalty is *death*, Isoc.8.50; ellipt., παιδίον κεκοσμημένον τὴν ἐπὶ θανάτῳ (sc. στολήν) Hdt.1.109; τὴν ἐπὶ θ. προσαγαγεῖν τινα Luc.*Alex.*44; but δῆσαί τινα τὴν ἐπὶ θανάτῳ (sc. δέσιν) Hdt.3.119; τὴν ἐπὶ θανάτῳ ἔξοδον ποιεῖσθαι to go to *execution*, Id.7.223; ἐπὶ θάνατον ἄγεσθαι Id.3.14; τοῖς Ἀθηναίοις ἐπιτρέψαι περὶ σφῶν αὐτῶν πλὴν θανάτου for any penalty short of *death*, Th.4.54; εὐθύνας εἶναι πλὴν φυγῆς καὶ θανάτου καὶ ἀτιμίας *IG*1².39.73; εἰργόμενον θανάτου καὶ τοῦ ἀνάπηρον ποιῆσαι short *of death* or maiming, Aeschin.1.183. 3. pl., θάνατοι *kinds of death*, Od.12.341; *the deaths* of several persons, S.*OT*1200, E.*Heracl.*628 (both lyr.); poet., of one person, A.*Ch.*53, S.*OT*496, *El.*206 (all lyr.); οὐχ ἑνός, οὐδὲ δυοῖν ἄξια θανάτοιν Pl.*Lg.*908e; πολλῶν θ., οὐχ ἑνὸς ἄξιος D.21.21, cf. 19.16, Ar.*Pl.*483, D.H.4.24; δεύτερος θ. *Apoc.*2.11, cf. Plu.2.942f; esp. of *violent death*, θ. αὐθένται A.*Ag.*1572 (lyr.), cf. *Th.*879 (lyr.); εἰς θανάτους ἰέναι Pl.*R.*399b. II. as pr. n., Θάνατος *Death*, Ὕπνῳ .. κασιγνήτῳ Θανάτοιο Il.14.231, cf. S.*Aj.*854, *Ph.*797, etc.; μόνος θεῶν γὰρ Θ. οὐ δώρων ἐρᾷ A.*Fr.*161; ὃν [ἰὸν] τέκετο Θ. S.*Tr.*834; character in E.*Alc.* III. *corpse*, θ. ἀτύμβευτος *AP*9.439 (Crin.).

θᾰνᾰτούσια (sc. ἱερά), τά, *a feast of the dead*, Luc.*VH*2.22.

θᾰνᾰτοφόρος, ον, = θανατηφόρος, πάθη A.*Ag.*1176 (lyr.).

θᾰνᾰτ-όω, fut. -ώσω A.*Pr.*1053 (anap.), etc.: pf. τεθανάτωκα Phld. *Rh.*1.359 S.:—Pass., fut. -ωθήσομαι Lxx 1*Ki.*14.45: fut. Med. in pass. sense θανατώσοιτο X.*Cyr.*7.5.31: aor. 1 ἐθανατώθην Id.*An.*2.6.4, Pl.*Lg.*865d: pf. τεθανάτωμαι Plb.23.4.14:—*put to death*, τινα Hdt.1.113, A.*Pr.* l.c.; esp. of the public executioner, Pl.*Lg.*872c, etc.: metaph., τεθανατωκέναι τὰς Ἀθήνας (sc. τοὺς ῥήτορας) Phld. l.c.:—Pass., *to be made dead*, *Ep.Rom.*7.4; ὁ -ωθεὶς the *murdered* man, Pl. *Lg.*865d. 2. Pass., of flesh, *to be mortified*, Hp.*Fract.*26:—metaph. in Act., *mortify*, τὰς πράξεις τοῦ σώματος *Ep.Rom.*8.13. II. *condemn to death by sentence* of law, Antipho 3.3.11, *Ev.Matt.*26.60:—Pass., X.*An.*2.6.4; οἱ τεθανατωμένοι those *condemned to death*, Plb. l.c. III. *to be fatal, cause death*, ὄφεις -οῦντες Lxx *Nu.*21.6; μυῖαι -οῦσαι ib.*Ec.*10.1; νόσος Ph.2.247 (-ῶσαν, -ώσασαν codd.). **-ώδης**, ες, *indicating death*, σημεῖον Hp.*Prog.*2. II. *deadly, fatal*, αὐχμοί Id.*Aph.*3.15; ἦρ ib.9; σπασμοί Ael.*NA*7.5. **-ωσις**, εως, ἡ, *putting to death*, Th.5.9; καταδίκαι καὶ -σεις πολιτῶν Plu.2.291c.

θᾶξαι· μεθύσαι, and **τεθαγμένοι**· μεμεθυσμένοι, and θαχμῆναι (cod., leg. θαχθῆμεν)· θωρηχθῆναι (Dor.), Hsch.; cf. *θώσσω.

***θάομαι**, a form needlessly invented to expl. the foll. Dor. forms of θεάομαι (q.v.), in which θᾱ- is contr. fr. θαε(ο)- and θαη-: 1 pl. θάμεθα Sophr.85: 2 pl. θᾶσθε (Megar.) Ar.*Ach.*770; imper. θάεο *APl.*4.306, *AP*6.354 (Nossis); part. θάμενος, ταὶ θάμεναι τὰ Ἴσθμια, title of mime by Sophron, Arg.Theoc.15; θασεῖσθε Call.*Cer.*3: fut. part. θασόμενος Theoc.15.23: aor. imper. θᾶσαι Epich.114, Theoc.1.149, 3.12; inf. θάσασθαι Id.2.72; part. θασάμενος *Tab.Heracl.*1.118. II. Act. only in part., θάοντα· διδάσκοντα, θεωροῦντα, Hsch., and Lacon. 1 pl. impf. ἔσᾱμεν (i.e. ἐθᾶμεν), = ἐθεωροῦμεν, Id.

θάπος, τό, dialectic form of τάφος (B), θάμβος, Eust.468.28: **θάπαν**· φόβον, Hsch. **θάπτα**· μυῖα (Cret.), Id.

θαπτέον, *one must bury*, τινα S.*Aj.*1140.

θαπτήριον, *sepultorium*, *Gloss.*

θάπτω, fut. θάψω Is.8.21:—Pass., fut. ταφήσομαι E.*Alc.*632, Lys.13.45, also τεθάψομαι S.*Aj.*577, 1141, E.*IT*1464: aor. 1 ἐθάφθην Simon.167 (cj.), Hdt.2.81, 7.228; more freq. aor. 2 ἐτάφην [ᾰ] Id.3.10, 55, and always in Att., as Ar.*Pl.*556; part. ἐν-θαφείς *CIG*2839 (Aphrodisias): pf. τέθαμμαι, Ion. 3 pl. τετάφαται v.l. τεθάφαται Hdt.6.103; imper. τεθάφθω Luc.*DMar.*9.1; inf. τεθάφθαι A.*Ch.*366 (lyr., prob. l.), Lycurg.113: plpf. Pass. ἐτέθαπτο Od.11.52, Hdt.1.113:—*honour with funeral rites*, ὅτε μιν θάπτωσιν Ἀχαιοί Il.21.323, cf. Hes.*Sc.*472; esp. by burial, οὐ γάρ πω ἐτέθαπτο ὑπὸ χθονός Od.11.52 (but freq. used later with ref. to cremation, D.S.3.55, App.*Hann.*35, Philostr.*Her.*10.11, etc.; πυρὶ θάπτειν Plu.2.286f, Philostr.*VS*2.20.3); θάπτειν .. γῆς φίλαις κατασκαφαῖς A.*Th.*1013, cf. E.*Supp.*545 (Pass.); θ. ἐς χῶρον Hdt.2.41; οὐ ἐβούλοντο Th.8.84; θ. ἐξ οἰκίας *to carry out to burial* from a house, Is.8.21; καταλείψει μηδὲ ταφῆναι not even his *burial expenses*, Ar.*Pl.*556; τῷ δ' εἶναι μηδὲ ταφῆναι Id.*Ec.*592.

θᾰρᾰπ-ευτής, = θεραπ-, *Annuaire des Études Grecques* 7.95 (Aenos). **-εύω**, = θεραπεύω, *IG*3.1296, *Schwyzer* 200 (Crete, ii B.C.). **-ηνα**, ἡ, Boeot., = θεράπαινα, ib.503ª.5 (iii/ii B.C.).

Θαργήλια (sc. ἱερά), ων, τά, a festival of Apollo and Artemis held at Athens in the month Thargelion, Hippon.37, Archil.113, Lex ap.D.21.10, *IG*2².1138, etc.:—also **Ταργ-**, *SIG*57.20 (Milet., V B.C.), *Schwyzer* 721.8 (Theb. ad Mycalen, iv B.C.): **Θαργηλιών**, ῶνος, ὁ, name of month at Athens, Antipho 6.42; also at Amorgos, *IG*12(7).62; and Andros, ib.135:—written **Ταργ-** at Delos, *BCH*5.26 (but Θαργ- *IG* 11(2).287 *A* 19 (iii B.C.)): Θαργήλιος and Ταργήλιος as pr. n., both in *GDI*5515 (Iasos); Ταργ- in Anacr.40.

θάργηλος ἄρτος, ὁ, = θαλύσιος, Crates Gr.ap.Ath.3.114a, dub. in *IG* 1².840; θάργηλος χύτρα prob. for θανατηγὸς χ. in Timocl.7.

θαρνεύει· ὀχεύει, σπείρει, φυτεύει, and **θάρνυσθαι**· ὀχεύειν, κυΐσκεσθαι, Hsch. (Cf. θόρνυμαι.)

θαρρᾰλέος, θαρρέω, θαρρητικός, θάρρος, θαρρύνω, Att. for θαρσ-.

θαρσᾰλ-έος, Att. **θαρρᾰλέος**, α, ον, (θάρσος) *daring*, πολεμιστής Il.21.589, etc.; ἦτορ 19.169; φωνά Pi.*N.*9.49; ἐλπίδες θ. *confident*, A.*Pr.*536 (lyr.): c. inf., ἀπὸ τῶν ἵππων πολεμεῖν θαρρ. Pl.*Prt.*350a; θ. περί τι Arist.*Rh.*1383ª15: Comp. -ώτερος Id.*PA*667ª16, Pl.*Prt.* l.c.; τὸ θαρσαλέον *confidence*, ἐν τῷ θαρσαλέῳ εἶναι Th.2.51, cf. Lys.21.25: so in Adv., θαρραλέως ἔχειν to be *of good courage*, πρὸς θάνατον Pl.*Ap.*34e; πρὸς τοὺς πολεμίους X.*An.*2.6.14: Comp. -ώτερον Isoc.*Ep.*7.3. 2. in bad sense, *overbold, audacious*, θ. καὶ ἀναιδής Od.17.449; θαρσαλέη, κύον ἀδεές 19.91; θ. καὶ θρασεῖς Pl.*Lg.*649c. Adv., ψευδῆ λέγειν θαρραλέως Is.10.1. II. *that which may be ventured on*, τὰ θ., opp. τὰ δεινά, Pl.*Prt.*359c, *La.*195c, al.; τἀληθῆ .. λέγειν ἀσφαλὲς καὶ θ. Id. *R.*450e. **-εότης**, Att. **θαρραλ-**, ητος, ἡ, *boldness, confidence*, Andronic.Rhod.p.578 M., Plu.*Aem.*36, 2.443d, Jul.*Or.*3.107b, Them. *Or.*2.30b; opp. θρασύτης, Ph.1.476.

θαρσ-έω, Att. **θαρρέω** (cf. pr. n. Θαρρίας *IG*1².847), Aeol. part. θέρσεισα (v.l. θαρσ-) Theoc.28.3: (θάρσος):—*to be of good courage*, τεθαρσήκασι λαοί Il.9.420, etc.; σὺν νοΐ, σὺν νῷ, Pl.*Men.*88b; in bad sense, *to be over-bold*, ὕβρει θ. Th.2.65: μάτην θ. Pl.*Tht.*189d:—Constr.: 1. abs., Il. l.c., etc.; θάρσει *fear not!* 4.184, A.*Supp.*732, etc.; θαρσεῖτε ib.600, 910; θάρσει, θυμέ Sopat.14; θάρρει Ar.*Pl.*328, al.:—in Epitaphs, θάρσει .. οὐδεὶς ἀθάνατος *CIG*5200b (Ptolemais), etc.: part. in an adverb. sense, θαρσήσας μάλα εἰπέ *with good courage*, Il.1.85, cf. A.*Ch.*666; κόμπασον θαρσῶν Id.*Ag.*1671, cf. *Pr.*916, S.*OC*491; θαρσέοντες πλούτου πέρι ἐρίζετε Hdt.5.49; πῖθι θαρρῶν Alex.232; λέγε τοίνυν θαρρῶν Pl.*Phdr.*243e; θαρρῶν πλείονα ἔθυεν ἢ ὀκνῶν ηὔχετο X.*Ages.*11.2; τὸ τεθαρρηκός *confidence*, Plu.*Fab.*26; τὸ θαρροῦν τῆς ὄψεως Id.*Cat.Mi.*44: in aor., *pluck up courage*, καὶ τότε δὴ θάρσησε Il.1.92. 2. c. acc., θάρσει τόνδε γ' ἄεθλον *fear not about* this contest, Od.8.197; later, *feel confidence against, have no fear of*, πάντα Hdt.7.50; θ. γέροντος χεῖρα E.*Andr.*993, cf. S.*OC*649; θάνατον Pl.*Phd.*88b; τὸ τοιοῦτον σῶμα .. οἱ μὲν ἐχθροὶ θαρροῦσιν .. Id.*Phdr.*239d; θ. τὸ ἀποκρίνασθαι Id.*Euthd.*275c; οὔτε Φίλιππος ἐθάρρει τούτους οὔτε οὗτοι Φίλιππον D.3.7; χωρίον Philostr.*Her.*1.3: c. acc. cogn., ἠλίθιον θάρρος θ. Pl.*Phd.*95c; αἰσχρὰ θάρρη θ. Id.*Prt.*360b; ταὐτὰ τισι θ. καὶ φοβεῖσθαι X.*HG*2.4.9; *venture*, θ. τὰς μάχας Id.*An.*3.2.20:—Pass., *to be risked*, Philostr.*Im.*1.17. b. c. acc. pers., also, *to have confidence in*, τινα X.*Cyr.*5.5.42, D.C.51.11. c. θ. τινί τι *entrust* to .., Marin.*Procl.*

9. 3. c. dat., *have confidence in*, τεθαρσηκότες τοῖσι ὄρνισι Hdt.3.76; ἑαυτῷ Plu.2.69c (s.v.l.); τοῖς χρήμασι *PGoodsp.Cair.*15.19 (iv A.D.). 4. with Preps., θ. περί.. *to be confident* about.., S.*Aj.*793, Pl.*R.*574b; ὑπὲρ ἑαυτῶν ib.566b; διά τι Isoc.3.55; ἐπί τινι Id.6.60; πρός τι Pl.*Prt.*350b; πρὸς ἐμαυτόν in myself, Ar.*Ec.*1060. 5. c. inf., *believe confidently that...*, S.*Ant.*668; also θ. ὅτι.. Th.1.81, etc.; θ. τὸ ἐξελέγξειν D.19.3. b. c. inf., *make bold, venture*, X.*Cyr.*8.8.6, Plu.*Per.*22, Ant.Lib.19.2. II. trans., *inspire with confidence*, [λόγοι] οἵ με θαρσοῖεν J.*AJ*19.1.9. **-ήεις**, εσσα, εν, = θαρσαλέος, Call.*Hec.*1.1.5, Nonn.*D.*13.562. **-ηρός**, ά, όν, = foreg., *Cat.Cod.Astr.*7.218. **-ησις**, εως, ἡ, *confidence in* a thing, ταῖς ναυσί f.l. in Th.7.49. **-ητέον**, *one must have confidence in*, ἀρετῇ Iamb.*Protr.*2. **-ητικός**, ή, όν, *courageous*, Arist.*Pr.*947^{b}26.

θαρσοποιός, όν, *making confident*, Eust.1344.12.

θάρσος, Att. **θάρρος**, Aeol. **θέρσος** (q.v.), εος, τό, (θρασύς) *courage*, Il.6.126; θ. τινός *courage to do* a thing, A.*Ch.*91, S.*OC*48: c. gen., *courage against..*, πολεμίων Pl.*Lg.*647b; πρὸς τοὺς πολεμίους X.*Cyr.*4.2.15; θ. ἴσχε *take courage!* S.*Ph.*807; θ. ἔχειν περί τινος Id.*El.*412; φρεσὶ θ. ἀέξειν Hes.*Sc.*96; αἴρειν πρός τι E.*IA*1598; λαβεῖν *Act.Ap.*28.15; but θ. ἔλαβέ τινας Th.2.92; θ. ἐμπνέειν Od.9.381; ἐνὶ φρεσὶ θεῖναι 3.76; τῷ δ' ἐνὶ θυμῷ θῆκε..θ. 1.321; ἐν κραδίῃ βάλλειν Il.21.547; παρασχεῖν, ἐμποιεῖν τινι, Th.6.68, X.*An.*6.5.17; θ. ἐγγίγνεται, ἐμπίπτει τινί, Id.*Cyr.*4.2.15, *HG*7.1.31; ἐμφύσεται Id.*Cyr.*5.2.32; οὔτ' ἐλπίδος γὰρ οὔτε του δόξης ὁρῶ θ. παρ' ἡμῖν ὡς.. E.*Hec.*371: pl., φόβοι καὶ θάρρη Arist.*EN*1107^{a}33, cf. Pl.*Prt.*360b. 2. *that which gives courage*, ὀλολυγμόν.., θάρσος φίλοις A.*Th.*270, cf. 184: pl., θάρση *grounds of confidence*, E.*IT*1281 (lyr.). II. rarely in bad sense, = θράσος, *audacity*, θάρσος ἄητον ἔχουσα Il.21.395; μυίης θάρσος ἐνὶ στήθεσσιν ἐνῆκεν the *reckless persistence* of a fly, 17.570.—On the diff. of θάρσος and θράσος, v. θράσος.

θαρσούντως, Att. **θαρρ-**, Adv. from gen. pres. part. of θαρσέω, *boldly*, X.*Smp.*2.11, Phld.*Rh.*1.325 S., Jul.*Or.*2.83a; θ. ἔχειν D.C.53.3.

θάρσῠνος, ον, = θαρσαλέος, Il.16.70: c. dat., *relying on* a thing, οἰωνῷ 13.823.

θαρσύνω [ῠ], Att. **θαρρύνω**, causal of θαρσέω, *encourage, embolden*, θάρσυνον (aor. imper.) δέ οἱ ἦτορ Il.16.242; θαρσύνεσκε παριστάμενος ἐπέεσσιν 4.233; θ. μύθῳ 10.190; θ. λόγοις, opp. φοβεῖν, A.*Pers.*216 (troch.); ἔργῳ καὶ λόγῳ X.*Cyr.*6.3.27, cf. Hdt.2.141, Th.2.59, etc. II. intr., = θαρσέω, ἀλλ', ὦ φίλη, θάρσυνε S.*El.*916.—Cf. θρασύνω.

Θαρσώ, οῦς, ἡ, name of Athena, Sch.Il.5.2.

θᾶσαι, θᾶσθε, v. *θάομαι.

Θάσιος [ᾰ], α, ον, *of* or *from Thasos*, Θάσιος (sc. οἶνος) *Thasian wine*, Hermipp.82.3, Ar.*Fr.*317, etc.; Θάσιον οἴνου σταμνίον Id.*Lys.*196, cf. *Ec.*1119; Θάσια κάρυα *almonds*, Chrysipp.Tyan.ap.Ath.14.647f, Aët.12.37; so Θάσια alone, Plu.2.1097d, Dsc.4.188, *Gp.*10.57 tit.: in sg., ib.76.6: ἡ Θασία ἅλμη *pickled sea-fish*, Cratin.6; and without ἅλμη, ἀνακυκᾶν Θασίαν to make *this pickle*, Ar.*Ach.*671. II. Θάσιος, ὁ (sc. μήν), name of month at Temnos, *Wiener Denkschr.*53.96 (prob.). 2. Θάσιον, τό, a measure in Egypt, *PCair.Zen.*12.19 (iii B.C.), al.

θᾶσσον, Att. **θᾶττον**, v. ταχύς. **θάσσουσα**· σπεύδουσα, Hsch.

θάσσω, Ep. **θαάσσω** (q.v.), *sit, sit idle*, στρατὸς δὲ θάσσει E.*Supp.*391; ἥσυχος θ. Id.*Ba.*622 (troch.); ἀμφὶ βωμόν Id.*Rh.*509; ἐπ' ἀκταῖς Id.*Hec.*36; τρίποδι ἐν χρυσέῳ Id.*IT*1253 (lyr.); πρὸς βάθροις Id.*HF*715: c. acc. sedis, θάσσειν θρόνον S.*OT*161 (lyr.); θ. τρίποδα E.*Ion*91 (anap.); θ. δάπεδον Id.*Andr.*117 (lyr.): c. acc. cogn., θ. δυστήνους ἕδρας *to sit* in wretched posture, Id.*HF*1214, cf. Ar.*Th.*889. (θάσσω contr. fr. θαάσσω (θᾰϝάκyω, cf. θάβακος): v. θᾶκος, θοάζω.)

θάσσων, Att. **θάττων**, v. ταχύς. **θάτας**· θῆτας (θύτας cod.), τοὺς δούλους (Cypr.), Hsch. **θατέρᾳ, θάτερον**, v. ἕτερος.

θᾱτέρως, Adv. *in the other way*, Simp.*in Ph.*210.10.

θᾱτήρ, ῆρος, ὁ, Dor. for *θᾱητήρ, = *θεατήρ, = θεατής, B.9.23, Hsch. **θᾱτύς**, ύος, ἡ, Dor. for *θαητύς, = *θεατύς, = θεωρία, Id. s.v. ἐς θατύν. **θαυλακίζειν**, = θυλακ-, Id. **θαυλέα**· οὐρά, κέρκος, Id. **θαύλια**, τά, a festival, Id.:—also **θαυλίζειν**, Id.: prob. connected with **Θαύλιος**, epith. of Zeus at Pharsalus, *Hermes*46.154, 286. (Possibly = *throttler*, cf. Καν-δαύλης = Κυνάγχης (q.v.).)

θαῦμα, ατος, τό, Ion. **θῶμα** (cf. θαυμάζω): (v. θεάομαι): I. of objects, *wonder, marvel*, in Ep. always in sg., Il.13.99, etc.; θαῦμ' ἐτέτυκτο πελώριον, of Polyphemus, Od.9.190; θαῦμα βροτοῖσι, of a beautiful woman, 11.287; ἄσπετόν τι θ., of Hercules, S.*Tr.*961 (lyr.), etc.: freq. c. inf., θ. ἰδέσθαι *a wonder* to behold, Il.5.725, etc.; θ. ἰδεῖν *h.Ven.*205, Hes.*Sc.*318; θ. ἰδεῖν εὐκοσμίας E.*Ba.*693; θ. ἀκοῦσαι Pi.*P.*1.26; θ. ἀνέλπιστον μαθεῖν S.*Tr.*673, etc.; θαῦμ' ὅτι... *strange* that.., Theoc.15.2; οὐ θαυμά [ἐστι] no *wonder*, Pi.*N.*10.50; so καὶ θ. γ' οὐδέν and no *wonder*, Ar.*Pl.*99; τὸ μὴ πείθεσθαι θ. οὐδέν Pl.*R.*498d, etc.; τί τοῦτο θ.; E.*Hipp.*439; ἦ μάλα θ. κύων ὅδε κεῖται Od.17.306; θῶμα ποιεῖσθαί τι Hdt.1.68; τί τινος Id.9.58; τινος Id.7.99; περί τινος Id.3.23: after Hom. in pl., θαύματ' ἐμοὶ κλύειν A.*Ag.*1166 (v.l. θραύματ'); θαύματ' ἀνθρώποις ὁρᾶν E.*Ion*1142; θαυμάτων κρείσσονα or πέρα things more than *wondrous*, Id.*Ba.*667, *Hec.*714. 2. in pl., also, *puppet-show, toy theatre*, θ. δεικνύναι, ἐπιδεικνύναι, Pl.*R.*514b, *Lg.*658c; ἐν θ. Thphr.*Char.*6.4, cf. 27.7, Ph.1.28; *mountebank-gambols*, X.*Smp.*2.1, cf. 7.3 (sg.); ἐν τοῖς θ. ὑπεκρίνετο μίμους in the *jugglers' booths*, Ath.10.452f; of menageries, Isoc.15.213; of mechanical devices, Arist.*Mech.*848^{a}11: metaph., ἔνιοι θ. ποιοῦσιν ἐν φιλοσοφίᾳ Phld.*Rh.*1.99 S.: sg., *puppet*, Pl.*Lg.*644d; *trick*, τὸ τῆς σοφιστικῆς δυνάμεως θ. Id.*Sph.*233a. II. *wonder, astonishment*, θ. μ' ἔχει ὡς.. Od.10.326, etc.; ἔσχον θ. S.*El.*897; θ. δ' ὄμμασιν πάρα A.*Eu.*407; θ. μ' ὑπέρχεται S.*El.*928; μ' ἐλάμβανε θ. Ar.*Av.*511; θαύματος ἄξιος worthy of *wonder*, E.*Hipp.*906, etc.; ἐν θώματι εἶναι to be *astonished*, Hdt.1.68, cf. Th.8.14; ἐν θώματι ἔχεσθαι, ἐνέχεσθαι, Hdt.8.135, 7.128; ἐν θ. ἐνέχεσθαί τινος *at* a thing, Id.9.37; ἐν θαύματι ποιεῖσθαι Plu.*Pomp.*14; διὰ θαύματος σχεῖν Hdn.2.2.7: pl., θαυμάτων ἐπάξια E.*Ba.*716, cf. Pl.*Lg.*967a.

θαυμ-άζω, Ion. **θωμ-**, Att. fut. θαυμάσομαι A.*Pr.*476, E.*Alc.*157, Pl.*Prm.*129c, Ep. θαυμάσσομαι Il.18.467; also θαυμάσω Hp.*Nat.Puer.*29, Plu.2.823f, etc. (in X.*Cyr.*5.2.12 θαυμάζουσι is restored for -σουσι, θαυμάσετε is v.l. for -σαιτε, Id.*HG*5.1.14): aor. ἐθαύμασα A.*Th.*772 (lyr.), etc., Ep. θαύμασα *h.Merc.*414: pf. τεθαύμακα X.*Mem.*1.4.2, etc.:—**Med.**, Gal.*Med.Phil.*2 (v.l.), Ael.*VH*12.30: aor. 1 ἐθαυμασάμην v.l. in Aesop.92; οὐκ ἂν θαυμασώμεθα (leg. -σαίμεθα) Procl.*in Prm.*p.750 S.; θαυμάσαιτο v.l. in J.*BJ*3.5.1:—**Pass.**, fut. -ασθήσομαι Isoc.6.105, Th.2.41: aor. ἐθαυμάσθην Id.6.12: pf. τεθαύμασμαι Plb.4.82.1. 1. abs., *wonder, marvel*, Il.24.394, Pl.*Hp.Ma.*282e, etc. 2. c. acc., *marvel at*, Il.24.631, etc.; πτόλεμόν τε μάχην τε 13.11; τύχη θαυμάσαι μὲν ἀξία S.*OT*777, cf. *OC*1152, *El.*393:—Pass., ὡς τέρας θ. Hdt.4.28; μὴ παρὼν -άζεται I *wonder* why he is not present, S.*OT*289. b. *honour, admire, worship*, once in Hom. (but cf. θαυμαίνω), οὔτε τι θαυμάζειν..οὔτ' ἀγάασθαι Od.16.203; freq. later, as Hdt.3.80, A.*Th.*772 (lyr.), S.*Aj.*1093, etc.; θ. τύμβον πατρός E.*El.*519; μηδὲ τὸν πλοῦτον μηδὲ τὴν δόξαν τὴν τούτων θαυμάζετε, ἀλλ' ὑμᾶς αὐτοὺς D.21.210; μηδὲν θ., Lat. *nil admirari*, Plu.2.44b; technically, of the *attendance* of small birds on the owl, Arist.*HA*609^{a}15; θ. πρόσωπον *to show respect to* a person, i.e. *comply with* their request, Lxx *Ge.*19.21; θ. τινά τινος *for* a thing, Th.6.36; θ. τινὰ ἐπὶ σοφίᾳ Pl.*Tht.*161c, X.*Mem.*1.4.2; ἀπὸ τοῦ σώματος τὸν νεανίσκον Plu.*Rom.*7:—Pass., *to be admired*, Hdt.7.204; ὑπό τινος Id.3.82; ἔν τινι Th.2.39; τῶν προγεγενημένων μᾶλλον -θησόμεθα Isoc.6.105; τοὺς ὁμοίως τεθαυμασμένους [ποιητάς] Phld.*Po.*5.31; διά τι Isoc.4.59: c. gen., τῆς ῥώμης Philostr.*VA*7.42; χάρις δ' ἀφ' ἡμῶν ὀλομένων -άζεται A.*Th.*703; τὰ εἰκότα θ. *to receive* proper *marks of respect*, Th.1.38; θ. τινί Id.7.63. c. *say with astonishment*, ἵνα μηδεὶς.. "εἶτα τότ' οὐκ ἔλεγες ταῦτα...;" θαυμάζῃ D.19.25. 3. c. gen., *wonder at, marvel at*, τούτου (cj. for τοῦτο) Lys.7.23: c. part., ὃ δ' ἐθαύμασά σου λέγοντος Pl.*Prt.*329c, cf. *Cri.*50c; θ. τῶν προθέντων αὖθις λέγειν Th.3.38; θ. τί τινος *to wonder* at a thing in a person, E.*Hipp.*1041; ὃ θ. τοῦ ἑταίρου Pl.*Tht.*161b, cf. *R.*376a: c. dupl. gen., θ. τούτου τῆς διανοίας Lys.3.44:—these phrases are used in Att. as a civil mode of expressing dissent. 4. rarely c. dat. rei, *to wonder at*, Th.4.85. 5. folld. by Preps., τὰ -όμενα περί τινος Pl.*Ti.*80c; θ. περί τινος τί τῇ τέχνῃ συμβάλλεται Sosip.1.37; ἐπί σου θαυμάζω, πῶς δύνῃ.. Plb.23.5.12; θαυμάσονται ἐπ' αὐτῇ Lxx *Le.*26.32. 6. freq. folld. by an interrog. sentence, θαυμάζομεν οἷον ἐτύχθη Il.2.320; θ. ὅστις ἔσται ὁ ἀντερῶν Th.3.38; θαυμάζοντες τί ἔσοιτο ἡ πολιτεία X.*HG*2.3.17; θ. ὡς οὔπω πάρεισιν Th.1.90, cf. X.*Cyr.*1.4.20, etc.; θ. ὅτι I *wonder at the fact that...*, Pl.*R.*489a; πολλάκις τεθαύμακα ὅπως.. *Com.Adesp.*22.46 D.; but more commonly, θ. εἰ.. I *wonder if..*, as a more polite way of saying I *wonder that..*, Hdt.1.155, S.*OC*1140, Pl.*Phd.*97a; ἐὰν..λέγω, μηδὲν θαυμάσῃς Id.*Smp.*215a; ὃ καὶ θαυμάζω, εἰ.. D.19.86; θαύμαζον ἀκούων, εἰ σὺ μὴ εἴης.., Lat. *mirum ni...*, Ar.*Pax*1292 (hex.).—This construction is freq. combined with one or other of the foregoing. b. c. acc., θαύμαζ' Ἀχιλῆα, ὅσσος ἔην οἷός τε Il.24.629; Τηλέμαχον θαύμαζον, ὃ θαρσαλέως ἀγόρευε they *marvelled at* Telemachus, that he spake so boldly, Od.1.382; τὸ δὲ θαυμάζεσκον (Ion. impf.), ὡς.. 19.229; θ. σοῦ γλῶσσαν, ὡς θρασύστομος A.*Ag.*1399, etc.: sts. without a connective, ἀλλὰ τὸ θαυμάζω· ἴδον.. Od.4.655; σοῦ..θαυμάσας ἔχω τόδε· χρῆν γάρ.. S.*Ph.*1362: sts. c. inf., θαυμάζομεν Ἕκτορα δῖον, αἰχμητὴν ἔμεναι Il.5.601. c. c. gen., θ. τινός, ἥντινα γνώμην ἔχων κτλ. Antipho 1.5; θ. τῶν..ἐχόντων ὅπως οὐ λέγουσιν Isoc.3.3; θ. αὐτοῦ τί τολμήσει λέγειν D.24.66; θαυμάζω τινὸς ὅτι.. Isoc.4.1; θ. τῶν δυναστευόντων εἰ ἡγοῦνται I *wonder at* men in power supposing, ib.170; ὑμῶν θ. εἰ μὴ βοηθήσετε X.*HG*2.3.53; also θ. αὐτοῦ..τοῦτο, ὡς.. Pl.*Phd.*89a. 7. c. acc. et inf., πενθεῖν οὔ σε θ. E.*Med.*268, cf. *Alc.*1130: after a gen., θαυμάζω δέ σου..κυρεῖν λέγουσαν A.*Ag.*1199. **-αίνω**, Ep. fut. θαυμανέω, = θαυμάζω 2, *admire, gaze upon*, ἀέθλια θαυμανέοντες Od.8.108; δένδρεα θαύμαινε (v.l. θάμβαινε) Pi.*O.*3.32, cf. Id.(?)*Parth.*ap.Sch.Il.*Oxy.*221 vii 11:—Pass., θαυμαίνονται καὶ φιλέονται Callicrat.ap.Stob.4.28.17, cf. Diotog.ap.eund.4.7.62. 2. abs., *wonder*, οὐδὲν δεῖ θαυμαίνεν (Dor. inf.), εἰ... Archyt.ap.eund.3.1.114. **-ακτρον**, τό, *money paid to see conjurers' tricks*, Sophr.120. **-ᾰλέος**, α, ον, *wondrous*, Hsch.

Θαύμας, αντος, ὁ, the father of Iris, Hes.*Th.*265; allegorized by Pl.*Tht.*155d.

θαυμάσι-ος [ᾰ], α, ον, Ion. **θωμ-**, rarely ος, ον Luc.*Im.*19: (v. θαῦμα):—*wonderful, marvellous*, ὅσσα *h.Merc.*443; χάρις Hes.*Th.*584 (nisi neut. pl.); [ὁδὸς] θωμασιωτέρη Hdt.2.21; θωμάσια *wonders, marvels*, ib.35: Sup. -ώτατα Id.6.47; θαυμάσια ἐργάζεσθαι Pl.*Smp.*220a; ἧττον θαυμαστά, καίπερ ὄντα θαυμάσια less *admired*, though *admirable*, Plu.2.974d: c. inf., τέρας θ. προσιδέσθαι Pi.*P.*1.26; οὐ θ. [ἐστι] c. inf., Ar.*Th.*468; ἔστιν δὲ..τοῦτο..θ., ὅπως... Id.*Pl.*340; θ. τοῦ κάλλους *marvellous* for beauty, X.*An.*2.3.9; πρὸς τὴν τόλμαν -ώτατε Aeschin.3.152: with interrog., θαυμάσιον ὅσον *exceedingly*, Pl.*Smp.*217a; θαυμάσι' ἡλίκα D.19.24; τὸ -ώτατον what is *most wonderful*, D.S.1.63. 2. Adv. -ίως *wonderfully*, i.e. *exceedingly*, Ar.*Nu.*

1240: freq. with ὡς, θ. ὡς ἄθλιος *marvellously* wretched, Pl.*Grg.*471a; θ. ἂν ὡς ηὐλαβούμην I should be *wonderfully* cautious, D.29.1. 3. *disposed to wonder*, in Adv., ὧν οὐ -ίως γ' ἔχουσι Hp.*Morb.Sacr.* 1. II. *admirable, excellent*, with slight irony, Pl.*Phdr.*242a, D. 19.113: freq. ὦ θαυμάσιε Pl.*R.*435c, al.; ὦ -ώτατε ἄνθρωπε, in scorn, X.*An.*3.1.27. III. θ. καὶ ἄλογον *strange* and absurd, Pl.*Grg.* 496a; θαυμάσια... ἐργαζομένους behaving *in an extraordinary manner*, Id.*Ap.*35a. **-ότης**, ητος, ἡ, *disposition to wonder*, Hp.*Morb.Sacr.*1, Arist.*Top.*126^{b}15. II. *marvellous nature* or *quality*, ὅσα ἔχει -ότητά τινα Clearch.69. 2. as a title, ἡ σὴ θ. your *Excellency*, *CIG* 3467.10 (Sardes, v A.D.). **-ουργέω**, v.l. for θαυματουργέω, X. *Smp.*7.2: **-ουργία**, ἡ, *jugglery*, Philostr.*VA*6.10: metaph., λέξεως θ. *wizardry* of language, Phld.*Rh.*2.94S.

θαυμ-ασμός, ὁ, *marvelling*, Phld.*Rh.*2.57S., Corn.*ND*2, Dius ap. Stob.4.21.16, S.E.*M.*9.17, Plu.*Aem.*39, etc. **-αστέος**, α, ον, *to be wondered at*, ἐκεῖνο θ., ὡς... Pl.*Plt.*302a. II. neut. θαυμαστέον *one must wonder*, εἰ.. E.*Hel.*85, cf. 499, Phld.*Rh.*2.27S., etc. **-αστής**, Ion. **θωμ-**, οῦ, ὁ, *admirer*, Ps.-Hdt.*Vit.Hom.*5 (θωυμ- codd.), Arist. *Rh.*1384^{b}37, al., Plu.*Cat.Mi.*25, Ph.Byz.*Mir.*4.2; ἑαυτοῦ Phld.*Vit.* p.14J. **-αστικός**, ή, όν, *inclined to wonder* or *admire*, Arist.*EN* 1125^{a}2, *Stoic.*2.62, Plu.2.41a; τινος Str.2.3.4. II. *expressing astonishment*, [ἐπιρρήματα] D.T.642.8. Adv. -κῶς, εἰπεῖν Ph.1.648; ἔχειν, διακεῖσθαι, Id.2.95, J.*AJ*8.6.5, cf. Phld.*Mus.*p.36K. **-αστοποιός**, *mirificus*, *Gloss.* **-αστός**, Ion. **θωμ-**, ή, όν, *wonderful*, *marvellous*, first in neut. as Adv., θαυμαστὸν γανόωντα *h.Cer.*10; ἔργα μεγάλα καὶ θ. Hdt.1 *Prooem.*; θ. καρπός Id.9.122; θ. λόχος γυναικῶν, of the Furies, A.*Eu.*46; οὐδὲν τούτων θαυμαστὸν ἐμοί S.*Ph.*191, etc.; ὁ πάντων -ότατον Pl.*Smp.*220a; θ. πλέγμα, Medic., the *rete mirabile*, Gal.5.196: c. acc., θαυμαστὴ τὸ κάλλος Pl.*Phd.*110c; πᾶσαν ἀρετήν Id.*Lg.*945e: c. gen., τῆς εὐσταθείας Plu.*Publ.*14; τῆς ἐπιεικείας Id. *Per.*39: c. dat., πλήθει Id.*Caes.*6; πλέοσι ἐσόμεθα θωμαστότεροι Hdt. 9.122; πρός τι Plu.2.980d: folld. by an interrog., εἰ, etc., θαυμαστὸν ὅσον..., Lat. *mirum quantum*, Pl.*Tht.*150d, etc.; θαυμαστὸν ἡλίκον D.24.122; θαυμαστά γ', εἰ.. X.*Smp.*4.3; οὐδὲν θ., εἰ.., Pl.*Phdr.*279a, *R.*390a; οὐ δὴ θ., εἰ... D.2.23. Adv. -τῶς Pl.*Lg.*633b; θαυμαστῶς ὡς σφόδρα Id.*R.*331a: neut. pl. as Adv., Id.*Smp.*192b; θαυμαστὰ ὡς S.*Fr.*960, E.*IA*943. II. *admirable, excellent*, πατήρ, υἱός, ὄλβος, Pi.*P.*3.71, 4.241, *N.*9.45; ἀνὴρ γὰρ οὐ στενακτὸς.., ἀλλ' εἴ τις βροτῶν θ. S.*OC*1665; iron., πράξας μὲν εὖ θ. ἂν γένοιτ' ἀνήρ A.*Pers.*212; *strange, absurd*, θ. καὶ γελοῖα Pl.*Tht.*154b; θαυμαστὰ δρῶντες ib.151a; θαυμαστὰ ἐργάζεται behaves in *an extraordinary way*, Id.*Smp.*213d, cf. θαυμάσιος III; θαυμαστὸν ποιεῖς, ὅς... X.*Mem.*2.7.13; ὦ θαυμαστέ Pl. *Plt.*265a; ὦ θαυμαστότατοι X.*An.*7.7.10. III. *to be worshipped*, οὐδείς μ' ἀρέσκει νυκτὶ θαυμαστὸς θεῶν E.*Hipp.*106. **-αστόω**, *magnify*, LXX *Ps.*4.4, al., *EM*443.37:—Pass., *to be regarded as a marvel*, ὑπό τινων Arist.*HA*633^{a}8, cf. Plu.*Per.*28.

θαυμᾰτ-ίζομαι, *marvel much*, Hsch. **-όεις**, εσσα, εν, = θαυμαστός, Man.6.402.

θαυμᾰτοποι-έω, *do wonders, play jugglers' tricks*, Luc.*Peregr.*17, 21: metaph., θ. τοῖς ὀνόμασιν Phld.*Po.*5.24, cf. Jul.*Or.*3.127c: c. acc., θ. παραπαίγνιον Porph.*Chr.*27. **-ία**, ἡ, *conjuring, juggling*, Pl.*R.*602d, Iamb.*Myst.*3.29. II. of orators, *a straining after the marvellous*, Isoc.10.7 (pl.). 2. *marvellous achievement*, D.C.57. 21. **-ικός**, ή, όν, *juggling*: ἡ -κή (sc. τέχνη), = foreg., Pl.*Sph.* 224a; τὸ θ. μόριον ib.268d. **-ός**, όν, *wonder-working*, ὄνειροι Luc. *Somn.*14; *acrobatic*, κοῦραι Matro *Conv.*121: as Subst., *conjurer, juggler*, Pl.*Sph.*235b, D.2.19: as fem., *IG*11(2).110.34 (Delos, iii B.C.), etc.; *puppet-showman*, Pl.*R.*514b, Phlp. *in GA*77.16.

θαυμᾰτός, ή, όν, poet. for θαυμαστός, Pi.*O.*1.28, *P.*10.30; esp. in Ep. phrase, θ. ἔργα *h.Merc.*80, 440, *h.Bacch.*34, Hes.*Sc.*165. (θαυμητός fr. θαυμαίνω (θαυμη-γω) as ἀκήρατος fr. κηραίνω.)

θαυμᾰτουργ-έω, = θαυματοποιέω, X.*Smp.*7.2; *work wonders* or *miracles*, Ph.2.18,185; but τὰ περίγεια θ. 'play tricks with', of Xerxes, Id.1.674; τὰ τεθαυματουργημένα *wonderful phenomena*, Pl.*Ti.* 80c. **-ημα**, ατος, τό, *wonder-work*, Ph.2.93 (pl.), Hld.10.39. **-ία**, ἡ, = θαυματοποιία, Pl.*Lg.*670a, Iamb.*Myst.*3.29; τοῦ θεοῦ Just.*Nov.* 40.1.1 (pl.). **-ός**, όν, = θαυματοποιός, γυναῖκες *acrobats*, Ath.4. 129d. II. *puppet-maker* or *-showman*, Hero *Aut.*1.7 (pl.).

θαῦνον· θηρίον, Hsch. **θαυσῆκρι**· θεωρεῖον, prob. f.l. for θατύς· ἰκρίον, θ., Id. **θαχθῆμεν**, v. θᾶξαι.

θαψία, ἡ, *deadly carrot, Thapsia garganica*, Arist.*Pr.*864^{a}5, Thphr. *HP*9.9.1,6, Dsc.4.153, Plin.*HN*13.124.

θάψῐνος, η, ον, *yellow-coloured, yellow, sallow*, γυνή Ar.*V.*1413; κρόκη *IG*1^2.330.17; χρῶμα Plu.*Phoc.*28; χιτών Callix.2.

θάψος, ἡ, *fustic, Rhus Cotinus, used for dyeing yellow*, brought from the island of Thapsos, Theoc.2.88, Nic.*Al.*570: θαψία ῥίζα Thphr. *Fr.*170.

***θάω**, v. θάομαι.

-θε, inseparable suffix, v. -θεν.

θεά, ἡ, in later Ep. **θεή** Call.*Dian.*119, dat. θεῇ A.R.3.549 codd. (Hom. has dat. pl. θεῇς, θεῇσι, Il.3.158, 8.305), Lacon. **σιά** Ar.*Lys.* 1263 (lyr.): fem. of θεός (q.v.) in Ep., Trag. (with imitations in Com., as Antiph.81, Eub.64), Att. in set phrases (v. infr.) and later Prose: —*goddess*, opp. γυνή, Il.14.315: with another Subst., θ. μήτηρ 1.280; θεαὶ νύμφαι 24.615; Παλλὰς θ. S.*Ant.*1184; θεοὶ θεαί τε A.*Th.*87 (lyr.); μὰ θεούς, μὰ θεάς Pl.*Smp.*219c; μὰ τοὺς θεοὺς καὶ τὰς θεάς D.19.67; τοῖς δώδεκα θεοῖς καὶ ταῖς σεμναῖς θεαῖς *IG*2^2.112.9, cf. Antiph.206.2, Anaxandr.2; τῷ θεῷ καὶ τῇ θεᾷ *IG*1^2.76.39: in dual, of Demeter and Persephone, μεγάλα θεά S.*OC*683 (in earlier Att. τὼ θεώ, v. θεός); αἱ θεαί *IG*2^2.661.28 (iii B.C.); αἱ σεμναὶ θ. the Erinyes, S.*OC*458, etc.; δειναί, ἀνώνυμοι θ., E.*El.*1270, *IT*944. II. name of third τόπος, Vett.Val.69.12, Paul.Al.*L.*3, cf. *Cat.Cod.Astr.*8(4).144. [⏑–, but sts. monosyll. in Trag., as E.*Andr.*978.]

θέᾱ, Ion. **θέη**, ἡ, (θεάομαι) *seeing, looking at*, θέης ἄξιος, = ἀξιοθέητος, Hdt.1.25, cf. X.*HG*6.2.34; θέαν λαβεῖν to take or get *a view*, S. *Ph.*536, 656; ἐς θέαν [τινὸς] ἔρχεσθαι, ἐπὶ θέαν τἀνδρὸς ἐλθεῖν, to go *to see*, E.*IA*427, Pl.*La.*179e; κατὰ θέαν ἀναβαίνειν τοῦ χωρίου Th. 5.7, cf. 9, 6.31; ἠγριωμένος ἐπὶ τῇ θέᾳ τινός at the *sight* of..., X. *Cyr.*1.4.24; βαδίζειν ἐπὶ κωμῳδῶν θέαν Id.*Oec.*3.7. b. of the mind, *contemplation*, ἡ τοῦ ὄντος θ. Pl.*R.*582c, cf. Arist.*Ph.*209^{b}20, etc. 2. *aspect*, διαπρεπὴς τὴν θ. E.*IA*1588; αἰσχρὰν θ. παρέχειν X.*Eq.*7.2; ἀπὸ τῆς θ. εἰκάζειν Luc.*VH*1.11; ὑποδῦσα θέαν ἀνθρώπου having assumed the *appearance* of a human being, Palaeph.48. II. *that which is seen, sight*, Ζηνὶ δυσκλεὴς θ. A.*Pr.*243; μάλ' ἄζηλος θ. S.*El.*1455; ὡς ἴδω πικρὰν θ. E.*Hipp.*809; ἀταρβὴς τῆς θ. without fear *of the sight*, S.*Tr.*23: pl., θέαι ἀμήχανοι τὸ κάλλος Pl.*R.*615a. 2. *spectacle, performance*, in a theatre or elsewhere, Thphr.*Char.*5.7, etc.; ἐν ταῖς θ. καὶ ἐν ταῖς πομπαῖς *CIG*3068*A*22 (Teos), cf. Plu.*Caes.* 55, *Brut.*21, Hdn.1.15.1 (pl.); μεγάλαι θ., = *Ludi Magni*, Plu.*Cam.* 5. III. *place for seeing from, seat in the theatre* (cf. αἴγειρος), θέαν εἰς τὰ Διονύσια καταvεῖμαι τοῖς πρέσβεσι Aeschin.2.55, cf. D.18. 28; θέαν καταλαμβάνειν to occupy one, Id.21.178; προκαταλαμβάνειν Luc.*Herm.*39; ἔχειν ἐν τῷ θεάτρῳ Plu.*Flam.*19, etc. 2. *auditorium*, *IG*2^2.1176. IV. αἴδεσσαί με θέας ὕπερ revere me *by thy countenance*, dub. in *h.Cer.*64 codd. (prob. θεὰν σύ περ).

θεαγγελεύς, έως, ὁ, *one who proclaims a festival*, Hsch.:—fem. **θεάγγελις**, ιδος, name of an intoxicating herb, used by the Magi, Plin. *HN*24.164.

θεαγενής· ὅσιος, θεοσεβής, Hsch. **θεάγισσα**, v. θεαγός.

θέαγον, = θεῖον (A) (at Salamis in Cyprus), Hsch.

θεᾱγός, ὁ, (θεός, ἄγω) *priest who carried images of the gods* in Egypt, *PPetr.*3 p.239 (iii B.C.), *PTeb.*61(*b*).59 (ii B.C.), *PRyl.*196.14 (ii A.D.), etc.:—fem. **θεάγισσα**, ἡ, *PSI*9.1039.45 (iii A.D.), al.

θεᾰγωγ-έω, *evoke gods*, Iamb.*Myst.*3.6:—hence **-ία**, ἡ, ib.2.10:— Adj. **-ός**, όν, λόγος *PMag.Par.*1.975, 985.

θεάζω, *to be divine*, Democr.21.

θέαινᾰ, ἡ, Ep. for θεά, *goddess*, in Hom. mostly in phrase πάντες τε θεοὶ πᾶσαί τε θέαιναι Il.8.5, cf. Od.8.341, al.; θεῶν τε καὶ θεαινῶν Antiph.81.3: in later Ep., Call.*Dian.*29.

θεαίτητος, ον, *obtained from God*, trans. of *Samuel*, J.*AJ*5.10.3: as pr. n. in Plato, etc.

θέ-ᾱμα, Ion. **θέημα**, ατος, τό, (θεάομαι) *sight, spectacle*, Semon.7.67, A.*Pr.*306, E.*Supp.*783, Ar.*Av.*1716, etc.; εἴ τις ὀρχοῖτ' εὖ, θέαμ' ἦν Pl.Com.130; opp. μάθημα, Th.2.39; freq. of a sight which gives pleasure, θεάματα καὶ ἀκροάματα ἥδιστα παρέχεις X.*Smp.*2.2, cf. 7.5; ὀρχήσεις καὶ θεάματα Phld.*Mus.*p.26K.; ἐμπλήσθητε τοῦ καλοῦ θ. Pl. *R.*440a; but also θ. δυσθέατον A.*Pr.*69, cf. S.*Aj.*992; ἑπτὰ θ. the seven *wonders of the world*, Str.14.2.5, Plu.2.983e: sg., of a marvellously engraved ring, Gal.*UP*17.1. **-άμων** [ᾱ], Ion. **θεήμων**, gen. ονος, ὁ, ἡ, *spectator*, *APl.*5.365.

θεανὴ νῆσος, f.l. for θεία νόσος (v. θεῖος A), S.*Fr.*650.

θεανῶσται· οἱ ξυστῆρες (Thess.), Hsch.

θεάομαι, Ep. and Ion. **θηέομαι** (v. infr.), Dor. **θᾱέομαι**, ***θάομαι** (qq.v.), imper. θεῶ Ar.*Ach.*262; opt. θηοῖο (for Att. θεῷο) Il.24.418; part. θηεύμενος Hdt.7.146: Ion. impf. ἐθηεῖτο, ἐθηεῦντο, Id.1.10, 3. 136; Ep. θηεῖτο Od.5.75, etc., θηεῦντο Il.7.444, al., ἐθηεύμεσθα Od.9. 218, ἐθεῆτο Hp.*Nat.Puer.*13, θηέσκετο Poet.ap.Parth.21.2: fut. θεάσομαι [ᾱ], Ion. -ήσομαι: aor. ἐθεασάμην, Ep. opt. θηήσαιο, θηήσαιτο, Od.17.315, 5.74; 3 pl. ἐθηήσαντο Euph.51.15; Ion. inf. θεήσασθαι (v.l. θεάσ-) Hdt.1.8: Att. pf. τεθέαμαι X.*Cyr.*7.5.7: codd. of Hdt. vary betw. θεη- and θηη-: a rare Ion. contr. of θηη- to θη- is found in θησαίατ' Od.18.191, θησάμενος *IG*1^2.826:—*gaze at, behold*, mostly with a sense of *wonder*, θηεῦντο μέγα ἔργον Il.7.444, cf. Od.2.13; λαοὶ δ' αὖ θηεῦντό τε θάμβησάν τε Il.23.728, cf. Hdt.1.8, 11, etc.; θ. τὰ καλά Democr.194; πάντες ὥσπερ ἄγαλμα ἐθεῶντο αὐτόν Pl.*Chrm.* 154c; θ. ὄμμασι E.*Ion*232 (lyr.); ζητεῖ τὸ κακὸν τεθεᾶσθαι Ar.*Th.*797 codd.; ἐθεᾶτο.. τὴν θέσιν τῆς πόλεως..., ὡς ἔχοι *reconnoitred* it, Th.5. 7; θ. κύκλῳ τὴν πόλιν X.*Cyr.*4.5.7: abs., θεᾷ; *do you see?* Men.*Epit.* 564. 2. of the mind, *contemplate*, τὸ ἀληθές Pl.*Phd.*84b, al. b. *see clearly*, ἵν' ἴδητε καὶ θεάσησθε ὅτι... D.4.3, cf. Pl.*Prt.*352a; with relat. clause, ὅση δεινότης ἦν ἐν τῷ Φιλίππῳ θεάσεσθε D.18.144. 3. *view as spectators*, esp. in the theatre, Isoc.4.44; οἱ θεώμενοι *the spectators*, Ar.*Ra.*2, cf. *Nu.*518, al. (but also, *onlookers, bystanders*, Antipho 3.3.7): metaph., θ. τὸν πόλεμον *to be spectators of* the war, Hdt. 8.116. 4. θ. τὸ στράτευμα *to review* it, X.*Cyr.*5.5.1. II. Act. **θεάω**, late, Baillet *Tombeaux des rois à Thèbes* 1080: elsewh. in imper. θέα Them.*Or.*3.44b, Jul.*Ep.*89b, Hsch.: aor. ἐθέαθην in pass. sense, Ps.-Callisth.2.42, *Ev.Marc.*16.11, Ap.Ty.*Ep.*49, Just.*Nov.*133.3.1: pres. θεῶνται Philostr.*Her.*2.9. (Orig. prob. θᾱϝέομαι and θᾱϝάομαι, cf. θαῦ-μα.)

θεάρεστος [ᾰ], ον, *pleasing to God*, Eustr. *in EN*35.34. Adv. -τως Sch.Iamb.*Protr.*13.

θεάριον [ᾱ], τό, Dor. for θεώριον (q.v.), *meeting-place of* θεωροί, Pi. *N.*3.70. II. **Θεάριος**, ὁ, Doric epith. of Apollo as god of oracles, *IG*4.748.16 (Troezen, iv B.C.), Paus.2.31.6.

θεᾱρίς, ίδος, fem. Adj. *of* or *for the* θεωροί, ὁδός *IGRom.*4.360.23 (Pergam., ii A.D.).

θεᾱροδόκος, **-δοκία**, Dor. for θεωρ- (q.v.).

θεᾱρός, ὁ, Dor. for θεωρός (q. v.): Θεαροί, οἱ, title of poem by Epich., Ath.9.408d.

θέασις, εως, ἡ, *contemplation*, Porph.*Abst.*4.6. II. *insight*, Gal. 1.52.

θεαστικός, ή, όν, (θεάζω) = ἐνθουσιαστικός, βῆμα *Mim.Oxy.*413.91.

θεᾱτ-έον, *one must see*, Pl.*Phd.*66e, *R.*390d. **-ής**, Ion. **θεητής**, οῦ, ὁ, (θεάομαι) *one who sees* or *goes to see*, τῆς χώρης Hdt.3.139, cf. E. *Ion* 301; in the theatre, *spectator*, Ar.*Nu.*575, al.; θ. σοφιστῶν Th. 3.38; *one who contemplates*, τἀληθοῦς Arist.*EN*1098a31. **-ικός**, ή, όν, *for seeing*, δύναμις θ. τινῶν Arr.*Epict.*1.6.3. **-ός**, ή, όν, *to be seen*, S.*Aj.*915; θ. σοφοῖς [Ἔρως] Pl.*Smp.*197d, cf. Isoc.2.49; μόνῳ νῷ Pl.*Phdr.*247c; cf. θαητός.

θεᾱτρ-εῖον, τό, = θέατρον, Suid. **-ια**, ἡ, fem. of θεατής, Com. ap.Poll.2.56. **-ίδιον**, τό, Dim. of θέατρον, Varro *RR*3.5.13. **-ίζω**, *to be* or *play on the stage*, Suid. II. Pass., *to be made a show of, held up to shame*, *Ep.Hebr.*10.33. **-ικός**, Ion. **θεητρικός**, ή, όν, *of* or *for the theatre, theatrical*, μουσική Arist.*Pol.*1342a18; ὄψις Plu.*Alex.* 19: **-κά**, τά, *properties*, etc., *OGI*510.7 (Ephesus, ii A.D.): **-κοί**, οἱ, *actors*, *BCH*44.88 (Lagina). Adv. **-κῶς**, εἰπεῖν Plu.2.1076c. 2. *pretentious*, Hp.*Medic.*4; θ. μέν... ἀνίατρον δέ Antyll.ap.Orib.10.23. 24; τὸ θ. Plu.2.7a, 15e. Adv. **-κῶς**, πολεμεῖν, στρατηγεῖν, Id.*Luc.* 11, *Lys.*21. 3. πόδες θ. dub. sens. in *IG*11(2).203 *B* 13 (Delos, iii B.C.), cf. *Inscr.Délos* 291 *b* 30. **-ισμός**, ὁ, *theatrical exhibition*, Vett.Val.18.1 (pl.), cf. Thom.Mag.p.283 R. **-ιστής**, οῦ, ὁ, *stage-player*, Hsch., Suid. s. v. ἠθολόγος.

θεᾱτρο-ειδής, ές, *like a theatre*, πέτρα Str.4.1.4, cf. D.S.19.45. Adv. **-δῶς** Str.16.2.41; *like the spectators in a theatre*, Crito ap.Gal. 12.458. **-κόπος**, ον, *courting applause*, Ptol.*Tetr.*165: **-κοπία**, ἡ, *courting of applause*, in pl., Artem.2.70. **-κορασία** (sic), = ὀχλοκορασία (sic), *EM*444.16 (better **-κρασία** in both words, Suid.; cf. sq.). **-κρᾰτία**, ἡ, *rule exercised by the spectators in a theatre*, Pl.*Lg.*701a. **-κῡνηγέσιον**, τό, in pl., *beast-hunts in the amphitheatre*, *Ausonia*6.9* (Gortyn), Just.*Nov.*105.1:—also **-κῡνήγιον**, τό, ibid. **-μᾰνέω**, *to be mad after stage-plays*, Man.4.277, Ph.2. 167. **-μορφος**, ον, = θεατροειδής, *theatre-shaped*, Lyc.600.

θέᾱτρον, Ion. **θέητρον**, τό, (θεάομαι) *place for seeing*, esp. *for dramatic representation, theatre*, Hdt.6.67, *IG*2².1176, al.; as a *place of assembly*, Th.8.93, Lys.13.32, *SIG*976.4 (Samos, ii B.C.), Posidon.36 J., *Act.Ap.*19.20, etc.; θ. κυνηγετικόν, of the Roman *amphitheatre*, D.C. 43.22; εἰς τὸ θ. εἰσφέρειν to bring upon *the stage*, Isoc.12.122; τὸ καλὸν τοῦ θ. a good place in the *theatre*, Ael.*VH*2.13, cf. Alciphr.3. 20. 2. collective for οἱ θεαταί, *the spectators*, '*the house*', Hdt.6. 21, Ar.*Eq.*233, al., Pl.*Smp.*194b, *Com.Adesp.*3 D.: metaph., ἐκάθηντο θέατρον αὐτῷ Lib.*Ep.*722.4. 3. = θέαμα, *spectacle*, θ. ἐγενήθημεν τῷ κόσμῳ 1*Ep.Cor.*4.9. 4. metaph., of *life*, τουτὶ τὸ θ. ὑπεκρίθημεν Porph.*Marc.*2.

θεᾱτρο-ποιός, όν, *making a theatre*, Anaxandr.34.9 (s. v. l.). **-πώλης**, ου, ὁ, *one who sells seats in a theatre*, Ar.*Fr.*562. **-τορύνη** [ῠ], ἡ, = τορύνη θεάτρου, *stage-pounder*, epith. of Melissa, who was a clumsy dancer, Ath.4.157a.

θεατρ-ώδης, ες, *theatrical*, in a bad sense, of persons, Vett.Val.14. 27. **-ώνης**, ου, ὁ, *lessee of a theatre*, Thphr.*Char.*30.6.

θεάφιον, τό, = θεῖον (A), *sulphur*, Hsch.: **θέαφος**, ὁ, Eust.1935.22.

θεάω, v. θεάομαι. **Θεδαίσιος**, v. Θεοδαίσια II.

θεειδής, ές, (θεός) = θεοειδής, [ἄνθρωπος] πάντων θηρίων θεειδέστατον Antipho Soph.48 (prob. l.).

θέεινος, η, ον, *sulphur-coloured*, *PTeb.*405.13 (iii A.D.).

θέειον, **θεειόω**, Ep. for θεῖον (A), θειόω (q.v.):—also **θέειος**, for θεῖος (A): **θεείω**· θαυμάζω, Suid.

θέη, ἡ, Ion. for θέα.

θεη-γενής, ές, poet. for θεογενής, Orph.*A.*1347, Q.S.6.9. **-γορέω**, *discourse of God*, Olymp.Alch.p.84 B. **-γόρος**, ὁ, *one who discourses of God*, Id.p.83 B.; but, *inspired by God*, Hld.2.4; μῦθος *spoken by a goddess*, Orph.*A.*541. **-δόχος**, ον, poet. for θεοδόχος, Nonn.*D.* 13.96.

θεήϊος, η, ον, Ion. for θέειος, θεῖος (A), *divine*, Bion *Fr.*15.9.

θεηκολ-έω, *to be a* θεηκόλος, *IG*2².1364 (i A.D.), prob. in *Inscr. Olymp.*468 (iii A.D.); παῖδας ἀοιδοπόλους Ζηνὶ -έοντας *BCH*50.529 (ii A.D.). **-εών**, ῶνος, ὁ, *dwelling of a* θεηκόλος, Paus.5.15.8. **-ος**, ον, = θεοκόλος, *priest*, ib.10, *IG*3.305, 487, *Inscr.Olymp.*123; *choirboy*, Luc.*Alex.*41 (pl.).

θεηκόρος, ὁ, = -κόλος, Ap.Ty.*Ep.*26 tit.

θεηλ-ᾰσία, ἡ, *visitation of God*, Sch.S.*Tr.*1235 (ἠλασία cod.). **-ᾰτέομαι**, *to be visited by God*, Hld.8.10. II. *complain of God's visitations*, Id.6.8. **-ᾰτος**, ον, (ἐλαύνω) *driven by a god*, θεηλάτου βοὸς δίκην A.*Ag.*1297; θ. δαίμονες Plu.2.830f. II. *sent* or *caused by a god*, of things evil in themselves or in their consequences, φθορή Hdt.7.18; ἔργον, πρᾶγμα, μάντευμα, S.*Ant.*278, *OT*255, 992; νόσους δ' ἀνάγκη τὰς θ. φέρειν Id.*Fr.*680; ἔκ τινος θεηλάτου from some *destiny*, E.*Ion* 1392. III. *built for the gods*, ἕδραι ib.1306.

θέημα, ατος, τό, Ion. for θέαμα, Semon.7.67.

θεημάχος [ᾰ], ον, poet. for θεομ-, *AP.*9.769 (Agath.); φῦλα Γιγάντων Procl.*H.*7.8.

θεημοσύνη, ἡ, *contemplation*: *a problem*, *AP*11.352.10 (Agath.).

θεήμων, ονος, ὁ, ἡ, Ion. for θεάμων, *APl.*5.365.

θεηπολέω, poet. for θεοπ-, Phot., Suid.

θεητής, **θέητρον**, Ion. for θεᾱτής, θέᾱτρον.

θέθμιον, τό, = θέσμιον, v. θέσμιος II:—also **θεθμός**, ὁ, Dor., = θεσμός (q. v.): and **θεθτμός**, *Schwyzer* 411 (Elis).

θεία, ἡ, *one's father's* or *mother's sister, aunt*, *POxy.*274.5 (i A.D.), Ammon.*Diff.*p.130 V., etc. (Late formation fr. θεῖος (B), replacing τηθίς.)

θει-άζω, (θεῖος A) *to be inspired, frenzied*, ὁπόσοι αὐτοὺς θειάσαντες ἐπήλπισαν as many as made them hope *by divinations*, Th.8.1; θ. καὶ θεοφορεῖται *is divinely inspired*, Ph.1.479; ὁπόσοι τελεταῖς ἐθείαζον *obtained inspiration* through ritual, Philostr.*Her.*5.3. 2. *prophesy*, ὅτι στρατοπεδεύσοιτο D.C.*Fr.*57.48:—Pass., [λόγος] ἐπὶ τῇ τελευτῇ τοῦ Ἀλεξάνδρου ἐθειάσθη Arr.*An.*7.18.6; λόγιον ὑπὸ τοῦ ὁμίλου θειασθέν D.C.62.18. II. *worship as divine*, Id.59.27; Πυθαγόραν καὶ Πλάτωνα Dam.*Isid.*36:—Pass., Max.Tyr.8.9. **-ασμός**, ὁ, *superstition*, ἄγαν θειασμῷ προσκείμενος, of Nicias, Th.7.50. II. *inspiration, frenzy*, θειασμοῖς κάτοχοι γυναῖκες D.H.7.68; θειασμοῦ [ἐπιρρήματα], such as εὐοῖ, D.T.642.17. **-αστής**, οῦ, ὁ, *worshipper*, Tz.*H.*8.347. **-αστικός**, ή, όν, *like one inspired*. Adv. **-κῶς** Poll.1.16.

θειάφιον, τό, *sulphur*, Tz.*H.*12.743.

Θείβᾱθεν, Adv., Boeot. for Θήβηθεν, *from Thebes*, Ar.*Ach.*862:—**Θείβᾱθι**, *at Thebes*, ib.868 codd. (**Θείβᾱθε** *from Thebes*, Elmsl.).

θείκελος, dub. l. in Ar.*Lys.*1252 codd. (σιοείκελοι Mein., συείκελοι Wilam.).

θεϊκός, ή, όν, late form for θεῖος (A), θρησκεία *Cat.Cod.Astr.*1.116; σοφία *MAMA*1.228 (Laodicea Combusta).

θειλο-πεδεύω, *dry in the sun*, σταφυλήν Dsc.5.6 (Pass.). **-πεδον**, τό, *sunny spot* in the vineyard where grapes were dried, Od.7.123, *AP*6.169, 9.586 (Comet.), Sch.E.*Or.*1492; θειλοπέδου τρόπον Dsc.1. 32; v. εἰλόπεδον.

Θειλούθιος, ὁ (sc. μήν), month in Boeotia, *IG*7.2861, al.: written **Θηλούθιος** ib.3326, al.

θεῖμεν, for θείημεν, 1 pl. aor. 2 opt. Act. of τίθημι.

θειμωνιαί· οἱ σωροὶ τῶν δραγμάτων, Hsch. (Boeot. for θημ-).

θεῖναι, aor. 2 inf. Act. of τίθημι.

θεινίον, v. θινίον.

θεϊνός, ή, όν, = θῖνος (q. v.), *GDI*4940.26 (Crete).

θείνω, Ep. inf. θεινέμεναι Od.22.443: impf. ἔθεινον A.*Pers.*418, etc.: fut. θενῶ Ar.*Ach.*564: aor. 1 part. θείνας Il.20.481 (ἔθεινε in 21.491 may be impf.); other moods from an aor. 2 ἔθενον (which does not occur in ind.); imper. θένε E.*Rh.*676, Ar.*Av.*54; subj. θένω E.*Rh.*687 (troch.), Ar.*Lys.*821 (lyr.), cj. in Theoc.22.66; inf. θενεῖν E.*Heracl.* 271; part. θενών Id.*Cyc.*7, Ar.*Eq.*640, *V.*1384, *Av.*1613, *Ra.*855 (these forms were freq. incorrectly written θένειν, θένων, as if from a pres. *θένω):—Pass., only in pres. and impf.:—poet. word, *strike*, τινα Od. 18.63; ξίφεσι 22.443; φασγάνῳ αὐχένα θείνας Il.20.481; μάστιγι.. θείνων 17.430; [τόξοισι] ἔθεινε παρ' οὔατα 21.491:—Pass., 1.588; θεινόμεναι βουπλῆγι 6.135; ἄορι 10.484; θεινομένου... πρὸς οὔδεϊ *dashed* to earth, Od.9.459; later σκάπτῳ θενών τινα Pi.*O.*7.28; ῥαιστῆρι A. *Pr.*56, cf. 76; τινὰ δι' ἀσπίδος E.*Heracl.*738; ἰτέαν εἰς μέσην Id.*Cyc.*7; τῷ σκέλει θένε τὴν πέτραν Ar.*Av.*54; τῷ πρωκτῷ θενὼν τὴν κιγκλίδ' Id. *Eq.*640; ποσσὶ θ. σκέλος, of a wrestler, Theoc.22.66: abs., θείνετε v.l. in E.*Or.*1303 (lyr.); θεῖν', ἀντέρειδε Id.*Supp.*702; θένε, θένε Id. *Rh.*676 (lyr.):—Pass., A.*Pers.*303, *Ch.*388 (lyr.). 2. metaph., θείνει δ' ὀνείδει μάντιν Id.*Th.*382. 3. intr., of corpses, θ. ἐπ' ἀκτᾶς Id.*Pers.*966. II. to the same Verb, but only with the meaning *slay*, belong the foll. forms formerly referred to a pres. *φένω, viz.: aor. 2 ἔπεφνον Il.21.55, Pi.*P.*10.46, B.17.19, S.*OT*1497; Ep. and Lyr. πέφνον Il.13.363, B.8.13; subj. πέφνῃς, ῃ, Od.22.346, Il.20.172; inf. πεφνέμεν 6.180; part. πεφνών 16.827 (parox. acc. to Aristarch., as if from a pres. πέφνω, which is found in late Ep., Opp.*H.*2.133): from the short form φᾰ (for φn̥) come pf. Pass. 3 sg. πέφαται Il.15. 140, al.; 3 pl. πέφανται 5.531; inf. πεφάσθαι 13.447: fut. Pass. πεφήσεαι ib.829, Od.22.217; ἢ πέφατ' ἢ .. πεφήσεται Il.15.140; later, part. πεφασμένος Lyc.269, 1374, Opp.*H.*5.122: Gramm. also give aor. 1 φάσαι Hsch. s. v. φάσγανον, Phot. s. v. πρόσφατος, Sch.Pi.*N.* 1.69: aor. 2 part. παφών Hsch.: aor. 2 Med. ἀπ-έφατο, = ἀπέθανεν, Id. Hence also φᾰτός *slain*, Id., found in compds. Ἀρεί-φατος, μυλή-φατος, ὀδυνή-φατος, πυρί-φατος. (I.-E. g^uhen- cf. Skt. *hánti*, pl. *ghnánti*, Hittite *kuenzi*, pl. *kunanzi* 'strike', 'kill'; g^uhon- in Gr. φόνος; g^uhn- in Skt. *ghn-ánti*, Gr. ἔ-πε-φν-ον (redupl.); g^uhn̥- in Skt. *-hata-*, Gr. -φατο-, πέφαται, etc.)

θειο-γενής, ές, = θεο-, *Gloss.* **-δάμη** [ᾰ], ἡ, (δαμάω) *she who tames the gods*, Suid.:—Adj. **-δᾶμος**, ἀνάγκαι Orac.ap.Porph.ap.Eus. *PE*5.8. **-δμητος**, ον, = θεό-, *AP*9.157 (v.l. θεοδηλήτου). **-δομος**, ον, *built by gods*, τεῖχος ib.7.138 (Acerat.), cf. 9.104 (Alph.).

θειόθεν, Adv., (cf. θεῖος (A) I. 4) *from the Emperor*, Just.*Nov.*82.9.

θειολόγος, ὁ, poet. for θεολόγος, *IG*3.770 (i A.D.).

θείομεν, Ep. for θέωμεν, θῶμεν, 1 pl. aor. 2 subj. Act. of τίθημι.

θεῖον (A), Ep. **θέειον** (in Od.22.493 **θήϊον**), τό, *brimstone*, used to fumigate and purify, δέπας.. ἐκάθηρε θεείῳ Il.16.228; οἶσε θέειον.., κακῶν ἄκος Od.22.481; δεινὴ δὲ θεείου γίγνεται ὀδμή, from a thunderbolt, Il.14.415; ἐν δὲ θεείου πλῆτο, of a ship struck by lightning, Od. 12.417; ἐμβαλόντες πῦρ ξὺν θ. Th.2.77, cf. 4.100; Κύριος ἔβρεξεν ἐπὶ Σόδομα καὶ Γόμορρα θ. καὶ πῦρ LXX *Ge.*19.24; as a natural product, Hp.*Aër.*7, Ph.2.21, 143, Ti.Locr.99c; θ. ἄπυρον Gal.12.903; opp. πεπυρωμένον, Dsc.5.107; cf. θεάφιον, θέαφος. (Perh. cogn. with θύω, θυμιάω, Lat. *suffīre*.)

θεῖον (B), τό, *the Divinity*, v. θεῖος (A) II.

θειο-πᾰγής, ές, *god-made*, ἱστός Orac.ap.Phleg.*Mir.*10; cf. θεοφανής. **-πόλος**, ὁ, *ministrant*, Maiist.43. **-πρόπος**, ὁ, poet. for θεοπρόπος, *IG*12(5).893.6 (Tenos, ii/iii A.D.); ἔγγονε θειοπρόπων, = θεοπροπίδης, Orac.ap.Porph.*Abst.*2.9.

θεῖος (A), α, ον: late Ep. **θέειος** Procl.*H.*2.16; **θεήϊος** Bion *Fr.*15. 9; late Aeol. **θήϊος** *Epigr.Gr.*989.4 (Balbilla); Lacon. **σεῖος** (v. infr. 1.3): Comp. and Sup. θειότερος, -ότατος, freq. in Pl., *Phdr.*279a, *Mx.* 244d, al.: (θεός): 1. *of* or *from the gods, divine*, γένος Il.6.180; ὀμφή 2.41; Ὄνειρος ib.22; ἐπιπνοίαις A.*Supp.*577, cf. Pl.*R.*499c; μάστιξ A. *Pr.*682; μανία S.*Aj.*611 (lyr.); νόσος ib.185 (lyr.) (but θ. νόσος, of a dust-storm, Id.*Ant.*421); κίνδυνοι And.1.139; θ. τινὶ μοίρᾳ by *divine* intervention, X.*HG*7.5.10; θ. τύχῃ γεγονώς Hdt.1.126; θ. τύχῃ χρεώμενος Id.3.139; θ. κάπόνῳ τύχῃ, of an easy death, S.*OC*1585; ἐκ θ. τύχης Id.*Ph.*1326; ἔμαθε ὡς θ. εἴη τὸ πρῆγμα Hdt.6.69; ὁ θ. νόμος Th.3. 82; φύσις θ. *SIG*1125.8 (Eleusis), cf. 2*Ep.Pet.*1.4; *appointed of God*, βασιλῆες Od.4.691; σκῆπτρον *given by God*, S.*Ph.*139 (lyr.); v. infr. 2. 2. *belonging* or *sacred to a god, holy*, ἀγών, χορός, Il.7.298, Od. 8.264; *under divine protection*, πύργος, δόμος, Il.21.526, Od.4.43; of heralds and bards, Il.4.192, Od.4.17, al.; so perh., of kings, ib. 691. 3. *more than human*, of heroes, Ὀδυσσεύς Il.2.335, al., Cratin. 144.4 (lyr.); θ. ἀνήρ Pi.*P.*6.38, A.*Ag.*1548 (lyr.), Pl.*R.*331e, *Men.*99d (esp. at Sparta (Lacon. σεῖος), Arist.*EN*1145^{a}29; ὦ θεῖε (in the mouth of a Spartan) Pl.*Lg.*626c); μετὰ σοῦ τῆς θείας κεφαλῆς Id.*Phdr.*234d, cf. Them.*Or.*9.128a, Lib.*Or.*19.66. b. of things, *excellent*, θεῖον ποτόν Od.2.341, 9.205; ἁλὸς θείοιο Il.9.214; θ. πρήγματα *marvellous* things, Hdt.2.66; ἐν τοῖσι θειότατον Id.7.137. 4. = Lat. *divinus* (or *sacer*), *Imperial*, διατάξεις prob. in *BGU*473.5 (200 A.D.), etc.; θησαυροί *PLips.*62 ii 14 (iv A.D.); θ. ὅρκος oath *by the Emperor*, *POxy.*83.6 (iv A.D.), etc.; θειότατος, of living Emperors, *Inscr.Prien.*105.22 (9 B.C.), etc. b. = Lat. *divus*, of deified Emperors, θ. Σεβαστός Edict.Claud. ap.J.*AJ*19.5.3, cf. *Inscr.Perg.*283 (iii A.D.), Lyd.*Mag.*2.3. II. as Subst., θεῖον, τό, *the Divinity*, Hdt.1.32, 3.108, al., A.*Ch.*958 (lyr.); τοῦ θ. χάριν Th.5.70; ἡμαρτηκότα εἰς τὸ θ. Pl.*Phdr.*242c. 2. in an abstract sense, *divinity*, κεκοινώνηκε..τοῦ θ. ib.246d; ἢ μόνον μετέχει τοῦ θ..., ἢ μάλιστα [ἄνθρωπος] Arist.*PA*656^{a}8, etc.; κατὰ θεῖον or κατά τι θ., Aen.Gaz.*Thphr.*p.37 B., p.4 B. 3. θεῖα, τά, *the acts of the gods, course of providence*, S.*Ph.*452, etc.; τὰ θ. θνητοὺς ὄντας εὐπετῶς φέρειν S.*Fr.*585; τὰ θ. μὴ φαύλως φέρειν Ar.*Av.*961. b. *matters of religion*, ἔρρει τὰ θ. *religion* is no more, S.*OT*910 (lyr.), cf. *OC*1537, X.*Cyr.*8.8.2, etc. c. *inquiries concerning the divine*, Pl.*Sph.*232c; τὰ φανερὰ τῶν θείων, i.e. the heavenly bodies, Arist.*Metaph.*1026^{a}18, cf. *GA*731^{b}24, *Ph.*196^{a}33 (Sup.), *EN*1141^{b}1. III. Adv. θείως *by divine providence*, θ. πως X.*Cyr.*4.2.1, etc.; θειοτέρως *by special providence*, Hdt.1.122; μᾶλλόν τι καὶ -οτέρον ib.174. 2. *divinely, excellently*, εὖ γε καὶ θ. Pl.*Tht.*154d; θείως εἰρῆσθαι Arist.*Metaph.*1074^{b}9.

θεῖος (B), ὁ, *one's father's* or *mother's brother, uncle*, E.*IT*930, Ar. *Nu.*124, And.1.18, 117, Pl.*Chrm.*154b, Men.5 D., etc.; ὁ πρὸς μητρὸς θ. Is.5.10; πρὸς πατρός Ph.2.172. (Cf. τήθη.)

θειό-στεπτος, -τελής, v. θεο-.

θειότης, ητος, ἡ, *divine nature, divinity*, Lxx *Wi.*18.9, *Ep.Rom.*1.20, *SIG*867.31 (Ephesus, ii A.D.), Plu.2.665a, etc. 2. f.l. for ὁσιότης, Isoc.11.26, Plu.2.857a, and so prob. in Id.*Sull.*6. II. as title of Roman Emperors, Orib.1.1.1, *SIG*900.23 (Panamara, iv A.D.), etc.

θειοφᾰνής, ές, *manifested by the gods*, Alex.162.14 (anap., v.l. -παγές).

θειόχροος, ον, contr. **-χρους**, ουν, *brimstone-coloured*, Dsc.5.101.

θειόω, Ep. **θεειόω**, (θεῖον A) *fumigate with brimstone*, ὄφρα θεειώσω μέγαρον Od.22.482; θειώσας τὰς ἀλλοτρίας ἐπινοίας, metaph., from the clothes-cleaner, who used sulphur, Lysipp.4:—Med., δῶμα θεειοῦται he *fumigates his* house, Od.23.50. 2. *purify, hallow*, θείου..θεσμὸν αἰθέρος μυχῶν dub. in E.*Hel.*866. 3. *smear with sulphur*, Gal.1.658 (Pass.); ἔριον τεθειωμένον *sulphurated*, Orib.*Fr.* 35, Paul.Aeg.3.33. II. in Alchemy, *sulphurate*, Ps.-Democr.ap. Zos.Alch.p.153 B. III. (θεῖος A) *hallow, consecrate*, Pl.*Lg.*771b, Ph.1.374.

θείω, Ep. for θέω, *run*. II. Ep. for θῶ, 1 sg. subj. aor. 2 of τίθημι.

θειώδης (A), ες, (θεῖον A) *sulphureous*, of waters, etc., Anon.Lond. 24.45, Antyll.ap.Orib.10.2.3, Archig.ap.Aët.3.167, Phlp.*in Mete.*7. 5; ὀδμή Str.1.3.18. 2. of colour, *yellow*, θώρακες *Apoc.*9.17.

θειώδης (B), ες, (θεῖος A) *divine*. Adv. -δως *by Imperial decree*, *PMasp.*451.42, 56 (vi A.D.).

θέκλεον· θαυμαστόν, Hsch. (fort. θέσκελον).

θελγεσίμῡθος [ῐ], ον, *soft-speaking*, *AP*9.525.9.

θέλγητρον, τό, (θέλγω) *charm, spell*, in pl., Hld.7.9: more usu. metaph., ὦ φίλον ὕπνου θ. E.*Or.*211; πόθων θέλγητρα Ath.5.220f; of music, Luc.*Im.*14; of a city, Id.*Scyth.*5; cf. θέλκτρον.

Θελγῖνες, = Τελχῖνες (q.v.), *wizards*, Hsch., Eust.1391.12.

θέλγμα, ατος, τό, = θέλγητρον, Sch.Pi.*P.*1.21; glossed by θαῦμα, Hsch.

θέλγω, Ion. impf. θέλγεσκεν Od.3.264: fut. θέλξω 16.298, A.*Pr.*865, Dor. -ξῶ Theoc.*Ep.*5.3: aor. ἔθελξα Il. (v. infr.):—**Med.**, Alc.*Supp.* 11.7:—Pass., fut. θελχθήσομαι Luc.*Salt.*85: aor. ἐθέλχθην Od.10. 326, Ep. 3 pl. -χθεν 18.212:—poet. Verb (used by Pl.*Smp.*197e, and in late Prose, as Phld.*Mus.*p.72 K., Jul.*Or.*4.150c, etc.), *enchant, bewitch*, [Ἑρμῆς] ἀνδρῶν ὄμματα θέλγει Od.5.47, al.; τὸν..Ποσειδάων ἐδάμασσε θέλξας ὄσσε φαεινά Il.13.435; [Κίρκη] οὐδ᾽ ὣς θέλξαι σε δυνήσεται Od.10.291, cf. 326 (Pass.); [Σειρῆνες] πάντας ἀνθρώπους θέλγουσιν, ὅτις σφέας εἰσαφίκηται 12.40; [θύελλα] θέλγε νόον *spell-bound* their senses, Il.12.255. 2. *cheat, cozen*, Od.16.195, 298, S.*Tr.*710: c. dat. modi, μήτε τί μοι ψεύδεσσι χαρίζεο μήτε τι θέλγε Od.14.387; μαλακοῖσι καὶ αἱμυλίοισι λόγοισι 1.57; ψεύδεσσι, δόλῳ, Il.21.276, 604; ἔπεσσιν Od.3.264. 3. metaph., *charm, beguile*, 17.521; οἱ ἐλπὶς ἔθελγε νόον *h.Cer.*37, cf. Pi.*P.*1.12, D.Chr.45.5; καί μ᾽ οὔτι μελιγλώσσοις πειθοῦς ἐπαοιδαῖσιν θέλξει A.*Pr.*174: σὺ δὲ θέλγοις ἂν ἄθελκτον Id. *Supp.*1055; θέλγει ἔρως E.*Hipp.*1274 (lyr.); ᾠδῆς.., ἣν ᾄδει θέλγων.. νόημα Pl.*Smp.*197e:—Pass., μήθ᾽ ὕπνῳ θελχθῇς E.*IA*142 (lyr.); τὰ δ᾽ οὔτι θέλγεται A.*Ch.*420 (lyr.); ἔρῳ δ᾽ ἄρα θυμὸν ἔθελχθεν Od.18.212; Μούσαισιν..τὴν φρένα θελγομένη (which may be Med.) *IG*14.1960. 4. c. inf., ἵμερος θέλξει τὸ μὴ κτεῖναι *will persuade* her not to kill, A.*Pr.* 865; ἔρως δέ νιν..θέλξειεν αἰχμάσαι τάδε S.*Tr.*355; ἕπεσθαι θ. Ael. *NA*10.14. 5. *produce by spells*, ἀοιδαὶ θέλξαν νιν (sc. εὐφροσύναν) Pi.*N.*4.3; [Γαλήνη] θ. ἀνηνεμίην *AP*9.544 (Adaeus). (Perh. cf. Lith. *žvelgiù* 'look', 'glance'.)

θελεμός, όν, epith. of πῶμα, A.*Supp.*1027 (lyr.): glossed by οἰκτρόν, ἥσυχον, Hsch.; but, = θελημός, acc. to Hdn.Gr.1.171, cf. *EM*103.48. Adv. -μῶς Hsch.

θέλ-εος, ον, *willing*, θ. ἀθέλεος, Lat. *nolens volens*, A.*Supp.*862 (lyr.). **-ημα**, ατος, τό, (θέλω) *will*, Antipho Soph.58 (pl.), Aen.Tact. 18.19, Lxx *Es.*1.8, al., *Ev.Matt.*7.21, *POxy.*924.8 (iv A.D.). II. ἔστιν μοι θ. ἔν τινι *pleasure* in.., Lxx *Ec.*12.1, cf. 5.3:—also **-ήμη**, ἡ, Theognost.*Can.*112. **-ηματικός**, ή, όν, *optional, voluntary, superfluous*. Adv. -κῶς Eust.920.19. **-ημάτιον**, τό, Dim. of θέλημα, ἔσχατον θ. last *will and testament*, *PLond.*1.77.12 (vi A.D.). **-ημός**, όν, *willing*, Emp.35.6. 2. *kindly*, ἄλσος B.16.85; glossed by ἥσυχος, Phot. **-ημοσύνη**, ἡ, = θέλησις, *PMag.Par.*1.2921 (pl.). **-ήμων**, ον, gen. ονος, *voluntary*, εἰρεσίη A.R.2.557. **-ησις**, εως, ἡ, *a willing, will*, *Stoic.*3.41, Lxx *To.*12.18, al., Phld.*Rh.*2.297 S., *Ep.Hebr.* 2.4; condemned by Poll.5.165: in Dor. pl. θελήσιες, *wishes*, Meliss. *Ep.* II. *goodwill, favour*, Lxx *Pr.*8.35. **-ητής**, οῦ, ὁ, *one who wills*, ἐλέους ib.*Mi.*7.18, cf. Hsch. II. *wizard* (by confusion of Hebr. *'ōbh* 'necromancer' with *'ōbheh* 'wishing'), Lxx 4*Ki.*21.6; = ἐγγαστρίμυθος, Cyr. **-ητός**, ή, όν, *wished for, desired*, Lxx 1*Ki.* 15.22, *Ma.*3.12.

θέλκ-ταρ, τό, = θέλγητρον, Hsch. (θέρκαλ cod.). **-τήρ**, ῆρος, ὁ, *soother, charmer*, θελκτὴρ ὀδυνάων, of Asclepius, *h.Hom.*16.4; cf. θέλκτωρ. **-τήριον**, τό, *charm, spell*, of the girdle of Aphrodite, ἔνθα τέ οἱ θ. πάντα τέτυκτο Il.14.215; of heroic lays, βροτῶν θελκτήρια Od.1.337; θεῶν θ. 8.509; πόνων θελκτήρια *means of lightening* toil, A.*Ch.*670 (s.v.l.); γλώσσης ἐμῆς μείλιγμα καὶ θ. Id.*Eu.*886; νεκροῖς θελκτήρια, of offerings to the Manes, E.*IT*166 (lyr.); ψυχῆς θ. Men. 559. **-τήριος**, ον, *enchanting, soothing*, μῦθοι, λόγοι, A.*Eu.*81, E. *Hipp.*478; ὄμματος θ. τόξευμα the eye's *magic* shaft, A.*Supp.*1004: c. gen., φίλτρα θ. ἔρωτος E.*Hipp.*509; μύθου μῦθος θ. speech *that heals* speech, A.*Supp.*447: in late Prose, θ. ἀγωνίσματα, of poems, Agath. *Praef.* **-τικός**, ή, όν, = foreg., δύναμις Sch.E.*Or.*211. **-τρον**, τό, = θελκτήριον, S.*Tr.*585, prob. in A.R.1.515 (nisi leg. **θελκτύν**). **-τωρ**, = θελκτήρ, A.*Supp.*1040 (lyr., θεάκτ- cod. M), cf. Suid. (θελκτῶ codd.).

θελξῐ-επής, ές, *speaking winning words*, γᾶρυς B.14.48. **-μβροτος**, ον, *charming men*, Κύπρις Id.5.175; ᾠδή Orph.*L.*320. **-μελής**, ές, *charming with music*, [φόρμιγξ] *IG*3.400. **-νοος**, ον, contr. **-νους**, ουν, *charming the heart*, φίλτρα *AP*6.88 (Antiphan.); ἔαρ ib.10.15 (Paul. Sil.); Ἔρωτες Musae.147. **-πικρος**, ον, *sweetly painful*, κνησμοναί *App.Anth.*3.158.

θέλξις, εως, ἡ, *an enchanting*, Ael.*NA*8.24, Plu.2.662a.

θελξίφρων, ον, gen. ονος, = θελξίνοος, Ἔρωτες E.*Ba.*404 (lyr.); παλμός *AP*9.505.17; of Apollo, ib.525.9.

θελοντής, οῦ, ὁ, = ἐθελοντής (q.v.), Hierocl.p.56 A., v.l. in Hdt. 6.92.

θέλυμνα, ων, τά, = θέμεθλα, *foundations* or *elements of things*, θ. τε καὶ στερεωπά cj. for θελημνά, θελημά, Emp.21.6. (Cf. προθέλυμνος, τετραθέλυμνος.)

θέλω, v. ἐθέλω and add ὅστις ἂν θέλῃ *IG*1^{2}.49.12; ἐὰν δέ τις θέλῃ ib.6.106; ἐάν τις μὴ θέλῃ ib.40.27.

θέμα, ατος, τό, (τίθημι) *that which is placed* or *laid down*: 1. *money deposited, deposit*, Ceb.31, *PCair.Zen.*22.11 (iii B.C.), *SIG*742. 58 (Ephesus, i B.C.), Plu.2.116a, b; also, of grain, *PRyl.*199.12 (i A.D.); ἐν θέματι ἔχειν παρά τινος *PTeb.*120.125 (i B.C.); *treasure*, Lxx *To.*4.9. 2. *pile*, of loaves, ib.*Le.*24.6, 7; θ. βρωμάτων παρακείμενα ἐπὶ τάφῳ ib.*Si.*30.18. 3. = θήκη, *coffer*, ib.1*Ki.*6.8. 4. *position, situation*, of land, *IG*14.217 (Acrae). 5. Astrol., *nativity*, '*horoscope*' (in mod. sense), Suet.*Aug.*94, Vett.Val.194.20, al., Man. 1.278. 6. either *common burial-place* or *common land*, *Michel* 995 *B* 50 (pl.); *private burial-ground*, ἡ σορὸς καὶ τὸ βαθρικὸν καὶ τὸ ὑποκείμενον θ. Judeich *Altertümer von Hierapolis* 208, cf. 124, al.; θέμα· ἕξις, τόπος, στάσις, μνῆμα, Hsch. II. *something proposed as a prize*, *IG* 9(1).12 (Ambryssus), *SIG*867.67 (Ephesus, ii A.D.), *Sammelb.*6222. 27 (iii A.D.). III. *case proposed for discussion, theme* of an argument, Quint.4.2.28, D.L.7.78. b. *proposition, premiss*, θ. ὁμολογούμενα Longin.32.8. c. *case*, in Law, Just.*Nov.*2.3 *Intr.*, 4.2 (pl.), dub. in *IG*4.364 (cf. *Supp.Epigr.*1.64). 2. *arbitrary determination*, opp. φύσις, ὁ κατὰ θέμα καλὸς λόγος Phld.*Rh.*1.151 S.; νόμοις καὶ θέμασιν διαφέρειν ib.259 S., cf. *Po.*5.22. 3. in Gramm., *primary* (non-derivative) *element* or *form*, A.D.*Pron.*11.21, al., cf. *Synt.*47.22; of the present tense, τὸ θ., ἀμύσσω· ὁ μέλλων, ἀμύξω *EM*88.13. 4. in Stoic Logic, *mode of reduction* of an irregular syllogism, *Stoic.*2.77, 83, al.

θεμᾰτ-ίζω, *deposit*, ἐπὶ τράπεζαν *BGU*1127.30 (i B.C.); πρὸς τοὺς τραπεζίτας *SIG*742.56 (Ephesus, i B.C.). 2. *place in order*, A.D. *Synt.*11.8:—Pass., κατὰ τύχην τεθεματίσθαι ib.1. II. *lay down, posit, assume*, Phld.*Rh.*1.152 S.:—Pass., *to be arbitrarily assumed*, ib.259S., cf. 124S. 2. Gramm., *assign arbitrarily* a meaning to a word, S.E.*M*.8.202; *determine arbitrarily* a gender, etc., ib.1.149, 152. **-ικός**, ή, όν, *of* or *for a* θέμα: I. *that in which a valuable prize is proposed*, ἀγὼν θ., opp. στεφανίτης and φυλλίτης, Poll.3.153, cf. *IG*3.128.20, *IGRom*.4.1432.20, 1442.8 (Smyrna), *LW*894.17 (Delph.); τρόπος θ. a style *calculated for effect*, Plu.2.1135c; cf. θεματίτης. II. *arbitrarily fixed, traditional*, παρατηρήσεις Phld. *Rh*.1.195S.: -κόν, τό, ib.151S. 2. Gramm., *primary*, not derivative, e.g. ἄμφω, which has no sg., *EM*91.33: θεματικά, τά, *elements*, ib.232.21: Comp., θεματικώτερα (μέρη) τοῦ λόγου ὀνόματά ἐστι καὶ ῥήματα *principal* parts, A.D.*Adv*.121.5; -ώτεραι αἱ πρωτότυποι ἐν τοῖς γένεσιν the personal pronouns *form* their genders *from different* θέματα, Id.*Pron*.110.24. Adv. Comp. -ώτερον, κλιθῆναι *by means of different* θέματα, e.g. ἐγώ, ἐμοῦ, Id.*Synt*.102.4. **-ιον**, τό, Dim. of θέμα I.5, Antig.Nic.ap.Heph.Astr.2.18. **-ισμός**, ὁ, *laying down*: hence, 1. *conventional arrangement*, Vitr.1.2.5. 2. Gramm., *arbitrary determination*, S.E.*M*.1.149. **-ίτης** [ῑ], ου, ὁ, *depositor*, *SIG*742.59 (Ephesus, i B.C.). 2. θ. ἀγών, ὁ, = θεματικὸς ἀγών, *IG*14.1102.33.

θεμᾰτοποιέω, *make into a* θέμα III. 3, Sch.Od.4.807 (Pass.).

θέμεθλα, τά, (τίθημι) *foundations, lowest part*, ὀφθαλμοῖο θ. *roots* of the eye, Il.14.493; στομάχοιο θ. 17.47; Ὠκεανοῖο θ. Hes.*Th*.816; Ἄμμωνος θ. *the place where* Ammon *stands*, i.e. his temple, Pi.*P*.4.16; Παγγαίου θ. *the roots* of Mt. Pangaeus, ib.180; θ. δίκης Sol.4.14; ἐκ θεμέθλων, Lat. *funditus*, Simm.25.4: dub. in sg., Call.*Dian*.248 (leg. θέμειλον).

θεμείλια, τά, = θέμεθλα, θεμείλια.. τὰ θέσαν μογέοντες Ἀχαιοί Il. 12.28; θ. τε προβάλοντο 23.255; διέθηκε θ. *h.Ap*.254; θ. καρτερὰ πήξας *AP*9.808 (Cyrus), cf. Call.*Del*.260, Opp.*H*.5.680: **θέμειλα**, *Epigr.Gr*.1078.3 (Adana): sg. **θέμειλον**, *AP*9.649 (Maced.), 14.115.

θεμελῐ-ᾰκός, ή, όν, *of* or *for the foundation*, Sch.Lyc.615. **-όθεν**, = Lat. *funditus*, Dosith.p.412K., *Gloss*. **-ος**, ον, *of* or *for the foundation*, λίθοι Ar.*Av*.1137; οἰκόπεδα D.S.5.66: abs., θεμέλιος (sc. λίθος), ὁ, *foundation-stone*, Arist.*Ph*.237b13, *Metaph*.1013a5: metaph., τῆς τέχνης θ. Machoap.Ath.8.346a; θ. ἀγνοίας Ph.1.266; οἱ θ. ἐκ παντοίων λίθων ὑπόκεινται the *foundations*, Th.1.93; τοὺς θ. ἐκ τῶν λίθων οἰκοδομεῖσθαι Arist.*PA*668a19: metaph., προλιπεῖν τοὺς προγονικοὺς θ. *SIG*888.70 (Scaptopara, iii A.D.): also neut. θεμέλιον Arist. *APo*.95b37 (s.v.l.), *PPetr*.3p.121 (iii B.C.), al.: pl., τὰ θ. Arist.*Ph*.200a 4, *PCair.Zen*.176.71 (iii B.C.), al., Paus.8.32.1: metaph., τὰ ὑποβληθέντα θ., of the *foundations* of the world, Epicur.*Ep*.2p.38U.: gender indeterminate, μὴ ὑποκειμένων.. θ. X.*Eq*.1.2; ἐκ τῶν θ. from the *foundations*, Th.3.68 (also sg., ἐνέπρησαν [οἰκίαν] ἐκ θεμελίου *BGU* 909.17 (iv A.D.)): metaph., ἐκ θ. ἐσφαλμένοι Plb.5.93.2, etc.; ἄρδην καὶ ἐκ θ. ἀπόλλυσθαι Hdn.8.3.2; also ἀνεκτίσθη τὸ τεῖχος ἐκ θεμελείων (sic) *Supp.Epigr*.2.480 (Kuban, iv A.D.). II. θεμέλια, τά, *building-sites*, Ptol.*Tetr*.174, cf. Vett.Val.82.24, al. III. Subst., *the fourth* τόπος, = ἀντιμεσουράνημα, Herm.Trism. in *Cat.Cod.Astr*.8(3).101, cf. 8(4).241. **-οῦχος**, ον, (ἔχω) *upholding the foundations*, Ποσειδῶν *Inscr.Délos* 290.116 (iii B.C.), Corn.*ND*22; ὁ θ. (sc. λίθος) Heraclit. *All*.48. **-όω**, *to lay the foundation of, found firmly*, πύργους.. φοίνιξι θεμελιώσας X.*Cyr*.7.5.11, cf. *IG*12(2).11.26 (Mytil.), Lxx *Jo*.6.25 (26), *Ep.Hebr*.1.10, etc.:—Pass., *have the foundations laid*, *IG*2².1343.15 (i B.C.); ἐπὶ τὴν πέτραν *Ev.Matt*.7.25: metaph., βασιλεία καλῶς θεμελιωθεῖσα D.S.11.68; ἡγεμονία κάλλιστα τεθεμελιωμένη Id. 15.1; ἐν ἀγάπῃ τεθ. *Ep.Eph*.3.18; τῇ πίστει *Ep.Col*.1.23. II. *destroy utterly*, in Pass., -ωθέντα (θεμειλωθ- cod.)· ἐκ ῥιζῶν ἀρθέντα, Hsch. **-ωσις**, εως, ἡ, *foundation*, Lxx 2*Es*.3.11, Ph.Byz.*Mir*.5.1; *paving*, *SIG*996.30 (Smyrna). **-ωτής**, οῦ, ὁ, *founder*, *Gloss*.

θέμεν, θέμεναι, v. τίθημι.

θέμερος, α, ον, = βέβαιος, σεμνός, εὐσταθής, Hsch.; θεμερώτερα *IG* 14.1018.3 (iv A.D.).

θεμερόφρων, ον, gen. ονος, *of grave and serious mind*, Hsch.

θεμερύνομαι (θεμαρ- cod.), = σεμνύνομαι, Hsch. s.v. θέμερον; also, = τρυφῶ, *Com.Adesp*.1017 (v.l.).

θεμερῶπις, ιδος, ἡ, *grave and sedate of look*, Ἁρμονίη Emp.122.2; θ. αἰδώς A.*Pr*.134 (lyr.).

θέμησις· δικαιοσύνη, παρὰ Πυτίᾳ, Hsch. (Fort. θέμισις, cf. sq.).

θεμίζω, (θέμις) *judge, punish*, imper. θεμιζέτω, = μαστιγούτω, νομοθετείτω (Cret.), Hsch.; θεμισσέτω Paus.Gr.*Fr*.202:—Med., aor. part. θεμισσάμενοι ὀργάς *controlling our* wills, Pi.*P*.4.141.

θεμινήσασα· πρακτική, ἀνυσίμη, ἀποτελεσίμη, Hsch. (post θεμιστός).

θεμί-ξενος, ον, *just to strangers*, ἀρετά Pi.*Pae*.6.131. **-πλεκτος**, ον, (πλέκω) *rightly plaited*, θ. στέφανος a *well-earned* crown (or, as Sch., *twined with due ceremony*), Pi.*N*.9.52.

θέμις, ἡ, old Ep. gen. θέμιστος (in Hom. the only declension): acc. θέμιστα Il.5.761, θέμιν A.*Ag*.1431, etc.: gen. pl. θεμιστέων Hes. *Th*.235: pr. n. Θέμις, Θέμιστος Od.2.68, Θέμιστα Il.20.4; dat. Θέμιστι 15.87; but Θέμιτος Pi.*O*.13.8, Θέμιδος A.*Pr*.18, etc., Θέμιος (v.l. -ιδος) Hdt.2.50, Θέμιν Hes.*Th*.16, *IG*2².1611.71: voc. Θέμι Il.15.93, E.*Med*.160 (anap.): I. *that which is laid down* or *established, law* (not as fixed by statute, but) *as established by custom*, θ. ἐστί 'tis *meet and right*, c. dat. pers. et inf., οὔ μοι θ. ἐστὶ ξεῖνον ἀτιμῆσαι Od.14.56; ἅ τε ξείνοις θ. ἐστὶν [παραθεῖναι] Il.11.779; ὃ οἱ Διόθεν θ. ἦεν [ἐκτελέσαι] Hes.*Sc*.22; γυναικὶ οὐ θ. *SIG*1024.9 (Myconos, iii/ii B.C.): without dat., Il.16.796, 23.44; οὐ θ. ἐν μοισοπόλων οἰκίᾳ θρῆνον ἔμμεν' Sapph.136; ὅτι δυνατὸν καὶ θ. αἰνεῖν A.*Ag*.98, cf. S.*Ant*.880 (lyr.), *Ph*.346, E.*Med*. 678, Pl.*Phdr*.250b, Isoc.4.92, etc.; ἡ γὰρ θ. for so 'tis *right* [to do], Od.24.286; freq. ἣ θ. ἐστί as *the custom* is, Il.2.73: c. dat. (= loc.), ἣ θ. ἐστὶν.. ἀγορῇ 9.33: c. gen., ἣ θ. ἀνθρώπων πέλει ib.134; ἣ θ. ἐστὶ γυναικός Od.14.130; also ᾗ θ. ἀνθρώποις κατὰ ἤθεα Hes.*Op*.137; θύειν τοὺς γεωργοὺς.. ᾗ (with ι) θέμις *IG*2².1364 (i A.D.); but ᾗ θέμις ἐστί is rejected for Hom. by Hdn.Gr.2.516, cf. A.D.*Adv*.148.28: indecl., πότερα κατ' ἔχθραν ἢ τὸ μὴ θέμις λέγεις; A.*Supp*.336; ὥστε μή.. θέμις σέ γ' εἶναι κεῖνον ἀντιδρᾶν κακῶς S.*OC*1191; οὐδὲ.. φασὶ θέμις εἶναι Pl. *Grg*.505c, cf. X.*Oec*.11.11, Ael.*NA*1.60. 2. *justice, right*, S.*Tr*.810; ὅσα τείνει πρὸς θέμιν Pl.*Smp*.188d; *penalty*, ἐκτίνειν ὁμοίαν θ. A.*Supp*. 436 (lyr.); *sanctity*, ὁρκίων ἐμῶν θ. Id.*Ag*.1431. II. = ἀγὼν θεματίτης, *IGRom*.3.319 (Pisid.); νικήσας θέμιν ἀνδρῶν ib.437 (Termessus). III. pl. **θέμιστες**, *decrees* of the gods, *oracles*, Διὸς θ. Od. 16.403; θέμισσιν *by oracles*, Pi.*P*.4.54, cf. *O*.10(11).24. 2. *dooms*, customary *laws*, *ordinances*, δικασπόλοι, οἵ τε θέμιστας πρὸς Διὸς εἰρύαται Il.1.238, cf. Hes.*Th*.235; τοῖσιν δ' (i.e. the Cyclopes) οὔτ' ἀγοραὶ βουληφόροι οὔτε θέμιστες Od.9.112; οὔτε δίκας εὖ εἰδότα οὔτε θέμιστας neither rights nor *laws*, ib.215: in sg., ὅς οὔ τινα οἶδε θέμιστα Il.5.761; ἵνα σφ' ἀγορή τε θέμις τε 11.807. 3. *judgements, decisions* given by the kings or judges, οἳ.. σκολιὰς κρίνωσι θέμιστας 16.387; σκολιῇς δὲ δίκῃς κρίνωσι θ. Hes.*Op*.221; διακρίνοντα θ. ἰθείῃσι δίκῃσιν Id.*Th*. 85. 4. *tribute, dues*, λιπαρὰς τελέουσι θέμιστας Il.9.156. IV. pr. n., *Themis*, ἥ τ' ἀνδρῶν ἀγορὰς ἠμὲν λύει ἠδὲ καθίζει 2.68, cf. Il.15. 87, 20.4, Hes.*Th*.16, A.*Pr*.18, etc.

θεμισκόπος, ον, *seeing to law and justice*, Pi.*N*.7.47.

θεμισκρέων, οντος, ὁ, *reigning by right*, Pi.*P*.5.29.

θέμιστα, θέμιστας, v. θέμις.

θεμιστ-εία, ἡ, *a giving of oracles*, Str.17.1.43. **-εῖος**, α, ον, *of law and right*, θ. σκᾶπτον the sceptre *of righteous judgement*, Pi.*O*. 1.12. **-ευτός**, ή, όν, *ordered by law* or *custom*, Hsch. **-εύω**, *declare law and right*, c. dat., Μίνωα ἴδον.. θεμιστεύοντα νέκυσσιν Od. 11.569: c. gen., *govern*, θ. δὲ ἕκαστος παίδων ἠδ' ἀλόχων 9.114. II. *give by way of answer* or *oracle*, νημερτέα βουλὴν πᾶσι θ. *h.Ap*.253, cf. Lys.*Fr*.23S.: abs., *deliver oracles*, E.*Ion* 371, D.S.5.67, Plu.*Alex*. 14; τινα Orac.ap.Ael.*VH*3.43; cf. θεμιτεύω. **-ιος**, ὁ, *patron of right*, of Zeus, Plu.2.1065e. II. name of month in Thessaly, etc., *IG*9(1).689, etc.

θεμιστοπόλος, ον, *ministering law and right*, epith. of kings and judges, *h.Cer*.103. II. *oracular*, σηκοί, of Delphi, *Klio*15.48 (Delph., iii B.C.).

θεμιστ-ός, ή, όν, = θεμιτός, A.*Th*.694 (lyr.). Adv. -τῶς cj. in Id.*Ch*. 645 (lyr.). II. *oracular*, ὕμνοι Pi.*Fr*.192; cf. θέμις III. 1. **-οσύνη**, ἡ, in pl., poet. for θέμιστες, Orph.*H*.79.6. **-οῦχος**, ον, (ἔχω) *upholding right*, βασιλῆες A.R.4.347.

θεμίστωρ, ορος, ὁ, *knowing right*, Hsch.

θεμῐτ-εύω, = θεμιστεύω, ὄργια θεμιτεύων *keeping lawful* orgies, E. *Ba*.79 (lyr., metri gr.). **-ός**, ή, όν, (θέμις) *allowed by the laws of God and men, righteous*, οὐ θεμιτόν [ἐστι], = οὐ θέμις, c. inf., οὐ θ. οἱ ἔφασκε πίνειν οἶνον *h.Cer*.207, cf. Pi.*P*.9.42, S.*OT*993, *OC*1758 (anap.), E.*Or*.97, Theoc.5.136, etc.: in Prose, Hdt.3.37, 5.72, Pl.*Ap*.30d, *IG* 2.1059.16, 14.1390; μηδὲ θεμιτὸν.. μηδ' ὅσιον D.21.148: in pl., τὰ μὴ θεμίτ' ἦν [ἰδεῖν] dub. l. in Call.*Lav.Pall*.78. Adv. -τῶς Phot., Suid. **-ώδης**, ες, *oracular*, Orac.ap.Eus.*PE*5.16.

θεμόω, only in phrase [νῆα] θέμωσε.. χέρσον ἱκέσθαι *drove* the ship *ashore*, *stranded* her, Od.9.486; but in ib.542, *drove* her landwards, i.e. towards her destination: cf. **θεμούς**· διαθέσεις, παραινέσεις, Hsch., who also has **θεμῶν**· θελήμων.

-θεν, old termin. of the gen., as in ἐμέθεν, Διόθεν, etc.: freq. with Ablatival sense, denoting *motion from* a place, as in Λεσβόθεν, Ἀβυδόθεν, ἄλλοθεν, οἴκοθεν, etc.: so with Preps., ἀπὸ Τροίηθεν Od.9.38; ἐξ οὐρανόθεν Il.8.19, cf. A.D.*Adv*.184.12 sq.: most of the forms in -οθεν were parox., exc. οἴκοθεν, ἄλλοθεν, πάντοθεν (sts. παντόθεν), ἔκτοθεν, ἔνδοθεν, ib.191.27 sq. (other exceptions in Hdn.Gr.1.500).

θέναρ, ᾰρος, τό, *palm of the hand*, πρυμνὸν ὕπερ θέναρος, i.e. just below the wrist, Il.5.339; χειρὸς τὸ ἐντὸς θέναρ Arist.*HA*493b32, cf. Poll.2.143. b. pl., *the two muscles forming the borders of the palm*, Gal.*UP*2.3. c. *ball of the thumb*, Ruf.*Onom*.87, Gal.18 (2).864. 2. *flat* of the foot, Hp.*Mul*.2.116 (pl.), Arat.718. 3. metaph., θ. βωμοῖο *hollow* in the top of the altar, on which the offerings are laid, Pi.*P*.4.206; ἁλὸς θ. *hollow bed* of the sea, Id.*I*.4(3).56. (Cf. OHG. *tenar* 'palm of the hand'.)

θεναρίζει· τύπτει, Hsch. **θένιοι**· οἱ προσήκοντες, Id.

θένω, v. θείνω. **θέο**, Ep. for θοῦ, v. τίθημι.

θεοβλάβ-εια [βλᾰ], ἡ, *infatuation sent by the gods, madness*, Aeschin.3.133, D.H.1.24, D.C.44.8 (-ία codd.). **-έω**, *to be* θεοβλαβής, A.*Pers*.831, Them.*Or*.4.56c. **-ής**, ές, *stricken of God, infatuated*, Hdt.1.127, 8.137, Ant.Lib.22.4. Adv. -βῶς Poll.1.22.

θεό-βουλος, ον, = θεόμητις, Phot., Suid.:—fem. -βούλη, of the Sibyl, Lact.*Inst*.1.6.7. **-βρότιον**, τό, = ἀείζων τὸ μικρόν, Ps.-Dsc. 4.89. **-γᾰμία**, ἡ, *marriage of gods*, Ph.2.205 (v.l. -μαχία): in pl., title of poem by Pisander, Suid., Zos.5.29. **-γάμια** [γᾰ], τά, name of festival in Sicily, Poll.1.37; at Athens, Plu. *in Hes*.85; at Nysa, *GDI*3661.11, Head *Hist.Num*.²654, al. **-γένaιος**, ὁ (sc. μήν), name of month in Egypt, *BGU*713.3 (i A.D.). **-γενής**, ές, *born of God*, Sch.rec.A.*Pr*.351, *Gloss*. **-γεννής**, ές, *begotten of a god*, S. *Ant*.834 (anap.).

θεό-γλωσσος, ον, *with the tongue of a god*, γυναῖκες, of poetesses, *AP*9.26 (Antip. Thess.). **-γνωσία**, ἡ, *the knowledge of God*, Hierocl. *in CA*20p.463M., Heph.Astr.1.1. **-γνωστος**, ον, *known of God*, ibid., *Gloss*.: as a complimentary term, ἡ θ. σου μνήμη *POxy*. 237 vi 29 (ii A.D.).

θεο-γονία, Ion. **-ίη**, ἡ, *genealogy of the gods*, title of Hesiod's poem; cf. Hdt.1.132, 2.53, Procl.*in Ti.*3.107 D. II. *generation* or *birth of gods*, Pl.*Lg.*886c, Ph.2.205,264, D.L.*Praef.*3. **-γονος**, ον, *born of God, divine*, E.*Or.*346. **-δαίμων**, ονος, ὁ, *inferior divinity*, *BCH*22.350 (Amphipolis).

Θεοδαίσια, τά, Cret. name for the Διονύσια, Call.*Aet.Oxy.*2080.88, *GDI*5075.43 (Crete), cf. Hsch.; also, at Rhodes, *SIG*1035c. II. Θεοδαίσιος, ὁ, epith. of Dionysus, Hsch.; also, (sc. μήν) name of month found in various forms: Cret. **Θιοδαίσιος** *GDI*5149; in Cos, Rhodes, etc., **Θευδαίσιος** ib.3593, al., etc.; at Mytilene, **Θεδαίσιος** *IG*11(4).1064*a* 2 (Delos).

θεο-δέγμων, ον, gen. ονος, = θεηδόχος, θῶκος *AP*7.363; *divine*, πηγή Archestr.*Fr.*13.8. **-δέκτωρ**, ορος, ὁ, ἡ, = θεηδόχος, Hsch. **-δήλητος**, ον, *by which the gods are injured*, μιαιφονίη v.l. in *AP*9.157. **-δίδακτος** [ῐ], ον, *taught of God*, 1*Ep.Thess.*4.9. **-δμής**, dat. -δμῆτι· θεόφρονι Cyr. (fort. θεόμητι). **-δμητος**, Dor. **-δμᾱτος**, ον, also α, ον Pi.*O.*6.59, *Fr.*87.1: (δέμω):—*god-built, founded by the gods*, πύργοι Il.8.519; Δᾶλος Pi. ll. cc.; πύλαι B.*Fr.*7 Bgk. (cf. p.437 Jebb); Ἀθῆναι S.*El.*707; βωμός E.*Hec.*23: metaph., θ. χρέος, ἀρεταί, Pi.*O.*3.7, *I.*6(5).11. **-δόνιον** or **-δώνιον**, τό, = γλυκυσίδη, dub. in Ps.-Dsc.3.140. **-δοσία**, ἡ, *a gift* or *offering to the gods*, Str.17.1.37 (pl.). **-δόσιος**, ον, *given by God*, Hsch.; f.l. in Aristeas 229. **-δότια**, τά, name of various eyesalves, Gal.12.784, Aët.7.118; *collyrium Theodoti*, Cels.6.6.6. **-δοτος**, ον, = θεόσδοτος, ἔργα Pi.*I.*5(4).23; εὐχαί B.7.50. II. θεόδοτον, τό, *remedy for coughs*, Alex.Trall.5.4. **-δρομέω**, *walk in God's ways*, Phot., Suid. **-δυτα**· ἱερόθυτα, Hsch. (leg. θεόθυτα). **-δώρητος**, ον, *given by God*, Iamb.*VP*2.6, 15.67, Asp.*in EN*25.28. II. θ. λίθος, of the ἀλαβαστρίτης λίθος, Zos.Alch.p.114 B. 2. ἡ θ. *a purgative*, Aët.13.112, Alex.Trall.1.15. **-είδεια**, ἡ, *godlike appearance*, φυσική Iamb.*VP*2.10. **-ειδής**, ές, *godlike*, in Hom. of form, Πρίαμος Il.24.217, al.; Ἀλέξανδρος, Τηλέμαχος, 3.16, Od.14.173, al.; Οὐρανίη Hes.*Th.*350; θ. πρόσωπον Pl.*Phdr.*251a; οἱ ποιηταὶ τοὺς καλοὺς θεοειδεῖς ὀνομάζουσιν Plu.2.988d, cf. Pl.*R.*501b. II. generally, *godlike*, θεοειδές τί ἐστιν ἡ ψυχή Id.*Phd.*95c, cf. Muson.*Fr.*17 p.91 H.; of things, λίθους, βοτάνας, ζῷα, ἀρώματα Iamb.*Myst.*5.23: Comp. -έστερος Pl.*Epin.*980d: Sup. -έστατος Eus.Mynd.33; κόσμος ἐπῶν Phalar.*Ep.*147.2: also irreg. θεειδ- (q.v.). Adv. -δῶς Herm.*in Phdr.*p.178 A., Suid. **-είκελος**, ον, *godlike*, of Achilles, Il.1.131, al.; of Telemachus, Od.3.416; of Hector and Andromache, Sapph.*Supp.*20c.6: in Prose, Pl.*R.*501b, Them.*Or.*6.79a. **-επής**, ές, (ἔπος) = θεσπέσιος, Hsch. **-εχθρία**, v. θεοισεχθρία.

θεόθεν, Adv. *from the gods*, θ. δ' οὐκ ἔστ' ἀλέασθαι (sc. θάνατον) death *at the hands of the gods*, Od.16.447, cf. Pl.Com.173.14 (hex.); εἴ τις ἄλλα θ. ἀνθρώποισι τέρψις *given by God* to man, *IG*3.171. 2. *by the will* or *favour of the gods*, Pi.*O.*12.8, *P.*11.50, A.*Th.*324, *Pers.*101 (both lyr.), etc.; *by the gods*, οἷς ἂν σεισθῇ θ. δόμος S.*Ant.*584.

θεο-θρέμμων, ον, gen. ονος, *maintained by God*, σιγή Orac.ap.Procl.*in Alc.*p.56 C. **-θρεπτος**, ον, = foreg., Sch.A.*Pers.*905. **-θῠτος**, ον, (θύω) *offered to the gods*: θεόθυτον, τό, *a victim*, Cratin.417 (pl.), cf. Poll.1.29 (pl.).

θεοίνια (sc. ἱερά), τά, an Attic feast of Dionysus, Jusj.ap.D.59.78, Lycurg.*Fr.*56: **θεοίνιον**, τό, his temple, Phot.

θέοινος, ὁ, *god of wine*, πάτερ θέοινε A.*Fr.*382, cf. Lyc.1247.

θεοισεχθρία, ἡ, *hatefulness to the gods, villainy*, D.22.59 (written θεοῖς ἐχθρίαν), prob. in Ar.*V.*418 (required by Cretic metre), in Archipp.35 (where the first two syll. coalesce), and in Luc.*Lex.*11: in the last three places codd. have θεοσεχθρία or θεὸς ἐχθρία (θεοσέχθρα v.l. Archipp. l. c.): θεοεχθρία is found in Sch.Ar.*Ra.*557, v.l. in Luc.*Lex.* l. c.; cf. θεοῖς ἐχθρός in D.19.95, 24.195.

θεο-κατάρᾱτος [ᾰρ], ον, *accursed of God*, Zos.Alch.ap.Olymp.Alch.p.101 B. **-κατασκεύαστος**, ον, *made by God*, ὕμνος Sch.Pi.*O.*3.11; gloss on θεότευκτον, Hsch. **-κέλευστος**, ον, *ordered by God*, gloss on θέσκελα, Id. **-κῆρυξ**, ῡκος, ὁ, *divine herald*: in pl., name of a family at Eleutherae *claiming descent from Talthybius*, Id. **-κίνητος** [ῑ], ον, *roused by the gods*, gloss on θέορτος, Sch.Pi.*O.*2.67. **-κλητέω**, f.l. for -κλῠτέω, Eust.805.36. **-κλητος**, ον, *sung by gods*, Nonn.*D.*5.92. **-κλῠτέω**, *call on the gods*, A.*Pers.*500, Plu.*Sull.*29, Ael.*Fr.*46, Porph.*Abst.*2.26, D.C.74.13: c. acc. pers., θ. Θέμιν E.*Med.*208; Κυρῖνον Plu.*Rom.*28: also, c. acc. rei, *ask in prayer*, Id.*Arist.*18. II. Pass., *to be inspired*, Id.2.592c:—so in Act., Hld.3.17. **-κλύτησις** [ῠ], εως, ἡ, *calling on the gods, invocation*, Plb.23.10.7 (pl.). **-κλῠτος**, ον, *calling on the gods*, θ. λιταί A.*Th.*143 (lyr.). II. Pass., *heard by God*, expl. of *Ishmael*, J.*AJ*1.10.4. **-κμητος**, ον, *wrought by a god*, βέλεμνα, πύργοι, Q.S.3.419, Tryph.40 (v.l. θεοδμ-). **-κόλος**, ὁ, = θεηκόλος, *servant of a god, priest*, *SIG*684.1 (Dyme, ii B.C.), 1021.3 (Olympia, i B.C.):—hence **-κολέω**, *serve as a priest*, θ. Ἀσκλαπιῷ *IG*9(1).1066 (Amphissa):—also **-κολεύω**, ib.417 (Aetol.):—**-κολία**, ἡ, *SIG*531.32 (pl., Dyme). **-κραντος**, ον, *accomplished* or *wrought by the gods*, A.*Ag.*1488. **-κρᾱσία**, ἡ, (κρᾶσις) *mingling with God*, Iamb.*VP*33.240, Dam.*Isid.*5. II. *Divine Mingling*, title of work by Pherecydes of Syros, Suid. **-κρᾰτία**, ἡ, (κράτος) *rule of God, theocracy*, J.*Ap.*2.16. **-κρήπῑς**, ῖδος, ἡ, *founded by a god*, of Athens, Nonn.*D.*24.96. **-κρῐτος**, ὁ, *judge of gods*, of Paris, Dosiad.*Ara* 10. **-κτητος**, ον, *acquired by God*, τρίποδες Aristonous 1.9. **-κτιστος**, ον (also -η, Dor. α, -ον *Trag.Adesp.*85), *created, established*, or *founded by God*, φλόξ l. c., cf. Limen.36; πόλις *OGI*168.4 (Egypt, ii B.C., v. corrigenda); νομοθεσία Lxx 2*Ma.*6.23. II. name of an eyesalve, Dessau *Inscr.Lat.Sel.* 8738. **-κτῖτος**, ον, = foreg. 1, Sol.36.6; γαῖα *Epigr.Gr.*223.5. **-κυνεῖ**· δόξαν θείαν ἔχουσαν, Hsch. (fort. -κυδῆ).

θεοληπτ-έομαι, Pass., *to be inspired*, Ph.1.143. **-ικός**, ή, όν, *belonging to one possessed* or *inspired*: ἡ θεοληπτική (sc. μαντεία) = θεοληψία, S.E.*M.*9.132. **-ος**, ον, *possessed, inspired*, Arist.*EE* 1214^{a}23, S.E.*P.*2.52, *Cat.Cod.Astr.*8(4).148; γνώμη App.*Hann.*42, cf. Sallust.3, etc.; θ. εἰς ἀρετήν Plu.2.1117a. 2. in bad sense, = θεοβλαβής, Man.4.80, Vett.Val.114.12. 3. *superstitious*, Plu.2.855b.

θεοληψία, ἡ, *inspiration*, Plu.2.763a. 2. *superstition*, ib.56e. 3. *frenzy, madness*, Vett.Val.210.4 (pl.).

θεολογ-εῖον, τό, in the theatre, *a place above the stage where gods appeared*, Poll.4.130. **-έω**, *discourse on the gods and cosmology*, Arist.*Metaph.*983^{b}29; περί τινων Id.*Mu.*391^{b}4, cf. Plu.2.614d, etc.; Δία αὐτὸν [τὸν Φαέθοντα] ζωογόνον θεολογοῦσι *call* him Ζεύς ζ. Antig.*Mir.*10b:—Pass., τὰ θεολογούμενα *discourses about the gods*, Plu.2.421e (v.l.), S.E.*M.*9.55; title of work by Asclepiades of Mendes, Suet.*Aug.*94; τρεῖς αἱ Μοῖραι θεολογοῦνται *Theol.Ar.*16. 2. *refer to a divine influence*, τοὺς τόκους Sch.Ptol.*Tetr.*103. **-ια**, τά, = *dei proverbia*, *Gloss.* **-ία**, ἡ, *science of things divine*, Pl.*R.*379a, Phld.*Piet.*72, Porph.*Marc.*15, Iamb.*Myst.*1.1, etc.; title of an Orphic work, Dam.*Pr.*124: in pl., Arist.*Mete.*353^{a}35. II. *oration in praise of a god*, *SIG*1109.115. 2. *incantation, invocation of a god*, *PMag.Par.*1.1037. **-ικός**, ή, όν, *theological*, φιλοσοφία θ., i.e. metaphysics, Arist.*Metaph.*1026^{a}19, cf. 1064^{b}3; γένος Str.10.3.23; πραγματεία D.H.4.62; [μῦθοι] Sallust.4; τὸ θ. Cleanth.*Stoic.*1.108; οἱ θ. Olymp.*in Mete.*129.19: Comp. -ώτερος Dam.*Pr.*135. Adv. -κῶς, opp. τραγικῶς, ἀποφαίνεσθαι Plu.2.568d, cf. Iamb.*Myst.*1.2. **-ος**, ὁ, (λέγω) *one who discourses of the gods*, of poets such as Hesiod and Orpheus, Arist.*Metaph.*1000^{a}9, S.E.*M.*2.31; of cosmologists (like the Orphics), Arist.*Metaph.*1071^{b}27, al., Cic.*ND*3.21.53; θεολόγοι καὶ ποιηταί Phld.*Piet.*48; of diviners and prophets, θ. καὶ μάντιες Philol.14; οἱ Δελφῶν θ. Plu.2.417f, cf. Luc.*Alex.*19, *BMus.Inscr.*4.481*.295 (Ephesus, ii A.D.), *IGRom.*4.1431 (Smyrna): fem., *CIG* 3199, 3200 (ibid.). 2. *theologian*: ὁ θ., = Moses, Ph.2.152,416.

θεολωβήτης, ου, ὁ, *blasphemer*, Man.4.234.

θεομᾰν-έω, *to be* θεομανής, Poll.1.19. **-ής**, ές, *maddened by the gods*, A.*Th.*653, E.*Ion* 1402; λύσσα θ. madness *caused by the gods*, Id.*Or.*845; πότμος ib.79. **-ία**, ἡ, *madness caused by God, inspiration*, cj. in Ph.1.571 (ἐνθεομανία, ἐνθέῳ μανίᾳ codd.).

θεομαντ-εία, ἡ, *spirit of prophecy*, D.C.62.18. **-εῖον**, τό, *spell for evoking a divine revelation*, *PMag.Leid.V.*5.13. **-ις**, εως, ὁ, *one who has a spirit of prophecy, an inspired person*, Pl.*Ap.*22c, *Men.*99c, Aristid.2.18 J., Gal.15.442.

θεομᾰχ-έω, *fight against God* or *the gods*, E.*Ba.*45, al., *IA*1408; μὴ θεομάχει Men.187, cf. Hp.*Ep.*14, Lxx 2*Ma.*7.19, Plu.2.168c, Arr.*Epict.*3.24.24. **-ία**, ἡ, *battle of the gods*, Pl.*R.*378d (pl.), cf. Il.20. tit. II. *fighting against God*, Arr.*Epict.*3.24.24. **-ος**, ον, *fighting against God*, Γίγαντες Scymn.637, cf. *Act.Ap.*5.39, Luc.*JTr.*45, Vett.Val.331.12.

θεο-μηνία, ἡ, *wrath of God*, Pall.*in Hp.*2.142 D., Steph.*in Hp.*1.72 D., Eust.891.24. **-μήστωρ**, ορος, ὁ, *like the gods in counsel*, A.*Pers.*655 (lyr.), *IG*14.1868. II. Pass., *devised by God*, θεομήστορος εἰκόνα κόσμου Alex.Eph.ap.Theon.Sm.p.141 H. (-μήτορος codd., em. Meineke); κόσμον Man.4.7 (-μήτορα edd. vett.). **-μητέω**, *to be divinely wise*, Hsch. **-μητις**, ιδος, ἡ, *divinely wise*, δίκη Maiist.54, cf. Suid. **-μήτωρ**, ορος, ἡ, *mother of a god*, of Olympias, mother of Alexander, Anon.Hist.(*FGrH*153) p.826 J. **-μῖμος**, ον, *imitating God*, θ. πρᾶγμα βασιλήα Diotog.ap.Stob.4.7.62. **-μῑσής**, ές, *hated by the gods*, opp. θεοφιλής, Pl.*Euthphr.*7a, *R.*612e, Them.*Or.*16.210a: Sup. -έστατος Pl.*Lg.*917a, Ph.1.653. Adv. -σῶς Poll.1.22. II. Act., *hating God*, Ar.*Av.*1548 (ubi v. Sch.), Ph.2.597, Suid. (θεομίσης v.l. in Ar. l. c.). **-μῑσητία**, ἡ, = θεοισεχθρία, Sch.Ar.*V.*416. **-μίσητος** [ῑ], ον, = θεομισής 1, Arist.(?) in *PLit.Lond.*112, Ph.2.202. **-μοιρία**, ἡ, *the god's portion* of a sacrifice, *SIG*1026.20 (Cos). **-μοιρος**, ον, *partaking of the divine nature*, Ecphant.ap.Stob.4.6.22; φύσις Dam.*Isid.*191. **-μόριος**, α, ον, Ep. θευμ-, collat. form of sq., θευμορίη νοῦσος, ἄτη, A.R.3.676,974. II. **θευμορίη**, ἡ, *destiny*, Call.*Ep.*32.4, *AP*7.367 (Antip.). 2. = θεοῦ μοῖρα, but also, *priest's share of the sacrifice*, Hsch.:—hence **θευμοριάζω**, Id. **-μορος**, ον, *destined by the gods, imparted by them*, ἀοιδαί Pi.*O.*3.10; γάμου θεόμορον γέρας Id.*I.*8(7).42. II. *blessed by the gods*, Id.*P.*5.5. **-μορφος**, ον, *of form divine*, *AP*12.196 (Strat.). **-μῡθία**, ἡ, *divine lore, mythology*, Procl.*Theol.Plat.*1.4: in pl., Herm.*in Phdr.*p.73 A., Marin.*Procl.*27. **-μῡσής**, ές, *abominable before the gods*, A.*Eu.*40. **-ξένιος**, ὁ, epith. of Apollo at Pellene, Paus.7.27.4: name of a month at Delphi, *GDI*1709, al. II. θεοξένια, τά, *festival in honour of Apollo* at Pellene, Paus. l. c., Sch.Pi.*O.*9.146; at Delphi, *Michel*995 *D*9, Polemo ap.Ath.9.372a, Plu.2.557f; and, *of the Dioscuri* at Agrigentum, Pi.*O.*3.tit.; also at Paros, *IG*12(5).129.61 (ii B.C.); gloss on Θεοδαίσια, Sch.Call.*Aet.Oxy.*2080.88:—hence **θεοξενιασταί**, οἱ, *the persons who celebrated such a festival*, *IG*12(5).872.114 (ii B.C.). **-παίγμων**, ονος, ὁ, ἡ, *sporting with the gods*, Nonn.*D.*30.210. **-παις**, παιδος, ὁ, ἡ, *child of the gods*, Ἔρως *AP*12.56 (Mel.); Βαβυλών Herodic.ap.Ath.5.222a; λάβραξ Archestr.*Fr.*45.2; Τύρος *AP*7.419 (Mel.). **-παιστος**, ον, *struck by a god*, κιθάρα Hsch. **-παράδοτος**, ον, *delivered by God*, Procl.*in Cra.*p.59 P.; λόγια Marin.*Procl.*26; σοφία Dam.*Pr.*311. **-πάτωρ** [ᾰ], ορος, ὁ, *son of God*, title of Parthian kings, *BMus.Cat.Coins Parthia* p.16, al. **-πειθής**, ές, *obedient to God*, ὑπακοή Hierocl.*in CA* 24 p.473 M. **–πεμπτος**, ον, *sent by the gods*, Arist.*EN*1099ᵇ15, Plb.32.15.14, D.H.1.14; ὄνειροι Ph.1.620, cf. Artem.1.6; ἀτυχία D.S.15.24; ἀγαθόν D.H.4.62. 2. *superhuman, extraordinary*, Longus 3.18. **–πιστος**, ον, *faithful to God*, *PMasp.*151.196 (vi A.D.). **–πλαστέω**, *make into a god*, Hld.9.9; θ. τὸν χρυσοῦν μόσχον Ph.1.559; *deify*, τὸν Νεῖλον Id.2.164. **–πλάστης**, ου, ὁ, *maker of gods*, i.e. *of their images*, Ar.*Fr.*787. II. *the divine Creator*, Ph.2.490. **–πληγής**, ές, v. –πλήξ. **–πληκτος**, ον, *stricken of God*, Hsch. (in Dor. form –πλακτος). **–πλήξ**, ῆγος, ὁ, ἡ, τό, = θεόπληκτος, θεοπλήγεσσιν ἐοικότας εἰδώλοισιν Maiist.60 (unless –πληγέσσιν from –πληγής, ές). **–πληξία**, ἡ, = θεοβλάβεια, Oenom.ap.Eus.*PE*5.36. **–πλοκος**, ον, = πρὸς θεοὺς προσπλεκόμενος, *Cat.Cod.Astr.*8(4).166. **–πνευστος**, ον, *inspired of God*, σοφίη Ps.-Phoc.129; ὄνειροι Plu.2.904f; πᾶσα γραφή 2*Ep.Ti.*3.16; δημιούργημα Vett.Val.330.19. **–πνοος**, ον, contr. **–ους**, ουν, = foreg., θ. γενόμενος *Corp.Herm.*1.30; θ. ὕδωρ Numen.ap.Porph.*Antr.*10; πρόσωπον, of the Sphinx, *Epigr.Gr.*1016.

θεοποι-έω, *make into gods, deify*, τὰ θνητά D.H.2.56, cf. Luc.*Scyth.*1; Πυθαγόραν S.E.*M.*7.94. II. *make divine*, ἄνθρωπον θ. αἱ ἐπιστῆμαι Hierocl.*in CA Praef.*p.417 M. **–ητικός**, ή, όν, *able to make gods*: ἡ –κή (sc. τέχνη) *the art of making statues of gods*, Poll.1.13. **–ητος**, ον, *made by the gods*, or *by God*, Isoc.7.62. **–ΐα**, ἡ, *making of gods*, Porph.*Abst.*4.9; *of their statues*, Poll.1.13. II. *being made divine*, ἵνα κατὰ ἀφαίρεσιν τοῦ βροτοῦ ἡ θ. ἡμῶν νοῆται Hierocl.*in CA* 27 p.483 M. **–ός**, όν, *making gods*, Ar.*Fr.*786; ἁ θ. τέχνα, = θεοποιητική, *AP*9.774 (Glauc.); οὐ θ. τις ἀλλ' ἀνθρωποποιὸς ὤν Luc.*Philops.*20. II. *making into gods, deifying*, Dam.(?)ap.Suid. s.v. ἀποκλήρωσις; παραγγέλματα Hierocl.*in CA* 19 p.462 M.

θεο-πολέω, *minister in things divine*, Pl.*Lg.*909d. **–πόλος**, ὁ, ἡ, *priest*; v. θεηπόλος. **–πομπεῖν**· ἐνθουσιᾶν, Hsch. (Fort. –προπεῖν.) **–πομπος**, ον, = θεόπεμπτος, τιμαί Pi.*P.*4.69; τύχα B.16.132 (– – ⏑); πόμα, as pr. n., Aët.11.11. II. pr. n. Θεόπομπος: hence, Adj. Θεοπόμπειον (sc. μέτρον), τό, Cretic pentameter used by Theopomp.Com., Heph.13.5. **–πόνητος**, ον, *prepared by the gods*, λέχη, of Helen, E.*Tr.*953, *Hel.*584.

θεοπρέπ-εια, ἡ, *divine majesty*, τῆς προσόψεως D.S.5.43, cf. 11.89. **–ής**, ές, *meet for a god*, Ἥρας δῶμα Pi.*N.*10.2; πεδίον D.S.11.89; πομπή, μορφή, Plu.*Dio* 28, 2.780a; ὀνόματα Max.Tyr.6.2; *marvellous*, θέαμα Plu.*Alc.*34, etc.; τὸ θ. τῶν διατεταγμένων Ph.2.137: Sup. –έστατος, ἄγαλμα Plu.2.780f. Adv. **–πῶς** *IG*5(1).1390.3 (Andania, i B.C.), D.S.4.2, Ph.1.154, al., Luc.*Alex.*15, etc. **–τος**, ον, = foreg., v.l. in A.*Pers.*905 (lyr.).

θεο-προπέω, *prophesy*, but only in part. masc., θεοπροπέων ἀγορεύεις Il.1.109, cf. Od.2.184, Pi.*P.*4.190, A.R.2.922. II. *to be a θεοπρόπος* II, in Boeot. form **θιοπρ–**, *IG*7.3207 (Orchom.). **–προπία**, ἡ, *prophecy, oracle*, Il.1.87, Od.1.415, etc. **–πρόπιον**, τό, = foreg., Il.1.85; θεοπροπίων εὖ εἰδώς 6.438: in Prose, ἐκ θεοπροπίου Hdt.1.7, 165, al.; κατὰ τὸ θ. ib.68, cf. Heraclid.Lemb.*Oxy.*1367.39, Ph.1.514 (pl.). **–πρόπος**, ον, *prophetic*, οἰωνιστής Il.13.70; ἔπος S.*Tr.*822 (lyr.); ἦτορ Q.S.12.534. 2. Subst., *seer, prophet*, Il.12.228, Od.1.416; of Moses, Ph.1.199. b. θεοπρόπον, τό, = θεοπροπία, Call.*Lav.Pall.*125 (pl.). II. *public messenger sent to inquire of an oracle*, Ion. for θεωρός, Hdt.1.48, al., A.*Pr.*659, *IG*12(5).141.9 (Paros, iii B.C.), *SIG*548.2 (Delph., iii B.C.), Plu.*Cim.*18: pl., as pr. n. of a family (= Θεοπροπίδαι, cf. D.L.2.125), Porph.*Abst.*2.9. (–προπο– assim. fr. –προκο–, cf. Lat. *procus, precor.*)

θεο-πρόσπλοκος, ον, *very religious*, as gloss on ἱεροπρόσπολος, Procl.*Par.Ptol.*224. **–πρόσπολος**, = foreg., Ptol.*Tetr.*71, 155 (where Procl. renders προσπλεκόμενοι πρὸς τὸ θεῖον (πρὸς θεούς)).

θεόπτ-ης, ου, ὁ, (ὁράω, ὄψομαι) *seeing God*, of Moses, Ph.1.579 (s.v.l.). **–ία**, ἡ, *divine vision*, Hsch. **–ικός**, ή, όν, *of* or *for a* θεόπτης: ἡ θ. δύναμις the power *of seeing God*, Herm.ap.Stob.1.3.52, 3.11.31; ἡ θ. ψυχή Iamb.*Myst.*8.6.

θεό-πτυστος, ον, *detested by the gods*, γένος A.*Th.*604. **–πῡρος**, ον, (πῦρ) *kindled by the gods*, φλόξ E.*El.*732 (lyr.). **–ρακτος**, ον, (ῥάσσω) *struck*, i.e. *maddened, by God*, nickname of Θεόμναστος, Cic. *Verr.*4.66.148.

θεόργητος, ον, = θεομανής, Sch.A.*Th.*653. **θεορέω**, v. θεωρέω.

θεό-ρρητος, ον, *spoken of God*, μέτρον *AP*9.505; εὐεπίαι Epic. in *BKT* 5(1) p.118. II. **Θεόρρητον**, τό, name of a building at Delos, *IG*11(2).199 *A* 103 (iii B.C.), *Inscr.Délos* 312.1; elsewh. τὸν οἶκον τὸν Θ–ου *IG*11(2).163 *Ba*6 (iii B.C.), al. **–ρρῦτος**, ον, *flowing from the gods*, λύθρος Opp.*H.*5.9.

θεόρτος, ον, (ὄρνυμαι) *sprung from the gods*, ὄλβος Pi.*O.*2.36; θεόρτον ἢ βρότειον A.*Pr.*765.

θεός, ὁ, Boeot. **θιός**, Lacon. **σιός** (v. infr.), Cypr., Cret. **θιός** *Inscr.Cypr.*135.27 H., *Leg.Gort.*1.1, Dor. also **θεύς** Call.*Cer.*58; acc. θεῦν v.l. ib.130; voc. (only late) θεός, also θεέ Lxx *De.*3.24, *Ev.Matt.*27.46, *PMag.Lond.*121.529, etc.; but classical in compd. names, Ἀμφίθεε, Τιμόθεε:—*God, the Deity*, in general sense, both sg. and pl. (εἰ καὶ ἐπὶ θεοὺς καὶ ἔτι μᾶλλον ἐπὶ θεὸν ἁρμόζει μεταφέρειν Plot.6.8.1), θ. δὲ τὸ μὲν δώσει τὸ δ' ἐάσει *God* will grant.., Od.14.444; οὐδέ κεν ἄλλως οὐδὲ θ. τεύξειε 8.177, cf. 3.231, Il.13.730 (also θεὸς Ζεύς Od.4.236, 14.327); θ. καὶ ἀγαθὴ τύχη Pl.*Lg.*757e, cf. Timocl.3 D.; σὺν θεῷ Il.9.49, S.*Aj.*765, etc. (less freq. ξὺν τῷ θ. ib.383); σὺν θ. εἰρημένον Hdt.1.86, cf. 3.153; σὺν θ. εἰπεῖν Pl.*Prt.*317b: so in pl., σύν γε θεοῖσιν Il.24.430; οὔ τοι ἄνευ θεοῦ Od.2.372; οὐ θεῶν ἄτερ Pi.*P.*5.76; ἐκ θεόφι Il.17.101; ὑπὲρ θεόν *against his will*, 17.327; ἂν θ. θέλῃ Alex.231; θ. θέλοντος Men.*Mon.*671: in pl., ἂν θεοὶ θέλωσιν Alex.247; θεῶν συνεθελόντων, βουλομένων, X.*Eq.Mag.*9.8, Luc.*Macr.*29; εἰ ὀρθῶς ἢ μή, θ. οἶδε Pl.*Phdr.*266b, cf. *R.*517b, etc.; in oaths, θ. ἴστω S.*OC*522 (lyr.), etc.; πρὸς θεῶν Hdt.5.49, D.1.15, etc.: τοὺς θεούς σοι *bless you! good heavens! for heaven's sake!* M.Ant.7.17, Arr.*Epict.*2.19.15, al.; τὸν θ. σοι ib.3.7.19, al.: qualified by τις, Od.9.142, etc.; οὐκ ἄνευ θεῶν τινος A.*Pers.*164 (troch.), E.*Ba.*764; κατὰ θεόν τινα Id.*IA*411, Pl.*Euthd.*272e; κατὰ θεόν πως εἰρημένα Id.*Lg.*682a: doubled in poets, θεὸν θεόν τις ἀγλαϊζέτω B.3.21, cf. Diagor.1; θεοὶ θεοὶ τῶν ἀδίκων μέλουσι E.*HF*772, cf. Paus.Gr.*Fr.*203; θεοί (Cret. θιοί) as an opening formula in Inscrr. (sc. τύχην ἀγαθὴν διδοῖεν), *Leg.Gort.*1.1, *IG* 1².52, etc.: sg., θ. τύχη ib.5(2).1, etc.: in Prose also with the Art., ὁ θ. πάντων ἂν εἴη αἴτιος Pl.*R.*379c, cf. *Lg.*716c, etc.; τὰ πρὸς τοὺς θ., τὰ παρὰ τῶν θ., X.*Mem.*1.3.1, 2.6.8. b. θεοί, opp. ἄνδρες, πατὴρ ἀνδρῶν τε θεῶν τε Il.1.544; ὃν Ξάνθον καλέουσι θ., ἄνδρες δὲ Σκάμανδρον 20.74: in Comparisons, θεοῖσιν ἶσ' ἔθελε φρονέειν 5.440; θεοῖς ἐναλίγκια μήδεα Od.13.89; also in sg., θεῷ ἐναλίγκιος αὐδήν Il.19.250; θεὸς ὥς 5.78; ὥς τε θεός 3.381: prov., θεὸς πρὸς ἀνθρώπους, of an 'angel's visit', Herod.1.9. c. of special divinities, νέρτεροι θ. A.*Pers.*622, S.*Ant.*602 (lyr.); ἐνέρτεροι θ. Il.15.225; οἱ κάτωθεν θ. S.*Ant.*1070; θ. οὐράνιοι *h.Cer.*55, A.*Ag.*90 (anap.); οἱ δώδεκα θ. Ar.*Eq.*235, X.*Eq.Mag.*3.2, *IG*2².30, etc.; μὰ τοὺς δώδεκα θ. Men.*Sam.*91; in dual, τὼ σιώ (Lacon.), of Castor and Pollux, ναὶ τὼ σ. X.*An.*6.6.34, *HG*4.4.10, Ar.*Lys.*81: so in Boeot., of Amphion and Zethus, νεὶ τὼ σιώ (leg. θιώ) Id.*Ach.*905. d. ὁ θ., of natural phenomena, ὁ θ. ὕει (sc. Ζεύς) Hdt.2.13; ὁ θ. ἐνέσκηψε βέλος Id.4.79; ἔσεισεν ὁ θ. (sc. Ποσειδῶν) X.*HG*4.7.4; of the sun, Hdt.2.24, A.*Pers.*502, E.*Alc.*722; δύνοντος τοῦ θ. App.*BC*4.79; the *weather*, τί δοκεῖ τὰ τοῦ θεοῦ; Thphr.*Char.*25.2. e. Astrol., θεοί, = ἀστέρες, Jul. Laod.in *Cat.Cod.Astr.*8(4).252. f. θεός (sc. Ἥλιος), name of the 9th τόπος, Rhetor.ib.163, etc. 2. metaph., of abstract things, τὸ δ' εὐτυχεῖν τόδ' ἐν βροτοῖς θεός τε καὶ θεοῦ πλέον A.*Ch.*60; ἡ φρόνησις ἀγαθὴ θ. μέγας S.*Fr.*922; θ. γὰρ καὶ τὸ γιγνώσκειν φίλους E.*Hel.*560; ὁ πλοῦτος τοῖς σοφοῖς θ. Id.*Cyc.*316; φθόνος κάκιστος θ. Hippothoon 2. 3. as title of rulers, θεῶν ἀδελφῶν (sc. Ptolemy II and Arsinoe), Herod.1.30, etc.; Πτολεμαῖος ὑπάρχων θεὸς ἐκ θεοῦ καὶ θεᾶς *OGI*90.10 (Rosetta, ii B.C.); Ἀντίοχος ὅτῳ θεὸς ἐπώνυμον γίγνεται App.*Syr.*65; θεὸς ἐκ θεοῦ, of Augustus, *OGI*655.2 (Egypt, 24 B.C.); θ. ἡμῶν καὶ δεσπότης *IPE*4.71 (Cherson., ii A.D.). b. = Lat. *Divus*, *Mon.Anc.Gr.*10.4, Str.4.1.1, etc.; οἱ ἐν θεοῖς αὐτοκράτορες, = *divi Imperatores*, *IG*12(1).786 (Rhodes). c. generally of the dead, καὶ ζῶντός σου καὶ εἰς θεοὺς ἀπελθόντος *PPetr.*2 p.45 (iii B.C.); θεοῖς χθονίοις, = Lat. *Dis Manibus*, *IG*14.30, al. 4. *one set in authority, judge*, τὸ κριτήριον τοῦ θ., ἐνώπιον τοῦ θ., Lxx *Ex.*21.6, 22.8; θεοὺς οὐ κακολογήσεις ib.22.28(27). II. θεός fem., *goddess*, μήτε θήλεια θεός, μήτε τις ἄρσην Il.8.7, cf. Hdt.2.35, al.; τοῖς θεοῖς εὔχομαι πᾶσι καὶ πάσαις D.18.1, cf. 141, Orac.ib.21.52; esp. at Athens, of Athena, Decr.ap.And.1.77, Pl.*Ti.*21a, etc.; ἁ Διὸς θεός, Ζηνὸς ἡ θ., S.*Aj.*401 (lyr.), 952 (ἡ Διὸς θεά ib.450); of other goddesses, ποντία θεός Pi.*I.*8(7).36; ἡ νερτέρα θ., = Περσεφόνη, S.*OC*1548, etc.; of Thetis, Pl.*Ap.*28c; of Niobe, S.*El.*150 (lyr.), *Ant.*834 (anap.): in dual, of Demeter and Persephone, τὰ τοῖν θεοῖν ψηφίσματα Ar.*V.*378 (lyr.); οὐδ' ἔδεισε τὼ θεώ And.1.125; freq. in oaths, νὴ τὼ θεώ Ar.*Lys.*112; μὰ τὼ θεώ Id.*Ec.*155, 532. III. as Adj. in Comp. θεώτερος, *divine*, θύραι θ., opp. καταιβαταὶ ἀνθρώποισιν, Od.13.111; χορὸς θ. Call.*Ap.*93, cf. *Dian.*249, D.P.257. (Derived by Hdt.2.52 fr. τίθημι (κόσμῳ θέντες τὰ πρήγματα), by Pl.*Cra.*397d fr. θεῖν. Etym. dub.) [In Ep. (twice in Hom.) and Trag. (E.*Ba.*47, 1347, al., not in Com.), as monosyll. by synizesis, θεοί Il.1.18, Thgn.142; θεῶν *h.Cer.*55, 259; θεοῖς Thgn.171; θεοῖσιν Od.14.251; θεούς *h.Cer.*325: even in nom. θεός before a vowel, E.*Or.*399 (cf. Pors. ad loc.), *HF*347; in Pi.*P.*1.56 apptly. a short monosyll.]

θεόσ-δοτος, ον, poet. and later Prose for θεόδοτος, *given by the gods*, Hes.*Op.*320; δύναμις Pi.*P.*5.13; εὐδαιμονία Arist.*EN*1099ᵇ12; ἀρετή Max.Tyr.38.4. **–δωρος**, ον, poet. for θεοδώρητος, a fiction of Tz. ad Lyc.47.

θεοσέβ-εια, ἡ, *service* or *fear of God, religiousness*, X.*An.*2.6.26, Pl.*Epin.*985c, 990a, Plu.*in Hes.*46, Iamb.*Protr.*20. **–έω**, *serve God*, Plu.*Fr.inc.*22, D.C.54.30; τὸ θ. *SIG*708.18 (Istropolis, ii B.C.). **–ής**, ές, *fearing God, religious*, Hdt.1.86, 2.37, S.*OC*260 (Sup.), Pl.*Cra.*394d, al.; θ. μέλος Ar.*Av.*897 (lyr.); τὸ θεοσεβές Pl.*Epin.*977e. Adv. –βῶς X.*Cyr.*3.3.58.

θεόσεπτος, ον, *feared as divine*, βροντή Ar.*Nu.*292; *holy*, Orac.ap. Jul.*Ep.*89b. II. Act., = θεοσεβής, Man.4.427.

θεοσέπτωρ, ορος, ὁ, = θεοσεβής, E.*Hipp.*1364 (anap.).

θεοσεχθρία, ἡ, v. θεοισεχθρία; cf. θεοεχθρία.

θεοσημεία, ἡ, *a sign from the gods*, Suid.:—also **θεοσημία**, ἡ, Hsch. s.v. εὐαμερία.

θεοσκνεῖ· θεοὺς τιμᾷ, Hsch.; cf. θυοσκέω.

θεοσοφ-έω, *have knowledge of things divine*, Porph.*Abst.*4.17. **–ία**, ἡ, *knowledge of things divine*, *PMag.Leid.W.*6.17; ἡ ἄγαν θ. Porph.*Abst.*4.9; Ἑλληνική, Χαλδαϊκὴ θ., Procl.*Theol.Plat.*5.35, Dam. *Pr.*350. **–ος**, ον, *wise in the things of God*, Porph.*Abst.*2.35, Iamb.*Myst.*7.1: pl., of the Γυμνοσοφισταί, Porph.*Abst.*4.17.

θεό-σπορος, ον, *sown by a god, divine*, κῦμα E.*Fr.*106. **–σσῦτος**, v. θεόσυτος.

θεόστᾰσις, εως, ἡ, *base* or *pedestal for statues of gods*, *CIL*2.1724 (Gades).

θεο-στήρικτος, ον, *supported by God*, σκῆπτρα *AP*15.15 (Const. Rhod.). **–στῐβής**, ές, *trodden by God*, δειράς Limen.21; πυλεῶνες

Procl.*H.*7.7. **-στῠγής,** ές, *hated of the gods*, E.*Tr.*1213, *Cyc.*602, Poll.1.21; *hated of God*, *Ep.Rom.*1.30 (where some take it Act., *hating God*). **-στύγητος** [ῠ], ον, = foreg. 1, ἄγος A.*Ch.*635 (lyr.). **-σύλης** [ῡ], ου, ὁ, (σῡλάω) *robbing God, sacrilegious*, Ael. *VH*5.16, *Fr.*124, Ph.ap.Eus.*PE*8.14. **-σῡλία,** ἡ, *sacrilege*, Ael. *NA*10.28: in pl., interpol. in Id.*VH*6.8.

θεοσύνδετος, ον, *united by God*, Hierocl.*in CA*26 p.478 M.

θεόσῠτος, ον, *sent by the gods*, θ. ἡ βρότειος; A.*Pr.*116; νόσος ib. 596 (lyr.):—also **θεόσσυτος** χειμών ib.643.

θεο-ταρπέ(ε)ς· θεὸν τέρποντες, Hsch. **-ταυρος,** ὁ, *god-bull*, a name for Zeus, Mosch.2.135. **-τείχης,** ες, *walled by gods*, of Troy, Epigr.ap.Certamen 311. **-τέρᾰτος,** ον, *with divine portents*, πλάναι θ., of Io's wanderings, dithyrambic phrase in Demetr.*Eloc.*91 codd. **-τερπής,** ές, of a dish, *fit for the gods*, Philox.2.9; *pleasing to God*, βιοτή *AP*9.197 (Marin.); cf. θεοταρπέες. **-τευκτος,** ον, *made by God*, πύργοι Simm.25, cf. Doroth.ap.Heph.Astr.1.1.

θεότης, ητος, ἡ, *divinity, divine nature*, *Ep.Col.*2.9, Plu.2.359d, Luc. *Icar.*9, etc.; διὰ θεότητα *for religious reasons*, Heliod.ap.Orib.50.7.1.

θεο-τίμητος [ῐ], Dor. **-ᾱτος,** ον, B.8.98:—*honoured by the gods*, θεοτιμήτους βασιλῆας Tyrt.4.3, cf. A.*Ag.*1337 (anap.); πόλις B. l. c. **-τῖμος,** ον, = foreg., ἄστυ Id.10.12 (trisyll.), cf. Pi.*I.*6(5).13, Orph.*H.*27.1. **-τόκος,** ἡ, *mother of God*, of the Virgin, *Cod. Just.*1.1.5.1, Just.*Nov.*3.1, *SIG*910 *B* (vi A.D.). **-τρεπτος,** ον, *turned by the gods*, θεότρεπτα τάδ' αὖ φέρομεν these *divine changes of fortune*, A.*Pers.*905 (-πρεπτα cod. M). **-τρεφής,** ές, *feeding the gods*, ἀμβροσίη *AP*9.577 (Ptol.), cf. Nonn.*D.*9.101.

θεούδεια, ἡ, *fear of God*, θεουδείῃ τ' ἐκέκαστο A.R.3.586; cf. sq.

θεουδής, ές, *fearing God*, Hom. only in Od., καί σφιν νόος ἐστὶ θεουδής 6.121, 8.576, 9.176; θεουδέα θυμὸν ἔχοντα 19.364; βασιλῆος .. ὅς τε θεουδὴς .. εὐδικίας ἀνέχῃσι 19.109, cf. *MAMA*1.171 (Laodicea Combusta), etc. Adv. -δῶς Orph.*Fr.*169. (θεο-δϝής contr. fr. θεο-δϝεής, compd. of θεός and δέος: but taken as if = θεοειδής by late Poets, as Q.S.1.65, 3.775.)

θεουργ-ία, ἡ, *divine work*, Jul.*Or.*7.219a. II. *sacramental rite, 'mystery'*, Porph.ap.Aug.*Civ.D.*10.9; ἱερατικὴ θ. Iamb.*Myst.*9.6; οἱ περὶ θεουργίαν δεινοί Procl.*in Alc.*p.92 C. **-ίασμα,** ατος, τό, = foreg. II, Dam.*Isid.*56. **-ικός,** ή, όν, *of* or *for a* θεουργός, τελεταί Porph.ap.Aug.*Civ.D.*10.9; κοινωνία Iamb.*Myst.*1.8; τέχνη ib.2.11. Adv. -κῶς Procl.*in Cra.*p.32 P.; opp. τεχνικῶς, Iamb.*Myst.*3.28: Comp. -ώτερον ib.2.11. **-ός,** ὁ, *divine worker*, of the δημιουργός, Dam.*Pr.*341. II. *performer of sacramental rites*, Jul.*Or.*5.173a, Procl.*in Alc.*p.150 C., Iamb.*Myst.*3.18. III. as Adj., ἡ θ. ἐνέργεια ib.20.

θεοφάν-εια, ἡ, *vision of God*, *Notiz.Arch.*4.236 (Cyrene). **-ια** (sc. ἱερά), τά, *festival at Delphi, at which the statues of Apollo and other gods were shown to the people*, Hdt.1.51, cf. Poll.1.34; at Chios, *SIG*1064.3 (Halic., i B.C.): generally, θ. ἄγειν τινί Philostr.*VA*4.31; θ. θύειν Ael.*NA*11.10.

θεό-φαντος, ον, *revealed by God* or *revealing God*, ὄργια Metrod. 38. **-φάντωρ,** ορος, ὁ, *a revealer of God, a priest*, Suid. s. v. Διονύσιος ὁ Ἀρεοπαγίτης. **-φᾰτος, -φᾰτίζω,** = θέσφατος, θεσφατίζω, Hsch. **-φημος,** ον, *declaring God's will*, ἀστρολόγοι Man.1.293, 4.128. **-φθεγκτος,** ον, *uttered by God*, Eust.1381.2.

θεοφίλ-εια [φῐ], ἡ, = θεοφιλία, Marin.*Procl.*32. **-ής,** ές, (φιλέω) *dear to the gods, highly favoured*, of persons, Hdt.1.87, Democr.217, Pl.*R.*382e, *Phlb.*39e, etc.; of Moses, Ph.2.218 (Sup.); as honorary epith. in Egypt, *Sammelb.*421 (Sup.), al.; also, of places, etc., πόλις Pi.*I.*6(5).66; Ἄργος B.10.60; πόλιν .. θεοφιλεστάτην Eup.307; χώρα A.*Eu.*869 (Sup.); τύχαι Id.*Fr.*350.3; ἑορτή Ar.*Ra.*446; μοῖρα X. *Ap.*32; ἐπιτήδευμα Isoc.8.35 (Comp.), cf. Pl.*Euthphr.*7a; θεοφιλές [ἐστιν] εἰ .. *'tis a mark of divine favour*, if .., Plu.2.30f. Adv. -λῶς, πράττειν to act *as the gods will*, Pl.*Alc.*1.134d: Comp. -έστερον, διαβεβιωκέναι Isoc.9.70. II. Act., *loving God*, Ph.2.415, Luc. *JTr.*47 (Sup.), Agath.3.13, *Cod.Just.*1.1.5.4 (Sup.). Adv. ἡ πόλις οὐ μόνον -λῶς ἀλλὰ καὶ φιλανθρώπως ἔσχεν Isoc.4.29, cf. Poll.1. 22. **-ητος,** η, ον, *loved by the gods*, Phint.ap.Stob.4.23.61[a] (hyperdor. -ᾱτος). **-ία,** ἡ, *the favour of God*, Oenom.ap.Eus.*PE*5.34, Sch.S.*OT*40. **-ιον,** τό, *eyesalve invented by Theophilus*, Aët.7.115, Alex.Trall.2. **-ος,** ον, = θεοφίλητος, epith. of a city, *BGU*924.1 (iii A.D.). **-ότης,** ητος, ἡ, *a being loved by God*, Men.Rh.pp.361, 362 S.

θεόφιν, Ep. gen. and dat., sg. and pl., of θεός.

θεό-φοβος, ον, *fearing God*, Porph.*Abst.*1.1, Hsch. **-φοιτος,** ον, *driven by divine frenzy*, of Cassandra, Tryph.374.

θεοφορ-έω, *deify*, τὸ πῦρ S.E.*M.*9.32. II. Pass., *to be possessed by a god, inspired*, Longin.13.2, Ph.2.146, al., Luc.*Philops.*38, S.E.*P.* 1.101; Θεοφορουμένη, name of a play of Menander, Ath.11.504a, cf. Arg.Men.*Oxy.*1235.46. **-ησις,** εως, ἡ, *divine possession, ecstasy*, in pl., D.H.2.19, Plu.2.278c. **-ητος,** ον, *possessed by a god, inspired*, A.*Ag.*1140 (lyr.), Str.12.2.3, Sor.1.88, Plu.2.54c; Θ., name of a play by Alexis. Adv. -τως Plu.2.45f. II. Act., *carrying a god* or *goddess*, Luc.*Asin.*37. **-ία,** ἡ, = θεοφόρησις, Phld.*Mus.*p.25 K., Iamb. *Myst.*3.5, al.: pl., Phld.*Mus.*p.49 K., Str.12.3.32, 16.2.36:—sg. in poet. form **θευφορίη** *AP*6.220.4 (Diosc.). **-ος** (-φόρ-), ον, (φέρω) *bearing* or *carrying a god*, πόδες A.*Fr.*225. II. θεόφορος, ον, *possessed by a god, inspired*, θ. δύαι the pains *of inspiration*, Id.*Ag.* 1150 (lyr.), cf. Phld.*D.*1.4. 2. θ. ὀνόματα names *derived from a god*, as Διόδωρος, Ath.10.448e.

θεοφρᾰδ-ής, ές, (φράζω) *speaking from God, prophetic*, Μουσαῖος Orph.*Fr.*271. II. Pass., *indicated by God*, κέλευθοι Procl.*H.*6. 8. **-ία,** ἡ, *a divine saying, oracle*, Hsch. **-μων,** ον, gen. ονος, = θεοφραδής I, Ph.1.516, 2.176.

θεο-φρονέω, = θεῖα φρονέω, Hld.2.11. **-φροσύνη,** ἡ, *godliness*, Hsch. **-φρουρος,** ον, *guarded by* (or perh. *guarding*) *the gods*, *IG*12(5).241 (Paros, i B.C.). **-φρων,** ον, gen. ονος, (φρήν) *godly-minded, holy*, Κάδμος Thebaïs *Fr.*2.3, cf. Pi.*O.*6.41. **-φύλαξ** [ῠ], ακος, ὁ, *guardian of a god*, gloss on θεωρός, Sch.Pi.*N.*3.122. **-χαρις·** *deo gratus*, *Gloss.* **-χολωσία,** ἡ, *the wrath of God*, Lyd.*Ost.*37, Sch.Od.8.232:—also **-χολωσύνη,** Sch.Luc.*Lex.*10. **-χόλωτος,** ον, *under God's wrath*, Arr.*Epict.*2.8.14, 3.1.37, Vett.Val.67.19. **-χρηστος,** ον, *delivered by God*, λόγια θ., of the Mosaic Law, Ph.2.577.

θεόω, *make into God, deify*, Oenom.ap.Eus.*PE*5.34:—Pass., ἔννοιαι θεωθεῖσαι Iamb.*VP*23.103. 2. *become divine*, γυῖα θεωθείς Call. *Dian.*159; καθ' ὅσον πάντα τεθέωται Procl.*in Prm.*p.490 S., cf. Jul. *Or.*5.178b. II. = θειόω I, Arar.12.

θέπτανος· ἁπτόμενος, Hsch. (perh. cogn. with Skt. *dáhati*, Lith. *degù* 'burn', Lith. *degtìnė* 'brandy').

θεράπαιν-α [ρᾰ], ἡ, fem. of θεράπων, *handmaid* or *female slave*, Hdt.3.134, Pherecyd.Syr.2, And.1.64, X.*Cyr.*6.4.11, Men.141, etc. **-ίδιον,** τό, Dim. of sq., Men.*Sam.*36, Parth.26.2, Plu.*Ant.* 29, Luc.*Pisc.*17, etc. **-ίς,** ίδος, ἡ, = θεράπαινα, Pl.*Lg.*808a, Men. 142, Parth.10.2.

θερᾰπ-εία, Ion. **-ηΐη** (-είη Hp.*Art.*80, al.), ἡ, *service, attendance*: I. of persons, θ. τῶν θεῶν *service paid* to the gods, Pl. *Euthphr.*13d, cf. E.*El.*744 (lyr.); θεῶν καὶ ἡρώων θεραπεῖαι Pl.*R.*427b, etc.; ἡ περὶ τοὺς θεοὺς θ. Isoc.11.24; ἀγυιάτιδες θ. *worship* of Apollo Agyieus, E.*Ion* 187; τὴν θ. ἀποδιδόναι τοῖς θεοῖς Arist.*Pol.*1329[a]32; θ. τῆς μήνιδος Jul.*Or.*5.159b: abs., πᾶσαν θ. ὡς ἰσόθεος θεραπευόμενος Pl.*Phdr.*255a, cf. Antipho 4.2.4; of parents, γονέων θεραπείας καὶ τιμάς Pl.*Lg.*886c, cf. Gorg.*Fr.*6 D.; of children, *nurture, care*, μικροὺς παῖδας θεραπείας δεομένους Lys.13.45; θ. καὶ ἐσθής X.*Mem.*3.11.4; θ. σώματος, ψυχῆς, Pl.*Grg.*464b, *La.*185e. 2. *service done to gain favour, paying court*, θ. τοῦ κοινοῦ καὶ τῶν αἰεὶ προεστώτων Th.3.11; ἐν θεραπείᾳ ἔχειν πολλῇ Id.1.55; πάσῃ θεραπείᾳ θεραπεύειν τινά X.*HG* 2.3.14; θεραπείαις προσαγαγέσθαι Isoc.3.22; τῇ θ. ψυχαγωγούμενος D.59.55. II. *medical* or *surgical treatment* or *cure*, χειρός, ποδός, Hp.l.c.; αἱ ὑπὸ τῶν ἰατρῶν θ. αἱ διὰ καύσεων γιγνόμεναι *cures* by cautery, Pl.*Prt.*354a; ἡ ἐκ τῶν γραμμάτων θ. *treatment* secundum artem, Arist.*Pol.*1287[a]40, cf. Gal.1.400, etc.; τῶν καμνόντων Pl.*Prt.* 345a, cf. Th.2.51, Phld.*Ir.*p.21 W.; τοῦ σώματος Id.*Lib.*p.19 O., *Vit. Philonid.*p.9 C.; *healing*, θεραπείας ἐπιτυχών *Sammelb.*1537*b*: in pl., *cures*, ἰατρὸς ποιεῖ -είας *POxy.*1[r].13. III. of animals, *care, tendance*, Pl.*Euthphr.*13a, Arist.*HA*578[a]7 (pl.). 2. of plants, *cultivation*, Pl.*Tht.*149e, Thphr.*HP*2.2.12. 3. *maintenance* or *repairs* of temples, *SIG*1106.49 (Cos, iv/iii B.C.), 1102.8 (ii B.C.). 4. *preparation* of fat for medical use, Dsc.2.76. IV. in collective sense, *body of attendants, retinue*, Hdt.1.199, 5.21, 7.184, LXX *Ge.* 45.16; σὺν ἱππικῇ θ. X.*Cyr.*4.6.1; ὁ ἐπὶ τῆς θ. τεταγμένος Plb.4.87. 5. **-ευμα,** ατος, τό, *a service done to another*: I. θ. θεοῦ divine *worship*, Pl.*Def.*415a. 2. *service paid* to a person, ξενικὰ θ. Id.*Lg.*718b, cf. Plu.2.1117c. II. *care* of the body, Pl.*Grg.*524b (pl.); of a child, E.*Hyps.Fr.*3(1)ii 12 (lyr., pl.). 2. *surgical treatment*, Hp.*Mochl.*40 (pl.), Arist.*EN*1181[b]3 (pl.); Ἀσκλαπιοῦ *IG*4.952. 96 (Epid.), etc. III. concrete, *preparations, drugs*, Hp.*Morb.*4. 34. **-ευσία,** ἡ, rarer form for θεραπεία II, Hsch. **-ευσις,** εως, ἡ, *treatment, attention*, Phld.*Lib.*p.20 O. **-ευτέον,** *one must do service to*, τοὺς θεοὺς X.*Mem.*2.1.28. 2. *one must court, flatter*, τοὺς ἀκούοντας ἐπαίνῳ Arist.*Rh.Al.*1436[b]32. II. *one must cultivate*, τὴν γῆν X.l.c. 2. *one must treat medically*, Pl.*R.*408b, Dsc.*Eup.*1.101. 3. *one must prepare* fat, Id.2.76. III. Adj. **θεραπευτέος,** α, ον, *to be courted*, Luc.*Merc.Cond.*38. **-ευτήρ,** ῆρος, ὁ, *attendant*, Aristox.*Fr. Hist.*15, Plu.*Lyc.*11, Charito 4.1; ὁ περὶ τὸ σῶμα θ. X.*Cyr.*7.5.65; τοῦ ἄντρου Max.Tyr.14.2 (pl.). **-ευτής,** οῦ, ὁ, *one who serves the gods, worshipper*, θ. Ἄρεως, θεῶν, Pl.*Phdr.*252c, *Lg.*740c; ὁσίων τε καὶ ἱερῶν ib.878a; τοῦ καλοῦ Ph.1.261; οἱ θ. worshippers of Sarapis or Isis, *UPZ*8.19 (ii B.C.), *IG*11(4).1226 (Delos, ii B.C.); title of play by Diphilus, ib.2.992 ii 9; name of certain ascetics, Ph.2.471; θ. ὁσιότητος, of the followers of Moses, ib.177. 2. *one who serves* a great man, *courtier*, οἱ ἀμφὶ τὸν πάππον θ. X.*Cyr.*1.3.7. II. *one who attends to anything*, c. gen., σώματος Pl.*Grg.*517e; τῶν περὶ τὸ σῶμα Id.*R.* 369d. 2. *medical attendant*, τῶν καμνόντων ib.341c. **-ευτικός,** ή, όν, *inclined to serve*, c. gen., τῶν φίλων X.*Ages.*8.1; εὐσέβεια δύναμις θ. θεῶν Pl.*Def.*412e; θεοῦ Ph.1.202 (but τὸ θ. γένος, = θεραπευταί, Id.2. 473); *inclined to court*, τῶν δυνατῶν, τοῦ πλήθους, Plu.*Lys.*2, *Comp.Lyc. Num.*2; τὸ θ. τῆς ὁμιλίας Id.*Lys.*4. 2. abs., *courteous, obsequious*, in good and bad sense, X.*HG*3.1.28 (Comp.), Plu.*Luc.*16; θ. παρρησία Id.2.74a. Adv. -κῶς Id.*Art.*4; θ. ἔχειν τινός Ph.1.186, cf. Str.6.4. 2. II. *inclined to take care of, careful of*, λόγου dub. l. in Men.402. 15. 2. esp. of medical treatment, ἕξις θ. a *valetudinarian* habit of body, Arist.*Pol.*1335[b]7; ἡ -κή, = θεραπεία, Pl.*Plt.*282a; also τὸ -κόν *therapeutics*, Dsc.*Ther.Praef.* (but also τὸ περὶ παθῶν θ., title of a work on *moral remedies* by Chrysippus, Phld.*Ir.*p.17 W.); περὶ θ. μεθόδου, title of work by Galen. **-ευτός,** όν, *that may be fostered* or *cultivated*, Pl.*Prt.*325b. 2. *curable*, Paul.Aeg.4.5. **-εύτρια,** ἡ, fem. of θεραπευτής *EM*47.45. **-ευτρίς,** ίδος, ἡ, = foreg., Ph.1.261, 655: pl., as title of certain female ascetics, Id.2.471. **-εύω,** later also **θᾰράπεύω** (q.v.), fut. -εύσω Th.2.51, etc.:—Med., fut. -εύσομαι *h.Ap.*390: aor. ἐθεραπευσάμην Nicostr.ap.Stob.4.23.65

codd., Gal.11.295:—**Pass.**, fut. -ευθήσομαι Id.10.617: fut. Med. in pass. sense, Antipho 4.2.4, Pl.*Alc.*1.135e: aor. ἐθεραπεύθην Id. *Chrm.*157b, etc.:—*to be an attendant, do service*, once in Hom., Od. 13.265:—Med., *h.Ap.*390. II. *do service to* the gods, ἀθανάτους, θεοὺς θ., Hes.*Op.*135, Hdt.2.37, X.*Mem.*1.4.13, etc.; δαίμονα Pi.*P.*3.109; Διόνυσον, Μούσας, E.*Ba.*82 (lyr.), *IT*1105 (lyr.); θ. Φοίβου ναούς *serve* them, Id.*Ion* 111 (anap.): abs., *worship*, Lys.6.51; *do service* or *honour to* one's parents, E.*Ion* 183 (lyr.), Pl.*R.*467a, *Men.*91a; *serve, wait upon* a master, Id.*Euthphr.*13d, cf. Ar.*Eq.*59, 1261, etc.; θ. τὰς θήκας *reverence* men's graves, Pl.*R.*469a. 2. in Prose, *pay court to*, [τινα] Hdt.3.80, etc.; in bad sense, *flatter, wheedle*, Th.3.12; θ. τὸ πλῆθος, τοὺς πολλούς, Id.1.9, Plu.*Per.*34; *conciliate*, τινὰ χρημάτων δόσει Th.1.137, cf. Hdn.2.2.8; τὸ θεραπεῦον, = οἱ θεραπεύοντες, Th.3.39; θ. γυναῖκα *pay* her *attention*, X.*Cyr.*5.1.18; also τὰς θύρας τινὸς θ. *wait at* a man's door, ib.8.1.6; αὐλὰς θ. καὶ σατράπας Men.897; αὐλὰς βασιλικὰς θ. D.L.9.63. 3. of things, *consult, attend to*, τὸ ξυμφέρον Th.3.56; ἡδονὴν θ. *indulge* one's love of pleasure, X.*Cyr.*5.5.41; θ. τὸ παρόν *look to, provide for* the present, S.*Ph.*149 (anap.); τὸ ναυτικόν Th.2.65; τὴν ἄνοιξιν τῶν πυλῶν Id.4.67; θ. τοὺς καιρούς D.18.307: c. inf., *take care that...*, θ. τὸ μὴ θορυβεῖν, μὴ λείπεσθαι, Th.6.61, 7.70; θ. ὅπως πολιτεύσουσι Id.1.19; θ. ὡς... Longus 4.1. 4. θ. τὸ σῶμα *take care of* one's person, Pl.*Grg.*513d; θ. αὐτούς Plu.*Eum.*9; θ. τὰς τρίχας Longus 4.4; μύροις χαίτην θ. Archestr.*Fr.*62.3; θ. τοὺς πόδας Lxx 2*Ki.*19.24: c. acc. et inf., θ. κόμην φαίνεσθαι λιπαράν Plu.*Lyc.*22. 5. *foster*, τὴν ψυχήν, τὴν διάνοιαν, Pl.*Cra.*440c, *R.*403d; θ. κάδεα *brood over* sorrows, Pi.*I.*8(7).8. 6. θ. ἡμέρην *observe* a day, *keep* it *as a feast*, Hdt.3.79; ἱερὰ -όμενα Th.4.98. 7. *treat medically*, Hp.*VM*9, Th.2.47,51; τοὺς τετρωμένους X.*Cyr.*3.2.12; τραύματα Phld.*Piet.*89; μὴ θεραπεύειν βέλτιον· θεραπευόμενοι γὰρ ἀπόλλυνται ταχέως Hp.*Aph.*6.38; ταύτην τὴν θεραπείαν θεραπεύσεσθαι Antipho 4.2.4; θ. νόσημα Isoc.19.28; σώματα -όμενα Pl.*Lg.*684c; ὀφθαλμούς Arist.*EN*1102^{a}19: abs., οἱ θεραπεύοντες Phld.*Ir.*p.29 W.: metaph., ὁ κοινὸς ἰατρός σε θεραπεύσει χρόνος Philippid.32; λύπην... οἶδε θεραπεύειν λόγος Men.591; τὰ πονοῦντα μέρη τῆς νεώς D.S.4.41; τὰς ὑποψίας *allayed*, Plu.*Luc.*22; ὑπόνοιαν Phlp. *in de An.*408.3; δυστυχίαν *assuage* it, Luc.*Ind.*6. 8. of animals, *train*, ἵππους Pl.*Grg.*516e. 9. of land, *cultivate*, X.*Oec.*5.12; of trees, *train*, Hdt.1.193; στέλεχος Thphr.*HP*2.7.3. 10. *prepare, dress*, food or drugs, Archestr.*Fr.*13.4, al., Dsc.2.76 (Pass.). 11. *mend* garments, *PGiss.*79 iv 3 (Pass., ii A.D.). -ητής, ἡ, Ion. for θεραπεία (q.v.):—also θεραπηΐας· βωμολοχίας, Hsch. -ήϊος, α, ον, Ion. and poet. for θεραπευτικός, in neut. pl. -ήϊα, νούσων *AP*7.158.8:—fem. **θεραπηΐς**, ΐδος, Orac.ap.Jul.*Ep.*88b. -ίδιον, τό, *means of cure*, Sch.Luc.*Alex.*21. -ιον, τό, Dim. of θέραψ, Hyp.*Fr.*99. -ίς, ίδος, ἡ, *paying court to, favouring*, πόλις τοῦ ἥττονος θ. Pl.*Mx.*244e. -νη, ἡ, poet., = θεράπαινα, *handmaid*, Ἑκατηβελέταο θ. *h.Ap.*157; Εὐρώπας θ. E.*Hec.*482 (lyr.), cf. A.R.1.786. II. *dwelling, abode*, E.*Tr.* 211 (lyr.), *Ba.*1043 (pl.), *HF*370 (lyr.), Nic.*Th.*486 (unless it be pr. n. in these places). III. as pr. n. **Θεράπνη**, a Laconian city, Pi.*P.* 11.63, Hdt.6.61, etc.; Lacon. **Σεράπνα** Alcm.4: in pl. **Θεράπναι** Isoc. 10.63. -νιον, τό, Dim. of foreg. 1, Hsch. -νίς, ίδος, ἡ, poet., = θεραπαινίς, *AP*9.603 (Antip.). -όντιον, τό, Dim. of θεράπων, D.L.4.59. -οντίς, ίδος, ἡ, *of a waiting-maid*, θ. φρενὴ A.*Supp.* 979 (anap.). -ουσία, ἡ, = θεραπεία IV, condemned by Poll.3. 75. -ων, οντος, ὁ, dat. pl. θεραπόντεσσι Pi.*P.*4.41; Aeol. θέραπων Sapph.74, gen. θερράποντος Choerob. in *An.Ox.*2.242 (θεράποντος cod., cf. Hdn.Gr.2.302):—*henchman, attendant*, Od.16.253, etc.; *companion in arms, squire*, 4.23, etc.; ἡνίοχος θ. Il.5.580, 8. 119; τώ οἱ ἔσαν κήρυκε.. καὶ θεράποντε 1.321; θεράποντε Διός Od. 11.255; θεράποντες Ἄρηος Il.2.110, etc.; Μουσάων θεράποντες *h.Hom.* 32.20, cf. Hes.*Th.*100, Thgn.769, Ar.*Av.*909 (lyr.); Ἔρως Ἀφροδίτης θ. Pl.*Smp.*203c, cf. Sapph. l.c.; *worshipper*, Ἀπόλλωνος Pi.*O.* 3.16, cf. Pl.*Phd.*85a; Ἄρεος *BMus.Inscr.*971 (Cypr., v B.C.): c. dat., οἶκος ξένοισι θεράπων *devoted to the service of* its guests, Pi.*O.*13.3; λωτὸς.. Μουσᾶν θ. E.*El.*717 (lyr.): c. gen., *attending upon*, τῶν ἀδίκως δυστυχούντων Gorg.*Fr.*6 D. II. *servant*, Hdt.1.30, 5.105, Ar.*Pl.*3, 5, And.1.12, Lys.7.34, etc.; at Chios, *slave*, Eust. ad D.P. 533.

θέραψ, ἄπος, ὁ, poet., = θεράπων, rare in sg., *Epigr.Gr.*415.3 (Alexandria): acc., Βακχιακὸν θέραπα (of Anacreon) *APl.*4.306.10 (Leon.), cf. *IGRom.*4.1655 (Notium): usu. in nom. pl., θέραπες E.*Ion* 94 (anap.), *Supp.*762, Ion Eleg.2.2, Maiist.14, *AP*12.229 (Strato): acc. pl. θέραπας in late Prose, Ant.Lib.13.4, 20.5.

θερεία, ἡ, *summer*; v. θέρειος.

θερεί-αυλος, ον, prob. *living in villeggiatura*, Theognost.*Can.* 96. -βοτος, ον, (βόσκω) *serving for a summer-pasture*, Eust.222. 20. -γενής, ές, *growing in summer*, Nic.*Th.*601. II. *hot*, ὕδατα Nonn.*D.*26.229. -λεχής, ές, *for sleeping under in summer*, πλάτανος Nic.*Th.*584. -νόμος, ον, *feeding in summer*, θ. πόα *summer*-pasture, D.H.2.2.

θέρειος, α, ον, also ος, ον Ael. (v. infr.): (θέρος):—*of summer, in summer*, αὐχμὸς θ. *summer*-drought, Emp.111.7; δρέπανον Orph.*H.* 40.11; καρποί ib.18; θέρειος ὥρα Ael.*NA*2.25. II. θερεία, Ion. -είη (sc. ὥρα), ἡ, = θέρος, *summer-time, summer*, Hdt.1.189, Arist. *Mir.*841^{a}25, Plb.5.1.3, al., *PTeb.*27.60 (ii B.C.), D.S.19.58 (θερίᾳ); θερείης *in summer*, Nic.*Fr.*81; μεσούσης θ. D.H.1.63; ὑπὸ τὴν θερείαν D.S.3.24: pl., θερείαις Pi.*I.*2.41. III. Sup. θερείτατος, η, ον, *very hot*, Arat.149, Nic.*Th.*460.—In Prose θερινός is the more common form.

θερείποτος, ον, (πίνω) *watered in summer*, γύαι Lyc.847.

θερείω, later poet. form of θέρω, in Med., Nic.*Th.*124, *Al.*567.

θερέσιμον· θεριστικόν, Hsch.

θέρετρον, τό, (θέρος) *summer-abode*, dub. in Hp.*Epid.*1.20, cf. Gal. 17(1).197.

θερηγᾰνον, contr. **θέρηγνον**, τό, (θέρος) *wicker body of the harvest-cart*, Hsch., *EM*447.14; perh. to be read in E.*Fr.*781.1.

θεριακός, ή, όν, *for summer*, ἱμάτια *POxy.*1901.37 (vi A.D.).

θερίδιον, τό, *summer residence*, Jul.*Ep.*4.

θερίζω, Boeot. inf. θερίδδειν Ar.*Ach.*947 (lyr.): fut. Att. -ιῶ Arist. *HA*601^{b}17: aor. ἐθέρισα S.*Aj.*239 (anap.), syncop. ἔθρισα A.*Ag.*536 (cf. ἀποθρίζω); poet. ἐθέρισσα *AP*9.451; later (subj.) ἐκθερίξω *Anacreont.*9.7:—Med. (v. infr.):—Pass., aor. ἐθερίσθην: pf. τεθέρισμαι (v. infr.): (θέρος):—*do summer-work, mow, reap*, σῖτον, κριθάς, Hdt.4. 42, Ar.*Av.*506, etc.: abs., *harvest*, Phld.*Mus.*p.71 K.: freq. metaph., joined with σπείρω, αἰσχρῶς μὲν ἔσπειρας κακῶς δὲ ἐθέρισας Gorg.*Fr.* 16 D., cf. Plu.2.394e; ἡ ῥητορικὴ καρπὸν ὧν ἔσπειρε θερίζει Pl.*Phdr.* 260d; οὐκ ἔστι μὴ σπείραντα θερίσαι κάρπιμα *Epigr.Gr.*1039.15:—Med., καρπὸν Δηοῦς θερίσασθαι Ar.*Pl.*515:—Pass., ἃ [δράγματα] ἔτυχεν... τεθερισμένα X.*HG*7.2.8. 2. metaph., *mow down*, Ἄρη τὸν.. θερίζοντα βροτούς A.*Supp.*637 (lyr.), cf. *Ag.*536; βίον θ. ὥστε κάρπιμον στάχυν E.*Hyps.Fr.*34(60).94; θ. Ἀσίαν *to plunder* it, Plu.2.182a. 3. *cut off*, κεφαλὴν καὶ γλῶσσαν ἄκραν S.*Aj.*239; κυνέας E.*Supp.*717; γλῶσσαν *AP*9.451: metaph., σελίδος νεαρῆς θ. στάχυν ib.4.2.3 (Phil.):—Pass., ἥτις [πῶλος].. θέρος θερισθῇ ξανθὸν αὐχένων ἄπο who *had her crop* of yellow mane *cut off*, S.*Fr.*659.4. 4. metaph., *reap a good harvest*, Ar.*Ach.*947 (lyr.); of bribes, Lib.*Or.*47.26. 5. ὁ θερίζων (with or without λόγος), a logical fallacy, Chrysipp.*Stoic.*2.94, D.L.7. 25: pl., ib.44. II. intr., *pass the summer*, X.*An.*3.5.15; θ. ἐν τοῖς ψυχροῖς, χειμάζουσι δ' ἐν τοῖς ἀλεεινοῖς Arist.*HA*596^{b}26, cf. 598^{a}25.

θερίκλειον· ποτήριον, κόνδυ, Hsch. (i.e. Θηρίκλειον).

θερῐνός, ή, όν, = θέρειος, Pi.*P.*3.50: the usu. form in Prose, ἀνατολή Hp.*Aër.*4, cf. *Aph.*2.25, Plb.3.37.4; θ. δύσεις, ἀνατολαί, Cleom. 1.9; θ. ζῴδια ib.6; μεσημβρία X.*Cyn.*6.26; ἥλιος Pl.*Lg.*915d; θ. τροπαί or τροπή, the summer solstice, ib.767c, Arist.*Mete.*364^{b}2; τροπέων τῶν θερινέων Hdt.2.19; θ. κύκλος, Tropic of Cancer, Ph.1.27; θ. τροπικός (sc. κύκλος) Euc.*Phaen.*p.34 M., Cleom.1.7, Gem.5.39, al.; θερινὸν ὑπηχεῖν to echo *summer-like*, Pl.*Phdr.*230c; θερινά the *summer-haunts* of the sun, Id.*Lg.*683c; ὄμβροι θ. Arist.*HA*601^{b}24; θ. ἄνεσις καὶ ἀπόλαυσις D.S.4.84; θ. ὥρα Oenopid.ib.1.41; *for summer use*, ἱμάτιον *PCair.Zen.*148 (iii B.C.); νομαί, opp. χειμεριναί, *PLond.*3.842.12 (ii A.D.).

θερ-ισμός, ὁ, *mowing, reaping*, X.*Oec.*18.3, *PHib.*1.90.5 (iii B.C.), *PFlor.*101.4 (i A.D.). II. *reaping-time, harvest*, Eup.202, Plb.5. 95.5, *Ev.Matt.*13.30, al. 2. *harvest, crop*, Lxx *Le.*19.9, *Ev.Matt.* 9.37. -ιστήρ, ῆρος, ὁ, *mower, reaper*, Lyc.840. -ιστήριον, τό, *reaping-hook*, Lxx 1*Ki.*13.20 (v.l. θέριστρον), Max.Tyr.30.6. -ιστής, οῦ, ὁ, = θεριστήρ, X.*Hier.*6.10, D.18.51, Arist.*HA*580^{b}20, *PCair.Zen.* 292.486 (iii B.C.): θερισταί, οἱ, a satyric play of Euripides, Arg.E. *Med.* -ιστικός, ή, όν, *of* or *for reaping*, δρέπανον *PMagd.*8.6 (iii B.C.); ὕμνος Suid. s.v. Λιτυέρσης: as Subst. θ., τό, *crop*, Str.17.3. 11. -ιστός, ή, όν, τὸ θ. a kind of *balsam*, Dsc.1.19 codd. (εὐθέριστον Wellm.).

θέριστος and **θεριστός**, ὁ, v. θέριτος.

θέριστρα, τά, *cost of reaping*, *POxy.*277.8 (i B.C.).

θερίστρια, ἡ, fem. of θεριστήρ, Ar.*Fr.*788.

θερίστριον, τό, *light summer garment*, Theoc.15.69, Aristaenet. 1.27.

θέριστρον, τό, = foreg., Lxx *Ge.*24.65, al., *PPetr.*1 p.37 (iii B.C.), *AP*6.254 (Myrin.), Ph.1.666. II. *sickle*, Lxx 1*Ki.*13.20 (v.l.).

θέριτος, ὁ, *harvest*, and **θεριτός**, ὁ, *harvest-time*, Tz. ad Hes.*Op.*571 (θέριστος and θεριστός cj. Spohn ad Niceph.Blemm.p.40).

θερίτροπος, ον, *turning in summer*, of the solstice, Tz. ad Hes.*Op.* 596.

θέρμᾰ, θέρμᾰν, alternative nom. and acc. sg. forms for θέρμη, θέρμην, Men.*Georg.*51, Ar.*Fr.*690, dub. in Pl.*Tht.*178c (θερμά codd., but Tim.*Lex.* and Phryn. perh. read θέρμη). II. pl. θέρματα, v. θρέμμα.

θερμάζω, = sq., Ep. aor. 1 opt. Med. θερμάσσαιο Nic.*Al.*587.

θερμαίνω, aor. ἐθέρμηνα Il.14.7, etc., later ἐθέρμᾶνα Arist.*GA*730^{a} 16: pf. τεθέρμαγκα Hsch. s.v. κεχλίαγκα: pf. Pass. τεθέρμασμαι Apollod.*Poliorc.*147.4, Eust.1573.47, (δια-) Hp.*Vict.*2.64: (θερμός):—*warm, heat*, εἰς ὅ κε θερμὰ λοετρὰ.. Ἑκαμήδη θερμήνῃ Il.14.7; ἥλιος θερμαίνων χθόνα E.*Ba.*679, cf. A.*Pers.*505; τὸ χαλκίον θέρμαινε Eup. 108:—Med., *cause to be warmed*, τῇ ἐρωμένῃ χαλκία δύο ὕδατος *PSI* 4.406.37 (iii B.C.):—Pass., *to be heated*, Od.9.376, Pl.*Phd.*63d; τὸ θερμαῖνον ψύχεται ὑπὸ τοῦ θερμαινομένου Arist.*GA*768^{b}18; *feel the sensation of heat*, Pl.*Tht.*186d; *to be* or *grow feverish*, Hp.*Epid.*1.26.ιβ'; *to be parched*, of roots, X.*Oec.*19.11. 2. metaph., θ. φιλότατι νόον Pi.*O.*10(11).87; ἕως ἐθέρμην' αὐτὸν φλὸξ οἴνου E.*Alc.*758; σπλάγχν' ἐθέρμαινον ποτῷ Id.*Cyc.*424; σπλάγχνα θ. κότῳ Ar.*Ra.*844; πολλὰ θερμαίνοι φρενί is prob. f.l. for π. θ. φρένα, A.*Ch.*990(1004); οὐ τοῦτο μή σε θερμήνῃ Herod.1.20:—Pass., κεναῖσιν ἐλπίσιν θερμαίνεται *glows* with hope, S.*Aj.*478; χαρᾷ θ. καρδίαν *have* one's heart *warm* with joy, E.*El.*402.

θέρμαν-σις, εως, ἡ, *heating*, Arist.*Metaph.*1067^{b}12, Gal.1.253, f.l. in Hp.*Liqu.*1. -τέον, *one must heat*, Gal.10.104. II. Adj. -τέος, α, ον, *to be heated*, Hp.*Art.*11. -τήρ, ῆρος, ὁ, *kettle* or *pot for boiling water*, Poll.6.89, 10.66. -τήριος, α, ον, *promoting warmth*, φάρμακα Hp.*Loc.Hom.*17. II. χαλκίον θ., = θερμαντήρ, *IG*4.39 (Aegina), 2^{2}.1416, Gal.13.663. **-τικός**, ή, όν, *capable of heating, calorific*, τὸ πῦρ θ. Arist.*Int.*22^{b}38; ὁ οἶνος Epicur.*Fr.*58, cf. 60; τὸ θ. πρὸς τὸ -τόν Arist.*Metaph.*1020^{b}29, cf. Thphr.*HP*6.3.6: Sup., Arist.*Cael.*307^{a}1, Dsc.1.19.4: c. gen., τὸ τῆς ψυχῆς θ. οἶνος Pl.*Ti.* 60a. **-τός**, ή, όν, *capable of being heated*, Arist.*Ph.*224^{a}30.

θερμᾰσία, ἡ, *warmth, heat*, Hp.*Aph.*5.63, Arist.*Pr.*860^{a}19, Epicur. *Ep.*2p.40 U., Thphr.*HP*8.11.7, Lxx *Je.*28(51).39, D.S.3.34, Paus.2. 34.6; *heating*, opp. ψῦξις, Arist.*GA*764^{b}7: pl., Plu.2.128f. (The pure Att. words are θερμότης and θέρμη, Thom.Mag.p.179 R., but θερμασία is used by X.*An.*5.8.15.)

θέρμασμα, ατος, τό, *warm fomentation*, Hp.*Acut.*16 (pl.), Gal.*UP* 4.8.

θέρμασσα, ἡ, = κάμινος, Hdn.Gr.1.267.

θερμάστιον, τό, = θερμαστρίς I, Aen.Tact.18.6, *IG*2^{2}.1425.379 (pl.).

θέρμαστις, ιδος, ἡ, perh. = θέρμαστρις, παρυφὴν ἔχει θέρμαστιν, of a garment, *IG*2^{2}.1514.29, 1515.21, 1516.8 (iv B.C.).

θερμάστρα, ἡ, *oven, furnace*, Call.*Del.*144 (-αυστραι codd.), Euph. 51.8 (pl.), Hsch. (nom. pl. proparox. cod. Hsch., codd. Call. vary in accent):—Adv. **θερμαστρῆθεν**, *from the furnace*, Hsch. (-στῆθεν cod.).

θερμαστρίς or **θέρμαστρις** (Hsch.), ἡ, *IG*2^{2}.1414.42; acc. θερμαστριν Roussel *Cultes Égyptiens* 220 (Delos, ii B.C.); gen. θερμαστρίδος Arist.*Mech.*854^{a}24: acc. pl. θερμάστρεις Lxx 3*Ki.*7.26(40), 31(45): for forms with -αυστρ- v. infr.:—*tongs* used by smiths to take hold of hot metal, Hsch.: generally, *pincers, pliers*, Arist. l. c. 2. metaph., *a violent dance*, in which the legs were crossed *tong-fashion*, Poll.4.102, Ath.14.630a, Hsch. (θαυμαστρίς codd. Poll., θαυμαστρεις cod. A Ath., θέρμαστρις Hsch.); cf. θερμαυστρίζω. II. *spike, clamp*, Ath.Mech.34.4. III. = θερμαντήρ, τὰς θερμάστρεις Lxx ll. cc.; θερμαυστρίς and θερμαστρίς Poll.10.66; acc. θέρμαυστριν (prob. in this signf.) Eup.228: in *IG* and Roussel ll. cc. the signf. may be I. 1 or III. (In signf. I prob. fr. θερμός, αὔω (A), cf. ἐξ-αύω: but the origin of signf. III and the form -αστρ- is not clear.)

θερμαύστρα, ἡ, f. l. for θερμάστρα (q. v.).

θερμαυστρίζω, *dance the* θερμαυστρίς (v. θερμαστρίς I. 2), Critias *Fr.* 36 D., Luc.*Salt.*34.

θερμαψίς, *fornax, Gloss.*

θέρμη, also **θέρμᾰ** (q. v.), ἡ, *heat*, Hp.*VM*19, Lxx *Si.*38.28, *Act. Ap.*28.3; τῆς θ. *when it is hot*, Olymp.*in Mete.*98.20; *feverish heat*, Pherecr.158, Pl.*Tht.*178c (θερμά codd.), Arist.*Pr.*862^{a}18: pl., Hp. *Epid.*7.51, Th.2.49, Arr.*An.*2.4.8. II. θέρμαι, αἱ, *hot springs*, *IG*14.455 (Catana), cf. 1055: name of a town in Sicily, Plb.1.24. 4. 2. *hot baths*, *POxy.*473.5 (ii A. D.), etc.

θερμ-ηγορέω, *speak warmly, hotly*, Orac. ap. Luc. *Peregr.* 30. **-ημερίαι**, ῶν, αἱ, *hot season, summer-time*, Hp.*Nat.Hom.*7, Arist. *HA*544^{b}11, Thphr.*HP*7.1.7.

θερμηρός, ά, όν, *for hot liquid*, ποτήριον Hsch. s. v. κελέβη: θερμηρόν (and -ητρον), expld. by *miliarium, Gloss.*

θερμίζω, *fall ill with fever*, *IG*12(9).1240.15 (Aedepsus).

θέρμῖνος, η, ον, (θέρμος) *of lupines*, ἄλευρα Dsc.2.110; πανοπλία Luc.*VH*1.27.

θέρμιον, τό, Dim. of θέρμος, *Stud.Pal.*22.75.11 (iii A. D.), *Gloss.*, condemned by Thom.Mag.p.183 R.

θερμο-βᾰφής, ές, *dyed hot*, opp. ψυχροβαφής, Thphr.*Od.*22. **-βουλος**, ον, *hot-tempered, rash*, σπλάγχνον E.*Fr.*858; parodied in Ar.*Ach.* 119; ἄνθρωπος Ael.*NA*8.17. **-δότης**, ου, ὁ, *one who brought the hot water at baths, Gloss.*:—fem. **-δότις**, ιδος, ἡ, *female bath-attendant*, *AP* 9.183 (Pall.): **-δοσία**, ἡ, Herod.Med.ap.Orib.5.30.19. **-ειδής**, ές, *of warm nature*, *EM*557.23. **-εργός**, ον, f. l. in A.*Eu.*560. **-κοίλιος**, ον, *hot-stomached*, Hp.*Epid.*6.4.19. **-κρᾱσία**, ἡ, *mixing of hot drink*, Aët.9.30. **-κύᾰμος** [ῠ], ἡ, *a leguminous plant*, of a kind between the θέρμος and the κύαμος, Diph.87.

Θερμολαῖος, ὁ (sc. μήν), name of month in Crete, *GDI*5075 *B* 3.

θερμο-λουσία, ἡ, *hot bathing*, Hp.*Insomn.*93, Aret.*CD*1.3, *Com. Adesp.*56, Thphr.*Sud.*16, Ph.2.548, Agathin.ap.Orib.10.7 tit. **-λουτέω**, *use hot baths*, Hermipp.76, Alex.75, Herod.Med.ap.Orib.10.39.6 (**-λουτρέω** is incorrect in Arist.*Pr.*863^{a}4). **-λούτης**, ου, ὁ, *one who uses hot baths*, Agathin.ap.Orib.10.7.9. **-λουτία**, ἡ, f. l. for -λουσίη, Hp.*Insomn.*93. **-λυχνον**, τό, *lamp-oil*, *IG*2^{2}.1368. 151. **-μιγής**, ές, *half-hot*, ἀήρ *Placit.*2.20.13. **-νους**, ουν, *heated in mind*, A.*Ag.*1172 (dub.).

θερμοπλ-άω, *have inflammation in the hoof*, of horses, *Hippiatr.* 53: **-ησις**, εως, ἡ, the disease itself, ibid.: **θερμόπλα** is dub. in Hsch.

θερμο-περίπᾰτος, ὁ, *sunny promenade*, *Rev.Arch.*1907 ii 418 (Nicopolis ad Istrum). **-ποιός**, όν, *producing heat*, Olymp.*in Mete.* 136.1, 244.14. **-ποσία**, ἡ, *drinking of hot liquid*, Sor.1.117. **-πότης**, ου, ὁ, *one who drinks hot drinks*, Ath.8.352b, Gal.10.828:—fem. **πότις**, ιδος, *cup for such drinks*, Pamphil.ap.Ath.11.475d, cf. Hsch. s. v. σκαμβίς. **-πρωκτος**, ον, *lascivious*, Sch.Ar.*V.*1030. **-πύλαι** [ῠ], ῶν, αἱ, *Thermopylae, 'gate of hot springs'*, Hdt.7.176, 201, Str.9.4. 12. **-πώλιον**, τό, *cook-shop*, in Lat. form *thermopolium*, Plaut. *Curc.*292, *Trin.*1013, but **θερμοπωλεῖον** is expld. by *lupinarium, Gloss.*

θερμός, ή, όν (but θερμὸς ἀϋτμή *h.Merc.*110, Hes.*Th.*696): (θέρω):—*hot*, θ. λοετρά Il.14.6, cf. Od.8.249; θ. λουτρά Pi.*O.*12.19, S.*Tr.*634 (lyr.), Pl.*Lg.*761c, etc.; δάκρυα Od.19.362; of water, ib.388; of glowing wood, 9.388; θ. καύματα Hdt.3.104 (Sup.); ἦν ἄρα πυρὸς ἕτερα -ότερα Ar.*Eq.*382: freq. in Att., of *hot* meals or drinks, Teleclid.1.8, 32, Pherecr.130.8, etc.; of blood, S.*OC*622, *Aj.*1411 (anap.); -οτάταν αἱμάδα Id.*Ph.*696; of fever, θ. νόσοι Pi.*P.*3.66; θ. σῶμα *feverish*, Th.2.49. II. metaph., *hot-headed, hasty*, freq. of persons, A.*Th.*603, *Eu.*560 (lyr.), Ar.*V.*918, etc.; θ. καὶ ἀνδρεῖος Antipho 2.4.5; of actions, πολλὰ καὶ θ. μοχθήσας S.*Tr.*1046; θ. ἔργον Ar.*Pl.* 415; δρᾶν τι νεανικὸν καὶ θ. Amphis 33.10; θ. ἐπὶ ψυχροῖσι καρδίαν ἔχεις S.*Ant.*88; θ. πόθος *AP*5.114 (Phld.); φάρμακον Alciphr.1.37 (Comp.): c. inf., θερμότερος ἐπιχειρεῖν Antipho 2.1.7: Sup., ὦ θερμόταται γυναῖκες Ar.*Th.*735. 2. *still warm, fresh*, ἴχνη *AP*9.371; ἀτυχήματα Plu.2.798f; θ. κακά, opp. ἕωλα, ib.517f; γάμοι θ. καὶ ἴσως αὔριον Philostr.*VA*4.25. III. τὸ θ., = θερμότης, *heat*, Hdt.1.142, Pl.*Cra.* 413c, etc. 2. θ. (sc. ὕδωρ), τό, *hot water*, θερμῷ λοῦσθαι, βάπτειν, Ar.*Nu.*1044, *Ec.*216; θερμῷ κεκραμένος οἶνος Gal.11.56; also, *hot drink*, Arr.*Epict.*1.13.2. 3. θερμόν, τό, *grace, favour*, θ. εὑρεῖν ἐν ἐρήμῳ Lxx *Je.*38(31).2. 4. τὰ θ. (sc. χωρία) Hdt.4.29; but (sc. λουτρά), *hot springs*, X.*HG*4.5.3; τὰ θ. τοῦ Ἡρακλέους Str.9.4.2. IV. Adv. -μῶς Pl.*Euthd.*284e: Comp. -ότερον, ἔχειν Eub.7.1: neut. pl. as Adv., θερμὰ θερμὰ πηδῶσαι Herod.4.61.

θέρμος, ὁ, *lupine, Lupinus albus*, Alex.162.11, 266.2 (pl.), Timocl. 18.4 (pl.), Thphr.*HP*8.11.2, Dsc.2.109, *PFlor.*379.47 (ii A. D.), *AP* 11.413 (Ammian.); εἰς τοὺς θ. to the *lupine-market*, Teles p.13 H.

θερμοσποδιά, ἡ, *hot ashes*, Dsc.2.170, Erot. s. v. μαρίλην, Archig. ap.Orib.8.2.30, Philum.ap.Aët.5.120.

θερμότης, ητος, ἡ, (θερμός) *heat*, Hp.*VM*16, Pl.*R.*335d, etc.: pl., Id.*Cra.*432c, Diocl.*Fr.*112. II. metaph., *heat, passion*, τοῦ Ἀχιλλέως Philostr.*Her.*12^{b}; ἐν τῷ λέγειν Ath.1.1b.

θερμοτρᾰγέω, *eat lupines*, Luc.*Lex.*5.

θερμουργ-ία, ἡ, *hasty act*, App.*Mith.*108. **-ός**, όν, *doing hot and hasty acts, reckless*, X.*Mem.*1.3.9 (Sup.), Luc.*Tim.*2.

θέρμουθις, ἡ, Egyptian pr. n. applied to the *asp*, *PMag.Par.*1. 2387, *PMag.Lond.*121.782, Ael.*NA*10.31.

θερμο-φόρον, τό, *saucepan*, *Gloss.*: **-φόρος**, ὁ, *boiler*, ib., *POxy.* 2145.15 (ii A. D.). **-φρων**, = δαήμων, Hsch. s. v. δαίμων. **-φύλαξ** [ῠ], ακος, ὁ, *kettle*, *Gloss.* **-χύτης** [ῠ], ου, ὁ, *vessel for hot drinks*, *AP*9.587 tit.

θερμόω, = θέρμω, *An.Ox.*2.448 (Pass.); τεθερμῶσθαι dub. l. in Ar. *Lys.*1079.

θέρμυδρον, τό, *a place with hot springs*, name of a harbour of Rhodes, Tz.*H.*2.385:—also **-υδρα**, τά, St.Byz.; **-υδραί**, αἱ, Apollod. 2.5.11.

θέρμ-ω, (θέρω) *heat, make hot*, only in pres. or impf. forms, θέρμετε δ' ὕδωρ Od.8.426, Ar.*Ra.*1339:—Pass., *grow hot*, θέρμετο δ' ὕδωρ Od. 8.437, Il.18.348; πνοιῇ ... μετάφρενον εὐρέε τ' ὤμω θέρμετ' 23.381; θέρμετο δὲ χθών Call.*Fr.anon.*24; μή πού τις ἐνὶ χροῒ θέρμετ' (Ep. for θέρμηται) ἀϋτμή Opp.*H.*3.522. **-ώδης**, ες, *lukewarm*, Aret.*CA* 2.3. **-ωλή**, ἡ, *feverish heat*, Hp.*Loc.Hom.*19, al.

θερόεις, εσσα, εν, *of* or *in summer*, Nic.*Al.*570.

θέρος, εος, τό, (θέρω) *summer*, χείματος οὐδὲ θέρευς Od.7.118; οὔτ' ἐν θέρει οὔτ' ἐν ὀπώρῃ 12.76; ἐν θέρει, opp. ἐν ψύχει, S.*Ph.*18; θέρει or θέρει, Il.22.151, Hes.*Op.*640; τὸ θέρος *during the summer*, Hdt.1.202; τοῦ θέρεος *in the course of it*, Id.2.24; τοῦ θέρους Ar.*Fr.*463; θέρεος or θέρους (without the Art.), Hes.*Op.*462, Pl.*Phdr.*276b, al.; τοῦ παρεστῶτος θέρους S.*Ph.*1340; τοῦ θ. εὐθὺς ἀρχομένου Th.2.47; κατὰ θέρους ἀκμήν X.*HG*5.3.19; θ. μεσοῦντος *about midsummer*, Luc.*Hist.Conscr.*1; esp. in Th., *campaigning-season*, ἅμα ἦρι τοῦ ἐπιγιγνομένου θέρους 4. 117, cf. 2.31, 6.8; τοσαῦτα μὲν ἐν τῷ θ. ἐγένετο 2.68. II. *summer-fruits, harvest, crop*, θ. ἀλλότριον ἀμᾶν Ar.*Eq.*392, cf. D.53.21, *AP*11. 365.3 (Agath.): pl., θέρη *crops*, *PFlor.*150.5 (iii A. D.); θέρη σταχύων the *ripe* ears, Plu.*Fab.*2: metaph., πάγκλαυτον ἐξαμᾷ θέρος A.*Pers.* 822, cf. *Ag.*1655; τὸ γηγενὲς δράκοντος .. θ. E.*Ba.*1026; of a horse's mane, v. θερίζω I. 3; of a youth's beard, Call.*Del.*298, *AP*10.19 (Apollonid.); also τέμνεται τὸ ἱερὸν καὶ ἀπόρρητον θ. τοῦ θεοῦ Γάλλου Jul.*Or.*5.168d. III. Astron., τὸ μέγα θ., ὅταν πάντες οἱ πλάνητες ἐν θερινῷ ζῳδίῳ γένωνται Olymp.*in Mete.*111.30. IV. metaph., in an epitaph for a *year* of life, *Supp.Epigr.*2.874.4 (Egypt).

θερσῐεπής, ές, (θέρσος) *bold of speech*, B.12.199:—so **Θερσίτης**, ὁ, as pr. n. in Hom.: pl., Ph.2.472.

θέρσος, Aeol. for θάρσος, Choerob.*in Theod.*1.166, *EM*447.24.

θερσός, ὁ, = ταρσός II. 1, *BGU*350.2 (ii A. D.).

θερτήρια· ἑορτή τις, Hsch.

θέρω, *heat, make hot*, θέρον αὐγαὶ ἠελίου Λιβύην A.R.4.1312; θέρων ἕλκος, = θεραπεύων, Nic.*Th.*687:—elsewh. only in Pass. **θέρομαι**, fut. Med. θέρσομαι Od.19.507: aor. 2 ἐθέρην (in Ep. subj. θερέω 17.23): poet. and later Prose, *become hot* or *warm*, νήησαν ξύλα πολλά, φόως ἔμεν ἠδὲ θέρεσθαι 19.64, cf. 507; ἐπεί κε πυρὸς θερέω *at* the fire, 17.23; θέρου *warm yourself*, Ar.*Pl.*953; ὁπόταν .. τις .. ποτὲ ῥιγῶν θέρηται Pl. *Phlb.*46c; εἶδον [Ἡράκλειτον] θερόμενον πρὸς τῷ ἰπνῷ Arist.*PA*645^{a}19: impf. ἐθέροντο Philostr.*VA*2.18, Alciphr.1.23; θέρεσθαι πρὸς τὴν εἵλην Luc.*Lex.*2: metaph., θέρεσθαι πυρί, of love, Call.*Ep.*27, cf. *APl.* 4.167 (Antip. Sid.). 2. of things, *become warm*, τὰ ψυχρὰ θέρεται Heraclit.126, cf. Archel.ap.Plu.2.954f; μὴ .. ἄστυ πυρὸς δηΐοιο θέρηται *be burnt* by fire, Il.6.331, cf. 11.667; *melt*, ἃ πέτρα θρυπτομένα θέρεται *AP*12.61. (g^{w}her-, cf. θερμός, Lat. *formus* and prob. Engl. *warm.*)

θέσις, εως, ἡ, (τίθημι) *setting, placing*, ἐπέων θ. *setting* of words in verse, Pi.*O.*3.8; πλίνθων καὶ λίθων Pl.*R.*333b, cf. *IG*7.3073.33 (Lebad.); θ. νόμων *lawgiving*, X.*Ath.*3.2, Pl.*Lg.*690d: in pl., νόμων θέσεις D.18.309, Arist.*Pol.*1289^{a}22; θ. ὀνόματος *giving* of a name,

Pl.*Cra.*390d; ἐπί τινος *application* of word to object, Demetr.*Eloc.* 145; θ. ἀγώνων *institution* of games, D.S.4.53; *ordinance, disposition,* S.*Ichn.*277 (only here in Trag.); *setting forth* in legal form, ἀσφαλειῶν *POxy.*1027.12 (i A.D.). **II.** *laying down,* ὅπλων, opp. ἀναίρεσις, Pl.*Lg.*814a; of diggers, *plunging* of the spade, opp. ἄρσις, *Gp.*2.45.5. **2.** *deposit* of money, preparatory to a law-suit, Ar.*Nu.*1191 (pl.): generally, *sum deposited* in a temple, *Inscr.Délos* 365.14 (iii B.C.), *IG*12(3).322 (pl., Thera). **3.** *pledging, giving as security,* D.33.12, Lys.8.10. **4.** *payment,* τελῶν Pl.*R.*425d (pl.). **III.** *adoption* of a child, κατὰ θέσιν υἱωνός Plb.18.35.9, cf. Ph.2.36, Philostr. *VA*6.11; Κρινοτέλην Πινδάρου, θέσει δὲ Φιλοξένου *IG*12(3).274 (Anaphe), cf. 12(7).50 (Amorgos); *adoption* as a citizen of a foreign state, Ἀλεξανδρεὺς θέσει, Ἀθηναῖος θ. (opp. φύσει), Suid. s. v. Ἀρίσταρχος, Ἀριστοφάνης Ῥόδιος. **IV.** *situation,* of a city, Hp.*Aër.*6; πόλις αὐτάρκη θ. κειμένη Th.1.37, cf. 5.7; ἡ θ. τῆς χώρας πρὸς τὰ πνεύματα Thphr.*CP*3.23.5; τόπων θ. Plb.1.41.7: Astron., θ. τῶν ἄστρων Herm. *in Phdr.*p.149 A.; *position, arrangement,* λεγομένων καὶ γραφομένων Pl.*Tht.*206a; τῶν μερῶν θέσεις Id.*Lg.*668e, cf. Epicur.*Ep.*1 p.11 U., *Fr.*30 (pl.). **2.** Math., *local position,* Arist.*GC*322ᵇ33; ἔχειν θ. Id.*APo.*88ᵃ34; θ. ἔχειν πρὸς ἄλληλα to have a *local* relation, Id. *Cat.*4ᵇ21, cf. Pl.*R.*586c; τῇ θ. μέσον Arist.*APr.*25ᵇ36: Geom., θέσει δεδόσθαι or εἶναι, to be given *in positon,* Archim.*Sph.Cyl.*2.3, Euc.*Dat.Def.*4, Apollon.Perg.*Con.*2.46, al.; παρὰ θέσει parallel to a straight line *given in position,* [Euc.]*Dat.Def.*15; εἰς δύο θέσεις τὰς ΑΒ, ΑΓ to meet the two *straight lines* ΑΒ, ΑΓ *given in position,* Hero *Metr.*3.10; κατὰ τὴν θ. τὴν πρὸς ἡμᾶς Arist.*Ph.*208ᵇ23, etc.; οὐ τῇ θ. διαφέροντα μόνον, ἀλλὰ καὶ τῇ δυνάμει ib.22; so in Music, of notes in a scale, κατὰ θέσιν, opp. κατὰ δύναμιν, Ptol.*Harm.*2.5. **V.** Philos., *thesis, position,* assumed and requiring proof, Pl.*R.*335a, Arist.*Top.*104ᵇ19, *APo.*72ᵃ15; θέσιν διαφυλάττειν to maintain *a thesis,* Id.*EN*1096ᵃ2; κινεῖν to controvert it, Plu.2.687b, cf. 328a, etc. **2.** *general question,* opp. ὑπόθεσις (*special case*), Aphth.*Prog.*13, Theon *Prog.*12, cf. Cic.*Top.*21.79, Quint.3.5.5 (but θ. includes ὑπόθεσις and ὁρισμός, Phlp.*in APo.*35.1; opp. ἀξίωμα, ib.34.9). **3.** *arbitrary determination,* esp. in dat. θέσει, τὰ ὀνόματα μὴ θ. γενέσθαι Epicur.*Ep.*1 p.27 U.; opp. φύσει, Chrysipp.*Stoic.*3.76, Str.2.3.7, etc.; τὰ θ. δίκαια, νόμιμα, Ph.1.50, 112; σημαίνειν θ. S.E.*P.*2.256. **4.** *affirmation,* opp. ἄρσις, ib.1.192, cf. 2.244, Plot.5.5.6, etc. **VI.** *a setting down,* opp. ἄρσις (*lifting*), πᾶσα πορεία ἐξ ἄρσεως καὶ θέσεως συντελεῖται Arist.*Pr.*885ᵇ6: hence, in rhythm, *downward beat,* opp. the *upward* (ἄρσις), Aristid.Quint.1.13, Bacch.*Harm.*98, etc. **VII.** in prosody, θέσει μακρὰ συλλαβή long by *position,* opp. φύσει, D.T.632.30, Heph. 1.3: orig. prob. in signf. v. 3, cf. Sch.D.T.p.206 H. **2.** θέσεις, αἱ, in punctuation, *stops,* Donat. in *Gramm.Lat.*4.372 K. **VIII.** part of a horse's hoof, ἡ θ. τοῦ ποδός *Hippiatr.*82.

θέσκελος, ον, Ep. Adj. perh. *set in motion by God* (κέλλω), and so *marvellous, wondrous,* always of things, θ. ἔργα deeds or works *of wonder,* Il.3.130, Od.11.610; θέσκελα εἰδώς Call.*Fr.anon.*385: neut. Adv., ἔικτο δὲ θέσκελον αὐτῷ it was *wondrous* like him, Il.23.107; prob. taken by later poets as, = *God-inspired* (κελεύω), θ. Ἑρμῆς Coluth.126.

θέσμιος, Dor. and Ep. **τέθμιος,** ον, or α, ον, (θεσμός) *fixed, settled, lawful,* ἑορτὰ τέθμιος Pi.*N.*11.27; τέθμιαι ὧραι Call.*Ap.*87; θέσμια τάδε καὶ πάτρια Lex ap.Arist.*Ath.*16.10; θέσμιον (sc. ἐστί) A.*Ag.*1564 (lyr.); θέσμιόν ἐστι, = θέμις ἐστί, A.R.2.12; *fitting,* θηρευτῆρσι σιγὴ τέθμιός ἐστι Opp.*C.*1.450. **II.** θέσμιον, Dor. and Ep. τέθμιον, τό, esp. in pl., *laws, customs, rites,* Hdt.1.59, A.*Eu.*491 (lyr.), S.*Aj.*712 (lyr.); θ. ἀναγράψαι Arist.*Ath.*3.4; προγόνων παλαιὰ θ. E.*Fr.*360.45, cf. Call.*Dian.*174: sg. in Pi.*I.*6(5).20, E.*Tr.*267 (anap.):—in form **θέθμιον** *IG*9(1).334.46 (Locr., v B.C.). **2.** *agreement,* τῶ τεθμίω ϝίστωρ ib.7.3172.165 (Orchom. Boeot.). **III.** Θέσμιος, title of Apollo, Paus.5.15.7; of Demeter, Id.8.15.4.

θεσμο-δότης, ὁ, *lawgiver,* cj. for -θέτης, Longin.9.9:—fem. **-δότειρα** Orph.Εὐχή 25. **-θεσία,** ἡ, *office of* θεσμοθέτης at Athens, *IG* 2².1368.133. **II.** *decree* of fate, Plu.2.573f.

θεσμοθετ-εῖον, τό, *hall in which the* θεσμοθέται *met,* Arist.*Ath.*3.5, Plu.2.613b (-θέτιον Suid. s. v. Πρυτανεῖον):—also **θεσμοθέσιον,** τό, Plu.2.714c, Sch.Pl.*Prt.*337d, Suid. s. v. ἄρχων. **-έω,** *to be a* θεσμοθέτης, Is.7.34, D.59.65. **-ης,** ου, ὁ, (τίθημι) *lawgiver, legislator,* of Moses, Longin.9.9. **II.** esp. at Athens, θεσμοθέται, οἱ, the *six junior archons,* *IG*1².39.75, al., Ar.*V.*775 (sg.), al., Antipho 6.35, Arist.*Ath.*3.4, al., Aeschin.3.38; also, title of magistrate in Amorgos, *IG*12(7).57.12 (iii B.C.). **-ις,** ιδος, ἡ, = θεσμοφόρος, title of Demeter, Corn.*ND*28; of Isis, *Hymn.Is.*20.

θεσμο-ποιέω, *make laws,* E.*Ph.*1645. **-πόλος,** ον, (πολέω) = θεμιστοπόλος, *AP*5.292.3 (Paul. Sil.).

θεσμός, Dor. **τεθμός** (v. infr.), **θεθμός** *IG*5(2).159 (Tegea, v B.C.), Isyll.12, Locr. **τετθμός** *Berl.Sitzb.*1927.8 (v B.C.): ὁ: pl. θεσμοί, poet. θεσμά S.*Fr.*92: (τίθημι):—*that which is laid down, law, ordinance,* once in Hom., λέκτροιο παλαιοῦ θεσμὸν ἵκοντο Od.23.296; εἰρήνης θεσμοί *the order* of peace, *h.Hom.*8.16; esp. of divine *laws,* θ. τὸν μοιρόκραντον ἐκ θεῶν A.*Eu.*391; ἵμερος.. τῶν μεγάλων πάρεδρος θ. S.*Ant.*800 (lyr.); οἱ τῶν θεῶν θ. X.*Cyr.*1.6.6; θ. Ἀδραστείας, οἱ τῆς εἱμαρμένης θ., Pl.*Phdr.*248c, Plu.2.111d; παρέβη θ. ἀρχαίους Ar.*Av.*331 (lyr.). **2.** of human *law,* οἱ πάτριοι θ. Hdt.3.31; at Athens, esp. of the laws of Draco, *IG*1².115.20, And.1.81, Decr. ib.83, Arist.*Ath.*4.1, etc., cf. Ael.*VH*8.10: used by Solon of his own laws, Sol.36.16, cf. 31.2, Plu.*Sol.*19; ὁ ταῦτα ἀπεργαζόμενος θ. νόμος ἂν ὀρθῶς εἴη κείμενος Pl.*Ep.*355c; ὁ τοῖς ἄλλοις τιθέμενος θεσμοὺς Δημήτριος Duris 10 J.; ὅδ' ὁ τεθμὸς πὲρ τῶν ἐντοφηΐων *GDI*2561 C19 (Delph.): in later poetry, θεσμοί, = *law, jurisprudence,* *Epigr.Gr.* 434.4, al.; θεσμῶν ταμίης, πρόμαχος, *IG*3.637, 638. **3.** generally, *rule, precept, rite,* S.*Tr.*682; θ. πυρός *the law* of the beacon-fire, A.*Ag.*304; τεθμὸς ἀέθλων Pi.*O.*6.69; στεφάνων τ. the *appointed* crowns, ib.13.29; θ. ὅδ' εὔφρων the cheering *strain* (cf. νόμος), A. *Supp.*1034 (lyr.); ὕμνον τεθμὸν Ὀλυμπιονίκαν Pi.*O.*7.88; μακάρων Id.*Pae.*4.47. **II.** *institution,* as the *tribunal* of the Areopagus, A. *Eu.*615; τεθμὸς Ἡρακλέος, Ποτειδᾶνος τεθμοί, the Olympian, Isthmian games, Pi.*N.*10.33, *O.*13.40. **III.** = θησαυρός, Anacr.58. **IV.** θεσμοί· αἱ συνθέσεις τῶν ξύλων, Hsch.

θεσμοσύνη, Dor. **-να,** ἡ, *justice,* *AP*7.593 (Agath.).

θεσμο-φόρια, ων, τά, women's festival at Athens and elsewhere, in honour of Demeter Θεσμοφόρος (q. v.), Hdt.2.171, Ar.*Av.*1519, *Th.* 80, 182, al.; θ. ἑστιᾶν τὰς γυναῖκας to furnish the women's feast *at the Th.,* Is.3.80; at Ephesus, Hdt.6.16. **-φοριάζω,** *keep the Thesmophoria,* X.*HG*5.2.29, *Gloss.Oxy.*1802.35; Θεσμοφοριάζουσαι, name of a play by Aristophanes. **-φόριον,** τό, *temple of Demeter* Θεσμοφόρος, Ar.*Th.*278, 880, *IG*2.1059.12; at Delos, ib.11(2).159 *A*17 (iii B.C.):—also **-εῖον** Theon *Prog.*5: **-φόριον** μέτρον, a form of dactylic metre, Mar.Vict.6.145 K.: **-φόριος,** ὁ, demoticon at Memphis, Mitteis *Chr.* 29.5 (ii B.C.); at Alexandria, *Supp.Epigr.*2.866. **II.** (sc. μήν) name of month at Rhodes, *IG*12(1).3.5; in Crete, *GDI*5149.58. **-φοριών,** ῶνος, ὁ, name of month at Heraclea ad Latmum, *SIG*633.55 (ii B.C.); in Crete, *Hemerolog.Flor.* **-φόρος,** ον, *law-giving,* epith. of Demeter, Hdt.6.91, 134, *IPE*2.13 (Panticapaeum, iv B.C.), Call.*Aet.Oxy.* 2079.10, D.S.1.14, etc.; σεμνὴ Θ. *AP*5.149 (Asclep.), cf. Luc.*Tim.*17; τὼ Θεσμοφόρω Demeter and Persephone, Ar.*Th.*83, al.; αἱ Θεσμοφόροι App.*BC*2.70, Plu.*Dio*56, etc.; πότνια Θ., of Persephone, Pi.*Fr.*37; also, as a title of Dionysus, Orph.*H.*42.1. **-φύλαξ** [ῠ], ακος, ὁ, *guardian of the law,* of Moses, Ph.1.171:—usu. in pl. **-φύλακες,** οἱ, a magistracy at Elis, Th.5.47, cf. D.S.5.67; at Alexandria, *PHal.*1.239 (iii B.C.); in Ceos, *IG*12(5).595 *B*16 (iii/ii B.C.); at Ptolemais, *PFay.*22.11 (i A.D.); Boeot. **τεθμοφούλαξ** *IG*7.3172.178 (Orchom.):—hence **-φῠλάκιον** [ᾰ], τό, their office, *PHal.*1.234 (iii B.C.): **-φῠλάκι(κ)ός,** ή, όν, νόμος Plu.2.292d.

θεσμῳδ-έω, *deliver oracular precepts*: τὰ θεσμῳδούμενα *oracles,* Ph. 1.650. **-ός,** ὁ, *giver of* θεσμοί, Id.ap.Eus.*PE*8.7, *BMus.Inscr.*4.481*.457 (pl.).

θέσπαλαι· αἱ Κῷαι, παρὰ Φιλητᾷ, καὶ αἱ φαρμακίδες, Hsch. (prob. Θεσσαλαί).

θεσπεσιανή, ἡ, name of an antidote, Orib.*Fr.*82.

θεσπέσιος, α, ον, also ος, ον E.*Andr.*296 (lyr.), Luc.*Sacr.*13: (perh. for θεσ-σπέσιος, cf. θεός, ἔσπον):—prop. of the voice, *divinely sounding, divinely sweet,* ἀοιδή Il.2.600; Σειρῆνες Od.12.158; ἔπεα Pi.*I.*4(3).39; ἀχέτας Ar.*Av.*1095 (lyr.). **2.** *divinely uttered* or *decreed,* dat. sg. fem. θεσπεσίῃ as Adv., Il.2.367. **b.** *oracular,* γένος Pi.*P.*12.13 (of the Graiae); δάφνα E. l. c.; θ. ὁδός the way *of divination,* of Cassandra, A.*Ag.*1154 (lyr.); εὐχαῖς ὑπὸ θ. with prayers *to the gods,* Pi. *I.*6(5).44. **c.** = θεῖος, βηλός Il.1.591; ἄντρον Od.13.363. **II.** *more than human*: hence, *awful,* of natural phenomena, θ. νέφος Il. 15.669; ἀχλύς Od.7.42; λαῖλαψ 9.68; *marvellous,* χάρις 2.12; θ. ἄωτον, χαλκός, 9.434, Il.2.457; θ. ὀδμή a smell *divinely sweet,* Od.9.211; ὀσμὴ θ. Hermipp.82.9; of human affairs, θ. φύζα, φόβος, Il.9.2, 17.118; πλοῦτος 2.670; ἠχή 8.159; βοή Od.24.49; θ. ὅμιλος Theoc. 15.66: also in Prose, τέχνη θ. τις καὶ ὑψηλή Pl.*Euthd.*289e; θ. βίος Id.*R.*365b; θ. καὶ ἡδεῖα ἡ διαγωγή ib.558a; σοφοὶ καὶ θ. ἄνδρες Id. *Tht.*151b, cf. Philostr.*Dial.*1; φύσεις Id.*VS*2.9.2; θ. τὴν γνώμην Luc. *Alex.*4. **III.** Adv. **-ίως,** θ. ἐφόβηθεν they trembled *unspeakably,* Il.15.637: neut. θεσπέσιον as Adv., θ. ὑλᾶν Theoc.25.70; also ἀπόζει θ. ὡς ἡδύ Hdt.3.113; ὠδώδει θ. οἷον Plu.*Alex.*20; θεσπεσίηθεν *divinely,* ἀρηρότα Emp.96.4.—Chiefly Ep., once in Hdt., twice in Trag. (lyr.), once in Ar. (lyr.).

θεσπεσιότης, ητος, ἡ, = θειότης, Eust.240.8.

θεσπῐ-αοιδός, όν, (θέσπις) poet. for θεσπιῳδός, Hsch. **-δαής,** ές, (δαίω A) *kindled by a god,* θ. πῦρ *portentous* fire, Il.12.177, 441, Od. 4.418, etc. (Ep. word.) **-έπεια,** (ἔπος) fem. Adj. *oracular, prophetic,* S.*OT*463 (lyr.).

θεσπίζω, fut. -ίσω, Att. -ιῶ, Ion. inf. θεσπιέειν v. l. in Hdt.8.135; Dor. aor. ἐθέσπιξα Theoc.15.63: (θέσπις):—*prophesy, foretell,* τι Hdt. 1.47, al.; τινί τι A.*Ag.*1210, E.*Andr.*1161:—Pass., τί δὲ τεθέσπισται; S.*OC*388, cf. Parth.35.2. **II.** Pass., c. acc., [χρησμοί,] οὓς ἐθεσπίσθη Μωυσῆς Ph.2.38. **III.** of the Emperors, = Lat. *sancire, decree,* Jul.*Ep.*75b, Wilcken *Chr.*6.8 (v A.D.), *OGI*521.9 (Abydus), *Cod.Just.*1.12.3 *Intr.*

θεσπῐόμαντις, Adj. *oracular,* ἕδρα Aristonous 1.3.

θέσπιος, ον, = θεσπέσιος, Hes.*Fr.*197, Orac.ap.Ar.*Av.*977.

θεσπιόφημον· παροιμίαν τινά, Hsch.

θέσπ-ις, ιος, ὁ, ἡ (acc. θέσπιδα Nonn.*D.*25.452, dat. ιδι ib.45.133): (cf. θεσπέσιος):—*filled with the words of God, inspired,* Hom. only in Od. in acc. θέσπιν; ἀοιδή 17.385; ἀοιδός 1.328, 8.498, E.*Med.*425 (lyr.); also θέσπιν αὐδάν S.*Ichn.*244 (lyr.). **2.** generally, *wondrous, awful,* θέσπις ἄελλα *h.Ven.*208. **II.** θέσπιδες· θυσίαι, θεοσέβειαι, Hsch. **-ισις,** εως, ἡ, *oracular utterance,* Sch.Ar.*Pl.* 11. **-ισμα,** ατος, τό, mostly in pl., *oracles, oracular sayings,* Hdt. 2.29, A.*Fr.*86, S.*OT*971: sg., E.*Ion* 405. **2.** *Imperial constitution,* Wilcken *Chr.*6.12 (pl., v A.D.), Just.*Nov.*113.1.1. **-ιστής,** οῦ, ὁ, *prophet,* Man.6.378.

θεσπῐῳδ-έω, *to be a* θεσπιῳδός, *sing in prophetic strain,* A.*Ag.*1161,

E.*Ph.*959, Ar.*Pl.*9, Pl.*Ax.*367d; χρησμοὶ τὸ κράτος τῆς οἰκουμένης -ῳδοῦσι Posidon.36 J. II. *hold office of* θεσπιῳδός, i.e. *versifier of oracles*, *OGI*530.6 (Amisus), *IGRom.*4.1588 (Claros), etc. -ός, όν, *singing in prophetic strain*, of persons, S.*Fr.*456, E.*Hel.*145; also ὀμφαλὸς γῆς θ. Id.*Med.*668; μαντική Philostr.*VS*1 *Praef.*: Subst. θεσπιῳδός, ἡ, = Lat. *Carmenta*, D.H.1.31. II. θ. φόβον *caused by prophecy*, A.*Ag.*1134 (lyr., s.v.l.).

Θεσσάλ-ειος [ᾰ], v. Θεσσαλός II. **-ία**, ἡ, *Thessaly*, Hdt.3.96, etc. **-ίζω**, Att. Θεττ-, *imitate the Thessalians*, Ael.*VH*4.15, St.Byz. s.v. Θεσσαλία; *speak like them*, Parth.24.2, D.Chr.11.23. **-ῐκέτης**, ου, ὁ, Att. Θεττ-, *serf in Thessaly*, Philocr.Hist.1. **-ικός**, Att. Θεττ-, ή, όν, *Thessalian*: Θ. ἕδος, a sort of *chair* or *couch*, Hp.*Art.*7; ὄρεα Hdt.7.128; δίφρος Eup.58, cf. Poll.7.112; Θ. ἔνθεσις Hermipp. 41; Θ. δεῖπνα Ar.*Fr.*492, cf. Antiph.34.3. Adv. -κῶς Crates Com. 19. 2. *of the Thessalian dialect*, ἔθος A.D.*Synt.*214.6; διαίρεσις ib.50.9. Adv. -κῶς Id.*Pron.*109.1: Comp. -ώτερον Id.*Synt.*159. 9. **-ιῶτις**, ιδος, ἡ, one of the four districts of Thessaly, Hellanic. 52 J., Hdt.1.57, Str.9.5.3. **-ός**, Att. Θεττ-, ή, όν, *Thessalian*, Hdt. 5.63, etc.: prov., Θ. σόφισμα a *Thessalian* trick, E.*Ph.*1407; Θ. νόμισμα, i.e. false money, Phot.; Thess. **Πετθαλός** *IG*9(2).258 (Cierium), 517.14 (Larissa); Boeot. **Φετταλός** (as pr. n.) ib.7.2430.8. II. pr. n. of a physician of the Methodic School:—hence Adj. **Θεσσάλειος**, α, ον, Gal.15.763, al. III. fem. **Θεσσαλίς**, ίδος, *Thessalian*, κυνῆ S.*OC*314: as Subst. Θετταλίς, ἡ, a kind of *shoe*, Lysipp.2.

θέσσασθαι, poet. aor. *pray for*, c. acc. θεσσάμενος γενεήν Hes.*Fr.* 201; γλυκερὸν νόστον Archil.11; παίδων γένος A.R.1.824, cf. Euph. 136: c. inf., τάν ποτ' εὔανδρον [εἶναι]..θέσσαντο *prayed that* this land might be.., Pi.*N.*5.10 (Hsch. also has θέσσεσθαι, θεσσόμενος, θῆσω, θησόμενοι, θησάμενοι):—hence Adj. **θεστός**, only in compds. ἀπόθεστος, πολύθεστος (q.v.), Boeot. pr. n. Θεόφειστος, Ion. Ἑρμόθεστος. (Perh. g^{w}hedh-, cf. πόθος (fr. φόθος), OIr. -*guidiu*, Welsh *gweddïo* 'pray', Lith. *gedėti* 'mourn'; θήσω, θησόμενοι, θησάμενοι seem to be analogical formations.)

θεσφᾰτηλόγος, ον, *prophetic*, A.*Ag.*1441.

θεσφᾰτ-ίζω, *prophesy*, Hsch.:—also **-όομαι**, Id. **-ος**, ον, (θεός, φημί) *spoken by God, decreed*, μόρος A.*Ag.*1321; ἥκει θ. βίου τελευτή S.*OC*1472: mostly in phrase θέσφατόν ἐστι, it is *ordained*, ὡς γὰρ θ. ἐστι Il.8.477, cf. E.*IA*1556: c. dat. pers. et inf., σοὶ δ' οὐ θ. ἐστι... θανέειν Od.4.561, cf. 10.473, Pi.*P.*4.71, Orac. in Ar.*Pax* 1073; so εἴ τι θ. πατρὶ..ἱκνεῖθ', ὥστε πρὸς παίδων θανεῖν S.*OC*969. 2. Subst. θέσφατα, τά, *divine decrees*, *oracles*, Od.11.151,297; παλαίφατα θ. 13. 172, cf. Pi.*I.*8(7).34: sg., E.*IT*121. II. generally, *wonderful*, *mighty*, ἀήρ Od.7.143.—Cf. θεσπέσιος, θέσκελος.

θετέος, α, ον, *to be counted as*, Pl.*Epin.*984a, Arist.*Pol.*1277^{b}38. II. θετέον, *one must establish*, ἆθλα Pl.*Lg.*832e; *one must assume*, X. *Mem.*4.2.15; *one must reckon, count*, τοὺς βαναύσους πολίτας Arist. *Pol.*1277^{b}35, cf. Satyr.*Vit.Eur.Fr.*39 xv6, etc.; ἐν ἁμαρτίᾳ Ph.2.171.

θετήρ, ῆρος, ὁ, *EM*177.24; = τολμητής, πράκτης, Hsch.: pl., etym. of θεοί, Corn.*ND*1.

θέτης, ου, ὁ, (τίθημι) *one who places*, ὀνομάτων θ. *name-giver*, Pl. *Cra.*389d. II. *mortgagor*, χωρίων Is.10.24. III. *adoptive father of a child*, Did.ap.Harp.

Θετίδειον [ῐ], τό, *temple of Thetis*, E.*Andr.*20, Plb.18.20.6, Str.9. 5.6.

θετικός, ή, όν, *fit for placing*, ὀνομάτων θ. *prompt at giving* names, D.H.*Comp.*16, cf. Ph.2.101. Adv. -κῶς *appositely*, D.H.*Rh.*3. 5. II. *concerning adoption*, νόμοι Arist.*Pol.*1274^{b}4. III. *belonging to a* θέσις, *disputable*, ὑπόθεσις Philostr.*VS*2.6; τὰ θ. τῶν χωρίων ib.29; so τὰ θ. alone, Phld.*Rh.*1.206 S.; θ. κεφάλαιον Theon *Prog.*2; τὴν ζήτησιν θ. ποιεῖσθαι to make the question *a matter of argument*, Str.2.3.7; Lat. *genus instituendi* θετικώτερον, *addressed to reason rather* than feeling, Cic.*QF*3.3.4. Adv. Comp. -κώτερον Aps. p.333 H. IV. *positive*, *affirmative*, opp. *negative* (ἀρνητικός), Numen.ap.Eus.*PE*14.8. Adv. -κῶς *positively*, *affirmatively*, D.L.9. 75; οὐ λίαν θ. not very *positively*, Phld.*Rh.*1.371 S. 2. Gramm., *positive*, τὸ θετικόν the *positive degree*, Sch.D Il.4.277. b. *expressing obligation*, of verbals in -τέον, D.T.642.16; θετικῶς· τὸ ὀφειλόμενον γενέσθαι, Hsch. V. *arbitrary*, χρῆσις τῶν ὀνομάτων S.E.*P.*2.256. Adv. -κῶς ib.1.38.

Θέτις, voc. Θέτῑ Il.24.88, acc. Θέτιν, gen. ιδος 4.512, Dor. ιος Pi.*I.* 8(7).30, dat. Θέτῑ: ἡ:—*Thetis*, Hom., etc.

θετός, ή, όν, (τίθημι) *placed*, *set*, E.*IA*251 (lyr.); *having position*, στιγμὴ οὐσία θετός Arist.*APo.*87^{a}36. II. *taken as one's child*, *adopted*, Pi.*O.*9.62, E.*Fr.*359, etc.; θετὸν παῖδα ποιεῖσθαι Hdt.6.57, cf. Pl.*Lg.*929c; θετὸς γενέσθαι τινί or ὑπό τινος, Plu.*Thes.*13, App.*BC* 1.5; θετός, ὁ, *adopted son*, dub. in Is.3.69; θετή *adopted daughter*, Hsch.; also θ. πατήρ *adoptive* father, D.S.10.11.

Θεττᾰλός, Θετταλικός, etc., Att. for Θεσσ-.

Θεττᾰλότμητον κρέας a lump of meat *such as you would cut for a hungry Thessalian*, Philetaer.10.

θεῦ, Dor. and Ion. for θέο, θοῦ, imper. aor. 2 Med. of τίθημι.

θευ-, Dor. and Ion. for θεο-, cf. Θευδαίσιος, θευμορία, θεύμορος:—hence **θευ-εργέσια**, τά, festival of a θεὸς εὐεργέτης, *Inscr.Délos* 363.53 (iii B.C.). **-κολέω**, = θεοκολέω, *IG*9(1).421 (Aetolia). **-ξένια**, = θεοξένια, Hsch. **-προπία**, ἡ, = θεοπροπία, B.9.41. **-φορία**, ἡ, = θεοφορία, *AP*6.220.4 (Diosc.).

θευγέσθαι, Cret., = θέλγ-, Hsch. **θευρός**, v. θεωρός.

θεῦσις, εως, ἡ, *running*, coined as etym. of θεός, Corn.*ND*1.

θεῦτις, = τευθίς, Hippon.115.

θέω (A), Ep. also **θείω**, Il.6.507, 10.437 (in Att. the syllables εο, εου, εω are not contr.); Ep. subj. θέῃσι 22.23; 3 sg. impf. ἔθει Od.12. 407 and later, ἔθεε Il.1.483, Hdt.1.43 (and in later Prose, D.S.16.94); Ep. θέε Il.20.275, Hes.*Sc.*224; Ion. impf. θέεσκον Il.20.229: fut. θεύσομαι 23.623, Ar.*Eq.*485, *Av.*205, (ὑπο-) Pi.*P.*2.84, (ἀντι-) Hdt. 5.22, (μετα-) X.*Cyn.*6.22; θεύσω Lyc.1119: aor. 1 ἔθευσα (δι-) Vett.Val.345.35, part. θεύσας *IGRom.*4.1740 (Cyme):—the other tenses are supplied by τρέχω and *δρέμω: (θεϝ-, Skt. *dhávate*):—*run*, ποσί, πόδεσσι, Od.8.247, Il.23.623; βῆ δὲ θέειν 17.698; θέῃσι τιταινόμενος πεδίοιο 22.23; ποῖ θεῖς; Ar.*V.*854; θᾶττον θανάτου θεῖ [ἡ πονηρία] Pl.*Ap.*39b; ὁ βραδέως θέων Id.*Hp.Mi.*373d; of horses, Id.*Cra.* 423a; ἐν Ὀλυμπίᾳ θεόντων ἵππων Id.*Lg.*822b: in part. with another Verb, ἦλθε θέων, ἦλθε θέουσα, came *running*, Il.6.54,394, etc.; ἷξε θέων, of a person on ship-board, Od.3.288; θέων Αἴαντα κάλεσσον *run and* call him, Il.12.343, etc. 2. περὶ τρίποδος γὰρ ἔμελλον θεύσεσθαι *to run* for a tripod, 11.701: metaph. (cf. τρέχω II.2), περὶ ψυχῆς θέον Ἕκτορος they *were running* for Hector's life, 22.161; θ. περὶ ὑμέων αὐτῶν Hdt.8.140.α'; θ. ⟨τον⟩ περὶ τοῦ παντὸς δρόμον ib.74; περὶ γυναικῶν καὶ παίδων Paus.6.18.3. 3. metaph., θ. ἐς νόσους Pl.*Lg.*691c; θ. ἐγγύτατα ὀλέθρου Id.*R.*417b; θεῖν παρὰ τὸν ἔσχατον κίνδυνον Plu. *Fab.*26. II. of other kinds of motion, as, 1. of birds, θεύσονται δρόμῳ Ar.*Av.*205. 2. of things, *run*; of ships, ἡ δ' ἔθεεν κατὰ κῦμα Il.1.483, cf. X.*HG*6.2.29; of a potter's wheel, Il.18.601; of a *rolling* stone, 13.141; of a quoit, ῥίμφα θέων ἀπὸ χειρός *flying* lightly .., Od.8.193. 3. metaph., δύναμις θαυμαστὴ ἐκεῖ θεῖ Plot.2.9.8, cf. 6.5.11. III. of things not actually in motion, [φλέψ] ἀνὰ νῶτα θέουσα διαμπερές Il.13.547; ἄντυξ ἣ πυμάτη θέεν ἀσπίδος 6.118; ἀμφὶ δέ μιν κίβισις θέε Hes.*Sc.*224; γραμμῆς περὶ [σημεῖον] θεούσης Plot.6. 5.11. IV. c. acc. loci, *run over*, τὰ ὄρη X.*Cyn.*4.6, cf. 5.17; μέσσα θέων πελάγευς *AP*7.273 (Leon.), cf. 10.23 (Autom.); πλωτῶν γένος ὑγρὰ θεόντων Opp.*H.*3.183.—The simple Verb is used in Trag. only by E.*Ion*1217.

θέω (B), *shine*, *gleam*, ὀδόντων λευκὰ θεόντων Hes.*Sc.*146 (λευκαθεόντων cj. Wackernagel); ὕλη χλωρὰ θεούσῃ cj. in Theoc.25.158; ποίην...χλωρὰ θέουσαν *IG*14.1389 ii 24; cf. θοός (B), Λευκαθέα, λευκαθίζω.

θεῶ, for θεάου, imper. of θεάομαι, *behold!*

θεώματα· περικαθαρτήρια, Hsch. (leg. θειώματα).

θεωρ-εῖον, τό, *place for seeing*, Hsch. s.v. θαυσήκρι. **-έω**:—**Pass.**, fut. -ηθήσομαι S.E.*M.*8.280: fut. Med. in pass. sense, ib.1.70, Ael.*VH* 7.10: (θεωρός):—*to be a* θεωρός I (q.v.), μαντεύεσθαι καὶ θ. Th.5.18; ἐγὼ δὲ τεθεώρηκα πώποτ' οὐδαμοῖ πλὴν ἐς Πάρον Ar.*V.*1188; of the states which sent θεωροί, οἱ Ἀθηναῖοι ἐθεώρουν ἐς τὰ Ἴσθμια Th.8.10. 2. *to be sent to consult an oracle*, Pl.*Ep.*315b. II. of spectators at games, τὰ Ὀλύμπια Hdt.1.59; ἀγῶνα Id.8.26, X.*An.*1.2.10; θ. τινά *to see* him *act*, Thphr.*Char.*11.3: abs., And.4.20, D.18.265; *to go as a spectator*, ἐς τὰ Ἐφέσια Th.3.104; ἐς Ὀλυμπίαν Luc.*Tim.*50; v. sub ὀβολός I. III. *look at*, *behold*, γῆν πολλήν Hdt.4.76; τύχας τινός A.*Pr.* 304; τὰ περὶ τὸν πόλεμον Pl.*R.*467c; *inspect*, *review* soldiers, X.*An.* 1.2.16, *HG*4.5.6: abs., *gaze*, *gape*, ἑστηκὼς θ. Thphr.*Char.*4.5: Astrol., = ἐπιθεωρέω 5, τὴν σελήνην Gal.19.542. 2. of the mind, *contemplate*, *consider*, αὐτῇ τῇ ψυχῇ αὐτὴν τὴν ψυχὴν θ. Pl.*Grg.*523e; τὰ ὄντα ᾗ ὄντα Arist.*Metaph.*1003^{b}15, cf. D.1.12, Epicur.*Nat.*2.6, etc.: folld. by an interrog., τοῦτο θ., εἰ τἀληθῆ λέγω D.3.3; θ. τινά, ὁποτέρου τοῦ βίου ἐστίν Aeschin.3.168; πόσας ἔχουσι διαφοράς Arist.*GA* 761^{a}11; θ. τίνας λέγομεν τοὺς φρονίμους Id.*EN*1140^{a}24; θ. τι ἔκ τινος *to judge of* one thing by another, τὴν ἔννοιαν ἐκ τῶν ἔργων Is.1.13, cf. Aeschin.3.160; θ. τι πρός τι *compare* one thing *with* another, D.18.17; πρὸς τοὺς πρὸ ἐμαυτοῦ...κρίνωμαι καὶ θεωρῶμαι; ib.315; τοὺς πρέσβεις θ. πρὸς τὸν καιρὸν καθ' ὃν ἐπρέσβευον Aeschin.2.80; θ. [τι τεκμηρίοις] D. 21.199. b. *observe*, θ. μᾶλλον τοὺς πέλας δυνάμεθα ἢ ἑαυτούς Arist. *EN*1169^{b}33, cf. *Pol.*1263^{b}25, al.; ταῦτα ἐμοῦ ἐθεωρήσατε, ὡς...ποιουμένου Lycurg.28:—Pass., τεθεώρηται τοῦτο μάλιστα ἐπὶ τῶν περιστερῶν Arist.*HA*562^{a}23, cf. 540^{b}19, al.; λόγῳ θεωρεῖσθαι, of objects not accessible to sense, Phld.*D.*3.10: abs., ὡς καὶ ἐπ' ἄλλων θεωρεῖται ib.1.13. c. *perceive*, c. inf., ἀναγκαῖον ὑπάρχειν D.S.13.88. d. abs., *speculate*, *theorize*, ἀκριβῶς, φορτικῶς, Arist.*Pol.*1280^{b}28, *Metaph.* 1001^{b}14; λογικῶς, φυσικῶς, Id.*APo.*88^{a}19, *Cael.*304^{a}25; περί τινος Id. *Metaph.*1004^{b}1, 983^{a}33 (Pass.); θ. ἔκ τινος *to conclude by observation from*..., ib.1029^{a}26; διά τινος Id.*Mete.*353^{b}18:—Pass., ἡ παρὰ τοῖς Ἕλλησι τεθεωρημένη μάθησις Ael.Tact.*Prooem.* (θεωρήσασα is prob. corrupt for ἑωρ- in S.*OC*1084 (lyr.).) **-ημα**, ατος, τό, *sight*, *spectacle*, λόγοι καὶ θεωρήματα D.18.68; θ. καὶ ἀκροάματα Aristox.*Fr. Hist.*15; θ. καὶ ἀκούσματα D.C.52.30: generally, *festival*, ὅσα Μουσῶν ὡσὶν ἔχεται θεωρήματα Pl.*Lg.*953a. 2. *object of contemplation*, τὸ ἐν ἡμῖν φάντασμα δεῖ ὑπολαβεῖν...εἶναι θ. Arist.*Mem.*450^{b}25; *vision*, Id.*Div.Somn.*463^{b}19; *intuition*, θ. κοινά Chrysipp.*Stoic.*3.72, al., cf. Phld.*Po.*5.25 (pl.). II. of the mind, *speculation*, *theory*, Arist. *Metaph.*1083^{b}18, *Top.*104^{b}1; τὰ κατὰ φυσιολογίαν θ. Metrod.*Herc.*831. 8; *speculative proposition*, M.Ant.1.8. b. *datum* or *rule of art*, Cic.*Fat.*6.11 (pl.); τέχνης θ. Phld.*Rh.*2.94 S., al. (pl.), cf. *Stoic.*3.51; ἰατρικῆς θ. Corn.*ND*33 (pl.); *scheme*, *plan*, Plb.6.26.10: pl., θεωρήματα, τά, *arts and sciences*, Id.10.47.12; αἱ τέχναι ἐκ -ημάτων εἰσίν Gal.1.106. c. Math., *theorem*, Archim.*Sph.Cyl.*1 *Prooem.*, al., Papp.30.6, al., Procl.*in Euc.*p.201 F.; also ἀστρονομικὰ θ. Phlp.*in Mete.*104.19. 2. *subject of investigation*, Plb.1.2.1, D.H.*Comp.* 2. b. *investigation*, Plu.2.1131c. **-ημᾰτικός**, ή, όν, *to be interpreted as seen*, ὄνειροι, opp. ἀλληγορικοί, Artem.4.1. II. *theoretic*, ἀρετή *Stoic.*3.48, cf. Iamb.*Protr.*21.λβ', D.L.3.49; *dogmatic*, epith. of

Metrodorus, Id.2.113; *contemplative*, βίος Jul.*ad Them.*265b; opp. πρακτικός, Id.*Or.*6.190a. -ημάτιον, τό, Dim. of θεώρημα, Arr. *Epict.*2.21.17, 3.5.15. -ήμων, ονος, ὁ, ἡ, *contemplative*, Choerob. in *An.Ox.*2.220. -ησις, εως, ἡ, *viewing*, τραγικαὶ θ. Pl.*Phlb.* 48a. -ητέον, *one must consider, investigate*, εἴτε.. εἴτε.. Id. *Lg.*815b; τίνι διαφέρει.. Arist.*Ph.*193^{b}23, etc. -ητήριον, τό, *seat in a theatre*, Plu.*CG*12 (pl.), *CIG*2782.20 (Aphrodisias). -ητής, οῦ, ὁ, *spectator*, ἐργάται τῶν καλῶν καὶ θ. Phld.*Oec.*p.63 J., cf. Hsch. s.v. θεωρούς. II. *overseer, director*, Sch.Opp.*H.*3.257. -ητικός, ή, όν, *able to perceive*, τοῦ περὶ τὰ σώματα κάλλους Arist.*Pol.*1338^{b}1; μὴ πάντων θ. ἀλλὰ ἐνίων Phld.*Rh.*2.108 S.; τῆς ἀφροσύνης S.E.*M.*11. 256. 2. of the mind, *contemplative, speculative*, ὁ περὶ τὴν.. οὐσίαν θ. Arist.*Metaph.*1005^{a}35; ὁ περὶ φύσεως θ. Id.*PA*641^{a}29: c. gen., μαντικὴ ἐπιστήμη θ. τοῦ.. μέλλοντος Pl.*Def.*414b; ἐπιστήμη θ., διάνοια, opp. πρακτική, ποιητική, Arist. *Metaph.*1064^{a}17, 1025^{b}25; νοῦς Id. *de An.*415^{a}11; θ. βίος *a contemplative* or *speculative* life (opp. ἀπολαυστικός, πολιτικός), Id.*EN*1095^{b}19, cf. Plu.*Cic.*3; θ. φιλόσοφος Id. *Per.*16: Comp. -ώτερος Herm. *in Phdr.*p.59 A. Adv. -κῶς Epicur. *Nat.*28.7, Poll.4.8, Iamb.*Comm.Math.*20. II. = θεωρικός, *Cod.Just.* 10.56.1.1. -ητός, ή, όν, *that may be seen*, D.S.14.60; ὄψει θ. Ael.*NA*9.4; θ. κατασκεύασμα Secund.*Sent.*1; of certain days in disease, *to be watched* (cf. ἐπίδηλος II. 1), Hp.*Aph.*2.24. 2. of the mind, *to be reached by contemplation*, τοὺς διὰ λόγου θ. χρόνους Epicur. *Ep.*1p.10 U.; θεοὺς λόγῳ θ. Id.*Fr.*355, cf. Phld.*Sign.*37; opp. ἐμφανής, Plu.2.722d; λόγῳ ib.876c. Adv. -τῶς Gal.18(1).363. -ητρα, ων, τά, *presents made by the bridegroom* to the bride, *when she first unveiled* herself, Eust.881.31, Harp. -ία, Ion. -ίη, Dor. **θεαρία** (v. infr.), Boeot. **θιαωρία** Ἐφ.Ἀρχ.1892.34: ἡ:—*sending of* θεωροί or *state-ambassadors* to the oracles or games, or, collectively, *the* θεωροί *themselves, embassy, mission*, θεωρίαν ἀπάγειν εἰς Δῆλον Pl.*Phd.*58b: pl., opp. στρατεῖαι, Id.*R.*556c; ἄγειν τῷ Διὶ τῷ Νεμείῳ τὴν κοινὴν ὑπὲρ τῆς πόλεως θ. D.21.115, cf. X.*Mem.*4.8.2, Decr.Byz.ap.D.18.91 (θεāρία), Plb.28.19.4. 2. *office of* θεωρός, *discharge of that office*, τῆς Ὀλυμπίαζε θ. Th.6.16, cf. Isoc.19.10, etc. II. *being a spectator at the theatre* or *games*, S.*OT*1491; οὔτ' ἐπὶ θεωρίαν πώποτε ἐκ τῆς πόλεως ἐξῆλθες Pl.*Cri.*52b; personified in Ar.*Pax* 523, al. III. *viewing, beholding*, θεωρίης εἵνεκεν ἐκδημεῖν to go abroad *to see the world*, Hdt.1.30; κατὰ θεωρίης πρόφασιν ib.29; ἐκπέμπειν τινὰ κατ' ἐμπορίαν καὶ κατὰ θεωρίαν Isoc.17.4, cf. Arist.*Ath.*11.1, Th.6.24; *pilgrimage*, E.*Ba.*1047. 2. of the mind, *contemplation, consideration*, Pl.*Phlb.*38b: pl., θεῖαι θ. Id.*R.*517d: c. gen., παντὸς μὲν χρόνου πάσης δὲ οὐσίας ib.486a; ἡ τῶν ἀρχῶν, ἡ τῶν ὅλων θ., Epicur.*Ep.*2 p.55 U., Phld.*Rh.*1.288 S.; θ. ποιεῖσθαι περί τινος Arist.*Metaph.*989^{b}25; ἡ περὶ φύσεως θ. Epicur.*Ep.*1 p.3 U., etc.: pl., τὰς σαθρὰς αὐτοῦ θ. Demetr.Lac.*Herc.*124.12. b. *theory, speculation*, opp. practice, Plb. 1.5.3; ἡ περὶ τὰ στρατόπεδα θ. Id.6.42.6; αἱ νυκτεριναὶ καὶ ἡμεριναὶ θ. *theoretic reckoning* of night and day, Id.9.14.6; ἡ μαθηματικὴ θ. Plu. *Rom.*12. 3. Pass., *sight, spectacle*, A.*Pr.*802, etc.; esp. *public spectacle at the theatre* or *games*, Ar.*V.*1005, X.*Hier.*1.12; ἡ τοῦ Διονύσου θ. the Dionysia, Pl.*Lg.*650a. 4. Rhet., *explanatory preface* to a μελέτη, Chor. in *Hermes* 17.208, etc.: so in Philos., *continuous exposition*, Olymp. in *Mete.*18.30, al. -ικός, ή, όν, *of* or *for* θεωρία (signfs. I and II), πεπλώματ' οὐ θεωρικά no *festal* robes, E.*Supp.*97; θ. σκηνή the tent *used by the* θεωροί, Henioch.5.8; θ. ὁδός, = θεωρίς I. 2, Poll.2.55. Adv. -κῶς Hsch. II. θεωρικόν, τό (θεωρικός, ὁ, seems to be an error in Phld.*Rh.*2.208 S.), at Athens, *fund for providing free seats at public spectacles*, οἱ ἐπὶ τὸ θ. Arist.*Ath.*43.1, cf. 47.2, D.18.113, *IG*2^2.223 C5; ἡ ἀρχὴ ἡ ἐπὶ τῷ θ. Aeschin.3.24: pl. (sc. χρήματα), D.3.11, Harp., etc., cf. Plu.*Per.*9: so elsewh. θεωρικά, with or without χρήματα, *fund for festivals*, *POxy.*1333 (ii/iii A.D.), 473.4 (ii A.D.). -ιος, v. θεάριος. II. θεώριον, τό, *box* at the amphitheatre, *PSI*8.953.62 (vi A.D.). -ίς, ίδος, ἡ, 1. (with and without ναῦς) *sacred ship, which carried the* θεωροί to their destination, Hdt.6.87, cf. Call.*Del.*314: metaph., ἄστολος θ., of *Charon's bark*, A.*Th.*858 (lyr.). 2. (sc. ὁδός) *road by which the* θεωροί *went*, Hsch. II. pl., = Βάκχαι, Id., cf. Plb.30.25.12; of attendants of Apollo, Nonn.*D.*9.261.

θεωροδοκ-έω, *act as* θεωροδόκος, *SIG*562.50 (Paros, from Magn. Mae.). -ία, ἡ, *office of* θεωροδόκος, *BCH*49.91 (Delph., iii B.C.), *SIG*608.5,10 (ib., ii B.C.): Dor. **θεāροδοκία**, τῶν Δηλίων *CIG*2329 (Delos). -ος, Dor. and Arc. **θεāροδόκος**, Thess. **θεουρο-** *Inscr. Magn.*26, Corc. **θιāρο-** ib.44: ὁ:—*one who receives the* θεωροί, *IG* 4.727 (Hermione, iv B.C.), 5(2).389 (Lusi), *SIG*608.7 (Delph., ii B.C.), etc.

θεωρός, ὁ (v. infr.), *envoy sent to consult an oracle*, S.*OT*114, *OC* 413; *to present an offering*, Orac.ap.D.21.53; *to be present at festivals*, θεωροὺς εἰς τὰ Πύθια πέμψαι D.19.128, cf. D.H.*Lys.*29, etc. 2. generally, *envoy*, sent to kings regarded as divine, Plu.*Demetr.*11, Ath.13.607c. II. title of a *magistrate* at Mantinea, Th.5.47; at Naupactus, *IG*9(1).360 (pl.), cf. ib.12(5).527 (found in Ceos); at Thasos, ib.12(8).267, etc. III. *spectator*, Thgn.805, A.*Pr.*118, *Ch.* 246, *Fr.*289; πολέμου Pl.*R.*467c, etc.; opp. ἀγωνιστής, Achae.3; *one who travels to see* men and things, Pl.*Lg.*951a, 953c; also λαμπάδα θ. εἰκάδων E.*Ion* 1076 (lyr., s.v.l.). (Uncontr. **θεαορός** *Schwyzer* 664.30 (Orchom. Arc., iv B.C.): contr. **θεāρός** in Dor. (*SIG*558.24, etc.), Arc. (*IG*5(2).4 (Tegea), etc.): **θεουρός** Thess. (*Inscr.Magn.*26): **θευρός** Thas. (*IG*12(8). l.c.); **θιāρός** Corc. (*Inscr.Magn.*44).) (Perh. fr. θεā-hopϝος, cf. θεη-κόλος and θυρωρός (θυρουρός) fr. θυρā-hopϝος.)

θεωροσύνη, ἡ, = θεωρία, Man.4.460.

θέωσις, εως, ἡ, (θεόω) *making divine*, Dam.*Pr.*100 (pl.).

θεώτερος, v. θεός III.

Θηβāγενής, ές, *sprung from Thebes, Theban*, Hes.*Th.*530: distd. fr. Θηβαῖος, Ephor.21 J.:—also **Θηβαιγενής**, E.*Supp.*136, D.P.623.

Θῆβαι, ῶν, αἱ, *Thebes*, Θ. Αἰγύπτιαι.. αἵ θ' ἑκατόμπυλοί εἰσι Il.9.381: also sg., Θήβης ἑπταπύλοιο (Boeotia) 4.406:—hence **Θήβασδε** *to Thebes*, 23.679; Att. Θήβαζε Sch.Il.3.29, al.; **Θήβησιν** *at Thebes*, Il. 22.479, Arist.*Rh.*1398^{b}2, Θήβησι Il.14.114: from the sg., **Θήβηθεν** *from Thebes*, Ephipp.15.7; poet. -θε *APl.*4.185; Boeot. **Θείβāθεν** *from Thebes*, Ar.*Ach.*862, also -āθε (-αθι codd.) ib.868:—Adj. **Θηβαιεύς**, έως, Ion. έος, ὁ, epith. of Zeus, *Theban*, Hdt.1.182, etc.: **Θηβαῖος**, α, ον, *Theban*, Od.10.492, etc.; Θηβαΐας (metri gr.) S.*Ant.* 1135 (lyr.): **Θηβαϊκός**, ή, όν, Hdt.2.4, etc.

Θηβαΐς, ΐδος, ἡ, *Thebais*, i.e. territory of Thebes (in Egypt), Hdt. 2.28; (in Boeotia), Id.9.65, Th.3.58:—hence **Θηβαΐτης** [ῑ], ου, ὁ, *dweller in the Egyptian Thebais*, Str.17.1.40. II. *Thebaid*, a poem on the siege of Thebes, which formed a portion of the Epic cycle, Paus.8.25.8.

Θηβάνας, ὁ, a name for *the north-east wind* (καικίας) in Lesbos, Arist.*Vent.*973^{a}9:—also **Θήβανις**, ὁ, St.Byz. s.v. Ἄδανα (because it blew from Hypoplacian Thebes), Hdn.Gr.1.95.

Θηβάρχης, ου, ὁ, *governor of the Thebaid*, *OGI*139.6 (pl., Philae, ii B.C.), 190.7 (ibid., i B.C.).

θῆβος (i.e. θῆϝος)· θαῦμα, and **θήγεια** (i.e. θήϝεια)· θαυμαστά, ψευδῆ, Hsch.

θηγᾰλέος, α, ον, (θήγω) *pointed, sharp*, στάλικες *AP*6.109 (Antip.); τρύφος ib.7.542 (Flacc.). II. Act., *sharpening*, c. gen. rei, ib.6. 68 (Jul. Aegypt.):—also **θηγάνεος**, Hsch.

θηγάν-η [ᾰ], ἡ, *whetstone*, A.*Ag.*1536 (lyr.), S.*Aj.*820: metaph., αἱματηρὰς θηγάνας *incentives* to bloodshed, A.*Eu.*859; θ. λάλης Luc. *Lex.*14:—also **θήγανον**, τό, Hsch. -ίτης [ῑ] λίθος, ὁ, a hard stone, used for *whetstones*, gen. θηγανεῖτα, *IG*14.317 (Therm. Himer.). -ω, = θήγω, restored by Herm. in A.*Ag.*1535 from Hsch., cf. *EM*450.13.

θήγη, ἡ, softer form of θήκη, Hsch. (v. διαθιγή).

θηγός, ή, όν, *sharp*, Hsch.

θήγω, Dor. **θάγω** [ᾱ] Ar.*Lys.*1256: fut. θήξω E.*Cyc.*242: aor. ἔθηξα Pi.*O.*10(11).20, E.*Or.*[51]:—Med., aor. ἐθηξάμην (v. infr.):—Pass., pf. τέθηγμαι (v. infr.):—poet. Verb (used by X. and later, v. infr.), *sharpen, whet*, Hom. (only in Il.), θήγων λευκὸν ὀδόντα 11.416, cf. 13.475, Hes.*Sc.*388; ὀδόντα Ar.*Ra.*815 (hex.); γένυν E.*Ph.*1380; θ. φάσγανον, ξίφος, μαχαίρας, A.*Ag.*1262, E.*Or.*1036, *Cyc.*242; ξίφη Onos.28; ὀϊστούς Jul.*Or.*7.229a:—Med., δόρυ θηξάσθω *let him whet his* spear, Il.2.382, cf. Phanocl.1.8. 2. metaph., *sharpen, excite*, Pi.*O.*10(11).20; ἰάμβων τοὺς ὀδόντας Babr.*Prooem.*2.14; *provoke*, τὰς ψυχὰς εἰς τὰ πολεμικά X.*Cyr.*2.1.20, cf. 1.2.10 (Pass.), *Mem.*3.3.7; τεθηγμένον τοί μ' οὐκ ἀπαμβλυνεῖς λόγῳ A.*Th.*715; λόγοι τεθηγμένοι *sharp, biting* words, Id.*Pr.*313; οὐ γάρ μ' ἀρέσκει γλῶσσά σου τεθηγμένη S.*Aj.*584; λῆμα τεθ. E.*Or.*1625; τῆς διανοίας ὀργῇ τεθ. Alcid. ap.Arist.*Rh.*1406^{a}10. II. intr., ὀργὴ γέροντος.. ἐν χειρὶ θήγει σὺν τάχει δ' ἀμβλύνεται dub. in S.*Fr.*894.

θηέομαι, Ion. form of θεάομαι. **θήης**, v. τίθημι.

θηητ-ήρ, ῆρος, ὁ, Ion. for θεατής, *one who gazes at, an admirer*, θ. τόξων Od.21.397; ἀκρασίης Perict.ap.Stob.4.28.19. -ής· ἀπατεών (cf. θηπητής), θεωρός, Hsch. -ός, ή, όν, Ion. for θεατός, Dor. **θāητός**, *gazed at, wondrous, admirable*, Hes.*Th.*31, Tyrt.10.29, Call. *Dian.*141; θ. ἀγών, γυῖα, Pi.*O.*3.36, *P.*4.80: in later Ion. Prose **θεητός** Aret.*CD*1.4.

θήϊον, τό, Ep. for θεῖον (A), *brimstone*, Od.22.493. **θήϊος**, Ep. for θεῖος (A); cf. θῆος.

θηκ-αῖος, α, ον, *like a chest* or *coffin*, οἴκημα θ. *burial* vault, Hdt.2. 86; perh. to be read in Plu.2.359a. II. Subst. θηκαῖον, τό, = θήκη, *SIG*1120 (pl., Cos). -άριον, τό, Dim. of θήκη, Sch.Opp.*H.* 2.356. -εῖον, τό, = θηκίον, *IG*5(1).813 (inc. loc.). -η, ἡ, (τίθημι) *case, chest*, χρυσοῦ θ. a money-*chest*, Hdt.3.130, 9.83, E.*Hec.*1147, cf. X.*Oec.*8.17, etc. 2. *grave, tomb*, A.*Pers.*405, S.*OC*1763 (anap.); νεκρῶν θήκας ἀνοίγειν Hdt.1.187, cf. 67, al.; αἱ θ. τῶν τεθνεώτων Th.1.8, 3.104; εἰς ἀναισχύντους θ. ἐτράποντο *modes of burial*, Id.2.52, cf. Pl.*R.*427b; θήκην ὀρύττειν X.*Cyr.*7.3.5. 3. ξίφους θ. sword-*sheath*, Poll.10.144; τόξου bow-*case*, *EM*333.41. -ίον, τό, Dim. of θήκη, *PFay.*104.5 (iii A.D.), *IG*12(3).1238 (Melos, iii/iv A.D.), Hsch.

θηκο-ποιέω, *store up*, *BGU*757.15 (i A.D.):—Pass., χόρτος τεθηκοποιημένος *PRyl.*142.16 (i A.D.). -ποιός, ὁ, *scabbard-maker*, Lyd. *Mag.*1.46. -φόρος, ὁ, = *cistophorus*, ib.3.8.

θηκτός, ή, όν, (θήγω) *sharpened, whetted*, A.*Th.*942 (lyr.), E.*Med.* 40, *AP*6.110 (Leon. or Mnasalc.), Pancrat.*Oxy.*1085.23.

θηλάζω, Dor. aor. I ἐθήλαξα Theoc.3.16 (v.l. -αζε): (θηλή): I. of the mother or nurse, *suckle*, Phryn.Com.29, Lys.1.9, Arist.*HA*576^b 10: abs., *give suck*, οἱ μαστοί, οἳ οὐκ ἐθήλασαν *Ev.Luc.*23.29:—also in Med., ἐπιμελεῖσθαι, ὅπως μέτριον χρόνον θηλάσονται Pl.*R.*460d, cf. Arist.*HA*566^{b}17; οὐ συλλαμβάνουσι θηλαζόμεναι Id.*GA*777^{a}13, cf. *IG*5(2).514.12 (Lycosura):—Pass., *to be sucked*, ὁ δελφὶς.. θηλάζεται ὑπὸ τῶν τέκνων Arist.*HA*504^{b}25. II. of the young animal, *suck*, Id.*GA*733^{b}29, etc.; ἐλέφαντος ὁ σκύμνος θ. τῷ στόματι Id.*HA*578^a 22; θηλάζων χοῖρος a *sucking* pig, Theoc.14.15; seldom of an infant, Orph.*Fr.*49.87. 2. c. acc., λεαίνας μασδὸν ἐθήλαξεν Theoc.3.16; ἐὰν μὴ τύχῃ τεθηλακὼς ὁ ὄνος ἵππον Arist.*HA*577^{b}16. (Written θελάσζ- *PSI*4.368.19 (iii B.C.).)

θηλᾰμινός, ὁ, *a suckling*, Hsch. (nisi leg. θηλαμόνος).

θηλᾰμών, όνος, ἡ, = θηλάστρια, Sophr.43, Thespis 4.2, Lyc.31; prob. for θηλονάς, Plu.2.278d.

θήλ-ασμα, ατος, τό, *mother's nursing, suckling*, *PMasp.*5.24 (vi A.D.), *PLond.*5.1708.82 (vi A.D.). **-ασμός**, ὁ, *giving suck, suckling*, Plu.*Rom.*4, *Aem.*14. **-άστρια**, ἡ, *one who suckles, wet-nurse*, S.*Fr.*98, Cratin.418, Eup.417.

θήλεα, θήλεια, v. θῆλυς. **θηλεογονία**, = θηλυγονία II, *Gloss.*

θηλέω, Dor. **θᾱλέω**, Ep. impf. θήλεον Od.5.73: fut. θηλήσω (ἀνα-) Il.1.236: Dor. poet. aor. θάλησα Pi.*N.*4.88; part. θηλήσας *AP*9.363 (Mel.): (τεθηλημένα is f.l. in Hp.*Insomn.*90):—poet. for θάλλω, *to be full of, abound in*, c. gen., λειμῶνες μαλακοὶ ἴου ἠδὲ σελίνου θήλεον Od.l.c.: c. dat., θάλησε σελίνοις Pi.l.c.; νικοφορίαις ἄστυ θάλησε ib.10.42. 2. abs., *grow luxuriantly, flourish*, A.R.3.221, *AP*l.c.; of a child, *IG*14.1971; prob. for ἐθάλλεον, Epigr.ap.Plu.2.110b. II. causal, *make to bloom*, Alex.Aet.3.9.

θηλή, ἡ, (θῆσαι) *teat, nipple*, E.*Cyc.*56 (lyr.), Hp.*Epid.*5.101, Pl.*Cra.*414a; τῶν μαστῶν ἡ θ., δι' ἧς..τὸ γάλα διηθεῖται Arist.*HA*493^{a}13; of animals, ib.500^{a}24; θ. πεφιλοτεχνημέναι dumb *teats*, Sor.1.115. II. *head* of a pole, κοντοὶ σὺν θηλαῖς σιδηραῖς *PLond.*3.1164^{h}9 (iii A.D.).

θηληνός, ή, όν, *quiet*, Cyr. **θηλητήρ**· κυνηγός, Hsch.

θηλοειδής, ές, *nipple-shaped*, *Gloss.*

θηλονή, v. θηλαμών.

θηλῠ-γενής, ές, *of female sex, womanish*, στόλος A.*Supp.*28, cf. E.*Ba.*1156; ὄχλος ib.117: Comp., Pl.*Lg.*802e. Adv. -νῶς Eust.10.27. **-γλωσσος**, ον, *with woman's tongue*, Νοσσίς *AP*9.26.7 (Antip. Thess.). **-γονέω**, *generate* or *promote the generation of females*, Thphr.*HP*9.18.5, Ph.1.262, Dsc.3.126. **-γονία**, ἡ, *generation of females*, opp. κουρογονίη, Hp.*Genit.*8; opp. ἀρρενογονία, Arist.*HA*585^{b}11, *GA*765^{a}30, S.E.*M.*5.7. II. *kin by the mother's side*, Hdn.1.7.4; = Lat. *cognatio*, Just.*Nov.*115.3.14. **-γόνος**, ον, *generating females*, Hp.*Steril.*230; καὶ γυναῖκες καὶ ἄνδρες..θ. εἰσίν Arist.*HA*585^{b}13; of animals, ib.573^{b}32, *GA*766^{b}32. II. θηλυγόνον, τό, a plant supposed *to promote the generation of females, dog-mercury, Mercurialis perennis*, Thphr.*HP*9.18.5; *a variety of* φύλλον, Dsc.3.125; = λινόζωστις θήλεια, Ps.-Dsc.4.189.

θηλυδρί-ας, ου, Ion. -ίης, εω, ὁ, *effeminate person*, Hdt.7.153, Ph.1.262, Luc.*DDeor.*5.3, S.E.*P.*3.217 (pl.), Lib.*Or.*64.83 (pl.); of animals, Arist.*HA*631^{b}17:—hence **θηλυδριάω**, *Gloss.* **-ώδης**, ες, *effeminate*, μέλος Ar.*Th.*131; λόγοι Sch.E.*Andr.*757. Adv. -δῶς Sch.D.T.p.247 H. **-ῶτις**, fem. Adj., = foreg., ῥαστώνη Prisc.p.332 D.

θηλῠκός, ή, όν, *woman-like*, ἄνδρες Arist.*GA*747^{a}1; *like the female*, of male animals, Id.*HA*589^{b}30: Comp., Id.*Pr.*961^{a}6. b. of women, *womanish, ultra-feminine*, opp. ἀρρενωπός, Id.*GA*728^{a}3. 2. Gramm., *feminine*, γένος D.T.634.17, D.H.*Amm.*2.11; μόριον ibid.; ὄνομα Ph.1.294. Adv. -κῶς Arist.*Fr.*499, Phld.*Piet.*12, Str.6.1.10, A.D.*Synt.*222.6, Alex.Aphr.*in Sens.*151.1. 3. = θῆλυς, *female*, *PCair.Zen.*166.2 (iii B.C.), Lxx *Nu.*5.3, *IG*14.872 (Cumae), Sor.1.32. b. θ. κεντήματα bites *of female* vipers, Philum.*Ven.*16.3. c. Astrol., applied to certain planets or figures of the Zodiac, Ptol.*Tetr.*20, 33.

θηλυ-κράνεια [κρᾰ], *the female* κράνεια, *dogwood, Cornus sanguinea*, Thphr.*HP*1.8.2, 3.3.1. **-κρᾰτής**, ές, *swaying women*, ἔρως A.*Ch.*599 (lyr.). **-κτόνος**, ον, *slaying by woman's hand*, Ἄρης θ. Id.*Pr.*860.

θηλῠκώδης, ες, *of effeminate nature*, Procl.*Par.Ptol.*265.

θηλύ-λᾰλος [ῠ], ον, = θηλύγλωσσος, Man.4.322. **-μᾰνέω**, *to be mad after women*, Ph.2.20, Man.4.164. **-μᾰνής**, ές, *mad after women*, *AP*5.18 (Rufin.); Πόθοι Id.9.16 (Mel.); of animals, ἵπποι θ. Lxx *Je.*5.8. II. Act., *maddening women*, κροτάλων θ. ὄτοβοι Antim.*Eleg.*17:—hence -μᾰνία, ἡ, Sch.Opp.*H.*1.536, *Cat.Cod.Astr.*2.177. **-μελής**, ές, *singing in soft strain*, Ἀλκμᾶνος ἀηδόνες *AP*9.184. **-μίτρης**, ου, ὁ, *with a woman's* μίτρα, *in woman's clothes*, Luc.*DDeor.*18.1: acc. -μίτρην prob. cj. for -μητριν, -μιτριν, Id.*Bacch.*3. **-μορφος**, ον, *woman-shaped*, E.*Ba.*353; *female in type*, Arist.*Phgn.*809^{b}37 (Comp.); ἰδέα Ph.2.261; θεότης Dam.*Pr.*204; of the number 4, Nicom.ap.Phot.*Bibl.*p.144 B. **-νοος**, ον, contr. **-νους**, ουν, *of womanish mind*, A.*Pr.*1003.

θηλύνω, Plu.2.999a: aor. ἐθήλῡνα E.*Fr.*360.29, Babr.*Prooem.*1.19, (ἐξ-) Str.5.4.13: pf. τεθήλῠκα Arist.ap.Stob.4.279 M.:—Pass., aor. ἐθηλύνθην (v. infr.), (ἐξ-) D.H.14.8: pf. τεθήλυσμαι Hp.*Aër.*15, J.*AJ*4.8.40, (ἐκ-) Gal.10.354; but -υμμαι (ἐκ-) Plb.36.15.2, Luc.*DDeor.*5.3; 3 sg. -υνται D.C.50.27; inf. -ύνθαι (ἐκ-) Plb.31.21.3: (θῆλυς):—*make womanish, enervate*, E.l.c.; τὴν ἡδονὴν Plu.l.c.; τοὺς ἄνδρας Vett.Val.76.6; *soften*, Ζέφυρος κῦμα θηλύνει *AP*10.4 (Marc. Arg.):—Pass., τῶν σωμάτων -ομένων X.*Oec.*4.2, cf. Porph.*Abst.*1.34; *become soft*, αἱ σάρκες -ονται Hp.*Art.*52; βαφῇ σίδηρος ὥς, ἐθηλύνθην στόμα S.*Aj.*651; οὔπω ἐθηλύνθης *gav'st* not yet *a sign of yielding*, *AP*5.250 (Iren.); θ. οἴκτοις ib.299 (Paul. Sil.); *play the coquette*, Bion 2.18; τᾷ μορφᾷ θηλύνετο Theoc.20.14; *muliebria pati*, Vett.Val.7.26, al.: Astrol., of planets, Ptol.*Tetr.*20.—Rare in Att.

θηλύ-πᾰθέω [ῠ], *muliebria pati*, prob. in Phld.*Herc.*312.4. **-παις**, παιδος, ἡ, *having borne a girl*, Lyc.851. **-ποιός**, όν, *making weak*, of the number 8, Nicom.ap.Phot.*Bibl.*p.144 B. **-πους**, ποδος, ὁ, ἡ, θ. βάσις the tread *of female foot*, [E.]*IA*421. **-πρεπής**, ές, *befitting a woman*, ποικίλματα Agath.3.28; *womanish*, οἰνοχόοι *AP*12.175 (Strat.), cf. Chor.*Lyd.*7: metaph., θεότης θ., of Difference, Dam.*Pr.*192. **-πρῖνος**, ἡ, Arc. name for φελλός, Eust.302.30. **-πρόσωπος**, ον, *with woman's face*, Suid. s. v. Σειρῆνας. **-πτερίς**, ίδος, ἡ, *bracken, Pteris aquilina*, Thphr.*HP*9.18.8, Dsc.4.185, Plin.*HN*27.78:—also **-πτέριον**, τό, Alex.Trall.*Verm.*p.597 P.

θῆλυς, θήλεια, θῆλυ: Ep. fem. θήλεα, acc. pl. -εας Il.5.269 (Hom. has regul. fem. θήλεια Il.8.7, al., but also θῆλυς as fem., 10.216, al., as in other poets, v. infr.): Ion. fem. θήλεα, θήλεαν, θηλέης, θηλέῃ, pl. θήλεαι, θηλέας, θηλέων, Hdt. and Hp.: gen. θήλυδος S.*Fr.*1054; acc. fem. θηλείην dub. l. in Nic.*Al.*42, neut. pl. θήλεια Arat.1068: Ep. also θηλύτερος indicating opposition rather than comparison (cf. ἀρρέντερος); θηλύτεραι δὲ γυναῖκες Il.8.520; θηλύτεραι δὲ θεαί Od.8.324; μάτε ἐρσεναιτέραν μάτε θηλυτέραν *Schwyzer* 424 (Elis, iv B.C.); in late Prose θηλύτερος, -ύτατος occur as Comp. and Sup. (v. infr. II): (θη- 'suckle', cf. θῆσαι):—*female*, θήλεια θεός a goddess, Il.8.7; Ἥρη θῆλυς ἐοῦσα being *female*, 19.97, cf. A.*Ag.*1231, S.*Tr.*1062, E.*IT*621; θήλειαι ἵπποι mares, Od.4.636, etc.; σύες θήλειαι sows, 14.16; ὄϊς θῆλυς a ewe, Il.10.216; θήλεια μῆλα Arat.1068; θήλεια ἔλαφος a hind, Pi.*O.*3.29; θήλεα κάμηλος Hdt.3.102; ἡ θ. ἵππος ib.86; θ. ὄρνις S.*Fr.*477; ζῷα θ. Pl.*Criti.*110c; ἄπαις θήλεος γόνου without *female* issue, Hdt.3.66; θῆλυς σπορά E.*Hec.*659; θήλειαι γυναῖκες Id.*Or.*1205; θ. κόραι Pl.*Lg.*764d: with masc. nouns, ὁ θῆλυς ὀρεύς the *she*-mule, Arist.*HA*577^{b}22; ἄνθρωπος θῆλυς Id.*PA*688^{b}31: masc. pl., θήλεις χοροί Critias 1.8 D.; but μὴ εἶναι θεοὺς ἄρρενας μηδὲ θηλείας Phld.*Piet.*12. b. ἡ θήλεα, Att. -εια, *the female*, Hdt.3.109, X.*Mem.*2.1.4; ἀλέκτωρ ὥστε θηλείας πέλας A.*Ag.*1671 (troch.). c. τὸ θ. γένος the *female* sex, *woman*-kind, E.*Hec.*885; τὸ θ. alone, Id.*HF*536, etc.; opp. τὸ ἄρρεν, Pl.*R.*454d, Arist.*Metaph.*988^{a}5; [ἡ δεῖνα] τέτοκεν θῆλυ *PTeb.*422.18 (iii A.D.), al. d. of plants and trees, Thphr.*HP*3.9.1; θ. κάλαμος Dsc.1.85; θῆλυς φοῖνιξ Ach.Tat.1.17; θῆλυ βούτομον Thphr.*HP*4.10.4. 2. *of* or *belonging to women*, κουράων θῆλυς ἀϋτή Od.6.122; θήλεα νοῦσος among the Scythians (cf. Ἐνάρεες), Hdt.1.105; νόμος A.*Ch.*821 (lyr.); φύσις Pl.*R.*453a; χάρις *APl.*4.287 (Leont.); θ. φόνος murder *by women*, E.*Ba.*796. II. metaph., of persons and things, 1. *soft, gentle*, θῆλυς ἐέρση Od.5.467, Hes.*Sc.*395; θ. νύξ (= ὑπόμβρος) S.*Fr.*1053. b. ὕδωρ θ. καὶ μαλακόν Thphr.*CP*2.6.3; θηλυτέρα ὀσμή ib.6.15.4; θηλύτατον πεδίον *most fruitful*, Call.*Fr.*296; θηλύτατον ὕδωρ, of the Nile, Id.*Sos.*vii 5. 2. *tender, delicate*, Φοίβου θήλειαι...παρειαί Id.*Ap.*37; θῆλυς ἀπὸ χροιῆς *delicate* of skin, Theoc.16.49; of temper or character, *soft, yielding, weak*, θῆλυς ηὕρημαι τάλας S.*Tr.*1075; γυνὴ δὲ θῆλυ κἀπὶ δακρύοις ἔφυ E.*Med.*928; θήλεια φρήν Ar.*Lys.*708, cf. E.*Andr.*181; δίαιτα θηλυτέρα ἢ κατ' ἄνδρα Plu.*Mar.*34; θηλύτατος Luc.*Im.*13; παλλακὴ -υτάτη Philostr.*VS*2.21.2; τὸ θῆλυ τῆς ψυχῆς *effeminacy*, Men.599. 3. in mechanics, those parts were called female *into which others fitted*, as the *female* vertebra, Poll.2.180; γίγγλυμος J.*AJ*3.6.3. 4. Gramm., *feminine*, θήλεα [ὀνόματα] Ar.*Nu.*682; θήλεα Arist.*Po.*1458^{a}10. 5. Pythag., of *even* numbers, Plu.2.264a, 288d. 6. Astrol., of planets, Ptol.*Tetr.*19; cf. θηλυκός 3 c. III. θήλειαι, αἱ, kind of cheese made in Crete, Seleuc.ap.Ath.14.650d.

θηλύσπορος, ον, *of female kind*, γέννα, of the daughters of Danaus, A.*Pr.*855.

θηλυστολ-έω, *wear women's clothes*, Str.10.3.8, 11.13.9. **-ία**, ἡ, *women's dress*, Eust.782.47. **-ος**, ον, *clad in women's clothes*: τὸ θ. *effeminacy*, Id.10.24.

θηλύτεκνος [ῠ], ον, *producing female children*, γάμοι *TAM*2(1).174 *Db*.

θηλύτης, ητος, ἡ, (θῆλυς) *womanhood, female nature*, Arist.*GA*775^{a}16; *sexual characters* of the female, Gal.4.570. 2. *womanishness, delicacy*, Corn.*ND*20, Plu.*Crass.*32; ἡ θ. τοῦ κάλλους *the womanish nature* of.., ib.24; also, *effeminacy*, ἐσθήτων Id.*Alc.*16 (pl.).

θηλῠτοκ-έω, *bear females*, Hp.*Genit.*7, Arist.*HA*574^{a}1, *GA*765^{a}24. **-ία**, ἡ, *bearing of females*, ib.767^{a}35: pl., J.*AJ*3.11.5. **-ος** (parox.), ον, *bearing females*, Arist.*GA*723^{a}27, *Pol.*1335^{a}13, Theoc.25.125.

θηλύ-τροπος, ον, *of womanish habit*: metaph., of the planet Venus, *Cat.Cod.Astr.*1.136. **-φᾰνής**, ές, *like a woman*, νεανίσκοι Plu.*Thes.*23; πάθος *AP*11.285 (Pall.). **-φθόριον**, τό, = ἀβρότονον, Ps.-Dsc.3.24. **-φόνος**, ον, *killing women*: θηλυφόνον, τό, *leopard's bane, Aconitum Anthora*, Thphr.*HP*9.18.2, Nic.*Al.*41, Plin.*HN*25.122, Dsc.4.76 (v.l. θηρο-). **-φρων**, ον, gen. ονος, *effeminate*, Ar.*Ec.*110 (= *Trag.Adesp.*51), Vett.Val.104.21. **-φωνος**, ον, *with woman's voice*, Ael.*NA*6.19; εὐγενὴς φιλοσοφία φεύγουσα τὸ θ. Eust.10.22. **-χειρ**, χειρος, ὁ, ἡ, *with woman's hand*, Id.550.37. **-χίτων** [ῑ], ωνος, ὁ, ἡ, *with woman's frock*, *AP*6.219 (Antip.), Orac.ap.Luc.*Alex.*27. **-χοίρα**, ἡ, = ὕαινα, Sch.Opp.*H.*5.31. **-ψῡχος**, ον, *of woman's spirit*, Ptol.*Tetr.*162.

θηλώ, όος, οῦς, ἡ, *wet-nurse*, Hsch.; = Lat. *Rumina*, Plu.2.278d.

θῆμα, ατος, τό, (τίθημι) *tomb*, S.*Fr.*541. II. = *prooemium*, *Gloss.*

θημολογέω, *collect in a heap*, shortd. from θημωνολογέω (metri gr.), ψαμμίτην δόρπον *AP*9.551 (Antiphil.).

θημών, ῶνος, ὁ, (τίθημι) *heap*, ἠΐων θημῶνα..καρφαλέων Od.5.368; θ. ἀχύρων Arist.*Mete.*344^{a}26; θημῶνα νῆσαι Opp.*H.*4.496, cf. Ph.ap.Eus.*PE*8.7: pl., Ph.2.97.

θημωνιά (not θημωνία), ἡ, = foreg., θ. ἅλωνος Lxx *Jb.*5.26; συνήγαγον αὐτοὺς θημωνιὰς θημωνιάς ib.*Ex.*8.14(10), cf. Eust.1539.16:—also **θειμωνειαι** and **θημονιαί**, Hsch.

θημωνοθετέω (θημον- codd.), *put in a heap*, Sch.Theoc.10.46.

θην, enclit. Particle (A.D.*Conj.*257.9) chiefly Ep. and Dor., rare in Trag., A.*Pr.*928:—*in truth, I ween*, freq. ironical, λείψετέ θ. νέας Il.13.620; ὥς θ. καὶ σὸν ἐγὼ λύσω μένος 17.29, cf. 21.568; strengthd., ἦ θ. *in very truth*, 11.365, 13.813; οὐ θ. *surely* not, 2.276, Od.5.211; οὐ θ. δή 3.352; καὶ γὰρ θ. Il.21.568: coupled with γα, Epich.34, Sophr. 24: freq. in Theoc., 1.97, al.; once in Call., *Aet.Oxy.*2079.46.

θήνιον· γάλα, Hsch.

θῆξις, εως, ἡ, = ῥοπή, στιγμή, τάχος, Hsch.; θήξει, = Lat. *momento*, *Gloss.*; but κατὰ θῆξιν is f.l. for κατὰ θίξιν in Archig.ap.Gal.12.577.

θηοῖο, Ep. for θεῷο, 2 sg. pres. opt. of θηέομαι.

θῆος, α, ον, Dor. for θεῖος (A), Callicr.ap.Stob.4.28.17, Euryph.ap. eund.4.39.27.

θηπαλέος· βωμολόχος, Hsch. **θηπέω**, *to be astonished*, Id. **θηπητής**, οῦ, ὁ, *deceiver*, Id. **θηπόν**· καταθύμιον, θαυμαστόν, Id. **θήπω**, *deceive*, Hippon.14.1; but also, = θαυμάζω, Hsch.; cf. θηπέω.

θήρ, θηρός, Ep. dat. pl. θήρεσσι, ὁ: later also ἡ, Ael.*NA*6.24, etc.: (v. sub fin.):—*beast of prey*, esp. a lion (so used in Cephallenia, Sch. Il.15.324), Il.15.586, etc.; ὁ Νέμειος θ. E.*HF*153: coupled with λέων, ib.465, Epimenid.2: with λέαινα, *AP*14.63.4 (Mesom.); of the wild boar, Ἐρυμάνθιος θ. S.*Tr.*1097; of Cerberus, Id.*OC*1569 (lyr.); ὁ θ., of a hind, Id.*El.*572: pl., generally, *beasts*, opp. birds and fishes, ἠέ που ἐν πόντῳ φάγον ἰχθύες, ἢ ἐπὶ χέρσου θηρσὶ καὶ οἰωνοῖσιν ἕλωρ γένετ' Od.24.291; ἰχθύσι μὲν καὶ θηρσὶ καὶ οἰωνοῖς πετεηνοῖς Hes.*Op.*277; ἐν θηρσίν, ἐν βροτοῖσιν, ἐν θεοῖς ἄνω S.*Fr.*941.12; ἐν ἄγρῃ θηρῶν Hdt. 3.129; ἄφοβοι θῆρες S.*Aj.*366: metaph., θῆρες ξιφήρεις, of Orestes and Pylades, E.*Or.*1272, cf. *Ph.*1296 (lyr.); ἡ σφοδρότης..θηρός (sc. Ἔρωτος) Alex.245.12: prov., ἔγνω θὴρ θῆρα Arist.*Rh.*1371^{b}16. 2. of any *living creature*, πλωτοὶ θῆρες, i.e. dolphins, Arion 1.5; of *vermin* killed by birds, Ar.*Av.*1064 (lyr.); of gnats, *AP*5.150 (Mel.); of the *sacred animals* in Egypt, ἀρχιστολιστὴς θηρῶν *Sammelb.*4011. 4. 3. any fabulous *monster*, as the Sphinx, A.*Th.*558 codd.; esp. of a centaur, S.*Tr.*556, 568 (cf. φήρ); of Satyrs, E.*Cyc.*624; οὐ θεῶν τις οὐδ' ἄνθρωπος οὐδὲ θ. A.*Eu.*70.—Less freq. than θηρίον in Prose, but found in Hdt. l.c. (v.l. θηρίων), X.*Cyr.*4.6.4, Pl.*R.*559d, *Sph.* 235a, Ael. l.c., etc.; ἄγριοι θῆρες Arist.*EE*1229^{a}25. (I.-E. *ĝhu̯ēr-*, cf. φήρ, Lith. *žvėris* 'wild beast'.)

Θήρα, ἡ, the island *Thera*, Pi.*P.*4.20, etc.:—hence **Θήρᾱθε**, *from Thera*, *Abh.Berl.Akad.*1925(5).20: **Θήρανδε**, *to Thera*, ib.21.

θήρα, Ion. **θήρη**, ἡ, *hunting of wild beasts*, *the chase*, βὰν δ' ἴμεν ἐς θήρην Od.19.429; αἵμονα θήρης Il.5.49; ἰέναι ἐπὶ τὴν θήρην Hdt.1.37, 4.114, cf. Ar.*Fr.*2 D.; ζῶσι ἀπὸ θ. Hdt.4.22, cf. Arist.*Pol.*1256^{a}35; ἐποίησε μεγάλην θήραν X.*Cyr.*1.4.14; θ. ποιεῖσθαι Arist.*HA*541^{a}20; τὰς θ. τῶν ὀρτύγων ἐποιοῦντο D.S.1.60; τοῦ πτηνοῦ γένους θ., = ὀρνιθευτική, Pl.*Sph.*220b; ἡ περὶ θάλατταν θ. *fishing*, Id.*Lg.*823d; κυνηγεσία καὶ ἡ ἄλλη θ. ib.763b: pl., πέρδικες εἰς τὰς θ. ἀγόμεναι, of decoy birds, Arist.*GA*751^{a}14, cf. Phld.*Ir.*p.42 W., Ant.Lib.41.2. b. in Ptolemaic Egypt, στρατηγὸς ἐπὶ τὴν θ. τῶν ἐλεφάντων *OGI*82, 86 (iii B.C.), cf. Str.16.4.5, 7, Wilcken *Chr.*385.14 (iii B.C.), *PPetr.*3 p.292 (iii B.C.), etc. 2. metaph., *eager pursuit* of anything, θήραν.. ἔχομεν τόξων, = θηρῶμεν τὰ τόξα, S.*Ph.*840; δυσμενῶν θήραν ἔχειν Id. *Aj.*564; θ. ἀνθρώπων Pl.*Sph.*222b,c; τοῦ ἡδέος Id.*Grg.*500d; ἐπιστημῶν Id.*Tht.*198a, etc. II. *prey*, *game*, αἶψα δ' ἔδωκε θεὸς μενοεικέα θήρην Od.9.158, cf. A.*Ch.*251, E.*Ba.*1144; πρὶν κινεῖσθαι τὴν θ. X. *Cyr.*2.4.25; θήραν καλήν, of a prisoner, S.*Ph.*609: in pl., ὦ πταναὶ θῆραι, of birds, ib.1146 (lyr.); τὴν θ. ἐπὶ τοῦ μέσου τηροῦσα watching its *prey*, of a spider, Arist.*HA*623^{a}13. III. *hunting-ground*, *preserve*, Ἀδριανοῦ θῆραι D.C.69.10. IV. in Roman times, *the games of the Circus*, *Epigr.Gr.*351.3 (Nicaea).

θηραγρ-έτης, ου, ὁ, *hunter*, E.*Ba.*1020 (lyr., s.v.l.), *AP*6.184 (Zos.). **-ία**, ἡ, *chase of wild beasts*, Poll.5.12. **-ος**, ον, (ἄγρα) *for catching wild beasts* or *game*, πέδη Ion Trag.40: name of a hound, dub. in *AP*7.304 (Pisand.).

Θηραϊκόν or **Θήραιον**, τό, a dress worn in the Satyric drama at Athens, *invented in the island Thera*, Thphr.*Fr.*119.

θήρ-ᾱμα, ατος, τό, (θηράω) *prey*, *spoil*, E.*Ba.*869 (lyr., s.v.l.), *Hel.* 192 (lyr.), *AP*6.105 (pl., Apollonid.), Plu.*Luc.*17: metaph., ἀρετὰ.., θ. κάλλιστον βίῳ Arist.*Fr.*675. **-αρχος**, ὁ, *commander of two elephants*, Ascl.*Tact.*9, Ael.*Tact.*23:—hence **-αρχία**, ἡ, *his command*, Ascl.*Tact.*9. **-άσιμος** [ᾱ], ον, *to be hunted down*, θηρεύοντες οὐ θηρασίμους γάμους A.*Pr.*858. **-άτειρα** [ᾱ], fem. of θηρατήρ, *huntress*, Call.*Del.*230. **-ᾱτέος**, α, ον, *to be pursued*, *sought eagerly*, S.*Ph.*116, X.*Mem.*2.6.8. II. θηρατέον *one must pursue*, Id.*Cyr.*2.4.10. **-ᾱτήρ**, Ion. **-ητήρ**, ῆρος, ὁ, poet. for θηρατής, Il. 5.51, etc.; ἀνδρὸς θηρητῆρος 21.574; κοῦροι θ. 17.726. **-ᾱτήριος**, α, ον, = θηρατικός, c. gen., ἴυγγα θ. ἔρωτος S.*Fr.*474.1. II. Subst. **-ατήριον**, τό, *hunting implement*, Hsch. s.v. ἄγκιστρον. **-ᾱτής**, οῦ, ὁ, (θηράω) *hunter*, Ael.*NA*13.12, *PSI*3.222.7 (iii A.D.): metaph., θ. λόγων Ar.*Nu.*358; δόξης D.L.8.8; τῶν ἀδήλων Philostr.Jun.*Im.* 1. **-ᾱτικός**, ή, όν, = θηρευτικός, σκύλακες Ph.1.628 (s.v.l.), cf. Gal.*Protr.*6; ἔργα Ael.*NA*14.5; θ. σημεῖα signals *given by the hunter*, Plu.2.593b; θ. φόρος tax *for game-licence*, dub. in *PSI*3.222 (iii A.D.). 2. *fit for winning*, τὰ θ. τῶν φίλων the arts *for winning* friends, X.*Mem.*2.6.33. 3. *fond of hunting*, Plu.2.960a, 965b. **-ᾱτός**, ή, όν, *to be caught*: metaph., *attainable*, τὴν ἕξιν ᾗ τὰ καλὰ θ. γίγνεται τοῖς ἀνθρώποις Plb.10.47.11; οὐδ' ὅλως ἐπιστήμῃ θ. ὁ καιρός, ἀλλὰ δόξῃ D.H.*Comp.*12; κριτήριον οὐδὲ στοχασμῷ θ. Phld.*Rh.* 1.167 S. **-ᾱτρον**, τό, *instrument of the chase*, *net*, *trap*, etc., X.*Mem.* 2.1.4, 3.11.7, Plu.2.961c (pl.), Ael.*NA*1.21: pl., *of spider's webs*, Max. Tyr.16.5: metaph., prob. in Lib.*Decl.*22.25. **-άτωρ** [ᾱ], Ion. **-ήτωρ**, ορος, ὁ, = θηρατήρ, θηρήτορας ἄνδρας Il.9.544; [κύων] θηράτωρ Nic. Dam.56 J. **-άφιον** [ᾱ], τό, Dim. of θηρίον, of insects, Damocr.ap.Gal. 14.91. **-άω**, fut. -άσω [ᾱ] S.*Ph.*958, E.*IT*1426, X.*An.*4.5.24, etc.: aor. ἐθήρᾱσα A.*Pers.*233, E.*Ba.*1215, X.*Cyr.*1.4.10: pf. τεθήρᾱκα ib. 2.4.16; Thess. pf. part. πεφειράκοντες *IG*9(2).536:—**Med.**, fut. θηράσομαι (which, acc. to Moer., is the true Att. fut.) E.*Ba.*228, *IT*1324: aor. ἐθηρᾱσάμην S.*Ph.*1007, E.*Hipp.*919:—**Pass.**, fut. -ᾱθήσομαι *Gp.* 12.9.2: aor. ἐθηράθην (v. infr. III): (θήρ, θήρα):—*hunt*, *chase*, λαγώς, σφῆκας, X.*An.* l.c., *HG*4.2.12, etc.; καί μ' οὓς ἐθήρων πρόσθε θηράσουσι νῦν S.*Ph.*958; of fishermen, *catch*, Arist.*Fr.*76: metaph., *catch* or *capture*, καί σ' εἷλε θηρῶνθ' ἡ τύχη S.*OC*1026, cf. *Ph.*1007, X.*An.*5.1.9: *captivate*, Id.*Mem.*2.6.28, 3.11.7; θ. πόλιν *seek to destroy* it, A.*Pers.* 233. 2. metaph., *hunt after* a thing, *pursue* it *eagerly*, τυραννίδα S.*OT*542; θηρᾶν οὐ πρέπει τἀμήχανα Id.*Ant.*92; μυρίαι κόραι θηρῶσι λέκτρον τοὐμόν E.*IA*960; ἥμαρτον ἢ θηρῶ τι; have I missed or *do I hit the quarry?* A.*Ag.*1194; τί χρῆμα θηρῶν; E.*Supp.*115; *reach*, *attain to*, τι Pi.*I.*4(3).46 (s.v.l.). 3. c. inf., *seek*, *endeavour* to do, θηρᾷ γαμεῖν με E.*Hel.*63; cf. II. 3. 4. = ἐκπράσσω III, θηρήτω δὲ ἁ θοιναρμόστρια *IG*5(1).1498 (Messenia, ii B.C.). II. Med. like Act., *hunt for*, *fish for*, ἐγχέλεις Ar.*Eq.*864: abs., οἱ θηρώμενοι *hunters*, X.*Cyn.*11. 2. 2. more freq. metaph., *seek after*, ἐμέτοισι θηρώμενοι τὴν ὑγιείην Hdt.2.77; μαστοῖς ἔλεον θ. E.*Or.*568; τὴν τῆς σωφροσύνης δόξαν D. 61.21, etc.; θ. πυρὸς πηγὴν *find*, *discover* it, A.*Pr.*109; *expect to derive*, τι παρά τινων Phld.*Rh.*1.263 S. 3. c. inf., *seek*, *endeavour*, ὅς με θηρᾶται λαβεῖν E.*Hel.*545; πεῖράν τιν' ἐχθρῶν ἁρπάσαι θηρώμενον S. *Aj.*2. III. Pass., *to be hunted*, *pursued*, πρὸς ἄτης θηραθεῖσαι A. *Pr.*1072; ὑπ' ἀνδρῶν E.*Ba.*732; Ἀλκιβιάδης διὰ κάλλος ὑπὸ γυναικῶν θηρώμενος X.*Mem.*1.2.24.—Cf. θηρεύω. **-εία**, ἡ, *hunting*, *Gloss.* **-ειος**, ον, also α, ον v.l. in Pl.*Phdr.*248d, *AP*5.265 (Paul. Sil.): (θήρ):—*of wild beasts*, δέρμα θ. λέοντος Panyas.1, cf. Hanno *Peripl.*9; μέλεα Emp.101; θήρειον γραφήν the figures *of animals* worked upon the cloak, A.*Ch.*232; θ. δάκος, = θήρ, E.*Cyc.*325; θ. βία, periphr. for ὁ θήρ, *the centaur*, S.*Tr.*1059; θ. κρέα *game*, X.*Cyr.* 1.3.6; so θήρεια, τά, Hp.*Aff.*52; θ. φύσις Pl. l.c.; θ. αὐλός (ἐκ νεβροῦ κώλων εἰργασμένος) Poll.4.75. II. θ. στόματα the entrance *of the Circus*, *IG*4.365 (Corinth).

θηρ-επῳδός, όν, *charming wild beasts*, Suid. s.v. σοφός. **-ευμα**, ατος, τό, (θηρεύω) *spoil*, *prey*, S.*Ichn.*285, E.*IA*1162. II. pl., *hunting*, Pl.*Lg.*823b. **-ευσις**, εως, ἡ, *hunting*, *the chase*, πεζῶν ib.824a: metaph., ὀνομάτων θηρεύσεις Id.*Tht.*166c. **-ευτέον**, *one must hunt after*, Plb.1.35.8. **-ευτήρ**, ῆρος, ὁ, = sq., Opp.*C.*1.449. **-ευτής**, οῦ, ὁ, *hunter*, used by Hom. (only in Il.) always as Adj., κύνεσσι καὶ ἀνδράσι θηρευτῇσιν hounds and *huntsmen*, Il.12.41; ἐν κυσὶ θηρευτῇσι 11.325; so θ. ἄνδρες Hes.*Sc.*303, 388; κύνες Thgn.1254, X.*Ages.*9.6: as Subst., Hdt.1.123, Satyr.*Vit.Eur.Fr.*39 xxi 14; of *a fisher*, Hdt.2.70; θ. πέρδιξ *a decoy* partridge, Arist.*HA*614^{a}10; θ. ἰξός *birdlime*, *AP*5.99. 2. metaph., θ. νέων καὶ πλουσίων Pl.*Sph.*231d, cf. Chor.p.67 B.; καλλίστων ὀνομάτων Ath.3.122c. **-ευτικός**, ή, όν, *of* or *for hunting*, κύνες θ. *hounds*, Ar.*Pl.*157, X.*Lac.*6.3; βίος θ. the life *of hunters*, Arist.*Pol.*1256^{b}2: ἡ -κή (sc. τέχνη) *hunting*, *the chase*, Pl.*Plt.*289a, cf. *Sph.*223b. 2. c. gen., *hunting after*, τῆς τροφῆς Arist.*HA*488^a 19: metaph., θ. τέχνη ἀνθρώπων Pl.*Euthd.*290b. **-ευτός**, ή, όν, = θηρατός, Arist.*Pol.*1324^{b}40. **-εύτρια**, fem. of θηρευτήρ, βοῦς *PCair.Zen.*292.298 (iii B.C.), cf. Hsch. s.v. θηρότις; θ. κύνες Them. *Or.*18.220b. **-εύτωρ**, ορος, ὁ, *hunter*, θ. ἄνδρες, of men engaged in Circus games, *IG*4.365 (Corinth). **-εύω**, aor. 1 ἐθήρευσα Pl. *Euthd.*290c: pf. τεθήρευκα Id.*Tht.*200a:—**Med.**, fut. -σομαι Id.*Sph.* 222a: aor. ἐθηρευσάμην Ar.*Fr.*51, Pl.*Tht.*197d:—**Pass.**, pf. τεθήρευμαι Lysipp.Com.7: aor. ἐθηρεύθην Hdt.3.102, A.*Ch.*493, Pl.*Sph.* 221a: (cf. θηράω):—*hunt*, θηρεύοντα *while hunting*, Od.19.465, cf. Hdt.4.112; θηρεύειν διὰ κενῆς, of the motions of the hands of dying persons, Hp.*Prog.*4. 2. *decoy*, Arist.*HA*614^{a}13. II. c. acc., *hunt after*, *chase*, *catch*, ἀττελέβους Hdt.4.172; θηρία, ὄρνιθας ἀγρίας, μῦν, X.*An.*1.2.7, Pl.*Tht.*197c, *PCair.Zen.*300.7 (iii B.C.); ἰχθῦς Arist. *HA*603^{a}7; [ἐλέφαντας] *OGI*54.11 (Adule, iii B.C.); of men, Hdt. 4.183; θ. ἀνθρώπους ἐπὶ θοίνην ἢ θυσίαν Arist.*Pol.*1324^{b}39, cf. X.*An.* 1.2.13; Τιτυὸν βέλος θήρευσε it *hit*, *struck* him, Pi.*P.*4.90:—Med., Ar.*Fr.*51, Pl.*Grg.*464d, *Euthd.*290b:—Pass., *to be hunted*, Hdt.3. 102; *to be preyed upon*, ib.108; *to be caught*, πέδαις A.*Ch.*493: metaph., *to be captivated*, Lysipp.Com.7. 2. metaph., *hunt*, *seek after*, κερδέων μέτρον Pi.*N.*11.47; γάμους A.*Pr.*858; ἀρετάν E.*IA*568 (lyr.); θ. νέους πλουσίους ὀρφανούς Aeschin.1.170; ἡδονάς, ἐπιστήμην, Isoc.1.16, Pl.*Tht.*200a, al.; [εὐδαιμονίαν] Arist.*Pol.*1328^{b}1; ὀνόματα, ῥήματα, Pl.*Grg.*489b, And.1.9, cf. Antipho 6.18; τὰς ἀρχὰς τῶν συλλογισμῶν Arist.*APr.*46^{a}11; θ. τὸν πλησίον, of an orator, Phld.*Rh.* 2.5 S., al.—Trag. preferred θηράω, exc. where metre demanded θηρεύω.

θηρεφόνος, ον, = θηροφόνος, Hdn.Gr.2.260.

θήρημα, θηρητήρ, -ήτειρα, -ήτωρ, Ion. for θήρᾱμα, etc.

θηρῑ-άζομαι, Pass., *pass into a beast*, of the soul, *Corp.Herm.*10. 20. **-ᾰκός**, ή, όν, (θηρίον) *concerning venomous beasts*, λόγος Dsc. *Ther.Praef.*; Φιλῖνος ⟨ὁ⟩ θ., the writer on this subject, Philum.*Ven.*6.1: ἡ -κή (sc. ἀντίδοτος) an antidote *against a poisonous bite*, Androm. ap.Gal.14.32, etc.; θ. φάρμακα Id.17(2).337; θηριακά, title of Nicander's poem on such antidotes; of other works, Gal.14.7; θ. ἄμπελος *Gp.*4.8.1, cf. Plin.*HN*14.117; θ. [οἶνος] Dsc.5.53. **-άλωσις** [ᾰ], εως, ἡ, *capture of wild beasts*, Sm.*Ge.*49.9. **-άλωτος** [ᾰ], ον, *caught by wild beasts*, Lxx *Le.*5.2, Ph.2.355.

θηρίαμβος, coined as etym. of θρίαμβος, Suid.

θηριάνθρωπος, ον, *beast-man*, ἔθνος Hdn.*Epim.*76.

θηρίδιον, τό, Dim. of θηρίον, in pl., *animalculae*, Thphr.*HP*2.8.3, Arr.*Epict.*2.9.6, Gal.16.162, *Gp.*5.53.6.

Θηρίκλειος, α, ον, or ος, ον, *made by Thericles*, a famous Corinthian potter (Eub.31, 43), Θ. κύλιξ Alex.96, Thphr.*HP*5.3.2 (pl.), Cleanth. *Stoic.*1.133; κρατήρ Alex.119, cf. *IG*11(2).124.43, al. (Delos, iii B.C.); ποτήρια Phalar.*Ep.*70; freq. Θηρικλεία (or -ος) alone, Alex.5, Men. 226, 324; Θ. ἡ μεγάλη Diox.4; τῶν Θηρικλείων εὐκύκλωτον ἀσπίδα Aristopho 14; ὅσα δ' ἐστὶν εἴδη Θηρικλείων τῶν καλῶν Dionys.Com.5.1.

θηριό-βρωτος, ον, = θηρόβορος, D.S.18.36. **-δεῖκται**, οἱ, *exhibitors of wild beasts*, Antioch.Astr. in *Cod.Astr.*7.118, 8(4).212. **-δηγμα**, ατος, τό, *bite of a serpent*, Dsc.2.79. **-δήκτης**, *marsus*, *Gloss.* **-δηκτος**, ον, *bitten by a wild beast*, esp. *by a serpent*, Damocr. ap.Gal.14.122, Dsc.1.103, 4.24. **-ειδής**, ές, *like a wild beast*, Adam. 1.4. **-κόμος**, ὁ, *keeper of wild beasts*, Procop.*Arc.*9. **-κτόνος**, ον, = θηροκτόνος, φάρμακον Eust.1416.14. **-μᾰχέω**, *fight with wild beasts*, D.S.3.43, 1*Ep.Cor.*15.32, Vett.Val.129.33, Ptol.*Tetr.*200, Artem.2.54. **-μάχης** [ᾰ], ου, ὁ, *one who fights with beasts*, D.S. 36.10. **-μᾰχία**, ἡ, *fighting with wild beasts*, in pl., = Lat. *venationes*, Str.2.5.33, Ph.1.602. **-μάχος** [ᾰ], ον, *fighting with wild beasts*, M.Ant.10.8, Luc.*Lex.*19. **-μῐγής**, ές, *half man half beast*, as Scylla, Tz. ad Lyc.45. **-μορφος**, ον, (μορφή) *in the form of a beast*, κώδων Eust.1139.57, cf. Procl.*Par.Ptol.*278.

θηρίον, τό (in form Dim. of θήρ), *wild animal*, esp. of such as are hunted, μάλα γὰρ μέγα θηρίον ἦεν, of a stag, Od.10.171,180 (never in Il.); in Trag. only in Satyric drama, S.*Ichn.*147 (dub. in A.*Fr.*26): used in Prose for θήρ, X.*An.*1.2.7, Isoc.12.163, etc.; of the spider's *prey*, Arist.*HA*623a27; freq. of elephants, Plb.11.1.12, al.: pl., *beasts*, opp. men, birds, and fishes, *h.Ven.*4, Hdt.3.108. 2. generally, *animal*, Id.1.119; νενόμισται πῦρ θ. εἶναι ἔμψυχον Id.3.16; of men, ἄνθρωπος πάντων θ. θεειδέστατον Antipho Soph.48; εἰς θηρίου βίον ἀφικνεῖσθαι Pl.*Phdr.*249b; also θ. ὕειον Id.*R.*535e; of the dog, Theoc.25.79; of fishes, Arist.*HA*598b1; of eels, Antiph.147.7; of leeches, *IG*4.951.101 (Epid.); of other small creatures, Arist.*HA* 552b11, 625b32, Hp.ap.Gal.19.103, Theoc.19.6; οὐκ ἔστιν οὐδὲν θ. τῶν ἰχθύων ἀτυχέστερον Antiph.161.1; opp. plants, Pl.*Smp.*188b: prov., ἢ θηρίον ἢ θεός, either above or below the nature of man, Arist. *Pol.*1253a29, cf. *EN*1145a25. 3. *beast*, esp. as hostile and odious to man, θηρία τε καὶ βοτά *carnivora* and *graminivora*, Pl.*Mx.*237d; *monster*, *creature*, of sharks, etc., Hdt.6.44; of Typhon, etc., Pl. *Phdr.*230a, *R.*588e; of the Satyrs, S.*Ichn.* l. c.; ταυτὶ ποδαπὰ τὰ θ.; Ar.*Nu.*184, cf. *Av.*93. b. *poisonous animal*, Dsc.1.75, *Act.Ap.* 28.4. II. Medic., = θηρίωμα, Hp.*Coac.*459, *Loc.Hom.*29, cf. Gal. l. c. III. as a term of reproach, *beast*, *creature*, ὦ δειλότατον σὺ θηρίον Ar.*Pl.*439, cf. *Eq.*273; κόλακι, δεινῷ θηρίῳ Pl.*Phdr.*240b; Κρῆτες, κακὰ θ. Epimenid.1; δυσνουθέτητον θ., of poverty, Men. *Georg.*78; ἡ μουσικὴ ἀεί τι καινὸν θηρίον τίκτει Anaxil.27, cf. Eup.132; τί δέ, εἰ αὐτοῦ τοῦ θηρίου ἠκούσατε; said by Aeschines of Demosthenes, Plin.*Ep.*2.3.10; θ. συνεστιώμενον, of woman, Secund. *Sent.*8. IV. Astron., the constellation *Lupus*, Eudox.ap.Hipparch.1.2.20, Vett.Val.6.13.

θηριο-νάρκη, ἡ, a plant *that benumbs serpents*, *Nerium Oleander*, Plin.*HN*24.163, 25.113. **-πληκτος**, ον, *struck by a poisonous animal*, *Cat.Cod.Astr.*8(4).150. **-ποιέω**, *make into wild beasts*, Tz. ad Lyc.815.

θηριότης, ητος, ἡ, *brutality*, Arist.*EN*1145a17, Metop.ap.Stob.3. 1.115.

θηριοτροφ-εῖον, τό, *park where wild beasts are kept*, Hortens. in Varro *RR*3.13.2 (*thero-* codd.). **-έω**, *train as a wild beast*, Alciphr. *Fr.*5 (Pass.). **-ος**, ον, (parox.) *abounding in wild beasts*, of a country, Str.2.5.33; *keeping wild beasts*, Procl.*Par.Ptol.*250. II. proparox., θηριότροφος, ον, Pass., *fed on reptiles*, Gal.11.143.

θηριόω, *make into a wild beast*, τοὺς πρὸς αὐτὴν ἀφικνουμένους ἡ Κίρκη θηριοῖ Phld.*Piet.*144:—Pass., *IG*14.1291. II. Pass., *come to the full size of a beast*, πρὶν θηριοῦσθαι τὸν γόνον Eub.107.14. 2. *become brutal*, θηριούμενος Pl.*Lg.*935a; πρός τινας Phld.*Lib.*p.25 O.; πρὸς ἀγριότητα Ph.2.53. 3. of seeds, *to be infested with worms*, Thphr. *CP*5.18.1. b. of places, *to be infested with reptiles*, Paul.Aeg. 5.1. 4. Medic., *become malignant*, ἕλκη ἐᾶσαι θηριωθῆναι Thphr. *Char.*19.3; τεθηριωμένον ἕλκος Dsc.3.9.

Θηρίτας, α, ὁ, Lacon. name of Ares, Paus.3.19.8, Hsch. (Lacon. for Θερσίτης).

θηρῐ-ώδης, ες, *full of wild beasts*, *infested by them*, of countries, ἡ θ. Λιβύη Hdt.4.181; ὄρεα -έστατα Id.1.110; ἐν τῇ θ. [χώρῃ] Id.4.174, cf. 2.32; -εστάτης ἐούσης τῆς θαλάσσης ταύτης *full of ravenous fishes*, Id.6.44. II. of beasts, *savage*, Arist.*PA*663a13; ἐπὶ τὸ -έστερον Id.*HA*502b4; τὸ θ., of a colt, E.*Tr.*671. 2. of men and manners, *brutal*, δίαιτα Hp.*VM*3; [βίοτος] E.*Supp.*202, cf. *SIG*704*E*11 (Delph., ii B.C.); ἡδονή Pl.*R.*591c; βρίμωσις Phld.*Ir.*p.58 W.; κατάστασις *OGI*424.3 (Palestine, i A.D.); ὁ θ. ἐν τοῖς ἀνθρώποις σπάνιος Arist.*EN* 1145a30; οἱ Λάκωνες .. θηριώδεις ἀπεργάζονται [τοὺς παῖδας] Id.*Pol.* 1338b12; ἡ θ. ἕξις Id.*EN*1145a24: Comp. -έστερος, ἄνθρωπος Plb.30. 12.3; τὸ θ. *brutality*, Pl.*Cra.*394e, al. Adv. -ωδῶς, διακεῖσθαι πρὸς ἀλλήλους Isoc.11.25, cf. Plb.15.20.3. 3. ζῴδια θ., = θηριόμορφα, Ptol.*Tetr.*200. III. Medic., *malignant*, of ulcers, Phld.*Ir.*p.44 W., Dsc.2.108, Plu.2.165e, Aret.*SA*2.8; also of intestinal worms, Hp. *Epid.*6.1.11, 6.2.11. **-ωδία**, ἡ, = θηριότης, v.l. in Arist.*EN*1145a 24, cf. Sch.E.*Or.*518 (written -ώδεια Asp. in *EN*130.7). **-ωμα**, ατος, τό, *malignant ulcer* (cf. θηρίον II), Cels.5.28.3, Dsc.2.109, Erot. s. v. τὸ θηριῶδες, Gal.17(1).948. **-ώνῠμος**, ον, *named after a wild beast*, Eust. ad D.P.976. **-ωσις**, εως, ἡ, *turning into a beast*, Luc. *Salt.*48.

θηρο-βολέω, *slay wild beasts*, S.*Ph.*165 (anap.), v.l. in *AP*6.186 (Diocl.). **-βορος**, ον, *eaten* or *torn by wild beasts*, κρέας Ps.-Phoc.147; θ. θάνατος death *by wild beasts*, Man.4.614. **-βοτος**, ον, *where wild beasts feed*, ἐρημοσύνη *AP*9.4 (Cyllen.), cf. Phalar.*Ep.* 34. **-βρομος**, ον, *heralded by the roar of wild beasts*, epith. of Hecate, Orph.*H.*1.6. **-βρωτος**, ον, = θηρόβοτος, Str.6.1.12 (v.l. θηριοβρ-). **-δηκτος**, ον, *stung by a serpent*, Sch.S.*Ph.*696. **-δῐδασκᾰλία**, ἡ, *taming*, *training of wild beasts*, Man.4.245. **-δίωξ** [ῐ], ωκος, ὁ, *hunter*, Choerob. in *Theod.*1.296, *EM*451.23. **-ειδής**, ές, *having the forms of wild beasts*, Hsch. **-ζῠγοκαμψῐμέτωπος**, ον, = ὁ θῆρας ζυγῶν καὶ κάμπτων τὰ μέτωπα, a word formed as part of a verse containing all the letters, *AP*9.538. **-θήρας**, ου or α, ὁ, *hunter*, Hsch. **-θῡμος**, ον, *with brutal mind*, *brutal*, *APl.*3.25 (Phil.). **-κόμος**, ον, *keeping wild beasts* or *camels*, Hld.10. 27. **-κτόνος**, ον, *killing wild beasts*, epith. of Heracles, *IG*5(2).91 (Tegea); of Artemis, E.*IA*1570, Corn.*ND*3, Porph.*Abst.*1.22; ἐν φοναῖς θ. in the chase, E.*Hel.*154. **-λέξης**, ου, ὁ, *word-chaser*, Hsch.

θηρ-ολετέω, *destroy wild beasts*, Eust. 561.3, Dosith. p.432 K. **-ολέτης**, ου, ὁ, *slayer of beasts*, Hsch.; ὄζος ὁ θ., of the club of Heracles, *APl.*4.104 (Phil.):—fem. **-ολέτις**, ιδος, cj. for θηρότις, Hsch.

θηρο-μᾰχία, ἡ, = Lat. *venatio*, *Mon.Anc.Gr.*19.7, *OGI*533.48 (Ancyra), *IGRom.*3.631 (Xanthus). **-μῐγής**, ές, *half-beast*, φῦλα θ., of centaurs, Opp.*C.*2.6; θ. τις ὠρυγή a cry *as of beasts*, Plu.*Mar.* 20. **-μικτος**, ον, = foreg., δαίμων Lyc.963. **-νόμος**, ον, *feeding* or *tending wild beasts*, of a mountain, *AP*6.111 (Antip.); of Pan, Castorio 2. 2. *guiding them*, μάστιξ Nonn.*D.*11.122. **-πεπλος**, ον, *clad in the skins of beasts*, Orph.*H.*69.7; θ. μανία the mad fancy *of wearing skins*, Cerc.10, Stratonic.ap.Timae.80. **-πλαστέω**, *to make beasts*, Tz. ad Lyc.673. **-πλαστος**, ον, *changing into beasts*, of Circe, Lyc.673. **-σκόπος**, ον, *looking out for wild beasts*, epith. of Artemis, *h.Hom.*27.11, B.10.107, *AP*6.240 (Phil.).

θηροσύνη, Dor. -να, ἡ, *the chase*, Opp.*C.*4.43 (pl.), *AP*6.167 (Agath.).

θηρότις· θηρεύτρια, Hsch.

θηρο-τόκος, ον, *producing beasts*, ἄγκεα *AP*6.186 (Diocl.). **-τροφέω**, = θηριοτροφέω, Aristaenet.2.20. **-τρόφος**, ον, *feeding wild beasts*, ἀνήρ *IGRom.*4.826 (Hierapolis); of places, E.*Ba.*556 (lyr.), A.R.4.1561, Longus 1.1; of Tethys, Orph.*H.*22.6. II. proparox., θηρότροφος, Pass., *feeding on beasts*, δράκων E.*Ph.*820 (hex.). **-τῠπος**, ον, *in the form of a beast*, Orph.*H.*24.5, 39.8. **-φᾰνής**, ές, *appearing like a beast*, Procl. ad Hes.*Op.*151. **-φονεύς**, έως, ὁ, *slayer of beasts*, Opp.*C.*1.538. **-φονέω**, *slay beasts*, ib.4.24. **-φόνος**, ον, also η, ον Thgn.11, prob. in Ar.*Th.*320:—*killing wild beasts*, epith. of Artemis, Thgn. l. c., Ar. l. c.; θεά E.*HF*378 (lyr.); of Apollo, *AP*9.525.9; θεός, i. e. Hadrian, Pancrat.*Oxy.*1085.31; κύνες E.*Hipp.*216 (anap.). II. θ., τό, v.l. for θηλυφόνον, Dsc.4. 76. **-φόρος**, ον, *producing game*, prob. l. *AP*14.24. **-φύλαξ** [ῠ], ἄκος, ὁ, *huntsman*, *PPetr.*3 p.321 (iii B.C.), *Sammelb.*286. 3. **-χλαινος**, ον, *clad in the skins of beasts*, Lyc.871.

θής, θητός, ὁ, *serf*, *bondsman*, θῆτές τε δμῶές τε Od.4.644; later, *hired labourer*, θῆτά τ' ἄοικον ποιεῖσθαι Hes.*Op.*602; μισθωτοὺς καὶ θῆτας Pl.*Plt.*290a; βάναυσοι καὶ θ. (opp. δοῦλοι) Arist.*Pol.*1278a 13. 2. at Athens, members of the fourth class in the constitution of Solon, *IG*1^2.45, Arist.*Ath.*7.3, Th.6.43, Poll.3.82. 3. v. θάτας. II. fem. **θῆσσα**, later Att. **θῆττα**, ἡ, *hired servant-girl*, opp. ἐπίκληρος, Posidipp.35; θ. γυνή A.R.1.193, cf. Ant.Lib.25.3. 2. as Adj., = θητική, θῆσσα τράπεζα *menial* fare, E.*Alc.*2; θ. ἑστία Id.*El.*205 (lyr.).

θῆσαι, aor. 1 inf. Act., *suckle*, Hsch.; elsewh. Med., *suck*; Hom. has pres. inf., ἀλλ' αἰεὶ παρέχουσιν ἐπηετανὸν γάλα θῆσθαι they give milk *to suck* the year round, Od.4.89: aor. 1, θήσατο μαζόν he *sucked* the breast, Il.24.58, cf. Call.*Jov.*48; part., θησάμενος *having sucked*, *h.Cer.*236; γάλα Call.*Sos.*vii.4; but, II. *suckle*, Ἀπόλλωνα θήσατο μήτηρ *h.Ap.*123. (I.-E. *dhē-* 'suck', cf. θηλή, θῆλυς, Lett. *dēt* 'suck', Skt. *dháyati*, Goth. *daddjan* 'suckle', Lat. *fēlare*, *filius*.)

θησαυρ-ίζω, *store*, *treasure up*, ἐν ἀσφαλείῃ τὰ χρήματα θ. Hdt.2. 121.α'; θ. τὸν νεκρὸν ἐν οἰκήματι *to lay* it *by*, ib.86; φάρμακα, σῖτα θ. παρ' αὐτῷ, X.*Cyr.*8.2.24, etc.; of fruits, *lay up in store*, *preserve*, *pickle*, [καυλοὺς] ἐν ἅλμῃ Thphr.*HP*6.4.10; τὸ ἔλαιον θ. [τὰς ὀσμάς] *preserves* its smell, Id.*CP*6.19.3:—Pass., ῥὰξ εὖ τεθησαυρισμένη S.*Fr.* 398.2; [ἡ ἐβένη] τὴν χρόαν οὐ -ομένη λαμβάνει τὴν εὔχρουν ἀλλ' εὐθὺς τῇ φύσει Thphr.*HP*4.4.6, cf. 3.12.5; ἡ τεθησαυρισμένη τῶν ἀρωμάτων ἀπόλαυσις Agatharch.97; τὸ θησαυρισθὲν *IG*14.423 ii 37 (Tauromenium). b. abs., *hoard*, *lay up treasure*, Phld.*Oec.*p.71 J., *Ep.Jac.* 5.3; ἑαυτῷ *Ev.Luc.*12.21. 2. metaph., θ. σεαυτῷ ὀργὴν *Ep.Rom.* 2.5; θ. θησαυροὺς ἐν οὐρανῷ *Ev.Matt.*6.20; θ. εὐτυχίαν *lay up a store of*.., App.*Samn.*4.3:—Med., *store up for oneself*, ἑαυτῷ ὑπομνήματα Pl.*Phdr.*276d, cf. Isoc.15.229:—Pass., τεθησαυρισμένος κατά τινος φθόνος D.S.20.36; χάριτας -ισθησομένας Id.1.90; *to be reserved*, πυρὶ 2*Ep.Pet.*3.7. **-ικός**, ή, όν, *of the public granary*, μέτρον *PLips.*97 v 7 (iv A.D.). 2. θησαυρικόν, τό, *charge for use of granary*, *PRyl.*213.3 (ii A.D.), al. 3. v. θησαυριστικός. **-ισμα**, ατος, τό, *store*, *treasure*, S.*Ph.*37, E.*El.*497, *Ion* 1394, Vett.Val.352.5: metaph., θ. κακῶν Democr.149. **-ισμός**, ὁ, *laying up in store*, χρημάτων Arist.*Pol.*1256b 28, cf. Phld.*Oec.*p.71 J.; *preservation*, *keeping*, ὀσμῶν Thphr.*Od.*14, cf. *HP*8.11.1; θ. φαντασιῶν, definition of memory, Zeno *Stoic.*1. 19. **-ιστέον**, *one must store up*, τὸ πλεονάζον τοῦ καρποῦ Ph.2. 57. **-ιστής**, οῦ, ὁ, *one who lays up in store*, Poll.3.115. **-ιστικός**, ή, όν, *accustomed to lay up in store*, [ζῷα] τροφῆς θησαυριστικά Arist. *HA*488a20; prob. l. for θησαυρικός (= *miserly*), Ptol.*Tetr.*158.

θησαυρο-ποιέω, *make stores*, Poll.3.116. **-ποιός**, *όν*, *laying up in store*, Pl.*R*.554a.

θησαυρός, ὁ, *store, treasure*, Ar.*Av*.599, etc.; θ. χθονός, of the silver-mines of Laureion, A.*Pers*.238 (troch.); θ. εὑρεῖν Arist.*Pol*.1303^{b}35; ἄνθρακες ὁ θ., prov., 'apples of Sodom', freq. in Luc.*Zeux*.2, al.; σποδὸς οἱ θ. γενήσονται Alciphr.2.3.13: metaph., θ. γλώσσης φειδωλῆς Hes.*Op*.719; θ. ὕμνων Pi.*P*.6.8; κακῶν E.*Ion*923, cf. Hp.*Lex*; κόμας.., ἱκτήριον θ. S.*Aj*.1175; Διὸς θ., of a tomb marking the fall of a thunderbolt, E.*Supp*.1010; οἰωνοῖς γλυκὺν θ., of a dead body, S.*Ant*.30; of learning, θ., οὓς κατέλιπον ἐν βιβλίοις X.*Mem*.1.6.14; σοφίας θ. Pl.*Phlb*.15e, *Ep.Col*.2.3; χρημάτων καὶ τιμῶν Pl.*Mx*.247b; καλὸς θ. παρ' ἀνδρὶ σπουδαίῳ χάρις Isoc.1.29; ἐκ τοῦ ἀγαθοῦ θ. τῆς καρδίας *Ev. Luc*.6.45. II. *strong-room, magazine*, Hdt.2.150, *SIG*419.17 (Delph., iii B.C.), Lxx *De*.32.34, etc.; esp. of the *treasuries* built at Delphi by Greek cities, *SIG*8 (vi B.C.), Hdt.1.14, al., X.*An*.5.3.5, Str.4.1.13, etc.; *vaults* of a bank, *PLips*.62 ii 14 (iv A.D.). 2. *granary*, *PCair.Zen*.232.4 (iii B.C.), Wilcken *Chr*.385.27 (iii B.C.), 192 (i A.D.), etc.; οἱ δημόσιοι θ. *PRyl*.90.9 (iii A.D.), cf. *POxy*.2119.3 (iii A.D.). 3. *receptacle* for valuables, *safe, casket*, Hdt.7.190, 9.106, *Ev.Matt*.2.11; θ. βελέεσσιν, of a quiver, A.*Pers*.1022 (lyr.). 4. *offertory-box* (for its form, v. *IG*9(2).590), *IG*7.235.23 (Oropus, iv B.C.), 12(3).443 (Thera, iii B.C.), *Jahrb*.16.162 note 13 (Rhodes, iii B.C.), *Schwyzer*89 (Argos, iii B.C.), *SIG*1015.30 (Halic.), *PTeb*.6.27 (ii B.C.), *IG*5(1).1390.89 (Andania, i B.C.); σπονδεῖον ἢ θ. *coin-in-the-slot machine* which sold holy water, Hero *Spir*.1.21. 5. *cavern*, S.*Ichn*.276; *subterranean dungeon*, Plu.*Phil*.19.

θησαυρο-φῠλᾰκέω, *lay by, store up*, ἀργύριον Ph.2.215; μνήμας Id. 1.237:—Pass., ib.338. II. *to be a treasurer*, D.S.19.15. **-φῠλᾰκικόν** or **-φῠλᾰκῑτικόν**, τό, *tax levied for the protection of granaries*, *PTeb*.68.89, 61(*b*).317 (ii B.C.). **-φῠλάκιον** [ᾰ], τό, *treasury*, Artem. 1.74, Them.*Or*.7.91d. **-φύλαξ** [ῠ], ἄκος, ὁ, *treasurer*, Lxx *Es*.5.14, D.S.18.58, Polyaen.4.9.4, Arr.*Ind*.12.7 (pl.), Vett.Val.85.23. II. *guard of the state-granaries*, *PCair.Zen*.292.155 (iii B.C.), *PTeb*.90.40 (i B.C.), *POxy*.522.9 (ii A.D.).

θησαυρώδης, ες, *filled with treasure*, τάφοι Philostr.*VA*7.23.1.

Θησεῖδαι, οἱ, *sons of Theseus*, i.e. *Athenians*, S.*OC*1066 (lyr.).

θησειομύζων, sine expl., Ar.*Fr*.459 (*Et.Gen.*).

Θησεῖον, τό, *temple of Theseus*, a sanctuary (ἄσυλον) for criminals and slaves, Ar.*Eq*.1312, *Fr*.567:—also **Θησέον**, Pherecr.49 (cf. *Et. Gen.*). II. **Θησεῖα**, τά, *festival of Theseus*, Ar.*Pl*.627:—also **Θησέα**, *SIG*1029.78 (iv B.C.). III. **θησεῖον**, τό, *holewort, Corydalis densiflora*, Thphr.*HP*7.12.3, Plin.*HN*21.107.

Θησειότριψ, ἴβος, ὁ, (τρίβω) *one who is always in the Theseum*, i.e. *a runaway slave*, Ar.*Fr*.458.

θησεύμεθα, Dor. fut. Med. of τίθημι.

Θησεύς, ὁ, gen. Θησέως [trisyll., S.*Ph*.562, *OC*1593, 1657, but disyll., ib.1003, 1103]:—*Theseus*, Il.1.265, etc.: pl. Θησέες Pl.*Tht*. 169b; Θησεῖς Alciphr.2.4.

Θησηΐς, ΐδος, contr. **Θησῆς**, ῆδος, fem. of *Θήσειος, *of Theseus*, χθών A.*Eu*.1026. II. Subst., *Theseid*, a poem on Theseus, Arist.*Po*. 1451^{a}20, D.L.2.59. 2. name of a mode of hair-cutting, used by Theseus, Plu.*Thes*.5.

θῆσθαι, v. θῆσαι.

θησομύζειν, f.l. for θησειομύζων, *EM*451.52.

θῆσσα, fem. of θής (q.v.). II. = Lat. *tensa, sacred car*, Plu.*Cor*.25.

θήσω· ἥσω, αἰτήσω (Boeot.), Hsch.; θησόμενοι· αἰτούμενοι, Id.; θησάμενοι· αἰτησάμενοι (Cret.), Id. (Prob. forms of θέσσασθαι, q.v.)

θῆτα, τό, indecl., *the letter* Θ (Hebr. *ṭêth*), Ar.*Ec*.685, etc.: gen. θήτατος Democr.20: nom. pl. θήτατες (*tetates*) Wessely *Schrifttaf. zur ält. lat. Paläogr*.No.8 (ii A.D.); nickname of Aesop (who was a θής), Ptol.Heph.ap.Phot.*Bibl*.p.151 B.

θηταλά· θαυμαστά, ψεύδεσιν ὅμοια, Hsch.

θητ-εία, ἡ, (θητεύω) *hired service, service*, S.*OT*1029, Isoc.14.48: in pl., ib.11.38, D.H.2.19. 2. *servility, sycophancy*, c. gen., θ. ὄχλων ἢ δυναστῶν Epicur.*Sent.Vat*.67. **-εῖον**, τό, = μίσθωμα, Μυστάκου θ., title of play by Sopatros, Ath.4.175c, al. (θητίον codd.). **-εύω**, *to be a serf* or *labourer*, Λαομέδοντι.. θητεύσαμεν εἰς ἐνιαυτόν Il.21.444, cf. Od.18.357; θητευέμεν ἄλλῳ, ἀνδρὶ παρ' ἀκλήρῳ 11.489, cf. E.*Alc*.6, *Cyc*.77 (lyr.), Pl.*Euthphr*.4c, *R*.359d, Phld.*Piet*.63; θ. ἐπὶ μισθῷ παρά τινι Hdt.8.137; θ. εἰς τὸ τεῖχος *labour* at it, Philostr.*Her*.12^a.3; θ. Παλλάδι καὶ Παφίῃ *serve*, *AP*5.292.12 (Paul. Sil.). **-ικός**, ή, όν, *of* or *for a hireling, menial*, ἔργον Arist.*Rh*.1367^{a}31; βάναυσος ἢ θ. βίος Id.*Pol*.1278^{a}21; -ωτέρα ἐργασία ib.1341^{b}14; θ. καὶ δουλικὸν πράττειν ib.1337^{b}21. 2. τὸ θ., = οἱ θῆτες, *the class of* θῆτες, ib.1274^{a}21, al.; θ. τελεῖν pay *on the assessment of a* θής at Athens, Id.*Ath*. 7.4, Lex ap.D.43.54; θ. τέλος Epigr.ap.Arist.*Ath*.7.4; τὸ θ. in an army, *servants, camp-followers*, etc., Arr.*Tact*.2.1. 3. *like a* θής, *servile*, πάντες οἱ κόλακες θ. Arist.*EN*1125^{a}2, cf. Luc.*Fug*.12.

θητόν· βωμόν, Hsch. **θῆττα**, ἡ, v. θῆσσα.

θητώνιον, τό, (θής, ὦνος) *hire, wages*, Suid.:—hence **θητωνέω**, *receive wages*, prob. in *IG*2^2.1013.54.

-θῐ, termin. of the locative case, Ἰλιόθι πρό Il.8.561; ἠῶθι πρό 11. 50. II. termin. of several locative Advs. formed from Substs., Adjs., and Prons., ἀγρόθι, οἴκοθι, ἄλλοθι, etc., cf. A.D.*Adv*.205.35, al.

θιαγών, όνος, ὁ, an Aetol. sacrificial cake, Nic.*Fr*.136, Hsch.

θιακχά· ἄνθη ἐν Σικυῶνι, Hsch. **θιάλλαι**· θῆμνες, Id. **θιάρατος** (i.e. *θεάρατος)· εὐκτός, Id. **θιαρός**, v. θεωρός. **θιάσαι**· χορεῦσαι, Id.

θῐᾰσ-αρχέω, *to be leader of a* θίασος, *OGI*529.5 (Sebastopolis, ii A.D.). **-άρχης**, ου, ὁ, *leader of a* θίασος, Luc.*Peregr*.11. **-εία**, ἡ, *Bacchic revel*, Procl.*H*.1.21. **-εύω**, *initiate into the* θίασος, *Epic.Alex.Adesp*. 9 i 2; ὅς με.. κόραις ἐθιάσευσ' E.*Ion*552; θ. χοροῖς Id.*Ba*.379 (lyr.):—Pass., -εύεται ψυχάν ib.75. II. *celebrate Bacchic rites*, Str.12.4. 3. **-ίτης** [σῑ], ου, ὁ, = θιασώτης, *IG*12(5).872.60 (Tenos), *SIG*1108 (Callatis), etc.:—fem. **-ῖτις**, ιδος, ἡ, Kastriotis Κατάλ. περιγραφικός, Γλυπτὰ τοῦ Ἐθνικοῦ Μουσ.(1908) No.1485 (pl., Nicaea, iii/iv A.D.). **-ῑτικός**, ή, όν, *belonging to a* θίασος, χρήματα *SIG*1108.9 (Callatis). **-ος** (proparox.), ὁ, *Bacchic revel, rout*, Hdt.4.79, E.*Ba*. 680, Ar.*Ra*.156, etc.; θ. ἄγειν E.*Ba*.115 (lyr.); τοὺς.. θ. ἄγων διὰ τῶν ὁδῶν τοὺς ἐστεφανωμένους τῷ μαράθῳ καὶ τῇ λεύκῃ D.18.260, cf. Ath. 5.185c, 8.362e. 2. *religious guild, confraternity*, *IG*2.986, 1663, 2^2. 1177, *SIG*1044.45 (Halic.), etc. II. generally, *company, troop*, used by Trag. in lyr., Κενταύρων E.*IA*1059; ἡλίκων Id.*IT*1146; Μουσῶν Ar.*Th*.41; ἐνόπλιος θ., of warriors, E.*Ph*.796; Κενταυρικὸς καὶ Σατυρικός Pl.*Plt*.303d; τοῦ σοῦ θ. of your *company*, X.*Mem*.2.1. 31; Ἀσιανῶν ἀκροαμάτων θ. Plu.*Ant*.24. III. *feast, banquet*, Id. 2.301f, *Cleom*.34. **-ώδης**, ες, *festive*, ἀμφίπολοι Βρομίου Nonn.*D*. 45.270. **-ών**, ῶνος, ὁ, *meeting-place of a* θίασος, Hsch. **-ώτης**, ου, ὁ, *member of a* θίασος, Ar.*Ra*.327 (lyr.), Is.9.30, *IG*2^2.1237.95; θ. καὶ ἐρανισταί Arist.*EN*1160^{a}19. 2. c. gen., θιασῶται τοῦ θεοῦ τούτου (sc. Ἔρωτος) *worshippers* of Love, X.*Smp*.8.1; Ἀφροδίτης οἱ θ. *IG*2^2.1261.23; ὁ ἐμὸς θ. my *fellow-reveller*, E.*Ba*.548 (lyr.); οἱ ἑαυτοῦ θ. *fellow-members* of his θ., *IG*2^2.1237.73. 3. of Bacchus, *leader of* θίασοι, *AP*9.524.9. 4. generally, *follower, disciple*, Luc.*Fug*.4; Πλάτωνος Them.*Or*.2.33c. **-ωτικός**, ή, όν, *belonging to a* θίασος, Arist.*Oec*.1346^{b}15, *BCH*50.233 (Thasos). **-ῶτις**, ιδος, ἡ, fem. of θιασώτης, Opp.*C*.4.298.

θίβεις· γυναῖκές τινες, Hsch.

θῖβις or **θίβις**, εως, ἡ, *basket* plaited from papyrus, *PPetr*.3 p.145 (iii B.C.), *PCair.Zen*.69 (iii B.C.), *PGrenf*.1.14.10 (ii B.C.), Lxx *Ex*.2. 3,6, Suid.: the form **θίβη** given by Hsch., Phot., v.l. in Suid., is false: **θῆβις** (sic) τῶν ἄρτων, correction of πρόθεσις τ. ἄ., *UPZ*149.21 (iii B.C.):—Hsch. also gives **θίβωνος** (extra ordinem)· κιβωτός (Cypr.), and **θίγωνος**· κιβωτοῦ. (Hebr. *tēbhāh*, from Egypt. *ḏbꜣt* 'box'.)

θιβρός or **θιμβρός** (v.l. in Nic.*Th*.35), ά, όν, *hot*, ὠεὰ θ. χελύνης (ἑψηθέντα ἐπ' ἀνθράκων Sch., cf. Hsch.), Nic.*Al*.555, cf. *Th*.35. II. *delicate, dainty, luxurious*, Κύπρις Call.*Fr*.267; θ. Σεμίραμις Euph. 81.—Only in Alex. poets. [ῐ in the Spartan pr. n. Θίβρων, Philosteph.Com.1.]

θιγάνα, ἡ, *cover, lid*, dub. in *Schwyzer*323 *C*39 (Delph.).

θιγγάνω, fut. προσ-θίξῃ prob. for -εις E.*Heracl*.652: 2 fut. τεθίξομαι Id.*Hipp*.1086: aor. 2 ἔθιγον Archil.71, E.*Ba*.304, etc.; Lacon. inf. σιγῆν Ar.*Lys*.1004:—Pass., aor. θιχθῆναι S.E.*M*.9.258:—*touch, handle*: abs., μὴ θίγγανε *IG*12(3).451 (Thera), etc.: usu. c. gen., οἴακος A.*Ag*. 663, etc.; χερσὶ or χερὶ θ. τινός, Id.*Th*.44, E.*Ba*.1318; δι' ὁσίων χειρῶν S.*OC*470: c. acc., χεῖρα (s.v.l.) Νεοβούλης θιγεῖν Archil. l.c.; χερσὶ γλαυκᾶς ἐλαίας θιγοῦ[σ' ὄζον] Limen.6 (dub. l.):—Pass., *to be touched*, Arist.*HA*495^{a}6. 2. *take hold of*, τινος S.*Aj*.1410 (anap.), etc.; θ. ὠλέναισιν τέκνου *embrace*, E.*Ph*.300 (lyr.); θ. γυναικός *have intercourse with*.., Id.*Hipp*.1044; θ. εὐνῆς ib.885, cf. S.*OC*329: abs., E.*El*.51; γλίχεται θιγεῖν καὶ συνεῖναι, of man's aspiration after God, Phld.*D*. 3.1. 3. *touch, attempt*, παντὸς.. λόγου κακοῦ γλώσσῃ θ. S.*Ph*.408; μή μοι λεπτῶν θίγγανε μύθων E.*Fr*.924; θ. πονηρίας Isyll.5; in hostile sense, *attack*, θηρός E.*Ba*.1183 (lyr.); σώματος τοῦ σοῦ Id.*IA*1351 (troch.). II. metaph., of the feelings, *touch*, θιγγάνει σέθεν τόδε; Id.*Hipp*.310; ψυχᾶς, φρενῶν, Id.*Alc*.108; πολλὰ θ. πρὸς ἧπαρ *reach* to the heart, A.*Ag*.432 (lyr.). 2. *touch upon*, in speaking or discussion, Arist.*Metaph*.988^{a}23, al., *Pol*.1323^{b}38; also of the mind, *apprehend*, νοῦς.. θιγγάνων καὶ νοῶν Id.*Metaph*.1072^{b}21, al. 3. *reach, win*, ἀγώνων Pi.*I*.1.18, etc.: also c. dat., θ. ἡσυχίᾳ, ἀρεταῖς, ψεύδει, Id. *P*.4.296, 8.24, 9.42; *reach, hit*, διαβολῇ θ. τινός Plu.*Alex*.10.—Not found in pure Att. Prose (ἅπτομαι being used), but used by X.*Cyr*.1. 3.5, al.: aor. 1 inf. θῖξαι v.l. for ψαῦσαι in Suid. s.v. θιγεῖν, θῖξαι v.l. for δεῖξαι in Arist.*EN*1111^{a}14.

θίγ-ημα [ῐ], ατος, τό, *touch*, prob. for φιλήματα in *AP*12.209 (Strat.). **-μα**, ατος, τό, = foreg., *IGRom*.4.503.11 (Pergam.). II. = μίασμα, Hsch. **-ωνος**, v. θῖβις.

θιδρακίνη, ἡ, = θριδακίνη, Hsch.

θίδραξ, v. θρίδαξ.

θιήϊον (θίκ- cod.)· θεῖον τὸ ὀρυκτόν (Cret.), Hsch. **θίημι**· ποιῶ, and **θιῆσαι**· ποιῆσαι, φιλῆσαι, Id. **θικέλιον**· τὴν γογγυλίδα (Lacon.), Id. **θίλα**· ὁ θημών, Id.

θιμβρός, ά, όν, v. θιβρός.

θινίον [θῐ], τό, Dim. of θίς I. 2, dub. in Phld.*D*.3.7. II. coined as etym. of ἀκροθίνιον, *AB*367.

θῖνος, Cret. for θεῖνος, *sacred*, *Leg.Gort*.10.42, *SIG*526.29 (iii B.C.), al.

θινώδης, ες, *like a sandy beach, sandy*, Str.8.3.14; θ. ἄγκιστρον an anchor *on the sand*, *Trag.Adesp*.379.

θίξις, εως, ἡ, *touching*, Hp.*Mul*.1.40, Arist.*GA*751^{a}19, *Ph*.202^{a}7, Gal.15.45, S.E.*P*.3.56, al.; ἄχρι τῆς Ἐρυθρᾶς θαλάσσης κατὰ θίξιν as far as the Red Sea, *which it touches*, Vett.Val.12.20, cf. 13.19; ὁ κατὰ θίξιν περισκυθισμός a scalp operation in which the edges of the wound were made to touch, *Arch.Pap*.4.270 (iii A.D.), cf. Archig.ap. Gal.12.577 (where θῆξιν). II. metaph., *apprehension* of the mind, Plot.5.3.10: pl., Procl. *in Prm*.p.628 S.

θῑπόβρωτος, v. θριπόβρωτος.

θίς [ῑ], θῑνός: ὁ Il.23.693, Od.12.45, Ar.*V*.696, Phld. (v. infr.); ἡ S.*Ant*.591, *Ph*.1124, Arist.*HA*548^{b}6, Call.*Fr*.126, D.H.3.44:—*heap*, πολὺς ὀστεόφιν θὶς Od.12.45; θῖνες νεκρῶν A.*Pers.*818: metaph., θὶς πημάτων Lyc.812; esp. of *sand-banks*, θῖνες ψάμμου Hdt.3.26; ἄμμου, γῆς, Plu.*Fab.*6, *Art.*18; τοὺς ἐν ἄμμῳ θῖνας Phld.*Piet.*20; ἐν ταῖς θ. Arist.*HA*548b6, cf. 537a25; θῖνας καὶ ψάμμους Porph.*Abst.*4.21; of the *sandy deserts* of Libya, A.R.4.1384; Νασαμώνων αὔλια καὶ δολιχὰς θ. Call.*Fr.*126. 2. usu. in Hom., etc., *beach, shore*, freq. in oblique cases, παρὰ θῖνα.. θαλάσσης Il.1.34, cf. Od.6.236, etc.; παρὰ θῖν' ἁλὸς ἀτρυγέτοιο Il.1.316, cf. 350, etc.; alone, ἐπὶ θινί Od.7.290; παρὰ θῖνα 9.46; later θῖν' ἁλός Ar.*V.*1521 (parod.); πόντου S.*Ph.*1124 (lyr.); θαλάσσας E.*Andr.*109 (eleg.); θαλαττία D.H.3.44. b. *sand-bank, bar* at the mouth of a river, Plb.4.41.6: pl., *banks* of a stream, D.S. 1.30. 3. *sand* or *mud* at the bottom of the sea, οἶδμα.. κυλίνδει βυσσόθεν κελαινὰν θῖνα S.*Ant.*591: metaph., ὥς μου τὸν θῖνα ταράττεις, i.e. trouble *the very bottom* of my heart, Ar.*V.*696, v. Sch. 4. *shore-weed*, θῖν' ἐν φυκιόεντι Il.23.693, cf. Arist.*HA*598a5; θινὸς ὄζειν ib.620a15. II. ἄκρης [πόλιος] θὶς *the temple that crowns* the Acropolis, dub. in Call.*Fr.anon.*332.

θίσβη· σορός, Suid. **θισπῶσαι·** εἰκάσαι, Hsch.

θιώτης (sc. ἄρτος?), ὁ, a kind of food (loaf?), *PFay.*117.10 (ii A.D.).

θλᾰδί-ας, ου, ὁ, *eunuch*, Lxx *Le.*22.24, Ph.2.261. **-άω**, *make* one *an eunuch*, Hsch. s. v. φλαδιᾶν.

θλάσις [ᾰ], εως, ἡ, (θλάω) *crushing, bruising*, Arist.*Mete.*386a18, *Pr.*890a2, Thphr.*Lass.*18, Dsc.2.170 (pl.), S.E.*M.*6.40.

θλάσμα, ατος, τό, *bruise*, Arist.*Mir.*841b11, Lxx *Am.*6.12(11), Ph. 2.488, Dsc.2.170; = κοίλωμα ἄνευ ῥήξεως, *dint*, Sor.*Fract.*9.

θλάσπις, εως, Ion. ιος, ἡ, (θλάω) *shepherd's purse, Capsella bursa-pastoris*, Hp.*Mul.*1.78, al.:—also **θλάσπι**, τό, Dsc.2.156, Plin.*HN* 27.140:—Dim. **θλασπίδιον**, τό, Ps.-Dsc.2.156.

θλάστ-ης, ου, ὁ, = ἐμβρυοθλάστης, Hp.ap.Gal.19.104. **-ικός**, ή, όν, *able to crush, crushing*, Arist.*Pr.*884b35. **-ός**, ή, όν, *crushed, bruised*, ἐλάα Ar.*Fr.*391, Diph.14.5, cf. *PSI*5.535.52. 2. *capable of being crushed* or *compressed*, opp. θραυστός (q. v.), Arist.*HA*523b7, cf. *Mete.*386a25.

θλάττω, late form of sq., f. l. in Gal.*UP*10.6, cf. Paul.Aeg.6.91 (Pass.).

θλάω, imper. θλῆ Herod. (v. infr.); inf. θλᾶν Gal.*UP*13.8; part. θλῶσα ib.13.3: 3 sg. impf. ἔθλα (συγκατ-) Macho ap.Ath.8.348f: fut. θλάσω [ᾰ] (ἐν-) Hp.*Int.*44: aor. ἔθλᾰσα, Ep. θλάσσα (v. infr.):—**Pass.**, fut. θλασθήσομαι Gal.*UP*12.15: aor. ἐθλάσθην Hp.*Ulc.*6: pf. τέθλασμαι (συν-) Alex.270, Ph.1.609, Theoc.22.45:—*crush, bruise*, θλάσσε δέ οἱ κοτύλην Il.5.307; ὀστέα δ' εἴσω ἔθλασεν Od.18.97; οὔτ' ἔρρηξε βαλὼν οὔτ' ἔθλασε Hes.*Sc.*140; [φωνὴν] ὥσπερ θλῶσαν [τὴν ἀκοήν] S.E.*M.*6.40: sens. obsc., αὐτὸς τὰ σαυτοῦ θλῆ Herod.2.83:—Pass., Arist.*Pr.*890a3, Herod.3.44; τεθλασμένος οὔατα πυγμαῖς Theoc. l. c.; ῥάβδος -μένη Lxx *4Ki.*18.21. 2. *overload* (?), τὰς ἅλως *PFay.*112.20 (i A.D.). 3. metaph., *oppress*, Lxx *Jd.*10.8, al. (Cf. φλάω.)

θλῖβ-ερός, ά, όν, (θλίβω) *chafing, rubbing*, Paul.Aeg.6.106. II. *oppressive*, Just.*Nov.*135.1. **-ή**, ἡ, *a rubbing*, Gal.18(2).923. **-ίας**, ου, ὁ, = θλαδίας, Str.13.4.1. **-ω** [ῑ], Ar.*Pax* 1239, etc.: fut. θλίψω (ἀπο-) E.*Cyc.*237: aor. ἔθλιψα Pl.*Ti.*60c, Call.*Del.*35: pf. τέθλῖφα Crobyl.4 (cj.), Plb.18.24.3:—**Med.**, fut. θλίψομαι (v. infr.):—**Pass.**, fut. θλῐβήσομαι v.l. in Sor.1.33: aor. 1 ἐθλίφθην Pl.*Ti.*91a, Arist.*Pr.* 925b20: aor. 2 part. θλῐβείς ib.13, v.l. in Dsc.3.7 (cf. subj. ἐκφλῐβῇ Hp. *Loc.Hom.*9): pf. τέθλιμμαι Arist.*Pr.*925b14, *AP*7.472.5 (Leon.):—*squeeze, chafe*, θλίβει τὸν ὄρρον [ὁ θώραξ] Ar.*Pax* 1239, cf. *Lys.*314; τοὺς ὄφεις θλίβων D.18.260; ὅπου με θλίβει where [the shoe] *pinches*, Plu.2.141a: metaph., δούλης ὦτα νωθρίῃ θλίβει Herod.4.53: abs., *exercise pressure*, Plot.3.6.6:—Pass., of a person heavy-laden, ὡς θλίβομαι! Ar.*Ra.*5, cf. *V.*1289:—Med., πολλῇς φλιῇσι παραστὰς θλίψεται (v.l. φλίψεται) ὤμους he *will rub his* shoulders against many doorposts, of a beggar, Od.17.221: χείλεα θλίβειν, of kissing, Theoc.20.4. II. *compress, straiten*, Pl.*Ti.*60c; *reduce, compress*, εἰς τὸ μὴ ὂν τὰ ὄντα θλίβοντες Epicur.*Ep.*1 p.16 U.:—Pass., *to be compressed*, Pl.*Ti.*91a; ὥστε ἐξωθεῖσθαι τὸ ἧσσον θλιβόμενον ὑπὸ τοῦ μᾶλλον θλιβομένου Archim.*Fluit.*1 *Prooem.*; θλιβομένα καλύβα *a small, close* hut, Theoc. 21.18; ὁδὸς τεθλιμμένη, opp. εὐρύχωρος, *Ev.Matt.*7.14; βίος τεθλ. a *scanty* subsistence, D.H.8.73, cf. *AP*7.472.5 (Leon.). 2. metaph., *oppress, afflict, distress*, ἀνάγκη ἔθλιψέ τινα Call.*Del.*35; θ. καὶ λυμαίνεσθαι τὸ μακάριον Arist.*EN*1100b28; θ. τὰς πόλεις τοῖς ὀψωνίοις *SIG* 700.25 (Macedonia, ii B.C.); *press hard* in battle, Plb.18.24.3:—Pass., θ. διὰ τὸν πόλεμον Arist.*Pol.*1307a1; ὑπό τινων *SIG*685.39 (ii B.C.); ὑπὸ τῆς ἀδοξίας Phld.*Lib.*p.61 O.—Once in Hom., never in Trag. **-ώδης**, ες, *oppressive*, Aq.*Ge.*32.7(8).

θλιμμός, ὁ, = θλῖψις, Lxx *Ex.*3.9.

θλιπτικός, ή, όν, *due to pressure*, πάθημα Gal.8.949. Adv. -κῶς *by pressure*, S.E.*M.*10.83.

θλῖψις, εως, ἡ, *pressure*, Arist.*Mete.*382a13, *Pr.*890a2; τῶν νεφῶν Epicur.*Ep.*2 p.49 U.; ἀντέρεισις καὶ θ. Str.1.3.6; of the pulse, Ruf. ap.Orib.8.24.61, cf. Gal.7.306; θ. στομάχου Orib.*Fr.*42; ὑστερικαὶ θ. Sor.1.42. 2. *crushing, castration*, πώλων *Hippiatr.*20. 3. metaph., *oppression, affliction*, Lxx *Ge.*35.3, al., *BGU*1139.4 (i B.C.), *Act.Ap.*14.22 (pl.), al., Vett.Val.71.16 (pl.), *POxy.*939.13 (iv A.D.).

θνάσκω, θνᾱτός, Dor. for θνήσκω, θνητός.

θνησ-είδιον, τό, *carcase of an animal*, ἐσθίειν κενέβρειόν τε καὶ θ. Ael. *NA*6.2 (θν. preferred to κ. by Phryn.*PS* p.75 B.); ἐσθῆτα ἀπὸ θνησειδίων φορεῖν Philostr.*VA*8.7.4; ἅψασθαι θνησειδίων Porph.*Abst.*4. 16, cf. D.L.8.33:—Aeol. **θνᾱσίδιον** *Schwyzer* 633.14 (Eresus, ii/i B.C.). **-ῐμαῖος**, α, ον, neut. as Subst. **-αῖον**, τό, = foreg., Lxx *3Ki.*13.25, al.; τῶν θ. οὐχ ἅψεσθε ib.*Le.*11.8, cf. Hierocl. *in CA*26 p.480 M.

θνῆσις, εως, ἡ, *mortality*, in a plague, Ruf.*Fr.*69; πολλὴ θ. γέγονε *Stud.Pal.*22.338 (i A.D.); νηπίων *Cat.Cod.Astr.*7.126.

θνήσκω (with ι *IG*2.2477.7,10,2494, Ἀρχ.Ἐφ.1910.73; θνείσκ- *IG* 2.4040b; [ἀποθν]ῄισκειν Pl.*Phdr.* in *PPetr.*1 p.18 (iii B.C.), but θνήσκω Did.ap.*EM*452.29, freq. in codd.), Aeol. **θναίσκω** Hdn.Gr.2.79, Dor. **θνᾱσκω** *Sammelb.*6754.22 (iii B.C.): fut. θᾰνοῦμαι Simon.85.9, S.*Ant.* 462, etc.; Ep. inf. -έεσθαι Il.4.12; later θνήξομαι *AP*9.354 (Leon.), Polyaen.5.2.22 codd.: aor. 2 ἔθᾰνον, Ep. θάνον Od.11.412, al.; inf. Ep. and Ion. θανέειν, as always in Hom., exc. Il.7.52, θανέμεν Pi.*P.*4.72: pf. τέθνηκα Il.18.12, etc.; subj. τεθνήκω Th.8.74: plpf. ἐτεθνήκειν Antipho 5.70, Lys.19.48; 3 pl. -ήκεσαν And.1.52: short forms of pf., 3 dual τέθνᾰτον X.*An.*4.1.19, 1 pl. τέθνᾰμεν Pl.*Grg.*493a, 3 pl. τεθνᾶσι Il.22.52, etc.; 3 pl. plpf. ἐτέθνᾰσαν Antipho 5.70, And.1.59, X.*HG*6.4.16; imper. τέθνᾰθι Il.22.365, τεθνάτω 15.496, *IG*1².10, Pl. *Lg.*933e, etc.; opt. τεθναίην Il.18.98, etc.; inf. τεθνάναι [ᾰ] Semon. 3, Hdt.1.31, Ar.*Ra.*1012, Pl.Com.68, Th.8.92, etc., τεθνᾶναι dub. l. in Mimn.2.10, A.*Ag.*539; Ep. τεθνάμεναι, -άμεν, Il.24.225, 15.497, etc.; Aeol. τεθνάκην Sapph.2.15; part. τεθνεώς Hdt.9.120, Ar.*Av.* 476, etc., fem. τεθνεῶσα Lys.31.22, D.40.27 (τεθνηκυῖα Hippon.29, E. *Or.*109), neut. τεθνεός Hdt.1.112, Hp.*Nat.Mul.*32 (τεθνηκός Pl.*Phd.* 71d, pl. τεθνεῶτα 72c); gen. τεθνεῶτος, etc., Hdt.5.68, etc. (once in Hom., dat. τεθνεῶτι Od.19.331); poet. τεθνεότος Archel.ap.Antig. *Mir.*89, Q.S.7.65; Dor. τεθνᾱότα Pi.*N.*10.74; Ep. τεθνηώς (v.l. -ειώς) Il.17.161, -ηυῖα Od.4.734, (κατα-) 11.141; gen. τεθνηῶτος Il.9. 633, etc.; also τεθνηότος 17.435, Od.15.23, al. [τεθνεῶτι is trisyll. Od.19.331, τεθνεώτων E.*Supp.*272 (hex.): disyll. forms are written in later Gr., nom. τεθνώς *BCH*18.438 (Argilus); gen. sg. τεθνῶτος *SIG*799.13 (Cyzicus, i A.D.); dat. sg. τεθνῶτι *Papers of the Amer. School* 3.334 (Pisid.); fem. τεθνώσῃ (and gen. pl. τεθνήτων) *Ath.Mitt.* 50.134 (Macedonia); acc. pl. fem. τεθνώσας Babr.45.9]: from τέθνηκα arose fut. τεθνήξω Ar.*Ach.*325, A.*Ag.*1279 (censured as archaic by Luc.*Sol.*7), later τεθνήξομαι Diogenian.Epicur.1.28, 3.52, Luc.*Pisc.* 10, Ael.*NA*2.46; part. τεθνηξόμενος Lib.*Ep.*438.7.—The simple Verb is regularly used in early Prose in pf. and plpf.; for pres., fut., and aor. the compd. ἀποθνήσκω is substituted: θνήσκει v.l. in Hp. *Mul.*1.9, σάρκες θνήσκουσι *Art.*69, ἔθνησκον Th.2.47, al., θνησκόντων ib.53, θνήσκοι Pl.*Phd.*72d, θνήσκομεν Epicur.*Ep.*1 p.20 U.: aor. part. θανών, subj. θάνῃ, *IG*12(5).593.2,20,23 (Iulis, v B.C.), *Berl.Sitzb.*1927. 166 (Cyrene), Phld.*Herc.*1649.4: aor. inf. θανεῖν ib.1418.13:—in pres. and impf., *die*, as well of natural as of violent death; in aor. and pf., *to be dead* (cf. τί τοὺς θανόντας οὐκ ἐᾷς τεθνηκέναι; Eup.12.3 D.; τέθνηκ' ἔγωγε πρὶν θανεῖν κακῶν ὕπο E.*Hec.*431), θανεῖν καὶ πότμον ἐπισπεῖν Il.7.52, etc.; ζωὸς ἠὲ θανών alive or *dead*, Od.4.553, cf. 15.350; ἢ ἤδη τέθνηκε 4.834; ὡς ἄμεινον εἴη τεθνάναι μᾶλλον ἢ ζώειν Hdt.1.31, cf. 7.46; τεθνάναι κρεῖττον ἤ.. D.9.65, cf. 10.25; ἄξιος τεθνάναι Ar.*Ra.* 1012, etc.; τεθνάτω *let* him *be put to death*, *IG*1².10.29; ἄτιμος τεθ. Lex ap.D.9.44: freq. in part., νέκυος πέρι τεθνηῶτος Il.18.173; νεκρὸν.. τεθνηῶτα a *dead* corpse, Od.12.10; οἱ τεθνηκότες, οἱ θανόντες, *the dead*, E.*Hec.*278, Eup. l. c., etc.; οὔτε τεθνεῶτα οὔτε ζῶντα Hdt.4.14; οἴχεται θανών (v. οἴχομαι); θανὼν φρουδος (v. φροῦδος); θανόντι συνθανεῖν S.*Tr.*798, *Fr.*953, cf. E.*Supp.*1007 (lyr.); ὁ θανών, opp. ὁ κτανών, S. *Ph.*336: pres. with pf. sense, θνήσκουσι γάρ, for τεθνήκασι, Id.*OT* 118, cf. E.*Hec.*695 (lyr.), *Ba.*1041 (lyr.), etc. 2. used like a pass. Verb, χερσὶν ὑπ' Αἴαντος θανέειν *to fall* by his hand, Il.15.289; θ. ὑπό τινος Pl.*Ep.*329c, Arist.*HA*625a16; ἔκ τινος Pi.*P.*4.72, S.*OT*1454; πρός τινος ib.292, E.*Hec.*773; θεοῖς τέθνηκε S.*Aj.*970: freq. c. dat. instrumenti, θ. χερί, δορί, Id.*OC*1388, A.*Th.*959 (lyr.); φαρμάκοισι E. *Fr.*464; also ἐν βρόχῳ A.*Ch.*558; τεθνάναι τῷ δέει, τ. τῷ φόβῳ, c. acc., *to be in mortal fear of*, D.4.45, 19.81, cf. Arr.*An.*7.9.4; προοίμιον σκοτεινὸν καὶ τεθνηκὸς δειλίᾳ Aeschin.2.34; θ. ἐπί τινι *to die* leaving one as heir, Luc.*DMort.*7.1. II. metaph., of things, *perish*, θνάσκει σιγαθὲν καλὸν ἔργον Pi.*Fr.*121; ἐσλῶν ὑπὸ χαρμάτων πῆμα θνάσκει.. δαμασθέν Id.*O.*2.19; λόγοι θνῄσκοντες μάτην A.*Ch.*846; θ. πίστις S. *OC*611; τὸ τρύβλιον τέθνηκέ μοι Ar.*Ra.*986 (lyr.): in Prose, τέθνηκε τὸ τοὺς ἀδικοῦντας μισεῖν D.19.289; τεθνηκός τι φθέγξασθαι D.C.40.54; τεθνηκὸς ὁρᾶν Callistr.*Stat.*14; τὸ τεθνηκὸς ὁ λίθος ὑπεδύετο ib.2.

θνητάδιος, sine expl., Hdn.Gr.2.924: **θνητίδια**, = νεκριμαῖα, Hsch. (θνιτ- cod.).

θνητο-γᾰμία, ἡ, *marriage with a mortal*, Eust.20.17. **-γενής**, Dor. **θνᾱτ-**, ές, *of mortal race*, S.*Ant.*835 (anap.), E.*HF*799 (lyr.). **-ειδής**, ές, *of mortal nature*, Pl.*Phd.*86a, Plu.2.1002c, Jul.*Or.*6.184a, etc.

θνητός, ή, όν, also ός, όν E.*Ion* 973, *IA*901, 1396: Dor. **θνᾱτός** (v. infr.): Aeol. **θνᾶτος** Sapph.*Supp.*13.7: (θνήσκω):—*liable to death, mortal*, opp. ἀθάνατος, freq. in Hom., Od.5.213, al.; θ. ἄνδρες Hes. *Th.*967; οὐδὲν.. θνητὸν ἐόν Hdt.8.98; ζῷα πάντα θ. καὶ φυτά Pl.*Sph.* 265c: as Subst., θνητοί *mortals*, Od.19.593, etc.; θνηταί *mortal women*, 5.213; πάντων τῶν θ. of all *mortal creatures*, Hdt.1.216, 2.68; εἴ τις φθόγγος (φθόγγον cod., but θ. is only used of living persons) εἰσακούεται θνητῶν παρ' Ἅιδῃ E.*HF*491: Comp., ἐν θνητῷ ὄντες, ἔτι θνητοτέρους ἑαυτοὺς ποιοῦντες Porph.*Abst.*4.20: Sup., θνητότατος πάντων Plot.5.1.1. 2. of things, *befitting mortals, human*, ἔργματα E.*Ba.* 1069; θνατὰ θνατοῖσι πρέπει Pi.*I.*5(4).16; θνατὰ χρὴ τὸν θνατόν.. φρονεῖν Epich.[263], cf. S.*Tr.*473; τὸ δαιμόνιον μεταξύ ἐστι θεοῦ τε καὶ θνητοῦ Pl.*Smp.*202e.

θνητότης, ητος, ἡ, *mortality*, Diog.Oen.36, Phlp.*in APo.*400.28.

θνητόψῡχος, ον, *maintaining the mortality of the soul*, Tz.*H.*8.222.

θοάζω (A), (θοός (A)) trans., *move quickly, ply rapidly*, πτέρυγας E.

IT 1142 (lyr.); τίς ὅδ' ἀγὼν .. θοάζων σε; what task is thus *hurrying* thee *on?* Id.*Or.*335; θοάζω Βρομίῳ πόνον ἡδύν *urge* it *on,* Id.*Ba.*65; θ. σῖτα γένυσι *dispatch* it *quickly,* Id.*HF*382 (lyr.). 2. intr., *move quickly, rush, dart,* θοάζων αἰθέρος ἄνω καπνός Id.*Or.*1542; ἐν δὲ δασκίοις ὄρεσι θ. Id.*Ba.*219; θ. δρόμῳ Id.*Tr.*307; κῆτος θοάζον ἐξ Ἀτλαντικῆς ἁλός Id.*Fr.*145. (Cf. θέω, θοός (A).)

θοάζω (B), = θάσσω, *sit,* σοφίης ἐπ' ἄκροισι Emp.4.8; ὑπ' ἀρχᾶς οὔτινος θοάζων [Ζεὺς] κρατύνει A.*Supp.*595; τίνας ποθ' ἕδρας τάσδε μοι θοάζετε; why *are ye in* this *suppliant posture?* S.*OT*2, cf. Plu.2.22e. (Cf. ἐπιθοάζω, θόωκος, θῶκος; v. θάσσω.)

θοάζω (C), v. θωάζω.

θόαξος· Ἀπόλλων, Hsch.

θοάς, ἄδος, ἡ, fem. Adj. *fleet, swift,* prob. in Pi.*Fr.*107.7.

θόασμα, ατος, τό, *a place for dancing,* etc., Orph.*H.*49.6.

θοδράκιον, v. θρόδαξ.

θοηρός· τεταραγμένος (i.e. θολερός), Hsch., *EM*453.20. **θοιά,** ἡ, *pair of mules,* Hsch., Theognost.*Can.*20. **θοίηβος,** ὁ, = θαῦμα, Cyr.; cf. θῆβος.

θοιν-άζω, rare form for θοινάω, X.*Ages.*8.7, Ael.*Fr.*267. **-ᾱμα,** ατος, τό, *meal, feast,* E.*Or.*814, *Ion* 1495 (both lyr.), Posidon.12 J. **-αρμόστρια,** ἡ, *mistress of the banquet,* cult-title, esp. in the worship of Demeter and Kore, in Laconia and Messenia, *IG*5(1).584,1498, etc.: spelt θυν- ib.583, σειναρμόστρηα ib.229. **-ᾱτήρ,** ῆρος, ὁ, *one who gives a feast,* χαλεπὸς θ. *lord of a* horrid *feast,* A.*Ag.*1502 (anap.). **-ᾱτήριον,** τό, = θοίνη, E.*Rh.*515. **-ᾱτικός,** ή, όν, *of* or *for a feast,* X.*Oec.*9.7 (v.l. -ητικός). **-άτωρ** [ᾱ], ορος, ὁ, *feaster,* E.*Ion* 1206, 1217. **-άω,** *feast on, eat,* δελφῖνες ἐθοίνων ἰχθῦς dub. l. in Hes.*Sc.*212. 2. Pass., *to be feasted upon,* i.e. *sacrificed,* ὗς τέλεος θοινῆται *IG*12(1).905 (Rhodes). II. *feast, entertain,* φίλους E.*Ion* 982; τὸ δεῖπνον, τό μιν ἐκεῖνος σαρξὶ τοῦ παιδὸς ἐθοίνησε (v.l. -ισε) the feast, which he *gave* him *upon* his son's flesh, Hdt.1.129. 2. more freq. in Med. and Pass., fut. -άσομαι E.*El.*836, *Cyc.*550, -ήσομαι (ἐκ-) A.*Pr.*1025 codd.: aor. 1 ἐθοινήθην (v. infr.): aor. 1 Med. -ησάμην Nonn.*D.*5.331, *AP*9.244 (Apollonid.): pf. τεθοίνᾱμαι E.*Cyc.*377 (prob.). a. abs., *to be feasted, feast, banquet,* once in Hom., ἐς δ' αὐτοὺς προτέρω ἄγε θοινηθῆναι lead them in *to feast,* Od.4.36; παρὰ κλαίουσι θοινᾶσθαι E.*Alc.*542; θ. καλῶς Cratin.164. b. c. acc., *feast on,* μῶν τεθοίναται ἑταίρους; E.*Cyc.*377; σὲ ὕστερον θοινάσομαι ib.550; θ. τὰ ζῷα Porph.*Abst.*2.2: c. acc. cogn., θ. παστήρια E.*El.*836: c. gen., ἅλις λεόντων ἐστί μοι θοινωμένῳ Id.*Cyc.*248; θοινήσατο θῆρης *AP*9.244 (Apollonid.); of an *eating* sore, σάρκα θοινᾶται ποδός E.*Fr.*792, cf. Arist.*Po.*1458^{b}24: **-η,** Dor. **θοίνα** (later **θοῖνα** Lxx *Wi.*12.6, perh. to be read in Epich.148.1), ἡ, *meal, feast,* Hes.*Sc.*114, Hdt.1.119, 9.82, A.*Fr.*350.7, etc.: in pl., Id.*Pr.*530 (lyr.), B.*Fr.*18; τὰς θ. κὰτ τὰν ὥραν ἀπάγεσθαι *Michel* 995 *D* 50; θοίνης δὲ καὶ εἰλαπίνῃσι Thgn.239; ἐκ θοίνας after *dinner,* Epich.148.2; εἰς θ. καλεῖν τινα E.*Ion* 1140; ἐπὶ θοίνην ἰέναι Pl.*Phdr.*247a; παρακαλεῖν ἐπὶ τὴν θ. Arist.*Fr.*549; σκευαζομένης θ. Pl.*Tht.*178d, cf. Arist.*Pol.*1282^{a}22; τραπέζας ἱερὰς πρεπούσης θ. γεμίζων *OGI*383.146 (Commagene, i B.C.); ἐν θ. λέγειν τινά to count as a guest, and generally to take into account, Pl.*Lg.*649a: metaph., Id.*Sph.*251b, *Phdr.*236e, X.*Cyr.*4.2.39. II. *food,* πτανοῖς E.*Ion* 504, cf. Tim.*Pers.*150; θ. παντοδαπή Parth.12.2. 2. *feeding upon,* c. gen., τῶν σαρκῶν Porph.*Abst.*2.47. (Cf. θῶσθαι.) **-ήτωρ,** ορος, ὁ, = θοινάτωρ, *AP*7.241 (Antip. Sid.). **-ίζω,** v.l. for θοινάω (q.v.).

θοινοδοτέω, *entertain at a banquet, Supp.Epigr.*3.774 (Crete, i B.C./i A.D.).

θοῖτο, for θεῖτο, 3 opt. aor. 2 Med. of τίθημι.

θολερεῖν· ταραχίζεσθαι, Hsch.

θολερ-ός, ά, όν, (θολός) *muddy, foul, turbid,* opp. καθαρός or λαμπρός, prop. of troubled water, Hdt.4.53, Hp.*Aër.*8, Th.2.102; θ. καὶ πηλώδης Pl.*Phd.*113b: metaph., λαμπρὸν δὲ θολερῷ δῶμα συμμείξας E.*Supp.*222; θ. οὖρα Hp.*Epid.*1.7; ἀήρ Pl.*Ti.*58d (Sup. -ώτατος); αἷμα Arist.*Somn.Vig.*458^{a}14 (Sup.); χυμοί Thphr.*CP*6.3.4 (Comp.); νεφέλαι *AP*9.277 (Antiphil.); χρώς Ael.*NA*14.9; πλίνθος Theoc.16.62; δύσμορφον ἢ ὗς καὶ θολερόν Plu.2.670a. 2. θ. πνεῦμα dub. l. in Hp.*Prorrh.*1.39 (v. θαλερός). II. metaph., *troubled by passion* or *madness,* θολεροὶ λόγοι *troubled* words of passion (compared to a torrent), A.*Pr.*885 (anap.); θολερῷ χειμῶνι νοσήσας with *turbid* storm of madness, S.*Aj.*206 (anap.); θολερῷ κυνόδοντι with *passionate* tooth, Nic.*Th.*130 codd. (θαλερῷ cj. Schneider). Adv. -ρῶς dub. in *Com.Adesp.*865. **-ότης,** ητος, ἡ, *turbidity,* Hp.*Epid.*2.3.11.

θολερόφρον· μέγα, Hsch.

θολερώδης, ες, dub. l. for θολώδης, Thphr.*Ign.*24.

θολία (Lacon. **σαλία** Hsch.), ἡ, (θόλος) *conical hat with broad brim,* or perh. *parasol,* Theoc.15.39. II. *chest with conical lid,* Poll.10.138; cf. θαλιοποιοί.

θολικός, ή, όν, *with a dome,* στοά Suid. s. v. Δαμιανός.

θολο-ειδής, ές, *like a* θόλος, Callix.1, Str.4.4.3; of the Roman Pantheon, D.C.53.27. Adv. -δῶς, κοιλανθεῖσα Dsc.4.153, cf. D.L.2.9. 2. *like a* θολία, cj. Scal. for θηλοειδῆ in Thphr.*HP*3.9.6 (fort. θολιοειδής). **-μῐγής,** ές, *mixed with dirt,* Onat.ap.Stob.1.1.39.

θόλος, ἡ, *round building with conical roof, rotunda,* Od.22.442, al., cf. Hsch. 2. at Athens, *the Rotunda,* in which the Prytaneis, etc., dined, Pl.*Ap.*32c, And.1.45, D.19.249, Arist.*Ath.*43.3, Alexand.Com.9, Paus.1.5.1; a similar building at Epidaurus, Id.2.27.3; at Magnesia on Maeander, *SIG*589.43 (ii B.C.). II. θόλος, ὁ, in public baths, *vaulted vapour-bath, PMagd.*33.3 (iii B.C.), Asclep.Myrl.ap.Ath.11.501d, Alciphr.1.23, *POxy.*2145.6 (ii A.D.), *PMag.Osl.*1.75. 2. *bandage* for the head, invented by Diocles, Heliod.ap.Orib.48.25 tit.

θολ-ός (A), ὁ, *mud, dirt,* esp. in water, Arist.*Fr.*311. 2. *menses,* Orph.*L.*490. II. *ink of the cuttle-fish,* Hp.*Morb.*2.73, Arist.*HA*524^{a}13, al. (v.l. θορόν in 544^{a}4). 2. *the vessel in which this ink is retained,* Id.*PA*679^{a}1, 681^{b}26.—On the accent, v. Hdn.Gr.1.154. **-ός** (B), ή, όν, = θολερός, Ath.10.420d, Olymp.*in Mete.*127.13, cf. Hsch. **-όω,** *make turbid,* prop. of water, θ. ἅπαντα, of the cuttle-fish, Antiph.26.2; of fishermen, Arist.*Fr.*311:—Pass., τεθολωμένα ὕδατα Hp.*Aër.*7; τεθ. ἀήρ Philyll.20. 2. metaph., θολοῖ δὲ καρδίαν E.*Alc.*1067; τεθολωμένος *confounded* by joy, Pherecr.115; θολοῦσθαί τι τῶν σπλάγχνων Philostr.*VA*8.7; γένος..τεθολωμένον γειτόνημα Procop.*Goth.*4.19. II. *soak,* σπόγγοις διὰ ψυχροῦ ὕδατος..τεθολωμένοις Orib.8.6.36. **-ώδης,** ες, *muddy, turbid,* of water, Hp.*Aër.*8 (Sup. -έστατος); ἐν τοῖς ἀμμώδεσι ἢ θολώδεσι Arist.*HA*620^{b}16; also θ. καπνός Vett.Val.345.21; πῦρ Iamb.*Myst.*2.4. **-ωσις,** εως, ἡ, *making turbid, troubling,* esp. of water, Arist.*PA*679^{a}7; also ἀέρος Gal.16.609.

θολωτός, ή, όν, *built like a* θόλος, τεῖχος Procop.*Aed.*4.11.

θονανία· ὀξεῖα, Hsch. (fort. θοὴ ἀνία).

θοός (A), ή, όν, (θέω) poet. Adj. *quick, nimble,* epith. of Ares and warriors, Il.5.430,571, 16.422,494, etc.: c. inf., θ. μάχεσθαι 5.536; of things, χείρ 12.306; βέλος Od.22.83; ἅρμα Il.17.458; μάστιξ ib.430; νῆες 14.410, etc.; νηυσὶ θοῇσι.. πεποιθότες ὠκείῃσι Od.7.34; νὺξ *swift* night, Il.10.394, Od.12.284, Hes.*Th.*481; θοὴν ἀλεγύνετε δαῖτα partake of a *hasty* meal, i.e. *in haste,* Od.8.38; later, of animals, Pi.*P.*4.17, E.*Ba.*977 (lyr.); also μάχαι Pi.*P.*8.26; γλῶσσα Id.*N.*7.72; θοὰ βάξις A.*Ag.*476 (lyr.); θ. εἰρεσίας ζυγόν S.*Aj.*249 (lyr.), cf. Orph.*A.*1037; πτέρυξ E.*Ion* 123 (lyr.), cf. A.*Pr.*129 (lyr.); σάκος A.R.1.743; ἀσπίδας.. θοὸν ἔχμα βολάων Id.4.201; πνοαί, αὖραι, E.*Andr.*479 (lyr.), *Tr.*454 (troch.): used adverbially with Verbs of motion, ἐκπρολιποῦσα θοὸν δόμον *quickly, in haste,* Antim.71 (expld. by *An.Ox.* from τίθημι); θοὰν νύμφαν ἄγαγες S.*Tr.*857 (lyr.). Adv. -ῶς *quickly, in haste,* Il.3.325, B.14.59, A.*Pr.*1060 (anap.), *Pers.*398, Hp.*Mul.*2.132; θοώτερον A.R.3.1406; *soon,* Od.15.216.

θοός (B), ή, όν, *pointed, sharp,* νῆσοι, name of certain of the Echinades (acc. to Str.8.3.26), Od.15.299; so later θ. γόμφοι, ὀδόντες, πελέκεις, A.R.2.79, 3.1281, 4.1683; ξίφος *AP*9.157; cf. sq.

θοόω, (θοός B) *make sharp* or *pointed,* Od.9.327; τεθοωμένος Nic.*Th.*228. II. metaph., in Pass., ἐν πυρὶ φωνὴν τεθοωμένος Hermesian.7.11; λύσσῃ τεθοωμένος Opp.*H.*1.557, 2.525.

θοραῖος, α, ον, (θορός) *containing the semen,* πτηρίν Nic.*Th.*586; ὁ θοραῖος, epith. of Apollo as *god of growth and increase,* Lyc.352.

θοράνας· τὸ ἔξω (Paph.), Hsch.

Θοράτης, ὁ, title of Apollo in Laconia, Hsch. (-τις cod.).

θόρε, θορεῖν, v. θρῴσκω.

θορή, ἡ, = θορός, Hdt.3.101, Alcmaeon *Fr.*3 D.

Θορῐκόνδε, Adv. to Thoricus, *h.Cer.*126.

θορικός, ή, όν, *of* or *for the semen,* πόροι θ. *ductus seminales,* Arist.*GA*720^{b}13, al.; [τὰ] θορικά *partes seminales,* ib.755^{b}20; τροφὴ θ. Ruf.*Sat.Gon.*12.

θορινεῦσαι· ὁ ξιφίας ἰχθύς, Hsch.

θορίσκομαι, Pass., *receive semen,* διὰ τῶν ὤτων Ant.Lib.29.3.

θόρισμα, ατος, τό, *bait* for fish, Hsch. **θόρναξ·** ὑποπόδιον (Cypr.), Id. (metath. of *θρόναξ).

θόρνυμαι, = θρῴσκω II, [S.]*Fr.*1127.9, Nic.*Th.*130: 3 pl. subj., ἐπεὰν θορνύωνται Hdt.3.109.

θορό-εις, εσσα, εν, *in embryo,* βρέφος θ. Opp.*C.*3.522. **-ποιός,** όν, gloss on θοῦρις, *EM*453.51 (v.l. φθορο-, θυρο-).

θορός, ὁ, *semen genitale,* Hdt.2.93, Hp.*Morb.*2.51, Arist.*HA*509^{b}20, Plu.2.637f, Porph.*Abst.*4.9. II. θορός· ἀφροδισιαστής, Hsch.

θόρραξ, v. θώραξ.

θορῠβ-άζομαι, Pass., *to be troubled, Ev.Luc.*10.41 (v.l. τυρβάζῃ): Act. in Gramm., Dosith.p.432 K., *EM*633.34. **-έω,** *make a noise, uproar* or *disturbance,* esp. of crowds, assemblies, etc., Hp.*Ep.*12, Ar.*Eq.*666, *V.*622, etc.; βλέπων εἰς τὸν ἀεὶ θορυβοῦντα τόπον τῆς ἐκκλησίας D.21.194. 2. *shout in token of approbation* or *the contrary*: a. *cheer, applaud,* Isoc.12.264, Pl.*Euthd.*303b:—Pass., λόγος τεθορυβημένος a *loudly cheered* speech, Isoc.12.233, cf. Arist.*Rh.*1356^{b}23. b. more freq. *raise clamour,* καί μοι μὴ θορυβήσητε pray *do not interrupt,* Pl.*Ap.*20e, cf. D.5.15; θ. ἐφ' οἷς ἂν λέγω Pl.*Ap.*30c; ὁ θορυβῶν, opp. ὁ θέλων λέγειν καὶ ἀκούειν, And.4.7:—Pass., *have clamours raised against one,* ὑπὸ τοιούτων ἀνδρῶν θορυβῇ S.*Aj.*164 (anap.). II. trans., *confuse by noise* or *tumult, bewilder,* Pl.*Phdr.*245b, *Prt.*319c, al.; *throw* [troops] *into confusion,* in battle, Th.3.78; θ. πρός τινας *cause excitement* amongst.., Id.6.61:—Pass., *to be thrown into disorder, confused,* Hdt.3.78, 4.130, Th.4.129, 8.50, Pl.*Ep.*348e, etc.; ὑπὸ τῶν λεγομένων Id.*Ly.*210e; τινι at a thing, D.18.35; ἐπί τινι Bato 7.2; περί τι Th.6.61; πρός τι Plu.*Cam.*29. **-ηθρον,** τό, = λεοντοπέταλον, Ps.-Dsc.3.96. **-ητικός,** ή, όν, *uproarious, turbulent,* Ar.*Eq.*1380.

θορῠβοποι-έω, *make an uproar,* Cic.*Fam.*16.23.2, D.S.13.111, App.*BC*2.74. **-ός,** όν, *making an uproar, turbulent,* πλῆθος Plu.*Mar.*28.

θόρῠβ-ος, ὁ, *noise,* esp. *the confused noise of a crowded assembly, uproar, clamour,* Pi.*O.*10(11).72, Th.8.92, etc.; θόρυβος βοῆς a confused clamour, S.*Ph.*1263; θ. στρατιωτῶν Ar.*Ach.*546; θ. Πυκνίτης *Com.Adesp.*45 D.; θ. παρέχειν ἐν ταῖς βουλαῖς καὶ ἐν ταῖς ἐκκλησίαις *OGI*48.9 (Ptolemais, iii B.C.); less freq. of an individual, E.*Or.*905;

of animals, θόρυβον δ' οὐκ ἐφίλησαν ὄνων Call.*Aet.Oxy.*2079.30. 2. esp. in token of approbation or the contrary, Pl.*R.*492b,c: a. *applause*, θ. Ληναΐτης Ar.*Eq.*547; θ. καὶ ἔπαινος Pl.*Prt.*339d, D.19. 195; θόρυβον καὶ κρότον ἐποιήσατε Id.21.14. b. *groans, murmurs*, And.2.15; μεγάλοι θόρυβοι κατέχουσ' ἡμᾶς great *murmurs* are abroad among us, S.*Aj.*142 (anap.). II. *tumult, confusion*, θ. παρασχεῖν τινι Hdt.7.181; ἐς θ. ἀπικέσθαι, καταστῆναι, Id.8.56, Th.4.104; ἐγένετο δ θ. μέγας, in a battle, ib.14; κραυγὴ καὶ θ. Phld.*Hom.*p.22 O.: pl., θ. ὀχλώδεις καὶ παροινίαι Men.*Mon.*239. 2. *confusion* of mind, θορύβους ἐνθυμηματικοὺς καὶ ἀποφθεγματικοὺς παρασκευάζειν Epicur. *Nat.*14.9; ὁ παρὰ κακὰς δόξας θ. Phld.*Rh.*2.31 S., cf. 40 S. III. c. inf., ἐς θόρυβον ἦλθον.. λευσθῆναι I ran a *risk* of being stoned, E. *IA*1349 (troch.). (Perh. cogn. with τονθορύζω.) **-ώδης**, ες, *uproarious, turbulent*, Pl.*Lg.*671a; *clamorous*, -ῶδες φθέγγεσθαι Arist. *HA*632^{b}18; θορυβώδεα ἐνυπνιάζεσθαι Hp.*VM*10. Adv. -δῶς Poll. 5.123, Iamb.*Myst.*3.25 (prob.): Comp. -έστερον, διατίθενται Plu.2. 656f. II. *causing alarm*, τῷ ἵππῳ θ. μηδὲν προσφέρειν X.*Eq.*9. 15. 2. *confusing*, δόξαι Demetr.Lac.*Herc.*1696.4.

θορώδης, ες, = θοραῖος, Gal.4.556, al.

θοῦ, aor. 2 imper. Med. of τίθημι.

θουρ-αῖος, α, ον, = θοῦρος, *violent, lustful*, Hsch.:—fem. **θουράς**, άδος, Nic.*Th.*131, Lyc.612. **-άω**, *rush* or *leap upon*, c. acc., Id. 85:—also **θουριῶν**· ἐνεργῶν, Hsch. **-ήεις**, εσσα, εν, = θουραῖος, Id. **-ης**, ου, ὁ, *male*, of animals, Id. (s. v. l.). **-ηταῖς**· αἱ τῶν ζῴων μίξεις, Id. **-ητρα**· ὀχεῖα, Id.

Θουριό-μαντις, εως, ὁ, *a Thurian prophet*, of the *seer* Lampon, Ar. *Nu.*332 (pl.); v. Sch. ad loc. **-πέρσαι**, οἱ, title of play by Metagenes, Ath.6.270a.

θούριος, α, ον, in Trag. (Com. in lyr.), = θοῦρος, λοχαγέται ἄρχων, A.*Th.*42, *Pers.*73 (lyr.); ὄρνις, τόξα, Id.*Ag.*112 (lyr.), *Eu.*627; Αἴας S.*Aj.*212 (anap.); λῆμα Ar.*Eq.*757 (lyr.).

θοῦρις, ιδος, ἡ, fem. of sq. (q. v.): in pl. **θούριδες**· νύμφαι, Μοῦσαι (Maced.), Hsch.

θοῦρος, ον, (θρῴσκω) *rushing, impetuous, furious*, Hom. (only in Il.), as epith. of Ares, 15.127, al. (of the planet Mars, Doroth.ap. Heph.Astr.1.1); Τυφών A.*Pr.*356, cf. *Fr.*199; δόρυ E.*Rh.*492; ἀνὴρ Γαλάτης *Eleg.Alex.Adesp.*2.14:—fem. **θοῦρις**, ῖδος, ἡ, epith. of ἀλκή, Od.4.527, Il.7.164, al.; θ. ἀσπίς, prob. the shield *with which one rushes to the fight*, 11.32; αἰγίς 15.308.

θούσχοινοι ἢ **θόσχοινοι**· ἅρπαγες, πλανῆτες, Hsch.

θόωκος, ὁ, Ep. form of θῶκος; v. θᾶκος.

θόωσα, ἡ, (θοός A) *speedy, swift*, as pr. n., Od.1.71, Emp.122.3.

θραγμός, ὁ, *crackling*, κυάμων ἐρεικομένων S.E.*P.*1.58; cf. θραύω.

θράζω, aor. 1 ἔθρᾶσα, = θραύω, Tz.*H.*9.34.

θραίειν· λοιδορεῖν (Lacon.), Hsch.

Θρᾴκ-η, ἡ, *Thrace*, Ar.*Ach.*136, Th.1.59, etc.: Ion. **Θρηΐκη** Hdt. 2.134, al.; Ep. and Trag. contr. **Θρῄκη** Il.13.301, A.*Pers.*509, etc.: —**Θρῄκηθεν**, *from Thrace*, Il.9.5, 72: **Θρῄκηνδε**, *to Thrace*, Od.8. 361. **-ίας** (sc. ἄνεμος), ὁ, = Θρασκίας (q. v.). 2. (sc. λίθος) stone said to take fire in water, Dsc.5.129, cf. Plin.*HN*33.94. **-ίζω**, *speak Thracian dialect*, A.D.*Adv.*162.4, St.Byz. s. v. Θρᾴκη. **-ικός**, ή, όν, = sq., Luc.*JTr.*21. **-ιος**, α, ον, *Thracian*, Th.5.10, etc.: Ion. **Θρηΐκιος**, η, ον, Il.10.559, Hdt.1.168 codd.:—contr. **Θρῄκιος**, α, ον (-ος, ον E.*Fr.*369.4 (lyr.)), A.*Ag.*654, E.*Hec.*36:—Σάμος Θρηϊκίη, = Σαμοθρᾴκη, Il.13.13. [Θρηΐκιος Hom.; Θρηΐκιος Phanocl.1.1, A.R.4. 905.] **-ιστί**, Adv. *in Thracian fashion*, κέκαρμαι Theoc.14. 46. II. *in the Thracian dialect*, Str.7.6.1, H.D.*Adv.*162.4.

Θρᾳκοφοίτης, ου, ὁ, *one who keeps going to Thrace*, like Ἁιδοφοίτης, Ar.*Fr.*149.7.

θρακτικόν· πορευτόν, and **θραξεῖται**· πορεύσεται, Hsch.: dial. forms for θρεκτ-, θρεξ-. **θραμβόν**· καπυρόν, Id. **θράμις**· κριός, Id.

θρᾱνεύομαι, Pass. with fut. Med. -εύσομαι, (θρᾶνος) *to be stretched on the tanner's board, tanned*, Ar.*Eq.*369; also, *to be crushed*, Hsch., Phot.

θρᾱνίας, ου, ὁ, a kind of fish, ξιφίαι θρανίαι τε Marcell.Sid.29 (cf. θρανίς):—also **θρανίαι**· θρόμβοι, Hsch.

θρᾱν-ίδιον, τό, Dim. of θρᾶνος, Ar.*Fr.*399. **-ίον**, τό, = foreg., Id.*Ra.*121, Ael.*NA*16.33; *the rower's bench*, Poll.1.94 (pl., with v. l. θρανεῖα). 2. *close-stool*, Hsch. 3. = θρᾶνος II. 1, 2, Id.

θρᾱνίς, ίδος, ἡ, *sword-fish*, = ξιφίας, Xenocr.17; cf. θρανίας.

θρᾱν-ίτης [ῑ], ου, ὁ, (θρᾶνος) *rower on the topmost of the three benches* in a trireme, Th.6.31, Ar.*Ach.*162, cf. Sch.Ar.*Ra.*1106. II. Adj. *of the topmost bench*, σκαλμὸς θ. the *topmost* bench, Plb.16.3.4:—fem. **θρᾱνῖτις** κώπη the oar *of a* θρανίτης, *IG*2^2.1604.52 (pl.), *EM*454. 12 (pl.). **-ῑτικός**, ή, όν, *of a* θρανίτης, κώπη Callix.1.

θραννομένη· προορῶσα, Hsch.

θρᾱνογράφος [γρᾰ], ὁ, = τοιχογράφος, Plb.15.25.32, Hsch.

θρᾶνος, ὁ, (θράομαι) *bench, form*, Ar.*Pl.*545 (gen. θράνους codd., θράνου Poll.). 2. *close-stool*, Hp.ap.Gal.19.104. II. Archit., 1. *wooden beam*, ὅσα κατέρρωγεν τοῦ τείχους ἐνδήσει θράνοις *IG*2^2.463.75; θράνους ἐπιθήσει διανεκεῖς, of *beams* supporting floors, ib.1668.81, cf. 1672.208. 2. ὁ θ. τοῦ νεώ the *top course* of masonry in a temple, ib.11(2).161 *A*49 (Delos, iii B. C.); θ. ποικίλος *PCair.Zen.*445.5 (iii B. C.).

θρᾶνυξ, v. θρῆνυξ.

θρᾱνύσσω, *break in pieces*, Lyc.664. (Cf. συνθρανόω, prob. cogn. with θραύω.)

Θρᾷξ, Θρᾳκός, ὁ, *Thracian*: Ep. and Ion. **Θρήϊξ**, ῖκος [ῐ, but ῑ in Nic.*Th.*49, Call.*Aet.Oxy.*2079.13, A.R.1.24, 632, etc.], Il.4.533, Hdt.1.28, etc.: Ep. and Trag. contr. **Θρῄξ**, Θρῃκός, Il.24.234, etc., to be read for Θρᾷξ in E.*Hec.*428, *Fr.*360.48; Ion. dat. pl. Θρήϊξιν [⏑ – ⏑] Archil.*Supp.*4.48:—fem. **Θρᾷσσα** (q. v.).

θρᾶξαι, θρᾶξον, v. θράσσω.

θράομαι (cf. θρᾶνος), *to be seated*, in Ion. aor. 1 Med. θρήσασθαι, πλατάνῳ γ(ρ)αίῃ ὕπο Philet.14.

θράσις, εως, ἡ, = θραῦσις, Hsch. **θράσκειν**· ἀναμιμνήσκειν, Id.

Θρασκίας, ου, ὁ, *the wind from NNW.*, Arist.*Mete.*363^{b}29, *Mu.* 394^{b}30, Thphr.*Vent.*42, Agathem.2.7, Lyd.*Mag.*3.32:—written **Θρᾳκίας**, Arist.*Vent.*973^{b}17, Thphr.*Sign.*35; **Θρᾱκίας** *IG*14.1308: —hence **θρασκικός**, ή, όν, *facing NNW.*, of windows, Zos.Alch. p.141 B.

θράσος [ᾰ], εος, τό, (θρασύς) = θάρσος (q. v.), *courage*, Il.14.416, A. *Pers.*394, E.*Med.*469, Ar.*Lys.*545 (lyr.); θ. πολέμων *courage* in war, Pi.*P.*2.63; θράσει *boldly*, B.16.63; but more freq. ἰσχύος θ. *confidence* in strength, S.*Ph.*104. II. in bad sense, *over-boldness, rashness, insolence*, ἐς τοῦτο θράσεος (v. l. θάρσεος) ἀνήκει Hdt.7.9.γ', cf. A.*Pr.*42, D.21.194, etc.; παμμάχῳ θράσει βρύων A.*Ag.*169 (lyr.), cf. *Pers.*831; προβᾶσ' ἐπ' ἔσχατον θράσους S.*Ant.*853 (lyr.); τόλμαις καὶ φρενῶν θράσει Id.*Aj.*46; πεπύργωσαι θράσει E.*Or.*1568; πανουργίᾳ τε καὶ θράσει Ar. *Eq.*331, cf. 637; θράσει ἀπίστῳ ἐπαιρόμενος Th.1.120; τοῦ θράσους ἐπισχεῖν τινα Pl.*Hp.Ma.*298a; τὸ τὴν τοῦ βελτίονος δόξαν μὴ φοβεῖσθαι διὰ θράσος Id.*Lg.*701b; ἀναίδεια καὶ θ. Aeschin.1.189; opp. αἰδώς, Arist.*Cael.*291^{b}26; θράσος μὲν γάρ ἐστιν ἄλογος ὁρμή, θάρσος δὲ ἔλλογος ὁρμή Ammon.*Diff.*p.71 V.; οἷον πέπονθε τὸ θάρσος πρὸς τὸ θράσος Arist.*EE*1234^{b}12, cf. Eus.Mynd.56, Luc.*Musc.Enc.*5.—This distn. holds good in Att. Prose: θάρσος is not found in Com.; θαρσύνω and θρασύνω are used indifferently; θρασέω and θαρσύς are not found; cf. θρασύς fin., θρασύτης.

Θρᾷσσα, ἡ, Att. **Θρᾷττα**, Trag. **Θρῇσσα**, fem. of Θρᾷξ, S.*Ant.*589, E.*Alc.*967 (both lyr.): **Θρηΐσσα** λᾶας, = Θρακίας λίθος, Nic.*Th.*45:— esp. as Subst., *Thracian slave-girl*, Ar.*Ach.*273, Pl.*Tht.*174a, etc.: **Θραΐσσα** [ᾰ] Theoc.*Ep.*20.1; Ion. **Θρεΐσσα** Herod.1.79.

θράσσω, Att. **θράττω**, pres. part. neut. θρᾶττον Pl.*Phd.*86e: aor. 1 inf. θρᾶξαι A.*Pr.*628, E.*Fr.*600:—*trouble, disquiet*, Pi.*I.*7(6).39, A. l. c., Cratin.363, Pherecr.39, S.*Fr.*177, Hp.*Mul.*1.70, E.*Rh.*863, Pl. l. c., *Phdr.*242c, etc.:—Pass., ὑπὸ ἐδωδῆς θράττεσθαι Jul.*Or.*6.192a: aor. 1 ἐθράχθη S.*Fr.*1055. 2. *disturb, destroy*, *APl.*4.255. 3. for pf. τέτρηχα, v. ταράσσω II.

θρασυ-βουλος [ῠ], ον, *bold in counsel*, Arist.*Rh.*1400^{b}19. **-γλωσσής**, ές, *bold of tongue*, Man.4.184. **-γλωττία**, ἡ, *boldness of tongue*, Poll.2.108. **-γυιος**, ον, *strong of limb*, Κλειτομάχοιο νίκα θ. Pi.*P.*8.37. **-δειλος**, ὁ, ἡ, *impudent coward, braggart, poltroon*, Arist.*EN*1115^{b}32, Vett.Val.40.14. II. name of a gem, Ps.-Plu. *Fluv.*17.2. **-εργός**, όν, *bold of deed*, Nonn.*D.*35.365. **-θῡμος**, ον, *bold-hearted*, Man.4.529; cf. θρασύμυθος. **-κάρδιος**, ον, *bold of heart*, Il.10.41, 13.343, Hes.*Sc.*448, Anacr.1.5, B.19.5. **-λογέω**, *speak boldly*, Sch.rec.S.*Aj.*1258. **-λόγος**, ον, *bold of speech*, *EM* 133.42. **-μᾰχος**, ον, *bold in battle*, Arist.*Rh.*1400^{b}20: as pr. n., *Thrasymachus*:—hence Adj. -μάχειος, α, ον, ἑρμηνεία style *of T.*, D.H.*Dem.*3. **-μέμνων**, ον, gen. ονος, (θρασύς, Skt. *mánma*, OIr. *menma* 'spirit', cf. Ἀγαμέμνων) *brave-spirited*, epith. of Heracles, Il. 5.639, Od.11.267; of Meleager, B.5.69. **-μήδης**, ες, *bold of thought* or *plan, daring, resolute*, Pi.*P.*4.143, *N.*9.13, B.15.15:—in Hom. only as pr. n. **-μητις**, ιδος, ὁ, ἡ, = foreg., *AP*6.324 (Leon. Alex.). **-μήχᾰνος**, Dor. -μάχᾰνος [μᾱ], ον, *bold in contriving, daring in design*, Ἡρακλέης Pi.*O.*6.67; λέοντες Id.*N.*4.62. **-μῡθος**, ον, *bold of tongue, saucy*, Id.*O.*13.10 (v. l. -θυμος).

θράσῡνος [ᾰ], = θρασύς, *EM*204.17.

θρᾰσύνω, (θρασύς) = θαρσύνω, *embolden, encourage*, A.*Ag.*222 (lyr.); πλήθει τὴν ἀμαθίαν θρασύνοντες *lending courage to* their ignorance by number, Th.1.142. 2. c. acc., *boast of*, τὴν ἰσηγορίαν Plb.4. 31.4. II. Pass. and Med., aor. 1 inf. θρασυνθῆναι A.*Supp.*772; ἐθρασυνάμην Isoc.4.12, Ph.2.557:—*to be bold, confident, take courage*, A.*Ag.*1188, etc.; οὐ.. ἀλόγως θρασυνόμεθα Th.5.104; πρὶν ὅρμῳ ναῦν θρασυνθῆναι before the ship *had got confidence in* her moorings, A. *Supp.* l. c.; ἐπί τι *make a bold bid* for.., Philostr.*VS*2.33.2; θ. τι πρός τινα *carry out a coup de main* against, Aen.Tact.9.1; more freq., 2. in bad sense, *to be over-bold, over-confident*, S.*Ph.*1387, E.*Hec.*1183, Ar.*Ra.*846, D.18.136; ἀλόγως Polystr.p.30 W.; ἐπί τινι Ar.*Ach.* 330; ᾐσχύνοντο ἐφ' οἷς ἐθρασύναντο Isoc.5.23; πρός τι Plu.2.794d, Luc.*Apol.*6; ἔκ τινων Polystr.p.22 W.: c. dat., λαιμαργίᾳ ἀθεότητι θρασυνομένη Plu.2.1125a.

θρᾰσυ-ξενία, ἡ, *the boldness of a stranger*, Pl.*Lg.*879e. **-πονος**, ον, *bold* or *ready for toil*, ἀκμαὶ ἰσχύος Pi.*O.*1.96. **-πτόλεμος**, ον, *bold in war*, *IG*9(1).871 (Corc.).

θρᾰσύς, εῖα, ύ, fem. θρασέα, metri gr., Philem.20 (s. v. l.):—*bold*, chiefly of persons, Il.8.89, etc.; also θ. πόλεμος 6.254, 10.28, Od.4. 146; θρασειάων ἀπὸ χειρῶν 5.434, Il.17.662, al.; θ. καρδία Pi.*P.*10.44; πούς Ar.*Ra.*330 (lyr.); ἐν τῷ ἔργῳ θρασύς Hdt.7.49; ἡ ἐλπὶς θρασεῖα τοῦ μέλλοντος *full of confidence*, Th.7.77; θρασὺς τὸ ἦθος Arist.*Pol.*1315^a 11. 2. more freq. in bad sense, *over-bold, rash*, σὺν δ' ὁ θ. εἵπετ' Ὀδυσσεύς Od.10.436 (Sch. προπετής); Γοργόνες Pi.*P.*12.7; *audacious, arrogant, insolent*, A.*Pr.*180 (lyr.), Ar.*Nu.*445 (anap.), etc.; Ἄρης.. πρὸς ἀλλήλους θ., of civil war, A.*Eu.*863; γλώσσῃ θ. S.*Aj.*1142; ἐν τοῖς λόγοις Id.*Ph.*1307; ἐπὶ τῶν λόγων D.*Prooem.*32; ἀνομίᾳ θ. E.*IT* 275; πονηρὸς εἶ καὶ θ. Ar.*Eq.*181; θρασεῖς καὶ ἄδικοι καὶ ὑβρισταί Pl.*Lg.* 630b; ἀλαζὼν ὁ θ. καὶ προσποιητικὸς ἀνδρείας Arist.*EN*1115^{b}29; [ὅμοιόν τι ἔχει] ὁ θ. τῷ θαρραλέῳ ib.1151^{b}7; τὸ μὴ θ. modesty, A.*Supp.*197:

Comp. -ύτερος Pl.*La.*184b, Phld.*Lib.*p.61 O.: Sup. -ύτατος Isoc.12.133, etc. II. of things, *to be ventured*, c. inf., θρασύ μοι τόδ' εἰπεῖν this I am *bold* to say, Pi.*N.*7.50; οὐκ ἄρ' ἐκείνῳ γ' οὐδὲ προσμεῖξαι θρασύ; S.*Ph.*106. III. Adv. -έως Ar.*V.*1031, etc.: Aeol. **θροσέως** Jo.Gramm.*Comp.*2.1: Comp. θρασύτερον *too boldly*, Th.8.103; -τέρως Phalar.*Ep.*34: Sup. θρασύτατα Th.8.84 and (with v.l. -άτως) D.S.17.44: neut. as Adv., ἀναιδὲς καὶ θρασὺ βλέπειν Cratin.24 D. (I.-E. *dhers-* in θέρσος (older than θάρσος and θράσος), *dhr̥s-* in θρασύς, Skt. *dhr̥ṣú-*, *dhr̥ṣṇú-* 'bold', cf. Engl. *dare, durst.*)

θρᾰσύσπλαγχνος, ον, *bold-hearted*, E.*Hipp.*424. Adv. -ως A.*Pr.*730.

θρᾰσυστομ-έω, *to be over-bold of tongue*, A.*Supp.*203, S.*Ph.*380, E.*Hec.*1286. **-ία**, ἡ, *insolence*, *AP*12.141 (Mel.). **-ος**, ον, *over-bold of tongue, insolent*, A.*Th.*612, *Ag.*1399, E.*Fr.*3.

θρᾰσύτης, ητος, ἡ, *over-boldness*, Hp.*Lex* 4, Th.2.61, Lys.3.45; θ., = τὸ σφόδρα θαρρεῖν, Arist.*Rh.*1390ᵃ31, cf. *EN*1108ᵇ31: pl., Isoc.4.77; ἀνδρεῖαι καὶ θ. D.*Prooem.*45.

θρᾰσύ-τολμος [ῠ], ον, *bold*, *Cat.Cod.Astr.*8(4).212. **-φρων**, ον, gen. ονος, *bold of mind*, Opp.*H.*1.112. **-φωνία**, ἡ, = θρασυστομία, Poll.2.112. **-φωνος**, ον, = θρασύστομος, ibid. **-χάρμης**, ου, ὁ, *bold in fight*, Q.S.4.502. **-χειρ**, χειρος, ὁ, ἡ, *bold of hand*, *AP*7.234 (Phil.); θ. μ[άχ]α, of boxing, B.2.4; in bad sense, θ. καὶ μιαίφονος Id.*Scol.Oxy.*1361 *Fr.*5.10, = *Scol.Oxy.*2081(*e*)10. **-χειρία**, ἡ, *boldness of hand*, Poll.2.148.

Θρᾰσώ, όος, contr. οῦς, ἡ, *Bold*, name of Athena, Lyc.936.

Θράσων, ωνος, ὁ, a name of a *braggart* soldier in New Com.

Θρᾷττα, ης, ἡ, Att. for Θρᾷσσα.

θρᾷττα, ἡ, *a small sea-fish*, Arist.*GA*785ᵇ23, Antiph.211, Mnesim.4.41:—Dim. **θραττίδιον**, τό, Anaxandr.27.

θράττης· ὁ λίθος, ὑπὸ Θρᾳκῶν, Hsch.; cf. Θρακίας. **θράττον**· ὕπερον, κόλουρον, Id. **θράττω**, Att. for θράσσω. **θραῦλος**, η, ον, *frangible, brittle*, Anon.ap.Suid. (Comp.):—also **θραῦρος**, Hsch.

θραῦμα, ατος, τό, (θραύω) *fragment*, A.*Pers.*425, *IG*7.3498.23 (Oropus, iii/ii B.C.), D.S.3.12. II. *breakage*, Jul.*Or.*2.60a. III. *destruction*, ἐχθρῶν Lxx *Ju.*13.5. IV. metaph., θραύματ' ἐμοὶ κλύειν A.*Ag.*1166 (lyr.). (Cf. θραῦσμα.)

θραύπαλος, ὁ, *joint fir, Ephedra campulopoda*, Thphr.*HP*3.6.4; ἡ, ib.4.1.3.

θραυπίς, ίδος, ἡ, *a small bird*, Arist.*HA*592ᵇ30 (v.l. θλυπίς).

θραυσάντυξ, ῠγος, ὁ, ἡ, (θραύω) *breaking* chariot-*rails*, τύχαι Ar.*Nu.*1264.

θραῦσις, εως, ἡ, (θραύω) *comminution*, opp. κάταξις, Arist.*Mete.*386ᵃ13, 390ᵇ7, *Placit.*3.3.7, Sor.*Fract.*12. II. *slaughter*, Lxx 2*Ki.*17.9; *destruction* by plague, ib.24.15, *Nu.*16.48. III. *falling off of hair in patches*, Gal.19.430. IV. = ὀργή, πληγή, σφῦρα ἡ τοὺς βώλους θραύουσα, Hsch.

θραῦσ-μα, ατος, τό, = θραῦμα I, Agatharch.25, Arist.*Mu.*394ᵇ4, Luc.*Hist.Conscr.*25. II. in leprosy, *scab*, Lxx *Le.*13.30. III. the best kind of ἀμμωνιακόν, Dsc.3.84. IV. *fracture*, *Hippiatr.*74 (pl.). **-μός**, ὁ, *breaking*, καρδίας Lxx *Na.*2.10(11). **-τήριος**, α, ον, *capable of dissolving*, λίθων Aët.2.19. **-της**, ου, ὁ, *one who breaks* or *crushes*, *POxy.*868.2 (nisi sub θραυστός ponendum). **-τός**, ή, όν, *frangible, brittle*, Ti.Locr.99c, Thphr.*HP*5.3.6; *capable of being broken down*, πύργος D.C.36.18, Asclep.ap.Gal.14.698, S.E.*P.*3.33. 2. *broken, crushed*, Epigr. in *PTeb.*3.4: θραυστόν, τό, = θραῦσμα III, Plin.*HN*12.107.

θραύω, Ep. impf. θραύεσκον Orph.*L.*140: fut. -σω Ar.*Av.*466: aor. 1 ἔθραυσα S.*El.*745, E.*HF*779 (lyr.):—Pass., fut. θραυσθήσομαι Gal.10.624: aor. ἐθραύσθην (v. infr.), (κατ-) Pl.*Ti.*56e: pf. τέθραυσμαι Thphr.*Sens.*11, (συν-) X.*Ages.*2.14, (παρα-) Pl.*Lg.*757e (v.l. -τεθραυμένον):—*break in pieces, shatter*, Simon.57, A.*Pers.*196, 416, Tim.*Pers.*99, etc.; θ. σάρκας E.*Hipp.*1239:—Pass., θραυομένης τῆς πέτρης *flying into pieces*, Hdt.1.174; σίδηρον θραυσθέντα καὶ ῥαγέντα S.*Ant.*476; πτερὰ θραύονται *have their* wings *broken*, Pl.*Phdr.*248b. II. metaph., *break down, enfeeble*, μὴ θραύσαι (-σοι codd.) χρόνος ὄλβον Pi.*O.*6.97, cf. E.*HF*779 (lyr.); διάτορον σφραγῖδα θ. στόματος Tim.*Pers.*160; ἔπος.., ὅ τι τὴν τούτων θραύσει ψυχὴν Ar.*Av.*466; θ. τὴν δύναμιν Plu.*Alc.*23; ἐλπίδα, etc., Hdn.3.2.2, etc.; θ. τι τῶν ἐκ χρόνου φυλασσομένων δικαίων *Supp.Epigr.*1.329.45 (Istrus, i A.D.), cf. Onos.32.10:—Pass., πόθος θραυσθεὶς Asp.ap.Ath.5.219e; θραυόμενος τὸν λογισμόν, Lat. *animo fractus*, Plu.*Ant.*17; θραυσθῆναι ἐπί τινα *to be grieved* for.., Lxx 1*Ki.*20.34.—Rare in Att. Prose.

Θρεΐσσα, ἡ, Ion. for Θρᾷσσα (q.v.).

θρεκ-τικός, ή, όν, (τρέχω) *able to run*, Att. for τροχαστικός, acc. to Moer.p.187 P.: Sup. -ώτατος Hsch. **-τός**, ή, όν, = τροχαῖος, θρεκτοῖσι νόμοις, f.l. for κρεκτ-, S.*Fr.*463:—also **θρεκτός**· δρόμος, Phot.

θρέμμ-α, ατος, τό, (τρέφω) *nursling, creature*, θ. Νηρεΐδων, of dolphins, Arion 1.9; mostly of tame animals, esp. sheep and goats, X.*Ages.*9.6, *Oec.*20.23, Plb.2.26.5, *Ev.Jo.*4.12, etc.; τὰ ἐν ταῖς ἀγέλαις θ. Pl.*Plt.*261d; τὰ ἀγελαῖα θ. ib.264a; ὑηνὰ θ. Id.*Lg.*819d; of game-cocks and quails, ὀρνίθων θ. ib.789b: generally, *animals*, τοῖς ἡμέροις καὶ ἀγρίοις.. θ. Id.*Criti.*118b, al. 2. of men, S.*OT*1143, *Ph.*243; Χαρίτων θ. Ar.*Ec.*973; δύσκολον τὸ θ. ἄνθρωπος Pl.*Lg.*777b, cf. *Tht.*174b; esp. of *domestic slaves*, = Lat. *verna*, τὸ Χρυσίππου θ. *GDI*2321.14 (Delph.), cf. *CIG*3113 (Teos). 3. generally, *creature*, ἄπλατον θ. κἀπροσήγορον, of a lion, S.*Tr.*1093 (cf. Pl.*Chrm.*155e); of Cerberus, S.*Tr.*1099; κακὰ θ., of a *swarm* of gnats, *AP*5.150 (Mel.); θ. Σελινοῦντος, of a fish, Archestr.*Fr.*12; Καρύστου θ., comic for a cup made at Carystus, Antiph.182.3; as a term of reproach, θρέμματ' οὐκ ἀνασχετά A.*Th.*182; ὦ θρέμμ' ἀναιδές S.*El.*622, cf. Ar.*Lys.*369; in periphr., ὕδρας θ., for ὕδρα, S.*Tr.*574; νεογενῆ παίδων θρέμματα Pl.*Lg.*790d; θρέμματα παλλακῶν *kept* mistresses, Plu.*Sol.*7. (Written θέρματα *BGU*478.15 (ii A.D.)). **-ατικός**, ή, όν, *of* or *for cattle-dealing*, ἐργασία Judeich *Altertümer von Hierapolis* 227 *b*7. **-άτιον**, τό, Dim. of θρέμμα 2, *CIG*2733 (Stratonicea), *SIG*1211 (Calymna, pl.), Keil-Premerstein *Dritter Bericht* 151 (ii/iii A.D.). **-ᾰτοτροφέω**, *keep cattle*, D.S.2.54, Str.15.1.41.

θρέξασκον, θρέξομαι, v. τρέχω.

θρέομαι, only in pres., *cry aloud, shriek*, always of women, θρέομαι φοβερὰ μεγάλ' ἄχη A.*Th.*78; elsewh. only in part., μινυρὰ θρεομένας Id.*Ag.*1165; πάθεα μέλεα θρεομένα Id.*Supp.*112, cf. E.*Hipp.*363; αὐτὴ θρεομένη σαυτῇ κακά Id.*Med.*51 (trim., elsewh. lyr.).—Act. only in Hsch. (I.-E. *dhreu-*, cf. θρο-έω, θρῦ-λος.)

θρέπτα, v. θρέπτρα, τά.

θρεπ-τάριον, τό, = θρεμμάτιον, *CIG*(add.)4303*h*6 (Lycia), *PPar.*p.422 (ii A.D.). **-τειρα**, ἡ, fem. of θρεπτήρ, E.*Tr.*195 (lyr.), *AP*5.105 (Diotim.), 6.51: metaph., Δίκη θ. πολήων Opp.*H.*2.680. **-τέος**, α, ον, (τρέφω) *to be fed, nurtured*, metaph., γυμναστικῇ Pl.*R.*403c. II. θρεπτέον *one must feed, keep*, Id.*Ti.*19a, X.*Lac.*9.5. 2. (from Pass.) ἢ ἐργαστέον ἢ ἀπὸ τῶν εἰργασμένων θρεπτέον *one must live* on what has been earned, Id.*Eq.Mag.*8.8. **-τήρ**, ῆρος, ὁ, *feeder, rearer*, of a parent or foster-parent, *IG*3.1401, *JRS*2.91 (Antioch in Pisidia), *AP*12.137 (Mel.): pl., *IG*14.1722: as Adj., θ. ἀγοστός Nonn.*D.*3.387. **-τήριος**, ον, *feeding, nourishing*, μαστός A.*Ch.*545. II. πλόκαμος Ἰνάχῳ θ. hair *dedicated as a thank-offering* to Inachus, ib.6. III. Subst. θρεπτήριον, τό, = θρεπτάριον, *PLond.*5.1708.248 (vi A.D.). 2. pl., θρεπτήρια, τά, *reward for rearing*, made to nurses by parents, *h.Cer.*168, 223; also, *return made by children for their rearing* (Att. τροφεῖα), Hes.*Op.*188, Ael.*VH*2.7. b. *nourishment*, τὰ ..νηδύος θ. S.*OC*1263. **-τήτωρ**, ορος, ὁ, *nourisher, feeder*, πενήτων *PMasp.*20.11 (pl., vi A.D.). **-τικός**, ή, όν, *able to feed* or *rear*, τινος Pl.*Plt.*267b, cf. 276b,c; *nourishing*, -ώτερα μῆλα Diph.Siph.ap. Ath.3.82f; -ώτατος οἶνος Mnesith.ib.1.32d. II. *of* or *promoting growth*, ἡ δύναμις τῆς ψυχῆς θ. καὶ γεννητική Arist.*de An.*416ᵃ19; ἡ θ. ψυχή ib.415ᵃ23; τὸ θ. *the principle of growth*, Id.*EN*1102ᵇ11; ἡ θ. καὶ αὐξητικὴ ζωή ib.1098ᵃ1; opp. φθαρτικός, Polystr.p.23 W. Adv. -κῶς Porph.*Gaur.*1.1. III. *causing to heal up*, ἑλκῶν Dsc.1.43. **-τός**, ή, όν, as Subst., **θρεπτός, θρεπτή**, *slave bred in the house*, Lys.*Fr.*215 S., Pherecr.125, Lxx *Es.*2.7, *IPE*1².709 (Olbia, ii B.C.), *POxy.*298.46 (i A.D.), etc.; οἱ θ. καὶ αἱ θ. *Inscr.Cos* 131; also of *adopted foundlings*, τὴν ἰδίαν θ. *SIG*1210 (Calymna), Plin.*Ep. ad Traj.*65, etc. II. *pupil*, Vett.Val.157.29. **-τρα** (A), τά, = θρεπτήριος III. 2, οὐδὲ τοκεῦσι θ. φίλοις ἀπέδωκε Il.4.478, 17.302; θρέπτα is dub. in *Epigr.Gr.*442.4 (ii A.D.), Q.S.11.89, Hsch. **-τρα** (B), ἡ, = θρέπτειρα, *a nurse*, *CIG*(add.)4300*d* (Antiphellos).

θρεσκός, v. θρῆσκος.

θρεττᾰνελό, *sound imitative of the cithara*, Ar.*Pl.*290.

θρέττε, τό, = τὸ θρασύ, οὐκ ἔνι μοι τὸ θ., barbarism in Ar.*Eq.*17.

θρεψίππας, ου, ὁ, = ἱπποτρόφος, as pr. n. in Apollod.2.7.8.

θρέψις, εως, ἡ, *nourishing*, σωμάτων S.E.*M.*11.97, cf. Alex.Aphr.*Pr.*2.66, Gal.1.655, etc.

θρηϊκή· ὑποδημάτων εἶδος Περσικῶν, Hsch.

Θρηϊκίη, Θρηΐκιος, η, ον, Ep. and Ion. for Θρᾴκιος (q.v.). **Θρῆϊξ**, ϊκος, ὁ, Ep. and Ion. for Θρᾷξ (q.v.). **Θρηΐσσα**, ἡ, poet. for Θρᾷσσα (q.v.). **Θρήκη**, ἡ, **Θρήκηθεν, Θρήκηνδε**, v. Θρᾴκη. **Θρήκιος**, v. Θρᾴκιος.

θρήν-ερως, ωτος, ὁ, ἡ, *a querulous lover*, Poll.6.189. **-εύω**, = θρηνέω, *Epigr.Gr.*406.9 (Iconium). **-έω**, fut. -ήσω A.*Ag.*1541 (anap.), S.*Aj.*632 (lyr.): aor. 1 -ησα E.*Tr.*[111]:—Med. (v. infr. 2): imper. in pf. Pass. (v. infr.): (θρῆνος):—*sing a dirge, wail*, Μοῦσαι δ' ἐννέα πᾶσαι ἀμειβόμεναι ὀπὶ καλῇ θρήνεον Od.24.61; τίς ὁ θρηνήσων; A.*Ag.* l.c.; τίς..ἔσθ' ὁ θρηνῶν; Ar.*Nu.*1260; θ. πρὸς τύμβον A.*Ch.*926; θ. καὶ ὀδύρεσθαι Pl.*Ap.*38d; πρὸς σφᾶς αὐτοὺς Isoc.8.128: c. acc. cogn., στονόεσσαν ἀοιδήν..ἐθρήνεον *were singing* a doleful dirge, Il.24.722¹; γόον θ. A.*Fr.*291; ὀξυτόνους ᾠδὰς S.*Aj.* l.c.; ἐπῳδάς ib.582; ὕμνους, of the nightingale, Ar.*Av.*211 (lyr.); φθόγγους ἀλύρους Alex.162.7:—Pass., ἅλις μοι τεθρήνηται γόοις S.*Ph.*1401; ἱκανῶς τεθρήνηται Luc.*Cat.*20. 2. c. acc., *bewail*, θ. πόνους A.*Pr.*615; τὸν θάνατον Pl.*Phd.*85a; ὅσα τὸν..ἐμὸν θρηνῶ πατέρα S.*El.*94 (anap.), cf. 530, *Ev.Luc.*23.27, etc.; τὸν φύντα E.*Fr.*449:—so also Med., ἄκος γὰρ οὐδὲν τόνδε θρηνεῖσθαι A.*Pr.*43:—Pass., *to be lamented*, S.*Aj.*852, *Fr.*653. **-ημα**, ατος, τό, *lament, dirge*, E.*Or.*132, *Hel.*174 (lyr.), etc. **-ήσιμος**, *flebilis*, Gloss. **-ητέον**, *one must lament*, Apollon.ap.Stob.4.56.35, Jul.*Or.*8.246b. **-ητήρ**, ῆρος, ὁ, *mourner, wailer*, A.*Pers.*938 (lyr.). **-ητήριος**, ον, = θρηνητικός, ᾠδαὶ θ. Eust.1372.26. **-ητής**, οῦ, ὁ, = θρηνητήρ, A.*Ag.*1075, *BGU*34 iv 4 (iii A.D.). **-ητικός**, ή, όν, *inclined to lament, querulous*, Arist.*EN*1171ᵇ10. 2. *of* or *for a dirge*, αὔλημα, μόναυλος, Poll.4.73, 75; τὸ θ. *matter for lament*, Plu.2.623a. Adv. -κῶς Poll.6.202. **-ήτρια**, ἡ, fem. of θρηνητήρ, Sch.E.*Ph.*1489. **-ήτωρ**, ορος, ὁ, = θρηνητήρ, Man.4.190.

θρηνο-λάλος [ᾰ], ον, *uttering laments*, Σειρῆνες *IG*12(8).445.5 (Thasos). **-λογέω**, *bewail*, τινα *IPE*2.197 (Panticapaeum). **-ποιός**, *luctificus*, Gloss.

θρῆνος, ὁ, (θρέομαι) *dirge, lament*, Il.24.721, Sapph.136, Pi.*I.*8(7).64, Hdt.2.79, 85, etc.; θ. οὑμός *for* me, A.*Pr.*390; εἰπεῖν..θ. θέλω ἐμὸν τὸν αὐτῆς Id.*Ag.*1322. 2. *complaint, sad strain*, *h.Pan.*18; Γοργόνων οὔλιον θ. Pi.*P.*12.8; θρῆνοι καὶ ὀδυρμοί Pl.*R.*398d, etc.: pl., *lamentations*, θρήνων ᾠδάς S.*El.*88 (lyr.), etc.; title of poems by Pindar, Stob.4.39.6, etc. (Distd. fr. ἐπικήδειον by Trypho ap.Ammon. *Diff.* p.54 V. (cf. Ptol.Asc.p.404 H.), ἐπικήδειον τὸ ἐπὶ τῷ κήδει, θ. δὲ ἐν ᾡδήποτε χρόνῳ.)

θρῆνυξ, υκος, ὁ, = sq., Euph.39; Boeot. **θρᾶνυξ** Corinn.38.

θρῆνυς, υος, ὁ, (θράομαι) *footstool*, ὑπὸ δὲ θρῆνυν ποσὶν ἥσει Il.14.240, cf. Od.19.57. II. θ. ἑπταπόδης the seven-foot *bench*, perh. *helmsman's bench* or *bridge*, Il.15.729.

θρηνῳδ-έω, *sing a dirge over*, τινα E.*IA* 1176. **-ημα**, ατος, τό, *dirge, lament*, Sch.S.*El.*92 (ed. T. Johnson, Oxon. 1705). **-ης**, ες, *like a dirge, fit for a dirge*, ἁρμονίαι Pl.*R.*398e, 411a; ὀδυρμός Tim. *Pers.*113; φθόγγος, μέλος, Plu.*Sull.*7, Hdn.4.2.5; τὸ θ. τῆς ψυχῆς *mournful mood*, Plu.2.822c. 2. = θρηνητικός, of persons, Pl.*Lg.* 792b; τὸ θ. Id.*R.*606b. **-ία**, ἡ, *lamentation*, ib.604d, Plu.2. 657a. **-ικός**, ή, όν, *appropriate to a dirge*, ἁρμονία ib.1136e. **-ός**, ὁ, ἡ, *one who sings a dirge, mourner*, Alciphr.1.36, Ptol.*Tetr.*180, Anon.*Oxy.*864, cf. Poll.6.202.

θρήνωμα, ατος, τό, = θρῆνος, εἰς τὸν Ὄσῖριν *PTeb.*140 (pl., i B.C.).

Θρῇξ, ῃκός, ὁ, Ion. for Θρᾷξ (q.v.); fem. Θρῇσσα, ἡ (q.v.).

θρήσασθαι, v. θράομαι.

θρησκ-εία, Ion. **-ίη**, ἡ, (θρησκεύω) *religious worship, cult, ritual*, ἡ περὶ τὰ ἱρὰ θ. Hdt.2.18, *IG*12(5).141.5 (Paros, iii B.C.), J.*AJ*17.9.3, etc.; τοῦ Ἀπόλλωνος *SIG*801 *D* (Delph., i A.D.); ἡ περί τινος θ. ib. 867.48 (Ephesus, ii A.D.): pl., *rites*, Hdt.2.37, D.H.2.63, *PGnom.* 185 (ii A.D.), Wilcken *Chr.*72 (iii A.D.). 2. *religion, service of God*, Lxx *Wi.*14.18, *Act.Ap.*26.5, *Ep.Jac.*1.26; θ. τοῦ θεοῦ μία ἐστί, μὴ εἶναι κακόν *Corp.Herm.*12 fin.; ἑκατέρα θ., i.e. Christianity and Paganism, Them.*Or.*5.69c; θ. τῶν ἀγγέλων *worshipping* of angels, *Ep.Col.*2. 18. 3. in bad sense, *religious formalism*, ἀντὶ ὁσιότητος Ph.1.195; θ. βιωτική vulgar *superstition*, Sor.1.4. **-ευμα**, ατος, τό, *religious worship*, *IG*2².1099.29 (Plotina), Just.*Nov.*103.2 (pl.). **-ευσις**, εως, ἡ, = foreg., Phint.ap.Stob.4.23.61ᵃ (pl.). **-ευτήριον**, τό, *place of worship*, Sch.Pi.*O.*7.33. **-ευτής**, οῦ, ὁ, *worshipper*, *BCH* 37.94 (Thessalonica), Ptol.*Tetr.*159, Sch.Pi.*O.*3.28. **-εύω**, *perform religious observances*, Hdt.2.64, *Sammelb.*991 (iii A.D.). II. c. acc., *worship*, θεούς D.H.2.23, *IG*5(2).268.42 (Mantinea), Porph. *Abst.*4.9, Hdn.1.11.1:—Pass., Dinon 17, Lxx *Wi.*14.16, Porph.ap. Eus.*PE*3.11: impers., εἴ τι ἄλλο -εύεσθαι νόμιμον ἦν D.H.1.76. III. *to be a devotee*, Plu.*Alex.*2. **-ια**, τά, *religious observances*, *OGI* 210.9 (Nubia, iii A.D.). **-ος**, ον, *religious*, *Ep.Jac.*1.26; in bad sense, *superstitious*, Hsch. (Hsch. has also **θρεσκός**.) **-ώδης**, ες, = foreg., Vett.Val.104.14.

Θρῇσσα, ἡ, Ion. for Θρᾷσσα.

θρήττανον· τῆς ἁμάξης ἐφ' ᾧ τὰ ἀγόμενα ἐπιτίθεται, Hsch.

Θρῖα, ἡ, *Thria*, name of an Attic deme, St.Byz., etc.: **Θριᾷ** *at Thria*, *IG*1².329, but **Θριᾶσι** X.*HG*5.4.21, Is.11.42: **Θριῶζε** *to Thria*, Th.1.114, *BCH*50.529 (ii A.D.): **Θριῶθεν** *from Thria*, *IG*2². 1672.109:—Adj. **Θριάσιος**, α, ον, πεδίον Hdt.8.65, etc.; πύλαι Plu. *Per.*30.

θριάζω, (θριαί) *to be rapt, possessed*, S.*Fr.*466, E.*Fr.*478; also glossed by φυλλολογεῖν (as if from θρῖον), Hsch., *EM*455.45:—also **θριάομαι**, = μαντεύομαι, *AB*265; cf. sq.

θρῖαί, ῶν, αἱ, *pebbles used in divination*, Philoch.196, Call.*Ap.*45, cf. Sch. ad loc., *EM*455.34. II. personified as nymphs of Parnassus, Philoch. l. c., Sch.Call. l. c., dub. cj. in *h.Merc.*552.

θρῐαμβ-ευτής, οῦ, ὁ, *one who enjoys a triumph*, Suid. **-ευτικός**, ή, όν, v.l. for θριαμβικός, Plu.*Cat.Ma.*24. **-εύω**, pf. τεθριάμβευκα Id. *Ant.*34: (θρίαμβος):—*triumph*, Plb.6.53.7, Posidon.1 J., Plu. *Pomp.*45, etc.; ἀπό τινος *triumph over*, Id.*Rom.*25, App.*Celt.*1; κατὰ τῆς πατρίδος Plu.*Cor.*35, cf. App.*BC*1.80; ἐπί τινι ib.4.31; also θ. ἐπὶ νίκῃ Hdn.3.9.1; ἀπὸ μάχης Plu.*Publ.*9: c. acc. cogn., θ. νίκην ἄδακρυν Id.2.318b; δεύτερον θρίαμβον Id.*Fab.*23. II. *lead in triumph*, of conquered enemies, τινα Id.*Comp.Thes.Rom.*4, *Ep. Col.*2.15:—Pass., -εύεσθαι ὑπό τινος Plu.*Cor.*35; μηδ' ἐν ἐμοὶ περιίδῃς -ευόμενον σεαυτόν Id.*Ant.*84. 2. *lead in triumph*, as a general does his army, metaph., ἡμᾶς ἐν Χριστῷ 2*Ep.Cor.*2.14. III. *divulge, noise abroad*, Phot., cf. Suid. s. v. ἐξεφοίτα. **-ικός**, ή, όν, *triumphal*, ἐσθής D.H.5.35, J.*BJ*7.5.4; κόσμος Str.5.2.2; πομπή, τιμαί, Plu.*Aem.* 30, *Sert.*18; κηδεύματα connexions *with triumphal families*, Id.*Cat. Ma.*24 (v.l. -ευτικῶν); ἄνδρες θ., Lat. *viri triumphales*, Id.*Cam.*21, cf. *Crass.*1. Adv. -κῶς, ἠμφιεσμένος App.*BC*2.106. **-ίς**, ίδος, pecul. fem. of θριαμβικός, στολή Anon.ap.Suid.

θρῐαμβοδιθύραμβος [ῠ], ον, epith. of Bacchus, Pratin.Lyr.1.16.

θρίαμβος [ῐ], ὁ, *hymn to Dionysus*, sung in festal processions to his honour, Cratin.36. 2. epith. of Dionysus, *Trag.Adesp.*140, D.S. 4.5, Ath.1.30b, Plu.*Marc.*22, Arr.*An.*6.28.2. 3. metaph., *scandal*, δεδιὼς τὸν ἐκ λόγων θ. Conon 31.1. II. = Lat. *triumphus* (which is borrowed fr. θ. through Etruscan), Plb.6.15.8, D.S.12.64, *Mon. Anc.Gr.*2.20, *SIG*804.9 (Cos, i A.D.), Plu.*Publ.*20, etc.; ὁ μέγας θ. the *triumph*, opp. ὁ ἐλάττων θ. *ovatio*, Id.*Marc.*22, cf. D.H.8.67; ὁ πεζὸς θ., = *ovatio*, Id.9.36. (For the termination perh. cf. ἴαμβος, διθύραμβος, but the origin of θρι- is unknown.)

θρίᾶσις [θρῖ], εως, ἡ, (θριάζω) *poetic rapture*, Suid. s. v. θρίαμβος.

θρῖαστής, οῦ, ὁ, (θρῖον) *planter of fig-trees*, Poll.7.140.

θριάτιον· ἁπαλωτέρα τροφή, Hsch.

θριγγίον, **-γός**, **-γόω**, later forms for θριγκίον, etc.

θριγκ-ίον, τό, Dim. of sq., Luc.*Gall.*22, App.*Mith.*71, Just.*Nov.* 133.1. **-ός**, ὁ, *topmost course of stones in a wall, cornice, coping*, mostly in pl., Od.17.267, S.*Fr.*506, Arist.*Ph.*246ᵃ18, *IG*7.3073.68 (Lebad.); of the row of slabs behind the frieze, *SIG*244 ii 61 (Delph., iv B.C.); δῶμα περιφερὲς θριγκοῖς E.*Hel.*430: sg., Id.*IT*47. b. *frieze*, θ. κυάνοιο Od.7.87; χρυσοῦς D.S.18.26. 2. metaph., *coping-stone, last finish*, θ. ἀθλίων κακῶν E.*Tr.*489; δοκεῖ ὥσπερ θ. τοῖς μαθήμασιν ἡ διαλεκτική.. ἐπάνω κεῖσθαι Pl.*R.*534e. II. *wall, fence* of any sort, E.*Ion* 1321, Ar.*Th.*58 (anap.), Paus.1.42.7, Plu.2.85f. 2. *row*, ὀδόντων Hp.*Ep.*23.—Later forms are **θριγγός** v.l. in Plu. l. c.; **θριγχός** v.l. in Dsc.4.85; **τριγχός**, Sch.Il.11.774, Eust.1570.17, *SIG* 1231.6 (Nicomedia, iii/iv A.D.). **-όω**, *surround with a* θριγκός, [αὐλὴν] ἐθρίγκωσεν ἀχέρδῳ *fenced* it with thorn-bushes, Od.14.10, dub. in *IG*1².111. II. *build even to the coping-stone*: metaph., *complete, make an end of*, ἄτας τάσδε θριγκώσων φίλοις A.*Ag.*1283; δῶμα -ῶσαι κακοῖς *to bring* the house *to the height* of misery, E.*HF* 1280; θριγκουμένη.. οἰκία Arist.*Ph.*246ᵃ19. **-ώδης**, ες, *like a coping*, Hsch. s. v. αἱμασιαί. **-ωμα**, ατος, τό, *coping, cornice*, cj. for τριχώμασιν, J.*AJ*15.11.3: metaph., θ. τῆς τροφῆς, of salt, Plu.2.685b.

θρῐδάκ-ηΐς, ΐδος, fem. Adj., *of the lettuce*, χαίτη Nic.*Th.*838. **-ίας**, ου, ὁ, = μανδραγόρας θῆλυς, Dsc.4.75. **-ίνη** [κῐ], ἡ, Att. form of Ion. and Dor. θρίδαξ (Ath.2.68f):—*lettuce*, Cratin.330, Hp.*Mul.*2. 136, Amphis 20, Eub.14, Thphr.*HP*1.12.2; ἡ πικρὰ θ. ib.9.11.10; in this signf., opp. θρίδαξ, Gal.13.387, Hellad.ap.Phot.*Bibl.*p.532 B. 2. *wild lettuce, Lactuca Scariola*, Id. l. c.; θ. ἥμερος ib.7.6.2. 3. *sea-lettuce*, a kind of sea-weed, Aët.12.42 (pl.). II. fem. Adj. (sc. μᾶζα), a kind of *cake*, Luc.*Lex.*3, Ath.3.114f, Hellad. l. c. **-ῖνίς**, ίδος, ἡ, = foreg., Stratt.66.6 (lyr.). **-ιον**, τό, Dim. of θρίδαξ, Plu.2. 349a (pl.). **-ίσκα**, ἁ, Lacon. for θριδακίνη, Alcm.20. **-ώδης**, ες, *lettuce-like*, Dsc.2.132 (Comp.).

θρίδαξ (Cypr. **θρόδαξ**, q.v.), ἄκος, ἡ, Ion. and Dor. for θριδακίνη, *lettuce*, Epich.158, Hdt.3.32, Hp.*Mul.*1.78, Thphr.*HP*7.2.4, *BGU* 1118.13 (i B.C.), *IG*4.955.8 (Epid.), etc.:—also **θρύδαξ**, *POxy.*1212 (ii A.D.); **θίδραξ**, Hsch. s. v. θιδρακίνη. [ῐ, Epich. l. c., *AP*9.412 (Phld.), 11.295 (Lucill.), 413 (Ammian.), cf. θριδακηΐς, -ίνη, -ινίς: the accentuation θρῖδαξ lacks authority.]

θρίζω, poet. syncop. for θερίζω, A.*Ag.*536. **θριήλοοι**· ἱερεῖς, Hsch.

θριῆσαι· καπρίσαι, Hsch. **θριληδεῖν**· θρυλλεῖν, Id. (prob. θρυλίζειν). **θριμμός**· γογγυσμός, Id.

θρῖνάκη, = θρῖναξ, Call.*Fr.*46 P. (nisi leg. θρίνακ' ἦν).

Θρῖνάκίη, ἡ, (θρῖναξ) a legendary island, Od.11.107, etc.: afterwards identified with Sicily and written Τρινακρία (from τρεῖς, ἄκραι) (q.v.); cf. Τριναχία:—also **Θρῖνακίς**, ίδος, ἡ, Str.6.2.1:—Adj. **Θρῖνάκιος**, α, ον, *Sicilian*, ῥίζα Nic.*Th.*529.

θρῖναξ, ἄκος, ἡ, *trident, three-pronged fork*, used to stir grain, etc., Ar.*Pax* 567, Nic.*Th.*114, *PFay.*120.3 (i/ii A.D.); as a signet, *Tab. Heracl.*1.5. [ῑ: later ῐ, *AP*6.95 codd. (Antiphil.).]

θρινία· ἄμπελος ἐν Κρήτῃ, Hsch.

θρίξ, ἡ, gen. τρῐχός, dat. pl. θριξί (τρίχεσιν J.*AJ*16.7.3 is f.l. for τρυχ-):—*hair*, Hom. only in pl., ὀρθαὶ τρίχες ἔσταν ἐνὶ.. μέλεσσι Il. 24.359; mostly, *hair of the head*, 22.77, Od.13.431; αἱ ἐν τῇ κεφαλῇ τρίχες Th.1.6; sheep's *wool*, Il.3.273, Hes.*Op.*517; pig's *bristles*, Il.19.254, Od.10.239; τρίχες ἄκραι οὐραῖαι, of a horse's tail, Il.23. 519; ἀνάστασις τῶν τριχῶν, of a lark's *crest*, Gal.12.361. II. later in sg. collectively, A.*Th.*535, *Ag.*562, S.*El.*451; τριχὸς πλόκαμος, βόστρυχος, A.*Th.* 564 (lyr.), *Ch.* 229; γενείου θρίξ Id. *Pers.*1056; κόμη θρίξ Lxx *Nu.*6.6; Ἐπαφρόδιτον.. τὴν παιδικὴν τρίχα Ὑγίᾳ (sc. ἀνέθηκεν) *IG*12(5).173 (Paros, i A.D.); of a horse's *mane*, S.*Fr.*475; of dogs, X.*Cyn.*4.8 (sg. and pl.). 2. *a single hair*, οὐδὲ τρίχ[α] Alc. *Supp.*14.10: prov., θρὶξ ἀνὰ μέσσον *only a hair's breadth* wanting, Theoc.14.9, cf. X.*Smp.*6.2; ἄξιον τριχός, i. e. good for nothing, Ar. *Ra.*614; οὐδ' ἂν τριχὸς πριαίμην Eup.7.18 D.; ἐκ τριχὸς κρέμασθαι to hang by *a hair*, Aristaenet.2.1, Zen.3.47; ἀπὸ τ. ἠρτῆσθαι *AP*5.229 (Paul. Sil.); ἐπὶ τριχὸς ἦν ἡ σωτηρία Procop.*Aed.*6.6; εἰς ἱερὴν τρίχα ἐλθεῖν, i. e. to come to life's end, v.l. in *AP*7.164 (Antip. Sid.), but cf. *Epigr.Gr.*248.13; μόνον οὐχὶ τῶν τ., φασί, λαμβάνεται 'saute aux yeux', S.E.*M.*7.257. III. Medic., *vein* on the right lobe of the liver, Hp.*Mul.*1.43 (v.l. ἡ σῦριγξ), Gal.19.104.

Θριξάλλιος, ὁ (sc. μήν), name of month at Lamia, *IG*9(2).74.

θρῖοβόλος, ὁ, (θριαί) *one who throws pebbles into the divining-urn, soothsayer*, Epic.ap.St.Byz. s.v. Θρῖα, Suid.

θρῖον, τό, *fig-leaf*, Ar.*Ec.*707, Sotad.Com.1.27: generally, *leaf*, Nic.*Al.*55; *petal*, ib.407. 2. prov., θρίου ψόφος, of empty threats, Ar.*V.*436. II. *mixture of eggs, milk, lard, flour, honey, cheese*, etc., wrapped in fig-leaves, θ. ταρίχους, δημοῦ, Id.*Ach.*1101, 1102; δημοῦ βοείου θρῖον Id.*Eq.*954; ἐγκεφάλου θρίω δύο (a pun on the fig-leaf-like hemispheres of the brain) Id.*Ra.*134, cf. Sch. ll. cc. [ῑ, Ar. *Eq.*954, al., Men.518.11; θρῖα, θρῖον are ff. ll. for θρύα, θρύον in Theoc. 13.40, *AP*9.723 (Antip. Sid.); cf. λεπτόθριος.]

θρῖπήδεστος, ον, (θρίψ, ἐδήδεσμαι) *worm-eaten*, ῥίζαι Thphr.*HP* 9.14.3, cf. *IG*2².1628.163, al., 1672.306; κεραῖαι θριπήδεσται ib.1628. 205, but -οι 1629.328. 2. σφραγίδια θ. seals *made of worm-eaten wood*, Ar.*Th.*427, cf. Sch. 3. metaph., = διεφθαρμένη, Hyp.*Fr.* 82. (Freq. corrupted to -έστατος, as in Ar.*Th.* l. c. (ap.Suid.), Hyp. l. c. (v.l.), Luc.*Lex.*13 (v.l.), cf. Paus.Gr.*Fr.*205, but a Sup. is never necessary exc. in Thphr.*HP*3.8.5 (v. θριπώδης).)

θρῖπό-βρωτος, ον, (βιβρώσκω) = foreg., Philosteph.ap.Hsch., Lyc. 508:—a form **θιπόβρωτος** (dissim.) is condemned by Hsch. **-φάγος** [φᾰ], ον, *eating wood-worms*, Arist.*HA*616ᵇ29.

θρῖπώδης, ες, *full of wood-worms*, in Sup. -έστατον, ξύλον Thphr. *HP*3.8.5 vulg.; θριπηδέστατον cod. Urb. (v. θριπήδεστος).

θρίσκειν· τὸν θροῦν, Hsch.

θρίσσα, Att. **θρίττα**, ἡ, *a fish*, = τριχίας, Anaxandr.41.52, Ephipp. 12.5, Arist.*HA*621^{b}16, *PCair.Zen.*40(iii B.C.), al., *Gp.*20.7.1 : **θρείσσα**, *BGU*816.20 (iii A.D.): **θρίσσος**, ὁ, is v.l. in *AP*6.304 (Phan.).

θρισσ-έμπορος, ὁ, *dealer in* θρίσσαι, *PCair.Zen.*261 (iii B.C.). **-ίον**, τό, Dim. of θρίσσα, *POxy.*1923.9 (v/vi A.D.).

θρίσσω, = τὸ κατὰ ψυχὴν ἐξίστασθαι, Ar.Byz.(?) ap.Erot.; Ion. acc. to Greg.Cor.p.571 S.

θρίττε, = θρέττε, Hsch.

θρίψ, gen. θριπός, ὁ (not ἡ, v.l. in Men.540.5), *wood-worm*, Thphr. *HP*5.4.4, *AP*12.190 (Strat.); ὁ θ. τὸ ξύλον (sc. λυμαίνεται) Men. l.c. II. metaph., *skinflint, miser*, Hsch. (Perh. connected with τρίβω.)

Θριώ· λίπος· ἑορτὴ Ἀπόλλωνος, καὶ ἡ σύντροφος αὐτοῦ, Hsch. **θρόδαξ**, Cypr. for θρίδαξ, Id.:—Dim. **θοδράκιον**, τό, Choerob. in *An.Ox.* 2.218 (sic cod.).

θροέω, aor. ἐθρόησα, poet. θρο– B.3.9, S.*Aj.*947, (δι–) Th.6.46:—Med. and Pass. (v. infr.): (θρόος):—*cry aloud*, B. l. c., S.*El.*1410; παρὰ νοῦν θ. Id.*Ph.*1195 (lyr.); πᾶσιν to all, Id.*Aj.*67, cf. *Tr.*531; *speak, say*, A.*Pr.*608 (lyr.); θρόει, τίς..; E.*Or.*187 (lyr.): c. acc. cogn., θ. αὐδάν A.*Ch.*829 (lyr.), E.*Or.*1248 (lyr.); λόγον S.*Ant.*1287 (lyr.); πολλά Id.*Aj.*592; εὔφημα, ψευδῆ, E.*IA*143 (lyr.), 1345 (troch.):—Med., τοῦτ' ἔπος –ούμενος A.*Eu.*510 (lyr.). 2. c. acc., *tell out, utter aloud*, τοὐμὸν πάθος Id.*Ag.*1137 (lyr.); νόμον ἄνομον ib. 1141 (lyr.), cf. 104; πᾶς τοῦτό γ' Ἑλλήνων θροεῖ S.*OC*597; θάνατόν τινι θ. ib.1425.—Rare, exc. in Trag.; in late Prose, J.*AJ*18.6.10, 19.1.16. II. causal, *scare, terrify*, Sch.E.*Hec.*180, al.:—Pass., *to be stirred, moved*, of joy, ἡ κοιλία μου ἐθροήθη ἐπ' αὐτόν Lxx *Ca.*5.4; of fear, μὴ θροεῖσθε *Ev.Matt.*24.6, cf. 2*Ep.Thess.*2.2.

θρομβ-εῖον, Ion. **-ήϊον**, τό, Dim. of θρόμβος, Nic.*Al.*295:—also **-ίον**, τό, Dsc.*Alex.*25.

θρομβο-ειδής, ές, *full of clots* or *lumps*, Hp.*Mul.*1.11,38. **-ομαι**, Pass., *to become clotted, curdled*, of blood, Nic.*Al.*315, Gal.18(1).33; of honey, Id.14.22. 2. *contain clots*, ἢν θρομβωθέωσιν αἱ μῆτραι Hp.*Mul.*2.165; of the breasts, Dsc.*Eup.*1.128:—Act., *cause to coagulate*, only as v.l. in Sch.Nic.*Th.*709.

θρόμβ-ος, ὁ, (τρέφω, τέτροφα) *lump*, Hdt.1.179; *clot* of blood, A. *Ch.*533, al., Pl.*Criti.*120a, etc.; χολῆς Hp.*Morb.*2.75; of milk, *curd*, αἰγῶν ἀπόρρους θ. Antiph.52.8; θρόμβοι ἁλῶν *coarse* salt, Suid. b. *drop*, θρόμβοι αἵματος καταβαίνοντες.. *Ev.Luc.*22.44. 2. *nipple*, *PLond.*1821.42. II. θ.· ὑψηλὸς τόπος, Hsch. **-ώδης**, ες, = θρομβοειδής, οὖρα Hp.*Aph.*4.69; ἀφροί S.*Tr.*702; σπέρματα Arist.*HA*582^{a}31. **-ωσις**, εως, ἡ, *becoming curdled*, αἵματος καὶ γάλακτος Dsc.5.13; αἵματος Antyll.ap.Orib.7.7.9, cf. Gal.8.408, Lyd.*Mens.*4. 116. 2. *blocked vein, thrombosis*, Cael.Aur.*TP*4.40.

θρον-ίζομαι, Pass., *to be enthroned*, Lxx *Es.*1.2. II. *to be initiated, consecrated*, τισι *PMag.Lond.*121.747. **-ιον**, τό, Dim. of θρόνος, *EM*456.28. II. part of the constellation Cassiopea, Ptol. *Alm.*8.2. **-ίς**, ίδος, ἡ, = foreg. I, Them.*Or.*31.353d. **-ισμός**, ὁ, *enthronement*, D.Chr.12.33, Man.4.104 (pl.). **-ιστής**, οῦ, ὁ, *enthroner*, *POxy.*1380.251 (ii A.D.). **-ῑτικός**, ή, όν, *throne-shaped*, συνψέλιον *TAM*2(1).210 (Sidyma).

θρονίτις· πρώτιστος, Hsch.

θρόνον, τό, only in pl. θρόνα, *flowers embroidered on cloth*, ἐν δὲ θρόνα ποικίλ' ἔπασσε Il.22.441, cf. Sch.Theoc.2.59, and v. τρόνα. II. *herbs used as drugs and charms*, Theoc.2.59, Nic.*Th.*493, 936, Lyc. 674, Aglaïas 7; used in sacrificial offering, *UPZ*96.4 (ii B.C.).

θρονοποιός, όν, *making thrones* or *seats*, Poll.7.182.

θρόνος, ὁ, *seat, chair*, Od.1.145, Ath.5.192e, *PMasp.*6 ii 63 (vi A.D.), etc. 2. *throne, chair of state*, θ. βασιλήϊος Hdt.1.14, cf. X. *HG*1.5.3, etc.; Ζηνὸς ἐπὶ θρόνον Theoc.7.93: metaph., Pl.*R.*553c: pl., ἐν θρόνοις ἥμενοι A.*Ch.*975; ἐκ τυραννίδος θρόνων τ' ἄϊστον ἐκβαλεῖν Id.*Pr.*910; Διὸς θρόνοι S.*Ant.*1041, cf. Ar.*Av.*1732; *king's estate* or *dignity*, σκῆπτρα καὶ θρόνους S.*OC*425, cf. 448; [γῆς] κράτη τε καὶ θρόνους νέμω Id.*OT*237, cf. *Ant.*166, etc.; in the Prytaneum, τῷ [Ἀπόλλωνι] θ. ἐξελεῖν *IG*1^{2}.78. 3. *oracular seat* of Apollo, E.*IT*1254, 1282 (both lyr.); μαντικοὶ θ. A.*Eu.*616, etc. 4. *chair of a teacher*, Pl. *Prt.*315c, Philostr.*VS*2.2, Lib.*Ep.*819, *AP*9.174 (Pall.). 5. *judge's bench*, Plu.2.807b, Him.*Ed.*10.9, 13.16. 6. Astrol., = ὕψωμα, *PMich.* in *Class.Phil.*22.22 (pl.). b. *favourable combination of planetary positions*, Ptol.*Tetr.*51. II. a kind of *bread*, Neanth.1 J. III. name of a lozenge, Paul.Aeg.3.42, 7.12.

θρόνωσις, εως, ἡ, = θρονισμός, *enthronement of the newly initiated*, at the mysteries of the Corybantes, Pl.*Euthd.*277d.

θρόος, Att. **θροῦς**, ὁ, (θρέομαι) *noise* as of many voices, οὐ γὰρ πάντων ἦεν ὁμὸς θ. Il.4.437; poet. of musical sounds, πολύφατος θ. ὕμνων Pi.*N.*7.81; θ. αὐλῶν Epic.ap.Plu.2.654f. 2. *murmur* of a crowd or assembly, Th.4.66, 8.79, D.H.6.57, etc. II. *report, rumour*, X.*Cyr.*6.1.37, Plu.*Galb.*26, D.C.44.18.

θροσέως, v. θρασύς.

θρυαλλ-ίδιον, τό, Dim. of sq., Luc.*Tim.*14. **-ίς**, ίδος, ἡ, *plantain, Plantago crassifolia*, used for making wicks, Thphr.*HP*7.11.2, Nic.*Th.*899, *BGU*1118.15 (i B.C.). II. *wick*, Ar.*Ach.*874, al., Philyll.26. b. κηρίνη θ. wax-*candle*, Archipp.3 D. III. = φλόμος, Ps.-Dsc.4.103, Plin.*HN*25.121.

θρύαλλον, τό, *shower of smuts* from a distant bonfire, Vett.Val. 345.22.

θρυαρίς· ψιαθής, Hsch. **θρυασμός**· φωνή, Id. (fort. θρυλισμός).

θρύβω, late form, = θρύπτω, Mich. in *PN*14.16.

θρῡγονάω, *tap at*, τὴν θύραν Ar.*Ec.*34 (v. l. τρυγον–, τρυγαν–); perh. to be read in Pherecr.10: cf. **θρυγανᾶ**· κνᾶται, ξύει, Hsch., **θρυγονᾶν** τὸ ξύειν Theognost.*Can.*20.

θρύ-ῐνος [ῠ], η, ον, (θρύον) *rushy*, Anon.ap.Suid., dub. in *PFlor.* 383.28 (iii A.D.). **-ῖτις**, ιδος, ἡ, *planted with rush*, γῆ *PFlor.*64.22 (iv A.D.), etc.

θρῡλ-έω, (θρῦλος) *make a confused noise, chatter, babble*, τὴν νύκτα θρυλῶν καὶ λαλῶν Ar.*Eq.*348; θρυλέοιμι trisyll., Theoc.2.142. II. c. acc., *repeat over and over*, θρυλοῦσ' ἅ γ' εἰπεῖν ἤθελον E.*El.*910; τὰ τοιαῦτα οἱ ποιηταὶ ἡμῖν ἀεὶ –οῦσιν, ὅτι.. Pl.*Phd.*65b; τὰ μυθώδη.., ἃ πάντες –οῦσιν Isoc.12.237; ὃ πάντες ἐθρύλουν τέως, δεῖν.. D.1.7, cf. 19.156; [τὴν τριήρη] θρυλήσει *will keep talking of* it, Id.21.160: abs., καθάπερ πάλαι θρυλῶ Epicur.*Nat.*109 G.; περὶ ἀγαθοῦ θ. Id.*Fr.*423: c. inf., *PSI*5.452.20 (iv A.D.):—Pass., *to be common talk*, τὸ –ούμενον, τὸ.. πανταχοῦ θ. E.*Fr.*285.1, cf. Isoc.*Ep.*6.7, Theopomp.Com.35, Antiph.246.2; τὸ θ. ποτε ἀπόρρητον D.2.6; ἡ ὑπὸ πάντων θρυλουμένη εἰρήνη Id.19.273; τὰ μὲν παλαιὰ καὶ θ. Anaxipp.1.4; περὶ τεθρυλημένου πολλοῖς Arist.*Rh.*1415^{a}3; αἱ τεθρ. καὶ κοιναὶ γνῶμαι ib.1395^{a}10; τὰ θ. περὶ τὸν βάτραχον Id.*HA*620^{b}11; τινῶν λόγων ὑπὸ τῆς μητρός μου θρυλησθέντων (sic) *UPZ*144.45 (ii B.C.). **-ημα**, ατος, τό, *common talk, by-word*, Lxx *Jb.*17.6. **-ητής**, οῦ, ὁ, *babbler*, *Gloss.* **-ητός**, ή, όν, *generally talked of*, Tz.*H.*12.36.

θρύλ-ιγμα [ῐ], ατος, τό, *fragment*, Lyc.880. **-ιγμός** or **-ισμός**, ὁ, *unmusical sound, false note*, D.H.*Comp.*11; ὅταν αὐλητὴς μὴ πιέσας τὸ στόμα θρυλισμὸν ἢ ἐκμελές τι αὐλήσῃ Porph. in *Harm.* p.204 W. **-ίζω**, *make a false note*, *h.Merc.*488 (θρυαλ– codd.).

θρῡλίσσω, *crush, shiver, smash*, θρυλίξας Lyc.487:—Pass., θρυλίχθη δὲ μέτωπον Il.23.396.

θρῦλος, ὁ, *noise as of many voices, murmur*, Batr.135, Orph.*Fr.* 286 (pl., = *Cat.Cod.Astr.*2.199), Demetr.Lac.*Herc.*1786.1 F., Anon. ap.Suid.—This word and its cognates are written with one λ in Papyri and best codd. (cf. Eust.1307.42), with λλ (as Batr. l. c.) in inferior codd., also in *PLips.*40 ii 10 (iv A.D.).

θρυμίς· ἰχθύς ποιός, Hsch.

θρύμμα, ατος, τό, (θρύπτω) *that which is broken off, bit*, Hp.*Mul.* 1.75, Ar.*Fr.*160, Aglaïas 20, Gal.6.343; ῥοιῆς θρύμματα *AP*6.232 (Crin.).

θρυμμᾰτίς, ίδος, ἡ, *a sort of cake*, Antiph.183.4, Philox.2.18, Luc. *Lex.*6.

θρυμνεύεται (θρημν– cod.)· ὑπερηφανεύεται, Hsch.; cf. θρύπτω II. 2.

θρῠό-εις, εσσα, εν, *rushy*, Nic.*Th.*200. **-κάλαμος** [κᾰ], ὁ, = θρύον I, *BGU*890 i 20. **-κοπέω**, *cut rushes*, *PLond.*1.131.80 (i A.D.), *POxy.*910.40 (ii A.D., Pass.). **-κοπία**, ἡ, *cutting of rushes*, *PLond.* 3.1171.58 (i B.C.), *POxy.*1628.18 (i B.C.).

θρύον [ῠ], τό, *reed, rush*, Il.21.351, Hp.*Steril.*246, Thphr.*HP*4.11. 12, Arist.*Mir.*844^{a}27: in sg. collectively, ἔπλεκεν Call.*Aet.*3.1.24, cf. D.S.3.10, Theoc.13.40 (pl.), *AP*9.723 (Antip. Sid.); [γῆν] καθαρὰν ἀπὸ θρύου (Pap. θρύου) *PTeb.*105.26 (ii B.C.), *POxy.*910.41 (ii A.D.): pl. written θρυία *UPZ*98.12 (ii B.C.). II. = στρύχνον μανικόν, *thorn-apple, Datura Stramonium*, Orph.*A.*916, Thphr.*HP*9.11.6 (θρύορον, βρύορον codd.), Dsc.4.73.

θρῠο-πώλης, ου, ὁ, *rush-seller*, *PLond.*1.125.39 (iv A.D.). **-πώλιον**, τό, *rush-seller's shop*, *UPZ*12.13 (ii B.C.). **-τίλλω**, *pluck rushes*, *PLond.*1.131.80 (i A.D., an incorrect formation).

θρύπτακον· κλάσμα ἄρτου (Cret.), Hsch.

θρυπτέον, *one must crumble*, Aët.9.12 (s. v.l.).

θρυπτικός, ή, όν, *able to break* or *crush*, λίθων Dsc.1.121, cf. Gal.8. 409. II. Pass., *easily broken*: metaph., *delicate, effeminate*, X. *Cyr.*8.8.15 (Comp.), *Mem.*1.2.5; σώματα cj. in Max.Tyr.10.2; θ. τι προσφθέγγεσθαι D.C.51.12. Adv. –κῶς Ael.*NA*2.11, Poll.6.185. 2. *saucy*, πρὸς τοὺς ἐραστάς Ael.*VH*3.12.

θρύπτω, aor. 1 ἔθρυψα (ἐν–) Hp.*Mul.*1.75:—Pass. and Med., fut. θρυφθήσομαι Arr.*An.*4.19.2; θρύψομαι Ar. (v. infr. II. 2c), Luc.*Symp.* 4: aor. 1 ἐθρύφθην Arist. *de An.*419^{b}26, (ὑπ–) dub. in *AP*5.293.15 (Agath.): aor. 2 ἐτρύφην [ῠ] (δι–) Il.3.363, ἐθρύβην Dsc.5.123: pf. τέθρυμμαι Hp.*Vict.*2.48: (akin to θραύω):—*break in pieces, break small*, Pl.*Cra.*426e, A.*Ag.*1595; Νεῖλος βώλακα θ. Theoc.17.80:—Pass., *to be broken small*, θρύπτεσθαι κερματιζόμενον ἀνάγκη πᾶν τὸ ὄν Pl. *Prm.*165b, cf. *AP*12.61; χιόνος τὰ μάλιστα θρυφθησόμενα Arr. l. c.; of dried leguminous seeds, *split*, Thphr.*HP*8.11.3, cf. *Sens.*51; of air, *to be dispersed*, Arist. *de An.* l. c., Theo Sm.p.50 H.: the literal sense is more common in compds. ἀπο–, διαθρύπτω, etc. II. metaph. in moral sense, *enfeeble*, esp. by debauchery and luxury, θ. τὰν ψυχάν Ti. Locr.103b; *corrupt*, [τινα] Pl.*Lg.*778a, Phld.*Mus.*p.79 K.; θ. τὰς ψυχὰς καὶ τὰ σώματα Jul.*Or.*1.10c; [οἱ κόλακες] ἀποκναίουσι τῶν κολακευομένων τὰ ὦτα θρύπτοντες Ph.1.453; θ. ἑαυτόν, = θρύπτεσθαι (v. infr.), Ael.*Ep.*9. 2. more freq. in Pass., with fut. Med., *to be enervated, unmanned*, μαλακίᾳ θρύπτεσθαι X.*Smp.*8.8; ἁπαλός τε καὶ τεθρυμμένος Luc.*Charid.*4; θρύπτεται ἡ ὄψις *is enfeebled*, Plu.2.936f; οἱ τεθρυμμένοι τὰς ὄψεις *weak*-sighted people, A.D.*Synt.*199.5. b. *wanton, riot*, ὅλην ἐκείνην εὐφρόνην ἐθρύπτετο f.l. in [S.]*Fr.*1127.9, cf. Luc.*Pisc.*31, *Anach.*29; *display moral weakness*, *POxy.*471.80 (ii A.D.); ἡδοναῖς ἀνάνδροις θ. Plu.2.751b; ἐπὶ τῷ κάλλει Phld.*Hom.*p.55 O.; ὄμμα θρυπτόμενον a *languishing* eye, *AP*5.286.8 (Agath.). c. *to be coy and prudish, bridle up*, esp. when asked a favour, θρύψομαι Ar.*Eq.*1163; ὡραζομένη καὶ θρυπτομένη Eup.358; ἁβρὰ καὶ θ. Charito 5.3; ἐθρύπτετο ὡς οὐκ ἐπιθυμῶν λέγειν Pl.*Phdr.*228c, cf. 236c, X.*Smp.*8.4; or when one *pretends to decline* an offer, Plu.*Mar.*14, *Ant.*12; θρύπτεσθαι πρός τινα *give oneself airs* toward him, Id.*Flam.*

18, Luc.DMeretr.12.1. d. grow conceited, τινι in or of a thing, AP 7.218.2 (Antip. Sid.); ἐσθῆτι πολυτελεῖ Ael.VH1.19, etc.; brag, Hld. 2.10.

θρυσέλινον, τό, an umbelliferous plant, Plin.HN25.141.

θρύσιος, ὁ, = θρύον, EM456.31:—written **θρύσις**, Sch.DIl.21.351. **θρύσκα**, τά, glossed by ἄγρια λάχανα, Hsch.

θρύψις, εως, ἡ, breaking in small pieces, οὔτε.. εἴη ἂν ἄπειρος ἡ θ. Arist.GC316^{b}30; dispersion, ἡ θ. τοῦ ἀέρος Id.de An.419^{b}23; coupled with διάλυσις, Chrysipp.Stoic.2.173. II. softness, weakness, σώματος Plu.Dem.4: esp. metaph., debauchery, X.Cyr.8.8.16, Plu.Lyc. 14: pl., Id.2.732e. 2. daintiness, κόμης ib.693b; θ. (cj. for τρίψις) ἐπικρατίδων Hp.Praec.10.

θρύψιχος, = θρυπτικός, Theognost.Can.20, Hsch.

θρυψίχρως, ωτος, ὁ, ἡ, of delicate skin, Hsch.

θρυώδης, ες, (θρύον) full of rushes, rushy, Str.8.3.24, Sch.Il.11.155.

θρῶναξ, ακος, ὁ, Lacon. for κηφήν, Hsch. **θρώπτει**· σκώπτει, Id.

θρῶσις, εως, ἡ, cord, line, Theognost.Can.20, Hsch.

θρῴσκω (so in Alc.Supp.12.9, but θρώσκω Did.ap.Hdn.Gr.2.522), Il.13.589, A.Ch.846, Eu.660: Ep. impf. θρῷσκον Il.15.314: fut. θοροῦμαι, Ion. 3 pl. θορέονται (ὑπερ-) 8.179, cf. A.Supp.873 (lyr.): aor. ἔθορον (ἐκ-) Il.7.182, etc., Ep. θόρον Il. (v. infr. 2), Hes.Sc.321, subj. θόρω Od. 22.303; inf. θορεῖν (ἀνα-) X.Lac.2.3, Ion. θορέειν (ὑπερ-) Il.12.53; later ἔθρωξα (ἀν-) Opp.H.3.293: pf. part. fem. τεθορυίης prob. in Antim.65: (cf. θορός: for the form cf. βλώσκω):—poet. Verb, leap, spring, χαμᾶζε θορών Il.10.528; ἐκ δίφροιο 8.320; ἀπὸ λέκτροιο Od.23.32; ἰχθὺς θρῴσκων κατὰ κῦμα Il.21.126; of arrows, ἀπὸ νευρῆφι δ' ὀϊστοὶ θρῷσκον 15.314, cf. 470, 16.773; of beans tossed from the winnowing shovel, ἀπὸ πτυόφιν θρῴσκωσιν κύαμοι 13.589; of the oar, S.OC718 (lyr.). 2. folld. by Prep., leap upon, assault, ἐπὶ Τρώεσσι θόρον Il.8.252, cf. 15.380; εἴς τινα A.R.1.1296; πλησίον τινός E.Or.257 (in this sense Hom. always uses aor.); of a recurring illness, attack, S.Tr.1028 (lyr.). 3. rush, dart, Pi.P.9.119; πεδίον over the plain, E.Ba.873 (lyr.); δόμους to the house, S.Tr.58: metaph., λόγοι πεδάρσιοι θρῴσκουσι leap up into air, i.e. melt away, A.Ch.846. II. trans., = θόρνυμαι, mount, impregnate, κνώδαλα Id.Fr.15; ὁ θρῴσκων the sire, Id.Eu.660; cf. θορός, θορή.

θρωσμός (θρῳσμός Apollon.ap.Hdn.Gr.2.522), ὁ, springing; of ground rising from the plain, ἐπὶ θρωσμῷ πεδίοιο Il.10.160, 11.56; ποταμοῖο A.R.2.823 (pl.).

θρώσσει· γεννᾷ, φοβεῖται, Hsch.

θύα, ἡ, = θύον I, Thphr.HP5.3.7.

θυάκτας, α, ὁ, sacrificing priest, IG4.757 B (Troezen, ii B.C.).

θυάλημα, v. θυήλημα. **θυαλόν**· τὸ θυτοῖς διαλαβεῖν, θυμιᾶσαι, Hsch. **θυάματα**· τὸ θύμον, καὶ θυμιάματα, Id.

θυανία, ἡ, prob. f.l. for ὑανία, Dor. for ὑην-, Epich.148.

θύανον· τὴν θυώνην (q.v.), ἐστὶ δὲ πέμμα ἀντὶ βοός, Hsch.

θύαρος, ὁ, = αἶρα II, Ps.-Dsc.2.100.

θυά(ρ)παξ, ἄγος, ὁ, ἡ, = ἱερόσυλος, Hsch.

θυάς, άδος, ἡ, (θύω) = θυιάς (q.v.). II. attack, πλευρωνίας Mich. in PN30.20. III. θύας· πηδήσας, Hsch.; cf. θύασσε· ἐπήδησε, Cyr.

θυαφόρος, ὁ, thurifer, SIG1025.52 (Cos, iv/iii B.C.).

θυάω, rut, of swine, Arist.HA546^{a}27, 573^{b}7.

Θυβριάς, άδος, ἡ, = Θυμβριάς, IG14.1389 i 1.

θυγατερεῖς, ίδος, ἡ, = θυγατριδῆ, Inscr.Magn.196.9.

θυγάτηρ [ᾰ], ἡ, gen. θυγατέρος contr. θυγατρός; dat. θυγατέρι, θυγατρί; acc. θυγατέρα Ep. θύγατρα Il.1.13; voc. θύγατερ: nom. pl. θυγατέρες, Ep. and lyr. θύγατρες 9.144, Sapph.Supp.20a.16: gen. pl. -τέρων IG2^{2}.832.19, Pl.R.461c, poet. -τρῶν: dat. pl. -τράσι Ep. -τέρεσσι Il.15.197; both sets of forms are found in poetry, θυγατρός, -τρί, -τράσι are used in Prose:—daughter, Il.9.148, 290, Od.4.4, etc.; θύγατρες ἵππων, of mules, Simon.7; θ. ταύρων, of bees, Philo Tars.ap.Gal.13.269: metaph., Μοισᾶν θυγατέρες, of Odes, Pi.N.4.3; πλάστιγξ ἡ χαλκοῦ θ. Critias 1.9 D.; θ. Σειληνοῦ, of the vine, Jul. Caes.25; ψήφου συμβολικῆς θ., of a λάγυνος, AP6.248 (Marc. Arg.); of villages dependent on a city, LXX Jd.1.27, 1Ma.5.8. II. later, maidservant, slave, Phalar.Ep.142.3. [ῠ in Ep. in the longer forms, metri gr.] (Cf. Skt. duhitár-, Engl. daughter, etc.)

θυγατρ-ιδῆ, ἡ, daughter's daughter, granddaughter, And.1.128, Lys.32.2, D.H.Lys.21: uncontr. nom. pl. **-δέαι** Euph.94.2. **-ιδοῦς**, οῦ, ὁ, daughter's son, grandson, Is.8.17, Arist.Fr.473, Ph.2.82,425, OGI529.23 (Sebastopolis): acc. -δῆ, as though from nom. -δεύς, ib. 377.5 (Smyrna, i A.D.):—Ion. -ιδέος Hdt.5.67,69. **-ίζω**, call one daughter, Araros 7. **-ιον**, τό, Dim. of θυγάτηρ, little daughter or girl, Stratt.63, Men.428, PPetr.3 p.155 (iii B.C.), Macho ap.Ath.13.581c, Com.Adesp.14.19 D., SIG364.55 (Ephesus, iii B.C.), Plu.Ant. 33, Jul.Or.7.226b.

θυγατρό-γᾰμος, ον, married to one's own daughter, Nonn.D. 12.73. **-γόνος**, ον, begetting or bearing daughters, ib.7.212, al. **-θετέω**, adopt as daughter, Tz. ad Lyc.183 (Pass.). **-μιξία**, ἡ, incest with a daughter, POxy.237 vii 26 (ii A.D.). **-ποιΐα**, ἡ, adoption of a daughter, GDI3706 vi 61 (Cos):—written **-ποία**, IG 12(1).818 (Rhodes). **-ποιός**, όν, begetting daughters, of Lot, Ph.1.382. **-τεκνον**, τό, a daughter's child, Tz.H.1.595.

θυεία, Ion. -είη Nic.Th.91: ἡ:—mortar, Ar.Nu.676, Ra.124, al., Lys.Fr.62a. 2. cup of the cottabus, Pl.Com.46.3.—Later **θυία**, **θυΐα**, Ph.Bel.88.49, Dsc.2.76.3 and 4; in the sense of oil-press, PFay.42(a) i 10 (ii A.D.): **θυίη** [ῑ], Androm.ap.Gal.14.41: **θυεῖον**, τό, PLond.2.193.23 (ii A.D.). II. θύεια, v. θυία I.

θυείδιον, τό, Dim. of θυεία, Ar.Pl.710; wrongly written θυΐδιον in cod. Rav., as in Damocr.ap.Gal.14.118.

θύελλ-α [ῠ], ἡ, (θύω, cf. ἄελλα from ἄημι) hurricane, squall (cf. Arist.Mu.395^{a}6), κακὴ ἀνέμοιο Il.6.346, al.; μισγομένων ἀνέμων.. θ. Od.5.317; πυρός τ' ὀλοοῖο θύελλαι, prob. thunderstorms, 12.68; κούρας ἀνέλοντο θ. 20.66; τοὺς δ' αἶψ' ἁρπάξασα φέρεν πόντονδε θ. 10.48, cf. S.El.1151; ποντία θ. Id.OC1660; in similes, φλογὶ ἶσοι ἠὲ θυέλλῃ Il. 13.39; ἴκελοι πυρὶ ἠὲ θ. Hes.Sc.345: metaph., ἄτης θύελλαι (nisi leg. θυηλαί, q.v.) A.Ag.819; ὀχλικὴ θ. Phld.Rh.1.184 S. **-ειος**, α, ον, = sq., στροφάλιγγες Orac.ap.Suid. s.v. Ἰουλιανός. **-ήεις**, εσσα, εν, stormy, Nonn.D.1.22, 2.532. **-ίζω**, pf. part. Pass. -ισμένον (-θυλλιαμένον cod.)· τεταραγμένον, Hsch.

θυελλό-πους, ὁ, ἡ, gen. ποδος, storm-footed, storm-swift, Nonn.D. 37.441. **-τόκος**, ον, producing storms, ib.28.277. **-φορέομαι**, Pass., to be carried by a storm, D.S.16.80.

θυελλώδης, ες, stormy, Sch.S.Ant.418.

Θυέστειος, α, ον, of Thyestes, ῥάκη Ar.Ach.433; δεῖπνον Porph.Chr. 69.

θυέστης, ου, ὁ, pestle, Dionys.Trag.12.

θυ-εστον, τό, drink made from bruised spices, Hsch.: **-ευτός**· ὁ ἐξ ὄμβρων ποταμός, dub. l. in Theognost.Can.20.

θυ-ήεις, εσσα, εν, (θύος) smoking with incense, fragrant, Ep. epith. of βωμός, Il.8.48, Od.8.363, Hes.Th.557; σπάργανα h.Merc.237. **-ηκόος**, ὁ, = θυοσκόος, Hsch.; cf. θυηχόος. **-ηλέομαι**, = θυλέομαι, prob. in Poll.1.27. **-ηλή**, ἡ, (θύω) part of a victim offered in burnt-sacrifice, usu. in pl., ὁ δ' ἐν πυρὶ βάλλε θυηλάς Il.9.220, cf. Philoch.172, Nic.Fr.62, Ath.13.566a: generally, sacrifice, ἄνευ θυηλῶν Ar.Av.1520; θυηλαὶ ἀναίμακτοι AP6.324.3 (Leon. Alex.); θυσίαι καὶ θ. D.S.3.62, Porph.Abst.2.59: metaph., θυηλὴ Ἄρεος an offering to Ares, i.e. the blood of the slain, S.El.1423; ἄτης θυηλαί cj. Herm. for θύελλαι, A. Ag.819; cf. θυάλημα, θύλημα. **-ήλημα**, ατος, τό, sacrificial offering, Thphr.Char.10.13:—Ion. **θυαλήματα** SIG57.38 (Milet., v B.C.); cf. θύλημα. **-ημα**, ατος, τό, (θύω) = foreg., in pl., Tim.Lex.: = ἀρώματα, Hp.ap.Erot.

θυηπολ-έω, perform sacrifices, A.Ag.262, E.Tr.330 (lyr.), Pl.R. 364e, Polystr.p.9 W.; θεοῖς E.El.665. 2. trans., sacrifice, γέρας βρότειον τῷ Κρόνῳ θ. S.Fr.126, cf. 522, Maiist.13:—Pass., θυηπολεῖται δ' ἄστυ μάντεων ὕπο is filled with sacrifices by them, E.Heracl. 401. **-ία**, Ion. -ίη, ἡ, sacrificing, A.R.1.1124, AP5.16 (Gaet.), D.H.1.21, Hld.3.2, prob. in Puchstein Epigr.Gr.36 (pl., Nubia): generally, mystic rites, Orph.A.470. **-ικός**, ή, όν, sacrificial, πῦρ, μέρος, Iamb.Myst.5.11,18; θεσμός Zos.4.59. **-ιον**, τό, altar, Dorieus ap.Ath.10.413a:—also **-εῖον**, τό, Rev.Ét.Gr.19.234 (Aphrodisias).

θυηπόλος, ον, also η, ον Suid., (τελέω, τέλλω) performing sacrifices, sacrificial, χείρ A.Pers.202: Subst., diviner, soothsayer, E.IA746, Ar.Pax1124; priest, Εὐμόλποιο IG3.1337.9, cf. Phld.D.1.4; αἱ θ. παρθένοι, of the Vestal Virgins, D.H.2.64, al.

θύ[η]σις [ῠ], εως, ἡ, sacrifice, IG5(2).514 (Lycosura, nisi leg. θύ[ω]σις).

θυητά [ῠ], τά, fumigations, Aret.CD1.4, CA2.10.

θυη-φάγος [ᾰ], ον, devouring offerings, φλόξ A.Ag.597. **-χόος**, contr. **-χοῦς**, ὁ, = θυηκόος, IG1^{2}.372.203, 3.244, Eust.1601.3.

θυία, ἡ, odorous cedar, Juniperus foetidissima, Thphr.HP1.9.3, 4.1.3; or **θυεία**, ib.3.4.2,6. II. = θύον I (q.v.), Dsc.1.26. III. v. θυεία.

Θυῖα, τά, (θύω) festival of Dionysus at Elis, Paus.6.26.1.

Θυῖαι, αἱ, = Θυιάδες, Str.10.3.10, prob. l. for Θυιάσιν, S.Ant.1151 (lyr.).

θυιάς, άδος, ἡ:—written **θυάς** Tim.Fr.3, A.Th.498 cod. Med.: (θύω):—inspired, possessed woman, esp. Bacchante, ll. cc., cf. A.Th. 836, Supp.564 (both lyr.), Plu.2.293f, etc.; cf. foreg. II. fem. Adj., frantic, mad for love, Lyc.143.

θυΐδιον, v. θυείδιον.

θυΐνος [ῠ], η, ον, of the tree θύον (q.v.), δένδρα, ξύλον, Str.4.6.2, v.l. in Dsc.1.22; made of this wood, Callix.1, Apoc.18.12.

θυϊόεν· πλῆρες, and **θυϊόεντες**· ἀνθοῦντες, Hsch.

θυῖον, τό, resin, Thphr.HP5.2.1.

Θυῖος, ὁ (sc. μήν), name of a month in Thessaly and Boeotia, IG 9(2).109 b 57 (Halus), 7.341, etc.; in Naupactus, ib.9(1).357:—also **Θῦος**, ib.9(2).515.3 (Larissa), al.:—Boeot. **Θούιος** or **Θιούιος**, ib.7. 517, 3172.116.

θυιόω, aor. part. Pass. θυιωθείς· μανείς, ὁρμήσας, Hsch.

θυΐς, ΐδος (-ίδος codd.), ἡ, = θυεία, Damocr.ap.Gal.14.130.

θυΐσκη, ἡ, censer, LXX 1Ma.1.22, al., J.AJ3.6.8, 3.8.10:—**θυΐσκος**, ὁ, v.l., ib.3.6.8:—also **θύσκη**, POxy.1657.13 (iii A.D.), Suid., EM 458.53: **θύσκος**, ib.52 (θύκος cod.).

θυΐτης [ῑ] (sc. λίθος), ου, ὁ, an Ethiopian stone, Dsc.5.136, Gal. 12.198.

θυίω, = θύω, to be inspired, subj. θυίωσι h.Merc.560. II. = θύω (B), Hes.Th.131 (Pap.), v.l. in A.R.3.755, Nic.Th.129.

θυλάκ-η [ᾰ], ἡ, = scrotum, Hippiatr.50. **-ίζω**, collect scraps in a wallet: hence, at Tarentum, beg, Hsch. **-ιον**, τό, Dim. of θύλακος, Hdt.3.105, Ar.V.314, Ra.1203 codd., PLille 10 ii 14 (iii B.C.), PCair. Zen.69.6 (iii B.C.). II. seed-capsule, Sch.Nic.Th.852. **-ίς**, ίδος, ἡ, Dim. of θύλακος, = θυλάκιον II, Ael.NA6.43, Nic.Th.852. **-ίσκος**, ὁ, = θυλάκιον I, bread-basket, Ar.Fr.545, Crates Com.14. II. = θυλάκιον II, Dsc.2.106. **-ίτης** [ῑ], ου, ὁ, = sq., only fem. θυλακῖτις μήκων the common poppy (cf. θυλακίς), Dsc.4.64; θ. νάρδος, = ὀρεινὴ ν., Id.1.9.

θῡλᾰκό-βολον, *verrutum*, *Gloss.* **-ειδής**, ές, *like a bag*, Arist. *HA* 543ᵇ13. **-εις**, εσσα, εν, = foreg., Nic.*Al.* 403. **-ομαι**, Pass., *become a bag*, Sch.Ar.*Pax* 198.

θύλᾰκος [ῠ], ὁ, *sack*, esp. to carry meal in, Hdt.3.46; ἄλφιτ' οὐκ ἔνεστιν ἐν τῷ θυλάκῳ Ar.*Pl.* 763; θ. δορκαδέων ἀστραγάλων *PCair.Zen.* 69.18 (iii B.C.); δερῶ σε θύλακον I'll make *a bag* of your skin, Ar.*Eq.* 370; contemptuous word for a garment, ὁ Τηλαύγους θ. prob. in Aeschin.Socr.42: metaph., of a person, θ. τις λόγων 'wind-bag', Pl.*Tht.* 161a; τῇ χειρὶ δεῖν σπείρειν, ἀλλὰ μὴ ὅλῳ τῷ θ. Corinn.ap.Plu. 2.348a. 2. *sack in which the eggs of the tunny are enveloped*, Arist. *HA* 571ᵃ14, cf. 552ᵇ19. II. in pl., slang term for the *loose trousers* of Persians and other Orientals, E.*Cyc.* 182, Ar.*V.* 1087. III. *ball* used for physical exercise, Antyll.ap.Orib.6.32.12.

θῡλᾰκο-τρώξ, ῶγος, ὁ, ἡ, *gnawing sacks*, Hsch., Hdn.Gr.2.37. **-φορέω**, *carry a sack* or *pouch*, Ar.*Fr.* 789. **-φόρος**, ον, *carrying a bag*, name for prospectors, Hsch., Phot.

θῡλᾰκώδης, ες, = θυλακοειδής, Thphr.*HP* 3.7.3, Dsc.1.90, Mnesith. Cyz.ap.Orib.*inc.* 15.8.

θῦλαξ, ἄκος, ὁ, = θύλακος, Arcesil.Com.1 D., Aesop.15; = προσκεφάλαιον, Hsch.; cited fr. Hom. by Poll.10.172; cj. in Sor.1.57.

θῡλάς, άδος, ἡ, = foreg., v. οὐλάς.

θῡλ-έομαι, *offer in sacrifice*, ἀλφίτων ὀλίγας δράκας Porph.*Abst.* 2. 17; θυηλήσασθαι shd. be read in Poll.1.27. **-ημα**, ατος, τό, *that which is offered*: mostly in pl., θυλήματα, *cakes*, *incense*, etc., Ar.*Pax* 1040, Thphr.*Fr.* 97.3, Pherecr.23.6, Telecl.33, Porph.*Abst.* 2.6,29; cf. θυάλημα, θυήλημα. (Cf. θύος, θύω (A), Lett. *dūlēt* 'smoke (bees)', Lat. *fuligo.*) [ῡ, Pherecr. l. c.]

θύλλα· κλάδους ἢ φύλλα, ἢ ἑορτὴ Ἀφροδίτης, Hsch.:—hence **Θυλλοφόρος**, title of Dionysus at Cos, *SIG* 1012.7 (ii/i B.C.).

θυλλίς, ίδος, ἡ, = θύλακος, Hdn.Gr.1.89, Hsch. **θύλον**· ὀλέθριον (leg. οὖλον), Id.

θῦμα, ατος, τό, (θύω A) *victim*, *sacrifice*, *SIG* 56.31 (Argos, v B.C.), A. *Ag.* 1310, S.*Ph.* 8, Ar.*Av.* 901, Wilcken *Chr.* 1 iii 3 (iii B.C.), etc.; τὸ θ. τοῦ Ἀπόλλωνος Th.5.53; θ. θύειν, θύσασθαι, Pl.*Plt.* 290e, *R.* 378a, etc.; usu. of animals, but πάγκαρπα θ. *offerings* of all fruits, S.*El.* 634; ⟨ἁγνὰ⟩ θ., opp. ἱερεῖα, expld. by Sch. as *cakes in the form of animals*, Th.1.126, cf. Pl.*Lg.* 782c, Poll.1.26: prov., θ. Δελφόν 'Barmecide's feast', Call.*Iamb.* 1.98. 2. pl., of *animals slaughtered* for food, Lxx *Ge.* 43.16. 3. metaph., of persons, θ. λεύσιμον, prob. of Clytemnestra, A.*Ag.* 1118 (lyr.); πρόκεισθε θύματα τῆς ἡμετέρας ἐξουσίας Hdn.2.13.5. II. *act of sacrifice*, ὧδ' ἦν τὰ κείνης θ. S.*El.* 573. [θῦμα only *Supp.Epigr.* 2.518 (Rome, iv A.D.), cf. Hdn.Gr.2.15.]

θῡμάγροικος, ον, *of clownish spirit*, Ar.*Fr.* 790.

θυμαδέων, Dor. for -ηδέων, = ἀθυμῶν (scr. εὐθ-), Hsch.

θῡμ-αίνω, Ep. impf. θυμαίνεσκον A.R.3.1326: (θυμός):—*to be wroth*, *angry*, Hes.*Sc.* 262, Ar.*Nu.* 610; τινι *at* one, ib.1478, Eup.191. **-αλγής**, ές, (ἀλγέω) *heart-grieving*, χόλος Il.4.513; λώβη 9.387, Od.20. 285; μῦθος, ἔπος, 8.272, 16.69, Hdt.1.129; μέρμηραι *IG* 14.1942. 11. II. Pass., *inly grieving*, [καρδία] A.*Ag.* 1031 (lyr.).

θῡμαλίς, v.l. for τιθύμαλλος in Nic.*Th.* 617.

θύμαλλος, ὁ, an unknown *fish*, Ael.*NA* 14.22.

θῡμάλωψ [ᾰ], ωπος, ὁ, *piece of burning wood* or *charcoal*, Ar.*Ach.* 321, *Th.* 729, Stratt.55, Luc.*Lex.* 24. (τύφω: for the termin., cf. αἰμάλωψ.)

θυμαμοργάς· ἡ νόσος (Eretr.), Hsch. **θῡμαντικός**, ή, όν, = *animosus*, *Gloss.*: **-άντρια**, ἡ, dub. sens., φασγάνων θ. *PMag.Par.* 1.2267.

θυμάρεστος, gloss on θυμαρής, Apollon.*Lex.*

θῡμᾱρ-έω, *to be well-pleased*, Theoc.26.9. **-ής**, ές, (θυμός, ἀραρίσκω) *suiting the heart*, i.e. *well-pleasing*, *delightful*, ἄλοχον θυμαρέα Il. 9.336, Od.23.232; σκῆπτρον θ. ἔδωκεν 17.199: irreg. acc. θυμάρην ὄλβον *IG* 14.433 (Tauromenium):—also **θυμήρης**, ες (on the accent v. Hdn.Gr.2.65, al.), Hom. only in neut. as Adv., θυμῆρες κεράσασα Od.10.362: as Adj., ἔπος A.R.1.705; ἑταῖραι Mosch.2.29: also in later Prose, Luc.*Am.* 43, Hdn.8.5.9: Comp., Lxx *Wi.* 3.14: Sup., Ph.2.36, Sch.Nic.*Al.* 577, and in form **θυμερέστατος** (sic) *BCH* 27. 330 (Bithynia). Adv. -ήρως Heph.Astr.3.11.

θῡμάρμενος, ον, = foreg., τέρας B.16.71, cf. Nic.*Al.* 577, Call.*Dian.* 167.

θύμαρνον, τό, = ἱππομάραθον, Ps.-Dsc.3.71.

θῡμάτιον, τό, Dim. of θῦμα, *Gloss.*

θυματῖτις, ιδος, ἡ, = πεντάφυλλον, v.l. in Ps.-Dsc.4.42.

θύμβρα, ἡ, (perh. from τύφω) *savory*, *Satureia Thymbra*, Eup.14.5, Thphr.*CP* 3.1.4, Dsc.3.37, Plin.*HN* 19.165:—also **θυμβραία**, ἡ, Hp. ap.Gal.19.104 (but θύμβρη or -ίην *Nat.Mul.* 32 codd.).

θυμβρεπίδειπνος, ον, *supping on bitter herbs*, i.e. *living poorly*, Ar. *Nu.* 421.

Θύμβρις, ιδος, ἡ, name of several rivers, esp. *the Tiber*, *AP* 9.352 (Leon. Alex.), D.P.352 sq.; cf. Θυβριάς.

θυμβρίτης [ῑ] οἶνος, ὁ, wine *flavoured with savory*, Dsc.5.50.

θύμβρον, τό, = θύμβρα, Thphr.*HP* 7.1.2, Sch.Ar.*Ach.* 253.

θυμβροφάγος [ᾰ], ον, *eating savory*, θυμβροφάγον βλέπειν to look *as if one had eaten savory*, 'make a *verjuice face*', Ar.*Ach.* 254.

θυμβρώδης, ες, *like savory*, Thphr.*HP* 6.7.5.

θῠμελαία, ἡ, prob. *spurge-flax*, *Daphne Cnidium*, Dsc.4.172, Plin. *HN* 13.114:—hence **-αΐτης** [ῑ] οἶνος, ὁ, wine *flavoured with* θυμελαία, Dsc.5.68.

θῠμέλ-η, ἡ, (θύω A) prop. *place of burning*, *hearth*, θυμέλαι οἴκων E.*Rh.* 234 (lyr.), cf. A.*Supp.* 669 (lyr.); Κυκλώπων θυμέλαι E.*IA* 152 (anap.); but usu. of *sacrificial hearths* or *altars*, δεξίπυροι θεῶν θ. Id.*Supp.* 64 (lyr.); ἁ Φοίβου θ. Id.*Ion* 114 (lyr.), cf. 46, al.; Ἑστία, δίδου.. ἀμφὶ σὰν θ. χορεύειν Aristonous 2.17; also of *braziers*, θυμέλαι ἐπίτναντο χρυσήλατοι E.*El.* 713 (lyr.); ἡ θ. τοῦ βωμοῦ the surface on which fire was kindled, *IG* 11(2).161 *A* 95 (Delos, iii B.C.). II. esp. of the *altar* of Dionysus which stood in the orchestra of the theatre, Διονυσιὰς θ. Pratin.Lyr.1. 2, cf. *EM* 743.37, etc.: hence in later writers, b. the *orchestra*, Phryn. 142, Sch.Aristid.p.536 D.: hence of the chorus, opp. actors, θυμέλῃσι καὶ ἐν σκηνῇσι τεθηλώς, of Sophocles, *AP* 7.21 (Simm.); cf. sq. c. the *stage*, Phryn.*PS* p.74 B., *EM* 653.8, etc. (hence generally, *platform*, *stage*, Plu.*Alex.* 67); so ὁ ἀπὸ τῆς θ., of a dramatic poet, Id. *Demetr.* 12, etc.; ὥσπερ ἐκ θ., i.e. theatrical, Id.2.405d; actuarii thymelae equorumque currulium, *Cod.Theod.* 8.7.21. d. αἱ ἐτήσιοι θ. annual *stage-performances*, Alciphr.2.3, cf. *POxy.* 1143.3 (i A.D.), *IG* 14.2342. III. of the θόλος at Epidaurus (containing a *hearth* or *altar*), ib.4.1485 *B* 162. IV. = θυλήματα, Pherecr.214. **-ικός**, ή, όν, *of* or *belonging to the thymele*, *theatrical*, θέαι, ἄνθρωποι, Plu.*Fab.* 4, *Sull.* 36; θ. ἔρις *Com.Adesp.* 57; τὸ θ. *theatrical*, *vulgar* style, Plu.2. 853b; of performances of music, dancing, etc., *in the orchestra* (cf. foreg. II.b); θ. ἀγών *SIG* 457.1 (Thespiae, iii B.C.), cf. D.S.4.5, *CIG* 3493.11 (Thyatira), etc.; θ. ἀκροάματα Corn.*ND* 30; οἱ θ. *the musicians*, opp. οἱ σκηνικοί, the actors, Plu.*Cat.Mi.* 46; opp. ὑποκριταί, Ptol. *Tetr.* 180 (but later of *actors*, Jul.*Ep.* 89b, *Cod.Just.* 1.4.14); ἡ θ. σύνοδος the company of θ., *IG* 2².1350, *OGI* 713, etc.

θῠμελο-ποιοί, οἱ, *board of curators of the* θυμέλη III at Epidaurus, *IG* 4.1485 *B* 142: also dat. pl. -ποίαις (from -ποίης) ib.134,139.

θῡμ-ηγερέων, (θυμός, ἀγείρω) *gathering breath*, *collecting oneself*, Od. 7.283. **-ηδέω**, Dor. -ᾱδέω (q.v.), *to be glad-hearted*, Semon.7. 103; ἐπί τινι Hld.10.3. **-ηδής**, ές, (ἥδος) *well-pleasing*, *dear*, χρήματα Od.16.389; νόστοιο τέλος A.R.1.249; τὰ λῷστα καὶ τὰ -έστατα A.*Supp.* 962; παῖδας *Epigr.Gr.* 403.7 (Sebastopolis); θ. ἀναθυμιάσεις cj. for θυμώδεις in Herod.Med.ap.Orib.10.40.1. **-ηδία**, Ion. -ίη, ἡ, *gladness of heart*, *rejoicing*, Eup.161, Call.*Fr.* 2 P., Plu.2.713d, Aret. *SD* 1.5, Chor. in *Rev.Phil.* 1.225: pl., Ph.2.548, Luc.*Abd.* 5, D.C.47. 1. **-ήρης**, v. θυμαρής.

θῡμία, Ion. -ίη, ἡ, = θυμίαμα, -ίησι κακώδεσι Aret.*SD* 2.11.

θῡμι-άζω, = -ιάω, *Gp.* 12.8.8. **-αίνω**, = -ιάω, *Gloss.* **-ᾱμα**, Ion. -ημα, ατος, τό, *incense*, Hdt.1.198, Amphis 27, *PTeb.* 112.22 (ii B.C.), Phld.*Vit.* p.37 J.; name of a particular kind (perh. = ἀμμωνιακόν), *Edict.Diocl.* in Ἀθηνᾶ 18.6 (Tegea): usu. in pl., *fragrant stuffs* for burning, Hdt.2.130, 7.54, S.*OT* 4, Ar.*Av.* 1716, Pl.*R.* 373c, *IG* 5(2). 514 (Lycosura), *Apoc.* 5.8; -ιάματα ἑρπετῶν *fumigations*, Philum.*Ven.* 6 tit. 2. *stuff for embalming*, Hdt.2.86, 4.71. **-ᾱσις**, εως, ἡ, *fumigating*, Dsc.1.98, Antyll.ap.Orib.10.19.1. II. *passing off in fumes*, Arist.*Mete.* 387ᵃ30; τῶν ἀπὸ γῆς Porph.*Abst.* 2.5. **-ᾱτέον**, *one must fumigate*, *Gp.* 6.10, Paul.Aeg.6.75. **-ᾱτεύω**, *fumigate*, τὴν ἐκκλησίαν Sch.Aeschin.1.23. **-ᾱτήριον**, Ion. θυμιητ-, τό, *censer*, Hdt. 4.162, Th.6.46, And.4.29, *POxy.* 521.19 (ii A.D.), etc. 2. *vessel for fumigation*, Aët.9.41. II. name of the constellation *Ara*, Eudox. ap.Hipparch.1.11.6, Ptol.*Tetr.* 28, etc. **-ᾱτίζω**, = θυμιάω, *Gp.* 6. 13.3:—Med., ib.6.12.1. **-ᾱτικός**, ή, όν, *good for burning as incense*, σώματα Pl.*Ti.* 61c. **-ᾱτός**, Ion. -ητός, ή, όν, *to be burnt as incense*, Hp.*Mul.* 2.114; πᾶν τὸ θ. Thphr.*Od.* 12; *capable of giving off fumes*, Arist.*Mete.* 387ᵇ7: pl., θυμιητά, = θυμιάματα, Aret.*SD* 2. 11. **-ᾱτρίς**, ίδος, ἡ, = θυμιατήριον, Dam.*Isid.* 188. **-ατρον**, τό, = foreg., *SIG* 577.31 (Milet., iii/ii B.C.). **-άω**, Ion. aor. ἐθυμίησα Hippon.92, Hdt.6.97:—Med., Ion. fut. -ήσομαι Hp.*Mul.* 2.126: aor. ἐθυμιησάμην ib.146, *Nat.Mul.* 7 (but -ασάμην *Morb.* 2.27):—Pass., fut. -ᾱθήσομαι Dsc.1.68.6: aor. ἐθυμιάθην ib.5:—*burn so as to produce smoke*, θ. τὴν στύρακα Hdt.3.107; λιβανωτοῦ τριηκόσια τάλαντα Id. 6.97; θυμιήματα Id.8.99; λιβάνου δάκρυα Pi.*Fr.* 122.4: abs., *burn incense*, Hermipp.8, Men.*Sam.* 264, Lxx 4*Ki.* 22.17, al., *OGI* 352.37 (ii B.C.), etc.; τινι in honour of any one, Ath.7.289f:—Med., Ael. *VH* 12.51:—Pass., *to be burnt*, [τὸ σπέρμα τῆς καννάβιος] θυμιᾶται (v.l. -ῆται) Hdt.4.75; λίθος..τεθυμιαμένος Ar.*Fr.* 635; *pass off in fumes*, Arist.*Mete.* 362ᵃ11; θυμιωμένων τινῶν Pl.*Ti.* 66d. 2. *smoke*, *fumigate*, τί τινι *PMag.Par.* 1.2970:—Med., Hp. ll. cc.:—Pass., θυμιώμεναι μέλισσαι Arist.*HA* 623ᵇ20. II. intr., *smoke*, ἄνθρακες θυμιῶντες Thphr.*Ign.* 75.

θῡμίδιον, τό, Dim. of θυμός, Ar.*V.* 878.

θῡμίζω, *taste of thyme*, Archig.ap.Orib.8.1.32:—Pass., *to be embittered*, θυμιχθείς· πικρανθείς, Hsch.

θῡμικός, ή, όν, (θυμός) *high-spirited*, of the dog, Arist.*HA* 488ᵇ21: τὸ ἄρρεν -ώτερον Id.*PA* 661ᵇ33: Sup., D.C.49.36. 2. = θυμοειδής 3, Pl.*Def.* 415e, Arist. *de An.* 432ᵃ25, Phld.*Oec.* p.33 J., Hierocl. *in CA* 26 p.480 M. 3. *irascible*, Ath.2.38b; θ. καὶ ὀξύθυμοι οἱ νέοι Arist.*Rh.* 1389ᵃ9. 4. Adv. -κῶς Plb.18.37.12: Comp. -ώτερον Id.7.13.3, Cic.*Att.* 10.11.5.

θύμῑνον [ῠ], τό (sc. μέλι), *honey made from thyme*, Colum.6.33, *Gloss.*, Apul.*Herb.* p.294 H.-S.

θύμιον, τό, = σμῖλαξ, Dsc.*Alex.* 12. II. *large wart*, Hp.*Ulc.* 14, Dsc.5.1, Plin.*HN* 32.128.

θῠμίτης [ῑ], ου, ὁ, (θύμον) *flavoured with thyme*, ἅλες Ar.*Ach.* 1099; οἶνος Dsc.5.49.

θῡμο-βᾰρής, ές, *heavy at heart*, *AP* 7.146 (Antip. Sid.):—fem. -βάρεια *EM* 458.24. **-βορέω**, *gnaw*, *vex the heart*, Hes.*Op.* 799. **-βόρος**, ον, (βιβρώσκω, βορά) *eating the heart*, θυμοβόρῳ ἔριδι Il.19.58, al.; λύα Alc.*Supp.* 23.10; Κῆρες A.R.4.1666; τῆς θυμοβόρου φρένα λύπης cj. for θυμοφθόρον in A.*Ag.* 103 (anap.). **-δᾰκής**, ές, *biting the heart*, θ. γὰρ μῦθος Od.8.185; ζάλου κέντρον *AP* 9.77 (Antip. Thess.): in late Prose, μῦθοι Aret.*CA* 1.1, cf. Jul.*Or.* 2.

96a. **-ειδής**, *ές*, *high-spirited*, τὸ θ. Hp.*Aër.*12; opp. ἄθυμος, Pl. *R.*456a; opp. ὀργίλος, ib.411c. **2.** *passionate, hot-tempered*, opp. πραΰς, ib.375c. **b.** of horses, *mettled*, X.*Mem.*4.1.3; opp. εὐπειθέστατος, Id.*Smp.*2.10: Comp., opp. βλακωδέστερος, Id.*Eq.*9.1. **3.** Philos., τὸ θ. *spirit, passion*, opp. τὸ λογιστικόν, τὸ ἐπιθυμητικόν, Pl. *R.*440e, al., cf. D.L.3.67. Adv. -δῶς Hdn.4.3.3.

θῡμόεις, εσσα, εν, *thymy*, Choeril.8.

θῡμο-κατοχέω, *nurse anger*, cj. for θυμω κατοχουντα in Epicur. *Sent.Vat.*62 (*Rh.Mus.*61.421). **-κάτοχος**, *ον*, *restraining anger*: neut. as Subst., *spell for this purpose*, *PMag.Lond.*121.941, *PMag. Osl.*1.35, *PMag.Par.*1.467,831; θ. πρὸς βασιλέας *PMag.Leid.W.*6. 38. **-λέαινα**, ἡ, fem. of θυμολέων, *AP*5.299 (Paul. Sil.). **-λεοντοφθόρος**, *ον*, *bold enough to slay a lion*, *PMasp.*2 iii 22 (vi A.D.). **-λέων**, *οντος*, ὁ, *lion-hearted*, of Achilles, Il.7.228, Hes.*Th.*1007; of Ulysses, πόσιν ἀπώλεσα θ. Od.4.724; of Hercules, 11.267, cf. Ar.*Ra.*1041 (anap.). **-λῑπής**, *ές*, (λείπω) = λιπόθυμος, Call.*Fr.*1.55P., Nonn.*D.* 37.540. **-μαντις**, *εως*, ὁ, ἡ, *prophesying from one's own soul*, A.*Pers.* 224 (troch.); cf. θυμόσοφος. **-μᾰχέω**, *to be angry*, Plb.9.40.4; ἐπί τινι Id.27.8.4; πρός τινας Plu.*Demetr.*22; τισι *Act.Ap.*12.20. **II.** *fight desperately*, D.S.17.33; *contend obstinately*, τινι D.H.5.11. **-μᾰχία**, ἡ, *desperate fight*, Polyaen.2.1.19.

θύμον [ῠ], τό, Arist.*HA*626^{b}21, *Pr.*925^{a}9, Thphr.*HP*6.2.3: dual θύμω Pherecr.167: pl., θύμα Eup.14.5, Antiph.179.4: gen. θύμων Ar.*Pl.*283; θυμέων *AP*9.226.2 (Zonas):—also **θύμος**, ὁ, Dsc.3.36:—*Cretan thyme, Thymbra capitata*, ll.cc., Hp.*Vict.*2.54, al.; τὸ μύρον φάσκειν οὐδὲν τοῦ θ. ἥδιον ὄζειν Thphr.*Char.*4.1. **b.** a marine plant, Id. *HP*4.7.2. **2.** *mixture of thyme with honey and vinegar*, eaten by the poor of Attica, Ar.*Pl.*253, cf. 283, Antiph.226.7, Luc.*Fug.*14, Hsch.

θῡμ-οξ-άλμη, ἡ, *drink of thyme, vinegar, and brine*, Dsc.5.16.

θῡμο-πληθής, *ές*, *wrathful*, A.*Th.*686 (lyr.). **-ποιέω**, *hearten, encourage*, τὸ πλῆθος Satyr.*Vit.Eur.Fr.*39 iv 31. **-ρραϊστής**, οῦ, ὁ, (ῥαίω) *life-destroying*, θάνατος Il.13.544, 16.414; δηΐων ὕπο θυμοραϊστέων ib.591. (**-ρραίστης** Glauc.ap.Sch.B Il.16.414.)

θύμος (A), ὁ, v. θύμον.

θύμος [perh. ῠ] (B), ὁ, *warty excrescence*, Hp.*Alim.*17, Dsc.2.28, Paul.Aeg.6.71; esp. in the anal or genital regions, Gal.7.731. **II.** *the thymus gland in the neck or breast* of young animals, Ruf.*Onom.* 168, Gal.*UP*6.4.

θῡμός, ὁ, *soul, spirit*, as *the principle of life, feeling and thought*, esp. *of strong feeling and passion* (rightly derived from θύω (B) by Pl.*Cra.* 419e ἀπὸ τῆς θύσεως καὶ ζέσεως τῆς ψυχῆς): **I.** in physical sense, *breath, life*, θ. ἀπηύρα, ἀφελέσθαι, ἐξαίνυσθαι, ὀλέσαι, freq. in Hom., Il.6.17, 5.852, 155, 1.205: c. dupl. acc., ἄμφω θ. ἀπηύρα 6.17; ἐπεί κε.. βεθέων ἐκ θ. ἔληται 22.68; λίπε δ' ὀστέα θ. 12.386; ἀπὸ δ' ἔπτατο θ. Od.10.163; ὀλίγος δ' ἔτι θ. ἐνῆεν Il.1.593; μόγις δ' ἐσαγείρετο θυμόν 21.417; ἄψορρόν οἱ θ. ἐνὶ στήθεσσιν ἀγέρθη 4.152; θυμοῦ καὶ ψυχῆς κεκαδών 11.334; of animals, 3.294, 12.150, etc.: less freq. in Trag., A. *Ag.*1388, E.*Ba.*620 (troch.). **2.** *spirit, strength*, τείρετο δ' ἀνδρῶν θ. ὑπ' εἰρεσίης Od.10.78; ἐν δέ τε θ. τείρεθ' ὁμοῦ καμάτῳ τε καὶ ἱδρῷ Il.17. 744. **3.** πάτασσε δὲ θ. ἑκάστου each man's *heart* beat high, 23.370, cf. 7.216. **II.** *soul*, as shown by the feelings and passions; and so, **1.** *desire* or *inclination*, esp. desire for meat and drink, *appetite*, πιέειν ὅτε θ. ἀνώγοι Il.4.263; πλησάμενος.. θυμὸν ἐδητύος ἠδὲ ποτῆτος Od.17.603: generally, τά με θ. ἐνὶ στήθεσσι κελεύει Il.7.68; βαλέειν δέ ἑ ἵετο θ. 8.301; αἲ γάρ με μένος καὶ θ. ἀνείη 22.346; θ. ἐποτρύνῃ [τινά] Od.9.139; θ. ἐπέσσυταί τινι, ἐφορμᾶται, Il.1.173, 13.73; ἤθελε θυμῷ he wished *in his heart* or *with all his heart*, 16.255, 21.65; ἵετο θυμῷ 2.589; so later θυμῷ βουλόμενοι wishing *with all their heart*, Hdt. 5.49; [ὄσσα ϝ]οι θ. κε θέλῃ γένεσθαι Sapph.*Supp.*1.3; θυμὸς ὥρμα Pi. *O.*3.25, cf. 38; θυμὸς ἡδονὴν φέρει S.*El.*286; ὧν ἐρᾷ θυμὸς Herod.7. 61; τῶν σφι θ. ἦν μάλιστα Hdt.1.1; ἄλλως σφι θ. ἐγένετο θεήσασθαι τὸν πόλεμον Id.8.116, etc.: with Verb omitted, σὲ γάρ μοι θῦμος ὔμνην Alc. 5; ἄρχ' αὐτὸς ὥς σοι θ. S.*El.*1319; ὅπου ὑμῖν θ. X.*Cyr.*3.1.37; βῆξαι θυμὸς ἐγγίνεται Hp.*Prog.*8. **2.** *mind, temper, will*, θ. πρόφρων, ἵλαος, Il. 8.39, 9.639; θ. ὑπερφίαλος καὶ ἀπηνής, νηλέα θ. ἔχοντας, σιδήρεος θ., 15. 94, 19.229, Od.5.191; ἕνα θ. ἔχειν to be of one *mind*, Il.15.710, etc.; οὐδὲ λύκοι τε καὶ ἄρνες ὁμόφρονα θ. ἔχουσιν 22.263; ἕτερος δέ με θ. ἔρυκε Od.9.302; ἐμὸν θ. ἔπειθεν ib.33; θωπείας κολακικάς, αἳ.. τοὺς θ. ποιοῦσιν κηρίνους Pl.*Lg.*633d. **3.** *spirit, courage*, μένος καὶ θ. Il.20.174; θ. ἐνὶ στήθεσσι λαβεῖν Od.10.461; πᾶσιν δὲ παραὶ ποσὶ κάππεσε θ. Il.15. 280; ψῦχρος ἔγεντο θ., of doves, Sapph.16; θ. ἔχειν ἀγαθόν Hdt.1. 120; θ. οὐκ ἀπώλεσεν S.*El.*26; ὁ θυμὸς εὐθὺς ἦν 'Αμυνίας Ar.*Eq.*570; ἴωμεν ῥώμῃ καὶ θυμῷ ἐπί.. X.*Cyr.*4.2.21; φρονήματός τε καὶ θυμοῦ ἐμπίπλασθαι Pl.*R.*411c: so in Philos., opp. λόγος, ἐπιθυμία, ib.440b, al., cf. Arist.*Pol.*1328^{a}7, 1327^{b}24, Phld.*Mus.*p.26K., etc.; personified, *Passion, Emotion*, opp. Λογισμός, Cleanth.*Stoic.*1.129. **4.** *the seat of anger*, χωόμενον κατὰ θυμόν Il.1.429; νεμεσιζέσθω ἐνὶ θυμῷ 17.254; θυμὸν ἐχώσατο 16.616, etc.: hence, *anger, wrath*, δάμασον θυμόν 9.496; εἴξας ᾧ θυμῷ ib.598; θυμὸς μέγας ἐστὶ.. βασιλήων 2.196; θ. ὀξὺς S.*OC* 1193; θ. κρείσσων τῶν ἐμῶν βουλευμάτων E.*Med.*1079, etc.; θυμῷ f.l. for θυμοῦ in S.*Ant.*718; οἱ τῷ θ. πραχθέντες φόνοι Pl.*Lg.*867b; opp. λογισμός, Th.2.11, etc.; ἐπανάγειν τὸν θ. Hdt.7.160; ἐκτείνειν And.3. 31; καταθέσθαι Ar.*V.*567; δακεῖν Id.*Nu.*1369; θυμῷ χρᾶσθαι Hdt.1. 137, al.; ὀργῆς καὶ θυμοῦ μεστοί Isoc.12.81 (so τὴν ὀργὴν καὶ τὸν θ., i.e. the outward manifestation of ὀ., Phld.*Ir.*p.90 W.); of horses, X.*Eq.* 9.2: pl. (not earlier than Pl., f.l. in S.*Aj.*718 (lyr.)), *fits of anger, passions*, περὶ φόβων τε καὶ θυμῶν Pl.*Phlb.*40e; οἵ τε θ. καὶ αἱ κολάσεις Id.*Prt.*323e, cf. Arist.*Rh.*1390^{a}11. **5.** *the heart*, as the seat of the emotions, esp. joy or grief, χαῖρε, γήθησε δὲ θυμῷ, Il.14.156, 7.189; θ. ἐνὶ στήθεσσι γεγήθει 13.494; μιν ἄχος κραδίην καὶ θ. ἵκανεν 2.171; ἄχνυτο θ. 14.39, etc.; δόκησε δ' ἄρα σφίσι θ. ὣς ἔμεν ὡς εἰ.. they felt as glad at *heart* as if.., Od.10.415; μηδ' ὀνίαισι δάμνα.. θ. Sapph.1.4; of fear, δέος ἔμπεσε θυμῷ Il.17.625, cf. 8.138; of love, τὴν ἐκ θυμοῦ φίλεον 9.343; ἐκ θυμοῦ στέργοισα Theoc.17.130; ἐμῷ κεχαρισμένε θυμῷ my *heart's* beloved, Il.5.243; reversely, ἀπὸ θ. μᾶλλον ἐμοὶ ἔσεαι wilt be alien from my *heart*, 1.562; ἐκ θ. πεσέειν, i.e. to lose thy favour, 23.595; ἔρωτι θυμὸν ἐκπλαγεῖσα E.*Med.*8; ἐκ θ. κλαῦσαι Philet. 11. **6.** *mind, soul, as the seat of thought*, ταῦθ' ὥρμαινε κατὰ φρένα καὶ κατὰ θ. Il.1.193, etc.; ᾔδεε γὰρ κατὰ θ. 2.409, cf. 4.163, etc.; φράζετο θυμῷ 16.646; ἐν θ. ἐβάλοντο ἔπος 15.566; τοὺς λόγους θυμῷ βάλε A.*Pr.*706; εἰς θ. βαλεῖν τι S.*OT*975; οὐκ ἐς θ. φέρω I bring him not into my *mind* or *thoughts*, Id.*El.*1347.

θῡμο-σοφικός, ή, όν, *clever*, Ar.*V.*1280 (Sup.). **-σοφος**, *ον*, *wise from one's own soul*, i.e. *naturally clever*, Id.*Nu.*877, Plu.*Art.*17; of animals, Arr.*Ind.*14.4, Ael.*NA*16.15; ὄρνεον -ώτερον ib.3; τὸ θ. Plu. 2.970e. **-φθορέω**, *to be tormented in soul*, S.*Tr.*142. **-φθόρος**, *ον*, *destroying the soul, life-destroying*, φάρμακα Od.2.329 (so, metaph. γράψας ἐν πίνακι θυμοφθόρα πολλά Il.6.169); ἰός Nic.*Th.*140 (v.l. γυιοφθ-). **2.** *heart-breaking*, τὴν δ' ἄχος ἀμφεχύθη θ. Od.4.716; κάματος 10.363; πενίη Hes.*Op.*717; of persons, *troublesome, annoying*, Od.19.323; cf. θυμοβόρος.

θῡμοφονέω, *to be in the death-agony*, gloss on βεβρυχότες, Hsch.

θῠμοφόρος, *ον*, *bearing thyme*, Eust.ad D.P.791; θ. ἡ 'Αττική Sch. Ar.*Pl.*283.

θυμοχεύων, = θυμὸν ἀχεύων (v. ἀχεύω), *Et.Gud.*267.34.

θῡμόω, *make angry, provoke*, Lxx *Ho.*12.14(15): once in Trag., ὥστε θυμῶσαι φρένας E.*Supp.*581. **II.** Med. and Pass., 2 sg. θυμοῖ Ar.*Ra.*584: fut. -ώσομαι A.*Ag.*1069, -ωθήσομαι Lxx *Jb.*21.4, Phld.*Ir.* p.89 W.: aor. ἐθυμωσάμην E.*Hel.*1343 (lyr.); more freq. ἐθυμώθην Hdt.3.1, al.; part. -θείς E.*Ph.*461, Pl.*Lg.*931b: pf. inf. τεθυμῶσθαι Hdt.3.52, A.*Fr.*478, Pl.*Ep.*346a:—*to be wroth* or *angry*, abs., Hdt. 3.1, A.*Ag.* l.c., Sor.1.88, etc.; θυμοῦ δι' ὀργῆς ἥτις ἀγριωτάτη S.*OT* 344; εἰς ἔριν θ. Id.*Aj.*1018; of animals, *to be wild, restive*, Id.*Ant.* 477, X.*Eq.*1.10; θυμοῦσθαι εἰς κέρας *vent fury* with the horns, Virgil's *irasci in cornua*, E.*Ba.*743; cf. ἀοιδὸς ἐς κέρας τεθύμωται Call.*Iamb.* 1.321; τὸ θυμούμενον *passion*, Antipho 2.3.3, Th.7.68; θυμοῦσθαί τινι *to be angry with* one, A.*Eu.*733, S.*Tr.*543, 1230, Pl.*Prt.*324a; ἔς τινα Hdt.3.52; περί τινος A.*Ag.*1368 (prob. for μυθοῦσθαι); βοῦς πρὸς τὸν ἐλαύνοντα -ωθείς Plu.*Dio*38; σοι θυγατέρος -ούμενος E.*Or.*751 (troch.): c. dat. rei, τῇ ξυντυχίᾳ Ar.*Ra.*1006.

θῡμώδης, *ες*, = θῡμοειδής 2, Arist.*Rh.*1389^{a}26, *EN*1149^{b}14, Plu.2. 462a; of animals, *fierce*, Arist.*HA*488^{b}14; θ. τὸ ἦθος Id.*PA*650^{b}34; = ἀνδρεῖοι, opp. ὀξύθυμοι and ὀργίλοι, Gal.17(1).188: Sup. **-έστατος** Ael.*NA*3.2. Adv. -δῶς, f.l. for μυθ-, Aristeas 168.

θῠμώδης, *ες*, *like thyme*, Thphr.*HP*6.7.2.

θῦμ-ωμα [ῡ], *ατος*, τό, *wrath, passion*, A.*Eu.*860 (pl.); θ. τὸ πόντου *Epigr.Gr.*339.6 (Cyzicus). **-ωσις**, *εως*, ἡ, *ebullition of anger*, Cic. *Tusc.*4.9.21.

θῡναρμόστρια, = θοιν- (q.v.).

θυνάσαι· ἀπολαῦσαι, ἐνθουσιάσαι, Hsch.

θῡνέω, = θύνω, only impf., *dart along*, δελφῖνες τῇ καὶ τῇ ἐθύνεον Hes.*Sc.*[210]; ἐν δ' Ἔρις, ἐν δὲ Κυδοιμὸς ἐθ. ib.156, cf. 257; νῶθ' ἵππων ἐπιβάντες ἐθύνεον ib.286, cf. eund.*Cat.Oxy.*1358 *Fr.*2.20. (Cf. Skt. *dhūnoti* 'shake', past part. *dhūtás*.)

θύνν-α, *ης*, ἡ, *female tunny*, θύνναν f.l. in Hippon.35.2: θύννης Antiph.129.4, Archestr.*Fr.*37.1. **-άζω**, *spear a tunny-fish, strike with a harpoon*, metaph., ἐς τοὺς θυλάκους Ar.*V.*1087. **-αῖος**, *α*, *ον*, = θύννειος, τὸ θ. *an offering of the first tunny-fish caught*, Antig. Car.ap.Ath.7.297e. **-αξ**, ἄκος, ὁ, Dim. of θύννος, Eriph.3. **-άς**, άδος, ἡ, Dim. of θύννα, Antiph.181. **-ειος**, *α*, *ον*, *of the tunny-fish*, ταρίχη θ. pickled *tunny*, Hices.ap.Ath.3.116e; τὸ θ. (sc. κρέας) Clearch.65; τὰ θ. (sc. κρέα) Ar.*Eq.*354. **II. θυννεῖον**, τό, *tunny-fishery*, *IG*4.752.7 (Troezen, pl.). **-ευτικός**, ή, όν, *for tunny-fishing*, σαγήνη Luc.*Sat.*24. **-ίζω**, = θυννάζω, Suid. **-ίς**, ίδος, ἡ, *young female tunny*, prob. l. in Hippon.35.2, Epich.74, Cratin. 161, Stratt.12, Archestr.*Fr.*37.1, Arist.*HA*543^{a}9, al. **-ίτης** [ῑ], *ου*, ὁ, *tunny-fisher*, *Rev.Arch.*28(1928).393 (Varna, θυνεῖται lapis).

θυννο-θήρας, *ου*, ὁ, *tunny-fisher*, title of Mime by Sophron, Ath.7. 303c, 306d, Ael.*NA*15.6. **-κέφᾰλος**, ὁ, *with the head of a tunny-fish*, Luc.*VH*1.35. **-λογέω**, *speak of the tunny-fish*, Eust.994.47.

θύννος, ὁ, *tunny-fish*, Orac.ap.Hdt.1.62, A.*Pers.*424, Arist.*HA* 571^{a}12, al., Ath.7.301e sqq.; θηρεύειν θύννον Phld.*Rh.*1.251 S. (The connexion with θύνω, suggested by the line θύννοι μὲν θύνοντες, ἐν ἰχθύσιν ἔξοχοι ὁρμήν Opp.*H.*1.181, is dub.)

θυννοσκοπ-εῖον, τό, *look-out to watch for shoals of tunnies*, Str.5. 2.6. **-έω**, *watch for tunnies*, metaph., τοὺς φόρους θ. Ar.*Eq.* 313. **-ία**, ἡ, *watch for tunnies*, Str.17.3.16 (s.v.l.). **-ος**, *ον*, *watcher for tunnies*, Arist.*HA*537^{a}19, Plu.2.980a.

θυννώδης, *ες*, *like a tunny-fish*, i.e. *stupid*, Luc.*JTr.*25.

θῦνος· πόλεμος, ὁρμή, δρόμος, Hsch.: θυνός acc. to Hdn.Gr.2.938.

θύνω [ῡ], only pres. and impf., = θυνέω, *rush, dart along*, θῦνε διὰ προμάχων Il.5.250, etc.; πάντῃ θῦνε σὺν ἔγχεϊ 20.493; ἀν' ὕλην ὠκὺς ἔθυνεν ὄρος *AP*6.217.8 ([Simon.]): c. part., βασιλῆες θῦνον κρίνοντες they *flitted* to and fro ordering the ranks, Il.2.446; μνηστῆρας ὀρίνων θῦνε κατὰ μέγαρον Od.24.449: c. acc. cogn., θ. ἀτραπὸν ἰθεῖαν Nic.*Th.* 264: metaph., ἐπ' ἄλλοτ' ἄλλον ὥτε μέλισσα θύνει λόγον *flits* from one tale to another, Pi.*P.*10.54 (θύνων· ὁρμῶν, Erot. is not in our text of Hp.). **II.** = θύω (B), Τρώων καὶ 'Αχαιῶν θῦνε μεσηγὺ ἱστάμενος *raged*, Il.11.570; οἱ δὲ λύκοι ὣς θῦνον ib.73; θῦνε γὰρ ἂμ πεδίον ποταμῷ πλήθοντι ἐοικὼς 5.87.

θῠο-δόκος, ον, (θύος) *receiving incense, full thereof*, of the Delphic temple, E.*Ion* 511, 1549; ἀνακτόρων Id.*Andr.*1157, cf. Hsch. **-εις**, εσσα, εν, (θύος) *laden with incense, fragrant*, νέφος Il.15.153; epith. of Eleusis, *h.Cer.*97, 318; ἄστεος ὀμφαλός, of an altar, Pi.*Fr.*75.3; βωμός Id.*Pae.*3.8, E.*Tr.*1061 (lyr.); Ἀστερίη Call.*Del.*300; ἀνάκτορον *AP*6.277 (Damag.).

θυοκόχθεις· μάντεις, Hsch.

θύον [ῠ], τό, (θύω A) *thyine-wood, citron-wood, Callitris quadrivalvis*, Od.5.60, Thphr.*HP*5.3.7, *BCH*6.26 (Delos, ii B.C.), Moschio ap.Ath. 5.207e, Plin.*HN*13.100, Ael.*VH*5.6; cf. θυία, θύα. II. = θύος, in pl. θύα, τά, *burnt-offerings* or *incense*, Sapph.*Supp.*8.2, prob. in *IG*5(1). p.vii (Delos, v B.C.), Pi.*Fr.*129.7 (θύματα codd. Plu.), *BCH*37.195 (Chios, iv B.C.), *SIG*1003.10 (Priene, ii B.C.), D.P.936, *EM*457.6.

θύος [ῠ], εος, τό, (θύω A) *burnt sacrifice*, A.*Ag.*1409; θύος ὅττι τάχιστον Call.*Aet.Oxy.*2079.23: but usu. in pl., σὺν θυέεσσι Il.6.270, cf. 9.499; σπονδῇσι θύεσσί τε ἱλάσκεσθαι Hes.*Op.*338, cf. Maiist.11; λίσσομ' ὑπὲρ θυέων Od.15.261; θύη πρὸ παίδων A.*Eu.*835, cf. *IG*12(5). 593.17 (Iulis, v B.C.), *Berl.Sitzb.*1927.170 (Cyrene); νιν ἐκ θυέων καταδήσομαι Theoc.2.10, cf. Euph.129. 2. later in pl., = θυμιάματα, Hp.ap.Gal.19.104. II. *a cake*, θύη πέττειν Eup.108.

θυοσκέω, *make burnt-offerings*, Hsch.; περίπεμπτα θυοσκεῖς prob. in A.*Ag.*87 (θυοσκινεῖς codd.). (For θυο-σκοέω, cf. sq.)

θυο-σκόος, ου, ὁ, *sacrificing priest*, Od.21.145, 22.318, 321, E.*Rh.*68; μάντιες θ. distd. from ἱερῆες, Il.24.221: fem., Μαινάδες θ. E.*Ba.*224: neut., θ. ἱρά *sacrificial* implements, *IG*14.1389i2. 2. pl., = Lat. *haruspices*, D.H.1.30. (θύος, σ-κοϝ-, cf. κοέω, *caveo*: the initial *s*- is found in OE. *scéawian*, OHG. *scauwôn* 'look at'.) **-σκοπία**, ἡ, = *haruspicina*, used as etym. of Θοῦσκος, Lyd.*Mag.Prooem.* **-σκόπος**, ου, ὁ, *inspecting the entrails*, Hsch., Phot., v.l. in E.*Rh.*68.

θυόω, (θύος) *fill with sweet smells*: pf. part. Pass. ἔλαιον τεθυωμένον *fragrant* oil, Il.14.172; εἵματα τεθ. Cypria *Fr.*4, cj. in *h.Ap.*184; τεθ. ἄλσος Call.*Lav.Pall.*63: aor. part. θυωθέν Hedyl.ap.Ath.11.486b.—Ep. word.

θύπτης· ὁ τυρός, Hsch.; cf. χθύπτης.

θύρα [ῠ], Ion. **θύρη**, ἡ, Ion. gen. pl. θυρέων Archil.127, Hdt.1.9:—*door*, Il.24.317, etc.: freq. in pl. of *double* or *folding doors*, θ. δικλίδες Od.17.267; θ. φαεινaί 6.19, al.; θυρῶν ζεῦγος καινῶν *IG*1².313.123, cf. 4.1488.25 (Epid.); ἡ δεξιὰ θ. the right *valve*, ib.2².1457.16; θ. μονόθυρος ib.1627.418; θύραι λίθιναι (including the framework) ib. 1².372.195; θύραι αὔλειαι, v. αὔλειος; ἡ θ. ἡ εἰς τὸν κῆπον φέρουσα D. 47.53, cf. κηπαῖος II; rarely for πύλαι, *gates*, Plu.*Cat.Mi.*65; of the *carceres* in the Roman circus, *barriers*, *Tab.Defix.Aud.*187.59.—Phrases: προσθεῖναι τὰς θ., προστιθέναι τὴν θ., Hdt.3.78, Lys.1. 13; ἐπισπάσαι X.*HG*6.4.36; κλείειν Aristopho 7, Pl.*Prt.*314d; ἐφέλκεσθαι Luc.*Am.*16; τὴν θ. βαλανοῦν, μοχλοῦν, bar *the door*, Ar. *Fr.*251, 369; θύραν κόπτειν, πατάσσειν, κρούειν, knock, rap at *the door*, Id.*Nu.*132, *Ra.*38, Pl.*Prt.*310b; ἀράττειν, ἐπαράξαι, Ar.*Ec.* 977, Pl.*Prt.*314d; τὴν θ. ἀνοιγνύναι open it, v. ἀνοίγνυμι; ὦσαι push *it* open, Lys.1.24; μικρὸν ἐνδοῦναι open *it* a little, Plu.2.597d; δόμου ἐν πρώτῃσι θύρῃσι στῆναι Od.1.255; ἷζε δ' ἐπὶ.. οὐδοῦ ἔντοσθε θυράων 17.339; θυρῶν ἔνδον S.*El.*78; πρὸ θυρῶν ib.109 (anap.); ἐπί or παρὰ Πριάμοιο θύρῃσι at Priam's *door*, i.e. before his dwelling, Il.2.788, 7.346: metaph., ἐπὶ ταῖς θύραις τῆς Ἑλλάδος εἶναι X. *An.*6.5.23, cf. D.10.34; τῆς πατρίδος Plu.*Sull.*29, *Arat.*37; ἐπὶ θύραις τῆς Πίστης Philostr.*VA*8.15; πυρετοῦ περὶ θύρας ὄντος being *at the door*, Plu.2.128f (but χειμῶνος ἐπὶ θύραις ὄντος Phlp. *in Mete.*130. 25). 2. esp. of kings and potentates, οἱ τῶν ἀρίστων Περσῶν παῖδες ἐπὶ ταῖς βασιλέως θύραις παιδεύονται are educated at *court*, X.*An.*1.9.3; γυνὴ φοιτῶσα ἐπὶ τὰς θύρας τοῦ βασιλέος, of a petitioner, Hdt.3.119, cf. X.*An.*2.1.8; αἱ ἐπὶ τὰς θ. φοιτήσεις dangling after *the court*, Id.*HG*1.6.7; ἐπὶ ταῖς τῶν πλουσίων θ. διατρίβειν Arist. *Rh.*1391ᵃ12; περὶ θύρας διατρίβειν Id.*Pol.*1313ᵇ7, Theopomp.Hist. 121; applied also to lovers, clients, disciples, etc., ἐπὶ τὴν θύραν (or τὰς θύρας) τινὸς βαδίζειν, ἰέναι, etc., Ar.*Pl.*1007, Pl.*R.*364b, cf. *Phdr.* 233e, etc.; ἐπὶ ταῖσι θύραις ἀεὶ καθῆσθαι Ar.*Nu.*467: metaph., Μουσῶν ἐπὶ ποιητικὰς θ. ἀφικέσθαι Pl.*Phdr.*245a. 3. prov., γλώσσῃ θύραι οὐκ ἐπίκεινται Thgn.421; οὐδέποτ' ἴσχει θ., of admirers of the Demos, Eup.265; ἐπὶ θύραις τὴν ὑδρίαν to break the pitcher *at the* very *door*, 'there's many a slip 'twixt cup and lip', Arist.*Rh.* 1363ᵃ7; τίς ἂν θύρας ἁμάρτοι; Id.*Metaph.*993ᵇ5; λόγος δικαστηρίου ἢ ἀγορᾶς οὐδὲ θύρας ἰδών D.H.*Dem.*23; τὸ κατὰ θύραν τερπνόν *vulgar* pleasures, Eun.*VS*p.496B.; παρὰ θύραν πλανᾶσθαι S.E.*M.*1.43; ἐκ θυρῶν εὐθέως τῆς.. ἀκροάσεως at the very *beginning*, Olymp. *in Mete.* 2.1. 4. *shutter* of a window, τὰς θ. τὰς ἐπὶ τῶν θυρίδων *IG*12(5). 872.37 (Tenos), cf. 2².1668.60. 5. pl., *door* of a chariot, X.*Cyr.* 6.4.9. 6. pl., *axle-trees*, Poll.1.146 (v.l. εὐραί). 7. θύρη καταπακτή trap-*door*, Hdt.5.16. 8. *frame of planks, raft*, Id.2.96; φραξάμενοι τὴν ἀκρόπολιν θύρῃσί τε καὶ ξύλοισι with *hurdles* and logs, Id.8.51, cf. Th.6.101. 9. in war, *fenced works* to obstruct landing-parties, in pl., Ph.*Bel.*94.37, 100.7. II. generally, *entrance*, as to a grotto, in pl., Od.9.243, al. 2. *sluice-gate*, *PPetr.*3p.134: pl., ib.2p.41 (iii B.C.). III. metaph., senses, as *the entrances to the soul*, τὸ σῶμα πολλαῖς θυρίσι καὶ θύραις ἀνοίγοντες Seren.ap.Stob.3. 6.17; ἐγγὺς τοῦ στόματος ἡ καρδία, ἡ δὲ ψυχὴ τῶν θ. Aristaenet.2.7. (I.-E. *dhur-*, cf. Lat. *foras, fores*, OE. *duru* 'door', etc.)

θῠραβάθρα, ἡ, *companion-ladder* in a ship, *PLond.*3.1164ʰ9 (iii A.D.).

θῠράγματα, τά, (θυράζω) = ἀφοδεύματα, Hsch.

θύρ-αζε [ῠ], Adv., for θύρασδε, *to the door*, and so, *out of doors*, ἐκ δὲ θ. ἔδραμον Il.18.29, cf. 416, Od.15.62; δόμων ἐξῆγε θ. ib.465. 2. generally, *out*, Il.5.694, Od.15.451, etc.; ἔκβασις.. ἁλὸς πολιοῖο θ. a way of getting *out of* the sea, 5.410; ἰχθῦν ἐκ πόντοιο θ. [ἕλκειν] Il. 16.408, cf. 21.237; ἐπὶ πρύμνῃσιν ἐείλεον οὐδὲ θ. εἴων ἐξιέναι 18.447; ἐξενεγκὼν θ. Ar.*Ach.*359; ἐξέλκειν τινὰ θ. Id.*Eq.*365; θ. ἐξιέναι Id.*V.* 70; ἐκχεῖν θ. empty *outside*, Id.*Fr.*306; καρδίαν θ. ἔχειν E.*Fr.*1063. 12; τὰ θ. *outside*, opp. τὰ ἔνδον, Id.*Or.*604; θ. ζῳοτοκεῖν or ᾠοτοκεῖν, Arist.*GA*718ᵇ32, 719ᵇ19; ῥεῖ διὰ τῶ σώματος ἔξω θ. τὰ πνεύματα Ti. Locr.102a. 3. c. gen., θ. τῶν νόμων *without* the law, E.*Ba.*331; θ. Ἀττικῶς, ἔξω Ἑλληνικῶς Moer.p.185P. **-άζω**, aor. inf. θυράξαι, *thrust out of doors*, Hsch. **-ᾱθεν**, Adv. *from outside the door*: and generally, *from without*, αἱ θ. εἴσοδοι E.*Andr.*952; θ. εἰκάσαι Id.*HF* 713; θ. ἐπεισιέναι Arist.*GA*736ᵇ28. 2. *outside the door, outside*, ἡ θ. ἡδονή E.*Fr.*1063.4; ὁ ἀὴρ ὁ θ. Arist.*Resp.*480ᵃ30, cf. *PA*642ᵇ1; οἱ θ. *foreigners, the enemy*, A.*Th.*68, 193. 3. metaph., opp. ἔνδοθεν (q.v.), S.*Tr.*1021 (hex.). **-ᾱθι**, Adv. *at the door*, *EM*25.17:—Ep. **θύρηθι**, *outside*, μάλα δ' ὦκα θύρηθ' ἔα I was soon *out* (of the sea), Od.14. 352. **-αῖος**, α, ον, also ος, ον S.*El.*313, E.*Alc.*805, Plu. (ll.cc. infr.): Aeol. **θύραος** *IG*12(2).14 (Mytil.): (θύρα):—*at the door* or *just outside the door*, A.*Ag.*1055, S.*Aj.*793; θ. οἰχνεῖν to go *to the door*, go *out*, Id.*El.*313; τόνδε βλέπω θ. ἤδη Id.*Tr.*595; θ. στίβος, opp. ἔναυλος, Id. *Ph.*158 (lyr.); θ. ἔστω πόλεμος A.*Eu.*864: metaph., θ. ἀμφὶ μηρόν round the *exposed, naked* thigh, S.*Fr.*872 (lyr.); θ. δόξα Plu.*Cat.Ma.* 18; θ. ὑποψίαι Id.2.38c. 2. *absent, abroad*, A.*Ag.*1608, *Ch.*115; θ. ἐλθεῖν to come *from abroad*, E.*Ion* 702 (lyr.); τοὺς δ' ἐν θυραίοις in *the public eye*, opp. τοὺς μὲν ὀμμάτων ἄπο, Id.*Med.*217. 3. *from out of doors, from abroad*, ἄνδρες θ. *strangers*, Id.*Hipp.*409; θυραῖα φρονήματ' ἀνδρῶν the thoughts *of strangers*, ib.395. 4. = ἀλλότριος, ὄλβος θ. the luck *of others*, A.*Ag.*837; πῆμα E.*Alc.*778; χείρ Id.*Ph.*848; παῖδες, i.e. *adoptive*, Id.*Fr.*491. II. *containing a door*, θ. τοῖχος *entrance*-wall, *IG*11(2).165.6 (Delos, iii B.C.), 12 l.c. (pl.), *Milet.*7.56 (Didyma). III. **θυραία**, ἡ, *doorway, opening*, Men.389, *IG*2². 1668.61 (pl.).

θῠρᾱμάχος [μᾰ], ον, *assaulting doors*, κῶμοι prob. l. in Pratin.Lyr. 1.8.

θῠρᾰνοίκτης, ου, ὁ, *door-opener*, A.D.*Synt.*324.8.

θύραξ· πύργος, χιτών, Hsch. (cf. θώραξ).

θύρᾱσι, -σιν [ῠ], Adv., (θύρα) *at the door, without*, Ar.*V.*891, *Pax* 942, 1023, al. 2. *abroad* (written θύραισι in codd.), E.*El.*1074, S. *OC*401.

θῠραυλ-έω, (αὐλή) *live in the open air, camp out*, Pl.*Plt.*272a, *Lg.* 695a, X.*Oec.*7.30, Isoc.6.76, etc.; esp. in war, *keep the field*, Arist.*Pol.* 1319ᵃ24, D.H.9.15, Plu.*Caes.*17, etc. II. *wait at another's door*, of visitors, *POxy.*471.72 (ii A.D.); freq. of lovers waiting on their mistresses, Plu.2.759b, Ph.1.306, etc.; ὁ θυραυλῶν Ἔρως Plot.6.5. 10. **-ία**, ἡ, *living out of doors, camping out*, Ti.Locr.103b (pl.), etc.; of soldiers, Plu.2.498c; of wild animals, Arist.*GA*783ᵃ 19. II. *waiting at the door*, of lovers, in pl., Ph.1.155, Philostr. *Ep.*29: sg., Luc.*Merc.Cond.*10. **-ος** (proparox.), ον, *living out of doors*, of shepherds, Hsch.

θῠρᾰωρός, όν, *warder of the gate*, v.l. for πυλαωρός, Il.22.69 (pl.); cf. θυρωρός.

θυργανᾶν· κρίνειν (fort. θρυγανᾶν· κρούειν), Hsch.

θύρδα, Arc. for θύραζε, = ἔξω, Hsch.

θῠρεᾱμᾰχία, ἡ, *contest in which shields were borne*, *SIG*1061.12 (Samos, ii B.C.).

θῠρέασπις, ιδος, ἡ, *large shield*, *AP*6.131 (Leon.).

θυρεᾱτικοὶ στέφανοι wreaths *worn to commemorate the victory at Thyrea*, Sosib.5.

θῠρεᾱφόρος, ον, = θυρεοφόρος, *Supp.Epigr.*3.351 (Thisbe, iii B.C.), Plb.5.53.8, Plu.*Aem.*19, Arr.*Tact.*4.4.

θύρεθρα· θύραι, Hsch.

θῠρεο-ειδής, ές, *shield-shaped*: χόνδρος θυρεοειδής (male θυροειδής) the *thyroid* cartilage (in the larynx), Gal.2.839, *UP*7.11, al.; νῆσος θ. Str.17.2.2; θ. τόπος prob. for θυρο- in *Hippiatr.*40. **-κοιλίτης** [ῑ], ου, ὁ, *soldier armed with hollow* θυρεός, *IPE*1².687 (Olbia).

θῠρεός, ὁ, (θύρα) *stone put against a door* to keep it shut, Od.9.240, 313. II. *oblong shield* (*shaped like a door*), *PSI*4.428.36 (iii B.C.), Inscr.ap.Plu.*Pyrrh.*26, Callix.2; hence, of the Roman *scutum* (opp. ἀσπίς, = *clipeus*), Plb.2.30.3, 6.23.2, D.H.4.16, cf. *Ep.Eph.*6.16, Apollod.*Poliorc.*163.2, Arr.*Tact.*3.2, etc. III. *disk* forming part of καθετήρ, *IG*11(2).287*B*68 (Delos, iii B.C.). IV. Math., *oval*, Procl. *in Euc.*1 *Deff.*3,8.

θῠρεοφορ-έω, *to be armed with the oblong shield*, Plb.10.13.2. **-ος**, ον, *armed with such a shield*, LXX 1 *Ch.*12.24, Plb.10.29.6, Ascl.*Tact.* 1.3, Plu.*Crass.*25; cf. θυρεαφόρος.

θυρεόω, *cover with a shield*, Aq.*Is.*31.5.

θῠρεπᾰνοίκτης, ου, ὁ, *door-opener*, of the philosopher Crates, *for whom all doors were open*, Plu.2.632e; or, *who forced all doors*, D.L. 6.86: pl., *burglars*, Vett.Val.202.6; cf. θυρανοίκτης.

θύρετρ-α [ῠ], τά, = θύρα, *door*, in pl., Il.2.415, Od.18.385, 21.49, Pi.*I.*7(6).6, E.*Ba.*448, *Or.*1474 (lyr.), Call.*Ap.*3, etc.; prop. the *door-casing, frame*, *IG*11(2).161*A*66 (Delos, iii B.C.); θύραις ἁρμοζούσαις τοῖς θυρέτροισι ib.12(2).14.7; θ. μαρμάρινα ib.6: so in sg., ib.4. 1484.30 (Epid.), *BCH*6.24 (Delos, ii B.C.), Plb.30.18.5, *AP*5.293.7 (Agath.), Ps.-Luc.*Philopatr.*4:—hence **-εᾶς**· φλιᾶς, Hsch. **-ικός**, ή, όν, *belonging to a door-frame*, πῆγμα *BCH*1.82 (Chios).

θυρευτής, οῦ, ὁ, *door-keeper*, *Gloss.* (dub.).

θύρη, θύρηθι, Ion. and Ep. for θύρα, θύραθι.

θῠρη-βόλιον· τὴν ἐπ' ἀγρῷ οἴκησιν, Hsch.; = ἔπαυλις, *EM*459.13: **-βόλος·** τέκτων, Suid.

θύρηφι [ῠ], Ep. dat. of θύρα, used as Adv., *outside*, Od.9.238, Hp. *Superf.*2, etc.; τὰ θ., opp. τὰ ἔνδοθι, Od.22.220; τὸ or τὰ θ., Hes.*Op.* 365, Naumach.ap.Stob.4.23.7.

θῠρῐδεύς, έως, ὁ, *window-frame*, *Inscr.Délos* 290.212 (iii B.C.).

θῠρίδιον, τό, Dim. of θύρα, *Gp.*15.6.2.

θῠρῐδ-όω, *make a window*, *PTheb.Bank* 11.10 (ii B.C.):—Pass., οἰκία τεθυριδωμένη *furnished with windows*, *BGU* 1116.15 (i B.C.). **-ωτός,** ή, όν, *having apertures*, κιβωτός Demioprat.ap. Poll.10.137; καταπάλτης *IG*2².1487.89.

θῠριοβόλος, ὁ, dub. sens. in *Cat.Cod.Astr.*8(4).126.

θύριον [ῠ] (not θυρίον, Eust.268.9), τό, Dim. of θύρα, *little door, wicket*, Ar.*Nu.*92, *Th.*26, *IG*11(2).154*A*26 (Delos, iii B.C.), Plu. *Cleom.*8, Alciphr.3.30: metaph., τὸ τοῦ λόγου θ. παραβαλοῦ *close the door* of discourse, Plu.2.940f, cf. 965b. 2. *small sluice*, *PLond.* 3.1177.243 (ii A.D.).

θῠρίς, ίδος, ἡ, Dim. of θύρα, *window*, Praxill.5, Ar.*V.*379, *Th.*797, Pl.*R.*359d, Arist. *deAn.*404ᵃ4, *Ath.*50.2, *IG*11(2).161*D*101 (Delos, iii B.C.), *BGU* 1116.23 (i B.C.), Plu.2.273b; *window-frame*, ἐναρμόσαι εἰς ἑκάστην τὴν θ. (*opening*) χαλκᾶς θ. (*frames*) *IG*2².1668.37. b. *audience-window* of the king or high officials in Egypt, *UPZ*15.7, 16.20, 53.5 (ii B.C.), Heraclid.Cum.4. 2. *opening* at each end of a bee's cell, Arist.*HA*624ᵃ7. 3. *valve* of a bivalve fish, ib.529ᵇ 7. 4. in pl., *embrasures* in battlements, *IG*2².463.55, al.; for artillery, D.S.20.91, D.C.74.10. II. in pl., *planks, boards*, Heraclid.Pont.ap.Ath.12.521f; *tablets*, Hsch. 2. *cell* of wasps, Arist. *HA*628ᵃ20, 629ᵃ30.

θυριώτης, ου, ὁ, *one found at the door*, Suid.

θυρξεύς, έως, ὁ, title of Apollo in Achaea, Paus.7.21.13.

θῠροειδής, ές, *like a door*, τόπος dub. in *Hippiatr.*40 (v. θυρεοειδής); τὸ θ. τρῆμα *the opening in the os pubis*, Gal.2.414.

θῠροιγός, ὁ, (οἴγνυμι) *door-keeper*, Hsch.

θῠροκιγκλίδες, ίδων, αἱ, *latticed doors*, *IG*2².1672.168.

θῠροκοπ-έω, *knock at the door, break it open*, esp. as a drunken feat, ἀπὸ γὰρ οἴνου γίγνεται καὶ θυροκοπῆσαι κτλ. Ar.*V.*1254; θυροκοπῶν ὦφλεν δίκην Antiph.239, cf. Chor.in *Hermes* 17.232. 2. metaph., *knock as at a door*, θ. τῇ χειρὶ τὴν πλευράν [τινος] Plu.2.503a; ὁ λιμὸς τὴν γαστέρα θ. Alciphr.3.70. **-ία,** ἡ, *knocking at the door*, Diph. 128, Lib.*Or.*11.47. **-ικός,** ή, όν, *of* or *like* θυροκοπία: θυροκοπικόν, τό, *tune played on the flute* (= κρουσίθυρον), Trypho ap.Ath.14.618c:—also **-ιστικόν,** τό, Hsch. **-ος** (parox.), ον, *knocking at the door, begging*, ψευδόμαντις A.*Ag.*1195.

θῠροκρουστία, ἡ, *knocking at a door*, dub. in *Sammelb.*4425 ii 24 (ii A.D.).

θυρουρός, ὁ, v. θυρωρός.

θῠρο-πηγία, ἡ, *making of doors*, Thphr.*HP*5.7.6. **-ποιός,** ὁ, *door-maker*, Poll.7.111; nickname of the Comic poet Aristomenes, Hsch., Suid.

θυρουλλεῖν, written for θυραυλεῖν, Hsch.

θῠροφύλαξ [φῠ], ᾰκος, ὁ, *door-keeper*, Sch.Il.22.69, prob. in Fronto *Ep.Gr.*5.1.

θῠρόω, (θύρα) *furnish with doors*, ἱερόν *IG*1².24.7; πρόπυλον ib.2². 1046.16; νεὼς.. θυρῶσαι χρυσαῖσι θύραις Ar.*Av.*614 (anap.): metaph., βλεφάροις θυρῶσαι τὴν ὄψιν X.*Mem.*1.4.6:—Pass., στεγόμενα καὶ τεθυρωμένα roofed and *furnished with doors*, *Tab.Heracl.*1.142, cf. *IG* 11(2).287*A*172 (Delos, iii B.C.), *PAmh.*2.51.14, 24 (i B.C.); *furnished with apertures*, πίναξ *JHS*41.195 (Delos, ii B.C.); πολλαῖς ἐξόδοις τεθυρῶσθαι *to be furnished* with many outlets, Luc.*Hipp.*8.

θυρσ-άζω, *bear* or *brandish the thyrsus*, θυρσαδδωᾶν Lacon. part. gen. pl. fem. for θυρσαζουσῶν, Ar.*Lys.*1313. **-άριον,** τό, Dim. of θύρσος, Plu.2.614a:—of vegetables, *head*, Orib.*Fr.*55. **-εχθής,** ές, of Bacchus, prob. f.l. for **-εγχής,** *with thyrsus-spear*, Orph.*H.*45.5 (Ruhnk.). **-ίαμβος** [ῐ], ὁ, coined as etym. of θρίαμβος, Lyd. *Mens.*1.2. **-ίνη,** = ὀροβάγχη, Dsc.2.142 (nisi leg. θυρσῖτιν, cf. θυρσίτης). **-ιον,** τό, = θύμον, Ps.-Dsc.3.36; also, = κατανάγκη, ib.4.131; symbolic of Aquarius, Herm.Trism. in *Rev.Phil.*32. 274. II. θυρσίον, Dim. of θύρσος, Hero *Spir.*2.9. **-ίτης** [ῑ], ου, ὁ, = ὠκιμοειδές, Ps.-Dsc.4.28 (with v.l. -ῖτις).

θυρσίων, ωνος, ὁ, part of a fish, Ath.7.310e; Lat. *tursio* (v.l. *thurs-*), = a dolphin-like fish, Plin.*HN*9.34.

θυρσο-ειδής, ές, *thyrsus-like*, Dsc.3.17. **-κόμος,** ὁ, *thyrsus-keeper*, a play of Lysippus, Suid. **-λογχος,** ὁ, *thyrsus-lance*, Callix. 2. II. as Adj., θ. ὅπλα *thyrsus-like* arms, Str.1.2.8. **-μᾰνής,** ές, *he who raves with the thyrsus*, epith. of Bacchus, E.*Ph.*792 (lyr.), Orph.*H.*50.8. **-πλήξ,** ῆγος, ὁ, ἡ, *thyrsus-stricken, frantic*, [ἑσμὸς] τεχνιτῶν Limen.19, cf. Hsch.

θύρσος, ὁ, in late Poets with heterocl. pl. θύρσα *AP*6.158 (Sabin.): —*wand wreathed in ivy and vine-leaves with a pine-cone at the top*, carried by the devotees of Dionysus, E.*Ba.*80 (lyr.), *SIG*1109.138, Hero *Spir.*2.9, etc.; also of the *devotees* themselves, Sch.E.*Hec.* 261. II. = κλάδος, ῥάβδος, Hsch. (Prob. a loan-word.)

θυρσο-τῐνάκτης, ου, ὁ, *thyrsus-shaker*, of Bacchus, Orph.*H.*52.4. **-φορέω,** *bear the thyrsus*, D.S.4.3. II. θ. θιάσους *assemble* or *lead* companies *with the thyrsus*, E.*Ba.*557 (lyr.). **-φορία,** ἡ, *bearing of the thyrsus*, Plu.2.671e. **-φόρος,** ον, *thyrsus-bearing*, Βάκχαι E.*Cyc.*64 (lyr.), cf. *AP*9.524.9. **-χᾰρής,** ές, *delighting in the thyrsus*, *Inscr.Magn.*215a.23, *AP*3.1 (Inscr.Cyzic.).

θυρσόω, *make into thyrsi*, λόγχαι τεθυρσωμέναι D.S.4.4.

θύρ-ωμα [ῠ], ατος, τό, *doorway* (including posts, sill, and lintel), *IG*1².372.78, 11(2).287*A*77 (Delos, iii B.C.), Thphr.*HP*3.14.1, Callix. 2, Hsch. s.v. θύρετρα; τὸ μέγα θ. *OGI*193.10 (Branchidae); τὸ πρόπυλον καὶ τὸ θ. ib.734 (Egypt, ii B.C.); διξὰ θ. Hdt.2.169: pl., also in Th.3.68, Lys.19.31, Pl.*Plt.*280d, D.21.167; τὰ θ. ἀποσπάσας Id. 29.3. II. *panel, tablet*, Diotog.ap.Stob.4.1.96; τὸν νόμον οὐκ ἐν οἰκήμασι καὶ θυρώμασι ἐνῆμεν δεῖ, ἀλλ' ἐν τοῖς ἤθεσι Archyt.ap.eund. 4.1.138. 2. in pl., *planks, boards*, D.S.20.86. III. *window*, Lxx 3*Ki.*7.42(5) (pl.). **-ών,** ῶνος, ὁ, *hall, antechamber*, S.*El.*328, *OT*1242, *Fr.*649.23, *IG*11(2).158*A*57 (Delos, iii B.C.), Plu.*Pyrrh.* 34, etc.

θῠρωρ-εῖον, τό, *porter's lodge*, Vitr.6.7.1 (dub.). **-έω,** *to be a door-keeper*, Plu.2.83cb. **-ός,** Cypr. **θυραϝωρός** dub. in *Inscr.Cypr.* 215 H., Ep. **θυραωρός** (q.v.), ὁ, ἡ:—*door-keeper, porter*, Sapph.98, Hdt.1.120, A.*Ch.*565, Pl.*Phlb.*62c, *Ev.Marc.*13.34, *BGU*1061.10 (i A.D.), Luc.*Vit.Auct.*7, etc.:—also **θυρουρός** *PCair.Zen.*292.76 (iii B.C.), *PRyl.*136.6 (i A.D.), *IG*3.1137 (ii A.D.), *PFlor.*71.380 (iv A.D.). (From θυρα-hopϝος, cf. οὖρος, ἐρύω (B): connected with ὠρέω by Corn. *ND*1.)

θύρ-ωσις [ῠ], εως, ἡ, *furnishing with a door*, τοῦ ἐργαστηρίου *IG*4. 1484.38 (Epid.). **-ωτός,** όν, *with a door* or *aperture*, στήθη Babr.59. 11: neut. as Subst., **-ωτόν,** τό, *doorway*, *IG*4.1484.304 (Epid., dual).

θῦσαι, ῶν, αἱ, like θυιάδες, *Bacchantes*, Lyc.106; v.l. θύστησιν, cf. θυστάς, θύστης.

θῠσᾰνηδόν, Adv. *fringe-like*, Ael.*NA*16.11.

θῠσᾰνο-ειδής, ές, *fringed*: τὸ τῶν στρωμάτων θ. Eun.*Hist.*p.239 D. **-εις,** Ep. **θυσσανόεις,** εσσα, εν, *tasseled, fringed*, Hom. (only in Il.), αἰγίδα θυσσανόεσσαν 15.229, 17.593, al.; ἀσπίδα (v.l. αἰγίδα) θ. 21.400.

θύσᾰνος [ῠ], ὁ, *tassel*: mostly in pl., *tassels, fringe*, Hom. (only in Il.), of the *tassels of the* αἰγίς, 2.448; ζώνῃ ἑκατὸν θυσάνοις ἀραρυίῃ 14.181, cf. Hes.*Sc.*225, Hdt.4.189; οἱ τῆς ὀθόνης θ. Ach.Tat.5.24; πέπλος ἄχρι τῶν θ. πεποικιλμένος Them.*Or.*18.222c; of the *tufts* of the golden fleece, Pi.*P.*4.231; of the *long arms* of the cuttle-fish, Opp.*H.*3.178; δικτυωτοὺς θ. D.S.18.26. (Possibly connected with θύσσομαι, θύω.)

θῠσάν-ουρος [ᾰ], ον, (οὐρά) *with a ragged tail*, Hsch. **-ώδης,** ες, = θυσανόεις, *tassel-like, bunched*, ῥίζα Thphr.*HP*1.6.4. **-ωτός,** ή, όν, = θυσανόεις, κιθών, αἰγέη, Hdt.2.81, 4.189; ἔνδυμα J.*BJ*5.5.7.

θῡσείω, Desiderat. of θύω, Hdn.*Epim.*249.

θύσθεν, Adv. for θύρθεν, = θύραθεν, *outside*, τᾶς κελεύθω *IG*5(2).3.23 (Tegea, iv B.C.).

θύσθλα, ων, τά, (θύω) *sacred implements of Bacchic orgies*, Il.6.134; θύσθλοις παιομένους Jul.*Or.*7.209d. II. *the Bacchic festival itself*, Opp.*C.*1.26: also in sg., Plu.2.501f. III. generally, *sacrifice*, θ. καταίθειν Lyc.459, cf. 720, 929, Orph.*A*.904, etc.

θῠσί-α, Ion. **-ίη,** ἡ, (θύω) prop. *burnt-offering, sacrifice*, mostly in pl., v.l. in Batr.176, cf. Emp.128.6, etc.; ἐν θυσίῃσι εἶναι Hdt.8.99; θυσίαισι δέκεσθαί τινα Pi.*P.*5.86, cf. *I.*5(4).30; θυσίῃσι ἱλάσκεσθαι τὸν θεόν Hdt.1.50, cf. 6.105; θυσίας ἔρδειν, ἐπιτελέειν, ἀνάγειν, Id.1.131, 2.63, 60: also in sg., θυσίαν ποιεῖσθαι, θύειν, Pl.*Smp.*174c, *R.*362c; ἄγειν Id.*Alc.*2.148e; θ. σωτηρίου, αἰνέσεως, τῆς τελειώσεως, Lxx *Le.*3. 1, 7.2, *Ex.*29.34; of the gods, θυσίαν δέχεσθαι A.*Th.*701 (lyr.). 2. *mode of sacrifice*, θ. ἡ αὐτὴ πᾶσι κατέστηκε Hdt.4.60, cf. 2.39. 3. *festival, at which sacrifices were offered*, Pl.*Phd.*61b, *Ti.*26e, al.; θ. καὶ διαγωγαὶ τοῦ συζῆν Arist.*Pol.*1280ᵇ37, cf. *EN*1160ᵃ20; περὶ τῶν ἐν Ῥόδῳ θ., title of work by Theognis Hist. b. generally, *rite, ceremony*, Plu.2.693f, *Thes.*20. II. *victim, offering*, Plu.2.184f, Luc. *Sacr.*12. **-άζω,** *sacrifice*, μῆλα Strato Com.1.21; θυσίαν, θυσίασμα, Lxx 2*Ch.*7.5, 2*Es.*6.3; ὑπέρ τινος dub. l. in Lys.6.4; ὑπὲρ τοῦ δήμου *OGI*339.36 (Sestos, ii B.C.); τῷ Διὶ ὑπὲρ τῶν πλοϊζομένων ib.199.36 (Adule); θ. τῷ θεῷ καὶ βακχεύειν D.S.4.3: abs., Lxx 1*Ch.*21.28, al., *IG*3.74.16, etc.: θυσιάζουσαι, αἱ, title of mime by Herodas. **-άς,** άδος, *frenzied*, φωνή Hsch.: pl. as Subst., = θυιάδες, Id. **-ασμα,** ατος, τό, = θυσία II, Lxx *Ex.*29.18 (v.l. θυμίαμα), 2*Es.*6.3. **-αστήριον,** τό, *altar*, ib.*Ex.*27.1, al., *Ev.Matt.*23.18, J.*AJ*8.4.1, *Cod.Just.*1.12. 3.2. **-αστήριος,** α, ον, *sacrificial*, [ὕμνος] Timae.154. **-αστής,** οῦ, ὁ, *a sacrificer*, Sch.E.*Hec.*224.

θύσῐμος [ῠ], ον, (θύω A) *fit for sacrifice*, κτήνεα Hdt.1.50, cf. Ar. *Ach.*784; τὸ θ. Plu.2.437a, cf. Porph.*Abst.*2.14.

θῠσῐουργός, ὁ, *sacrificer, slaughterer*, Ptol.*Tetr.*179.

θύσις or **θῦσις,** εως, ἡ, (θύω B) *raging*, ἀπὸ τῆς θ. καὶ ζέσεως τῆς ψυχῆς Pl.*Cra.*419e.

θύσκα· κύρια, Hsch. **θυσκάριον,** τό, Dim. of sq., *EM*458.53 (cod. Voss.). **θύσκη, θύσκος,** v. θυΐσκη.

θυσμικός, ή, όν, *sacrificial*, ἔτος *IG*12(5).141 (Paros), 903 (Tenos).

θυσπολίαι· θυηπολίαι, Hsch.

θυσσᾰνόεις, Ep. for θυσαν-.

θυσσάς, άδος, ὁ, = θυιάς, epith. of Bacchus, *IG*12(5).972 (Tenos).

θύσσομαι, = τινάσσομαι, Hsch.

θυστάς, άδος, ἡ, (θύω A) *sacrificial*, θ. βοή the cry *uttered in sacrificing*, A.*Th.*269; θ. λιταί the prayers *accompanying a sacrifice*, S. *Ant.*1019. II. as Subst., = θυτήρ, Sch.Opp.*H.*5.417; = θυιάς, Hsch. 2. *sacrificial robe*, E.*Fr.*1101.

θυστήριον· ὁρμητήριον, Suid.; but θυστηρίοις· θυμιατηρίοις, Hsch. **θυστήριος,** ὁ, epith. of Dionysus, *EM*455.31. **θύστης,** ου, Dor. **-τας,** α, ὁ, *sacrificing priest* (Cret.), Hsch. **θύστινον·** τρίχινον, οἱ δὲ μεσοτριβῆ, Id. **θύστρα,** τά, = θύματα, *SIG*1026.24 (Cos).

θῠτ-εῖον, τό, (θύω A) *place for sacrificing*, Aeschin.3.122. **-έον**, *one must sacrifice*, Ar.*Av.*1237, Pl.*R.*365e, Porph.*Abst.*2.13; τῇ ἀληθείᾳ Luc.*Hist.Conscr.*39. **-ήρ**, ῆρος, ὁ, *sacrificer, slayer*, A.*Ag.* 224,240 (both lyr.), S.*Tr.*613, al.: coupled with μάντις, Call.*Iamb.*1. 221. **-ήριον**, τό, = θῦμα, E.*IT*243. II. = θυσιαστήριον, as name of the constellation *Ara*, Arat.403, Q.S.4.554. III. = θυμιατήριον, Phot. **-ης**, ου, ὁ, *sacrificer* or *diviner*, *SIG*589.18 (Magn. Mae., ii B.C.), D.S.17.17, Onos.10.25, Arr.*Epict.*1.17.18, *IG*14.617.6 (Rhegium), App.*Hisp.*85, Hdn.4.12.3: Thess. **θύτας** *IG*9(2).1234 (Phalanna). **-ικός**, ή, όν, *of* or *for sacrifice*, μαχαιρίδιον Luc.*Pisc.*45: ἡ -κή (sc. τέχνη), the *art of the diviner*, Ph.2.221, Onos.10.28, Ath.14. 659d, Hdn.8.3.7, Porph.*Abst.*2.53; τὸ θ. *Placit.*5.1.3; θ. μαντεία Sch. rec.A.*Pr.*496. II. *given to sacrificing*, Str.3.3.6. **-ις**, ιδος, fem. of θύτης, Hsch. s.v. ἱρήτειρα: **-ρια**, fem. of θυτήρ, Suid. s.v. ἱέρεια.

θῦψαι, θύψω, v. τύφω.

θῦψις, εως, ἡ, (τύφω) *burning*, Suid. s.v. θυμάλωπες (= Sch.Ar.*Ach.* 320).

θύω (A), impf. ἔθυον, Ep. θύον Od.15.222, Ion. θύεσκον Hippon.37: fut. θύσω [ῡ] E.*El.*1141, Pl.*Lg.*909d, Henioch.5.10, Dor. θυσῶ Theoc. 2.33; 3 pl. θυσέοντι *IG*12(3).452 (Thera): aor. ἔθῡσα Od.9.231, etc., Ep. θῦσα 14.446: pf. τέθυκα Ar.*Lys.*1062, Pl.*R.*328c:—**Med.**, fut. θύσομαι E.*Heracl.*340 (as Pass., Hdt.7.197): aor. ἐθυσάμην Th.4. 92, (ἐκ-) Hdt.6.91, etc.:—**Pass.**, fut. τῠθήσομαι D.S.16.91, Luc. *DDeor.*4.2: aor. ἐτύθην [ῠ] Hdt.1.216, A.*Ch.*242, Philem.155.2 (part. written θυθέν Men.*Sam.*185, cf. τὴν βοῦν τὴν θυθεῖσαν *IG*12(7).241 (Amorgos, iii B.C.), etc.): pf. τέθῠμαι A.*Eu.*341 (lyr.), Ar.*Av.*1034, X. *HG*3.5.5 (in med. sense, 5.1.18, *An.*7.8.21): plpf. ἐτέθυτο Id.*HG*3. 1.23. [ῡ in fut. and aor., ῠ in pf. Act. and Pass., and aor. Pass.; ῡ generally in pres. and impf., exc. in trisyll. cases of part., θύοντα Od.15.260, θύοντες *h.Ap.*491, but θύεσκε Hippon.37; ἔθυε, θύων, Pi. *O.*10(11).57, 13.69; θύειν, at the end of a line, E.*El.*1141 (s.v.l., fort. θύη), *Cyc.*334, Ar.*Ach.*792 (spoken by a Megarian); θύεις, θύω, Strato Com.1.19,20; θύωντι 3 pl. pres. subj., Theoc.4.21.] I. Act., *offer by burning* meat or drink to the gods (τὸ θύειν δωρεῖσθαί ἐστι τοῖς θεοῖς Pl.*Euthphr.*14c), θεοῖσι δὲ θῦσαι ἀνώγει Πάτροκλον.., ὁ δ' ἐν πυρὶ βάλλε θυηλάς Il.9.219, cf. Aristarch.ap.Sch.ad loc., *Com.Adesp.*7D. (ap. Phryn.*PS*p.74 B.); ἦ ῥα καὶ ἄργματα θῦσε θεοῖς, of a drink-offering, Od.14.446, cf. 15.260; so ἔνθα δὲ πῦρ κήαντες ἐθύσαμεν (sc. τῶν τυρῶν) *made an offering* of cheese, 9.231; θ. ἀκρόθινα Pi.*O.*10(11).57; πέλανον, δεῖπνα, A.*Pers.*204, *Eu.*109; πυρούς, ναστούς, Ar.*Av.*565, 567: c. dat. rei, θ. τούτῳ ὅ τι ἔχοι ἕκαστος (with v.l. τοῦτο) Hdt.1. 50. 2. *sacrifice, slay* a victim, [τῷ ἡλίῳ] θ. ἵππους (v.l. ἵπποισι) ib. 216; ταῦρον Pi.*O.*13.69; αὐτοῦ παῖδα A.*Ag.*1417, cf. S.*El.*532, etc.; ἱρά Hdt.1.59; ἱερεῖα Th.1.126, etc.; θ. θῦμα, θυσίαν, Pl.*Plt.*290e, *R.* 362c, etc.; θ. διαβατήρια, ἐπινίκια, etc., Plu.*Luc.*24, Pl.*Smp.*173a, etc.:—Pass., τὰ τεθυμένα *the flesh of the victim*, X.*HG*4.3.14, etc.; τὰ τεθ. ἱερά ib.3.5.5; τὰ θυόμενα Id.*Lac.*15.3. b. simply, *slaughter*, Hdt.1.126, Ar.*Lys.*1062, LXX *Is.*22.13. 3. abs., *offer sacrifice*, Hdt.1.31, al., A.*Ag.*594, *Fr.*161.2, S.*OC*1159; τοῖσι θεοῖσι θ. Pherecr. 23, cf. Hdt.4.60, 8.138; θεῶν ἕνεκα Men.129.1. 4. *celebrate* with offerings or sacrifices, σῶστρα θ. Hdt.1.118; γενέθλια Pl.*Alc.*1.121c; Λύκαια, Ἡράκλεια, X.*An.*1.2.10, D.19.86; ἐλευθέρια Henioch.5.10; γάμους Plu.*Pomp.*55. 5. c. dupl. acc., εὐαγγέλια θ. ἑκατὸν βοῦς *sacrifice* a hundred oxen *for* the good news, Ar.*Eq.*656. 6. Ἑστίᾳ θύειν, prov. of niggards, because sacrifices to Hestia admitted no one to share the offering, Theopomp.Com.28. II. Med., *cause* a victim *to be offered*, τῶν θυμάτων ὧν δεῖ θύεσθαι καὶ παρίστασθαι *IG*5(1). 1390.65 (Andania, i B.C.), etc.: hence freq. abs., *consult the gods*, Hdt.7.189, E.*Heracl.*340; ἐπὶ Κρότωνα, ἐπὶ τῷ Πέρσῃ, i.e. on marching *against*.., Hdt.5.44, 9.10, cf. X.*An.*7.8.21; θύεσθαι ἐπ' ἐξόδῳ ib. 6.4.9; ὑπὲρ τῆς μονῆς ib.5.6.27: c. inf., θ. ἰέναι *offer sacrifice* [to learn] whether to go or not, ib.2.2.3; also ἐθυόμην εἰ βέλτιον εἴη ib.6.1.31 (so in Act., ἔθυε (v.l. ἐθύετο) τῷ Διί.. πότερά οἱ λῷον καὶ ἄμεινον εἴη.. ib.7.6.44); διαβατήρια θύεσθαι, as in Act., Th.5.54. 2. metaph., *tear in pieces*, of wild beasts, A.*Ag.*137 (lyr.). (Hence θυμός, cf. Skt. *dhūmás*, Lat. *fumus* 'smoke', θυμιάω, θύος, θυήλημα, τύφω, perh. θεῖον (A), Lat. *suffire*; cf. sq.)

θύω (B) [ῡ], aor. ἔθυσα Call.*Fr.*82:—*rage, seethe*, ἄνεμος μὲν ἐπαύσατο λαίλαπι θύων Od.12.400; Ζέφυρος μεγάλῃ σὺν λαίλαπι θύων ib. 408, cf. Hes.*Op.*621, *Th.*874; of a swollen river, ὁ δ' ἐπέσσυτο οἴδματι θύων *seething*, Il.21.234; ὑψόσε θύων ib.324; of a wind-swept sea, ὁ δ' ἔστενεν οἴδματι θύων 23.230, cf. Hes.*Th.*109, 131; of the wake of a ship, κῦμα δ' ὄπισθε πορφύρεον μέγα θῦε Od.13.85; δάπεδον δ' ἅπαν αἵματι θῦεν the ground *seethed* with blood, 11.420, 22.309; of persons, *storm, rage*, ἦ γὰρ ὅ γ' ὀλοιῇσι φρεσὶ θύει Il.1.342; ἔγχεϊ θῦεν 11. 180; κασιγνήτα μένει θύοισα Pi.*P.*3.33; θύουσαν Ἅιδου μητέρα A.*Ag.* 1235; πυκνὰ δέ οἱ κραδίη ἔντοσθεν ἔθυεν A.R.3.755 (v.l. ἔθυιεν): c. inf., *desire eagerly*, ἐνισπεῖν ib.685; of a horse, Call.*Fr.*82; of a serpent, Nic.*Th.*129 (v.l. θυίησι). [ῡ always: for θύμενος [ῡ] is f.l. for σύμενος in Pratin.Lyr.1.4.] θυίω (q.v.) should perh. be preferred in later Ep., and is cj. in Pi. l.c. (Cf. Lett. *dusmas* (pl.) 'anger', *dusēt* 'puff', 'pant', Lat. *fūro* (fr. *dhūs-*), θύελλα, θυίω, θυιάς (orig. *madwoman*); prob. cogn. with foreg.)

θυ-ώδης, ες, (θύος, ὄδ-ωδα, cf. εὐώδης, δυσώδης) *smelling of incense, fragrant*, εἵματα.. θυώδεα Od.5.264; θαλάμοιο θυώδεος 4.121; βωμός *h.Ap.*87; νηός *h.Ven.*59; ναοί Theoc.17.123; Οὔλυμπος *h.Merc.*322; λίβανος Emp.128.6; καπνός E.*Andr.*1026 (lyr.): Comp. -έστερος, τέρμινθος Thphr.*HP*3.15.3. II. (θύον I) *belonging to the tree* θύον, ib. 5.4.2. **-ώεις**, εσσα, εν, = θυόεις, Hsch. **-ωμα**, ατος, τό, *that which is burnt as incense*: pl., *spices*, Heraclit.67, Semon.16, Hdt.2.40,86, Luc.*Syr.D.*20.

Θυώνη, ἡ, (θύω B) epith. of Semele, *h.Hom.*1.21, Sapph.*Supp.* 6.10, Pi.*P.*3.99, D.S.3.62, etc.:—Adj. **Θυωναῖος** Διόνυσος Opp.*C.* 1.27. II. **θυώνη**, Dor. -ᾱ, ἡ, *portion of sacrifice*, acc. pl. -ας *Abh. Berl.Akad.*1928(6).12 (Cos); cf. Hsch. s.v. θύανον.

θυωρ-εῖσθαι· θυωθεῖσθαι, εὐωχεῖσθαι, Hsch. **-ίς** (sc. τράπεζα), ίδος, ἡ, *a table for offerings*, Poll.4.123; cf. θυωρός. **-ίτης**· τραπεζίτης, Hsch.: metaph., θ. κάλλους *an examiner* of beauty, of Paris, Lyc.93; expld. by ἀργυρογνώμων, *EM*457.50. **-ός**, όν, (θύος) *taking care of offerings*: as Subst. (sc. τράπεζα), = θυωρίς, Call.*Dian.*134, *BCH* 11.161 (Lagina); οἱ θεοὶ τὴν τράπεζαν θυωρὸν καλοῦσιν Pherecyd.Syr. 12. II. (θύος) *perfumer*, Nic.*Th.*103.

θώ, ὁ, apocop. for θώραξ, *AP*6.85 (Pall.).

θωάζω, Elean **θωάδδω**, (θωή) *pay the penalty*, βοῖ *Schwyzer*412.1 (Elis): **θωάω**, *penalize, fine*, *IG*1^2.4.7,12:—Delph. **θωέω** *Michel*995 *D*19:—Cret. **θωαίω** *GDI*4977 (Gortyn):—Pass., διπλείῳ θωιήστω (imper.), *IG*9(1).333.9 (Locr., v B.C.).

θωή, ἡ, *penalty*, θωὴν ἐπιθήσομεν Od.2.192; θωὴν ἀλέεινεν Ἀχαιῶν a *penalty* imposed by them, Il.13.669:—Att. **θωά**, ἡ, *IG*1^2.114.42:—Ion. also **θωϊή** Archil.109, *BCH*50.214 (Thasos, v B.C.), prob. l. in Democr.262: **θωιιή**, *SIG*58.12 (Milet., v B.C.): Att. gen. pl. θῳῶν with ι acc. to Choerob.*in Theod.*1.405, but v. supr. and cf. θωάω. (I.-E. *dhō-*, in OE. *dóm* 'doom', cf. *dhē-* in τίθημι.)

θωίασις, εως, ἡ, *infliction of penalty*, *Michel*995*D*23 (Delph.).

θωκέω, Ion. and Dor. for θᾱκέω. **θωκίζω**, *establish, settle*, Hsch. **θῶκος**, Ion. for θᾶκος. **θῶμα, θωμάζω, θωμάσιος**, Ion. for θαυμ-, Hdt. **θῶμαι**, v. θῶσθαι.

θωμεύω, (θωμός) *heap up*, Hsch.

θῶμιγξ, ιγγος, ἡ, *cord, string*, Hdt.1.199, *AP*9.343 (Arch.), Polyaen.6.50, Ael.*VH*3.26; *bow-string*, A.*Pers.*461, *Eu.*182, *Trag. Adesp.*215; *a fishing-line*, Opp.*H.*3.76, etc. (Perh. cognate with Lat. *fūnis.*)

θωμίζω (also -ίσσω, Hsch.), *whip, scourge*, νῶτον μάστιγι θωμιχθείς Anacr.21.10, cf. *EM*459.54:—also, *bind*, Hsch., Suid.

θώμισσον· τὸν μισθόν, Hsch. (leg. θῶμισσον· τὸ ἥμισσον).

θωμός, ὁ, *heap*, A.*Ag.*295, Ar.*Lys.*973, Thphr.*HP*8.11.4, *AP*6.299 (Phan.): metaph., θ. ψηφισμάτων Ar.*Fr.*217. (Like θημών, fr. I.-E. *dhē-*, τί-θημι.)

θωός, ὁ, a kind of *bird*, Hsch.

θωπ-εία, ἡ, *flattery*, E.*Or.*670, Jul.*Or.*3.102c, etc.: pl., Ar.*Eq.* 890; θωπεῖαι λόγων Pl.*Lg.*906b; θ. κολακικαί ib.633d. **-ευμα**, ατος, τό, *piece of flattery*, Ar.*V.*563: in pl., *endearments*, E.*Supp.*1103; *flatteries*, Pl.*R.*590c, Plu.2.823c:—Dim. **-ευμάτια**, τά, *bits of flattery*, Ar.*Eq.*788. **-ευτικός**, ή, όν, *disposed to flatter, fawning*, of dogs, Arist.*HA*488^{b}21; τὰ θωπευτικά *flattery*, Pl.*Lg.*634a. Adv. **-κῶς** D.C.69.6, Gal.14.600. **-εύω**, (θώψ) *flatter, wheedle*, τινα S.*OC* 1003, 1336, E.*Heracl.*983, Ar.*Ach.*657, *Eq.*48; σὺ ταῦτα θώπευ' *be it* thine to *flatter* thus, S.*El.*397; θ. τὸν δεσπότην λόγῳ Pl.*Tht.*173a; τὸν δῆμον Aeschin.3.226; τὰς πόλεις Phld.*Rh.*2.170S.; καιρὸν θ. *to be a time-server*, Ps.-Phoc.93; ἵνα μὴ ἄλλους θωπεύωμεν σοῦ ὑγιαίνοντος *serve* others (in good sense), *PSI*5.525.16 (iii B.C.); of dogs, *fawn*, Arist.*Phgn.*811^{b}38; *caress, pat* a horse, X.*Eq.*10.13, *Cyn.*6. 21; of disease, *soothe*, τὴν χολήν Sever.*Clyst.*p.37 D.:—Pass., Ar. *Eq.*1116. **-ικός**, ή, όν, (θώψ) = θωπευτικός, Id.*Lys.*1037, Max.Tyr. 9.7. Adv. **-κῶς** Suid. **-τω**, = θωπεύω, c. acc., θῶπτε τὸν κρατοῦντ' ἀεί A.*Pr.*937: fut. θώψεις Id.*Fr.*234.

θωρᾱκ-εῖον, τό, = θωράκιον II, *breastwork, parapet*, or *dwarf-wall* of an enclosure, A.*Th.*32, *IG*2^2.463.86, *IGRom.*4.293^{a}139 (Pergam., ii B.C.), 1465, 1474 (Smyrna), D.S.17.44 (v.l. -ίοις); the *breast-high part* of a wall-surface, ἵνα γραφῇ.. θ. ὀροβοειδές *PCair.Zen.*445 (iii B.C.). 2. *gunwale* of a trireme, *IG*2^2.1604.31. II. *cuirass*, *PCair. Zen.*14.12 (iii B.C.). **-ίζω**, prose form of θωρήσσω, *arm with a breastplate* or *corslet*, θωρακίσας αὐτοὺς καὶ ἵππους X.*Cyr.*8.8.22:—Med., *put on one's breastplate*, Id.*An.*2.2.14:—Pass., θωρακισθείς ib.3.4.35; τεθωρακισμένοι *cuirassiers*, Th.2.100, X.*An.*2.5.35; ἄγαλμα τεθ. *OGI*332. 7 (Elaea, ii B.C.). II. generally, *cover with defensive armour*, τοὺς ἡνιόχους ἐθωράκισε πλὴν τῶν ὀφθαλμῶν X.*Cyr.*6.1.29; ὄγκῳ.. χαλινίδος εὖ τεθωρακισμένος Ephipp.14.10: metaph., θ. ἑαυτούς, of wild boars, *to sheathe* themselves *in mud*, preparatory to fighting, Arist. *HA*571^{b}16; of the ichneumon, θωρακισθεὶς πηλῷ Str.17.1.39. **-ικός**, ή, όν, *suffering in the chest*, Aët.8.63. II. **-ικά**, τά, with or without μόρια, *region of the thorax*, Pall. *in Hp.*2.97, 102 D. **-ιον**, τό, Dim. of θώραξ, Luc.*Par.*49. II. *breastwork, parapet*, Plb.8.4.4, D.S.17.44 (v.l. for -είοις), J.*BJ*5.7.4, Ph.2.324; *shield* for those who worked the battering-ram, Ath.Mech.18.11; or for those who attempted to burn the enemy's engines, D.S.14.51; λύγου θ. Menodot. 1; also, *the tower on the back of elephants*, or rather *the upper part thereof*, [Plb.]*Fr.*162^b, D.S.2.17, Ael.*NA*13.9; *a crow's-nest at the masthead*, in which javelin-men were stationed, Asclep.Myrl.ap.Ath.11. 475a. III. δυστυχὲς θ. dub. sens. in *Com.Adesp.*15.29 D. **-ίς**, = θώραξ, *Gloss.* **-ισμός**, ὁ, *arming with breastplates*, LXX *2 Ma.*5. 3. **-ίτης** [ῑ], ου, ὁ, *soldier with breast-armour only*, Plb.10.29. 6, al.:—fem. **-ῖτις**, as Adj., ζώνη *cuirass*-belt, prob. in *PPetr.*3 p.12 (iii B.C.).

θωρᾱκο-ειδής, ές, *breastplate-shaped*, ὕφασμα Ph.2.226. **-ζώνη**, ἡ, *cuirass-belt*, Sch.Il.11.234. **-ποιός**, ὁ, *maker of breastplates*, X. *Mem.*3.10.9, *IG*2^2.1261.3, *PTeb.*278.18 (i A.D.). **-πώλης**, ου, ὁ, *dealer in breastplates*, Ar.*Pax* in Ind. personarum. **-φόρος**, Ion.

θωρηκ-, ον, *wearing a breastplate, cuirassier*, Hdt.7.89,92, 8.113, X. *Cyr.*5.3.36, Jul.*Or.*2.63c; τὸ θ. D.C.47.43.

θώραξ, ᾱκος, Ep. and Ion. **θώρηξ**, ηκος, Aeol. **θόρραξ** Alc.15 (codd. Ath.), ὁ:—*corslet*, θ. χάλκεος Il.23.560; παναίολος 11.374; πολυδαίδαλος 4.136, cf. 11.19, etc.; δεκάμνουν θώρηκος κύτος Ar.*Pax*1224; ἔξαιρε παῖ θώρακα..τὸν χοᾶ Id.*Ach.*1133; θ...γυάλοισιν ἀρηρώς Il.15.529 (γύαλα expld. as front- and back-piece fastened with περόναι, Paus.10.26.5); θώρηκος γύαλον Il.5.99; ὅθι διπλόος ἤντετο θ. 4.133; κατὰ ζώνην θώρηκος ἔνερθε 11.234; linen *jerkin* (not worn by Homeric Greeks acc. to Sch.Il.2.529, but cf. λινοθώρηξ), θόρρακες νέω λίνω Alc. l. c., cf. Hdt.2.182, 3.47, *Chron.Lind.*C.36, Paus.6.19.7. 2. *coat of mail, scale armour*, θ. χρύσεος λεπιδωτός Hdt.9.22, cf. 74; φολιδωτός Posidipp.26.7, cf. Paus.1.21.6; of chain mail, v. ἁλυσιδωτός. b. *slough* of a serpent, καθάπερ ὄφις παλαιὸν ἀποδύεται θ. Porph.*Chr.*88. II. *part covered by the* θώραξ I, *trunk*, Hp.*de Arte*10, E.*HF*1095, Arist.*HA*493^{a}5; κεφαλῆς καὶ θώρακος καὶ τῆς κάτω κοιλίας Id.*Pr.*962^{a}34; sts. taken as extending below the midriff, Pl.*Ti.*69e; ἀπ' αὐχένος μέχρι αἰδοίων Arist.*HA*491^{a}30, cf. *PA*686^{b}5; ἐν τῷ κάτω θώρακος χωρίῳ, of the abdominal cavity, Gal.16.448; but also of the *chest, thorax*, Arist.*HA*493^{a}17:—there is a play on signfs. I and II in Ar.*V.*1194 sq. b. *thorax* of crustaceans, Arist. *HA*601^{a}13, al. 2. *bandage for the chest*, Heliod.ap.Orib.48.48 tit., Sor.*Fasc.*33, cf. Gal.18(1).817. III. = θωράκιον II, Hdt.1.181, D.C.74.10.

θωρηκοφόρος, ον, Ion. for θωρακοφόρος.

θωρηκτής, οῦ, ὁ, (θωρήσσω) *armed with* θώραξ, Ἀργείοισι θωρηκτῇσι Il.21.429; Λυκίων, Τρώων πύκα θωρηκτάων *armed with* stout *cuirass*, 12.317, 15.689.

θώρηξ, ηκος, ὁ, Ion. and Ep. for θώραξ.

θώρηξις, εως, ἡ, *drinking to intoxication*, Hp.*Aph.*2.21, 7.48, Gal. 17(2).498, 18(1).154, Aret.*SD*2.6: pl., Hp.*Morb.*2.66.

θωρήσσω, Ep. aor. θώρηξα, subj. θωρήξομεν (for -ωμεν) Il.2.72:—*arm with a* θώραξ: generally, *arm*, θωρῆξαί ἑ κέλευε..Ἀχαιούς Il. 2.11; Μυρμιδόνας..θώρηξεν Ἀχιλλεύς 16.155:—more freq. in Med. and Pass., θωρήσσομαι, fut. -ξομαι: aor. ἐθωρήχθην:—*arm oneself, put one's harness on*, αὐτίκα θωρήσσοντο Il.19.352; σὺν τεύχεσι θωρηχθέντες 8.530, etc.; ἐς πόλεμον ἅμα λαῷ θωρηχθῆναι 1.226; τεύχε' ἐνείκω θωρηχθῆναι I will bring you arms *to arm yourselves withal*, Od.22.139; ἐθωρήσσοντο δὲ χαλκῷ 23.369; ἐν τῷδε (sc. θώρακι) πρὸς τοὺς πολεμίους θωρήξομαι Ar.*Ach.*1134; to which Dicaeopolis replies, ἐν τῷδε (sc. χοΐ) πρὸς τοὺς συμπότας θ., with reference to signf. II. II. *fortify with drink*, Hp.*Epid.*2.5.10; ποτῷ φρένα θωρηχθέντες Nic.*Al.* 32; τεθωρηγμένος Ruf.ap.Orib.6.38.23; *make drunk, intoxicate*, Thgn.842:—Med. and Pass., *get drunk*, οἴνῳ Id.470: abs., Id.413, Pi.*Fr.*72; θωρηχθεὶς ὑπὸ οἴνου Hp.*Morb.*4.56, cf. Duris 27 J. III. Med. in causal sense, τὸν μὲν..νέκταρι θωρήξαιο Nic.*Al.*225.

θώς, θωός, ὁ, also ἡ, prob. *jackal, Canis aureus*, Τρῶες ἕπονθ' ὡς εἴ τε δαφοινοὶ θῶες..ἀμφ' ἔλαφον Il.11.474, cf. Arist.*HA*610^{a}14, 630^{a}9; θώων παρδαλίων τε λύκων τ' ἦϊα Il.13.103; θ. καὶ πάνθηρες Hdt.4.192; ἔχει ὁ θ. πάντα τὰ ἐντὸς ὅμοια λύκῳ Arist.*HA*507^{b}17; a large kind in India, Arr.*Ind.*15.3: pl., θώαντες *IG*14.1302 (mosaic at Praeneste). 2. *hunting dog, Lycaon pictus*, Opp.*C.*3.338, al. 3. *panther*, Cyr.

θῶσθαι, = δαίνυσθαι, εὐωχεῖσθαι (Dor.), A.*Fr.*49, *EM*461.1; cf. θῶται· εὐθηνεῖται, θοινᾶται, and θῶνται· θοινῶνται κτλ., Hsch.: fut. θωσούμεθα Epich.139: aor. 1 inf. θώσασθαι· εὐωχηθῆναι, Hsch.:—Pass., θωθῆναι· φαγεῖν, γεύσασθαι, Id.

***θώσσω**, = θωρήσσω II, aor. 1 θῶξαι, Dor. θᾶξαι Hsch.: aor. Pass. part. θωχθείς S.*Fr.*173, Dor. inf. θαχθῆμεν Hsch.

θωστήριον, τό, = εὐωχητήριον, ἑορτή, Alcm.23.81, Hsch. (pl.).

θωτάζω, = τωθάζω, Hsch.

θωϋκτήρ, ῆρος, ὁ, *barker, roarer*, *APl.*4.91.

θωῦμα, θωυμάζω, etc., less correct forms for θῶμα, θωμάζω, v. θαυμ-.

θωΰσσω, of a dog, *bark, bay*, Hom.*Fr.*25; of a gnat, *buzz*, A.*Ag.* 893: generally, *cry aloud, shout*, S.*Aj.*308, E.*Tr.*153 (anap.), *Or.* 168 (lyr.): c. acc. cogn., τόνδ' ἐθώϋξας λόγον A.*Pr.*395; τάσδ' ἀγγελίας ἐθώϋξεν ib.1041 (anap.); τήνδε θωΰσσει βοήν S.*Aj.*335. 2. c. acc. pers., *call on, call*, φθέγμα..τινὸς θώϋξεν αὐτόν Id.*OC*1624: c. dat., θ. κυσί *shout* to dogs, E.*Hipp.*219 (anap.), cf. *Ba.*871 (lyr.). b. *lament, bewail*, dub. in *IG*12(3).9 (Syme).

θώψ, gen. θωπός, ὁ, *flatterer, false friend*, Hdt.3.80; θ. πλούτου Antipho Soph.65, cf. Them.*Or.*20.237d. II. as Adj., θῶπες λόγοι *fawning* speeches, *Trag.Adesp.*24, Pl.*Tht.*175e, Ph.2.52 (cf. τέ-θηπα, θάμβος).

I

I ι, ἰῶτα, τό, indecl., tenth (later ninth) letter of the Gr. alphabet: as numeral ι' = 10, but ͵ι = 10,000.

The ι 'subscript' of modern texts was said προσγράφεσθαι, cf. D.T.639.14, A.D.*Pron.*87.10, Ael.Dion.*Fr.*192 (also τὸ ληιστής (disyll.)..ἔχει προσκείμενον τὸ ῑ Hdn.Gr.2.946), and this mode of writing is found in Papyri, Inscrr., and some medieval Mss. (e.g. cod. A of Plato, saec. ix, which has τῶι = τῷ, etc.); the present mode is found as early as the tenth century, and came into use in the thirteenth. This ι was prob. always pronounced up to ca. 150 B.C., but thereafter dropped in pronunciation, cf. D.T. l.c.; hence called ι ἀνεκφώνητον Choerob.*in Theod.*1.143 and freq. omitted in Pap. and Inscrr. (cf. Epigr.ap.Str.14.1.41, = *SIG*766), later freq. restored in writing, sts. in the wrong place (v. ῥάθυμος). From ca. 150 B.C. (at Argos from ca. 450 B.C., v. *SIG*56.13) ει was pronounced ι and the sound is written indifferently ει or ι.

-ί, *iota demonstrativum*, in familiar Att. (not in Trag.), is attached to demonstr. Prons., to strengthen their force, and as it were point out the individual, as οὑτοσί, αὑτηΐ, τουτί, ἐκεινοσί, ὁδί, ταδί, τοσουτονί, τοσονδί, τυννουτοσί, etc.; also with the Particles γε δέ μέν inserted, as τουτογί, τουτοδί, ταυτηνδί, τηδεδί, τουτομενί, for τουτί γε, ταυτηνὶ δέ, etc.: also to demonstr. Advs., as οὑτωσί, ὡδί, ἐνθαδί, δευρί, νυνί, and νυνδί for νυνὶ δέ.—Of these forms, such as end in σί are sts. written in codd. with ν ἐφελκυστικόν before a vowel, as οὑτοσίν, ἐκεινοσίν, οὑτωσίν, etc.: such forms are recognized by A.D.*Pron.*59.24, 82.11, but are not found in best codd., e.g. of Pl. and D. [ῑ with the acute accent; a long vowel or diphthong before it is shortd., as αὑτηΐ, οὑτοΐ.]

ἵ, nom. of the reflex. Pron. οὗ, *sui* (q.v.), S.*Fr.*471, cj. Wackernagel in Il.24.608, Bekk. in Pl.*Smp.*175c, 223d: dat. ἵν αὐτῷ, *sibi ipsi*, Hes.*Fr.*11; ἱν (enclit.) prob. in Pi.*P.*4.36; ϝιν αὐτῷ *Leg.Gort.* 2.40. [ῑ S. l. c., ἵν Pi. l. c.]

ἶ, Argive, = εἶ, *SIG*56.29 (V B.C.), *Schwyzer*90.12, al., 91.31 (iii B.C.).

ἴ, Cypr. for ἤ, *or*, before a vowel, *Inscr.Cypr.*135.24 H.

ἰά [ῑ], Ion. **ἰή**, ἡ, = ἰωή, *voice, cry*, Orac.ap.Hdt.1.85, A.*Pers.*937 (lyr.); σύριγγος ἰά E.*Rh.*553 (lyr.).

ἴᾰ, ἰῆς, ἰῇ, ἴαν, Ep. fem., = *one*, v. εἷς.

ἰά [ῐ], τά, heterocl. pl. of ἰός, *arrow*, Il.20.68.

ἴα [ῐ], τά, pl. of ἴον, *violet*, *h.Cer.*6.

ἰάζω (A), (Ἰάς) = ἰωνίζω, Dicaearch.3.2, A.D.*Adv.*134.31, Hermog. *Id.*2.4.

ἰάζω (B), (ἰά) *cry aloud*, Theognost.*Can.*18.

ἰάζω (C), (ἴον) *to be of a violet colour*, Hld.2.30. II. (ἰός C) *to be green*, of bile, Gal.18(2).141.

ἰαθενεῖ· διαπορεῖ ἐπὶ κακῷ (Coan), Hsch.:—also **ἰηθενέουσα**· ἐκπεπληγμένη καὶ ἀποροῦσα, Id. **ἰαθμός**, v. ἰανθμός. **ἴαθος**· πρόθυμος, Id.

ἰαί, 1. barbarous exclam. of sorrow, S.*Fr.*631. 2. of triumph, Ar.*Lys.*1292; ἰαὶ ἰαί Id.*Ec.*1180.

ἰαιβοῖ [ῐ], Comic exclam. for αἰβοῖ, Ar.*V.*1338.

ἰαίνω, Ion. impf. -εσκον Q.S.7.340: aor. ἴηνα Od.8.426, Dor. ἴᾱνα Pi.*O.*7.43:—Pass., aor. ἰάνθην Il.23.598, etc. [ῐ, exc. in augm. tenses, in Hom.; but at the beginning of a verse ῑ without augm., Od.22.59: ῑ freq. in later Poets, *AP*12.95 (Mel.), Q.S. l. c., 4.402, 10.327, Orph.*L.*268, etc.]:—*heat*, ἀμφὶ δέ οἱ πυρὶ χαλκὸν ἴηνατε Od. 8.426:—Pass., ἰαίνετο δ' ὕδωρ 10.359. 2. *melt*, ἰαίνετο κηρός 12.175: metaph., θυμὸν ἰαίνειν *melt* the heart, Il.24.119. b. *relax by warmth*, Hp.*Mul.*1.69 (Pass.). 3. more freq. (cf. Plu.2.947d) *warm, cheer*, κραδίην καὶ θυμὸν ἰαίνειν *h.Cer.*435; θυμὸν ἰαίνειν τινί Od.15.379, Pi.*O.* l. c., cf. Theoc.7.29; καρδίαν Alcm.36, Pi.*P.*1.11; νόον ib.2.90:—more freq. in Pass., ἵνα..σὸ φρεσὶ σῇσιν ἰανθῇς Il.19.174; θυμὸς ἐνὶ στήθεσσιν ἰάνθη Od.4.549; εἰς ὅ κε σὸν κῆρ ἰανθῇ 22.59; ἦτορ ἰανθέν *Anacreont.*48.2: c. dat., σοὶ..μετὰ φρεσὶ θυμὸς ἰάνθη Il.23.600, cf. 24.321, etc.; θυμὸν ἰάνθης Od.23.47; χοροῖσι φρένα ἰανθείς B.16.131; μέτωπον ἰάνθη her brow *unfolded*, Il.15.103: c. dat. rei, *take delight in*, σφιν ἰαίνομαι εἰσορόωσα Od.19.537; σφισι θυμὸς αἰὲν εὐφροσύνῃσιν ἰαίνεται 6.156; καρδίην ἰαίνεται Archil. 36; ἰανθεὶς ἀοιδαῖς Pi.*O.*2.13; cf. εὐφροσύνη: later ἰαίνειν τινά τινι Man.3.184. II. later, = ἰάομαι, *heal, save*, τινὰ ὀδυνάων Q.S.10.327; ὑπὲκ κακοῦ ἰαίνονται Id.4.402.—Ep. and Lyr. word; Trag. only Phryn.Trag.1, ἰαίνεται· χολοῦται, πικραίνεται, παρὰ τὸν ἰόν (cf. Hsch.).

Ἰᾰκός, ή, όν, (Ἰάς) *Ionic*, ἀσωτία Plb.32.11.10; τὸ Ἰακόν *the Ionic form*, Ath.9.400c; ἡ Ἰ. ἔγκλισις A.D.*Pron.*98.8. Adv. -κῶς ib.4.21.

Ἰακυνθοτρόφος, ἡ, epith. of Artemis, *Schwyzer*265 (Cnidus); cf. Ὑακινθοτρόφια.

ἴακχα, ης, ἡ, Sicyonic name of *a perfumed garland*, Philet.ap.Ath. 15.678a, Timach.ibid., Hsch.

Ἰακχ-άγωγός [ῐ], όν, *bearing the image of Bacchus* on his festivals, *IG*2^{2}.1092 *B*31 (written Ἰαχχ-), *IG*3.162, 262, Poll.1.35. **-άζω**, *shout* Ἴακχος, Longus 3.11 (cj. for ἰακχεύσαντες): c. acc. cogn., ἰακχάζειν φωνήν Hdt.8.65. II. generally, = ἰαχέω, of birds, ἰακχ. ἀοιδήν Orph.*L.*46. **-αῖος**, α, ον, *Bacchanalian*, στέφανος Philet. 27. **-εῖον**, τό, *temple of Bacchus*, Plu.*Arist.*27, Alciphr.3.59.

ἰακχέω, ἰακχή, v. ἰαχ-.

Ἰακχιαστής, οῦ, ὁ, *worshipper of* Ἴακχος, Benndorf-Niemann *Reisen in Lykien* No.134b.

Ἴακχος, ὁ, *Iacchos*, mystic name of Dionysus, S.*Fr.*959, *Trag. Adesp.*140 (lyr.), Ar.*Ra.*398, Paus.1.2.4, etc.; ἡ Ἐλευσῖνι τοῦ Ἰαάκχου (sic) ὑποδοχή *IG*2^{2}.847.21; τὸν Ἴακχον ἐξελαύνειν lead forth a Bacchic procession, Plu.*Alc.*34; τὸν Ἴ. προπέμψαι *IG*2^{2}.1028.10. 2. *song* in his honour, ὁ μυστικὸς ἴ. Hdt.8.65, cf. Athenio ap.Posidon.36 J., Anon.ap.Suid.; ᾄδειν τὸν Ἴ. Hsch. s. v. Διαγόρας: as Adj., ἴακχος ᾠδά E.*Cyc.*69 (lyr.). 2. in pl., *Epigr.Gr.*985 (Philae): generally, *chorus*, νεκρῶν ἴ. E.*Tr.*1230; τυμπάνων ἴ. dub. in Id.*Fr.*586.4 (lyr.). II. used by the tyrant Dionysius for χοῖρος, Athanis 1 (= Dionys.Trag.12).

ἰᾰλεμ-έω [ῐ], = sq., Hdn.Gr.2.236. **-ίζω**, Ion. **ἰηλ-**, (ἰάλεμος) *bewail*, Call.*Fr.*176. **-ίστρια**, Ion. **ἰηλ-**, ἡ, *wailing woman*, A.*Ch.*424 (lyr., Herm., from Hsch.). **-ος**, Ion. **ἰήλ-**, ὁ, *lament, dirge*, used by Trag. in lyr., A.*Supp.*115, E.*Rh.*895, *Tr.*1304, *Ph.*1033, etc.; τὸν ἰ. ἀρίστευσε Theoc.15.98: rare in Prose, Metrod.*Herc.*831.17 (s. v. l.):

prov., ἰαλέμου ψυχρότερος, of something tedious and dull, Zen.4.39. II. as Adj., *melancholy*, γόοι E.*HF*109 (lyr., s. v. l.); but usu., 2. *tedious, dull, stupid*, ποιηταί Luc.*Pseudol.*24; ἰατροί Gal.14.617: as Subst., *dullard, oaf*, Men.236, Hermog.*Id.*2.6; title of play by Amphis, Ath.2.69b. (Perh. from the cry ἰή.) **-ώδης**, ες, *like an* ἰάλεμος, *wretched*, Phot., Suid.

ἰαλία, ἡ, Cret. for φωνή, Hsch. **ἰάλιον**· ἐρέβινθον ἢ τὴν θάλασσαν (Cret.), Id.

ἰάλλω, Att. **ἰάλλω** acc. to Hdn.Gr.1.539, cf. ἐφιάλλω: fut. ἰᾰλῶ (ἐπ-) Ar.*Nu.*1299: aor. ἴηλα Il.15.19, Dor. **ἴᾱλα** Sophr.14. [ῐ, unless augmented; Hom. never uses the augm.]:—*send forth*, ὀϊστὸν ἀπὸ νευρῆφιν ἴαλλεν Il.8.300, 309, cf. *AP*5.187 (Leon.): used by Hom. mostly in phrase, ἐπ' ὀνείατα χεῖρας ἴαλλον *they put forth* their hands to the dishes, Od.1.149, al.; ἐπὶ σίτῳ χ. ἰ. 10.376; ἑτάροις ἐπὶ χεῖρας ἴ. *laid* hands upon his comrades, 9.288; περὶ χερσὶ δὲ δεσμὸν ἧηλα *threw* chains around thy arms, Il.15.19; ἐπὶ δεσμὸν ἧηλε Od.8.447; so later ὑλακὴν *give* tongue, *AP*7.69 (Jul. Aegypt.); ἴχνος *set down, plant* the foot, Nic.*Al.*242. 2. c. acc. obj., ἄριστον ἀτιμίῃσιν ἰάλλειν *assail* him with insults, Od.13.142. 3. later, *send, dispatch*, ἄγγελον Thgn.573, cf. A.*Ch.*45 (lyr.); ἐπὶ Δωδώνης.. θεοπρόπους ἴαλλεν Id.*Pr.*659; Δίκην ἴαλλε σύμμαχον Id.*Ch.*497; ἄρτον τοῖς παιδίοις Sophr. l. c.; τινὰ παρά τινα Id.61; Φθίᾳ ἐλεύθερον ἦμαρ ἰ. *AP*7.529 (Theodorid.). 4. = εὑρίσκω, Hsch. s. vv. ἴᾱλαι, ἰάλλει. II. intr. (sc. ἑαυτόν) *send oneself on*, i. e. *flee, run*, Hes.*Th.*269. (Cf. Skt. *i-yarti* 'set in motion'.)

ἰαλτός [ῐ], ή, όν, *sent forth*, ἐκ δόμων A.*Ch.*22 (lyr.).

Ἰᾰλυσός, Ion. **Ἰηλυσός**, ἡ, one of the three Dorian cities of Rhodes, Il.2.656, Hdt.1.144, Pi.*O.*7.74, Timocr.1.7, Str.14.2.12: **Ἰαλυσία**, ἡ, its territory, D.S.5.57:—Adj. **Ἰηλύσιος**, α, ον, D.P.505. [ῡ in Hom., ῠ in D.P., doubtful in Pi.; ῑ exc. in Timocr. l. c. and Ἰαλυσοῖο (– ∪ ∪ – ∪) *AP*7.716 (Dionys.).]

ἴᾱμα, Ion. **ἴημα**, ατος, τό, (ἰάομαι) *remedy, medicine*, Hdt.3.130, Hp.*Acut.*6, Th.2.51, Pl.*Lg.*771c, etc.; στεναγμοί, τῶν πόνων ἰάματα v.l. in A.*Fr.*385. II. = ἴασις, ἰάματα τοῦ Ἀπόλλωνος καὶ τοῦ Ἀσκλαπιοῦ *IG*4.951.2 (Epid.), cf. 1*Ep.Cor.*12.9 (pl.). 2. *soothing, pacification*, Lxx *Ec.*10.4.

ἰαμβαυλεῖν· τὸ δι' αὐλοῦ παριαμβίζειν τῇ κιθάρᾳ καὶ ᾠδῇ, Hsch. (emended).

ἰαμβειογράφος, v. ἰαμβειοφάγος.

ἰαμβεῖος [ῐ], ον, (ἴαμβος) *iambic*, μέτρον Arist.*Po.*1448^{b}31. II. as Subst. ἰαμβεῖον, τό, *iambic verse*, Ar.*Ra.*1133, 1204, Pl.*R.*602b, Arist.*Po.*1458^{b}19, *Sammelb.*6308 (iii B. C.), etc.: in pl., *iambic poem*, Luc.*Salt.*27: generally, *verse, line*, Ath.8.355a (of anapaests). 2. *iambic metre*, Arist.*Rh.*1404^{a}31.

ἰαμβειοφάγος [ῐ, φᾰ], ὁ, *glutton at iambics*, or perh. *mouther, murderer of them*, applied to Aeschines by D.18.139 (v. l. -γράφος):—also **ἰαμβο-φάγος**, ὁ, *AB*190.

ἰαμβ-έλεγος [ῐ], ὁ, an asynartete verse, formed by substituting an iambic penthemimer for the former half of a pentameter, Heph.15.11. **-ιάζω**, = sq., *AP*7.405 (Phil.). **-ίζω**, *assail in iambics, lampoon*, τινα Gorg.ap.Ath.11.505d, Arist.*Po.*1448^{b}32, D.H.7.72. II. abs., *talk in iambic verse*, Luc.*JTr.*33 (s. v. l.). 2. etym. of θρίαμβος, Corn.*ND*30. **-ικός**, ή, όν, *of invective*, ἰδέα Arist.*Po.*1449^{b}8; in metric, *iambic*, D.H.*Comp.*18, Heph.5, etc.: ἡ -κή (sc. ὄρχησις) Ath.15.629d. Adv. -κῶς Phld.*Po.*2.29. **-ίς**, ίδος, ἡ, cited without interpr. from A.(*Fr.*81) by Hsch. **-ιστής**, οῦ, ὁ, *one who writes iambics, libeller*, Ath.5.181c.

ἰαμβο-γράφος [ῐ, γρᾰ], ὁ, *writer of iambics*, Suid. s. v. Σωτάδης, v.l. in *EM*424.23. **-ειδής**, ές, *like an iambus*, Aristid.Quint.1.17. **-ποιέω**, *parody*, Arist.*Po.*1458^{b}9. **-ποιός**, ὁ, *writer of lampoons*, ib.1451^{b}14; *of iambics*, Phld.*Po.*2.29, Ath.8.359e.

ἴαμβος [ῐ], ὁ, *iambus*, the metrical foot ∪ –, Pl.*R.*400b, etc.; ὁ ἴ. αὐτή.. ἡ λέξις ἡ τῶν πολλῶν Arist.*Rh.*1408^{b}33; δάκτυλος ὁ κατὰ ἴαμβον, = ∪ – ∪ –, Anon.Rhythm.*Oxy.*2.3, Aristid.Quint.1.17. II. *iambic verse*, Archil.22 (pl.), Pl.*Ion* 534c, etc.; ἴαμβος τρίμετρος Hdt.1.12; ἴ. Ἱππώνακτος Ar.*Ra.*661, cf. Arist.*Rh.*1418^{b}29, *Po.*1448^{b}33. III. *iambic poem*, such as those of Callimachus, Str.8.3.30; esp. *lampoon*, mostly in pl., Pl.*Lg.*935e, Arist.*Pol.*1336^{b}20; ἐφ' ὑβριστῆρας ἰάμβους *AP*7.352 (Mel.(?)): also in Prose, οἱ καταλογάδην ἴ. Ath.10.445b. b. of the persons lampooned, Luc.*Pseudol.*2. 2. *a kind of extempore play* got up by αὐτοκάβδαλοι, who themselves had the same name, Semus 20. (For the termination perh. cf. διθύραμβος, θρίαμβος.)

ἰαμβύκη [ῡ], ἡ, *musical instrument*, distinct from the σαμβύκη, acc. to Hsch., Eup.139, Phillis ap.Ath.14.636b.

ἰαμβύλος [ῐ, ῠ], ὁ, *libeller*, Hdn.Gr.1.164, Hsch. (-βηλος cod.).

ἰαμβώδης [ῐ], ες, *iambic, scurrilous*, ἐπίδειξις Philostr.*VA*6.11.

ἰᾰμεναί, late form of εἰαμεναί, Hsch.

ἴαμνοι, ων, οἱ, = foreg., Nic.*Th.*30, al.; glossed by θάμνοι, κοῖται, νομοί, Hsch. (ἴαμβοι cod.).

Ἰάν, ὁ, in pl. Ἰᾶνες, contr. for Ἰάων, Ἰάονες, *Ionian*, A.*Pers.*950, al.

ἴανα (ἴαννα cod.)· τὰ βαλλόμενα, ἀπὸ τοῦ ἱέναι, Hsch.

ἰάνθῐνος, η, ον, (ἴον, ἄνθος) *violet-coloured*, ἱμάτιον Str.15.3.19, cf. Plin.*HN*21.27, Aq., Sm.*Ex.*25.5:—Subst. **ἴανθος**, ὁ, or **ἴανθον**, τό, = ἴον, Hsch., Theognost.*Can.*18.

ἰᾰνο-γλέφᾰρος [ῐ], ον, = μαλακο-βλέφαρος, prob. l. in Alcm.23.69: **-κροκα**· λεπτά, Hsch.: but **ἰανο-κρήδεμνος** (sic), ον, is expld. by ἴοις ὅμοιον τὸ ἐπικράνισμα, Id.; ὁ στέμμα ἐξ ἴων φορῶν, Suid. (Prob. compds. of a dialectic form of ἑανός, wh. (viz. ἑανός) is glossed μαλακός, λεπτός, λαμπρός in Sch.Il.18.613.) **ιανόφρυς**, prob. f.l. for κυαν-, *PMich.*11.13.

ἰάομαι, imper. ἰῶ (v. infr.), Ion. inf. ἰᾶσθαι Hp.*Loc.Hom.*24 (ἰῆσθαι v. l. in Id.*Morb.Sacr.*13), Cypr. ἰյᾶσθαι *Inscr.Cypr.*135.3 H.: fut. ἰάσομαι E.*HF*1107, Aeschin.3.69; Ion. and Ep. ἰήσομαι Od.9.525, Archil.13, (ἐξ-) Hp.*Morb.*1.6: aor. ἰασάμην E.*Fr.*1072, Pl.*Phd.*89a; Ion. ἰησάμην Il.5.899, Hp.*Int.*2:—**Pass.** (v. infr.). [ῑ- in Hom., etc.; also ῐ, E.*Hipp.*597]:—*heal, cure*, in pres. and impf., *attempt to cure, treat*, of persons or bodies, etc., τινα Il.12.2, Hdt.3.134, etc.; τοὺς κάμνοντας Pl.*Plt.*299a, cf. 293b; ὀφθαλμόν Od.9.525; τὸ σῶμα S.*Tr.*1210: abs., Od.9.520, Il.5.899: prov., ὁ τρώσας ἰάσεται *Mantiss.Prov.*2.28. 2. *cure, treat*, of diseases, νόσους Pi.*P.*3.46, cf. E.*Hipp.*597, Pl.*Prt.*340e, *Chrm.*156b, etc.; σμύρνῃσι ἰ. τὰ ἕλκεα Hdt.7.181: metaph., *remedy*, δύσνοιαν, ἀδικίαν ἰᾶσθαι, E.*HF*1107, *Or.*650; ἀτυχίας Isoc.6.101; δωροδόκημα Aeschin.3.69; ἀσάφειαν Arr.*Tact.*1.3: prov., μὴ τῷ κακῷ τὸ κακὸν ἰῶ, i. e. do not make bad worse, Hdt.3.53, cf. Th.5.65; μὴ κακοῖς ἰῶ κακά A.*Fr.*349; κακοῖς ὅταν θέλωσιν ἰᾶσθαι κακά S.*Fr.*77: abs., οὔτε τι γὰρ κλαίων ἰήσομαι Archil.13. 3. *cure the effects of, counteract*, ἄκρατος ἰ. τὸ κώνειον Plu.2.653a. 4. *repair*, τὸ βλαβέν Pl.*Lg.*933e; τὴν φύσιν τὴν ἀνθρωπίνην Id.*Smp.*191d; θυσιαστήριον Lxx 3*Ki.*18.32; δίκελλαν Lib.*Decl.*27.3. II. Act. only aor. I ἰάσαμεν Gal.10.453; part. ἰάσαντες Sch.E.*Hec.*1236: aor. ἰάθην is always Pass., *be healed, recover*, And.2.9, *AP*6.330 (Aeschin.), *IG*4.951.113 (Epid.), etc.; ἀπὸ τῶν νόσων *Ev.Luc.*6.17; Ion. ἰήθην Hp.*Mul.*1.3, *Int.*1: fut. ἰαθήσομαι Luc.*Asin.*14, *Gp.*12.25.3, Gal.10.377; ἰάσομαι Aristid.2.317 J.: pf. ἴᾱμαι *Ev.Marc.*5.29.

Ἰᾱοναῦ [ῐ], barbarism for Ἰάον (voc.), *O Ionian*, Ar.*Ach.*104.

Ἰάονες [ῐᾱ], οἱ, = Ἴωνες, *Ionians*, Il.13.685, *h.Ap.*147, etc.; in the mouth of a Persian = Ἕλληνες, A.*Pers.*178, 563 (lyr.): sg., Ἰάων rare, Theoc.16.57:—fem. **Ἰαονίς**, ίδος, Νύμφαισιν Ἰαονίδεσσιν Nic.*Fr.*74.8: **Ἰαονίηθε**, *from Ionia*, ib.2: **Ἰαόνιος**, α, ον, *Greek*, A.*Supp.*69 (lyr.), *Pers.*899 (lyr., Herm. for Ἰόνιον); *Athenian*, Orac.ap.Plu.*Sol.*10.

ἰαόντυς, Boeot., = Att. ἐῶσιν (dat. pl.), *Schwyzer* 462 *A* 5 (Tanagra, iii B. C.).

ἰαππᾰπαιάξ [ῐ], exclamation of astonishment, Ar.*Th.*945.

ἰάπτω (A) [ῐ], *hurt, spoil* (= βλάπτω, Hsch.), ὡς ἂν μὴ κλαίουσα κατὰ χρόα καλὸν ἰάπτῃ *mar* her beauty, Od.2.376, cf. 4.749; ναυτιλίην A.R.2.875; of a spear, *wound, pierce*, τοῦ δ' οὐ χρόα καλὸν ἴαψεν Q.S.6.546; Ἔρως.. ὅς με κατασμύχων καὶ ἐς ὀστέον ἄχρις ἰάπτει Theoc.3.17; βροτῶν, οὓς αὐτίκα γῆρας ἰάπτει *AP*11.389 (Lucill.); ἃ δειλὸς χαλεποῖς ἐνὶ πένθεσι γῆρας ἰάψει Q.S.3.455; ἐπεὶ ἦ νύ με κῆδος ἰάπτει λευγαλέον ib.481:—Pass., ὃς δὲ.. μελλόντων χάριν ἐὸν ἰάπτεται κέαρ B.*Fr.*7.5; ἰάπτομαι ἄλγεσιν ἦτορ Mosch.4.39; ὥς μοι περὶ θυμὸς ἰάφθη Theoc.2.82. (Perh. cf. ἴπτομαι.)

ἰάπτω (B) [ῐ], fut. -ψω A.*Th.*525 (lyr.): aor. ἴαψα S.*Aj.*700 (lyr.): —*send, drive on*, of missiles, *send forth, shoot*, τόξοις βέλη εἴς τινα A.*Ag.*510; χερμάδα ἐπί τινι Id.*Th.*299 (lyr.); πρόσθε πυλᾶν κεφαλὰν ἰ. to *throw* his head before the gates, i. e. lose it, ib.525 (lyr.): metaph., ἐπιτύμβιον αἶνον ἐπ' ἀνδρὶ θείῳ.. ἰάπτειν Id.*Ag.*1548 (lyr.); μακάρεσσιν ἔπι ψόγον αἰνὸν ἰ. Rhian.1.4; ἰ. ὀρχήματα *begin* the dance, S. l. c.:—Pass., ἐπί τινι ἰάπτεται βέλη A.*Th.*544. 2. c. acc. objecti, λόγοις ἰάπτειν τινὰ *assail* one with words, S.*Aj.*501. II. intr. (sc. ἑαυτόν), *rush, hurry*, A.*Supp.*547 (lyr.). (Perh. cf. Lat. *jacio.*)

Ἰᾶπυξ, Ion. **Ἰῆπυξ**, ῡγος, ὁ, *the NW.* (or rather *WNW.*) *wind*, = ἀργέστης, Arist.*Vent.*973^{b}14, *Mu.*394^{b}26. II. **Ἰάπῡγες**, Ion. **Ἰήπῡγες**, οἱ, a people of Southern Italy, Hdt.7.170: ἡ **Ἰαπῡγία**, Ion. **Ἰηπῡγίη**, their *country*, ibid.:—Adj. **Ἰαπύγιος**, α, ον, *Iapygian*, ἄκρα Th.6.30.

ἴαρ· αἷμα, and **ἰαροπότης**· αἱμοπότης, Hsch.; cf. ἔαρ, εἶαρ.

ἰάραξ, Dor. for ἱέραξ, Hsch., perh. to be read in Epich.68.

ἰαράρχας and other words beginning with ἰαρ- = ἱερ-, v. ἱερ-.

ἰαριγμόν· χαράν, καὶ θροῦν, Hsch. **ἰαροχρείαν**· τὴν ὀσφῦν (Ital.), Id.:—also **ἰαροχρής**· καθαρός, θύσιμος, Id. (For ἱερο-.) **ἰαρπάλαμος**· ἀκρόχειρος, Id. **ἰάρωμα**· κοσμάριον παιδικόν, Id.

Ἰάς, άδος, ἡ, Adj. fem. *Ionic*, στρατιή, ἐσθής, Hdt.5.33, 87; [γυνή] Id.1.92; τῇ Ἰάδι συγγενείᾳ Th.4.61; διάλεκτος A.D.*Adv.*189.5, Str.8.1.2; γλῶττα ibid.: as Subst., Luc.*Hist.Conscr.*16. 2. *the Ionian flower*, = ἴον, Nic.*Fr.*74.2. [ῐ, but ῑ in arsi, *App.Anth.*2.21.]

ἴᾱσι [ῐ], 3 pl. pres. of εἶμι (*ibo*). **ἰᾶσι** [ῑ], for ἱέασι, 3 pl. pres. of ἵημι.

ἰάσιμος [ῑᾱ], Ion. **ἰήσιμος**, ον, (ἰάομαι) *curable*, of persons, φαρμάκοις A.*Pr.*475, cf. Hp.*Morb.Sacr.*11; opp. ἀνίατος, Pl.*Lg.*941d, etc.; διαφθείρεσθαι ἰάσιμος ὤν Antipho 4.2.4: metaph., *appeasable*, θεός E.*Or.*399. 2. of wounds, τραῦμα ἰ. Pl.*Lg.*878c: metaph., ἰ. ἁμάρτημα Id.*Grg.*525b; κακά Id.*Lg.*731d; ἰ. τὸ πάθος Alex.124.4.

ἴᾱσις [ῑ], Ion. **ἴησις**, εως, ἡ, (ἰάομαι) *healing, mode of healing, remedy*, Hp.*Aph.*2.17, S.*OT*68, Pl.*Smp.*188c; οἷς [πήμασιν] ἴ. οὐκ ἔνεστ' ἰδεῖν S.*El.*876; [ἀδίκημα] οὗ μὴ ἔστιν ἴ. Arist.*Rh.*1374^{b}31, cf. Antipho 5.94, Arr.*An.*7.29.2; ἔλεγχος ἰ. τοῦ λόγου Arist.*Metaph.*1009^{a}21: pl., *cures*, ἰάσεις ἀποτελῶ *Ev.Luc.*13.32. 2. *mending, repairs*, ζυγάστρου *SIG*244 I 53 (Delph., iv B. C.). 3. Alch., *cupellation, refining*, *PLeid.X.*21.

ἰασιώνη, ἡ, *bindweed, Convolvulus sepium*, Thphr.*HP*1.13.2, cf. Plin.*HN*21.105.

ἰάσκειν· ἄγειν, Hsch.: **ἰασσεῖν**· θυμοῦσθαι, δάκνειν, Id. (Prob. connected with ἰάπτω.)

ἴασμη, ἡ, *jessamine, Jasminum officinale*, Aët.ap.Ps.-Dsc.1.63 (fr. Pers. *yāsam*): **ἰάσμῐνον**, τό, *oil of jasmine*, ibid.:—also **ἰασμέ-**

λαιον, τό, Aët.1.119 (who states that ἴάσμη = ἰάσμινον = ἰασμέλαιον was prepared ἐκ τῶν ἀνθῶν τῶν λευκῶν τοῦ ἴου, καὶ ἐλαίου σησαμίνου).

ἰασπ-ἀχάτης [ῐ, χᾱ], ου, ὁ, *jasper-like agate*, Aët.2.37, Plin.*HN* 37.139. **-ίζω**, *to be like a jasper*, Dsc.5.136. **-ις**, ιδος (but acc. ἴασπιν Orph.*L*.267,613), ἡ, *jasper*, Pl.*Phd*.110d, *IG*2^{2}.1388.88, 7.2420 (Thebes, iii B.C.), Thphr.*Lap*.23, *AP*9.746 (Polemo). II. = χρυσόγονον, Dsc.4.56. (Cf. Hebr. *yāšpheh*.) **-όνυξ**, ὕχος, ὁ, *jasper-like onyx*, Plin.*HN*37.118.

Ἰαστί [ῐ, τῐ], Adv., (Ἰάς) *in the Ionic mode* (of music), Pratin.Lyr. 5, Pl.*R*.398e; κρούων Ἰ. *Com.Adesp*.415; ἡ Ἰ. ἁρμονία Heraclid. Pont.ap.Ath.14.524f: metaph., opp. Δωριστί, Pl.*La*.188d. 2. *in the Ionic dialect*, Call.*Iamb*.1.354, Str.13.4.8, A.D.*Adv*.134.31, Luc. *Herod*.2. 3. = Ἑλληνιστί, Hsch.

Ἰαστιαιόλιος, ον, *Ionic-Aeolic*, of a scale, Ptol.*Harm*.2.1.

Ἰάστιος, α, ον, *Ionic*, in Music, Max.Tyr.7.1.

Ἰᾱσώ, Ion. Ἰησώ, όος, contr. οῦς, ἡ, voc. Ἰασοῖ, (ἰάομαι) *Iaso, the goddess of healing and health*, Ar.*Pl*.701, *Fr*.21, Herod.4.6, Paus.1. 34.3.

ἰά-τειρα [ῑᾰ], Ion. ἰητ-, ἡ, *healing*, φύσις Marc.Sid.1. **-τέον**, *one must heal*, Hp.*Flat*.1, Gal.10.220. **-τήρ** [ῑ], Cypr. acc. sg. ἰjατῆραν *Inscr.Cypr*.135.3 H., Ep. ἰητήρ, ῆρος, ὁ, poet. for ἰατρός, in Hom. mostly, *surgeon*, Il.2.732, Od.17.384, cf. Pi.*P*.3.65, etc.: generally, *healer*, νόσων Theoc.*Ep*.8: metaph., ἰ. κακῶν S.*Tr*.1209; πένθεος *AP*7.466.8 (Leon.): abs., *deliverer*, Pi.*P*.4.270. **-τήριον**, Ion. ἰητήριον, τό, *mode of cure, cure*, Hp.*Epid*.2.3.7 (cf. 6.2.4), Aret. *CA*1.4; ἰητήρια νούσων Q.S.7.61. **-τής**, οῦ, ὁ, = ἰατήρ, Lxx *Jb*. 13.4, *PCair.Preis*.20.26 (iv A.D.). **-τικός**, ή, όν, *healing*, Ἀπόλλων Str.14.1.6; ἰκτέρου Dsc.3.75, cf. 5.123, Gal.18(2).394, Max.Tyr. 28.7. **-τορία**, Ion. ἰητορίη, ἡ, *art of healing* or *of medicine*, B.1. 39; χειροτέχνης ἰατορίας, of a surgeon, S.*Tr*.1001 (lyr.), cf. *IGRom*. 4.507*a* 18, *b* 7 (Pergam.).

ἴᾱτον [ῐ], τό, *drink prepared from honey, wine and violets*, [Orib.] 5.33.6, Alex.Trall.1.16; ἔλαιον ἰ. Aët.1.118.

ἰᾱτός [ῑ], ή, όν, *curable*, Pi.*I*.8(7).15, Pl.*Lg*.862c, al.

ἴατρ-α [ῐ], Ion. ἴητρα, τά, *doctor's fee*, ἴητρα νούσων ἐποιεύμεσθα Herod.4.16, cf. Hsch. II. *thank-offering for cure*, *IG*4.951.45 (Epid.), al.; Ὑγιείᾳ, τῷ Τελεσφόρῳ ἴ., ib.1321, 1334; ἴατρων ἀντί ib. 5(1).1119 (Geronthrae). **-ᾰλείπτης**, ου, ὁ, (ἀλείφω) *surgeon who practises by anointing, friction, and the like*, Plin.*Ep*.10.5(4), Cels.1.1, Gal.13.104, Paul.Aeg.3.47:—hence **-ᾰλειπτική** (sc. τέχνη), *practice of an ἰατραλείπτης*, Plin.*HN*29.4. **-εία**, Ion. ἰητρείη, ἡ, (ἰατρεύω) *healing, medical treatment*, Hp.*Fract*.34, al., Plu.*Pyrrh*.3, *Epigr.Gr*. 305.1 (Smyrna), *Sammelb*.1934 (Serapeum). 2. metaph., *curing, correcting*, ἐπιθυμίας Arist.*Pol*.1267^{a}7; τῆς ἁμαρτίας ib.1272^{b}2, cf. 1284^{b} 19, Plu.2.510c; ἰατρείας ἕνεκεν Arist.*EN*1152^{b}32: pl., ib.1104^{b}17, al. **-εῖον**, Ion. ἰητρεῖον, τό, *surgery*, Hp.*Off*.2, Pl.*R*.405a, Aeschin.1.40, *BGU*647.3 (ii A.D.); κατ' ἰητρεῖον ἀνόσως διάγειν not to be so ill *as to need medical advice*, Hp.*Epid*.1.1: metaph., ψυχῆς ἰ. D.S. 1.49. 2. *remedy*, Androm.ap.Gal.13.832. II. pl., = ἴατρα 1, *doctor's fee, expense of a cure*, Lxx *Ex*.21.10, Poll.4.177, 6.186. 2. = ἴατρα II, -εῖα θεοῖς ἐπηκόοις Roussel *Cultes Égyptiens* 94, al. (Delos, ii/i B.C.). **-ευμα**, ατος, τό, = ἴαμα, παθῶν Dam.*Isid*.189 (pl.): Rhet. in pl., '*specifics*' for allaying prejudice, etc., Arist.*Rh*.1415^{a}25. **-ευσις**, εως, ἡ, = ἰατρεία, Pl.*R*.357c, Arist.*Ph*.193^{b}14, al. **-ευτέον**, *one must treat*, Gal.10.209, Alex.Trall.*Febr*.3. **-ευτικός**, ή, όν, = ἰατικός, φάρμακα Sch.Ar.*Ach*.1211. **-εύω**, Ion. pf. ἰήτρευκα Hp.*Art*.46: (ἰατρός):—*treat medically, cure*, ἕκαστα Id.*Acut*.2; οὐδὲν ἰ. τῆς λύπης Phld.*Mus*.p.69 K.; τινα Hp.*Art*. l. c., Pl.*Lg*.857d, al.:—Pass., *to be under medical care*, Id.*R*.357c, *Grg*.478b sq., al.; *to be cured*, *IG*14.2283 (Bononia). 2. abs., *practise medicine*, Hp.*Art*. 72; τίς ὀρθῶς ἰάτρευκεν; Arist.*Pol*.1281^{b}40. II. metaph., *remedy, correct*, Id.*PA*665^{a}8. **-ια**, ἡ, fem. of ἰατήρ, Alex.318. **-ικός**, Ion. ἰητρ-, ή, όν, *of* or *for an* ἰατρός, καρκίνος *IG*2^{2}.47.16 (iv B.C.): -ικόν (sc. τέλος), τό, tax *for maintenance of doctor*, *SIG*437 (Delph., iii B.C.), *PSI*4.371, 388 (iii B.C.); so perh. τὰ ἰατρικά *PCair.Zen*.36.4, 13 (iii B.C.); but -ικόν, τό, Milit., *medical corps*, Arr.*Tact*.2.1: ἡ -κή (sc. τέχνη), *surgery, medicine*, Hdt.2.84, 3.129, Hp.*VM*1, Pl.*Grg*.478b, Epicur.*Fr*.221, etc. Adv. -κῶς *in medical terms*, ἐκφέρεσθαι Phld. *Po*.5.29, etc. II. *skilled in the medical art*, Pl.*R*.455e, etc.; ἰ. ἐκ τῶν συγγραμμάτων γίνεσθαι by rule, Arist.*EN*1181^{b}2, etc.: Comp. -ώτερος ib.1097^{a}10; -ώτερον τῶν ἰατρικῶν Phld.*Mus*.p.6 K.: Sup. -ώτατος Pl.*Smp*.186d, Gal.*Protr*.10. Adv. -κῶς Alex.124.13, etc. 2. metaph., ἰ. περὶ τὴν ψυχήν Pl.*Prt*.313e. 3. of drugs, *efficacious*, φάρμακα Hp.*Ep*.16 (Sup.). III. ἰατρικός (sc. δάκτυλος), ὁ, *forefinger*, *PLond*.1821.300. **-ίνη** [ῑν], ἡ, *midwife*, *IG*3.134, al., J.*Vit*. 37, Gal.8.414, Alex.Aphr.*Pr*.2.64, *POxy*.1586.12 (iii A.D.).

ἰατρο-κλύστης, ου, ὁ, *physician who uses douches*, *UPZ*148.7 (ii B.C.). **-λογέω**, *lecture on medicine*, D.L.8.78. **-λογία**, ἡ, *study of medicine*, Ph.1.302. **-μᾰθημᾰτικοί**, οἱ, *those who practised medicine in conjunction with astrology*, esp. in Egypt, Ptol.*Tetr*. 16, Heph.Astr.*Praef*., *Cat.Cod.Astr*.1.126. **-μαια**, ἡ, *midwife*, Dessau *Inscr.Lat.Sel*.7806, *CIL*6.9478. **-μαντις**, εως, ὁ, *physician and seer*, of Apollo and Aesculapius, A.*Supp*.263, cf. *Eu*.62: metaph., φρενῶν ἰ. A.*Ag*.1623. **-νίκης** [νῑ], ου, ὁ, *conqueror of physicians*, Inscr. in Plin.*HN*29.9 (epitaph of Thessalus).

ἰᾱτρός, Ion. ἰητρός, ὁ, (ἰάομαι) like ἰατήρ, *one who heals, physician* or *surgeon*, Il.16.28, al., Hdt.3.130 sq.; ἰητρὸς ἀνήρ Il.11.514; φὼς ἰ. A.*Supp*.261; ἥρως ἰ., worshipped at Athens and elsewhere, D. 19.249, *IG*2^{2}.840, *AB*263, etc.; οὐ πρὸς ἰατροῦ σοφοῦ θρηνεῖν ἐπῳδὰς πρὸς τομῶντι πήματι S.*Aj*.581; ἰατρῶν παῖδες, for ἰατροί, Luc.*Hist. Conscr*.7; as a name of Apollo, Ar.*Av*.584 (anap.), Lyc.1207, *IPE*2.6 (Panticapaeum); ἰ. ὀφθαλμῶν, κεφαλῆς, ὀδόντων Hdt.2.84: as fem., of Artemis, Diog.Trag.1.5; of Aphrodite, Plu.2.143d: pl., of certain Nymphs in Elis, Hsch.; *midwife*, Hellad.ap.Phot.*Bibl*.p.531 B., Hsch. s. v. μαῖα. II. metaph., εὐφροσύνα πόνων ἰ. Pi.*N*.4.2; ὦ θάνατε, . . τῶν ἀνηκέστων κακῶν ἰ. A.*Fr*.255; ὁ θάνατος λοῖσθος ἰ. νόσων S.*Fr*.698; ὀργῆς νοσούσης εἰσὶν ἰατροὶ λόγοι A.*Pr*.380, cf. *Ch*.699; [ἀτυχίας] Antipho 2.2.13; τῆς πόλεως ⟨κακῶς⟩ βουλευσαμένης Th.6. 14; λύπης ἰ. χρόνος Diph.117; τῆς ὕβρεως Ath.14.627e: Comically, βουλιμίας, of a table, Timocl.13.3; γῆς ἰ., of a farmer, Secund.*Sent*. 16. [ῑᾱ Trag., also Antiph.259, Diph.88, Men.497, etc.: ῐᾱ in [Emp.]157, E.*Fr*.1072, Ar.*Ec*.363, *Pl*.406, Philem.11, Men.282, etc.: ῐᾱ monosyll., *TAM*2(1).369.]

ἰᾱτρο-σοφιστής, οῦ, ὁ, *professor of medicine*, Dam.ap.Suid. s. v. Γέσιος. **-τέχνης**, ου, ὁ, *practiser of medicine*, Ar.*Nu*.332 (anap.). **-τομεύς**, έως, ὁ, *doctor who uses the knife, surgeon*, *Princeton Exp.Inscr*.787 (Syria). **-φῐλόσοφος**, ὁ, *scientific doctor*, Baillet *Inscr. des tombeaux des rois* 1298.

ἴαττα, Cret. pres. part. fem. of εἰμί (q. v.).

ἰατταταῖ, ἰαττᾰταιάξ, exclamations of astonishment, Ar.*Eq*.1.

ἰᾱτύς, ύος, ἡ, *medical attendance*, Hsch. (prob.).

ἰάτωρ [ῑᾱ], Ion. ἰήτωρ, ορος, ὁ, = ἰατρός, Alcm.23.89, *IG*9(2).317 (Tricca), Hsch.

ἰαῦ, a shout in answer to one calling, *ho! holla!* Ar.*Ra*.272.

ἰαυθμός, ὁ, (ἰαύω) *sleeping-place*, esp. of wild beasts, *den, lair*, Lyc. 606 (pl.). II. *sleep*, Hsch.

ἰαυοῖ, exclamation of sorrow, Ar.*Ra*.1029.

ἴαυος· κοίτη, Hsch.; cf. ἰαύω. **ϝιαυτοῦ**, v. ἑαυτοῦ. **ἴαυχεν**, v. ἰάχω.

ἰαύω [ῐ], poet. Verb, mostly used in pres. and impf. (Trag. only in lyr.): Ep. impf. ἰαύεσκον Od.9.184, Perdrizet-Lefebvre *Graffites Grecs du Memnonion d'Abydos* 528: fut. ἰαύσω Lyc.101, 430: aor. 1 ἴαυσα Od.11.261, Call.*Aet*.3.1.2:—*sleep, pass the night*, Ζηνὸς . . ἐν ἀγκοίνῃσιν ἰαύεις Il.14.213, cf. Od.11.261; ἀΰπνους νύκτας ἴαυον Il.9. 325, Od.19.340; of beasts, ἔνθα δὲ πολλὰ μῆλ' . . ἰαύεσκον 9.184; ἄρσενες ἐκτὸς ἴαυον 14.16; δεμνίοις δύστανος ἰαύων E.*Ph*.1537 (lyr.): c. acc. cogn., ἐννυχίαν τέρψιν ἰαύειν *enjoy* the night's sleep, S.*Aj*.1204 (lyr.); ὑπασπίδιον κοῖτον ἰαύειν, of a soldier *sleeping* under arms, E. *Rh*.740 (anap.); ὕπνον Theoc.3.49, Call. l. c. II. c. acc. et gen., Lyc.101. (Prob. redupl. form of αὔω (c), cf. ἄω (A) II, αὐλή.)

ἰᾰφέτης [ῑ], ου, ὁ, (ἰός, ἀφίημι) *archer*, of Apollo, *AP*9.525.10.

ἰᾰχ-έω, aor. 1 ἰάχησα *h.Cer*.20, *AP*7.745 (Antip. Sid.):— = ἰάχω, *cry, shout*, used by Trag. in lyr., E.*Heracl*.752, *El*.1150, *Or*.826, 965, etc.: c. acc. cogn., ἰαχεῖν μέλος, αἴλινον, Id.*Tr*.515, *HF*349; [ἀοιδάν] Ar.*Ra*.217; χρησμόν *IG*7.4240*b*2. 2. rarely c. acc. obj., *bewail*, νέκυν ὀλόμενον E.*Ph*.1295, cf. [1523]:—Pass., κατ' ἰαχήθης . . ἄδικος *thou wert proclaimed . . .*, Id.*Hel*.1147 (prob. for καὶ ἰαχῇ σῇ . .). II. of things, *sound*, γαῖα σμερδαλέον ἰάχησεν *h.Hom*.28.11; τρίποδες ἰαχεῦσι Call.*Del*.146, cf. Orph.*A*.997, etc.; ὀλολύγματα ἰαχεῖ E.*Heracl*. 783. [ᾰ in Ep.: ᾱ in Trag. (it is unnecessary to write ἰακχ- when α is long): ᾱ in *IG* l. c.: ϝῐ, cf. sq.] **-ή**, ἡ, *cry, shout*, both of victor and vanquished, Il.15.396, etc.; *wail, shriek*, Od.11.43; also, *a joyous sound*, ἰαχὰ ὑμεναίων Pi.*P*.3.17, cf. E.*Tr*.337 (lyr., pl.); κροτάλων τυπάνων τε *h.Hom*.14.3; αὐλῶν *Lyr.Adesp*.96; συρίγγων E.*IA* 1039 (lyr.): in pl., generally, *shouts of joy*, Thgn.779, E.*Ba*.149 (lyr.); but πολυδάκρυς ἰ. A.*Pers*.940, cf. E.*El*.142, *Ph*.1302 (all lyr.). (ϝι-, cf. Il.4.456: a vowel is not elided before it in Ep. exc. in *h.Hom*. 14.3, Hes.*Th*.708, *Sc*.404: Trag. only in lyr.; for the quantity cf. foreg.) **-ημα**, ατος, τό, *cry, shout*: *hissing* of a serpent, E.*HF*884 (lyr., pl.); *sound* of an instrument, ῥόπτρων *AP*6.165 (Phalaec.).

ἰαχρός [ῐ], ά, όν, *melted, softened*: metaph., *at ease, tranquil*, Hsch.

ἰάχω [ῐ, ᾰ, v. sub fin.], Ion. impf. ἰάχεσκε Hes.*Sc*.232; Aeol. ἴαυχεν, = ἴαχεν, Aristarch.ap.Eust.1654.28:—*cry, shout*, ἰάχοντες ἐπεσσύμεθ' Od.4.454, etc.; of battle-shouts, Ἀργεῖοι δὲ μέγα ἴαχον Il.17. 317; σμερδαλέα ἰάχων 19.41, Od.22.81; *shriek* in alarm or pain, πρὸς κόλπον . . τιθήνης ἐκλίνθη ἰάχων Il.6.468, cf. 5.343, Od.10.323; δμωαὶ . . θυμὸν ἀκηχέμεναι μεγάλ' ἴαχον Il.18.29; γοηρὸν ἴαχεν *Epigr.Gr*. 790.7 (Dyme, iii B.C.); sts. of articulate speech, of a herald, E.*El*. 707 (lyr.); of the ship Argo, A.R.4.581, 592, cf. *AP*5.298.10 (Agath.). 2. of things, *ring, resound*, of an echo, περὶ δ' ἴαχε πέτρη Od.9.395, cf. Il.21.10, Limen.15; of waves, ἀμφὶ δὲ κῦμα στείρῃ . . μεγάλ' ἴαχε Il.1.482, Od.2.428, cf. Il.2.394; of fire, *roar*, 23.216; of a bowstring, *twang*, 4.125; of hot iron in water, *hiss*, Od.9.392; of a struck shield, Hes.*Sc*.232; also μέλαθρον ὑπὸ μολπᾶς ἴαχεν *AP*7.194 (Mnasalc.). 3. c. acc. cogn., ἰ. μέλος *sound forth* a strain, Call.*Cer*.40; ἄνδρες ἐπήρατον ἴαχον ὄρθιον Sapph.*Supp*. 20c.4; [λογίων ὁδόν] τινι *proclaim* it to him, Ar.*Eq*.1016: c. acc. pers., *sound* one's *praises*, ἴαχον Ἀπόλλω *were sounding* his *praises*, Id. *Av*.772; με Νεμέα ἴαχεν ἀθλοφόρον *Epigr.Gr*.932*a*.—Ep. only 3 sg. and pl. impf. and part.: pres. ἰάχει E.*El*.707: pf. only in part. of the compd. ἀμφιαχυῖα (q. v.): ἰαχέω (q. v.) is commoner in Att. Poets. (ϝιϝάχω, cf. Od.4.454, al.; when ϝ is observed ι is short and the sense pres. or impf.; when a preceding vowel is elided ι is long and the sense aor., as in μεγάλ' ἴαχε Il.1.482, al.: hence in the latter places μεγάλα ϝϝάχε etc. (καὶ εὔαχε (ἔϝϝαχε) in 20.62, ἐν πρώτοισι ϝαχών in 19.424) is prob. cj.: -ᾰ-, exc. in impf. ἴᾱχον (v. l. ἴακχον) Ar.*Av*. l. c.: *wāgh-* perh. cogn. with *swāgh-* in ἠχέω, ἀχέω B.)

Ἰάων, ονος, ὁ, v. Ἴαονες. **ἶβα**· σιώπα, Hsch.

ἰβανατρίς, ίδος, ἡ, *rope of a draw-well*: **ἰβανέω**, *draw water* (nisi leg. ἰβανᾷ): **ἰβάνη**, ἡ, **ἴβανον**, τό, *water-bucket*, all in Hsch. **ἰβάρβιον**· χαλεπόν, ἀνυπόστατον, Id.

ἴβδης, ου, ὁ, *cock* or *plug in a ship's bottom*, Eust.525.34, 858.38.

ἴβη, ἡ, = σορός, Hsch. **ἴβηνα**, Cret. word for *wine*, Id. **ἴβηνος**, ὁ, = σορός, Id.:—also **ἴβηνος**· πλησμονή, Id.: **ἴβηρ**, name of an animal, etym. of Ἴβηρες, Id.

ἰβηρίς, ίδος, ἡ, *pepperwort, Lepidium graminifolium*, Damocr.ap. Gal.13.350; = λεπίδιον, Aët.ap.Ps.-Dsc.2.174. (Prob. from its place of growth.)

ἴβιβυος· παιανισμός, Hsch. **ἴβινος**· ἀετός, Id.

ἰβῐο-βοσκός [ῑβ], ὁ, *keeper of the sacred ibis*, *PCair.Zen.*270.7 (iii B.C.), *Sammelb.*1178*a,b* (iii B.C.), *PTeb.*72.410 (ii B.C.), al. **-πρόσωπος**, ον, *ibis-faced*, *PMag.Leid.V.*5.6. **-στολιστής**, οῦ, ὁ, *maker of shrouds for the sacred ibis*, *PFay.*246 (i/ii A.D.). **-ταφεῖον**, τό, *tomb of the sacred ibis*, *Sammelb.*3937 (iii B.C.), *PTeb.*88.53 (ii B.C.). **-τάφος** [ᾰ], ὁ, *ibis-burier*, *PGrenf.*2.15(2).7 (ii B.C.).

ἶβις [ῑβ, Timocl.1], ἡ, gen. ἴβιος Hdt.2.76, etc., ἴβεως Ael.*NA*10.29, Porph.*Abst.*4.9, *Gp.*13.8.5, ἴβιδος Suid.; acc. ἶβιν Hdt.2.75: pl. ἴβιες Arist. (v. infr.), Ion. acc. ἴβις Hdt.2.67,75; gen. pl. ἰβίων *PTeb.*5.70 (ii B.C.); dat. pl. ἴβεσι Ph.2.570, Paus.8.22.5:—*ibis*, an Egyptian bird, of which there were two species, *white ibis, I. religiosa*, and *black ibis, Plegadis falcinellus*, Hdt.2.75, Ar.*Av.*1296, Arist.*HA*617ᵇ27, etc.; ἰβίων τροφή *PPetr.*3p.229 (iii B.C.).

ἰβίσκος, ὁ, Lat. *hibiscus*, = ἀλθαία, v.l. in Ps.-Dsc.3.146, Erot. s. v. ῥίζη ἀλθαίης; also written **ἐβίσκος**, q. v.

ἰβιών [ῑβ], ῶνος, ὁ, *chapel of the sacred ibis*, *PTeb.*62.23 (ii B.C.), *BGU*1216 (ii B.C.).

ἰβρίκαλοι· χοῖροι, Hsch.; cf. ὀβρ-.

ἰβύ, *loudly*, Phot.: hence aor. 1 inf. **ἰβυκινῆσαι**, *shout*, Teleclid.58 (**ἰβυκηνίσαι** *EM*464.44): but Subst. **ἰβυκανητής**, οῦ, ὁ, = βυκανητής, *trumpeter*, read by Suid. in Plb.2.29.6 (βυκανητῶν, βυκανιτῶν codd.). Ion. words, acc. to Hsch.: derived from the poet Ibycus, Suid.

Ἰβύκειον σχῆμα, τό, use of the termination -σι in 3 sg. of Subj., Hdn.*Fig.*p.101 S. (From the poet Ibycus.)

Ἰβύκινον, τό, *musical instrument named after the poet Ibycus*, Suid.

ἰβυκτήρ, ῆρος, ὁ, in Cretan, *one who begins a war-song*, Hsch. (-βηκ- cod.). **ἰβύκχα**· σεμνότης, ἢ σωρὸς κρεῶν, Id. (-υηχ- cod.). **ἶβυξ**, υκος, = ἶβις, Id. **ἴβυς**, υος, ὁ, = εὐφημία, στιγμή, Id. **ἰβύω**, *shout*: *strike*, Id.; cf. **ἰβῶν**· εὐφημῶν, στάζων, Id. **ἴγα**, in Cretan, = σίγα, Id. **ἴγγι** τινί· ἐπιθυμίᾳ τινὶ ἑλκομένη, Id. (leg. ἴυγγι). **ἴγγια**· εἶς (Cypr.), Id. **ἴγδην** and **ἴγνην**· ἄρσην, Id.

ἰγδίον, τό, Dim. of sq., *Gp.*12.19.5, Paul.Aeg.3.59.

ἴγδις, εως, ἡ, *mortar*, Sol.39, Damocr.ap.Gal.14.130, Dsc.5.89, *AP* 9.642 (Agath.): cited as obsol. for θυεία by S.E.*M.*1.234:—the form **ἴγδη** in Hdn.Gr.2.523, Hp.*Mul.*1.103, Gal. l. c., Ps.-Democr.Alch. p.55 B. is prob. incorrect. II. = sq., Antiph.127, *Com.Adesp.*140. (Cf. Lat. *ico*.)

ἴγδισμα, ατος, τό, (from ἰγδίζω, which is not found) *pounding*: hence, *a dance, in which the loins were moved like a pestle*, *EM*464.51, Suid.

ἰγδοκόπᾰνον, τό, *a pestle*, Sch.Il.11.147 (ap.Valck.*Animadv. ad Ammon.*p.140, ὀγδ- cod.). **ἰγδόλης**· ὁ ἐπὶ μέρει γεωργῶν, Hsch. **ἴγκρος**, ὁ, = ἐγκέφαλος, Hdn.Gr.1.204, Hsch. **ἶγμαι**, **ἱγμένος**, pf. of ἱκνέομαι. **ἰγμαλέος**, α, ον, = ἰκμ-, Hdn.Gr.2. 523. **ἰγμή**· βοή, Hsch. (for ἰυγμή or ἰυγή). **ἴγνην**, v. ἴγδην.

ἴγνητες, ων, οἱ, = αὐθιγενεῖς, Rhodian word, A.D.*Pron.*56.4 (who derives it, as ἴγνητες, from the Pron. ἵ), Choerob.*in Theod.*1.161, Hsch.; as pr. n., coupled with Τελχῖνες, Simm.11: sg., *EM*465.1.

ἰγνύα, Ion. **ἰγνύη**, ἡ, *the part behind the thigh and knee, ham*, κατ' ἰγνύην βεβλημένος Il.13.212; παρ' ἰγνύῃσιν ἕλιξε κέρκον Theoc.25.242, cf. 26.17, *AP*12.176 (Strat.), *APl.*4.253: also in Prose, Hp.*Fract.*13, Ruf.*Onom.*121; τὸ μόριον τὸ τῆς ἅλσεως κύριον (καλεῖται δὲ τοῦτο ἰγνύα) Arist.*HA*515ᵇ8: acc. sg. ἰγνύαν Phld.*Acad.Ind.*p.50 M.; περὶ τὴν ἰγνύαν Plu.*Art.*11: dat. pl. ἰγνύαις Lxx 3*Ki.*18.21, Luc.*VH*1.23.—From a nom. **ἰγνύς**, ύος, ἡ, we find dat. pl. ἰγνύσι *h.Merc.*152, v.l. in Luc. l. c.: acc. ἰγνύν Arist.*HA*494ᵃ8 (v.l. -ύην), Agatharch.53; dat. ἰγνύϊ Gal.10.902: gen. pl. ἰγνύων Arist.*HA*512ᵇ22, Herod.1.14: acc. pl. ἰγνύας is indeterminate, Plu.*Galb.*26. [ῡ in ἰγνύη, v. ll.cc.; but ῠ in ἰγνύων, ἰγνύσι.]

ἴγνυς, v. ἴκνυς. **ἰγχηρέω**, v. ἐγχειρέω.

Ἰδαῖος, α, ον, *of Ida*, v. Ἴδη.

ἰδάλιμος [ῑ], ον, (ἶδος) *causing sweat*, καῦμα Hes.*Op.*415.

ἰδαλίς, ἡ, a bird, Hsch. **ἰδάλτα**· ἰδιά τινα (leg. ἴδ' ἄττα), Id.

ἰδᾰνικός [ῐ], ή, όν, (ἰδεῖν, ἰδέα) *existing in idea*, κόσμος Ti.Locr.97d.

ἰδᾰνός [ῐ], όν, (ἰδεῖν) *fair, comely*, χάριτες Call.*Fr.*535.

ἰδᾰνόχροος [ῐ], ον, *with lovely colour*, ἄνθη *Epic.Alex.Adesp.*9 iii 10.

ἴδδιος, v. ἴδιος.

ἰδέ [ῐ], Ep. Conj., = ἠδέ, *and*, Il.4.147, al., Emp.20.7, etc., prob. l. in S.*Ant.*969 (lyr.). II. Cypr., *then, in that case*, *Inscr.Cypr.*135. 12 H. (Prob. fr. the demonstrative stem *i-* (cf. Lat. *is*) and δέ.)

ἴδε (A) (Att. **ἰδέ** Hdn.Gr.1.431), aor. 2 imper. of εἶδον, *behold*, Il. 17.179, etc.: folld. by ὅτι.., Pl.*Phd.*72a; used by Trag. in lyr., A.*Supp.*350, S.*Tr.*222, E.*Or.*1541.

ἴδε (B), Ep. 3 sg. of aor. 2 εἶδον, he saw, Hom.

ἰδέα [ῐ], Ion. **ἰδέη**, ἡ, (ἰδεῖν) *form*, ἰδέᾳ καλός Pi.*O.*10(11).103, cf. Theoc.29.6; τὴν ἰ. πάνυ καλός Pl.*Prt.*315e; τὴν ἰ. μοχθηρός And.1.100, cf. Ar.*Av.*1000; ἰδέην ὀρέων Hdt.1.80; opp. χρῶμα, Id. 4.109; opp. μέγεθος, Pl.*Phd.*109b (pl.); ἡ ἰ. αὐτοῦ ἦν ὡς ἀστραπή *Ev.Matt.*28.3, etc.; of the elementary *shapes*, ἄτομοι ἰδέαι Democr. ap.Plu.2.1111a codd., cf. *Fr.*141 D.; of the four *elements*, Philistion ap.Anon.Lond.20.25. 2. *semblance*, opp. reality, γνώμην ἐξαπατῶσ' ἰδέαι *outward appearances* cheat the mind, Thgn.128. 3. *kind, sort*, φύλλα τοιῆσδε ἰδέης Hdt.1.203; φύσιν παρέχονται ἰδέης τοιῆνδε [οἱ ποτάμιοι ἵπποι] Id.2.71; ἐφρόνεον διφασίας ἰ. they conceived two *modes* of acting, Id.6.100, cf. 119; τὰ ὄργι' ἐστὶ τίν' ἰ. ἔχοντά σοι; what is their *nature* or *fashion?* E.*Ba.*471; ἑτέραν ὕμνων ἰ. Ar.*Ra.*384; καινὰς ἰ. εἰσφέρειν new *forms* of comedy, Id.*Nu.* 547; τίς ἰ. βουλεύματος; Id.*Av.*993; πᾶσα ἰ. θανάτου every *form* of death, or death in every *form*, Th.3.81, cf. 83, 2.51; πολλαὶ ἰ. πολέμων Id.1.109; ἡ ὑπάρχουσα ἰ. τῆς παρασκευῆς Id.4.55; πᾶσαν ἰδέαν πειράσαντες having tried every *way*, Id.2.19; τῇ αὐτῇ ἰ. Id.3. 62, 6.76; οὐκ ἐν ταῖς αὐταῖς ἰ. not in the same *relations*, Isoc.3.44: εἰς μίαν τινὰ ἰ. into one *kind of existence*, Pl.*Tht.*184d; ἄλλη ἰ. πολιτείας Id.*R.*544c, etc.; ἀγοραίας.. ἰδέας τοῦ βίου Epicur.*Fr.*196. 4. esp. in Rhet., etc., of literary *form*, ἀμφοτέραις ταῖς ἰδέαις κατεχρήσαντο πρὸς τὴν ποίησιν Isoc.2.48, cf. 15.47,183; ἡ ἰαμβικὴ ἰ. Arist. *Po.*1449ᵇ8, cf. 1450ᵇ34, *Rh.Al.*1425ᵃ9, etc.; ἡ ἐν τῷ λέγειν ἰ. Phld. *Rh.*2.258 S. b. *style*, Πλατωνική, Δημοσθενικὴ ἰ., Syrian.*in Hermog.* 1.112 R. c. *a quality of style* (e.g. σαφήνεια, γοργότης, etc.), Hermog.*Id.*tit., etc. II. in Logic, = εἶδος, *class, kind*: hence, *principle of classification*, ἔφησθα.. μιᾷ ἰδέᾳ τά τε ἀνόσια ἀνόσια εἶναι καὶ τὰ ὅσια ὅσια Pl.*Euthphr.*6d, cf. *Phdr.*265d, *Sph.*253d, etc. 2. pl. in Platonic Philosophy, *ideal forms, archetypes*, τὰς.. ἰ. νοεῖσθαι μέν, ὁρᾶσθαι δ' οὔ Id.*R.*507b, cf. 596b, al., Arist.*Metaph.*990ᵃ34, al., *EN*1096ᵃ17: also in sg., ἡ τοῦ ἀγαθοῦ ἰ. Pl.*R.*508e, al., cf. εἶδος. 3. *notion, idea*, προάγειν τὸν ἀποκρινόμενον ἐπὶ τὴν ἰ. ἀγνοουμένου πράγματος Nausiph.2. (Written εἰδέα in later Greek, as *PGen.*16.17 (iii A.D.), v.l. in *Ev.Matt.*28.3.)

ἰδέατος· ἰδήρατος (Sicel), Hsch.

ἴδεδρος [ῐ], ον, = ἰδίων τὴν ἕδραν, Did.*in D.*11.22.

ἰδεῖν, Ep. **ἰδέειν**, Dor. **ἰδέμεν**, aor. 2 inf. of ὁράω, v. εἴδω.

ἰδέν, dub. sens. in *PStrassb.*24.16, al. (ii A.D.).

ἰδέρως [ῐ], ωτος, ὁ, ἡ, *one who loves at first sight*, Hsch., Suid.

ἴδεσκον, ες, ε, Ion. for εἶδον, Il.3.217. **ἰδέω**, v.l. for εἰδέω, Ep. for εἰδῶ, subj. of οἶδα, *know*, 14.235, Od.16.236.

ἴδη [ῑ], Dor. **ἴδα**, ἡ, *timber-tree*, in pl., χώρη ὑψηλή τε καὶ ἴδῃσι συνηρεφής Hdt.1.110; ὄρεα.. ἴδῃσι παντοίῃσι συνηρεφέα Id.7.111, cf. 4.109,175: in sg., *wood*, ἐν τῇ ἴδῃ τῇ πλείστῃ in the thick of *the wood*, Id.4.109; ἴδαν ἐς πολύδενδρον Theoc.17.9; ἴδη ναυπηγήσιμος *timber* for.., Hdt.5.23: never in Att.: also in late Prose, Philostr. *Dial.*2, *VA*3.4 (s. v.l.). II. pr. n., **Ἴδη**, *Ida*, i. e. *the wooded hill*, 1. in the Troad, Il.2.821, etc.: **Ἴδηθεν**, *from Ida*, 4.475; Ἰ. μεδέων ruling *from I.*, 3.276:—Adj. **Ἰδαῖος**, α, ον (Aeol. **Ἴδαος** as pr. n., Sapph.*Supp.*20a.3), Ζεύς Il.16.605; ὄρεα 8.170, etc.; Ἰ. ῥίζα, a plant, *Ruscus Hypoglossum*, Dsc.4.44: also Ἰδαία alone, = δάφνη Ἀλεξάνδρεια, ib.145: Ἰ. Δάκτυλοι, prop. 'dwarfs *of the forest*', Hes.*Fr.*176, Pherecyd.47 J., Hellanic.89 J., etc.; but Ἰ. δάκτυλος is a name for one of the fingers, *PMag.Lond.*46.455. 2. in Crete, D.P.502, Paus.5.7.6.

ἴδη, ἡ, *sheen of metal*, etc., v.l. for σίδη in Philostr.*Im.*1.28, 2.32.

ἴδηαι, 2 sg. aor. 2 subj. Med. of εἰδόμην, Ep. for ἴδῃ. **ἴδημα**, ατος, τό, = ὅραμα, Hsch.: **ἰδήμων**, = εἰδ-, Id.: **ἰδήρατος**, ον, *beautiful*, Id. **ἰδησῶ**, Dor. fut. of εἶδον, I *shall see*, Theoc.3.37. **ἰδίᾳ**, v. ἴδιος VI. 2.

ἰδῐ-αζόντως [ῐδ], Adv. *in a special* or *peculiar way*, *Stoic.*3.94, D.S.19.99, S.E.*P.*1.182, *Cod.Just.*1.3.35.3, etc.; *separately*, opp. κοινῇ, *Sammelb.*7033.53 (v A.D.). **-άζω**, (ἴδιος) *to be alone*, Hdn. 4.12.7, 7.6.7, D.C.66.9; ἰδιάζουσαι Herod.6 tit.; δωμάτιον ἰδιάζον *secluded*, Hld.7.12; ἰ. πρός τινα *to be alone* with.., ib.25; ἰ. θεῷ *to be alone with* God, Ph.1.95; ἰ. πράγματι *devote oneself* to a thing, *Com. Adesp.*414:—so in Med., of members of a chorus, *sing independently*, Arist.*Pr.*922ᵃ35. II. *to be peculiar*, ἰδιάζοντα γένη λίθων Phld. *Sign.*28, cf. Jul.*Gal.*143a; ἰ. τῇ φύσει D.S.2.58; ἰδιάζουσα φύσις Id.3. 46, Hld.2.28; ἰδιάζον συμπόσιον Ath.1.12a; αἱ ἰδιάζουσαι ἀρχαί *special* principles, Dam.*Pr.*134; of drugs, ἰδιάζων *special, superior*, Dsc.1.14; ἃ ἂν ἰδιάσωμεν, ψευδόμεθα S.E.*M.*7.133; ἰ. τινί *to be peculiarly adapted* to.., Ael.*NA*6.19; βωμὸς τῷ Διονύσῳ ἰδιάζων *appropriated* to D., Hld.10.6: c. gen., *to be the property of*, J.*AJ*16.7.3. b. ἡ -άζουσα θερμασία its *proper* heat, Herod.Med.ap.Orib.5.30.12. 2. Gramm., *to be peculiar to an individual*, τὰ κτητικὰ -άζει κατὰ τὸν κτήτορα A.D. *Pron.*105.4, cf. *Synt.*128.13, al.:—so in Med., [ὁ βασιλεὺς] μᾶλλον -άζεται τοῦ Πτολεμαίου ib.84.20. **-αίτερος, -ατος**, Comp. and Sup. of ἴδιος (q. v.). **-ασμός**, ὁ, *peculiarity*, Iamb.*VP*35.255. 2. *particularity*, ὁ τοῦ ἑνὸς ἀπεστενωμένος ἰ. Dam.*Pr.*28 bis. **-αστής**, οῦ, ὁ, *recluse*, D.L.1.25.

ἰδικός [ῐδ], ή, όν, (εἶδος) late form of εἰδικός (q. v.), *special*, Stob.2. 7.11ⁿ, Ath.9.373b, Gal.1.333 (Sup.), Wilcken *Chr.*6.14 (V A.D.), etc.; τὰ ἰ. τῶν γενῶν Ascl.*Tact.*12.11, etc. 2. [ῐδ] (ἴδιος) *proper, one's own*, *AP*5.105 (Diotim.), Man.5.122. Adv. -κῶς Herm.*in Phdr.* p.185 A.; opp. κοινῶς, Simp.*in Ph.*848.21: Comp. -ώτερον Ath.7. 299d.

ἰδῐο-βουλέω [ῐδ], *follow one's own counsel, take one's own way*, Hdt.7.8.δ' (v.l. -εύειν), D.C.43.27. **-γενής**, ές, *mating only with its kind*, opp. κοινογενής, Pl.*Plt.*265e. 2. *peculiar in kind*, Herm. ap.Stob.1.49.44, Dsc.2.66. **-γλωσσος**, ον, *of distinct, peculiar tongue*, πόλις Str.5.2.9. **-γνωμονέω**, *hold one's own opinion, be* *self-opinionated*, Phld.*Vit.*p.30 J., cf. D.C.45.42, 53.21: **-γνωμέω** is f.l. in Id.43.27. **-γνώμων**, ον, gen. ονος, *holding one's own opinion*, Hp.*Aër.*24, Phryn.Com.18, Arist.*EN*1151^{b}12. **-γονία**, ἡ, *breeding only with one's own kind*, opp. κοινογονία, Pl.*Plt.*265d. **-γρᾰφία**, ἡ, *autograph*, dub. in *BGU*1135.10 (i B.C.). **-γρᾰφος**, ον, *written with one's own hand, autograph*, liber Vergilii, Gell.9.14.7, cf. *POxy.*250.13 (i A.D.), etc.:—Subst. -γραφον, τό, *autograph*, *PFlor.* 27.13 (iv A.D.), etc. 2. *specially* or *separately written*, ψαλμὸς ἰ. εἰς Δαυίδ Lxx *Ps.*151 tit. **-θάνᾰτος** [θᾰ], ον, *dying a natural death* (cf. ἴδιος I. 6b), Vett.Val.19.2. **-θᾰνέω**, *die a natural death*, Procl.*Par.Ptol.*277. **-θηρευτικός**, ή, όν, *hunting by* or *for oneself*: ἡ -κή (sc. τέχνη) *private hunting*, Pl.*Sph.*222d: **-θηρία**, ἡ, ib. 223b. **-θρονέω**, Astrol., of a planet, *enjoy its proper dignity*, Ptol.*Tetr.*51, Paul.Al.*S.*4. **-κρᾱσία**, ἡ, *peculiar temperament*, Procl.*Par.Ptol.*13 (nisi leg. -συγκρασίαν). **-κρῖτος**, ον (-κοιτον cod.), = ἰδιόρρυθμος, Hsch. **-κτήμων**, gen. ονος, ὁ, *private owner*, *PTeb.*124.32 (ii B.C.), Heph.Astr.1.1. **-κτητος**, ον, *held as private property*, Hp.*Ep.*26 (dub.l.); γῆ *BGU*1216.83 (ii B.C.), Str.14.6.5, *PFay.*342 (ii A.D.), *Cod.Just.*10.3.7; ἡ ἰ. (sc. γῆ) *PTeb.*5.111 (ii B.C.); ἰ. πανευτυχίη *won all by himself*, *Epigr.Gr.*443 (Namara); ἀρετή Onos. 1.25. **-λογέω**, *develop one's own ideas*, prob. in Phld.*Acad.Ind.* p.4 M.:—Med., *converse in private with*, ἄττα σοι Pl.*Thg.*121a; θεῷ Ph.1.197; πρός τινα Charito 6.7. **-λογία**, ἡ, *subjective theorizing*, dub. cj. in Epicur.*Ep.*2 p.36 U. (ἰδιαλογίας, ἤδη ἀλογίας codd.). II. *private conversation*, Charito 4.6. **-μήκης**, ες, *of their own length*, i.e. *of the same length each way*, of square numbers, Nicom.*Ar.*2. 18. **-μορφος**, ον, *of peculiar form*, Thphr.*HP*9.13.6, Str.4.6.10, Plu.*Mar.*25.

ἴδιον, τό, v. ἴδιος.

ἰδῐο-ξενία [ῐδ], ἡ, *private friendship*, Anon.ap.Suid. **-ξενοδόκος**, ὁ, *private* (opp. official) *guarantor of an alien*, *Rev.Epigr.*2.227 (Doliche). **-ξενος**, ον, *private friend* in a foreign state (opp. πρόξενος), D.S.13.5, Luc.*Phal.*2.1, etc.: as Adj., ἰ. ἄνδρες D.H.1.84: Locr. ϝιδιόξενος (nisi leg. ϝιδίō ξένō) *IG*9(1).333.12 (v B.C.).

ἰδῐόομαι [ῐδ], (ἴδιος) Med., *make one's own, appropriate*, Pl.*R.*547c, *Lg.*742b; of literary plagiarism, Phld.*D.*1.9. 2. *make one's friend*, τινα D.C.39.29. II. Pass., *to be specifically constituted*, Dam.*Pr.*34.

ἰδῐο-πάθεια [ῐδ, πᾰ], ἡ, Medic., *affection having a local origin*, Gal. 8.31, al., Alex.Aphr.*Pr.*2.35. **-πᾰθέω**, *suffer from a local affection*, Gal.8.31. **-περιόριστος**, ον, *specially defined* or *limited*, φύσις Suid. s.v. Θεόδωρος. **-πλαστος**, ον, *self-formed*, ἀγαθόν Secund.*Sent.* 3, 14. **-ποιέω**, *make separately*, ἐπίδειξίν τινι Gal.2.672. 2. prob. f.l. for εἰδοπ-, τὴν γραφήν Str.15.1.14. II. *appropriate, plagiarize*, Vett.Val.96.26 (Act., s.v.l.):—elsewh. Med., *appropriate to oneself*, Phld.*Herc.*1788.1, D.S.5.13, etc.; *win over*, Id.15.29, Lxx *2Ki.*15.6. III. Pass., *to be invested with a specific character*, Dam. *Pr.*75. **-ποίημα**, ατος, τό, *act of appropriation*, *Gloss.* **-ποιός**, όν, *creating particularity*, Dam.*Pr.*36; ἰ. ἐπιστροφή ib.76. **-πρᾱγέω**, *act independently*, Plb.8.26.9, Phld.*Ind.Sto.*60; *pursue one's own interest*, D.S.18.39,64, Str.12.3.28; εἰερεὺς ὢν ἰδιοπραέων (if written for ἰδιοπραγέων) *MAMA*1.237 (Laodicea Combusta); ἰδιοπραγεῖ· τὰ ἴδια πράσσει, ἡσυχάζει, Hsch. **-πρᾱγία**, ἡ, *pursuit of private interests*, πλεονεξία καὶ ἰ. Pl.*Lg.*875b; πρὸς -πραγίαν ὡρμημένος on a *private venture*, D.S.18.52. **-πραγμονέω**, = ἰδιοπραγέω, Sch.Th.1.32, Sch.E.*Med.*217. **-πράγμων**, ον, gen. ονος, *minding one's own business*, opp. πολυπράγμων, D.L.9.112, Ptol.*Tetr.*161; βίος Vett. Val.185.6. **-προσωπέω**, Astrol., of a planet, *possess its proper aspect* (i.e. that of its 'house') with respect to sun and moon, Ptol. *Tetr.*114:—hence **-προσωπία**, ἡ, ib.155: **-πρόσωπος**, ον, ib. 50. **-ρρυθμία**, ἡ, = ἰδία τάξις, Cyr. **-ρρυθμος**, ον, = ἰδιότακτος, Hsch.: gloss on αὐθέκαστος, Thom.Mag.p.25 R.

ἴδιος [ῐδ], α, ον, Att. also ος, ον Pl.*Prt.*349b, Arist.*HA*532^{b}32 (v. sub fin.): I. *one's own, pertaining to oneself*: hence, 1. *private, personal* (opp. κοινός): twice in Hom., πρῆξις δ' ἥδ' ἰδίη οὐ δήμιος this business is *private*, not public, Od.3.82; δήμιον ἢ ἴδιον; 4.314; ἴδιος ἐν κοινῷ σταλείς embarking *as a private man* in a public cause, Pi.*O.* 13.49; ἰ. στόλῳ χρᾶσθαι, opp. δημοσίῳ, Hdt.5.63; γῆς.. νοσούσης ἴ. κινοῦντες κακά S.*OT*636; κοινὸν ἐξ ἰδίας ἀνοίας κακόν E.*Hec.*641 (lyr.), cf. *Or.*766 (troch.); ἴδια πράσσων ἢ στρατοῦ ταχθεὶς ὕπο; Id.*IA*1363 (troch.); ἴ. κέρδεα Hdt.6.100; συμφορά Antipho 2.1.11; πρόσοδος And.4.11; τὰ ἴ. διάφορα Th.2.37; πλοῦτος ἴ. καὶ δημόσιος Id.1.80, cf. Pl.*R.*521a; ὁ οὐ κοινὸς πόνος ib.535b, cf. 543b; ξυμβόλαια ib.443e; ἰ. ἢ πολιτικὴ πρᾶξις Id.*Grg.*484d; πόλεις καὶ ἴ. οἶκοι Id.*Lg.*890b, cf. 796d, etc.; τὰ ἱρά, opp. τὰ ἴ., temples, opp. *private buildings*, Hdt. 6.9, 8.109; τὸ ἐν ἰδίοις discussion among *private persons*, Pl.*Sph.* 225b. 2. *one's own*, opp. ἀλλότριος, ἐπικώμια Pi.*N.*6.32; ἡ ἰ. ἐλευθερίη Hdt.7.147; Ζεὺς ἰδίοις νόμοις κρατύνων A.*Pr.*404 (lyr.); ἰδίᾳ γνώμᾳ ib.543 (lyr.); οὔτοι τὰ χρήματ' ἴ. κέκτηνται βροτοί E.*Ph.* 555; φίλων οὐδὲν ἴ., = κοινὰ τὰ τῶν φίλων, Id.*Andr.*376: with Pron., χωρίον ἡμέτερον ἴδιον D.55.8. 3. τὰ ἴ. *private interests*, opp. public, Th.1.82, 2.61, etc.; *one's own property*, Id.1.141, etc.; τὰ ἴ. πράττειν mind *one's own business*, in later Gr., Phryn.405, cf. *1Ep. Thess.*4.11; μένειν ἐπὶ τῶν ἰ. Plb.2.57.5; εἰς τὸ ἴ. καταθέσθαι for *self*, X.*An.*1.3.3, etc.: with Pron., τοὐμὸν ἴ. εἰπεῖν my *personal* opinion, Isoc.6.8; τὰ ἐμὰ ἴ. D.50.66; τὰ αὑτοῦ ἴ. Thgn.440 (dub.l.), cf. Antipho 5.61, Isoc.8.127; τὰ ὑμέτερα ἴ. D.19.307; τὰ ἴ. σφῶν αὐτῶν, τὰ ἴ. τὰ σφέτερα αὐτῶν, And.2.2, 3.36; ἔγωγε τοὐμὸν ἴ. I *for my own part*, Luc.*Merc.Cond.*9. 4. of persons, *personally attached* to one, ἴδιοι Σελεύκου Plb.21.6.4, cf. Arist.*Pol.*1315^{a}36, *UPZ*146.38 (ii B.C.), 109.18 (i B.C.); ἄνθρωπος ἴδιος τῇ εὐνοίᾳ τῇ πρὸς.. *PCair.Zen.*32 (iii B.C.); ταῖς εὐνοίαις ἴδιοι D.S.11.26; ἴδιοι, οἱ, *members of one's family, relatives*, *BGU*665 ii 1 (i A.D.), Vett.Val.70.5, etc. 5. ἡ ἰ. (sts. with κώμη added, *BGU*15.13 (ii A.D.)), one's *place of origin*, *PTeb.* 327.28 (ii A.D.), etc.: pl., καταπορεύεσθαι εἰς τὰς ἰ. ib.5.7 (ii B.C.). 6. in later Gr., almost as a possessive Pron., = ἑαυτοῦ, ἑαυτῶν, ἡ ἰ. φιλαγαθία *IG*2^2.1011.71 (ii B.C.), etc.; χρῶνται ὡς ἰδίοις *UPZ*11.14 (ii B.C.); περὶ τῶν ἰ. βιβλίων, title of work by Galen. b. ἴ. θάνατος *one's own*, i.e. a *natural* death, Ramsay *Cities and Bishoprics* No. 133; ἰδίοις τελευτῶσι θανάτοις Ptol.*Tetr.*199; also ἰδίᾳ μοίρῃ Ramsay op.cit. No.187. II. *separate, distinct*, ἔθνος ἴ. καὶ οὐδαμῶς Σκυθικόν Hdt.4.18, cf. 22; ἴδιοί τινές σοι [θεοί]; Ar.*Ra.*890; ἑκάστῳ τῶν ὀνομάτων ὑπόκειταί τις ἴδιος οὐσία Pl.*Prt.*349b; πόλεις.. βαρβάρους καὶ ἰδίας Decr.ap.D.18.183; ὁ βάτραχος ἰδίαν ἔχει τὴν γλῶτταν, τὴν ἰ. ἀφίησι φωνήν, a *peculiar* kind of tongue, ..its *peculiar* note, Arist. *HA*536^{a}8, 11: folld. by ἤ, ἴδιον ἔπασχεν πάθος ἢ οἱ ἄλλοι *unique and different* from others, Pl.*Grg.*481c; so ἴδιον παρὰ τὰ ἄλλα Thphr.*HP* 6.4.10. b. ἴ. λόγος, in Ptolemaic and Roman Egypt, *private account*, δεδώκαμεν Πύρωνι τὸν ἔσχατόν σου ἴ. λόγον *PCair.Zen.*253 (iii B.C.), cf. *PGrenf.*1.16 (ii B.C.), etc.; later, *special account*, a branch of the fiscal administration, Wilcken *Chr.*162 (ii B.C.), *PAmh.*2.31 (ii B.C.), *PGnom.Prooem.* (ii A.D.), etc.; ὁ γνώμων τοῦ ἰ. λόγου *OGI*669.44 (i A.D.); also as the title of the Controller, Str. 17.1.12 codd., *OGI*408 (ii A.D.), Mitteis *Chr.*372 vi 1 (ii A.D.). 2. *strange, unusual*, ἰδίοισιν ὑμεναίοισι κοὐχὶ σώφροσιν E.*Or.*558; *peculiar, exceptional*, περιττὸν καὶ ἴ. γένος Arist.*GA*760^{a}5; τὰ περιττὰ καὶ ἴ. τῶν δένδρων Thphr.*CP*2.7.1; παράδοξον εἰπεῖν τι καὶ περιττὸν καὶ ἴ. Plu.2.1068b; *eccentric*, of persons, ib.57e; ἴ. τις ἐν πᾶσι βουλόμενος εἶναι Id.*Them.*18. 3. *peculiar, appropriate*, ἴδια ὀνόματα *proper, specific* words, opp. περιέχοντα, class-names, Arist. *Rh.*1407^{a}31; ὄνομα ἴ. τινος Pl.*R.*580e; τὸ ἴ. τοῦ ἐπαίνου Luc.*Pr.Im.* 19. III. ἴ. λόγοι *ordinary private* conversation, opp. ποίησις, Pl. *R.*366e, cf. *Euthd.*305d; v. infr. VI. 2b. IV. τὸ ἴ. *characteristic property* of a species, Arist.*Top.*102^{a}18, 103^{b}11, Chrysipp.*Stoic.*2.75, Plot.5.5.13; but also, *distinguishing feature* in a relative sense, ἴ. πρός τι Arist.*Top.*128^{b}25. V. regul. Comp. ἰδιώτερος Isoc.12.73, Thphr.*HP*3.1.6: Sup. -ώτατος D.23.65, Thphr.*HP*1.14.2; also ἰδιαίτερος, -αίτατος, Arist.*PA*656^{a}26, 658^{b}33; -αίτατος but not -αίτερος acc. to Thom.Mag.p.189 R. VI. Adv. **ἰδίως**, *peculiarly*, Isoc.5.108; *severally*, Pl.*Lg.*807b: Comp. ἰδιωτέρως Thphr.*HP*1.13. 4; ὡς -ώτερον εἰπεῖν Phld.*Oec.*p.68 J.; ἰδιαίτερον Hdn.7.6.7: Sup. ἰδιώτατα (v.l. -αίτατα) D.S.19.1; ἰδίως καλεῖσθαι to be called *specifically*, Arist.*Mu.*394^{b}28; -αίτατα λέγεσθαι Id.*Mete.*382^{a}3; ἰδίως, opp. κοινῶς, λέγεσθαι Demetr.Lac.*Herc.*1014.41 F. (but in Gramm., to be used *as a proper name*, D.T.634.13); *in a peculiar sense* or *usage*, Sch. Ar.*Pl.*115; ἰ. Αἰσχύλος τὸν Ἀγαμέμνονα ἐπὶ σκηνῆς ἀναιρεῖσθαι ποιεῖ A. *Ag.*Arg., cf. Sch.E.*Ph.*1116; also, = *extra versum*, τὸ "φεῦ" ἰδίως Sch. Ar.*Nu.*41 (v.l. ἰδίᾳ). 2. **ἰδίᾳ**, Ion. -ίῃ, as Adv., *by oneself, privately, on one's own account*, θύοντι ἰδίῃ μούνῳ Hdt.1.132, cf. 192, Ar.*Eq.*467; οὔτε ἰδίᾳ οὔτε ἐν κοινῷ Th.1.141; καὶ ἰ. καὶ δημοσίᾳ Id.3.45, Pl.*Ap.*30b; καὶ ἰ. καὶ κοινῇ Arist.*Ath.*40.3; ἰδίᾳ ἕκαστος Th.8.1, cf. Pl.*Lg.*946d, etc.: c. gen., ἰ. τῆς φρενός *apart from*.., Ar.*Ra.*102. b. *in ordinary talk*, opp. ὑπὸ ποιητῶν, Pl.*R.*363e, cf. 606c; v. supr. III. 3. κατ' ἰδίαν *in private*, Philem.169; κατ' ἰδίαν εἰπεῖν τινι D.S.1.21; κατ' ἰ. λαβεῖν τινα to take him *aside*, Plb.4.84.8; also, *separately, apart*, Plu.2.120d; οἱ κατ' ἰ. βίοι Plb.1.71.1. (ϝίδιος *Tab.Heracl.*1.13, al., *Schwyzer* 324.4 (Delph., iv B.C.), *IG*9(1).333.12 (Locr., v B.C.), etc.; with spiritus asper, ἐκ τοῦ hιδίου *Jahresh.*14 *Beibl.*141 (Argos, v B.C.); καθ' ἰδίαν *IG*2^2.891.6, 5(1).6 (Lacon.), 9(2).66 (Lamia), Aët.3.159, etc.; καθ' ἰδδίαν prob. in *IG*9(2).461.26 (Thess.).)

ἰδῐό-σημος [ῐδ], ον, *peculiar in signification*, ὀνόματα Sch.Hermog. in Rh.7.195 W. **-σπορέομαι**, Pass., of land, *to be sown by one's own labour*, *PFlor.*64.34 (iv A.D.). **-σπορία**, ἡ, *sowing carried out by one's own labour*, *PRyl.*142.18 (i A.D.), *PAmh.*2.131.10 (ii A.D.). **-σπορος**, ἡ (sc. γῆ), *land sown by the landlord's own employees*, *PCair.Zen.*292.508: so -σπορα, τά, ib.60, al. (iii B.C.). **-στολος**, ον, *equipped at one's own expense*, τριήρης Plu.*Alc.*1; *hired for one's own use*, πλοῖον Ath.12.521a, cf. Philostr.*VA*5.20; ἰ. πλεῦσαι sail *in one's own ship*, Plu.*Thes.*26. **-συγκρᾱσία**, ἡ, (κρᾶσις) *peculiar temperament* or *habit of body, idiosyncrasy*, Ptol.*Tetr.*12, Gal.10.169, al.:—also **-σύγκρᾱσις**, εως, ἡ, Ptol.*Tetr.*142:—also **-συγκρῐσία**, ἡ, Sor.2.56 (cj.), Herod.Med.ap.Orib.6.20.24, S.E.*P.*1.79 (pl.): **-σύγκρῐσις**, εως, ἡ, Dsc.*Alex.Praef.* (pl.). **-σύγκρῐτος**, ον, *peculiarly composed*, Herm.ap.Stob.1.49.44. **-συστᾰσία**, ἡ, *peculiar constitution*, prob. in Sor.2.56. **-τακτος**, ον, gloss on ἰδιόρρυθμος, Hsch.

ἰδιότης [ῐδ], ητος, ἡ, (ἴδιος) *peculiar nature, property, specific character*, Damox.2.41, Epicur.*Ep.*1 p.17 U.; ἡ ἰ. τῆς ἡδονῆς X.*An.*2.3. 16; τῶν πράξεων Pl.*Plt.*305d; τοῦ πολιτεύματος Plb.1.13.13, etc.; εἰκὼν τῆς ἰδίας ἰ. Lxx *Wi.*2.23; of a mountain, Agatharch.81: pl., *peculiarities*, Plb.9.22.7, Demetr.Lac.*Herc.*1012.41 F.; ἰ. ἐθνικαί, of language, Phld.*Rh.*1.154 S.; ῥυθμῶν Id.*Mus.*p.49 K. 2. Gramm., ἰδιότητός τινων μετέχειν D.T.639.31, cf. A.D.*Synt.*16.14, al.; εἰς ἰδιότητα *as a proper name*, St.Byz. s.v. Θεσσαλία, Sch.Il.18.319. 3. *particular existence*, Chrysipp.*Stoic.*2.126; *individuality*, ἀεὶ πρότερα τὰ ὀλίγης ἰδιότητος Dam.*Pr.*280. 4. *relationship*, *POxy.*1644.21 (i B.C.).

ἰδῐο-τοπέω [ῐδ], Astrol., *occupy a congenial position in the zodiac*,

Vett.Val.71.7: -τοπία, ἡ, ib.276.17. -τοπος, ον, *of their own district*, βασιλεῖς cj. in *Peripl.M.Rubr.*47. -τροπία, ἡ, *peculiar quality*, Cleom.2.4, Ptol.*Tetr.*1, Heph.Astr.1.20, etc. 2. *specific form* or *manner*, Simp. *in Ph.*1073.19; *peculiarity*, Dam.*Pr.*90; *idiosyncrasy*, ib.388. -τροπος, ον, *peculiar, distinctive*, ἑνότης, ἡδονή, Epicur. *Ep.*1 p.13 U., *Fr.*186; φύσις, νόσοι, D.S.3.35, 5.10; *of a peculiar species*, ὁ νυκτικόραξ Str.17.2.4. Adv. -πως D.S.3.19, Dam.*Pr.*40: Comp., Marcellin.*Puls.*506. -τρόφος, ον, *feeding individuals*, Pl.*Plt.*261d. II. ἰδιότροφος, ον, *feeding on a peculiar diet*, opp. παμφάγος, Arist.*HA*488^{a}15. -τῠπος, ον, *of a peculiar form*, Herm.ap.Stob.1.49.44. -φεγγής, ές, *self-shining*, of the moon, v.l. in *Placit.*2.28.4. -φυής, ές, *of peculiar nature*, ib.1.7.20; σάλπιγγες D.S.5.30; τὰ ἰ., title of work by Archelaus, D.L.2.17. -φῠτον, τό, = κῆμος, Ps.-Dsc.4.133. -χειρος, ον, *autographed*, ἀπογραφή Just.*Nov.*48.1 *Intr.*: Subst. -χειρον, τό, ib.49.2.1. -χρεος, ον, *carrying a personal obligation*, σύμβολα *Sammelb.*4638.15 (ii B.C.). -χροιος, ον, *of peculiar colour*, Ptol.*Tetr.*103 (v.l. -χρονος):—also -χρωμος, ον, *of natural colour, not dyed*, Artem.2.3, *BGU*327.6 (ii A.D.), *PHolm.*24.32, etc.

ἰδιόω, v. ἰδιόομαι.

ἴδῐσις [ῐδ], εως, ἡ, *sweating, perspiring*, Arist.*Pr.*965^{a}2.

ἰδίω [ῐδ], aor. 1 ἴδισα Arist.*HA*521^{a}14, Thphr.*Sud.*28: (ἶδος):—*sweat*, of the cold sweat of terror, ἴδιον, ὡς ἐνόησα Od.20.204; πρὶν ἂν ἰδίῃς καὶ διαλύσῃς ἄρθρων ἶνας Ar.*Pax*85, cf. *Ra.*237, Eub.53, Hp.*Mul.*1.38, Diocl.*Fr.*142; ἴδισαν αἱματώδη ἱδρῶτα Arist. l.c., cf. Thphr.*HP* 5.9.8; ἱδρόω is more common in Prose. [Second ι in pres. and impf. short in Ep., long in Att., in aor. always long.] (Perh. cogn. with Skt. *svidyati*, Lat. *sudo*, Engl. *sweat.*)

ἰδί-ωμα [ῐδῐ], ατος, τό, (ἰδιόω) *peculiarity, specific property, unique feature*, Epicur.*Ep.*1 p.25 U., *Stoic.*2.25, etc.; τὰ τῶν χρωμάτων ἰ. Epicur.*Ep.*2 p.51 U.; τῆς πολιτείας Plb.2.38.10; τοῦ νόμου *BGU*12.18 (ii A.D.); τὸ καθ' αὑτὸν ἰ. τηρεῖν Plb.2.59.2; τὰ περὶ τὴν χώραν, περὶ αὐτοὺς ἰ., Id.2.14.3, 6.3.3; τὸ ἐξαίρετόν τινος ἰ. A.D.*Synt.*15.19; ἀγαθότητος ἰ. Procl.*Inst.*133; ὕλης Id.*Theol.Pl.*5.35; *property*, φαρμάκου Heras ap.Gal.13.785, cf. Dsc.1.71; of the properties of numbers, *Theol.Ar.*5, al.; τὸ ἰ. τοῦ ἑνός Dam.*Pr.*5: *special subject*, τῆς πραγματείας Sor.1.126. II. *peculiarity of style*, D.H.*Amm.*2 tit., al. 2. *idiom*, ἰ. Ὁμηρικόν A.D.*Synt.*157.9. 3. *style*, παιανικὸν ἰ. Ath.15.696e. -ώνῠμος, ον, *appropriate*, προσηγορία Dam.*Pr.*40. -ωσις, εως, ἡ, *isolation*, opp. κοινωνία, Pl.*R.*462b; *appropriation*, Plu.2.644d.

ἰδιωτ-εία [ῐδ], ἡ, *private station*, opp. τυραννίς, X.*Hier.*8.1; opp. βασιλεία, Pl.*Lg.*696a: pl., opp. ἀρχαί, Id.*R.*618d; ἐν ἰ., opp. ἐν φιλοσοφίᾳ, Phld.*Rh.*2.277 S. II. *uncouthness, want of education*, Luc. *Hist.Conscr.*27, *Abd.*7. III. *defenceless condition*, τῆς ἰ. ἡμῶν καταφρονοῦντες *SIG*888.65 (Scaptopara, iii A.D.). -εύω, *occupy a private station*, opp. δημοσιεύω, Pl.*Ap.*32a, *R.*579c; opp. ἄρχω, X. *Hier.*8.5; opp. τυραννεύω, Isoc.2.4; opp. πολιτεύεσθαι, Aeschin.1.195; of a country, *to be of no consideration*, X.*Cyr.*8.7.7. II. *practise privately*, of a physician, opp. ὁ δημοσιεύων, Pl.*Plt.*259a, cf. *Grg.*514e sq. III. c. gen. rei, τῆς ἀρετῆς ἰ. *to be unpractised, unskilled in*.., Id.*Prt.*327a. IV. in Lit. Crit., *to be vulgar*, of expressions, Longin.31.2. -ης, ου, ὁ, (ἴδιος) *private person, individual*, opp. the State, ξυμφέροντα καὶ πόλεσι καὶ ἰδιώταις Th.1.124, cf. 3.10, *SIG*37.3 (Teos, v B.C.), Pl.*Smp.*185b, X.*Vect.*4.18, etc.; opp. γένος, *SIG*1013.6 (Chios, iv B.C.); opp. φατρία, ib.987.28 (ibid., iv B.C.). II. *one in a private station*, opp. to one holding public office, or taking part in public affairs, Hdt.1.59,123, al., cf. Decr. ap.And.1.84, Th.4.2, etc.; opp. βασιλεύς, Hdt.7.3; opp. ἄρχων, Lys.5.3, Pl.*Plt.*259b, *SIG*305.71 (iv B.C.); opp. δικαστής, Antipho 6.24; opp. πολιτευόμενος, D.10.70; opp. ῥήτωρ, Hyp.*Eux.*27; *private soldier*, opp. στρατηγός, X.*An.*1.3.11, cf. *PHib.*1.30.21 (iii B.C.); *layman*, opp. priest, *OGI*90.52 (Rosetta, ii B.C.), *PGnom.*200 (ii A.D.), 1*Ep.Cor.*14.16: as Adj., ἰ. ἄνδρες Hdt.1.32,70, Th.1.115; ἰ. θεοί *homely* (with play on ἴδιος), Ar.*Ra.*891. 2. *common man, plebeian*, οἱ ἰ. καὶ πένητες Plu.*Thes.*24; ἰ. καὶ εὐτελής, opp. βασιλεύς, Hdn.4.10.2. 3. as Adj., ἰ. βίος *private* station, Pl.*R.*578c; ἰ. λόγος *everyday* speech, D.H.*Dem.*2, cf. Longin.31.2. III. *one who has no professional knowledge, layman*, καὶ ἰατρὸς καὶ ἰ. Th.2.48, cf. Hp.*VM* 4, Pl.*Tht.*178c, *Lg.*933d; ἰ. ἤ τινα τέχνην ἔχων Id.*Sph.*221c; of prose-writers, ἐν μέτρῳ ὡς ποιητής, ἢ ἄνευ μέτρου ὡς ἰ. Id.*Phdr.*258d, cf. *Smp.*178b; ἰ. καὶ μηδὲν αὐλήσεως ἐπαΐων Id.*Prt.*327c; opp. to a professed orator, Isoc.4.11; to a trained soldier, X.*Eq.Mag.*8.1; ἰδιώτας, ὡς εἰπεῖν, χειροτέχναις (-νας codd.) ἀνταγωνισαμένους Th.6.72; opp. ἀσκητής, X.*Mem.*3.7.7, cf. 12.1; opp. ἀθλητής, Arist.*EN* 1116^{b}13; opp. a professed philosopher, Id.*Pol.*1266^{a}31, Phld.*Lib.* p.51 O., *D.*1.25; in Music, Id.*Mus.*p.42 K.; opp. δημιουργός, Pl.*Prt.*312a, *Thg.*124c: as Adj., ὁ ἰ. ὄχλος, opp. artificers, Plu.*Per.*12. 2. c. gen. rei, *unpractised, unskilled in* a thing, ἰατρικῆς Pl.*Prt.*345a, cf. *Ti.*20a; ἔργου X.*Oec.*3.9; ἰ. κατὰ τοὺς πόνους, κατὰ τὸν ὕπνον, Id.*Cyr.*1.5.11; ἰ. τὰ ἄλλα Hdn.4.12.1; ἰ. ὡς πρὸς ἡμᾶς ἀγωνίζεσθαι X.*Cyr.* l.c., cf. Luc.*Herm.*81. 3. generally, *raw hand, ignoramus*, ἄν τε δεινοὶ λάχωσιν ἄν τε ἰδιῶται.. D.4.35; παιδάρια καὶ ἰ., of slaves, S.E. *M.*1.234 (cf. ἰ. οἰκέται Luc.*Alex.*30); ἀμαθὴς καὶ ἰ., opp. τεχνίτης, Id.*Ind.*29; voc. ἰδιῶτα, as a term of abuse, Men.*Sam.*71. 4. '*average man*', opp. a person of distinction, Plu.2.1104a. IV. ἰδιῶται, οἱ, *one's own countrymen*, opp. ξένοι, Ar.*Ra.*459. -ίζω, *pronounce in the local manner*, Eust.145.10 (Pass.). -ικός, ή, όν, *of* or *for a private person, private*, σῖτος καὶ ἑωυτοῦ καὶ ἰ. Hdt.1.21; πύργος Id.4.164; opp. δημόσιος, ἱερά *SIG*1015.9 (Halic.); opp. κοινός, οἰκίαι ib.987.5 (Chios, iv B.C.); opp. βασιλικός, Pl.*Criti.*117b, cf. Isoc.9.72; ἰ. σύγγραμμα, opp. πολιτικόν, Pl.*Phdr.*258d; ἰ. τριήρεις, opp. the Paralos, D.21.174; οἰωνὸς οὐκ ἰ., i.e. indicating royalty, X.*An.*6.1.23; ἰ. τράπεζα *private* bank, *PLond.*3.1168.21 (i A.D.); δάνεια, opp. δημόσια, ib.932.8 (iii A.D.); συμβόλαια D.H.10.57; ἰ. λόγοι speeches *in private suits*, Id.*Dem.*56; καθαρὸς ἀπὸ δημοσίου ἢ ἰ. free from public or *private* encumbrance, *BGU*446.15 (ii A.D.); ἰ. κανών impost *on private land*, *POxy.*2124.10 (iv A.D.). II. *not done by rules of art, unprofessional, amateurish*, Pl.*Euthd.*282d; φαῦλον καὶ ἰ. Id.*Hp.Ma.*287a, *Ion* 532e; λέξις S.E.*M.*1.234; λήμματα Gal.5.213; of language, *commonplace, everyday*, τὸ ἰ. Arist.*Po.*1458^{a}21, 32, cf. D.L.10.13 (Sup.); but also, *vulgar*, Phld.*Po.*2.71, Longin.43.1. Adv., μὴ φαύλως μηδὲ -κῶς Pl.*Lg.*966e; ἰ. καὶ γελοίως Id. *Euthd.*278d; ἰ. ἔχειν Id.*Cra.*394a; ἰ. τὸ σῶμα ἔχειν, i.e. to neglect gymnastic exercises, Id.*Lg.*839e, X.*Mem.*3.12.1; also, *in a special way*, Phld.*D.*3.8. III. of persons, *unprofessional*, Apollon.Cit.3. IV. ἄρτοι ἰ. *common* bread, *UPZ*94.17 (ii B.C.). V. ἰ. βίος *cloistered* life, Marcellin.*Puls.*138. -ις, ιδος (nom. pl. -ώτιες *IG* 5(1).1390.17 (Andania, i B.C.)), ἡ, fem. of ἰδιώτης, J.*AJ*8.11.1; opp. φιλόσοφος, Muson.*Fr.*3 p.11 H.; ἰδιώτιες, opp. ἱεραί, *IG* l.c.; ἰ. πόλις, opp. ἡγεμονίς, App.*BC*4.16,95. II. *unskilled, uninstructed*, Luc. *Im.*13, Alciphro 2.4; ἰ. ἀκοαί *unlearned* ears, Dam.*Pr.*5. -ισμός, ὁ, *way* or *fashion of a common person*, Epict.*Ench.*33.6, S.E.*M.*1.67, Dam.*Isid.*223; in language, *homely, vulgar phrase*, Phld.*Po.*2.71, Longin.31.1, D.L.7.59. 2. Rhet., *argumentum ad hominem*, usu. in the form of a hypothetical question, Rufin.*Fig.*10.

ἰδιωφελής [ῐδ], ές, *of private benefit*, opp. κοινωφελής, νόμος Archyt. ap.Stob.4.1.138, cf. Alex.Aphr. *in Top.*234.16, Sch.Arr.*Epict.*4.10.12.

ἰδμάν, ᾶνος, ὁ, *one who knows*, Hdn.Gr.1.13: **ἰδμή**, ἡ, = ἰδμοσύνη, Hsch.

ἴδμεν, Ion., Aeol., Dor. for ἴσμεν: **ἴδμεν, ἴδμεναι**, Ep. for εἰδέναι; v. οἶδα.

ἰδμοσύνη, ἡ, *knowledge, skill*, *APl.*4.273 (Crin.): in pl., Hes.*Th.*377.

ἴδμων, ον, gen. ονος, (ἴδμεν, = εἰδέναι) *having knowledge of* a thing, εὐνομίης ἴ. πόλις *AP*7.575 (Leont.).

ἰδνόομαι, Pass., *bend oneself, double oneself up*, esp. for pain, ἰδνώθη Il.2.266; ἰδνώθη δὲ πεσών 13.618; ἰδνωθεὶς ὀπίσω, of a snake in the clutches of an eagle, 12.205; also, of one throwing up a ball perpendicularly, Od.8.375, cf. *APl.*4.97; of the womb, ἢν.. ἰδνωθῇ Hp. *Mul.*1.2; ἰδνοῦται ib.10:—Act., ἰδνῶ only in Hdn.Gr.1.451.

Ἰδογενής [ῑ], ές, *born on Ida*, Orac.ap.Paus.10.12.3.

ἶδοι· ὀφθαλμοί, Hsch.

ἰδομαλιάδαι, = οἱ τὰς ὄψεις κοσμούμενοι, Alc.150 (ap.Hsch.); v. εἰδομαλίδας.

ἶδος, εος, τό, *sweat*: pl., *sweats*, Hp.*Coac.*105 (s.v.l.). 2. *warmth*, Emp.62.5, prob. in Id.21.4; *violent heat*, Hes.*Sc.*397, Call. *Fr.*124 (prob.), D.P.966; cf. ἰδίω.

ἰδός· ὁδός, σῶμα, Hsch.

ἰδοῦ (ἴδου Hdn.Gr.ap.Choerob. *in Theod.*2.140), aor. 2 imper. Med. of ὁράω; but, II. **ἰδού** (on the accent v. Hdn.Gr.1.417, al.), as Adv., *lo! behold!* (even with words of hearing, ἰδοὺ δοῦπον αὖ κλύω τινά S.*Aj.*870 (lyr.), cf. *El.*1410): 1. with Nouns and Prons., ἰ. χελιδών Klein *Meistersign.*133 (Attic vase, vi B.C.), etc.; ἰ. ἐγώ *here am* I, Lxx *Ge.*27.1, al.; ἰ. ἡ μνᾶ σου *Ev.Luc.*19.20; οὐκ ἰ. Ἀαρών; Lxx *Ex.*4.14. 2. with Verbs, a. in the imper., ἰ. θεᾶσθε S.*Tr.*1079, Ar.*Ach.*366; esp. in offering a thing, *take it!* ἰ. δέχου παῖ S.*Ph.*776. b. in ind. of all tenses, ἰ. πείθομαι E.*Or.*143 (lyr.): freq. in Lxx and *NT* with past tenses, *Ge.*24.15, al., *Ev.Matt.*27.51, al.; in the middle of a sentence, *Ev.Luc.*13.16. 3. with questions, ἰ., τί ἔστιν; Ar.*Nu.*825, *Eq.*157. 4. in repeating another's words quizzingly, as ἰδού γ' ἄκρατον wine, *quotha!* ib.87; ἰ. λέγειν ib.344; ἰδού γε κλέπτειν Id. *Th.*206, cf. *Ec.*136.

ἰδρεία, Ion. -είη, ἡ, (ἴδρις) *knowledge, skill*, ἰδρείῃ πολέμοιο Il.16.359; οὐδέ τι ἰδρείῃ (Aristarch. for vulg. οὐδέ τ' ἀϊδρείῃ) 7.198, cf. A.R.2.72, Q.S.4.226, Theoc.22.85.

ἴδρ-ις, gen. ἴδριος, Att. ἴδρεως, ὁ, ἡ, neut. ἴδρι: voc. ἴδρι *AP*9.559 (Crin.), prob. in ib.6.182 (Alex. Magnes.): pl. ἴδριες; also ἴδριδα S.*Fr.*1056, ἴδριδες Phryn.Com.90 (= Phryn.Trag.22), cf. πολυ-ΐδριδι Sapph.166 (but these forms are censured by Hdn.Gr.2.40): (οἶδα):—poet. Adj. *experienced, knowing, skilful*, ἀνὴρ ἴδρις Od.6.233: c. inf., ἴδριες.. νῆα θοὴν ἐνὶ πόντῳ ἐλαυνέμεν 7.108: c. gen. rei, πόνου καὶ ὀϊζύος Hes.*Sc.*351; καλῶν Pi.*O.*1.104; ἔργων Archil.39, cf. A.*Ag.*446 (lyr.), S.*El.*608, *Ichn.*124, Call.*Jov.*74, etc.: in late Prose, ἴ. τῶν οὐρανίων Vett.Val.4.19: with Preps., κατὰ γνώμαν ἴδρις S.*OT*1087 (lyr.); οὐδὲν ἴδρις Id.*OC*525 (lyr.); ἐν πολέμοισι D.P.857. 2. as Subst., *the provident one*, i.e. *the ant*, Hes.*Op.*778. -ίτας, ου, ὁ, = ἴδρις, dub. l. in *AP*6.182 (Alex. Magnes.).

ἱδροσύνη, ἡ, *sweating, toil*, σώματος *IGRom.*4.607 (pl., Phrygia).

ἱδρόω [ῑ by nature, cf. ἀφίδρωσον *Com.Adesp.*3 D.], v. sub fin.: fut. -ώσω Il.2.388: aor. ἵδρωσα 4.27, X.*Cyr.*8.1.38: pf. ἵδρωκα Luc.*Merc. Cond.*26:—Pass., pf. ἵδρωται Id.*Herm.*2: (ἶδος):—*sweat, perspire*, esp. from toil, τὸν δ' ἱδρώοντα Il.18.372; ἵππους λῦσαν.. ἱδρώοντας Od.4.39; of a hunted deer, ἤϊξε... σπεύδουσ' ἱδρώουσα Il.11.119; ἱδρώσει.. τελαμὼν ἀμφὶ στήθεσφιν it *shall reek with sweat*, 2.388: c. acc. cogn., ἱδρῶ θ' ὃν ἵδρωσα μόγῳ 4.27; διὰ τί τὸ πρόσωπον μάλιστα ἱδροῦσιν; Arist.*Pr.*867^{b}34, cf. 866^{b}28.—The contr. forms (really from ἱδρώ-ω) have ω, ῳ for ου, οι (cf. ῥιγόω), fem. part. ἱδρῶσαι Il.11.598; 3 pl. ἱδρῶσι Thphr.*Sud.*36; opt. ἱδρῴη Hp.*Aër.*8: codd. of X.

vary between ἱδροῦντι and ἱδρῶντι, *HG*4.5.7, *Cyr.*1.4.28, but ἱδροῦντι *An.*1.8.1, ἱδροῦσι Arist. ll. cc.; ὡς ἂν ἱδρῶντες, corrupted to ὡσανεὶ δρῶντες, Ph.1.490: pres. ἱδρώω in Luc.*Syr.D.*10,17; Ep. part. ἱδρώουσα, -οντα (v. supr.), -οντας Ar.*Pax*1283 (hex.).

ἵδρ-ῡμα, ατος, τό, *establishment, foundation*, Ἰάσονος ἵ. Str.6.1.1, cf. Plu.*Marc.*20; Ποιῆσσαν Χαρίτων ἵ. Call.*Aet.*3.1.73. 2. *temple, shrine*, θεῶν Hdt.8.144, A.*Ag.*339, cf.*Ch.*1036, E.*Ba.*951, Pl.*Lg.*717b, etc.; *statue*, δαιμόνων ἵ. A.*Pers.*811, cf. Arr.*Epict.*2.22.17. 3. τὸ σὸν ἵ. πόλεως the *stay, support* of thy city, of chieftains, E.*Supp.*631 (lyr.). [ἵδρῠμα Call. l. c. (s. v.l.); ῑ by nature, Lyc.1032.] **-ῡσις**, εως, ἡ, *founding, foundation*, esp. of temples, ἱερῶν -σεις Pl.*R.*427b, cf. *IG*2².337 (iv B.C.): abs., Pl.*Lg.*909e; ἵ. ξοάνων *setting up* of statues, D.H.2.18; πόλεως ἵδρυσιν λαμβανούσης Plu.*Rom.*9. 2. Ἑρμέω ἱδρύσιες *statues* of Hermes, *AP*6.253 (Crin.). II. *settlement, abode*, Str.8.7.1, Plu.2.408a: metaph., οὐκ ἔχειν ἵ. ib.651d, etc. [ῠ only in later Poets, *AP* l. c.] **-ῡτέον**, *one must set up*, of a statue, Ar. *Pax*923, Max.Tyr.8 tit. II. intr., οὐχ ἱ. *one must* not *sit idle*, S.*Aj.* 809. **-ύω**, fut. -ύσω (καθ-) E.*Ba.*1339: aor. ἵδρῡσα Il.15.142, E. *Ba.*1070: pf. ἵδρῡκα (καθ-) Arist.*PA*665ᵇ20:—Med., fut. -ύσομαι E. *Heracl.*397, Ar.*Pl.*1198: aor. ἱδρῡσάμην Hdt.6.105, Anacr.104, Ar. *Pl.*1153:—Pass., fut. ἱδρυθήσομαι D.H.*Comp.*6: aor. ἱδρύθην Ar.*Fr.* 245, etc.; freq. written ἱδρύνθην in codd., as Il.3.78, Hp.*Coac.*309, A.R.3.1269: pf. ἵδρῡμαι, used both in pass. and med. sense (v. sub fin.). [ῐ by nature, E.*Ba.*1070, Ar.*Fr.*26 D., etc., but freq. lengthd. by position, E.*Hipp.*639, Ar.*Pl.*1153, etc.: ῠ by nature, even in ἱδρύεται E.*Heracl.*786; but ἵδρῠε Il.2.191; καθίδρῠε Od.20.257: ῡ in fut. and aor. 1, exc. in late Poets, as *AP*7.109 (ἐν-, ⟨D. L.⟩), Man.3. 80 (dub.), *Arch.Pap.*2.570, Nonn.*D.*4.22: pf. Pass. ἵδρῡμαι A.*Supp.* 413, E.*Heracl.*19, *Hel.*820, Theoc.17.21, etc.:—*make to sit down, seat*, αὐτός τε κάθησο καὶ ἄλλους ἵδρυε λαούς Il.2.191; ἵδρυσε θρόνῳ ἔνι θοῦρον Ἄρηα 15.142, cf. Od.3.37; ἱ. τινὰ εἰς θρόνους E.*Ion*1573; ὄζων ἔπι Id. *Ba.*1070; ἵδρυσε τὴν στρατιὴν ἐπὶ ποταμῷ *encamped* the army, Hdt. 4.124, cf. Th.4.104:—Pass., *to be seated, sit still*, τοὶ δ' ἱδρύνθησαν ἅπαντες Il.3.78; κατ' οἶκον ἵδρυται γυνή E.*Hipp.*639; of an army, *lie encamped*, Hdt.4.203, al., Th.7.77, al.; Πελοπόννησος ἀσφαλέως ἱδρυμένη *secure*, Hdt.6.86.α'; ἐν θεῶν ἕδραισιν ὧδ' ἱδρυμένας A.*Supp.*413; ἡ στρατιὰ βεβαίως ἔδοξεν ἱδρῦσθαι seemed *to have got a firm footing*, Th. 8.40; ἱ. ἐπὶ τῶν ἵππων Ael.*Tact.*2.4. 2. *settle* persons in a place, εἰς τόνδε δόμον E.*Alc.*841; ἐν τοῖς ἀστοῖσιν Ἄρη ἐμφύλιον ἱ. *to give a footing to*, i. e. *excite*, intestine war, A.*Eu.*862; ἱ. πολλοὺς ἐν πόλει Plu.*Pomp.* 28:—Pass., *to be settled*, Hdt.8.73; ποῦ κλύεις νιν ἱδρῦσθαι χθονός; S. *Tr.*68; ἐς Κολωνὰς ἱδρυθεὶς Th.1.131; μεταξὺ φρενῶν ὀμφαλοῦ τε ἱδρῦσθαι Pl.*Ti.*77b; of local diseases, πόνος ἐς στῆθος ἱδρυνθεὶς Hp.*Coac.* 309; τὸ ἐν κεφαλῇ.. ἱδρυθὲν κακόν Th.2.49. 3. Med., *establish*, τινὰ ἄνακτα γῆς E.*Ph.*1008; τινὰ ἐς οἶκόν τινος Id.*Hel.*46; ἱδρύσασθαι τοὺς βίους *to choose settled* modes of life, D.H.1.68; ἱ. οἴκησιν Pl. *Smp.*195e. 4. pf. Pass. ἵδρυμαι, of places, *to be situated, lie*, of a city, Hdt.2.59, cf. A.*Pers.*231, Pl.*Lg.*745b. 5. Pass., *settle down, become quiet*, Hp.*Epid.*3.17.ιε'. II. *set up, found*, esp. in Med., *dedicate* temples, statues, etc., Anacr.104, Simon.140, etc.; Πανὸς ἱρὸν Hdt.6.105, cf. 1.105, al.; βρέτας E.*IT*1453; βωμούς Pl.*Prt.*322a, al.; ἱδρύσασθαι [Ἑρμῆν] *set up a statue of* H., Ar.*Pl.*1153; Εἰρήνην Id. *Pax*1091: also c. dat., τὴν δαίμον' ἣν ἀνήγαγον ἐς τὴν ἀγορὰν ἄγων ἱδρύσωμαι βοΐ Id.*Fr.*26 D.:—Pass., ἐξ οὗ τὸ ἱρὸν ἵδρυται Hdt.2.44, cf. 1.172; βωμὸς -ύθη Ar.*Fr.*245; [Πλοῦτος] -υμένος Id.*Pl.*1192; at Athens, ἥρωες κατὰ πόλιν ἱδρυμένοι the heroes *who had statues erected to them*, Lycurg.1: pf. Pass. in med. sense, Hdt.2.42, Men.202.

ἵδρωα or **ἱδρῶα**, τά, (ἱδρώς) *heat-spots, pustules*, Hp.*Aph.*3.21, cf. Gal. ad loc. II. v. ἱδρώιον.

ἱδρ-ώδης, ες, *accompanied by perspiration*, Hp.*Epid.*5.73, 7.51. **-ώεις**, εσσα, εν, *causing sweat*, πόνος B.12.57. **-ώιον** or **-ῷον**, τό, *cloth for wiping perspiration*, as a piece of harness, *PLond. ined.*2383 *B* (iii B.C.), *PSI*5.527 (iii B.C.), dub. in *PTeb.*116.34 (ii B.C.). **-ώς** (v. fin.), ῶτος, ὁ, and Aeol. ἡ, Sapph.2.13; dat. ἱδρῶτι, acc. ἱδρῶτα; Hom. has dat. ἱδρῷ (not ἱδρῷ as Choerob. *in Theod.*1.248) Il.17.385,745; acc. ἱδρῶ 11.621, 22.2, cf. A.R.2.87, 4.656: (ἴδος):— *sweat*, Hom. (v. infr.), etc.; μετὰ ἱδρῶτος Pl.*R.*350d; κατὰ δ' ἱ. ἔρρεεν ἐκ μελέων Od.11.599; ἱ. ἀνήει χρωτί S.*Tr.*767; στάζειν ἱδρῶτι (v. στάζω); ῥέεσθαι ἱδρῶτι Plu.*Cor.*3; of *sweat* as the sign of toil, τῆς ἀρετῆς ἱδρῶτα θεοὶ προπάροιθεν ἔθηκαν Hes.*Op.*289; ἱδρῶτα παρέχειν X.*Cyr.*2.1.29: pl., Hp.*Aph.*4.36, Arist.*Pr.*867ᵃ13, etc.; ἱδρῶτες ξηροί, opp. the effect of baths, Pl.*Phdr.*239c. 2. *exudation* of trees, *gum, resin*, σμύρνης E.*Ion*1175; δρυὸς Ion Trag.40; Βρομιάδος ἱδρῶτα πηγῆς, of wine, Antiph.52.12. II. metaph., *anything earned by the sweat of one's brow*, οὐ γὰρ τὸν ἐμὸν ἱδρῶτα.. ἐκβαλῶ Ar.*Ec.*750, cf. Chor.p.270 B. (pl.). [ῑ in Ep. and Lyr.: ῐ in E. l. c.] (Cf. ἰδίω.) **-ωσις**, εως, ἡ, *sweating*, Philostr.Jun.*Im.*11 (s. v.l.), Olymp. *in Mete.*103.5. **-ώσσω**, Att. **-ττω**, = ἱδρόω, Gal.16.778, Sch.Ar.*Ra.*238. **-ωτάρια**, τά, = ἵδρωα, Orib.*Fr.*117. **-ωτήριον**, τό, *sudatorium*, *Gloss.*: pl., *sudorifics*, Paul.Aeg.3.74. **-ωτίδες**, αἱ, = ἵδρωα, Steph. *in Hp.*2. 370 D. **-ωτικός**, ή, όν, *sudorific*, Hp.*Vict.*3.72, Orib.2.58.78; δύναμις Gal.11.711. II. *apt to perspire*, Thphr.*Sud.*36, Gal.14.290 (Comp.). Adv. Comp. -κωτέρως, διακεῖσθαι Arist.*Pr.*870ᵇ7. **-ώτιον**, τό, Dim. of ἱδρώς, Hp.*Epid.*7.5. **-ωτοειδῶς**, Adv. *after the manner of sweat*, κενοῦσθαι Steph. *in Hp.*1.112 D.

ἱδρωτοποι-έω, *induce perspiration*, Orib.*Fr.*128:—Pass., *to be made to perspire*, Arist.*Pr.*870ᵇ31: hence **-ποιΐα**, ἡ, ib.38 (pl.), Philum.*Ven.*4.9, Paul.Aeg.5.3. **-ός**, όν, *sudorific*, Dsc.3.68, Philum.ap.Aët.9.12.

ἰδύβολαι· προφαίνεται, Hsch.

ἰδυῖα [ῐ], ἡ, Ep. for εἰδυῖα, part. fem. of οἶδα; v. εἴδω.

ἴδυιοι, Att. **ἴδυοι**, = συνίστορες, μάρτυρες, Lex Solon.ap.Ar.*Fr.*222, Paus.Gr.*Fr.*151; = οἱ τὰς φονικὰς δίκας κρίνοντες, Hsch.; cf. βιδιαῖοι.

ἰδύλευμα· μάθημα, Hsch. **ἰδυλιτρίχες**, sine expl., Id. **ἰδυναγής**· μάντις, Id. **ἴδυξ**, υκος, ὁ, = ἴκτις, Alex.Mynd.ap.Hdn.Gr. 1.44.

ἰέ, shortd. form of ἰή, in Paeans, Aristonous 1.4, al., Isyll.37, al., cf. Ephor.31(*b*) J.

ἴε, ἴεν, Ep. 3 sg. impf. of εἶμι (*ibo*); also as imper., Hsch. **ἵει**, Ion. and Att. 3 sg. impf. of ἵημι. **ἱείας**· τὰς κυρίας, οἰκογενεῖς, Hsch. **ἰείη**, Ep. for ἴοι, 3 sg. pres. opt. of εἶμι (*ibo*). **ἴελος**, = ἴλεος (i.e. εἰλ-), Id. **ἱέμεν, ἱέμεναι**, Ep. pres. inf. of ἵημι: **ἱέμενος**, pres. part. Pass.:—hence Adv. **ἱεμένως**, *eagerly*, Sch.A.R.3. 890. **ἴεν**, Ep. 3 pl. impf. of ἵημι.

ἱερά, ἡ, a kind of *serpent*, v.l. for ἱερόν, Arist.*HA*607ᵃ31. II. a name for many medicines in the Greek pharmacopoeia, Gal.13. 126, al.; of a plaster, ib.778; esp. of aloes, Id.6.354; ἱερὰ πικρά Id. 13.129. III. v. ἱερός.

ἱερ-άγγελος, ὁ, *one who proclaims a festival*, Hsch. **-ᾱγέω**, *carry offerings*, *Sammelb.*6753a (iii B.C.). **-ᾱγωγός**, όν, *carrying offerings*, μύσται Hedyl.ap.Ath.11.497d; ναῦς Plb.31.12.11; ἄνδρες D.H.16.3: as Subst., *Inscr.Délos* 291ᵇ8 (iii B.C.), *IG*12(1).1035 (Carpathos), 12(8).190.45 (Samothrace). **-άζω**, *serve as priest*, τοῖς Διοσκόροις ib.12(5).129.56 (Paros); τῷ Ἀσκληπιῷ *SIG*²588.43 (Delos, ii B.C.): also c. gen., τοῦ Ἀσκλ. ib.45: abs., *IG*12(7).237. 27 (Amorgos):—Boeot. **ἱαρειάδδω** ib.7.3169 (Orchom.): aor. part. ἱαρειάξασα ib.1816.2 (Leuctra, iv/iii B.C.), 2876.3 (Coronea, ii B.C.), *BCH*50.409, al. (Thespiae); ἱερεάξασα ib.26.292 (ibid.).

ἱερᾱκ-άριος [ῐε], ὁ, = ἱερακοτρόφος, *Cat.Cod.Astr.*8(4).217. **-εῖον**, τό, *shrine of the hawk*, *PTeb.*5.70 (ii B.C.). **-ειος**, α, ον, *of a hawk*, πρόσωπον Porph.ap.Eus.*PE*3.12. **-ία** βοτάνη, = ἱεράκιον 1, Horap.1.6. **-ιάς**, άδος, ἡ, = foreg., Alex.Trall.2. **-ιδεύς**, έως, ὁ, *young hawk, eyass*, Eust.753.56. **-ίδιον**, τό, *statuette of a hawk*, Roussel *Cultes Égyptiens* 219 (Delos, ii B.C.). **-ίζω**, *behave like a hawk*, Thphr.*Sign.*16, Arist.*Fr.*253. **-ιον**, τό, *hawk-weed*: ἱ. τὸ μέγα, = *Urospermum picroides*, ἱ. τὸ μικρόν, = *Hymenonema graecum*, Ps.-Dsc.3.64. II. *a compound eyesalve*, Gal.12.783. **-ίσκος**, ὁ, Dim. of ἱέραξ, Ar.*Av.*1112. **-ιστί**, Adv. *in hawks' language*, *PMag.Leid.W.*2.42. **-ίτης** [ῑτ], ου, ὁ, *stone of the colour of a hawk's neck*, Plin.*HN*37.167, Gal.12.207, *PMag.Par.*2.221. II. = ἱεράκιον 1, ib.1.901.

ἱερᾱκο-βοσκός, ὁ, *hawk-feeder, falconer*, *PPetr.*3 p.239 (iii B.C.), Ael.*NA*7.9. **-κτόνος**, ον, *hawk-killing*, Hsch. s.v. φαβοκτόνος. **-μορφος**, ον, *hawk-shaped*, of the Egyptian god Phrê (the Sun), represented with a hawk's head, Ph.Bybl.ap.Eus.*PE*1.10, Horap.1.6, S.E.*P.*3.219, *PMag.Leid.W.*9.43. **-πόδιον**, τό, = λυχνὶς ἀγρία, Ps.-Dsc.3.101. **-πρόσωπος**, ον, *hawk-faced*, *PMag. Leid.W.*1.39, Porph.ap.Eus.*PE*3.12. **-τάφος** [ᾰ], ὁ, *one who buries sacred hawks*, *PStrassb.*91.5 (i B.C.), etc. **-τρόφος**, ον, = ἱερακοβοσκός, *Cat.Cod.Astr.*7.118, al. II. *pupil of Hierax*, Eun.*Hist.* p.268 D.

ἱερᾱκώδης, ες, *hawk-like*, Eun.*Hist.*p.206 D.

ἱεράμοιβοι· προφῆται θεῶν, Hsch.

ἱερανθεσία, ἡ, only Dor. **ἱαρ-**, *dedication*, i.e. *manumission*, *IG*9 (1).193.31, al.

ἱερᾱνομέω, *hold office as commissioner of sacred rites*, *Mon.Ant.*23. 179 (Iotape).

ἱέραξ [ῐ], ᾱκος, ὁ, Ion. and Ep. **ἴρηξ** [ῑ], ηκος (the longer form first in Alcm.28, E.*Andr.*1141, Ps.-Orac.ap.Ar.*Eq.*1052):—*hawk, falcon*, ἴρηξ ὠκύπτερος Il.13.62, cf. 819, Od.13.86, Hes.*Op.*212, Hdt.2.65, Arist.*HA*620ᵃ17; sacred to Apollo, Ar.*Av.*516. II. a kind of *fish*, Epich.68 (in Dor. form **ἱάραξ**), Epaenet.ap.Ath.7.329a. III. name for a grade of initiates in Mithras-worship, Porph.*Abst.*4. 16. IV. name of a *bandage*, Sor.*Fasc.*12.

ἱεράοιδός, ὁ, *sacred bard*, Hsch.

ἱεράομαι, Ion. **ἱρ-**, fut. -άσομαι [ᾱ] J.*AJ*4.2.3; Ion. -ήσομαι *SIG* 1003 (Priene, ii B.C.): aor. -ησάμην ib.708.34 (Istropolis, ii B.C.); pf. part. ἱερημένος ib.5:—**Pass.**, aor. 1 part. ἱεραθεῖσα *Philol.*71.41 (Delph.):—*to be a priest or priestess*, θεοῦ Hdt.2.35, cf. *SIG*1037.4 (Milet., iv/iii B.C.), al.; θεᾶς D.H.2.19; θεῷ Paus.6.11.2, cf. *Philol.* l. c.: abs., Th.2.2, Ph.2.157, al.; c. acc. cogn., ἱερωσύνην ἱεράσασθαι Aeschin.1.19 (v. l. ἱερώσασθαι): freq. in Inscrr., ἱερασάμενος τῇ πατρίδι *CIG*4069 (Ancyra), etc.; cf. ἱερόω.

ἱερᾱ-πολέω, *to be a* ἱεραπόλος, *IG*4.1444, 1536; of a woman, Ἀρχ. Δελτ.2.app.49 (Palaerus). **-πόλος**, ὁ, (πέλλω) *chief priest*, Pi. *Parth.*1.6, *IG*14.256 (Gela), 5(1).29 (Sparta): **ἱερηπόλος** *TAM*2(1). 174 *E*9 (Sidyma).

ἱεράρχης, ου, ὁ, *president of sacred rites, high-priest*, *IG*7.303 (Oropus), 9(1).32 (Stiris): Boeot. **ἱᾰράρχᾱς** *Schwyzer*515.4, al.:—hence Boeot. **ἱαραρχίω**, *to be high-priest*, ib.544.4.

ἱερᾱτ-εία, ἡ, *priesthood*, Arist.*Pol.*1328ᵇ13, *OGI*90.52 (Rosetta, ii B.C.), Lxx *Ex.*29.9, *Ev.Luc.*1.9, *IG*5(2).516 (Lycosura, i A.D.), etc.: Ion. **ἱρητήη** *Schwyzer*692 (Chios, v B.C.); later **ἱερητείη** and **-α** *GDI* iv pp.885-6 (Erythrae, iv B.C), *SIG*1014.14 (ibid., iii B.C.), 1015.5 (Halic.). **-εῖον**, τό, *a sanctuary*, Procop.*Aed.*1.4. **-ευμα**, ατος, τό, *priesthood*, Lxx *Ex.*19.6, 1*Ep.Pet.*2.9. 2. *body of priests*, ib. 5. **-εύω**, Ion. **ἱερητ-** *GDI*5394 (later also in Northern Greece, Boeot., *IG*7.3097 (perh. i B.C.); Phoc., ib.9(1).32.40 (Stiris, ii B.C.), al.; Thess., ib.9(2).333 (i A.D.), cf. *SIG*²588.110 (Delos, ii B.C.); Lesb. **ἰρητεύω** *IG*12(2).527.45):—*to be priest* or *priestess*, θεῶν *OGI* 90.51 (Rosetta, ii B.C.); Καίσαρος prob. ib.767.4 (Cyrene); τοῦ Διὸς τοῦ Σωτῆρος *IG*7.2727 (Acraeph., i B.C.); τᾷ Ἀθάνᾳ ib.9(1).65 (Daulis), cf. Hdn.5.6.3: abs., *SIG*1044.19 (Halic., iv/iii B.C.), al., Lxx *Ex.* 28.1, *Ev.Luc.*1.8:—also **-εύομαι**, *IGRom.*4.539 (Cotiaeum). II. Pass., *to be made holy*, Zos.Alch.p.108 B. **-ικός**, ή, όν, *priestly*, *sacerdotal*, θυσίαι Arist.*Pol.*1285ᵇ10; ὑπομνήματα Plu.*Marc.*5; στέφανος, ἁγιστεῖαι, Id.2.34e, 729a; ὀνόματα Luc.*Philops.*12; λόγος Ptol.*Tetr.* 87 (-ατητικός codd.); βίος Jul.*Ep.*89b; ἡ ἱ. (sc. τέχνη), = ἱερατεία, Pl.*Plt.*290d; οἱ ἱ. the *priestly caste*, Hld.7.11, cf. Dam.*Pr.*399. Adv. **-κῶς** *in a sacerdotal sense*, ib.256; ἱ. ζῆν *as a priest should*, Jul. l.c.; σεμνῶς καὶ ἱ. κρίνειν δίκας Just.*Nov.*79.1. 2. ἱ. βύβλος, χάρτης, name of a kind of papyrus, Str.17.1.15, *PMag.Par.*1.2105; κόλλημα, πιττάκιον, made of this material, ib.2068, 3142. II. *devoted to sacred purposes*, τὰ ἱ. the *sacred fund*, *IGRom.*3.1137 (Syria, iii A.D.). III. **-ικόν**, τό, name of a *plaster*, Gal.13.183.

ἱεραύλης, ου, ὁ, *flute-player at sacrifices*, *IG*3.1041.19, 1048.14, al.

ἱερᾱφορία, ἡ, *bearing of holy vessels*, D.H.16.3.

ἱερᾱφόρος, ὁ, *bearer of holy vessels*, Plu.2.352b, *SIG*²754 (Pergam.): **ἱεροφόρος**, *IG*9(1).486.16 (ii/i B.C.), Ptol.*Tetr.*181.

ἱέρεια, ἡ, Ion. **ἱρείη**, as v.l. in Hdt.5.72, 8.104: scanned -εῐα in Trag., S.*Fr.*456, E.*Or.*261 (with v.l. ἱερίαι), *Ba.*1114, and perh. to be written **ἱερέα**, as in *IG*1².4.13, 843*a*3, etc., and prob. in Pi.*P.*4.5: Ep. **ἱερέη** Call.*Ep.*41: **ἱερῆ**, *Schwyzer*725 (Milet., vi B.C.), *GDI*5562 (Panticapaeum), 5584 (Priene), al.: **ἱαρέα** or **ἰάρεα** (pl. ἰάρεαι) ib. 4847: **ἰάρεια** dub. in *IG*7.2465 (Thebes):—fem. of ἱερεύς, *a priestess*, τὴν.. ἔθηκαν Ἀθηναίης ἱέρειαν Il.6.300, al., cf. Ar.*Th.*758, Th.4.133, Pl.*Phdr.*244b, al., *BCH*6.24 (Delos, ii B.C.), etc.

ἱερεία, ἡ, (ἱερεύω) *sacrifice, festival*, Lxx 4*Ki.*10.20. II. = ἱερατεία, *CIG*3491.23 (Thyatira). III. Cypr. ἰερηϝίjα, *sanctuary*, τᾶς Ἀθάνας *Inscr.Cypr.*135.20 H. (v B.C.).

ἱερειάζω, v. ἱεράζω.

ἱερεῖον, τό, Ion. **ἱερήϊον** or **ἱρήϊον** (the former in Hom. (pl. written ἱερήια *SIG*57.14 (Milet., v B.C.)), the latter in Hdt.), Dor. **ἰαρήϊον** *Berl.Sitzb.*1927.159 (Cyrene), prob. in *Leg.Gort.*10.38:—*victim, animal for sacrifice*, ἱρεύειν ἱερήϊον Od.14.94; ἱερήϊα πολλὰ παρεῖχον ib.250; ἐπεὶ οὐχ ἱ. οὐδὲ βοείην ἀρνύσθην Il.22.159 (prov. for 'no trifling stake', Cic.*Att.*1.1.4), cf. Hdt.1.132, 6.57, Ar.*Lys.*84, *Pax* 1091, And.1.126; opp. (ἁγνὰ) θύματα, Th.1.126; ἱερεῖον καὶ ἱερά *Test.Epict.*5.35; freq. of sheep, *OGI*214.62 (Didyma, iii B.C.), *IPE*1².76 (Olbia, perh. iv B.C.); of pigs, *PCair.Zen.*161 (iii B.C.). 2. in Od.11.23 (pl.), *offering for the dead*, for which, acc. to Sch., τόμιον or ἔντομον was more correct. II. *cattle slaughtered for food*, Hp.*Aff.*52, Mnesith.ap.Orib. 2.68.6: in pl., X.*Cyr.*1.4.17; of sucking-pigs, Gal.1.578, 10.489.

ἱερειτεύω, later spelling of ἱεριτεύω. II. Thess. spelling of ἱερητεύω, *Schwyzer*616ᵃ (Phalanna).

ἱερεῖτις, v. ἱερῖτις. **ἱερεόομαι**, v. ἱερόω.

ἱερ-εύς [ῐ], έως, Ion. **-ῆος**, Cypr. **-ῆϝος** *Inscr.Cypr.*59 H., ὁ, Att. pl. ἱερῆς: gen. sg. and pl. written ἱερέως, ἱερέων, *PStrassb.*83.2, 9 (ii B.C.):—Ion. nom. **ἱρεύς** Il.5.10, 16.604, Od.9.198: Dor. **ἰᾱρεύς** *IG* 4.1182, al. (gen. ἰαρέος ib.1580); acc. pl. τὸς ἰαρές *Schwyzer*236 (Cyrene); nom. pl. οἱ ἰαρές ibid.; nom. sg. ἰαρές *GDI*4846 (Cyrene):—also **ἱέρεως** (Att. and proparox. acc. to Choerob. *in Theod.*1.253) *SIG*1037.4 (Milet., iv/iii B.C.); gen. ἱέρεω *IPE*1².32 *A* 23, al. (Olbia, iii B.C.); dat. Ἱρέῳ *Schwyzer*692 (Chios, v B.C.); acc. ἱέρεω *Milet.* 1(7).203 *b* 3 (ii B.C.): **ἱερής** *IG*5(2).115.1 (Tegea, iv/iii B.C.), cf. *Inscr. Cypr.*100 H.:—Arc. **ἰαρής** *IG*5(2).13.10 (iii B.C.): acc. ἱερήν ib.3.1 (Tegea, iv B.C.): (ἱερός):—*priest, sacrificer, diviner*, Il.1.62, 16.604, Pi.*P.*2.17, Hdt.2.2, And.1.124, etc.; ἐφ' ἱερέως, as a date, *SIG*332.1 (Potidaea, iv/iii B.C.), etc. (freq. unaspirated, ἐπ' ἱερέως *IG*12(1). 890, etc. (Rhodes)); of the Jewish High Priest, D.S.34/5.1; ἱ. ὁ μέγας Lxx *Le.*21.10, Ph.2.591; ἱ. ὁ χριστός Lxx *Le.*4.5; at Rome, = *pontifex*, *Mon.Anc.Gr.*6.9; ἱ. ὁ μέγιστος, = *pont. maximus*, D.S.27. 2. 2. metaph., ἱ. τις ἄτας *a minister* of woe, A.*Ag.*735 (lyr.); comically, λεπτοτάτων λήρων ἱερεῦ Ar.*Nu.*359; ἱ. Διονύσου, of a winebibber, Eup.19; ἱ. φιλοσοφίας Lib.*Or.*52.42. **-εύσιμος**, ον, *fit for sacrifice*, Plu.2.729d. **-ευσις**, εως, ἡ, *slaying, sacrificing*, Sch.E.*Hec.* 224. **-ευτικός**, ή, όν, *belonging to a* ἱερόν, [γῆ] *PTeb.*5.236 (ii B.C.): **-κά**, τά, ib.257. **-εύω**, Ion. **ἱρεύω** Od.14.94, al.; Ion. impf. ἱρεύεσκον 20.3: 3 sg. plpf. Pass. ἱέρευτο Il.24.125: (ἱερός):—*sacrifice*, βοῦς.. ἧνις ἠκέστας ἱερευσέμεν 6.94; ταύρους [ποταμῷ] 21.131; τοῖσι δὲ βοῦν ἱέρευσε... Ζηνί Od.13.24, etc.: abs., *offer sacrifice*, τῇ θεῷ Ant. Lib.20.2. 2. *slaughter* for a feast, βοῦς ἱερεύοντες... εἰλαπινάζουσιν Od.2.56; ἄξεθ' ὑῶν τὸν ἄριστον, ἵνα ξείνῳ ἱερεύσω 14.414, cf. 8.59; also δεῖπνον δ' αἶψα συῶν ἱερεύσατε ὅς τις ἄριστος 24.215:—Med., βοῦς ἱρεύσασθαι oxen *to slaughter for themselves*, 19.198; μῆλα A.R.2. 302. 3. *consecrate, devote to* a god, ἱερευομένη παρθένος Paus.3.18. 4. 4. *sacrifice*, i.e. *slay*, Ph.2.34, Procop.*Goth.*2.25.

ἱερεωσύνη, v. ἱερωσύνη.

ἱερή, ἡ, = ἱέρεια, *AP*7.733 (Diotim., nisi leg. ἱερῆ): Att. **ἱερά** Pl. ap.*AB*100.

ἱερήϊον, τό, Ion. for ἱερεῖον, Hom.

ἱερηΐς, ΐδος, ἡ, poet. for ἱέρεια, *IG*7.113 (Megara).

ἱερής, v. ἱερεύς. **ἱερητεία, ἱερητεύω**, Ion. for ἱερᾱτ-. **ἱερία**, Ion. **-ίη**, v. ἱέρεια.

ἱερ-ίζω, *consecrate, purify*, Hsch. s. v. ἁγνίτης. **-ίς**, ίδος, ἡ, = ἱέρεια, *priestess*, dub. in Plu.2.435b. **-ισμός**, ὁ, *sacred service*, εἰς -ισμόν *Inscr.Délos*338 *Aa*19 (iii B.C.), *BCH*6.23 (Delos, ii B.C.). **-ισσα**, ἡ, = ἱέρεια, *PStrassb.*84.14 (ii B.C.), *BGU*994 ii 8, *PLond.*3.880.7 (ii B.C.), *CIG*4009*b* (Iconium). **-ιστής**, οῦ, ὁ, *one who presides at* σπονδαί, *IG*11(2).145 (iv B.C.), 161 *A* 88 (iii B.C.), cf. Hsch. s. v. ἁγνίτης (prob.). **-ῖτεύω**, *serve as priest*, τᾷ Δάματρι *IG* 5(2).266 (Mantinea, i B.C.): Dor. **ἰᾱριτεύω** *GDI*5117 (Crete, iv/iii B.C.), 4841 (Cyrene): pf. part. ἰαριτευκότες *Abh.Berl.Akad.*1925 (5).7 (ibid.): later **ἱερειτεύω** *GDI*4842 (ibid.). **-ῖτις**, ιδος, ἡ, = ἱκέτις, A.*Fr.*93 ap.Hsch. (-είτην cod., cf. Theognost.*Can.*45).

ἱερο-βόαι, οἱ, dub. l. in Hsch. s. v. ἄφετοι. **-βοτάνη** [ᾰ], ἡ, = ἱερὰ βοτάνη (cf. βοτάνη), Isid.*Etym.*17.9.55.

ἱερογλῠφ-έω, *represent hieroglyphically*, ζῴδια Eust.632.52; ὀρίγανον Horap.2.34. **-ικός**, ή, όν, *hieroglyphic*: ἱερογλυφικά, with or without γράμματα, τά, D.S.3.4, Plu.2.354f, Ps.-Luc.*Philopatr.*21, Dam.*Isid.*98, etc. Adv. **-κῶς** *PMag.Leid.V.*8.29: **-ιστί**, *in hieroglyphic characters*, *PMag.Leid.W.*2.37, al. **-ος**, ὁ, *carver of hieroglyphics*, *UPZ*81 iv 2 (ii B.C.), *POxy.*1029 (ii A.D.), *Sammelb.*3570 (Fayûm), Ptol.*Tetr.*180.

ἱερο-γλωσσόκομον, Dor. **ἰᾱρο-**, τό, *sacred deed-box*, *Hermes*64.64 (Epid., ii A.D.). **-γλωσσος**, ον, *of prophetic tongue*, Epigr.ap.Paus.6. 17.6: **-γλωσσον**, τό, *sacred formula*, *PMag.Berol.*2.69. **-γραμμᾰτεύς**, έως, ὁ, *sacred scribe*, a lower order of the Egyptian priesthood, Eudox. *Ars* 3.21, *OGI*56.4 (Canopus, iii B.C.), 90.7 (Rosetta, ii B.C.), Luc. *Macr.*4, J.*Ap.*1.32, al., Heras ap.Gal.13.776, Aët.15.13, etc. **-γρᾰφικός**, ή, όν, γράμματα *sacred* signs, Man.Hist.p.512 M. **-δακρυς**, υ, gen. υος, epith. of λίβανος, *with hallowed tears* or *gum*, Melanipp. 1. **-δῐδάσκᾰλος**, ὁ, *teacher of holy things* at Rome, = *pontifex*, D.H. 2.73 (pl.). **-δόκος**, ον, *receiving sacrifices*, or **ἱερόδοκος**, *received in temples*, A.*Supp.*363 (lyr., dub. l.). **-δουλεία**, ἡ, *company of* ἱερόδουλοι, *IG*14.914 (Ostia):—also **-δουλία**, ib.1024 (Rome). **-δουλος**, ὁ, ἡ, *temple-slave*, *PCair.Zen.*451 (iii B.C.), *PHib.*1.35.3 (iii B.C.), *UPZ*34.13 (ii B.C.), *PTeb.*6.25 (ii B.C.), *SIG*996.29 (Smyrna), *BMus. Inscr.*986.4 (Cyprus), *OGI*383.174 (Nemrud Dagh, i B.C.), etc.; νεωκόροι καὶ ἱ. Ph.2.420; of the Nethinim, Lxx 1*Es.*1.2, al.; esp. of *temple-courtesans* at Corinth and elsewhere, Str.8.6.20, 6.2.6; also of men, Id.11.4.7, al. **-δρομος**, ον, *flowing in a sacred stream*, ὕδωρ *Epigr. Gr.*835ᵇ4 (Berytus): poet. **ἱρό-**, *running in sacred races*, Philox. 15. **-εργός**, όν, v. ἱερουργός. **-θαλλής**, ές, *blooming holily*, Orph. *H.*40.17 (Herm. -θηλής). **-θέσιον**, τό, *monument, mausoleum*, *OGI*383.36 (Nemrud Dagh), 403.1 (Kara Kush, i B.C.). **-θετέω**, *ordain sacred rites*, f.l. in *EM*468.57. **-θήκη**, ἡ, *depository for holy things, sanctuary*, *Gloss.* **-θρησκεία**, ἡ, *divine worship*, Edict. Maximini ap.Eus.*HE*9.7. **-θροος**, contr. **-θρους**, ουν, *of mystic sound*, *Mim.Oxy.*413.90. **-θύσιον** [ῠ], τό, *place of sacrifice*, Paus.4. 32.1. **-θῠτεῖον**, τό, = foreg., *IG*12(1).847 (Rhodes), 1033 (Carpathos). **-θῠτέω**, *sacrifice*, βοῦς Heraclit.*Incred.*39, cf. Ἀρχ.Ἐφ. 1911.59, *IG*14.290 (Segesta), 12(1).67 (Rhodes): Arc. pres. part. nom. sg. masc. ἱεροθυτές ib.5(2).3.7 (Tegea, iv B.C.). **-θύτης** [ῠ], ου, Dor., etc. **-τᾱς**, α, ὁ, *sacrificing priest*, *IG*5(2).3.5 (Tegea, iv B.C.), *SIG*492.5 (Euboea, iii B.C.), Paus.8.42.12, cj. in Theopomp. Hist.76: as title of magistrate, *IG*14.952 (Agrigentum): pl., ib. 12(3).1270 (Syme). **-θῠτος**, ον, *devoted, offered to a god*, καπνός smoke *from the sacrifices*, Ar.*Av.*1265; θάνατος death *as a sacrifice for one's country or any holy cause*, Pi.*Fr.*78; ὑποδήματα δερμάτινα ἱ. *IG*5(1).1390.23 (Andania, i B.C.); οἷς ἱ. *SIG*624.43 (ii B.C.): **-θυτα**, τά, *sacrifices*, Theopomp.Hist.76 (s.v.l.), Arist.*Oec.*1349ᵇ13, Plu.2. 729c; of meats *offered to idols*, 1*Ep.Cor.*10.28. **-καυτέω**, *sacrifice as a burnt-offering*, Phryn.*PS*p.88 B.:—Pass., *to be burnt as a sacrifice*, D.S.20.65. **-κηρῡκεύω**, *to be a* ἱεροκῆρυξ, Aristeas 184, *SIG*444.6 (Delph., iii B.C.): **-κηρῡκεία**, *IGRom.*3.711 (Lycia, iii A.D.). **-κῆρυξ**, ῡκος, ὁ, *herald* or *attendant at a sacrifice*, D.59.78, Herm.Hist.2, prob. in *IG*1².6.89, cf. *Supp.Epigr.*2.258.23 (Delph., iii B.C.), *SIG*577.33 (Milet., iii/ii B.C.), *OGI*332.43 (Elaea, ii B.C.), etc.: Dor. **-κᾱρυξ** *IG*12(1).155.31 (Rhodes, ii B.C.). **-κόμος**, ὁ, *one who takes charge of a temple*, ib.14.621 (Rhegium). **-κορᾰκικά**, τά, *symbols of the* κόρακες, in the cult of Mithras (cf. κόραξ), *CIL*6.751*b* (iv A.D.). **-κτίστης**, ου, ὁ, *founder of a sanctuary*, *Cat. Cod.Astr.*8(4).165. **-κτῖτος**, ον, *established as a sanctuary*, πέτρα, of Delphi, Aristonous 1.1.

ἱερόλας, ὁ, = ἱερεύς, S.*Fr.*57 (dub.; for the termination cf. μαινόλης).

ἱερό-ληπτος, ον, *inspired*, Man.4.227. **-λογέω**, Ion. **ἱρολ-**, *recount a* ἱερὸς λόγος, Luc.*Syr.D.*26; *prophesy*, *EM*468.14. **-λογία**, Ion. **ἱρολογίη**, ἡ, *mystical language*, Luc.*Astr.*10. **-λόγοι**, οἱ, *authors of* ἱεροὶ λόγοι, Dam.*Pr.*38. **-μαντις**, εως, ὁ, *holy seer*, *Cat.Cod.Astr.*8(4).148. **-μας**· τῶν ἱερῶν ἐπιμελούμενος, Hsch.; uncontr. **ἰαρόμαορ** *Schwyzer*414, cf. 411 (Elis). **-μηνία**, ἡ, (μήν) *sacred month*, during which the great festivals were held and hostilities suspended, ἱ. Νεμεάς, of the Nemean games, Pi.*N.*3.2; ἱ. ἁ Πυθιάς *IG*2².1126.44 (Amphict.); ἐν σπονδαῖς καὶ προσέτι ἱερομηνίᾳ Th.3. 56; ἐν σπονδαῖς καὶ ἱερομηνίαις ib.65 (s.v.l.); ἱ. ἄγειν D.24.29: in pl., *sacrifices offered during the sacred month*, *IG*11(2).154.11 (Delos, iii B.C.); = Lat. *supplicatio*, App.*BC*5.130: pl., D.C.39.53 (**-μήνια**, τά, of the Κάρνεια (q.v.), is prob. f.l. in Th.5.54). **-μηνιακός**, ή, όν, *of the* ἱ., ἡμέραι *Inscr.Mus.Alex.*47 (i A.D.).

ἱερο-μνημονέω, Dor. **-μνᾱμονέω**, *to be* ἱερομνήμων, Ar.*Nu.*624, Plb. 4.52.4, *SIG*545.2 (Delph., iii B.C.), etc. **-μνημονικός**, Dor. **-μνᾱμ-**, ή, όν, *of a* ἱ., ψᾶφος ib.554.21 (Thermon, iii B.C.). **-μνημοσύνη**, Dor. **-μνᾱμοσύνα**, ἡ, *right to appoint a* ἱερομνήμων, *Klio*16.162, 163 (ii B.C.). **-μνήμων**, Dor., Arc. **-μνάμων** [ᾱ], ονος, ὁ, *mindful of sacred* things, ὅρκων Alciphr.2.4. II. as Subst., 1. *representative sent by each Amphictyonic state* to the Delphic Council, D.18.148, Jusj.ap. eund.24.150, *IG*2^2.1126.10, 1299.80, etc.; also at the Amphictyony of Calauria, ib.4.842 (ii B.C.). 2. *magistrate who had charge of temples* or *religious matters*, ib.4.823 (Troezen, iv B.C.), 5(2).3.22, 26 (Tegea), 14.423.3 (Tauromenium), Decr.Byz.ap.D.18.90, etc. b. at Rome, = *pontifex*, D.H.8.55, 10.57, Str.5.3.2. 3. generally, *recorder, registrar*, Arist.*Pol.*1321^{b}38. **-μοσχοσφρᾶγιστής**, οῦ, ὁ, *sealer of sacred calves* for sacrifice, *PGen.*32.4 (ii A.D.). **-μυρτος**, ἡ, = μυρσίνη ἀγρία, Ps.-Dsc.4.144. **-μύστης**, ου, ὁ, *one who initiates in sacred things*, Phot., Suid.

ἱερόν, τό, v. ἱερός III. 2.

ἱερο-νίκης [νῑ], ου, ὁ, *conqueror in the games*, *OGI*332.34 (Elaea, ii B.C.), *SIG*1073.4 (Olymp., ii A.D., in form -νείκης), Phld.*Mus.* p.105 K., Luc.*Hist.Conscr.*30, etc.: Dor. **-νίκας** *IG*5(1).668 (Laconia). **-νομέω**, *to be a* ἱερονόμος, *SIG*982.2 (Pergam.), 1219.1 (Gambreum, iii B.C.). **-νόμοι**, οἱ, *temple-wardens*, ib.982.23, *IGRom.* 4.461 (Pergam., sg.), *OGI*219.20 (Sigeum, iii B.C.); of the *pontifices* at Rome, D.H.2.73. **-νουμηνία**, ἡ, *feast of the new moon*, coined by Sch.Pi.*N.*3.1. **-όστεον**, τό, = ἱερὸν ὀστοῦν, prob. in *PMag. Lond.*121.212. **-παρέκτης**, ου, ὁ, (παρέχω) *priest's attendant*, *IG* 14.617, 621 (Rhegium). **-πλοκος**, ον, *religious*, *Cat.Cod.Astr.* 8(4).212 (s.v.l.).

ἱεροποι-έω, *serve as* ἱεροποιός, -ποιῶν καὶ θύων ὑπὲρ τῆς δημοκρατίας Antipho 6.45, cf. Pl.*Ly.*207d, *IG*11(2).144*A* (Delos, iv B.C.); τῇ Ἀθηνᾷ ib.2^2.1257 (iv B.C.); τῷ Ἀπόλλωνι *SIG*1037.6 (Milet., iv/iii B.C.), etc.: c. acc., ἱ. εἰσιτητήρια ὑπὲρ τῆς βουλῆς D.21.114; οἱ τὰ μυστήρια -ποιήσαντες *IG*2.872; ἱ. τὰ Ἀπολλώνια *BCH*36.413 (Delos, ii B.C.). II. *deify*, Aristid.1.191 J. **-ημα**, ατος, τό, *sacrifice*, *Jahresh.*23*Beibl.* 27, 28 (Maeonia, iii A.D.). **-ία**, ἡ, *sacred service, festival*, Aen. Tact.17.1 (pl.), *BSA*24.154 (Halimus, iv B.C., pl.); αἱ εἰς τὸν θεὸν ἱ. Decr.Halic.ap.J.*AJ*14.10.23, cf. Arist.*Rh.Al.*1423^{b}13 (pl.), Str.5.2.9, Porph.*Abst.*2.18; ἱερεὺς πεντεκαιδέκανδρος ἐπὶ τῶν -ποιῶν, = *XVvir sacris faciundis*, *IGRom.*3.172 (Ancyra). **-ον** (for -ποίιον), τό, *office of* ἱεροποιοί, *IG*11(2).144*A* 104 (Delos, iv B.C.); **-ποῖον** *Inscr. Délos* 316.69 (iii B.C.). **-ός**, ὁ, (ποιέω) *overseer of temples and sacred rites*, title of magistrates at Athens and elsewhere, *IG*1^2.5, al., D.4. 26, Arist.*Pol.*1322^{b}24, *Ath.*54.6, Decr.ib.30.2, *IG*12(8).264 (Thasos, iv B.C.), *SIG*410 (Erythrae, iii B.C.), *Inscr.Prien.*14.25 (iii B.C.), etc.; ἱεροποιοὶ τῶν σεμνῶν θεῶν were different, D.21.115, Din.*Fr.*8.1. II. *sacrificer*, D.H.1.40. 2. as Adj., ἱ. νεανίσκος, παρθένοι, ib.80, 9.40.

ἱερό-πολις, εως, ἡ, *holy city*, Ph.2.146; of the cities of refuge, ib. 308, 321. **-πομπός**, ὁ, *one who conveys the sacred tribute*, ib.224, 578. **-πρακτος**, ὁ, = ἱεροποιός, *Cat.Cod.Astr.*8(4).138 (s.v.l., fort. **-πράκτωρ**). **-πρεπής**, ές, *beseeming a sacred place, person* or *matter*, ὄνομα Pl.*Thg.*122e; τέχνη, of cookery, Men.130; κνῖσα Luc. *Sacr.*13; of persons, -έστατος τῶν προγεγενημένων X.*Smp.*8.40, cf. D.C.56.46, Lxx 4*Ma.*9.25, *Ep.Tit.*2.3. Adv. -πῶς *Michel* 163.21 (Delos, ii B.C.), *Inscr.Prien.*109.216 (ii B.C.), Str.12.5.3, Beros.ap.J. *Ap.*1.19. **-πρόσπολος**, ὁ, *sacred attendant, priest*, Ptol.*Tetr.*159.

ἱερόπτης, ου, ὁ, = Lat. *haruspex*, D.C.52.36, 64.5.

ἱερός (v. sub fin.), ά, όν, also ός, όν in the phrase ἱερὸς ἀκτή Hes. *Op.*597, 805, Orac.ap.Hdt.8.77: Ion. and poet. **ἱρός**, ή, όν (v. sub fin.): Dor. and N. Greek **ἱαρός** *IG*2^2.1126.20, etc.: Aeol. **ἶρος** Sapph.*Supp.*23.25, Alc.*Supp.*8.4, but **ἴαρος** (corr. from ἱερ-) Sapph. *Supp.*20a.6: Sup. ἱερώτατος Ar.*Eq.*582 (lyr.), Pl.*Lg.*755e. I. *filled with* or *manifesting divine power, supernatural*, ἱ. ἲς Τηλεμάχοιο Od.2.409, al.; ἱ. μένος Ἀλκινόοιο 8.421, etc.; ἄλφιτον, ἀλωαί, Il.11. 631, 5.499; Δημήτερος ἱερὸς ἀκτή Hes.*Op.* ll. cc.; of natural objects or phenomena, rivers, Od.10.351, Il.11.726, E.*Med.*410 (lyr.); λιβάς, of the Spercheus, S.*Ph.*1215 (lyr.); ἱεραὶ βῆσσαι Κίρκης 'faery', Od.10.275; ἱ. ἦμαρ, κνέφας, Il.8.66, 11.194; φάος Hes.*Op.* 339; ἱερὸς δίφρος (where δ. perh. = ἵπποι) Il.17.464; after Hom., ἱ. χεῦμα θαλάσσης A.*Fr.*192 (anap.); ἱ. κῦμα E.*Hipp.*1206, cf. *Cyc.* 265; ὄμβρος S.*OT*1428; δρόσοι E.*Ion*117 (lyr.); ὕπνος, of death, Call.*Ep.*11; ἔστι μὲν οὐδὲν ἱ. *no great* matter, Theoc.5.22. II. of divine things, *holy*, ἱεροῖς ἐν δώμασι Κίρκης Od.10.426; ἱ. γένος ἀθανάτων Hes.*Th.*21; λέχος, of Zeus, ib.57; δόσις the gift *of God*, ib. 93; πόλεμος *holy* war, *'crusade'*, Ar.*Av.*556, etc. 2. of earthly things, *hallowed, consecrated*, βωμοί Il.2.305; ἱ. δόμος, of the temple of Athena, 6.89; ἱ. ἑκατόμβη 1.99, 431, etc.; ἐλαίη Od.13.372; χοαί S.*OC*469, etc.; ἱρὰ γράμματα *hieroglyphics*, Hdt.2.36; but ἱ. γράμματα of the *Holy* Scriptures, 2*Ep.Tim.*3.15; ἱ. βύβλοι *OGI*56.70 (Canopus, iii B.C.); ἱ. ἄγαλμα, τρίπους, S.*OT*1379, E.*Ion*512, etc.; χρήματα Pl.*R.*568d, etc.; ἱ. τὸ σῶμα τῷ θεῷ δίδωμ' ἔχειν E.*Ion* 1285; ἱ. σώματα, of ἱερόδουλοι, Str.6.2.6; χῆνες Plu.2.325c; of animals regarded as 'taboo', [κριοὶ] εἰσί σφι ἱ. διὰ τοῦτο Hdt.2.42; so perh. ἱ. ἰχθύς Il.16.407; of the Roman Tribunes, = Lat. *sacrosanctus*, ἱ. καὶ ἄσυλος Plu.*TG*15, etc.; of Augustus, *Mon.Anc.Gr.* 5.17; ἱ. νόμος law *of sacrifice*, D.21.35, cf. *SIG*685.81 (ii B.C.); ἱ. λόγος *legend*, Hdt.2.81, etc.; οἱ παλαιοὶ καὶ ἱ. λόγοι Pl.*Ep.*335a; ἱ. γάμος *mystical* marriage, a religious ceremony, Men.320, Phot. s.v.; opp. βέβηλος, as *sacred* to *profane*, D.H.7.8, *AB*223; but more freq. ἱ. καὶ ὅσιος Th.2.52, X.*Vect.*5.4, etc.; cf. ὅσιος. 3. *under divine protection*, freq. of places, Ἴλιος Il.5.648, Alc.*Supp.*8.4; Πύλος Od. 21.108; Θήβη Sapph.*Supp.*20a.6; Τροίης ἱερὸν πτολίεθρον, Τροίης ἱερὰ κρήδεμνα, Od.1.2, Il.16.100; Ἀθῆναι Od.11.323, cf. Pi.*Fr.*75, S. *Aj.*1221 (lyr.), Ps.-Orac.ap.Ar.*Eq.*1037; Σούνιον ἱρόν Od.3.278; ἱ. κύκλος the judge's seat *under the protection of Zeus*, Il.18.504: with gen. of the divinity, ἄλσος ἱρὸν Ἀθηναίης, ἄντρον ἱρὸν νυμφάων, Od.6. 322, 13.104, cf. Hdt.1.80, 2.41, Ar.*Pl.*937, X.*An.*5.3.13, etc.; γῆ καὶ ἑστία ἱερὰ πᾶσι πάντων θεῶν Pl.*Lg.*955e; χωρίον ὡς -ώτατον ib.755e, cf. *Ti.*45a; with gen. of a human being, Γναθίου . . ἱ. εἰμι *IG*1^2.920. b. of persons, φυλάκων ἱ. τέλος Il.10.56; ἱ. πυλαωροί 24.681; στρατός Od.24.81; βασιλέες Pi.*P.*5.97; ἱ. εὐσεβής τε, of Oedipus, S.*OC*287; ἄνθρωπος ἱ. *initiated*, Ar.*Ra.*652; c. gen. of a divinity, *devoted, dedicated*, E.*Alc.*75, Pl.*Phd.*85b. c. under the Roman Empire, = *sacer*, *Imperial*, ἐκ τῶν ἱερῶν τοῦ Καίσαρος γραμμάτων *IGRom.*4.571 (Aezani, ii A.D.); ὁ -ώτατος φίσκος, τὸ -ώτατον ταμιεῖον, ib.3.727 (Lycia), *SIG*888.10 (Scaptopara, iii A.D.), etc.; τὸ -ώτατον βῆμα (of the *praefectus Aegypti*), *PHamb.*4.8 (i A.D.): generally, *worshipful*, ἱ. σύνοδος *OGI*713.9 (Egypt, iii A.D.), etc. III. as Subst., 1. **ἱερά**, Ion. **ἱρά**, τά, *offerings, victims*, ἱερὰ ῥέξας Il.1.147, etc.; ἔρδειν Hes.*Op.*336; διδόναι Od.16.184; ἀλλ' ὅ γε δέκτο μὲν ἱρά Il.2.420, cf. 23.207: less freq. in sg., ὄφρ' ἱρὸν ἑτοιμασσαίατ' Ἀθήνῃ 10.571; θῦσαι ἱρά Hdt.1.59, 8.54, etc.; θυσίας καὶ ἱρὰ ποιέειν Id.2.63; αἴθειν S. *Ph.*1033; ἱ. πατρῷα A.*Th.*1015; ἱ. ἐπιχώρια Democr.259. b. after Hom., *omens afforded by sacrifice*, τὰ ἱρὰ οὐ προεχώρεε χρηστά Hdt. 5.44; τὰ ἱερὰ καλὰ [ἦν] X.*An.*1.8.15; simply οὐκ ἐγίγνετο τὰ ἱ. ib. 2.2.3. c. generally, *sacred objects* or *rites*, Hdt.1.172, 4.33; τῶν ὑμετέρων ἱ. καὶ κοινῶν μετεῖχον D.57.3; of *cult-images*, *IGRom.*3.800 (Syllium). 2. after Hom., **ἱερόν**, Ion. **ἱρόν**, τό, *holy place*, Hdt.5. 119, al.; opp. νηός, Id.2.170, cf. Th.4.90, 5.18; freq. of a *temple*, ἔστι δὲ ἐν τῷ τεμένεϊ...ἱρόν κτλ. Hdt.2.112; of the Jewish temple, Lxx 1*Ch.*29.4, Plb.16.39.4, Str.16.2.34, *Ev.Matt.*24.1. 3. ἱερὸν τῆς δίκης *a sacred principle* of right, E.*Hel.*1002. 4. **ἱερός**, ὁ (sc. μήν), name of month at Delos, *IG*1^2.377.22, 11(2).203*A* 31 (iii B.C.). 5. **ἱεροί**, οἱ, members of a religious college or guild, ib.5(1).1390.1, al. (Andania, i B.C.), prob. in *SIG*1010.7 (Chalcedon), etc.; also of women, **ἱεραί**, αἱ, *IG*5(1). l.c., cf. 1511 (Sparta). b. = ἱερόδουλος, ib. 1356 (Messenia, v B.C.), *Inscr.Perg.*572, *GDI*5702.39 (Samos). IV. special phrases, post-Hom., 1. prov., ἱ. ἄγκυρα *one's last hope*, Plu. 2.815d, Luc.*JTr.*51, *Fug.*13, Poll.1.93, Gal.11.182. 2. ἱ. βόλος, name of a throw at dice, Eub.57.1. 3. ἱ. βοτάνη, v. βοτάνη. 4. ἱ. (sc. γραμμή) (cf. γραμμή III. 1), *last line* of draught-board, κινήσαις τὸν ἀπ' ἱρᾶς . . λίθον Alc.82, cf. Epich.225, Sophr.127; τὴν ἀφ' ἱερᾶς (v.l. τὴν ἱεράν) Plu.*Cor.*32. 5. ἱ. ἰχθύς, = ἀνθίας, Arist.*HA* 620^{b}35, cf. Ath.7.282e, Plu.2.981d. 6. ἱ. λόχος, v. λόχος. 7. ἱερά (sc. νίκη), ἡ, *drawn contest, dead heat* (because the prize was assigned to the god), *SIG*1073.48 (Olymp.); ποιῆσαι ἱεράν, of the competitor, Wood *Ephesus*, *App.*vi p.70; so ἱ. ἀθλήματα *Inscr. Olymp.*56; ἱερὸς ὁ στέφανος ἐκρίθη *IG*9(2).525 (Larissa); τὸ παγκράτιον ἱ. ἐγένετο ib.527 (ibid.); ἱερός (sc. ἀγών) ib.7.2727.19, 24 (Acraeph.): metaph., ἱερὸν ποιῆσαι τὸν στέφανον 'divide the honours', Plb.1.58.5, 29.8.9. 8. ἱ. νόσος *epilepsy*, Hdt.3.33, Hp.*Morb. Sacr.* tit., Thphr.*HP*9.11.3, etc., cf. Call.*Aet.*3.1.14: metaph., τὴν οἴησιν ἱ. νόσον ἔλεγε Heraclit.46 (= Epicur.*Fr.*224). 9. ἡ ἱ. ὁδός *the sacred road* to Delphi, Hdt.6.34; also, from Athens to Eleusis, Cratin. 61, Paus.1.36.3, Harp. s. v.; and that from Elis to Olympia, Paus. 5.25.7. 10. ἱ. ὀστέον, *os sacrum*, the last bone of the spine, Hp. *Art.*45, Plu.2.981d, Gal.*UP*5.8, etc. 11. ἱ. συμβουλή *sacred duty of an adviser*, Pl.*Ep.*321c, X.*An.*5.6.4, cf. Pl.*Thg.*122b, Luc.*Rh.Pr.* 1. 12. ἱ. σῦριγξ *spinal canal*, Poll.2.180. 13. ἱερὰ τριήρης, of the Delian ship, or one of the state-ships (Salaminia or Paralos), D.4. 34. 14. freq. in geographical names, e. g. ἱ. ἄκρα, in Lycia, Str. 14.3.8; ἱ. ἀκρωτήριον, in Spain, *Cape St. Vincent*, Id.2.4.3; ἱ. κώμη, in Lydia, Plb.16.1.8; ἱ. νῆσος, one of the Liparean group, Th.3.88; one of the *insulae Aegates*, Plb.1.60.3. V. Adv. -ρῶς *holily*, ἀποθανεῖν v.l. in Plu.*Lyc.*27. [ῐ by nature, but sts. ῑ in Ep., esp. in endings of hexameters, ἱ. ἰχθύς, ἱ. ἦμαρ, ἱερὰ ῥέξας, ἀλφίτου ἱεροῦ ἀκτή, Il.16.407, 8.66, 1.147, 11.631; ῑερόν in the first foot of a hex., Theoc.5.22; also in compds. ἱεραγωγός, ἱεροθαλλής, ἱερόφωνος: ῑ always in contr. form ἱρός wh. is used in Ep., Hdt., and some Ion. Inscrr., as *IG*12(8).265.9 (Thasos), cf. Semon.7.56, Herod.4.79, al., but is rarely found in codd. of Hp. (never in Heraclit. or Democr.); also in Trag., A.*Th.*268, etc., but never required by metre in lyr. of Com.]

ἱερο-σαλπικτής, οῦ, ὁ, *trumpeter at a sacrifice*, Poll.4.87 (v.l. **-ιγκτής**), *CIG*1969 (Thessalonica), 2983 (Ephesus): **-ιστής** *IG*14. 617 (Rhegium). **-σέβαστος** (sc. μήν), ὁ, name of month in Ionian calendar, *Hemerolog.Flor.* **-σκοπέομαι**, *inspect victims, divine therefrom*, Plb.34.2.6; ἱ. μόσχῳ *divine by* the entrails of a calf, D.S. 1.70. **-σκοπία**, ἡ, *divination by inspection of victims*, ib.73, Iamb. *VP*19.93: Ion. -ίη Hp.*Acut.*8, Dio ap.Orph.*Fr.*219. **-σκόπος**, ον, *inspecting victims*, Θέμις ἱ. ἀνδρῶν Orph.Εὐχή 23, cf. Porph.*Abst.* 2.50. II. = Lat. *haruspex*, D.H.2.22, D.S.32.12. III. dub.l. in *Cat.Cod.Astr.*8(4).145 (fort. -σκώπτης). **-στάτης** [ᾰ], ου, ὁ, *governor of the temple*, Lxx 1*Es.*7.2.

ἱερο-στολικά, τά, *title of poem on sacred vestments*, Suid. s.v. Ὀρφεύς. **-στολιστής**, οῦ, ὁ, = sq., Chaerem.ap.Porph.*Abst.*4.8, *Sammelb.*5553. **-στολος**, ὁ, an Egyptian priest *who had charge of the sacred vestments*, = στολιστής, Plu.2.352b.

ἱεροσῦλ-έω, pf. ἱεροσύληκα *SIG*417.8 (Delph., iii B.C.):—*rob a temple, commit sacrilege*, Ar.*V.*845, Antipho 5.10, Pl.*R.*575b. II. c. acc., ἱ. τὰ ὅπλα *steal the sacred* arms, D.57.64, cf. Lycurg.136; ἱ. τὰ ἱερά *rob* or *plunder* the temples, Plb.30.26.9; θεούς Phalar.*Ep.* 84.1. **-ημα**, ατος, τό, *sacrilegious plunder*, Lxx 2*Ma.*4.39; *sacrilege*, Hsch. **-ησις**, εως, ἡ, *temple-robbery, sacrilege*, f.l. in D.S.

16.14. **-ία**, ἡ, = foreg., X.*Ap.*25, *SIG*1017.18 (Sinope, iii B.C.), etc.: pl., Pl.*R.*443a. **-ος**, ὁ, (proparox.) *temple-robber*, or generally, *sacrilegious person*, Ar.*Pl.*30, Lys.30.21, Pl.*R.*344b, Men.*Epit.*560, etc.: fem., ib.504; ἱερόσυλε γραῦ ib.524: neut. as Adj., ἱ. θηρία Id.*Pk.*176. II. of things, *got by sacrilege*, παροψίδες Eub.7.4.

ἱερο-τᾰμίας, ου, ὁ, *temple-treasurer*, *IG*9(1).32.25 (Stiris), 12(1).890 (Rhodes): pl., *Chron.Lind.*A.8, *Supp.Epigr.*2.828 (Damascus). **-τᾰμιεύω**, *to be temple-treasurer*, *SIG*804.16 (Cos, i A.D.). **-τέκτων**, ονος, ὁ, *temple-carpenter*, *POxy.*579 (ii A.D.), *Sammelb.*789 (iii A.D.), *Cat.Cod.Astr.*8(4).165. **-τελεστία**, ἡ, *solemnization of sacred rites*, interpol. in Suid. s. v. ἁγίασμα. **-τεύκτης**, ου, ὁ, *temple-builder*, Vett.Val.4.11. **-τροχος**, ον, ἅρμα ἱ. *sacred* car, Orph.*H.*14.2. **-υλίζω**, of wine, τὸν παλαιὸν καὶ ἱερουλίζοντα dub. sens. in Alex.Trall.10.

ἱερουργ-έω, *perform sacred rites*, *IG*1².4.4,8, Ph.2.94, etc. II. c. acc., ἱ. τὴν κλίνην, Lat. *lectisternium facere*, *CIG*(add.)4528 (Lebanon); ἱ. ζῷα *sacrifice* them, gloss on σφάξαι, Ammon.*Diff.*p.127 V.; ἱ. τὸ εὐαγγέλιον *minister* the gospel, *Ep.Rom.*15.16; τὸν νόμον v.l. in Lxx 4*Ma.*7.8:—Med., ἱερουργίας ἱερουργεῖσθαι Plu.*Alex.*31:—Pass., τὰ ἱερουργηθέντα *victims offered*, Hdn.5.5.9, cf. Palaeph.51; -ούμεναι τελεταί *celebrated*, Iamb.*VP*3.14; ἱερουργούμενοι βωμοί *consecrated*, Porph.*Marc.*18. **-ημα**, ατος, τό, *sacrifice, offering*, J.*AJ*8.4.5 (pl.), Iamb.*VP*28.147 (pl.). **-ία**, ἡ, *religious service, sacrifice*, Hdt.5.83 (in Ion. form ἱροργίαι, with vv.ll.), Pl.*Lg.*775a, *PTeb.*293.20 (pl., ii A.D.), etc. **-ικός**, ή, όν, *ceremonial*, Iamb.*Myst.*5.14; μάχαιρα Sch.E.*Or.*194. **-ός**, ὁ, *sacrificing priest*, Call.*Fr.*450 (in Ep. form ἱεροεργός), Ammon.*Diff.*p.90 V.; ἱερουργοὶ τῆς Ἀθηνᾶς, members of a religious college, *IG*12(7).241.3 (Amorgos, iii B.C.): Dor. **ἱερω[ργός]** prob. in *Schwyzer*288.91 (Rhodes, iii/ii B.C.).

ἱεροφαντ-έω, *to be a* ἱεροφάντης, Luc.*Alex.*39, *SIG*869.19 (Eleusis, ii A.D.). 2. *initiate, instruct in mysteries*, Ph.2.403, al.: c. dat., Id.1.146:—Pass., -ουμένη ψυχή Id.2.187. II. trans., *expound as a hierophant*, τελετάς Heraclit.*All.*64:—Pass., τοὺς ἱεροφαντηθέντας λογισμοὺς θεοῦ *inspired*, Ph.1.194. **-ης**, Ion. ἱρ-, ου, ὁ, (φαίνω) *hierophant, one who teaches rites of sacrifice and worship*, ἱ. τῶν χθονίων θεῶν Hdt.7.153; of *the initiating priest* at Eleusis, *IG*1².76.24, al., Lys.6.1, Is.7.9, Plu.*Alc.*33; at Rome, = *pontifex*, D.H.2.73, 3.36; of the *pontifex maximus*, Plu.*Num.*9; of the Jewish High Priest, Ph.2.322; of Moses, Id.1.117; later, *mystical expounder*, ἱ. τῆς τετρακτύος Hierocl.*in CA*20p.466 M. **-ία**, ἡ, *office of hierophant*, Plu.*Alc.*34, Luc.*Alex.*38 (pl.), Theo Sm.p.15 H. **-ικός**, ή, όν, *of a hierophant*, στέμμα Luc.*Alex.*60; βίβλοι ἱ., = Lat. *libri pontificales*, Plu.*Num.*22. Adv. -κῶς Luc.*Alex.*39. **-ις** (parox.), ιδος, fem. of -φάντης, *IG*2².1092 *B*35, Plu.*Sull.*13, *Cat.Cod.Astr.*1.115, Jul. *Or.*7.221c. **-ρια**, ἡ, fem. of ἱεροφάντης, *hierophantria deae Hecatae*, *CIL*6.1780, cf. 1779. **-ωρ**, ορος, ὁ, = ἱεροφάντης, Suid. s. v. Ἰουλιανός.

ἱερο-φοιτάω, *visit temples*, Ptol.*Tetr.*158 (-οῦντας codd.). **-φόρος**, v. ἱεραφ-. **-φῠλάκιον** [ᾰ], τό, *treasury for sacred vessels*, D.H.2.70. **-φύλαξ** [ῠ], poet. ἱρ-, ᾰκος, ὁ, *guardian of a temple*, E.*IT*1027 (cj. Markl.), *IG*14.291 (Segesta). 2. = Lat. *pontifex*, D.H.2.73. **-φωνος**, ον, *with sacred voice*: as Subst., prob. *utterer of oracles*, *CIG*4684 (Egypt), *IG*14.914 (Ostia); prob. read for ἠεροφώνων in Il.18.505 by Suid., Phot. (expld. by μεγαλοφώνων); f.l. for ἱμερο- in Alcm.26.1. **-φωρέω**, = ἱεροσυλέω, *SIG*530.5 (Achaia, iii B.C.). **-χθων**, poet. ἱρ-, ὁ, ἡ, gen. ονος, *of hallowed soil*, βῶλος *IG*14.1389 ii 27. **-ψάλτης**, ου, ὁ, *singer in the temple*, Lxx 1*Es.*1.15, al., *OGI*737.16 (Egypt, ii B.C.), Antioch.ap.J.*AJ*12.3.3. **-ψῡχος**, ον, *of holy, pious soul*, Lxx 4*Ma.*17.4.

ἱερ-όω, Dor. **ἱᾰρ-**, (ἱερός) *consecrate, dedicate*, Pl.*Lg.*771b; [τὰν γᾶν] ἃν Ἀμφικτίονες ἱάρωσαν *IG*2².1126.16 (Amphict.); ηιαρόντο (= ἱερούντων) Ἀπόλλονος Ἐχέτο ἄγαλμα *Berl.Sitzb.*1927.8 (Locr., v B.C.); Thess. part. ἱερούοντος *Schwyzer*553: pf. Pass. ἱερῶσθαι Th.5.1, *SIG*1006.4 (Cos, iii B.C.), etc.; ἱερωσύνην ἱερώσασθαι (v.l. ἱεράσασθαι) *to be consecrated* to a priesthood, Aeschin.1.19:—also **ἱερεόομαι**, τὴν ἱερωσύνην ἀξίως ἱερεώσατο τοῦ θεοῦ *IG*2².1271.13 (iii B.C.); τῷ θεῷ οὗ ἂν ᾖ ἱερειωμένος ib.1183.32 (iv B.C.); Δωρίδος ἱερεωμένης (perh. pres. part. of ἱεράομαι = ἱερωμένης) *IG*2.1561 (iv B.C.). **-ωμα**, ατος, τό, *consecrated object, offering*, ἱαρώματα *Supp.Epigr.*1.414.7 (Crete, v/iv B.C., nisi leg. ἀρώματα); ἱαρ[ώ]ματα *IG*4.917 (Epid., iv B.C.), cf. Lxx 2*Ma.*12.40, J.*AJ*1.19.10, Dam.*Isid.*71. II. = σκόλλυς (Lacon.), Hsch. **-ωνία**, ἡ, dub. sens. in *PTeb.*119.32 (ii B.C.). **-ώνῠμος**, ον, (ὄνομα) *of hallowed name*, Luc.*Lex.*10. **-ωσις**, εως, ἡ, *consecration*, cj. for ἵδρυσις in D.C.*Fr.*13.3. **-ωστί**, Ion. ἱρωστί, Adv. *in holy sort, piously*, Anacr.149. **-ωσύνη**, in Att. Inscrr. **ἱερεωσύνη** *IG*2².1235.8, al., also *SIG*²554.22 (Magn. Mae.), *SIG*³1068.22 (Patmos, iii/ii B.C.), *Milet.*7.28, etc.: ἡ:—*priesthood*, Hdt.3.142, etc.; ἱερωσύνης μετασχεῖν D.59.92: in pl., *priestly services, sacrifices*, Sch.Ar.*Pax*923. **-ωσύνιον**, *sacerdotium, sacrimonium*, *Gloss.* **-ώσυνος**, η, ον, in Att. Inscrr. both **ἱερώσ-** *IG*2².1358.15, al. and **ἱερεώσ-** ib.1356, 1361; **ἱερειώσ-** ib.1359:—*priestly*: ἱερώσυνα, τά, *the parts of a victim which were the priest's perquisites*, *IG* ll. cc., cf. *SIG*1038.12 (Eleusis, iv/iii B.C.), Amips.7, Phryn.*PS*p.77 B. **-ωτεία**, **-ωτεύω**, = ἱερατ-, *SIG*1009.12, 1010.3 (Chalcedon), *BCH*44.251 (Boeotia, i B.C.). **-ωτός**, ή, όν, Thess. **ἱαρωτός**, **ἱαρουτός**, *consecrated*, Ἀρχ.Ἐφ.1919.52 (Pharsalus, v/iv B.C.), *IG*9(2).461 (Crannon).

ἴεσις, εως, ἡ, (εἶμι) *going*, coined by Pl.*Cra.*426c (v.l. ἵεσις; fort. ἕσις).

ἵεσις, εως, ἡ, (ἵημι) *throwing*, *EM*469.54.

ἴεσσα· βαδίζουσα, Hsch. **ἰέττας**· πατέρας, ἢ τοὺς ἀγρίους τράγους (Cret.), Id.

ἰεῦ, an ironical exclamation, *whew!* Ar.*V.*1335.

ἱζαίνω, = sq., *lodge, settle*, v.l. in Aret.*SD*1.15.

ἱζάνω, (ἵζω): I. causal, *make to sit*, ἵζανεν εὐρὺν ἀγῶνα Il.23.258. II. intr., *sit*, ἐν τῷ [κλισίῳ]..ἵζανον Od.24.209, cf. Sapph.2.3; *settle*, οὔ μοι ἐπ' ὄμμασι νήδυμος ὕπνος ἱζάνει Il.10.92; ἡ δρόσος ἱ. ἐπὶ δόνακας Philostr.*Her.*19.19. 2. of soil, *settle down, subside*, ἐπὶ τὸ κενούμενον Th.2.76.

ἰζέλα· ἀγαθὴ τύχη (Maced.), Hsch.: **ἰζέλος**· ὁ θαλάττιος σκορπίος, Id.

ἵζημα, ατος, τό, *subsidence, sinking*, ἰσθμὸς ἵ. λαμβάνει Str.1.3.17, cf. 2.3.6, Plu.2.434c (pl.): metaph., of language, ὕψη ἱζήματα μηδαμοῦ λαμβάνοντα Longin.9.13.

ἱζημᾰτίας (sc. σεισμός), ου, ὁ, earthquake *which causes subsidence*, Lyd.*Ost.*53; v.l. for χασματίαι in Arist.*Mu.*396ᵃ4.

ἰζίνες· οἰωνοί, ὄρνιθες, προχόοι, λέβητες, τρίποδες, Hsch. **ἰζοῦνα**· βοόστασις, Id.

ἵζω, imper. ἵζε (not ἷζε) Od.24.394, E.*Hec.*145 (anap.): impf. ἷζον Il.20.15, E.*Alc.*946, Ion. ἵζεσκον Od.3.409: aor. εἷσα Il.23.359, Hdt.3.61, *IG*3.701, *Hymn.Is.*5, etc.; imper. εἷσον Od.7.163 codd.; part. ἕσας 10.361, Cyren. acc. ἕσσαντα (v. infr.); inf. ἕσσαι Pi.*P.*4.273 (the only tenses in Hom.): aor. ἵζησα D.C.50.2, 58.5, etc.: pf. ἵζηκα (ἐν-) Gal.2.691, 15.452, (συν-) Philostr.*Im.*2.20:—Med., v. infr. I and III, and cf. ἕζομαι.—Mostly in Poets and late Prose, the Att. Prose form being καθίζω: (Redupl. *si-sd-ō*, aor. (augmented) *e-sed-s-*, cf. ἕζομαι, ἕδος): I. causal, *make to sit, seat, place, set*, μή μ' ἐς θρόνον ἵζε Il.24.553, cf. Hdt.3.61; βουλὴν ἷζε Il.2.53; ἵζει μάντιν ἐν θρόνοις A.*Eu.*18; ὅς μ' ἐπὶ βουσὶν εἷσ' *set* me over the oxen, Od.20.210; σκοπὸν εἷσε *set* as a spy, Il.23.359; λόχον εἷσαν *laid* an ambush, 4.392; εἷσεν δὲ (v.l. δ' ἐν) Σχερίῃ *settled* [them] in Scheria, Od.6.8, cf. Il.2.549; ἐπὶ χώρας ἕσσαι Pi.*P.* l. c.; ἐπὶ τὸ δεῖπνον ἵζειν τοὺς βασιλέας Hdt.6.57; ἕσσαντα ἐπὶ τῷ ὠδῷ *having caused* (the suppliant) *to sit* on the threshold, *Berl.Sitzb.*1927.170 (Cyrene): rare in Trag., σὺ γάρ νιν εἰς τόδ' εἷσας αὔχημ' for *thou didst throne* her in this pride, S.*OC*713 (lyr.). 2. later in aor. 1 Med. εἱσάμην, 3 sg. εἵσατο *IG*12(5).615 (Iulis, v B.C., written εσατο), 2.1298.4 (ii B.C.), 1336.1 (ii B.C.):—*set up and dedicate* temples, statues, etc. in honour of gods, Thgn.12, Hdt.1.66; τέμενος ἕσσαντο Pi.*P.*4.204; ἕσσατο βωμόν Id.*Oxy.*408.37: Dor. 3 sg. ἡίσατο *IG*9(1).704 (Corc., vi B.C.), ἵσσατο ib.4.569 (Argos); 3 pl. [ἧ]σσαντο *BCH*33.171 (ibid., iii B.C.); part. ἑσσάμενος *IG*4.840.7, 841.23 (Calauria, iii B.C.): Att. part. prob. ἑσάμενος, θυσίας τὰς πατρίους τῶν ἑσαμένων (ἑσσ-, ἐσσ-, εἰσ- codd.).. ἀφαιρήσεσθε Th.3.58; later εἱσάμενος *IG*2².1364 (i A.D.), Plu.*Them.*22, *Thes.*17, *Pyrrh.*1, Luc.*Syr.D.*1, also Hdt.1.66 codd.: late fut. εἵσομαι ἱερόν A.R.2.807. II. intr., *sit, sit down*, Il.2.96, 792, etc.; ἷζε ἐν μέσσοισι he *sat* in the midst, 20.15; ἵζειν ἐς θρόνον Od.8.469, Hdt.5.25; ἐς θᾶκον S.*Ant.*1000; ἐπὶ θρόνου Il.18.422, cf. Od.17.339; ἐπὶ [λίθοισιν] 3.409; ἐπ' ἄκριας ἠνεμοέσσας 16.365; ἐπὶ κώπην, of rowers, Ar.*Ra.*199; ἐπὶ κώπᾳ πηδαλίῳ τε E.*Alc.*441 (lyr.); ἐπὶ τοὺς νεώς Epicr.3.12; νέφεσσι..Ὀλύμποιο..ἵζων Ζεύς Pi.*Pae.*6.93: c. acc. loci, ἵζειν θρόνον A.*Ag.*982 (lyr.); βωμόν E.*Ion*1314: c. acc. cogn., ἵ. κλωπικὰς ἕδρας Id.*Rh.*512. 2. *sit still, be quiet*, *h.Merc.*457 (dub.). 3. metaph., *sink*, εἰς ὀχετὸν ἄτας ἵζοισαν πόλιν *sink* into.., Pi.*O.*10(11).38; εἰς ἑτέραν ἵζει ἕδραν Pl.*Ti.*53a. III. Med. in signf. II, *sit*, πάροιθ'..ἵζευ ἐμεῖο Il.3.162; Διὸς..ποτὶ βωμὸν ἑρκείου ἵζοιτο Od.22.335; ἰσσάμενος ἐπὶ τῷ δαμοσίῳ ἰαρῷ *Berl.Sitzb.*1927.169 (Cyrene); late fut. εἵσεται Phylarch.44 J.: Dor. pres. imper. ἵσδευ *Papers of Amer.Sch.at Athens* 3 No.437 (Pisidia); *lie in ambush*, ἔνθ' ἄρα τοί γ' ἵζοντ' Il.18.522; freq. of an army, *take up a position*, ἵζεσθαι ἀντίοι τινί Hdt.9.26; ἵζεσθαι ἐν τῷ Τηϋγέτῳ, ἐς τὸ Τηΰγετον, Id.4.145, 146; ἐν τῷ Ἰσθμῷ, ἐς τὸν Ἰσθμόν, Id.8.71; of a fleet, Id.6.5: generally ἐς ἱρὸν Ἀφροδίτης Id.1.199; ἐς τὰ πρόθυρα Id.3.140; in Trag., ἐν ἁγνῷ ἵζεσθε A.*Supp.*224; ἐς θρόνους E.*Ion*1618: c. acc., ἵζεσθαι κρήνας Id.*IA*141 (lyr.). 2. of things, *settle down, subside*, ἡ νῆσος ἱζομένη Pl.*Ti.*25c.

ἰή [ῑ], exclam. of joy or enthusiasm, ἰή, ἰή, ἰή, Ar.*Pax*195; esp. used in the cult of Apollo, ἰὴ παιών ib.453, al.; ἰὴ παιῆον Call.*Ap.*21, 103, *Hec.*1.1.10; ἀλαλαὶ ἰὴ παιήων Ar.*Lys.*1291; cf. ἰέ. 2. of grief, A.*Pers.*1004, *Supp.*114, *Ag.*1485 (all lyr.). (ἵη v.l. in Call.*Ap.* ll. cc., where it is associated with ἵει, imper. of ἵημι.)

ἰή, ἡ, v. ἰά, ἡ.

ἰηγορεῖν· ἐγρηγορέναι (Lacon.), Hsch. **ἰηδών**, όνος, ἡ, (ἰαίνω) *joy*, formed like ἀλγηδών, Id. (pl.); cf. ἰαίνω. **ἰηθενέουσα**, v. ἰαθενεῖ.

ἰήϊος, α, ον, also ος, ον (v. infr. II), epith. of Apollo, the god *invoked with the cry* ἰή or ἰὴ παιών (v. ἰή), ἰήϊε παιάν Pi.*Pae.*2.35, cf. A.*Ag.*146, S.*OT*154 (both lyr.), 1096, Ar.*V.*874, A.R.2.702, Duris 79 J. II. *mournful, grievous*, ἰήϊοι κάματοι S.*OT*174 (lyr.); ἰήϊος βοά, γόος, a cry *of mourning*, E.*Ph.*1036, *El.*1211 (both lyr.). (From the cry ἰή, as Εὔιος from εὐοῖ; but also associated with ἰάομαι, Hsch. (hence applied to Asclepius, *IG*3.171); and, as ἱήϊος, with ἵημι, Hsch., Macr.*Sat.*1.17.16.)

ἴηλα, v. ἰάλλω. **ἰήλεμος, ἰηλεμίζω, ἰηλεμίστρια, Ἰηλυσός**, Ion. for ἰαλ-. **ἰηλενές**· πορφυροῦν, μέλαν, Hsch.

ἴημα, Ion. for ἴαμα; but found in *IG*2².1121.15 (iv A.D.).

ἵημι, ἵης (v.l. ἵεις S.*El.*596, Castorio 2), ἵησι, 3 pl. ἱᾶσι, Ion. and Ep. ἱεῖσι; imper. ἵει Il.21.338, E.*El.*593 (lyr.); subj. ἱῶ; opt. ἱείην (also ἀφ-ίοιμι, X.*HG*6.4.3); inf. ἱέναι; part. ἱείς:—thematic forms of the pres. (as if from **ἱέω**) are also found, esp. in compds., cf.

μεθίημι, σύνιημι: also, as if from ἵω, 3 sg. pres. ἵει A.R.4.634, imper. ξύν-ιε Thgn.1240b codd.: impf. 3 sg. ἵει Il.1.479, Dor. ἀν-ίη *SIG*1 (Abu Simbel, vi B.C.); 3 pl. ἵεσαν E.*Ba.*1099, ἵεν Il.12.33, ξύν-ιεν (v.l. -ιον) 1.273; also 2 sg. ἵεις Ar.*V.*355; Ion. impf. ἵεσκε (ἀν-) Hes.*Th.*157: fut. ἥσω Il.17.515, etc.: aor. 1 ind. ἧκα Il.5.125, etc., Ep. ἕηκα 1.48 (mostly in compds.); 3 sg. subj. ἥσι 15.359; 3 sg. opt. εἵη 3.221; inf. εἷναι Ar.*Ra.*133, Ep. ἐξ-έμεναι Od.11.531: pf. εἷκα, only in compds. (ἀφ-, καθ-, παρ-, συν-), also ἕωκα (ἀφ-) *PCair. Zen.*502.4 (iii B.C.), Hdn.Gr.2.236:—**Med.**, pres. ἵεμαι Od.2.327, etc.; also 3 pl. προ-ίονται *PCair.Zen.*151.4 (iii B.C.): impf. ἱέμην Ar.*Eq.*625, etc.: fut. ἥσομαι (μετ-) Hdt.5.35, (προ-) D.1.12, (ἐξαν-) E.*Andr.*718: aor. 1 ἡκάμην (only in compds. προσ-, προ-): aor. 2 εἵμην, Ep. and Ion. ἕμην, of which we find εἷτο (ἐφ-) S.*Ph.*619, (ἀφ-) X.*Hier.*7.11, ἕτο (συν-) Od.4.76, ἕντο (ἐξ-) Il.9.92, etc.; imper. ἕο (ἐξ-) Hdt.5.39, οὗ (ἀφ-) S.*OT*1521; subj. ὧμαι (συν-) Il.13.381; opt. εἵμην (ἀφ-) Ar.*Av.*628, or οἵμην (προ-) Pl.*Grg.*520c; inf. ἕσθαι (προσ-) Ar.*V.*742; part. ἕμενος (προ-) Th.6.78, Isoc.4.164, etc.:—**Pass.**, fut. ἑθήσομαι (ἀν-) Th.8.63: aor. εἵθην (only in compds. ἀφ-, καθ-, παρ-): pf. εἷμαι (only in compds.); also ἕωμαι in compds. ἀν-, ἀφ-, ἐφ- (q.v.): plpf. εἵμην (only in compds.).—Of the Pass. and Med. Hom. has only pres., impf., and 3 pl. aor. 2 Med. ἕντο.—For varieties peculiar to special compds., v. ἀν-, ἀφ-, ὑφ-ίημι. (Perh. cogn. with Lat. *ja-c-io* or with Lat. *sēmen*:—Med. ἵεμαι prob. from Ϝῑ-, cf. εἴσομαι II, Skt. *véti* (pl. *vyánti*) 'press forward, desire', Lat. *vīs* (2 sg.), *invitus*.) [ῐ generally in Hom. and Ep., ῑ in Att.; sts. ῑ in Hom., ἵει Il.16.152, etc.; ἱεῖσαι Od.12.192; also in inf. ἱέμεν, ἱέμεναι, part. ἱέμενος, etc., ξυν-ίετε Archil.50: ῐ sts. in Trag., ἵησι A.*Th.*309 (lyr.), ἱέντα ib.493, ἱείς, ἱεῖσα, E.*IT*298, *IA*1101, *Hec.*338; ἱεῖσαν Id. *Supp.*281; in Com., συνῑημι Ar.*Av.*946 (s.v.l.), Strato Com.1.3: with variation of quantity, πλεῖστον οὖλον ἵει [ῑ], ἴουλον ἵει [ῐ] *Carm.Pop.* 1.]:—*release, let go*, ἧκα.. πόδας καὶ χεῖρε φέρεσθαι Od.12.442; ἧκε φέρεσθαι *let* him *float off*, Il.21.120; *let fall*, κὰδ δὲ κάρητος ἧκε κόμας *made* his locks *flow* down from his head, Od.6.231; [ἐθείρας] ἵει λόφον ἀμφί Il.19.383; ἐκ δὲ ποδοῖιν ἄκμονας ἧκα δύω I *let* two anvils *hang* from his two legs, 15.19; ἐκ δ' ἄρα χειρὸς φάσγανον ἧκε χαμᾶζε Od.22.84, cf. Il.12.205; ἵεις σαυτὸν κατὰ τοῦ τείχους Ar.*V.*355; ἧκαν ἑαυτούς *let* themselves *go*, X.*An.*4.5.18; ἵεσαν φυγῇ πόδα E.*Rh.*798. 2. of sounds, *utter*, ὄπα Il.3.152, Od.12.192; ἔπεα Il.3.221; γλῶσσαν Hdt. 1.57; Ἑλλάδα γλῶσσαν ἱ. *to speak* Greek, Id.9.16; Δωρίδα, Ἀττικὴν γλῶσσαν, Th.3.112, Sol.36.10; φωνὴν Παρνησίδα A.*Ch.*563; δύσθροα βάγματα Id.*Pers.*636 (lyr.); ἐκ στηθέων ἄλγος Id.*Th.*865 (lyr.); μέγαν κωκυτόν S.*Aj.*851, etc.; but πᾶσαν γλῶσσαν ἱ. *to let loose* every kind of speech, Id.*El.*596; πᾶσαν (τὸ λεγόμενον) φωνὴν ἱέντα Pl.*Lg.* 890d; τὸ τᾶς εὐφάμου στόμα φροντίδος ἱέντες, i.e. speaking not in words, but in silent thought, S.*OC*133 (lyr.); ἧκε abs. (sc. φωνήν), Plu.2.973e; of instruments, ἄλλα μέλη τῶν χορδῶν ἱεισῶν Pl.*Lg.* 812d. 3. *throw, hurl*, λᾶαν, βέλος, δόρυ, Od.9.538, Il.4.498, E.*Rh.* 63; ἱέναι (sc. τινά) πέτρας ἄπο E.*HF*320, cf. S.*Tr.*273: c. gen. pers., *to throw* or *shoot* at one, ὀϊστόν τινος Il.13.650; ἐπ' ἀλλήλοις ἵεσαν βέλεα Hes.*Th.*684: metaph., ἐκ μαλθακᾶς φρενὸς ὀϊστοὺς ἱέντες Pi.*O.*2.90. b. abs., *throw, shoot*, τόσσον γὰρ ἵησιν Od.9.499, cf. 8.203, Il.17.515, Pl.*Tht.*194a, etc.; ἄνω ἱέντες X.*An.*3.4.17; δίσκοισιν τέρποντο... ἱέντες Il.2.774, al.: c. gen. objecti, τῶν μεγάλων ψυχῶν ἱεὶς *shooting* at great spirits, S.*Aj.*154; ἐπὶ στόχον (στοίχον codd.) at a mark, X. *Ages.*1.25: c. dat. instr., ἵησι τῇ ἀξίνῃ Id.*An.*1.5.12. 4. of water, *let flow, spout forth*, ῥόον Il.12.25; [Ἀξιὸς] ὕδωρ ἐπὶ γαῖαν ἵησι 21.158; ῥέος A.*Pr.*812: abs., [ποταμὸς] ἐπὶ γαῖαν ἵησιν the river *pours* over the land, Od.11.239; [κρήνη] ἵησι 7.130; of tears, δάκρυον ἧκε χαμᾶζε 16. 191; of fire or smoke, ἵει νᾶμα παμφάγου πυρὸς E.*Med.*1187; λιγνὺν A.*Th.*493. 5. *send*, of living beings, τίς γάρ σε θεῶν ἐμοὶ ἄγγελον ἧκε; Il.18.182; Αἰνείαν.. ἐξ ἀδύτοιο ἧκε 5.513; of omens or portents, τοῖσι δὲ δεξιὸν ἧκεν ἐρῳδιόν 10.274; ἔλαφον.. εἰς ὁδὸν αὐτὴν ἧκεν Od. 10.159; τέρας 21.415; generally of things, ἱκμενον οὖρον τινι Il.1. 479, etc. II. Med., *speed oneself, hasten*, freq. in part. with Advs., πρόσω ἵεσθε Il.12.274; ἐνθένδ' ἱέμην Ar.*Eq.*625; ἱ. Τροίηνδε, Ἐρεβόσδε, Od.19.187, 20.356: with Preps., ἵεσθαι κατὰ τὴν φωνήν Hdt. 2.70; πρός τινα Id.9.78; δρόμῳ ἵεσθαι ἐς τοὺς βαρβάρους Id.6.112; ἵετ' εὐθὺ πρὸς τὰ νυμφικὰ λέχη S.*OT*1242; ἐς ὄρεα E.*Ba.*140 (lyr.); εἰς Κολωνόν Pherecr.134; ἱ. ἐπί τινα *spring* upon, of the lion, Arist.*HA* 629^{b}24: abs., ἰδόντες ἱέμεσθα S.*Ant.*432; ἱέμενος ῥεῖ *rushing*, Pl.*Cra.* 420a, etc. 2. metaph., *to be eager, desire to do* a thing, c. inf., ἵετο γὰρ βαλέειν Il.16.383; βαλέειν δέ ἑ ἵετο θυμός 8.301; ἵετο θυμῷ τείσασθαι.. 2.589: c. gen., *to be set upon, long for* a thing, in part., ἱέμενοι πόλιος, νίκης, 11.168, 23.371; νόστοιο Od.15.69; λεχέων S.*Tr.*514 (lyr.); ἱέμενος ποταμοῖο ῥοάων *setting thyself toward*, Od.10.529: abs. in part., ἱέμενός περ *eager* though *he was*, 1.6, etc.

ἵηνα, aor. 1 Act. of ἰαίνω.

Ἰηπαι-ήων, ονος, ὁ, epith. of Apollo, from the cry ἰὴ παιῆον, *h.Ap.* 272. II. *hymn* sung to him, ib.500, 517. **-ωνίζω**, *cry* ἰὴ παιών! Ar.*Eq.*408.

ἱήρια, τά, = ἱατήρια, dub. in *Supp.Epigr.*1.414.4 (Crete, v/iv B.C.).

ἴῃσι, Ep. 3 sg. pres. subj. of εἶμι (*ibo*). **ἰήσιμος, ἴησις**, Ion. for ἰασ-.

Ἰησοῦς, οῦ, dat. οῖ, *Joshua*, LXX *Jo.*1.1, al., *Act.Ap.*7.45; in *NT*, with dat. -οῦ, JESUS, *Ev.Matt.*9.27, al.

ἰήτειρα, ἰητέον, ἰητήρ, ἰητόριον, ἰητρός, etc., Ion. for ἰατ-.

ἰήτης· τοξότης, ἰοβόλος, Hsch.

ἰθᾱγενής [ῑ], ές, or **ἰθαιγ-**, Od.14.203 (v.l.), Hdt.2.17 (v.l.), A. *Pers.*306 (v.l.), Alex.Aet. (v. infr.):—*born in lawful wedlock*, ἀλλά με ἶσον ἰθαγενέεσσιν (so most codd. and A.D.*Adv.*187.24: v.l. ἰθαιγ-) ἐτίμα honoured me like *his true-born sons*, of a νόθος, Od. l.c., cf. A.R.*Fr.*12.2 (ἰθαγ- cod.), Alex.Aet.3.2 (ἰθαιγ- cod.). 2. of a nation, *from the ancient stock, aboriginal*, opp. ἔπηλυς, ἰ. Αἰγύπτιοι Hdt.6.53, cf. A.*Pers.*306; οὐχ ὑπ' ἰθαγενῶν ἤρχοντο Str.7.7.8, cf. Agath.2.15,25. 3. ἰ. κύημα, opp. an abortion, Hp.*Mul.*1.71; of some mouths of the Nile, *natural, original*, opp. ὀρυκτά, Hdt.2.17; ἰ. νότος, ζέφυρος, *genuine*, Arist.*Mete.*364^{a}16,18. (Glossed αὐτόχθων by Hsch., αὐθιγενής by Erot.; *originalis, indigena*, by *Gloss.*; perh. ἰθᾰ-γενής [ᾱ metri gr.], cf. Skt. *ihá*, Avest. *iδa* (fr. **idhá*) 'here'; cf. pr. n. Ἰθαγένης Plu.*Per.*26, Ps.-Hdt.*Vit.Hom.*1, but Ἰθαιγένης *IG* 12(9).192 (iv B.C.).)

ἰθαίνω, = εὐφρονῶ, Hsch.: etym. of ἰθαγενής, A.D.*Adv.*187.25; ἴθαινε θυμόν Anon.ap.*An.Ox.*1.61 (cf. ἰθαινάθυμος Theognost.*Can.* 81). (Cogn. with ἰθαρός.)

Ἰθάκη [ῐ, ᾰ], ἡ, *Ithaca*, Od.1.18, etc.: **Ἰθακήσιος**, ὁ, *Ithacan*, Il. 2.184, Od.2.25, B.*Fr.*25, etc.:—**Ἰθάκηνδε**, *to Ithaca*, Od.16.322; -ηθεν, *from it*, Q.S.7.187.

ἴθανα· σχοινία, Hsch. **ἶθαρ**, = εἶθαρ, Id.

ἰθᾰρός [ῐ], ά, όν, *cheerful, glad*, in Comp. -ώτερος Alc.*Supp.*4. 18. II. *pure*, κρᾶναι Simm.25.6; cf. ἰθαραῖς· ταχείαις, κούφαις, ἱλαραῖς, καλαῖς, καθαραῖς, Hsch.

ἰθείη, ἡ, = ἅμαξα (Thess.), Hsch. **ἰθή**, ἡ, = εὐφροσύνη, Id.

ἴθῐ, imperat. of εἶμι (*ibo*), *come, go* (q.v.): used as Adv. of encouragement, *come! well then!* Il.4.362; ἴ. νυν Ar.*Ra.*519, etc.

ἰθίτας· ὁ βλεννὸς καὶ μωρός, Hsch.

ἴθμα, ατος, τό, (εἶμι *ibo*), always in pl., *step, motion*, πελειάσιν ἴθμαθ' ὁμοῖαι Il.5.778, *h.Ap.*114. II. *feet*, Call.*Cer.*58.

ἰθμαίνω· ἀσθμαίνω, Hsch. **ἰθμία**· ἡ τῶν μελισσῶν ἐρυθρὰ κόπρος, Id. **ἰθμίν** (sic)· περιστόμιον, περιτραχήλιον, ἢ στεφανίς, Id. (cf. ἴσθμιον).

ἴθρῐς, ὁ, *eunuch*, restored from Hsch. for ἴδρις in *AP*6.219 (Antip.).

ἰθύ-βῐος [ῑθῠ], ον, *straightforward, honest*, *IG*5(2).474 (Megalopolis, ii/iii A.D.; ἐιθ- lapis). **-βόλος**, ον, *straight-hitting*, ἀκόντιον Apollod.3.15.1: Sup. -ώτατος, ἀκοντιστής J.*BJ*1.21.13: metaph., *sagacious*, φύσις Dam.*Isid.*160. **-γραμμος**, ον, *rectilinear*, σχήματα Agath.5.9. **-δίκης** [δῐ], ου, ὁ, *giving right judgement*, Hes. *Op.*230, *APl.*4.35. **-δῐκος**, ον, *righteous*, *Epigr.Gr.*906 (Gortyn). **-δρομία**, ἡ, *straight course*, διὰ τῶν πόρων Harp.Astr. in *Cat. Cod.Astr.*8(3).148. **-δρόμος**, ον, *straight-running*, πρίων *AP*6.103 (Phil.). **-θριξ**, τρῐχος, ὁ, ἡ, *straight-haired*, opp. οὐλόθριξ (woolly-haired), Hdt.7.70, Hp.*Epid.*1.19. **-κέλευθος**, ον, *straight-going*, Nonn.*D.*15.365. **-κρήδεμνος**, ον, epith. of ships, prob. *with canvas set*, Pamphos ap. Paus.7.21.9. **-κτέᾰνον**· τὸ ἰθὺ πεφυκὸς καὶ ὀρθὸν δένδρον, Hsch.; cf. sq. and εὐκτέανος (B). **-κτίων**, v. ἰθυπτίων. **-κῡφος**, η, ον, of parts of the normal spine, *frontally concave*, Hp.*Art.*45 (-κῡφής, ές, *Mochl.*1); opp. **ἰθύ-λορδος**, η, ον (ος, ον *Mochl.* l.c.), *frontally convex*, ll. cc., cf. Gal.18(2).542. **-μᾰχία**, Ion. -ίη, ἡ, *fair, stand-up fight*, ἰ. ποιέεσθαι Hdt.4.120; ἰθυμαχίῃ διώσασθαι στρατόν ib.102. **-μάχος** [ᾰ], ον, *fighting fairly and openly*, Simon.137.

ἴθυμβος, ὁ, *Bacchic dance and song*, Poll.4.104, Hsch., Phot. (For the termination cf. ἴαμβος, διθύραμβος.)

ἴθῡνα, ης, ἡ, = εὔθυνα, *penalty, fine*, *SIG*986.12 (Chios, v/iv B.C.), *GDI*5654 (ibid.).

ἰθύν-τατα [ῑ], Adv., Sup. of ἰθύς (A) (q.v.). **-τειρα**, ἡ, fem. of sq., as epith. of Δίκη, Orph.*A.*352. **-τήρ**, ῆρος, ὁ, *guide, pilot*, A.R. 4.209, 1260, *IG*9(1).390 (Naupactus), Jul.*Or.*1.25c; *shepherd*, Theoc. *Syrinx* 2; ἰ. πυρός, of Hephaestus, v.l. in Coluth.54; *ruler*, Ἑσπερίης χθονὸς *Epigr.Gr.*905 (Gortyn); προτέρων ὑπέρτερος ἰθυντήρων *Milet.* 1(9).340. **-τήριος**, α, ον, *guiding, directing*, S.*Ichn.*73. II. Subst. -τήριον, τό, *laurel-bough*, used by diviners, Hsch.; = *regimen*, *Gloss.* 2. -τηρία, ἡ, = *canalis*, ib. (prob.). **-τής**, οῦ, ὁ, = ἰθυντήρ, Hsch. s. v. διϊθυντής; = *rector*, *Gloss.*: -τωρ, Orph.*A.*122; ἰθύντορος ἀνθυπάτοιο *IG*4.1603 (Corinth). **-ω**, Ion. impf. ἰθύνεσκον Q.S.1.273, al., *Hymn.Is.*153: aor. 1 ἴθυνα Od.23.197:—**Med.** (v. infr. 2), aor. 1 inf. ἰθύνασθαι Q.S.14.500:—Pass., aor. 1 ἰθύνθην Il.16.475: pf. ἴθυμμαι D.P.341, ἀπ-ίθυνται Hp.*Fract.*7: (ἰθύς A). [ἰθῡνω: ῐ- only in *APl.* 74]:—Ion. and Ep. for εὐθύνω (sts. used in Trag., generally with v.l. εὐθυν-; never in Com. or Att. Prose), *make straight, straighten*, ἐπὶ στάθμην ἴθυνεν by the rule, Od.5.245, 23.197, al.:—Pass., ἐκ στάθμης ἰθυμμένος D.P. l.c. 2. *guide in a straight line*, ἵππους τε καὶ ἅρμ' ἰθύνομεν (Ep. for -ωμεν) *let us drive* them *straight*, Il.11.528; νῆα θοὴν ἰθύνει [the pilot] *keeps* it *straight*, 23.317; τὴν δ' ἄνεμός τε κυβερνήτης τ' ἴθυνε Od.11.10, etc.; τρόπιν *Hymn.Is.* l.c.; ἰ. δρόμον, κῶλον, E.*Hipp.* 1227 (v.l. εὐθ-), *Or.*1016 (lyr.); κέντρα Id.*Ph.*178 (lyr.); βέλος δ' ἴθυνεν Ἀθήνη she *sped* it *straight*, Il.5.290: in late Prose, λεπτοὶ ὕπνοι ἰθύνοντες τὰ σιτία Philostr.*Gym.*48:—Med., *guide* or *steer for oneself*, of missiles, ἐπ' Ἀντινόῳ ἰθύνετο πικρὸν ὀϊστόν *aimed his* arrow *straight* at.., Od.22.8; πηδαλίῳ ἰθύνετο (sc. σχεδίην) 5.270; ἡνίοχος ἰθύνετο ἅρμα Hes.*Sc.*324: c. gen., ἀλλήλων ἰθυνομενάων.. δοῦρα *as they drove* their spears *straight at* each other, Il.6.3:—Pass., *run straight* or *evenly*, of horses yoked abreast, τὼ δ' ἰθυνθήτην Il.16.475 (but, *to be guided*, οὐ γὰρ ἄτερ μάστιγος ἰθύνεται ἵππος *APl.* l.c.); of a boat, *to be steered*, Hdt.1.194. 3. *guide, direct, rule*, Ζεὺς.. πάντ' ἰθύνει Il.17. 632; ἀμηχανίῃ ἰ. νόον Parm.6.6; ἰ. στρατόν (corr. from ηὔθ- in cod. M) A.*Pers.*773; ἰ. ἑορτὰς Orac.ap.D.21.52; ζωὴν *AP*6.68 (Jul. Aegypt.); of a judge, μύθους ἰ. *put straight, rectify* unjust judgements, Hes.*Op.* 263 (dub.), cf. Call.*Jov.*83; ἰ. τὸ πλέον τινὶ *adjudge* the greater part to him, Theoc.5.71:—Pass., ἰθύνεσθαι θανάτῳ *to be visited with the penalty* of death, Hdt.2.177.

ἰθῠπετεῖν [ῐ] (ἰθυνπ- cod.)· ἐπ' εὐθείας ὁρμῆσαι, Hsch.

ἰθῠ-πορέω [ῐ], *go straight on*, Hp.*Oss*.15. **-πόρος**, ον, *going straight on*, γραμμή, γραφίδες, *AP*6.64 (Paul. Sil.), 68 (Jul. Aegypt.). **-πτίων** [πτῖ], ωνος, ὁ, ἡ, only in Il.21.169 μελίην ἰθυπτίωνα Ἀστεροπαίῳ ἐφῆκε, from πέτομαι, *straight-flying* (cf. ἰθύς (A) II):—Zenod. read **ἰθυκτίωνα**, *straight-fibred* (fort. -κτείωνα, cf. εὐθυκτέανον, κτηδών).

ἰθύρ· τὸ σιδήριον τοῦ ἄξονος τὸ τριβόμενον, Hsch.

ἰθύρροπος [ῐ], ον, (ῥοπή) *hanging perpendicularly*, Hp.*Art*.44.

ἰθύς (A) [ῐ], ἰθεῖα, ἰθύ, Ion. fem. ἰθέα Hdt.2.17, Eus.Mynd.63 (but ἰθείης, ῃ, αν are prob. in oblique cases): Comp. ἰθύντερος Hdn.Gr.2.927: Sup. ἰθύντατος or -ύτατος (v. infr.):—Ion. and Ep. form of Att. εὐθύς: 1. *straight*, used by Hom. in this sense only in Adv. ἰθύς (infr. II); ἰθείῃ τέχνῃ *straightway, forthwith*, Hdt.9.57; ἰθέα ὁδὸς Id.2.17; ἰθεῖαν (sc. ὁδὸν) *straight on*, Id.7.193; ἐκ τῆς ἰθείης *outright, openly*, Id.2.161, al.; ἰ. ἀτραπός Nic.*Th*.265, cf. *AP*10.3; ἰθύντατον ἴχνος D.P.651; γραφίδες ἰθύταται *AP*6.63 (Damoch.); ἰθύτατον ὄρος *steepest*, App.*Hisp*.1. 2. in moral sense, *straight-forward, just*, εἰ δ' ἄγ' ἐγὼν αὐτὸς δικάσω, . . ἰθεῖα γὰρ ἔσται [ἡ δίκη] Il.23.580; ἰθείῃσι δίκῃσιν *h.Cer*.152, Hes.*Th*.86, cf. *Op*.36; opp. σκολιαὶ δίκαι, ib.224: in Sup. Adv., δίκην ἰθύντατα εἰπεῖν to give judgement *the most fairly*, Il.18.508; later οὔποτε δουλείη κεφαλὴ ἰθεῖα πέφυκεν Thgn.535; πρήξιες ἰθύτεραι Id.1026; Δίκα ἰθεῖα B.14.54; ἰθύς τε καὶ δίκαιος Hdt.1.96; λόγος ἰ. ib.118. II. ἰθύς, or less freq. ἰθύ, as Adv., *straight at*, mostly c. gen. objecti, βῆ ῥ' ἰθὺς Διομήδεος Il.5.849, cf. 16.584; ἰθὺς κίεν οἴκου went *straight towards* the dwelling, 24.471, cf. Od.15.511; ἰθὺ βέλος πέτετ' οὐδ' ἀπολήγει Il.20.99; ἔπλεε ἰθὺ τοῦ Ἴστρου Hdt.4.89; ἰθὺ τῆς ἀρχῆς τῆς Τομύριος 1.207, cf. 6.95, al.; ἰθὺ βαδίζειν Semus 20; ἰθὺς πρὸς τεῖχος ἔκιον Il.12.137; ἰθὺς ἐπὶ Θεσσαλίης Hdt.5.64. 2. abs., ἰθὺς φρονέων resolving to go *straight on*, Il.12.124, cf. 13.135; ἰθὺς μεμαώς 11.95, etc.; of a bird's flight, *SIG*1167.7 (Ephesus, vi B.C.); ἰθὺς μαχέσασθαι to fight *face to face*, Il.17.168; μένος χειρῶν ἰθὺς φέρον 5.506; also τέτραπτο πρὸς ἰθύ οἱ (v.l. πρὸς ἰθύν, cf. sq.) he fronted him *face to face*, 14.403; κατ' ἰθὺ γούνασιν *opposite*, i.e. *vertically below*, the knees, Hp.*Off*.3; of Time, *straightway*, Hdt.3.58. 3. regul. Adv. ἰθέως Id.2.121.β', al.; πλέειν ἰθέως ἐπὶ τὸν Ἑλλήσποντον Id.8.108.

ἰθύς (B) [ῐθῡ], ἡ, used by Hom. only in acc. ἰθύν: 1. ἀν' ἰθύν, = *against*, πρὸς ῥόον ἀΐσσοντος ἀν' ἰθύν *against* the stream, Il.21.303; ἐπεὶ δὴ σφαίρῃ ἀν' ἰθὺν πειρήσαντο in throwing *straight upwards*, Od.8.377; πρὸς ἰθύν v.l. in Il.14.403. 2. *enterprise*, οἵσι μάλιστα πεποίθεα πᾶσαν ἐπ' ἰθύν Od.4.434; ἄριστοι πᾶσαν ἐπ' ἰθὺν ἐστὲ μάχεσθαί τε φρονέειν τε Il.6.79; γυναικῶν γνώομεν ἰθύν their *mood, designs*, Od.16.304; ἐμὴν ἰ. dub. in *h.Ap*.539.

ἰθυ-σκόλιος [ῐθ], ον, *curved in one direction, though straight in another*, of the normal spine, Hp.*Art*.45. **-τένεια**, ἡ, *extension in length*, Ptol.*Geog*.1.2.4. **-τενής**, ές, *straight*, ibid.; κανών *AP*6.65 (Paul. Sil.); στάθμη ib.103 (Phil.); γραμμή Simp. *in Cael*.180.11; στοά Chor.p.85 B.; ξύλα Agath.5.21; *upright, perpendicular*, ῥόπαλον *APl*.4.261 (Leon.): metaph., ἰ. κνήμη Aristaenet.1.27.

ἰθύτης [ῐ], ητος, ἡ, (ἰθύς A) *straightness*, ὁδοῦ Aret.*CA*2.6.

ἰθυ-τμής [ῐ], ῆτος, ὁ, ἡ, *straight-cut*, Nonn.*D*.2.451, 5.282. **-τόνος**, ον, = ἰθυτενής, στάλικες *AP*6.187 (Alph.; v.l. -τενῶν). **-τρηυ** (neut. sg.), = ἰθύτρητον, *bored straight*, Democr.128. **-φαλλικός**, ή, όν, *ithyphallic*, of metre, Heph.15.2, Hermog.*Id*.1.6; τὰ ἰ. *poems in such metre*, D.H.*Comp*.4 (ἰθυφάλλια codd.), Poll.4.53. **-φαλλος**, ὁ, *fascinum erectum, the phallos carried in the festivals of Bacchus*, Cratin.14, etc. II. *ode and dance* performed at such festivals, Hyp.*Fr*.50, Duris 13 J. III. *one who danced in such dance*, Hippoloch.ap.Ath.4.129d, Semus 20, Democh.2 J.: metaph., *lewd fellow*, D.54.14. **-φάνεια** [φᾰ], ἡ, *direct incidence of light*, κατ' ἰθυφάνειαν Damian.*Opt*.12:—Adj. **-φᾰνής**, ές, in phrase κατ' ἰθυφανές, = κατ' ἰθυφάνειαν, ibid. **-φορικός**, ή, όν, *moving in a straight line*, Phlp. *in Mete*.30.18.

ἰθύω [ῐ], aor. ἴθῡσα (v. infr.), *go straight, press right on*, rare in pres., ὁ δέ, κρειῶν ἐρατίζων, ἰθύει [ῠ] Il.11.552; ἔνθα καὶ ἔνθ' ἴθυσε μάχη πεδίοιο the tide of war *set straight* over the plain.., 6.2; ἰθύει τάχιστα δελφίς Pi.*Fr*.234; ἰθύει τὸ ἔμβρυον πρὸς τὸ ἧπαρ Hp.*Mul*.1.32, cf. 2.145 vulg.: c. gen. objecti, ὡς Ἕκτωρ ἴθυσε νεὸς *dashed straight at* it, Il.15.693; ἴθυσαν δ' ἐπὶ τεῖχος 12.443; ἴθυσαν πρός.. Hdt.4.122. II. c. inf., *to be eager, strive* to do, τῶν ὁπότ' ἰθύσειε.. ἐπὶ χερσὶ μάσασθαι Od.11.591; ἴθυσέν ῥ' ὀλολύξαι 22.408; ὅκῃ ἰθύσειε στρατεύεσθαι whichever way he *purposed* to march, Hdt.1.204, cf. 3.39; ἰθύοντα στρατεύεσθαι Id.7.8.β'. 2. c. acc., *desire eagerly*, τι μετὰ φρεσίν A.R.2.950. 3. abs., τί μακρὰν γλῶσσαν ἰθύσας ἐλαύνω ἐκτὸς ὁδοῦ; why *in my zeal* do I drive, etc., B.9.51. (Signf. I never in Od., signf. II never in Il.)

ἰθυωρίη [ῐθ], ἡ, Ion. for εὐθυωρία, *direction, straightness*, of a limb, etc., Hp.*Off*.15 (pl.), *Fract*.30, al.

ἰθών· πυγή, λαγαρός, καὶ πρωκτός, Hsch. (fort. ἴθων).

ἰίζω, (ἰός) *to be like rust, ferruginous*, Dsc.5.75, 103.

ἱκᾰνο-δοσία [ῐκ], ἡ, = Lat. *satisdatio*, *Cod.Just*.2.12.27.2 (also in pl.), Just.*Nov*.131.15 *Intr*. **-δοτέω**, = Lat. *satisdare*, *POxy*.259.29 (i A.D.). **-δότης**, ου, ὁ, *one who gives security*, *BGU*1189.3. II. *one who requites*, ὁ ἰ. θεός *PMasp*.6 ii 82 (vi A.D.). **-ποιέω**, *make satisfaction*, *Gloss*.

ἱκᾰν-ός [ῐ], ή, όν, (ἱκνέομαι) *sufficing, becoming, befitting*; prose Adj., used two or three times by Trag. (v. infr.): I. of persons, *sufficient, competent to do* a thing, c. inf., Hdt.3.45, Antipho 1.15, etc.; ἰ. τεκμηριῶσαι *sufficient* to prove a point, Th.1.9; -ώτατος [εἰπεῖν] καὶ γνῶναι Lys.2.42; τίς σοῦ -ώτερος πεῖσαι; X.*Cyr*.1.4.12; ἰ. ζημιοῦν *with sufficient power* to punish, Id.*Lac*.8.4; ἰ. βοηθεῖν Pl.*Phdr*.277a, cf. *R*.365a; ἰ. ὥστε γνῶναι Id.*Lg*.875a, cf. *Phdr*.258b; ἰ. κατὰ τὴν ἐπιφάνειαν Plb.25.3.6, al.: c. acc. rei, ἀνὴρ γνώμην ἰ. a man of *sufficient* prudence, Hdt.3.4; ἰ. τὴν ἰατρικὴν *sufficiently versed in* medicine, X.*Cyr*.1.6.15: c. dat. rei, ἰ. ἐμπειρίᾳ καὶ ἡλικίᾳ Pl.*R*.467d; οἱ τοῖς χρήμασιν -ώτατοι X.*Eq*.2.1: c. dat. pers., *a match for, equivalent to*, εἷς ἔχων ἰατρικὴν πολλοῖς ἰ. ἰδιώταις Pl.*Prt*.322c, cf. *Tht*.169a: abs., ἰ. Ἀπόλλων S.*OT*377; οἱ -ώτατοι τῶν πολιτῶν Isoc.12.132; κριτὴς -ώτερος Id.10.38; ἰ. σοφιστής Pl.*Ly*.204a; αὐληταὶ ἰ. ὡς πρὸς ἰδιώτας *very tolerable* in comparison with.., Id.*Prt*.327c; γυνὴ ἰ. μέν, ἄγροικος δέ Luc.*DDeor*.20.3; ὁ Ἰ. *the Almighty*, Lxx *Ru*.1.21. 2. in bad sense, *capable*, ἰ. εἶ λαλῶν κατακόψαι πάντα Men.*Sam*.69. II. of things, in amount, *sufficient, adequate*, τὰ ἀρκοῦνθ' ἰ. τοῖς γε σώφροσιν E.*Ph*.554; ἰ. τὰ κακὰ καὶ τὰ παρακείμενα Ar.*Lys*.1047; ἱκανὰ τοῖς πολεμίοις ηὐτύχηται they have had successes *enough*, Th.7.77; ἰ. εἴς, ἐπί, πρός τι, X.*Hier*.4.9, Pl.*R*.371e, *Prt*.322b; [πρόβατα] ἰ. ἐς φορβήν Hdt.4.121; of size, *large enough*, οὐχ ἱκανῆς οὔσης τῆς Ἀττικῆς Th.1.2; οὐδ' ἦν ἱκανά σοι.. μέλαθρα.. ἐγκαθυβρίζειν not *large enough* to riot in, E.*Tr*.996; χώρα ἰ. τρέφειν τοὺς τότε Pl.*R*.373d, al.; of number or magnitude, *considerable*, λῦπαι Antipho 2.2.2; μέρος τῶν ὄντων ib.2.1.6, etc.; of Time, *considerable, long*, ἰ. χρόνον Ar.*Pax* 354 (lyr.); ἰ. χρόνος τινὶ ἐπιλαθέσθαι Lys.3.10; ἱκανόν ἐστί τινι Damox.1.1: with personal constr., ἔφη ἱκανὸς αὐτὸς ἀτυχῶν εἶναι Is.2.7. 2. *sufficient, satisfactory*, ἰ. μαρτυρίαν παρέχεσθαι Pl.*Smp*.179b; ἰ. λόγῳ ἀποδεῖξαι Id.*Hp.Mi*.369c; τὸ ἰ. λαμβάνειν to take *security* or *bail*, *Act.Ap*.17.9, *OGI*629.100 (Palmyra, ii A.D.); τὸ ἰ. ποιεῖν give *security*, Plb.32.3.13, D.L.4.50, Just.*Nov*.86.4 (but simply, *satisfy*, τῷ ὄχλῳ *Ev.Marc*.15.15); ἰ. δοῦναι *PSI*6.554.23 (iii B.C.), *POxy*.294.23 (i A.D.); ἐφ' ἱκανόν, = ἱκανῶς, Plb.11.25.1, D.S.11.40. III. Adv. -νῶς *sufficiently, adequately*, Th.6.92, etc.; λαγόνες λαπαραὶ ἰ. X.*Cyn*.5.30, cf. Arist.*Phgn*.807b26; ἰ. εἴρηται περί τινος Id.*EN*1096a3, al.; later, *considerably, amply*, Philostr.*VA*3.6, *VS*1.8.3, Ant.Lib.7.7; *fully*, μιᾶς ὥρας ἰ. παρελθούσης Ptol.*Alm*.4.6. b. *excessively*, οὔτε γὰρ ἰ. ὑγρόν ἐστι not *too* moist, Gal.6.765, cf. 767,768; ἰ. βλαβερά Id.*Vict.Att*.8; παχὺ ἰ. αἷμα ibid. 2. ἰ. ἔχειν to be *sufficient*, Th.1.91, etc.; ἰ. ἐχέτω let this be *enough*, Pl.*Sph*.245e; ἰ. ἔχει πρός τι Id.*R*.430c, cf. X.*Cyr*.6.3.22; περί τινος Pl.*R*.402a; ἰ. ἔχειν τινί to be *sufficiently* supplied *with*.., Id.*Grg*.493c; ἰ. ἔχειν τοῦ βάθους Id.*Tht*.194d; ἐπιστήμης Id.*Phlb*.62a; ἰ. πεφυκέναι πρὸς τἄλλα Id.*Chrm*.158b: abs., Antipho 2.1.1: Sup. -ωτάτως Hp.*de Arte* 12; -ώτατα Pl.*Phlb*.67a. **-ότης**, ητος, ἡ, *sufficiency, fitness*, Id.*Ly*.215a. II. *a sufficiency*, παίδων Id.*Lg*.930c. **-όω**, *make sufficient, qualify*, 2*Ep.Cor*.3.6:—Pass., *to be empowered*, *PTeb*.20.8 (ii B.C.); *to be made complete, brought to perfection*, of the soul, τῷ περιέχοντι Hierocl.p.9 A. II. Pass., *to be satisfied, content*, τινι D.H.2.74: abs., Telesp.39 H., cf. Lxx *Ma*.3.10; ἱκανούσθω ὑμῖν, c. inf., *let it suffice you*.., i.e. do it no more, Lxx 3*Ki*.12.28, al.: abs., ib.*Nu*.16.7.

ἵκαντι, v. ἵκω. **ἱκάντιν**· εἴκοσιν, Hsch. (cf. ϝίκατι).

ἱκάνω [ῑκᾰ], impf. ἵκᾰνον [ῑ by the augm.], used only in these tenses, the fut., aor., and pf. being supplied by ἱκνέομαι:—lengthd. form of ἵκω, found in Ep. and Lyr., sts. in Trag., *come*, ἐς Χρύσην, ἐς Σκαιάς.. πύλας, Il.1.431, 9.354; ἐπὶ νῆας 2.17; ἐνθάδε Od.15.492; so οἴκαδε A.*Ag*.1337 (anap.); οἳ ἱκάνομεν S.*El*.8; πρὸς ἐσχατιὰν Pi.*O*.3.43, cf. B.10.96: in Hom. mostly c. acc., *to come to*, ἱκάνω νῆας Ἀχαιῶν Il.24.501; ἱκανέμεν ἡμέτερον δῶ Od.4.139; later ἰ. δόμους A.*Pers*.159 (troch.): abs., ἦ φίλοι ἄνδρες ἱκάνετον Il.9.197; εὖ ἱκάνεις S.*El*.1102. 2. *reach, attain to*, [ἐλάτη] δι' ἠέρος αἰθέρ' ἵκανεν Il.14.288; φωνὴ δέ οἱ αἰθέρ' ἵκανεν 15.686; [ἄνεμος] αἰπὺν ἰ. οὐρανόν Sol.13.21; ἥβης μέτρον ἰ. Od.18.217, 19.532. II. c. acc. pers., esp. of grief, hardship, etc.; με πένθος ἱκάνει Od.6.169; μέγα πένθος Ἀχαιΐδα γαῖαν ἱκάνει Il.1.254; τάφος δέ οἱ ἦτορ ἵ. Od.23.93; ἄλγος, γῆρας, δύη, κάματος, κῆδος, ὀϊζύς, μόρος, ἱκάνει τινά, 2.41, Il.4.321 (v.l.), Od.18.81, 5.457, Il.15.245, Od.5.289, Il.18.465; ὅτε μιν γλυκὺς ὕπνος ἱκάνοι 1.610; με παλαίφατα θέσφαθ' ἱκάνει they *are fulfilled* upon me, Od.9.507: c. dupl. acc., μιν ἄχος κραδίην καὶ θυμὸν ἰ. Il.2.171: rarely c. dat., σφῶϊν ἐελδομένοισιν ἱκάνω Od.21.209. 2. of a suppliant, σόν τε πόσιν σά τε γούναθ' ἱκάνω 7.147, al. III. Med., in signf. I.1, οἶκον ἱκάνεται 23.7; in signf. II.1, χρειὼ γὰρ ἱκάνεται Il.10.118; in signf. II.2, τὰ σὰ γούναθ' ἱκάνομαι 18.457, Od.3.92, 4.322. (Fr. ἱκ-άνϝ-ω, ἱκ-ηϝ-ω (cf. ἱκνέομαι); Aeol. ἴκᾰνε dub. in Alc.*Supp*.34, [ἴκᾰ]νε prob. in Sapph.*Oxy*.2076.16; ἵκανον f.l. in Od.15.101.)

Ἰκάριος [ῑκᾰ], α, ον, *Icarian*, πόντος Il.2.145; πέλαγος Hdt.6.96.

ἰκάς [ῑ], άδος, ἁ, Dor. etc. for εἰκάς, *twentieth* of the month, *SIG*1025.47 (Cos), *IG*9(2).517.10 (Larissa); hικάς ib.12(3).1324 (Thera, vi/v B.C.). (ϝικ- in pr. n. Ϝικάδιος ib.5(2).271.8 (Mantinea).)

ϝίκατι, v. εἴκοσι:—hence **ἰκαστός**, = εἰκοστός, *IG*5(2).4.18 (Tegea, iv B.C.): **Ϝῑκατίδειος**, ὁ, *twenty feet broad*, [ἄντομος] *Tab.Heracl*.2.18, al. **Ϝικατιϝέτης**, v. εἰκοσαέτης. **Ϝῑκατίπεδος**, ον, v. εἰκοσίπεδος.

ἴκελος [ῐ], η, ον, poet. and Ion. form of εἴκελος, *like, resembling*, τινι Il.11.467, al., Hes.*Sc*.198, Sapph.*Supp*.20b.1, B.*Fr*.19, Hdt.3.81, Hp.*Epid*.3.4, Ar.*Av*.575, Theoc.2.51, etc.; ὀργαῖς ἀλωπέκων ἰ. *like* foxes in disposition, Pi.*P*.2.77; ἐπιθυμίῃ κυνὶ ἰ. Democr.224: c. gen., θέας ἰκέλαν dub. in Sapph.*Supp*.25.4. Adv. -λως, c. dat., *in the same way as*, Hp.*Gland*.8, Diotog.ap.Stob.4.1.133.

ἰκελόω [ῐ], *make like*, *AP*9.83 (Phil.).

ἰκενάς· ὀρχήσεις, Hsch. (cf. σικανοί, σίκιννις).

ἱκεσ-ία, ἡ, (ἱκέτης) (replaced by ἱκετεία in Att., cf. Phryn.3, *PS* p.77 B., but found in *IG*1².434; used later, *SIG*781.11 (Nysa, i B.C.), 888.11 (Scaptopara, iii A.D.), etc.):—*the prayer of a suppliant, supplication*, E.*Or.*1337, Plu.*Sol.*12, J.*AJ*11.8.4, *AP*5.215 (Agath.); πρὸς παντοίαν ἱ. τραπῆναι D.S.20.14: pl., Ph.2.2; ἱκεσίαισι σαῖς at thy *entreaties*, E.*Ph.*91; ἱκεσίας ποιεῖσθαι, on behalf of the state, Aeschin. 3.121; = Lat. *supplicatio*, D.H.8.43. 2. = ἱκέτευμα, Plu.*Them.*24. [ῐ, but ῑ metri gr. in *AP*l.c., Procl.*H.*1.36.] **-ιος**, α, ον, or ος, ον (v. infr.), *of* or *for suppliants*, epith. of Zeus, their protector, A.*Supp.* 616, S.*Ph.*484, E.*Hec.*345, *SIG*929 (Cos); also Ἱκέσιος alone, *IG*12 (3).402 (Thera); πρὸς Ἱκεσίου Luc.*Pisc.*3; ἱκεσία Θέμις Διός A.*Supp.* 360 (lyr.). 2. *of* or *consisting of suppliants*, παρθένων ἱ. λόχος Id. *Th.*111 (lyr.). 3. *suppliant*, ἱκεσίους πέμπων λιτάς S.*Ph.*495; ἱκεσίαν..προστροπάν E.*Heracl.*108 (lyr.); ἱκεσίοις σὺν κλάδοις Id.*Supp.* 102; ἱκεσίᾳ χερί ib.108; ἀνάγκας ἱκεσίους λῦσαι ib.39; of persons, ἱκέσιός σε λίσσομαι S.*Ant.*1230; ἱκεσία τε γίγνομαι E.*Med.*710: ἱκέσιος, ὁ, as Subst., *suppliant*, *Berl.Sitzb.*1927.167 (Cyrene). II. ἡ Ἱκέσιος (sc. ἔμπλαστρος), name of a *plaster*, Paul.Aeg.3.62, 7.17; ἡ Ἱκεσίου Id.3.64. [ῐκ-, exc. metri gr. in A.R.2.215.]

ἱκετᾱδόκος, ον, *receiving suppliants*, σκοπή A.*Supp.*713.

ἱκετ-εία [ῐ], ἡ, more Att. form of ἱκεσία (q.v.), *supplication*, Th.1. 24; ἱκετείαν ποιεῖσθαί τινος to supplicate him, Id.3.67; ἱκετεῖαι θεῶν *addressed to* them, Lys.2.39; ἐφ' ἱκετείαν τραπόμενος Pl.*Ap.*39a; μετὰ δεήσεως καὶ ἱ. *PPetr.*2p.60(iii B.C.), cf. *SIG*1181.12 (Jewish): pl., -είας ποιεῖσθαι Pl.*Smp.*183a, etc. **-ευμα**, ατος, τό, *mode of supplication*, μέγιστον ἱ. Th.1.137, cf. D.C.68.21. **-ευσις**, εως, ἡ, = ἱκεσία, Suid. **-ευτέος**, α, ον, *to be besought* or *entreated*, Luc.*Merc.Cond.*38. **-ευτικός**, ή, όν, *supplicatory*, Sch.S.*OT* 143; = *precarius*, *Gloss.* Adv. -κῶς Hsch. s.v. ἀντήδης. **-εύω**, fut. -σω E.*IA*462 (cj. Markl.), Isoc.7.69: aor. 1 ἱκέτευσα: used by Hom. only in impf. and aor. with ῐ metri gr., but in Trag. ῑ from the augm.:—Med. and Pass. (v. infr.):—*approach as a suppliant*, ἐπεί σε φυγὼν ἱκέτευσα Od.15.277, al.; ἐς Πηλῆ' ἱκέτευσε Il.16. 574; ἐς Θήβας ἱ. Hes.*Sc.*13; ἱ. σε τῶνδε γουνάτων, πρὸς γονάτων σε, E.*Hec.*752, *Med.*854 (lyr.): abs., Hdt.3.48, Isoc.7.69, Phld.*Piet.* 63. 2. *supplicate, beseech*, c. acc. pers. et inf., ὁ δέ με μάλα πόλλ' ἱκέτευεν ἱππόθεν ἐξέμεναι Od.11.530, cf. Hdt.1.11, S.*OC*1414, E.*Ion* 468 (lyr.); δέομαι ὑμῶν καὶ ἱ. καὶ ἀντιβολῶ.. βοηθῆσαι D.27. 68; δεόμενον καὶ ἱκετεύοντα σοφίας μεταδιδόναι Pl.*Euthd.*282b; ἱ. τὸν θεόν, ἵνα.. Aristeas 233; ἱκετεύεις ἵνα ἀφεθῇς Arr.*Epict.*3.24.76; ἱ. ὡς.. Luc.*Anach.*1: c. gen. pers. et inf., *beg of* one that.., E.*IA* 1242: c. dat., interpol. in Is.2.8:—Pass., τοῦ θεοῦ ἱκετευθέντος ὑπὸ σοῦ J.*AJ*6.2.2. 3. c. acc. rei, ὑπὲρ οἴκου..ἱ. τάδε E.*Or.*673; ὅσα πρὸς ἱεροῖς ἱκέτευσαν Th.2.47; περὶ ὧν ἔδοξεν ἔννομα ἱκετεύειν ἐν τῇ βουλῇ *IG*2².218.8, cf. 337.34:—Pass., τὰ -όμενα Aristeas 192. 4. in Trag., freq. parenthetic, ἱκετεύω or ἱκετεύω σε, S.*Ph.*932, 1183 (lyr.), E.*Hec.*97 (anap.), cf. Ar.*Nu.*696, al.:—Med., Id.*Ec.*915 (lyr.). **-ήριος**, poet. **ἱκτήριος**, α, ον, as Adj. in the latter form only, *of* or *fit for suppliants*, ἱ. θησαυρός, of hair offered to a god, S. *Aj.*1175; κλάδοι Id.*OT*3; ἱκτήριοι, = ἱκέται, ib.327; φωτῶν ἱκτήρια, = φῶτας ἱκτηρίους, Id.*OC*923. II. ἱκετηρία, poet. ἱκτηρία, Ion. -ίη (sc. ῥάβδος), ἡ, *olive-branch which the suppliant held in his hand* as a symbol of his condition, λευκοστεφεῖς ἱκτηρίας A.*Supp.*192; ἱκετηρίην λαβεῖν, φέρειν, Hdt.5.51, 7.141; ἱκετηρίαν ἔχειν Ar.*Pl.*383; καταθεῖναι ἐν τῷ Ἐλευσινίῳ And.1.110, cf. *UPZ*1.9 (iv B.C.); esp. of petitions laid before the Athenian people, ἱ. θεῖναι And. l.c., Arist.*Ath.*43.6 (less correctly θέσθαι Poll.8.96, wh. is a later use, cf. *SIG*²666.6 (Samos)); ὑπὲρ θυγατρὸς ἱ. τιθεμένη *PTeb.*326.3 (iii A.D.); ἱ. ἔθηκεν παρ' ὑμῖν, = ἱκέτευσεν ὑμᾶς, D.18.107, cf. 24.12; ὑπὲρ τοῦ μισθοῦ ἱ. θεῖναι εἰς τὴν βουλήν Aeschin.1.104, cf. 2.15; later ἱ. πέμπειν, προβάλλεσθαι, Plu.*Pomp.*28, Ael.*VH*3.26; ἱκετηρίας προσενέγκας, ἱκετηρίαν προσάγειν, *Ep.Hebr.*5.7, *POxy.*71 i 3 (iv A.D.): metaph., ἱκετηρίαν δὲ γόνασιν ἐξάπτω σέθεν τὸ σῶμα τοὐμόν, where the suppliant represents herself as the olive-branch, E.*IA*1216; νομίζετε τὸν παῖδα τουτονὶ ἱκετηρίαν προκεῖσθαι D.43.83. 2. = ἱκεσία, v.l. in Isoc.8. 138 (pl.), cf. Plb.3.112.8 (pl.), Jul.*ad Ath.*275c, Hld.7.7. **-ηρίς**, ίδος, ἡ, pecul. fem. of ἱκετήριος, Orph.*H.*3.13, 34.27. **-ης**, ου, ὁ, (ἱκνέομαι) *one who comes to seek aid* or *protection, suppliant*; freq. in Hom. of *one who comes to seek for purification after homicide*, ἀνὴρ ἱ. Il. 24.158, cf. Od.9.270, al.: later generally, ἱκέται ἱζόμενοι τοῦ θεοῦ Hdt.2.113, cf. 5.71; ἱ. σέθεν ἔρχομαι Pi.*O.*5.19, cf. S.*OC*634, Th.1. 136; ἱ. πατρῴων τάφων Id.3.59; δέξασθαι ἱκέτην A.*Supp.*27 (anap.); of pilgrims to a healing shrine, ἐγκεκοιμισμένων τῶν ἱκετᾶν *IG*4.951. 90 (Epid.); ὑβρίζειν..εἰς ἱκέτας Phld.*Ir.*p.35 W.:—wrongly expld. as *protector of suppliants* by some Gramm. in Od.16.422. **-ήσιος**, α, ον, epith. of Zeus, = ἱκέσιος, 13.213. II. *suppliant*, Nonn. *D.*36.379. **-ικός**, ή, όν, = ἱκετήριος, Ph.2.546, Aq.*Pr.*27.6. Adv. -κῶς Sch.Par.A.R.1.824, Sch.E.*Hec.*147. **-ις** (parox.), ιδος, ἡ, fem. of ἱκέτης, Hdt.4.165, 9.76, A.*Supp.*350, 428 (both lyr.), S.*OT* 920, *IG*4.951.4 (Epid.), A.R.4.743, etc.

ἱκετοδόχος, ον, = ἱκεταδόκος, Eust.1807.9.

ἱκετώσυνα (sc. ἱερά), τά, *purifications*, Hsch.

ἵκηαι, Ep. for ἵκῃ, 2 sg. aor. 2 subj. of ἱκνέομαι.

ἴκκος, ὁ, = ἵππος, *EM*474.12; cf. ἵππος sub fin.

ἰκμ-ᾰδώδης, ες, *moist, wet*, Hsch. s.v. ἴκμενος, dub. in Sch.Arat. 1065: **ἰκματώδης** in Ach.Tat.*Intr.*34. **-άζω**, = sq., Nic.*Fr.*70. 17. II. *filter through, ooze*, Alex.Aphr. *in Mete.*87.27. III. *evaporate moisture, dry up*, ἰκμασθέντος δὲ τούτου Plu.2.954e codd.; ἰκμάζειν· κατασκελετεύειν, Hsch. **-αίνω**, *moisten*, Nic.*Al.*112:—Med., δέμας ἰκμαίνεσθαι *anoint one's* body, A.R.3.847:—Pass., *to be wetted, to be wet*, Nic.*Fr.*70.8, A.R.4.1066. **-αῖος**, ὁ, (ἰκμάς) epith. of Zeus, *god of rain*, Id.2.522, Nonn.*D.*5.270. **-ᾰλέος**, α, ον, *damp, wet*, Ath.Med.ap.Orib.*inc.*23.23, Aret.*SD*2.1, Opp.*H.*3.595. 2. *full of fluid*, of the liver, Hp.*Mul.*1.7.

ἴκμαρ, τό, = sq., Hsch. (Rather ἰκμάρ, if Lacon.) II. v.l. ant. for ἴκταρ (B), Erot.

ἰκμ-άς, άδος, ἡ, *moisture*, e.g. of oily leather, Il.17.392; ἰκμάδος ἐστὶ ἐν αὐτῇ [τῇ Λιβύῃ] οὐδέν Hdt.4.185; ἀνιεὶς ἐκ τοῦ σώματος ἰκμάδα, of a corpse exposed to the sun, Id.3.125, cf. Hp.*Aër.*8; of *moisture* in the soil, *Ev.Luc.*8.6; also θανόντων ἰσὶν οὐκ ἔνεστ' ἰκμάς no *blood*, A.*Fr.*229 (prob.); of the bodily *humours*, Hp.*Morb.*4.40; of all kinds of *animal juices* or *moist secretions*, τὸ περίττωμα τῆς ὑγρᾶς ἰ. ὃν καλοῦμεν ἱδρῶτα Arist.*PA*668ᵇ4; ἡ τῶν καταμηνίων ἰ. Id.*GA*727ᵇ11, cf. *HA*556ᵇ27, al.: com. metaph., τὴν ἰ. τῆς φροντίδος Ar.*Nu.*233; ἰ. Βάκχου, i.e. wine, *AP*5.133 (Posidipp.); ἰ. δρυός, i.e. gum, ib.6.109 (Antip.). **-ᾰσία**, ἡ, = ἰκμάς, Hsch., *Gloss.*

ἰκμάω (A), = λικμάω, Hsch. (Act. and Pass.):—also **ἰκμάσαι·** ἐφορμῆσαι, Id. (For νικμάω, ν being lost by dissimilation; v. νεικητήρ.)

ἰκμάω (B), in Pass., Cypr. acc. pl. masc. pf. part. ἰκμαμένος *wounded*, *Inscr.Cypr.*135.3 H. (or ἰγμ- as *Schwyzer* 679.3). (Perh. cogn. with Lat. *ico.*)

ἴκμενος, only in the phrase ἴκμενος οὖρος, of *a fair* breeze, Il.1.479, Od.2.420, al.; not *moist*, as Hsch. (Perh. not related to ἵκω, ἱκνέομαι.)

ἴκμη, ἡ, (ἰκμάς) *a plant growing in moist places, duckweed, Lemna minor*, Thphr.*HP*4.10.1.

ἴκμιος, α, ον, *moist*, Nonn.*D.*2.490. 2. = ἰκμαῖος, as epith. of Aristaeus, Call.*Aet.*3.1.34.

ἰκμόβωλον, τό, *wet clod of earth*, Dsc.2.106.

ἰκμώδης, ες, *moist, wet*, Sch.rec.A.*Pr.*88.

ἰκνά· τροφεῖα, **ἰκνεῖαν·** τροφεῖαν, **ἰκνεῖος·** τροφεύς (Rhodian words), Hsch.

ἱκνέομαι, lengthd. form of ἵκω (q.v.), ἱκάνω, wh. are the Homeric forms of the pres. (exc. ἱκνεύμεναι, ἱκνεύμεσθα, Od.9.128, 24.339), first in Alc.98 (s.v.l.): impf. ἱκνεῖτο S.*OC*970: fut. ἵξομαι Il.6.502, Parm. 3.2, A.*Supp.*159 (lyr.); Dor. ἱξοῦμαι *AP*9.341 (Glauc.): aor. 2 ἱκόμην Il.8.149, etc.; inf. ἵκεσθαι Sapph.*Supp.*1.2 [ῐ, exc. when lengthd. by the augm.]; for part. ἴκμενος v. sub voce: pf. ἷγμαι S.*Tr.*229, part. ἱγμένος Id.*Ph.*494: non-thematic aor. 2 ἶκτο Hes.*Th.*481, [Simon.]179.4, Euph.2: (ἀφικνέομαι is used in early Prose, exc. in signf. III; ἵκοντο is f.l. in Th.5.40, ἵκηται is a poet. reminiscence in Pl.*Phdr.*276d; but ἵκετο is found in Hdt.1.216, ἵκηται Hp.*Loc.Hom.* 47; also in later Prose, Luc.*Salt.*5, *DDeor.*6.4, Procop.*Pers.*1.4, 2.21):—*come*, αἶψα δ' ἵκοντο Il.18.532; ὁππότε Κρήτηθεν ἵκοιτο when he *came* to us.., 3.233; ὑπότροπον οἴκαδ' ἱ. Od.22.35; ἐς χῶρον Il.4. 446; ἐπὶ νῆας 6.69; κατὰ λειμῶνα Od.24.13; πρὸς γούνατα Hes.*Th.* 460; ὑπὸ πτόλιν Il.11.182; εἰς δμόν Parm.8.46; πρὸς ὁμοῖον Emp.62. 6; τυῖδ' ἵκεσθαι Sapph.l.c.: freq. in Hom., c. acc., *arrive at*, ἵκετο νῆας Il.8.149; τέλος ἵκεο μύθων 9.56; οἶκον..καὶ σὴν ἐς πατρίδα γαῖαν Od.23.258; later ἱκέσθαι γαῖαν Pi.*P.*4.118 codd.; βένθος Emp.35.3; ἄλσος A.*Supp.*556 (lyr.); στέγας S.*OT*534, etc. 2. *reach, attain to*, ποσὶν οὖδας ἱ. Od.8.376; οὐδ' ἵκετο χρόα καλόν, of a spear, Il.11.352; οὐδ' ὀστέον ἵκετο Od.19.451 (v. ὑπερείπω); so of things, ἠχή, καπνὸς αἰθέρ' ἱ., Il.13.837, 18.207; ἔμπης ἐς γαῖάν τε καὶ οὐρανὸν ἵκετ' ἀϋτμή 14. 174; ἐς πόλιν ἵκετ' αὐτή Od.14.265; of Time, ἥβης μέτρον or ἥβην ἱ., Il.11.225, 24.728, etc.; γήραος οὐδόν Od.15.246; so ἐπὶ γῆρας 8.227; ἠῶ ἱ. *live till* morn, 17.497; also ὀλέθρου πεῖραθ' ἱ. Il.6.143; λέκτροιο παλαιοῦ θεσμὸν ἵκοντο Od.23.296, cf. 354; φίλην ἐπὶ γένναν ἵ. Emp. 110.9; ἐς ἄπειρον Xenoph.28; ἐς τὸ τυθῆναι Hdt.1.216; εἰς τὸ λήθης γῆρας Pl.*Phdr.* l.c.:—in various phrases, ἱ. μετὰ κλέος *come in* quest of glory, Il.11.227; ἐς χεῖρας ἱ. *come* into one's power, 10. 448; ὅ τι χεῖρας ἵκοιτο whatever *came* to hand, Od.12.331; ἱ. ἐς γενεάν τινος into his family, Pi.*N.*10.14; ἐς λόγους τοὺς σοὺς ἱ. to speak with thee, S.*El.*315; ἐνθάδ' ἵξομαι *shall come* to this *at last*, Id.*Aj.* 1365; ἤν ποτε δασμὸς ἵκηται if ever a division *come about*, Il.1. 166. II. with a person as object, τινα ib.139, etc.; ἔς τινα Od. 6.176; but also, *come to his house*, 20.372; Πηλεΐωνάδ' ἵ. *to the hut* of the son of P., Il.24.338; μετὰ Τρῶας ἱ. 3.264: rarely c. dat., ἐπειγομένοισι δ' ἵκοντο *came to* them at need, 12.374; cf. ἱκάνω II. 2. of suffering, desire, anger, etc., *come upon*, Ἀχιλλῆος ποθὴ ἵξεται υἷας Ἀχαιῶν Il.1.240; τί σε φρένας ἵκετο πένθος; ib.362; ὅν τιν' ἵκηται ἄλη καὶ πῆμα καὶ ἄλγος Od.15.345; ὁππότε μιν κάματός τε καὶ ἱδρὼς γούναθ' ἵκοιτο Il.13.711; ἄδος, σέβας ἵ. τινα θυμόν, 11.88, 18.178; με ἵ. ἄχος κραδίην 23.47. 3. *approach as suppliant*, τὴν ἱκόμην φεύγων 14.260, cf. 22.123; τὰ σὰ γοῦνα ἱκόμεθ' Od.9.267; θεοὺς προστροπαῖς ἱκνουμένη A.*Pers.*216 (troch.); Ζῆνα..ἱξόμεσθα σὺν κλάδοις Id.*Supp.*159 (lyr.); [θεὸν] θυέεσσιν ἱκνεῖσθαι *approach* a god with offerings and prayer, Theoc.*Ep.*8.3. b. Poet. in pres., *supplicate, beseech*, τάσδε τὰς θεὰς καλῶν ἱκνοῦμαι S.*OC*1011; καί σε πρὸς τοῦ σοῦ τέκνου καὶ θεῶν ἱκνοῦμαι μή.. Id.*Aj.*588, cf. *OC*275, *Ph.*470; ταύτης ἱκνοῦμαί σ' E.*Or.*671: c. inf., πάντες σ' ἱκνοῦνται..θάψαι νεκρούς Id.*Supp.*130: freq. parenthetic, S.*Ph.*932, *El.*136 (lyr.), Ar.*Ec.*958, Tim.*Pers.*139. III. pres. and impf., *it becomes, befits, pertains to*, c. acc. et inf., φαμὲν ἡμέας ἱκνέεσθαι ἡγεμονεύειν Hdt.9.26; τοὺς μάλιστα ἱκνέεται (sc. κεκάρθαι) Id.2.36; ἱκνέεται *it is usual* that.., Hp.*Art.*63; later, not impers., οὗ ἡ ἱερουργία ἱκνεῖτο D.C.*Fr.*25.5; ὅ[σα τᾶς δίκας ἱ]κνεῖται *SIG*953.46

(Cnidos, ii B.C.). **b.** αὐτὸς καὶ ὧν ἱκνεῖται, of a man and *those to whom he belongs*, i.e. his family, ib.46.25, al. (Halic.). **2.** freq. in part., τὸ ἱκνεύμενον *that which is fitting, proper*, Hdt.6.84; ὁ ἱ., with or without χρόνος, *the fit, proper* time, Hp.*Aer.*7, Hdt.6.86.α'; ἐν ἱκνουμένᾳ ἁμέρᾳ Orac.ap.D.43.66; τὸ ἱ. ἀνάλωμα *the quota* of expense, Th.1.99; κατὰ τοὺς ἱ. χρόνους Arist.*GA*750ᵇ13 (also of *the latter days*, D.H.1.66); ἱ. καιροί Thphr.*CP*1.13.3; τὰ -ούμενα μεγέθη Arist.*GA*772ᵃ8; ἡ ἱ. ἐπιστήμη Id.*Pol.*1288ᵇ16; τῆς ἱ. ἡλικίας τυχεῖν ib.1332ᵇ41; also ἱκνούμεναι ἀποδείξεις *convincing* proofs, Phld.*Piet.*79; οὐδὲν εἴρηται ἱ. S.E.*M.*1.205; λόγος τινὶ ἱκνούμενος *favourable*, *SIG*679.77 (Magn. Mae., ii B.C.). Adv. ἱκνουμένως, Ion. -ευμένως, *fittingly, aright*, Hdt.6.65, Hp.*Mul.*2.135, M.Ant.5.12.

ἴκνυς, υος, ἡ, *dust* or *ashes*, τὰν ἴκνυν ἀπὸ τῶ βωμῶ.. ἀφελὲν ἐς καθαρὸν *Berl.Sitzb.*1927.159 (Cyrene); cf. **ἴκνυον**· κονίαν, σμῆμα, Hsch.; τὴν ἴγνυν οἴνῳ διατρίψας, δοῦναι πιεῖν Hp.*Nat.Mul.*88 (v.l. ἴγδην).

ἴκρια, τά (sg. v. infr. III; for the accent v. Hdn.Gr.1.357), *half-deck* at the stern of a ship, νηῶν ἴκρι' ἐπῴχετο μακρὰ βιβάσθων Il.15.676; [κυβερνήτης] κάππεσ' ἀπ' ἰκριόφιν Od.12.414; εἰς ἴκρια νηὸς ἔβαινον πρῴρης (i.e. from the prow) ib.229; νηὸς ἐπ' ἰκριόφιν καταλέξεται 3.353; εὐπάκτων ἐπ' ἰκρίων σταθεὶς ὄρουσε B.16.83: wrongly expld. by Eust. as = ἐγκοίλια in Od.5.252, but perh. so used by Nonn. *D.*40.447,452; expld. as = κεραία in A.R.1.566 by Sch., but prob. wrongly, cf. Lyc.751. **II.** generally, *platform, stage*, ἴκρια ἐπὶ σταυρῶν ὑψηλῶν.. ἔστηκε Hdt.5.16, cf. Str.12.3.18, Hsch. **2.** *scaffolding*, *IG*1².94.28 (prob. in 374.151), 4.39 (Aegina, v B.C.), *BCH*6.27 (Delos, ii B.C.). **3.** *benches* in a theatre, Cratin.323, Ar.*Th.*395, Ath.4.167f. **4.** dub. sens. in Thphr.*HP*5.6.2. **III.** sg., = ἱστός, *mast*, Eust.1533.31; *pole*, dub. l. in Nic.*Th.*198; set up on a cenotaph, Marcellin.*Vit. Thuc.*31.

ἰκριάς, ἡ, = *pergula*, *Gloss.* (dub.).

ἴκρινον, τό, = *tabulum*, *Gloss.* (dub.).

ἰκριο-ποιέω, = ἰκριόω I, *Rev.Phil.*50.69 (Didyma, ii B.C.), *Inscr. Délos* 290.241 (iii B.C.). **-ποίησις**, εως, ἡ, *erection of scaffolding*, ib.240 (prob.). **-ποιός**, ὁ, *maker of scaffolding* or *benches*, Poll. 7.125.

ἰκρι-όω, *erect scaffolding*, *IG*1².371.22, 374.74 (ἰκ-). **II.** *furnish with benches*, θέατρον D.C.43.22:—Pass., ib.59.7. **-ωμα**, ατος, τό, *scaffold*, *IG*1².374.67 (ἰκ-), Hsch. s.v. κατῆλιψ. **II.** in pl., = ἀντηρίδες, Eust.903.54. **-ωτήρ**, ῆρος, ὁ, *upright* supporting a gallery or loft, *IG*2².1668.78: pl., ib.1².313.110 (ἰκ-). **II.** in pl. -ῆρες, οἱ, *flooring of the deck*, ib.2².1629.1156, 1631.339 (or perh. *joists* which support it). **2.** = ἰκριώματα, Demioprat.ap.Poll.10.157.

ἰκταῖος, α, ον, = ἱκέσιος, A.*Supp.*385 [lyr., with penult. short].

ἴκταρ (A), Adv. *close together, thickly* (= πυκνῶς, Hsch.), κεραυνοὶ ἴ. ἅμα βροντῇ τε καὶ ἀστεροπῇ ποτέοντο Hes.*Th.*691. **II.** Prep. c. gen., *close to, hard by*, ἴ. μελάθρων A.*Ag.*116 (lyr.); ἴ. ἥμενοι Διός Id.*Eu.*998 (lyr.): c. dat., Alcm.23.80: abs., ταῦτα πρὸς τύραννον.. οὐδ' ἴ. βάλλει do not strike even *near* him, are quite wide of the mark, prov. in Pl.*R.*575c, cf. Ael.*NA*15.29.

ἴκταρ (B), τό, = *pudendum muliebre*, Hp.*Mul.*2.174 (restored fr. Erot. and Gal.19.105: ἧπαρ (ἦπαρ) codd. Hp.).

ἴκταρ (C), ὁ, some kind of *fish*, Call.*Fr.*38:—also **ἰκτάρα**, ἡ, Hsch.; = *albula*, *Gloss.*; cf. κτάρα.

ἰκτέα· ἀκόντιον, Hsch.

ἰκτερ-ίας λίθος, ὁ, *a yellowish* kind of *stone*, Plin.*HN*37.170. **-ιάω**, (ἴκτερος) *to be ill of the jaundice*, v.l. in Dsc.3.1, M.Ant.6.57, Hld.3.8, S.E.*P.*1.44, Gal.18(1).250. **-ικός**, ή, όν, *jaundiced*, Gal.*Nat. Fac.*1.13, *Gp.*12.17.9; *for jaundice*, φάρμακον Ruf.ap.Orib.7.26.142. **-ις**, = *aurugo*, *Gloss.* **-ίτης**, = *rosmarinum*, ib.; but **-ῖτις**, Ps.-Dsc.3.75, Apul.*Herb.*80 (v.l. *-es*): **-ιώδης**, ες, = ἰκτερικός, Hp.*Aph.*5.72, Dsc.3.1; and **-όεις**, εσσα, εν, χλόος Nic.*Al.*475. **-όομαι**, Pass., *have the jaundice*, Hp.*Prorrh.*1.32, Gal.16.574. **-ος**, ὁ, *jaundice*, Hp.*Aph.*4.62 (pl.), *Morb.*2.38, *Int.*35 (pl.), etc. **II.** *a bird of a yellowish-green colour*, by looking at which a jaundiced person was cured—the bird died! Plin.*HN*30.94 (who identifies it with *galgulus*, the *golden oriole*). **-ώδης**, ες, = ἰκτερικός, Hp.*Epid.*3.17.ιγ'.

ἰκτευ· κρατεῖς (Lacon.), Hsch. **ἰκτή**, = ἰκτίν, Ruf.*Fr.*79.

ἴκτηρ, ερος, ὁ, = ἴκτερος, acc. ἴκτερα v.l. in Lxx *Le.*26.16.

ἱκ-τήρ, ῆρος, ὁ, = ἱκέτης, *a suppliant*, S.*OT*185 (lyr.), E.*Heracl.*764 (lyr.): as Adj., ἱ. κλάδοι S.*OT*143; θαλλὸς E.*Supp.*10. **II.** Ζεὺς ἱκτὴρ *the protector of the suppliant*, A.*Supp.*479. **-τήριος**, α, ον, v. ἱκετήριος. **-της**, ου, ὁ, = ἱκέτης, Lyc.763, Hsch., Theognost. *Can.*15.

ἰκτίδεος, α, ον, (ἰκτίν) v. κτίδεος.

ἰκτίν, ῖνος, ὁ, = sq., Lyr. in *Philol.*80.336 (-τειν Pap.): acc. sg. ἰκτῖνα Ar.*Fr.*628, Pl.Com.243, Jul.*Mis.*366a: gen. sg. ἰκτῖνος ibid.: nom. pl. ἰκτῖνες Paus.5.14.1: dat. pl. ἰκτῖσι Ctes.*Fr.*57.11: nom. sg. also **ἰκτίς**, *Gloss.*, prob. in Hsch. (Pamph.).

ἴκτινος (Sch.Il.*Oxy.*1087.60 (i B.C.), Choerob.*in Theod.*1.267, but **ἰκτῖνος** Hdn.Gr.1.183), ὁ, *kite, Miluus regalis*, Semon.12, Hdt.2.22, S.*Fr.*111, 767, Ar.*Av.*502, al., Pl.*Phd.*82a, Men.926; ἰκτίνου ἀγχιστρόφου ἦθος Thgn.1261; φεύγεις ἰκτίνου σχέτλιον ἦθος ἔχων Id. 1302. **II.** a kind of *wolf*, Opp.*C.*3.331. (Cf. Arm. *çin* 'kite'.)

ἰκτίς, ῖδος (ἰκτῖδας is f.l. in Ar.*Ach.*880), ἡ, *the* γαλῆ ἀγρία or *yellow-breasted marten*, Ar. l.c., Arist.*HA*612ᵇ10, Nic.*Th.*196, cf. Sch. ad loc., Aret.*SD*1.15. (ι is prothetic, cf. κτίδεος.)

ἰκτορεύω, poet. for ἱκετεύω, S.*Fr.*58.

ἰκτός, in neut. **ἰκτόν**· τὸ ἐοικός, and **ἰκτύς**· ὁμοίωμα, εἰκών, Theognost.*Can.*15, 16.

ἵκτωρ, ορος, ὁ, = ἱκέτης, but used of women in A.*Supp.*653 (lyr.).

ἵκω [v. sub fin.], chiefly Ep., Lyr., and Dor., never in Hdt. or Trag. (in A.*Supp.*176 Pors. restored ἥκετε); cf. ἱκάνω, ἱκνέομαι; Dor., Arc. **ἵκω** *IG*4.329 (Corinth), 952.16 (Epid.), *Schwyzer* 323 *C*37 (Delph.), *IG*5(2).3.12 (Tegea), written εἵκω in Epich.35.13 codd., but ἵκει correctly in Ar.*Lys.*87; 3 pl. ἵκαντι, = ἥκουσιν, Hsch. (cf. παρίκω): impf. ἶκον Il.1.317: poet. fut. inf. ἱξέμεν Pi.*Pae.*6.116; Dor. fut. ἱξῶ Megar. in Ar.*Ach.*742: Ep. aor. ἶξον (v. infr.); also aor. 1 ἶξα Q.S.12.461 (v.l.): for ἵξομαι, ἵγμαι, v. ἱκνέομαι:—*come*, of persons, ἐς δόμον ἵκει Od.18.353; ἶξεν δ' ἐς Πριάμοιο Il.24.160, cf. 122; εἰ δέ κεν οἴκαδ' ἵκωμι φίλην ἐς πατρίδα γαῖαν 9.414; ἐς Ῥόδον ἶξεν ἀλώμενος 2.667; ἐπὶ Θρηκῶν.. τέλος ἶξον ἰόντες 10.470; ἶξε δ' ἐπ' ἐσχατιὴν 20.328; ποταμοῖο κατὰ στόμα.. ἶξε νέων Od.5.442: in Hom. freq. c. acc., *come to*, δόμον Il.18.406, etc.; Μαλειάων ὄρος Od.3.288; εἰ Θεμίστιον ἵκεις ὥστ' ἀείδειν Pi.*N.*5.50, cf. *O.*5.9; αἴ κ' αὐτὸς ἵκῃ, ἀνελέσθω prob. in *IG*5(2).159.2 (*Class.Phil.*20.134). **2.** of things, Φρυγίην.. κτήματα περνάμεν' ἵκει *come* or *are brought to*.., Il.18.292; also ὁπότε χρόνος ἶξε δικασπόλος Maiist.52. **3.** *attain to, reach*, κνίση δ' οὐρανὸν ἷκεν Il.1.317, cf. 2.153, 14.60; αἴγλη δι' αἰθέρος οὐρανὸν ἷκε 2.458; ὀρυμαγδὸς.. οὐρανὸν ἷκε δι' αἰθέρος 17.425; κλέος οὐρανὸν ἵκει Od.9.20; ὕβρις τε βίη τε.. οὐρανὸν ἵκει 15.329; Ἰθάκης γε καὶ ἐς Τροίην ὄνομ' ἵκει 13.248; ἵκῃ τ' ἐς ἄκρον ἀνδρείας Simon.58.6. **4.** of sufferings, feelings, etc., ὅτε κέν τινα.. χόλος ἵκοι *come upon* him, Il. 9.525; τοι πινυτὴ φρένας ἵκει Od.20.228; χρειὼ ἵκει τινά 2.28, 5.189: abs., χρειὼ τόσον ἵκει Il.10.142. [In ἵκω, ῑ always; in ἱκάνω, and the unaugmented moods of ἱκόμην, ῐ always.—ἵκοντ' is prob. for ἵκοντο [ῐ] in Pi.*P.*2.36.] (Prob. cogn. with ἥκω.)

ἴλᾱ [ῑ], ἡ, Dor. for ἴλη.

ἰλᾰδόν [ῑ], Adv., (ἴλη) *in troops*, Il.2.93, Hdt.1.172 (vv.ll. ἰλ-, εἰλ-): generally, *in abundance*, κακότητα καὶ ἱ. ἔστιν ἑλέσθαι Hes. *Op.*287.

ἱλάειρᾰ, ἡ, *mildly-shining*, φλὸξ ἱλάειρα [ῑλᾰ] Emp.85; ἱλάειρα [ῑλᾰ] σελήνη Id.40: as pr. n., Cypr.*Fr.*8. (Prob. from ἱλαρός.)

ἱλάεις, εντος, ὁ, contr. **ἱλᾶς** (q.v.), Ion. **ἱλῆς** (q.v.), Aeol. **ἰλλάεις**, = ἵλαος, ἰλλάεντι θύμῳ Alc.*Supp.*4.19: for ἱλάεος· ἱδαρός, Hsch., read ἱλάεις· ἱλαρός. [ᾱ by nature.]

ἵλαθι, v. ἵλημι.

Ἱλαῖος, ὁ (sc. μήν), name of month at Delphi, *SIG*²847.2, al. (Perh. connected with ἴλη.)

ἵλᾰμαι, = ἱλάομαι, ἵλαμαι δέ σ' ἀοιδῇ *h.Hom.*19.48, 21.5; Ἄρτεμιν ἵλασθαι θέλξαι θ' ὑπερήνορα θῆρα Orph.*A.*944; cf. ἵλημι. [ῑ in *h.Hom.*, ῐ in Orph.]

ἱλάομαι [ῑλᾰ], Ep. pres. for ἱλάσκομαι, ταύροισι καὶ ἀρνειοῖς ἱλάονται Il.2.550; ἱλάεσθαι A.R.2.847:—also **ἱλέομαι**, A.*Supp.*117 (lyr.): **ἱλεόμαι**, Pl.*Lg.*804b and later Prose, as Luc.*Salt.*17, Porph.*Antr.*20, D.C.59.27, Procop.*Aed.*3.6, Ps.-Callisth.1.6:—also **ἱλαόομαι**, *MAMA*1.230 (Laodicea Combusta).

ἵλαος [v. sub fin.], ον, Ep. and Lyr. (incl. lyr. of Trag., A.*Eu.*1040, S.*OC*1480, Ar.*Th.*1148): irreg. gen. ἱλάονος *UPZ*1.8 (iv B.C.); Att. and later **ἵλεως**, ων (also in Herod.4.25, v.l. for ἵλεον in Hdt.6.91), dual ἵλεω Pl.*Euthd.*273e; nom. pl. ἵλεῳ S.*OC*44, X.*Mem.*1.1.9 (later ἵλεως indecl. as nom. pl., *SIG*985.47 (Philadelphia, ii or i B.C.), as acc. sg., Lxx 2*Ma.*7.37, 10.26, as gen. sg., ib.2.22); neut. ἵλεα Pl. *Phd.*95a: **ἵλεος**, ον, Hdt.4.94, 6.91 (v. supr.); also Cret., *SIG*527.92 (Dreros, iii B.C.), *GDI*5039.26 (Hierapytna), Hsch.: **ἵληϝος**, dub. in *IG*5(1).1562 (Olymp., vi or v B.C., = Epigr.ap.Paus.5.24.3, where ἱλάῳ); Aeol. **ἴλλαος** Hdn.Gr.2.524, cf. ἱλάεις:—of gods, *propitious, gracious*, ἔπειθ' ἵλαος Ὀλύμπιος ἔσσεται ἡμῖν Il.1.583, cf. Hes.*Op.*340, Thgn.782, Archil.75, Pi.*O.*3.34, Trag. et Ar. ll. cc., Theoc.5.18: in Prose, Pl.*Lg.*712b, Lxx *Ge.*43.23, al., *UPZ*78.24 (εἵλ-, ii B.C.), *Ep. Hebr.*8.12, etc.; in deprecation, ἵλεώς σοι, κύριε (sc. ὁ θεός), i.e. be it far from thee, *Ev.Matt.*16.22; ἵ. ἡμῖν Πλάτων καὶ ἐνταῦθα *OGI*721.10 (Egypt, iv A.D.). **2.** of things, *propitious, blameless, atoned for*, ἵλαον ἦναι, opp. ἰνμενφὲς ἦναι, *IG*5(2).262 (Mantinea, v B.C.). **II.** of men, *gracious, kindly*, σὺ δ' ἵλαον ἔνθεο θυμόν Il.9.639; σοι.. θυμὸς ἐνὶ φρεσὶν ἵ. ἔστω 19.178; ἵλεως κλύειν S.*El.*655; δέξασθαι Id. *Aj.*1009, cf. *Tr.*763; ποιῆσαί θ' ἱλαρὸν.. κἀπέδειξεν ἵλεων Ephipp.6.7: sts. almost, = ἱλαρός, μειδῆσαι γελάσαι τε καὶ ἵλαον σχεῖν θυμὸν *h.Cer.*204, cf. Pl.*Smp.*206d; ὁ οἶνος τὸν ἄνθρωπον ποιεῖ ἵλεων Id.*Lg.*649a. **III.** Adv. ἱλάως and ἱλέως, Hsch. [ῑ always: ᾰ Il.1.583, *h.Cer.*204, Hes. and A. ll. cc., Euph.12, *Pae.Erythr.*19, Theoc.5.18, Epigr.ap.Paus. l.c., *IG*12(2).476, Parth.*Fr.*4; elsewh. ᾰ, v. supr., also Id.*Fr.*32, etc.]

ἱλᾰρ-εία [ῐ], ἡ, *rejoicing*; in pl., = ἱλάρια, τά, Sallust.4. **-εύομαι**, *to be joyful, exult*, Sm.*Ca.*1.4, al., Dosith.p.431 K. (prob.). **-ία**, ἡ, (ἱλαρός) = ἱλαρότης, Herod.Med.ap.Orib.5.27.20, Vett.Val.3.27, *PFlor.*391.43 (iii A.D.), dub. in Luc.*Am.*17; μετὰ πάσης χαρᾶς καὶ ἱλαρίας *Sammelb.*991 (iii A.D.). **II.** pet name for a γαλῆ, interpol. in Artem.3.28. **-ια** (sc. ἱερά), τά, = Lat. *hilaria, festival of rejoicing* in various cults, e.g. Isis, *CIL*1².p.334; esp. of Magna Mater, Jul.*Or.*5.168d, Macr.*Sat.*1.21.10, Dam.*Isid.*131.

ἱλᾰροποιέω [ῐ], *gladden*, *Gloss.*

ἱλᾰρός [ῐ], ά, όν, (ἵλαος) *cheerful, merry*, φέγγος Ar.*Ra.*456 (lyr.); ἱλαροὶ ἀντὶ σκυθρωπῶν X.*Mem.*2.7.12; ἱλαρὸς ἴσθι Thphr.*Char.*17.9; ἱλαρὸν βλέψαι *AP*12.159 (Mel.), cf. Phld.*Mus.*p.85 K., Philostr.*Im.*1.16; ἱ. δότης 2*Ep.Cor.*9.7, cf. Lxx *Pr.*22.8: in later Greek, = ἵλεως, *gracious*, *PMag.Leid.W.*14.12, etc.: τὸ ἱ., = ἱλαρότης, Plu.*Sull.*34,

Heraclid.Pont.ap.Ath.14.624d; -ωτέρα ἀγγελία *more cheerful* news, *Jahresh.*23*Beibl.*283 (Ephesus). Adv. -ρῶς X.*Ap.*33, Lxx *Jb.*22.26, Phld.*Mus.*l. c., Plu.*Ages.*2. II. of blood, *quick-pulsing*, Philostr. *Gym.*48 (Comp.). III. of imitation gold, *bright*, *PLeid.X.*17 (iii/iv A.D.). Adv. ἱλαρῶς (leg. ἱλαρῷ) ib.87.

ἱλᾰρότης [ῐ], ητος, ἡ, *cheerfulness, gaiety*, Lxx *Pr.*18.22, D.S.3.17, *Ep.Rom.*12.8, Plu.*Ages.*2, Alciphr.3.43; ἱ. ἡ πρὸς πάντας *Vit.Philonid.* p.10C.: pl., Phld.*Mus.*p.85K.

ἱλᾰροτρᾰγῳδία [ῐ], ἡ, *burlesque tragedy*, invented by Rhinthon, Suid. s. v. Ῥίνθων.

ἱλᾰρ-όω [ῐ], *gladden, brighten*, Lxx *Si.*7.24, al., Aristeas 108; λόγους Phld.*Mus.*p.99 K.:—also -ύνω, Lxx *Ps.*103(104).15:—Pass., fut. -υνθήσομαι, aor. -ύνθην, *PMag.Leid.W.*12.30, 5.20.

ἱλ-άρχης (later written εἰλ-, cf. βειλάρχας), ου, ὁ, (ἴλη) *commander of a troop of horse*, *PPetr.*3p.8 (iii B.C.), al., Ascl.*Tact.*7.2, Plu.*Tim.* 31 (pl.), Arr.*An.*2.7.3; = Lat. *praefectus turmae*, Plb.6.25.1, 6.35.8. II. *commander of eight elephants*, Ascl.*Tact.*9, Ael.*Tact.*23:—hence -αρχέω, Boeot. Fιλαρχίω, *command cavalry*, *IG*7.3087 (Lebad.), 3206 (Orchom.), 2466 (Thebes). II. at Rome, *to be sevir equitum*, D.C.55.10. -αρχία, ἡ, *contingent of eight elephants*, Ael.*Tact.*23. -αρχος, ὁ, = ἰλάρχης I, *IG*4.487.2, al. (Nemea, iii B.C.); = *praefectus turmae*, App.*Hisp.*43.

ἱλᾰρ-ῳδός [ῐ], ὁ, (ᾠδή) *singer of joyous* (not 'comic') *songs*, Aristocl.Hist.8:—hence -ῳδέω, Id.7; -ῳδία, Aristox.*Fr.Hist.*58, cf. Ath.14.621c. -ῶπις, ἡ, *of gracious aspect*, prob. in *PMag.Lond.* 121.382.

ἱλᾶς [ῑ], ᾶντος, ὁ, = εὐμενής, Hdn.Gr.2.657, cf. 318, al.: pl. ἱλᾶντες (ἱλάντες cod.) Hsch. (contr. fr. ἱλάεις -εντος, q. v.).

ἱλᾰσ-ία [ῐ], ἡ, = ἱλασμός, *IGRom.*3.1297 (Arabia). -ιμος, ον, *placable*, πρόνοια M.Ant.12.14. -κομαι, fut. ἱλάσομαι [ᾰ] Pl. *Phd.*95a, Ep. ἱλάσσομαι Orac.ap.Paus.8.42.6, also ἱλάξομαι A.R. 2.808: aor. 1 ἱλᾰσάμην, Ep. part. ἱλασσάμενοι Il.1.100, Ep. subj. 2 sg. ἱλάσσεαι 1.147, -ηαι A.R.3.1037; inf. ἱλάσσασθαι Ant.Lib.25.2 codd.; also ἱλάξασθαι A.R.1.1093:—Pass. (v. infr. II). [ῑ regularly (written ι, not ει, *SIG*1044.6,9 (Halic., iv/iii B.C.)); ῐ Il.1.100,147]: (ἵλαος):—*appease*, in Hom. always of gods, θεὸν ἱ. ib.386, cf. 100, al., Od.3.419; μολπῇ θεὸν ἱλάσκοντο Il.1.472; σπονδῇσι θύεσσί τε ἱλάσκεσθαι (sc. θεούς) Hes.*Op.*338; ὄφρ' ἡμῖν ἑκάεργον ἱλάσσεαι Il.1.147; c. part., ἱλάσκομαι πέμπων by presenting, Pi.*O.*7.9; τοῦτον (sc. θεὸν) ἱλάσκου ποιῶν μηδὲν ἄτοπον Men.*Epit.*558; of the dead as hero-ized, θυσίῃσί τινα ἱ. Hdt.5.47. 2. of men, *conciliate*, ἱ. τινὰ χρήμασι Id.8.112; πῶς ἱλασόμεθα καὶ τίνι λόγῳ; Pl.*Phd.*l. c.; ἱ. τὴν ὀργήν τινος Plu.*Cat.Mi.*61. 3. *expiate*, τὰς ἁμαρτίας *Ep.Hebr.*2.17. II. Pass. with fut. ἱλάσομαι, also ἱλασθήσομαι v.l. in Lxx 4*Ki.*5.18: aor. 1 ἱλάσθην ib.*Ex.*32.14, al.:—*to be merciful, gracious*, τινι ll. cc.; ἱλάσθητί μοι τῷ ἁμαρτωλῷ *Ev.Luc.*18.13; ταῖς ἁμαρτίαις τινῶν Lxx *Ps.*77(78).38: c. inf., ἱλάσθη κύριος περιποιῆσαι τὸν λαόν ib.*Ex.*32.14. -μα, ατος, τό, *propitiation*, Orac.ap.Phleg.*Macr.*4. -μός [ῐ], ὁ, *a means of appeasing*, in pl., Plu.*Sol.*12, Orph.*A.*39, 554, etc. 2. *atonement, sin-offering*, Lxx *Ez.*44.27, 2*Ma.*3.33, 1*Ep.Jo.*2.2, 4.10, Ph.1.121. -τήριος, α, ον (ος, ον *PFay.*337 (ii A.D.)), *propitiatory, offered in propitiation*, μνῆμα J.*AJ*16.7.1; θάνατος Lxx 4*Ma.*17.22; θυσίαι *PFay.* l. c. II. ἱλαστήριον ἐπίθεμα, *the mercy-seat*, covering of the ark in the Holy of Holies, Lxx *Ex.*25.16(17): ἱλαστήριον alone as Subst., ib.*Le.*16.2, al., *Ep.Hebr.*9.5, cf. Ph.2.150. 2. (sc. ἀνάθημα) *propitiatory gift* or *offering*, *Ep.Rom.*3.25; of a monument, *Inscr.Cos* 81, 347. 3. *monastery*, Men.Prot.p.15 D. -τής, οῦ, ὁ, *propitiator*, Aq., Thd.*Ps.*85(86).5, f.l. in Lxx 1*Es.*8.53.

ἱλᾰτ-εύω, = ἱλήκω, Lxx *Da.*9.18. -ήριον, τό, *expiatory* or *propitiatory offering*, *Chron.Lind.*B.49.

ἱλεας, τάς, dub. sens. in *Abh.Berl.Akad.*1928(6).16 (Cos): perh. Coan for τὰς ἴλας (ἴλη) or τὰς ἱλέας (ἵλεως).

ἱλέομαι, ἱλεόομαι [ῑ], v. ἱλάομαι. **ἱλεός** [ῑ], ὁ, = εἰλεός I and II, Hsch. **ἵλεος**, = ἵλαος; and **ἵλεως**, ων, Att. for ἵλαος (q. v.).

ἱλέ-ωσις [ῑλ], εως, ἡ, *propitiation*, Plu. *in Hes.*26. -ωτήριον, τό, = ἱλαστήριον, Phot., Suid.

ἴλη [ῐ], Dor. **ἴλᾱ** (Boeot. Fιλ- in Fιλαρχίω), ἡ, *band, troop* of men, Hdt.1.73, 202; εὔφρονες ἶλαι merry *companies*, Pi.*N.*5.38; also ἴλα λεόντων E.*Alc.*581 (lyr.). 2. as a military term, *troop of horse*, prop. of sixty-four men, cf. Arr.*Tact.*18.2; but varying in number, Ascl.*Tact.*7.2; = Lat. *turma*, Plb.6.25.1, al., D.H.6.12, al., Plu.*Caes.* 45, al.; later, = Lat. *ala*, *IGRom.*3.272 (Galatia), *BGU*69 (ii A.D.), J.*AJ*17.10.9, etc.; κατὰ ἴλας, = ἰλαδόν, opp. κατὰ τάξεις, X.*An.*1.2.16: generally, *troop* or *company of soldiers*, S.*Aj.*1407 (anap.). 3. at Sparta, subdivision of the ἀγέλα (q. v.), X.*Lac.*2.11; κατ' ἴλην Plu. *Lyc.*16.

ἰληδόν [ῑ], Adv., = ἰλαδόν, Q.S.1.7, al.

ἱλήκω [ῑ], (ἱλάσκομαι) *to be gracious*, of a god, once in Hom. in subj., εἴ κεν Ἀπόλλων ἡμῖν ἱλήκῃσι Od.21.365; elsewh. in opt., ἱλήκοι Ἀπόλλων *h.Ap.*165; ἱλήκοις, Δέσποινα *AP*5.72 (Rufin.); ἱλήκοις, Πολιοῦχε ib.9.154 (Agath.); θεοὶ μάκαρες, ἱλήκοιτε Alciphr.3.68, cf. Hld. 8.11, 9.25. (Prob. εἰλ-, cf. sq.)

*__ἵλημι__ [ῑ], = foreg., only in imper. ἵληθι, in prayers, *be gracious!* Od.3.380, 16.184, *h.Hom.*20.8, etc.: Aeol. **ἔλλᾱθι** (q. v.): Dor. **ἵλᾱθι** Theoc.15.143, Luc.*Epigr.*22; both together, ἵλαθ', ἄναξ, ἵληθι *AP* 12.158 (Mel.): pl., ἵλᾰτε A.R.4.984, Man.6.754. (Prob. pf. imper. fr. *se-sl-*; Aeol. ἐλλ- points to εἶλ- as the true Ion. spelling; Dor. pf. part. dat. ἱλαότι (leg. εἰλ-) Hsch.: ῑ is genuine in ἵλεως, ἱλάσκομαι [fr. *si-sl-*].)

ἶληοι· θηρία διὰ φρυγάνων, κτλ., Hsch. (fort. θηρίδια φ.; cf. εἰλύϊος, ἐλειός III).

ἰλῆς [ῑ], Ion. contr. fr. ἰλήεις, = ἱλάεις (q. v.), prob. for εἰλῆς (q. v.).

ἶλια· δῶρα γυναικεῖα, Hsch.

Ἰλιάδαι [ῑλ], οἱ, *descendants of Ilos*, i. e. *Trojans*, Sapph.*Supp.* 20a.13, *AP*9.77 (Antip. Thess.): as Adj., Ἰ. βασιλῆες E.*Andr.*1023 (lyr.).

Ἰλιακός [ῑλ], ή, όν, *Ilian, Trojan*, μῦθοι *AP*9.192 (Antiphil.); πόλεμος Str.1.2.9; *concerning the Iliad*, προσῳδία, title of work by Hdn. Gr. II. **ἰλιακά**, τά, word of doubtful meaning in *PTeb.*61(*b*).319, cf. 68.88, al. (ii B.C.).

Ἰλιάς [ῑ], άδος, ἡ, pecul. fem. of Ἰλιακός, χώρη Hdt.5.94, cf. A.*Ag.* 453 (lyr.), E.*Hec.*102 (anap.), 923 (lyr.), etc.; epith. of Athena, Hdt. 7.43, *IG*9(1).350 (ii B.C.). II. as Subst., 1. (sc. γῆ) *Troy, the Troad*, Hdt.5.122. 2. (sc. γυνή) *a Trojan woman*, E.*Hel.*1114 (lyr.), *Tr.*245 (lyr.), etc. 3. (sc. ποίησις) *the Iliad* of Homer, Hdt.2.116, Arist.*Po.*1448b38, al.: prov., κακῶν Ἰλιάς, i. e. *an endless string* of woes, D.19.148, D.S.36.6, etc. III. a kind of *thrush*, perh. *the redwing*, *Turdus iliacus*, Arist.*HA*617a21 (s. v. l.); cf. ἰλλάς III.

ἰλιγγ-ιάω [ῑ], *become dizzy, lose one's head*, as when one looks down from a height, ἰλιγγιῶν ἀφ' ὑψηλοῦ κρεμασθείς Pl.*Tht.*175d; from drunkenness, ψυχὴ ἰ. ὥσπερ μεθύουσα Id.*Phd.*79c; ἰ. κάρα λίθῳ πεπληγμένος Ar.*Ach.*1218; ἰ. καὶ χασμᾶσθαι Phld.*Rh.*2.176 S.; from perplexity, ἐσκοτώθην καὶ ἰλιγγίασα Pl.*Prt.*339e; ἰ. ὑπὸ τῆς τοῦ λόγου ἀπορίας Id.*Ly.*216c; ὑπὸ τοῦ δέους Ar.*Ach.*581; ἐπί τινι Luc.*Tox.*30; πρὸς τὴν θέαν Hld.5.6:—also written εἰλιγγιάω, freq. in codd. of Pl., cf. *AP*7.706 (Diog.), Plu.*Alex.*74; ἰλ- Phld. l. c.; εἰλιγγιάω but ἴλιγγος acc. to Sch.Ar.*Ach.*581, Suid. s. v. εἰλιγγιῶ. -ος, ὁ, (ἴλλω, εἴλω) *spinning round*; esp. *swimming* in the head, Hp.*Aph.* 3.17 (pl.), Pl.*R.*407c (pl.); σκοτοδινίαν ἴλιγγόν τε ἐμποιεῖν τινι Id.*Lg.* 892e; also, *disturbance of the bowels*, Nic.*Al.*597. 2. in pl., *eddies* or *wreaths* of smoke, A.R.4.142. 3. *whirlpool*, Procop.*Goth.*4.6. 4. *agitation of mind*, Plu.2.1068c:—also written εἴλιγγος, A.R. l. c., Nic. l. c., Plu.*Caes.*60, and codd. Pl. -ιώδης (εἰλ- cod.), ες, = *verticulosus*, Gloss.

ἴλιγξ, ιγγος, ἡ, *whirling, whirlpool*, D.S.17.97, Alex.Aphr.*Pr.*2.71. 2. v. l. for ἴλιγγος I, Gal.*UP*7.13. (Written **ἶλιξ** in Hsch.:—also **ἰλίγγη**, ἡ, Id.)

ἶλιον· τὸ τῆς γυναικὸς ἐφήβαιον δηλοῖ, καὶ κόσμον γυναικεῖον παρὰ Κῴοις, Hsch.

Ἰλιοπόρος [ῑλ], ον, *faring to Ilium*, Tim.*Pers.*132.

Ἰλιορραίστης, f. l. for Ἰλοραίστης (q. v.).

Ἴλιος [ῑλ], ου, ἡ, *Ilios* or *Ilium*, *the city of Ilus, Troy*, Il.5.210, al., Alc. *Supp.*8.4, E.*Andr.*103 (eleg.): **Ἴλιον**, τό, Hom. only in Il.15.71, but always in Trag. (exc. E. l. c.):—hence Ep. genitives, **Ἰλιόθεν**, *from Troy*, Il.14.251, Od.9.39; **Ἰλιόθι** πρό *before Troy*, 8.581, etc.; **Ἰλιόφι** κλυτὰ τείχεα the walls *of Troy*, Il.21.295. II. as Adj., **Ἴλιος**, α, ον, *Ilian, Trojan*, Ἀθάνα E.*Hec.*1008: -ος, ον is f.l. in Id.*Hel.*1164 (lyr.).

ἶλις, = *volumen*, Gloss. (dub.); ἰλίς sine expl., Hsch.; cf. ἰλλίς.

Ἰλισός [ῑλ], οῦ, ὁ, *the Ilissus*, in Attica, Pl.*Criti.*112a, Hdn.Gr.1.213, etc.: **Ἰλισός**, *the god I.*, *IG*1^{2}.324.89, cf. 310.206: **Ἰλισσός** freq. f.l. in codd., as Hdt.7.189, Str.9.1.24, A.R.1.215, D.P.424: Εἰλισσός f.l. in Paus.1.19.5.

ἰλίσσαι· κατωχῆσαι, Hsch. (fort. εἰλῦσαι· καταχῶσαι).

ἰλλάεις, v. ἰλάεις.

ἰλλάζω, *bind up, make into a bundle*, Hsch. **ἶλλαι**· συστροφαί, Id.

ἰλλαίνω, *look awry, squint*, Hp.*Epid.*3.1.γ'; of the eyes, *to be distorted*, Id.*Coac.*214, *Epid.*4.12:—so also in Pass., **ἰλλαίνομαι**, Id. *Morb.*3.12. **ἴλλαος**, v. ἵλαος.

ἰλλάς, άδος, ἡ, (ἴλλω, εἴλω) *rope, band*, βοῦς, τόν τ' οὔρεσι βουκόλοι ἄνδρες ἰλλάσιν . . δήσαντες ἄγουσιν Il.13.572. II. as Adj., *close-packed, herding together*, of cattle, ἰλλάδες γοναί S.*Fr.*70, E.*Fr.*837. III. = Ἰλιάς III, Ath.2.65a, Eust.947.8.

ἰλλ-ίζω, *look askance, leer*, glossed by διανεύω, Suid. -ίς, ίδος, ἡ, fem. of sq., Hsch. -ός, ὁ, (ἴλλω) *squinting* (acc. to Moer., Att. for στραβός), ἰ. γεγενῆσθαι to get a *squint*, Ar.*Th.*846: Comp. ἰλλότερος Sophr.158, cf. Gal.17(1).680. -ος, ὁ, Ion. = ὀφθαλμός, Poll. 2.54. -ωψ, ωπος, ὁ, ἡ, coined as etym. of ἔλλοψ, Ath.7.308b, c, cf. Plu.2.728e.

Ἰλλυριοί, οἱ, *Illyrians*, Hdt.1.196, etc. (Ἰλλ- *IG*1^{2}.329.24): **Ἰλλυρία**, ἡ, *Illyria*, St.Byz.:—also **Ἰλλυρίς**, ἡ, Ptol.*Geog.*2.16.1, App. *Ill.*6; γονή S.*Fr.*601:—Adj. **Ἰλλυρικός**, ή, όν, *Illyrian*: -κή, (sc. ἱστορία), ἡ, title of work by Appian: -κόν, τό, the *region* or *province of Illyria*, *Ep.Rom.*15.19: **Ἰλλυρίζω**, *speak the Illyrian language*, St. Byz. s. v. Ἰλλυρία:—hence Adv. **Ἰλλυριστί**, ibid.

ἴλλω, v. εἴλω: aor. 1 Med. ἰλλάμην, *plait*, πλοκάμους *IG*5(2).472.11 (Megalopolis, ii/iii A.D.).

ἰλλ-ώδης, ες, *squinting, distorted*, ὄμματα Hp.*Mul.*1.41. -ωπέω, -ωπίζω, = ἰλλίζω, *squint*, both in Sch.Ar.*Eq.*292, cf. Suid.: -ώπτω, *Com.Adesp.*1019, Adam.1.23, Hsch. (For the termination cf. γοργώψατο.) -ωσις, εως, ἡ, *distortion*, ὀφθαλμῶν Hp.*Prorrh.*1.69, cf. Aret.*SD*1.7.

ἴλμη· δεσμός, σειρά, Theognost.*Can.*15 (ἰλμηδεσμός cod.).

Ἰλοραίστης, Dor. -τᾱς, α, ὁ, (ῥαίω) *destroyer of Ilus*, i. e. *of Troy*, prob. in Dosiad.*Ara* 17.

Fίλσις, ιος, ἁ, *distress*, *Schwyzer* 686.2 (Pamphylia, iv B.C.).

ἴλῡμα [ῐ], ατος, τό, *sediment* deposited in water, Gal.13.45 (sed leg. λύματα).

ἰλῠόεις [ῐ], εσσα, εν, (ἰλύς) *muddy*, ποταμός A.R.2.823; ζάλος Nic. *Th*.568: metaph., ἀχλὺς ἰ., of the soul's material envelope, *App. Anth*.3.146 (Theon).

ἰλῡός [ῐ], ὁ, = εἰλεός II, εἰλυός, *den, lair*, Call.*Jov*.25.

ἰλύς [ῐ], ύος, ἡ, *mud, slime*, τεύχεα... κείσεθ' ὑπ' ἰλύος κεκαλυμμένα Il.21.318, cf. *IG*1^2.94.20,23, Zeno *Stoic*.1.29, *Inscr.Délos* 354.19, etc.; of alluvial soil, Hdt.2.7; ἰ. καὶ ψάμμος Hp.*Aër*.9. 2. *dregs, sediment*, Id.*Mul*.1.66; of wine, Arist.*GA*753^{a}24, al. 3. *impurity*, αἵματος Gal.1.603, cf. 616; στέρνων Androm.ap.eund.14.35. [ἰλῡς -ῡν Choerob.*in Theod*.1.331; gen. ἰλῠος *APl*.4.230 (Leon.), A.R. 1.10, but ἰλῡος (metri gr. Hdn.Gr.2.117) Il. l.c.] (Cf. Russ. *il*, Polish *ił* 'mud', 'potter's clay'.)

ἰλυσπ-άομαι [ῐ], *crawl*, like a worm, Hp.*Genit*.5, Pl.*Ti*.92a, Meno *Iatr*.37.32, J.*AJ*1.1.4, *BJ*3.7.21, Plu.2.567b, Max.Tyr.26.6, Ael. *NA*8.14, 9.32. (εἰλυσπ- Meno l.c., v.l. in Pl. l.c.) **-ᾰσις**, εως, ἡ, *crawling*, Arist.*IA*709^{a}28. **-αστικός**, ή, όν, *of* or *for crawling*, Id.*HA*487^{b}21.

ἰλύ-ω [ῐ], (ἰλύς) *cover with slime* or *dirt*, Hsch. II. = εἰλύω, Id. **-ώδης**, ες, *muddy, slimy*, Hp.*Coac*.512, Max.Tyr.41.3, S.E. *M*.5.75; ὕδωρ Str.4.1.6; πηλός Arr.*Ind*.41.3; περίττωμα Gal.1.616; τὸ -ῶδες Plu.2.935a.

ἰμ- in compds., = ἰν, Arc., Cypr., Cret. for ἐν.

ἶμα, ατος, τό, = εἷμα, Hsch.

ἱμαῖος [ῐ], α, ον, (ἱμάω) *of* or *for drawing water*, ἱμαῖον (sc. μέλος) *song of the draw-well*, Call.*Hec*.1.4.12, cf. Trypho ap.Ath.14.618d.

Ἱμάλιος, ὁ (sc. μήν), v. sq.

ἱμαλίς, ίδος, ἡ, Syrac. epith. of Demeter, Polem.Hist.39:—hence **ἱμαλιά**, ἡ, = τὸ ἐπίμετρον τῶν ἀλεύρων, Hsch.: **ἱμάλιος**, α, ον, *abundant*, Id.: as name of a month at Hierapytna, *GDI*5040.4. II. Dor. word for ὁ νόστος καὶ τὰ ἐπίμετρα τῶν ἀλεύρων Trypho ap.Ath.14. 618d; = ἐπιμύλιος ᾠδή, Hsch., Poll.4.53.

ἱμανήθρη [ῑ], ἡ, = ἱμονιά, Herod.5.11.

ἱμαντ-άριον [ῐ], τό, Dim. of ἱμάς, *BCH*29.536 (Delos, ii B.C.), *POxy*.326 (i A.D.). 2. *halyard*, Hsch. **-ελιγμός**, οῦ, ὁ, *pricking the tape*, '*fast and loose*', a trick practised at fairs, etc., Poll.9.118, Eust.979.28. **-ελικτής**, οῦ, ὁ, (ἑλίσσω) *pricker of tapes* (cf. foreg.): metaph., '*thimble-rigger*', of sophists, Democr.150. **-ηρις** (sic cod., fort. -ῆρες), = *corrigiae*, *Gloss*. **-ίδιον**, τό, Dim. of ἱμάς, *EM* 671.8. **-ῐνος**, η, ον, *of leathern thongs*, Hdt.4.189, Hp.*Art*. 78. **-ιον**, τό, Dim. of ἱμάς, *strap*, Id.*Mochl*.41. II. = ἱμάς II, Aret.*SA*1.8. **-ίσκος**, ὁ, Dim. of ἱμάς, Herod.6.71. **-ισμός**, ὁ, in building, *insertion of bonding courses*, *PTeb*.402.32 (ii A.D.).

ἱμαντό-δεσμος [ῐ], ὁ, *leathern band*, Hsch. s.v. ζεύγλας. **-δετος**, ον, *bound with thongs*, gloss on τρητοῖσι, Sch.Od.1.440. **-μάχος** [μᾰ], ον, *fighting with the caestus*, Orac. in Tz.*H*.7.422. **-πάροχος**, ὁ, *purveyor of straps*, etc., for the races, *CIG*2758 *D* 6 (Aphrodisias). **-πέδη**, ἡ, *leathern noose*, of a polypus' leg, *AP*9.94 (Isid. Aeg.). **-πους**, ποδος, ὁ, (ἱμάς III) *spindle-shanked*; esp., 1. name of a tribe of Ethiopians, Plin.*HN*5.46, Apollod.ap.Tz.*H*.7. 767. 2. kind of *water-bird*, Dionys.*Av*.2.9. **-σκελής**, ές, = foreg., Tz. l.c. **-τομέω**, *cut straps*, Poll.7.81,83.

ἱμαντ-όω [ῐ], *furnish with straps*, in Pass., Hsch. s.v. πυξ(ίνην). **-ώδης**, ες, *fibrous*, of the hair, Pl.*Ti*.76c; φλοιός, κλῶνες, Dsc.1.84, 3. 15; of asbestos, Id.5.138. 2. of hair, *ropy*, Gal.1.615; of the uvula when diseased, Id.10.988. II. *sinewy, wiry*, of athletes, Philostr. *Gym*.37. **-ωμα**, ατος, τό, *hawser*, Hsch. s.v. σίρα. **-ωσις**, εως, ἡ, *binding with thongs*, Id.; of the *straps of a car*, Poll.1. 142. II. *piece of timber used instead of a bond-stone*, Lxx *Si*.22.16, Phot., etc.

ἱμάοιδός [ῐ], ὁ, *one who sings the* ἱμαῖον μέλος, Poll.4.53, Hsch. (ἰλ- cod.).

ἱμάς, ὁ, gen. ἱμάντος (not ἱμᾶς, ἱμᾶντος Hdn.Gr.2.939): Ep. dat. pl. ἱμάντεσσι:—*leathern strap* or *thong*, Il.10.262, etc.; ἱμάντα βοός 3. 375; βοέους ἱμάντας 22.397: mostly in pl., in various senses: a. *traces*, 10.475,499, al. b. *reins*, 23.324, etc.; τμητοῖς ἱμᾶσι S.*El*. 747, cf. E.*Hipp*.1222. c. *straps* on which the body of the chariot was hung, Il.5.727. d. *lash* of a whip, formed by several thongs, 23.363. e. *boxing-glove*, consisting of *several straps put round the hand*, ib.684, Pi.*N*.6.35, Pl.*Prt*.342c; ἱ. πυκτικοί Eup.22 D. 2. in sg., the magic *girdle* of Aphrodite, Il.14.214,219. b. *chin-strap* of the helmet, 3.371. c. *thong*, by which the bolt was shot home into the socket, Od.1.442, cf. 4.802, 21.46. d. after Hom., *thong* or *latchet* of a sandal, X.*An*.4.5.14, Ephipp.14.9, Men.109.2, *Ev.Marc*.1.7. e. *rail-rope*, Aristag.5. f. *well-rope*, Poll.10.31, Moer. g. *dog-leash*, X.*Cyn*.7.6: prov., ἦσθ' ἱμὰς κύνειος you were tough as a dog-*leash*, Ar.*V*.231; also σὺν τῷ κυνὶ καὶ τὸν ἱμάντα Phot. h. *whip, scourge*, ἔξω τις δότω ἱμάντα Antiph.74.8, cf. Men.*Sam*.106; ἡ διὰ τῶν ἱ. αἰκεία *POxy*.1186.2 (iv A.D.), cf. *Act. Ap*.22.25; ἱμάντες παιδαγωγῶν Lib.*Ep*.911.2. i. *cord*, Gal.10.1001, cf. 1.616. II. *diseased condition of the uvula*, Id.17(1).379. III. ἱμάντες, in Archit., *planks* laid on rafters, *IG*1^2.372.82, 373.236, al., 2^2. 1668.55, 1672.305; on στρωτῆρες (q.v.), ib.463.66. (Cf. Skt. *sināti* 'bind', Lat. *saeta*.) [⏑ –, usually; but also ῑ in Ep., Il.8.544, etc.: in derivs. and compds. always ῐ.]

ἱμάσθλη [ῐ], ἡ, (ἱμάς) *thong* of a whip, *whip*, Il.23.582, Od.13.82, *Eranos* 13.88 (pl.): metaph., νηὸς ἱ., i.e. ship's *rudder*, *AP*6.28 (Jul.); later, *any thong*, Opp.*C*.4.217.

ἱμάσκω, dub. sens., perh. *flog* or *imprison* (ἱμάς), *Schwyzer* 409 (Elis).

ἱμασσία, ἡ, perh. = *scaffolding* (cf. ἱμάς), or = αἱμασιά, *IG*4.823.26 (Troezen).

ἱμάσσω [ῐ], fut. ἱμάσω [ᾰ]: aor. ἵμᾰσα: (ἱμάς):—*flog* horses, τοὺς ἵμασ' Ἀντίλοχος Il.5.589, cf. 11.531; of men, εἰ.. σε πληγῇσιν ἱμάσσω 15.17, cf. Hes.*Th*.857; ἵμασε χθόνα χειρί *smote* it, *h.Ap*.340; ὅτε.. γαῖαν ἱμάσσῃ when he *smites* it *with lightnings*, Il.2.782:—Pass., ἱμασσόμενος δέμας αὔραις *AP*7.696 (Arch.), cf. Nonn.*D*.42.491.

ἱμᾰτ-εύομαι [ῐ], *to be a clothier*, *IGRom*.4.1209 (Thyatira) (nisi leg. πραγματ-). **-ηγός**, όν, *loaded with apparel*, ναῦς Thphr.*Lap*. 68. **-ῐδάριον**, τό, Dim. of ἱμάτιον, Ar.*Fr*.90. **-ίδιον** [ῐδ], τό, Dim. of ἱμάτιον, Id.*Pl*.985, Lys.*Fr*.316 S., *BGU*1103.12 (i B.C.); by crasis with the Art., θαἰματίδια Ar.*Lys*.401. **-ίζω**, fut. -ιῶ, *furnish with clothing*, *UPZ*2.14 (ii B.C.), etc.:—Pass., τοῦ παιδὸς τρεφομένου καὶ -ομένου *POxy*.275.14 (i A.D.); γυνὴ ἱματισμένη ἔχιδνα Secund.*Sent*.8; ἱματισμένος *Ev.Marc*.5.15.

ἱμᾰτιο-θήκη [ῐμ], ἡ, *wardrobe*, *IG*2^2.1672.229,309, Hsch. s.v. κανδυτάναι. **-κάπηλος** [κᾰ], ὁ, *clothes-seller*, Luc.*Merc.Cond*.38, *Pseudol*.21. **-κλέπτης**, ου, ὁ, *clothes-stealer*, D.L.6.52. **-μίσθης**, ου, ὁ, *one who lets out actor's costumes*, *IG*12(9).207.22 (Eretria, iii B.C.), *SIG*424.85 (Delph., iii B.C.), Poll.7.78, *AB*100. **-μισθωτής**, οῦ, ὁ, = foreg., Poll.7.78.

ἱμάτιον [ῐμᾰ-], τό, in form a Dim. of ἷμα (i.e. εἷμα), *a piece of dress*; in usage always of *an outer garment*, formed by an oblong piece of cloth worn above the χιτών, Ar.*Ec*.333, *IG*2^2.1524.205, al., D.24. 114, etc.; λαμπρὸν ἱ. ἔχων Epich.[277]; θοἰμάτιον by crasis for τὸ ἱμ-, Ar.*Nu*.179, al.; θοἰμάτιον καθεὶς ἄχρι τῶν σφυρῶν D.19.314; ἱματίων ἕλξεις Pl.*Alc*.1.122c; of the Roman *toga*, Plu.*Brut*.17, *Cor*.14: hence ἐν ἱματίοις, of civilians, = *togati*, Id.*Cam*.10; but ἱ. Ἑλληνικόν, opp. the toga, Luc.*Merc.Cond*.25. 2. ἱμάτια, τά, generally, *clothes*, Hdt.1.9, Pl.*Plt*.279e, D.27.10; by crasis, θαἰμάτια Hippon.83.1, Ar.*V*.408 (lyr.), *Lys*.1093; of *grave-clothes*, ἐν εἱμ. τρισὶ [θάπτειν] *IG* 12(5).593.2 (Iulis, v/iv B.C.), cf. Plu.*Sol*.21. 3. metaph., ἱμάτια πόλεως τείχη Eust.1871.50. II. generally, *cloth*, Hdt.4.23, D.S. 14.109, Ael.*VH*8.7, Iamb.*VP*21.100. [ἱμ- in Att. Inscrr., *IG*1^2.427, 386.18, 2^2.1514.16, etc.; εἱμ- ib.12(5) l.c. (εμ- lap.), 5(1).1390.16, al. (Andania, i B.C.), which is easier to explain, v. εἷμα, εἱματισμός.]

ἱμᾰτιο-παραλήμπτης [ῐ], ου, ὁ, *collector of deliveries in kind in the form of clothing*, *BGU*1564.1 (ii A.D.). **-πλύτης** [ῠ], ου, ὁ, = κναφεύς, dub. in ib.118 iii 7 (ii A.D.). **-ποιΐα**, ἡ, *clothes-making*, *Gloss*. **-πράτης** [ᾱ], ου, ὁ, = sq., *Stud.Pal*.22.95.2 (iii A.D.). **-πώλης**, ου, ὁ, *clothes-dealer*, Critias *Fr*.64 D., *UPZ*8.32 (ii B.C.), *AJP* 38.418 (Egypt), *Ephes*.3 p.146 (εἱμ-), Ptol.*Tetr*.179:—also in form **εἱματοπ.**, *Gloss*.:—fem. **-πωλις**, ιδος, *IG*2.3650, Ath.3.76a; ἡ ἱ. ἀγορά Poll.7.78: **-πωλικόν** (sc. τέλος), τό, *tax on clothes-dealers*, *PLeipz*.5.7 (*Ber.Sächs.Ges.d.W*.37.245 (iii A.D.)).

ἱμᾰτιουργικός [ῐ], ή, όν, *skilled in making clothes*: ἡ -κή (sc. τέχνη) *the tailor's art*, Pl.*Plt*.280a, Gal.*Thras*.26.

ἱμᾰτιο-φόριον, τό, = sq., *Sammelb*.7033.42,43 (v A.D.). **-φορίς**, ίδος, ἡ, *portmanteau*, *POxy*.116.10 (ii A.D.), Ammon.*Diff*.p.135 V. (cf. Ptol.Ascal.p.406 H.), Ael.Dion.*Fr*.206. **-φῠλᾰκέω**, *take care of clothes*, Luc.*Hipp*.8. **-φῠλάκιον**, τό, *wardrobe*, *Gloss*.:—also in form **εἱματοφ-**, ib. **-φύλαξ** [ῠ], ᾰκος, ὁ, ἡ, *keeper of the wardrobe*, Lxx 4 *Ki*.22.14:—in form **εἱματο-**, *Gloss*.

ἱμᾰτισμός [ῐ], ὁ, *clothing, apparel*, Thphr.*Char*.23.8, Aen.Tact.31. 15, *SIG*1015.35 (Halic., iii B.C.), *PHib*.1.54 (iii B.C.), *PCair.Zen*.28. 1 (iii B.C.), *BCH*6.24 (Delos, ii B.C.), Plb.11.9.2, *Ev.Luc*.7.25, Plu. *Alex*.39: **εἱμ-** *PEleph*.1.4 (iv B.C.), *IG*5(1).1390.15 (Andania, i B.C.), etc.

ἱμάω, Att. inf. ἱμῆν Phot.:—*draw up*, esp. water from a well, Ath.8.352a; κάδῳ Orib.*Eup*.1.1.2:—Pass., *to be tapped of, yield*, γάλα Arist.*HA*522^{b}12, *PA*688^{b}10. (From ἱμάς 2f, acc. to Ael.Dion. *Fr*.211; ἱμάω has ῑ (v. καθιμάω), like ἱμονιά, ἱμανήθρη, but ἱμαῖος has ῐ.)

ϝιμβάναι (γιμβ- cod.)· ζεύγανα, Hsch. **ἴμβηρις**, = ἔγχελυς, at Methymna, Id. (cf. Lith. *ungurỹs* 'eel').

Ἴμβρος, ὁ, the island of Imbros, Il.13.33, etc.: also, epith. of Pelasgian Hermes, St.Byz. s.v.: hence **Ἴμβριοι**, οἱ, *the Imbrians*, *IG*1^2. 198.101.

ἱμείρω [ῑ], Aeol. **ἰμέρρω** Sapph.1.27, Alc.*Supp*.26.5, cf. Hdn.Gr. 2.949: (ἵμερος):—*long for, desire*, c. gen., τί κακῶν ἱμείρετε τούτων...; Od.10.431, cf. 555, Hes.*Sc*.31; μεγάλων B.1.62; μάχης A.*Ag*.940; βίου S.*Fr*.952, cf. Ar.*Nu*.435: c. inf., *long* or *wish* to do, Alc. l.c., Sol.13.7, A.*Pers*.233, S.*OT*587, *Ichn*.128; ὄσσα μοι τέλεσσαι θῦμος ἰμέρρει Sapph. l.c.: c. Adj. neut., γνωτὰ κοὐκ ἄγνωτά μοι προσήλθεθ' ἱμείροντες S.*OT*59: abs., Id.*El*.1053; ἀσμένοις.. καὶ ἱμείρουσιν... τὸ φῶς ἐγίγνετο Pl.*Cra*.418d. II. Med. **ἱμείρομαι**, aor. 1 ἱμειράμην Il.14.163:—Pass., aor. 1 ἱμέρθην Hdt.7.44: c. gen., ὁππότ' ἂν ἠβήσῃ τε καὶ ἧς ἱμείρεται αἴης (Ep. aor. subj.) Od.1.41; χρημάτων ἱ. μεγάλως Hdt.3.123: c. inf., εἴ πως ἱμείραιτο παραδραθέειν φιλότητι (cf. ἵμερος) Il.14.163, cf. Od.1.59, Hdt.6.120, S.*OT*386.—Ep., Ion. (Hdt. and Hp.*Morb*.4.39), and Trag. word: never in Att. Prose; introduced as etym. in Pl.*Cra*. l.c.

ἴμεν, ἴμεναι [ῐ], Ep. inf. of εἶμι (*ibo*).

ἱμέρα, ἡ, old collat. form of ἡμέρα, acc. to Pl.*Cra*.418c,d.

ἱμεράμπυξ [ῑ], ῠκος, ἡ, *with lovely diadem*, θεά B.16.9.

ἱμερό-γυιος [ῑ], ον, *with lovely limbs*, B.12.137. **-εις**, εσσα, εν, (ἵμερος) *exciting desire, lovely, charming*, in Hom. always of things, ἱμερόεντα.. ἔργα γάμοιο Il.5.429, etc.; χροὸς ἱμερόεντος 14.170; ἀοιδή, ἔπεα, Od.1.421, 17.519; γόος (cf. ἵμερος) 10.398; Χαρίτων χορὸν ἱμερόεντα 18.194, cf. Il.18.603; ἱμερόεν κιθάριζε ib.570; so later κισσός D.P.947; ἔρωτες *AP*5.277 (Agath.); of persons, Pi.*Fr.*87 (Sup.), Thgn.1365 (Sup.), Theoc.7.118; νύμφη Coluth.295. **-θαλής**, ές, (θάλλω) Dor. for -θηλής, *sweetly blooming*, ἔαρ *AP*9.564 (Nicias): vulg. ἡμεροθ–. **-νους**, ουν, *lovely of soul*, Orph.*H.*56.8. **-ομαι**, Pass., of a female, *have sexual intercourse with*, τοῦ ἀνδρός, or abs., Hp.*Mul.*1.12,24. **-πνους**, πνουν, *breathing sweetness*, *BMus. Inscr.*1084.

ἵμερος [ῑ], ὁ, *longing*, *yearning after*, c. gen. rei, σίτου.. περὶ φρένας ἵμερος αἱρεῖ Il.11.89, etc.; γόου ἵμερον ὦρσε raised [in them] *a yearning* after tears, i.e. a desire of the soul to disburden itself in grief, 23.14; ὑφ' ἵμερον ὦρτο γόοιο Od.16.215, etc.: with gen. obj. added, πατρὸς ὑφ' ἵμερον ὦρσε γόοιο *for* his father, 4.113; ἵμερον ἔχειν, = ἱμείρεσθαι, c. inf., Hdt.5.106, 7.43; ἵμερος ἔχει με... ἰδεῖν S.*OC*1725 (lyr.), cf. Sapph.*Supp.*24.11; ἵ. ἐπείρεσθαί μοι ἐπῆλθέ Hdt.1.30, cf. 9.3; τῶν (sc. δενδρέων) γλυκὺς ἵ. ἔσχεν.. φυτεῦσαι Pi.*O.*3.33: in pl., πολλοὶ γὰρ εἰς ἓν ξυμπίτνουσιν ἵ. various *impulses* or *emotions*, A. *Ch.*299, cf. Phld.*Ir.*p.37 W., *Piet.*20. 2. abs., *desire*, *love*, ὥς σεο νῦν ἔραμαι καί με γλυκὺς ἵ. αἱρεῖ Il.3.446; δὸς νῦν μοι φιλότητα καὶ ἵ. 14.198; δαμέντα φρένας ἱμέρῳ Pi.*O.*1.41, cf. Sapph.*Supp.*25.16; ἱμέρῳ πεπληγμένος A.*Ag.*544; ἱμέρου νικώμενος Id.*Supp.*1005, cf. *Pr.*649, S.*Tr.*476, Ar.*Ra.*59; βλεφάρων ἵ. S.*Ant.*796 (lyr.). 3. personified, Χάριτές τε καὶ Ἵ. Hes.*Th.*64; Ἔρως.. χαρίτων, ἱμέρου, πόθου πατήρ Pl.*Smp.*197d, cf. Luc.*DDeor.*20.15, Nonn.*D.*1.68, al. II. as Adj., only in neut. as Adv., ἵμερον αὐλήσαντι *AP*9.266 (Antip.); ἵμερα μελίζεσθαι, δακρῦσαι, ib.7.30 (Antip. Sid.), 364 (Marc. Arg.).— Poet., exc. in Pl. and Ion. and later Prose, as Hdt. ll. cc., Hp.*Aër.* 22, Phld. ll. cc., *Acad.Ind.*p.56 M. (Sts. derived fr. *is-mero–*, cf. Skt. *iṣṭás* 'desired', *iṣmás* 'god of love', but Aeol. texts have ἴμερος, ἰμέρρω, never ἰμμ–; cf. ἠμερτόν· ἐπέραστον, Hsch. (s.v.l.).)

ἱμερό-φρων [ῑ], ονος, ὁ, ἡ, *lovely in spirit*, Doroth.ap.Heph.Astr.3. 9. **-φωνος**, ον, *of lovely voice* or *song*, ἀηδών Sapph.39, Alcm.26 (vulg. ἱεροφ–), Theoc.28.7.

ἰμέρρω [ῐ], Aeol. for ἱμείρω (q.v.).

ἱμερτός [ῑ], ή, όν, (ἱμείρω) *longed for*, *desired*, *lovely*, Τιταρήσιος Il. 2.751; ὕδατα A.R.2.939; Σαλαμίς Sol.1.1; κίθαρις *h.Merc.*510; στέφανοι Hes.*Th.*577; κόμα Sapph.119; λέχος Pi.*P.*3.99; ἀοιδαί, δόξα, Id.*O.*6.7, *P.*9.75; ἱ. ἡλικίη *dear* life, Simon.115; of persons, *AP*5. 297 (Jul.); epith. of Apollo and Dionysus, ib.9.524.10, 525.10.— Poet. and later Prose, as Epicur.*Fr.*165, Luc.*DDeor.*20.15: ἱμερτόν, τό, Plu.2.926f; ἐφ' ἱμερτοῖσιν prob. from a poet, ib.394b.

ἱμερώδης [ῑ], ες, = ἱμερόεις, Callistr.*Stat.*11.

ἰμέσος, Prep., c. gen., *between*, ἰ. Πελειᾶν *Schwyzer*664.17 (Orchom. Arc., iv B.C.); also ἰμέσουν τοῖς Διδύμοιυν ib.25; prob. fr. ἰν (= ἐν)-μεσ–.

ἵμεστος· δίκη (Sicel), Hsch. **ἱμητός** [ῑ], ή, όν, (ἱμάω) *drawn out as from a well*, Id. **ἱμιτραόν**· ὑπόζωσον (–στον cod.) (Cypr.), Id.

ἰμμεμφής (ἰνμενφ– lap.), v. ἐμμεμφής.

ἴμμεναι, poet. for ἴμεναι, ἰέναι, inf. of εἶμι (*ibo*).

ἱμονιά [prob. ῑ, cf. *An.Ox.*1.217], ἡ, (ἱμάς) *well-rope*, Alex.174.9, Apollod.Gel.1 (pl.), Ph.2.89 (pl.), Luc.*Icar.*7, *JConf.*8, Hsch.; ἱμονιάν (abs.) *a rope's length*, i.e. as long as a bucket takes to go down and come up a well, Ar.*Ec.*351.

ἱμονιοστρόφος, ὁ, *water-drawer*, Ar.*Ra.*1297.

ἵμοροι· πόλεμοι, Hsch. **ἵμπασις**, v. ἔμπασις. **ἰμπάταον**· ἔμβλεψον (Paph.), Id. **ἰμπλατία**, ἡ, Arc. for ἐμπλ–, a sacrificial *cake*, *IG*5(2).4 (Tegea, iv B.C.). **ἰμπολά**, v. ἐμπολή. **ἰμπόλης**· λῃστής, Hsch. (perh. Arc. for ἐμπολεύς). **ἵμπτω**, v. ἴπτω. **Ἴμψιος**, epith. of Poseidon in Syria, Hsch. **ἵν**, dat. and acc. of the old pers. Pron. ἵ (q.v.). **ἰν**, Arc., Cypr., and Cret. for ἐν (q.v.).

ἵν or **εἵν**, gen. εἱνός, τό, an Egyptian and Jewish liquid measure, Lxx*Ex.*29.40, al., J.*AJ*3.9.4, Eust.1282.51 (indecl. in Lxx ll. cc.); cf. ἵνιον.

ἵνα, A. Adv., I. of Place, 1. *in that place*, *there*, once in Hom., ἵ. γάρ σφιν ἐπέφραδον ἠγερέθεσθαι Il.10.127 (acc. to Eust.). 2. elsewh. relat., *in which place*, *where*, 2.558, Od.9.136, Hdt.2.133, 9. 27,54, Pi.*O.*1.95, B.10.79, A.*Pr.*21, al., S.*El.*22,855, Ar.*Ra.*1231, etc.: rarely in Att. Prose, Lys.13.72 (v. infr.), Pl.*Ap.*17c, *Phlb.*61b; ἵ. ἡ Νίκη (sc. ἐστίν) *IG*2².1407.13: rare in later Greek, Arr.*An.*1.3. 2, Luc.*Cont.*22, *Ind.*3: with particles, ἵ. τε Il.20.478; ἵ. περ 24.382, Od.13.364, Lys. l.c.; ἵν' ἂν c. subj., *wherever*, S.*OC*405, E.*Ion*315; as indirect interrog., Hdt.1.179, 2.150, E.*Hec.*1008. b. after Hom., like other Advs. of Place, c. gen., ἵ. τῆς χώρης Hdt.1.98; ἔμαθε ἵ. ἦν κακοῦ *in what* a calamity, Id.1.213; οὐδ' ὁρᾶν ἵν' εἶ κακοῦ S.*OT*367; ἵν' ἕσταμεν χρείας ib.1442; ἵν' ἦμεν ἄτης Id.*El.*936; ὁρᾷς ἵν' ἐσμὲν αὐτοῦ πέρι τῆς ἀπορίας Pl.*Sph.*243b. c. with Verbs of motion, *whither*, Od.4.821, al.; ὁρᾷς ἵν' ἥκεις S.*OT*687, al., Din.2.10; ἵναπερ ὥρμητο Th. 4.74. II. of circumstance, γάμος.., ἵ. χρή *at which*, *when*, Od.6. 27; ἵ. μὲν ἐξῆν αὐτοῖς.., ἐνταῦθα.. *when* it was in their power, Antipho6.9. 2. = ἐάν, dub. in Il.7.353 (v.l. ἵν' ἄν, cf. Sch.), Archil. 74.7 codd., v.l. in Din.1.1, and Pl.*Chrm.*176b.

B. Final Conj., *that*, *in order that*, from Hom. downwards, mostly first word in the clause, but sts. preceded by an emphatic word, Pl.*Chrm.*169d; ἵ. δὴ Il.7.26, 23.207, Hdt.1.29, Pl.*R.*420e, 610c: never with ἄν or κε (if found, these particles belong to the Verb, as in Od.12.156, E.*IA*1579). I. general usage: 1. with subj., a. after primary tenses of ind., also subj. and imper.: pres. ind., Il.3. 252, Od.2.111, X.*Mem.*3.2.3, *Cyr.*1.2.11, Isoc.3.2: pf. ind., Il.1.203, Isoc.4.129: fut., Od.2.307, 4.591, X.*Cyr.*1.2.15; subj., S.*OT*364; imper., Il.19.348, al., A.*Pr.*61, S.*Ph.*880, Ar.*Ra.*297, Pl.*R.*341b, *Men.*71d. b. after historical tenses, in similes, where the aor. is gnomic, Od.5.490 (αὔοι codd.); where aor. is treated as equiv. to pf., Il.9.99, Od.8.580, Hdt.5.91, Lys.1.4, D.9.26: when the purpose is regarded from the point of view of the speaker's present, σὲ παῖδα ποιεύμην ἵ. μοι.. λοιγὸν ἀμύνῃς Il.9.495, cf. Hdt.1.29, 6. 100, Th.1.44, al., Lys.1.11,12, al. c. after opt. and ἄν, when opt. with οὐκ ἄν is used with sense of imper., Il.24.264, Od.6.58; after βουλοίμην ἄν.., Lys.7.12. d. after impf. with ἄν, D.23. 7. 2. with opt., a. after historical tenses, Il.5.3, Od.3.2, A. *Th.*215, Lys.3.11, Pl.*Prt.*314c, etc.: after the historical pres., E. *Hec.*11: sts. both moods, subj. and opt., follow in consecutive clauses, Od.3.77, Hdt.8.76, 9.51, D.23.93, 49.14. b. after opt., Od.18.369, S.*Ph.*325; βούλοιντ' ἂν ἡμᾶς ἐξολωλέναι, ἵνα.. λάβοιεν Ar. *Pax*413. c. rarely after primary tenses, by a shifting of the point of view, Od.17.250, Ar.*Ra.*24, Pl.*R.*410c. 3. with past tenses of ind., a. after unfulfilled wishes, Id.*Cri.*44d. b. after ind. with ἄν, to express a consequence which has not followed or cannot follow, S.*OT*1389, Pl.*Men.*89b, D.29.17: esp. after ἐβουλόμην ἄν.., Ar. *V.*961, Lys.4.3. c. after such Verbs as ἐχρῆν, ἔδει, E.*Hipp.*647, Pl.*Prt.*335c, *Smp.*181e, *Euthd.*304e, Isoc.9.5, D.24.48, Men.349.5, etc.: when an unfulfilled obligation is implied, τεθαύμακα ὅτι οὐκ εἶπεν (= ἔδει εἰπεῖν).. ἵ... Pl.*Tht.*161c; ἀντὶ τοῦ κοσμεῖν (= δέον κοσμεῖν) .. ἵ... D.36.47. d. after pres. ind. in general statements (including the past), οὐδὲ γὰρ τὸ εἶναι ἔχει ἡ ὕλη, ἵ. ἀγαθοῦ ταύτῃ μετεῖχεν Plot.1.8.5. 4. ἵ. μή as the neg. of ἵνα, *that not*, Il.19.348, etc. II. special usages: 1. like ὅπως, after Verbs of command and entreaty, is common only in later Gr. (but cf. Od.3.327 with ib.19), ἀξιοῦν ἵ... Decr.ap.D.18.155; δεήσεσθαι ἵ... D.H.1.83; παρακαλεῖν ἵ... Arr.*Epict.*3.23.27: freq. in *NT*, ἐκήρυξαν ἵ. μετανοήσωσιν *Ev. Marc.*6.12, al.; of will, ὅσα ἐὰν θέλητε ἵ. ποιῶσιν.. ib.25: hence ἵ. c. subj. stands for infin., ἐν τούτῳ ἵ. καρπὸν φέρητε (= ἐν τῷ φέρειν) *Ev. Jo.*15.8, etc.; πρῶτόν ἐστιν ἵ. κοιμηθῶ Arr.*Epict.*1.10.8, cf. M.Ant.8. 29; also for ὥστε, Lxx*Ge.*22.14, al., Plu.2.333a, Porph.*Abst.*2.33, etc. 2. *because*, ἵ. ἀναγνῶ ἐτιμήθην I was honoured *because* I read, Anon.ap.A.D.*Synt.*266.5, cf. *Conj.*243.21, Choerob. *in Theod.*2.257, al.; not found in literature. 3. elliptical usages, a. where the purpose of the utterance is stated, Ζεὺς ἔσθ', ἵν' εἰδῇς 'tis Zeus,— [I tell thee this] *that* thou may'st know it, S.*Ph.*989; ἵ. μὴ εἴπω ὅτι οὐδεμιᾷ Pl.*R.*507d; ἵ. συντέμω D.45.5; ἵν' ἐκ τούτων ἄρξωμαι Id.21.43; ἵ. δῶμεν.. *granted that*.., S.E.*P.*2.34, cf. 1.79. b. in commands, introducing a principal sentence, ἵ. συντάξῃς *order* him..., *PCair.Zen.* 240.12 (iii B.C.); ἵ. λαλήσῃς *PSI*4.412.1 (iii B.C.); ἵ. ἐλθὼν ἐπιθῇς τὰς χεῖρας αὐτῇ *Ev.Marc.*5.23, cf. 2*Ep.Cor.*8.7, Lxx 2*Ma.*1.9, Arr.*Epict.*4. 1.41, Did.ap.Sch.S.*OC*156. c. ἵ. τί (sc. γένηται); *to what end?* either abs. or as a question, Ar.*Ec.*719; or with a Verb following, Id.*Pax* 409, cf. Pl.*Ap.*26d, etc.; ἵ. δὴ τί; Ar.*Nu.*1192. d. in indignant exclamations, *to think that*...! Σωκράτης ἵ. πάθῃ ταῦτα Arr.*Epict.*1.29. 16. III. in later Gr. with ind., Lxx*Ex.*1.11, al., *Ep.Gal.*2.4, 4. 17, etc.

ἰναία, ἡ, *force*, *strength* of a swell or current at sea, *Peripl.M.Rubr.* 46 (ἰνδίᾳ cod.), Hsch.

ἰναλίνω, v. ἐναλίνω.

ἴναντι [ῐν], Cret., = ἔναντι, *GDI*5125 a 1.

ἰνάριον [ῐ], τό, Dim. of ἴς, *strand*, *fibre*, ἰ. λεπτὸν καὶ μακρόν Phlp. *in Mete.*61.31.

ἰνάσσω, fut. -άσω, = ἰνόω, ἰσχὺν παρέχω, Choerob. in *Theod.*2.154, *EM*100.39, Suid.; ὅταν μ' ἰνάσσατο (sic cod.) Call.*Fr.anon.*126.

Ἴνᾰχος [ῐ], ὁ, *Inachus*, a river of Argolis, A.*Fr.*168, E.*El.*1. II. son of Oceanus, king of Argos, A.*Pr.*663, al.:—Adj. **Ἰνάχειος**, α, ον, ib.590.

-ίνδα, adverbial termin. of words signifying a game or sport, mostly with παίζειν, Poll.9.110, Theognost.*Can.*164.

ἰνδαλίμη, epith. of the Moon, dub. sens. in *PMag.Par.*1.2273.

ἰνδάλλομαι, almost always used in pres. and impf.: aor. ἰνδάλθην Lyc.597, 961, Max.163:—*appear*, *seem*, ἄλλοι μοι δοκέουσι παροίτεροι ἔμμεναι ἵπποι, ἄλλος δ' ἡνίοχος ἰνδάλλεται Il.23.460; ἰνδάλλετο δέ σφισι πᾶσι τεύχεσι λαμπόμενος μεγαθύμου Πηλεΐωνος 17.213 (-θύμῳ -ωνι Aristarch., cf. 2), cf. Od.3.246, *h.Ven.*178: ὥς μοι ἰνδάλλεται ἦτορ as my memory *seems* to me, or perh., as my heart *pictures him*, Od.19. 224; also in Att., ὥστ' ἔμοιγ' ἰνδάλλεται ὁμοιότατος κλητῆρος εἶναι πωλίῳ Ar.*V.*188; τοῦτο γάρ μοι ἰ. διανοουμένη [ἡ ψυχή], οὐκ ἄλλο τι ἢ διαλέγεσθαι it *seems* to me to be merely engaged in a dialogue, Pl. *Tht.*189e; τὰ δι' ὀφθαλμῶν ἰνδαλλόμενα ἡμῖν Arist.*Mu.*397ᵇ18, cf. Iamb.*Myst.*2.3; *flash on one's mind*, ἀμφὶ δὲ.. μεληδόνες ἰνδάλλοντο *appeared*, A.R.3.812, cf. 2.545. 2. c. dat., *resemble*, θεοῖ ξένοις -όμενοι Pl.*R.*381e, cf. *Lg.*959a; ἀργύρῳ Theoc.22.39; κύκνοις Lyc. 597. (Never in Trag.; connected with *vid–*, *εἴδω.)

ἴνδαλ-μα, ατος, τό, *form*, *appearance*, Lxx*Wi.*17.3, Ael.*NA*17.35; ἰ. ψυχῆς, = εἴδωλον, *IG*3.1403: pl., ἰ. ζωῆς Plot.1.4.3; κρυφίων ἰνδάλματα πυρσῶν *AP*5.250 (Iren.); *mental image*, ἰ. καὶ δόκησις ψυχῆς Them.*Or.*26.327d: in pl., *hallucinations*, Luc.*Gall.*5, Aret.*SD*1. 6. **-ματίζομαι**, = ἰνδάλλομαι, dub. in Lib.*Descr.*30.1. **-μός**, ὁ, = ἴνδαλμα, in pl., Hp.*Ep.*18: title of work by Timon, D.L.9.65, 105.

ἰνδάριον, τό, name of an *eye-salve*, Aët.7.118.

ἰνδέα· μεσημβρία (Maced.), Hsch. **ἰνδικάζω**, **ἴνδικος**, v. ἐνδ–.

ἰνδικοπλάστης (–πλεύστης cod.), *dyer, Gloss.*

Ἰνδικός, ή, όν, *Indian*: ἡ Ἰ. χώρη Hdt.3.98: Sup. –ώτατος Philostr. *VA*1.10:—fem. **Ἰνδίς**, ίδος, f.l. in Nonn.*D*.17.377. II. Ἰνδικὸν φάρμακον *a kind of pepper*, Hp.*Mul*.1.81; but, *indigo* (cf. infr. 2), *PHolm*.11.2; also called ἰ. μέλαν ib.9.8. 2. the plant *indigo, Indigofera tinctoria*, Dsc.5.92. 3. name of an *eye-salve*, Gal.12.780, al.

Ἰνδιστί, Adv. *in the Indian language*, Ctes.*Fr*.57.4.

Ἰνδογενής, ές, *born in India*, Man.1.297.

Ἰνδολέτης, ου, ὁ, *Indian-killer*, of Dionysus, *AP*9.524.

Ἰνδός, ή, όν, *Indian*, Hdt.3.38, al., cf. A.*Supp*.284; esp. of the drivers of elephants, Phylarch.36J., Plb.1.40.15, al. 2. **Ἰνδός**, ὁ, the river *Indus*, Hdt.4.44, etc. 3. name of a *fallacy*, Plu.2.133b. II. as Adj., = Ἰνδικός, *Indian*, *AP*9.544.1 (Addaeus). 2. **Ἰνδή**, ἡ, (sc. ἔμπλαστρος) name of a *plaster*, Orib.*Fr*.88.

Ἰνδοσκῦθία, ἡ, *the country on the banks of the Indus*, Ptol.*Geog*.7.1.

ἴνδουρος, ὁ, *mole* (ἀσπάλαξ), Hsch.

Ἰνδοφόνος, ὁ, = Ἰνδολέτης Nonn.*D*.17.387.

Ἰνδῷος, α, ον, = Ἰνδικός, Nonn.*D*.17.380, St.Byz.

Ἰνεῖον, τό, *sanctuary of Ino*, Sch.Euph.*Oxy*.2085*Fr*.1.15.

ἰνεύει· τείνει, Hsch.

ἰν-έω or –άω, *carry off by evacuations*, Ion. word, Hsch., Phot.: fut. Med. ἰνήσομαι Hp.*Mul*.1.52, and prob. l. ib.119; in pass. sense, Id.*Loc.Hom*.27:—Pass., ἰνῶνται, –ώμενος, ibid., ib.33.

ἴνϝοικος, ὁ, Arc. for ἔνοικος, *IG*5(2).343 (Orchom. Arc., iv B.C.).

ἴνη [ῑ], ἡ, = ἴς (A), ταῖς ἀπὸ τῶν καλάμων ἴναις *Peripl.M.Rubr*.65.

ἰν-ηθμός, ὁ, *emptying, purging*, Hp.*Loc.Hom*.16, 33. –ησις, εως, ἡ, = foreg., ib.20 (νῆσις codd., cf. Erot. s. v. ἰνήσεται), Pherecyd.66J.

ἰνίον [ῐν], τό, (ἴς A) *occipital bone, occiput*, [τοῦ τριχωτοῦ κρανίου] .. τὸ ὀπίσθιον [ἐστὶν] ἰνίον Arist.*HA*491ᵃ33, cf. Gal.*UP*9.17, al.; κεφαλῆς κατὰ ἰνίον Il.5.73; διὰ ἰνίου ἦλθεν [δόρυ] 14.495, cf. Hp.*Aph*.3.26, Pherecyd.66J., Theoc.25.264, Euph.41, Plu.*Mar*.33. (ἰ– codd., κατ' ἰν– Gal. l. c., but cf. ἐφινίους· τὰς ἐπὶ τοῦ ἰνίου σάρκας, Hsch.)

ἵνιον, τό, Dim. of ἵν (q.v.), an Egyptian measure of capacity, *PSI* 4.333.6 (iii B.C.), Kalbfleisch *Ind.Lect.Rost*.1902.10 (ii A.D.), *PLond. ined*.186 (ii A.D.), Gal.19.769.

ἶνις, ὁ, *son*, A.*Eu*.323, *Supp*.42, prob. in Id.*Ag*.717, cf. E.*Tr*.571, *HF*354, Lyc.570, Isyll.53 (dub.), Call.*Aet*.3.1.63, *IG*12(8).p.vii (Egypt):—fem. ἶνις, ἡ, *daughter*, E.*IA*119.—Trag. only in lyr.; Prose only in Cypr. dialect, *Inscr.Cypr*.101, al.

ἰνκαπάταόν· ἐγκατάβλεψον, Hsch.

ἰνμενφής, v. ἐμμεμφής.

ἴννην· κόρην μικράν, καὶ τὴν ἐν τῷ ὀφθαλμῷ, Hsch.

ἴννος, ὁ, = γίννος (q. v.):—also **ἴννους**· παῖδας, Hsch.

ἰνόω [ῑ], (ἴς) *make strong and nervous*, Hdn.*Epim*.49:—Pass., ἰνῶνται (also ἰννοῦνται), glossed by ζῶσιν, Hsch.

ἴντῠβος, ὁ, (ἴντουβος *Edict.Diocl*.6.3) = ἔντυβος, *endive*, Gal.6.628:—also **ἰντῠβολάχᾰνον**, τό, [Id.]14.321.

ἰνύεται (ἰνν– cod.)· κλαίει, ὀδύρεται, Hsch.:—also **ἰνύεσθαι**· κοσμεῖν, ἱδρύνεσθαι, and **ἰνύρετο**· ἐμύρετο, Id. **ἴνυξ**, = ἴυγξ, Id. **ἰνφορβίειν, ἰνφορβισμός**, v. ἐμφ–.

Ἰνώ [ῑ], όος contr. οῦς, ἡ, *Ino*, daughter of Cadmus, worshipped as a sea-goddess by the name of Leucothea, Od.5.333, Hes.*Th*.976, Alcm.84, Pi.*O*.2.30, etc.: prov., Ἰνοῦς ἄχη Zen.4.38.

ἰνώδης [ῑ], ες, *fibrous*, of parts of animals, X.*Cyn*.4.1, Arist.*HA* 497ᵃ21; ἰνωδέστατον αἷμα Id.*PA*651ᵃ3; of vegetables, φλοιός, φύλλον, Thphr.*HP*3.12.1,5, cf. Dsc.4.20; *sinewy*, X.*Cyn*.4.1.

Ἰνωπός, ὁ, name of a stream on Delos; also of a building at its source, *IG*11(2).144*A*72 (iv B.C.):—hence **Ἰνωποφύλαξ** [ῠ], ἄκος, ὁ, *warden of the I.*, ib.142.52, 144*C*10 (iv B.C.).

ἴξ (on the accent v. Hdn.Gr.1.396), ἰκός, ἡ, *worm* or *grub that destroys the vine-buds*, Alcm.43. (ἴ, perh. cogn. with ἴψ.)

ἰξᾰλῆ (ἰζάλη in codd., but ἰζαλῆ Ael.Dion.*Fr*.398), ἡ, *goat's skin* (τελείας αἰγὸς δέρμα, Erot.), Hp.*Fract*.29, cf. Gal.19.106; used as a dress for actors in satyric dramas, Poll.4.118. (**ἰζάλη** Hsch., **ἰζάνη** Poll. l. c., **ἰσάλη** Sch.Ar.*Nu*.72; cf. the forms **ἰσσέλα, ἰτθέλα, ἰσθλῆ** Hsch., **ἰσσέλη** Theognost.*Can*.14: cf. sq.)

ἴξᾰλος, ον, epith. of the Ibex, = τέλειος acc. to Ar.Byz.ap.Eust. 1625.33, or *bounding, springing* (as Sch.Il., Hsch., etc.), or = τομίας (as Porph.ap.Sch.Il.), ἰξάλου αἰγὸς ἀγρίου Il.4.105, cf. *AP*6.32 (Agath.), 113 (Simm.), 9.99 (Leon.). (Perh. borrowed fr. Asia Minor.)

ἰξ-ευμα, ατος, τό, = *aucupium, Gloss.* –ευτήρ, ῆρος, ὁ, *fowler*, Man.4.339. –ευτήριος, α, ον, *like birdlime*, v. ἰξεύτρια. II. ἰξευτήριον, τό, = *aucupium, Gloss.* –ευτής, οῦ, ὁ, *fowler, bird-catcher*, Lyc.105, Lxx *Am*.8.1, *AP*9.824 (Eryc.), *Cat.Cod.Astr*.1.166, Apollod.*Poliorc*.152.2, Porph.*Abst*.1.53; ἰ. κῶρος Bion *Fr*.9. II. as Adj., *catching with birdlime*, ἰ. κάλαμοι *AP*6.152 (Agis). –ευτικός, ή, όν, *of an* ἰξευτής, Artem.2.19; τὰ Ἰ., title of lost poem by Opp.: ἡ –κή (sc. τέχνη) Poll.7.139. –εύτρια, ἡ, fem. of ἰξευτήρ, epith. of Τύχη, Plu.2.322f:—written **ἰξευτηρία**, ib.281e (s. v. l.). –εύω, (ἰξός) *catch by birdlime*, Artem.2.19, *EM*471.53:—Med., Poll.7.135.

ἰξία, ἡ, = ἰξός I, Thphr.*HP*3.16.1, *CP*2.17.1, prob. in Dsc.3.89. II. = χαμαιλέων λευκός, *pine-thistle, Atractylis gummifera*, Dsc.3.8, Plin. *HN*22.45; ἡ ἰ. ἡ ἐν Κρήτῃ Thphr.*HP*9.1.3. 2. = sq., Sch.Nic.*Al*. 279. III. = κιρσός, *varicocele*, Arist.*HA*518ᵇ25, *Pr*.878ᵇ37, Plu.2.202b.

ἰξίας, ου, ὁ, = χαμαιλέων μέλας, *chamaeleon-thistle, Cardopatium corymbiferum*, Dsc.3.9, *Alex*.21, Gal.14.140.

ἰξίνη [ῑ], ἡ, = ἰξία II, *pine-thistle, Atractylis gummifera*, Thphr.*HP* 6.4.3; ἄκανθα ἡ ἰ. ib.9.1.2, al.: confused with ἐλξίνη by Plin.*HN*21.94, 22.41.

ἰξιόεις, εσσα, εν, *made from* ἰξίας, πῶμα Nic.*Al*.279.

ἰξίον, τό, *leaf of* χαμαιλέων λευκός (= ἰξία II), Gal.19.106.

Ἴξιος, ὁ, epith. of Apollo in Rhodes, from a place **Ἰξίαι**, Artem.ap. St.Byz. s. h. v.

ἴξις, Ion. **ἶξις**, εως, ἡ, (ἵκω) *coming*, E.*Tr*.396 (prob. l.); οὐ πτύσις ἀλλ' ἀναγωγὴ καλέεται, τῆς ἄνω ἴξιος [τῆς ὁδοῦ] τοὔνομα ἔχουσα Aret. *SA*2.2; οἶνος ὠκὺς ἐς τὴν ἄνω ἴξιν Id.*CA*2.4. 2. *passage through*, οὐδαμῇ.. κατὰ τὴν τοῦ θώρηκος ἴ. Hp.*Acut*.15 (but perh. simply, 'at no point *in the* θ.'); ἴξιν παρέχεσθαι allow *free passage*, dub. in Sch. Epicur.*Ep*.1 p.8 U. (fort. εἶξιν). II. *direction, straight line*, esp. *vertical line*, καθημένῳ πόδες ἐς τὴν ἄνω ἴ. κατ' ἰθὺ γούνασι his feet when he is seated should be *vertically* opposite his knees, Hp.*Off*.3; ἐπιδεῖν δεξιὰ ἐπ' ἀριστερά, ἀριστερὰ ἐπὶ δεξιά, πλὴν κεφαλῆς· ταύτην δὲ κατ' ἴξιν *vertically*, ib.9; βάλλεσθαι χρὴ τὸ ὀθόνιον κατ' αὐτὴν τὴν ἴ. τοῦ ἕλκεος directly *over* the wound, Id.*Fract*.26; τοὺς νάρθηκας.. μὴ κατὰ τὴν ἴ. τοῦ ἕλκεος προστιθέναι ibid.; ὁκόσα κοινωνεῖ τοῖσι τῆς κνήμης ὀστέοισι καὶ αὐτέῃ τῇ ἴξει ib.9 codd. (κατὰ τὴν ἴξιν Gal.18(2).423; κατ' αὐτὴν τὴν ἴ. Ermerins). 2. κατ' ἴξιν c. gen., *corresponding to, on the same side as*, ἤλγησεν κατὰ βουβῶνα, σπληνὸς κατ' ἴ., i. e. on the spleen or left side of the body, Hp.*Epid*.1.26.γ', cf. 4.35,37, *Art*.33, *Fract*.16, 18, *Mul*.1.17; τῶν ὀδόντων τῶν τε ἄνω καὶ τῶν κάτω κατ' ἴ. Id.*Art*.31; = *ex ipsa parte*, Cass.Fel.37; ἐν πυρετοῖσι ἀπὸ σπληνὸς καὶ ἥπατος διὰ ῥινῶν αἱμορραγέουσι, κατ' ἴ. τοῦ σπλάγχνου τοῦ μυκτῆρος ῥέοντος the nostril *corresponding to* the organ in question, Aret.*SA* 2.2; ἡ κατ' ἴ. κληῒς the *corresponding* (i.e. liver or right side) collarbone, ib.2.7, cf. *CA*1.10; κατὰ τὴν ὄπισθεν ἴ. *at the back* of the leg, Hp.*Art*.60. 3. more generally, *in line with*, κατ' ἴ. τοῦ πυγαίου ποιησάμενον τὴν σανίδα ib.75; κατ' ἴ. τῇ ἐντομῇ τῇ ἐς τὸν τοῖχον ib.47.

Ἰξίων [ῑ], ονος, ὁ, *Ixion*, Pi.*P*.2.32, etc.: perh. connected with ἱκέτης, cf. A.*Eu*.441: pl., Ἰξίονες *tragedies on the subject of I.*, Arist. *Po*.1456ᵃ1.

ἰξο-βολέω, *practise bird-liming*, οὐκ ἰδίην –βολῶν μελέτην *AP*9.273 (Bian.). –βόλος, ον, *setting limed twigs*: as Subst., *fowler*, Man. 4.243. –βόρος, ον, (βορά) *eating mistletoe-berries*, ἡ ἰ. (sc. κίχλη) *missel-thrush, Turdus viscivorus*, Arist.*HA*617ᵃ18; cf. ἰξοφάγος. –ειδές, τό, = *viscidum, Gloss.* –εργός, ὁ, *one who uses birdlime, fowler*, *AP*9.264.5 (Apollonid. vel Phil.), 273 tit.

ἶξον, ες, ε, aor. of ἵκω.

ἰξόομαι, Pass., *to be smeared with birdlime*, Thphr.*Ign*.61.

ἰξοποιέω, *make viscous* like birdlime, of a plaster, Paul.Aeg.2.43.

ἰξός, ὁ, *oak-mistletoe, Hozanthus europaeus*, Arist.*GA*715ᵇ30, Dsc. 3.89. 2. *mistletoe-berry*, Thphr.*CP*2.17.8. II. *birdlime* prepared from the mistletoe-berry, E.*Cyc*.433; θηρευτὴς ἰ. *AP*5.99. b. *oak-gum*, used for the same purpose, Ath.10.451d, cf. Plu.*Cor*.3, Philox.ap.Gal.13.742. c. *any sticky substance*, Hp.*Mul*.1.74, *IG* 1².314.42 (ἰ–), 2².1673.63. 2. metaph., ἰ. ὀμμάτων of one who causes the eyes to be *fixed* upon him, Tim.Com.2; ἐκφυγὼν τὸν ἰ. τὸν ἐν πράγματι Luc.*Hist.Conscr*.57; καθάπερ ἰξῷ τινι προσέχεται τοῖς τοιούτοις ἡ ψυχή Id.*Cat*.14. b. *skinflint, miser*, Ar.*Fr*.718. (Prob. ϝιξός, cf. Lat. *viscum, viscus*.)

ἰξο-φάγος [ᾰ], ον, = ἰξο-βόρος, Ath.2.65a. –φορεύς, έως, ὁ, *limed*, δόνακες ἰξοφορῆες *AP*9.209. –φόρος, ον, *having mistletoe growing thereon*, δρύες S.*Fr*.403: read by Agathocl. in Il.14.398. II. *limed*, δόναξ Opp.*H*.1.32.

ἰξύα, ἡ, = ἰξύς, *EM*770.13; ἰξύη ib.636.24.

ἰξυόθεν, Adv. *from the loins*, Arat.144; prob. l. for ἰξυόφιν in Opp. *C*.2.6.

ἰξύς, ύος, ἡ, *waist*, of women, περὶ δὲ ζώνην βάλετ' ἰξυῖ (contr. for ἰξύϊ) Od.5.231, cf. Longus 1.4; of a man, Arat.310; of centaurs, Opp. *C*.2.6; of a deer, *APl*.4.96: pl., ἰξύες, οἱ, *loins*, Hp.*Fract*.20, cf. Gal. 19.106: sg., = ὀσφύς, [Id.]14.706. (Perh. akin to ἰσχύς, cf. ἰσχίον.) [ῡ in nom. and acc. sg., Choerob. *in Theod*.1.331; ῠ in trisyll. cases.]

ἰξώδης, ες, *like birdlime, sticky, clammy*, Hp.*Ulc*.12, Luc.*Tim*.29.

Ἰοβάκχ-εια [ῐ], τά, *festival in honour of Bacchus*, Jusj.ap.D.59.78. –ιος, ὁ (sc. μήν), name of month at Astypalaea, *IG*12(3).169.15, 170.14; at Amorgos, ib.12(7).67*A*6. –ος, ὁ, *Bacchus invoked with the cry of* ἰώ, *APl*.4.289, Max.496, Corn.*ND*30, Hsch. 2. in pl., *worshippers of the God*, name of a guild at Athens, *SIG*1109.35, al. (ii A.D.). 3. *hymn beginning with* ἰὼ Βάκχε, such as were ascribed to Archilochus, Heph.15.9.

ἰο-βάπτης [ῐ], ου, ὁ, *violet-dyer, Gloss.* –βαφής, ές, *violet-coloured*, Democr.Eph.1; of water, Ath.2.42e. –βλέφᾰρος, Dor. ἰογλέφ–, ον, *violet-eyed*, Pi.*Fr*.307; Χάριτες, Μοῦσαι, B.18.5, 8.3, cf. Man.5.145, Luc.*Im*.8.

ἰο-βολέω [ῐ], *shoot arrows, dart*, A.R.4.1440, *AP*5.187 (Leon.); ἐς ἐμὴν κραδίην ib.5.9 (Alc.). II. *emit poison*, *Gp*.2.47.12. –βόλος, ον, (ἰός) *shooting arrows*, τόξον *AP*6.34 (Rhian.). II. *shedding venom, venomous*, of animals, Numen.ap.Ath.7.304f, Hdn.3.9.5: Sup., J.*AJ*17.5.5; ἰοβόλα, τά, *venomous animals*, Arist.*HA*607ᵃ28; περὶ ἰοβόλων ζῴων, title of work by Philumenus; τὰ τῶν ἰ. ἄκη Philostr.*VA*3.44. 2. of arrows, *poisoned*, Orph.*H*.12.16; αἷμα *AP*11.237 (Demod.): metaph., ἰ. γέννες, of Momus, *APl*.4.266. 2. –βόρος, ον, (ἰός B) *poison-eating*, Opp.*C*.3.223; of a serpent, διψάς *IG*4.620 (Argos). II. *eating venomously*, πυθεδόνες Nic.*Th*. 467.

ἰο-βόστρῠχος [ῐ], ον, *dark-haired*, Μοῦσαι Pi.*I*.7(6).23. –γληνος, η, ον, *dark-eyed*, Hsch. **-δετος**, ον, (δέω) *violet-twined*, στέφανοι Pi.*Fr.*75.6. **-δνεφής**, ές, (δνόφος) *dark as the flower* ἴον (v. ἴον IV), *purple-dark*, εἶρος Od.4.135, 9.426.

ἰοδόκος [ῑ], ον, (ἰός A) *holding arrows*, φαρέτρη Il.15.444, Od.21.12, Pittac.Lyr.1: **ἰοδόκη** (sc. φαρέτρα), ἡ, *quiver*, A.R.2.679, 3.156, 279, *AP*6.296 (Leon.), 12.45 (Posidipp.): **ἰοδόχη**, Hsch., Phot. II. *containing poison*, ὀδόντες ἰ. *poison*-fangs, Nic.*Th.*184.

ἰοειδής [ῐ], ές, (ἴον) *like the flower* ἴον I, *purple*, in Hom. always of the sea, ἰοειδέα πόντον, whether calm or stormy, Il.11.298, Od.5.56, 11.107, Hes.*Th.*844; κρήνη ib.3. II. (ἰός B) *poisonous*, κέντρον Nic.*Th.*886; λοιγός ib.243. [Nic. makes ῐ short, as conversely he has ῑάσι from ἴον (q.v.).]

ἰόεις [ῐ], εσσα, εν, (ἴον) *violet-coloured, dark*, ἰόεντα σίδηρον Il.23.850, cf. Phoronis *Fr.*2, Q.S.6.48; ἰόεντα θάλασσαν Nic.*Al.*171. II. **ἰόεις**, (ἰός B) *poisonous*, ἄκανθαι Androm.ap.Gal.14.38 [who makes ῐ short; cf. foreg. II].

ἰό-ζωνος [ῐ], ον, (ζώνη) *with purple girdle*, Hsch., dub. in Call. in *Stud.Ital.*7(1929).9. **-θᾰλής**, ές, *blooming with violets*, στέφανοι Philox.2.42. **-κολπος**, ον, = ἰόζωνος, Alc.63 (Sapphus est), Sapph. *Supp.*17.5. **-κουρος**, ὁ, = βιόκουρος, *Ephes.*3p.165.

ἰολόχευτος [ῑ], ον, (ἰός B) *born of venom*, Procl.*H.*1.41.

ἴομεν, Ep. for ἴωμεν, 1 pl. pres. subj. of εἶμι (*ibo*).

ἰομῐγής [ῑ], ές, (ἰός B) *tainted with poison*, θηλή *AP*9.1 (Polyaen.).

ἰόμωροι, οἱ, twice in Hom., Ἀργεῖοι ἰόμωροι, ἐλεγχέες Il.4.242; Ἀργεῖοι ἰόμωροι, ἀπειλάων ἀκόρητοι 14.479. (Expld. by Sch. as *caring for arrows* (cf. μέριμνα), but ῑ is against this: perh. *noisy* (cf. ἰά).)

ἴον [ῐ], τό, heterocl. dat. pl. ἴασῐ [ῐᾰ] Nic.*Fr.*74.2:—*violet, Viola odorata*, στέφανοι ἴων Sapph.*Supp.*23.12, cf. Pi.*O.*6.55, etc.; καὶ τὸ ἴον μέλαν ἐντί Theoc.10.28, cf. *AP*4.1.21 (Mel.); κυαναυγές ib.5.73 (Rufin.); ἴ. τὸ μέλαν Thphr.*HP*1.13.2, *CP*1.13.12; ἴον alone, Dsc. 4.121:—in Od.5.72, λειμῶνες μαλακοὶ ἴου ἠδὲ σελίνου θήλεον, there were vv.ll. σίου (Ptol. Euerg.) and θρύου. II. ἴον τὸ λευκόν (= λευκόϊον, q.v.) *gilliflower, Matthiola incana*, Thphr.*HP*6.6.3; also ἴον alone, ib.6.8.1. III. = κρίνον, Philin.ap.Ath.15.681b. IV. generally, any *flower*, *EM*473.10. V. a precious stone of dark colour, Plin.*HN*37.170. (Ϝίον, cf. γία· ἄνθη, Hsch., Lat. *viola*.)

ἰονθάς, άδος, ἡ, *shaggy*, epith. of the wild goat, Od.14.50.

ἴονθος, ὁ, *root of a hair, young hair*, ἰόνθους ἐκθλιβομένους Phld. *Sign.*13, cf. Eun.*Hist.*p.250 D., Phryn.*PS* p.77 B. II. *eruption on the face, which often accompanies the first growth of the beard*, etc., Hp.*Epid.*1.26.β', Arist.*HA*556ᵇ29, *Pr.*963ᵇ40, Erot. s.v. ὀλοφλυκτίδες:—hence **ἰονθώδης**, ες, ἐπάρσεις Thphr.*Sud.*16, cf. Gal.12.824.

Ἰόνιος [ῑ], α, ον, (Ἰώ) *of* or *called after Io*, epith. of the sea between Epirus and Italy, at the mouth of the Adriatic sea, across which Io swam, πόντιος μυχὸς..Ἰόνιος κεκλήσεται, τῆς σῆς πορείας μνῆμα A.*Pr.*840; another expl. in Theopomp.Hist.125; Ἰ. κόλπος Hdt.6.127, Th.1.24; θάλασσα, πόρος, Pi.*P.*3.68, *N.*4.53; also simply ὁ Ἰόνιος Th. 6.30; later Ἰόνιον πέλαγος *AP*6.251 (Phil.).

ἰόομαι, Pass., (ἰός C) *become* or *be rusty*, Arist.*Col.*793ᵇ6, Thphr. *Char.*10.14, Dsc.5.78, Antig.*Mir.*151. 2. *become acrid, embittered*, Hsch.:—Act. **ἰόω**, only late, *rust*, ὁ σίδηρος μᾶλλον ἰοῖ Olymp. *in Mete.* 266.26, cf. 270.14; *convert into* ἰός, Zos.Alch.pp.148, 238 B.

ἰό-πεπλος [ῐ], ον, *with violet robe*, Hsch. **-πλόκᾰμος**, ον, *with dark locks*, Μοῖσαι Pi.*P.*1.1, cf. Simon.18. **-πλοκος**, ον, = foreg., Alc.55; κόρα, Νηρήιδες, B.8.72, 16.37; Μοῖσαι *Lyr.Adesp.*53; of Apollo, *AP*9.524.10.

ἰοποίησις [ῑ], εως, ἡ, = ἴωσις, Zos.Alch.p.252 B.

ἰόππα· μιξόδης, Hsch. **ἴορκος**, ὁ, v. δορκάς.

ἰός (A) [ῑ], ὁ, pl. ἰοί, heterocl. ἰά Il.20.68 (Cypr., acc. to *AB*1095):—*arrow*, ἰὸν ἧκε Il.1.48; βλήμενος ἢ ἰῷ ἢ ἔγχεϊ 8.514, cf. A.*Pers.*461; ἧκεν κομήτην ἰόν S.*Tr.*567. (Cf. Skt. *iṣus* 'arrow'.)

ἰός (B) [ῑ], ὁ, *poison*, as of serpents, A.*Eu.*478, S.*Tr.*771, E.*Ion* 1015, Plu.2.562c, etc.; *venom* of a mad dog, Ruf.*Fr.*118; ἰὸς ἀμεμφὴς μελισσῶν, of honey with which snakes fed Iamos, Pi.*O.*6.47: metaph., of envy, A.*Ag.*834. (Cf. Skt. *viṣám* 'poison', Lat. *vīrus*.)

ἰός (C) [ῑ], ὁ, *rust* on iron, or *verdigris* on copper and bronze, Sapph.141 (dub.), Thgn.451, Pl.*R.*609a, *Ti.*59c, Theoc.16.17; ἰ. σιδήρου Dsc.5.80; ἰ. χαλκοῦ Hp.*Mul.*1.75, Dsc.5.79, Gal.12.218; *patina* on bronze statues, ὅπως καθαρὸς ἰοῦ ἔσται ὁ ἀνδριάς *SIG*284.15 (Chios, iv B.C.), cf. Plu.2.395b. (Perh. identical with ἰός B.)

ἰός [ῐ], ἴα, ἰόν, *one*, commonest in fem. (v. εἷς): neut. ἰῷ κίον ἤματι Il.6.422: masc. dat. ἰῷ, = ἐκείνῳ, *Leg.Gort.*8.8; but, = ἑνί, ib.7.23; acc., τόν γ' ἰὸν ἐνιαυτόν the *same* year, *IG*5(1).1390.126 (Andania, i B.C.); ἰός, = μόνος, acc. to Trypho ap.A.D.*Pron.*56.4.

ἰός, Boeot. for ἑός (q.v.).

ἰο-σάκχαρ [ῐ], τό, *sugar of violets*, Ruf.*Fr.*80. **-στέφᾰνος**, ον, *violet-crowned*, epith. of Aphrodite, *h.Hom.*6.18, Sol.19.4; of the Muses, Thgn.250; esp. of Athens, Pi.*Fr.*76, cf. B.5.3, Ar.*Ach.*637, *Eq.*1323.

ἰότης [ῐ], ητος, ἡ, *will, desire*, Ep. and Lyr. almost always in dat., θεῶν ἰότητι *by the will* of the gods, Il.19.9, Od.7.214, al., cf. Alc.13 A; μητρὸς ἐμῆς ἰότητι *at* her *will*, Il.18.396; κακῇς ἰ. γυναικός Od.11. 384; μνηστήρων ἰ. 18.234; ἀλλήλων ἰ. Il.5.874; ἀναιδήτῳ ἰ. with shameless *will*, A.R.4.360: acc. only in Il.15.41 δι' ἐμὴν ἰ. II. once in Trag., *for the sake of*, ἰότατι γάμων A.*Pr.*558 (lyr.).—Hsch. explains it by βουλήσει, αἰτίᾳ, ὀργῇ, χάριτι.

ἰο-τόκος [ῑ], ον, (ἰός B) *poison-bearing, venomous*, Opp.*C.*3. 73. **-τῠπής**, ές, (ἰός A) *arrow-stricken*, *AP*5.86 (Rufin.), 9.265 (Apollonid. or Phil.).

ἰού or **ἰοῦ** (v. sub fin.), Interj., a loud cry expressive of sorrow, joy, or surprise, 1. of grief or annoyance, usu. twice repeated, ἰοὺ ἰού D.19.209; ἰ. ἰ. δύστηνος or δύστηνε, S.*Tr.*1143, *OT*1071; ἰ. ἰ. βοᾶν, κεκραγέναι, Ar.*Nu.*543, *Pax* 345: c. gen., ἰ. ἰ. τῶν..κιγκλίδων Jul. *Caes.*330d: rarely once, φῦ (φεῦ codd.), ἰ. τῆς ἀσβόλου Ar.*Th.*245; or thrice, Id.*Pax* 110: with other Interj., ἰ. ἰ. ὢ ὢ κακά A.*Ag.*1214; ἰ. ἰ. πόπαξ Id.*Eu.*143 (lyr.). 2. of joyful surprise, *hallo!, hurrah!*, Id.*Ag.*25, E.*Cyc.*464, 576, Ar.*Eq.*1096, Pl.*R.*432d, *Grg.*499b, *Smp.* 223a. (Sch.Ar.*Pax* 345, 316 says that ἰοὺ ἰού is of woe, ἰοῦ ἰοῦ of joy: the rule is not observed in codd. In Att. Poets it sts. stands extra versum, A.*Ag.*25, Ar.*Nu.*1.)

Ἰουδαῖος, ὁ, *a Jew*: **Ἰουδαία**, *a Jewess*; ἡ Ἰουδαία (sc. γῆ) *Judaea*: —**Ἰουδα-ϊκός**, ή, όν, *Jewish*, Lxx 2*Ma.*8.11, etc. Adv. **-κῶς** J.*BJ*6.1. 3, *Ep.Gal.*2.14, *Cod.Just.*1.1.7.4: **-ΐζω**, *side with* or *imitate the Jews*, Lxx *Es.*8.17, *Ep.Gal.* l.c.: **-ισμός**, ὁ, *Judaism*, Lxx 2*Ma.*2.21, *Ep. Gal.*1.13: **-ϊστί**, *in the Hebrew tongue*, Lxx 4*Ki.*18.26.

ἴουκαι· πεπόρευται, Hsch.

Ἰουλαῖος, ὁ (sc. μήν), name of month in Lesbos (?), *CIG*6850*A*; in Cyprus, *Cat.Cod.Astr.*2.139:—also **Ἰουλίηος**, *CIG*2827, 2836 (Aphrodisias): **Ἰούλιος**, = Lat. *Julius*, *Hemerolog.Flor.*

ἰουλίζω [ῑ], *become downy* or *hairy*, Tryph.53, cf. Phot.

ἰουλίς [ῑ], ίδος, ἡ, *rainbow-wrasse, Coris iulis*, Arist.*HA*610ᵇ6, *AP* 7.504.5 (Leon.), Numen.ap.Ath.7.304f, Artem.1.14.

ἰουλόπεζος [ῑ], ον, (ἴουλος IV) *footed like the centipede*, i.e. *many-footed, many-oared*, of a ship, Lyc.23.

ἴουλος [ῑ], ὁ, *down, the first growth of the whiskers and beard*, in pl., πρίν σφωϊν ὑπὸ κροτάφοισιν ἰούλους ἀνθῆσαι Od.11.319: later in sg., στείχει δ' ἴ. ἄρτι διὰ παρηΐδων A.*Th.*534; πρᾶτον ἴ. ἀπὸ κροτάφων καταβάλλειν Theoc.15.85; ἔτι χνοάοντας ἰούλους ἀντέλλων A.R.2.43; ὑπὸ κροτάφοισιν ἰούλους ἐκρέμενος *AP*6.198 (Antip. Thess.); ἰούλοις πλῆσαι παρειάς *IG*14.1601. II. *corn-sheaf*, whence Demeter is said to be named Ἰουλώ, Semus 19, *Carm.Pop.*1. 2. *song in honour of Demeter*, Semus l.c., Apollod.Hist.149 J., Eratosth.*Fr.*10. III. *catkin*, Thphr.*HP*3.5.5, 3.7.3; *tendril*, ib.3.18.11. IV. *creature like the centipede*, prob. the *wood-louse*, Arist.*HA*523ᵇ18, *PA*682ᵇ3, Thphr.*Sign.*19, Arat.959; *earthworm*, Numen.ap.Ath.7.305a. V. = ἰουλίς, Eratosth.*Fr.*12 (pl.). (Perh. cogn. with οὖλος, q.v.)

ἰουλοφόρος [ῑ], ον, *downy*, γένυς Demitsas Μακεδ.No.410 (Thessalonica, ii A.D.).

Ἰουλώ [ῑ], οῦς, ἡ, *goddess of sheaves*, epith. of Demeter, Semus 19; cf. ἴουλος II.

ἰουλώδης [ῑ], ες, *scolopendra-like*, Arist.*PA*682ᵃ5.

ἰόφ, prob. corrupt in A.*Supp.*828: interj. expressing aversion, acc. to Sch.

ἰο-φόρος [ῑ], ον, (ἰός B, φέρω) *poison-bearing*, Opp.*C.*3.433. **-χέαιρα**, ἡ, (ἰός A) *arrow-pourer, shooter of arrows*, epith. of Artemis, Il.5.53, etc.; ἰ. παρθένος Pi.*P.*2.9: as Subst., Ἰοχέαιρα Il.21.480, Od. 11.198, *Schwyzer*758 (vi B.C.), *IG*14.1389 i 53; later ἰ. φαρέτρα *AP* 6.9 (Mnasalc.). II. (ἰός B) *poison-shedding*, of serpents, Nic.*Fr.* 33. (-χέϜαιρα from χέω, not as expld. by Apollon.Lex. etc. from χαίρω.) [ῑ as in ἰός: yet ῐ in Pi. l.c.]

Ἴοχια, τά, name of a festival, perh. *Parilia* (*parelia, pardia* codd.), *Gloss.*

ἴπαμα· κάμινη, Hsch. **ἶπαρ**, Aeol. for ὕπαρ, Jo.Gramm.*Comp.* 3.15. **ἰπνασία**· γαστήρ (Tarent.), Hsch.

ἰπνευ-τής, οῦ, ὁ, = *furnarius*, *Gloss.*; prob. for ἰπνίτης in *AP*6.299 (Phan.). **-ω**, (ἰπνός) *dry* or *bake in the oven*, Hsch., prob. in *IG* 1².4.15 (*hιπν*-).

ἴπνη, ἡ, *woodpecker*, Ant.Lib.21.6; cf. ἴππα (ἴπτα cod.)· = δρυοκόλαψ, Hsch.: **ἰπνή**· ἐφιππίς (Sicel), Id.

ἰπν-ίον, τό, Dim. of ἰπνός, Dieuch.ap.Orib.4.5.2. **-ιος**, α, ον, (ἰπνός I) *of an oven*:—hence **ἴπνια**, τά, *soot*, Hsch., cf. Sch.Ar.*V.* 832. II. (ἰπνός IV) *of a dunghill*, Call.*Fr.*216. **-ίτης** [ῑτ], ου, ὁ, *baked in the oven*, οἱ ἰ. ἄρτοι Hp.*Vict.*2.42, Polem.Hist.86, *IG*5 (1).363.18 (Sparta, i A.D.: written -είταν): without ἄρτος, Timocl. 33; ἰ. φθοΐς *AP*6.299 (Phan., sed leg. -ευτής).

ἰπνο-δόμαν· τὴν φρυγίαν (Cret.), Hsch. **-κᾰής**, ές, (καίω) *baked in the oven*, Luc.*Lex.*6. **-καύστης**, = *furnarius*, *Gloss.* (also **-καύτης**, ibid.). **-κήιον**· φρύγιον, οἱ δὲ τὴν ὑπόκαυσιν τοῦ ἰπνοῦ, Hsch. **-λέβης**, ητος, ὁ, *boiler, cauldron*, Luc.*Lex.*8, Ath.3. 98c. **-λεβήτιον**, τό, Dim. of foreg., Poll.10.66.

ἴπνον, τό, *mare's-tail, Hippuris vulgaris*, Thphr.*HP*4.10.1.

ἰπνοπλάθος [ᾰ], ὁ, (πλάσσω) *oven-maker, fire-clay moulder, worker in terra-cotta*, much like κοροπλάθος (q.v.), Pl.*Tht.*147a:—later **ἰπνοπλάθης**, Poll.7.163, Tim.*Lex.*, Harp.:—also **-πλάστης**, ου, ὁ, Gal.*Thras.*43: **-ποιός**, όν, Luc.*Prom.Es* 2, Them.*Or.*21.256d.

ἰπν-ός, ὁ, *oven, furnace*, Hdt.5.92.η', Hp.*Morb.*2.47, Antiph.176.4, Diph.Siph.ap.Ath.2.54a, Archestr.*Fr.*46; esp. for heating water for the bath, Ar.*V.*139, *Av.*437 (ἴπν-). II. *the place of the oven*, i.e. *the kitchen*, Semon.7.61, Ar.*V.*837, Lycurg.*Fr.*73. III. *lantern*, Ar.*Pax* 841, *Pl.*815, *SIG*1027.13 (Cos, iv/iii B.C.), Ael.*NA*2. 8. IV. = κοπρών, *dunghill, privy*, Ar.*Fr.*353, Hsch. (Prob. cogn. with Engl. *oven*.) **-ών**, ῶνος, ὁ, *kitchen*, *IG*11(2).287 *A* 147, al. (Delos, iii B.C.).

ἰποκτόνος [ῑ], ον, (ἴψ) *killing the worms in vines*, epith. of Heracles at Erythrae, Str.13.1.64.

ἶπ-ος, ἡ (so in Pi. l.c.) or τό (Eust.844.39), in a mouse-trap, *the piece of wood that falls and catches* the mouse, Ar.*Pl.*(815?) ap.Poll. 10.155, Id.7.41, Eust.16.40, etc. cf. εἶπος. 2. *any weight, fuller's* *press*, Archil.169 ; ἵ. ἀνεμόεσσα, of Aetna as the weight which holds Typhoeus down, Pi.*O*.4.8 ; *press* used in surgery, Hp.*Mochl*.38. (Perh. cf. ἵπτομαι.) **-όω,** *press, squeeze*, Cratin.91 ; esp. in surgery, Hp.*Art*.47 ; ἱ. τὴν κεφαλὴν τοῦ βραχίονος Heliod.ap.Orib.49. 13.8 :—Pass., *to be weighed down*, ἰπούμενος ῥίζαισιν Αἰτναίαις ὕπο A. *Pr*.365 ; ἰπούμενος ταῖς ἐσφοραῖς Ar.*Eq*.924.

ἵππα, ἡ, v. sub ἵππη : as pr. n. Ἵππα, *Hippa*, nurse of Dionysus, Orph.*H*.48.4.

ἱππ-αγρέται, ῶν, οἱ, (ἀγρέω) three officers at Lacedaemon, *who chose* 300, the flower of the ἔφηβοι, *to serve as a body-guard for the kings* (v. ἱππεύς II. 1), X.*HG*3.3.9, *Lac*.4.3, Archyt.ap.Stob.4.1.138 : sg., Th.4.38 (unless it be pr. n.). **-αγρος,** ὁ, = ἵππος ἄγριος, *wild horse*, Opp.*C*.3.252. **-ᾰγωγός,** όν, *carrying horses* ; esp. of ships used as *cavalry transports*, πλοῖα Hdt.6.48 ; νέες ib.95 ; ναῦς Th.2.56, 4.42, Arr.*An*.2.19.1 ; τριήρεις D.4.16, D.S.11.3 ; ἱππαγωγοί alone, Ar.*Eq*.599, D.4.21 : Ἱππαγωγός as pr. n. of a ship, *IG*2^2.1623. 14. **-άζομαι,** Dor. fut. 3 sg. ἱππασεῖται *Dialex*.6.4 :—*drive horses, drive a chariot*, Ἀντίλοχ', ἀφραδέως ἱππάζεαι Il.23.426 ; later, *ride*, Hdt.4.114, Hp.*Aër*.17, Ar.*Nu*.15, etc. ; ἱ. ἐφ' ἵππων Hdt.4.110 ; ἵππῳ X.*Eq*.10.1 : metaph., ἁ ξυσμὰ ἐκ ποδὸς εἰς κεφαλὰν ἱππάζεται Sophr. 53 :—rare in Act., ἱππάσαι πῶλον ap.Poll.1.182. 2. Pass., of the horse, *to be ridden* or *driven*, Pl.*Ion* 540e ; *to be broken in for riding*, X.*Eq*.3.1. II. c. acc. loci, ἱππάζεσθαι χώραν *ride over* a country, Plu.*Cam*.23 ; τὰς ὁδούς D.S.13.88. **-ᾱΐς,** ΐδος, ἡ, hyperdor. for ἱππηΐς, fem. of ἱππικός I. 3, *of a knight*, πόρπα, i. e. *fibula* which fastened the *trabea* of a Roman *eques*, *Epigr.Gr*.985.1 (Philae). **-αιχμία,** ἡ, *cavalry-action*, Sch.Pi.*N*.1.23 (pl.). **-αιχμος,** ον, *fighting on horseback, equestrian*, Pi.*N*.1.17. **-άκη** [ᾰ], ἡ, *mare's-milk cheese*, used by the Scythians, Hp.*Aër*.18, A.*Fr*.198, Theopomp.Hist.48, Thphr.*HP*9.13.2, Dsc.2.71 :—also **ἱππάκης,** ου, ὁ, Eust.916.16. 2. *horse's rennet*, Dsc.2.75. II. *a leguminous plant*, Ph.*Bel*.86.25, Plin.*HN*25.83. **-ᾰκοντιστής,** οῦ, ὁ, *mounted javelineer*, Ael. *Tact*.2.13, Arr.*An*.4.4.7, Poll.1.131. **-άκοπον,** τό, (cf. ἄκοπος) *remedy for horses*, *Hippiatr*.130. **-ᾰλεκτρυών,** όνος, ὁ, *horse-cock, gryphon*, a fabulous animal in A.*Fr*.134, cf. Ar.*Ra*.932, *Av*. 800. **-ᾰλέος,** α, ον, poet. for ἱππικός, Opp.*C*.1.169, 242, etc. **-ᾰλος,** ὁ, name of the *monsoon* in the Indian Ocean (from the name of the pilot who observed it), prob. in *Peripl.M.Rubr*.57. **-αναβάτης** [βᾰ], ου, ὁ, *mounted man*, *PLond*.1821.80. **-άνθρωπος,** ὁ, *centaur*, Gal.*UP*3.1, Eust.1909.53.

ἱππᾶπαῖ, a cry of the Ἱππεῖς, a parody of the boatmen's cry (ῥυππαπαῖ), Ar.*Eq*.602.

ἱππ-άριον, τό, Dim. of ἵππος, *pony*, *PCair.Zen*.30, al. (iii B.C.), Arr.*Tact*.19.3. 2. *wretched horse*, in contempt, X.*Cyr*.1.4.19, Plu. *Phil*.7, Them.*Or*.24.306d. 3. *statuette of a horse*, *IG*11(2).203*B* 84 (Delos, iii B.C.). **-αρμοστής,** οῦ, ὁ, Laced. for ἵππαρχος, *commander of cavalry*, X.*HG*4.4.10, 5.12 ; cf. ἱπφαρμος.

ἱππαρχ-εῖον, τό, *head-quarters of the* ἵππαρχος, *IG*2^2.895 (ii B.C.). **-έω,** *to be* ἵππαρχος, *command cavalry*, c. gen., τῆς ἵππου Hdt.9.20, 69 ; ἱππαρχηκὼς ἀνδρῶν καλῶν κἀγαθῶν Din.3.12 ; ἱππέων D.21.164 : abs., X.*Ages*.2.4, Lys.26.20, D.21.172 ; οἱ ἱππαρχηκότες Hyp.*Lyc*. 17 ; of the Roman *magister equitum* and *praefectus equitum*, D.C.43. 48, App.*BC*5.8 :—Pass., *serve under an* ἵππαρχος, Arist.*Pol*.1277^b 10. **-ης,** Dor. **-άρχας,** Ion. gen. **-άρχεω** *IG*12(8).194.7 (Samothrace), *Michel*596 (Cyzicus), ὁ, = ἵππαρχος, *OGI*217 (Caria, iii B.C., pl.), Plb.10.22.6 (Achaean), 18.22.2 (Macedonian), cf. Lxx 2*Ki*.1.6, *PTeb*.54.2 (i B.C.), Plu.*Tim*.32 ; at Sparta, *IG*5(1).32^A, al. ; = Lat. *magister equitum*, Plb.3.87.9, D.H.5.75, Nic.Dam.130.17 J., etc. ; = *praefectus equitum*, App.*BC*2.102 ; = *praefectus alae*, J.*BJ*2.14.5. **-ία,** ἡ, *office of* ἵππαρχος, X.*Ath*.1.3 (pl.) ; of the *magister equitum*, D.C. *Fr*.36.26, Lyd.*Mag*.2.13. II. *a squadron of horse such as he commands*, Plb.10.23.4, D.S.17.57, Str.17.1.12, Plu.*Eum*.7, Arr.*An*. 1.24.3 ; consisting of 512 men, Ascl.*Tact*.7.11, etc. **-ικός,** ή, όν, *of* or *for a* ἵππαρχος, ἡγεμονία ἱ., = ἱππαρχία, Suid. s. v. ἵππαρχος ; ἱ. ἐστί it is *part of his duty*, X.*Eq.Mag*.5.1 : -ικός, ὁ (sc. λόγος), title of treatise by Xenophon. **-ος,** ὁ, *ruling the horse*, epith. of Poseidon, Pi.*P*.4.45. II. *commander of cavalry*, τῆς ἵππου Hdt.7.154 ; at Athens, *IG*2^2.116.15 (iv B.C.), Ar.*Av*.799, Lys.16.8, Pl.*Lg*.755c, 880d, X.*Eq.Mag*.1.7, al. ; ἱ. εἰς Λῆμνον χειροτονεῖν Hyp.*Lyc*.17, cf. D. 4.26 ; in other states, Th.4.72, *IG*7.2466 (Thebes, iii B.C.), etc. ; in the Achaean league, ib.5(2).344.7 (Orchomenus), etc. ; = Lat. *magister equitum*, D.S.12.64, Plu.*Cam*.5, etc. ; = *praefectus equitum*, App.*Hisp*.47 ; cf. ἱππάρχης.

ἱππ-άς, άδος, ἡ, pecul. fem. of ἱππικός, ἱ. στολή *a riding-dress*, Hdt. 1.80 ; = Lat. *equester*, ἱ. ἐσθής D.C.38.14. II. as Subst., ἡ ἱ. (sc. τάξις) *the order of knights* (ἱππεῖς) at Athens, Arist.*Pol*.1274^{a}21 ; θυσίαι, βοῦς ἱππάδες of sacrifices *offered by the knights*, Hsch. ; πύλαι ἱ., name of a gate at Athens, Plu.2.849c. 2. *knights' tax*, ἱππάδα τελεῖν Is.7.39, Arist.*Ath*.7.4, Plu.*Sol*.18 ; θητικοῦ ἀντὶ τέλους ἱππάδ' ἀμειψάμενος Epigr.ap.Arist.*Ath*. l. c. 3. at Rome, = *ordo equester*, D.C.40.57, al. ; in full ἡ ἱ. τάξις Hdn.5.1.5. 4. a boy's game, Poll. 9.122. 5. = ἵππος, ἡ, *mare*, Opp.*C*.1.162, *Hippiatr*.14, *BGU*2 iiii 8 (iv A.D.). **-ᾰσία,** ἡ, *riding, horse-exercise*, Ar.*Ach*.1165 (lyr.) ; ἱ. ποιεῖσθαι, = ἱππάζεσθαι, to take a *ride*, X.*Eq*.8.9, cf. *An*.2.5.33 ; ἱ. ἱππάσασθαι Id.*Oec*.11.17 ; *horsemanship*, Id.*An*.2.5.33 ; as a subject of competition, *IG*7.3087 (Lebad.). 2. *chariot-driving*, Luc. *DDeor*.12.1, etc. II. *cavalry*, Arr.*An*.4.4.7. **-άσιμος** [ᾰ], η, ον, *fit for horses, fit for riding*, Αἴγυπτον τὸ πρὶν ἐοῦσαν ἱππασίμην καὶ ἁμαξευομένην, opp. ἄνιππος, Hdt.2.108, cf. 5.63, 9.13, X. *Cyr*.1.4.14, Aen.Tact.6.6, Plb.10.49.5, Onos.31.1, etc. ; τὸ ἱππάσιμον, i.e. τὸ πεδινόν, X.*HG*7.2.12 ; τὰ ἱ. τῆς χώρας ἄνιππα ποιεῖν Aen.Tact.8.4 : metaph., τοῖς κόλαξιν ἑαυτὸν ἀνειχὼς ἱππάσιμον allowing himself *to be ridden* by flatterers, Plu.*Alex*.23. **-άσιον,** τό, Dim. of ἵππος, Theognost.*Can*.125. **-ασμα,** ατος, τό, *a ride*, Ach. Tat.1.13. **-ασμός,** ὁ, *riding*, Sch.E.*Hel*.1355. **-αστήρ,** ῆρος, ὁ, = sq., metaph. of the μύωψ, *AP*5.202 (Asclep.) ; κημός ib.7.424 (Antip. Sid.). **-αστής,** οῦ, ὁ, = ἱππευτής, Luc.*Am*.46. II. as Adj., *fit for riding*, of a horse, X.*Eq*.10.17. **-αστί,** Adv. *like a horseman*, καθίζειν Hsch. **-αστικός,** ή, όν, *fond of riding*, Plu.*Alc*.23. **-αστός,** ή, όν, *that can be ridden*, Arist.*HA*576^b 17. **-άστριαι** κάμηλοι, αἱ, *dromedaries*, Plu.*Eum*.15. **-άφεσις,** εως, ἡ, *starting-post in a race-course*, Plb.*Fr*.52 (pl.), *Abh.Berl.Akad*. 1904(2).9 (Pap., ii B.C.), D.H.3.68 (pl.), Epigr.ap.Paus.6.20.14 (Olymp.), prob. in *SIG*251*H* ii 63, 253*U* (Delph., iv B.C.) :—also **ἱππάφια,** τά, *Tab.Defix.Aud*.234.21 (Carthage, i A.D.). **-αφίδες,** *caballi ammissi, carceres*, *Gloss*. (prob. -αφέσεις). **-εία,** ἡ, (ἱππεύω) *riding* or *driving* of horses, *horsemanship, racing*, S.*El*.505 (lyr.) : pl., E.*HF*374 (lyr.). II. *cavalry*, X.*An*.5.6.8, *Ages*.1.23. III. *breed of horses*, ἐνδόξου γενομένης ἐνθένδε ἱ. Str.5.1.9. **-ειος,** α, ον, (ἵππος) *of a horse* or *horses*, ζυγόν, φάτνη, Il.5.799, 10.568 ; κάπαι Od. 4.40 ; ἵ. λόφος *horse-hair* crest, Il.15.537 ; ἔντεα Pi.*N*.9.22 ; γένος, μάνδραι, S.*Ant*.341 (lyr.), *Fr*.659.3 ; ἔθειραι Theoc.16.81 ; τὸ ἵππειον [γάλα] Arist.*HA*522^{a}28, Posidon.ap.Gal.19.712 ; κάλω ἱππείω δύο *IG* 1^2.330.19. Adv. -είως Dam.*Pr*.58. 2. ἵππειος, ὁ (sc. μήν), name of month at Thronion, *Klio*16.176 (Delph.). (ἵππιος is the usual form in Trag., ἱππικός in Prose.) **-ελάτειρα** [ᾰ], fem. of sq., Orph.*H*.32. 12. **-ελάτης** [ᾰ], ου, ὁ, *driver* or *rider of horses*, Opp.*C*.1.95. **-έλᾰφος,** ὁ, lit., *horse-deer*, perh. *nylghau, Portax picta*, Arist.*HA*498^{b}32 ; ἡ θήλεια ἱ. οὐκ ἔχει κέρατα ib.499^{b}2. **-εραστής,** οῦ, ὁ, *lover of horses*, Ael.*NA*2.28. **-ερος,** ὁ, *horse-fever*, formed after ἴκτερος, ὕδερος, etc., with a pun on ἔρος (= ἔρως), Ar.*Nu*.74. **-ευμα,** ατος, τό, *ride on horseback* or *journey in a chariot*, E.*IT*1428 ; [Νύξ], μακρὸν ἵ. διώκεις Id.*Fr*.114 (lyr.). **-εύς,** gen. έως (-έω dub. in Hsch.), Ep. ῆος, ὁ, (ἵππος) *one who fights from a chariot*, Hom. (only in Il.), opp. πεζός, 2.810 ; either of *the driver* or of *the hero who fights*, 12.66, 15.270 ; also of *one who drives in a chariot-race*, 23.262. 2. *horseman, rider, cavalryman*, ἰππήων στρότος Sapph.*Supp*.5.1, cf. Hdt.3.88, 9.49, A. *Pers*.14 (anap.), Arist.*Pol*.1270^{a}29, etc. ; τῆς πολιτείας ἱ. a public *courier*, Aristaenet.1.26. 3. *groom*, *Class.Rev*.27.12 (Laodicea Combusta), 24.12, *JHS*18.108 (near Lysias). II. ἱππεῖς, in social and political sense, *knights*, forming an aristocracy in early Greek communities, Arist.*Pol*.1297^{b}18, etc. ; at Eretria, ib.1306^{a}35, *Ath*. 15.2 ; at Sparta, a royal bodyguard, Hdt.8.124, cf. 1.67, etc. ; esp. at Athens, the Second Class in Solon's constitution, Arist.*Ath*.7.3 ; later, an aristocratic corps of cavalry, Ar.*Eq*.225, And.3.5, Philoch. 100, etc. 2. of the Roman *equites*, D.S.37.8, D.H.4.24, App. *BC*1.22, etc. ; ἱππεὺς Ῥωμαίων, = Lat. *eques Romanus*, *Mon.Anc.Gr*. 7.17, *IG*3.768*a*, *IGRom*.3.204 (Ancyra), *OGI*547.2 (ibid.), 645.7 (Palmyra), prob. in *IGRom*.4.1213 (Thyatira). III. *nimble* kind of *crab*, Arist.*HA*525^{b}8. IV. kind of *comet*, Plin.*HN*2.90, Lyd. *Ost*.11. V. *girl's ornament*, Hsch., cf. *Ostr*.323 (ii B.C.). VI. a *measure*, πυρῶν, ἀμυγδάλων, ἀλεύρων, *Supp.Epigr*.2.710 (Pednelissus). **-ευσις,** εως, ἡ, *riding*, in pl., Sch.E.*Ph*.791. **-ευτήρ,** ῆρος, ὁ, = sq., πῶλος, ἱ. πεδίων, οὐχ ἁλός *AP*9.295 (Bianor). **-ευτής,** οῦ, ὁ, *rider, horseman*, Pi.*P*.9.123 : as Adj., Τρῶες B.12.160 ; στρατός E.*HF*408 (lyr.). **-εύω,** *to be a horseman* or *rider, ride*, Hdt.1.136, etc. ; ἱ. ταῖς κυούσαις ἵπποις Arist.*HA*576^{a}21 ; ἱ. ἐπ' ὄνου Luc.*Bacch*.2 ; of a people, ἱππεύει ταῦτα τὰ ἔθνη Hdt.7.84, cf. 87 :—also in Med., Id.1.27, 79. 2. metaph., of the wind, ζεφύρου πνοαῖς ἱππεύσαντος E.*Ph*.212 (lyr.) ; σελάνα ἱππεύουσα δι' ὀρφναίας Id.*Supp*.994 (lyr.) ; also, *rush*, πρὸς φόνον Id.*HF*1001. II. *serve in the cavalry*, Lys.14. 7, X.*HG*3.1.4, Pl.*Lg*.756b, etc. 2. at Rome, *to be an eques*, D.C. 49.12 ; τὸ -εῦον the *ordo equester*, Id.60.7. III. of a horse, as we say '*the horse rides* (i.e. *carries his rider*) well', X.*Eq*.1.6, 3.4, 10.3. IV. *drive* a team, Ar.*Nu*.1406. **-ηγέτης,** ου, ὁ, *driver of horses*, of Poseidon, Lyc.767. **-ηγός,** όν, (ἄγω) = ἱππαγωγός, νῆες (expressed or understood) Philoch.132, Plb.1.27.9, D.S.20.83 ; τριήρης Ἱππηγός as pr. n., *IG*2^2.1628.423, 1629.944. **-ηδόν,** Adv. *like a horse*, A.*Th*.328 (lyr.), *Supp*.431 (lyr.). II. *like a horseman*, Ar.*Pax*81. **-ηλᾰσία,** ἡ, (ἐλαύνω) *driving* or *riding of horses*, Hld. 8.14, Them.*Or*.15.188a, 18.216d :—Adj. **-ηλάσιος,** α, ον, *fit for riding* or *driving*, ἱ. ὁδός *chariot*-road, Il.7.340.

ἱππηλᾰτ-έω, *ride* or *drive*, Ar.*Av*.1443. **-ης,** ου, ὁ, *driver of horses, one who fights from a chariot*, Hom. (always in Ep. form ἱππηλάτα, and only in nom.), as an epith. of honour, *Knight*, ἱ. Τυδεύς, γέρων ἱ. Πηλεύς, Φοῖνιξ, Οἰνεύς, Il.4.387, 7.125, 9.432, 581 ; Νέστωρ Od.3.436 : generally ἱππηλάται E.*Rh*.117 : as Adj., ἱ. λεώς, opp. πεδοστιβής, A.*Pers*.126 (lyr.). **-ος,** ον, *fit for horsemanship* or *driving*, νῆσος Od.4.607 ; γαῖα 13.242 ; ὁδὸς ἱ. *chariot*-road, Luc.*Rh.Pr*.3, Poll.9.37 ; ἱ. οἶδμα Nonn.*D*.20.157 ; θάλασσα Agath.4.29, cf. 5.11 ; ἱ. ἔργον Ἀθήνης, i. e. the Trojan horse, Tryph.2 ; τὸ δι' ἡδονῆς καθάπερ ἱ. τι χωρίον Porph.*Marc*.6.

ἱππημολγ-ία, ἡ, *milking of mares*, Scymn.855 (pl.). **-οί,** οἱ, (ἀμέλγω) *the Mare-milkers*, a Scythian or Tartar tribe, Il.13.5, cf. Str. 7.3.2 ; Σκύθαι ἱ. Hes.*Cat.Oxy*.1358*Fr*.2.15 ; ἱ. Κιμμέριοι Call.*Dian*.252.

Ἱππιάζω, *ape Hippias*, Philostr.*VS*2.21.3.

ἱππιάναξ [ᾱν], ακτος, ὁ, *king of horsemen*, A.*Pers*.996 (lyr.).

ἱππίας, ου, ὁ, = ἱππεύς IV, Apul.ap.Lyd.*Mens*.4.7.

ἱππιατρ-ός (on the accent v. Hdn.Gr.1.229), ὁ, *veterinary surgeon, farrier*, *IG*9(2).69.5 (ii B.C.), *PGen.*42.35 (iii A.D.), *Hippiatr.*12, etc.; cf. ἱπποϊατρός :—Adj. **-ικός**, ή, όν, *of* or *for farriery*: ἱππιατρικόν, τό, *a work on farriery*, Suid. s. v. Χείρων: -κά, τά, title of extant compilation: also -κόν, τό, *tax on farriers*, *PHib.*1.45.21 (iii B.C.).

ἱππίδιον, τό, *a kind of fish*, Epich.44.

ἱππικός, ή, όν, (ἵππος) *of a horse* or *horses*, freq. in Trag., ἱ. ἐκ πλευμόνων A.*Th.*61; ἱ. φρυάγματα ib.245, cf. S.*El.*717, 719; ὀχήματα, ἄντυγες, ib.740, *Aj.*1030; φάτναι E.*Ba.*509. 2. *of horsemen* or *chariots*, ἀγών Hdt.1.167, And.4.26 (pl.); in ἱππικῶν ἀγών S.*El.*698, ἱππικῶν is prob. neut. (v. infr. IV); δρόμος ib.754; ναυάγια ib.730; ἆθλον Pl.*Lg.*949a. 3. = Lat. *equester*, τάξις, ἀξίωμα, D.H.12.1, Plu.*Pomp.*23; of persons, *of equestrian rank*, ἱ. ἄνδρες Str.3.4.20, cf. *IGRom.*3.474 (Lycia, iii A.D.), etc. II. *of riding* or *horsemanship, equestrian*, X.*HG*5.3.20; ἱ. ἄσκησις training *in horsemanship*, *IG*2².1042.21, al.; ἱ. ἡγήτωρ leader *of the knights*, ib.3.693; *skilled in riding*, opp. ἄφιππος, Pl.*Prt.*350a, al.: Comp., Satyr.1, Phld.*Mus.*p.6 K.: Sup., Arr.*Tact.*16.9. 2. ἡ -κή (sc. τέχνη), *horsemanship, riding*, Ar.*Nu.*27, etc.; περὶ -κῆς, title of treatise by Xenophon; ἱ. ἐπιστήμη Pl.*La.*193b; ἱ. λόγοι X.*HG*5.3.20; τὰ ἱ. [πράγματα] Pl. *Alc.*1.124e, cf. *Thg.*126a; ἡ ἐμὴ ἱ. this *riding* of mine, Lys.24.10. III. *fit for riding*, Sup. -ώτατον, χρῆμα γυνή Ar.*Lys.*677. IV. τὸ ἱ. the *horse, cavalry*, Hdt.7.87, E.*Supp.*682, X.*An.*6.5.29, etc.; τὰ ἱ. Plb.3.114.5. 2. *course* or *space of four stadia*, Plu.*Sol.*23. b. the *circus* at Rome, *Tab.Defix.Aud.*187.59. V. Adv. -κῶς *like a horseman*: Sup. -κώτατα *with best horsemanship*, X. *Oec.*21.7.

ἵππιος, α, ον, (ἵππος) poet. form of ἵππειος (q. v.), *of a horse* or *horses*, λόφοι crests *of horsehair*, Alc.15.2; σθένος ἵ. Pi.*P.*2.12; Ἄργος ἵ. (cf. ἱππόβοτος) Id.*I.*7(6).11, B.18.15; δρομεύς, prob. l. in E.*El.*825; ἄνασσα ἵ. *Queen of the Amazons*, Id.*Hipp.*307; epith. of Poseidon as creator of the horse, B.16.99, A.*Th.*130 (lyr.), Ar.*Eq.*551, *Nu.*83, *IG* 1².310.142, etc.; hence, of Colonos as sacred to him, Arg.S.*OC*, Paus.1.30.4 (but cf. Pherecr.134); also of Athena, Pi.*O.*13.82, S.*OC* 1070 (lyr.), Harp.; of Hera, at Olympia, Paus.5.15.5; of Ares, Id. 5.15.6, cf. Tryph.105. II. *of horsemen* or *the horse-race*, ἵ. νόμος Pi.*O.*1.101; ἱππίαν ἔσοδον Id.*P.*6.50; ἄεθλα *AP*6.312 (Anyte); sc. ἀγών *SIG*1064.8 (Halic., i B.C.). III. Ἵππιος, ὁ (sc. μήν), month at Rhegium, *IG*14.612.

ἱππιο-χαίτης, ου, ὁ, *shaggy with horsehair*, λόφος Il.6.469. **-χάρμης**, ου, ὁ, *one who fights from a chariot*, 24.257, Od.11.259, Hes. *Fr.*7; later, *horseman, rider*, A.*Pers.*29 (anap.). II. as Adj., ἱ. κλόνοι the tumult *of the horse-fight*, ib.105; cf. ἱπποχάρμης.

ἱππ-ίσκος, ὁ, Dim. of ἵππος, name of a play by Alexis, Ath.3.120b. 2. *small statue of a horse*, *Michel*832.41 (Samos, iv B.C.). II. *an ornament for the head* (cf. ἱππεύς v), Cratin.Jun.5, Hsch. **-ιστί**, Adv., = ἱππηδόν, *astride*, Ἀφροδίτη ἱ. καθημένη ἐπὶ Ψυχῆς *PMag.Par.*1.1724. **-ίτας**· ἱπποφορβός, Hsch. **-ιών**, ῶνος, ὁ (sc. μήν), month at Eretria, *IG*11(4).1066*b*21 (found in Delos).

ἱππο-βάμων [ᾰ], ον, gen. ονος, (βαίνω) *going on horseback, equestrian*, Ἀριμασπὸν ἱπποβάμονα στρατόν A.*Pr.*805; στρατὸς ἱ., of centaurs, S.*Tr.*1095. 2. *trotting like a horse*, or *used for riding*, κάμηλοι A.*Supp.*284 (cj. Turneb.). 3. metaph., ῥήματα ἱ. *high-paced* words, *bombast, fustian*, Ar.*Ra.*821. **-βάτης** [ᾰ], ου, ὁ, *horseman*, A.*Pers.*26 (anap.). II. ἱ. ἵππος or ὄνος, *stallion*, Str.8.8.1, *Hippiatr.*14; cf. ἱπποβότης.

Ἱππόβῑνος, ὁ, (βινέω) comic distortion of the pr. n. Ἱππόνικος, = ἱππόπορνος, Ar.*Ra.*433.

ἱππο-βόσιον, τό, *horses' keep*, Theognost.*Can.*125. **-βοσκός**, όν, (βόσκω) *feeding horses*, Ael.*NA*6.10, Suid., *Gloss.* **-βότης**, ου, ὁ, (βόσκω) *feeder of horses*, Ἀτρεύς E.*Or.*1000 (lyr., but prob. -βῶτα), *IA*1059 (but prob. -βάτας). II. ἱπποβόται, οἱ, at Chalcis in Euboea a social class (cf. ἱππεύς II), *Knights*, Hdt.5.77, 6.100; ἡ ἱπποβοτῶν πολιτεία Arist.*Fr.*603. **-βοτος**, ον, (βόσκω) *grazed by horses*, Od.4.606, E.*Andr.*1229 (anap.), *IG*1².1034, Just.*Nov.*25.1; ἡ ἱ., at Chalcis, Ael.*VH*6.1 (cf. foreg.); esp. of the plain of Argos, from the rich pastures of Lerna, Il.2.287, al., B.10.80, E.*Supp.*365 (lyr.). **-βουκόλος**, ὁ, *horse-herd, horse-keeper*, S.*Fr.*1057, E.*Ph.*28. **-βροτοι** ὠδῖνες pangs that gave birth *to a horse and man* (Pegasus and Chrysaor), Lyc.842. **-γέρᾰνοι**, οἱ, *crane-cavalry*, Luc.*VH*1.13. **-γνώμων**, ον, gen. ονος, *judging well of horses*: hence generally, *quick in judging*, τινος A.*Fr.*243, cf. Hsch. **-γῦποι**, οἱ, *vulture-cavalry*, Luc.*VH*1.13. **-δᾰμαστής**, οῦ, ὁ, = ἱππόδαμος, Poll.1.181, Hsch. **-δάμνοις**· ἐφίππων, Id. **-δᾰμος**, ον, (δαμάω) *tamer of horses*, Hom., epith. of heroes, Il.2.23, Od.3.17; Τρῶες Il.4.352, etc.; Γερηνοί Hes.*Fr.*15; ἥρωες Pi.*N.*4.29:—fem. Ἱππο-δάμεια, as pr. n., *Hippodamia*, Il.2.742, etc. **-δάσεια** [ᾰ], ἡ, fem. Adj., Ep. epith. of κόρυς and κυνέη, *bushy with horsehair*, 3.369, Od.22.111, etc. **-δεσμα**, ων, τά, *horse-bands, reins*, E.*Hipp.*1225: Adj. δακτύλιοι ἱππόδεσμοι, *snaffle-rings*, *IG*2².1542.25. **-δέτης**, ου, ὁ, *binding horses*, ῥυτήρ S.*Aj.*241 (anap.); epith. of Heracles at Thebes and Onchestos, Paus.9.26.1. **-δίνητος** [ῑ], ον, *whirled in chariots*, Συρακόσιοι, B.5.2. **-διώκτης**, ου, ὁ, Dor. -τας, = ἱππηλάτης, *driver* or *rider of steeds*, Theoc.14.12, Hsch.; a kind of gladiator, *IGRom.*4.1455 (Smyrna). **-δρομία**, ἡ, *horse-race* or *chariot-race*, Pi.*P.*4.67, *I.*3.13, X.*Smp.*1.2, Pl.*Ion* 537a, Arist.*Ath.*60.1, *IG*2².784 (iii B.C.), *SIG*730.30 (Olbia, i B.C.); ἱ. ἄγειν Ar.*Pax* 900; ποιεῖν Th.3.104; ἱ. παιδική, ἣν καλοῦσι Τροίαν, = Lat. *ludus Troiae*, Plu.*Cat.Mi.*3. **-δρομικός**, ή, όν, *of horse-racing*, ἀγών Sch.Il.23.757. **-δρόμιος**, ον, *of the horse-race*: -δρόμιος, ὁ (sc. μήν), name of month in Boeotia, *IG*7.531, al. (Tanagra), cf. Plu.*Cam.*19; at Delphi, *GDI*1987, al.; at Naupactus, *IG*9(1).359. II. epith. of Poseidon (cf. ἵππιος), Pi. *I.*1.54. **-δρομος**, ὁ, *chariot-road*, λεῖος δ' ἱ. ἀμφίς Il.23.330. 2. *race-course* for chariots, Pl.*Criti.*117c, D.47.53; at Olympia, Paus. 6.20.15; at Delphi, *SIG*636.24 (ii B.C.); at Andania, *IG*5(1).1390.31; at Rome, the *circus*, D.H.1.79; ὁ μέγας ἱ., = *circus maximus*, Id. 5.36, *Mon.Anc.Gr.*10.8: comic metaph., ἱ. οὗτός ἐστί σου μαγειρικῆς Posidipp.26.23. II. **ἱπποδρόμος**, ὁ, *light horseman*, ἱ. ψιλοί Hdt. 7.158. **-ζώνη**, ἡ, acc. -ζώνην, f.l. for ὑπὸ ζώνην, *Hippiatr.*26; the gloss in Hsch. is missing.

ἱππόθεν, Adv., (ἵππος) *forth from the horse*, of the heroes descending from the Trojan horse, Od.8.515, 11.531. **-θήλεια**, ἡ, = *equa*, *Gloss.*

ἱππο-θήλης, ου, ὁ, *ass which has been suckled by a mare*, such being kept for the stud, acc. to Arist.*HA*577ᵇ17. **-θοος**, ον, *swift-riding*, Hsch.: in Il. only as pr. n. **-θόρος**, ὁ, (θόρνυμι) *covering mares*, esp. of a he-ass kept for breeding mules, Hsch. II. as Adj., ἱ. νόμος a tune *played to a mare, while she was being covered*, Plu. 2.138b, 704f. **-θοώντειον**, τό, *sanctuary of Hippothoon*, Hsch. **-θῠτέω**, *sacrifice horses*, τῷ Ἡλίῳ Str.11.8.6. **-ίατρος**, = ἱππιατρός, *Hippiatr.*27, *CIG*1953 (Maced.), *POxy.*92 (iv A.D.). **-κάμπιον**, τό, Dim. of ἱππόκαμπος, Epich.115. II. A kind of *ear-ring*, Poll.5.97. **-καμπος**, ὁ, *monster with horse's body and fish's tail*, on which the sea-gods rode, Men.831; ἑστήκει Ποσειδῶν χάλκεος, ἔχων ἱ. ἐν τῇ χειρί Str.8.7.2, cf. Philostr.*Im.*1.8. 2. a small fish, *the sea-horse*, Dsc.2.3, Ael.*NA*14.20, Gal.12.362. **-καμπτος**· στρουθίον τι, Hsch. **-κάνθᾰρος**, ὁ, *horse-beetle*, Com. word in Ar.*Pax*181. **-κέλευθος**, ον, *travelling by means of horses*: *driver of horses*, epith. of Patroclus, Il.16.126, 584, 839; *rider*, *AP*9.210. **-κενταύρειος**, α, ον, *of a centaur*, S.E.*M.*9.125. **-κένταυρος**, ὁ, *horse-centaur, half-horse half-man*, Pl.*Phdr.*229d, X.*Cyr.*4.3.17: also as fem., θήλειαν ἱ. ἐποίησεν Luc.*Zeux.*3. **-κέντωρ**, ορος, *stinging horses*, Tz.*H.*9 No.290 tit. **-κλείδης**, ου, ὁ, (κλείω) *pudenda muliebria*, Ar.*Fr.*703. **-κοινάριον**, τό, *stable*, *Raccolta Lumbroso* 374. **-κομέω**, *groom horses*, ἱ. κάνθαρον *groom* his beetle, Ar.*Pax*74. **-κόμος**, ὁ, (κομέω) *groom, esquire, who attended the* ἱππεύς *in war*, Hdt.3.85, 88, X.*HG*2.4.6: generally, *groom*, Pl.*Plt.*261d, *PSI*4.371.13 (iii B.C.), Plb.13.8.3, etc.; ἱ. τῶν καμήλων Philostr.*VA*2.1. II. Adj. **ἱππό-κομος**, ον, (κόμη) *decked with horsehair*, epith. of a helmet (not in Od.), κόρυς Il.13.132, cf. S.*Ant.*116 (anap.); πήληξ Il.16.797; τρυφάλεια 13.339. **-κόρῠθος**, ον, coined as compd. of ἵππος and κόρυς, Porph. ad Il.2.1 (v.l. -κόρυθες as nom. pl.). **-κορυστής**, οῦ, ὁ, *marshaller, arranger of chariots*, ἀνέρες ἱπποκορυσταί Il.2.1, 24.677; epith. of the Paeonians, 16.287, 21.205. **-κόσμια**, τά, *horse-trappings*, Hsch. s.v. φάλαρα, Charis. p.549 K., *Gloss.* **-κούριος**, ὁ, *tender of horses*, epith. of Poseidon at Sparta, Paus.3.14.2. **-κράτειος**, α, ον, *Hippocratic*, διδασκαλία Gal.6.753, cf. 15.147; ἀπολίνωσις Paul.Aeg.6.78. Adv. -ως Gal. *UP*8.3. **-κρᾰτέω**, *to be superior in horse*, D.19.148, Plb.3.66.2, Onos.31.1:—Pass., *to be inferior in horse*, Th.6.71. **-κρᾰτία**, ἡ, *victory in a cavalry action*, X.*Cyr.*1.4.24. **-κράτωρ** [ᾰ], ορος, ὁ, the constellation *Centaurus*, Teucer in Boll *Sphaera* 20. **-κρημνος**, ον, *tremendously steep*, ἱ. ῥῆμα *a neck-breaking* word, Ar.*Ra.*929. **-κρήνη**, ἡ, = Ἵππου κρήνη, the spring of Pegasus on Helicon, v.l. in Str.9.2.25. **-κροτος**, ον, *sounding with the tramp of horses*, ὁδός Pi.*P.*5.92; γυμνάσια E.*Hipp.*229 (anap.); ἱ. δάπεδα γυμνάσιά τε Id.*Hel.*207 (lyr.), cf. *AP*12.131 (Posidipp.): in late Prose, Chor.*Lyd.*17. **-κύων** [ῠ], -κῠνος, ἡ, *half-mare half-bitch*, epith. of the moon-goddess, *PMag.Par.*1.2614. **-λάπᾰθον** [λᾰ], τό, *Rumex aquaticus, dock-sorrel*, Dsc.2.115, Gal.12.56. **-λειχήν**, ῆνος, ὁ, *a sort of moss* used in farriery, Sch.Nic.*Th.*945.

ἱππολέτας, ου, ὁ, (ὄλλυμι) *destroyer of horses*, Hdn.*Epim.*211.

ἱππο-λεχής, ές, *having given birth to a horse*, Δηώ Orac.ap.Paus.8.42.6. **-λήπτρας**· τὰς τριχίνους σειρὰς Πάρθοι οὕτω καλοῦσιν, Hsch. (-ληπρα cod., fort. -λήμπτρας). **-λούστρας**· ἔνθα τοὺς ἵππους ἀπένιζον, Id. **-λοφία**, ἡ, *horse's mane*, Iamb. post Polem.p.50 Hinck. **-λοφος**, ον, *with horsehair crest*, κόρυς *IG*12(2).129 (Mytilene); ἱ. λόγοι, by comic metaph., Ar.*Ra.*818. **-λῦτος**, ον, *letting horses loose*, dub. l. in *APl.*4.44 (fort. ἱππελάτης). **-μᾰνέω**, *to be a-horsing*, of mares, Arist.*HA*572ᵃ10. **-μᾰνής**, ές, *abounding in, swarming with horses* (cf. καρπο-, ὑλο-, φυλλο-μανής), λειμών S.*Aj.*143 (anap.); variously expld. by Sch. II. as Subst., ἱππομανές, έος, τό, an Arcadian plant, *thorn-apple, Datura stramonium*, *of which horses are madly fond*, or *which makes them mad*, Theoc.2.48; f.l. for -φαές in Thphr.*HP*9.15.6. b. = κάππαρις, Dsc.2.173; = ἀπόκυνον, Ps.-Dsc.4.80. 2. *small black fleshy substance on the forehead of a new-born foal*, which, if procured before it was eaten off by the dam, was held to be a powerful φίλτρον, Arist.*HA*577ᵃ9, 605ᵃ2, Thphr.*Fr.*175, Ael.*NA*3.17, 14.18. 3. *mucous humour that runs from mares a-horsing*, used for like purposes, Arist.*HA*572ᵃ21, Paus.5.27.3. **-μᾰνία**, ἡ, *mad love for horses*, Luc.*Nigr.*29. **-μάρᾰθον** [μᾰ], τό, *horse-fennel, Prangos ferulacea*, Diocl.*Fr.*155, Thphr. *HP*6.1.4, Dsc.3.71, Zopyr.ap.Orib.14.64.1, etc.: sts. misspelt -μάραθρον in codd.

ἱππομᾰχ-έω, *fight on horseback*, Th.4.124, X.*Cyr.*6.4.18; ἱ. πρὸς ὁπλίτας *to fight*, cavalry against infantry, Id.*Ages.*2.3. **-ία**, ἡ, *horse-fight, action of cavalry*, Th.2.22, 4.72, Pl.*La.*193b, etc. **-ικός**, ή, όν, *of a horse-fight*, νίκη St.Byz. s. v. Ἀλάβανδα. **-ος**, ον (parox.,

Hdn.Gr.1.230), *fighting on horseback, trooper*, Il.10.431 (v.l. -δαμοι), Simon.107.8 (= *IG*7.53), Luc.*Macr.*17, *IG*9(1).871 (Corc., iii/ii B.C.).

Ἱππο-μέδων, οντος, ὁ, *horse-ruler*, as a pr. n., A., etc. [In *Th.*488, with the 2nd syll. long, metri gr.] **-μητις**, ὁ, ἡ, *skilled in horses* or *in riding*, Pi.*I.*7(6).12. **-μῐγής**, ές, *partly a horse, half-horse half-man*, Ael.*VH*9.16. **-μολγία, -μολγός**, ff. ll. for ἱππη-. **-μορφος**, ον, *horse-shaped, horse-like*, Pl.*Phdr.*253c. **-μύρμηξ**, ηκος, ὁ, *horse-ant*, dub. in Arist.*HA*606^{a}5. II. pl., *ant-cavalry*, Luc.*VH* 1.12. **-νῖκος**, ον, *victorious in the chariot-race*, *Gloss.*, prob. l. in B.13.22: freq. as pr. n. **-νομεύς**, έως, ὁ, *horse-keeper*, *Gloss.* **-νόμος**, ον, *keeping horses*, Poll.1.181. II. **ἱππόνομα**, τά, prob. *horse-hire*, Hsch. **-νώμας**, ου, ὁ, *guiding* or *keeping horses*, S.*Aj.*232 (lyr., Pors. for ἱππονόμους), E.*Hipp.*1399, Ar.*Nu.*571 (lyr.).

ἱππόομαι, Pass., *have the concept* or *idea of a horse*, opp. its real existence, Plu.2.1120d,1121a; cf. ἀνθρωπόομαι.

ἱππο-πάρηος [ᾰ], ον, *with large cheeks*, Apollon.*Lex.* s.v. ἱππόβοτον. **-πέδη**, ἡ, *horse-fetter*, *Hippiatr.*106. II. a name given by Eudoxus to a *figure-of-eight curve described by a planet*, Simp.*in Cael.*497.3, Procl.*in Euc.*pp.127,128 F. **-πῆραι**, ῶν, αἱ, *saddle-bags*, Sen.*Ep.*87.7. **-ποδες**, οἱ, *horse-hoofed men*, name of a fabulous tribe in Sarmatia, D.P.310. **-πόλος**, ον, *herding horses*, of the Thracians, Il.13.4, 14.227. (Cf. αἰ-πόλος, βου-κόλος.)

ἵπποπορ, prob. corrupt for ἵππορ, Lacon. for ἵππος, Hsch.: **ἱππόπορι**· κοιλάς, αὐλή, δῶμα, Id.

ἱππό-πορνος, ὁ, ἡ, *excessive prostitute*, Ath.13.565c, Alciphr.1.38, al.; cf. ἵππος VII; also, *one on horseback*, Diog.ap. Eust. 1909.63. **-πότᾰμος**, ὁ, *hippopotamus*, Dsc.2.23, Gal.14.241, Dam.*Isid.*98:—also **-ποτάμις** (for -ποτάμιος), ὁ, *POxy.*1220.21 (iii A.D.). **-πρόσωπος**, ον, *horse-faced*, epith. of the Moon-goddess, *PMag.Par.*1.2549; of a fabulous tribe, *Peripl.M.Rubr.*62.

ἵππος, ὁ, *horse*, ἡ, *mare*, most freq. fem. in Poets; in full θήλεες ἵπποι Il.5.269; ἵπποι θήλειαι 11.680, Od.4.635; ἄρσενες ἵπποι 13.81, cf. Hdt.3.86, Pl.*Hp.Ma.*288b: pl., ἵπποι *team of chariot-horses*, Il.16.370, al.: freq. in dual, 5.237, 8.41, al.: hence, of *the chariot* itself, ἀφ' ἵπποιιν, ἀφ' ἵππων, from *the chariot*, Il.5.13,19, al.; καθ' ἵππων ἆλτο, ἐξ ἵππων βῆσε, ib.111,163; ἵππων ἐπιβησόμενος intending to mount *his chariot*, ib.46; opp. πεζοί, πλῆτο δὲ πᾶν πεδίον πεζῶν τε καὶ ἵππων Od.14.267, cf. 9.49; ἵπποι τε καὶ ἀνέρες Il.2.554; λαός τε καὶ ἵπποι 18.153; of riders, νῶθ' ἵππων ἐπιβάντες ἐθύνεον Hes.*Sc.*286; freq. of race-horses, ἵ. ἀκαμαντόποδες Pi.*O.*3.4; ἀελλόποδες Simon.7; ἀθληταί Lys.19.63: metaph., ἁλὸς ἵ., of ships, Od.4.708, cf. Secund.*Sent.*17. 2. the constellation *Pegasus*, Eudox.ap.Hipparch.1.2.12, Ptol.*Tetr.*27, Vett.Val.12.11. 3. title of Hecate in the Mithraic cult, Porph.*Abst.*4.16. 4. perh. an instrument of torture, Lat. *eculeus*, Plu.*Luc.*20(pl.). II. as Collective Noun, ἵππος, ἡ, *horse, cavalry*, ἡ τῶν Θεσσαλῶν ἵ. Hdt.5.64, etc.: always in sg., even with numerals, ἵ. χιλίη a thousand *horse*, Id.7.41; μυρίη ibid.; μυρία, τρισμυρία, A.*Pers.*302,315; ἡ διακοσία ἵ. Th.1.62; ἵππον ἔχω εἰς χιλίαν X.*Cyr.*4.6.2. III. *a sea-fish*, Antim. et Numen.ap.Ath.7.304e; but ὁ ἵ. ὁ ποτάμιος *the hippopotamus*, Hdt.2.71, Arist.*HA* 502^{a}9; ὁ ἵ. τοῦ Νείλου Ach.Tat.4.2. IV. *lewd woman*, Ael.*NA* 4.11. b. *pudenda muliebria et virilia*, Hsch. V. *a complaint of the eyes*, such that they are always winking, Gal.16.611, al. (also in Hp., acc. to [Gal.]19.436). VI. title of ministrants ('chuckers-out') in certain religious ceremonies, *IG*2^2.1368.144 (Athens, ii A.D.), 3.1280*a*. VII. in compds., to express *anything large* or *coarse*, as in our *horse-chestnut, horse-laugh*, v. ἱππό-κρημνος, -λάπαθον, -μάραθον, -πορνος, -σέλινον, -τυφία, and cf. βου-. (From ἴκϝος, v. ἴκκος; cf. Skt. *aśvas*, Lat. *equus*: the ἵ- (in place of ἐ-) and the aspirate are unexplained; the latter acc. to Gell.2.3.2 was confined to Attic; cf. Λεύκ-ιππος, Γλαύκ-ιππος.)

ἱππο-σείρης, ου, ὁ, *one who leads a horse by the rein*, Anacr.75.6. **-σέλῑνον**, τό, *Alexanders, Smyrnium olus-atrum*, Thphr.*HP*2.2.1, Arist.*Pr.*923^{a}34, Dsc.3.67: metaph., γελᾶν ἱπποσέλινα Pherecr.131.4. **-σκελής**, ές, *with horse's legs*, ἄνθρωπος Gal.*UP*3.1. **-σκόπος**, ὁ, *inspector of horses*, *PPetr.*3 pp.157,158 (iii B.C.). **-σόας**, ου, ὁ, (σεύω) *driving horses*, ἄνδρες Pi.*P.*2.65; Ἰόλαος Id.*I.*5(4).32:—fem. **ἱπποσόα**, epith. of Artemis, Id.*O.*3.26 (as Subst., *Pae.*9.7):—also **ἱπποσσόος**, ον, Nonn.*D.*37.320. **-στάσιον** [ᾰ], τό, = sq., Lys.*Fr.*56 S.: pl., App.*Pun.*95, *Mith.*84:—also **-στᾰσία**, ἡ, *Hippiatr.*29. **-στᾰσις**, εως, ἡ, *stable*, Plb.13.8.3, Ph.2.307(pl.), Poll.1.184, Anon.*Oxy.*1368.46: metaph., Ἀελίου κνεφαία ἱππόστασις the dark *stable* of the Sun, i.e. the West, E.*Alc.*594 (lyr.); but Ἕω φαεννὰς Ἡλίου θ' ἱπποστάσεις, of the East, Id.*Fr.*771.5.

ἱπποσύνη, ἡ, (ἵππος) *the art of driving the war-chariot*: generally, *driving, horsemanship*, ἱπποσύνῃ .. πεποιθώς Il.4.303, cf. 11.503; ἔξοχοι ἱπποσύνᾳ Simon.108 (= *IG*1^2.946): in pl., λελασμένος ἱπποσυνάων Il.16.776, Od.24.40; ἱπποσύνας ἐδίδαξαν Il.23.307. II. = ἵππος II, *horse, cavalry*, Orac.ap.Hdt.7.141.

ἱππόσῠνος, η, ον, = ἱππικός, Δαρδανία E.*Or.*1392 (lyr.); unless ἱπποσύνα is Dor. gen. from nom. ἱπποσύνης, ὁ, cf. Sch., or ἱπποσύνᾳ be read.

ἱππότᾰ, ὁ, Ep. form of ἱππότης.

ἱππο-τακτικά· ἵππων τάξεις μισθοφόρων, Hsch. **-ταυρος**, ὁ, *horse-bull*, Hld.10.29. **-τέκτων**, ονος, ὁ, *maker of the Trojan horse*, Lyc.930.

ἱππότης (A), ου, ὁ, *driver* or *rider of horses, horseman, knight*, Hdt.7.55, 9.49,69; in Hom. always in Ep. nom. ἱππότᾰ, as Γερήνιος ἱππότα Νέστωρ Il.2.336, etc.; ἱππότης Κολωνός S.*OC*59; ἱππότης *on horseback*, Luc.*Tox.*47; τοὶ ἱππότη, Boeot. for οἱ ἱππεῖς, *IG*7.3087 (Lebad.), cf. Ascl.*Tact.*10.2. II. Adj., ἱππόται λαοί Pi.*P.*4.153; ἱ. λεώς *the horse*, A.*Th.*80 (lyr.); λεὼν ἄνιππον ἱ. τε S.*OC*899; ἱ. ὄχλος E.*Supp.*660; στρατός Plu.*Aem.*9.—Never used in correct Att. Prose.

ἱππότης (B), ητος, ἡ, *horse-nature, the concept of horse*, Antisth. et Pl.ap.Simp.*in Cat.*208.30,32, Sch.Aristid.p.167 F.

ἱππό-τιγρις, ιδος, ὁ, *a large* kind of *tiger*, D.C.77.6; cf. ἵππος VII. **-τῖλος**, ὁ, (τιλάω) *diarrhoea of horses*, *Hippiatr.*56.

ἱππότις, ιδος, fem. of ἱππότης, Tryph.670, Nonn.*D.*1.172.

ἱππο-τόκος, ον, *horse-bearing*, of Medusa, Nonn.*D.*47.693. **-τοξεία**, ἡ, *the art of the ἱπποτοξότης*, Tz.*H.*6.996,998. **-τοξότης**, ου, ὁ, *mounted bowman, horse-archer*, Hdt.9.49, 4.46; employed as police at Athens, Th.2.13, Lys.15.6: Com., ἱέρακας ἱ. Ar.*Av.*1179. **-τρᾰγέλᾰφος**, ὁ, *horse-goat-stag*, a fabulous monster: used of a *cup made to represent it*, Philem.87.

ἱπποτροφ-εῖον, τό, *place for horse-breeding, stud-stable*, Str.5.1.4, 16.2.10 (-τρόφιον). **-έω**, aor. -τρόφησα Paus.3.8.1: pf. -τρόφηκα D.L.8.51, (καθ-) Is.5.43; but ἱπποτετρόφηκα Lycurg.139 codd.:—*breed* or *keep horses*, Lycurg. l. c., Isoc.16.33, Hyp.*Lyc.*16, Satyr.1; ἱπποτροφοῦσα πόλις Aen.Tact.26.4; *feed horses*, ποᾷ χλωρᾷ Dsc.4.15 (v.l. πόαν χλωράν). **-ία**, ἡ, *breeding* or *keeping of horses*, esp. for racing, ἱ. γὰρ οὐ Ζακύνθῳ. . ὀπαδεῖ Simon.15: freq. in pl., ἱπποτροφίας νομίζειν Pi.*I.*2.38, cf. X.*Oec.*2.6, Pl.*Lys.*205c, Arist.*Pol.*1289^{b}35, Anon.*Oxy.*664.27: sg., Th.6.12, Plu.*Ages.*20. 2. as a liturgy, ἀτελὴς ἔσται..-ίας *SIG*1003.26 (Priene, ii B.C.). **-ικός**, ή, όν, *of* or *for horse-keeping*: **-κόν**, τό, *allowance made to* ἱπποτρόφοι, *PTheb.Bank*6.8 (ii B.C.). **-ος**, ον, (parox.) *horse-feeding, abounding in horses*, of Thrace, Hes.*Op.*507; of Argos, Pi.*N.*10.41; πόλις B.10.114. II. of persons, *breeding and keeping race-horses*, Pi.*I.*4(3).32, etc.; μέγας καὶ λαμπρὸς ἱ. D.18.320, cf. Plu.*Them.*5, Paus.6.2.1. 2. generally, *horsebreeder*, *POxy.*2110.6 (iv A.D.), *Hippiatr.*34.

ἱπποτῦφία, ἡ, (τῦφος) *horse-pride*, i.e. *excessive pride* or *conceit*, Luc.*Hist.Conscr.*45, Pl.ap.D.L.3.39.

ἱππούρ-αιον, τό, = ἵππουρος, *horse-tail*, Arat.438. **-εύς**, έως, ὁ, = ἵππουρος, Hices.ap.Ath.7.304c. **-ις**, ιδος, ἡ, (οὐρά) as fem. Adj., *horse-tailed, decked with a horse-tail*, freq. in Hom. (esp. Il.), in nom. and acc. ἵππουρις, -ιν, κόρυς Il.6.495; τρυφάλεια 19.382; κυνέη Od.22.124. II. as Subst., *horse-tail*, Ael.*NA*16.21; *Satyr's tail*, Phryn.*PS*p.77 B. 2. a water-plant, *horse-tail, Equisetum silvaticum*, Dsc.4.46, Ps.-Democr. in *Gp.*2.6.27; also, = *Equisetum maximum*, Dsc.4.47. 3. *a complaint in the groin*, caused by constant riding, dub. in Hp.*Epid.*7.122. **-ος**, ον, (οὐρά) *horse-tailed*: as Subst., 1. a sea-fish, *Coryphaena hippurus*, Epich.51, Arist.*HA* 543^{a}23, Numen.ap.Ath.7.304d, Opp.*H.*1.184. 2. *a* kind of *insect*, Ael.*NA*15.1. 3. = ἵππουρις II. 2, *Hippiatr.*27.

ἱπποφάγοι [ᾰ], οἱ, *horse-eaters*, name of a Scythian tribe, Ptol.*Geog.*5.9.

ἱπποφαές, έος, τό, a kind of *spurge, Euphorbia spinosa*, used for carding cloth, Asclep.ap.Gal.*Nat.Fac.*1.13, Dsc.4.159 (also **ἱππόφαος** ibid., **ἱπποφανής** Ps.-Dsc.ibid.). 2. = sq., Ps.-Dsc.4.160; = ἱππόφεως, Gal.19.106; as a drug, Thphr.*HP*9.15.6.

ἱππόφαιστον, τό, a plant, *Centaurea spinosa*, Dsc.4.160, Plin.*HN* 27.92, Ruf.ap.Orib.7.26.37.

ἱππό-φεως, εω, ὁ, *spurge, Euphorbia acanthothamnos*, gen. -φεω (v.l. -φαέως, -φέως) Hp.*Int.*13,25,26; nom. -φεως Thphr.*HP*6.5.2. 2. = ἐπίθυμον, Plin.*HN*26.55, *Gloss.* **-φλομος**, ὁ, *giant φλόμος*, i.e. *belladonna, Atropa belladonna*, Plin.*HN*25.148. **-φοβάς**, άδος, ἡ, *horse-fear*, a fabulous plant, Ps.-Democr.ap.Plin.*HN*24.161.

ἱπποφορβ-εύς, έως, ὁ, = ἱπποφορβός, Poll.7.185:—fem. **-άς**, άδος, Sch.Luc.*Ind.*5: **-έω**, = *keep horses*, Choerob.*in Theod.*2 lxxxv. **-ία**, ἡ, *horse-keeping*, Pl.*Plt.*299d. **-ιον**, τό, *herd of horses*, Hdt.4.110, X.*HG*4.6.6, Arist.*HA*576^{a}20. II. = ἱπποτροφεῖον, E.*El.*623, Arist.*HA*576^{a}25, Ph.2.307. **-ός**, όν, (φέρβω) *horse-keeper*, Pl.*Plt.*261d, Arist.*HA*577^{a}15, Jul.*Or.*7.227c: as Adj., ἱ. γῆ D.H.1.37. 2. αὐλὸς ἱ. a flute *used by* ἱπποφορβοί, made of laurel bark, Poll.4.74.

ἱππο-χάρμης, ου, ὁ, = ἱππιοχάρμης, Pi.*O.*1.23, *Pae.*2.104. **-χθων**, ονος, dub. sens., *Tab.Defix.Aud.*38.29 (Alexandria, iii A.D.).

ἱππ-ώδης, ες, *horse-like*, X.*Eq.*1.11 (Comp.), Poll.1.192; κεφαλή *Hippiatr.*14. **-ώκης**, ες, *riding in a swift chariot*, ἀέλιος B.10.101. **-ών**, ῶνος, ὁ, *place for horses*: 1. *stable*, *IG*1^2.336 (pl.), X.*Eq.*4.2, Moschio ap.Ath.5.207f, *PCair.Zen.*193.5 (iii B.C.). 2. *posting-house, station*, X.*Cyr.*8.6.17, *Supp.Epigr.*2.481 (Scythia, iii A.D.).

ἱππ-ωνέω, (ὠνέομαι) *buy horses*, X.*Eq.Mag.*1.14, *Eq.*11.13. **-ωνία**, Ion. -ίη, ἡ, *buying of horses*, Id.*Eq.Mag.*1.12 (with v.l. ἱππωνεία, which is found in codd. of *Eq.*1.1, 3.1), Poll.1.182. II. *tax on sale of horses*, *SIG*4 (Cyzicus, vi B.C.).

ἵπταμαι, = πέτομαι, Mosch.3.43, Babr.65.4, Jul.*Or.*2.72a, etc.; censured by Luc.*Sol.*7, *Lex.*25.

***ἵπτομαι**, fut. ἴψομαι: aor. 1 ἰψάμην:—*press hard, oppress*, μέγα δ' ἴψαο λαὸν Ἀχαιῶν Il.1.454, 16.237; τάχα δ' ἴψεται υἷας Ἀχαιῶν 2.193: generally, *hurt, harm*, σὺ τόνδε μηρὸν ἴψω; Theoc.*Adon.*19, cf. Str.8.6.7:—Act., **ἴπτω**, = βλάπτω, only in *EM*481.3; ἶψαι, ἴψας, Hsch. (Perh. related to ἰάπτω (B) or to ἶπος.)

ἰπύα, ἡ, = σιπύα, Hsch. (prob. ἰπύα).

ἴφαρμος· ἀρχή τις, Hsch. (prob. = ἱππαρμοστής).

ἴπ-ωσις [ῑ], εως, ἡ, (ἰπόω) *pressing hard, squeezing*, esp. in reducing dislocations, Hp.*Art.*47, Heliod.ap.Orib.49.27.5 and 32.7. **-ωτήριον**, τό, *olive-* or *wine-press*, *l.* ληνοῦ, *Gloss.*; ὅλμοι καὶ *l.* *PRev.Laws* 49.13, cf. 51.2 (iii B.C.). II. in surgery, *bougie*, Heliod.ap.Orib. 50.9.7, Antyll.ap.eund.44.23.61, Meges ap.eund.44.24.9. 2. name of a plaster, Heracl.Tarent.ap.Gal.13.725, Orib.*Fr.*52. **-ωτρίς**, ίδος, ἡ, *for pressing in* dislocated joints, σπάθη Heliod.ap.Orib.49.32. 4 and 17.9.

ἶραι, ῶν, αἱ, v.l. for εἶραι, Il.18.531; v. εἴρη.

ἱράνα, v. εἰρήνη. **ἱράνθεμον**, τό, = ἠράνθεμον, *Hippiatr.*44.

ἱράομαι, Ion. for ἱεράομαι. **ἱρέα, ἱρέη, ἱρεία, ἱρηΐη**, v. ἱέρεια. **ἵρερος**, v.l. for εἴρερος. **ἱρεύς, ἱρεύω, ἱρήϊον**, Ion. and Ep. for ἱερ-.

ἱρήν, ένος, ὁ, Ion. for εἰρήν, prob. in Hdt.9.85.

ἴρηξ, ηκος, ὁ, Ion. and Ep. for ἱέραξ.

ἱρήτειρα, ἡ, (ἱεράομαι) *priestess*, Hsch.

ἰρίζω [ῑ], *to be iridescent*, *PHolm.*7.6.

ἱρικάν· ἵππος οἰνωπὸς χρώματι, Hsch.

ἰρίνεος [ῑρῐν], α, ον, = ἴρινος, Nic.*Al.*203, 241.

ἰρῐνόμικτος [ῑ], ον, *mixed with iris-oil*, Philox.2.40.

ἴρῐνος [ῑ], η, ον, *made from the iris*, μύρον Pl.Com.69.7, Cephisod. 3.2, Alex.62.8, Thphr.*HP*9.9.2, Plb.30.26.2.

ἰριοειδής [ῐρ], ές, *rainbow-like*, Luc.*Hist.Conscr.*19, Olymp.*in Mete.*230.21, al.

Ἶρις, ιδος, ἡ, acc. Ἶριν, voc. Ἶρι:—*Iris*, the messenger of the gods among themselves, Il.8.398 (never in Od.), Hes.*Th.*780, etc. (Perh. fr. *Ϝῖρις, cf. ὠκέα Ἶρις Il.2.786, al., Hes. l. c.; ὦκα δὲ Ἶρις Il.23.198 (Pap.); possibly also fr. *Ἐϝῖρις: Εἶρις is the name of a ship, *IG*2^2. 1611 c 137 (iv B.C.), but ἶρις is written in *Michel* 832 (Samos, iv B.C.): allegorized as προφορικὸς λόγος and derived from εἴρω by *Stoic.*2. 43.) II. as Appellat., **ἶρις**, ἡ, gen. ἴριδος Thphr.*CP*6.11.13, also εως Androm.ap.Gal.14.43, *POxy.*1088.34 (i A.D.), *Gp.*6.8.1; acc. ἶριν *Michel* l. c., Plu.2.664e, ἴριδα Nic.*Al.*406; Ep. dat. pl. ἴρισσιν (v. infr.):—*rainbow*, δράκοντες..., ἴρισσιν ἐοικότες, ἅς τε Κρονίων ἐν νέφεϊ στήριξε, τέρας μερόπων ἀνθρώπων Il.11.27, cf. Arist.*Mete.*375^{a}1, Epicur. *Ep.*2 p.51 U. 2. any *bright-coloured circle* surrounding another body, as *the* lunar *rainbow*, Arist.*Mete.*375^{a}18; *halo* of candle, Thphr.*Sign.*13; round the eyes of a peacock's tail, Luc.*Dom.*11; *the iris* of the eye, Ruf.*Onom.*24, [Gal.] 14.702; also, *section through the ciliary region*, Gal.*UP*10.2. 3. *iridescent garment*, *Michel* l. c. 4. various species of the botanical genus *iris*, e.g. *the purple Iris*, *I. germanica* or *pallida*, εὐάνθεμον ἶριν *AP*4.1.9 (Mel.); τὸ ἄνθος πολλὰς ἔχει ἐν αὑτῷ ποικιλίας Arist.*Col.*796^{b}26, cf. Plin.*HN*21.40; also, *the white variety of it*, *I. florentina*, from the rhizome of which *the orris-root* of commerce is made, Thphr.*HP*1.7.2, *CP*6.11.13, etc.; ἶρις Ἰλλυρική Dsc.1.1, cf. Plin.*HN*13.14: in this sense some wrote it oxyt. **ἰρίς**, ίδος, Eust.391.33, Sch.Nic. l. c. 5. a precious stone, Plin.*HN* 37.136.

ἰριώδης, ες, *like the rainbow*, Arist.*Mete.*374^{a}28.

ἱρμοφόρος, ὁ, perh. *sack-bearer*, *Schwyzer* 230 (vi B.C.).

ἱρο-, Ion. and Ep. contr. for ἱερο-.

ἱροδρόμος, ὁ, poet. for ἱεροδρ- (q. v.).

ἱρόν, τό, Ion. for ἱερόν: **ἱοργίη**, v. ἱερουργία.

ἱροπόλος, ὁ, ἡ, *priest* or *priestess*, *IG*3.736, 5(2).461 (Megalop.).

ἱρός, Ion. and Ep. for ἱερός, but also in Att. Poets, v. ἱερός sub fin.: ἶρος, Aeol. for ἱερός.

Ἶρος, ὁ, *Irus*, a name given by the suitors to the Ithacan beggar Arnaeus because he carried messages (cf. Ἶρις), Od.18.5 sq.: hence, later as Appellat., *an Irus*, i.e. *a beggar*, Lib.*Or.*18.140: pl., Ἶροι Luc.*Nav.*24.

ἱρο-φάντης, ὁ, Ion. for ἱεροφ-. **-χθων**, ὁ, ἡ, gen. ονος, *of sacred earth*, βῶλος *IG*14.1389 ii 27.

ἱρών, ῶνος, ὁ, perh. = *region*, dub. word in *Inscr.Cypr.*135.8, 31 H. (where *toironi* may be τοῖ οἰρῶνι; v. οἰρών).

ἱρωστί, Ion. for ἱερωστί, *in sacred fashion*, Anacr.149.

ἱρωσύνη, ἡ, Ion. for ἱερωσύνη, *priesthood*, v.l. in Hdt.4.161.

ἴς (A) [ῑ], ἡ, gen. ἰνός, acc. ἶνα, nom. pl. ἶνες, dat. ἴνεσι Il.23.191, also ἰσίν Sor. (v. infr.), Suid. s. v. ἶνες, cj. Nauck for εἰσίν in A.*Fr.*229:—*sinew, tendon*, sg. once in Hom., ὡς δ' ὅτ' ἂν.. ἀνὴρ... ἶνα τάμῃ διὰ πᾶσαν Il.17.522: usu. in pl., *sinews*, οὐ γὰρ ἔτι σάρκας τε καὶ ὀστέα ἶνες ἔχουσιν Od.11.219, cf. Il.23.191; ἶνες ἄρθρων Ar.*Pax* 86, cf. Archil.138; ἶνες αὐτὸ μόνον καὶ λεπτὴ δορά, of a person wasted by disease, Ph.2.432; δοράς, σάρκας, ἶνας ib.527: metaph., Τρωίας ἶνας ἐκταμὼν δορί Pi.*I.*8(7).57. 2. later, *the fibrous vessels in the muscles*, Pl.*Ti.*84a, Arist.*HA*515^{b}27, al.; in blood, *fibrine*, Id.*PA*650^{b}14, cf. Pl.*Ti.*82c, Meno *Iatr.*17.34: metaph., of metals, Plu.2.434b. 3. *rib* in the leaves of plants, Thphr.*HP*3.12.7 (sg.). 4. *strip* of papyrus, ταῖς τῶν χαρτῶν ἰσίν Sor.1.13: sg., Gal.10.1000. b. λεπτὴ ἲς a small *fibre* of papyrus, Id.17(1).795.

ἴς (B) [ῑ], ἡ, three times in acc. sg. ἶνα (elided ἶν') Il.5.245, 7.269, Od.9.538, freq. in instr. ἶφι (q. v.), elsewh. only nom. sg.:—*strength, force*, of persons, ἀλλ' ἄρα καὶ ἲς ἐσθλή Il.12.320; ἐπέρεισε δὲ ἶν' ἀπέλεθρον 7.269; ἥ μοι ἔτ' ἐστὶν ἴς, οἵη πάρος.. Od.21.283, cf. 11.393, 18.3: freq. in periphr., ἱερὴ ἲς Τηλεμάχοιο the *strong* Telemachus, 2.409; κρατερὴ ἲς Ὀδυσῆος Il.23.720; ἲς Ἡρακλῆος Hes.*Th.*951; and in twofold periphr., ἲς βίης Ἡρακληείης ib.332; also of things, ἲς ἀνέμου or ἀνέμοιο, Il.15.383, 17.739, Od.9.71; ἲς ποταμοῖο Il.21.356; κράται' ἴς was read by Ptol.Asc. in Od.11.597; v. κρατύς. (Ϝι-, cf. γίς· ἰσχύς, Hsch., pr. n. Ϝιφιάδας *IG*7.3172.70, Lat. *vis, vim*; prob. cogn. with ἵεμαι but not with ἴς (A).)

ἰσ-άγγελος, ον, *like an angel*, *Ev.Luc.*20.36, Hierocl.*in CA*4 p.425 M. **-άδελφος** [ᾰ], ον, *like a brother*, of Pylades, E.*Or.*1015 (anap.); εὔνοια *IPE* 1^2.359. **-άζω**:—Pass., fut. ἰσασθήσομαι Arist.*EE* 1243^{b}31: aor. 1 ἰσάσθην Id.*EN*1133^{a}14: pf. ἴσασμαι ib.^{b}5: (ἴσος):—*make equal, balance*, of a person holding scales, σταθμὸν... καὶ εἴριον... ἀνέλκει ἰσάζουσ' Il.12.435; *l.* τὰς κτήσεις *to equalize* them, Arist.*Pol.* 1265^{a}38; *l.* τὸ ἄνισον Id.*EN*1132^{a}7; τὴν φιλίαν ib.1163^{b}33:—Med., *make oneself equal to another*, οὕνεκ' ἄρα Λητοῖ ἰσάσκετο (sc. Νιόβη) Il. 24.607:—Pass., *to be made* or *to be equal*, θεοῖς Pl.*Ti.*41c: abs., Arist. *EN*1133^{a}14, al.; μήκει ποδὸς ἴχνος ἰσάζεται Nic.*Th.*286; δίστιχα ψήφοισιν ἰσάζεται *AP*9.356 (Leon.). II. intr. in Act., *to be equal*, Pl.*Lg.*773a, Arist.*EN*1154^{b}24; ἀλλήλοις Id.*Pol.*1304^{a}39. 2. *to be even, normal*, Hp.*Morb.*4.49. [ῑ in Hom.; ῐ in Nic.*Th.*286, 886.] **-αθάνᾰτος** [ᾰθᾰ], ον, *equal to the Immortals*, καρπός Arist. *Fr.*675.7 as quoted by Did. in D.(6.37). **-αίομαι**, poet. for ἰσάζομαι, *resemble*, Nic.*Al.*399, *Fr.*74.56; *to be made equal*, Arat.235, 513:—Act., **ἰσαίω** is implied in ἰσῄ (Boeot. for ἰσαίει)· ἰσοῖ, ἰσάζει, Hsch. **-αῖος** [ῐ], α, ον, late poet. form of ἴσος, Nic.*Th.*360:—ἡ ἰσαία (sc. μοῖρα), *equality*, ἐπ' ἰσαίῃ Call.*Jov.*63, cf. Philostr.Jun.*Im.* 3; τὰ ἰσαῖα (ἰσεα lapis) *an equal share*, *SIG*57.10 (Milet., v B.C.).

ἰσαίτερος, ἰσαίτατος, v. ἴσος.

ἰσάκις [ῐσᾰ], Adv. from ἴσος, *the same number of times, as many times*, Str.3.5.8; *l.* πολλαπλάσιος c. gen., *the same* multiple of..., Euc.7 *Def.*21, al.; *l.* πολλαπλάσια *equimultiples*, Id.5 *Def.*5, al.; *l.* ἴσος, of a number, *equal multiplied by equal*, i.e. *square*, Pl.*R.*546c, *Tht.* 147e, 148a, Euc.7 *Def.*19, Ph.1.11, etc.; *l.* ἴσος *l.* *equal multiplied by equal multiplied by equal*, i.e. *cube number*, Euc.7 *Def.*20, etc.

ἰσάκτιος, ον, *ranking with the Actian games*, *CIG*4472.11 (Laodicea ad Mare).

ἰσᾱμέριος, ον, Dor. for ἰσημέριος, *lasting an equal time*, φύλλοις αἰγείρου S.*Fr.*593.2.

ἴσᾱμι, v. *εἴδω (B), and add: ἴσαμι Theoc.5.119; ἴσαις (2 sg.) Id. 14.34; ἴσατι Id.15.146; ἴσᾰτε Periand.ap.D.L.1.99; ἴσαντι Theoc. 15.64; inf. γισάμεναι (i.e. ϝισ-)· εἰδέναι, Hsch.; Arc. ἰσάμεν (ισμεν lapis), *IG*5(2).357.12; 3 pl. subj. ἴσαντι *Schwyzer* 190 (Cretan).

ἰσ-άμιλλος [ᾰ], ον, *equal in the race*: neut. pl. as Adv., ἰσάμιλλα δραμεῖν τινι *AP*9.311 (Phil.). **-άμμορος**· δύσμορος, Hsch. (leg. κάμμορος).

ἴσαν, *they went*, 3 pl. impf. Ep. of εἶμι (*ibo*), Hom. II. *they knew*, 3 pl. plpf. Ep. of οἶδα, Il.18.405, Od.4.772.

ἰσάναν· ἰσάνιον, ῥητίνην, Hsch.

ἰσ-ανάτολος, ον, *taking the same time to rise*, ζῴδια Vett.Val.142. 27:—also **-ανάφορος**, ον, ibid., cf. Paul.Al.*E.*4, *S.*2. **-ανδρος**, ον, (ἀνήρ) *like a man*, Hsch. **-άνεμος** [ᾰ], ον, *swift as the wind*, E.*IA* 206 (lyr.). **-άξιος**, ον, *of equal worth*, Porph.*Abst.*2.55; τῷ Διί Procl.*in Cra.*p.50 P.; τοῖς θεοῖς Iamb.*Myst.*3.21; *adequate*, πρός τι Dam.*Pr.*43, cf. 28. Adv. -ίως Iamb.*Myst.*9.7. **-άργῠρος**, ον, *worth its weight in silver*, πορφυρᾶς *l.* κηκῖδα A.*Ag.*959, cf. Achae.5, Ephipp.21.4. **-ᾰριθμέω**, *to be equal in number*, τινι Tz.*H.*1. 939. **-ᾰρίθμιος**, ον, = sq., c. gen., Μουσῶν *IG*14.1747. **-άριθμος** [ᾰ], ον, *equal in number with*, ψυχαὶ *l.* τοῖς ἄστροις Pl.*Ti.*41d, cf. *Lg.*845a, Arist.*EN*1156^{a}7, al., Call.*Del.*175, Puchstein *Epigr.Gr.*p.9; εἰσαρίθμοις ἔπεσι, = ἰσοψήφοις, *IG*5(1).257 (Laconia): poet. ἰσήριθμος, *AP*6.84 (Paul. Sil.), 328 (Leon.), Lyc.1258. Adv. ἰσαρίθμως Gal.19.469, Them.*Or.*33.367b. II. Gramm., *of the same grammatical number*, A.D.*Synt.*170.13. Adv. -μως ib.143.9. **-άρχαιος**, ον, *equally ancient*, Choerob.*in Theod.*2.55. **-άρχων**, οντος, ὁ, *equitable ruler*, *POxy.*41.12, 28 (iii/iv A.D.).

ἰσάσκετο [ῑ], Ep. 3 sg. impf. Med. of ἰσάζω, Il.24.607.

ἰσασμός [ῐ], ὁ, *equalization*, Epicur.*Nat.*15.21 (pl.).

ἰσάστερος, ον, *like a star, bright as a star*, Lxx 4 *Ma.*17.5.

ἰσαστικός, ή, όν, *equalizing, handicapped*, στάθμη, in a race, Eust. 1023.5.

ἰσάτις, ιδος, Hp.*Ulc.*11, *Michel* 832 (Samos, iv B.C.) (but -ιος Hp. *Aff.*38, -εως *POxy.*101.12): ἡ:—a plant producing a dark blue dye, *woad*, Lat. *Isatis tinctoria*, Hp. ll. cc., Thphr.*Sens.*77, Dsc.2.184, Plin.*HN*20.59.

ἰσατώδης, ες, *like woad*, Hp.*Epid.*4.45, 2.3.1; χολή Aret.*CD*1.15.

ἰσαύδης [ῐ], ες, (αὐδή) *of the same name*, Theoc.*Syrinx* 9.

ἰσᾰχῶς [ῐ], Adv., (ἴσος) *in the same number of ways*, Arist.*Metaph.* 1013^{a}16, al.; παρακολουθεῖν *l.* τινί ib.1054^{a}14; τἀγαθὸν *l.* λέγεται τῷ ὄντι *in as many ways as*, Id.*EN*1096^{a}23.

ἰσγίνη, ἰσγένη, v. ὕσγινον.

Ἰσεῖα, τά, and **Ἰσεῖον**, τό, v. Ἰσιεῖα, Ἰσιεῖον.

ἰσεννύω, *to be of an intermediate age*, ἰσεννύουσαι Hp.*Mul.*2.111 (so Gal.19.106; ἴσαι νῦν ἐοῦσαι Hp. codd.; ἴσενοι ἐοῦσαι cj. Schneider (cf. ἕνος)).

ἰσήβας [ῑ], ου, ὁ, (ἥβη) = ἰσῆλιξ, Tim.*Pers.*226.

ἰσηγορ-έομαι, *speak as an equal*, v.l. in Lxx *Si.*13.11:—Act. **-έω**, Sch.D Il.1.187, Hsch., Phot. **-ία**, Ion. -ίη, ἡ, *equal right of speech*, and generally, *political equality*, Hdt.5.78, Eup.291, X.*Cyr.*1.3.10, Zeno *Stoic.*1.54, Phld.*Hom.*p.20 O., etc.; *l.* καὶ ἐλευθερία D.21.124; *l.* καὶ παρρησία Jul.*Or.*1.17b. **-ος**, ον, *enjoying equal right of speech, freedom of speech*, Poll.6.174.

ἰσ-ήλῐκος, η, ον, *equal in magnitude*, τάφρος Ph.*Bel.*91.21; *equal in age*, Procl.*in Prm.*p.944 S., al., Dam.*Pr.*316. **-ῆλιξ**, ῐκος, ὁ, ἡ, *of the same age with*, τινι X.*Smp.*8.1, *Com.Adesp.*874: c. gen., *l.* χρόνος κόσμου Ph.1.6: abs., Id.2.303. **-ημερία**, ἡ, *equinox*, *l.* ἐαρινή, μετοπωρινή, ὀπωρινή, Arist.*Mete.*364^{b}1, 2, 371^{b}30; φθινοπωρινή

Id.*HA*570^{b}14, etc.: in pl., Hp.*Aër.*11, Pl.*Ax.*370c, Porph.*Antr.* 24. **-ημερινός**, ή, όν, *equinoctial*, ἀνατολή, δυσμή, Arist.*Mete.*363^{a}34,^{b}1, cf. Str.2.1.11; σκιά Hipparch.1.3.6, cf. Str.2.1.20; ζῴδιον Ptol.*Tetr.*31; ὧραι *standard* hours (opp. καιρικός, q.v.), each = $\frac{1}{24}$ of the νυχθήμερον, Hipparch.1.1.10, Ptol.*Alm.*2.9, Gal.10.479, etc.; πυρὸς ἰ. wheat *sown at that time*, Thphr.*CP*4.11.4; ὁ ἰ. κύκλος *celestial equator*, Arist.*Mete.*345^{a}3, Euc.*Phaen.*p.4 M., Plu.2.429f, etc.; ὁ ἰ. (sc. κύκλος), Hipparch.1.10.22, Str.1.1.21, etc.; ἁψίς Jul.*Or.*5.168c; ἰ. χρόνοι time-degrees [each = 4 time-minutes] *of the equator*, Ptol. *Alm.*1.16.

ἰσημέριον, τό, = *aequinoctium*, *Gloss.* **ἰσήμερος**, ον, = *aequidialis*, ib. **ἰσήμορτεν**· ἀπέθανεν, Hsch.

ἰσήρετμος [ῐ], ον, *with as many oars as*, τινι E.*IA*242 (lyr.).

ἰσήρης, ες, = ἴσος, ἰ. ψῆφοι E.*IT*1472, cf. Nic.*Th.*643 [ῐσ]: c. dat., ῥαιβοῖσιν ἰσήρεες [ῐσ] ib.788.

ἰσήριθμος, ον, poet. for ἰσάριθμος.

ἴσθι, *know*, imper. of οἶδα. **II.** **ἴσθι**, *be*, imper. of εἰμί.

ἰσθλῆ, v. ἰξαλῆ.

ἴσθμα, = ἆσθμα, and **ἰσθμαίνω**, = ἀσθμαίνω, Hsch. (also **ἰσμ-**, Id.).

Ἴσθμ-ια, ων, τά, v. ἴσθμιον IV. **-ιάζω**, *attend the Isthmian games*: prov., *to be unhealthy*, Suid., Hsch. **II.** (ἰσθμός I) *drink*, Phot. **-ιακός**, ή, όν, = Ἰσθμικός (q.v.): Ἰσθμιακά, τά, a kind of *garlands*, Ar.*Fr.*491. **-ιάς**, άδος, pecul. fem. of foreg., νίκα Pi.*I.*8(7).3; αἱ Ἰ. σπονδαί Th.8.9. **II.** ἡ Ἰ. (sc. ἑορτή) the *Isthmian festival*, Pl.Com.46.10: pl., αἱ Ἰσθμιάδες, = τὰ Ἴσθμια, Pi.*O.*13.33; *a period of two years*, between each celebration of the games, Apollod.2.7.2. **-ιαστής**, οῦ, ὁ, *spectator of the Isthmian games*: Ἰσθμιασταί, οἱ, title of a play by Aeschylus. **-ικός**, ή, όν, *of the Isthmus*, ἀγών, σπονδαί, Str.8.6.20, Paus.5.2.1.

ἴσθμιον, τό, (ἰσθμός) *anything belonging to the neck* or *throat*, *necklace*, Od.18.300. **2.** ἴσθμια, τά, *pharynx*, *fauces*, Hp.*Dent.*21, Nic.*Al.*191,615, unless = παρίσθμια. **II.** *neck of a bottle*, ἴσθμιον ἀμφιφορῆος Poet.ap.Suid.; *big-bellied bottle with a long neck*, Cypr. word in Pamphil.ap.Ath.11.472e; v. ἴσφνιον. **2.** *curb-stone* of a well, Phot., Moer. **3.** part of dagger, perh. the *guard*, Philet.ap.Ath. 15.677c. **III.** *isthmus*, Hsch. **IV.** Ἴσθμια (sc. ἱερά), τά, *the Isthmian games*, held on the Isthmus of Corinth, Ar.*Pax*879, etc.; Ἴσθμι' ἐνίκα Simon.153, cf. *IG*1^2.606; Ἴσθμια... ἐστεφανώθην Simon. 188; στέφος Ἴσθμι' ἑλών Id.158.

Ἰσθμιονίκης [νῑ], ου, ὁ, *conqueror in the Isthmian games*, B.9.26 (also **-νῖκος**, ὁ, Id.1.46): Ἰσθμιονῖκαι, οἱ, title of one book of Pindar's odes, A.D.*Synt.*156.11, etc.

ἴσθμιος, α, ον, also ος, ον E.*Tr.*1098 (lyr.):—*of* or *belonging to the Isthmus*, *Isthmian*, Ποτειδᾶν Pi.*O.*13.4; χθών S.*OT*940.

ἰσθμοειδής, ές, *like an isthmus*, αὐχήν *Peripl.M.Eux.*58.

Ἰσθμ-όθεν, Adv. *from the Isthmus*, *AP*9.588 (Alc.). **-όθι**, Adv. *on the Isthmus*, ib.6.259 (Phil.). **-οῖ**, loc. of Ἰσθμός II. 2, Ar.*Fr.* 14 D.:—usu. *on the Isthmus*: *at the Isthmian games*, *IG*1^2.77, Pi. *O.*13.98, Lys.19.63, Timocr.1.10; also ἐν Ἰσθμοῖ Simon.125 cod. [Ἰσθ- *IG*1^2.77,829; Ἰθμοῖ *SIG*36*A* (Delph., iv B.C.), but Ἰσθμοῖ ib.*B* (Olymp., v B.C.); cf. Ἰσθμός.] **-ός**, οῦ, ὁ (ἡ *Inscr.Délos* 353*A*29, 34 (iii B.C.), but ὁ 354.29, and v. infr. II), *neck*, *narrow passage*, esp. of the body, *neck*, Emp.100.19; ἰ. καὶ ὅρος τῆς τε κεφαλῆς καὶ τοῦ στήθεος Pl.*Ti.*69e: metaph., βίου βραχὺν ἰσθμόν S.*Fr.*568 (lyr.). **2.** *pharynx*, *fauces*, Gal.18(2).961, Aret.*SA*1.6. **II.** *neck of land* between two seas, *isthmus*, ὁ ἰ. τῆς Χερσονήσου Hdt.6.36; of Athos, Id.7.22; Κιμμερικός A.*Pr.*729; ὁ ἰ. τῆς Παλλήνης Th.1.56; ὁ Λευκαδίων ἰ. Id.3.81. **2.** Ἰσθμός (also **Ἰθμός** *SIG*507 (Delph., iii B.C.), cf. foreg.) ὁ (ἡ in Pi., as *O.*7.81, 8.48), *the Isthmus* of Corinth, Hdt.8.40, etc.; Ἰσθμοῦ δειράς, αὐχὴν Ἰσθμοῦ, Pi.*I.*1.9, B.2.7; dat. Ἰσθμῷ prob. f.l. for Ἰσθμοῖ (q.v.) in Th.5.18, *AP*13.15; but ἐν Ἰσθμῷ correctly in Hdt.9.27,81. **3.** *narrow ridge*, of the Caucasus, between Caspian and Euxine, Arist.*Mu.*393^{b}25, D.P.20. **4.** of the sea, *strait*, *narrow channel*, *Inscr.Délos* ll. cc., App.*Hann.*34. (Perh. fr. εἶμι (*ibo*), cf. ἴθμα, εἰσ-ίθμη, and the spellings Ἰθμός (supr.), Ἰθμο-νίκα *IG*4.951.10.) **-ώδης**, ες, = ἰσθμοειδής, Th.7.26: Sup., Scymn.926.

ἴσι· γνῶσιν, Hsch.

Ἰσ-ῐᾰκός [ῑ], ή, όν, *of* or *for Isis*, σύνοδος *IGRom.*1.1303 (Philae, i B.C.): Subst. **-κός**, ὁ, *priest of Isis*, Dsc.3.23, Plu.2.352b. **-ιασταί**, οἱ, *guild of worshippers of Isis*, at Rhodes, *IG*12(1).157,165 (i B.C.). **-ῐδεῖον**, τό, *temple of Isis*, Roussel *Cultes Égyptiens* 223 (Delos, ii B.C.), *Sammelb.*3926 (Ptolemais Hermiu, i B.C.):—also Ἰσιεῖον, τό, *SIG*^{2}588.230 (Delos, ii B.C.); pl. **Εἰσιεῖα**, τά, *festival of I.*, *PCair.Zen.*154 (iii B.C.):—later **Ἰσεῖον**, τό, *temple of I.*, Plu.2. 352a, prob. in *AP*11.212 (Lucill., pl.); pl. **Ἰσεῖα**, τά, *festival of I.*, D.S.1.14,87.

ἰσικιάριος [ῐσ], ὁ, *sausage-maker*, *PStrassb.*46 (vi A.D.).

ἰσικιομάγειρος [ῐσ], ὁ, = foreg., *Wien.Stud.*24.129 (vi A.D.).

ἰσίκιον [ῐσῑ], τό, or **ἴσῐκος**, ὁ, *a dish of mince-meat* (formed from Lat. *insicium* acc. to Macr.*Sat.*7.8.1), Ath.9.376b, *POxy.*1730 (iv A.D.):—also **ἴσικος**, ὁ, Alex.Aphr.*Pr.*1.22, Alex.Trall.*Febr.*1: pl., Olymp.*in Grg.*p.360 J.

ἰσινδίη· καθίνη, Hsch.

ἴσιον, τό, purgative bark, Aët.3.37,104.

Ἰσιονόμος, ὁ, *warden of the temple of Isis*, *PCair.Zen.*172.14 (iii B.C.), *BGU*993 (ii B.C.).

Ἶσις, ἡ, voc. Ἶσιν *UPZ*81 ii 19 (ii B.C.), gen. Ἴσιδος *BGU*993 ii 10 (ii B.C.), Plu.2.353f, etc.; Ion. and later Ἴσιος Hdt.2.41, *PPetr.*3 p.216 (iii B.C.), etc. (written Ἔσιος *Schwyzer*749 (v B.C.)), dat. Ἴσιδι *OGI*175.4 (ii B.C.), etc., Ἴσῑ or Ἴσει Hdt.2.59, *OGI*61.4 (iii B.C.); acc. Ἶσιν:—*Isis*, Hdt. ll. cc., Call.*Ep.*58, Apollod.2.1.3, Plu.2.351f, *POxy.*1380 (ii A.D.), etc.; Ἴσιδος τρίχες, name of a *plant*, Plu.2. 939d, cf. Plin.*HN*13.142. **II.** name of a *plaster*, Gal.11.126, 13. 774. **III.** Pythag. name for the δυάς, *Theol.Ar.*12.

ἴσκαι, ῶν, αἱ, *fungus growing on oaks and walnut-trees*, used as a cautery, Aët.7.91, Paul.Aeg.6.49, Alex.Trall.12.

ἰσκάνδιον· σαλπίγγιον, Hsch. **ἰσκανδοτόν**· σαλπιγγωτόν, Id. **ἴσκλος**, ὁ, v. ὕσκλος. **ἰσκός**· κλέπτης, Id.; cf. κίσκος.

ἴσκω (A), iterat. pres. of εἶμι, *go*, ἐνς πόλεμον *Schwyzer*180 (Crete).

ἴσκω (B), = ἐΐσκω (q.v.), only 3 sg. impf. ἴσκε(ν) in early Ep., *make like*, φωνὴν ἴσκουσ' ἀλόχοισιν *she made* her voice *like* (the voice of) their wives, Od.4.279; *feign*, ἴσκε ψεύδεα πολλὰ λέγων ἐτύμοισιν ὁμοῖα 19.203. **II.** *think like*, ἐμὲ σοὶ ἴσκοντες *thinking* me *like* (i.e. taking me for) you, Il.16.41; σὲ τῷ ἴσκοντες 11.799 (εἴσκ- Aristarch.). **2.** *guess*, *imagine*, ἴσκεν ἕκαστος ἀνήρ Od.22.31; *suppose*, c. acc. et inf., Simon.130. **III.** in Alex. Poets, through a misinterpretation of Hom., *speak*, *say*, A.R.2.240, al.: 1 sg. ἴσκον Theoc.22.167, part. ἴσκων Lyc.574.

ἴσμα, ατος, τό, (ἵζω) *foundation*, *seat*, Lyc.731.

ἰσμα, ἰσμαίνω, v. ἴσθμα.

ἰσμή, ἡ, (οἶδα, ἴσμεν) *knowledge*, Hsch.

ἰσο-αχθής, ές, *equal in weight*, Nic.*Th.*44. **-βᾰθής**, ές, *of equal depth*, Thphr.*CP*3.4.2, Heliod.(?)ap.Orib.46.8.2. **-βᾰρέω**, *to be of equal weight*, τὰ -βαρέοντα τῷ ὑγρῷ Archim.*Fluit.*1.3, cf. Sch.Il.17.742. **-βᾰρής**, ές, *of equal weight*, Arist.*Cael.*273^{b}24, 308^{b}34, Chrysipp.*Stoic.*2.175, Archim.*Fluit.*1.3, Luc.*Vit.Auct.* 27. **-βᾰσῐλεύς**, έως, ὁ, ἡ, *equal to a king*, Plu.*Alex.*39. **-βῐος**, ον, *holding office for life*, γραμματεύς *IGRom.*4.1675 (Belevi). **-βοιος**, ον, (βοῦς) *worth an ox*, Hsch. s. v. ἀντίβοιος. **II.** ἰσόβοιον, τό, a poppy-like flower, Id.

ἰσοβόλων· ἰσοστασίων, Hsch., Phot.

ἰσό-γαιος, ον, *of equal height in relation to the land*, θάλασσαι Luc. *Ner.*5: Att. **-γεως**, *even with the ground*, τέμνειν ἰσόγεων Thphr.*CP* 3.7.3:—written **-γειως**, *IG*2^2.1665 (iv B.C.).

ἴσογκος [ῐ], ον, *equal in bulk*, Archim.*Fluit.*1.7, 2.4.

ἰσο-γλώχῑν, ῖνος, ὁ, ἡ, *equiangular*, Nonn.*D.*6.23. **-γονία**, ἡ, *equality of birth*, Pl.*Mx.*239a, D.C.52.4. **-γρᾰφος** or **-γράφος**, ον, *writing like*: metaph., ἰ. τέττιξιν *musical* as the cicada, of Plato, Timo 30.2 (s.v.l.): **-γρᾰφή**, ἡ, name of a work by Antisthenes, D.L. 6.15: **-γρᾰφον**, τό, *copy*, Men.Prot.p.24 D. (pl.). **-γώνιος**, ον, *equiangular*, τετράγωνα Arist.*Metaph.*1054^{b}2, cf. Plu.2.427a, etc.; πεντάγωνον Gal.5.67. **-δαίμων**, ον, gen. ονος, *godlike*, A.*Pers.*634 (lyr.), Ariphron 1.4, Hierocl.*in CA*4 p.425 M. **II.** *equal in fortune* or *happiness*, ἰ. βασιλεῦσι Pi.*N.*4.84. **-δαίτης**, ου, ὁ, (δαίω) *dividing equally*, *giving to all alike*, epith. of Dionysus and Pluto, Plu.2.389a, Luc.*Ep.Sat.*32; of Pluto, Hsch. (ἰσοδέτης cod.). **II.** Subst., name of a δαίμων, Hyp.*Fr.*177. **-δᾱμιοργός**, ὁ, (Ϝισο- lapis) *enjoying the privileges of a* δαμιοργός (cf. δημιουργός), at Elis, *Schwyzer* 415.4 (Olymp.). **-δενδρος**, ον, *equal to that of a tree*, ἰσοδένδρου.. αἰῶνος Pi.*Fr.*165. **2.** *as big as a tree*, Thphr.*HP*3.1.1. **-δέξιος**, ον, *ambidextrous*, Philostr.*Gym.*41. **-δίαιτος** [ῐ], ον, *living on an equal footing*, πρός τινα with one, Th.1.6; τινι Luc.*Bis Acc.* 33. **-διάστατος**, ον, *equal in dimension*, of the surfaces of a cube, Nicom.*Ar.*2.16, cf. Iamb.*in Nic.*p.93 P., Eust.ad D.P.2. **-δομος**, ον, of walls, *built in equal courses*, Vitr.2.8.6, Plin.*HN*36.171. **-δοξος**, ον, gloss on ἰσοκλεής, Hsch., Phot., Suid. **-δουλος**, ον, *like a slave*, Sch.A.*Ch.*135. **-δρομέω**, *keep pace with*, τινι Arist.*Pr.* 913^{a}38; ἰσοδρομεῦσα χελιδόσι (Ion. part.) Nic.*Fr.*74.33. **2.** metaph., *concur with*, τοῖς οὐρανίοις ἔργοις Longin.15.4: abs., *to be concurrent*, Arist.*GA*727^{b}10. **-δρομος**, ον, *keeping pace with*, τινι Pl.*Ti.*38d, Ti.Locr.96e, Ph.1.469; τινος Arist.*Mu.*399^{a}8: abs., ἰ. μῆκος a course of equal length, *AP*7.212 (Mnasalc.). **II.** ἡ ἰσοδρόμη Μήτηρ, i. e. Cybele, Str.9.5.19.

ἰσοδῠνᾰμ-έω, *have equal power*, τὸ ψεῦδος ἰ. πρὸς τὴν ἀλήθειαν Plb.2.56.2; *to be equivalent to*, τινι *Stoic.*3.9, Ph.2.291, etc.; ἀλλήλοις Arr.*Epict.*1.8.1; esp. in meaning, A.D.*Pron.*41.15, al.: Math., Ptol.*Alm.*2.7: abs., Chrysipp.*Stoic.*2.83, Lxx *Si.Prol.*13; of sounds in speech, Phld.*Po.Herc.*994 *Fr.*22; of drugs, etc., *possess the same properties*, Dsc.1.70, 5.75: Astrol., *to be equipollent*, Ptol.*Tetr.*36, Vett.Val.142.27. **-ία**, ἡ, *equal force* or *power*, Ti.Locr.95b. **2.** *equivalence in meaning*, A.D.*Conj.*244.17. **3.** Astrol., *equipollence*, Ptol.*Tetr.*132, Vett.Val.296.11. **-ος**, ον, *equal in force* or *power*, Alex.Aphr.*Pr.*1.135; of drugs, Paul.Aeg.2.30; *equivalent in meaning*, Men.Prot.p.24 D.: generally, *equivalent*, c. dat., Lxx 4 *Ma.*3.15. Adv. -μως, ἔχειν Eust.72.33, cf. Gal.18(2).483.

ἰσο-ελκής, ές, *equal in weight*, Nic.*Th.*41, v.l. ib.44. **-επίπεδος**, *equal in plane surface*, Iamb.*in Nic.*p.93 P. **-έτηρος**, ον, *equal in years*, Nonn.*D.*21.177 [ῑ]. **-ετής**, ές, = foreg., gloss on οἰέτεας, Apollon.*Lex.*, Sch.Il.*Oxy.*1086 i 21. **II.** ἰσοετές, τό, = ἀείζωον τὸ μικρόν, Plin.*HN*25.160. **-ευρής**, ές, *equal in breadth*, Phot.

ἰσοζῠγ-έω, *make equal in weight*, Nic.*Th.*908. **-ής**, ές, *evenly balanced*: *equal*, *AP*10.16.3 (Theaet.). **-ος**, ον, Gramm., *of the same number and person*, ῥῆμα A.D.*Pron.*69.8. **II.** gloss on ἀντίζυγα, Hsch.

ἰσο-θάνᾰτος [θᾰ], ον, *like death*, S.*Fr.*359; ἀρρωστία *PHaw.*65. 19; κίνδυνος Vett.Val.293.4; censured by Poll.6.174. **-θεος**, ον, *equal to the gods*, *godlike*, of heroes, ἰ. φώς Il.2.565, Od.1.324, A. *Pers.*80 (lyr.); Δαρεῖος ib.857 (lyr.); οἱ ἰ. S.*Ant.*837 (anap.); γένος

E.*IA*626, cf. Pl.*Phdr.*255a, Isoc.2.5, etc.; ἰητρὸς φιλόσοφος ἰ. Hp. *Decent.*5: Com., νομίσαι τ' ἰσόθεον τὴν ἔγχελυν Antiph.147.2. 2. of things, ἰ. τυραννίς E.*Tr.*1169; δόξα Isoc.5.145; εἴσοδος Epicur. *Fr.*165; τιμαί Men.*Mon.*378, Plb.10.10.11, *IG*5(2).432.4 (Megalop.); χάριτες *OGI*666.21 (Egypt, i A.D.); freq. of medicines or remedies, Gal.13.65,279, Aët.7.11: neut. -θεον as Adv., *PMag.Par.*2.220. [ῑσ- in Hom. and Trag. (always lyr.); hyperaeol. ἰσσο- *Schwyzer*647.15 (Cyme, i A.D.).] **-θεόω,** *make equal to the gods,* in Pass., Aesop.160.

ἰσόθι, Arc. Adv. *within,* ἰ. πλέθρω *SIG*306.13 (Tegea, iv B.C.).

ἰσό-θροος, ον, *sounding like,* Ἠχώ Nonn.*D.*36.473. **-θῡμος,** ον, *equal in spirit,* Sch.Il.7.295. **-καινος,** ον, *as good as new,* Hsch. s.v. ἀντίκαινον. **-κάμπᾱνος,** ον, *equal in weight,* Sch.Od. 4.129; cf. κάμπανος. **-κᾰπῑτώλιος,** ον, *ranking with the* Καπιτώλια, ἀγών *BGU*1074.16 (iii A.D.). **-κατάληκτος,** ον, *ending alike,* Eust.1839.43: -ληκτα, τά, Gell.18.8.1. **-κέλευθος,** ον, *walking alike, keeping up with,* Nonn.*D.*48.316 [ῐ]. **-κέφᾰλος,** ον, *like-headed,* dub. in Ibyc.16. **-κίνδῡνος,** ον, *facing equal risks,* Th. 6.34; τισί D.C.41.55. **-κιννάμωμος** [ᾰ], ον, *like cinnamon,* of cassia (prob. = ἄχυ, q.v.), Plin.*HN*12.98. **-κλεής,** ές, *equal in glory,* Hsch., Phot. **-κληρονόμος,** ον, *inheriting equally,* Sch. Hermog. in Rh.4.169 W. **-κληρος,** ον, *equal in property,* Plu. *Lyc.*8. **-κλῑνής,** ές, *evenly balanced,* Arist.*Mu.*400ᵇ28. **-κνημος,** ον, *with the legs on a level,* Erot. **-κοιλος,** ον, *with equal cavities,* αὐλός Plu.2.1021a, Theo Sm.p.60 H. (pl.). **-κόρῠφος,** ον, *equally high* or *eminent,* πόλεις D.H.3.9. **-κρᾱής,** ές, *equally mixed,* prob. l. (for -κρατεῖ) Hp.*Morb.*2.42. **-κραιρος,** ον, *with equal horns,* Nonn.*D.*27.24. **-κράς,** ὁ, ἡ, = ἰσοκραής, Hdn.Gr.1. 525. **-κράτεια** [κρᾰ], ἡ, = ἰσοκρατία, *equilibrium, equivalence,* Gal. *Hist.Phil.*126.

Ἰσοκράτειος [ᾰ], ον, *of Isocrates,* λόγοι Phld.*Rh.*1.100 S.; ἀγωγή D.H.*Isoc.*20:—also **Ἰσοκρᾰτικός,** ή, όν, Id.*Vett.Cens.*3.3: **-κοί,** οἱ, *followers of I.,* Phld.*Rh.*1.148 S.

ἰσοκρᾰτ-έω, *to be of equal force,* S.E.*M.*10.81. **-ής,** ές, *of equal power, possessing equal rights with others,* ἰσοκρατέες...αἱ γυναῖκες τοῖσι ἀνδράσι Hdt.4.26; ἰ. καὶ ὁμότιμοι Plu.2.827b: generally, *evenly balanced,* ἡ ἰσημερία ἐστὶ χειμὼν καὶ θέρος ἰσοκρατής Arist.*Pr.*942ᵇ37; ἰ. οἶνος *half-and-half,* Hp.*Morb.*2.42 (nisi leg. ἰσοκραής); ἐκ τῆς ἀμφοῖν -οῦς μίξεως Gal.6.528; ἰ. κράσεις *normal* temperaments, Ruf.ap. Orib.8.24.61. Adv. -τῶς, ἀπομάχεσθαι Ph.1.198; *with even balance,* Zeno *Stoic.*1.27, Iamb.*in Nic.*p.79 P. **-ία,** ἡ, *equality of strength* or *power,* Ti.Locr.95c. 2. = ἰσονομία, *equality of rights, republic,* opp. τυραννίς, Hdt.5.92.α' (pl.).

ἰσό-κρᾰτος, ον, = ἰσοκραής, Praxag.ap.Ruf.*Onom.*226. **-κρῑθος,** ον, *equal to barley in price,* Plb.2.15.1. **-κτῐτος,** ον, (κτίζω) *made alike,* Hsch., Phot. **-κτῠπος,** ον, *sounding like,* τινι Nonn.*D.*27. 92. **-κυκλος,** ον, *equally round,* Philox.2.10. **-κωλία,** ἡ, *equality of members* or *clauses,* Hermog.*Id.*1.12 (pl.). **-κωλος,** ον, *of equal members* or *clauses,* Arist.*Top.*148ᵇ33; τὸ ἰ. *a sentence consisting of equal members,* Demetr.*Eloc.*25, Plu.2.350e: in pl., D.S. 12.53, Ath.5.187c. 2. *formed of an equal number of strands,* χορδαί Nicom.*Harm.*6. **-λᾰχής,** ές, = ἰσόμοιρος, cj. in Philol. 6. **-λεκτοι** *versus, antithetically composed,* Diom.p.498 K. **-λεχής,** ές, *with the same bed,* Apollon.*Lex.Hom.* **-λογέω,** *speak freely with,* τινι Sch.E.*Hipp.*702. **-λογία,** ἡ, = ἰσηγορία, Plb.30. 31.16; -λογίαν ἔχειν πρός τινα Id.24.10.9. II. in pl., *counter-balancing arguments,* S.E.*M.*1.144. **-λόγχητος,** ον, = ὁ τὰ ἴσα λαχών (cf. λόγχη), dub. in *IG*9(1).309 (Thronium).

ἰσολύμπιος, ον, *like those rendered to the Olympians,* τιμαί Ph. 2.181, cf. 567. II. *ranking with the Olympic games,* [ἀγὼν] γυμνικός *SIG*630.13 (Delph., ii B.C.), cf. *IG*12(7).506.7 (Nicuria), etc.

ἰσό-λῠρος, ον, *like the lyre,* Sch.S.*Tr.*643. **-μάτωρ** [ᾰ], Dor. for -μήτωρ, ὁ, ἡ, *like one's mother* or *dam,* ἀμνός Theoc.8.14; said to be Cret. by Hsch. **-μᾰχος,** ον, *equal in the fight,* D.H.3.52; ἀρετή, κίνδυνος, D.S.16.12, 17.83: τισι Ant.Lib.14.2. **-μεγέθης,** ες, *equal in size,* X.*Cyn.*5.29, Plb.10.44.2, Phld.*Mort.*3, Herod.Med.ap. Orib.10.8.2: c. dat., κύστις ἰ. ληκύθῳ Aen.Tact.31.10; ἰ. γῇ Jul.*Gal.* 135c. Adv. -θῶς Aristid.Quint.3.6. **-μέρεια,** ἡ, *equality,* ἐξ -μερίας *Sammelb.*6266.17 (vi A.D.). **-μερής,** ές, *equally divided,* δόσεις *BGU*1122.12 (i B.C.); *of equal length,* ib.393.12 (ii A.D.): generally, *equal,* κέρδος Just.*Nov.*97.1. **-μέτρητος,** ον, *of equal measure* or *weight,* εἰκών Pl.*Phdr.*235d, Plu.*Sol.*25; τινι D.C.59.11, cf. Max.Tyr.31.2. **-μετρία,** ἡ, *equality of measure,* Arist.*Fr.* 47. **-μετρος,** ον, = ἰσομέτρητος, Ephipp.14.9, Palaeph.30; λίθοι, prob. in *IG*2².463.46; σφηνίσκος Sever.ap.Aët.7.92: c. dat., ἰ. τῇ προτέρᾳ δοῦναι προῖκα Just.*Nov.*97.5; *of equal perimeter,* περὶ ἰ. σχημάτων, title of work by Zenodorus; *in the same latitude,* Nech. in *Cat.Cod.Astr.*7.149: Subst., ἰσόμετρον, τό, *life-size statue,* τινος *BCH* 48.484 (Delos, iv B.C.). **-μέτωπος,** ον, *with equal forehead* or *front,* X.*HG*4.5.16. **-μήκης,** ες, *equal in length,* Arist.*HA*506ᵇ 14; τῇ Ἀττικῇ Str.9.2.1; of numbers, *having a common factor,* Pl.*R.* 546c. **-μῑλήσιος,** α, ον, *of Milesian fashion,* ἱμάτιον D.S.12.21.

ἰσομοιρ-έω, *have an equal share,* Th.6.39, X.*Cyr.*2.3.17; τινος of a thing, D.48.19; τινὸς πρός τινα Th.6.16; πρὸς ἀλλήλους Isoc.5. 39; τινός τινι Is.1.2, D.H.6.66. II. Astrol., *occupy the same degree,* *Cat.Cod.Astr.*5(1).219. **-ία,** Ion. -ίη, ἡ, *equal share,* κακοῖσιν ἐσθλοὺς ἰσομοιρίαν [ῑσ-] ἔχειν Sol.ap.Arist.*Ath.*12.3; τινος in a thing, Th.7.75. 2. = ἰσονομία, Nymphod.21, D.C.52.4. 3. *equability,* of climate, Hp.*Aër.*12; τῶν κράσεων Gal.1.534. 4. Astrol., *equivalence of degree,* Vett.Val.139.16. **-ικός,** ή, όν, of *equivalent positions,* κανονογραφία Id.336.11. **-ος,** ον, Cret. ϝισϝόμοιρος *Leg.Gort.*10.53, *GDI*4974 (Gort.): (μοῖρα) *sharing equally* or *alike,* c. gen. rei, πάντων X.*Cyr.*4.6.12, etc.; τῶν ἄλλων ἰ. ἔστω *SIG*1044. 40 (Halic., iv B.C.); γῆς ἰσόμοιρ' ἀήρ air that *sharest* earth *equally* [with light], S.*El.*87 (anap.): c. dat., τιμαῖς ἰσόμοιρον ἔθηκεν τὰν ὁμόλεκτρον ἥρωσιν *IG*12(3).1190.3 (Melos); ἰσόμοιρον, τό, *equal portion,* Nic.*Th.*592: abs., ἰσόμοιρα...ἐν τῷ κόσμῳ φῶς καὶ σκότος D.L.8.26. Adv. -ρως Eust.161.20. 2. *equivalent, corresponding,* c. dat., κίβισιν, βάκτρῳ ἅρπην ἰσόμοιρον *AJA*9.320 (Sinope). 3. Astrol., *occupying the same degree,* αἱ κατ' ἰσόμοιρον στάσεις Vett.Val.70.31, cf. Man.4.194; τὴν Ἀφροδίτην ἰσόμοιρον οὖσαν ἡλίῳ Procl.*Hyp.*1.21. Adv. -ρως *Cat.Cod.Astr.*5(1).219.

ἰσόμορος, ον, = ἰσόμοιρος, used by Poseidon of himself in relation to Zeus, Il.15.209: generally, *like,* τινι *AP*6.206 (Antip.Sid.); ἰσόμορον, τό, *equal portion,* Nic.*Th.*105, Androm.ap.Gal.14.41. [ῑσ- Il. cc.]

ἰσόνειρος, ον, *dream-like, empty,* A.*Pr.*549 (lyr.) [perh. ῑ].

ἰσό-νεκυς, υος, ὁ, ἡ, *dying equally* or *alike,* E.*Or.*200 (lyr.), ubi v. Sch. **-νέμεος,** ον, *ranking with the Nemean games,* ἀγών *SIG*402.10, al. (Delph., iii B.C.), *IG*2².680.17 (prob.):—also **-νέμειος** *Klio*14. 275 (Delph., iii B.C.).

ἰσονομ-έομαι, Pass., *have equal rights,* μετά τινος Th.6.38. **-ία,** Ion. -ίη, ἡ, *equal distribution, equilibrium, balance,* δυνάμεων Alcmaeon 4, cf. Ti.Locr.99b, Epicur.*Fr.*352. II. *equality of political rights,* Hdt.3.80,142; ἰ. ποιεῖν Id.5.37; opp. δυναστεία, Th.4.78; ἰ. πολιτική Id.3.82; ἰ. ἐν γυναιξὶ πρὸς ἄνδρας καὶ ἀνδράσι πρὸς γυναῖκας Pl.*R.*563b. **-ικός,** ή, όν, *devoted to equality,* ἀνήρ ib.561e. **-ος,** ον, *where all have equal rights,* ἰσονόμους τ' Ἀθήνας ἐποιησάτην *Scol.* 12; ὀλιγαρχία ἰ. Th.3.62; δίκαιος καὶ ἰ. πολιτεία Pl.*Ep.*326d; ἐν ἰσονόμῳ πολιτεύειν App.*BC*1.15; ζῷον ἰ. θεῷ M.Ant.8.2; Γαλατία ἰ. *enjoying full citizen rights,* of Gallia Cisalpina, Nic.Dam.130.28 J. II. χαλκὸς ἰ. copper *at par* (24 obols = 1 stater), opp. χαλκὸς οὗ διαλλαγή (copper at a discount), *UPZ*112 v 19 (ii B.C.), *PTeb.*99.4 (ii B.C.), *PPetr.*3 p.193, al. (ii B.C.).

ἰσονύκτιον, τό, *equinox, Gloss.*:—Adj. **-νύκτιος,** ον, *equinoctial,* Gal.16.407.

ἴσοξ, ὁ, a fish, Hsch. (Celtic word, cf. Welsh *ehawc, eog* 'salmon', Lat. *esox*.)

ἰσό-ξῠλος, ον, *like wood,* Hsch. s.v. ὀξυλον. **-ογκος,** ον, *of equal bulk* or *volume,* Simp.*in Cael.*691.35, *in Ph.*1016.23. **-παις,** ὁ, ἡ, *like a child, as of a child,* ἰσχύς A.*Ag.*75 (lyr.). **-πάλαιστος** [ᾰ], ον, *a span long,* *AP*6.287 (Antip.). [ῑ..ᾰ] **-πᾰλής,** ές, *equal in the struggle, well-matched,* μαχομένων...καὶ γενομένων ἰσοπαλέων Hdt. 1.82, cf. 5.49; *evenly balanced,* μάχη Ctes.*Fr.*29.31. 2. generally, *equivalent, equal,* ἰ. πάντῃ Parm.8.44; ἰ. κίνδυνοι Th.2.39; πλήθει ἰ. τισί Id.4.94; οὔτι ὥριφος ἰ. τοι Theoc.5.30; ἰ. ἤματι νύξ *AP*9.384.18, cf. Orph.*Arg.*1014. Adv. -λῶς Sch.Arat.364. **-πᾰλος,** ον, = foreg., Luc.*Nav.*36, D.C.40.42, Poll.3.149, 5.157, Hsch.; prob. in Ibyc.14, X.*Ages.*2.9. **-πᾰχής,** ές, *of equal* or *even thickness* or *density,* Arist.*HA*527ᵃ7, Thphr.*HP*3.5.6, Dsc.5.90, Gal.10.431, Nicom.*Harm.*6:—late nom. sg. **-πᾰχυς** Herod.Med.ap.Orib.8.4.3 codd. **-πεδής,** ές, = ἰσόπεδος, *Gloss.* **-πεδον,** τό, *level ground, a flat,* Il.13.142, X.*Cyr.*3.1.5; φυλάττειν ἐπὶ τοῦ ἰσοπέδου ἑαυτήν Luc.*Im.*21. **-πεδος,** ον, *of even surface, level,* ἐξ ἰ. χωρίου Hp.*VC*11, cf. Luc.*Hipp.*4; ἰ. τῷ δέρματι Gal.10.1011; ἰ. χρώματα *flat in appearance,* opp. κοῖλα, Alex.Aphr.*Pr.*1.49. 2. c. dat., *level* or *even with,* χοῦν ποιέων τῇ ἄλλῃ γῇ ἰσόπεδον Hdt.4.201, cf. D.S. 19.94, Plu.*Num.*10. **-πέλεθρος,** ον, *of the same number of* πλέθρα, Hsch. **-πενθής,** ές, *in equal distress,* Sch.A.*Eu.*783. **-πέραστος** or **-πέρατος,** ον, *equally bounded,* Sch.Od.1.98. **-περίμετρος,** ον, *of equal perimeter,* Damian.*Opt.*3, Hero *Def.*82, Procl.*in Ti.*2.71 D., al. **-πετρος,** ον, gloss on ἀντίπετρος, Sch.S.*OC*192. **-πηχυς,** υ, *of the length of a cubit,* Philostr.*Gym.*12, Opp.*H.*1.213. **-πλαστος,** ον, gloss on ἀντίπλαστος, Hsch. **-πλᾰτής,** ές, *equal in breadth,* Arist.*Oec.*1345ᵃ33, Archimel.ap.Ath.5.209c; ἄρτος ἰ. Hippoloch.ap. Ath.4.128d (-πλατυς codd.): c. dat., ἰ. τῷ τείχει Th.3.21. **-πλάτων,** ωνος, ὁ, *a second Plato,* *AP*11.354. [ῑ...ᾰ] **-πλευρος,** ον, *with equal sides,* πλαίσιον X.*An.*3.4.19, etc.: freq. in Geom., *equilateral,* τρίγωνον Pl.*Ti.*54a,e; ἐπίπεδον ib.55e; τετράγωνον Plb.6.31.10. II. of numbers, *square,* opp. ἑτερομήκης, Pl.*Tht.*148a, Arist.*APo.*73ᵃ40. Adv. -πλεύρως Nicom.*Ar.*2.13. III. Rhet., of periods, Hermog. *Inv.*4.3. **-πληγής,** ές, *struck in the same way,* χορδή Porph. *in Harm.*p.296 W. **-πληθής,** ές, *equal in number* or *quantity,* ἡήρ Hp.*Morb.*2.4; ἱππεῖς X.*Ages.*2.9: Math., *equal in number,* Euc.12. 4, al.; σχήματα τὰς πλευρὰς ἰ. ἔχοντα Papp.332.14: c. dat., τινι to a person or thing, Th.6.37, D.C.50.33; ἰ. θαλάσσῃ ποταμοί Poll.3.103. Adv. -θῶς Euc.12.5. **-πληθόπλευρος,** ον, *having an equal number of sides,* εὐθύγραμμα, σχήματα, Anon.Geom. in Papp.1142.21.

ἰσοπολῑτ-εία, ἡ, *equality of civic rights,* Arist.*Fr.*575; granted to individuals, *IG*7.4264 (Oropus, iii B.C.), 5(2).11 (Tegea, iii B.C.), etc.; or to communities, *SIG*472.11 (Phigalea, iii B.C.), Plb.16.26.9, D.S.15.46, etc. 2. esp. *reciprocity of such rights* (guaranteed by treaty between two states), *GDI*5040 (Crete), *OGI*265 (Pergam., iii B.C.), etc.; Λεβαδεῦσίν ἐστιν ἰ. πρὸς Ἀρκάδας Plu.2.300b. **-ης,** ου, ὁ, *enjoying equal political rights,* τινὰς τοῖς Μακεδόσιν ποιήσας ἰ. J. *AJ*12.1.1, cf. Lxx 3*Ma.*2.30, *GDI*5183.25 (Crete), *Inscr.Magn.*34.28, al., *IPE*1².357. 2. *enjoying reciprocity of rights,* of the citizens of Roman *municipia,* D.H.8.76:—fem. **-πολῖτις,** ιδος, of cities *enjoying such rights,* αἱ ἰ. πόλεις, = *municipia,* App.*BC*1.10. 3. *equitable citizen,* *POxy.*41.28 (iii/iv A.D.).

ἰσο-πραξία, ἡ, *a faring equally, like condition*, Eust.662.35. **-πρέσβυς**, υ, *like an old man*, A.*Ag*.78 (anap.). **-προικον**, τό, *wedding-gift* of bridegroom to bride, *CPR*30 ii 10 (vi A. D.), etc. 2. *as good as given away*, Hsch. s. v. ἀντίπροικα. **-πρόξενος**, ον, (ϝισο- lapis) *enjoying the privileges of a* πρόξενος, *Schwyzer*415.3 (Olymp.). **-πτερος**, ον, gloss on ἄπτερος, Sch.A.*Ag*.276 :—also ἰσόπτεροι· ἰσότιμοι, Hsch.

ἰσο-πτυχής, ές, *with similar folds*, χιτώνιον *IG*2².1518.82,84. **-πτωτος**, ον, (πτῶσις) *with like cases*, A.D.*Pron*.90.6. **-πύθιος** [ῡ], ον, *ranking with the Pythian games*, ἀγών *SIG*402.24 (Delph., iii B. C.), prob. in *IG*2².680.16; στέφανος *SIG*557.29 (Magn. Mae.); ἱερὰ Αὐγουστεῖα ἰ. *IGRom*.4.1265 (Thyatira). **-πυκνος**, ον, *equally condensed* (by tension), χορδή Porph. *in Harm*.p.296 W. (comment on πυκνοτέρας in Ptol.*Harm*.1.8). **-πυργος**, ον, gloss on ἀντίπυργος, Hsch. **-πῦρον**, τό, *fumitory*, *Fumaria capreolata*, Dsc. 4.120, Plin.*HN*27.94, Gal.11.891. **-πῦρος**, ον, *reckoned as of equal value with wheat*, λωτός, κρότων, *PLond.ined*.2360. **-ρρεπής**, ές, = ἰσόρροπος, Nic.*Th*.646, Poet. *de Herb*.98.

ἰσορροπ-έω, *to be equally balanced, in equipoise*, Pl.*Ti*.52e, *Lg*.733c, 794e; τινι *with*.., Plb.1.11.1. **-ησις**, εως, ἡ, *equipoise, equilibrium*, Hero *Spir*.1.1. **-ία**, ἡ, *equipoise, equilibrium*, Pl.*Phd*. 109a: metaph., ἰ. τοῦ χρόνου Agath.4.25. **-ικά**, τά, title of *work on equilibrium* by Archimedes. **-ος**, ον, (ῥοπή) *in equipoise*, of the balance, Pl.*Phd*.109a, *Plt*.270a (Sup.), etc.; τάλαντα βρίσας οὐκ ἰσορρόπῳ τύχῃ A.*Pers*.346; ἰσορρόπου τοῦ πήχεως (sc. τοῦ ζυγοῦ) γινομένου *IG*2².1013.34. 2. generally, *well-balanced, well-matched*, ἰ. αὐτὸς ἑαυτῷ of a man *with his legs of the same length*, Hp.*Fract*.19; of a nose, *flattened, but not awry*, Id.*Art*.37; of a bone, *cylindrical*, ib. 34; δέρμα ἰ., opp. περιρρεπής, ib.50; ἰ. ἀγών *evenly balanced*, E.*Supp*. 706; μάχη Th.1.105; δυνάμεις Pl.*Ti*.52e; βίος Id.*Lg*.733c; τιμή Arist.*EN*1164ᵇ4: c. dat., τὸ γένος τὸ Ἀττικὸν ἰ. τῷ ἑωυτῶν ἂν γίνοιτο would become *a match for* their own, Hdt.5.91; ἰ. Ῥωμαίοις Hdn.6. 7.8; ἰ. καταστῆναί τινι *IPE*1².40.18 (Olbia, ii A. D.); ἰ. ὁ λόγος τῶν ἔργων *in precise equipoise with*.., Th.2.42; ἰ. πρός τι Hdn.6.3.2. 3. *of equal weight*, χρυσίον *Inscr.Délos*313ᵃ.45 (iii B. C., -ορο-). II. Adv. -όπως, ἀφιέναι Hp.*Art*.43; πορεύεσθαι Pl.*Phdr*.247b; ἀγωνίσασθαι D.C.41.61: neut. pl. ἰσόρροπα as Adv., Tim.*Pers*.47.

ἰσόρυθμος, ον, perh. *of like form*, Pi.*Pae*.*Fr*.90.

ἴσος, η, ον, Ep. **ἶσος** and **ἐΐσος** (v. infr.); Cret., Arc. ϝίσϝος *GDI* 4998 ii 2, 4982.2, *Schwyzer*665, cf. γισγόν· ἴσον, Hsch.; later **ἴσος** *Schwyzer*708ᵃ(1) (Ephesus, iv B. C.), *Tab.Heracl*.1.175, etc.:—*equal* in size, strength, or number, c. dat., κύματα ἶσα ὄρεσσιν Od.3.290, etc.; freq. of appearance, *like*, ἶσος ἀναύδῳ 10.378; ἴσος Ἄρευι Sapph.91 (dub.); ἴσος θεοῖσιν Ead.2.1: freq. abs., ἴσην .. βίην καὶ κῦδος Il.7.205; ἶσον θυμὸν ἔχειν to be of *like* mind, 13.704, 17.720: neut. as Adv., ἶσον ἐμοὶ φρονέουσα 15.50; θεοῖσιν ἶσ' ἔθελε φρονέειν 5.441, cf. 21.315, etc.; ἴσος τινὶ τὸ μέγαθος, ὕψος, Hdt.2.32,124; τὸ μῆκος, τὸ πλάτος, X.*An*. 5.4.32; ἀριθμόν E.*Supp*.662; ἴσα τὸν ἀ. Pl.*R*.441c; ποτὴν ἴσον *equal* in flight of song, Alex.Aet.5.5; ἴσον, τό, *copy* of a document, *PLond*. 3.1222.5 (ii A. D.), etc.: with dat. pers. in place of an object of comparison, οὐ μὲν σοί ποτε ἶσον ἔχω γέρας (i. e. τῷ σῷ γέραϊ) Il.1.163; τοῖσδ' ἴσας ναῦς (i. e. ταῖς τῶνδε) E.*IA*262 (lyr.); ἴσα τοῖς νῦν στρατηγοῖς ἀγάθ' εἰργασμένους D.13.21: folld. by a relative word, ἐμοὶ ἴσον.., ὅσονπερ ὑμῖν *the same* to me as to you, Ar.*Ec*.173; τὰ ἐκεῖ ἴσα, ὥσπερ τὰ ἐνθάδε Lys.19.36 codd. (fort. σᾶ); τὰ ἴσα ὅσαπερ.. Lex ap.D.23. 44; ἴσον .. ὅπερ Pl.*Erx*.405b. 2. repeated to denote equal relations, ἴσα πρὸς ἴσα tit for tat, Hdt.1.2; ταχθέντες ἴσοι πρὸς ἴσους S. *Ant*.142 (anap.); ἴσους ἴσοισι .. ἀντιθεὶς E.*Ph*.750; ἴσα ἀντὶ ἴσων λαμβάνειν, ἐκδοῦναι Pl.*Lg*.774c; ἴσος ἴσῳ (sc. οἶνος ὕδατι) Cratin.184, *Com.Adesp*.107, etc.; κύλικος ἴσον ἴσῳ κεκραμένης (where ἴσον is adverbial) Ar.*Pl*.1132; διδόναι γάλα καὶ οἶνον πίνειν ἴσον ἴσῳ Hp. *Epid*.2.5.1: metaph., 'fairly blended', μηδὲν ἴσον ἴσῳ φέρων Ar.*Ach*. 354. 3. of persons, *equal in rights*, βούλεται ἡ πόλις ἐξ ἴσων εἶναι καὶ ὁμοίων Arist.*Pol*.1295ᵇ25; ἡ πολιτικὴ ἐλευθέρων καὶ ἴσων ἀρχή ib. 1255ᵇ20; τὸ κατ' ἀξίαν ἴ. ib.1307ᵃ26, al. II. *equally divided* or *distributed*, ἴση μοῖρα Il.9.318; ἴση alone, *one's equal share*, μή τίς μοι ἀτεμβόμενος κίοι ἴσης Od.9.42 (ἴσσης cj. Fick, cf. ἰσσασθαι); τὴν ἴ. ἔχων Cratin.250; οὐ μὴν ἴ. ἔτεισεν (sc. τίσιν) S.*OT*810; ἄχρι τῆς ἴ. up to *the point of equality*, D.5.17: neut., μὴ ἴσον νεῖμαι ἑκατέρῳ Pl.*Prt*.337a; οὐ μόνον ἴσον, ἀλλὰ καὶ πλέον ἔχειν Isoc.17.57; οὐκ ἀνέξῃ δωμάτων ἔχων ἴσον καὶ τῷδε νεῖμαι; E.*Ph*.547; τὰ ἴσα *fair measure*, τὰ ἴ. νέμειν Hdt. 6.11; μὴ ἴσων ἕκαστον τυγχάνειν ἀλλὰ πλεονεκτεῖν, X.*Cyr*.2.2.20; προστυχεῖν τῶν ἴ. to obtain *fair terms*, S.*Ph*.552; κἂν ἴσαι (sc. ψῆφοι) γένωνται *equally divided*, Ar.*Ra*.685. 2. *based on equality of rights*, ἴ. καὶ ἔννομος πολιτεία Aeschin.1.5; τὴν πολιτείαν ἰσαιτέραν καθιστάναι Th.8.89; τὰ ἴ. *equal rights, equality*, freq. joined with τὰ ὅμοια or τὰ δίκαια, ὡς τῆς πολιτείας ἐσομένης ἐν τοῖς ἴ. καὶ ὁμοίοις X.*HG*7.1.45; τῶν ἴ. καὶ τῶν δικαίων ἕκαστος ἡγεῖται ἑαυτῷ μετεῖναι ἐν τῇ δημοκρατίᾳ D.21.67; οὐ μέτεστι τῶν ἴ. οὐδὲ τῶν ὁμοίων πρὸς τοὺς πλουσίους τοῖς λοιποῖς ib.112; τῶν ἴ. μετεῖχε τοῖς ἄλλοις ib.96; also ἡ ἴ. καὶ ὁμοία (sc. δίκη), τῆς ἴ. καὶ ὁμοίας μετέχειν Th.4.105; ἐπ' ἴ. τε καὶ ὁμοίῃ on *fair* and equal terms, Hdt.9.7,α', cf. Th.1.145; ἐπὶ τῇ ἴ. καὶ ὁμοίᾳ ib.27, cf. *SIG*312.27 (Samos, iv B. C.), *OGI*229.44 (Smyrna, iii B. C.), etc.: generally, *just, fair*, ἐκ ποίας ἴ. καὶ δικαίας προφάσεως; D.18.284. 3. of persons, *fair, impartial*, S.*Ph*.684 (lyr.), *OT*677; ἴ. δικαστής Pl.*Lg*. 957c; ἴ. καὶ κοινοὶ ἀκροαταί D.29.1, cf. 18.7; ἴ. καὶ κοινὸν δικαστήριον Id.7.36; κοινοὺς μὲν.., ἴ. δὲ μή Pl.*Prt*.337a; ἴ. ἴσθι κρίνων Men.*Mon*. 266, cf. 257; κριταὶ ἴ. καὶ δίκαιοι Plb.24.15.3, etc. 4. *adequate*, ἡ ἴ. φρουρά Th.7.27 (expld. by Sch. as *regular*, τεταγμένη); ἴσος τοῖς παροῦσι Id.1.132. III. of ground, *even, flat*, εἰς τὸ ἴ. καταβαίνειν, of an army, X.*An*.4.6.18 (but ἐν ἴσῳ προσιέναι to advance *with even step*, ib.1.8.11); λέουσιν εἰς τὸ ἴ. καθιστάμενοι μάχεσθαι, opp. μετὰ πλεονεξίας ἀγωνίζεσθαι, *on even terms*, Id.*Cyr*.1.6.28; ἴ. τοῖχος, opp. κεκλικώς, *perpendicular*, Phlp. *in APo*.2.27. IV. Adv. ἴσως (v. sub voc.): but also, 1. neut. sg. and pl. from Hom. downwds. (v. sub init.), ἶσον.. ἀπήχθετο κηρὶ μελαίνῃ *even as* Death, Il.3.454; ἶσον ἐμοὶ βασίλευε be king *like* me, 9.616; ἶσον γάρ σε θεῷ τίσουσιν Ἀχαιοί ib. 603; ἶσον ἐμῇ κεφαλῇ 18.82; τὸν.. ἶσα θεῷ .. εἰσορόωσιν Od.15.520; ἶσα φίλοισι τέκεσσι Il.5.71, cf. 13.176, Od.1.432, 11.304, etc.: later abs., *alike*, δείλαιε τοῦ νοῦ τῆς τε συμφορᾶς ἴσον S.*OT*1347; τὴν Σάμον καὶ Ἡρακλέας στήλας ἴσον ἀπέχειν Hdt.8.132: c. dat., ἴσον ναοῖς θεῶν E.*Hel*.801; ἴσον ἄπεσμεν τῷ πρίν *equally* as before, Id.*Hipp*.302 (v. l. τῶν πρίν); ἴσα τοῖς πάνυ D.C.*Fr*.70.6; ἴσα καί.. *like as, as if*, S.*OT* 1187 (lyr.), E.*El*.994 (anap.), Th.3.14; ἴσον ὡς.. E.*Ion* 1363; ὥσπερ .. S.*El*.532; ὥστε.. E.*Or*.882; ἅτε.. Id.*HF*667 (lyr.); ὅσονπερ.. D.15.1. 2. with Preps.: ἀπὸ τῆς ἴσης *equally*, Th.1.15; ὁ ἀπὸ τῆς ἴ. ἐχθρός Id.3.40; ἀπ' ἴσης εἶναι D.14.6; ἀφ' ἴσου *SIG*426.14 (Teos, iii B. C.); δι' ἴσου D.C.43.37; at *equal* distance, Pl.*R*.617b: also in Math., *ex aequali*, of proportions, Euc.5 *Def*.17, al.; δι' ἴ. ἐν τεταραγμένῃ ἀναλογίᾳ *ex aequali* in disturbed proportion, Archim. *Sph.Cyl*.2.4, al., Papp.932.11; ἐν ἴσῳ *equally*, Th.2.53, 4.65; ἐν ἴσῳ ἐστί it matters not, E.*IA*1199; ἐν ἴσῳ [ἐστὶ] καὶ εἰ.. Th.2.60; ἐν τῷ ἴσῳ εἶναι Id.4.10; ἐξ ἴσης Pl.*Lg*.861a: more freq. ἐξ ἴσου Hdt.7.135, S.*OT*563, etc.; ἐξ ἴ. τινί Id.*Ant*.516, 644, Antipho 5.1, Pl.*Grg*.517a; *evenly*, εὐθεῖα γραμμή ἐστιν ἥτις ἐξ ἴ. τοῖς ἐφ' ἑαυτῆς σημείοις κεῖται Euc. 1 *Def*.4; ἐξ ἴ. καί.. S.*OC*254; ὡς.. Id.*OT*61; οἱ ἐξ ἴ. persons *of equal station*, Pl.*Lg*.777d, cf. 919d; ὁ ἐξ ἴ. κίνδυνος Plb.9.4.4; ἐκ τοῦ ἴ. γίγνεσθαί τινι Th.2.3; τοῖς ἐκ τοῦ ἴσου ἡμῖν οὖσι X.*Hier*.8.5; ἐξ ἴσου τισὶ τῆς πολιτείας μεταδιδόναι Lys.25.3; ἐκ τοῦ ἴ. μάχεσθαι *to be evenly matched*, X.*HG*2.4.16; ἐξ ἴ. πολεμεῖν D.8.47; κατὰ μῆνα τὸ αἱροῦν ἐξ ἴ. the sum due in *equal* monthly instalments, *PAmh*.2.92.14, etc.; ἐπὶ or ἐπ' ἴσης, ἐπὶ ἴ. διαφέρειν τὸν πόλεμον Hdt.1.74; τοῦτο ἐπ' ἴσης ἔχει Id.7.50, cf. S.*El*.1062 (lyr.), etc.; ἐπ' ἴσου Plb.1.18.10; ἐπ' ἴσον Id. 6.38.4, cf. Docum.ap.D.18.106, Phld.*Ir*.p.21 W.; ἐπὶ ἶσα μάχη τέτατο Il.12.436; cf. κατὰ ἶσα μάχην ἐτάνυσσε 11.336; κατ' ἴσον Dsc.1.68.6, Gal.*UP*1.19; μετ' ἴσου *equally*, Demetr.Lac.*Herc*.124.12. V. Comp. ἰσαίτερος E.*Supp*.441, Th.8.89, X.*HG*7.1.14: Sup. ἰσότατος Timo 68; ἰσαίτατος Ph.1.462. Adv. ὡς ἰσαίτατα Pl.*Lg*.744c, but ὡς ἰσότατα *SIG*531.30 (Dyme). [ῑ in early Ep. (exc. Hes.*Op*.752), cf. Sol.24.1: ῐ first in Thgn.678, Sapph.2.1 (but ἶσος Ead.91 s. v. l.), B. 5.46 (but ἶσον 1.62, *Fr*.2.2), and always in Pi. (exc. in compd. ἰσοδαίμων) and Trag. (A.*Fr*.216 is dub. l.) exc. in compd. ῑσό-θεος (q. v.); dub. in ἰσ-όνειρος. Both quantities are found in later poetry, sts. in same line, ἔχοισαν ἴσον κάτω, ἶσον ἄνωθεν Theoc.8.19; πρέσβυν ἴσον κούροις, ἶσον ἀδόντα κόραις *APl*.4.309.]

ἰσοσθέν-εια, ἡ, *equipollence*, [τῶν αἰσθήσεων] Epicur.*Fr*.36, cf. Chrysipp.*Stoic*.2.37, S.E.*P*.1.8, D.L.9.74. **-έω**, *possess equal force*, [κινήσεων] κατ' ἴσον ἀμφοῖν -σθενουσῶν Gal.*UP*1.19; of arguments, D.L.9.73; *to be equal in strength*, of military forces, Ascl. *Tact*.3.2,4. **-ής**, ές, *equal in force* or *power*, πενίαν ἰ. πλούτῳ ποιεῖν Democr.284; ἀδάμαντος ἰ. ἄορ Opp.*H*.2.466; μύες τὴν ῥώμην ἰ. Gal.*UP*7.14; *evenly balanced*, μάχαι Id.1.364; διαφωνία S.E.*P*.1.26; τὸ ἰ. D.L.9.107. Adv. -νῶς Gal.9.81.

ἰσοσκελ-εια, ἡ, *having two sides equal*; κατ' -ειαν *in trine aspect*, Ptol.*Tetr*.125. **-ής**, ές, *with equal legs*, esp. in Geom., *having two sides equal, isosceles*, τρίγωνον Pl.*Ti*.54a, etc.; τὸ ἰ. Arist.*APo*.41ᵇ 14. 2. of numbers, *that can be divided into two equal parts, even* (as 6 = 3 + 3), opp. σκαληνός, odd (as 7 = 4 + 3), Pl.*Euthphr*.12d. 3. Rhet., of periods, *containing equal members*, Hermog.*Inv*.4.3. 4. Medic., *having equal tails*, of a bandage, Heliod.ap.Orib.48.62 tit.

ἰσόσπριος, ον, *bean-like*; ὄνος ἰ. an insect *that rolls itself up like a bean*, the *wood-louse*, S.*Fr*.363.

ἰσο-στάδην [ᾰ], Adv., (ἵστημι) = ἰσοστασίως, with marginal gloss ἢ συστάδην, Suid. s. v. ἀνταγωνιστής. **-σταθμέω**, *to be equal in weight*, Id. s. v. ἄγουσαν. **-σταθμος**, ον, *equal in weight*, Dsc.1.44, Orib.*Fr*.106, App.*Sic*.3; *even*, σφυγμός [Gal.]19.641; gloss on σύσταθμος, ib.143:—also **-σταθμής**, ές, Ptol.*Tetr*.98. **-στάσιος** [ᾰ], ον, *equal in weight*, χρυσός, χρυσίον, Str.4.4.5, Plu.*CG*17; *equivalent* or *adequate*, τινι Hp.*Ep*.16, Luc.*DMort*.10.5, D.C.44.40, Max.Tyr.6.6; τίς σοι ἰ. νεκρός; Polem.*Call*.46, cf. 31; ἆρα οὖν ἰ. τῷ Κρόνῳ ὁ Ζεύς; Dam.*Pr*.91; ἰσοστάσιον, τό, prob. name of a ἑταίρα, title of a play by Alexis. 2. *equally poised, in equilibrium*, metaph., Dam.*Pr*.122. Adv. -ίως Poll.8.11: neut. pl. as Adv., βαίνειν Ph.1.462. **-στατέω**, = ἰσοσταθμέω, Lib.*Decl*.43.2. **-στοιχέω**, = ἀντιστοιχέω, Sch.D.T. p.44 H.; *to be co-ordinate*, Simp. *in Ph*.408.13. **-στοιχος**, ον, *occupying a corresponding place*, of terms in parallel series, Id. *in Cael*. 156.18; gloss on ἀντίστοιχος, Sch.E.*Andr*.745. **-στροφή**, ἡ, *correspondence*, Ammon. *in APr*.35.23, Phlp. *in APr*.40.3. **-στροφος**, ον, *equally twisted, even*, χορδαί Nicom.*Harm*.6. II. = ἀντίστροφος, S.E.*M*.7.6, Ammon. *in APr*.35.26: coupled with ἀντίστρ., Herm. *in Phdr*.p.189 A.; ἀνάγκη πᾶν πρὸς πᾶν ἢ ἰ. εἶναι ἢ ἕτερον Dam. *Pr*.312. **-σύγκρῐτος**, ον, gloss on ἀμφήριστος, Sch.Opp.*H*.1.90.

ἰσοσυλλᾰβ-έω, *have the same number of syllables*, A.D.*Pron*.11. 20, al., *PLit.Lond*.183. **-ία**, ἡ, *equality of syllables*, A.D.*Adv*.174. 16. **-ος**, ον, *having the same number of syllables*, Plu.2.739a, Hermog.*Id*.1.12, A.D.*Pron*.11.8, etc. Adv. -βως St.Byz. s. v. Ἄβαι, *EM*552.34.

ἰσο-σώμᾰτος or **-σωμος**, ον, glosses on ἀντίστοιχος, Sch.E.*Andr*.

745. **–τᾱγής**, ές, *corresponding in order*, Philol.6(v.l.); χῶραι *Theol.Ar.*51. **–τάλαντος** [τᾰ], ον, gloss on ἀτάλαντος, Hsch. **–ταυρος**, ον, *like a bull*, cj. in S.*OT*478 (lyr.).

ἰσοτάχ-εια [τᾰ], ἡ, *equal velocity*, Simp.*in Ph.*1019.23. **–έω**, *travel with equal velocity*, Thphr.*Fr.*89.11; τινι Ph.1.463, Hld.8.17. **–ής**, ές, *possessing equal velocity*, Arist.*Ph.*216ª20, al., Plb.10.44.9, Cleom.2.1, Ph.1.588; ἄτομοι Epicur.*Ep.*1 p.18 U., *Nat.*2.2; πλοῖα Ph.*Bel.*73.21; τινι Arist.*Ph.*240ª8: generally, *equally swift*, νίκης κρίσις *Epigr.Gr.*939.2 (Synnada). Adv. –χῶς Arist.*Mech.*848ª16, Sch.Epicur.*Ep.*1 p.8 U. II. *uniform in rate*, of the pulse, Gal. 8.459, Plb.10.44.13, Str.1.2.17. Adv. –χῶς Gal.9.454.

ἰσοτέλ-εια, ἡ, *condition of an* ἰσοτελής, *equality in tax and tribute*, X.*HG*2.4.25, *Vect.*4.12, *IG*2².109*b* 20, 276.13, al., *GDI*3077 (Mesembria), Ph.1.160, etc.: freq. in Boeot. Inscrr., **ϝισοτέλια** *IG*7.505, al. (Tanagra). **–εστος**, ον, (τελέω) *made exactly like, exact*, ἰ. μίμημα Nonn.*D.*18.247. 2. *coming at the last to all alike*, ἐπίκουρος, of Death, S.*OC*1220 (lyr.). **–ευτον**, τό, *leading to the same result*, Sch.Hermog. in Rh.4.169 W.

ἰσοτελής, ές (gen. sg. ἰσοτελοῦ (sic), *Epigr.Gr.*48), (τέλος) *bearing equal burdens*; at Athens and elsewh., of a favoured class of μέτοικοι, subject to the same taxation as the citizens, Lys.*Fr.*225 S., Is.*Fr.*45, D.20.29, Arist.*Ath.*58.2, *IG*2².276.15, al., cf. *SIG*742.44 (Ephesus, i B.C.); of freedmen, *IG*9(1).412 (Aetolia), Hsch. II. metaph., of Hera, [τῷ Διΐ] ἰ. his *consort*, Orph.*Fr.*163.

ἰσο-τενής, ές, *level*, [ἵπποι] τὰ νῶτα ἰσοτενεῖς Tim.Gaz.ap.Ar.Byz. *Epit.*147.4. **–τετράγωνος** [ᾰ], ον, *of four equal rectangles*, συναγωγή Ps.-Hero *Poliorc.*p.238 W. **–τεχνος**, ον, *equal in art* or *skill*, τινι *Epigr.Gr.*532 (Perinthus); τοῖν ἰ. αὐλητοῖν Plu.*Nob.*9.

ἰσότης, ητος, ἡ, (ἴσος) *equality*, Arist.*Metaph.*1054ᵇ3, etc.: in pl., Pl.*Lg.*733b; ἰ. χρόνου Id.*Prm.*140e: Math., ἰ. γεωμετρική *equality of ratios, proportion*, Id.*Grg.*508a; ἀναλογία ἰ. λόγων Arist.*EN*1131ª31. 2. esp. *political equality* or *justice*, personified in E.*Ph.*536, cf. Pl.*Lg.*757a; ἰ. πολιτική Plb.6.8.4, etc.: in dual, Pl.*Lg.*757b, cf. Arist.*Pol.*1302ª7, Isoc.7.21. II. *fair dealing, impartiality*, Men. *Mon.*259, Plb.2.38.8, *Ep.Col.*4.1. III. *equiformity*, of the earth, Epicur.*Nat.*11.10. (On the accent v. Hdn.Gr.1.83, 2.945; ἰσοτής is said to be Hellenistic by Moer.202.)

ἰσοτίμ-ημα [τῑ], gloss on ἰσωνία (–ονία cod.), Hsch. **–ία**, ἡ, *equality of privilege*, opp. πλεονεξία, X.*Hier.*8.10, cf. Str.8.5.4, Ph.1.160; ἐξ ἰσοτιμίας διαλέγεσθαί τινι to converse with him *as his equal*, Luc.*Pisc.*34. **–ος**, ον, *equal in honour* or *privilege*, Ἀπόλλων (i.e. sharing the honours paid to Zeus) *OGI*234.25 (Delph., iii B.C.), *CRAcad.Inscr.*1906.419 (Alabanda); ὁ θεὸς .. –ον παρέχι τράπεζαν τοῖς ὁποθενοῦν ἀφικνουμένοις *BCH*51.73 (Panamara); πίστις 1*Ep. Pet.*1.1; οἱ πρῶτοι καὶ ἰ. Plu.*Lys.*19, cf. Wilcken *Chr.*13.10 (i A.D.), Luc.*DMort.*24.3, etc.; πόλεις τισί D.Chr.41.2: Comp. –ότεροι, τοῖς κρατοῦσιν Id.39.4; τὸ ἰ., = ἰσοτιμία, Ph.2.246; of a person, *maintaining equality of privilege*, Hdn.2.4.9. Adv. –μως, τινάς τισιν ἄγειν Ath.5.177c; ζῶντα δικαίως καὶ ἰ. *OGI*544.34 (Ancyra, ii A.D.), cf. *CIG*4032.5 (ibid.), *IGRom.*3.195 (ibid.); ἰ. ἔχουσι πρὸς ἀλλήλους οἱ ὅροι Phlp.*in APr.*167.14, cf. Alex.Aphr. *in Metaph.*241.11. 2. generally, *equal in value*: hence, *equal*, ἁμάρτημα ἀκούσιον ἰ. ἑκουσίῳ Ph.2.248; τὸ ἰ. δυσέφικτον ἐν ταῖς ἀμοιβαῖς Hdn.2.3.6; ἰ. μάχη *evenly balanced*, Ael.*NA*10.1. 3. as title of rank at the Ptolemaic court, τῶν ἰσοτίμων τοῖς πρώτοις φίλοις *PRyl.*66 intr., 253 (ii B.C.), *Arch.Pap.* 6.372.

ἰσό-τοιχος, ον, *with equal walls* or *sides*, of ships, gloss on ἐΐσας, Hsch. **–τονία**, ἡ, in Music, *uniformity of pitch, level pitch*, Ptol. *Harm.*1.4 (pl.), Porph. *in Harm.*p.287 W. **–τονος**, ον, *pulling evenly*, βρόχος Gal.18(1).351, Paul.Aeg.6.102. II. *bearing the same accent*, Hermog.*Id.*1.12. 2. in Music, *of level (unvarying) pitch*, Ptol.*Harm.*1.4; but, *in unison*, ib.7, 2.1. III. generally, *equal, even*, ἰ. τῇ συγκρίσει τοῦ χρώματος Dsc.5.123. Adv. –νως *equally*, θυμιᾶσθαι Id.68.6. **–τράπεζος** [ᾰ], ον, *equal to the table*, i.e. *large enough to fill it*, κάκκαβος Antiph.182.2, cf. Philox.2.15. **–τρῑβής**, ές, in A.*Ag.*1443, σελμάτων ἰσοτριβής (cj. Pauw. pro ἰσοτρ–) *pressing* the benches *like others*. **–τῡπος**, ον, *shaped alike*, Nonn.*D.*1.448. II. *executed in duplicate*, ὁμολογία *PLond.*1.113 i65 (vi A.D.), cf. *PMasp.*32.79 (vi A.D.); misspelt σοιτυπος *POxy.*2134.29 (ii A.D.): Subst., ἰσότυπον, τό, *copy, counterpart* of a legal instrument, Just. *Nov.*7.12 *Ep.* **–τύραννος** [ῠ], ον, *despotic, absolute*, ἀρχή Arist. *Pol.*1270ᵇ14, D.H.5.70.

ἰσ-ουράνιος [ᾰ], α, ον, *high as heaven*, δόξα *Arch.Pap.*1.220 (Ptol.). **–ουργός**, όν, (ἔργον) *doing like things*, Phot.

ἰσο-ϋψής, ές, *of equal height*, Euc.11.34, al.; τείχει, νεῷ, Plb.8.4.4, Str.17.1.28:—also **–ϋψος**, ον, Gal.18(1).757. **–φᾰνής**, ές, *appearing like*, Nonn.*D.*9.233.

ἰσοφᾰρίζω [ῐ], = ἀντιφερίζω, *match oneself with, vie with*, οὐδέ τίς οἱ δύναται μένος ἰσοφαρίζειν Il.6.101; ἔργα δ' Ἀθηναίῃ .. ἰσοφαρίζοι 9.390; μνήμην οὔτινά φημι Σιμωνίδῃ –φαρίζειν Simon.146, cf. Theoc.7.30: generally, *to be equal to*, τινι Il.21.194, Hes.*Op.*490. II. trans., *make equal*, Nic.*Th.*572.

ἰσό-φθογγος, ον, *sounding equally*, Nonn.*D.*6.202. **–φονος**, ον, gloss on ἀντίφονος, Sch.A.*Th.*895. **–φορία**, ἡ, *equal* or *regular movement*, ὀρχηστοῦ Poll.4.97. **–φόριος**, ον, dub. sens. in *POxy.* 1684.4 (iv A.D.). **–φόρος**, ον, *bearing* or *drawing equal weights, equal in strength*, βόες .. ἥλικες, ἰσοφόροι Od.18.373; τὰ σκέλη τοῖς ὤμοις –φόρα ἔχειν X.*Smp.*2.20. II. proparox., *moving regularly*, Poll.4.97.

ἴσοφρυς, ὁ, name of a *plant*, Herm.Trism. in *Rev.Phil.*32.252.

ἰσό-φρων, ονος, ὁ, ἡ, *fair-minded*, εὐθυντήρ *IG*9(1).877 (Corc., i B.C.). **–φυής**, ές, *of equal growth*, i.e. *symmetrical*, coined as etym. of ὀσφύς, Arist.*HA*493ª23. 2. *like in character*, Thphr.*HP* 3.7.4. **–φωτον**, τό, name of an *eyesalve*, Aët.7.112 (109 Lat. vers.). **–χειλής**, ές, *level with the brim*, κριθαὶ ἰσοχειλεῖς grains of malt *floating level with the brims* of the vessels, i.e. on the surface of the liquor, X.*An.*4.5.26; ζωρὸν κεράσας ἰσοχειλέα *AP*6.105 (Apollonid.); ἰ. τὴν κάτω σιαγόνα ποιήσας [ὁ βάτραχος] *level with the surface of the water*, Arist.*HA*536ª16: c. dat., Εὐφράτης ἰ. τῇ γῇ Arr.*An.*7.7.5; *equally full*, Max.Tyr.31.2. **–χειλος**, ον, = foreg., τῇ γῇ *Gp.* 12.19.4, cf. 13.15.8. **–χειρ**, χειρος, ὁ, ἡ, *ambidextrous*, Philostr. *Gym.*41. **–χνοος**, ον, *equally woolly with*, τινι *AP*6.252 (Antiphil.). **–χοιρον**, Achaean for βούθουτον (i.e. βούθυτον), Hsch. s.h.v. **–χοος**, ον, *of the same number of* χόες, ὄξος ἰ. ὕδατι Hp. *Morb.*2.26. **–χορδος**, ον, *with like strings*, Hsch. s.v. ἀντίχορδα.

ἰσοχρον-έω, *to be as old as*, τινι Luc.*Syr.D.*3; *to have the same period* of maturity, τὸ μὴ –χρονεῖν τὰ σπέρματα καθάπερ καὶ τὰ ζῷα Thphr.*CP*4.11.9. II. Gramm., *have the same number of time-units*, of syllables, A.D.*Synt.*257.16; of feet, –χρονοῦντες πόδες Aristid.Quint.1.23. **–ιος**, ον, = sq., Thphr.*CP*4.11.2, Euc.*Phaen.* p.4 M., al., Hero *Dioptr.*38; στροφή Cleom.2.4; διαστήματα Ptol. *Tetr.*36: c. dat., τὸ –χρόνιον εἶναι τὸ παρὰ φύσιν τῷ κατὰ φύσιν Simp. *in Cael.*430.6. Adv. –ίως Ptol.*Alm.*13.2, Heph.Astr.1.10; τῷ ἡλίῳ Theo Sm.p.171 H. **–ος**, ον, *equal in period of revolution*, οἱ ἀπλανεῖς ἀστέρες ἰσόχρονοί εἰσιν ἀλλήλων Eudox.*Ars*16.15; *equal in period* of maturity, cj. in Thphr.*CP*1.18.3 (περισσόχρονος codd., παρισό– Schneid., alternatively). 2. *contemporary*, *Gloss.*; τινος *Vit. Theoc.* 3. *even, regular*, σφυγμός Gal.8.830. 4. Adv. –νως Eudox.*Ars*5.8, Gem.6.27, S.E.*M.*5.83, Ruf.*Syn.Puls.*3. II. Gramm., *consisting of the same number of time-units*, A.D.*Synt.*272.23, Hermog.*Id.*1.12, Aristid.Quint.1.23.

ἰσό-χροος, ον, *of uniform colour*, Dsc.2.146. **–χρῡσος**, ον, *like gold, worth its weight in gold*, Archipp.49, Archestr.*Fr.*15.3. II. ἰσόχρυσον, τό, name of an *eyesalve*, *CIL*13.10021.85, Gal.12.785. **–ψηφία**, ἡ, *equality of votes*, D.H.7.64. II. *equal right to vote*, Plu.*CG*9. **–ψηφιστής**, οῦ, ὁ, *valuer*, cj. for –ψίστης in *Gloss.* **–ψηφος**, ον, *with* or *by an equal number of votes*, ἢν ἰ. κριθῇ A.*Eu.*741; ἰ. δίκη ib.795. II. *having an equal vote with* others, ξύμμαχοι Th.1.141, cf. 3.11; of a commander, ib.79; ποιεῖν [δύναμιν] ἰσόψηφόν τινι Pl.*Lg.*692a; of communities, *possessing an equal franchise*, ἐλευθερώσας τήνδ' ἰ. πόλιν E.*Supp.*353. 2. *voting alike*, D.H.4.20. III. *equal in numerical value*, of words *in which the values of letters added together make up the same sum*, "Δαμαγόραν" καὶ "λοιμὸν" ἰσόψηφόν τις ἀκούσας (both words make up 270), *AP*11.334; ἰσόψηφος δυσὶ τούτοις "Γάϊος" ὡς "ἅγιος", ὡς "ἀγαθὸς" προλέγω *IGRom.*4.743 (Eumenia), cf. Gell.14.6.4, Artem.3.34, 4.24; for examples cf. the epigrams of Leonidas, *AP*6.321 sqq. 2. ἰ. ἐστία, name of a plaster, containing a number of drachms *equal to the numerical value* of its name, Nech.ap.Aët.15.13. **–ψιστος** and **–ψίστης**, = *aestimator*, *Gloss.* (dub.). **–ψῡχος**, ον, *of equal spirit*, κράτος ἰ. A.*Ag.*1470 (lyr.). Adv. –χως, μάχεσθαι Eust.831.52. 2. *of like soul* or *mind*, *Ep.Phil.*2.20.

ἰσόω [ῑ, exc. in Od. l.c.], *make equal*, τινί τι S.*El.*686, Ar.*V.*565 (dub.l.), Hp.*Morb.*4.39:—Med., ὄνυχας χεῖράς τε ἰσώσαντο *they made* their nails and hands *alike*, i.e. used them in like manner, Hes.*Sc.* 263:—Pass. (with aor. 1 Med.), *to be made like* or *equal to*, τοῖσίν κεν ἐν ἄλγεσιν ἰσωσαίμην Od.7.212; θεοῖσι μέν νυν οὐκ ἰσούμενόν σ' .. κρίνοντες S.*OT*31, cf. 581, Hp. l.c.: abs., ἰσούμενος, opp. κρείττων, Pl. *Phdr.*239a; *to be made level*, of a bank, *POxy.*1674.7 (iii A.D.).

Ἱσπᾱνία, ἡ, *Spain*, *Mon.Anc.Gr.*16.1, Str.3.4.19, Agathem.7; ἀπὸ τῆς Ἰβηρίας ἢ Ἱσπανίας ἢ ὅπως ἄν τις ὀνομάζειν ἐθέλῃ Gal.12.388; τὴν Ἰβηρίαν τε καὶ **Σπανίαν** (v.l. Ἱσπανίαν) ὀνομαζομένην Id.6.613, cf. 12.428, D.S.5.37.

Ἱσπᾱνός, ή, όν, *Spanish*, μάχαιραι Ph.*Bel.*71.14, etc.: **Ἱσπανόν**, τό, a kind of oil, in form **Σπᾶνον** or **Σπανόν**, Gal.10.551, 790, 822, 12.513, *POxy.*2052 (vi A.D.), *Gp.*9.26; ἡ **Σπάνη** [λιθάργυρος] Dsc.5.87.

ἰσσα, exclam. of malicious triumph over another's distress, Pl. Com.66, Men.36; ἰσσᾷ Herod.3.94. (Onomatop.; cf. σίττα.)

ἴσσασθαι· κληροῦσθαι, Λέσβιοι, Hsch.

ἰσσέλα, ἰτθέλα, v. ἰξαλῆ.

ἰσσόθεος, v. ἰσόθεος fin.

ἴσσυπος, = ὕσσωπος, *PGoodsp.Cair.*30.42 (ii A.D.).

ἱστάνω, later collat. form of ἵστημι, first in inf. ἱστάνειν, (ἀνθ–) *PPetr.*2 p.120 (iii B.C.), (καθ–) *Michel*1006.22 (Teos, ii B.C.), (συν–) Plb.3.108.4, (ἀποκαθ–) Ascl.*Tact.*10.9, cf. Dsc.4.43, etc.; cf. ἱστάναι Ἀττικοί, ἱστάνειν Ἕλληνες Moer.200; part. (ἐφ)ιστάνοντες Plb.11.2.5; τὸ ἱστάνον Simp.*in Ph.*1257.34: ind. ἱστάνει Philistio ap.Ath.3.115e, ἱστάνομεν *Ep.Rom.*3.31, (παρ)ιστάνουσι Phld.*Rh.*1.266 S., etc.: impf. (συν)ἵστανον Plb.4.5.6, (δι–) App.*Hisp.*36, etc.:—Pass., ἱστανόμενος *IG*2².1343.26 (i B.C.):—introduced by the copyists into Lys. 25.3, Is.2.29, etc.

ἱστάριον, τό, Dim. of ἱστός, Men.142, *PLond.*5.1728.13 (vi A.D.), Choerob. *in Theod.*1.332.

ἱστάρχης, ου, ὁ, = ἱστωνάρχης, *Ostr.*1155.

ἱστάω, collat. form of ἵστημι, 3 sg. pres. ἱστᾷ Hdt.2.143, 4.103: impf. ἵστα Id.2.106 (v.l. ἵστη): freq. in later Gr., (καθ–) *UPZ*18.11 (ii B.C.), Aristeas 228, (συν–) Str.9.5.16, cf. Dsc.1.129 (v.l. in 4.43), Aesop.340, Them.*Or.*23.292c, etc.

ἱστεῖον, τό, = ἱστεών, *PCair.Zen.*176.323 (iii B.C.): gen. pl. written ἱστέων *BGU*1359, al., *PTeb.ined.*703.90.

ἰστέον, (*εἴδω, οἶδα) *one must see*, ἰστέον δή Pl.*Tht.*202e; *ἰ.* ἤδη τί ἐστι τὸ πρᾶγμα Id.*Smp.*217c. II. *one must know*, Gal.5.480, Sch. Nic.*Th.*11.

ἱστεών, ῶνος, ὁ, *weaving-shed*, Men.*Sam.*19: censured by Phryn. 144.

ἵστημι (cf. ἱστάω, ἱστάνω), I. causal, *make to stand*, imper. ἵστη Il.21.313, E.*Supp.*1230, καθ-ίστα Il.9.202: impf. ἵστην, Ep. ἵστασκε Od.19.574; 3 pl. ἵσταν B.10.112: fut. στήσω, Dor. στασῶ Theoc.5.54: aor. 1 ἔστησα, Ep. 3 pl. ἔστᾰσαν for ἔστησαν dub. in Od.18.307, 3.182, 8.435, al. (v. ἔστᾰσαν): hence, in late Poets, ἔστᾰσας, ἔστᾰσε, *AP*9.714, 708 (Phil.): aor. 1 Med. ἐστησάμην (never intr.), v. infr. A. III. 2, 3: pf. ἕστᾰκα Cerc.3, (καθ-) Hyp.*Eux.*28, *UPZ* 112.5 (ii B.C.), (περι-) Pl.*Ax.*370d, (ἀφ-) Lxx *Je.*16.5, (παρ-) Phld.*Rh.* 1.9 S., al., (συν-) S.E.*M.*7.109; also ἕστηκα (v. infr.) in trans. sense, (δι-) Arist.*Vent.*973ᵃ18, (ἀφ-) v.l. in Lxx l. c.; ἑστακεῖα trans. in *Test. Epict.*1.25. II. intr., *stand*, 1. Act., aor. 2 ἔστην, Ep. στάσκον Il.3.217; 3 pl. ἔστησαν, more freq. in Hom. ἔσταν, στάν [ᾰ]; imper. στῆθι, Dor. στᾶθι Sapph.29, Theoc. 23.38; subj. στῶ, Ep. 2 and 3 sg. στήῃς, στήῃ (for στῇς, στῇ), Il.17.30, 5.598; 1 pl. στέωμεν (as disyll.) 22.231, στείομεν 15.297; opt. σταίην, Ep. 3 pl. σταίησαν 17.733; inf. στῆναι, Ep. στήμεναι 17.167, Od.5.414, Dor. στᾶμεν Pi.*P.*4.2; part. στάς: pf. ἕστηκα: plpf. ἑστήκειν, sts. with strengthd. augm. εἱστήκειν, as E.*HF*925, Ar.*Av.*513, Th.1.89, etc.; Ion. 3 sg. ἑστήκεε Hdt. 7.152:—from Hom. downwds. the shorter dual and pl. forms of the pf. are preferred, ἕστᾰτον, ἕστᾰμεν, ἕστᾰτε, ἑστᾶσι (*IG*12(8).356 (Thasos, vi B.C.), etc.), in Hdt. ἑστέᾱσι; imper. ἕστᾰθι Aristomen. 5; subj. ἑστῶ; opt. ἑσταίην; inf. ἑστάναι, Ep. ἑστάμεν, ἑστάμεναι (ἑστηκέναι only late, as Ael.*VH*3.18); part. ἑστώς (ἑστηκώς rare in early Gr., Hdt.2.126, Pl.*Men.*93d, *Lg.*802c, Arist. (infr. B. II. 2), Alex.126.16, εἱστηκότα *IG*1².374.179), fem. ἑστῶσα (not ἑστυῖα; but συνεστηκυιῶν prob. in Hp.*Aër.*10), neut. ἑστός Pl.*Ti.*40b, *Tht.* 183e, *SIG*1234 (Lycia), etc., (καθ-) *POxy.*68.32 (ii A.D.), (ἐν-) *PRyl.* 98(*a*).10 (ii A.D.), (παρ-) Ar.*Eq.*564 (-ώς freq. v.l. as in Pl. and Ar. ll. cc., preferred by Choerob. *in Theod.*2.313); gen. ἑστῶτος; Ion. ἑστεώς, ἑστεός, ῶτος; Ep. ἑστηώς Hes.*Th.*747; dat. pl. ἑστηῶσι cj. in Antim.16.5, cf. Call.*Dian.*134; Hom. does not use the nom., but has gen. ἑστᾰότος, acc. ἑστᾰότα, nom. pl. ἑστᾰότες, as if from ἑσταώς: so also plpf. ἑστάτην, ἕστᾰμεν, ἕστᾰτε, ἕστᾰσαν: late pres. ἑστήκω, formed from pf., Posidipp.ap.Ath.10.412e: hence, fut. ἑστήξω Hom. *Epigr.*15.14, X.*Cyr.*6.2.17, Hegesipp.1.25, ἑστήξομαι X.*Cyn.*10.9 codd. 2. **Pass.**, ἵσταμαι: imper. ἵστασο Hes.*Sc.*449, ἵστω S.*Ph.* 893, Ar.*Ec.*737: impf. ἱστάμην: fut. στᾰθήσομαι And.3.34, Aeschin. 3.103: more freq. στήσομαι Il.20.90, etc.: aor. ἐστάθην Od.17.463, etc.; rarely ἔστην, Dor. 3 sg. ἔσστα *SIG*56.43 (Argos, v B.C.): pf. ἕσταμαι (δι-) v.l. in Pl.*Ti.*81d, κατεστέαται v.l. in Hdt.1.196. (From I.-E. *sthā-*, cf. Skt. *sthā-* (aor. *á-sthā-t*), Lat. *stare*, etc.; Gr. redupl. pres. and pf. fr. *si-sthā-*, *se-sthā-*.)

A. Causal, *make to stand, set up*, πελέκεας ἑξείης Od.19.574; ἔγχος μέν ῥ' ἔστησε φέρων πρὸς κίονα *he set* it against the pillar, 1.127, cf. Il. 15.126; *ἱ.* ἱστόν *set up* the loom, or *raise* the mast (v. ἱστός I and II); κρητῆρας στήσασθαι *to have* bowls *set up*, Od.2.431; θεοῖς.. κρητῆρα στήσασθαι in honour of the gods, Il.6.528; στῆσαί τινα ὀρθόν, στ. ὀρθὰν καρδίαν, Pi.*P.*3.53, 96; ὀρθῷ στ. ἐπὶ σφυρῷ Id.*I.*7(6).13; ἐς ὀρθὸν *ἱ.* τινά E.*Supp.*1230; ὁ Ξανθίας τὸν φαλλὸν ὀρθὸν στησάτω Ar.*Ach.*243; ὀρθὸν οὖς ἵστησιν S.*El.*27; στῆσαι λόγχας, for battle, Id.*Ant.*145 (lyr.); esp. *raise* buildings, statues, trophies, etc., *ἱ.* ἀνδριάντα Hdt.2.110; τροπαῖα S.*Tr.*1102; τροπαῖον *ἱ.* τῶν πολεμίων Isoc.4.150, cf. *IG*2².1457.26; τροπαῖον στησάμενοι X.*HG*2.4.7; τροπαῖον ἂν στήσαιτο τῶν ταύτης τρόπων Ar.*Pl.*453; τὰ μακρὰ στῆσαι τείχη Th.1.69; *ἱ.* τινὰ χαλκοῦν *set* him *up* in brass, *raise* a brazen statue to him, D.13.21, 19.261 (so in pf., *stand*, οὗτος ἕστηκε λίθινος Hdt.2.141:—Pass., σφυρήλατος ἐν Ὀλυμπίᾳ σταθήτι Pl.*Phdr.*236b; σταθῆναι χαλκοῦς Arist.*Rh.*1410ᵃ33). II. *set, place*, of things or persons, τρίποδ' ἔστασαν ἐν πυρί Od.8.435, etc.; ὥς σ' ἄγχι γῆς στήσωσι Καδμείας S.*OC*399, etc.; *fix*, τοὺς ὀφθαλμοὺς εἰς τὴν γῆν Philostr.*VA*1.10; esp. *set* men *in order* or *array*, πεζοὺς δ' ἐξόπιθε στῆσεν Il.4.298, cf. 2.525, etc.; στῆσαί τινας τελευταίους X. *Cyr.*6.3.25, etc. III. *bring to a standstill, stay, check*, λαὸν δὲ στήσον Il.6.433; νέας, ἵππους, ἡμιόνους στῆσαι, Od.3.182, Il.5.755, 24. 350; μύλην στῆσαι *to stop* the mill, Od.20.111; στῆσεν ἄρ' (sc. ἡμιόνους) 7.4; στῆσε δ' ἐν Ἀμνισῷ (sc. νῆα) 19.188; βᾶριν Iamb.*Myst.*6. 5; στῆσαι τὴν φάλαγγα *halt* it, X.*Cyr.*7.1.5; ἵστησι ῥοῦν Pl.*Cra.*437b, etc.; *ἱ.* τὴν ψυχὴν ἐπὶ τοῖς πράγμασιν ib.437a; στ. τὰ ὄμματα *fix* them, of a dying man, Id.*Phd.*118; στ. τὸ πρόσωπον *compose* the countenance, X.*Cyr.*1.3.9; στήσαντες ἐπὶ τούτων τὴν διήγησιν Plb. 3.2.6: esp. in Medic., *ἱ.* κοιλίαν Dsc.1.20; τὰς κοιλίας Philotim.ap. Orib.4.10.1; αἱμορραγίας Dsc.1.129: abs., Arist.*HA*605ᵃ29:—Med., ἱστάμενος τῷ νοσήματι Hp.*Ep.*19 (*Hermes* 53.65). 2. *set on foot, stir up*, κονίης.. ἱστᾶσιν ὀμίχλην Il.13.336; ἵστη δὲ μέγα κῦμα 21. 313; νεφέλην ἔστησε Κρονίων Od.12.405, cf. Il.5.523; of battle, etc., φυλόπιδα στήσειν *stir up* strife, Od.11.314; ἔριν στήσαντες 16.292 (so intr. φύλοπις ἕστηκε the fray *is on foot*, Il.18.172):—also in Med., στησάμενοι δ' ἐμάχοντο ib.533, Od.9.54; πολέμους ἵστασθαι Hdt.7. 9.β', 175, 236; so ἱστάναι βοήν A.*Ch.*885; κραυγήν E.*Or.*1529 (Pass., θόρυβος ἵσταται βοῆς *arises*, S.*Ph.*1263); also of passions and states of mind, μῆνιν, ἐλπίδα στῆσαι, Id.*OT*699, E.*IA*788 (lyr.). 3. *set up, appoint*, τινὰ βασιλέα Hdt.1.97; τύραννον S.*OT*940, cf. *OC*1041, *Ant.*666:—Med., ἐστάσαντο τύραννον Alc.37A; φύλακας στησόμεθα Pl.*R.*484d:—Pass., ὁ ὑπὸ Δαρείου σταθεὶς ὕπαρχος Hdt.7.105, cf. *IG* 9(1).32.23 (Stiris, ii B.C.). 4. *establish, institute*, χορούς, παννυχίδα, Hdt.3.48, 4.76 (so στήσασθαι ἤθεά τε καὶ νόμους Id.2.35; ἀγῶνα *h.Ap.*150); στῆσαι χορόν, Ὀλυμπιάδα, ἑορτάν, Pi.*P.*9.114, *O.*2.3, 10(11).58; κτερίσματα S.*El.*433; χορούς B.10.112, D.21.51; οὐχ ὑγιῶς ἱστάμενος λόγον *setting up* a bad argument, Anon.Lond.26. 34:—Pass., ἀγορὴ ἵσταταί τινι Hdt.6.58. 5. = Lat. *statuere, determine*, γνῶναι καὶ στῆσαι D.H.8.68; διαγεινώσκειν καὶ ἱστάναι *Not. Arch.*4.21 (Aug.):—Pass., τὰ ὑπό τινος σταθέντα *OGI*665.27 (Egypt, i A.D.); τὰ ἑσταμένα Wilcken *Chr.*167.27 (ii B.C.). 6. *fix by agreement*, ὁ σταθεὶς τόκος *PGrenf.*1.31.1 (i B.C.), cf. *PFlor.*14.11 (iv A.D.); τὸ ἑσταμένον ἐνοίκιον *BGU*253.15 (iii A.D.). 7. *bring about, cause*, ἀμπνοάν Pi.*P.*4.199; στῆσαι δύσκηλον χθόνα *make* its case desperate, A.*Eu.*825. IV. *place in the balance, weigh*, Il.19.247, 22.350, 24.232, Ar.*V.*40; [ἐκπώματα] Thphr.*Char.*18.7; ἀριθμοῦντες καὶ μετροῦντες καὶ ἱστάντες X.*Cyr.*8.2.21, etc.; ἱστάναι τι πρὸς ἀργύριον *weigh* a thing against silver, Hdt.2.65; ἀγαθὸς ἱστάναι good *at weighing*, Pl.*Prt.*356b; τὸ ἐγγὺς καὶ τὸ πόρρω στήσας ἐν τῷ ζυγῷ ibid., cf. Lys.10.18; ἐπὶ τὸ ἱστάναι ἐλθεῖν have recourse to *the scales*, Pl.*Euthphr.*7c:—Pass., ἵστασθαι ἐπὶ ζυγοῦ Arr.*Epict.*1. 29.15; σταθεὶς *weighed*, *IG*11(2).161*B*113 (Delos, iii B.C.). 2. *weigh out, pay*, Lxx 3*Ki.*21.39, cf. *Za.*11.12, *Ev.Matt.*26.15.

B. Pass. and intr. tenses of Act., *to be set* or *placed, stand*, Hom. etc., ἀγχοῦ, ἆσσον, Il.2.172, 23.97; ἄντα τινός 17.30; ἐς μέσσον Od.17. 447; σταθεὶς ἐς μέσον Hdt.3.130; ἀντίοι ἔσταν, ἐναντίοι ἔστησαν, Il.1. 535, Od.10.391: prov. of critical circumstances, ἐπὶ ξυροῦ ἵσταται ἀκμῆς Il.10.173: freq. merely a stronger form of εἶναι, *to be* in a certain place or state, ἀργύρεοι σταθμοὶ ἐν χαλκέῳ ἕστασαν οὐδῷ Od.7. 89, etc.; ἑστάτω for ἔστω, S.*Aj.*1084; τὰ νῦν ἑστῶτα, = τὰ νῦν, Id. *Tr.*1271 (anap.); ἐμοὶ δ' ἄχος ἕστᾰκεν Id.*Aj.*200 (lyr.): with Adv., ξυμφορᾶς ἵν' ἕσταμεν, ἵν' ἕστ. χρείας, in what case or need *we are*, Id. *Tr.*1145, *OT*1442; ποῦ τύχης ἕστηκεν; Id.*Aj.*102; later also ἀδίκως, ὀρθῶς, εὐλαβῶς ἵστασθαι, *behave* wrongly, etc., Plb.18.3.2, 33.6.3, 18.33. 4. 2. *take up an* intellectual *attitude*, ὡς ἵστασθαι δεῖ περὶ χρημάτων κτήσεως Phld.*Oec.*p.38 J.; οὐκ ὀρθῶς *ἱ.* Id.*Rh.*1.53 S. 3. in pregnant sense, στῆναι ἐς.. Hdt.9.21; στ. ἐς δίκην E.*IT*962; στ. παρά τινα Il.24. 169 (but οἱ μὴ στάντες παρὰ τὰ δεινά those who did not *face* the danger, D.H.9.28): c. acc. loci, τί τοῦτ' αἰθερίαν ἕστηκε πέτραν; E.*Supp.*987 (lyr.); στῆτε τόνδε τρίβον Id.*Or.*1251: c. acc. cogn., ποίαν μ' ἀνάστασιν δοκεῖς.. στῆναι; S.*Ph.*277. II. *stand still, halt*, ἀλλ' ἄγε δὴ στέωμεν Il.11.348, cf. Od.6.211, 10.97; opp. φεύγω, 6.199, etc.; *stand idle*, Il.4.243, al.; ἑστάναι *to be stationary*, opp. κινεῖσθαι, Pl.*R.*436c, etc.; κατὰ χώρην ἑστάναι Hdt.4.97; οὐ μὴν ἐνταῦθ' ἕστηκε τὸ πρᾶγμα *does* not *rest* here, D.21.102, cf. 10.36; ἐὰν ἡ κοιλία στῇ if the bowels *are constipated*, Arist.*HA*588ᵃ8: c. part., οὐ στήσεται ἀδικῶν D.10.10; *come to a stop, rest satisfied*, ἄν τις ὀρθῶς ἐπιβάλῃ, ἔπειτα σταθῇ Epicur. *Fr.*423; οὐχ ἱστάμενοι Plot.3.1.2: impers., ἵσταται *there is a stop, one comes to a stop*, Arist.*APr.*43ᵃ37, al.; οὐκ ἔστη ἐνταῦθα κακοῖς γενομένοις ἀποθανεῖν Plot.3.2.8; also ἵστασθαι μέχρι τοῦ γένους Them.*in APo.* 55.8, al. 2. metaph., *stand firm*, X.*HG*5.2.23; τῇ διανοίᾳ Plb.21. 11.3; of arguments or propositions, *hold good*, Phld.*Rh.*1.83, 2.192 S.: part., ἑστηκὼς *fixed, stable*, Arist.*GA*776ᵃ35, *EN*1104ᵃ4, *Metaph.* 1047ᵃ15; δεῖ τὸ κρίμα ἑστηκὸς καὶ κύριον εἶναι *SIG*826 ii 29 (Delph., ii B.C.); λογισμὸς ἑστὼς καὶ νουνεχής Plb.3.105.9; τέχναι οὐκ ἔχουσαι τὸ ἑστηκός, ἀλλὰ τὸ στοχαστικόν Phld.*Rh.*1.71 S. (so Adv. ἑστηκότως, opp. στοχαστικῶς, ib.70 S.), cf. Iamb.*Protr.*21.κ'; χρεία ἑστηκυῖα καὶ τεταγμένη Plb.6.25.10; ἑστηκότα θεωρήματα, ἑστηκότες σκοποί, Phld.*Rh.*1.2 S., *Po.*5.22; of age, ἑστηκυῖα ἡλικία Pl.*Lg.*802c; τιμαὶ ἑστηκυῖαι *fixed* prices, *PTeb.ined.*703.177. III. *to be set up* or *upright, stand up, rise up*, κρημνοὶ ἕστασαν Il.12.55; ὀρθαὶ τρίχες ἔσταν 24.359, cf. A.*Th.*564 (lyr.), Pl.*Ion* 535c, etc.; κονίη ἵστατο Il.2.151; ἵστατο κῦμα 21.240; of a horse, ἵστασθαι ὀρθός *to rear*, Hdt.5.111; ἵστασθαι βάθρων *from* the steps, S.*OT*143. 2. *to be set up, erected*, or *built*, στήλη, ἥ τ' ἐπὶ τύμβῳ ἑστήκῃ Il.17.435; ἕστακε τροπαῖον A. *Th.*954 (lyr.); μνημεῖον Ar.*Eq.*268, etc.; v. supr. A. II. 3. generally, *arise, begin*, ἵστατο νεῖκος Il.13.333; cf. A. III. 2. 4. in marking Time, ἔαρος νέον ἱσταμένοιο when spring *is* not long *begun*, Od.19.519; ἕβδομος ἑστήκει μείς the seventh month *was begun*, Il. 19.117; τοῦ μὲν φθίνοντος μηνός, τοῦ δ' ἱσταμένοιο as one month ends and the next *begins*, Od.14.162, cf. Hes.*Op.*780; later μὴν ἱστάμενος, μεσῶν, φθίνων, first in Hdt.6.57, 106, cf. And.1.121, Aeschin.3.67; σχεδὸν ἤδη μεσημβρία ἵσταται Pl.*Phdr.*242a. 5. *to be appointed*, στῆναι ἐς ἀρχήν Hdt.3.80; v. supr. A. III. 3.

ἱστία, ἱστία, ἱστίη, Ἱστίη, Ἱστιαία, v. ἑστία. **Ἱστιαϊκός**, ή, όν, *Histiaean*, of currency, *BCH*2.579, 6.51, 35.260 (Delos). **ἱστίασις**, εως, ἡ, = ἑστίασις, *POxy.*471.53 (ii A.D.). **ἱστιατορία**, ἡ, = ἑστ., *feast*, *PTeb.*584 (ii A.D.). **ἱστιάτωρ**, v. ἑστιάτωρ. **ἱστιητόριον**, and **-ᾱτόριον**, v. ἑστιατόριον.

ἱστιο-δρομέω, *run under full sail*, Hp.*Ep.*17, Plb.1.60.9, D.S.3. 28. **-κωπος** (sc. ναῦς), ἡ, *with oars and sails*, a type of boat, Gell. 10.25.5.

ἱστίον, τό (Dim. of ἱστός in form only), *web, cloth, sheet*: hence in pl., *hangings*, Lxx *Ex.*27.9, 15; as a measure, *piece*, *PRyl.*70.25 (ii B.C.); but, II. from Hom. downwds., *sail*, mostly in pl. ἱστία, ἕλκον δ' ἱστία λευκὰ.. βοεῦσιν they hauled *them* up with ox-hide ropes, Od.2.426; τέταθ' ἱστία *the sails* were spread, 11.11, cf. Pi. *N.*5.51; ἱστία στέλλεσθαι, μηρύεσθαι, καθελεῖν, to lower or furl *sail* (v. sub vocc.): λύειν Od.15.496; ἱστίοισι χρᾶσθαι Hdt.4.110; ἄκροισι χρώμενος τοῖς ἱστίοις Ar.*Ra.*1000: prov., πλήρεσιν *ἱ.* under full *sail*, with all one's might, Philostr.*VS*1.25.5, cf. Suid.: rarely in sg., ἐν δ' ἄνεμος πρῆσεν μέσον ἱστίον Il.1.481; ἐξίει ἱ. ἀνεμόεν Pi.*P*.1.92; ἱστίῳ καταπετάσαι τινά Pl.*Prm*.131b, cf. *PMagd*.11.7 (iii B.C.).

ἱστιο-πετής, *velivolus*, Gloss. **-ποιέομαι**, Pass., *to be furnished with sails*, of ships, Str.15.1.15. **-ρράφος** [ᾰ], ὁ, (ῥάπτω) *sail-patcher*, *CIG*9175, Poll.7.160. 2. metaph., *tricky*, *cheating fellow*, Ar.*Th*.935:—also **ἱστιαρράφος**, Gramm. in Reitzenstein *Ind.Lect. Rost*.1892/3 p.4.

ἱστο-βοεύς, έως, Ion. ῆος, ὁ, *plough-tree* or *pole*, Hes.*Op*.435, cf. A.R.3.1318: prov., ἱστοβοῆι γέροντι νέην ποτίβαλλε κορώνην put a new tip on the old *plough*, of an old man marrying a young wife, Orac.ap.Paus.9.37.4.—Acc. ἱστοβόην, prob. f.l. for ἱστοβοῆ, *AP*6.104 (Phil.). **-δόκη**, ἡ, *mast-holder*, a piece of wood standing up from the stern, on which the mast rested when let down, Il.1.434; glossed by **-θήκη**, Sch.D ad loc., *EM*478.30. **-κεραία**, ἡ, *sail-yard*, Orph.*A*.696, Artem.1.35. **-πέδη**, Dor. **-πέδα**, ἡ, *a piece of wood* set in the keel *to which the mast was bound*, or, *a hole* in the keel *for stepping the mast*, Od.12.51,162, Alc.18.6. **-ποδες**, οἱ, = κελέοντες, *the long beams of the loom*, between which the web was stretched, *AP*7.424 (Antip. Sid.): sg., Eub.145, *POxy*.264.5 (i A.D.). **-ποιία**, ἡ, *loom-making*, Sch.Nic.*Th*.11. **-πόνος**, ον, *working at the loom*, *AP*6.48, Man.4.423; Παλλάς *AP*6.247 (Phil.); κερκίδες ib.9.778 (Id.); v.l. for ἱστότονος, Ar.*Ra*.1315.

ἱστορ-έω, (ἵστωρ) *inquire into* or *about* a thing, τι Hdt.2.113, A.*Pr*.632, etc.; περί τινος Plb.3.48.12; also, *inquire about* a person, τινα S.*OT*1150, 1156; ὅδ' εἴμ' Ὀρέστης..ὃν ἱστορεῖς E.*Or*.380, cf. *Tr*.261: folld. by relat. clause, Αἴγισθον ἔνθ' ᾤκηκεν ἱστορῶ S.*El*.1101. 2. *examine*, *observe*, χώραν, πόλιν, Plu.*Thes*.30, *Pomp*.40, cf. J.*AJ*1.11.4; τὴν τοῦ Μέμνονος [σύριγγα] *OGI*694.7; τὴν σύνεσίν τινος Plu.*Cic*.2, etc.; τινὰς ἀπολουμένους Gal.11.109: hence, *to be informed about*, *know*, κακῶς τὸ μέλλον ἱστορῶν A.*Pers*.454; πατέρα ἱστορεῖς καλῶς Id.*Eu*.455, cf. Hp.*Praec*.12: metaph., εἴ τις ἀκτὶς ἡλίου νιν ἱστορεῖ βλέποντα *has news of* him, A.*Ag*.676: folld. by relat., τὴν πορείαν ἱστορῶν, ὡς δυσδίοδος ὑπάρχει Plb.3.61.3; *read in history*, Id.1.63.7. 2. c. acc. pers., *inquire of*, *ask*, ἱστορέων αὐτοὺς ἥντινα δύναμιν ἔχει ὁ Νεῖλος Hdt.2.19, cf. 3.77; *inquire of an oracle*, E.*Ion* 1547; *visit* a person for the purpose of inquiry, Κηφᾶν *Ep.Gal*.1.18:—Pass., *to be questioned*, κληθέντας ἱστορέεσθαι εἰ.. Hdt.1.24; ἱστορούμενος S.*Tr*.415, E.*Hel*.1371. b. c. dupl. acc., *inquire of* one *about* a thing, τί μ' ἱστορεῖς τόδε Id.*Ph*.621, cf. Lyc.1. 4. abs., *inquire*, ἀκοῇ ἱ. Hdt.2.29, etc.; esp. in part., ἱστορέων εὕρισκε Id.1.56, etc.; οὔθ' ὁρῶν οὔθ' ἱστορῶν S.*OT*1484; folld. by a relat. word, ἱστορεόν τε ὅτεῳ τρόπῳ περιγένοιτο Hdt.1.122. II. *give an account of what one has learnt*, *record*, τοὺς βίους τῶν χερσαίων Thphr.*HP*4.13.1, cf. Luc. *Hist.Conscr*.7, etc.; ἱστοροῦσί τινες.. *it is stated that*.., Dsc.4.75, etc.:—freq. in Pass., ὁ καρπὸς.. ἐπιληπτικοὺς ἱστορεῖται ὠφελεῖν Id.1.83; περί τινος ἱστορεῖται διότι Phld.*Mus*.p.18 K.; ἱστορεῖται περὶ Γοργοῦς τοιοῦτον Plu.2.227e, cf. Id.*Cic*.1, Ael.*Tact*.34.3, etc.; Ἀπολλόδωρος εἴρηκεν ἀπελθόντας Ὕαντας ἱστορεῖσθαι *are represented* as having gone, Str.10.3.4; τῶν ἱστορουμένων οὐδενὸς ἧττον πολυπράγμων the most industrious person *on record*, Phld.*Mus*.p.108 K. **-ημα**, ατος, τό, *narrative*, *tale*, φευκτὸν ἱ. *Anacreont*.4.9; μυθικὰ ἱ. D.H.2.61, cf. Plu.*Per*.1: pl., μαθήματα καὶ ἱ. Aristid.*Or*.46(3).28. **-ητέον**, *one must relate*, λόγον Plu.2.882b. **-ία**, Ion. **-ίη**, ἡ, *inquiry*, ἱστορίῃσι εἰδέναι τι παρά τινος Hdt.2.118, cf. 119; ἡ περὶ φύσεως ἱ. Pl.*Phd*.96a; αἱ περὶ τῶν ζῴων ἱ. Arist.*Resp*.477^{a}7, al.; ἡ ἱ. ἡ περὶ τὰ ζῷα Id.*PA*674^{b}16; ἡ ζωικὴ ἱ. ib.668^{b}30; περὶ φυτῶν ἱ., title of work by Theophrastus; *systematic* or *scientific observation*, Epicur.*Ep*.1 p.29 U.: abs., of *science* generally, ὄλβιος ὅστις τῆς ἱ. ἔσχε μάθησιν E.*Fr*.910 (anap.); of *geometry*, Pythag.ap.Iamb.*VP*18.89: in empirical medicine, *body of recorded cases*, Gal.1.144; *mythology*, Ἡσίοδον πάσης ἤρανον ἱστορίης Hermesian.7.22. 2. *knowledge so obtained*, *information*, Hdt.1 *Praef*., Hp.*VM*20; ὄψις ἐμὴ καὶ γνώμη καὶ ἱ. Hdt.2.99; πρὸς ἱστορίαν τῶν κοινῶν for *the knowledge of*.., D.18.144; ἡ τῆς ψυχῆς ἱ. Arist.*de An*.402^{a}4. II. *written account of one's inquiries*, *narrative*, *history*, prob. in this sense in Hdt.7.96; αἱ τῶν περὶ τὰς πράξεις γραφόντων ἱ. Arist.*Rh*.1360^{a}37, *Po*.1451^{b}3, Plb.1.57.5, al.; ἐκ τῶν ἱστοριῶν καὶ ἐκ τῶν ἄλλων μαρτυριῶν *OGI*13.12 (iii B.C.); αἱ Μαιανδρίου ἱ. *Inscr. Prien*.37.105; κοινὴ ἱ. general *history*, D.H.1.2; ἱ. Ἑλληνική, Ῥωμαϊκή, Plu.2.119d; restricted by some to contemporary history, Lat. *rerum cognitio praesentium*, Verr.Flacc.ap.Gell.5.18: generally, *story*, *account*, Call.*Aet*.3.1.7.

ἱστοριαγράφος, v. ἱστοριογράφος.

ἱστορικός, ή, όν, *exact*, *precise*, *scientific*, μίμησις Pl.*Sph*.267e; τῶν παρὰ τοῖς ἄλλοις εὑρημένων ἱ. *well-informed respecting*.. or *able to recount*.., Arist.*Rh*.1359^{b}32; ἀποδείξεις ἱστορικῶν Phld.*D*.1.23. Adv. **-κῶς** *scientifically*, *accurately*, Arist.*GA*757^{b}35; *by personal observation*, καταμαθεῖν τι Gal.14.275. II. *belonging to history*, *historical*, πραγματεῖαι D.H.1.1; τύπος (opp. λογικός) Id.*Dem*.24; ἀναγραφή Id.1.4; γράμματα Plu.*Them*.13: Subst., *historian*, Arist.*Po*.1451^{b}1, Aristeas 31, Phld.*Rh*.1.200 S., D.H.4.6, D.S.1.6, etc.; -ώτατος βασιλέων Plu.*Sert*.9. Adv. **-κῶς**, ἱ. καὶ διδασκαλικῶς Str.1.1.10; ἱ. καὶ ἐξηγητικῶς, opp. ἀποδεικτικῶς, Phld.*Mus*.p.12 K.; but ἐξηγητικώτερον ἢ -ώτερον, of Aristotle's method in *HA*, Antig.*Mir*.60.

ἱστοριογράφ-έω, *write history*, D.H.*Th*.42. **-ία**, ἡ, *history-writing*, interpol. in J.*Ap*.1.19. **-ικός**, ή, όν, = ἱστορικός II, Sch. D.T.p.167 H. **-ος**, ὁ, *writer of history*, *historian*, *Inscr.Prien*.37.107 (ii B.C.), Plb.2.62.2, Phld.*Rh*.1.359 S., D.S.1.9, Ath.Mech.7.2, etc.: *chronicler*, as distd. from συγγραφεύς (writer of contemporary history), Sch.D.T.p.168 H.; Ἔφορος ὁ ἱ., opp. Ἡρόδοτος ὁ συγγρ., *Placit*.4.1.6:—Dor. **ἱστοριαγράφος**, οἱ ἱ. οἱ συγγεγραφότες τὰς Μαγνήτων πράξεις *SIG*560.13, cf. 702.3 (Delph., ii B.C.), 685.93 (Crete).

ἱστόρ-ιον, τό, (ἵστωρ) *fact* or *illustration in proof*, Hp.*Nat.Puer*.31, *Morb*.4.54, *Ep*.19 (*Hermes* 53.66). **-ισμα**, ατος, τό, *clinical history*, Gal.17(1).648 (pl.). **-ιώδης**, ες, *like history*, Tz.*H*.8 No.231 tit.

ἱστός, ὁ, (ἵστημι) *anything set upright*: I. *mast*, ἱστὸν.. στῆσαν ἀείραντες they stepped *the mast*, Od.15.289, cf. Il.23.852, etc.; ἱστοὺς στησάμενοι Od.9.77. cf. Il.1.480; ἱστὸν αἴρεσθαι X.*HG*6.2.29; opp. καθαιρεῖν, κὰδ δ' ἕλον ἱστόν took *it* down, unstepped *it*, Od.15.496; κεραία καὶ ἱ. *IG*2².657.14: generally, *rod*, *pole*, ἱστὸς χάλκεος Hdt.8.122; *beam*, *IG*2².1672.306 (pl.). II. *beam* of a loom, which stood upright, instead of lying horizontal as in our looms; πόσσω κατέβα τοι ἀφ' ἱστῶ; (sc. τὸ ἐμπερόναμα) Theoc.15.35; later ἱ. ὄρθιος (opp. the horizontal loom), Artem.3.36: generally, *loom*, ἱστόν τ' ἠλακάτην τε Il.6.491, *Schwyzer*180 (Crete), etc.; ἱ. στήσασθαι to set up *the beam* and so begin a web, Hes.*Op*.779; ἱ. ἐποίχεσθαι to traverse *the loom*, because the weaver was obliged to walk to and fro, Il.1.31, Od.5.62. 2. *warp fixed to the beam*: hence, *the web* itself, ἱστὸν ὕφαινε Il.3.125, etc.; ἠματίη μὲν ὑφαίνεσκεν μέγαν ἱ., νύκτας δ' ἀλλύεσκεν Od.2.104; ἱ. μεταχειρίζεσθαι Pl.*Phd*.84a; ὁ ἐκτετμημένος ἱ. *the web* cut from the loom and finished, opp. ὁ πρὸς ἐκτομήν, Artem. l. c.; *web of a certain size*, *piece*, *PHib*.1.67.12 (iii B.C.), etc.; ὀθονίων ἱ. τρισχίλιοι Plb.5.89.2; τρεῖς ἱ. καθελεῖν Str.8.6.20. 3. ἱ. ἀραχνᾶν spiders' *webs*, B.3.7. 4. *comb* of bees, Arist.*HA*624^{a}5. III. *shin-bone*, *leg*, Opp.*C*.1.408. IV. a constellation, Aët.3.164.

ἱστό-τονος, ον, *stretched on the loom*, πηνίσματα v.l. in the codd. other than Rav. for ἱστόπονα, Ar.*Ra*.1315; κερκίς E.*Hyps.Fr*.1 ii 10 (lyr.). **-τρίβής**, v. ἱσοτριβής.

ἱστουργ-εῖον, τό, = ἱστών, Gloss. **-έω**, *work at the loom*, S.*OC*340, Trypho ap.Ath.14.618d (Epit.), Orph.*Fr*.192. **-ία**, ἡ, *weaving*, Pl.*Smp*.197b, Alciphr.3.41. **-ικός**, ή, όν, *of* or *for weaving*, Poll.7.35, 10.126; ἡ ἱ. (sc. τέχνη), = foreg., Phld.*Mus*.p.24 K. Adv. **-κῶς** Poll.7.35. **-ός**, ὁ or ἡ, *worker at the loom*, *weaver*, *PSI*4.371.8 (iii B.C.), J.*BJ*1.24.3.

ἱστοφόρος, ον, *bearing a mast*, Hsch.

ἵστραξ, a kind of *bird*, Hsch. (fort. τέτραξ).

Ἴστρος, ὁ, *Ister*, *Danube*, Hes.*Th*.339, etc.; **Ἴστρος**, ἡ, *Milesian colony at its mouth*, St.Byz.; also called **Ἰστρία**, ἡ, Arr.ap.eund., Ion. **-ίη**, Hdt.2.33:—Adj. **Ἰστριᾱνός**, Ion. **-ηνός**, ή, όν, *of* or *from Istria*, Hdt.4.78, St.Byz., etc.; Ἰστριανὰ πρόσωπα *tattooed* masks, like the faces of Scythian slaves, Ar.*Fr*.88; Ἰστριαναὶ ζειραί *Scythian* tunics, prob. for ἰσπνιᾶται σειραί (glossed ἰστρηνίδες), Theognost. *Can*.14; ἰστριανά, τά, covers for the baskets carried by κανηφόροι, Poll.10.191:—fem. **Ἰστριᾱνίδες**, of these garments and covers, Hsch.; but also Ἰστριανίδων ὕφη S.*Fr*.210.67.

ἰστρίδες, αἱ, a kind of *garment* (perh. f.l. for foreg. (or for ϝεστρ-)), Hsch. **ἰστυάζει**· ὀργίζεται, Id.; cf. οἶστρος. **ἰστυλόν**· τὸ στυχηδόν (leg. στοιχηδόν), Id. **ἴστω**, 3 sg. imper. of οἶδα; cf. ἴττω.

ἱστών, ῶνος, ὁ, = ἱστεών (q. v.), *weaving-shed*, Varro *RR*1.2.21.

ἱστων-άρχης, ου, ὁ, *controller of weaving*, *PGiss*.12, *Ostr*.1154, al. **-αρχία**, ἡ, *his office*, *PRyl*.98.5 (ii A.D.), *BGU*753 iv 4 (iii A.D.).

ἵστωρ or **ἴστωρ**, Boeot. **ϝίστωρ** *Schwyzer*491, etc., ορος, ὁ, ἡ:—*one who knows law and right*, *judge*, ἐπὶ ἵστορι πεῖραρ ἑλέσθαι Il.18.501; ἵστορα δ' Ἀτρεΐδην Ἀγαμέμνονα θείομεν ἄμφω 23.486; **ϝίστορες** *witnesses*, *IG*7.1779 (Thespiae); τῶ τεθμίω ϝίστωρ *Schwyzer*523.64 (Orchom. Boeot.); θεοὺς πάντας ἵστορας ποιεύμενος Hp.*Jusj*.init., cf. Poll.8.106. II. Adj. *knowing*, *learned*, Hes.*Op*.792; ἴ. τινός *knowing* a thing, *skilled in* it, ᾠδῆς *h.Hom*.32.2; ἐγχέων B.8.44; κἀγὼ τοῦδ' ἴ. ὑπερίστωρ S.*El*.850 (lyr), cf. E.*IT*1431, Pl.*Cra*.406b. (From ϝιδ-τωρ, cf. *εἴδω, οἶδα: ἴστωρ acc. to Hdn.Gr.2.108, etc.)

ἰσφαίνειν· μεριμνᾶν, Hsch.

ἴσφνιον, τό, prob. f.l. for ἴσθμιον, *neck of a jar*, E.*Fr*.656: prov., χαλεπὸς βίος ἴσφνι' ἄγοντος, expld. of a potter's life, cod.Par.ap. Nauck l. c., nisi leg. Ἴσθμι' (cf. ἰσθμιάζω).

ἴσφωρες· λῃσταί, κλέπται (Lacon.), Hsch.

ἰσχάδιον [ᾰ], τό, Dim. of ἰσχάς, Ar.*Pl*.798.

ἰσχᾰδο-κάρῠον [κᾰ], τό, *mixture of figs and almonds*, Arr.*Epict*.4.7.23: pl., ib.3.9.22, 4.7.22. **-πώλης**, ου, ὁ, *dealer in figs*, Pherecr.4, Nicoph.19:—fem. **-πωλις**, ιδος, Ar.*Lys*.564. **-φάγος** [φᾰ], ον, *eating figs*, Hsch. s. v. κραδοφάγος.

ἰσχᾰδώνης, ου, ὁ, *buyer of figs*, Pherecr.4.

ἴσχαιμος, ον, (ἴσχω, αἷμα) *staunching blood*, Thphr.*HP*9.13.1, Dsc.4.43; *styptic*, Luc.*Tim*.46, Aret.*CA*2.6 (dat. pl. -αίμασι codd.), *POxy*.1088.19. 2. ἴσχαιμος, ἡ, *plant used as a styptic*, *Andropogon ischaemum*, Thphr.*HP*9.15.3, Sch.Il.11.846.

ἰσχαίνω, f.l. for ἰσχάνω or ἰσχναίνω (qq. v.).

ἰσχᾰλέος, α, ον, poet. for ἰσχνός, *dried*, κρομύοιο λοπὸν ἰσχαλέοιο Od.19.233; *thin*, *paltry*, περόναι Man.6.434:—later **ἰσχνᾰλέος**, Eust.1863.60.

ἰσχαλεῦσαι· θηλάσαι, Hsch. (Cf. ἀνίσχαλος.) **ἰσχαλωμέναι**· δεδερματωμέναι, Id. (cf. ἴξαλος).

ἰσχᾰνάω, Ep. lengthd. form of ἰσχάνω (cf. sq.): Ion. impf. ἰσχανάασκον Il.15.723:—*hold back*, *stay*, 5.89; νῦν δ' ἐπεὶ ἰσχανάᾳς (sc. με) Od.15.346:—Pass., *hold back*, *wait*, νηυσὶν ἔπι.. ἐελμένοι ἰσχανόωντο Il.12.38; σὸν μῦθον ποτιδέγμενοι ἰσχανόωνται Od.7.161, cf. Il.19.234; *to be stayed*, A.R.2.864. II. intr., c. gen., *cling to*, and so, *long after*, *desire eagerly*, μέγα δρόμου ἰσχανόωσαν Il.23.300; ἰσχανόων φιλότητος Od.8.288 : c. inf., [μυῖα]..ἰσχανάᾳ δακέειν Il.17.572; ἰσχανόωσιν ἰδεῖν Procl.*h.Ven.*2.6. (ἰχαν- is v. l. in Il.23.300, Od.8.288, and shd. prob. be preferred; cf. ἰχανάω.)

ἰσχάνω [ᾰ], Ep. lengthd. form of ἴσχω (v. foreg.), *hold in check, hinder*, δέος ἰσχάνει ἄνδρας Il.14.387; Αἴαντ' ἰσχανέτην ὥς τε πρὼν ἰσχάνει ὕδωρ 17.747; τὸν δ' οὐκ ἴσχανε δεσμά *h.Bacch.*13 : c. gen., *keep back from*, κρύος ἀνέρα ἔργων ἰσχάνει Hes.*Op.*495; so in Prose, ὁ ἥλιος..ἰσχάνει [τὸν σῖτον] *checks* its growth, Thphr.*CP*4.13.6 (v.l. ἰσχαίνει, fort. ἰσχναίνει). II. *get, obtain, have*, ἀπεμνημόνευεν ἢ ἀνάλογον τῇ ἀπομνημονεύσει πάθος ἴσχα[νε] *had* an experience.., Epicur.*Nat.*27 G., cf. 51 G.; περὶ..δάκτυλον (δακτύλων codd.) πάθος ἰσχάνουσιν Vett.Val.65.13; μᾶλλον ἐκ τῶν πραγμάτων ἢ ἐκ τῶν λόγων τὰς λαβὰς ἰσχάνουσι Phld.*Herc.*873.6; ἐμέθεν πέρι θυμὸν ἀρείω ἴσχανε A.R.1.902.

ἰσχάριον, τό, Dim. of ἰσχίον, *hip*, Hero *Aut.*29.

ἰσχάς, άδος, ἡ, (ἰσχνός) *dried fig*, Ar.*Eq.*755, Hermipp.63.16, Alex.162.15, Arist.*HA*577^{a}10, *IG*2^{2}.1013.24, *PCair.Zen.*110 (iii B.C.), Theoc.1.147, etc.; ἰσχάδος ἐγκώμιον *POxy.*2084; also, of *over-ripe olives*, Eust.1963.55. 2. *spurge, Euphorbia Apios*, Thphr.*HP*9.9.6, Dsc.4.175, Plin.*HN*26.72. II. (ἴσχω) *that which holds, anchor*, S.*Fr.*761, Luc.*Lex.*15.

ἴσχαυδαι· ἰσχ[ν]όφωνοι, Hsch.

ἰσχέ-γᾱον, τό, (ἴσχω, γῆ) *retaining wall*, *SIG*241 A 7, 247 I^{2} 14 (Delph., iv B.C.). **-θῡρον**, τό, perh. *frame of a window*, *IG*11(2).165.10, al. (Delos, iii B.C.). **-πλινθα**, τά, *uprights* (perh. *door-jambs*), *SIG*247 I^{2} 15 (Delph., iv B.C.).

ἰσχερώ· ἑξῆς, Hsch. (Cf. σχερός.)

ἰσχητήριος, α, ον, (ἴσχω) *astringent*, Hp.*Loc.Hom.*20, cf. Erot.

ἰσχῐ-ᾰδικός, ή, όν, (ἰσχίον) *of the hips*, φθίσις Hp.*Coac.*140. II. of persons, *subject to sciatica*, Dsc.1.30.6, Gal.13.986. III. *good for sciatica*, ἐπίπλασμα Dsc.2.174 (as v.l.), cf. Gal. l. c. **-άζω**, *move the hips*, of a rider, Procop.*Goth.*4.31; of a woman, Id.*Arc.*9; in walking, Suid., Phot. II. Pass., καὶ ἰσχιασθέντα, of a bandage, prob. f. l. for καὶ σχισθέντα, Gal.18(1).786. **-ᾰκός**, ή, όν, = ἰσχιαδικός, Thphr.*Fr.*87, *Cat.Cod.Astr.*7.241. **-άς** (sc. νόσος), άδος, ἡ, *hip-disease*, Hp.*Aph.*6.59,60. 2. *sciatica*, ib.3.22 (pl.), Id.*Aër.*22 (pl.), Thphr.*HP*9.13.6 (pl.); ἰ. χρονία Dsc.1.10. II. = λευκάκανθα, Id.3.19, cf. Gal.12.58. **-ᾱσις**, εως, ἡ, *hip-disease*, Pall.*in Hp.*2.13 D. **-οίδης** (οἰδέω)· ὁ μεγάλα ἰσχία ἔχων, Com.Adesp.1022. **-ον** (parox.), τό, *hip-joint*, in which the thigh turns, κατ' ἰσχίον, ἔνθα τε μηρὸς ἰσχίῳ ἐνστρέφεται, κοτύλην δέ τέ μιν καλέουσιν Il.5.305, cf. 11.339, Od.17.234, etc.; later τὸ κατ' ἰσχίον ἄρθρον Gal.*UP*15.8; also, the intra-capsular ligament of the hip-joint, Poll.2.186; = κεφαλὴ τοῦ μηροῦ, Hp.*Art.*53,58, Cael.Aur.*TP*4.38. 2. in pl. (dual, Autocr.1.6), *fleshy parts round the hip-joint, haunches*, of a boar, ἰσχία τε γλουτούς τε Il.8.340; of a lion, πλευράς τε καὶ ἰσχία 20.170; of a horse, Pl.*Phdr.*254c, cf. e; freq. of men, ἐκ τῶν μηρῶν ἔς τε τὰ ἰ. καὶ τὰς λαπάρας Hdt.6.75, cf. X.*Eq.*7.7; ἰσχίων φύσιν..πρὸς τὰς ἀναπαύσεις χρήσιμον Arist.*PA*689^{b}15; τὰ ἰ. σαρκώδη ἐποίησεν [ἡ φύσις] ib.^{b}14: hence, other animals are said to have no ἰ., ib.^{b}6,33. II. later, *the projecting part of the os innominatum*, upon which man rests when sitting, Gal.2.772.

ἰσχιορρωγικός, ή, όν, (ῥώξ) *with broken hips, limping*, μέτρον ἰ. an iambic trimeter ending in five long syllables ascribed to Ananius, Gramm. Harl. in Studemund *Ind. Lect. Vratisl.* 1887/8 p.16 :—also **ἰσχιορρώξ** (sc. στίχος), ῶγος, ὁ, Tz. in *An.Ox.*3.310.

ἰσχν-αίνω, fut. -ᾰνῶ (συν-) E.*IA*694 codd.: aor. ἴσχνᾱνα A.*Eu.*267, Ar.*Ra.*941; Ion. -ηνα Hdt.3.24, Hp.*Off.*13 :—**Med.** (v. κατισχναίνω) :—**Pass.**, aor. ἰσχνάνθην Id.*Coac.*369, 407 : (ἰσχνός) :—*make dry, wither*, ἐπεὰν τὸν νεκρὸν ἰσχνήνωσι, of a mummy, Hdt.3.24, cf. Hp.*Aph.*5.22, A.*Eu.*267, Pl.*Grg.*522a, etc.; ἰ. τὸ σῶμα Hp.*Art.*33, cf. Pl.*Plt.*293b, Arist.*Metaph.*1048^{b}27; ἔπινε βρῦτον ἰσχναίνων χρόα A.*Fr.*124. 2. *reduce* a swelling, Hp.*Liqu.*6, *Aph.*5.25 : metaph., σφυδῶντα θυμὸν ἰ. *to bring down* a proud stomach, A.*Pr.*382; τὸ δεινὸν καὶ διαφθαρὲν φρενῶν ἴσχναινε E.*Or.*298; τὴν τέχνην οἰδοῦσαν ἴσχνανα I *reduced* the swollen art (Tragedy), Ar.*Ra.*941.— In the metaph. sense, ἰσχαίνω is a constant v.l. (as in the compds. κατισχναίνω, συνισχναίνω); cf. ἰσχάνω fin. **-ᾰλέος**, v. ἰσχαλέος. **-ανσις**, εως, ἡ, *emaciation*, Paul.Aeg.3.69, Aët.16.80(75), Mich.*in PN*46.6. **-αντικός**, ή, όν, *fit for reducing*, Arist.*Pr.*885^{a}28, Dsc.1.24. **-ᾰσία**, Ion. -ίη, ἡ, *thinness, leanness*, Hp.*Aff.*12, Arist.*Metaph.*1013^{b}1, 1048^{b}29. **-ασμός**, ὁ, *reducing treatment*, τοῦ σώματος Hp.*Fract.*14.

ἰσχνεῦσαι· ὑφεῖναι, θηλάσαι, Hsch. (Cf. ἰσχαλεῦσαι.) **ἰσχνίδες**· ἄγκυραι, ἰσχάδες· καὶ φιλήματος εἶδος, Id.

ἰσχνο-κᾰλᾰμώδης, ες, *with slender reed*, Eust.1165.12. **-κωλος**, ον, *with thin limbs*, Antyll.ap.Orib.7.16.15. **-μῡθέω**, = λεπτολογέω, and **-μῡθία**, ἡ, *subtle dispute*, Hsch. **-πους**, ποδος, ὁ, ἡ, gloss on ταναύποδα, Sch.Od.9.464.

ἰσχνός, ή, όν, *dry, withered*, φυλλεῖα Ar.*Ach.*469; ἰ. τυρός, opp. χλωρός, Poll.6.48, *POxy.*1338 (V A.D.). 2. of persons, *thin, lean*, Hp.*Aph.*2.44, Theoc.10.27, etc.; ἰσχνοὶ καὶ σφηκώδεις Ar.*Pl.*561; ἰσχνοὶ καὶ ἄσιτοι Pl.*Lg.*665e; ἰ. ἕξεις a *spare* habit of body, Plu.*Lyc.*17; of roots, -ότεραι Dsc.1.9,10; of the voice, ἰσχνὸν φθέγγεσθαι to speak *thin* or *small*, Luc.*Nigr.*11. 3. *weak, feeble*, σφυγμός Gal.8.506. 4. *reduced*, of a swelling, οὕτω ἂν τάχιστα ἰσχνὸν τὸ οἴδημα γένοιτο Hp.*Fract.*21, cf. *Epid.*4.26. Adv. -νῶς, ἑστηκὼς *without external swelling*, Id.*Coac.*481. 5. *light, thin*, of clothing materials, *POxy.*1535 B 9 (ii/iii A.D.), etc.: metaph., of style, *spare, plain, unadorned*, ἰ. χαρακτήρ D.H.*Pomp.*2, cf. Demetr.*Eloc.*190, Quint.12.10.58, Plu.2.42d. Adv. -νῶς, εἰπεῖν to speak *plainly*, Plb.1.2.6; -νῶς ἰδεῖν τὴν ἀρετήν dub. l. in Lycurg.80. (Perh. cogn. with Lat. *vescus* : a connexion with ἴσχω was imagined by the Greeks; cf. ἰσχνόφωνος II.)

ἰσχνοσκελής, ές, *lean-shanked*, D.L.5.1, Gal.6.322.

ἰσχνότης, ητος, ἡ, *thinness, leanness*, σαρκός Hp.*Aër.*21; σώματος Arist.*HA*581^{b}26; φύσιος Aret.*SA*1.7. 2. of style, *spareness*, i. e. *plainness*, ἰ. φράσεως, of Lysias, D.H.*Vett.Cens.*5.1; cf. Phld.*Rh.*1.165 S., Demetr.*Eloc.*14. 3. *thinness, weakness* of pronunciation, opp. πλατειασμός, Quint.1.5.32.

ἰσχνουργής, ές, *finely wrought*, gloss on εὐϋφής, Sch.S.*Tr.*602.

ἰσχνο-φωνία, Ion. -ίη, ἡ, *hesitancy of speech*, Hp.*Epid.*2.5.1, Arist.*Pr.*895^{a}16, 902^{b}25. **-φωνος**, ον, *thin-voiced, weak-voiced*, Phld.*Po.*2.25, Gal.17(1).186; of Isocrates, Plu.2.837a; of partridges, Antig.*Mir.*6; but, II. *having an impediment in one's speech* (connected by the Greeks with ἴσχω), οἱ ἰ...ἴσχονται τοῦ φωνεῖν Arist.*Pr.*903^{a}38, cf. 895^{a}15, 905^{a}21, *AB*100; ἰ. καὶ τραυλός Hdt.4.155, cf. Hp.*Epid.*1.19; ἰ. καὶ βραδύγλωσσος Lxx *Ex.*4.10, cf. Ezek.*Exag.*114; also of metals, etc., χρυσὸς καὶ λίθος ὑπὸ πληρότητος ἰ. καὶ δυσηχῆ Plu.2.721c : metaph., ἡ φιλία ἰ. γέγονεν ἐν τῷ παρρησιάζεσθαι ib.89b. Adv. -φώνως Zos.Alch.p.108 B.

ἰσχν-όω, = ἰσχναίνω, *make dry*, Arist.*Pr.*885^{a}19; *put on low diet*, Orib.*Syn.*9.37.4. **-ωσις**, εως, ἡ, *drying up*, μαστῶν Sor.1.59; of the body, Id.2.36. **-ωτικός**, ή, όν, *of* or *for drying up* or *reducing*, δύναμις Dsc.5.109 (interpol.).

ἰσχομένως, Adv., (ἴσχω) *with checks* or *hindrances*, Pl.*Cra.*415c.

ἰσχουρ-έω, *suffer from retention of urine*, Aret.*SD*2.4, Herod.Med. ap.Orib.10.37.2. **-ία**, ἡ, *retention of urine*, Sor.2.6, Gal.8.403, Herod.Med.ap.Orib.10.37.16.

ἰσχῡρ-ιείω, Desiderat. from sq., *venture to affirm*, Hp.*Art.*1, cf. Gal.18(1).309. **-ίζομαι**, fut. -ιοῦμαι Lys.6.35, Isoc.17.24 : aor. ἰσχῡρῐσάμην Th.5.26, Pl.*Grg.*489c :—*make oneself strong, be strong*, ἰσχυριζόμενος ὑφ' ἵππων σίδηρος *gaining force* from the impetus of the horses, X.*Cyr.*6.4.18. II. *use one's strength*, τῷ σώματι Pl. l. c.; esp. in overcoming resistance, πρὸς τὸ πολὺ ἧττον Arist.*Pr.*951^{a}13; εἰς τοὺς ἀσθενεῖς Id.*EN*1124^{b}23; *contend stoutly*, ὑπὲρ ἄθλων Ael.*NA*15.15; *persist* or *continue obstinately in* doing.., c. part., Th.7.49 : abs., ibid.; esp. by word of mouth, *maintain stiffly, obstinately*, c. acc. et inf., Id.3.44, Is.11.1; ταῦτα Pl.*Grg.*495b; ὅτι.., ὡς.. Th.4.23, 6.55, Pl.*Tht.*172b; περί τινος Id.*Sph.*249c. 2. *put firm trust in* a thing, *rely on* it, τῷ ξυνῷ πάντων Heraclit.114; λόγῳ Lys.6.35; διαθήκαις Is.1.3; τῷ νόμῳ Hyp.*Eux.*4, D.33.27; παρασκευῇ Id.44.3, cf. Isoc.17.24; *feel confidence*, Antipho 5.76. **-ικός**, ή, όν, *stubborn*, Pl.*Tht.*169b (Comp.), prob. l. in Alex.194, cf. Phot. **-ιστέον**, *one must maintain stoutly*, Pl.*R.*533a. **-ιστικῶς** ἔχω, *to be inclined to affirm*, gloss on ἰσχυριείω, Gal.18(1).309.

ἰσχῡρο-γνωμοσύνη, ἡ, *obstinacy*, Ph.1.653, J.*Ap.*1.22. **-γνώμων**, ον, gen. ονος, *stiff in opinion*, Arist.*EN*1151^{b}5, D.L.2.24 : Sup., Ph.*Fr.*23 H.: metaph., λογισμός Id.2.413. **-δετος**, ον, *fast-bound*, Sch.A.*Pr.*148. **-θώραξ**, ᾱκος, ὁ, ἡ, gloss on χαλκοχιτώνων, Hsch. **-κάρδιος**, ον, gloss on τλήθυμος, Id. **-πᾰθέω**, = δεινοπαθέω, Sch.Arat.71. **-παίκτης**, ου, ὁ, *one who plays valiantly*, *IG*14.1535, *Delph.*3(1).216, Vett.Val.4.17. **-πλήκτης**, ου, ὁ, *wounding severely*, gloss on διοπλῆκταν, Hsch. **-ποιέω**, *strengthen*, τὴν δύναμιν D.S.17.65; τὰς ἐπικρατείας τινός Plb.28.20.7; τόπον J.*AJ*15.8.5; στόμαχον [Gal.]14.752; *establish*, τὰς διατριβὰς τῶν ῥητορικῶν Phld.*Rh.*1.192 S. :—Med., Onos.21.2 :—Pass., ἰσχυροποιεῖται τὰ μέσα Ascl.*Tact.*10.16; τῆς δυναστείας -ουμένης D.S.14.9, cf. Arr.*Epict.*2.18.7; of assertions, Vett.Val.333.7; *to be valid*, ἡ ἀναλογία οὐκ -εῖται S.E.*M.*1.201. **-ποίησις**, εως, ἡ, *strengthening*, τῶν ἀσθενούντων μορίων Aët.12.21. II. *confirmation, corroboration*, Gloss. **-ποιός**, όν, *strengthening*, *EM* 480.12, Sch.A.*Ch.*415, etc. **-πότης**, ου, ὁ, gloss on ζαπότης, Hsch. **-πους**, ποδος, ὁ, ἡ, *strong-footed*, gloss on χαλκόποδας, Id. **-πράγμων**, ον, gen. ονος, *doing mighty deeds*, Paul.Al.*O.*1; gloss on ὀβριμοεργός, Sch.D Il.5.403. **-ρριζος**, ον, (ῥίζα) *with strong root*, Thphr.*CP*2.12.3, etc.

ἰσχῡρός, ά, όν, (ἰσχύς) *strong*, esp. of personal strength, S.*Ph.*945, E.*Fr.*290, etc.; of things, ἰ. βέλος Alc.15.4; ῥεύματα Hdt.8.12; ἰ. χθὼν *hard*, A.*Pers.*310; of food, *indigestible*, Hp.*Art.*50; of taste, *strong*, Thphr.*HP*7.6.1; of armies, ἰσχυροτέρα φάλαγξ X.*Cyr.*7.1.30; of places, Th.4.9, X.*An.*4.6.11, etc.; τῆς χώρης τὸ -ότατον Hdt.1.76; τὸ ἑαυτοῦ ἰ., opp. τὰ τοῖς πολεμίοις ἰ., X.*Eq.Mag.*8.24; τὰ ἰσχυρότατα your *strongest points*, Th.5.111; τὰ τῆς πόλεως ἰ. *that in which the strength* of the state *lies*, Aeschin.3.66; ὁρῶντες οὐδὲν ἰ. ἀπὸ τῶν Λεσβίων no *show of strength*, Th.3.6; ἰ. τι πρὸς τὸ πρᾶγμ' ἔχειν a *strong* point, Men.*Epit.*130; -ότατον τεκμήριον *SIG*685.84 (Crete, ii B.C.). 2. *powerful*, ἄλοχος Διός A.*Supp.*302; πόλις E.*Supp.*447; θεός Ar.*Pl.*946; ἰ. τὸ πολλόν Hdt.1.136; οἱ ἰ. ἐν ταῖς πόλεσιν X.*Ath.*1.14 : Comp. -ότερος, ἐς πειθώ Democr.51; ὁ ὀπίσω μου ἐρχόμενος -ότερός μου ἐστίν *Ev.Matt.*3.11. 3. *forcible, violent, severe*, σιτοδείη, ψύχη, Hdt.1.94, 4.29; λιμός *Ev.Luc.*15.14; ἀναγκαίη Hdt.1.74; αἱ λίαν ἰ. τιμωρίαι *violent, excessive*, Id.4.205; ὅρκος -ότατος, ἀνάγκαι -όταται, Antipho 5.11, 6.25; νόσημα Hp.*Acut.*(*Sp.*)4; βήξ Th.2.49; γέλως, ἐπιθυμίαι, etc., Pl.*R.*388e, 560b, etc.; νόμος ἰ. *severe*, Hdt.7.102, Lys.15.9; ἔχθρα Pl.*Phdr.*233c; γνώμη -οτέρη *more positive*, Hdt.9.41; τρόπῳ ᾧ ἂν δύνωνται -οτάτῳ Foed.ap.Th.5.23; κατὰ τὸ ἰσχυρὸν *by main force*, opp. δόλῳ, Hdt.4.201, cf. 9.2. 4. of literary style, *vigorous*, D.H.*Comp.*22; also of syllables, *strong*, ib.16; στάσεις λαμβάνειν ἰ. ib.22. II. Adv. -ρῶς *strongly, with all force*, ἐγκεῖσθαι Th.1.69, etc.; φυλάττειν τινάς X.*An.*6.3.11. 2. *very much, exceedingly*, with Adjs., Hdt.4.108; ἔθνος μέγα ἰ. ib.183; διώρυγες ἰ. βαθεῖαι X.*An.*[1.7.15], etc.; ἰ. χλωρόν Hp.*Progn.*11; κίνησις νωθὴς ἰ. Arist.*HA*503^{b}9; ἰ. φιλοπλάτων Phld.*Ind.Sto.*61: with Verbs, ἰ. ἥδεσθαι, ἀνιᾶσθαι, X.*Cyr.*8.3.44; ἀπήγγειλεν ὅτι πάντα δοκοίη ἰ. τῷ εὐνούχῳ ib.5.3.15: Comp. -οτέρως Heraclit.114, Hdt.3.129; -ότερον X.*Cyr.*4.5.12, etc.: Sup., in answers, ἰσχυρότατά γε *most certainly*, Id.*Oec.*1.15.

ἰσχῡροσώματος, ον, gloss on ὀβριμοεργός, Sch.Opp.*H.*1.360.

ἰσχῡρότης, ητος, ἡ, *strength*, Ph.1.128; v.l. for ἐχ-, D.H.3.65, for ὀχ-, Ph.1.644.

ἰσχῡρό-φρων, ονος, ὁ, ἡ, *strong-minded*, D.C.*Fr.*43.25. **-φωνος**, ον, *strong-voiced*, Antyll.ap.Orib.6.10.10. **-χρως**, ωτος, ὁ, ἡ, gloss on ταλαύρινος, Sch.Il.5.289. **-ψῡχος**, ον, *strong-souled*, Hsch. s.v. λάσιον κῆρ.

ἰσχῡρόω, *strengthen*, Lxx *Is.*41.7.

ἰσχ-ύς [v. sub fin.], ύος, ἡ, *strength* of body, Hes.*Th.*146, 823, etc.; ἀκμαὶ ἰσχύος Pi.*O.*1.96; δεινὸν ἰσχύος θράσος S.*Ph.*104; τὴν ἰ. δεινὰ καὶ τὴν ῥώμην Pl.*Smp.*190b; πρὸς ἰσχὺν ὀφθαλμοὶ ἄριστα πεφυκότες X.*Smp.*5.5: pl., ἰσχύες καὶ ἀσθένειαι Pl.*R.*618d; κατὰ σωμάτων ἰσχὺς καὶ εὐμορφίας Id.*Lg.*744c; of places, ἰσχὺς γῆς S.*OC*610; of a fortified place, Th.4.35. 2. *might, power*, θεοῦ, θεῶν, A.*Th.*226 (lyr.), S.*Aj.*118; ἰ. βασιλεία A.*Pers.*590 (lyr.), cf. 12 (anap.); ὅπου γὰρ ἰ. συζυγοῦσι καὶ δίκη *might* and right, Id.*Fr.*381; φύσεως ἰ., of Themistocles, Th. 1.138; ἐπὶ μέγα ἐλθεῖν ἰσχύος to a great height *of power*, Id.2.97, cf. 1.85, etc.; παρὰ ἰσχὺν τῆς δυνάμεως Id.7.66; ἰ. μάχης fighting *power*, Id.2.97; ἰ. τῆς ἐλπίδος Id.4.65, cf. 2.62; ἡ τῶν νόμων ἰ. *POxy.*67.14 (iv A.D.); *validity*, *PGrenf.*2.71 ii 11 (iii A.D.), etc. 3. *brute force*, κατ' ἰσχὺν *perforce*, opp. δόλῳ, A.*Pr.*214; πρὸς ἰσχύος κράτος S.*Ph.*594; πρὸς ἰσχύος χάριν E.*Med.*538; ὑπὸ τῆς ἰσχύος Epicr.3.10; κατέχοντες ἰσχύϊ τὸ πλῆθος Th.3.62; εἴ τι ἰσχύϊ πράττεται, ἰσχυρῶς πράττεται Pl.*Prt.*332b. 4. *motive force*, Arist.*Ph.*250^{a}6; ἡ κινοῦσα ἰ. Id.*Cael.*275^{b}20, al. 5. in Lit. Crit., *vigour* of style, D.H.*Pomp.*3, *Comp.*2, al. II. in Tactics, the *main body* of troops, οὔπω ἡ ἰ. πάρεστιν X.*Cyr.*1.4.19. [ῠ in gen., etc.: in nom. and acc. sg. ῠ in Pi.*N.*11.31 (acc.): ῡ in Trag. and Com., A.*Th.*1080 (anap.), *Ch.*721 (anap.), S.*Aj.*118, Men.449.] (Perh. ϝισχύς, cf. βίσχυν, γισχύν.) **-ῡσις**, εως, ἡ, mistranslation of Hebr., Lxx *Ca.*2.7, 3.5 prob. for diff. root; prob. f.l. for χύσις (cj. Wendl.) in Ph.1.354. **-ύω** (ἰσχύς), Batr.279: impf. ἴσχυον Ar.*V.*357, X.*HG*6.4.18: fut. ἰσχύσω Ar.*Av.*1607, etc.: aor. ἴσχῡσα S.*Aj.*502, etc.: pf. ἴσχῡκα Aeschin.1.165, Cerc.17. 34:—Pass., aor. κατ-ισχύθην D.S.15.87: (ἰσχύς):—*to be strong* in body, S.*Tr.*234; ὅπως ὑγιαίνοιεν καὶ ἰσχύοιεν X.*Cyr.*6.1.24; ὃς μέγιστον ἴσχυσε στρατοῦ S.*Aj.*502; ἰ. τοῖς σώμασιν X.*Mem.*2.7.7; τοῦ σώματος ἰσχύοντος Antipho 5.93; ἴσχυόν τ' αὐτὸς ἐμαυτοῦ, i.e. I *had* all my *strength*, Ar.*V.*357; ἰ. ἐκ νόσου *to be recovering*, X.*HG*6.4. 18. 2. *to be powerful, prevail*, μηδὲν μεῖον ἰ. Διός A.*Pr.*510, etc.; πλέον, μεῖζον ἰ., E.*Hec.*1188, Ar.*Av.*1607; later ἰ. πρός τινα *prevail* against, Lxx *Ps.*12(13).4; ἐπί τινας ib.1*Ma.*10.49; ἰ. τινί *to be strong in* a thing, σοφίᾳ ἀνὴρ ὑπὲρ ἀνδρὸς ἰσχύει Pi.*Fr.*61; θράσει E.*Or.*903; ἐν τῇ ποιητικῇ Phld.*Po.*5.9; ἰ. τινὶ πρὸς τοὺς πολεμίους Th.3.46; ἰ. ἐκ πονηρίας D.2.9; ὅθεν ἰσχύομεν, ἧπερ ἰσχύουσι, Th.1.143, 2.13; ἰ. παρά τινι *have power* or *influence* with one, Id.8.47, Aeschin.2.2, D.38.20, etc. b. of things, *prevail*, ὅρκος οὔτι Ζηνὸς ἰ. πλέον A.*Eu.*621; τἀληθὲς γὰρ ἰσχῦον τρέφω S.*OT*356; τὸ δίκαιον ἐν πᾶσιν ἰ. D. 37.59; *have force*, ἃ ὡρίσω σὺ δίκαια, ταῦτα.. καὶ κατὰ σοῦ προσήκει τοῖς ἄλλοις ἰσχύειν D.19.241, cf. 25.71; ὁ λόγος δόξειεν ἂν ἰσχύειν Arist.*Pol.*1280^{a}28; νομὴ ἄδικος οὐδὲν ἰ. *is of* no *force*, *PTeb.*286.7 (ii A.D.); ἰσχῦόν τι something *permanent*, prob. in Epicur.*Ep.*1 p.7 U.: c. inf., ὁ καιρὸς ἰσχύει.. πράττειν D.17.9, cf. Lxx 2*Ch.*2.6(5), al., Plu.*Pomp.*58; οὐκ ἰ. ἀρτιστομεῖν Str.14.2.28, cf. *Ev.Marc.*5.4, D.Chr.33.22, etc. 3. *to be worth* or *equivalent to*, ἡ μνᾶ ἰσχύει λίτρας δύο καὶ ἥμισυ J.*AJ*14.7.1, cf. *PGnom.*106, Ptol.*Tetr.*134; αἱ ψῆφοι τάλαντον ἰσχύουσιν (prob. for ἴσχουσιν) Plb.5.26.13. 4. Act., *condense*, νεφέλας Lxx *Si.*43.15. b. ἄρτον πᾶσαν ἡδονὴν ἰσχύοντα *making strong*.., ib.*Wi.*16.20 (*in se habentem*, Vulg.). 5. -ύοντες ἀστέρες those *in dominating positions*, Serapion in *Cat.Cod.Astr.*8(4).226. [ῡ in Batr. l.c., Trag. and Com., S.*Aj.*1409, *OT*356, Ar.*V.*357, *Av.*488, 1606; later, ῠ sts. in pres. and impf., *AP*5.166 (Asclep.), 211 (Mel.).]

ἴσχω, redupl. form of ἔχω (only found in pres., and impf. Act. and Pass., Ep. inf. ἰσχέμεναι, ἰσχέμεν, Od.20.330, Il.17.501), but in Hom. and Hes. almost always with a limited sense, *keep back, restrain* (v. infr. II), δέος ἴσχει τινά Il.5.812, 817, etc.; ἴ. τινὰ ἀνάγκῃ Od.4.558; θυμὸν ἴ. ἐν στήθεσσι Il.9.256; Ζεὺς ἴσχεν ἑὸν μένος Hes.*Th.*687; οὐδ' ἔτι σηκοὶ ἴσχουσι (the calves) Od.10.413; [πρὼν] ἴσχει ῥέεθρα Il.17. 750; ἵππους ἴ. 15.456, etc.; ἶσχον βουλομένους τοὺς ἑπτὰ ἐς τὸ πρόσω παριέναι Hdt.3.77; μηδὲν ἡμᾶς ἰσχέτω Ar.*V.*1264; οὐδέποτέ γ' ἴσχει θύρα, prov. of those who keep open house, Eup.265; ἴσχε στόμα E.*HF*1244; ἴσχε δακὼν στόμα σόν S.*Tr.*976 (anap.); τὸ ἴσχον τὴν πορείαν X.*An.*6.5.13; χείμαρρον.. ἕρκεα ἴσχει ἀλωάων *keep* it *back*, Il.5.90: c. gen., ξίφος ἴ. τινός *to keep* it *from* him, E.*Hel.*1656; ἴ. τῆς ῥοῆς, τοῦ ἰέναι, Pl.*Cra.*416b, 420e: folld. by inf., ἴ. τινὰ μὴ πράσσειν E.*IA*661:—Pass., *to be checked*, Gal.*UP*15.3: also impers., ἐν τούτῳ ἴσχετο here *the matter stopped*, X.*An.*6.3.9. 2. abs., ἴσχε *hold, stay, stop!* A.*Ch.*1052, S.*Ichn.*95; of ships, *put in*, v.l. in Th.2.91; πρὸς ταῖς πόλεσι Id.7.35, cf. A.R.2.390; of rivers, *stop*, Arr.*An.*5. 9.4:—in this sense Hom. uses Med. or Pass., ἴσχεσθ' Ἀργεῖοι, μὴ φεύγετε Od.24.54, cf. Il.3.82; ἴσχεο *check thyself, be calm*, 1.214, 2. 247, Od.22.356, etc.; *keep quiet*, 11.251: c. gen., ἴσχεσθαί τινος *desist from* a thing, 18.347, 24.323. II. *hold fast, hold*, once in Hom., [κανόνα] ἀγχόθι στήθεος Il.23.762, cf. S.*Aj.*575, *Ph.*1111 (lyr.): metaph., *keep, maintain*, εὐφημίαν Id.*Tr.*178; ἐλπίσιν ἴ. τι ib.138; γνώμαν Id.*Ph.*853 (lyr.); ἐπιστήμην λαβόντα ἴσχειν Pl.*Tht.*198a; of outward matters, ὀδύνη ἴ. τὴν γαστέρα *affects* it, Hp.*Nat.Mul.*14; τὸν αἶσ' ἄπλατος ἴσχει S.*Aj.*256 (lyr.); αἱ ἄτομοι τὸν παλμὸν ἴσχουσι *keep up*, Epicur.*Ep.*1 p.8 U.:—Pass., φθόῃ ἴσχεσθαι Isoc.19.11 (s.v.l., σχόμενον Blass); also τὸ ἰσχόμενον κατὰ διαφοράν that which *is permanent* in distinction, Chrysipp.*Stoic.*2.128. III. after Hom., *hold* or *have in possession*, v.l. in Hdt.3.39, Th.3.58; *have a wife*, Hdt.5.92.β'; of women, ἴ. ἐν γαστρί or simply ἴ. *to be pregnant*, Hp.*Epid.*2.2.18, etc.; μετὰ τοῦτον ἴ. Κλεόμβροτον *conceives* Cl., Hdt.5. 41: generally, like ἔχω, ἴσχε κάμοῦ μνῆστιν S.*Aj.*520; λῆστιν ἴ. to be forgetful, Id.*OC*584; ἄλγος ἴ. Id.*OT*1031; γνώμαν ἴ., = γνῶναι, Id.*El.*214 (lyr.); ἴ. δοῦλον βίον Id.*Tr.*302; νοῦν Pl.*Smp.*181d; ἐπωνυμίαν Id.*Prm.*130e; χρώματα Hp.*Prog.*12; κακώσιας Id.*Art.*61; *receive*, [πεμπάδα] *SIG*57.35 (Milet., v B.C.); ἰσχέτω δίκην καὶ ὑπεχέτω ib. 286.15 (iv B.C.), cf. *IG*5(2).357.23 (Stymphalus, iii B.C.): c. dupl. acc., ἴ. τινὰ ξύνευνον S.*Aj.*1301; θεὸν οὐ λήξω προστάταν ἴσχων Id.*OT*882 (lyr.). 2. *have in it, involve*, ὄλβος ἴ. φθόνον Pi.*P.*11.29; μετάστασιν ἴ. *to be susceptible, capable of* cure, Hp.*Aph.*5.7; ἀνάληψιν μετ' εὐπετείας Pl.*Ti.*83e; *to be worth*, dub. l. in Plb.5.26.13; v. ἰσχύω 3. 3. intr., *to be*, like ἔχω, ἀπολέμως ἴσχοντες Pl.*Plt.*307e; εὖ ἴ. τὸ σῶμα Id.*R.*411c; ὧδε Id.*Phil.*38c; τοῖς πᾶσι χαλεπώτερον Th.7.50.

ἰσωνία, ἡ, (ὠνή) *the same price, cost price*, τῆς ἰ. Ar.*Pax*1227; τᾶς ἰ. ἀπολυσάτω he shall release him at *the original price*, *Milet.*3 No.140. 55 (Crete).

ἰσωνῠμ-ία, ἡ, rejected as a name for a *pronoun* by A.D.*Pron.*9. 7. **-ος**, ον, (ὄνομα) *bearing the same name as*, c. gen., καλεῖν τινα ἰσώνυμον ἔμμεν μάτρωος Pi.*O.*9.64; ἠελίοιο τροπαῖς ἰσώνυμον [ῑ] ἔρνος, i.e. ἡλιοτρόπιον, Nic.*Th.*678.

ἴσως, Lacon. ϝίωρ (v. βίωρ), Adv. of ἴσος, *equally, in like manner*, Sapph.*Supp.*25.11, S.*Ph.*758, Pl.*Lg.*805a, etc.; ὡς ἰσαίτατα ib.744c; *evenly*, Hp.*Off.*3. II. *equally, with reference to equality*, τὸ ὀρθὸν ληπτέον ἴσως Arist.*Pol.*1283^{b}40; *fairly, equitably*, ἴ. καὶ κοινῶς Aen.Tact.22.24; οὐκ ἴ. οὐδὲ πολιτικῶς D.10.74; μηδὲν ἴ. καὶ δικαίως φρονοῦντας D.H.10.40; οὐκ ἴσως χρήσασθαί τινι Plb.23.2.7. III. *probably, perhaps*, Alc.*Supp.*33, Hdt.6.124, A.*Pr.*319, S.*Ph.*144, Pl.*Grg.*473b, etc.; ἴ. που E.*El.*518; οὔτε συμφόρως οὔτ' ἴ. καλῶς D.5.10; οὐκ ἴσως, ἀλλ' ὄντως Pl.*Lg.*965c: ironical, σμικρά γε ἴ. προσθήκη Id.*R.*339b: freq. joined with ἄν or τάχ' ἄν, e.g. S.*Aj.*691, 1009, Pl.*Ap.*31a; ἀμφισβητοῦντες προστιθέασιν ἀεὶ τὸ ἴσως καὶ τάχα Arist.*Rh.*1389^{b}18: ἴσως without ἄν c. opt. is f.l. in A.*Supp.*727, E.*IT*1055; ἴ. μέν.., ἴ. δέ.. *perhaps* so or so, X.*Cyr.*4.3.2: repeated ἴ., ἴ. Ar.*Nu.*1320, D.3.33: used to soften or qualify a positive assertion, S.*OC*661, Ar.*Ra.*224, Pl.*Phd.*61c, *Phdr.*233e, Arist.*Metaph.*987^{a}26, etc. IV. with numerals, *about*, Ar.*Pl.*1058, Damox.3.2.

ἴσωσις, εως, ἡ, (ἰσόω) *making equal, comparison*, *Gloss.*

ἴταλα· ἱστία εἰς ἃ τοὺς ἱστοὺς διατείνουσιν, Hsch. (Cf. ἰτλαί.)

Ἰτᾰλ-ία, Ion. -ίη, ἡ, *Italy*, Hdt.1.24, etc. [Ῑτ-, S.*Ant.*1119 (lyr.), Call.*Dian.*58.] **-ιάζω**, Dor. fut. -άξω, *live in Italy*, Hsch., Phot. **-ίδης**, ου, ὁ, poet. for Ἰταλιώτης, *AP*9.344 (Leon.), Call.*Fr.*448. **-ικός**, ή, όν, *Italian*, Pl.*Lg.*659b, etc.; αἵρεσις *Placit.*1.3.9; σπεῖρα, = *Cohors Italica*, *Act.Ap.*10.1; Ἰταλικοί, οἱ, *Italians* resident at Delos, *SIG*726.4 (i B.C.), etc.:—pecul. fem. -ίς, ίδος [ῐ], *AP*7.373 (Thall.); ἡ Ἰταλίς (sc. γῆ), = Ἰταλία, D.C.54.22 codd. **-ιώτης**, ου, ὁ, *Greek inhabitant of Italy*, Hdt.4.15, Th.6. 44, etc.; cf. Σικελιώτης:—fem. -ιῶτις, ιδος, Adj. *Italian*, νῆες, πόλεις, Th.8.91, Str.5.4.4: Adj. -ιωτικός, ή, όν, Pl.*Ep.*326b, Luc.*Hist. Conscr.*15. **-ός**, ὁ, *Italian*, Parth.7.1, Str.5.1.1: as Adj., Ἰ. αἰχμητής [ῐ] *AP*7.741 (Crin.), etc.

ἰτᾰλός, ὁ, = ταῦρος, D.C.*Fr.*4.2, Hsch.; whence Italy is said to be called, Timae.12, cf. Fest. s.v. Ἰταλία. (ϝιταλός, cf. Lat. *vitulus*, Osc. *Viteliú* (*Italia*).)

ἰτᾰμ-εύομαι [ῐ], *to be* ἰταμός, interpol. in Jul.*Or.*7.210c. **-ία**, ἡ, = ἰταμότης, Lxx *Je.*29.17(49.16). **-ός**, ή, όν, (εἶμι *ibo*, ἴτης) *headlong, hasty, eager*, κύνες A.*Fr.*282, Alex.234; ἰ. πρόσωπον Nicol.Com.1. 28; *bold, reckless*, ἰταμὸν καὶ τολμηρὸν ἡ πονηρία D.25.24; ἀναιδὴς καὶ ἰ. Men.*Epit.*311; ἰ. πρὸς τὸ πράττειν Arist.*Pr.*953^{b}4; πρὸς τὰ δεινά Plu.*Galb.*25; πρὸς λόγους ἰταμώτερος Id.2.1041a: Sup. -ώτατος Phld.*Rh.* 1.341 S., Luc.*Icar.*30; τὸ ἰ., = ἰταμότης, Plu.*Fab.*19, etc.; *vigour* of style, Diog.Oen.12; τὸ ἰ. τῆς ψυχῆς Plu.*Rom.*7; ἰ. τι δεδορκώς Luc.*Fug.*19; ἰ. ἀντιβλέπειν Ael.*NA*17.12. Adv. -μῶς Alex.105, Euphro 1.25, Men.*Pk.*306, Plu.2.93b, Gal.11.232; οἱ ἰ. πολιτευόμενοι D.8. 68: Comp. -ώτερον Pl.*Lg.*773b; -ώτερον τῷ βίῳ χρῆσθαι D.19. 233. **-ότης**, ητος, ἡ, *initiative, vigour*, Pl.*Plt.*311a; *effrontery*, Plu.2.715e, Jul.*Or.*7.225c; συγγραφέως Plb.12.9.4.

ἴτας· ὅρκος, καὶ ὁ ᾅδης, Hsch.

ἰτέα [ῐ], Ep. and Ion. ἰτέη, also ἰτείη (A.R.4.1428): ἡ:—*willow*, Il. 21.350, Hecat.292(a) J., Hdt.1.194, *PTeb.ined.*703.195, etc.; ἰ. λευκή, = *Salix alba*, ἰ. μέλαινα, = *Salix amplexicaulis*, Thphr.*HP*3.13.7. II. *wicker shield, target*, E.*Heracl.*376 (lyr.), *Supp.*695, *Tr.*1193, *Cyc.*7, Ar.*Fr.*65. III. ἰ. δένδρος, = ἵππουρις, Ps.-Dsc.4.46. (Εἰτέα, the Attic deme-name, is a different word; cf. ἰτέϊνος, ἰτεόφυλλος; prob. cogn. with Lat. *viēre*, *vīmen*, Lith. *výti* 'twist', 'wind', *vytìs* 'willow-twig', OE. *wiþig* 'willow'.)

ἰτέϊνος [ῐτ], η, ον, *of willow*, ἰ. ῥάβδος Hdt.4.67, cf. Thphr.*HP*5.3.4, *PCair.Zen.*353.5 (iii B.C.); τὰ ἰ. *Sammelb.*5807.3. II. *made of withy rods, wicker*, ἰ. σάκεα Theoc.16.79.

ἰτέον [ῐ], (εἶμι *ibo*) *one must go*, Hp.*Acut.*38, Pl.*R.*394d, *Lg.*803e, etc.

ἰτεόφυλλος [ῐ], ον, *decorated with a pattern of willow-leaves*, φιάλη *Annuario* 4/5.463 (Halic., iii B.C.).

ἰτεών [ῐ], ῶνος, ὁ, *willow-ground*, *Gp.*3.6.6.

ἴτηλος, η, ον, expld. by Hsch. as ἔμμονος, οὐκ ἐξίτηλος, A.*Fr.* 42.

ἰτ-ήριος [ῐ], coined as etym. of ἐξιτήριος, *EM*348.45. **-ης**, ου, ὁ, = ἰταμός, Ar.*Nu.*445, Pl.*Smp.*203d; ἴτας γε ἐφ' ἃ οἱ πολλοὶ φοβοῦνται ἰέναι Id.*Prt.*349e, cf. 359c; ἴ. καὶ πολυπράγμων D.C.55.18. **-ητέον**, = ἰτέον, Ar.*Nu.*131, Diph.31. **-ητικός**, ή, όν, = ἰταμός, Max.Tyr. 41.5: Comp., Id.21.2: Sup. -ώτατον ὁ θυμὸς πρὸς τοὺς κινδύνους *most ready to encounter* dangers, Arist.*EN*1116^{b}26.

ἶτθαι· ἧσθαι, Hsch. **ἰτθέλαν**· διφθέραν, Id. (cf. ἰξαλῆ). **ἰτλαί**· οἷς ⟨ἐν⟩τείνουσι τὰς ᾤας τοῦ ὑφαινομένου μυγελεῖς (fort. Πυγελεῖς)· οἱ δὲ τοὺς μίτους, Id.

ἶτον, τό, Thracian name for a kind of *mushroom*, Thphr.*Fr.*167, Plin.*HN*19.36; prob. fr. ϝίτον, cf. οἰτόν, οὐιτόν.

ἰτός, ή, όν, (εἶμι *ibo*) *passable*, ὁδός *AP*7.480 (Leon.).

ἴτριον (on the accent v. Hdn.Gr.1.357, al.), τό, a kind of *cake* (πεμμάτιον λεπτὸν διὰ σησάμου καὶ μέλιτος γινόμενον Ath.14.646d, but cf. πλακοῦντες, σησαμοῦντες, ἴτρια Ar.*Ach.*1092, μελιτώμασι καὶ ἰτρίοις Dsc.4.63), Anacr.17, Hp.*Acut.*(*Sp.*)72, Anon.Lond.*Fr.*2.3, *POxy.* 736.50: freq. in pl., Sol.38, S.*Fr.*199, Archipp.9, prob. in Herod.3. 44; ἴτρια, τραγήμαθ' ἧκε, πυραμοῦς, ἅμης Ephipp.8.3; later, of any cake, ἴτρια καρποῦ πεποιημένα πυρίνου D.H.1.55; of the Roman *libum*, πλακοῦς ἐκ γάλακτος ἰτρίων καὶ μέλιτος Ath.3.125f.

ἰτρίνεος [ῑν], α, ον, *like* ἴτρια, *AP*6.232 (Crin.).

ἰτριοπώλης, ου, ὁ, *dealer in* ἴτρια, prob. in Poll.7.30.

ἴττα, dialect word for δρυοκόλαψ, Hsch. **ἰττέλα**, v. ἰξαλῆ. **ἴττιον**· οὐσία (Elean), Id. **ἴττον**· ἕν (Cret.), Id. **ἴττυγα**· ἐκπληκτικά A.*Fr.*427 (ap. Hsch.).

ἴττω, Boeot. for ἴστω, 3 sg. imper. of οἶδα, esp. in phrase ἴττω Ζεύς Zeus *be witness!* says Cebes the Theban in Pl.*Phd.*62a; Θήβαθεν ἴττω Δεύς, and ἴττω Ἡρακλῆς, says the Boeotian in Ar.*Ach.*911, 860, cf. Pl.*Ep.*345a.

Ἴτῠλος [ῐ], ὁ, *Itylus*, son of Zethus and Aëdon, Od.19.522, Pherecyd.124J.: expld. as, = μόνος, ὀρφανός, νέος, ἁπαλός by Hsch.

ἴτυξ, a bird, Phot., Suid.; cf. ἴδυξ.

ἴτῠς [ῐ], υος, ἡ, in Hom. (only in Il.) always of the *felloe* of a wheel, ὄφρα ἴτυν κάμψῃ Il.4.486 (made of poplar), cf. 5.724, *PMasp.*303.14 (vi A.D.); *outer edge* or *rim* of a shield, Hes.*Sc.*314, Hdt.7.89: hence, *the round shield* itself, Tyrt.15.3, E.*Ion*210 (lyr.), *Tr.*1197, X.*An.*4.7.12; ἴ. βλεφάρων *arch* of the eyebrows, *Anacreont.*15.17; ἀγκίστρων ἴ. *AP*6.28 (Jul.), cf. Opp.*H.*5.138; ἴ. τῆς πλευρᾶς *border* of rib, Gal.2.681; *rim* of joint-socket, Id.*UP*2.17; *guard* of trepan, Id.10.448. (Aeol. ϝίτυς Ter.Maur.658.)

Ἴτυς, υος, ὁ, *Itys*, son of Tereus and Procne, A.*Ag.*1144 (lyr.), Ar.*Av.*212, etc. [ῐτῠ-, but ἃ Ἴτῡν αἰὲν Ἴτῡν ὀλοφύρεται S.*El.*148 (lyr.), cf. Ar. l. c.]

ἴτω [ῐ], 3 sg. imper. from εἶμι (*ibo*); in Trag. almost an exclam., *go to!* S.*Ph.*120; *well, well!* E.*Med.*798.

Ἴτων [ῐ], ὁ, St.Byz., and **Ἴτωνος**, ὁ, Str.9.5.8, a town in Thessaly:—hence **Ἰτωνία**, ἡ, title of Athena who was worshipped there, Hecat. 2J., Paus.1.13.3, 10.1.10; χρυσαιγίδος Ἰτωνίας ναός B.*Fr.*11.2; also at Coronea, Plb.4.25.2, 25.3.2, Str.9.2.29, Paus.9.33.1; at Athens, *IG* 1^{2}.310.217; at Amorgos, ib.12(7).33 (ii B.C.):—also **Ἰτωνιάς**, ἡ, Call. *Cer.*75, *AP*9.743 (Theodorid.): **Ἰτωνίς**, ἡ, A.R.1.551, *AP*6.130 ((Leon.)).

Ἰτώνιος, ὁ (sc. μήν), name of month in Thessaly, *IG*9(2).259.5, al.: **Ἰτώνια**, τά, festival of Athena Itonia, ib.12(7).22, al. (Amorgos), cf. Polyaen.2.54.

ἰῦ, exclam. of surprise, Hdn.Gr.1.506.

Ἰυγγίης, ὁ, epith. of Dionysus, Hsch.

ἰυγγικός, ή, όν, (ἴυγξ) *of the* ἴυγγες (cf. ἴυγξ 3), φύσις Dam.*Pr.*112, 119.

Ἰύγγιος, ὁ (sc. μήν), name of month in Thessaly, *IG*9(2).258.5 (cf. p.xii); cf. Ἰυγγίης.

ἰυγγοδρομέω, = βοηδρομέω, βοηθέω, (Boeot.) Hsch. (leg. ἰυγο-).

ἰυγή, ἡ, = ἰυγμός, *howling, shrieking*, as of men in pain, Orac.ap. Hdt.9.43, S.*Ph.*752; = γυναικῶν οἰμωγαί *AB*267; but also of the *shout* of heralds, Tim.*Pers.*233; the *hissing* of snakes, Nic.*Th.*400, Opp.*H.* 1.565. [ῑυ- Orac.ap.Hdt. l. c., Nic.; ῐυ- in S. l. c.]

ἰυγμός, ὁ, (ἰύζω) *shout of joy*, Il.18.572; also, *a cry of pain, shriek*, A.*Ch.*26 (lyr.), E.*Heracl.*126. [ῑ in Il.; ῐ in Trag.]

ἴυγξ, ἴυγγος, ἡ, (ἰύζω, cf. Dam.*Pr.*213), *wryneck, Iynx torquilla*, Arist.*HA*504^{a}12, *PA*695^{a}23, Ael.*NA*6.19; used as a charm to recover unfaithful lovers, being bound to a revolving wheel, ἴ. τετράκναμος Pi.*P.*4.214, cf. *AP*5.204; ἕλκειν ἴυγγα ἐπί τινι X.*Mem.*3.11. 18; ἴ. ἕλκε τὺ τῆνον ἐμὸν ποτὶ δῶμα Theoc.2.17: metaph., ἕλκομαι ἴυγγι ἦτορ *as by the magic wheel*, Pi.*N.*4.35; ὥσπερ ἀπὸ ἴυγγος τῷ κάλλει ἑλκόμενος Luc.*Dom.*13. 2. metaph., *spell, charm*, τῇ σῇ ληφθέντες ἴυγγι Ar.*Lys.*1110, cf. S.*Fr.*474 (prob. cj.), Lyc.310, D.L. 6.76, Plu.2.1093d (prob. cj. in 568a), Philostr.*VA*8.7 (pl.), Hld.8.5; *passionate yearning for*, ἀγαθῶν ἑτάρων A.*Pers.*989. 3. in pl., name of certain 'Chaldaic' divinities, Procl.*in R.*2.213K., *in Cra.*p.33P., Dam.*Pr.*111, al.: in sg., ἡ πρώτη ἴ. ib.217, cf. 213. 4. = σῦριγξ μονοκάλαμος, *EM*480.1. [ῑ Ep. and Pi.; ῐ Att.]

ἰύζω, aor. ἴυξα Pi.*P.*4.237:—*shout, yell*, in order to scare beasts, πολλὰ μάλ' ἰύζουσιν Il.17.66; οἱ δ' ἰύζοντες ἕποντο Od.15.162; later, *yell* from grief or pain, *cry out*, ἴυξεν ἀφωνήτῳ ἄχει Pi. l. c.; used by A. in lyr., only in imper., ἴυζ' ἄποτμον βοάν *Pers.*281, cf. 1042, *Supp.* 808, 872; part., ἰύζων S.*Tr.*787; ἰύζων ἀν' ὄρος Call.*Fr.*512 (perh. here = *piping*, cf. sq.); of bees, *buzz*, Q.S.1.440. (From the Interjection ἰῦ, q. v. (from ἰού acc. to *EM*480.6): ϝι-, cf. ἀβίυκτος, ἐκβιούζει.) [ῑ Ep. and Pi.; ῐ in S.*Tr.*787, and prob. in A.]

ἰυκτής [ῐ], οῦ, ὁ, (ἰύζω) *one who shouts* or *yells*: *singer, piper*, Theoc.8.30, in poet. form ἰυκτά [ᾰ].

ἴυρκες· αἶγες ἀγρίαι, ὑστριχίδες, Hsch. **ἰυχμός**, ὁ, = ἰυγμός, Id. **ιφειομαχω**, = *ario*, *Gloss.* (dub., fort. κριομαχῶ, = *arieto*).

Ἴφθῖμις, ὁ, Egyptian deity (prob. Nefertem) identified with Prometheus, *PHib.*1.27.86 (iii B.C.).

ἴφθῖμος, η, ον, also ος, ον (v. infr.), *stout, strong*, of bodily strength, ὤμοις ἰ. Il.18.204; κρατὶ ἐπ' ἰ. 3.336; ἰ. ποταμῶν 17.749; βοῶν ἴ. κάρηνα 23.260; of heroes, ἴ. ψυχαί, κεφαλαί, 1.3, 11.55; of Hades, Od. 10.534; also, of women, *comely, stately*, ἰ. βασίλεια 16.332; ἄλοχος Il.5.415, Theoc.17.128; παράκοιτις Od.23.92, etc.; θυγάτηρ 15.364; Πηρώ 11.287: later, generally, *strong, powerful*, ἰφθίμης φιλότητος D.P.655:—Hom. uses ἰφθίμη of women; but ἴφθιμοι ψυχαί, κεφαλαί, speaking of men. (No ϝ-; prob. not cogn. with ἴς, ἶφι.)

ἶφι (A) (instrum. of ἴς, q. v.), Ep. Adv. *by force* or *might*, freq. in Hom., but only with four Verbs, ἶ. ἀνάσσειν Il.1.38, etc.; ἶ. μάχεσθαι 1.151; ἶ. δαμῆναι 19.417, Od.18.156; βοὸς ἶ. κταμένοιο Il.3.375; later ἶ. βιησάμενος Euph.90, etc.—Freq. in prop. names, e. g. Ἰφιάνασσα, Ἰφιγένεια, Ἰφιγόνη, Ἰφιδάμας, Ἴφικλος, ϝιφιάδας, etc.

ἶφι (B), an Egyptian measure, prob. = $\frac{1}{4}$ and $\frac{1}{8}$ artaba, *PMasp.*138, 139, al. (vi A.D.), *PLond.*5.1687.11 (vi A.D.):—hence **ἴφιον** μέτρον *PMasp.*308.3 (vi A.D.): written οἶφιν Hsch.

ἰφῐ-γένειᾰ [ιφ], ἡ, *strong-born, mighty*, epith. of Artemis, Paus. 2.35.1, Hsch. II. pr. n., *Iphigeneia*, Agamemnon's daughter, the Homeric Ἰφιάνασσα (but distd. by S.*El.*158), Stesich.27, etc.; also called Ἰφιγόνη, E.*El.*1023; Ἶφις Lyc.324. [-ειᾱ A.*Ag.*1526 (lyr.).] **-γένητος**, ον, *produced by might*, πῦρ Orph.*Fr.*247.28.

ἴφικλος· δυσχερής, Hsch.: as pr. n., Il.2.705, al.:—hence Adj., Ἰφίκλειος, α, ον, σφυρόν Call.*Aet.*3.1.46.

Ἰφικρᾰτίδες, αἱ, a kind of *shoes*, called from the Athen. general Iphicrates, D.S.15.44, Alciphr.3.57, Dam.*Isid.*89.

ἰφίν· καλήν, Hsch. **ἰφιντάν**· κρύφα λαλοῦσαν, αἰνιγματωδῶς, Id.

ἴφιος [ῑφ], α, ον, Ep. Adj., freq. in Hom., but only in phrase ἴ. μῆλα *fat, goodly* sheep, Il.5.556, al., cf. D.P.753, etc.

ἶφις· ταχύς, Hsch. **ἰφίτην**· ἁγνίτην, Id. **ἴφλημα**· τραῦμα, Id. (i. e. ἰφλ-, cf. σίφλωμα).

ἴφυον [ῐ], τό, *spike-lavender, Lavandula Spica*, Ar.*Th.*910 (pl.), *Fr.* 560 (pl.), Epich.161, Thphr.*HP*6.6.11, 6.8.3.

ἰχαίνω [ῐ], = sq., ὅσσα δ' ἐμεῖο σέθεν παρὰ θυμὸς ἀκοῦσαι ἰχαίνει Call. *Aet.*1.1.22, cf. *EM*568.7.

ἰχᾰνάω [ῐ], *crave, yearn*, v. l. for ἰσχ- in Il.23.300, Od 8.288; τυροῦ ἀλώπηξ ἰχανῶσα Babr.77.2:—Med., ἰχανᾶσθ' ἐπαυρέσθαι Herod. 7.26, cf. Hsch., *EM*478.44. (Cf. sq.; **Ἴχανα**, name of a town in Sicily, is derived from the root by St.Byz.: prob. cogn. with ἀχήν, ἠχήν; Avest. *āzi-* 'craving', Skt. *īhate* 'crave'.)

ἶχαρ (ἴχαρ codd.), τό, *vehement desire*, dub. l. in A.*Supp.*850 (lyr.), cf. Sch.

ἴχθον· ἄστρον, ἐγχειράδιον, ξυλοφάνιον, Hsch.

ἰχθύ-α [ῠ], Ion. -ύη, ἡ, (ἰχθῦς) *dried skin of the fish* ῥίνη, like our *shagreen*, Hp.*Foet.Exsect.*1, Archig.ap.Gal.12.406; of *fish-skin* in general, Ruf.ap.Orib.4.2.16. II. *pot*, perh. for pickled fish, *CIG* 8345*c* (Nola, vase). III. *fishing, fishery*, *BGU*1123.9 (i A.D.), *PSI*3.160.8 (ii A.D.). IV. ταριχηρὰ ἰ. pickled *fish*, *PLond.*3.856. 20 (i A.D.). **-ἀγωγός**, v. ἰχθυόνερ. **-άζομαι**, = ἰχθυάω, *AP* 7.693 (Apollonid.). **-ᾰκός**, ή, όν, = ἰχθυϊκός, ζῴδια, *Cat.Cod. Astr.*1.160. II. **-ᾰκὴ** πύλη, ἡ, *fish*-gate, Aq., Sm., Thd.*Ze.*1.10: cf. ἰχθυϊκός. **-άω**, *fish, angle*, mostly in Ep. pres. and impf., ἰχθυάασκον γναμπτοῖς ἀγκίστροισιν Od.4.368: c. acc., *fish for*, αὐτοῦ δ' ἰχθυάᾳ.. δελφῖνας 12.95, cf. Opp.*H.*1.426:—Med., Lyc.46. II. *sport* (like fish), δελφῖνες.. ἐθύνεον ἰχθυάοντες Hes.*Sc.*210. III. Pass., *to be made of fish*, ἰχθυώμενος ἄρτος (vulg. ἄργος) Horap.1.14.

ἰχθῠβολ-εύς, έως, ὁ, = ἰχθυβόλος 2, Nic.*Th.*793, Call.*Del.*15, *AP*7. 504 (Leon.), 10.9, cf. Ps.-Hes.ap.Ath.3.116a. **-έω**, *strike, harpoon fish*, *AP*7.381 (Etrusc.), 635 (Antiphil.). **-ος**, ον, (parox.) *striking fish, catching fish*, ἰ. μηχανή of the trident, A.*Th.*132 (lyr.); αἴθυιαι *AP*6.23. 2. Subst., *fisher, angler*, ib.7.295 (Leon.), 9.227 (Bianor). II. Pass., (proparox.) ἰ. θήρα a spoil *of speared fish*, ib.6.24; ἰ. δεῖπνα Opp.*H.*3.18.

ἰχθῠ-βόρος, ον, *fish-eating*, λαρίδες *AP*7.652 (Leon.). **-βοτος**, ον, *fed on by fish*, Opp.*H.*2.1, Epic.*Oxy.*213^{v}.15. **-γόνος**, ον, *producing fish*, Nonn.*D.*26.275.

ἰχθύδιον, τό, Dim. of ἰχθύς, *little fish*, freq. in Com. (v. infr.), Chrysipp.*Stoic.*2.208, *PFlor.*119.7 (iii A.D.), Jul.*Mis.*350b, etc. [ῡ, Ar.*Fr.*387.8, Theopomp.Com.62.3, Anaxil.19, Cratin.Jun.13, *POxy.* 784 (i B.C.), etc.; but ῠ in dact., *AP*11.405 (Lucill.), Archestr.*Fr.* 45.18.]

ἰχθῠ-δόκος, ον, (δέχομαι) *holding fish*, σπυρίδες *AP*6.4 (Leon.). **-εῖον**, τό, *fish-market*, dub. in *IG*12(2).646^{a}.49 (Nesos). **-η**, ἡ,

Ion. for ἰχθύα. **-ήματα, τά,** (ἰχθύα) *fish-scales*: hence, *scrapings, shavings,* λωτοῦ Hp.*Ulc.*13, al.: sg. only, ib.21. **-ηρός,** ά, όν, (ἰχθύς) *fishy, scaly,* i.e. *foul, dirty,* πινακίσκοι Ar.*Pl.*814, *Fr.*532; ἔλαιον Ph.*Bel.*90.19; ζωμός Luc.*Lex.*5; οὐκ ἔστιν ἰχθυηρόν nothing *of the fish kind,* Diph.32.21; ἡ πύλη ἡ ἰ. the *fish*-gate, Lxx *Ne.*3.3:—Subst., **ἰχθυηρά,** ἡ, *tax on fish, UPZ*110.98 (ii B.C.), *PFay.*42(*a*)^{v}2 (ii A.D.). **-ία,** ἡ, *fishing,* Procl.*Vit.Hom.*p.25 W. **-ικός,** ή, όν, = ἰχθυηρός, πύλη Lxx 2*Ch.*33.14; ζῴδια Ptol.*Tetr.*152:—Subst., **-ική,** ἡ, *fishery toll, Inscr.Magn.*116.42, *OGI*496.9 (Ephesus): **-ικά,** τά, *Ostr.*343 (iii B.C.):—also **-ϊνος,** η, ον, Ael.*NA*17.32. **-κεντρον,** τό, *trident,* Poll.10.133, Paus.Gr.*Fr.*216: **ἰχθυόκεντρον,** Hsch., Suid. **-μέδων,** οντος, ὁ, *king of fish,* Marc.Sid.54. **-νόμος,** ον, *ruling-fish,* Opp.*H.*1.643.

ἰχθῠο-βολεύς, -βόλος, = ἰχθυβ-, Phot., Eust.191.33. **-βρωτος,** ον, *eaten by fish,* Plu.2.668a, *SIG*997.7 (Smyrna). **-ειδής,** ές, *fish-like,* λεπίς Hdt.7.61. **-εις,** εσσα, εν, *full of fish, fishy,* πόντος, Ἑλλήσποντος, Il.9.4,360; ἰ. κέλευθα, i.e. the sea, Od.3.177; μυχὸς ἰ., of the Bosporus, Ar.*Th.*324; *fish-like,* δέμας Opp.*H.*3.548. II. *consisting of fish,* θήρη ib.1.666; βόλος *AP*6.223 (Antip.). **-θήρα,** = κυκλάμινος, Ps.-Dsc.2.164. **-θήρας,** ου, ὁ, *fisherman,* Sch.Lyc.1200: also **-θηρευτής,** οῦ, ὁ, Man.4.243: **-θηρητήρ,** ῆρος, ὁ, *AP*7.702 (Apollonid.). **-θηρία,** ἡ, *fishing,* Eust.1165.3: ἡ ἰχθυοθηρική (sc. τέχνη) Poll.1.97. **-κένταυρος,** ὁ, ἡ, *half-man and half-fish,* of Triton, Tz. ad Lyc.34. **-κολλα,** ἡ, *fish-glue,* i.e. *isinglass,* Dsc.3.88, Gal.13.662, cf. Plin.*HN*32.84:—also **-κολλον,** τό, *Gloss.* **-λογέω,** *discourse of fish,* Ath.7.308d, 8.360d. **-λύμης** [ῡ], ου, ὁ, *plague of fish,* Com. epith. of a fish-eater, Ar.*Pax* 814. **-μαντις,** εως, ὁ, *one who prophesies by means of fish,* Ath.8.333d. **-μετάβολος,** ὁ, *fishmonger, PRyl.*196.7 (ii A.D.).

ἰχθυόνερ· ἰχθυαγωγοί, Hsch.

ἰχθῠοπράτης [ᾰ], οῦ, ὁ, = -πώλης, *PLond.*1.113.5^{b}4 (vi A.D.), etc.

ἰχθῠοπτρίς (v.l. **-οπτίς**), ίδος, fem. Adj. *for broiling fish,* ἐσχάρα Poll.6.88, 10.95.

ἰχθῠο-πώλαινα, irreg. fem. of -πώλης, Pherecr.64. **-πωλέω,** *sell fish,* Poll.7.26. **-πώλης,** ου, ὁ, *fishmonger,* freq. in Com., Ar.*Fr.*387.10, Antiph.68.7, Alex.56.1; also in Pap., *BGU*330.10, etc.:—fem. **-πωλις** ἀγορά *fish*-market, Plu.2.849e, Maiuri *Nuova Silloge* 440 (Cos). **-πωλία,** ἡ, *fishmongering,* Ath.7.276f, Plu.2.668a (nisi leg. τὰ ἰχθυοπώλια). **-πώλιον,** τό, *fish-market, IPE*I^2.32*B*4 (Olbia), *PFlor.*119.9 (iii A.D.), Sch.Ar.*Ra.*1068: **-πωλεῖον,** Hsch. **-ρροος,** ον, contr. **-ρους,** ουν, (ῥέω) *swarming with fish,* ποταμός Timocl.15.1. **-τροφεῖον,** τό, *fish-pond,* Moschio ap.Ath.5.208a, D.S.11.25: **-τρόφιον,** τό, *SIG*997.13 (Smyrna). **-τροφικός,** ή, όν, *of* or *for keeping fish, Gp.*20.1 tit. **-τρόφος,** ον, *feeding fish*: *full of fish,* διαδρομαί Plu.*Luc.*39.

ἰχθῠουλκός, ὁ, (ἕλκω) *angler,* Phot., Suid.:—written **-ολκός** in Hsch.

ἰχθῠοφᾰγ-έω, *feed on fish,* Arist.*HA*616^{a}32, Str.11.8.7. **-ία,** ἡ, *fish diet, PMag.Berol.*1.290, Eust.135.19. **-ος,** ον, *eating fish,* Clearch.74; ἔθνη Porph.*Abst.*1.13; οἱ Ἰ. ἄνδρες the *Fish-eaters,* a tribe on the Arabian Gulf, Hdt.3.19, cf. Str.16.4.4, Paus.1.33.4; another on the Persian Gulf, Str.15.2.1.

ἰχθῠοφορ-έω, *convey fish,* εἰς Ἀρκαδίαν, Ἀρχ.Ἐφ.1918.168 (Epid.). II. *produce fish, EM*117.26. **-ος,** ον, *producing fish,* κρηνῖδες Ctes.*Fr.*57.10. 2. *carrying fish,* πλοῖα Sm.*Jb.*40.26(31): Subst. -φόρος, ὁ, Ἀρχ.Ἐφ.1918.168 (Epid.).

ἰχθῠ-πᾰγής, ές, *piercing fish,* ἀγκίστρων στόματα *AP*6.27 (Theaet.). **-πόρος,** ὁ, (πείρω) *harpoon, Inscr.Délos* 354.60 (iii B.C.).

ἰχθῦς (so Hdn.Gr.2.936, -ῦς and -ύς freq. in codd.), ύος, ὁ, acc. ἰχθύν Pi.*Fr.*306, cf. Hdn.Gr.1.416, Choerob. *in Theod.*1.383, in late Poets also ἰχθύα *AP*9.227 (Bianor), Theoc.21.45: voc. ἰχθύ Erinn.1, Crates Com.14: pl. ἰχθύες Pl.*Phd.*109e, etc., ἰχθῦς Alex.261.9, acc. ἰχθύας, contr. ἰχθῦς Od.5.53, both forms being used in Com., -ῦς Ar.*Ra.*1068, Archipp.29, -ύας Antiph.68.12, Ephipp.21; codd. vary in Arist.*HA*564^{b}19, *PA*644^{a}21, D.S.5.3, Str.8.3.19, etc.; -ῦς *SIG*997.1 (Smyrna, perh. i B.C.); -ύας *BGU*1123.9 (Aug.), etc.: dual ἰχθῦ Antiph.194.15:—*fish,* ὠμηστής Il.24.82, cf. 21.122, al., cf. Hes.*Op.*277, Hdt.2.93, S.*Aj.*1297, etc.: prov., ἀφωνότερος τῶν ἰχθύων Luc.*Gall.*1, cf. S.E.*M.*2.18: metaph., of *a stupid fellow,* Plu.2.975b. II. in pl., οἱ ἰχθύες *the fish-market* at Athens, παρὰ τοὺς ἰχθῦς Ar.*Ra.*1068; ἐν τοῖς ἰχθύσι Id.*V.*789, Antiph.125.1. III. pl., the constellation *Pisces,* Eudox.ap.Hipparch.1.2.3; ἰ. Διός Porph.*Antr.*22. (ἰχθύς Att. acc. to Gell.2.3.2.) [ῡ in disyll. cases, nom. -ῦς Il.21.127, Damox.2.20, Archestr.*Fr.*52 (ἰχθῦς οὖσα shd. be read for ἰχθὺς ἐοῦσα in Matro *Conv.*35), acc. -ῡν Pherecr.120, Antiph.166.7, Archestr.*Fr.*28, but -ῠν Theoc.21.49, and apptly. Pi. l.c.: ῠ in trisyll. cases and in all compds.] (Cf. Lith. *žuvìs,* Arm. *jukn,* 'fish'.)

ἰχθῠσιληϊστήρ, ῆρος, ὁ, *a stealer of fish, AP*7.295 (Leon.).

ἰχθυ-στεφής, ές, *fish-crowned,* κόλποι Ἀμφιτρίτας Tim.*Pers.*38. **-φάγος** [ῠ, ᾰ], ον, = ἰχθυοφάγος, *AP*9.83 (Phil.). **-φόνος,** ον, *killing fish,* Opp.*C.*2.444. **-ώδης,** ες, = ἰχθυοειδής, Arist.*PA*697^{b}5, al. Adv. -δῶς Id.*HA*536^{a}9. 2. *full of fish,* λίμνη Hdt.7.109, Arr.*Ind.*41.1. II. (ὄδ-ωδα) *fishy, smelling* or *tasting of fish,* ἐρυγή Aret.*SD*1.5, Gal.7.76; πρόβατα Philostr.*VA*3.55, cf. Arr.*Ind.*26.7.

ἴχλα· κίχλα, Hsch. **ἴχματα·** ἴχνια, Id. (Perh. for ἴθματα.)

Ἰχν-αῖος, α, ον, *of Ichnae in Thessaly,* of Themis, *h.Ap.*94; of Nemesis, *AP*9.405 (Diod.), Lyc.129: Ἴχναι (in Thessaly), ὅπου ἡ Θέμις Ἰ. τιμᾶται Str.9.5.14. **-άομαι,** = ἰχνεύω, Hsch., Suid. **-εία,** ἡ, *casting about for the scent,* of hounds, X.*Cyn.*3.7 (pl.). **-ελάτης,** v. ἰχνηλάτης. **-ευμα,** ατος, τό, *track,* Poll.5.11. **-εύμων,** ονος, ὁ, *tracker*: hence, 1. an Egyptian animal of the weasel-kind, *which hunts out* crocodile's eggs (asp's eggs, Ael.*NA*6.38), *Herpestes ichneumon,* Arist.*HA*612^{a}16, Eub.107.12, Nic.*Th.*190, Plu.2.966d, *PLond.*3.904 (ii A.D.); cf. ἰχνευτής II. 2. a small kind of wasp, *that hunts* spiders, *Pelopaeus spirifex,* Arist.*HA*552^{b}26, 609^{a}5, cf. Plin.*HN*10.204. 3. a bird, Ant.Lib.14. **-ευσις,** εως, ἡ, *tracking,* X.*Cyn.*3.4, 10.5, Poll.5.11. II. *method of investigation,* cj. in Epicur.*Ep.*2 p.42 U. **-εύτειρα,** ἡ, fem. of ἰχνευτήρ, τέχνα *IG*9(1).880.9 (Corc.). **-ευτέος,** α, ον, *to be searched out,* δικαιοσύνη Philostr.*VA*6.21. **-ευτήρ,** ῆρος, ὁ, = sq., Opp.*C.*1.76, 450, 468; as Adj., ἰ. ταρσός Nonn.*D.*46.115. **-ευτής,** οῦ, ὁ, *tracker, hunter,* Poll.5.10; of dogs which hunt by scent, ib.17: metaph., Κύπριδος ἰχνευτὰς ἀργυρέους σκύλακας, of money given to a ἑταίρα, *AP*5.15 (Marc. Arg.): Ἰχνευταί, οἱ, title of a satyric play by Sophocles (cf. v. 298). 2. *detective* who *traces* missing persons, *PRyl.*188.22 (ii A.D.). II. = ἰχνεύμων I, Hdt.2.67, Nic.*Th.*195. **-ευτικός,** ή, όν, *good at tracking,* κύων Ael.*NA*6.59, Arr.*Epict.*1.2.34, Ph.2.38. **-εύω,** *track out, hunt after,* S.*Aj.*20, *OT* 221, 476 (lyr.); ἰ. θῆρας κυσίν E.*Cyc.*130; κύνες ἰχνεύουσαι *hunting by scent,* Pl.*Lg.*654e: metaph., κατὰ σοῦ τὴν ψῆφον ἰ. *seeking for* a vote of condemnation, Ar.*Eq.*808; ἰ. τὰ λεχθέντα Pl.*Prm.*128c; τὴν τοῦ καλοῦ φύσιν Id.*R.*401c; [σοφίαν] Lxx *Si.*51.15; ἰχνεύεις.. τίς εἴμ' ἐγώ..; *Epigr.Gr.*227 (Teos); *follow on the track of, emulate,* ματραδελφεούς Pi.*P.*8.35. 2. ἰ. ὄρη *to hunt* the mountains, X.*Cyn.*4.9.

ἰχνηλ-ᾰσία, ἡ, (ἐλαύνω) *tracking out, search,* Them.*Or.*13.165d. **-ᾰτέω,** *track out,* τἀληθὲς λόγῳ Ph.1.12, cf. 2.475, al. **-άτης** [ᾰ], ου, ὁ, *tracker,* [ἀληθείας] Plu.2.762b:—poet. **ἰχνελάτης** *AP*6.183 (Zos.), *APl.*4.289. **-ᾰτία** or **-εία,** ἡ, = ff.ll. for -ηλασία in Poll.5.11. **-ᾰτικός,** ή, όν, = ἰχνευτικός, Sch.S.*Aj.*8.

ἴχνιον, τό (Dim. of ἴχνος only in form, cf. Hdn.Gr.2.903, but written ἰχνίον by Eust.233.44), *track, footprint,* ἴχνι' ἐρευνῶντες κύνες ἤϊσαν Od.19.436; μετ' ἴχνια βαῖνε θεοῖο followed on her *track,* 5.193; μετ' ἀνέρος ἴχνι' ἐρευνῶν Il.18.321; κατ' ἴχνιά τινος ἐφέπεσθαι A.R.1.575; ἴχνια ἵππων X.*An.*1.6.1 (v.l. ἴχνη): less freq. in sg., τὸ ἰ. μοῦνον λέλειπται τῶν ποδῶν Democr.228; ἰ. ὀξέος ἵππου Call.*Aet.*3.1.86; ἕπεσθαί τινι κατ' ἴχνιον Q.S.8.361; ἰ. ἑδράσασθαι to plant one's *step, AP*6.70 (Maced.). 2. metaph., *trace, remnant,* προτέρης ἀγλαΐης ib.58 (Isid.).

ἴχνιππος· ὅπου οἱ λίθοι τρίβονται, ἀκόνη, Hsch.

ἰχνο-βάτης [ᾰ], ου, ὁ, *going on the track,* name of a hound, Ov.*Met.*3.207. **-βλᾰβής,** ές, *hurt in the foot,* Man.4.500. **-γρᾰφία,** ἡ, *tracing out*: *ground-plan,* Vitr.1.2.2. **-πέδη,** ἡ, a kind of *fetter* or *trap, AP*6.109 (Antip.), 7.626. **-ποιέω,** *track out,* ταῖς ῥισὶν ἰ. τὰ θηρία *EM*395.39.

ἴχνος, εος, τό, *track, footstep,* Od.17.317, Hes.*Op.*680, Hdt.4.82; of the *spoor* of game, X.*Cyn.*6.15, etc.: metaph., *track, trace,* κατ' ἴχνος πλατᾶν ἄφαντον A.*Ag.*695 (lyr.); ἐς ταὐτὸν ἐλθὼν.. λόγων ἴ. Id.*Pr.*845; ἴ. κακῶν ῥινηλατούσῃ Id.*Ag.*1184; ἴ. παλαιᾶς δυσεκμάρτου αἰτίας S.*OT*109; ἴ. τειχέων E.*Hel.*108; ἴχνη τῶν πληγῶν Pl.*Grg.*524c; τὰ τῶν κονδύλων ἴ. Aeschin.3.212: with neg., not *a trace,* μαζῶν οὐδὲ ἴχνη Aret.*SD*1.8; ἴ. ποδὸς θεῖναι, Lat. *vestigia ponere,* E.*IT*752, cf. *Or.*234; θέσθαι *AP*7.464 (Antip.); λεπτὸν ἴ. ἀρβύλης τίθετε step softly, E.*Or.*140 (lyr.); ἴ. ἐπαντέλλειν ποδός Id.*Ph.*105 (lyr.); ἴ. ἐρείδειν *AP*5.300 (Paul. Sil.); ἐν ἴχνεσί τινος πόδα νέμειν (metaph.) Pi.*N.*6.15; ἰχνῶν τινος ἔχεσθαι Lib.*Or.*64.4; τοῖς στοιχοῦσι τοῖς ἴχνεσι τῆς πίστεως *Ep.Rom.*4.12; κατ' ἴχνος ᾄσσειν, κατ' ἴχνη διώκειν, S.*Aj.*32, Pl.*R.*410b, cf. E.*Hec.*1059 (lyr.); εἰς ἴχνος τινὸς ἰέναι Pl.*Ep.*330e; ἴ. μετιέναι, μετελθεῖν, Id.*Phdr.*276d, *Tht.*187e; ἴχνους προσάπτεσθαι hit upon a *trail,* Id.*Plt.*290d; τοῖς ἀρχαίοις ἴ. ἐς τὰ θεμέλια χρωμένους Jul.*Or.*2.66b; ἴχνη ὑποψίας εἴς τινα φέρει Antipho 2.3.10; μήτ' ἴ. μήτ' αἴθυγμα..παραδιδόντων Phld.*Sign.*29, cf. *Rh.*1.91 S. 2. poet., *foot,* E.*Ba.*1134, Herod.7.20. 3. *hard sole of the foot,* Lxx *De.*11.24, al., Gal.10.876, Orib.47.9.7; *sole of a shoe,* Hp.*Art.*62, Arr.*Ind.*16.5; *sandal, POxy.*1449.51 (pl., iii A.D.). 4. τὰ ἴ. τῶν χειρῶν the *palms* of the hands, Lxx 1*Ki.*5.4. 5. ἴ. ἀνθρώπινον, as a measure of length, Ruf.*Anat.*31. 6. *track, route* in the desert, *PRyl.*197.8 (ii A.D.). 7. pl., *representations of footprints* as votive offerings indicating the presence of a God, ἀνέθηκαν... κατὰ τὴν τοῦ θεοῦ ἐνέργιαν ἴχνη αὐτοῦ χρύσεα τέσσερα *BCH*51.106 (Panamara), etc.

ἰχνοσκοπ-έω, *look at the track* or *traces,* ἐν στίβοισι τοῖς ἐμοῖς A.*Ch.*227, cf. S.*Ichn.*7; ἰ. καὶ στιβεύειν τὸ μέλλον Plu.2.399a. **-ία,** ἡ, *looking at the tracks,* Plu.2.917f.

ἰχώρ [ῑ], ῶρος, ὁ, *ichor, the juice,* not blood, that flows in the veins of gods, Il.5.340, etc.: Ep. acc. ἰχῶ ib.416: in pl., of the Giants, Str.6.3.5; later simply, *blood,* A.*Ag.*1480 (anap.). II. *the watery part* of animal juices, *serum* (cf. Gal.15.345), of the blood, Hp.*Cord.*11, Pl.*Ti.*83c, Arist.*HA*521^{b}2 (also in pl., v.l. in 521^{a}18), *PA*651^{a}18; of gall, χολάδεας ἰχῶρας Hp.*Acut.*(*Sp.*)1; of milk, *whey,* Arist.*HA*521^{b}27; *gravy* of underdone meat, Archestr.*Fr.*57.6; *juice* of burning logs, Dsc.1.119, *Eup.*1.120. 2. *serous* or *sero-purulent discharge,* Hp.*VC*19, Arist.*HA*630^{a}6 (pl.), Gal.10.184, etc.; ἰχῶρες ὑδαρεῖς ὕπωχροι, from women in childbirth, Arist.*HA*586^{b}32; of the *putrefied blood* of a viper, Id.*Mir.*845^{a}8; of *naphtha* (prob.), regarded in legend as due to the putrefaction of Giants' corpses, ib.838^{a}29.

ἰχωρο-ειδής [ῑ], ές, *serous,* αἷμα Hp.*Nat.Hom.*12, Arist.*HA*521^{a}13, Alex.Trall.12. **-ρροέω,** (ῥέω) *run with serous matter,* Hp.

*Coac.*501, Erot. s.v. δακρυῶδες ἕλκος :—later **ἰχωρροέω**, ὦτα ἰχωρροοῦντα Dsc.3.23, cf. Archig.ap.Orib.46.26.2.

ἰχωρώδης [ῑ], ες, = ἰχωροειδής, Hp.*Morb.*3.16, v.l. in Arist.*HA*586ᵃ 29.

ἴψ (on the accent v. Hdn.Gr.1.404), ὁ, gen. ἰπός [ῐ], nom. pl. ἶπες : (ἴπτομαι):—*wood-worm*, Od.21.395, Thphr.*HP*8.10.5; found in vines, Id.*CP*3.22.5, *Lap.*49, Str.13.1.64. (Cf. ἴξ.)

ἴψαο, v. ἴπτομαι.

ἴψ-ηλος, α, ον, Aeol. for ὑψηλός, *Lyr.Adesp.*60. **-οθεν**, Aeol. for ὑψόθεν, Jo.Gramm.*Comp.*3.15. **-οι**, Aeol. for ὑψοῦ, Sapph.91.

ἴψον (ἴπτομαι)· τὸ δεσμωτήριον, Hsch.

ἴψος (A) or **ἰψός**, ὁ, *cork-oak*, *Quercus Suber* (?), Thphr.*HP*3.4.2. 2. at Thurii, = κισσός, Hsch.

ἴψος (B), τό, Aeol. for ὕψος, Hdn.Gr.2.928; cf. ἴψοι.

ἴω, subj. of εἶμι (*ibo*). **ἰῶ**, contr. for ἰάου, imper. of ἰάομαι.

ἰώ, an exclam., chiefly in dramatic poetry (lyr.); freq. repeated twice, rarely three times, as A.*Supp.*125; esp. in invoking aid, ἰ. μάκαρες, ἰ. θεοί, Id.*Th.*96, S.*Ph.*736; ἰ. ἰ. Παιάν Id.*Tr.*222; ἰ. Βάκχαι E.*Ba.*578. 2. freq. also of grief or suffering, *oh! ἰ.* δύστανος S.*Ant.*850; ἰ. μοί μοι Id.*OC*199, etc.; ἰ. κακοπάρθενε Μοῖρα *AP*7.468 (Mel.); ἰ. Σπάρτα ib.434 (Diosc.): c. gen., ἰ., πάτερ, σοῦ τῶν τε.. τέκνων A.*Ag.*1305; ἰ. μοι πόνων E.*Ph.*1290; ἰ. ἰ. τραυμάτων Ar.*Ach.*1205. 3. rarely in Prose, ἰ., φασί τινες, of an objector, Gal.*Thras.*32. II. with other Interj., ἰ. ὤ ὤ S.*OC*224; ἒ ἒ ἰ. Id.*El.*840. [ῐ: yet sts. ῑ, in anap., A.*Ag.*1455, S.*El.*149, E.*Alc.*741.]

Ἰώ [ῑ], Ἰοῦς, ἡ, acc. Ἰοῦν Hdt.1.1; voc. Ἰοῖ A.*Pr.*635, etc.:—*Io*, daughter of Inachus. II. name of *the moon* at Argos, Eust. ad D.P.92.

ἰωά (A), = ἰώ, A.*Pers.*1070 (lyr.). **ἰωά** (B), ἡ, *smoke*, prob. in Call.*Fr.*1.40P.

ἰώγα, v. ἐγώ.

ἰωγή, ἡ, Ep. word, *shelter*, Βορέω ὑπ' ἰωγῇ under *shelter* from the north wind, Od.14.533.

ἰώδης [ῑ], ες, (ἰός) *like verdigris, green*, Hp.*Prog.*11, Dsc.5.79, Gal.10.871; of bile, Id.18(1).107; κακόνοια.. τουτὶ τὸ ἰῶδες.. ἀφίησιν Plu.2.565c. 2. *rust-coloured, ferruginous*, Thphr.*Lap.*37, Call.*Hist.*4, Dsc.5.152. 3. *poisonous*, ὕδωρ Ath.2.42a, cf. Gal.11.327; ὀδόντες, of serpents, Philostr.Jun.*Im.*5: metaph., of persons, *virulent*, Ptol.*Tetr.*158. II. (ὄδ-ωδα) *acrid*, ὀξύτητες Hp.*VM*19; ἆσθμα Philum.*Ven.*36.3, etc.

ἰωεῖ· βέλει, Hsch.

ἰωή, ἡ, *any loud sound*: *shout*, or *cry* of men or women, περὶ φρένας ἤλυθ' ἰωή Il.10.139; ὦρτο δ' ἰ. λεπταλέη ὀδυρομένων A.R.3.708; ἰ. δενδρώδης (of Daphne) Nonn.*D.*15.300; *sound* of the lyre, περὶ δέ σφεας ἤλυθ' ἰωὴ φόρμιγγος Od.17.261; of the wind, ὑπὸ Ζεφύροιο ἰωῆς by *the roaring blast* of Zephyrus, Il.4.276, cf. 11.308; of fire, πυρὸς δηΐοιο ἰωήν 16.127; of footsteps, ποδῶν αἰπεῖα ἰ. Hes.*Th.*682; *clang* of arms, Coluth.56.—Ep. word, once in Trag., βοᾷ τηλωπὸν ἰωάν S.*Ph.*216 (lyr.).

ἰωκή, ἡ (for διωκή acc. to A.D.*Conj.*256.27, v. sq.), *rout, pursuit*, οὔτε βίας.. ὑπεδείδισαν οὔτε ἰωκάς Il.5.521: personified, with Ἔρις and Ἀλκή, 5.740:—metaplast. acc., πόνον αἰπὺν ἰῶκά τε δακρυόεσσαν 11.601.

ϝιώκω, = διώκω, *GDI*3153 (Corinthian vase).

ἰωλία, ἡ, (ἰά) = φήμη, δειλή, Hsch. **ἰῶλκα**, = αὔλακα, Id., Cyr.; cf. ὦλκα. **ἴωλον**· μέλαν, Hsch. **ἰών, ἰώνγα, ἰώνει**, Boeot. for ἐγώ, ἔγωγε, ἐγώνη, v. ἐγώ.

Ἴων, ωνος, ὁ, *Ion*, Hdt.7.94, 8.44, E.*Ion* 74, etc.: **Ἴωνες**, οἱ, *the Ionians*, v. Ἰάονες; of those who spoke the Ionic dialect, A.D.*Pron.*4.22, al.: **Ἰωνία**, ἡ, *their country*, A.*Pers.*771.

ἰωνᾶς· περιστερά, Hsch.

ἰωνιά, ᾶς, ἡ, (ἴον) *violet-bed*, Ar.*Pax* 577; ἰ. λευκή *gilliflower, Matthiola incana*, Thphr.*HP*6.8.5; ἰ. μέλαινα *violet, Viola odorata*, ib. 6.6.2. II. *ground-pine, Ajuga Chamaepitys*, Apollod.ap.Ath.15.681d, Dsc.3.158; ἰ. ἀγρία Sch.Nic.*Al.*55. III. ἐς ἰωνιάν· ἐς κοπρῶνα, Hsch.

Ἰωνίζω, *speak Ionic*, A.D.*Adv.*162.7.

Ἰωνικολόγος, ὁ, *reciter of* Ἰωνικά, Ath.14.620e.

Ἰωνικός, ή, όν, *Ionic, Ionian*: -κοί, οἱ, = Ἴωνες, Philostr.*VS*1.21.5: -κόν (sc. ὑπόδημα), τό, a kind of *shoe*, Herod.7.59; esp. with the connotation, *effeminate*, Ar.*Pax*46, Pl.Com.69.14, etc. Adv. -κῶς *in the Ionic fashion*, i.e. *softly, effeminately*, Ar.*Th.*163. 2. Ἰ. μέτρον, συζυγία, *Ionic*, defined in Heph.11, cf. D.H.*Comp.*4, etc.; πούς Heph.1.9, cf. Aristid.Quint.1.15: -κά, τά, poem in this style, Ath.14.620e. Adv. -κῶς, prob. in D.H.*Dem.*43. 3. Ἰ. ἔθος, of the *Ionic dialect*, A.D.*Pron.*74.9. Adv. -κῶς Sch.Porph.*Abst.*2.36: Comp. -ώτερον A.D.*Adv.*135.1.

Ἰώνιος, α, ον, = foreg., τρόπος, of the *Ionic* dialect, Philostr.*VA*7.35:—fem. **Ἰωνίς**, ίδος, *Ionian*, Paus.6.22.7, etc.: as Subst., Call.*Ep.*27, Plu.*Luc.*18: **Ἰωνιάς**, άδος, Nic.*Fr.*74.4, Str.8.3.32.

ἰωνίς, ίδος, ἡ, *a water bird*, Ar.Byz.*Epit.*5.5.

ἰωνίσκος, ὁ, Ephes. name for the fish χρύσοφρυς, Archestr.*Fr.*12.

Ἰωνιστί, Adv. *in Ionic dialect*, A.D.*Adv.*162.8.

Ἰωνο-κάμπτης, ου, ὁ, *one who sings with soft Ionic modulations*, Tim.*Fr.*27. **-κῦσος**, ὁ, *debauchee*, Cratin.419.

ἰωνός, ὁ, a kind of *fish*, Hsch. **ἴωξις**, εως, ἡ, = ἰωκή (q.v.), Id., *EM*481.30, Suid. **ἰωπάτερ**· τὰ ἐν τοῖς ἱματίοις σημεῖα (Lacon.), Hsch. **ἴωπι**· δεῦρο (Lydian), Id.

ἰωρός, ὁ, Att. for ὁ αὐτῆς τῆς πόλεως φύλαξ acc. to A.D.*Pron.*55.26 (pl., derived from ἴ), cf. Hdn.Gr.1.200, Hsch., Phot.; but ἐντὸς (ἐν τοῖς) and ἐκτὸς ἰωροῦ, of the *ban* placed on manslayers, Prov.ap.Suid., *App.Prov.*4.39.

ἴωσις [ῑ], εως, ἡ, (ἰόω) *refinement* (because freq. due to oxidization of impure substances), χρυσοῦ *PMag.Leid.V.*6.18, cf. Olymp.Alch.p.94B., Zos.Alch.p.145B., al. 2. *making of a tincture*, ib. p.219B.

ἰῶτα [ῐ], τό, indecl., (Hebr. *yôd*) *the letter* ι, Pl.*Cra.*418b, Aen.Tact.31.18, Call.Gramm.ap.Ath.10.453d, etc. 2. *line, stroke*, on a sundial, *Bull.Soc.Alex.*4.83 (iii B.C.). 3. prov., of anything very small, *smallest letter, jot*, *Ev.Matt.*5.18.

ἰωτᾰκισμός, οῦ, ὁ, doubling of *i*, as in *Troiia, Maiia*, Quint.1.5.32, Isid.*Etym.*1.32.7. II. *repetition of i*, as *Iunio Iuno Iovis iure irascitur*, Mart.Cap.§514.

ἰωτογρᾰφέω, *write with iota*, Sch.Ar.*V.*926 (Pass.), etc.

ἰωχμός [ῑ], ὁ, = ἰωκή, ἦλθον ἀν' ἰωχμόν through *the rout*, Il.8.89,158; ἰωὴ ἀσπέτου ἰωχμοῖο Hes.*Th.*683, cf. Theoc.25.279.

ἴωψ [ῐ], ωπος, ὁ, *a small fish*, Dorio ap.Ath.7.300f, Nic.*Fr.*18, Call.*Fr.*38, Ael.*NA*1.58, Hdn.Gr.1.247.

K

K κ, κάππα, τό, indecl., eleventh (later tenth) letter in Gr. alphabet: as numeral κ' = 20, but ͵κ = 20,000. The numeral κα' (21) is perh. used as one syll. in a metrical (?) Inscr., *IG*12(7).296 (Minoa), like ζήσασα ἔτη ε', at the end of a hexam. (?), *CIG*3025 (Lydia).

κᾱ, Dor. for Ep., Aeol. κε(ν), = Att., Arc. ἄν, *SIG*9 (Olympia, vi B.C.), Epich.35, al., *Leg.Gort.*1.9, *Foed.Delph.Pell.*2 A 9, Ar.*Ach.*737, 799, *Lys.*117, Th.5.77, Theoc.1.4. [Although long, the α is elided in Epich.170.12, al., *SIG*56.8 (Argos, v B.C.), *Leg.Gort.*1.1, etc.]

κᾰ, shortd. form of κατά used before the article, κα τὸν νόμον *IG*5(2).16 (Arcadia); κα τῶνυ ib.262; κα τοὺς νόμους *SIG*²860.9 (Delph., ii B.C.), etc.; κα τὰ τῆς συγκλήτου δόγματα *SIG*705.12 (ibid.) κα τὰ δόξαντα.. τῇ βουλῇ *Inscr.Magn.*179.33 (ii A.D.): also in compds., cf. καβαίνων, etc. II. Cypr., = κάς, *Inscr.Cypr.*135.5 H., *Schwyzer* 683.8.

κἀ, crasis for καὶ ἐ, i.e. καὶ ἐμ (= ἐν), Herod.2.62 (κῆμ corr. m.rec.).

κααρτίας· βάτραχος, Hsch. **κάαυκα**· περιδέραια, πλόκια, Id. (leg. κάλυκας).

καβάδης, ὁ, *military garment named after the Persian king* Καβάδης, Tz.*H.*12.792.

καβαθα (accent dub.), ἡ, prob. = Lat. *gabata, dish*, *Edict.Diocl.*15.51: also as neut. pl., καβαθα β' *UPZ*149.40 (iii B.C.); [γ]αβαθα τρία Cumont *Fouilles de Doura-Europos* p.372 No.13; cf. γαβαθόν, ζάβατος II.

κᾰβαίνων, Dor. for καταβ-, Alcm.38.

κάβαισος [ᾰ], ὁ, *gluttonous fellow*, Cratin.103. (Derived by Gramm. fr. κάβος and αἶσα and said to be a pr. n.; cf. Κάβαισος *IG*5(2).271.9 (Mantinea, iv B.C.).)

κᾰβάλλειον, τό, = sq., κ. καὶ ἐργάτας δεκαπέντε *Rev.Arch.*1925.63 (Callatis): **καβάλλιον**, Hsch.

κᾰβάλλης, ου, ὁ, *nag*, Lat. *caballus*, Plu.2.828e; = ἐργάτης ἵππος, Hsch.:—hence **καβαλλαρικός**, ή, όν, *of* or *for a horse*, μύλος *Edict.Diocl.*15.52; τάπης 19.22: **καβαλλάτιον**, τό, = κυνόγλωσσον, Ps.-Dsc.4.127.

κάβαξ, = πανοῦργος, Phot., *EM*482.26, Suid.

Κάβαρνος, ὁ, *priest of Demeter* at Paros, *IG*12(5).292 (iii A.D.): pl., Hsch. (From Κάβαρνις, a poetical name of Paros, St.Byz.)

κάβασα and **καβάσας**, both perh. nom. sg., name of an unknown object in temple inventories, *Inscr.Délos* 298 A 111, 300 B 16, *IG*11(2).287 B 89 (Delos, iii B.C.). (Perh. fr. Κάβασα in Egypt.)

κάβᾱσι [κᾰ], Lacon. for κατάβηθι, Hsch.

καβάτας, = καταιβάτης (q.v.), title of Zeus in Laconia, *IG*5(1).1316 (Thalamae).

καββᾰλικός, ή, όν, Lacon. for καταβλητικός, *good at throwing*, of wrestlers: in Comp. καββαλικώτερος Plu.2.236e, Gal.*Thras.*45: metaph., *more ready to trip up* one's neighbour, M.Ant.7.52: καββαλική (sc. τέχνη), ἡ, *art of wrestling*, Gal. l.c.

καββάλλω, Aeol. for καταβάλλω, Alc.343; **κάββαλε**, Ep. for κατέβαλε, aor. 2 of καταβάλλω:—also **κάβαλεν**· κατέβαλεν, Hsch. **καββάς**, v. καταβαίνω. **καββασία**, v. καταβασία. **καββιόρνους**· κατεσθίων, Id. **κάββλημα**· περίστρωμα (Lacon.), Id.

Κάβειροι [ᾰ], οἱ, *the Cabeiri*, divinities worshipped especially in Lemnos, Samothrace, and Boeotia, Pi.*Fr.*74ᵇ Schr., Hdt.2.51, 3.37, Str.10.3.15, etc.; at Miletus, Nic.Dam.52 J., *Milet.* (v. infr.), *BCH*1.288; title of play by Aeschylus, Ath.10.428f, Sch.Pi.*P.*4.303: sg., Κάβειρος Pi. l.c.; freq. in Boeotian Inscrr. (written -βιρ-), *IG*7.2457, al., cf. *AP*6.245 (Diod.), Q.S.1.267: **Καβειρίδες** Νύμφαι, and **Καβειρώ**, ἡ, *the sisters* and *mother of the Cabeiri*, Acus.20 J., Pherecyd.48 J.:—Adj. **Καβειρικός**, ή, όν, fem. **Καβειριάς**, άδος, *Cabeiric*, St.Byz.:—also **Καβειραῖος**, α, ον, Id., Paus.9.25.8: **Καβειρία**, ἡ, epith. of Demeter at Κάβειροι, Id.9.25.5 codd.: **Καβείριον**, τό, *sanctuary of the C.*, Id.9.26.2; more correctly **Καβείρ[ε]ιον** *IG*11(2).144 A 90

(Delos, iv B.C.): **Καβείρια,** τά, *their mysteries, Inscr.Perg.*252, Hsch.:—hence **Καβειριάζομαι,** *celebrate these mysteries,* St.Byz.: **Καβῑριάρχας,** ὁ, *IG*7.2428 (Boeot.): **-αρχίω** (= -έω), ib.2420. (The spelling -βειρ- is correct, ib.11(2).l.c., Hdn.Gr.2.411: the form -βιρ- is Boeot. (v. supr.) and late Gr., *Milet.*6.26 (i A.D.), Alexio and Philox.ap.*Et.Gud.*289.30.) (The connexion with the Semitic root *KBR 'great'* (cf. the title Μεγάλοι Θεοί) is not certain; nor is that with Skt. *Kúbera-* (name of a divinity), fr. **Kabera-*, cf. Patron. *Kāberaká-*.)

κάβειος· νέος (Paph.), Hsch. **κάβηλος·** ὁ ἀπεσκολυμμένος τὸ αἰδοῖον, ἢ ὄνος, Id.

καβιδάριος, ὁ, *gem-engraver,* Lat. *cabidarius, Gloss.,* Rhetor. in *Cat.Cod.Astr.*8(4).216.

καβιτᾶς, ὁ, dub. sens. (apptly. a nomen agentis), *PLond.*1821.368.

καβλέει· καταπίνει, Hsch. **καβλής·** μάνδαλος τῶν θυρῶν (Paph.), Id.

καβολά, ἁ, = Dor. καταβολή, *Schwyzer*110^8 (Argos).

κάβος, ὁ, (Hebr. *ḳab*) *corn-measure,* = 4 ξέσται, Lxx 4*Ki.*6.25; f.l. in *Gp.*7.20.1.

κάγ, poet. form for κατά before γ, κὰγ γόνυ for κατὰ γόνυ, Il.20.458; κὰγ γόνων Sapph.44; κὰγ γᾶν dub. in *SIG*179.9 (Boeot., iv B.C.).

καγκαίνω, *parch, dry,* Hsch.:—also **κάγκω,** metaph. in Pass., καγκομένης· ξηρᾶς τῷ φόβῳ (cf. αὖος), Id. (Cf. κέγκω.)

κάγκαμον, τό, *Bissa Bol, Balsamodendron Katuf,* an Arabian gum, Dsc.1.24, Plin.*HN*12.98:—also **κάγκαλον,** τό, Hsch.

κάγκανον, τό, = κακκαλία (q.v.), Gal.12.8, Paul.Aeg.7.3.

κάγκᾰνος, ον, (καγκαίνω) *dry,* ξύλα κ. Il.21.364, Od.18.308, Theoc.24.89; κάγκανα κᾶλα *h.Merc.*112: κ. κῆλα Epich. in *Arch.Pap.*7 p.7; σταχύς Lyc.1430: **καγκαλέα·** κατακεκαυμένα, Hsch.: **καγκάνεος,** Man.4.324.

κάγκελλον μέτρον, a system of measures of capacity, μέτρῳ τῷ κ. ἀρτάβας ἕνδεκα τέταρτον *POxy.*1447 (i A.D.), cf. 133.15 (vi A.D.), etc.

κάγκελος, ὁ, = Lat. *cancelli, barrier, starting-gate,* in races, Sch. Theoc.8.57, Hsch.:—also **κάγκελλοι,** οἱ, *IG*7.1681 (Plataea), *POxy.*2146.12 (iii A.D.):—whence **καγκελλάριος,** ὁ, orig. *usher* at the (lattice-work) bar of a court, then = λογοθέτης, Lyd.*Mag.*3.36,37, *PMasp.*5.19, al. (vi A.D.): **κάγκελον,** τό, *bar,* τοῦ δικαστηρίου Sch. Ar.*Eq.*641,675: **κάγγελλον,** *railing, balustrade, PRyl.*233.4 (ii A.D.):—hence **καγκελο-ειδῶς,** Adv. *like a grating, criss-cross, Hippiatr.*117 (v.l. -λλ-): **-θυρίς,** ίδος, ἡ, = κιγκλίς, *EM*513.4:—also **καγκελωτὴ** θύρα Sch.Ar.*V.*124, Poll.8.124; διαβάθρα **καγγελλωτὴ** *furnished with a railing, PRyl.*233.3 (ii A.D.).

καγκές· πτύελος, Hsch.

καγκύλη, ἡ, Aeol. for κηκίς, Hsch. **καγρᾶ⟨ς⟩·** καταφαγᾶς (Salam.), Id. (prob. l.).

καγχάζω, later form for καχάζω (q.v.).

καγχᾰλάω, *rejoice, exult,* καγχαλόωσι...Ἀχαιοί, κτλ. *rejoice* because a Trojan champion has been chosen for his looks, Il.3.43; καγχαλόων 6.514, 10.565; καγχαλόωσα Od.23.1,59; καγχαλάασκε A.R.4.996; ἐπακτὴρ καγχαλῶν ἀγρεύματι Lyc.109; καγχαλάασκον ἐτώσια μητιόωντι Q.S.8.12; ἐνὶ φρεσὶ -όωντες κρύβδ' Ἥρης Id.3.136, cf. 200, al., Opp.*C.*4.377, *H.*5.234; of hounds, deer, Id.*C.*1.523, 2.237; of pards, οἴνῳ μέγα -όωσι ib.3.80; of a polypus, Id.*H.*4.281.

καγχαλίζομαι, καγχάομαι, = foreg., Hsch. **κάγχαμος,** ὁ, in Crotoniate dialect, = κισσός, Id. **κάγχαρμον·** τὸ τὴν λόγχην ἄνω ἔχειν (Maced.), Hsch.

καγχ-ασμός, ὁ, *loud laughter,* Poll.6.199; v. καχασμός. **-αστής,** οῦ, ὁ, *loud laugher,* Phryn.*PS* p.78 B., Poll.6.29.

καγχλάζω, = καγχάζω, Ath.10.438f, Aq.*Jb.*41.23, Hsch.

καγχρύδιον, κάγχρυς, etc., v. καχρύδιον, κάχρυς, etc.

κἀγώ [ᾱ], Att. crasis for καὶ ἐγώ.

κάδ, Ep. for κατά before δ, κὰδ δώματα Od.4.72; κ. δύναμιν Hes. *Op.*336; before δέ, Il.2.160, etc.; κ. δ' ἔβαλε by tmesis for κατέβαλε δέ, Od.4.344.

καδᾰλέομαι, Dor. for καταδηλέομαι (q.v.). **καδαλίων,** ὁ, *one who walks on stilts;* and **κάδαλοι,** οἱ, *stilts,* Hsch. **κάδαμος·** τυφλός (Salam.), Id. **καδαρόν·** θολερόν, Id.

καδδαιμονέστερος, = κακοδ-, Epich. 1 Demiańczuk.

κάδδιον, v. κάδιον.

κάδδῐχος, ὁ, (κάδος) *jar,* κάδδιχος καλεῖται τὸ ἀγγεῖον εἰς ὃ τὰς ἀπομαγδαλίας ἐμβάλλουσι Plu.*Lyc.*12: hence, *voting-urn,* whence **κεκαδδίχθαι,** *to be rejected on a vote,* ibid.; also, a *measure,* = ἡμίεκτον, Hsch., cf. *Tab.Heracl.*1.52, *IG*5(1).1447.10 (Messene, iii/ii B.C.):—Lacon. **καδίκορ,** Hsch. s.v. ἐνδεκαδίκορ.

κάδδος, = κάδος (q.v.). **καδδρᾰθέτην,** v. καταδαρθάνω. **καδδῦσαι,** Ep. nom. pl. fem. aor. 2 part. Act. of καταδύω. **κᾱδεστής,** Dor. for κηδεστής. **κάδης·** ἁγιασμός, Hsch.

καδικεύω, perh. *hold a priesthood,* dub. in *Rev.Phil.*35.302 (Pharsalus).

κάδ-ιον [ᾰ], τό, Dim. of κάδος, *IG*11(2).287*A*64 (Delos, iii B.C.), Lxx 1*Ki.*17.40; = ὑδρία (Salam.), Hsch. (pl.): **κάδδιον** Sch.D.T. p.195 H.:—also **κάδιν,** ἔλαιον καὶ κάδιν *Abh.Berl.Akad.*1925(5).31 (Cyrene, ii/iii A.D.). **-ίσκιον,** τό, Dim. of sq., *part of a spice-box,* Nicoch.2. **-ίσκος,** ὁ, Dim. of κάδος, Cratin.193, Stratt.22, *BCH* 35.286 (ii B.C.), Ph.2.89, Gal.11.555. II. *voting-urn* used in law-courts, ὁ δὲ κ... ὁ μὲν ἀπολύων οὗτος, ὁ δ' ἀπολλὺς ὁδί Phryn.Com.32, cf. Ar.*V.*853, Lys.13.37, Lycurg.149; καδίσκων τεττάρων τεθέντων κατὰ τὸν νόμον (in a civil cause), D.43.10, cf. Is.11.21.

καδμεία (in codd. **καδμία**) (sc. γῆ), ἡ, *cadmia, calamine,* Dsc.5.74, Gal.1.413, al., *PTeb.*273.14 (ii/iii A.D.):—written **καδμήα,** *POxy.*1088.4 (i A.D.).

Καδμει-ῶνες, οἱ, = Καδμεῖοι, Il.4.385, etc. **-ώνη,** ἡ, *daughter of Cadmus,* i.e. Semele, *IG*14.1389 i 59.

Καδμῖλος (on the accent v. Hdn.Gr.1.162), ὁ, name of one of the Cabiri in Samothrace, St.Byz. s.v. Καβειρία, Hdn.Gr.2.446:—also **Κασμ-,** Dionysodor.ap.Sch.A.R.1.917, cf. *IG*12(8).74 (Imbros, ii A.D.), Call.*Fr.*409; identified with Hermes, ibid., Hdn.Gr.1.162, Sch.Lyc.162: with Lat. *camillus* (*casm-*), Varr.*LL*7.3, cf. Plu.*Num.*7; Καδμῖλοι is prob. for Κάδωλοι, title of ministrants in the cult of the Curetes and Μεγάλοι Θεοί, D.H.2.22.

Καδμογενής, ές, *Cadmus-born,* A.*Th.*302, S.*Tr.*116, E.*Ph.*808 (all lyr.).

Κάδμος, ὁ, *Cadmus,* Od.5.333, Hes.*Th.*937, etc.:—Adj. **Καδμεῖος,** α, ον, Ion. **Καδμήιος,** η, ον, *Cadmean,* Hes.*Th.*940, etc.:—fem. **Καδμηίς,** ίδος, ἡ, *h.Bacch.*57, Hes.*Op.*162, Th.1.12, prob. in *Trag. Adesp.*177:—poet. **Καδμέῐος,** Pi.*I.*3(4).71, S.*Ant.*1115 (lyr.): Καδμεῖοι, οἱ, *the Cadmeans* or *ancient inhabitants of Thebes,* Il.4.388, Hes. *Th.*326, Hdt.5.57, etc.: Καδμεία, ἡ, *the citadel of Thebes,* X.*HG*6.3.11; also, Pythag. name for *eight, Theol.Ar.*54: prov., Κ. νίκη a victory involving one's own ruin (from the story of the Σπαρτοί, or that of Polynices and Eteocles), Hdt.1.166, cf. Pl.*Lg.*641c, Plu.2.488a, Suid. (but = a *great* victory, Arr.*Fr.*21 J.); so Κ. κράτος *AP*5.178 (Mel.): metaph., Κ. παιδεία Pl. l.c.; Κ. γράμματα the alphabet, supposed to have been brought by Κ. from Phoenicia, Hdt.5.59. (The spelling Κάσσμος is found on a vase of Rhegium, Roscher *Lex.d.Gr.u.Röm.Myth.*2(1).842.)

κάδμος· δόρυ, λόφος, ἀσπίς (Cret.), Hsch.

κᾰδοποιός, όν, *making pails* or *vessels,* Sch.Ar.*Pax* 1202.

κάδος [ᾰ], ὁ, *jar* or *vessel for water* or *wine,* Anacr.17, Archil.4, Hdt.3.20, S.*Fr.*534.3 (anap.), Ar.*Ach.*549, etc.; κ. ἀντλητικός *CPR* 232.12 (ii A.D.); said to be Ion. for κεράμιον, Clitarch.Gloss.ap.Ath. 11.473b. 2. a liquid measure, = ἀμφορεύς, Philoch.155a; ἐλαίου Lxx 2*Ch.*2.10(9) (cod. A), cj. in Simon.155.4 (*Hermes* 64.274); πίνει τετραχόοισι κάδοις Hedyl.ap.Ath. l.c.; later, *half an* ἀμφ., *Script. Metrol.*1.257, 2.144 Hultsch. II. = καδίσκος II, Ar.*Av.*1032. III. *funerary urn, Jahresh.*8.154.—The metre usu. requires κάδος, never κάδδος which is written in Them. in *Ph.*268.2, al.; cf. κάδδιχος.

κᾶδος, Dor. for κῆδος. **κάδουσα·** εἶδος σταφυλῆς, Hsch. **καδρανές** (perh. for καπρανές, i.e. κατα-πρηνές)· κατωφερές, Id. **κάδυρος·** κάπρος ἔνορχις, Id.

καδύτας, ου, ὁ, a parasitic plant, *dodder, Cassyta filiformis* (Arabic *kašūth*), Thphr.*CP*2.17.3.

Κάδωλοι, v. Καδμῖλος.

Κάειρα [ᾰ], ἡ, fem. from Κάρ, *Carian woman,* Il.4.142, Hdt.1.92, al. II. Adj. fem., = Καρική, ἐσθής Hdt.5.88.

κᾱείς, κᾱήμεναι, v. καίω. **κάζελε,** Arc. for κατέβαλε, Hsch. **κάηνα·** τὰ εὖ καιόμενα ξύλα, Id.

κᾰθά [θᾰ], Adv. for καθ' ἅ, *according as, just as, IG*1^2.90.43, 116.27, Men.*Mon.*551, *PCair.Zen.*188.8 (iii B.C.), Plb.3.107.10, Lxx *Ge.*7.9, etc.; ὁ κ. παρατεταγμένος σφυγμός the (*so to speak*) 'regular' pulse (a military metaphor), Archig.ap.Gal.8.626. II. also **καθάπερ,** Ion. **κατάπερ,** Philol.14, Democr.164, Hdt.1.182, al., Ar.*Eq.*8, *Ec.*61, *IG*1^2.39.42, al., D.37.16, etc.: freq. in legal instruments, ἡ πρᾶξις ἔστω κ. ἐκ δίκης *PEleph.*1.12 (iv B.C.), etc.: with a part., like ὡς, ἅτε, D.C.37.54 (nisi leg. καίπερ):—strengthd., **καθάπερ εἰ** (Ion. κατάπερ εἰ, Hdt.1.170), *like as if, exactly as,* Pl.*Phlb.*22e, 59e, al.; **καθάπερ ἂν** (for ἐάν) D.23.41; **καθάπερ ἂν εἰ** Pl.*Lg.*684c, Arist.*Ph.*240^{b}10, Plb. 3.32.2, etc.:—μάχαιραν κ. *like* a knife, Porph.*Chr.*31. Cf. καθό, καθώς.

καθᾰγ-ιάζω, = sq., Lxx *Le.*27.26, 2*Ma.*1.26; ὁ σοφὸς -άζει ψυχὴν Ph.1.115:—Pass., Iamb.*Myst.*5.24. **-ίζω,** Att. fut. -ιῶ: Ion. fut. inf. κατ-αγιεῖν Hdt.1.86:—*devote, dedicate,* ἀκροθίνια θεῶν ὅτεῳ δὴ l.c.; νήττη πυροὺς Ar.*Av.*566, cf. *Lys.*238, Pl.*Criti.*120a, Men. 319.13, etc.; esp. of a burnt offering, θυμιήματα κ. Hdt.2.130; κ. πυρί ib.47; κ. ἐπὶ πύρης Id.7.167; ἐπὶ τοῦ βωμοῦ Id.1.183; ἀρκεύθου ξύλοις Paus.2.10.5: abs., Hdt.2.40, etc.; *make offerings* to the dead, Luc. *Luct.*9:—Pass., cj. in Ph.1.190 (καταγιζ- Pap., καθαγνιζ- codd.), 558 (καθαγνιζ- codd.). II. generally, *burn,* καταγιζομένου τοῦ καρποῦ τοῦ ἐπιβαλλομένου [ἐπὶ τὸ πῦρ] Hdt.1.202; esp. *burn* a dead body, τὸ σῶμα τοῦ Καίσαρος ἐν ἀγορᾷ κ. Plu.*Ant.*14, cf. *Brut.*20; so (as cj. for καθήγνισαν) ὅσων σπαράγματ' ἢ κύνες καθήγισαν whose mangled bodies dogs *have buried,* i.e. devoured, S.*Ant.*1081 (= μετὰ ἄγους ἐκόμισαν, Sch.). **-ισμός,** ὁ, *funeral rites,* Luc.*Luct.*19. **-νίζω,** Att. fut. -ιῶ, *purify, hallow,* τὸν τόπον θείῳ καὶ δᾳδί Id.*Philops.*12; μήτηρ πυρὶ καθηγνισται δέμας, i.e. has been burnt on the funeral-pyre, E.*Or.*40. II. *offer as an expiatory sacrifice,* πέλανον ἐπὶ πυρὶ καθαγνίσας Id.*Ion* 707 (lyr.).—On S.*Ant.*1081, Ph.1.190,558, v. καθαγίζω.

καθαιμ-ακτός, όν, *bloodstained,* φόνος E.*Or.*1358 (lyr.). **-άσσω,** *make bloody, sprinkle* or *stain with blood,* τινα A.*Eu.*450; χρόα, δέρην, E.*Hec.*1126, *Or.*1527; σκήπτρῳ κ. κάρα Id.*Andr.*588; τὴν γλῶτταν Pl.*Phdr.*254e. **-ᾰτόω,** = foreg., E.*Hel.*1599, *HF*234, 256, *Ph.*1161, Ar.*Th.*695:—Pass., Luc.*Ind.*9. **-ος,** ον, *bloody,* τραύματα, σῖτα, E.*IT*1374, prob. in *HF*383 (lyr.).

καθαίρ-εσις, εως, ἡ, *pulling down, demolition,* Th.5.42, Isoc.7.66, X.*HG*2.2.15, *IG*2^2.1672.75 (iv B.C.), *PMagd.*9.6 (iii B.C.), etc.: metaph., τινῶν, opp. οἰκοδομή, 2*Ep.Cor.*10.8; ἀναστήσωμεν τὴν κ. τοῦ λαοῦ ἡμῶν Lxx 1*Ma.*3.43: in concrete sense, αἱ καθαιρέσεις *the débris*, Ph.*Bel.*92.31. 2. generally, *overthrow, subjugation*, Jul.*Caes.* 320d; τῆς ἀνέτου ἐξουσίας Hdn.2.4.4; Ἰουλιανοῦ Id.3.1.1; *killing*, Plu.*Ant.*82. 3. *reduction, diminution*, opp. πρόσθεσις, Arist.*Ph.* 207^{a}23: Medic., *bringing down superfluous flesh, lowering, reducing*, Hp.*Epid.*6.3.1, cf. Gal.17(2).368; τῶν σωμάτων Arist.*GA*738^{a}31; τῶν ὄγκων Pl.*Ti.*58e. 4. *eclipse* of sun or moon (with reference to the magical process of *drawing down* those bodies), Sch.A.R.3.533 (pl.). **-ετέος**, α, ον, *to be put down*, Th.1.118. II. καθαιρετέον *one must put down, overthrow*, κ. καὶ καταγωνιστέον τινάς Aristid. 1.445 J.; κ. ἐξ ἀκροπόλεως τὴν τυραννίδα Them.*Or.*21.256a. **-έτης**, ου, ὁ, *overthrower*, πολεμίων Th.4.83; Καίσαρος D.C.44.1. II. *house-breaker*(?), *BGU*14 v 12 (iii A.D.). **-ετικός**, ή, όν, *destructive*, c. gen., Corn.*ND*30, Ph.2.548. 2. *reducing, catheretic*, φάρμακα, of mild caustics, Gal.11.756; σπληνὸς καθαιρετικόν Dsc.2.112; *putting a stop to*, παλμῶν Gal.7.600: generally, ὑγίεια κ. παθῶν Ph.*Fr.* 103 H. **-ετός**, ή, όν, *able to be achieved*, ὃ ἐκεῖνοι ἐπιστήμῃ προύχουσι, καθαιρετὸν ἡμῖν ἐστὶ μελέτῃ Th.1.121 (v.l. καθαιρετέον, but cf. D.C.*Fr.*43.11). **-έω**, Ion. **κατ-**, Aeol. **κατάγρημι**, q.v.: fut. -ήσω Il.11.453, etc.: fut. 2 καθελῶ *APl.*4.334 (Antiphil.): aor. 2 καθεῖλον, inf. καθελεῖν: aor. 1 καθεῖλα Lxx 3*Ki.*19.14: Ion. pf. part. Pass. καταραιρημένος Hdt.2.172:—*take down*, καθείλομεν ἱστία Od. 9.149; κὰδ δ' ἀπὸ πασσαλόφι ζυγὸν ᾕρεον Il.24.268; κ. ἄχθος *take it down*, i.e. off one's shoulders, Ar.*Ra.*10; κ. τὸ σημεῖον And.1.36; κ. τῶν ἐκ τῆς στοᾶς ὅπλων some of them, X.*HG*5.4.8; κ. εἰκόνα ἐξ ἀκροπόλεως Lycurg.117; κ. τινά, from the cross, Plb.1.86.6, Ph.2. 529:—Med., κατελέσθαι τὰ τόξα *take down one's* bow, Hdt.3.78; τοὺς ἱστοὺς Plb.1.61.1. 2. *put down, close* the eyes of the dead, ὄσσε καθαιρήσουσι θανόντι περ Il.11.453; ὀφθαλμοὺς καθελοῦσα Od.24.296; χερσὶ κατ' ὀφθαλμοὺς ἑλέειν 11.426. 3. of sorcerers, *bring down* from the sky, σελήνην Ar.*Nu.*750, Pl.*Grg.*513a. 4. κατά με πέδον γᾶς ἕλοι may earth *swallow* me! E.*Supp.*829 (lyr.). II. *put down by force, destroy*, ὅτε κέν μιν μοῖρ' ὀλοὴ καθέλῃσι Od.2.100, 19.145, cf. 3. 238, etc.; μὴ καθέλοι μιν αἰών Pi.*O.*9.60; φῶτ' ἄδικον καθαιρεῖ A.*Ag.* 398 (lyr.); μοῖρα τὸν φύσαντα καθεῖλε S.*Aj.*517, cf. E.*El.*878 (lyr.), etc.; *kill, slay*, ταῦρον ib.1143, cf. Stesich.23, S.*Tr.*1063, *Fr.*205; ἐάν τις ἀποκτείνῃ.. ἐν ὁδῷ καθελών Lex ap.D.23.53:—Pass., of criminals, *to be executed*, Plu.*Them.*22. 2. *put down, reduce*, κ. Κῦρον καὶ τὴν Περσέων δύναμιν Hdt.1.71, etc.; καθαιρεθῆναι, opp. ἀρθῆναι, D.2.8; esp. *depose, dethrone*, Hdt.1.124, etc.; κ. τὸ λῃστικὸν ἐκ τῆς θαλάσσης *remove it utterly* from.., Th.1.4, cf. *POxy.*1408.23 (iii A.D.); κ. ὕβριν τινός Hdt.9.27, Lxx *Za.*9.6; ὄλβον S.*Fr.*646.4; ὑπερηφάνους Aristeas 263:—Pass., καθῃρημένος τὴν αἴσθησιν *bereft* of sense, Plu.*Per.*38; καθαιρεῖσθαι τῆς μεγαλειότητος ['Αρτέμιδος] *Act.Ap.*19.27. 3. *raze to the ground, demolish*, πόλεις Th.1.58, al., Lxx *Is.*14.17; τείχη Pl. *Mx.*244c; τῶν τειχῶν a part of the walls, X.*HG*4.4.13:—Pass., Th. 5.39, etc.; καθῃρέθη.. Οἰχαλία δορί S.*Tr.*478. 4. *cancel, rescind*, τὸ Μεγαρέων ψήφισμα Th.1.140, cf. 139, Plu.*Per.*29; ἔργον κ. λόγῳ Philem.140. 5. as law-term, *condemn*, ἡ καθαιροῦσα ψῆφος a verdict of *guilty*, Lys.13.37: c. inf., ἐμὲ πάλος καθαιρεῖ.. λαβεῖν S. *Ant.*275; so prob. κατά με.. Ἀΐδας ἕλοι πατρὶ ξυνθανεῖν Id.*OC*1689 (lyr.), cf. E.*Or.*862; simply, *decide*, ὅ τι ἂν αἱ πλείους ψῆφοι καθαιρῶσι D.H.7.36,39; in book-keeping, ἃν καθαιρῶσιν αἱ ψῆφοι whatever the counters (or accounts) *prove*, prob. in D.18.227. 6. *reduce*, τῶν αὐξανομένων καὶ καθαιρουμένων γραμμῶν Arist.*Ph.*237^{b}9; τοῦ ἀποστήματος πεφυκότος ἐπὶ πολὺ καθαιρεῖν τὰ μεγέθη Phld.*Sign.*9; of mild caustics, τὰ ὑπερσαρκέοντα καθαιρεῖ (prob. for καθαίρει) Hp.*Ulc.*14, cf. Gal.11.756; τὸ σῶμα κ. διαίταις Plu.*Ant.*53: Rhet., *minimize*, Arist.*Rh.*1376^{a}34. III. *overpower, seize*, κὰδ δέ μιν ὕπνος ᾕρει Od. 9.372; κ. τινά *overtake*, X.*Cyr.*4.3.16; κ. τινὰ ἐν ἀφροσύνῃ *catch* in the act of folly, S.*Ant.*383 (anap.): c. gen. partis, κ. τῶν ὤτων *seize by*.., Theoc.5.133:—Pass., κ. ὑπό τινος Hdt.6.29. IV. *fetch down as a reward* or *prize*, καθαιρεῖν ἀγῶνας Plu.*Pomp.*8: metaph., *achieve*, ἀγώνων.. εὖχος ἔργῳ καθελών Pi.*O.*10(11).63: fut. inf. καθαρεῖν, παστόν, μίτραν, Epigr. in *Berl.Sitzb.*1894.908 (Asia Minor):—Med., φόνῳ καθαιρεῖσθ', οὐ λόγῳ, τὰ πράγματα E.*Supp.*749:—Pass., Hdt.7. 50. V. less freq. like the simple αἱρεῖν, *take and carry off*, Id.6. 41, cf. 5.36 (Pass.). Cf. καθαίρω.

καθαίρω, fut. καθᾰρῶ X.*Oec.*18.6, prob. in Pl.*Lg.*735b, etc.: aor. 1 ἐκάθηρα Od.20.152, Th.3.104, Hp.*Mul.*1.47, *IG*2^{2}.1672.47 (ἀνα-), Theoc.5.119, etc.; ἐκάθαρα is found in codd. of Antipho 6.37, X.*An.* 5.7.35, Hp.*Acut.*(*Sp.*)11, and commonly in later Gr., Thphr.*Char.* 16.7, *BCH*6.23 (Delos, ii B.C.), (ἀνα-) *PPetr.*3 p.141 (iii B.C.), (συνανα-) *IG*11(2).163*A*56 (Delos, iii B.C.), cf. διακαθαίρω, ἐκκαθαίρω, etc., and Phryn.16; v. infr. Med.: pf. κεκάθαρκα (ἐκ-) Sch.Ar.*Pax* 752:—Med., fut. καθαροῦμαι Pl.*Cra.*396e, Hp.*Morb.*2.38 (in pass. sense, ib. 2.13, *Nat.Mul.*13, *Mul.*2.160): aor. ἐκαθηράμην A.*Fr.*354, Hp.*Epid.* 5.43, Pl.*Lg.*868a, *IG*11(2).146*A*78 (Delos, iv B.C.), 153.9, 154*A*37 (ibid., iii B.C.); later ἐκαθᾰράμην ib.146*A*80 (iv B.C.), *Inscr.Délos* 290. 79, al. (iii B.C.), etc., (ἀνα-) *IG*2^{2}.1668.8 (iv B.C.):—Pass., fut. καθαρθήσομαι Ruf.ap.Orib.7.26.64, Gal.7.222: aor. ἐκαθάρθην Hdt.1.43, Th. 3.104, Hp.*Epid.*5.2, etc. (aor. 2 ἀποκαθαρῇ is f.l. in Arr.*Cyn.*27.1): pf. κεκάθαρμαι Hp.*Nat.Mul.*8, Pl.*Phd.*69c, etc.: (καθαρός): I. *cleanse*, of things, καθήρατε δὲ κρητῆρας Od.20.152; τραπέζας ὕδατι.. καθαίρειν 22.439; καθήραντες χρόα καλὸν ὕδατι 24.44; κ. οἰκίαν Antipho l.c., Thphr. l.c.; of wounds, Hp.*Ulc.*6, al. (cf. καθαιρέω II. 6): c. gen., ἵππον αὐχμηρᾶς τριχός S.*Fr.*475; κ. σῖτον X.*Oec.*18.6; γῆν *clear* of weeds, ib.20.11, cf. *PLille* 5.24 (iii B.C.), etc.; χρυσὸν *purify, refine*, Pl.*Plt.*303d: metaph., *purge, clear* a land of monsters and robbers, S.*Tr.*1012 (hex.), 1061, Plu.*Thes.*7; κ. λῃστηρίων τὴν ἐπαρχίαν Id.*Mar.*6: c. acc. cogn., καθαρμὸν κ. Pl.*Lg.*735b:—Pass., τὴν νηδὺν ἀνασχισθεῖσαν καὶ καθαρθεῖσαν Hdt.4.71. 2. in religious sense, *purify*, [δέπας] ἐκάθηρε θεείῳ by fumigating with sulphur, Il.16.228; κ. τινὰ φόνου *purify* him *from* blood, Hdt.1.44, cf. *Berl.Sitzb.*1927. 160 (Cyrene); Δῆλον κ. Hdt.1.64, cf. Th.1.8; στόλον κ., Lat. *classem lustrare*, App.*BC*5.96: abs., *IG*5(1).1390.68 (Andania, i B.C.):—Med., *purify oneself, get purified*, Hdt.4.73; οἱ φιλοσοφίᾳ καθηράμενοι Pl.*Phd.*114c, cf. *Phdr.*243a, *Cra.*396e; καθαίρεσθαι καθαρμοὺς Id.*Lg.* 868e; καθήρασθαι στόμα *keep one's* tongue *pure*, A.*Fr.*354:—Pass., κεκαθαρμένος καὶ τετελεσμένος Pl.*Phd.*69c. 3. Medic., *purge, evacuate*, either by purgatives or emetics, κ. κάτω ἢ ἄνω Hp.*Mul.*1.64 (Pass.), cf. Thphr.*HP*9.11.11, etc.:—Med., κατὰ κύστιν ἐκαθήρατο Hp.*Epid.* 1.15:—Pass., ib.5.2, etc.; also of menstruation, Id.*Superf.*33; of the after-birth, τὰ λοχεῖα κ. Id.*Mul.*1.78; καθαίρων, ὁ, name for ἶρις, Ps.-Dsc.1.1. 4. *prune* a tree, i.e. *clear* it of superfluous wood, *Ev.Jo.* 15.2. 5. *sift, winnow* grain, *PTeb.*373.10 (ii A.D.). 6. metaph., = μαστιγόω, Theoc.5.119. II. of the thing removed by purification, *purge away, wash off*, λύματα πάντα κάθηρεν Il.14.171; ἐπεὶ πλῦνάν τε κάθηράν τε ῥύπα πάντα Od.6.93; *clear away*, τὰ λῃστικά D.C.37. 52: metaph., φόνον κ. A.*Ch.*74 (lyr.); also perh., *clear up, explain* an action, τὴν σύστασιν Epicur.*Nat.*66 G., cf. 73 G. III. c. dupl. acc., αἷμα κάθηρον.. Σαρπηδόνα *cleanse* him *of* blood, *wash* the blood *off* him, Il.16.667:—Pass., καθαίρομαι γῆρας I *am purged of* old age, A. *Fr.*45; ὁ καθαρθεὶς τὸν φόνον Hdt.1.43.

κάθακα, τά, apptly., = καθήκοντα, πάντα τὰ κ. ποιήσασα *BSA*18.148 (Beroea).

καθάλλομαι, fut. -ᾰλοῦμαι: aor. part. -αλόμενος or -αλάμενος (both readings in X.*HG*4.5.7):—*leap down*, ἀπὸ τοῦ ἵππου, ἀπ' ὄχθων, Id. l.c., *Eq.*3.7; ἐντὸς τοῦ τείχους Luc.*DMort.*14.5: abs., App.*Hisp.*22: metaph., of a storm, *rush down*, καθαλλομένη ἰοειδέα πόντον ὀρίνει Il. 11.298; of convulsions, Anon.ap.Gal.7.624.

καθαλμ-άω, (ἅλμη) *become crusted with salt*, κέραμον τὸν καθηλμηκότα *IG*11(2).287*A*112 (Delos, iii B.C.). **-ής**, ές, *salt, saltish*, Nic. *Al.*514.

κάθᾰλος, ον, (ἅλς A) *full of salt, over-salted*, Diph.17.13: comically, of the cook, Posidipp.1.7.

καθᾰμαξεύω, *wear with wheels*: metaph., ἕτεροι κατημάξευσαν (sic) τάσδε τὰς τρίβους Nech.ap.Vett.Val.354.2; *crush*, καθημάξευσε ταῖς συμφοραῖς Eun.*Hist.*p.240 D.: elsewh. in pf. part. Pass., καθημαξευμένος, η, ον, metaph., γύναιον κ. ὑπὸ παντὸς τοῦ προσιόντος, of a *common* prostitute, Ael.*Fr.*123: but almost always written **κατημ-**, *hackneyed, stale, trite*, ἀντιλογίαι D.H.10.41, cf. *Th.*11.2; ἔθη κ. Ph. 1.513; πρόχειρον καὶ κ. ib.426; τὰ κοινὰ καὶ κ. Ath.15.677a, cf. Artem.1.31 (in marg.), Simp.*in Cat.*424.13, Sch.Pi.*N.*6.91 (ind., [ὁ λόγος] κατημάξευται Conon 46). Adv. καθημαξευμένως *in a trite way*, Ael.Dion.*Fr.*218.

κάθαμμα, ατος, τό, (καθάπτω) *knot*: metaph., κ. λύειν λόγον (dub. l.) to solve a *knotty point*, E.*Hipp.*671 (lyr.); κ. λύειν, proverb from the Gordian knot, to overcome a difficulty, Zen.4.46, Suid.

καθαμματίζω (κατ- cod.), *innodo*, *Gloss.*

καθαμμίζω, *cover with sand*, ἑαυτά Arist.*HA*620^{b}29, prob. in Antig.*Mir.*48.

καθᾰνύω, Att. for κατανύω, acc. to Hdn.Gr.1.541; καθήνυσαν cited by Phryn.*PS*p.23 B.; καθανύσαι· συντελέσαι, Hsch.: but codd. of Att. writers have only **κατανύω**, q.v. (καθήνυσαν is cj. in S.*El.*1451 (Dobree), καθανύσαι, -σας, -σειν, in X.*HG*7.1.15, 5.4.49, 20 (Cobet)).

καθάπαν [ᾰπ], Adv. *on the whole*; better divisim καθ' ἅπαν, cf. Lxx 2*Ma.*15.30.

καθάπαξ [ᾰπ], Adv. *once for all*, Od.21.349, D.18.231, Phld.*D.*3 *Fr.*23, Jul.*Or.*2.70c; *out-and-out, absolutely*, οἱ κ. ἐχθροί D.18.197; κ. ἄτιμος γέγονεν Id.21.87, cf. 25.30; κ. σπουδαῖος, opp. κατά τι, Phld. *Po.*5.16, cf. Ph.2.6; opp. πρός τι, Archig.ap.Gal.8.626; οἱ κ. μὴ συναπτόμενοι not *at all*, Ocell.4.4; οὕτω κ. πέπρακεν ἑαυτόν D.19. 118; οὐδὲ κ. not even *once*, Plb.1.2.6, 1.20.12, etc.; οὐδὲ τὸ κ. S.E.*M.* 11.97; πάντως δ', οὐ κ. not merely *in a single case*, Demetr.Lac.*Herc.* 1055.22; *singly*, Plb.3.90.2. II. *each time*, = ἑκάστοτε, *PMag. Par.*1.326.

καθάπερ, καθαπερεί, καθαπερανεί, v. καθά.

καθαπλόω, *spread over*, τοῦ αὐχένος, of the hair, Aristaenet.2.4.

καθαπτής, οῦ, ὁ, or -ή, ἡ, a kind of vase, in pl., γάστρας καὶ καθαπτάς *PSI*4.420.26 (iii B.C.).

καθαπτός, ή, όν, *bound with, equipped with*, θύρσοισι καὶ νεβρῶν δοραῖς E.*Fr.*752. II. κ. ὄργανον *percussion* instrument, e.g. cymbal or drum, Aristocles ap.Ath.4.174c.

καθάπτω, Ion. **κατ-**, *fasten* or *fix on, put upon*, καθῆψεν ὤμοις.. ἀμφίβληστρον S.*Tr.*1051; κ. τι ἀμφί τινι E.*Ion* 1006; τι ἐπί τι X.*Cyn.* 6.9; τι εἴς τι Plb.8.6.3; τι ἔκ τινος Plu.2.647e; ἄγκυραν καθάψας *having made it fast*, Philem.213.10; τὰ ὀστέα καθάπτει τὰ νεῦρα Arist. *Spir.*483^{b}31:—Med., κισσὸν ἐπὶ κρατὶ καθάπτεσθαι Theoc.*Ep.*3.4:—Pass., βρόχῳ καθημμένος S.*Ant.*1222, cf. Theoc.*Adon.*11. 2. *equip* by fastening or hanging on, in Med., σκευῇ σῶμ' ἐμὸν καθάψομαι E.*Rh.*202, cf. *AP*9.19 (Arch.):—Pass., νεβρίνῃ καθημμένος δορᾷ *with* a fawn-skin *slung round him*, S.*Ichn.*219; καθημμένοι νεβρίδας Str.15.1.71. 3. intr., *attach itself*, εἴς τι, πρός τι, Arist.*HA*514^{b} 30, 515^{a}3; later = II. 5, *fasten upon*, τῆς χειρός τινος *Act.Ap.*28.3, cf. Poll.1.164. II. used by Hom. only in Med., καθάπτεσθαί τινα ἐπέεσσι, in good or bad sense, as, σὺ τόν γ' ἐπέεσσι καθάπτεσθαι μαλακοῖσι *do* thou *accost* him.., Il.1.582; μαλακοῖσι καθαπτόμενος ἐπέεσσιν Od.10.70; μειλιχίοις ἐπέεσσι κ. 24.393; but also ἀντιβίοις ἐπέεσσι καθαπτόμενος *assailing*.., 18.415, 20.323; χαλεποῖσι κ. ἐπέεσσι Hes.*Op.*332: without a qualifying Adj., *accost, assail*, ἐπέεσσι καθάπτετο θοῦρον Ἄρηα Il.15.127, cf. Od.2.240; without ἐπέεσσι, γέροντα καθαπτόμενος προσέειπεν 2.39, cf. 20.22, Il.16.421. 2. after Hom., c. gen., *upbraid*, Hdt.6.69, Th.6.16, Pl.*Cri.*52a, X.*HG* 1.7.4: abs., Th.6.82. 3. in military sense, *attack*, καθαψάμενοι τῆς οὐραγίας Plb.1.19.14. 4. *appeal* to, θεῶν...καταπτόμενος *appealing* to them, Hdt.6.68; Δημαρήτου καὶ ἄλλων μαρτύρων Id.8.65. 5. *lay hold of*, τυραννίδος Sol.32.3; βρέφεος χείρεσσι Theoc.17.65; τῆς θαλάσσης *take to* the sea, Philostr.*VA*3.23: Act., καθάπτων τοῦ τραχήλου Arr.*Epict.*3.20.10 (cf. 1.3). 6. *to be sensitive in respect of*, ψόφου Hp.*Prorrh.*1.16.

καθάρβυλος, v. κατάρβυλος.

κᾰθάρ-ειος, later **καθάριος** [θᾰ], ον, (καθαρός) of persons, *cleanly, neat, tidy*, τοὺς καθαρείους περὶ ὄψιν, περὶ ἀμπεχόνην, περὶ ὅλον τὸν βίον Arist.*Rh.*1381b1: -ιώτατόν (v.l. -ειότατόν) ἐστι τὸ ζῷον (i.e. the bee) Id.*HA*626a24; καθάρειοι ταῖς διαίταις D.S.5.33 (καθάριοι codd.); οἱ καθαρειότεροι *decent, respectable* men, Phld.*Rh.*2.150S., Hierocl. p.63A. (-ριώτ-, -ρώτ- codd., em. Meineke); of things, ἐὰν ἡ σκευασία καθάρ(ε)ιος ᾖ Men.*Phasm.Fr.*2; καθαριώτερα (or -ειότερα) ὅπλα Plb. 11.9.5; τὸ κ., *daintiness*, of food, Plu.2.663c; κ. ἄρτος *white* bread, *Sammelb.*5730 (iv/v A.D., sg.), *PMag.Lond.*46.230 (pl.); βίος, δίαιτα καθάρειος, *refined*, Ath.3.74d, *Carm.Aur.*35; εἰς τὰ καθάρεια λιμὸς εἰσοικίζεται Men.841 (καθαρά codd.). Adv. -είως *cleanly, tidily*, ἐγχέουσιν X.*Cyr.*1.3.8, cf. Posidon.15J., Dsc.1.44; *neatly*, κ. εἰργασμένος Ph.*Bel.*76.27; *clearly*, ὑποδεῖξαι Plb.15.5.5; also, *frugally*, μὴ πολυτελῶς, ἀλλὰ καθαρείως Eub.110.1, Ephipp.15.3, Nicostr.6.2; ἔχειν καθαρ(ε)ίως ἐγχελύδιον Amphis 35; μονοτροφοῦντες καθαρίως καὶ λιτῶς Str.3.3.6; *irreproachably*, ἀναστραφεὶς ἀνδρήως καὶ καθαρήως (sic) *AJA*17.31 (Sardes, i B.C.). II. Gramm. of language, *pure, correct*, ὄνομα Sch.Ar.*Ach.*244; οἱ κ. *purists*, Archig.ap.Gal.8.578. [-ειος is written in Phld.*Rh.* l.c. (Comp.), *PSI*3.158.50 (Comp., iii A.D.), Phld.*D.*3.8, *PMag.Lond.* l.c., and required by metre in Eub., Nicostr., *Carm.Aur.*, ll. cc.: -ιος never.] **-ειότης**, later **καθᾰριότης**, ητος, ἡ, *cleanliness, neatness*, Hdt.2.37, X.*Mem.*2.1.22; *purity*, διαφέρει ἡ ὄψις ἁφῆς καθαρειότητι Arist.*EN*1176a1, cf. 1177a 26; τοῦ ἀέρος Thphr.*Sens.*48; *purity* of language, Plu.*Lyc.*21, S.E. *M.*1.176. 2. *scrupulousness, moral integrity*, *IG*4.1 (Aegina, ii B.C.), *OGI*339.14 (Sestos, ii B.C.). 3. *elegance, refinement*, τῇ κ. Κυπρίους...[ὑπερέβαλε] Duris 10J.; opp. περιεργία, Plu.2.693b, cf. 142a, *Crass.*3; opp. λιτότης, Hierocl. *in CA*17 p.457M.; also, *simplicity, frugality*, τῆς διαίτης Plu.2.644c; *economy of movement* in a surgeon's hand, ib.67e. **-εσις**, εως, ἡ, perh. Dor. for καθάρισις, στέγας *IG*4.1484.293 (Epid.). **-ευσις**, εως, ἡ, gloss on ἁγιασμός, Hsch., cf. *EM*10.38. **-ευτέον**, *one must keep oneself clean*, τινος *from* a thing, Luc.*Hist.Conscr.*6; περὶ ἀφροδίσια Epict.*Ench.* 33.8. **-εύω**, (καθαρός) *to be clean* or *pure*, Pl.*Phd.*58b, *Lg.*759c, Phld.*Lib.*p.9O., Porph.*Abst.*4.6; of *sifted* grain, *PPetr.*2 p.2 (iii B.C.): c. gen., *to be clean* or *free from*, φόνου Pl.*Ep.*357a; [κακιῶν] Phld.*Rh.*1.218S.; ἁμαρτημάτων Plu.*Cat.Mi.*24; ὀνείδους Luc.*Am.* 22; κ. πυρετοῦ *to be free from* fever, Gal.7.503: hence ἡμέραι -εύουσαι ibid.; κ. ἀπ' αὐτοῦ (sc. τοῦ σώματος) Pl.*Phd.*67a; κ. γνώμῃ *to be pure* or *clean* in mind, Ar.*Ra.*355; περί τι Plb.6.56.15. 2. Rhet., of a writer, *to be pure, correct* in language, κ. τὴν διάλεκτον D.H. *Lys.*2; οἱ καθαρεύοντες *purists*, Hdn.Gr.2.224. 3. Gramm., *to be preceded by a vowel*, to be '*pure*' (cf. καθαρός I.5b), A.D.*Pron.*99.24, Theodos.*Can.*p.70H.; *contain a* '*pure*' *syllable*, Hdn.Gr.2.923, Id. ap.Eust.1859.13. **-ιεύω**, *to be* καθάριος, in Med., Alex.Aphr. *Pr.*2.53. II. = καθαρεύω 3, Hdn.Gr.ap.Choerob.*in Theod.*1.232, Theognost.*Can.*28, etc. **-ίζω**, fut. -ιῶ *Ep.Hebr.*9.14:—*cleanse*, θυσιαστήριον Lxx *Ex.*29.36, cf. *Ev.Matt.*23.25, *Act.Ap.*10.15; *sift* grain, *PStrassb.*2.11 (iii A.D.); *prune away*, περισσὰ βλαστήματα *PLond.*1.131r192 (i A.D.); *clear* ground of weeds, etc., *PLips.*111. 12 (iv A.D.); *keep* a precinct *clear*, ἀπό τινων *IG*5(1).1390.37 (Andania, i B.C.):—in Med., fut. -ιοῦμαι, of the menses, Hp.*Superf.* 43. II. of persons, *purify*, ἀπὸ ἁμαρτίας Lxx *Si.*38.10; ἀπὸ παντὸς μολυσμοῦ 2*Ep.Cor.*7.1; τὴν συνείδησιν ἀπὸ νεκρῶν ἔργων *Ep. Hebr.*9.14; *cleanse* from leprosy, *Ev.Matt.*8.2 (and in Pass., of the disease, ib.3):—Pass., -ιζέστω ἀπὸ γυναικὸς κτλ. *IG*2².1366.4, cf. 1365. **-ιος**, v. καθάρειος. II. καθάριον, τό, *purgative medicine*, *POxy.*116.15 (ii A.D.). **-ιόω**, *purify*, in Pass., Lxx *La.*4.7, prob. in *PTeb.ined.*703. **-ῐσις**, εως, ἡ, = κάθαρσις, *PHeid.*1.6.18 (iv A.D.), v.l. in Lxx *Le.*12.4,6, Aq.ibid.; cf. καθάρεσις. **-ισμός**, ὁ, later form for καθαρμός, Lxx *Ex.*29.36, *Ev.Luc.*2.22, *Ev.Jo.*2.6, Luc. *Asin.*22, *PLond.*2.168.11 (ii A.D.). **-ιστήριον**, τό, *place for purifying, sifting*, Harp. s.v. Κεγχρεών. **-ιστής**, οῦ, ὁ, *tree-pruner*, *Gloss.*

κάθαρμα [κᾰ], ατος, τό, (καθαίρω) *that which is thrown away in cleansing*: in pl., *offscourings, refuse of a sacrifice*, A.*Ch.*98; *residuum* of ore after smelting, *slag*, Str.3.2.8: sg., = κάθαρσις II, Hp.*Epid.* 5.2. 2. = φαρμακός, Sch.Ar.*Pl.*454, Sch.Id.*Eq.*1133: hence metaph., of persons, *outcast*, Ar.*Pl.*454; αἱρούμενοι καθάρματα στρατηγούς Eup.117.8; τοὺς μὲν καθάρματα, τοὺς δὲ πτωχούς, τοὺς δ' οὐδ' ἀνθρώπους ὑπολαμβάνων εἶναι D.21.185, cf. 199, 18.128, Aeschin.3. 211, etc. II. in pl., = κάθαρσις, *purification*, E.*IT*1316; ποντίων καθαρμάτων...ἀμοιβάς in return *for clearing* the sea (of pirates), Id. *HF*225. III. ἐντὸς τοῦ καθάρματος within *the purified ground* where the assembly was held, Ar.*Ach.*44.

κᾰθαρματώδης, ες, *connected with* καθαρμοί, ὄνομα *EM*512.7.

καθαρμόζω, *join* or *fit to*, βρόχον δείρᾳ E.*Hipp.*771 (lyr.); [πλόκαμον] ὑπὸ μίτρᾳ Id.*Ba.*929; βάσιν χερσὶ προσθίαν καθαρμόσας *fitting* its forefeet to my hands, Id.*Rh.*210; *fit clamps* into their places, *IG*7. 3073.72 (Lebad.):—Med., Ph.1.342.

κᾰθαρμός, ὁ, (καθαίρω) *cleansing, purification*, from guilt, νίψαι καθαρμῷ τήνδε τὴν στέγην S.*OT*1228: hence, *purificatory offering, atonement, expiation*, καθαρμὸν τῆς χώρης ποιέεσθαί τινα Hdt.7.197: freq. in pl., μύσος ἐλαύνειν καθαρμοῖς A.*Ch.*968 (lyr., dub. l.), cf. *Th.* 738, *Eu.*277, 283, *Berl.Sitzb.*1927.156 (Cyrene): sg., S.*OT*99; θεοῦ νῦν καθαρμὸν δαιμόνων make *an offering to avert* their wrath, Id.*OC*466; καθαρμὸν θύειν E.*IT*1332; λύσεις τε καὶ καθαρμοὶ ἀδικημάτων Pl.*R.* 364e; ὁ περὶ τὴν διάνοιαν κ. Id.*Sph.*227c; κ. ποιεῖσθαι τῆς δυνάμεως, Lat. *lustrare exercitum*, Plb.21.41.9, Plu.*Caes.*43; of the Roman *lustrum*, D.H.4.22; κ. ὅπλων, σάλπιγγος, = Lat. *armilustrium, tubilustrium*, Lyd.*Mens.*4.34,60. 2. *purificatory rite* of initiation into mysteries, Pl.*Phd.*69c, *Phdr.*244e; ἀνιστὰς ἀπὸ τοῦ καθαρμοῦ D.18. 259, cf. Plu.2.47a: hence in pl., as title of poem by Empedocles, Ath.14.620d; by Epimenides, Suid. s.h.v. 3. *purgation* by ordeal, *PMag.Lond.*46.180,196. II. *purging, evacuation, discharge*, Arist.*HA*587b1, Plu.2.134d. 2. metaph., *purge, clearance* of unhealthy animals, Pl.*Lg.*735b. III. = κάθαρμα I.2, Plu. 2.518b.

καθάρμοσις, εως, ἡ, *precise adaptation*, *Theol.Ar.*54.

κᾰθᾰρο-λογέω, *to be precise* or *accurate in language*, Eust.352. 35. **-ποιέω**, *cleanse*, ἕλκη Gal.11.683. 2. *sift, winnow*, gloss on πτίσσειν, Sch.Ar.*Ach.*506. II. *clear* property from debts and encumbrances, *PMasp.*97.32 (vi A.D.):—hence **-ποίησις**, εως, ἡ, ib. 151.122 (vi A.D.).

κᾰθᾰρ-ός, ά, όν, Dor. **κοθαρός** *Tab.Heracl.*1.103, Orph.*Fr.*32c.1, Aeol. **κόθ-** Alc.*Supp.*7.3; cf. ἀνακαθαίρω, κάθαρσις: 1. *physically clean, spotless* (not in Il.), εἵματα Od.6.61, Archil.12, cf. E.*Cyc.*35, 562, etc.; of persons, *cleanly*, κ. περὶ ἐσθῆτα Arist.*VV*1250b28, cf. *Rh.*1416a 23 (nisi leg. καθάριος). 2. *clear of admixture, clear, pure*, esp. of water, Βορυσθένης ῥέει καθαρὸς παρὰ θολεροῖσι Hdt.4.53; κ. ὕδατα E. *Hipp.*209 (anap.); ὕδωρ κ. ζῶν Lxx *Nu.*5.17; δρόσοι E.*Ion*96 (anap.); κ. καὶ διαφανῆ ὑδάτια Pl.*Phdr.*229b; οὖρον Hp.*Epid.*1.3; διαχώρημα Id.*Coac.*640; κ. φάος, φέγγος, Pi.*P.*6.14, 9.90; πνεῦμα κ. οὐρανοῦ E.*Hel.*867; κ. ἄρτος Hdt.2.40; of *white* bread, Wilcken *Chr.*30 ii 17 (iii/ii B.C.), Lxx *Ju.*10.5, Gal.6.482, 19.137; ἄλευρον κ. Diocl.*Fr.*139; χρυσίον, ἀργύριον -ώτατον, Hdt.4.166, cf. Theoc.15.36, Ph.1.190, etc.; σῖτος X.*Oec.*18.8; σῖτος κ. ἀπὸ πάντων *PHib.*1.84(a).6 (iv/iii B.C.): freq. of grain, *winnowed*, πυρὸς κ. ἄδολος *POxy.*1124.11 (i A.D.), cf. *PTeb.*93.36 (ii B.C.), etc.; of metals, etc., σίδηρος *Sammelb.*4481.13 (v A.D.), etc.; ἀρωμάτων, καθαρῶν, λαχάνων, dub. sens. in *PLond.*2.429. 6 (iv A.D.); ἄκρατος καὶ κ. νοῦς X.*Cyr.*8.7.30; χρόαι Arist.*Sens.*440a5; φωναί Id.*Aud.*801b28; of feelings, *unmixed*, μῖσος τῆς ἀλλοτρίας φύσεως Pl.*Mx.*245d, cf. Thgn.89; *serene*, φρήν E.*Hipp.*1120 (lyr.). 3. *clear of objects, free*, ἐν καθαρῷ (sc. τόπῳ) in an *open* space, ἐν κ., ὅθι δὴ νεκύων διεφαίνετο χῶρος Il.8.491; ἐν κ., ὅθι κύματ' ἐπ' ἠϊόνος κλύζεσκον 23.61, cf. Ph.2.535 (Sup.); πάξαις Ἄλτιν ἐν κ. in *a clearing*, Pi.*O.*10 (11).45; ἐν κ. βῆναι to leave the way *clear*, S.*OC*1575 (lyr.); ἐν τῷ κ. οἰκεῖν live in *the clear sunshine*, Pl.*R.*520d; διὰ καθαροῦ ῥέειν, of a river whose course is *clear and open*, Hdt.1.202: with Subst., κελεύθῳ ἐν κ. Pi.*O.*6.23; χῶρος κ. Hdt.1.132; ἐν κ. λειμῶνι Theoc.26.5; ἐν ἡλίῳ κ. in the *open* sun, opp. σκιά, Pl.*Phdr.*239c; ὥς σφι τὸ ἐμποδὼν ἐγεγόνεε κ. was *cleared away*, Hdt.7.183; κ. ποιεῖσθαι τὰς ἀρκυστασίας set up the nets *in open ground*, X.*Cyn.*6.6; freq. of land, *free* from weeds, etc., παραδώσω τὸν κλῆρον κ. ἀπὸ θρύου καλάμου ἀγρώστεως κτλ. *PTeb.*105.59 (ii B.C.); παραδώσω τὰς ἀρούρας κ. ὡς ἔλαβον *BGU*1018.25 (iii A.D.): c. gen., γλῶσσα καθαρὴ τῶν σημηΐων *clear* of the marks, Hdt.2.38; καθαρὸν τῶν προβόλων, of a fort, Arr.*An.*2.21.7; of documents, *free from mistakes*, *POxy.*1277.13 (iii A.D.); χειρόγραφον κ. ἀπὸ ἐπιγραφῆς καὶ ἀλείφαδος *free* from interlineation and erasure, *PLond.*2.178.13 (ii A.D.). b. metaph., *free, clear* of debt, liability, etc., κ. ἀπὸ δημοσίων καὶ παντὸς εἴδους *BGU*197.14 (i A.D.); κ. ἀπό τε ὀφειλῆς καὶ ὑποθήκης καὶ παντὸς διεγγυήματος ib.112.11 (i A.D.); γῆ κ. ἀπὸ γεωργίας βασιλικῆς *POxy.*633 (ii A.D.); καθαρὰ ποιῆσαι to give a *discharge*, *PAvrom.*1 A 22; in moral sense, *free from pollution*, καθαρῷ θανάτῳ an *honourable* death, Od.22.462; θάνατον οὐ κ., τὸν δι' ἀγχόνης Ph.2.491; ψυχαὶ ἀρηΐφατοι καθαρώτεραι ἢ ἐνὶ νούσοις Heraclit.136; freq. *free from guilt* or *defilement, pure*, χεῖρες A.*Eu.* 313 (anap.); καθαρὸς χεῖρας Hdt.1.35, Antipho 5.11, And.1.95; κ. παρέχειν τινὰ κατὰ τὸ σῶμα καὶ κατὰ τὴν ψυχήν Pl.*Cra.*405b; ἔρχομαι ἐκ κοθαρῶν κοθαρά Orph.*Fr.*32c.1, al.; of ceremonial *purity*, καθαρὰ καὶ ἁγνή εἰμι ἀπό τε τῶν ἄλλων τῶν οὐ καθαρευόντων καὶ ἀπ' ἀνδρὸς συνουσίας Jusj.ap.D.59.78, cf. *UPZ*78.28 (ii B.C.), Lxx *Nu.*8.7, al.; ἀπὸ τάφου καὶ ἐκφορᾶς καθαροί *SIG*982.9 (ii B.C.); esp. of persons *purified* after pollution, ἱκέτης προσῆλθες κ. A.*Eu.*474, cf. S.*OC*548, etc.; also of things, βωμοί, θύματα, δόμος, μέλαθρα, A.*Supp.*654 (lyr.), E. *IT*1163, 1231 (troch.), 693: c. gen., *clear of* or *from*.., κ. ἐγκλημάτων Antipho 2.4.11; ἀδικίας, κακῶν, Pl.*R.*496d, *Cra.*404a; ὁ τῶν κακῶν κ. τόπος Id.*Tht.*177a; κ. τὰς χεῖρας φόνου Id.*Lg.*864e; Κόρινθον...ἀποδεῖξαι τῶν μιαιφόνων καθαράν X.*HG*4.4.6; κ. εἰμι ἀπὸ τοῦ αἵματος πάντων *Act.Ap.*20.26, cf. D.C.37.24; κ. ἀπὸ ὅρκου Lxx *Ge.*24.8; *ceremonially pure*, of food, ὄσπριον Hdt.2.37; of victims, Lxx *Ge.*7.2, al., *PGen.*32.9 (ii A.D.), etc.; κ. ἡμέραι, opp. ἀποφράδες, Pl.*Lg.*800d. c. in act. sense, *purifying, cleansing*, λέβης Pi.*O.*1.26; θέειον Theoc. 24.96. 4. of birth, *pure, genuine*, σπέρμα θεοῦ Pi.*P.*3.15; πόλις

E.*Ion*673; τῶν Ἀθηναίων ὅπερ ἐστράτευε καθαρὸν ἐξῆλθε, i.e. were *citizens of pure blood*, Th.5.8; οἱ τῷ γένει μὴ κ. Arist.*Ath.*13.5; κ. ἀστοί Sch.Ar.*Ach.*506; καθαρόν a *real, genuine* saying, Ar.*V.*1015; κ. Τίμων *a* Timon *pure and simple*, Id.*Av.*1549; κ. δοῦλος Antiph.9 (glossed by ἀπηκριβωμένος, *AB*105); ζημία κ., of a person, Alciphro 3.21. 5. of language, *pure*, ὀνόματα, λέξις, D.H.*Comp.*1,3; διάλεκτος Id.*Dem.*5; so of writers, [Λυσίας] κ. τὴν ἑρμηνείαν Id.*Lys.*2; [Ξενοφῶν] κ. τοῖς ὀνόμασι Id.*Pomp.*4; also, *clear, simple*, σεμνὸς καὶ κ. Jul.*Or.*2.77a. b. Gramm., *preceded by a vowel, pure*, D.T. 635.10, 639.5, Hdn.Gr.2.930, al.; *containing a 'pure' syllable*, ib. 928. 6. *without blemish, sound*, ὁ κ. στρατός, τὸ κ. τοῦ στρατοῦ, the *sound portion* of the army, Hdt.1.211, 4.135; v. supr. 4. 7. *clear, exact*, ἂν κ. ὦσιν αἱ ψῆφοι if the accounts are *exactly balanced*, D.18.227 (sed cf. καθαιρέω II. 5). II. Adv. *purely*, ἁγνῶς καὶ καθαρῶς *h.Ap.*121, Hes.*Op.*337: Comp. -ωτέρως Porph.*Abst.*2.44. 2. of birth, κ. γεγονέναι Hdt.1.147; αἱ κ. Ἑλληνίδες Sor.1.112, cf. Luc.*Rh. Pr.*24. 3. *with clean hands, honestly*, σὺν δίκῃ.. καὶ κ. Thgn.198; δικαίως καὶ κ. D.9.62; κ. τε καὶ μετρίως τὸν βίον διεξελθεῖν Pl.*Phd.* 108c. 4. *clearly, plainly*, λέγειν Ar.*V.*631, cf. E.*Rh.*35 (anap.); λέξις κ. καὶ ἀκριβῶς ἔχουσα Isoc.5.4; κ. γνῶναι Ar.*V.*1045, Pl.*Phd.*66e; εἴσεσθαι ibid.; καθαρώτατα ἀποδεῖξαι Id.*Cra.*426b. 5. of language, *purely, correctly*, -ώτερον διαλέγεσθαι Plu.2.1116e, cf. Luc.*Im.*15. 6. *entirely*, Ar.*Av.*591; κ. τις ὢν ἀόργητος Phld.*Ir.*p.71 W.; κ. ἐς ἐφήβους τελεῖν D.C.36.25, cf. *Cod.Just.*1.4.34.9: Sup. -ώτατα *in its purest form*, Phld.*Piet.*66. **-ότης**, ητος, ἡ, *purity* of αἰθήρ as compared with ἀήρ, Pl.*Phd.*111b: metaph., [ἡ σοφία] χωρεῖ διὰ πάντων διὰ τὴν κ. Lxx *Wi.*7.24; ἡ τῶν εἰδῶν κ. Dam.*Pr.*308; ἄμικτος καὶ ἀσύγχυτος κ. ibid. 2. *cleanliness*, of a town, Pl.*Lg.*778c. 3. *clearness*, ὀφθαλμῶν Hp.*Coac.*213. 4. moral *purity*, ψυχῆς Aristeas 234. 5. *honesty*, ἡ περὶ τὰ χρήματα κ. Plb.31.25.9; ἐπιείκεια καὶ κ. *POxy.*67.6 (iv A.D.); πίστις καὶ κ. *Michel* 545.18 (Phrygia, ii B.C.). 6. *purity, lucidity*, of literary style, Sch.Hermog. in Rh.7.81 W. 7. as a title, *Rectitude, Holiness*, *POxy.*2110.16 (iv A.D.).

κᾰθᾰρουργ-(ε)ῖον, τό, *bakery for fine bread*, *CPR*207.12 (ii A.D.). **-ία**, ἡ, *artistic work* (the exact sense is dub.), *CIG*4558 (Syria). II. *baking of fine bread*, *POxy.*2128.10 (ii A.D.). **-ικός**, ή, όν, *sifted, fine*, γῦρις *Gp.*20.35. **-ός**, ὁ, *baker of fine bread*, *Sammelb.*984.5 (pl., i A.D.), *PLond.*2.454a (iv A.D.).

καθαρο-φόνος and **-φόντης**, glosses on Ἀργειφόντης, Hsch.

καθαρπ-ἀγή (κατ- cod.), ἡ, *direptio*, *Gloss.* **-άζω**, *snatch down*, ἐκ δεξιᾶς ξίφη, τεύχη πασσάλων, E.*Andr.*813, 1122; *seize, appropriate*, τὰ ἀλλότρια Str.16.2.37:—Pass., Ph.2.7, *PThead.*23.14 (iv A.D.).

κᾰθάρ-σιος, ον, (καθαίρω) *cleansing* from guilt or defilement, *purifying*, Ζεύς Hdt.1.44, cf. Arist.*Mu.*401ᵃ23, etc.; of Dionysus, μολεῖν καθαρσίῳ ποδί S.*Ant.*1144 (lyr.); of sacrifice, αἷμα A.*Eu.*449, *Th.*680; πῦρ E.*HF*937, *IA*1112, J.*AJ*20.8.5, al.; φλόξ E.*Hel.*869; προχύται Id.*IA*1471: c. gen., [Λοξίας] δωμάτων κ. A.*Eu.*63; ἱερὰ κ. οἴκων E. *HF*923; also κ. φόνου *cleansing from...*, A.*Eu.*578. II. as Subst., 1. καθάρσιον (sc. ἱερόν), τό, *purificatory offering*, Aeschin. 1.23, cf. Phot.: pl., *BMus.Inscr.*481*.280: hence, *expiation*, καθαρσίου ἐδέετο κυρῆσαι Hdt.1.35, cf. Jul.*Or.*2.58d. 2. (sc. φάρμακον) *purge*, Alex.Trall.1.15, *POxy.*1384.1 (v A.D.), Phlp. in *Ph.*318. 12. III. καθάρσια, τά, = Lat. *illuvies*, *Gloss.* (nisi leg. ἀκαθαρσία). **-σις**, εως, ἡ, Elean **κόθαρσις** *Schwyzer* 412, *cleansing* from guilt or defilement, *purification*, Hdt.1.35, Pl.*Cra.*405a, etc.; κάθαρσις... τὸ χωρίζειν ὅτι μάλιστα ἀπὸ τοῦ σώματος τὴν ψυχήν Id.*Phd.*67c, cf. *Sph.*227c (pl.); *cleansing* of the universe by fire, Zeno and Chrysipp.*Stoic.*2.184; *cleansing* of food by or before cooking, Diocl. *Fr.*138. 2. *clarification*, φυσικῶν προβλημάτων Epicur.*Ep.*2 p.36 U.; καθάρσεως δεῖται needs *explanation*, Phld.*Lib.*p.22 O. II. Medic., *clearing off of morbid humours*, etc., *evacuation*, whether natural or by the use of medicines (cf. Gal.17(2).358), Hp.*Aph.* 5.36, cf. *Acut.*(*Sp.*)31, etc.; ἰατρικὴ κ. Pl.*Lg.*628d; καθάρσεις, the menses in women, Hp.*Aph.*5.60; καθάρσεις καταμηνίων Arist. *HA*572ᵇ29; so κάθαρσις alone, Id.*GA*775ᵇ5; κ. μετὰ τόκον Hp.*Aër.* 7; ἡ ἐν τοῖς τόκοις κ. Arist.*HA*574ᵇ4; κ. αἵματος αὐτομάτη μοι... συνέβη D.54.12. b. τραγῳδία... δι' ἐλέου καὶ φόβου περαίνουσα τὴν τῶν τοιούτων παθημάτων κ. Arist.*Po.*1449ᵇ28, cf. *Pol.*1341ᵇ 38. III. *pruning* of trees, Thphr.*CP*3.7.12. IV. *winnowing* of grain, in pl., *PTeb.*92.10 (ii B.C.); κ. πυροῦ *PRyl.*71.9 (i B.C.); τοῦ καρποῦ Ph.2.57 (sg.). V. *clearing* of land, *PSI*6.577.13 (iii B.C.), *PPetr.*3 p.122 (iii B.C.), etc. **-τέος**, α, ον, *to be purged*, Gal. 10.971. II. **-τέον**, *one must purge*, Hp.*Loc.Hom.*23. 2. *one must prune*, δένδρον *Gp.*10.77.2. **-τήρ**, ῆρος, ὁ, = καθαρτής, Man. 4.251; a name given to ὄροβος at Tralles, Plu.2.302b. **-τήριος**, ον, *purificatory*, θυσίαι D.H.9.40; τὰ κ. Poll.1.32. II. **-τήριον** (sc. φάρμακον), τό, *drug which effects* κάθαρσις, λοχείων, ἐπιμηνίων, Hp.*Mul.*1.78; *purgative*, Aret.*CA*1.4, Gal.11.354; κ. κατωτερικόν Aet.16.52. **-τής**, οῦ, ὁ, *cleanser, purifier*, μάγοι καὶ κ. Hp.*Morb. Sacr.*1, cf. D.Chr.4.89 (pl.); οὐ γὰρ ἔρχομαι... κ. S.*El.*70; στρατοῦ κ. Id.*Fr.*34; τῆς χώρας Ar.*V.*1043; ποταμῶν Plu.*Luc.*26; θηρίων, of Heracles, Max.Tyr.21.6: metaph., δοξῶν... περὶ ψυχὴν κ. εἶναι Pl.*Sph.* 231e; as occupational name, *IG*5(1).209.25 (i B.C.). **-τικός**, ή, όν, *of, fit for cleansing* or *purifying*, ἐλαίου καὶ γῆς Pl.*Ti.*60d; τὰ μέλη τὰ κ. (v. κάθαρσις II) Arist.*Pol.*1342ᵃ15; τὰ κ. *purgatives*, Phld.*Sign.* 25; κ. ἀρεταί Hierocl. in *CA*2 p.422 M.: ἡ -κή (sc. τέχνη) Pl.*Sph.* 231b. Adv. -κῶς Marin.*Procl.*19. II. Medic., *promoting* κάθαρσις, πρόσθετον Hp.*Mul.*1.74; usu.. *purgative*, δύναμις Gal.11.768 (metaph., Cebes 14); φάρμακον Plu.2.999f, cf. Gal.5.128; οἶνος Dsc.5.66 (Comp.); κ. alone, Hp.*Fract.*24, S.E.*M.*8.480. **-τρια**, ἡ, fem. of καθαρτής, Sch.Pi.*P.*3.139. **-υλλος**, ον, Com. Dim. of καθαρός, *dainty*, ἄρτοι Pl.Com.86. Adv. -λλως Cratin.27. **-ώδης**, ες, *clear*, ὄμμα v.l. for καρώδης, Hp.*Epid.*5.99.

καθαναίνω, v. καταναίνω.

κάθαψις, εως, ἡ, *good reaction*, produced by friction after the bath, ἄχρι πολλῆς κ. Agathin.ap.Orib.10.7.18.

κάθε· ἐπίδος, Hsch.

καθέδρ-α, ἡ, *seat*, κ. τοῦ λαγῶ a hare's *seat* or *form*, X.*Cyn.*4.4; *chair*, Herod.Med.ap.Orib.6.25.1, *CPR*22.8 (ii A.D.), Hdn.2.3.7; opp. κλίνη, Plu.2.714e; of rowers' *seats*, Plb.1.21.2; κ. λοιμῶν, πρεσβυτέρων, Lxx *Ps.*1.1, 106(107).32. 2. *sitting part, posteriors*, Hp.*Int.*47, Poll.2.184, *PRyl.*63.10 (iii A.D.). 3. *base* of a column, Str.17.1.46. II. *sitting posture*, Arist.*Cat.*6ᵇ11, *PA*689ᵇ21, Thphr.*Lass.*5,7, Plu.2.45c, etc. 2. *sitting idle, inaction*, ἐν τῇ καθέδρᾳ Th.2.18; κ. καὶ σχολή Plu.*Cam.*28. 3. *session*, Luc. *JTr.*11. III. *chair* of a teacher, ἐπὶ τῆς Μωυσέως κ. ἐκάθισαν *Ev. Matt.*23.2; *professorial chair*, ἐπὶ τῆς κ. σοφιστής *SIG*845 (Eleusis, iii A.D.). IV. imperial *throne*, τὸν ἐπὶ τῇ κ. τοῦ Αὐτοκράτορος, the Emperor's representative, *BSA*27.234 (Sparta, ii A.D.). **-άριον**, τό, Dim. of foreg., *POxy.*963 (ii/iii A.D.). **-ιος**, ον, *of* or *for sitting*, σχῆμα Antyll.ap.Orib.9.14.6, Aët.15.5; καθέδριόν τινα σχηματίζειν ib.7; -ιος σχηματιζέσθω Id.8.51. 2. *sedentary*, βίος Sor. 1.27. II. Subst. **-ιον**, τό, *small chair*, ib.106; gloss on διέδριον, Zonar. **-ωτός**, όν, *provided with seats*, καρρίον *Gloss.*

καθέζομαι (v. infr.), impf. ἐκαθεζόμην in Prose, X.*An.*1.5.9, *Cyr.*5.3. 25 (but freq. as aor. 2, And.1.44, Th.4.110, Pl.*Euthd.*272e); in Poets, καθεζόμην Od.9.417, A.*Eu.*6, Ar.*Lys.*1139: fut. καθεδοῦμαι Id.*Ra.*200, *Av.*727 (anap.), And.1.111, Pl.*Tht.*146a, D.5.15; later καθεδήσομαι D.L.2.72, καθεσθήσομαι Lxx *Le.*12.5: aor. καθεσθείς *AP*9.644.5 (Agath.), Paus.9.3.4, Charito 3.2, but v. Luc.*Sol.*11 (καθίζομαι, Pass. of καθίζω, which supplies the trans. sense, is more common in pres. and impf., but we have κατ' ἄρ' ἕζεαι Od.10.378, καθεζόμεσθα E.*Heracl.* 33, καθέζονται Lys.13.37, etc.):—*sit down, take one's seat*, ἀγορήνδε καθεζώμεσθα κιόντες Od.1.372; εἰνὶ θύρῃσι καθέζετο 9.417, cf. Il.24. 126, etc.; κατ' ἄρ' ἕζεν ἐπὶ θρόνου ib.522; κατ' ἄρ' ἕζετ' ἐπὶ... λίθοισιν Od.3.406; καθεζομένη πρόχνυ (v. πρόχνυ); so κ. ἐν... εὐναστηρίοις S. *Tr.*918; ἐπὶ ζυγοῖς ἀρχῆς E.*Ph.*75; ἐς θρόνον A.*Pr.*231; *preside*, Lys. l.c., Aeschin.3.73; ἐνθαδί Ar.*Ra.*200; οὐ λαχόντες προεδρεύειν, ἀλλ' ἐκ παρασκευῆς καθεζόμενοι *taking their seats*, Aeschin.3.3: Medic., Hp.*Epid.*7.3. 2. *sit down in, occupy*, a country, *encamp*, Th.2. 18, 7.77; *settle*, εἰς χώραν *OGI*201.13 (Nubia, vi A.D.). II. *remain seated*, in various senses: 1. *sit still*, with collat. notion of inaction, τίφθ' οὕτως κατ' ἄρ' ἕζεαι ἶσος ἀναύδῳ; Od.10.378, cf. 6.295. 2. *sit* as suppliants, ἱκέται καθεζόμεσθα βώμιοι E.*Heracl.* l.c.; πρὸς τὰ ἱερὰ ἱκετῶν καθεζομένων Th.3.70, cf. Ar.*Lys.*1139, D.18.107. 3. *sit* for one's portrait, Porph.*Plot.*1. 4. of a teacher, πρὸς ὑμᾶς ἐκαθεζόμην διδάσκων *Ev.Matt.*26.55.

καθείατο, Ep. for ἐκάθηντο, 3 pl. impf. of κάθημαι.

καθείμαρται, pf. Pass., used impers., *it is ordained by fate*, esp. to one's ruin, Ps.-Luc.*Philopatr.*14; τινι c. inf., ib.16, Arr.*Epict.*2.6.10: plpf., καθείμαρτο Chrysipp.*Stoic.*2.292; also pers., βραχὺς χρόνος ὁ τοῦ ζῆν ἑκάστῳ καθείμαρται Luc.*Am.*19; part., πάλαι καθειμαρμένων τούτων *having been ordained by fate*, Plu.*Alex.*52.

καθείργνῡμι, and in Luc.*Am.*39 **καθείργω** (= **κατείργω**, q.v.): aor. 1 καθεῖρξα E.*Ba.*618 (troch.), etc.:—*shut in, confine*, usu. of animals or persons, κατὰ συφεοῖσιν ἐέργνυ Od.10.238; οὗ καθεῖρξ' ἡμᾶς E.*Ba.* l.c.; τὸν πατέρα... ἔνδον καθείρξας Ar.*V.*70, cf. Cratin.72, Lys. *Fr.*75.4, Pl.*Tht.*197e; κηρίνοις πλάσμασι κ. ib.200c; ἐν τῷ σταυρώματι X.*HG*3.2.3; ἐν οἰκίσκῳ D.18.97. 2. rarely of things, καθεῖρξαι χρυσὸν ἐν δόμοις Anan.3; τὴν σελήνην... ἐς λοφεῖον Ar.*Nu.*751; τὴν μακρολογίαν κ. *confine it within bounds*, Pl.*Grg.*461d.

κάθειρξις, εως, ἡ, Att. for κάτειρξις, *shutting in, confining*, Plu.2. 366d, Ael.*NA*15.27, Aristid.*Or.*48(24).58.

καθεῖς, for καθ' εἷς, *one by one, one after another*, Lxx 3*Ma.*5.34; εἷς καθεῖς *Ev.Marc.*14.19, etc.: formed backwards from the neut. ἓν καθέν, noted by Luc.*Sol.*9.

καθεῖσα, v. καθίζω:—but καθεῖσαν 3 pl. aor. 2 of καθίημι.

καθειστόν· εἶδος φιλήματος, Hsch.

καθεκ-τέον, (κατέχω) *one must keep back, restrain*, Plu.*Cat.Mi.*63, etc. **-της**, ου, ὁ, *trap-door*, *Gp.*14.6.6. **-τικός**, ή, όν, *capable of holding* or *retaining*, ἡ μνήμη ἕξις κ. ὑπολήψεως Arist.*Top.*125ᵇ18; κ. δύναμις Gal.1.654, Alex.Aphr.*Pr.*2.60; τὸ κ. καὶ ἰξῶδες Artem.2.14: c. gen., κ. τοῦ πνεύματος, opp. προετικός, Arist.*Pr.*963ᵃ21 (Comp.). Adv. -κῶς, ἔχειν τῶν μαθημάτων Marin.*Procl.*5. **-τός**, ή, όν, (κατέχω) *to be held back, checked*, θρασὺς καὶ βδελυρὸς καὶ οὐδὲ κ. ἔτι D. 21.2, cf. Plu.*Fab.*10, *Pomp.*66; τῶν πραγμάτων οὐκέτι πολλοῖς ὄντων καθεκτῶν since power *could* not *be retained in the hands of* many, Id. *Brut.*47; ἐν τῷ κ. εἶναι to *contain oneself*, Philostr.*Im.*2.6. Adv. οὐ -τῶς *so as* not *to be restrained*, μάχεσθαι Id.*Her.*10.5. II. *in the grip of*, λύπῃσι χαλεπῇσιν Corinn.*Supp.*1.28.

καθελίσσω, Ion. **κατειλίσσω**, Att. aor. part. **κατειλίξας** (v. infr.), *wrap with bandages*, κατειλίσσουσι πᾶν τὸ σῶμα σινδόνος... τελαμῶσι, of mummies, Hdt.2.86; of wounds, Id.7.181; σώματα σπαργάνοις καθειλίξαντες Max.Tyr.36.2 (v.l. κατ-); καττίτερον.. κατειλίξας ἐρίοις *IG*2².204.32 (iv B.C.); καθελίξας, v.l. κατειλ-, κατελ-, Hp.*Nat.Mul.* 32:—Pass., τὰς κνήμας ῥάκεσι... κατειλίχατο (3 pl. plpf.) Hdt.7.76; κατειλίχθαι ταινίῃ Hp.*Art.*5; ἐρίοις... καθείλικτο Gal.*UP*4.9; ὅταν κατελιχθῇ Ath.Mech.24.8. II. of a serpent, *drag down in its coils*, συνέσφιγγεν ἅπαντα, καθελίττων ἐς τὴν ἑαυτοῦ χειάν Eun.*Hist*.p.257 D.

καθελκόομαι, Pass., *break out into ulcers*, χείλεα καθηλκωμένα Hp. *Epid*.7.11; but καθελκωθεὶς *covered with wounds*, Arist.*HA*621^{a}20.

καθελκυσμός, ὁ, *launching*, Moschio ap.Ath.5.207a. II. *collapse*, Marcellin.*Puls*.293.

καθέλκω, fut. καθέλξω Ar.*Ra*.1398, καθελκύσω Luc.*DDeor*.21.1: aor. part. καθελκύσαντες Th.6.34: pf. καθείλκυκα D.5.12:—Pass., aor. and pf. (v. infr.): 1. of ships, *draw to the sea, launch*, E.*Hel*. 1531, Ar.*Ach*.544, *Eq*.1315, Isoc.4.118; καθεῖλκον ναῦς ἐς τὸν Πειραιᾶ Th.2.94: abs., Phld.*Mus*.p.15 K., al.:—Pass., τῶν νεῶν κατελκυσθεισέων ἐς θάλασσαν Hdt.7.100; εἴ τι ναυτικόν ἐστι καθειλκυσμένον Th.6.50. 2. *draw down, depress* the scale, Ar.*Ra*.1398: metaph., *outweigh*, καθέλκει δρῦν πολὺ τὴν μακρὴν ὅμπνια Θεσμοφόρος Call.*Aet. Oxy*.2079.9; [ἡ τροφὴ] τοῖς λοιποῖς... ἰσοσθενεῖ καὶ κ. τὰ πάντα Gal. 19.190. 3. in building, *carry down*, τὰ σκέλη καθειλκυσται the long walls *have been carried down to the sea*, Str.8.6.22. II. metaph., *drag down*, τὸ χεῖρον... καθελκυσθὲν συνεφελκύσασθαι τὸ μέσον Plot.2.9.2, cf. Luc.*Apol*.11. 2. *constrain, compel*, *BGU*648.12 (ii A.D.), *POxy*.899.25 (iii A.D.); τινὰ εἰς φιλανθρωπίαν Lib.*Or*.15.29 (Pass.).

κάθεμα, ατος, τό, (καθίημι) *necklace, collar*, Lxx *Is*.3.19:—written **κάθημα** in Antiph.319.

κάθεμεν, Ep. 1 pl. aor. 2 of καθίημι. **καθέν**, for καθ' ἕν, v. κατά B. II. 3.

καθέννυμι, *clothe*, v. καταέννυμι. **καθένς**, v. κατατίθημι.

καθεξῆς, Adv., = the more usu. ἐφεξῆς, *Ev.Luc*.1.3, Plu.2.615c, Ael.*VH*8.7, *IGRom*.4.1432.9 (Smyrna); poet. κατὰ θ' ἑξείης Opp. *C*.3.59.

κάθεξις, εως, ἡ, (κατέχω) *holding, retention*, τῆς ἀρχῆς Th.3.47; ἐν μνήμῃ καὶ καθέξει Plu.2.968c; *possession*, Plot.6.1.23. 2. *holding in, restraining*, τοῦ πνεύματος Arist.*Somn*.456^{a}16; [θυμοῦ] Id.*EE* 1223^{b}20. 3. *retentive power*, of the bladder, Aret.*CA*1.4.

καθέξω, fut. of κατέχω.

κάθερμα, ατος, τό, in pl., = ἕρματα (v. ἕρμα II), Anacr.21.12.

καθέρπω, aor. 1 καθεῖρπυσα Ar.*Ra*.485:—*creep, steal down*, ἀπ' ὀρθίων πάγων καθεῖρπεν ἔλαφος S.*Fr*.89; καθέρπυσόν νυν ἐς Κεραμεικόν Ar.*Ra*.129, cf. 485: metaph., παρὰ τὰ ὦτα ἄρτι ἴουλος καθέρπει X. *Smp*.4.23. II. *return* from exile, *SIG*306.54 (Delph., from Tegea, iv B.C.): in this signf. the aor. part. is κατενθών ib.4; pf. part. κατηνθηκώς ib.39.

κάθες, aor. 2 imper. of καθίημι. **καθέσαι**, aor. 1 inf. of καθίζω.

καθέσιμον (sc. ἀργύριον), τό, (καθίζω) *fee for attendance* at the βουλή, *IG*2^{2}.956.14, al.

κάθεσις, εως, ἡ, (καθίημι) *letting down*, τῆς κόμης D.L.1.109; of a diving-bell, Arist.*Pr*.960^{b}33. 2. *production* of a play, Sch.Ar. *V*.1317, prob. in Sch.*Ra*.1060, Sch.*Lys*.1096. 3. *insertion*, τοῦ αὐλίσκου Ruf.*Ren.Ves*.7; of a finger, Antyll.ap.Orib.44.23.1; of a lancet, Orib.7.5.12. II. (from Pass.) *descent*, Arist.*Mete*.356^{a}11; κ. νέφους εἰς τοὺς κάτω τόπους Epicur.*Ep*.2 p.47 U.

κάθεσσαν, καθέσσαντο, aor. 1 of καθίζω.

καθεστέον, (καθέζομαι) *one must sit down*, Pherecr.215.

καθεστηκότως, Adv. pf. part. Act. of καθίστημι, *fixedly, steadily*, κ. ἔχειν πρός τι Arist.*Pol*.1340^{b}3.

καθεστήξω, fut. 3 of καθίστημι, with intr. sense.

καθεστήριον, τό, *guest-room* of a monastery, *PMasp*.110.36 (vi A.D.).

καθεστιάω, v. καθιστιάω.

καθεστῶτα, ων, τά, neut. pl. pf. part. of καθίστημι.

καθεστώτως, Adv. = καθεστηκότως, *steadily*, πορεύεσθαι prob. in D.Chr.31.162.

καθέσω, v. καθίζω.

καθετ-ήρ, ῆρος, ὁ, (καθίημι) *anything let down into, inserted*: 1. *plug of lint, pessary*, Hp.*Mul*.2.157 ap.Gal.19.107 (καθετηρίῳ codd. Hp.). 2. *surgical instrument* for emptying the bladder, Gal.1. 125, al., Sor.2.59; κ. ἀρρενικὸς Ruf.*Oss*.12. 3. *fishing-line*, Artem. 2.14. 4. = κάθεμα, Nicostr.Com.33, *IG*11(2).287 *B*68 (Delos, iii B.C.). **-ηρίδιον**, τό, Dim. of foreg. 4, *BCH*35.286 (ib., ii B.C.). **-ηρίζω**, *treat with the* καθετήρ 2, Orib.*Fr*.64. **-ήριον** (sc. ὄργανον), τό, = καθετήρ 1, f.l. in Hp.*Mul*.2.157; τὸ ὄργανον τὸ κ. Aret.*CA*2.9. **-ηρισμός**, ὁ, *insertion of the* καθετήρ, Ruf.ap.Aët. 11.27, Paul.Aeg.6.59. **-ηριστέον**, *one must treat with the* κ., Ruf. ap.Aët.11.21. **-ης**, ου, ὁ, prob. *portcullis* (v. πτερόν III. 9), Sch. E.*Ph*.114. II. *plummet*, Aen.Tact.32.6 cod., *Gloss*. **-ικός**, ή, όν, *perpendicular*, Sch.Arat.881. **-ος**, ον, (καθίημι) *let down, perpendicular*, πρὸς τὴν γῆν Arist.*Mech*.857^{b}28; καθέταν is f.l. in Alc. 39: usu. Subst., 1. κάθετος (sc. γραμμή), ἡ, *perpendicular*, Arist.*Mete*. 373^{a}11, Ti.Locr.98b, etc., al.; *plumb-line*, Aen.Tact.32.6; πρὸς τὴν κ. δ' ἐμετρήθη Epigr.ap.Plu.*Aem*.15; κατὰ κάθετον *vertically, perpendicularly*, Ph.*Bel*.69.22, Heliod.ap.Orib.49.13.1, *Placit*.2.24.1, Apollod.*Poliorc*.155.9; κατὰ κ. τοῦ ὀμφαλοῦ *vertically below*, Paul.Aeg.6. 50; πρὸς κ. Plu.2.938a; *perpendicular height*, τριῶν ἥμισυ σταδίων ἔχειν τὴν κ. Str.8.6.21. 2. (sc. ὁρμιά), ἡ, *fishing-line*, Opp.*H*.3. 77,138, *AP*7.637 (Antip., v.l. καθέτης). 3. (sc. ἀμνός or βοῦς), ὁ, *an animal let down into the sea* as an offering to Poseidon, Lys. *Fr*.227 S., cf. Phot., Suid.

καθευδητέον, *one must sleep*, Pl.*Phdr*.259d.

καθεύδω, so also in Ion., Hdt.2.95 codd.: impf. καθεῦδον (καθηῦδον) Il.1.611, Ar.*Av*.495, Pl.*Smp*.217d, al.; ἐκάθευδον Lys.1.13,23, X.*Oec*.7.11: fut. καθευδήσω Ar.*Ec*.419, X.*Cyr*.6.2.30, etc.: aor. ἐκαθεύδησα (not in Att.), Luc.*Asin*.6; inf. καθευδῆσαι Hp.*Int*.12:—*lie down to sleep, sleep*, Il.1.611, Od.3.402, etc.; opp. ἀγρυπνέω, ἐγρήγορα, Thgn.471, Pl.*Phd*.71c, etc.; καλὸς νέκυς, οἷα καθεύδων Bion 1.71; κ. μάτην A.*Ch*.881; νυκτὸς κ. *to sleep* by night, Pl.*Phdr*. 251e; κ. τὰς νύκτας *to sleep* all one's nights, Bato 4; μαλακῶς, σκληρῶς κ., Antiph.187.6, Timocl.16.2; of male and female, ἵνα τώ γε καθεύδετον ἐν φιλότητι Od.8.313; κ. μετά τινος Pl.*Smp*.219d: generally, *pass the night*, τὴν βουλὴν εἰς ἀκρόπολιν ἰέναι κἀκεῖ κ. And.1.45; κ. ἐπὶ ξύλου *roost*, of a fowl, Ar.*Nu*.1431; ἐκ τοῦ καθεύδοντος from *a sleeping state*, Pl.*Phd*.72b. II. metaph., *lie asleep, lie idle*, χερί A. *Ag*.1357, cf. X.*HG*5.1.20, *An*.1.3.11, D.19.303; κ. τὸν βίον *to be asleep* all one's life, *sleep away* one's life, Pl.*R*.404a; opp. ἐνεργεῖν, Arist.*EN*1157^{b}8; opp. προσέχειν τοῖς πράγμασι, Plu.*Pomp*.15. 2. of things, *lie still, be at rest*, ἐλπίδες οὔπω κ. E.*Ph*.634; καθεύδειν ἐᾶν ἐν τῇ γῇ κατακείμενα τείχη Pl.*Lg*.778d: τοὺς νόμους ἐᾶν κ. Plu.*Ages*. 30. 3. of the *sleep* of death, καθεύδοντες ἐν τάφῳ Lxx *Ps*.87(88).6, cf. *Da*.12.2, 1 *Ep.Thess*.5.10.

καθεύρεμα, ατος, τό, *invention*, Lxx *Si*.32(35).10(12) (but prob. καθ' εὕρεμα).

καθευρεσῐλογέω, *invent reasons*, Plb.12.25^{k}.9.

καθευρίσκω, *discover*, Luc.*Ocyp*.68:—Pass., καθευρέθη κοσμοῦσα *she was found* in the act of adorning..., S.*Ant*.395 (prob. f.l. for καθηρέθη *she was caught*).

καθεφθ-έος, α, ον, = sq., prob. cj. in Nic.*Al*.573 (κατεφθέος, καθεψίοιο, καθεψέος codd.). **-ος**, ον, *boiled down*, Hp.*Mul*.2.110, Achae. 7, Diocl.*Fr*.139 (κάτ– codd.), Mnesith.ap.Orib.*Inc*.15.18, Dieuch. ap.Orib.4.7.31, Diph.Siph.ap.Ath.2.59b.

καθέψησις, εως, ἡ, *a boiling down*, Hp.*Vict*.2.42, D.S.1.40.

καθεψιάομαι, *mock at*, c. gen., ὡς σέθεν αἱ κύνες αἵδε καθεψιόωνται Od.19.372.

καθέψω, fut. -εψήσω, *boil down*, in Pass., Dsc.*Alex*.6, Plu.2.555b; of plants, *to be dried up* by the sun, cj. in Thphr.*HP*7.5.2; of a person, ἡλίῳ -ψεῖσθαι (sic) *to be broiled, swelter*, Luc.*Asin*.25; of a river, to be *softened* (sweetened) by boiling, D.S.1.40: Act., -ψοντες ἑαυτούς, by hot baths, Gal.6.185. II. metaph., *soften, temper*, joined with πραΰνειν, X.*Eq*.9.6. 2. *digest*, ἀργύριον Ar.*V*.795 codd. (prob. καταπέψεις).

κάθη, Att. for κάθησαι, 2 sg. pres. of κάθημαι.

καθηγεμ-ονία, ἡ, *headship* of a philosophical school, *IG*2^{2}.1099.35 (Plotina): generally, *primacy, leadership*, Phld.*Piet*.76. **-ών**, Ion. κατηγ–, Dor. καθᾱγ–, όνος, ὁ, ἡ, *leader, guide*, τῆς ὁδοῦ Hdt.7. 128, cf. Plb.3.48.11; *pilot*, Id.4.40.8; of a statesman, Ἀράτῳ καθηγεμόνι χρησάμενος περὶ τῶν ὅλων Id.7.14.4; of the founders of the Epicurean school, Phld.*Rh*.1.49 S., *Ir*.p.89 W., al.; of Crates, Jul. *Or*.6.202d; κ. τῆς ἀρετῆς *in* or *to* virtue, Plu.*Dio* 1; as a title of gods, Διόνυσος κ. *CIG*3068 (Teos); τᾷ εὐεργέτιδι καὶ καθαγεμόνι τᾶς πόλιος *SIG*559.36 (Arc., from Magn. Mae., iii B.C.); Ἀφροδίτην κ. ποιεῖσθαι Plu.*Thes*.18; of divinities, τῷ Διί, καθηγεμόνι τούτῳ τῆς τῶν ὄντων διοικήσεως ὄντι *Stoic*.1.43; καθηγεμόνες εὐτυχοῦς ἀρχῆς *OGI* 383.86 (Nemrud Dagh, i B.C.): metaph., κ. ταττόμενοι τὸν θυμόν Lxx 2 *Ma*.10.28.

καθηγ-έομαι, Ion. κατηγ–, *act as guide, lead the way*, abs., Hdt. 9.40,66, 6.135, Th.6.4; οἱ κατηγεόμενοι the *guides*, Hdt.7.130; σὺ καθηγοῦ, ἕψομαι δ' ἐγώ Pl.*Ep*.312b; κατ. τινὶ ἐς χώρους Hdt.4.125, cf. 6.102; ἐπὶ Φωκέας Id.7.215; also κατ. τινὶ ὁδόν Id.9.104. 2. c. acc. rei, *show, explain, indicate*, τὸ ἕρμα κατ. τινί Id.7.183, cf. X. *An*.7.8.10; ὁ τὸν ποταμὸν κ. *he who was explaining* it, i.e. showing where it was fordable, Pl.*Tht*.200e. 3. c. gen., κ. τοῦ λόγου *to begin* the discourse, Id.*Smp*.199c; ὧν καθηγήσαιτ' ἂν τοῦτο of which this *would be the beginning*, Id.*La*.182c. b. *lead, command, exercise authority over*, κ. τῆς στρατείας, τοῦ πολιτεύματος, Plu.*Cam*.15, *Thes*.35. 4. *to be the first to do, establish, institute*, Hdt.2.49,56: c. part., οὐ κατηγήσομαι νόμον τόνδε τιθείς I *will* not *begin* establishing this law, Id.7.8.α'. 5. *instruct, teach*, abs., Phld.*Lib*.p.21 O., al.; κ. γραμματιστοῦ τρόπον Diog.Oen.11; ὁ καθηγησάμενος the *teacher*, Plu.2.120a: c. gen. pers., *to be teacher of*..., Str.14.5.14, D.H.*Is*.1, *Amm*.5. 6. in Logic, *to be antecedent*, *Stoic*.2.72. **-ησις**, εως, ἡ, *rule, principle*, αἱ τοῦ τακτικοῦ κ. Ascl. *Tact*.12.11, cf. Ael.*Tact*.42.2; also f.l. in Antig.*Mir*.171. **-ητής**, οῦ, ὁ, *guide*, Numen.ap.Ath.7.313d. 2. *teacher, professor*, Phld.*Ir*. p.43 W., al., D.H.*Th*.3, *Ev.Matt*.23.10, Plu.2.70e, Philum.*Ven*.5.6, *OGI*408 (Theb. Aegypt., ii A.D.), *POxy*.930.6 (ii/iii A.D.), etc.:—also **-ητήρ**, ῆρος, ὁ, Man.2.300, Dor. καθᾱγ–, κελεύθου *IG*12(1).44 (Rhodes):—fem. **-ήτειρα** Call.*Fr*.33 P., Orph.*H*.76.6. **-ητικός**, ή, όν, *able to guide, guiding*, c. gen., Gal.*Phil.Hist*.16, 19.

καθηδύνω [ῡ], *sweeten*, αἱ μέλιτται κ. τὸ πόμα Max.Tyr.27.6; ζωμὸς καθηδυσμένος περιττῶς Ath.4.140a. 2. *gratify*, τινα Eun.*VS* p.458 B.

καθηδῠπᾰθέω, *squander in luxury* or *revelling*, τοὺς δαρεικοὺς X. *An*.1.3.3; τὰς εὐπορίας D.H.20.8; τὸν χρόνον κ. καὶ ἀναλίσκειν Plu. *Ant*.28; τοὺς τοῦ πολέμου καιροὺς κ. Luc.*DMort*.12.6: abs., Ph.2. 106,357, Alciphr.1.21.

καθηκόντως, v. sq. II. 4.

καθήκω, Ion. κατήκω, (v. ἥκω) *come* or *go down*, esp. to fight, A. *Ch*.455 (lyr.). 2. *come down to, reach to*, ἐς θάλασσαν Hdt.7.22, 130; ἐπὶ θάλ. Id.2.32, 5.49, Th.2.27; πρὸς τὸν Μηλιακὸν κόλπον Id.3. 96; κέρκος.. εἰς λεπτὸν καθήκουσα *tapering* away, Arist.*HA*503^{a}20: metaph., of descent, ὃ [γένος] εἰς αὐτὸν κ. Arr.*An*.1.11.8. 3. *come* *in due course* to any one, καθῆκεν ἐς ἡμᾶς ὁ λόγος the turn of speaking *came* to us, Aeschin.2.25; παρὰ τετάρτην ἡμέραν ἑκάστῃ σημαίᾳ καθήκειν τὴν λειτουργίαν Plb.6.33.9, cf. *PCair.Zen.*218.24 (iii B.C.); τῆς βολῆς καθηκούσης ἐς αὐτόν Plu.*Alc.*2; ἐν τῷ ξυμποσίῳ... ἐπὶ τὸν Θεσμόπολιν καθῆκε τὸ σκῶμμα Luc.*Merc.Cond.*34. **4.** of Time, ὁπότε καθήκοι ὁ χρόνος X.*HG*4.7.2; ὅταν οἱ χρόνοι καθήκωσι Arist. *HA*591^{a}8; πρότερον ἢ τὴν ὥραν καθήκειν *PRev.Laws*41.14 (iii B.C.); in part., τοῦ καθήκοντος χρόνου the *normal* time, S.*OT*75, D.4.35, cf. Aeschin.3.126; αἱ κ. ἡμέραι the *regular*, *proper* days, D.59.80; ἐν τῇ κ. ὥρᾳ Arist.*HA*568^{a}17; ἐν τοῖς κ. καιροῖς ib.573^{a}30; of events, ἑορτῆς εἰς τὰς ἡμέρας ἐκείνας καθηκούσης as the festival *fell* on those days, Plu.*Fab.*18, cf. Plb.4.7.1; ἐκκλησίαν ποιῆσαι, ὅταν ἐκ τῶν νόμων καθήκῃ when it is legally *due*, D.19.185; ἡ κ. σύνοδος or ἐκκλησία, Plb.4.14.1, 1.15.8, etc. **II.** *to be meet, fit, proper*, τοῖς κ. [νομίμοις] Arist.*Pol.*1325^{a}13; τὰς ἐσθῆτας τὰς κ. ἀεὶ ταῖς περιθεταῖς *suiting* them, Plb.3.78.3; ὁ καθήκων ἐκ τῶν νομίμων ἀριθμός *a quorum*, D.C.39.30; also καθῆκόν ἐστιν αὐτὸν ἐπαινεῖσθαι *Inscr.Prien.*114.32 (i B.C.). **2.** impers., καθήκει μοι *it belongs* to me, *is* my *duty*, c. inf., οἷς καθήκει ἀθροίζεσθαι X.*An.*1.9.7, cf. *Cyr.*8.1.4, etc.: in later writers, impf. καθῆκε in pres. sense, *it is meet, proper*, οὐδ' ἅψασθαι καθῆκέ τινων Aristeas 149; οὐ κ. αὐτὸν ζῆν *Act.Ap.*22.22: freq. in part., τὰ καθήκοντα *one's due* or *duty*, X.*Cyr.*1.2.5; τὰ κατήκοντα Σπαρτιήτῃσι Hdt.7.104; ποιεῖν τὸ κ. Men.575: esp. in Stoic philos. (from signf. I. 3 acc. to D.L.7.108, cf. κατά B.I. 3), περὶ τοῦ κ., title of work by Zeno, cf. *Stoic.*1.55, etc.: freq. in pl., ib.3.30, etc.; μὴ κ. *unbecoming*, *Ep.Rom.*1.28. **3.** τὰ κατήκοντα the *present crisis*, Hdt. 1.97, 5.49; τὰ κ. πρήγματα Id.8.19, 40, 102. **b.** τὰ καθήκοντα the *payments due*, *UPZ*42.15 (ii B.C.); τὴν -ουσαν ἡμῖν δίδοσθαι σύνταξιν τῶν δεόντων ib.6. **4.** Adv. pres. part. καθηκόντως *fittingly, properly*, Epicur.*Ep.*2 p.53 U., *OGI*90.28 (Rosetta, ii B.C.), Plb.5.9.6, v.l. in D.S.1.93; πρός τι Porph.*Abst.*1.43; *consistently with duty*, *Stoic.*3.188, Plu.2.448e; *appropriately*, c. dat., τῷ τόπῳ Aristeas 81; κ. ἔχειν πρός τι Id.87. **III.** τὸ καθῆκον the *precise proportion*, Thphr.*Lap.*46.

καθηλιάζω, *bring the sun upon, illuminate*, νύκτα Luc.*Epigr.*19.

καθῆλιξ, λῐκος, ὁ, ἡ, *contemporary*, *Inscr.Prien.*117.56 (i B.C.).

καθηλ-όω or **κατηλόω** (cf. ἧλος), *nail on*, παραβλῆματα κατηλῶσαι *IG*2^2.1604.31 (iv B.C.); τι πρός τι Plu.*Alex.*24; περί τι Apollod.1.9.1, cf. *IG*2^2.463.79, 1668.57; οἷον κ. τὴν ψυχὴν πρὸς τὴν ἀπόλαυσιν Porph. *Abst.*1.38:—Pass., κλῖμαξ σανίσι καθηλωμένη with boards *nailed thereto*, Plb.1.22.5, cf. Apollod.*Poliorc.*189.5; καθηλωθήσεται σύριγξι καμαρικαῖς Ath.Mech.36.5; λεπίδες καθηλωμέναι *nailed on*, D.S.20.91, cf. Orib.49.4.51; χάλκωμα συμμαχίας... ἐν Καπετωλίῳ κατηλωθῆναι *IG* 12(3).173.7 (Astypalaea, ii B.C.). **II.** by confusion of Hebr. *sāmar* 'bristled' with *sāmar*, imper. *sĕmōr* 'nail thou', καθήλωσον ἐκ τοῦ φόβου σου τὰς σάρκας μου Lxx *Ps.*118(119).120. **-ωμα**, ατος, τό, *that which is nailed on*, *revetment*, ib.3*Ki.*6.20. **-ωσις**, εως, ἡ, *nailing on*, ἀσθενὴς [τῶν ἥλων] γίνεται ἡ κ. Hero *Bel.*95.6, cf. Sm., Thd.*Ez.*7.23, *PLond.*3.1177.239 (ii A.D.). **-ωτής**, οῦ, ὁ, *one who nails on*, *Gloss.*

κάθημα, v. κάθεμα.

κάθημαι, Ion. κάτ-, 2 sg. κάθησαι (Ion. κάτ- Hdt.3.134) X.*Cyr.*3.1. 6, prob. in Call.*Sos.* vi 4, κάθῃ Hyp.*Fr.*115, *Act.Ap.*23.3, dub.l. in *Com. Adesp.*1203, (προ-) Them.*Or.*13.171a codd.; 3 sg. κάθηται Ar.*Lys.* 597, Pl.*Ap.*35c, D.9.70, *SIG*987.26 (Chios, iv B.C.); Ion. 3 pl. κατέαται Hdt.2.86; imper. κάθησο Il.2.191, E.*IA*627; κάθου Ar.*Fr.*620, Anaxandr.13, Men.1017, Alex.224; κάθουσο Sch.Theoc.11.42; 3 sg. καθήσθω A.*Pr.*916; 3 pl. καθήσθωσαν *IG*9(2).1109.38 (Thess.); subj. καθῶμαι, κάθῃ Cratin.277, καθῆται Ar.*Eq.*754; opt. καθοίμην Id.*Ra.*919, prob. in Id.*Lys.*149; inf. καθῆσθαι; part. καθήμενος: impf. ἐκαθήμην Ar. *Ec.*152, D.48.31, etc., ἐκάθητο *h.Bacch.*14, Ar.*Av.*510, Th.5.6, ἐκάθησθε Ar.*Ach.*638, ἐκάθηντο, Ion. ἐκατέατο v.l. in Hdt.3.144, 8.73; also without syll. augm. καθῆστο Il.1.569, E.*Ba.*1102, *Ph.*1467, Pl.*R.*328c, Is.6.19, καθῆτο D.18.169, 217; Ion. κατῆστο Hdt.1.46, καθῆσθε D. 25.21 (with vv. ll.), καθῆντο Ar.*Ec.*302, v.l. in Th.5.58; Ep. καθήατο Il.11.76; Ion. κατέατο Hdt.3.144, 8.73, 9.90 (v.l. καθ-): the later fut. καθήσομαι Lxx *Le.*8.35, *Ev.Luc.*22.30 is corrupt in E.*Fr.*960:—*to be seated, sit*, αὐτός τε κάθησο καὶ ἄλλους ἵδρυε λαούς Il.2.191; κάθησ' ἑδραία E.*Andr.*266: freq. in part., πέτρῃ ἔπι προβλῆτι καθήμενος Il.16.407; ἐπ' ἀκτῆς κλαῖε κ. Od.5.82; κ. οἷος ἐν Ἴδῃ Il.8.207; ἐν ἀγῶνι κ. 23.448; κλαῖον δ' ἐν λεχέεσσι κ. Od.10.497; θύρῃσι κ. 17.530; ἐπὶ ταῖσι θύραις Ar.*Nu.*466; αὐτόθεν ἐκ δίφροιο κ. even from his seat *as he sat there*, Od.21.420; καθήμεθ' ἄκρων ἐκ πάγων S.*Ant.*411; ἐκ μέσου κατῆστο *sate* aloof, remained neutral, Hdt.3.83, cf. 4.118, 8.73; ἐν θρόνῳ κ. Id.2.149; θρόνῳ κ. E.*El.*315; κ. πρὸς τάφῳ Id.*Hel.*1084; πρὸς τὸ πῦρ Ar.*V.*773; ἐπὶ δίφρου Pl.*R.*328c; ἐπὶ τῶν ἵππων X.*Cyr.*4. 5.54; ἐπὶ τοῦ ἅρματος *Act.Ap.*8.28; ἐς τοὐργαστήριον Alciphr.3.27: c. acc. cogn., ἕδραν κ. E.*Heracl.*55: c. acc. loci, *sit on*, ὀφρύην ib. 394. **2.** esp. of courts, councils, assemblies, etc., *sit*: οἱ καθήμενοι *the judges, the court*, And.1.139, D.6.3, etc.; δικαστὰς οὐχ ὁρῶ καθημένους Ar.*Nu.*208; ὑμεῖς οἱ καθήμενοι you *who sit as judges*, Th. 5.85; οὐκ ἐπὶ τούτῳ κ. ὁ δικαστής Pl.*Ap.*35c; κ. ὑπὲρ τῶν νόμων D.58. 25; of the βουλή, And.1.43; βουλῆς περὶ τούτων καθημένης D.21.116; of an assembly, X.*An.*5.10.5; οἱ κ. *the spectators in a theatre*, Hegesipp.1.29. **3.** *sit still, sit quiet*, ὕψι περ ἐν νεφέεσσι καθημένω Od. 16.264; σφοῖσιν ἐνὶ μεγάροισι καθήατο (for ἐκάθηντο) Il.11.76; ἐν πένθεϊ μεγάλῳ κατῆστο Hdt.1.46; μετὰ κόπον κ. *rest* after labour, S.*Fr.* 479.3: and, in bad sense, *sit doing nothing, lie idle*, Il.24.403, Hdt. 3.134; of an army, Id.9.56, Th.4.124; of a boat's crew, *PCair.Zen.* 107.6 (iii B.C.); οὐδὲν ποιοῦντες ἐνθάδε καθήμεθα, μέλλοντες ἀεί D.11. 17, cf. 2.23, S.*Fr.*142.20, etc.; also, of an army, *to have its quarters, be encamped*, περὶ τὰς Ἀχαρνάς Th.2.20, cf. 101; ἐχθρῶν ὑπ' αὐτοῖς τείχεσιν καθημένων E.*Ph.*752. **4.** *reside* in a place, Lxx *Ne.*11.6; λαὸς καθήμενος ἐν σκοτίᾳ *Ev.Matt.*4.16; *settle*, εἰς Σινώπην Muson.*Fr.* 9 p.43 H. **5.** *lead a sedentary, obscure life*, ἐν σκότῳ καθήμενος Pi. *O.*1.83; ἔσω καθημένη A.*Ch.*919; αἱ βαναυσικαὶ [τέχναι] ἀναγκάζουσι καθῆσθαι X.*Oec.*4.2; *to be engaged* or *employed*, esp. in a sedentary business, ἐπ' αὐτῷ τούτῳ Hdt.2.86; κ. ἐπὶ τῇ τραπέζῃ, of bankers, D.49.42, cf. 45.33; ἐπ' ἐργαστηρίου Id.59.67; ἐπὶ τοῦ... ἰατρείου Aeschin.1.40; καθῆσθαι ἐν πόλει, opp. ζῆν ἐν χωρίῳ, Muson.*Fr.*11 p.59 H. **6.** *sit* as a suppliant, ἐν Δελφοῖσι Hdt.5.63, cf. Orac.ib. 7.140. **7.** of districts and countries, *lie*, χωρία ὁμοίως καθήμενα Thphr.*HP*8.8.7. **b.** *to be low-lying*, τὰ λεῖα καὶ καθήμενα Ael.*VH* 3.1, cf. *NA*16.12; πεδίον κ. Him.*Or.*14.17; πόπανον... κ. δωδεκόμφαλον prob. *flat* in the middle, *IG*2^2.1367. **8.** of a statue, *to be placed*, Pl.*Smp.*215b, Arist.*Pol.*1315^{b}21. **9.** of things, *to be set* or *placed*, λαγῳοῖς ἐπ' ἀμύλῳ καθημένοις Telecl.32, cf. Pherecr.108.17; τὸ πηδάλιον κ. πλάγιον Arist.*Mech.*851^{a}4, cf. ib.13.

καθημαξευμένως, Adv. pf. part. Pass. of καθαμαξεύω (q. v.).

καθημερ-εία, ἡ, *daily business*, Plb.6.33.4 (pl.). **-ιος**, Dor. **καθᾱμ-**, α, ον, *day by day, daily* (καθ' ἡμέραν), neut. as Adv., E.*Ph.* 229 (lyr.); μοῖρα κ. S.*El.*1414 (dub., lyr.):—later also **καθημερινός**, ή, όν, δίαιτα Lxx *Ju.*12.15, cf. Plu.2.141b, al.; διακονία *Act.Ap.*6.1; γυμνασία Ael.*Tact.*3.1, Plu.*Lyc.*10, Ath.1.10c; of fevers, *quotidian*, later word for ἀμφημερινός (q.v.), esp. of *non-remittent quotidians*, Gal.7.354, 17(1).221; ῥῖγος *PTeb.*275.21 (iii A.D.); φρίξ *POxy.*924. 3 (iv A.D.). **-ίσια**, τά, *daily wages*, *IG*1^2.373.245.

καθημεροθύτης [ῠ], ου, ὁ, *priest who offers daily sacrifice*, *SIG*1021. 22 (Olymp.).

καθημερόω, *soften, tranquillize*, τὴν ψυχήν Porph.*VP*32:—Med., *smooth down*, κύματα v.l. in Ps.-Callisth.1.1:—Pass., καθημερούμενα ζῷα Hierocl.p.59 A.

κᾰθῆραι, καθήρας, aor. 1 inf. and part. of καθαίρω.

καθησῠχάζω, strengthd. for ἡσυχάζω, Plb.9.32.2, Ph.2.71, *BGU* 36.14 (Trajan):—Med., fut. καθησυχάσομαι *Lyr.Alex.Adesp.*4.24.

καθθηρᾱτόριον, τό, Lacon. (for *καταθηρατόριον), *contest in hunting* at Sparta, *IG*5(1).278, etc.; cf. κασσηρατόριν.

καθιγνῦσαι· νεκροῖς θῦσαι, Phot. (Apptly. corrupt for καθαγνίσαι.)

κάθιδοι· ὑδρίαι (Arc.), Hsch.

κάθιδρος, ον, *sweating violently*, Lxx *Je.*8.6, Hsch., Phot.

καθίδρ-ῡμα, ατος, τό, = ἵδρυμα, *Gloss.* **-ῡσις**, εως, ἡ, = ἵδρυσις, ἑαυτῆς, of Artemis, D.S.4.51; ἀγαλμάτων Iamb.*Myst.*5.23 (pl.), cf. Poll.1.11, *Cat.Cod.Astr.*8(4).252; ἀνδριάντων *Cod.Just.*1.4.26.6 (pl.); *foundation-festival*, *BGU*1.28 (ii/iii A.D.). **-ύω**, causal of καθέζομαι, *make to sit down*, Ὀδυσῆα καθίδρυε Od.20.257; μακάρων ἐς αἶαν σὸν καθιδρύσει βίον *will carry* thee to the land of the Blest that thou mayst live there, E.*Ba.*1339:—Pass., *sit down, settle*, Ar. *Av.*45; ἐν πόλει, ἐν τῷ ὄρει, Pl.*Sph.*224d, Th.4.46; κ. ἐς Ἀργὼ *take one's seat* in.., Theoc.13.28; *to be quartered*, of troops, *PLond.*3. 1313.11 (vi A.D.). **2.** *establish, place*, ἐν τοῖς τιμιωτέροις τὸ τιμιώτερον (sc. τὴν καρδίαν) καθίδρυκεν ἡ φύσις Arist.*PA*665^{b}20; ἐφ' ἑνὸς τόπου κ. τὴν ἱστορίαν *to limit* it, D.H.*Th.*6:—Pass., κ. ἐς τὴν ἑωυτῶν χώρην *to be restored, replaced*, Hp.*Fract.*31, cf. *Prorrh.*2.19; ἐν αἷς [ἱστορίαις] καθιδρῦσθαι τὴν ἀλήθειαν ὑπολαμβάνομεν D.H.1.1. **3.** *consecrate, dedicate*, aor. 1 Med. καθιδρῡσάμην E.*IT*1481; -ῠσάμην *IG*14.882 (Capua): pf. Pass. in act. sense, E.*Cyc.*318:—Pass., Ποσειδῶνος τοῦ κατιδρυθέντος ὑπὸ .. *SIG*1020.5 (Halic., i B.C.); τεμένη -ύετο τῷ θεῷ Luc.*Cal.*17. **4.** *found*, γυμνάσιον Lxx 2*Ma.* 4.12.

καθιέρ-ευσις, εως, ἡ, *consecration, deification*, ζῴων Plu.2.380d (pl.). **-εύω**, *sacrifice, offer*, αὐτοὺς Pl.*Phdr.*252c; τὴν μητέρα Arist. *EN*1148^{b}26; τὸν ἱκέτην D.H.8.1: cf. κατιαραίω. **-ουργέω**, = foreg., D.S.20.14 (Pass.). **-όω**, Ion. **κατιρόω**, *dedicate, devote*, Hdt.1.92, 164; τῇ μὲν γὰρ Ἀθηναίᾳ καθιέρωσεν εἰς ἀναθήματα... πεντακισχιλίους στατῆρας Lys.19.39; τὸ λαχὸν μέρος ἑκάστῳ τῷ θεῷ Pl.*Lg.*745d; χώραν Aeschin.3.109; ἑαυτοὺς ὑπὲρ τῆς πατρίδος τῷ δαίμονι κ. Plu.*Cam.*21; τὸ θέατρον D.C.39.38, cf. *SIG*791 *B*5 (Delph., i A.D.), etc.:—Pass., ἐμοὶ τραφεὶς τε καὶ καθιερωμένος [ῐ] A.*Eu.*304; ἡ Κιρραία χώρα καθιερώθη *was consecrated*, D.18.149; καθιερωμένα ἀναθήματα Plb.7.14.3, cf. 3.22.1; οἱ καθιερούμενοι τῷ Διί his priests, S.E.*P.*3.224. **2.** *set up, establish as sacred*, τὴν φήμην Pl.*Lg.*838d:—Pass., νόμιμον καθιερωθέν ib.839c; δίκαια ἐν στήλῃ καθιερωμένα Plb.9.36.9.—Prose word, used once by A. **-ωσις**, εως, ἡ, *dedication*, Aeschin.3.46, D.H. 6.1, J.*AJ*19.7.5, Ph.2.234, Plu.*Publ.*15, *BMus.Inscr.*481*.21 (pl.), etc.: Dor. **καθιάρωσις** *Schwyzer* 203.9 (Crete, from Teos, iii/ii B.C.). **-ωτέος**, α, ον, *to be dedicated*, Pl.*Lg.*809b. **-ωτικός**, ή, όν, *dedicatory*, λόγος Sopat. in Rh.5.14 W.

καθίεψεν· ἐξέθετο, Hsch.

καθιζάνω, Aeol. **κατισδάνω** Sapph.*Supp.*19.5, irreg. impf. ἐκαθίζανον (παρ-) *IG*2^2.1011.22 (ii B.C.):—*sit down*, θῶκόνδε καθίζανον *they went* to the council *and took their seats*, Od.5.3; μάντις ἐς θρόνους κ. A.*Eu.*29; παρά τινα Polyaen.8.64: abs., σὺ δὲ καθίζανε Pherecr.172; of bees, birds, etc., *settle, perch*, μέλιτταν ἐφ' ἅπαντα βλαστήματα καθιζάνουσαν Isoc.1.52, cf. Arist.*HA*601^{a}7; ἐπὶ δονάκων, πέτραις, ib. 593^{b}10, 619^{b}8.

καθίζω, Ion. κατ-, impf. κάθιζον Il.3.426, al.; in Prose ἐκάθιζον X.*HG*5.4.6, Din.2.13: fut. καθέσω Eup.12.11 D.; καθίσω (intr.) Apollod.Com.5; Ion. κατίσω (trans.) Hdt.4.190; Att. also καθιῶ X.*An.*2.

1.4, D.24.25, 39.11, *IG*2².778.13 (iii B.C.); Dor. καθιξῶ Bion *Fr.*10.16: aor. 1 καθεῖσα Il.18.389, al., subj. καθέσω *h.Ap.*ap.Th.3.104; inf. καθέσαι *IG*2².46*aB** 21,25 (v/iv B.C.); poet. κάθεσσα Pi.*P.*5.42 codd.; this aor. καθεῖσα has Ms. authority in E.*Hipp.*31 (ἐγκαθ–, Med.), *Ph.* 1188, Hdt.1.88, 4.79, Th.7.82, but we also find Ep. κάθῖσα, Ion. κάτ– (for which κάθεσα, κάτεσαν, etc., shd. perh. be restored), Il.19.280 (v.l. κάθεσαν), al., Hdt.1.89, 2.126, καθῖσα Ar.*Ra.*911, Th.6.66 (leg. καθεῖσα), later ἐκάθισα X.*Cyr.*6.1.23, Men.544, etc., cf. Poll.3.89; also Ep. part. καθίσσας Il.9.488; Dor. καθίξας Theoc.1.12, subj. καθίξῃ ib.51; late part. καθιζήσας, subj. –ζήσῃ, D.C.54.30, 37.27: pf. κεκάθικα D.S.17.115, *Ep.Hebr.*12.2, A.D.*Synt.*323.23:—**Med.**, impf. ἐκαθιζόμην Ar.*V.*824, κὰδ..ἵζ– Il.19.50: fut. καθιζήσομαι Pl.*Phdr.*229a, *Euthd.*278b, (προσ–) Aeschin.3.167, later καθίσομαι *Ev.Matt.*19.28, Plu.2.583f, –ιοῦμαι Lxx *Ma.*3.3, al.: aor. 1 καθεσσάμην Anacr.111; also ἐκαθισάμην *SIG*975.6 (Delos, iii B.C.), Hsch., (ἐπ–, παρ–) Th.4.130 codd., D.33.14; Ep. ἐκαθισσάμην Call.*Dian.*233, καθισσάμην A.R.4.278, 1219:—**Pass.**, aor. 1 part. καθιζηθείς D.C.63.5: **I.** causal, *make to sit down, seat*, ἄλλους μὲν κάθισον Τρῶας Il.3.68; μή με κάθιζ' 6.360; σ' ἐπ' ἐμοῖσιν ἐγὼ γούνεσσι καθίσσας 9.488; κὰδ δ' εἷσ' ἐν θαλάμῳ 3.382; τὴν μὲν.. καθεῖσεν ἐπὶ θρόνου 18.389; κατίσαι τινὰ ἐπ' οἰκήματος Hdt.2.121.ε'; καθεῖν τινα εἰς τὸν θρόνον, i.e. to make him king, X.*An.*2.1.4; ἐπὶ θρόνου Phld.*Vit.*p.22 J. **2.** *set, place*, τὸν μὲν.. καθεῖσεν ἐπ' ἠϊόεντι Σκαμάνδρῳ Il.5.36; κὰδ δ' ἐν Ἀθήνῃς εἷσεν 2.549; Κρόνον.. Ζεὺς γαίης νέρθε καθεῖσε 14.204; καθίζειν τινὰ εἰς δόμον E.*Ion* 1541; κ. στρατόν *encamp* it, Id.*Heracl.*664, cf. Th.4.90; κ. τὸ στράτευμα ἐς χωρίον ἐπιτήδειον Id.6.66; σύλλογον εἰς χωρίον κ., χωρὶς μὲν τοὺς ὁπλίτας, χωρὶς δὲ τοὺς ἱππέας Pl.*Lg.*755e. **b.** *post* watchers, guards, etc., σκοπὸς ὅν ῥα καθεῖσεν Αἴγισθος Od.4.524; κατίσαι φυλάκους *set* guards, Hdt.1.89, cf. X.*Cyr.*2.2.14; ἄλλους κάτισον ἀγαγὼν κατὰ τὰς.. πύλας Hdt.3.155; κ. ἐνέδραν Plu.*Publ.*19: rarely of things, τι ἐπὶ τηγάνοις Pherecr.127. **3.** *set up*, ἀνδριάντα κάθεσσαν Pi.*P.*5.42 codd.:—Med., καθέσσασθαι Anacr.111, A.R.4.1219. **4.** *cause* an assembly, court, etc., *to take their seats, convene*, ἀγορὰς ἠμὲν λύει ἠδὲ καθίζει Od.2.69; ὅταν καθέσωσιν ἀγῶνα *h.Ap.*ap.Th.3.104; κ. τὸ δικαστήριον Ar.*V.*305, cf. D.39.11, *IG*2².778.13; νομοθέτας D.24.25, prob. in Id.3.10; but κ. τινὶ δικαστήν *appoint* a judge to try a person, Pl.*Lg.*874a; ἐάν τε χιλίους ἐάν θ' ὁποσουσοῦν ἡ πόλις καθίσῃ D.21.223; *constitute, establish*, δικαστήρια Pl.*Plt.*298e; βουλὴν ἐπίσκοπον πάντων Plu.*Sol.*19. **5.** *put into a certain condition*, esp. in the phrase κλαίοντά τινα κ. *set* him a-weeping, κλάοντα καθέσω σ' Eup. l. c., cf. Pl.*Ion* 535e, X.*Cyr.*2.2.15; but ib.14 κλαίειν τινὰ κ. *to make* him weep: for Theoc.1.51, v. ἀκράτιστος. **6.** *marry*, γυναῖκας ἀλλοτρίας Lxx *Ne.*13.27, cf. 23. **II.** intr., *take one's seat, sit*, abs., Il.3.394, etc.; μετ' ἀθανάτοισι, ἐν θρόνοισι καθίζειν, 15.50, Od.8.422; ἐν [θώκοισι] Hdt.1.181; ἐπὶ τοῖς ἐργαστηρίοις or τῶν –ίων, Isoc.18.9, 7.15; ἐπὶ σκίμποδα Ar.*Nu.*254; ἐπὶ δένδρου Arist.*HA*614ª34 (but κ. ἐπὶ κώπην, of rowers, Ar.*Ra.*197); of suppliants, κ. ἐπὶ τὸν βωμόν Th.1.126, Lys.13.24; εἰς γόνυ D.S.17.115: in Poets also c. acc., κ. τρίποδα E.*Ion* 366, *El.*980; βωμόν, ὀμφαλόν, ἱερά, Id.*HF*48, *Ion* 6, 1317. **2.** *sit, recline at meals*, X.*Cyr.*8.4.2. **3.** *sit as judge*, Hdt.1.97, 5.25, Pl.*Lg.*659b, Ph.1.382; *hold a session*, of the πρόεδροι, D.24.89, cf. *Hermes* 17.5 (Delos). **4.** *reside*, μετά τινος Lxx *Ru.*2.23 (3.1); ἐν πόλει ib.*Ne.*11.1. **5.** *settle, sink down*, ἐπὶ τὰ ἰσχία καθίσαι τῷ ἵππῳ Pl.*Phdr.*254c; καθίσας ὁ φελλὸς ἀνοίξει τὸν κρουνόν Hero *Spir.*1.20. **6.** of ships, *run aground, be stranded*, Plb.1.39.3, Str.2.3.4. **III.** Med. in intr. sense, Il.19.50 (in tmesi), Theoc.15.3, etc.; εἰς τὸν αὐτὸν θᾶκον Pl.*R.*516e; ἐὰν δὲ καθίζεσθαι κελεύσῃ if he order them *to take their seats* (among the spectators in the theatre), D.21.56 (nisi leg. καθέζεσθαι, as also ib.162, both readings are found ib.119); καθίζεσθαι ἢ κατακλινῆναι Pl.*Phdr.*228e. **2.** of birds, *settle, alight*, Arist.*HA*614ᵇ23. **3.** *leave goods purchased* in a market, *SIG*975.6 (Delos, iii B.C.).—Att. in this signf. acc. to Hsch.

καθίημι, Ion. **κατ–**, fut. καθήσω A.*Eu.*555 (lyr.): aor. 1 καθῆκα, Ep. καθέηκα Il.24.642: 2 dual aor. 2 κάθετον *h.Ap.*487: pf. καθεῖκα Lysipp.1, D.29.46: (v. ἵημι):—*let fall, drop, send down*, κὰδ δὲ [κεραυνὸν].. ἧκε χαμᾶζε Il.8.134; κατὰ δ' ὑψόθεν ἧκεν ἐέρσας 11.53; οἶνον λαυκανίης καθέηκα I *have sent* the wine *down* my throat, 24.642; καθίετε ἵππους ἐν δίνῃσι *sink* them in the stream, as an offering to the river-god, 21.132; [ἱστία] ἐς νῆας κάθεμεν we *let* them *down, lowered* them, Od.9.72; λαῖφος καθήσειν A.*Eu.* l.c.; σχοίνῳ σπυρίδα κ. *let* it *down* by a cord, Hdt.5.16; σῶμα πύργων κ. E.*Tr.*1011; κοντὸν ἐς [τὴν λίμνην] κ. Hdt.4.195; ἐμαυτὸν εἰς ἅλα E.*Hel.*1614; ὅπλα εἰς ἅλα ib.1375; καθεῖσαν δέλεάρ μοι φρενῶν Id.*IT*1181 (so metaph. τοῦτον τὸν λόγον καθεῖκε D.29.46); κ. τι ἐς πῶμα E.*Ion* 1034; νάρθηκ' ἐς πέδον Id.*Ba.*706; κ. σπονδὰς *pour* them, Id.*IA*60; τὸν κλῆρον ἐς μέσον καθείς, of putting lots into a helmet or urn, S.*Aj.*1285; ἄγκυραν Hdt.7.36; τὰ δίκτυα Arist.*HA*533ᵇ18; κατιεμένην καταπειρητηρίην, of a sounding-line, Hdt.2.28: abs., καθιέναι *reach by sounding, sound*, οὐδεὶς καθεὶς ἐδυνήθη πέρας εὑρεῖν Arist.*Mete.*351ª13: Medic., [αὐλίσκον] *pass* a catheter, Ruf.*Ren.Ves.*7.11; οἵαν πρόφασιν καθῆκε (παρὰ προσδοκίαν for οἷον ἄγκιστρον) Ar.*V.*174; λόγους συμβατηρίους κ. *make* offers of peace, D.C.41.47; κ. πεῖραν *make* an attempt, Ael.*VH*2.13, *NA*1.57; εἰς ὤμους κ. κόμας *let* one's hair *flow loose*, E.*Ba.*695, cf. *IT*52; κ. πώγωνα *let* one's beard *grow long*, Ar.*Ec.*100, cf. *Th.*841, Arr.*Epict.*2.23.21 (Pass., τὰς τρίχας καθειμέναι Crates Com.27; πώγωνα καθειμένος Plu.*Phoc.*10; τὸ γένειον αὐτῷ καθεῖτο Ael.*VH*11.10); [αἱ ὄϊες] μείζω τὰ οὔθατα καθιᾶσιν Arist.*HA*596ª24 (Pass., of a mare's udder, Hdt.4.2); also τείχη καθεῖναι ἐς θάλασσαν *carry* them *down* to the sea, Th.5.52 (Pass., καθεῖτο τείχη 4.103); καθῆκε τὰ σκέλη *let down* his legs, of one who had been lying, Pl.*Phd.*61c; κατ' ἀμφοῖν ἄμφω (sc. τὰ σκέλη) καθέντος, of a wrestler, Gal.6.143; κ. δόρατα *let down* one's pike, *bring* it *to the rest*, X.*An.*6.5.25; κ. τὰς κώπας *let down* the oars, so as to stop the ship's way, Th.2.91; rarely of striking, δι' ὀμφαλοῦ καθῆκεν ἔγχος E.*Ph.*1413; καθῆκε ξύλον παιδὸς ἐς κάρα Id.*HF*993; κ. πρὸς γαῖαν γόνυ to kneel down, Id.*Hec.*561; ἐς δὲ γῆν γόνυ καμάτῳ καθεῖσαν Id.*IT*333; κ. τινὰ ἐς ὕπνον *let* him *fall* asleep, Id.*HF*1006; εἰς κίνδυνον ἐμαυτόν D.H.5.27; [πώλους] ἐς λειμώνων χλόην E.*IA*423; of a general, κ. στρατόπεδα εἰς.. *let* them *march* into.., Plb.3.70.11; εἰς τὸ πεδίον τὴν δύναμιν Id.3.92.7; κ. ἐπί τινας τόπους ἐνέδρας *lay* an ambush, Id.4.63.9:—Pass., *stretch down seawards*, ὄρεα μέχρι πρὸς τὴν θάλατταν καθειμένα Pl.*Criti.*118a; ἕως γῆς τοῦ πρηστῆρος καθειμένου Epicur.*Ep.*2 p.47 U., cf. p.51 U.; τὸ καθειμένον τῆς φωνῆς *low tone* of voice, Hdn.5.2.3. **2.** *send down into the arena, enter for racing*, ἅρματα, ζεύγη, Th.6.16, Isoc.16.34; of plays, *produce*, Eratosth.ap.Sch.Ar.*Nu.*552 (Pass.); διδασκαλίαν Plu.*Cim.*8; so ἔδοξε τοῖς πρυτάνεσι.. γνώμας καθεῖναι (Com. for προθεῖναι) Ar.*Ec.*397; κατὰ τὴν ἀγορὰν λογοποιοὺς κ. D.24.15: freq. in later Greek in a general sense, *set in motion, employ*, Luc.*DMeretr.*7.4; κ. ἔς τινας ὑποψίας Philostr.*VA*6.38; φίλους καὶ ῥήτορας κ. *employ* them, Plu.*Per.*7, cf. Philostr.*VA*4.42:—Pass., *to be put in motion*, ἡ στρατηλασίη κατίετο ἐς πᾶσαν τὴν Ἑλλάδα Hdt.7.138. **3.** *allow to return* from exile, φυγάδας X.*HG*2.2.20. **II.** intr., *swoop down* like a wind, λαμπρὸς καὶ μέγας καθιείς Ar.*Eq.*430; of rivers, *run down*, ἐκατέρωσε μέχρι τοῦ μέσου Pl.*Phd.*112e; κ. εἰς γόνυ *sink* on the knee, Plu.*Ant.*45; κ. εἰς ἀγῶνα, Lat. *descendere in arenam*, Id.2.616d, Luc.*Alex.*6; κ. ἐς Ῥόδον *arrive* there, v.l. for κατῆγεν, Polyaen.5.17.2.

καθῐκετεύω, Ion. **κατ–**, strengthd. for ἱκετεύω, *entreat earnestly*, κατικ. τινί Hdt.6.68; πολλὰ κ. τινά Hld.6.14; τινα c. inf., Plu.*Cat.Mi.*32, cf. Parth.5.2, Ph.2.384:—also in Med., E.*Or.*324 (lyr.).

καθικμαίνω, = κατικμαίνω (q.v.).

καθικνέομαι, fut. –ίξομαι Plb.5.93.5, etc., dub. in *IG*5(2).4.13 (Tegea, iv B.C.): aor. –ῑκόμην (v. infr.): pf. part. καθιγμένον Hsch.:—*come down to*: in Hom. only metaph., *reach, touch*, με μάλιστα καθίκετο πένθος ἄλαστον Od.1.342, μάλα πώς με καθίκεο θυμὸν ἐνιπῇ thou *hast touched* me *nearly*, Il.14.104; later, of any down-stroke, κάρα.. κέντροισί μου καθίκετο *came down upon* my head, S.*OT*809; εἰς ὦμους κ. ὑπέροις Paus.5.18.2: abs., ἐπανατεινάμενος τὸ ξίφος καθικνεῖται Parth.8.9: generally, *take effect*, Phld.*Mus.*p.85 K.; *attack, affect*, τῆς ὀπτήσεως καθικνουμένης καὶ ἐξατμιζούσης τὸ τροφῶδες Ath.Med.ap.Orib.1.9.1: freq. in Prose, c. gen., κ. τῆς πηγῆς Paus.7.21.12; κ. τῆς ψυχῆς *reach* or *touch* it, Pl.*Ax.*369e; ἡμῶν ὁ λόγος καθίκετο Luc.*Nigr.*35; ἡ ὕβρις οὐ μετρίως μου καθίκετο Id.*Tox.*46; κ. τινὸς πικρότατα Ael.*VH*14.3; κ. τινὸς σκύτεσι, κονδύλῳ, *strike* one with a strap, etc., Plu.*Ant.*12, *Alc.*7. **2.** κ. τῆς ἐπιβολῆς *attain* one's purpose, Plb.2.38.8, cf. 4.50.10; ποιεῖν [πόλιν] τηλικαύτην ἡλίκην καὶ τειχίζειν ἐπιβαλλόμενοι καθίξονται *they will succeed*, Id.5.93.5. **3.** κατικόμενον, τό, *that which comes to one*, one's share of an inheritance, *IG*9(1).334.30 (Locr., v B.C.).

καθῑλᾰρ-εύομαι, c. gen., and **–ύνω**, c. dat., sine expl., Suid.

καθιλύσας· ἀθροίσας, Hsch. (fort. καθειλήσας = κατ–).

καθῑμ-άω, *let down by a rope*, αὐτόν Ar.*V.*379, 396; κάδον Arist.*Mech.*857ᵇ4; τὸν τράχηλον.. καθιμήσας, of the heron, Babr.94.3:—Pass., ἐς τὸ Καπιτώλιον ἐκ τοῦ οὐρανοῦ καθιμῆσθαι D.C.45.2. **–ησις**, εως, ἡ, *a letting down by a rope*, Plu.2.264f. **–ονεύω**, = καθιμάω, Hsch.

καθίννυμαι, by-form of καθίζομαι, Hp.*Fract.*3,8; *take a hip-bath*, ἐν ὕδατι θερμῷ Id.*Mul.*1.84, cf. 2.154, al.; cf. ἰνύεσθαι.

κάθιξις, εως, ἡ, *arrival* at a point, τῆς συναφῆς Vett.Val.244.35.

καθιξῶ and **καθίξω**, Dor. fut. and aor. 1 subj. of καθίζω.

καθιππ-άζομαι, Ion. **κατ–**: **I.** trans., *ride down, overrun with horse*, χώρην Hdt.9.14. **2.** metaph., *trample under foot*, δαίμονας A.*Eu.*150 (lyr.); νόμους ib.779 (lyr.), cf. 731: later c. gen., κ. φιλοσοφίας D.L.4.47. **II.** Pass., pf. καθιππάσθαι Macho ap.Ath.13.581d (sens. obsc.). **III.** intr., *ride*, Polyaen.1.3.5. **–ευσις**, εως, ἡ, *charging down*, of cavalry, D.H.9.9 (pl.). **–εύω**, *ride over, overrun with horse*, τὰ πεδία Id.3.26, cf. Hdn.6.2.5; *ride upon*, οἶδμα *Hymn.Is.*154; of fish, κῦμα κ. Opp.*H.*2.515:—Pass., of frozen rivers, *to be ridden over*, Arist.*Mir.*846ᵇ32, Hdn.6.7.6. **2.** *ride down, trample under foot*, Ἀργείων στρατόν E.*Ph.*732. **3.** *conquer by means of a horse* (i.e. the δούρειος ἵππος), Tryph.174.

καθιππο-κρᾰτέω, *conquer with horse*, Poll.1.164, 9.141. **–μᾰχέω**, = foreg., ibid. **–τροφέω**, *squander* a fortune *in keeping horses*, Is.5.43.

καθίππαμαι, v. καταπέτομαι.

καθίππαξις (leg. καθίππασις), εως, ἡ, *cavalcade* (Lacon.), Hsch.

κάθῐσις, εως, ἡ, *sitting*, καθίσεις ἄμορφοι Plu.2.609c, cf. Gal.*UP*3.9 (pl.). **II.** *causing to sit down*, Plu.2.158b.

κάθισμα, ατος, τό, *part on which one sits*: in pl., *buttocks*, Sch.Aeschin.1.126. **2.** *seat*, Simp.*in Ph.*347.9, Pall.*in Hp.Fract.*12.278C. **3.** *base* of a still, Zos.Alch.p.224 B. **II.** *sinking, settling down*, of a wall, Apollod.*Poliorc.*150.1. **2.** *sediment*, Sch.Nic.*Al.*95.

καθιστάνω, = καθίστημι, inf., Is.2.29, Lys.26.15, 28.7, *CIG*3065.22 (Teos), etc.: impf., D.S.15.33, etc.:—also **καθιστάω**, *SIG*531.32 (Dyme, iii B.C.); inf. –ιστᾶν D.S.19.15; part. –ιστῶν Lxx *De.*17.15, –ιστῶντες (v.l. –ιστάνοντες) *Act.Ap.*17.15.

καθίστημι, **A.** in causal sense:—**Act.**, in pres., impf., fut., and pf. καθέστᾰκα Hyp.*Eux.*28, Lxx *Je.*1.10, D.H.*Dem.*54, D.S.32.11, etc.; once καθέστηκα *PHib.*1.82 i 14 (iii B.C.): plpf. -εστάκει Demetr. Sceps.ap.Ath.15.697d:—also in **Med.**, fut. (Paus.3.5.1), aor. 1, more rarely pres. (infr. A. II. 2):—*set down*, κρητῆρα καθίστα Il.9.202; νῆα κατάστησον *bring* it *to land*, Od.12.185; κ. δίφρους *place, station* them, before starting for the race, S.*El.*710; ποῖ [δεῖ] καθιστάναι πόδα; E.*Ba.*184; κ. τινὰ εἰς τὸ φανερόν X.*An.*7.7.22; *set up, erect*, of stones, *Inscr.Cypr.*94, 95 H.:—Med., [λαῖφος] κατεστήσαντο βοεῦσι *steadied* it, *h.Ap.*407. **2.** *bring down* to a place, τούς μ' ἐκέλευσα Πύλονδε καταστῆσαι Od.13.274: generally, *bring*, κ. τινὰ ἐς Νάξον Hdt.1.64, cf. Th.4.78; esp. *bring back*, πάλιν αὐτὸν κ. ἐς τὸ τεῖχος σῶν καὶ ὑγιᾶ Id.3.34; κ. τοὺς Ἕλληνας εἰς Ἰωνίαν πάλιν X.*An.*1.4.13; without πάλιν, *replace, restore*, ἐς φῶς σὸν κ. βίον E.*Alc.*362; ἃς (sc. τὰς κόρας) οὐδ' ὁ Μελάμπους.. καταστήσειεν ἄν *cure* their squint, Alex.112.5; ἰκτεριῶντας κ. Dsc.4.1; τὸ σῶμα *restore* the general health, Hp.*Mul.* 2.133:—Med., κατεστήσαντο (v.l. for κατεκτήσαντο) εὐδαιμονίαν Isoc. 4.62:—Pass., οὐκ ἂν ἀντὶ πόνων χάρις καθίσταιτο *would be returned*, Th. 4.86. **3.** *bring before* a ruler or magistrate, Hdt.1.209, *PRyl.*65.10 (i B.C.), etc.; τινὰ ἐπί τινα *PCair.Zen.*202.6 (iii B.C.), *POxy.*281.24 (i A.D.). **II.** *set in order, array*, of soldiers, X.*An.*1.10.10; *set* as guards, προφυλακάς ib.3.2.1, etc. **2.** *ordain, appoint*, κατέστησε τύραννον εἶναι παῖδα τὸν ἑωυτοῦ Hdt.5.94, cf. 25: usu. without the inf., κ. τινὰ ὕπαρχον Id.7.105; ἄλλον [ἄρχοντα] ἀντὶ αὐτοῦ X.*Cyr.*3.1.12, etc.; βασιλέα ἐπί τινας Lxx 1*Ki.*8.5, al.; τινὰ ἐς μοναρχίαν E.*Supp.* 352; ἐπὶ τὰς ἀρχάς Isoc.12.132; τινὰ τύραννον Ar.*Av.*1672; κ. ἐγγυητάς Hdt.1.196, Ar.*Ec.*1064; δικαστάς, ἐπιμελητάς, νομοθέτας, Id.*Pl.* 917, X.*Cyr.*8.1.9, D.3.10 (sed leg. καθίσατε, cf. καθίζω I. 4); of games, etc., γυμνικοὺς ἀγῶνας κ. Isoc.4.1: rarely c. inf., οἱ καθιστάντες μουσικῇ.. παιδεύειν Pl.*R.*410b:—so in Pass., κυβερνᾶν κατασταθεὶς X. *Mem.*1.7.3: aor. Med., *appoint for oneself*, τύραννον καταστησάμενοι παρὰ σφίσι αὐτοῖσι Hdt.5.92.α'; ἄρχοντας X.*An.*3.1.39, etc. **b.** esp. of laws, constitutions, ceremonies, etc., *establish*, νόμους, τελετάς, E.*Or.*892, *Ba.*21, etc.; πολιτείαν, δημοκρατίαν, Arist.*Ath.*7.1, Decr.ib. 29.3; ὀλιγαρχίαν Lys.12.42; also, *set in order, arrange*, πολιτείαν Pl. *R.*590e:—also in Med., τοῦτο βουλευτήριον φρούρημα γῆς καθίσταμαι A.*Eu.*706; τὴν Ἱππίου καθίσταμαι τυραννίδα Ar.*V.*502; καθίστατο τὰ περὶ τὴν Μυτιλήνην ᾗ αὐτῷ ἐδόκει Th.3.35; πόλεις ἐπὶ τὸ ὠφέλιμον Id. 1.76; [Εὔβοιαν] ὁμολογίᾳ ib.114; πρὸς ἐμὲ τὸ πρᾶγμα καταστήσασθαι *settle* it with me, D.21.90. **3.** *bring into a certain state*, τινὰ ἐς ἀπόνοιαν Th.1.82; ἐς ἀπορίαν Id.7.75; εἰς ἀνάγκην Lys.3.3; εἰς αἰσχύνην Pl.*Sph.*230d; εἰς ἐρημίαν φίλων Id.*Phdr.*232d; εἰς ἀγῶνα Id.*Ap.*24c; τινὰ εἰς ἀσφάλειαν Isoc.5.123; τίνας εἰς ἀγῶνα καθέστακα; Hyp.*Eux.* 28, cf. Lycurg.2; κ. τινὰ ἐν ἀγῶνι καὶ κινδύνῳ Antipho 5.61; τὴν πόλιν ἐν πολέμῳ Pl.*Mx.*242a; τοὺς φίλους ἐν ἀκινδύνῳ X.*Cyr.*4.5.28; κ. ἑαυτὸν ἐς κρίσιν *present* himself for trial, Th.1.131, cf. Lycurg.6; κ. τινὰ εἰς τοὺς ἀρχικοὺς *reckon* him as one of..., X.*Mem.*2.1.9. **4.** c. dupl. acc., *make, render so and so*, ψευδῆ γ' ἐμαυτὸν S.*Ant.*657; ἡ ἐπιθυμία κ. τινὰ ἀμνήμονα Antipho 2.1.7; τὸ πιστὸν ὑμᾶς ἀπιστοτέρους κ. Th.1.68; κ. τι φανερόν, σαφές, Id.2.42, 1.32; τινὸς ἐπίπονον τὸν βίον κ. Isoc.10.17: c. part., κλαίοντα καθιστάναι τινά *bring* one to tears, E.*Andr.*635: rarely c. inf., κ. τινὰ φεύγειν *make* him fly, Th.2.84, cf. E.*Alc.*283, Luc.*Charid.*8:—Pass., ἀνάγκη τὴν ναυμαχίαν πεζομαχίαν καθίστασθαι Th.2.89. **5.** Med., *get for oneself*, τὴν ζόην καταστήσασθαι ἀπ' ἔργων ἀνοσιωτάτων Hdt.8.105. **6.** *make*, in periphrases, πάννυχοι.. διάπλοον καθίστασαν A.*Pers.*382:—Med., κρυφαῖον ἔκπλουν οὐδαμῇ καθίστατο ib.385.

B. intr. in aor. 2, pf. καθέστηκα, and plpf. of Act. (also fut. καθεστήξω Th.3.37,102), and all tenses of Med. (exc. aor. 1) and Pass.: pf. καθέσταμαι in later Greek, *IG*2².1006.24 (ii B.C.), Lxx *Nu.*3.32, etc.:—*to be set, set oneself down, settle*, ἐς [Αἴγιναν] Hdt.3.131, cf. Th.4.75; [ὀδύναι] καθίσταντο ἐς ὑπογάστριον Hp.*Epid.*7.97; of joints, ἐξίσταται ἀνωδύνως καὶ κ. goes out of joint and *in again*, Id. *Art.*8; κ. ἐς Ῥήγιον *to make* R. *a base* of operations, Th.3.86; simply, *to be come to* a place, ὅποι καθέσταμεν S.*OC*23. **b.** *come before* another, *stand in* his *presence*, Pi.*P.*4.135; λέξον καταστάς A.*Pers.* 295 (unless it be taken in signf. 4), cf. Hdt.1.152; κ. ἐς ὄψιν τινός Id.7.29; καταστάντες ἐπὶ τοὺς ἄρχοντας ἔλεγον Id.3.46, cf. 156; καταστὰς ἐπὶ τὸ πλῆθος ἔλεγε Th.4.84. **2.** *to be set* as guard, ὑπό τινος Hdt.7.59, cf. S.*OC*356, X.*An.*4.5.19, etc.; *to be appointed*, δεσπότης .. καθέστηκα E.*HF*142; στρατηλάτης νέος καταστάς Id.*Supp.*1216; κ. χορηγὸς εἰς Θαργήλια, στρατηγός, etc., Antipho 6.11, Isoc.4.35, etc.; οἱ πρόβουλοι καθεστᾶσιν ἐπὶ τοῖς βουλευταῖς Arist.*Pol.*1299ᵇ37; δικτάτωρ.. καθε[στάμενος τὸ τέταρτον], = Lat. *dictator designatus quartum*, of Caesar, *IG*12(2).35 b 7 (Mytil.). **3.** *deposit a sediment*, Hp. *Epid.*1.2,7. **4.** also, *stand* or *become quiet* or *calm*, of water, ὅταν ἡ λίμνη καταστῇ Ar.*Eq.*865, cf. *PHolm.*16.3; θάλασσα γαληνὴ καὶ κ. Plb.21.31.10; πνεῦμα λεῖον καὶ καθεστηκός calm and *settled*, Ar.*Ra.* 1003; ὁ θόρυβος κατέστη *subsided*, Hdt.3.80; of laughter, Philostr. *VA*3.4; of a swelling, Hp.*Prog.*7; ἕως τὰ πράγματα κατασταίη Lys. 13.25; also of persons, καταστάς *composedly*, A.*Pers.*295 (but v. supr. I b); [ἡ ψυχὴ] καθίσταται καὶ ἠρεμίζεται Arist.*Ph.*248ᵃ2; δρῶμεν [τοὺς ἐνθουσιαστικοὺς].. καθισταμένους Id.*Pol.*1342ᵃ10; καθεστηκυίας τῆς διανοίας Ocell.4.13; καθεστῶτι προσώπῳ with *composed, calm* countenance, Plu.*Fab.*17; μαίνεσθαι καὶ ἔξω τοῦ καθεστηκότος εἶναι Luc.*Philops.*5; τίς ἂν καθεστηκὼς φήσαιε; what person *of mature judgement* would say..? Phld.*Po.*5.15; ἡ καθεστηκυῖα ἡλικία *middle* age, Th.2.36; ἡλικία μέση καὶ κ. Pl.*Ep.*316c; οἱ καθεστηκότες *those of middle age*, Hp.*Aph.*1.13: also, with metaphor from wine, *mellow*, of persons, Alex.45.8. **5.** *come into a certain state, become*, and in pf. and plpf., *to have become, be*, ἀντὶ φίλου πολέμιόν τινι κ. Hdt. 1.87; οἱ μὲν ὀφθαλμῶν ἰητροὶ κατεστέασι, οἱ δὲ κεφαλῆς Id.2.84; ἔμφρων καθίσταται S.*Aj.*306; τῶν ἄνωθεν ὑπόπτων καθεστώτων Epicur. *Sent.*13; ἐς μάχην Hdt.3.45; ἐς πόλεμον ὑμῖν καὶ μάχην κ. E.*HF* 1168; ἐς πάλην καθίσταται δορὸς τὸ πρᾶγμα Id.*Heracl.*159; ἐς τὴν ἴησιν Hp.*Prorrh.*2.12; ἐς τὸ αὐτό they *recover*, Id.*Coac.*160 (later abs., καταστῆναι καὶ μηδενὸς ἔτι φαρμάκου δεηθῆναι Gal.*Vict.Att.*1); ἐς τοὺς κινδύνους Antipho 2.3.1; ἐς φόβον Hdt.8.12, Th.2.81; ἐς δέος, λύπην, Id.4.108, 7.75; ἐς φυγήν Id.2.81; ἐς ἔχθραν τινί Isoc.9.67; εἰς ὁμόνοιαν, εἰς πολλὴν ἀθυμίαν, Lys.18.18, 12.3; καταστῆναι ἐς συνήθειάν τινος τὴν πόλιν ποιεῖν make the city *become* accustomed to it, Aeschin.1.165; ἀντιστασιώτης κατεστήκεε *had been*, Hdt.1.92, cf. 9.37; ἐν δείματι μεγάλῳ κατέστασαν Id.7.138; καταστάντων σφι εὖ τῶν πρηγμάτων ib.132; τίνι τρόπῳ καθέστατε; in what case *are ye?* S.*OT*10; φονέα με φησὶ.. καθεστάναι ib.703; ἄπαρνος δ' οὐδενὸς καθίστατο Id.*Ant.*435; κρυπτὸς καταστάς E.*Andr.*1064; οἱ ἐν τούτῳ τῆς ἡλικίας καθεστῶτες ἐν ᾧ.. Antipho 2.1.1; ἐν οἵῳ τρόπῳ [ἡ τῶν Ἀθηναίων ἀρχὴ] κατέστη how it *came into being*, Th.1.97, cf. 96; ἀρξάμενος εὐθὺς καθισταμένου (sc. τοῦ πολέμου) from its first *commencement*, Id.1.1. **6.** *to be established* or *instituted, prevail*, καί σφι μαντήϊον Διὸς κατέστηκε Hdt.2.29; ἄγραι.. πολλαὶ κατεστᾶσι ib.70, cf. 1.200; ὅδε σφι νόμος κατεστήκεε ib.197; βροτοῖσιν ὃς καθέστηκεν νόμος E. *Hipp.*91: c. inf., θεὸν Ἀμφιάραον πρῶτοις Ὠρωπίοις κατέστη νομίζειν Paus.1.34.2: pf. part., *existing, established, prevailing*, τὸν νῦν κατεστεῶτα κόσμον Hdt.1.65; ἦν κατεστηκὸς οὐδὲν φόρου πέρι Id.3.89; τοὺς κατεστεῶτας τριηκοσίους the *regular* 300, Id.7.205; οἱ καθεστῶτες νόμοι S.*Ant.*1113, Ar.*Nu.*1400; τὰ καθεστῶτα the *present state of life*, S.*Ant.*1160; also, *existing laws, usages*, τὰ τότε κ., τά ποτε κ., Pl.*Lg.* 798b, Isoc.7.56; ἐπὶ τοῖσι κατεστεῶσι ἔνεμε τὴν πόλιν Hdt.1.59. **7.** of purchases, *cost*, πλέον ἢ ὅσου ἐμοὶ κατέστησαν more than *they stood* me in, And.2.11, cf. Plu.2.349a. **8.** *stand against, oppose*, πρός τινα dub. l. in Plb.23.18.5:—Pass., Τιτήνεσσι κατέσταθεν Hes. *Th.*674.

C. aor. 1 Med. and sts. pres. Med. are used in trans. sense, v. supr. A. II. 2 sq.

καθιστήριον, τό, *seat*, Sch.Ar.*Ec.*729, Hsch. s. v. δίφρον.

καθιστ-ῐᾰσις, εως, ἡ, *expenditure on feasts*, *IG*7.2710 (Acraeph.). **-ιάω**, *spend on feasts*, τόκον ib.12(7).237.25, cf. 56 (Amorgos).

καθιστορέω, *observe*, *Gp.*15.2.31.

καθίστρα, ἡ, = καθέδρα (?), *Supp.Epigr.*2.727 (Pednelissus).

καθό, Adv. for καθ' ὅ (which shd. perh. be written), *in so far as, according as*, Lys.34.5, Arist.*Metaph.*1022ᵃ14, D.S.31.16, 2*Ep.Cor.* 8.12, etc.; κ. μεγέθει καὶ κ. ποιότητι *in respect of...*, Phld.*Ir.*p.91 W. **II.** *wherefore*, Pl.*Sph.*267d, Plu.2.51b.

καθοδηγ-έω, *guide*, Lxx *Jb.*12.23, Plu.*Cat.Ma.*13: c. acc., Id.2. 558d. **-ησις**, εως, ἡ, *guidance*, Th.*Is.*38.15. **-ία**, ἡ, = foreg., Str.2.3.4. **-ός**, ὁ, *guide*, Hellanic.51 J., Str.15.2.6, Orph.*H.*8.8, Apollod.3.4.1; τῆς Ἴσιδος *PMag.Osl.*1.338.

καθόδιον, τό, *expenses of return journey*, *Milet.*3 No.152.106 (Eresus, ii B.C.).

καθοδοιπορέω, strengthd. for ὁδοιπορέω, Erot.*Fr.*36.

κάθοδος, Ion. **κάτοδος**, ἡ, *descent*, esp. of Demeter, Plu.2.378e; represented in mysteries, Herod.1.56; and so of a *procession*, ἥρωος κ. Call.*Aet.*1.1.26: generally, *going down*, τῶν ἐδεστῶν ἐν τῇ κ. ἡ ἡδονή Arist.*PA*690ᵇ30, cf. Luc.*Nec.*2; *way down*, Id.*DMort.*27.1; of planets, *declination*, Simp.*in Cael.*510.29. **2.** ἡ κ. ἡ ἐπὶ θάλασσαν, = κατάβασις, Arr.*An.*1.2.4. **3.** *journey down* the Nile, *POxy.* 1119.27 (iii A.D.), etc. **II.** *coming back, return*, E.*HF*19, Th.3. 114; esp. of an exile to his country, Hdt.1.60, 61, al., Th.3.85, 5.16, etc.; κ. καὶ ἄδεια Id.8.81. **III.** *cycle, recurrence*, χιλίων ἐτῶν κ. a thousand years *twice told*, in pl., Lxx *Ec.*6.6, cf. Phot.; also τρεῖς καθόδους three *times*, Lxx 3*Ki.*9.25, cf. Aq.*Ex.*34.24, al.; ἄχρι δύο καθόδων *twice over*, Alex.Trall.1.17.

καθολικός, ή, όν, (καθόλου) *general*, ὕδερος Hp.*Int.*26; καθολικόν, τό, *generic description*, *Stoic.*2.74; καθολικά, τά, title of work by Zeno, ib.1.14; ἔμφασις (v. sub voc.) Plb.6.5.3, cf. 1.57.4; κ. καὶ κοινὴ ἱστορία Id.8.2.11; κ. περίληψις D.H.*Comp.*12; κ. παραδόσεις Phld. *Rh.*1.126 S.; κ. θεώρημα Cic.*Att.*14.20.3; κ. *praecepta*, Quint.2.13. 14; -ώτεροι λόγοι *general*, opp. εἰδικοί, S.E.*P.*2.84, cf. Hermog.*Meth.* 5; κ. προσῳδία, title of work by Hdn.Gr. on accents; νόμος -ώτερος Ph.2.172; κ. ἐπιστολή an epistle *general*, 1*Ep.Pet.* tit.; *of general interest*, *BGU*1915 (ii A.D.); *universal*, κ. τίς ἐστιν καὶ θεία ἡ ταυτότης καὶ ἡ ἑτερότης Dam.*Pr.*310. Adv. -κῶς *generally*, ἀποφήνασθαι Plb. 4.1.8; εἰπεῖν *in general terms*, Str.17.3.10, cf. Phld.*Rh.*1.161 S.; κ. εὑρίσκεταί τι Hermog.*Inv.*3.11; κ., opp. πληθικῶς ('in the majority of cases'), *OGI*669.49 (Egypt, i A.D.); *universally*, Porph.*Sent.*22: Comp. -ώτερον Plb.3.37.6, Gal.18(1).15; -ωτέρως Tz.ad Lyc.16. **II.** as Subst., **καθολικός**, ὁ, *supervisor of accounts* (οἱ καθόλου λόγοι), = Lat. *procurator a rationibus*, Εὐφράτης ὁ κ. Gal.14.4, cf. *Jahresh.*23 *Beibl.*269 (Ephes., ii A.D.); in Egypt, = Lat. *rationalis*, *PLond.*3.1157 (iii A.D.), *IGRom.*1.1211 (Diocletian), *POxy.*2106.25 (iv A.D.), etc.; also, = *consularis*, *Gloss.*; in cent. iv, also, = *rationalis summarum*, Γεωργίῳ κ. Jul.*Ep.*188, 189 tit.

καθολκ-εύς, έως, ὁ, (καθέλκω) *a kind of bandage*, Gal.18(1).785. **-ή**, ἡ, *drawing down* of ships to sea, opp. ἀνολκή, Aen.Tact.10.12, cf. *IG*2².1028.37 (pl.), Callix.1, Hero *Aut.*22.3. **-ός**, ὁ, = καθολκεύς, Gal.18(1).786.

καθόλου, Adv. *on the whole, in general*, = καθ' ὅλου (as it shd. perh. be written), Epist.Philipp.ap.D.18.77; κ. γράφειν, opp. κατὰ μέρος,

Plb.3.32.8; κ. εἰπεῖν Arist.*Top.*156^{a}13, Plu.2.397c, etc.; οἱ κ. λόγοι *general* statements, opp. οἱ ἐπὶ μέρους, Arist.*EN*1107^{a}30 (but in Roman times, accounts *kept by the central government*, = Lat. *summae rationes*, *OGI*715.3 (Alexandria), D.C.79.21, etc.); τοῦτο γάρ ἐστι κ. μᾶλλον too *general*, Arist.*Pol.*1265^{a}31, cf. *GA*748^{a}8; ἡ τῶν κ. πραγμάτων σύνταξις *general* history, Plb.1.4.2; τὸ κ. D.S.1.77, Plu.2.569f; τὸ κ. τῆς μοχθηρίας, opp. τὸ πρὸς ἡμᾶς, ib.468e; οὐδ' οὗτος ἀποφαίνει κ. τὸ καταλειφθέν the *whole* amount left, D.27.43; ἐν τῷ κ. *in general, speaking generally*, Ath.1.30e, Arr.*Epict.*1.8.8, al. 2. in the Logic of Arist., of terms, τὸ κ. *general*, opp. τὸ καθ' ἕκαστον (singular), λέγω δὲ κ. μὲν ὃ ἐπὶ πλειόνων πέφυκε κατηγορεῖσθαι, καθ' ἕκαστον δὲ ὃ μή *Int.*17^{a}39, cf. *Metaph.*1023^{b}29; opp. τὸ κατὰ μέρος, *Rh.*1357^{b}1, al.; hence, τὰ κ. *universal* truths, ἡ ποίησις μᾶλλον τὰ κ., ἡ δ' ἱστορία τὰ καθ' ἕ. λέγει *Po.*1451^{b}7; = γνῶμαι, ib.1450^{b}12; esp. *commensurate* predicate, ὃ ἂν κατὰ παντός τε ὑπάρχῃ καὶ καθ' αὑτὸ καὶ ᾗ αὐτό *APo.*73^{b}26; as Adj., of propositions, λόγος κ. a *universal* statement, opp. ἐν μέρει, κατὰ μέρος (particular), ἀδιόριστος (infinite), *APr.*24^{a}17 sq.; of inference, ἡ κ. ἀπόδειξις *universal* proof, opp. κατὰ μέρος, *APo.*85^{a}13; hence, as predicate, κ. εἰσὶν [αἱ ἀρχαί] *Metaph.*1003^{a}7; as Adv., κ. ἀποφαίνεσθαι ἐπὶ τοῦ κ. *Int.*17^{b}5, al. 3. *completely, entirely*, Plb.1.20.2; οὐδὲ κ. μακρὸν πλοῖον no warships *at all*, ib.13, cf. Lxx *Da.*3.50, al.; μηδὲ τέχνην εἶναι τὸ κ. τοῦ πείθειν Phld.*Rh.*1.327 S. (Written κατὰ ὅλου Pl.*Men.*77a.)

κάθομα, f.l. for καθ' ὁμά, Call.*Fr.*293, = Id.*Oxy.*2079.26.

καθομηρ-εύω, *express in Homeric language*, Hsch. s.v. καθωμηρευμένα. **-ίζω**, *describe Homerically*, Aristaenet.1.3,12. II. intr., *speak in the style of Homer*, Eustr. *in EN*268.33.

καθομῑλέω, *conciliate by daily intercourse, win the favour of*, τοὺς γνωρίμους Arist.*Pol.*1315^{b}4, cf. Plu.2.52e, *Caes.*15, App.*BC*5.63: c. dat., κ. τῷ πλήθει (nisi leg. τὰ πλήθη) D.S.14.70; κ. τοὺς καιρούς Ath.12.513b, v.l. in Sch.Ar.*Ra.*1001, v.l. in Suid. s.v. ἀγχίστροφοι (nisi leg. τοῖς καιροῖς, as in Sch.Ar.*Ra.*47,546):—Pass., ὑπὸ Δημάδου καθομιληθείς D.S.16.87. II. Pass., *to be used in daily intercourse, to be current*, esp. in pf. part. Pass., ἡ καθωμιλημένη δόξα Plb.10.5.9; κ. φράσεις Phld.*Rh.*1.161 S.; κ. ὄνομα Alex.Aphr. *in Mete.*7.9, cf. Antig.*Mir.*8; also Σαρδόνιος γέλως καθωμίληται *has become a proverb*, Dsc.*Alex.*14: c. dat., νόμοι οὐ -μένοι τῷ τῶν πολλῶν ἔθει which *have* nothing *to do* with.., Max.Tyr.23.2.

καθομοιόω, *assimilate*, Simp. *in Cat.*328.30.

καθομολογ-έω, *confess, allow*, esp. to one's detriment, Pl.*Cri.*49d, *Grg.*499b. 2. *consent*, abs., And.1.42. b. *consent to accept in payment*, τόκους D.56.14. II. *promise, engage, vow*:—Pass., ἀνάθημα τῷ θεῷ Luc.*Phal.*2.1, cf. Philostr.*VA*5.30. 2. *betroth*, τινὰ τῷ υἱῷ Lxx *Ex.*21.9 (Med.); Κλαυδίαν ἀνδρί Plu.*TG*4:—pf. Pass. in med. sense, τὴν ἀδελφὴν.. γυναῖκά τινι καθωμολογημένος Id.*Crass.*33; but in pass. sense, Id.*Pomp.*47: plpf. καθωμολόγητο Parth.13.2. 3. *pledge, mortgage*, ὑποθήκην κ. τί τινι Alciphr.3.3. III. Med. in sense of Act. II. 1, c. fut. inf., Parth.9.4. **-ία**, ἡ, *engagement, agreement*, *Foed.Delph.Pell.*2 A 3.

κάθομον, f.l. for καθ' οἶμον, Hsch.

καθόπερ, = καθ' ὅπερ: Ion. **κατόπερ**, *just as*, *SIG*45.43 (Halic., v B.C.), 57.11 (Milet., v B.C.).

καθοπλ-ίζω, *equip, arm fully*, τῇ πανοπλίᾳ Aeschin.3.154, cf. Decr. ap.D.18.116, Aristeas 14:—Med., *arm oneself fully*, Batr.122,160, Plb.3.62.7, Plu.*Phil.*9, etc.; παντοπλίας κ. *arm oneself in*.., Lxx 4*Ma.*3.12:—Pass., *to be so armed*, X.*Cyr.*2.1.11; καθωπλισμένοι εἰς τὰ Μακεδονικά D.S.19.27; θυμιατηρίῳ καθωπλισμένος *furnished with*.., Lxx 4*Ma.*7.11: metaph., καλοκἀγαθίᾳ ib.11.22. II. *array, set in order*: metaph., τὸ μὴ καλὸν καθοπλίσασα δύο φέρειν so *ordering* that which is not well as to.., S.*El.*1087 (lyr., Sch. καταπολεμήσασα τὸ αἰσχρὸν καὶ νικήσασα). **-ῖσις**, εως, ἡ, *arming, making of arms*, Philoch.ap.Anon.*Oxy.*1241 v 6; *mode of arming, armour*, Plb.6.23.14, Ael.*Tact.*2.7:—so **-ισμός**, ὁ, Plb.11.32.7, Ael.*Tact.*2.9, *SIG*569.33 (Halasarna, iii B.C.); οἱ ἐν τοῖς βαρέσι κ. Plb.3.113.7; κοῦφοι κ. D.S.5.34.

καθοπτεύει· καθορᾷ, Hsch.; cf. κατοπτεύω.

καθορ-ᾱτικός, ή, όν, *able to see into*: *keen-sighted*, Poll.9.151. **-άω**, Ion. κατ-, impf. καθεώρων X.*Cyr.*3.2.10, Ion. 3 sg. κατώρα Hdt.7.208: pf. καθεώρακα Pl.*Lg.*905b: fut. κατόψομαι Hdt.3.17: 3 sg. pf. κατῶπται Pl.*R.*432b: aor. 1 κατώφθην Id.*Phlb.*46b: for aor. Act., v. κατεῖδον:—*look down*, ἐξ Ἴδης καθορῶν Il.11.337; ἐπί τινος Hdt.7.44:—Med., ἐπὶ Θρῃκῶν καθορώμενος αἶαν Il.13.4. II. trans., *look down upon*, ὅσους θνητοὺς ἥλιος καθορᾷ Sol.14, cf. Thgn.168,616, X.*Cyr.*3.2.10; ὑψόθεν τὸν τῶν κάτω βίον Pl.*Sph.*216c, etc.: metaph., φρένα Δίαν κ., ὄψιν ἄβυσσον A.*Supp.*1058 (lyr.):—Med., Τροίην κατὰ πᾶσαν ὁρᾶται Il.24.291. 2. *have within view, see distinctly, descry*, Hdt.7.208, 9.59, Ar.*Nu.*326, Pl.*R.*516a, etc.:—Pass., Th.3.20,112, Pl.*Phlb.*38d, etc. 3. *behold, observe, perceive*, Pi.*P.*9.49, E.*Fr.*910.5 (anap.); καθορᾶν τι ἔν τινι *to observe* something therein, Pl.*Lg.*905b, cf. *Grg.*457c; τι ἐν τῇ ζητήσει Id.*R.*368e; ἵν' ἃ πανουργεῖς μὴ καθορᾷ σου that he *may* not *observe* thy knavish tricks, Ar.*Eq.*803; also κ. τὰς τρίχας εἰ.. *to look and see* whether.., Hdt.2.38. 4. *explore*, τὰ ἄλλα Id.3.17, cf. 123. 5. *regard, reverence*, τὸ τοῦ θεοῦ κράτος Lxx 3*Ma.*3.11.

καθορ-ίζω, *determine*, τὰς αἰτίας τινός Phld.*D.*1.14; *bound, define*, Hsch.:—Med., *lay claim to*, τόπους *Sammelb.*5240.9 (i A.D.). **-ιστικῶς**, Adv. *definitely*, οὐδὲν κ. δογματίζειν Anon. *in Tht.*61.12.

καθορμ-ίζω, *bring* a ship *into harbour, bring to anchor*, καθώρμισαν πρός τι πολισμάτιον Plb.1.53.10 codd. (dub.); τὸν στόλον εἰς τὸ νεώριον Plu.*Cat.Mi.*39:—Pass., with aor. Med., *come into harbour, put in*, ἐς τὴν Ἔφεσον Th.3.32, cf. 6.97, etc.: aor. 1 Pass., Anon.Hist. (*FGr.H*160) ii 20 (iii B.C.), Plb.1.21.5, Plu.*Sull.*26; ὑπ' Ἀκραγαντίνων (Cobet ὑπ' ἄκραν τινὰ) καθωρμίσθησαν Polyaen.6.16.4. 2. metaph., ἐς τάσδε σαυτὸν πημονὰς καθώρμισας *hast brought* thyself to such miseries, A.*Pr.*965; κ. ἑαυτὸν εἰς ἡσυχίαν Plu.2.455c:—Pass., καθώρμισται ἡ κύστις ἐκ τῶν νεφρῶν *is suspended* from them, Arist.*PA*671^{b}25: metaph., γένος ἐν μεταιχμίῳ ἀρετῆς καὶ κακίας -ισμένον Max.Tyr.30.3; of logical dependence, τὰ αἴτια τὰ νοητά, εἰς ἃ διὰ νοῦ -ίζεται ἡ ἐπιστήμη Simp. *in de An.*124.23. **-ιον**, τό, = ὅρμος, *necklace*, *PMagd.*42.5 (iii B.C.), Lxx *Ho.*2.13(15), Phot., Suid.; κάθορμον Hsch. **-ισις**, εως, ἡ, *bringing to land*, Dion.Byz.40.

καθόσι-ος, ον, in Sup. -ώτατος *devotissimus*, Gloss. **-ότης**, ητος, ἡ, *defunctio*, Gloss. **-όω**, *dedicate*, ἄγαλμα Poll.1.11, cf. *OGI* 383.109, al. (Commagene, i B.C.), *SIG*799.6 (Cyzicus, i A.D.):—Med., ὃν τοῖσδε βωμοῖς θεὰ καθωσιώσατο E.*IT*1320:—Pass., ἐπεὶ δὲ βωμῷ πόπανα καὶ προθύματα καθωσιώθη Ar.*Pl.*661, cf. D.H.2.23; καθωσιωμένος τινί *devoted*, of a person, Hdn.7.6.4; **-ωμένοι** νόμοι Ph.2.581; στρατιῶται Just.*Edict.*13.9. 2. *betroth*, J.*BJ*1.24.5. 3. κ. πόλιν καθαρμοῖς *purify*, Plu.*Sol.*12. **-ωσις**, εως, ἡ, *dedication*, [ἀγαλμάτων] Poll.1.11. 2. *devotion, fidelity*, *POxy.*2106.9 (iv A.D., written κατοσ-), Just.*Nov.App.*4.1; as a title, ἡ ἐμὴ κ., *SIG*905.11 (Chalcis, iv A.D.), cf. *Arch.Pap.*1.298 (iv A.D.). II. *crimen laesae majestatis*, Just.*Nov.*95.1.1, cf. Suid. s.v. εὐνοῦχος. **-ωτέον**, *one must dedicate oneself*, c. dat., *Theol.Ar.*50.

καθότι, Ion. κατ-, for καθ' ὅ τι (which shd. perh. be written) *in what manner*, *IG*1^{2}.24.8, al., Hdt.7.2, Th.1.82, etc.; κ. γέγραπται *as* is written, *SIG*577.18 (Milet., iii/ii B.C.), etc.; *so far as, inasmuch as*, Plb.4.25.3, al.

καθοῦ, aor. 2 imper. Med. of καθίημι. **κάθου**, imper. of κάθημαι.

καθουφήν· ἀλώπεκα, Hsch.; cf. κοθοῦριν.

καθυβρίζω, Ion. κατ-, *treat despitefully, insult*, c. acc., S.*El.*522; σῶμ' ἐμόν E.*El.*698, cf. *PHal.*1.210 (iii B.C.), Ph.2.574, etc.; κ. ταῦτα αὐτόν E.*Ba.*616 (troch.); τὸν δῆμον Ar.*Ach.*631, cf. *PLit.Lond.*52.2: c. acc. cogn., πολλὰ κ. Plu.*Crass.*29: also c. gen., S.*OC*960, *Ph.*1364: abs., Id.*OC*1535:—Pass., Phld.*Vit.*p.12 J.; καθυβρίζεται τοιαῦτα τῶν χειρωνακτέων ὑπὸ τῶν ἀνθρώπων such *are occasions of* the practitioners *being mocked*, Hp.*Acut.*44. 2. c. dat., Hdt.1.212, Paus.4.27.3; also κ. εἰς θυγατέρας dub. l. in D.H.11.2.

καθυγρ-αίνω, *moisten well*, Arist.*Pr.*863^{b}23, Thphr.*CP*6.18.10, Plu.*Luc.*32:—Pass., Thphr.*CP*1.13.6; of the bowels, *to be relaxed*, Hp.*Aph.*4.27, etc. II. *liquefy*, in Pass., Plu.2.953e. **-ασμός**, ὁ, *moistening*, Sor.1.120, Aët.5.118. **-ος**, ον, *very wet*, Hp.*Aph.*5.62; χώρα, γῆ, *Gp.*2.13.1, Porph.*Antr.*28; of plants which grow in wet places, Thphr.*HP*1.4.2; χωρίον v.l. in Plb.5.24.4; Γαλάται ταῖς σαρξὶ κ. with *flowing* muscles, D.S.5.28. 2. *connected with water* or *the sea*, πράγματα Vett.Val.82.32; ζῴδια Ptol.*Tetr.*181.

κάθυδρος [ῠ], ον, *very watery, full of water*, κ. κρατήρ S.*OC*158 (lyr.); χωρίον v.l. in Plb.5.24.4.

καθῠλακτέω, *bark at* one, Plu.2.969d:—also **καθυλάσσω** (written κατ-), Gloss.

καθῡλίζω, *strain, filter*, τὸν οἶνον Ath.10.420d; of a drug, *clarify*, τὸ αἷμα κ. Archig.ap.Aët.3.114, cf. 9.31.

καθῠλομᾰνέω, *run all to wood*, Hp.*Ep.*13.

καθυμνέω, *sing of much* or *constantly, descant upon*, Cleanth.1.6, Phld.*Rh.*1.221 S., D.S.11.11, J.*BJ*1.31.3, Plu.2.1117a; *make a hymn of*, τὸν αὐτῶν βίον Epicur.*Fr.*605.

καθύομαι [ῡ], Pass., *to be rained upon*, σφοδροῖς ὄμβροις St.Byz. s.v. Ὑηττός.

καθυπ-ᾰκούω, *consent*, σῖτον ἀποδόσθαι τῆς καλῶς ἐχούσης τιμῆς *IG* 7.4262.4 (Oropus, iii/ii B.C.). **-άρχω**, strengthd. for ὑπάρχω, Plu.*Cic.*23. **-είκω**, strengthd. for ὑπείκω, Nicom.*Harm.*3.

καθυπερ-ᾱκοντίζω, *overshoot completely*, ἵν' οἱ θεοὶ τοὺς Γηγενεῖς.. καθυπερηκόντισαν Ar.*Av.*825. **-βάλλω**, v.l. for ὑπερβάλλω, Ruf. ap.Orib.7.26.35. **-έχω**, *to be much superior*, -έχων, opp. ἥττων, Aristeas 257: c. gen., ἀλόγων ζῴων κ. τῷ ἀρετᾶς ἐπιμοίρος ἦμεν Euryph. ap.Stob.4.39.27; τινι *in* or *by* a thing, Plb.2.25.9; γένει Callicrat. ap.Stob.4.28.18: rarely c. acc., ἐξουσίαν κ. Theano *Ep.*5.4: c. acc. pers. et dat. rei, τὼς ἄλλως ἀρετᾷ Diotog.ap.Stob.4.7.62:—Pass., Ps.-Philol.ap.Stob.1.20.2. **-ηφᾰνέω**, strengthd. for ὑπερηφανέω, Arg. Ar.*Ach.*: c. gen., *treat with disdain*, τῶν φιλοσόφων Phld.*Vit.*p.7 J.:—also **-ηφᾰνεύομαι**, Hsch. s.v. κατεπλατύνετο, Eust.561.1:—hence Subst. **-ηφᾰνία**, ἡ, Phld.*Vit.*p.28 J.

καθύπερθε [ῠ], poet. before a vowel **-θεν** (also v.l. in Th.5.59, S.*El.*1090 (lyr.)); Ion. **κατύπερθε**: Adv.:—*from above, down from above*, δεινὸν δὲ λόφος κ. ἔνευεν Il.3.337, cf. 22.196, Od.12.442, etc.; κ. μελαθρόφιν 8.279; ἐκ μὲν τοῦ πεδίου.., κ. δέ.. Th.5.59, cf. *IG*1^{2}.398: c. gen., πυρός Nic.*Th.*691. 2. *atop, above*, opp. ὑπένερθε, Od.10.353; κ. ἐπιρρέει floats *atop*, Il.2.754; κ. τῶν ὅπλων τοῦ τόνου Hdt.7.36; of geographical position, Λέσβος ἄνω.., καὶ Φρυγίη καθύπερθε Il.24.545: c. gen., καθύπερθε Χίοιο *above*, i.e. *north of*, Chios, Od.3.170: in Prose, Κέρκιος κατύπερθε *SIG*1.3 (Abu Simbel, vi B.C.); ἡ χώρη ἡ κ. Hdt.4.8; ἡ κ. ὁδός Id.1.104, etc.; τὰ κ. *the upper country*, i.e. farther inland, τὰ κ. τῆς λίμνης Id.2.5; τὰ κ. τῆς θηριώδεος ib.32; τοῖσι κ. Ἀσσυρίων οἰκημένοισι Id.1.194. 3. *above, having the upper hand of*, κ. γενέσθαι τινός, prop., of a wrestler *who falls atop of* his opponent, ib.67, 8.60.γ'; κ. χερὶ πλούτῳ τε τῶν ἐχθρῶν S.*El.* l. c. (lyr.); also, of affairs, ἐλογίζετο.. κ. οἱ τὰ πρήγματα ἔσεσθαι τῶν Ἑλληνικῶν Hdt.8.136; κακοὶ δ' ἀγαθῶν καθύπερθεν Thgn.679; μόχθου κ. *superior* *to* misery, unconquered by it, Pi.*P*.9.31; also κ. ἤ... Hdt.8.75. II. of Time, *before*, c. gen., Id.5.28.

καθυπερτερ-έω, Astrol., of planetary influences, *prevail*, Heph. Astr.1.16, Porph.*in Ptol.*188: c. gen., Ptol.*Tetr.*119: c. acc., *overcome*, Vett.Val.102.14, al.:—Pass., Ptol.*Tetr.*88 (but expld. by ἐπαναφερομένου *PSI*3.158.22): generally, c. gen., *prevail over*, ἐχθρῶν Vett. Val.11.8, cf. M.Ant.8.8, Man.6.687 (s.v.l.): abs., Herm.ap.Stob.1.42. 7 (prob.). **–ησις**, εως, ἡ, Astrol., *prepollence*, Antioch.Astr. in *Cat. Cod.Astr.*8(3).106, Ptol.*Tetr.*193, Vett.Val.5.15, al.: generally, *prevalence*, prob. in Herm.ap.Stob.1.42.7. **–ητικός**, ή, όν, *prevalent*, *prepollent*, δύναμις Vett.Val.102.14. **–ία**, ἡ, = καθυπερτέρησις, *Cat. Cod.Astr.*4.6. **–ος**, α, ον, Ion. **κατ–**, η, ον, Comp. Adj.: (καθύπερθε):—*above*, Σεληναίης Man.6.604. II. commonly metaph., *having the upper hand, superior*, κ. γίνεσθαι τῷ πολέμῳ Hdt.1.67: abs., Th.5.14; κ. τῶν Περσέων γινόμενα τὰ πρήγματα Hdt.7.233, cf. Th.7.56; θεοῦ δ' ἔτ' ἰσχὺς κ. A.*Th.*226(lyr.); κ. Ζεύς Theoc.24.99: c. gen., πόλις κ. τῶν ἀντιπάλων X.*Mem.*4.6.14, cf. Theoc.24.100, etc.: neut. καθυπέρτερον as Adv., = καθύπερθε, Id.2.60 (s. v. l.):—Sup. **καθυπέρτατος**, η, ον, *highest*, ἐν τῇ κατυπερτάτῃ τῆς γῆς Hdt. 4.199. 2. Astrol., *prevalent, prepollent*, ἀστέρες Vett.Val.98.27.

καθυπερτίθεμαι, *communicate*, [τί] τινι Nic.Dam.66 J.

καθυπηρετέομαι, *assist*, τῇ ἀποκρίσει Sor.1.25; τῷ τάχει... καθυπηρετούμενας χεῖρας *keeping up with*.., Sch.Pl.*Phdr.*244b.

καθυπισχνέομαι, strengthd. for ὑπισχ–, Luc.*Herm.*6, *Rh.Pr.*25, Hsch.

καθυπν-ής, ές, = κάθυπνος, Nic.*Al.*434. **–ιος**, ον, *happening in sleep*, Oenom.ap.Eus.*PE*5.25. **–ος**, ον, *fast asleep*, Parmeno 1, Arist.*Pr.*876^{a}21. **–όω**, Ion. **κατ–**, *fall fast asleep*, Hdt.4.8, 7.12, al., X.*Mem.*2.1.30, Aen.Tact.18.17, Phld.*Hom.*p.25 O., *IG*4.952.51 (Epid.): Ep. part. καθυπνώοντι dub. in Maiist.16:—Pass., κατυπνωμένος *asleep*, Hdt.3.69, 7.14, 17. **–ωσις**, εως, ἡ, *falling asleep*, Arist. *Pr.*900^{b}37.

καθυπο-βαίνω, pf. –βέβηκα, *occupy a lower place than*, τῶν ἐπάνω Ach.Tat.*Intr.Arat.*18. **–βάλλω**, *subject*, Heliod. *in EN*109.20, Eust.1406.41; τινὰς τῇ τοῦ τετραπλασίου ἀποδόσει Just.*Nov.*161.1. 3:—Pass., ποιναῖς ib.134.7. II. *place underneath*, τοὺς δακτύλους τῇ ἕδρᾳ Aët.16.110 (= 100). **–γράφω**, *describe*, Eust.974. 13; *append signature* to a document or edict, *Sammelb.*5251.4 (ii B.C.), *PFlor.*36.22 (iv A.D.), *Cod.Just.*1.1.7.11, etc. **–δύομαι**, strengthd. for ὑποδ–, Eustr.*in EN*372.27. **–κειμαι**, strengthd. for ὑπόκ–, *to be 'in being', 'in evidence'*, Artem.1.1. **–κρίνομαι** [ῑ], *subdue by histrionic arts*, D.19.337; κ. καὶ διαφθείρουσι τὰς βουλήσεις τῶν ποιημάτων destroying *by bad acting*, D.H.*Dem.*53. II. c. inf., κ. εἶναι.. *pretend* to be some one else, Luc.*DMar.*13.2; κ. μειδιᾶν Ph. 2.280: c. acc., *counterfeit*, φιλίαν ib.520; τὴν σεμνότητα Him.*Ecl.*3. 2. **–νοέω**, *suspect*, c. acc. et inf., *PRyl.*127.15 (i A.D.); *harbour suspicions*, εἴς τινα *POxy.*1465.7 (i B.C.): c. acc., Iamb.*Myst.*5.10: abs., Procl. *in Prm.*p.586 S. II. *form a vague conception of*, τῷ γνωστῷ τὸ ἄγνωστον κ. Dam.*Pr.*29: c. acc. et inf., *suppose*, Sor.2.64; *perceive, understand*, πρὸς τίνος ἂν μάλιστα σῴζοιτο Phld.*Rh.*2.18 S.

καθυποπτεύω, *suspect*, f.l. in Arist.*Rh.Al.*1426^{b}28 (Pass.) (ὑπ– *PHib.*1.26.302).

καθυπο-στῐβίζω, *paint underneath with* στίβι (v. στίμμι), in Pass., –ισμένος τὼ ὀφθαλμώ Nic.Dam.4 J. **–τάσσω**, Att. **–ττω**, *subject*, Phleg.*Fr.*17 J., *PMag.Lond.*123.4. II. = καθυπογράφω, *PFlor.* 377.7 (vi A.D.). **–τοπέομαι**, *place a sinister construction upon*, *EM*762.15 (nisi leg. καχ–).

καθυπουργέω, *render service*, Eustr.*in EN*387.8.

καθυστερ-έω, *fall behind*, κ. πολὺ τῇ διώξει Plu.*Crass.*29: metaph., *fall short*, τῇ φύσει Plb.23.7.5. 2. of Time, κ. τῆς ἑορτῆς *come too late for*.., *PSI*6.607.7 (iii B.C.); κ. τῆς καταστάσεως τῶν ὑπάτων Plb. 11.33.8; πάντων Id.5.17.7; τῆς ἐκτάξεως Id.10.39.5, cf. D.S.5.53, Str.14.2.5: c. acc., ἀπαρχὰς ἅλωνος οὐ –ήσεις *shalt* not *be slow to offer*, Lxx*Ex.*22.29(28): abs., ξενίας ἀεὶ φρόντιζε, μὴ καθυστέρει Men.*Mon.* 396; *delay*, Plb.5.16.5; of growing plants, *to be later*, Thphr.*CP*1. 17.2. 3. *fare badly*, ἐν αἷς (sc. πρεσβείαις) ἐν οὐδενὶ καθυστέρησεν ὁ δῆμος *OGI*339.22 (Sestos, ii B.C.): c. gen., *come short of*, πάσης τροφῆς Lxx*Si.*37.20; *lack*, ἀγαθοῦ νοῦ Phld.*Rh.*2.61 S.; δικαίου μηθενὸς κ. *SIG*568.13 (Halasarna, iii B.C.); *fail in*, πράξεων Ph.*Bel.*103. 11. 4. c. dupl. gen., *fail* a person *in*, ἐλιπάρεον [τὸν Ἀσκληπιὸν] μὴ –έειν μου τῆς θεραπείης Hp.*Ep.*15. 5. *to be kept waiting for* a thing, c. gen., ἐντονίων Ph.*Bel.*58.3; θανάτου Ps.-Luc.*Philopatr.* 16. **–ίζω**, = foreg. 2, περὶ τὴν σποράν *Gp.*2.13.2. **–ικῶς**, Adv. *behind* their *time*, Ptol.*Phas.*p.11 H.

καθῠφαίνω, *interweave, weave in*, Lxx*Ex.*28.17:—Med., aor. 1 part. καθυφηνάμενος *Lyr.Alex.Adesp.*10.15:—Pass., *to be inwoven*, Lxx*Ju.*10.21.

καθύφ-εσις, εως, ἡ, *collusion*, Poll.8.143; *praevaricatio*, *Gloss.* **–έτης**, ου, ὁ, *praevaricator*, ib. **–ίημι**, *give up, surrender treacherously*, [καιρὸν] ἐάν τις ἑκὼν καθυφῇ τοῖς ἐναντίοις καὶ προδῷ D.19.6, cf. 16.18, al.; τὰ τῆς πόλεως Id.58.6, cf. Luc.*Prom.*5; esp. in a lawsuit, κ. τὸν ἀγῶνα *conduct* it *collusively, compromise* it, D.21.151; οὐ μόνον τῷ μὴ καθυφεῖναι ταῦτα σεμνύνομαι Id.18.107: abs., καθυφέντων τῶν κατηγόρων *when* they *let the action drop*, Id.23.96. II. Med., καθυφίεσθαί τινι *give way, yield*, c. dat. pers., X.*HG*2.4.23; ἔν τινι *slacken*, ἐν μάχαις Polyaen.8.24.1: abs., Luc.*Abd.*7. 2. Med., with pf. Pass., used trans. like the Act., εἰ καθυφείμεθά τι τῶν πραγμάτων D. 3.8; καθυφεῖντο ἑαυτούς Plb.3.60.4; ἐπ' ἀργυρίῳ τὸ τίμημα καθυφειμένος Plu.*Cic.*8; οὐδὲν.. καθυφηκάμην J.*BJ*2.16.4; –ίενται τὴν τοῦ ἑνὸς τιμήν Ph.2.220. **–ίσταμαι**, pf. inf. καθυφεστάναι *to be really existent*, Jul.*Or.*4.163d.

κάθω, barbarism for καθίζω, Tim.*Pers.*168.

καθωπλισμένως, Adv. pf. part. Pass. (καθοπλίζω), *like armed warriors*, Sch.Ar.*Pl.*325.

καθωραΐζομαι, = ὡραΐζομαι, Phot. (ubi κατωρ–), Suid.

καθώς, Adv. = καθά, Hdt.9.82 codd., Arist.*Pr.*891^{b}34, *IG*5(2).344. 20 (Arc., iii B.C.), Wilcken *Chr.*11 *A* 53 (ii B.C.), *IG*2^2.1030.22 (i B.C.), al.; *even as*, *Ev.Jo.*15.12. 2. *how*, ὑπομιμνήσκειν κ... Aristeas 263, cf. *Act.Ap.*15.12. II. of Time, *as, when*, ib.7.17, Lxx2*Ma.*1.31, Aristeas 310. (Condemned by Phryn.397, Moer.212.)

καθώσπερ, Adv. = foreg., Him.*Or.*1.20.

καί, Conj., copulative, joining words and sentences, *and*; also Adv., *even, also, just*, freq. expressing emphatic assertion or assent, corresponding as positive to the negative οὐ (μή) or οὐδέ (μηδέ).

A. copulative, *and*, I. joining words or sentences to those preceding, ἦ, καὶ κυανέῃσιν ἐπ' ὀφρύσι νεῦσε Κρονίων Il.1.528, etc.: repeated with two or more Nouns, αἱ δὲ ἔλαφοι κ. δορκάδες κ. οἱ ἄγριοι οἶες κ. οἱ ὄνοι οἱ ἄγριοι X.*Cyr.*1.4.7; joining only the last pair, Cleom.2.1 (p.168.5 Z.), Phlp. *in APr.*239.30, etc., v.l. in Arist.*Po.*1451^{a}20; ὁ ὄχλος πλείων κ. πλείων ἐπέρρει more *and* more, X.*Cyr.*7.5.39; to add epithets after πολύς, πολλὰ κ. ἐσθλά Il.9.330; πολλὰ κ. μεγάλα D.28. 1, etc. 2. to add a limiting or defining expression, πρὸς μακρὸν ὄρος κ. Κύνθιον ὄχθον to the mountain *and specially* to.., *h.Ap.*17, cf. A.*Ag.* 63 (anap.), S.*Tr.*1277 (anap.) (sts. in reverse order, πρὸς δῶμα Διὸς κ. μακρὸν Ὄλυμπον Il.5.398); to add by way of climax, θεῶν.. κ. Ποσειδῶνος all the gods, *and above all*.., A.*Pers.*750, etc.; ἐχθροὶ κ. ἔχθιστοι Th.7.68; τινὲς κ. συχνοί Pl.*Grg.*455c; freq. ἄλλοι τε καί.., ἄλλως τε καί..., v. ἄλλος II.6, ἄλλως I.3; ὀλίγου τινὸς ἄξια κ. οὐδενός little *or* nothing, Id.*Ap.*23a: joined with the demonstr. Pron. οὗτος (q.v.), εἶναι.. δούλοισι, κ. τούτοισι ὡς δρηπέτῃσι Hdt.6.11, cf. 1.147; κ. ταῦτα *and* this *too*.., γελᾶν ἀναπείθειν, κ. ταῦθ' οὕτω πολέμιον ὄντα τῷ γέλωτι X.*Cyr.*2.2.16, etc. II. at the beginning of a sentence, 1. in appeals or requests, καί μοι δὸς τὴν χεῖρα Il.23.75; καί μοι λέγε.., καί μοι ἀπόκριναι.., Pl.*Euthphr.*3a, *Grg.*462b; freq. in Oratt., καί μοι λέγε.. τὸ ψήφισμα, καί μοι ἀνάγνωθι.., D.18.105, Lys.14.8, etc. 2. in questions, to introduce an objection or express surprise, κ. τίς τόδ' ἐξίκοιτ' ἂν ἀγγέλων τάχος; A.*Ag.*280; κ. πῶς...; *pray* how..? E. *Ph.*1348; κ. δὴ τί..; *but* then what..? Id.*Hel.*101; κ. ποῖον..; S.*Aj.* 462; κ. τίς εἶδε πώποτε βοῦς κριβανίτας; Ar.*Ach.*86; κἄπειτ' ἔκανες; E.*Med.*1398 (anap.); κ. τίς πώποτε χαριζόμενος ἑτέρῳ τοῦτο εἰργάσατο; Antipho 5.57, cf. Is.1.20, Isoc.12.23, Pl.*Tht.*163d, al. 3. = καίτοι, *and yet*, Ar.*Eq.*1245, E.*HF*509. 4. at the beginning of a speech, Lys.*Fr.*36a. III. after words implying sameness or likeness, *as*, γνώμῃσι ἐχρέωντο ὁμοίῃσι κ. σύ they had the same opinion *as* you, Hdt.7.50, cf. 84; ἴσον or ἴσα κ..., S.*OT*611, E.*El.*994; ἐν ἴσῳ (sc. ἐστὶ) κ. εἰ.. Th.2.60, etc. 2. after words implying comparison or opposition, αἱ δαπάναι οὐχ ὁμοίως κ. πρίν Id.7.28; πᾶν τοὐναντίον ἔχει νῦν τε κ. ὅτε.. Pl.*Lg.*967a. 3. to express simultaneity, ἦν ἦμαρ δεύτερον.., κἀγὼ κατηγόμην S.*Ph.*355, cf. Th.1.50; παρέρχονταί τε μέσαι νύκτες κ. ψύχεται [τὸ ὕδωρ] Hdt.4.181, cf. 3.108; [οἱ Λακεδαιμόνιοι] οὐκ ἔφθασαν τὴν ἀρχὴν κατασχόντες κ. Θηβαίοις εὐθὺς ἐπεβούλευσαν Isoc.8.98. IV. joining an affirm. clause with a neg., ἀλλ' ὥς τι δράσων εἶπε κοὐ θανούμενος S.*Tr.*160, etc. V. καί..., καί... correlative, *not only*.., *but also*.., κἀεὶ κ. νῦν, κ. τότε κ. νῦν, Pl.*Grg.*523a, *Phlb.*60b; κ. κατὰ γῆν κ. κατὰ θάλατταν X.*An.*1.1. 7. VI. by anacoluthon, ὡς φαμένη κ. κερδοσύνῃ ἡγήσατ' Ἀθήνη, for ὡς ἔφη κ..., Il.22.247; ἔρχεται δὲ αὐτῇ τε.. κ. τὸν υἱὸν ἔχουσα, for κ. ὁ υἱός, X.*Cyr.*1.3.1; ἄλλας τε κατηγεόμενοί σφι ὁδούς, κ. τέλος ἐγίνοντο Hdt.9.104; τοιοῦτος ὤν, κἀτ' ἀνὴρ ἔδοξεν εἶναι Ar.*Eq.*392, cf. *Nu.*624.

B. *even, also, just*, 1. τάχα κεν κ. ἀναίτιον αἰτιόῳτο *even* the innocent, Il.11.654, cf. 4.161, etc.; δόμεναι κ. μεῖζον ἄεθλον an *even* greater prize, 23.551, cf. 10.556, 5.362: with numerals, κ. πέντε *full* five, 23.833; γενομένης κ. δὶς ἐκκλησίας Th.1.44, cf. Hdt.2.44, 60, 68, al. (but ἐτῶν δύο κ. τριῶν two *or* three, Th.1.82, cf. X.*Eq.*4. 4). 2. *also*, κ. ἐγώ I *also*, Il.4.40; κ. αὐτοί they *also*, X.*An.*3.4. 44, etc.; Ἀγίας καὶ Σωκράτης κ. τούτω ἀπεθανέτην *likewise* died, ib. 2.6.30; in adding surnames, etc., Ὦχος ὁ κ. Δαρειαῖος Ctes.*Fr.*29. 49 (sed Photii est): Ptol. Papyri have nom. ὃς κ., gen. τοῦ κ. etc., Πανίσκος ὃς κ. Πετεμῖνις *PLond.*2.219(*b*)2 (ii B.C.); dat. τῷ κ. ib.(*a*)^{v}2, *PRein.*26.5 (ii B.C.); nom. ὁ κ. first in *PTeb.*110.1 (i B.C.), freq. later, *BGU*22.25 (ii A.D.), etc.; Ἰούδας ὁ κ. Μακκαβαῖος J.*AJ*12.6.4; Σαῦλος ὁ κ. Παῦλος *Act.Ap.*13.9: with ἄλλος, λαβέτω δὲ κ. ἄλλος Od.21.152; εἴπερ τι κ. ἄλλο, ὥς τις κ. ἄλλος, X.*Mem.*3.6.2, *An.*1.3.15, cf. Pl. *Phd.*59a, Ar.*Nu.*356: freq. in antithetic phrases, οὐ μόνον.., ἀλλὰ καὶ..., not only.., but *also*.., v. μόνος; οὐδὲν μᾶλλον.. ἢ οὐ καὶ.. Hdt.5.94, al. b. freq. used both in the anteced. and relat. clause, where we put *also* in the anteced. only, εἰ μὲν κ. σὺ εἶ τῶν ἀνθρώπων ὧνπερ κ. ἐγώ Pl.*Grg.*458a, cf. Il.6.476, X.*An.*2.1.21. 3. freq. in apodosi, after temporal Conjs., ἀλλ' ὅτε δή ῥα.., κ. τότε δή.. Il.1. 494, cf. 8.69, Od.14.112; also after εἰ, Il.5.897: in Prose, ὡς δὲ ἔδοξεν, κ. ἐχώρουν Th.2.93: as a Hebraism, κ. ἐγένετο.. κ... Lxx *Ge.*24.30, al., *Ev.Luc.*1.59, etc. 4. with Advs., to give emphasis, κ. κάρτα Hdt.6.125; κ. λίην *full* surely, Il.19.408, Od.1.46; κ. μᾶλλον Il.8.470, cf. E.*Heracl.*386; κ. πάλαι, κ. πάνυ, S.*OC*1252, Pl. *Chrm.*154e; κ. μάλα, κ. σφόδρα, in answers, Ar.*Nu.*1326, Pl.*La.* 191e. 5. with words expressing a minimum, *even so much as, were it but, just*, ἱέμενος κ. καπνὸν ἀποθρῴσκοντα νοῆσαι Od.1.58; οἷς ἡδὺ κ. λέγειν Ar.*Nu.*528; τίς δὲ κ. προσβλέψεται; who will *so much as* look at you? E.*IA*1192, cf. Ar.*Ra.*614, Pl.*Ap.*28b, 35b. **6.** *just*, τοῦτ' αὐτὸ κ. νοσοῦμεν 'tis *just* that that ails me, E.*Andr.*906, cf. *Ba.*616, S.*Tr.*490, Ar.*Pax*892, *Ra.*73, Pl.*Grg.*456a, *Tht.*166d: freq. with a relat., τὸ κ. κλαίουσα τέτηκα Il.3.176; διὸ δὴ καὶ... Th.1.128, etc.: also in interrogations (usu. to be rendered by emphasis in intonation), ποίου χρόνου δὲ καὶ πεπόρθηται πόλις; and *how long ago* was the city sacked? A.*Ag.*278; ποῦ καὶ σφε θάπτει; *where* is he burying her? E.*Alc.*834, cf. S.*Aj.*1290, al., X.*An.*5.8.2, Ar.*Pax*1289, Pl. *Euthphr.*6b, D.4.46, etc. **7.** *even, just*, implying assent, ἔπειτά με κ. λίποι αἰών thereafter let life *e'en* leave me, Il.5.685, cf. 17.647, 21.274, Od.7.224. **8.** κ. εἰ *even if*, of a whole condition represented as an extreme case, opp. εἰ κ. *although, notwithstanding that*, of a condition represented as immaterial even if fulfilled, cf. Il.4.347, 5.351, Od.13.292, 16.98 with Il.5.410, Od.6.312, 8.139, etc.; εἰ κ. ἠπιστάμην if I *had* been able, Pl.*Phd.*108d, cf. *Lg.*663d. (This remark does not apply to cases where εἰ and καί each exert their force separately, as εἴ περ ἀδειής τ' ἐστί, καὶ εἰ.. *and if*.. Il.7.117, cf. Hdt.5.78, etc.) **9.** before a Participle, to represent either καὶ εἰ.., or εἰ καί.., *although, albeit*, Ἕκτορα κ. μεμαῶτα μάχης σχήσεσθαι ὀΐω, for ἢν κ. μεμάῃ, *how much soever* he rage, *although* he rage, Il.9.655; τί σὺ ταῦτα, κ. ἐσθλὸς ἐών, ἀγορεύεις; (for εἰ κ. ἐσθλὸς εἶ) 16.627, cf. 13.787, Od.2.343, etc.; κ. τύραννος ὢν ὅμως S.*OC*851.

C. Position: καί *and*, is by Poets sts. put after another word, ἔγνωκα, τοῖσδε κοὐδὲν ἀντειπεῖν ἔχω, for καὶ τοῖσδε οὐδέν A.*Pr.*51, cf. Euph.51.7, etc. **2.** καί *also*, sts. goes between a Prep. and its case, ἐν κ. θαλάσσᾳ Pi.*O.*2.28. **3.** very seldom at the end of a verse, S.*Ph.*312, Ar.*V.*1193.

D. crasis: with ᾰ, as κἄν, κἀγαθοί, etc.; with ε, as κἀγώ, κἄπειτα, etc., Dor. κἠγώ, κἤπειτα, etc.; with η, as χἠ, χἡμέρη, χἠμεῖς, etc.; with ῐ in χἰκετεύετε, χἰλαρή; with ο, as χὠ, χὤστις, etc.; with υ in χὑμεῖς, χὑποχείριον, etc.; with ω in the pron. ᾧ, χᾧ; with αι, as κᾀσχρῶν; with αυ, as καὐτός; with ει, as κεἰ, κεἰς (but also κἀς), κᾆτα; with εὐ-, as κεὐγένεια, κεὐσταλής; with οι in χοἰ (χᾠ *EM*816.34); with ου in χοὖτος, κοὐ, κοὐδέ, and the like.

καιάδας, ου, Dor. α, ὁ, *a pit* or *underground cavern* at Sparta, into which state-prisoners or their corpses were thrown, Th.1.134, Paus. 4.18.4:—the forms **καιάτας** and **καιέτας** are found in Eust.1478.45: —also **καιετός**, ὁ, *fissure produced by earthquake*, Str.8.5.7: hence Λακεδαίμονα **καιετάεσσαν** *full of hollows* or *abysses*, read by Zenod. for κητώεσσαν in Od.4.1: but Εὐρώτας καιετάεις Call.*Fr.*224, is expld. by καλαμινθώδης in Str.l.c.; cf. **καιέτα**· καλαμίνθη (Boeot.), Hsch.; **καιέτας** in Apollon.*Lex.* s.v. κητώεσσαν; gen. pl. **καιατῶν** Anon. Lond.36.57.

καὶ γάρ, *for also, for in fact*, combining καί (in various senses) with γάρ, Il.3.188, Od.18.261, Hdt.3.15, etc.; also, *for else*, Arist.*Pol.* 1280^{a}36: with strengthening Particles, κ. γ. δή *for of a surety*, Il. 16.810; in Ep., κ. γ. ῥα 1.113; in Att., κ. γ. καί, κ. γ. οὖν, Pl.*Prt.* 317c, X.*An.*1.9.8, etc.

καὶ...γε, v. γε II.1. **καὶ δέ**, v. δέ II.2b. **καὶ δή, καὶ δὴ καί**, v. δή IV.4. **καὶ εἰ**, by crasis **κεἰ**, v. καί B.8, D.

καιετάεις, καιέτας, καιετός, v. sub καιάδας.

καἶκα, by crasis for καὶ αἶκα (v. αἰ), Theoc.3.27.

καικίας, ου, ὁ, *north-east wind*, Arist.*Mete.*363^{b}17, *Pr.*940^{a}18, *Mu.* 394^{b}22, *IG*14.1308, Plu.*Sert.*17, *Gp.*1.11.2; καικίας καὶ συκοφαντίας πνεῖ Ar.*Eq.*437. (Derived from the river Κάϊκος by Ach.Tat.*Intr. Arat.*33.)

καιλοῖα, v. κελοῖα. **καὶ μήν**, v. μήν II.2.

καίμιον, τό, *fowl*, *POxy.*1656.14 (iv/v A.D.). (Coptic *gaime.*)

καινέω, prob. misspelling for καινίζω in aor. 1 part. καινήσασα, *PThead.*19.11 (iv A.D.).

καινία· νίκη, Hsch.

καινίζω, (καινός) prop. *make new* or *strange*, but usu. in deriv. senses, καί τι καινίζει στέγη the house *has* something *new, strange* about it, S.*Tr.*867; κ. εὐχάς *offer new, strange* prayers, E.*Tr.*889; ἀμφίβληστρον ὡς ἐκαίνισαν (corr. Blomf. for ᾧ σ' ἐκαίνισαν) how they *devised a new, strange* net, A.*Ch.*492; ὅστις τόνδ' ἐκαίνισεν λόγον E. *Fr.*598 (= Critias 21 D.); so later, *innovate*, καθολικόν τι καινίζει *OGI*669.47:—Pass., ib.62 (Egypt, i A.D.), Just.*Nov.*7.12 *Ep.*; πολλὰ τῷ βίῳ κ. Vett.Val.270.27; in Poets, esp. *use for the first time, handsel*, καίνισον ζυγόν *try on* thy *new* yoke, A.*Ag.*1071; πρῶτος τὸν ταῦρον ἐκαίνισεν first *handseled* the bull [of Perilaus], Call.*Fr.*119; κ. δόρυ *first to feel* the spear, Lyc.530.

καινίς, ίδος, ἡ, *knife*, v.l. for κοπίς, Luc.*Asin.*40, cf. Hdn.*Epim.*63.

καίν-ισις, εως, ἡ, *renovation*, ἡ τῶν πατρίων κ. καὶ μεταβολή J.*AJ* 18.1.1; v.l. for -ωσις in Ph.2.45. **-ισμός**, ὁ, *renewal*, *PLond.* 2.354.16 (ii B.C.). **2.** *innovation*, Vett.Val.192.15, Just.*Nov.*20.4, 118.6. **-ιστής**, οῦ, ὁ, = *innovator*, *Gloss.*

καινίτα· ἀδελφή, and **καινίτας**· ἀδελφοὺς καὶ ἀδελφάς, Hsch. (For καίνιτα, -ιτας, i.e. κασιγνήτα, -ήτας.)

καινό-γρᾰφος, ον, *written in a new style*, σύνθεσις prob. for -γραφής in Philic.ap.Heph.9.4. II. parox., καινογράφος, ὁ, *composer in a new style*, prob. in Anon.Metr.*Oxy.*220 vi 3. **-κουφον**, τό, *new cask*, *POxy.*1911.181 (vi A.D.). **-λεκτος**, ον, *new-fangled*, Hdn. *Epim.*3. **-λογέω**, *tell new* or *strange tales*, cj. for κενο- in J.*Ap.* 1.24; *say something new*, Anon.Lond.34.7. **-λογία**, ἡ, *strange language* or *phraseology*, Plb.38.9.2, D.H.*Lys.*3; *telling of strange tales*, κ. τίς ἐστιν ὁ μῦθος Str.1.2.8. **-λόγος**, ον, *using new phrases*, ποιητής Eust.1801.27.

καινόν, τό, v. καινός.

καινο-πᾰγής, ές, v. καινοπαθής. **-πᾰθέω**, *suffer things unheard of*, Plu.2.1106a. **-πᾰθής**, ές, *new-suffered*: *unheard of*, πήματα S.*Tr.*1277 (anap., v.l. -παγῆ). **-πηγής**, ές, *newly put together, new-made*, A.*Th.*642. **-πήμων**, ονος, ὁ, ἡ, *new to misery*, δμωΐδες ib. 363 (lyr.). **-ποιέω**, pf. κεκαινοποίηκα Plb.4.2.4:—*make new, renew*, τὴν θεραπείαν Id.15.25.17; κ. ἐλπίδας *gives new life to* hopes, Id.3. 70.11; κ. τά τινος ἁμαρτήματα *renew the memory of*..., Id.30.4.17:— Pass., ἐκαινοποιήθη τὰ τῆς ὀργῆς Id.21.31.3, cf. 11.4.5, 31.28.9; of a plaster, Philum.*Ven.*7.9. II. *make changes, innovate*, πολλὰ κ. [ἡ τύχη] Plb.1.4.5, etc.: abs., Luc.*Prom.Es* 3, etc.:—Pass., τί καινοποιηθὲν λέγεις; what *new-fangled, strange* words are these? S.*Tr.*873, cf. Plb.9.2.4; τὰ καινοποιηθέντα *innovations*, *OGI*669.44 (Egypt, i A.D.), cf. *POxy.*237 viii 42 (ii A.D.). **-ποιητής**, οῦ, ὁ, *inventor of new pleasures*, X.*Cyr.*8.8.16. **-ποιΐα**, ἡ, *complete change*, περί τι Plb.4.2. 10: c.gen., Vett.Val.48.10 (pl.), al. **-ποιός**, *novator*, *Gloss.* **-πρᾱγέω**, Gramm., *coin new forms* or *phrases*, in Pass., Eust.36.16. **-πρᾱγία**, ἡ, *innovation*, f.l. for κοινοπραγία in D.S.15.8. **-πρέπεια**, ἡ, *novelty*, τοῦ σχήματος Eust.93.31. **-πρεπής**, ές, *novel*, σχήματα Hermog.*Id.*1.12; of innovations in law, κ. πρὸς τὸ πρότερον Just. *Nov.*105.1. Adv. -πῶς *in a new-fangled manner*: Comp. -πεστέρως, λέγειν Arist.*Metaph.*989^{b}6: Sup. -πέστατα D.C.79.11.

καινός, ή, όν, *new, fresh*, ἔργα οὔτ' ὦν κ. οὔτε παλαιά Hdt.9.26; κ. ὁμιλία A.*Eu.*406; κ. λόγους φέρειν to bring *news*, Id.*Ch.*659; τί δ' ἐστὶ κ.; S.*OC*722, cf. *Ph.*52; τὰ κ. τοῖς πάλαι τεκμαίρεται Id.*OT*916; θυγῆρα καινῷ καινὸν ἐν πεπλώματι Id.*Tr.*613; ἢ βούλεσθε περιιόντες πυνθάνεσθαι, "λέγεταί τι κ.;" D.4.10; γένοιτ' ἄν τι -ότερον ἤ.. ibid.; ἐκ καινῆς (sc. ἀρχῆς) *anew, afresh*, Th.3.92, Thphr.*CP*5.1.11, *Jahresh.*23 *Beibl.*91 (Pamphyl., i A.D.), etc. (also ἐκ καινοῦ *CPR*244.14 (iii A.D.)); esp. of *new* dramas, τραγῳδῶν γιγνομένων καινῶν Aeschin.3.34; briefly τραγῳδοῖς κ. at the representation of the *new* tragedies, Docum.ap.D. 18.54; τραγῳδῶν τῇ κ. [ἐπιδείξει] ib.55; καινῇ κωμῳδῶν, τραγῳδῶν, *CIG*2759 iii (Aphrodisias); but κ. κωμῳδία, τραγῳδία, of a *new style* of drama, *IG*7.1773 (Thebes, ii A.D.). **2.** *newly-made*, κύλικες, τριήρης, ὀθόνια, οἶνος, *SIG*1026.26 (Cos, iv/iii B.C.), *IG*2^{2}.1623.289, *PLond.*2.402^{v}12 (ii B.C.), *Ostr.*1142.4 (iii A.D.). **3.** Adv. -νῶς *newly, afresh*, Alex.240.4. II. *newly-invented, novel*, καινότεραι τέχναι Batr.116; κ. προσφέρειν σοφά E.*Med.*298; ἔνθα τι κ. ἐλέχθη Philox.3.23; οὐκ ἀείδω τὰ παλαιά, καινὰ γὰρ ἀμὰ κρείσσω Tim.*Fr.*21; κ. θεοί *strange* gods, Pl.*Euthphr.*3b; κ. δαιμόνια Id.*Ap.*24c; κ. τινες σοφισταί Id.*Euthd.*271b; κ. καὶ ἄτοπα ὀνόματα Id.*R.*405d; καινὰ ἐπιμηχανᾶσθαι *innovations*, X.*Cyr.*8.8.16; οὐδὲν -ότερον εἰσέφερε τῶν ἄλλων he introduced *as little of anything new as* others, Id.*Mem.*1.1.3, cf. Pl.*Phd.*115b; πεπόνθαμεν -ότατον D.35.26; τὸ κ. τοῦ πολέμου prob. f.l. for κενόν (v. κενός), Th.3.30; οὐ καινόν nothing *to be surprised at*, Hp.*Int.*17; τὸ -ότατον *what is strangest*, parenthetically, Luc.*Nigr.*22, al.; εἰ χρὴ -ότατα μᾶλλον ἢ κακουργότατα εἰπεῖν Antipho 2.4.2. Adv., μὴ σὺ -νῶς μοι λάλει *in new, strange style*, Alex.144, cf. Pl.*Phdr.*267b: Comp. -οτέρως, νοῆσαι περί τινος Arist.*Cael.*308^{b}31; *without precedent*, -νῶς κατακριθῆναι *OGI*669.46, 49 (Egypt, i A.D.). III. κ. ἄνθρωπος, = Lat. *novus homo*, Plu.*Cat.Ma.*1; πράγματα κ., = *res novae*, Id.*Cic.*14, cf. 2.212c.

καινό-σπουδος, ον, *fond of novelty*, τὸ περὶ τὰς νοήσεις κ. Longin.5. 1. **-σχημάτιστος**, ον, *newly* or *strangely formed*, Eust.141. 32. **-σχήμων**, ον, gen. ονος, = foreg., Id.1479.57, Sch.rec.S.*Aj.* 1398. **-τάφια**· νεκροτάφια, Hsch. (leg. κενο-). **-τάφον** σχῆμα, for καινὸν σχῆμα τάφου, *AP*7.686 (Pall.).

καινότης, ητος, ἡ, *newness, freshness*, Plu.*Per.*13; αἱ τῶν δερμάτων -τητες Philostr.*Ep.*18. **2.** *novelty*, λόγου Th.3.38; τῶν εὑρημένων Isoc.10.2; χρὴ γὰρ εἰς ὄχλον φέρειν... ὅσ' ἄν τις καινότητ' ἔχειν δοκῇ Anaxandr.54.6; ἡ ἐν τοῖς σχηματισμοῖς κ. D.H.*Amm.*2.3: pl., καινότητες *novelties*, Isoc.2.41; αἱ κ. καὶ αἱ ὑπερβολαὶ τῶν τιμῶν D.C. 44.3.

καινο-τομέω, *cut fresh into*, in mining, *open a new vein*, X.*Vect.*4.27 sq., Phot.; in road-making, metaph., ἀτραπὸν ἄλλην Ph.2.445, cf. J. *BJ*5.9.4, Luc.*Rh.Pr.*10 (Pass.). II. mostly metaph., *begin something new, institute anew*, τελετήν τινι Ar.*V.*876 (anap.): abs., *make changes* or *innovations* in the state, Id.*Ec.*584 (anap.), Arist.*Pol.* 1305^{b}41, 1316^{b}19, Plb.15.30.1, *PLips.*35.19 (iv A.D.), etc.: generally, μὴ καινοτομεῖν Phld.*Mus.*p.9K.; κ. τι νέον Pl.*Lg.*797c, cf. 709a; κ. περὶ τὰ θεῖα Id.*Euthphr.*3b, 16a; περὶ τῶν θείων ib.5a; τὰ θεῖα Jul.*Or.* 5.159b; κ. τὴν περὶ τὰ τέκνα κοινότητα Arist.*Pol.*1266^{a}35; οὐθὲν κ. εἰς [τὰ γινόμενα περὶ θεῶν σεβασμούς] D.H.7.70, cf. *Comp.*25:—Pass., Pl.*Lg.*797b, D.59.75. **-τόμημα**, ατος, τό, *innovation, new form*, ἐγκλημάτων Procop.*Arc.*21 (pl.). **-τομητέον**, *one must be an innovator*, Ath.Mech.8.2. **-τομία**, ἡ, *opening of new mines*, Hyp. *Eux.*36 (pl.), *IG*2^{2}.1587.5 (prob.), Poll.3.87, 7.98 (pl.). II. mostly metaph., *making anew, inventing*, ὀνομάτων Pl.*Lg.*715d; *innovation*, κ. περὶ τοὺς λόγους Plu.*Cic.*2: in Music, Satyr.*Vit.Eur.Fr.*39 xxii 5; μηδεμίαν κ. γίγνεσθαι Mitteis *Chr.*96 ii 19 (iv A.D.): pl., *innovations* in the state, Lat. *res novae*, Pl.*Lg.*950a; κ. τῆς πολιτείας Plb.13.1.2: in Law, *interference* with another's right or easement, Just.*Nov.*7.5.1: pl., ib.63 tit. **2.** = καινότης, *novelty, strangeness*, ἡ κ. τοῦ συμβαίνοντος Plb.1.23.10: pl., Plu.*Alex.*72. **-τόμος**, ον, (τέμνω) *innovating*, ἔχουσι... οἱ τοῦ Σωκράτους λόγοι.. τὸ κομψὸν καὶ τὸ κ. are marked by cleverness and *novelty*, Arist.*Pol.*1265^{a}12; of persons, Hermog.*Inv.*3.5: metaph., -τόμον πρᾶγμα ὁ πόλεμος ibid. **-τροπία**, ἡ, *strangeness*, Eust.1200.56. **-τροπος**, ον, *new-fashioned, unusual*, μῦθος [E.]*Fr.*1132.49 (lyr.); χειμών App.*BC*5.90.

καινουργ-έω, *make new*, Alciphr.3.3; *re-create*, τινα Zos.Alch. p.108B. 2. *begin something new*, τι Hp.*VM*21; τί καινουργεῖς; what *new plan art thou meditating?* E.*IA*2 (anap.); κ. λόγον *speak new, strange* words, ib.838; *coin*, ὄνομα Dam.*Pr.*439: abs., ἐπὶ τὸ κ. φέρου Antiph.29: usu. in bad sense, *make innovations*, περί τι X.*HG*6.2.16, cf. D.H.11.21:—Pass., τὰ καινουργούμενα *all attempts at alteration*, Arist.*Mu.*398ᵃ35. **-ής**, ές, *newly made*, τρίποδες Sch.Il.9.122. **-ησις**, εως, ἡ, *new manufacture*, Suid. s.v. καταβολή. **-ία**, ἡ, *making new*: *innovation* in the state, ταραχὴ καὶ κ. Isoc.6.50; of Christianity, prob. in *OGI*569.18 (Arycanda, iv A.D.); *renewal, re-creation*, τοῦ ὅλου Max.Tyr.41.4; of *manufacture*, J.*AJ*12.2.9, cf. D.H.*Isoc.*9, Hierocl.p.52A. **-ιος**, α, ον, *newly made*, *Sammelb.* 7033.44 (v A.D.), *Gloss.*; χύτρα Aët.8.6. **-ισμός**, ὁ, = καινουργία, Suid. (v.l. -ησμός). **-ός**, όν, (ἔργον) *producing changes*, πόλεμος Hld.9.5; κ. βασάνων *inventing new* tortures, Lxx 4*Ma.*11.23. II. Pass., τὸ κ. *novelty*, Luc.*Prom.Es*3; τῶν κολάσεων τὸ πρὸς ὠμότητα κ. Id.*Cat.*26.

καινο-φᾰνής, ές, *appearing new*, λέξεις Eust.39.16. **-φῐλος**, ον, *often changing one's friends*, Phot., Suid. **-φωνέω**, *use new words*, Eust.67.6. **-φωνία**, ἡ, *vocum novitas*, *Gloss.*, cf. Phlp. *in APo.* 11.7. **-φωνος**, ον, *new-sounding*, λέξεις Eust.1761.23, etc. **-χωρισμός**, ὁ, *renewed execution*, συναλλάξεως *POxy.*1644.19 (i B.C.).

καινόω, (καινός) *make new, change*, τὰ ἐπιβουλεύματα D.C.47.4; of language, D.H.*Th.*21:—Pass., of political changes, Th.1.71; καινοῦσθαι τὰς διανοίας in *inventing new* devices, Id.3.82, cf. Ph.1.326, 2.156. II. = καινίζω, *use for the first time, handsel*, Hdt.2.100. III. *renew*, φόβον Ph.2.78.

καί νύ (κε), *and now*, κ. νύ κεν.. ἄσπετον ἤρατο κῦδος, εἰ μὴ.. Il. 3.373, cf. 8.90, Od.24.50; so κ. νύ κε δὴ Il.17.530: also folld. by εἰ without μή, Od.11.317; by ἀλλά, ib.630: with no protasis, κ. νύ κεν ἐς δεκάτην γενεὴν ἕτερόν γ' ἔτι βόσκοι 14.325.

καίνῡμι, *overcome*, Act. only in imper. καινύτω, μή σ' ἀπάτη φρένα κ. Emp.23.9:—elsewh. **καίνυμαι**, *surpass, excel*, in impf., c. acc. pers. et inf. modi, ἐκαίνυτο φῦλ' ἀνθρώπων νῆα κυβερνῆσαι he *surpassed* mankind in steering, Od.3.282: c. dat. rei, ἣ φῦλον γυναικῶν φῦλον ἐκαίνυτο... εἴδεΐ τε μεγέθει τε Hes.*Sc.*4: more freq. in pf. and plpf. κέκασμαι, ἐκεκάσμην, Dor. κέκαδμαι, *excel* one in a thing, c. acc. pers. et dat. rei, ἐγχείῃ δ' ἐκέκαστο Πανέλληνας Il.2.530; ὃς ἡλικίην ἐκέκαστο ἔγχεΐ θ' ἱπποσύνῃ τε 16.808; ὃς ἀνθρώπους ἐκέκαστο κλεπτοσύνῃ θ' ὅρκῳ τε Od.19.395: c. inf. pro dat. rei, ὁμηλικίην ἐκέκαστο γνῶναι *surpassed* them all in knowledge, 2.158; ἐκέκαστο ἰθύνειν A.R.2.867: c. dat. rei only, δόλοισι κεκασμένε *excellent* in wiles, Il.4.339; παντοίῃς ἀρετῇσι κεκασμένον ἐν Δαναοῖσιν Od.4.725; μαντοσύνῃ 9.509, cf. Il.5.54; [ἀγλαΐῃ] μετὰ δμῳῇσι κέκασσαι Od.19.82; ἐκ πάντων τέχνῃσι κεκασμένος Οὐρανιώνων Hes.*Th.*929: c. gen., τῶν σε... πλούτῳ τε καὶ υἱάσι φασὶ κεκάσθαι *above* all these (as if ἐκ τούτων), Il.24.546. II. later, *to be adorned, equipped*, ἐλέφαντι ὦμον κεκαδμένον Pi.*O.*1.27; φρουραῖς κέκασται *is well furnished* with..., E.*El.*616; πανουργίαις μείζοσι κεκασμένον Ar.*Eq.*685; μῦθος ἀληθείῃ κέκασται *AP*3.18.1 (Inscr. Cyzic.): abs., εὖ κεκασμένον δόρυ a *well-armed* band, A.*Eu.* 766.—Poet. word (Pl.*R.*334b is borrowed from Od.19.395; κεκασμένος etym. of κεστός Corn.*ND*24.)

καὶ νῦν, *so now*, Hom., mostly to confirm a general statement by an example, e.g. Il.1.109; ὡς κ. ν. Od.1.35; κ. ν. ἦ τοι 4.151.

καίνω, A.*Ag.*1562, *Ch.*886: fut. κᾰνῶ E.*HF*1074 (lyr.): aor. 2 ἔκᾰνον A.*Ch.*930; inf. κανεῖν, Dor. κανῆν Theoc.24.92: pf. κέκονα S. *Fr.*1058:—Pass., A.*Th.*347 (lyr.), E.*IT*27:—*kill, slay*, A.*Th.*630 (lyr.), S.l.c., Timocr.1.9, Theoc. l.c.: once in X., *Cyr.*4.2.24 (nisi leg. κατακ-, q.v.).

καίνωσις, εως, ἡ, *renewal*, ὧν ὑπέμεινε Ph.2.45 (v.l. -ισις); τῶν λόγων *news*, J.*AJ*18.6.10.

καίπερ, in Hom. always with a word between (exc. καί περ πολλὰ παθόντα Od.7.224); but one word in Pi. and Prose, and usu. in Trag. I. *even*, καὶ αὐτοί περ πονεώμεθα Il.10.70. II. *although, albeit*, usu. c. part., καὶ αὐτῇ περ νοεούσῃ 1.577; καὶ ἀχνύμενός περ ἑταίρου 8.125; καὶ πρίν περ θυμῷ μεμαώς 5.135; καὶ κήδεά περ πεπαθυίῃ Od.17.555: so in later Poets, κ. ἀχνύμενος Pi.*I.*8(7).4, cf. *N.*6.6; καὶ θουρός περ ὤν A.*Fr.*199.2; κ. αὐθάδη φρονῶν Id.*Pr.*907; κ. οὐ στέργων ὅμως Id.*Th.*712; κ. οὐ δύσοργος ὤν S.*Ph.*377: preceded by ὅμως, Pl. *R.*495d: the part. must freq. be supplied, καὶ θεός περ [ὤν] A.*Ag.* 1203; γιγνώσκω σαφῶς, κ. σκοτεινὸς [ὤν], τήν γε σὴν αὐδὴν ὅμως S.*OT* 1326; also εἰ μέμονάς γε, καὶ ὀψέ περ [ἐρυόμενος], ... ἐρύεσθαι Il.9.247; ἐπιμνησαίμεθα χάρμης, καὶ πρὸς δαίμονά περ [μαχούμενοι] 17.104; λέγεις ἀληθῆ, κ. ἐκ μακροῦ χρόνου [λέγων] S.*OT*1141; ἀλλ' ἔστιν ὧν δεῖ, κ. οὐ πολλῶν ἄπο, = καίπερ οὐ πολλῶν ὄντων, Id.*Ph.*647: with finite Verbs only as dub. l., κ. ἔχει (leg. καίπερ) Pi.*N.*4.36; κ. (leg. καίτοι) ἐκεῖνό γε ᾤμην τι εἶναι Pl.*Smp.*219c.

καίπετος· ἀξίνη, Hsch.

καί ῥα, Ep., to make a transition, *and so*, Il.1.360,569, etc.

καίραμα· μέρος νεός, ἢ ἀμφίεσμα, Hsch.

καιρία, ἡ, *tape* or *cord* used for ligatures, etc., Archig.ap.Orib.47.13.7, Heraclas ib.48.1.1. (From κείρεσθαι or καῖρος acc. to Sch. Orib.4p.537D.; cf. κειρία.)

καιρ-ικός, ή, όν, *timely*, ἀπαγγελίαι *IG*3.769. 2. *appropriate to certain times* or *seasons, seasonable*, ἄνθη *PMag.Leid.W.*24.1. b. Astrol., *belonging to the* καιρός or *chronocratory*, κ. χρόνοι Ἀφροδίτης Nech.ap.Vett.Val.289.37. c. Astron., ὧραι κ. hours of the kind *that vary in length with the season*, opp. ἰσημεριναί, Ptol.*Alm.*4.11, 7.3, *Tetr.*76. 3. Gramm., *temporal*, Eust.17.3. 4. καιρικαὶ βαφαί, dub. sens. in Zos.Alch.p.246B., cf. p.228, 239, al. **-ῖμος**, η, ον, = καίριος, dub. in Macho ap.Ath.13.581b, cf. Al.*Le.*16.21; -ώτερος οἶνος *PFlor.*143.2 (iii A.D.).

καιριολεκτέω, (λέγω) *use a word appropriately*, Eust.909.17 (Pass.).

καίριος, α, ον, also ος, ον Thgn.341, A.*Ch.*1064, S.*Ph.*637, Luc.*Nigr.* 35: I. (καιρός II) in Hom. always of Place, *in* or *at the right place*, hence of parts of the body, καίριον *a vital part*, Il.8.84,326; ἐν καιρίῳ 4.185; ὁ αὐχὴν ἐστι τῶν καιρίων X.*Eq.*12.2, cf. 8 (Sup.); of wounds, *mortal*, καιρίῃ (sc. πληγῇ) τετύφθαι Hdt.3.64; πέπληγμαι καιρίαν πληγήν A.*Ag.*1343; καιρίας πληγῆς τυχεῖν ib.1292, cf. X.*Cyr.*5.4.5; καιρίας (v.l. -ίους) σφαγάς E.*Ph.*1431; ἔχειν τὴν καταφορὰν κ. Plb.2.33.3; but also, *grave, serious*, νουσήματα, τρώματα, Hp.*Morb.*1.5: generally, καιριωτάτης τετευχέναι χώρας *Theol.Ar.*44. II. of Time, *in season, timely*, εὕρισκε ταῦτα καιριώτατα εἶναι Hdt.1.125, cf. Emp.111.6; χρὴ λέγειν τὰ κ. A.*Th.*1, cf. *Ch.*582; καίριοι συμφοραί ib.1064; εἴ τι κ. λέγει S.*Ant.*724; δρᾶν, φρονεῖν τὰ κ., Id.*Aj.*120, *El.*228 (lyr.); καίριος σπουδή Id.*Ph.*637; -ωτέρα βουλή E.*Heracl.*471; κ. ἐνθύμημα X. *HG*4.5.4; τὸ ἀεὶ κ. Id.*Cyr.*4.2.12, etc.; πρὸς τὸ κ., = καιρίως, S.*Ph.* 525; *critical*, αὐτὰ τὰ κ. ἔχων ἑκκαίδεκα (sc. ἔτη) *AP*12.22 (Scyth.); agreeing with the subject, καιρίαν δ' ἡμῖν ὁρῶ στείχουσαν Ἰοκάστην coming *at the right time*, S.*OT*631; καίριος ἤλυθες E.*El.*598; καιρία (Dind. for καὶ δορία) πτώσιμος falling *at the exact* or *fatal moment*, A. *Ag.*1122 (lyr.); τὰ κ. *timely circumstances, opportunities*, Th.4.10; *emergencies*, D.C.*Fr.*70.8. 2. *lasting but for a season*, *AP*12.224 (Strato). III. *chief, principal*, τὰ καιριώτατα τῶν κλημάτων Thphr. *CP*3.15.4, cf. 6.4.2. IV. Adv. -ίως *in season, seasonably*, κ. εἰρημένον A.*Ag.*1372; σκοπεῖν E.*Rh.*339: Comp. -ωτέρως X.*Cyr.*4.5.49. 2. *mortally*, οὐτασμένος A.*Ag.*1344, cf. Plb.2.69.2.

καιροδᾰπιστής, οῦ, ὁ, (καῖρος, δάπις) *carpet-weaver*, Judeich *Altertümer von Hierapolis* 342 (pl.).

καιρόεις, v. καιροσέων.

καιρομᾰνέω, prob. f.l. for **καιρονομέω**, *guide in season*, εἰς τέχνην ὄρνιν ἐκαιρονόμεις (-μάνεις cod.) *AP*9.272 (Bianor).

καιροπτία or **-εία**, ἡ, as if from *καιρόπτης, διὰ καιροπτείας by *watching their opportunity*, J.*Ap.*2.11.

καιρός, ὁ, *due measure, proportion, fitness* (not in Hom.), καιρὸς δ' ἐπὶ πᾶσιν ἄριστος (which became a prov.) Hes.*Op.*694, Thgn. 401; κ. παντὸς ἔχει κορυφάν Pi.*P.*9.78; κ. χάριτος A.*Ag.*787 (anap.) (cf. ὑποκάμπτω II); εἰ ὁ κ. ἦν σαφής the *distinction*, the *point*, E.*Hipp.* 386; ἡ ἀπορία ἔχει τινὰ κ. has some *point* or *importance*, Arist. *Metaph.*1043ᵇ25; καιροῦ πέρα beyond *measure, unduly*, A.*Pr.*507; μείζων τοῦ κ. γαστήρ X.*Smp.*2.19; καιροῦ μεῖζον E.*Fr.*626 codd.; προσωτέρω or πορρωτέρω τοῦ κ., X.*An.*4.3.34, *HG*7.5.13; ὀξύτερα τοῦ κ. Pl.*Plt.*307b; νωθεστέρα τοῦ κ. ib.310e; ὑπερβάλλων τῇ φιλοτιμίᾳ τὸν κ. Plu.*Ages.*8, cf. Hp.*Loc.Hom.*44. II. of Place, *vital part* of the body (cf. καίριος I), ἐς καιρὸν τυπείς E.*Andr.*1120. III. more freq. of Time, *exact* or *critical time, season, opportunity*, χρόνου κ. S.*El.* 1292: usu. alone, κ. [ἐστιν] ἐν ᾧ χρόνος οὐ πολὺς κτλ. Hp. *Praec.*1, cf. Chrysipp. et Archig.ap.Daremberg *Notices et extr. des MSS. médicaux* 1p.200; κ. ὀξύς Hp.*Aph.*1.1; κ. πρὸς ἀνθρώπων βραχὺ μέτρον ἔχει 'time and tide wait for no man', Pi.*P.*4.286; κ. ὄλβου, = καίριος ὄλβος, Id.*N.*7.58; δηλοῦν, ὅ τι περ δύναται κ. Ar.*Ec.*576 codd. (sed leg. δύνασαι); τίνα κ. τοῦ παρόντος βελτίω ζητεῖτε; D.3.16; κ. δόσιος *for* giving, Hp.*Acut.*20; κ. τοῦ ποτισμοῦ, τῆς τρύγης, *BGU*1003.12 (iii B.C.), *PStrassb.*1.8 (v A.D.); τὰ ἐκ τοῦ κ. προγινόμενα Plb.6.32.3; καιρὸν παριέναι to let *the time* go by, Th.4.27 (so in pl., τοὺς κ. παριέναι Pl.*R.*374c; τοὺς κ. ὑφαιρεῖσθαι Aeschin.3.66); κ. τῶν πραγμάτων τοῖς ἐναντίοις καθυφιέναι καὶ προδοῦναι D.19.6; καιροῦ (τοῦ κ.) τυχεῖν E.*Hec.* 593, Pl.*Lg.*687a, Men.*Mon.*281; καιρὸν εἰληφέναι Lys.13.6 (but καιρὸς ἐλάμβανε Th.2.34; cf. καιροῦ διδόντος Lib.*Or.*45.7); καιροῦ λαβέσθαι Luc.*Tim.*13; καιρὸν ἁρπάσαι Plu.*Phil.*15; κ. τηρεῖν Arist.*Rh.* 1382ᵇ11; καιρῷ χρήσασθαι Plu.*Pyrrh.*7; καιρῷ χειμῶνος ξυλλαβέσθαι co-operate with the *occurrence* of a storm, Pl.*Lg.*709c; ἔχει κ. τι it happens *in season*, Th.1.42, etc.; κ. ἔχειν τοῦ εὖ οἰκεῖν to be *the chief cause* of..., Pl.*R.*421a; ὑμέας καιρός ἐστι προβοηθῆσαι Hdt.8.144, cf. A.*Pr.*523, etc.; νῦν κ. ἔρδειν S.*El.*1368: sts. c. Art., ἀλλ' ἔσθ' ὁ κ. ... ξένους ... τυγχάνειν τὰ πρόσφορα A.*Ch.*710; ὁ κ. ἐστι μὴ μέλλειν ἔτι Ar. *Th.*661, cf. *Pl.*255. b. adverbial phrases, ἐς καιρόν *in season*, Hdt. 7.144, E.*Tr.*744, etc.; ἐς κ. ἐπείγεσθαι Hdt.4.139; ἐς αὐτὸν κ. S.*Aj.* 1168; εἰς δέοντα κ. Men.*Sam.*294; ἐν καιρῷ A.*Pr.*381, Th.4.59, etc.; ἐν κ. τινί Pl.*Cri.*44a; ἐπὶ καιροῦ D.19.258, 20.90, etc.; κατὰ καιρόν Pi.*I.*2.22; ὡς οἱ κατὰ κ. ἦν Hdt.1.30 (but also οἱ κατὰ κ. ἡγεμόνες in office *at the time*, *BGU*15.10 (ii A.D.), etc.); παρὰ τῷ ἐντυχόντι αἰεὶ καὶ λόγου καὶ ἔργου κ. Th.2.43; πρὸς καιρόν S.*Aj.*38, *Tr.*59, etc.; σὺν καιρῷ Plb.2.38.7: without Preps., καιρῷ S.*OT*1516; καιρόν, abs., S.*Aj.*34, E.*Fr.*495.9 (in Comp. form καιρότερον, Achae.49); κ. γὰρ οὐδὲν ἦλθες E.*Hel.*479; opp. ἀπὸ καιροῦ *out of season*, Pl.*Tht.*187e; ἄνευ καιροῦ Id.*Ep.*339d; παρὰ καιρόν Pi.*O.*8.24, E.*IA*800 (lyr.), Pl. *Plt.*277a; πρὸ καιροῦ *prematurely*, A.*Ag.*365 (anap.); ἐπὶ καιροῦ also means *on the spur of the moment*, ἐπὶ κ. λέγειν Plu.*Dem.*8, cf. *Art.*5; ἐξενεγκεῖν πόλεμον Id.*Ant.*6. 2. *season*, πᾶσιν καιροῖς at all *seasons* of the year, *IG*14.1018, cf. Lxx *Ge.*1.14, Ph.1.13, Porph.ap. Eus.*PE*3.11; κ. ἔτους, later Gr. for Att. ὥρα ἔτους, acc. to Moer.424; *time of day*, Philostr.*VA*6.14. b. *critical times, periodic states*, καιροὶ σωμάτων Arist.*Pol.*1335ᵃ41. 3. generally, *time, period*, κατὰ τὸν κ. τοῦτον Plb.27.1.7; κατ' ἐκεῖνο καιροῦ Conon 3, al.: more freq. in pl., κατὰ τούτους τοὺς κ. Arist.*Ath.*23.2, al., cf. Plb.2.39.1; τὰ κατὰ καιροὺς *chronological sequence* of events, Id.5.33.5; ἐν τοῖς πάλαι, ἐν τοῖς μεταξὺ κ., Phld.*Rh.*1.28,363 S. 4. in pl., οἱ καιροί *the times*, i. e. *the state of affairs*, freq. in bad sense, ἐν τοῖς μεγίστοις κ. at the most *critical times*, X.*HG*6.5.33, cf. D.20.44; περιστάντων τῇ πόλει κ. δυσκόλων *IG*2^{2}.682.33, etc.: also in sg., X.*An.*3.1.44, D.17.9; ὁ ἔσχατος κ. extreme *danger*, Plb.29.27.12, etc.; καιρῷ δουλεύειν *AP*9.441 (Pall.). IV. *advantage, profit*, τινος *of* or *from* a thing, Pi.*O.*2.54, *P.*1.57; εἴ τοι ἐς κ. ἔσται ταῦτα τελεόμενα to his *advantage*, Hdt.1.206; ἐπὶ σῷ κ. S.*Ph.*151 (lyr.); τίνα κ. με διδάσκεις; A.*Supp.*1060 (lyr.); τί σοι καιρὸς.. καταλείβειν; what *avails* it...? E.*Andr.*131 (lyr.); τίνος εἵνεκα καιροῦ; D.23.182; οὗ κ. εἴη where it was *convenient* or *advantageous*, Th.4.54; ᾗ κ. ἦν ib.90; χωρίον μετὰ μεγίστων κ. οἰκειοῦταί τε καὶ πολεμοῦται with the greatest *odds*, the most *critical results*, Id.1.36. V. Pythag. name for *seven*, *Theol.Ar.* 44.

καῖρος, ὁ (on the accent v. Eust.907.13), *row of thrums* in the loom, to which the threads of the warp are attached, *ravel*, Ael. Dion.*Fr.*400, Phot.:—hence **καιρ-όω**, *make fast these threads*: **-ωσις**, εως, ἡ, *act of fastening* them, Poll.7.33, Hsch.: **-ωμα**, ατος, τό, = καῖρος, Ael.Dion.l.c.; of the *web so fastened*, Call.*Fr.*295: **-ωστρίς** or **-ωστίς**, ίδος, ἡ, *woman-weaver*, ib.356, Hsch.

καιροσέων, (καῖρος) *close-woven*, only in gen. pl. fem., καιροσέων ὀθονέων ἀπολείβεται ὑγρὸν ἔλαιον Od.7.107. (Archaic spelling of καιρουσσέων (trisyll.), Ion. gen. pl. of καιρόεις, like Τειχιόσης for Τειχιούσσης in *SIG*3*d* (Milet., vi B.C.).)

καιρο-σκοπέω, gloss on καιροφυλακέω, Hdn.*Epim.*63; prob. (for καιρῷ σκόπει) in Men.*Mon.*307. **-σπάθητος** [ᾰ], ον, (καῖρος) *close-woven*, ὕφασμα Hermipp.5. **-τηρέω** τὰς μεταβολάς *observe the seasons* of change, D.S.19.16, cf. 13.22: generally, *lie in wait for*, τινὰς ἀσχολουμένους *PAmh.*2.35.8 (ii B.C.), cf. *UPZ*19.26 (ii B.C.):—also in Med., -τηρησάμενός με ἐξερχόμενον *BGU*909.6 (iv A.D.): **-τηρησία**, ἡ, Aristeas 270. **-φῐλος**, ὁ, *lover* or *observer of times*, epith. of an astrologer, Vett.Val.271.25. **-φῠλᾰκέω**, *watch for the right time*, c. acc., τὴν πόλιν D.23.173, Hyp.*Phil.*8; τὴν χρῆσιν Arist.*Pol.*1337^{b}41; ἔχθραν παλαιάν Olymp.Hist.p.460 D.: abs., App. *Pun.*88, *Mith.*70; also, *attend on*, Luc.*Abd.*16:—Pass., καιροφυλακεῖται Metrod.*Fr.*60.

καιρόω, καίρωμα, καίρωσις, καιρωστίς or **-τρίς**, v. καῖρος.

Καῖσαρ, ᾰρος, ὁ, (said to be Punic, = *elephant*, Lyd.*Mens.*4.102) *Caesar*, a *cognomen* of the Gens Julia; esp. of Julius Caesar, D.S. 5.22, Str.4.5.3, etc.; Κ. ὁ θεός prob. in *OGI*767.5; also of Augustus, ib.458.9 (9 B.C.), Nic.Dam.*Vit.Caes.* tit., etc.; ὁ νεὸς Κ., opp. ὁ πρεσβύτερος Κ., ib.6; in general, *the Emperor*, *OGI*473.8, etc.; Καίσαρος ἀπελεύθερος ib.629.90, etc.; Πρῖμος Καίσαρος, i. e. P. *the Emperor's slave*, Wilcken *Chr.*112.4; ἀπόδοτε τὰ Καίσαρος Καίσαρι *Ev.Luc.*20.25: pl., οἱ Καίσαρες *OGI*516.21: as title of the designated successor, Καίσαρα ἀποδεικνύει Hdn.2.15.3, etc.; name of month in the province of Asia, *OGI*458.54, etc.:—hence **Καισάρειος**, ον, *of, belonging to Caesar*, οἱ Κ. *his household* or *officials*, *POxy.*477.5 (ii A.D.), D.C. 52.24, al.; οἶκος Κ., hall in Herod the Great's palace, J.*BJ*1.21.1; τὸ Κ. *temple of Julius Caesar* at Alexandria, Str.17.1.9: **Καισάρεια** (-ηα), τά, *games in honour of Gaius Caesar* at Cos, *SIG*1065.9 (Cos); at Corinth and elsewhere, *IG*7.1856 (Thespiae), etc.: **Καισάρειος**, or **-ιος**, ὁ (sc. μήν), name of month in Egypt and elsewhere, *POxy.*45.17 (i A.D.), *Hemerolog.Flor.*, etc.:—also **Καισαρεών**, ῶνος, ὁ, *Rev.Ét. Gr.*19.268 (Κεσ-, Aphrodisias): **-εύω**, *play the Caesar*, D.C.66.8: **Καισαριανοί**, οἱ, *the Caesarian party*, App.*BC*3.91:—also, = Καισάρειοι, *PGnom.*241 (ii A.D.): **Καισαριασταί**, οἱ, *worshippers of Caesar*, *IGRom.*4.1348 (Mostene).

καισάραι· περικεφαλαῖαι, Hsch. **καισεκπρώπιον**· δρέπανον, ξηροκόπιον, Id.

καιτάεις, f.l. for καιετάεις in Sch.Od.4.1.

καί τοι, *and indeed, and further*, freq. in Hom. with one or more words between, Il.1.426, al.; καὶ σύ τοι E.*Med.*344; καὶ τἄλλά τοι X.*Cyr.*7.3.10: once in Hom. as one word, Il.13.267. II. after Hom. usu., *and yet*, to mark an objection introduced by the speaker himself, freq. in Rhetorical questions, καίτοι τί φημι; A.*Pr.*101; κ. τί φωνῶ; S.*OC*1132, cf. Isoc.4.99, etc.: without a question, κ. φύγοιμ' ἂν E.*Cyc.*480; κ. καὶ τοῦτο... D.4.12, 18.122: strengthd., καίτοι γ' Ar.*Ach.*611, E.*Fr.*953.10, X.*Mem.*1.2.3, Ph.1.274, etc.: mostly separated, καίτοι...γε E.*Or.*77, Ar.*Ra.*43, X.*Mem.*3.12.7, etc. (καίτοι is f.l. in A.*Eu.*849); so καίτοι περ v.l. in Hdt.8.53. III. with a participle, much like καίπερ, Simon.5.9, Ar.*Ec.*159, Pl.*R.* 511d, Plb.22.8.13, Phld.*Ir.*p.22 W., Luc.*Alex.*3: once in the Att. Oratt., Lys.31.34; also καίτοι γε διαχλευάζων Pl.*Ax.*364b.

καίτρεαι· ὅπλα Ἰβηρικά· οἱ δὲ κυρτίας, Hsch. (Cf. Lat. *caetra.*)

καιφος (corrected to **κεφος**), = *sparrow*, *PLond.*1821.162 (fort. κέπφος).

καίω, Att. **κάω** [ᾱ], impf. ἔκαιον Od.9.553, Att. ἔκᾱον, Ep. καῖον Il. 21.343: fut. καύσω X.*Cyr.*5.4.21, (ἐπι-) Pl.Com.186.4, (κατα-) Ar. *Lys.*1218; also καύσομαι Id.*Pl.*1054: aor. 1 ἔκαυσα Id.*Pax*1088, Th. 7.80 (bis), Pl.*Grg.*456b, etc.; Ep. ἔκηα (certain Act. and Med. forms have κει- in codd. of Hom., v. infr.), ἔκηα Il.1.40, al.; 3 sg. ἔκηε(ν) 22. 170, 24.34, al.; unaugm. κῆεν 21.349; 3 pl. ἔκηαν (v.l. ἔκειαν) Od.22. 336; imper. κεῖον 21.176 codd.; 1 pl. subj. κείομεν Il.7.333 (κατα-), 377, 396 (better attested than κήομεν); opt. κήαι, κήαιεν, 21.336, 24.38; inf. κῆαι Od.15.97 (v.l. κεῖαι), κατα-κῆαι 10.533, 11.46, κακκῆαι ib.74 (v.l. κακκεῖαι); part. κείαντες 9.231, 13.26, Att. κέαντες A.*Ag.*849, S.*El.*757, (ἐκ-) E.*Rh.*97, ἐκκέας Ar.*Pax*1133 (lyr.), ἐγκέαντι *IG*1^{2}.374.96, 261: pf. κέκαυκα (κατα-, προσ-) X.*HG*6.5.37, Alex.124.3:—**Med.**, aor. 1 ἐκαυσάμην (ἀν-) Hdt.1.202, 8.19; Ep. κείαντο, κειάμενοι, Il.9.88, 234; κειάμενος Od.16.2, 23.51:—**Pass.**, fut. καυθήσομαι Hp.*Nat.Mul.*107, (κατα-, ἐκ-) Ar.*Nu.*1505, Pl.*R.* 362a; late κἀήσομαι 1*Ep.Cor.*3.15: aor. 1 ἐκαύθην Hp.*Epid.*4.4, *Int.* 28, (κατ-) Hdt.1.19, Th.3.74; Ep. and Ion. aor. 2 ἐκάην [ᾰ] Il.9.212 (κατ-), Od.12.13, (δι-) Hp.*Loc.Hom.*40, (κατ-) Hdt.2.180; inf. καήμεναι Il.23.210, καῆναι Parth.9.8: pf. κέκαυμαι E.*Cyc.*457, Th.4.34, etc., κέκαυσμαι Hp.*Int.*28; inf. κεκαῦσθαι Arist.*Mete.*343^{a}9. (From κᾰϝ-yω.) I. *kindle*, πυρὰ πολλά Il.9.77; πῦρ κείαντες Od.9.231; πῦρ κῆαι 15.97, etc.:—Med., πῦρ κείαντο *they lighted them* a fire, Il.9. 88, cf. 234, Od.16.2:—Pass., *to be lighted, burn*, πυραὶ νεκύων καίοντο Il.1.52; θεείου καιομένοιο 8.135; καιομένοιο πυρός 19.376, cf. Hdt.1. 86, Ar.*V.*1372, etc.; φῶς πυρὸς καόμενον Pl.*R.*514b; αἱ φλόγες αἱ καιόμεναι...περὶ τὸν οὐρανόν the meteors *which blaze*, Arist.*Mete.*341^{b} 2; of ore, *to be smelted*, Id.*HA*552^{b}10. II. *set on fire, burn*, μηρία, ὀστέα, Od.9.553, Hes.*Th.*557; νεκρούς Il.21.343; δένδρεα ib. 338:—Pass., νηυσὶν καιομένῃσιν 9.602. 2. *make hot*, of the sun, ἀνθρώπους Hdt.3.104: abs., ibid., Pl.*Cra.*413b; [χείμαρρος] ἠελίῳ κεκαυμένος *smelted*, *AP*9.277 (Antiphil.). 3. of extreme cold, ἡ χιὼν καίει τῶν κυνῶν τὰς ῥῖνας X.*Cyn.*8.2, cf. 6.26 (Pass.); κάειν λέγεται..τὸ ψυχρόν, οὐχ ὡς τὸ θερμόν Arist.*Mete.*382^{b}8. 4. Pass., of fever-heat, τὰ ἐντὸς ἐκάετο Th.2.49: metaph., of passion, esp. of love, *to be on fire*, ἐν φρασὶ καιομένα Pi.*P.*4.219; κάομαι τὴν καρδίαν Ar.*Lys.*9; ἔρως... ὕβρει καόμενος Pl.*Lg.*783a; καίεσθαί τινος (sc. ἔρωτι) Hermesian.7.37, Charito 4.6, cf. Parth.14.2; also καομένη Ἑλλάς Greece *being in a fever* of excitement, Lys.33.7. 5. *suffer from inflammation*, ἐκαύθη ἔσω Hp.*Epid.*4.20, cf. 4. III. *burn and destroy* (in war), τέμνειν καὶ κ., κ. καὶ πορθεῖν, *waste with fire* and sword, X.*HG*4.2.15, 6.5.27. IV. of surgeons, *cauterize*, ὤμους Hp.*Art.*11:—in Pass., Id.*Aph.*6.60: abs., τέμνειν καὶ κάειν *to use* knife and *cautery*, Pl.*Grg.*480c, 521e, X.*An.*5.8.18, etc.: rarely reversed, κέαντες ἢ τεμόντες A.*Ag.*849. V. *burn* or *bake* pottery, κανθάρους dub. in Phryn.Com.15.

κάκ (A), name of the letter κ, κάμηλος θήλεια κεχαραγμένη κὰκ λὰλ ἄλφα *PLond.*3.909*a*7 (ii A.D.), cf. *BGU*153.17 (ii A.D.).

κάκ (B), apocop. for κατά before κ, in Hom. mostly κὰκ κεφαλῆς, κὰκ κεφαλήν, Il.18.24, 16.412, al.; also κὰκ κόρυθα 11.351; κὰκ κορυφήν 8.83; cf. κάγ, κάδ.

κἀκ, crasis for καὶ ἐκ. **κάκα**· κακία ἢ ὄρνεον, Hsch. **κακάβη**, ἡ, **κάκαβος**, ἡ, **κακάβιον**, τό, v. κακκ-.

κᾰκαγγελ-έω, *bring evil tidings*, *Trag.Adesp.*122. **-ία**, ἡ, *evil tidings*, Antig.*Mir.*12, prob. in Man.4.556, cf. Hp.ap.Gal.19. 107. **-ος**, ον, *bringing ill tidings*, γλῶσσα A.*Ag.*636, cf. Plu.2. 241b, Ant.Lib.15.4. **-τος**, ον, *caused by ill tidings*, κ. ἄχη the sorrow *of ill tidings*, S.*Ant.*1286 (lyr.).

κακᾱγόρος, κακᾱγορία, Dor. for κακηγ-, Pi.*O.*1.53, *P.*2.53.

κακαλία, v.l. for κακκαλία II (q. v.) in Dsc.4.122; cf. **κακαλίς**· νάρκισσος, Hsch.

κάκαλον, τό, = τεῖχος, A.*Fr.*166. (Perh. connected with ποδοκάκκη.)

κᾰκανδρία, ἡ, *unmanliness*, S.*Aj.*1014, E.*Rh.*814.

κακάνειν, v. κακκανῆν.

κᾰκ-ανθήεις, εσσα, εν, *with noxious blossom*, Nic.*Al.*420. **-ανθέω**, *bear such blossom*, Sch. ad loc.

κᾰκάω, cf. κακκάω. **κἀκεῖ, κἀκεῖθεν, κἀκεῖνος**, Att. crases for καὶ ἐκ-.

κάκεις or **κακεῖς**, οἱ, a kind of *Egyptian loaves*, Str.17.2.5.

κᾰκ-ελκής, ές, *suffering from malignant ulcer*, Hp.*Aff.*20; cf. κακοελκής. **-ελπιστέω**, *have ill hopes*, Arr.*Epict.*4.5.27. **-έμφᾰτος**, ον, *ill-sounding*, κακέμφατόν ἐστι τὸ "ὑπεξαίρεσις" Demetr.Lac.*Herc.* 1012.23; esp. of words *used in a vulgar* or *equivocal sense*, Quint.8.3. 44, Sch.Luc.*Lex.*21; τὸ κ. Sch.Ar.*Ach.*258, al. Adv. -τως Sch.Ar. *Ra.*48, 426, etc. II. = ἄδοξος, Hsch. **-εντρέχεια**, ἡ, *activity in mischief*, Plb.4.87.4. **-εντρεχής**, ές, *active in mischief*, Epich. [259], Plb.22.19.3, Str.7.3.7; κ. τῇ διανοίᾳ Vett.Val.17.5. **-επίθυμος** οἴνου *fatally fond* of wine, Hsch. s. v. οἰνόφλυξ. **-εργᾰσία**, ἡ, *bad effect*, prob. f.l. for κατ-, Thphr.*Sud.*10. **-εργέτης**, ου, ὁ, *evil-doer*, nickname of Ptolemy Euergetes II, Ath.4.184c: **-εργέτις**, ιδος, ἡ, Herm. *in Phdr.*p.75 A. (written κακοεργ- Porph.*Antr.*30, s.v.l.): —also **-γάτις** [ᾰ], Them.*Or.*2.33d. **-έρως**, ωτος, ὁ, ἡ, *fatally in love*, Hdn.*Epim.*206. **-εστώ**, οῦς, ἡ, *ill-being*, opp. εὐεστώ, Hsch., cj. in Democr.182.

κάκη [ᾰ], ἡ, (κακός) *wickedness, vice*, E.*Hipp.*1335, Ar.*Av.*541, etc.; of a horse, Pl.*Phdr.*247b. 2. *baseness of spirit, cowardice, sloth*, ἄψυχον κάκην A.*Th.*192; λήματος κάκῃ ib.616; δειλίαν καὶ κ. E.*IT*676, cf. *Med.*1051; εἴκοντας κάκῃ Pl.*Mx.*246b; διὰ κάκην Id.*R.* 468a.

κᾰκηγορ-έω, *speak ill of, abuse, slander*, τινα Pl.*Smp.*173d, *R.* 395e, al.; τινὰ πρός τινα (v.l. παρά τινι) Ps.-Phoc.226: abs., ἀπεχόμενος...τοῦ κακηγορεῖν from *evil-speaking*, Pl.*Lg.*934e, cf. Arist.*EN* 1129^{b}23, Hyp.*Fr.*246:—Pass., *to be abused*, Pl.*R.*368b. **-ία**, ἡ, *evil-speaking, abuse, slander*, Pi.*P.*2.53 (pl.), Arist.*EN*1131^{a}9, Phld. *Ir.*p.52 W. (pl.); κ. τινός *abuse* of one, Pl.*Phdr.*243a,b; κακηγορίας δίκη action *for abusive language*, D.21.32, cf. 81; κακηγορίας δικάζεσθαι Lys.10.2, etc.; ἔνοχος κακηγορίᾳ D.57.30. **-ίου** δίκη, = foreg., Test.ap.D.21.93. **-ος**, ον, Dor. **κᾰκᾱγόρος**, (ἀγορεύω) *evil-speaking, abusive, slanderous*, Pi.*O.*1.53; γλῶττα Pl.*Phdr.*254e; κ. τινος *abusive of* one, Ath.5.220a: Comp. κακηγορίστερος Pherecr.96: Sup. -ίστατος Ecphant.5. Adv. -ρως Poll.8.81.

κᾰκήθης, ες, = κακοήθης, Hp.*Mul.*2.141, Nic.*Th.*152.

κᾰκηλόγος, ον, *evil-speaking*, Men.*Mon.*117.

κᾰκηπελ-έων, *in evil plight*, Ep. part., formed after Homer's ὀλιγηπελέων (q.v.), Nic.*Th.*878, *Al.*93. **-ία**, Ep. **-ίη**, ἡ, *evil plight*, opp. εὐηπελία, Id.*Th.*319, Doroth.ap.Heph.Astr.3.36.

κάκησις [ᾰ], εως, ἡ, *taedium*, *Gloss.*

κᾰκία, ἡ, (κακός) *badness* in quality, opp. ἀρετή (excellence), Thgn. 322, S.*OT*512 (lyr.), Pl.*Smp.*181e, *R.*348c, etc.; κακίᾳ ἡνιόχων by their *incapacity*, Id.*Phdr.*248b: pl., κακίαι *defects*, Luc.*Hist.Conscr.* 6. 2. *cowardice*, *faint-heartedness*, Th.2.87, Pl.*R.*556d; κ. καὶ ἀνανδρία Id.*Cri.*46a. 3. *moral badness*, *vice*, μετ' ἀρετῆς ἀλλ' οὐ μετὰ κακίας And.1.56; ἡ ἀρετή, ὡσαύτως δὲ.. καὶ ἡ κ. Pl.*Men.*72a, etc.; personified in the Fable of Prodicus, X.*Mem.*2.1.26: pl., περὶ κακιῶν, title of treatise by Philodemus. 4. Philos., *Evil*, ὕλη κακίας αἰτία Plot.1.8.14. II. *ill-repute*, *dishonour*, κ. ἀντιλαβεῖν Th.3.58. 2. *hurt*, *damage* done or suffered, Lxx 1*Ki.*6.9, 1*Ma.* 7.23, *Ev.Matt.*6.34.

κᾰκιζότεχνος, ον, *finding fault with one's craftsmanship*, *meticulous*, of the sculptor Callimachus, v.l. in Paus.1.26.7; cf. κατατηξίτεχνος.

κᾰκίζω, (κακός) *abuse*, *reproach*, τινα Hdt.3.145, D.34.2; κ. τινὰ ὅτι οὐκ.. Th.2.21; νουθετεῖν τε καὶ κ. Pl.*R.*560a; τὴν τύχην κ. D.18. 306, cf. 21.73: abs., Epicur.*Nat.*28.12,72 G.:—Pass., *to be reproached*, ὑπό τινος Th.1.105. II. *make cowardly*, E.*IA*1435:—Pass., *play the coward*, οὔ ἑ κακιζόμενόν γε κατέκτα Il.24.214; καὶ μὴ κακισθῇς E. *Med.*1246, cf. *El.*982, Pl.*Mx.*247c; κακιζόμενοι τύχῃ *worsted* by fortune alone, Th.5.75.

κακιθά· λιμηρά, Hsch. **κακιθής**· ἄτροφος ἄμπελος, and **κακιθές**· χαλεπόν, λιμηρές, Id. **κακίμην**· τὴν ἀτυχῆ, Id. **κακῑότερος**, v. κακός.

κάκ-ισις [ᾰ], εως, ἡ, *blame*, ἐν τοῖς διαπραττομένοις Vett.Val.182.20 (pl.). **-ισμός**, ὁ, = foreg., Phld.*Vit.*p.10 J., Str.9.3.10. **-ιστέον**, *one must bring reproach on*, c. acc., E.*IT*105.

κάκιστος, **κᾰκίων**, v. κακός. **κακίω**, v. κηκίω.

κακκάβη [ᾰ] (A), ἡ, *three-legged pot* (= χύτρα, Ath.4.169c), Ar.*Fr.* 215, Antiph.217.3, Dorio ap.Ath.8.338a: **κάκκᾰβος**, ὁ, Nicoch.14, Antiph.182.4, 249: **κάκαβος**, ἡ, Alex.Trall.3.7: **κακάβη**, ἡ, Gal.14. 309.

κακκάβη [ᾰ] (B), *partridge*, so called from its cry, Ath.9.390a.

κακκᾰβίζω, *cackle*, of partridges, Arist.*HA*536ᵇ14, Thphr.*Fr.*181; of doves and partridges coupled, Chrysipp.*Stoic.*3.180; of owls, *hoot*, Ar.*Lys.*761 (v.l. -άζω):—also **κακκάζω**, Hsch. Cf. κικκαβαῦ.

κακκάβ-ιον, τό, Dim. of κακκάβη (A), Eub.38, Orib.5.33.3 (-βιν), *PLond.*5.1657.6 (iv A.D.): also **κακάβιν** Aët.1.130. **-ίς**, ίδος, ἡ, collat. form of κακκάβη (B), Alcm.25. **-ος**, v. κακκάβη (A).

κακκαλία, ἡ, = στρύχνον ὑπνωτικόν, Dsc.4.72. II. *Mercurialis tomentosa*, ib.122, Plin.*HN*25.135; v. κακαλία.

κακκανῆν, Lacon. inf., perh. *stir up*, *incite*, νέων ψυχὰς dub. in Leonidas ap.Plu.*Cleom.*2, cf. 2.235f (κακάνειν codd.), 959b (κακύνειν codd.).

κακκάω, *cacare*, Ar.*Nu.*1384, 1390.

κακκεῖαι, v. κατακαίω. **κακκεῖναι**· κατακόψαι (Cypr.), Hsch.

κακκείοντες, Ep. for κατακείοντες, part. of κατακείω.

κάκκη, ἡ, *human ordure*, Ar.*Pax*162. **κακκῆαι**, v. κατακαίω.

κακκόρ· ὁ μικρὸς δάκτυλος, Hsch. (Lacon. for κασκός, q.v.)

κακκρύπτω, Ep. for κατακρ-, Nic.*Fr.*78.

κακκώνιον· σκαφίον, Hsch.

κᾰκο-ανάστροφος, ον, *of bad conversation*, Procl.*Par.Ptol.*233. **-ανδρος**, ον, = ἄνανδρος, Sch.E.*Med.*436. **-αυλος**, ον, = ἄναυλος, Sch.E.*Ph.*790. **-βάκχευτος**, ον, = ἀβάκχευτος, Sch.E.*Or.*316, 319. **-βας**· ἐπὶ κακῷ ἥκων, Hsch. **-βῖος**, ον, *living poorly*, *living a hard life*, Hdt.4.95, X.*Cyr.*7.5.67 (Sup.), Arist.*HA*616ᵇ31, Str.17.2. 1. **-βίωτος** [ῐ], ον, = ἀβίωτος, Sch.Ar.*Pl.*970. **-βλαστέω**, *sprout ill* or *with difficulty*, Thphr.*CP*4.7.3. **-βλαστής**, ές, *sprouting ill* or *with difficulty*, ib.1.20.6, 4.7.2: Comp. κακοβλαστότερος Id.*HP*4.14. 1. **-βλητος**, ον, *ill-thrown*, *missed*, Suid. s.v. ἀβλῆτα βέλη. **-βολέω**, *have unlucky throws* (with dice), Sch.Ar.*Ra.*1001 (prob.), Suid. s.v. Θηραμένης. **-βόρος**, ον, *eating bad food*, Ael.*NA*10.29 (Sup.).

κᾰκοβουλ-εύομαι, Pass., *to be ill-advised*, ψυχὴ κακοβουλευθεῖσα E. *Ion*877 (anap.); but the form is incorrect and corrupt. **-ία**, ἡ, *ill-advisedness*, J.*BJ*2.11.3, D.L.7.93, Quint.*Ps.*138(139).20, prob. in *POxy.*1101.7 (iv A.D.). **-ος**, ον, *ill-advised*, *foolish*, φροντὶς S. *Fr.*592 (lyr.); φῶτες E.*Ba.*401 (lyr.), cf. Ar.*Eq.*1055 (hex.), Ph.2.280 (Sup.), D.Chr.31.50, Vett.Val.66.3: Comp., Sch.Th.1.120. II. Act., *giving bad advice*, opp. εὔβουλος, Pl.*Sis.*391c.

κᾰκό-γαμβρος γόος distress *for her wretched brother-in-law*, E. *Rh.*260 (lyr.). **-γᾰμία**, ἡ, *bad marriage*, *Cat.Cod.Astr.*8(4). 159. **-γᾰμίου** δίκη, action *for forming an unlawful* or *improper marriage* at Sparta, Plu.*Lys.*30; ζημία punishment for that offence, Aristo *Stoic.*1.89. **-γᾰμος**, ον, *marrying unlawfully*, μνηστῆρες Eust.1415.47; κ. γάμος an *ill-starred* marriage, Sch.Triclin.S.*OT* 1214, cf. Paul.Al.*O.*2. **-γείτων**, ον, gen. ονος, *a bad neighbour*, Call.*Cer.*118. 2. οὐδέ τιν' ἐγχώρων κακογείτονα *neighbour to* his *misery*, S.*Ph.*692 (lyr.). **-γένειος**, ον, *with a poor beard*, Suid. s.v. εἰς Τροιζῆνα. **-γενής**, ές, *base-born*, τὸ κ. D.C.44.37. **-γηρως**, αος, ὁ, ἡ, *unlucky in old age*, Hdn.*Epim.*205. **-γλωσσία**, ἡ, *slanderousness*, Sch.Pi.*P.*4.504. **-γλωσσος**, ον, *ill-tongued*, βοὴ κ. a cry *of misery*, E.*Hec.*661. II. *bringing evil* [on oneself] *by one's tongue*, of Niobe, Call.*Del.*96. **-γνωμονέω**, *to be ill-disposed*, Quint.*Ps.*30(31).14. **-γνωμοσύνη**, ἡ, = κακοβουλία, Aesop.417b, Thd.*Ps.*25(26).10: pl., Sch.E.*Ph.*1727. **-γνώμων**, ον, gen. ονος, *ill-judging*, *wanting in judgement*, Sm.1*Ki.*25.3, D.C.77.11. **-γονία**, ἡ, *evil birth*, Iamb.*in Nic.*p.82 P. **-γονος**, ον, *born to ill*, Sch.S.*OT* 26. **-γρᾰφος**, ον, *badly written*, γραμματεῖον Phlp.*in de An.*533. 30. **-γύναιος** [ῠ], ον, *bringing ills to women*, Procl.*Par.Ptol.*228.

κᾰκοδαιμον-άω, *to be tormented by an evil genius*, *possessed by an evil spirit*, Ar.*Pl.*372, X.*Mem.*2.1.5, D.8.16 (-οῦσι codd.), Din.1.91, v.l. for sq. in M.Ant.2.8. **-έω**, *to be unfortunate*, *unhappy*, X. *Hier.*2.4, Epicur.*Fr.*485, Phld.*Vit.*p.34 J., J.*BJ*1.22.1, Plu.2.76a, Arr.*Epict.*1.25.13. II. Astrol., *occupy the region of* κακὸς δαίμων, Doroth.ap.Heph.Astr.3.9, Ptol.*Tetr.*195, *Cat.Cod.Astr.*8(4). 130. **-ημα**, ατος, τό, Astrol., *occupation of the region of* κακὸς δαίμων, Vett.Val.74.6, *Cat.Cod.Astr.*8(2).119, 8(4).126, al. **-ία**, Ion. **-ίη**, ἡ, *unhappiness*, *misfortune*, opp. εὐδαιμονία, Hdt.1.87, Antipho 5.79, X.*Mem.*1.6.3, Arist.*Po.*1450ᵃ17, Phld.*Rh.*1.220 S., etc. II. *possession by an evil spirit*, Ar.*Pl.*501, X.*Mem.*2.3.19, D.2.20. **-ίζω**, *deem unhappy*, Phld.*Mort.*33, Str.11.11.8, Ph.1.219. **-ικός**, ή, όν, *bringing unhappiness* or *misfortune*, πικρία Phld.*Ir.*p.56 W., cf. D.L. 7.104, S.E.*M.*9.176. **-ιστής**, οῦ, ὁ, *worshipper of the* κακὸς δαίμων, *member of a 'Satanist' club*, Lys.*Fr.*53.2.

κᾰκοδαιμ-οσύνη, ἡ, = κακοδαιμονία II, Hippod.ap.Stob.4.1.95, Ael. *Fr.*110. **-ων**, ον, gen. ονος, *possessed by an evil genius*, Antipho 5.43; ὁ κ. Σωκράτης Ar.*Nu.*104; *ill-starred*, E.*Hipp.*1362 (anap.), Max.Tyr.36.4: freq. in Com., ὦ κακόδαιμον *poor devil!* Ar.*Pl.*386; οἴμοι κακοδαίμων Pherecr.117, etc.; -ονος ἔπαρμα Phld.*Mort.*31: Comp. -έστερος Luc.*Lex.*25: Sup., Id.*Deor.Conc.*7. Adv. -μόνως Id. *Vit.Auct.*7. II. *evil genius*, τοῦ δαίμονος δέδοιχ' ὅπως μὴ τεύξομαι κακοδαίμονος Ar.*Eq.*112, cf. Arr.*Epict.*4.4.38.

κᾰκο-δάκρῡτος, ον, *producing inferior gum*, of trees, Hsch. s.v. δύσ⟨σ⟩τακτον. **-δεκτεύω**, = κακῶς δέχομαι, Id. **-δερκής**, v. κακολ⟨α⟩ῆ. **-δερμος**, ον, *with a bad skin*, Sch.Theoc.4.63. **-δήνης**, ες, *ill-counselling*, Epic.in *Arch.Pap.*7 p.5.

κᾰκοδία, ἡ, opp. εὐοδία, = κακὴ ὁδός, *Et.Gud.App.*672.5.

κᾰκο-δῑαιτησία, ἡ, *bad habit of life*, Sor.1.92. **-διάκονος** [ᾱ] (-διάβολος cod.)· κακοικονόμος (Lacon.), Hsch. **-δῐδασκᾰλέω**, *instruct in evil*, τοὺς πολλοὺς S.E.*M.*2.42, cf. *Tab.Defix.* in *IG*12(7).p.1 (Amorgos). **-δῐκία**, ἡ, *corruption of justice*, Pl.*Lg.*938b.

κάκοδμος [ᾰ], ον, (ὀδμή) Ion. for κάκοσμος, Hp.*Prog.*11.

κᾰκοδοξ-έω, *to be in ill repute*, X.*Mem.*1.7.2, Muson.*Fr.*9 p.47 H., Sch.E.*Andr.*777. **-ία**, ἡ, *bad repute*, X.*Ap.*31, Pl.*R.*361c. II. *heretical opinion*, Just.*Nov.*109 *Praef.* **-ος**, ον, *in ill repute*, *of low reputation*, Thgn.195, X.*Ages.*4.1: Comp. -ότερος Pl.*Min.*321a; of things, *inglorious*, νίκα E.*Andr.*778 (lyr.).

κᾰκο-δουλία, ἡ, *badness of slaves*, D.Chr.38.15. **-δουλος**, ὁ, *ill-treating one's slaves*, Cratin.81. II. *bad slave*, Ps.-Luc.*Philopatr.*7. **-δρομία**, poet. **-ίη**, ἡ, *bad passage* (by sea), *AP*7. 699. **-δωρος**, ον, gloss on ἄδωρος, Suid. **-ειδής**, ές, *ill-featured*, D.C.78.9 (Sup.). **-ειμονία**, ἡ, *bad clothing*, Sch.A.R. 1.308. **-είμων**, ον, gen. ονος, *ill-clad*, πτωχοί Od.18.41, cf. Ps.-Luc.*Philopatr.*21, Hsch. s.v. λιναγερτουμένη. **-ελκής**, ές, *badly festering*, Man.1.54.

κᾰκο-εξία, ἡ, (ἔχω) = καχεξία, ἐπὶ κ. f.l. for καρδίᾳ in Lxx *Si.*19. 5. **-έπεια**, ἡ, *bad language*, *blasphemy*, Suid., (in form -πία) Phot. **-εργᾰσία**, ἡ, = κακεργασία, Lesb.Rh.3.7. **-έργετα** (neut. pl.), = sq., πήματα, prob. for -είργετα, Antioch.Astr. in *Cat.Cod.Astr.* 1.109. **-εργέτις**, ιδος, ἡ, *evil-doing*, ψυχή Porph.*Antr.*30; cf. κακεργέτις. **-εργής**, ές, poet., = κακοεργός, *IG*12(5).229.15 (Paros), Man. 1.249. **-εργία**, **-εργός**, = κακουργία, -γος, v. sub vocc. **-ζηλία**, ἡ, *unhappy imitation* or *rivalry*, v.l. for -ζηλωσία, Plb.10.22.10 (ap. Suid. s.v. Φιλοποίμην). II. Rhet., of style, *affectation*, Luc.*Salt.* 82, Demetr.*Eloc.*189. **-ζηλος**, ον, *having bad taste*: hence in Rhet., *using a bad*, *affected style* (cf. ζῆλος), ῥήτωρ D.L.1.38; τὸ κ., = κακοζηλία, Longin.3.4, cf. Demetr.*Eloc.*186, Hermog.*Inv.*4.12. Adv. κακοζήλως, εἰπεῖν Gal.18(1).180. **-ζηλωσία**, v. κακοζηλία. **-ζωία**, ἡ, *evil life*, Procl.*in Alc.*p.58 C., Herm.*in Phdr.*pp.90, 179 A.: poet. **κακοζοΐα**, *miserable life*, Sapph.120.

κᾰκοήθ-εια, Ion. **-ίη**, ἡ, *bad disposition*, *malignity*, Pl.*R.*348d, 401a, Hyp.*Eux.*32 (-ηθία), *Ep.Rom.*1.29; κ. τὸ ἐπὶ τὸ χεῖρον ὑπολαμβάνειν ἅπαντα Arist.*Rh.*1389ᵇ20: pl., κ. ὑπὲρ τοῦ πράγματος λεγόμεναι Aeschin.1.166, cf. Isoc.15.284, D.C.*Fr.*96.2. II. *bad manners* or *habits*, X.*Cyn.*13.16. III. Medic., *malignant character*, τῆς νόσου Epicur.*Fr.*471: in pl., *malignant diseases* or *growths*, Dsc.3. 92 (v.l. for τὰ -ήθη). **-ευμα**, ατος, τό, *malicious deed*, Plu.*Pomp.* 37. **-εύομαι**, *act maliciously*, *play a scurvy trick*, Men.*Epit.*334; πρὸς τὸν δῆμον Sch.Ar.*Lys.*313. II. Medic., *to be malignant*, Gal.18(2).464. **-ης**, ες, (ἦθος) *ill-disposed*, *malicious*, opp. εὐήθης, Ar.*Pax*822 (Comp., 823), D.18.11, Pl.*Ep.*360c, Ph.1.529, etc.; of animals, κ. ὄρνεον καὶ πανοῦργον Arist.*HA*613ᵇ23; esp. *thinking evil*, *prone to put the worst construction on everything*, Id.*Rh.*1389ᵇ20; τὸ κακόηθες *malice*, *wickedness*, Pl.*R.*401b, Men.653, Ph.1.684, etc. Adv., πανούργως καὶ -ήθως Men.*Epit.*318; κ. πολιτεύεσθαι Philipp.ap. D.18.78, cf. J.*AJ*13.11.1: Comp. -εστέρως Poll.4.148. II. of things, *infamous*, *abominable*, κλειδία κρυπτὰ -έστατα Ar.*Th.*422. 2. Medic., of sores, fevers, etc., *malignant*, Hp.*Aph.*6.4, *Prog.*20 (Sup.); ἐξάνθημα Phld.*Ind.Sto.*26. Adv. -θως Hp.*Art.*41 codd. **-ίζομαι**, = κακοηθεύομαι, Arr.*Epict.*3.16.4, etc. II. *put a bad construction on* things, κ. τὴν φιλοσοφίαν (sed leg. κ. ⟨εἰς⟩ τὴν φ.) Stob.2.7.2. **-ίη**, ἡ, v. κακοήθεια. **-ιστέον**, *one must put a bad construction*, ἐπὶ τὸ χεῖρον ἐκλαμβάνοντι Arist.*Rh.*1416ᵇ10.

κᾰκο-ηχής, ές, *ill-sounding, dissonant*, Phld.*Po*.2.42: Comp. ἠχῇ -εστέρᾳ Adam.2.42:—also **-ηχος**, ον, Suid. s. v. ἐκμελές. **-θαλπής**, ές, (θάλπω) *warming badly*, Hsch. s. v. δυσθαλπέος. **-θᾰνᾰσία**, ἡ, *miserable death*, Paul.Al.*M*.4, Vett.Val.126.10, al. **-θάνᾰτος** [θᾰ], ον, *dying miserably*, Plu.2.22c (as expl. of ῥιγεδανός), cf. Vett.Val. 128.19, Sch.E.*Hipp*.1143. **-θέλεια**, ἡ, *malevolence*, *Gloss*. **-θελής**, ές, *malevolent*, Adam.2.19. **-θέλω** (incorrect form), *to be ill-disposed*, *PMasp*.151.177 (vi A.D.). **-θεος**, ον, *having bad gods*, Thphr.ap.Porph.*Abst*.2.7. **-θερᾰπεία**, Ion. **-είη**, ἡ, *bad treatment*, Hp.*Aff*.20, 22. **-θέρειος**, ον, *with a bad summer*, Tz.*Proll.Hes*. p.12. **-θερής**, ές, *unfitted to endure summer heat*, φύσεις Sor.1. 41. **-θημοσύνη**, ἡ, *disorderliness*, Hes.*Op*.472. **-θηνέω**, *to be in a bad state, to be weakly*, of sheep, Arist.*HA*574a15. **-θῐγία**, ἡ, (θιγγάνω) *aimlessness*, γνώμης Democr.223. **-θροος**, ον, contr. **-θρους**, ουν, *evil-speaking, slanderous*, S.*Aj*.138 (anap.). **-θῡμία**, ἡ, *malevolence*, πρὸς ἀλλήλους Plu.*Lyc*.4. **-θῡμος**, ον, *ill-disposed*, Man.4.564, Adam.2.24. **-θυρσος**, ον, gloss on ἄθυρσος, Sch.E. *Or*.1492. **-θῦτος**, ον, *offering bad sacrifices*, Thphr.ap.Porph. *Abst*.2.7. **-ῑδρῡτος**, ον, gloss on ἀΐδρυτος, Hsch.

κᾰκοικονόμος, ὁ, *bad manager*, Ph.2.269.

Κᾰκοΐλιος [ῑλ], ἡ, *unhappy Ilios*, Κακοΐλιον οὐκ ὀνομαστήν Od.19. 260, al.

κᾰκο-καρπία, ἡ, *bearing bad* or *imperfect fruit*, Thphr.*HP*1.4.1, al. **-κέλᾰδος**, ον, gloss on δυσκέλαδος, Procl. ad Hes.*Op*. 196. **-κέρδεια**, ἡ, *base love of gain*, Thgn.225 (pl.). **-κλεής**, ές, (κλέος) *ill-famed*, Tryph.127. **-κνημος**, Dor. **-κνᾱμος**, ον, (κνήμη) *weak-legged, thin-legged*, Theoc.4.63, Call.*Fr*.472. **-κοίμητος**, ον, gloss on δυσηλεγής, Hsch. **-κρᾱτος**, ον, *badly tempered*, τὸ κ. (sc. τοῦ αἵματος) Gal.17(1).565. **-κρῐσία**, ἡ, *bad judgement*, *AP*7.236 (Antip. Thess.); ἀπειρία καὶ κ. Plb.12.24. 6. **-κρῖτος**, ον, = δύσκριτος, Gal.17(2).575, al. **-κτερής**, ές (-οτερής cod.)· κακῶς θάπτων (κακοθ- cod.), Hsch. **-κτέριστος**, ον, gloss on ἀκτέριστος, Sch.S.*Ant*.1207. **-λ⟨α⟩ῆ**· κακοδερκῆ, Hsch. **-λεκτρος**, ον, = κακόγαμος, Opp.*C*.1.261. **-λῐμένιστος**, ον, gloss on ἄνορμος, Sch.rec.S.*OT*423.

κᾰκολογ-έω, *revile, abuse*, τινα Lys.8.5, Isoc.6.98, Hyp.*Fr*.25, Lxx *Ex*.21.16(17), *Ev.Matt*.15.4, al.: abs., D.36.61:—Pass., Gorg. *Hel*.7, *PFay*.12.15 (ii B.C.). **-ία**, ἡ, *coarse expression, bad style*, Pl.*R*.401a: but usu. *abuse, reviling*, Hdt.7.237, X.*Cyr*.1.2.6, Hyp. *Fr*.247, Thphr.*Char*.28, etc. **-ικός**, ή, όν, *vituperative*, τὸ κ. Arist.*Rh.Al*.1440b5. **-ος** (parox.), ον, *evil-speaking, slanderous*, Pi.*P*.11.28, Men.256, Arist.*Rh*.1381b7; τινος *of* one, Id.*EN* 1125a8.

κᾰκό-λῡρος, ον, gloss on ἄλυρος, Sch.E.*Ph*.1028. **-μᾰθής**, ές, *bad at learning*, Anaxandr.8. **-μᾰνέω**, *to be exceeding mad*, Ph.2.501. **-μαντις**, εως, ὁ, ἡ, *prophet of evil*, Ἐρινύς A.*Th*.722 (lyr.); θυμός Id.*Pers*.10 (anap.). II. abs., *sorry prophet*, A.R.3. 936. **-μᾰχέω**, *fight unfairly*, Plu.2.32b, Luc.*Demon*.49. 2. *fight against odds, use desperate expedients*, Phlp. *in GC*16.28. **-μέλετος**, ον, (μελέτη) *busied with evil, full of evil augury*, κ. ἰά A.*Pers*. 937 (lyr.).

κᾰκομετρ-έω, *give bad measure*, Luc.*Herm*.59. **-ητος**, ον, *ill-measured*: τὸ κ., = sq., Eust.1644.32. **-ία**, ἡ, *short measure*, *POxy*. 1447.6 (i A.D.). II. *false metre*, Sch.Heph.p.106 C. (pl.), Eust. ad D.P.739. **-ος**, ον, *in bad metre, unmetrical*, Plu.2.747f, etc.; τὸ κ. Phld.*Po.Herc*.1676.8.

κᾰκο-μηδής, ές, (μῆδος) *contriving ill, deceitful*, *h.Merc*.389. **-μήτης**, ου, ὁ, = foreg., pl. -μῆται Orph.*Fr*.119. **-μητίη** [ῐ], ἡ, *cunning*, Man.2.308. **-μητῐς**, ὁ, = -μήτης, E.*Or*.1403 (lyr., -μήτας codd.); pl. -μήτιες, Astrol., = κακοποιοί, ἀστέρες Doroth.ap.Heph. Astr.3.30. **-μήτωρ**, ορος, ἡ, *mother of ill*, gloss on ἀμήτωρ, Hsch.:—but prob. **-μήστωρ** (= κακόμητις) shd. be read in Man. 4.307.

κᾰκομηχᾰν-έω, *practise base arts*, περί τινα Plb.13.3.2. **-ία**, ἡ, *practising of base arts, mischief*, Luc.*Phal*.1.12, Adam.1.5. **-ος**, Dor. **-μάχᾰνος** [μᾱ], ον, *mischief-plotting*, Il.6.344, Od.16.418; λῃσταί B.17.8; κῶρος Mosch.*Fr*.3.7; of things, *mischievous, baneful*, ἔρις Il.9.257. Adv. -νως Phot.*Bibl*.p.292 B.

κᾰκομῑλία, ἡ, *bad intercourse* or *society*, D.S.12.12 (nisi leg. καχομιλία, q.v.).

κᾰκό-μισθος, ον, *ill-rewarded*, Sch.A.*Ch*.733. **-μοιρία**, ἡ, *ill fate*, Sch.S.*Tr*.850, Sch.E.*Ph*.156. **-μοιρος**, ον, *ill-fated*, ὠδῖνες *AP*7.375 (Antiphil.), cf. Maiuri *Nuova Silloge*630. **-μορος**, ον, = foreg., Hsch. s. v. ἄμμορον, Suid. s. v. ἄμμορος. Adv. -ως *Cat.Cod. Astr*.8(4).129, 142. **-μορφία**, ἡ, *ill shape, ugliness*, *Gloss*.; gloss on δυσχλαινία, Sch.E.*Hec*.240. **-μορφος**, ον, *misshapen*, Sor. 1.39, 47, *AP*5.88 (Marc. Arg.). **-μουσία**, ἡ, *corruption of music*, Plu.2.748c. **-μουσος**, ον, *unmusical*, χορεία Sch.E.*Ph*.786 (Sup.). **-μοχθος**, ον, *working ill* or *perversely*, Lxx *Wi*.15.8.

κάκονες· κακὸς ὄλεθρος, Hsch.

κᾰκο-νοέω, *to be ill-disposed, bear malice*, Lys.29.10. **-νόητος**, ον, = κακόνοος, Polem.*Phgn*.10. **-νοια**, ἡ, *ill-will, malice*, opp. εὔνοια, Lys.22.16, X.*An*.7.7.45, *Cyr*.3.1.38, D.21.204, Ph.2.120, al.

κᾰκονομ-έομαι, Pass., *to be badly governed*, Ocell.4.8. **-ία**, ἡ, *bad system of laws and government*, opp. εὐνομία, X.*Ath*.1.8. **-ος**, ον, *with bad laws, ill-governed*, opp. εὔνομος, in Sup., Hdt.1.65, Ph. 2.268.

κᾰκό-νοος, ον, contr. **-νους**, ουν: Att. pl. κακόνοι:—*ill-disposed, disaffected*, opp. εὔνους, Antipho Soph.109, Ar.*Pax*496 (lyr.), 671; εὐνοεῖν τοῖς κακόνοις X.*Cyr*.8.2.1; τινι Id.*An*.2.5.16; τῇ πόλει Th.6. 24; τῷ πλήθει Lys.25.7; τῷ δήμῳ κακόνους ἔσομαι, oligarchical oath in Arist.*Pol*.1310a9; εἰς τὰ ὑμέτερα πράγματα Lys.20.20: Sup. κακονούστατος Id.7.28, D.23.6. Adv. κακονόως Sch.E.*Or*.108; κακόνως Poll.5.115: Sup. -νούστατα ib.116.

κᾰκονύμφ-ευτος, ον, gloss on ἀνύμφευτος, Sch.rec.S.*Ant*.980. **-ιον** ἔργον *the work of an evil bride*, Nonn.*D*.3.308. **-ος**, ον, *ill-married*, κακονυμφοτάτα ὄνασις *most unprofitable wedlock*, E.*Hipp*.756 (lyr.). II. Subst., *unhappy bridegroom*, Id.*Med*.206, 990 (both lyr.).

κᾰκό-νωτος, ον, *with foul back*, of fish, Antiph.129.7. **-ξενία**, ἡ, *inhospitality*, Charond.ap.Stob.4.2.24, Plu.*Cat.Mi*.12. **-ξενος**, Ion. **-ξεινος**, ον, *unfortunate in guests*, in Ep. Comp., οὔ τις σεῖο κακοξεινώτερος ἄλλος Od.20.376. II. *unfriendly to strangers, inhospitable*, E.*Alc*.558 (v.l. for ἐχθρόξ-), *AP*7.699, Lyc.1286: Comp., Σκυθῶν -ώτεροι Jul.*Ep*.89b. **-ξύνετος**, ον, *wise for evil*, οὐκ ἀξυνετωτέρου, κακοξυνετωτέρου δέ not less wise, but *more wise for evil*, Th. 6.76. **-οινία**, ἡ, *bad quality of wine*, opp. καλλιοινία, *Gp*.5.43 tit.

κᾰκοπᾰθ-εια [πᾰ], ἡ, *distress, misery*, Hp.*VM*10, Antipho 3.2.11, Isoc.6.55, Arist.*Pol*.1278b28; σώματος Antipho 5.18; of plants or trees, Thphr.*CP*3.7.8; *strain, stress*, on the parts of a machine, Hero *Bel*.93.1: pl., Hp.l.c.; ταῖς παρὰ τὴν ἀξίαν νῦν κακοπαθείαις your present unmerited *sufferings*, Th.7.77:—later, usu. written **-παθία**, *IG*2².900.16 (ii B.C.), *SIG*685.30 (Magnesia, ii B.C.), *BGU* 1209.7 (i B.C.), *Ep.Jac*.5.10: pl., *IG*12(7).386.24 (Amorgos, iii B.C.), Phld.*Piet*.86, etc.; *laborious toil, perseverance*, *BGU* l.c. (i B.C.). **-έω**, fut. -παθήσομαι *PLond*.1.98r73 (i/ii A.D.): pf. κεκακοπάθηκα Aen.Tact.26.7:—*to be in ill plight, be in distress*, Th.1.78, X.*Mem*.2.1.17, And.2.26, Lys.6.28, D.18.146; πολλὰ κ. *PCair.Zen*. 93.17 (iii B.C.); τινι *by* or *from* a thing, τοῦ χωρίου τῇ ἀπορίᾳ Th.4.29; ὑπό τινος Id.2.41; πρός τι Phld.*Oec*.p.53 J.; of sickness, Hp.*VM*19; κ. σώματι *suffer in* body, Antipho 5.2, 18, Isoc.2.46; τῇ ψυχῇ Democr. 191; of plants or trees, Thphr.*CP*3.4.4, al. **-ής**, ές, (πάθος) *miserable, in evil plight*, Vett.Val.2.5. Adv. -θῶς *in patient wretchedness*, Arist.*Pol*.1269b10; διάγειν Vett.Val.121.34. II. *troublesome, difficult*, Hero *Aut*.5.1. **-ητικός**, ή, όν, *miserable*, Arist.*EE* 1221a31. **-ος**, ον, = κακοπαθής, *miserable*, βίος D.H.8.83. 2. *troublesome, laborious*, κατασκευή Ph.*Bel*.56.46; μεταλλεῖαι Posidon. 48 J. (cod. Ath.), cf. A.D.*Synt*.187.24. 3. of persons, *laborious, persevering*, γυνή Muson.*Fr*.3 p.11 H.

κᾰκο-παρθενεύτως, gloss on ἀπαρθένευτα, Sch.E.*Ph*.1740. **-πάρθενος**, ἡ, *accursed maiden*, Sch.E.*Hec*.612. II. Adj. *unbecoming a maid*, Μοῖρα *AP*7.468 (Mel.). **-παστος**, ον, dub. in A.D.*Synt*.187. 23. **-πατρίδης**, ου, Aeol. **-ας**, α, ὁ, *base-born* (cf. εὐπατρίδης), prob. in Alc.*Supp*.28.11; cf. sq. **-πατρις**, ιδος, ἡ, *base-born*, Thgn.193; masc. in Alc.37 A. codd. (leg. -ίδαν). **-περίπᾰτος**, ον, *walking ill*, of horses, *Hippiatr*.115. **-πέτης**, ες, (πέτομαι) *flying badly*, Arist. *HA*616b11. **-πηρος**, ον, *with a bad wallet* or *scrip*, *EM*670. 56. **-πῑνής**, ές, *filthy, loathsome*, κακοπινέστατόν τ' ἄλημα S.*Aj*. 381 (lyr.); οὐ μόνον τοῖς ἤθεσιν ἀλλὰ καὶ ἕξει Ath.13.565e. Adv. **-νῶς**, διακείμενος Archig.(?) ap.Aët.3.114. **-πιστοτέρως**, Adv. Comp. *with misplaced confidence*, Phld.*D*.3 *Fr*.75. **-πλαστος**, ον, *ill-conceived*, Hermog.*Stat*.1.1. Adv. -τως Tz. ad Lyc.805. **-πλοέω**, *sail badly*, Str.15.1.15. **-πλοος**, ον, contr. **-πλους**, ουν, *ill for sailing*, θάλασσα Sch.Philostr.*Her*.p.478 B. **-πνευστος**, ον, gloss on δυσαής, Sch.D Od.13.99. **-πνοια**, ἡ, *difficulty of breathing*, Gal. 17(1).757. **-πνοος**, ον, Att. **-πνους**, ουν, (πνοή) *breathing with difficulty*, Poll.1.197.

κᾰκοποι-έω, *do ill, play the knave*, A.*Fr*.111, Ar.*Pax*731; *manage one's affairs ill*, X.*Oec*.3.11. II. trans., *do mischief to, injure*, πολλὰ μὲν τὴν βασιλέως χώραν κ. Id.*Mem*.3.5.26, cf. Plb.4.6.10; τὰς νῆας Id.13.4.1:—Pass., Id.27.7.6. **-ησις**, εως, ἡ, = κακοποιΐα, Lxx 3*Ma*.3.2, 2*Es*.4.22. **-ητικός**, ή, όν, *prone to do evil*, τρόπος Aristeas 163, cf. Andronic.Rhod.p.572 M., Hierocl.p.49 A.: Astrol., *maleficent*, ἰδιοτροπία Ptol.*Tetr*.210. **-ΐα**, ἡ, *evil-doing*, Arist. *Rh.Al*.1432a9, Chrysipp.*Stoic*.2.249: pl., *injuries*, Isoc.12.122; opp. εὐεργεσίαι, Id.1.26. **-ός**, όν, *doing ill, mischievous*, ὄνειδος Pi.*N*. 8.33; σκεῦος, of a man, Plb.15.25.1; κακοποιοί *evil-doers*, Arist.*EN* 1125a18; esp. of poisoners and sorcerers, 1*Ep.Pet*.4.15; of things, *noxious*, χυλός Thphr.*CP*2.6.4, etc.; φάρμακα *PSI*1.64.21 (i B.C.); τὸ κ. [τῆς ὕλης] Arist.*Ph*.192a15: Astrol., *maleficent*, Ptol.*Tetr*.19, Artem.4.59, etc.

κᾰκο-πολῑτεία, ἡ, *bad government*, Plb.15.21.3, Plu.*Pomp*.75: pl., Id.*Lyc*.7, Ph.1.41, 601. **-πονητικός**, ή, όν, *unfit for toil*, ἕξις Arist.*Pol*.1335b7. **-ποτμος**, ον, *ill-fated, ill-starred*, B.5.138; τύχαι A.*Ag*.1136 (lyr.); ἐμὲ κ. E.*Hel*.694 (lyr.); κ. ὄρνις ἢ κρέξ Arist. *HA*616b21. **-πους**, ὁ, ἡ, πουν, τό, gen. ποδος, *with bad feet*, ἵππος X.*Mem*.3.3.4, *Eq*.1.2; εὔπτερα μέν, κακόποδα δέ Arist.*HA*487b26.

κᾰκοπρᾱγ-έω, *fare ill, fail in an enterprise*, Th.4.55; *to be in ill plight*, Id.2.43; κ. ἀναξίως Arist.*Rh*.1386b26, cf. Aphth.*Prog*.1, al.: in physical sense, ἥπατος ἢ γαστρὸς κακοπραγούντων Gal.10.789, al. **-ής**, ές, *evil-doing*, Hsch. **-ία**, ἡ, *misadventure, failure*, αἱ κατ' οἶκον κ. Th.2.60; ἡ ἐκ τῆς Σικελίας κ. Id.8.2; κ. γίγνεται Arist. *Pol*.1296a17; ἡ τοῦ πέλας κ. Corn.*Rh*.p.393 H.: pl., κ. ἀνάξιαι Arist. *Rh*.1386b10, cf. Plb.8.12.8, Phld.*Herc*.1251.11, Artem.4.56, etc. b. *bad physical condition*, Gal.10.255. II. *ill-doing*, Lxx *Wi*.5.24, J.*AJ*2.4.4: pl., *misdeeds*, Isoc.15.300. **-μονέω**, *do ill*, Plb.3.2.8, al. **-μοσύνη**, ἡ, *evil-doing*, Democr.297, D.25.101, Plb.4.23.8, al., Phld.*Acad.Ind*.p.54 M. **-μων**, ον, gen. ονος, *doing evil, mis-*

chievous, X.*HG*5.2.36, Isoc.15.225,236, Arist.*Ath.*35.3: Sup. -έστατος, περί τι Plb.8.9.3. Adv. -μόνως *Klio* 16.163 (Delph.).

κăκο-πρόσωπος, ον, *ugly-faced*, Posidipp.43, Plu.2.1058a; τὸ κακοπρόσωπον Xenocr.ap.Stob.4.40.24. **-πτερος**, ον, *with bad wings, weak in the wing*, opp. εὔπτερος, Arist.*HA*617^{b}4, al.; of the Sphinx, as *a bird of ill omen*, Epigr.ap.Sch.E.*Ph.*50. **-πώγων**, ωνος, ὁ, *with a thin beard*, *PPetr.*3 p.23 (iii B.C.).

κακόρας· κατακόψας, Euclus ap.Hsch. (Perh. for κα-κορά⟨α⟩ς, cf. κοραίω.) **κακόρδαζε**· ἀπεχώρει, Hsch.

κăκορέκτης, ου, ὁ, (ὀρέγω) *with evil yearnings*, ἀνήρ Adam.2.39.

κăκο-ρρăφεύς, έως, ὁ, = κακοποιός, Hsch. **-ρρăφία**, ἡ, *contrivance of ill, mischievousness*, κακορραφίῃς ἀλεγεινῆς Il.15.16; κακορραφίῃσι νόοιο Od.2.236; μή τι κακορραφίῃ ἀλεγεινῇ ... ἀλγήσετε 12.26. **-ρρέκτης**, ου, ὁ, (ῥέζω) *evil-doer*, A.R.3.595. **-ρρημοσύνη**, ἡ, *evil-speaking*, Plb.8.10.3; *slander*, Poll.8.80. **-ρρήμων**, ον, gen. ονος, (ῥῆμα) *telling of ill, ill-omened*, A.*Ag.*1155 (lyr.). 2. *a poor speaker*, D.C.77.11. II. τὸ κ., = foreg., Suid. s. v. Ἀρχίλοχος. Adv. -όνως Poll.8.81. **-ρροθέω**, = κακολογέω: c. acc., *abuse, revile*, E.*Hipp.*340, *Alc.*707, Ar.*Ach.*577, *Th.*896. **-ρροος**, ον, contr. **-ρρους**, ουν, *bringing a grievous flux*, of disease, dub. in Ἀρχ.Ἐφ. 1920.80 (Crete, vi B.C.). **-ρρυγχος**, ον, *with ugly muzzles*, παιδία Arr.*Epict.*3.22.77. **-ρρυθμος**, ον, *in bad rhythm* (κακόρυθμ-), Phld.*Rh.*1.162 S.; τὸ κ. Id.*Po.Herc.*1676.8; of the pulse, Gal.19.409. **-ρρῦπος**, ον, *filthy*, Aesop.73 (= Babr.10.1).

κăκός, ή, όν, *bad*: I. of persons, 1. of appearance, *ugly*, εἶδος μὲν ἔην κακός Il.10.316, cf. Paus.8.49.3. 2. of birth, *ill-born, mean*, γένος ἐστὲ διοτρεφέων βασιλήων.., ἐπεὶ οὔ κε κακοὶ τοιούσδε τέκοιεν Od.4.64; Ζεὺς δ' αὐτὸς νέμει ὄλβον.. ἐσθλοῖς ἠδὲ κακοῖσι 6.189; οὐ κακὸν οὐδὲ μὲν ἐσθλόν 22.415; οὐδ' ἐὰν.. φανῶ τρίδουλος, ἐκφανῇ κακή S.*OT*1063; κακός τ' ὢν κἀκ κακῶν ib.1397. 3. of courage, *craven, base*, Il.2.365, 6.489; κακοῦ τρέπεται χρὼς ἄλλυδις ἄλλη (called δειλὸς ἀνήρ in the line above) 13.279; Ἕκτωρ σε κ. καὶ ἀνάλκιδα φήσει 8.153, cf. Od.3.375; κ. καὶ ἀνήνορα 10.301; οἵτινες... ἐγένοντο ἄνδρες κ. ἢ ἀγαθοὶ ἐν τῇ ναυμαχίῃ Hdt.6.14; κ. καὶ ἄθυμος Id.7.11; οὐδαμῶν κακίονες ib.104; κακοὺς πρὸς αἰχμήν S.*Ph.*1306; κακή τ' ἐς ἀλκὴν καὶ σίδηρον εἰσορᾶν E.*Med.*264; οὐδενὶ ἐπιτρέψοντας κακῷ εἶναι X.*An.*3.2.31. 4. *bad* of his kind, i.e. *worthless, sorry, unskilled*, ἡνίοχοι Il.17.487; [τοξότης] ἢ κ. ἢ ἀγαθός ib.632; νομῆες Od.17.246; κ. ἀλήτης a *bad* beggar, ib.578; ἰατρός A.*Pr.*473; κυβερνήτης, ναύτης, E.*Supp.*880, *Andr.*457; μάγειρος Pl.*Phdr.*265e: c. acc. modi, πάντα γὰρ οὐ κακός εἰμι I am not *bad* in all things, Od.8.214; κ. γνώμην S.*Ph.*910: also c. dat., κακοὶ γνώμαισι Id.*Aj.*964: c. inf., κ. μανθάνειν Id.*OT*545; [νῆσος] φυτεύεσθαι κακή *Trag.Adesp.*393; cf. II. 5. in moral sense, *base, evil*, Od.11.384, Hes.*Op.*240; opp. χρηστός, S.*Ant.*520; ὦ κακῶν κάκιστε Id.*OT*334, *Ph.*984; πλεῖστον κάκιστος Id.*OC*744; κ. πρός τινας Th.1.86; εἰς φίλους E.*Or.*424 codd.; περὶ τὰ χρήματα Pl.*Clit.*407c. 6. *wretched*, Herod.3.42. II. of things, *evil, pernicious*, freq. in Hom., etc., as δαίμων, θάνατος, μοῖρα, αἶσα, κῆρες, νοῦσος, ἕλκος, φάρμακα, ὀδύναι, Od.10.64, Il.3.173, 13.602, 1.418, Od.2.316, Il.1.10, 2.723, 22.94, 5.766; χόλος, ἔρις, Il.16.206, Od.3.161; πόλεμος, ἔπος, ἔργα, Il.4.82, 24.767, Od.2.67, al.; ἦμαρ, ἄνεμος, Il.9.251, Od.5.109; of omens and the like, *unlucky*, ὄρνις, ὄναρ, σῆμα, Il.24.219, 10.496, 22.30: also in Trag., κ. τύχη, δαίμων, μόρος, S.*Tr.*328, A.*Pers.*354, 369, etc.; of words, *abusive, foul*, κ. λόγοι S.*Ant.*259, cf. *Tr.*461; κ. ποιμήν, i.e. the storm, A.*Ag.*657: Astrol., *unlucky*, τόποι Heph.Astr.1.12; κ. τύχη, name for the sixth region, Paul.Al.*M.*1.

B. κακόν, τό, and κακά, τά, as Subst., *evil, ill*, δίδου δ' ἀγαθόν τε κακόν τε Od.8.63; ἀθάνατον κακόν 12.118; ἐκ μεγάλων κακῶν πεφευγέναι Hdt.1.65; so κ. ἄμαχον, ἄπρηκτα, Pi.*P.*2.76, *I.*8(7).8; ἔκπαγλον, ἄφερτον, ἀμήχανον, etc., A.*Ag.*862, 1102, E.*Med.*447, etc.; κακὸν ἥκει τινί there's *trouble* in store for some one, Ar.*Ra.*552; δυοῖν ἀποκρίνας κακοῖν the least of two *evils*, S.*OT*640, cf. *OC*496; κακῶν Ἰλιάς, v. Ἰλιάς; κακόν τι ῥέξαι τινά to do *harm* or *ill* to any one, Il.2.195, etc.; πολλὰ κάκ' ἀνθρώποισιν ἐώργει Od.14.289; κακὰ φέρειν, τεύχειν τινί, Il.2.304, Hes.*Op.*265; κακόν τι (or κακὰ) ποιεῖν τινα (v. δράω, ποιέω, ἐργάζομαι); κακὸν πάσχειν ὑπό τινος to suffer *evil* from one, Th.8.48, etc.: in Trag. freq. repeated, κακὰ κακῶν, = τὰ κάκιστα, S.*OC*1238 (lyr.); εἴ τι πρεσβύτερον ἔτι κακοῦ κακόν Id.*OT*1365 (lyr.); δεινὰ πρὸς κακοῖς κακά Id.*OC*595, cf. *Ant.*1281; δόσιν κακὰν κακῶν κακοῖς A.*Pers.*1041 (lyr.). 2. κακά, τά, *evil words, reproaches*, πολλά τε καὶ κακὰ λέγειν Hdt.8.61, cf. A.*Th.*571, S.*Aj.*1244, *Ph.*382, etc. 3. Philos., κακόν, τό, *Evil*, *Stoic.*3.18, al., Plot.1.8.1, al. 4. of a person, *pest, nuisance*, τουτὶ παρέξει τὸ κ. ἡμῖν πράγματα Ar.*Av.*931; also, comically, ὅσον συνείλεκται κακὸν ὀρνέων what a *devil* of a lot of birds, ib.294.

C. degrees of Comparison: 1. regul. Comp. in Ep., κακώτερος Od.6.275, 15.343, Theoc.27.22, A.R.3.421, etc.: also in late Prose, Alciphr.3.62: irreg. κακίων, ον [with ῐ], Od.2.277, Thgn.262, etc., with ῑ in Trag., exc. E.*Fr.*546 (anap.); κακιότερος *AP*12.7 (Strato). 2. Sup. κάκιστος Hom., etc.—Cf. also χείρων, χείριστος, and ἥσσων, ἥκιστος.

D. Adv. κακῶς *ill*, ἢ εὖ ἦε κακῶς Il.2.253, etc.; κακῶς ποιεῖν τινα to treat one *ill*; κακῶς ποιεῖν τι to hurt, damage a thing; κακῶς ποιεῖν τινά τι to do one any evil or harm; κ. πράσσειν to fare *ill*, A.*Pr.*266, etc.; κάκιον ἢ πρότερον πράττειν And.4.11; κ. ἔχειν Ar.*Ra.*58, etc.; of illness, *Ev.Matt.*4.24; rarely κακῶς πάσχειν A.*Pr.*759, 1041 (anap.); χρῆν Κανδαύλῃ γενέσθαι κ. Hdt.1.8; κ. ὄλοισθε S.*Ph.*1035, etc.; with play on two senses, ὡς κ. ἔχει ἅπας ἰατρός, ἂν κ. μηδεὶς ἔχῃ Philem.Jun.2; κ. ἐρεῖν τινά, λέγειν τὴν πόλιν, Mimn.7.4, Ar.*Ach.*503; κ. εἰδότες, = ἀγνοοῦντες, X.*Cyr.*2.3.13, Isoc.8.32, cf. Hyp.*Eux.*33; κακῶς ἐκπέφευγα I have *barely* escaped, D.21.126: Comp. κάκιον Hdt.1.109, S.*OT*428, And. l. c., Pl.*Mx.*236a, etc.: Sup. κάκιστα Ar.*Ra.*1456, *Pax* 2, Pl.*R.*420b, etc. 2. Adv. and Adj. freq. coupled in Trag., Att., etc., κακὸν κακῶς νιν.. ἐκτρῖψαι βίον S.*OT*248; κακὸς κακῶς ταφήσῃ E.*Tr.*446 (troch.); ἀπό σ' ὀλῶ κακὸν κακῶς Ar.*Pl.*65, cf. *Eq.*189, 190, D.32.6, Procop.*Pers.*1.24; κακοὺς κακῶς ἀπολέσει αὐτούς *Ev.Matt.*21.41; κακοὺς κάκιστα S.*Aj.*839; in reversed order, ὥσπερ ἀξία κακῶς κακὴ θανεῖται E.*Tr.*1055; with intervening words, κακῶς.. ἀπόλλυσθαι κακούς S.*Ph.*1369, cf. E.*Cyc.*268, Ar.*Eq.*2. (Perh. cogn. with Avest. *kasu-*, Comp. *kasyah-*, Sup. *kasišta-* 'small', Lith. *nukašěti* 'grow feeble, thin', Germ. *hager*.)

κăκό-σημος, ον, gloss on ἄσημος, Sch.rec.S.*Ant.*1013. **-σῖνος**, ον, *very harmful*, in Sup. -ώτατος (v.l. -ώτερος) Hp.*Fract.*46. **-σῑτία**, Ion. -ίη, ἡ, *lack of appetite*, Archig.ap.Orib.8.23.3, Poll.6.36; κ. στομάχου Aret.*SD*2.6. **-σῖτος**, ον, *eating badly*, i.e. *having a poor appetite, fastidious*, Hp.*Steril.*215, Eub.17; ὁ περὶ τὰ σιτία δυσχερής Pl.*R.*475c, Ael.*NA*3.45, cf. Arr.*Cyn.*8.2. 2. metaph., *fastidious*, πρὸς Κύπριν οὐ κ. (of Priapus), Ἀρχ.Δελτ.2 *App.*47 (Thyrrheum). **-σκελής**, ές, *with bad legs*, ἵππος X.*Mem.*3.3.4. **-σκήνης**, ες, *of a bad, mean body*, *AP*7.401 (Crin.).

κăκοσμ-ία, ἡ, *a bad smell*, Poll.2.75. **-ος**, ον, *ill-smelling*, A.*Fr.*180.2, S.*Fr.*565, Ar.*Pax* 38.

κăκό-σπερμος, ον, *with bad seed*, Thphr.*HP*7.4.4. **-σπλαγχνος**, ον, *faint-hearted*, A.*Th.*237. **-σπορία**, poet. -ίη, ἡ, *impious sowing*, *AP*7.175 (Antiphil.). **-στăθέω**, *to be in bad case*, Nic.*Th.*431; of the wind, *to be contrary*, ib.269. **-στένακτος**, ον, *sighing lamentably*, Sch.Ar.*Th.*1068, Sch.rec.A.*Th.*856. **-στέφăνος**, ον, gloss on ἀστέφανος, Sch.E.*Andr.*1020. **-στόμăτος**, ον, *foul-mouthed*, sens. obsc., = Lat. *fellator*, *AP*11.155 (Lucill.).

κăκοστομăχ-έω, *have a sensitive stomach*, S.E.*M.*11.212. **-ία**, ἡ, *bad state of the stomach*, Gal.14.735. **-ος**, ον, *having a sensitive stomach*, Cic.*Fam.*16.4.1, Aët.8.45; f.l. in *AP*11.155; cf. κακοστόματος. II. Act., *bad for the stomach, unwholesome*, Heraclid. Tarent.ap.Ath.3.120c, Philistion Locr.ap.eund.3.115d, Dsc.1.127, al., Sor.1.94, Gal.6.641: Comp. -ώτερος Diph.Siph.ap.Ath.2.56b.

κăκοστομ-έω, *revile*, τινα S.*El.*597. **-ία**, ἡ, *faulty pronunciation*, Str.14.2.28. **-ος**, ον, *foul-mouthed*, λέσχαι E.*IA* 1001. 2. *lacking in eloquence*, Ptol.*Tetr.*166. II. *bad to pronounce, ill-sounding*, Longin.43.1.

κăκό-στρωτος, ον, *ill-spread*, i.e. *rugged*, A.*Ag.*556. **-συμβίβαστος** [ῐ], ον, *hard to reconcile*, Eust.1946.13. **-σύμβουλος**, = *malesuadus*, Gloss. **-συνάντητος**, ον, gloss on δυσαντής, Sch. Opp.*H.*1.370. **-σύνετος**, ον, *of bad understanding*, Eustr.*in EN* 368.31; cf. -ξύνετος. **-συνθεσία**, ἡ, gloss on κακορραφία, Hsch.:—also **-σύνθεσις**, εως, ἡ, Phot., Suid. **-σύνθετος**, ον, *ill-composed*, in Rhet., Quint.8.3.59; ἔπη Luc.*Cal.*14; λόγος Sch.E.*Or.*674; *ill put together*, κ. τὸ σῶμα Sch.Ar.*V.*818. Adv. -τως Sch.E.*Hec.*801, al. **-συνταξία**, ἡ, *bad grammar*, Eust.210.29, al. **-σφαιρος**, ον, *ill-rounded*, Tz.*H.*11.492. **-σφυκτος**, ον, *with a bad pulse*, Gal.9.831. **-σφυξία**, Ion. -ίη, ἡ, *bad pulse*, Aret.*SA*2.8, Gal.6.238. **-σχημος**, ον, *badly formed*, of a period, Sch.E.*Or.*307, cf. Hdn.*Epim.*177. **-σχήμων**, ον, gen. ονος, *unseemly*, only in Adv. -νως Lib.*Or.*25.15; Sup. -ονέστατα Pl.*Lg.*728b.

κăκοσχολ-εύομαι, *play mischievous tricks*, Porph.*Ep.Aneb.*26; in mal. part., Hsch. s. v. ὀρχιπεδίζειν. **-έω**, of children, *to be mischievous*, Chrysipp.*Stoic.*3.77; πρὸς ἡδονήν Theano *Ep.*4.3. **-ία**, ἡ, *mischief, malpractice*, *Delph.*3(1).362 i 32 (ii B.C.), Plu.2.274d. **-ος**, ον, (σχολή) *mischievous, frivolous*, Arr.*Epict.*2.19.15; κακόσχολε *naughty!* *AP*5.103 (Marc. Arg.). Adv. -λως, οἰκονομεῖν act *with frivolous delay*, Ptol.Philad.ap.Aristeam 24; *frivolously*, προσφιλονεικεῖν, ἐγκαλεῖν, Simp.*in Cat.*67.15, *in Ph.*433.7; τὰ καλῶς λεγόμενα -λως ἐκδεχόμενον ἀδόκιμα δεικνύναι Id.*in Cat.*7.27; also, = κακεμφάτως, Tryph.*Trop.*p.193 S., *EM*634.6, Sch.Ar.*Ach.*397, Eust.1638.17. II. Act., κ. πνοαί winds *that enforce harmful idleness*, A.*Ag.*193 (lyr.).

κăκό-τακτος, ον, gloss on δύστακτος, Hsch. **-τάφος**, ον, gloss on ἀτύμβευτος, Sch.Opp.*H.*5.346. **-τεκνία**, ἡ, *having bad children*, Phryn.*PS*p.80 B. **-τελεύτητος**, ον, *ending ill*, Sch.A.*Pers.*910. **-τέρμων**, ον, gen. ονος, *ending ill* or *with difficulty*, ψυγμός Poet.*de Herb.*94.

κăκοτεχν-έω, *use base arts, deal fraudulently*, ἔς τινα Hdt.6.74, *PEleph.*1.9 (iv B.C.); περὶ τὰς δίκας D.46.25: abs., Antipho 1.22, D.29.11, 35.56. 2. Rhet., *use false artifices* of style, Demetr.*Eloc.*28, 250. II. trans., *misuse*, τινὰ περὶ τὸ σῶμα Arr.*Epict.*4.6.4; *mislead*, τοὺς νέους Aristaenet.2.18. 2. *falsify*, οὐ κακοτεχνησῶ οὐδὲν τῶν.. γεγραμμένων *GDI*5039.19 (Hierapytna); *counterfeit, imitate*, [αἱματίτης] κεκακοτεχνημένος Dsc.5.126. **-ημα**, ατος, τό, *base art*, Oenom.ap.Eus.*PE*5.24. **-ής**, ές, = κακότεχνος, Luc.*Cal.*10 (Comp.). **-ία**, ἡ, *base artifice, malpractice*, Heraclit.[129], *PRein.*16.26 (ii B.C.), *OGI*669.55 (Egypt, i A.D.), *CIG*2712.15 (Mylasa), Ph.1.636, Iamb.*Myst.*10.2 (pl.): freq. in pl., as law-term, *fraudulent* or *malicious conspiracy*, κακοτεχνιῶν διαδικάζεσθαι Pl.*Lg.*936d; esp. *subornation of perjury*, D.47.1, 49.56; δόλοι καὶ ἐπιορκίαι καὶ κ. Luc.*Alex.*4. II. *bad art*, applied to forensic oratory by Epicur.*Fr.*51: generally, Plu.2.228b: esp. in Rhet., *false artifice*, Demetr.*Eloc.*27, 247, Luc.*Par.*27, Ath.14.631f: pl., ἡδονὰς καὶ κ. εἰσάγων Str.7.3.7. **-ίζω**, = κακοτεχνέω, Alc.Com.7. **-ίου** (sc. δίκη), = κακοτεχνιῶν, Lys.*Fr.*116. **-ος**, ον, (τέχνη) *using evil practices, artful*, δόλος Il.15.14: esp. in mal. part., *lascivious*, *AP*5.

128 (Autom.): Sup., ib.131 (Phld., v.l. κατατ–); of songs, Plu.2.706d. Adv. –νως *with bad art*, Ph.1.195.

κᾰκότης, ητος, ἡ, (κακός) *badness*: I. of moral character, *baseness, cowardice*, Il.2.368, 13.108, Od.24.455; ἀτιμίη καὶ κ. Tyrt.10.10; κ. καὶ δειλία Th.5.100; οὐδεμιῇ κ. λειφθῆναι τῆς ναυμαχίης not through *cowardice*, Hdt.7.168. 2. *wickedness, vice*, τείσασθαι Ἀλέξανδρον κακότητος Il.3.366, cf. Hes.*Op*.287, Democr.178; κακότητος ἄπειροι Emp.112.3; κακότητ' ἀσκεῖν A.*Pr*.1066 (anap.); ἄνευ κακότητος [συμφορά] Antipho 6.1: pl., Emp.145. II. of condition, *evil case, distress, misery*, ἐκφυγέειν κακότητα Od.5.414, cf. 290, 379, 397, Pi.*P*.2.35, Hdt.2.128, 6.67, S.*El*.236 (lyr.); esp. in war, Τρῶες ἀνέπνευσαν κακότητος Il.11.382, cf. 12.332, Hdt.8.109, etc.: pl., *distresses, miseries*, Alc.59, E.*Fr*.303 codd. (lyr.); αἱ ἐντὸς κ. Pl.*Ax*.366a. III. of quality, *badness*, τῶν οὔρων Hp.*Epid*.3.10: pl., *bad qualities*, Id.*Acut*.57.

κᾰκοτράχηλος [τρᾰ], ον, gloss on ἀτράχηλος, Apollon.*Lex*. s.v. ἀ.

κᾰκοτροπ-εύομαι, *deal perversely*, πρός τινα Plb.5.2.9, cf. *AB* 354. –έω, *become malignant*, of ulcers, Hp.*Mul*.1.38. –ία, ἡ, *badness of habits, mischievousness*, Th.3.83, D.C.54.21, Artem.4.63; in argument, *malice, unfairness*, Simp. *in Cael*.156.27. –ος, ον, *malignant*, D.C.52.2, Vett.Val.74.12, *PMasp*.97 ii 20 (vi A.D.): Comp., D.C.*Fr*.85.1: Sup., Zen.5.41. Adv. –πως D.C.47.4. 2. of animals, *mischievous*, κτήνη *Hippiatr*.129. II. Medic., *malignant*, Antyll.ap.Orib.9.23.13.

κᾰκοτροφ-έω, *have poor nourishment*, κακοτροφήσας Thphr.*HP* 5.2.2:—also in Pass., κακοτροφηθείς ibid. II. Pass., *to be ill cared for*, of vines, Theano *Ep*.4.4. –ία, ἡ, *poor nourishment*, Thphr.*HP*5.2.3; *malnutrition*, Gal.7.73.

κᾰκοτῠχ-έω, *to be unfortunate*, Th.2.60, D.C.*Fr*.36.15. II. Astrol., *occupy the region named* κακὴ τύχη, Vett.Val.66.7. –ής, ές, *unfortunate*, used by E. in lyr., *Med*.1274, *Hipp*.669: Sup., ib. 679; τὸ κ., = sq., Id.*HF*133; κ. καὶ ἄθλιον γένος Sch.rec.A.*Pers*.1013, cf. *Cat.Cod.Astr*.8(4).142. –ία, ἡ, *misfortune*, Eust.1422.44.

κακουβαι, gloss on *uniones* (*onions*), *Gloss*. (dub. l.).

κάκουλοι· κακοί, σκληροί, κύαμοι, Hsch.

κακόϋπνος, ον, gloss on ἄϋπνος, Hsch.

κᾰκοϋπονόητος, ον, (ὑπονοέω) gloss on δυστόπαστος, Suid.

κᾰκουργ-έω, *do evil, work wickedness*, E.*Or*.823 (lyr.), etc.; κ. τι Antipho 2.3.2; μηδὲν κ. Pl.*Prt*.326a; περί τινας Id.*R*.416d; ἵππος ἣν κακουργῇ *be vicious*, X.*Oec*.3.11; ἀδικεῖν καὶ κ. Ar.*Nu*.1175; κ. καὶ ἐξαμαρτάνειν Pl.*Hp.Mi*.375d:—Pass., εὑρέν τι –ηθέν found that *a fraud had been committed*, *POxy*.1468.19 (iii A.D.). 2. of discussion, κ. ἐν τοῖς λόγοις *use captious* or *unfair arguments*, Pl.*Grg*.489b, cf. 483a, Arist.*Rh*.1404ᵇ39. 3. of things, ὁ...ἱδρὼς κακουργεῖ X.*Mem*.1.4.6. II. c. acc. pers., *maltreat, injure*, A.*Fr*.266, E.*Supp*.537; κ. ἀλλήλους καὶ ἀδικεῖν Pl.*Lg*.679e. 2. c. acc. rei, *ravage* a country, τὴν Εὔβοιαν Th.2.32, cf. 3.1; κ. τὴν χώραν καὶ τὰ κτήματα Pl.*Lg*.760e, etc.; κ. τὸν λόγον *spoil* the argument, Id.*R*.338d. 3. *corrupt, falsify*, τοὺς νόμους D.24.65:—Pass., τὰ ἀληθῆ καὶ μὴ κακουργούμενα τῶν πραγμάτων Id.31.8. 4. c. dat., κ. τοῖς προβάτοις, of dogs, Pl.*R*.416a. –ημα, ατος, τό, *knavish trick, fraud*, Id.*Lg*.933e, D.18.31, 24.86, etc.; τὰ ἐν τοῖς συμβολαίοις κ. Pl.*R*.426e; *crime*, Antipho 5.10, etc. –ία [ῐ], Ep. κακοεργίη [ῑ metri gr.], ἡ, *wickedness, villainy, malice*, ὡς κακοεργίης εὐεργεσίη μέγ' ἀμείνων Od.22.374, cf. Th.1.37, etc.; of a horse, *vice*, X.*Eq.Mag*.1.15: in pl., *malpractices*, τὰ κιβδηλεύματά τε καὶ κ. τῶν πωλούντων Pl.*Lg*.917e: κ. καὶ ἀπάται καὶ δολώσεις X.*Cyr*.1.6.28, etc. II. *bad workmanship*, only in form κακοεργία Pl.*R*.422a. III. *injury*, τῆς ἑαυτοῦ πόλεως ib.434c: pl., *ill effects*, ἀποκρούειν τὰς τῶν φαρμάκων κ. Dsc.1.90. –ικός, ή, όν, *malicious*, ἀδικήματα Arist.*Rh*.1391ᵃ18. –ος, Ep. κακοεργός (also late Prose, Porph.*Abst*.2.38; δαιμόνια κακοεργά Aen.Gaz.*Thphr*.p.60 B.), ον, (ἔργον) *doing ill, mischievous, knavish*, once in Hom., ἀλλά με γαστὴρ ὀτρύνει κακοεργός *importunate*, Od.18.54; freq. later, κλῶπες κακοῦργοι Hdt.1.41; κ. ἀνήρ S.*Aj*.1043; also κακουργότατος λόγος D.20.125; κ. μάχαιρα *AP*11.136 (Lucill.); –ότατα εἰπεῖν Antipho 2.4.2. Adv. –γως Poll.3.132. 2. as Subst., *malefactor, criminal* in the eye of the law, Ps.-Phoc.133, Th.1.134, *PLille* 1.7.20 (iii B.C.), *Ev.Luc*.23.32, etc.; οὐδεὶς κακοεργός Theoc.15.47; at Athens, technically, *thief, robber*, ὁ τῶν κακούργων νόμος Antipho 5.9, cf. 16, Lys.13.78, D.22.28, 24.102. II. c. gen., *doing harm to*, κ. μὲν τῶν ἄλλων, ἑαυτοῦ δὲ πολὺ –ότερος, X.*Mem*.1.5.3, cf. Pl.*R*.421b: abs., *harmful*, κ. ἐπιθυμίαι ib.554c; καρτερία Id.*La*.192d; ἄγνοια –οτάτη καὶ αἰσχίστη Id.*Alc*.1.118a.

κᾰκουχ-έω, (ἔχω) *wrong, injure*, αὐτόν Telesp.34 H.; *maltreat*, esp. a wife, Mitteis *Chr*.284.6 (ii B.C.), *POxy*.281.17 (i A.D.), etc.:—Pass., *to be afflicted* or *injured*, Lxx 3*Ki*.2.26; ὑπὸ τοῦ δηγμοῦ D.S.3.23; κακουχουμένους τελευτῆσαι τὸν βίον Plu.2.114e. –ία, ἡ, *maltreatment*, Pl.*R*.615b; of a wife, *BGU*1105.18 (Aug.); '*mobbing*', Plb.5.15.6 (dub. l.); ἐν χθονὸς κ. *devastation*, A.*Th*.668. II. = καχεξία, *bad condition*, Alex.80; *misery, distress*, Plb.3.64.8, Vett.Val.127.13: pl., of ascetic practices, μάτην ἑαυτοὺς καταικισάμενοι ταῖς κ. Plu.2.117f.

κᾰκό-φᾰτις, ιδος, ἡ, *ill-sounding, ill-omened*, βοά A.*Pers*.936 (lyr.). –φημία, ἡ, *evil report*, ἡ ἐκ τῶν πολλῶν κ. Ael.*VH*3.7. –φημίζω, = *inclamo*, *Gloss*. –φημος, ον, *ill-sounding, ominous*, Sch.S.*Aj*.214; τὸ κ. *evil* or *ominous words*, J.*BJ*6.5.3; of persons, *foul-mouthed*, Ptol.*Tetr*.166. Adv. –μως *with evil words, abusively*, Man.5.323. –φθαρτος, ον, *wasted away*, Hsch. s.v. κακόκνημος. –φθόρος, ον, *destructive, deadly*, Nic.*Th*.795, *Al*.168: heterocl. gen. κακοφθορέος (as if from –φθορεύς) ib. 465. –φῐλος, ὁ, *bad friend*, Phld.*Lib*.p.24 O., *Cat.Cod.Astr*.8(4).146. –φλοιος, ον, *with bad rind*, v.l. for κακό-χλοος (q.v.), Nic.*Al*.331. –φονος, ον, gloss on ἀπόφονος, Sch.E.*Or*.163. –φορεσία, ἡ, gloss on δυσχλαινία, Sch.E.*Hec*.240.

κᾰκοφρᾰδ-ής, ές, (φράζομαι) poet. word, *bad in counsel, foolish*, Αἶαν, νεῖκος ἄριστε, κακοφραδές Il.23.483, cf. A.R.3.936: neut., κακοφραδές, as Adv., *foolishly*, Euph.98.2. –ία, Ion. –ίη, ἡ, *folly*, κακοφραδίῃσι τιθήνης *h.Cer*.227: sg., Nic.*Th*.348, Q.S.12.554. –μοσύνη, ἡ, = foreg., Democr.273, Orph.*Fr*.285.41 (pl.).

κᾰκοφράσμων, ον, gen. ονος, = κακοφραδής, prob. in Theoc.4.22; v. –χράσμων.

κᾰκό-φραστος, ον, *ill-conceived*, Sch.E.*Or*.674. –φρονέω, *bear ill-will* or *malice*, A.*Ag*.1174 (lyr.). II. *to be foolish*, Sch.E.*Or*.821. –φρονίζω, *stultify*, Aq.2*Ki*.15.31. –φροσύνη, ἡ, *folly*, Lxx *Pr*.16.18, Opp.*H*.3.363 (pl.). –φρων, ον, gen. ονος, (φρήν) *ill-minded, malignant*, πραπίδων καρπός Pi.*Fr*.211, cf. E.*Heracl*.372 (lyr.), *Supp*.744; κ. [μέριμνα] A.*Ag*.100 (anap.): in late Prose, Porph.*Abst*.2.7. II. *imprudent, heedless*, S.*Ant*.1104, E.*Or*.824 (lyr.).

κᾰκοφῠ-ής, ές, (φυή) *of bad natural qualities*, κατὰ τὴν ψυχήν Pl.*R*.410a. II. (φύομαι) *growing ill*, Thphr.*HP*8.11.8; σπόρος *PTeb*.61(*b*).370 (ii B.C.). –ΐα, ἡ, *bad natural qualities*, Pl.*Def*.416.

κᾰκοφων-έω, *speak ill*, opp. καλλιφωνέω, prob. in Phld.*Rh*.1.176 S. –ία, ἡ, *ill-sound*, of a name, Str.13.2.4; *cacophony*, Demetr.*Eloc*.255, A.D.*Conj*.228.20; opp. εὐφωνία, Phld.*Po.Herc*.994.23: dist. fr. δυσφωνία, Gal.7.59. –ος, ον, *ill-sounding, not producing agreeable sounds*, τὰ ξηρὰ κ. Arist.*Aud*.802ᵇ23; *with a bad voice*, τραγῳδός D.T.631.21, Phlp. *in de An*.533.32; opp. εὔφωνος, Phld.*Po.Herc*.994 *Fr*.11; of words, *cacophonous*, D.H.*Comp*.12, cf. 16 (Sup.), D.T.631.20; τὸ κ., = κακοφωνία, Sch.Ar.*Eq*.248.

κᾰκό-χαρτος, ον, *rejoicing in evil*, Ἔρις, ζῆλος, Hes.*Op*.28, 196, cf. Hsch. –χείμερος, ον, *unfitted to endure winter*, Sor.1.41. –χλοος, ον, *with poor foliage*, Nic.*Al*.331 (–χλοίοιο metri gr., Schneid.). –χορος, ον, gloss on ἄχορος, Hsch. –χρήσμων, Dor. –χράσμων, ον, gen. ονος, (χράομαι) *difficult to live with*, v.l. for –φράσμων, Theoc.4.22, cf. Sch. ad loc. –χρηστος, ον, *ill-used*, Sch.Philostr.*Her*.p.412 B. –χροέω, *to be of a bad complexion*, Dsc.1.128. –χροια, ἡ, *bad complexion*, Ruf.ap.Orib.45.30.48, Gal.17(2).215; of a corpse, Phld.*Mort*.30: pl., *blotches*, Dsc.3.1, Gal.6.814. –χροος, ον, contr. –χρους, ουν, *of bad complexion*, Hp.*Prorrh*.2.42, *Aff*.20; *of bad coloration*, Arist.*HA*616ᵇ31; *of bad colour*, κύμη Nic.*Fr*.85.5; ὀφθαλμοί Gal.17(2).214; of urine, Id.19.598. –χῡλος, ον, *with bad juice* or *flavour*, μῆλα Diph.Siph.ap.Ath.2.54a: Comp., ib.68f, 3.80c, Diocl.*Fr*.138; of meat, Sor.1.94. –χῡμία, ἡ, *unhealthy state of the humours*, Gal.6.553, 10.891: pl., Dsc.2.87. 2. *unwholesomeness*, τροφῶν Gal.6.749. –χῡμος, *with unhealthy juices*, Arist.*Pr*.954ᵃ10, Ath.1.24f (Sup.), Hices.ib.7.309b, Dsc.2.88; τὸ κ. Alex.Aphr.*Pr*.2.10. 2. *unwholesome*, of foods, Gal.6.641. 3. *having an unpleasant taste*, S.E.*P*.1.52.

κάκοψις [ᾰ], ιδος, ἡ, *short-sighted*, *PLips*.1.9 (ii B.C.), *PGrenf*.2.28 (ii B.C.); *sinister*, Vett.Val.14.23.

κᾰκό-ψογος, ον, *malignantly blaming, censorious*, πόλις Thgn.287, cf. Ptol.*Tetr*.166. –ψῡχία, ἡ, = κακοφυΐα, *bad natural qualities*, opp. εὐψυχία, Pl.*Lg*.791c.

κᾰκόω, *maltreat, distress*, in Hom. always of persons, κεκακωμένοι ἐν Πύλῳ ἦμεν, ἐλθὼν γάρ ῥ' ἐκάκωσε βίη Ἡρακληείη Il.11.689; μηδὲ... κάκου κεκακωμένον *afflict* not the *afflicted*, Od.4.754; ἧμεν κυδῆναι... βροτὸν ἠδὲ κακῶσαι 16.212, cf. 20.99; ὅσοι παθόντες εὖ κακοῦσί μ' ἐκδίκως A.*Pr*.976; κ. [θεὸς] δῶμα Id.*Fr*.156; κ. τοὺς ἀναιτίους E.*HF* 1162; τοὺς Ἀθηναίους Th.8.32; τὸν δῆμον Lys.13.91; ἑαυτούς Pl.*Mx*.248c:—in Pass., *to be in ill plight, be distressed*, κεκακωμένος ἅλμῃ *befouled* with brine, Od.6.137 (v. supr.): generally, Hdt.1.170, al., A.*Pers*.728 (troch.), S.*OC*261, And.2.16, Th.4.25; πρὸς θεῶν κακοῦται E.*Hel*.268; ἐκάκωτο ὑπὸ τῆς πορείας X.*An*.4.5.35; ἐκ πυρετοῖο *AP*11.382.1 (Agath.). 2. of things, *spoil, ruin*, τὰ κοινά Hdt.3.82; τὸ ναυτικόν Th.8.78; of the air, *injure* a plant, Thphr.*CP*2.11.2; τὰ κακούμενα τῆς χώρας Aen.Tact.15.1: Astrol., *render unpropitious*, Vett.Val.70.22 (Pass.): physically, *injure, paralyse*, τὰς ἀρχὰς τῶν νεύρων Gal.2.690:—Pass., κακοῦται πᾶν τὸ σκέλος *deteriorates*, Hp.*Art*.58.

κακτάμεναι, κάκτανε, κάκτεινε, v. κατακτείνω.

κάκτος, ἡ, *cardoon, Cynara Cardunculus*, Thphr.*HP*6.4.10, Philet.16, Theoc.10.4, Antig.*Mir*.8, Dsc.*Alex*.33. 2. κάκτος, ὁ, *the fruit*, μακωνίδες, μάραθα, τραχέες τε κάκτοι Epich.159; also the edible leaf, Thphr. l.c.

κάκυνσις [ᾰ], εως, ἡ, *corrupting*, Sch.E.*Hec*.251.

κᾰκύνω, *damage*, in prov., κ. τὸν πηλόν· τὸν ἄξιον ὕβρεως ὑβρίζειν, Suid.; τὰς τύχας Antioch.Astr. in *Cat.Cod.Astr*.8(3).105:—Pass., *turn bad*, Thphr.*Od*.56. 2. in moral sense, *corrupt*, *Com.Adesp*.138:—usu. in Pass., *to be corrupted*, D.C.60.2: esp. *become bad*, E.*Hec*.251, Pl.*Ti*.42c; of soldiers, *show cowardice*, v.l. for μαλακύνω, X.*Cyr*.6.3.27. 3. Pass. also, *to be reproached*, E.*Hipp*.686.

κακχαδίαι· ἰσχνόφωνοι, Hsch. **κακχάζω**, = καχάζω, Id. **κάκχαρτος**· κατάχαρτος, Id.

κακχεῦαι, Ep. for καταχεῦαι, aor. 1 inf. of καταχέω. **κακχύδην**, poet. for καταχύδην (q.v.).

κᾰκώδ-ης, ες, (ὄζω) *ill-smelling*, Hp.*Mul*.2.204, Arist.*Pr*.867ᵇ10 (Comp.), Thphr.*Od*.2. –ία, ἡ, *stench*, ibid., *Sud*.5, 9, al.

κᾰκώλεθρος, ον, *very destructive*, Sch.rec.S.*El*.492.

κᾰκωνῠμ-ία, ἡ, *bad name, ill report*, Sm.*Ex*.32.25. **-ος**, ον, (ὄνομα) gloss on δυσώνυμος, Suid., cf. Paul.Al.*N*.3.

κάκ-ωσις [ᾰ], εως, ἡ, (κακόω) *ill-treatment*, τοῦ ἡγεμόνος X.*An*.4.6.3, cf. *Stud.Pal*.1.8.10 (v A.D.); *oppression*, τοῦ λαοῦ Lxx *Ex*.3.7. 2. esp. in Law, *ill-usage*, of persons by their natural protectors, ὁ τῆς κ. νόμος Lys.13.91, cf. Is.8.32, D.10.40, etc.; γραφὴ κακώσεως Id.58.32, Men.328; κ. γονέων, ὀρφανῶν, ἐπικλήρου, οἴκου ὀρφανικοῦ, Arist.*Ath*.56.6; τοκέων κ. Lycurg.147; also κ. ἐπαρχίας *misgovernment*, of the Rom. *actio repetundarum*, Plu.*Caes*.4. II. *suffering, distress*, Th.2.43; πληρωμάτων Id.7.4; αἰκίαι σωμάτων καὶ κακώσεις Arist.*Rh*.1386^{a}8, cf. 1385^{a}24; of the effects of disease, Hp.*VM*17: pl., Id.*Aër*.19; αἱ τᾶς σαρκὸς τακομένας κακώσιες Ti.Locr.102c, cf. Phld.*Mort*.21, Sor.1.31. **-ωτής**, οῦ, ὁ, *one who ill-treats, oppressor*, Ph.1.544, Ptol.*Tetr*.159; γυναικῶν Vett.Val.49.4. **-ωτικός**, ή, όν, *hurtful, noxious*, Ph.2.557, Herm.ap.Stob.1.41.6; τινος Dsc.1.94, cf. Gal.6.260, Sch.D Il.1.10; κ. τι παθεῖν Chor.p.221 B.; κ. αἰτία, ἀκτίς, Vett.Val.49.11, 151.6. Adv. -κῶς, διάγειν Id.165.34, cf. Sch.Epict.*Ench*.42.

καλαβάς· καλαβώτης, Hsch. **Καλαβίδια, Καλαβίς**, v. Καλλαβίς. **καλαβοίδια** (i.e. καλαϝοίδια), τά, hymns in honour of Artemis, Id. (καλαβοῦτοι cod.); cf. Καλαοίδια. **κᾰλαβρίζω, κᾰλαβρισμός**, v. κολαβρ-. **καλαβρός**· βάρβαρος, Id. **καλαβύστας**· τοὺς κωλώτας (Argive), Id.

κᾰλᾰβώτης, ου, ὁ, = ἀσκαλαβώτης, Lxx *Le*.11.30, *PMag.Lond*.121.186.

καλαδία· ῥυκάνη, Hsch. **καλάζει** (fort. καλα(μά)ζει)· ὀγκοῦνται (Achaean), Id. **κάλαθα**· λάλαβοι, οἱ δὲ ἄνθη, Id. **καλάθαρβα**· παροινία, Id.

κᾰλᾰθηφόρος, ον, *basket-carrying*, Hsch.: Καλαθηφόροι, title of play by Eubulus.

κᾰλάθ-ιον [λᾰ], τό, Dim. of κάλαθος, Poll.10.125, Sch.Call.*Cer*.1; part of a surgical machine, in the shape of a κάλαθος, Orib.49.4.41:—also -ίς, ίδος, ἡ, Hsch. s.v. πλαγγών. **-ίσκιον**, τό, = foreg., Anon. *in Rh*.108.30: also -ίσκον, τό, Roussel *Cultes Égyptiens* 232 (Delos, ii B.C.). **-ίσκος**, = foreg., ὁ, Ar.*Th*.822, *Lys*.535, 579, *Jahresh*.16 *Beibl*.51 (iv B.C.), Theoc.21.9. 2. Archit., = κόφινος, of the *coffers, panels* of a ceiled roof, Chor.p.118 B. II. a kind of *dance*, Apolloph.1, Men.1018, Poll.4.105; prob. l. for -ισμός, Ath.14.629f.

κᾰλᾰθο-ειδής, ές, *basket-shaped, narrow at the base*, Cleom.2.2, Gal.18(1).822, Theo Sm.p.196 H., Simp.*in Cael*.546.31. Adv. -δῶς Heraclit.*All*.46. **-πλόκος**, ὁ, *basket-weaver*, P.cit. ad *PFlor*.13.9. **-ποιός**, όν, *making baskets*, A.D.*Adv*.189.7.

κάλᾰθος [κᾰ], ὁ, *basket narrow at the base*, Ar.*Av*.1325 (lyr.); esp. for wool, Hsch.; for fruit, Arist.*Rh*.1413^{a}21; carried in procession in honour of Demeter, Call.*Cer*.1, cf. *Gloss.Oxy*.1802 *Fr*.3.30. 2. Archit., *capital of a column*, in this form, Callix.1, cf. Vitr.4.1.9. II. *wine-cooler*, = ψυκτήρ, Hsch. III. *mould for casting iron*, Id. IV. *reservoir* of an oil-lamp, Hero *Spir*.2.22.

κᾰλάθωσις [λᾰ], εως, ἡ, *coffering* of a ceiled roof, *Gloss*.; cf. καλαθίσκος I. 2.

κᾰλάϊνος or **καλλάϊνος**, η, ον, *like the* κάλαϊς, *shifting between blue and green*, κ. πτέρυξ, of the cock, *AP*7.428.2 (Mel.); χρῶμα κ., of jasper, Dsc.5.142; = *venetus*, Lyd.*Mens*.4.30, *Tab.Defix.Aud*.15.5, 16.13 (Syria, iii A.D., written καλλαεινου and καλαεινου); κ. λίθος, = sq., *Peripl.M.Rubr*.39 (καλλεανός cod.); πλινθίς *AP*6.295.6 (Phan.). II. κ. κέραμος *glazed* pottery made at Alexandria, *EM*486.51, Suid.; κ. ὄστρακον Gal.12.866; τὰ καλάϊνα *PSI*4.396.9 (iii B.C.).

κάλαϊς or (in Plin. l. c.) **κάλλαϊς**, ιδος, ἡ, *precious stone of a greenish blue, turquoise*, Plin.*HN*37.151. II. *cock*, *IG*4.914.3 (Epid., v B.C.). III. = ἱστίον, Hsch.

καλακάνθη, ἡ, = χαλκάνθη, *Gp*.13.11.1.

κάλαμα· ὄγκος, ἰχθύς, Hsch.

κᾰλᾰμ-άγρωστις, εως, ἡ, *Dactyloctenium aegyptiacum*, Dsc.4.30. **-αῖος**, α, ον, *of* or *in the cornstalks* (καλάμαι): **κᾰλᾰμαία**, ἡ, a kind of *grasshopper*, μάντις ἁ κ. Theoc.10.18, cf. Sch., Hsch.: **κᾰλᾰμαῖον**, τό, a small τέττιξ, Paus.Gr.*Frr*.87,401, Hsch. s.v. κερκώπη. II. **Καλαμαῖα**, τά, festival of Demeter and Persephone at Eleusis, *IG*2^{2}.949.9 (ii B.C.).

Κᾰλᾰμαιών, ῶνος, ὁ (sc. μήν, cf. foreg. II), name of month at Miletus, *SIG*683.42 (ii B.C.); at Olbia, *IPE*I^{2}.49; at Cyzicus, *CIG*3663^{A}.

καλαμανθήλη, ἡ, = ἀνθήλη, *Edict.Diocl*.18.6.

κᾰλᾰμ-άομαι, (καλάμη) *gather cornstalks, glean*, Cratin.420; κ. τὰ ὀπίσω Lxx *De*.24.20: metaph., [Alexander] ἐθέριζε τὴν Ἀσίαν, ἐγὼ δὲ [Antigonus] καλαμῶμαι Plu.2.182a; *gather up* the stragglers of an army, Lxx *Jd*.20.45; οἱ πράκτορες καλαμῶνται ὑμᾶς ib.*Is*.3.12. **-άριον**, τό, (κάλαμος) *reed-case, pen-case*, Lyd.*Mag*.2.14, *PLond*.3.1007.5 (vi A.D.). II. = τευθίς, Sch.Opp.*H*.3.166. **-αύλης**, ου, ὁ, *one who plays on a reed-pipe*, Ath.4.176d. **-αυλητής**, οῦ, ὁ, = foreg., Hedyl.ap.Ath.ibid. **-αυλος**, ὁ, = foreg., *Cat.Cod.Astr*.8(4).217. **-εία**, ἡ, *reeds*, in a collective sense, *PTeb*.5.199 (ii B.C.); *crop of reeds* (in form -μία), *PLond*.2.163.22 (i A.D.). 2. (sc. γῆ) *reed-land*, *PTeb*.457 (ii A.D.). **-ειφύή**, ἡ, *growth of reeds*, *POxy*.1141.4 (iii A.D.). **-εύς**, έως, ὁ, *angler*, Pancrat.ap.Ath.7.305c. **-ευτής**, οῦ, ὁ (as if from *καλαμεύω), *reaper, mower*, Theoc.5.111. II. = καλαμεύς, *AP*6.167 (Agath.), 10.8 (Arch.). **-εών**, ῶνος, ὁ, = καλαμών, condemned by Phryn.144. **-η**, ἡ, (v. κάλαμος) *stalk*, esp. *the stalk* or *straw of corn*, metaph. in Hom., αἶψά τε φυλόπιδος πέλεται κόρος ἀνθρώποισιν, ἧς τε πλείστην μὲν καλάμην χθονὶ χαλκὸς ἔχευεν, ἄμητος δ' ὀλίγιστος, i.e. when there is much *straw* and little harvest, much *slaughter* and little profit, Il.19.222; κ. πυρῶν wheat-*straw*, Hdt.4.33; σῖτος σὺν τῇ καλάμῃ ἀποκείμενος X.*An*.5.4.27; καλάμαν τε καὶ ἱερὰ δράγματα.. ἀσταχύων Call.*Cer*.20; prov. of a greedy farmer, πυροὺς ἐπὶ καλάμῃ ἀροῦν to exhaust ground by one corn-crop after another, Lys.*Fr*.77: pl., σῖτος ἐπὶ ταῖς κ. D.H.5.13. 2. *stubble*, Arist.*Mete*.341^{b}27, *PSI*4.380.6 (iii B.C.), 1*Ep.Cor*.3.12, etc.: metaph., of an old man, καλάμην γέ σ' ὀΐομαι εἰσορόωντα γιγνώσκειν thou mayst still, I ween, perceive *the stubble* (i.e. *the residue*) of former strength, Od.14.214; τὸ γῆρας καλάμη Arist.*Rh*.1410^{b}14; τὴν κ. δωρῇ, δοὺς ἑτέροις τὸ θέρος *AP*11.36 (Phil.); Ῥήσου κ. *the remains* of Rhesus, i.e. his *corpse*, Orac.ap.Polyaen.6.53; ἀπὸ τῆς κ. τεκμαίρεσθαι to judge from *the remains*, Luc.*Alex*.5. 3. κολχὶς κ., = λίνον, Call.*Fr*.265. II. = κάλαμος, Hld.8.9. **-ηδόν**, Adv. *like a broken reed*, of a kind of fracture, Sor.*Fract*.10, Paul.Aeg.6.89. **-ημα**, ατος, τό, *gleanings*, Thd.*Ob*.5.

κᾰλᾰμη-τομία, Ep. -ίη, ἡ, *cutting of stalks, reaping*, *AP*6.36 (Phil.). **-τόμος**, ον, *cutting stalks, reaping*, ἅρπη A.R.4.987. **-τρια**, ἡ, *gatherer of stalks, gleaner*, Plu.2.784a (nisi leg. -τρίδας). **-τρίς**, ίδος, ἡ, = foreg., Hsch. **-φάγος** [φᾰ], ον, *devouring reeds*, i.e. *cutting* or *trimming pens*, χάλυψ *AP*6.65.3 (Paul.Sil.). **-φορέω**, *bring a corn-token* in order to receive a ration of corn (cf. κάλαμος VI), Them.*Or*.23.292a. **-φόρος**, ον, *carrying reeds*, X.*HG*2.1.2 (v. l. καλαμοφ-).

κᾰλᾰμία, v. καλαμεία.

κᾰλᾰμ-ίζω, (κάλαμος) *pipe on a reed*, Ath.15.697c (**καλαβίζω** cj. Lobeck, cf. Καλλαβίς). **-ικός**, ή, όν, *made of reeds*, σφυρίδιον *PTeb*.120.77 (i B.C.).

κᾰλᾰμίνδαρ· πλάτανος ἡδονιεῖς (sic), Hsch.

κᾰλᾰμίνθη (so Hsch., but -μίνθα Philum.*Ven*.7.9, 14.6, Phot.), ἡ, = καλάμινθος, Ar.*Ec*.648 (gen. sg.), Thphr.*CP*2.16.4 (pl.).

κᾰλᾰμινθίνη, ἡ, = foreg., Zopyr.ap.Orib.14.62.1 codd.

Κᾰλᾰμίνθιος, ὁ, *Minty*, comic name of a frog, Batr.224.

κᾰλᾰμινθ-ίτης [ῑ] οἶνος, ὁ, wine *flavoured with mint*, Dsc.5.52. **-ος**, ἡ, (μίνθα) *catmint, mint*, Nic.*Th*.60. **-ώδης**, ες, *full of mint*, Str.8.5.7, Apollon.*Lex*. s.v. κητώεσσαν.

κᾰλάμ-ῐνος [λᾰ], η, ον, *of reed*, οἰκίαι Hdt.5.101; ὀϊστοί, τόξα, Id.7.61, 65; χάραξ *PSI*4.393.6 (iii B.C.); σῦριγξ, αὐλός, Ar.*Fr*.719, Ath.4.182d; κ. πλέγμα cheese-*crate*, Poll.7.173: σκελετός, ἄπυγος, καλάμινα σκέλη φορῶν with legs *like reeds*, Pl.Com.184.3. II. *of cane, bamboo*, πλοῖα κ. Hdt.3.98. **-ιον**, τό, Dim. of καλάμη, Hsch. (pl.). II. of κάλαμος: 1. = sq. I, *POxy*.1631.14 (iii A.D.): without diminutive sense, κ. μεγάλα ib.1742.4 (iv A.D.). 2. = κάλαμος II. 8, Eust.1181.53. 3. καλάμια τῶν ὑποδέσεων, = ἀναγωγεῖς, Id.995.30: sg., Sch.Ar.*Pl*.784. 4. *splint*, Paul.Aeg.6.8. **-ίς**, ίδος, ἡ, (κάλαμος) *limed twig*, acc. -ῖδα (perh. metri gr.) *AP*10.11 (Satyr.). 2. *case for a writing-reed, pen-case*, Poll.10.59, Hsch.; *pen* (?), Phld.*Po*.2.41. 3. *toothpick* or *toothbrush*, Dsc.1.70; = κάλαμος II. 7, Id.*Eup*.1.60, Paul.Aeg.6.24; also of *quills* used as *splints* for broken noses, ib.91. 4. = κάλαμος II. 8, Poll.5.96, Hsch. 5. pl., καλαμίδες (sic *AB*269), αἱ, *reeds put in layers* to strengthen buildings, *IG*11(2).144*A* 61, 62 (Delos, iv B.C.), *Inscr.Délos* 366 *A* 36 (iii B.C.), *IG*2^{2}.1672.64, cf. *AB* l. c.; also, *bundles*, ibid. 6. at Cerynea, = καλαμαία, Hsch. **-ίσκος**, ὁ, Dim. of κάλαμος, used as a tube or phial, Ar.*Ach*.1034, *Gp*.20.24.1; in Surgery, Antyll.ap.Orib.44.23.39, Gal.2.873, Paul.Aeg.6.88. 2. *branch of a candlestick*, Lxx *Ex*.25.30(31). **-ιστρος**, ὁ, *stipula*, *Gloss*. **-ίτης** [ῑ], ου, ὁ, = καλάμινος, *reed-like*, στύραξ Alex.Trall.5.4, al., Aët.1.133. II. ὁ κ. ἥρως, perh. the hero *of the probe* or, *of the splints*, nickname of Aristomachus, a surgeon who had a statue at Athens, called ὁ ἥρως ὁ ἰατρός, D.18.129, cf. 19.249. **-ῖτις**, ιδος, ἡ, = καλαμαία, *AP*7.198 (Leon.).

κᾰλᾰμο-βόας, α, ὁ, *noisy with the pen*, nickname of Antipater, who dared not argue *viva voce* with Carneades, Plu.2.514d. **-γλῠφέω**, *cut reeds, make pens*, Hdn.Gr.1.468. **-γλύφος** [ῠ], ον, *making pens*, *EM*485.35. **-γραφία**, Ep. -ίη, ἡ, *writing with a reed* or *pen*, Man.4.72. **-δύτης** [ῠ], ου, ὁ, (δύω) a kind of bird, perh. *the reed-warbler*, Ael.*NA*6.46. **-ειδής**, ές, *reed-like*, Dsc.3.142. **-εις**, εσσα, εν, *of reed*, συρίγγων καλαμοεσσᾶν E.*IA*1038 (lyr.). **-θήκη**, ἡ, *reed-case*, *Gloss*. **-θήρας**, ου, ὁ, *angler*, Procl.*in Cra*.p.40 P. **-κεντρῖτις** (sc. γῆ), ιδος, ἡ, land *overgrown with prickly rush*, *POxy*.1911.101 (vi A.D.). **-κόπιον**, τό, *reed-bed for cutting*, *Gp*.2.6.31. **-κόπος**, ὁ, *reed-cutter*, *BGU*1529.2 (iii B.C.). **-κρῖνον**, τό, prob. = κάλαμος ἀρωματικός, Aët.1.132. **-πώλης**, ου, ὁ, *reed-seller*, *PCair.Zen*.398.5 (iii B.C.).

κάλᾰμος [κᾰ], ὁ, *reed*, used for thatching or wattling, Hdt.5.101, al., Th.2.76; for wreaths, κ. λευκός Ar.*Nu*.1006 (anap.); for bedding, Plu.*Lyc*.16; for fuel, *PCair.Zen*.85 (iii B.C.); various species, κ. εὐώδης, ἀρωματικός, *sweet flag, Acorus Calamus*, Thphr.*HP*4.8.4, 9.7.1, *Od*.33, Dsc.1.18; κ. αὐλητικός *pole-reed, Arundo Donax*, Thphr.*HP*4.11.1, 9; κ. εἰλετίας *marram, Ammophila arundinacea*, ib.13; κ. ἐπίγειος *bush-grass, Calamagrostis epigeios*, ibid.; κ. Ἰνδικός *bamboo, Bambusa arundinacea*, ibid., Dsc.5.92, *PLond*.2.191.11 (ii A.D.), *Gp*.2.6.23, cf. Hdt.3.98; κ. Ἰνδικὸς ὁ ἄρρην *male bamboo, Dendrocalamus strictus*, Thphr.*HP*4.11.13; κ. κύπριος, = δόναξ, Asclep.ap.Gal.12.414; κ. πλόκιμος *spear-grass, Phragmites communis*, Thphr.*HP*4.11.1; κ. χαρακίας, *Arundo Donax*, ibid. II. applied to various uses, 1. *reed-pipe, flute*, Pi.*O*.10(11).84, *N*.5.38, E.*El*.702 (lyr.), *IT*1126 (lyr.). 2. *fishing-rod*, Pl.Com.11, Theoc.21.43, Luc.*DMort*.27.9; κ. ἁλιευτικός Arist.*PA*693^{a}23. 3. *limed* *twig* used by fowlers, Bion *Fr.*10.5, Aesop.171, 296. 4. *shaft* of an arrow, Ptol.*Alm.*7.5; made of κ. τοξικός or Κρητικός, Thphr.*HP*4.11.11. 5. *reed-pen*, Lxx *Ps.*44(45).1, 3*Ep.Jo.*13, Plu.*Dem.*29, Luc.*Hist.Conscr.*38; κάλαμοι γραφικοί *PGrenf.*2.38.7 (i B.C.); κ. γραφεῖς Poll.10.61. 6. *measuring-rod*, *Apoc.*11.1, al.: hence, a definite measure, *IG*9(1).61.50 (Daulis, ii A.D.); = 5 πήχεις, Hero *Geom.*4.11; = 6⅔ πήχεις, ib.23.13. 7. Medic., *tube* for insufflation, Aret.*CA*1.9, Asclep.ap.Gal.12.985; for fumigation, Dsc.*Eup.*1.56; for extraction, Cels.7.5.2; also, *splint*, Pall. *in Hp.Fract.*12.282 C. 8. ornament of female dress, *AP*6.292 (Hedyl.). 9. *stake* to which vines were tied, *PFlor.*369.4 (ii A.D.), Jul.*Or.*3.125b, etc. III. collectively, 1. *reed*, i.e. *reeds*, Arist.*Mete.*359^{b}1, *POxy.*742.2 (i B.C.), etc.: in pl., *reed-beds*, Plb.3.71.4. 2. of plants, which are neither shrub nor bush (ὕλη), nor tree (δένδρον), X.*An.*1.5.1. 3. *mat of reeds*, Pl.*R.*372b; *roof of reeds* (Coan), Hsch. IV. = καλάμη, *stalk* of wheat, X.*Oec.*18.2. V. ὁ κ. τοῦ σκέλους the *shin-bone*, Sch.Luc.*VH*1.23. VI. *ticket* for obtaining corn-rations, = *tessera frumentaria*, *Gloss.* (Cf. Lat. *culmus*, OHG. *halm*, etc.)

κᾰλᾰμο-στᾰσία, ἡ, *fixing of vine-poles*, *PGiss.*56.12 (vi A.D.). **-στεφής**, ές, *covered with reed*, βύρσαι Batr.127. **-σφάκτης**, ου, ὁ, *one who kills with a pen*, Ph.2.536. **-τομος**, ον, *furnished with reeds cut for vine-poles*, κτῆμα *BGU*863.16 (ii A.D.). **-τύπορ** [ῠ], ὁ, *one who catches birds with limed twigs* (Lacon.), Hsch. (-ον cod.).

κᾰλᾰμουργ-έω, *set up poles for vines*, *PTeb.*120.141 (i B.C.), *PSI* 4.317.6 (i A.D.):—hence **-ία**, ἡ, *PLond.*2.163.24 (i A.D.).

κᾰλᾰμό-φθογγος, ον, *played on a reed*, of tunes, Ar.*Ra.*230 (lyr.). **-φόρος**, ον, cf. καλαμηφ-. **-φυλλος**, ον, *with leaves like those of reeds*, Thphr.*HP*1.10.5. II. Subst. -φυλλα, τά, = καλάμου φύλλα, *Gp.*10.44, *Hippiatr.*129.

κᾰλᾰμόχνοος, contr. **-χνους**, ὁ, = ἀδάρκη, Plin.*HN*32.140.

κᾰλᾰμ-όω, *bind a fractured bone with a splint of reed*, Gal.14.561. II. Pass., *grow into stalk*, Thphr.*HP*8.2.4. **-ώδης**, ες, *rushy*, *full of reeds*, τὰ κ. Arist.*HA*550^{b}7, 568^{a}21; κ. λίμνη *AP*7.365 (Zonas); κ. τόπος D.C.63.28; *of a reedy character*, Thphr.*HP*1.6.7, al. **-ών**, ῶνος, ὁ, *reed-bed*, Posidipp.(?) in *PLit.Lond.*60.21, *Gp.*3.6.6, Paus.Dam.p.160 D., Sch.Il.18.576. **-ωτή**, ἡ, *fence* or *edging of reed*, Eust.1533.51; cf. καλαμῶται· εἶδος ἐσχάρας, Hsch.

κᾰλάνδαι, ῶν, αἱ, = Lat. *Calendae*, D.H.6.49, Plu.*Cic.*2, etc.:—hence **καλανδικά**, τά, *new year's allowances*, *POxy.*1869 (vi A.D.), Just.*Edict.*13.3.

κάλανδρος, ὁ, a kind of *lark*, Dionys.*Av.*3.15.

καλάνι, for καλή, barbarism in Ar.*Av.*1678.

καλαντίων, dub. sens. in *PCornell* 33 (iii A.D.).

Καλαοίδια, τά, festival of Artemis in Laconia, Hsch.; cf. καλαβοίδια.

κᾰλάπους, ποδος, ὁ, (κᾶλον) *shoemaker's last*, Pl.*Smp.*191a, Poll.10.141:—also **κᾱλόπους**, v.l. in Pl. l. c., cf. Poll.2.195, Gal.*Thras.*43, *Edict.Diocl.*9.1a, *EM*486.6. II. a kind of *servant*, Suid. s.v. ὄνον ὄρνιν, οἰωνοί (= Sch.Ar.*Av.*722).

κᾰλαπόδιον, τό, Dim. of foreg. I, Gal.6.364 (v.l. καλοπόδιον, q.v.).

καλαρῖνες· ὀχετοί (Lacon.), Hsch.

κάλαρις, ὁ, a small *bird*, preyed on by the αἰγώλιος and birds of prey generally, Arist.*HA*609^{a}27.

καλαρρυγαί· τάφροι, Amerias ap.Hsch.:—Ambraciot word, acc. to Sch.Gen.Il.21.259 (in form **καλαρύα**).

κᾰλάσῖρις [λᾰ], ιος, ἡ, *a long Egyptian garment*, with tassels or fringe at bottom, Hdt.2.81, Cratin.30; also, *a Persian garment* of like kind, Democr.Eph.1; used in the Mysteries of Andania, *IG*5(1).1390.17 (in form **καλάσηρις**):—title of a Comedy of Alexis. Cf. τρυφοκαλάσιρις. II. as pr. n., Καλασίριες, οἱ, a branch of the military caste in Egypt, Hdt.2.164, etc.

καλασίριτα· τὰ λοχία ἃ καλοῦσιν ᾠά, Hsch.

καλαυνεῖ· τρυφᾷ, ἐμπίπλαται, and **καλαυρεῖ**· τρυφᾷ, Hsch.

Κᾰλαύρεια, ἡ, *Calauria*, an island off Troezen, A.R.3.1243, *IG*4.752.18 (Troezen, ii B.C.), etc.; later **Καλαυρία**, Str.8.6.3, etc.: **Κᾰλαυρῖα**, ἡ, D.P.499:—hence **Κᾰλαυρεάτης**, ου, Dor. **-τᾶς**, α, ὁ, *citizen of C.*, *IG*4.839 (Calauria, iv B.C.); **Καλαυρῖτις** λιθάργυρος, f.l. for σκαλαυθρῖτις, Dsc.5.87.

κᾰλαυρόπιον, τό, Dim. of καλαῦροψ, Artem.4.72.

κᾰλαυρόφις· βακτηριοφόρος, Hsch.

κᾰλαῦροψ, οπος, ἡ, *shepherd's staff* or *crook*, which was thrown so as to drive back the cattle to the herd, Il.23.845, Antim.61, A.R.2.33, *AP*6.106 (Zonas), *APl.*4.74, D.H.1.39, Longus 1.8, *BSA*16.107 (Pamphylia, ii/iii A.D.). (Prob. καλά-ϝροψ, from *ϝρέπω, v. ῥέπω: but the first part of the word is uncertain.)

κάλαφος, ὁ, = ἀσκάλαφος (Magnesia), Hsch.

καλβάτεινος, = καρβάτινος, Ephor.(?) in *PLit.Lond.*114.

καλέας or **καλλέας**, ὁ, = δορύκνιον, Crateuas ap.Dsc.4.74.

καλειάς, v. καλιάς.

καλεσάνδρα, ἡ, *summoner of men*, epith. of ἄρκτος, *PMag.Lond.*121.696 (καδ- Pap.).

κάλεσις, εως, ἡ, v. κλῆσις III.

κᾰλεσίχορος [ῐ], ον, only in Ep. form **καλεσσ-**: *calling forth the dance*, *calling to the dance*, Βρόμιος Orph.*L.*718.

κᾰλεστής, οῦ, ὁ, gloss on κλητήρ, Sch.rec.A.*Th.*574: **κᾰλεστός**, ή, όν, = κλητός, *Gloss.*

καλεύειν· λιθοβολεῖν, Hsch. (κα- for κατα-). **καλέχες**· κατάκεισο (Paph.), Id. (cf. foreg. and λέχομαι). **κάληβος**, = κάβηλος, Id. **καλημνεῖ**· καλεῖ σαφῶς, Id.

κᾰλέω, Aeol. **κάλημι** (q.v.), Ep. inf. καλήμεναι Il.10.125: Ion. impf. καλέεσκον 6.402; 3sg. κάλεσκε A.R.4.1514: fut., Ion. καλέω Il.3.383, Att. καλῶ Pl.*Smp.*175a, X.*Smp.*1.15, etc.; later καλέσω Lxx *Ge.*16.11, al., Ph.1.69, (παρα-) D.8.14 codd., *SIG*656.40 (Teos, ii B.C.), (ἐγ-) v.l. in D.19.133, cf. 23.123 codd. (καλέσω in S.*Ph.*1452 (anap.), Ar.*Pl.*964, etc., is aor. 1 subj.): aor. 1 ἐκάλεσα, Ep. ἐκάλεσσα, κάλεσσα, Od.17.379, Il.16.693 (late Ep. ἔκλησα Nic.*Fr.*86, late Prose ἐκάλησα Ps.-Callisth.3.35): pf. κέκληκα Ar.*Pl.*260, etc.:—Med., Att. fut. καλοῦμαι Id.*Nu.*1221, *Ec.*864; in pass. sense, S.*El.*971, E.*Or.*1140, etc.; later καλέσομαι (ἐκ-, ἐπι-) dub. l. in Aeschin.1.174, Lycurg.17: aor. 1 ἐκαλεσάμην Hdt.7.189, Pl.*Lg.*937a; Ep. καλεσσάμην Il.1.54, 3 pl. καλέσαντο ib.270:—Pass., fut. κεκλήσομαι Il.3.138, A.*Th.*698 (lyr.), *Pr.*840, etc.; κληθήσομαι Pl.*Lg.*681d, Lxx *Ge.*48.6, v.l. in E.*Tr.*13: aor. ἐκλήθην Archil.78, S.*OT*1359, Ar.*Th.*862, etc.: pf. κέκλημαι, Ep. 3 pl. κεκλήαται A.R.1.1128, Ion. κεκλέαται Hdt.2.164; Ep. 3 pl. plpf. κεκλήατο Il.10.195; opt. κεκλῄμην, κεκλῇο S.*Ph.*119, κεκλῄμεθα Ar.*Lys.*253: late pf. κεκάλεσμαι Suid. s.v. κλητή. I. *call*, *summon*, εἰς ἀγορὴν καλέσαντα Od.1.90; ἐς Ὄλυμπον Il.1.402; ἀγορήνδε, θάλαμόνδε, θάνατόνδε, Il.20.4, Od.2.348, Il.16.693: c. acc. only, κεκλήατο (for -ηντο) βουλήν *they had been summoned* to the council, 10.195: folld. by inf., αὐτοὶ γὰρ κάλεον συμμητιάασθαι ib.197; καιρὸς καλεῖ.. S.*Ph.*466; κἄμ' ὑπηρετεῖν καλεῖς Id.*El.*996; κ. τινὰ εἰς ἕ, ἐπὶ οἷ, Il.23.203, Od.17.330, etc.; εἰς μαρτυρίαν κληθείς Pl.*Lg.*937a; ἐμὲ νῦν ἤδη καλεῖ ἡ εἱμαρμένη Id.*Phd.*115a; *demand*, *require*, ἡ ἡμέρα 'κείνη εὔνουν καὶ πλούσιον ἄνδρα ἐκάλει D.18.172: aor. Med., καλέσασθαί τινα *call to oneself*, freq. in Ep., Il.1.270, Od.8.43, etc.; φωνῇ Il.3.161; ἀγορήνδε λαόν 1.54; *call* a witness, Pl.*Lg.* l.c. 2. *call to one's house* or *to a repast*, *invite* (not in Il.), Od.10.231, 17.382, al., 1*Ep.Cor.*10.27; later usu. with a word added, κ. ἐπὶ δεῖπνον Hdt.9.16 (Pass.), X.*Cyr.*2.1.30, etc.; ἐς ἔρανον Pi.*O.*1.37; ἐς θοίνην E.*Ion* 1140; ὑπὸ σοῦ κεκλημένος Pl.*Smp.*174d, etc.; κληθέντες πρός τινα *invited* to his house, D.19.196; ὁ κεκλημένος the *guest*, Damox.2.26. 3. *invoke*, Δία Hdt.1.44, cf. Pi.*O.*6.58, A.*Th.*223; at sacrifices, Sch.Ar.*Ra.*482; μάρτυρας κ. θεούς S.*Tr.*1248, cf. D.18.141:—Med., τοὺς θεοὺς καλούμεθα A.*Ch.*201, cf. 216; also μαρτύριά τε καὶ τεκμήρια καλεῖσθε Id.*Eu.*486; but ἀράς, ἅς σοι καλοῦμαι which I *call down* on thee, S.*OC*1385:—Pass., of the god, *to be invoked*, A.*Eu.*417. 4. as law-term, *summon*, of the judge, καλεῖν τινας εἰς τὸ δικαστήριον *cite* or *summon* before the court, D.19.211, etc.; simply καλεῖν ib.212, Ar.*V.*851, etc.; ἐὰν μὲν καλέσῃ D.21.56; also ὁ ἄρχων τὴν δίκην καλεῖ *calls on* the case, Ar.*V.*1441:—Pass., ἡ πατροκτόνος δίκη κεκλῆτ' ἂν αὐτῷ S.*Fr.*696; πρὶν τὴν ἐμὴν [δίκην] καλεῖσθαι before it *is called on*, Ar.*Nu.*780; καλουμένης τῆς γραφῆς D.58.43; but, b. of the plaintiff in Med., καλεῖσθαί τινα *to sue* at law, *bring before the court*, Ar.*Nu.*1221, al., D.23.63; κ. τινὰ ὕβρεως Ar.*Av.*1046; κ. τινὰ πρὸς τὴν ἀρχήν Pl.*Lg.*914c; ὁ καλεσάμενος the *plaintiff*, *PHal.*1.224 (iii B.C.). 5. with an abstract subject, *demand*, *require*, καλεῖ ἡ τάξις c. inf., *CP Herm.*25 ii 7 (iii A.D.). 6. metaph. in Pass., καλουμένης τῆς δυνάμεως πρὸς τὴν συναναληψίαν *called forth*, *summoned*, Sor.1.29. II. *call by name*, *name*, ὃν Βριάρεων καλέουσι θεοί Il.1.403, cf. Od.5.273, etc.; κοτύλην δέ τέ μιν καλέουσι Il.5.306; ὥς σφας καλοῦμεν Εὐμενίδας S.*OC*486, cf. A.*Pr.*86, etc.; ὄνομα καλεῖν τινα *call* him by a name, εἴπ' ὄνομ' ὅττι σε κεῖθι κάλεον Od.8.550, cf. E.*Ion* 259, Pl.*Cra.*383b, etc. (in Pass., οὔνομα καλέεσθαι Hdt.1.173, cf. Pi.*O.*6.56): without ὄνομα, τί νιν καλοῦσα τύχοιμ' ἄν; A.*Ag.*1232; τοῦτο αὐτὴν κάλεον Call.*Fr.*66b; τούτοις τὸ ὄνομα "ἱμάτια" ἐκαλέσαμεν Pl.*Plt.*279e (Pass., τύμβῳ δ' ὄνομα σῷ κεκλήσεται *shall be given* to thy tomb, E.*Hec.*1271); κ. ὄνομα ἐπί τινι *give* a name to something, Pl.*Prm.*147d; but *call* (a man) a name *because of* some function, Id.*Sph.*218c; κ. τινὰ ἐπὶ τῷ ὀνόματι τοῦ πατρός *Ev.Luc.*1.59; ἐπ' ὀνόματος καλεῖν τινα Plb.35.4.11:—Pass., *to be named* or *called*, Μυρμιδόνες δὲ καλεῦντο Il.2.684; εἰ τόδ' αὐτῷ φίλον κεκλημένῳ A.*Ag.*161 (lyr.); ὁ καλούμενος the *so-called*, ἐν τῇ Θεράπνῃ καλεομένῃ Hdt.6.61; ὁ κ. θάνατος Pl.*Phd.*86d; οἱ "τῶν ὁμοτίμων" κ. X.*Cyr.*2.1.9; κεκλημένος τινός *called from* or *after* him, Pi.*P.*3.67; καλεῖσθαι ἐπί τινι Lxx *Ge.*48.6; κέκληνται δέ σφιν ἕδραι Pi.*O.*7.76. 2. Pass., *to be called*, almost = εἰμί, esp. with words expressing kinship or status, ἐμὸς γαμβρὸς καλέεσθαι Od.7.313, cf. A.*Pers.*2 (anap.); ἀφνειοὶ καλέονται Od.15.433; esp. in pf. Pass. κέκλημαι, οὕνεκα σὴ παράκοιτις κέκλημαι because I *am* thy wife, Il.4.61; φίλη κεκλήσῃ ἄκοιτις 3.138; αἲ γὰρ ἐμοὶ τοιόσδε πόσις κεκλημένος εἴη Od.6.244; ἠγάγετ' ἐς μέγα δῶμα φίλην κεκλῆσθαι ἄκοιτιν Hes.*Th.*410; σὴ κεκλημένη..ῆα *h.Ap.*324; μηδ' ἔτι Τηλεμάχοιο πατὴρ κεκλημένος εἴην Il.2.260; οὗτινος δοῦλοι κέκληνται A.*Pers.*242, cf. S.*El.*366, etc. 3. special constructions, a. Ἀλησίου ἔνθα κολώνη κέκληται where *is* the hill *called* the hill of Alesios, Il.11.758; ἵνα κριοῦ καλέονται εὐναί A.R.4.115; ἔνθα ἡ Τριπυργία καλεῖται X.*HG*5.1.10, etc.:—so in Act., ἔνθα Ῥέας πόρον ἄνθρωποι καλέοισιν where *is* the ford men *call* the ford of Rhea, Pi.*N.*9.41, cf. κικλήσκω, κλῄζω, κλέω. b. folld. by a dependent clause, ἐκάλεσσέ νιν ἰσώνυμον ἔμμεν *said that* his *name* should be the same, Id.*O.*9.63; καλεῖ με πλαστὸς ὡς εἴην πατρί, i.e. καλεῖ με πλαστόν S.*OT*780; καλοῦμέν γε παραδιδόντα μὲν διδάσκειν *we say* that one who delivers teaches, Pl.*Tht.*198b, cf. *Smp.*205d; τὰς ἀμπέλους τραγᾶν καλοῦσιν Arist.*HA*546^{a}3.

κάλη, καλήτης, v. κήλη, κηλήτης.

καλήγιον, v. καλίγιον.

καλήζω, Cypr., = καλέω, Hdn.Gr.1.444.

κᾰλήμερος, ον, *bringing a fair day* (opp. κακήμερος), *AP*9.508 (Pall.); καλήμερε, χαῖρε *Mim.Oxy.*413.67.

κάλημι [ᾰ], Aeol. for καλέω, Sapph.1.16 (v.l. -ημμι), *Supp.*21.4: 3 sg. impf. ἐκάλη Alc.*Supp.*10.5.

κᾰλήτωρ, ορος, ὁ, (καλέω) *crier,* κήρυκα καλήτορα τοῖο γέροντος Il.24.577: pr.n. in 15.419.

κᾰλιά, Ion. -ιή, ἡ, *wooden dwelling, hut,* Hes.*Op.*374, 503, Call.*Fr.*131; esp. *barn, granary,* Hes.*Op.*301, 307; bird's *nest,* Theoc. 29.12, Ps.-Phoc.84, A.R.1.170, 4.1095, Luc.*Syr.D.*29, *Anacreont.* 25.7; *lair,* ὕστριχος Call.*Dian.*96; *shrine* or *grotto,* containing the image of a god, *AP*6.253 (Crin.), *IG*12(2).484.15 (Mytil.). Cf. καλιός. [ῑ in Hes., etc.; ῐ in Theoc. and Ps.-Phoc.]

κᾰλῑάδιον, τό, Dim. of sq., *model of a hut,* κ. ἐλεφάντινον *JHS*41.196 (Delos, ii B.C.).

κᾰλῑάς, άδος, ἡ, = καλιά, *hut,* *AP*11.44 (Phld.), Plu.2.418a; *chapel, shrine,* *IG*2^2.1533.5 (iv B.C.), D.H.3.70, Plu.*Num.*8, etc.; *nest,* in form καλειάς, Max.Tyr.16.5 (pl.).

κᾰλίγιον [ῐγ], τό, Dim. of Lat. *caliga, boot,* *PSI*8.886 (iv A.D.), Anon. *in Rh.*123.21; written καλήγιον Aët.7.101.

κᾰλίδιον [ῑδ], τό, Dim. of καλιά, Eup.42, prob. in *Com.Adesp.* 1335:—also **καλίδια**· ἔντερα (Cypr.), Hsch.

κᾰλῑδόω, v. κηλιδόω.

κᾰλίζομαι, (καλιά) *live in huts,* in Lacon. aor. 1 ἐκαλίξαντο, Hsch.

κάλιθος· οἶνος, Ameriasap.Hsch.

κάλικα, ἡ, only in gen. pl. καλικῶν, = Lat. *caliga, boot,* *Edict. Diocl.*9.5, al.:—hence **κᾰλῐκαρικός,** ή, όν, *belonging to boots,* φόρμαι ibid.

καλίκιοι, οἱ, = Lat. *calcei,* Plb.30.18.3.

κάλικον· βόθρον, Hsch.

κᾰλινδ-έομαι, only in pres. and impf., = κυλινδέομαι (q.v.), *roll about, wallow,* ἀποθνῄσκοντες ἐν ταῖς ὁδοῖς ἐκαλινδοῦντο, of plague-stricken persons, Th.2.52; of birds, κ. ἐν τῇ γῇ, κ. τοῖς πτεροῖς πρὸς τὴν κόνιν, Arist.*HA*612^{a}20, ^{b}24; ⟨ἐν⟩ ῥεύμασι Plu.*Tim.*28; ἐπὶ ἐλαίου, as a form of exercise, Gal.6.220, cf. 324; *roam,* κατὰ τὰς νάπας X.*An.*5.2.31; ἐν τῇσι στοιῇσι Hdt.3.52: metaph., ἐν θιάσοις καὶ μεθύουσιν ἀνθρώποις κ. D.19.199: hence, *to be continually busy with, pass one's time in* a thing, ἐν τῷ πειρᾶσθαι X.*Cyr.*1.4.5 (v.l. κυλινδ-); περὶ τὰς ἔριδας, περὶ τὰ δικαστήρια, Isoc.13.20, 15.30; κ. ἐπὶ τοῦ βήματος Id. 5.81 (v.l. κυλ-); ἐν ἀγοραῖς S.E.*M.*2.27. **-ήθρα,** ἡ, = ἀλινδήθρα, *place for horses to roll after exercise,* Ael.*NA*3.2. **-ησις,** εως, ἡ, = κυλίνδησις, *a throw of the dice,* Alciphr.3.42 (pl.).

κάλῐνος [ᾱ], η, ον, (κᾶλον) *wooden,* Lyc.1418, Epich.100a, A.R.2.381a; κολοσσός *Berl.Sitzb.*1927.167 (Cyrene).

κάλιον, τό, Dim. of κᾶλον, Hsch.

κᾰλῑός, ὁ, *cabin, hovel,* Epich.39. 2. *fowl-coop,* Cratin.72. 3. *prison,* Hsch.

καλιότερος, irreg. Comp., = καλλίων, *BGU*948.8.

καλίς· σκέπαρνον, Hsch.

κᾰλίστρα, ἡ, = κυλίστρα, f.l. in X.*Eq.*5.3.

κᾰλιστρέω, = καλέω, D.47.60 (restored fr. Harp. s.v. ἐκαλίστρουν), Call.*Dian.*67, *Cer.*98.

καλιῶσαι· πρᾶξαι (fort. ἀρᾶξαι), πατάξαι, Hsch.

κάλκιος, = κάλτιος, *PGen.*80.9 (iv A.D.).

κάλλα ἢ κάννα· κάλαμος, Hsch.

καλλά, Adv., Dor. for καλά, Alcm.98, cf. A.D.*Adv.*155.10.

Καλλᾰβίς, ίδος, ἡ, *a wanton dance,* Καλλαβίδας βαίνειν Eup.163 (lyr.), cf. Phot.:—written **Καλαβίς** in Hsch.

καλλαινιοποιοῖς (dat. pl.), prob. *makers of blue dye,* *PBodl.ined.* c.88 (P.).

καλλάϊνος, v. καλάϊνος.

κάλλαιον, τό, *cock's comb,* Arist.*HA*631^{b}10, 28: pl., κάλλαια, τά, *wattles,* Ar.*Eq.*497, Ael.*NA*5.5, 15.2, Paus.9.23.4. 2. *cock's tail-feathers,* Ael.Dion.*Fr.*219.

κάλλαϊς, v. κάλα-.

καλλαμβάνω, aor. part. Pass. καλλάφθεις, Aeol. for καταληφ-, *IG* 12(2).526.20 (Eresus).

καλλᾰρίας, ου, ὁ, a kind of *cod-fish,* Archestr.*Fr.*14, Opp.*H.*1.105, Hsch. s.v. λαζίνης.

καλλαροί· βάρβαροι, Hsch. **καλλέας,** v. καλέας. **καλλείπω,** Ep. for καταλείπω. **κάλλειψιν**· κατάλειψιν, Id. **κάλλης**· καρπίμου, Id.

καλλῐ-, in compds., *beautiful*: καλο- is later and less common. 2. like a mere Adj. with its Subst., as καλλίπαις, = καλὴ παῖς.

καλλῐ-άζω, *to be a member of the* κάλλιον (q.v.) at Cyzicus, *IGRom.*4.153, 157:—also **-αρχέω,** *to be president of the* κάλλιον (q.v.) at Cyzicus, *CIG*3661.

καλλῐᾰρία, ἡ, Dor. for *καλλιερία, *auspicious sacrifice* (cf. καλλιερέω), *Abh.Berl.Akad.*1928(6).16 (Cos).

καλλίας, ου (Lacon. **καλλίαρ** Hsch.), ὁ, = πίθηκος, *tame ape,* Din.*Fr.*6.2; Ion. **καλλίης** Herod.3.41: a euphemism, cf. Gal.18(2).236, 611.

καλλῐαστράγᾰλος [ᾰγ], ον, *with fine ankle,* Arist.*HA*499^{b}22.

καλλιβάντες· ὅμοια σμιλίοις καὶ ψαλίσιν, ἐν αἷς τὰς ὀφρῦς κοσμοῦσιν αἱ γυναῖκες, Hsch.

καλλι-βλέφᾰρος, ον, *with beautiful eyelids*: *beautiful-eyed,* E.*Ion* 189 (lyr.). II. as Subst., κ. (sc. φάρμακον), τό, *paint for the eyelids and eyelashes,* Dsc.1.69, 1*Enoch*8.1, Gal.12.211: as Adj., κ. δυνάμεις ib.62. **-βόας,** α, ὁ, *beautiful-sounding,* αὐλός Simon.46.3, S.*Tr.*640 (lyr.), Ar.*Av.*682 (lyr.). **-βολος,** ὁ, name of a *throw at dice,* Poll. 7.204. **-βοτος,** ον, *with fine pastures,* Nonn.*D.*35.59. **-βοτρυς,** υ, *beautiful-clustering,* νάρκισσος S.*OC*682 (lyr.). **-βωλος,** ον, *with rich soil,* Ἴδας ὄρος E.*Or.*1382 (lyr.). **-γάληνος,** Dor. **-γάλᾱνος** [γᾰ], ον, *beautiful in its calm,* πρόσωπα Id.*Tr.*837 (lyr.). **-γᾰμος,** ον, *of happy marriage,* λέκτρα *AP*9.765 (Paul. Sil.). **-γένεθλος,** ον, *beautifully formed,* καρπός prob. in Poet. *de herb.*104. II. Act., *having a fair offspring,* Corinn.23, Procl.*H.*6.1. **-γένεια,** ἡ, *bearer of a fair offspring,* name by which Demeter was invoked in the Thesmophoria, Ar.*Th.*299, Alciphr.2.4, cf. *IG*14.205 (Acrae); or her nurse, Ar.ap.Phot.; epith. of the Moon, *Hymn.Mag.*5.31; of the Earth, Apollod.ap.Phot.:—neut. pl., **Καλλιγένεια** θύειν offer *sacrifice to Demeter K.,* Alciphr.3.39 (nisi leg. τῇ Κ.). **-γέφῡρος,** ον, *with beautiful bridges,* ποταμός E.*Rh.*349 (lyr.). **-γλουτος,** ον, = καλλίπυγος, Nic.*Fr.*23. **-γονος,** ον, *of noble race,* Porph.ap.Eus. *PE*3.11 (v.l. καλλιγόνης); τέκνων καλλιγόνους σταχύας *IG*12(3).1188 (Melos):—fem. **Καλλιγόνη,** ἡ, epith. of Demeter at Pergamon, *Ath. Mitt.*37.288.

καλλιγρᾰφ-έω, *write beautifully,* in point of style, metaph. in Med., κ. τὴν ἀπομίμησιν τοῖς τῆς ἀρετῆς στοιχείοις Arist.*Rh.Al.*1420^{b}17: pf. Pass. in act. sense, Longin.33.5; in pass. sense, κεκαλλιγραφημένοι λόγοι J.*Ap.*2.31, cf. D.L.7.18: later use for Att. εἰς κάλλος γράφειν, Phryn.99. II. *paint beautifully,* τὸ πρόσωπον Poll.5.102. **-ία,** ἡ, *beautiful writing,* whether of the characters or the style, cf. Plu. 2.397c with 145f; as a subject of competition in schools, *good handwriting,* *CIG*3088 (Teos): in pl., *elegances* of style, D.L.3.66. **-ικός,** ή, όν, *suited for fine penmanship,* ἐργαλεῖον Suid. s.v. κανονίς; but σφάλμα κ. *copyist's* error, Steph. *in Hp.*2.407 D. **-ος** (parox.), *penman, copyist,* *Edict.Diocl.* in *IG*5(1).1406 (Asine), Hdn. post Moer. p.477 P., *An.Ox.*2.397, Pall. *in Hp.*2.102 D.

καλλῐ-γύναιξ [ῠ], ὁ, ἡ, gen. αικος, *with beautiful women,* poet. word, only in obl. cases, Ἑλλάδα καλλιγύναικα, Ἀχαιΐδα κ., Σπάρτην κ., Il.2.683, 3.75, Od.13.412: gen., Sapph.[26]: dat., Pi.*P.*9.74. **-δενδρος,** ον, *with fine trees,* of places, Plb.5.19.2 (Sup.), Sch. Pi.*O.*9.27. **-δίνης** [δῑ], ου, Dor. **-ᾱς,** α, ὁ, *with beautiful eddies,* Πηνειός E.*HF*368 (lyr.). **-διφρος,** ον, *with beautiful chariot,* πῶλοι Id.*Hec.*467 (lyr.). **-δόναξ,** ὁ, ἡ, gen. ἄκος, *with beautiful reeds,* Εὐρώτας Id.*Hel.*493. **-δώρα**· καλλιονύμφη, Hsch. **-έθειρος,** ὁ, ἡ, *with beautiful hair,* Orph.*H.*50.7: pecul. fem. καλλιέθειρα Nonn. *D.*27.248. **-έλαιος,** ἡ, *garden olive,* opp. ἀγριέλαιος, *Ep.Rom.* 11.24:—fem. **-ελαία,** ἡ, *Arch.Pap.*2.218 (iii/iv A.D.): as Adj., κ. ἐλαία *PCair.Zen.*125.3 (iii B.C.), *Gp.*9.8; φυτόν ib.9.10.6.

καλλῐέπ-εια, ἡ, *beautiful language,* Herm. *in Phdr.*p.68 A., Hsch. **-έομαι,** *say in fine phrases,* κ. ὡς . . εἰκότως ἄρχομεν Th.6.83; εἰ δοῦλος καλλιεποῖτο *use fine language,* Arist.*Rh.*1404^{b}16; ῥημάτων ὧν οἱ δεξιοὶ περὶ τὰς δίκας -εποῦνται Pl.*Hipparch.*225c:—Pass., λόγοι κεκαλλιεπημένοι ῥήμασί τε καὶ ὀνόμασι Id.*Ap.*17b:—later in Act., **καλλιεπέω,** Them.*Or.*20 p.285 D. **-ής,** ές, *elegant in diction,* Ar. *Th.*49 (of Agathon), 60, D.H.*Comp.*18; etym. of Καλλιόπη, Corn. *ND*14.

καλλῐεργ-έω, in Pass., *to be worked beautifully,* Phlp. *in Ph.*327.1; of land, *to be well-cultivated,* *Sammelb.*5168.27 (ii A.D.). **-ία,** ἡ, *good work,* of improvements made by a tenant, Just.*Nov.*64.1: generally, *good cultivation,* *Sammelb.*4481.16 (v A.D.), etc. **-ος,** ον, f.l. for καλεῖ ἔργον (cj. Bernays) in Ph.2.490.

καλλῐερ-έω, pf. κεκαλλιέρηκα Ph.1.319: plpf. ἐκεκαλλιερήκειν X. *Cyr.*6.4.12: (ἱερόν):—*have favourable signs in a sacrifice, obtain good omens,* of the person, κἂν καλλιερῇτε Pl.Com.51, cf. X. l. c., *IG*1^2.45. 5, etc.:—also in Med., Hdt.6.82, Isoc.14.60, X.*An.*5.4.22, etc.; ἐς τὸν (sc. ποταμὸν) . . ἐκαλλιερέοντο σφάζοντες ἵππους (where ἐς τόν is constructed with σφάζοντες) Hdt.7.113. 2. c. acc., *sacrifice with good omens,* ταῖς Νύμφαις τὰν ἀμνόν Theoc.5.148; καλλιερεῖν βοῦν prob. l. in Orac.ap.D.21.53; ἑαυτὸν τῷ πατρίῳ νόμῳ Plu.*Alex.*69: abs., κ. τοῖς θεοῖς X.*Eq.Mag.*3.1, cf. Pl.*Lg.*791a:—Med., Ar.*Pl.*1181:—Pass., ἐὰν καὶ καλλιερηθῇ τοῖς θεοῖς Men.319.8; τοὺς ξένους τῇ Ἀρτέμιδι καλλιερεῖσθαι S.E.*P.*1.149. II. of the offering, *give favourable omens,* καλλιερησάντων [τῶν ἱρῶν] Hdt.9.19; καλλιερῆσαι θυομένοισι οὐκ ἐδύνατο (sc. τὰ ἱρά) Id.7.134: c. inf., οὐκ ἐκαλλιέρεε ὥστε μάχεσθαι Πέρσῃσι Id.9.38; οὐκ ἐκαλλιέρεε οὐδαμῶς διαβαίνειν μιν Id. 6.76:—Med., ὡς οὐδὲ ταῦτα ἐκαλλιερεῖτο X.*HG*3.1.17. **-ημα,** ατος, τό, *auspicious sacrifice,* Hsch., *EM*487.14. **-ησις,** εως, ἡ, = foreg., *IG*1^2.98.23, Onos.10.26. **-ία,** v. καλλιαρία.

καλλι-ζῠγής, ές, *beautifully yoked,* ἅρμα E.*Andr.*278 (lyr.). **-ζωνος,** ὁ, ἡ, *with beautiful girdles,* γυναῖκες Il.7.139, 24.698, Od.23.147; Ἥρα B.5.89: in late Prose, κόραι Hld.3.2. **-θέμεθλος,** ον, *with beautiful foundations,* νηός Musae.71. **-θριξ,** τρῐχος, ὁ, ἡ, *with beautiful manes,* καλλίτριχας ἵππους Il.5.323, Od.3.475, etc.; of sheep, *with fine wool,* καλλίτριχα μῆλα νομεύων 9.336, cf. 469: in late Prose, *with beautiful hair,* Herm.ap.Stob.1.49.45. II. Subst., **καλλίθριξ,** *waterwort, Asplenium trichomanes,* Plin.*HN*25.132. **-θῠτέω,** *offer in auspicious sacrifice,* κάπρον *AP*6.240 (Phil.). **-θῠτος,** ον, *offered auspiciously,* αἶγες *Epigr.Gr.*872 (Patmos).

καλλῐκαρπ-έω, *bear fine fruit,* Thphr.*HP*3.15.2, *Gp.*3.3.6. **-ία,** ἡ, *beauty of fruit,* Thphr.*HP*1.4.1, *Gp.*10.1.4. **-ος,** ον, *rich in fine fruit,* of places, Σικελία A.*Pr.*371, cf. E.*HF*464, Str.17.3.21: Comp. -ότερος Thphr.*HP*3.8.1: Sup. -ότατος, τόπος Plb.5.19.2. 2. of trees, *bearing fine fruit,* μῖλαξ E.*Ba.*108 (lyr.), cf. Thphr.*CP*1.17.10 (Comp.). II. Διόνυσος κ., identified with Domitian, *Jahresh.*18 *Beibl.*55 (Anazarba).

καλλῐκέλᾰδος, ον, *beautiful-sounding,* Suid.

καλλῐ-κέρας, -κέρα, *with beautiful horns,* δάμαλις B.18.24. **-κε-**

ρως, = foreg., *ταῦρος, ἔλαφος, AP*7.744 (D.L.), 9.603 (Antip.). II. = *τῆλις*, Gal.12.426.

καλλίκλιον, τό, *inkstand*, Lyd.*Mag*.2.14. (Lat. *caliculus*, late Lat. *callicula*.)

καλλί-κοκκος [ῐ], ον, *with beautiful seeds*, *ῥόα* Thphr.*CP*1.9.2. **-κολώνη**, ἡ, *Fair-hill*, a hill near Troy, on the Simois, Il.20.53, 151:—also **Καλλικόλωνος**, ὁ, Demetr.Sceps.ap.Sch.Il.20.53. **-κόμας**, ὁ, = sq., *πλόκαμος* E.*IA*1080 (lyr.). **-κομος**, ὁ, ἡ, *beautiful-haired*, of women, Il.9.449, Od.15.58, Pi.*P*.9.106; *Ὧραι* Hes.*Op*.75, cf. *Th*.915; *Ἀφροδίτη* Epimenid.19; *Μοῖσαι* Sapph.60; *Χάριτες* Ar.*Pax* 798 (lyr.), *IG*1².821; also of trees, *with beautiful foliage*, *IG*2.3412. **-κοττᾰβέω**, = *καλῶς κοτταβίζω*, S.*Fr*.537.2. **-κρεας**, gen. *κρέως*, τό, = *πάγκρεας*, Gal.2.781. **-κρήδεμνος**, ὁ, ἡ, *with beautiful head-band*, *ἄλοχοι* Od.4.623; *θεά* B.*Scol.Fr*.5 i 22. **-κρηνος**, Dor. **-κρᾱνος**, ον, *with beautiful spring*, Pi.*Fr*.198. **-κριτα· χελώνην, οἱ δὲ φώκην**, Hsch. **-κτῐτος**, ον, *beautifully built*, Nonn.*D*.26.85. **-λαμπέτης**, ου, ὁ, *beautifully shining*, *Ἥλιος* Anacr.27. **-λεκτέω**, *use elegant diction*, S.E.*M*.2.55, D.L.5.66. **-λεξία**, ἡ, *beauty of language*, Herm.*in Phdr*.p.191 A., Simp.*in Epict*.p.129 M. **-λογέω**, *express in elegant diction, embellish*, D.H.8.32, *Comp*.3 (Pass.):—Med., *use specious phrases*, Luc.*Tox*.35. **-λογία**, ἡ, *elegance of language*, D.H.*Comp*.16; *ἡ Προδίκου κ.* Max.Tyr.23.1. **-μάρτυς**, ὁ, *one who gives good evidence*, Hdn.*Epim*.186. **-μᾰχος**, ον, *fighting nobly*, Lib.*Or*.18.280 (sed fort. pr. n.). **-μηρος**, ον, *with beautiful thighs*, Herm.ap.Stob.1.49.45. **-μορφος**, ον, *beautifully formed*, *δέμας* E.*Andr*.1155; *χορὸς τέκνων* Id.*HF*925; *ταῶς* Antiph.175.5.

κάλλῐμος, ον, poet. for *καλός*, *beautiful*, *δῶρα* Od.4.130, 8.439; *οὖρος* 11.640; *χρόα, ὄπα κάλλιμον*, 11.529, 12.192.

καλλί-νᾱος [ῐ], ον, *beautifully flowing*, *Κηφισός* E.*Med*.835 (lyr.), cf. *Alc*.589 (lyr.); *κρήνη* A.R.1.1228: Sup., Hsch. (*καλλινοτάτη* cod.). **-νῖκος**, ον, (*νίκη*) *gloriously triumphant*, *τήνελλα ὦ καλλίνικε χαῖρ' ἄναξ Ἡράκλεες* Archil.119, cf. *IG*12(5).234 (Paros); *κῦδος κ.* the glory *of noble victory*, Pi.*I*.1.12; *χάρμα κ.* ib.5(4).54; *καλλίνικος ἅρμασι* Id.*P*.1.32: c. gen., *τῶν ἐχθρῶν triumphant over* one's enemies, E.*Med*.765; *ἐραστῶν* Pl.*Alc*.2.151c; epith. of Helios, *IG* 12(2).127 (Mytil.); of kings, as Seleucus II, Plb.2.71.4, Str.16.2.4, etc.; of martyrs, *Cod.Just*.1.3.35.3 (Zeno). II. *adorning* or *ennobling victory*, *μέλος, ὕμνος*, Pi.*P*.5.106, *N*.4.16 codd.; *ᾠδά, μοῦσα*, E.*El*.865 (lyr.), *Ph*.1728 (lyr.); *στέφανος, στέφη*, Id.*IT*12, *Alex*. in *Gött. Nachr*.1922.10; *κ. ἠλαίη* Call.*Iamb*.1.283; *τὸ κ.* *the glory of victory*, Pi.*N*.3.18; so *καλλίνικος* (sc. *ὕμνος*) Id.*O*.9.2; *καλλίνικον οἴσεται* E.*Med*.45; *τὸν καλλίνικον μετὰ θεῶν ἐκώμασε* Id.*HF*180; also *τὰν Ἡρακλέους κ.* (sc. *ᾠδὰν*) *ἀείδω* ib.681 (lyr.). III. *τὸ κ.* *an air for the flute*, Trypho ap.Ath.14.618c. **-οινία**, ἡ, *goodness of wine*, *Gp*.6.3.10, 5.2.19.

κάλλιον (A), neut. of *καλλίων*, used as Adv., v. sub *καλός* c.

κάλλιον (B), τό, precinct used as a Court at Athens, *AB*269, cf. Androt.ap.Poll.8.121 (**Κάλλειον**, fr. *Καλλίας*, Phot.); at Cyzicus, apptly. a *board* or *bench of magistrates*, *ἄρχων τοῦ κ. IGRom*.4.153 (ii A.D.); cf. *καλλιάζω, καλλιαρχέω*.

Καλλιόπη, ἡ, (*ὄψ*) *Calliope, the beautiful-voiced*, name of the Epic Muse, Hes.*Th*.79, *h.Hom*.31.2, Sapph.82, etc.; *ἡμετέρη Κ.* my *Muse*, Call.*Aet*.3.1.77:—also **Καλλιόπεια**, *AP*4.3b.61 (Agath.): as Adj., *κούρα καλλιόπα*, of Echo, Theoc.*Syrinx*19.

καλλιοπλία, ἡ, *possession of fine armour*, subject of competition at Priene, *Inscr.Prien*.112.109 (i B.C.).

καλλίουλος [ῐ], ὁ, a song to Demeter, Semus 19; cf. *ἴουλος*.

καλλῐ-ουργέω, *work artistically*, in Pass., Them.*Or*.20.237d: **-ούργημα**, ατος, τό, *work of art*, Jul.*Ep*.205 (pl.).

καλλιόω, *make more beautiful*, Lxx *Ca*.4.10 (Pass.).

καλλί-παις [ῐ], παιδος, ὁ, ἡ, *with beautiful children, blessed with fair children*, *Λητώ Trag.Adesp*.178; *κ. πότμος* A.*Ag*.762 (lyr.); *κ. στέφανος* E.*HF*839: also in Prose, Pl.*Phdr*.261a, Arist.ap.Ael.*VH*1.14, Aristid.*Or*.17(15).20. II. *beautiful child*, *Περσέφασσα κ. θεά* E.*Or*.964 (lyr.). **-πάρηος** (so, not **-ηος**, in most codd., cf. *εὐπάραος*) [πᾰ], ον, *beautiful-cheeked*, *Χρυσηΐς, Ἑλένη*, Il.1.143, Od.15.123; *Λητώ* Il.24.607, al., cf. B.19.4 (prob. l.), *AP*9.96 (Antip. Thess.):—written **-πάρειος** Poll.2.87. **-πάρθενος**, ον, *with beautiful nymphs*, *Νείλου.. κ. ῥοαί* E.*Hel*.1; *δέρη κ.* neck *of a beauteous maiden*, Id.*IA*1574:—later **-παρθένιος**, ον, *πηγή Inscr.Magn*.252.

κάλλῐπε, Ep. for *κατέλιπε*, inf. **καλλιπέειν**, v. *καταλείπω*.

καλλῐ-πέδῐλος, ὁ, ἡ, *with beautiful sandals*, *h.Merc*.57. **-πεπλος**, ὁ, ἡ, *with beautiful robe, beautifully clad*, of women, Pi.*P*.3.25, E.*Tr*.338 (lyr.). **-πέτᾰλον**, τό, = *πεντέφυλλον*, Dsc.4.42. **-πέτηλος**, ον, *with beautiful leaves*, *AP*9.64 (Asclep. or Arch.), 10.16 (Theaet.). **-πηχυς**, υ, gen. εως, *beautiful* arm, *κ. βραχίων* E.*Tr*.1194; *with beautiful arms*, *παρθένος* Alciphr.3.67. **-πλόκᾰμος**, ὁ, ἡ, *with beautiful locks*, *Δημήτηρ, Θέτις*, Il.14.326, 18.407; *Ἑλένα* Pi.*O*.3.1; *Πιερίδες* E.*IA*1040 (lyr.); *χρυσέαν ἄρνα κ.* Id.*El*.705 (lyr.). **-πλουτος**, ον, *adorned with riches*, *πόλιες* Pi.*O*.13.111. **-πνοος**, ον, contr. **-πνους**, ουν, *beautifully breathing*, *αὐλός* Telest.2.1; also of smell, *κ. ἄνθη* Hsch. s.v. *κρίνα*, prob. in Porph. *in Ptol*.182. **-πολις**, εως, ἡ, *fair city*, Pl.*R*.527c: freq. as pr. n.:—hence **Καλλιπολῖται**, οἱ, Hdt.7.154, etc.

κάλλῐπον, Ep. for *κατέλιπον*, v. *καταλείπω*.

καλλῐ-πόταμος, ον, *of beautiful rivers*, *νοτίς* E.*Ph*.645 (lyr.). **-πους**, ποδος, ὁ, ἡ, *with beautiful feet*, Hsch. s.v. *ἀργυρόπεζα*. **-πρόβᾰτος**, ον, *with beautiful sheep*, Suid. s.v. *εὔρηνος*, *EM*395.54. **-πρόσωπος**, ον, *with beautiful face*, *Γαλάτεια* Philox.8. **-πρῳρος**, ον, (*πρῷρα*) *with beautiful prow*, of ships, E.*Med*.1335: metaph., of men, *with beautiful face, beautiful*, *βλάστημα* A.*Th*.533; *στόμα κ.* Id.*Ag*.235 (lyr.). **-πῡγος**, ὁ, ἡ, *with beautiful πυγή*, Cerc.14; epith. of Aphrodite, Ath.12.554c: Comp., ibid. **-πῠλος**, ον, *with beautiful gates*, *Θήβη Epigr.Gr*.993. **-πυργος**, ον, *with beautiful towers*, *ἄστυ* E.*Ba*.1202; *τὰ κ. πεδία*, of Thebes, Id.*Supp*.618 (lyr.); *κ. σοφία* *high-towering*, Ar.*Nu*.1024. **-πύργωτος**, ον, = foreg., E.*Ba*.19. **-πῡρος**, ον, dub. sens. in *Epic.Alex.Adesp*.9 ii 22. **-πωλος**, ον, *with beautiful steeds*, Pi.*O*.14.1. **-ρέεθρος**, ον, *beautifully flowing*, *κρήνη* Od.10.107; *Ἴστρος* Hes.*Th*.339; *Δίρκα* E.*HF*784 (lyr.).

καλλί-ροος, ον, poet. for *καλλίρροος* (q.v.):—also **καλλῐρόας**, B.10.26, 96, *Inscr.Prien*.376. **-ρραβδος**, ὁ, ἡ, *with beautiful wand*, Hsch. s.v. *ἀκαλαυρόπις*. **-ρρημονέω**, *speak beautifully*, Eust.829.50. **-ρρημοσύνη**, ἡ, *elegance of language*, D.H.*Th*.23, Luc.*JTr*.27. II. *braggart language*, Id.*DDeor*.21.2. **-ρρήμων**, ον, gen. ονος, *elegant*, *λέξις* D.H.*Comp*.3; *λέξεως μόρια* ib.16. **-ρροος**, ον, poet. also **καλλίροος** [ῐ] (contr. **καλλίρους** S.*Fr*.649.39), *beautiful-flowing*, *ὕδωρ, κρουνώ*, Il.2.752, 22.147; *ποταμοῖο κατὰ στόμα καλλιρόοιο* Od.5.441; *κρήνην καλλίροον* 17.206; *πηγή* A.*Pers*.201; *Ὠκεανός* Orph.*Fr*.15: metaph., of the voice, *καλλιρόοισι πνοαῖς* Pi.*O*.6.83:—fem., *Καλλιρόη*, one of the Oceanids, *h.Cer*.419, Hes.*Th*.288, etc. II. pr. n., *Καλλιρρόη*, a famous spring at Athens, later *Ἐννεάκρουνος*, Th.2.15, Pl.*Ax*.364a. **-στάδιος** [στᾰ], ον, *with a fine race-course*, *Ἀχιλλῆος δρόμοι* E.*IT*437 (lyr.). **-στάφῠλος** [στᾰ], ον, *with fine grapes*, gloss on *ἐριστάφυλος*, Hsch.

καλλιστεῖον, τό, (*καλλιστεύω*) *offering of what is fairest*, E.*IT*23: pl., name of a festival and *beauty-contest* at Lesbos, Sch.Il.9.129: in pl. also, *the fairest prize*, *τὰ πρῶτα κ. ἀριστεύσας στρατοῦ* S.*Aj*.435 (cf. Sch.); *τῶν φαλύρων τὰ κ. SIG*56.9 (Argos, v B.C.); so in sg., *IG* 12(9).189.36 (Eretria, iv B.C.), 207.19 (ibid., iii B.C.). II. *beauty-prize*, of the apple of Paris, Luc.*DDeor*.20.1.

καλλίστερνος, ὁ, ἡ, *beautiful-breasted*, Nonn.*D*.5.553.

καλλίστ-ευμα, ατος, τό, *offering of what is most beautiful*, E.*Ph*.215 (lyr., pl.); *the fairest prize*, Id.*Or*.1639. II. *τὰ δευτερεῖα καλλιστευμάτων* second *prize for beauty*, Lyc.1011. **-εύω**, (*κάλλιστος*) *to be the finest* or *most beautiful*, Hdt.1.196, al., E.*Tr*.226 (lyr.); of animals, Hdt.4.72, 163: c. gen., *καλλιστεύσει πασέων τῶν γυναικῶν* Id.6.61, cf. 7.180:—Med., *δῶρ' ἃ καλλιστεύεται τῶν νῦν ἐν ἀνθρώποισι* E.*Med*.947, cf. *Ba*.409 (lyr.), *Hipp*.1009: pf. part. Pass., *ἀγώνων τῶν κεκαλλιστευμένων* E.*Oen*.p.39 A.; *κεκ. θέαμα* Procop.*Aed*.1.1.

καλλιστέφᾰνος, ον, *beautiful-crowned*, of Demeter, *h.Cer*.251, 295; of Hera, Tyrt.2; *εὐφροσύναι* E.*Ba*.376 (lyr.); *Λιβύη* Orac.ap. D.S.8.29. II. *κ. ἐλαία* the wild olive tree at Olympia, *from which the crowns of victory were taken*, Arist.*Mir*.834ᵃ12, Paus.5.15.3.

κάλλιστος, η, ον, Sup. of *καλός*; v. *καλός* B.

καλλιστρᾰτεύω, *win glory in war*, *Cat.Cod.Astr*.7.227.

καλλιστρούθια, τά, name of a kind of *fig*, Ath.3.75e: *callistruthis* in Colum.10.416.

καλλίσφῠρος, ὁ, ἡ (fem. **-σφύρα** Sch.B.*Scol.Fr*.5 i 24), *beautiful-ankled*, of women, *καλλισφύρου εἵνεκα νύμφης* Il.9.560, cf. 14.319, Od.5.333; *Νίκη* Hes.*Th*.384; *Ἥβη* Poet.ap.Luc.*DMort*.16.1.

καλλῐτεκν-έω, *have beautiful children*, *OGI*308.9 (Hierapolis, ii B.C.). **-ία**, ἡ, *possession of beautiful children*, *IG*12(7).397 (Amorgos), Parth.33.1. **-ος**, ον, *with beautiful children*, Arist.*Eleg*.2, *IG*12(7).477 (Amorgos), *Inscr.Prien*.225 (Aug.): Comp., Luc.*DDeor*.16.1: Sup., Plu.*Aem*.5:—also **καλλῐτέξ**, ἡ, Hdn.*Epim*.186.

καλλῐτέχν-ης, ου, ὁ, *beautiful artist*, *Anacreont*.4.1: pl., **-τέχνεις** *Epigr.Gr*.796. **-ία**, ἡ, *beauty of workmanship*, Plu.*Per*.13, Ath.5.191b. **-ος**, ὁ, ἡ, *making beautiful works of art*, Str.1.2.33, 16.2.24, Them.*Or*.4.56b.

καλλῐ-τόκεια, ἡ, pecul. poet. fem. of sq., Opp.*C*.1.6. **-τοκος**, ον, = *καλλίτεκνος*, Hsch. **-τοξος**, ὁ, ἡ, *with beautiful bow*, E.*Ph*.1162. **-τράπεζος** [ᾰ], ον, *with beautiful*, i.e. *well-spread, table*, Call.Com.5, Amips.19. **-τρῐχον**, τό, = *ἀδίαντον*, Ps.-Dsc.4.134, Ael.*NA*1.35, Archig.(?)ap.Gal.14.321. **-τρῐχος**, ον, later form for *καλλίθριξ*, Opp.*C*.1.321. II. *producing luxuriant hair*, Dsc.1.125. **-φεγγής**, ές, *beautiful-shining*, *ἡλίου σέλας, Ἕως*, E.*Tr*.860, *Hipp*.455, cf. Theodect.10.1. **-φθογγος**, ον, *beautiful-sounding*, *ᾠδαί* E.*Ion*169 (lyr.); *ἱστοί* Id.*IT*222 (lyr.). **-φλοξ**, ὁ, ἡ, gen. φλογος, *auspiciously burning*, *πέλανος* Id.*Ion*706 (lyr.). **-φυής**, ές, *of beautiful growth* or *shape*, Nonn.*D*.15.171. **-φυλλον**, τό, = *ἀδίαντον*, Hp.*Epid*.7.59 (**-φυτον** Gal.19.107). **-φυλλος**, ον, *with beautiful petals*, *ῥόδον Anacreont*.42.3. **-φῠτος**, ον, *bringing beauty to birth*, *ὧραι* Orph.*Fr*.183; *καλλιφύτων κοίρανον ἡμερίδων* lord of the *beautiful* vine, Nonn.*D*.47.38.

καλλῐφων-έω, *speak beautifully*, opp. *κακοφωνέω*, Phld.*Rh*.1.176 S.; *pronounce euphoniously*, *ὁ τὴν τετράπεζαν -φωνήσας εἰς τράπεζαν* Eust.664.41. **-ία**, ἡ, *beauty of sound* or *pronunciation*, D.H.*Rh*.1.5, 4.1, Luc.*Pisc*.22. 2. Gramm., *euphony*, D.T.(*Suppl*.)675.14. **-ος**, ὁ, ἡ, *with a fine voice*, *ὑποκριταί* Pl.*Lg*.817c; expl. of *Καλλιόπη*, Corn.*ND*14.

καλλίφως, *shining gloriously*, epith. of a divinity, *PMag.Par*.1.594.

καλλί-χειρ [ῐ], χειρος, ὁ, ἡ, *with beautiful hands*, *ὠλέναι* Chaerem.14.7. **-χέλωνος**, ον, *with a beautiful tortoise on it*, *ὀβολός* Eup.141.

κάλλιχθυς, υος, ὁ, *beauty-fish*, = *ἀνθίας*, Arist.*Fr*.316, cf. Hedyl.

ap.Ath.8.344f, Numen.ap.eund.7.295b; but distd. from it by Dorion ib.282e, cf. Opp.*H*.3.335.

καλλί-χοιρος [ῐ], ον, *with fine pigs*, ὗς Arist.*HA*573^{b}12. **-χορος**, ον, *with fair dancing-grounds*, epith. of cities, Od.11.581, *h.Hom*.15.2, Pi.*P*.12.26, E.*Heracl*.359 (lyr.); of Olympia, B.10.32; ἀγορή Simon. 164.2. II. *of* or *for beautiful dances*, στέφανοι, ἀοιδαί, E.*Ph*.786 (lyr.), *Fr*.453.7 (lyr.); τρόπον τὸν καλλιχορώτατον παίζοντες Ar.*Ra*.452 (lyr.); ὁ κ., a sacred spring near Eleusis, *the fount of goodly dances*, *h.Cer*.272, cf. E.*Ion* 1075 (lyr.), *Supp*.392, 619 (lyr.). 2. *beautiful in the dance*, of Apollo, Id.*HF*690 (lyr.); κ. δελφῖνες Id.*Hel*.1454 (lyr.). **-χροος**, ον, *beautiful-coloured*, νάρκισσος prob. l. in Cypr. *Fr*.4.6.

καλλίων, ον, gen. ονος, Comp. of καλός; v. καλός B.

καλλῐώνῠμος, ον, *with beautiful name*: as Subst., a kind of fish, *Uranoscopus scaber*, Hp.*Vict*.2.48, Arist.*HA*598^{a}11, Men.31, Anaxipp.2.2: sens. obsc., *Com.Adesp*.1023.

καλλονάριον, τό, *broom, besom*, *Gloss*.

καλλονή, ἡ, *beauty*, rarer form of κάλλος, Hdt.3.106, 7.36, E.*Tr*. 977, *Ba*.459, *IA*1308 (lyr.), Pl.*Smp*.206d, Herod.1.35, *Lyr.Alex. Adesp*.4*B*4, etc.; [κιόνων] *IG*5(2).268.51 (Mantinea, i B.C./i A.D.): metaph., κ. βίου Hp.*Decent*.1; *fine quality*, of pitch, Thphr.*HP*9.2.4; οἴνου *PFlor*.65.12 (vi A.D.).

καλλοποιός, όν, *producing beauty*, ἄνθος κάλλους κ. Plot.6.7.32, cf. Procl.*in Ti*.1.269 D., *in Prm*.p.543 S.; cf. καλοποιός.

κάλλος, εος, Att. ους, τό, (καλός) *beauty*, esp. of body, Il.9.130, 20. 235, etc.; κάλλεΐ τε στίλβων καὶ εἵμασιν 3.392; κάλλεϊ καὶ χάρισι στίλβων Od.6.237; περί τ' ἀμφί τε κ. ἄητο *h.Cer*.276: in a concrete sense, as though external to the body, κάλλεϊ μέν οἱ πρῶτα προσώπατα καλὰ κάθηρεν ἀμβροσίῳ, οἵῳ Κυθέρεια χρίεται Od.18.192: freq. in Trag. and Prose, γυναῖκε..κάλλει ἀμώμω A.*Pers*.185; κ. σώματος Democr.105; opp. αἶσχος, Pl.*Smp*.201a: in a general sense, τῶν ἔργων τῷ μεγέθει καὶ τῷ κάλλει χαλεπὸν ἐξισῶσαι τοὺς ἐπαίνους Isoc.12.36; χώρη κάλλεϊ καὶ ἀρετῇ μέγα ὑπερφέρουσα Hdt.8.144, cf. Pl.*Chrm*.157e, D.S.1.30; of ships, Th.[3.17]; ἀρετὴ ἂν εἴη κ. ψυχῆς Pl.*R*.444d; τὸ τῶν μαθημάτων κ. Id.*Grg*.475a; ἐς κάλλος with an eye to *beauty*, so as to set off her *beauty*, E.*El*.1073; οὐ γὰρ ἐς κ. τύχας δαίμων δίδωσιν so as to regard *beauty* or *show*, Id.*Tr*.1201; ὁ εἰς κ. βίος, opp. αἰσχρουργία, X. *Ages*.9.1; ἐς κ. ζῆν Id.*Cyr*.8.1.33; but ἐς κ. κυνηγετεῖν hunt for *pleasure*, Arr.*Cyn*.25.9: in pl., σωμάτων κάλλη, opp. ψυχῶν ἀρετή, Pl. *Criti*.112e. 2. concrete, of persons, κ. κακῶν ὕπουλον S.*OT*1396; of a bird, Clitarch.21 J. codd.; mostly of women, *a beauty*, τὴν θυγατέρα, δεινόν τι κάλλος καὶ μέγεθος X.*Cyr*.5.2.7; Γαλάτεια, κάλλος Ἐρώτων Philox.8 (nisi leg. θάλος); Ἑλένη καὶ Λήδα καὶ ὅλως τὰ ἀρχαῖα κάλλη Luc.*DMort*.18.1, cf. *Im*.2. 3. in pl., *beautiful things*, as garments and stuffs, ἐν ποικίλοις..κάλλεσιν βαίνειν A.*Ag*.923; βάπτειν τὰ κ. Eup.333, cf. Pl.*Phd*.110a, Poll.7.63, Hsch. s. v.; κυπαρίττων ὕψη καὶ κάλλη Pl.*Lg*.625c; μεγέθεσιν κάλλεσίν τε ἔργων Id. *Criti*.115d, etc.; τὰ κ. τῆς ἑρμηνείας *beauties* of style, Longin.5.1 (also in sg., τὸ κ. τῆς ἑρμ. D.H.*Comp*.3); κάλλεα κηροῦ *beautiful works* of wax, i.e. honeycombs, *AP*9.363.15 (Mel.); κάλλη τοιαῦτα καὶ τοσαῦτα ἱερῶν D.3.25; κ. οἰκοδομημάτων, = καλὰ οἰκοδομήματα, Plu.2. 409a, cf. 935a, D.C.65.15. 4. Pythag. name for *six*, Iamb.*in Nic*. p.34 P.

καλλοσύνη, Dor. -σύνα, ἡ, poet. for κάλλος, in lyr., E.*Or*.1386, *Hel*.383; also eleg., *Supp.Epigr*.1.570; κ. ἐπέων, title of work by Democr.

κάλλυν-θρον, τό, *sweeper, duster* made of palm-leaves, κ. φοινίκων Lxx *Le*.23.40, *BGU*1120.17 (i B.C.). **-τήριος**, ον, *of* or *for beautifying*: hence τὰ κ., a festival on the 19th Thargelion, *when the statue of Athena Polias was fresh adorned*, Phot., *EM*487.13. **-τής**, οῦ, ὁ, *sweeper, cleaner*, esp. in temples, οἱ ἐκ τοῦ ἱεροῦ κ. *UPZ*8.6 (ii B.C.). II. = κουρεύς, Hsch. **-τρον**, τό, *broom, brush*, Cleanth.*Stoic*.1.130, Plu.*Dio* 55; ἀντὶ τοῦ δόρατος κ. φέρων Anon.ap. Suid. II. an unknown shrub, Arist.*HA*553^{a}20. **-ω**, (καλός) *beautify*, νέα πρόσωπα S.*Fr*.871.6:—Pass., Plot.6.1.20; λίθῳ Λακαίνῃ Them.*Or*.18.223a. 2. metaph., *gloss over*, ὅταν ἐν κακοῖσί τις ἁλοὺς ἔπειτα τοῦτο καλλύνειν θέλῃ S.*Ant*.496; εὐδιάβολον κακὸν κ. Pl. *Lg*.944b. 3. Med., *pride oneself in* a thing, Id.*Ap*.20c; ἐπί τινι Ael.*VH*3.19. II. *sweep clean*, Arist.*Pr*.936^{b}27, *UPZ*79.17 (ii B.C.); ὡς φαίνηται καὶ καλλύνηται [ἡ πλατεῖα] Plb.6.33.4.

κάλλυσμα, ατος, τό, *sweeping*, in pl., *IG*12(5).593*A*22 (Ceos), prob. in Thphr.*Char*.10.6, cf. Hsch. s. v. σάρματα.

καλλωπ-ίζω, (ὤψ) prop. *beautify the face*: hence, *give a fair appearance to* a thing, *embellish*, κ. ὄνομα Pl.*Cra*.408b, cf. 409c (Pass.), Phld. *Hom*.p.58 O.; τὴν πόλιν, ὥσπερ γυναῖκα Plu.*Per*.12; τὸ λογικόν Arr. *Epict*.3.1.26:—Pass., οἰκία..δαπάνῃ κεκαλλωπισμένη X.*Hier*.11.2, cf. *Oec*.9.4; κεκ. τὸ χρῶμα, i.e. painted, Id.*Mem*.2.1.22: metaph., λόγος κεκ., opp. καθαρός, Hermog.*Id*.1.3; λέξις κεκ. S.E.*M*.2. 55. II. Med., *adorn oneself, make oneself fine* or *smart*, Pl.*Smp*. 174a. 2. metaph., *pride oneself in* or *on* a thing, τινι Id.*Phdr*. 252a, X.*Ages*.11.11; ἐπί τινι Pl.*R*.405b: also κ. ὅτι.. Id.*Prt*.317c; ὡς.. c. part., Id.*Cri*.52c, *Tht*.195d: abs., *make a display, show off*, Arist.*Rh.Al*.1421^{a}4; of a horse, X.*Eq*.10.5: c. acc. cogn., πολλὰ πρὸς αὐτούς Phld.*Rh*.1.238 S.; ταῦτα -ίζεται *makes a fair show*, Iamb. *Protr*.20. 3. *to be coy* or *mock-modest*, τινι or πρός τινα towards another, Pl.*Prt*.333d, *Phdr*.236d: c. inf., κ. παραιτεῖσθαι *affecting* to deprecate, Plu.*Caes*.28, cf. Phalar.*Ep*.92. **-ισμα**, ατος, τό, *ornament*, χρυσᾶ, ἀργυρᾶ κ., Plu.*Lyc*.9; τραπέζης Porph.*Abst*.3.19; *source of pride*, Luc.*Merc.Cond*.36. 2. *ornament of speech*, D.H.*Th*. 46. 3. metaph., *fair show, pretence*, Pl.*Grg*.492c (pl.). **-ισμός**, ὁ, *adorning oneself, making a display*, Id.*R*.572c; *showing off*, ὁ πρὸς ἵππους κ. X.*Eq*.10.16, cf. Jul.*Mis*.349c. II. *ornamentation*, κ. φορτικός Hp.*Medic*.2; εἰς κ. for *ornament*, X.*An*.1.9.23; καλλωπισμοὶ οἱ περὶ τὸ σῶμα Pl.*Phd*.64d. 2. *making euphonious*, of words, Id.*Cra*.414c, 426d. b. Rhet., *embellishment*, φράσεως Steph. *in Hp*.2.419 D. **-ιστεία**, ἡ, *beauty of style, poetica* κ. Serv. ad Verg.*Aen*.1.223. **-ιστής**, οῦ, ὁ, *one who adorns himself, dandy*, opp. φιλόκαλος, Isoc.1.27, cf. Arist.*Rh*.1401^{b}24, Phld.*Vit.Herc*.1457. 9. **-ιστικός**, ή, όν, = καλλυντήριος, c. gen., Arr.*Epict*.2.23.14: ἡ -κή (sc. τέχνη) *the art of embellishment*, Gal.14.766. **-ίστρια**, ἡ, fem. of καλλωπιστής, Muson.*Fr*.3 p.10 H., Plu.2.140c.

καλλωσόν, τό, (Lat. callosum) *rind of pork, crackling*, Orib.3.5.2, 3.16.7; = κόλλοψ, *Gp*.19.6.3.

κᾰλοᾰγόραστος, ον, *well-bought, cheap*, Zonar.

κᾰλο-βάμων [βᾰ], ονος, ὁ, (κάλως) *tight-rope walker*, Man.4.287. **-βᾰτέω**, *walk on the tight-rope*, Porph.*Abst*.3.15. **-βάτης** [βᾰ], ου, ὁ, *tight-rope walker*, *SIG*847.5 (Delph.), Man.5.146; = *funambulus*, *Gloss*.

κᾰλό-βῐος, ον, *living decorously*, Paul.Al.*N*.4. **-βουλία**, ἡ, = εὐβουλία, *Gloss*. **-γένειος**, ον, gloss on ἠϋγένειος, Hsch. **-γηρος**, ον, *venerable*; esp. of monks, *EM*230.48. **-γηρυς**, υος, ὁ, ἡ, *with a fine voice*, as etym. of κρήγυον, Suid. s. h. v. **-γνώμων**, ον, gen. ονος, *noble-minded*, Ptol.*Tetr*.158. **-δῐδάσκᾰλος**, ὁ, *teacher of virtue*, *Ep.Tit*.2.3. **-ειδής**, ές, *of beautiful form*, στροφαί Sopat. in Rh.8.56 W. **-έργαστος**, ον, *well-wrought*, gloss on εὐεργής, Zonar. **-εργέτις**, ιδος, ἡ, *doing good*, ψυχή Porph.*Antr*.30. **-εργός**, όν, *well-doing, good*, Man.1.256. **-ετής**, unexplained Adj. in *EM* 435.42. **-ήθης**, ες, *well-disposed*, M.Ant.1.1, Procl.*Par.Ptol*.232, Procop.*Arc*.22. **-θέλεια**, ἡ, *goodwill*, *Gloss*. **-θελής**, ές, *benevolent*, ib. Adv. -λῶς *PLond*.5.1674.68 (vi A.D.). **-θριξ**, τριχος, ὁ, ἡ, = καλλίθριξ, Suid. s. v. εὐχαίτης ἵππος.

καλοΐς· βασιλεύς, Hsch. (Perh. Lydian.)

κᾰλοιώνιστος, ον, *of good omen*, gloss on Augustus, Lyd.*Mag*.1. 23; name of certain θεράποντες, Sch.Ar.*Av*.722.

κᾰλοκᾰγᾰθ-έω, *practise noble arts*, καλοκἀγαθεῖν ἀσκοῦντας dub. cj. in Ar.*Fr*.198.8. **-ία**, ἡ, *the character and conduct of a* καλὸς κἀγαθός (v. καλοκἀγαθός), *nobleness, goodness*, X.*Mem*.1.6.14, Arist.*EN* 1124^{a}4, al., Poll.4.10; freq. in Inscrr., ἀ ποτὶ τοὺς Ἕλλανας κ. *SIG* 558.15 (Ithaca, found at Magn. Mae.); ἀρετᾶς ἕνεκεν καὶ κ. τᾶς εἴς τινας ib.649 (Olymp.); τῆς πόλεως κ., opp. ἡ Φιλίππου κακία, D.18.93, cf. Isoc.1.6, D.25.24; opp. ῥᾳδιουργία, X.*Ages*.11.6: pl., ἀρεταὶ καὶ κ. Phld.*Rh*.2.33 S. **-ικός**, ή, όν, *beseeming a* καλὸς κἀγαθός, *honourable*, προαίρεσις Plb.7.11.9. Adv. -κῶς *BMus.Inscr*.925*b*8 (Branchidae), Plu.*Phoc*.32. 2. *inclined to* καλοκἀγαθία, Id.*Them*.3, 2.225f: Comp., Muson.*Fr*.14 p.76 H. **-ος**, ον, an adject. form, perh. only in Poll.4.11 (in all early writers written divisim καλὸς κἀγαθός); καλὸς κἀγαθός orig. denotes a *perfect gentleman*, Hdt.1.30, Ar.*Eq*.185, 735, al., Th.4.40, 8.48, X.*HG*5.3.9, Arist.*Pol*.1293^{b}39, etc.; καλῷ τε κἀγαθῷ X.*An*.4.1.19; but later in a moral sense, a *perfect character*, Arist.*MM*1207^{b}25; also applied to qualities, actions, etc., οὐδὲν καλὸν κἀγαθὸν εἰδέναι Pl.*Ap*.21d; τῶν καλῶν τε κἀγαθῶν ἔργων X. *Mem*.2.1.20; καρτερία κ. κ. Pl.*La*.192c; καρδία κ. καὶ ἀ. *Ev.Luc*.8. 15; πάντα ἔμοιγε δοκεῖ τὰ καλὰ καὶ τἀγαθὰ ἀσκητὰ εἶναι X.*Mem*.1.2. 23, cf. *Cyr*.2.1.17; of things, *admirable, splendid*, ib.3.3.6; πᾶν ὅ τι κ. καὶ ἀ. ἔστιν ἐν Σάρδεσιν ib.7.2.12; μαντεῖαι πολλαὶ καὶ καλαὶ κἀγ. καὶ ἀληθεῖς D.*Ep*.1.16: Sup., ὅ τι κάλλιστον καὶ ἄριστον ἔχετε X.*An*. 2.1.9, cf. 5.6.28: rarely with words between, ἦν καὶ κ., ὦ δέσποτα, καὶ ἀ. v.l. in Id.*Cyr*.4.6.3; ἅμα μὲν κ., ἅμα δὲ ἀ. Pl.*Ti*.88c; κ. μὲν γὰρ ἦν καὶ ἀ. ὁ Βρασίδας Plu.*Lyc*.25.

κᾰλοκαιρ-ία, ἡ, = εὐετηρία, Melamp.p.30 D., Hsch. **-ιανός**, ὁ, name of an eye-salve, Orib.*Fr*.102. **-ῖνός**, ὁ, name of an ἐγχυματισμός, *Hippiatr*.129.8. **-ος**, ὁ, = *bonum tempus*, *Gloss*.

κᾰλο-κάρφωτος, ον, gloss on εὐγόμφωτος, Sch.Opp.*H*.1.58. **-κέραστος**, ον, *well-mixed*, gloss on εὔζωρον, Zonar.

κᾱλοκοπέω, *cut wood*, Hsch.

κᾰλολαΐγξ [λᾱ], ιγγος, ἡ, *beautiful pebble*, Tz.*H*.7.254.

κᾰλολογέω, = εὐλογέω, Sch.E.*Ph*.967.

κᾶλον, τό, *wood*, κᾶλον ἐν ἱαρῷ πεφυκός *Berl.Sitzb*.1927.157 (Cyrene); elsewh. only in pl. κᾶλα, = ξύλα, *logs*, for burning, κάγκανα κ. *h.Merc*.112; παλαίφατα κ. Call.*Fr*.66c; τὰ κ. καὶ τοὺς ἄνθρακας Ion Trag.29; also, *timber* for joiner's work, ἐπικαμπύλα κ. Hes.*Op*.427; esp. of ships, ποττὰ κᾶλα (κάλα cod.) Ar.*Lys*.1253; ἔρρει τὰ κᾶλα the *ships* are lost (καλά codd.), X.*HG*1.1.23, Plu.*Alc*.28. (κᾶλον and κῆλον (q. v.) perh. fr. *κᾱϝελος, cf. καίω.)

κᾱλόνης· εἴρων (Rhodian), Hsch.

κᾰλοπαίκτης, ου, ὁ, (κάλως) *trapeze-artist*, *PSI*8.953 (vi A.D.), prob. cj. for calopettas in *GGM*ii 519 (*Arch.Lat.Lex*.13.552).

κᾱλοπέδῐλα, τά, (κᾶλον) *wooden shoes*, prob. *a hobble tied to a cow's legs* to keep her still while milking, Theoc.25.103.

κᾰλοπλόκος, ὁ, *one who plaits* or *weaves*, *Gloss*.

κᾱλοπόδιον, τό, = καλάπους, Gal.6.364 (v.l.), Suid.:—hence **κᾱλοποδάριαι** φόρμαι *lasts*, *Edict.Diocl*.9.1.

κᾰλοποι-έω, *do good*, 2*Ep.Thess*.3.13, Ph.1.698, *Gp*.2.22.3. **-ός**, όν, *making beautiful*, c. gen., τὸ δίκαιον κ. τῆς ψυχῆς Procl. *in Alc*. p.327 C.; *creating beauty*, Dam.*Pr*.33, *Cat.Cod.Astr*.7.101, *PMag. Leid.V*.9.3; cf. καλλοποιός.

κᾱλόπους, ὁ, v. καλάπους.

κᾰλό-πους, ὁ, ἡ, πουν, τό, gen. ποδος, *with beautiful feet*, Suid.: but

καλοπούς (leg. καλωπούς)· εὐοφθάλμους, Hsch. **-πρᾱγέω,** = καλῶς πράσσω, Sch.E.*Hec.*951, 984. **-πρᾱγία,** ἡ, = καλοποιΐα, Sch.A.R.3.68. **-πρόσωπος,** ον, *with fair face*, Sch.D Il.1.310. **-ρρημοσύνη,** ἡ, = καλλιρρημοσύνη, Hsch. s. v. εὐηγορία.

κάλος, ὁ, v. κάλως.

καλός, ή, όν, Aeol. **κάλος** (v. infr.), α, ον, Boeot. **καλϝός** *Schwyzer* 538 (vi B.C.) :—*beautiful*, of outward form, freq. of persons, κάλλιστος ἀνὴρ ὑπὸ Ἴλιον ἦλθεν Il.2.673 : in Hom. usu. in the phrase κ. τε μέγας τε Il.21.108, al.; μέγας καὶ κ. Od.9.513 ; καλή τε μεγάλη τε 13.289, 15.418 ; καλὸς δέμας *beautiful* of form, 17.307 ; κ. ἰδέᾳ Pi.*O.*10(11).103 ; εἶδος κάλλιστος X.*Cyr.*1.2.1 ; κ. τὸ σῶμα Id.*Mem.*2.6.30 ; τὰς ὄψεις Theopomp.Hist.195 ; χορῷ καλή *beauteous* in the dance, Il.16.180 : c. inf., καλλίονες καὶ μείζονες εἰσοράασθαι Od.10.396 ; ἐσορᾶν κ. Pi.*O.*8.19 : freq. of parts of the body, *fair, shapely*, κ. πρόσωπα, ὄμματα, παρήϊα, σφυρά, Il.19.285, 23.66, Od.19.208, Il.4.147 ; χρώς 5.354, al. ; of clothes, εἵματα, φάρεα, χιτών, χλαῖνα, πέδιλα, Od.6.111, 24.277, Il.2.43, Od.10.365, 1.96 ; πέπλος κάλλιστος ποικίλμασιν ἠδὲ μέγιστος Il.6.294 ; of arms and armour, κνημῖδες, ἀσπίς, σάκος, κόρυς, φάσγανα, ἔντεα, 3.331, 11.33, 22.314, 18.612, 15.713, Od.19.18 ; of buildings, manufactured articles, etc., αὐλὴ κ. τε μεγάλη τε 14.7 ; κ. δώματα, τεῖχος, πόλιες, 3.387, Il.21.447, 18.491 ; ἅμαξα, τράπεζα, θρόνος, 24.267, 11.629, Od.1.131 ; also τέμενος, ἀγρός, Il.12.314, Od.24.206 ; so after Hom., Λύδιον κ. ἔργον Sapph.19, etc. ; ἐέρσα κ. ead.*Supp.*25.12. **2.** in Att. added to a name in token of love or admiration, as Ἀρίσημος κ. *IG*1².921, etc. ; ἐν τοῖσι τοίχοις ἔγραφ' "Ἀθηναῖοι καλοί" Ar.*Ach.*144, cf. *V.*98 ; Ἀλκιβιάδης ὁ καλός, Σαπφὼ ἡ καλή, Pl.*Alc.*1.113b, *Phdr.*235c. **b.** ἡ Καλή or Καλλίστη, as epith., A.*Ag.*140 (lyr.), Paus.1.29.2, *CIG*4445 (Beroea). **c.** Καλοί, οἱ, divinities worshipped in childbirth, *IG*5(1).1445 (Messene, ii B.C.). **3.** τὸ καλόν *beauty*, Sapph.79, E.*IA*21 (anap.), etc. ; τὰ καλά *the proprieties* or *elegancies* of life, Hdt.1.8,207 ; ἁπάντων καλῶν ἄμμορος Pi.*O.*1.84 ; αἱ τέχναι ἃς πηγάς φασι τῶν κ. εἶναι X.*Cyr.*7.2.13. **II.** with ref. to use, *good, of fine quality*, κ. λιμήν Od.6.263 ; Βορέῃ ἀνέμῳ.. καλῷ *fair*, 14.253,299 ; κ. ἀργύριον, opp. κίβδηλον, *genuine* silver, X.*Mem.*3.1.9 ; opp. ἀποτετριμμένον, *good* silver currency, *PCair.Zen.*21.33 (iii B.C.) ; ἐλαῖαι *PHib.*1.49.12 (iii B.C.) ; γῆ *Ev.Luc.*8.15 ; κ. οἶνος *PFay.*133.8 (iv A.D.) ; στρατόπεδον κάλλιστον Th.5.60 ; ἀνταπεδώκατε πονηρὰ ἀντὶ καλῶν LXX *Ge.*44.4 ; κ. ἐς στρατιάν X.*Cyr.*3.3.6 ; πρός τι Pl.*Hp.Ma.*295c, *Grg.*474d, etc. : c. inf., λόφος κάλλιστος τρέχειν X.*An.*4.8.26 ; ἐν καλῷ [τόπῳ] in a *good* place, καθίζεσθαι, ὁρμεῖν, Ar.*Th.*292, X.*HG*2.1.25 ; ἐν καλῷ μὲν τοῦ κόλπου καὶ τῶν πόλεων, ἐν κ. δὲ τοῦ τὴν χώραν βλάπτειν, ib.6.2.9 ; ἐν καλῷ under *favourable circumstances*, Th.5.59,60 ; ἐν κ. (sc. χρόνῳ) in *good time, in season*, E.*IA*1106 ; ἐν οὐ κ. Id.*Or.*579 ; ἐν καλῷ [ἐστι] c. inf., S.*El.*384 (so καλόν ἐστι c. inf., Id.*Ph.*1155 (lyr.), Ar.*Pax* 278, Th.8.2) ; ἐς καλόν S.*OT*78, Pl.*Men.*89e, *Smp.*174e ; τί γὰρ ἐμοὶ ζῆν καλόν; what is the *good* of life to me ? Ph.2.594 ; καλῇ πίστει, = Lat. *bona fide*, *PTeb.*418.14 (iii A.D.). **2.** of sacrifices, *auspicious*, σφάγια A.*Th.*379 ; οἰωνοί E.*Ion* 1333 ; ἱερά Th.4.92 ; τὸ τέλος κ. τῆς ἐξόδου X.*An.*5.2.9 ; κ. τὰ ἱερὰ ἦν αὐτῷ Id.*Cyr.*3.2.3 : c. inf., ἰέναι..κ. ἡμῖν τὰ ἱερὰ ἦν Id.*An.*2.2.3 : Com., τὰ τῆς πυγῆς κ. (for τοῦ θεοῦ) Ar.*Pax* 868. **III.** in a moral sense, *beautiful, noble, honourable*, in Hom. only in neut., οὐ καλὸν ἔειπες Od.8.166, cf. 17.381 ; μεῖζον κλέος ..καὶ κάλλιον 18.255 ; freq. καλόν [ἐστι] c. inf., κ. τοι σὺν ἐμοὶ τὸν κήδειν ὅς κ' ἐμὲ κήδῃ Il.9.615 ; οὐ γὰρ ἔμοιγε κ. (sc. ἄρχειν) 21.440 ; οὐ κ. ἀτέμβειν οὐδὲ δίκαιον Od.20.294 ; so in Trag., καλόν μοι τοῦτο ποιούσῃ θανεῖν S.*Ant.*72, etc. ; μάθετε καλὸν ποιεῖν LXX *Is.*1.17 : Comp., οὐ μέν τοι τόδε κάλλιον οὐδὲ ἔοικε Od.7.159, cf. Il.24.52 ; after Hom. freq. of actions, etc., κάλων κἄσλων Sapph.*Supp.*2.4 (unless of persons here) ; κ. ἔργματα *noble* deeds, Pi.*I.*4(3).42, cf. S.*Fr.*839, etc. ; ἀναστροφὴ κ. 1*Ep.Pet.*2.12 : in pl., *excellences*, πλῆθος καλῶν Pi.*O.*13.45 ; πολλῶν καλῶν δεῖ τῷ καλῶν τι μωμένῳ S.*Fr.*938 ; τὰ τοῦ παιδὸς κ. X.*Smp.*8.17. **2.** τὸ κ. *moral beauty, virtue, honour*, opp. τὸ αἰσχρόν, Id.*Mem.*1.1.16, cf. Pl.*Smp.*183d, etc. ; ὅττι καλόν, φίλον ἐστί, τὸ δ' οὐ καλὸν οὐ φίλον ἐστίν Thgn.17, cf. E.*Ba.*881 (lyr.), Pl.*Ly.*216c ; οὐ ταὐτὸν ἡγῇ σύ, ὡς ἔοικας, κ. τε καὶ ἀγαθὸν καὶ κακὸν καὶ αἰσχρόν Id.*Grg.*474d, cf. *Smp.*201e ; τοὐμὸν κ. E.*Supp.*300. **3.** of persons, in early writers coupled with ἀγαθός, v. καλοκἀγαθός ; later κ. ποιμήν *Ev.Jo.*10.11 ; κ. στρατιώτης 2*Ep.Tim.*2.3. **IV.** in Att. and Trag. freq. ironically, *fine, specious*, γέρας κ. A.*Eu.*209 ; κ. γὰρ οὑμὸς βίοτος ὥστε θαυμάσαι S.*El.*393, cf. E.*Ba.*652 ; κ. χάρις D.9.65 ; κ. ὕβριν ὑβρισμένοι Id.23.121 ; καί σοι.. θωπεῦσαι καλόν S.*OC* 1003 ; μετ' ὀνομάτων καλῶν Th.5.89.

B. Degrees of Comp. : Comp. καλλίων, ον, Il.24.52, Od.10.396, etc. : neut. κάλιον [ᾰ] Alc.134 : Sup. κάλλιστος, η, ον, Il.20.233, etc. ; late καλλιώτερος or -ότερος, *POxy.*1672.6 (i A.D.), Sch.E.*Tr.*966 ; also καλώτερος Hdn.*Epim.*69.

C. Adv. :—Poets freq. use neut. καλόν as Adv., κ. ἀείδειν Il.18.570, Od.1.155 ; καλά Il.6.326 ; later τὸ κ. Theoc.3.3,18, Call.*Ep.*53, Herod.1.54. **II.** regul. Adv. **καλῶς** (Dor. **καλώς** Sophr.22), *well, rightly*, οὐδ' ἔτι κ. οἶκος ἐμὸς διόλωλε Od.2.64 ; κ. ζῆν, τεθνηκέναι, etc., S.*Aj.*479, etc. ; κ. φρονεῖν to be in one's *right* mind, Id.*Fr.*836 ; οὐ κ. ταρβεῖς Id.*Tr.*457 ; κ. ἀγωνιεῖσθαι *fairly, on the merits of the case*, Lys.13.88 ; χρήματα δατῆθθαι κ. *Leg.Gort.*4.39 ; κ. εἰρημένα S.*Fr.*576.6 ; κάλλιον λέγεις Pl.*Tht.*161b ; κάλλιστ' ἂν εἴποι S.*OT*1172 : freq. in phrase καλῶς καὶ εὖ, καλῶς τε καὶ εὖ, Pl.*Prt.*319e, *Prm.*128b, etc. **2.** of good fortune, *well, happily*, κ. πράσσειν, = εὖ π., A.*Pr.*979, S.*Ant.*271 ; κ. καὶ εὖ πράττειν Pl.*Chrm.*172a ; κ. ἔχειν to be *well*, A.*Th.*799, etc. ; κ. ἔχει σοι Ar.*Ach.*946, cf. S.*El.*816 ; κ. ἔχει c. inf., 'tis *well* to.., X.*Mem.*3.11.1 : c. gen., κ. ἔχειν τινός to be *well off in respect to* a thing, Hp.*Superf.*29 ; κ. παράπλου κεῖσθαι Th.1.36 ; εἰ κ. σφίσιν ἔχοι Id.4.117 ; οὔτε τοῖς θεοῖς ἔφη κ. ἔχειν, εἰ.. X.*Mem.*1.3.3 ; καλλιόνως ἔχει Pl.*Tht.*169e, etc. ; κάλλιστα ἕξει Id.*Hp.Ma.*295b. **3.** καλῶς, = πάνυ, *thoroughly, altogether*, τὸν κ. εὐδαίμονα A.*Fr.*317, = S.*Fr.*934 ; κ. ἔξοιδα Id.*OC*269, cf. *OT*1008 ; κ. ὑπὸ τοῦ πυρὸς διεφθάρθαι D.S.13.108 : Comp., κάλλιον εἰδέναι Pl.*Hp.Ma.*300d ; κάλλιον ἐοικέναι to be *just* like, Hp.*Genit.*8. **4.** κ. ἀκούειν to be *well* spoken of, Men.*Mon.*285, Plu.2.177e. **5.** κ. ποιῶν *rightly, deservedly*, κ. ποιῶν ἀπόλλυται Ar.*Pl.*863, cf. D.1.28, al., Aeschin.3.232 ; in requests, κ. ποιήσεις πριάμενος, etc., *PPetr.*3 p.143 (iii B.C.), etc. ; also c. inf., κ. π. γράψαι *BGU*1203.7 (i B.C.), etc. **6.** in answers, to approve the words of the former speaker, *well said!* E.*Or.*1216, D.39.15 ; also, to decline an offer courteously, *no, thank you!* Ar.*Ra.*888 ; κ. ἔχει Antiph.165, Men.*Pk.*266 ; πάνυ κ. Ar.*Ra.*512 ; ἀμέλει κ. ib.532 : Sup., κάλλιστ', ἐπαινῶ ib.508 ; ἔχει κάλλιστα Theoc.15.3. **7.** ironically, *finely*, καλῶς ἐρήμης γ' ἂν σὺ γῆς ἄρχοις μόνος S.*Ant.*739, cf. E.*Med.*588, Ar.*Eq.*344, Din.1.69. **8.** κ. ὁ ἱερεύς *hurrah for the priest!* *SIG*1109.14 (Athens, ii A.D.). **9.** repeated with the Adj., καλὴ καλῶς Ar.*Ach.*253, *Pax* 1330, *Ec.*730 ; καλὸς κάλλιστά τε ῥέξαις Pi.*O.*9.94. **10.** Comp. καλλιόνως Pl.*Tht.* l. c., *Lg.*660d : Sup. καλλίστως *PMag.Par.*1.2443,2465, Sch.E.*Hec.*310.

D. for compds., v. καλλι-, καλο-.

E. Quantity : ᾱ in Ep. and early Iamb. Poets (exc. *h.Ven.*29, Hes.*Op.*63, *Th.*585) : ᾰ in Lyr. (exc. κᾱλῶς B.12.206) and Trag. (A.*Fr.*314, S.*Ph.*1381 are corrupt).—In Eleg., Epigr., and Bucol. Poets ᾰ or ᾱ (the latter usu. in thesi) ; τὰ μὴ κᾰλὰ κᾱλὰ πέφανται Theoc.6.19, cf. Herod.7.115, Call.*Jov.*55.—In Comp., ῐ in Hom., ῑ in Trag. and later.

κᾰλο-σύμβουλος, ον, *giving good counsel*, Ptol.*Tetr.*163. **-σύντῠχος,** ον, *sociable*, Zonar. s. v. εὔθειος. **-σχηματίζομαι,** Pass., Astrol., *to be grouped in propitious lineation*, *Cat.Cod.Astr.*6.61. **-τεχνία,** ἡ, = καλλιτεχνία, Sopat. in Rh.4.51 W.

κᾰλότης, ητος, ἡ, = κάλλος, *beauty*, a word formed by Chrysipp. *Stoic.*3.60.

κᾰλο-τίθηνος [ῐ], ον, *well-reared*, Hsch. **τράχηλος** [τρᾰ], ον, *with beautiful neck*, *Cat.Cod.Astr.*8(4).181. **-τροπος,** ον, *well-mannered*, *Gloss.* **-τροφος,** ον, gloss on καλοτίθηνος, Hsch.

κᾱλοτύπος [ῠ], ὁ, (κᾶλον) *woodpecker*, Hsch.

κᾰλο-ῠφαντος [ῠ], ον, *beautifully woven*, Sch.rec.S.*Tr.*602. **-φῐλος,** ον, gloss on εὔξεινος, Sch.Opp.*H.*1.627.

κᾱλοφόρος, ον, (κᾶλον) *wood-carrier*, one of a soldier's attendants, Dosiad.Hist.1.

κᾰλό-φρων, ον, gen. ονος, gloss on εὔφρων, Hsch. **-φυλλος,** ον, *with beautiful leaves*, Thphr.*HP*5.3.2. **-ψῡχος,** ον, = εὔψυχος, Hsch. s. v. εὔθυμος.

καλπ-άζω, (κάλπη A) *trot*, of a horse, A.*Fr.*145A, Aq.*Je.*8.6, Suid. **-ασμός,** ὁ, *trotting*, ὁ ἐν ἀναβολῇ κ. Philum.ap.Orib.45.29.36.

κάλπᾰσος, ἡ, = κάρπασος, *PMag.Par.*1.2046, al.

κάλπη (A), ἡ, *trot* : κάλπης δρόμος the *trotting*-race in the Olympic games, Paus.5.9.1 ; ὁ τῆς κ. ἀγών Plu.2.675c, cf. *Hippiatr.*34. (Perh. cogn. with OHG. *hlaufan*, Germ. *laufen*.)

κάλπη (B), ἡ, = κάλπις, Hsch. ; κάλπην v.l. for κάλπιν in Aristaenet.2.4, Plu.*Marc.*30, Hdn.3.15.7 :—of a *pitcher*, Aristaenet. l. c. ; of a *cinerary urn*, Plu., Hdn. ll. cc. **II.** Astron., name of a group of stars in Aquarius, Vett.Val.12.29, v.l. in Gem.3.6.

κάλπιον, τό, Dim. of foreg. (B), Pamphil.ap.Ath.11.475c.

κάλπις, ιδος, ἡ, acc. κάλπιν Od.7.20, κάλπιδα Pi.*O.*6.40 :—*pitcher* (Thess. word for ὑδρία, acc. to *AB*1095), Od. and Pi. ll. cc., *h.Cer.*107, E.*Hipp.*123 (lyr.), Ar.*Ra.*1339 (lyr.), *Lys.*358, etc. ; a kind of *cup*, Philem.Gr.ap.Ath.11.468f ; *box* for unguent, Antiph.106.2, Plb.30.25.17 ; *urn for drawing lots* or *collecting votes*, Luc.*Herm.*40,57 ; *cinerary urn*, Plu.*Demetr.*53 : with play on the original sense, *AP* 12.74 (Mel.), 7.384 (Marc. Arg.) ; *Panathenaic vase*, Call.*Fr.*122 ; = κάλπη (B) II, Gem.3.6, S.E.*M.*5.92 :—in Hsch. also **κάλπη,** ἡ (q. v.), and **κάλπος,** ὁ.

κάλτιος, ὁ, Sicil. form of Lat. *calceus*, *shoe*, Rhinth.5, Plu.*Aem.*5, 2.813e, *Edict.Diocl.*9.7 :—**κάλτοι·** ὑποδήματα κοῖλα, ἐν οἷς ἱππεύουσι, Hsch. :—**καλίκιοι,** Plb.30.18.3 codd. :—**κάλσιοι,** *Gloss.*

κᾰλῠβ-εύς, έως, ὁ, *cottager*, *Gloss.* **-η,** ἡ, *hut, cabin*, Hdt.5.16, Th.1.133, 2.52, Theoc.21.7,18, Agatharch.47, etc. ; σχοινῖτις κ. *AP*7.295.7 (Leon.) ; ἡ ἱερὰ κ. *CIG*4591 (Palestine). **2.** *bridal bower*, A.R.1.775. **3.** *sleeping-tent* on roof of house, *PFlor.*335.2 (iii A.D.). **II.** *cover, screen*, Theopomp.Hist.195. **-ιον,** τό, Dim. of foreg., Phld.*Acad.Ind.*p.54 M., D.H.10.19, Plu.*Pomp.*73, Alciphr.1.1, D.L.4.19. **-ίτης** [ῑ], ου, ὁ, *living in a hut*, Str.7.5.12.

κᾰλῠβο-ποιέομαι, Med., *make oneself a cabin*, Str.4.5.2. **-ποιΐα,** ἡ, *making of cabins*, Id.15.2.13.

κᾰλῠβός, ὁ, = καλύβη, *chamber*, *Epigr.Gr.*260 (Cyrene), Hsch.

κάλυγες· τὰ ἔμβρυα, Hsch. **καλυδίλα·** γέφυρα, Id.

κᾰλύδριον, τό, Dim. of κάλως, *small cable*, *BCH*29.543 (Delos, ii B.C.).

κᾰλῠκ-άνθεμον, τό, = κλύμενον, Ps.-Dsc.4.13 ; = περικλύμενον, ib.14. **-ειος** λίθος, ὁ, stone found in the head of the fish σάλπης, Hsch. **-η,** ἡ, name of a song, Aristox.*Fr.Hist.*72. **-ίζειν·** ἀνθεῖν, Hsch. **-ιον,** τό, Dim. of κάλυξ, Dsc.ap.Orib.11.1.50, Hsch.

κᾰλῠκοστέφᾰνος, ον, *crowned with flower-buds*, B.5.98, 10.108, *AP* 6.55 (Barbuc.) ; ὧραι Emp.(?)154.2.

κᾰλῠκ-ώδης, ες, *cup-shaped*, ἄνθος Thphr.*HP*3.5.6, 3.10.4. **II.** dub. sens., ἐνθάδε Κλειτόριος κεῖται δρῖλον καλυκῶδες κτλ. *Raccolta*

Lumbroso 257 (iii B. C.). **-ῶπις**, ιδος, ἡ, (ὤψ) *like a budding flower in face*, i. e. *blushing*, *roseate*, *h.Cer.*8,420, *Ven.*284, B.*Scol.Oxy.Fr.*5 i 11, Orph.*Fr.*49 ii 23, *H.*79.2.

κάλυμμα [ᾰ], ατος, τό, (κᾰλύπτω) *head-covering*, *hood*, *veil*, κ. κυάνεον dark *veil* worn in mourning, Il.24.93, *h.Cer.*42; χρύσεον κ. B. 16.38; ὁ χρησμὸς οὐκέτ' ἐκ καλυμμάτων ἔσται δεδορκὼς νεογάμου νύμφης δίκην A.*Ag.*1178 (but metaph., δείξω τάδ' ἐκ καλυμμάτων 'I will lift the *veil*', S.*Tr.*1078); λεπτῶν ὄμμα διὰ καλυμμάτων ἔχουσ' E.*IT* 372, cf. Ar.*Lys.*532, *Fr.*320.5, Dicaearch.1.18; κάρα καλύμμασι κρυψάμενον S.*Aj.*245 (lyr.); χαλᾶτε πᾶν κάλυμμ' ἀπ' ὀφθαλμῶν Id.*El.*1468; Μωυσῆς ἐτίθει κ. ἐπὶ τὸ πρόσωπον 2*Ep.Cor.*3.13. **2.** *fishing-net* shaped like a sack, Opp.*H.*3.82; βουλευτοῖσιν ἐν καλύμμασιν, of the garment thrown by Clytaemnestra over her husband, A.*Ch.* 494. **3.** *skull* (as the brain's covering), Nic.*Th.*906. **4.** *grave*, *AP*7.227 (Diotim.). **5.** in animals, *the covering* of the gills of fishes, Arist.*HA*505ᵃ2; *operculum* of testaceans, ib.547ᵇ5; *eyelid*, Poll.2.66. **6.** *covering of honeycomb*, Arist.*HA*624ᵇ31. **7.** *shell* of fruit, Nic.*Al.*269. **8.** *shutter*, D.S.20.91. **9.** *sheathing-planks* for a roof, *IG*2².1668.57; but, *slabs* for closing coffers, ib.4. 1484.57 (Epid., iv B. C.), 11(2).144*A* 42 (Delos, iv B. C.). **10.** perh. *paving-slab*, *Milet.*7.60.53.

κᾰλυμμάτιον, τό, Dim. of κάλυμμα 9, Ar.*Fr.*73.

κάλυξ [ᾰ], ῠκος, ἡ, also ὁ v.l. in Dsc.2.143: (perh. cogn. with καλύπτω):—*covering*, used only of flowers and fruits: **1.** *seed-vessel*, *husk*, *shell* or *pod*, of the water-lily, Hdt.2.92; of rice, Id.3.100; of wheat, πρὶν ἂν ἐν τῇ κάλυκι γένηται [ἡ στάχυς] Thphr.*HP*8.2.4, cf. 8.4.3; κάλυκος ἐν λοχεύμασι, i.e. when the fruit is setting, A.*Ag.* 1392, cf. S.*OT*25, Ar.*Av.*1065 (lyr.). **2.** *cup* or *calyx of a flower*, ἀνεμωνῶν κάλυξι.. ἠριναῖς Cratin.98; κισσοῖο καλύκεσσι Theoc.3.23; ὅσα ἐν κάλυκι ἀνθεῖ Arist.*HA*554ᵃ12; [φύλλοις] τοῖς τῶν ῥόδων ὅταν ἐν κάλυξιν ὦσι Thphr.*HP*4.10.3; ῥόδου κ. ibid.; so in Poets, *rose-bud*, *h.Cer.*427, *AP*12.8 (Strato), etc.: metaph., σταθερὰ.. κ. νεαρᾶς ἥβης Ar.*Fr.*467. **II.** in pl., *women's ornaments*, perh. *ear-rings shaped like flower cups*, Il.18.401 (other expl. in Sch.), cf. *h.Ven.* 87. **III.** = ἄγχουσα, Dsc.4.23.

κάλυξις [ᾰ], εως, ἡ, = foreg. I. 1, Hsch.; also, = foreg. II, Id.

κᾰλύπτ-ειρα, ἡ, fem. of sq., = καλύπτρα, *veil*, *AP*6.206 (Antip. Sid.). **-ήρ**, ῆρος, ὁ, *covering*, *sheath*, Hp.*Haem.*4; νάρθηκας ἢ κ. Arist.*Pr.*923ᵇ25, cf. Thphr.*CP*5.6.4. **2.** *cover*, Lxx *Nu.*4.13; *lid*, D.S.18.26: metaph., γῆ ᾅδου κ. Secund.*Sent.*15. **3.** pl., *tiles*, *IG*2².463.71, D.H.6.92; κ. ἀνθεμωτοί *IG*2².1627.306 (sg.), *BCH*35. 76 (Delos, ii B. C.), *IG*7.3498.61 (Oropus, ii B. C.), Demioprat.ap. Poll.10.157. **4.** metaph., οἱ τῆς πόλιος κ. 'pillars of society', Herod.2.31. **-ηρίζω**, *cover with tiles*, Att. fut. -ιῶ, *IG*2².463.71: **-ηριάζω**, *Gloss.* **-ήριον**, τό, *covering*, ib. **-ης**, ου, ὁ, *tile*, ib. **II.** *one who hides* or *conceals*, τῶν φανερῶν *PMag.Leid.V.*7.9 (pl.). **-ός**, ή, όν, *covered*, S.*Fr.*534.4 (anap.), Ar.*Th.*890, Arist. *Fr.*308; τεύτλῳ περὶ σῶμα κ. Eub.35. **II.** (from καλύπτω II) *put round so as to cover*, καλυπτῆς ἐξέκειντο πιμελῆς from the *enfolding* fat, S.*Ant.*1011. **-ρα**, Ion. -ρη, ἡ, *veil* or *head-dress*, ἀπὸ δὲ λιπαρὴν ἔρριψε καλύπτρην Il.22.406, cf. Od.5.232, Parm.1.10, A.*Pers.*537 (anap.), *Supp.*122; κ. πλοκάμων Archil.18; esp. *bride's veil*, Euph.107.4: metaph., δνοφερὰ κ. the dark *veil* of night, A.*Ch.* 811 (lyr.). **2.** land given to queens as *veil-money* (cf. ζώνη I. 3), Pl.*Alc.*1.123c, Aristid.*Or.*19(41).4. **II.** *cover*, *lid*, φαρετρέων Hdt. 4.64 (pl.); θυμιατηρίου *IG*2².1396.31 (iv B. C.). **2.** *seed-capsule*, *Gp.*11.11.2. **-ω**, Ep. impf. κάλυπτον Il.24.20: fut. -ψω A.*Th.* 1045: aor. ἐκάλυψα, Ep. κάλ- Il.23.693:—**Med.**, fut. καλύψομαι (ἐγ-) Ael.*NA*7.12, (συγ-) Aristid.2.59 J.: Ep. aor. καλυψάμην Il.3.141, al.:—**Pass.**, fut. καλυφθήσομαι Paus.8.11.11, Aristid.1.130 J., Gal. *UP*9.3, (δια-) D.11.13: aor. ἐκαλύφθην Od.4.402, E.*Supp.*531: aor. 2 part. καλῠφείς *CPR*239.5 (iii A. D.): pf. κεκάλυμμαι Il.16.360, X.*Cyr.* 5.1.4, Aen.Tact.26.3: plpf. κεκάλυπτο Il.21.549.—Rare in Prose, exc. in compds. (Cf. κέλυφος, καλύβη, Lat. *oc-culo*, *celo*.) **I.** *cover*, freq. c. dat. instr., παρδαλέῃ.. μετάφρενον εὐρὺ κάλυψε Il.10.29; σάωσε δὲ νυκτὶ καλύψας 5.23 (but in 13.425, ἐρεβεννῇ νυκτὶ καλύψαι is *to kill*); simply, *cover*, μέλαν δὲ ἑ κῦμα κάλυψεν 23.693; ἐπισκύνιον κάτω ἕλκεται ὄσσε καλύπτων 17.136; [πέτρον] περὶ χεὶρ ἐκάλυψεν his hand *covered*, *grasped* a stone, 16.735; of death, τὼ.. τέλος θανάτοιο κάλυψεν 5.553; τὸν δὲ σκότος ὄσσε κάλυψεν 4.461,503, etc.; τὸν δὲ κατ' ὀφθαλμῶν ἐρεβεννὴ νὺξ ἐκάλυψεν 13.580; τὼ δέ οἱ ὄσσε νὺξ ἐκάλυψε μέλαινα 14.439; so τὸν δ' ἄχεος νεφέλη ἐκάλυψε 17.591; ἑ πένθος ὀφθαλμοὺς ἐκάλυψε 11.250: freq. in Lyr. and Trag., ὅταν θανάτοιο κυάνεον νέφος καλύψῃ B.12.64; κ. χθονὶ γυῖα, i. e. *to be buried*, Pi.*N.*8.38; but χθονί, τάφῳ κ., *bury*, A.*Pr.*582 (lyr.), S.*Ant.*28; γῇ, χέρσῳ, E.*Ph.*1633, *Hel.*1066: abs., καὐτὴ καλύψω A.*Th.*1045: rare in Prose, μὴ καλύπτειν τὰ δολοσχερέα τοῖς εἱματίοις *SIG*1218.7 (Ceos, v B. C.); of armour, *protect*, X. *Eq.*12.5:—Med., *cover* or *veil oneself*, ἀργεννῇσι καλυψαμένη ὀθόνῃσιν Il.3.141; κρηδέμνῳ δ' ἐφύπερθε καλύψατο 14.184; λευκοῖσιν φαρέεσσι καλυψαμένω (fem. dual) χρόα καλόν Hes.*Op.*198: abs., καλυψάμενος δ' ἐνὶ νηῒ κείμην Od.10.53:—Pass., ἀσπίδι ταυρείῃ κεκαλυμμένος.. ὤμους Il.16.360; ἐν χλαίνῃ κεκ. 24.163; χαλκῷ, ἠέρι, 13.192, 21.549; οἰὸς ἀώτῳ Od.1.443; φρικὶ καλυφθείς, of the sea, 4.402: in Prose, τὸν νεκρὸν κεκαλυμμένον φερέτω σιγᾷ *Michel* 995 *C* 32 (Delph., v/iv B. C.); [βράγχια] καλυπτόμενα καλύμματι Arist.*HA*505ᵃ6; κεκαλυμμένος *veiled* *IG*5(2).514.10 (Lycosura). **2.** *hide*, *conceal*, κεκαλυμμένοι ἵππῳ *concealed* in it, Od.8.503:—Act., Hippon.52, etc.; ἔξω μέ που καλύψατε S.*OT*1411, cf. *Ev.Luc.*23.30; κρυφῇ κ. καρδίᾳ τι S.*Ant.* 1254; σιγῇ κ. E.*Hipp.*712: metaph., ἐκάλυψας τὰς ἁμαρτίας αὐτῶν Lxx *Ps.*84(85).2, cf. *Ep.Jac.*5.20. **3.** *cover with dishonour*, *throw a cloud over*, σὺ μὴ κάλυπτε τὰς εὐδαίμονας ἔργοις Ἀθήνας ἀνοσίοις S. *OC*282. **II.** *put over as a covering*, πρόσθε δέ οἱ πέπλοιο πτύγμ' ἐκάλυψεν Il.5.315; τόσσην οἱ ἄσιν καθύπερθε καλύψω I *will put* mud *over* him, 21.321; ἀμφὶ Μενοιτιάδῃ σάκος εὐρὺ καλύψας 17.132; πρόσθεν δὲ σάκος στέρνοιο κάλυψε 22.313.

κᾰλῠφή, ἡ, (καλύπτω) *submerged land*, *CPR*32.5 (iii A. D.), *BGU* 640.7 (iii A. D.). **II.** etym. of καλύβη, *EM*486.22.

κᾰλύφιον (Dim. of κᾶλον)· ξυλήφιον, Hsch. (-ύριον cod.).

κάλυψ [ᾰ], ῠβος, ὁ, = καλύβη, S.*Fr.*574.6.

κάλυψις [ᾰ], εως, ἡ, *covering*, Sch.Ar.*Pl.*22 (pl.), Hsch. s. v. στρέφωσις.

Κᾰλυψώ, όος, contr. οῦς, ἡ (prob. from καλύπτω, 'she that conceals'), *Calypso*, Od.1.14, Hes.*Th.*359, etc.

καλχαίνω, (κάλχη) prop. *make purple*:—Pass., *to be purple*, Nic. *Th.*641. **II.** metaph. (cf. πορφύρω), *make dark and troublous* like a stormy sea, *ponder deeply*, κ. ἔπος S.*Ant.*20; ἀμφὶ τέκνοις E.*Heracl.* 40: c. inf., *long*, *desire*, Lyc.1457; cf. sq.

Κάλχας, αντος, ὁ, voc. Κάλχαν or Κάλχα Il.1.86:—*Calchas*, the Greek Seer at Troy, ib.69, al.: prob. connected with foreg. II.

κάλχη, ἡ, (perh. a loan-word) *murex*, *purple limpet*, = πορφύρα, Nic.*Al.*393. **2.** *purple dye*, Str.11.14.9. **II.** *rosette* on the capitals of columns, *IG*1².372.90, 4.1484.83 (Epid., iv B. C.), 11(2). 161 *A* 73 (Delos, iii B. C.), Hsch.:—written **χάλκη** *IG*1².374.317, al., **χάλχη** ib.374.103. **III.** *purple flower*, *Chrysanthemum coronarium*, Alcm.39, Nic.Dam.76 J.:—written **χάλκη** in Nic.*Fr.*74.60, cf. Ps.-Dsc.4.58.

κάλχιον, τό, *purple dye*, Sch.Nic.*Al.*393.

κᾰλῴδιον (ῳ *IG*2².1632.3, 1648.13, *EM*486.15), τό, Dim. of κάλως, *small cord*, Eup.313, Ar.*V.*379, Th.4.26, Apollod.*Poliorc.*171.8.

κᾰλωνῠμ-έομαι, *to be in good repute*, *bear a good name*, Heph.Astr. 2.32. **-ος**, ον, *bearing a fair name*, εὐσέβεια *IG*5(1).1331 (Laconia), cf. *EM*143.22.

κᾰλωπός, ή, όν, (ὤψ) *with beautiful eyes*, prob. in Hsch.

καλῶς, Adv. from καλός (q. v.).

κάλως [ᾰ], ὁ, gen. κάλω, acc. κάλων: Ep. and Ion. **κάλος**, ου, ὁ, Od.5.260, Hdt.2.36, also Aen.Tact.11.6; Att. Inscrr. have nom. dual κάλω *IG*1².330.19, nom. (and acc.?) pl. κάλως ib.2².1610.13, 1611.57, 1612.68: as nom. sg. (?) ib.1673.18; late Ep. nom. pl. κάλωες A.R.2.725; acc. κάλωας Orph.*A.*255, Opp.*H.*2.223; dat. κάλωσι Orph.*A.*239:—*reefing rope*, *reef*, Od. l. c.; τῶν ἱστίων τοὺς κάλους Hdt.2.36, cf. Aen.Tact. l. c.; κάλως ἐξιέναι let out *the reefs*, i. e. *set sail*, ὅταν στράτευμ' Ἀργεῖον ἐξίῃ κάλως E.*Tr.*94; ἐχθροὶ γὰρ ἐξιᾶσι πάντα δὴ κάλων are letting out every *reef*, i. e. using every effort, Id. *Med.*278, cf. Ar.*Eq.*756 (and Sch. ad loc.); τοὺς κάλως ἔκλυε καὶ χάλα πόδα Epicr.10.5; πάντας ἔσεισε κάλους *AP*9.545 (Crin.); φόνιον ἐξίει κάλων let murder *loose*, E.*HF*837; πάντα κάλων ἐκτείναντα Pl.*Prt.* 338a; ἐφέντες Id.*Sis.*389c; κινεῖν Luc.*Scyth.*11; γαστρὶ πάντας ἐπιτρωπῶσι κάλωας Opp.*H.*2.223; κάλων τείνας οὔριον εὐφροσυνᾶν *IG*14. 793.8 (Naples). **II.** generally, *rope*, *line*, κάλον (v.l. -ων) κατεῖναι let down *a sounding-line*, Hdt.2.28; ἀπὸ κάλω παραπλεῖν to be towed along shore, Th.4.25; *cable*, Hdt.2.96; πρυμνήτης κ. E.*Med.* 770; οἱ ἐπὶ τὸν κ. βαίνοντες tight-*rope* walkers, Luc.*Rh.Pr.*9.

κᾰλωστρόφος, ὁ, *rope-twister*, *rope-maker*, Plu.*Per.*12.

κάμ, Ep. and Lyr. shortd. form for κατά before μ, Il.11.172, etc.

κᾰμᾰκ-ίας σῖτος, ὁ, corn *which makes too much straw*, Thphr.*HP* 8.7.4. **-ῐνος**, ον, *made of reed* or *cane*, δόρυ κ., opp. κρανέϊνον, X. *Eq.*12.12. **-ιον**, τό, Dim. of κάμαξ, Sch.E.*Ph.*188.

καμάν· τὸν ἀγρόν (Cret.), Hsch. (i. e. χαμάν, cf. χαμαί).

κάμαξ [κᾰ], ᾰκος, ἡ (ὁ in A.*Fr.*171, *AP*6.165, cf. infr. 3), *vine-pole*, *vine-prop*, Il.18.563, Hes.*Sc.*299. **2.** *any pole* or *shaft*, κ. πεύκης A.*Fr.*171; θύρσου χλοερὸν κ. *AP*l. c. (Phal.); in an engine of war, Apollod.*Poliorc.*171.8, al. **3.** *shaft of a spear*, A.*Ag.*66 (anap.), E. *Hec.*1155, *El.*852, Ar.*Fr.*404; χαλκέαι κάμακες, with rings at the top, *J.AJ*3.6.2 (masc. in this sense, acc. to *EM*487.38). **4.** *tiller*, Luc. *Nav.*6. **5.** = κερκίς I, *AP*6.247 (Phil.). **6.** in pl., *steering-paddles*, Alc.*Supp.*4.16. **7.** *tent-pole*, Gal.2.218. **8.** *perch* for fowls, *Gp.*14.7.2, 14.24.5.

κᾰμάρ-α, Ion. -η [μᾰ], ἡ, *anything with an arched cover*, *covered carriage*, Hdt.1.199, D.C.36.49; *covered boat* or *barge*, Str.11.2.12, cf. Gell.10.25; *vaulted chamber*, Agatharch.62, *PStrassb.*91.5 (i B. C.), D.S.18.26, *BGU*731 (ii A. D.); *vault* of a tomb, *CIG*2241 (Chios), 3007 (Ephesus), 3104 (Teos), *IG*7.2725.4 (Acraeph.); *vault* of heaven, Lxx *Is.*40.22; *vaulted ceiling*, τοῦ ἑπτακλίνου *PCair.Zen.*445.9 (iii B. C.); *tester-bed*, Arr.*An.*7.25.4; *vaulted sewer*, as gloss on ψαλίς, Sch.Pl.*Lg.* 947d, Hsch. **II.** Medic., *hollow near the auditory meatus*, Poll. 2.86. **III.** pl., = ζῶναι στρατιωτικαί, Hsch. (Cf. Avest. *kamarā* 'girdle', Lat. *camurus*, unless Carian, cf. καμαρός II.) **-εύω**· σωρεύω, φιλοπονῶ, πορίζω, κακοπαθῶ, συνάγω, and **καμαρεύουσα**· φιλοπονοῦσα, πορίζουσα, Hsch. **-ικός**, ή, όν, = καμαρωτός, Ath.Mech. 36.5: **-ικά**, τά, *treatise on vaulting*, title of work by Hero, Eutoc.*in Archim.Sph.Cyl.*3.84 H. **-ικῶς** λέγει· παροιμιακῶς λέγει, ἀποτόμως, ἀνδρείως, Hsch. **-ιον**, τό, Dim. of καμάρα, *Papers of Amer. Sch. at Athens* 1 No.71 (Assus). **2.** Medic., *fornix* of the brain, Gal.*UP*8.11. **-ίς**, ἡ, woman's ornament, Hsch.

κᾰμᾰροειδής, ές, *like a vault*, *vaulted* or *arched*, Dsc.5.79, Erot. s. v. κοτυληδόνας, Ruf.*Oss.*25.

κάμαρος, ὁ, v. κάμμαρος. **II. καμαρός**, ά, όν, Carian word, = ἀσφαλής, κάμαρα (sic codd.) λέγεσθαι τὰ ἀσφαλῆ Apollon.ap.Sch.

Orib.46.21.7. **III. κάμαροι·** στῆλαι ἐν αἷς ἀναγέγραπται ὁ περιορισμὸς τῆς Ἀσίας, Hsch.

κᾰμᾰρόω, *furnish with a vault*, *BGU*1545.8 (iii B.C.):—Pass., *to be vaulted*, *PGrenf.*1.21.9 (ii B.C.), *IG*4.203.25 (Corinth.).

κᾰμάρ-ωμα [μᾰρ], ατος, τό, *vault, arch*, Str.16.1.5, Gal.10.449. **-ωσις,** εως, ἡ, *building of a vault* or *cellar*, *PPetr.*3 p.143 (iii B.C.). II. Medic., *arched fracture* (opp. depressed fracture), Sor.*Fract.* 4. **-ωτικός,** ή, όν, *used in vaulting*, πήχεις *POxy.*921 (iii A.D.); ὠλέναι *BGU*1545.5 (iii B.C.). **-ωτός,** ή, όν (-ός, όν Erot. s. v. καμμάρῳ), *vaulted, arched*, Str.16.1.5; στέγη Callix.2; ἅρματα Ath.4.139f.

κᾰμᾰσῆνες, ων, οἱ, *fish*, Emp.72,74; a special kind of fish, *AP*11.20 (Antip. Thess.): sg., Hdn.Gr.2.923.

καμάσιον, τό, *shirt*(?), κ. Δαμάσκινον ἕν *Sammelb.*7033.41 (v A.D.); sine expl., *Gloss.*

καμασός· βάραθρον, Hsch. **II. κάμασος,** = ἀμφίμαλλος, *Gloss.* (Cf. late Lat. *camasus.*) **καμάσσυται·** πτερύσσεται, Hsch.

κᾰμάσσω, *shake* (from κάμαξ 3), Hsch.: καμάσαι is prob. f. l. for καμάξαι, cf. ἐκάμαξεν, διεκάμαξεν, Id.

καμαστίς· μέτρον τι, Amerias ap.Hsch.

κᾰμᾰτ-άω (κάματος), = κοπιάω, Hsch. **-εύω,** aor. ἐκαμάτευσε· μετὰ κακοπαθείας εἰργάσατο, καὶ ἔφυγεν, Id. **-ηδόν,** Adv. *laboriously*, Man.4.622. **-ηρός,** ά, όν, *toilsome, wearisome*, γῆρας *h.Ven.*246; κόπος Ar.*Lys.*542; καματηρὸν ἀϋτμένα φυσιόωντε A.R.2.87; καματηρὸν τὸ ἄρχειν Arist.*Mu.*400ᵇ9. 2. *tiring, exhausting*, σφοδρὰ καὶ κ. πηδήματα Luc.*Salt.*34. II. Pass., *bowed down with toil, broken down, worn out*, Hdt.4.135; κ. σώματα D.H.10.53, cf. Arr.*An.*5.16.1, *Cat.Cod.Astr.*2.166. 2. *hard-working, toiling*, βόες Porph.*Chr.* 29. **-ος,** ὁ, (κάμνω) *toil, trouble*, ἄτερ καμάτοιο Od.7.325; ἄνευ καμάτου Pi.*P.*12.28; κ. ἵππων A.*Fr.*192.6 (anap.); οὐδέποτ' ἐκ καμάτων ἀποπαύσομαι S.*El.* 231, cf. 130 (both lyr.); of the pangs of childbirth, Id.*OT*174 (lyr.); εὐκάματος E.*Ba.*67 (lyr.): pl., καμάτων ἅλις *AP*9.359 (Posidipp. or Pl.Com.): rare in early Prose, κ. ἐστι τοῖς αὐτοῖς μοχθεῖν Heraclit.84, cf. 111; of the *pains* of disease, Hp. *de Arte* 3 (pl.); κ. ὁ πολύς Luc.*Herm.*71; freq. later, Arist.*Mu.*397ᵇ23, *OGI* 717.8 (pl., iii A.D.), *POxy.*913.15 (pl., v A.D.). 2. *the effect of toil, weariness*, ὁππότε κέν μιν γυῖα λάβῃ κ. Il.4.230, cf. 13.85,711, etc.; κ. πολυάϊξ γυῖα δέδυκεν 5.811; αἴθρῳ καὶ κ. δεδμημένον Od.14.318; ὕπνῳ καὶ κ. ἀρημένος 6.2; κ. τε καὶ ἄλγεσι θυμὸν ἔδοντες 9.75, cf. Sapph. *Supp.*19.4, etc.: in Prose, Aen.Tact.26.8, Parth.1.1, Jul.*Or.*2.87b. 3. *illness*, Simon.85.10 (= Semon.29 Diehl): pl., D.H.10.53. II. *the product of toil*, ἡμέτερος κ., viz. the pigs we have reared, Od.14.417; ἀλλότριον κ. σφετέρην ἐς γαστέρ' ἀμῶνται Hes. *Th.*599, cf. Thgn.925; τόρνου κ. *a thing wrought* by the lathe, A.*Fr.*57.3 (anap.), cf. *AP*6.206 (Antip. Sid.); κ. μελίσσης, of honey, Nic.*Al.*71 (pl.), cf. 144. **-ώδης,** ες, *toilsome, wearisome*, θέρεος καματώδεος ὥρη Hes.*Op.*584; πλαγαί, μέριμναι, Pi.*N.*3.17, *Fr.*218.1; καματωδέστερος Thphr.*Lass.*13.

καμβατηθείς· καταπονηθείς, Hsch. **κάμβει·** παύεται, Id.

καμβολίαι· κακολογίαι, λοιδορίαι, Hsch.

κάμε, Ep. aor. 2 of κάμνω; but, 2. **κἀμέ,** crasis for καὶ ἐμέ.

κάμηλα [κᾰ], ἡ, = Lat. *camella*, *Edict.Diocl.*15.51.

κᾰμηλ-άριος, ὁ, *camel-driver*, *PLond.*5.1796.15 (vi A.D.). **-ᾰσία** (for *καμηλελασία), ἡ, *camel-driving*, *Dig.*50.4.1.2. **-άσιον,** τό, *wages of camel-driver*, *PLond.*5.1904.7 (v/vi A.D.). **-άτης** (for *καμηλελάτης), ου, ὁ, *camel-driver*, *PBasel* 2.2 (ii A.D.), *BGU*14 vi 12 (iii A.D.). **-ειος,** α, ον, *of a camel*: καμήλεια (sc. κρέα) *camel's flesh*, Porph.*Abst.*1.14 fin., cf. Gal.8.183; κ. οὖρον *PHolm.* 15.18. **-έμπορος,** ὁ, *one who carries his wares on a camel*, of merchants travelling in caravans, Str.17.1.45. **-ίζω,** *to be like a camel*, Hld.10.27. **-ικός,** ή, όν, *of* or *for a camel*, γόμοι *OGI* 629.16 (Palmyra, ii A.D.); *transportable by camels* (cf. ὀνικός), λίθοι *POxy.*498.8 (ii A.D.). **-ιον,** τό, Dim. of κάμηλος, *PHamb.*1.54.7 (ii/iii A.D.), etc. **-ίτης** [ῑ], ου, ὁ, *camel-driver*, Arist.*HA*630ᵇ35, *POxy.*710.4 (ii B.C.), etc.; *camel-rider*, Hld.10.5, Hdn.4.15.2. 2. also, = καμηλέμπορος, Str.1.2.32, 16.1.27. II. κ. βοῦς, prob. *buffalo*, Suid.

κᾰμηλο-βοσκός, ὁ, *camel-herd*, Str.16.4.2. **-κόμος,** ον, *keeping camels*, Eust.ad D.P.954. **-πάρδᾰλις,** εως (or ιδος), ἡ, *camelopard, giraffe*, Agatharch.72, Lxx *De.*14.5, Callix.2, D.C.43.23, Hld. 10.27. **-πόδιον,** τό, = πράσιον, Ps.-Dsc.3.105.

κάμηλος [ᾰ], ὁ and ἡ (as in Ar.*Av.*1563), *camel*, *Camelus bactrianus* and *C. dromedarius* (cf. Arist.*HA*499ᵃ13), A.*Supp.*285, etc.; τοὺς ἔρσενας τῶν κ. Hdt.3.105; κ. ἀμνός *a camel*-lamb, i.e. young camel, Ar.*Av.*1559 (lyr.); κ. δρομάς Plu.*Alex.*31: prov., κάμηλον καταπίνειν *Ev.Matt.*23.24; cf. κάμιλος. 2. ἡ κ. *camelry*, Hdt.1.80. (Semitic word, cf. Hebr. *gāmāl.*)

κᾰμηλο-τροφέω, *feed, keep camels*, D.S.3.45. **-τρόφος,** ὁ, *camel-keeper*, *BGU*607.12 (ii A.D.), etc.

κᾰμηλ-ώδης, ες, *camel-like*, Gal.6.664. **-ών,** ῶνος, ὁ, *stable for camels*, *POxy.*507.26 (ii A.D.), *BGU*393.15, etc.

κάμῑλος, ὁ, *rope*, Sch.Ar.*V.*1030, Suid. (Perh. coined as an emendation of the phrase εὐκοπώτερόν ἐστι κάμηλον διὰ τρυπήματος ῥαφίδος διελθεῖν ἢ πλούσιον εἰς τὴν βασιλείαν τοῦ θεοῦ εἰσελθεῖν *Ev.Matt.*19.24: but cf. Arab. *jummal* 'ship's cable'.)

κᾰμῑν-αία, ἡ, *furnace*, Lxx *Ex.*9.10. **-αῖος,** α, ον, *of* or *from a furnace*, τέφρα Ezek.*Exag.*136. **-εία,** ἡ, *furnace-work*, Thphr. *HP*5.9.6 (-ίας codd.), Gal.12.220. **-εύς,** έως, ὁ, *furnace-worker, smith* or *potter*, D.S.20.63. **-ευτήρ,** ῆρος, ὁ, = foreg.; αὐλὸς κ. the pipe *of a smith's bellows*, *AP*6.92 (Phil.):—fem. **-εύτρια** Aristarch. ap.Eust.1835.41, Hsch. s. v. καμινοῖ. **-ευτής,** οῦ, ὁ, = καμινεύς, *PPetr.*3 p.173 (dub., iii B.C.), Luc.*Sacr.*6. II. title of priests at Ostia, *IG*14.914. **-ευτικός,** ή, όν, *of* or *for a furnace*, Suid. s. v. κοδομήϊον. **-εύω,** *heat in a furnace*, Arist.*Mir.*833ᵇ25, Thphr. *Lap.*69, etc.; σίδηρος καμινευόμενος Str.5.2.6. **-η,** ἡ, = κάμινος, *PLond.*3.994.11 (vi A.D.). **-ιον,** τό, Dim. of κάμινος, *Gp.*2.3.9, Olymp.Alch.p.76 B. **-ιος,** α, ον, *of* or *for a furnace*, Thphr.*HP* 5.9.6. **-ίτης** [ῑ], ὁ, *baked in an oven*, ἄρτος Philistion ap.Ath.3.115e. **-ίων,** ωνος, ὁ, *furnace-attendant*, *IG*5(2).50.82 (ii A.D.).

κᾰμῑνο-γρᾰφία, ἡ, *treatise on furnaces*, i. e. *alchemy*, title of work by Maria, Olymp.Alch.p.90 B. **-θεν,** Adv. *from a furnace*, Nic. *Th.*707, Call.*Dian.*60. **-καύστης,** ου, ὁ, *one who heats a furnace* or *oven*, *Gloss.* (fem. **-καύστρια** Sch.Od.18.27). II. κ. γύψου *one who burns* gypsum *in a kiln*, *BGU*952.8 (ii/iii A.D.).

κάμῑν-ος [ᾰ], ἡ, *oven, furnace*, or *kiln*, for smelting, baking, burning earthenware and bricks, Hom.*Epigr.*14, Hdt.1.179, 4.164, A.*Fr.* 281, Critias 2.13 D., *PPetr.*3 p.141 (iii B.C.), etc.: pl., of Hephaestus' forge, *Anacreont.*27A2; *flue* for warming a room, Gal.6.332, cf. 10.843; *alcove*, Lxx *Nu.*25.8: prov. of one who ate hot dishes, κάμινος οὐκ ἄνθρωπος Crobyl.8; κάμινον ἔχων ἐν τῷ πνεύμονι, of a drunkard, *Com.Adesp.*633. (Perh. cogn. with καμάρα, q. v.) **-ώ,** οῦς, ἡ: γρηῢς κ. an old *furnace*-woman, i. e. an old woman *who worked at a furnace*, Od.18.27. **-ώδης,** ες, *like an oven* or *furnace*, ἀναπνοαί Str.5.4.6.

καμίσιον, τό, *shirt*, *Stud.Pal.*20.245.10 (vi A.D.), etc.:—also **κάμισον,** τό, *PGen.*80.1 (*Arch.Pap.*3.404, iv A.D.). [ῑ inferred from Romance languages; κάμασος and καμάσιον are perh. different.]

κάμμα, ατος, τό, (κάπτω) *that which is supped up*, in pl., = ψαιστά, Nicocl.2; cf. καμματίδες.

κάμμᾰρος, ὁ, a kind of *lobster*, Epich.60, Sophr.26, Rhinth.18:—also **καμμαρίς,** ίδος, ἡ, Gal.6.735. II. a kind of *aconite*, used as a cooling medicine, Hp.*Loc.Hom.*27, Stratt.21, Dsc.4.76, Nic.*Al.*41; also, = δελφίνιον, Ps.-Dsc.3.73; = μανδραγόρα ἄρρεν, Id.4.75. (Meaning and spelling are dub. in Hp., cf. Erot. s. v.: **κάμαρος** and **κάμμορον** were variants, the latter is v. l. in Dsc. l. c., cf. Sch.Nic. l. c.)

κάμμαρψις· μέτρον σιτικόν, τὸ ἡμιμέδιμνον (Aeol.), Hsch.

καμματίδες, ων, αἱ, (κάπτω) *laurel leaves* used for supping up κάμματα, Nicocl.2.

κάμμει· καθέζει, Hsch.

καμμονίη, ἡ, Ep. for καταμονή, *steadfastness, endurance* (ἡ ἐκ καταμονῆς νίκη Sch., cf. Plu.2.22c), *steady courage*, αἴ κεν ἐμοὶ Ζεὺς δώῃ καμμονίην Il.22.257, cf. 23.661, *APl.*4.221.4 (Theaet.).

κάμμορον, τό, variant for κάμμαρος II (q. v.): expld. as, = κακόμορον, Erot. s. v. καμμάρῳ, cf. Sch.Nic.*Al.*41; but, = κώνειον, Zeno Herophileus ap.Gal.19.108.

κάμμορος, ον, Ep. for κατάμορος, *subject to destiny*, i. e. *ill-fated* (not in Il.), περὶ πάντων κάμμορε φωτῶν Od.11.216, cf. 2.351, 5.160, A.R. 4.1318. (Cf. κάσμορος, ἤμορος.)

κάμμυσις, εως, ἡ, = κατάμυσις, *Corp.Herm.*1.30; cf. sq.

καμμύω, Ep. for καταμύω, v.l. in Batr.191: also in later Gr., τοὺς ὀφθαλμοὺς ἐκάμμυσαν Lxx *Is.*6.10, al., cf. Ph.1.645, Hero *Aut.*22.1, *PMag.Lond.*121.855 (iii A.D.), Paul.Aeg.3.22.29: pf. κεκάμμυκα A.D.*Synt.*323.22: cited from Alex.319 by Phryn., but censured as un-Attic.

κάμνω, fut. κᾰμοῦμαι, καμῇ, A.*Eu.*881, S.*Tr.*1215; καμεῖται Il.2.389, Pl.*Lg.*921e; Ep. inf. -έεσθαι A.R.3.580: aor. 2 ἔκᾰμον, Ep. κάμον Il.4.187, al.; inf. καμεῖν, Ep. subj. redupl. κεκάμω, κεκάμῃσι, κεκάμωσιν, Il.1.168, 17.658, 7.5 (but Aristarch. read κε κάμω, etc., prob. rightly): pf. κέκμηκα Il.6.262, etc.: plpf. ἐκεκμήκεσαν Th.3.98; Ep. part. κεκμηώς, κεκμηῶτι, κεκμηῶτα, Il.23.232, 6.261, Od.10.31; κεκμηῶτας Il.11.802; κεκμηῶτας is v.l. for κεκμηκότας in Th.3.59:—Med., aor. 2 ἐκαμόμην Od.9.130, Ep. καμ- Il.18.341. I. trans., *work*, μίτρη, τὴν χαλκῆες κάμον ἄνδρες *wrought* it, 4.187, 216; ἐπεὶ πάνθ' ὅπλα κάμε 18.614; σκῆπτρον.., τὸ μὲν Ἥφαιστος κάμε τεύχων 2.101, cf. 8.195; κ. νῆας Od.9.126; πέπλον Il.5.338, cf. Od.15.105; ἵππον 11.523; λέχος 23.189; ἄστυ *build*, A.R.1.1322: also in aor. Med., ἱρόν Id.2.718. 2. aor. Med., *win by toil*, τὰς (sc. γυναῖκας) αὐτοὶ καμόμεσθα βίηφί τε δουρί τε μακρῷ Il.18.341. 3. aor. Med., *labour, till*, οἵ κέ σφιν καὶ νῆσον.. ἐκάμοντο Od.9.130; οἴκους Philet.8. II. intr., *toil, labour*, τινι *for* one, Od.14.65; ὑπὲρ τῆς πόλεως Th.2.41: then, from the effect of continued work, *to be weary*, ἀνδρὶ δὲ κεκμηῶτι μένος μέγα οἶνος ἀέξει Il.6.261, cf. 11.802: with acc. of the part, οὐδέ τι γυῖα.. κάμνει nor *is* he *weary* in limb, 19.170, etc.; περὶ δ' ἔγχεϊ χεῖρα καμεῖται 2.389; ὁ δ' ἀριστερὸν ὦμον ἔκαμνεν 16.106: freq. c. part., κ. πολεμίζων, ἐλαύνοντες, ἐρεθίζων, *is weary* of fighting, rowing, etc., 1.168, 7.5, 17.658, etc.; οὐ μέν θην κάμετον.. ὀλλῦσαι Τρῶας 8.448; ἔκαμον δέ μοι ὄσσε πάντῃ παπταίνοντι Od.12.232; but οὐδέ τι τόξον δὴν ἔκαμον τανύων I *did* not long *strain over* stringing the bow, i. e. did it without *effort*, 21.426, cf. Il.8.22: later freq. with neg., οὔτοι καμοῦμαι.. λέγουσα I *shall* never *be tired* of saying, A.*Eu.*881; μὴ κάμῃς λέγων E.*IA*1143; οὐκ ἂν κάμοιμι τὰς κακὰς κτείνων Id.*Or.*1590; οὔποτε κάμοιμ' ἂν ὀρχουμένη Ar.*Lys.*541 (lyr.); κ. εὐεργετῶν, ἐπαινῶν, Pl.*Grg.*470c, *Lg.*921e: c. dat., κ. δαπάναις *to grow tired* in spending, spare expense, Pi.*P.*1.90. 2. *to be hard-pressed, worsted*, in battle or contest, ib.1.78, 80; τὸ κάμνον στρατοῦ E.*Supp.* 709. 3. *to be sick* or *suffering*, τί πάσχεις; τί κάμνεις; Ar.*Nu.*708; οἱ κάμνοντες *the sick*, Hdt.1.197, cf. S.*Ph.*282, And.1.64, Pl.*R.*407c, *Ep.Jac.*5.15, etc.; of a doctor's *patients*, Hp.*Acut.*1, D.18.243, *SIG*943.10 (Cos); καμοῦσα ἀπέθανε *having fallen sick*, And.1.120: c. acc. cogn., κάμνειν νόσον E.*Heracl.*990, Pl.*R.*408e; [τὴν ποδάγραν] v.l. in Arist.*HA*604ᵃ23; τοὺς ὀφθαλμούς Hdt.2.111; τὰ σώματα *to be ill* or *distempered* in body, Pl.*Grg.*478a; ὠσίν τε κῶμμασιν Herod.3.32; πάθᾳ Pi.*P.*8.48; νοσήμασι Arist.*HA*603ᵃ30; ἀπὸ τοῦ τραύματος Luc.*Tox.*60; ὑπὸ νόσου Hdn.3.14.2. 4. generally, *to be distressed, meet with disaster*, στρατοῦ καμόντος A.*Ag.*670; τῷ πεποιημένῳ κ. μεγάλως Hdt.1.118, cf. A.*Ag.*482 (lyr.), E.*Med.*1138, *HF*293; οὐ καμῇ τοὐμὸν μέρος *wilt* not *have to complain*.., S.*Tr.* 1215; κ. ἔν τινι E.*Hec.*306, *IA*966; of a ship, νεὼς καμούσης ποντίῳ πρὸς κύματι A.*Th.*210: c. acc. cogn., οὐκ ἴσον καμὼν ἐμοὶ λύπης not *having borne* an equal share of grief, S.*El.*532. 5. in aor. part., of the dead, i.e. either *outworn*, or *those whose work is done*, or *those who have met with disaster*, οἳ ὑπένερθε καμόντας ἀνθρώπους τίνυσθον Il.3.278, cf. Theoc.17.49; βροτῶν εἴδωλα καμόντων Od.11.476; εἴδωλα κ. 24.14, Il.23.72, cf. A.*Supp.*231, etc.: also in pf. part. in Trag. and Prose, κεκμηκότες S.*Fr.*284, E.*Supp.*756, Th.3.59, Pl.*Lg.*718a, 927b, Arist.*EN*1101ᵃ35; ἱερὰ τῶν κ. E.*Tr.*96; also in the finite Verb, ὅπη ἄνθρωπος ἔκαμε *Berl.Sitzb.*1927.158 (Cyrene).—The pf. is always intr. (Cf. Skt. *śamnīte* 'work hard', 'serve zealously', *śamitár*– 'sacrificing priest', Gr. εἰρο-κόμος, κομέω, κομίζω.)

κάμορος· κλῆθρα τὸ δένδρον, Hsch.

καμπαγών, ῶνος, ὁ, a kind of *boot*, *IG*2².1120 (*Edict.Diocl.*).

καμπᾰλέος, α, ον, (καμπή) = καμπτός, Hsch.

καμπανίζω, *weigh*, *PLond.*5.1708.130 (vi A.D.).

κάμπανος, ὁ, *weighing-machine, steelyard*, *PMasp.*325 iv*A* 37 (vi A.D.), *Gloss.* (Lat. *campana*).

καμπεσί-γουνος [ῐ], ον, *bending the knees*, Ἐρινύς Hsch. **-γυιος**, ον, *bending the limbs*, παίγνια κ. *puppets*, Orph.*Fr.*34.

καμπή, ἡ, (κάμπτω) *winding*, of a river, Hdt.1.185; Εὐβοΐδα κ., of the Euripus, A.*Fr.*30; τὰς κ. τῶν χωρίων Aen.Tact.15.6; τόπους καμπὰς ἔχοντας Ael.*Tact.*35.4. 2. *flexion, bending*, τὰ ἄποδα δυσὶ χρώμενα προέρχεται καμπαῖς Arist.*IA*707ᵇ9, cf. *HA*490ᵃ31. 3. *curved part*, Hero *Spir.*2.16, Sor.2.62. II. *turning-post in a race-course*, περὶ ταῖσι καμπαῖς ἡνίοχοι πεπτωκότες Ar.*Pax*905; καμπαῖσι δρόμων E.*IA*224 (lyr.); εὐλαβηθῆναι περὶ τὴν κ. Pl.*Ion*537a: metaph., μῦθον ἐς καμπὴν ἄγε bring a speech to *its goal* (cf. καμπτήρ II), E.*El.* 659; καμπὴν ποιεῖσθαι Pl.*Phd.*72b. III. in Music, *turn, sudden change*, εἴ τις κάμψειέν τινα καμπήν Ar.*Nu.*969; ἐξαρμονίους κ. Pherecr. 145.9, cf. ib.28; καμπαὶ ᾀσμάτων Philostr.*VS*2.28. 2. Rhet., *rounding off* of a period, Cic.*Att.*1.14.4 (pl.), Demetr.*Eloc.*10, 17. IV. *bend* or *flexure* of a limb, τῶν ὤμων, τῶν ἰσχίων, τῶν δακτύλων, etc., Arist.*HA*498ᵃ25 sqq., cf. Pl.*Ti.*74e; of the skull, οὐκ ἔχουσα καμπάς ib.75c; οὐλὴ καμπῇ (= –ῇ) χιρὸς δεξιᾶς *Sammelb.*7031.5 (i A.D.).

κάμπη, ἡ, *caterpillar*, Hp.*Superf.*28, Aristopho 10.4, Lxx *Am.*4.9, etc.; of the *silk-worm*, Arist.*HA*551ᵇ11, Thphr.*HP*4.14.9. 2. *ornament* of this shape, dub. in *IG*12(5).134.13 (Paros). II. *a fabulous Indian monster*, D.S.3.72, Nonn.*D.*18.237; cf. κάμπος.

κάμπῖμος, η, ον, (καμπή) *bent, turning*, δρόμος E.*IT*81:—also **κάμπιος**, Ptol.*Tetr.*150: **κάμπειος**, Hsch.

κάμπος, εος, τό, *a sea-monster*, Lyc.414. II. = ἱπποδρόμος (Sicel), Hsch. **καμπουλίρ**· ἐλαίας εἶδος (Lacon.), Id. (–ούληρ cod.).

καμπ-τήρ, ῆρος, ὁ, *bend, angle*, X.*Cyr.*7.1.6, Str.14.2.14. II. *turning-point in the* δίαυλος, which was *the goal* in the single race (cf. καμπή II), Arist.*Rh.*1409ᵃ32, *BCH*23.567 (Delph., iii B.C.), Babr.29. 4: pl., as works of art, Plin.*HN*36.25: metaph., κ. βίου *the 'last lap'* of life, Herod.10.3; κ. πύματος, of the colophon which marks the last page, *AP*12.257.1 (Mel.). **-τηρία**, ἡ, = foreg. II, Tz.*H.*8.27:—also **-τήριος** (sc. νύσσα), Sch.Opp.*H.*1.205. **-τικός**, ή, όν, *bending, flexible*, δακτύλου τὸ κ. the *joint*, Arist.*HA*493ᵇ28; κίνησις ἡ κ. Id.*Spir.*484ᵇ13; φωνάριον Poll.4.64. **-τός**, ή, όν, *flexible*, Pl. *Ti.*44e, Arist.*Mete.*385ᵃ13, al. II. masc. as Subst., = καμπτήρ II, Aq.*Pr.*2.9, Sch.Ar.*Nu.*28, v.l. in *EM*609.29 and Choerob.*in Theod.* 2.151. 2. *flank*, *Hippiatr.*32. **-τρα**, ἡ, *case, chest* (cf. κάμψα), *IG*5(1).1390.11 (Andania, i B.C.), *BGU*781.12 (i A.D.), *Gloss.*:—Dim. **-τρίον**, τό, *Gp.*10.21.10, *Gloss.*; cf. καπτρίον. **-τρον**, τό, *turning-point* in the race-course, ib. s.v. *intermetium*. II. = κάμπτρα, ib.; cf. κάπτρον.

καμπτρο-ποιός, ὁ, *basket-maker*, *Gloss.* **-φόρος**, ὁ, = *capsarius*, ib.

κάμπτω, fut. κάμψω Il.7.118, S.*OC*91: aor. 1 ἔκαμψα Od.5.453, Pi.*P.*2.51, etc.:—**Pass.**, fut. καμφθήσομαι D.Chr.77.33, Gal.*UP*2.15: aor. ἐκάμφθην A.*Pr.*513, Th.3.58: pf. inf. κεκάμφθαι Hp.*Art.*67, part. κεκαμμένος Arist.*Metaph.*1016ᵃ12, (ἐπι–, συγ–) Hp.*Prog.*3, X. *Eq.*7.2. (Cogn. with Lith. *kam̃p-as* 'corner', *kum̃p-as* 'curved', and prob. Lat. *campus*):—*bend, curve*, ὄφρα ἴτυν κάμψῃ that he *may bend* it into a chariot-rail, Il.4.486 (so metaph., κ. νέας ἁψῖδας ἐπῶν Ar.*Th.*53): freq. in phrase, γόνυ κ. *bend* the knee so as to sit down and rest, φημί μιν ἀσπασίως γόνυ κάμψειν Il.7.118, cf. 19.72; ὁ δ' ἄρ' ἄμφω γούνατ' ἔκαμψε χεῖράς τε στιβαράς Od.5.453; οὐ κάμπτων γόνυ, i.e. never resting, A.*Pr.*32; ἄσμενος τἂν.. κάμψειεν γόνυ ib. 398; ἵζω.. κάμψας γόνυ E.*Hec.*1150; so κ. κῶλα S.*OC*19; then κάμπτειν alone, *sit down, rest*, ib.85, E.*Hec.*1080 (lyr.); also γόνυ κ. *bend* the knee in worship, Lxx *Is.*45.23, etc.:—Pass., *bend oneself*, opp. ἐκτείνεσθαι, Pl.*Ti.*74b; ὥσπερ ξύλον καμπτόμενον εὐθύνουσιν Id.*Prt.* 325d; ἡ κεκαμμένη (sc. γραμμή) a *bent* line, Arist.*Metaph.* l.c. II. *turn* or *guide* a horse or chariot *round* the turning-post (cf. καμπτήρ II), κάμψαι διαύλου θάτερον κῶλον πάλιν *to double* the post and return along the second half of the δίαυλος, A.*Ag.*344; κ. δρόμον B. 9.26; κάμπτοντος ἵππου as the horse *was turning*, S.*El.*744; κ. περὶ νύσσαν Theoc.24.120: metaph., κ. βίον *to make the last turn in the course* of life, S.*OC*91; κ. βίου τέλος E.*Hipp.*87, *El.*956; ὅταν κάμψῃς καὶ τελευτήσῃς βίον Id.*Hel.*1666; ἑξηκοστὸν ἥλιον κ. Herod.10.1; διὰ λόγου κάμψαι κακά *to end* evils by reasoning, E.*Supp.*748. 2. of seamen, *double* a headland, Ἡρακλέας στήλας Hdt.4.42; τὸ ἀκρωτήριον, τὴν ἄκρην, Id.4.43, 7.122; ὡς δὲ τὴν ἄκραν κάμπτοντας ἡμᾶς εἶδον Men. 15, cf. Aeschrio 8.3; Μαλέαν κ. Poet.ap.Str.8.6.20, D.S.13.64, etc.; κ. περὶ ἄκραν Ar.*Ach.*96; κ. κόλπον *wind round* the bay, Hdt.7.58. 3. abs., πάλιν κ. *turn* back, E.*Ba.*1225, *Rh.*234 (lyr.); ἐγγὺς τῶν ἐμῶν κάμπτεις φρενῶν (κάμπτῃ codd.) thou *comest* near my meaning, Id.*IT* 815. III. in Music, κάμπτων με καὶ στρέφων ὅλην διέφθορεν (sc. Phrynis) with his *turns* and twists, Pherecr.145.15; κ. καμπήν Ar.*Nu.* 969; κ. ᾠδάς Philostr.*VA*4.39. IV. metaph., κάμπτειν τινά *bow down, humble*, Pi.*P.*2.51; ὁ χρόνος μ' ἔκαμψε Crates Theb.17:—Pass., *to be bent* or *bowed down*, πημοναῖσι A.*Pr.*239, 308, cf. 513; κάμπτομαι I *submit*, Pl.*Prt.*320b, etc.; κάμπτεσθαι καὶ ἕλκεσθαι πρὸς φιλοσοφίαν Id.*R.*494e; πολλὰ κάμπτονται καὶ συγκλῶνται are *warped*, Id.*Tht.* 173b: abs., *to be moved to pity*, Th.3.58 (in full κ. εἰς ἔλεον Lib.*Or.* 59.85).

καμπ-ύλη [ῠ] (sc. βακτηρία), ἡ, *crooked staff*, Ar.*Fr.*128, Plu.2. 790b, Alciphr.3.3. **-ῠλιάζω**, = sq., Phot., Suid. **-ύλλω**, Ion. for κάμπτω, *bend, crook*, Hp.*Art.*60 (Pass.):—Med., ib.46: **-υλεύομαι**, Pass., Erot., Aret.*SA*1.6.

καμπῠλο-ειδής, ές, *appearing crooked*, φαντασία Plu.2.1121c. **-εις**, εσσα, εν, poet. for καμπύλος, ἴτυς *AP*6.28 (Jul. Aegypt.). **-ομαι**, Pass., *become curved*, Antyll.ap.Aët.7.74. **-πρυμνος**, ον, *with rounded stern*, Sch.D Il.2.392, Hsch. s.v. κορωνίς. **-ρρῖν**, ῖνος, ὁ, ἡ, *hook-nosed*, *EM*395.36, Hsch. s.v. γρυπός.

καμπύλος [ῠ], η, ον, (κάμπτω) *bent, curved*, opp. εὐθύς, of a bow, κ. τόξα Il.3.17, etc.; ἅρμα 5.231; κ. κύκλα, of wheels, ib.722; ἄροτρα *h.Cer.*308, Sol.13.48; δίφρος Pi.*I.*4(3).29; ὄχημα A.*Supp.*183; σελίς *IG*1².374.57; κῦμα *BMus.Inscr.*1012 (Chalcedon); κ. ἐς τὸ ἔξω Hp. *Art.*1; καμπύλα τε καὶ εὐθέα Pl.*R.*602c: metaph., κ. μέλος an ode *of varied metre*, Simon.29; cf. καμπύλη.

καμπῠλοσαλπιστής, οῦ, ὁ, *horn-blower*, = Lat. *cornicen*, *Gloss.*

καμπῠλότης, ητος, ἡ, *crookedness, curvature*, Hp.*Coac.*214, Arist. *Cat.*10ᵃ13, *PA*643ᵃ33, Gal.4.796.

καμπύλοχος [ῠ], ον, *with curved carriage*, κερκίδες, i.e. ploughs, Orph.*Fr.*33.

κάμψα, ης, ἡ, *basket, case*, Hsch.:—also **κάψα** (cf. Lat. *capsa*), Phot., Suid.:—Dim. **καμψίον**, τό, *PMasp.*6 ii 90 (vi A.D.), Hsch.:—also **καμψάκης** or **καψάκης**, ου, ὁ, *cruse, flask*, ἐλαίου Lxx *Ju.*10.5, cf. 3*Ki.*17.12,16; μέλιτος καψάκαι *PSI*4.428.64 (iii B.C.), cf. *PCair. Zen.*12.107, al. (iii B.C.); **καμψάκιον**, τό, *BGU*387 ii 19 (ii A.D.), Cumont *Fouilles de Doura-Europos* 372; **καψάκιον**, Hsch.

καμψάνεμα, gender and declension unknown, = λιβανωτίς, Dsc. 3.74.

καμψάριος, ὁ, = Lat. *capsarius*, *Edict.Diocl.*7.75.

κάμψη, ἡ, = *ebulus*, *Gloss.*

καμψῐδίαυλος [δῐ], ον, *turning the post* (καμπτήρ II) *so as to run the whole* δίαυλος: metaph., of a harp-player, *running quickly up and down* the strings, χεὶρ κ. Telest.4.

καμψικίζω, = βαρβαρίζω, Hsch. **καμψίον**, τό, v. κάμψα.

καμψί-ουρος [ῐ], ον, *bending the tail*, v. σκίουρος. **-πους**, ὁ, ἡ, πουν, τό, gen. ποδος, *bending the foot*, in running, i.e. *swift-running*, Ἐρινύς A.*Th.*791 (lyr.).

κάμψις, εως, ἡ, (κάμπτω) *bending*, Pl.*Ti.*74a, Gal.*UP*12.4; κάμψιν ἔχειν εἰς τὸ πλάγιον to have a *bend*, of joints, Arist.*HA*498ᵃ18; κ. δέχεσθαι Thphr.*HP*4.11.11.

καμψός, ή, όν, (κάμπτω) *crooked, bent*, Hsch.

κάμων [ᾰ], ωνος, = σκαμμωνία, Nic.*Al.*484.

κάν, poet. for κατά before ν, κὰν νόμον Pi.*O.*8.78, prob. in Alc. *Supp.*19. **κἀν**, crasis for καὶ ἐν.

κἄν (not κἂν), by crasis, I. for καὶ ἄν.., v.l. in Hes.*Op.*357, freq. in Att.: not often when καί is simply copul., Pl.*Phd.*79a, *Grg.* 514d; but freq. when καί is intens., ὅ γε κ. μέγα δοίη *even* a great thing, Hes. l.c.; κακὸν δὲ κ. ἐν ἡμέρᾳ γνοίης μιᾷ S.*OT*615, cf. 591, *Aj.*45, Ar.*Nu.*1130, Th.7.61, etc.; sts. repeated after or before a Verb with ἄν, ἐπεὶ κ. σύ.., εἴ τίς σε διδάξειεν.., βελτίων ἂν γένοιο Pl. *Prt.*318b, cf. *R.*515e; freq. in the phrase κ. εἰ, where καί properly belongs to εἰ, *even if*, and ἄν to the Verb that follows in apodosi, νῦν δέ μοι δοκεῖ, κ. ἀσέβειαν εἴ καταγιγνώσκοι, τὰ προσήκοντα ποιεῖν (for καὶ εἰ καταγιγνώσκοι, ποιεῖν ἄν) D.21.51: hence, 2. even when the Verb in apodosi was of a tense that could not be joined with ἄν, κ. εἰ πολλαὶ [αἱ ἀρεταί].. εἰσιν, ἕν γέ τι εἶδος ταὐτὸν ἅπασαι ἔχουσι Pl.*Men.* 72c; κ. εἰ μή τῳ δοκεῖ Id.*R.*473a, 579d, cf. 408b, *Phd.*71b, *Sph.*247e, Arist.*Top.*136ᵃ31, al. 3. in later Gr. without εἰ, simply as a stronger form of καί, *even*, εἴσελθε κ. νῦν Men.342; κ. νεκρῷ χάρισαι τὰ σὰ χείλεα Theoc.23.41, cf. 35 (v.l.) (and so with εἷς, μία, ἕν, κ. μίαν ἡμέραν δόντες αὐτοῖς v.l. in X.*HG*1.7.19; εἰ κ. ἕν τι φαίνοιτο S.E. *P.*2.195, cf. Ph.2.29); ἐὰν ἅψωμαι κ. τῶν ἱματίων *Ev.Marc.*5.28; κ. νῦν now *at any rate*, *POxy.*2151.7 (iii A.D.); κἂν ὡς *even* so, *nevertheless*, ib.123.7 (iii/iv A.D.); οἷς οὐδὲ κ. ὄνος ὑπῆρξε πώποτε Luc.*Tim.*20 codd., cf. *DDeor.*5.2, etc. II. for καὶ ἄν (= ἐάν), *even if*, with the same moods as ἐάν, S.*Aj.*15, Pl.*Prt.*319c, etc.: freq. used ellipt., ἄνδρα χρὴ δοκεῖν πεσεῖν ἂν κ. (sc. πέσῃ) ἀπὸ σμικροῦ κακοῦ S.*Aj.*1078, cf. Ar.*V.*92, *Ach.*1021, and so prob. in S.*El.*1483: later folld. by ind., κἂν γὰρ οὕτω φαμέν A.D.*Synt.*70.22. 2. κἄν.., κἄν.., *whether*.., *or*.., κἂν μεγάλην πόλιν οἰκῶσι κἂν μικράν D.25.15.

κανάβευμα, v. κιν–.

κανάβῐνος, η, ον, *of* or *for a block-figure*, κηρός Hsch.; σῶμα κ. a body *so lean as to be a mere skeleton*, *AP*11.107 (Lucill.): κανάβιον codd. in ll. cc.; κᾰ- in *AP*l.c. (nisi leg. καννν-).

κανᾰβιουργός, ὁ, *maker of* κάναβοι, *Tab.Defix.*87^{a}7 (iv B.C.).

κάνᾰβος or **κάννᾰβος**, ὁ, *wooden framework* round which artists moulded wax or clay, *block-figure*, Hsch., Poll.7.164, 10.189. 2. *mannikin* or *rough drawing of the human frame*, Arist.*HA*515^{a}35, *GA*743^{a}2 (wrongly expld. as *cistern* by Phlp. *in GA*109.27). 3. metaph., *lean person*, '*skeleton*', Stratt.20, Hsch. (Spelling and quantity undetermined: cf. κίναβος.)

κάναδοι· σιαγόνες, γνάθοι, Hsch. **καναδόκα**· χεῖλη ὀϊστοῦ (Lacon.), Id.; cf. κανδόχα.

κάναθρον or better **κάνναθρον**, τό, (κάννα) *cane* or *wicker carriage*, X.*Ages.*8.7, cf. Hsch., Eust.1344.44.

κάνακις· ξίφος, Hsch.

κάνασθον, τό, = κάναστρον, *Schwyzer*748.3 (Naucratis).

κᾰνάσσω, only in aor. inf. and part. κανάξαι, -άξας, *pour with a gurgling sound*, Hsch.; τὸ ἐκκενῶσαι ἢ ἐκπιεῖν κανάξαι λέγουσι Poll. 10.85: elsewh. only in compds. δια-, ἐγ-, ἐκ-κανάσσω; cf. καναχέω.

καναστραῖα· κοῖλά τινα ἀγγεῖα, Suid.

κάναστρον [κᾰ], τό, = κάνεον, *wicker basket*, *GDI*5087.9 (Crete), dub. in *Supp.Epigr.*1.414 (Crete), cf. Hsch.: **καναῦστρον**, *IG*1^{2}.330. 11 (cited as **κάναστρον** and **κάνυστρον** by Poll.10.86), cf. *Carm.Pop.* 41.9; **κάνιστρον** (?), *PLond.*5.1657.9 (iv/v A.D.). II. *earthen vessel, dish*, = τρύβλιον, Hom.*Epigr.*14.3, Nicopho 24.

καναφόρος· μεσόδμη, Hsch.

κᾰνᾰχ-έω, a Verb expressing various sounds, κανάχησε δὲ χαλκός *rang, clashed*, Od.19.469; καναχοῦσι πηγαί *plash*, Cratin.186; καναχῶν ὀλόφωνος ἀλέκτωρ *crowing*, Id.259: c. acc. cogn., κ. μέλος *to let a song ring loud*, A.R.4.907. **-ή**, Dor. **-χά**, ἡ, (κανάσσω) *sharp sound*; esp. *ring* or *clang* of metal, δεινὴν..πήληξ βαλλομένη καναχὴν ἔχε Il.16.105, cf. 794; κ. δ' ἦν ἡμιόνοιιν *loud* rang their *tramp*, Od.6.82; ὀδόντων μὲν κ. πέλε *gnashing* of teeth, Il.19.365, Hes.*Sc.*164: pl., ib. 160; κ. [χαλκ]όκτυπος B.13.15; χρυσοῦ κ. S.*Ant.*130 (lyr.); κ. αὐλῶν *sound* of flutes, Pi.*P.*10.39 (pl.), B.2.12, cf. S.*Tr.*642 (lyr.); of the lyre, *h.Ap.*185. **-ηδά**, Adv. *with a loud noise*, ποταμοὶ καναχηδὰ ῥέοντες Hes.*Th.*367, cf. A.R.3.71, Call.*Del.*45; of flutes, v. μίτρα. **-ηδής**, ές, *resounding*, ἀνθερεών Jo.Gaz.2.162 (s. v. l.). **-ηδόν**, Adv., = καναχηδά, D.P.145, Aret.*SD*1.3. **-ήπους**, ποδος, ὁ, ἡ, *with sounding feet*, of the horse, Certamen 100, Opp.*C.*2.431; Dor. acc. sg. masc. **-άποδα** [ᾰ] Alcm.23.48. **-ής**, ές, of water, *plashing*, κ. δάκρυ A.*Ch.*152 (lyr.). **-ίζω**, = καναχέω, κανάχιζε δὲ δούρατα Il. 12.36; δῶμα σμερδαλέον κανάχιζε v.l. in Od.10.399; κανάχιζε πόσ' εὐρεῖα χθών Hes.*Sc.*373. **-ός**, ή, όν, *noisy*, κ. βάτραχοι Nic.*Th.*620.

κανδαλιστής, οῦ, ὁ, *acrobat*, *Delph.*3(1).226 (sed leg. σκανδ-).

κάνδαλοι· κοιλώματα, βάθρα, κωλοβάθραι, Hsch. **κάνδαρος**, ὁ, = ἄνθραξ, Id. (Cf. *candeo.*)

Κανδαύλης, ὁ, Lydian name for Hermes, expld. as *dog-throttler*, Hippon.1; name of a Lydian king, Hdt.1.7, al.

κάνδαυλος, ὁ, a *Lydian dish*, of which there were several varieties, Nicostr.Com.17, Alex.172.1, Philem.60, Men.462.11:—also **κάνδῠλος**, Id.518.6, Euang.1.8, [Cerc.]18 ii 15, Plu.2.664a, *PGiss.* 93.12 (ii A.D.), Sch.Ar.*Pax* 122 (v.l.), Hsch.; **κάνδυτος** f.l. (cod. Phot.) in Ar.*Fr.*791.

κανδήλη, ἡ, Lat. *candela*, *candle, torch*, Ath.15.701b:—hence **κανδηλο-σβέστης**, ου, ὁ, fem. **-σβέστρια**, ἡ, *moth*, Sch.Nic.*Th.*763, Sch.Opp.*H.*1.404.

κανδοφόρους· μελανειμοῦντας, Hsch. **κανδόχα**· κήλη (Lacon.), Id.; cf. καναδόκα. **κανδύλη**, v. κανδύταλις. **κάνδυλος**, v. κάνδαυλος.

κάνδυς, υος, ὁ, *Median double* or *upper garment with sleeves*, X.*Cyr.* 1.3.2, *An.*1.5.8, Luc.*DMort.*14.4, Them.*Or.*2.36c; κ. ποικίλος *IG*2^{2}. 1514.19.

κανδύτᾰλις [ῠ], ὁ, *clothes-press*, Maced. word in Diph.40, Men.82: **κανδύλη** or **κανδυτάνη**, Hsch.: pl. **κανδύτανες** prob. in Ael.*NA*17. 17, cf. Poll.7.79, Phot. (who also explains it as a kind of *fish*, or = αἰδοῖον).

κάνδυτος, v. κάνδαυλος.

κάνειον, τό, Ep. for sq. II. *lid of a vessel*, Hp.*Mul.*1.11, 2.133.

κάνεον [ᾰ], τό, Ep. also **κάνειον**, Att. contr. **κανοῦν** *IG*1^{2}.313.136, 2^{2}.1414.20, al.; dual κανώ ib.1^{2}.280.10; pl. κανᾶ ib.2^{2}.1414.38:—*basket of reed* or *cane*, esp. *bread-basket*, καλοῖς ἐν κανέοισιν Il.9.217; περικαλλέος ἐκ κανέοιο Od.17.343, cf. Hdt.1.119, etc.; χάλκειον κάνεον Il.11.630; χρύσεια κάνεια Od.10.355; esp. used for the sacred barley at sacrifices, ἔχεν οὐλὰς ἐν κανέῳ 3.442; κανοῦν ἐνῆρκται E.*El.* 1142, cf. *HF*926, Aeschin.3.120, Men.*Sam.*7; τὸ κανοῦν ὀλὰς ἔχον Ar.*Pax*948, cf. *Ach.*244, al., Pherecr.137, etc.; carried in procession, Men.*Epit.*222; as a votive offering (perh. a vessel of basket-shape), *IG*11(2).161*B*34, al. (Delos, iii B.C.), 7.2424 (Thebes), *CIG* 2855.21 (Branchidae).

κανῆν, Dor. aor. 2 inf. of καίνω (q.v.).

κάνης [ᾰ], ητος, ὁ, *a mat of reeds* such as the Athen. women took with them when they went out, Lex Solonis ap. Plu.*Sol.*21: generally, *mat*, D.H.2.23 (pl.): prov., ὁ κ. τῆς κοίτης ὑπερέχει, of those who make a show abroad with poverty at home, Crates Com.12, cf. Phot. s. v. II. = λίκνον, Poll.6.86.

κᾰνήτιον, τό, = κανίσκιον, Poll.6.86.

κᾰνητοποιός, ὁ, *maker of reed-mats*, prob. in Hippon.116, cf. Poll. 10.184 (καννηνο- cod.).

κᾰνηφορ-έω, *carry a basket*, Ph.2.55, al.; esp. *carry the sacred basket in procession*, Ar.*Lys.*646, al., *IG*2.1204, al., 3.921; κ. Παναθηναίοις Arist.*Ath.*18.2; also κ. Δήλια καὶ Ἀπολλώνια Durrbach *Choix d'Inscriptions de Délos* 115 (ii B.C.); τῷ Διὶ τῷ βασιλεῖ Plu.2.772a; Ἴσιδι *CIG*2298 (Delos), cf. 3602 (Ilium). **-ία**, ἡ, *office of κανηφόρος*, Pl.*Hipparch.*229c. **-ικός**, ή, όν, *of the* Κανηφόροι, κόσμος *IG* 2^{2}.333c10. **-ος** (parox.), ον, *carrying a basket*: Κανηφόροι, αἱ, at Athens, title of maidens who carried baskets in procession at festivals, Ar.*Ach.*242 (sg.), al. (cf. Sch. ad loc.), Hermipp.26, *IG*2^{2}.896.9 (sg.); represented in works of art, Cic.*Verr.*4.3.5, Plin.*HN*36.25; elsewh., as title of priestess, κ. θεᾶς Ἀρτέμιδος *CIG*4362 (Pisid.); κ. Ἀρσινόης Φιλαδέλφου *PCair.Zen.*3 (iii B.C.), *PTeb.*176 (iii/ii B.C.), cf. *PStrassb.*83.10 (ii B.C.), etc.

κανθάρ-εως or **-εος** [θᾰ], ὁ, name of a kind of *vine*, Thphr.*CP*2.15.5: **-ιος** Hsch. **-ιον**, τό, Dim. of κάνθαρος II, *IG*2^{2}.1517.10, 101, Plu.2.461e. **-ίς**, ίδος, ἡ, a kind of *beetle*, prob. *blister-beetle*, *Cantharis vesicatoria*, Arist.*HA*531^{b}25, 542^{a}9; used in medicine, Hp.*Nat.Mul.*32, Plu.2.22a: pl., *POxy.*1088.14 (i A.D.); *beetle hurtful to corn*, Pl.Com.37, Thphr.*HP*8.10.1, Nic.*Al.*115; also to fruits, etc., Arist.*HA*552^{b}1; so prob. in Gal.12.363. II. a kind of *fish*, Numen.ap.Ath.7.326f. **-ίτης** [ῑ] οἶνος, ὁ, *wine from the vine* κανθάρεως, Plin.*HN*14.75.

κανθᾰροποιός, ὁ, *maker of* κάνθαροι II, *IG*12(9).292 (Eretria).

κάνθᾰρος, ὁ, *dung-beetle*, *Scarabaeus pilularius*, Arist.*HA*490^{a} 15, al., Ael.*NA*10.15, Ar.*Lys.*695, Crates Theb.10.6, Theoc.5.114, Aesop.7, etc.; Αἰτναῖος κ., a specially large kind, A.*Fr.*233, S.*Ichn.* 300, cf. Epich.76: prov., κανθάρου σκιαί, of some paltry fear, Hsch., Diogenian.5.88; so ἀθυμῶν ὅτι αὐτοῦ καταθέουσι δύο κανθάρω Lib.*Ep.* 91.4. II. a sort of *drinking-cup* with large handles, Phryn.Com. 15, Amips.2, Axionic.7. III. a kind of *Naxian boat*, Ar.*Pax* 143, Sosicr.2, Nicostr.Com.10. IV. *black sea-bream*, *Cantharus lineatus*, Arist.*HA*598^{a}10. V. in Egypt, *mark* or *knot* on the tongue of the Apis-bull, Hdt.3.28. VI. *woman's ornament*, prob. a gem in scarab-form, Antiph.61.

κανθᾰρ-ώδης, ες, *like a beetle*, ζῷον Sch.Ar.*Ach.*920. **-ώλεθρος**, ὁ, *death-to-beetles*, name of a district in Thrace, Arist.*Mir.*842^{a}6, Str. 7*Fr.*30, Plu.2.473f.

κανθήλη, ἡ, = καλαμανθήλη, *rush used for candle-wicks*, *Edict. Diocl.*18.6.

κανθήλ-ια, ων, τά, *panniers* at the sides of a pack-saddle, Ar.*V.* 170: hence, *any large baskets*, for carrying grapes at the vintage, Artem.4.5, *Gp.*6.11.1, Hsch.: generally, *pack-saddle*, κ. καμηλικά prob. in *PGoodsp.Cair.*30 xxxiv 18 (ii A.D.). II. *wooden frame that rises in a curve at a ship's stern*, Hsch. III. sg., **κανθήλιον**, τό, in Archit., *rafter*, *IG*2^{2}.463.73. (Lat. *cantherius*, Vitr.4.2.3.) **-ικός**, ή, όν, *belonging to a pack-saddle*, σαγή prob. in *PGoodsp.Cair.*30 xxxviii 16 (ii A.D.).

κανθήλιος, ὁ, *pack-ass*, Ar.*Lys.*290 (lyr.), Luc.*Pseudol.*3, *POxy.* 1733.4 (iii A.D.); ὄνος κ. Hermipp.9, X.*Cyr.*7.5.11, Pl.*Smp.*221e, etc.: metaph., *ass, blockhead*, Lysipp.7, Luc.*JTr.*31.

κανθίαι· σπυρίδες, Hsch. **κανθίς**, ίδος, ἡ, *ass's dung*, Id.

κανθός, ὁ, *corner of the eye*, Arist.*HA*491^{b}23, *PA*657^{b}18, Nic.*Th.* 673, *CPR*29.10 (ii A.D.). 2. poet., *eye*, Call.*Fr.*150, Cerc.7.2, *IG*12(9).954.8 (Chalcis), *Supp.Epigr.*3.543 (Philippopolis, iii(?) B.C.), *AP*6.62 (Phil.), 5.218 (Paul. Sil.), Moschio Trag.9.9, Opp.*C.* 4.118, etc. II. *tyre of a wheel*, *Edict.Diocl.*15.36, *EM*364.29, Sch. Il.5.725. III. *chimney*, Hsch. IV. *pot, pan*, Id. (Lat. *cantus* (in signf. II) is said to be African or Spanish by Quint.1.5.8.)

κανθύλη, ἡ, *swelling, tumour*, A.*Fr.*220.

κανθώδης, ες, *curved*, prob. in Call.*Fr.*204.

κάνθων, ωνος, ὁ, = κανθήλιος, *pack-ass*, Ar.*V.*179, *AP*11.383 (Pall.), 399 (Apollinar.), Apion ap.J.*Ap.*2.9; of Trygaeus' beetle (with play on κάνθαρος), Ar.*Pax* 82 (anap.).

κανίας, ου, ὁ, = κάλαθος, dub. in Hsch. **κᾰνίδιον**, τό, *little basket* (unless = κνίδιον), *PPar.Wess.*p.245, *Sammelb.*7243.12 (iv A.D.).

κᾰνις, crasis for καὶ ἄνις, = ἄνευ, Megar.ap.Ar.*Ach.*834.

κᾰνίσκιον, τό, Dim. of κάνεον, Ar.*Fr.*160, *IG*2^{2}.1472.41, Ptol. Euerg.7 J., Babr.108.20:—also **κᾰνίσκος**, ὁ, *Gloss.*: **κᾰνισκώδης**, ες, *basket-like*, πλέγμα Sch.Ar.*V.*672.

κάνιστρον, τό, v. κάναστρον:—also **κάνιτρον**, = κανίσκιον, Hsch., Phot.

κάννα or **κάννη**, ης, ἡ, *pole-reed*, *Arundo Donax*, Plb.14.1.15; κάννας τιμά (prob. for making pens) *SIG*241.103 (Delph., iv B.C.). 2. *reed-mat*, Cratin.197, Eup.228, dub. in *IG*1^{2}.330.12: in pl., *reed-fence*, Ar.*V.*394, Pherecr.63. (Cf. Bab. *ḳanû*, Hebr. *ḳāneh* 'reed'.)

καννᾰβάριος, ὁ, (Lat. *canabae*) *booth-keeper, stall-holder*, *Jahresh.* 24 *Beibl.*31 (Ephesus). II. = *stupparius*, *Gloss.*

καννάβ-ῐνος [ᾰβ], η, ον, *like hemp*, κράμβη *AP*11.325 (Autom.); *hempen*, Apollod.*Poliorc.*159.5; σφήκωμα *Hippiatr.*24. **-ιον**, τό, = sq., Ps.-Dsc.3.148, *Gp.*13.11.9. **-ις**, ἡ, gen. ιος Hdt.4.74, εως Sor.2.46, Gal.6.549; acc. κάνναβιν Moschio ap.Ath.5.206f, κανναβίδα (sic codd.) Hdt. l. c., Paus.6.26.6:—*hemp*, *Cannabis sativa*, S.*Fr.*243, Hdt. l. c., Dsc.3.148, etc. (but κ. ἀγρία *hemp-mallow*, *Althaea cannabina*, ib.149): in pl., -ίδες *hemp-seed*, Ephipp.13.6; burnt and used to medicate vapour baths, Hdt.4.75:—hence **κανναβισθῆναι** *take a vapour-bath*, Hsch. (Cf. OE. *hænep* 'hemp', Skt. *śaṇás* 'a kind of hemp', etc.; borrowed perh. fr. Ugro-Finnish, cf. Čeremissian *keñe*, *kiñe* 'hemp' and Syrianian *piš* 'hemp'.) **-ίσκα**, τά, *hempen shoes*, Herod.7.58. **-ος**, ἡ, = κάνναβις, Poll.10.176. II. v. κάναβος.

κάνναθρον, τό, = κάναθρον. **καννεύσας**, Ep. for κατανεύσας, Od.15.464. **κἀννεώσασθαι**, poet. for καὶ ἀνανεώσασθαι. **κάννη**, v. κάννα. **κάννηκες**· πλέγματα ταρσῶν, Hsch.

καννοχερσαία, ἡ, = ἑλξίνη, Ps.-Dsc.4.39.

Κάννωκος, ὁ, title of Zeus Panamaros, *BCH*12.261.

κᾰνον-ίας, ου, ὁ, *one as straight as a* κανών, Hp.*Aër*.24. **-ίζω**, (κανών) *measure* or *judge by rule*, Longin.16.4; *measure, regulate*, τὰς πράξεις ἡδονῇ καὶ λύπῃ Arist.*EN*1105^{a}3, cf. S.E.*M*.7.158; τῇ πείρᾳ τὴν ἐνέργειάν τινος Dsc.*Praef*.2; τὴν ψυχὴν Procl.*Par.Ptol.* 16:—Pass., πάντα κεκανόνισται πρὸς δικαιοσύνην Aristeas 168; ἡδονῇ κανονιζόμενον Phld.*Po*.5.25; τοῖσιν [τοῖς πλάνησι] κανονίζεται αἰών *App.Anth*.3.147 (Theon or Hermes). 2. *prescribe rules for*, c. acc., Simp.*in Ph*.980.23. II. *assess* for taxation, *PLond*.5.1674.34 (Pass., vi A.D.). III. Gramm., κανονίζεται *the rule is..*, A.D. *Pron*.21.20: generally, Heliod.ap.Orib.46.9.4. 2. Act., *conjugate, give the paradigm* of a verb, Sch.E.*Hec*.1293:—Pass., Sch.Opp. *H*.1.259, etc.; *to be parsed as..*, εἰς ἀόριστον Sch.E.*Ph*.1188.

κᾰνονικάριος, ὁ, *collector of an Imperial tax*, *Cod.Just*.10.19.9, Just.*Nov*.30.7.1.

κᾰνον-ικός, ή, όν, (κανών) *of* or *belonging to a rule*, ἀρχή A.D.*Adv*. 141.29; *regular, according to rule*, διαφοραί Gal.7.417; ἀναλογία Eust. 113.40, etc. Adv -κῶς Artem.1.1a. 2. *connected with assessment* (cf. κανών II. 6), *PMasp*.131.13 (vi A.D.). II. ἡ -κή (sc. τέχνη) *the mathematical theory of music* (Pythag., cf. Ptolemais ap. Porph. *in Harm*.p.207), based on the division of the monochord (cf. κανών I. 10), Gell.16.18; κ. θεωρία, τέχνη, Ph.1.22, Procl. *in Euc*.p.40F. 2. *belonging to an astronomical table*, Vett.Val.141.14; κανονικοί, οἱ, *constructors of such tables*, Cleom.2.6. 3. κανονικόν, τό, the equivalent of Logic in Epicurean philosophy, D.L.10.30: pl., τὰ κ. S.E.*M*.7. 22; title of work by Antiochus, ib.201; ὁ κ. λόγος dub. in Phld.*Ir*. p.65 W. **-ιον**, τό, *small bar* or *rod*, Ph.*Bel*.74.11, Hero *Spir*.1.5, al., Apollod.*Poliorc*.182.6, Hero *Bel*.77.1. II. *compass*, S.E.*M*. 10.149,153. III. = σταμίς, Poll.1.92. IV. *tabulation, table*, Ptol.*Harm*.2.15, Gaud.*Harm*.22, Vett.Val.321 sq. V. *correct list*, *PLond*.2.259.126 (i A.D.). VI. Dim. of κανών I. 10, Ptol.*Harm*.1. 15 (pl.), 2.13. **-ίς**, ίδος, ἡ, acc. to Suid., = ἐργαλεῖον καλλιγραφικόν, *ruler*, dub. in *AP*6.62 (Phil.), dub. in *IG*2^{2}.1678.4. II. *frame with parallel cross-ledges*, Arist.*Ath*.64.2; *door-frame*, *IG*2^{2}.1672.155 (pl.). 2. in pl., *cross-bars* for strengthening an engine, Ph.*Bel*. 57.11. III. pl., *profile-stones* running along the top of a wall, *IG*2^{2}.1666 *A* 16: sg., *row of such stones*, ib.1672.186. [ῐ *AP* l.c., s.v.l.] **-ισμα**, ατος, τό, *ruler*, *AP*6.295 (Phan.). II. *grammatical rule*, Eust.439.26. **-ισμός**, ὁ, perh. *the frieze* of a building, in pl., Man.1.299, 4.151. **-ιστέον**, *one must regulate*, κἂν ἡδονῇ κ. ἢ τὰ ἀρεστά Muson.*Fr*.24 p.119 H., cf. Luc.*Hist.Conscr*.9. **-ιστικός**, ή, όν, *regulative*, οἱ κανόνες τῶν ὑγιῶν, οὐ τῶν πεπονθότων εἰσὶ -κοί Choerob. *in Heph*.p.226 C.

κᾰνονο-γρᾰφία, ἡ, *construction of astronomical tables*, Ptol.*Alm*. 2.9, Vett.Val.336.12:—also **-ποιΐα**, ἡ, Ptol.*Alm*.3.1, Theon *in Ptol. Alm*.p.109 H., Vett.Val.353.14.

κᾰνονωτός, ή, όν, *furnished with cross-bars*, θυρίδες *PSI*5.547.4 (iii B.C.); ἀγγεῖον, ζωγρεῖον κ., a *cage* for pigs, Sch.Ar.*V*.840 ed. Ald. (v.l. κανωτόν). 2. *made straight* or *even*, ῥάβδοι Eust.707.59.

κάντορες· οἱ κρατοῦντες, Hsch. (Fort. κράντορες.)

κανυσῖνος, ὁ, *dress of Canusian wool*, Ath.3.97e; cf. **κανύσια** ἔρια *PHolm*.22.26.

κάνυστρον, τό, v. κάναστρον.

Κάνωβος [ᾰ], ὁ (**Κάνωπος** St.Byz., cf. Scyl.106, Luc.*Nav*.15, Ath. 7.326a), *Canopus* in lower Egypt, A.*Pr*.846, Hdt.2.15, D.C.50.27; name of the star *Canopus*, Hipparch.1.11.7 (Κάνωπος), Ptol.*Alm*.8.1 (Κάνωβος), etc.:—hence **Κανωπίτης** [ῑ], *of Canopus*, αἰγιαλός Call. in *PSI*9.1092.58; also epith. of Sarapis, who had a temple there, Id. *Ep*.56.1; or **Κανωβεύς**, Orac.ap.Paus.10.13.8:—Adj. **Κανωβικός**, ή, όν, στόμα, i.e. the westernmost mouth of the Nile, Hdt.2.17,113; ἡ πύλη ἡ Κανωβική Str.17.1.10 and 16; Κανωπικά, τά, a kind of *cake*, Chrysipp.Tyan.ap.Ath.14.647c: **Κανωβισμός**, *luxurious living*, Str. 17.1.16.

κανών, όνος, ὁ, *straight rod, bar*, esp. to keep a thing straight: 1. in pl., *staves* which preserved the shape of the shield, [ἀσπίδα] δύω κανόνεσσ' ἀραρυῖαν Il.13.407, cf. 8.193, Them.*Or*.21.257a. 2. *weaver's rod*, to which alternate threads of the warp were attached, Il. 23.761, Ar.*Th*.822 (anap.), Plu.2.156b, Nonn.*D*.37.631. 3. *ruddled line* used by masons or carpenters, πύργους.. ὀρθοῖσιν ἔθεμεν κανόσιν E.*Tr*.6; βάθρα φοίνικι κανόνι.. ἡρμοσμένα Id.*HF*945; also κ. λίθινος *rule, straight-edge*, *IG*1^{2}.313.113, 373.217, al., cf. Pl.*Phlb*.56b, X.*Ages*.10.2, *AP*11.120 (Callicter); ὥστε τέκτονος παρὰ στάθμην ἰόντος ὀρθοῦται κ. S.*Fr*.474.5; κανόνα προσφέρειν Aeschin.3.199; ποιῶν ὀρθὰ πάντα πρὸς κανόνα *IG*7.3073.108 (Lebad., ii B.C.); κανόνεσσι.. μετρήσασθαι A.R.1.724, cf. Ar.*Av*.1004; μολίβδινος κ., i.e. a flexible *rule* that cannot be depended on for straight measurement, Arist.*EN*1137^{b}31 (unless = κῦμα); κανόνα ποιῆσαι στρεβλόν Id. *Rh*.1354^{a}26. b. *ruler*, *AP*6.63.2 (Damoch.). c. metaph., κανόνες καὶ πήχεις ἐπῶν Ar.*Ra*.799; λαμπρὰ μὲν ἀκτὶς ἡλίου, κ. σαφής E.*Supp*.650. 4. *beam* or *tongue of the balance*, στῆσαι ἐκ κανόνος *AP*11.334, cf. Sch.Ar.*Ra*.811. 5. *curtain-rod*, Chares *Fr*. 4 J. 6. in pl., *reeds* of a wind-organ, *AP*9.365 (Jul. Imp.). 7. *bed-post*, Lxx *Ju*.13.6. 8. in pl., *poles* from which the *ancilia* were suspended when carried, D.H.2.71. 9. pl., *bars* of a window, *PSI*5.547.9 (iii B.C.). 10. in Music, *monochord*, κατατομὴ κανόνος, title of work by Euc., cf. Phld.*Mus*.p.100 K., Ptol.*Harm*. 1.8, 2.12; ὀκτάχορδος, πεντεκαιδεκάχορδος κ., ib.2.2, 3.1 tit. 11. *cross-bar of* κιθάρα, Porph. *in Harm*.p.207. II. metaph., *rule, standard*, κανόνι τοῦ καλοῦ μαθών E.*Hec*.602; γνώμης πονηροῖς κανόσιν ἀναμετρούμενος τὸ σῶφρον Id.*El*.52; κανόνα προσάγειν Luc.*Hist. Conscr*.5; of the law, Lycurg.9; ὁ σπουδαῖος.. ὥσπερ κ. καὶ μέτρον αὐτῶν (sc. καλῶν καὶ ἡδέων) ὤν Arist.*EN*1113^{a}33, cf. Arr.*Epict*.3.4.5; τὴν ἐλευθερίαν καὶ τὸ μηδέν' ἔχειν δεσπότην αὑτῶν, ἃ τοῖς προτέροις Ἕλλησιν ὅροι τῶν ἀγαθῶν ἦσαν καὶ κανόνες D.18.296; ὡς κανόνι τῷ πάθει πᾶν ἀγαθὸν κρίνοντες Epicur.*Ep*.3 p.63 U.; ὁ Ἐπικούρου κ. his treatise on Logic, Id.*Fr*.34, Damox.2.15; ὁ τῆς φιλοσοφίας κ. Lxx 4 *Ma*.7.21: Κανόνες, οἱ, title of treatise by Democritus; of a philosophic *principle*, Dam.*Pr*.312. 2. in Art, *model, standard*, ὁ κ., a statue by Polyclitus which furnished a model of proportions, Plin.*HN*34.55; also his treatise on the same, Chrysipp.*Stoic*.3.122 (adnot.); also in Literature, Ἡρόδοτος τῆς Ἰάδος ἄριστος κ., Θουκυδίδης δὲ τῆς Ἀτθίδος D.H.*Pomp*.3. c. of a person, *severe critic*, *κ. scriptorum*, Cic.*Fam*. 16.17.1. 3. Gramm., *general rule*, *AB*1180, Choerob. *in Theod*.2 p.xxi; *paradigm*, οἱ κ. τῶν ὀνομάτων A.D.*Adv*.141.25. b. metrical *scheme* showing all possible forms of a verse, Heph.14.1, al. 4. in Astronomy and Chronology, *table of dates*, κανόνες χρονικοί Plu. *Sol*.27; sg., κανών, ὁ, *system of chronology*, D.H.1.74. b. astrological *table*, κανόνων καὶ εἰσόδων πήξεις Vett.Val.108.19. 5. *limit, boundary*, expl. as τὸ μέτρον τοῦ πηδήματος, Poll.3.151. b. *'province'*, *sphere of action*, 2 *Ep.Cor*.10.15. 6. *assessment* for taxation, *PLond*.1.99.5 (iv A.D.), etc.; οἱ δεσποτικοὶ κ. the Imperial *taxes*, ib.234.9 (iv A.D.); ἰδιωτικὸς κ. *POxy*.2124.10 (iv A.D.). 7. *tariff*, *Stud.Pal*.20.143.5 (v/vi A.D.).

Κανωπικόν, τό, = πιτύουσα, Dsc.4.165. II. a kind of *cake*, *POxy*. 1774.15 (iv A.D.); cf. Κανωβικός.

κάνωπον, τό, *elder-flower*, Paul.Aeg.7.3; *elder-bark*, Alex.Trall.12.

Κάνωπος, ὁ, v. Κάνωβος.

κάος [ᾰ], εος, τό, (καίω) *that which burns*, etym. of χάος, Corn.*ND*17.

κάπ, Ep. for κατά before π, φ, κὰπ πεδίον Il.6.201; κὰπ φάλαρα 16. 106; also Thess., *IG*9(2).517.20 (Larissa).

κᾰπαῖος, α, ον, *of the crib* or *manger*, epith. of Zeus, Antiph.111.

καπαλευτής, οῦ, ὁ, = ὀνηλάτης, Hsch.:—also **καπαλαί**· κάπηλοι, φάτναι, and **καπαλίζω**, = ζευγηλατέω, Id.

κᾰπάνη [πᾱ], ἡ, *chariot*, Thess. for ἀπήνη, Xenarch.11. (Prop. *the cross-piece in a chariot seat, the side-pieces* being **καπάνακες**, Poll. 1.142.) II. = κάπη, Hsch.; also, *a felt helmet*, Id.

καπανῆται, sine gl., Suid. **καπάνια**· ἀρπεδόνες, Hsch.

κᾰπᾰνικός, ή, όν, (καπάνη) dub. in τὰ Θετταλικὰ (sc. δεῖπνα) μὲν πολὺ καπᾰνικώτερα Ar.*Fr*.492: expld. by Ath.9.418d as, = ἁμαξιαῖα, *enormous*, by Hsch. as χορταστικώτερα, *more foodful, more plenteous* (from καπάνη = κάπη).

καπανοι· ἀλφίτων εἶδος, Phot. (sine accentu).

καπαρδεῦσαι· μαντεύσασθαι, Hsch.; cf. σκαπαρδεύω.

καπάριον, κάπαρις, written for καππ- (q.v.).

κάπατα (sic)· κατακόψεις (Paph.), Hsch. **κάπατας**· καθορῶν, Euclus ap.Hsch. (leg. καπατάς, cf. ἰμπάταδον, ἰνκαπάταδον).

καπέτις, ιος, ἡ, a Persian measure, $\frac{1}{48}$ *of the* ἀρτάβη, Polyaen.4.3. 32; = χοῖνιξ, Hsch.; cf. καπίθη.

κάπετον, Dor. for κατέπεσον, Pi.*O*.8.38.

κάπετος [ᾰ], ἡ, (for σκάπετος, from σκάπτω) *ditch, trench*, ὄχθας καπέτοιο βαθείης Il.15.356, cf. 18.564; *hole, grave*, ἐς κοίλην κάπετον θέσαν [ὀστέα] 24.797, cf. S.*Aj*.1165, 1403 (both anap.); *groove* for lever, Hp.*Art*.72, 74. II. *shovel, spade* (?), *GDI*4992 *a* ii 6 (Gortyn).

Κᾰπετώλιον, τό, = Lat. *Capitolium*, D.H.1.34 (v.l.), etc.:—hence **Κᾰπετώλιος**, ὁ, = *Capitolinus*, epith. of Zeus = Jupiter, Paus.2.4.5, *SIG*694.24 (Elaea, ii B.C.), etc.: **Κᾰπετωλιονίκης** [νῑ], ὁ, *victor in the Ludi Capitolini*, *Sammelb*.5725: **Κᾰπετώλιος**, ὁ (sc. μήν), name of month of *December*, *Gloss*., cf. *Cat.Cod.Astr*.2.140: **Κᾰπετώλια**, τά, = *Ludi Capitolini*, *IG*3.129.

κάπη [ᾰ], ἡ, (κάπτω) *crib, manger*, [ἵππους] κατέδησαν ἐπ' ἀμβροσίῃσι κάπῃσιν Il.8.434; ἐφ' ἱππείῃσι κάπῃσι Od.4.40; βουσταθμου κάπης S.*Ichn*.8; ἀντὶ κάπης Lyc.95: **κάπηθεν** as Adv., Suid.

κᾰπηλ-εία, ἡ, *retail trade*, esp. *provision-dealing, tavern-keeping*, Pl.*Lg*.849d, 918d, Arist.*Pol*.1256^{a}41: in pl., *petty trades*, ib.1291^{a}6; κ. ἀσκεῖν προσώπῳ, of women who paint, Poll.5.102. **-εῖον**, τό, *shop of a* κάπηλος, freq. of a *tavern*, *Com.Adesp*.493 (in a parody of Sophocles), Ar.*Lys*.427, *Ec*.154, Lys.1.24, Eub.80, Isoc.7.49, cf. Theopomp.Hist.65, *Tab.Defix*.87 (iv B.C.), Ἀρχ.Ἐφ.1923.39 (pl., Orop., iv B.C.), *PTeb*.43.18 (ii B.C.), *POxy*.2109.11 (iii A.D.): pl., καπηλεῖα, τά (prob. l. for κάπηλα), the *meat-market* at Tarentum, Hsch. **-ευτικός**, ή, όν, = καπηλικός, Pl.*Lg*.842d. **-εύω**, *to be a retail-dealer, drive a petty trade*, Hdt.1.155, 2.35, Isoc.2.1, Nymphod.21, *IG*11(2).161 *A* 16 (Delos, iii B.C.), *BGU*1024 vii 23 (iv A.D.); δι' ἀψύχου βορᾶς σίτοις καπήλευ' *drive a trade, chaffer* with your vegetable food, E.*Hipp*.953. II. c. acc., *sell by retail*, τὸν ἔρπιν Hippon.51. 2. metaph., κ. τὰ πρήγματα, of Darius, Hdt.3.89; κ. τὰ μαθήματα *sell* learning *by retail, hawk it about*, Pl. *Prt*.313d; κ. τὸν λόγον τοῦ θεοῦ 2 *Ep.Cor*.2.17; so ἔοικεν οὐ καπηλεύσειν μάχην will not *peddle in* war, i.e. fight half-heartedly, A.*Th*. 545; κ. τῇ χάριτι τὴν ἀμοιβὴν Epicur.*Sent.Vat*.39; κ. τὴν πολιτείαν *traffic in* grants of citizenship, D.C.60.17; κ. τῆς ὥρας ἄνθος or τὴν ὥραν, of prostitutes, Ph.2.394,576; εἰρήνην πρὸς Ῥωμαίους χρυσίου κ. Hdn.6.7.9; τύχη καπηλεύουσα.. τὸν βίον *playing tricks with* life, *corrupting* it, *AP*9.180 (Pall.). -η, ἡ, *steersman's seat, hold*, or *belaying-pin*, Hsch. **-ικός**, ή, όν, *of* or *for a* κάπηλος, ζυγόν Dinol. 2 (fort. καπανικόν); ἀργύρωμα *IG*11(2).110 (Delos, iii B.C.), cf. 111; *mercenary*, ἦθος M.Ant.4.28; σοφιστής Poll.4.48; ἡ -ική (sc. τέχνη), = καπηλεία, Pl.*Sph.*223d, Arist.*Pol.*1257ᵃ18: καπηλικόν, τό, *camp-followers, sutlers* of an army, Arr.*Tact.*2.1; but also, *tax on retail-traders*, *BGU*1237 (iii/ii B.C.). 2. *like a petty trader, knavish, cozening*, κ. μέτρα φιλεῦσα *AP*9.229 (Marc. Arg.); ὕθλος Porph.*Chr.* 49. Adv. -κῶς, ἔχειν to be *vamped up for sale*, Ar.*Pl.*1063; τὰ πράγματα κ. διανέμων Plu.2.369c; *in a mercenary spirit*, Gal.14.216: Comp. -ώτερον Numen.ap.Eus.*PE*14.8. -ιον, τό, = καπηλεῖον, *Tab.Defix.Aud.*70 (iii B.C.). **-ίς**, ίδος, ἡ, fem. of κάπηλος, Ar.*Th.* 347, *Pl.*435, 1120, *Com.Adesp.*567, Aeschin.Socr.4, *PFay.*12.23 (ii B.C.): Καπηλίδες, αἱ, title of play by Theopomp. Com.:—accented κάπηλις, acc. to Hdn.Gr.1.91, cf. Oenom.ap.Eus.*PE*6.7:—late **καπήλισσα**, ἡ, Sch.Ar.*Pl.*426.

κᾰπηλο-γείτων, ονος, ὁ, = *attubernalis*, *Gloss.* **-δύτης** [ῠ], ου, ὁ, (δύω) *tavern-haunter*, *Cat.Cod.Astr.*7.242, Hsch.

κάπηλος [ᾰ], ὁ (also ἡ, *AP*9.180 (Pall.)), *retail-dealer, huckster*, Hdt. 1.94, 2.141, Sophr.1, etc.; opp. ἔμπορος, Lys.22.21, X.*Cyr.*4.5.42, Pl.*R.*371d, *Prt.*314a; also opp. the producer (αὐτοπώλης), Id.*Sph.* 231d, *Plt.*260c; applied to Darius, Hdt.3.89; κ. ἀσπίδων, ὅπλων, *a dealer in..*, Ar.*Pax* 447, 1209. 2. esp. *tavern-keeper*, Ar.*Th.*347, Lys.*Fr.*1, *PMagd.*26.2 (iii B.C.), *PTeb.*612 (i/ii A.D.), Luc.*Herm.*58, etc. 3. metaph., κ. πονηρίας *dealer in petty* roguery, D.25.46. II. as Adj., ος, ον, = καπηλικός, βίος D.H.9.25; esp. *cheating, knavish*, κ. προσφέρων τεχνήματα A.*Fr.*322; κ. φρόνημα *Com.Adesp.*867.

καπήλτια· γυναικεῖα ἱμάτια, Hsch. (leg. καππάτια). **κάπηξ**, *projecting piece at a ship's stern*, Id. **κᾰπητόν**, τό, (κάπη) *fodder*, Id. II. in pl., = *wicker baskets*, Lyd.*Mag.*1.46.

κάπια, τά, *onions* (at Cerynea), Hsch.

καπίθη, ἡ, *a Persian measure containing two* χοίνικες, X.*An.*1.5.6; = *two Attic* κοτύλαι, Hsch.

καπίστριον, τό, *halter*, Hsch.

καπν-αύγης, ου, ὁ, *smoke-observer, diviner*, *IG*14.617 (Rhegium): pl. -αῦγαι ib.618 (ibid.). **-ειος** (sc. ἄμπελος), ἡ, vine *with smoke-coloured grapes*, Thphr.*HP*2.3.2, *PCair.Zen.*33.14 (iii B.C.):—written **κάπνεος** in Arist.*GA*770ᵇ20; **καπνέως** in Thphr.*CP*5.3.1 (cod. Urb., v.l. **κάπνεος**); **καπνία** in Suid., Sch.Ar.*V.*151; **καπνός** in cod. Hsch. s.v. καπνίας; **κάπνιος** in *App.Prov.*3.43. **-είω**, poet. for καπνίζω, *turn into smoke*, Nic.*Th.*36. **-έλαιον**, τό, *oily resin* from trees, Gal.13.626, Alex.Trall.3.2. II. = καπνιστὸν ἔλαιον, *Edict.Diocl.Delph.* **-εος, -έως**, v. κάπνειος. **-η**, ἡ, = καπνοδόκη, Eup.88, Ar.*V.*143, Alex.173.13. II. = καπνιαῖος λίθος, *PHolm.* 5.11. **-ηλός**, όν, *smoky*, ὀδμή Nic.*Th.*54. **-ία**, ἡ, = κάπνη I, Moer.292, *Gloss.* **-ιαῖος** λίθος *smoky* quartz, *PHolm.*10.9, cf. 4.6. **-ίας**, ου, ὁ, (καπνός) *smoky*, nickname of the Comic poet Ecphantides, Sch.Ar.*V.*151. II. as Subst., 1. κ. οἶνος, ὁ, expl. by Hsch., Phot. as wine *that had a smoky taste* from having been long hung up in smoke, Pherecr.130.6, Anaxandr.41.71 (anap.), Pl.Com. 244: perh. rather to be expld. as *made from the vine* κάπνειος. 2. κ. (sc. λίθος), ὁ, a kind of *jasper*, Dsc.5.142, Plin.*HN*37.118. **-ιάω**, *smoke* a bee-hive, A.R.2.131. **-ίζω**, *make smoke*, i.e. *make a fire*, Ep. aor. 1 κάπνισσαν Il.2.399; *use as a fumigation*, τροχίσκον Paul.Aeg.3.28. II. *smoke, blacken with smoke*, D.54.4, Sopat.6.9, *PMasp.*141 ii *a*25 (vi A.D.):—Pass., *to be smoked*, ὁ ἠπίολος φεύγει -όμενος Arist.*HA*605ᵇ16; of the eyes, *suffer from smoke*, Id.*Pr.*957ᵇ 33, cf. 896ᵇ8; of cookery, καπνιζομένη τυραννίς empire *of the smoke*, Demetr.Com.Nov.1.4; κλίβανος -όμενος *smoking* furnace, Lxx *Ge.*15. 17. 2. intr. in Act., *to be black with smoke*, pf. κεκάπνικα Ar.*Pax* 892; τὸ ὄρος τὸ καπνίζον Lxx *Ex.*20.18; κρύσταλλος ἡ -ίζουσα *smoky* quartz, *PHolm.*6.38: metaph., [θυμὸν] καπνίζοντα (v.l. -ιῶντα) καὶ διακαιόμενον Plu.2.454e. **-ιος** (sc. ἄμπελος), ἡ, v. κάπνειος. II. κάπνιος, ἡ, = καπνός II, Gal.12.8. **-ισις**, εως, ἡ, *exposure to smoke*, Arist.*Pr.* 896ᵇ9. **-ισμα**, ατος, τό, *offering of smoke*, i.e. *incense*, *AP*9.174.5 (Pall.). **-ιστέον**, *one must smoke*, 'gas', τοὺς ἐν τοῖς μετάλλοις ὄντας Ph.*Bel.*99.18. **-ιστήριον**, τό, perh. *vapour-bath*, *Inscr.Prien.*112. 98 (i B.C.). **-ιστός**, ή, όν, *smoked*, κρέα Posidon.1 J.; but τροχίσκος κ. *for use as a fumigation*, Paul.Aeg.3.28; κ. ἔλαιον *fragrant* oil, Aët. 1.138; κ. μύρον Id.16.66(67). **-ίτης** [ῑ] λίθος *smoky* quartz, Alex. Trall.1.15. II. fem. **-ῖτις** (v.l. -ίτης), = καπνός II, Ps.-Dsc.4.109.

καπνο-βάτης [βᾰ], ου, ὁ, epith. of a pastoral people, dub. in Posidon.104 J. **-γόργιον**, τό, = καπνός II, Ps.-Dsc.4.109. **-δόκη**, ἡ, prop. *smoke-receiver*, i.e. *hole in the roof for the smoke to pass through*, Hdt.4.103, 8.137, Pherecr.141, Eup.133:—later **-δόχη** Lxx *Ho.*13.3 codd. AQ, Luc.*Icar.*13, Gal.2.727. **-δοχεῖον**, τό, = foreg., *Gloss.* **-δόχος**, ον, *receiving smoke*, ib. **-ειδής**, ές, *smoke-coloured*, Ael.*NA*6.20. **-κορτῠάζομαι**, *leap, frisk*, Epich. 195. **-μαντις**, εως, ὁ, *smoke-diviner*, Lact.ad Stat.*Theb.*4. 411. **-ομαι**, Pass., *to be turned into smoke, burnt to ashes*, Pi.*P.* 5.84, E.*Supp.*497, *Tr.*8.

καπνοόν· τὰ πνέοντα, Hsch.

καπνοποιός, όν, *making smoke, smoky*, Sch.Ar.*V.*145.

καπνός, ὁ, *smoke*, Il.1.317, etc.; κνισάεντι καπνῷ Pi.*I.*4(3).66; καπνῷ πυρὸς A.*Ag.*497; *spray*, καπνοῦ καὶ κύματος ἐκτὸς ἔεργε νῆα Od. 12.219 (hence metaph., Porph.*Abst.*1.47): prov., καπνοῦ σκιά, of things worth nothing, A.*Fr.*399, S.*Ph.*946; τἄλλ' ἐγὼ καπνοῦ σκιᾶς οὐκ ἂν πριαίμην Id.*Ant.*1170; also περὶ καπνοῦ στενολεσχεῖν Ar.*Nu.* 320; κ. καὶ φλυαρία Pl.*R.*581d: and in pl., γραμμάτων καπνοί learned *trifles*, E.*Hipp.*954; καπνοὺς..καὶ σκιάς Eup.51; nickname of a man, Id.122: metaph. also of envy, ὕδωρ καπνῷ φέρειν to throw water *on the smoking embers*, Pi.*N.*1.24: prov., ἐς αὐτὸ τὸ πῦρ ἐκ τοῦ καπνοῦ βιαζόμενος 'out of the frying-pan into the fire', Luc.*Nec.*4, al. II. *fumitory, Fumaria officinalis*, Anon.Lond.36.58, Dsc.4.109.

καπν-οσφράντης, ου, ὁ, *smoke-sniffer*, of a miser or a parasite, *Com.Adesp.*1025: as pr. n., Alciphr.3.49. **-οῦχος**, ὁ, *chimney*, *Gloss.* **-ώδης**, ες, *smoky*, opp. ἀτμιδώδης, Arist.*Mete.*360ᵃ10, al.; [φλόξ] Thphr.*Ign.*76; κ. καὶ συννεφὴς ἀήρ Plb.9.16.3. Adv. -δῶς Gal. 4.507. 2. of colour, *dark, dusky*, Thphr.*CP*5.3.2, Luc.*Philops.* 16; φύλλον δριμὺ καὶ κ. D.Chr.66.5. **-ωτήριον**, τό, *altar*, *Gloss.*

κᾶπος, Dor. for κῆπος.

κάπος, ὁ, *breath*, Eust.1280.34, Hsch.:—also **κάπυς**, Id.; **κάφος**, Eust. l. c. **κάπουπλος**· φάρυγξ, Hsch.

κάππα, τό, v. sub Κ κ.

Καππαδόκαι, ῶν, οἱ, *Cappadocians*, Hdt.5.49, etc.:—also **Καππάδοκες**, ων, Str.6.4.2, etc.:—fem. **Καππαδόκισσα** Id.14.2.17:—hence **Καππαδοκία**, Ion. -ίη, ἡ, *Cappadocia*, Hdt.1.71, etc.; **Καππαδοκίζω**, *favour the Cappadocians*, App.*Mith.*53:—Pass., *to be Cappadocianized* (with pun on Joannes Cappadox), [Demod.]5.

καππάριον, τό, Dim. of sq., *Gloss*; πρὸς καππάριον ζῆν prov. in *Com.Adesp.*459: **καπάριον**, *PGen.*62.17 (iv A.D.).

κάππᾰρις, εως, Ion. ιος, ἡ, *caper-plant, Capparis spinosa*, or its fruit, *caper*, Hp.*Fist.*10 (v.l. καπαρ-), Arist.*Pr.*924ᵃ1, Antiph.62, Timocl. 23, Alex.127.6, Thphr.*HP*6.5.2, *PCair.Zen.*488 (iii B.C.), Lxx *Ec.* 12.5, Dsc.2.173, etc.; ὁ Ζήνων ὄμνυε τὴν κ. Empedus ap.Ath.9.370c.

κάππαρος, ὁ, a kind of *fish*, *PCair.Zen.*83 (iii B.C.).

κάππαστον (i.e. κατάπαστον)· ποικίλον, Hsch. **καππάτια**· γυναικεῖα ἱμάτια, Id.

κάππεσον, Ep. aor. 2 Act. of καταπίπτω.

καππῠρίζω, for καταπυρίζω, *catch fire*, aor. 1 part. καππυρίσασα dub. in Theoc.2.24.

Καππώτας, α, ὁ, Ζεὺς Κ., Doric name given to a large unworked stone at Gythium on which Orestes was said to have sat down and recovered his sanity (παύσασθαι τῆς μανίας), Paus.3.22.1.

κάπρα· αἴξ, Τυρρηνοί, Hsch.; but **κάπρας**· ἀκολασίας, Id.

κάπρ-αινα, ἡ, fem. of κάπρος, *wild sow*: metaph., *lewd woman*, Phryn.Com.33, Hermipp.10: dub. sens. in Lyr. in *Philol.* 80. 334. **-άω**, of sows, *want the boar*, Arist.*HA*572ᵇ24: metaph., *to be lecherous*, καπρῶσα γραῦς Ar.*Pl.*1024, cf. Men.917. **-ειος**, α, ον, *of the wild boar*, ὀδόντες Nonn.*D.*18.245. **-ία**, ἡ, *the ovary of sows*, cut out to prevent their breeding, Arist.*HA*632ᵃ21. II. *virus in sows*, like ἱππομανές in mares, ib.572ᵃ21, 573ᵇ2. III. *dance in armour*, Hsch. IV. = κάππαρις, Dsc.2.173. **-ιάω**, = καπράω, used of mares, Ar.Byz.*Epit.*145.12. **-ίδιον**, τό, Dim. of κάπρος, Ar.*Fr.*506.2. **-ίζω**, = καπράω, Arist.*HA*572ᵃ16. **-ίολος**, *furcilla*, *Gloss.* **-ιος**, ὁ, poet. for κάπρος, *wild boar*, Il.11.414, 12. 42, A.R.1.126; σῦς κάπριος Il.11.293, 17.282. II. Adj. κάπριος, ον, = κάπρειος, *like a wild boar*, καπρίους ἔχειν τὰς πρῴρας Hdt.3. 59. **-ίσκος**, ὁ, Dim. of κάπρος, Crobyl.7, Diph.Siph.ap.Ath.5.355f.

καπροβόλ⟨ι⟩ον, τό, gloss on συβίνη, Hsch.

κάπρος [ᾰ by nature], ὁ, *boar*, esp. *wild boar*, Il.17.725, Pl.*La.* 196e, etc.; also σῦς κ. Il.5.783, 17.21, cf. Ar.*Lys.*202 (ubi v. Sch.); ἧπαρ κάπρου Id.*Fr.*318.5: in fem. sense, *sow*, ὀχευομένους τοὺς κάπρους Anaxandr.47. II. a *sea-fish, Capros aper*, Philem.79. 21, Arist.*HA*505ᵃ13; a species found in the Achelous, ib.535ᵇ18. (Cogn. with Lat. *caper*, ONorse *hafr* 'he-goat', but not with Lat. *aper.*)

καπροσύρη· περικάθαρσις, Hsch.

καπρο-φάγος [φᾰ], ον, *eating boar's flesh*, epith. of Artemis at Samos, Hsch. **-φόνος**, ον, *killing wild boars*, κύων *AP*9.83 (Phil.).

καπρ-ῴζομαι, *rut*, of the boar, Sciras 1. **-ών**, ῶνος, ὁ, *pig-sty*, *IG*11(2).154*A*41 (Delos, iii B.C.).

καπτρ-ίον, τό, = καμπτρίον, Anon. in *Rh.*74.11, *Gloss.* **-ον**, = κάμπτρον II, ib.

κάπτω, fut. κάψω (v. infr.), *gulp down*, ἐμπίδας Ar.*Av.*245 (lyr.), cf. Sophr.64; [ἄλφιτα] Nicocl.2; of liquids, Xenarch.9 codd. Ath., Arist.*HA*593ᵃ21; ἀφρόν ib.620ᵃ13; κ. αὔρας Eub.10: c. gen. partit., κ. τῶν θυλημάτων Telecl.33: abs., ἄχρις ἑσπέρης κ. Herod.7.41; expressing greater greediness than φαγεῖν, Ar.*Ec.*687; ἡ ἄρκτος οὐδὲ σπάσει οὐδὲ λάψει ἀλλὰ κάψει Arist.*HA*595ᵃ10: metaph., σεν τὸ ὥριον τέφρη κάψει Herod.1.38. (Cogn. with Lat. *capio*, Germ. *haben*, *Heft.*)

καπυκτά· πνέοντα, Hsch. **καπύνιοι**· ἀκόλουθοι, Id.

κᾰπῠρ-ίδια, ων, τά, a kind of *cakes*, Chrysipp.Tyan.ap.Ath.3.113d codd.:—perh. **καπύρια** (καπήρια Suid.), cf. *POxy.*1655.3 (iii A.D.); **καπύριον**, *crustulum*, *Gloss.* **-ίζω**, *live riotously, revel* (cf. καπυρός II), Str.17.1.16. **-ις**, *Persian gown with sleeves*, Poll.7. 58. **-ιστής**, οῦ, ὁ, *debauchee*, Str.14.2.26. **-όομαι**, Pass., *become dry* or *parched*, Id.4.4.1; *become crackly*, Orib.*Fr.*74. **-ός**, ά, όν, *dried by the air*, κάρυα Epich.150; χοιρίων σκέλη Antiph.185; ἄλφιτον κ. Arist.*Pr.*927ᵃ24, cf. Dieuch.ap.Orib.4.7.3; τυρός *Test. Epict.*5.36; χαῖται (of thistle-down) Theoc.6.16. b. *brittle*, ὀστέον Hp.*VC*19 (v.l. εὔπριστον); cj. in Thphr.*HP*3.13.4 and 7 (Comp.); *crisp, crackly*, Diocl.*Fr.*147. 2. Act., *drying, parching*, κ. νόσος, of love, Theoc.2.85. II. of sound, *crackly*, καπυρὸν ψοφεῖν Gal.6.434: metaph., κ. γελάσας laughing *loud*, *AP*7.414 (Nossis), cf. Longus 2.5; κ. γέλως Alciphr.3.48; κ. στόμα *clear-sounding*, of Poets, Theoc.7.37; κ. συρίζειν to play *clearly* on the syrinx, Luc.*DDeor.*

22.3; καπυρώτεραι ᾠδαί *rude* songs, opp. ἐσπουδασμέναι, Ath.15.697b. **-ώδης**, ες, *dry*, Hsch. s. v. ἴτρια, *EM*479.39.

κάπυς, v. κάπος.

καπύω, *breathe forth*, Ep. aor. I κάπυσσεν Q.S.6.523; cf. κεκαφηώς.

κάπων, ωνος, ὁ, *capon*, *Gloss.*

κάρ, for κατά before ῥ, κὰρ ῥόον Il.12.33; κάρ ῥα 20.421.

***κάρ** (A), a word of uncertain gender, nom. form, and meaning, typifying what is worthless, τίω δέ μιν ἐν κἀρὸς αἴσῃ I value him at *a ..'s worth*, Il.9.378: καρός is variously expld. by Ar.Byz. etc. ap. Sch., e.g. as = κηρός or as pr. n. Καρός. **II.** = κάρα, ἐπὶ κάρ *head*-long (nisi junctim scrib.), Il.16.392; ἀνὰ κάρ *upwards*, Hp.ap.Gal.19.79.

κᾶρ (B), τό, Aeol. for κήρ (q. v.).

Κάρ, ὁ, gen. Κᾱρός, pl. Κᾶρες (contr. fr. Κάερ-), *Carian*, Il.2.867, etc.:—fem. **Κάειρα** [ᾰ] (q. v.): employed as mercenaries, καὶ δὴ 'πίκουρος ὥστε Κὰρ κεκλήσομαι Archil.24, cf. Ephor.12 J.: hence prov., ἐν τῷ Καρὶ κινδυνεύειν (cf. *experimentum facere in corpore vili*), E.*Cyc.* 654, cf. Sch.Pl.*La.*187b, *Euthd.*285c; ἐν Καρὶ τὸν κίνδυνον.. πειρᾶσθαι Cratin.16, cf. Philem.18; δεῖ ἐν Καρὶ τὴν πεῖραν, οὐκ ἐν τῷ στρατηγῷ γίνεσθαι Plb.10.32.11; ἐν τῷ Καρὶ καὶ οὐκ ἐν τοῖς ἑαυτῶν σώμασι τὰς πείρας ποιούμενοι Aristid.1.163 J. **II.** v. Κήρ.

κάρᾱ (A), Ep. and Ion. **κάρη** [ᾰ], τό, poet. for κεφαλή, Luc.*Lex.*5:—*head*, of men or animals, πολιόν τε κάρη πολιόν τε γένειον Il.22.74; ὑψοῦ κάρη ἔχει [ἵππος] 6.509; περὶ πόδα περὶ κάρα from *head* to foot, A.*Eu.* 165 (lyr.): metaph., ἐν δ' ἐμῷ κάρᾳ θεός μ' ἔπαισεν S.*Ant.*1272, cf. *OC* 564; of *the face*, γέλωτι φαιδρὸν κ. Id.*El.*1310; μου κ. τὸ δυσπρόσοπτον Id.*OC*285. **2.** *peak, top*, κάρη νιφόεντος Ὀλύμπου Hes.*Th.*42; of a tree, S.*Fr.*23; *edge, brim* of a cup, Eub.56.6. **3.** in Trag., as periphr. for *a person*, Οἰδίπου κάρα, i. e. Οἰδίπους, S.*OT*40, 1207 (lyr.); αὐτάδελφον Ἰσμήνης κ. Id.*Ant.*1; ὦ κασίγνητον κ., for ὦ κασίγνητε, Id.*El.*1164; ὦ φίλον κ. Id.*OC*1631; φίλον κ. A.*Ag.*905.—Hom. uses nom. acc. κάρη, gen. dat. κάρητος, κάρητι, Od.6.230, Il.15.75; also καρήατος, καρήατι, 23.44, 19.405, nom. pl. καρήατα 11.309 (whence was formed nom. sg. κάρηαρ, Antim.76); acc. pl. κάρη Il.10.259 (but perh. sg.), nom. acc. pl. κάρᾱ Sannyr.3, perh. S.*Ant.*291; κάρᾱ ἐξεπεφύκει *h.Cer.* 12; dat. pl. κάρησι f. l. in Tryph.602:—post-Homeric Poets inflected κάρη as if it were of decl. 1, gen. κάρης Mosch.4.74, Call.*Fr.*125; dat. κάρῃ Thgn.1024, Nic.*Th.*249; acc. κάρην D.P.562, Nic.*Th.*131; Trag. dat. κάρᾳ with neut. Prons., A.*Ch.*230, etc.; late acc. κάραν *Anacreont.*50.9. (Cf. Skt. *śiras* (neut.) 'head', gen. *śīrṣṇás*, abl. *śīrṣatás*: κάρηνα (fr. κάρᾱσ-ν-α) and κράατα (perh. fr. κρᾱσ-ṇ-τα) are forms of this word, v. κάρηνον, κράς, κρανίον: cogn. with Lat. *cerebrum* (fr. *ceres-ro–*), ONorse *hjarne* 'brain', and prob. κέρας, κόρση.)

κάρα (B), ἡ, *tame goat* (Cret.), Hsch.; also, *fig*, Id. **καραβαία**· δίκρουν ξύλον, Id.

κᾱράβιον [ρᾰ], τό, Dim. of κάραβος III, Hsch. s. v. ἐφόλκια, Sch.E. *Hec.*631.

κᾱρᾰβίς, ίδος, ἡ, = κάραβος I (Methymn.), Hsch. **II.** = κάραβος II, Sch.Opp.*H.*1.261; but distd. by Gal.19.686.

κᾱρᾰβο-ειδής, ές, *of the* κάραβος *kind*, Arist.*HA*526^{b}26, *PA*679^{a}31. **-πρόσωπος**, ον, *with the face of a* κάραβος, Luc.*VH*1.35.

κάρᾰβ-ος [κᾰ], ὁ, *horned* or *cerambycid beetle*, Arist.*HA*531^{b}25, 551^{b}17 (with vv.ll. καράβιοι, καράμβιοι). **II.** a prickly crustacean, *crayfish*, Epich.57, Ar.*Fr.*318.7, Gal.12.313, etc.: distd. from καρκίνος, Arist.*PA*684^{a}1, cf. *HA*525^{b}32, 590^{b}20; μαλακόστρακος ib.490^{b}11, cf. Speus.ap.Ath.3.105b; an Eastern species, Nearch.ap.Arr. *Ind.*29.14. **III.** a *light ship*, *EM*490.31. **VI.** Maced., *gate*, Hsch. **-ώδης**, ες, = καραβοειδής, Arist.*HA*607^{b}4, *GA*758^{a}12.

καραγος· ὁ τραχὺς ψόφος, οἷον πρί⟨οντ⟩ων, Hsch. **καραδάλη**· ἁρμενοθήκη, Id.

κᾰρᾰδοκ-έω, *wait for the outcome of*, κ. τὴν μάχην, τὸν πόλεμον τῇ πεσέεται, *wait to see* how the battle will end, Hdt.7.163,168; τὸν πόλεμον κῇ ἀποβήσεται Id.8.67; τἀκεῖθεν οἷ προβήσεται E.*Med.*1117; ἀδήλους ἐλπίδας *Trag.Adesp.*16; τἀνθένδε E.*Heracl.*279; ἀγῶνας Id. *Hel.*739; κ. ὅταν στράτευμα.. ἐξίῃ κάλως Id.*Tr.*93: simply, *wait for*, αὔραν ἱστίοις κ. ib.456 (troch.); παρουσίαν τινός Id.*IA*1432; τἀπιόντα τραύματα Id.*IT*313, etc.; τὰ προσταχθησόμενα X.*Mem.*3.5.6: freq. in later Prose, κ. τὸν καιρόν Plb.1.33.11, al.; τὸ μέλλον Cic.*Att.*9.10.8; τινα Zos.3.15, *PMasp.*2.2 (vi A. D.); also κ. εἴς τινα *look expectantly* at one, Ar.*Eq.*663. **-ητής**, οῦ, ὁ, gloss on ὔποπτος, Sch.E.*Hec.* 1135. **-ία**, ἡ, *eager expectation*, Aq.*Ps.*38(39).8, *Pr.*10.28.

καραιβαράω, v. καρηβαρέω.

Κᾰραιός, ὁ, (κάρα A) name of Zeus in Boeotia, *IG*7.3208 (Orchom.), Hsch., cj. Mein. in Cratin.111; cf. Κάριος.

κᾱράκαλλον [ρᾰ], τό, *hood*, *AP*11.345, *Edict.Diocl.*26.120:—Dim. **-κάλλιον**, τό, *Sammelb.*7033.37 (v A. D.), *PMasp.*6ii64 (vi A. D.), *Gloss.*

καράμβας· ῥάβδον ποιμενικήν, Hsch.

καράμβιος, ὁ, = κάραβος I, prob. in Ar.Byz.*Epit.*9.11, v.l. in Arist. *HA*551^{b}17.

κᾱρᾱν-ιστήρ, ῆρος, ὁ, ἡ, *beheading, touching the head*, κ. δίκαι A.*Eu.* 186:—also **-ιστὴς** μόρος E.*Rh.*817.

κάραννος· κεκρύφαλος, κρήδεμνον, ἢ ἔριφος (cf. κάρνος), ἢ ζημία (cf. κάρηνη, αὐτόκαρνος), Hsch.

κάρᾱνον, τό, v. κάρηνον.

κάρᾱνος [ᾰ], ὁ, (κάρα A) *a chief*, X.*HG*1.4.3, cj. in *Anacreont.*15.3.

κᾱρᾱνόω, like κεφαλαιόω, *achieve*, A.*Ch.*528 (Pass.), 705.

καρανώ, ἡ, *goat* (Cret.), Hsch. **κάραξι**· στρώσω, Id. **καραρύες**, Scythian *travelling-wagons*, Id. **καράς**· ὁ ἀποσπερματισμός, Id. **καραταί**· κεφαλαί, Id.

κᾱρᾱτομ-έω, *behead*, E.*Rh.*586, J.*BJ*1.17.8, al.:—Pass., Lyc.313, Agath.1.12. **-ος** (proparox.), ον, (τέμνω) *beheaded*, Γοργών E. *Alc.*1118 (dub. l.); κ. ἐρημία νεανίδων, i. e. their slaughter, Id.*Tr.*564 (lyr.); so Ἕκτορος.. κ. σφαγαί Id.*Rh.*606. **2.** *cut off from the head*, κ. χλιδαί one's *shorn* locks, S.*El.*52. **II.** parox., Act., *beheading*, c. gen., Ἑλλάδος Lyc.187.

καρβάζω and **καρβανίζω**, = βαρβαρίζω, Hsch.

κάρβᾰνος, ον, = βάρβαρος, *outlandish, foreign*, A.*Supp.*914; χείρ Id.*Ag.*1061, cf. Lyc.1387: also **καρβάν**, Hsch. s. v. ἐκαρβάνιζεν; acc. καρβᾶνα, αὐδάν A.*Supp.*129 (lyr.).

καρβάρεοι· κάραβοι, Hsch.

Κάρβας, name in Cyrene for the wind Εὖρος, Arist.*Vent.*973^{b}4 (ἀπὸ τῶν Καρβανῶν τῶν κατὰ Φοινίκην): Phoenician word, acc. to Thphr.*Vent.*62.

καρβάτινος [βᾰ], η, ον, *made of hide*, οἰκίαι Ph.*Bel.*101.31:—esp. **καρβάτιναι**, αἱ, *shoes of undressed leather, brogues*, X.*An.*4.5.14, Arist.*HA*499^{a}30, Luc.*Alex.*39:—also **καρπάτινον**, τό, Hsch.

καρβᾰτιών, ῶνος, ὁ, *engine* of war, βάλλοντες λίθοις ἀπὸ τῶν κ. Ph. *Bel.*92.28 codd. (fort. καρβατίνων (sc. οἰκιῶν)).

κάρβις· μαστροπός, Hsch.

κάρβων, ωνος, ὁ, Lat. *carbo*, *coal*, *PMasp.*58viii14 (vi A. D.): pl., Anon. *in EN*428.13.

κάρδακες, οἱ, Persian name for *foreign mercenaries*, Theopomp. (Hist. or Com.) ap.Paus.Gr.*Fr.*222, Plb.5.79.11 and 82.11: derived by Str.15.3.18 from Pers. κάρδα, = τὸ ἀνδρῶδες καὶ πολεμικόν.

καρδᾰμ-άλη, ἡ, Persian *loaf* or *cake made of* κάρδαμον, Trypho ap. Ath.3.114f, Hsch., Phot.:—also **καρδάμη** Poll.6.76; **παρδαμάλη** Phot. **-ίζω**, *to be like cress*, τί καρδαμίζεις; why *chatter so much about cresses*, i. e. about nothing? Ar.*Th.*617. **-ίνη**, ἡ, = σισύμβριον, Dsc.2.128. **2.** = ἰβηρίς, Aët.12.1. **3.** = κάρδαμον, Ps.-Dsc. 2.155. **-ίς**, ίδος, ἡ, = κάρδαμον, Nic.*Al.*533, Plu.2.466d. **-ον**, τό, *nose-smart*, *Lepidium sativum*, of which the seed was eaten like mustard, X.*Cyr.*1.2.8, *POxy.*1429.5, Ael.*VH*3.39: pl., Ar.*Nu.*234; κάρδαμ' ἐσκευασμένα Eub.36: metaph., βλέπειν κάρδαμα look *sharp and stinging*, Ar.*V.*455: prov. of worthless things, ὅσῳ διαφέρει σῦκα καρδάμων Henioch.4.2.

καρδᾰμύσσω, = σκαρδαμύσσω, Hsch., *EM*490.53.

καρδάμωμον [ᾰ], τό, *cardamum*, *Elettaria Cardamomum*, Thphr. *HP*9.7.2, Dsc.1.6, etc. **II.** = γεράνιον, Ps.-Dsc.3.116. (For καρδαμάμωμον.)

καρδάνη, = κάρδαμον, *Gloss.*

καρδί-α, ἡ, Ion. **καρδίη**, Ep. **κρᾰδίη** (καρδίη in Hom. only in καρδίῃ ἄλληκτον πολεμίζειν ἠδὲ μάχεσθαι Il.2.452, al., καρδία always in Trag., exc. in some dact. and anap. verses, A.*Pr.*881, *Th.*781, E.*Med.*99, *Hipp.*1274); Aeol. **κάρζα** *EM*407.21 (but **καρδία** Sapph.2.6); Cypr. **κορζία** (Paph.), Hsch. (fort. κόρζα):—*heart*, ἐν δέ τέ οἱ κραδίη μεγάλα στέρνοισι πατάσσει Il.13.282; κραδίη δέ μοι ἔξω στηθέων ἐκθρῴσκει, of one panic-stricken, 10.94; πηδᾷ ἡ κ. Pl.*Smp.*215e, cf. Ar.*Nu.*1391 (lyr.): esp. as the seat of feeling and passion, as rage or anger, οἰδάνεται κραδίη χόλῳ Il.9.646; τέτλαθι δή, κραδίη Od.20.18, cf. E.*Alc.* 837; καρδίης πλέως full of *heart*, Archil.58.4; of fear or courage, κυνὸς ὄμματ' ἔχων, κραδίην δ' ἐλάφοιο Il.1.225; [σφηκῶν] κραδίην καὶ θυμὸν ἔχοντες 16.266; ἐν μέν οἱ κραδίῃ θάρσος βάλε 21.547, etc.; ὀρχεῖται καρδία φόβῳ A.*Ch.*166; θερμὴν ἐπὶ ψυχροῖσι κ. ἔχεις S.*Ant.* 88; τὸν νέον τίνα οἴει κ. ἴσχειν; what do you think are his *feelings*? Pl.*R.*492c; of sorrow or joy, ἐν κραδίῃ μέγα πένθος ἄεξε Od.17. 489; κ. καὶ θυμὸς ἰάνθη 4.548; ἄχος κραδίην καὶ θυμὸν ἵκανεν Il.2.171, cf. 10.10, B.10.85, etc.; καρδίην ἰαίνεται Archil.36; κεκαινόχρως.. πάλλεταί μου κ. A.*Supp.*785; ὦ τάλαινα κ. ψυχή τ' ἐμή E.*Or.*466; of love, Sapph. l. c., etc.; ἐκ τῆς κ. φιλεῖν Ar.*Nu.*86; φιλέειν ἀπὸ κ. Theoc.29.4 (but ἐρεῖν τἀπὸ κ. to speak *freely*, E.*IA*475); λαλῆσαι ἐπὶ καρδίαν τινός speak *kindly* to.., Lxx *Jd.*19.3. **2.** *inclination, desire, purpose*, ἐμ' ὀτρύνει κραδίη καὶ θυμὸς Il.10.220; πρόφρων κ. ἐν πάντεσσι πόνοισι ib.244; καρδίας δ' ἐξίσταμαι S.*Ant.*1105. **3.** *mind*, ὡς ἄνοον κραδίην ἔχες Il.21.441; κραδίη πόρφυρε Od.4.572; κραδίη προτιόσσετ' ὄλεθρον 5.389; εἰ θεάσῃ τοῖς τῆς καρδίας ὀφθαλμοῖς *Corp.Herm.* 4.11, cf. 7.2; διαλογισμοὶ ἀναβαίνουσι ἐν τῇ κ. *Ev.Luc.*24.38. **II.** *cardiac orifice of the stomach*, Th.2.49, Hp.*Prorrh.*1.72, Gal.8.338, al. **III.** *heart in wood, pith*, Thphr.*HP*3.14.1; = ἐντεριώνη, ib. 1.2.6; ἀρτεμισίας μονοκλώνου καρδίας ζ' *PMag.Berol.*1.245, cf. *PMag. Leid.V.*13.24; λαβὼν βάϊν χλωρὰν καὶ τῆς κ. κρατήσας σχίσον εἰς δύο *PMag.Leid.W.*6.51. **IV.** metaph., κ. θαλάσσης *depths* of the sea, Lxx *Ez.*27.4. **V.** Κ. Λέοντος, name of the star *Regulus*, Gem.3.5. (I.-E. *kr̥d–*, cf. Lat. *cor(d)–*, Lith. *širdis* 'heart', etc.) **-ακός**, ή, όν, *of* or *belonging to the heart*, πῦρ Rhet.ap.Eust.801.36: in Medic. sense, κ. πάθος Diog.Oen.66; συγκοπαί Gal.8.302; νόσος Alex. Aphr.*de An.*98.23. Adv. **-κῶς** Gal.8.368; κ. κινδυνεύειν S.E.*P.*1. 84. **II.** of persons, *suffering from heart disease*, Archig.ap.Gal. 9.19; but prob. = καρδιαλγής, Dsc.1.112, Ath.1.10d.

καρδῐαλγ-έω, *suffer from heartburn*, Hp.*Epid.*2.2.1. **-ής**, ές, *suffering from heartburn*, Id.*Acut.*30, Gal.6.604. **-ία**, ἡ, *heartburn*, Id.8.343, al., Ruf.ap.Orib.7.26.8. **-ικός**, ή, όν, *afflicted with heartburn*, Hp.*Epid.*3.17.ι'.

καρδιᾶτις, ιδος, ἡ, Pythag. name for *five*, *Theol.Ar.*32.

καρδιάω, = καρδιαλγέω, in Ep. part. καρδιόωντα, Nic.*Al.*581.

καρδῐηβολέω, *lay to heart*, Herod.4.52 (s. v.l.).

καρδικός, ή, όν, *heart-shaped* (?), *PMag.Berol.*2.68.

καρδῐο-βολέομαι, Pass., *to be stricken in heart, grieved*, Hsch. **-βόλος**, ον, *affecting the cardia* (v. καρδία II) *injuriously*, βρώματα

Aret.*SA*2.3; φάρμακον Ruf.ap.Orib.7.26.86. **-γνώστης**, ου, ὁ, *knower of hearts*, *Act.Ap.*1.24, 15.8. **-δαιτος**, ον, *feasting on* men's *hearts*, *PMag.Par.*1.2865. **-δηκτος**, ον, *gnawing the heart*, κ. ἐκ γυναικῶν κράτος (prob. for καρδίᾳ δηκτόν) A.*Ag.*1471 (lyr.). **-ειδής**, ές, *heart-shaped*, σχῆμα Herm. *in Phdr.*p.199 A.

κάρδιον, τό, Dim. of καρδία, *heart-shaped ornament*, *IG*11(2).161 *B* 116 (pl., Delos, iii B.C.).

καρδῐό-πληκτος, ον, gloss on ἐμβρόντητος, Sch.X.*An.*3.4.12 (ed. L. Dindorf). **-της**, *praecordia*, *Gloss.* **-τρωτος**, ον, *wounded in the heart*, Gal.1.112.

καρδῐ-ουλκέω, (ἕλκω) *draw the heart of the victim* at a sacrifice, Luc. *Sacr.*13. II. κ. φοινίκινα perh. *extract the pith* (cf. καρδία III), *Sammelb.*7188.43 (ii B.C.). **-ουλκία**, ἡ, *drawing out the heart*, Hsch. (pl.). **-ουργέω**, = καρδιουλκέω, Id. s. v. καρδιοῦσθαι.

καρδιοφύλαξ [ῠ], ἄκος, ὁ, *breastplate*, Plb.6.23.14.

καρδῐ-όω, *hearten*, Lxx *Ca.*4.9. II. in Med., = καρδιουργέω, Hsch., *EM*492.12. **-ωγμός**, ὁ, = καρδιαλγία, Hp.*Prog.*24, *Aph.* 4.17 (pl.), Dsc.1.7, Alex.Aphr.*Pr.*2.35, etc. **-ώσσω**, Att. **-ττω**, = καρδιαλγέω, *have heartburn* or *stomach-ache*, Hp.*Prog.*24, *Mul.* 1.9, Arist.*Pr.*873^{b}29, Ael.*NA*9.11, Aret.*SA*2.3, prob. l. in Ar.*Fr.* 362. II. in Sicil. Greek, = βουλιμιάω, Epich.202.

καρδοπεῖον, τό, *cover of a kneading-trough*, Hsch. II. = πανσικάπη, *muzzle*, Ar.*Fr.*301.

καρδοπογλύφος [ῠ], ον, *scooping out kneading-troughs* or other *wooden utensils*, Crates Com.6.

κάρδοπος, ἡ, *kneading-trough*, Eup.228 (pl.), Ar.*Ra.*1159; κ. πλατεῖα Pl.*Phd.*99b: generally, *wooden vessel*, Hom.*Epigr.*15.6; *mortar*, Nic.*Th.*527: Com. fem. **καρδόπη**, ἡ, coined by Ar.*Nu.*678.

κάρδος, ἡ, = κάκτος, Ath.2.70e.

κᾰρέα, ἡ, = καρύα, Phlp. *in GA*23.7, al.

κάρειον [ᾰ], τό, poet. for κάρα (A), Nic.*Fr.*74.51 (fort. καρήνοις).

Κάρειος, ὁ (sc. μήν), name of month in Western Locris, *IG*9(1). 331, *BCH*22.10.

κάρζα, Aeol. for καρδία (q. v.). **κάρη, κάρηαρ**, v. κάρα (A).

κᾰρηβᾰρ-έω, *to be heavy in the head*, *drowsy*, τὴν κεφαλὴν κ. Arist. *PA*653^{a}14; [ἰχθύδια] κ. ὑπὸ τοῦ ψόφου *bewildered*, Id.*HA*534^{a}4; *stagger* as one drunken, Ph.2.123; τῷ σώματι κ. καὶ σφάλλεσθαι Plu.*Art.* 11, cf. *Ant.*85, Q.S.6.266; *to be top-heavy*, of a spindle charged with yarn, *AP*6.160 (Antip. Sid.); μῆλα -έοντα κορύμβοις ib.5.257 (Paul. Sil.); *have a headache*, ναυτιῶντα καὶ -οῦντα ὑπὸ τοῦ σάλου Luc.*Herm.* 28:—also **-άω** Pherecr.218 (καραι- codd. Eust.), Thphr.*Od.*46 (but -βαρεῖν *HP*9.8.6), v.l. in Luc.*Lex.*13; and **-ιάω** v.l. in Ar.*Fr.*792, prob. l. in Telecl.44, cf. Sch.Opp.*H.*3.368:—the form **κάρηβοάω**, = ἰλιγγιάω is quoted by Ael.Dion.*Fr.*221, and καρηβορᾶν, καρυβοᾶν are vv.ll. in Ar. l.c. **-ής**, ές, *drowsy*, *comatose*, prob. l. in Hp. *Epid.*3.6, cf. Gal.16.579. II. *producing drowsiness*, νότος Sch. Arat.786. **-ησις**, εως, ἡ, *heaviness in the head* or *headache*, Polem. Hist.83. **-ία**, Ion. **-ίη**, ἡ, = foreg., Hp.*Acut.*49, *Aph.*5.22, Arist. *Somn.*456^{b}29, Porph.*Abst.*1.28, Agath.2.38; κ. βάκτρου, paraphrase for a 'knobby' stick, *AP*9.249 (Maec.). **-ικός**, ή, όν, *subject to headache*, Hp.*Epid.*3.17.ς´; τὸ -κόν, = καρηβαρία, Telecl. 47. II. *causing headache*, οἶνος Hp.*Acut.*50, Arist.*Fr.*106; νότος Hp.*Aph.*3.5:—so **-ίτης** [ῑ], ου, ὁ, οἶνος Sch.Ar.*Pl.*808.

κᾰρηκομόωντες, οἱ, (κομάω) *with hair on the head*, *long-haired*, epith. of the Achaians, Il.2.11, al. (sed divisim scrib.): Com. metaph., ἐχῖνοι κ. ἀκάνθαις Matro *Conv.*18:—hence Verb **καρηκομόω**, coined by Diog.*Ep.*19.

κᾰρῆναι, aor. 2 inf. Pass. of κείρω.

κάρηνον [ᾰ], τό, Dor. **κάρᾱνον** A.*Ch.*396 (lyr.), Mosch.1.12 (Ion. κάρηνον 2.87); in derivs. the ᾰ prevails: (v. κάρα A):—*head*, mostly in pl. (as always in Hom.), ἀνδρῶν κάρηνα, periphr. for ἄνδρες, Il.11.500; νεκύων ἀμενηνὰ κ. Od.10.521, etc.; βοῶν ἴφθιμα κ. Il.23.260; ἵππων ξανθὰ κ. 9.407: metaph., of mountain *peaks*, Οὐλύμποιο κ. 1.44, etc.; of towns, πολλάων πολίων κατέλυσε κάρηνα 2.117, 9.24; Μυκάλης αἰπεινὰ κ. 2.869: in pl., of a single person, κάρηνα.. Μελανίππου σπάσας E.*Fr.*537: sg. in *h.Hom.*8.12, 28.8, Mosch. ll. cc., Coluth.264, *Anacreont.*1.11.

κάρητος, κάρητι, v. κάρα (A).

καρθμός, ὁ, = κίνησις (i.e. = σκαρθμός), Hsch.

κάρθρα, τά, *wages for clipping* or *shearing*, *Edict.Diocl.*7.20; cf. κάρτρα.

κάρι, τό, dub. sens. in Hdn.Gr.1.354; ἀπὸ κάρεως ἀναθυμίασις perh. *caraway*, Gal.17(1).563; cf. κάρον, καρώ.

κᾱρῑδάριον, τό, Dim. of καρίς, Anaxandr.27 (anap.):—also **κᾱρίδιον**, τό, Arist.*HA*547^{b}17.

κᾱριδόω, (καρίς) *wriggle*, *twist about like a shrimp*, Anaxandr.37. [ῑ prob.]

καρίεντο, barbarism in Ar.*Th.*1210, for χαρίεν.

Κᾱρίζω, *act like a Carian*, Diogenian.7.65. II. *speak like a Carian*, i.e. *barbarously*, Str.14.2.28.

Κᾱρικοεργής, ές, *of Carian work*, ὄχανον Anacr.91.

Κᾱρικός, ή, όν, *Carian*, λόφος Alc.22, cf. Hdt.1.171, al.; used for εὐτελής, *worthless*, κ. τράγοι S.*Fr.*540. II. Κ. ἔλαιον a kind of *salve*, Ophel.5; Κ. φάρμακον Hp.*Ulc.*16. III. Καρικὴ μοῦσα *funeral song*, *dirge*, Pl.*Lg.*800e; Κ. αὐλήματα Ar.*Ra.*1302; Κ. μέλος Pl.Com.69.12 (dub. l.). IV. Καρική (καρίκη cod.)· ἀσύνθετος (leg. ἀσύνετος), καὶ ἄμπελος, Hsch. V. Καρικόν, τό, *Carian quarter* in Memphis, *PSI*4.409.21 (iii B.C.).

καριμοίρους· τοὺς ἐν μηδεμιᾷ μοίρᾳ, ἢ μισθοφόρους, Hsch.; cf. *κάρ.

Κᾱρίνη [ῑ], ἡ, *Carian woman*, Phan.Hist.6; Κ. παρθένος Plu.2. 246e; Κ. κύνες Poll.5.37. 2. esp. *woman hired to sing Carian dirges*; title of plays by Antiphanes and Menander.

Καρινός, ὁ (sc. μήν), a month at Byzantium, = November, dub. in *Philol.*2.248.

καριόθρεπτος, ον, dub. sens. in *PRyl.*1.35 (iii A.D.).

Κάριος [ᾱ], α, ον, = Καρικός, Hdt.8.135; esp. as epith. of Zeus, Id.1.171, 5.66, Str.14.2.23: worshipped in Thessaly and Boeotia, Phot. (Possibly from κάρα (A), cf. Καραιός.)

καριόω, aor. ἐκαρίωσα, *kill*, Hsch.

κᾱρίς (v. sub fin.), ἡ, prob. a general term for small crustaceans, incl. *shrimp* (*Crangon*) and *prawn* (*Palaemon*), Anan.5, Arist.*HA* 525^{a}33, Luc.*Merc.Cond.*3; Dor. **κουρίς** Epich.31, Sophr.26, cf. Hsch., or **κωρίς** Epich.89. [ῐ in Anan. l. c., Ar.*V.*1522 (lyr.), Cratin.283, Eup.7, 107: later ῑ, gen. ῖδος, Arar.8, Anaxandr.22, Eub.78, Archestr. *Fr.*25, Numen.ap.Ath.7.287c.]

κάρισο, barbarism in Ar.*Th.*1195, for χαρίσω.

Κᾱριστί, Adv. *in Carian language*, *barbarously*, Str.14.2.28.

Κᾱρίων, ωνος, ὁ, prop. Dim. of Κάρ, common name of slaves in Comedy, as in Ar.*Pl.*

καρκάδων, ονος, gender unknown, *the fee paid to Charon by the dead*, Phot., Suid.:—expld. by some Gramm. as name of a plant.

καρκαίρω, *quake*, of the earth, κάρκαιρε δὲ γαῖα πόδεσσιν ὀρνυμένων Il.20.157. II. ἐκάρκαιρεν· ἐπλήθυεν, and ἐκάρκαιρον· ψόφον τινὰ ἀπετέλουν, Hsch.

κάρκαρα, τά, = πίτυρα (ἐπιτυρά cod.), Semon.33.

καρκαρίς, ἡ, *load of timber*, Hsch. **κάρκαροι**· τραχεῖς, Id.

κάρκᾰρον, τό, *prison*, Sophr.147:—also **κάρκᾰρος**, ὁ, D.S.31.9: indeterm. in Vett.Val.68.26: pl. κάρκαροι, = δεσμοί, and κάρκαρα, = μάνδραι, Hsch.

καρκῐν-άς, άδος, ἡ, Dim. of καρκίνος I, Gal.6.717, Ael.*NA*7.31, Artem.2.14, Opp.*C.*2.286, *H.*1.320. **-ευτής**, οῦ, ὁ, *crab-catcher*, Artem.2.14. **-ηθρον**, τό, = *Polygonum*, *Gloss.*; f.l. for -ωθρον, Dsc.4.4. **-ίας**, ου, ὁ, *crab-coloured gem*, Plin.*HN*37.187. **-ιον**, τό, Dim. of καρκίνος, *hermit-crab*, *Pagurus*, Arist.*HA*529^{b}20; a smaller species, ib.547^{b}17. II. = καρκίνος III, Hp.*Morb.*2.37. III. a kind of *slipper*, in pl., Herod.7.128.

καρκῐνο-βάτης, ου, ὁ, *walking like a crab*, Aristonym.2 (sed leg. -βήτης). **-ειδής**, ές, *of the crab kind*, τὰ κ. Arist.*PA*684^{a}14, cf. Ael.*NA*6.20. II. *like a still*, Zos.Alch.p.140 B. (cf. *intr.* p.149 B.). **-πους**, πουν, gen. ποδος, *crab-footed*, i.e. *lame*, *IG*3. 171*a*.

καρκίνος [ῐ], ὁ, heterocl. pl. καρκίνα (v. sub fin.: on the accent v. Hdn.Gr.2.926):—*crab*, Epich.53, Hellanic.103 J., S.*Ichn.*298, Ar. *Eq.*608, Pl.*Euthd.*297c, Batr.299; κ. ποδήνεμοι Crates Com.29.3: various species distinguished, Arist.*HA*525^{a}34, cf. 601^{a}17, al.: prov., οὔποτε ποιήσεις τὸν καρκίνον ὀρθὰ βαδίζειν Ar.*Pax* 1083; εἴς μ' ὁρεῦσα καρκίνου μέζον 'with saucer-eyes', Herod.4.44. II. *Cancer*, as a sign in the zodiac, Eudox.ap.Hipparch.1.2.18, Euc. *Phaen.*p.10 M., Arat.147, etc. III. *eating sore* or *ulcer*, *cancer*, = καρκίνωμα, Hp.*Aph.*6.38, D.25.95, Gal.10.83. IV. from likeness of shape to crab's claws, 1. *pair of pincers*, Aen.Tact.20.3, 32.5, *IG*11(2).165.11 (Delos, iii B.C.), *AP*6.92 (Phil.), Ath.10.456d; κ. σιδηροῦς *POxy.*521.14 (ii A.D.); used as an instrument of torture, D.S.20.71: in Surgery, *forceps*, κ. ἰατρικός *IG*2^{2}.47.16: metaph., λήψεται τὸν τράχηλον ἐντόνως ὁ κ. E.*Cyc.*609. 2. = ζυγώματα, bones of the temples, Poll.2.85. 3. a kind of *shoe*, Pherecr.178. 4. a kind of *bandage*, Heliod.ap.Orib.48.54 tit., Gal.18(1).777. 5. *pair of compasses*, Ph.*Bel.*55.25, Ph.2.192, Gal.*Opt.Doctr.*3, S.E.*M.* 10.54: heterocl. pl., καρκίνα σπειροῦχα *AP*6.295.5 (Phan.). 6. *still*, implied in καρκινοειδής II (q. v.). V. pr. n. of Attic tragedian, hence prov., Καρκίνου ποιήματα, = τὰ αἰνιγματώδη, Men.525; Megarian pr. n. **Κερκίνος** *SIG*201.12 (iv B.C.). (Cf. Lat. *cancer*, Skt. *karkaṭas* 'crab'.)

καρκῐνόχειρες, ων, *with crab's claws for hands*, Luc.*VH*1.35.

καρκῐν-όω, *make crab-like*, κ. τοὺς δακτύλους *crook* one's fingers *like crab's claws*, Antiph.55.15:—Pass., of roots, *spread crab-wise*, Thphr.*HP*1.6.3, *CP*3.21.5:—also in Act., *cause to spread*, ὁ χειμὼν πιλώσας καὶ καρκινώσας τὰς ῥίζας ib.3.23.5. II. in Pass., also, *suffer from cancer*, Hp.*Nat.Mul.*31; *become cancerous*, ἐκινδύνευσεν καρκινωθῆναι τὰ ἕλκεα Id.*Mul.*1.40. **-ώδης**, ες, = καρκινοειδής, Arist.*PA*683^{b}31, Plu.2.980b. II. *cancerous*, Dsc.*Eup.*2.72, Ruf. ap.Orib.45.11.1; ὄγκος Gal.18(1).80, Alex.Aphr.*Pr.*1.92. **-ωθρον**, τό, = ψίλωθρον, Sch.Nic.*Th.*902; = πολύγονον ἄρρεν, prob. in Dsc. 4.4. **-ωμα**, ατος, τό, = καρκίνος III, Hp.*Epid.*5.101, 7.111, Xenophon Med.ap.Ruf.ap.Orib.45.11.2, Dsc.2.10, Plu.2.65d. **-ωσις**, εως, ἡ, *formation of a cancerous growth*, Aët.16.41 (pl.).

Καρκώ· Λαμία, Hsch.

κάρμα, ατος, τό, (κείρω) *wool shorn off*, Hsch.; *cream skimmed off*, Id.

κάρμορον· τὸν κηριγμεμορημένον, Hsch.

καρναβάδιον, τό, *caraway*, *Carum Carvi*, *Gp.*9.28.2.

Καρνεᾶται, οἱ (cf. sq.), unmarried ministrants of Apollo, Hsch.

Καρνειάσιον, τό, (sc. ἄλσος) *grove sacred to Apollo Carneus*, *IG* 5(1).1390.54, al. (Andania, i B.C.): written **Καρνάσιον** in Paus.4.33. 5, al.

Κάρνειος, ὁ, (κάρνος) title of Apollo in Peloponnesus, Pi.*P.*5.80, Call.*Ap.*71, etc.:—hence **Κάρνεια**, τά, (Κάρνεα metri gr., Theoc.5. 83) *festival held in his honour* by Dorians, esp. by the Spartans, Hdt.

7.206, Th.5.75, SIG735.25 (Argos, i B.C.), etc.; τὰ Κ. νικᾶν Ath.14.635e; πανηγυρίζειν Plu.2.873e:—**Κάρνειος** or **Καρνήϊος**, ὁ (sc. μήν), name of month in which the festival was held, E.Alc.449 (lyr.), Th.5.54, cf. IG4.1485 (Epid.), GDI5009 (Crete), etc.; Κάρνειαι θυσίαι at Argos, IG4.620.

κάρνειος Δωρικός dub. l. in Thphr.HP3.16.4.

Καρνεονίκης [ῑ], ου, Dor. -ας, α, ὁ, victor in the Carnean games, IG 5(1).82,209 (Sparta): in pl., K., οἱ, title of work by Hellanicus.

κάρνη· ζημία, Hsch.

κάρνον, τό, Gallic horn, Hsch. II. cart, PFlor.140.2, al. (iii A.D.):—hence **καρνάριος**, ὁ, carter, ib.207.5, al.

κάρνος, ὁ, (cf. κέρας) expld. by Hsch. as βόσκημα, πρόβατον, i.e. ram:—hence **καρνοστάσιον**, τό, pen, fold, Id. II. = φθείρ, Id.

κάρνυξ, ὁ, = κάρνον I, Celtic word in Sch.T Il.18.219, Eust.1139.57.

κάροινον, τό, sweet wine boiled down, καροίνου Μεονίου Edict.Diocl. 2.13 (v.l. καρυηνου), cf. Hippiatr.2, Gloss.; οἶνος **Καρύϊνος** produced in Maeonia, Gal.15.632, 6.801, al. II. ἀβόλλης, χιτὼν καροΐνος perh. = καρύϊνος, nut-brown, Stud.Pal.20.46.13 (iii A.D.), cf. POxy. 929.9 (ii/iii A.D.), unless a geographical name, cf. I.

καρόκερκος, ὁ, name of constellation, Head and Tail of Dragon (Οὐροβόρος), Cat.Cod.Astr.7.123.

κάρον [ᾰ], τό, = καρώ, Theb.Ostr.135 (i A.D.); also v.l. for καρώ, Dsc.3.57. II. = μεγάλη ἀκρίς, Hsch.

κάροπερ· ἔπακμος παῖς, Hsch. **καρορύς**· ὕδρα (Cret.), Id.

κάρος [ᾰ], ὁ, heavy sleep, torpor, κ. καὶ κραιπάλη Arist.Pr.873^{b}14, cf. A.R.2.203, Phld.D.1.18, Str.16.4.19, Max.Tyr.16.1, Gal.8.231; κάρῳ προσφερὴς κατάληψις Iamb.Myst.3.2: pl., μελαγχολίαι καὶ κάροι καὶ λήθαργοι Stoic.3.57; drowsiness, Luc.Am.39.

καρός· κωφός, οἱ δὲ σκοτόδινος, Hsch. **κάρουα**, Lacon., = κάρυα, Id.

καροῦχα, ἡ, Lat. carruca, carriage, Sm.Is.66.20, Sch.E.Ph.847:—also -οῦχον, τό, Edict.Diocl.15.37:—Dim. -ούχιον, τό, PFlor.335.8 (iii A.D.), Gloss.:—also -ουχάριος, cisiarius, mulio, ib.

καροῦχος· εὐχερής, εὔκολος, Hsch.

κᾰροφόρος, ον, soporiferous, Gloss.

κᾰρόω, plunge into deep sleep or torpor, stun, stupefy, πληγαὶ καροῦσαι Hp.Art.30; of wine, Antipho Soph.34, Anaxandr.3, cf. Ath.1.33a; ὀδμὴ καροῦσα a stupefying smell, Id.15.675d:—Pass., to be stupefied, ὑπὸ βροντῆς, of certain fish, Arist.HA602^{b}23; ὑπὸ μύρου, of bees, Id.Mir.832^{a}3; ὑπὸ τῶν εὐωδιῶν Str.16.4.19; θανάτῳ κεκαρωμένα..πέλωρα Theoc.24.59; τραύμασι D.H.3.19, cf. Plu.Art.11; τὴν διάνοιαν D.H.Th.34; of drunken sleep, Lxx Je.28(51).39.

καρπαία, ἡ, mimic dance of the Thessalians, in which a peasant scuffles with a cattle-stealer, τὴν καρπαίαν..ἐν τοῖς ὅπλοις ὀρχεῖσθαι X.An.6.1.7, cf. Ath.1.15f:—also **κάρπεα**, ἡ, Maced., acc. to Hsch.

καρπᾰ́λῐμος [πᾰ], ον, (κάλπη A) Ep. Adj. swift, πόδες Il.16.342,809, A.R.3.280, cf. Ar.Th.957 (lyr.): more freq. in Adv. -μως swiftly, Il.1.359, etc. 2. eager, ravenous, γέννες Pi.P.12.20.

καρπαλίον· κάρπημα, Hsch.

καρπάσινος [πᾰ], η, ον, made of κάρπασος, Lxx Es.1.6, Str.7.2.3, D.H.2.68.

καρπάσιον, τό, flax, CPR61.13 (iii A.D.):—but λίνον **Καρπάσιον**, asbestos (from Carpasia in Cyprus), Paus.1.26.7.

κάρπᾰσος, ἡ, with heterocl. pl. κάρπασα, AP9.415.6 (Antiphil., with play on the meanings 'sails' and 'clothes'); also **κάλπᾰσος** (q.v.):—flax, Linum usitatissimum (or perh. L. angustifolium), D.H.2.68, Sch.Ar.Lys.736. 2. cotton, Peripl.M.Rubr.41 (cf. Skt. karpāsas). II. **κάρπασον**, τό, white hellebore, Veratrum album, Orph. A.922; ὀπὸς καρπάσου Archig.ap.Gal.12.445, Dsc.Alex.13; sucus carpathi, Plin.HN32.58; cf. ὀποκάρπασον, καρπησία.

καρπαστῖναι· σκορπισθῆναι, Hsch.

καρπάτινον, v. καρβάτινος.

καρπ-εία, ἡ, usufruct, enjoyment, Plb.31.21.8, Test.Epict.3.5, v.l. in Ph.2.380; τῶν κρεῶν IG12(5).721 (Andros): in pl., profits or emoluments of an office, PEleph.14.13 (iii B.C.), PTeb.6.34 (ii B.C.), etc. -εῖον, τό, = καρπός (A), Nic.Al.277: pl., Ar.Fr.177; = καρπεία, Πρακτικὰ τῆς Ἀκαδ. Ἀθηνῶν 1928.109 (Epid., iii/ii B.C.). -ευμα, ατος, τό, fruit, in pl., dub. in Sosith.2.17. -εύω, enjoy the fruits of, χώραν Hyp.Fr.107, IG9(1).693.3 (Corc.), cf. Plb.10.28.3: generally, profit by, Gal.9.790: abs., SIG1044.18 (Halic., iv/iii B.C.):—Med., Supp.Epigr.3.378B30 (Delph., ii/i B.C.).

καρπέω, inf. καρπεῖν· πληθώττειν, Hsch. **κάρπη**· τὰ σπέρματα· καὶ τήγανα ὀβελίσκους ἔχοντα, Id. **κάρπημα**, ατος, τό, gloss on καρπαλίον, Id.

καρπήσιον, τό, an aromatic plant, Valeriana Dioscoridis, chiefly brought from Asia, Gal.12.15, Alex.Trall.9.1:—but **καρπησία**, ἡ, = κάρπασος II, Paul.Aeg.5.44.

καρπ-ίζω (A), (καρπός A) enjoy the fruits of, IG12(5).243 (Paros):—elsewh. always in Med., κ. γῆν Theopomp.Hist.217b; κλῆρον PFrankf.7.7 (iii B.C.), cf. Hyp.Fr.119, Lxx Jo.5.12, IG5(2).419.14 (Phigalea, iii B.C.), ib.7.413.28, al. (Oropus, i B.C.), etc.; χρόνον Epicur.Ep.3 p.61 U.; but also, exhaust the soil, καρπίζεται τὴν γῆν μάλιστα πυρός Thphr.HP8.9.1, cf. CP4.8.1: metaph., δόξαν ἐσθλὴν E.Hipp.432; κῦδος ἐκαρπίσατο Epigr.Gr.516.4 (Aegae), cf. Supp. Epigr.3.781 (Gortyn); exploit, BGU1571 (i A.D.); βέλτιον ἐμὲ (sc. τὴν σοφίαν) καρπίζεσθαι ὑπὲρ χρυσίον Lxx Pr.8.19. II. make fruitful, fertilize, E.Ba.408 (lyr.), Hel.1328 (lyr.). -ίζω (B), (κάρφος II) enfranchise a slave by touching him with the rod, καρπίζομαι ἐπὶ ἐλευθερίᾳ, = Lat. adseror, Gloss. -ιμος, ον, fruit-bearing, fruitful, θέρος A.Pr.455; στάχυς, πέδον, E.Supp.31, Or.1086; καρπίμους ἐτῶν κύκλους Id.Hel.112; μυρρίναι Ar.Pax1154; κισσοῦ κλάδοι Alex.119.5; ξύλον Lxx Ge.1.11; κάρπιμα πρῷα early crops, Ar.V.264; θερίσαι κάρπιμα to reap the fruits, CIG4310.15 (Limyra), cf. PSI4.292.13 (iii A.D.); κ. [ἀγαθά] property that yields a produce, opp. ἀπολαυστικά, Arist.Rh.1361^{a}17; opp. ἄκαρπα, Id.EN1125^{a}12: metaph., ἀμέλγεις τῶν ξένων τοὺς κ. from whom money can be wrung, Ar.Eq.326.

καρπίον, τό, Dim. of καρπός (A), Thphr.Od.32, BGU1120.50 (i B.C.). II. vulgar name for ἐλλέβορος, Hippiatr.11. III. καρπία· κλονία (fort. κλωνία), Hsch.

κάρπιον, τό, screw-pine, Pandanus odoratissimus, Ctes.Fr.57.28.

Κάρπιος, ὁ, variant for Ἐπικάρπιος, title of Zeus in Arist.Mu.401^{a}19 (ap.Stob.1.1.36).

καρπ-ισμός (A), ὁ, (καρπίζω A) exhaustion, τῆς γῆς Thphr.CP4.8.2. II. profit, Arist.Pr.952^{b}6. -ισμός (B), ὁ, (καρπίζω B), -ιστεία and -ιστία, ἡ, = Lat. vindiciae, Gloss. -ιστής, οῦ, ὁ, emancipator, Arr.Epict.3.24.76, 4.1.113. -ιστικός, ή, όν, connected with emancipation, Gloss.; of a suit, = liberale judicium, ib.

καρπο-βάλσᾰμον, τό, the fruit of the balsam, Gal.14.166, v.l. in Dsc.1.58. -βόλον· τὸ σιτοβόλον ἀγγεῖον, Hsch. -βρωτος, ον, with edible fruit, ξύλον Lxx De.20.20. -γένεθλος, ον, = καρπογόνος, epith. of Apollo, AP9.525.11.

καρπογον-έω, to be productive, bear fruit, Thphr.HP9.1.1, CP3.9.2, Porph.Abst.4.20. -ία, ἡ, productiveness, X.Smp.2.25, Thphr.CP 1.5.5, Sor.1.42 (pl.), Lib.Or.25.67, Aen.Gaz.Thphr.p.54B. -ος (parox.), ον, bearing fruit, Dsc.5.141, prob. in Lyr. in Philol.80.338.

καρπο-δαιστάς, ᾶ, ὁ, Cret., distributor of produce, GDI4993 (Gortyn). -δεσμα, ων, τά, chains for the arms, armlets, Luc.Lex.10: -δεσμος, ὁ, bandage for wrist, Sor.Fasc.50, Cass.Fel.24. -δέσμιος, ον, wearing a knee-halter, Horap.2.78. II. Subst. -δέσμιον, τό, armlet, POxy.1153.13 (i A.D.). -δότειρα, ἡ, giver of fruit, Orph.H.43.9. -δόχος, ον, v. καρπολόχος.

καρπολογ-έω, gather fruit, SIG1000.29 (Cos):—in Pass., of trees, Thphr.CP1.15.1. -ία, ἡ, gathering of fruit, Gp.10.78.1. -ος (parox.), ον, gathering fruit, Polyaen.3.10.9. II. title of magistrates at Thasos, BCH45.147 (iv B.C.).

καρπο-λόχος, ον, bearing fruit, of Demeter, cj. for καρποδόχος in AP12.225 (Strat.). -μᾰνής, ές, running to fruit, luxuriant, S.Fr.652. -ποιός, όν, making fruit, of Demeter, E.Rh.964:—later -ποιητικός Phlp. in GA193.21.

καρπός (A), ὁ, fruit, in Hom. and Hes. (only in sg.), usu. of the fruits of the earth, corn, ἀρούρης κ. Il.6.142; κ. δ' ἔφερε ζείδωρος ἄρουρα Hes.Op.117; κ. Δήμητρος Hdt.1.193, etc.; Δηοῦς Ar.Pl.515; κ. ἀρούρης, also of wine, Il.3.246; ἀμπέλινος κ. Hdt.1.212; so κ. alone, Ar.Nu.1119 (codd. and Sch.); but of corn, opp. Βάκχιον νᾶμα, Id.Ec.14; καρποῦ ξυγκομιδή harvest, Th.3.15; κ. λωτοῖο, κρανείης, Od.9.94, 10.242; μελιηδέα κ., of grapes, Il.18.568; κ. ἐλαίας Pi.N.10.35; τὸν ἐπέτειον κ. the crops of the year, Pl.R.470b: generally, produce, κ. ὑγρός, of honey, Porph.Abst.2.20; also κ. εὐανθὴς μήλων, of wool, Opp.H.2.22: pl., καρπῶν ἐστερήθητε διξῶν robbed of two years' produce, Hdt.8.142; καρπῶν ἀτελεῖς Id.6.46; κ. ὑγροὶ καὶ ξηροὶ produce of trees and fields, X.Oec.5.20; ξύλινοι, σιτικοὶ κ., Str.5.4.2; of fruits offered in sacrifice, BMus.Inscr.975.7 (Amathus), cf. κάρπωσις II; also of taxes paid in kind, opp. χρυσικά, PHib.1.47.5 (iii B.C.), al. 2. seed, X.Oec.16.12; defined as seed with seed-vessel, Thphr.HP1.2.1. 3. of children, Δῖοι κ. offspring of Zeus, E.Ion922 (lyr.). II. returns, profits, οἱ κ. οἱ ἐκ τῶν ἀγελῶν γενόμενοι X.Cyr.1.1.2; τῶν ἀνηλωμένων..τοὺς κ. Is.5.29. III. of actions, fruit, profit, εἰ κ. ἔσται θεσφάτοισι Λοξίου if his oracles shall bear fruit, i.e. be fulfilled, A.Th.618; γλώσσης ματαίας κ., i.e. curses, Id.Eu.831 codd.; ὁμιλίας κακῆς κάκιον οὐδέν, κ. οὐ κομιστέος Id.Th.600; οὐκ ἐξάγουσι καρπὸν οἱ ψευδεῖς λόγοι S.Fr.834, cf. Pl.Phdr.260d: freq. in Pi., κ. ἐπέων οὐ κατέφθινε, i.e. poesy, I.8(7).50; κ. φρενῶν wisdom, P.2.74; κ. φρενός, of his own ode, O.7.8; ἥβας κ., of the bloom of youth, ib.6.58, P.9.109; later, reward, profit, ἐπιτηδευμάτων Epicur.Sent.Vat.27; ὅπου ὁ κίνδυνος μέγας, καὶ ὁ κ. Diog.Oen.27; κ. νίκης Hdn.8.3.6: freq. in NT, κ. εἰρηνικὸς δικαιοσύνης Ep.Hebr.12.11, etc. (Cf. Lat. carpo, Engl. harvest.)

καρπός (B), ὁ, wrist, Il.24.671, Od.24.398, Hp.Fract.3, Arist.HA 494^{a}2, etc.; ἐπὶ καρπῷ χερός E.Ion1009; καρποὶ χειρῶν ib.891, cf. X.Cyr.6.4.2. (Perh. cf. ONorse huerfa 'turn round'.)

καρπο-σπόρος, ον, sowing fruit, Man.4.256. -τελής, ές, bringing fruit to perfection, fruitful, A.Supp.688.

καρποτόκ-εια, ἡ, poet. fem. of καρποτόκος, Nonn.D.21.26. -έω, bear fruit, Thphr.CP5.2.3, Ph.1.444. -ία, ἡ, bearing of fruit, Thphr.HP1.2.1, CP2.1.2 (pl.). -ος (parox.), ον, bearing fruit, epith. of Demeter, v.l. in AP12.225 (Strat.), of Isis, APl.4.264: metaph., Ph.1.53.

καρπο-τρόφος, ον, rearing or ripening fruit, δρῦς Lyc.1423: metaph., ἥβαι E.Ion475 (lyr.); epith. of Demeter, Milet.7.64; of the clouds, Orph.H.21.1. -φᾰγέω, live on fruit, Arist.HA593^{a}15; κ. πρώτης δρυὸς Porph.Abst.2.5. -φάγος [φᾰ], ον, living on fruit, opp. σαρκοφάγος, παμφάγος, ζῷα Arist.HA488^{a}15, cf. Pol.1256^{a}25, Max.Tyr.35.7. -φθόρος, ον, spoiling fruit, δένδρων AP9.256 (Antiphan.), cf. Orph.Fr.285.55.

καρποφορ-έω, bear fruit, X.Vect.1.3, Arist.GA755^{b}10, Ph.1.602, al., Orph.Fr.255: metaph., of virtue, Ph.1.154; τῷ θεῷ Ep.Rom.7.4; also τῷ θανάτῳ ib.5:—Med., Ep.Col.1.6, BMus.Inscr.918

(Halic.):—Pass., Ptol. *Tetr.*80. **-ημα**, ατος, τό, *fruit borne*, Eust. 1572.33. **-ία**, ἡ, *fruit-bearing*, Ocell.4.9 (pl.), Ph.1.105, *Cod.Just.* 1.3.38.2 (pl.). **-ος** (parox.), ον, *fruit-bearing, fruitful*, of trees, Hdt. 1.193, 2.156, X.*Cyr.*6.2.22, etc.; of lands, Λιβύα, πεδία, Pi.*P.*4.6, E. *Hel.*1485 (lyr.); τῇ κ. γαίῃ *Sammelb.*6598 (iii A.D.), al.; of Demeter, τὴν κ. βασίλειαν Ar.*Ra.*384 (lyr.), cf. Paus.8.53.7, *CIG*4082 (Pessinus), *IG*12(5).226 (Paros), *SIG*820.5 (Ephesus, i A.D.): hence of Agrippina, *IG*12(2).212 (Mytilene), *IGRom.*4.1300 (Aeolis, in fem. -φόρα); κ. καιροί *Act.Ap.*14.17.

καρπο-φύλαξ [ῠ], ἄκος, ὁ, *watcher of fruit*, *AP*6.22 (Zonas). **-φυλλον**, τό, = δάφνη Ἀλεξανδρεία, Plin.*HN*15.131.

καρπόχειρ, late word for μετακάρπιον, Eust.1572.38.

καρπόω, *bear fruit* or *bear as fruit*, metaph., ὕβρις γὰρ ἐξανθοῦσ' ἐκάρπωσε στάχυν ἄτης A.*Pers.*821:—Pass., τὰ πλεῖστα τῶν ῥιζοφύτων καρπωθέντα Ocell.1.13. 2. *offer* by way of sacrifice, Lxx *Le.*2.11; ἐπὶ τοῦ βωμοῦ, of burnt-offerings, *SIG*1025.33 (Cos, iv/iii B.C.):—so in Pass., ib.997.9 (Smyrna), cf. Hsch. II. *take as fruit* or *produce*, Lxx *De.*26.14:—elsewh. in Med., καρπόομαι *get fruit for oneself*, i.e., 1. *reap crops from*, c. acc. rei, [ἀρούρας] Hdt.2.168; χθόνα A.*Pr.*851, *Supp.*253; δὶς τοῦ ἐνιαυτοῦ τὴν γῆν καρποῦσθαι *to crop* the land twice a year, Pl.*Criti.*118e: metaph., βαθεῖαν ἄλοκα διὰ φρενὸς καρπούμενος A.*Th.*593: hence, *exhaust, drain, exploit*, καρπουμένῳ τὴν Ἑλλάδα Ar.*V.*520, cf. Isoc.4.133, 166; οὐσίας D.19.249. 2. *enjoy the usufruct* or *interest* of money, ἔδωκεν ἑβδομήκοντα μνᾶς καρπώσασθαι Id.27.5; τοὺς λιμένας καὶ τὰς ἀγορὰς καρποῦσθαι *to derive profits from*..., Id.1.22; ἔθνη X.*HG*6.1.12; ἰδίᾳ κ. τὰς τῆς πόλεως συμφοράς Lys.25.25; [πλεονεξίαν] D.23.126: in pf. Pass., τὸ ἐργαστήριον κεκαρπωμένος *having enjoyed the profits of* the shop, Id.27.47: abs., *make profit*, Ar.*Ach.*837. 3. *enjoy the free use of*, τὰ αὐτοῦ ἀγαθὰ γιγνόμενα Th.2.38; τὴν τῶν πολεμίων [χώραν], τὰς τῶν θεῶν τιμάς, X. *Ages.*1.34; τὴν οἰκείαν ἀδεῶς κ. D.1.25, cf. 28. 4. simply, *enjoy*, ἄελπτον ὄμμα.. φήμης S.*Tr.*204; τἀμὰ.. λέχη E.*Andr.*935; ἐλευθερίαν Th.7.68; τὴν σοφίαν Pl.*Euthd.*305e; ἡδονὴν ταύτην Id.*Phdr.* 252a, cf. 240a, etc.; ἀσφάλειαν καὶ εὔκλειαν X.*Cyr.*8.2.22; τὴν δόξαν τινός D.20.69; τὴν ἡλικίαν Id.59.19; δωρεάς Plu.*Them.*31: in bad sense, ἰδίας καρποῦσθαι λύπας Hp.*Flat.*1; φρενῶν τὴν ἁμαρτίαν A.*Ag.* 502; τὰ ψευδῆ καλά ib.621; πένθη E.*Hipp.*1427; ἄπαιδα κ. βίον Id. *Fr.*571.3; τὰ μέγιστα ὀνείδη Pl.*Smp.*183a; λοιδορίας Phld.*Vit.* p.34 J.

καρπύλη, ἡ, an *Indian plant*, Clitopho ap.Stob.4.36.22.

καρπυραί· ξύλων ξηρῶν κοῖται, Hsch.; cf. καρφηρός.

καρπ-ώδης, ες, *fruitful*, ἔλαιον Orac.ap.Phleg.*Fr.*1 J., cf. *Gloss.* **-ωμα**, ατος, τό, *fruit*, A.*Supp.*1001; *profit*, Hsch. II. *offering of fruits*, Lxx *Nu.*18.9; cf. κάρπωσις II. **-ώνης**, ου, ὁ, *buyer of fruit*, *IG*2².1100 (ii A.D.), *PFay.*133.12 (iv A.D.). **-ωνία**, ἡ, *fruit-buying*, *PLond.ined.*2338 (iii B.C.), *BGU*830.8 (i A.D.). **-ώσιμος**, ον, *yielding fruit, profitable*, Hermipp.Hist.81. **-ωσις**, εως, ἡ, *use, profit*, X.*Cyr.*4.5.16. II. *offering of fruits*, Lxx *Le.*4.10, al., *IG* 3.77 (pl., ii A.D.); *sacrifice* to Aphrodite at Amathus, Hsch. **-ωτός**, όν, (καρπός B) *reaching to the wrist*, κ. χιτών a coat *with sleeves down to the wrist*, Lxx 2*Ki.*13.18, 19.

καρρέζουσα, Ep. for καταρρέζουσα, Il.5.424.

καρρ-ικός, ή, όν, *sufficient to fill a wagon*, γόμος *OGI*629.16 (Palmyra, ii A.D.). **-ίον** καθεδρωτόν, *covinnus*, *Gloss.*

κάρρον, τό, *car, cart*, Lxx 1*Es.*5.55 (cod. A), *PGoodsp.Cair.*30 xxix 21 (ii A.D.), *Edict.Diocl.*15.38a: **κάρρος**, ὁ, ib.39:—hence **καρροπηγός**, ὁ, and **-ποιός**, ὁ, *coach-builder*, *Gloss.*

κάρρων, ον, gen. ονος, *stronger, better*, Dor. for κρείσσων, Alcm.89, Epich.165, Sophr.59, Ti.Locr.94c, *AP*7.413.7 (Antip.), Plu.*Lyc.*25; κάρρον ἐστίν c. inf., it is *better* to.., Cerc.5.13:—hence **καρρόθεν**, Adv. *from something better*, Dam.ap.Suid. s. v. κάρρων.

κάρσιος, α, ον, *crosswise*, Hsch. Adv. -ίως Suid.; cf. ἐγκάρσιος.

κάρτᾰ (cf. κράτος), Adv., freq. in Ion. and Trag., rare in Com. and Att. Prose (v. infr.):—with Adjs. and Advbs., *very, extremely*; with Verbs, *very much*; κ. κακῶς ῥιγῶ Hippon.16; ἐσθλοὺς κ. μαχητάς Aristeas Epic.*Fr.*3; κ. ἀπὸ θερμέων χωρέων *very* hot, Hdt.2.27; κ. θεραπεύειν τινά, opp. μετρίως, Id.3.80; κ. δεόμενος Id.8.59; κ. ὀξὺ Hp. *Acut.*58; κ. πρευμενεῖς A.*Ag.*840; κ. ἰδεῖν ὁμόπτερος Id.*Ch.*174; εἰ καὶ μακρὰ κ. ἐστίν S.*Tr.*1218; ὥς σου κ. νῦν μνείαν ἔχω E.*Med.*328, cf. 222, etc.; once in Pl., πηλοῦ κ. βραχέος *Ti.*25d; ληρεῖς ἔχων κ. Ar. *Av.*342 (troch.). 2. *surely, in very deed*, κ. δ' ἔστ' ἐγχώριος A.*Th.* 413; κ. δ' ὢν ἐπώνυμος *true* to thy name, Id.*Eu.*90, cf. *Th.*658; κ. δ' εἰμὶ τοῦ πατρός *all* on the father's side, Id.*Eu.*738; κ. δ' εἴσ' ὅμαιμοι Id.*Th.*939 (lyr.); ἦ κ. Id.*Ag.*592, 1252, S.*El.*312, 1278, etc.; σὺ δὲ κ. φείδῃ Amips.22. 3. καὶ κ., used to increase the force of a previous statement, τὰ ἀνέκαθεν λαμπροί, ἀπὸ δὲ Ἀλκμέωνος.. καὶ κ. λαμπροί Hdt.6.125; esp. in dialogue, *yes, verily*, ἦ γάρ τινες ναίουσι..; Answ. καὶ κ.. S.*OC*65; ἆρ' ἄν τί μου δέξαιο..; Answ. καὶ κάρτα γ' E.*Hipp.* 90; once in Ar., καὶ κ. μέντἂν.. καθείλκετε *Ach.*544; in Hdt. also, τὸ κ. 1.71, 4.181; esp. with a slightly iron. sense, *with a vengeance*, ἐς ὃ δὴ καὶ τὸ κ. ἐπύθοντο 1.191, cf. 3.104, 6.52.

καρτάζω (in Pass.) and **καρταίνω**, = καρτύνω, Hsch.

καρτάζωνος, ὁ, = μονόκερως, Ael.*NA*16.20.

καρταίπους, ὁ, ἡ, πουν, τό, gen. ποδος, = κραταίπους (q.v.), Pi.*O.* 13.81: neut. pl., **καρταίποδα**, τά, *larger cattle, beasts*, *Leg.Gort.*4. 36, al.: sg., **καρταῖπος**, τό, *GDI*4998 i 17 (Gortyn), al.

καρτάλαμον, τό, = περίζωμα, Lyd.*Mag.*2.13:—Dim. **-άμιον**, τό, = *fiscella*, *Gloss.*

κάρταλλος, ὁ, *basket with pointed bottom*, Lxx 4*Ki.*10.7, al., *Sammelb.*6801.4 (iii B.C.), Ph.1.694, Hsch.; also, of a *feast*, Ph.2.298 (κάρταλος cod.):—Dim. **καρτάλλιον**, τό, *Sammelb.*6801.26 (iii B.C.), *Gloss.*; cf. κερτύλλιον.

καρτέον, (κείρω) *one must shear*, Muson.*Fr.*21 p.115 H.

καρτερ-αίχμης, -αύχην, v. κρατερ-.

καρτερ-έω, *to be steadfast, patient*, S.*Ph.*1274, Men.*Sam.*112, etc.; ῥᾷον παραινεῖν ἢ παθόντα καρτερεῖν E.*Alc.*1078, cf. Th.7.64; κ. μάχῃ E.*Heracl.*837; κ. ἐλπίδι τινός Th.2.44: freq. with a Prep., κ. πρός τι *to hold up* against a thing, e.g. πρὸς ἡδονάς τε καὶ λύπας Pl.*R.*556c; πρὸς λιμὸν καὶ ῥῖγος X.*Cyr.*2.3.13; ἐπὶ τοῖς παροῦσι Isoc.6.48, cf. Pl. *La.*194a; κ. ἐν ταῖς ἡδοναῖς *to be patient* or *temperate* in.., Id.*Lg.* 635c; ἐν πολέμῳ Id.*La.*193a; κ. ἀπὸ τοῦ ὕπνου *refrain* therefrom, Ael.*NA*13.13: c. part., *persevere* in doing, οἱ δ' ἐκαρτέρουν πρὸς κῦμα λακτίζοντες E.*IT*1395; κ. ἀναλίσκων ἀργύριον φρονίμως Pl.*La.*192e; ἀκούων Aeschin.3.241; κ. ἐν ἐπιτηδεύμασιν Isoc.2.32; also τὰ δείν' ἐκαρτέρουν *was* strangely *obdurate* or *obstinate*, S.*Aj.*650: in later Prose meaning little more than *wait*, καρτέρει καὶ θεώρει *wait* and see, Lxx 2*Ma.*7.17; οὐ κ. μέχρι θαλάμων ἐλθεῖν S.E.*M.*1.291. II. c. acc. rei, *bear patiently, endure*, τὰ δ' ἀδύναθ' ἡμῖν καρτερεῖν οὐ ῥᾴδιον E.*IA*1370; κ. θεοῦ δόσιν Id.*Alc.*1071; τῷ σώματι τὰ συντυγχάνοντα X.*Mem.*1.6.7; τὸν τῶν ὑπεροπτικῶν ὄγκον Isoc.1.30; πολλὴν κακοπάθειαν Arist.*Pol.*1278ᵇ27:—Pass., κεκαρτέρηται τἀμά my *time for patience is over*, E.*Hipp.*1457.—In Hsch., οὐ καρτεριάδδει· οὐ φρόνιμος εἶ, should prob. be οὐ καρτερίδδει (Lacon. for καρτερίζει). **-ημα**, ατος, τό, *act of endurance*, Pl.*Men.*88c (pl.). **-ησις**, εως, ἡ, *bearing patiently, patience*, Id.*La.*193d: in pl., Id.*Lg.*637b. 2. c. gen., *patient endurance of* a thing, αἱ τοῦ χειμῶνος κ. Id.*Smp.*220a; αἱ κ. τῶν ἀλγηδόνων Id.*Lg.*633b. **-ία**, ἡ, *patient endurance, perseverance*, opp. μαλακία, X.*Cyr.*8.8.15, cf. Pl.*La.*192b, al.; κ. ἡ περὶ τοὺς πόνους D.H.2.28; distd. from ἐγκράτεια (self-control), Arist.*EN*1150ᵇ1: pl., εἴ πού τινες.. κ. πρὸς ἅπαντα.. λέγονται Pl.*R.*390d. **-ιάζω, -ίζω**, v. καρτερέω (sub fin.). **-ικός**, ή, όν, *capable of endurance, patient*, Amips.9, Isoc.8.109, etc.; πρὸς χειμῶνα X.*Mem.*1.2.1 (Sup.); ῥώμη κ. πρὸς ἀρετήν Pl.*Def.*412a: Sup., Luc.*Anach.*38; opp. μαλακός and distd. from ἐγκρατής (cf. καρτερία), Arist.*EN*1150ᵃ33. Adv. -κῶς ib. 1179ᵇ33, Marin.*Procl.*12.

καρτερο-βρόντης, ου, ὁ, *thundering mightily*, Pi.*Fr.*155. **-εις**, εσσα, εν, = καρτερός, *Epic.Alex.Adesp.*9 iv 7. **-θῡμος**, ον, *strong-hearted*, of heroes, Od.21.25, Il.13.350; Μυσοί 14.512; [Ζεύς], Ἔρις, Hes.*Th.*476, 225: generally, *strong, mighty*, ἄνεμοι ib.378. **-πληγής**, ές, *striking fiercely*, D.S.5.34 (v.l. -πλῆγες, nom. pl.). **-πονος**, ον, *bearing labours stoutly*, Sch.Opp.*H.*1.35.

καρτερός, ά, όν, (κάρτος) = κρατερός (q.v.), *strong, staunch*, φάλαγγες Il.5.592; καὶ εἰ μάλα κ. ἐστιν [Hector] 13.316; Ἡρακλῆς ὁ κ. Ar.*Ra.*464: c. inf., κ. ἐστι μάχῃ ἔνι φῶτας ἐναίρειν Il.13.483; πολέμῳ ἔνι κ. ἐσσι 9.53; Ζεὺς Τυφῶ -ώτερος μάχῃ A.*Th.*517; τὰ καρτερώτατα *the strongest*, S.*Aj.*669. 2. c. gen., *possessed of, in control of, master of*, Ἀσίης Archil.26; οὐκέτι τῆς αὐτοῦ γλώσσης κ. οὔτε νόου Thgn.480; ἁμῶν Theoc.15.94; παθῶν D.H.5.8; γῆς καὶ οἰκίων *SIG*45. 28 (Halic., v B.C.); Θηβαίων Arr.*Fr.*91 J. 3. = καρτερικός, *steadfast, patient*, πρὸς πάντα X.*Cyr.*1.6.25; *obstinate*, -ώτατος ἀνθρώπων πρὸς τὸ ἀπιστεῖν Pl.*Phd.*77a; κ. πρὸς τὸ λέγειν *mighty* in disputation, Id. *Tht.*169b. 4. of things, *mighty, potent*, ὅρκος Il.19.108; κ. ἔργα deeds *of might*, 5.872; κ. ἕλκος *severe*, 16.517; κ. μάχη *strongly contested, sharp, severe*, Hdt.1.76, Th.4.43; ναυμαχίη Hdt.8.12; ἀγών Plb.1.27.11; ἀλαλά, μέριμναι, Pi.*I.*7(6).10, 8(7).13; λίθος Id.*O.*1.58, E.*Fr.*1044; κτύπος A.*Pr.*923; -ώτατον βέλος Pi.*O.*1.112; τὸ κ. *force, violence*, A.*Supp.*612; but τόλμης εἶμι πρὸς τὸ κ. *the utmost verge of*.., E.*Med.*394; κατὰ τὸ κ. in Adv. sense, Hdt.1.212, 3.65, Ar.*Ach.*622, etc.; πρὸς τὸ κ. A.*Pr.*214: abs., τὸ κ. Theoc.1.41. 5. of place, *strong*, Hdt.9.9, Th.4.3; τὸ -ώτατον τοῦ χωρίου Id.5.10; λόφος κ. Id.4.131. 6. = κύριος, *fixed, determined*, τοῦτο κ. εἶναι *SIG*45.22 (Halic., v B.C.). II. Adv. -ρῶς *strongly, violently*, Lxx 4*Ma.*15. 31, Arr.*An.*2.23.7, Luc.*Somn.*6; κ. ὑπνοῦσθαι to sleep *sound*, Hdt. 3.69. 2. *resolutely*, Ach.Tat.8.17; κ. ὑπόμενε Luc.*Prom.*21.

καρτερούντως, Adv. of καρτερέω, *strongly, stoutly*, Pl.*R.*399b, Iamb.*VP*32.220.

καρτερό-φρων, ονος, ὁ, ἡ, *stout-hearted*, *EM*745.8. **-χειρ**, χειρος, ὁ, ἡ, *strong-handed*, Ἄρης *h.Hom.*8.3; βασιλεύς *AP*9.210. 4. **-ψῡχία**, ἡ, *strength of spirit*, Lxx 4*Ma.*9.26.

καρτερόω, *strengthen*, ὄνυξι καὶ ὅπλαῖς Herm.ap.Stob.1.49.69, cf. Aq.*Ps.*30(31).25, al.

καρτερῶνυξ, καρτερώνυχος, v. κρατερ-.

κάρτη, η, a kind of *garment*, Juba Hist.85.

κάρτιστος, η, ον, Ep. for κράτιστος. **καρτομιστής**, ὁ, = κερτ-, Hsch.

καρτός, ή, όν, (κείρω) *shorn smooth*, opp. rough, of cloths, *IG*2². 1514.40. II. *chopped, sliced*, esp. of the leaves of the leek, πράσον κ. Dsc.2.149, *Eup.*2.123; also κ. κρόμμυα Gal.10.815; τὸ κ. abs., *Gp.*2.6.32. (On the accent v. Hdn.Gr.1.216.)

κάρτος, εος, τό, Ep. and Dor. for κράτος (for which it is v.l. in Hdt.8.2), *strength, vigour*, καρτεϊ καὶ σθένεϊ σφετέρῳ Il.17.322; κάρτος τε βίη τε Od.6.197; *violence, force*, κάρτεϊ νικήσας πατέρα Hes.*Th.* 73; κάρτεϊ, = βίᾳ, *Leg.Gort.*2.3, al.

κάρτρα, τά, = κάρθρα, *PLond.*1.131ʳ 111 (i A.D.).

καρτύνω, Ep. for κρατύνω (q.v.).

κάρτων, Dor. for κρείττων, *Leg.Gort.*1.15.

κᾰρύα [ῠ], ἡ, *nut-bearing tree* of various kinds, S.*Fr.*759 (pl.), Lxx *Ca.*6.10(11), Plu.2.647b, etc.; esp. *hazel, Corylus Avellana*, Thphr.

*HP*1.12.1, 3.2.3; κ. Περσική *walnut, Juglans regia*, ib.3.6.2, 3.14.4; κ. Εὐβοϊκή *sweet chestnut, Castanea vesca*, ib.5.4.2; κ. Ἡρακλεωτική *filbert*, variety of *Corylus Avellana*, ib.1.3.3; -ῶτις ib.3.3.8; cf. κάρυον.

Κᾰρύαι [ῠ], ῶν, αἱ, *Caryae*, a place in Laconia with a famous temple of Artemis, Th.5.55, etc.:—hence **Κᾰρῠᾶτις**, ιδος, ἡ, μέλισσα (prob. priestess of Artemis) St.Byz.; as Subst. esp. **1.** *Artemis*, Paus.3.10.7. **2.** *dance in honour of Artemis*, Poll.4.104; cf. καρυατίζω 2. **II. Κᾰρῠᾱτῖδες**, ων, αἱ, *priestesses of Artemis at Caryae*, Pratin.Lyr.4. **2.** Archit., *female figures used as bearing-shafts*, Lync.ap.Ath.6.241e, Vitr.1.1.5. **3.** a kind of *ear-rings*, Poll.5.97.

Κᾰρῠάτεια [ᾱτ], τά, festival of Artemis Καρυᾶτις, Phot.

κᾰρῠατίζω, *play with nuts*, Ph.1.11. **2.** dance the Καρυᾶτις, Luc.*Salt.*10.

κᾰρύδιον [ῠ], τό, Dim. of κάρυον, *small nut*, Philyll.19.

κάρυδοι· κορυδαλλοί (καρύδαλοι cod.), Hsch.

καρυδόω, *castrate* a horse, and **καρύδωσις**, εως, ἡ, *castration*, *Hippiatr.*99.

κᾰρῠ-ερία (sc. κυβεία), ἡ, *dicing for nuts*, dub. l. in Max.Tyr.6.6. **-ηδόν**, *like a* κάρυον: κ. κάταγμα fracture *like a broken nut*, i. e. *comminuted fracture*, Sor.*Fract.*10, Gal.14.792, Paul.Aeg.6.89. **-ήματα**, τά, *nuts* (Lacon.), Hsch.

καρυηνόν, τό, or **Καρυηνός**, ἡ, όν, v. κάροινον.

κᾰρῠ-ηρός, ά, όν, *nut-like*, σπέρματα Thphr.*HP*1.11.3, cf. 3.11.4. **-ῐνος**, η, ον, *of nuts*, ἔλαιον Gal.11.871; κ. χρῶμα *nut-brown*, Thphr.*Sens.*78; cf. καρύϊνος. **II.** *made of walnut-wood*, σανίδες *IG*11(2).203*B*100 (Delos, iii B.C.); ῥάβδος Lxx *Ge.*30.37, cf. *Je.*1.11. **III.** καρυΐνη, ἡ, *narrow jar*, *Gp.*13.7.2. **IV.** Καρύϊνος οἶνος, v. κάροινον. **-ΐσκος**, ὁ, Dim. of κάρυον, Lxx *Ex.*25.32, al. (pl.). **-ΐτης** [ῑ], ου, ὁ, *like a nut*, τιθύμαλλος κ., *Euphorbia Myrsinites*, Dsc.4.164.

κᾰρῠκ-άζω· ταράττω, Hsch.; cf. sq. 2. **-εία**, ἡ, *cooking with* καρύκη: hence, *rich cookery*, Ath.14.646e (pl.), Luc.*Symp.*11, *Lex.*6, Ael.*NA*4.40; ἄνευ γάρου καὶ τῆς ἄλλης κ. Gal.6.298. **2.** metaph., *meddling*, Hsch. (pl.). **-ευμα**, ατος, τό, *savoury dish*, Poll.6.56 (pl.), Phlp.*in de An.*601.16, Sch.Ar.*Eq.*342, Hsch. **-εύω**, *dress with rich sauce*, ἱερεῖα Ath.4.173d:—more freq. in Pass., ὄψα κεκαρυκευμένα Alex.163.6, cf. Men.462.7, Sor.1.51, Alciphr.3.53; ἐς ταὐτὸν κ. *make up* into one *sauce*, Men.518.7: metaph., κ. λόγον *season* a story *well*, Plu.2.55a; [ἡ ἱστορία] κ. τὰς ἀπαγγελίας τῇ ποικιλίᾳ τῶν παραδειγμάτων Agath.*Praef.* **2.** metaph., *embroil*, Erot. s.v. καρυκοειδέα, Hsch. **-η**, ἡ, *rich sauce*, invented by the Lydians, *composed of blood and spices*, Pherecr.181, Ath.12.516c, Gal.8.568, Max.Tyr.3.9, Luc.*Tim.*54: in pl., Ath.4.160b, Plu.2.664a. (Freq. written καρύκκη in codd. (as also in derivs.), and this spelling is preferred by Hdn.Gr.1.317.) **-ινος**, η, ον, *of the colour of* καρύκη, *dark-red*, X.*Cyr.*8.3.3.

κᾰρῡκο-ειδής, ές, *like* καρύκη, *of the consistency and appearance of* κ., Hp.*Epid.*4.25. **-ποιέω**, *make a* καρύκη, Ar.*Eq.*343. **-ποιός**, ὁ, *maker of a* καρύκη, Achae.12.

καρυμνόν· μέλαν, Hsch. **κάρυννος**, ὁ, a throw of the dice, Phot. **κᾶρυξ**, Dor. for κῆρυξ.

κᾰρῠο-βᾰφής, ές, *stained with walnut-juice*, *EM*492.55, cf. Hsch. s.v. καρυχρ(οῦς). **-δενδρον**, τό, *walnut-tree*, *Gloss.* **-κατάκτης**, ου, ὁ, *nut-cracker*, Pamphil.ap.Ath.2.53b, Hsch. s.v. μουκηροβαγός.

κάρῠον [ᾰ], τό, any kind of *nut*, Ar.*V.*58, *Pl.*1056, Theoc.9.21; κάρυα, = ἀκρόδρυα, Ath.2.52a (but τὰ κ. ἢ...τὰ ἀκρόδρυα Thphr.*Char.*11.4); κ. πλατέα, i. e. *filberts*, X.*An.*5.4.29; esp. of *walnuts*, Batr.31, Epich.150, Philyll.25, Gal.6.609; but this is prop. κ. βασιλικόν, Thphr.*CP*4.2.1, Agatharch.96, *PCair.Zen.*13.6 (iii B.C.), Dsc.1.125; or Περσικόν ibid.; κ. Εὐβοϊκόν *sweet chestnut*, Thphr.*HP*1.11.3, 4.5.4; also κασταναϊκόν ib.4.8.11, Agatharch.43; κ. Ἡρακλεωτικόν *filbert*, Thphr.*CP*4.2.1, *IG*2².1013.19; also κ. Ποντικόν *PCair.Zen.*12.48 (iii B.C.), Dsc.1.125, Ruf.ap.Orib.8.47.20; κ. πικρά *almonds*, Archig.ap.Gal.12.409, Erot. s.v. νίωπον; so κ. alone, Lxx *Nu.*17.8, Ph.2.162. **2.** *nut-shaped boss* as ornament, *OGI*214.49 (Branchidae, iii B.C.). **II.** *stone, kernel*, Thphr.*HP*3.9.5; κ. κοκκυμήλου ib.4.2.5. **2.** *seed* of conifers, Id.*CP*1.19.1; κ. πιτύϊνα pine-*kernels*, Diocl.*Fr.*127. **III.** = ἠρύγγη, Dsc.3.21.

κᾰρῠο-ναύτης, ου, ὁ, *one who sails in a nut*, Luc.*VH*2.38. **-πώλης**, ου, ὁ, *nut-seller*, *Jahresh.*16 *Beibl.*51, prob. rest. in *IG*2².10. **-τομία**, ἡ, dub. sens. in *Gloss.* **-φυλλον**, τό, *dried flower-bud of the clove-tree, Eugenia caryophyllata*, Alex.Trall.1.17, *Febr.*7, Paul.Aeg.7.3.

κᾱρύσσω, Dor. for κηρύσσω. **καρυστεῖναι**· κεκραγέναι (Lacon.), Hsch. **καρυτίζομαι**, = εὐφραίνομαι, Id.

κᾰρυ-χρ.̃. (sic cod.)· καρυοβαροῦς, Hsch. (fort. καρυκοχροῦς (gen. of *κᾰρῡκοχρής)· καρυοβαφοῦς). **-ώδης**, ες, *like a walnut*, σπέρμα Thphr.*CP*1.19.1; τὰ κ. Str.12.3.15. **-ῶτις**, ιδος, ἡ, *date*, Dsc.1.109. **-ωτὸς** [φοῖνιξ], ὁ, *date*-palm, *date, Phoenix dactylifera*, Str.17.1.15, Dsc.*Eup.*2.31, Gal.6.607. **II.** φιάλη καρυωτή cup *adorned with a nut-shaped boss*, *IG*11(2).161*B*30, al. (Delos, iii B.C.), *OGI*214.31 (Branchidae, iii B.C.), Semus 16; also κ. λαμπάδια Lxx *Ex.*38.16(37.19).

καρφ-ᾰλέος, α, ον, (κάρφω) *dry, parched*, ὡς ἄνεμος ἠΐων θημῶνα τινάξῃ καρφαλέων Od.5.369; δέρμα Hp.*Aph.*5.71, *Prog.*2, Gal.10.674; ἀστάχυες, ἄρουρα, *AP*9.384.14, Orph.*L.*269; κ. δίψει *AP*9.272 (Bianor), 7.536 (Alc.); of sound, καρφαλέον δέ οἱ ἀσπὶς..ἄϋσεν the shield rang *dry*, i. e. *sharply*, Il.13.40 **II.** Act., *drying, parching*, πῦρ v. l. for καρχ- (q. v.), Nic.*Th.*691. **-ᾱμάτιον** (fort. -ατρον), τό, (ἀμάω) prob. *rake for collecting fallen ears of corn*, Hsch. **-εῖα**, τά, *ripe fruit* or (as Sch.) *chips*, κέδρου Nic.*Al.*118. **-η**, ἡ, *hay*, X.*An.*1.5.10, Arr.*An.*1.3.6. **-ηρός**, ά, όν, (κάρφος) *of dry straw*, εὐναῖαι καρφηραί *nests*, E.*Ion* 172:—misquoted as **καρφυραί**, Hsch.; cf. καρπυραί.

κάρφινος, = Lat. *carpineus*, Apollod.*Poliorc.*176.5.

καρφ-ίον, τό, Dim. of κάρφος, Dsc.4.102, Ruf.ap.Orib.8.47.20. **2.** in pl., *suckers* of a polypus, Sch.Opp.*H.*2.312. **-ισμός**, ὁ, *gleaning*, *CIG*2700*e* (Mylasa). **-ίτης** [ῑ], ου, ὁ, *built of* κάρφη (pl.): θάλαμος κ., of a swallow's nest, *AP*10.4 (Marc. Arg.).

καρφο-ειδής, ές, *like dry sticks*, κλῶνες, κλωνία, Dsc.4.42, *Gp.*2.6.29. **-λογέω**, prop. *gather dry twigs*: hence, *pick bits of hair*, etc., off a person's coat, Thphr.*Char.*2.3, Gal.8.227, 18(2).74:—hence **-λογία**, ἡ, Id.14.733.

κάρφος, εος, τό, *any small dry body*, esp. *dry stalk*, as of the *dry sticks* of cinnamon, Hdt.3.111; of *rice-straw*, Polyaen.4.3.32, cf. Luc. *Herm.*33: generally, in pl., *dry twigs, chips, straws, bits of wool*, such as birds make their nests of, Ar.*Av.*643, Sophr.32, Arist.*HA*612^{b}23, *AP*10.14 (Agath.): collectively in sg., A.*Fr.*24, Arist.*HA*560^{b}8, Ath.5.187c: in sg., *chip* of wood, Ar.*V.*249; *toothpick*, Alciphr.1.22: prov., κινοῦσα μηδὲ κ. 'not stirring an inch', Ar.*Lys.*474, cf. Herod. 3.67; οὐδὲ κ. ἐβλάβη *Epigr.Gr.*980.9 (Philae); ἀπὸ τῆς κύλικος κάρφος τῷ μικρῷ δακτύλῳ ἀφαιρετεῖν Ion Hist.1. **II.** = Lat. *festuca*, Plu.2.550b. **III.** *a small piece of wood* on which the watchword was written, Plb.6.36.3. **IV.** in pl., *ripe fruit*, Nic.*Al.*230, 491, *Th.*893, 941. **V.** = τῆλις, Dsc.2.102. (σκάρφος is v. l. (perh. right) in A. l. c., Plb. l. c.: perh. cogn. with Engl. *sharp.*)

καρφόω, = κάρφω, *AP*7.385 (Phil., Pass.). **II.** *nail*, Sch.Ar. *Ra.*844 (Pass.).

καρφυκτοί· φρύγιοι (leg. φρυκτοί) (Rhod.), Hsch. **καρφύνω**, = καρφόω, Id. **κάρφυροι**· νεοσσοί, Id.; cf. καρφηρός.

κάρφ-ω, poet. Verb, *dry up, wither*, κάρψω μὲν χρόα καλὸν *will wither* the fair skin, *wrinkle* it, Od.13.398, cf. 430; ἠέλιος χρόα κάρφει Hes. *Op.*575:—and in Pass., [χρὼς] κάρφεται ἤδη Archil.100; πυρὶ καρφόμενα Euph.50; περὶ χροῒ καρφομένη θρὶξ Nic.*Th.*328. **2.** metaph., ἀγήνορα κάρφει Ζεὺς Zeus *withers* the proud of heart, Hes.*Op.*7; κάματοι κάρφοντες γυῖα Nic.*Al.*383:—Pass., οἴτῳ κάρφεσθαι A.R.4.1094; v. κάρφος. **-ώδης**, ες, *full of* κάρφη, *of uncleansed* wool, *Gloss.*

κάρχαι· καρκίνοι, καὶ ⟨κ⟩όχλοι (Sicel), Hsch.

καρχᾰλέος, α, ον, *rough*, δίψῃ καρχαλέοι *rough in the throat* with thirst, Il.21.541 (v. l. καρφαλέοι), cf. A.R.4.1442, Nonn.*D.*14.426. **II.** *rough, fierce*, κύνες A.R.3.1058; λύκοι Tryph.615 (v. l. καρχαρέος); of sounds, χρεμετισμός, ἱμάσθλη, Nonn.*D.*29.199, 48.307; of fire, *fierce*, Nic.*Th.*691 (v. l. καρφ-, q. v.). (Redupl. of *khar*-, cf. Skt. *khára*- 'rough, sharp'.)

καρχᾰρ-έος, α, ον, = κάρχαρος, κύνες *EM*493.1; cf. foreg. II. **-ίας**, ου, ὁ, a kind of *shark*, so called from its saw-like teeth, Pl.Com.173.13, Mnesim.4.36 (anap.), Thphr.*HP*4.7.2, Numen.ap.Ath.7.327a: metaph., ἁ γαστὴρ ὑμέων κ. Sophr.46. **-όδους**, ὁ, ἡ (neut. -όδουν Plot.6.7.9), gen. -όδοντος, *with saw-like teeth*, καρχαρόδοντε δύω κύνε Il.10.360; κυνῶν ὕπο κ. 13.198; ἅρπην κ. Hes.*Th.*180; applied to Cleon, Ar.*Eq.*1017, *V.*1031; καρχαρόδοντα.. ὅσα ἐπαλλάττει τοὺς ὀδόντας τοὺς ὀξεῖς Arist.*HA*501^{a}18; opp. χαυλιόδους, Id.*PA*661^{b}19; of the lobster's claws, Id.*HA*526^{a}19. **-όδων**, οντος, ὁ, ἡ, = foreg., λύκος Theoc.24.87. **-ος**, ον, and α, ον Alcm.140:—*saw-like, jagged*, so *with saw-like jagged teeth*, κύων Lyc.34, Luc.*Luct.*4, cf. Ael.*NA* 16.18; στόμα Opp.*C.*3.142; ἕρκος Id.*H.*1.506; ὀδόντες Philostr.*Im.* 2.18; δῆγμα Luc.*Trag.*302; κάρχαρον μειδήσας, of the wolf, Babr.94.6. **2.** metaph., *harsh*, of sounds or language, καρχάραισι φωναῖς Alcm. l. c., cf. Luc.*Hist.Conscr.*43; ῥήτωρ Id.*Merc.Cond.*35; nick-name of Thrason, Bato Sinop.3; *rough, rude*, [ἦθη] κ. καὶ σκολιά Plu. 2.468c.

Καρχηδονίζω, *side with the Carthaginians*, Plu.*Marc.*20.

Καρχηδών, όνος, ἡ, *Carthage*, Hdt.3.19, S.*Fr.*602:—Adj. **Καρχηδόνιος**, α, ον, *Carthaginian*, Hdt. l. c., etc.; **Καρχηδονιακός**, ή, όν, κόλπος Str.17.3.13.

καρχήματα· θέλγητρα, Hsch.

καρχήσιον, Dor. **-άσιον** [χᾱ], τό, *drinking-cup* narrower in the middle than at the top and bottom, Sapph.51.3, Pherecyd.13 J., Cratin.38, Herodor.16 J., S.*Fr.*660, Callix.3, *IG*1².265, al., 2².47, 12(8).51.25 (Imbros, ii B.C.). **II.** *mast-head of a ship*, through which the halyards worked, ζυγὸν καρχασίου *sailyard*, Pi.*N.*5.51, cf. Hp.*Art.* 43, Luc.*Merc.Cond.*1 (interpol.), Asclep. Myrl. ap. Ath.11.474f: in pl., E.*Hec.*1261, Plu.*Them.*12; cf. sq.—In Epicr.10 there is a play on the double meaning (I and II). **III.** *triangular instrument used in carpentry*, Hsch. **IV.** *cage* or *chamber* in a torsion-engine, Ph.*Bel.*74.15, Hero *Bel.*88.5 (χαλκ- codd.), Ath.Mech.35.4. **V.** *crane* for unloading ships, Vitr.10.2.10, 10.16.3.

καρχήσιος, ὁ, in pl., *halyards of a ship*, Gal.19.109. **2.** *cords* used in surgical operations, Id.18(1).351, 522.

καρώ, ἡ, *caraway*, Dsc.3.57, Orib.3.2.3: perh. to be read in Ath. 9.371e.

κᾰρώδης, ες, *drowsy, heavy*, ὄμματα Hp.*Epid.*7.30; τὸ καρῶδες, = κάρωσις, Id.*Prorrh.*1.63; τὰ καρώδεα *fits of stupor*, ib.103, cf. *Coac.* 523. **II.** *causing stupor*, Id.*Art.*31; *soporific*, Aret.*CA*2.1. Adv. -δῶς Gal.14.4, Alex.Trall.*Febr.*7.

Καρώνιος, ὁ (sc. μήν), name of month at Cnossus, prob. in *SIG* 712.21 (ii B.C.).

κάρωσις [ᾰ], εως, ἡ, (κᾰρόω) *heaviness in the head, drowsiness,* νωθρὴ κ. Hp.*Art.*31, cf. Philonid.ap.Ath.15.675b, Aët.9.31.

κᾰρωτίδες, ων, αἱ, *carotid arteries,* Aret.*SA*2.11, Gal.*UP*16.12: derived fr. καρόω by Ruf.*Onom.*210: sg., τὴν καρωτὶν (sic) ἀρτηρίαν Antyll.(?) ap.Orib.45.17.6.

κᾰρωτικός, ή, όν, *stupefying, soporific,* κ. ὁ κρίθινος Arist.*Fr.*106, cf. Dsc.4.64; κ. φάρμακα Gal.10.817; δυνάμεις, ἐπιβροχαί, Id.11.711, 14.733, cf. Porph.*Abst.*1.27.

κᾰρωτόν, τό, *carrot,* dub. in Diph.Siph.ap.Ath.9.371e; but, = *gleanings of grapes, PLond.*1821.202.

κάς, *skin,* Hsch. II. Cyprian for καί, Id., cf. *Inscr.Cypr.*135.1 H. (Idalion); also Arc., *IG*5(2).261,262 (Mantinea, v B.C.).

κἀς, crasis for καὶ εἰς or καὶ ἐς, Ar.*Ach.*184, etc.

κάσα, ἡ, prob. = Lat. *casa, cot,* dub. in Ath.Mech.25.7, cf. Hsch.

κᾰσαλβ-άζω, *behave like a strumpet,* Hermipp.Com.71. 2. c. acc., κ. τοὺς στρατηγοὺς *abuse* them *in strumpet fashion,* Ar.*Eq.* 355. **-άς**, άδος, ἡ, *strumpet,* Id.*Ec.*1106, *Fr.*478; cf. κασαύρα, κασωρίς. **-ιον**, τό, v.l. for κασώριον in Id.*Eq.*1285 (ap.Sch.).

κάσαμον, τό, = κυκλάμινος, Aët.16.146(136).

κασάνδρα, gloss on ἐπάγων, Hsch. **κασᾶς**, v. κασῆς. **κασαύρα** and **κασαυράς**, ἡ, = κασαλβάς, Id.

κασαυρεῖον, τό, *brothel,* Hsch. (pl.), prob. for κασαυρίοισι in Ar. *Eq.*1285; cf. κασώριον.

κάσεν (indecl.?), Lacon. for κάσις or κάσιος (v. κάσιοι), denotes relationship of a Spartan boy to the βουαγός (ἀγελάρχης) of his class (ἀγέλη): usu. c. dat., *IG*5(1).60, al., but c. gen., ib.298.

κασέρηνον· κάθελε (Lacon.), Hsch. (fort. κασαίρηδν).

κασῆς, ὁ (on the accent v. Hdn.Gr.1.63), *skin* used as a *saddle* or *horse-cloth,* acc. sg. κασᾶν X.*Cyr.*8.3.8; acc. dual κασᾶ ib.8.3.7; acc. pl. κασᾶς ib.8.3.6 (καλέσας codd.), Agatharch.20; nom. sg. κασῆς *PTeb.*38.22 (ii B.C.); abbreviated in *PLond.*2.402^{v}5 (ii B.C.): written κασσ- by Poll.7.68; cf. κάσσος, κασσοποιός. (Ethiopian word, Agatharch. l. c.; cf. Hebr. *kāsāh* 'covered'.)

κάσης· ἡλικιώτης, Hsch.

κᾰσία, Ion. **-ίη**, ἡ, *cassia, Cinnamomum iners,* Sapph.*Supp.*20c.2, Hdt.2.86, 3.110, Thphr.*HP*9.4.2, *Od.*30, *OGI*214.59 (Branchidae, iii B.C.), etc.; λίβανον εὐώδεις τε φοίνικας κασίαν τε.., τέρενα Συρίας σπέρματα Melanipp.1, cf. Mnesim.4.58. (Cf. Hebr. *qĕṣīʿāh,* Assyr. *kasîa*: sts. written κασσία, as in Dsc.1.13, Str.16.4.25, cf. κασσίζω.)

κᾰσιγνήτ-η, ἡ, fem. of κασίγνητος, *sister,* Il.4.441, etc.; dual **-τα** A.*Pers.*185: metaph., συκῆ ἀμπέλου κ. Hippon.34, cf. 70^A; λάγυνε, ..κ. νεκταρέης κύλικος *AP*6.248 (Marc. Arg.):—Cypr. **κασινήτα** *Gött.Nachr.*1914.95, and **καίνίτα** (q.v.): Aeol. **κασιγνήτα** Sapph. *Supp.*1.9 (prob.). **-ικός**, ή, όν, *brotherly* or *sisterly,* Eust.775.2. **-ος**, ὁ, (κάσις, γενέσθαι, cf. γνήσιος) *brother,* Od.8.585, *IG*9(1).867.6 (Corc., prob. vi B.C.), etc.; esp. of those *born from the same mother,* κ. καὶ ὄπατρον Il.11.257: later as fem., *sister,* τώδε τὼ κασιγνήτω these two *sisters,* S.*El.*977, cf. Ps.-Luc.*Philopatr.*11: in more general sense, *cousin,* κ. τε ἔται τε Il.16.456, cf. 15.545: Astrol., *Gemini,* Doroth.ap.Heph.Astr.3.36. II. as Adj., κασίγνητος, η, ον, *brotherly, sisterly,* κασίγνητον κάρα S.*Ant.*899, 915, *El.*1164, dub. l. in E.*Or.*294; κασιγνήτοιο φόνοιο a *brother's* murder, Il.9.567. (Mostly poet.; also Aeol., Sapph.*Supp.*1.2 (prob.), *IG*12(2).526*d* 19 (Eresus), and Cypr., *Inscr.Cypr.*135.3 H. (Idalion): Thess. **κατίγνειτος** *IG*9(2).894 (Larissa).)

κασίδιον, τό, Dim. of Lat. *cassis, helmet, Sammelb.*7247.25, al. (iii/iv A.D.).

κᾰσιοβόρος, ον, *eating cassia,* of a worm, Hsch.

κάσιοι [ᾰ], οἱ, *brothers* or *cousins belonging to the same* ἀγέλη (q.v.) at Sparta, Hsch.

κᾰσιόπνους, ουν, *breathing of cassia,* Antiph.52.14.

κάσις [ᾰ], ὁ, gen. κάσιος first in Orph.*A.*1229; dat. pl. κασίεσσι Nic.*Th.*345:—*brother,* A.*Th.*674, etc.; voc. κάσι S.*OC*1440: ἡ, *sister,* E.*Hec.*361, Call.*Aet.*3.1.23: metaph., λιγνύν, αἰόλην πυρὸς κ. A.*Th.*494; κ. πηλοῦ..κόνις Id.*Ag.*495.

Κασιωτικόν (sc. πλοῖον), τό, kind of *boat used by the inhabitants of Kasion, PCair.Zen.*289.7, al. (iii B.C.).

κασκαλίζεται· γαγγαλίζεται, Hsch. **κάσκανα**, τά, (κάς I) = κασσύματα, Id. **κασκάνδιξ**· ἡ γηθυλλίς, Id. (Redupl. and dissim. from σκάνδιξ.) **κασκός**, ὁ, *little finger,* Id. (cf. κακκόρ). **κάσμορος**· δύστηνος, Id.; cf. κάμμορος.

κασοποιός, ὁ, (κασῆς, κάσσος) *maker of thick garments, PPetr.*2 p.108 (iii B.C.), *Ostr.*1616, al. (ii B.C.):—also **κασσοποιός** (q.v.).

κασπολέω, Aeol. fut. = καταστελῶ, or perh. aor. subj. Pass. = κατασταλῶ, Sapph.81; cf. **κασπέλη**· στορνύει, Hsch. (leg. κασπέλλει).

κάσσα, ἡ, = κασαλβάς, Lyc.131: **κασσαβάς**, *EM*493.28.

κάσσει· νεοσσειᾷ, Hsch. **κασσία**, ἡ, v. κασία.

Κασσιέπεια, ἡ, the constellation *Cassiopea,* Eudox.ap.Hipparch. 1.2.13.

κασσίζω, *look, taste,* or *smell like cassia,* Dsc.1.14.

κασσιτερᾶς, ᾶτος, ὁ, *tinker, BGU*9 iv 22, 1087 iv 9 (iii A.D.).

Κασσῐτερίδες, ων, αἱ, *the Cassiterides* or *tin-islands,* prob. the Scilly Islands, Hdt.3.115, cf. Str.2.5.15 and 30, etc.

κασσῐτέρινος, Att. **καττ-**, η, ον, *made of tin,* ἐνῴδια *IG*2^2.1388.78, cf. Arist.*SE*164^{b}24, Plu.2.1075c.

κασσῐτεροποιός, ὁ, = κασσιτερουργός, Ptol.*Tetr.*180.

κασσίτερος [ῐ], Att. **καττ-**, ὁ, *tin* (never in Od.), Il.11.25, 23.503, *SIG*247 i 3 (Delph., iv B.C.), etc.; ἐτήκετο κασσίτερος ὣς τέχνῃ ὑπ' αἰζηῶν Hes.*Th.*862, cf. Il.18.474; χεῦμα κασσιτέροιο a plating of *tin,* 23.561; κ. πάνεφθος Hes.*Sc.*208; κνημῖδας ἑανοῦ κ. Il.18.613; δύο καττιτέρω two *plates of tin, IG*2^2.204.23, cf. Hdt.3.115. (Elamite word, cf. Bab. *kassi-tira*: hence Skt. *kastīram.*)

κασσῖτερ-ουργός, ὁ, *tinker, Gloss.* **-όω**, *plate with tin,* λέβης κεκασσιτερωμένος Dsc.1.30.5.

κασσοποιός, ὁ, = κασοποιός, *Ostr.*1081, al. (ii B.C.).

κάσσος, ὁ (cf. κασῆς), *thick garment,* Hdn.Gr.1.208, Hsch.

κάσσ-ῦμα, Att. **κάττ-**, ατος, τό (cf. sq.), *anything stitched of leather,* esp. *sole of a shoe* or *sandal,* Hp.*Epid.*5.45, Ar.*Ach.*301 (ubi v. Sch.), *Eq.*315, 869, Crates Com.29.4; of cork soles, Dsc.*Eup.*2.30; ὑποδήσασθαι ἐχθρῶν παρ' ἀνδρῶν καττύματα to put on *shoes* made by an enemy, Ar.*V.*1160. II. metaph., in pl., *patchings, botchings,* of bad music, Plu.2.1138b. **-ύω** [ῡ], Att. **κατт-**, (καττύς) *stitch, sew together like a shoemaker,* Pl.*Euthd.*294b; πέδιλα Nic.*Fr.*85.6:—Med. (nisi leg. καττύομεν), Pherecr.178. II. metaph., *stitch up* a plot, οἶδ' ἐγὼ τὸ πρᾶγμα τοῦθ' ὅθεν πάλαι καττύεται (says Cleon the tanner), I know the shop that this piece of leather comes from, Ar.*Eq.*314; καττύειν διαβολάς Alciphr.3.58.

Κασταλία, Ion. **-ίη**, ἡ, the spring of the Muses on Mt. Parnassus, Hdt.8.39, Pi.*P.*1.39, etc.

κάστᾰνα, ων, τά, *sweet chestnuts,* Mnesith.ap.Ath.2.54b, v.l. in Gal.6.621, v.l. in Dsc.1.106:—also **κάστανοι**, αἱ, Gal.*Vict.Att.*10; **καστανίαι** (οἱ or αἱ?) Dsc. l. c.; **καστάναια**, τά, *IG*2^2.1013.19; **καστάνεια**, τά, Heracleon ap.Ath.2.52b (καστάν⟨ε⟩ιος as Adj., φλοιός v.l. in Dsc.*Eup.*2.49); βάλανοι **καστανικαί** Gal.6.777, 791; **καστηνοῦ** (gen. sg.) Nic.*Al.*269. **καστανέα**, ἡ, *chestnut-tree, Gp.*2.8.4:—also **κάστανος**, ἡ, Hsch. s.v. καρύαι; **κάστανον**, τό, *Gp.*10.63.1; derived by the ancients from **Κασταvέα**, a place in Asia Minor (πόλις Μαγνησίας), *EM*493.26 (cf. **Καστανὶς** αἶα Nic.*Al.*271); but cf. Armen. *kask*: for κάρυον **καστανаϊκόν**, v. κάρυον. **καστᾰνεών**, ῶνος, ὁ, *chestnut-grove, Gp.*3.15.7.

καστεία, ἡ, (Lat. *castus*) in pl., *ascetic practices,* Marin.*Procl.*19.

κάστον· ξύλον (Athaman.), Hsch.

Καστόρειος, α, ον, *of* or *belonging to Castor*: τὸ Κ. μέλος a martial song, set to the flute, used in celebrating victories in the horse or chariot races, Pi.*P.*2.69; ὁ Κ. ὕμνος Id.*I.*1.16; also, of a battle-march, Plu.*Lyc.*22, cf. 2.1140c, Phld.*Vit.*p.25 J. II. **καστόρειος** or **-όριος**, α, ον, *of the beaver,* ὄρχεις Hsch. s.v. κάστωρ; αἷμα Dsc.2.24:—esp. **καστόρειον** or **-όριον**, τό, *castor,* secretion found in the body of the beaver, used in medicine, Anon.Lond.37.51, *POxy.*1088.27 (i A.D.), Plu.2.55a, Sor.2.29, Phlp.*in GC*65.29, etc.

καστορ-ίδες, αἱ, a famous Laconian breed of *hounds,* said to be first reared by Castor, *AP*6.167 (Agath.), cf. Poll.5.39:—also **καστόριαι** κύνες X.*Cyn.*3.1. II. *sea-calves, seals,* Opp.*H.*1.398, Ael.*NA*9.50. **-ίζω**, *to be like castor,* τῇ ὀσμῇ Dsc.2.8, 3.84; τῇ χρόᾳ Vett.Val.2.23. **-ιον**, τό, v. καστόρειος. **-ιος**, v. καστόρειος, καστορίδες.

καστορνῦσα, Ep. for καταστορνῦσα, v. καταστόρνυμι.

Κάστωρ, ορος, ὁ, *Castor,* Il.3.237, etc.

κάστωρ, ορος, ὁ, *beaver, Castor fiber,* Hdt.4.109, Arist.*HA*594^{b}31, Hierocl.p.17 A., Ael.*NA*6.34. II. = καστόρειον, Hp.*Mul.*2.157, Aret.*CA*2.10. III. = κρόκος, Ps.-Dsc.1.26.

κασύας· ὄρκυνος (Perg.), Hsch. **κασύτας**, ου, ὁ, prob. = καδύτας (q.v.), Id. **κασφυράσσεται**· κατασπείρει, Id. **κάσχεθε**, Ep. for κατέσχεθε, κατέσχε, v. κατέχω.

κᾰσωρ-εύω, *fornicate,* Lyc.772. **-ικὸς** δόμος *brothel,* cj. in Hippon.74:—also **-ιον**, τό, Ar.*Eq.*1285 ap.St.Byz. s.v. Κασώριον (κασωρεῖον Hsch.); cf. κασαυρεῖον. **-ίς**, ίδος, ἡ, = κασαλβάς, Lyc. 1385, St.Byz. **-ίτης** [ῑ], ου, ὁ, *fornicator,* Id. **-ῖτις**, ιδος, ἡ, = κασωρίς, Hippon.117, Antiph.320.

κασωτός, ή, όν, (κασῆς) *thick,* ἐσθῆτες, opp. στρεπταί, Diog.Oen.10.

κάτ, for κατά before τ, v. καττά.

κατά [κᾰτᾰ], poet. καταί acc. to A.D.*Synt.*309.28, found in Compds., as καταιβάτης: Prep. with gen. or acc.:—*downwards.*

A. WITH GEN., I. denoting motion from above, *down from,* βῆ δὲ κατ' Οὐλύμποιο καρήνων, κατ' Ἰδαίων ὀρέων, βαλέειν κ. πέτρης, Il. 22.187, 16.677, Od.14.399; κατ' οὐρανοῦ εἰλήλουθας Il.6.128; καθ' ἵππων ἀΐξαντε ib.232; δάκρυα..κ. βλεφάρων χαμάδις ῥέε 17.438; ἵεις σαυτὸν κ. τοῦ τείχους Ar.*V.*355; ἁλόμενοι κ. τῆς πέτρας X.*An.*4.2.17; κ. τῶν πετρῶν ὦσαι Pl.*Phdr.*229c; κ. κρημνῶν ῥιφέντες Id.*Lg.*944a:—for κατ' ἄκρης v. ἄκρα: Μοῖσα κ. στόματος χέε νέκταρ Theoc.7.82 (but perh. in sense II. 1). II. denoting *downward motion,* 1. *down upon* or *over,* κ. χθονὸς ὄμματα πήξας Il.3.217; of the dying, κατὰ..ὀφθαλμῶν κέχυτ' ἀχλύς a cloud settled *upon* the eyes, 5.696, cf. 20.321; τὸν δὲ κατ' ὀφθαλμῶν..νὺξ ἐκάλυψεν 13.580; φᾶρος κὰκ κεφαλῆς εἴρυσσε *down over..,* Od.8.85; [κόπρος] κ. σπείους κέχυτο.. πολλή 9.330; ὕδωρ κ. χειρός, v. χείρ; μύρον κ. τῆς κεφαλῆς καταχέαντες Pl.*R.*398a; νάρκη μου κ. τῆς χειρὸς καταχεῖται Ar.*V.*713; κ. τῆς τραπέζης καταπάσας τέφραν Id.*Nu.*177; ξαίνειν κ. τοῦ νώτου πολλὰς [πληγάς] D.19.197; ἐσκεδασμένοι κ. τῆς χώρας Plb.1.17.10; οἱ κ. νώτου πονοῦντες Id.3.19.7; ῥόπαλον ἦλασα κὰκ κεφαλῆς Theoc.25.256; κ. κόρρης παίειν, = ἐπὶ κόρρης, Luc.*Cat.*12, al. b. Geom., *along, upon,* πίπτειν κατ' [εὐθείας] Archim.*Sph.Cyl.*1 *Def.*2; αἱ γωνίαι κ. κύκλων περιφερειῶν ἐνεχθήσονται will move *on..,* ib.1.23, al., cf. Aristarch.Sam.1. 2. *down into,* νέκταρ στάξε κ. ῥινῶν Il.19.39; of a dart, κ. γαίης ᾤχετο 13.504, etc.; ἔθηκε κατ' ὄχθης μείλινον ἔγχος 21.172; ψυχὴ κ. χθονὸς ᾤχετο 23.100; κ. γᾶς *under*ground, Pi.*O.*2.59; κατ' ὕδατος *under* water, Hdt.2.149; [ποταμὸς] δὺς κ. τῆς γῆς Pl.*Phd.*

113c, cf. *Ti.*25d; κ. γῆς σύμεναι A.*Eu.*1007 (anap.); κ. χθονὸς κρύψαι to bury, S.*Ant.*24; ὁ κ. γῆς one dead and buried, X.*Cyr.*4.6.5; οἱ κ. χθονὸς θεοί A.*Pers.*689, etc.; θεοὶ (οἱ) κ. γᾶς Id.*Ch.*475 (lyr.), etc.; so κ. θαλάσσης ἀφανίζεσθαι, καταδεδυκέναι, Hdt.7.6,235; also βᾶτε κατ' ἀντιθύρων go *down by* or *through*.., S.*El.*1433. 3. later, *towards* a point, τοξεύειν κ. σκοποῦ to shoot *at*, Hdn.6.7.8; κατ' ἰχνῶν τινος ὁδεύειν Luc.*Rh.Pr.*9. 4. of vows or oaths, *by*, καθ' ἡμῶν ὀμνύναι D.29.26, cf. 54.38; ἐπιορκήσασα κ. τῶν παίδων Lys.32.13; esp. of the victims, etc., *over* which the oath is taken, ὀμνυόντων τὸν ἐπιχώριον ὅρκον καθ' ἱερῶν τελείων Foed.ap.Th.5.47, cf. Arist.*Ath.*29.5, *Foed.Delph.Pell.*1 *A* 9, etc.; κ. τῶν νικητηρίων εὐξάμενοι D.*Ep.*1.16; also κατ' ἐξωλείας ὀμνύναι to imprecate destruction on oneself, Id.21.119; κατ' ἐξ. ἐπιορκεῖν Id.57.22. b. to make a vow *towards*, i.e. make a vow of offering.., κ. χιλίων εὐχὴν ποιήσασθαι χιμάρων Ar.*Eq.*660. 5. in hostile sense, *against*, A.*Ch.*221, S.*Aj.*304, etc.; κ. πάντων φύεσθαι D.18.19; esp. of judges giving sentence *against* a person, A.*Th.*198, S.*Aj.*449, etc.; ψεύδεσθαι κατά τινος Lys.22.7; λέγειν κατά τινος κακά S.*Ph.*65, cf. X.*HG*1.5.2, etc.; of speeches, [λόγος] κ. Μειδίου, etc. (opp. πρὸς Λεπτίνην, in reply to L.); δῶρα εἰληφέναι κατά τινος Din.3.6, cf. 18. 6. of Time, *for*, μισθοῦν κ. εἴκοσι ἐτῶν *IG*1^2.94.37; κ. βίου *for* life, *Tab.Heracl.*1.50; κἀπ παντὸς χρόνοι *IG*9(2).517.20 (Larissa) (but κ. παντὸς τοῦ χρόνου σκέψασθε D.22.72 falls under 7); κ. παντὸς τοῦ αἰῶνος ἀείμνηστον Lycurg.7. 7. *in respect of, concerning*, μὴ κατ' ἀνθρώπων σκόπει μόνον τοῦτο Pl.*Phd.*70d; κ. τῶν ἄλλων τεχνῶν τοιαῦτα εὑρήσομεν Id.*Sph.*253b; οἱ κ. Δημοσθένους ἔπαινοι praises *bestowed on* D., Aeschin.3.50; ἐρεῖν or λέγειν κατά τινος to say *of* one, Pl.*Ap.*37b, *Prt.*323b, etc.; εἰ κ. θηλείας φαίης A.D.*Synt.*198.10; εἴπερ ἕν γέ τι ζητεῖς κ. πάντων Pl.*Men.*73d, cf. 74b; ὅπερ εἴρηται καθόλου κ. πασῶν τῶν πολιτειῶν Arist.*Pol.*1307^{b}2; freq. in the Logic of Arist., κατά τινος λέγεσθαι or κατηγορεῖσθαι to be predicated *of*.., *Int.*16^{b}10, *Cat.*1^{b}10, etc.; καταφῆσαί (or ἀποφῆσαί) τι κατά τινος to affirm (or deny) *of*.., *Metaph.*1007^{b}21; so κ. τινὸς ὑπάρχειν *Int.*16^{b}13: and in Adv. καθόλου (q.v.).

B. WITH ACC., I. of motion *downwards*, κ. ῥόον *down* stream, Od.14.254, Il.12.33; opp. ἀνὰ τὸν ποταμόν, Hdt.2.96; κ. τὸν ποταμόν, κ. τὸ ὑδάτιον, Id.1.194, Pl.*Phdr.*229a; κατ' οὖρον ἰέναι, ῥεῖν, *down* (i.e. *with*) the wind, A.*Th.*690, S.*Tr.*468; κ. πνεῦμα, κατ' ἄνεμον ἵστασθαι *to leeward*, Arist.*HA*535^{a}19, 560^{b}13, Dsc.4.153. 2. with or without signf. of motion, *on, over, throughout* a space, freq. in Hom., καθ' Ἑλλάδα καὶ μέσον Ἄργος Od.1.344; κατ' Ἀχαιΐδα, κ. Τροίην, Il.11.770, 9.329; κατ' ἠερόεντα κέλευθα Od.20.64; κ. πόντον, κῦμα, ὕλην, Il.4.276, 6.136, 3.151; κ. πτόλιν Od.2.383; κ. ἄστυ, οἶκον, Il.18.286, 6.56; κ. ὅμιλον, στρατόν, 3.36, 1.229; κ. κλισίας τε νέας τε ib.487; πόλεμον κάτα δακρυόεντα 17.512; κ. ὑσμίνην, μόθον, κλόνον, 5.84, 18.159, 16.331; τὸ ὕδωρ κ. τοὺς ταφροὺς ἐχώρει X.*Cyr.*7.5.16, etc. (in later Gr. of motion *to* a place, κ. τὴν Ἰταλίαν Zos.3.1); καθ' Ἑλλάδα A.*Ag.*578; κ. πτόλιν Id.*Th.*6; αἱ σκηναὶ αἱ κ. τὴν ἀγοράν D.18.169; τὰ κατ' ἀγροὺς Διονύσια Aeschin.1.157, etc.; κ. τὸ προάστιον Hdt.3.54; τύμβον κατ' αὐτόν A.*Th.*528, cf. *Supp.*869 (lyr.): Geom., *at* a point, Euc.1.1, al.; τέμνειν [σφαῖραν] κ. κύκλον *in* a circle, Archim.*Aren.*1.17; also, *in the region of*, οἱ κ. τὸν ἥλιον γινόμενοι ἀστέρες Gem.12.7: freq. in Hom. in describing the place of a wound, βαλεῖν κ. στῆθος, γαστέρα, etc., Il.11.108, 16.465, al.; νύξε κ. δεξιὸν ὦμον 5.46; οὔτασε κατ' ἰσχίον 11.339; so βαλεῖν κατ' ἀσπίδα, κ. ζωστῆρα, 5.537,615; βέλος κ. καίριον ἦλθεν struck *upon* a vital part, v.l. in 11.439: metaph., ἄχος κ. φρένα τύψε 19.125: generally, κ. φρένα καὶ κατὰ θυμόν *in* heart and soul, 4.163, al. 3. *opposite, over against*, κ. Σινώπην πόλιν Hdt.1.76, cf. 2.148, Th.2.30, etc.; ἀνὴρ κατ' ἄνδρα A.*Th.*505; μολὼν.. μοι κ. στόμα Id.*Ch.*573; κατ' ὀφθαλμούς τινος Lxx 2*Ki.*12.11; οἱ μὲν Ἀθηναῖοι κ. Λακεδαιμονίους ἐγένοντο X.*HG*4.2.18; κατ' Ἀχαιοὺς ἀντετάχθησαν ibid.; ἐν συμποσίῳ.., περίμενε, μέχρις ἂν γένηται κατὰ σέ Epict.*Ench.*15, cf. D.L.7.108. II. *distributively*, of a whole divided into parts, κρῖν' ἄνδρας κ. φῦλα, κ. φρήτρας *by* tribes, *by* clans, Il.2.362; κ. σφέας μαχέονται *by* themselves, *separately*, ib.366, cf. Th.4.64; ἐσκήνουν κ. τάξεις X.*Cyr.*2.1.25; αὐτὴ καθ' αὑτήν A.*Pr.*1013; κ. κώμας κατοικημένοι *in separate* villages, Hdt.1.96; κατ' ἑωυτοὺς ἕκαστοι ἐτράποντο each *to his own* home, Id.5.15; κ. πόλεις ἀποπλεῦσαι, διαλυθῆναι, Th.1.89, 3.1: στρατιὰ κ. ἕνδεκα μέρη κεκοσμημένη Pl.*Phdr.*247a; later οἱ κατ' ἄνδρα λόγοι *PLond.*2.259.72 (i A.D.), cf. D.*Chr.*32.6, etc.; ἡ κατ' οἰκίαν ἀπογραφή *PLond.*3.904.20 (ii A.D.), etc.; κατ' ἔπος word *by* word, Ar.*Ra.*802; κατ' ὄνομα *individually*, 3*Ep.Jo.*15, etc.; παῖδα κ. κρήνην *at each* fount a boy, *Lyr.Alex.Adesp.*37.13, cf. *POxy.*2108.9 (iii A.D.). 2. of Time, καθ' ἡμέραν, κατ' ἦμαρ, day *by* day, daily, v. ἡμέρα III; καθ' ἐνιαυτόν, κατ' ἔτος, *Test.Epict.*6.24, *Ev.Luc.*2.41, etc.; κ. μῆνα *POxy.*275.18 (i A.D.). 3. of Numbers, *by* so many *at a time*, καθ' ἕνα one *at a time, individually*, Hdt.7.104 (later τὸ καθ' ἕν *detailed list*, *PTeb.*47.34 (ii B.C.), etc.); κ. μίαν τε καὶ δύο *by* ones and twos, Hdt.4.113; δύο μνέαι τεταγμέναι κατ' ἄνδρα αἰχμάλωτον ἕκαστον Id.6.79; ἐκ τῶν συμμάχων ἐξελέγετο κατ' ὀλίγους Id.8.113; κ. τὰς πέντε καὶ εἴκοσι μνᾶς πεντακοσίας δραχμὰς εἰσφέρειν to pay 500 drachmae *on every* 25 minae, D.27.7; κ. διακοσίας καὶ τριακοσίας ὁμοῦ τι τάλαντον διακεχρημένον *in separate sums of* 200 and 300 drachmae, Id.27.11; of ships, κ. μίαν (sc. ναῦν) *in column*, Th.2.90; κ. μίαν ναῦν ἐπιτάττειν Plb.1.26.12, cf. Th.2.84: Geom., μετρεῖν, μετρεῖσθαι κατά.., measure, be measured a certain number of times, Euc.7 *Def.*8,9, al.; μετρεῖν κ. τὰς ἐν τῷ Β μονάδας *as many times as* there are units in B, Id.7.16. III. of direction *towards* an object or purpose, πλεῖν κ. πρῆξιν *on* a business, *for* or *after* a matter, Od.3.72, 9.253; πλάζεσθαι κ. ληΐδα to rove *in search of* booty, 3.106; κ. ληΐην ἐκπλῶσαι Hdt.2.152; ἔβη κ. δαῖτα Il.1.424; ἐπιδημεῖν κατ' ἐμπορίαν *IG*2^2.141.32, cf. Arist.*Ath.*11.1; κ. χρέος τινὸς ἐλθεῖν come to seek his help, consult him, Od.11.479, etc.; ἵεται κ. τὴν φωνήν Hdt.2.70; κ. θέαν ἥκειν to have come *for the purpose of* seeing, Th.6.31; κ. πλοῦν ἤδη ὤν Id.7.31; καθ' ἁρπαγὴν ἐσκεδασμένοι X.*An.*3.5.2; κ. τί; *for* what purpose? why? Ar.*Nu.*239. 2. of pursuit, κ. πόδας τινὸς ἐλαύνειν Hdt.9.89; simply κ. τινά *after* him, Id.1.84; ἰέναι κ. τοὺς ἄλλους Id.9.53; κατ' ἴχνος *on* the track, S.*Aj.*32, A.*Ag.*695 (lyr.); ὥσπερ κατ' ἴχνη κ. τὰ νῦν εἰρημένα ζῆν Pl.*Phd.*115b. 3. Geom., in adverbial phrases, κ. κάθετον *in the same* vertical line, Archim.*Quadr.*6; κατ' εὐθεῖάν τινι *in the same* straight line with.., Papp.58.7. IV. of fitness or conformity, *in accordance with*, κ. θυμόν Il.1.136; καθ' ἡμέτερον νόον *after* our liking, 9.108; κ. νόον πρήξωμεν Hdt.4.97; κ. μοῖραν *as is* meet and right, Il.1.286; κατ' αἶσαν, κ. κόσμον, 10.445,472; κ. νόμον Hes.*Th.*417; κὰν νόμον Pi.*O.*8.78; κ. τοὺς νόμους *IG*2^2.1227.15; αἰτίαν καθ' ἥντινα *for* what cause, A.*Pr.*228; κατ' ἔχθραν, κ. φθόνον, *for* (i.e. *because of*) hatred, envy, Id.*Supp.*336, *Eu.*686; καθ' ἡδονήν τι δρᾶν, ποιεῖν, do *as* one pleases, Th.2.37,53; κ. τὸ ἔχθος τὸ Θεσσαλῶν Hdt.8.30, cf. 9.38; κ. φιλίαν, κατ' ἔχθος, Th.1.60,103, etc.; κατ' ἄλλο μὲν οὐδέν, ὅτι δὲ.. *for* no other *reason* but that.., Pl.*Phdr.*229d; κ. δύναμιν *to the best of* one's power, Hdt.3.142, etc. (κὰδ δ. Hes.*Op.*336); κ. τρόπον διοικεῖν arrange *suitably*, Isoc.2.6, al.; κατ' εὐνοίην *with* goodwill, Hdt.6.108; κ. τὰ παρηγγελμένα X.*An.*2.2.8, etc.; in quotations, *according to*, κατ' Αἰσχύλον Ar.*Th.*134; κ. Πίνδαρον Pl.*Phdr.*227b, etc. 2. *in relation to, concerning*, τὰ κατ' ἀνθρώπους = τὰ ἀνθρώπινα, A.*Eu.*930, 310; τὰ κ. τὸν Τέλλον Hdt.1.31; τὰ κ. τὴν Κύρου τελευτήν ib.214; τὰ κ. πόλεμον *military* matters, Aeschin.1.181; αἱ κ. τὴν πόλιν οἰκονομίαι (opp. αἱ πολεμικαὶ πράξεις) the management of *public* affairs, Din.1.97; τὰ κ. τὰς θυσίας *SIG*506.7 (Delph., iii B.C.); so τὸ κατ' ὑμέας *as far as concerns* you, Hdt.7.158; τὸ κατ' ἐμέ *as far as* I *am concerned*, D.18.247; κ. τοῦτο *in* this *respect*, Hdt.5.3, etc.; κ. ταὐτά *in* the same *way*, Id.2.20; καθ' ὅτι *so far as*, Th.1.82, etc. 3. in Comparisons, *corresponding with, after the fashion of*, κρομύοιο λοπὸν κ. *like* the coat of an onion, dub. in Od.19.233; μέλος κ. Φοίνισσαν ἐμπολὰν πέμπεται Pi.*P.*2.67; κ. Μιθραδάτην *answering to the description of* him, Hdt.1.121; τὴν ἰδέαν κ. πνιγέα *like* an oven in appearance, Ar.*Av.*1001; κηδεῦσαι καθ' ἑαυτόν to marry *in* one's own *rank* of life, A.*Pr.*890; οὐ κατ' ἄνθρωπον φρονεῖν Id.*Th.*425; λέγω κατ' ἄνδρα, μὴ θεόν, σέβειν ἐμέ Id.*Ag.*925; οὐ κατὰ σέ none *of* your *sort*, Chionid.1 (but ἵνα προσείπω σε κατὰ σέ to address you *in* your own *style*, Pl.*Grg.*467c); τὸ κατ' ἐμὲ καὶ οὐ κατ' ἐμέ Arr.*Epict.*1.28.5; οὐ κ. τὰς Μειδίου λητουργίας D.21.169; ἡ βασιλεία κ. τὴν ἀριστοκρατίαν ἐστί Arist.*Pol.*1310^{b}3: freq. after a Comp., μέζων ἢ κατ' ἀνθρώπων φύσιν Hdt.8.38, cf. Pl.*Ap.*20e, etc.; μείζω ἢ κ. δάκρυα too great for tears, Th.7.75; ἤθεα βαθύτερα ἢ κ. Θρήϊκας more refined than *was common among* the Thracians, Hdt.4.95. V. *by the favour of* a god, etc., κ. δαίμονα Pi.*O.*9.28, cf. *P.*8.68; κ. θεὸν Ar.*Eq.*147 codd. (κ. θεὸν Cobet); κ. τύχην τινά D.48.24. VI. of round numbers (v. infr. VII. 2), *nearly, about*, κ. χίλια ἑξακόσια ἔτεα 1600 years *more or less*, Hdt.2.145, cf. 6.44, al.; κατ' οὐδέν *next to* nothing, Pl.*Plt.*302b. VII. of Time, *during* or *in the course of* a period, κ. τὸν πόλεμον Hdt.7.137; καθ' ἡμέραν, κατ' ἦμαρ, *by* day, A.*Ch.*818, *Ag.*668; κατ' εὐφρόνην Id.*Pers.*221; κ. χειμῶνα, κ. θερείαν, *PLille* 1^{r}14 (iii B.C.), *PTeb.*27.60 (ii B.C.). 2. *about*, κ. τὸν αὐτὸν τοῦτον χρόνον Hdt.3.131, etc.; κ. τοὺς θανάτους τῶν βασιλέων Id.6.58; esp. with names of persons, κ. Ἄμασιν βασιλεύοντα *about the time of* Amasis, Id.2.134; κ. τὸν κ. Κροῖσον χρόνον Id.1.67; οἱ κατ' ἐκεῖνον (sc. τὸν Ἀλκιβιάδην) ὑμέτεροι πρόγονοι D.21.146 (v.l. κατ' ἐκ. τὸν χρόνον); κ. τοὺς Ἡρακλείδας X.*Lac.*10.8; οἱ καθ' ἑαυτοὺς ἄνθρωποι their contemporaries, Id.*Mem.*3.5.10. 3. καθ' ἔτος *this* year, *SIG* 284.24 (Erythrae, iv B.C.), *OGI*458.64 (i B.C./i A.D.), *CIG*3641 *b* 5,38 (Lampsacus). VIII. periphrastically with abstract Subst., κατ' ἡσυχίην, κ. τάχος, = ἡσύχως, ταχέως, Hdt.1.9, 7.178; κ. κράτος *by* force, X.*HG*2.1.19, etc.; κ. μέρος *partially*, Arist.*Po.*1456^{a}16; *individually, severally*, Pl.*Tht.*157b, *Lg.*835a; κ. φύσιν *naturally*, Hdt.2.38, Pl.*R.*428e; κ. τὴν τέχνην *skilfully*, Luc.*DDeor.*20.7; οὔτ' ἐμοὶ λέγειν καθ' ἡδονὴν [ἐστι] it is not *pleasant* for me to tell you, A.*Pr.*263.

C. POSITION: κατά may follow both its cases, and is then written with anastr. κάτα, as Il.20.221, etc.; so also in tmesi, when it follows its Verb, 17.91.

D. abs. as ADV. in all the above senses, esp. like κάτω, *downwards, from above, down*, freq. in Hom.

E. κατά in COMPOS., I. *downwards, down*, as in καταβαίνω, καταβάλλω, κατάκειμαι, καταπέμπω, καταπίπτω, καταπλέω I. II. *in answer to, in accordance with*, as in κατᾴδω (*occino*), καταινέω, καταθύμιος. III. *against*, in hostile sense (cf. A. II. 5), as in καταγιγνώσκω, κατακρίνω, καταψηφίζομαι: more rarely with a Subst., as καταδίκη. IV. *back, back again*, as in κάτειμι, καταπορεύομαι, καταπλέω II. V. freq. only to strengthen the notion of the simple word, as in κατακόπτω, κατακτείνω, καταφαγεῖν, etc.; also with Substs. and Adjs., as in κατάδηλος, κάτοξος. VI. sts. to give a trans. force to an intr. Verb, our *be-*, as in καταθρηνέω *be*wail. VII. implying *waste* or *consumption*, as in καταλειτουργέω, καθιπποτροφέω, καταζευγοτροφέω: and generally in a *disparaging* sense, as in καταγιγνώσκω I.

F. κατά as a Prep. was shortd. in some dialects, esp. in Ep., into κάγ, κάδ, κάκ, κάμ, κάν, κάπ, κάρ, κάτ, before γ, δ, κ, μ, ν, π (or φ), ρ, τ (or θ), respectively; see these forms in their own places. Mss. and the older Edd. join the Prep. with the following word, as καγγόνυ, καδδέ, κακκεφαλῆς, καππεδίον, καπφάλαρα, καρρόον, καττάδε, καττόν, etc. In compd. Verbs, κατά sts. changes into καβ, καλ, καρ, κατ, before β, λ, ρ, θ, respectively, as κάββαλε, κάλλιπε, καρρέζουσα, κάτθανε; and before στ, σχ, the second syll. sts. disappears, as in καστορνῦσα, κάσχεθε, as also in the Dor. forms καβαίνων, κάπετον.

κατά, = κατὰ τά, *IG*2².334.15; cf. κά. **κᾆτα**, Att. crasis for καὶ εἶτα, v. εἶτα sub fin. **κατάβα**, for κατάβηθι, aor. 2 imper. of καταβαίνω.

καταβάδην [βᾰ], Adv. *with one's feet down* (coined as opp. to ἀναβάδην, q. v.), Ar.*Ach.*411.

καταβαθμός, ὁ, *descent*, a name of the *steep slope* which separates Egypt and Nubia, and causes the Cataracts, A.*Pr.*811 (in Att. form **Καταβασμός**), Plb.31.18.9, Str.17.1.5, *Abh.Berl.Akad.*1925(5).6 (Cyrene).

καταβαίνω, Dor. **κᾰβαίνω** Alcm.38: fut. -βήσομαι Hes.*Th.*750, etc.: pf. -βέβηκα; Boeot. part. καταβεβάων *IG*7.3055: aor. κατέβην Il.10.541, Pi.*O.*9.43, etc.; poet. 3 pl. κατέβαν Il.24.329, κατέβησαν Lxx 2*Ki.*23.13; imper. κατάβηθι Od.23.20, Ar.*Lys.*873, Lacon. κάβασι Hsch., κατάβᾱ Ar.*V.*979, *Ra.*35; Ep. 1 pl. subj. καταβήομεν (v.l. -βείομεν) Il.10.97; late 3 sg. opt. καταβοι Lxx 2*Ki.*1.21 (cod. B), Conon 45.2 J.; poet. part. καββάς Pi.*N.*6.51; Ep. inf. καταβήμεναι Il.14.19:—Med., Ep. aor. 1 κατεβήσετο 6.288, 13.17, Od.2.337, al. (with v.l. κατεβήσατο); imper. καταβήσεο Il.5.109:—*go* or *come down from*.., c. gen., πόλιος κ. 24.329; οὐρανόθεν κ. 11.184; Παρνασοῦ Pi.*O.*9.43, etc.: also with Preps., ἐξ ὄρεος Il.13.17; ἐς πεδίον 3.252, etc.: also c. acc. loci, θάλαμον κατεβήσετο Od.2.337; κ. Ἀΐδαν, Ἀΐδα δόμον, S.*Ant.*822 (anap.), E.*Heracl.*913 (lyr.); but κατέβην δόμον Ἄϊδος εἴσω Od.23.252 (later abs., *die*, Lib.*Or.*38.16); ἔσω κ. Hes.*Th.*750: also c. acc. in quite different senses, κατέβαιν' ὑπερῷϊα she *came down from* the upper floor, Od.18.206, 23.85; κλίμακα κατεβήσετο *came down* the ladder, 1.330 (κ. κατὰ τῆς κλίμακος Lys.1.9); ξεστὸν ἐφόλκαιον καταβάς *having got down by* the lading-plank, Od.14.350: abs., καταβαίνειν δ' οὐ σχολή *come downstairs*, Ar.*Ach.*409; esp. 1. *dismount* from a chariot or from horseback, δίφρου Il.5.109; ἐκ τῆς ἁρμαμάξης Hdt.9.76; ἀφ' ἁρμάτων Pi.*N.*6.51; ἀπὸ τοῦ ἵππου X.*Cyr.*5.5.6; but κ. ἀπὸ τῶν ἵππων *give up* riding, D.42.24, cf. Arist.*Ath.*49.1:—hence in Pass., ἵππος καταβαίνεται the horse *is dismounted from*, X.*Eq.*11.7. 2. *go down from the inland parts to the sea*, esp. from central Asia (cf. ἀναβαίνω II. 3), Hdt.1.94, etc.; also from Athens, κ. ἐς Πειραιᾶ, ἐς λιμένα, Pl.*R.*327a, *Tht.*142a. 3. *go down into the scene of contest*, γυμνὸν ἐπὶ στάδιον κ. Pi.*P.*11.49; κ. ἐπ' αὐτὸ τοῦτο (sc. τὸ ἀεθλεύειν) Hdt.5.22: abs., = Lat. *in certamen descendere*, Pi.*N.*3.42, S.*Tr.*504 (lyr.), X.*An.*4.8.27; cf. καταβατέον; μέτρῳ καταβαίνειν 'seek no more contests' (μέτρῳ by litotes for μή), Pi.*P.*8.78; μεθ' ὅπλων κ. Pl.*Lg.*834c. 4. of an orator, *come down from the tribune*, Lys.12.92, D.19.23, etc.; rarely in full, κ. ἀπὸ τοῦ βήματος ib.113; so κατάβα.—καταβήσομαι Ar.*V.*979; later, also κ. ἀπὸ τοῦ λόγου, ἀπὸ τῶν ἰαμβείων, *to cease* from.., Luc.*Tox.*35, *Nec.*1. 5. less freq. of things, πρὶν.. καταβήμεναι ἐκ Διὸς οὖρον Il.14.19; of tears, E.*Andr.*111 (eleg.); of streams, Pl.*Criti.*118d; of the womb, Arist.*HA*582ᵇ24; πόσσω κατέβα τοι ἀφ' ἱστῶ; at what price did [the robe] *come down* from the loom? Theoc.15.35; of the heavenly bodies, *set*, Vett.Val.31.3. II. metaph., 1. *attain*, πόμπιμον κατέβαινε νόστου τέλος Pi.*N.*3.25; κ. ἐπὶ τελευτήν Pl.*R.*511b: abs., *attain one's end*, ἐν φάει κ. Pi.*N.*4.38; simply, *come to, arrive* at in course of speaking, κατέβαινε ἐς λιτάς he *ended* with prayer, Hdt.1.116: usu. c. part., κατέβαινε αὖτις παραιτεόμενος ib.90, cf. 118, 9.94; καταβάς, of a writer, Eun.*VS*p.454 B. 2. κ. εἰς.. *conform to*, εἰς τοὺς χρόνους κ. τούτους Arist.*Pol.*1335ᵃ11. 3. *condescend*, Timocl.1.2 D. 4. *fall in value*, *POxy.*1223.33 (iv A.D.), cf. Poll.1.51. 5. λέγεται μηδὲν αὐτοῖς τούτων καταβαίνειν, of abusive language, does not *affect* them or *get home*, Chrysipp.*Stoic.*2.242.

καταβακχιόομαι, Pass., *to be full of Bacchic frenzy*, καταβακχιοῦσθε δρυὸς.. κλάδοισι in oak-wreaths *rave with Bacchic rage*, E.*Ba.*109 (lyr.).

καταβάλλω, fut. -βᾰλῶ: aor. κατέβᾰλον; Ep. 3 sg. κάββαλε Od.6.172, Hes.*Th.*189, etc.; imper. καββαλόντων *Foed.Delph.Pell.*1 *B* 14:—*throw down, overthrow*, κατὰ πρηνὲς βαλέειν Πριάμοιο μέλαθρον Il.2.414; ἐς μέσσον κ. τι 15.357; ἐνὶ πόντῳ Hes.*Th.*189; ἐπ' ἀκτῆς Il.23.125 (tm.); ἐπὶ χθονί Hes.*Sc.*462, etc.; κ. [τινὰ] ἐνθάδε Od.6.172; κ. τὰ οἰκήματα, τὰ ἀγάλματα, Hdt.1.17, 8.109; τεῖχος Th.7.24; κ. τινὰ ἀπὸ τοῦ ἵππου X.*HG*5.2.41; ἀπ' ἐλπίδος Pl.*Euthphr.*15e; κ. ἐς τὸ μηδέν *to bring down* to nothing, opp. ἐξᾶραι ὑψοῦ, Hdt.9.79; κάββαλλε τὸν χείμωνα *confound, defy* the storm, Alc.34.3. 2. κ. ἑαυτόν *throw* oneself *down* to sleep, Plu.*Caes.*38. 3. *strike down* with a weapon, *slay*, Il.2.692 (tm.), Hdt.4.64, etc.; by a blow, κ. πατάξας Lys.13.71; esp. of slaying victims, E.*Or.*1603, Isoc.2.20; κ. θῦμα δαίμοσιν E.*Ba.*1246. b. Pass., *to be stricken*, νόσῳ *POxy.*1121.9 (iii A.D.). 4. *throw* into prison, κ. τινὰ ἐς ἑρκτήν Hdt.4.146: generally, *throw, bring* into a certain state, κ. [τινὰ] ἐς ξυμφοράς E.*IT*606, Antipho Soph.58; εἰς ἀπορίαν, εἰς ἀπιστίαν, Pl.*Phlb.*15e, *Phd.*88c, etc. 5. *overthrow, refute*, οἱ -βάλλοντες (sc. λόγοι), title of work by Protagoras: κ. τινά Democr.125; δόξαν Gal.*UP*6.20. 6. *abuse, bully*, Phld.*Rh.*2.164 S. 7. *cast down* or *away, cast off, reject*, Isoc.12.24: metaph., *forget*, Ael.*Fr.*111; κ. εἴς τι *throw away* upon a thing, Pl.*Lg.*960e:—Pass., οἱ καταβεβλημένοι *despicable fellows*, Isoc.12.8; cf. καταβεβλημένως. II. *let fall, drop*, ἀπὸ ἕο κάββαλεν υἱόν Il.5.343; κάββαλε νεβρόν, of an eagle, 8.249; of a fawning dog, οὔατα κάββαλεν ἄμφω Od.17.302; ἴουλον ἀπὸ κροτάφων κ. Theoc.15.85; of sails, καθ' ἱστία λευκὰ βαλόντες Thgn.671; τἀκάτια Epicr.10; κατ' ὀφθαλμοὺς βαλεῖ A.*Ch.*574; τὰς ὀφρῦς κ. E.*Cyc.*167; κ. τὰ κέρατα *droop* their feelers, Arist.*HA*590ᵇ26: in Politics, *abandon* a measure, καταβάλλοντ' ἐὰν ἐν ὑπωμοσίᾳ D.18.103. 2. *lay down, set down*, κρεῖον μέγα κάββαλεν ἐν πυρὸς αὐγῇ Il.9.206, cf. Ar.*Ach.*165, *V.*727, etc. 3. *lay down, lay in* stores, κ. σιτία Hdt.7.25:—Pass., κὰτ ἄσπιδες βεβλήμεναι *stored up*, Alc.15.5. 4. *pay down, yield, bring in*, ἡ λίμνη καταβάλλει ἐπ' ἡμέρην ἑκάστην τάλαντον ἐκ τῶν ἰχθύων Hdt.2.149; τὰς ἐπικαρπίας τῇ πόλει And.1.92, cf. Lexib.93. b. *pay*, τἀργύριον Th.1.27; τριώβολον Amips.13; ἀρραβῶνα Men.743, cf. *PRev.Laws* 48.10 (iii B.C.), etc.; τιμήν τινι ὑπέρ τινος Pl.*Lg.*932d, Luc.*Vit.Auct.*25; τέλη *GDI*5018ᵃ17 (Gortyn), *PHib.*29.6 (iii B.C.); λύτρα *GDI* 5151.8 (Cret., found at Delphi); καταβαλὼν σοι δραχμὴν τῶν βοτρύων for them, Philostr.*Her.Praef.*1; κ. ζημίαν *pay up, discharge* a fine, D.24.83, cf. 59.27:—later in Med., μισθὸν καταβαλέσθαι Alciphr.1.12. 5. *put in, deposit*, in Pass., εἰ ἡ μαρτυρία κατεβάλλετο ἐνταῦθα D.34.46:—but usu. in Med., *deposit*, γράμματα εἰς κιβωτόν *BCH*25.100 (Tlos), cf. *IG*12(1).3.15 (Rhodes); ψευδεῖς γραφὰς εἰς τὰ δημόσια γράμματα Docum.ap.D.18.55; λόγους *IG*7.2850 (Haliartus); δόγμα *GDI*5182.10 (Cret., found at Teos). 6. *throw down* seed, *sow*, Men.*Georg.*37, cf. καταβλητέον; κ. τὸ σπέρμα, of the male, Epicur.*Nat.*908.1:—Pass., *Placit.*5.7.4, Sor.1.33, Ocell.4.14: metaph., σπέρμα κ. τοιούτων πραγμάτων D.24.154; κ. φάτιν ὡς.. *spread abroad* a rumour, Hdt.1.122, cf. E.*HF*758 (lyr.). 7. *lay down as a foundation*, mostly in Med., τὴν τῆς ναυπηγίας ἀρχὴν καταβαλλόμενος Pl.*Lg.*803a: esp. metaph., -βαλλομένα μέγαν οἶκτον *beginning* a lament (cf. infr. 8), E.*Hel.*164 (lyr.); Ἀρίστιππος τὴν Κυρηναϊκὴν φιλοσοφίαν κατεβάλετο Str.17.3.22; καταβαλέσθαι τοὐπτάνιον Sosip.1.39; ἐξ ἀρχῆς καινὴν νομοθεσίαν D.S.12.20; τὴν Στωϊκῶν αἵρεσιν Plu.2.329a: hence generally, *to be the author of, commit to writing*, ἱστορικὰς καταβαλόμενοι πραγματείας D.H.1.1; λόγον Darius ap.D.L.9.13; φλυαρίας Gal.7.476:—Pass., ὅταν δὲ κρηπὶς μὴ καταβληθῇ.. ὀρθῶς E.*HF*1261: freq. metaph., δεδημοσιωμένα που καταβέβληται Pl.*Sph.*232d; πολλοὶ λόγοι πρὸς αὐτὰ -βέβληνται Arist.*EN*1096ᵃ10; καταβεβλημέναι μαθήσεις *fundamental, established*, Arist.*Pol.*1337ᵇ21; τὰ κ. παιδεύματα ib.1338ᵃ36, cf. Phld.*Rh.*1.27 S. 8. c. inf., γάμον καταβάλλομ' ἀείδειν I *begin* my song of, Call.*Fr.*196. III. Pass., *lie down*, εἰς εὐνάν Theoc.18.11. 2. like καταβαίνω II. 1, *arrive* at in a course of lectures, εἰς Γοργίαν Dam.*Isid.*54. B. intr., *fall*, εἰς φθόνον καὶ ἀπορίαν Pl.*Ep.*344c.

καταβαπτ-έον, *one must dip*, εἰς ἔλαιον Sor.2.16. **-ίζω**, *dip, drown*, of wine, κ. τὴν ζωτικὴν δύναμιν Alex.Aphr.*Pr.*1.17; τὴν ψυχήν Ach.Tat.1.3:—Pass., *to be submerged, overwhelmed*, ὑπὸ τῆς ὑγρότητος Steph.*in Gal.*1.278 D.; καταβαπτισθήσεταί μοι τὸ ζῆν Alciphr.2.3. **-ω**, *dip*, εἰς ζεστὸν ὕδωρ Sor.1.50; εἰς γλεῦκος *Gp.*8.23.1; *soak*, ὄξει βαφικῷ *PHolm.*1.3. II. *dye, colour*, πρόσωπον ἐρυθήματι Eun.*Hist.*p.267 D.; χρυσόν *produce it by dyeing*, Ps.-Democr.Alch.p.45 B.:—in Pass., Luc.*Im.*16: Medic., οὖρον καταβεβαμμένον *deep-coloured*, Pall.*Febr.*15; ἀπὸ αἵματος -ομένου τοῦ οὔρου Gal.19.604.

καταβαρβᾰρόω, *make quite barbarous*, τὴν τέχνην Tz.*H.*12.230.

καταβᾰρ-έω, *weigh down, overload*, v.l. for καταπονέω in Luc.*DDeor.*21.1: metaph., *impose a burden on*, τινας 2*Ep.Cor.*12.16; κ. τὴν Ἰταλίαν ἐσφοραῖς App.*BC*5.67; ἀθληταὶ -βαροῦσι τοὺς τεχνίτας Plu.*Cleom.*27; τῶν -βαρούντων τὸ σῶμα καμάτων Ps.-Plu.*Vit.Hom.*207:—Pass., *to be overborne, crushed*, καταβαρεῖσθαι τῇ μάχῃ Plb.11.33.3; τοῖς ὅλοις Id.18.21.8; ὑπὸ τοῦ πάθους D.S.19.24; ἐν ταῖς λειτουργίαις *POxy.*487.10 (ii A.D.); also, *to be outweighed*, ὑπὸ τοῦ συμφέροντος Arr.*Epict.*2.22.18. **-ής**, ές, *heavy-laden*, πλάστιγγες Poll.4.172; νῆες, πλοῖα, D.C.39.42, 74.13. **-ησις**, εως, ἡ, *weighing down, oppression*, Demoph. in *Cat.Cod.Astr.*5(1).189 (pl.), *Gloss.* 2. ὀχλικὴ κ. mob *violence*, *Rev.Ét.Gr.*19.234 (Aphrodisias). **-ύνω**, = καταβαρέω, Thphr.*Vert.*9:—in Pass., Lxx 2*Ki.*13.25, al.; of sleep, *Ev.Marc.*14.40: metaph., κ. τὸν βίον Antip.ap.Stob.4.22.25, cf. *Corp.Herm.*2.9 (Pass.).

καταβᾰσᾰνίζω, strengthd. for βασανίζω, *examine thoroughly*, Hp.*Prorrh.*2.3.

κατα-βᾰσία, v. καταιβασίη. **-βάσιον** [βᾰ], τό, = κατάβασις, *a way down*, esp. to the nether world, Dam.*Isid.*131; εἰς Ἅιδου Suid. s. v. πορθμήϊον. **-βάσιος** [βᾰ], ον, = καταιβάσιος, πῦρ Lxx *Wi.*10.6. **-βᾰσις**, εως, ἡ, opp. ἀνάβασις, *way down, descent*, Hdt.1.186 (pl.), 7.223, etc.; ἡ εἰς Ἅιδου κ. Isoc.10.20, Str.8.6.12, cf. Hdt.2.122; title of work by Dicaearchus, Cic.*Att.*13.31.2; cf. καταίβασις. 2. *descent from* central Asia, X.*An.*5.5.4; ἡ ἐπὶ θάλατταν κ. D.S.14.25. 3. metaph., *descent* of an idea into the mind, Chrysipp.*Stoic.*2.242. 4. *steep ground, declivity*, Demetr.*Eloc.*248 (pl.). 5. ἔργον καταβάσεως *hanging* work, Lxx 3*Ki.*7.16(29).

καταβασκαίνω, strengthd. for βασκαίνω, Plu.2.680c, 682b, Hld.3.8; τῇ θέᾳ τινά Id.4.5.

καταβασμός, v. καταβαθμός.

καταβᾰτ-έον, (καταβαίνω) *one must descend*, Ar.*Lys.*884, Pl.*R.*520c. **-εύω**, *tread* or *walk upon*, Sch.S.*OC*467. **-ης**, ου, ὁ, *one who dismounts* and fights on foot, Pl.*Criti.*119b. **-ικός**, ή, όν, *affording a means of descent*, Porph.*Antr.*22. Adv. -κῶς *by a descending* or *deductive process*, ψυχὴ -κῶς νοοῦσα τὰ πράγματα, opp. ἀθρόως, Olymp.*in Alc.*p.78 C. **-ός**, ή, όν, *descending, steep*, ὁδὸς Sch.A.R.2.353, cf. Porph.*Antr.*23; v. καταιβατός. II. καταβατόν, τό, = σελίς, Hdn.*Epim.*2, 122, cf. Hsch. s. v. σελίς.

καταβαΰζω, *bark at*, prob. in Heraclit.97; τινος *AP*7.408 (Leon., καταβαΰξας metri gr.).

καταβαυκᾰλ-άω, *lull to sleep*, Ael.*NA*14.20, Poll.9.127. **-ησις**, εως, ἡ, *lullaby*, Ath.14.618e (pl.). **-ίζω**, = καταβαυκαλάω, *Com. Adesp.*1030. II. (βαύκαλις) *gulp down*, Sopat.25.

κατα-βᾰφή, ἡ, *tincture*, in alchemy, Zos.Alch.p.228 B. **-βᾰφής**, ές, *soaked*, δρώπακι Paul.Aeg.1.30.

καταβεβαι-όομαι, *affirm strongly*, Plu.*Caes.*47. **-ωσις**, εως, ἡ, *strong asseveration*, in pl., D.S.9*Fr.*10.5, Plu.2.1120d.

καταβεβλημένως, Adv. pf. part. Pass. of καταβάλλω, *contemptibly*, Isoc.15.305.

καταβελής, ές, *stricken by many arrows*, D.H.2.42, 5.24.

καταβῐάζω, *subdue by force*, Anon.Hist.(*FGrH*160)*Fr.*1 i 2 (iii B.C.); τὴν ψυχήν Ph.1.685 :—more freq. in Med., *constrain*, καταβιάσασθαι παρὰ γνώμην τοὺς πολλούς Th.4.123; τὴν πόλιν App.*BC*2.28, cf. Eun.*Hist.*p.259 D.; χάρισι τὴν δόξαν Plu.2.385e; τὰ πράγματα πρὸς τὰς ὑποθέσεις ὁμολογεῖν μὴ πεφυκότα κ. ib.75f. 2. *contend, strive to show*, ὧν εὐνοῦχος ἀνὴρ εἶναι κατεβιάζετο Eun.*Hist.*p.256 D. II. Pass., *to be forced*, Plu.*Thes.*11, Id.2.639f; [νούσημα] ἤδη ὑπὸ χρόνου πολλοῦ καταβεβιασμένον, of a *chronic* disease, Hp.*Morb. Sacr.*2.

καταβῐβ-άζω, causal of καταβαίνω, *make to go down, bring down*, τινὰ ἀπὸ τῆς πυρῆς Hdt.1.87, cf. 86; τοὺς ἐκ τοῦ καταστρώματος ἐς κοίλην νέα Id.8.119; στρατιώτας.. εἰς τὴν χώραν τῶν Φρυγῶν *Hell.Oxy.*16.3; τὴν πόλιν πρὸς τὴν θάλασσαν Plu.*Them.*4; *bring from town to country*, Id.*Cam.*10; down into a mine, Th.7.86, Plu.2.262d: metaph., *bring down, lower*, κ. σεαυτὸν ἀπὸ αὐχημάτων εἰς τὸ δημοτικώτερον D.H.7.45 :—Pass., κωμῳδία -βιβασθεῖσα εἰς τὸ λογοειδές Str.1.2.6. 2. *force to come down*, εἰς τὸ ὁμαλὸν τὸ στρατόπεδον X.*HG*4.6.7, cf. Th.5.65; *drive away*, Hp.*Prorrh.*1.143. II. *bring down*, τὴν διήγησιν ἐπὶ τὴν ἀρχὴν τοῦ πρώτου Φοινικικοῦ πολέμου D.H.1.8; τὸν λόγον ἐπὶ τὰ νῦν καθεστῶτα Luc.*Rh.Pr.*20. III. *bring down* the accent, i.e. *throw* it *forward*, A.D.*Synt.*213.16, *EM*774.34. IV. Astron., ὁ -βιβάζων (sc. σύνδεσμος) *the descending node*, Vett.Val.30.6, Procl.*Hyp.*5.101. **-άσκω**, frequentat. of καταβαίνω, *trespass*, *Schwyzer* 126a (Corinth, v B.C.). **-ασμός**, ὁ, *decrease*, = ὑπόβασις, Procl.*Par.Ptol.*67. II. *throwing* of the accent *forward*, Sch.Od.5.248, Eust.1361.39 :—also **καταβίβᾰσις**, εως, ἡ, *EM*610.24. **-αστέος**, α, ον, *to be brought down*, Pl.*R.*539e.

καταβιβρώσκω (pres. not found, v. ἐσθίω), aor. κατέβρων *h.Ap.*127: pf. Pass. καταβέβρωμαι: aor. κατεβρώθην (v. infr.) :—*eat up, devour*, *h.Ap.* l.c.; καταβεβρωκὼς σιτία ἴσως ἐλεφάντων τεττάρων Antiph.82: metaph., καταβεβρώκασι.. τὰς οὐσίας Hegesipp.Com.1.30; τὰ ὄντα Hyp.*Fr.*249 :—Pass., ὑπὸ εὐλέων κατεβρώθη Hdt.3.16; κατεβρώθη ὑπὸ τῶν ἰδίων κυνῶν Palaeph.6; καταβέβρωται Hdt.4.199; ὑπ' ἰχθύων prob. in Phld.*Mort.*32; *to be corroded*, Pl.*Phd.*110a.

καταβῑνέω, = βινέω; 3 sg. καταβηνῆσι, barbarism in Ar.*Th.*1215.

καταβῐ-όω, aor. κατεβίων Pl.*Prt.*355a, later κατεβίωσα Plb.12.28.6, Plu.*Dem.*24 :—*pass one's life*, τὸ ἡδέως καταβιῶναι τὸν βίον Pl. l.c., cf. *R.*578c, Ph.1.627: c. part., κ. ξενιτεύων, σοφιστεύων, Plb. l.c., Plu. l.c.; κ. διώξαντες ἕτερον ἢ καὶ φυγόντες ὑφ' ἑτέρου Phld.*Rh.*2.166 S.; κ. γεωργοῦντες Str.13.4.10. 2. *bring one's life to an end, die*, λέγεται ἄρτιος καταβιῶναι καὶ τὰς αἰσθήσεις ἡβῶν Philostr.*VS*1.9.3. **-ωσις**, εως, ἡ, *decline of life*, Cic.*Att.*13.1.2. 2. *residence*, D.S.18.52, App.*BC*4.16.

καταβλᾰβεύς, έως, ὁ, *damager*, prob. in *IG*14.432.9 (Tauromenium), = *Supp.Epigr.*4.58.

καταβλᾱκεύω, *treat carelessly, mismanage*, Hp.*Art.*52 (sed leg. καταμβλ-), X.*An.*7.6.22 :—in Pass., καταβλακευόμενοι ἄνθρωποι *negligent, slothful*, Just.*Nov.*95.1.2.

καταβλάπτω, *hurt greatly, damage*, *h.Merc.*93, Pl.*Lg.*877b, Lex ap.D.23.28, etc.; βλάβην κ. τινά *inflict* damage upon him, Pl.*Lg.*864e; κατεβλαφότες τὰς προσόδους *IG*7.303.51 (Oropus); ὅ κα καταβλάψῃ for whatever *damage* he *may have done*, ib.9(1).694.102 (Corc.) :—Pass., πολλὰ καταβλαβῆναι μέρη Str.1.3.20.

καταβλέθει· καταπίνει, Hsch.

καταβλέπω, *look down at*, Lxx *Ge.*18.16; ἄνωθεν εἰς.. Plu.*Arat.*32; *view*, Id.2.680d. b. metaph., *despise*, *BGU*15 ii 5 (ii A.D.). 2. *examine, contemplate*, Call.*Del.*303; τὸ σεαυτοῦ κακόν Plu.2.469b.

καταβλεφᾰρίζω, gloss on κατιλλώπτω, Hsch.

κατά-βλημα, ατος, τό, *overthrow*, in argument, πτῶμά τοι τὸ κ. Democr.125. II. *anything let down*: hence, 1. in ships, *tarpaulin* for keeping off missiles, *IG*2².1629.409, 1631.262, al. 2. *curtain, drop-scene* of a theatre, in pl., Poll.4.127, 131. 3. *skirt, fringe*, Duris 14 J. 4. *outer wrapper*, Hp.*Art.*33. III. *payment*, dub. in *IG*1².354. **-βλής**, ῆτος, ὁ, = ἐπιβλής, *bolt*, Hsch. **-βλητέον**, (καταβάλλω) *one must sow*, εἰς ποίαν γῆν ποῖον σπέρμα κ. Pl.*Tht.*149e. 2. *one must pay*, χρέος (metaph. of life), Plu.2.107a. **-βλητικός**, ή, όν, *fit for throwing off horseback*, X.*Eq.*8.11; *of throwing* in wrestling, τέχνη Gal.*Thras.*45: c. gen., κ. τοῦ μεγέθους τῆς Ἑλλάδος D.H.*Th.*19: metaph., *fond of confuting*, τῶν πέλας Gal.9.217; *abusive*, Phld.*Lib.*p.18 O.

καταβληχάομαι, strengthd. for βληχάομαι, Theoc.5.42.

καταβλώσκω, poet. for κατέρχομαι, *go down* or *through*, ἄστυ καταβλώσκοντα Od.16.466; πόληος νόσφι A.R.1.322; of seamen, Lyc.1068 (in irreg. fut. -βλώξω); of a stream, A.R.4.227.

καταβο-άω, fut. -βοήσομαι Ar.*Eq.*286; Ion. -βώσομαι Hdt.6.85: strengthd. for βοάω :—*bawl*, οὐ μόνον βοᾶν, ἀλλ' ἤδη καὶ καταβοᾶν Ph.1.475: but usu. 2. c. gen., *cry out, inveigh against*, τινὸς περί τινος Hdt. l.c.; κ. τινῶν ὅτι σπονδὰς λελυκότες εἶεν Th.1.67, cf. 115, 5.45 :—Pass., *have clamour raised against one*, ὑπό τινων App.*BC*5.13. II. c. acc., *shout down*, Ar.*Ach.*711, *Eq.*286. III. c. acc. cogn., κατά μοι βόασον.. ὅπα τοῖς Ἀτρείδαις *carry down* my voice.., S.*El.*1067 (lyr.). IV. *call for help*, τινὶ περί τινος *PSI*6.551.2 (iii B.C.), *PMagd.*42.5 (iii B.C.): c. gen. et inf., *demand clamorously from*.., κ. τινὸς κολάζειν τὸν στρατιώτην J.*BJ*2.12.1. 2. Pass., *to be loudly entreated*, Nic.Dam.4 J. **-ή**, ῆς, ἡ, *outcry against* any one, c. gen. pers., Th.1.73, 8.85; κ. ἡ ἐς Λακεδαίμονα ib.87, cf. *UPZ*1.6 (iv B.C.); κ. ποιήσασθαι J.*AJ*15.10.3, cf. Men.Prot.p.29 D. **-ησις**, εως, ἡ, = foreg., αἰτίαι καὶ κ. Plu.*Pomp.*67, cf. 2.420f, *IG*12(3).325.34 (Thera, ii A.D., pl.). II. *shouting*, Ph.2.537 (pl.); *loud cry*, κ. ἀγαθαί, κακαί, Artem.1.24. III. *divulgation*, τῶν ἔξωθεν Philostr.*Ep.*7.

καταβολ-άδας· κλάδους, Hsch. **-αῖον**, τό, *storehouse*, *PFay.*110.6, 30 (i A.D.). **-εύς**, έως, ὁ, *founder*, Sch.Pi.*O.*3.1. II. *one who pays*, *Gloss.* III. in pl., officers *who collect payments* due to the state, *IG*5(2).357.9 (Stymphalus, iii B.C.). **-ή**, ἡ, *throwing down*: hence, *sowing*, *Corp.Herm.*9.6; esp. of *begetting*, κ. σπέρματος, σπερμάτων, Philol.13, Luc.*Am.*19, cf. *Ep.Hebr.*11.11, Arr.*Epict.*1.13.3; ἡ Ῥωμύλου σπορὰ καὶ κ. Plu.2.320b. b. *congenital defect*, ἀπὸ ξυγγενικῆς αἰτίας καὶ κ. Plu.*Tim.*37. c. Astrol., *nativity*, ἡ ἐξ ἀρχῆς κ. Vett.Val.220.29, al. 2. *paying down*, esp. by instalments, καταβάλλειν τὰς κ. D.59.27; τὸ ἀργύριον ἔφερε καταβολὴν τῇ πόλει paid money as *a deposit* (by way of caution), Docum.ib.37.22, cf. *IG*12(7).515.26 (Amorgos, ii B.C.), *UPZ*112 v 12 (pl., ii B.C.), etc.; ἔχειν τῆς γῆς.. καταβολήν *liability for rent*, *PEleph.*23.17 (iii B.C.): pl., *instalments*, *PLips.*12.17 (iii A.D.), etc. II. *laying of a foundation*: hence, *building, structure*, Lxx 2*Ma.*2.29; τῆς ἀρχιτεκτονίας Bito 49.2; ἔργου J.*AJ*12.2.9: but usu. metaph., 1. *foundation, beginning*, ἱερῶν ἀγώνων Pi.*N.*2.4; τῆς περιόδου Arist.*Mete.*352ᵇ15; κ. ἐποιεῖτο καὶ θεμέλιον ὑπεβάλλετο τυραννίδος Plb.13.6.2; κ. κόσμου *Ev.Matt.*13.35, *Ep.Eph.*1.4; κ. κοσμική *Cat.Cod.Astr.*8(3).138 (Thessal.); ἡ πρώτη κ. τῆς φιλοσόφου θεωρίας Procl. *in Alc.Praef.*p.8 C.; ἐκ καταβολῆς from *the foundations*: hence, *anew*, σκάφη ἐκ κ. ἐναυπηγοῦντο, of *fresh* construction, Plb.1.36.8; ἐκ κ. πλάττων, of *pure* invention, Id.15.25.35: hence, of *set purpose, deliberately*, Id.1.47.7, 24.8.9. 2. = θυσία, τελετή, Hsch., cf. κατηβολή. III. *periodical attack* of illness, *fit*, τῆς ἀσθενείας Pl.*Grg.*519a, cf. κατηβολή; πυρετοῦ D.9.29, Ph.1.399, 2.563, cf. Aristid.*Or.*50(26).59, Id.2.166 J.; *trance*, Poll.1.16; cf. Lat. *catabolicus*. IV. *detraction, abuse*, Phld.*Rh.*2.56 S.: pl., Ph.2.571 codd. V. perh. *outer wrapper* (cf. κατάβλημα II. 4) of a bandage, Hp.*Off.*9.

καταβόλ-ια, *confectores* (sic), *Gloss.* **-ος** (proparox.), ὁ, *stewpond, oyster-bank*, Xenocr.ap.Orib.2.58.96. II. *naval station*, = ἐπίνειον, Sch.Th.1.30; *entrepôt*, = ἐμπόριον, *EM*336.21.

καταβομβέω, in Pass., *to be deafened*, τῇ σάλπιγγι τὸ Ἐνυάλιον ἐπηχούσῃ Agath.2.1.

καταβορβόρωσις, εως, ἡ, *wallowing in mud*, Plu.2.166a (pl.).

καταβόρειος, ον, (Βορέας) = sq., Thphr.*HP*2.8.1.

κατάβορρος, ον, *sheltered from the north*, i.e. *facing the south*, ἀπὸ τῶν ἄρκτων κ. Pl.*Criti.*118b, cf. Thphr.*CP*2.9.7; [οἰκία] κ. Arist.*Oec.*1345ᵃ33.

καταβόσκησις, εως, ἡ, *feeding down* or *off*, Sm.*Is.*6.13.

καταβόσκω, *feed flocks upon* or *in* a place, ἀγρόν Lxx *Ex.*22.5(4); χὠ τὰν Σαμίαν καταβόσκων the *shepherd* of Samos, Theoc.15.126, cf. *PSI*4.346.5 (iii B.C.) :—Med., with aor. 1 Med. and Pass., fut. Pass., of the flock, *feed upon*, Longus 2.16; καταβοσκηθήσονται βοτάνην *Gp.*2.39.2; *devour, consume*, of disease or pestilence, Call.*Dian.*125; δέμας καταβόσκεται ἄτη Nic.*Th.*244; ἡσυχίῃ δὲ πόλιν κ. *reigns throughout*.., Tryph.503.

καταβόστρῠχος, ον, *with flowing locks*, νεανίας E.*Ph.*146 (lyr.), cf. Aristaenet.2.19, Hld.7.10.

καταβουκολέω, *lead astray, beguile*, Them.*Or.*26.330a (Pass.).

καταβρᾰβεύω, *give judgement against* one as βραβεύς, and so, *deprive one of the prize, deprive one of one's right*, c. acc., *Ep.Col.*2.18, Sch.Il.1.399 :—Pass., ὑπὸ Μειδίου καταβραβευθέντα *being cast in his suit* by means of Meidias, Test.ap.D.21.93, cf. *Sammelb.*4512 B 58 (ii B.C.). 2. c. gen., *rule over*, ἡ γῆ κ. τῶν λοιπῶν Vett.Val.344.29.

καταβρᾰδύνω, *retard*, Asclep.ap.Gal.12.413.

καταβράζει· καταβοᾷ, Hsch. (sed leg. -κράζει).

κατα-βρεκτέον, *one must drench*, τὸν στόμαχον οἴνῳ Alex.Trall.9.3. **-βρεξις**, εως, ἡ, *soaking*, *Gloss.* **-βρέχω** :—Med., fut. -βρέξομαι v.l. in Hp.*Mul.*2.133 :—Pass., aor. 1 κατεβρέχθην Ar.*Nu.*267: aor. 2 κατεβράχην [ᾰ] Thphr.*CP*6.17.2 :—*drench, soak, steep*, μὴ καταβρεχθῶ Ar. l.c.; δρῦς ἐν τῷ ὕδατι -βρεχομένη Thphr.*HP*5.4.3; σμύρνα -βραχεῖσα μελικράτῳ Id.*CP* l.c.; Ἀσκληπιὸς κατέβρεξεν [τὴν Θασίαν ἄμπελον?] *watered* the Thasian vine, i.e. gave it its healing property, Antid.4.4: metaph., κ. τινὰ κάδοις Χίου Hedyl.ap.Ath.10.473a; μέλιτι πόλιν κ. Pi.*O.*10(11).99; καύχημα κ. σιγᾷ *steep* boasting in silence, i.e. be silent instead of boasting, Id.*I.*5(4).51. *inundate*, *PPetr.*3 p.108 (iii B.C.).

καταβρίζω, *fall asleep*, Hsch.

καταβρίθω [ῑ], intr., *to be heavily laden, weighed down* by a thing, ὄϊες μαλλοῖς καταβεβρίθασι Hes.*Op.*234; ὄρπακες βραβύλοισι καταβρίθοντες ἔραζε Theoc.7.146. II. trans., *weigh down, outweigh*, ὄλβῳ μὲν πάντας κε καταβρίθοι βασιλῆας Id.17.95.

καταβρῐμάομαι, strengthd. for βριμάομαι, Corinna 18 (s.v.l.).

καταβροντάω, fut. -ήσομαι, *to thunder down*, τοὺς ῥήτορας Longin.34.4; καταστράψουσι καὶ -ήσονται Them.*Or.*27.337d; κατέσεισεν ἅπαντα καὶ κατεβρόντησεν Eun.*Hist.*p.256 D.

καταβρόξειε, v. *βρόχω 2. **καταβροτόω**, *soil with gore*, Hsch.

καταβροχή, ἡ, *soaking, steeping*, Dsc.1.54 (pl.), Thd.*Pr*.3.8, Orib. 10.15.2.

καταβροχθίζω, *gulp down*, Hp.*Coac*.62, Ar.*Eq*.357, 826; ὀβολόν Id.*Av*.503, cf. Antiph.190.6; τὴν Πελοπόννησον ἅπασαν Hermipp. 45: metaph., λόγους κ. Ath.6.270b.

καταβροχίζω (-βρογχ- codd.), *tie up, ligature*, Orib.*Fr*.38.

κατάβροχος, ον, *inundated*, *PMagd*.3.5 (iii B.C.), etc.

καταβρύκω [ῡ], aor. 1 κατέβρυξα Nic.*Th*.675:—*bite in pieces, eat up*, Hippon.36, *AP*6.263 (Leon.), Nic. l.c.

καταβρύω, *to be overgrown*, κισσῷ καταβρύουσαν, of a cup with ivy ornament, Eub.56.6 (s. v. l.).

κατάβρωμα, ατος, τό, *that which is eaten, food*, Lxx*Nu*.14.9, al., *EM*453.53.

καταβρώξειε, v. *βρόχω 2.

κατάβρωσις, εως, ἡ, *eating up, devouring*, Lxx*Ge*.31.15.

καταβρώσομαι, fut. of καταβιβρώσκω.

καταβῡθ-ίζω, *cause to sink*, Hp.*Ep*.17, Thphr.*HP*5.4.7 (Pass.); ναῦν D.S.15.34: metaph., κ. αὐτάνδρους τοὺς βίους Longin.44.6:—Pass., πολέμοις -βυθισθεῖσαν πόλιν *IPE*1^{2}.34.7 (Olbia, i B.C.). **-ισμός**, ὁ, *sinking*, *Gloss*.

καταβυρσόω, *cover with hides*, ναῦς Th.7.65. 2. *sew up in a skin*, Plu.*Cleom*.38.

καταβυσσόω, *bury*, in Pass., εἴδωλα καταβυσσούμενα ἐν τῷ ὀφθαλμῷ Alex.Aphr.*in de An*.135.19.

καταγαΐδιοι θεοί gods *of the underworld*, = Lat. *di manes*, *IG*14. 581 (Centuripa).

κατάγαιος, ον, Ion. for καταγειος.

κατ-ᾰγᾰπάω, strengthd. for ἀγαπάω, *to be content with, accept*, Epicur.*Ep*.2 p.55 U.: pf. part. κατηγαπηκώς ib.p.41 U.

κατάγαστρον, τό, *stomach-band*, *Gloss*.

κατάγαστρος, ον, *gluttonous*, *Cat.Cod.Astr*.7.212.

κατ-αγγειόομαι, *to be furnished with blood-vessels*, Ruf.*Anat*.13, Heliod.ap.Orib.50.47.3 (-γι- codd.); cf. κατηγγειωμένως.

καταγγελ-εύς, έως, ὁ, *one who proclaims, herald*, ἀγώνων *IG*12(2). 58a10 (Mytilene, i B.C.), cf. *BSA*26.163 (Sparta, ii A.D.); ξένων δαιμονίων *Act.Ap*.17.18. **-ία**, ἡ, *proclamation*, πολέμου Luc.*Par*.42; esp. of games or festivals, ἐκ καταγγελίας ἐπιτελεῖν ἀγῶνα Plu.*Rom*. 14; τὴν κ. ἐποιήσαντο πρεπόντως *OGI*319.13 (Magn. Mae., ii B.C.), cf. *CIG*3656.6 (Cyzicus, ii B.C.); τὰν κ. ἀποδέχεται ib.12. II. *denunciation*, J.*AJ*10.7.4 (pl.).

κατ-αγγέλλω, *announce, proclaim, declare*, πόλεμον κατηγγέλκασι Lys.25.30, cf. D.S.14.68, Plu.*Pyrrh*.26; κ. ῥύσιά τινι Plb.4.53.2; δεῖπνον Plu.2.727b: freq. in *NT*, κ. τὸ εὐαγγέλιον, Χριστόν, 1*Ep.Cor*. 9.14, *Ep.Phil*.1.17: c. inf., κ. ἱκέσθαι *report* one's arrival, *Berl.Sitzb*. 1927.170 (Cyrene). 2. *recite, recount*, ἀγῶνα Luc.*Par*.39. 3. *denounce*, τινὸς τὴν ἐπιβουλήν X.*An*.2.5.38; δοῦλοι ὅσοι δεσπότας κ. Hdn.5.2.2; *lay an information*, πρός τινα *CIG*3641 b.32 (Lampsacus): metaph., κ. ἀπειρίαν τοῦ ποιητοῦ A.D.*Pron*.78.20. 4. of symptoms, *threaten*, σπασμόν Antyll.ap.Orib.10.2.6.

κατάγγελ-ος, ὁ, = μυρσίνη ἀγρία, Ps.-Dsc.4.144 (nisi leg. κακ-). **-σις**, εως, ἡ, *giving of information*, *Gloss*. **-της**, ου, ὁ, *informer*, ib. **-τικός**, ή, όν, *announcing*, c. gen. rei, Hld.3.1. **-τος**, ον, *denounced, betrayed*, κ. γίγνεσθαί τινι Th.7.48, cf. D.C.*Fr*.11.14.

καταγγ-ίζω, *put into a vessel, bottle*, Dsc.5.6.7, *POxy*.2153.6 (iii A.D., Pass.): **-ισμός**, ὁ, *packing*, λάρδου *PLond.ined*.2147 (iv A.D.); ἄνθρακος *PBaden*29.8 (v A.D.).

κατάγειος, Ion. **κατάγαιος**, ον, *under the earth, subterranean*, θησαυρός Hdt.2.150; οἰκήματα Id.3.97, etc.; οἰκίαι X.*An*.4.5.25; οἴκησις Pl.*R*.514a, *Prt*.320e; ἐκ τοῦ κ. from *below ground*, Id.*R*.532b; οἰκίσκος κ. v.l. in Paul.Aeg.6.21. II. *on the ground*, τὰ κ. *ground-floor* rooms, opp. ὑπερῷα, D.H.10.32; στρουθοὶ κ. ostriches, Hdt.4. 175, 192; cf. κατώγειος. 2. Subst., κατάγειον or κατάγαιον, τό, *cellar*, *POxy*.75.19 (ii A.D.), etc.

Καταγέλα, ἡ, Comic name of a town, with a play on the Sicil. *Gela*, Γέλα καὶ Καταγέλα Ar.*Ach*.606, cf. Ath.7.314f.

καταγελάσ-ιμος, ον, *ridiculous*, with play on the name Γελάσιμος, Plaut.*Stich*.631. **-τής**, οῦ, ὁ, *mocker*, *Gloss*. **-τικός**, ή, όν, *satirical*, ὕμνοι Men.Rh.p.337 S. (Comp.). Adv. -κῶς *scoffingly*, Poll. 5.128. **-τος**, ον, *ridiculous, absurd*, κ. εἶ Ar.*Nu*.849; ὦ καταγέλαστ' Id.*Ra*.480; κ. δῆτ' ἔσει..ἔχων Id.*Th*.226; Πέρσας ποιῆσαι κ. γενέσθαι Ἕλλησι *ridiculous* in their eyes, Hdt.8.100, cf. Pl.*Ap*.35b; of things, κ. τὸ χρῆμα γίγνεται Id.*Grg*.485a; φοβοῦμαι οὔ τι μὴ γελοῖα εἴπω ἀλλὰ μὴ καταγέλαστα Id.*Smp*.189b, cf. Epicur.*Nat*.28.5, etc.: c. gen., τῆς ἀλλαγῆς because of.., Max.Tyr.2.3: Comp., Pl.*Ep*.314a: Sup., Isoc.10.9, 15.56, Pl.*Plt*.296d. Adv. -τως X.*Mem*.1.7.2, Pl.*Lg*. 781c, Aeschin.1.31, D.H.*Comp*.18, etc.: Sup. -τότατα Pl.*Sph*.252b.

καταγελάω, fut. -άσομαι Lys.3.9, late -γελάσω Hsch. s. v. κατακριδεύσει:—Pass., fut. -γελασθήσομαι Epict.*Ench*.22: pf. -γεγέλασμαι Luc.*DMort*.1.1: plpf. κατεγεγέλαστο Id.*Icar*.19:—*laugh, jeer at*, c. gen., Hdt.5.68, Ar.*Ach*.1081, And.4.29, Pl.*Grg*.482d: also c. dat., Hdt.3.37, 4.79, al.: abs., *laugh scornfully, mock*, E.*IA*372 (troch.), Ar. *Eq*.161, X.*An*.1.9.13, Pl.*Prt*.319c, D.21.151; ἅπαντες καταγελῶσιν, ὅταν τις.. Epicur.*Nat*.28.9; ἐπί τινι Them.*Or*.22.272b. 2. c. acc., *laugh down, deride*, E.*Ba*.286, Lxx*Si*.7.11:—Pass., *to be derided*, ὑπό τινος A.*Ag*.1271, Ar.*Ach*.680; καταγελάμενος (Dor.pres. part. Pass.) ὑπὸ τῶν ἄλλων *IG*4.951.123 (Epid.); τὸ εὔηθες καταγελασθὲν ἠφανίσθη Th.3.83; τὸ καταγελᾶσθαι γὰρ πολὺ αἴσχιόν ἐστι Men.*Epit.Fr*.7, cf. Pl.*Euthphr*.3c, al.

κατ-άγελος [ᾰ], ον, (ἀγέλη) *rich in herds*, Hdn.*Epim*.206.

κατάγελως, ωτος, ὁ, *derision*, τί δῆτ' ἐμαυτῆς καταγέλωτ' ἔχω τάδε; these ornaments *which bring ridicule* upon me? A.*Ag*.1264, cf. Ar. *Ach*.76; -γέλωτος ἄξιος X.*Oec*.13.5; κ. πλατύς sheer *mockery*, Ar. *Ach*.1126; κατάγελων..φίλοις παρασχεθεῖν Id.*Eq*.319; διπλοῦν προσλήψῃ -γέλωτα Epict.*Ench*.22; κ. τῆς πράξεως *the crowning absurdity* of the matter, Pl.*Cri*.45e; κατάγελων ἡγούμην πάντα Philostr.*VA* 7.23. 2. of persons, *laughing-stock*, οὗτος κ. νομίζεται Men. 160.4.

καταγεμίζω, *load heavily*, σκάφη D.C.74.13.

καταγέμω, only pres. and impf., *to be full of*, c. gen., -γέμοντος τοῦ στρατοπέδου τῆς λείας Plb.14.10.2, cf. D.S.5.43, J.*BJ*6.5.1, Luc. *Somn*.6: c. dat., J.*BJ*4.3.10.

καταγενής, ές, in Comp. -έστερος, prob. f. l. for μεταγ- (q. v.), Procl.*in Prm*.p.850 S.

καταγεύομαι, *taste*, οἴστρου Orac.ap.Phleg.37 J. 2. Medic., *examine, probe*, τοῦ βάθους Heliod.ap.Orib.46.11.13. II. also as Pass., *to be conquered in taste*, Phot., Suid.

καταγεύστριον, τό, dub. sens. in *PLond*.3.1164*h*17 (iii A.D.).

καταγεωμετρέω, *geometrize, turn into geometry*, τὴν φύσιν Simp. *in Ph*.1341.20.

καταγεωργέω, *bring into tillage*, Str.9.3.4.

καταγεώτης, ου, ὁ, *grave-digger*, Hsch.

καταγηρ-άσκω, Od.19.360 (= Hes.*Op*.93), E.*Med*.124 (anap.), Hyp.*Lyc*.12, Arist.*HA*622a26, etc.:—also **-άω**, Pl.*Criti*.112c, Is.2. 22 (-γηράναι Dobree): fut. -γηράσομαι [ᾱ] Ar.*Eq*.1308, etc., -άσω Pl.*Lg*.949c (aor. subj. in *Smp*.216a): aor. -εγήρᾱσα Hdt.2.146, Pl. *Tht*.202d, Ath.14.633b:—from *-γήραμι (cf. γηράσκω) come inf. -γηράναι or -γηρᾶναι (Att., acc. to Moer.p.115 P., v. supr.) Ath.5. 190e, and prob. -εγήρα Od.9.510, Hdt.6.72: pf. καταγεγήρᾱκα Isoc. 10.1:—*grow old*, ll. cc.; αἶψα..ἐν κακότητι βροτοὶ καταγηράσκουσιν Od.19.360; μαντευόμενος κατεγήρα Κυκλώπεσσιν 9.510, cf. Hdt.6. 72. **-ασμός**, ὁ, *old age*, *Hippiatr*.13.

καταγῑγαρτίζω, *take out the kernel*: metaph., *deflower*, Ar.*Ach*. 275 (lyr.).

καταγίγνομαι, Ion. and later **-γίνομαι** [ῐ], *abide, dwell*, ἐν [χρυσοχοείῳ] Test.ap.D.21.22, cf. Teles p.27 H., *PMagd*.9.3 (iii B.C.), Lxx *Ex*.10.23, *OGI*666.14 (Egypt, i A.D.), etc. 2. *busy oneself* about, *be concerned* with a thing, ἔν τινι Plb.31.29.6; ἐν ἀριθμοῖς καὶ προσώποις A.D.*Synt*.226.28 (but κ. ἐν δοτικῇ *to be constructed* with the dative case, 298.10); ὑφ' ὧν καὶ δι' ὧν καὶ περὶ ὧν τὸ χειρουργικὸν μέρος τῆς τέχνης καταγίνεται Gal.18(2).667; περί τι Phld.*Mus*.p.40 K., Arr.*Epict*.3.2.6; περὶ τὸ ποιὸν μᾶλλον ἢ τὸ ποσόν Ptol.*Geog*.1.1.4, cf. S.E.*M*.4.1; τὴν γεωμετρίαν οὐ περὶ μεγέθη ἀλλὰ περὶ ποιότητα κ. Plot. 6.3.14; εἴς τι A.D.*Synt*.298.21; πρός τι ib.280.15; πρὸς τὸ οἴκοι ἐνδιατρίβειν Agatharch.101. 3. = διάγω II. 2, οὕτω, ἐν τρυφῇ, Id.40, 101.

καταγιγνώσκω, Ion. and later **-γῑνώσκω**, fut. -γνώσομαι Pl. *Euthphr*.2b:—*remark, observe*, esp. something *to one's prejudice*, c. gen. pers.: I. generally, καταγνοὺς τοῦ γέροντος τοὺς τρόπους *having observed* his foibles, Ar.*Eq*.46; πολλήν γέ μου δυστυχίαν κατέγνωκας I have been very unfortunate *by your way of it*, Pl.*Ap*.25a; πολλὴν ἡμῶν ἐρημίαν Is.1.2; οὐκ ἐπιτήδεα κατά τινος κ. *having formed* unfavourable *prejudices* against one, Hdt.6.97: c. inf., of an unfavourable judgement, κ. ἑαυτοῦ μὴ περιέσεσθαι Th.3.45, cf. 7.51; αὐτὸς ἐμαυτοῦ κατέγνων μὴ ἂν καρτερῆσαι X.*Cyr*.6.1.36, cf. Pl.*Ti*.19d: folld. by ὅτι, ὡς, ἐμοῦ κατέγνωκας ὅτι εἰμὶ ἥττων τῶν καλῶν Pl.*Men*. 76c; οὐκ ἂν καταγνοίην ὑμῶν οὐδενὸς ὡς..ἀμελήσετε D.21.4 (but κατεγνωκότες ὅτι..ἐφθείρομεν *despising* us because.. Th.6.34, cf. *PMagd*. 42.4 (iii B.C.), Jul.*Or*.3.108b): c. part., κ. τινὰ πράττοντα X.*Oec*.2.18, cf. *Cyr*.8.4.9; τὸ χωρίον νοσερὸν ⟨ὂν⟩ καταγνόντες D.L.2.109:—Pass., *to be judged unfavourably, lightly esteemed*, παρολιγωρεῖσθαι καὶ καταγινώσκεσθαι Plb.5.27.6; κατεγνωσμένος *despised*, Philostr.*VS*2. 29. II. c. acc. criminis, *lay as a charge against* a person, κ. ἑωυτῶν ἀνανδρείην Hp.*Aër*.22; κ. τινὸς μηδὲν ἀνόσιον Antipho 2.2.12; δειλίαν, δωροδοκίαν κ. τινός, Lys.14.16, 21.21; οὐδὲν ἀγεννὲς ὑμῶν καταγιγνώσκω D.21.152; ἑαυτῶν ἀδικίαν And.1.3; πολλὴν μανίαν, μωρίαν, Isoc.4.133, 5.21; σκληρότητα ἡμῶν καὶ ἀγροικίαν Pl.*R*.607b; τοσαύτην ὑμῶν εὐήθειαν D.30.38: with gen. understood, οὐ γὰρ ἐκεῖνό γε (sc. σοῦ) καταγνώσομαι, ὡς.. Pl.*Euthphr*.2b; later κ. κατά τινος τὸν φόνον Porph.*Abst*.2.30:—Pass., καταγνωσθεὶς δειλίαν *being convicted* of cowardice, D.H.11.22; κ. ἐπὶ λογοκλοπίᾳ D.L.8.54; κατεγνωσμένος *self-condemned*, *Ep.Gal*.2.11. 2. c. gen. criminis, παρανόμων κ. τινός D.25.67; παρανοίας ὑμῶν αὐτῶν Id.*Prooem*.35: c. acc. pers., κ. τινὰ φόνου *pronounce a verdict* of murder *against*.., Lex ap. Lys.1.30; μὴ καταγιγνώσκωμεν τὸ (fort. τοῦ) μηδὲν εἰρηκέναι τὸν ἀποφηνάμενον Pl.*Tht*.206e. 3. c. inf., κ. σφῶν αὐτῶν, ἑαυτοῦ ἀδικεῖν, *charge* oneself *with*.., Lys.20.6, Aeschin.2.6, cf. D.21.175, 206; κ. ὡς.. Isoc.9.78:—so in Pass., καταγνωσθεὶς νεώτερα πρήσσειν *being suspected* of doing, Hdt.6.2; κ. αὐθέντης (sc. εἶναι) Antipho 3.3.11; *to be detected*, ἔν τινι *PFlor*.175.16 (iii A.D.); also κατέγνωσται μελίκρητον ὑπὸ τῶν ἀνθρώπων ὡς καταγυιοῖ τοὺς πίνοντας Hp.*Acut*.56. 4. c. gen. pers. only, *condemn*, τοῦ ἀνθρώπου Pl.*Demod*.382e. III. c. acc. poenae, *give judgement* or *sentence against* a person, κ. τινὸς θάνατον *pass sentence* of death *on* one, Th.6.60; Μηδισμοῦ κ. τινὸς θάνατον *for* Medism, Isoc.4.157; κ. τινὸς φυγήν And.1.106; φυγὴν αὐτοῦ καταγνούς Lys.14.38: c. inf., κ. αὐτοῦ ἀποτεῖσαι τὰ χρήματα D.56.18; later θάνατον, φυγὴν κ. κατά τινος, D.S.18.62, 19.51:—Pass., θάνατός τινος κατέγνωστο Antipho 5.70, cf. Lys.13.39, Jusj.ap.D.24.149;

later καταγνωσθεὶς θανάτῳ Ael.*VH*12.49: abs., κατεγνώσθησαν *they were condemned*, Th.4.74, cf. And.4.8; τὸ ἀδίκημα κεκριμένον ἐστὶ καὶ κατεγνωσμένον Lycurg.52. 2. *decide* a suit, δίκην Ar.*Eq.*1360:—Pass., A.*Eu.*573 codd.; δίκη μὴ ὀρθῶς -γνωσθεῖσα Antipho 6.3.

κατ-ᾰγίζω, Ion. for καθαγίζω, Hdt.1.86, al.

κατ-ᾰγῑνέω, Ion. for κατάγω, *bring down*, Od.10.104. II. *bring back, recall*, Hdt.6.75.

κατ-αγλᾰΐζω, *glorify*, *AP*11.64.8 (Agath.); ναὸν λίθοις J.*AJ*8.5.2:—Pass., κατηγλαϊσμένοι *splendidly attired*, *Com.Adesp.*1275.

καταγλισχραίνω, strengthd. for γλισχραίνω, Hp.*Acut.*53:—Pass., ib.16.

κατάγλισχρος, ον, *viscous*, Alex.Trall.8.2.

καταγλῠκαίνω, *sweeten*, Gal.14.753:—metaph. in Med., ἐν ἐννέ' ἂν χορδαῖς κατεγλυκάνατο Chionid.4.

κατά-γλυμμα, ατος, τό, *sculptured ornament*, *IG*4.1485.94 (pl., Epid.). **-γλυπτόν**· εἶδος φιλήματος, Hsch. **-γλῠφή**, ἡ, (γλύφω) *incision, groove*, Hp.*Art.*72, *Mochl.*38 (**-γλῠφος**, ἡ, ibid., is doubtful). 2. *carving*, λίθων *IG*4.1485.117 (pl., Epid.); γάστρων, σχοινίδος, *Milet.*7.59.4 and 17. **-γλῠφος**, ον, *carved*, σοροί Judeich *Altertümer von Hierapolis* 323. **-γλύφω** [ῠ], *scoop out, groove*, pf. part. Pass. -γεγλυμμένος Hp.*Mochl.*38. 2. *carve*, κυμάτια *IG* 11(2).199*A* 76 (Delos, iii B.C.); σπεῖραν *Milet.*7.59.14.

καταγλωττ-ίζω, *bill, kiss wantonly by joining mouths and tongues*, *Com.Adesp.*882: hence, μέλος κατεγλωττισμένον *wanton, lascivious* song, Ar.*Th.*131. II. *use the tongue against* another, ψευδῆ κ. τινός Id.*Ach.*380. III. κ. τινά *talk* one *down*, hence in Pass., πόλιν ὑπὸ σοῦ κατεγλωττισμένην σιωπᾶν Id.*Eq.*352. IV. (γλῶσσα II. 2) in pf. part. Pass., *composed of far-fetched words*, λέξις Philostr.*VA* 1.17, Eun.*VS* p.496.25 D. **-ισμα**, ατος, τό, *lascivious kiss*, Ar.*Nu.* 51. **-ισμός**, ὁ, = foreg., *Com.Adesp.*1027. **-ος**, ον, *glib, fluent*, ἐν τῇ σχολῇ γοργοὶ καὶ κ. Arr.*Epict.*2.16.20; *babbling, garrulous*, Gell.1.15.17. II. *written in rare* or *far-fetched language*, ποιήματα *AP*11.218 (Crates), prob. l. in Luc.*Lex.*25; τὸ κ. τῆς λέξεως D.H.*Th.*53.

κάταγμα (A), ατος, τό, (κατάγω) *wool drawn* or *spun out, worsted*, Pl.*Plt.*282e; *flock of wool*, S.*Tr.*695, Ar.*Lys.*583, Philyll.22, Chor. p.92 B. [τᾰ by nature, Ammon.*Diff.*p.78 V.]

κάταγμα (B), ατος, τό, Ion. **κάτηγμα**, later **κατέαγμα** (cf. κατάγνυμι), *fragment*, *BCH*35.286 (Delos, ii B.C.); later μικρὰ κατεάγματα λίθου *BGU*647.13 (ii A.D.); πλίνθων κατάγματα dub. cj. in Alc. 153. II. *breakage*, *PAmh.*2.93.19 (ii A.D., in form -αίαγμα = -έαγμα); esp. 2. Medic., *fracture*, Hp.*Aph.*5.22, Thphr.*HP*4. 8.6, Sor.*Fract.*1, al., Gal.10.423; μελῶν Vett.Val.110.5. [τᾰ by nature, Ammon.*Diff.*p.78 V.]:—hence **-αγματικός**, ή, όν, *liable to fracture*, Vett.Val.110.23; but usu. 2. *of* or *for fracture*, ἔμπλαστρος Asclep.ap.Gal.13.536; ἀγωγή Pall.*in Hp.Fract.*12.279 C.; ἐπίδεσις Gal.18(2).441. Adv. -κῶς ib.536.

καταγνάμπτω, *bend down*, *AP*4.3^b.5 (Agath.).

καταγνάφω [γνᾰ], *lacerate*, v.l. for καταγράφω, Hdt.3.108.

κατ-αγνοέω, strengthd. for ἀγνοέω, Phld.*Lib.*p.16 O.

κατ-άγνῡμι, inf. -ύναι [ῠ] Th.4.11, Pl.*Phdr.*265e; **καταγνύω** Eub. 107.14, X.*Oec.*6.5; late pres. **κατάσσω, κατεάσσω** (qq. v.): fut. κατάξω Eup.323: aor. κατέαξα Hom., etc. (v. infr.); Ion. κατῆξα Hp.*Epid.*5.26; 3 sg. subj. κατάξει *SIG*38.37 (Teos, v B.C.); part. κατάξας (Dobree for κατεάξας) Lys.3.42, Plu.2.526b (v.l. κατεάξας, κατάγξας); Ep. opt. καυάξαις = κατϝάξαις for κατ-Ϝάξαις, Hes.*Op.* 666, 693:—**Pass.**, κατάγνῠμαι Hp.*Fract.*45, *Art.*67, Ar.*Pax* 703: impf. κατεάγνυτο Epicur.*Nat.*113 G.: aor. 2 κατεάγην [prob. ᾰ] Ar. *V.*1428, subj. κατ-ᾰγῶ (contr. fr. κατᾰ-Ϝᾰγ-) Id.*Fr.*604, prob. in Id. *Ach.*928, opt. καταγείην ib.944; part. καταγείς [prob. ᾰ] *IG*2^2.1673. 33, 39, al., later κατᾰγέντος *APl.*4.187: fut. καταγήσομαι *Cat.Cod. Astr.*8(4).129: pf. κατέᾱγα, Ion. κατέηγα Hp.*Art.*67 (in pass. sense); part. κατεαγώς, written κατειαγώς *IG*2^2.1673.55, contr. κατηγώς Phoenix 5.1: pf. Pass. κατέαγμαι Luc.*Tim.*10, Paus.8.46.5, Artem. 5.32: aor. 1 κατεάχθην Lxx *Je.*31(48).25; inf. καταχθῆναι Arist.*PA* 640^{a}22; part. καταχθείς Anon.Lond.26.52, D.Chr.11.82.—The forms κατέαξα, κατεάγην led the copyists to insert the ε in unaugmented forms, as κατεάξας Lys. l. c., κατεαγῇ Hp.*Art.*50, κατεαγῆναι Pl.*Grg.*469d, and such forms were in use in later Gr., as κατεάξει *Ev. Matt.*12.20, κατεαγῶσιν *Ev.Jo.*19.31, κατέαξαν *BGU*908.25 (ii A.D.):—*break in pieces, shatter*, κατὰ θ' ἅρματα ἄξω Il.8.403; ἄξονα Hes.*Op.* 693; τὸ (sc. ἔγχος) γὰρ κατεάξαμεν Il.13.257; νέα μέν μοι κατέαξε Ποσειδάων Od.9.283, cf. Hes.*Op.*666; εἴ τινες μαχεσάμενοι ἔτυχον ἀλλήλων κατάξαντες τὰς κεφαλάς Lys.3.42; κατάξειέ τις αὐτοῦ μεθύων τὴν κεφαλήν Ar.*Ach.*1166 cod. R (v.l. τῆς κεφαλῆς, cf. οὐ γὰρ κατάξει τῆς κεφαλῆς τὰ ῥήματα Eup.323, κατῆξε τῶν πλευρέων Hp.*Epid.* 5.26, v. sub fin.); κατάξω τὴν κεφαλήν, ἄνθρωπέ, σου Men.*Sam.*173; γυνὴ κατεάξ' ἐχῖνον Ar.*V.*1436; Ναξίαν ἀμυγδάλην κατᾶξαι Phryn. Com.68; τὰς ἀμυγδαλᾶς.. κάταξον τῇ κεφαλῇ σαυτοῦ λίθῳ Ar.*Fr.*590: metaph., *break up* into species, μὴ κ. μηδὲ κερματίζειν τὴν ἀρετήν Pl.*Men.*79a. 2. *weaken, enervate*, πατρίδα θ', ἣν αὔξειν χρεὼν καὶ μὴ κατᾶξαι E.*Supp.*508; τὰς ψυχὰς καταγνύουσι X.*Oec.*6.5: abs. in pf. part. κατεαγώς *effeminate*, D.H.*Comp.*18, Ath.12.524f; αὐλητὴς τῶν κ. Plu.*Dem.*4; κ. μουσική S.E.*M.*6.14. II. Pass. with pf. Act., *to be broken*, δόρατα κατεηγότα Hdt.7.224; ὀστέα Hp. *Fract.*8; κληῒς Id.*Art.*14; περὶ δ' ἐμῷ κάρᾳ κατάγνυται τὸ τεῦχος S. *Fr.*565.3; κατέαγεν ἡ χύτρα Ar.*Th.*403; esp. καταγῆναι τὴν κεφαλήν *have* one's head *broken*, And.1.61, Lys.3.14; τὴν κεφαλὴν κατεαγέναι D.54.35: Com., στάμνου κεφαλὴν κατεαγότος Ar.*Pl.*545; τὸ κρανίον E.*Cyc.*684; τὸ σκάφιον Ar.*Fr.*604; κατεαγέναι or κατάγνυσθαι τὰ ὦτα, of pugilists, Pl.*Grg.*515e, *Prt.*342b; τὴν κλεῖν κατεαγώς D.18.67: also c. gen. partit. (οὐ πᾶσαν τὴν κεφαλὴν ἀλλὰ μέρος τι αὐτῆς Hdn.*Philet.* p.448 P.), τῆς κεφαλῆς κατέαγε περὶ λίθῳ πεσών Ar.*Ach.*1180; κατεάγη τῆς κ. Id.*V.*1428; τῆς κ. καταγῆναι (-εαγῆναι, -εαγέναι codd.) δεῖν Pl.*Grg.*469d; κατέαγα τοῦ κρανίου Luc.*Tim.*48: metaph., *to be shattered*, of an argument, Epicur. l. c.

καταγνῡπόομαι, Pass., *to be weak*, in pf. Pass. κατεγνυπῶσθαι, Hsch., *EM*236.40; κατεγνυπωμένον cj. in Plu.2.753c. Adv. κατεγνυπωμένως *lazily*, Men.1020; cf. γνύπετος.

κατά-γνωσις, εως, ἡ, *thinking ill of, low* or *contemptuous opinion of*.., κ. ἀσθενείας τινός Th.3.16; *moral condemnation, blame, censure*, Ephor.1 J., Plb.6.6.8, Phld.*Vit.Herc.*1457.9. II. *judgement given against* one, *condemnation*, Th.3.82, Arist.*Ath.*45.1 (pl.), D.21.175; τοῦ θανάτου *to* death, X.*Mem.*4.8.1. III. *dereliction of duty*, *PFlor.* 313.5 (v A.D.), *POxy.*140.17 (vi A.D.). **-γνωσμα**, ατος, τό, = foreg. II, *PTeb.*5.4 (ii B.C.), 124.24 (ii B.C.). **-γνωστέον**, *one must condemn*, τι Ph.1.698; τινος Luc.*Salt.*80; τινων Gal.13.793; κ. τῶν ἀξιούντων τι ὅτι.. *one must reject* the view of.., on the ground that.., Phld.*Po.*5.35. **-γνωστικός**, ή, όν, *damnatory*, Gal.8.656.

καταγογγύζω, *murmur against*, τινος Lxx 1 *Ma.*11.39.

καταγοητεύω, *bewitch*: hence, *cheat* or *blind by trickery*, τινα X. *Cyr.*8.1.40; ἡδονὴ τὸ σῶμα -γεγοήτευκεν Plu.2.986e:—Pass., v. l. in X.*An.*5.7.9, M.Ant.10.13; κρέως καρυκείᾳ καταγοητευθέντος meat *disguised* by sauce, Ael.*NA*4.40.

κατάγομος, ον, *deep-laden, heavy-laden*, πλοῖα Plb.9.43.6, D.S.5. 35; ἅμαξαι Id.3.34: c. gen., *laden with, full of*, στρατοῦ λαφύρων καταγόμου App.*Syr.*21; ψευσμάτων J.*Ap.*2.9: also c. dat., ἀπῄεσαν κ. ταῖς ὠφελείαις D.S.31.45.

καταγομφόω, strengthd. for γομφόω I, Sch.Od.5.248.

κατᾰγορ-άζω, Dor. aor. inf. -αγοράξαι, σῖτον *IG*5(1).1379.21 (Thuria, ii/i B.C.):—**Pass.**, aor. 1 subj. -αγορασθῇ ib.13:—*buy up, purchase*, φορτία D.34.7, cf. Ephipp.21 (sed leg. κατ' ἀγ-); ἐκ τῶν ἰδίων ταῦρον *Milet.*1(9).368. **-αξις**, εως, ἡ, *buying up, purchase*, *IG*5(1). 1379.22 (Thuria, ii/i B.C.). **-ασμός**, ὁ, = foreg., *Milet.*7.28 (ii B.C.); σίτου *IG*12(9).900*c*2 (Chalcis, ii B.C.), D.S.16.13. **-ευσις**, εως, ἡ, *declaration*, Plu.2.428f. 2. *denunciation*, J.*AJ*17.3. 2. **-ευτικός**, ή, όν, *declaratory, definitive*, D.L.7.70; περὶ τῶν κ., title of work by Chrysippus, ib.190. **-εύω** (aor. in use κατεῖπον, hence καταγορεύῃ shd. be restored for -εύσῃ in Ar.*Pax* 107), *tell, announce*, τί τινι Ar. l. c.; cf. κατερῶ. 2. more freq. *denounce*, Th.4.68, 6.54; τι πρός τινα X.*HG*3.3.4. II. *accuse*, τινος Arist. *Pol.*1314^{a}22, Ael.*NA*7.15. III. Pass., *to be predicated*, αἱ κατηγορίαι ὠνομάσθησαν ἀπὸ τοῦ -εύεσθαι Dexipp.*in Cat.*6.27.

κατα-γραπτέον, *one must describe, draw*, of a figure, Ph.*Bel.*52. 33; ἐν πίνακι ἐπιπέδῳ κ. Str.2.5.10. **-γραπτος**, ον, *striped, variegated*, Περσικά, σῦκα, ἀμύγδαλα, *Gp.*10.14 tit., 47 tit., 60 tit., cf. Eust.852.11.

καταγρᾰφ-εύς, έως, ὁ, *cataloguer*, τῶν ἐθνικῶν Eust.335.41. **-ή**, ἡ, *drawing, delineation*, τῆς σφαίρας D.S.3.60; *drawing of maps*, Ptol.*Geog.*1.2.5; ποιεῖσθαι τὴν τῆς οἰκουμένης κ. ib.1.4; of the celestial globe, Gem.5.45; *diagram, figure*, Ael.*Tact.*18.1, Simp.*in Cael.* 652.10. 2. *delineation in profile*, in bas-relief, οἱ ἐν ταῖς στήλαις καταγραφὴν ἐκτετυπωμένοι Pl.*Smp.*193a. 3. *marking out*, τῆς χώρας D.H.8.69. 4. *engraving* of an inscription, *Abh.Berl.Akad.* 1925(5).21 (Cyrene, iv B.C.). II. *list, register*, ὀνομάτων Plu.2. 492b (pl.); esp. *roll of soldiers*, in pl., Plb.2.24.10, D.H.4.19; ἡ τῶν συνέδρων κ. the *roll* of the Senate, D.S.20.36. III. *conveyance* of land or houses, *BGU*1131 21 (Aug.), *POxy.*306 (i A.D.), *Annuario* 4/5.469 (Halic.), etc.; also of slaves, etc., *BGU*1114, Charito 1.14. **-ος**, ον, = κατάγραπτος, Alex.Mynd.ap.Ath.9.387f, Dsc.3. 156, Luc.*Alex.*12, *Hippiatr.*14. II. *drawn in profile*, Hipparch. 1.4.5; κατάγραφα, τά, = Lat. *obliquae imagines*, Plin.*HN*35.56. **-ω**, *scratch, lacerate*, Hdt.3.108 (v.l. καταγνάφω), Ael.*VH*10.3; ἰὸς δένδρεα κ. *marks* them, Nonn.*D.*21.329; κατέγραφεν ἠέρα ταρσῷ *grazed* it, ib.4.407, cf. Tryph.669:—Pass., καταγεγράφθαι ταῖς ῥυτίσι *EM*239. 31. 2. *engrave, inscribe*, εἰς τοὺς τοίχους στίχον Plb.5.9.4:—Pass., νόμοι κατεγράφησαν (for Att. ἀνεγρ-) εἰς ἄξονας Plu.*Sol.*25. 3. *draw in outline, delineate*, Paus.1.28.2. 4. *describe*, Ptol.*Geog.*1.2.2, D.P. 707, Aret.*CA*1.5 (Pass.): in Geom., ἑξάγωνον κ. Simp.*in Cael.*653. 7. 5. *paint over*, τοίχων ἀμορφίαν βαφαῖς Luc.*Am.*34. II. *fill with writing*, [σανίδας] E.*Alc.*969 (lyr.):—Pass., Luc.*VH*1.7. 2. *register, record*, μνήμας εἰς τὸν ἔπειτα χρόνον -γεγραμμένας Pl.*Lg.*741c; ὠνάς *BGU*1213.9 (iii B.C.); κατεγράφησαν ἄνδρες οὓς ἔδει θνῄσκειν Plu. *Cic.*46; esp. *enroll*, ναύτας Plb.1.49.2; δυνάμεις D.S.11.1; τινὰς εἰς φυλὰς καὶ φρατρίας D.H.2.35:—Pass., τμηθέντων τῶν ὁρκίων... καὶ καταγραφέντων, ...τοὺς ὁμήρους.. τούς.. καταγραφέντας, Plb.29.3.6; σύγκλητος ὑπὸ τῶν τιμητῶν καταγραφεῖσα D.S.20.36; Σαπφὼ ἐν Μούσαις δεκάτη καταγράφεται *AP*9.571. 3. *summon by a written order*, [χορηγούς] κ. τινάς Arist.*Oec.*1352^{a}7; κοινοβούλιον Plb.28.19.1. b. *prescribe, ordain*, c. acc. et inf., Luc.*Am.*19. 4. *convey, transfer by deed*, Plu.2.482c; οἰκίαν εἴς τινα *PPetr.*2 p.70 (iii B.C.), cf. *BGU*50.8 (Pass., ii A.D.), *POxy.*1703 (iii A.D.), etc. (also in Med. of the purchaser, *have conveyed* to one, *Annuario* 4/5.469 (Halic.)):—Pass., ὁ καταγραφείς the person *to whom* property *is conveyed*, *POxy.*472.19 (ii A.D.)): generally, *assign*, ἑαυτῷ λύτρα Ael.*Fr.*71: c. inf., *reckon* that.., Id.*NA*7.11. 5. *devote* to the infernal gods, *curse*, *IG*9(1). 977 (Corc.), *Tab.Defix.*p.vii; so prob. in Plu.*Cic.*32.

κατ-άγρημι, Aeol. = καθαιρέω, Sapph.43, Alc.*Supp.*16.9; imper.

κατάγρεντον *IG*12(2).6.15 (Mytilene): irreg. Pass. part. καταγρόμενος Theoc.*Ep.*3.6 (dub. l.).

καταγρῡπόω, *curl the nose*: αὐστηρὸν καὶ κατεγρυπωμένον *scornful*, Plu.2.753c codd. (κατεγνυπωμένον Schneid.).

κατ-αγυιόω, *enfeeble*, Hp.*Acut.*56.

καταγυμν-άζω, *train, discipline*, τὰ σώματα Luc.*Anach.*24; πολλὰ κ. τινὰ Id.*Merc.Cond.*42: c. inf., τοὺς νέους ἀντέχειν καταγυμνάζωσιν Id.*Nigr.*27. II. Med., *squander in gymnastic exercises and games*, Hsch. **-ᾰσία**, ἡ, = γυμνασία, Orib.*Fr.*59.

καταγυμνόω, *strip naked*, Aristaenet.1.7 (Pass., s. v. l.).

καταγύναιος [ῠ], ον, = sq., *Gloss.*

κατάγῠνος, ον, *much given to women*, Arist.*Mir.*837ᵃ34.

καταγυψόω, *plaster with gypsum*, κεράμια Gal.17(2).164.

κατ-άγχουσα, ἡ, = ἄγχουσα, Ps.-Dsc.4.23.

κατ-άγχω, *strangle*, Thd.*Jd.*11.35. II. κατάγξας f.l. for κατάξας in Plu.2.526b.

κατ-άγω [ᾰγ], fut. -ξω Th.1.26, etc.: aor. κατήγᾰγον Od.11.164, Epig.7: rarely aor. 1 κατῆξα v.l. in X.*HG*2.2.20, *PGrenf.*2.44 (ii A.D.), Philum.*Ven.*10.4: Ep. aor. inf. -αξέμεν Il.6.53: pf. καταγήοχα Decr.ap.D.18.73:—*lead down*, esp. *into the nether world*, ψυχὰς μνηστήρων κατάγων Od.24.100; εἰς Ἀΐδαο 11.164, cf. Pi.*O.*9.34, Paus. 3.6.2: generally, *bring down* to a place, Od.20.163; τὴν ἐκ τῶν ὀρῶν ὕλην εἰς τὸ ἄστυ Pl.*Criti.*118d, etc.; *bring down* a river or canal, *PGrenf.* l. c.:—Pass., *POxy.*708.3 (ii A.D.). 2. *draw down*, κατῆγεν ἦγεν ἦγεν ἐς μέλαν πέδον E.*Ba.*1065; esp. by magic arts, κ. τὸν Δία Plu.*Num.*15; ἀετόν ib.8, dub. sens. in Thphr.*CP*2.9.4. 3. *bring down to the sea-coast*, κατάγειν κοίλας ἐπὶ νῆας Il.5.26, cf. 6.53; ἐπὶ θάλατταν τὸ στράτευμα X.*Ages.*1.18. b. *launch*, σκάφος εἰς τὴν θάλασσαν Callix.1. 4. *bring down from the high seas to land*, τὸν Κρήτηνδε κατήγαγε ἴς ἀνέμοιο Od.19.186: abs., *put in to shore*, 3.10 Aristarch. (κατάγοντο codd.); esp. for purposes of exacting toll or plundering, X.*HG*4.8.33, *An.*5.1.11, D.5.25, al.; κ. ναῦς ἐς τοὺς ἑαυτῶν συμμάχους X.*HG*5.1.28; also κ. τοὺς ἐμπόρους Plb.5.95.4, cf. D.S.20.82; κ. σαγήνην *draw* it *to land*, Plu.*Sol.*4; τοῦ πνεύματος κλύδωνα κατάγοντος πολὺν *bringing in* a heavy swell *from the sea*, Id.*Mar.*36; ὥρα πνεῦμα λαμπρὸν ἐκ πελάγους κατάγουσα Id. *Them.*14:—Pass., *come to land, land*, opp. ἀνάγεσθαι, of seamen as well as ships, Od.3.178; ἐπ' ἀκτῆς νηῒ κατηγαγόμεσθα 10.140, cf. Hdt.4.43; Σίγειον οὐρίῳ πλάτῃ κατηγόμην S.*Ph.*356; κατάγεσθαι ἐς τὸν Μαραθῶνα Hdt.6.107, cf. 8.4, Pl.*Mx.*240c; εἰς τὸν λιμένα X.*HG*6.2.36. b. κατάγεσθαι παρά τινι *turn in and lodge* in a person's house, Eup.344, X.*Smp.*8.39, *PFlor.*248.11 (iii A.D.); ὥς τινα D.52.22; εἰς οἰκίαν Id.49.22; εἰς πανδοκεῖον Plu.2.773e. 5. *draw down* or *out, spin*, Pherecr.46, Epig.7, Pl.*Sph.*226b; κατάγουσα, ἡ, *spinning-girl*, statue by Praxiteles, Plin.*HN*34.69: metaph., κ. λόγον Pl.*Men.*80e. 6. *reduce* to a state, ἐς κίνδυνον φανερὸν κ. τὴν πόλιν Th.4.68; ὁ οἶνος εἰς ὕπνον κ. Ael.*VH*13.6. 7. *bring home, gain*, θρίαμβον καὶ νίκην τῇ πατρίδι Plb.11.33.7; ἐκ πολέμων Plu.*Fab.* 24; *escort*, ἐπὶ τιμητείαν Id.*Aem.*38, etc. 8. κ. γένος *derive* a pedigree, ἀπό τινος Id.2.843e, Nic.Dam.61 J.:—Pass., τὰ στέμματα κατάγεται εἴς τινα *are traced down* to.., Plu.*Num.*1; φᾶμαι κατάγοντο Call.*Fr.*1.39 P.; of persons, *to be descended*, ἀπό τινος Olymp. *Vit.Pl.*p.1 W. 9. *derive* a word, S.E.*M.*1.242 (Pass.): generally, *derive*, ὅθεν δεῖ κατῆχθαι καὶ πῶς ἀποδεικνύειν Phld.*Rh.*1.203 S.; κ. [βοάν] *lower* the voice, E.*Or.*149 (lyr.): metaph., *bring down, lower*, πρὸς αὑτόν to one's own standard, D.Chr.40.11. 10. Medic., *couch* a cataract, Gal.18(2).680. 11. *wind up* a torsion-engine, Ph.*Bel.*76.13:—Pass., Hero *Bel.*79.6; ὁ κατάγων τὴν χεῖρα Ph.*Bel.*75.9. 12. καταγόμενος *current*, ἐνιαυτός Vett.Val.27.16. II. *bring back*, κατὰ δὲ φρόνιν ἤγαγε πολλήν *brought back* much news [of Troy], Od.4.258; esp. from banishment, *recall*, Hdt.1.60, Th.1.26, A.*Th.* 647, 660, etc.; κ. οἴκαδε X.*An.*1.2.2: generally, *restore*, τυραννίδας ἐς τὰς πόλις Hdt.5.92.α'; εἰς τὰς πατρίδας.. εἰρήνην Plb.5.105.2; ἐκ ταλαιπωρίας Jul.*Or.*2.58c:—Pass., *return*, ἐπὶ τὸ στρατόπεδον X.*An.* 3.4.36.

κατᾰγωγ-εύς, έως, ὁ, *cattle-drover*, *BGU*92 (ii A.D.). **-ή**, ἡ, *bringing down from* the high sea, *landing*, Th.6.42 (pl.); ποιεῖσθαι τὴν κ. Str.8.3.26. 2. *bringing down* a river, *PMagd.*11.10 (iii B.C.), *PCair.Zen.*518 (iii B.C.), etc. 3. *bringing down* from a height, ὑδάτων J.*BJ*2.9.4. 4. concrete, *halting-place, inn*, like καταγώγιον, Hdt.1.181, al.; *place of rest*, καλὴ ἡ κ. Pl.*Phdr.*230b; *lodging, residence*, *IGRom.*4.1209 (Thyatira); τῶν ἀρχόντων Lib.*Or.*51.4; *shelter* for cattle, *PFlor.*103.12 (iv A.D.). 5. metaph., κ. τοῦ γένους *genealogy, pedigree*, Plu.2.843e. II. *bringing back* from banishment, *restoration*, Plb.32.12.1, D.S.5.4. 2. *winding up* of a torsion-engine, Ph.*Bel.*58.8 (pl.), Hero *Bel.*84.1; *stringing* of a stomach-bow, ib.79.2. 3. Medic., *couching* for cataract, Paul.Aeg.6. 21. III. *anything reaching downwards*, of the nose, Thom.Mag. p.323 R. **-ιμον**, τό, = καταγώγιον II, *PTeb.*35.5 (ii B.C.). **-ιον**, τό, *lodging, inn, resting-place*, Th.3.68, Pl.*Phdr.*259a, X.*Vect.*3.12; Μουσῶν κ. Plu.*Luc.*42; κ. ἀσωτίας Id.*Eum.*13; *official residence* of a magistrate, Procop.*Arc.*29, al.; τὸ τῶν δαιμόνων κ. *OGI*610.1 (Zorava, vi A.D.):—the form **-γεῖον** is required by metre in Antiph.53.5, Macho ap.Ath.8.337d. II. *extra payment for transport*, *PEleph.*14.11 (iii B.C.), *PTeb.*35.18 (ii B.C.). III. in pl., τὰ καταγώγια *festival of the return*, opp. ἀναγώγια, Ath.9.395a, *SIG*1109.114 (ii A.D.). **-ιος**, ὁ, *returned*, epith. of Dionysus, ib.1003.5 (Priene, ii B.C.). **-ίς**, ίδος, ἡ, *winding-mechanism* of a torsion-engine, Ph.*Bel.*75.46. 2. *curved end* of a stomach-bow (used for stringing it), Hero *Bel.*78.3. II. *woman's dress*, Sapph.*Supp.*14.5, cf. Poll.7.49, Hsch. **-ός**, όν, *seductive*, Σειρήνων μέλος *AP*15.12 (Leo Phil.). 2. *lowering*, ψυχῆς, opp. ἀναγωγός, Iamb.*Myst.*3.25; τὸ κ. ἔθνος τῶν δαιμόνων Procl. *in Alc.*p.45 C.; *debasing*, παθήματα Iamb.*VP*32.228, cf. Hierocl. *in CA* 24p.472 M. 3. = κατωφερής, Iamb.*Myst.*5.11. II. *fit for ships to put in at*, of a harbour, Sch.Il.2.494.

κατᾰγων-ίζομαι, *prevail against*, τινας Plb.2.42.3, al., *OGI*553.7 (Xanthus); τὰ αἰσχρὰ τῶν παθῶν Metrod.*Herc.*831.19; κ. Ὀδυσσέα περὶ στεφάνου Luc.*VH*2.22; ἕλκη διαίτῃ Dam.*Isid.*122:—Pass., καταγωνισθῆναι τὰ ὅλα Plb.3.4.12; ὑπό τινος Luc.*Symp.*19. 2. *contend against*, τὴν ἀλήθειαν Plb.13.5.5, cf. 12.25ᵈ.6. II. *win by a struggle*, βασιλείας *Ep.Hebr.*11.33. **-ισις**, εως, ἡ, *conquest*, *Gloss.*, Hsch. (κατάγωσις cod.). **-ισμός**, ὁ, = foreg., Poll.9.142. **-ιστής**, οῦ, ὁ, *conqueror*, Iamb.*VP*14.63. **-ιστικός**, ή, όν, *arguing for victory, polemical*, Procl. *in Prm.*p.706 S.

καταδαίνυμαι, only in aor. 1 κατεδαισάμην, *devour, consume*, νιν φλὸξ κατεδαίσατο Phryn.Trag.6, cf. Is.*Fr.*152, Theoc.4.34, Ael.*NA* 12.6, Ath.9.399a.

κατάδαιτον, corrupt word in Orac.ap.Phleg.*Fr.*36.10 J.

καταδαίω, *burn up*, in aor. 2 Pass. κατεδάη, Hsch.

καταδάκνω, *bite*, v.l. in Batr.45; κέντρα Ael.*NA*1.32:—Pass., κατὰ χρόα πάντ' ὀνύχεσσι δακνόμενος Theoc.7.110.

καταδακρύω, *bewail*, τὴν ἑαυτοῦ τύχην X.*Cyr.*5.4.31; τινας Id.*HG* 2.4.22; τινος *for* one, Suid.: abs., *weep bitterly*, E.*Hel.*673 (lyr.), Tim. *Pers.*151, Plu.*Caes.*41, etc. II. causal, *make weep, move to tears*, App.*Pun.*70, *BC*4.114.

καταδακτῠλ-ίζω, *feel with the finger*, sens. obsc., Phryn.*PS* p.83 B., Sch.Ar.*Pax* 548. **-ικός**, ή, όν, *inclined thereto*, Ar.*Eq.*1381.

καταδᾰμάζω, *subdue*, aor. 1 Act. κατεδάμασα Lxx *Jd.*14.18: aor. inf. Med. καταδαμάσασθαι Th.7.81: aor. Pass., D.C.50.10, 78.39.

καταδάμναμαι, = foreg., *h.Merc.*137.

καταδάνειος [δᾰ], ον, *burdened with mortgages*, D.S.17.109.

καταδᾰπᾰν-άω, *squander*, τὴν οὐσίαν Arist.*Pol.*1316ᵇ23; τὸ στρωμάτων βάρος κ. εἰς τἀπιτήδεια X.*Cyr.*6.2.30:—Pass., [τὰ χρήματα] κατεδεδαπάνητό σφι Hdt.5.34:—Med., *to be prodigal*, Pyrrho ap.Ath. 10.419e. II. *consume*, of an army, X.*An.*2.2.11; τὸν Ὅμηρον λιμὸς κατεδαπάνησεν Sotad.15.16:—Pass., καταδαπανᾶσθαι ἐν τῇ κακίᾳ Lxx *Wi.*5.13; κατεδαπανῶντο ταῖς μάστιξι τὰ σώματα Eun.*Hist.* p.269 D. 2. *absorb, do away with*, Aët.7.91. **-η**, ἡ, *absorption, drying up*, τῆς ὑγρᾶς τροφῆς Alex.Aphr.*Pr.*2.75. **-ητικός**, ή, όν, *tending to consume*, *EM*110.2.

καταδάπτω, *devour*, μή με ἕα.. κύνας καταδάψαι Ἀχαιῶν Il.22.339; κύνες τε καὶ οἰωνοὶ κατέδαψαν Od.3.259; of fire, *consume*, Q.S.1.2, *Rev.Phil.*46.129 (Isaura): metaph., καταδάπτετ' ἀκούοντος φίλον ἦτορ, like δαίεται ἦτορ, Od.16.92.

καταδαρδάπτω, = foreg., Hsch.

καταδαρθάνω, aor. κατέδαρθον (Att. inf. -δάρθειν acc. to Sch.Ar. *Nu.*38), Ep. κατέδρᾰθον, subj. καταδράθω Od.5.471; part. -δαρθόντα Ar.*Pl.*300 (-δαρθέντα codd.): aor. 1 Pass. κατεδάρθην is found in later writers, as Philostr.*VA*2.36, and 3 pl. κατέδαρθεν A.R.2.1227: pf. καταδεδάρθηκα Pl.*Smp.*219c:—*fall asleep*, mostly in aor., *to be asleep*, ἐν θαλάμοισι κατέδραθον Od.7.285, cf. 23.18; τὼ δ' ἐς δέμνια βάντε κατέδραθον 8.296; καδδραθέτην, for κατεδραθέτην, 15.494; εἰ δέ κεν.. καταδράθω 5.471; ἔασον.. καταδαρθεῖν τί με Ar.*Nu.*38; ὁ μακαρίτης οἴχεται, κατέδαρθεν Ar.*Fr.*488.11, cf. Hp.*Epid.*5.37, X.*Ages.* 9.3: in pres., *to be falling asleep*, opp. ἀνεγείρεσθαι (to be waking), Pl.*Phd.*71d, 72b. 2. *pass the night*, κατέδαρθον ἐν Θησείῳ ἐν ὅπλοις Th.6.61: so in pf., Pl.*Smp.* l. c.

καταδᾰτέομαι, fut. -δάσομαι (v. infr.):—Med., *divide among themselves, tear and devour*, κύνες κατὰ πάντα δάσονται Il.22.354:—Pass., ὑπ' ἰχθύων καταδασθῆναι (nisi leg. κατεδεσθῆναι) Luc.*Demon.* 35; καταδέδασται· καταβέβρωται, καταμεμέρισται, Hsch. II. τὰν γᾶν κατεδασσάμεθα *divided, allotted* it, *Tab.Heracl.*2.28.

καταδεδίττομαι, = καταφοβέομαι, Hsch.

καταδεής (A), ές, (καταδέω B) *wanting in, lacking*, c. gen., χρημάτων κ. ἀγγήϊα Hdt.2.121.β'; abs., of persons, *needy*, v.l. for ἐπιδεής, D.10. 36; κ. τάφος a *sorry, shabby* burial, Pl.*Lg.*719e; κ. τὴν ἡλικίαν *under* age, *POxy.*54.2 (iii A.D.). 2. more freq. in Comp., καταδεέστερος *weaker, inferior*, Isoc.2.7, D.27.2, Phld.*Piet.*7, etc.; καταδεέστερός τινος τῷ τάχει, πρὸς τὸ φρονεῖν, Isoc.3.5, 5.18, cf. Thphr. *Char.Prooem.*3. II. Adv. -δεῶς, mostly in Comp., καταδεέστερον Isoc.5.84, 6.67; -τέρως Id.12.37; -τέρως ἔχειν περί τι to be *very ill off* in a thing, D.48.55; τῶν ἀντιδίκων -τέρως ἔχειν πρὸς τὸ λέγειν Arist. *Rh.Al.*1442ᵃ16.

καταδεής (B), ές, (καταδείδω) *timid*, ἵππος Poll.1.197, cf. 3.136. Adv. -δεῶς ib.137.

καταδεῖ, impers., *there is wanting*, v. καταδέω (B).

καταδείδω, only in aor. -δεῖσαι, and (in Phalar. infr. cit.) fut. -δείσειν:—*fear greatly*, τι Ar.*Pax* 759 (anap.), And.4.1, Th.2.93; τὸν Ἀχιλλέα Jul.*Or.*2.53b; περί τινος Ph.2.102; μή.. ib.590. II. *put into great fear, scare*, Phalar.*Ep.*91.

καταδείκνῡμι, Ion. aor. κατέδεξα, *discover and make known*, τὸν Ταρτησσὸν οὗτοί εἰσι οἱ καταδέξαντες Hdt.1.163; Νεκῶ.. πρώτου καταδέξαντος (sc. τὴν Λιβύην περίρρυτον ἐοῦσαν) Id.4.42: folld. by a Conj., κατέδειξεν ἐναργῶς, ὡς.. Arist.*Fr.*673:—Pass., c. part., κατεδέδεκτο ἐοῦσα οὐδὲν χρηστή *had been proved* to be.., Hdt.7.215. 2. *invent and teach, introduce*, προαγωγούς Ar.*Ra.*1079 (anap.); τέχνην Antiph. 123.1, cf. Diod.Com.2.4; ἰατρικὴν Pl.*R.*407d, cf. 406c; τελετάς D.25. 11; τὸν οἶνον τοὺς θεοὺς θνητοῖς καταδεῖξαι *Com.Adesp.*106.2: c. inf., *show how* to do, ἐπὶ τὰ κράνεα λόφους ἐπιδέεσθαι Κᾶρές εἰσι οἱ καταδέξαντες Hdt.1.171; οἱ πατέρες ἡμῶν ἐν ταῖς φονικαῖς δίκαις κατέδειξαν τέμνοντας τὰ τόμια ἐξορκίζεσθαι Aeschin.2.87; κ. τοῖς λαοῖς θεοὺς σέβεσθαι D.S.1.45: both constr. joined, τελετάς θ' ἡμῖν κατέδειξε φόνων τ' ἀπέχεσθαι Ar.*Ra.*1032, cf. 1062.

καταδειλιάω, *show cowardice,* D.61.28; *spoil by cowardice,* οὐδέν X.*An.*7.6.22.

καταδειμαίνω, *fear,* τὸ μέγεθος τῆς φύσεως Eun.*VS* p.487 B.

καταδειπν-έω, *eat at a meal,* τὸν Ἆπιν Plu.2.355c; ταῦρον Ael.*VH* 1.24. **-ον,** τό, = δεῖπνον, οἰωνῶν Man.4.200 (pl.).

καταδεκ-τέον, *one must accept,* Ps.-Gem. in Iriarte *Cat.Cod.Matr.* 389. **-τικός,** ή, όν, *receptive,* Simp. *in Cat.*247.34.

κατάδενδρος, ον, *thickly wooded,* Nymphod.12, D.S.17.68, Ael. *Tact.*35.4; τὰ κ. [τῶν ὀρέων] *Gp.*2.6.1.

καταδέομαι, *entreat earnestly,* c. gen. pers., Pl.*Ap.*33e, Lxx *Ge.* 42.21, al.

καταδέρκομαι, aor. 1 κατεδέρχθην S.*Tr.*999 (anap.): aor. 2 κατέδρακον Opp.*H.*1.10 (tm.):—poet. for καθοράω, *look down upon,* αὐτοὺς Ἠέλιος.. καταδέρκεται ἀκτίνεσσιν Od.11.16; μανίας ἄνθος καταδερχθῆναι S. l. c., cf. *Lyr.Adesp.*87; ἐπὶ χθόνα κ. ἀκτίνεσσι *h.Cer.*70.

καταδερμᾰτόω, in Pass., *to be covered with hide,* Hsch. s. v. κατερρινωμένον.

καταδέρω, *flay*: hence, in Pass., *to be subject to extortion,* aor. 2 inf. καταδᾰρῆναι Anon. *in Rh.*117.35.

κατάδεσις, εως, ἡ, *binding fast,* Plu.2.771a. II. *binding by magic knots*: hence, *spells, enchantments,* in pl., Pl.*Lg.*933a.

κατάδεσμα, ατος, τό, = κατάδεσμος II, *PMag.Lond.*121.299 (pl., abbrev.):—but pl. **κατάδεσμα,** τά, = κατάδεσμος I, *IG* 1².314.43.

καταδεσμ-εύω, *bind up,* τραύματα Lxx *Si.*30.7. 2. *bind on, Gp.* 12.21 (Pass.). II. *inhibit by means of a spell,* τινα *PMag.Lond.* 46.321; τὸν νοῦν τινος ib.326. III. *bind fast, retain,* κ. δίς *repeat,* Lxx *Si.*7.8. **-έω,** = foreg., *Gloss.* **-ος,** ὁ, *tie, band,* κ. ἥβης *bathing-drawers,* Theopomp.Com.37. II. = κατάδεσις II, -δέσμοις τοὺς θεοὺς πείθοντες Pl.*R.*364c, cf. Plot.4.4.40 (pl.), *PMag.Par.*1.2176 (pl.); κ. καὶ φαρμακεῖαι Artem.1.77.

καταδέτης, ου, ὁ, *cross-beam, tie,* Apollod.*Poliorc.*141.10.

καταδεύω, *wet through,* κατέδευσας ἐπὶ στήθεσσι χιτῶνα οἴνου ἀποβλύζων Il.9.490; μήποτέ σ'.. νέφος ἀμφικαλύψῃ.. κατὰ θ' εἵματα δεύσῃ Hes.*Op.*556; ἵν' οὔατα μὴ καταδεύῃ that [the rain] *may not wet* your ears, ib.546; of a river, *water,* πεδίον E.*Ph.*827 (anap.). II. metaph., ὁ -όμενος τῇ καρδίᾳ he whose heart *is easily melted,* Lxx *Ex.* 35.5.

καταδέχομαι, Arc. **κατυ-** *SIG*306.58 (iv B.C.):—*receive, admit,* τι εἰς τὴν ψυχήν Pl.*R.*401e; [τὸν θεὸν] τῇ σκηνῇ J.*AJ*3.8.1; πάσαις ταῖς πύλαις τὴν ἡδονήν Luc.*Nigr.*16; esp. of food, τοὺς φακοὺς Eup. 350; πόμα Hp.*Epid.*7.41; τροφήν Pl.*Ti.*84b, cf. Arist.*Resp.*476ᵃ29:—Pass., -δεχθῆναι ἐπὶ γάμον Luc.*Tox.*44. 2. *receive back, take home again,* esp. from banishment, And.3.3, Lys.6.13, D.26.6, etc.: aor. Pass. καταδεχθῆναι in pass. sense, Luc.*Bis Acc.*31, D.C.78.39: fut. καταδεχθήσεσθαι ib.40.40. 3. *accept, admit the truth of,* τὸ γενεθλιαλογεῖν Str.16.1.6. 4. *allow, permit of,* ἀναβολήν Suid. s. v. εἰσαγγελία; τὴν μῖξιν Phlp. *in GC*189.6.

καταδέω (A), fut. -δήσω, *bind on* or *to, bind fast,* πρυμνήσια, ἱστόν, Il.1.436 (tm.), Od.2.425 (tm.); ἵππους μὲν κατέδησαν.. ἱμᾶσι φάτνῃ ἐφ' ἱππείῃ Il.10.567; ἐπ' ἀμβροσίῃσι κάπῃσιν 8.434; ἐμὲ μὲν κατέδησαν.. ἐνὶ νηΐ Od.14.345; κ. λάρνακας Hdt.3.123:—Pass., καταδεδεμένος τοὺς ὀφθαλμούς Hdt.2.122; ἐν φόβῳ καταδεθεῖσα E.*Ion* 1498 (lyr.) (so μανίη καταδεῖ τινα Hermesian.7.85); καταδεῖται ψυχὴ ὑπὸ σώματος Pl. *Phd.*83d; γλῶττα -δεδεμένη Arist.*HA*492ᵇ32:—Med., *bind to oneself,* ἀγχόνιον βρόχον κατεδήσατο E.*Hel.*687 (lyr.); σπόγγους περὶ τὰ ὦτα Arist.*Pr.*960ᵇ15: metaph., ἀριθμῷ καταδήσασθαι *tie up for oneself* in lots, D.H.*Rh.*11.3; καταδησαμένη τινὰ ὁρκίοις Parth.12.3. b. κ. τι ἀπό or ἔκ τινος, metaph., *establish securely,* τὴν διὰ πάντων διήκουσαν ὠφέλειαν ἀπὸ [τοῦ συλλογισμοῦ] Procl. *in Alc.*p.252 C., cf. Simp. *in de An.*15.34. 2. *bind up,* θραῦμα, τραύματα, Lxx *Si.*27.21, *Ev. Luc.*10.34. 3. *put in bonds, imprison,* Hdt.3.143, Th.8.15, Pl.*Ti.* 70e, etc.; κ. τὴν ἐπὶ θανάτῳ (sc. δέσιν) Hdt.5.72. 4. *convict of* a crime, opp. ἀπολύω, c. inf., κ. τινὰ φῶρα εἶναι Hdt.2.174, cf. 4.68. II. *tie down, stop, check,* ἀνέμων κατέδησε κελεύθους or κέλευθα, Od.5.383, 10.20; ὅς μοι ἐφορμήσας ἀνέμους κατέδησε κελεύθου 7.272, cf. 4.380; τοῦ γε θεοὶ κατὰ νόστον ἔδησαν 14.61. III. *bind by spells, enchant* (with fut. -δήσομαι Theoc.2.3), Din.*Fr.*6.7 (Pass.), *SIG*1175.2 (iv/iii B.C.), etc.; κ. τὸ ἐργαστήριόν τινος *Tab.Defix.*71.2 (iii B.C.); κ. τινὰ γλῶτταν καὶ ψυχὴν καὶ λόγον *Tab.Defix.Aud.*49.1 (iv/iii B.C.); γοητεῦσαι καὶ κ., of Cleopatra, D.C.50.5:—Pass., *Tab.Defix.*107ᵃ2, Clearch.38, Plu.2.378f; cf. καταδηνύω, καταδίδημι.

καταδέω (B), *lack, need,* c. gen., esp. of numbers, ἡ [ὁδὸς] καταδέει πεντεκαίδεκα σταδίων [ὡς] μὴ εἶναι πεντακοσίων Hdt.2.7; πυραμίδα.. εἴκοσι ποδῶν καταδέουσαν τριῶν πλέθρων *wanting* 20 feet of 3 plethra, ib.134; ἕνδεκα μυριάδες ἦσαν, μιῆς χιλιάδος.. καταδέουσαι Id.9.30, cf. 70; [τὸ ναυτικὸν] δύο νεῶν κατέδεε ἐς τὸν ἀριθμόν *there was a lack* of two ships, 8.82 (unless κατέδεε be impersonal). 2. *come after, be behind,* Θῆβαι ἀνδρὸς ἰδιώτου καταδέουσιν εἰς εὐδαιμονίαν Paus.8.33.2.

καταδηῐόω, contr. **-δηόω,** *ravage, waste,* in Pass., D.H.11.42 (interpol.).

καταδηλέομαι, *injure, violate,* Men.Prot.p.108 D.: Elean forms καδαλέοιτο, καδαλήμενοι, *Schwyzer* 413.8,6; καζαλήμενον ib.418.19.

κατάδηλος, ον, *manifest, visible,* τούτοις οὐ κ. ἦν ἡ μάχη ὑπὸ τοῦ.. ὄρους Th.4.44; κ. γενέσθαι *to be discovered,* Hdt.1.5, 3.68; κ. μᾶλλον.. τὰ τῶν Χίων ἐφάνη Th.8.10; κατάδηλον ποιῆσαι make *known, discover,* Hdt.3.88, cf. Phld.*Vit.Herc.*1457.10: c. part., φυλάσσων κ. ἔσται S.*OC*1214 (lyr.); κ. γίγνονται προσποιούμενοι Pl.*Ap.*23d, etc.; κ. ὦσιν ὅτι.., κ. ἔσται ὡς.., Id.*Prt.*342b, 355b, cf. Arist.*Top.*109ᵇ2, *Ep.Hebr.*7.15, etc. Adv. -λως Poll.6.207.

κατάδημα, ατος, τό, *band, fastening,* Arist.*Pr.*938ᵃ14.

καταδημᾰγωγέω, *conquer by the arts of a demagogue,* τινα Plu.2. 482d, cf. Arr.*Fr.*150 J.:—Pass., Plu.*Per.*9; *to be won by such arts,* Id. *Cleom.*13, etc.

καταδημο-βορέω, *consume,* λαοῖσι δότω -δημοβορῆσαι Il.18.301. **-κοπέω,** *overcome by courting popularity,* τοὺς πολεμίους App.*Mith.*19.

καταδηνύω, = καταδέω (A) III, *Tab.Defix.*75ᵃ1 (iii B.C.).

καταδήω, = foreg., *Tab.Defix.Aud.*73.1.

καταδιαίρ-εσις, εως, ἡ, *division,* τοῦ κανόνος Phld.*Mus.*p.100 K.; τοῦ κλήρου *PTeb.*376.27 (ii A.D.). **-έω,** *divide,* τὴν Ἐρυθρὰν θάλασσαν Lxx *Ps.*135(136).13; τὸν κύκλον εἰς δώδεκα μοίρας S.E.*M.*5.23:—Pass., κ. ἐς τὰ μέρη Asclep.*Tact.*10.22. 2. *distribute,* τὸ πλῆθος εἰς λόχους D.H.4.19, cf. *CPR*22.25 (ii A.D.):—Med., *distribute among themselves,* Lxx *Jo.*3(4).2, Plb.2.45.1, D.S.3.29. 3. *analyse,* τὰς συνδρομάς Gal.1.158.

καταδῐαιτάω, *decide as arbitrator against* one, *give judgement against,* opp. ἀποδ-, ὁ διαιτητὴς οὐ κατεδιῄτα, ἀλλ' ἀπιὼν ᾤχετο ἀποδιαιτήσας τούτου τὴν δίαιταν D.49.19, cf. 21.84; οἷός τ' ἦν πείθειν αὐτόν, ἣν κατεδεδιῃτήκει, ταύτην ἀποδεδιῃτημένην ἀποφαίνειν ib.85; ἔρημον κ. τινὸς [δίκην] *give judgement* in default *against* one, Id.21. 92, cf. 40.17, Luc.*Pr.Im.*15: metaph., *condemn,* c. gen., Alciphr.1. 31:—Med., καταδιαιτᾶσθαι δίαιτάν τινος *to be the cause of an arbitration being given against* one, Lys.25.16.

καταδιαλλάσσω, *reconcile again,* aor. 2 Pass. -διηλλάγην Ar.*V.* 1284.

καταδια-σπλεκόω, strengthd. for σπλεκόω, v.l. in Sch.Ar.*Pl.* 1082. **-φθείρω,** *squander,* τὰ πατρῷα Eup.44. 2. in Pass., *to be consumed,* ἐν πυρί Luc.*Tim.*44 (s.v.l.). **-χέω,** *diffuse completely,* Arist.*Spir.*483ᵇ21 (Pass.).

καταδίδημι, = καταδέω (A) III, *Tab.Defix.*42.1 (iii B.C.), al.: Dor. **καδδίδημι** ib.74.1.

καταδίδωμι, *assign,* τὰ ἀριστεῖα τῆς ἐν λόγοις δεινότητός τινι D.H. *Comp.*18. II. intr., of a channel, *open into,* ἡ Προποντὶς καταδιδοῖ ἐς τὸν Ἑλλήσποντον Hdt.4.85, cf. Plu.*Fab.*6.

καταδιήγησις, εως, ἡ, *pure narrative,* Fortunat.*Rh.*2.19.

καταδιΐστημι, strengthd. for διΐστημι, Hsch., Phot.

καταδῐκ-άζω, *give judgement* or *sentence against* a person, *condemn,* opp. ἀποδικάζω:—Constr.: c. gen. pers. et acc. rei, κ. τινὸς θάνατον Hdt.1.45; τὴν διπλασίαν (sc. ζημίαν) Lex ap.D.24.105; πολλὴν μοχθηρίαν J.*Ap.*1.24; πολλὴν τὴν ἀπόγνωσιν Luc.*Merc.Cond.*11: c. gen. pers. et inf., κ. σεαυτοῦ τὰ ἔσχατα παθεῖν X.*Cyr.*3.1.9, cf. *An.* 6.6.15: c. gen. pers. only, Luc.*DMort.*29.2: abs., Pl.*Lg.*958c; τᾶν ψάφων ταὶ -δικάζουσαι *SIG*953.83 (Calymna, ii B.C.):—Med., *get sentence given against* a person, δίκην καταδικάσασθαί τινος Th.5.49, D.21. 176; κ. τινός, without acc., Lys.23.14, D.47.18; κ. τινὸς χρημάτων *get* a person *condemned* [to a payment] of money, Paus.6.3.7: abs., Pl. *Lg.*857a, *PHal.*1.65 (iii B.C.), etc.:—Pass., καταδικασθεὶς *condemned,* Pl.*Lg.*958c; ὑπὸ ἐχθρῶν Phld.*Ir.*p.51 W.; ἐπὶ φόνῳ *for* murder, D.S. 4.76; ἐπὶ κακουργίᾳ Id.3.12; later καταδικασθῆναι θανάτῳ *to be condemned* to death, Id.13.101, etc.; θάνατον D.C.68.1; τὴν ἐπὶ θανάτῳ Artem.4.60; φυγήν App.*Ital.*3; εἰς ἀλαβαστρῶνα *Sammelb.*4639. 2 (iii A.D.); εἰς δοῦλον, εἰς νῆσον, Artem.4.65, 5.21: c. inf., καταδικάζεται ἀποθανεῖν Luc.*VH*1.29; of the sentence, ἀντέλεγον μὴ δικαίως σφῶν καταδεδικάσθαι *that judgement had been given against* them unjustly, Th.5.49; later -δικασθείσης αὐτοῦ δίκης *PHal.*1.44 (iii B.C.), cf. *PLille* 29.6 (iii B.C.); of fines imposed, τὰ -θέντα ἐκπραξέω *IG*2². 1126.5 (Amphict. Delph.). II. Med., *have judgement given in one's favour,* Is.4.9, 10.24. III. *declare by express judgement,* ὅτι.. X.*An.*5.8.21. IV. Pass., *to be bound by* a law, Men.Prot.p.39 D. **-αστής,** οῦ, ὁ, *one who condemns,* τοῦ πατρός Iamb.*VP*25. 113. **-αστικός,** ή, όν, *condemnatory,* Sch.Ar.*V.*167. **-η,** ἡ, *judgement given against* one, *sentence,* Epich.148.5, Plb.25.3.1 (pl.), Lxx *Wi.*12.27, Phld.*Rh.*1.12S., *Act.Ap.*25.15, Plu.*Cor.*29, *PGnom.*208 (ii A.D.); κ. εἰς μονομάχους Artem.4.65. 2. *damages* or *fine,* Th.5. 49,50, D.47.52, *PHal.*1.52 (iii B.C.); μετεῖναι αὐτῷ τὸ ἥμισυ τῆς κ. *IG* 12(8).267.16 (Thasos, iii B.C.), cf. *Tab.Heracl.*1.156 (pl.). **-ος,** ον, (δίκη) *having judgement given against* one, *found guilty, condemned, SIG*484.1 (Delph., iii B.C.): c. gen., φυγῆς *to* banishment, D.S.13.63; θανάτου Id.27.1; *mulcted in,* μυρίων στατήρων *GDI*2516.7 (Delph.): abs., J.*AJ*5.1.14, Arr.*Epict.*4.11.24, App.*BC*1.2, *CIG*2759*b* (Aphrodisias).

καταδιφθερόω, *cover over with skins,* Plu.2.664c.

καταδιφρεύω, *throw down from a chariot,* Eust.183.38.

καταδίχιον, τό, = *καδδίχιον, Dim. of κάδδιχος, *IG*14.427 i 15, al. (Tauromenium).

καταδίψιον· εἶδος καύματος, Hsch. (fort. κατὰ δ. ἴδος· (ὥρᾳ) κ.).

καταδιωκτικός, ή, όν, *pursuing,* τινος Horap.2.90.

καταδιώκω, *follow hard upon, pursue closely,* Th.1.49, 2.84, Lxx *Ps.*17(18).38, *PCair.Zen.*439 (Pass., iii B.C.), Phld.*Ir.*p.29 W., etc.: metaph., *try to gain,* Plb.6.42.1. 2. *search for,* τινα *Ev.Marc.*1. 36. 3. *overdrive* cattle, Lxx *Ge.*33.13.

καταδοκέω, prop. *think* or *suppose* a thing *to* any one's *prejudice,* c. inf., κ. τινὰ ποιέειν τι *suspect* one *of..,* Hdt.3.27; σφέας κ. εἶναι κλῶπας Id.6.16: with inf. understood, Id.1.22, 3.69: c. dat. pers., τοῖσι κατεδόκεον νεοχμὸν ἄν τι ποιέειν Id.9.99: c. acc. neut., τάδε καταδόξας . . σφέας ἐθελοκακέειν Id.8.69 :—Pass., *to be suspected*, ὑφ' ὑμῶν Antipho 2.2.3: also c. inf., καταδοχθεὶς φονεὺς εἶναι Id.2.2.2; later in good sense, καταδόξαντα [ὑπέρμεγαν] εἶναι τοῖς τότε ἀνθρώποις *who was recognized* to be great by his contemporaries, Numen.ap.Eus.*PE*14.8. 2. generally, *guess*, οὐ γὰρ ἄν κοτε κατέδοξα ἔνθεν ἦν *should* never *have guessed* whose son he was, Hdt.1.111.

κατ-ᾰδολεσχέω, *chatter at, weary by chattering*, καταδολεσχήσει ἐπ' ἐμὲ ἡ ψυχή μου Lxx *La*.3.20; τινος Plu.2.22a; ταῦτα ἴσως -ηδολέσχησά σου Jul.*Ep*.32: pf. -ηδολέσχηκα Plu.2.503b: abs., *PSI*5.495.3:—Pass., pf. part. κατηδολεσχημένος Suid. s. v. διατεθρυλημένος τὰ ὦτα.

καταδοξάζω, = καταδοκέω, X.*An*.7.7.30, D.S.32.10:—Pass., ibid. 2. *form a wrong opinion*, Epicur.*Nat*.2.9, *Herc*.1413.4; ὑπέρ τινος D.H.6.10.

κατάδοσις, εως, ἡ, *instalment* of a payment, *POxy*.1632.21 (iv A.D.).

καταδουλ-εύομαι, *reduce to slavery*, Sm.*Le*.27.17, f. l. in Eus. Mynd.*Fr*.10 (v. καταδουλόω I. 2). **-ίζω**, = foreg., *IG*9(1).119 (Elatea):—but usu. Med., -ίζομαι *GDI*1701.7, al. (Delph.): aor. καταδουλίξασθαι *IG*9(1).42 (Stiris). **-ισμός**, ὁ, *enslavement*, ἅπτεσθαι or ἐφάπτεσθαί τινος ἐπὶ καταδουλισμῷ, *GDI*1685.5, 1686.8, al. (Delph.). **-ος**, ὁ, *slave*, κ. παῖς *PStrassb*.40.24 (vi A.D.). **-όω**, *reduce to slavery, enslave*, Ἀθήνας Hdt.6.109; τὴν Ἑλλάδα Id.8.144; Ἀθηναίοις κ. Κέρκυραν Th.3.70; νῆσον βασιλεῖ Isoc.9.20:—Pass., κατεδεδούλωντο Hdt.5.116; κατεδουλώθησαν Id.6.32; καταδεδουλωμένος ὑπό τινος Pl.*Smp*.219e: abs., Lys.18.5. 2. more freq. in Med., *make a slave to oneself, enslave*, τὴν μητρόπολιν Hdt.7.51, cf. Pl.*R*.351b; τινας X.*Mem*.2.1.13, cf. *GDI*4982 (Gortyn), *PEleph*.3.3 (iii B.C.), etc.; ἡ τύχη τὸ σῶμα κατεδουλώσατο Philem.95.8; τὸ κρέσσον τῷ χείρονι -εύμενοι (Ion. for -ούμενοι) Eus.Mynd.*Fr*.10; κ. τὸν Ἰσραὴλ δουλείαν Lxx 1*Ma*.8.18; ἔργα ὧν κατεδουλοῦντο αὐτοὺς ib.*Ex*.1.14. II. metaph., *enslave in mind*, παιδισκάριόν με καταδεδούλωκ' εὐτελές Men.338, cf. 2*Ep.Cor*.11.20; κ. τὴν ψυχὴν *PMag.Lond*.123.4 (iv/v A.D.); *break in spirit*, καταδουλοῖ τὴν τόλμαν ἡ ἀνάγκη App.*Pun*.81. 2. more freq. in Med., ἡ ἀνάγκη καταδουλοῦται τὴν γνώμην Hp.*Fract*.15; οἴει τι μᾶλλον καταδουλοῦσθαι ἀνθρώπους τοῦ ἰσχυροῦ φόβου; X.*Cyr*.3.1.23, cf. E.*IA*1269; κ. τὰς ψυχάς Isoc.12.178; τὸ λογιστικόν Pl.*R*.553d; τὰς ἐπιθυμίας Aristox.*Fr.Hist*.15. **-ωσις**, εως, ἡ, *enslavement*, Th.3.10, 7.66, Pl.*Lg*.776d, *GDI*1869.7 (Delph.), *Mémoires de la mission arch. de Perse* 20.85 (Susa, ii B.C.).

καταδουπέω, *fall with a loud heavy sound, crash*, aor. 2, τυπεὶς κατέδουπε κεραυνῷ *AP*7.637 (Antip.).

Κατάδουποι, ων, οἱ, *the first Cataract* of the Nile, Hdt.2.17 (in gen. -δούπων), Thphr.*Lap*.34, Philostr.*VA*6.23, Plin.*HN*5.54; *Catadupa*, neut. pl., Cic.*Somn.Scip*.5.

καταδοχή, ἡ, *receiving back, restoration* of exiles, Pl.*Lg*.867e; *reception* of soul by body, Porph.*Sent*.35; τοῦ θεοῦ Id.*Marc*.19. II. *receptacle*, Gal.14.713.

καταδράθω, v. καταδαρθάνω.

καταδράσσομαι, *lay hold of*, τῆς φθοροποιοῦ δυνάμεως -δραξαμένης τῶν σωμάτων Dsc.*Ther.Praef*.; *grasp, apprehend*, τῆς ἀληθείας Procl. *in Prm*.p.534 S.; τῆς λέξεως τοῦ Πλάτωνος Id.*in Ti*.3.107 D.; [τοῦ ὅλως ἀγαθοῦ] Id. *in Alc*.p.153 C., cf. Olymp.*in Alc*.p.194 C.

καταδρέπω, *strip off*, τῶν δενδρέων τὰ φύλλα Hdt.8.115.

καταδρομή, ἡ, *inroad, raid*, Th.1.142; ἐνέδραι καὶ κ. Id.5.56; καταδρομὰς ποιεῖσθαι Id.7.27, etc.; κ. γενομένης Lys.20.28; ὥσπερ κ. ἐποιήσω ἐπὶ τὸν λόγον μου Pl.*R*.472a; *charge*, of troops in battle, Lxx 2*Ma*.5.3; *assault*, *PRein*.18.19 (pl., ii B.C.). 2. metaph., *attack, invective*, κ. μέλλει περὶ ἐμοῦ ποιεῖσθαι Aeschin.1.135, cf. D.H.*Th*.3; κατά τινος Plb.12.23.1; ἐν καταδρομῆς μέρει λέγεται περί τινος S.E.*M*.2.43. II. *recourse*, κ. γίγνεται ἐπί... A.D.*Pron*.25.15. III. *lurking-place, lair, den*, δακέτου Ael.*NA*2.9, cf. 5.49 (pl.); ὕπαντροι ἢ λοχμώδεις κ. ib.9.1. 2. perh. = *cryptoporticus*, *IGRom*.4.159.23 (Cyzicus).

κατάδρομος, ον, *overrun, wasted*, μέλαθρα πυρὶ κ. E.*Tr*.1300 (lyr.). II. Subst., *course* or *lists for exercising in*, Suet.*Ner*.11.

καταδροσίζω, *drench*, v. l. in Sch.Pi.*O*.6.88 (Pass.).

κατάδρυμμα, ατος, τό, (καταδρύπτω) *tearing, rending*, σαρκῶν . . καταδρύμματα χειρῶν *of* flesh *with* hands, E.*Supp*.51.

κατάδρυμος, ον, *thickly wooded*, Str.4.5.2.

καταδρύπτω, *tear in pieces, rend*, τὸ πρόσωπον *AP*5.42 (Rufin., v. l. for -τρίψεις); παρειάς ib.7.487 (Pers.), cf. M.Ant.6.20:—Med., κατὰ δ' ἐδρύπτοντο παρειάς Hes.*Sc*.243.

καταδρῠφάσσω, *hedge* or *fence in*, Lyc.239.

καταδῠναστ-εία, ἡ, *oppression*, Lxx *Ex*.6.7, al., Aristeas 23. **-εύω**, *oppress*, τινα Lxx *Ex*.1.13, al.; τοὺς πτωχοὺς ἀπὸ τῆς γῆς ib.*Am*.8.4: metaph., δέδοικα μὴ πλοῦτός με -εύσῃ X.*Smp*.5.8; τινος D.S.13.73, *Ep.Jac*.2.6: abs., Str.16.1.26, Ph.1.421, Plu.2.367d:—Pass., *to be oppressed*, *PPetr*.3 p.74 (iii B.C.), Lxx *Ne*.5.5, D.S.37.8; ὑπὸ τινος Str.6.2.4; ὑπὸ τοῦ διαβόλου *Act.Ap*.10.38; ταῦτα -εύετο ἕκαστα these districts *were under their* several *rulers*, Str.7.7.8. 2. *get control*, abs., of mutineers, Ps.-Ptol.*Centil*.56.

καταδύνω, v. καταδύω.

κατά-δῠσις, εως, ἡ, *dipping*: hence, *setting*, of stars, in pl., Hipparch.2.6.1, Ptol.*Tetr*.140: metaph., κ. εὐλογιστίας, opp. ἀνατολὴ ἀφροσύνης, Ph.1.415. 2. of a river, *descent into* an underground course, Str.8.8.4. 3. generally, *going down into, descent*, Luc.*VH*1.33. II. *hiding-place, hole*, Id.*Am*.34, Ph.1.315, Ath.11.477d, Gal.11.167 (pl.). 2. *depth*, Sm.*Ps*.68(69).3. 3. = θαλάμη, Erot. s. v. ὕποφρον. III. *present world* (as subject to *decline*), Aq.*Ps*.16(17).14, Id., Sm.*Ps*.48(49).2; so of *human life*, Aq.*Ps*.38(39).6. IV. rendering of Hebr. *miphleseth* 'a thing to shudder at', Lxx 3*Ki*.15.13. V. (καταδύω II. 2) *ducking* of the head in a bath, Orib.*Fr*.48. **-δυστής**, οῦ, ὁ, *one who dips under*, Hsch. s. v. καταυστής.

καταδῠσωπέω, strengthd. for δυσωπέω, *put to the blush* by earnest intreaty, τινα Luc.*Sacr*.3.

κατάδῠτος, ἡ, = κατάδυσις II. 2, Quint.*Ps*.87(88).7. 2. = κατάδυσις III, Al.ib.48(49).2.

καταδύω or **-δύνω**: I. intr., in Act. pres. καταδύνω and Med. καταδύομαι: fut. -δύσομαι: aor. -εδῡσάμην, Ep. 2 and 3 sg. -δύσεο, -δύσετο:—Act., aor. 2 κατέδυν: pf. καταδέδῡκα:—*go down, sink, set*, esp. of the sun (as Hom. always in aor. 2 Act.), ἠέλιος κατέδυ Il.1.475, etc.; ἅμα . . ἠελίῳ καταδύντι ib.592; ἐς ἠέλιον καταδύντα Od.10.183; ἠελίοιο -δυομένοιο *h.Merc*.197; καταδεδυκέναι τὴν [νῆσον] κατὰ θαλάσσης Hdt.7.235; also of ships, *to be sunk* or *disabled*, Id.8.90, Th.2.92, 7.34, X.*HG*1.6.35, etc.; also οἱ ἱππεῖς καταδύνοντες ἐν τέλμασιν Plb.5.47.2; κ. ὑφ' ὕδατι *duck* under water, Batr.89; καταδεδυκώς *having popped down*, Ar.*V*.140. 2. *go down, plunge into*, c. acc., καταδῦναι ὅμιλον Il.10.231, etc.; κατεδύσετο πουλὺν ὅμιλον ib.517; καταδύσεο μῶλον Ἄρηος 18.134; so μάχην, δόμον, πόλιν καταδύμεναι, 3.241, 8.375, Od.4.246: folld. by Prep., μυῖαι καδδῦσαι (Ep. for καταδ-) κατὰ . . ὠτειλάς Il.19.25; σπάργαν' ἔσω κατέδυνε *h.Merc*.237; καταδυσόμεθ' . . εἰς Ἀΐδαο δόμους we *shall go down* into . ., Od.10.174; so καταδύνειν ἐς ὕλην Hdt.9.37, cf. 4.76; εἰς φάραγγας, of hares, X.*Cyn*.5.16; εἰς ἅπασαν [τὴν πόλιν] Pl.*R*.576e; κατὰ τῆς γῆς Hdt.4.132; κατὰ τέφρας πολλῆς Plu.*Cam*.32; of souls, εἰς βυθὸν κ. Plu.2.943d: c. dat., *sink into*, ταῖς ὁμοιοπαθείαις Metrod.*Fr*.38: freq. with a notion of secrecy, *insinuate oneself, steal into*, καταδύεται εἰς τὸ ἐντὸς τῆς ψυχῆς ὅ τε ῥυθμὸς καὶ ἁρμονία Pl.*R*.401d; ἡ ἀναρχία εἰς τὰς ἰδίας οἰκίας κ. ib.562e; κ. ἡ ψῦξις ἕως πλείστου the cold *penetrates* most, Gal.15.90, cf. 6.178. 3. *slink away and lie hid*, καταδύεσθαι ὑπὸ τῆς αἰσχύνης X.*Cyr*.6.1.35, cf. D.21.199 (so abs., *to be overcome with shame*, ἐπὶ τῇ ἀγνοίᾳ Zos.5.40); καταδεδυκὼς ἐν τῇ οἰκίᾳ Pl.*R*.579b; εἰς ἄπορον ὁ σοφιστὴς τόπον καταδέδυκεν Id.*Sph*.239c, etc. 4. *get into, put on*, κατέδυ κλυτὰ τεύχεα Il.6.504, cf. Od.12.228; καταδύσετο τεύχεα καλά Il.7.103; εἵματα Mosch.4.102. II. causal, *make to sink*, rare in pres., ἐμπίπτων καὶ καταδύων Pherecr.12; ἐμὲ καταδύουσι τῷ ἄχει X.*Cyr*.6.1.37: mostly in aor. 1, γαύλους καταδύσας Hdt.6.17; in naval warfare, καταδῦσαι ναῦν *cut it down to the water's edge, disable* it, Id.8.87, al., Ar.*Ra*.49, Th.1.50; ἥλιον ἐν λέσχῃ κατεδύσαμεν we *let* the sun *go down* in talk, Call.*Ep*.2, cf. Aristaenet.1.24. 2. *duck*, τὴν κεφαλήν, in a bath, Herod.Med.ap.Orib.10.37.13.

κατ-ᾴδω, uncontr. **-αείδω**, *sing to*: hence, I. trans., *charm, appease by singing*, τινα D.H.4.29, Plu.2.745e, Luc.*JTr*.39, *Philops*.31: c. dat., *sing a spell* or *incantation* (ἐπῳδή) to . ., καταείδοντες . . τῷ ἀνέμῳ Hdt.7.191:—Pass., *to be induced by charms* to do a thing, c. inf., Ael.*NA*5.25 (dub. l.). b. κ. δεῖπνον *enliven* a repast *by song*, Id.*VH*7.2. 2. *sing in mockery*, Luc.*DMort*.2.2:—Pass., *to have* another *sing before one*, Id.*Bis Acc*.16. 3. *fill with song*, τὰς λόχμας Longus 1.9: c. gen., ἀηδὼν κ. τῶν ἐρημαίων χωρίων Ael.*NA*1.43. II. c. acc. cogn., *sing by way of incantation*, κατῇδε βάρβαρα μέλη μαγεύουσ' E.*IT*1337. III. intr., *sing from above* or *sing throughout* a place, of birds or insects, Ael.*VH*3.1, *NA*1.20.

καταδωροδοκέω, *betray in return for bribes*, Ar.*V*.1036, Lys.27.3:—Med., Ar.*Ra*.361, Arist.*Pol*.1271ᵃ3.

καταείδω, v. κατᾴδω. **καταειδώς**, v. κάτοιδα.

καταειμένος, η, ον, pf. part. Pass., 1. of καταέννυμι, Od.13.351. 2. of καθίημι, *hanging down over*, A.R.1.939, 3.830.

καταείσατο, 3 sg. aor. Med. (cf. εἴσομαι II, ἐπιείσομαι), ὅθι οἱ κ. γαίης where it *had sped* to earth, Il.11.358: also expld. as fr. εἴδω (εἴδομαι), where it *was visible* to him (he *descried* it) on the ground, Sch. l. c.

καταέννῡμι or **-εινύω**, Ep. Verb, not found in the form καθέννυμι because of the digamma, only in impf., aor. Act., and pf. Pass.:—*clothe, cover*, θριξὶ δὲ πάντα νέκυν καταείνυσαν (aor., v. l. -είνυον) Il.23.135; νηοὺς αἵματι καπνῷ τε . . κατείνυον Opp.*H*.2.673:—Pass., ὄρος καταειμένον ὕλῃ Od.13.351, 19.431, *h.Merc*.228, *h.Ven*.285; ἕδος κ. ὕλῃ *h.Ap*.225.

καταέρρω, Aeol. for καταίρω, Alc.41 (tm.).

καταϝελμένος, v. κατειλέω. **καταϝέργω**, v. κατείργω. **καταϝοικίδδω**, v. κατοικίζω.

κατ-αζαίνω, *make dry, parch up*, καταζήνασκε δὲ δαίμων (Ion. aor. 1) Od.11.587.

καταζάω, v. καταζῶ.

κατάζευγ-μα, ατος, τό, *cross-beams*, ὀροφῆς *IG*11(2).161 *A* 113 (Delos, iii B.C., pl.). **-νῡμι** and **-νύω**, *yoke together*, ἐν ἅρματα κ. σθένος ἵππιον Pi.*P*.2.11:—Pass., δύο πλοῖα κατεζευγμένα (v. l. χελώνας -μένας) D.S.20.85: metaph., *to be united*, ταῖς πρῶτον οὕτω καταζευγνυμέναις πόλεσιν Pl.*Lg*.753e; of marriage, Ael.*VH*4.1. 2. in Pass., *to be straitened, confined*, ὑπ' ἀναγκαίης κατέζευχθε Hdt.8.22; ἐν τυμβήρει θαλάμῳ κατεζεύχθη S.*Ant*.947. 3. Pass., of a right angle, *to be made acute*, κἂν μικρῷ τινι μᾶλλον κατεζευγμένη ᾖ ἡ εὐθεῖα γωνία Asp.*in EN*19.32. II. intr., *fix one's quarters, halt, encamp*, ταῖς δυνάμεσι Plb.3.95.3, cf. Plu.*Sull*.25, etc.

καταζευγοτροφέω, *squander money on teams of horses*, Is.5.43.

κατάζευξις, εως, ἡ, *yoking*, τοῦ ζυγοῦ *Hippiatr*.103; βοῶν Porph.

*Abst.*3.18: metaph., of marriage, Plu.2.750c. II. opp. ἀνάζευξις, *encamping*, Id.*Sull.*28, etc.

καταζηλόω, *create prejudice against*, τινας Epicur.*Nat.*14.6.

καταζήνασκε, v. καταζαίνω.

καταζητέω, *search out*, Iamb.*VP*29.158 (Pass.); *hold inquiry into*, τι Just.*Nov.*123.18.1, cf. *Cod.Just.*1.3.41.26 (Pass.).

καταζοφόω, in Pass., *to be darkened*, Sch.E.*Hec.*912.

καταζῡγίς, ίδος, ἡ, iron *connecting-rod* in a torsion-engine, Ph. *Bel.*60.5 (s.v.l.), 64.31. II. as Adj., λίθοι κ. *connecting* stones, *PCair.Zen.*499.21 (iii B.C.).

κατάζῡμος, ον, *fermented*, ἄρτος Dieuch.ap.Orib.4.7.10.

καταζῶ, *live one's life out, live on*, ἐν ἀνακτόροις θεοῦ καταζῇ δεῦρ' ἀεὶ σεμνὸν βίον E.*Ion* 56, cf. Pl.*Smp.*192b, Arist.*EN*1100^{b}16, Plu.2.194a; ἐν ἡσυχίᾳ Phld.*Rh.*2.162 S., Plu.*Cic.*4.

καταζωμεύω, *sup up*, Hsch.

κατα-ζώννῡμι, *gird fast*:—Med., *gird for oneself*, δορὰς ὄφεσι κατεζώσαντο E.*Ba.*698; ἐν ἱματίοις κ. τοὺς χιτωνίσκους Plu.*Pyrrh.*27:—Pass., χιτῶνας μίτραις κατεζωσμένοι D.H.2.70. **-ζωσμα**, ατος, τό, gloss on ἔλατρον, Hsch. II. *body of initiates wearing a special girdle* (cf. καταζωστικός), prob. to be read in Buresch *Aus Lydien* p.12. **-ζώστης**, ου, ὁ, *girth, strap*, Hsch. **-ζωστικός**, ή, όν, *of* or *for girding*: τὸ κ. *work on the girding of sacred robes*, Suid. s.v. Ὀρφεύς.

κατ-άημι, Ep. aor. part. καταέσσας, = κατακοιμηθείς (cf. ἄεσα), Hsch.: fut. καταήσεται· καταπνεύσει, Id.

καταθᾰλαττόω, *throw into the sea*, Tz. ad Lyc.712.

καταθάλπω, strengthd. for θάλπω, Plu.2.367d, D.L.7.152, Alciphr. 3.41.

καταθαμβέομαι, Pass., *to be astonished at*, c. acc., Plu.*Num.*15, *Fab.*26.

καταθάπτω, Ep. aor. inf. κατθάψαι Il.24.611:—*bury*, 19.228, A. *Ag.*1553 (lyr.), Lys.6.47, Isoc.19.22, Luc.*Philops.*24.

καταθαρσ-έω, later Att. **-θαρρέω**, *to be confident*, in pf. part., Plb. 1.40.3; κ. τοῖς ὅλοις *looking forward confidently to* a complete victory, Id.3.86.8; κατεθάρσησεν ὁ λαὸς ἐπὶ τοῖς λόγοις Lxx 2*Ch.*32.8: c. inf., *make bold to..*, παρεπιδείκνυσθαι δημοσίᾳ τὸ ἀνοσιούργημα Ph.2.220; τοῖς ὕδασι παραδοῦναι σφᾶς αὐτούς Agath.3.20. 2. c. gen., *behave boldly against*, τῆς τῶν Σπαρτιατῶν δυνάμεως D.S.15.34; χώρας Str. 12.8.6. 3. Pass., *to be confirmed*, *Cod.Just.*9.4.6.5. **-ύνω**, *embolden, encourage against*, τινὰ πρὸς τὸ μέλλον Plu.*Luc.*29:—Pass., in form **καταθρασύνομαι**, = foreg., Ph.1.41, Luc.*DMort.*21.2, D.L.2. 127: c. gen., πρὸς τοὺς ἀλόγως -ομένους τῶν ἐν τοῖς πολλοῖς δοξαζομένων, title of work by Polystr., cf. Them.*Or.*34 p.464 D.

καταθε-άομαι, *look down upon, watch from above*, τὰ γιγνόμενα κ. ἀπὸ λόφου X.*An.*6.5.30; κ. εἰς τοὺς πολεμίους ib.1.8.14: abs., Id. *Cyr.*3.2.1: generally, *contemplate*, φορὰς ἄστρων Plu.2.426d: metaph., with the mind, X.*Cyr.*8.2.18. **-ᾱτέον**, *one must observe*, τὴν τάξιν Procl. *in Prm.*p.537 S.

καταθείω, καταθείομαι, καταθείομεν, v. κατατίθημι.

καταθέλγω, *subdue by spells* or *enchantments*, τοὺς αὐτὴ κατέθελξεν (sc. Circe) Od.10.213, cf. Luc.*Ind.*12, etc.

κατάθελξις, εως, ἡ, *enchantment*, Luc.*Philops.*9.

κατάθεμα, ατος, τό, = ἀνάθεμα, *accursed thing*, *Apoc.*22.3. II. *curse*, *Tab.Defix.Aud.*22.23 (Curium, iii A.D.).

καταθεματίζω, = ἀναθεματίζω, *Ev.Matt.*26.74.

καταθεμελιόω, in Pass., *to be founded, based*, εἰς τὴν Γῆν Lyd.*Mens.* 4.51.

κατάθεος, ον, *godly*, ὑφηγήσεις Ph.2.298, cf. Poll.1.20; *superstitious*, Phot. s.v. ὄλολυν.

κατα-θερμαίνω, strengthd. for θερμαίνω, dub.l. in Philagr.ap.Orib. 5.21.1. **-θερμος**, ον, strengthd. for θερμός, Aët.9.1, Sch.Pi.*O.*3.42.

κατά-θεσις, εως, ἡ, *layering* of branches for propagation, κ. κλάδων D.S.2.53; φυτῶν ἐν τῇ γῇ *Gp.*9.5.1: generally, *planting*, χορτασμάτων *PStrassb.*10.10 (iii A.D.). 2. *paying down, payment*, Ph.2.224, Poll.4.47, 5.103, dub. in *CIG*2826.17 (Aphrodisias). 3. *laying down* or *affirming, positive statement*, δύο στερήσεις κ. ποιοῦσιν *EM* 97.38. 4. *laying aside, giving up*, τοῦ πολέμου Anon.ap.Suid. s.vv. καταθέσει, κτηματίτην. 5. in Surgery, *position*, '*putting up*' of a limb, Erot. s.v. κατατεῖναι, Pall. *in Hp.Fract.*12.273 C. 6. in Law, *promise, covenant*, Just.*Nov.*85.3.1, 94.2; also, *disposition*, *POxy.*243.11 (i A.D.), *Sammelb.*5679.18 (iv A.D.). 7. *burial*, *POxy.*475.31 (ii A.D.). **-θετέον**, *one must lay down*, Them.*Or.* 16.199c. 2. *one must layer*, *Gp.*4.12.15.

καταθέω, *run down*, ἀπὸ λόφων Th.3.97, cf. X.*Cyr.*3.2.1; of ships, *run into port*, εἰς Πειραιᾶ Id.*HG*1.1.35. II. *make inroads*, εἰς πόλεις ib.5.2.43: c. acc., κ. χώραν *overrun, ravage*, Th.7.27, X.*Cyr.* 5.4.15; κ. θάλατταν Polyaen.1.23.1. 2. metaph., *attack, persecute*, Parth.13.3 cod.; τοὺς τετελευτηκότας Lib.*Or.*63.42; esp. *in argument*, '*run down*', Pl.*Tht.*171c; cf. κατατρέχω: c. gen., *treat insultingly*, τῆς τοῦ αὐτοκράτορος ἡλικίας Procop.*Pers.*1.2.

καταθεωρ-έω, *observe, contemplate*, in Pass., ἡ ἰατρικὴ ὑπὸ ψυχῆς κ. Pl.*Grg.*465d. **-ησις**, εως, ἡ, *observation*, Apollod.*Poliorc.*139.2.

καταθήγω, *sharpen, whet*, ἐν βύβλοισι καθήξετ' ὀδόντα (sc. μύες) *AP*6.303 (Aristo); = παροξύνω, Hsch.: Dor. aor. inf. κατθᾶξαι, = παρακονῆσαι, μεθύσαι, Id.

καταθήκη, ἡ, *deposit*, prob. f.l. for παρακαταθ- in Lys.*Fr.*70 tit., Isoc.17.27.

καταθηλύνω, *make womanish*, Luc.*Peregr.*19, *DMeretr.*5.3; καρποὶ κατατεθηλυσμένοι *softened*, f.l. in Hp.*Aër.*15.

***καταθήπω**, v. κατατέθηπα.

καταθηρατόριον, v. καθηρ-.

καταθλάττειν, gloss on φλᾶν, Cyr.

καταθλάω, aor. 1 -έθλασα, *crush in pieces*, ὀστᾶ Lxx *Ps.*41(42).11: metaph., τινὰς ὡς γῆν ib.*Is.*63.3.

κατ-αθλέω, *wrestle down, overcome*, τινα Plu.*Cleom.*27: metaph., τὴν ἀμαθίαν Id.2.47f; ἀσκήσει τὸ ἄλογον ib.459b. 2. *master by practice*, τοῦτον τὸν τόπον Arr.*Epict.*2.17.31. 3. *train, exercise*, τινὰς ἐν ἀκοντισμοῖς Plu.2.8d:—Pass., -ηθλημένοι ἐν πολέμοις D.H. 13.12. II. intr., *exercise oneself, train*, Plu.2.2e; -ηθληκότες *well-trained*, of soldiers, Id.*Mar.*26.

κατα-θλίβω [ῑ], *press down*, τοὺς δαλούς Thphr.*Ign.*23; [τοὺς μαστούς] Sor.1.76; τὸ πνεῦμα Plu.2.133d; καταθλῐβεῖσα ἀναθυμίασις Id. *Aem.*14. **-θλιψις**, εως, ἡ, *pressing down*, *Gloss.*

καταθνήσκω, Aeol. **κατθναίσκω** Sapph.62 (καταθνάσκ- codd.): fut. -θανοῦμαι: aor. κατέθᾰνον, Ep. κάτθᾰνον; late poet. aor. 1 κάθθανα Maiuri *Nuova Silloge* 48: pf. -τέθνηκα (v. infr.):—poet. Verb, *die away, be dying*, τὸν δὲ καταθνήσκων προσέφη Il.22.355; κάτθανε καὶ Πάτροκλος *died*, 21.107: in pf., *to be dead*, κατατεθνήκασι, opp. ζώουσι, 15.664: freq. in pf. part., ἀνδρὸς.. κατατεθνηῶτος 7.89, 22. 164; νέκυι κατατεθνηῶτι 16.565; νεκροὺς κατατεθνηῶτας 18.540, etc.: used by Trag. only in sync. fut. κατθανοῦμαι, E.*Med.*1386, *Alc.*150, etc.; and in inf. and part. of sync. aor. κατθανεῖν, κατθανών, A.*Ag.* 1290, 873, etc.: once in ind., κάτθανε ib.1553 (anap.). 2. metaph., *perish*, μέλι.. κάτθανε ἐν κηρῷ λυπεύμενον Mosch.3.34; κάτθανε δ' ἁ μορφὰ σὺν Ἀδώνιδι Bion 1.31.

καταθνητός, ή, όν, *mortal*, Il.5.402, *h.Ap.*464, etc.: fem., *h.Ven.* 39, 50.

καταθοινάω, *feast upon*, Hsch.:—aor. Med., Aesop.14, Diogenian. 7.52:—aor. Pass. in med. sense, Pancrat.ap.Ath.7.283b.

καταθορεῖν, v. καταθρῴσκω.

καταθορῠβέω, *shout down*, ἕως ἂν ἀποστῇ ὁ ἐπιχειρῶν λέγειν καταθορυβηθείς Pl.*Prt.*319c:—Act. in Numen.ap.Eus.*PE*14.6: also c. acc. cogn., τὴν ἀπὸ ἁμάξης πομπείαν πᾶσαν κ. ibid.

καταθρᾰσύνομαι, v. καταθαρσύνω.

κατά-θραυσις, εως, ἡ, *breaking up*, τοῦ φλέγματος Steph.*in Hp.*1. 176 D. **-θραυστος**, ον, *broken in pieces*, f.l. in Dsc.5.87. **-θραύω**, *break in pieces, shatter*, Pl.*Plt.*265d, *Ti.*56e (Pass.), Plu.2.949c; εἰς λεπτά Gal.18(1).471.

κατ-αθρέω, *look down on from above*, Man.4.421. 2. *examine*, Alex.Aphr.*in SE*176.11. 3. = καθοράω, κατανοέω, Anon.ap.Hsch.

καταθρηνέω, *bewail*, E.*El.*1326 (anap.), prob. in Phld.*Mort.*24: c. acc., τὴν Ἀλεξάνδρου τελευτήν D.S.17.118; ἀποθνῄσκοντας Plu.2. 1103a; ἑαυτούς App.*Pun.*81.

καταθροέω, = καταθορυβέω, Poll.8.154.

καταθρύβω, = καταθρύπτω, λάγανον Bilabel Ὀψαρτ. p.11.

καταθρῡλέω, = καταθορυβέω, Poll.8.154.

κατάθρυπτος, ον, (cf. θρύπτω II.2c) *mincing, affected*, Eub.108.

καταθρύπτω, *break in pieces*, γυῖα Nic.*Al.*61; λάγανον Artem.ap. Ath.14.663e; κ. ἄρτους εἰς γάλα D.S.1.83, cf. Dieuch.ap.Orib.*Syn.* 5.33 (Pass.).

καταθρῴσκω, aor. 2 κατέθορον, *leap down*, κὰδ δ' ἔθορ' ἐς μέσσον Il. 4.79: c. acc., κ. τὴν αἱμασιήν *leap down* the wall, Hdt.6.134; καταθορόντες ἀπὸ τῶν ἵππων Id.3.86: c. gen., Nonn.*D.*23.220.

καταθῡμέω, *to be cast down, lose heart*, X.*HG*3.2.7.

καταθύμιος [ῡ], α, ον, also ος, ον Eumel.13:—*in the mind* or *thoughts*, ὄφρα ἔπος εἴπωμι τό μοι καταθύμιόν ἐστιν Od.22.392; μηδέ τί τοι θάνατος κ. ἔστω let not death sit *heavy on thy heart*, Il.10.383, cf. 17.201. II. *according to one's mind*, τῷ Ἰθωμάτᾳ κ. ἔπλετο Μοῖσα Eumel. l.c.; οὔτι μάλ' ἀνθρώποις κ. πάντα τελεῖται Thgn.617, cf. 1086; Μαρδονίῳ τὰ σφάγια οὐ δύναται κ. γενέσθαι Hdt.9.45; ἐούσης ταύτης [γυναικὸς] οἱ καταθυμίης Id.5.39; τί γὰρ ἥδιον ἀνθρώπῳ γυναικὸς καταθυμίας; Antipho Soph.49, cf. Muson.*Fr.*14 p.74 H.; παῖς κ. Democr.277; ὄρνις *Lyr.Alex.Adesp.*4 *B*16; ποιοῦντες τὰ κ. αὐτῶν Lxx *Is.*44.9, cf. *Mi.*7.3, D.C.37.56.

καταθῡμοβορέω, strengthd. for θυμοβορέω, [ζωὴν] κ. Pythag.ap. Ps.-Plu.*Vit.Hom.*154 (= ap.Stob.4.56.24).

καταθύω, *sacrifice*, πρόβατα Hdt.8.19, cf. X.*An.*4.5.35, *Milet.*1(9). 368, D.C.65.13, etc.; [τοῖς θεοῖς] πάντα Anon.*Oxy.*2151 9; of incense, *burn as an offering*, λιβανωτοῦ χίλια τάλαντα Jul.*Or.*2.79b. 2. *offer, dedicate*, τὴν δεκάτην Inscr.ap.X.*An.*5.3.13, D.S.4.21. 3. simply, *kill*, αἶγα Aret.*CD*2.12. II. Med., φίλτροις καταθύσομαι *will compel by* magic *sacrifices*, Theoc.2.3 (-δήσομαι Sch.).

καταθωπεύω, strengthd. for θωπεύω, δώροις τοὺς πολεμίους Agath. 5.14, cf. Sch.Theoc.6.30.

καταθωρᾱκίζομαι, Pass., *wear protective armour*, ἵπποι -ισμένοι X. *Cyr.*6.2.17.

καταί, rare poet. form for κατά, A.D.*Synt.*309.28.

καται-βᾰσία, Ep. -ίη, ἡ, poet. for κατάβασις, Q.S.6.484 (pl.). II. καταιβασίαι *thunderbolts*, Plu.2.555a. **-βάσιος** [βᾰ], ον, *descending*, epith. of the thunderbolt, κ. Διὸς ἔγχος Orac.ap.Porph.ap.Eus. *PE*6.3; cf. καταβάσιος. II. of Apollo, as *invoked by those who prayed for a return* (κατάβασις) to their country, Sch.E.*Ph.*1408, Zen.4.29. **-βᾰσις**, εως, ἡ, poet. for κατάβασις, *AP*11.23 (Antip.). **-βάτης** [ᾰ], ου, ὁ, a name of Zeus as *descending in thunder and lightning*, Ar.*Pax* 42, Clearch.9, Lyc.1370, *IG*2.1659*b*, 12(3). 1360 (Thera), 1093 (Melos), *BCH*50.245 (Thasos), Ἀρχ.Ἐφ.1924. 146 (Thess.), Paus.5.14.10, Corn.*ND*9: applied by Athenian flattery to Demetrius, Plu.*Demetr.*10; also κ. κεραυνός, σκηπτός, A.*Pr.*361,

Lyc.382. 2. of Hermes, *who led souls down* to the nether world, Sch.Ar.*Pax*649. 3. of Ἀχέρων, *that to which one descends, downward*, E.*Ba.*1360. 4. of a person, *descending underground*, Dam. *Isid.*131. 5. καταιβάται, οἱ, members of a thiasos of worshippers of Dionysus, *Inscr.Magn.*215 *a* 36.—In these senses the form καταβάτης never occurs; cf. καταιβάσιος, καταιβάτις, etc. **-βάτις** [ᾰ], ιδος, ἡ, fem. of foreg., ζῶσ' ἐς Ἅιδην ἵξεται κ. Lyc.497. 2. κ. κέλευθος *steep, downward* path, A.R.2.353, 3.160; τρίβος Lyc.91. II. Act., *that brings down*, κόρη σελήνης κ. *that brings down* the moon by spells, Sosiph.1. **-βᾰτός**, ή, όν, poet. for καταβατός, θύραι.. καταιβαταὶ ἀνθρώποισιν gates *by which* men *descend*, Od.13.110.

κατ-ᾱΐγδην, Adv. *coming violently down*, A.R.1.64, Opp.*H.*3.574, Orph.*L.*508, etc.

καταιγ-ῐδώδης, ες, *tempestuous*, πνοαί, ἄνεμοι, Sch.A.R.1.1016, Eust.1414.38. **-ίζω**, *rush down like a storm*, πρὶν καταιγίσαι πνοὰς Ἄρεως A.*Th.*63, cf. Str.16.4.5, J.*AJ*3.5.2, Hld.1.22; στρόμβος καταιγίζων *a rushing roaring* sound, A.*Fr.*195; ἐκνεφίας καταιγίσας ἐς τὴν ἀγοράν Alex.46.5; εἰς τοὔψον Id.247.3; of the sea, *AP*10.16.9 (Theaet.): metaph., of pain and sickness, Hp.*Morb.*3.7,16; of love, *AP*12.88; of rumour, Ach.Tat.6.10; of drunken frenzy, τὴν καταιγίζουσαν ἐκ μέθης ζάλην *Com.Adesp.*1227. 2. Pass., *to be visited by storms*, of places, τοῖς βορέαις Str.7.4.3, cf. 9.3.15: metaph., ὁλκὰς θορύβοις -ομένη Hld.5.24; also, of the sea, ὅταν ὑπ' ἀνέμου -ίζηται ὁ πόντος Gal.6.709. **-ίς**, ίδος, ἡ, (αἰγίς II) *squall descending from above, hurricane*, Democr.14, Arist.*Mu.*395^{a}5, *AP*7.273 (Leon.), Corn.*ND*9, Erot. s. v. πόνος, Gal.18(2).178, D.C.74.12, Lib.*Or.*59. 138: metaph., of *gusts* of passion (cf. sq.), Phld.*Herc.*1251.6; of battles, Tz.*H.*1.984 (pl.). **-ισμός**, ὁ, = foreg., in pl., *gusts* of physical passion, Epicur.*Fr.*413.

καταιδέομαι, fut. -έσομαι: aor. Pass. -ηδέσθην in act. sense:—*feel shame* or *reverence before* another, *stand in awe of* him, c. acc., Hdt.3.72,77, S.*OT*654, E.*Or.*682; δαίμονα καταιδεσθεῖσα Id.*Hipp.* 772 (lyr.); καταιδέσθητι πατρῷον Δία Ar.*Nu.*1468 (paratrag.): c. inf., *to be ashamed to do* a thing, E.*Heracl.*1027: abs., Id.*Hel.*805, D.C. 38.3. II. later in Act., **καταιδέω**, *put to shame*, Hld.4.18, Them. *Or.*15.191b, f.l. in Plu.2.801f, cf. Hsch., Phot.

καταιέτια γεῖσα *raking* cornices *of a pediment* (cf. ἀετός IV), *IG*2^2. 1668.39.

καταιθᾰλόω, *burn to ashes*, δόμους..καταιθαλώσω A.*Fr.*160; ὃν Ζεὺς κεραυνῷ πυρπόλῳ καταιθαλοῖ E.*Supp.*640; Μίμαντα πυρὶ Id.*Ion* 215 (lyr.); σῶμα καὶ δόμων περιπτυχὰς κ. Ar.*Av.*1242, cf. 1248; γαῖαν Lyc.1376: metaph., of love, καταιθαλώσεις τῶν νεωτέρων τινά Ar. *Av.*1261:—Pass., [Τροίας] πυρὶ κατηθαλωμένης E.*Tr.*60; ὑπ' ἀσβόλου κατηθαλωμένος *all burnt* and sooty, Luc.*DDeor.*5.4, cf. Artem.2.10; ἱερῶν -ουμένων Hp.*Ep.*27.

καταιθύσσω, *wave* or *float down*, πλόκαμοι..νῶτον καταίθυσσον Pi.*P.*4.83; εὐδίαν ὃς καταιθύσσει ἑστίαν *sheds* fair weather *down upon* the hearth, ib.5.11:—hence **καταῖθυξ** ὄμβρος, *Trag.Adesp.* 216.

καταίθω, *burn down, burn to ashes*, καταίθουσα..δαλόν (Canter for κ' αἴθουσα) A.*Ch.*607 (lyr.); σὺ δ' οὖν κάταιθε E.*Andr.*258; ὕφαπτε καὶ κάταιθε Ar.*Th.*730; πυρὶ καταίθεται τέραμνα E.*Tr.*1296 (lyr.). 2. metaph., *kindle, rouse*, Lyc.249; ἔρως με καταίθει Theoc.7.56:—Pass., καταίθεσθαι ἐπί τινι Id.2.40:—A.*Fr.*359 is corrupt.

καταικίζω, *maltreat*, τεύχεα..κατῄκισται the arms *have been disfigured* [by smoke and soot], Od.16.290:—Med., σῶμα σὸν καταικιῇ (fut. Att.) E.*Andr.*828 (lyr.), cf. D.S.18.47:—Pass., βασάνοις -αικισθέντες D.H.3.73: metaph., μουσικὴ -ῃκισμένη τὸ σῶμα Plu.2.1141d.

καταίν-εσις, εως, ἡ, *betrothal*, Plu.*TG*4. **-έω**, poet. aor. 1 -ησα Pi. (v. infr.):—*agree* to a thing, *approve of* it, opp. ἀναίνομαι, c. acc. rei, Hdt.4.80, 6.62; κ. [τι] ἐπί τινι to *agree* to it on conditions, Id.3.53: c. dat. rei, Th.4.122: abs., οὐ καταινέσαμεν ἀλλὰ ἀπειπάμεθα Hdt.9.7.α'. 2. *agree, promise to* do, c. aor. inf., γάμον μεῖξαι Pi.*P.*4.222: c. fut. inf., καταίνεσον μή ποτε προδώσειν S.*OC* 1633, cf. 1637; also τοῦτον κ. βασιλέα σφίσι εἶναι *agree that* he should be king, Hdt.1.98; κ. τινὰ ταγόν (sc. εἶναι) *AP*9.98 (Stat. Flacc.). 3. *grant, promise*, τοὔτ' ἐμοὶ πόλις τὸ δῶρον..κατῄνεσεν S.*OC*432, cf. *Ichn.*158; esp. *promise in marriage, betroth*, παῖδά τινι E.*IA*695, cf. Plu.*Pomp.*47; κ. πρὸς γάμον Nic.Dam.10 J.

κατ-αΐξ [τᾱ], ῖκος, ἡ, = καταιγίς, Eumel.9 (pl.), A.R.1.1203, Call. *Dian.*114.

καταιον-άω, *pour upon* or *over, foment*, of ailing parts, Hp.*Mul.* 1.68, Plu.2.74d: metaph., κ. τινὰ σοφίᾳ D.C.38.19:—Pass., Luc. *Lex.*5. **-ημα**, ατος, τό, *fomentation*, Ael.*NA*8.22, Alex.Trall.1. 13. **-ησις**, εως, ἡ, = foreg., D.Chr.17.6, M.Ant.5.9, Poll.4.180, Gal.12.675; αἱ κατὰ κεφαλῆς κ. Ath.1.24d.

καταίρεσις, -αιρέω, Ion. for καθαίρεσις, -αιρέω.

καταίρω, *take down*, only in Aeol. form **κατ-αέρρω** for κατ-αείρω (q. v.): elsewh. II. intr., *come down, swoop*, of birds, ἐς τὰ βιβλία Ar.*Av.*1288; ἐς Δελφούς Paus.10.15.5; ἀφ' ἑτέρας τινὸς γῆς ἐνταῦθα Plu.*Rom.*9; of bees, ἐπὶ τὸν θύμον κ. Id.2.41f; of persons, κ. ἀπ' ὄχθων X.*Eq.Mag.*6.5; ἐκεῖσε E.*Ba.*1294; εἰς τὰς Ἀθήνας Pl. *Hp.Ma.*281a; εἰς τὰς τῶν πολεμίων χεῖρας Plu.*Phil.*14. 2. of ships, *put into port, put in*, ἐς Καῦνον Th.8.39; εἰς τὴν χώραν *Hell.Oxy.*16.1; ἐπὶ νῆσον, πρὸς τὴν Πανορμῖτιν, Plb.1.60.3, 1.56.3; ἀπὸ τῆς Συρίας δευρί Alciphr.1.38.

καταισθάνομαι, *perceive*, τι S.*OT*422.

καταίσιμ-ος, ον, = αἴσιμος, Hsch. **-όω**, *consume utterly*, Eub. 15.6 (Pass.); κ. πῶμα *to drink* it *off*, Epin.1.10.

καταίσιος, ον, = αἴσιος, *righteous*, ἔργον οὐ κ. A.*Ag.*1598, cf. Cerc. 18.36, Hsch.

κατ-ᾱΐσσω, fut. -ΐξω, *rush down from*, ἔκποθεν ὀλέθρου A.R.2.224; opp. ἀναΐσσω, Herm.ap.Stob.1.49.68:—Med., *rush in from above*, αἰθὴρ καταΐσσεται Emp.100.7. II. c. acc., *rush, dart through*, φρὴν..κόσμον..καταΐσσουσα Id.134.5.

καταϊσχαλέος, α, ον, = ἰσχαλέος, dub. l. in Od.19.233.

καταισχόφιλος, v. κατασκάφιλος.

καταισχρεύομαι, *speak* or *act foully*, Tz.*H.*6.32.

καταισχυμμός, ὁ, *shaming, disgrace*, Sm.*Mi.*2.6.

καταισχυν-τήρ, ῆρος, ὁ, *dishonourer*, δόμων A.*Ag.*1363. **-ω**, fut. -αισχῠνῶ Id.*Th.*546:—*dishonour, put to shame*, μή τι καταισχύνειν πατέρων γένος Od.24.508; καταισχύνητέ τε δαῖτα 16.293; τὰ πρόσθε ἐργασμένα Hdt.7.53, cf. A.*Supp.*996, D.18.101, etc.; τὴν σὴν οὐ κ. φύσιν I *put* not thy nature *to shame*, i.e. show myself not unworthy of thee, S.*El.*609; κ. τὸ Τρωϊκὸν κλέος E.*Hel.*845; τὸ γένος οὐ καταισχυνῶ Ar.*Av.*1451; κ. τὴν πατρίδα Id.*Nu.*1220; τοὺς προγόνους Pl.*La.*187a; ὑποσχέσεις Id.*Smp.*183e; τὰς εὐγενείας ταῖς αὑτῶν ..κακίαις Isoc.7.76, etc. 2. *dishonour* a woman, ἀλλοτρίας γυναῖκας Lys.1.49; also of a male, D.45.79. 3. ὁ μέλλων χρόνος ἐμὸν καταίσχυνε..χρέος *covered* me *with dishonour* in that my debt remained unpaid, Pi.*O.*10(11).8. 4. = καταχέζειν, χαίτην Babr. 82.8. II. Med., *feel shame before*, θεούς S.*Ph.*1382, cf. *OT*1424:—aor. Pass., καταισχυνθέντες τὴν ἀρετὴν αὐτῶν Isoc.4.97: c. inf., *to be ashamed* to..., ἰητρεύειν Hp.*Art.*42; καταισχυνθῆναι..ὅπως μὴ δόξει..*to be ashamed* of being thought.., Th.6.13.

καταΐσχω, Ep. for κατίσχω, κατέχω, Od.9.122 (Pass.).

καταιτι-άομαι, *accuse, arraign*, ἀλλήλους Hdt.6.14; τί σαυτὸν ἀδικῶν τὴν τύχην καταιτιᾷ; Men.618; τινὰ περί τινος D.57.27; τινὰς ἀσεβείας D.C.68.1, cf. J.*AJ*8.13.3; τινα c. inf., χρήματα εἰληφέναι D.C.*Fr.*104.3; τινος X.*Cyr.*6.1.4 (v.l.): abs. in med. sense, *accuse one another*, Hdt.5.92.γ':—Pass., *PTeb.*64(*a*).84 (ii B.C.). 2. c. acc. rei, *lay* something *to one's charge, impute*, ἀμαθίαν Th.3.42; καταιτιώμενος ταῦτα D.21.118. II. aor. 1 part. Pass. καταιτιαθεὶς in pass. sense, *accused person, defendant*, οἱ κ. Th.6.60, Plb.30.32.11; οἱ ἐκ τοῦ Περσικοῦ πολέμου κ. Id.3.5.4: c. inf., καταιτιαθεὶς ταῦτα πρᾶξαι X.*HG*1.1.32; so also οἱ κατητιαμένοι Plb.32.3.14; κατητιᾶσθαι τὴν κλοπήν D.S.4.31. **-ᾱσις**, εως, ἡ, *accusation*, Plu.2.546f (pl.), M.Ant.1.16. **-ασμός**, ὁ, = foreg., Vett.Val.2.8 (pl.), al., *Cat.Cod. Astr.*2.161 (pl.).

καταῖτυξ, ῠγος, ἡ, *leathern helmet*, without φάλος or λόφος, Il.10. 258.

καταίφλεξ, *burning with heat*, Hsch. s. v. καταῖθυξ.

καταιχμάζω, *strike down*, c. gen., Nonn.*D.*21.6, al.

καταιωρέομαι, Pass., *hang down*, θύσανοι κατηωρεῦντο Hes.*Sc.*225.

κατακαγχάζω, *laugh aloud at*, τινος *AP*5.215.6 (Agath.), cf. Anon. ap.Suid. s. v. ἀνατεινάμενος.

κατακαῆμεν, κατακαιέμεν, v. κατακαίω.

κατακαίνυμαι, pf. -κέκασμαι, *to be adorned*, κεφαλῇ κατὰ γυῖα κέκασται Emp.134.1.

κατακαίνω, = κατακτείνω, *kill*, in early writers in aor. 2 κατέκανον, X.*Cyr.*4.6.5 (v.l. -καίνων), *An.*3.2.12; 3 sg. subj. κατακάνῃ Anon. in *PSI*9.1091.4; κατέκανον (for -έκτανον) is required by the metre in S.*Ant.*1340: pf. part. -κεκονότες (cf. καίνω) shd. be read in X.*An.* 7.6.36: pres. in later Prose, Parth.7.2, Arr.*Ind.*11.10, App.*Pun.*1, Eun.*Hist.*p.212 D.; Hsch. has κατακαινιῶ· ἀποκτενῶ (fort. leg. κατακενίω, Dor. fut.).

κατακαίριος, ον, = καίριος, Il.11.439, *AP*9.227 (Bianor).

κατακαίω, Att. -κάω [ᾱ], Ep. inf. κατακαιέμεν Il.7.408: fut. -καύσω Ar.*Lys.*1218: aor. κατέκαυσα Th.7.25; Ep. 3 sg. κατέκηε Il.6.418; 1 pl. subj. κατακήομεν (v.l. -κείομεν) Il.7.333; inf. κατακῆαι Od.11. 46, κακκῆαι ib.74 (v.l. -κεῖαι): pf. -κέκαυκα X.*HG*6.5.37, Phld. *Acad.Ind.*p.69 M.:—Pass., fut. -καυθήσομαι Ar.*Nu.*1505, -καήσομαι 1*Ep.Cor.*3.15: aor. κατεκαύθην (the Att. form) Hdt.4.69, 6.101, κατεκάην Id.1.51, 2.107; Lacon. inf. -καῆμεν Plu.*Lyc.*20; -εκαύσθην *Chron.Lind.*D.41: pf. -κέκαυμαι And.1.108:—*burn completely*, in Hom. of sacrifices and dead bodies, κατακήομεν αὐτούς Il.7.333; μιν κατέκηε σὺν ἔντεσι 6.418; κ. τοὺς μάντιας *burn* them *alive*, Hdt. 4.69; ζῶντα κατακαυθῆναι Id.1.86, cf. 2.107; of cities and houses, etc., κατὰ μὲν ἔκαυσαν..πόλιν Id.8.33; κατεκαίετο ὁ ἐν Δελφοῖσι νηός Id.1.50; [οἰκίη] κατεκάη Id.4.79; κατακαυθέντων ἱρῶν Id.6.101; τείχη -κεκαυμένα And. l. c.; γῆ κατακεκαυμένη *burnt* earth, Arist. *Mete.*358^{a}14; Κατακεκαυμένη, name of the upper valley of the Hermus, in Lydia, Str.13.4.11, cf. κατακεκαυμενίτης; of the fingers, *to be burnt* with hot food, Porph.*Abst.*4.15; also κ. τὴν κοιλίαν *PMagd.*33.4 (iii B.C.). 2. of hot winds, *parch*, τὰ ἐκ τῆς γῆς *PHib.*1.27.73 (iii B.C.), al. 3. metaph., ὁ ἔρως ἐμέ..κατακέκαυκεν *Lyr.Alex.Adesp.*8(*c*):—Pass., τὰ στόματα -κάεται ἐπὶ τέχνην Anaxandr.33.6; -καίομαι καταλελειμμένη *Lyr.Alex.Adesp.*1.24. II. Pass., of fire, κατὰ πῦρ ἐκάη *had burnt down, burnt out*, Il.9.212.

κατακᾰλέω, *call down*, Plu.*Oth.*18; but usu. *summon*, ἐκ τῆς μητροπόλεως κατακληθεὶς Th.1.24; δοῦλοι -κεκλημένοι ἐπ' ἐλευθερίᾳ Str. 14.1.38:—Med., κ. Ἀθήναζε Plu.*Sol.*24; *call upon* for performance, *BGU*1185.25 (i B.C.). II. *call upon, invoke*, τοὺς θεούς App.*Pun.* 81; κατακαλέσασθαι v.l. Isoc.10.61, cf. Plu.*Them.*13. 2. *appeal to*, τοὺς ἐπιδώσοντας *SIG*591.3 (Lampsacus, ii B.C.). III. *call back, recall*, εἰς τὴν Μακεδονίαν Plb.25.3.1, cf. Oenom.ap.Eus.*PE*5.34.

κατακαλλύνω, *clear away*, κόπρον *IG*11(2).287 *A* 62 (Delos, iii B.C.).

κατακάλυμμα [κᾰλ], ατος, τό, *covering, veil*, Lxx*Ex*.26.14, J.*BJ*5.12.3 (dub. l.).

κατακᾰλύπτω, *cover up*, κατά τε κνίσῃ ἐκάλυψαν (sc. μηρούς) Il.1.460, cf. Hdt.2.47(tm.); με τεθνηῶτα.. κατὰ γαῖα καλύπτοι Il.6.464; κατὰ δὲ σκότος ὄσσε κάλυψεν 16.325; Ἴδην δὲ κατὰ νεφέεσσι κ. 17.594; κἀμὲ θανάτου κατὰ μοῖρα καλύψαι A.*Pers*.917 (anap.), cf. Hes.*Op*.121, E.*Tr*.1315 (lyr.), etc. :—Med., κατὰ κρᾶτα καλυψάμενος γοάασκεν *having covered his* head, Od.8.92; so -καλυψάμενος alone, Hdt.6.67; κἂν κατακεκαλυμμένος τις γνοίη even one *veiled* would perceive, Pl.*Men*.76b; λογισμῷ κατακαλυψάμενος Id.*Ep*.340a.

κατακάλυψις [κᾰλ], εως, ἡ, *covering, concealment*, Longin.17.3; τὰ ἐν -καλύψει ἀποστήματα Scrib.Larg.ap.Gal.13.99, Cass.Fel.21.

κατακᾰμᾰρόω, *cover with a vault*, Hsch.

κατακάμπτω, *bend down*, so as to be concave, ἐξ ὀρθοῦ κ. Pl.*Ti*.71c; εἰς ἓν κύκλῳ ib.36b; κ. τὰς στροφάς, v. στροφή 1.3 :—Pass., opp. ἀνακάμπτομαι, Arist.*Mete*.386^{a}1; φλὲψ ἐπὶ τὴν ῥάχιν -ομένη Gal.15.530: pf. part. Pass. -κεκαμμένος *bending over*, cj. in Thphr.*HP*3.18.8. **II.** *cover with a vault*, λίθῳ κατακαμφθέντες Str.5.3.8. **III.** metaph., κ. ἐλπίδας *bend down, overthrow* hopes, E.*Tr*.1252 (Burges, -γναψε codd., anap.) :—Pass., *to be bent* (by entreaty), Aeschin.1.187.

κατάκαμψις, εως, ἡ, *bending down*, κλάδων Str.3.5.10; *bending into a concave form*, opp. ἀνάκαμψις, Arist.*Mete*.386^{a}5.

κατακάρδιος, ον, *in* or *to the heart*, πληγαί Hdn.7.11.3.

κατακάρπ-ιον, τό, = περικάρπιον, Thphr.*HP*4.10.3 codd. (dub. l.). **-ος**, ον, *fruitful*, Aristodem.ap.Ath.11.495f, Lxx*Ho*.14.7. Adv. **-πως** *abundantly*, κ. κατοικηθήσεται Ἱερουσαλήμ ib.*Za*.2.4(8). **-όω**, *offer burnt-sacrifices*, esp. *of fruits*, Suid. **-ωσις**, εως, ἡ, *ashes of a burnt-sacrifice*, Lxx*Le*.6.10(3), 11(4).

κατακαρφής, ές, *dried*, φλοιός (of a turnip) Nic.*Fr*.70.9.

κατακάρφω, fut. -κάρψω, *parch up*, Hsch. :—Pass., *wither, fall into the sere*, A.*Ag*.80 (anap.).

κατάκασσα or **-κᾶσα**, ἡ, = κάσσα, Call.*Fr*.184 (κατακάσαι Hsch.).

κατά-καυμα, ατος, τό, *anything burnt*: pl., *burnt parts*, Paul.Aeg.4.13. **2.** *fiery inflammation*, Hp.*Coac*.154, Lxx*Le*.13.24,25; *burns*, in pl., Thphr.*Ign*.57, Dsc.5.123, Crito ap.Gal.13.800, *Gp*.12.17.11. **II.** *burning*, Lxx*Ex*.21.25, Luc.*Asin*.6. **-καύσιμος**, ον, *combustible*, ξύλα Hsch. s.v. ἄθινα. **-καυσις**, εως, ἡ, *burning*, Gal.19.542, Porph.*Abst*.4.15. **-καύτης**, ου, ὁ, *one who burns* (a corpse), Plu.2.296b.

κατακαυχάομαι, *boast against* one, *exult over* him, τινος *Ep.Rom*.11.18, Eust. ad D.P.*Prooem*.p.67 B.; κατά τινος *Ep.Jac*.3.14: metaph., -καυχᾶται ἔλεος κρίσεως ib.2.13; κ. ἔν τινι *to glory* in it, Lxx *Za*.10.12.

κατακαχρύω, fut. -ύσω Hsch., Phot.: aor. inf. -ῦσαι Paus.Gr.*Fr*.227 :—prop. *grind roasted corn*: metaph., *grind, crush*, ll. cc.

κατακεῖαι, -κείομεν, v. κατακαίω.

κατάκειμαι, Ep. 3 pl. κατακείαται Il.24.527: Ion. plpf. κατεκέατο Hdt.7.229; subj. -κέωμαι Pl.*Smp*.213b :—Pass., only in pres. and impf. with fut. Med. -κείσομαι :—*lie down*, μῆλα τὰ δὴ κατάκειτ' ἐσφαγμένα Od.10.532; ἐπὶ πλευρὰς κ. Il.24.10; νέκυς κ. Tyrt.11.19; ἐφ' ἁρμαμαξῶν μαλθακῶς κατακείμενοι Ar.*Ach*.70. **2.** *lie hid*, ἐν λόχμῃ.. κατέκειτο μέγας σῦς Od.19.439; θάμνῳ ὕπ' ἀμφικόμῳ κατακείμενος Il.17.677. **3.** *lie stored up*, δοιοὶ γάρ τε πίθοι κατακείαται ἐν Διὸς οὔδει Il.24.527; τό γ' ἐν οἴκῳ κατακείμενον ἀνέρα κήδει Hes.*Op*.364: metaph., ἄλγεα.. ἐν θυμῷ κ. Il.24.523. **b.** *to be deposited*, of deeds in a registry, *POxy*.1040.32 (iii A.D.), etc. **4.** *lie sick, keep one's bed*, Hdt.7.229, *Ev.Marc*.1.30, etc.; *lie in bed*, Ar.*Ec*.313; ἐφ' ὃ κατέκειτο *Ev.Luc*.5.25. **5.** *lodge, reside*, Hp.*Epid*.1.26.ε', 3.1.γ', al. **6.** *to be idle*, X.*An*.3.1.14; of things, *lie neglected*, καθεύδειν ἐᾶν ἐν τῇ γῇ κατακείμενα τὰ τείχη Pl.*Lg*.778d. **7.** *recline at meals*, πῖνε, κατάκεισο Ar.*Ach*.985, cf. Hdt.3.121, Pl.*Smp*.185d, *Ev.Marc*.14.3. **8.** of land, *lie sloping to the sea*, πρῶνες ἔξοχοι -κειται Pi.*N*.4.52. **9.** ἀρετᾷ κατάκειται πᾶσαν ὀργάν *is expended* in every impulse *on*.., Id.*I*.1.41.

κατακείρω, fut. -κερῶ (v. infr.), *shear, clip close*, τὸν πώγωνα Plu.2.52c (Pass.): Com., ὁ κουρεὺς.. ὑπὸ τῆς ὑπήνης κατακερεῖ τὴν εἰσφοράν Eup.278 :—Med., κ. τὰς κεφαλὰς *crop their* heads *close*, Hdt.1.82. **II.** in Hom. only metaph., *cut away, waste*, βίοτον κατακείρετε πολλόν Od.4.686; ὅτι μοι κατεκείρετε οἶκον 22.36; μῆλα δ' ἅ μοι μνηστῆρες.. κατέκειραν 23.356.

κατακείω, = κατάκειμαι, used in imperat. and as fut., δαισάμενοι κατακείετε οἴκαδ' ἰόντες Od.7.188, 18.408; σπείσαντες κατακείομεν οἴκαδ' ἰόντες ib.419; κακκείοντες, Ep. part., in phrases οἱ μὲν κακκείοντες ἔβαν οἶκόνδε, κλισίηνδε ἕκαστος, Il.1.606, 23.58.

Κατακεκαυμένη, ἡ, v. κατακαίω :—hence **κατακεκαυμενίτης** οἶνος, wine from that district, Str.13.4.11.

κατακεκλεισμένως, Adv. pf. part. Pass. (κατακλείω), κ. ἔχειν Hsch. s.v. κατεκλάζετο.

κατακελευ-σμός, ὁ, *calling to one, encouraging*, name of a part of the Πυθικὸς νόμος, Str.9.3.10, Poll.4.84. **-ω**, *command silence*, Ar.*Av*.1273: generally, *command*, c. inf., Plu.*Oth*.18 (s. v. l.). **2.** of the boatswain, *give the time in rowing*, Ar.*Ra*.207.

κατακενόω, strengthd. for κενόω, σάκκους Lxx*Ge*.42.35; φάρμακον εἰς τὸ πῦρ J.*BJ*1.30.6, cf. Androm.ap.Gal.13.886.

κατακεντ-έω, *pierce through*, Pl.*Ti*.76b; *prick*, Gal.12.323 (Act. and Pass.); *stab severely*, D.S.3.37; *cut down, stab*, δόρασι καὶ ξίφεσι Zos.4.49, cf. 5.23 :—Pass., Ctes.*Fr*.29.54. **2.** *shoot down*, Zos.5.21. **3.** metaph., πάθη κ. τινάς Ph.1.299 :—Pass., ὑπὸ ἀπιστίας κατακεντούμενοι ib.287 :—later form **κατακεντάννυμι** Palaeph.1, Ps.-Luc.*Philopatr*.4 (Pass.). **-ημα**, ατος, τό, *puncture*, Pl.*Ti*.76b. **-ίζω**, *slay with a spear*, Ael.*NA*7.2. **-ρόομαι**, Pass., *to be furnished with spikes*, D.S.18.71.

κατακέραμα, *sarta tecta*, Gloss.

κατα-κεράννῡμι, *mix, temper*, in Pass., Arist.*Pr*.949^{a}38, Sor.1.53, Plu.2.132d :—Act., *dilute, weaken*, δριμύτητα Dsc.5.11; cf. κατακίρνημι :—also -ύω, Poll.10.149. **-κέρᾰσις**, εως, ἡ, *process of mixing*, κατακεράσει αὐξάνεται Arist.*GA*723^{a}18. **-κεραστέον**, *one must mix, temper*, Aët.4.6. **-κεραστικός**, ή, όν, *demulcent, restoring normal* κρᾶσις, Gal.8.41, 10.486; τροφή Herod.Med.ap. Aët.5.129: c. gen., οὔρων δριμέων *Gp*.12.19.8.

κατακεραυνόω, *strike down by thunder*, Ps.-Luc.*Philopatr*.4.

κατακερδαίνω, *make gain of* a thing *wrongly*, X.*Oec*.4.7.

κατακερκίζω, *divide into* κερκίδες, στάδιον -ίζων τοῖχος *LW*141 (Ephesus), cf. *Jahresh*.15 *Beibl*.181 (ibid.).

κατακερματ-ίζω, (κέρμα) *chop up, cut into pieces*, freq. metaph., κ. αὐτὴν (sc. ἀρετὴν) κατὰ μόρια Pl.*Men*.79c; τὴν μίαν τέχνην εἰς πολλὰς Gal.*Thras*.24; κ. τὴν τέχνην εἰς μικρά *fritter* it *away*, Demetr.*Eloc*.76; τὴν μουσικήν Plu.2.1142b; τοὺς ἀγῶνας Str.4.4.2; τὸν λόγον Gal.1.246 :—Pass., *to be cut up*, φαίνεται εἰς σμικρότερα κατακεκερματίσθαι ἡ τοῦ ἀνθρώπου φύσις Pl.*R*.395b; κατακεκερμάτισται.. ὡς οἷόν τε σμικρότατα Id.*Prm*.144b; κατακεκ. ἐρωτήσεσι πρὸς ἀποκρίσεις *cut up* into questions and answers, Id.*Sph*.225b, cf. 257c, 258e, Plot.3.9.2; διήγησις εἰς μικρὰς κ. τομάς D.H.*Th*.9; σύνθεσις κατακεκομμένη καὶ -ισμένη Demetr.*Eloc*.4; ἄντικρυς μικρὰ καὶ -ισμένα Longin.42; τοῦ πυρετοῦ.. κατακερματιζομένου *gradually becoming slighter*, Hp.*Acut*.(*Sp*.)13: seldom in lit. sense, Porph.*Marc*.10 (Pass.); also, *change into smaller coin*, *POxy*.1411.12 (iii A.D.). **-ισμός**, ὁ, *dividing into small parts*, Porph.*Sent*.35.

κατακερτομέω, *rail violently*, Hdt.1.129; τινα *at* a person, Id.2.135, Ph.2.440; τινος Nic.Dam.3 J., Polyaen.1.34.2, Longus 2.20.

κατακερχνόομαι, strengthd. for κερχνόομαι, Hsch.

κατακεύθομαι, *to be hidden*, εἰς δνοφερὸν τύμβον *AP*15.29 (Ignat.).

κατακέφᾰλα, Adv., for κατὰ κεφαλῆς, *head downwards*, Teucer in Boll *Sphaera* p.17, *Gp*.10.30; *from head to foot*, λούσασθαι *IG*2^2.1365, 1366.

κατακεφάλαιον [φᾰ], τό, *poll-tax*, dub. in *PTeb*.119.6 (ii B.C.).

κατακηλ-έω, *charm, cast a spell over*, τήνδ' ἄτην S.*Tr*.1002 (anap.) :—Pass., Pl.*Cra*.403e, Plu.*Num*.20, Ath.4.174b, Dam.*Isid*.48. **-ητικός**, ή, όν, *fit for enchanting*, τινος Ael.*NA*17.19.

κατακηλῑδόω, strengthd. for κηλιδόω, v.l. in D.C.*Fr*.39.7.

κατακήομεν, v. κατακαίω.

κατακηρόω, *cover with wax*, Hdt.1.140, v.l. in X.*Eq*.10.7 (ap.Poll.1.207) :—Pass., κατακεκηρωμένον τὸ σῶμα Hdt.4.71.

κατακηρύσσω, Att. **-ττω**, *proclaim* or *command by public crier*, σιωπήν *IG*12(7).237.36 (Amorgos); σιγήν v.l. in X.*An*.2.2.20 :—Pass., *to be promulgated*, Plb.22.4.6. **2.** Pass. also, *to be summoned by crier*, Poll.8.61. **II.** at auction, κ. τι εἴς τινα *order* it *to be knocked down* to one, Plu.*Comp.Lys.Sull*.3.

κατακίκκας, v. κατακόκκας. **κατακικλάσκω**, = κατακλάω, Phot. s.v. κατεκίκλασκε.

κατακῑνέω, strengthd. for κινέω, in Pass., f.l. in Sch.Theoc.5.116.

κατακίρνημι, = κατακεράννυμι, in Pass., Longin.15.9, *AP*9.362.12, Iamb. *in Nic*.p.119 P.: —also **-κιρνάω**, Id.*Protr*.21.ιε'.

κατακισηρίζω, *rub smooth with pumice-stone*, pf. part. Pass., of an effeminate youth, Ctes.*Fr*.20.

κατακισσᾶν (-κίσσαν cod.)· προσποιεῖσθαι, Hsch.

κατάκισσος, ον, *ivy-wreathed*, *Anacreont*.41.5.

κατακλᾰδαίνω, aor. 1 -εκλάδᾱνα, = ἀναιρέω, Hsch.; cf. κλαδάω.

κατάκλᾰδος, ον, gloss on κατάπρεμνος, Hsch.

κατακλᾴζω, v. κατακλείω.

κατακλαίω, Att. -κλάω [ᾱ], *bewail loudly, lament*, τινα Ar.*V*.386: —Med., E.*El*.156 (lyr.), *IT*149 (lyr.). **2.** abs., *wail aloud*, Id.*El*.113 (lyr.). **II.** c. gen. pers., *lament before* or *to* another, Herod.1.59, Arr.*Epict*.1.23.4, etc.; κ. αὐτὸς ἑαυτοῦ ib.3.13.4.

κατάκλᾰσις, εως, ἡ, *forced position*, τῶν ἄρθρων Hp.*Epid*.6.1.15 (pl.). **2.** κ. ὄμματος *drooping* of the eyelid, Id.*Prorrh*.1.84 (vv. ll. -κλισις, -κλεισις), cf. *Epid*.6.1.15, Gal.16.675. **II.** *refraction* of light or sound, opp. ἀνάκλασις (reflexion), Arist.*Pr*.901^{b}20, 904^{b}30, Cleom.2.6.

κατάκλαυσις, εως, ἡ, (κατακλαίω) *bewailing*, *Gloss*.

κατακλάω (A) [ᾱ], Att. for κατακλαίω (q. v.).

κατακλάω (B) [ᾰ], impf. κατέκλων Il.20.227, Hdt.9.62: aor. 1 -έκλᾰσα Pl.*Phd*.117d :—Pass., pf. and aor. (v. infr.) :—*break short, snap off*, ἐπ' ἀνθερίκων καρπὸν θέον οὐδὲ κατέκλων Il. l. c.; κατεκλάσθη δ' ἐνὶ καυλῷ ἔγχος 13.608; τὰ δόρατα κατέκλων Hdt. l. c., cf. Pi.*P*.5.34; φυτευτήρια ἐλαῶν D.53.15; κατὰ δ' αὐχένα νέρθ' ἐπὶ γαίης κλάσσε *bowed* it *down*, Theoc.25.146; κ. τὸν ὀφθαλμόν *ogle*, Phryn.*PS*p.79 B.; but ὄμματα κατακεκλασμένα eyes *with drooping lids*, Arist.*Phgn*.808^{a}8; τὸ σῶμα.. -κέκλασται *has been crushed*, *PMasp*.77.12 (vi A.D.). **II.** metaph., *break down*, οὐδένα ὅντινα οὐ κατέκλασε he *broke* us all *down*, Pl.*Phd*. l. c.; πάθος, εἴτ' οἶκτος εἴτ' αἰδώς, κατέκλασε τὴν διάνοιαν Plu.*Tim*.7; [Ἔρως] κατακλάσας τὸ σοβαρόν Id.2.767f :—more freq. in Pass., ἐμοί γε κατεκλάσθη φίλον ἦτορ, κλαῖον δ' ἐν ψαμάθοισι καθήμενος Od.4.538; of fear, ἡμῖν δ' αὖτε κατεκλάσθη φίλον ἦτορ δεισάντων 9.256, cf. 10.198; τὸ θράσος κατεκέκλαστο Plu.*Fab*.11; of passion, ἐρώτων.. νόσῳ φρένας.. κατεκλάσθη E.*Hipp*.766 (lyr.); of pity, οὐδὲ κατεκλάσθης Call.*Del*.107; of persuasion, D.L.7.114. **2.** Pass., κατακεκλασμένος *reduced by fever*, Hp.*Coac*.510:

metaph., of character, *to become enfeebled, degenerate*, Aristeas 149: in pf. part. Pass., *enervated, effeminate*, of men, *Com.Adesp.*339.2; γραφαὶ κ. D.H.*Comp.*18:—Act., κ. ἑαυτόν, of an effeminate dancer, Luc.*Symp.*18, *Salt.*27. III. Pass., of light, *to be refracted*, opp. ἀνακλᾶσθαι (to be reflected), ὄψεως -κλωμένης *Placit.*3.18.1; of sound, αἱ κατακλώμεναι φωναὶ μετὰ φαρμακείην *broken, feeble* voice, Hp.*Coac.*246.

κατα-κλείδιον, τό, Dim. of κατακλείς I. 3, Bito 65.11. **-κλειμμα**, ατος, τό, f.l. for κατάλημμα (q.v.). **-κλείς**, εῖδος, or **κατάκλεις**, ειδος, Ion. and Ep. **-κληΐς**, ῗδος, ἡ, *instrument for shutting* or *fastening doors*, distd. from the bolt (μοχλός) and bolt-pin (βάλανος), Ar.*V.*154, *IG*11(2).158*A*65 (Delos, iii B.C., pl.); αἱ κ. τῶν ἀξόνων *linch-pins*, prob.l. in D.S.17.53. 2. *pawl, check-hook*, Ph.*Bel.*68.5, Hero *Bel.*79.13. 3. κατακληῒς βελέμνων *case* for arrows, quiver, Call.*Dian.*82; *cap* or *case* fitted to an engine, Bito 59.3; also, *socket* for the arrow in the γαστραφέτης, Id.62.9. 4. pl., *locks* on a canal, *PPetr.*2 p.43 (iii B.C.). 5. *sheath for a pin*, in pl., Sch.Od.18.294, Aristeas 65, cf. Hsch. s.v. κληῗδα. II. = ἀκρώμιον, Heliod.ap.Orib.48.48.1, Sor.2.62, Gal.2.766. 2. *first rib*, Id.18(2).956. 3. *clavicular region*, Id.14.703, Hdn.4.13.5. III. *final remark, conclusion*, Cic.*Att.*9.18.3, prob. l. in ib.2.3.3. 2. *close of a verse* or *set of verses*, Heph.5.1, 6.6, Aristid.Quint.1.27, Sch.Ar.*Ach.*659. **-κλεισις**, εως, ἡ, *shutting up, closing*, Gal.19.445. II. *completion*, Nicom.ap. *Theol.Ar.*43. III. *beam* resting on the pillars of the χελώνη, Ath. Mech.18.9 (pl.). **-κλειστος**, ον, *shut up*, of women, Call.*Fr.*118, cf. Lxx 2*Ma.*3.19, Luc.*Tim.*15, Hsch.; οἶκοι κατάκλειστος ἦν D.L.6.94; κ. εἶχεν τὰ βιβλία Str.13.1.54; *precious*, τίμιον ἢ κ. S.E.*P.*1.143. **-κλείω**, old Att. -κλῄω Th. (v. infr.): a rare fut. κατακλιῶ dub. in Eup.287, cf. Hero *Bel.*107.13:—**Med.**, aor. -εκλεισάμην X.*Cyr.*7.2.5:—**Pass.**, aor. -εκλῄσθην, -εκλείσθην (v. infr.); Ion. -εκληΐσθην Hdt.2.128; Dor. -εκλᾴσθην Theoc.7.84: pf. -κέκλημαι Ar.*Pl.*206. I. c. acc. pers., *shut in, enclose*, e.g. a mummy in its case, Hdt.2.86: freq. of blockading, τοὺς Ἕλληνας ἐς τὴν νῆσον κ. Th.1.109; κ. ἑαυτοὺς εἰς ἔρυμα X.*Cyr.*4.1.18; κατακλείειν τοὺς γυμνῆτας εἴσω τῶν ὅπλων Id.*An.*3.4.26; κ. εἰς πολιορκίαν, εἰς δυσχωρίας, D.H.6.74, 11.26; κ. τινὰ ἐν φυλακῇ *Ev.Luc.*3.20, cf. *OGI*669.17 (Egypt, i A.D.): metaph., κ. ἑαυτὸν εἰς πολιτείαν, i.e. not to be a cosmopolite, X.*Mem.*2.1.13:—Pass., ἐς τὸ τεῖχος κατακλῄεσθαι Th.4.57; ναυσὶ κατεκλῄσθησαν Id.1.117, cf. X.*An.*3.3.7; ὅταν ἐς [νεφέλας] ἄνεμος κατακλῃσθῇ Ar.*Nu.*404; εἰς μικρὸν τόπον -κεκλῃμένοι Isoc.4.34; διὰ τοῦ ζῆν . . κ. ἐν Ἀπόλλωνος ἢ Ἀθηνᾶς Phld.*D.*1.17:—Med., *shut oneself up*, ἐν τοῖς βασιλείοις X.*Cyr.*7.2.5; also κατεκλᾴζετο *shut up* the bride *with oneself* [in the bridal-chamber], Theoc.18.5:—Pass., κατεκλᾴσθης Id.7.84. 2. metaph., νόμῳ κ. *shut up*, i.e. *compel, oblige*, ἂν . . πᾶσαν τὴν δύναμιν νόμῳ κατακλείσητε ἐπὶ τῷ πολέμῳ μένειν D.4.33, cf. And.3.7, Antiph.190.15. 3. metaph., τῆς πόλεως εἰς κίνδυνον μέγιστον κατακεκλειμένης *being reduced*, D.26.11; εἰς σπάνιν κατακλεισθῆναι D.S.20.74: generally, *confine*, ἐν τῷ κατὰ φύσιν πέρατι -κέκλειται τἀγαθόν Metrod.*Herc.*831.8; πᾶσαι αἱ ἐπιχειρήσεις εἰς μίαν ἀπόδειξιν -κλείονται Phld.*Rh.*2.283 S.; κατακλείειν τὸ πᾶν τῆς τέχνης εἰς . . *confine* the whole business of art to . ., Hld.3.4. II. c. acc. rei, *shut up, close*, τὰς πυλίδας Hdt.1.191; τὰ ἱρά Id.2.124, cf. 128 (Pass.); τὸ ἐργαστήριον Id.4.14; τὸν δίφρον X.*Cyr.*6.4.10; εὑρὼν ἅπαντα κατακεκλῃμένα Ar.*Pl.*206:—in Pass., of humours in the body, Hp.*Loc.Hom.*27. 2. *clamp down, make fast*, of stones in masonry, *IG*7.3073.158 (Lebad.); also κ. [τὴν δεξιάν] Luc.*Prom.*2. 3. *close* a speech, *conclude*, D.L.10.138; εἰς ἀπειλὴν κ. τὸν λόγον with a threat, D.H.7.14, cf. A.D.*Synt.*234.17; οὐ κ. διάνοιαν *give* no *complete* sense, Id.*Adv.*119.6 (δ. shd. be supplied, Id.*Synt.*179.13); *conclude* an argument or inference, Phld.*Sign.*15, 33.

κατακλῇθρον, τό, = κατακλείς I. 1, *IG*11(2).144*A* 41 (Delos, iv B.C., pl.).

κατακληΐς, ῗδος, ἡ, Ion. for κατακλείς.

κατακληρο-δοτέω, *seize and parcel out*, τὴν γῆν αὐτῶν v.l. in Lxx 1*Ma.*3.36, *De.*1.38, *Act.Ap.*13.19. **-νομέω**, I. c. acc. rei, 1. *obtain as one's assured possession*, Lxx *Si.*4.16. 2. *leave as an inheritance*, τοῖς υἱοῖς τὰ ὑπάρχοντα ib.*De.*21.16. 3. *assign as a possession*, ib.3.28, 12.10, *Act.Ap.*13.19. II. c. acc. pers., *make one's heir*, Lxx 2*Ki.*7.1.

κατακληρ-ουχέω, *receive as one's portion*, esp. of a conquered country, *divide among themselves, portion out*, τὴν χώραν Plb.2.21.7; τὰς οὐσίας Id.7.10.1; τὴν Σικελίαν D.S.13.30; τὴν νῆσον Str.8.6.16; τὴν γῆν εἰς κλήρους Ael.*VH*6.1. 2. *assign as a portion*, τισὶ τὴν ἀρίστην τῆς χώρας D.S.1.54, cf. *PLond.*2.383.2 (Pass., iii A.D.); *portion out to colonists*, πᾶσαν ὀλίγου δεῖν τὴν Ἰταλίαν Plu.*Ant.*55. **-όω**, = foreg. 2, D.S.13.2 codd., *PSI*4.344 (iii B.C.):—Med., *receive as one's portion*, Plu.*Pomp.*41; *draw the lot*, Lxx 1*Ki.*14.42; but also ὃν ἂν κατακληρώσηται κύριος, ἀποθανέτω ibid.

κατα-κλησία, ἡ, = sq. 2, Poll.8.116, Hsch. **-κλησις**, εως, ἡ, *summoning by name*, Ph.2.388. 2. *summoning of the whole body of citizens, incl. rural population*, πρὸς ἐπίσκεψιν μείζονα τῶν πραγμάτων, opp. ἐκκλησία, Ammon.*Diff.*p.47 V. 3. *invocation* of the gods, Ph.2.342, Arr.*An.*5.2.7, Poll.1.29. II. *recalling*, D.S.13 Arg. (nisi leg. μετάκλησις); ἡ [τῆς θεοῦ] κ. *CIG*6850^A. **-κλητικός**, ή, όν, *for invoking*: -κλητικόν, τό, *invocatory spell*, *PMag.Par.*1.2373. **-κλητος**, ον, *specially summoned*, ἐν κ. ἁλίᾳ *Tab.Heracl.*1.11, 2.10.

κατα-κλινής, ές, *bed-ridden*, Hp.*Epid.*3.17.β′, *PRyl.*124.26 (i A.D.), dub.l. in Plb.31.13.7. II. *sloping*, ἀταρπός Leonid.ap.Stob.4.52.28; γεώλοφος D.H.5.38. 2. *hanging down*, Thphr.*CP*2.9.11. **-κλινοβάτης**, ές, *making one lie abed*, ποδάγρα Luc.*Trag.*198 (in voc. -βατές, prob. f.l. for -βάτις). **-κλίνω** [ῑ], *lay down*, [δόρυ] κατακλίνας ἐπὶ γαίῃ Od.10.165; κ. τοὺς Πέρσας ἐς λειμῶνα *having made* them *recline* (for dinner) in a meadow, Hdt.1.126, cf. Pl.*R.*363c, 420e, *Ev.Luc.*9.14, *Milet.*1(9).368; κ. παιδίον *put* it *to bed*, Ar.*Lys.*19, cf. Plu.*Lyc.*3; κ. τινὰ ἐν ἁρμαμάξῃ X.*Cyr.*6.4.11; also, *cause* one *to take to his bed*, i.e. *strike with disease*, *PMag.Par.*1.2075; of animals, X.*Cyn.*9.3; κ. τινὰ εἰς Ἀσκληπιοῦ *lay* a sick person in the temple of Asclepios, Ar.*Pl.*411, *V.*123; ταύταν ὀβολῷ κ. (sens. obsc.) Cerc.5.31:—Pass. (with aor. 2 Att. -εκλίνην, aor. 1 -εκλίθην Att. and in other dialects), *lie at table*, κατακλιθέντας πίνειν Hdt.2.121.δ′; κατακλινήσομαι Ar.*Eq.*98, cf. *V.*1208; generally, *lie down*, κατακλινεὶς δευρί Id.*Nu.*694; κατακλίνεσθαι παρά τινα *lie* at table *next* him, Pl.*Smp.*175a; but, παρά τινι *lie with* him sexually, ib.203c; κατακλίνηθι μετ' ἐμοῦ Ar.*Lys.*904; κ. ἐπὶ ταῖς κοίταις, ἐπὶ στιβάδος, Ar.*V.*1040, X.*Cyr.*5.2.15; of a sick man, *take to one's bed*, Hp.*Epid.*1.2; simply, *lie in bed*, Id.*Prog.*3, Diocl.*Fr.*141; κατακλιθέντα ἐς τὸ ἱερόν Hyp.*Eux.*18; κατεκλίθη ὕπτιος Pl.*Phd.*117e codd.; κατακεκλιμένος, of a corpse, Plb.6.53.1. II. *cause to incline, bend downwards*, ἕως ἂν κατακλίνῃ [ὁ ἐλέφας τοὺς φοίνικας] Arist.*HA*610^a23: metaph., *lay prostrate, overthrow*, τύραννον Thgn.1181. III. Pass., of ground, *slope*, ἠπειρόνδε A.R.2.734. 2. of the sun, *set*, Poll.4.157. 3. of crabs' eyes, *turn sideways*, Arist.*HA*529^b28. 4. *kneel*, ὅταν κατακλιθῇ εἰς γόνατα [κάμηλος] ib.499^a17. 5. c. dat., *to be set under, made subject to*, ὅταν κατακλιθῇ τὸ θητικὸν τῷ προπολεμοῦντι Herm.*in Phdr.*p.157 A. **-κλίσις**, εως, ἡ, *making* one *to lie down, seating* him *at table*, opp. ὑπανάστασις, Pl.*R.*425b, Arist.*EN*1165^a28; ἡ κ. τοῦ γάμου the *celebration* of the marriage *feast*, Hdt.6.129. II. (from Pass.) *lying at table, sitting at meat*, Arist.*Pol.*1336^b9, 21; παρά τινι Pl.*Smp.*175e; τὸ σχῆμα τῆς κ. Plu.2.679f, cf. Porph.*Abst.*2.61. 2. *way of lying in bed*, τὴν κ. ποιείσθω ἐπὶ τὴν ὑγιᾶ γνάθον Hp.*Art.*33, cf. *Prog.*3 (pl.). b. *taking to one's bed*, of a sick person, Id.*Epid.*4.31, J.*AJ*4.8.33, etc. c. *causing* one *to take to his bed*, i.e. *striking with disease*, *PMag.Par.*1.2496. d. Astrol., *horoscope cast at the hour when a patient takes to his bed*, Gal.19.529, *Cat.Cod.Astr.*1.20, 8(4).57. **-κλιτέον**, *one must cause to lie down, put to bed*, Sor.1.78, Herod.Med.ap.Orib.6.20.5. **-κλιτον**, τό, *couch, chaise-longue*, Suid., Phot. **-κλιτος**, ον, perh. *flowing down*, of light summer garments, θέριστρα κ. Lxx *Is.*3.23; cf. κατάκλιτος· τελευταία, Hsch.

κατα-κλύζω, fut. -κλύσω [ῠ], poet. -κλύσσω Pi.*O.*10(11).10: pf. κατακέκλυκα *PMagd.*28.10 (iii B.C.):—*deluge, inundate*, τὴν γῆν Hdt.2.13 (of the Nile), cf. 99 (Pass.), Pi.*O.*9.50, Th.3.89, Pl.*Ti.*22d, *OGI*90.24 (Rosetta, ii B.C.):—Pass., *PPetr.*2 p.15 [= 3 p.xv] (iii B.C.), etc.; ὑπ' ὄμβρων -κλυζόμενος Isoc.11.12; κόσμος ὕδατι -κλυσθείς 2*Ep.Pet.*3.6. 2. metaph., *deluge, overwhelm*, τοίους γὰρ κατὰ κῦμα . . ἔκλυσεν Archil.9.3; τὴν Φρυγῶν πόλιν . . ἤλπισας κατακλύσειν δαπάναισιν E.*Tr.*995; ἅπαντα . . κατακλύσει ποιήμασιν Cratin.186; κ. ἀφθονίᾳ δίαιταν *make* life *overflow* with plenty, X.*Oec.*2.8; κατακλύσαι δεινῶν πόνων *deluge* with sufferings, E.*Or.*343 (lyr.); εἰ καὶ μέλλει γέλωτι . . ὥσπερ κῦμα . . κατακλύσειν Pl.*R.*473c:—Pass., ἀλλοδαπῶν κύματι φωτῶν -κλυσθῆναι, of a city, A.*Th.*1084 (anap.); -κλυσθεὶς ὑπὸ τοῦ τοιούτου ψόγου ἢ ἐπαίνου Pl.*R.*492c; χρυσίῳ -κεκλυσμένος Plu.*Dem.*14; -κλυσθέντα πλήθει κακῶν Lib.*Ep.*5.1. II. *wash down* or *away*, κῦμα κ. ψάφον ἑλισσομέναν Pi.*O.*10(11).10, cf. Thphr.*CP*3.22.3. 2. *wash out*, τὰ ἴχνη τοῦ λαγώ X.*Cyn.*5.4. III. *fill full of water*, τὴν πύελον Ar.*Pax*843. IV. *clean out* a bath, Gal.15.198. **-κλῦσις**, εως, ἡ, *douche*, Hp.*Hum.*1, cf. Gal.16.162. **-κλυσμα**, ατος, τό, *purge* or *clyster*, Hp.*Salubr.*5. **-κλυσμός**, ὁ, *flood*, Pl.*Lg.*679d, Arist.*Ph.*222^a23, *Stoic.*2.337, *Marm.Par.*6, etc.; *inundation*, *PMagd.*28^v.4 (iii B.C.): pl., Pl.*Ti.*25c, *Lg.*677a. 2. metaph., κ. τῶν πραγμάτων political *deluge*, D.18.214. II. Medic., *affusion, douche*, Cael.Aur.*TP*4.1.1. **-κλυστρον**, τό, = Lat. *compluvium*, *Gloss.*

κατακλύω [ῠ], *hear of*, θαῦμα S.*Ichn.*224 (v.l. κατήλυθεν Theon ap. Sch.).

κατακλῶθες, αἱ, *the Spinners*, v. κλῶθες.

κατακλώθω, *spin one's fate*, *CIG*6870:—Med., Lyc.145.

κατακναίω, = sq., metaph., *wear out*, ἑαυτόν Them.*Or.*32.362b.

κατακνάω, *scrape away*, ἀπόκριναι . ., εἰ μὴ κατέκνησας τοῖς στρατιώταις ἅλαβες whether you did not *scrape away, make away with* . ., Ar.*V.*965; -κνήσας (-κνίσας codd.) [τοῦ κηροῦ] τὸ λευκόν Dsc.2.83:—Pass., κατακνησθείην Ar.*Eq.*771; κηρὸς -κεκνησμένος wax *scrapings*, Asclep.ap.Gal.13.1022. 2. v. κατακνίζω II. 3.

κατακνήθω, = foreg., Nic.*Th.*944.

κατάκνημος, ον, *thin-legged*, *UPZ*121.20 (ii B.C.).

κατακνῆστις, ιδος, ἡ, = τυροκνῆστις, Hsch.

κατακνιδεύω, (κνίδη) = καταξύω, Hsch. (prob. f.l. for Lacon. κατέκνιδδεν, cf. sq.).

κατακνίζω, *chop up, mince*, τι εἰς λεπτά Ath.9.376d. 2. metaph., *pick to pieces*, λόγους Isoc.12.17; τὰ τοῦ Ὁμήρου κ. λεπτά Luc.*Hes.*5. II. *scratch, irritate, stimulate* the scalp, Asclep.ap.Gal.12.420:—Pass., v.l. in Dsc.2.123; *to be prurient*, ἐγὼ δὲ κατακέκνισμαι Ar.*Pl.*973. 2. *cut grooves in, score*, ξύλα καὶ λίθους τραχύνουσι -ζοντες Diocl.*Fr.*26. 3. *scarify, let blood from*, -κνίσω (prob. for -κνήσω) σου τὸν πόδα Luc.*Ocyp.*91:—Pass., -κνισθεὶς τὸ σκέλος Orib.7.20.8 (= Gal.19.524, where -κνήσας).

κατακνισμός, ὁ, = κνισμός, Sch.Ar.*Pl.*975.

κατακνώσσω, *fall asleep*, A.R.3.690, Orph.*L.*321.

κατακοιμ-άω (on the Hom. usage v. infr. II. 2): I. intr., *sleep*, *pass the night*, ξεῖνόν τινα χρήμασι πείσας κατεκοίμησε (v. l. -ισε) ἐς Ἀμφιάρεω he *went to sleep* there, Hdt.8.134: freq. v. l. for -κοιμίζω II (q. v.). II. causal, *put to sleep*, οὐδὲ..λάθα κατακοιμάσῃ (sc. τοὺς νόμους) S.*OT*871 (lyr.); κατεκοίμησα τοὐμὸν ὄμμα ib.1222 (lyr.); v.l. for -κοιμίσαντ' in Pl.*Smp*.223d:—Pass., -κοιμηθεὶς ὑπὸ μέθης Them. *Or*.26.326b; θυμὸς κ. ὑπὸ λογισμοῦ ib.8.110c. 2. used by Hom. only in aor. Pass., *sleep*, κατακοιμηθῆναι Il.2.355, Hdt.2.121.δ'; κατακοιμηθήτω Il.9.427; κατακοιμηθέντες ἐν τῷ ἱρῷ Hdt.1.31; ὃς ἂν ὑπαίθριος κατακοιμηθῇ Id.4.7, cf. Plb.3.67.2 (v.l.); imper. pres. κατακοιμάσθω Ar.*Th*.46 (anap.). -ησις, εως, ἡ, *sleeping, lodging*, τῆς πενίας παρὰ τῷ πόρῳ Them.*Or*.13.162b. -ητικός, ή, όν, *of* or *for lulling to sleep*, Arg.Theoc.18. -ίζω, = κατακοιμάω II (for which it is a constant v.l.), *lull to sleep*, τὴν φυλακήν Hecat.33 J.; τὰ δυσυπνοῦντα τῶν παιδίων Pl.*Lg*.790d, cf. *Smp*.223d (v.l. -κοιμήσαντ'), Luc.*VH*2.34, *Asin*.6: metaph., κ. τὸν λύχνον Phryn.Com.24; ὀργάς *Com.Adesp*.521; τοὺς πολεμίους Plu.2.346c:—Pass., *go to sleep*, Plb.3.67.2; of troublesome questions, ἵνα..ἀεὶ ἂν κατακοιμισθῶσιν *IG*2^2.1121.26. II. *sleep through*, τὴν φυλακήν *sleep out* one's watch, Hdt.9.93, Ael. *NA*1.15, al.; τῆς ἡμέρας τὸ χρησιμώτατον -κοιμίζουσα X.*Mem*.2.1.30. -ισμός, ὁ, *putting to sleep*, τῶν βρεφῶν Phld.*Po*.2.47 (pl.). -ιστής, οῦ, ὁ, *one who puts to bed, chamberlain*, D.S.11.69, Ph.2.571, Plu.2.173e, Jul. *ad Ath*.272d, prob. in Ephor.191.131 J.

κατακοινωνέω, *make one a partaker, give one a share*, τισι D.32.25; κ. τὰ τῆς πόλεως *share* the public property *among themselves*, Aeschin.3.66 (v.l. κατακοινώσαντες).

κατακοιρᾰνέω, *govern*, Hsch., cf. Sch.Il.5.332.

κατάκοιτος, ον, *in bed*: *at rest, quiet*, Ibyc.1.7.

κατακόκκας ἢ **κατακίκκας**· κατάπλασμα, Hsch.

κατακολλάω, *glue* or *fasten upon, inlay*, θύρας χρυσῷ J.*AJ*8.3.3:—Pass., ὀθονίῳ..κατακεκολλήσθω..τὸ ξύλον Hp.*Art*.7; θύραι κατεκεκόλληντο σανίσιν Callix.1. 2. *glue together*, Arist.*Pr*.889b14.

κατάκολλος, ον, *mixed with glue*, μέλαν Aen.Tact.31.10.

κατακολλῠβίζω, = κατακερματίζω, *AB*104.

κατ-ᾰκολουθ-έω, *follow after*, ὀπίσω τινός Lxx *Je*.17.16, cf. Longus 3.15 codd.: c. gen., Dioxipp.2 (s. v.l.); *comply with*, εἰ ταῖς τῶν ἀνθρώπων εὐχαῖς ὁ θεὸς κατηκολούθει Epicur.*Fr*.388; *obey*, νόμῳ, προστάγμασιν, Lxx *Da*.9.10, 1*Ma*.6.23; λόγῳ Plu.*Lys*.25; *follow* a historical or philosophical authority, Phld.*Rh*.2.146 S.; Ἀράτῳ, Δημοκρίτῳ, Plb. 2.56.2, Plu.2.1108f; in fortification, κ. ταῖς ὀχυρότησι τῶν τόπων Plb.6.42.2; *emulate, imitate*, ἀδυνάτοις ἐπιβολαῖς Hegetor ap.Apollon.Cit.3; κ. τοῖς ἱεροῖς, mistranslation of *prosecuisset*, as though *prosecutus esset*, Plu.*Cam*.5: abs., *obey instructions*, *PAmh*.2.31.12 (ii B.C.). -ητέον, *one must follow*, κριτηρίῳ, τέχνῃ, S.E.*M*.1.186, 11.175. -ία, ἡ, *compliance* with instructions, *CPHerm*.97.8a (iii A.D.). -ος, ον, *following*, of persons, c. dat., Vett.Val.220.4; of things, Id.125.31.

κατακολούω, *cut short*, Poll.8.154.

κατακολπ-ίζω, *run into a bay*, κ. ἐς Αἴγιναν Th.8.92, cf. Str.8.3.33. -ισις, εως, ἡ, *putting into a bay*, Anon.ap.Suid. s. v. ἐπιβάθρα.

κατακολυμβ-άω, *dive down*, Th.7.25, Arist.*HA*620b34, Luc.*JTr*.48. -ητής, οῦ, ὁ, *diver*, Arist.*HA*631a31, Ath.7.296e.

κατακομάω, *wear the hair long*, Procop.*Arc*.7: metaph., of a ship, κ. τοῖς ἀναθήμασι Id.*Aed*.1.4.

κατακομ-ῐδή, ἡ, *bringing down to the sea-shore for exportation*, opp. ἀντίληψις (importation), Th.1.120. 2. *bringing home*, σώματος D.S.18.3. -ίζω, *bring down*, esp. *from the inland to the coast*, σῖτον τῷ στρατεύματι Th.6.88; ⟨ὕλην⟩ ποταμοῖς κ. Str.11.2.17, cf. *OGI*132.10 (Egypt, ii B.C.), Hdn.8.2.3 (Pass.), etc.:—Med., *cause to be brought down*, ὡραῖα πλοίοις Pl.*Criti*.118e. 2. *bring into harbour*, ναῦν D.50.55; ναῦν Ἀθήναζε Id.56.27; εἰς τὸν Πειραιᾶ ib.20; *bring home*, τριήρεις Aeschin.2.71. 3. *bring into a place of refuge*, κ. τὰ ἐλεύθερα σώματα καὶ τοὺς καρποὺς ἐν τῇ πόλει Aen.Tact.10.3; κ. γυναῖκας ἐκ τῶν ἀγρῶν D.19.125; κ. τὰ ἐκ τῶν ἀγρῶν Decr.ap.eund.18.38; παῖδας καὶ γυναῖκας ἐκ τῶν ἀγρῶν εἰς τὰ τείχη Lycurg.16, cf. D.S.12.39. 4. *import*, κεράμου πανταχόθεν -ομένου Ath.11.784c. 5. *bury*, prob. in *Berl.Sitzb*.1927.161 (Cyrene).

κατάκομος, ον, *with falling hair* or *beard*, E.*Ba*.1187 (lyr.); πρόσωπον ἐχίδναις κ. Luc.*DDeor*.19.1, cf. Poll.4.140.

κατακομπολᾰκῠθέω, *boast loudly*, Tz.*H*.10.278.

κατακομψεύομαι, *speak elegantly* or *boastfully*, Sch.Luc.*Apol*.6.

κατᾰκονά, ἡ, (κατακαίνω) *destruction*, κατακονὰ ἀβίοτος βίου E.*Hipp*.821 (lyr.).—The v.l., supported by Sch. (cf. *EM*50.25, Eust.381.22), κατακονᾷ..βίος, implies a Verb **κατ-ᾰκονάω**, *wear away*, as is done in whetting steel.

κατακονδῠλ-ίζω, strengthd. for κονδυλίζω, Aeschin.3.212 (Pass.), Lxx *Am*.5.11; ὄχλος -ισμένος τὴν ψυχήν Ph.1.387. -ιστος, ον, *well cuffed*, Hsch. s. v. ἐπικόρριστον. -όω, = κατακονδυλίζω, Id. s. v. κρομβότατον (Pass.).

κατ-ᾰκοντίζω, Att. fut. -ιῶ, used also by Hdt.9.17:—*shoot down*, Id. l. c., Th.8.108, D.18.151, Lxx *Ju*.1.15: pf. inf. Pass. κατηκοντίσθαι Phld.*Piet*.34; θηρία -όμενα Luc.*Tox*.59.

κατάκοος, v. κατήκοος.

κατα-κοπή, ἡ, *cutting back, pruning*, δένδρων Thphr.*CP*2.12.6 (pl.); *cutting in pieces*, πρὸς κατακοπὴν ἱερεῖα Theopomp.Hist.283a; τραύματα καὶ κ. Artem.1.50. -κοπος, ον, *very weary*, κ. τῷ σώματι Lxx *Jb*.3.17, al.; ἐξ ὁδοῦ μακρᾶς D.H.6.29; ὑπὸ τῆς μάχης D.S.13.18, cf. Plu.*Arat*.8. II. *wearisome, tedious*, Phld.*Rh*.1.173 S. -κόπτης, ου, ὁ, *cutter up*, σπλάγχνων Sch.Lyc.35 (ed. Bachm.). -κοπτικός, ή, όν, dub. sens. in *PMag.Lond*.121.430. -κόπτω, *cut down, fell*, of trees, in Pass., Thphr.*HP*3.15.1, *CP*2.15.4, etc. 2. *cut in pieces, cut up*, Hdt.1.48,73, 2.42, Ar.*Av*.1688 (Pass.), etc.; κρέα Pl.*Euthd*.301c; κατακοπεὶς *cut in pieces*, Hdt.8.92. 3. *cut down, massacre, butcher*, Id.6.75, Th.7.29:—Pass., ὥσπερ βόες κατεκόπησαν Phld.*Rh*.1.235 S. 4. in a military sense, *cut in pieces*, '*cut up*', τὴν μόραν D.13.22:—Pass., κατακοπῆναι X.*An*.1.2.25; κατακεκόψεσθαι ib.1.5.16. 5. κ. πληγαῖς τινα *PLips*.37.20 (iv A.D.), etc. 6. generally, *break in pieces, destroy*, στεφάνους D.22.70; κέραμον Plb.5.25.3; ἔρια ὑπὸ τῶν σέων κατακοπτόμενα *fretted in pieces*, Ar.*Lys*.730, cf. Luc.*Ind*.1: metaph., κ. τὴν ἀρχήν Plu. *Demetr*.30; κατακέκοπται οἱ τὸ τῆς ψυχῆς γαῦρον Id.2.762f; κατεκόπημεν ἂν we *should have been made mince-meat of*, Pl.Com.35. 7. *weary, bore*, Anaxipp.1.23, Men.*Sam*.70, 77. 8. Rhet., λέξις -κεκομμένη '*staccato*', *jerky* composition, Demetr.*Eloc*.4. 9. in Med., μαστοὺς κατεκόψατο, in vehement grief, *Epigr.Gr*.316 (Smyrna). II. *strike with a die, coin* bullion *into money*, Hdt.3.96; τὸν θρόνον ὄντα ἀργυροῦν X.*HG*1.5.3; τὰς χρυσᾶς πλίνθους εἰς νόμισμα D.S.16.56, cf. Demetr.*Eloc*.281, Lib.*Or*.14.45.

κατακόπωσις, εως, ἡ, *wearying*, Gloss.

κατακορᾰκόω, *fasten up, close* a sarcophagus, *BSA*17.225 (Pamphyl.), *Jahresh*.23 *Beibl*.101 (ib., ii A.D.).

κατακορέω, = ἐκλύω, Hp.ap.Gal.19.109 (s. v.l.).

κατακορής, ές, *satiated, glutted*, οἴνῳ Phryn.*PS* p.83 B.; σιτίοις Procop.*Arc*.13. 2. of solutions, *saturated, strong*, φάρμακον Hp. *Epid*.5.15, cf. Gal.19.108; ἅλμη Id.5.111. 3. of colours, *deep*, μέλαν κατακορές Pl.*Ti*.68c, cf. Arist.*Col*.795a3; χρῶμα ὅμοιον ῥόδῳ κ. Thphr. *HP*4.8.7, cf. S.E.*P*.1.105; διαχώρημα Hp.*Coac*.596, cf. *Epid*.4.20; τὰ κ. πονηρά Id.*Coac*.601; ἐρύθημα Id.*Epid*.7.7; στήθεα κ. dub. sens. ib.2.6.14, cf. Gal.19.108. 4. of harmony, *complete*, τῆς κοσμικῆς συμφωνίας κ. τι καὶ παναρμόνιον φθεγγομένης Nicom.*Harm*.3; -κορεστάτῃ συμφωνίᾳ ἡ διὰ πασῶν ib.5; -κορέστερον μέλος, of the spheres, Iamb.*VP*15.65. II. metaph., *intense, violent*, δίψα, ῥύσις, Hp. *Epid*.7.11, *Medic*.6; βήξ Id.*Epid*.7.26; *profound*, ὕπνος ib.7.2. b. metaph., βαθὺ καὶ κ. αἴνιγμα a *profound* problem, Ph.1.659; ἀμετάβλητος καὶ κ. γνώμη a *deep* resolve, Id.1.78. 2. *immoderate, wearisome*, παρρησία, συνουσία, Pl.*Phdr*.240e, *Lg*.776a; ἂν ᾖ κατακορῆ [τὰ ἐπίθετα] Arist.*Rh*.1406a13, cf. Demetr.*Eloc*.303; κατακορῆς ἀπείλει Tim.*Pers*.79; τοῦ τῶν γυναικῶν γένους λάλου καὶ κ. ὄντος Plb. 31.26.10, cf. 32.2.5; ὁ Δημοσθένης..ἐν τῷ γένει τούτῳ -έστατος Longin.22.3; -εστέραις κέχρηται ταῖς αὐστηραῖς ἁρμονίαις D.H.*Dem*.45. III. Adv. -κορῶς, Ion. -ρέως, *deeply, intensely*, κ. δίαιμον *deeply* tinged with blood, Aret.*SA*1.10. 2. *to excess*, διαχωρήματα μᾶλλον τοῦ καιροῦ -έως χολώδεα Hp.*Acut*.54; cf. κατάκορος.

κατακορμ-ίζω, *cut wood into logs* or *pieces*, Paus.Gr.*Fr*.224:—also -άζω, Hsch.

κατάκορος, ον, = κατακορής, Poll.5.151, Thom.Mag.p.105 R.; κ. χρῆσις ἀφροδισίων Steph. *in Gal*.1.239 D.:—in Adv., of colours, *deeply*, κ. μέλας *Gp*.16.2.1. II. metaph., *immoderate*, κ. καὶ περίεργοι ἱερουργίαι Plu.*Alex*.2. Adv. -ρως, *to excess*, ᾧ -κόρως χρῶνται οἱ λογογράφοι Arist.*Rh*.1408a33; τῇ τύχῃ κ. χρώμενος Decr.ap.D.18.182, cf. Plu.*Cic*.5; κ. χρώμενοι τῇ κραυγῇ Plb.4.12.9, cf. Phld.*Rh*.1.157, 366 S., Dsc.2.52, Iamb.*Protr*.21.κ'.

κατακοσμ-έω, *set in order, arrange*, ἐπὴν..δόμον κατακοσμήσησθε Od.22.440; ἐπὶ νευρῇ κατεκόσμει πικρὸν ὀϊστόν *was fitting* it on the string, Il.4.118; πόλιν καὶ ἰδιώτας κ. v.l. in Pl.*R*.540b; εἰς τάξιν κ. τινὰ πρὸς ἄλληλα Id.*Ti*.88e:—Med., κ. εἰς τὴν γνώμην τινός Plu. *Comp.Per.Fab*.3:—Pass., Pl.*R*.560a, *Lg*.685d; ὅπως πεπαινόμενον τὸ ἦθος δύναιτο -κοσμεῖσθαι Diotog.ap.Stob.4.1.96, cf. 133. 2. *fit out, equip*, ὅπλοις κατακεκοσμημένος X.*Hier*.11.3; σεμνοτέροις πράγμασι Ar.*V*.1473 (lyr.); κ. τινὰ οἷον ἄγαλμα *adorn*, Pl.*Phdr*.252d. II. *reduce to order, regulate*, Plu.*Num*.14; ἑαυτούς Id.*Rom*.23:—Pass., Pl.*Plt*.273a. -ησις, εως, ἡ, *arrangement*, ib.271e; *order*, Id. *Ti*.47d. 2. *adornment*, ναῶν Andronic.Rhod.p.572 M. 3. metaph., πλάσις καὶ κ., of an *assumed demeanour*, Plu.2.712d. -ητέος, α, ον, *to be adorned*, ἱερόν Porph.*Marc*.11. -ος, ον, *adorned*, θρόνοι App.*Mith*.115.

κατακοττᾰβίζω, *squirt* or *throw wine over* any one, τινος Ar.*Fr*.152.

κατακούρην· τοῦ ξυροῦ τὴν τομήν, Gal.19.109.

κατ-άκουσις [ᾰκ], εως, ἡ, *hearing*, Arr.*An*.5.7.5. -ακουστής, οῦ, ὁ, *listener*, Gloss. -ακούω, *hear and obey, be subject*, Ἀράβιοι οὐδαμὰ κατήκουσαν ἐπὶ δουλοσύνῃ Πέρσῃσι Hdt.3.88, cf. App.*Syr*.55; τινος D.1.23, Arr.*Fr*.7 J., App.*Mith*.57, Hierocl. *in CA*19 p.461 M. 2. *give ear, listen* to one, D.6.35; of eavesdroppers, Str.14.1.32. 3. *hear plainly*, τι E.*Rh*.553 (lyr.), Th.2.84, Pl.*R*.531a; τίνος; Ar.*Ra*.312, cf. Pl.*Prt*.330e; ὁ θυρωρὸς..κατήκουεν ἡμῶν *overheard* us, ib.314c; κ. αὐλοῦντος Arist.*EN*1175b4: abs., Th.3.22.

κατακράζω, fut. -κεκράξομαι, *cry down, outdo in crying*, Ar.*Eq*.287.

κατακραιπᾰλάω, strengthd. for κραιπαλάω, Procop.*Goth*.4.19.

κατακρᾱνία, ἡ, *an affection of the head*, Hippiatr.103.

κατάκρας, Ion. -άκρης, v. ἄκρα.

κατάκρᾱσις, εως, ἡ, = κατακέρασις, Plu.2.688c, Gal.1.212. II. Arith., *multiplication*, opp. παράθεσις (addition), *Theol.Ar*.10,12; ἄρσενος καὶ θήλεος κ., i. e. *multiplication* of two by three, Iamb. *in Nic*. p.34 P.

κατακρᾰτ-έω, *prevail over*, c. gen. pers., κατακρατεῖν ἀνδρὸς εἴωθεν γυνή Men.646, cf. Thphr.*CP*2.14.4; τῶν πολεμίων Plb.16.30.5: metaph., of pleasure, κ. τοῦ οἴκου *Stoic*.3.98; also c. acc., τοὺς ἄλλους ἀρετῇ κ. D.C.54.29; ὁ ἵππος πρεσβύτερος ἤδη ὢν οὐ κ. τὰς θηλείας *PCair.Zen.*225.8 (iii B.C.):—Pass., *to be overcome*, ὑπὸ νόμου βελτίονος Zaleuc.ap.Stob.4.2.19. 2. abs., *prevail, gain the mastery, gain the victory*, κατὰ μοῖρ' ἐκράτησεν A.*Pers.*101 (lyr.), cf. Hdt.7.168, Th. 6.55, Pl.*Lg.*840e; ὁ Πηνειὸς τῷ οὐνόματι κατακρατέων ἀνωνύμους τοὺς ἄλλους [ποταμοὺς] εἶναι ποιέει Hdt.7.129; of an opinion, D.C.57.15; of planetary influence, *predominate*, Procl.*Par.Ptol.*18, al. II. c. acc. rei, *gain the mastery over*, ἀμάχους ῥώμας, εὔνοιαν, Ph.2.117, 438; *win*, στέφανον D.Chr.9.13: c. gen. rei, τῆς προθέσεως *become master of* one's purpose, Plb.5.38.9; τοῦ γενέσθαι τι Id.28.13.13; τῶν ὅλων Id.3.81.10; *retain possession of*, τῆς πόλεως Id.1.8.1; *master*, τῆς Ἑλληνικῆς διαλέκτου Id.39.1.4, cf. Cleom.1.10; ἰδιότητος Porph.*Sent.*33. 2. *digest, concoct*, τὰς τῶν σίτων τροφάς Pl. *Lg.*789d, cf. Arist.*Pr.*$930^{b}31$:—Pass., τῇ εὐχυλίᾳ Sor.1.53 (fort. -κραθῇ). **-ησις**, εως, ἡ, *subduing*, Poll.9.142.

κατακρᾱτικός, ή, όν, *fit for tempering*, Philagr.ap.Orib.5.21.10 (Comp.); v.l. for κατακεραστικός in Archig.ap.Aët.9.35 (9.56 cod. Laud.Gr.60).

κατακραυγάζω, = κατακράζω, τινος Arr.*Epict.*4.4.28.

κατακρέμ-ᾰμαι, Pass., *hang down, be suspended*, Hdt.4.72, Cratin. 164; τινος *from* a thing, Plu.2.672a. **-άννυμι**, *hang up*, κὰδ δ' ἐκ πασσαλόφι κρέμασεν φόρμιγγα Od.8.67; τὸν νέκυν κατὰ τοῦ τείχεος κ. Hdt.2.121.γ'; δίκτυα Aen.Tact.11.6: in med. sense, κατακρεμάσασα..τόξα *having hung* the bow *on herself*, *h.Hom.*27.16: Ep. Subj., ὄφρα -κρεμάησιν Nic.*Fr.*74.42:—Pass., *hang down, be suspended*, Hp.*Fract.*21; κατακεκρέμαστο στέμμα D.S.18.26. **-ασμός**, ὁ, *hanging down*: κ. τῆς κιονίδος *relaxation* of the uvula, Apollon.ap. Gal.12.981. **-αστος**, ον, *hanging, pendent*, βότρυες Thphr.*HP* 3.18.12.

κατακρεουργέω, Ion. -οργέω, *hew in pieces, as a butcher does* meat, Hdt.7.181 (Pass.), Xanth.12.

κατάκρεως, unexplained word in Hdn.*Epim.*206.

κατακρῆθεν, Adv., better written divisim κατὰ κρῆθεν, v. κράς II.

κατακρήμνᾰμαι, Pass., = κατακρέμαμαι, Hp.*Morb.*2.10, Ar.*Nu.* 377: impf. κατεκρημνῶντο (from -κρημνάομαι) *h.Bacch.*39, prob. in Dsc.4.46, J.*AJ*3.7.5.

κατακρημν-ίζω, fut. -ιῶ *Carm.Pop.*46.33: (κρημνός):—*throw down a precipice*, ἑαυτούς Phld.*Ir.*p.56 W., cf. Plu.*Mar.*45, 2.825b, *Ev.Luc.* 4.29: with a word added, ἀπὸ τοῦ ἄκρου τοῦ κρημνοῦ Lxx 2*Ch.*25. 12:—Pass., D.19.327, Plu.*Sull.*1, etc.: pf. part., *having fallen over a precipice*, X.*Cyr.*8.3.41. 2. generally, *throw headlong down*, ἐκ τριηρέων X.*HG*2.1.31; ἀπὸ τῶν ἵππων Plb.3.116.12; ἀπὸ τοῦ πύργου D.S.4.31:—Pass., X.*Cyr.*1.4.7. **-ισμός**, ὁ, *throwing headlong*, Ath.Mech.37.6. **-ιστής**, οῦ, ὁ, *one who throws headlong down*, *Gloss.* **-ος**, ον, *steep and rugged*, χῶρος Batr.154, cf. *Gp.*18. 18.2.

κατάκρης, Adv., Ion. for κατάκρας (q. v.).

κατ-ακρῑβόω, strengthd. for ἀκριβόω: pf. part. Pass. -ωμένος *careful, precise*, Men.Prot.p.40 D.

κατ-ακρῐδεύω, *chatter like a swarm of locusts*, Hsch., Phot.

κατά-κρῐμα, ατος, τό, *condemnation, judgement*, D.H.6.61. 2. *punishment, fine, damage*, *CPR*1.16 (i A.D.), *PAmh.*2.114.8 (ii A.D.), *Ep.Rom.*5.16, 8.1. **-κρίνω**, Arc. κακρίνω (v. infr.) [ῑ], *give as sentence against*, τὸ τελευτῆσαι πάντων ἡ πεπρωμένη κατέκρινε Isoc.1.43:—Pass., τοῖσι κατεκέκριτο θάνατος *sentence* of death *had been passed upon* them, Hdt.7.146; κατακεκριμένων οἱ τούτων *when* this *sentence has been given against* him, Id.2.133; φυγὴν κατακριθείς Suid. s. v. Ἱεροκλῆς: impers., ἂν κατακριθῇ μοι if *sentence be given against* me, X.*Apol.*7: Arc., c. dat. pers. et gen. rei, ὀσέοι ἂν χρηστήριον κακρίνη ἢ γνωσίαι κακριθέη τῶν χρημάτων anyone whom the oracle *has condemned* or who by judicial process *has been condemned* to forfeit his property, *IG*5(2).262.14, 15 (Mantinea, v B.C., = *Class.Phil.*20.137). 2. c. acc. pers., *condemn*, v.l. in Antipho 4. 4.2: c. acc. et inf., κατέκρινάν μιν ἔκδοτον ἄγεσθαι Hdt.6.85, cf. 9.93, Theoc.23.23 (ubi sc. βαδίζειν); κ. τινὰ θανάτῳ *Ev.Matt.*20.18, cf. J. *BJ*5.13.1; εἴκοσι δραχμαῖς *IG*5(1).1390.161 (Andania, i B.C.): c. acc. rei, *deem guilty of* a thing, κ. πολλὴν ἄνοιάν τινων Arist.*Rh.Al.*1423^{b} 29; ψευδολογίαν τινός J.*AJ*3.14.4:—Pass., *to be condemned*, X.*HG* 2.3.54; ψήφῳ θανάτου E.*Andr.*496 codd. (anap.), cf. Phld.*Herc.*1251. 18; ἀποθνήσκειν X.*Hier.*7.10; also of the crime, τὰ ὁμολογούμενα τῶν πραγμάτων ὑπὸ τοῦ νόμου -κέκριται Antipho 3.1.1; -κεκρίσθαι τὰ ὑπὸ ἰδιωτῶν πραχθέντα *OGI*669.27 (Egypt, i A.D.). II. Pass., simply, *to be judged, deemed*, κατεκρίθη θνατοῖς ἀγανώτατος ἔμμεν Pi. *Fr.*149. **-κρίσιμος** [κρῐ], ον, *condemned*: κατακρίσιμοι *convicts*, *Peripl.M.Rubr.*59. II. of a case, *ready to be judged*, *Sammelb.* 5230.18 (i A.D.). **-κρῐσις**, εως, ἡ, *condemnation*, 2*Ep.Cor.*3.9, 7.3, Vett.Val.108.4, 117.35 (pl.). 2. *judgement*, κ. ψευδής a *false estimate*, Gal.5.76. **-κρῐτος**, ον, *condemned, sentenced*, κ. γενόμενος ἐπί τινι D.S.33.2, cf. Plu.2.188b; θανάτου to death, Luc.*Am.* 52, cf. 23, 36; ἡ κ. γενεά Ph.2.411.

κατ-ακροάομαι, *listen attentively to*, μου τὰ μουσοδονήματα Eup. 245; τινος J.*BJ*4.1.5, Anon. in *Gött.Nachr.*1922.33.

κάτ-ακρος, ον, strengthd. for ἄκρος, Sch.D Il.15.536. Adv. -ως Anon.*Prog.* in Rh.1.627 W.

κατακροτᾰλίζω, *make a loud rattling noise*, πόδεσσιν Call.*Dian.* 247.

κατακροτέω, *applaud excessively*, Hsch., Phot.

κατάκροτος, ον, *noisy*, Hld.1.30.

κατακρουν-ίζω, *pour down over*, Archestr.*Fr.*13.8; of a douche or shower-bath, Philum.*Ven.*5.3, Gal.10.935:—Pass., *to have water poured over one*, D.L.6.41. **-ισμός**, ὁ, *douche*, Sor.2.15, al.

κατά-κρουσις, εως, ἡ, *downward pressure*, Arist.*Pr.*$874^{b}12$, 963^{b} 9. II. *shock*, λαμβάνειν κ. ἐκ πληγῆς Ph.*Bel.*80.6. **-κρουστικός**, ή, όν, *exercising downward pressure*, οἶνος Arist.*Pr.*$873^{b}26$. **-κρούω**, *knock*, τι ἐς τρύπημα *Gp.*10.61. 2. *make narrow incisions* or '*stabbings*', Hp.*Ulc.*24, 25, *Medic.*7. 3. *beat copper pans*, etc., in order to entice bees, Pl.*Lg.*843e. 4. in Archit. perh., = διακρούω, *IG* 7.4255.14.

κατα-κρύβδην, Adv. *in private, in secret*, opp. ἀναφανδόν, Ptol. *Tetr.*64. **-κρύπτω**, Ep. aor. part. κακκρύψας Nic.*Fr.*78.5: aor. 2 κατέκρυβον Plu.*Crass.*23:—Pass., aor. 2 κατεκρύβην [ῠ] Id.2.310e, Alciphr.3.47:—*hide, conceal*, μή τι κατακρύψειν Il.22.120; τοὺς δ' ἄρ' Ἀθήνη νυκτὶ κατακρύψασα..ἐξῆγε Od.23.372; κατακρύψας ὑπὸ κόπρῳ 9.329; ὑπὸ κόλπῳ 15.469; σπέρμα -κρύπτων Hes.*Op.*471; ὑπὸ τὴν θύρην Hdt.1.12; ἐς κυψέλην Id.5.92.δ'; εἰς τὴν γῆν X.*Cyr.*3.3.3; ἐν μεγάρῳ πλοῦτον κ. Pi.*N.*1.31; ἐν ἀδήλῳ *put away* (euphem.) Pl.*R.* 460c: metaph., κόνις οὐ κ. χάριν Pi.*O.*8.79; ἄστυ..πένθει δνοφερῷ κ. A.*Pers.*536 (anap.). II. abs., *use concealment, conceal oneself* or *one's true nature*, οὔ τι κατακρύπτουσιν, of the gods, Od.7.205; ἄλλῳ δ' αὐτὸν φωτὶ κατακρύπτων ἤϊσκε 4.247. **-κρῠφή**, ἡ, *means of concealment*, οὐ γὰρ ἔχω κ. S.*OC*218 (lyr.). **-κρύφω** [ῠ], = κατακρύπτω, Q.S.2.478, Nonn.*D.*25.476.

κατακρώζω, *croak at, croak down*, like jackdaws, μίσει σφε κ. κολοιοί Ar.*Eq.*1020.

κατακτάμεν and **-κτάμεναι**, v. κατακτείνω.

κατακτάομαι, fut. -κτήσομαι Lxx 2*Ch.*28.10:—*get for oneself, win*, κράτος, νοῦν, S.*Aj.*768, 1256; ἐγκλήματα, πλούτους, Th.4.86, Isoc.4. 182: metaph., *win over, gain completely*, τὸ θέατρον Ael.*VH*3.8: aor. 2 Act. κατέκτην (as if from κατάκτημι) dub. in *IG*14.1934. II. Pass., τοῖς ἰδιώταις -κτώμενα *possessed* by.., Phld.*Vit.Herc.*1457.10: aor., D.S.16.56.

κατακτάς, κατακτάμενος, v. κατακτείνω.

κατακτεᾰτίζομαι, Ep. fut. -ίσσομαι, Med., = κατακτάομαι, A.R. 3.136.

κατακτείνω, Ep. fut. -κτενέω, in 3 sg. -κτενεῖ Il.23.412; -κτᾰνέω 6.409: aor. 1 κατέκτεινα Hom. (in all moods but ind.), *SIG*58.7, al. (Miletus, v B.C.): aor. 2 κατέκτᾰνον Il.6.204, etc., Ep. imper. κάκτανε ib.164: poet. aor. 2 κατέκτᾰν, ας, α, Il.4.319, al., A.*Eu.*460, *Fr.*181, 221; Ep. inf. κακτάμεναι Hes.*Sc.*453, κατακτάμεν Il.15.557; part. κατακτάς ib.335, Od.15.224, A.*Th.*965 (lyr.), E.*IT*715: pf. κατέκτονα A.*Eu.*587:—Pass., fut. Med. in pass. sense κατακτανέεσθε Il.14.481 codd. (-κτενέεσθε Cobet): aor. κατεκτάθην [ᾰ], 3 pl. -θεν 5.558, etc.; part. Med. κατακτάμενος (in pass. sense) Od.16.106; but καθανεῖν is freq. used as Pass. to this Verb:—*kill, slay*, freq. in Ep. and Trag., ll. cc.; rare in Prose, Heraclit.56, Hdt.2.75, *SIG* l. c., X.*Hier.*6.14, 7.12, etc.

κατακτεν-ίζω, *comb, dress carefully*, κατεκτενισμένοι τὰς κόμας Duris 60 J. **-ισμός**, ὁ, *careful combing*, Herod.Med.ap.Orib. 10.17.1. **-ος**, ον, *carefully combed* or *dressed*, Hsch.

κατάκτης, ὁ, (κατάγω I. 4 b) *visitor, guest* at an inn, Poll.7.16.

κατάκτησις, εως, ἡ, *acquisition*, πραγμάτων, χώρας, γῆς, Plb.4.77.2, Str.8.3.33, Plu.*Caes.*22; αὐτονομίας D.S.17.74; δυνάμεως ῥητορικῆς Phld.*Rh.*2.261 S.

κατακτός, ή, όν, (κατάγνυμι) *capable of being broken*, Arist.*Mete.* $385^{a}14$; θραυστὸν καὶ κ., ἀλλ' οὐ θλαστόν Id.*HA*$523^{b}10$. II. (κατάγω) *to be sunk* or *let down*, of a kind of κότταβος, Pherecr.66, Ar.*Pax* 1244, cf. Ath.15.667e.

κατάκτρια, ἡ, *spinning woman* (κατάγω I. 5), Hsch.

κατακτῠπ-έω, *make a loud noise, roar against*, κατεκτύπουν ἡμῶν οἱ ἄνεμοι Alciphr.1.23. **-ησις**, εως, ἡ, *making a noise at*, Eust.1602. 18. **-ος**, ον, gloss on κατάδουπος, Zonar.

κατακῠβεύω, pf. -κεκύβευκα D.C.45.28:—*gamble away*, τὰ ὄντα Lys.14.27:—Pass., Aeschin.1.95. II. Pass., also, *to be beaten in play*, Eust.1396.54.

κατακῠβιστάω, *turn a somersault*, Ael.*NA*5.54.

κατακῠκάω, *beat up*, as white of egg in water, Hp.*Morb.*3.17.

κατακυκλόω, *encompass, encircle*, in Pass., J.*BJ*3.8.6 (v.l. κυκλωθέντα), Gal.18(1).787.

κατακῠλίνδω or **-κυλίω** (J.*BJ*6.1.6:—Med., v. infr.), *roll down*, D.H.11.26, Lxx *Je.*28(51).25:—Med., λίθους κατακυλιομένους Arr. *Tact.*11.6:—Pass., *to be rolled down* or *thrown off*, Hdt.1.84, 5.16; κατακεκυλισμένοι ἀπὸ τῶν ἵππων X.*Cyr.*5.3.1:—pres. **κατακῠλινδέω** J.*BJ*4.1.10; impf. κατεκυλίνδουν D.C.56.14.

κατακύλλωμα, ατος, τό, *a particular case of lameness* (κύλλωμα), Eust.1599.13. II. metaph., *turning-point*: hence, *extreme point*, = τὸ πέρας τῶν κακῶν, Phot., Suid. (post τοκάς), cf. *EM*761.38.

κατακῡμοτάκής, ές, *melting the waves*, αὖραι Tim.*Pers.*144.

κατακυνῶν ἢ κατακύων· ὅταν τὸ σχοινίον ἑλίγκας (fort. ἑλίξας) τῶν ἄκρων προσκατακλείσῃς, Hsch.

κατακύπτω, *bend down, stoop*, πρόσσω γὰρ κατέκυψε Il.16.611, cf. Aristeas 91, *Ev.Jo.*8.8; *to be bowed down* by shame, *AP*12.8 (Strato). 2. *look down* from a window, Lxx 4*Ki.*9.32; *stoop down and look*, εἰς τὸν βυθόν Arr.*Epict.*2.16.22; κ. εἴσω τοῦ χάσματος Luc.*DMort.*21.1; κ. ἐς τὸ ἄστυ Id.*Pisc.*39, cf. *Icar.*15.

κατακῡριεύω, *gain* or *exercise complete dominion*, Lxx *Ps.*71(72). 8. 2. κ. τινός *gain dominion over, gain possession of*, ib.*Ps.*9.26 (10.5), 1*Ep.Pet.*5.3; [πλοίου] D.S.14.64.

κατάκυψις, εως, ἡ, *stooping*, Ruf.ap.Orib.*inc.*20.7 (pl.).

κατακῡρόω, *confirm, ratify*, Arist.*Ath.*47.2 ; κ. τὴν ὠνήν *confirm* a contract with a tax-farmer, J.*AJ*12.4.4 :—Pass., *to be ratified*, Thphr. *Fr.*97.1 ; *to be fulfilled*, S.*Ant.*936 (anap.) ; ψήφῳ θανάτου κατακυρωθείς *condemned* to death, E.*Or.*1013 (anap.).

κατακωκύω, *wail, shriek loudly*, Hsch., Phot.

κατακωλύω, *hinder from doing*, c. acc. et inf., Simon.41, cf. Ar. *Ach.*1088 ; *detain, keep back*, τινα X.*Oec.*12.1, D.53.5 ; κ. ἔξω τινάς X.*An.*5.2.16 ; ἄχθεται.. τῷ κατακωλύοντι Pherecr.153.7 :—Pass., c. gen. rei, κατεκωλύθη τοῦ ἐς Σικελίαν πλοῦ D.33.13.

κατακωμάζω, *burst riotously in upon*, τὸ δαιμόνιον κατεκώμασε δώμασιν E.*Ph.*352.

κατακωμῳδέω, *attack in comedy*, Tz.*H.*6.869, Sch.Ar.*V.*61 (Pass.).

κατακωχή, κατακώχιμος, incorrect forms for κατοκωχή, -χιμος.

καταλᾰβ-εύς, έως, ὁ, *holder, nail*, in pl., Hsch., Phot. **-ή**, ἡ, *grasping, comprehension*, Pl.*Def.*412c.

κατάλαβρος, ον, strengthd. for λάβρος, Eup.293.

καταλαγνεύομαι, Pass., *to be very lewd*, καταλαγνευθείς Hsch.

καταλαγχάνω, *hold possession of*, χῶρον dub. l. in Ael.*NA*9.35.

κατ-ᾰλαζονεύομαι, *boast, brag largely*, πρός τινα D.21.169 ; ὡς.. Plu.*Luc.*22. 2. *exaggerate invidiously*, Isoc.15.5,31. 3. also, *depreciate invidiously*, Thphr.ap.D.L.5.40. II. κ. τινός *to boast against* one, Ph.1.339, 2.85, Sm.*Ps.*136(137).3, Suid. s. v. Ἀδράστεια.

καταλαθισταί· ἐξηγηταί, ἢ ἐνδεικνύοντες τὰ δημόσια, Hsch.

καταλακτίζω, *inculco, Gloss.*

κατ-ᾰλᾰλάζω, *shout, exult*, Aq.*Ps.*146.7.

καταλᾰλ-έω, pf. -λελάληκα A.D.*Synt.*323.7 :—*talk, babble loudly*, τοῖς θύραζε ταῦτα κ. Ar.*Ra.*752 ; τινος *before* another, Luc.*Asin.* 12. II. *talk down, rail at*, ἡμᾶς *IG*9(2).338.6 (Thess.) ; τινὰ πρὸς πάντας Plb.3.90.6 ; τὸ δόγμα Id.18.45.1 ; τινος D.S.11.44 ; ὑμῶν ὡς κακοποιῶν 1*Ep.Pet.*2.12 ; τινὸς ψευδῆ Lxx*Ho.*7.13 ; κατά τινος ib. *Ps.*49(50).20 :—Pass., ἐπί τινι Plb.27.13.2 ; *to be outdone in speech*, ὑπ' ἰδιωτῶν Phld.*Rh.*1.343S. 2. *weary by talking*, gloss on καταγλωττίζειν, Phryn.*PS*p.79B. 3. simply, *interview, address* a person, *PHib.*1.151 (iii B. C.). **-ητέον**, *one must talk against*, cj. in Thom.Mag.p.224R. (who censures it). **-ιά**, ἡ, *evil report, slander*, Lxx*Wi.*1.11, 1*Ep.Pet.*2.1 (pl.). **-ος**, ὁ, *slanderer*, *Ep. Rom.*1.30, *POxy.*1828ʳ.3.

καταλαμβάνω, fut. -λήψομαι Pl.*Prt.*311a (in pass. sense, A.D.*Synt.* 48.9), Ion. -λάμψομαι Hdt.6.39, Aeol. -λᾶμψομαι dub. in Alc.*Supp.* 5.9 (v. λαμβάνω) : pf. -είληφα Pl.*Phdr.*250d, etc. (καθ- *SIG*129.18 (Carpathos, iv B. C.)), -λελάβηκα Pherecyd.Syr.ap.D.L.1.122, Hdt.3. 42 (v. l. -λελαβήκεε) :—Pass., Ion. aor. -ελάμφθην Id.5.21 ; -ελάφθην *SIG*279.7 (Zelea, iv B. C.) : pf. in med. sense, D.S.17.85 :—*seize, lay hold of*, c. acc., τοῦ κατὰ νῶτα λαβών Od.9.433, cf. Ar.*Lys.*624, etc. ; κατέλαβε τὴν ἀκρόπολιν Th.1.126, cf. Hdt.5.71, Ar.*Lys.*263 (lyr., tm.), Isoc.4.153, etc. (metaph., τὴν τοῦ νέου τῆς ψυχῆς ἀκρόπολιν κ. Pl.*R.* 560b) ; πάντα φυλακαῖς κ. Plu.*Per.*33 ; κ. ἕδρας Ar.*Ec.*21, 86 ; φάσκων Ποσειδῶ πρότερον Ἀθηνᾶς καταλαβεῖν αὐτήν (sc. τὴν πόλιν) Isoc.12.193 ; later, simply, *arrive at* a place, *POxy.*1829 (vi A. D.), etc. :—Med., *seize for oneself*, τὰ πρήγματα Hdt.6.39 ; τὰ ἄλλοι οὐ κατελάβοντο matters which others *had* not *preoccupied*, ib.55 : freq. in Plb., κ. λόφον 1.19. 5, al. :—Pass., of a person, ὑπὸ τοῦ θεοῦ καταληφθείς *possessed*, Plot. 5.8.11. 2. of death, fatigue, disaster, etc., τὸν δὲ κατ' ὄσσε ἔλλαβε.. θάνατος Il.5.82 ; Ἄργον.. κατὰ μοῖρ' ἔλαβεν.. θανάτοιο Od.17. 326 : c. dupl. acc., εὖτ' ἄν μιν κάματος κατὰ γυῖα λάβῃσιν 1.192 ; Δίκη καταλήψεται ψευδῶν τέκτονας Heraclit.28 ; *befall, overtake*, συμφορὰ κ. πόλεις E.*Hipp.*1161 : freq. in Hdt., θεῖα πρήγματα καταλαμβάνει τοὺς αἰελούρους 2.66 ; πένθεα μεγάλα τοὺς Αἰγυπτίους κ. ibid., cf. 3.42 ; ὅσα φεύγοντας ἐκ τῆς πατρίδος κακὰ ἐπίδοξα καταλαμβάνειν may be expected to *befall* them, 4.11 ; ἤν τι καταλαμβάνῃ νεώτερον τὸν πεζόν 8.21 : folld. by inf., νοῦσός τινα κ. νοσῆσαι 3.149, cf. 3.75 ; πρίν τι ἀνήκεστον ἡμᾶς κ. Th.4.20 ; κίνδυνος κ. τινά D.18.99 ; rarely of good fortune, τοῦτον κατέλαβε εὐτυχίη τις Hdt.3.139. 3. *seize with the mind, comprehend*, Pl.*Ax.*370a, Chrysipp.*Stoic.*2.39, Plb.8.2.6, *Ev. Jo.*1.5 (perh. *overcome*) ; κάλλος διὰ τῆς [ὄψεως] Pl.*Phdr.*250d ; ἐκ τοῦ φάσματος ὅτι.. D.H.5.46, cf. Arr.*Epict.*1.5.6 :—so in Med., D.H.2. 66, S.E.*M.*7.288 ; ὅτι.. *Act.Ap.*4.13 ; τί τὸ πλάτος *Ep.Eph.*3.18 :—Pass., Phld.*Sign.*22, *Mus.*p.62K., Numen.ap.Eus.*PE*14.8. 4. *accept*, παρὰ τοῦ βασιλέως.. δωροδοκήματα dub. l. in Pl.Com.119.1 (κἀτ' ἔλαβον Mein.). II. *catch, overtake, come up with*, τοὺς φεύγοντας Hdt.1.63, cf. 2.30, etc. :—Pass., Id.7.211, Plb.1.47. 8. 2. *find on arrival*, c. part., τινὰ ζῶντα Hdt.3.10 ; τὰ πλεῖστα.. προειργασμένα Th.8.65 ; πάντα ἔξω Id.2.18 ; ἀνεῳγμένην τὴν θύραν Pl. *Smp.*174d ; τοὺς ἄρχοντας ἐξιόντας D.21.85 ; τινὰ ἔνδον Pl.*Prt.*311a ; τῶν φορτίων πολλὴν ἀπρασίαν D.34.8 ; τι ὑπάρχον Arist.*Top.*131ᵃ 29 ; *detect*, ἐπ' αὐτοφώρῳ ἐμαυτόν Pl.*Ap.*22b :—Pass., κατελήφθη σοῦ λάθρα πωλῶν τὰ σά E.*Cyc.*260, cf. *Ev.Jo.*8.3, etc. ; κατείληπτο σοφιζόμενος D.21.164 ; *to be taken by surprise*, Plu.*Publ.*20. III. impers., καταλαμβάνει τινά c. inf., *it happens to* one, *it is* one's *fortune* to.., καταλαμβάνει μιν φεύγειν Hdt.2.152, cf. 3.118 ; καταλελάβηκέ με.. τοῦτο.. ἐκφῆναι Id.3.65, cf. 4.105, 6.38. IV. abs., πρὸς τὴν καταλαβοῦσαν συμφορήν *that had befallen*, Id.4.161 ; τὰ καταλαβόντα, = τὰ συμβάντα, *what had happened, the circumstances*, Id.9.49 ; ἢν πόλεμος καταλάβῃ Th.2.54, cf. 18 ; εἰ -λαμβάνοι ἀναχώρησις Id.4.31 ; τῆς νυκτὸς -λαμβανούσης as night *was coming on*, D.S.20.86 ; χειμῶνος ἤδη -λαμβάνοντος Hdn.7.2.9. V. *hold down, cover*, τῇ χειρὶ τὸν ὀφθαλμόν Pl.*Tht.*165b ; τὰς χεῖρας Plu.*Sert.*26 ; *fasten down*, κ. πῶμα γόμφοις Id.2.356c, cf. Gal.13.358 (so in Med., D.S.3.37) :—Pass., *to be compressed*, opp. διαλύεσθαι, Arist.*Pr.*870ᵇ11 ; τὰς φλέβας -λαμβανόμενοι Id.*Somn.*455ᵇ7. 2. *keep under, repress, check*, κ. τινῶν αὐξανομένην τὴν δύναμιν Hdt.1.46 ; κ. τὸ πῦρ *get* it *under*, ib.87 ; ἴσχε καὶ κ. σεωυτόν Id.3.36 ; κ. τὰς διαφοράς *put an end to* them, Id.7.9.β' ; κ. ἐρίζοντας *stop* their quarrelling, Id.3.128 : folld. by inf., κ. τοὺς Αἰγυπτίους ταῦτα μὴ ποιέειν Id.2.162 ; ὁ τῶν Περσέων θάνατος καταλαμφθεὶς ἐσιγήθη inquiries about their death *being checked*.., Id.5. 21. b. κ. τὸ πνεῦμα *hold* the breath, Gal.6.176, al. 3. *bind*, κ. πίστι καὶ ὁρκίοισι Hdt.9.106 ; ὅρκοις Th.4.86, etc. :—Pass., εἴ τινι -λέλαμμαι ὅρκῳ *SIG*360.41 (Chersonesus) ; νόμοις, ἔθεσι κατειλημμένα *enforced*, Arist.*Pol.*1324ᵇ22 ; ζημίαις Pl.*Lg.*823a ; [τὰς σπονδὰς] ηὗρε κατειλημμένας he found the treaty *concluded*, Th.5.21 codd. 4. *compel, constrain* one *to do*, c. inf., ἀναγκαίῃ μιν κ. φαίνειν *forces* him to bring out the truth, Hdt.3.75 :—Pass., ἀναγκαίῃ καταλαμβανόμενος *being constrained*, Id.2.65, cf. Th.7.57. 5. *convict, condemn*, Antipho 2.4.11 ; opp. ἀπολύειν, Id.4.4.9 ; ἐὰν καταληφθεὶς ἀποθάνω Id.2.2.9, cf. *IG*12(2).526ᴬ20 (Eresus, iv B. C.) ; of the prosecutor, *secure a conviction*, *Rev.Phil.*1928.192 (Erythrae, v B. C.) ; ὁ -λαβών *SIG*578.58 (Teos, ii B. C.), etc.

κατάλαμπρος, ον, *very bright*, Gal.19.576, *EM*790.29.

καταλαμπρύνω, *make splendid*, νεὼν κάλλει τε καὶ μεγέθει Procop. *Aed.*1.6.

καταλᾰμπτέος, α, ον, Ion. for καταληπτέος, *to be arrested*, θανάτῳ by death, Hdt.3.127.

καταλάμπω, *shine upon* or *over*, c. gen., ὧν ὁ ἥλιος κ. Pl.*R.*508d : also c. acc., κ. τοὺς στενωπούς *to light them*, Plu.*Cic.*22 ; ἡμέρα κατέλαμψεν αὐτόν Id.*Ages.*24, cf. Luc.*Prom.*19 :—Pass., ὑπὸ τοῦ ἡλίου καταλαμπόμενοι X.*Mem.*4.7.7, cf. E.*Tr.*1070 (lyr.), *Ion* 87 (anap.). II. abs., *shine*, of the sun, Hp.*Aër.*5, E.*El.*464 (lyr.), v. l. in *h.Merc.*141.

κατάλαμψις, εως, ἡ, *bright reflection*, κ. ἀντίρροπος v. l. in Iamb.*VP* 15.67 ; *illumination*, Ptol.*Alm.*13.7 (pl.).

καταλαπριώσει· ἀποκτενεῖ, καταδέξεται, κατατρυπήσει ἢ καταπερήσει, Hsch.

καταλγ-έω, *feel sore pain*, S.*Ph.*368, Plb.3.80.4. **-ύνω**, *grieve very much*, in Pass., Hsch.

καταλεαίνω, fut. -λεᾰνῶ Lxx*Da.*7.23 :—*grind down*, Plu.2. 802b :—Pass., -ομένη τροφή Anon.Lond.24.23. II. *smooth down, placate*, Just.*Nov.*129 *Praef.*

κατάλεγμα, ατος, τό, *dirge*, Sm.*Ez.*2.10, Al.*Is.*16.9.

καταλέγω (A), *lay down* ; v. καταλέχομαι.

καταλέγω (B), *recount, tell at length and in order*, Hom., always in fut. or aor. 1, ταῦτα μάλ' ἀτρεκέως καταλέξω Il.10.413, al. ; τόδε εἰπὲ καὶ ἀτρεκέως κατάλεξον ib.384, al. ; πᾶσαν ἀληθείην κατάλεξον 24.407 : freq. in Hdt., as 4.83, 114 ; ἑξῆς κ. Ath.13.610b ; κ. τὰς προσηγορίας ib.c :—Pass., τούτων ὧν τῶν καταλεχθέντων of those *which have been recounted*, Hdt.4.50, cf. 23, al. :—Med., Ps.-Hdt.*Vit.Hom.*21 : folld. by interrog. Adv., κατάλεξον ὅπως ἤντησας Od.17.44, 3.97 ; κεῖνον ὀϊζυρὸν κατάλεξον, ἤ που ἔτι ζώει.. *tell* me *the tale of* that unhappy man, 4.832. b. *repeat, recite*, τῶν χρησμῶν Hdt.7.6 ; τετράμετρα πρὸς τὸν αὐλόν X.*Smp.*6.3 ; τὰς πατρίους εὐχάς Herm.Hist.2 ; καταλέγεσθαι· ὀδύρεσθαι τὸν τεθνεῶτα, Hsch. ; cf. κατάλεγμα, καταλογή III. 2. *reckon up, tell in full tale*, μνηστῆρας ἀριθμήσας κατάλεξον Od.16.235 ; of a line of kings or ancestors, κατέλεγον οἱ ἱρέες ἐκ βύβλου.. βασιλέων τ' καὶ λ' οὐνόματα Hdt.2.100 ; τοὺς αἰεὶ πατέρας Id. 6.53 ; κ. ἑωυτὸν μητρόθεν *reckoned up* his pedigree, Id.1.173 ; κ. τοὺς ἄρχοντας Pl.*Hp.Ma.*285e, cf. *Ep.*327e, X.*Mem.*2.4.4 :—later in Med., Ph.1.187, 2.593, Ath.11.504f. b. *reckon, count as*, οὓς οἱ πολλοὶ πλουσίους κ. Pl.*Lg.*742e, cf. X.*An.*2.6.27 : so perh. in Pass., χήρα -έσθω 1*Ep.Ti.*5.9. c. *conclude by enumeration*, ὡς.. Arist.*Rh. Al.*1429ᵇ35. 3. with pf. κατείλοχα Paus.10.24.1 :—Pass., aor. (v. infr.) : pf. κατείλεγμαι ; 3 pl. plpf. κατειλέχατο J.*AJ*19.1.15 :—*enumerate, draw up a list*, hence, *enrol, enlist*, ἄνδρας οἳ δορυφόροι μὲν οὐκ ἐγένοντο Πεισιστράτου, κορυνηφόροι δέ Hdt.1.59 ; στρατιώτας, ὁπλίτας, Ar.*Ach.*1065, *Lys.*394, etc. ; ἱππέας Arist.*Ath.*49.2 ; κ. εἰς ὁπλίτας Lys.15.7 ; εἰς τὸν κατάλογον Ἀθηναίων Id.25.16 ; ἐς τὰς ναῦς Th.3.75 : generally, τοὺς πεντακισχιλίους Arist.*Ath.*29.5 ; κ. τὸν Ἡρακλέα εἰς τοὺς δώδεκα θεούς D.S.4.39 : c. dat., κ. τινὰ τοῖς δημοσίᾳ ἱππεύουσιν Philostr.*VS*1.22.3, cf. 1.25.3 (nisi leg. ἐγκατ-) : c. inf., τοὺς πλουσιωτάτους ἱπποτροφεῖν κ. X.*HG*3.4.15 :—in Med., *enrol for oneself*, δορυφόρους, ὁπλίτας, Hdt.1.98, Th.7.31 :—Pass. (aor. 2 κατελέγην more common in Att. than aor. 1, cf. *IG*2².896.9, Pl.*Lg.*762e, 943a), *to be enlisted* or *enrolled*, Hdt.7.1 ; τῶν τρισχιλίων κ. *to be enrolled* of their number, Lys.30.8 ; κ. στρατιώτης Id.9.4 ; κατειλεγμένος ἱππεύειν Id.16.13 ; καταλεγεὶς τῶν τριηράρχων Is.7.5 ; ὁ κατειλεγμένος D.39.8 ; εἰς τὴν σύγκλητον κ. Plu.*Pomp.*13 ; ἀγορανόμον -λεγέντα, = Lat. *adlectum inter aedilicios*, *Ann.Epigr.*1905.120. 4. later, *select*, τοῖς παισὶ τοὺς διδασκάλους *AB*105 :—Med., τὸν πλωτικὸν [βίον] Pl.*Ax.*368b. II. = μηνύειν, τῷ βασιλεῖ τὴν ἐπιβουλήν J. *AJ*15.3.2 : c. gen., *inform against*, ib.19.6.3 ; *accuse*, μάρτυς ἄδικος -λέγων αὐτοῦ ἀσέβειαν Lxx*De.*19.16.

καταλείβω, *pour down* : hence, *cause to waste away*, δέμας E.*Andr.* 131 (lyr.) :—Pass., *drop down*, γλυκίων μέλιτος καταλειβομένοιο Il.18. 109 ; [ὕδωρ] ἐκ πέτρης καταλείβεται Hes.*Th.*786 ; δάκρυά τ' ἐκ δακρύων καταλείβεται E.*Tr.*605 (lyr.) ; *melt away* (in tears), καταλειβομένης ἄλγεσι πολλοῖς Id.*Supp.*1119 (anap.) ; also καταλείβεσθαί νιν καὶ καταρρεῖν ὥσπερ τοὺς κολοσσούς, in an imprecation, *Abh.Berl.Akad.* 1925(5).21 (Cyrene).

κατάλειμμα, ατος, τό, *remnant*, Lxx*Ge.*45.7, al. 2. v. κατάλημμα.

καταλειπτέον, *one must leave behind*, Ph.*Bel.*100.37, Antyll.ap. Orib.45.2.9.

κατ-άλειπτος [ᾰλ], ον, *anointed*, σμύρνῃ Ar.*Eq.*1332; μύρῳ Id.*Pax* 862.

καταλείπω, later **καταλιμπάνω** (q.v.), Ep. also **καλλείπω** Il.10. 238: fut. καλλείψω 14.89: aor. κάλλῐπον 12.92: aor. 1 subj. καλλείψῃς Q.S.10.299; part. καλλείψας Nonn.*D.*32.130; καταλείψας Luc. *DMeretr.*7.3; Ion. iterat. καταλίπεσκε (κατελίπεσκε, καταλειπέεσκε codd.) Hdt.4.78: pf. -λέλοιπα Ar.*Lys.*736:—**Med.**, fut. καταλείψομαι (in pass. sense) X.*An.*5.6.12: aor. 2 -ελιπόμην Hdt.3.34, Pl. *Smp.*209d (in pass. sense, *Berl.Sitzb.*1927.161 (Cyrene)):—**Pass.**, fut. καταλειφθήσομαι Isoc.15.7, 17.1:—*leave behind*, πὰρ δ' ἄρ' ὄχεσφιν ἄλλον.. κάλλιπεν Il.12.92; esp. of persons dying or going into a far country, κὰδ δέ με χήρην λείπεις ἐν μεγάροισι 24.725; οὖρον.. κατέλειπον ἐπὶ κτεάτεσσιν Od.15.89; οἷόν μιν Τροίηνδε κιὼν κατέλειπεν Ὀδυσσεύς 17.314; so later, τὴν στρατιὴν καταλίπεσκε ἐν τῷ προαστίῳ Hdt.4.78; φύλακον κ. τινά Id.1.113, cf. 2.103:—Med., καταλείπεσθαι παῖδας *leave behind one*, Pl.*Smp.* l. c., cf. Hdt.3.34, etc.:— Pass., *to be left, remain behind*, κατελέλειπτο ἐν Πέρσῃσι Hdt.1.209, cf. 7.170, X.*An.*5.6.12: c. gen., [στρατὸς] καταλελειμμένος τοῦ ἄλλου στρατοῦ a force *left behind* the rest, Hdt.9.96. 2. *bequeath*, [τόξον] παιδὶ κάλλιπ' ἀποθνήσκων Od.21.33: metaph., ἐμοὶ δ' ὀδύνας τε γόους τε κάλλιπεν 1.243, cf. 11.279; δόκησιν ἰσχύος καὶ ξυνέσεως ἐς τὸ ἔπειτα Th.4.18; τοῖς θρέψασι λύπας Lys.2.70; παισὶν αἰδῶ οὐ χρυσὸν κ. Pl.*Lg.*729b: c. inf., εἰ καταλείψει μηδὲ ταφῆναι not enough to be buried with, Ar.*Pl.*556:—Pass., [χρήματα] καταλειφθέντα Is.1. 45. b. κ. διαθήκας *leave* a will (when going on service), Id.9. 14. 3. Med., *leave* in a certain state, κόλπον βαθὺν καταλιπόμενος τοῦ κιθῶνος Hdt.6.125. II. *forsake, abandon*, οὕτω δὴ μέμονας Τρώων πόλιν.. καλλείψειν; Il.14.89, cf. 22.383; πολλοὺς καταλείψομεν we *shall leave* many *upon the field*, 12.226; ὤ μοι, εἰ μέν κε λίπω κάτα τεύχεα 17.91; κὰδ δέ κεν εὐχωλὴν Πριάμῳ καὶ Τρωσὶ λίποιεν Ἀργείην Ἑλένην 2.160: c. inf., κάλλιπεν οἰωνοῖσιν ἕλωρ καὶ κύρμα γενέσθαι Od.3.271; σχεδίην ἀνέμοισι φέρεσθαι κ. 5.344; μέλη.. θηρσὶν βοράν E.*Supp.*46 (lyr.); μή ποτ' ἐμὸν κατ' αἰῶνα λίποι θεῶν πανάγυρις A. *Th.*219; μή με καταλίπῃς μόνον S.*Ph.*809; οἰκίας τε καὶ ἱερά Th. 2.16; πατέρας καὶ ξυγγενεῖς ἀτίμους κ. Id.3.58; κ. τὴν δίαιταν *not to appear at* the trial, Test.ap.D.21.93. 2. *let drop, give up*, τὰ αὐτῶν ἔργα X.*Cyn.*3.10, cf. 10.15; εἰ ἐνταῦθα -λίποιμι τὸν λόγον Isoc. 9.33. III. *leave remaining*, ὀκτὼ μόνον X.*An.*6.3.5 codd.; κ. ἄφοδον *leave* an exit, ib.4.2.11:—Med., κ. στενὴν διέξοδον Pl.*Ti.*73e; -λείπεσθαι ἑαυτῷ *reserve* for oneself, X.*Mem.*1.1.8; ὑπερβολὴν οὐ κ. χαρᾶς Plb.16.23.4, cf. 16.25.6:—Pass., *to be left, remain*, τίς ἔτι ἡδονὴ -λείπεται; Lys.2.71, cf. *Ep.Hebr.*4.1, etc.; of the *remainder* in calculations, *PPetr.*3 p.326, al. (iii B.C.), Nicom.*Ar.*1.13.13, etc.: impers. καταλείπεται c. inf., *it remains that*.., τὸν κόσμον κ. ἀθάνατον εἶμεν Aristaeus ap.Stob.1.20.6, cf. D.Chr.37.16, etc.; -λείπεται μάχη *yet remains to be fought*, X.*Cyr.*2.3.11. 2. *leave alone*, opp. περιαιρέω, Id.*Mem.*3.2.4, cf. Arist.*Pol.*1342^{a}34. b. *leave undisputed*, τὰς παραλλαγάς Phld.*Sign.*24: hence, *admit, allow the truth of* a doctrine, Id.*Po.*5.34, Demetr.Lac.*Herc.*1055.13:—Pass., Phld.*Piet.* 80. c. *omit*, c. inf., Alex.Aphr.*in SE*118.10.

καταλειτουργέω, Att. **-λητουργέω**, *spend one's substance in bearing the public burdens*, D.36.39:—Pass., prob. in Is.*Fr.*130S. (=29 T.); τὰ ἴδια πατρίδι χρήματα *BCH*44.91 (Lagina).

κατ-ᾰλείφω, *besmear*, τὸ κηρίον Arist.*HA*627^{a}10; πηλῷ φράγματα Aen.Tact.37.9; κατήλειψε τὸν χηραμὸν τῷ πηλῷ Ael.*NA*3.26: abs., *apply an ointment*, Hp.*Liqu.*6:—Med., dub. l. in Arist.*HA*555^{a} 14:—Pass., καταλήλειπταί τινι ib.551^{b}5; ὅταν καταλειφθῇ ib.554^{a} 30, cf. Poll.9.112, Gal.1.657. 2. *plaster*, τέγη *IG*12(7).62.26 (Amorgos, iv B.C.); ὀροφήν *Inscr.Délos* 290.97 (iii B.C.).

καταλείψᾰνον, τό, *remnant*, *PMag.Par.*1.1405a.

κατάλειψις, εως (poet. **κάλλειψις** only in Hsch.), ἡ, *leaving behind*, συγγραμμάτων Pl.*Phdr.*257e, cf. Arist.*Fr.*151; ἐκ χρημάτων καταλείψεως by a *legacy*, *CIG*4369 (Sagalassus), cf. *POxy.*75.12 (ii A.D.), *IG Rom.*4.671 (Prymnessus, ii A.D.), Vett.Val.177.22, al. II. *posterity*, Lxx *Ge.*45.7.

καταλεκτέον or **-έα**, *one must reckon*, τοῦτον ἐς τοὺς κόλλοπας Eub. 11. II. καταλεκτέος, α, ον, *to be drawn up*, κ. ἂν εἴη κατάλογος Pl. *Lg.*968c. 2. *to be reckoned*, ἐν τῷ αὐτῷ ἀριθμῷ Plu.*Nob.*7.

κατάλεκτος, *catalectum*, *Gloss.*

καταλέκτρια, ἡ, perh. = θαλαμηπόλος, Βύνης -ιαι αὐδηέσσης Call. (*Fr.anon.*82) ap.*EM*217.5, Tz.ad.Lyc.107.

κατάλεξις, εως, ἡ, *levying*, = Lat. *dilectus*, App.*Hisp.*49.

καταλεπτολογέω, *refine away by talk*, '*pulverize*', πνευμόνων πολὺν πόνον Ar.*Ra.*828 (lyr.).

κατάλεπτον, τό, and **κατάλεπτα**, τά, '*petty cash*', *minor expenses*, *PTeb.*120.85 (i B.C.), *POxy.*1729.6, 13 (iv A.D.).

καταλεπτύνω, *make very thin*, in Pass., τὸ πρόσωπον -λελεπτύνσθαι Hp.*Aër.*7; οἱ μάλιστα -λελεπτυσμένοι Arist.*PA*668^{a}22, cf. Gal.18(2). 18, 25.

καταλευγαλέα· κάθυγρος, Hsch.

καταλευκόω, *whiten*, [πινάκιον] Aen.Tact.31.15.

κατα-λεύσιμος, ον, *worthy to be stoned*, Din.*Fr.*8.3. **-λεύω**, *stone to death*, Hdt.1.167, al., Ar.*Ach.*285, Th.1.106, etc.:—Pass., Aeschin.1.163, Ph.2.165, Luc.*Anach.*39. II. *condemn to work in mines*, Hsch. (Pass.).

κατ-αλεύω, strengthd. for ἀλεύω, in aor. inf. καταλεῦσαι, Hsch.

καταλέχομαι, pres. only in Cypr. imper. **καλέχες** (fort. καλέχεο), = κατάκεισο, Hsch. (cf. λέγω A); Ep. only in Med. and Pass. fut. and aor.:—*lie down, go to bed*: aor. 1 κατελέξατο Il.9.690, Od.10. 555: non-thematic aor. (or impf.) Pass. κατέλεκτο Il.9.662, etc.; part. καταλέγμενος Od.22.196; inf. καταλέχθαι 15.394: fut. καταλέξομαι Hes.*Op.*523.

κατ-ᾰλέω, aor. 1 κατ-άλεσα, *grind*, κατὰ πυρὸν ἄλεσσαν Od.20.109; κριθὰς ἐς τὸ πῶμα Hecat.323 J., cf. Hdt.4.172, Hp.*VM*3, Ph.*Bel.*88. 46, Str.6.1.8; κ. [μόσχον] λεπτόν Lxx *Ex.*32.20:—Pass., καταλεσθείς Ph.1.257.

καταλήγω, *leave off, stop*, πρὶν καταλῆξαι.. ἄχος A.*Ag.*1479 (anap.): ποῖ καταλήξει μένος ἄτης; at what point *will* it *cease*? Id.*Ch.*1075 (anap.); κ. ἐν.. *to end* at or with.., Plu.2.791c; ἐπί τι D.S.14.2, Arr.*Epict.*6.20.21, M.Ant.4.20; [ἡδοναὶ] περὶ τὸ σῶμα κ. Plu.2.705a; πρός τι Arist.*Mete.*340^{b}9; εἴς τι D.S.20.2, Hierocl.*in CA*19 p.462 M., Porph.*Sent.*37: abs., Thphr.*Ign.*50; τὰ καταλήγοντα *limits* of a district, Plu.*Fab.*6, *Arist.*11; πόλεως J.*BJ*3.7.34: in sg., τὸ κ. τοῦ πελάγους *extremity*, Plb.5.59.5, cf. Poll.2.71, 177. 2. esp. in Metric and Rhetoric, of feet, verses, or periods, κρητικοῦ εἰς σύμφωνον -λήγοντος A.D.*Pron.*50.17; εἰς τὸ αὐτὸ ὄνομα Demetr.*Eloc.* 154, cf. 4, Hermog.*Id.*1.6. II. trans., *close, finish*, ναυμαχίᾳ εἰς ἣν Θουκυδίδης κατέληξε τὴν πραγματείαν D.S.14.84.

καταλήθομαι, *forget utterly*, τινος Il.22.389.

καταληΐζομαι, *plunder*, τοὺς ὑπηκόους Procop.*Arc.*21, cf. Hsch., Phot.

καταληκτ-έον, *one must end*, ἢ ἐπ' ἄπειρον [ἰτέον] ἢ εἴς τινας ἑνάδας κ. Procl.*in Prm.*p.948 S. **-ικός**, ή, όν, *leaving off*; esp. in Metric, of verses *having the last foot incomplete*, Heph.4.2, Anon.Metr.*Oxy.* 2201 x 19, etc.; τὸ κ. Heph. l. c.; of feet, κ. [εἶδος παίωνος] Demetr. *Eloc.*38. II. Adv. -κῶς *disinterestedly*, διδόναι τι M.Ant.9.42, cf. 7.13 (-ληπτ- codd.), Arr.*Epict.*2.23.46.

κατάλημμα, ατος, τό, *comprehension*, D.L.7.45. 2. *outer bandage*, Orib.48.19.24 (prob.), Heliod.ap.eund.48.20.4; written κατάλειμμα in Gal.18(2).740; κατάκλειμμα Id.18(1).836.

κατάληξις, εως, ἡ, *ending, termination*, S.E.*M.*10.61, Nicom.*Ar.* 1.13.13; ἡ εἰς ὃ κ. A.D.*Pron.*29.17. 2. *cadence* or *close* of a period, Longin.41.2, Demetr.*Eloc.*19; *final syllable*, D.H.*Comp.*18.

καταληπ-τέος, α, ον, (καταλαμβάνω) *to be seized* or *occupied*, Plu. *Caes.*32; *to be comprehended*, Vett.Val.272.30; Ion. καταλαμπτέος (q.v.). 2. **-τέον**, *one must cover* with a plaster, Philum.ap.Orib. *Syn.*8.3, Philum.*Ven.*3.5. **-τήρ**, ῆρος, ὁ, *strap for holding fast*, Hsch. s.v. μαχαιροδέτης. 2. *clamp*, *BCH*29.468 (Delos). 3. Archit., *top course of stylobate*, *IG*2^{2}.1682.11; *coping laid on ὀρθοστάται*, ib.11(2).287 *A*120 (Delos, iii B.C.). **-τικός**, ή, όν, *able to check*, τοῦ θορυβητικοῦ Ar.*Eq.*1380. 2. *conveying direct apprehension* of an object, κ. φαντασία *Stoic.*2.26, etc.; κ. λόγος Phld.*Rh.* 2.120S.; τὸ -κόν M.Ant.4.22. Adv. -κῶς *by direct apprehension*, *Stoic.*2.27; *manifestly*, φαίνεσθαι Cleom.1.8. **-τός**, ή, όν, *seized*, D.S.24.1; *capable of being seized*, Procop.*Goth.*3.24; *liable*, θανάτῳ Id.*Vand.*1.4. 2. *to be achieved*, ὅσον.. τὰ πράγματα ἐφαίνετο κ. Th.3.11; ὅ τι ἂν ἔσω δέκα ἡμερέων ἐμβάλλῃς, πᾶν κ. whatever joint you set within ten days, is *manageable*, i.e. *curable*, Hp.*Art.*67; σοφίᾳ κ. ἅπαντα Philostr.*Her.*10.4. 3. *capable of being apprehended* or *grasped*, κ. τὸ ἦθος ἐξ εἴδους Cleanth.*Stoic.*1.137, al.; λόγῳ, αἰσθήσει κ., Phld.*Po.*5.20, Diog.Oen.4 (-λημπτ-). 4. *certain*, opp. εὔλογος, Herod.Med.ap.Aët.9.37. II. Act., πένθος θεόθεν κ. grief *that falls on us* from the gods, E.*Hipp.*1346 (anap.).

καταληρέω, *lose by idle talking*, τὴν ἐξωμίδα Eub.53. II. *overpower with talk*, τινος Jul.*Ep.*32: abs., Ach.Tat.7.11.

καταλήψιμος, ον, *to be seized and condemned*, opp. ἀπολύσιμος, Antipho 4.4.9.

κατάληψις, εως, ἡ, *seizing*, οὐκέτι ἐν καταλήψει ἐφαίνετο to be within one's *grasp*, Th.3.33. 2. *seizing, assaulting*, Ar.*Nu.*318. 3. *taking possession, occupation*, τῆς βασιλείας Isoc.9.69; χωρίων Pl. *Grg.*455c, *R.*526d (pl.); ἱεροῦ D.19.21; καταλήψεις πολέμου prob. f.l. for πολέων, App.*BC*4.14. 4. Philos., *direct apprehension* of an object by the mind, Zeno *Stoic.*1.20, Luc.*Par.*4, al.; τῶν μετεώρων Philostr.*Her.*10.9; ἀκριβὴς κ. *certainty*, Herod.Med.ap.Aët.9. 37: pl., *perceptions*, *Stoic.*2.30, Luc.*Herm.*81, etc.; introduced into Latin by Cicero, Plu.*Cic.*40. II. *holding, grip*, with the fingers, bandages, or instruments, Hp.*Off.*9; τὰς -λήψιας ποιεῖσθαι ibid., cf. *Art.*11 (in pl. also = *ligatures*, *Medic.*8); ὁ ὕπνος τοῦ.. αἰσθητηρίου κ. *compression*, Arist.*Somn.*458^{a}29. 2. *stoppage*, οὔρων Gal.17 (1).423; σπέρματος Ruf.ap.Orib.6.38.4; *holding*, πνεύματος Gal.6. 152. 3. in Music, *stopping* of the strings of an instrument, Sch. Ar.*Nu.*317. III. later, *catalepsy*, Gal.8.485, al.

καταλῐθάζω, = καταλιθόω, Ev.Luc.20.6.

καταλῐθοβολέω, *throw stones at, stone*, Lxx *Ex.*17.4.

κατάλῐθ-ος, ον, *set with precious stones*, ὕφασμα Lxx *Ex.*28.17. **-όω**, *stone to death*, D.18.204, Paus.6.9.7 (Pass.), Philostr.*VA*1.16, al. II. gloss on καταχρυσόω, Hsch.

καταλιμπάνω, = καταλείπω, Hp.*Mul.*1.78, Th.8.17, Antiph.35, *PPetr.*3 pp.4, 12 (iii B.C.), Lxx *Ge.*39.16, Ocell.4.13, etc.

κατ-ἄλιναι· κατ-αλεῖψαι (-μῖξαι cod.), Hsch., cf. Phot.

καταλῐπαίνω, *make very fat*, Hsch.

καταλῐπᾰρέω, *entreat earnestly*, Luc.*DDeor.*25.2, *Cat.*4.

καταλίπᾰρος [ῐ], ον, *very greasy*, [κηροῦ] τὸ κ. Dsc.2.83. II. v. κατάλυπρος.

κατ-ᾰλιφή, ἡ, *plastering, whitewashing*, *IG*2^{2}.1664.12 (iv B.C.), *OGI*737.10 (Memphis, ii B.C.).

καταλιχμ-άζομαι, *lick all over*, Opp.*C*.2.389 (tm.). **-άομαι**, *lick up, eat*, S.E.*P*.1.57.

καταλλ-άγδην, Adv. *reciprocally*, Hsch. **-ἄγή**, ἡ, *exchange*, esp. of money, Arist.*Oec*.1346b24, *PHib*.1.100.4 (iii B. C.). 2. *money-changer's profit, agio*, D.50.30, Diph.66.14, Euphro 3.4. 3. *freight, merchandise*, metaph., [ἀραὶ] βαρεῖαι κ. A.*Th*.767 (lyr.). 4. *change, difference*, Phld.*Mus*.p.74K. II. *change from enmity to friendship, reconciliation*, καταλλαγὰς ποιεῖσθαι πρός τινας D.1.4; κ. πολέμου Ar.*Av*.1588. 2. *reconciliation* of sinners *with God*, 2*Ep.Cor*.5.18; κόσμου *Ep.Rom*.11.15. **-αγμα**, ατος, τό, = foreg. II, Hsch. s. v. καταλλαγὴν δορός. **-ακτήριος**, ον, *reconciliatory*, συμβάσεις Ph. 1.673; fem. -ία as epith. of Aphrodite, *Milet*.7.19. **-άκτης**, ου, ὁ, *money-changer*, *EM*137.24. II. *reconciler, mediator*, J.*AJ*3.15.2, D.C.*Fr*.72.1 (pl.). **-ακτικός**, ή, όν, *easy to reconcile, placable*, Arist. *EE*1222b2, *Rh*.1367b17 (Comp.): c. dat., κ. τοῖς ὑπηκόοις prob. in Muson.*Fr*.33 p.122 H. **-αξις**, εως, ἡ, *varied exercise*, νεύρων Antyll. ap.Orib.6.35.1. **-άσσω**, Att. -ττω, *change* money, Plu.*Arat*. 18, etc. (also in Med., D.19.114:—Pass., Matreas ap.Ath.1.19b, with a play on signf. II); *change* or *give away*, τὴν χάριν τῶν νόμων for the laws, Din.3.21 (s. v. l.); καταλλάσσειν τὸν βίον *to leave* life, Ael.*VH*5.2. b. abs., *transgress, contravene* regulations, *IG*5(2). 3.2 (Tegea). 2. Med., *exchange* one thing *for* another, ἡδονὰς πρὸς ἡδονάς Pl.*Phd*.69a; ἀντί τινος πάντα ibid., cf. Phld.*Vit.Herc*.1457. 10; βίον πρὸς μικρὰ κέρδη Arist.*EN*1117b20; τι ἐπ' ἀργυρίῳ Hdn. 2.13.6: abs., *exchange prisoners*, D.C.*Fr*.57.36. II. *change* a person *from enmity to friendship, reconcile*, σφέας Hdt.5.29, cf. 95, 6.108; κ. τινὰς πρὸς ἀλλήλους Arist.*Oec*.1348b9; θεὸς κόσμον κ. ἑαυτῷ 2*Ep.Cor*.5.19:—Med., καταλλάσσεσθαι τὴν ἔχθρην τινί *to make up one's* enmity with any one, Hdt.1.61, cf. 7.145:—Pass., esp. in aor. κατηλλάχθην or κατηλλάγην (former preferred by Trag., latter in Prose), *to become reconciled*, τινι E.*IA*1157, X.*An*.1.6.1, etc.; πρὸς ἀλλήλους Th.4.59; θεοῖσιν ὡς καταλλαχθῇ χόλου that *he may be reconciled* to them after his anger, S.*Aj*.744; κ. πρός τινα ἐκ διαφορᾶς Ael.*VH*2.21. 2. Pass., of an offence, *to be atoned for*, φόνον ἐπιγαμίαις μὴ καταλλάσσεσθαι μηδὲ χρήμασιν *OGI*218.105 (Ilium, iii B. C.).

καταλληλ-ία, ἡ, *systematic construction*, τῆς τεχνολογίας Nicom. *Ar*.1.20.2. **-ος**, ον, *set over against one another, correspondent*, πόροι Arist.*Pr*.905b8, cf. Thphr.*CP*6.9.2; φύσει ἅμα κατάλληλα τελειοῦται· διὸ καὶ ἀκούει τε ἅμα καὶ φωνεῖ [τὰ παιδία] Arist.*Pr*.902a 11; γλῶσσα κ. τῷ στόματι Artem.1.32, cf. Str.2.1.29; κ. κεῖσθαι to be *parallel*, of lines, S.E.*M*.3.100; τὰ κ. the *corresponding states*, Id. *P*.1.238; κ. λόγος D.H.*Th*.37; τὸ κ. τῆς διανοίας ib.31; φαντασίαι δόγμασι κ. M.Ant.7.2; τοῖς στρατιωτικοῖς ἔργοις καταλληλότερος D.C. 71.1. 2. *appropriate*, κ. καὶ κατὰ φύσιν Arr.*Epict*.1.9.9, cf. Zos.4. 53; πρὸς ὑγίειαν M.Ant.5.8. Adv. -λως, κ. λέγεσθαι prob. f.l. for κατ' ἀλλήλων, Arist.*Metaph*.1041a33, cf. *Stoic*.3.42; κ. τῇ φύσει Arr. *Epict*.1.22.9. 3. Gramm., *rightly constructed, congruent*, A.D. *Synt*.4.3, al.; also, *well-arranged, in good order*, of the text of Aristotle, Alex.Aphr.*in Metaph*.172.13 (Comp.). Adv. Comp. -ότερον ib. 37.20. II. *one after another, in succession*, neut. pl. κατάλληλα, as Adv., Plb.3.5.6, 5.31.5; *in a row*, ἑπτὰ κεφαλὰς κ. J.*AJ*3.6.7; ληφθέντα κατάλληλα taken *in corresponding order*, Euc.5.4. **-ότης**, ητος, ἡ, Gramm., *correct construction*, A.D.*Synt*.3.5, al.

κατ-ἄλοάω, *crush in pieces, make an end of*, c. acc., X.*Cyr*.7.1.31, Aeschin.2.140:—Pass., κατηλόηται Eub.15.5; τὴν ὀφρὺν κατηλοημένος Luc.*Icar*.15; cf. καταλοιάω.

καταλοβεύς, έως, ὁ, *cornice over a door*, *IG*4.1485.94 (Epid.). II. *course* laid on ὀρθοστάται, *GDI*5045 (Hierapytna).

καταλογάδην, Adv. *by way of conversation, in prose*, κ. συγγράφειν, διηγεῖσθαι, Pl.*Smp*.177b, *Ly*.204d; τὰ κ. συγγράμματα, opp. τὰ μετὰ μέτρου ποιήματα, Isoc.2.7; οἱ κ. ἴαμβοι Ath.10.445b, cf. Ph.1.694, Plu.2.316d, *IG*7.418 (Oropus), Jul.*Or*.1.3a. 2. *in detail, long-windedly*, Steph. *in Hp*.2.238 D.

καταλογεῖον, τό, *record office*, *POxy*.73.34 (i A. D.), 2134.2 (ii A. D.).

καταλογεύς, έως, ὁ, (καταλέγω (B) I. 3) *officer who enrols* citizens, Lys.20.13, Arist.*Ath*.49.2.

κατ-ἄλογέω, v. κατηλογέω.

καταλογ-ή, ἡ, (καταλέγω (B) I. 3) *enrolment, enlistment*, στρατιωτῶν D.Chr.43.10. II. (καταλέγω (B) I. 2 b) *regard, respect*, Plb.22.12. 10 codd. (-δοχῇ Reiske), cf. *SIG*739.9 (Delph., i B. C.); καταλογῆς [ἕνεκα], *honoris causa*, with gen., *IG*7.413.37 (Oropus); καταλογή σοι εἴη 'saving your reverence', prob. for καταλογισθείη, Hsch.; εἰς τὴν ἐμὴν κ. on my *recommendation*, used in letters of introduction, *PStrassb*.117.5 (i A. D.), *POxy*.787 (i A. D.), etc.; ὅπως.. κ. αὐτῶν γένηται *IG*14.951.9; condemned by Phryn.403. III. (καταλέγω (B) I. 1 b) *recitation*, opp. music, *IG*9(2).531.12 (Larissa, i B. C./i A. D.), Hsch. **-ίζομαι**, *count up, reckon*, X.*An*.5.6.16, *HG*3.2.18; κ. εὐεργέτημα πρός τινα *put* it *down to* his *account*, D.7.6; μηδ' ἐν ἀρετῇ τοῦθ' ὑμῶν μηδεὶς -λογιζέσθω let no one *impute* it as a virtue, Aeschin.3.202: c. inf., κατελογίσατο τῇ βουλῇ τὴν Ἰταλίαν ἡμερῶσαι App.*Ill*.16. II. *count, reckon among*, τοὺς ἀχαρίστους ἐν τοῖς ἀδίκοις X.*Mem*.2.2.1:—Pass., ἔν τισι -λογισθῆναι Lxx *Is*.14.10, *Wi*. 5.5. III. *recount in order*, τισὶ τὰ ἔργα τὰ ἑαυτοῦ App.*Syr*.61, cf. *Mac*.19. **-ος**, ὁ, *enrolment, register, catalogue*, Pl.*Tht*.175a, *Lg*.968c; ὀσπρίων Diocl.*Fr*.117; κ. νεῶν *the catalogue* of ships in Il. 2, Plu.*Sol*.10: prov., of a long story, νεῶν δὲ κατάλογον δόξεις μ' ἐρεῖν Apollod.Com.13.17. 2. at Athens, *register of citizens* liable for service, ὁπλίτης ἐντεθεὶς ἐν κ. Ar.*Eq*.1369; [ὁπλῖται] ἐκ καταλόγου those on *the list for service*, Th.6.43, al.; ἐκ κ. στρατευόμενος κατατέτριμμαι X.*Mem*.3.4.1; οἱ ἐν τῷ κ. Id.*HG*2.4.9; οἱ ὑπὲρ τὸν κ. the *superannuated*, opp. οἱ ἐν ἡλικίᾳ, D.13.4; of trierarchs, Id.18. 105; καταλόγους ποιεῖσθαι make up *the lists for service*, Th.6.26, D. 50.6; εἰς τὸν κ. καταλέξαι Lys.25.16; καταλόγοις χρηστοῖς ἐκκριθέν, of picked troops, Th.6.31; προγράφειν στρατιᾶς κ. Plu.*Cam*.39; τὸν κ. ἀποδιδράσκειν Luc.*Nav*.33; κ. ἀνδρῶν χιλίων *authority to conscript* 1000 recruits, Polyaen.3.3. b. *list of the* βουλή, ἐκ τοῦ κ. ἐξαλείφειν X.*HG*2.3.51. c. κατάλογοι βουλᾶς, οἱ, committee of the βουλή at Epidaurus, *IG*4.925, al.

κατ-ἄλοιάω, = καταλοάω, Phot.

καταλοιδορέω, *rail violently against*, τινα App.*Mith*.59.

κατάλοιπος, ον, *left remaining*, τὸ κ. ἀπεργάζεσθαι Pl.*Ti*.39e; ἐκ τοῦ κ. Arist.*HA*548b18, cf. *Michel*829.23 (i B. C.), etc.; τὰ κ. τῆς διεξόδου Phld.*Rh*.1.120 S.; τοῦτο.. κατάλοιπόν [ἐστι] c. inf., Strato Com. 1.10; ἡ κ. εἰσβολή Plb.3.91.9; ἡ κ. the *other* of two, Gal.7.314.

κατ-ἄλοκίζω, *cut into furrows*, κατὰ μὲν ὄνυξιν ἠλοκισμεθ' E.*Supp*. 826 (lyr.).

κατα-λούομαι, Med., *spend in bathing*, καταλόει [prob. cj. for -λούει] μου τὸν βίον Ar.*Nu*.838. **-λουστικοί**, οἱ, *members of a guild which performed ceremonial ablutions*, Keil-Premerstein *Zweiter Bericht* 183 (Lydia, ii A. D.).

καταλοφάδεια [ἄδ], Adv., (λόφος) = κατὰ τὸν λόφον, *on the neck*, βῆν δὲ καταλοφάδεια φέρων (sc. τὸν ἔλαφον) Od.10.169: by metrical lengthening for καταλοφάδια (cf. κατωμάδιος), v. Eust. ad loc.—Perh. to be read divisim, cf. λοφάδεια.

καταλοχ-ία, ἡ, = καταλοχισμός, v.l. in Lxx 2*Ch*.31.18. **-ίζω**, *form into* λόχοι, τὴν φάλαγγα Ascl.*Tact*.2.1. 2. *distribute into* λόχοι, Ael.*Tact*.2.4, Arr.*Tact*.5.2: generally, *distribute*, εἰς τάξεις D.S.18.70; εἰς ἀγέλας Plu.*Lyc*.16; εἰς τοὺς ὁπλίτας Id.*Sull*.18; εἰς τοὺς... ποιητάς Lib.*Ep*.36.1 (-ελόχησας codd.):—Pass., Plu.*Cic*. 15. **-ισμός**, ὁ, *register, enrolment*, Lxx 1*Ch*.4.33, Plu.*Cic*.15, Ael.*Tact*.15.1, Luc.*Hist.Conscr*.29: in pl., *muster-rolls*, *OGI*229.45, 47 (Smyrna, iii B. C.), *POxy*.2129.6, al. (iii A. D.). 2. *register of grants of land to military settlers*, φυλακιτῶν καὶ ἐφόδων τῶν ἐν κ. *PPetr*.3 p.230 (iii B. C.), cf. *POxy*.45 (i A. D.), etc.

κατ-αλσής, ές, (ἄλσος) *woody*, Str.5.3.11:—later **-αλσος**, ον, Eust. ad D.P.321.

καταλῠγίζω, = λυγίζω, Hsch. (Pass.).

καταλῠκουργίζω, *press the laws of Lycurgus against*, τῆς ἀνθρωποπαθείας Alciphr.2.1.

κατάλῠμα, ατος, τό, *lodging*, Plb.2.36.1 (pl.), *UPZ*120.5 (ii B. C.), Lxx *Ex*.4.24, Aristeas 181 (pl.), *Ev.Marc*.14.14, Iamb.*Bab*.13; δημόσιον κ. D.S.14.93; *billet* for troops, *PSI*4.341.8 (iii B. C.): in pl., *provision of quarters*, *IG*5(2).515 (Lycosura, i B. C./i A. D.):—Dim. **-λῠμάτιον**, τό, *PCair.Zen*.205 (iii B. C.).

καταλῠμαίνομαι, Dep., *ruin utterly, destroy*, τὸν οἶκον, τὰ σώματα, X.*Oec*.2.13, 6.5; τὰς ὀροφάς Plb.5.9.3.

καταλῠμᾰκόομαι, (λῦμαξ) Pass., *to be silted up*, *Tab.Heracl*.1.56.

καταλύμανσις [ῠ], εως, ἡ, *ravaging*, *Gloss*.

κατάλυπρος, ον, *sad*, ὄμμα κ., στίλβον, dub. in Herod.Med. in *Rh. Mus*.58.96 (v. l. ὄμματα καταλίπαρα).

κατα-λύσιμος [ῠ], ον, *to be dissolved* or *done away*, κακόν S.*El*.1247 (lyr.). **-λῠσις**, εως, ἡ, *dissolution, putting down*, esp. of governments, ἡ τῶν τυράννων κ. ἐκ τῆς Ἑλλάδος Th.1.18; τοῦ δήμου And.1. 36, Lys.13.20; τῆς παρούσης πολιτείας Pl.*Lg*.864d; τῆς ἀρχῆς X.*Cyr*. 8.1.47, cf. Arist.*Pol*.1305b3, al.; Κρόνου Phld.*Piet*.94: generally, τὴν τῶν πονηρῶν ὁμιλίαν κ. εἶναι ἀρετῆς X.*Mem*.1.2.20; κ. χρείας Gal.9. 44. 2. *dismissal, disbanding* of a body of men, στρατιᾶς X.*Cyr*. 6.1.13; κ. τριήρους *breaking up* of a ship's crew, D.50.11; εἰς κατάλυσιν till *dismissal*, of soldiers at a review, X.*Eq.Mag*.3.12. 3. κ. πολέμου *pacification*, Th.8.18, X.*Mem*.2.8.1, Isoc.6.51. 4. generally, *end, termination*, συμποσίου X.*Smp*.9.7; βίου Id.*Ap*.30, *PMagd*. 8.10 (iii B. C.). 5. *settlement* of disputes, *IG*5(2).357.21 (Stymphalus, iii B. C.). 6. *feebleness, impotence*, χειρῶν καὶ σκελέων Hp. *Epid*.4.53. II. *resting, lodging*, δεξώμεθ' οἴκων καταλύσεις E. *El*.393; κ. ποιεῖσθαι to *rest*, Plb.2.15.5. 2. = κατάλυμα, *resting-place, guest-chamber, quarters, lodging*, σταθμοὶ καὶ καταλύσιες (Ion.) κάλλισται Hdt.5.52; ξένοις κ. ποιεῖν Pl.*Prt*.315d, cf. *Lg*.919a (pl.), Antiph.15, Alex.2.2, Dicaearch.1.6 (pl.), *IG*4.203 (Corinth); κ. βασιλική *PPetr*.3 p.137 (iii B. C.). 3. pl., *billets* for troops, *PHal*. 1.168 (iii B. C.). **-λῠτέος**, α, ον, *to be put down*, τύραννος κ. ἐστίν Chio *Ep*.15.2. II. neut., *one must put down*, κ. ἐστὶ τύραννον D.S.14.65. 2. *one must rest*, Suid. s. v. διασκηνητέον. **-λῠτήρ**, ῆρος, ὁ, *arbitrator*, *IG*5(2).357.36 (Stymphalus, iii B. C.). **-λῠτήριον**, τό, = κατάλυμα, Poll.1.73. **-λύτης** [ῠ], ου, ὁ, *lodger, stranger*, Plb. 15.6, Plu.*Sull*.25. II. *arbitrator*, *IG*5(2).357.15. **-λῠτικός**, ή, όν, *able to dissolve* or *put an end to*, ὑδέρων Antyll.ap.Orib.6.28.1; ποιότητες κ. τῶν δυνάμεων Gal.11.97. **-λύω**, fut. -λύσω Od.4.28: 3 pl. plpf. -λελύκεσαν Hdn.8.4.2:—Pass., fut. -λυθήσομαι Pl.*Lg*.714c, D. 38.22 (fut. Med. in pass. sense, v. infr. I. 2 a): pf. -λέλῠμαι Th.6.36:—*put down, destroy*, πολλάων πολίων κατέλυσε κάρηνα Il.2.117, 9.24; τείχη, [πτόλιν], E.*Tr*.819, 1080 (both lyr.); γέφυραν *break it up*, Hdn. l. c. 2. of political or other systems, *dissolve, break up, put down*, κ. ἀρχήν, βασιληΐην, ἰσοκρατίας, Hdt.1.53, 54, 5.92.α'; τοῦ Διὸς τὴν δύναμιν Ar.*Pl*.142; τὸ κράτος τῆς βουλῆς Plu.*Per*.7; τὰς προσόδους τὰς Μιλησίων *SIG*633.40 (Milet., ii B. C.): freq. in Att., κ. τὸν δῆμον Ar.*Ec*. 453, Th.3.81; τὴν δημοκρατίαν Ar.*Pl*.948; τὰς πολιτείας Decr.ap.D. 18.182:—Pass., καταλελυμένης τῆς δημοκρατίας Lex ap.And.1.96, cf.

95, Lys.13.4, Arist.*Pol.*1292ᵃ29: fut. Med. as Pass., καταλύσεται..ἡ ἀρχή (Cobet καταλελύσεται) X.*Cyr.*1.6.9. b. c. acc. pers., *put down, depose*, κ. τύραννον Th.1.18, etc.; κ. τινὰ τῆς ἀρχῆς X.*Cyr.*8.5.24:—Pass., τῶν ἄλλων καταλελυμένων στρατηγῶν *having been dismissed*, Hdt.6.43; καταλυθῆναι τῆς ἀρχῆς Id.1.104, cf. 6.9. c. *dissolve, dismiss, disband* a body, καταλύειν τὴν βουλήν, τὸν στόλον, Id.5.72, 7.16.β'; τῶν πόλεων τά τε βουλευτήρια καὶ τὰς ἀρχὰς Th.2.15; τὸ ναυτικόν D.18.102 (Pass.). d. *abolish* or *annul* laws, customs, etc., δίκην Gorg.*Pal.*17; νόμους Isoc.6.66 (Pass.), Plb.3.8.2, cf. *Ev.Matt.*5.17; ψήφισμα *Michel*725.20 (ii B.C.); also κ. τὸν ἱππέα *render* him *useless*, X.*Eq.*12.5. e. τὴν φυλακὴν κ. *neglect* the watch, Ar.*V.*2, cf. Arist.*Pol.*1308ᵃ29; τὴν φρουράν Pl.*Lg.*762c; τὴν κοινὴν φυλακὴν καταλυθῆναι βούλεται Din.1.112. f. κ. τὴν τριηραρχίαν *lay* it *down*, Isoc.18.59; τὴν ἄσκησιν, v. infr. 3a. 3. *bring to an end*, τὸν βίον X.*Ap.*7; ἐς Ἅιδαν καταλύσουσ' ἔμμοχθον βίοτον E.*Supp.*1004 (lyr.); μώμου ἀδικίαν καὶ δόξης ἀμαθίαν Gorg.*Hel.*21; ἐλπίδα Th.2.89; δόξα, ἣν αἰσχρόν ἐστιν ἐν σοὶ -λῦσαι D.10.73; κ. τὸ πλεῖν, τὴν ἄροσιν, Id.33.4, Ael.*NA*13.1; κ. τὰς θυσίας Lys.30.17, Isoc.6.68; τὰ γυμνάσια And.4.39; τὸν λόγον Aeschin.2.126, Isoc.12.176; τοὺς λόγους περὶ τὰ μέγιστα κ. ib.199: abs., *make an end*, ὥρᾳ κ. *die* in good time, Diocl.Com.14, cf. Philostr.*VA*8.28; πύκτης ὢν κατέλυσε *retired* from the ring, *AP*11.79 (Lucill.), cf. 161 (Id.) (in full -λῦσαι τὴν ἄσκησιν Gal.*Protr.*14); καθάπερ ἐν τοῖς χοροῖς ἐν τῷ καταλύειν in the *ending*, Arist.*Pr.*921ᵃ20: also pf. part. Pass. καταλελυμένος *disused, obsolete*, Phld.*Mus.*p.68 K. b. κ. τὴν ὑπάρχουσαν εἰρήνην *break* the peace, Aeschin.3.55; but, c. more commonly, κ. τὸν πόλεμον *end* the war, make peace, Ar.*Lys.*112, Th.7.31, X.*An.*5.7.27, etc.; δίκας *settle* disputes, *IG*5(2).357.15 (Stymphalus, iii B.C.): abs. (sc. τὸν πόλεμον), Foed.ap.Th.5.23; πρός τινα Foed.ib.8.58:—more freq. in Med., καταλύσασθαι τὰς ἔχθρας, *componere inimicitias*, Hdt.7.146; τὸν πόλεμον And.3.17, Th.6.36; στάσιν Ar.*Ra.*359: abs., *make peace*, Hdt.8.140.α', Th.1.81, X.*HG*6.8.6, etc.; καταλύεσθαί τινι *come to terms with* one, Hdt.9.11, etc. 4. Pass., ἤδη καταλελυμένης τῆς ἡλικίας in the *decay* of life, Arist.*Pol.*1335ᵃ34. II. *unloose, unyoke*, καταλύσομεν ἵππους Od.4.28; τὸ σῶμα τοῦ ἀδελφεοῦ κ. *take* it *down* from the wall where it was hung up, Hdt.2.121.γ':—Pass., *to be taken down* from hanging, Hp.*Aph.*2.43. 2. intr., *take up one's quarters, lodge*, παρ' ἐμοὶ καταλύει he *is* my *guest*, Pl.*Grg.*447b, cf. *Prt.*311a, D.18.82: abs., Pl.*Prt.*315d: c. acc., κ. παρά τινα *turn off* the road to a person's house, *go and lodge* with him, Th.1.136; κ. εἰς πανδοκεῖον Aeschin.2.97; Μεγαροῖ Pl.*Tht.*142c; ἐν τῷ ἱαρῷ *SIG*978.8 (Cnidos, iii B.C.):—Med., θανάτῳ καταλυσαίμαν *may I take my rest* in the grave, E.*Med.*146 (anap.).

καταλωβάω, *mutilate*, Plb.15.33.9.

καταλωφάω, Ion. -έω, *rest from* a thing, κάδ δέ κ' ἐμὸν κῆρ λωφήσειε κακῶν Od.9.459. II. trans., *give rest from*, κούρην δ' ἐξ ἀχέων ..καταλώφεεν ὕπνος A.R.3.616.

καταμαγγᾰνεύω, *subdue by sorceries*, gloss on καταγοητεύω, Hsch. (prob.).

καταμάγεῖον, τό, (μάσσω) *cloth for wiping*, Artem.1.64.

καταμᾰγεύω, *bewitch*, Luc.*Nec.*7.

καταμᾰθημᾰτικεύω, *reduce to mathematical terms*, in Med., -εύσατο τὴν φύσιν Phlp.*in de An.*481.34.

καταμάθ-ησις [μᾰ], εως, ἡ, *thorough knowledge*, Hermog.*Id.*2.7, Plot.3.8.6. **-ητέον**, *one must learn thoroughly, observe closely*, Hp.*Aph.*6.5. **-ητικός**, ή, όν, *apt at learning*, Poll.9.152.

καταμαίνομαι, aor. Pass. -εμάνην [ᾰ], *do mad acts against*, τῶν Ἰουδαίων Ph.2.542, cf. J.*BJ*7.8.1.

καταμάκτης, ου, ὁ, (μάσσω) *one who wipes off*, Gloss.

κατάμακτος, ον, *cast, moulded*, of votive offerings, σῶμα, οὖς, *IG*2².1534.45,48.

καταμᾰλᾰκίζω, in Pass., *to be* or *become soft* or *effeminate*, X.*Oec.*11.12, Arist.*MM*1202ᵇ37, 1203ᵇ7.

καταμᾰλάσσω, Att. -ττω, *soften*, σώματα ἐλαίῳ Luc.*Anach.*24: metaph., *appease*, Id.*JTr.*24, Ach.Tat.6.19; τοῦ θυμοῦ τὸ φλεγμαῖνον Hld.7.21.

καταμαλθᾰκίζομαι, Pass., *to be enervated*, Pl.*Ep.*329b.

καταμαλθάσσω, = καταμαλάσσω, Hsch.

καταμανθάνω, pf. -μεμάθηκα Hp.*Art.*8, X.*Cyr.*1.1.1:—*observe well, examine closely*, τὴν στρατιήν Hdt.7.146; τὸν Οἰνέα Timocl.6.16, cf. 10; τὸ τραῦμα Plu.*Dio* 34; *look to, inspect*, τὸν ἐλαιῶνα *PFay.*114.11 (100 A.D.); κ. ἥν που.. X.*Oec.*12.3. 2. *learn, acquire knowledge of*, Pl.*Tht.*198d, etc.; ὑπακούειν how to obey, v.l. in X.*Oec.*13.7. 3. *perceive with the senses, observe*, Arist.*Pr.*960ᵃ7: more commonly with the mind, *understand, perceive, observe*, οὐκ ὀρθῶς κ. Pl.*Prm.*128a; εἰ ἄρα μου καταμανθάνετε ὃ λέγω Id.*Lg.*689c; ἐκ τῶν νόμων κ. τοὺς λόγους εἰ ὀρθῶς.. Antipho 5.14; κ. ὁπόσα θνητῇ φύσει δυνατὰ Pl.*Epin.*986c; κ. ὅτι.. Hp. l. c.; ῥᾴδιον τοῦτο κ., ὅτι.. Arist.*Pol.*1285ᵃ1: pf., *to be aware*, Λυκοῦργον -μεμάθηκας ὅτι.. X.*Mem.*4.4.15: c. acc. et part., κ. πολλοὺς ἔχοντάς τι Id.*Cyr.*1.1.1; καταμαθόντες μιν ἀγοράζοντα Hdt.4.164; κ. τινὰ θύοντα X.*Mem.*1.4.2; καταμαθὼν δὲ..καταστασιαζόμενος that a party was being formed against him, Id.*HG* 1.6.4: καταμαθεῖν τοῦ Κύρου δοκοῦμεν, ὡς.. Id.*Cyr.*8.1.40. 4. *consider*, τι Id.*An.*3.1.44; ὅτι.. Id.*Cyr.*7.5.80, etc.

καταμαντ-εία, ἡ, *divination*, Jul.Laod. in *Cat.Cod.Astr.*5(1).190 (pl.). **-εύομαι**, *foretell against* or *about* one, τι τῶν ἐχθρῶν J.*BJ* 4.4.6; ⟨αὐτὸς⟩ αὐτοῦ σιωπὴν κ. Ath.15.686c; τοῦτο τῇ πόλει, c. fut. inf., App.*Pun.*77. 2. *divine, surmise*, ἐκ τῶν προγεγονότων τὰ μέλλοντα -μαντευόμενοι κρίνομεν Arist.*Rh.*1368ᵃ31; κ. τὸ μέλλον Plb.2.22.7, etc.: c. gen., ἰητροῦ ἐστι -μαντεύσασθαι τῶν τοιούτων Hp.*Art.*9; κ. τῆς τῶν ποιημάτων διανοίας Ath.14.634d; τοῦ εἰκότως συμβαίνοντος Hierocl. *in CA*10 p.437 M.; κ. περὶ τῶν γυναικῶν, ὁποῖαι.. Nicostr. ap.Stob.4.22.102, cf. Gal.15.907; ὑπέρ τινος Onos.36.2.

κατ-ᾰμαξεύω, v. καθαμαξεύω.

καταμᾰραίνω, aor. -εμάρανα Ph.1.266:—*cause to wither*, Thphr.*Ign.*10, Ph. l. c.; *make lean*, Luc.*Tim.*17:—Pass., *die away*, of dropsical swellings, Hp.*Prorrh.*2.6; τὸ πῦρ κ. Arist.*Resp.*479ᵃ14, cf. Thphr.*HP*5.9.3, etc.; τὸ πάθος (sc. τοῦ σεισμοῦ) κ. Arist.*Mete.*368ᵃ7; of persons, πρὶν ἀνθῆσαι..κ. Plu.2.804e.

καταμαργάω, Ion. -έω, *to be stark mad, rave*, φθόνῳ Hdt.8.125.

καταμάρπτω, *catch*, ὥς κεν ἔμ' ἔντοσθεν πόλιος καταμάρψῃ ἐόντα Il.6.364; esp. *catch, overtake* one running away, ὅτε δὴ κατέμαρπτε διώκων 5.65, cf. 16.598, Pi.*N.*3.35; κατὰ γαῖ' αὐτόν τέ νιν καὶ..ἵππους ἔμαρψεν Id.*O.*6.14; ἐπεὶ κατὰ γῆρας ἔμαρψεν Od.24.390; ἄλλον δ' οὐ -έμαρψε δίκη Thgn.207; κρέσσον ἔσφαλε τέχνα -μάρψαισ' Pi.*I.*4(3).35; κατὰ ματέρα πότμος ἔμαρψε *IG*14.1389 i 17.

καταμαρτῠρέω, *bear witness against*, τινος Antipho 2.4.10, D.19.120, 29.9, Mitteis *Chr.*31 v 33 (ii B.C.), etc.; κατά τινος D.28.3, etc.: c. acc. rei, ψευδῆ κ. τινός Id.45.46 (Docum.), 29.2, Is.5.12, cf. *Ev.Matt.*26.62: abs., αὐτὸ τὸ ψήφισμα τῆς βουλῆς—μαρτυρήσει Lys.13.28:—Pass., *have evidence given against* one, μὴ πιστῶς καταμαρτυρηθείς Antipho 2.4.7; κ. ὑπὸ τοῦ βίου τοῦ ἑαυτοῦ *to be convicted*, Aeschin.1.90. 2. Pass., of evidence, *to be given against* one, ἃ καταμαρτυρεῖται αὐτοῦ Is.5.25, cf. 6.15: abs., D.29.55. II. *assert concerning*, οὐδὲν κ. τῶν οὐ παρόντων Plot.5.5.13. III. Astrol., *exercise malign influence over*, '*aspect*', Vett.Val.104.2.

καταμαρτύρομαι [ῡ], *bear witness against*, *IG*2.4322.34.

καταμᾰσάομαι, *chew, bite*, γλῶσσαν Hp.*Epid.*5.53 (= 7.74): metaph., ἅπαντα κ. Alex.105.

καταμάσσω, *wipe off*, Hld.1.2, Palaeph. in Westermann Μυθογράφοι p.310; *wipe*, τὰς χεῖρας *EM*587.48, cf. *PMag.Osl.*1.213:—Med., Luc.*Asin.*10. 2. *rub, shampoo* after a bath, *Edict.Diocl.*7.75 (Pass.).

καταμαστῑγόω, *scourge*, v.l. in Lib.*Decl.*26.20 (Pass.).

καταμαστίζω, *reverbero*, Gloss.

κατάμαστρος, ον, (μαστροί) = ὑπεύθυνος, *liable to condemnation*, ἱερῶν χρημάτων φωρᾶς *GDI*2642.21 (Delph.).

καταματτεύομαι, Pass., *to be tickled*, πτερῷ (as an emetic) Hp.*Int.*6, 27 (v.l. **-ματευόμενος**):—also **-ματέομαι** Gal.19.109; **-μάττομαι** Hp.*Int.*12 (v.l. **-ματτεόμενος**).

καταμάχ-ησις [μᾰ], εως, ἡ, *subduing, conquest*, Gloss. **-ομαι**, pf. -μεμάχημαι Plu.*Flam.*3:—*subdue by fighting, conquer*, τινα l. c.; πύκτην Paus.6.11.2: metaph., *overcome*, τὴν ὑπερβολὴν τῆς εὐωδίας D.S.3.47.

κατ-ᾱμάω, once in Hom. in Med., *scrape up, heap up*, τήν ῥα (sc. τὴν κόπρον) κυλινδόμενος καταμήσατο χερσὶν ἑῇσι Il.24.165; τὸν χοῦν καταμήσονται (Mein. for κατακοιμήσονται) Pherecr.121: c. gen., *heap upon*, καταμώμενοι τῆς κεφαλῆς κόνιν J.*BJ*2.15.4, v.l. ib.2.21.3. II. κατ' αὖ νιν..νερτέρων ἀμᾷ κοπίς (Jortin for κόνις) *cuts* it *down, reaps* it *like corn*, S.*Ant.*601 (lyr.); if κόνις is retained, καταμᾷ must be rendered *covers over*.

καταμβλᾰκεύω, = καταβλ–, Aret.*CD*1.1, Apollon.Cit.3.

καταμβλ-ύνω, *blunt, dull*, κατημβλύνθη κέντρον *AP*5.219 (Agath.): metaph., παρεὶς καὶ καταμβλύνων κέαρ S.*OT*688. **-υόω**, = foreg., τὸ κατημβλυωμένον Diph.18.7.

καταμεγᾰλ-αυχέομαι, strengthd. for μεγαλαυχέομαι, in aor., Hsch. **-ύνομαι**, *exalt oneself against*, τινος Aq., Thd., Sm.*Ps.*40(41).10.

καταμεθύσκω, aor. -εμέθυσα, causal, *make drunk*, Hdt.1.106, 2.121.ε', Pl.*Grg.*471b, etc.; εὐτυχία -ύσκουσα τοῖς ἀγαθοῖς τὰν διάνοιαν Archyt.ap.Stob.3.1.114:—Pass., *to be made quite drunk*, ὑπό τινος D.S.4.84: abs., *get drunk*, Plb.5.39.2.

καταμεθύω, *rave in drunken style against*, τινος Ph.1.361.

κατ-ᾰμείβω, in Pass., *to be divided between*, -μειφθεὶς δύο τισίν f.l. in *EM*358.44 (fort. -μερισθείς).

καταμείγνῡμι or -ύω, *mix in, combine*, καταμειγνύντας τούς τε μετοίκους κτλ. Ar.*Lys.*580; τὴν φροντίδα καταμείξας..εἰς τὸν ὅμοιον ἀέρα Id.*Nu.*230; τὴν προῖκα εἰς τὴν οὐσίαν D.30.10; τινὰ εἰς ὑμᾶς αὐτοὺς Id.25.63; συμπόταις ἑαυτόν Plu.2.148a; δένδρα τοῖς φυτοῖς ib.648c; τοῖς ἀλαιοῖς ἀρετῆς τινα ζῆλον Id.*Lyc.*27:—Pass., [ὕδωρ] καταμεμειγμένον ἐς τὸν ἠέρα Hp.*Aër.*8; τούτοις καταμεμεῖχθαι τοιαύτην δύναμιν Arist.*Spir.*485ᵇ10; οἱ στρατιῶται εἰς τὰς πόλεις κατεμείγνυντο, i.e. *were mingled* with the citizens, X.*An.*7.2.3; εἰς γένος Plu.*Cat.Ma.*20.

καταμειδιάω, *smile at, despise*, θανάτου J.*BJ*3.7.33.

καταμεικτέον, *one must mix*, Paul.Aeg.3.14.

καταμειλίσσομαι, Att. -ττομαι, *appease*, τὸν θυμόν τινος J.*AJ*6.13.7.

κατάμειξις, εως, ἡ, *admixture*, Arist.*Pr.*868ᵇ4, Anon.Rhythm. *Oxy.*4.12, Dsc.*Alex.Praef.* (pl.); ἡ πρὸς τὸ σῶμα κ. τοῦ οἴνου Plu.2.1110a (-μειξ– Anon.Rhythm. l. c., -μιξ– freq. in codd.).

καταμελαίνω, *make black, darken*, in Pass., ὁ ἀὴρ -εμελαίνετο Agath.5.3.

καταμελεϊστί, Adv. *limb by limb*, Arat.624 [κατᾰ–, metri gr.].

καταμελετάω, *train fully, exercise*, τινα Pl.*Phlb.*55e:—Pass., ib.57a; τὴν ἀνδρείαν ἐν τοῖς φόβοις δεῖ -μελετᾶσθαι Id.*Lg.*649c. 2. *study carefully*, for the purpose of composing, τὸν ἔπαινον περί τινος Id.*Clit.*410b; ῥητορικήν Phld.*Rh.*1.236 S.; λόγον Them.*Or.*26.312b.

κατ-ᾰμελέω, *give no heed to*, c. gen., ὁδοιπορίης, ἐδωδῆς, Hp.*Art.*14, cf. X.*Oec.*4.7, J.*AJ*18.6.9 (Med.); *neglect*, τῶν προσηκόντων ἔργων

BGU195.19 (ii A.D.): folld. by relat. clause, ὁπόθεν δὲ καταφαγεῖν ἔχοι, τούτου κατημέληκεν Eup.352: abs., *pay no heed*, S.*Aj*.45,912 (lyr.), Pl.*Ti*.44c, D.S.29.3 (nisi leg. -μέλλ-), etc.: c. acc., *ruin by neglect*, μηδὲν κ. X.*HG*6.2.39; τὰ πράγματα Antipho Soph.76:—Pass., *to be neglected*, Hp.*Art*.60: pf. part. κατημελημένος Isoc.12.8.

καταμελῐτόω, *spread with honey*: metaph., of the nightingale's voice, κατεμελίτωσε τὴν λόχμην ὅλην Ar.*Av*.224.

καταμέλλω, *procrastinate*, Plb.4.30.2, al., Phld.*Herc*.1251.8.

κατάμεμπτος, ον, *blamed by all, abhorred*, γῆρας S.*OC*1235 (lyr.): neut. pl. as Adv., οὔ τοι κατάμεμπτ' ἔβητον ye have fared not *so as to have cause to find fault*, ib.1696 (lyr.).

καταμέμφομαι, fut. -μέμψομαι Phld.*Oec*.p.74 J.: aor. Pass. -εμέμφθην in act. sense, Pi.*N*.11.30; also in pass. sense, *Sammelb*.5357.11 (v A.D.):—*find fault with*; esp. with a sense of *distrust in oneself*, ἰσχὺν Pi. l. c.; τὴν δύναμιν τὴν σφετέραν αὐτῶν Isoc.15.61, cf. 5.110; σφᾶς αὐτοὺς Th.8.106, cf. D.22.27; ἐμαυτόν, ὡς.. Pl.*Men*.71b; τὴν ἐμαυτοῦ ἡλικίαν D.29.1: more generally, *blame, censure*, τὴν τυραννίδα ἔν τινι X.*Hier*.8.6; τὴν ἱστορίαν D.S.20.43; ὑμᾶς αὐτοὺς ταῖς ξυμφοραῖς *blame for*.., Th.7.77; ἐπί τινι Plb.5.87.4; τινος Plu.*Dio*8, Sch.Arat.147 (v. l.), Nicom.*Exc*.4 (v. l.); ὅτι.. D.S.15.6: c. dat. rei, *AP*11.57 (Agath.), Anon.ap.Suid., Longus 2.21, Ps.-Luc.*Philopatr*.27; *disparage*, Σωκράτην Phld.*Piet*.77.

κατάμεμψις, εως, ἡ, *blaming, finding fault with*, κ. σφῶν αὐτῶν πολλὴ ἦν Th.7.75, cf. Plu.*Mar*.39; οὐκ ἔχει τινὶ κατάμεμψιν it leaves him no *ground for censure*, Th.2.41, cf. J.*AJ*6.6.3.

καταμένω, fut. -μενῶ Men.*Epit*.197:—*stay*, Thgn.1373, Hdt.2.103,121.δ', etc.; ἐνθάδ' αὐτοῦ κ. Ar.*Pl*.1187; ἐνταῦθα X.*Cyr*.1.4.17; κ. ἐν τοῖς δήμοις Lys.31.18; παρά τινι Eub.21; *reside*, *PHal*.1.183 (iii B.C.), *Act.Ap*.1.13; ἐν ἐποικίῳ *PFay*.24 (ii A.D.), etc. 2. *remain fixed, continue* in a state, ἐν τοῖς ὑπηρετικοῖς ὅπλοις X.*Cyr*.2.1.18; ἐπὶ τῶν αὐτῶν Gal.6.328; ἔν τινι Id.2.27; ἐπὶ τοῖς ὑπάρχουσι Nymphod.21: abs., τῆς εἰωθυίας ἀρχῆς καταμενούσης X.*Cyr*.3.1.30.

κατ-ᾰμέργω, strengthd. for ἀμέργω, Poll.1.225.

καταμερ-ίζω, *cut in pieces*, [τὸν Πλοῦτον] εἰς πολλά Luc.*Tim*.12; λίθους εἰς μεγέθη D.S.5.13: metaph., εἰς πολλὰς ταλαιπωρίας τὸν θάνατον Id.3.40:—Pass., of flavours, *to be resolved* into components, Thphr.*Od*.65. 2. *distribute*, τὰ βοεικὰ ζεύγη τοῖς λοχαγοῖς κατεμερίσθη X.*An*.7.5.4; κ. εἰς λόχους, = καταλοχίζω, Ascl.*Tact*.2.1:—Med., ἕκαστόν τι εἰς τὴν ἑαυτοῦ φύσιν Thphr.*CP*5.2.5. **-ισις**, εως, ἡ, *division into parts*, Epicur.*Ep*.2 p.48 U.; *distribution*, τῶν μερῶν Metrod.*Herc*.831.10. **-ισμός**, ὁ, = foreg., Lxx *Jo*.13.14.

καταμέστ-ιος, ον, poet. for sq., *quite full*, Nic.*Al*.45. **-ος**, ον, strengthd. for μεστός, gloss on κατάπαστος, Sch.Ar.*Eq*.500. **-όω**, *fill quite full of* a thing, τινος Pherecr.145.28.

καταμετρ-έω, *measure out*, [σῖτον] τοῖσι ἐπικούροισι Hdt.3.91; of a garden, X.*Oec*.4.21; μεγέθη, πέρατα, Epicur.*Ep*.1 p.17 U., *Sent*.19; ὑμῖν αὐτοῖς τὰ ὅρια Lxx *Nu*.34.10:—Med., ἐν τῷ -μετρεῖσθαι ὑμᾶς τὴν γῆν ib.*Ez*.45.1; of castrametation, Plb.6.41.4; *assign* land held by military tenure, τῶν -μεμετρημένων [κλήρων] *PPetr*.2 intr.p.22 (iii B.C.), cf. *PCair.Zen*.245.2 (iii B.C.), al.; also of the grantees, τοὺς -μεμετρημένους ἱππεῖς *PHal*.15.5 (iii B.C.), cf. *PLille* 14.3 (iii B.C.). 2. *measure exactly, be the measure of*, μόριον ὃ -μετρήσει τὴν ὅλην Arist.*Ph*.237^{b}28 (for wh. ἀναμ- is used 238^{a}22); τὰ -μετροῦντά τινων *aliquot parts*, Id.*Metaph*.1023^{b}15:—Pass., ὁ λόγος -μετρεῖται συλλαβῇ Id.*Cat*.4^{b}33: esp. in Metric, of feet or rhythms, D.H.*Comp*.17, cf. *Dem*.39. **-ημα**, ατος, τό, *unit of measurement*, Epicur.*Ep*.1 p.17 U. **-ησις**, εως, ἡ, *measuring out*, Plb.6.41.5, S.E.*M*.1.46; τῆς τοῦ σώματος ἰδέας Iamb.*Myst*.10.5. **-ητέον**, *one must measure*, S.E.*M*.6.65. **-ητικός**, ή, όν, *of* or *for measuring*, ἡμερῶν καὶ νυκτῶν Epicur.*Herc*.1413.10; πλάτους S.E.*M*.3.73, 9.427.

καταμηγγές· παρακμὴ σώματος, Hsch. (Corruption of Od.14.214.)

καταμηκύνω, *lengthen out*, Gal.1.246; ἀκτῖνας Ptol.*Tetr*.100.

καταμηλόω, *put in the probe*, so as to sound wounds, Suid., Phot., etc.; or to produce vomiting, ἔμει καταμηλῶν Phryn.Com.62: metaph., κημὸν κ. *use* the funnel of the ballot-jar *as a probe*, i.e. *make* a peculator *disgorge* what he has stolen, Ar.*Eq*.1150 (lyr.). 2. κ. τὰ ἔρια *plunge* them into dyestuff, Poll.7.169.

καταμηνι-αῖα, τά, (μήν) = sq. II. 2, *Gloss*. **-ος**, ον, *monthly*, of wages, *IG*1^{2}.339.30, al.; καθάρσεις Ph.1.45; αἷμα Gal.*UP*14.3. 2. *hired by the month*, *BGU*1521 (iii B.C.), *POxy*.2155.8 (iv A.D.). II. Subst. καταμηνίη, ἡ (sc. κάθαρσις), = καταμήνια, τά, prob. in *IG*12(5).646 (Ceos). 2. τὰ κ. *menses of women*, Hp.*Aph*.3.28, Arist.*GA*727^{a}18, al., Plot.2.9.12, etc.: sg. -μήνιον, τό, Arist.*HA*573^{a}16, Gal.8.423, Speus.ap.Alex.Aphr.*in Metaph*.699.31. **-ώδης**, ες, *subject to menstruation*, Arist.*GA*748^{a}20. 2. *menstruous*, περίττωμα ib.751^{a}3.

καταμήν-ῡσις, εως, ἡ, *information*, Him.*Ecl*.4.18; as law-term, Just.*Nov*.115.3.7. **-υτής**, οῦ, ὁ, *informer*, *Cod.Just*.10.11.8 *Intr*. **-ύω**, *point out, make known*, κ. διὰ γραμμάτων τοὺς οὔρους Hdt.7.30; τόδ' ἐγὼ καταμηνύσω A.*Pr*.176 (anap.), cf. Plu.*Them*.23, etc.; κ. ἑωυτὸν ὡς εἴη Ἱστιαῖος Hdt.6.29; τὸν Ὅμηρον ὅτι.. Phld.*Hom*.p.54 O.:—Pass., Jul.*ad Ath*.273d. 2. *inform against*, τινος Lys.13.49, cf. D.24.60; also τινὰς πρός τινα D.H.4.43:—Pass., ὑπό τινος -μηνυθεὶς ib.62, cf. *Cod.Just*.10.11.8.4. 3. of a god, *give a sign*, X.*HG*3.3.2.

καταμηρίζω, = διαμηρίζω, Suid. s.v. καταγιγαρτίσαι.

καταμήσας· καθάπαξ, Hsch.

καταμηχᾰνάομαι, *plan and execute*, Plot.4.4.31.

καταμῐαίνω, *defile*, ψεύδεσιν -μιάναις γένναν Pi.*P*.4.100; [τὰ καλὰ] Pl.*Lg*.937d; τὸ φῶς Luc.*Cat*.27:—Pass., *wear squalid garments* as a sign of grief, Hdt.6.58.

καταμῐαιφονέομαι, *defile oneself with bloodshed*, Heraclit.*Ep*.7.6.

καταμίγας, f.l. for κατὰ μόνας, Gal.18(2).774.

καταμίγνυμι, later spelling of καταμείγνυμι.

καταμιεῖ· καταπίνει, κατεσθίει· μιεῖν γὰρ τὸ ἐσθίειν, Hsch.

καταμῑμέομαι, *burlesque*, c. acc., D.H.7.72.

καταμιμνήσκομαι, = μιμνήσκομαι, Lxx 4*Ma*.13.12.

κατάμιξις, v. κατάμειξις.

καταμίσγω, = καταμείγνυμι, Str.1.2.9:—Med., Nic.*Al*.353:—Pass., *h.Pan*.26.

καταμισθο-δοτέω, *corrupt by high pay*, D.H.4.31. **-φορέω**, *spend in paying* δικασταί, ἐκκλησιασταί, etc., Ar.*Eq*.1352, v. Sch.; κ. τὰ ὑπάρχοντα *in paying mercenaries*, Aeschin.2.131; κ. προσόδους Theopomp.Hist.90; πλοῦτον εἰς τοὺς πολεμίους D.H.*Dem*.20: c. dat., ξενικοῖς στρατεύμασι Id.4.23.

κατάμῐτον, Adv. *in a series, one after another*, παντὸς ὀργάνου κ. ἧπται Protagorid.2. (Perh. rather κατὰ μίτον, cf. μίτος, μίττος.)

κατάμιττα or **κατὰ μίττα**, perh. = εὐτενῆ, of dressing stones, *IG* 2^{2}.1670.18; cf. foreg. and μίτος, μίττος.

καταμνημονεύω, *call to mind*, Plu.2.748f, 974e, Gal.17(1).515.

καταμνίω, = κατεσθίω, Phot.; cf. καταμιεῖ.

καταμοιχ-εύω, *seduce*, *PMasp*.4.17 (vi A.D.). **-ος**, ὁ, *adulterer*, Vett.Val.117.9.

καταμολύνω, *defile utterly*, in Pass., Sch.E.*Hec*.912.

κατάμομφος, ον, *liable to blame, inauspicious*, A.*Ag*.145 (lyr.).

καταμόνᾱς, Adv. *alone, apart*, better divisim κατὰ μόνας, v. μόνος B.III.

καταμονή, ἡ, *a remaining*, Plb.3.79.12, Ael.*NA*9.46, A.D.*Synt*.310.19, Artem.5.70.

καταμονίη, ἡ, = foreg., only found in poet. form καμμονίη (q.v.).

καταμονομᾰχέω, *conquer in single combat*, Plu.*Thes*.11, Ael.*VH*10.22.

κατάμονος, ον, *permanent*, *SIG*141.8 (Corc. Nigr., iv B.C.); τιμαί Plb.39.3.9, *IG*5(1).1432.16 (Messene, i B.C.); ψαφίσματα *SIG*563.8 (Aetol., from Teos, iii B.C.). 2. ἐψηφίσατο τὸν πόλεμον κ. εἶναι should *continue*, Plb.18.12.1, cf. 21.2.6, al.

καταμόσχ-ευσις, εως, ἡ, *propagation by suckers*, *Gloss*. **-εύω**, *propagate by suckers*, ib.

καταμουσίζω, *charm with song*, Men.Rh.p.408 S.

κατάμουσον· κατάκρυψον, Hsch. (i.e. -μυσον).

καταμουσόω, *embellish*, Jul.*Ep*.10.

κατ-άμπελος, ον, *wine-growing*, χώρα Str.4.1.5.

κατ-αμπέχω and **-ίσχω**, *encompass*, εὔψυχον ἄνδρα κούφη καταμπίσχουσιν ἐν τύμβῳ χθονί, i.e. bury him, E.*Hel*.853; μηκάδων μέλη, χλόην καταμπέχοντα *full of* green herbs, i.e. either *fed on grass* or *stuffed with herbs*, Antiph.1; *cover*, τὰ κράνη -αμπέχοντες Plu.*Crass*.11.

κατ-αμπῠκόω, *cover with a fillet*, κρᾶτα S.*Fr*.402.

καταμῡθολογέω, *amuse with fables*, τινα Philostr.*Her*.1.1.

καταμυκτηρίζω, *mock with upturned nose*, gloss on κατιλλώπτειν, Paus.Gr.*Fr*.209:—Pass., Hsch. s.v. κατιλλάνθη.

κατ-ᾰμύνω [ῡ], *ward off*, βίαν prob. in *PCair.Preis*.4.17 (iv A.D.):—Med., *avenge oneself*, dub. in Ael.*NA*5.11.

κατάμῠσις, εως, ἡ, *closing of the eyes*, Plu.*Cam*.6 (pl.): κ. ὀφθαλμῶν A.D.*Synt*.291.16. 2. *winking*, γέλωτι καὶ λαλιῇ καὶ κ. Aret.*SD*1.7.

κατ-ᾰμύσσω, *tear, scratch*, κατὰ δὲ χρόα καλὸν ἀ. Theoc.6.14; καλὸν ἄμυξε κάτα ῥέθος *AP*7.218 (Antip. Sid.): c. acc. cogn., μεγάλας ἀμυχὰς κ. Phryn.Com.3.6 (anap.):—Med., καταμύξατο χεῖρα ἀραιήν she *scratched her* hand, Il.5.425; μέτωπον καὶ ῥῖνα καταμύσσονται Hdt.4.71; κὰδ δέ σ' ἀμυξάμεναι *AP*7.491 (Mnasalc.):—Pass., καταμυχθεὶς τὴν κνήμην ὑπὸ κυνοσβάτου Did.ap.Ath.2.70d.

καταμυττωτεύω, *make mincemeat of*, in pf. Pass., Ar.*Pax*247.

καταμύω, Ep. aor. inf. καμμῦσαι v.l. in Batr.191; καμμύειν, aor. ἐκάμμυσα, etc., also in later Gr., v. καμμύω:—*close the eyes*, κ. τὰ βλέφαρα X.*Cyn*.5.11; τὰ ὄμματα Hp.*Epid*.7.83; τοὺς ὀφθαλμούς Lxx (v. καμμύω); τὸ τῆς ψυχῆς ὄμμα Ph.1.645, cf. 2.414; κ. τῷ νοερῷ ὄμματι M.Ant.4.29: more freq. alone, *close the eyes*, Str.6.1.14; κ. ὑπ' ἐκπλήξεως Philostr.*VA*6.11: hence, *drop asleep, doze*, Batr. l. c., Ar.*V*.92: euphem. for καταθνήσκειν, Luc.*DMer*.7.2, D.L.4.49. [ῡ in pres., Hedyl.ap.Ath.8.345a: in aor., Batr. l. c.; v. μύω.]

καταμφι-έννῡμι, *clothe completely, cover all round*, τοίχους πριστῷ [λίθῳ] J.*AJ*8.5.2. **-κᾰλύπτω**, strengthd. for ἀμφικαλ-, *put all round*, κεφαλῇ δὲ κατὰ ῥάκος ἀμφικαλύψας Od.14.349.

καταμωκ-άομαι, *mock at*, c. gen., Plu.*Demetr*.13, Epict.*Ench*.22: c. acc., Anon.ap.Suid.: abs., Lxx 2*Ch*.30.10, Hld.7.25, Sch.A.R.3.791. **-ημα**, ατος, τό, = sq., Hsch. s.v. χήνημα. **-ησις**, εως, ἡ, *mockery*, Plb.12.26^{c}.1, Ath.2.55d.

καταμωλύνομαι, Pass., = καταμαραίνομαι, of ulcers, Hp.*Prorrh*.1.170, f.l. in Id.*Epid*.2.2.6.

καταμωλωπίζω, *cover with weals* or *stripes*, Suid.

καταμωραίνω, *waste through folly*, τὰ πατρῷα Antiph.239.

καταμώσας· καθεὶς ἕνεκα τοῦ ζητῆσαι, κτλ., dub. l. in Gal.19.109.

καταναῖ· κατὰ νοῦν, Hsch.; cf. ἐγκατάνα.

καταναγιγνώσκω, *read through*, πᾶσαν τὴν ἱστορίαν Ath.13.610d.

κατᾰναγκ-άζω, *force back*, esp. of dislocated or fractured limbs, *force* them *into their place*, Hp.*Fract*.8, al. II. *overpower by force, constrain*, δεσμοῖς ἦν κατηναγκασμένος E.*Ba*.643; κ. τὸ σῶμα *torture*,

Luc.*Nec*.4. 2. *coerce*, τινὰ ἐς ξυμμαχίαν Th.4.77; τινά τι Luc.*Laps*. 8; τινὰ ποιεῖν τι Is.7.38, cf. *PGen*.49.24 (iv A. D.):—Pass., ὅσα -άζεται πρὸς μικρότητα καὶ μέγεθος Thphr.*CP*1.16.11; κινήσεις τινὲς ὑπὸ φαρμάκων -άζονται Gal.6.150; κατηναγκασμένος *necessary, inevitable*, ὁμολογούμενον καὶ κ. ἅπασι Plb.3.4.3, cf. A.D.*Synt*.43.1, al.; αἱ -ασμέναι ὑπηρεσίαι τοῦ βίου Ph.*Fr*.101 H. **-ἄσις**, εως, ἡ, *reduction* of dislocated limbs, Hp.*Art*.48, al. **-αστικός**, ή, όν, *conclusive, cogent*, λόγος *EM*239.43. **-η**, ἡ, *means of constraint*: *spell*, βιαιότεραι κ. cj. in Hld.6.14. II. kind of *vetch, Ornithopus compressus*, used in making philtres, Dsc.4.131, Plin.*HN*27.57, *PMag.Osl*.1.370. 2. = κῆμος, Ps.-Dsc.4.133.

καταναγραφέω, *ordain duly*, καθά κα ἁ βουλὰ καταναγραφήσῃ *IG* 14.256.29 (Phintias). **-θεμα**, ατος, τό, *curse*, *Apoc*.22.3; and **-θεμᾰτίζω**, *curse*, *Ev.Matt*.26.74, both vv. ll. for καταθ-.

κατ-αναιδεύομαι, *behave impudently to*, τινος Eust.69.22.

κατ-αναισῐμόω, *use quite up*, in Pass., Hp.*Art*.11, *Gland*.3.

καταναίω, *make to dwell, settle*:—Act. only in poet. aor., κατένασσε πατὴρ ἐς πείρατα γαίης Hes.*Op*.168; κ. ὑπὸ χθονὸς Id.*Th*.620; γουνοῖσιν Νεμέης ib.329, cf. B.3.60:—aor. Med., δυσαρέστους δαίμονας αὐτοῦ καταναssαμένη A.*Eu*.929 (anap.):—Pass., only in aor., *take up one's abode, dwell*, ὑπὸ δειράσι Παρνασοῦ κατενάσθη E.*Ph*.207 (lyr.); ἐν τῇ χώρᾳ κατένασθεν (3 pl.) Ar.*V*.662: so in aor. Med., ἐν Κέῳ κατενάσσατο A.R.2.520. 2. *establish*, βωμόν B.10.41.

κατανᾰλ-ίσκω, impf. -ανάλισκον Isoc.1.18: plpf. -ανηλώκει (intr.) Pl.*Ti*.36b: but aor. -ηνάλωσα Isoc.9.60:—**Pass.**, aor. -αναλωθῆναι Pl.*Phd*.72d; subj. -αναλωθῇ Hp.*Epid*.2.4.1; indic. -ηναλώθησαν ib. 2: pf. -ανήλωμαι Isoc.3.31 codd.; inf. κατηναλῶσθαι Plu.2.112a:—*use up, spend, lavish*, χρήματα X.*Mem*.1.2.22; εἴς τι upon a thing, εἰς τὴν στρατείαν τάλαντα μύρια Isoc.9.60; τὴν σχολὴν εἰς φιληκοΐαν Id.1.18; τὰς δυνάμεις εἰς τὰ ἄλογα Pl.*Prt*.321c; τέσσαρας μνᾶς εἰς ὀψοφαγίαν Ister ap.Ath.8.345d; of space in a treatise, Phld.*Herc*. 1508.10; also κ. πολλὰ ἡδοναῖς D.S.17.108; τὸ πλεῖστον τοῦ βίου ἐν ὁμιλίᾳ Ael.*VH*3.13:—Pass., with plpf. Act., *to be lavished*, Pl.*Ti*. l. c.; εἴς τι Id.*Phd*. l. c.; πάσας [τιμὰς] κατηναλῶσθαι ἄλλοις Plu. l. c. 2. *consume*, τὴν τροφήν Arist.*GA*763ᵃ13, Plu.2.160b; *devour* fuel, of fire, Arist.*Juv*.469ᵇ29; later, *eat*, [ἰχθύν] Agatharch.109; [ῥοιᾶς κόκκον] Apollod.1.5.3:—Pass., ἡ τροφὴ κ. εἰς τὴν αὔξησιν, εἰς τὸ σῶμα, Arist.*GA*771ᵃ28, 725ᵇ31, cf. Hp.*VM*11; ἐπιστήμη οὐ κ. ὑπὸ πόνων Andronic.Rhod.p.578 M. **-ωσις**, εως, ἡ, *waste, consumption*, Plu.2.678f. **-ωτέον**, *one must expend*, τὴν σπουδὴν εἰς τὰ μηδενὸς ἄξια Arist.*Rh.Al*.1420ᵇ22.

καταναρκάομαι, Ion. **-έομαι**, Pass., *grow quite numb*, Hp.*Art*.48; *to be reduced to a torpid condition*, Phld.*Lib*.p.52 O. II. Act., καταναρκᾶν τινος *to be slothful towards, press heavily upon...*, 2*Ep.Cor*. 11.9, 12.13.

κατανάσσω, *stamp, beat down firmly*, κατανάξαντες τὴν γῆν Hdt. 7.36:—Pass., -νενασμένος σφυγμός *firm* pulse, Archig.ap.Gal.8.662.

καταναυμᾰχέω, *conquer in a sea-fight, beat at sea*, βασιλέα And.3.5, cf. D.20.68, X.*HG*7.1.10, Din.1.75, *TAM*2(1).265 (Xanthos):—Pass., ὑπὸ τῆς βασιλέως δυνάμεως Isoc.12.105, cf. Luc.*Hist.Conscr*.38.

κατ-ανδρᾰποδίζω, *enslave*: metaph., in Pass., ἐννοίαις Just.*Nov*. 42 *Praef*.

κατ-ανδρᾰφύσσω, *slay*, in aor. κατηνδράφυξα, Hsch.

κατ-ανδρίζομαι, *fight manfully against*, expld. by καταπαλαῖσαι, Hsch.

κατανδρίζω, (κατ' ἄνδρα) *place on a list*, *BGU*1095.14 (i A. D.).

κατανεᾱνιεύομαι, *prevail over by youthful vigour*, or *exult over*, Hsch.

κατανείφω, fut. -νείψω (v. infr.), *snow all over, cover with snow*, κατένειψε χιόνι τὴν Θρᾴκην [ὁ θεός], i. e. *snow fell over all* Thrace, Ar. *Ach*.138:—Pass., Plu.*Luc*.24: metaph., *sprinkle as with snow*, Luc. *VH*2.14; κατανείψων ἀπὸ γλώσσης ἅπαντας Id.*Lex*.15. II. abs., κατανείφει *it snows*, κεἰ κριμνώδη κατανείφοι even *were it to snow* thick as meal, Ar.*Nu*.965.

κατανεκρόω, *kill*, prob. in *Tab.Defix.Aud*.16 *Fr*.x 13. 2. *deaden*, τὴν ζῳογόνον φύσιν ἐν τῷ χειμῶνι -ωθεῖσαν Lyd.*Mens*.4.67.

κατανέμησις, εως, ἡ, *pasturage*, διὰ τῶν προβάτων *PRyl*.141.16 (i A. D.), cf. Sch.Pi.*O*.7.61.

κατ-άνεμος, ον, f.l. for κατήνεμος, Poll.1.101.

κατανέμω, *distribute, allot*, freq. of pasture land, κ. χώρην τισί Hdt. 2.109, cf. Isoc.3.28; τὴν ὀργάδα D.H.1.79, etc.; θέαν τινί D.18. 28. 2. *distribute, divide into portions*, δεκα(χα) δὲ καὶ τοὺς δήμους κατένειμε ἐς τὰς φυλάς *distributed* or *apportioned* them in ten groups among the tribes, Hdt.5.69, cf. Decr.ap.D.59.104: without Prep., τὸ στράτευμα κατένειμε δώδεκα μέρη X.*Cyr*.7.5.13; τὴν νῆσον δέκα μέρη κ. Pl.*Criti*.113e; of a single person, κ. τινὰ εἰς τὴν τάξιν *assign* him to his post, Aeschin.1.155:—Pass., δεῖ τὸ πλῆθος ἐν συσσιτίοις κατανενεμῆσθαι Arist.*Pol*.1331ᵃ20. 3. *graze*, τὰ πρόβατα τὰ -νενεμηκότα τὰ ἐκεῖ *BGU*885.6 (ii A. D.); *occupy grazing land*, *PHib*.1.52.3 (iii B. C.); of shepherds, *pasture*, [πρόβατα] Eust.212.39. II. Med., *divide among themselves*, Th.2.17, Pl.*R*.547b. 2. with aor. and pf. Pass., *occupy, overrun*, esp. with cattle, *feed* or *graze land*, τὴν χώραν ἡμῶν -νενέμηνται Isoc.14.7, cf. ib.20 (also in Act., βοσκήμασι κ. [τὴν χώραν] Decr.ap.D.18.154); γέρανοι -ενέμοντο χώρην Babr. 26.1: hence, *plunder, ravage*, πᾶσαν τὴν Λιβύην Ath.15.677e. 3. metaph., of a plague, ἡ λοιμώδης φθορὰ -ενεμήθη τὴν ἀκμάζουσαν ἡλικίαν Plu.*Per*.34; ἀλφὸς κ. τὸ σῶμα *spreads over*, Plu.*Art*.23; so of fire, *spread*, εἰς τὰς πρώτας σκηνάς Plb.14.4.6.

κατανέναι· κατανεῦσαι, Hsch.

κατάνευρος, ον, *full of nerves* or *sinews*, μέρη, τόπος, *Hippiatr*.57, 96.

κατάνευσις, εως, ἡ, *assent*, J.*AJ*17.9.5; αἰτήσεων ibid. (pl.).

κατανεύω, fut. -νεύσομαι Il.1.524, Pl.*R*.350e: aor. κατένευσα Il.1. 558, etc.; Ep. part. καννεύσας Od.15.464:—*nod assent*, κεφαλῇ κατανεύσομαι Il.1.524; χαίταις Pi.*N*.1.14; κατανεύσομαι καὶ ἀνανεύσομαι Pl.*R*. l. c., cf. *Euthd*.277c, Ar.*Ec*.72: abs., of granting a request, ὑπέστην καὶ κατένευσα Il.4.267, cf. Hdt.9.111, Ar.*Th*.1020: c. acc. rei, *grant, promise*, ὅτι μοι κατένευσε Κρονίων νίκην καὶ μέγα κῦδος Il.8.175: later c. dat., *consent to*, *BGU*1119.24 (i B. C.): c. fut. inf., δωσέμεναι κατένευσε Il.10.393; ὑπέσχετο καὶ κατένευσεν Ἴλιον ἐκπέρσαντ' εὐτείχεον ἀπονέεσθαι 2.112: later c. aor. inf., Bion *Fr*.5.8: generally, *make a sign by nodding the head*, ὁ δὲ τῇ -ένευσε σιωπῇ Od.15.463. II. *bow down*, εἰς γῆν v. l. in Ach.Tat.7.14; ἐπειδὰν -νεύσῃ τὸ ἀγγεῖον *Gp*. 2.4.2; κ. τὴν κεφαλήν Poll.1.205: pf. part. -νενευκώς *downcast*, Vett. Val.2.4. III. Astron., *tilt downward*, of the pole, Eudox.*Ars* 6.31. [κατᾰνεύων Od.9.490.]

κατανεφόω, *overcloud*, Plu.*Tim*.27.

κατανέω (A), aor. -ένησα, *heap, pile up*, Hdt.6.97.

κατανέω (B), *spin out*, in pf. Pass., Hsch. s. v. λίνοιο.

κατάνη, ἡ, = τυρόκνηστις, Sicil. word in Plu.*Dio* 58.

κατανήχομαι, *swim down stream*, Sch.A.R.4.937.

κατ-ανθίζομαι, Pass., *to be decked with bright colours*, χρώμασι παντοδαποῖς κατηνθισμένος D.S.18.26; πέδιλον κατήνθιστο χρυσῷ Callistr.*Stat*.7; οἰκία πολυτελέσι λίθοις κατηνθισμένη Hierocl. *in CA* 17 p.458 M. (Act. perh. to be read in Plu.2.789c.)

κατανθρᾰκ-ίζω, = sq.: metaph., of love, *AP*12.99. **-όω**, fut. -ώσομαι, *burn to cinders*, στέγην πυρώσω καὶ κατανθρακώσομαι A.*Fr*.281.4. II. elsewh. only in Pass., δέμας φλογιστὸν ἤδη καὶ κατηνθρακωμένον S.*El*.58; ἅπαν κατηνθρακώθη θῦμ' ἐν.. φλογί E. *IA*1602; κατηνθρακώμεθ' ὀφθαλμοῦ σέλας *I have it burnt out*, Id.*Cyc*. 663.

κατανθρωπ-ίζω, *treat in a friendly manner*, *BGU*1141.5 (i A. D.). **-ισμός**, ὁ, *hospitality, entertainment*, τινος *POxy*.736.11, al. (i A. D.).

κατ-ᾰνιάω, strengthd. for ἀνιάω, Hsch. s. v. κατήφησας:—also **κατανιάζω**, Id. s. v. κατηφήσας (Pass.).

κατανίζω (pres. -νίπτω Ph.2.45), *wash well*, ὄξει πάντα κ. Hp.*Ulc*. 27, cf. 24; τὸν κηρόν Gal.13.743; γάλακι καταν̣ενιμμένος Pherecr.108. 18. II. *wash out, purge*, αἱ διάρροιαι..-νιφθεῖσαι πεπαύσονται Hp. *Prorrh*.2.23; κατανίζεται τὸ σῶμα τοῖς οἴνοις Mnesith.ap.Ath.11. 484a.

κατανῑκάνδρα, ἡ, *she that subdues men*, epith. of Ἄρκτος, *PMag. Lond*.121.762.

κατανῑκάω, strengthd. for νικάω, ὅταν οἵ γ' ἀγαθοὶ πρὸς τῶν ἀγενῶν -νικῶνται S.*Fr*.84, cf. J.*AJ*3.2.2, *PFlor*.338.11 (iii A. D.); ὑπὸ τῆς φθοροποιοῦ δυνάμεως Philum.*Ven*.4.3.

κατάνιμμα, ατος, τό, *water for washing in*, Ath.1.19a (pl.).

κατανίπτης, ου, ὁ, *washer*: at Athens, *he who washed the peplos of Athena Polias*, *AB*269, *EM*494.25.

κατανίσσομαι, *go* or *come down from*, ἐξ ὀρέων A.R.2.976. II. *go through*, c. acc., Hermesian.7.65.

κατ-ανίσταμαι, aor. κατανέστην: pf. κατανέστηκα:—*rise up against*, τῶν πολεμίων, τῶν ἀρχόντων, Plb.1.46.10, 38.12.7: abs., Id. 38.13.1; ἐπὶ τὴν συναγωγήν Lxx *Nu*.16.3.

κατανίφω, late spelling of κατανείφω (q. v.).

κατανο-έω, *observe well, understand, apprehend*, ὡς ἐμὲ κατανοέειν Hdt.2.28, cf. 93; οὐ χαλεπὸν τῷ βουλομένῳ κ. Lys.25.34; οὐ.. κατανοῶ τὸ νῦν ἐρωτώμενον Pl.*Sph*.233a; κ. ὅ τι λέγω Id.*Grg*.455b; οὐ πάνυ κατανοῶ Id.*Phlb*.48a; κ. ὅτι.. Id.*Sph*.264b; κατανοεῖς τίς ποτ' ἐστίν..; Antiph.33.1; ἐκεῖνο, ὅτι.. Epicur.*Ep*.1 p.30 U.; ἐκ τίνων.. καὶ πότε.. καὶ πῶς.. Plb.1.12.9:—Pass., of a doctrine, *to be grasped and* hence *accepted*, μᾶλλον μᾶλλον κ. Epicur.*Nat*.138 G.; εἰς καρδίαν -εῖται *is understood* of.., Heph.Astr.1.1. 2. *perceive*, τῷ κατανοουμένῳ τὸ κατανοοῦν ἐξομοιῶσαι *the percipient to the perceived*, Pl.*Ti*.90d, etc.: c. part., κ. οὐ πολλοὺς ὄντας Th.2.3. 3. *learn*, τῆς Περσίδος γλώσσης ὅσα ἐδύνατο κατενόησε Id.1.138. 4. *consider*, περί τινος X.*Cyr*.1.6.20. 5. *look at, view*, τὴν οἰκίαν Ath. 5.179a. II. *to be in one's right mind, in one's senses*, Hp.*Epid*.1. 26.γ', 5.39. **-ημα**, ατος, τό, *purpose, contrivance*, τὸ τῶν θεῶν τοῦ κόσμου κ. Pl.*Epin*.987d; κ. χρηματιστικόν Arist.*Pol*.1259ᵃ7. **-ησις**, εως, ἡ, *observation, consideration*, Pl.*Ti*.82c, *Criti*.107d, Lxx *Si*.41. 21; ἡ αὐτοῦ κ. *introspection*, Plot.5.3.1; ἑαυτῆς (sc. ψυχῆς) Id.4.7. 10; of sense perception, ἡ δι' αἰσθήσεως κ. Id.6.2.4. 2. *means of observing*, πολλὴν ἑαυτοῦ παρέχειν κ. Plu.*Rom*.6. **-ητέον**, *one must observe, learn*, Pl.*Plt*.305c, Porph.*Marc*.27; *one must consider*, πάλιν περί τινος Ph.1.83. **-ητικός**, ή, όν, *observant, intelligent*, Poll.9.151.

κατ-ανοίγνυμι, strengthd. for ἀνοίγω, Lxx *Ps*.4.4, Philostr.*Dial*.2.

κατ-άνομαι [ᾰ], Pass., (ἄνω) *to be used up* or *wasted*, πολλὰ κατάνεται Od.2.58; μέτρα κατανομένων ἐνιαυτῶν *completed*, Arat.464.

κατανομή, ἡ, *pasture*, προβάτων *PIand*.26.33 (i A. D.), cf. Sch.Ar. *Av*.769, Sch.S.*Tr*.13 (pl.).

κατανομ-ίζω, *recognize*, *PGrenf*.1.11 ii 2 (ii B. C.). **-ιστεύω**, *melt down into coin*, J.*BJ*1.18.4.

κατανομοθετέω, *legislate*, Pl.*Lg*.861c.

κατανοστέω, *return from banishment*, Plb.4.17.10.

κατανοσφίζομαι, Med., *embezzle*, τὰ δημόσια D.H.4.11.

κατανοτιαῖος, α, ον, *with south aspect*, ἐξέδριον *CIG*2554.124 (Cret., dub.).

καταvοτίζω, *bedew*, κατὰ δὲ γόος ἅμα χαρᾷ τὸ σὸν νοτίζει βλέφαρον E.*IT*833 (lyr.).

κάταντ-α, Adv. *downhill*, πολλὰ δ' ἄναντα κ. πάραντά τε δόχμιά τ' ἦλθον Il.23.116, cf. Luc.*Merc.Cond.*26: c. gen., *below*, prob. in *PFlor.*370.7 (ii A.D.). **-άω**, *come down to, arrive*, εἰς τὰ βασίλεια, ἐπὶ κοίτην, D.S.4.52, 3.27, cf. *PTeb.*59.3 (i B.C.), etc.: metaph., ἐπὶ τὴν φυσικὴν ὁδὸν Vett.Val.259.3, cf. 185.16, 251.30. 2. in a speech or narrative, *come to, arrive at* a point, εἰς τὴν ἔκπτωσιν Plb. 4.1.8; ἐπί τινας λογισμούς Id.10.37.3; κ. ἐπὶ τὸν ὅρκον D.S.1.79, cf. J.*AJ*3.10.4, etc.; *have recourse to*, ἐπὶ [τὴν ἡδονήν] Epicur.*Ep.*3 p.63 U.; ἐπὶ τὰ δάκρυα Phld.*Lib.*p.62 O. 3. of persons, κ. εἰς ἑαυτοὺς *attack, commence hostilities against* each other, Plb.30.11.3. 4. of events, *come upon*, πᾶς δ' ἀγὼν ἐπ' ἐμὲ κατήντα Alex.261.13; κ. εἴς τινα *affect* him, Phld.*Ir.*p.83 W.; of blood-guiltiness, *fall*, ἐπὶ κεφαλήν τινος Lxx 2*Ki.*3.29. b. *turn out, result*, ποῦ καταντήσει πάλιν Plb.6.4.12; τὸ πρᾶγμα κ. εἰς ὑπόνοιαν D.S.1.37; εἰς τὸ μηδέν Plb.4. 34.2; so of numbers, *to be reduced*, εἰς μόνους ἄνδρας δέκα *BGU*903.14 (ii A.D.), etc. 5. of an inheritance, κ. εἴς τινα *fall* to one's share, 1*Ep.Cor.*10.11, *POxy.*75 (ii A.D.), etc. II. trans., *make to come back, bring back*, τινα Palaeph.2; εἰς ἑαυτὸν τὴν ἀρχιερωσύνην Lxx 2*Ma.*4.24 (so intr. in pf., *return*, εἰς τὸν αὐτὸν κατηντηκέναι βίον *BGU* 1101.5 (i B.C.)). **-ημα**, ατος, τό, *end, goal*, Lxx *Ps.*18(19).7, Sch. Ar.*Ra.*1026; κ. σκέψεως Sch.E.*Hec.*744; *result*, *PSI*6.698.5 (iv A.D.). **-ην**, Adv., = κάταντα, Them.*Or.*13.168b. **-ης**, ες, (ἄντα) *downhill, steep*, opp. ἀνάντης, κ. ἀτραπός Ar.*Ra.*127; ἐς τὰ κατάντεα *downwards*, Hp.*Off.*9; ἐπὶ κάταντες, = κάταντα, Pl.*Ti.*77d; εἰς τὸ κάταντες X.*Eq.*8.8; ἐν τῷ κατάντει Id.*HG*4.8.37; ἀπὸ τοῦ κατάντους ib.3.5.20; ἐν τοῖς κατάντεσι Diocl.*Fr.*142: neut. as Adv., κάταντες κινεῖσθαι Arist.*Ph.*248ᵃ22; τὰ κατάντη ἁμιλλώμενοι X.*Eq.* 8.6; τὰ κ. ἐλαύνεσθαι Id.*Eq.Mag.*8.3; θεῖν Id.*Cyn.*5.17; φέρεσθαι Arist.*HA*567ᵃ7; καταβαίνειν Thphr.*Lass.*11. II. metaph., *prone, inclined*, πρός τι E.*Rh.*318, Epicur.*Nat.*908.4, Plu.2.53e. **-ησις**, εως, ἡ, *recourse*, ἐπὶ τὴν ἀρετὴν Phld.*Rh.*1.265 S. II. Astrol., *encounter*, of planetary influences, Vett.Val.247.26 (pl.). **-ητέον**, *one must have recourse*, ἐπὶ φλεβοτομίαν Aët.5.115. **-ία**, ἡ, *hanging downwards*, Hp.*Off.*3. II. καταντία, v. καταντίον.

κατ-αντιβολέω, *entreat earnestly*, τινα Ar.*Fr.*625: c. inf., J.*BJ* 1.6.4, al.

κατ-αντικρύ, Prep. c. gen., *straight down from*, καταντῖκρὺ τέγεος πέσε Od.10.559, cf. 11.64. 2. in Att., = Homeric ἀντικρύ, *over against, right opposite*, πρυτάνεων καταντῖκρύ Ar.*Ec.*87; τὰ κ. Κυθήρων the parts *opposite* Cythera, Th.7.26, cf. X.*HG*4.8.5; κ. ᾗ.. ἐξέπεσεν *exactly opposite* to the point at which.., dub. l. in Pl. *Phd.*112d: c. dat., κ. τῇ θέσει Arist.*Mete.*356ᵃ10; τῷ ἡλίῳ D.C.60. 26. II. Adv. of Place, *right opposite*, ἡ ἤπειρος ἡ κ. Th.1.136; ἐν τῷ κ. προσστῆναί τινι Pl.*Euthd.*274c, cf. *Prt.*315c; τὸ κ. αὐτῶν τοῦ σπηλαίου Id.*R.*515a; ἐκ τοῦ κ. from the *opposite* side, ib.b; κ. ὁρᾶν look *right in the face*, Id.*Chrm.*169c; ἐπὶ τὸ κ. in the *opposite* direction, Arist.*HA*528ᵇ10 (but εἰς τὸ κ. towards the *opposite* end, Pl.*Phd.* 72b); πρὸς τὸ κ. κείμενος Plb.4.39.6. b. *in opposition, to the contrary*, κατὰ τὴν κ. ἢ ὡς Γλαύκων λέγει Arist.*Po.*1461ᵃ35. 2. *straight forward*, Id.*HA*591ᵇ24; opp. πλάγια, Pl.*Tht.*194b. 3. *outright, downright*, Th.7.57 (nisi leg. καὶ ἄντικρυς); παραβάλλειν.. μὴ κ. Arist.*Rh.*1419ᵇ36. [On the quantity v. ἀντικρύ: the form **καταντροκύ** is found in Att. Inscrr., *IG*2².1668.88.]

κατ-αντίον, Adv. *over against, right opposite*, c. gen., Hdt.6.103, 118, 8.52: c. dat., Id.7.33: abs., χὼ κ. θανὼν *facing him*, S.*Ant.*512, cf. *APl.*4.95 (Damag.): **καταντία**, πόντου κ. κυμαίνοντος Agesianax ap.Plu.2.921b, cf. Opp.*H.*2.555.

κατ-αντιπέρας, = καταντικρύ II, c. gen., X.*An.*1.1.9; **κατ' ἀντιπέραν** is found ib.4.8.3, Luc.*JTr.*42; **καταντίπερα** Man.4.188:—also **-πέρην** Id.2.22, al.

καταντλ-έω, *pour* water or liquid *down* one's throat, Alex.85; *pour over*, εἰς τὰ λοιπὰ μέρη τοῦ σώματος κατήντλουσαν (3 pl. impf.) *PSI* 3.168 (ii A.D.): metaph., *pour a flood of words over*, ταῦτά τινος Ar. *V.*483; κ. λόγον κατὰ τῶν ὤτων Pl.*R.*344d; φιλοσοφίας γέλωτα κ. ib. 536b; τὰ ποιήματα ἡμῶν κ. Id.*Ly.*204d:—Pass., metaph., -ούμενος ταῖς τῶν βασάνων τρικυμίαις Lxx 4*Ma.*7.2. 2. *bathe*, κ. τι ἐλαίῳ Gal.8.366; τὴν ὁδὸν αἵματι J.*AJ*8.4.1:—Pass., μύροις Id.*BJ*4.9. 10. **-ημα**, ατος, τό, *douche*, Dsc.1.104. **-ησις**, εως, ἡ, = foreg., Hp.*Medic.*3, Antyll.ap.Orib.9.23.1, Gal.10.237. **-ητέον**, *one must douche*, Antyll.ap.Orib.9.23.4, Archig.ap.Aët.3.191, *Gp.* 16.7.1. **-ητικός**, ή, όν, *of* or *for douching*, Herod.Med. in *Rh. Mus.*58.113. **-ος**, ον, = ὑπέραντλος, Poll.1.113.

καταντροκύ, v. καταντικρύ.

κατα-νυκτικός, ή, όν, *pricking at heart*, Suid. s. v. γοερόν. **-νυξις**, εως, ἡ, *stupefaction, bewilderment*, ἐπότισας ἡμᾶς οἶνον -νύξεως Lxx *Ps.* 59(60).3, cf. *Is.*29.10. 2. *contrition*, Just.*Nov.*137.6 *Intr.* **-νύσσω**, *stab, gouge*, τοὺς ὀφθαλμούς τινος Phleg.36.4 J.:—elsewh. in Pass., with fut. -νῠγήσομαι Lxx *Si.*20.21: aor. -ενύγην [ῠ] (v. infr.); *to be sorely pricked*, metaph., κατενύγησαν τὴν καρδίαν *Act.Ap.*2.37, cf. Lxx *Ge.* 34.7: hence, *to be bewildered, stunned*, κάθισον -νενυγμένη Lxx *Is.*47. 5, cf. *Ps.*4.5, al.; *keep silence*, ib.*Le.*10.3.

κατανυστάζω, aor. κατενύσταξα Poll.2.67:—*doze, fall asleep*, Alex. 286. II. trans., *lull asleep*, dub. in Ael.*NA*14.20.

κατ-ἀνύω, Att. καθ- (q.v.) (-ύτω [ῠ] X.*Cyr.*8.6.17):—Pass. (v. infr. II):—*bring to an end*; esp. 1. *accomplish, cover* a certain distance, τὸν προκείμενον δρόμον Hdt.8.98; νηῦς -ανύει ἐν μακρημερίῃ ὀργυιὰς ἑπτακισμυρίας Id.4.86; δυοῖν ἡμέραιν ὁδὸν ἐν μιᾷ X.*HG*5.4.49, etc.; then, 2. intr., *arrive at* a place, νηῒ κατανύσας ἐς Λῆμνον Hdt.6.140, cf. X.*HG*5.4.20: c. gen., φίλης γὰρ προξένου (sc. ἐς οἶκον) κατήνυσαν they *have come to* a kind hostess's, S.*El.*1451: metaph., πρὶν σᾶν.. κατανύσαι φρενῶν before thou *arrivest at* thy purpose, E. *Hipp.*365 (s. v. l., lyr.). II. *accomplish, perpetrate*, τάδε Id.*El.*1163 (lyr.); αἷμα γενέθλιον κ. Id.*Or.*89:—Med., πολλὰ τῇ πατρίδι κ. *IPE* 1².40.10 (Olbia, ii/iii A.D.):—Pass., *to be fulfilled*, τὸ τέρας αὐτῷ εἰς τὴν ὑπατικὴν ἀρχὴν κατηνύσθη Dam.*Isid.*64. III. *procure*, ὑποζυγίοις χόρτον Plb.9.4.3. IV. *slay*, Sch.E.*Ph.*1062.

κατανωτ-ίδιος (v.l. **-ιαῖος**), ον, *on the back*, Poll.1.148. **-ίζομαι**, *carry on one's back*, Plu.2.924d, Luc.*Lex.*5, Longus 1.20. II. *turn one's back upon*: hence, *ignore, disdain, reject*, *BGU*1296.9 (iii B.C.), *PFay.*11.21 (ii B.C.), Phld.*Mort.*35; of critics, Simp. *in Ph.*1036.17, al., Dam.*Isid.*150. **-ιστής**, οῦ, ὁ, *one who despises*, παντὸς δικαίου Dicaearch.1.14.

καταξαίνω, fut. -ξᾰνῶ Lxx *Jd.*8.7:—*card, comb well*, καταξῆναι Pl. Com.245:—Pass., εἴρια κατεξασμένα Hp.*Ulc.*24; πέτρα κατεξαμμένη *hollowed out*, D.S.17.71 (hence καταξάνωσι cj. Dind. Id.1.98). 2. *tear in pieces, rend in shreds*, πλόκους κόμης E.*Ion* 1267; πολλοὺς αἱ σαὶ καταξανοῦσι.. χέρες Lyc.300; σάρκας Lxx l. c.; κεφαλὴν Plu.*Agis* 2; so κ. τινὰ εἰς φοινικίδα *pound* him (by stoning) to red rags, Ar. *Ach.*320:—Pass., πέτροισι.. καταξανθεὶς θανεῖν *crushed to atoms*, S. *Aj.*728; πρὶν κατεξάνθαι βολαῖς E.*Ph.*1145; πέτραις καταξανθέντες ὀστέων ῥαφάς Id.*Supp.*503; πυρὶ καταξανθέντας Id.*HF*285; λύγου ξηρᾶς πληγαῖς -εξασμένης Longus 2.1. 3. *wear, waste away*, πνοαὶ.. τρίβῳ κατέξαινον ἄνθος Ἀργείων A.*Ag.*197 (lyr.); τὴν σάρκα Epicur. *Sent.Vat.*51; νόσοι κ. ὅλα δι' ὅλων Ph.2.432:—Pass., κατεξάνθην πόνοις E.*Med.*1030; δακρύοις Id.*Tr.*509; κατέξανται δέμας Id.*Hipp.* 274; ὅπλα κατεξάνθαι *were worn out by use*, D.S.17.94; ἐν τοῖς ὀρύγμασι καταξαινόμενοι τὰ σώματα Id.5.38.

καταξενόομαι, Pass., *to be received as a guest, hospitably treated*, κατεξενωμένος A.*Ch.*706.

κατα-ξέσματα, τά, *chips, filings*, Suid. s. v. μύγματα. **-ξεστικῶς**, Adv., gloss on ἀμύξ, Sch.Nic.*Th.*131. **-ξέω**, *polish smooth*, τοὺς ὀρθοστάτας -ξοῦντι *IG*1².374.221, cf. 12(2).10.22 (Mytil.); λίθον *Milet.*7.59:—Pass., κατεξέσθη τὸ ὑπέρθυρον Haussoullier *Milet* p.163, cf. Plu.2.953b: metaph., of style, τῇ λέξει -εξεσμένον Ps.-Plu.*Vit. Hom.*72. II. *carve*, in Pass., Arist.*Mir.*838ᵇ15.

καταξηρ-αίνω, *dry up*, Arist.*GA*772ᵃ12; θάλατταν Lxx *Jo.*2.10:—Pass., Pl.*Ti.*76a, Arist.*Mete.*340ᵇ1. **-ος**, ον, *very dry, parched*, γλῶσσαι Hp.*Prorrh.*1.3, cf. Arist. *de An.*422ᵇ5, Thphr.*CP*6.18.3, etc.; τὸ κ. τῆς βώλου Alciphr.3.35: metaph., ψυχὴ κ. Lxx *Nu.*11.6; τὸ κ. τῆς ἐπιθυμίας Alciphr.1.22; of persons, κ. γινομένους πρός τι ἀπαγορεύειν *stale*, Plu.2.8c. Adv. -ρως, πυρέσσειν Antyll.ap.Orib.9. 23.6.

κατ-αξιοπιστέομαι (-εύομαι Suid.), *demand implicit belief to the prejudice of*, τινος Plb.12.17.1.

κατάξι-ος, ον (fem. -αξία *Inscr.Prien.*109.220 (ii B.C.), al.), strengthd. for ἄξιος, *quite worthy*, c. gen., S.*Ph.*1009: abs., E.*El.*46; κρίσις Lxx *Es.*16.18; χάριτας τὰς κ. ἀποδιδόναι *IG*12(1).155.11 (Rhodes), cf. *GDI* 3585.22 (Iasos); τὰς κ. τιμάς τισι ἀπονέμειν *OGI*763.24 (Milet., ii B.C.): neut. pl. as Adv., *AP*3.14 (Inscr.Cyzic.). Regul. Adv. -ίως S.*OC*911, *El.*800, *SIG*577.87 (Milet., 200 B.C.), Plb.1.88.5, etc. **-όω**, *deem worthy*, c. acc. et inf., D.59.111; *hold in honour*, Plb.4.86.8: c. gen. rei, *deem worthy of* a thing, τάξεως τὸν κίνδυνον Id.1.23.3; τινὰ μεγάλης ἀποδοχῆς D.S.2.60:—Med., οὔτε νιν.. Δίκη προσεῖδε καὶ κατηξιώσατο did not regard and *hold in high esteem*, A.*Th.*667:—Pass., *to be held worthy*, πρεσβείας Plb.12.10.8, cf. Iamb.*VP*36.265; ἔργον ἐπιφανὲς καὶ κατηξιωμένον Plb.5.83.4. II. *command, bid*, πολλὰ χαίρειν ξυμφοραῖς καταξιῶ A.*Ag.*572; σύ τοι κατηξίωσας thou *didst decree it so*, S.*Ph.*1095 (lyr.). III. *deign, vouchsafe*, c. inf., Luc. *Ind.*3, Jul.*Ep.*204, *PLond.*2.232.14 (iv A.D.), *POxy.*1214 (v A.D.), etc. IV. in bad sense, τῶν ἐν μέρους εἴδει πεφυκότων μηδενὶ καταξιώσωμεν *let us* not *degrade it by likening it to*.., Pl.*Ti.*30c. V. in argument, *claim, maintain*, Phld.*Sign.*30, al.:—Med., c. inf., Id. *Rh.*1.32 S.

κάτ-αξις, εως, Ion. **-ηξις**, ιος, ἡ, *fracture*, including all forms of skull injury, Hp.*VC*9, al.; *breaking into large fragments*, distd. from θραῦσις, Arist.*Mete.*386ᵃ12, Thphr.*Lass.*18.

κατ-αξίωσις, εως, ἡ, *high esteem, reputation*, Plb.1.78.1.

κατα-ξοή, Dor. **-ξοά**, ἡ, *polishing, smoothing*, *IG*4.1484.56, al. (Epid.), *Rev.Phil.*50.70 (Didyma, ii B.C.). **-ξὐή**, ἡ, = foreg., πλίνθου ib.67 (ibid., ii B.C.).

κατάξῠλ-ος, ον, gloss on ἄξυλος, Sch.D Il.11.155. **-ωσις**, εως, ἡ, = δόκωσις, *IG*4.1485.130 (Epid.); κ. ἐπὶ στέγης, *tignatio*, *Gloss.*

καταξῠράω, *shave close*, κατεξυρημένος τὸν πώγωνα Ctes.*Fr.*20 M.: abs., Nic.Dam.4 J.

κατάξῠροι θυρίδες, (ξυρόν) *embrasures*, Ph.*Bel.*81.12.

κατά-ξῠσις, εως, ἡ, *scraping*, Apollon.*Lex.*s.v. γραπτῦς (pl.). **-ξυσμα**, ατος, τό, *scraping, filing*, Sch.E.*Andr.*826, *Gloss.* **-ξυσμή**, ἡ, gloss on δρυφή, Hsch. **-ξυσμός**, ὁ, *scarification*, Sor.ap.Gal. 12.415. **-ξυστικῶς**, v.l. for -ξεστικῶς (q. v.). **-ξύω**, *scrape down*, Hp.*VC*19, Sor.2.12, Gal.10.132. 2. *scratch, mark*, Luc. *Nigr.*27; γραφίδεσσι κ. *inscribe*, *Hymn.Is.*11. II. *polish, smooth, plane down*, Thphr.*HP*3.15.2, D.S.2.13:—Pass., σανὶς -εξυσμένη εἰς εὐθεῖαν τομήν Agatharch.27; γλῶσσα -εξυσμένη ὑπὸ τέκτονος Lxx *Ep.Je.*8. III. Pass., of land, *to be eroded*, *PTeb.*74.52 (ii B.C.), etc. IV. Pass., *to be worried*, πράγματι *POxy.*525.4 (ii A.D.); καταξύομαι μὴ ὁρῶν σε ib.1676.24 (iii A.D.).

κατάορος [ᾱ], ον, Dor. for κατήορος, E.*Tr.*1090 (lyr., s. v. l.); cf. καταορᾷ· καταντεῖ, Hsch.

καταπάγιος [πᾰ], ον, *solidly built*, of persons, Sor.1.34; *fixed*, cf. καταπάγιον (-πάτιον cod.)· ἀσαλές, ἢ ἀθροῦν, Hsch.: **-πάγιον**, τό, *fixed payment*, *IG*12(5).572 (Ceos). Adv. -ίως *constantly*, πόλιν κ. οἰκεῖν Isoc.15.156.

καταπαγκρᾰτιάζω, *conquer in the* παγκράτιον, Ph.1.681; τινα Id. 2.348.

καταπαιγμός, ὁ, *mockery*, Apollon.*Lex.* s. v. μωμήσονται.

καταπαιδεραστέω, *waste in* παιδεραστία, οἶκον Is.10.25.

καταπαιδεύω, *chastise*, Sm.*La.*1.13.

καταπαίζω, fut. -παίξομαι (v. infr.), *jest, mock at*, c. gen., καταπαίζεις ἡμῶν Ar.*Fr.*166, cf. Lxx 4*Ki.*2.23, *AP*5.39 (Nicarch.); τῶν δογματικῶν S.E.*P.*1.62: c. acc., D.L.2.136. 2. *deceive*, ἕκαστος κατὰ τοῦ φίλου -παίξεται Lxx *Je.*9.5(4). II. Med. in sense of Act., ἐπί τινι πράξει τινῶν κ. Hdn.*Fig.*p.92 S.

κατάπαις, *puerarius*, *Gloss.*

καταπαίω, *strike hard*, Hsch.

καταπακτός, ή, όν, (καταπήγνυμι) only in the phrase καταπακτὴ θύρα, a door *shutting downwards*, *trap*-door, Hdt.5.16. [Cf. πακτός, πακτόω (ἐμ-, ἐπι-), with ᾰ by nature.]

καταπᾰλαιόομαι, Pass., *grow very old*, Gal.18(2).475.

καταπᾰλαίω, *throw in wrestling*, Εὐάθλους δέκα Ar.*Ach.*710: metaph., *overthrow*, λόγοι -παλαίουσιν λόγους E.*IA*1013; τὰ ῥηθέντα Pl. *R.*362d; κ. πάθος λόγῳ S.E.*M.*8.475:—Pass., καταπαλαισθεὶς ὑπὸ τοῦ Θανάτου Luc.*Cont.*8.

καταπαλλᾰκεύω, *make a concubine of*, Nic.Dam.51 J.

καταπάλλομαι, Pass., *dart down*, ἅρπῃ ἐϊκυῖα.. οὐρανοῦ ἐκ κατέπαλτο (Ep. aor. 2) Il.19.351 (but this form shd. perh. be referred to κατεφάλλομαι, q. v.); Νὺξ φυγὰς οὐρανόθεν καταπάλλεται *PMag.Berol.* 2.95: aor. 1, ἑοῦ κατεπήλατο δίφρου *leapt down from*, Nonn.*D.*18. 13.

καταπάλμενος· καταπηδήσας, Hsch.; of a waterfall, *AP*9.326 cod. (Leon.): nisi leg. κατεπ-, v. κατεφάλλομαι.

καταπαλτ-αφεσία, ἡ, *discharging of catapults, artillery practice*, *IG* 2^{2}.1006.65, 12(5).647.25 (Ceos). **-αφέτης**, ου, ὁ, *artilleryman*, ib.30, 2^{2}.665.27, al., (-πελτ-) Ph.*Bel.*82.13. **-ης**, ου, ὁ, (πάλλω) *engine of war for hurling bolts, catapult*, *IG*2^{2}.120.37, 554.15, 12(5). 647.36 (Ceos):—freq. written **-πέλτης** in literary texts, Mnesim.7. 10, Timocl.12.5, Onos.42.3, etc.; καταπάλτην ἀφιέναι Arist.*Ath.*42. 3, *EN*1111^{a}11, cf. *Aud.*800^{b}13, Ath.Mech.8.7, Ael.*VH*6.12; used as an instrument of torture, D.S.20.71, Charito 3.4, Lxx 4*Ma.*8.13. 2. *bolt, shot*, (-πέλτης) Hp.*Epid.*5.95, 7.121, (-πάλτης) Hsch.:—hence **-ικός**, ή, όν (in literary texts -πελτ-), *of* or *belonging to catapults*, βέλη *IG*2^{2}.1487.102; ὄργανα καὶ βέλη Plb.11.11.3, cf. Str.17.3.15, Bito 62.4; τὰ κ., = καταπάλται, Plb.9.41.5; τὸ κ. *artillery*, D.S.14. 42.

καταπαλτός, ή, όν, *hurled down*, ἐξ αἰθέρος ὕδωρ A.ap.Aristid.*Or.* 36(48).53.

καταπαννῠχίζω, *pass the night in revelry*, Alciphr.1.39.

καταπᾰνουργ-εύομαι, *devise villainously*, ἐπὶ τὸν λαὸν κ. γνώμην Lxx *Ps.*82(83).3. **-εύω**, *act villainously*, Suid.

κατ-άπαξ, = καθάπαξ, *Ath.Mitt.*49.3 (Attica, iv B. C.).

καταπάομαι, *gain possession of*, in aor. 1 -επάσατο, Hsch.

καταπαραλλήλως, Adv. *along a parallel of latitude*, κινεῖσθαι *Vit. Pyth.*ap.Phot.*Bibl.*p.440 B.

κατα-παρμός, ὁ, (καταπείρω) *piercing, boring*, Sor.2.62. **-παρσις**, εως, ἡ, = foreg., ib.61, Aët.16.23, Paul.Aeg.6.64. **-παρτέον**, *one must pierce*, ib.74.

κατά-πασμα, ατος, τό, *powder*, Antyll.ap.Orib.10.31.1, Paul.Aeg. 7.13. **-πασμός**, ὁ, prob. f. l. for κατασπασμός, Cael.Aur.*TP*1. 166.

καταπασσᾰλεύω, Att. **-παττ-**, *nail down*: hence, *bewitch*, *SIG* 1261.17 (Attica, iv/iii B. C.).

κατα-πάσσω, Att. **-ττω**, fut. -άσω [ᾰ] (v. infr.): aor. 1 -έπᾰσα Men. 708:—*besprinkle, bespatter with*, πάντα καταπάσω βουλευματίων Ar. *Eq.*99: usu. c. dat. rei, ἀψινθίῳ κ. μέλι Men. l. c.; γῇ τὰς κεφαλὰς κ. Lxx 2*Ma.*10.25: also abs., *pour out*, κ. χύδην Pherecr.168:—Pass., καταπαττόμενος Ar.*Nu.*262:—Med., κ. τὰς κεφαλὰς πηλῷ *their own* heads, v. l. in D.S.1.72, 91. II. c. acc. rei, *sprinkle, strew over*, ἄνθος χαλκοῦ Hp.*Fist.*3; ἄλευρα Arist.*HA*627^{b}20; κατὰ τῆς τραπέζης κ. τέφραν Ar.*Nu.*177:—Med., καταπασάμενος τῆς κεφαλῆς κόνιν *on his own* head, J.*BJ*2.21.3 (v. l. καταμησάμενος); γῆν ἐπὶ τῆς κεφαλῆς v. l. in Lxx *Jb.*1.20; τῶν στρωμάτων ῥόδα πολλὰ κατεπέπαστο Luc.*Asin.*7. **-παστέον**, *one must sprinkle*, Orib.*Fr.* 38. **-παστος**, ον, *besprinkled, bespattered with*, στεφάνοις Ar.*Eq.* 502; ἡδυσματίοις Telecl.1.11; σαργὸν τυρῷ κ. Archestr.*Fr.*36.3. 2. *suitable for use as a powder*, Asclep.ap.Gal.13.159, etc. 3. *embroidered*, ἁλουργίς Ar.*Eq.*968; χιτὼν χρυσῷ κ. D.C.72.17; χρυσαῖς ἀκτῖσι Hld.3.4, cf. 10.9, Aristid.*Or.*17(15).10.

καταπᾰτάκτην, v. l. καταπατηκτην, prob. ff. ll. for καταπακτήν or καταπηκτήν (sc. θύραν) *trap-door*, i. e. *dungeon*, Aq.*Je.*29(36).26.

καταπᾰτ-έω, *trample under foot*, Th.7.84, etc.; ὑσὶ τὸ σπέρμα κ. *trample down* the seed (i. e. *have it trampled down*) by swine, Hdt. 2.14:—Pass., Id.7.173, 223, Th.5.72, D.34.37; τὸν ἐγκέφαλον ἐν ταῖς πτέρναις -πεπατημένον φορεῖν Id.7.45. 2. metaph., κατὰ δ' ὅρκια πιστὰ πάτησαν Il.4.157; κ. τοὺς νόμους Pl.*Lg.*714a; τὰ γράμματα Id.*Grg.*484a; τὸν υἱὸν τοῦ θεοῦ *Ep.Hebr.*10.29; ὅρκον Lib.*Ep.*14. 1. **-ημα**, ατος, τό, *that which is trampled under foot*, Lxx *La.*2.8, al. **-ησις**, εως, ἡ, *trampling on*, ib.4*Ki.*13.7. 2. *perambulation, inspection*, χωρίων καὶ παραδείσων *CPHerm.*7 ii 6 (ii A. D.). **-ητέος**, α, ον, *to be trampled down*, *Gp.*6.13.1. **-ητής**, οῦ, ὁ, gloss on κατάσκοπος, Sch.E.*Hec.*239.

καταπάτιον, v. καταπάγιον.

κατά-παυμα, ατος, τό, *means of stopping*, δειλοῖσι γόου κ. γενοίμην Il.17.38. II. *rest*, Lxx *Si.*36.15(18). **-παυσις**, εως, ἡ, *stopping*: metaph., *putting down, deposing*, τυράννων Hdt.5.38; τῆς βασιληΐης *deposition* from.., Id.6.67; Κολλατίνου D.C.46.49. II. *rest, calm*, Lxx *Is.*66.1, al.; *place of rest*, ib.*Ps.*94(95).11, al.; αἱ κ. τῶν πνευμάτων Thphr.*Vent.*18: metaph., *allaying*, στάσεως Phld. *Mus.*p.86 K. **-παυστέον**, *one must stop, staunch*, τὴν φορὰν [τοῦ αἵματος] Antyll.(?)ap.Orib.50.3.7. **-παυστήριον**, τό, *means of putting to rest*, gloss on κηλητήριον, Sch.S.*Tr.*575. **-παυστικός**, ή, όν, *causing to cease*, ταραχῶν Phld.*Mus.*p.20 K.; κακοῦ Eust.138. 2. **-παύω**, poet. **καππαύω** Pi.*N.*9.15, B.*Scol.Oxy.Fr.*1.2:—*put an end to, stop*, κατέπαυσα θεῶν χόλον Od.4.583; μηνιθμὸν καταπαυσέμεν (Ep. fut. inf.) Il.16.62; πόλεμον καταπαυσέμεν ἀνδρῶν 7.36; νεῖκος κ. Hes.*Th.*87; τὴν ναυπηγίην Hdt.1.27; νόσους A.*Supp.*586 (lyr.); λιγυρὰν γᾶρυν B. l. c.; αἱμορραγίαν Gal.16.777; *bring to a close*, τὸν λόγον Plb.2.8.8; τὸ σύγγραμμα Phld.*Po.*5.26; κ. τὸν πρῶτον λόγον εἰς.. *conclude* the first section *and proceed* to.., Olymp.*in Mete.*78.9:—Med., πόνους -παυόμενοι E.*Hel.*1154 (lyr.):—Pass., -παύεται τὰ ἀρρωστήματα τοῖς τῶν ἰατρῶν εὑρήμασι D.26.26. II. c. acc. pers., *put an end to*, i. e. *kill*, τάχα κέν σε.. ἔγχος ἐμὸν κατέπαυσε Il.16.618; σοῦ κ. τὰς πνοάς Ar.*Av.*1397. 2. *make one stop from* a thing, *hinder, check*, μιν καταπαύσῃ ἀγηνορίης ἀλεγεινῆς Il.22.457; παῖδας καταπαυέμεν ἀφροσυνάων Od.24.457; so κ. τινὰ δρόμου Pl.*Plt.*294e: c. part., κ. ταύτην λαλοῦσαν Men.66.5: c. acc. only, *keep in check*, τινα Od.2.244 (cf. 168), Il.15.105. 3. *depose from* power, κ. τινὰ τῆς ἀρχῆς, τῆς βασιληΐης, Hdt.4.1, 6.64; τοὺς τυράννους Id.5.38, cf. 2.144, 7.105; Μούσας *depose* them *from their honours, cease to worship* them, E. *HF*685 (lyr.):—Pass., τῆς βασιληΐης κατεπαύσθη Hdt.1.130, cf. 6. 71. b. *put down*, τὴν ἑωυτοῦ ἀρχήν Id.1.86; τὴν Κύρου δύναμιν ib. 90; δῆμον Th.1.107; τοὺς τετρακοσίους Id.8.97; τιμὰς ἐνέρων E.*Alc.* 31 (anap.). III. Pass. and Med. (fut. -πάήσομαι *PMag.Lond.* 121.916), *leave off, cease*, Ar.*Eq.*1265; λόγος κ. ἐν.. Pl.*Phlb.*66c: c. part., οὐ -παήσεται ἐρχομένη *PMag.* l. c. IV. Act. used intr. like Med., μολπᾶν δ' ἄπο.. καταπαύσας πόσις.. ἔκειτο E.*Hec.*918 (lyr., s. v. l.); εὐημερῶν κατάπαυσον *rest* while you are well off, *Com.Adesp.* 110.8, cf. Lxx *Ge.*8.22, al.; κ. τοῦ πορευθῆναι ib.3*Ki.*12.24.

καταπεδάω, *fetter, hamper*, κατὰ δ' οὖν ἕτερόν γε πέδησε Il.19.94; θεοῦ κατὰ μοῖρ' ἐπέδησεν Od.11.292 (μοῖρα πέδησεν Aristarch.), cf. Mosch.2.4 (tm.).

καταπεζεύω, *dismount*, ἐξ ἵππων Eust.866.14.

καταπεζομᾰχέω, *conquer by land*, Poll.9.141.

καταπειθ-ής, ές, *obedient*, τινι Ph.2.118, J.*AJ*2.4.2, al., Plu.2. 5c. **-ησις**, εως, ἡ, *persuasion*, Sch.E.*Hec.*816. **-ω**, *persuade*, Lxx 2*Ki.*17.16, Luc.*Charid.*16:—Pass., Sch.Ar.*Pl.*507.

κατ-ᾰπειλέω, strengthd. for ἀπειλέω, κ. ἔπη *use threatening* words, S.*OC*659; ἀκραιφνεῖς τῶν κατηπειλημένων *by the threats uttered*, ib. 1147.

κατάπειρ-α, ἡ, *attack*, of disease, πάθους, νόσου, Philum.*Ven.*1.4, Orib.*Fr.*76, Paul.Aeg.3.78, 5.3. **-άζω**, fut. -πειράσω Lys.30.34:—*make an attempt on*, τήν τινος ψῆφον Lys. l. c.; τοὺς τόπους Lxx 2*Ma.* 13.18; τοὺς στρατηγούς *Inscr.Prien.*111.135 (i B. C.). 2. c. gen., *make trial of*, τῶν πολεμίων, τῆς πόλεως, Plb.4.11.6, 4.13.5, cf. *PAmh.*2. 134.3 (ii A. D.):—also in Med., Herod.Med.ap.Orib.10.40.5. **-άομαι**, Pass., *to be much tried*, -αθεὶς ὑπ' ἀρρωστίας D.S.17.107. II. Med., v. l. for κατασπείρασαι in Ph.2.567. **-ασμός**, ὁ, *attack*, of disease, τοῦ συμπτώματος Dsc.*Ther.*3, cf. Philum.*Ven.*4.11: in pl., *skirmishes*, Anon.ap.Suid. s. v. χειραψίαι. **-ᾱτηρία**, Ion. **-πειρητηρίη**, ἡ, *sounding-line*, Hdt.2.5, 28; *catapirātes* in Lucil.*Fr.*1191 Marx; *anchor-cable*, prob. in *CIL*8.27790 (Althiburos).

καταπείρω, *insert*, ἐμβρυουλκὸν εἰς τόπον Sor.2.62; τοῖς κατὰ τοὺς βουβῶνας τὰ σκέλη Hld.10.32:—Pass., -πεπαρμένον ἐν ποδὶ σκόλοπα Gal.*Nat.Fac.*1.14; -παρεῖσαι (aor. 2 part.) τῇ φάρυγγι ἄκανθαι Paul. Aeg.6.32; of persons, -παρέντες εἰς τὴν 'Ιμεραίων θηρόβοτον ἄχρι τῶν στηθῶν Phalar.*Ep.*147.4. (καταπείραντες (-ροντες cod.)· καταδύσαντες (-δήσ- cod.), dub. in Hsch.)

κατάπεισις, εως, ἡ, *persuasion*, Hdn.*Epim.*110, Sch.E.*Or.*705.

καταπελεκάω, *hew with an axe*, in Pass., Sch.Il.16.642.

καταπελεμίζω, strengthd. for πελεμίζω, A.R.2.91 (tm.).

καταπελμᾰτόομαι, Pass., *to be cobbled, clouted*, of shoes, Lxx *Jo.* 9.5.

καταπελτάζω (cf. πελταστής), *overrun with light-armed troops*, καταπελτάσονται τὴν Βοιωτίαν ὅλην Ar.*Ach.*160.

κατα-πελταφεσία, -πελταφέτης, -πέλτης, -πελτικός, v. καταπαλτ-.

κατάπεμνοι· καθαπτόμενοι, Hsch. **καταπεμπάμενα**· καθημένηα, Id. (fort. καταπεπταμένα· καθημμένα).

καταπεμπ-τέος, α, ον, *to be sent down*, Luc.*DDeor.*5.4. **-τος**, ον, *sent down*, ἀνὴρ κ. ἐκ θεῶν Attic.ap.Eus.*PE*11.2. **-ω**, *send down*, εἰς ἔρεβος Hes.*Th.*515; esp. from the inland to the sea-coast, X.*HG*5.1.30, *An.*1.9.7 (Pass.); in Egypt, *down* the Nile, *PEleph.* 10.7 (iii B. C.), etc. II. *send from head-quarters, dispatch*, λῃστάς D.12.13; στρατηγὸν κ. τινά as general, Plu.*Flam.*15; ἐς ἐπισκοπήν τινος Luc.*DDeor.*20.6; γράμματα Hdn.2.12.3.

καταπενθέω, *bewail*, *AP*7.618, Lxx *Ex.*33.4.

καταπεπαίνω, *ripen*, καρποὶ -πεπανθέντες Ph.2.429; cj. in Thphr. *HP*3.13.6.

καταπεπλᾰνημένως, *erroneously*, f.l. for sq., in Poll.4.51. **καταπεπλασμένως**, *affectedly*, ibid.

καταπεπτηυῖα, Ep. fem. pf. part. of καταπτήσσω.

καταπέπτω, late form of καταπέσσω, πάθος Iamb.*VP*31.196.

καταπεπῠκασμένως, (πυκάζω) *covertly, slily*, f.l. in Poll.4.51.

κατάπερ, Ion. for καθάπερ (q.v.).

καταπεραι-όω, *conclude, close*, εἰς πόδα ἀμφίμακρον Eust.13.14, cf. 81.3. **-ωσις**, εως, ἡ, *conclusion, close*, τῆς λέξεως εἰς τέλειον ib.5.

καταπέρδομαι, only in aor. 2 Act. κατέπαρδον:—*break wind at*, τινος, in sign of contempt, Epicr.11.28 (anap.), Ar.*Pax*547; τοῦ σοῦ δίνου Id.*V*.618; τῆς Πενίας Id.*Pl*.618 (anap.).

καταπερί-ειμι, *surpass, have the advantage of*, τινος Plb.5.67. 2. **-ῐστημι**, intr. in aor. 2, *surround*, *Sammelb*.4638.18 (ii B.C.). **-ξῠσις**, εως, ἡ, v.l. for κατάξυσις, *scarification*, Sch.Od. 24.229 (pl.).

καταπερονάω, *rivet*, λαβίσι Plb.6.23.11.

καταπερπερεύομαι, = περπερεύομαι, *Com.Adesp*.1031.

καταπέσημα, ατος, τό, *downfall*, *Com.Adesp*.621 (dub. l.).

καταπέσσω, Att. -ττω Thphr.*CP*2.11.10, later -πτω (q.v.), *digest* food, Diocl.*Fr*.141:—esp. in Pass., Arist.*GA*756b11; ἕως ἂν καταπεφθῇ [ἡ τροφή] Id.*Somn*.457b19, cf. *Hippiatr*.46. 2. metaph., *digest, keep from rising*, χόλον Il.1.81; -πέψαι μέγαν ὄλβον, i.e. *bear* great fortune *meekly*, Pi.*O*.1.55.

καταπετάννῡμι, *spread out over*, κατὰ λῖτα πετάσσας Il.8.441, cf. E.*Hel*.1459 (lyr., tm.); δέρρεις πρό τινος κ. Ph.*Bel*.91.13, cf. D.S. 20.9. II. *spread* or *cover with*, τὴν αὐλὴν δικτύοις Ar.*V*.132; τὴν κεφαλὴν φοινικίδι Id.*Pl*.731; ἱστίῳ ἀνθρώπους Pl.*Prm*.131b; ἵπποι ἱματίοις καταπεπταμένοι X.*Cyr*.8.3.16.

καταπέτασμα, ατος, τό, *curtain, veil*, Hld.10.28, *PGrenf*.2.111.7 (v/vi A.D.); esp. *the veil of the Temple*, Lxx*Ex*.26.31, Aristeas 86, *Ev.Matt*.27.51, etc.; prop. *the inner veil*, the outer being τὸ κάλυμμα, cf. Ph.2.148: metaph., κ. δόξης Id.1.270. 2. κ. τραπέζης *table-cover*, *Michel*832.25 (Samos, iv B.C.).

καταπέτομαι, *fly down*: fut. καταπτήσομαι Luc.*Prom*.2: aor. κατέπτᾰτο Ar.*Av*.789, al. codd.; part. καταπτάμενος Hdt.3.111 (v.l. -πετομένας, -πετεωμένας), Ar.*V*.16, *Av*.1624 codd.; subj. and opt. κατάπτωμαι, -πτοῖο, Luc.*Icar*.13, *Bis Acc*.8: aor. 2 Act. κατέπτην, part. καταπτάς Arist.*HA*614b21, Ph.2.318, Luc.*Charid*.7, Porph. *Abst*.1.25: pf. κατέπτηκα Men.*Kol*.39: aor. 1 Pass. κατεπετάσθην Lxx*Pr*.27.8, D.S.2.20.

καταπετροκοπέω, *dash against rocks*, D.S.16.60.

καταπετρόω, *stone to death*, X.*An*.1.3.2 (Pass.). II. *throw down from a rock*, Str.3.3.7.

καταπεφνών, v. κατέπεφνον.

καταπεφρονηκότως, Adv. pf. part. Act. of καταφρονέω, *contemptuously*, D.17.29, D.S.14.17, etc. II. Adv. pf. part. Pass. **-πεφρονημένως**, *despisedly*, v.l. for -μένως in Sch.Luc.*Ind*.10.

καταπηγάζω, (πηγή) *form a spring*, *Stoic*.2.197.

καταπήγνῡμι and -ύω (Arist.*Pol*.1324b20), *stick fast* in something, *plant firmly*, ἔγχος μὲν κατέπηξεν ἐπὶ χθονί Il.6.213; ἐν δὲ σκόλοπας κ. 7.441, cf. Hdt.4.72, Ar.*Av*.360, *PPetr*.3p.121 (iii B.C.), etc.; εἰς τὴν γῆν κ. τὸν καυλόν Arist.*HA*555b20; τὸ κέντρον ἐπὶ δένδρον Philum.*Ven*.37.1:—Pass., -παγέντος σκόλοπος S.E.*P*.1.238, cf. Thphr.*HP*3.1.1. 2. metaph., *fix, crystallize*, τὴν χύσιν τῆς ἀπειρίας τῷ περατοειδεῖ δεσμῷ Dam.*Pr*.57. II. Pass., with pf. and plpf. Act., *stand fast* or *firm in*, ἰὸς ἐν γαίῃ κατέπηκτο Il.11.378; ἱστὸς -πεπηγώς Hp.*Art*.43; στήλη -πεπηγυῖα Hdt.7.30. 2. *become congealed, freeze*, Plb.3.55.5; of fish, ὑπὸ τοῦ ψύχους κ. Arist. *HA*601b31.

καταπηδάω, *leap down*, ἀπὸ τοῦ ἵππου X.*Cyr*.7.1.38, cf. Lxx*Ge*.24.64, *BGU*1201.12 (i A.D.), Plu.*Caes*.49; ἐκ τοῦ ἵππου Charito 5.3; ἀφ' ὑψηλῶν Aen.Tact.22.19.

καταπημαίνω, *hurt, damage*, in aor. 1 opt. καταπημήνειε, Hsch., Phot.

κατάπηξ, πηγος, ὁ, ἡ, *fixed in the ground*, *EM*194.24. II. as Subst. **καταπήξ**, πῆγος, ὁ, *pivot* of door-post, J.*BJ*6.5.3; *post*, *PPetr*. 3p.121 (iii B.C.), Apollod.*Poliorc*.189.9, Sm.*Jb*.38.6. 2. *graft*, *Gp*.10.65.2.

κατάπηρος, ον, *maimed, mutilated*, Hp.ap.Erot. s.v.

καταπήττω, = καταπήγνυμι, Str.4.3.5, D.H.3.22, Apollod.*Poliorc*. 166.16 (Pass., -πησσ-).

καταπῑαίνω, *fatten*, in Pass., -πεπιασμένον ζῷον Pl.*Lg*.807a, cf. Ael.*VH*9.13, *PFlor*.130.1 (iii A.D.).

κατα-πιέζω, *compress*, Thphr.*Ign*.23. **-πίεσις** [ῐ], εως, ἡ, *compression*, τοῦ ψύχους Id.*CP*2.1.4.

καταπῐθᾰνεύομαι, *use probable arguments*, S.E.*M*.8.324.

κατάπικρος, ον, *very bitter*, τῇ ψυχῇ Lxx*2Ki*.17.8, cf. Sm.*Jb*.6.3; χολή *PLeid.X*.62.

καταπῑλέω, lit. *wrap up in felt*:—Pass., *wrap oneself close*, πόκοις Alciphr.2.2.

καταπῑμελ-ής, ές, = sq., Xenocr.ap.Orib.2.58.148 (Sup.). **-ος**, ον, *very fat* or *rich*, of persons or lands, Dsc.1.24, Antyll.ap.Orib.7.16.4, Gal.19.451; στέαρ Dsc.2.76.

καταπίμπλημι, *fill quite full*, dub. l. in Lync.1.16. II. c. acc. et gen., *fill full of*, κ. [τινὰ] φρονήματος Plu.2.715a; βίον πολέμων Ph. 1.411, cf. 2.558:—Pass., καταπιμπλάμενοι ἀνομίας Pl.*R*.496d: also c. dat., ἡδύσμασιν.. καταπεπλησμέν' Antiph.183.4:—Med., πηλοῦ κατεπίμπλαντο τὰς σκηνάς *their own* tents, Plu.*Brut*.47.

καταπίμπρημι, fut. -πρήσω D.C.39.9: pf. -πέπρηκα Id.59.16:—*burn to ashes*, *AP*11.131 (Lucill.), Ph.1.516, Plu.*Cam*.22, Polyaen.8.65, Hdn.8.1.4, Jul.*Or*.2.62d:—Pass., κατεπρήσθησαν Plb.14.4.10; καταπρησθέντας Luc.*Par*.57 (nisi leg. -πτισθέντας).

καταπίνω [ῑ], fut. -πίομαι Ar.*Eq*.693, later -πιοῦμαι Plu.*Alc*.15: aor. κατέπιον *IG*4.951.102 (Epid.); poet. κάππιον Hes.*Th*.p.45 R.: pf. -πέπωκα Ar.*Av*.1137:—*gulp, swallow down*, both of liquids and solids (οὐδ' ἐν τῷ καταπίνειν ἢν πάντως τὸ πίνειν Ph.1.478), τοὺς μὲν κατέπινε Κρόνος (sc. υἱούς) Hes.*Th*.459, cf. 467, E.*Cyc*.219; ὁ τροχίλος.. καταπίνει τὰς βδέλλας Hdt.2.68, cf. 70; τεμάχη Ar.*Nu*.338; λίθους Id.*Av*. l.c.; [κίχλας] Pherecr.108.24; [μάζας] Telecl.1.5; of the sea, μὴ ναῦν κατὰ κῦμα πίῃ Thgn.680, cf. Arist.*Pr*.931b39 (Pass.); τὸ στόμα [τῆς γῆς] -πίεται αὐτοὺς Lxx*Nu*.16.30:—Pass., τὸ -ποθὲν ὕδωρ (sc. by the earth) Pl.*Criti*.111d; of rivers *that disappear underground*, Arist.*Mete*.351a1; ὑφ' ἄμμου D.S.1.32; of cities *swallowed* by an earthquake, Str.1.3.17; πόλις καταποθεῖσα ὑπὸ τῆς θαλάττης Plb.2.41.7. 2. abs., *swallow*, μόλις καταπίνειν δύνηται Hp.*Aph*. 4.35, cf. Gal.*Nat.Fac*.3.6. II. metaph., τὸν ἡμίοπον ὁ μέγας [αὐλὸς] κ. A.*Fr*.91; καταπιοῦνται ὑμᾶς οἱ Ἀθηναῖοι Plu.*Alc*.15:—Pass., *to be absorbed*, of knots in wood, Thphr.*HP*5.2.2; τῆς -πεπομένης ὑπ' αὐτοῦ φύσεως Dam.*Pr*.10. b. κ. Εὐριπίδην *drink in* Euripides, i.e. *imbibe* his spirit, Ar.*Ach*.484, Luc.*JTr*.1:—Pass., τὸ τεχνίον ἀεὶ τοῦτό μοι κατεπίνετο Antid.2.4. c. *swallow, absorb*, τὰς τέχνας Chrysipp.*Stoic*.2.257 (Pass.); but, *swallow* one's anger, ib.242. 2. *swallow up, consume*, [the robe] ἐρίων τάλαντον καταπέπωκε ῥᾳδίως Ar.*V*.1147; ὁ δικαστὴς αὐτὰ [the revenue] καταπίνει μόνος Id.*Ra*.1466; τὸν ναύκληρον αὐτῷ σκάφει κ. Anaxil.22.19; τι Men. *Epit*.151. 3. *spend, waste in tippling*, [τὴν οὐσίαν] οὐ μόνον κατέφαγεν, ἀλλὰ..καὶ κατέπιεν Aeschin.1.96, cf. D.C.45.28.

καταπιπράσκω, *sell outright*, καταπρᾱθείς Luc.*Sat*.16.

καταπίπτω, fut. -πεσοῦμαι: aor. κατέπεσον, poet. κάππεσον (the only tense used by Hom.), Dor. κάπετον (q.v.), also κατέπετον *IG* 4.951.80 (Epid.); late 3 sg. opt. -πέσειεν Apollod.*Poliorc*.168.5 (v.l. -οιεν): pf. -πέπτωκα:—*fall, drop*, καππεσέτην Il.5.560; κάππεσον ἐν Λήμνῳ 1.593; κάππεσον ἐν κονίῃσι 12.23; πρηνὴς ἐπὶ γαίῃ κάππεσε 16.311,414; πρηνὴς ἁλὶ κάππεσε Od.5.374; ἀφ' ὑψηλοῦ πύργου Il. 12.386; ἀπὸ τῶν ἡμιπλινθίων Hdt.1.50; ἀπὸ τῆς κλίμακος Ar.*Av*. 840; ἀπ' ὄνου Id.*Nu*.1273; ἀφ' ἵππου X.*Oec*.1.8; ἐς μέσους τοὺς ἄνθρακας E.*Cyc*.671; ἐπὶ τῆς γῆς X.*Cyr*.4.5.54; πληγεὶς κ. Lys.1.27; οἰκίαι καταπεπτωκυῖαι And.1.108, *BGU*282.7 (ii A.D.), etc.: used as Pass. of καταβάλλω, πρὸς ἡμῶν κάππεσε, = κατεβλήθη, A.*Ag*.1553 (lyr.). 2. metaph., παραὶ ποσὶ κάππεσε θυμός their spirit *fell*, Il. 15.280; μήτε καταπεσὼν ὀδύρεο Archil.66.5; πρὸς τὴν φήμην τῆς ἐφόδου -πεσόντες J.*BJ*7.4.2, cf. Paus.10.20.1; κ. τὴν ψυχήν v.l. in J. *AJ*6.14.2: freq. in pf. part. καταπεπτωκώς, *base, contemptible*, λόγος Aristeas 144; γένος ἄτιμον καὶ κ. Plu.*Phoc*.4; ἀγεννεῖς καὶ καταπεπτωκότες Lib.*Decl*.30.45; ταῖς ψυχαῖς καὶ τοῖς σώμασι Them.*Or*.10. 136b. b. κ. εἰς ἀπιστίαν Pl.*Phd*.88d; εἰς ἀπορίαν Id.*Men*.84c; πρὸς τὸ χεῖρον J.*AJ*2.16.1. 3. τὰ -πίπτοντα the *accidents* of fortune, Vett.Val.40.15. 4. τὰς νυνὶ -πεπτωκυίας [ἐμβολάς] which *have* just *been rejected*, Hegetor ap.Apollon.Cit.3. 5. ἄλλα, ἃ -πέπτωκε τούτοις which *fall under the same head*, Gal.5.723. II. *have the falling sickness*, Luc.*Tox*.24, *Philops*.16.

καταπισσόω, Att. -ττόω, *cover with pitch*, as was done to wine-jars, etc., Cratin.189 (Pass.), Ar.*Ec*.1109, Gal.17(2).164: metaph., *paint black*, opp. καταχρυσόω (in v. 826), κατεπίττου πᾶς ἀνὴρ Εὐριπίδην Ar.*Ec*.829. II. *tar and burn* (as a punishment), Heraclid. Pont.ap.Ath.12.524a:—Pass., Pl.*Grg*.473c.

καταπιστ-ευτέον, *one must trust*, Sor.1.33. **-εύω**, *trust*, ταῖς ἰδίαις δυνάμεσι Plb.2.3.3; τινι Hld.4.13: c. pres. or fut. inf., Id.6.7, 1.23; ἐν φίλοις Lxx*Mi*.7.5: abs., *feel confidence*, Plu.*Lys*.8, Gal.12. 692. II. *entrust*, τινὶ τὴν ἄμυναν, τὴν διοίκησιν, Zos.1.36, 3.2; ἑνὸς ἀνδρὸς ἐξουσίᾳ τοσαύτης ἀρχῆς κίνδυνον Id.1.5; τινι c. inf., *Sammelb*. 5273.4 (v A.D.):—Pass., *to be entrusted*, *POxy*.136.8 (vi A.D.): also in pf. part., *devoted*, ἀνὴρ ταῖς Μούσαις -πεπιστευμένος Phalar.*Ep*.93. 1. **-όομαι**, Med., *become security*, ὑπέρ τινος πρός τινα for one to another, Plu.*Cleom*.21. **-ωσις**, εως, ἡ, *assurance, pledge of faith*, καταπιστώσεις ποιεῖσθαι, of lovers, Arist.*Fr*.97, cf. Plu.2. 258b.

καταπιττόω, Att. for καταπισσόω.

καταπλᾰγής, ές, *panic-struck, scared*, κ. γενέσθαι τὴν ἔφοδον Plb. 1.7.6; κ. μή.. Id.2.69.6.

καταπλᾰκών, aor. 2 part. (v. ἀμπλακεῖν); the gloss of Hsch. (καταπλακών· καταπλήξας, διαμαρτών) shd. be corrected thus: καταπλακών· διαμαρτών:—καταπτακών· καταπτήξας.

καταπλᾰνάω, strengthd. for πλανάω, *deceive, mislead*, *App.Prov*. 1.50 (cod. C).

κατά-πλᾰσις, εως, ἡ, *plastering* or *poulticing*, Hp.*VC*13, cj. in Sor.1.73. **-πλασμα**, ατος, τό, *plaster, poultice*, Hp.*Art*.40 (pl.), Ar.*Fr*.320.12, Arist.*Pr*.863a6, Thphr.*HP*9.11.4, *Od*.59, *PLit.Lond*. 170 (pl., i A.D.), etc. **-πλασμάτιον**, τό, Dim. of foreg., Sor.1. 50. **-πλασμός**, ὁ, = κατάπλασμα, Anon.Lond.36.58. **-πλάσσω**, Att. -ττω, fut. -πλάσω [ᾰ], *plaster over*, πηλῷ κατ' ὧν ἔπλασε τοὺς ὀφθαλμούς Hdt.2.70, cf. Arist.*HA*612a18; ὄξει τὰ βλέφαρα Ar.*Pl*. 721; τὰ ὦτα κηρῷ Plu.2.15d:—Pass., καταπεπλασμένη ψιμυθίῳ Ar. *Ec*.878; κηρῷ Arist.*HA*624a13:—Med., τὴν κεφαλὴν κατ' ὧν ἐπλάσατο *plastered her own* head, Hdt.2.85, cf. D.S.1.72,91; τοῦτο καταπλάσσονται πᾶν τὸ σῶμα this they *plaster over their* whole body, Hdt.4.75:—Pass., καταπλαττομένων ἢ ἐπιπλαττομένων Phld.*Mus.* p.52 K. 2. Medic., *plaster* or *poultice*, Hp.*VC*13, al.; also, *apply as a plaster* or *poultice*, in Pass., Dsc.4.87,88: metaph., c. gen., θεὸς κ. τῶν ψυχῆς τραυμάτων Ph.1.455. 3. metaph., καταπεπλασμένος, = καταπλαστός II, Aristid.*Or.*28(49).101; τὸ κ. the *artificial sound* produced by stopping the higher notes in a flute, Quint.1.11.6. **-πλαστέον**, *one must plaster*, Antyll.ap.Orib.7.16.4, Archig.ap.Aët.3.191. **-πλάστης**, ου, ὁ, *one who plasters*, Ph. 2.478. **-πλαστός**, όν, *plastered over*, φάρμακον καταπλαστόν, = κατάπλασμα, *plaster*, Ar.*Pl.*717; opp. χριστά and ποτά, v. Sch. ad loc. II. metaph., *affected*, ἀπαμφιεῖ τὸ κ. σου ἡ μέθη your *false assumptions*, Men.339; κ. βαρύτης Plu.2.44a. **-πλαστύς**, ύος, ἡ, Ion. for κατάπλασμα, Hdt.4.75.

καταπλᾰτύνω, strengthd. for πλατύνω, Gal.2.298: **-πλᾰτύς**, εῖα, ύ, for πλατύς, Tz.*H.*11.855.

καταπλέκω, *entwine, plait*, [φλοῦν] φορμοῦ τρόπον κ. Hdt.3.98. b. in Anatomy, Pass., perh. *inosculate, anastomose*, in aor. -επλάκην [ᾰ], Hp.*Oss.*18 (aor. part. Pass. -πλεκεῖσι Hsch.); also, *to be entwined, matted*, Sor.1.88. c. *twine round*, τὰ εὐώνυμα μέρη Meno *Iatr.*16.16; *compose*, τὸν ὄσχεον Paul.Aeg.6.63. 2. metaph., *implicate*, κ. τινὰ προδοσίῃ Hdt.8.128 (as v.l.):—Pass., πόλεμος.. καταπεπλεγμένος τῇ ποικιλίᾳ in the variety of its events, *complicated*, Arist. *Po.*1459^{a}34; *to be involved*, ἐν τούτῳ ψεῦδος κατεπέπλεκτο S.E.*M.* 2.71. 3. c. dat. pers., *entangle, involve in contradictions*, *POxy.* 1673.20 (ii A.D.), 903.35 (iv A.D.). II. *finish twining*: hence metaph., *bring to an end*, τὴν ζόην, τὴν ῥῆσιν, Hdt.4.205, 8.83.

καταπλεονεκτέω, *to have mastered*, ἃ -εῖ νῦν ἡ ἰητρική Hp.*Decent.*6.

κατάπλεος, ον, Att. -πλεως, ων, gen. ω, *quite full*, τινος of a thing, Ph.2.568, Plu.2.498f: *fouled, stained with*, γῆς τε κατάπλεων τὸ γένειον καὶ αἵματος X.*Cyr.*8.3.30, cf. *IG*4.952.44 (Epid.); [πηλῷ] D.H.1. 79: c. dat., *filled with*, λύχνος ὥσπερ κέγχροις πολλοῖς κ. Thphr.*Sign.* 42; χωρίον ὀχετοῖς κατάπλεων App.*Pun.*117.

καταπλέω, Ion. -πλώω Hdt.2.93 codd.: aor. -έπλωσα Id.1.2, al.:—*sail down*; i.e., 1. *sail from the high sea to land, put in*, ἔνθα κατεπλέομεν Od.9.142: abs., Hdt.6.97, 7.137, Lys.28.5, etc.; ἐς Αἶαν Hdt.1.2, cf. 8.132; ἐπὶ Ἑλλησπόντου ib.109, 9.98; ἐπ' Ἀρτεμίσιον Id.7.195; τὰς ἐκ Πόντου ναῦς Ἀθήναζε κ. X.*HG*5.1.28; ἕως ἂν δεῦρο -πλεύσωμεν Test.ap.D.21.168; ἐνταῦθα κ. Id.32.14; *sail home*, Lys. 21.3, Phoenicid.2.3; νεωστὶ καταπεπλευκώς having lately *come ashore*, Pl.*Euthd.*297c; of things, *to be brought by sea*, πυρὸς Ἀθήναζε -πλέων Thphr.*CP*4.9.5; ἡ -πλέουσα ἀγορά App.*Pun.*100. 2. *sail down stream*, [ἐς] τὸν Εὐφρήτην Hdt.1.185; in Egypt, *down the Nile*, κ. εἰς τὴν πόλιν (sc. Alexandria) *PMagd.*22.4 (iii B.C.), cf. *PTeb.*58.44 (ii B.C.), etc.; of fish, *swim down stream*, κ. ἐς θάλασσαν Hdt.2.93, cf. Arist.*HA*598^{b}16. II. *sail back*, Hdt.1.165, 3.45, And.2.13, Phld.*Acad.Ind.*p.102 M., etc.

κατάπλεως, ων, gen. ω, Att. for κατάπλεος.

κατα-πληγία, ἡ, *panic fear*, Poll.3.137. **-πληγμός**, ὁ, = κατάπληξις, Lxx *Si.*21.4. **-πλήγνυμι**, = καταπλήσσω, Dam.*Isid.* 284. **-πληκτέον**, οὐ κ. *one must* not *be terrified*, Din.1. 108. **-πληκτικός**, ή, όν, *striking, astonishing*, εὐπρόσωπος καὶ κ. Macho ap.Ath.13.578c; εὐπρέπεια κ. Phld.*Hom.*p.58 O.; *terrible*, προσβολαί Plb.3.13.6; πρόσοψις, διήγησις, κραυγή, Id.3.114.4, 4.28.6, 11.16.2; τὰ εἰς πόλεμον κ. D.S.2.16; but expressly opp. φοβερός in Muson.*Fr.*33p.122 H. (nisi leg. καταλλακτικός). Adv. -κῶς Plb.3.41. 3, D.S.3.35, etc. **-πληκτος**, ον, *astonishing*, f.l. for foreg., Id.31. 8. **-πλήξ**, ῆγος, ὁ, ἡ, *stricken, struck*, ὑπὸ τῶν γυναικῶν Theopomp.Com.59: usu. metaph., *stricken with amazement, astounded*, ὑπὸ τῶν τούτου ἁμαρτημάτων Lys.6.50; ἄτολμος καὶ κ. Plu.2.7b; κ. καὶ περιδεής ib.814f; μὴ ὦσιν οἱ ἵπποι καταπλῆγες Ael.*NA*16.25. 2. *shy, bashful*, opp. ἀναίσχυντος, Arist.*EN*1108^{a}34, *EE*1233^{b}28, Jul. *Or.*7.233b. 3. c. gen., *nervous, apprehensive of*, πολλῶν Plu. *Fab.*14 codd. 4. Medic., *fixed*, ὀφθαλμός (in paralysis) Hp.*Epid.* 5.50. **-πληξις**, εως, ἡ, *amazement, consternation*, Th.7.42, 8.66, *BGU*1209.16 (i B.C.), etc.; κ. ὀμμάτων *fixation*, Hp.*Epid.*7.56. 2. *extreme shyness*, Arist.*MM*1193^{a}1. **-πλήσσω**, Att. -ττω, fut. -ξω D.21.194:—*strike down*, τινὸς εἰς τὴν κατακλεῖδα [ξίφος] *PMag.Par.* 1.300: usu. metaph., *strike with amazement, astound, terrify*, κατέπλησσεν ἐπὶ τὸ φοβεῖσθαι Th.2.65; ὁ φόβος κ. τὰς ψυχάς X.*Cyr.*3.1.25; καταπλήξειν ᾤετο τὸν δῆμον D. l. c.; κ. τοὺς ἀκροατάς, of orators, Arist.*Rh.*1408^{a}25; -πλῆξαί τινα τῇ προδοσίῃ *tax* him with his treachery, Hdt.8.128 (v.l. -πλέξαι); *browbeat, bully*, *POxy.*237 viii 10 (ii A.D.):—Med., -πλήξασθαι τοὺς ὑπεναντίους Plb.3.89.1, cf. D.S. 11.77, Jul.*Or.*6.191a, etc.:—Pass., *to be panic-stricken, astounded*, most freq. in aor. 2 and pf. (pres., Eup.159.10), κατεπλήγη φίλον ἦτορ Il.3.31; -πλαγῆναι τῷ πολέμῳ Th.1.81; τῷ πλήθει Id.4.10; μὴ -πέπληχθε ἄγαν Id.7.77: c. acc., πάνυ τοῦτ' ἐπαινῶ καὶ -πλήττομαι Eup. l. c.; τὴν ἀπειρίαν τὴν αὐτοῦ -πεπλῆχθαι Isoc.*Ep.*4.11; μηδὲν -πλαγέντες τὸν Φίλιππον Decr.ap.D.18.185; -πεπλῆχθαι τὸν βίον Id.37. 43 codd.; -πεπληγμένοι τὸν στόλον Plb.1.20.6; *to be amazed at*, τὴν ἀπαθίαν τινῶν Phld.*Sto.Herc.*339.7: later intr. in pf. -πέπληγα, plpf. -πεπλήγη App.*Mith.*19, Paus.10.22.2, Luc.*DMeretr.*13.2: esp. in part., -πεπληγότες τὸ τῶν Ῥωμαίων τάχος D.H.6.25, etc.; τὸ περιδεὲς καὶ -πεπληγός *abject terror*, Plu.*Comp.Pel.Marc.*1.

καταπλίσσομαι, Pass., *to be tripped up*, ἡμῶν ἴσως σὺ καταπλῐγήσει (fut. 2) τῷ χορῷ *will be tripped up, beaten* by our chorus, dub. in Ar. *Fr.*198.3, cf. Hsch. s. v. καταπλιγήσει.

καταπλοκή, ἡ, *entwining, interlacing*, τοῦ νεύρου καὶ τοῦ δέρματος Pl.*Ti.*76d; *complication*, τῶν πραγμάτων Artem.2.5. II. in Music, *descending progression*, opp. ἀναπλοκή, Ptol.*Harm.*2.12.

κατάπλοος, contr. -πλους, ὁ, *sailing down, bearing down*, Th.4. 10; *sailing to land, putting ashore*, ib.26; ὁ Σικελικὸς κ. the *arrival* of the corn-fleet from Sicily, D.56.9. 2. *sailing down stream*, esp. *down the Nile*, ὁ κατ' ἐνιαυτὸν εἰς Ἀλεξάνδρειαν κ. *OGI*90.17 (Rosetta, ii B.C.), cf. *PTeb.*27.103 (ii B.C.). II. *sailing back, return*, ὁ οἴκαδε κ. X.*HG*1.4.11; παρῆν τις ἐκ κ. one *who had just returned*, Plb.15.23.3.

καταπλουτίζω, *enrich greatly*, τινα Hdt.6.132, X.*Oec.*4.7; τινὰ εὐεργεσίαις Ph.2.588.

καταπλουτομᾰχέω, *conquer by money*, D.S.5.38.

κατα-πλυντηρίζω, *drench with foul abuse*, *Com.Adesp.*715. **-πλύνω** [ῡ], *drench*, ὕδατι τὴν κεφαλήν X.*Eq.*5.6. II. *wash out, remove by washing*, [ἁλμυρόν τι] Arist.*Mete.*357^{b}5:—Pass., καταπλῠθείσης τῆς ἅλμης Thphr.*CP*3.24.3: metaph., καταπέπλῠται τὸ πρᾶγμα the affair *is washed out, has become worthless*, Aeschin.3.178, cf. Poll.7. 38. **-πλῠσις**, εως, ἡ, *bathing in water*, τῶν σκελῶν X.*Eq.*5.9.

κατά-πλωσις, εως, ἡ, Ion. for κατάπλους, *home-coming by sea*, Herod.1.68: **-πλώω**, Ion. for καταπλέω.

καταπνέω, Ep. -πνείω, *blow* or *breathe upon* or *over*, τί τινος, χώρας (Reisk. for χώραν) καταπνεῦσαι ἡδυπνόους αὔρας E.*Med.*839 (lyr.); Ἔρως ἵμερον κ. ἡμῶν κατὰ τῶν κόλπων Ar.*Lys.*552: with gen. understood, Arist.*HA*541^{a}29, 594^{b}27: also c. acc., κ. τόπον εὐωδίᾳ *fill* the place with fragrance, Hld.3.2: c. acc. cogn., ἡδὺ κ. *h.Cer.* 238:—Pass., σπινθὴρ -πνευσθείς Ph.1.455; -πνευσθέντες ὑπὸ ἀνέμων ψυχρῶν *blown upon* by.., Gal.12.599; στρατόπεδον οὐ -πνεόμενον ἐκ τῆς θαλάσσης App.*Pun.*99: abs., ὅταν Βορρᾶς -πνεύσῃ Cratin. 207. 2. *inspire*, θεόθεν καταπνείει πειθὼ.. ξύμφυτος αἰών A.*Ag.* 105 (s. v.l., lyr.); θεοῦ ὁμόνοιαν, ὀργὴν δικαίαν -πνέοντος, Ael.*NA*12. 2,7: c. acc. pers., θεὸς καταπνεῖ σε E.*Rh.*387:—Pass., -πνευσθείς Ph.1.411. 3. *blow upon*, c. dat., τοῖς πρὸς ἄρκτον οἰκοῦσι.. κ. ὁ νότος Arist.*Pr.*945^{a}36: metaph., μή σοι νέμεσις θεόθεν καταπνεύσῃ Pl. Com.173.14. II. Pass., *to be blown up*, φλόξ Plu.2.474d.

κατα-πνίγω [ῑ], *choke, smother*, γόγγρον ἐν ἅλμῃ Sotad.Com.1.21; ὁ ὕπνος κ. τὸ θερμόν Arist.*Fr.*233; ταῦτα κ. τὰ δένδρα Thphr.*CP*2. 18.3; τὴν αὔξησιν Plu.2.806c; πνεῦμα Nic.*Al.*286; λύγγας Arist. *Pr.*962^{a}7:—Pass., *to be choked up*, of the secretions, ib.967^{a}6; of a fire, opp. ἐγκρύπτω 2, Id.*Juv.*470^{a}16; καταπεπνιγμένοι τόποι *choked up, close*, opp. εὐπνούστεροι, Id.*Pr.*869^{a}35; φωναὶ καταπεπν. *stifled* utterances, Id.*Aud.*800^{a}15, cf. Poll.4.114. 2. κ. τὰς φύσας *close* the bellows, Arist.*Resp.*474^{a}15. **-πνιξις**, εως, ἡ, *choking, smothering*, opp. εὔπνοια, ib.966^{b}36, cf. Thphr.*HP*5.9.4, *Sud.*9.

κατα-πνοή, ἡ, *blowing*, ἀνέμων Pi.*P.*5.121 codd. **-πνοος**, ον, contr. -πνους, ουν, *blown upon*, Poll.1.240.

καταποδίζω, *obstruct, hamper*, Phld.*Lib.*p.15 O.

καταπόθρα, ἡ, *gullet, pharyngeal region*, Paul.Aeg.6.32, *Hippiatr.* 16.

καταποιέω, *depress*, Hp.*Mochl.*2 (v.l. κακοποιεῖ).

καταποικίλλω, *deck with various colours* or *in divers modes, mottle*, τὸ σῶμα Pl.*Ti.*85a; θάλαμος, ὃν αἱ Χάριτες κατεποίκιλαν Men.Rh. p.407 S.; διττὰ ὑφάσματα Ph.2.226:—Pass., ὑπὸ τῶν γραφέων τὰ ἱερὰ ἡμῖν καταπεποίκιλται Pl.*Euthphr.*6c; ὀροφὴ ἀστέρας καταπεποικιλμένη D.S.1.47. 2. metaph., of style, κ. τὸν λόγον Isoc.13.16, Phld. *Rh.*1.167 S.; also κ. τὰ γεγενημένα, of historians, Agath.*Praef.* p.136 D.

καταπολεμ-έω, *war down*, i.e. *exhaust by war, reduce*, τὴν Πελοπόννησον Th.2.7, cf. 4.1, And.3.15, X.*HG*7.1.10: pres., *attempt to subdue*, ἐγκλήμασι Th.4.86:—Pass., ἐλπίζοντες αὐτὴν [τὴν πόλιν] καταπεπολεμῆσθαι Id.6.16, cf. Pl.*Mx.*243c,d. II. simply, *make war against*, τινα Phld.*Piet.*54: abs., *carry on warfare*, τοῖς ὅλοις Plu. *Caes.*26. **-ησις**, εως, ἡ, *subduing*, condemned by Poll.9.142.

καταπολεύω, *revolve*, ὁ ἰσημερινὸς τῷ βορείῳ κύκλῳ -εύοντι βραδυτέρω(ς).. ὁμοχρόνως κινεῖται Sch.Arat.147; of the constellation Ἄρκτος, *move downwards in an orbit*, opp. ἀναπολεύω, *PMag.Par.*1.702.

καταπολιός, όν, *white-haired*, *Gloss.*

καταπολῑτεύομαι, *subdue* or *reduce by policy*, τινα D.19.315, Plu. *Pomp.*51, *Galb.*20, etc.

καταπομα, ατος, τό, *drink*, Aq., Sm.*Je.*51(28).44.

καταπομπ-εύω, *scoff at*, τινος Luc.*Am.*37. **-ή**, ἡ, *delivery, rendering* of goods or returns, *POxy.*1415.7, *BGU*362 viii 15 (both iii A.D.). II. *sending back*, Afric.ap.Eus.*DE*8.2. **-ός**, ὁ, *one who conveys* or *delivers*, c. gen., *POxy.*1415.5 (iii A.D.), etc.

καταπον-έω, *subdue*, τῇ ἐνδείᾳ τῆς τροφῆς τὴν ἀλκὴν τοῦ θηρίου D.S.3.37, cf. Heraclit.*Incred.*11: in fut. Med., τὰς ὀλίγας ναῦς ταῖς πολλαπλασίαις D.S.11.15; *worst* in a lawsuit, *POxy.*1101.9 (iv A.D.):—Pass., *to be subdued, reduced, worn out*, δῆμος -πεπονημένος Aeschin.2.36, cf. Plb.29.27.11, D.S.11.6; πάντα ταῖς ἐνδελεχείαις -πονεῖται πράγματα Men.744; *to be exhausted*, τῷ θάλπει Gal.10. 715. 2. *handle roughly, crush, damage*, τὰ -πονούμενα καὶ συμπατούμενα Thphr.*HP*8.7.5; *maltreat, oppress*, esp. in Pass., ὑπὸ τῶν τυράννων, ὑπὸ τῶν τελωνῶν, Arist.*Fr.*575, *BGU*1188.17 (Aug.), cf. *Act.Ap.*7.24, Diog.Oen.1. 3. *digest* food, Sor.2.32 (Pass.). II. intr. in pf. part. -πεπονηκώς *ruinous*, Procop.*Aed.*1.4,8. **-ησις**, εως, ἡ, *affliction*, Sm.*Ex.*3.7. **-ος**, ον, *tired, wearied*, ἀθλητής Plu. *Sull.*29; *worn out, exhausted*, of cattle, *PLond.*3.1170^{v}462 (iii A.D.); ὑπ' ἀλλήλων Plu.*Alc.*25. II. *laboured*, of poetry or works of art, Id.*Tim.*36; *wearisome*, λατρεία Lxx 3*Ma.*4.14; κ. βάρος Phld.*D.* 3.13.

καταποντ-ίζω, *throw into the sea, plunge* or *drown therein,* τινα Lys. 14.27, D.23.169, Plu.2.403c, etc.: metaph., Axiop.6(Pass.); κ. τὰς βουλάς Lib.*Or.*49.10:—Pass., v.l. in Plb.2.60.8; καταποντισθεὶς ὑπὸ τῆς θαλάσσης D.S.18.20; ἐν τῷ πελάγει *Ev.Matt.*18.6; εἰς τὸ πέλαγος Plu.*Tim.*13; *sink, Ev.Matt.*14.30; of a ship, *PPetr.*2 p.135 (iii B.C.). **-ισμός,** ὁ, *drowning,* Isoc.12.122 (pl.), Lxx *Ps.*51(52).4(6); ὁ κ. τῶν χρημάτων App.*Mac.*16. **-ιστής,** οῦ, ὁ, *one who throws into the sea,* of pirates, λῃσταὶ καὶ κ. Isoc.12.226, D.23.166,167, cf. Jul. *Or.*6.201b: metaph., καταποντισταὶ τῆς Ἑλλάδος Paus.8.52.3, cf. Lib.*Or.*63.17. **-όω,** = καταποντίζω, Hdt.1.165, 4.154, Xenarch.2.5, etc.; κ. ἐς τὴν θάλασσαν Hdt.3.30; εἰς ποταμόν Polem.Hist.54; τὴν οὐσίαν Philostr.*VA*1.13:—Pass., Antipho 5.28, Pl.*Grg.*511e, Ph.1.264,394, Plu.*Cat.Mi.*11.

καταπορεύομαι, *come back* from banishment, Plb.4.17.8, *OGI*90.19 (Rosetta, ii B.C.). 2. *return home,* Lxx 2*Ma.*11.30, 3*Ma.*4.11. 3. κ. εἰς τάξιν, = Lat. *regredi in ordinem, IG*7.2225.42 (Thisbe).

κατ-απορέω, *fail in treating*:—hence in Pass., κατηπορήθη ὀστέα ἐμπεσεῖν *there was a failure in* reducing the fracture, Hp.*Fract.*33; οἷσι ἂν ὦμος κ. ἐμβληθῆναι Id.*Art.*12, cf. 61.

καταπορθέω, *ravage utterly, Gloss.*

καταπορθμίας, ὁ, *an East wind, blowing down the Straits* of Messina, Arist.*Vent.*973ᵃ25.

καταπορίζω, = *remeo, Gloss.*

καταπόρν-ευσις, εως, ἡ, *prostitution,* θυγατέρων παρθένων Plu.*Tim.* 13 (pl.). **-εύω,** *prostitute,* τὰ θήλεα τέκνα Hdt.1.94,196:—Pass., Str.11.14.16. II. *violate, treat as prostitutes,* Plu.2.821d, Ael.*VH* 9.8:—Pass., prob. in *POxy.*1241 iii 11. III. *squander on courtesans,* D.C.45.28.

καταπορνοκοπέω, = foreg. III, Poll.3.117.

καταπόρφῠρος, ον, *all-purple,* Lyd.*Mag.*2.13.

καταπόσια, τά, = *ludi Florales, Gloss.*

κατάποσις, εως, ἡ, *gulping down, swallowing,* Pl.*Ti.*80a, Arist. *PA*690ᵇ28, Gal.10.506; τῆς τροφῆς Aret.*CA*1.4; τοῦ Κρόνου τῶν παίδων Sallust.4(pl.); [τέχνης] Chrysipp.*Stoic.*2.257. II. *gullet,* Muson.*Fr.*18ᴬ p.97 H., Epict.*Gnom.*22, Dsc.3.80, Sor.1.86, Xenocr. ap.Orib.2.58.93, Aret.*SD*1.7.

κατ-αποστέλλω, *send down* (to Alexandria), *UPZ*110.137 (ii B.C.).

καταποτάομαι, *fly down,* v.l. in Lib.*Or.*11.86.

κατα-πότης, ου, ὁ, = λάρυγξ, Hsch. s.v. βρόγχος, Suid. **-ποτον,** τό, *pill, bolus,* v.l. for καταπότια in Hp.*Acut.*(*Sp.*)70, *Mul.*2.133, cj. for κατὰ ποτόν in Thphr.*HP*9.20.2: in pl., *things swallowed,* Aret. *CA*2.2:—Dim. **-πότιον,** *little pill,* Hp. ll.cc., Thphr.*HP*9.8.3, Ruf. ap.Orib.7.26.125, Archig.ib.8.2.30, *POxy.*2144.4 (iii A.D.), etc.

κατ-αποφαίνομαι, *pronounce dogmatically,* Diog.Oen.8.

κατ-αποχή, ἡ, *receipt, Arch.Pap.*3.418 (vi A.D.).

καταπραγμᾰτεύω, Act. and Med., c. gen., sine expl., Suid.

καταπραιδεύω, (Lat. *praeda*) *ravage,* Suid. s.v. καταδῃοῦν.

καταπρακτικός, ή, όν, *fitted for accomplishing,* τῶν νοηθέντων Muson.*Fr.*8 p.39 H. II. Subst. **-κόν,** τό, *spell for achieving* success, *PMag.Par.*1.2373.

καταπρᾱνής, ές, Att. for καταπρηνής, πρόσχωσις J.*AJ*4.8.5, cf. Hsch.

κατάπραξις, εως, ἡ, *execution,* τῶν βεβουλευμένων J.*AJ*19.1.4.

καταπράσσω, Att. -ττω, *accomplish, execute,* τινί τι X.*An.*7.7.46; τι τῶν ἐπειγόντων Plu.*Per.*5; κ. ὥστε τι γίγνεσθαι X.*HG*7.4.11. b. *construct, build,* ἡρῷον *IG*12(7).478.2 (Amorgos). 2. *achieve, gain,* ἀρχήν X.*Cyr.*7.5.76:—Med., *achieve for oneself,* dub. in Id.*An.*7.7.27, cf. Zos.1.44; ὅπως καταπράξεται τὸν γάμον Men.242; ἰδίαν ἀσφάλειαν D.H.6.68:—Pass., τὰ καταπεπραγμένα X.*Cyr.*7.5.35; τὴν ἡγεμονίαν -πραχθῆναι Id.*Vect.*5.5.

καταπρᾱτικόν, τό, (πιπράσκω) *tax on sales, Inscr.Magn.*116.42.

καταπρᾱΰν-σις, εως, ἡ, *placation, Gloss.* **-ω,** fut. -πραΰνῶ Hsch.: Ep. and Ion. **-πρηΰνω**:—*soften,* opp. τραχύνω, Pl.*Ti.*67a: usu. metaph., *soften down, appease,* Pl.*Euthd.*288b, A.R.1.265, Q.S.14.328; κ. τοὺς ἀκροατάς, of an orator, Isoc.4.13, cf. Arist.*Rh.*1380ᵇ30; κ. τὴν ταραχήν Plb.5.52.14; κ. τινὰ τῆς ὀργῆς Plu.*Them.*31:—Pass., *to be pacified,* of animals, Phld.*Mus.*p.20 K.; *to be allayed,* of emotions, Id.*Rh.*1.370 S.

κατάπρεμνος, ον, *with many branches,* Hsch.

καταπρεσβεύω, *undertake an embassy against,* τινος Str.17.1.11: abs., Plb.22.11.8.

καταπρην-ής, ές, *down-turned,* opp. ὕπτιος, in Hom. always of the hand as used in striking or grasping, πλῆξεν.. χειρὶ καταπρηνεῖ *with the flat of* his hand, Il.16.792, cf. Od.13.164; πεπλήγετο μηρὼ χερσὶ καταπρηνέσσι Il.15.114; χείρεσσι κ. λαβοῦσα Od.19.467; ἐς τὸ κ. ῥέποντα Hp.*Fract.*40. (Ion. for καταπρανής, q.v.) **-ίζω,** *throw headlong down,* ἁλιῆας.. κατεπρήνιξεν ἐπάκτρου εἰς ἅλα Nic.*Th.*824, cf. Nonn.*D.*4.395. **-όω,** = foreg., τινὰ πόντῳ καταπρηνώσασθαι *AP* 7.652 (Leon.).

κατά-πριστος, ον, *sawn,* ἐλέφας prob. in Hermipp.63.15. **-πρίω** [ῑ], *saw up,* κορμοὺς ξύλων Hdt.7.36; *saw asunder,* Lxx *Su.*59. 2. *cut* or *bite into pieces,* κύμινον Theoc.10.55; γλῶσσαν κυνόδοντι Nic. *Al.*283.

καταπρο-βάλλω, *prostrate,* prob. f.l. for προκατα-, Gal.19.622. **-δίδωμι,** *betray utterly, leave in the lurch,* Hdt.7.157, 8.94, Ar.*V.*1044, Th.1.86, 7.48, etc.; τὰς Ἀφίδνας τινί Hdt.9.73; τὰ πράγματα Lys.20.6:—Pass., Hdt.9.7.α', Th.3.111. **-θῡμέομαι,** strengthd. for προθυμέομαι, c. acc., Suid. **-ίεμαι,** Med., *throw away, abandon,* τοὺς καιρούς Plb.1.77.3, etc.; τοὺς ἰδίους βίους Id.3.81.4, cf. *PRev.Laws* 27.11 (iii B.C.), *PTeb.*27.61 (ii B.C.); τὸ ζῆν Phld.*Mort.*5; πολλὰ τῶν κοινῶν τοῖς κλέπτουσιν Plu.*Arist.*4; ἀλλήλω Procop.*Arc.*1 (ἀλλήλων codd.): aor. καταπροηκάμην Poll.8.143.

καταπροΐξομαι, Att. -προίξομαι, in early writers only fut., later also aor. 1 (v. infr.): used with neg., and usu. c. part., οὐ γὰρ δὴ ἐμέ γε ὧδε λωβησάμενος καταπροΐξεται he *shall* not *escape unpunished for* thus insulting me, Hdt.3.156; οὐ καταπροΐξονται ἀποστάντες Id.5.105, cf. 7.17; οὔτοι καταπροίξει τάλαντα πολλὰ κλέψας Ar.*Eq.*435; οὔτοι καταπροίξει τοῦτο δρῶν you *shall* not *escape unpunished for* doing this, Id.*V.*1366; οὔτοι.. καταπροίξει λέγουσα ταυτί Id.*Th.*566: abs., ἐκείνους οὐ καταπροΐξεσθαι ἔφη *should* not *get off scot-free,* Hdt.3.36: without a neg., Them.*Or.*2.25b: in aor. 1, οὐ μὴν ἐκεῖνός γε παντελῶς κατεπροίξατο Plu.2.10c (-πράξ- codd.), cf. Hsch. 2. c. gen. pers., ἐμεῦ δ' ἐκεῖνος οὐ καταπροΐξεται he *shall* not *escape* me *unpunished,* Archil.92; οὔτοι ἐμοῦ.. καταπροίξει Ar.*Nu.*1240; οὔτοι.. καταπροίξει Μυρτίας Id.*V.*1396. 3. both constructions combined, οὐ καταπροίξῃ αὐτὸς μεθύων νηφούσης γυναικός Hdn.1.17.5.—Ion. word, used in colloquial Att. of Com. (Glossed προῖκα ἐκφύγοι in Suid., δωρεὰν καταγνώσεται in *EM*495.34, and connected by both with προΐσσομαι, προΐκτης; but perh. rather from κατα-προ-ἱκνέομαι.)

καταπρολείπω, *forsake utterly,* A.R.3.1164.

καταπρονομεύω, *carry off as booty,* Lxx *Nu.*21.1, *Jd.*2.14.

κατάπροσθεν, = ἔμπροσθεν, *IG*11(2).161 *A* 45, 165.22 (Delos, iii B.C.); **κατάπροσθε** ib.163.51.

καταπροτείνομαι, *hold out as a pretence,* Gal.5.92.

καταπροτερέω, *get the better of,* τινος D.S.17.33; κ. τὸν καιρόν *seize a favourable* opportunity, Men.Prot.p.102 D.:—Pass., *to be beaten, yield,* τοῖς ἐπιβατικοῖς, ταῖς εὐχειρίαις, Plb.1.47.9, 16.19.1.

καταπροχέω, *pour down over,* δάκρυα παρειῶν A.R.3.1118.

κατάπρωκτος, ον, = καταπύγων, dub. l. in Ar.*Ec.*364.

κατάπτερ-ος, ον, *winged,* A.*Pr.*798, E.*Or.*176 (lyr.). **-όω,** *furnish with wings,* ἱππείᾳ τριχί E.*Melanipp.Sap.Prol.*15, cf. Apollod. 1.6.3 (Pass.).

καταπτήσομαι, fut. of καταπέτομαι.

καταπτήσσω, fut. -πτήξω (v. infr.): 3 dual Ep. aor. 2 καταπτήτην Il.8.136: poet. aor. part. καταπτᾰκών A.*Eu.*252 (cf. καταπλακών): pf. κατέπτηκα Lxx *Jo.*2.24 (v.l. -έπτηχε), Did. *in D.*11.25, Them.*Or.*24.309b, or κατέπτηχα D.4.8, Plu.*Per.*25, Gal.5.510; Ep. part. καταπεπτηώς (v. infr.):—*crouch, cower,* esp. from fear, καταπτήτην ὑπ' ὄχεσφι Il.8.136; καταπτήξας ὑπὸ θάμνῳ 22.191; κατὰ δ' ἔπτηξαν ποτὶ γαίῃ Od.8.190; λιμῷ καταπεπτηυῖα Hes.*Sc.*265: also in Prose, κατέπτηχε μέντοι ταῦτα πάντα νῦν D. l.c., cf. D.H.7.50; ταπεινοὶ -πτήξετε πρὸς τὸ μέλλον Plu.*Aem.*27; διὰ τὸ μέγεθος Id.*Sull.*7. 2. c. acc., *cower beneath,* ἐξουσίαν D.H.11.18; τὸ θεοῦ κράτος Ph.1.677, cf. 322, 2.600; of a breach in a wall, ἀπειλουμένην ὅσον οὔπω κατεπτηχέναι τὴν ἐπίκλυσιν Hld.9.5.

καταπτίσσω, *grind to powder,* Plu.2.449e, Nic.Dam.118 J.

καταπτοέω, *frighten,* Ps.-Luc.*Philopatr.*29.

καταπτύρομαι, *to be terrified,* Aq.*Ge.*41.8.

κατάπτυσμα, = *putacilla, Gloss.*

κατάπτυστος, ον, also η, ον Anacr.152; *to be spat upon, abominable,* Anacr. l.c., A.*Ch.*632 (lyr.), *Eu.*68; ὦ κ. κάρα E.*Tr.*1024: also in Com. and Prose, Anaxil.22.6, D.18.33, etc.

καταπτῠχής, ές, *with ample folds,* ἐμπερόναμα Theoc.15.34.

καταπτύω, *spit upon* or *at,* esp. as a mark of abhorrence or contempt, c. gen., τίς οὐχὶ κατέπτυσεν ἂν σοῦ; D.18.200, cf. Aeschin.3.73, Luc.*Cat.*12, etc.; κ. δωροδοκίας Aeschin.2.23; πλούτου Luc.*Icar.* 30: abs., Ar.*Ra.*1179. [On the quantity, v. πτύω.]

κατά-πτωμα, ατος, τό, *downfall,* Lxx *Ps.*143(144).14. 2. τὸ κ. τοῦ ὄντος μὴ ὄν the Not-Being which forms the *lower limit* of Being, Porph.*Sent.*26. II. *debility, collapse,* Alex.Trall.9.2. **-πτωσις,** εως, ἡ, *fall,* Hp.*Art.*42; ἐξ ὀχήματος Gal.7.560; λίθου Simp. *in Ph.*261.17. 2. Medic., *collapse,* ἡ συγκοπή ἐστι κ. δυνάμεως Gal. 10.837; of epileptic *seizures,* Alex.Aphr.*Pr.*2.64, cf. Vett.Val.38.13 (pl.): hence of a spell which induces a *trance, PMag.Par.*1.850. 3. *downfall, calamity,* Lxx 3*Ma.*2.14.

καταπτώσσω, = καταπτήσσω, τίπτε καταπτώσσοντες ἀφέστατε; Il. 4.340, al.; of dogs, *Gp.*19.2.11.

καταπτωτικός, ή, όν, *liable to fits,* Vett.Val.112.34.

καταπτωχεύω, *reduce to beggary, beggar,* Plu.*Cat.Mi.*25:—Pass., *to be* or *become beggared,* Id.*Cic.*10; τύχαι κατεπτωχευμέναι *beggared* fortunes, D.H.9.51.

καταπῡγίζω, *to be* or *act like a* καταπύγων, Phot.

καταπυγμομαχέω, *conquer in boxing,* Sch.*AP*11.80 (Lucill.).

κατάπῡγ-ος, ον, = καταπύγων (q.v.), Hsch., Phot., prob. in Gerhard *Phoinix* p.7 (cf. p.153): Comp. -ότερος Sophr.63: Sup. -ότατος *Epigr.Gr.*1131. **-οσύνη,** ἡ, *unnatural lust,* Cratin.53, Ar.*Nu.*1023 (anap.), *Fr.*130, Luc.*Gall.*32. **-ων,** ονος, ὁ, ἡ, neut. κατάπυγον Ar. *V.*687: (πυγή):—*given to unnatural lust*: generally, *lecherous, lewd,* Id.*Ach.*79, al., Luc.*Tim.*22, Alciphr.3.45, etc.; ὦ κατάπυγον Ar.*Th.* 200.—The oblique cases are sts. wrongly written -πύγωνος, cf. Hdn. Gr.2.725: irreg. Comp. -πυγωνέστερος (metri gr.) Ar.*Lys.*776. II. in Att., *the middle finger* (used in an obscene gesture), Poll.2.184.

καταπύει· ἐνέπλησε, κατ. γνόει, Hsch.

καταπύθω [ῡ], *putrefy,* τὴν.. κατέπυσ' ἱερὸν μένος Ἠελίοιο *h.Ap.* 371:—Pass. (with pf. -πέπυθα Hsch. (-οιθα cod.)), *become putrefied,* ξύλον.. · τὸ μὲν οὐ καταπύθεται ὄμβρῳ Il.23.328.

καταπυκάζω, *cover over,* Hsch. s.v. κατερρινωμένον (Pass.): metaph., μύθοις τὴν ἱστορίαν Eust.1379.12.

κατάπυκν-ος, ον, strengthd. for πυκνός, *thick, tufted*, ἕρπυλλος Theoc.*Ep.*1.1. 2. Milit., ἐν κ. στάσει in *close* formation, Ascl. *Tact.*5.1. II. Medic., *very costive*, κοιλίη Hp.*Acut.*(*Sp.*)56. III. κ. εἰς σχηματισμόν *often using* a formation, A.D.*Adv.*186.2; ἡ διάλεκτος κ. ἐπὶ τὴν χρῆσιν Id.*Synt.*50.18. **-όω**, *stud thickly*, τρήμασι τὸ τεῖχος Plb.8.5.6; θύρας ἥλοις D.S.18.71; τοῖς ἀφώνοις τὰς συλλαβάς D.H.*Comp.*16; παραδειγμάτων πλήθει τὴν πόλιν Plu.*Lyc.*27; τοῖς ὑπερβατοῖς Phld.*Rh.*1.160S.:—Pass., of the sky, καταπεπυκνῶσθαι.. πλήθει ἀστέρων Arist.*Mete.*346ᵃ29; of a country, ἐλαίαις καταπεπυκνῶσθαι *to be thickly planted with*.. (v.l. for -πεφυτεῦσθαι), D.S. 3.44: metaph., βίος ἐν θαλίαις -πεπυκνωμένος Porph.*Plot.*23. II. *force into a small compass, compress, condense*, Ἐπίκουρος οὕτω κατεπύκνου τὴν ἡδονήν Damox.2.62; τάλαντ' ἐγώ σοι κατεπύκνωσα τέτταρα *spent* four talents *in a lump*, ib.4; to illustrate this is cited the dogma of Epicur., *Sent.*9, εἰ κατεπυκνοῦτο πᾶσα ἡδονὴ κτλ., cf. καταπύκνωσις; ὁ Λυκοῦργος τοὺς πολίτας τῇ σιωπῇ πιέζων συνῆγε καὶ κατεπύκνου Plu.2.510f:—Pass., -πεπύκνωται ἡ πραγματεία Porph. *Plot.*14; also εἰ μὴ -πυκνοῦταί σοι τὸ ἀπὸ δογμάτων ὀρθῶν ἕκαστα πράσσειν that your *habit* of acting.. *is not consolidated*, M.Ant.5.9. 2. in Music, κ. τὸ διάγραμμα *fill up* the intervals in a scale (with smaller intervals), Aristox.*Harm.*p.7 M.:—Pass., Theo Sm.p.91 H., Nicom. *Exc.*7. III. Pass., *to be condensed*, of complex forms of inference (cf. πυκνόω V), Arist.*APo.*79ᵃ30. **-ωσις**, εως, ἡ, *condensation* (v. καταπυκνόω II), τοῦ ἡδομένου *densification, solidification* of pleasure by filling in unoccupied gaps in time and completing the penetration of the organism, Epicur.*Fr.*432: pl., Dam.*Pr.*354. 2. in Music, *close packing* of the intervals in a scale, Aristox.*Harm.*p.7 M., Nicom.*Harm.*11. **-ωτέον**, *one must fill up*, of intervals in music, Theo Sm.p.91 H.; cf. καταπυκνόω II.2.

καταπυκτεύω, *conquer in boxing*, Sch.A.R.2.98 (Pass.), cj. in Pl. Com.124.

καταπῠρίζω, v. καππυρίζω.

καταπῠρόω, *dry*, ἕως ἂν..-ωθῇ [τὸ ἔριον] *PHolm.*20.24 (fort. καπυρωθῇ).

καταπυρπολέω, *waste with fire*, Ar.*Th.*243 (Pass.), Plb.5.19.8, Palaeph.52 (Pass.), Phalar.*Ep.*104.

κατάπυρρος, ον, *very red, deep red*, Dsc.5.77; f.l. for καπυρός, Id. 2.154.

καταπώγων, ον, gen. ωνος, *with a long beard*, D.S.3.63, Str.16. 4.10.

καταπωλέω, *sell*, *BGU*8iii 13 (iii A.D.), *PThead.*16.18 (iv A.D.).

καταπωμάζω, *close up*, ὀπήν Hero *Aut.*28.5.

κατ-άρα [ᾰρ], Ion. **-άρη**, ἡ, *curse*, κατάρας ποιέεσθαί τινι to lay *curses* upon one, Hdt.1.165; ἐποιήσαντο νόμον τε καὶ κατάρην μὴ.. θρέψειν κόμην.. μηδένα ib.82; ἐκ κατάρης τευ in consequence of.., Id.4.30; διδόναι τινὰ κατάρᾳ E.*Hec.*945 (lyr.), cf. *El.*1324 (pl., anap.), A.*Th.*725 (pl., lyr.); opp. εὐχή, Pl.*Alc.*2.143b (pl.), cf. *SIG*1241 (Lyttus, iii A.D.), etc.; opp. εὐλογία, *Ep.Jac.*3.10; κατάραι γίγνονται κατά τινος Plb.23.10.7; τὴν κ. ἀναγράψαι, στηλιτεῦσαι, D.S.1.45, Plu.2.354b; *cursing*, κ. καὶ λοιδορία Phld.*Lib.*p.11 O.

κατ-ᾰραιρημένος, Ion. pf. part. Pass. of καθαιρέω, q.v.

κατ-άρακτοι θυρίδες, *shutters*, *IG*2².463.76; cf. καταρράκτης.

κατάρ-ᾱμα [ᾰρ], ατος, τό, *curse*, Sch.E.*Ph.*1355. **-άομαι** [ᾱρ Ep., ᾰρ Att.], *call down curses upon*, τῷ δὲ καταρῶνται πάντες βροτοὶ ἄλγε' ὀπίσσω Od.19.330; πολλὰ κατηρᾶτο he *called down* many *curses*, Il.9.454; κεφαλῇ πολλὰ κ. Hdt.2.39; κ. ὁ κῆρυξ "εἴ τις ἐξαπατᾷ" λέγων D.23.97; κ. τὴν Ἶσίν τινι *AP*11.115 (Nicarch.): c. inf., καταρῶνται δ' ἀπολέσθαι they *pray* that he may perish, Thgn.277; κ. μήτε πλοῖα στεγανὰ γενέσθαι Arist.*Fr.*554, cf. 148: c. dat., *curse, execrate*, τῷ ἡλίῳ Hdt.4.184, cf. Ar.*Nu.*871, *Ra.*746, D.19.292 codd., etc.: c. acc., Lxx *Ge.*12.3, al., *Ev.Marc.*11.21, Plu.*Cat.Mi.*32 codd., Luc. *Asin.*27: abs., Ar.*V.*614, D.18.283:—Pass., aor. κατηράθην [ᾰ] Lxx *Jb.*3.5: pf. part. κατηραμένος *accursed*, ib.4*Ki.*9.34, *Ev.Matt.*25.41, Plu.*Luc.*18: also pf. κεκατήραμαι with double redupl., Lxx *Nu.*22.6; part. κεκατηραμένος ib.*Si.*3.18, al. **-άσιμος** [ᾰσ], ον, *accursed*, Suid. s.v. ἀράσιμος. **-ᾱσις**, εως, ἡ, *cursing*, Lxx *Jd.*5.23.

κατ-ᾰράσσω, Att. **-ττω**, *dash down, break in pieces*, ὁ παῖς ἐμπεσὼν κατήραξε (sc. τὴν κύλικα) Hippon.38:—Pass., ἡ θύρη κατήρακται Herod.2.63: metaph., διασείειν καὶ κ. τὰ βουλεύματα cj. for ταράττειν in Luc.*Dem.Enc.*38; esp. of a broken and routed army, τοὺς λοιποὺς κατήραξεν ἐς τὸν Κιθαιρῶνα Hdt.9.69; κ. εἰς τὴν θάλασσαν ἅπαντας D. 23.165; τὸ στράτευμα κατηράχθη εἰς τὰ τειχίσματα Th.7.6, cf. D.H.9. 58, Arr.*An.*5.17.2: fut. Med. in pass. sense, Plu.*Caes.*44. II. of sea-birds, κ. αὑτοὺς εἰς τὰς κεφαλὰς αὐτῶν *dash down* head foremost, Arist.*Mir.*836ᵃ13: but more freq. 2. intr., *fall down, fall headlong*, Clearch.44; of rain, Arist.*Mu.*392ᵇ10; of rivers, εἰς τὸ χάσμα κ. D.S.17.75, cf. Plb.10.48.7, Str.14.4.1: c. gen., τοῦ ἀγγείου, of a stream of water, Gal.10.554. (Freq. written καταρρ-, augm. κατερρ-, in part perh. correctly, if fr. κατα-ρράσσω, cf. ῥάσσω, ἐπιρράσσω.)

κατ-άρᾱτος [ᾰρ], ον, Ion. **κατ-ήρητος** Herod.5.44, but **κατάρητος** *Schwyzer*702.11 (Erythrae, iv B.C.):—*accursed, abominable*, E.*Med.* 112 (anap.): freq. in Com., ὡς σεμνὸς ὁ κ. Ar.*Ra.*178, cf. *Pax*33; ὦ κατάρατε Id.*Lys.*530, etc.: Comp. καταρατότερος D.18.212: Sup. -ότατος S.*OT*1345 (lyr.).

καταρᾰχίζω, *make a rough surface* on masonry, dub. in *IG*2².1665. 12 (iv B.C.).

καταραψῳδῆσαι· φλυαρῆσαι, Hsch.

κατ-άρβῠλος, ον, (ἀρβύλη) *reaching down to the shoes*, χλαῖναι S.*Fr.* 622:—also **καθάρβυλος**, χλανίς Hsch.

καταργ-έω, *leave unemployed* or *idle*, χέρα E.*Ph.*753; κατηργηκέναι τοὺς καιρούς *to have missed* the opportunities, Plb.*Fr.*176; κ. τὴν γῆν *make* the ground *useless, cumber* it, *Ev.Luc.*13.7. 2. *cause to be idle, hinder* in one's work, Lxx 2*Es.*4.21, *POxy.*38.17 (i A.D.):—Pass., Lxx 2*Es.*6.8; *to be rendered* or *lie idle*, *PFlor.*176.7 (iii A.D.), etc. II. *make of no effect*, *Ep.Rom.*3.3, 31, al.:—Pass., *to be abolished, cease*, ib.6.6, 1*Ep.Cor.*2.6, etc.; κ. ἀπὸ τοῦ νόμου *to be set free* from.., *Ep.Rom.*7.2; *to be parted*, ἀπὸ Χριστοῦ *Ep.Gal.*5.4. **-ησις**, εως, ἡ, *making null, abolishing*, cj. in Sm.*Ps.*45.9, *La.*1.7. **-ητέον**, *one must abolish, cancel*, τὰ πάθη Iamb.*Protr.*5. **-ία**, ἡ, *reduction to inactivity, inhibition*, τῶν αἰσθήσεων *Corp.Herm.*10.5.

κάτ-αργμα, ατος, τό, only pl. κατάργματα, *first offerings* (cf. κατάρχω II.2), χέρνιβάς τε καὶ κατάργματα E.*IT*244, cf. Plu.*Thes.*22.

κατάργῠρ-ος, ον, *covered with silver, silvered*, Callix.2, Socr. Rhod.1, J.*BJ*5.5.3, Plu.2.828e. **-όω**, *cover with silver, silver over*, Philoch.138:—Pass., καταργυρωμένους (Ion. for κατηργ-) ἔχων τοὺς προμαχεῶνας Hdt.1.98, cf. D.S.1.57. II. *buy* or *bribe with silver*, ἄθρησον εἰ κατηργυρωμένος λέγω S.*Ant.*1077.

κατάρδ-ευτος, = *irriguus*, *Gloss.* **-εύω**, = sq., Sch.A.*Pr.*813. **-ω**, *water*, Θρῄκην (-ης codd. Ath.) Antiph.105, cf. D.H.2.2. 2. *besprinkle*, πολυτελείᾳ τῶν ἀλειμμάτων J.*AJ*11.6.2 (Pass.): metaph., *besprinkle with praise*, Ar.*Ach.*658; also, *to be swept along*, χειμάρρῳ οἷα -αρδόμενα, of the poetry of Aeschylus, *AP*7.411 (Diosc.).

καταρέζω, poet. for καταρρέζω.

κάταρϝος, ον, (ἀρά) *accursed*, *IG*5(2).3.4 (Tegea, iv B.C.).

κατάρης ἄνεμος, ὁ, a wind *rushing from above*, Alc.135, Sapph. 160 (v.l. κατώρης).

καταρθεία and **-θία**, v. καταρτεία.

καταρῑγηλός, ή, όν, *making* one *shudder, horrible*, λυγρά, τά τ' ἄλλοισίν γε καταριγηλὰ πέλονται [κατᾱρ-] Od.14.226.

κατᾰριθμ-έω, *count* or *reckon among*, μετά τινων E.*Tr.*872 (Pass.); ἔν τισι Pl.*Plt.*266a, cf. D.S.4.85, Plu.*Sol.*12; εἰς εὐδαιμονίαν κ. *reckon* as.., Ath.1.9d: c. dupl. acc., Pl.*Sph.*266e:—Pass., Arist.*Pol.* 1329ᵃ27; μετά τινων ib.1293ᵇ26; ἔν τισι *Act.Ap.*1.17, Phld.*Rh.*1. 239S. 2. *recount in detail*, τὴν ἀτοπίαν σου Pl.*Smp.*215a:—Med., *recount, enumerate*, Id.*Phlb.*27b, *Grg.*451e, Isoc.1.11; τι πρός τινα Aeschin.3.54: pf. Pass. in med. sense, τὰς τῶν πολλῶν κατηριθμημένοι δόξας *having summed up*.., Arist.*Top.*101ᵃ31:—Pass., Phld. *Ir.*p.78 W.; τὰ συμβεβηκότα -ηρίθμηται S.E.*M.*7.281. 3. Med., *count* or *reckon* so and so, εὐδαιμονέστατον κ. τινά Pl.*Phlb.*47b; ἐν ἀδικήματι κ. τὴν πρᾶξιν Plb.5.67.5. II. abs., *count, reckon*, διὰ τί πάντες ἄνθρωποι εἰς τὰ δέκα κ.; Arist.*Pr.*910ᵇ24. **-ησις**, εως, ἡ, *computation*, χρόνων J.*Ap.*1.21; *enumeration, list*, Herod.Med.ap. Orib.5.30.29, M.Ant.4.45, Gal.6.95. **-ητέον**, *one must count*, Ph. 2.488.

καταρῑνάω or **-έω**, v. καταρρ-.

καταρίπτω, = καταρρίπτω, Man.3.55.

κατ-ᾰριστάω, *squander in breakfasts*: generally, *squander*, Antipho Soph.73:—Pass., *Com.Adesp.*1032.

καταριστήν, = τὴν χάλαζαν, dub. in Call.*Fr.*357.

καταρκ-έω, *to be fully sufficient*, χώρη οὐδεμία καταρκέει πάντα ἑωυτῇ παρέχουσα Hdt.1.32; ἐμοὶ δὲ φῶς ἐν ἡλίου καταρκέσει E.*Rh.*447; πρὸς τὰς παρασκευάς Jul.*Or.*1.29c: impers., *it is enough*, καταρκεῖ τοῦδε κεκλῆσθαι πατρός S.*Fr.*86. **-ής**, ές, *fully sufficient*, Hsch. (-χής cod.).

κατ-αρκτικός, ή, όν, *forming the beginning*, ἡ δυὰς ἑτερότητος κ. Nicom.*Ar.*2.17; ἡ Δημήτηρ πόλεως -κή, οἱονεὶ ἡ γῆ Lyd.*Mens.*4.63, cf. Eust.432.3.

καταρμόζω, Ion. for καθαρμόζω.

καταρν-έομαι, *deny strongly, persist in denying*, φῄς, ἢ καταρνῇ μὴ δεδρακέναι τάδε; S.*Ant.*442, cf. *PFlor.*181.5 (ii A.D.). **-ητικός**, ή, όν, *prone to deny* or *raise objections*, Sch.Ptol.*Tetr.*18 (Comp.).

κάτ-αρξις, εως, ἡ, *beginning*, τοῦ πάθους Archig.ap.Aët.12.1.

κατ-ᾰρόω, *plough up*, τὴν γῆν Ar.*Av.*582: fut. -αρόσω Jusj.ap. Poll.8.106: 2 sg. aor. κατήροσας Hsch.

καταρρᾰγή, ἡ, *collapse, falling in*, τοῦ σώματος Hp.*Mul.*1.1. 2. *rending*, καταρραγαὶ πέπλων Lyc.256.

καταρρᾱθῡμέω, *to be remiss* or *idle*, X.*Mem.*3.5.13, D.24.210, *PHib.* 1.44.4 (iii B.C.), Porph.*Abst.*2.46, etc.:—also in Med., Ammon.*in Cat.*7.12. II. trans., *neglect*, τι *Cod.Just.*1.2.24.16: also c. gen., Just.*Nov.*22.45.3. 2. *lose through negligence*, μηδὲν κ. X.*HG*6.2. 39:—Pass., τὰ κατερραθυμημένα πάλιν ἀναλήψεσθε will recover *ground lost through negligence*, D.4.7. 3. *make languid*, -θυμοῦντος τὴν χεῖρα τοῦ ὕπνου Philostr.*Im.*1.2:—Pass., Philostr.Jun.*Im.*2.

καταρραίνω, *besprinkle*, οἴνῳ καὶ ἐλαίῳ Hp.*Art.*63; βίβλους ζωμῷ D.S.34.1: without dat., Ath.10.453a:—Pass. (pf. part. καταρερασμένος), Apollon.ap.Gal.12.504; of a spotted snake, κατέρρανται στιγμαῖς Philum.*Ven.*23.1. II. *sprinkle*, ὕδωρ *Gp.*2.32.1 (Pass.):—Pass., S.E.*P.*1.55.

καταρρᾰκόω, *tear into shreds*: pf. part. Pass. κατερρακωμένος *in rags*, S.*Tr.*1103.

καταρρακ-τήρ, ῆρος, ὁ, *down-swooping*, κίρκος Lyc.169, cf. 539. **-της**, ου (from καταρράσσω), or **κατ-ᾰράκτης** (from καταράσσω, cf. Eust.1053.5); ὦ κατάρακται *Epigr.Gr.*979.7 (Philae). I. as Adj., *down-rushing*, ὄμβρος Str.14.1.21. 2. *sheer, abrupt*, τὸν καταρράκτην ὀδόν S.*OC*1590 (cf. Sch.; καταφράκτην Suid. s.v. ὀδός). II. as Subst., *waterfall, cataract*, esp. of the Nile, D.S.1.32, 17.97, Str.17.1.2 and 49, *Epigr.Gr.* l.c.:—Ion. **Καταρρήκτης**, name of a river in Phrygia, Hdt.7.26. 2. *portcullis*, Plu.*Ant.*76, *Arat.*26, D.H.8.67. 3. *trap-door*, οἱ κ. τοῦ οὐρανοῦ ἠνεῴχθησαν Lxx *Ge.*7.11, cf. 4*Ki.*7.2. 4.

movable bridge, for boarding ships, App.*BC*5.82; for attacking elephants, D.H.20.1. **5.** *sluice*, Hld.9.8. **6.** a sea-bird, prob. so called from *swooping down* upon its prey, Ar.*Av.*887, Arist.*HA*509ᵃ4, 615ᵃ28, Juba 68a, Dionys.*Av.*2.2, 3.22; *cormorant*, Hebr. *shālākh*, Lxx *De.*14.16(17), al.; of an eagle, S.*Fr.*377; of the Harpies, ib. 714. **–τικῶς**, Adv. *rushing down, swooping*, Eust.688.52.

καταρραντέον, *one must besprinkle*, *Gp.*6.10.

καταρραντίζω, = καταρραίνω, Philum.*Ven.*14.2 (Pass.).

καταρρᾰπιστέον, *one must strike*, Eust.512.20.

καταρραπτέον, *one must stitch up*, Antyll.(?)ap.Orib.45.3.8.

καταρραπτίτης [ῑ] (sc. ἀγών), ου, ὁ, contest at Rhodes, Gorgon 2.

καταρράπτω, *stitch on* or *over*, θύρη κατερραμμένη ῥιπὶ καλάμων a frame *lashed to* a crate, Hdt.2.96. **II.** *stitch tight*, τι ἔς τι Hp. *Acut.*21; *sew up*, Thphr.*HP*9.5.3; λίθον εἰς τὴν ζώνην κ. Plu.*Ant.*81; in Surgery, Gal.14.783:—Pass., Aen.Tact.31.4; καταρραφῆναι ἐν μηρῷ Agatharch.7; τοῖς δέρμασι Sor.1.68. **2.** metaph., *devise, compass*, Πενθεῖ καταρράψας μόρον A.*Eu.*26.

καταρράσσω, Att. **–ττω**, v.l. for καταράσσω (q.v.) Ph.2.98, etc.; ἐκτραχηλίζειν καὶ καταρράττειν Id.1.676; ἐπάρας κατέρραξάς με Lxx *Ps.*101(102).10; cf. καταρρήσσω (B). **II.** = καταρρήγνυμι II. 4, Ael. *NA*3.18 (s. v. l.).

καταρρᾳστωνεύω, strengthd. for ῥᾳστωνεύω, Sch.Luc.*Par.*41 (Pass.).

καταρρᾰφή, ἡ, *stitching*, of an operation on the eyelid, Leonid.ap. Aët.7.72. **II.** *hem*, Lyd.*Mag.*2.13.

κατάρρᾰφος, ον, *sewn together, patched*, Luc.*Ep.Sat.*28.

καταρρᾰχίζω, strengthd. for ῥαχίζω, Anon. in Rh.3.577 W.

καταρρέζω, Ep. impf. καταρρέζεσκε Opp.*H.*5.481:—*pat, stroke, caress*, χειρί τέ μιν κατέρεξεν (Ep. for κατέρρ–) Il.1.361, al., cf. A.R.4. 687: abs., καρρέζουσα (Ep. for καταρρ–) Il.5.424, cf. Call.*Dian.*29.

κατάρρειθρον, = *endoriguum*, *Gloss.*

καταρρεμβεύω, *lead astray*, Lxx *Nu.*32.13 codd. AF.

καταρρεπής, ές, = ἑτερορρεπής, Hsch.

καταρρέπω, *sink down* or *to one side, hang down*, Hp.*Art.*43; opp. ἰσορροπέω, Plb.6.10.7: metaph., *incline, fall back upon*, ἐπὶ τὸν μοναχὸν τρόπον Epicur.*Ep.*2 p.41 U.; ἐπὶ τὴν αὐτὴν γνώμην *OGI*315.51 (Pessinus, ii B.C.). **II.** trans., *cause to incline, make to fall*, τύχη γὰρ ὀρθοῖ καὶ τύχη καταρρέπει τὸν εὐτυχοῦντα τόν τε δυστυχοῦντ' ἀεί S.*Ant.*1158.

καταρρέω, pf. –ερρύηκα: aor. –ερρύην (v. infr.):—*flow down*, αἷμα καταρρέον ἐξ ὠτειλῆς Il.4.149, 5.870; κατὰ δὲ νότιος ῥέεν ἱδρὼς ὤμων καὶ κεφαλῆς 11.811; κατὰ δ' αἷμα... ἔρρεε χειρός 13.539; ποταμοὶ κατ' ὄρεσφι ῥ. 4.452; καταρρέον φλέγμα ἐκ τῆς κεφαλῆς Hdt.4.187; of rivers, παρὰ τὴν Ἄλτιν κ. X.*HG*7.4.29; τὸ καταρρέον ὕδωρ D.55.10. **2.** of men, *stream, rush down*, ἀθρόοι καταρρέοντες Ar.*Ach.*26; οἱ δὲ ἐμπαλασσόμενοι κατέρρεον, i. e. into the river, Th.7.84; μὴ σφαλεὶς καταρρυῇς Ar.*Pax* 146, cf. 71; *sink down*, κ. ἀπὸ τῆς κλίνης ἐπὶ τοὺς πόδας Hp.*Prog.*3; εἰς τοὺς ὁμαλοὺς τόπους Plb.8.14.6; διὰ τοῦ τέγους κ. Luc.*Tim.*41: c. acc., τὴν ἀτραπὸν κατερρύην Ar.*Fr.*47. **3.** of fruit, leaves, etc., *fall, drop off*, X.*Cyr.*1.5.10, Thphr.*CP*4.13.3, etc. **4.** *fall in ruins*, τὰ τοιαῦτα.. περὶ αὑτὰ καταρρεῖ D.2.10: metaph., κατερρύη τὸ τῆς πόλεως ἀνδρεῖον Arist.*Fr.*557; σιγᾷ κατερρύη μέλος dub. in Pi. *Fr.*177; of a crater, *fall in*, Plb.34.11.12; of a roof, Paus.1.44.3, etc.; νεκροῦ κατερρυηκότος τὰς σάρκας *having collapsed*, Id.10.2.6; καταλείβεσθαί νιν καὶ κ. ὥσπερ τοὺς κολοσσούς *Abh. Berl. Akad.*1925(5).21 (Cyrene). **5.** κ. ἔς τινα *come to, fall to the lot of*, Theoc.1.5, Bion 1.55. **6.** *burrow*, εἰς τὴν γῆν Arist.*HA*556ᵇ5. **7.** metaph., *fall* into, ἐπὶ τὸν μῦθον Epicur.*Ep.*2 p.36 U. **II.** *run down, drip with*, φόνῳ E.*Tr.*16:—and in Pass., αἵματι, ἱδρῶτι καταρρεῖσθαι, Plu.*Galb.* 27, Luc.*Nigr.*35.

κατα-ρρήγνῡμι and **–ύω**, fut. –ρήξω E.*HF*864: late pf. κατέρρηχα *Arch.Pap.*2.125ᵇ10 (ii A. D.):—*break down*, τὴν γέφυραν Hdt.4.201; μέλαθρα E. l. c. **2.** *tear in pieces, rend*, κατερρήγνυε.. τὰ ἱμάτια D. 21.63; τὸ διάδημα D.S.19.34; τὴν ἐσθῆτα Luc.*Pisc.*36:—Med., κατερρήξαντο τοὺς κιθῶνας they *rent their* coats, Hdt.8.99, cf. X.*Cyr.*3.1.13, etc. **3.** metaph., τροπὰς καταρρήγνυσι [ἡ ἀναρχία] *breaks up* armies *and turns them to* flight, S.*Ant.*675. **4.** κ. τινῶν γέλωτας *make* them *burst out* laughing, Ath.4.130c; cf. II. 2. **II. Pass.**, esp. in aor. κατερράγην [ᾰ], with pf. Act. κατέρρωγα:—*to be broken down*, κρημνοὶ καταρρηγνύμενοι Hdt.7.23; καταρρήγνυσθαι ἐπὶ γῆν *to be thrown down and broken*, Id.3.111; τὸ οἴκημα κατερράγη Th.4.115; ἄκρας κατερρωγυίας εἰς τὴν θάλασσαν Str.5.2.6. **2.** *fall, rush down*, of storms, waterfalls, etc., Hp.*Aër.*8; *break* or *burst out*, χειμὼν κατερράγη Hdt. 1.87; ὄμβροι καταρραγέντες Arist.*Mu.*400ᵃ26; of tears, ἐξ ὀμμάτων πηγαὶ κατερρώγασι E.*Alc.*1068: c. gen., τοῦ ῥεύματος –ρηγνυμένου τῶν ὀρῶν Philostr.*VA*6.23 (also intr. in Act., of a river, –ρηγνὺς ἐς τὴν θάλατταν 3.52); of wind, Plu.*Fab.*16: metaph., ὁ πόλεμος κατερράγη Ar.*Eq.*644, cf. *Ach.*528; γέλως Ph.2.598; κρότος Plb.18.46.9 (but κατερρήγνυτο πᾶς ὁ τόπος ὑπὸ τοῦ κρότου 15.32.9); βροντή Luc.*VH*2. 35. **3.** *to be broken in pieces*, Αἴγυπτος μελάγγαιός τε καὶ καταρρηγνυμένη *with comminuted, crumbling soil*, Hdt.2.12; γῆ κατερρωγυῖα Arist.*HA*556ᵃ5; *to be ruinous*, ὅσα κατέρρωγεν τοῦ τείχους *IG*2².463. 75. **4.** Medic., *have a violent discharge, suffer from diarrhoea*, καταρρήγνυται ἡ κοιλίη Hp.*VM*10, cf. καταρράσσω II; of persons, κατερρήγνυντο τὰς γαστέρας App.*Hisp.*54; ἢν μὴ φῦσαι –ρραγέωσιν Hp.*Aph.*4.73. **b.** of menstruation, τοῖς θήλεσιν.. τὰ καταμήνια κ. Arist.*HA*581ᵇ1. **5.** of tumours, *break, burst*, Hp.*Coac.*613, *Epid.* 6.8.18, al. **6.** of parts of the body, *fall in, collapse*, οἵ τε μαζοὶ καὶ τὰ ἄλλα μέλεα κ. Id.*Nat.Puer.*30, cf. *Mul.*1.1; κατερρωγότα τὰ στέρνα [ἔχων] *flat*-chested, Jul.*Or.*6.198a; of the lips or tongue, *to be fissured*, Antyll.ap.Orib.10.27.13, Aët.5.118. **–ρρηκτικός**, ή, όν, Medic., *promoting discharge*, φυσέων Hp.*Acut.*23 (Comp.); οὔρων Aret.*CA* 1.2: abs., *purgative*, Hp.*Acut.*51. **–ρρηξις**, εως, ἡ, Medic., κ. κοιλίης *violent diarrhoea*, Id.*Coac.*235: abs., Id.*Epid.*4.26. **2.** *rupture* of membranes, Id.*Nat.Puer.*30.

κατάρρησις, εως, ἡ, *accusation*, Jul.*Or.*2.85d, *PLond.*5.1680.9 (vi A. D.), Hsch.; *condemnation*, Suid.

καταρρήσσω (A), Att. –ρρήττω, = καταρρήγνυμι, in Med., τὰς ἐσθῆτας D.S.1.72.

καταρρήσσω (B), Ion. for καταρράσσω, Hsch.

καταρρητορεύω, *overcome by rhetoric*:—Pass., *to be so overcome*, Hyp.*Dem.Fr.*7, Plu.2.801f, Luc.*Anach.*19, Agath.5.7. **II.** = Lat. *peroro*, *Gloss.*

καταρρῑγέω, *shudder greatly*, ἰδέσθαι A.R.3.1132.

κατάρριζ-ος, ον, *having roots below*, Thphr.*HP*1.6.8. **–όω**, *make rooted, plant firmly*, τὸ θνητὸν γένος Pl.*Ti.*73b; ἑαυτὸν εἰς τὴν πολιτείαν Plu.2.805f; λᾶα *AP*9.708 (Phil.):—Pass., *take root*, Pl.*Ti.*76c, 77c, etc.; σύριγγος –ερριζωμένης *planted, terminated*, Antyll.ap.Orib. 44.22.10.

καταρρικνόομαι, *to be shrivelled*, in pf. part. Pass., S.*Ichn.*295; also glossed by συνεστραμμένον, καμπύλον γενόμενον, Suid.

κατάρρῑν, ῑνος, ὁ, ἡ, *hook-nosed*, *PPetr.*1 p.51 (iii B. C.).

καταρρῑνάω or **–έω**, (ῥίνη) *file down, make thin*, ἰσχναίνων καὶ καταρινῶν τὰ συγκρίματα Antyll.ap.Stob.4.37.16: metaph., κατερρινημένον τι λέγειν *polished, elegant*, Ar.*Ra.*901; of men, βραχίον' εὖ κατερρινημένους, i. e. *having had all superfluous flesh worked off*, A. *Supp.*747 (κατερρινωμένους *covered with shields*, Wellauer; cf. **κατερρινωμένον·** καταπεπυκασμένον, καταδεδερματωμένον, Hsch.).

καταρρῑπισμός, ὁ, *treatment by a blast of air*, Sor.2.41.

καταρριπτ-άζω, in Pass., *to be blown away, scattered*, Hsch. **–ω** (later –ριπτέω Man.4.288:—Pass., καταρειπτούμενα *IG*12(3).325.41 (Thera, ii A. D.), also pf. part. κατηρειμμένος ib.326.20), *throw down, overthrow*, εἴ τε δημόθρους ἀναρχία βουλὴν καταρρίψειεν A.*Ag.*884; τὰ βασίλεια Plu.*Luc.*34, cf. Luc.*Salt.*9; κ. τοὺς πολεμίους, opp. ἐπαίρω, Id.*Hist.Conscr.*7. **2.** *bring into disrepute*, μάθησιν Vett.Val. 238.31; ἑαυτούς Id.2.2. **3.** *despise*, δόξαν, ἔπαινον, D.S.13.15, 22.

καταρροή, ἡ, *flowing down, defluxion*, Aesop.145 Chambry.

καταρροια, ἡ, = foreg., Aq.*Ps.*77(78).44. **II.** = κατάρροος II, Arr.*Epict.*1.26.16, Plu.2.128a, prob. in Cass.Fel.34.

καταρροιβδέω, *swallow up*, Hsch. (–ρυβδήσας cod., fort. recte, v. ἀναρροιβδέω).

καταρροιζέω, *rush hurtling against*, τινος Nonn.*D.*1.217, 6.116.

καταρρο-ίζομαι, *have a catarrh*, Dsc.1.40 (as v.l.), Gal.6.548. **–ῐκός**, ή, όν, *of a catarrh, catarrhal*, Hp.*Aph.*5.24; κ. νοσήματα Pl.*Ti.* 85b. **II.** *subject to catarrh*, Arist.*Pr.*967ᵇ20. **–ῐστικός**, ή, όν, = foreg. II, cj. ib.929ᵇ27 (–ιτικοί, –ητικοί codd.). **–ος**, ον, contr. **–ρους**, ουν, *down-flowing*, Νεῖλος Philostr.*VA*6.23. **2.** *full of streams*, νῆσος Id.*Im.*2.17. **II.** Subst., *running from the head, catarrh*, Hp.*Aph.*3.12 (pl.), Pl.*R.*405d (pl.), *Cra.*440c, etc.: distd. from κόρυζα etc. by Gal.7.263: metaph., Pl.*Cra.*440d.

καταρροπ-ή (v. l. –ροπίη), ἡ, *weight of a hanging body*, opp. ἀναρροπίη, Hp.*Art.*43. **–ος**, ον, *inclining downwards*, κ. ποιεῖν τι ib. 69; ἐπὶ τὸ κ. ῥέπειν ibid.; *pendent*, φύματα Id.*Epid.*6.1.10, cf. Gal. 7.567, 15.330. **2.** *sloping*, κλίνη Antyll.ap.Orib.9.14.6. **3.** *tending to descend*, νοῦσος Hp.*Hum.*5, 7.

καταρροφ-άνω, *gulp* or *swallow down*, Hp.*Morb.*2.54, 59. **–έω**, = foreg., Id.*Loc.Hom.*17, X.*Cyr.*1.3.9, Arist.*Pr.*876ᵃ27, Herm.Iamb. 4; τινος some of.., Orib.8.6.16:—Pass., Ruf.*Sat.Gon.*18:—later –ροφάω, Alex.Trall.11.2, Sm.*Jb.*39.30. **–ησις**, εως, ἡ, *swallowing*, Sor.2.41, Dsc.*Eup.*2.5.

καταρροώδης, ες, *subject to catarrh*, Hp.*Vict.*1.32.

καταρρυής, ές, *slipping away*: hence, *dripping with fat*, μηροί S. *Ant.*1010.

καταρρυθμ-ίζω, *bring into rhythm*, Hld.3.3; τὰ κατερρυθμισμένα passages *over-rhythmical*, Longin.41.2: metaph., κ. τινὰ (neut.) ἐς τὴν τοῦ δικαίου δόξαν Philostr.*VA*7.18:—Pass., γέροντα εἰς βίον ἥμερον Ath.5.179a. **–ος**, ον, *very rhythmical*, Longin.41.1. **II.** κατάρυθμος, prob. f. l. for κακόρρυθμος in Paul.Aeg.2.11.

καταρρῠπ-αίνω, fut. –ρυπᾰνῶ Isoc.12.63:—*defile, sully*, ταῖς κατηγορίαις τὰς εὐεργεσίας l. c., cf. Pl.*Lg.*919e, 937d; ἑαυτόν Arist.*Ath.* 6.3, cf. Lib.*Or.*64.41; ἀκόλαστα ῥήματα τοὺς λέγοντας κ. Plu.2.456c; βραχείᾳ κηλῖδι τοὺς πόνους κ. Chor.*Milt.*64. **–όω**, = foreg., David *Proll.*40.20: metaph., δικαστήριον Lyd.*Mag.*3.66:—Pass., *to be soiled and dirty*, of a dress, *SIG*1219.6 (Gambreum, iii B. C.). **2.** κατερρυπωμένος, = *destitutus*, *Gloss.*

κατάρρῠσις, εως, ἡ, *flowing down*, of soap into the eyes, Philum. ap.Orib.45.29.60; of phlegm, Mich. *in PN*78.17. **2.** *sinking down*, Gal.18(2).702.

καταρρῠσόομαι, Pass., *become wrinkled*, *EM*737.1.

κατάρρῠτος, ον, *irrigated, watered*, κῆπος E.*El.*777; νάπη χιόνι κατάρυτα Id.*Tr.*1067 (lyr.), cf. *Andr.*215; γῆ ἔνδροσός τε καὶ κ. Ael. *NA*10.37; λίμνη κ. αἵματι Lxx 2*Ma.*12.16; ὄρος κ. *channelled by streams*, *OGI*199.12 (Adule). **2.** *flowing*, ὕδωρ Olymp. *in Mete.* 128.32. **II.** *carried down by water, alluvial*, of the Delta, Hdt.2. 15. **III.** *with a steep slope*, of a testudo, Plb.28.11.2.

κατ-αρρωδέω, Ion. for κατορρωδέω, *fear, dread*, τι Hdt.1.34, 80, al.; τινας Id.9.8; ὑπέρ τινος Id.7.178: abs., Id.8.75, 103; κ. μή.. Id.9.45.

καταρρώξ, ῶγος, ὁ, ἡ, *jagged, broken*, πέτραι S.*Ph.*937; of earth, *friable*, prob. l. in Hsch. (-ρόγεα cod.).

κάταρσις, εως, ἡ, (καταίρω) *landing, bringing to land*, opp. ἄπαρσις, Poll.1.102; but usu. *landing-place*, Th.4.26, Plu.*Pomp.*65, D.C. 60.11, Ael.*VH*9.16.

κάταρσον· κατάκλεισον, Hsch.

καταρτ-άω, *hang up, suspend*, Plu.*Rom.*16; τι ἔκ τινος Id.*Marc.* 8:—Pass., *to be suspended*, Arist.*Pr.*874ᵃ18; κατήρτηντο βότρυσιν *were hung thick with* grapes, Luc.*Am.*12. II. *fasten, adjust*, χρῆμα κατηρτημένον a *well-adjusted* or *convenient* thing, Hdt.3.80; κατήρτητο *became normal, recovered sense*, Hp.*Epid.*1.26.η′; οὐδὲν -ημένον λέγειν to talk no *connected sense*, Id.*Acut.*(*Sp.*)16:—later in Act., τῇ θεῷ κατάρτησον σαυτήν Herod.1.62. -εία or -ία, ἡ, = ἐξαρτία, *PSI*9. 1030.6 (ii A. D.), *POxy.*1208.14 (iii A. D.); written **καταρθία** and -εία *PLond.*3.1164(*h*)17,25 (iii A. D.), *PSI*9.1072.10 (iii A. D.). II. v.l. for -άρτιος, Artem.2.53. -ίζω, *adjust, put in order, restore*, πάντα ἐς τὠυτό Hdt.5.106; Μίλητος νοσήσασα στάσι, μέχρι οὗ μιν Πάριοι κατήρτισαν ib.28, cf. 30; τὸν δῆμον Plu.*Marc.*10; ἵνα καταρτισθῇ [ἡ πόλις] D.H.3.10; κ. δίκτυα *mend*, *Ev.Matt.*4.21; *set* a dislocated limb, in Pass., Apollon.Cit.2, Heliod.ap.Orib.49.1.3 (Act. and Pass.); but κ. τὴν ὀσφὺν καὶ τοὺς ὤμους *form* them by exercise, Arr.*Epict.*3.20.10: metaph., *restore to a right mind*, *Ep.Gal.* 6.1; κ. τινὰ εἰς τὸ συμφέρον Plu.*Cat.Mi.*65; *reconcile*, φίλους διαφερομένους Eus.Mynd.1; *make good*, τὰ ὑστερήματα τῆς πίστεως 1*Ep. Thess.*3.10:—Med., ἠσθένησε, σὺ δὲ κατηρτίσω αὐτήν Lxx*Ps.*67(68). 10. II. *furnish, equip*, τετρήρη πληρώμασι Plb.1.47.6, al., cf. *PTeb.*6.7 (ii B. C., Pass.), D.S.13.70, etc.:—Pass., πλοῖα ταῖς εἰρεσίαις κατηρτισμένα Plb.5.2.11; κατηρτισμένος abs., *in battle array*, Hdt. 9.66; *instructed*, *Ev.Luc.*6.40; *prepare, make ready*, σφενδόνην Ph.*Bel.*78.24:—Med., Lxx*Ex.*15.17, al.; σῶμα κατηρτίσω μοι *Ep. Hebr.*10.5; ὁ τὸν κόσμον καταρτισάμενος *PMag.Par.*1.1147: c. inf., κατηρτίσατο δίδοσθαι *OGI*177.10 (Egypt, i B. C.):—so in Pass., ib.179. 8 (ibid., i B. C.): abs. in imper., καταρτίζεσθε 2*Ep.Cor.*13.11. 2. *compound, prepare* dishes, medicines, etc., Dsc.*Alex.Praef.* codd. (v. καταρτύω):—Med., Nic.*Th.*954. -ιον, τό, *mast*, *EM*478. 23:—also -ιος, ἡ, but distd. from ἱστός, Artem.2.12,53, *EM* l. c., *Gloss.* 2. *part of the loom*, Artem.3.36. -ισις, εως, ἡ, *restoration*, 2*Ep.Cor.*13.9. II. *training, discipline*, Plu.*Alex.*7. III. = καταρτισμός II, Paul.Aeg.6.99. -ισμα, ατος, τό, *finished product*, *Gloss.* (pl.). -ισμός, ὁ, *restoration, reconciliation*, Sm.*Is.*38.12. II. *setting* of a limb, Heliod.ap.Orib.49.1.1 (pl.), Sor.1.73 (pl.). III. *furnishing, preparation*, αὐλῆς *PTeb.*33.12 (ii B. C.); ἱματίου *PRyl.* 127.28 (i A. D.). IV. *training, discipline*, τῶν ἁγίων *Ep.Eph.*4. 12. -ιστήρ, ῆρος, ὁ, *one who restores order, mediator*, Hdt.4.161, 5.28, Them.*Or.*4.61c. -ῡσις, εως, ἡ, *training, discipline*, παιδεία καὶ κ. Plu.*Them.*2; ψυχῶν Iamb.*VP*16.68, cf. 20.95. 2. = *confectio*, *Gloss.* -ύω, *prepare, dress*, of food, Luc.*Hist.Conscr.*44; τὴν ξεινίην Hp.*Ep.*12:—Pass., τὰ -τυμένα τῶν ἐδεσμάτων restored in Dsc. *Alex.Praef.* fr. Paul.Aeg.5.28. 2. *train, discipline*, τὴν φύσιν Plu. 2.38d: c. inf., καταρτύσων μολεῖν *to procure* his coming, S.*OC*71:—Pass., καταρτύεται νόος ἀνδρός Sol.27.11; σμικρῷ χαλινῷ δ' οἶδα.. ἵππους καταρτυθέντας S.*Ant.*478; παῖς ἔχει πηγὴν τοῦ φρονεῖν μήπω κατηρτυμένην Pl.*Lg.*808d; μανθανόμενα καὶ καρτυόμενα Id.*Men.* 88b; τὸ πρεσβύτερον καὶ κατηρτ. Junc.ap.Stob.4.50.9. 3. *equip*, λέμβος.. ἐρέταις κατηρτυμένος Alciphr.1.8. II. intr. in pf. part., κατηρτῡκώς *thoroughly furnished, full-grown*, used of horses which have lost their foal's-teeth, Hsch., cf. E.*Fr.*41, *AB*105 (so in pres. οἱ καρτύοντες τῶν ἵππων Philostr.*VA*7.23); κάμηλος τῷ σώματι κατηρτυκώς *BGU*13.5 (iii A. D.); also of men, τὸ κατηρτυκέναι Philostr.*VA* 5.33: metaph., κατηρτυκὼς.. ἱκέτης προσῆλθες *a perfected* suppliant, one *who has done all that is required*, or one *that is broken in* like a horse *tamed*, A.*Eu.*473: c. gen., ἀμβλύς εἰμι καὶ κατηρτυκὼς κακῶν *tamed, broken in spirit* by them, E.*Fr.*821.5. [ῠ, exc. in Sol. l. c.]

καταρυβδήσας, v. καταρροιβδέω. **κατάρῠτος**, ον, = κατάρρυτος (q. v.).

κατ-αρχαιρεσιάζω, *beat in an election*, esp. by unfair means, τινα Plu.*CG*11:—metaph. in Pass., *to be corrupted as by office*, Longin.44.9.

καταρχ-ή, ἡ, *beginning*, πράγματος *BGU*1209.11 (i B. C.), cf. Callicr. ap.Stob.4.28.16, Plb.2.12.8; κ. διαφορᾶς Id.22.4.14, al.; ἀνέμου *Mim. Oxy.*413.213. II. Astrol., *forecast of an undertaking, voyage*, etc., Serapio in *Cat.Cod.Astr.*1.99, Vett.Val.187.15 (pl.); περὶ καταρχῶν, title of poems by Maximus and Heph. Astr. III. *part of victim first offered*, *IG*2².1359. IV. *primacy, sovereignty*, τοῦ ἀθρόου Epicur.*Fr.*314; *starting-point, basis*, Chrysipp.*Stoic.*2.246; τὰς Χάριτας [εἶναι] τὰς ἡμετέρας κ. Phld.*Piet.*14. -ης, voc. -άρχα, ὁ, *founder, creator*, γῆς *PMag.Par.*1.713. -ικός, ή, όν, *pertaining to* καταρχαί II, *Cat.Cod.Astr.*2.41. -ω, *make beginning of* a thing, c. gen., τίνες κατῆρξαν.. μάχης; A.*Pers.*351; ὁδοῦ κατάρχειν *lead* the way, S.*OC*1019; δεινοῦ λόγου Id.*Tr.*1135; λόγων χρησίμων Ar.*Lys.*638, cf. Pl.*Prt.*351e, etc.; τραυμάτων Ascl.*Tact.*7.1; τὸ κατάρχον αἰσθήσεως, τῆς κινήσεως, the *source* of perception, of motion, Gal. 5.588: rarely c. acc., *begin* a thing, θαυμαστόν τινα λόγον Pl.*Euthd.* 283b: c. part., *begin* doing, X.*Cyr.*1.4.4, 4.5.58: abs., Pl.*Smp.*177e, Arist.*Mu.*399ᵃ15. 2. θανόντα δεσπόταν γόοις κατάρξω I *will lead* the dirge over.., E.*Andr.*1199 (lyr., with reference to the religious sense, infr. II. 2). II. Med., *begin*, like Act., c. gen., ἐχθρᾶς ἡμέρας κατάρχεται Id.*Ph.*540; τοῖς κατηργμένοις τῆς πορείας Pl.*Phdr.*256d; κ. τῆς προσβολῆς Plb.2.67.1; τοῦ λόγου Plu.2.151e: c. acc., κ. νόμον, στεναγμόν, E.*Hec.*685 (s. v. l.), *Or.*960 (both lyr.): abs., κατάρχεται μέλος *is beginning*, Id.*HF*750 (lyr.), cf. 891 (lyr.); τὸ -άρξασθαι Ael. *Tact.*17. 2. in religious sense, *begin the sacrificial ceremonies*, once in Hom., Νέστωρ χέρνιβά τ' οὐλοχύτας τε κατήρχετο Nestor *began* [*the sacrifice*] *with* the washing of hands and sprinkling the barley on the victim's head, Od.3.445: abs., Hdt.4.60,103, And.1.126; κατάρχομαι μέν, σφάγια δ' ἄλλοισιν μέλει I *begin the rite*, but leave the slaughter of the victim to others, E.*IT*40; ἐπὶ τῶν θυσιῶν κριθαῖς κ. D.H.2.25: c. gen., κατάρχεσθαι τοῦ τράγου *make a beginning of* the victim, i. e. *consecrate* him *for sacrifice* by cutting off the hair of his forehead, Ar.*Av.*959; ἐπεὶ δὲ αὐτοῦ (sc. Ἡρακλέος) πρὸς τῷ βωμῷ κατάρχοντο Hdt.2.45; πῶς δ' αὖ κατάρξῃ θυμάτων; E.*Ph.*573, cf. *IT*56,1154; κατάρξασθαι τῶν ἱερῶν D.21.114: metaph., σκυτάλην λαβών μου κατήρξατο Luc.*Somn.*3, cf. Plu.*Caes.*66:—so later in Act., Hld.2.34, al. b. *sacrifice, slay*, ξίφει, φασγάνῳ κ., E.*Alc.*74, *El.*1222 (lyr.):—Pass., ᾗ (sc. τῇ θεᾷ) σὸν κατῆρκται σῶμα *hath been devoted*, Id.*Heracl.* 601. III. Act., *rule, govern*, c. gen., Alciphr.3.44 (s. v. l.). IV. κατάρξω ὑμᾶς ἐν σκορπίοις *will chastise* you.., Lxx 3*Ki.*12.24r.

κατ-ᾰσᾰμινθεύω, *throw into a bath*, ἐσθῆτας *PMasp.*9 ii 29 (vi A. D.).

κατάσαρκ-ος, ον, *fleshy, plump*, Agatharch.*Fr.Hist.*7 J., Sor.2.57, Antyll.ap.Orib.7.12.8, Alciphr.*Fr.*5.3; gloss on σωμασκίας, Hdn. *Epim.*130. -ωσις, εως, ἡ, *plumpness*, Eust.1656.42.

κατασάττω, *stamp down*, τὴν γῆν Thphr.*CP*5.6.2: pf. part. Pass. κατασεσασμένα, glossed by κατασεσεισμένα, Hsch.

κατα-σβέννῡμι or -ύω, Ion. aor. inf. -σβῶσαι Herod.5.39:—*put out, quench*, κατέσβεσε θεσπιδαὲς πῦρ Il.21.381, cf. 16.293 (tm.), E. *Or.*697, etc.: metaph., ἔστιν θάλασσα, τίς δέ νιν κατασβέσει; who *shall dry* it *up*? A.*Ag.*958, cf. *Th.*584; κ. βοήν, ἔριν, *quell* noise, strife, S.*Aj.*1149, *OC*422; ἀνομίαν Critias 25.40 D.; τὰς ἡδονάς Pl. *Lg.*838b; τὴν δυσχέρειαν Id.*Prt.*334c; τὴν ταραχήν X.*Cyr.*5.3.55; χολὴν Herod. l. c.; κ. τὰ τραύματα *heal* them, Luc.*DMar.*11.1. II. Pass., fut. -σβήσομαι (v. infr.), with aor. 2 and pf. Act., *go out, be quenched*, καιόμενον τὸν χρυσὸν κατασβῆναι (aor. 2) Hdt.4.5; κατασβεσθῆναι τὴν πυρήν Id.1.87; ὁ κάνθαρος (i. e. the Sun) -σβήσεται *PMag.Leid.V.*2.18: metaph., κλυμάτων πηγαὶ.. κατεσβήκασι A.*Ag.* 888; of tumours, κατέσβη Hp.*Epid.*1.1; κατασβεννύμενος, of passion, Pl.*R.*411c; κατασβεσθεὶς ταῖς ἐλπίσιν Plu.2.168f; of the wind, Id. *Tim.*19. -σβεσις, εως, ἡ, *putting out*, D.C.54.2. -σβεστέον, *one must quench*, Plu.2.787f.

κατά-σεισις, εως, ἡ, *shaking*, Hp.*Art.*43; τῆς κεφαλῆς Gal.10. 1019. -σεισμός, ὁ, = foreg., Sor.1.60 (pl.), Archig.ap.Gal.12. 657, Aët.6.87. -σειστέον, *one must shake*, Sor.1.65. -σείω, fut. -σείσω Hp.*Art.*43: pf. -σέσεικα Philem.84:—*shake down, throw down*, οἰκοδομήματος ἐπὶ μέγα Th.2.76; τεῖχος, τοῦ τείχους ἐπὶ μέγα, Arr.*An.*1.19.2, 2.23.1; σεισμὸς κ. τὴν πόλιν Ael.*VH*6.7:—Pass., *fall down*, Ph.2.512; of a lion's mane, αὐχένος ἐκ λασίοιο χαίτη -εσείετο Pancrat.*Oxy.*1085.21: metaph., κ. ἀκροατοῦ ὦτα Philostr.*VS*2.29; νόμους Procop.*Arc.*27.33; κατέσεισεν ἅπαντα καὶ κατεβρόντησε Eun. *Hist.*p.256 D.; ἕως κατέσεισε until he *laid* him *on the floor* (with drinking), Men.8, cf. Philem. l. c., Ath.10.431c. 2. *impel, drive headlong*, νεανίσκον εἰς τὸν μανιώδη καὶ σφαλερὸν τῆς βασιλείας ἔρωτα Eun.*Hist.*p.235 D., cf. p.267 D.:—Pass., πρὸς τὸ λέγειν κ. ib. p.223 D. 3. in Surgery, *treat by shaking*, Hp.*Art.*42:—Pass., ib. 43. 4. κατασείσας τὴν χεῖρα *with a motion* of the hand, *Act.Ap.* 19.33; κ. ἱκετηρίας J.*BJ*2.21.8; κ. τὰ ἱμάτια, by way of signal, Plu. *Pomp.*73: more freq. c. dat., κ. τῇ χειρὶ *beckon* with the hand, Plb. 1.78.3, Hld.10.7; κ. τῇ χειρὶ σιγᾶν *Act.Ap.*12.17; κ. τῷ λύχνῳ ἅμα λέγων τὸν λόγον *PMag.Lond.*46.453; κ. ὀθόναις Hld.9.6: abs., κ. τινί *beckon* to another, as a sign for him to be silent, X.*Cyr.*5.4.4; κ. τισὶν ἐπεξιέναι J.*AJ*17.10.2; but also, *shake the head* in token of contempt, Phld.*Vit.*p.37 J.

κατ-ασελγαίνω, *to be libidinous*, Suid. s. v. καταπυγῶν.

κατασεύομαι, Pass., *rush down along*, c. acc., κῦμα κατέσσυτο καλὰ ῥέεθρα Il.21.382: abs., *rush down*, κατεσσύμενος Q.S.4.270. 2. *rush against*, κατεσσεύεσθε λεόντων Nonn.*D.*5.353.

κατασήθω, aor. -έσησα, *strain through a sieve*, Hp.*Mul.*2.133:—Pass., aor. part. -σησθεῖσα *Gp.*12.17.1. 2. *strew*, ναόν [τέφρᾳ] Thd.*Bel.*14.

κατασημ-αίνομαι, Med., *cause to be sealed up*, ὄφεις.. ἐν κίστῃ που κατασήμηναι Ar.*Fr.*28; [ἐχίνους] Arist.*Ath.*53.2; χρυσίον Pl.*Men.* 89b; ὑδρίαν *IG*2².204.39:—Pass., ib.41; τὰς ἐπισκήψεις φυλάττειν -σεσημασμένας ὑπ' ἀμφοῖν Pl.*Lg.*937b. II. *cause to be noted down*, ib.756c:—Pass., τὰ κατασημανθέντα ὀνόματα ib.756e, cf. Arist.*Ath.* 49.2. -αντικός, ή, όν, *marking distinctly*, Longin.32.5. -ειόομαι, Pass., = κατασημαίνομαι I, *Klio* 17.187 (Delph., i A. D.), cf. Hsch.

κατασήπω, *cause* or *allow to rot*, X.*Cyr.*8.2.21:—Pass., *rot away*, ib.8.2.22; μή.. κατὰ χρόα πάντα σαπήῃ Il.19.27; ἕως ἂν κατασαπῇ Pl. *Phd.*86d; -σαπέντων τῶν καρπῶν *CPHerm.*6.16 (iii A. D.): so in pf. -σέσηπα Ar.*Pl.*1035, Philetaer.9. 2. metaph., *cause* or *allow to linger*, τοὺς ἀνθρώπους ἐν τοῖς πάθεσι Gal.10.264:—Pass., *pine away*, -σήπεσθαι ἐπὶ τῆς κλίνης ib.263; πρὸς ταῖς ἀλλοτρίαις θύραις -σαπῆναι Arr.*Epict.*4.10.20.

κατ-ασθενέω, *to be* or *grow weak*, οἱ κατησθενηκότες Aët.9.42, cf. Sor.2.11, Erot. s. v. κατηπέδανον. 2. later causal, *weaken*, κνησμονάς *App.Anth.*3.158.

κατ-ασθμαίνω, *pant, struggle against*, c. gen., ἵππος χαλινῶν ὡς κατασθμαίνων μένει A.*Th.*393.

κατασῑγ-άζω, *put to silence*, Arist.*HA*614ᵃ20, Ael.*VH*14.9; τὸν δῆμον Hdn.1.9.3; σάλπιγγα Ael.*NA*16.23:—Pass., Posidon.36 J.; τὰ Πινδάρου ἤδη κατασεσιγασμένα *not* now *perused*, Ath.1.3a (cf. Eup.

366). **-αίνω**, *silence, calm*, Hsch. s. v. πραΰνει. **-αστικός**, ή, όν, *of* or *for silencing*, Eust.197.48. **-άω**, *remain silent*, Pl.*Phd.* 107a. II. = κατασιγάζω, *CPHerm.*25 ii 2, Luc.*JTr.*13 (v.l. -σιώπησον).

κατασῐδηρόω, *plate with iron*, κριοὶ κατασεσιδηρωμένοι D.S.13.54, cf. Bito 53.7, Str.15.3.11.

κατασῐκελίζω τυρόν, *Sicilize* the cheese (in allusion to the *peculations* of Laches in Sicily), Ar.*V.*911, cf. Sch. ad loc.

κατασιλλαίνω, *mock at*, Hp.*Praec.*8.

κατάσῑμος, ον, = σιμός, *Gloss.*

κατασίνομαι [ῐ], *injure, damage*, Hsch.: aor. 1 part., κατασινάμενος τὰ κάλλιστα τῆς χώρας prob. l. in Malch.p.407 D.

κατασῑτέομαι, *eat up, feed on*, c. acc., Hdt.1.216, 3.38, Str.15.2.14, D.S.3.36.

κατασιωπ-άω, *keep silence*, Isoc.8.38, Arist.*Rh.*1413ᵇ7, J.*Ap.*2.33, etc.; εἰδότες κ. Arist.*Ath.*14.2; πρός τι D.41.23. 2. c. acc. rei, *keep silent, pass over*, τὸ γεγονός D.S.32.10:—Pass., Isoc.4.27. 3. *condemn by silence*, πόλιν D.Chr.32.98. II. causal, *make silent, silence*, τὴν γυναῖκα X.*HG*5.4.7, cf. Luc.*Bis Acc.*17, *Anach.*19, *Dom.* 16:—Med., *cause silence*, X.*HG*2.4.20; κατασιωπήσασθαι διὰ τοῦ σαλπιγκτοῦ τὸν θόρυβον Plb.18.46.9. **-ητέον**, *one must keep silence*, Isoc.12.96.

κατασκαίρω, *bound up and down*, Opp.*H.*4.322.

κατασκάπτω, pf. -έσκᾰφα Isoc.14.35:—*dig down*, ἐπὶ θάτερα τῆς ἀμπέλου Thphr.*HP*4.13.5; but usu., II. *destroy utterly, raze to the ground*, τὸ ἄστυ Hdt.7.156; Τροίαν κ. βίᾳ S.*Ph.*998, cf. A.*Ag.* 525; πάτραν S.*OC*1421; δόμους E.*HF*566; πόλιν *SIG*344.7 (Teos, iv B.C.), cf. D.18.71; το τέγος Ar.*Nu.*1488; τὰ τείχη ἐς ἔδαφος Th. 4.109, cf. Lys.12.40, Isoc. l. c., Arist.*Ath.*37.1; τὸν λιμένα Aeschin. 3.123; τὰ θυσιαστήρια Lxx 3*Ki.*19.10; τὴν οἰκίαν εἰς ἔδαφος Plu.*Publ.* 10, etc.:—Pass., ϝοικία κατασκαπτέσθω *Berl.Sitzb.*1927.8 (Locr., v B.C.); τὰ οἰκία οἱ κατεσκάφη Hdt.6.72; πατρῷα ἑστία κατεσκάφη E. *Hec.*22; τὰ κατεσκαμμένα ἀναστήσω Lxx *Am.*9.11.

κατασκᾰρῑφάω, *peck at*, Ath.11.507c.

κατασκᾰφ-ή, ἡ, *razing to the ground, destruction*, S.*OC*1318, Th. 5.63; τειχῶν Lys.13.8; ἀκροπόλεως *SIG*285.9 (Erythrae, iv B.C.): more freq. in pl., Ἰλίου κ. E.*Hel.*196 (lyr.); ἰὼ κ. δόμων A.*Ch.*50 (lyr.); πόλει κατασκαφὰς θέντες Id.*Th.*46; πύργων κ. E.*Ph.*1196; τειχῶν Aeschin.3.157. II. *that which is dug*, esp. *grave*, in pl., θάπτειν..γῆς..κατασκαφαῖς A.*Th.*1013, cf. 1042; ἐς θανόντων..κατασκαφάς S.*Ant.*920. **-ής**, ές, *dug down*, κ. οἴκησις the *deep-dug* dwelling, i.e. the grave, ib.891.

κατασκάφιλος· καταισχύνων τοὺς φίλους, Hsch. (leg. καταισχόφιλος).

κατασκεδ-άζω, = sq., Suid.:—Pass., Sch.E.*Hec.*916. **-άννῡμι** and -ύω (D.54.4 codd.), Att. fut. -σκεδῶ Antiph.25:—*scatter, pour upon* or *over*, κατάχυσμα..κατεσκέδασαν θερμὸν τοῦτο καθ' ὑμῶν Ar.*Av.* 536, cf. *PMagd.*33.4 (iii B.C.); τὰς ἀμίδας D. l. c.: usu. c. acc. et gen., τὴν μεγίστην ἀρύταιναν ὑμῶν Antiph. l. c., etc.; ὥσπερ ἑωλοκρασίαν τινά μου τῆς πονηρίας -σκεδάσας D.18.50; κ. ὕβριν τινός *pour* abuse *upon* one, Plu.2.10c; λῆρον κ. τινός Luc.*Salt.*6; ὅλας ἁμάξας βλασφημιῶν κ. τινός Id.*Eun.*2, etc. 2. κ. φήμην *spread* a report *against* one, Pl.*Ap.*18c:—Pass., ἡ φήμη κατεσκέδασται τοῦ Μίνω Id.*Min.*320d; ὁ λόγος ἐν τῇ πόλει κατεσκέδασται (prob. l. for -σκεύασται) Lys.10. 23; τοῦ πόνου πλείονος -ασμένου τῆς σαρκός Hp.*Medic.*7. 3. Med., *pour, sprinkle about*, X.*An.*7.3.32 (Suid., Phot.: συγκατ- codd.). 4. *overthrow, destroy*, *IG*12(9).1179.9 (Euboea).

κατασκελετ-εύω, *reduce to a skeleton*, ἑαυτούς Plu.2.7d; τὸ σῶμα Sch.Ar.*Ra.*153:—Pass., *to be wasted away*, '*desiccated*', μὴ περιιδεῖν τὴν φύσιν -ευθεῖσαν Isoc.15.268, cf. Ph.1.198, al., Onos.1.5 (Act.), D.L.8.41: metaph., τὰ φυσικὰ ἔργα ταῖς τεχνολογίαις -ευόμενα Longin.2.1. **-όω**, = foreg., Phot. (Pass.).

κατασκελής, ές, *meagre*, of style, D.H.*Isoc.*2; τὸ τῶν παρ' ἡμῖν ἐπιτεχνημάτων κ. the *meagreness* or *inadequacy* of human contrivances, Ptol.*Alm.*13.2. II. *hard, difficult*, μέθοδος Id.*Harm.*2. 13, cf. 2.2.

κατασκέλλομαι, Pass., *become a skeleton, wither away*, φαρμάκων χρείᾳ κατεσκέλλοντο A.*Pr.*481: mostly in pf. Act. κατέσκληκα, Thphr. *CP*6.14.11, Luc.*Gall.*29, Gal.*UP*8.7, etc.; ὑπὸ τῶν πόνων Alciphr.3. 19, cf. Luc.*Bis Acc.*34: plpf., λιμῷ κατεσκλήκει Babr.46.8; *to be hard* or *frozen*, Thphr. l. c.: metaph., -εσκληκὼς *austere*, Philostr.*VS*1.18.1.

κατασκένω, Cret., = κατακτείνω, *GDI*4998 i 14.

κατασκεπ-άζω, *cover entirely*, Aen.Tact.37.3, Thphr.*HP*9.3.2, J. *AJ*8.4.1: pf. inf. Pass. κατεσκεπάσθαι Artem.2.32. 2. metaph., μοχθηρὰ ἤθη λόγοις ἐπιεικέσιν κ. Ph.2.341. **-ασμα**, ατος, τό, *covering*, Al.*Ex.*26.36. **-αστέον**, *one must cover*, Herod.Med. in *Rh.Mus.*58.85. **-αστός**, όν, *covered*, Aq.*Nu.*7.3.

κατάσκεπος, ον, v. κατάσκοπος II.

κατασκέπτομαι, later pres., = κατασκοπέω (q. v.), Just.*Nov.*22 *Praef.*: impf., Plb.3.94.7.

κατασκέπω, = κατασκεπάζω, *AP*5.59 (Rufin.), Muson.*Fr.*19 p.106 H.

κατασκευ-άζω, fut. -σκευάσω, Att. -σκευῶ *SIG*1097.9 (Athens, iv B.C.), *IPE*1².32 *B*53 (Olbia, iii B.C.): Dor. aor. -εσκεύαξα Ti. Locr.94d, *Test.Epict.*1.14, also κατεσκέαξα *Africa Italiana* 1.330 (Cyrene): Boeot. aor. inf. -σκευάττη *SIG*1185.13 (Tanagra, iii B.C.): pf. -εσκεύακα D.42.30: fut. Med. 3 sg. -ᾶται *SIG*1015.28 (Halic.): Dor. aor. Med. -εσκευαξάμην *Test.Epict.*1.9:—*equip, furnish fully with*.., [πᾶσι] κ. τὸ πλοῖον *with* all appliances, D.18.194:—Med., τοὺς ἵππους χαλκοῖς..προβλήμασι κ. X.*Cyr.*6.1.51:—freq. in Pass., ἱρὸν θησαυροῖσί τε καὶ ἀναθήμασι κατεσκευασμένον Hdt.8.33, cf. 2.44; κατασκευὴ χρυσῷ τε καὶ ἀργύρῳ κατεσκ. Id.9.82; οἷς ἡ χώρα κατεσκεύασται Th.6.91. 2. without dat., *furnish, equip fully*, τὴν χώραν X.*An.*1.9.19; κ. τινὰ ἐπὶ στρατιάν Id.*Cyr.*3.3.3; [ἐλέφαντας] κ. πρὸς τὴν πολεμικὴν χρείαν *OGI*54.12 (Adule, iii B.C.):—Med., κ. τοὺς ὄνους *having got his* asses *ready*, Hdt.2.121.δ', etc.:—Pass., τῆς Ἀντάνδρου μελλούσης -σκευάζεσθαι Th.4.75, cf. 8.24; ἔργα -ασμένα *cultivated* farms, Anaxag.4; of persons, *to be under treatment*, Phld. *Lib.*p.30., al. 3. *construct, build*, γέφυραν Hdt.1.186 (Pass.); διδασκαλεῖον Antipho 6.11; πόλιν Pl.*R.*557d; γυμνάσια Id.*Lg.*761c; ἱερὰ θυσίας τε αὐτοῖς κ. Id.*Criti.*113c; ἐπιτείχισμ' ἐπὶ τὴν Ἀττικὴν D. 18.71: generally, *prepare, arrange, establish*, κ. δημοκρατίαν X.*HG* 2.3.36; δύναμιν τῇ πόλει And.3.39; συμπόσιον Pl.*R.*363c; ἰσότητα τῆς οὐσίας Id.*Lg.*684d, cf. Arist.*Pol.*1265ᵃ39; ὀλιγαρχίαν Id.*Ath.* 37.1; ναύτας D.50.36; κ. τινὰς μελέτῃ *train* them, X.*Cyr.*8.1. 43, etc.; *turn out*, πολιτικούς Phld.*Rh.*2.264 S., al.:—Med., κατασκευάζεσθαι ναυμαχίαν *prepare* it, *make ready for* it, v.l. for παρασκ- in Th.2.85; *make for oneself*, esp. *build* a house *and furnish* it, opp. ἀνασκευάζομαι Id.1.93, 2.17; *unpack*, opp. ἀνασκ., X.*Cyr.*8.5.2; κ. ἐρημίαν αὐτῷ Pl.*Lg.*730c, etc.; κ. τράπεζαν *set up* a bank, Is.*Fr.*66; κατασκευάζομαι τέχνην μυρεψικὴν *I am setting up* as a perfumer, Lys.*Fr.* 1.2; τοὺς ἐγγυτάτω τῆς ἀγορᾶς κατεσκευασμένους Id.24.20; [πρόσοδον] οὐ μικρὰν κατεσκευάσαντο *made themselves* a good [income], D.27.61, cf. And.4.11. 4. of fraudulent transactions, *fabricate, trump up*, πρόφασιν X.*Cyr.*2.4.17; τὸ ἀπόρρητον κατασκευάσαι D.2.6; λιποταξίου γραφὴν κατεσκεύασεν Id.21.103, cf. 92; χρέα ψευδῆ Id.42.30, cf. 45. 22 (Pass.); of persons, *suborn*, λογοποιούς Din.1.35; *set up*, ἤ..ἐπιτίθενται αὐτοὶ ἢ κατασκευάζουσιν ἕτερον Arist.*Pol.*1306ᵃ1; οἱ κατεσκευασμένοι τῶν Θετταλῶν men *prepared for the purpose*, D.18.151; κατεσκ. δανεισταί Id.42.28: c. inf., τὸν ἀνεψιὸν..κατεσκεύασεν ἀμφισβητεῖν Id.55.1. 5. c. dupl. acc., *make, render*, [φρούρια] κ. ὡς ἐχυρώτατα X.*Cyr.*2.4.17; ἀριστερὰ δεξιῶν ἀσθενέστερα κ. Pl.*Lg.*795a; φοβερὸν κ. τὸ αὐτόχειρα γενέσθαι D.20.158; ἀνομοθέτητον ἑαυτῷ τὸν βίον Duris 10 J.; κ. τινὰ τοιοῦτον.. Arist.*Rh.*1380ᵃ2 (also with Adv., πρὸς ἑαυτὸν κ. εὖ τὸν ἀκροατὴν *render* the audience favourably disposed towards oneself, 1419ᵇ11). 6. *represent as* so and so, κ. τινὰς παροίνους, ὑβριστάς, ἀγνώμονας, D.54.14, cf. 45.82; εἰ μὴ Γοργίαν Νέστορά τινα κατασκευάζεις unless you *make out* a Gorgias *to be* Nestor, Pl.*Phdr.* 261c. 7. in argument, *maintain, prove*, τῶν ἐν Εὐβοίᾳ πραγμάτων.. ὡς ἐγὼ αἴτιός εἰμι, κατεσκεύαζε *tried to make out* that.., D.21.110; κ. ὅτι.. Arr.*Epict.*3.15.14, S.E.*P.*1.32; κ. τῷ λόγῳ *establish* a proposition by reasoning, Damian.*Opt.*5; διὰ λόγου -σκευασθήσεται Phld. *Sign.*6. 8. in Logic, *construct* a positive argument, opp. ἀναιρέω, ἀνασκευάζω (of negative arguments), Arist.*Rh.*1401ᵇ3, cf. Plu.2.1036b, etc.: Philos., κ. τῶν ἀριθμῶν ἰδέαν *construct, postulate*, Arist.*EN*1096ᵃ 19, cf. *Metaph.*984ᵇ25, al. 9. Geom., *construct*, Euc.5.7 (Pass.), Archim.*Sph.Cyl.*2.6 (Pass.); *solve by a construction*, πρόβλημα Papp. 54.25. 10. Rhet., *frame*, ὀνόματα D.H.*Comp.*16; *elaborate*, κατεσκεύασται τὸ δοκοῦν εἶναι ἀφελὲς Id.*Is.*7; λόγος κατεσκευασμένος Str. 1.2.6. 11. abs. in Med., *prepare oneself* or *make ready for* doing, ὡς πολεμήσοντες Th.2.7; ὡς οἰκήσων X.*An.*3.2.24; ὡς εἰς μάχην Paus. 5.21.14. 12. Pass., of disease, *to become established*, -σκευαζομένου τοῦ πάθους Gal.8.332. **-ᾰσία**, ἡ, *preparation* of drugs, Suid. s. v. κῦφι. **-ασμα**, ατος, τό, *that which is prepared* or *made, work of art*, τὰ Κορίνθια κ. Hippoloch.ap.Ath.4.128d, cf. Plb.4.18.8, Aristeas 52, J.*BJ*7.5.5, Arr.*Epict.*2.19.26; surgical *apparatus*, Orib.49. 24.2; esp. *building, structure*, D.23.207, *SIG*330.39 (pl., Ilium, iv B.C.), Plb.10.27.9, D.H.3.27, D.S.1.50; οἰκητήριον κ. Cleanth.*Stoic.*1. 132; θεωρητὸν κ., of the world, Secund.*Sent.*1: in pl., *engines of war*, Plb.1.48.5; *furniture*, ἱεροῦ *SIG*330.4 (Ilium, iv B.C.). II. *arrangement, contrivance*, D.23.13; τὸ κ. τῶν συσσιτίων Arist.*Pol.*1271ᵃ 33; τὰ [τυραννικὰ] κ. ib.1319ᵇ27; σοφιστοῦ Phld.*Rh.*1.183 S.; ἐκ κατασκευάσματος, Lat. *ex composito*, D.C.52.7. **-ασμάτιον**, τό, Dim. of foreg., Hero *Spir.*1.7. **-ασμός**, ὁ, *contrivance*, D.24.16; ἐκ κατασκευασμοῦ, Lat. *ex composito*, D.C.38.9, al. **-αστέος**, α, ον, *to be prepared* or *made*, X.*Ages.*1.23, Gal.14.262. II. neut., *one must prepare, make*, etc., Pl.*Lg.*964d, X.*HG*3.4.15, etc.; κ. ἔθος πρὸς τὸν ἔμετον Philum.ap.Aët.9.23. 2. *one must construct a proof* or *argument*, Aphth.*Prog.*6, Theon *Prog.*3. **-αστής**, οῦ, ὁ, *contriver*, Hsch. and Suid. s. v. μηχανορράφος. 2. *one who makes provision, commissariat officer, quartermaster*, Just.*Nov.*30.7.1. **-αστικός**, ή, όν, *fitted for providing*, τινος Arist.*VV*1250ᵇ29; *fitted for bringing about*, τοῦ μὴ πλανᾶν Phld.*Rh.*1.347 S. 2. in Logic, *constructive, positive*, opp. destructive (λυτικός, ἀνασκευαστικός), Arist.*Rh.*1403ᵃ25, Theon *Prog.*12, etc.: c. gen., λόγος κ. ζητήματος Corn.*Rh.*p.377 H., cf. Nicol. *Prog.*p.29 F. Adv. -κῶς, opp. ἀνασκευαστικῶς, Arist.*APr.*52ᵃ31. 3. (κατασκευή VIII) *systematic*, γυμνάσια Gal.6.177. **-αστός**, ή, όν, *artificial*, opp. αὐτοφυής, τὸ κ. D.H.*Is.*11; ἡ κατασκευαστὴ δόξα, opp. ἡ σιωπωμένη ἀλήθεια, Id.1.76; εἰκὼν κ. Plu.2.210d. Adv. -τῶς *under artificial conditions*, Theon *Intr.* ad Euc.*Opt.*p.146 H. 2. *suborned*, ἄνδρες Arist.*Oec.*1348ᵃ7. **-άστρια**, ἡ, fem. of κατασκευαστής, *she who prepares*, Sch.Lyc.578 (ed. Bachm.). **-ή**, ἡ, *preparation*, ὄντων ἐν κατασκευῇ τοῦ πολέμου being engaged in *preparing for* it, Th. 8.5; *construction*, λιμένων ἢ νεωρίων Pl.*Grg.*455b; *fitting out*, πλοίων Plb.1.21.1, etc. 2. *unpacking*, X.*Cyr.*8.5.5. 3. *training*, *Stoic.* 3.89. II. *permanent* or *fixed assets*, opp. what is movable or temporary (παρασκευή), *fixtures, plant*, etc., Th.1.10; ἀνειληφότες τὰς κ. having repaired their *estates*, Id.2.16; ἡ περὶ τὸν κλῆρον κ. Pl.

Lg.923d; τῆς ἄλλης κ., ἐν ᾗ κατοικοῦμεν καὶ μεθ' ἧς πολιτευόμεθα καὶ δι' ἣν ζῆν δυνάμεθα the aggregate of our possessions, Isoc.4.26; αἱ κ. αἱ ἐπὶ τῶν ἀγρῶν ἢ αἱ ἐντὸς τείχους Id.7.52; but also, like παρασκευή, any *furniture* or *fittings*, τὴν Μαρδονίου κ., i.e. his *tent and its furniture*, Hdt.9.82; κ. πολυτελέσι χρησαμένων Th.6.31; φιάλας τε.. καὶ θυμιατήρια καὶ ἄλλην κ. ib.46; ἡ κ. τῆς οἰκίας D.47.54; τῇ τῶν θεῶν κ. χρῆσθαι *whatever* the gods *provided*, X.*Ages*.9.5. III. *state, condition, constitution* of a thing, θεοῦ κ. βίῳ δόντος τοιαύτην E.*Supp*.214; αἱ.. κ. τῆς ψυχῆς Pl.*R*.544e; ἡ τοῦ βίου κ. Id.*Lg*.842c; ἡ τῶν νόμων κ. ib.739a; ἐν πάσῃ κ. πολιτικῇ ib.736b; ἐν χρημάτων κ. in *the constitution* of a man's fortune, Id.*Grg*.477b; ἐν σώματος κ. ibid.; κ. τις παρὰ φύσιν, definition of νόσος, Gal.6.837. IV. *device, trick*, τέχναι καὶ κ. Aeschin.2.1, v.l. in Din.1.34; ἄνευ κατασκευῆς ᾄδειν *artlessly*, Ael.*NA*5.38. V. in Logic, *constructive reasoning*, opp. ἀνασκευή, D.H.*Lys*.24, Hermog.*Prog*.5, etc.: in pl., Cic.*Att*.1.14.4, Longin.11.2, Quint.2.4.18. VI. Rhet., *artistic treatment*, κ. ποιητική Str.1.2.6, D.H.*Comp*.1; *manipulation*, συλλαβῶν, γραμμάτων, ib.15,16; *elaboration*, Id.*Pomp*.2, etc.; *correct style*, opp. ἰδιωτισμός, Diocl.*Stoic*.3.214; *technical resources*, πλάσμα καὶ ἡ ἄλλη κ. δημηγόρου Phld.*Rh*.1.199 S. VII. Geom., *construction*, Archim.*Sph.Cyl*.2.4, cf. Procl. *in Euc*.p.203 F.; κ. ὀργανική *solution by* mechanical *construction*, Papp.174.17. VIII. *system of gymnastic exercise*, as t.t., Gal.6.169. **-ος**, ον, *furnished*, οἶκος dub. l. in *IG*12(3).185 (Astypalaea). **-όω**, Dor. = κατασκευάζω, aor. κατεσσκέωσα *IG* 14.241 (Neëtum): pf. κατεσκεύωκα *Test.Epict*.4.13:—Med., εἴ τι κα -σκευώσωνται *GDI*1874.26 (Delph.).

κατάσκεψις, εως, ἡ, *careful examination*, χωρίων Str.6.1.12.

κατ-ασκέω, *practise*: pf. part. Pass. κατησκημένος *regular, ascetic*, δίαιτα Plu.*Ages*.33.

κατασκην-άω, = sq., aor. -εσκήνησα X.*An*.3.4.32, *HG*4.5.2, etc.:—Med., κατασκηνᾶσθαι Pl.*R*.614e. **-όω**, *take up one's quarters, encamp*, εἰς.. X.*Cyr*.4.5.39, *Hell.Oxy*.16.2, etc.; ἐν.. Lxx 1*Ch*.23.25; ἔνθα κατεσκηνώκατε X.*Cyr*.6.2.2: generally, *rest*, ἐπ' ἐλπίδι Lxx *Ps*.15(16).9; *settle*, of birds, ἐν κλάδοις *Ev.Matt*.13.32: metaph., οὐ ψυχὴ ἐν μόνῳ ἀνθρώπῳ κ. Porph.*Abst*.4.9. **-ωμα**, ατος, τό, *covering, veil*, A.*Ch*.985. 2. gloss on αὔλιον, Sch.Opp.*H*.2.524, cf. 3.5. **-ωσις**, εως, ἡ, *encamping, taking up one's quarters*, Lxx 1*Ch*.28.2, al.; καλεῖν τινα πρὸς κατασκήνωσιν Plb.11.26.5; διδόναι εἰς κ. to give them as *quarters*, *OGI*229.57 (Smyrna, iii B.C.); ἐν κ. in *camp*, Onos.11.6: pl. -σκηνώσεις βασιλέων *Gp*.11.2.9. 2. of birds, *resting-place, nest*, *Ev.Matt*.8.20 (pl.).

κατα-σκήπτω, fut. -ψω E.*Hipp*.1418:—*rush down* or *fall upon*, Arist.*Mu*.395^{a}25, D.S.16.80, etc.; of the rainbow, Arist.*HA*553^{b}30; of divine visitations, τοῖσι Λακεδαιμονίοισι μῆνις κατέσκηψε Ταλθυβίου Hdt.7.134; ἐς ἀγγέλους ib.137; ἣν κατασκήψῃ ἐς τὴν Πελοπόννησον, of an omen, Id.8.65; ὀργαὶ κ. ἐς τὸ σὸν δέμας E. l. c.; τίς κατέσκηψεν τύχη; A.*Supp*.327; ἐς Οἰδίπου παῖδε Ἄρης κ. Ar.*Fr*.558; of Nemesis, D.H.3.23; esp. of sickness, *attack*, [ἡ νόσος] κατέσκηπτε ἐς ἄκρας χεῖρας καὶ πόδας Th.2.49, cf. Hp.*Epid*.3.8; εἰς γυναῖκας D.H.9.40; ῥεῦμα κ. τινὶ ἐς τὰ νεῦρα Paus.6.3.10, cf. Gal.1.286; ἡ ξανθὴ [χολὴ] ὀδόντι Alex.Aphr.*Pr*.1.40, etc. 2. c. acc., *fall upon*, τινα dub. l. in E.*Med*.94 (fort. τινί):—Pass., κατασκηφθέντα χωρία *struck by lightning*, Hsch. s.v. ἐνηλύσια. II. causal, εἰς ὅ τι -σκήψει τέλος ὁ δαίμων νέμεσιν Plu.*Aem*.27. III. κ. λιταῖς *storm* or *importune* with prayers, c. inf., S.*OC*1011. IV. abs., *break out, go forth*, of a report, App.*BC*3.25; κ. εἰς τέλος *come* to an issue, of a war, D.H.3.54. **-σκηψις**, εως, ἡ, *attack*, τῶν παθῶν Dsc.*Ther.Praef.*

κατασκῐ-άζω, fut. -σκιάσω, Att. -σκιῶ S.*OC*406:—*overshadow, cover over*, κατὰ δ' ἐσκίασαν βελέεσσι Τιτῆνας Hes.*Th*.716; ἡ δέ οἱ κόμη ὤμους κ. Archil.29; σαρξὶν πάντα κατεσκίασεν ἄνωθεν Pl.*Ti*.74d; *spread awnings*, E.*Ion* 1142; κόνει *bury* one, S. l. c.; θανόντα.. γαῖα κατεσκίασε *IG*7.580 (Tanagra). **-άω**, poet. for foreg., Od.12.436:—Pass., Opp.*H*.3.467.

κατασκίδναμαι, Pass. of κατασκεδάννυμι, Plu.2.776f.

κατάσκῐος, ον, *shaded* or *covered with*, λάχνῃ δέρμα κ. Hes.*Op*.513, cf. Hdt.2.138, A.*Ag*.493, S.*El*.422; *shaded*, νῶτον Pi.*Pae*.6.139: later c. gen., αἰγείροιο *AP*9.333 (Mnasalc., v.l. αἰγείροισι): metaph. in Astrol., ἀργὸς καὶ κ. τόπος, of a region, Vett.Val.77.25; name of second τόπος, Id.179.13; of third, *Cat.Cod.Astr*.8(4).144. II. trans., *overshadowing*, λόφοι A.*Th*.384, Ar.*Ach*.965 codd., cf. E.*Ph*.654 (lyr.).

κατασκῑρόομαι, Pass., *become hard* or *dry* through age, κατεσκιρωμένης (-σκηρ- cod.)· πεπαλαιωμένης, Hsch., cf. eund. s.v. κατεσκληκότα (ubi -σκληρ- cod.). II. pf. inf. κατεσκιρῶσθαι (sic cod. Patm., -σκειρῶ- cod. Phot.), = λελευκάνθαι, Apollod.Hist.*Fr*.107(*c*) J. (nisi leg. κατεσκυρῶσθαι eodem sensu).

κατασκιρτάω, *leap upon*, τοῦ βήματος Plu.2.790c. 2. *leap about*, Ael.*NA*5.6. II. metaph., *show contempt for*, τινος ib.2.6, Polyaen.8.23.7, etc.

κατασκλῆναι, v. κατασκέλλομαι.

κατασκληρ-αίνω, *harden*, Hsch. s.v. καταμαλάσσοντα (dub.). **-όομαι**, pf. part. Pass. κατεσκληρωμένα, gloss on κατεσκληκότα, Id. (fort. κατεσκιρωμένα). **-ος**, *very hard*, Ph.*Bel*.71.30, *Hippiatr*.96. **-ύνομαι** [ῡ], Pass., *become hard*, Thphr.*CP*4.12.9, Gal.11.531.

κατασκόπ-ευσις, εως, ἡ, *reconnoitring*, Eust.69.37. **-εύω**, = sq., Lxx *Ex*.2.4, al., *PTeb*.230 (ii B.C.). **-έω**, fut. -σκέψομαι: aor. -εσκεψάμην:—*view closely, spy out, reconnoitre*, κ. ὅποι.. E.*Hel*.1067; τὰ ἀγγελλόμενα *reconnoitre*, Aen.Tact.23.10; εἴ πῃ.. X.*Cyr*.7.1.39, cf. Th.6.50, al.; τῶν πολεμίων Plu.*Sol*.9; *keep a look-out*, of ships, Plb.3.95.6:—Med., -σκοπεῖσθαι ἑαυτήν X.*Mem*.2.1.22; αὐτὸς ἑαυτὸν κ. Arist.*MM*1213^{a}5; *inspect*, τὰς πανοπλίας Plb.10.20.2; γραφὴν *POxy*.1414.4 (iii A.D.); of a medical examination, Gal.1.293. **-ή**, ἡ, *viewing closely, spying*, πέμπειν τινὰ εἰς κατασκοπήν S.*Ph*.45; μολεῖν εἰς κ. E.*Ba*.838; ἐπὶ κατασκοπήν X.*Cyr*.6.2.9, cf. *HG*1.4.11, Arist.*Ath.Fr*.4, Plb.3.95.8; ἐπὶ -σκοπῇ τῶν πραγμάτων Aeschin.2.28; κατασκοπῆς ἕνεκα X.*An*.7.4.13; ἔχειν κ. Plu.*Fab*.12; κατασκοπαῖς χρωμένους Th.6.34; ἐς τὴν κ. τῶν χρημάτων *to inspect* the money, ib.46. **-ησις**, εως, ἡ, = foreg., *Gloss.* **-ία**, ἡ, fem. of κατάσκοπος, epith. of Aphrodite at Troezen, Paus.2.32.3. **-ικός**, ή, όν, *for scouting*: -κά, τά (sc. πλοῖα), Plu.*Cat.Mi*.54. **-ιον**, τό, *look-out ship*, Gell.10.25 (sed leg. -σκοπικόν). **-ίς** (sc. ναῦς), ίδος, ἡ, = foreg., *Gloss.* **-ίσκος**, ὁ, = foreg., *CIL*8.27790 (Althiburos). **-ος**, ὁ, *one who reconnoitres, scout, spy*, Hdt.1.100, 112, al.; κατάσκοπον πολεμίων πέμπειν E.*Rh*.125; πεμφθεὶς Ἰλίου κ. ib.505, cf. *Hec*.239, Th.6.63; τριήρεις πέμψαι κ. Plu.*Lys*.10; τῶν λόγων κ. Ar.*Th*.588, cf. X.*Cyr*.6.1.31; πραγμάτων Men.*Pk*.105. 2. *examiner, inspector*, Th.4.27, cf. 8.41; τῆς προσόδου ἐκ σίτου *Fouilles de l'Institut Français d'Arch. Orientale du Caire* 4(2).p.74: metaph., κ. βίου Secund.*Sent*.7. II. κατάσκοπος, ον, *closely covered*, Sch.Opp.*H*.3.636 (sed leg. -σκεπος).

κατασκορπίζω, *scatter abroad*, D.S.24.1.

κατασκοτίζω, *veil in darkness*, Gal.*UP*10.3.

κατασκυθρωπ-άζω, *look gloomy*, J.*AJ*11.5.6. **-άω** or **-έω**, = foreg., c. gen., Suid.

κατασκώπτω, *make jokes upon*, τινα Hdt.2.173; mostly in bad sense, *jeer, mock*, Id.3.37,151.

κατασμῑκρ-ίζω, *disparage, depreciate*, Arist.*EN*1163^{a}14, Phld.*Vit*.p.37 J. **-ολογέω**, *speak disparagingly of, accuse as niggardly*, τὴν φύσιν Hp.*Ep*.17. **-ύνω**, *lessen, abridge*, τὴν τοῦ λόγου σεμνότητα Demetr.*Eloc*.44, cf. Luc.*Gall*.14, Porph.*Sent*.40:—Pass., *to be made small*, Lxx 2*Ki*.7.19; *become less*, Marcellin.*Puls*.310: metaph., M.Ant.8.36. II. = κατασμικρίζω, *belittle*, -σμικρῦναι καὶ διαφαυλίσαι Hierocl.p.59 A., cf. Max.Tyr.22.2, Ath.8.359a, Simp. *in Epict*.p.102 D. III. = κατακερματίζω, εἰς λεπτὰ καὶ ἀγεννῆ μόρια Max.Tyr.34.1 (Pass.).

κατάσμυρνος, ον, *smelling of myrrh*, Dsc.1.27.

κατασμύχω [ῡ], *burn with a slow fire, burn up*, κατά τε σμῦξαι πυρὶ νῆας Il.9.653: metaph., ὅς με κατασμύχων, of love, Theoc.3.17:—in Pass., of a disappointed rival, *waste away*, Id.8.90, cf. Phalar.*Ep*.144.4; ἐσσηρός τι καὶ κατεσμυγμένον ὑποβλέπειν Hld.7.21.

κατασμώχομαι, Med., *rub in pieces, bruise*, Nic.*Th*.860, *Al*.332.

κατασοβᾰρεύομαι, *regard haughtily*, τινος J.*BJ*3.1.1, D.L.1.81, Men.Prot.p.32 D.

κατασοβέω, *frighten away, scare*, τοὺς ὄρνιθας Arist.*Mir*.841^{b}22; *drive down*, εἰς βαθὺ φρέαρ Parth.14.3.

κατασοφ-ίζομαι, *outwit by sophisms* or *fallacies*, c. acc. pers., Lxx *Ex*.1.10, Luc.*DDeor*.1.1, etc.; ταῖς εὑρησιλογίαις κ. τὴν δύναμιν τῆς πεπρωμένης D.S.17.116; τὸν νόμον διὰ τῆς ἑαυτοῦ κακουργίας κ. Just.*Nov*.72.5: c. gen., Ael. in Ar.Byz.*Epit*.58.6:—also as Pass., *to be outwitted*, Plu.2.80c, Alex.Aphr. *in SE* 43.22, Luc.*DDeor*.16.2, Longin.17.1. 2. κ. τι περί τινων *evade by quibbling*, *CIG*(add.)4224*d* 10 (Anticragus). 3. *falsify*, J.*AJ*8.15.5. **-ισμός**, ὁ, *outwitting, trickery*, Alex.Aphr. *in SE*48.10, Eust.1695.36, Sch.Hermog. in Rh.4.215 W. **-ιστεύω**, = κατασοφίζομαι, c. gen., Suid.

κατ-ασπάζομαι, *embrace, kiss*, τινα Plu.*Cor*.9; σορόν Id.*Ant*.85; *treat lovingly*, φιλήμασι, θρήνοις, Hld.5.11, 7.7. 2. *do homage to* a king, J.*AJ*7.10.5.

κατασπαθάω, v.l. for σπαθάω, Alciphr.3.50.

κατασπᾰράσσω, Att. -ττω, *tear in pieces*, Ar.*Eq*.729; βυβλίον Plb.23.14.8, D.S.29.21; κατεσπαραγμένη τὴν ἐσθῆτα Luc.*Asin*.22.

κατασπαργᾰνόω, *wrap in swaddling-clothes*, βρέφη Ph.2.495.

κατά-σπᾰσις, εως, ἡ, *drawing down*, Arist.*Mete*.369^{b}20; ἐντέρων dub. in Herod.Med. in *Rh.Mus*.58.108. **-σπασμα**, ατος, τό, in pl., *vibrations* of the reed-tongue of a pipe, Thphr.*HP*4.11.5. II. *part, fragment*, τῆς στρατιᾶς J.*BJ*5.12.1 (dub. l.), cf. Hsch. and Suid. s.v. κάταγμα. **-σπασμικός**, ή, όν, of a drug, *curing* κατασπασμός, *POxy*.1088.68 (i A.D.). **-σπασμός**, ὁ, = κατάσπασις, ὑγρῶν Plu.2.650c; ὑποχονδρίων Sor.2.36; *pulling down, demolition* of buildings, Nech. in *Cat.Cod.Astr*.7.136 (pl.), *PRyl*.125.6 (i A.D.). 2. *plucking, gathering* of fruit-crops, ib.97.6 (ii A.D.), etc. 3. *stroking* or *rubbing down*, cj. for -πασμός in Cael.Aur.*TP*1.166. II. metaph., *depression of spirits*, Plu.2.78a (pl.). III. *lowering* of the voice, Antyll.ap.Orib.6.8.5. **-σπαστικός**, ή, όν, *fitted for drawing down*, γάλακτος Dsc.2.136, cf. Antyll.ap.Orib.6.31.6 (v.l. -παυστικός); κ. δύναμις Philum.*Ven*.10.4.

κατασπᾰτᾰλάω, *live wantonly, wanton*, Lxx *Pr*.29.21, *Am*.6.4, Luc.*Epigr*.50.

κατασπάω, fut. -άσω [ᾰ]: pf. -έσπακα Ar.*Eq*.718:—*draw, pull down*, μολυβδὶς ὥστε δίκτυον κατέσπασεν S.*Fr*.840; κατασπάσαι τινὰ τῶν τριχῶν *drag* one *down by* the hair, Ar.*Lys*.725; τινὰ τοῦ σκέλους Antiph.86.3; κ. τὰς πεντηκοντέρους *haul* them *down to the sea, set* them *afloat*, Hdt.1.164, cf. 7.193; τὰ σημεῖα κατεσπάσθη (in token of defeat), Th.1.63; κ. τινὰ ἀπὸ τοῦ ἵππου X.*An*.1.9.6; κατεσπακὼς τὰς ὀφρῦς, of one frowning, Alciphr.3.3:—Pass., *to be drawn down*, τὰ κατασπώμενα.. κἀνασπώμενα, of the limbs of puppets, X.*Mem*.3.10.7; κατεσπασμέναι ὀφρύες, of one frowning, Arist.*HA*491^{b}17; κατασπᾶσθαι ἐς ὕπνον, ἐς δάκρυα, Luc.*DMar*.2.2, *Anach*.23. b. *gather* fruit from, τὸν ἐλαιωνοπαράδεισον, prob. in *PSI*1.33.26 (iii A.D.). 2. Pass., *to be displaced downwards*, of a dislocated bone, Hp.*Mochl.*

4, 5; *to be convulsed, suffer a spasm*, Id.*Epid*.3.17.β′ (or perh. *to be drawn*, as in facial paralysis); *fall into a trance*, *PMag.Lond*.121.549. II. *draw down* or *forth*, τὰ γυναικεῖα Hp.*Epid*.6.8.32, cf. Arist.*GA*750ᵇ35; γάλα Dsc.3.58; *draw off*, τὸ τὴν νοῦσον παρέχον Hp.*Loc.Hom*.30 (Pass.); χυμοὺς κ. [τὸ λουτρόν] *App.Anth*.3.158. III. *quaff, swallow down*, Ar.*Eq*.718, *Ra*.576, Antiph.204.13. IV. *pull down*, οἶκον, ἄλση, Lxx 2*Ch*.24.7, 34.7; τὰ ὑψηλά ib.31.1, cf. *PTeb*.5.134 (ii B.C., Pass.); τὴν Σμύρναν Str.14.1.37, cf. 16.2.30 (Pass.); κ. τὰς τάξεις *break* the ranks, Plb.1.40.13: metaph., Phld.*D*.1.17. V. *lower*, τὴν φωνήν Antyll.ap.Orib.6.9.5. VI. *precipitate*, Zos.Alch.p.195 B. (Pass.). VII. v. κατασπεύδω.

κατασπειράω, in pf. part. Pass., τοῦ ἀπὸ τῶν ἄστρων κατεσπειραμένου φωτός dub.l. in Epicur.*Ep*.2 p.45 U.; fort. κατεσπαρμένου (*scattered, given out*).

κατασπείρω, fut. -σπερῶ Lxx (v. infr.):—*sow, plant*, εἰς μήτραν ζῷα Pl.*Ti*.91d: metaph., ἀνίας μοι κατασπείρας S.*Aj*.1005:—Pass., ὁ κατεσπαρμένος σπόρος *PMagd*.7.8 (iii B.C.). 2. *beget*, τινα E.*HF* 469, Phint.ap.Stob.4.23.61ᵃ; τὸν κατασπείραντα *him that begat* me, Diph.93. II. *spread as in sowing*, τοῦ χάρακος κ. [πυροβόλα] *scatter* them *over*.. Plu.*Cam*.34; αὐτοῖς αὔραν τινὰ κ. ἡ χώρα νότιον Id.*Dio* 25:—Pass., *to be spread abroad, dispersed*, εἰ μὴ κατεσπαρμένοι ἦσαν οἱ τοιοῦτοι λόγοι ἐν τοῖς πᾶσιν Pl.*Lg*.891b. III. *plant*, ἀμπελῶνα Lxx *De*.22.9; γῆν *PMagd*.28.3 (iii B.C.), Ph.2.262: metaph., [νόσοι] χωρία καὶ πελάγη κατασπείρασαι τῶν ἀβουλήτων Id.2.567; πλούτῳ Ἑλλάδα κ. D.H.*Dem*.29. IV. *besprinkle*, ἤδη καὶ λευκαί με κατασπείρουσιν ἔθειραι *AP*11.41 (Phld.).

κατάσπεισις, εως, ἡ, *besprinkling with holy water*, Plu.2.438a (pl.). II. *self-devotion*, of Spanish retainers, Id.*Sert*.14; cf. κατασπένδω II. 3.

κατασπένδω, fut. -σπείσω E.*Or*.1187:—*pour as a drink-offering*, c. acc. cogn., χοὰς ὑπὲρ μητρὸς τάφῳ E. l. c.; κ. κατὰ τῆς κεφαλῆς ἀρυβάλλῳ ἀμβροσίαν κατὰ σοῦ Ar.*Eq*.1094: abs., *pour drink-offerings*, Hdt.2.151; τοῖς θεοῖς Plb.3.11.6:—Pass., -σπένδεται (-τε lapis) ἀκρήτῳ *SIG*57.26 (Milet., v B.C.). II. c. acc., *wet*, λιβάσι κ. παρηΐδα *Trag.Adesp*.548. 2. c. acc. pers., κ. τινὰ δακρύοις *honour with offerings* of tears, E.*Or*.1239; simply, κ. τινά *lament with tears*, *AP* 7.260 (Carph.). 3. c. acc. pers., *offer up, devote, consecrate*, τινα D.S.5.31; κατασπένδειν ἑαυτοὺς *devote* themselves, of Spanish retainers, Str.3.4.18; cf. κατάσπεισις II:—Pass., ἄνθρωπος κατεσπεισμένος Id.4.4.5; πρόβατα κ. Plu.*Alex*.50; Μούσαισι.. κατεσπείσθη πᾶς ὁ τεὸς βίοτος *AP*7.27 (Antip. Sid.), cf. Longus 2.6; of a priest, *to be consecrated*, ἐπὶ τὰ ἱερά prob. in *OGI*331.20 (Pergam., ii B.C.).

κατασπέρχω, *urge on*, λῃστὰς δορί with a spear, Ar.*Ach*.1188; ἐλάτῃσι νῆα Opp.*H*.4.91; ὁ ἄνεμος ἰσχυρῶς -έσπερχε *drove* [them] *on*, D.C.41.46; κατασπέρχον, of circumstances, *urgent, pressing*, Th.4.126:—Pass., *to be driven on*, J.*BJ*4.2.4.

κατασπερχωτήν· ἐπὶ τὴν οἰκίαν, ἢ ἐπὶ τὴν ἑστίαν κεκαυμένη, Hsch.

κατα-σπεύδω, *urge, hasten on*, πρᾶγμα Aeschin.3.67, cf. Lxx *Ex*.5.13:—Pass., of words, *to be urgent* or *rapid*, κατεσπεῦσθαι τὴν φράσιν D.H.*Comp*.20 (Upton for κατεσπάσθαι); κατεσπεῦσθαι (v.l. -εσπάσθαι) τὴν λέξιν Gal.16.548; τὰ κατεσπευσμένα Longin.19.2; ἡ ἁρμονία οὐ κ. Id.40.4. 2. *agitate, dismay*, τινα Lxx *Da*.4.16(19). II. intr., *make haste, hasten*, ib.*De*.33.2. **-σπευσις**, εως, ἡ, *haste*, Thd.*Pr*.1.27.

κατασπῐλ-άζω, (σπιλάς B) *spot, stain*, Hsch. 2. = κατακρύπτω, Anon.ap.*EM*495.42. II. (σπιλάς C) *swoop down upon*, as a sudden storm, Ph.*Fr*.28 H., Suid. s. v. κατεσπίλασεν. **-ος**, ον, *blemished*, βοῦς Porph.*Abst*.4.7.

κατασπλεκόω, = σπλεκόω, Hsch.

κατασποδέω, *throw down in the dust, make to bite the dust*, τὸν ἄνδρα τῷ πελέκει κατεσπόδησεν Ar.*Th*.560; κατεσποδημένῳ A.*Th*.809.

κατασπορ-ά, ἡ, *sowing*, *PTeb*.341.5 (ii A.D.), *POxy*.2121.42 (iii A.D.), Sch.Pl.*Lg*.853d, Phot. s. v. κερασβόλα. **-εύς**, έως, ὁ, *sower*, *PFay*.118.11 (ii A.D.), *PLond*.1821.217. **-εύω**, = κατασπείρω, dub. in *BGU*12.10 (ii A.D.).

κατασπουδ-άζομαι (with aor. and pf. Pass.), *to be earnest, serious*, Hdt.2.173; οὐδαμῶς κατεσπουδασμένος ἀνήρ ib.174; κατεσπουδασμέναι δεήσεις D.H.11.61, cf. 4.67:—later in Act., ἐὰν αὐτός τις.. φαίνηται -εσπουδακώς Phld.*Mort*.31: also c. dat., *take a serious interest in*, βλαβεροῖς κ. Id.*Mus*.p.56 K.: abs., Apollon.*Lex*. s. v. ἐπείγετον. II. as Pass., *to be troubled*, Lxx *Jb*.23.15, Aq.2*Ki*.4.1, al. 2. *to be oppressed*, ὑπὸ μειζόνων Vett.Val.254.16. **-αζόντως**, Adv. *eagerly*, Hsch. s. v. ἠπειγμένως (ἐπηγ- cod.). **-αίως**, Adv. = foreg., *BGU* 1206.7, 1207.10 (i B.C.). **-ασμός**, ὁ, *trouble, amazement*, Aq.*Ze*.1.18.

κατάσσῠτος, ον, *rushing down*, ἰχώρ, πῦρ, Nonn.*D*.4.388, 45.338.

κατάσσω, later for κατάγνυμι, impf. κατέασσε Aesop.7:—Pass., Apollod.*Poliorc*.189.6, App.*Pun*.129, Artem.1.66, *PHolm*.6.40. [ᾰ by nature, Hdn.Gr.2.109.]

κατασταγμός, ὁ, *running at the nose*, Cels.4.5.2, Orib.*Fr*.27; κ. ἀρτηρίας *tracheitis*, Gal.13.92.

καταστάζω, *shed, drip*, I. of persons, 1. c. acc. rei, *let fall in drops upon, shed over*, κ. δάκρυ τινός E.*Hec*.760; ἀφρὸν καταστάζετ᾽ εὐτρίχου γενειάδος Id.*HF*934; also of a garment, νώτου καταστάζοντα βύσσινον φᾶρος S.*Fr*.373.3: c. acc. only, *let fall in drops* (sc. αἷμα), A.*Fr*.327. 2. c. dat. rei, *run down with* a thing, νόσῳ κ. πόδα to have one's foot *running* with a sore, S.*Ph*.7. II. of the liquid, 1. intr., *drip, trickle down*, βωμοῦ from the altar, E.*IT*72; τάφου Id.*Hel*.985; δάκρυα κ. τὰ μὲν κατὰ τῶν πέπλων, τὰ δὲ ἐπὶ τοὺς πόδας (v.l. for στάζω) X.*Cyr*.5.1.5; αἷμα κ. εἰς τὴν γῆν Luc.*VH*1.17; ὁ ἄκρατος κ. πρὸς ἡμᾶς Id.*Luct*.19. 2. trans., *bedew, wet*, ἱδρώς γέ τοί νιν πᾶν καταστάζει δέμας S.*Ph*.823, cf. E.*Hec*.241; ἀφρῷ Id.*Supp*.587.

κατασταθμ-εύω, *put into a stable* or *stall*, Str.4.5.2:—Pass., *to be oppressed by having soldiers quartered upon* one, ὑπό τινος Id.16.1.16. **-ησις**, εως, ἡ, *accurate measurement*, Epicur.*Nat*.11.5. **-ισμός**, ὁ, *weighing out*, Dsc.1.59.

καταστᾰλάω, = καταστάζω I, Nonn.*D*.38.434.

κατασταλτικός, ή, όν, *fitted for checking*, opp. ἐγερτικός, c. gen., S.E.*M*.6.19; ὑπερσαρκωμάτων Dsc.2.4, cf. Antyll.ap.Orib.6.23.2; κ. φάρμακα Gal.14.763. II. *sedate*, τὸ θηλύτερον -σταλτικώτερον Ptol.*Tetr*.172. III. -κή, ἡ, *the plant* βατράχιον, Apul.*Herb*.8.

κατασταμνίζω, *draw off wine into a smaller vessel* (στάμνος), *rack off, bottle*, οἶνος κατεσταμνισμένος wine *in bottle*, Thphr.*CP*2.18.4; λάγυνοι κατεσταμνισμένοι bottles of wine, Nicostr.Com.11:—Act., Com.ap.Poll.7.162.

κατάσταξις, εως, ἡ, *dropping down, dripping*, Gal.19.140.

καταστᾰσι-άζω, *overpower by forming a counter-party*, τινα Theopomp.Hist.233, D.S.19.36, etc.; ἐν τῷ δήμῳ κατεστασίασε τὴν βουλήν Plu.*Per*.9:—Pass., *to be factiously opposed* or *overpowered*, ὑπό τινος X.*HG*1.6.4; ὑπὸ παρατάξεως D.44.3; κατὰ γάμους ἢ δίκας Arist.*Pol*.1306ᵃ33. 2. = στασιάζω, Lxx *Ex*.38.22(1), J.*BJ Prooem*.7, *BGU* 836.5 (vi A.D.). **-αστικός**, ή, όν, *factious*, Hld.7.19.

κατά-στᾰσις, εως, ἡ, I. trans., *settlement, establishment, institution*, χορῶν A.*Ag*.23, cf. Ar.*Th*.958; πραγμάτων ἀρχὴ καὶ κ. πρώτη D.18.188; αὕτη ἡ κ. τῆς δημοκρατίας *mode of establishing* democracy, Pl.*R*.557a; ἐπιτροπῆς κ. *constitution* of a wardship, Arist.*Ath*.56.6: also c. gen. agentis, δαιμόνων κ. their *ordinance, decree*, E.*Ph*.1266. 2. *appointment* of magistrates, ἀρχόντων, δικαστῶν, etc., Pl.*R*.414a, 425d; τῶν τετρακοσίων Arist.*Ath*.41.2, etc.; αἱ περὶ τὰς ἀρχὰς κ. Pl.*Lg*.768d. b. at Athens, *payment on enrolment* in the cavalry, Eup.268, Pl.Com.165, Lys.16.6 (pl.). 3. *bringing* of ambassadors *before* the senate or assembly, *introduction, presentation*, Hdt.3.46, 8.141, 9.9. 4. κ. ἐγγυητῶν *bringing* one's bail *forward*, D.24.83, 84; ἐμφανῶν *production* of goods, etc., in dispute, Id.53.14, Arist.*Ath*.56.6, Is.6.31. 5. *pleading* of a case, τὰ πρὸς τὴν κ. δικαιώματα *PPetr*.3 p.55 (iii B.C.), cf. *PAmh*.2.33.7 (ii B.C.), etc.; opp. ἀφήγησις, Aps.p.251 H.; opp. διήγησις, Corn.*Rh*.p.371 H., cf. Syrian.*in Hermog*.2.64 R.; αἱ κ. τῶν δημηγοριῶν Arist.*Rh.Al*.1438ᵃ2; f.l. for προκατάστασις, Hermog.*Inv*.2 tit. 6. *settling, quieting, calming*, εἰς ἠρεμίαν καὶ κ. ἐλθεῖν Arist.*Ph*.247ᵇ27; ἔστω πραΰνσις κ. καὶ ἠρέμισις (-ησις codd.) ὀργῆς Id.*Rh*.1380ᵃ8; πρᾳότης κ. κινήσεως τῆς ὑπ᾽ ὀργῆς Pl.*Def*.412d; κατάστασιν ὥσπερ ἐκ μανίας ὁ πότος ἐλάμβανεν Plu.2.704e; opp. μανία, S.E.*M*.7.404: hence, of disease, opp. παροξυσμός, Hp.*Aph*.1.12 (pl.), *Epid*.1.25 (pl.). 7. *restoration*, opp. διαφθορά, Pl.*Phlb*.46c; εἰς δέ γε τὴν αὑτῶν φύσιν ὅταν καθιστῆται, ταύτην αὖ τὴν κ. ἡδονὴν ἀπεδεξάμεθα ib.42d; [ἡ ἡδονὴ] κ. εἰς τὴν ὑπάρχουσαν φύσιν Arist.*Rh*.1369ᵇ34. 8. rarely, *setting* of fractures, Hp.*Fract*.31, cf. Gal.18(2).590. II. intr., *standing firm, settled condition, fixedness*, κ. γένοιτ᾽ ἂν οὐδενὸς νόμου S.*Aj*.1247. 2. *state, condition*, οὕτω δὴ ἀνθρώπου κ. so is *the condition* of man, Hdt.2.173; ἐν ἀνθρώπου φύσι καὶ καταστάσι Id.8.83; ἡ αὐτὴ κ. ἐστι τῇ πρὸ τῆς γενέσεως ἡ μετὰ τὴν τελευτήν Epicur.*Fr*.495; of climatic and seasonal conditions, Hp.*Epid*.1.3, 20; αἱ κ. τοῦ ἐνιαυτοῦ Id.*Aph*.3.15; ἀέρος Thphr.*HP*8.8.7; λοιμικὴ κ. Plb.1.19.1, Dsc.4.115 (pl.); νηνεμία καὶ κ. *settled weather*, Plu.2.281b; θαυμαστή τις εὐδίας κ. Luc.*Halc*.4; κ. τοῦ χρώματος καὶ σώματος Hp.*Prorrh*.2.4; κ. ὀμμάτων, προσώπου, E.*Med*.1197, Plu.2.260c; κ. κακῶν E.*Hipp*.1296; νυκτὸς ἐν κ. in the *stillness* of night, Id.*Rh*.111; ἐν τοιαύτῃ κ. τῆς ἡλικίας at such a mature age, Hyp.*Fr*.205; τὰς ψυχὰς ἐπὶ τὴν ἀρχαίαν κ. ἄγειν Pl.*R*.547b; οὐ τὴν αὐτὴν ἔχει κ. Arist.*HA*601ᵇ7; equiv. to διάθεσις, Id.*Rh*.1370ᵃ2; *state of affairs*, Isoc.4.115, D.18.62, Plb.2.71.2; also τὴν προσήκουσαν ἔχειν κ. the proper *attitude*, Carneisc.*Herc*.1027.10. 3. *settled order* or *method, system*, ἀπὸ φύσιος καὶ κ. ἀρχαίης Democr.278; esp. of political constitutions, ἐχρᾶτο καταστάσι πρηγμάτων τοιῇδε Hdt.2.173; Κορινθίοισι ἦν πόλιος κ. τοιήδε Id.5.92.β′; ἡ κ. τῆς πόλεως Pl.*R*.426c; κ. πολιτείας Id.*Lg*.832d, Arist.*Ath*.42.1; εἴπερ ἐστὶ... τὴν ποίαν κ. ὀλιγαρχίαν; Pl.*R*.550c; ἡ παροῦσα κ. Isoc.3.55, cf. 26, Arist.*Pol*.1292ᵃ35; τῆς περὶ τοὺς ἀγῶνας κ. *CIG*2741 (Aphrodisias); ἡ πρώτη κ. τῶν περὶ τὴν μουσικὴν ἐν τῇ Σπάρτῃ Plu.2.1134b. 4. *position* of troops in battle, Plb.2.68.9. 5. Gramm., *construction*, ἡ δέουσα κ. A.D.*Synt*.132.3 (but τῆς κ. οὕτως ἐχούσης *the state of the case* being as follows, Id.*Adv*.157.1). **-στᾰτέον**, *one must appoint*, ἄρχοντα, ταξιάρχους, Pl.*R*.414a, X.*Cyr*.8.1.10. 2. *one must lay down, define*, A.D.*Synt*.238.26; κ. πῶς.. Id.*Adv*.135.21. 3. Gramm., *one must construct*, Did. *in D*.7.2. **-στᾰτήρια**, τά, = ἀποπεμπτήρια, καταπαυστήρια, Hsch. **-στάτης** [ᾰ], ου, ὁ, *establisher, restorer*, δόμων S.*El*.72. 2. in dual, καταστάτω (Elean), as official title, *Schwyzer*418.13 (Olympia). **-στᾰτικός**, ή, όν, *fitted for calming*, ἔννοιαι Eust.1041.20; τὸ κ. *power to calm*, of music, Plu.*Lyc*.4; cf. καταστηματικός II. 2. = ἀποκαταστατικός I, μοῖρα τοῦ Ἡλίου Rhetor. in *Cat.Cod.Astr*.8(1).247. 3. -κόν, τό, perh. banker's *charge for weighing*, *PPetr*.3 p.191 (iii B.C.). Adv. -κῶς, = ἀνηπλωμένως καὶ ἀφηγηματικῶς, Aps.p.243 H., al.: Comp. -ώτερον, διηγεῖσθαι Sch.E.*Hipp*.392; διαβάλλειν ib.616. **-στᾰτόν**, τό, *kind of cake*, gloss on ἄμυλον, Sch.rec.Theoc.9.21 (Mod.Gr. καταστατός = *starch*).

καταστεγ-άζω, *cover over*, ῥιψί [τὸν νεκρόν] Hdt.4.71, cf. Pl.*Criti*.115e; κ. τάφρον χόρτῳ Arist.*HA*603ᵃ5; *roof over*, *IG*2².463.52:—Pass., *Gp*.13.14.7. **-ασμα**, ατος, τό, *covering*, τῆς ὀροφῆς Hdt.2.155. **-νόομαι**, Pass., *to be closely covered*, Moschio ap.Ath.5.207d, v.l. in *Gp*.13.14.7. **-νος**, ον, *close-covered*, Myia *Ep*.4. **-ος**, ον, (στέγη) *covered in, roofed*, αὐλαὶ κατάστεγοι Hdt.2.148; ἐν τῷ κ. δρόμῳ Pl.*Euthd*.273a; [νεοττιαὶ ἀλκυόνος] Arist.*HA*616a25, cf. Men. *Sam*.76, Ph.*Bel*.80.32, Plb.9.41.9; ὁδοί Lib.*Or*.9.8.

καταστείβω, *tread down*, τὰν ὐάκινθον πόσσι Sapph.94. II. *tread*, κατέστειψας πέδον S.*OC*467 (vv. ll. κατέστεψας, κατάστεψον).

κατάστειρος, ον, *barren*, Vett.Val.14.26.

καταστείχω, aor. 2 -έστῐχον, = κατέρχομαι, *AP*9.298 (Antiphil.); *return from exile*, *IG*2^{2}.1113.12.

καταστέλλω, fut. -στελῶ E.*Ba*.933 (for Aeol. forms v. καστολέω):—*put in order, arrange*, [πλόκαμον] E. l. c.; *equip, clothe, dress*, κ. τινὰ τὰ περὶ τῷ σκέλει Ar.*Th*.256, cf. Plu.2.69c. II. *let down, lower*, τὰς ῥάβδους D.H.8.44; κ. τὰ βράγχια *shut* them, Plu.2.979c; *press down*, τὴν γλῶσσαν Gal.15.792. 2. *repress, restrain*, οἶκτον E.*IA*934; τὸν ὄχλον *Act.Ap*.19.35, cf. Wilcken *Chr*.10 (ii B.C., prob.); κ. τὰς ἐπιθυμίας Phld.*Rh*.2.284S., cf. Arr.*Epict*.3.19.5; τοὺς νέους Plu.2.207e, cf. 547b, etc.:—Pass., ἅπαντα λήξει καὶ καταστα λήσεται Apollod.Com.18; of persons, *to be placed under restraint, reduced to order*, *PTeb*.41.21 (ii B.C.), *BGU*1192.5 (i B.C.); also κατεσταλμένοι τοῖς ἤθεσι *of calm, sedate character*, opp. τολμηρός, D.S.1.76, cf. Arr.*Epict*.4.4.10; κατεσταλμένον ἦθος D.S.10.3; κατέσταλται πρὸς τὸ κόσμιον Plu.*Comp.Lyc.Num*.3, cf. Ael.*NA*4.29, Arr. *Epict*.3.23.16. 3. Medic., *reduce*, τὰ ὑπερσαρκοῦντα Dsc.2.1.

κατάστελμα, ατος, τό, *grain dropped* in transport, *PMasp*.2 iii 11 (vi A.D.).

καταστέλξαι· καταγαγεῖν τὸν βοῦν, Hsch.

κατάστεμα, τό, late form of κατάστημα (q.v.).

καταστεν-άζω, *sigh, mourn*, Lxx *Ex*.2.23, al.:—Pass., δυστυχεῖς καὶ κατεστεναγμέναι τῶν ἐραστῶν χάριτες Alciphr.1.36. **-ᾰχέω**, *mourn for*, θύγατρα *Epigr.Gr*.205 (Halic., ii B.C.).

καταστενοχωρέω, *drive into a narrow space*, Zos.5.16 (Pass., sed leg. κατὰ στ.).

καταστένω, *sigh over, lament*, c. acc., S.*OC*1440, E.*Tr*.317 (lyr.), *HF*1141; κατὰ σὲ δακρύοις στένω ib.1045 (lyr.); ὑπέρ τινος Id.*IA*470; ὧν κατέστενες κακῶν (gen. by attraction) S.*El*.874.

καταστερεόω, strengthd. for στερεόω, Steph.*in Hp*.1.174D. (Pass.).

κατ-αστερ-έω, = sq., in Pass., Nech.ap.Vett.Val.59.28. **-ίζω**, *place among the stars*, [στέφανον] Pherecyd.148J.; τὸν ἐν οὐρανῷ στέφανον κ. D.S.4.61, cf. Plu.2.308a, Heph.Astr.1.1:—Pass., D.H.1.61, Theo Sm.p.130H. 2. *mark out* a constellation, τὴν Πλειάδα δι' ἑπτὰ ἀστέρων -ίζομεν Ps.-Alex.Aphr. *in Metaph*.832.34. II. pf. part. Pass., *adorned with stars*, κατηστερισμένα ζῴδια Hipparch.1.1.9, Gem.1.4; κ. σφαῖραι Id.5.65; ποτήριον Asclep.Myrl.ap.Ath.11.489e. **-ῐσις**, εως, ἡ, = sq., *Gloss*. **-ισμός**, ὁ, *placing among the stars*: Καταστερισμοί, οἱ, title of treatise on constellations by Hipparchus, Suid.; also of an extant work wrongly attributed to Eratosthenes; cf. Plin.*Epp*.5.17.1, Ps.-Alex.Aphr. *in Metaph*.833.2. **-όω**, f.l. for καταστερίζω I, Palaeph.51:—Pass., οἱ κατηστερωμένοι ἄνδρες prob. in Phld.*D*.3.9, cf. Sch.E.*Or*.1631.

καταστεφᾰν-όω, *crown*, τινὰ ῥόδοις *AP*12.189 (Strat.):—Pass., D.S.12.9. **-ωσις**, εως, ἡ, *crowning*, of a cult-statue, *IG*12(5).946.11 (Tenos).

κατα-στεφής, ές, *crowned*, S.*Tr*.178, A.R.3.220, etc. **-στέφω**, *deck with garlands, crown, wreath*, κ. βωμόν (with branches wreathed in wool) E.*Heracl*.124; κ. νεκρόν (with libations) Id.*Ph*.1632; πλόκαμος ὅδε καταστέφειν here are my tresses for you *to crown*, Id.*IA*1478 (lyr.); ἅπτομαί σε καὶ κ. χεροῖν *encircle* thee, Id.*Heracl*.226; κατέστεψας πέδον and κατάστεψον π. are vv.ll. in S.*OC*467, cf. καταστείβω; κ. τὰς πρῴρας D.C.51.5; οὔρεα Epic. in *Arch.Pap*.7 p.7:—Pass., κατεστέφθαι Aeschin.3.164; δάφνῃ κατεστεμμένος τὰς κόμας D.H.2.34; κλάδος ἐρίῳ κατεστ. Plu.*Thes*.18: metaph., πεδία λῄοις κατεστεμμένα Men.Rh.p.345S.; ὁ πόλος ἀστέρας κατέστεπται Hp.*Ep*.12. **-στεψις**, εως, ἡ, *crowning*, Theo Sm.p.15H.

καταστηλῑτεύω, *post up, publish* a name, etc., Luc.*DMeretr*.4.2, cf. Hsch. s.v. κατεστήριξεν:—Pass., δόγματα κατεστηλιτευμένα Ph.*Fr*.54H., cf. Poll.8.73.

καταστηλόω, *mark with pillars*, ὁδὸς κατεστηλωμένη Plb.34.12.2a ap.Str.7.7.4 (-στηλοθετημένη in Str.*Chr*.).

κατάστημα, ατος, τό, later **κατάστεμα** Lxx 3*Ma*.5.45:—*condition, state*, not necessarily permanent: 1. bodily or mental *condition*, τὸ εὐσταθὲς σαρκὸς κ. Epicur.*Fr*.68, Metrod.*Fr*.5, cf. Diog.Oen.29, Asp. *in EN*143.22; τὸ κατὰ φύσιν καὶ οἰκεῖον κ. Dsc.*Alex.Praef*., cf. Sor. 1.36; τῆς ψυχῆς ib.39; τὸ κατὰ μέθην κ. Ath.2.38e; κ. μανιῶδες Lxx l.c. 2. *weather*, Diocl.*Fr*.30, Ptol.*Alm*.3.1; τὸ θερινὸν κ. Ps.-Plu. *Fluv*.12; κ. χειμέριον Polyaen.5.12.3; αἰθρίου ὄντος τοῦ κ. Dsc.*Praef*. 6, cf. Cleom.2.1, Sabin.ap.Orib.9.15.1; *direction of wind*, νοτίου τοῦ κ. ὄντος Alex.Aphr. *in Mete*.47.2; *time, season*, κ. νυκτερινόν A.D.*Synt*. 198.27; τὰ ἐνιαύσια κ. Ptol.*Tetr*.93. 3. *demeanour, behaviour*, *Ep. Tit*.2.3, Porph.*Abst*.4.6; τὸ σύνηθες κ. Plu.*Marc*.23; ἀτρεμαῖον κ. J. *AJ*15.7.5; τὸ τῆς εὐσεβείας, τῆς ἀρετῆς κ., Aristeas 210, 278; τὸ μέσον κ. Id.122. 4. *political condition, constitution*, τὸ Λακωνικὸν κ. Plb.6.50.2, cf. *OGI*669.3 (Egypt, i A.D.). 5. generally, *state of the case, state of affairs*, A.D.*Pron*.25.18. 6. Astrol., *position* of the heavens, Vett.Val.71.23. 7. *physical constitution*, τὸ κοσμικὸν κ., i.e. the four elements and four winds, Id.175.10; ἐν στερεῷ τινι καὶ οὐσιώδει κ. Dam.*Pr*.124; of the Intelligible World, ib.119; ὑποστάσεως κατάστημα Simp. *in Ph*.232.1.

καταστηματικός, ή, όν, *pertaining to a state* or *condition* (cf. foreg. 1), opp. κατὰ κίνησιν, ἡδοναί Epicur.*Fr*.2, cf. Metrod.*Fr*.29. II. (cf. καθίστημι B.4) *sedate*, of persons, Plu.*TG*2; διάθεσις τῆς ψυχῆς Simp. *in Epict*.p.114D.; of musical instruments, *calming*, v.l. for -στατικά in Procl. *in Alc*.p.198C.

κατάστημον, τό, = στημόνιον, Hsch. s.h.v.

καταστηρίζω, *establish*, Nonn.*D*.38.424; *prove*, Lyd.*Mens*.1.14:—Pass., *to be propped* or *stayed*, ἐπί τινι E.*Fr*.382.9; *to be firmly fixed* or *established*, Lxx *Jb*.20.7; κατεστηριγμένος, opp. ἀβέβαιος, Arist. *Mu*.395b16. II. intr., κ. εἰς .. *settle* in a spot, of disease, Hp. *Aff*.15, cf. 11.

κατά-στιγμα, ατος, τό, *point, spot*, Sch.D.P.443 (*GGM* ii p.415). **-στίζω**, *cover with marks*, βιβλία Hdn.Gr.1.10; *brand*, τινὰς χαρακτῆρσι D.S.34/5.2.27: freq. in pf. Pass., *to be marked* or *spotted*, ᾠὰ κατεστιγμένα *spotted*, Arist.*HA*559a24, cf. Dsc.5.143; κυανέαις σταγόσι κατέστικται Ael.*NA*12.24; τὴν χρόαν κατέστ. D.C.43.23; χρυσοειδῆ ἰνδάλματα ἐπ' αὐτῶν κατέστ. *are marked* upon them, Ael.*NA*10.13: metaph., *to be spotted and stained*, Philostr.*VA*1.11. **-στικτος**, ον, *spotted, speckled, brindled*, κύων S.*Fr*.11; δορά E.*Ba*.697; ὁ κνιπολόγος Arist.*HA*593a13; of garments, *IG*2^{2}.1514.11, al.; ἐσθής Arr.*Ind*.5, cf. Men.1019; *tattooed*, Str.7.5.4: metaph., *dotted*, χώρα κ. οἰκήσεσι Id.2.5.33; κατοικίαις μικραῖς Id.17.3.1; *studded*, κ. ἄστροις τιάραν Jul.*Or*.5.171a.

καταστίλβω, *send beaming forth*, σέλας *h.Mart*.10. 2. *irradiate*, πάντα *AP*12.254 (Strat.).

κατάστιξις, εως, ἡ, *dotting*, of Argus' eyes, Sch.E.*Ph*.1115.

καταστοιβάζω, in pf. part. Pass. -ασμένος *packed, compressed*, of the style of Thucydides, Anon. in *Rhet*.p.212H.

καταστοιχ-ειόομαι, Pass., *to be reduced to its elements*, τύπος κατεστοιχειωμένος Epicur.*Ep*.1 p.3U. **-ίζω**, *instruct in the rudiments*, Chrysipp.*Stoic*.2.39.

καταστολ-ή, ἡ, *equipment, dress*, 1*Ep.Ti*.2.9, J.*BJ*2.8.4: metaph., κ. δόξης Lxx *Is*.61.3. II. *putting down, checking*, D.S.15.94; *reduction, subjugation*, Θηβαΐδος Wilcken *Chr*.12.15 (i B.C.). 2. *modesty, reserve*, Hp.*Decent*.5, 8; *moderation*, κ. περιβολῆς in dress, Plu.*Per*.5: abs., *dignity, restraint*, κ. καὶ εὐσχημοσύνη *Inscr.Prien*.109.186 (ii B.C.), cf. Aristeas 284; ἡ τοῦ βίου σώφρων κ. *IGRom*.4.1756.66 (Sardes, i B.C.), cf. Arr.*Epict*.2.10.15, 21.11, Porph.*Abst*.4.6. 3. *conclusion, 'finale'*, *Mim.Oxy*.413.95; δράματος Sch.Ar. *Pax*1203; *remission*, τῆς ὀδύνης Orib.*Fr*.74. **-ίζω**, *clothe, dress*, Plu.2.65d (Pass.), Eun.*Hist*.p.248D.

καταστομ-ίζω, v.l. for ἐπι-, *put to silence*, Plu.*Arist*.4. **-ιον**, τό, *mouth* of a pipe or tube, Hero *Spir*.1.25. **-ίς**, ίδος, ἡ, *mouthpiece of a flute*, Hsch.

καταστονᾰχέω, *bewail*, c. acc., *AP*7.574 (Agath.).

κατάστοργος, ον, *of love*, γόμφοι Emp.87.

κατα-στορέννῡμι, part. καστορνῦσα (as if from καταστόρνυμι) (v. infr.): fut. -στορέσω: aor. Pass. κατεστορέσθην Hp.*VM*19: pf. κατεστόρεσται Them.*Or*.15.194d:—*spread, cover with* a thing, [κάπετον] λάεσσι κατεστόρεσαν μεγάλοισι Il.24.798. II. *spread upon*, κώεα καστορνῦσα θρόνοις ἔνι δαιδαλέοισι Od.17.32, cf. 13.73. III. *throw down, lay low*, κατεστόρεσαν αὐτῶν ἑξακοσίους Hdt.9.69; κ. κύματα *smooth* the waves, *AP*7.668 (Leon.): metaph., of morbid humours, Hp. l. c. (Pass.); κ. τὴν ἀνωμαλίαν Plu.*Comp.Lyc.Num*.2; τὴν φιλοτιμίαν, τὰ πάθη, Id.*Luc*.5, 2.101c; τὸν θυμόν Ael.*Fr*.103. IV. *layer*, κλῆμα *Gp*.4.3.2, cf. 4.1.7. **-στόρεσις**, εως, ἡ, *layering*, ἀμπέλων ib.3.3.8.

καταστοχ-άζομαι, *aim at*, τὸ συμφέρον Alex.Trall.*Febr*.6: hence, *hit, guess, infer*, τι Plb.12.13.4; τὸ μέλλον D.S.19.39; τινος Ath.9.391b, Procl. *in Alc*.p.46C., Phlp. *in Ph*.640.3: abs., Heph.Astr.3.4:—Act. is f.l. in Suid. s.v. προφητεία, and dub. cj. for καταστοχέω (q.v.):—Pass., τὸ -ασμένον εἰκότως Phld.*Rh*.1.362S.; κατεστοχάσθαι, gloss on ἐσκευωρῆσθαι, *EM*385.15. **-ᾰσις**, εως, ἡ, = sq., τῆς ἀνατολῆς τῶν ἄστρων Phlp. *in APo*.385.23. **-ασμός**, ὁ, *conjecture*, D.S.1.37. **-αστέον**, *one must guess*, c. acc., Ptol.*Tetr*.176, Heph.Astr.3.37. **-αστής**, οῦ, ὁ, *one who guesses*, cj. for -στοχάσαι in Suid. s.v. προφητεία. **-αστικός**, ή, όν, *of conjecture*, δύναμις Phld.*Rh*.2.12S. **-έω**, *hit the mark*, τινος, i.e. succeed in bribing him, *PTeb*.58.35 (ii B.C.).

καταστραγγίζω, fut. -ιῶ, *squeeze out*, τὸ λοιπὸν τοῦ αἵματος -ιεῖ Lxx *Le*.5.9.

κατ-αστράπτω, *hurl down lightning, flash lightning*, κατ' Οἰταῖον νάπος S.*Tr*.437: abs., καταστράπτει *it lightens*, Plu.*Galb*.23. II. trans., *strike with lightning, dazzle*, τὰς ὄψεις Id.*Tim*.28; τινα Them. *Or*.27.337d; τινὰ τῷ κάλλει Hld.1.21; ὅπλοις κ. τὸ πεδίον *make* it *gleam* with arms, Id.9.14.

καταστρᾰτεύω, *take the field against, make war upon*, τινος Suid. II. Med., *overrun in war*, τὸν Πόντον Chio *Ep*.2.

καταστρᾰτηγ-έω, *overcome by generalship* or *stratagem*, τινα Plb.3.71.1 (dub. l.), D.S.11.21, D.H.3.26, Str.4.4.2, etc.; τινος Sopat. in Rh.8.201W.: metaph., *out-general, outwit*, D.S.16.11, D.H.4.10; τοὺς δικαστάς Id.*Is*.3, cf. Ph.2.203:—Pass., D.S.4.9, Onos.11.5; ὑπὸ τῆς τύχης Charito 2.8. II. *counteract by stratagem*, διαμαρτίαν Zos.3.24. **-ία**, ἡ, *conquest by stratagem*, Tz.*H*.9.70 (pl.).

καταστρᾰτοπεδ-εία, ἡ, *pitching a camp*: *living in camps*, Phylarch.41J. (pl.), Ael.*VH*9.3 (pl.). **-εύω**, *encamp*, τοὺς ἑαυτοῦ X.*Cyr*.7.2.8, cf. Onos.6.12; *station*, τὸ ναυτικόν X.*HG*6.2.7. II. intr., *take up quarters*, εἰς [πόλιν], ἐν μέρεσι τῆς πόλεως, πρὸ τῆς πόλεως, Plb.1.30.15, 1.18.2, 3.77.1: abs., Ph.*Bel*.103.48:—Med., X.*An*.3.4.18, Arr.*An*.5.9.1. III. *march*, εἰς Φοινίκην Lxx 2*Ma*.4.22.

καταστρεβλόω, *put to torture*, Plu.*Art*.19, 2.105b (Pass.).

καταστρεπτικῶς, Adv. *so as to end*, ἐπ' αὐτά, opp. ἀνεκτικῶς (fort. κατενεκτικῶς) ἐφ' ἕτερα, *Stoic*.3.34 ap.Sch.Luc.*Bis Acc*.22 (v.l. κατατρεπτικῶς).

καταστρέφω, pf. κατέστραφα (trans.) Plb.23.11.2:—**Pass.**, fut. -στρᾰφήσομαι D.C.42.42: pf. imper. κατεστρέφθω Epicur. (v. infr.): plpf. 3 sg. -έστραπτο Hdn. (v. infr.); 3 pl. -εστράφατο D.C.39.5:—*turn down, trample on*, ποσσί *h.Ap*.73; *turn the soil*, X.*Oec*.17.10; κάνθαρον κ. *turn* it *upside down*, so as to drain it, Alex.115, cf. Sotad. Com.1.33, Lxx 4*Ki*.21.13; κατεστραμμένῳ τῷ ὀστράκῳ Arist.*HA* 622^{b}8. **II.** *upset, overturn*, τὴν πόλιν κ. Ar.*Eq*.274; τὰς εἰκόνας D.L.5.82; *ruin, undo*, βίον καὶ τέκνα καὶ πόλεις Plb.23.11.2; τινα *AP* 11.163 (Lucill.):—Pass., τὰ προάστεια κατέστραπτο Hdn.8.4.8. **2.** Med., *subject to oneself, subdue*, πολέμῳ Hdt.1.64, cf. 71, al., Th.3.13, D.18.244, etc.; νόσον E.*Hipp*.477; τοὺς μὲν κατεστρέψατο ἐς φόρου ἀπαγωγήν *subdued and made* them *tributary*, Hdt.1.6: c. inf., Ἰωνίην κατεστρέψατο δασμοφόρον εἶναι Id.7.51. **3.** Pass., in aor. and pf., *to be subdued*, Id.1.130, 68: plpf., Th.5.29: c. inf., ἀκούειν σοῦ κατέστραμμαι *am constrained* to hear, A.*Ag*.956: pf. Pass. also in sense of Med., Hdt.1.171; πάντα κατέστραπται καὶ ἔχει D.4.6, cf. X.*HG*5. 2.38, Isoc.5.21. **III.** of a floating solid, *right itself*, Archim.*Fluit*. 2.9 (Pass.). **b.** intr., *return*, εἰς ταὐτόν Arist.*Pr*.921^{a}26, cf. *Mech*. 856^{b}17. **IV.** *turn round, direct*, [καταπάλτην] *train* it on the enemy, Ph.*Bel*.82.14; esp. towards an end, ποῖ καταστρέφεις λόγων τελευτήν; A.*Pers*.787; οὕτω κατέστρεψεν ἡ τύχη ταῦτα, ὥστ' ἐναντία γενέσθαι τοῖς προσδοκωμένοις Din.1.32; κατέστρεψεν εἰς φιλανθρωπίαν τοὺς λόγους *guided* the conversations *to* a friendly *end*, Aeschin.2. 39: hence, *bring to an end*, κ. τὴν βίβλον, τὸν λόγον, Plb.3.118.10, 22.9.4 (Pass., ταῦτα μὲν αὐτοῦ κατεστρέφθω Epicur.*Nat*.14.6); esp. κ. τὸν βίον Cebes 10, Ael.*NA*13.21, Plu.*Thes*.19, etc.; ὑπὸ τῶν πολεμίων Id.*Comp.Sol.Publ*.1: abs., *come to an end, close*, Plb.4.2.1; τοῦ ἐνιαυτοῦ -στρέφοντος Plu.*Caes*.51; esp. *end life, die*, Epicur.*Ep*.3 p.61 U., Plu.*Them*.31, Arr.*An*.7.3.1, Hdn.5.8.10; κ. εἰς ἀπώλειαν *end* in.., Alciphr.3.70; τοὺς λόγους ἐπὶ τὰ πράγματα -στρέφειν οἰόμενος Plu. *Phil*.4; ἡ ἡμέρα κ. εἰς ὥραν δεκάτην *inclines* towards.., Id.*Sull*. 29. **2.** Rhet., metaph., λέξις κατεστραμμένη *periodic* style, opp. εἰρομένη, Arist.*Rh*.1409^{a}26, cf. Demetr.*Eloc*.12, 21. **V.** *screw* or *stretch tight*, αἱ κατεστραμμέναι χορδαί Arist.*Aud*.803^{a}28.

καταστρηνιάω, *behave wantonly towards*, τοῦ Χριστοῦ 1*Ep.Ti*. 5.11.

καταστροφ-εύς, έως, ὁ, *one who ruins* or *spoils* his work, *bungler*, *Mim.Oxy*.413.102; = *eversor, tergiversator*, *Gloss*. **2.** *subverter*, τοῦ πολιτεύματος Lyd.*Mag*.3.69. **-ή**, ἡ, *overturning*, θεσμίων A.*Eu*.490 (lyr., pl.). **2.** *subjugation, reduction*, Hdt.1.6, 92, etc.; καταστροφὴν ποιήσασθαί τινος Id.6.27; ἐπὶ Λιβύων καταστροφῇ πέμπεσθαι Id. 4.167; ἐπ' ἄλλων καταστροφῇ ἐξιέναι Th.1.15: pl., καταστροφαὶ ἐθνῶν Phld.*Rh*.1.255 S. **3.** *return* of vibrating string to axial position, Arist.*Pr*.921^{a}17 (pl.). **II.** *end, close, conclusion*, ἄνευ δὲ λύπης οὐδαμοῦ καταστροφή A.*Supp*.442; κ. βίου, i.e. death, S.*OC*103, cf. Plb.5. 54.4, etc.; κ. τοῦ ζῆν Men.*Pk*.12: without βίου, Th.2.42, Epicur.*Sent*. 35; ποία κ. εὐδαιμονεστέρα; Arr.*Epict*.4.10.17; τὸ τέλος αὐτῶν τῆς κ. the event of their *life's end*, Plb.6.8.6; κ. καὶ συντέλεια τῶν γεγονότων Id.3.1.9; κ. λαμβάνειν Id.3.47.8; τὴν κ. τῆς βίβλου ποιεῖσθαι εἰς.. Id.1.13.5; in the drama, *dénouement, ending*, Antiph.191.19, Hero *Aut*.22.6, Luc.*Alex*.60, al., Euanth. et Donat. in *CGF* pp.67, 69 K.: pl., αἱ κ. τῶν δραμάτων Plb.3.48.8. **III.** *ruin, undoing*, κ. γῆς (of a person) Men.548.8. **IV.** *crane*, *Stud.Pal*.10.259. 13 (pl., vi A.D.). **-ικῶς**, Adv. *by way of conclusion*, Ath.10. 453c.

κατά-στρωμα, ατος, τό, *that which is spread upon* or *over*: in a ship, *deck*, Hdt.8.118, 119, Th.1.49, X.*HG*1.4.18, Pl.*La*.184a, Thphr.*Char*. 22.5, etc.; καταστρώματα διὰ πάσης [τῆς νεὼς] Th.1.14; οἱ ἀπὸ τῶν κ., i.e. the fighting men, opp. the rowers, Id.7.40. **II.** part of the constellation Argo, Hipparch.1.8.1, Ptol.*Alm*.8.1. **III.** πλίνθινα κ. a tile *roof*, *AB*269, cf. *LW*3.141 (Ephesus). **IV.** *floor, pavement*, Ath.Mech.13.4, *Gp*.6.2.10. **-στρώννῡμι**, also -ύω Lxx *Jb*.12.23, Mitteis *Chr*.31 viii 18 (ii B.C.): fut. -στρώσω:—Pass., fut. -στρωθήσομαι Lxx *Ju*.7.14: aor. -εστρώθην (v. infr.):—*spread out*, κλίνην Hierocl.p.63 A. **II.** *spread over, cover*, οἶκον ... ῥόδοις Ael.*VH*9.8:—Pass., πεδίον νεκρῶν κατεστρώθη *was strewed with*.., D.S.14.114; σκορπίων κανθήλιον -εστρωμένον Str.14.2.26. **III.** *lay low*, δάμαρτα καὶ παῖδ' ἑνὶ κατέστρωσεν βέλει E.*HF*1000, cf. X. *Cyr*.3.3.64:—Pass., ὡς δὲ Ἕλλησι κατέστρωντο οἱ βάρβαροι Hdt.9. 76, cf. 8.53, 1*Ep.Cor*.10.5. **IV.** *layer*, in Pass. of vines, *Gp*.5. 17.11. **2.** βοτάνιον κατὰ τοῦ ἐδάφους -εστρωμένον *prostrate*, Dsc. 2.130. **-στρωσις**, εως, ἡ, *spreading, laying*, τρικλίνου Aristeas 319. **-στρωτέον**, *one must pave*, ἔδαφος πλίνθοις *Gp*.6.2. 10. **-στρωτήρ**, ῆρος, ὁ, *pavement-slab*, *IG*7.3073.91, al. (Lebad.). **-στρώτης**, ου, ὁ, = *scansor*, *Gloss*.

καταστῠγ-έω, aor. κατέστῠγον Il.17.694:—*to be horror-struck*, κατέστυγε μῦθον ἀκούσας l.c.: c. acc., *abhor, abominate*, κατὰ δ' ἔστυγον αὐτήν Od.10.113; δόρπα Nic.*Al*.476: later aor. κατεστύγησα Eun. *VS*p.471 D., Apollon.*Lex*. s.v. κατέστυγε. **II.** causal in aor. 1 κατέστυξα, *make abominable*, *EM*731.26 (but in Hsch. = μισῆσαι): pf. part. Pass. κατεστυγημένος Phot., Suid.; f.l. -μένως in Hsch. **-νάζω**, pf. -εστύγνᾰκα, *to be of sad countenance*, Apollon. *Lex*. s.v. κατέστυγε; ὄμμα -νακός Sch.E.*Or*.1317:—Pass., pf. part., Sch.E.*Med*.1009. **-νόομαι**, Pass., = καταστυγνάζω, Hsch. s.v. ἔστυγμαι. **-νος**, ον, *of sad countenance*, Ath.13.585d, Vett.Val. 2.5, Sch.E.*Alc*.800.

κατα-στύφελος [ῠ], ον, *very hard* or *rugged*, πέτρη, χῶρος, *h.Merc*. 124, Hes.*Th*.806. **-στυφλος**, ον, = foreg., Hsch.

καταστύφω [ῡ], *astringe*: metaph. in Pass., of a person, αὐστηρὸς καὶ κατεστυμμένος Men.Rh.p.389 S.; τὸ κατεστ. *sourness, harshness*, Plu.*Cat.Mi*.46.

καταστωμύλλομαι, *chatter*, οἷα κατεστωμύλατο οὐκ ἄκαιρα (Dind. κἀστωμύλατο) Ar.*Th*.461: pf. part. κατεστωμυλμένος *a chattering fellow*, Id.*Ra*.1160, Numen.ap.Eus.*PE*14.5. **II.** in pass. sense, τὰ κατεστ. *things blabbed out*, *EM*524.31.

καταστῠβωτέω, *fatten like a pig*, τὴν ψυχὴν ἡδοναῖς Plu.2.1096d.

κατασυγκρίνω, *reduce* the pores *to a proper state*, Steph. *in Gal*.1. 337 D.

κατασῡκοφαντέω, *criticize captiously*, τὸν Εὐριπίδην Sch.E.*Andr*. 733.

κατασυλλογίζομαι, Pass., *have a conclusion drawn against one*, Arist.*APr*.66^{a}25.

κατασυμβαίνω, dub. l. in Iamb. *in Nic*.p.12 P.

κατασυν-ηγορῆσαι, f.l. for κατηγορῆσαι in Sch.B D Il.21.79 (v. Sch.Gen. l.c. ii p.190). **-ήθεια**, ἡ, *customary gift*, *PMasp*.136.3 (vi A.D.).

κατασῡρίζω, in Pass., of the monochord, *to be subdued by an accompaniment of the syrinx*, Ptol.*Harm*.2.12.

κατασύρω [ῡ], aor. 1 κατέσῡρα (v. infr.):—**Med.**, aor. 1 κατεσῡράμην Pherecyd.158 J.:—**Pass.**, aor. 2 κατεσύρην [ῠ] (v. infr.):—*draw, pull down*, Philum.ap.Aët.9.12 (Pass.): usu. with a notion of violence, τὰ [ἀεροπόρα] ἐκ τοῦ οὐρανοῦ D.C.*Fr*.30.4: metaph., ἐπιθυμία κ. τὸν ἡνίοχον λογισμόν Ph.1.58, cf. 1.627 (Pass.): esp. *lay waste, ravage*, τὰς [πόλιας] ὅσας πρότερον οὐ κατέσυραν Hdt.6.33; κατὰ μὲν ἔσυραν Φάληρον, κατὰ δὲ.. πολλοὺς δήμους Id.5.81; ὡς πλείστην τῆς χώρας Aen.Tact.16.8, cf. Plb.1.56.3, al. **2.** *drag, carry off*, λείαν Pherecyd. l.c.; γυναῖκας Parth.19; τινὰ πρὸς τὸν κριτήν *Ev.Luc*.12.58: metaph., τινὰ εἰς ἐκμελῆ πολιτεύματα Phalar.*Ep*.93.1. **3.** *sweep away*, πελάγη κ. πόλεις Ph.2.142:—Pass., metaph., σκολιὰ ῥεῖθρα ὑφ' ὧν οἱ πολλοὶ -σύρονται, ὡς τὰ λόγιά φησιν *Orac.Chald*.ap.Procl. *in Ti*. 3.326 D.; εἰς τὸ πλῆθος ὑπὸ τοῦ μερισμοῦ καὶ τῆς διαστάσεως τῶν ὄντων Id. *in Prm*.p.551 S., cf. Hierocl. *in CA*19 p.461 M. **b.** Pass., *rush down*, of rivers, etc., D.P.296, Alciphr.3.13, *Gp*.5.2.17. **4.** *drag out*, οὐρανὸς.. δρόμον ἀΐδιον -σύρων *Orac.Chald*.ap.Dam.*Pr*.284. **5.** Pass., *to be reduced*, σωμάτων λοιμῷ -συρέντων Lib.*Or*.61.19 (v.l. συρέντων). **II.** *draw down, launch*, τὸ σκαφίδιον Alciphr.1.1; τοὺς φελλοὺς κ. ὑφάλους, of a net, ibid.

κατασυστάδην, Adv., = συστάδην, ἡ κ. χειρονομία Hld.9.16.

κατασφᾰγή, ἡ, *slaughtering*, Nech. in *Cat.Cod.Astr*.7.143 (pl.).

κατασφάζω, later **-σφάττω** Luc.*Sacr*.12 (Pass. -σφάττεσθαι Jul. *Or*.5.174a): fut. -ξω Lxx *Ez*.16.40:—*slaughter, murder*, Hdt.6.23, 8.127, Lxx l.c., al., *Ev.Luc*.19.27, D.C.40.48: freq. in aor. Pass. κατεσφάγην [ᾰ] A.*Eu*.102, S.*OT*730, X.*An*.4.1.17, etc.

κατ-ασφᾰλίζομαι, *fortify*, Men.Prot.p.15 D. **2.** *confirm*, τοὺς πραττομένους Lyd.Mag.3.12; ὅρκοις πρᾶγμα Just.*Nov*.102 *Praef*.; *assure oneself of*, τι Steph. *in Hp*.1.76 D. **3.** abs., *take refuge*, εἰς τὸ ἐνδότερον Aesop.196. **II.** Pass., *to be made fast*, Lxx 3*Ma*.4.9, Aesop.376; δεῖ κατησφαλίσθαι τὸν νοῦν εἰς.. S.E.*M*.7.23.

κατασφηκόω, *nail fast, fasten*, in Pass., ἑλίκεσσι χελώνης Tryph. 88, cf. Hsch.

κατασφηνόομαι, Pass., *to be wedged, bound tight*, Hp.*Nat.Puer*.24.

κατασφίγγω, *bind tightly*, Plu.2.983d:—Pass., J.*AJ*3.7.2.

κατασφρᾱγίζω, Ion. and Ep. **-σφρηγίζω**, *seal up*, Lxx *Jb*.9.7, 37. 7: mostly pf. part. Pass. κατεσφρηγισμένος *sealed up, made fast, secured*, ὅρκοις Emp.115.2, cf. A.*Supp*.947, E.*Fr*.762, Pl.*Erx*.400a, etc.: impf. Pass. κατεσφρηγίζετο Tryph.68: fut. -σφραγισθήσομαι *Hermes* 64.64 (Epid., ii A.D.): aor. κατεσφραγίσθην Lxx *Wi*.2.5, Hsch.:—Med., κ. τὰς θύρας Arist.*Mir*.842^{a}29, cf. *UPZ*6.21 (ii B.C.): Ep. aor. 1 -ίσσατο Nonn.*D*.45.188.

κατα-σχάζω, *slit, cut open*, στελέχη Thphr.*HP*2.7.6; συκῆ κατασχασθεῖσα Id.*CP*1.17.10, al.; κ. φλέβα *open* a vein, let blood, Gal. 19.139:—also **-σχάω**, *scarify*, Hp.*Int*.22, Heliod.ap.Orib.46.29. 2. **-σχᾰσις**, εως, ἡ, *scarification*, Archig.ap.Orib.44.26. 6. **-σχασμα**, ατος, τό, *incision* of a poisoned wound, Dsc.*Ther. Praef*. **-σχασμός**, ὁ, = κατάσχασις, Gal.11.321, Antyll.ap.Orib. 7.16.15, Orib.7.18 tit. **-σχαστέον**, *one must scarify*, Archig.ap. Orib.44.26.8, Dsc.*Ther*.2; cf. κατασχιστέον. **-σχαστήρ**, ῆρος, ὁ, = σχαστήρ, prob. in *IG*11(2).165.11 (Delos, iii B.C.).

κατασχεδιάζω, *affirm rashly of*, τῆς οἰκουμένης Plb.12.26^d.3; θεοῦ J.*BJ*3.8.9.

κατα-σχεθεῖν, inf. of κατέσχεθον, poet. aor. 2 of κατέχω (v. *σχέθω): —*hold back*, κατὰ δ' ἔσχεθε λαὸν ἅπαντα Od.24.530; κάσχεθε (Ep. for κατέσχεθε) Il.11.702; χειρὶ παιωνίᾳ κατασχεθών A.*Supp*.1066 (lyr.); κατασχεθόντες ἱππικὸν δρόμον S.*El*.754; also ὀργάς, θυμὸν κατασχεθεῖν, Id.*Ant*.1200, E.*HF*1210 (lyr.). **II.** νηΐ θοῇ Θορικόνδε κατέσχεθον *put in at* Th., *h.Cer*.126. **-σχεσις**, εως, ἡ, *holding back, restraining, retention*, πνεύματος Hp.*Vict*.2.64. **II.** *possession*, Lxx *Le*.25.25, *Za*.11.14, al., *Act.Ap*.7.5. **III.** *relation, attitude*, κ. φιλικὴ πρὸς τῶν πέλας *Stoic*.3.24. **-σχετέος**, α, ον, *to be held fast*, Sch.Ar.*Ach*. 258. **2.** **-σχετέον**, abs., *one must hold back, delay*, Sch.E.*Ph*. 1279.

κατασχετλιάζω, *complain indignantly*, J.*BJ*1.32.4.

κατάσχετος, ον, poet. for κάτοχος, *held back, kept back*, κατάσχετόν τι καλύπτειν S.*Ant*.1253. **II.** *held fast, possessed*, κακίαις Phld. *Lib*.p.27 O.; κ. δαιμονίῳ πνεύματι D.H.1.31; θείᾳ μέθῃ Ph.1.103;

[ταῖς θεαῖς] Phalar.*Ep.*93.1; οἴστρῳ *AP*5.225 (Paul. Sil.); λύσσῃ Paus.8.19.3; ἐκ Νυμφῶν Id.10.12.11: abs., *inspired*, Str.11.4.7.

κατασχημᾰτίζω, *dress up* or *invest with* a certain form or appearance, σφᾶς αὐτοὺς οὕτως Isoc.11.24; κ. ἑαυτὸν σχήματί τινι Plu.*Rom.* 26:—Pass., *to be conformed, modelled*, Id.*Lyc.*27.

κατ-ασχημονέω, *act indecently*, Phot. s. v. σινωπῆσαι; *act indecently towards*, τινος App.*Sam.*7, Sch.Ar.*Ra.*153.

κατα-σχίζω, fut. -σχίσω X.*An.*7.1.16:—*cleave asunder, split, slit*, Ar.*V.*239, cj. in Hp.*Mochl.*36 (Pass.); κ. τὰς πύλας, τὰς θύρας, *burst them open*, X. l.c., D.21.79; *tear*, τοὺς χιτωνίσκους Phld.*Ir.*p.39 W.:—Med., κατεσχίσω τὸ ῥάκος Ar.*Ra.*405 (lyr.):—Pass., of nerves or veins, *branch*, Gal.2.390, 8.65; of leaves, Dsc.2.130. **-σχῐσις**, εως, ἡ, *splitting up*, Gal.2.851, Dsc.3.60. **-σχιστέον**, *one must slit*, κύκλῳ Archig.ap.Aët.9.28 (melius -σχαστέον cod. Laud.Gr.60).

κατασχολάζω, *pass the time in idleness, loiter*, χρόνου τι κ. *tarry* somewhat too long, S.*Ph.*127; κ. ἐν ἀγρῷ Plu.*Tim.*36. II. κατεσχόλαζε τῆς Γναθαινίου λέγων, for ἐσχόλαζε λέγων κατὰ τῆς Γν., Macho ap.Ath.13.581d.

κατ-ασχολέομαι, *to be engaged*, περὶ τῶν ἐόντων, of sciences, Perict. ap.Stob.3.1.121; τὸ κατησχολημένον περὶ τὸν ἀνθρώπινον βίον *Placit.*1 *Prooem.*, cf. Archyt.ap.Iamb.*Comm.Math.*8, Apollon.*Mir.*7, *Theol. Ar.*18; *to be concerned, worried* about, περί τι *PRein.*18.18 (ii B.C.), Phld.*Rh.*2.139 S.

κατασχόμενος, aor. part. Med. used in pass. sense, v. κατέχω C. II.

κατασῴζω, *restore*, κατεσῴσαμες *Tab.Heracl.*1.51; -εσῴξαμες ib. 2.30.

κατασωρεύω, *heap up*, πλῆθος ὅπλων Plu.*Mar.*22, cf. *Cat.Ma.*20 (Pass.).

κατ-ασωτεύομαι, *squander on profligate living*, τὰς οὐσίας J.*BJ* 4.4.3.

κατασώχω, *rub in pieces, pound*, κ. περὶ λίθον τρηχὺν τῆς κυπαρίσσου pieces of cypress-wood, Hdt.4.75.

κατατᾰγή, ἡ, (κατατάσσω) *replacing* of dislocated bones, Heliod. (?) ap.Orib.49.30.8. II. *placing* in position of names on a map, Ptol.*Geog.*1.18.5.

καταταινιόω, *bind with a* ταινία, Anon.ap.Suid. s. v. ἐταινίωσε (s. v. l.).

κατατάκερος [τᾰκ], ον, *softened much*, Gal.6.669.

κατατακ-τέον, *one must place, class*, τινὰ ἔν τισι Artem.2.34. **-τι-κῶς**, Adv., = *ordinate*, *Gloss.*

κατατάκω [ᾱ], Dor. for κατατήκω.

κατατᾰνύω, = κατατείνω, *h.Bacch.*34 (in Ep. aor. 1 καττάνῠσαν), Hp. *Fract.*14, 44.

κατάτᾰξις, εως, ἡ, *ordering, arranging*, Arr.*Epict.*4.1.53, Porph. ap.Iamb.*Myst.*1.8; κ. ἀστεροειδής Hierocl. *in CA*27 p.488 M.; *classification*, Crinis *Stoic.*3.268. 2. *ordinance, regulation*, *Milet.*3 No. 152.102 (Eresus, ii B.C.). II. Medic., *reduction* of dislocations, Heliod. (?) ap.Orib.49.29.5; of rupture, Heliod.ib.50.47.7.

καταταρᾰ́σσω, f.l. for καταράσσω, *Gloss.*

καταταρτᾰρ-όω, *hurl down to Tartarus*, Orph.*Fr.*57, Corn.*ND*7, S.E.*P.*3.210; οἱ μυθικοὶ τὸν Κρόνον -οῦσιν Lyd.*Mens.*4.159:—Pass., Apollod.1.1.3, Sch.E.*Med.*1296:—hence **-ωσις**, εως, ἡ, Procl. *in Ti.* 1.188 D., Lyd. l.c.

κατάτᾰσις, εως, ἡ, *stretching*, κ. τῶν χορδῶν (κατάστασις codd.) Arist.*Aud.*803^{a}37. 2. esp. for the purpose of setting broken or dislocated bones, Hp.*Fract.*13 (pl.), *Mochl.*38. 3. *torture, torment*, D.H.7.68, Ael.*Fr.*276; κατατάσεις τῆς ψυχῆς Ph.2.599. 4. *violent exertion*, μετὰ φιλονικίας καὶ κ., cj. for -στάσεως in Pl.*Lg.* 796a. II. *extension* in space, *spreading*, Id.*Ti.*58e (-στασιν cod.). 2. = ὁλκὴ εἰς τοὺς κάτω τόπους, Gal.19.461.

κατατάσσω, Att. -ττω, pf. -τέτᾰχα Plb.8.9.5, al.:—*draw up in order, arrange*, τὴν στρατιάν X.*Cyr.*3.3.11, cf. *Oec.*9.13; esp. *place in, refer to* a class, εἰς φυλήν Lys.13.79; τινὰ εἰς τοὺς δικαστάς Plu.2.178f; τινὰ μετά τινος Ath.8.335b:—Pass., εἰς τοὺς ἀσεβεῖς -ταχθεὶς D.S. 4.74; ἐς τοὺς ἱππεύοντας -ταγεὶς Hdn.6.8.1: Geog., *insert* in a map, Ptol.*Geog.*1.18.4: in Surgery, *replace*, τὸν δίδυμον Heliod.ap.Orib. 50.47.6: pf. part. Pass. -τεταγμένος *in an ordered series*, opp. ἀόριστος, μονάδες Procl. *in Prm.*p.561 S.; opp. ἐξηρημένος, μονάδες ib.p.573 S. 2. *appoint*, ἐπί τι to do a thing, D.25.13; κ. τινὰ εἰς τάξιν ἡντινοῦν Pl.*Lg.*945a; εἰς λειτουργίαν *POxy.*1415.18 (iii A.D., Pass.); κ. τινὰ εἰς.. *appoint* one to go to a place, Plb.3.33.12. 3. *pay* into a treasury, εἰς τὸ βασιλικόν *PSI*5.510.13 (iii B.C.):—Pass., *to be allocated* to a fund, *SIG*459.6 (Beroea, iii B.C.). II. *set down in order, narrate* or *describe fully*, ἐν τοῖς ὑπομνήμασι Plb.2.47.11, cf. Phld.*Ir.* p.74 W., etc.; κ. εἰς τὴν ἀπόκρισιν διότι.. Plb.24.10.7, etc. III. κατατάξασθαι τοῖς φυλέταις ὑπέρ τινος *make arrangements* with..., D. 58.17. IV. *assimilate* food, in Pass., Sor.1.37; of things inhaled, Anon.Lond.23.31, al.

καταταχέω, *accelerate*, *PTeb.*19.13 (ii B.C.):—Pass., ib.24.29 (ii B.C.). II. *outstrip, overtake*, τινὰ τῇ παρασκευῇ Plb.8.3.3; *escape by superior speed*, Id.1.47.8; κ. τινά c. part., *anticipate* in doing, Id. 3.16.5, 4.68.5:—Pass., κ. ὑπὸ τῆς ὀξύτητος τοῦ καιροῦ D.S.14.72. 2. abs., *to be first, arrive first*, πρὸς τὴν πύλην Plb.9.17.4, cf. 1.86.8; *come in time*, Id.3.86.3, 9.18.3: c. part. only, do *quickly* or *in good time*, Id.2.18.6, 3.16.4, etc.

κατατέγγω, *wet thoroughly*, σπόγγον Hp.*Mul.*2.113:—Pass., Phld. *Mort.*29.

κατατεθαρρηκότως, Adv. pf. part. Act. of καταθαρρέω, *boldly, confidently*, Plb.1.86.5, Plu.*Ant.*27.

κατατέθηπα, pf. with pres. sense, *to be astonished at*, Hsch. (with inf. -τεθήπειν), Suid.

κατατεθνεώς, and (in Hom.) -ηώς, pf. part. of καταθνήσκω.

κατατείνω, fut. -τενῶ E.*IA*336: aor. -έτεινα (v. infr.):—*stretch, draw tight*, κατὰ δ' ἡνία τεῖνεν ὀπίσσω Il.3.261, 311; κ. χαλινοὺς Hdt.4. 72; κ. τὰ ὅπλα *draw* the cables *taut*, Id.7.36; τὰ νεῦρα εἰς τὸ ἐξόπισθεν κ. Pl.*Ti.*84e. 2. *stretch for the purpose of setting* a bone, Hp.*Fract.* 15:—also Med., ib.5:—Pass., μῦς κατατεταμένος ib.8. 3. *rack, torture*, κατατεινόμενος ὑπὸ τῆς βασάνου προσωμολόγησε D.48.18, cf. Ael. *Fr.*176; κατατείνειν ταῖς κολάσεσι Id.*Fr.*279: metaph., κ. τὴν ψυχήν Id.*Fr.*60; κατέτεινέ με διηγούμενος Lib.*Decl.*33.25; κατατείνεσθαι ὑπὸ ποδάγρας Phylarch.40 J., cf. *AP*11.128 (Poll.). 4. *stretch out* or *draw in a straight line*, κατέτεινε σχοινοτενέας ὑποδέξας διώρυχας, i.e. he marked out the ditches by drawing straight lines, Hdt.1.189; δόλιχον κ. τοῦ λόγου *make a very long* speech, Pl.*Prt.*329b; μακρὸν λόγον, πολλοὺς καὶ μακροὺς ἐλέγχους, Phlp. *in APr.*262.10, *in APo.*243.19; φεύγουσι κατατείναντες τὴν κέρκον Arist.*HA*629^{b}35:—Pass., *extend throughout*, Id.*PA*650^{a}29. 5. Pass., *to be tightly bound*, ὑπὸ δεσμοῦ Plu.*Luc.*24. 6. *stretch on the ground, lay at full length*, [ὁ ἐλέφας] τοὺς φοίνικας κ. ἐπὶ τῆς γῆς Arist.*HA*610^{a}24; κ. τινὰς ἐπὶ τοὔδαφος Plu. *Publ.*6:—Pass., *to be extended over* a space, ἐπὶ γῆν Pl. *Ti.*58e; πρὸς γῆν πᾶν τὸ σῶμα ib.92a; σκέλη ἐπὶ τῇ γῇ -τεταμένα Arist.*IA*713^{a}19. 7. metaph., *strain, exert*, κ. τὴν ῥώμην ὅλην Plb.21.34.7 (s. v. l.):—Pass., *to be strained*, μᾶλλον, ἧττον -τείνεσθαι, Pl.*Ti.*63c; λόγοι κατατεινόμενοι words *of hot contention*, E.*Hec.*130 (anap.); δρόμημα συνεχῶς -τεταμένον Arist.*HA*629^{b}19; κ. τῷ προσώπῳ *strain* with the muscles of *one's* face, Plu.*Ant.*77; cf. infr. II. 2. b. *overwork*, τοὺς γεωργοὺς *PTeb.* 61^{b}197 (ii B.C.). II. intr., *extend* or *run straight towards*, τάφρον -τείνουσαν ἐκ τῶν Ταυρικῶν ὀρέων ἐς τὴν Μαιῆτιν λίμνην Hdt.4.3, cf. 9.15; γῆ κ. πρὸς ἑσπέρην ἐπὶ ποταμὸν Ἀγγίτην it *stretches* westward up to.., Id.7.113, cf. 4.19, X.*HG*4.4.7: abs., *extend*, ταύτῃ κ. Hdt.8. 31. b. *extend downwards*, Plu.2.566d. c. metaph., *tend*, εἴς τι Metrod.*Fr.*6. 2. *strive earnestly, be vehement*, E.*IA*336; ἰσχυρῶς κ. X.*An.*2.5.30; opp. χαλάω, Pl.*R.*329c; κ. ἡ ὀδύνη v.l. for κατακτείνει in Hp.*Fract.*43, cf. Gal.6.311: freq. in aor. part. with adverb. sense, *with all one's force* or *might*, κατατείνας ἐρῶ Pl.*R.*358d, cf. 367b; ὁ λέων τρέχει κ. Arist.*HA*629^{b}18; ᾠχόμην κ. Luc.*Lex.*3; ὄρνεις κατατείνασαι ἐκπτήσονται Id.*Sat.*35.

κατατειχίζω, *fortify*, Sch.D Il.19.99 (Pass.).

κατατειχογρᾰφέω, f. l. for κατατοιχ- (q. v.).

κατατελευτάω, *terminate*, εἰς τοὺς νεφρούς Arist.*PA*671^{b}13.

κατατελέω, *contribute*, φόρον dub. in *IG*1^{2}.231.

κατατέμνω, Ion. -τάμνω, fut. -τεμῶ Ar.*Ach.*301: aor. κατέτεμον (v. infr.); Ion. and Dor. κατέταμον Hdt.4.26, *Tab.Heracl.*1.14:—*cut in pieces, cut up*, κρέα Hdt. l. c., cf. Ar.*Pax* 1059; ἑαυτόν X.*Mem.*1.2.55; τὴν κεφαλήν Aeschin.3.212; γέρρα X.*An.*4.7.26:—Med., κ. δέραν ὄνυχι *lacerate*, E.*El.*146 (lyr., tm.):—Pass., τελαμῶσι κατατετμημένοις with regularly *cut* bandages, Hdt.2.86; σπλάγχνα κατατετμημένα Ar.*Av.* 1524; χώρη ἐς διώρυχας -τέτμηται *is cut up* into ditches or canals, Hdt. 1.193, cf. 2.8; κατετέτμηντο ἐξ αὐτῶν (sc. τῶν διωρύχων) τάφροι ἐπὶ τὴν χώραν X.*An.*2.4.13. b. metaph., τι ἐν τοῖς λόγοις κ. Pl.*Hp.Ma.* 301b. 2. c. dupl. acc., κ. τινὰ καττύματα *cut* him *up* into strips, Ar.*Ach.*301; σῶμα κατατεμὼν κύβους *having cut it up* into cubes, Alex.187.4; τὴν βατίδα τεμάχη κατατεμὼν Ephipp.22; ὅτι σμικρότατα τὸ σῶμα Pl.*R.*610b; κ. (sc. τὰν γᾶν) μερίδας τέτορας *Tab.Heracl.* l. c.:—Pass., κατατμηθείην λέπαδνα *may I be cut up* into straps, Ar.*Eq.* 768. 3. κ. τὸν Πειραιᾶ *lay* it *out* in streets, Arist.*Pol.*1267^{b}23:—Pass., τὸ ἄστυ κατατέτμηται τὰς ὁδοὺς ἰθέας *has its* streets *cut* straight, Hdt.1.180. 4. *cut into* the ground, κ. τοῦ χωρίου βάθος τρεῖς πόδας *IG*2^{2}.1668.7; τὰ κατατετμημένα *places where mines have already been worked*, opp. τὰ ἄτμητα, X.*Vect.*4.27. 5. *cut down, pare*, [τὸ δέρμα] ὁμαλῶς Hp.*Fract.*11. 6. *abuse, revile*, Pl.*R.*488b, Hyp.*Ath.*12.

κατατέρπω, *delight greatly*, in Pass., Lxx *Ze.*3.14.

κατατεταγμένως, Adv. pf. part. Pass., (κατατάσσω) *in order*, D.S. 9.10 (sed leg. -τεταμένως (κατατείνω), *eagerly*).

κατατετραίνω, found as pres. only in the form -τιτράω Gal.11. 402: aor. 1 -έτρησα Plu.2.689c:—*bore through, perforate*, ll. cc.: usu. in pf. Pass., σήραγγας κατατετρημένας cavities *bored through* it, Pl. *Ti.*70c, cf. Str.15.1.36; ὁ πλεύμων πόροις κατατέτρηται Plu.2.699a.

κατατεύχω, *make, construct*, ἰδίην σορόν *Epigr.Gr.*460 (Trachonitis); [ἐγκώμιον] Phld.*Rh.*1.215 S. (Pass.). II. *make, render*, αὐτοὺς θαρσαλέους Q.S.7.676.

κατατεφρόω, *cover with ashes*, τὴν Λιπαραίων πόλιν, of the volcano, Arist.*Mete.*367^{a}7:—Pass., Str.5.4.8.

κατατεχνέω, *frame artificially*, Ph.1.608 codd. (κακο- Wendl.).

κατάτεχνος, ον, *artificial*, κίνημα (v. l. κακο-) *AP*5.131 (Phld., Sup.); τὸ κ. Plu.2.79b; epith. of Callimachus the sculptor, Vitr.4.1.10 codd. (sed leg. κατατηξίτεχνος); cf. κακιζότεχνος.

κατατήκω, Dor. -τάκω [ᾱ], *melt* or *thaw away*, and in Pass., *to be melted* or *thawed*, ὡς δὲ χιὼν κατατήκετ'.. ἥν τ' Εὖρος κατέτηξεν Od.19. 205; κ. ὦπας δάκρυσι Theoc.*Ep.*6; ψυχὴν λύπαις D.L.8.18; κατατήκεσθαι τὸ θυμοειδὲς Phld.*Mus.*p.103 K. 2. *dissolve*, λίτρον κ. τὰς σάρκας Hdt.2.87, cf. *POxy.*40.8 (ii/iii A.D.); ἀέρα κ. πῦρ, i.e. rarifies it, Pl.*Ti.*61a; κ. ὁ χρόνος Arist.*Ph.*221^{a}31; τὸ αἷμα *dilute* it, Gal.6. 262. 3. metaph., κ. τέχνην εἴς τι *waste* art and skill upon a thing, D.H.*Dem.*51. II. Pass., with pf. Act. κατατέτηκα, *melt away*, κατατήκομαι ἦτορ Od.19.136; τὰ σπλάγχνα κατατετηκότα ἐξάγειν *dissolved*, Hdt.2.87; κατατάκομαι S.*El.*187 (lyr.), cf. *Ant.*977 (lyr., tm.), ὑπὸ τοῦ.. ἄλγους κατατέτηκα Ar.*Pl.*1034; ἔρωτι κατατήκεσθαι X.*Smp.*

8.3, Eub.104: so with gen. added, τούτω κατετάκετο.. ἔρωτα Theoc. 14.26; κ. ἐν ψήφοις *wear oneself away* in.., Luc.*Epigr*.12.

κατατηξίτεχνος [ῐ], ον, *enfeebling his art*, epith. of the artist Callimachus, Paus.1.26.7 (v.l. κακιζότεχνον), prob. in Plin.*HN*34.92 (*calat*–, *catot*–, codd.), and in Vitr.4.1.10 (*catatechnos*, *catathecnos*, codd.).

κατατίθημι, fut. -θήσω: Hom. freq. uses the Ep. aor. forms, Act. κάτθεμεν, κάτθετε, κάτθεσαν, inf. καθθέμεν (Dor. καθθέμειν prob. in Epich.71, Aeol. κά(θ)θηκε *Schwyzer*647ᵃ (Naucratis, vi B.C.)), Med. κατθέμεθα, κατθέσθην, κατθέμενοι (sg. κάτθετο A.R.3.867); also καταθείομεν, aor. subj. for καταθῶμεν, Od.21.264; καταθείομαι, aor. subj. Med. for καταθῶμαι, Il.22.111, Od.19.17:—*place, put, lay down*, folld. by various Preps., κ. ἄρνας ἐπὶ χθονὸς Il.3.293; κόρυθ' ἐπὶ χθονὶ 6.473; κ. τινὰ ἐν Λυκίης δήμῳ or εἰς Ἰθάκην, *set* him *down in*.., 16.683, Od.16.230; τινὰ ἐν λεχέεσσι Il.18.233; τεύχε' ἐς θάλαμον Od.24.166; ἐς μέγαρον ἐπὶ θρόνου 20.96; κλισίῃν τινὶ παρὰ πυρί 19.55; τι ὑπὸ ζυγά 13.20; τι ἐκ καπνοῦ *take down* out of the smoke, 16.288, 19.7. 2. *put down, offer as a prize*, ἄπυρον κατέθηκε λέβητα Il.23.267, cf. 885 (tm.); κ. ἄεθλα Od.24.91; but κ. ἄεθλον *ordain* a contest, 19.572; εἰς τὴν ἀγορὰν γράμματα κ. *set up* as a public notice, Pl.*Lg*.946d; so also κ. τι ἐς μέσον *put* it *down* in the midst, i.e. for common use, E.*Cyc*.547, cf. Ar.*Ec*.602; οὐσίαν, χρήματα κ., ib.855, 871; τὰ ὅπλα εἰς τὸ μέσον X.*Cyr*.2.1.14; but ἐς μέσον Πέρσῃσι κ. τὰ πρήγματα *communicate* power to them, *give* them *a common share of* it, Hdt. 3.80; ἐς μέσον Κῴοισι κ. τὴν ἀρχήν Id.7.164; τὸ αὑτῶν ἔργον ἅπασι κοινὸν κ. Pl.*R*.369e; κ. εἰς τὸ μέσον or εἰς τὸ κοινόν, *propose* for common discussion, Id.*Phlb*.14b, *Cra*.384c. 3. *put down as payment, pay down*, Hdt.9.120, Ar.*Ra*.176, *Nu*.246, Th.1.27, Pl.*Prt*.314b, *Lg*. 921d, etc.; τέλη Antipho 5.77; μετοίκιον Lys.31.9; τὸ ὄφλημα D. 21.99, cf. 151; τὰς συμβολάς Antiph.26.8; *put down as paid* (in accounts), X.*Oec*.9.8; τί.. τουτοιὶ καταθῶ σοι..; what *shall I pay* you for these? Ar.*Pax* 1214: generally, *pay, perform* what one has promised, νικῶντί γε χάριν κ. Pi.*N*.7.76; ἃ δ' ὑπέσχεο ποῖ καταθήσεις; S. *OC* 227 (anap.):—also in Med., v. infr. II.7. b. *dedicate*, *Schwyzer* 647ᵃ (Naucratis, vi B.C.), 682(2) (Cypr.), al. 4. *deposit*, παρακαταθήκην ἐς.. Hdt.5.92.η'; ἐνέχυρα *IG*5(2).344.18 (Orchom. Arc., iii B.C.):—in this sense usu. in Med., cf. II.4. b. *mortgage*, *Leg.Gort*.6.19, *Test.Epict*.2.13, etc. 5. *deposit* in the tomb, *bury*, v.l. in *Ev.Marc*. 15.46. 6. *sow* seed, *POxy*.1031.17 (iii A.D.). 7. κ. ὁδόν *lay down, make* a road, Pi.*P*.5.90. 8. *dish up, serve*, Epich.71. 9. in late form κατατίθω, *consign*, ἀγγέλοις καταχθονίοις *Tab.Defix.Aud*. 75.1. II. Med., *lay down from oneself, put off, lay aside*, esp. of arms, τεύχεα.., τὰ μὲν κατέθεντ' ἐπὶ γαίῃ Il.3.114, cf. Od.22.141 (hence, comically, θυμὸν κατάθου παρὰ τὴν ὀργὴν ὥσπερ ὁπλίτης Ar.*Av*. 401); χλαίνας μὲν κατέθεντο κατὰ κλισμούς Od.17.86; ζώναν καταθηκαμένα, of a maiden, Pi.*O*.6.39; θοἰμάτιον, etc., Ar.*Pl*.926, etc.; τὴν χλαμύδα (of the ἔφηβος) prob. in Philem.34; τὴν μοναρχίαν *lay down*, Plu.*Fab*.9. 2. metaph., *put an end to, settle*, τὸν πόλεμον Th.1.121, Lys.33.6, D.19.264:—Pass., ξυμφορᾶς μετρίως κατατιθεμένης *being arranged* on tolerable terms, Th.4.20. b. *put aside, leave out of the question*, τοὺς ποιητάς Pl.*Prt*.348a, cf. *Ti*.59c, Democr.3; κ. ἐν ἀμελείᾳ *treat* negligently, X.*Mem*.1.4.15. 3. *lay down* in a place; of the dead, *bury*, Od.24.190; κ. πηδάλιον ὑπὲρ καπνοῦ Hes.*Op*.45; τὰς μαχαίρας ἐνθαδί Ar.*Eq*.489; [τὰ στρώματα] Id.*Ra*.166; ὤμοισι κατ' ἄμβροτα θήκατο τεύχη on one's shoulders, Q.S.12.303; *put on shore, disembark*, Luc.*Alex*.57; ποῖ δὴ ἡμᾶς ὁ ἀνὴρ -θήσεται; Plu.*Caes*.37: metaph., πολλὰ αἱ μακραὶ ἁμέραι κατέθεντο λύπας ἐγγυτέρω *have brought* them *nearer*.., S.*OC* 1216 (lyr.). 4. *deposit for oneself, lay by, lay up in store* (v. supr. I.4), [γαστέρας] ἐπὶ δόρπῳ for supper, Od.18.45; ἔντεα ἐς θάλαμον 19.17; ὅπλα εἰς τὰς ἄκρας X.*Cyr*.7.5.34; βίον Hes.*Op*.601; σμικρὸν ἐπὶ σμικρῷ ib.361; καρποὺς ἐς φορβήν Hdt.1.202; παραθήκην Id. 6.73; χρήματα Antipho Soph.54; θησαυρὸν παισί Thgn.409; θησαυροὺς ἐν οἴκῳ X.*Cyr*.8.2.15; μυρίους δαρεικοὺς εἰς τὸ ἴδιον ἐμοί Id.*An*.1.3.3; [σῖτον] *hoard it up* in hope of high prices, Lys.22.9. b. metaph., κλέος *lay up store of* glory, Hdt.7.220, 9.78, Pl.*Smp*.208c; ἀΐδιον δόξαν κ. Th. 4.87; κ. ἀποστροφήν τινι X.*An*.7.6.34: freq. χάριτα or χάριν κατατίθεσθαί τινι or πρός τινα, *lay up a store of* gratitude or favour, Hdt.6.41, 7.178, Antipho 5.61, Th.1.33, D.59.21, etc.; εὐεργεσίαν κ. ἐς βασιλέα Th.1.128 (so in Pass., μεγάλων μοι κατατεθεισῶν ἐς αὐτὸν εὐεργεσιῶν Hdn.3.6.2, cf. 1.4.3); also ἔχθραν καταθέσθαι πρὸς ἐκείνους ὑπὲρ αὐτῶν Lys.2.22; κατέθετο μῖσος διπλάσιον τῆς οὐσίας Men.626; but κ. ὀργὴν εἴς τινας *vent* one's fury upon.., X.*Cyn*.10.8. 5. *deposit in a place of safety*, τοὺς πρέσβεις κατέθεντο εἰς Αἴγιναν Th.3.72; τὴν λείαν ἐς τοὺς Βιθυνούς X.*HG*1.3.2; κ. εἰς τὸ οἴκημα D.56.4; οἴκαδε Pl.*Prt*. 314a; διαθήκην παρά τινι Is.6.27; φιλίαν παρὰ θεούς X.*An*.2.5.8; [Διόνυσον] ἐν Δρακάνῳ Theoc.26.34:—Pass., of prisoners, ἐν τῷ δεσμωτηρίῳ κατατεθῶσιν Lex ap.D.24.63, cf. D.C.58.1. 6. *lay up in memory* or *as a memorial*, χρὴ.. γνώμην ταύτην (ταύτῃ Bgk.) καταθέσθαι Thgn.717; μνημεῖον παρά τινι Pl.*Tht*.209c; κ. εἰς μνήμην *record, register*, Id.*Lg*.858d; κ. τι ἐς βιβλίον D.61.2; γνώμην -θέσθαι εἰς μέσον D.H.*Rh*.9.4. 7. *pay* (cf. I.3), ἐκφόριον *BGU* 1059.22 (i B.C.), cf. *PTeb*.329.7 (ii A.D.), etc. b. *employ, spend*, τὴν ἀκμὴν ..πρὸς τί κατατιθέμενος on what he is *employing* the prime of life, Apollod.Com.13.4; τὸν βίον εἴς τι Phld.*Rh*.1.244S.; κ. τὴν σχολὴν εἰς καλόν τι *employ* one's leisure in.., Plu.2.135d; τὴν τοῦ λέγειν δύναμιν εἰς τὴν τῶν ἀδικουμένων βοήθειαν D.S.9.13; σπουδὴν -τιθέμενοι Polystr.p.19 W. 8. *impose*, ὄνομα Parm.19.3, cf. 8.39; but μορφὰς κατέθεντο δύο γνώμας ὀνομάζειν *recorded their decision, decided* to name, ib.53. 9. in Law, *depose, aver*, ἐν ὑπομνήμασι *PLips*.35.16 (iv A.D.), cf. *Cod.Just*.1.5.16.1, etc. b. = συγκατατίθεμαι, Eust. 1261.19. c. *make* a testamentary *disposition*, κ. διαθηκιμαίαν βούλησιν *PMasp*.151.43, al. (vi A.D.).—Freq. in Hom. and familiar Att.; rare in Trag.

κατατῑλάω, *make dirt over*, τῆς στήλης, τῶν Ἑκαταίων, Ar.*Av*.1054, *Ra*.366:—Pass., τοῖς ὄρνισι κατατιλώμενοι Id.*Av*.1117; κατὰ τῆς κεφαλῆς κατατετιλῆσθαι Artem.2.26.

κατατίλλω, aor. 1 -έτῖλα, *pull to pieces*, ῥάκος Hp.*Nat.Mul*.32: metaph., κ. ἑαυτὸν ἐπὶ θρήνου Hsch. s.v. δρύπτεται.

κατατῑμωρέω, *punish*, *Tab.Defix.Aud*.76.7 (Attica).

κατατιτρ-άω, v. κατατετραίνω. -**ησις**, εως, ἡ, = κατάτρησις, Crito ap.Gal.13.883.

κατατιτρώσκω, *wound*, X.*An*.3.4.26; λίθοις καὶ τοξεύμασι ib.4.1. 10; ἑαυτόν D.L.1.60, cf. Plb.33.9.6, Plu.*Sol*.30, etc.:—Pass., Id. *Caes*.66: metaph., πάθη κ. τινάς Ph.1.299; κατατετρωμένοι τὰς ψυχὰς ἐκ νοσημάτων Id.1.156. 2. *open an abscess*, ἔμπλαστρος -σκουσα Aët.15.17.

κατατῐτύσκομαι, *aim at*, ἀλλήλων Eust.1331.14.

κατατλάω, strengthd. for *τλάω, in med. form κατετλᾶτο, Hsch. **κατατοιόντα**· κατασκευάζοντα, Id. (fort. καταρτύοντα).

κατατοιχογρᾰφέω, *write upon a wall*, κ. τί τινος *write up libels against* a person, Str.14.5.14; v.l. κατατειχ-.

κατατοκίζω, *beggar by usurious interest*, τινας Anon.*Vit.Thuc*.:—Pass., *to be thus beggared*, Arist.*Pol*.1316ᵇ16.

κατατολμάω, *behave boldly towards*, τῶν πολεμίων Plb.3.103.5; *make an insolent attack upon*, τῆς πόλεως Id.12.8.2; κ. τῆς κοινῆς πίστεως S.E.*M*.7.27; ὁ πρῶτος -ήσας θαλάττης Philostr.*Ep*.38; ἐρωμένης ib.16; ἀλλοτρίων ἔργων Jul.*Or*.1.3c; κ. τοῦ καλῶς ἔχοντος *presume beyond* propriety, Plb.39.1.9: also c. gen., *make a bold bid for*, τῆς τῶν ὅλων ἀρχῆς Id.15.25.28. II. strengthd. for τολμάω: abs., Id.1.47.10, *UPZ*42.20 (ii B.C.); κατατετολμηκότες *desperate, reckless persons*, Phld.*Sto.Herc*.339.12: c. inf., Plb.2.13.5, Lxx 2*Ma*. 3.24, Gal.14.644: c. acc., κ. ἔφοδον Hld.7.24.

κατατομή, ἡ, *incision, notch, groove*, Thphr.*HP*4.8.10, Sm.*Je*.31 (48).37; ἄνευ -τομῆς *uncarved, smooth*, *IG*1².372.134, cf. 373.231: pl., Artem.1.67. II. *part of a theatre*, Hyp.*Dem.Fr*.3: variously expld. as = ὀρχήστρα or διάζωμα, *AB*270, cf. Phot. 2. *face* of rock, ἐπέγραψεν ἐπὶ τὴν κ. τῆς πέτρας Philoch.138; μέταλλον καὶ κ. perh. a mine and a *quarry-face*, *IG*2².1582.70. III. = καταγραφή, *profile*, Hsch. (s.h.v.). IV. *mutilation*, opp. true *circumcision*, a παρονομασία in *Ep.Phil*.3.2.

κατάτονος, ον, *stretching down*: *depressed*, i.e. less high than broad, opp. ἀνάτονος, Vitr.10.10.6.

κατατοξ-ευσις, εως, ἡ, gloss on βολή, Sch.Opp.*H*.4.559 (pl.). -**εύω**, *strike down with arrows, shoot dead*, τινα Hdt.3.36, Th.3.34, etc.; ῥηματίοισιν καινοῖς αὐτὸν καὶ διανοίαις κ. Ar.*Nu*.944:—Pass., X. *HG*4.7.6, Phld.*Piet*.34: metaph., κ. τινὰ τὸ περιττὸν τῆς τρυφῆς Eun. *Hist*.p.263 D.

κατατορνεύω, *turn*, in Pass., κ. τὴν ἐντὸς ἐπιφάνειαν πρὸς ἐμβολέα Hero *Spir*.1.28.

κατατρᾰγεῖν, aor. 2 inf. Act. of κατατρώγω.

κατατρᾰγῳδέω, *describe tragically, exaggerate*, κάλλος Ach.Tat.6.4: also c. gen., ὅσα κατετραγῴδησέ μου *uttered in tragic phrase against*, Id.8.9.

κατατραυματίζω, Ion. -τρωματίζω, *wound*, ἑαυτόν Arist.*Ath*.14.1, D.S.13.95; opp. ἀποκτείνειν, Plb.3.67.3:—Pass., Hdt.7.212, Th.7. 80, etc. II. of ships, *disable, cripple*, ib.41, 8.10.

κατατρεπτικῶς, v. καταστρεπτικῶς.

κατατρέπω, *put to flight*, *PMasp*.4.13 (vi A.D.).

κατατρέχω, aor. 1 inf. καταθρέξαι only in Hsch.: aor. 2 κατέδρᾰμον Ar.*Ec*.961, etc.: pf. -δεδράμηκα [ᾰμ] X.*HG*4.7.6:—Pass., aor. inf. καταδρᾰμηθῆναι Heph.Astr.1.21:—*run down*, Ar. l. c.; ἀπὸ τῶν ἄκρων Hdt.7.192; κάτω Id.3.156; ἐπὶ θάλατταν X.*An*.7.1.20; ἐπί τινας *Act.Ap*.21.32. 2. of seamen or passengers by sea, *run to land, disembark*, X.*HG*5.1.12; εἰς ἐμπόρια Plb.3.91.2: metaph., κ. ξένιον ἄστυ *come to a haven in*.., f.l. in Pi.*N*.4.23. II. trans., *run down, inveigh against*, τὴν Σπάρτην Pl.*Lg*.806c, cf. Diog.Oen.12, D.C.50.2, etc.: more freq. c. gen., Phld.*Vit*.p.42 J., etc.; κ. τῶν μάντεων D.L.2.135; τῶν συνόντων τοῖς δυνάσταις D.C.61.10; τῆς ῥήσεως Ath.1.10e; Ἀλκιβιάδου ὡς οἰνόφλυγος Id.5.220c, cf. A.D.*Synt*.100.19; κατὰ τῆς βουλῆς, κατὰ τῆς μοναρχίας, D.C.36.44, 66.13. 2. *overrun, ravage, lay waste*, τῆς Σαλαμῖνος τὰ πολλά Th.2.94, cf. 8.92, Dionys. Com.3.5, D.S.2.44, Luc.*Alex*.2, etc.; *oppress*, τοὺς γεωργούς *PTeb*. 41.30 (ii B.C.). 3. *run over*, c. gen., κὰδ δ' ἄρα οἱ βλεφάρων βαρὺς ἔδραμεν ὕπνος Theoc.22.204. 4. *pursue*, Lxx *Le*.26.37. 5. *hurry*, Plu.2.512e. 6. *slip down*, of a bandage, Gal.18(1).829.

κατάτρησις, εως, ἡ, *aperture*, mostly pl., Epicur.ap.*Placit*.2.20.14, Dsc.5.102, Gal.7.728, al., Erot. s.v. σπόγγοι.

κατατρῐακοντουτίζω, Com. word in Ar.*Eq*.1391, alluding to the σπονδαὶ τριακοντούτιδες, personified upon the stage as courtesans, with an obscene pun upon ἀκοντίζω (i.e. περαίνω).

κατα-τρῐβή, ἡ, *wasting, squandering*, τὴν Πλάτωνος διατριβὴν κ. [ἔλεγε ὁ Διογένης] D.L.6.24. -**τρίβω** [ῑ], fut. -ψω X.*Cyr*.8.4.36: pf. -τέτρῐφα Isoc. (v. infr.):—Pass., fut. -τρῐβήσομαι X.*HG*5.4.60:—*rub down* or *away*: hence, 1. of clothes, *wear out*, ἀμφὶ πλευρῇσι δοράς Thgn.55, cf. Ar.*Fr*.345, Pl.*Phd*.87c, Metrod.*Fr*.55: hence metaph., πολλὰ σώματα κατατρίψασα ἡ ψυχή Pl.*Phd*.91d, cf. 87d; οἱ τὰ βήματα κατατετριφότες, i.e. *constant frequenters* of the tribune, Isoc.*Ep*.8.7; ὁ σταλαγμὸς κ. Arist.*Ph*.253ᵇ15: metaph., κ. τὸ τῆς ἀρετῆς ὄνομα *to have* it *always on one's tongue*, Luc.*Par.*43. b. *press downwards*, -ομένης πάτῳ τῆς ῥίζης Thphr.*HP*6.6.10. c. *rub* or *roll* thread, περὶ γούνατι νῆμα χειρί Theoc.24.77. 2. of persons, *wear out, exhaust*, αὐτοὺς περὶ ἑαυτοὺς τοὺς Ἕλληνας κ. Th.8.46 :—Pass., *to be quite worn out*, c. part., κατατετρίμμεθα πλανώμενοι Ar.*Pax*355, cf. X.*Mem.*1.2.37; -τριβήσοιντο ὑπὸ πολέμου Id.*HG*5.4.60; ἐν τοῖς στρατοπέδοις Isoc.15.115; περὶ τὸν πόλεμον Plu.*Fab.*19. 3. of Time, *spend, consume*, κατέτριψε τὴν ἡμέραν δημηγορῶν D.57.9, cf. Aeschin. 2.14, Men.*Epit.*54, Plu.*Caes.*13; τὰς ἡμέρας περὶ τῶν τυχόντων Arist. *EN*1117^{b}35, cf. Plb.5.62.6, etc.; κ. τὸν βίον *employ* it *fully*, X.*Mem.* 4.7.5, Nicol.Com.1.23, cf. Phld.*Rh.*1.38 S. :—so in Med., τὸ πολὺ τοῦ βίου ἐν δικαστηρίοις φεύγων τε καὶ διώκων κ. *waste* the greater part of one's life in..., Pl.*R.*405b : in pf. Pass. (later in aor. 2 -τρῐβέντες *Cod.Just.*1.5.16.5), *wear away one's life, pass one's whole time*, c. part., αὐλοῖς καὶ λύραισι κατατέτριμμαι χρώμενος Ar.*Fr.*221; κ. στρατευόμενος X.*Mem.*3.4.1; ἐπί τινι Them.*Or.*26.312c. 4. of property, etc., *squander*, ἅπαντα X.*Cyr.*8.4.36; τὸν λόγον περί τι D.H.*Comp.* 11.

κατατρῐδομέω, perh. *lay three layers of stones*, *IG*12(2).11.18 (Mytil.).

κατατρίζω, strengthd. for τρίζω, Batr.88.

κατατρίχιος [τρῐ], ον, *fine as a hair*, Hsch.

κατάτριψις, εως, ἡ, *a being worn out*, τῶν ὀργάνων Hp.*Epid.*6.3.1.

κατα-τροπά, ᾶ, Dor. name of a part of the νόμος κιθαρῳδικός, Poll. 4.66. **-τροπος**, ον, = κατάντης, *steep*, prob. in Hsch. **-τροπόω**, *put to flight*, Aesop.291^b :—also in Med., Id.21.

κατατροχ-άζω, *cause to run smoothly*: hence, *promote*, τὴν εὐανδρίαν *OGI*339.84 (Sestos, ii B.C.). II. = κατατρέχω II.2, Nech. in *Cat.Cod.Astr.*7.141 (Pass.). **-ίζω**, *upset* from a chariot, Sch. A.R.1.752; *break on the wheel*, condemned by Phryn.*PS*p.114B. (Pass.).

κατατρύζω, *chatter against*, τινος *AP*11.321 (Phil.).

κατατρῡπάω, *bore through*, *Gloss.*

κατατρῠφάω, *make merry, be insolent*, Luc.*JTr.*53; = κατασπαταλάω, Hsch. II. c. gen., *delight in*, τοῦ Κυρίου Lxx*Ps.*36(37).4; ἐπὶ πλήθει εἰρήνης ib.11.

κατατρύχω [ῡ], *wear out, exhaust*, δώροισι κατατρύχω καὶ ἐδωδῇ λαοὺς Il.17.225; ἵνα μή σε κ. καὶ ἑταίρους Od.15.309, cf. 16.84; τίς τυ κατατρύχει; Theoc.1.78, cf. *AP*7.630 (Antiphil.), Luc.*Herm.*77, *Dips.*4, *PLond.*5.1677.50 (vi A.D.) :—Pass., μελέτῃ κατατρυχόμενοι E.*Med.*1100 (anap.).

κατατρύω, = foreg., in Med., κατατρύσαιο δὲ γυῖα Nic.*Al.*593 :—Pass., pf. inf. -τετρῦσθαι prob. l. in X.*Cyr.*5.4.6.

κατατρώγω, fut. -τρώξομαι Cratin.143: aor. 2 κατέτρᾰγον Ar.*Ach.* 809 :—*eat up*, esp. fruits and vegetables, ll.cc., Thphr.*HP*9.11.9, Lxx*Pr.*24.23(29.27), Theoc.5.115, Luc.*Apol.*5: c. gen., Plu.*Art.*3, etc.: aor. 1 part. κατατρώξαντες Timo 66.6 :—Pass., Arist.*Pr.*925^{a}31.

κατατρωματίζω, Ion. for καταστραυμ-.

κατατυγχάνω, *hit one's mark, reach the object of*.., [τῆς ἐλπίδος] Demad.6, cf. Diocl.*Fr.*138; τῆς στρατείας D.S.13.3; τῆς σπουδῆς Ael. *NA*3.25. 2. abs., *to be lucky* or *successful*, opp. ἐξαμαρτάνω, D.18. 178; τὴν θέσιν εὔχεσθαι δεῖ κατατυγχάνειν as to the situation of the city, one must hope *to be successful*, Arist.*Pol.*1330^{a}37. 3. c. dat., *fall to the lot of*, Procop.*Arc.*4. 4. Pass., in abs. sense, τὸ κ. Euryph.ap.Stob.4.39.27. II. *to be in office at the time*, ὁ κ. ἀρτυτήρ *Test.Epict.*4.37, cf. *IG*12(3).249.36 (Anaphe).

κατατυμβοχοέω, *heap a funeral mound over*, Call.*Fr.anon.*262 (dub.).

κατατύπτω, *pound, crush*, Sch.E.*Hipp.*977 :—Med., *beat one's breast*, καττύπτεσθε, κόραι Sapph.62: c. acc., *beat one's breast for*, Εὔκλειτον.. κατετύψατο μήτηρ *Supp.Epigr.*4.190 (Halic., iv B.C.).

κατατῠραννέω, *to be tyrant over*, c. gen., Sm.*Nu.*16.13.

κατάτῡρος, ον, *covered with cheese*, Archestr.*Fr.*57.8.

κατατωθάζω, *jeer, scoff at*, τινος Hld.6.2, cf. Lib.*Descr.*5.6.

κατ-αναίνω, fut. -ανᾰνῶ Archil.61 :—*wither up*, l.c. :—later **καθαναίνω** Lyc.397, Luc.*Am.*12.

καταυγ-άζω, *shine upon, illuminate*, c. acc., Lxx *Wi.*17.5, Str.2.5. 42, Corn.*ND*32, S.E.*M.*9.247, Hld.1.1 :—Pass., Id.7.7, Ph.1.150; ὑπὸ μεταρσίου φωτὸς Heraclid.Pont.ap.*Placit.*3.2.5. 2. *outshine, occult*, of the Sun or Moon, Theo Sm.p.193H. (Act. and Pass.), Jul.*Or.*3.109c (Pass.): metaph., ἡ ἀγαθοεργία σου κ. πάντας Them. *Or.*15.192a. II. intr., *shine brightly*, Hld.5.31. III. Med., *gaze at, see*, A.R.4.1248, *AP*9.58 (Antip.). **-ασμα**, ατος, τό, *radiance*, *PMag.Par.*1.1130. **-ασμός**, ὁ, *shining brightly*, Plu.*Nic.* 23 (pl.). **-άστειρα**, ἡ, as if fem. of *καταυγαστήρ, *illuminator*, of the Moon, Orph.*H.*9.6. **-εια**, ἡ, *illumination, brightness*, Aristeas 307. **-έω**, in Pass., ὑπὸ τοῦ ἡλίου, *to be occulted*, of planets near the Sun, Gem.12.7, al.

καταυδ-άω, *speak out, speak plainly*, S.*Ant.*86. **-ησις**, εως, ἡ, *loud speaking, shouting*, Hp.*Praec.*14.

κατ-αυθᾰδίζω, *act* or *speak obstinately against*, τινος Suid. :—Med., Men.Prot.p.102 D. :—also **-ιάζομαι**, *defy*, τῶν νόμων Just.*Nov.*12.1.

κατ-αῦθι, Adv. *again, once more*, A.R.1.1079, 2.528; in Od.10.567, 21.55 κατ' belongs to the Verb.

κατ-αυλέω, *charm by flute-playing*, τινος Pl.*Lg.*790e, cf. *R.*411a; τινα Alciphr.2.1: metaph., σε...-ήσω φόβῳ I will *flute to* you on a ghastly flute, E.*HF*871 (troch.) :—Pass., of persons, μεθύων καὶ καταυλούμενος drinking wine *to the strains of the flute*, Pl.*R.*561c; κ. πρὸς χελωνίδος ψόφον *to be played to on the flute* with lyre accompaniment, Posidon.10 J., cf. Call.*Fr.*10.3P., Phld.*Mus.*p.49K. 2. c. gen. loci, *make* a place *sound with flute-playing*, Thphr.*Fr.*87 :—Pass., *resound with flute-playing*, νῆσος κατηυλεῖτο Plu.*Ant.*56. II. in Pass., [τὸν μονόχορδον κανόνα] παρέχειν ταῖς αἰσθήσεσι..καταυλούμενον *subdued by a flute accompaniment*, Ptol.*Harm.*2.12: metaph., *to be piped down, ridiculed*, γελώμενοι καὶ -ούμενοι Anon.ap.Suid., cf. Porph.*Chr.*34. III. c. acc. rei, *play on the flute*, τὰ μητρῷα Duris 16 J. :—Pass., *to have played to one as an accompaniment on the flute*, -ούμενοι πρὸς τῶν ἑπομένων τὰ μητρῷα μέλη D.H.2.19.

κατ-αύλημα, ατος, τό, *residence*, Lyd.*Mag.*2.21 (nisi leg. -ίσματα).

κατ-αύλησις, εως, ἡ, *flute-playing*, Thphr.*HP*4.11.5, Apollon.*Mir.* 49; *treatment by music*, Sor.2.29.

κατ-αυλίζομαι, aor. κατηυλίσθην Hippon.63 (dub. l.), S.*Ph.*30, E. *Rh.*518, X.*An.*7.5.15; later κατηυλισάμην Plu.*Pyrrh.*27, etc. :—*to be under shelter of a hall, house, tent*, ll.cc.

κάταυλον· καταυλημένον (sic), ἀναπεπταμένον, Hsch.

κατ-αύστηρος, ον, *very harsh* or *morose*, Arr.*Epict.*1.25.15.

καταυστής· καταδυστής, Hsch.; cf. καταύω.

κατ-αυτόθι, Adv. *on the spot*, A.R.2.16, 776, etc.; but in Hom. κατ' αὐτόθι shd. be read, for κατά belongs to the Verb, v. Hdn.Gr.(2.71) ad Il.10.273 on the accent.

κατ-αυτοί, *by themselves*, αὐτοὶ καταυτοί *PCair.Zen.*294.2 (iii B.C.).

κατ-αυχένιος, ον, *on* or *over the neck*, πλόκαμοι *AP*5.72 (Rufin.).

κατ-αυχέω, *exult in*, πλήθει καταυχήσας νεῶν A.*Pers.*352.

κατ-αύω, = καθαιρέω, *destroy*, τὰν Μῶσαν καταύσεις Alcm.95; cf. καθαῦσαι· ἀφανίσαι, καταῦσαι· καταυλῆσαι (καταντλῆσαι Lobeck), καταδῦσαι, Hsch.; cf. αὔω (A), ἐν- (A), ἐξ- (B), προσ-αύω.

καταφᾰγᾶς, ᾶ, ὁ, v. κατωφαγᾶς.

καταφᾰγεῖν, serving as aor. 2 to κατεσθίω (q.v.); Dor. inf. -ῆμεν Epich.42.4: later fut. καταφάγομαι Lxx 3*Ki.*12.24m, *PLand.*26.23, 34 (i A.D.), *Gloss.* :—*devour, eat up*, αὐτὰρ ἐπεὶ κατὰ τέκν' ἔφαγε Il.2.317, cf. Hdt.2.141 (tm.), 3.25, Eup.352, Luc.*Merc.Cond.*17. 2. *spend in eating, waste*, μή τοι κατὰ πάντα φάγωσι κτήματα Od.3.315, 15.12; τὴν πατρῴαν οὐσίαν Aeschin.1.96; πατρῴαν γῆν Men.349.4.

καταφαίνω, Dor. aor. 1 -έφᾱνα, *declare, make known*, τοῦτον λόγον Pi.*N.*10.11. II. Pass., fut. -φᾰνήσομαι dub. in E.*Fr.*781.65 (lyr.) :—*become visible, appear*, *h.Ap.*431, Hdt.7.51, Th.5.6, E. l.c., Plu.*Luc.* 27 :—also intr. in Act., Orph.*A.*370, 762. 2. *to be clear, plain*, τῷ Ὀτάνῃ μᾶλλον κατεφαίνετο τὸ πρῆγμα Hdt.3.69, cf. Plu.2.40c, 682a; *seem, appear*, ὥς γε κ. ἐμοί Pl.*Phlb.*16c; ὅτι μοι ἄτοπ' ἄττα κ. περὶ σωφροσύνης Id.*Chrm.*172c, cf. Plu.2.802f, etc.: also c. inf., ὡς ἐμοὶ καταφαίνεται εἶναι Hdt.1.58, cf. 6.13; κατεφάνη τῷ Δαρείῳ τεχνάζειν, i.e. Darius *well knew* that he was evading, Id.3.130; ταὐτόν σοι πάθος -φαίνομαι πεπονθέναι Pl.*Lg.*712e; πάντων μοι μετριώτατοί γε εἶναι κατεφάνησαν ib.811d: c. part., ὀρθῶς ἔτι μοι κατεφάνης λέγων ib. 631a, cf. *Sph.*232b; δαιμονία..τις ἔμοιγε κ. τὸ μέγεθος Id.*Grg.*456a, cf. *Sph.*217e; τοιαύτη ἡ ἕξις τοῦ σώματος κ. X.*Oec.*7.2; οἱ ἀντιλέγοντες ὄχλος καὶ βασκανία κατεφαίνετο D.19.24.

καταφάν-εια [ᾰν], ἡ, *clearness*, κ. καὶ γαλήνη Plu.2.914f. II. *manifestness*, κ. ποιεῖν ἐν τοῖς λόγοις ib.715f. **-ής**, ές, *clearly seen, in sight*, οὔπω κ. ἦσαν οἱ πολέμιοι X.*An.*1.8.8, cf. *Eq.Mag.*7.8; ἐν κ. στρατοπεδεύεσθαι in *an open place*, Id.*Cyr.*3.3.28. 2. *manifest, evident*, κ. ποιέειν τι Hdt.2.120, cf. Isoc.11.4, Pl.*Grg.*453c, X.*Cyr.*1.6.14, etc.; κ. ἐστί τι, γίγνεταί τι Hp.*Off.*3: Comp., Pl.*Lg.*812a: Sup., Id. *Tht.*186e, etc.: freq. c. part., καταφανέες εἰσὶ ἁμαρτάνοντες Hp.*VM* 1; κ. ἦν τῇ βουλῇ αὐτὸς θεὶς τὴν ἱκετηρίαν And.1.116, cf. Aeschin.2.39, Isoc.2.1; κ. ἐγένοντο οὐχ ὅσιοι ὄντες Antipho 5.82, cf. Plb.7.12.8; καταφανέστερος εἶναι κακουργῶν Th.5.16; κ. ἐστί τις, ὅτι.. Pl.*Plt.* 265d, *R.*506b; κ. γίγνονται, ὅτι.. X.*Oec.*1.20; κ. ποιεῖν τινα Antiph. 235.6. Adv. -νῶς *evidently, plainly*, Ar.*Eq.*943, D.35.27; καταφανέστερον ἢ ὥστε λανθάνειν *too manifestly* to escape detection, Th.8.46.

κατ-αφᾰνίζω, strengthd. for ἀφανίζω, Hsch. s.v. καταδηώσαντες, Sch.E.*Hec.*1142.

καταφαντ-άζομαι, *to be like*, τινι Herm.ap.Stob.1.49.44 codd. **-ικός**, ή, όν, v.l. for -φατικός, Numen.ap.Eus.*PE*14.8. **-ός**, ή, όν, *to be affirmed*, opp. ἀποφαντός, D.L.7.65, Suid. s.v. ἀξίωμα.

κατάφαρκτος, ον, = κατάφρακτος (q.v.).

καταφαρμᾰκεύω, *dose with drugs*, Alex.Trall.9.3, *Febr.*7. II. *anoint with drugs* or *charms*, τὰ πρόσωπα φαρμάκοις Luc.*Am.*39: hence, 2. *enchant, bewitch*, Pl.*Phdr.*242e (Pass.), Plu.2. 141b. III. *poison*, Id.*Dio* 3.

καταφαρμάσσω, *bewitch with drugs*, κατά με ἐφάρμαξας Hdt.2.181: metaph., τῷ Πλάτωνος λόγῳ Διονύσιον κ. Plu.*Dio* 14.

κατάφᾰσις, εως, ἡ, *affirmation, affirmative proposition*, opp. ἀπόφασις, Pl.*Def.*413c, Arist.*Int.*17^{a}25, al., *EN*1139^{a}21. 2. *affirmative particle*, A.D.*Adv.*124.9, *Synt.*245.22.

καταφάσκω, = κατάφημι, Phld.*Piet.*123, Ph.1.104; περί τινος Gal. 10.37, al.; *answer in the affirmative*, ἐρώτησιν Id.7.526 :—Pass., A.D. *Synt.*245.12.

καταφᾰτίζω, *declare*, Arist.*Ath.*7.1, Plu.*Sol.*25.

καταφᾰτικός, ή, όν, *affirmative*, opp. ἀποφατικός, λόγος Arist.*APr.* 24^{a}16; προτάσεις ib.25^{a}3; ἀξίωμα *Stoic.*2.56, al.; τὸ κ. Plu.2.1047d, A.D.*Adv.*122.13. Adv. -κῶς Arist.*APr.*64^{a}15, Gal.16.328, Eust.92. 22. 2. *emphatic*, A.D.*Pron.*49.11 (Comp.).

καταφαυλίζω, *depreciate*, Plu.*Alex.*28.

καταφέγγω, *illuminate*, in Pass., Max.Tyr.19.6. 2. *dazzle, overpower* by oratorical brilliance, Longin.34.4 (prob. l.).

καταφέρ-εια, ἡ, *proneness*, ἡδονῆς to pleasure, Ath.7.352c: abs., *lechery*, Eust.827.31. **-ής**, ές, *going down*, εὖτ' ἂν κ. γίνηται ὁ ἥλιος when the sun is *near setting*, Hdt.2.63; of ground, *sloping*, X.*Cyn*.10.9, *PLille* 1ᵛ1 (iii B.C.); κ. ἐπί τι *inclined* towards.., Hp.*Art*. 57; πρός τι, opp. εὐθεῖα, ib.75; κ. φυγή *downhill*, Plb.2.68.7; κ. κοιλία, of *diarrhoea*, Dieuch.ap.Orib.4.7.21: metaph., *headlong*, *rapid*, ῥύσις τῆς λέξεως D.H.*Dem*.40. II. *inclined*, *prone*, esp. to sensual pleasures, εἰς λίθων βολάς prob. in Phld.*Ir*.p.31 W.; πρὸς οἶνον, πρὸς τἀφροδίσια, Plu.*Alex*.23, Ath.13.589d: abs., *lecherous*, D.L.4.40, Sor.1.38 (Comp.), Phot. s. v. μύραινα: freq. written κατωφερής (q. v.).

καταφέρω, fut. κατοίσω Plu.*Per*.28, -οίσομαι Il.22.425: aor. 1 κατήνεγκα Lxx *Ge*.37.2, inf. -ενεγκεῖν Plb.1.62.9; Dor. κατέφειρα *GDI* 2317.8 (Delph.):—*bring down*, once in Hom., οὗ μ' ἄχος ὀξὺ κατοίσεται Ἄϊδος εἴσω *will bring* me *down* to the grave, Il. l. c.; βαρυπεσῆ καταφέρω ποδὸς ἀκμάν A.*Eu*.370 (lyr.); of rivers, κ. χρυσίον, γῆν, Arist.*Mir*.833ᵇ17, *Pr*.935ᵃ16: Com., ὁ Κρᾶθις ἡμῖν κ. μάζας Metag. 6.1; esp. of cutting instruments, κ. τὴν σμινύην Ael.*NA* 11.32; τὴν δίκελλαν, τὴν σφῦραν, Luc.*Tim*.7, *Prom*.2: c. dat. obj., κ. τὸ ξίφος τῷ πολεμίῳ *let* it *fall upon* him, Plu.2.236e: c. gen., τὴν ἅρπην τῆς ἰξύος Ach.Tat.1.3; τῶν γνάθων τὸ ξυρόν Alciphr.3.66: metaph., ψόγον τινός Lxx *Ge*.37.2: abs., *hew downwards*, *deal a blow*, Luc.*DDeor*. 8, *Somn*.3; κ. πληγήν Id.*Tim*.40, cf. D.S.11.69 (but also κατήνεγκε πληγαῖς τὴν κεφαλήν *PTeb*.138 (ii B.C.)). b. *pull down*, *demolish*, πύργους Plb.4.64.11; ἥλους (warts) Philum.*Ven*.10.4. c. *pay down*, *discharge*, Arist.*Oec*.1348ᵃ2, Plb.1.62.9, 33.13.6, *GDI* 1754 (Delph.), Plu.*Per*.28. d. *pass*, *evacuate*, τὰ σπλάγχνα μετὰ τῶν σιτίων J.*BJ*5.9.4. e. *refer* a thing, ἀπό τινος ἐφ' ἕτερον, v.l. for μεταφέρειν, Lexap.D.21.94. f. *carry down*, in reckoning, etc., πλῆθος ἀμήχανον ἐτῶν Plu.*Num*.18; τὸ τῆς εὐδαιμονίας εἰς τὰ ζῷα Plot. 1.4.1. 2. Pass., *to be brought down* by a river, of gold dust, Hdt. 1.93; from an upper story, D.47.63; *to move downwards with violence*, *to be discharged*, of humours, Hp.*Epid*.6.8.18; *to be couched*, of a cataract, -ενεχθέντος τοῦ ὑποχύματος Gal.7.89. b. *descend*, *sink*, Arist.*HA*590ᵇ8; κ. ὁ ἥλιος, ἡ σελήνη, ἡ ἡμέρα, ib.552ᵇ21, Plu.*Nic*.21, *Tim*.12; κ. ὁ λύχνος *is near going out*, Id.*Caes*.69; κ. [ἡ ἄμπελος] *is perishing*, Thphr.*HP*4.13.5; of dancers, κ. ἐπὶ γῆν Critias 36 D., cf. Democr.228; of a sick person, κ. καθάπερ νεκρόν Gal.7.591; but ἐπὶ πόδας, of a patient in bed, Id.18(2).60. c. *fall*, *flow down*, of rain or rivers, *Gp*.5.2.16, Hsch. s. v. Πεντέλεια. d. *tumble down*, αἱ οἰκίαι κ. ἐπί τινα.. Plu.*Dio* 44; ἀφ' ὕψους -ενεχθεῖσα γυνή Sor.2.84. e. *to be weighed down*, ἐν τοῖσιν ὕπνοισι v.l. in Hp.*Epid*.4.45, cf. 5.50; κ. καὶ νυστάζειν Arist.*Somn.Vig*.456ᵇ31; ἐς ὕπνον Luc.*DMeretr*.2.4; ὕπνῳ βαθεῖ *Act.Ap*.20.9, cf. Philostr.*Gym*.54; ὑπὸ μέθης Ath.11.461c: abs., *drop asleep*, opp. ἐγείρεσθαι, Arist.*GA*779ᵃ9, *Insomn*.462ᵃ10; *to be semi-comatose*, ἀγρυπνεῖν τε ἅμα καὶ -εσθαι Gal.16.497. II. *carry back*, *carry home*, Ar.*Ach*.955. 2. of a storm, *drive to land*, ὁ χειμὼν κατήνεγκε τὰς ναῦς ἐς τὴν Πύλον Th.4.3, cf. Plb.3.24.11:—Pass., καταφέρεται χειμῶνι ἐς τὸ Ἀθηναίων στρατόπεδον Th.1.137, cf. 3.69: generally, in Pass., *to be landed*, *discharged*, of cargoes, *PFlor*. 278 ii 13 (iii A.D.), etc. III. Pass., metaph., *to be brought* to a point, ἐπὶ γνώμην, ἐλπίδα, etc., Plb.30.19.13, 6.9.3, Plot.2.6.1; ἐπὶ τὰς αὐτὰς διανοίας D.H.*Lys*.17, cf. Phld.*Mort*.29, al.: abs. (cf. καταφορά II. 3), ib.30:—also Act., *have recourse*, ἐπ' οὐθὲν ψεῦδος Id.*Rh*.1.159 S. 2. *tend*, ἡ [σύνταξις] ἐπὶ τὸ προστακτικὸν φύσει κ. A.D.*Synt*.232.8; τῶν ῥημάτων -φερομένων εἰς τὴν ἐπὶ τέλους βαρεῖαν ib.134.25. 3. *enter the lists*, like Lat. *descendere in arenam*, Lib.*Or*.59.67. IV. *bring against*, τὴν διαβολήν κ. τινός Arist.*Rh.Al*.1437ᵃ19. V. intr. in Act., *to be prone*, *inclined*, κ. εἰς τὰς γυναῖκας *POxy*.465.146.

κατα-φεύγω, fut. -φεύξομαι D.8.41:—*flee for refuge*, ἐς τὸ [ἱρόν] Hdt. 2.113, cf. 1.145; ἐπὶ Διὸς βωμόν Id.5.46: c. acc., οὐκ ἔχω βωμὸν κ. E.*IA* 911 (troch.); -πεφευγέναι ἐν τόπῳ *flee and take refuge* in.., Pl.*Sph*. 260c, cf. X.*HG*4.5.5; ἐκεῖ, ἐνθάδε κ., Th.3.71, Isoc.14.28; ὅποι.. X. *Mem*.3.8.10; κ. εἴς τινα *flee for protection* to him, ὃς ἂν φεύγων καταφύγῃ ἐς τούτους Hdt.4.23; εἰς ὑμᾶς κ. καὶ ἀντιβολῶ And.1.149; ἐπί τινα D.18.19, etc.; πρὸς ὑμᾶς Id.8.41; παρ' ἡμῖν Isoc.12.194. 2. ἐκ τῆς μάχης κ. *escape* from.., Hdt.6.75: abs., ἄνω μάλ' εἰσὶ καταφυγών (sc. ὁ ἀτμός) Alex.124.17. 3. *have recourse*, εἰς ἔλεον Antipho 3.2.2; εἰς σωτηρίαν Id.2.4.1; εἰς τοὺς λόγους Pl.*Phd*.99e, cf. 76e; εἰς ὅρκον Arist.*Rh.Al*.1432ᵃ38; ἐπὶ τὰς μηχανάς Pl.*Cra*.425d; ἐπὶ τὸν δικαστήν Arist.*EN*1132ᵃ20; ἐπὶ τὸν λόγον ib.1105ᵇ13; ἐπὶ Καρχηδονίους Plb.1. 10.1, cf. Plu.*Cam*.7; πρὸς θεῶν εὐχάς Pl.*Phdr*.244e; ὥς τινας Plb.24. 10.11: c. dat., τῇ μητρί Ctes.*Fr*.29.57. 4. εἰς τὴν τοῦ βίου μετριότητα κ. *fall back* upon, *appeal* to.., D.25.76; ἐπὶ τὸ φάσκειν.. Phld. *D*.3.8. **-φευκτέον**, *one must fall back upon*, *have recourse to*, ἐπὶ τὰς ἀτυχίας Arist.*Rh.Al*.1429ᵃ14; ἐπί τινα Luc.*Pisc*.3. **-φευξις**, εως, ἡ, *flight for refuge*, κ. ποιεῖσθαι ἐς τὸν ὅρμον Th.7.41. II. *place of refuge*, ib.38.

κατάφημι, *assent*, S.*OT*506 (lyr., μεμφομένων is gen. abs.); opp. ἀπόφημι, in aor. 1 inf. -φῆσαι, Arist.*Metaph*.1007ᵇ21; οἷον -φᾶσα ἢ ἀποφᾶσα [ἡ ψυχή] διώκει ἢ φεύγει Id.*de An*.431ᵃ9:—Pass., aor. inf. -φάθῆναι Id.*Int*.18ᵇ39. II. *promulgate*, νόμοι οὓς κατέφησεν θεὸς Ἰουδαίοις f.l. in J.*BJ*3.8.4 (v. κατηφέω).

καταφημ-ίζω, aor. -εφήμισα, Dor. -εφάμιξα Pi.*O*.6.56:—Pass., pf. -πεφήμισμαι (v. infr.):—*spread abroad*, *announce*, κατεφάμιξεν καλεῖσθαί νιν Pi. l. c.; λίμνη Μαιῶτις, ἣν μητέρα..τοῦ Πόντου κ. *made it known as*.., Dion.Byz.2:—Pass., καταπεφήμισται *it is rumoured*, Plb.16.12.3; of persons, *become notorious* or *infamous*, Vett.Val.118. 5. II. *assign* or *dedicate* to a god, τὰ τοῖς θεοῖς καταπεφημισμένα Plb.5.10.8; θρόνος Ἀλεξάνδρῳ -ισμένος Plu.*Eum*.13, cf. Jul.*Or*.4. 156c. **-ος**, ον, *infamous*, *Gloss*.

καταφθάνω [φθᾰ], *fall upon unawares*, ἐπί τινα Lxx *Jd*.20.42. II. c. inf., κ. τεκεῖν bring forth a child *first*, *BGU*665 ii 14 (i A.D.): also c. acc., *pay in advance*, κατέφθακα ἀρτάβας ιβ *POxy*.1482.10 (ii A.D.).

καταφθᾰτόομαι, (φθάνω) *take first possession of*, γῆν καταφθατουμένη A.*Eu*.398; cf. καταφ(θ)ατουμένη· κατακτωμένη, Hsch.

καταφθέγγω, *sound loudly*, βροντήν, ἧς οὐδὲν -ει μεῖζον Horap. 1.29.

καταφθείρω, fut. -φθερῶ Plu.2.240d:—*destroy*, *bring to naught*, στρατόν, πόλιν, ἔθνη, A.*Pers*.345, S.*OT*331, Pl.*Lg*.697d, cf. Democr. 159; ἔργα νομήων Theoc.25.122; κατέφθαρται ὄλβος A.*Pers*.251; ἐπεὶ δέ χ' εἵκω οἴκαδις καταφθερεὶς *in sorry plight*, Epich.35.13; -φθαρεὶς τὸν βίον Men.*Epit*.429, cf. *Raccolta Lumbroso* 17 (iii B.C.); δένδρα -εφθαρμένα *IG*9(2).1109.74 (Coropa, ii B.C.), cf. *PMagd*.11.9 (iii B.C.), etc. 2. *corrupt*, τινα Plu. l.c.

καταφθῐνύθω [ῠ], = καταφθίω, *h.Cer*.353, Emp.111.4; cf. sq.

καταφθίνω [ῐ, sed v. infr.], *waste away*, *decay*, Pi.*I*.8(7).51, Hdt. 2.123; κ. νόσῳ, γήρᾳ, S.*Ph*.266, E.*Alc*.622: in later Att. Prose, Thphr.*HP*9.16.5: aor. part. καταφθινήσας Plu.2.117c: pf. part. κατεφθινηκώς ib.621f, Arr.*Epict*.4.11.25: καταφθίνουσι trans. is f.l. in Theoc.25.122.

καταφθίω (pres. only in the simple φθίω): I. causal in fut. καταφθίσω [ῑ] Od. (v. infr.), aor. 1 κατέφθῐσα Trag. (v. infr.):—*ruin*, *destroy*, οὐ μὲν δή σε καταφθίσει Od.5.341; παλαιὰς διανομὰς -φθίσας A.*Eu*.727; κατὰ μὲν φθίσας τὰν γαμψώνυχα παρθένον S.*OT*1198 (lyr.). II. Pass., aor. κατεφθίμην, part. καταφθίμενος, inf. καταφθίσθαι; poet. καππφθίμενος restored in anapaestic and choriambic verses of E., *Rh*.378, *Supp*.984, *El*.1299:—*waste away*, *perish*, κεν ἤϊα πάντα κατέφθιτο καὶ μένε' ἀνδρῶν *would all have been consumed*, *spent*, Od.4.363; ὡς καὶ σὺ καταφθίσθαι σὺν ἐκείνῳ ὤφελες 2.183; σεῖο καταφθιμένοιο *if* thou *shouldst die*, Il.22.288; νεκύεσσι καταφθιμένοισιν ἀνάσσειν Od.11.491, cf. *h.Cer*.347; νόμοι περὶ τῶν -φθιμένων *IG* 12(5).593 *A* 1 (Ceos); ἐκεῖ κατέφθιτο there he *died*, A.*Pers*.319, cf. S. *Ph*.346; τὠμῷ πόθῳ κ. Id.*OT*970; φέγγος ἡλίου κατέφθιτο the sun's light *died away*, A.*Pers*.377.

καταφθορά, ἡ, *destruction*, *death*, *ruin*, λεύσιμοι καταφθοραί E.*Ion* 1237 (lyr.); κ. τῶν ἀνδρῶν, τῆς Ἑλλάδος, Plb.1.49.4, 11.5.1; χώρας Id. 4.67.1, cf. 1.48.9; τῶν ἰδίων *OGI*339.5 (Sestos, ii B.C.), cf. *UPZ*110. 126 (ii B.C.). 2. metaph., *confusion*, *perturbation*, φρενῶν A.*Ch*. 211.

κατ-αφίημι, *let slip down*, κατηφίει (impf.) τὸ δόρυ διὰ χειρός f.l. in Pl.*La*.184a; λέβητα (sc. εἰς θάλασσαν) Arist.*Pr*.960ᵇ32.

καταφῐλ-έω, *kiss*, *caress*, δίφρον X.*Cyr*.6.4.10; χεῖρας καὶ πόδας τινός ib.7.5.32, cf. Men.*Epit*.56, Arr.*Epict*.4.10.20; τοὺς μὲν καλοὺς φιλήσοντος, τοὺς δ' ἀγαθοὺς καταφ. X.*Mem*.2.6.33, cf. Arist.*Fr*.553, Lxx *Ru*.1.9, *Ev.Matt*.26.49; dist. from φιλεῖν, Ph.1.478; esp. of an amorous kiss, Luc.*Am*.13. **-ημα**, ατος, τό, *kiss*, f.l. for φίλημα in Ph.1.480.

καταφῐλονεικέω, sine expl., Suid.

καταφῐλοσοφέω, *overcome in philosophizing*, τινος Ael.*NA*6.56; but -σοφήσαντες· διὰ τῆς σιγῆς νικήσαντες, Hsch., cf. Phot., Suid. II. *prove philosophically*, κ. ὅτι.. Arr.*Epict*.4.1.167.

καταφῑμόω, *conticisco*, *Gloss*.

καταφλάω, *press*, *crush*, Hsch.:—Pass., dub. l. in Str.4.1.7.

κατάφλεβος, ον, *full of veins*, *vascular*, Ruf.*Onom*.153.

κατα-φλέγω, fut. -φλέξω Il.22.512: aor. -έφλεξα Hes.*Sc*.18:—*burn up*, *consume*, πυρί ll. cc., cf. Arist.*Mu*.400ᵃ31 (v.l. προσ-), Plu. *Caes*.68, Diog.Oen.38, etc.; of a caustic drug, Paul.Aeg.6.31: metaph., of love, θεὸς ἄνδρα κ. *AP*5.9 (Alc.):—Pass., *to be burnt*, aor. 1 -εφλέχθην Th.4.133, D.S.8 *Fr*.11, Philostr.*VA*8.15: aor. 2 -εφλέγην J.*AJ*13.4.4, D.Chr.46.1. **-φλεκτος**, ον, *burnt*, Hld. 1.1. **-φλεξίπολις** [ῐ], ὁ, ἡ, *inflamer of cities*, of a courtesan, *AP* 5.1. **-φλεξις**, εως, ἡ, *burning*, Luc.*Salt*.39, Ptol.*Tetr*.86.

καταφλογίζω, *set on fire*, Lxx *Ps*.17(18).8.

καταφλῠαρέω, *keep on chattering*, τι Ps.-Luc.*Philopatr*.20, 25: c. gen., ὀνόματα ἅπερ Ἑλλάνικος καὶ Ἡρόδοτος -εφλυάρησαν ἡμῶν Str. 12.3.21, cf. D.L.5.20, *Corp.Herm*.1.29.

καταφοβ-έω, *strike with fear*, Th.7.21, Luc.*DMeretr*.13.5, D.C.39. 36:—Pass., c. fut. Med., *to be greatly afraid of*, τι Ar.*Ra*.1109 (lyr.): abs., καταφοβηθεὶς Th.6.33. **-ος**, ον, *fearful*, *afraid of*, κ. ἦν, = κατεφοβεῖτο, c. acc., ἐλέφαντας Plb.1.39.12; τὸ μέλλον Id.3.107.15; κ. ἦν μή.. Id.10.7.7: abs., κ. γίγνεσθαι Lxx *Pr*.29.16, cf. Ath.Med.ap. Orib.*Inc*.21.3; κ. βίος Plu.*Dio*4. II. Act., *terrifying*, μήνυσις *PSI*6.684.17 (iv/v A.D.).

καταφοινίσσω, *dye red*, Hsch., Phot., Suid.

καταφοιτάω, Ion. -έω, *come down constantly* or *regularly*, as wild beasts from the mountains to prey, Hdt.7.125 (-τῶντες, -τέωντες, -τέοντες codd.).

καταφονεύω, *slaughter*, Hdt.1.106, 165, al., E.*Ba*.1178 (lyr.):—Pass., Id.*Or*.536.

καταφορ-ά, ἡ, (καταφέρω) *conveyance*, of materials to the sea, *IG*2². 1672.125. 2. *bringing down*, esp. of a sword, *downward stroke*, Plb. 2.33.3, etc.; ἐκ καταφορᾶς *cutting*, opp. *thrusting*, Id.3.114.3; τραῦμα ἐκ κ. γεγενημένον a sword wound, Plu.*Dio* 34. 3. metaph., *attack*, *tirade*, Phld.*Lib*.p.48 O. (pl.), cf. Hermog.*Inv*.4.5: c. gen., against.., Anon.*in Rh*.53.9. 4. *payment*, *SIG*230 *C* 26, 252.70 (Delph., iv B.C.). II. (from Pass.) *downward motion*, Epicur.*Nat*.15.26, 27; *descent*, *fall*, καταφοραὶ ὄμβρων Pl.*Ax*.370c; χαλάζης J.*AJ*6.5.6; αἱ κ. πέντε, ὑετοῦ, χιόνος, δρόσου, χαλάζης, πάχνης *Theol.Ar*.31; *sinking*, κ. ἡλίου *sunset*, Thphr.*Vent*.12, Anon.Hist.(*FGr.Hist*.160)p.887 J.;

ἡ ἰσημερινὴ κ. Plb.3.37.5, etc.; *setting* of a zodiacal sign, Ptol.*Tetr.* 134: pl., Longus 2.24. 2. Medic., κ. κοιλίης *diarrhoea*, Hp.*Aph.* (*Sp.*)7.86, cf. Ath.2.53d (pl.). b. *lethargic attack*, Hp.*Epid.*3.6, cf. Plu.*Aem.*37(pl.); κ. πρὸς ὕπνον Gal.9.476; κ. πόνους παρέχουσα *PHerc.* 1041.2. 3. in reasoning, *deduction*, τὴν κ. ἐκ τῶν φαινομένων μεθοδεύειν Hp.*Praec.*1. 4. *sloping surface*, *IG*2^2.463.66,1668.51,7.4255.16 (Oropus, iv B.C.). -έω, = καταφέρω, of a river, *carry down*, ψῆγμα χρυσοῦ κ. ἐκ τοῦ Τμώλου Hdt.5.101, cf. 3.106 (Pass.): metaph., ἀμήχανον.. λογισμὸν καταπεφόρηκας τῆς διαφορότητος.. you *have poured forth* a wonderful *stream* of calculation of the difference.., Pl.*R.* 587e; πολλὰ.. κατεφόρει τῆς προνοίας he *went on inveighing* much against.., Plu.2.548c. -ικός, ή, όν, *violent, vehement*, σφοδρὸς καὶ κ. λόγος Hermog.*Id.*1.1. Adv. -κῶς Olymp.*in Grg.*p.370 J.; opp. εὐλαβῶς, Simp.*in Cat.*1.21. II. *lethargic, somnolent*, Hp.*Dent.*8; *causing lethargy*, ψύξεις, νοσήματα, Gal.8.161,162. III. Adv. -κῶς *by evacuation*, prob. in Hsch. -ος, ον, *rushing down, tempestuous*, τὸ κ. τῆς θαλάσσης, opp. τὸ γαληνίζον, Arist.*Pr.*936^{b}6 (dub. l.). b. *having a downward tendency*, τὸ ψυχρὸν ἀεὶ κ. Olymp.*in Mete.*85.5. 2. *inclined, tending* to.., ἐπὶ τὸ παροξύνεσθαι A.D.*Adv.*189.28, cf. *Synt.* 134.1. II. *bearing down, lethargic*, ὕπνος prob. in Hsch. III. of a burial-ground, *accessible*, Judeich *Altertümer von Hierapolis* 336. 21 (fort. κατάφωρα; καταφωορα lapis).

καταφορτ-ίζω, *load heavily*, ὄνους τοῖς ἐπιτηδείοις J.*AJ*7.9.3 (Pass.): metaph., *weigh down*, τὰν ψυχὰν κακοῖς Hipparch.ap.Stob.4.44.81; *weary, burden*, τινὰς τοῖς Πλάτωνος λόγοις Jul.*Or.*2.69b; of financial burdens, κ. τὸ δημόσιον χρέεσι Just.*Nov.*148 *Praef.* (Pass.). -ος, ον, *laden with*, τινος J.*Vit.*26.

καταφράζω, *declare*, τὸ σαφανές Pi.*O.*10(11).55:—Med., with aor. Pass. and Med., *consider, think upon, weigh*, καταφράζεσθε καὶ αὐτοὶ τήνδε δίκην Hes.*Op.*248; καταφρασθεὶς αὐτὸν ταῦτα ποιεῦντα *having observed*.., Hdt.4.76; κατεφράσατο Sol.13.38; εἰ τήνδε -φράσσαιο κέλευθον D.P.884.

κατα-φράκτης, ου, ὁ, *coat of mail*: a kind of *bandage*, so called from its likeness, Gal.18(1).816. -**φρακτος**, ον, *covered, shut up*, ἐν δεσμῷ S.*Ant.*958 (lyr., in old Att. form **κατάφαρκτος**); πλοῖα κ. *decked* vessels, Th.1.10 codd., cf. Plb.1.20.13; ἔν τε ταῖς ἀφράκτοις καὶ ταῖς κ. ναυσί *IG*12(1).41 (Rhodes, i B.C.); ἡ κ. ἵππος cavalry *clad in full armour, mailed*, Plb.30.25.9, cf. Arr.*Tact.*4.1, 19.4; ἱππεῖς Plu. *Crass.*21; τὰ κ. *coat of mail*, *PMagd.*13.6 (iii B.C.): metaph., *encased* in ignorance of the future, ψυχαί Ion Trag.6. -**φραξις**, εως, ἡ, *stopping up*, τῆς χοινικίδος *Hippiatr.*96. -**φράσσω**, *fortify, protect*, in Pass., -φρασσόμενοι ἐν ταῖς φάλαγξιν Lxx 1*Ma.*6.38; πύργος σιδήρῳ -πεφραγμένος J.*BJ*7.8.5; τόπους ὅπλοις -πεφραγμένους καὶ ἵπποις Plu. *Alex.*16; ἵπποι κ. χαλκοῖς καὶ σιδηροῖς σκεπάσμασιν Id.*Crass.*24: metaph., πολλοῖς ἱππεῦσι καταπεφραγμένος Id.*Alex.*33.

καταφρίσσω, pf. -πέφρικα, strengthd. for φρίσσω, Hsch.

καταφρον-έω, *look down upon, think slightly of*, τινος Hdt.4.134, Th.7.63, etc.; τῶν παρόντων καταφρονῶν, τῶν ἀπόντων ἐπιθυμῶν Lys. 12.78; κ. τοῦ κινδύνου Pl.*Ap.*28c; τῆς τέχνης Id.*Grg.*512c, al.; καύματος καὶ ψύχους Ephor.149 J.; κυνηγεσίων X.*Cyn.*1.18; θεῶν E.*Ba.* 199, Antiph.262; τῶν πτωχῶν Men.301.10; οὐ δεῖ διαβολῆς κ. Id.88. 1. 2. c. acc., *regard slightly, despise*, E.*Ba.*503; τοὺς ἐπιόντας Th.6.34:—Pass., *to be despised*, ὑπό τινων Pl.*R.*556d; εἰς τὰ πολεμικὰ καταφρονούμενοι X.*HG*7.4.30: fut. -φρονηθήσομαι Isoc.6.95, Aeschin. 1.176: also in med. form -φρονήσομαι Pl.*Hp.Ma.*281c: aor. -εφρονήθην Isoc.6.108, Pl.*Euthd.*273d. 3. abs., *to be disdainful, deal contemptuously*, Th.2.11, Amphis 1.3, Arist.*Rh.*1378^{b}15; τὸ -φρονοῦν *contempt*, D.H.5.44. 4. c. inf., *think contemptuously that.., presume*, καταφρονήσαντες Ἀρκάδων κρέσσονες εἶναι Hdt.1.66; καταφρονοῦντες κἂν προαισθέσθαι Th.3.83: also c. acc., -φρονήσαντες ταῦτα Hdt.8.10. 5. c. acc. et gen., like καταγιγνώσκω, κ. τῶν Ἀθηναίων ἀδυνασίαν Th.8.8. II. c. acc. rei, *fix one's thoughts upon, aim at*, τὴν τυραννίδα Hdt.1.59; τοὺς βύστακας μὴ καταφρόνει do not *think of* your moustache, *do* not *aim at having* one (because the Spartans had to shave the upper lip, cf. μύσταξ), Antiph.44. III. *come to one's senses*, Hp.*Morb.Sacr.*15, *Nat.Mul.*3 (prob. l.), Plu.2.165f. -ημα, ατος, τό, *contempt*, μὴ φρονήματι μόνον, ἀλλὰ κ. not only spirit, but *a spirit of disdain*, Th.2.62, cf. J.*AJ*19.1.16, al., D.C.51.9. -ησις, εως, ἡ, *contempt, disdain*, Th.1.122, Pl.*R.*558b, Arist.*Rh.*1378^{b}14, D.S.1.93, etc.; *disregard, neglect*, *PMasp.*94.13 (vi A.D.), etc.; εἰς κ. ἄγειν τοὺς λόγους D.H.*Orat.Vett.*2; περὶ ἀλόγου κ., title of work by Polystratus: also without any bad sense, opp. αὔχημα, Th.2. 62. -ητέον, *one must despise*, τινος Ath.14.625d: also in pl., -φρονητέα, τοῦ τυράννου Philostr.*VA*6.22. -ητής, οῦ, ὁ, *despiser*, νόμων Arr.*Epict.*4.7.33; θανάτου Plu.*Brut.*12; πλούτου J.*BJ*2.8.3: abs., Lxx *Hb.*1.5, *Ze.*3.4, Vett.Val.47.33. -ητικός, ή, όν, *contemptuous, disdainful*, Arist.*EN*1124^{b}29, *Rh.*1379^{b}31, 1388^{b}25, Plu. 2.40f: c. gen., Phld.*Herc.*1457.10, Porph.*Abst.*3.27. Adv. -κῶς Pl. *Tht.*161c, X.*HG*4.1.17, 5.3.1, D.43.72 (καταφρονικός Gal.17(1).188, and Adv. -κῶς v.l. in App.*BC*2.45, are incorrectly written). -ητος, ον, *despicable*, Phld.*Rh.*2.175 S.

καταφροντίζω, used in a Com. phrase, [θοἰμάτιον] οὐκ ἀπολώλεκ', ἀλλὰ καταπεφρόντικα I have not lost it, but I'*ve thought* it away, *spent* it *in the schools*, Ar.*Nu.*857. II. *attend to*, τι Plb.28.13.10 (dub. l.).

καταφρυάττομαι, *snort at*, prop. of a horse: metaph., *behave insolently*, M.Ant.7.3; τινι Id.9.41; τινος Suid.

καταφρύγω [ῡ], *burn away, burn to ashes*, of lightning, Ar.*Nu.* 396:—Pass., of love, v.l. in Theoc.14.26 (Pap. ined.). 2. *parch, consume*, of disease, Alex.Trall.*Febr.*4:—Pass., *to be dried up*, γλῶσσαι καταπεφρυγμέναι Ruf.ap.Aët.5.95: fut. -φρυγήσομαι Hsch.:—also -**φρύσ(σ)ω**, -**φρύττω**, Id., Olymp.*in Mete.*299.11.

κατα-φῠγᾱς, ᾶ, ὁ, *runaway*, Hdn.Gr.2.657 cod. (-φαγᾶς Lentz). -**φυγγάνω**, = καταφεύγω, Hdt.6.16, Aeschin.3.208, *PCair.Zen.*495.10 (iii B.C.). -**φυγή**, ἡ, *place of refuge*, Hdt.7.46; ἔχει γὰρ καταφυγὴν θὴρ μὲν πέτραν, δοῦλος δὲ βωμούς E.*Supp.*267; κ. σωτηρίας a safe *retreat*, Id.*Or.*724; μηδεμίαν ἔχειν κ. Isoc.14.55; μόνην οἴονται κ. εἶναι τοὺς φίλους Arist.*EN*1155^{a}12; κύριος κ. μου Lxx *Ex.*17.15; ἐπί τινα κ. πεποιῆσθαι *Sammelb.*4638.29 (ii B.C.), etc. 2. c. gen. obj., κ. κακῶν *refuge from*.., E.*Or.*448 (pl.); τῶν ἀκουσίων ἁμαρτημάτων κ. εἶναι τοὺς βωμούς Th.4.98; κ. ποιεῖσθαι εἰς τέκνα E.*Or.*567 (pl.), cf. Antipho 1.4; ηὕρισκον κ. αὐτοῖς εἰς θεούς Pl.*Lg.*699b, etc.; ἡ εἰς τοὺς νόμους κ. Hyp.*Eux.*10; ἐμοὶ πόλις ἐστὶ καὶ κ. καὶ νόμος ὁ δεσπότης Men. 581. II. *way of escape, excuse*, μεγάλων ἀδικημάτων D.46.9, cf. 54.21 (pl.). -**φύγιον** [ῠ], τό, Dim. of foreg., Democr.180, Sch. Hermog. in Rh.4.172 W.

καταφῡλᾰδόν, Adv. *in tribes, by clans*, Il.2.668, Opp.*H.*3.644.

καταφῠλάσσω, *watch, guard well*, Ar.*Ec.*482.

καταφυλλορο-έω, *shed the leaves*: metaph., *lose its splendour*, τιμὰ κατεφυλλορόησε Pi.*O.*12.15.

κατάφυλλος, ον, *leafy*, κ. ἀνὰ κήπους Stratt.66.1.

καταφύξει· κατασβέσει, Hsch.

καταφύξιμος, ον, *to which one can fly for refuge*, Plu.2.290c.

καταφῡσάω, *spray, besprinkle*, σμῆνος οἴνῳ Arist.*HA*627^{b}15; [ἰσχίον] οἴνῳ καὶ ἐλαίῳ *Hippiatr.*30. 2. *discharge*, κ. τὸν θορόν (sc. τῇ θηλείᾳ) Arist.*HA*544^{a}4 (v.l. θολόν).

κατάφῠσις, εως, ἡ, *insertion* of tendons, Gal.*UP*1.17, al. II. = ψύλλιον, Ps.-Dsc.4.69.

καταφῠτ-εία, ἡ, *planting*, *BGU*1120.20 (ii B.C.). -**ευσις**, εως, ἡ, = foreg., Lxx *Je.*38(31).22. -**εύω**, *plant*, ib.*Ex.*15.17, al.; ἀγορὰν πλατάνοις Plu.*Cim.*13, cf. Luc.*VH*2.42; λαὸν εἰς τόπον Lxx 2*Ma.*1.29. II. *transplant, acclimatize*, τοὺς πέραν Εὐφράτου καρποὺς ἐπὶ τὰ κάτω τῆς Ἀσίας μέρη *SIG*22.13 (Epist. Darei), cf. Posidon. 68 J., Str.15.3.11. -**ος**, ον, *full of plants* or *trees*, τόποι Plb.18. 20.1: c. dat., *planted* with.., κηπεύμασι καὶ καρποῖς D.S.2.37; δένδροις Str.12.2.1; ἀσφοδέλῳ Luc.*Nec.*11.

καταφύω, aor. 1 -έφῡσα, *implant, insert*, [ἡ φύσις νεῦρα] εἰς τὰς σάρκας κατέφυσε Gal.*UP*1.18, cf. 4.11:—Pass., aor. 2 κατέφυν Hsch. (also in part. -φυέν Id.): pf. -πέφυκα Plu.2.442c:—*to be inserted*, of muscles, nerves, etc., Gal.5.563, 7.185, *UP*13.12 (pres. Act. in same sense, Id.2.240); *penetrate*, εἰς τὴν πεπονθυῖαν σάρκα Id.18(2).599: generally, *to be produced*, περὶ τὸ σῶμα Plu. l.c. II. Med., *overrun* a country, Suid., Phot.

καταφωνεῖ· ταράσσει, Hsch.

καταφωρ-άω, *catch in a theft*: generally, *detect*, Th.8.87, Luc.*Gall.* 28; κ. τινὰς ἐπιβουλεύοντας Th.1.82; [ψυχὴν] ὡς οὖσαν κ. *discover* its existence, X.*Cyr.*8.7.17: aor. Pass., καταφωραθῆναι τῆς κακοηθείας J.*AJ*16.10.1. -**ος**, ον, *detected*, Onos.39.2, J.*AJ*20.11.1, Plu.2.301b, App.*BC*1.25, Chariton 1.1, Ach.Tat.2.17, *POxy.*71.11 (iv A.D.). II. *evident, manifest*, D.H.*Rh.*9.5; κ. τῆς γνώμης γεγονέναι Plu.*Cat.Mi.* 54. III. v. κατάφορος III.

καταφωτ-ίζω, *illuminate, light up*, *AP*9.178 (Antiphil.), Sch.E. *Hec.*367. -**ισμός**, ὁ, *illumination*, Hero *Deff.*135.12.

καταχαίρω, fut. -χᾰροῦμαι Lxx *Pr.*1.26:—*exult over*, ἐόντι αἰχμαλώτῳ.. κ. Hdt.1.129; εἴτε εὐνοίῃ.., εἴτε καὶ καταχαίρων *with malicious joy*, Id.7.239. II. *rejoice much*, Alciphr.2.4, *IG*14.2410.11, *Supp. Epigr.*2.844 (Syria).

καταχᾰλαζάω, *shower down like hail upon*, λίθους τινός Luc.*Gall.* 22.

καταχᾰλάω, *let down*, τινὰς διὰ θυρίδος Lxx *Jo.*2.15.

καταχαλκ-εύω, *work* or *mould in bronze*, ἀνδριὰς καταχαλκευόμενος Plu.2.559d; ὅπως μὴ καταχαλκεύοιτο that [the coin] *might* not *be worked up*, Id.*Lys.*17. -**ος**, ον, *overlaid with bronze* or *copper*, ἰτέα E.*Heracl.*376 (lyr.); κ. ἅπαν πεδίον ἀστράπτει flashes *with gleaming armour*, Id.*Ph.*110 (lyr.); δράκων κ. a serpent *lapt in mail*, i.e. scales, Id.*IT*1246 (lyr.); κ. πανοπλίαι Onos.1.20. 2. *alloyed with bronze*, χρυσός Thphr.*Lap.*46. -**όω**, *cover* or *point with bronze*, τὰ κέρεα Hdt.6.50:—Pass., θυρώματα -κεχαλκωμένα χαλκῷ Lxx 2*Ch.*4.9. II. κ. τόπον θυρίσι *block up with bronze* doors, Heraclid.ap.Ath.12.521f; στοὰς ὅπλοις D.S.12.70.

καταχᾰράσσω, *scratch all over*, τὰ πρόσωπα ταῖς μαχαίραις Men. Prot.p.89 D.:—Pass., ἵνα μὴ -χαράσσωνται τὰ βιβλία Sch.D.T.p. 139 H.

καταχᾰρίζομαι, *corruptly make* one *a present of* a thing, τινὶ λάφυρα, λείαν, D.H.6.30, 7.63. 2. *surrender* a thing *corruptly*, τι Lys. 27.14; τὸν ἀγῶνα Aeschin.3.53; κ. τὰ δίκαια *give* judgement *by private interest*, Pl.*Ap.*35c, cf. Din.1.105, J.*AJ*4.8.14; κ. καὶ προέσθαι D.26.20; καταδωροδοκεῖσθαι καὶ κ. πολλὰ τῶν κοινῶν Arist.*Pol.*1271^{a}3; κ. τἀληθὲς τοῖς πολίταις Ael.*VH*14.5, cf. 11.9; κ. ταῖς γυναιξὶ τοὺς προδότας Plu.*Publ.*7. 3. *show favour*, c. dat. pers., κ. Ἀνδοκίδῃ Lys.6.3; ταῖς ὑμετέραις γνώμαις Isoc.8.10: abs., μὴ καταχαριζόμενον, ἀλλὰ διαμαχόμενον Pl.*Grg.*513d, cf. Phld.*Lib.*p.53 O.; πάντα ταῦτα κ. D.41.12; [ἡ δόξα] τὰ μὲν κ., τὰ δὲ ψεύδεται Ael.*VH*1.23.

κατάχαρμα, ατος, τό, *mockery*, ἐχθροῖς Thgn.1107.

καταχάσκω, aor. 1 -έχηνα, *gape, jeer at*, Hsch.

καταχασμ-άομαι, = foreg., Hsch. s.v. ἐγχαλεῖν. II. Pass., *split, burst open*, Thphr.*CP*4.12.11. -**ησις**, εως, ἡ, gloss on καταχήνη, Hsch., Phot.

καταχέζω, fut. -χέσομαι Ar.*Fr.*152: aor. κατέχεσα Id.*Nu.*174, κατέχεσον Alc.Com.4 :—*befoul*, τινος ll. cc.

καταχειρ-ίζομαι, *make away with*, D.C.77.6. II. *take in hand*, Ptol.*Tetr.*206 (Pass.). **-ιος**, ον, *fitting the hand*, ἐρετμός A.R.1. 1189. **-όομαι**, *subject to oneself, conquer*, Hsch.

καταχειροτον-έω, *vote by show of hands against, vote in condemnation of* or *so as to commit for trial*, τινος D.21.2, Din.2.20, etc.: c. inf., ἀδικεῖν Εὐάνδρου κατεχειροτόνησεν ὁ δῆμος D.21.175, cf. 51.8; καταχειροτονηθὲν αὐτοῦ καὶ ταῦτ' ἀσεβεῖν *a vote of condemnation having been passed against* him, and that for sacrilege, Id.21.199; κ. θάνατόν τινος *vote* the death-penalty *against* him, Lys.29.2, D.19.31, Pl.*Ax.* 368e; καταχειροτονίαν κ. τινός Aeschin.3.52:—Pass., *to be condemned*, πανδήμῳ φωνῇ D.S.18.67, cf. Plu.*Tim.*23. **-ία**, ἡ, *condemnation*, esp. *by show of hands*, καταχειροτονίαν ὁ δῆμος ἐποιήσατο D.21.6, cf. Aeschin.3.52, Arist.*Ath.*59.2 (pl.), Harp., *EM*481.46.

καταχεύω, Ep. for sq.:—Med., τέττιξ καταχεύετ' ἀοιδήν Hes.*Op.* 583.

καταχέω, Il.6.496 (tm.), al.: aor. 1 κατέχεα, Ep. and Lyr. κατέχευα (v. infr.):—**Med.**, Ep. aor. 1 κατεχεύατο Call.*Hec.*1.1.11; inf. -χέασθαι Hdt.1.50:—**Pass.**, pf. κατακέχυμαι Orac.ap.Hdt.7.140 (tm.): aor. -εχύθην E.*Hipp.*854 (lyr.): Ep. aor. Pass. (freq. in tm.) κατέχυντο, κατέχυντο, Il.20.282, Od.12.411, *h.Ven.*228:—*pour down upon, pour over*, c. dat., κὰδ δέ οἱ ὕδωρ χεῦαν Il.14.435; so ἥ ῥά οἱ ἀχλὺν θεσπεσίην κατέχευε Od.7.42; ὄρεος κορυφῇσι Νότος κατέχευεν ὀμίχλην Il.3.10; τῷ γε χάριν κατέχευεν Ἀθήνη Od.2.12, etc.; σφιν..πλοῦτον κατέχευε Κρονίων Il.2.670; μὴ σφῶϊν ἐλεγχείην καταχεύῃ 23.408, cf. Od.14.38; οἱ..κατ' αἶσχος ἔχευε 11.433; ἐμῇ κεφαλῇ κατ' ὀνείδεα χεῦαν 22.463; νεφέλαν κρατὶ κατέχευας Pi.*P.*1.8; ἀντιπάλοις φόνον Epigr.ap.Plu. *Marc.*30:—Pass., κὰδ δ' ἄχος οἱ χύτο ὀφθαλμοῖσι Il.20.282; κατὰ.. ὀρόφοισιν αἷμα..κέχυται Orac.ap.Hdt. l. c.; δάκρυσι βλέφαρα -χυθέντα E. l. c.; οἱ -χυθέντες J.*BJ*3.7.29:—also Act. c. gen., rarely in Hom., ὃς σφῶϊν..ἔλαιον χαιτάων κατέχευε Il.23.282, cf. 765: freq. later, καταχέουσι αἷμα τοῦ ἀκινάκεος Hdt.4.62; κατάχει σὺ τῆς χορδῆς τὸ μέλι Ar.*Ach.*1040; ἔτνος τοὐλατῆρος ib.246; τοῦ δήμου καταχεῖν..πλουθυγίειαν Id.*Eq.*1091; ἱππερόν μου κατέχεεν τῶν χρημάτων Id.*Nu.*74, cf. *Pl.*790; βλασφημίαν τῶν ἱερῶν κ. Pl.*Lg.*800d; also κὰδ δὲ χευάτω μύρον..κὰτ τὼ στήθεος Alc.36, cf. Pl.*R.*398a:—Med., κατὰ τῶν ἱματίων καταχεόμενοι [ἄκρατον] *letting* it *be poured over*.., Id.*Lg.*637e:—Pass., κατὰ τοῖν κόραιν ὕπνου τι καταχεῖται γλυκύ Ar.*V.*7. 2. simply, *pour, shower down*, χιόνα, νιφάδας ἐπὶ χθονί, Od.19.206, Il.12.158; ψιάδας κ. ἔραζε 16.459; so κατὰ δ' ἠέρα πουλὺν ἔχευεν 8.50; κατὰ δ' ὕπνον ἔχευεν Od.11.245:—Med., νότος..χύσιν κατεχεύατο φύλλων Call. l. c.:—Pass., ἴδρως κακχέεται Sapph.2.13. b. *throw, cast down*, θύσθλα χαμαὶ κατέχευαν Il.6.134; κατὰ δ' ἡνία χεῦεν ἔραζε 17. 619; ὅπλα τε πάντα εἰς ἄντλον κατέχυνθ' Od.12.411; πέπλον μὲν.. κατέχευεν ἐπ' οὔδει *let* the robe *fall upon* the floor, Il.5.734; τείχος..εἰς ἅλα πᾶν κ. 7.461:—Med., Pl.*Ti.*41d; χαίταν *let fall*, Call.*Cer.* 5. c. metaph., κοινολογίας..ἡδονὴν -χεούσης Phld.*D.*3.14. 3. Pass., *to be poured over* the ground, *be there in heaps*, ὁ χῶρος, ἐν ᾧ αἱ ἄκανθαι [τῶν ὀφίων] κατακεχύαται Hdt.2.75; of persons, *to be spread, dispersed*, Eun.*Hist.*p.239 D. II. *cause to flow, run*, [χρυσὸν] ἐς πίθους τήξας κ. Hdt.3.96:—Med., χρυσὸν καταχέασθαι *to have* it *melted down*, Id.1.50.

καταχήνη, ἡ, *flouting, mockery*, Ar.*V.*575, *Ec.*631; Καταχῆναι, αἱ, title of play, *IG*14.1097.8. II. *amulet in the shape of a locust* offered in the Acropolis of Athens, Hsch.

καταχηρεύω, *pass in widowhood*, τὸν βίον D.29.26.

καταχής, ές, Dor. for κατηχής, *sounding*, ὕδωρ Theoc.1.7.

καταχθ-έω, *weigh down, afflict*, J.*AJ*18.6.7: pf. part. Pass. -ηχθημένος, = βεβαρημένος, Phot. (-ισμένος Hsch.). **-ής**, ές, (ἄχθος) *loaded with*, καρποῖο Arat.1044; *laden, surcharged*, γαστήρ Nic.*Al.* 322. II. *heavy*, λᾶαν Nonn.*D.*40.517.

κατ-αχθίζομαι, *to be hateful*, Hsch.

καταχθον-ίζω, *devote to the infernal gods*, *Tab.Defix.*ap.Herwerden *Lex.Suppletorium* s. h. v. **-ιος**, ον, also η, ον A.R.4.1413:—*subterranean*, Ζεὺς καταχθόνιος, i. e. Pluto, Il.9.457 (but Ζεὺς κ., = *Veiovis*, D.H.2.10); of Pluto, Demeter, Persephone, and the Erinyes, *IG*3. 1423; δαίμονες κ. Hierocl. *in CA*1 p.419 M.; = Lat. *Di Manes*, *AP*7. 333; κ. θεοί, = Lat. *Di Manes*, freq. in sepulchral Inscrr., *IG*14.1660, al. **-ος**· ὁ λιπαρός, ὁ τρόφιμος, Hsch.

καταχιονίζω, *cover with snow*, in Pass., Hsch. s. v. κατανίφεται.

καταχλαινόω, *clothe with a* χλαῖνα, Anon.ap.Suid.

καταχλευ-άζω, *scoff, jeer*, D.H.*Comp.*25, Poll.6.199: c. gen., τῆς παρακλήσεως J.*BJ*2.18.7:—Pass., f. l. in Ph.2.598. **-αστικός**, ή, όν, *derisive*, Poll.6.200. Adv. -κῶς v. l. ibid.

καταχλιαστέον, (χλιαίνω) *one must warm thoroughly*, Sor.1.69.

καταχλιδάω, Ion. -έω, *to be effeminate*, Hp.*Praec.*7 (v.l. -χλιδευσιν): c. gen., *display pomp* or *luxury by way of insult over*, τινος Posidon.36 J.

καταχλοάζομαι, *to be covered with green weed*, of rocks, Sch.Opp. *H.*1.131.

κατ-αχλυόομαι, *to be dimmed*, Cerc.4.21.

κατάχολος, ον, *very bilious*, ὑποχωρήματα Hp.*Epid.*7.14, cf. Aët.8.74.

καταχορδ-εύω, *mince up as for a sausage*, κ. [τὴν γαστέρα] Hdt.6. 75; κ. τινὰ ἐν βασάνοις Them.*Or.*21.261d. **-έω**, = foreg., Ael. *Fr.*280.

καταχόρ-ειον, τό, = sq., μέρος τὸ λεγόμενον -ηον (sic) Demetr.Lac. *Herc.*1014.53 F. **-ευσις**, εως, ἡ, *song*, finale of the Πυθικὸς νόμος, representing Apollo's *dance of triumph*, Poll.4.84. **-εύω**, *dance in triumph over*, τινος Ael.*NA*1.30: metaph., *insult*, τῶν Ῥωμαϊκῶν συμφορῶν Anon.ap.Suid.

καταχορηγέω, *lavish as* χορηγός, ὑπέρ τινος πεντακισχιλίας δραχμάς Lys.19.42: generally, *spend* or *contribute lavishly*, οὐσίας τισί D.H.3.72; τὰ οἰκεῖα Plu.*Lys.*9; *squander upon*, τι εἰς δεῖπνα Id.*Eum.* 13; εἰς τὸ θέατρον Id.2.348f; κ. τοῖς στρατεύμασιν ἀφειδῶς τῶν χρημάτων Id.*Cat.Ma.*3.

καταχόρηον, v. καταχόρειον.

καταχραίνω, *befoul*, οὔπω νιν ὑπὸ προτέρων ἵππων κατέχρᾶνεν κόνις B.5.44, cf. Eustr. *in EN*316.34:—also in Med., *sprinkle*, γάλακτι with milk, *AP*7.657 (Leon.).

καταχράομαι, Delph. -χρέομαι *SIG*672.32 (ii B. C.), al.: fut. -χρήσομαι Pl.*Mx.*247b: pf. -κέχρημαι both in act. and pass. senses (v. infr.): aor. -εχρήσθην (v. infr. II. 4):—*make full use of, apply*, τινὶ εἰς.., ἐπί.., πρός τι, Pl.*Lg.*700c, *R.*520a, *Cra.*426e; μάρτυσι κ. πρὸς τὸ.. Id.*Phlb.* 51a; κ. ἡ φύσις ἐν παρέργῳ τῇ..ἀναπνοῇ πρὸς τὴν ὄσφρησιν Arist.*Resp.* 473^a23, cf. *Sens.*444^a25; λόγους..οἷσπερ νυνὶ κατακέχρηται (in act. sense) D.35.44; ἐν καιρῷ [πράξεσι] κ. Isoc.4.9; κενῇ προφάσει ταύτῃ κατεχρῶ D.18.150: c. acc., τὴν..ὑπερβολὴν ἐπὶ βοήθειαν κ. ἡ φύσις Arist.*PA*663^b33; σχολὴν ἐς ἀκρόασιν Luc.*Prom.*4; τι εἴς τι *IG*2^2. 1672.307 (iv B. C.), cf. J.*BJ*5.9.1: abs. in pf. part. in pass. sense, ἐξεύρημα..Ἀθήνησιν..κατακεχρημένον ἐν συμποσίοις ἰδίᾳ 'στί *is fashionable* at private banquets there, Amphis 14.4. II. *do what one likes with* a person or thing, καταχρήσασθέ μοι, εἰ δοκῶ τοιοῦτος εἶναι Aeschin.1.122. 2. *use up, consume*, of money, etc., c. acc., Lys. 19.22 (bis); στέαρ *PRev.Laws* 50.14 (iii B. C.); τὰ κρέα ἐν τὰν δαμοθοινίαν *SIG*671 *A*7 (Delph., ii B. C.); *lay out, apply* money, εἴς τι D.49. 4, *IG*9(1).694.34 (Corc., ii B. C.), 12(1).155.86 (Rhodes); ἐνταῦθα on this, D.47.50: pf. in act. sense, ὅσα κατακέχρημαι Ἀθήνησι D.L.5. 69:—Pass., *to be spent, consumed*, Isoc.4.74; πλίνθου τῆς -χρησθείσης εἰς τοὺς τοίχους *PPetr.*3 p.139 (iii B. C.). 3. *misuse, abuse*, D. 19.277: c. dat., τῇ τῶν προγόνων δόξῃ μὴ -χρησόμενοι Pl.*Mx.* l. c.; κ. ὀνόματι *use* it *in a wrong sense, misapply* it, Arist.*Cael.*270^b24, Phld. *Rh.*1.43 S., cf. Str.5.1.2 (also abs., Phld.*Rh.*1.59 S.; *fall into an error*, Olymp. *in Mete.*279.11): c. acc., κ. τὴν σχολὴν εἰς τοῦτο Dionys. Com.4; τοῦ ἀρχαίου τι κ. *misappropriate*, *Test.Epict.*8.8. 4. of persons, in bad sense, *make away with, destroy, kill*, c. acc., Hdt. 1.82, 117, 4.146, al., Plb.1.85.1:—Pass., aor. -χρησθῆναι, ἐδέοντό μιν κ. requested that he might *be put to death*, Hdt.9.120. III. *pretend, allege*, ὡς.. D.43.39; ὅτι.. Id.48.44.

B. Act. **καταχράω** only Ion., used only in 3 sg., ἀντὶ λόφου ἡ λοφιὴ κατέχρα the mane *sufficed them* for a crest, Hdt.7.70; elsewh. impers., *it suffices*, οὐδέ οἱ καταχρήσει..ὑμέων ἀπέχεσθαι nor *will he be satisfied* to keep his hands off you, Id.4.118; ὥς οἱ καταχρᾷ εἰ βούλονται that *it is sufficient* for him, if.., Id.1.164; καταχρήσει *it will suffice*, Phoen.2.21.

κατ-αχρειόομαι, Pass., *to be ill-treated*, κατηχρειωμένη *AP*9.203 (Phot. or Leo).

καταχρέμπτομαι, *spit upon*, τινος Ar.*Pax* 815.

κατάχρεος, ον, also -χρεως, of persons, *involved in debt*, Plb.13.1.1, Agatharch.*Fr.Hist.*16 J., D.S.19.9, App.*Mith.*48, etc.; -χρεως δανείοις S.E.*M.*5.101: metaph., -χρεος ἁμαρτίας *involved in*.., Lxx *Wi.* 1.4. II. of things, τὰ κ. *that which is owing, debts*, *IG*14.759.20 (Naples); τὸ κ. κεφάλαιον dub. in Philem.88.9.

καταχρηματ-ίζω, *deal with*, *SIG*1023.73 (Cos, iii/ii B. C.), *GDI* 3624^a32 (ibid.): *dispose of* property, *POxy.*506.42 (ii A. D.), etc. **-ισμός**, ὁ, *deed, instrument* dealing with property, ib.237 iv 7 (ii A. D.), *PFlor.*381.11 (ii A. D.).

κατά-χρησις, εως, ἡ, *excessive use* or *consumption*, *PTeb.*61(*b*).305 (ii B. C.), Gal.19.679. II. *analogical application* of a word (e. g. γόνυ καλάμου, ὀφθαλμὸς ἀμπέλου), Arist.ap.Cic.*Orat.*27.94, Demetr.Lac. *Herc.*1014.49, D.H.*Comp.*3 (pl.), Quint.8.6.34, Sch.D.T.p.459 H., etc.: pl., Suid. s. v. Γοργίας; ἐκ -χρήσεως Gal.6.136. **-χρηστέον**, *one must use*, τινὶ εἴς τι Luc.*Am.*17. **-χρηστικός**, ή, όν, *misused, misapplied*, of words and phrases, ὑπάκουσις Phld.*Rh.*1.89 S., cf. S.E. *M.*8.129. Adv. -κῶς *by a misuse of language*, Str.7.7.11, S.E.*P.*1. 191, etc.; opp. κυρίως, D.T.632.24, Phld.*Po.*5.15, Ph.1.68: Comp. -ώτερον A.D.*Synt.*4.26, S.E.*M.*6.2. 2. *serviceable*, τὰ κ. καὶ συνεργατικὰ πρός τι Ptol.*Tetr.*80.

κατά-χρῖσις, εως, ἡ, *smearing on*, Alex.Aphr.*Pr.*2.59, Hld.6. 11. **-χρισμα**, ατος, τό, *salve, ointment*, Antyll.ap.Orib.10.27. 1. **-χριστέον**, *one must anoint*, *Gp.*16.18.2, Aët.7.24. **-χριστος**, ον, *for use as ointments*, τροχίσκοι Antyll.ap.Orib.10.24.10, cf. Dsc.5. 106; φάρμακον *Tab.Defix.Aud.*8. **-χρίω** [ῑ], *anoint, smear, coat*, Arist.*HA*625^b31; τέγη *IG*11(2).203 *A*54 (Delos, iii B. C.); τὰ τείχη τῆς σκηνῆς ib.199 *A*102 (ibid.); θῖβιν ἀσφαλτοπίσσῃ Lxx *Ex.*2.3; πηλῷ πρόσωπον Luc.*Anach.*9; θρόνους ἀσβόλῳ Ael.*VH*2.15:—Med., -κεχρῖσθαι τὸ πρόσωπον Artem.4.41:—Pass., Dsc.2.70; βολβίτῳ -κεχρισμένος M.Ant.3.3; ἐλαίῳ κ. Ph.2.158; κατακεχριμένα, = *oblita*, *Gloss.*

κατάχρους, ουν, = εὔχρους, ἔριφος *IG*12(1).892 (Netteia, dub., cf. *Arch.f.Relig.*19.285).

κατάχρυσ-ος, ον, *overlaid with gold-leaf, gilded*, *IG*1^2.280.78, 2^2. 1388.75, *SIG*1106.125 (Cos, iv/iii B. C.), Onos.1.20, Plu.2.753f, Luc. *Alex.*13; κόμη κ. τῇ χροιᾷ Ach.Tat.5.13. 2. metaph., of persons, *gilded*, Diph.60.1. 3. *rich in gold*, ψάμμος Poll.7.97. 4. metaph., *spurious*, Phld.*Po.*5.15. Adv. -σως *speciously*, Id.*Piet.*17. **-όω**, *cover with gold-leaf, gild*, Hdt.2.129, 3.56, 4.26:—Pass., Id.1.98, 2.63, *IG*2^2.1388.77. II. metaph., *make golden* (i. e. *splendid*), τὴν πόλιν

Plu.*Per.*12; κατεχρύσου πᾶς ἀνὴρ Εὐριπίδην *plastered* him *with gold* (opp. κατεπίττου), Ar.*Ec.*826.

κατα-χρώννῦμι, Poll.7.169, Suid.: impf. **κατέχρωζεν** Anon.ap. Suid. (s.h.v.):—*colour*, -χρῶσαι τὴν κόμην Poll.2.35, cf. Alex.Aphr. *in SE*9.3:—Pass., metaph., κατὰ δὲ κηλῖδα..κέχρωσαι E.*Hec.*911 (lyr.). **-χρωσις**, εως, ἡ, *colouring*, Poll.7.169.

κατα-χύδην [ῠ], Adv. *pouring down, profusely*, πίνειν Anacr.90. 3. **-χῦμα**, ατος, τό, *bath-water*, Ammon.*Diff.*p.78 V.; κ., = *perfusio* and κ. ζωμοῦ, = *tucca*, *Gloss.*: but in pl., = καταχύσματα, Them.*Or.* 23.293c. **-χύννω**, late form of καταχέω, *Gloss.* **-χῠσις**, εως, ἡ, *pouring on* or *over*, πολλοῦ ψυχροῦ Hp.*Aph.*5.21; *affusion, besprinkling*, Id.*Art.*27; ἡ τοῦ θερμοῦ κ. *Gp.*13.14.11. II. *vase for pouring*, later Gr. for Att. πρόχους, Moer.p.296 P., cf. Hsch. s.v. προχοΐδια. III. mistransl. of Hebr. *mûṣaq* 'straitness', as if *mûṣāq* 'smelting', Lxx *Jb.*36.16. IV. = ἀήρ, Hsch. **-χυσμα**, ατος, τό, *that which is poured over, sauce*, Ar.*Av.*535 (anap.), 1637; βολβοὺς.. καταχύσματι δεύσας Pl.Com.173.9; τὰ κ. ὄξος οὐκ ἔχει Philonid.9. 2. καταχύσματα, τά, *handfuls* of nuts, figs, etc., *showered over* a bride, τὰ κ. κατάχει τοῦ νυμφίου Theopomp.Com.14; also on a new slave, by way of welcome, Ar.*Pl.*768 (cf. Sch. adloc.), D.45.74; cf. κατάχυμα. **-χυσμάτιον**, τό, Dim. of foreg., *sauce for pouring over* a dish, Pherecr.108.11, Poll.6.68. **-χῠτήρια**, τά, festival in Egypt at the inundation of the Nile, *PCair.Zen.*176.39 (iii B.C.), Eudox.*Ars* 3.24. **-χυτλον**, τό, *watering-pot, portable shower-bath*, κατάχυτλον τὴν ῥῖν' ἔχεις Eup.283; ἐν καταχύτλοις λεκάναισι Pherecr.108.19.

καταχυτρίζω, = ἐγχυτρίζω, Ar.*Fr.*793.

κατάχωλος, ον, *dead lame*, Alc.Com.2.

καταχών-ευσις, εως, ἡ, *melting down*, *BCH*35.243 (Delos, ii B.C.). **-εύω**, *melt down*, D.22.76, Din.1.69, Str.9.1.20, etc.; [ἀνδριάντας] εἰς ἀμίδας Plu.2.820f; τοῦ στόματος κατεχώνευσε χρυσίον *poured molten* gold down his throat, App.*Mith.*21.

καταχώννῡμι (-ύω *Gp.*2.42.5, *Hippiatr.*34), fut. -χώσω Pl.*Tht.* 177c:—*cover with a heap, overwhelm, bury*, ὁ νότος κατέχωσέ σφεας *buried* them in sand, Hdt.4.173; κ. τινὰ λίθοις Ar.*Ach.*295 (tm.); σφέας..κατέχωσαν οἱ βάρβαροι βάλλοντες Hdt.7.225; ἐν λίθοις σφενδόνης Lxx *Za.*9.15; ἐν κοπρίᾳ *Hippiatr.*l.c.:—Pass., Lib.*Or.*61.15. 2. *silt up, dam up*, τὸ στόμιον τοῦ λιμένος D.S.24.1. 3. metaph., ἐπιρρέοντα καταχώσει...τὸν ἐξ ἀρχῆς λόγον with fresh streams they *will choke up the channel of* our original argument, Pl.l.c.; κ. τινὰ λόγοις Id.*Grg.* 512c; τὴν ἐρώτησιν Plu.2.512e:—Pass., *to be buried in obscurity*, τὰ πρῶτα ὀνόματα -κέχωσται ὑπὸ τῶν βουλομένων τραγῳδεῖν αὐτά Pl.*Cra.* 414c; ἐνθυμήσεις μυστικῶς -κεχωσμέναι Vett.Val.301.9. 4. *overwhelm, ruin*, Lib.*Or.*63.19.

καταχωρ-έω, *yield* or *give up to* a person *in* a thing, τινί τινος D.L. 5.71; τινί τι Plu.2.312b. II. = κάτειμι III, τοὺς τόκους -εῖν..ἐς τὸ θεῖον *Supp.Epigr.*2.481 (Scythia, iii A.D.). **-ίζω**, Att. fut. -ιῶ *OGI* 229.75 (iii B.C.), Apollon.Cit.2:—*place in position*, freq. in X., as *Cyr.* 4.3.3, al.; mostly of soldiers, as *An.*6.5.10, *Cyr.*2.2.8: generally, *place*, κατ' ἀξίαν Plot.3.2.12:—Pass., *take up a position*, ὅπου δέοιτο X.*Cyr.*8.5.2. II. *enter in a register* or *record*, κ. εἰς μνημόσυνον ἐν τῇ βιβλιοθήκῃ Lxx *Es.*2.23; εἰς τὴν τῶν ὑπομνημάτων δέλτον *IG*7.413.31 (i B.C.); ὑπόμνημα *PAmh.*2.35.36 (ii B.C.), etc.:—Pass., *POxy.*515.3 (ii A.D.), etc.; τὰ ἐν τῷ ψηφίσματι -κεχωρισμένα *SIG*618.6 (Heraclea ad Latmum, ii B.C.), cf. *Supp.Epigr.*3.378 C13 (Delph., ii/i B.C.); -εχωρίσθη ὁ ἀριθμὸς ἐν βιβλίῳ Lxx 1 *Ch.*27.24; [διαμαρτυρίαν] -κεχωρισμένην ἐν στασίμῳ Satyr.*Vit.Eur.Fr.*39 xvii 27. 2. *assign*, τινὰς εἰς φυλὰς *OGI*l.c.; εἰς τὸ στρατιωτικὸν σύνταγμα Aristeas 36. b. *invest, allocate* funds, etc., μισθὸν εἴς τι D.S.5.17 cod., cf. *PSI*4.372.10 (iii B.C.); of confiscated property, τὰ ὑπάρχοντά τινος κ. εἰς τὸ βασιλικόν *PAmh.*2.33.36 (ii B.C.):—Pass., τὰ εἰς τὸ ναυτικὸν -ισμένα Wilcken *Chr.*385.30 (iii B.C.), cf. *SIG*578.44 (Teos, ii B.C.). 3. *convey by deed*, τινι *PAmh.*2.52 (ii B.C.). III. *set down in a book, place on record*, Phld.*Po.*994 *Fr.*48, al.; εἰς τὴν ποίησιν Str.1.2.3; ἐν τοῖς ποιήμασι D.S.5.5, cf. 1.31, D.H.1.6; Κτησίβιος κατεχώρισεν, ὥστε... Ath. Mech.29.10; οὕτως -κεχώρικεν (sc. ὁ Ἱπποκράτης) Apollon.Cit.1:—Pass., Id.3; ἐν ἱστορίαις κ. *Inscr.Prien.*37.54 (ii B.C.), cf. Demetr.Lac. *Herc.*1647.27 F.; παρά τισι Phld.*Rh.*1.160 S. **-ισμός**, ὁ, *registration, deposit in a registry*, *PAmh.*2.35.37 (ii B.C.), *POxy.*514.4 (ii A.D.), etc.: *setting in order*, πράξεων Andronic.Rhod.p.576 M. (pl.). **-ιστέον**, *one must assign a place to*, ἐν τάξει Dam.*Pr.*252.

κατάχωσις, εως, ἡ, *covering up, burying*, *Gp.*4.3.2.

καταψαίρουσι· κινοῦνται, Hsch.

καταψακάζω, Att. for καταψεκ- (q.v.).

καταψάλλω, *play stringed instruments to*, [συμπόσιον] καταυλεῖν καὶ κ. Plu.2.713e:—usu. in Pass., *have music played to one, enjoy music*, ib.785e; of places, *resound with music*, Id.*Ant.*56. 2. Pass., *to be buried to the sound of music*, Procop.*Pers.*2.23. 3. metaph., καταψάλλεται..ὁ δημιουργός *is drummed out*, Porph.*Chr.*34.

κατάψᾱσις, v. κατάψησις.

καταψάω, *stroke, caress*, καταψῶσα τοῦ παιδίου τὴν κεφαλήν Hdt.6. 61; καταψῶν αὐτὸν [τὸν κάνθαρον] ὥσπερ πωλίον Ar.*Pax* 75, cf. X.*Ap.* 28; τὸ φαλακρόν Herod.6.76:—Pass., Asclep.ap.Gal.12.411; *to be stroked the right way*, Sch.Gen.Il.21.474. 2. metaph., *smooth down*, Plb.2.13.6, 10.18.3; *cajole, wheedle*, *BGU*1011.13 (ii B.C.). 3. *scrape down*, τοὺς τοίχους *IG*11(2).199 A 48 (Delos, iii B.C.); *rub down*, ἅτερος τὸν ἕτερον Luc.*Anach.*1.

καταψεκ-άζω, Att. **καταψᾰκ-**, *wet by continual dropping*, δρόσοι κατεψάκαζον A.*Ag.*561; κ. φαρμάκῳ Plu.*Alex.*35:—hence **-αστέον** *Gp.*5.39.2.

καταψελλίζομαι, Pass., *to be made to lisp*, κατεψελλισμένοι τὴν φωνὴν ὑπὸ τοῦ οἴνου Philostr.*Im.*1.25.

κατα-ψεύδομαι, fut. -ψεύσομαι: pf. -έψευσμαι D.55.8, *Ep.*3.35: also in pass. sense, as also aor. -εψεύσθην, v. infr. II:—*tell lies against, speak falsely of*, τινος Ar.*Pax* 533, Lys.16.8, Antipho 2.4.7, Pl.*R.*381d, D.21.134, etc.; κ. τινὸς πρός τινα *accuse falsely* to another, Plu. *Them.*25, *Phoc.*33: abs., Hyp.*Lyc.*8. 2. *allege falsely against*, τί τινος And.1.8, Pl.*Euthd.*283e, *R.*391d; τὰ πλεῖστα κατεψεύσατό μου D.18.9; ἑαυτοῦ μωρίαν D.H.4.68. 3. *say falsely, pretend*, ὡς.. E.*Ba.*334; *feign, invent*, τι D.18.11. 4. c. gen., *make a pretence of*, ὕπνου Luc.*Asin.*7; *give a false account of*, γένους Arist.*Pr.*950^{b}6; τῶν πραγμάτων J.*BJ Prooem.*1. II. Pass., *to be falsely reported*, Ἑλληνικὸς ὅρκος -ψεύδεται Theon *Prog.*2; τὰ κατεψευσμένα *false allegations*, Antipho 5.19; *to be falsely accused*, προδότης εἶναι κατεψεύσθη Philostr.*Her.*10.7, cf. *VA*5.24. 2. of writings, *to be falsely attributed*, τινος to one, Ael.*VH*12.36: abs., *to be spurious*, Ath.15.697a, Plu.2.833c. 3. *to be wrong, in error*, Phld.*Mus.*p.103 K., Str.9.2. 33: c. gen., *about*.., Sor.1.14, 2.4. **-ψευδομαρτῠρέω**, *bear false witness against*, τινος X.*Ap.*24:—Med., D.29.6:—Pass., *to be borne down by false evidence*, Pl.*Grg.*472a, Is.5.9, D.21.136. **-ψευσις**, εως, ἡ, *false account*, τῶν τόπων Str.1.3.18. **-ψευσμα**, ατος, τό, *false accusation*, Metrod.*Fr.*18: generally, *fiction, falsity*, Arr.*Epict.* 2.20.23. **-ψευσμός**, ὁ, *slander, calumny*, Lxx *Si.*26.6. **-ψεύστης**, ου, ὁ, = *commentor*, *Gloss.*

καταψέφω, = κατασκοτίζω, Hsch.

καταψηλᾰφάω, = ψηλαφάω, Luc.*Asin.*14.

κατάψησις, Dor. -ᾱσις, εως, ἡ, *raking over*, *BCH*23.566 (Delph., iii B.C.).

καταψηφ-ίζομαι, fut. -ιοῦμαι Lys.12.90:—*vote against* or *in condemnation of*, τινος Antipho 1.12, Lys.10.31, Pl.*Ap.*36a, 41d, X.*Ap.* 32: metaph., τῆς ψυχῆς Democr.159; κ. τινὸς θάνατον *pass a vote* of death *against* him, Lys.12.100; κατεψηφισμένοι αὐτοῦ θάνατον X. *HG*1.5.19; κ. τινὸς δειλίαν, κλοπήν, *find* him *guilty* of cowardice, of theft, Lys.14.11, Pl.*Grg.*516a; ἀδικίαν ὑμῶν αὐτῶν Isoc.15.297: abs., οἱ -ψηφισάμενοι δικασταί Pl.*Lg.*878d: later in pf. Act. κατεψήφικα D.H.4.58, 5.8. 2. Pass. (so always in aor.), *to be condemned*, ἑάλωκεν ἤδη καὶ κατεψήφισται D.21.151; θανάτου ἢ φυγῆς καταψηφισθῆναι *to* death or exile, Pl.*R.*558a, cf. *Plt.*299a. b. of the sentence, *to be pronounced against* a person, δίκη κατεψηφισμένη τινός Th.2.53; κατεψηφισμένος ἦν μου ὁ θάνατος X.*Ap.*27, cf. 23; τὰ ὑφ' ὑμῶν -ψηφισθέντα Lys.14.12. 3. Med., *carry measures adverse to* a person, Plu.*Caes.*29. II. *vote in affirmation*, opp. ἀποψηφ-, Arist. *Pol.*1298^{b}39; generally, *come to a determination*, Id.*Po.*1461^{b}2:—so in Pass., τὰ κοινῇ τοῖς Ἀχαιοῖς -ψηφισθέντα εἰς τιμήν τινος D.S.29. 18. 2. metaph., ἀείμνηστον ἡμῶν δόξαν Vett.Val.351.28. **-ισις**, εως, ἡ, *voting against, condemnation*, Antipho 1.3, D.C.36.38 (pl.):—also **-ισμός**, ὁ, Poll.8.149. **-ιστέον**, *one must condemn*, τινος X. *HG*2.4.9, cf. Democr.262.

καταψήχω, *rub down, pound in a mortar*, Nic.*Th.*898. 2. *wear away, consume*, χρόνος πάντα κ. cj. in Simon.176:—Pass., *crumble away*, ῥεῖ πᾶν ἄδηλον καὶ κατέψηκται S.*Tr.*698, cf. Pl.*Ti.*84a. II. *stroke, caress*, ἵππους E.*Hipp.*110; χεῖρα Clearch.25; κόμην Luc.*Am.* 44; ἄκρα γενείου *AP*11.354.12 (Agath.): metaph., ὣς φάτο μειλιχίοισι καταψήχων ὀάροισι A.R.3.1102.

καταψῐθῠρίζω, *whisper against*, τινὸς πρός τινα Plu.2.483c. 2. abs., ἡ ἐπιδίφριος καὶ -ψιθυρίζουσα λέξις *in a low, conversational tone*, Hieronym.ap.Phld.*Rh.*1.199 S.

καταψῑλόω, *strip bare*, in Pass., D.S.20.96.

καταψίω, *crush, grind small*, *EM*818.35.

καταψοφέω, *make a loud noise*, θεὸς κ. βρονταῖς J.*AJ*6.2.2.

κατα-ψυκτικός, ή, όν, *cooling*, Arist.*Resp.*479^{a}31. **-ψυξις**, εως, ἡ, *cooling* or *becoming cold, chill*, αἱ μετὰ καταψύξιος δυσφορίαι Hp. *Prorrh.*1.27, cf. *Coac.*337, al.: freq. in Arist., ὁ φόβος κ. δι' ὀλιγαιμότητά ἐστι *PA*692^{a}23, cf. *Rh.*1389^{b}32; simply, *cold*, Thphr.*HP*6.8. 4. II. = κώνειον (from its effect), Ps.-Dsc.4.78. **-ψῡχος**, ον, = *opacus*, *Gloss.* **-ψυχραίνω**, gloss on σβέννυμι, Sch.Opp.*H.*2. 76. **-ψυχρος**, ον, *very cold*, Hp.*Art.*67, S.E.*P.*1.125, etc.; τόπος Dsc. 2.76; χειμών *Gp.*1.12.33; of character, Vett.Val.11.32, al. **-ψύχω** [ῡ], *cool, chill*, ὕδωρ κ. τὴν ξηρὰν ἀναθυμίασιν Arist.*Mete.*361^{a}2, cf. 368^b 34; ὁ φόβος καταψύχει Id.*PA*650^{b}28, cf. *Pr.*954^{b}13, al.; αἱ ἄτομοι.. κατέψυξαν [τὸ σῶμα] Epicur.*Fr.*60:—Pass., fut. -ψῠγήσομαι Vett.Val. 73.21: pf. -έψυγμαι: aor. -εψύχθην, also -εψύγην [ῠ] Arist.*Pr.*897^a 22:—*to be chilled, become cold*, Hp.*Aph.*4.40, Arist.*HA*531^{b}31, etc.; of persons, κατεψυγμένοι, opp. θερμοί, Id.*Rh.*1389^{b}30. 2. metaph., οὐ -έψυξαν τὴν ὁρμὴν *did* not *allow* their ardour *to cool*, J.*BJ*1.2.7:—Pass., κατέψυκτο τὸ πρακτικόν Plu.*Pomp.*46, cf. Critodem. in *Cat.Cod. Astr.*8(1).259, Vett.Val.l.c. 3. *cool, refresh*, καταψύχει πνοή A. *Fr.*127. II. *dry* land after irrigation, *PCair.Zen.*155 (iii B.C.):—Pass., of a country, χώρα κατεψυγμένη *dried* or *parched up*, D.S.1.7, cf. Plu.*Pomp.*31. III. intr., *cool down*, of persons, Lxx *Ge.*18.4.

κατέᾱγα, κατεάγην [ᾰ], **κατέαξα**, v. κατάγνυμι.

κατ-έαγμα, ατος, τό, later form of κάταγμα, *BGU*647.12 (ii A.D.), *PAmh.*2.93.19 (ii A.D.), *Gloss.* **-εακτέος**, α, ον, = *perfringendus*, ib. **-έαξις**, εως, ἡ, = *confractio*, ib. **-εάσσω**, later form of κατάγνυμι, *break*, ib.:—Pass., Arist.*Mech.*852^{b}22 (though καταγνύῃ, καταγνύμενον occur ib.23, 28), Aesop.179c; cf. κατάσσω.

κατεβλᾰκευμένως, Adv. pf. part. Pass. of καταβλακεύω, *slothfully, tardily*, Ar.*Pl.*325, *AP*4.3a.16 (Agath.).

κατεγγῠ-άω, aor. κατηγγύησα D.33.10, κατενεγύησα J.*AJ*16.7.6, etc.:—*pledge, betroth*, τινά τινι E.*Or.*1079, 1675; γάμον θυγατρός τινι J.*AJ*6.10.2:—Med., Parth.5.3. II. as law-term, *make responsible, compel to give security*, τινὰ πρὸς τὸν πολέμαρχον or πρὸς τῷ -χῳ, D.32.29, 59.40, cf. Pl.*Lg.*871e, *PTeb.*490 (i B.C.), etc.; κ. τινὰ πρὸς εἴκοσι τάλαντα *make* him *give security* to the amount of 20 talents, Plb.5.15.9; πρὸς δίκην τινά Plu.*Tim.*37:—Pass., *to be held to bail*, D.59.49; [ἐγγύην] κ. Pl.*Lg.*872b. 2. *sequester, put an embargo upon*, πυρόν *PAmh.*2.35.23 (ii B.C.). 3. *seize as a security*, ὑπὲρ ἀργυρίου τὴν ναῦν καὶ τοὺς παῖδας D.33.11: metaph., *bind, subject*, τὸ ζῆν λύπαις αὐθαιρέτοις κ. Thales ap.Stob.4.22.65:—Pass., πατρίοις ἔθεσιν κατηγγυημένος Apion ap.J.*Ap.*2.2. 4. in Pass., *undertake* to do, c. inf., Plb.3.5.8. -εύω, *give security*, ποτὶ τοὺς ἱερούς *IG*5(1).1390.69 (Andania, i B.C.). -η, ἡ, *giving of security*, D.25.60. -ησις, εως, ἡ, = *taking of pledges, sequestration*, *PTeb.*148 (ii B.C.), *PRyl.*119.13 (i A.D.). -ητικά, ῶν, τά, *betrothal*, *Gloss.*

κάτεγγυς, Adv. *near*, c. gen., prob. in Hippon.42.

κατέγ-κειμαι, v.l. for κάτω ἔγκ., Hp.*Mul.*2.137. -**κλημα**, ατος, τό, *accusation*, Eust.922.46. -**κονέω**, *to be in great haste*, Hsch. -**κρᾰτεύομαι**, strengthd. for ἐγκρατ-, c. acc., Suid.

κατεγνῡπωμένως, Adv., v. καταγνυπόομαι.

κατεγχειρέω, *treat fully, discuss thoroughly*, Phld.*Mort.*4, *Lib.*p.27 O. II. *plot against* one, abs., Them.*Or.*19.232a.

κατεγχλῐδάω, *look haughtily down upon*, τινι Macho ap.Ath.13.577e.

κατεδᾰφίζω, *dash to earth*, Suid.:—Pass., Sch.E.*Hec.*21.

κατέδω, Homeric pres., = κατεσθίω, *eat up, devour*, μυίας αἵ ῥά τε φῶτας .. κατέδουσιν Il.19.31; εὐλαὶ .. φῶτας ἀρηϊφάτους κ. 24.415: metaph., οἶκον, βίοτον, κτῆσιν κ., *eat up* house, goods, etc., Od.2.237, 19.159,534; ὃν θυμὸν κατέδων *eating* one's heart for grief, Il.6.202:—later in Pass., ὑπὸ ὄφεως κατέδεσθαι Arist.*Fr.*145.—For fut. κατέδομαι and other tenses, v. κατεσθίω.

κατεζητημένως, Adv. pf. part. Pass. from καταζητέω, *in a far-fetched, recondite style*, Vett.Val.301.29.

κατεηγώς, Ion. pf. 2 part. of κατάγνυμι, for κατεαγώς.

κατεθίζω, aor. -είθισα Plb.4.21.3:—*make customary*, τινί τι l.c.:—Pass., τὰ -ειθισμένα ἱερεῖα D.S.12.30, cf. *EM*752.38. 2. *accustom, habituate*, ῥαθυμίᾳ τινάς Ath.Med.ap.Orib.*inc.*21.1.

κατείβω, poet. for καταλείβω, *let flow down, shed*, τί νυ δάκρυ κατείβετον Od.21.86:—Med., *flow apace*, θαλερὸν δὲ κατείβετο δάκρυ παρειῶν Il.24.794; τὸ κατειβόμενον Στυγὸς ὕδωρ Styx's *downward flowing* water, Od.5.185: metaph., κατείβετο δὲ γλυκὺς αἰών life *was flowing, passing away*, ib.152: rare in Att., τί δάκρυον κατείβεται; Ar.*Lys.*127 (paratrag.). II. trans., *flood, overflow*, metaph., Ἔρος κατείβων καρδίαν Alcm.36:—Pass., *overflow with*, γλυκερῇ κατείβετο θυμὸν ἀνίῃ, A.R.3.290; κατείβετο θυμὸς ἀκουῇ ib.1131.

κατεῖδον, inf. κατιδεῖν, part. κατῐδών, aor. 2 with no pres. in use, καθοράω being used instead:—*look down*, Περγάμου ἐκ κατιδών Il.4.508 (nisi leg. ἐκκατ-). II. c. acc., *look down upon, view*, τὰς νήσους ἁπάσας ἐν κύκλῳ Ar.*Eq.*170. 2. *see, behold, regard*, Thgn.905, A.*Pers.*1026 (lyr.); *catch sight of*, τὰς νέας Hdt.7.194, cf. E.*Supp.*1044; κατιδεῖν βίον *to live*, A.*Ag.*474 (lyr.). 3. of mental vision, *perceive, discern*, S.*OT*338, Pl.*Euthphr.*2c. III. Med. in act. sense, aor. 2 κατειδόμην, inf. κατιδέσθαι, τι Hdt.4.179, 7.208, S.*El.*892, etc.; κατιδέσθαι ἔς τι Hdt.5.35.

κατείδωλος, ον, *full of idols, given to idolatry*, *Act.Ap.*17.16.

κατεικάζω, *liken to*, κατεικάζουσιν ἡμᾶς ἰσχάδι Eup.345:—Pass., *to be* or *become like*, ὦ.. τοῖς ἐν Αἰγύπτῳ νόμοις φύσιν κατεικασθέντε S.*OC*338. II. *guess, surmise*, Hdt.6.112; ἐν ὑπονοίῃ κ. Hp.*Ep.*17; *suspect*, Hdt.9.109.

κατεικής, ές, = ἐπιεικής, Hsch.

κατεικονίζω, *imaginor*, *Gloss.*

κατειλάδα· ἡμέραν χειμερινήν, Hsch.; cf. κατουλάς.

κατειλ-έω, *force into a narrow space, coop up*, in Pass., ἐς τὸ τεῖχος Hdt.1.80; ἐς τὸ ἄστυ ib.176; ἐς Διὸς ἱρόν Id.5.119, cf. Onos.42.19, Parth.32.2; εἰς χωρία προσάντη Plu.*Cam.*41; ἐν ὀλίγῳ χώρῳ.. πολλαὶ μυριάδες κατειλημέναι Hdt.9.70, cf. J.*AJ*14.16.2, al.; ἐρευγμὸς εἴσω κατειλούμενος Hp.*Coac.*622, cf. Arist.*Pr.*869[a]21; τοιαύτην δίνην κατειληθῆναι τοῖς ἄστροις Epicur.*Ep.*2 p.40 U. b. καταϝελμένων τῶν πολιατᾶν *when* the citizens *are assembled*, *Leg.Gort.*10.35, 11.13. 2. *wrap up*, X.*Eq.*10.7, Ael.*NA*5.3, 15.10 (Pass.); ταινίᾳ κατειλημένος τὴν ὀσφύν Diocl.*Fr.*142; κατειλημένος ταινίαις τὴν κεφαλήν Luc.*Symp.*47; τελαμῶνι τὸν μηρὸν -ειλημένον Paus.8.28.6. 3. *roll up*, βιβλίον Luc.*Alex.*20. II. v. κατίλλω. -ησις, εως, ἡ, *crowding, compression*, Epicur.*Ep.*2 pp.46,54 U. 2. *wrapping*, εἰρίων Aret.*CA*2.9, cf. Herod.Med.ap.Orib.10.18.1; -ησία is f.l. in Archig.ap.Gal.13.168. -ητέον, *one must wrap*, Antyll.ap.Orib.7.21.8.

κατείλια (fort. -είλεα)· τὰ ἐσώτερα οἰκήματα (Erythr.), Hsch.

κατειλίσσω, v. καθελίσσω.

κατειλυσπάομαι, Pass., *wriggle down*, Ar.*Lys.*722.

κατειλύω, *cover up*, κὰδ δέ μιν αὐτὸν εἰλύσω ψαμάθοισιν Il.21.318; ἐν βοείαις A.R.3.206; ὄρος πέτρινον ψάμμῳ κατειλυμένον Hdt.2.8.

κατειλωτισμένος, (Εἵλωτες) *reduced to serfdom*, Suid.

κάτειμι, Dor. 3 sg. [κάτε]ιτι *Berl.Sitzb.*1927.166 (Cyrene), part. fem. κατίασσα ibid.: Ep. impf. κατήϊεν Od.10.159: (εἶμι *ibo*):—*go, come down*, ποταμόνδε Od. l.c.; Ἴδηθεν Il.4.475: in Trag., as fut. to κατέρχομαι, E.*Alc.*73, etc.; esp. *go down* to the grave, κατίμεν δόμον Ἄϊδος εἴσω Il.14.457; Ἀϊδόσδε 20.294; εἰς Ἅιδου δόμους E. l.c.; so κάτειμι alone, S.*Ant.*896; of a ship, *sail down* to land, νῆα.. κατιοῦσαν ἐς λιμέν' ἡμέτερον Od.16.472; of a person, *travel down* the Nile, κ. ἐπὶ or εἰς Ἀλεξάνδρειαν, *PLips.*45.12,14 (iv A.D.); of a river, ποταμὸς πεδίονδε κάτεισι χειμάρρους Il.11.492; of a wind, *come sweeping down*, Th.2.25, 6.2; ὡς τὸ πνεῦμα κατήει Id.2.84: metaph., ὀνείδεα κατιόντα ἀνθρώπῳ φιλέει ἐπανάγειν τὸν θυμόν Hdt.7.160; ἅμα ταῖς πολιαῖς κατιούσαις Ar.*Eq.*520. II. *come back, return*, ἀγρόθεν Od.13.267; ἐς ἄστυ 15.505; of exiles, *return home*, Hdt.1.62, 3.45, 5.62, A.*Ag.*1283, And.1.80, etc.; ἐκ τῶν Μήδων Hdt.4.3:—as Pass. of κατάγω, E.*Med.*1015; ὑπὸ τῶν ἑταίρων παρακληθεὶς κάτεισι Th.8.48. III. *come in*, of revenue, *PFay.*20.7 (iii/iv A.D.).

κατεῖναι, Ion. for καθεῖναι, aor. 2 inf. of καθίημι.

κατείνυον, v. καταέννυμι.

κατειπεῖν, inf. κατειπεῖν, used as aor. to the pres. καταγορεύω (κατερῶ (v. κατερέω) being the fut.):—also in form **κατεῖπα** Hdt.2.89, Ar.*Pax* 20:—*speak against* or *to the prejudice of, accuse, denounce*, τινος Ar.*Pax* 377, *Th.*340; κ. τινὸς πρός τινα Pl.*Tht.*149a, cf. X.*Mem.*2.6.33: abs., *give information*, Hdt.2.89; πρὸς τοὺς βασιλέας *SIG*986.7 (Chios, v/iv B.C.). II. c. acc., *declare, report*, εἴ σοι γάμον κατεῖπον E.*Med.*589; κ. τοῖς θεαταῖς τὸν λόγον Ar.*V.*54; τὰν Σάμῳ ib.283 (lyr.); πατέρα κ. *make* him *known*, E.*Ion* 1345; κ. τοὺς ποιήσαντας, τὰ γεγενημένα, *denounce* them, And.2.7: c. acc. et part., κ. σῷ κασιγνήτῳ πόσιν ἥκοντα E.*Hel.*898; *enumerate*, φύλλα δένδρων *Anacreont.*13.2. 2. abs., *tell*, κάτειπέ μοι *tell* me, Ar.*Nu.*155, *Pl.*86: folld. by interrog., κ. ὅκως.. Hdt.1.20; πόθεν.. Ar.*Pax* 20; ὅ τι σιωπᾷς, κ. μοι ib.657; πρὸς σὲ κ., ἐφ' οἷς ἐλύπησάν με Isoc.5.17, etc.

κατεῖρα· ἀσπίς, πέλτη, Hsch. (fort. καιτρέα).

κατειργᾰθόμην, poet. aor. Med. of κατείργω, A.*Eu.*566.

κατείργω, Ion. -έργω (v. ἔργω), Cypr. aor. 2 κατέϝοργον *Inscr. Cypr.*135.1 H.:—also -έργνυμι (v. infr.), Att. also **καθείργω, καθείργνυμι** (q.v.): fut. -είρξω, Ion. -έρξω:—*drive into, shut in*, τοὺς περιγενομένους ἐς τὰς νέας κατεῖρξαν Hdt.5.63; κατεργνῦσι [αὐτοὺς] ἐς μέσα τὰ φρύγανα *shut* them *up* into the middle of the fire-wood, Id.4.69: generally, *press hard, reduce to straits*, κατέργοντες πολλὸν τοὺς Ἀθηναίους Id.6.102; *besiege*, πτόλιν *Inscr.Cypr.* l.c.:—Pass., *to be hemmed in, kept down*, ὑπὸ τοῦ δυνατωτέρου Th.1.76; ὑπ' ἀνάγκης D.H.6.2; ὅρκοις -ειργόμενοι ib.45; τὸ πολέμῳ καὶ δεινῷ τινι -ειργόμενον *what is done under stress of*.., Th.4.98. II. *hinder, prevent*, τινα E.*Med.*1258 (lyr.): c. acc. et inf., κατείργοντας νεκροὺς τάφου.. λαχεῖν Id.*Supp.*308: abs., *delay*, Id.*Alc.*256 (lyr.); *limit*, τὴν φιλαρχίαν Plu.*Pomp.*53.

κατειρωνεύομαι, *use irony towards, banter*, τινας Plu.2.211d, cf. *Cat.Ma.*11; τινος J.*BJ*7.8.1, al., Jul.*Or.*6.198b; τῆς ἀγνοίας J.*BJ*4.3.1: abs., -όμενος *jestingly*, Parth.7.2, cf. Plu.*Agis* 18. 2. *treat in a spirit of raillery*, τι Id.*Comp.Dem.Cic.*1. II. *feign*, πένθος J.*BJ*2.2.5. 2. *conceal, dissimulate*, τὴν ἐξουσίαν, τὸν χρησμόν, Plu.*Phoc.*29, *Comp.Ages.Pomp.*1; ὑπόσχεσιν Aristaenet.1.4.

κατεισ-άγω [ᾰγ], *display to one's own loss*, μωρίαν *AP*10.91 (Pall.). -**ᾰγωγεύς**, έως, ὁ, *magistrate's clerk*, *POxy.*2154.7 (iv A.D.). -**ᾰγωγή**, ἡ, *disparagement*, Phld.*Vit.*1457.9 (pl.). -**έρχομαι**, *return*, *Sammelb.*4284.8, etc.

κατεκλύω, *cause to relax in* one's *effort*, τὸν Ἀντίοχον Plb.5.63.2.

κατέκτᾰθεν, Aeol. and Ep. 3 pl. aor. 1 Pass. of κατακτείνω (q.v.).

κατεκτός, Adv. *outside*, c. gen., τοῦ σώματος *Corp.Herm.*2.8.

κατέλαιος, ον, *oily*, Archestr.*Fr.*57.9.

κατελαύνω, *drive down*, τὰς ἀγέλας Longus 2.10; τὰς ναῦς *bring* them *in*, Plu.*Nic.*14. 2. *push down*, τὴν σπαθίδα [ἐς τὴν λήκυθον] Ar.*Fr.*205. 3. sens. obsc., κ. γυναικός, = Lat. *subagitare*, Id.*Pax* 711, *Ec.*1082; τινα Theoc.5.116. 4. κατελάσαι· καταπῆξαι, Hsch.

κατελέγχω, *convict of falsehood, belie*, σὲ δὲ μή τι νόον κατελεγχέτω εἶδος Hes.*Op.*714, cf. Tyrt.10.9 (tm.); ἔργῳ οὐ κατ' εἶδος ἐλέγχων Pi.*O.*8.19:—Pass., ὑπό τινος *PSI*4.442.20. II. *disgrace*, Pi.*P.*8.36; ἀνδρῶν ἀρετάν Id.*I.*3.14. III. *betray*, ὑλακῇ τινας, of dogs, Poll.5.42.

κατελεέω, strengthd. for ἐλεέω, *have compassion* upon, τινα or τι, Pl.*R.*415c, And.2.15, Lys.6.3; τὰς συμφορὰς Plb.2.6.2: abs., Arist.*HA*631[a]19.

κατελίσσω, v. καθελίσσω. **κατέλκω**, Ion. for καθέλκω.

κατελπ-ίζω, *hope* or *expect confidently*, κ. εὐπετέως τῆς θαλάσσης κρατήσειν Hdt.8.136, cf. Plb.2.31.8; μηδὲν ἄγαν κ. D.S.15.33, cf. Phld.*Oec.*p.73 J.: c. gen., *base* one's *hopes upon*, τῆς αὐτῶν δυνάμεως J.*AJ*5.1.20:—Pass., ἀποβαίνειν οἷα κατηλπίσθη Phld.*Lib.*p.27 O. -**ισμός**, ὁ, *confident hope*, Plb.3.82.8.

κατεμβλέπω, strengthd. for ἐμβλέπω, LXX *Ex.*3.6. II. *look down upon, despise*, c. dat., Phld.*Vit.*p.37 J.

κατεμέω, aor. 1 -έμεσα, *vomit, be sick over*, τινος Ar.*Fr.*152, Ael.*NA*4.36, Luc.*Sat.*38.

κατεμμᾰτέω, = ἐμματέω, ἐμματεύω, Nic.*Al.*536.

κατεμπάζω, = καταλαμβάνω, ὁππόταν χρειώ σε -εμπάζῃ Nic.*Th.*695.

κατέμπαρσις, v. κατέπαρσις.

κατεμπείρω, = καταπείρω, τὴν τοῦ ἐμβρυουλκοῦ καμπήν Philum.ap. Aët.16.23 (s.v.l.).

κατεμπορεύομαι, sine expl., c. gen., Suid.

κατεμφορέομαι, Med., *take one's fill of*, τινος Eun.*Hist.*p.256 D.

κατεναίρομαι, *slay, murder*, κατενήρατο χαλκῷ Od.11.519, cf. Nic.*Al.*401: aor. Act. κατήνᾰρον S.*Ant.*871 (lyr.), Call.*Ap.*101, *AP*7.201 (Pamphil.); -ένηρα Orph.*A.*666.

κατ-έναντα, Adv. *over against, opposite*, c. gen., Cydias 1, Pancrat. *Oxy.*1085.24, Q.S.1.552, Man.3.176: c. dat., Id.6.277: abs., Id.3.132:—also -**έναντι** LXX *Ex.*19.2; πύλη ἡ κ. ib.*Ez.*11.1; κώμη ἡ κ. ὑμῶν *Ev.Marc.*11.2, cf. *UPZ*79.11 (ii B.C.), *Inscr.Prien.*37.170 (ii

B.C.). -εναντίον, = foreg., τινι Il.21.567; ἀλλήλοισιν AP9.132, Man.1.215, etc.; ἐκείνου (v.l. ἐκείνῳ) Hes.Sc.73, cf. A.R.2.360; τῆς ἀκροπόλιος Hdt.3.144: abs., Man.1.285:—also -εναντία, νήσου A.R. 2.1116: abs., κ. κεῖνται D.P.114. -εναντιόω, pf. part. Pass. -ηναντιωμένος in opposition to, τοῖς προειρημένοις Phld.Po.Herc.1676.3.

κατενᾰρίζω, strengthd. for ἐναρίζω, kill outright: aor. Pass. κατηναρίσθης A.Ch.347 (lyr.): pf. part. Pass. κατηναρισμένος S.Aj.26.

κατένασσε, v. καταναίω.

κατένεξις, εως, ἡ, (κατενεγκεῖν) = καταφορά, Suid. s. v. καταλύσας, Eust.152.14.

κατενεχῠρ-άζω, pledge, pawn, Poll.3.84 (v.l. -ιάζω), 8.148. -ᾰσία, ἡ, pledging, Jahresh.18 Beibl.287 (Ephesus, i B.C.). -ασμός, ὁ, = foreg., Poll.8.148.

κατενήνοθεν, 3 sg. and pl. plpf., covered, πολλὴ δὲ κόνις κ. ὤμους Hes.Sc.269; ξανθαὶ δὲ κόμαι κ. ὤμους h.Cer.279; cf. ἐπενήνοθε.

κατενιαύσιος, ὁ, title of an annual magistrate at Gela, IG14.256, 257.

κατεν-ισχύω, become firmly established, ἐπὶ τῆς βασιλείας v.l. in Lxx 1Ch.29.30 (2Ch.1.1). -τείνομαι, strengthd. for ἐντείνομαι, M.Ant.4.3. -τευκτής, οῦ, ὁ, accuser, Lxx Jb.7.20. -τρῠφάω, c. gen., = ἐντρυφάω κατά τινος, Iamb.Bab.11. -τυγχάνω, seek an interview with, τινι PGen.31.4 (ii A.D.). II. plead against, accuse, Suid. and Phot. s. v. κατεντευκτήν. III. κ(ατ)εντευχθέντα· κατεντυχηθέντα, Hsch.

κατένωπα (cf. Hdn.Gr.2.94, κατενῶπα or κατ' ἐνῶπα Aristarch. ap.Hdn.Gr. l. c.), over against, right opposite, c. gen., Il.15.320, Orph. L.132, 464: c. acc., Puchstein Epigr.Gr.p.76 (Memphis):—also -ενώπιον, τινος Lxx Jo.1.5, Ep.Eph.1.4, al., BGU954.6 (vi A.D.).

κατεξᾰγιάζω, assay, Arch.Anz.38/39.154 (Pass.).

κατεξ-ανάστᾰσις, εως, ἡ, rebellion against, resistance to, τινος Longin.7.3; δόξης καὶ πλούτου Iamb.VP16.69. -αναστᾰτικός, ή, όν, fit for resisting, ἀλγηδόνων, ὀχληρῶν, S.E.M.11.104, 106; ἀρετὴ κ. δικαιοσύνης M.Ant.8.39. -ανίσταμαι, aor. 2 Act. κατεξανέστην, rise up against, struggle against, τινος Ph.2.47, Plu.Alex.6; τῆς τύχης Eun. Hist.p.256 D.; τοῦ πάθους D.S.10.7; κατεξαναστῆναι τοῦ μέλλοντος to be on one's guard against.., Plb.Fr.172; τοῦ πολέμου Plu.Demetr.22; παντὸς δεινοῦ D.S.17.21. 2. rise, -ιστάμενα [νέφη] Cat.Cod.Astr. 8(1).139. -εράω, vomit upon, τὸ φλέγμα κ. τινός Arr.Epict.3.13.23: metaph., [χόλιά] τινος ib.3.21.6. -ετάζω, decide, try, δίκην Cod. Just.1.4.29 Intr.; examine carefully, Agath.5.9 (Pass.). -ευμᾰρίζω, strengthd. for ἐξευμαρίζω, Hsch. -ουσία, ἡ, sovereignty, dominion, τῶν νερτέρων θεῶν IG14.1047.5 (= Tab.Defix.Aud.188): c. gen., power over, τοῦ βιοθανάτου πνεύματος PMag.Par.1.1949; also δὸς αὐτῷ τὴν κ. κατὰ τῶν ἐχθρῶν αὐτοῦ CIG4710 (Egypt). -ουσιάζω, exercise authority over, τινος Ev.Matt.20.25, Ev.Marc.10.42; τῶν ὅλων Jul. Gal.100c.

κατεπ-αγγελία, ἡ, promise, Gloss. -αγγέλλομαι, Med. with pf. Pass., make promises or engagements, τινι with one, D.32.11; τὸ παρὸν λυμαινόμενος, τὸ δὲ μέλλον κ. Aeschin.3.223; promise, c. acc., τινὶ τιμήν J.AJ8.14.4; κ. τῇ φιλίᾳ τὴν πολιτείαν devote it to..., Plu. 2.807b: c. pres. inf., τέχνας -όμενος διδάσκειν Aeschin.1.117, cf. Ph. 2.316: c. fut. inf., κ. πρός τινας λήσειν Aeschin.1.173; προκαταλήψεσθαι τὰς παρόδους D.S.11.4: abs., μέχρι τοῦ -αγγείλασθαι Phld. Rh.2.3 S.:—Pass., ἡ -ομένη ζημία J.AJ6.5.3. -άγω [ᾰγ], bring down upon, τιμωρίαν τινί Plu.2.551d (sed leg. -επείγει): κατεπάγων is f.l. for κἆτ' ἐπ. in Ar.Eq.25. -ᾴδω, subdue by song or enchantment, τινα Pl.Grg.483e, Men.80a, Plu.Dio14, Lib.Or.64.91; τὰς τῶν νέων ψυχάς Max.Tyr.23.3; overcome by a spell, Phld.Lib.p.29 O.; soothe, τινος Ach.Tat.7.10. 2. sing by way of enchantment, Id.2. 7. II. to be always repeating, Ph.2.304, Anon.ap.Suid., Hld.7. 10, Ach.Tat.2.19. -αίρομαι, Pass., to be arrogant towards, c. gen., Sm.Ps.60(61).3, Just.Nov.129 Praef. -άλληλος, ον, = ἐπάλληλος, κίνησις dub. l. in Sch.A.R.3.1018. -άλμενος, -αλτο, v. καταπάλλομαι, κατεφάλλομαι. -ᾰμύνω, strengthd. for ἐπαμύνω, c. acc., Suid.

κατέπαρσις, εως, ἡ, insertion, ἀγκίστρων Sor.2.40 cod. (pl., leg. κατέμπ– vel κατάπ–).

κατεπ-είγω, press down, χαλεπὸν κατὰ γῆρας ἐπείγει Il.23.623. 2. press hard, οἱ χρῆσται κατήπειγον αὐτόν his creditors were pressing him hard, D.33.6, cf. Th.1.61; κατεπείγει ὕδωρ ῥέον the ebbing water (of the clepsydra) urges him on, Pl.Tht.172e; ἡ φιλοτιμία κατήπειγεν αὐτόν Id.Ep.338e: c. acc. et inf., οὐδὲν ἡμᾶς ἐστὶ τὸ κατεπεῖγον τὸ μὴ.. σκοπεῖν Id.Lg.781e; οὐδὲν ὑμᾶς κ. ἀκοῦσαι D.24.18; τὸ -επεῖγον πράττειν X.Mem.2.1.2; τὰ ἀναλώματα τὰ -επείγοντα PFlor.161.5 (iii A.D.); τὸ κ. alone, the urgent symptom, Gal.17(2). 426; οὔτε τι κωλύει οὔτε -επείγει Hp.Fract.14; τὰ μάλιστα -επείγοντα Isoc.8.132, cf. Plb.1.66.6; τῶν ἐν ἐκείνῳ μὲν τῷ χρόνῳ πραχθέντων, ῥηθῆναι δὲ νῦν οὐ -επειγόντων not urgently requiring mention, Isoc.12. 192; τῆς ὥρας -επειγούσης Plb.3.99.9; θόρυβος φόβος μετὰ φωνῆς -επείγων Stoic.3.98:—Pass., to be pressed, Hyp.(?)Oxy.1607.43, Phld.Rh.1.138 S.; περί τινος PCair.Zen.530 (iii B.C.). II. intr., hasten, make haste, ἕπου κατεπείγων Ar.Ec.293: c. inf., Βοιωτοὶ οὐδέν τι κατήπειγον ξυνάψαι were in no haste, X.HG4.2.18; οὐδέν κω κατεπείγων αὐτὸς ἥκειν prob. in Hdt.8.126. III. Med., hasten, ἐκ Κορίνθου Ἀθήναζε Alciphr.3.51. 2. c. gen., to be anxious, long for.., Plb.5.37.10, 30.5.9: also c. dat., press for, τῷ ἐφοδίῳ PSI6.603. 22 (iii B.C.). -ειξις, εως, ἡ, bustling, hurrying, Stoic.3.98.

κατεπεμβαίνω, overflow to its injury, θάλασσα κ. τῆς γῆς Sch.Opp. H.2.34. II. plant one's foot firmly upon, κορυφαιότητι Corp.Herm. 18.16.

κατέπεφνον, Ep., Lyr., and Trag. (in lyr.) aor. 2 with no pres. in use (v. θείνω), kill, slay, καταπέφνῃ Il.3.281; κατέπεφνε 6.183, 24. 759, Od.3.252, 4.534, S.El.486; κατέπεφνες Id.Aj.901, Pi.Fr.171 (tm.); καταπεφνών Il.17.539.

κατεπι-γάστριος, ον, abdominal, μύες Gal.7.199. -δείκνῦμαι, Med., show off before another, M.Ant.11.13. -δέω, bandage afresh, Gal.18(2).387. -θεσις, εως, ἡ, = δόλος, Aq.Ps.31(32).2, 119(120). 3. -θῡμέω, strengthd. for ἐπιθυμέω, Eun.VS p.477 B., Phot. and Suid. s. v. λίχνος. -θύμιος [ῡ], ον, desirable, Gloss. -θῡμος, ον, very eager, c. inf., Lxx Ju.12.16. -κειμαι, Pass., lie, rest upon, IG14.1888, CIG4152d (Amastris). -κύπτω, bow down upon, Lxx Es.15.10 (v.l. ἐπέκυψεν). -ορκέω, commit perjury against, τῶν θεῶν Nicol.Prog. in Rh.1.348, 365 W. II. Med., effect by perjury, οὐ κατεπιορκησόμενος τὸ πρᾶγμα D.54.40.

κατεπίσταμαι, know fully, Ael.Fr.284.

κατεπιτηδεύω, finish too elaborately, of style, D.H.Th.42.

κατεπι-φύω, in Med., = καταφύω II, Hsch. -χειρέω, lay hands upon, attempt, τοῦ πράγματος AB154, cf. Eustr. in EN51.21.

κατεποικοδομέω, build over or upon, in Pass., CIG3281 (Smyrna).

κατεπτηχότως, Adv., (καταπτήσσω) in abject fear, Poll.3.137.

κατεράω, pour out, pour off, Str.17.1.38, Plu.2.968d; εἰς ἀγγεῖον Agatharch.28, Dsc.1.30. II. pour over, δυσφημίαν κ. τοῦ δικαστηρίου Demetr.Eloc.302; κατὰ τῶν ξηρῶν Gal.13.53.

κατεργ-άζομαι, fut. -άσομαι, later 3 sg. -ᾶται PTeb.10.2 (ii B.C.): aor. κατειργασάμην, and (in pass. sense) κατειργάσθην (v. infr.): pf. κατείργασμαι both in act. and pass. sense (v. infr.):—effect by labour, achieve, πρήγματα μεγάλα Hdt.5.24; πᾶν S.El.1022; μόρον.. ἐπαλλήλοιν χεροῖν Id.Ant.57; ταὖθ' ἁπινοεῖς Ar.Ec.247; τὰ δυνατά Th.4.65; τὰ πρὸς εὐδαιμονίαν Phld.Rh.2.31 S.; μεγάλα μὲν ἐπινοεῖτε, ταχὺ δὲ κατεργάζεσθε X.Hier.2.2; κ. εἰρήνην τινί And.3.8; ἣν κατεργάσῃ if you do the job, Ar.Eq.933: pf. κατείργασμαι, μέγιστα ἔργα X.Mem. 3.5.11: in pass. sense, to have been effected or achieved, Hdt.1.123, 141, 4.66, E.IT1081, etc.; κατειργασμένη ὠφέλεια Antipho 2.1.4; ἐλθεῖν ἐπὶ κατειργασμένοις Lys.31.9: aor. -ειργάσθην Luc.Herm.5. b. earn, gain by labour, acquire, τὴν ἡγεμονίην Hdt.3.65; πόλει σωτηρίαν E. Heracl.1046; μεγάλα τῇ πόλει Aeschin.3.229; τοῦτο D.45.66; ὁ κατειργασμένος τὴν τυραννίδα Pl.Grg.473d: in pass. sense, ἀρετὴ ἀπὸ σοφίης κατεργασμένη Hdt.7.102. c. abs., achieve one's object, be successful, αὐτὸς ἑωυτῷ Id.5.78; simply, work, ἐν τοῖς ἐργαστηρίοις PTeb.ined.703.148. 2. c. acc. pers., make an end of, finish, kill, ἑωυτόν Hdt.1.24, cf. E.Hipp.888, etc.; λέοντα βίᾳ S.Tr. 1094. b. overpower, subdue, conquer, Hdt.6.2, Ar.Eq.842, Th.4. 85, Isoc.9.59, etc.; τὴν Ἑλλάδα Hdt.8.100; ποσὶ καὶ στόματι κ. [τινά] attack him, of a horse, Id.5.111: in pass. sense, of land, μακέλλῃ τῇ κατείργασται πέδον is subdued, brought under cultivation, A.Ag. 526; κατεργαζομένη ἡ γῆ Thphr.CP3.1.3; later trans., cultivate, PTeb.10.2 (ii B.C.), etc. c. prevail upon, κατεργάσατο καὶ ἀνέπεισε Ξέρξην, ὥστε.. Hdt.7.6, cf. X.Mem.2.3.16, Parth.13.1, Plu.Fab.21; κ. τινὰ πειθοῖ Str.10.4.2:—Pass., οὐκ ἐδύνατο κατεργασθῆναι [ἡ γυνή] could not be prevailed upon, Hdt.9.108. d. c. dupl. acc., do something to one, καλόν τι τὴν πόλιν And.2.17 (but κ. τὴν πόλιν carry on business in the city, SIG899 (Mesambria, iii A.D.)). II. till, cultivate land, PSI6.632.9 (iii B.C.), etc.; work up for use, freq. of food, by chewing or digestion, ὀδόντας ἔχει οἷς κ. τὴν τροφήν Arist.HA501b 30, cf. Juv.469a31, Spir.482b16, Gal.11.649 (Pass.); τὸ -αζόμενον ἔχειν εὔρωστον a strong digestion, Id.17(2).430; κ. τὰ ἐδέσματα Sch. Ar.Eq.714; by grinding (of corn), Longus 3.30, cf. D.H.5.13 (Pass.); by ripening (of fruits), κατειργασμένα ἐπὶ τοῦ δένδρου Gal.11.367; κ. μέλι make.., Hdt.4.194; κ. τὴν κόπρον prepare it, Arist.HA552a 24; σίδηρον D.27.10; ξύλα -ειργασμένα Thphr.CP5.17.2; στίππυον τὸ κατειργαζμένον PCair.Zen.472.9 (iii B.C.); λίθους D.S.1.98. 2. turn bullion into coin, PCair.Zen.21.6 (iii B.C.). III. work at, practise, ἄλλην μελέτην κ. Pl.Ti.88c. IV. κ. ὄρη level them, J.AJ 11.3.4 (fr. Lxx 1Es.4.4). -ᾰσία, ἡ, working up, freq. of food, by digestion or by chewing, Arist.PA675b5, Pr.931a32, etc.; ἡ τοῦ πυρὸς κ. stewing, boiling, Mnesith.ap.Ath.2.59b: generally, production, χυμῶν (in the body) Hp.Praec.9; κοιλωμάτων Epicur.Ep.1 p.9 U. (pl.); σίτου Phld.Oec.pp.51, 55 J.; working or manufacture, ἐλαίου Thphr. CP1.19.4; cultivation of land, ib.1.16.6 (pl.), 3.20.1, PTeb.61(b).129 (ii B.C.), etc.; καρπῶν D.S.1.14; of mines, Str.3.2.10; ξύλων Bito 52. 2; παραδείγματος Lxx 1Ch.28.19; τυγχάνειν κατεργασίας ἀφ' ἡλίου, of vapour, D.L.7.153; completion, κ. λαμβάνειν Thphr.HP1.12. 2. -ασμα, ατος, τό, work, achievement, Aq.Ps.45(46).9, Pr.8. 22. -αστέον, one must promote digestion, Xenocr.ap.Orib.2.58.90; one must combat, counteract, of poison, Dsc.Ther.Praef. -αστικός, ή, όν, of or for accomplishing, effective, δύναμις Thphr.CP1.8.4. II. likely to wear out, consume, Hp.Coac.472; of fire, Vett.Val.345.18 (Comp.).

κατεργολᾰβέω, exact tribute, Phld.Rh.1.224 S.

κάτεργος, ον, worked, cultivated, χώρα Thphr.CP5.14.5. II. κάτεργον, τό, wages, PHib.1.119 (iii B.C.), PRev.Laws45.8 (iii B.C.), PCair.Zen.472.6 (iii B.C.), etc.; labour-costs, τὸ εἰς τὴν πλίνθον κ. γεινόμενον PSI4.365.4 (iii B.C.), cf. PLille1.50 (iii B.C.); εἰς κ. τῆς σκηνῆς for the service of the tabernacle, Lxx Ex.30.16; εἰς πάντα τὰ κ. αὐτῆς ib.35.21.

κατέρεαι· κάθισαι (Paph.), Hsch.

κατερέθω, irritate, provoke, in Pass., Hsch.

κατερείδω, intr., swoop down, of a storm, D.Chr.74.7.

κατερείκω, bruise, grind, κάχρυς κατηριγμέναι Demon 22: metaph., θυμὸν κατερεῖξαι *crush, subdue*, Ar.*V*.649 :—Med., *rend one's garments*, in token of sorrow, κίθωνας Sapph.62, cf. Hdt.3.66, A.*Pers.* 538 (anap.).

κατερειπ-όω, = sq., in pf. part. Pass., D.S.32.14, Hld.9.5, Porph. *Plot.*12, *Gloss.* **-ω**, *throw* or *cast down*, Ἴλιον κατερεῖψαι Pi.*Pae.* 8.33; κατὰ γάρ μιν ἐρείπει πῦρ Orac.ap.Hdt.7.140; σεισμοὶ κατήρειψαν πολὺ τῆς κατοικίας Str.6.1.6, cf. Max.Tyr.1.3: metaph., κ. τινά *ruin, corrupt* him, Plu.*Sol.*6 :—Pass., *fall in ruins*, of Troy, E.*Hec.*477 (lyr.); [τὸ τεῖχος] κατερήρειπτο Hdn.8.2.4 codd.; κατερηρειμμένα *IG* 5(1).538.22 (Sparta); κατηριμμένα ib.12(5).1097.11 (Ceos, ii A.D.), 12(3).324.17 (Thera, ii A.D.). II. intr. in aor. 2, *fall down, fall prostrate*, [ὑπὸ ποταμοῦ] ἔργα κατήριπε κάλ' αἰζηῶν Il.5.92; κ. ἐς μέλαν ὕδωρ Theoc.13.49: pf., τεῖχος μὲν γὰρ δὴ κατερήριπεν Il.14.55. **-ωσις**, εως, ἡ, *overthrow*, Suid. (-ρίπ- codd.).

κατερεύγομαι, aor. 2 -ήρῠγον, *belch over* or *upon*, θερμόν τί τινος Ar.*V*.1151.

κατερεύθω, *make all red*, κατὰ δ' αἵματι πόντον ἐρ. Opp.*H.*2.612.

κατερευνάω, *lay bare, uncover*, τὸν Ἡσαῦ Lxx *Je.*29(49).10 (-εραυν-, v.l. κατέσυρα); κατερευνᾷ, = *dirimat*, *Gloss.*

κατερέφω, *cover over, roof*, τὰς σκηνὰς κλήμασιν Plu.*Caes.*9; ἀλλήλους τοῖς θυρεοῖς Id.*Ant.*49 :—Med., *roof over for oneself* or *what is one's own*, κατηρέψασθε κεράμῳ τὸ νῶτον Ar.*V*.1294; ὡς ὅτε τις κεράμῳ κατερέψεται ἑρκίον ἀνήρ A.R.2.1073.

κατερέω, Att. **κατερῶ**, serving as fut. of aor. κατεῖπον: pf. κατείρηκα :—*speak against, accuse*, τινος X.*Cyr.*1.4.8; τινὸς πρός τινα Pl.*R.* 595b; τινὸς ἐναντίον τινός Id.*Thg.*125a. 2. c. acc., *denounce*, τινὰ πρός τινα Hdt.3.71: abs., κατερῶ Ἀθηναίοισι *IG*1².39.25. II. *declare*, πόθεν.. Pi.*Pae.*6.129; *tell plainly*, κ. ἐν τῷ κεῖται χώρῳ ἡ παρακαταθήκη Hdt.5.92.η'; κατερῶ πρὸς ὑμᾶς ἐλευθέρως τἀληθῆ Ar.*Nu.*518, cf. E.*Med.*1106 (anap.); κ. τοὔνομ' ὅτι ποτ' ἐστί σοι Ar.*Pax* 189 :—Pass., κατειρήσεται *shall be declared*, Hdt.6.69.

κατερημόω, *strip entirely off*, τὰ πτερά Aesop.6.

κατερήρῖπε, v. κατερείπω.

κατερητύω, fut. -ύσω [ῡ] S.*Ph.*1416 (anap.):—*hold back, detain*, κατερήτυον ἐν μεγάροισι Il.9.465, Od.9.31; φωνῇ...κατερήτυε 19.545; κατερητύσων ὁδόν S. l. c.; κ. αὐδήν, θυμόν, Orph.*A.*1170, 1177.

κατερῑθεύομαι, *overcome by intrigue*, Plb.*Fr.*173 (dub.).

κατ-ερικτός or -ερεικτός, ή, όν, *bruised, ground*, of pulse, Ar.*Ra.* 505, cf. Phryn.*PS*p.14B., *EM*387.15.

κατέρνης, ες, *with luxuriant branches*, Orph.*A.*918.

κατερυθρ-αίνομαι, *turn red*, Dsc.5.79. **-ιάω**, *blush deeply*, Hld. 10.18.

κατερῡκ-άνω [ᾰ], lengthd. form of κατερύκω, μή μ' ἐθέλοντ' ἰέναι κατερύκανε Il.24.218. **-τικός**, ή, όν, *restraining, inhibiting*, *PMag. Lond.*121.450. **-ω**, *hold back, detain*, μάλα δή σε καὶ ἐσσύμενον κατερύκω Il.6.518; κ. καὶ ἔσχεθεν ἱεμένω περ Od.4.284, cf. 1.315, 15.73; μηδένα...ἀέκοντα μένειν κατέρυκε Thgn.467: rare in Att., τῶν ἀγαθῶν οἵων ἀποκλείεις καὶ κατερύκεις Ar.*V*.601 :—Pass., κατερύκεται εὐρέϊ πόντῳ Od.1.197, 4.498.

κατερύω, Ion. -ειρύω, *draw, haul down*, freq. in Od. of ships, τήν γε [σχεδίην] κατείρυσεν εἰς ἅλα δῖαν 5.261 :—Pass., νηῦς τε κατείρυσται 8.151, etc.; so κατειρύσαντες ἐς Σαλαμῖνα τὰ ναυήγια Hdt.8.96; also κ. οὔθατα μόσχου *to draw* or *milk* them, Nic.*Th.*552; τόξα κ. *draw* a bow, *AP*9.16 (Mel.) :—Med., κὰδ δ' ἄρα λαῖφος ἐρυσσάμενοι *unfurling*, A.R.2.931.

κατέρχομαι, fut. κατελεύσομαι Od.1.303, Hdt.5.125, Arr.*An.*6.12.3 (but in good Att. κάτειμι, as also κατῄειν is always used for the impf.): aor. κατήλῠθον or κατῆλθον, inf. κατελθεῖν; Dor. subj. κατένθῃ *Berl. Sitzb.*1927.165 (Cyrene); Arc. part. κατενθών, pf. part. κατηνθηκώς, v. καθέρπω II: pf. κατελήλυθα *SIG*675.24 (ii B.C.) :—*go down*, Οὐλύμποιο κατήλθομεν Il.20.125, etc.; τιν' ἀθανάτων ἐξ οὐρανοῦ ἀστερόεντος.. κατελθέμεν 6.109; *go down to the grave*, κ. Ἄϊδος εἴσω, Ἀϊδόσδε, ib. 284, 7.330; εἰς Ἅιδου E.*HF*1101, etc.: rarely c. acc., τίς..σκότου πύλας ἔτλη κατελθεῖν; Ar.*Fr.*149.2 (parod.); from high land to the coast, ἐπὶ νῆα θοὴν κατελεύσομαι Od.1.303; from country to town, 11. 188; *down* the Nile, εἰς Ἀλεξάνδρειαν *PLille* 3.80 (iii B.C.), etc. 2. of things, κατερχομένης ὑπὸ πέτρης by the *descending* rock, Od.9.484, 541; of a river, κατέρχεται ὁ Νεῖλος πληθύων *comes down* in flood, Hdt.2.19; κατελθόντος αἰφνιδίου τοῦ ῥεύματος Th.4.75. 3. κ. εἰς τὸν ἀγῶνα, Lat. *descendere in certamen*, S.E.*M.*7.324. 4. c. acc., *come to* a place, ὑμέτερον δῶ Od.24.115; ἀφθονία κατελήλυθε τὴν πόλιν Lyd.*Mag.*3.76. 5. of property, *pass* to, *PRein.*42.28 (i/ii A.D.), *POxy.*1704.5 (iii A.D.). II. *come back, return*, esp. *come back from exile*, Hdt.4.4, al., A.*Ag.*1647, *Ch.*3, *Eu.*462, S.*OC*601, Ar.*Ra.*1165, 1167, Pl.*Ap.*21a, *OGI*90.20 (Rosetta, ii B.C.), etc.; φυγὰς κατελθών S.*Ant.*200; ὃς ἂν κατέλθῃ τήνδε γῆν E.*IT*39: in pass. sense, ὑπ' ὀλιγαρχίας κατελθεῖν *to be brought back* by.., Th.8.68; cf. κάτειμι II, καθέρπω II.

κἀτέρωτᾰ, Aeol. crasis for καὶ ἀτέρωτα (ετερωτα cod. A.D.*Adv.* 194.5), = καὶ ἄλλοτε, Sapph.1.5, Hsch. s. v. κἀτέρωτα.

κατεσθίω, poet. and later -έσθω *APl.*4.240 (Phil.), *Ev.Marc.*12. 40, *Dialex.*2.14 (Pass., 1.5, *PMag.Lond.*46.279 (iv A.D.)): fut. κατέδομαι Il.22.89, Od.21.363, Ar.*Av.*588: aor. κατέφαγον (v. καταφαγεῖν): pf. κατεδήδοκα Id.*V*.838, *Pax*386, etc.; part. κατα..εδηδώς Il.17.542 :—Pass., pf. κατεδήδεσμαι Pl.*Phd.*110e, Antiph.161.3: aor. κατηδέσθην Pl.Com.35 :—*eat up, devour*, in Hom. freq. of animals of prey, λέων κατὰ ταῦρον ἐδηδώς Il.17.542; of a serpent, [νεοσσοὺς] κατήσθιε 2.314, cf. Od.12.256; of a dolphin, κατεσθίει ὅν κε λάβῃσιν Il.21.24; also of men, οἳ κατὰ βοῦς..ἤσθιον Od.1.8; τοὺς γονέας Hdt.3.38, cf. 8.115, E.*Cyc.*341; [τυρὸν] αὐτοῖς τοῖς ταλάροις κ. Ar.*Ra.*560; κατεδηδόκασι τὰ λάχαν' Alex.15.12: c. gen. partit., κ. πολλῶν πουλύπων Amips.6. 2. *eat up, devour* one's substance, τὰ κοινά, τὰ πατρῷα, Ar.*Eq.*258, Antiph.239; τὰ ὄντα D.38.27; πατρῴαν οὐσίαν Anaxipp.1.32. 3. *corrode*, [ῥεύματα] κ. γνάθους Hp.*VM*19; λίθοι κατεδηδεσμένοι ὑπὸ σηπεδόνος Pl. l. c., cf. *Dialex.*1.5 (Pass.); of the wind, κ. τὰ ἄνθη Thphr.*CP*2.7.5 :—Pass., *to be gnawed*, ib.5.17. 7. 4. *bite*, τοῦ παλαιστοῦ τὸ οὖς Philostr.*Im.*1.6. 5. κ. ἑαυτόν, metaph., of remorse, Lib.*Or.*29.32, *Ep.*256.

κατέσκληκα, v. κατασκέλλομαι.

κατεσκολιωμένως, Adv. pf. part. Pass. as if from *κατασκολιόω, *crookedly*, Antyll.ap.Orib.44.23.1.

κατεσπευσμένως, Adv., (κατασπεύδω) *hastily*, Dsc.*Ther.Praef.*, Plu.2.522d.

κατεσπουδασμένως, Adv., (κατασπουδάζομαι) *earnestly*, Procop. *Pers.*2.21.

κατεστραμμένως, Adv., (καταστρέφω) *reversely*, *Placit.*5.14.2.

κατεστράφατο, v. καταστρέφω. **κατέσχεθον**, v. κατέχω.

κάτευγμα, ατος, τό, always in pl., *vows*, A.*Ch.*218, *Eu.*1021. 2. *imprecations, curses*, Id.*Th.*709, E.*Hipp.*1170. II. *symbols of prayer*, S.*OT*920.

κατευ-δαιμονίζω, strengthd. for εὐδαιμ-, J.*BJ*1.33.8. **-δοκέω**, *to be well content with*, τινι Plb.21.33.2. **-δοκῐμέω**, *surpass in reputation*, τινος D.S.33.1.

κατεύδω, for καθεύδω, barbarism in Ar.*Th.*1193.

κατευ-εργετέω, strengthd. for εὐεργ-, Tz.*H.*10.811 (Pass.). **-ημερέω**, *to be influential*, κατευημερηκὼς παρ' ὑμῖν Aeschin.2.89. **-θικτέω**, *hit exactly*, τῇ πληγῇ Lxx 2*Ma.*14.43.

κατευθύ, Adv. *straight forward*, τὸ κ. ὁρᾶν X.*Smp.*5.5, cf. Luc. *Jud.Voc.*11; τὴν κ. ἔρχεσθαι Paus.2.11.3: c. gen., κ. τινός Plu.2.3b; *on the same side* (cf. ἰθύς), ὁ κ. δίδυμος Ruf.(?)ap.Paul.Aeg.3.45. (Better written κατ' εὐθύ.)

κατευθυν-τηρία, ἡ, *carpenter's line*, Sch.Il.15.410, *EM*740.42. **-ω**, poet. impf. κατευθύνεσκον *IGRom.*4.507b (Pergam.) :—*make* or *keep straight*, τὴν πτῆσιν Arist.*IA*710ᵃ2; ναῦν τῷ πηδαλίῳ D.Chr.13.18; βιοτῆς οἴακα κατευθύνεσκες ἐν οἴκῳ *IGRom.* l. c. :—Pass., αἱ περιφοραὶ κατευθυνόμεναι Pl.*Ti.*44b. 2. *guide, direct*, τὰς φύσεις Id.*Lg.* 809a; τινὰ εἰς τὸν αὐτοῦ δρόμον ib.847a; [τὸν ἐλέφαντα] τῷ δρεπάνῳ Arist.*HA*610ᵃ28; [ναῦν] Id.*Fr.*11; κ. τὰς πράξεις ὁ θεός Aristeas 18; τὰ παρόντα πρὸς τὸ τέλος Plu.*Cam.*42; πρὸς τὰ βελτίονα τοὺς νέους Id.2.20d; τὴν ψυχήν ib.780b; τὸν λόγον πρός τι Gal.17(2). 362. 3. κ. τινός *demand* an account *from* one, *condemn*, Pl.*Lg.* 945a, cf. *IG*2².1183.10 (prob.), Poll.8.22. II. intr., *make straight towards*, κατεύθυναν αἱ βόες ἐν τῇ ὁδῷ εἰς ὁδὸν Βαιθσάμυς Lxx 1*Ki.*6. 12; κ. τῇ πτήσει ὄρθιον ἐπὶ τοὺς πολεμίους Plu.*Alex.*33. 2. *prosper*, Lxx *Si.*29.18: c. gen., *succeed* in doing.., οὐ κατεύθυνε τοῦ λαλῆσαι οὕτως ib.*Jd.*12.6. 3. οἱ -ευθύνοντες the *righteous*, ib.*Pr.*15.8.

κατευ-καιρέω, *find a good opportunity*, Plb.12.4.13. **-κηλέω**, *calm, quiet*, A.R.4.1059.

κατευκ-τικός, ή, όν, *entreating*. Adv. -κῶς Sch.S.*Aj.*831 (s. v. l.). **-τός**, ή, όν, *vowed*, Hsch.

κατευ-λογέω, strengthd. for εὐλογέω, Plu.2.66a, Lxx *To.*11. 1. **-μᾰρίζω**, strengthd. for εὐμαρίζω, Hsch., Suid., Phot. **-μεγεθέω**, = καταδυναστεύω, Hsch.

κατευν-άζω, aor. -ήνᾰσα (v. infr.), *put to bed, lull to sleep*, Ἅλιον, ὃν αἰόλα νὺξ...τίκτει κατευνάζει τε S.*Tr.*95 (lyr.); of death, με δαίμων κατευνάζει Id.*Ant.*833 (lyr.); ἐκτὸς αὐτὸν τάξεων κατηύνασεν *assigned* him *quarters* outside the army, E.*Rh.*614: metaph., *quiet, calm*, πόντον A.R.1.1155 (tm.); θηρὸς ἐρωήν Opp.*C.*3.374 (tm.); μόχθων οὐδ' Ἀίδης με κατεύνασεν *gave* me *no rest* from.., *AP*7.278 (Arch. Byz.); [κίνημα] Hierocl.*in CA* 24p.474M. :—Pass., *lie down to sleep*, ἐν τρητοῖσι κατεύνασθεν λεχέεσσιν Il.3.448; *to be quieted*, ἔρως δοκῶν κατευνάσθαι λογισμοῖς Plu.*Ant.*36. **-ασμός**, ὁ, *lulling to sleep*, Id.2.378f (pl.). **-αστήρ**, ῆρος, ὁ, *chamberlain*, Agath.1.19 (pl.). **-αστής**, οῦ, ὁ, = foreg., Plu.*Alex.*40, *Oth.*17, Them.*Or.*10.138a, etc.: metaph., of Hermes, Plu.2.758b. 2. generally, *servant*, ib.945d. **-αστικός**, ή, όν, *lulling to sleep*, βοῆς Eust.1424.6; κ. λόγος, ποίημα, *epithalamium*, Men.Rh.p.405S. **-άστρια**, ἡ, *female chamberlain*, Eust. 1943.58. **-άω**, = κατευνάζω, ἄλλον μέν κεν ἔγωγε θεῶν..ῥεῖα κατευνήσαιμι Il.14.245, cf. 248: metaph., of stanching blood, αἱμάδα... ἠπίοισι φύλλοις κατευνάσειεν S.*Ph.*699 (lyr.) :—Pass., τὸν μὲν ἐπὴν.. κατευνηθέντα ἴδησθε Od.4.414, cf. 421. **-ησις**, εως, ἡ, *putting to rest*, ἀνέμων Iamb.*VP*28.135 (pl.). **-ήτειρα**, ἡ, *she who lulls*, κυδοιμοῦ Nonn.*D.*33.225.

κατευοδ-όω, = εὐοδέω, Lxx *Jd.*18.5 cod. A :—also in Pass., ib.*Pr.* 17.23, *Gp.Prooem.*11. 2. *bring prosperity*, ἡμῖν Lxx *Ps.*67(68). 20. **-ωσις**, εως, ἡ, *good success*, *Gloss.*

κατευ-ορκέω, *swear right solemnly*, an exaggerated word used by Gorgias, Arist.*Rh.*1406ᵃ1. **-πᾰθέω**, *waste in dissipation*, in Pass., Phryn.*PS*p.80B. **-ποιέω**, *do much good to*, τοὺς φίλους Tz.*H.* 3.638. **-πορέω**, *to be sufficiently provided*, τοῖς βοηθήμασι D.S. 17.45.

κατευρύνω, *widen*, τοὺς πόρους *EM*482.10 :—Pass., Hsch.

κατευ-στοχέω, strengthd. for εὐστοχέω, *to be quite successful*, ἐν πᾶσιν D.S.2.5: abs., Plu.*Aem.*19. **-τελίζω**, strengthd. for εὐτελίζω, Id.2.1097c, Sch.E.*Or.*414. **-τονέω**, strengthd. for εὐτονέω, *have the power to..*, c. inf., Hp.*Ep.*17. II. abs., *to be finely tempered*, Ph.*Bel.*71.24. **-τρεπίζω**, *put in order*, Ar.*Ec.*510, X. *Cyr.*8.6.16. **-τῠχέω**, *to be quite successful, prosper*, Arist.*EE*1229ᵃ

19 (cj. ib.$1247^{b}31$), Phld.*Rh.*1.132 S.; τὰ πλεῖστα Plu.*Sert.*18:—also in Pass., τούτων κατευτυχηθέντων D.S.20.46. **-φημέω**, *applaud, extol*, τινα Lxx 3*Ma.*7.13, Plu.*Sert.*4, *Cic.*9, *Epigr.Gr.*430.12 (Egypt): abs., τὸ -φημοῦν Plu.2.487b; περὶ τᾶς ἰδίας πατρίδος πολλὰ κατευφάμηκε *OGI*234.18 (Delph., iii B.C.):—Pass., D.H.3.18:—also **-φημίζω**, Hsch. s.v. Τραυσός. **-φραίνω**, strengthd. for εὐφραίνω, τινα Luc.*Am.*1. **-χειρίζω**, gloss on κατευμαοίζω, Phot., Suid.

κατ-ευχή, ἡ, *prayer, vow*, A.*Ch.*477 (anap.), Plu.*Dio* 24 (pl.); κ. καὶ σπονδαί *OGI*309.7 (Teos, ii B.C.), cf. *SIG*589.7 (Magn. Mae., ii B.C.). **-εύχομαι**, fut. -εύξομαι E.*IA*1186:—*pray earnestly*, c. inf., τοῖσι Πέρσῃσι κατεύχεται εὖ γίνεσθαι Hdt.1.132; τί σοι κατεύξῃ τἀγαθόν (sc. γενέσθαι); E.l.c. 2. c. acc. et inf., A.*Ch.*139, *Eu.*922 (lyr.), S.*OC*1575 (lyr.); κ. τινί *pray* to one, A.*Ch.*88, E.*Andr.*1105; κ. τῇ θεῷ ἀπάξειν Ath.13.573e; κ. τινά c. inf., *entreat* a person to..., Theoc. 2.71. 3. abs., *make a prayer* or *vow*, Hdt.2.40, 4.172, A.*Ag.*1250, S.*Tr.*764, etc. 4. c. gen., *pray over*, τῶν ἱερῶν *IG*7.235.25 (Oropus, iv B.C.). II. in bad sense, 1. c. gen. pers., *pray against* one, *imprecate* curses *on* one, τινῶν πρὸς τὸν θεόν Pl.*R.*393a: c. acc. rei, οἵας ἀρᾶται καὶ κ. τύχας A.*Th.*633, cf. S.*Aj.*392; πολλὰ καὶ δεινὰ καθ' αὐτῶν Plu.*Num.*12. 2. c. acc. et inf., τὸν δεδρακότα κακῶς.. ἐκτρῖψαι βίον S.*OT*246; κ. τεῖσαι τοὺς Ἀχαιοὺς τὰ ἃ δάκρυα Pl.*R.* 394a. 3. abs., μηδὲν κατεύχου E.*IT*536, cf. Pl.*Lg.*934e. III. *boast*, c. fut. inf., Theoc.1.97.

κατευωχέομαι, *feast and make merry on*, ἑψήσαντες τὰ κρέα κατευωχέονται Hdt.1.216, cf. 3.99, Str.3.3.7; βοῦν Plu.2.363c. 2. later in Act., *feast, entertain*, τινα J.*AJ*11.6.1:—Pass., ib.6.1.3, al.

κατεφ-άλλομαι, *leap down against*, ἐξ ἵππων κατεπάλμενος ἀντίος ἔστη Il.11.94 (where Sch.A read κατ-απ-άλμενος); *swoop down upon*, κῦμα..νηὸς ὑπὲρ πάσης κατεπάλμενον A.R.2.583, cf. Opp.*C.*3.120; κατέπαλτο *leapt upon* him, Tryph.478; *leapt down*, οὐρανόθεν Nonn. *D.*48.614; cf. καταπάλλομαι, καταπάλμενος, καταπαλτός.

κατεφθός, όν, *boiled*, Philum.ap.Aët.9.12.

κατεφίσταμαι, *rise up against*, in aor. Act., κατεπέστησαν τῷ Παύλῳ *Act.Ap.*18.12.

κατεχθραίνω, *hate inveterately*, τινα Jul.*Or.*5.171b.

κατεχμάζω, *hold fast, keep back*, Hsch.

κατεχομένιον, τό, = κώνειον, Ps.-Dsc.4.78.

κατέχω, fut. καθέξω (of duration) Il.18.332, κατασχήσω (of momentary action) Hdt.5.72, Th.4.42: aor. κατέσχον, poet. κατέσχεθον Hes.*Th.*575, S.*El.*754; Ep. 3 sg. κάσχεθε Il.11.702, Aeol. κατέσκ[εθε] Alc.*Supp.*1a.12; imper. κατάσχες E.*Ba.*555 (lyr.), later κατάσχε Philostr.*Ep.*38 (v.l.), *PMag.Lond.*97.404; late aor. κατέσχα *PGen.* 54.22 (iv A.D.). I. trans., *hold fast*, καλύπτρην χείρεσσι Hes.*Th.* 575. b. *hold back, withhold*, εἴ με βίῃ ἀέκοντα καθέξει Il.15.186, cf. 11.702, Od.15.200; ἐν κολεῷ ξίφος Pi.*N.*10.6: *check, restrain, bridle*, ἑωυτόν Hdt.6.129, cf. Pl.*Chrm.*162c, Men.*Sam.*112; [γυναῖκε] A.*Pers.* 190; ἱππικὸν δρόμον S.*El.*754; δάκρυ A.*Ag.*204 (lyr.); ὀργήν, θυμόν, ὕβριν, etc., S.*El.*1011, *OC*874, E.*Ba.*555 (lyr.), etc.; δύνασιν S.*Ant.* 605 (lyr.); τὴν διάνοιαν Th.1.130; κ. τὴν ἀγωγήν *put* it *off*, Id.6.29; κ. τὸ πλῆθος ἐλευθέρως, ἰσχύϊ, Id.2.65, 3.62; κ. τινὰ πολέμῳ Id.1.103; τὰ δάκρυα Pl.*Phd.*117d, al.; τὸν γέλωτα X.*Cyr.*2.2.5, Pl.*La.*184a, Thphr.*Char.*2.4; οὖρον *hold in*, Gal.8.407 (but -όμενα [οὖρα] as a disease, Hp.*Prorrh.*1.59, cf. Gal.16.639); ἑαυτὸν κατέχει μὴ ἐπιπηδᾶν *restrains* himself *from*.., Pl.*Phdr.*254a:—Pass., *to be held down*, γλῶσσα κατείχετο Hp.*Epid.*5.50; ἐπιθυμίας -ομένας Pl.*R.* 554c; *to be bound*, ὁρκίοισι μεγάλοισι Hdt.1.29; ὑποσχέσει *PAmh.* 2.97.17 (ii A.D.); τοῖς τινων ὀφειλήμασιν *PRyl.*117.13 (iii A.D.); of a nation, *to be kept under* (by tyrants), Hdt.1.59. c. *detain*, κ. [αὐτοὺς] ἐνιαυτόν Id.6.128, cf. 8.57, Th.8.100; κ. [αὐτοὺς] ὥστε μὴ ἀπιέναι X. *Mem.*2.6.11:—Pass., *to be detained, stay*, Hdt.8.117, S.*Tr.*249; περὶ Κρήτην Th.2.86, etc. d. in imprecations, *inhibit* (cf. καταδέω (A) III), *Tab.Defix.Aud.*50.11 (iv B.C.), *PMag.Par.*1.2077; Μανὴν καταδῶ καὶ κατέχω *Tab.Defix.*109. e. *place under arrest*, *PFlor.*61.60 (i A.D.), etc. f. *keep* an oath, ὅρκον *SIG*526.39 (Itanos, iii B.C.). 2. c. gen., *gain possession of, be master of*, τῶν ἐπιστημῶν μὴ πάνυ κ. Arist.*Cat.*$9^{a}6$; τῆς ὀργῆς Philem.185 codd. Stob.; τῆς παραποταμίας βίᾳ κατέσχον D.S.12.82, cf. Plb.14.1.9; τῆς Ἀσίας ἐθνῶν App.*Praef.* 9; *control*, τινων Lxx 1*Ma.*6.27; ἑαυτῶν Erot. s.v. προπετής; μηκέτι κατέχων ἑαυτοῦ Hdn.1.15.1, cf. 1.7.3; *cling to*, τῶν κεράτων τοῦ θυσιαστηρίου Lxx 3*Ki.*1.51. II. *possess, occupy*, esp. of rulers, A.*Th.* 732 (lyr.), E.*Hec.*81 (anap.); σῴζειν ἅπερ ἂν ἅπαξ κατάσχωσι whatever they *have got*, Isoc.12.242; esp. of property, *enjoy possession of*, *PTeb.*5.47 (ii B.C.), etc. (but also, *sequestrate*, *PLille* 3.16 (Pass., iii B.C.), etc.); ὡς μηδὲν ἔχοντες καὶ πάντα κατέχοντες 2*Ep.Cor.*6. 10. b. *dwell in, occupy*, Ὀλύμπου αἴγλαν S.*Ant.*609 (lyr.); esp. of tutelary gods, Παρνασίαν ὃς κ. πέτραν, of Dionysus, Ar.*Nu.*603 (lyr.), cf. X.*Cyr.*2.1.1, *SIG*662.10 (Delos, ii B.C.), Luc.*Alex.*10; of a place, μέσον ὀμφαλὸν γᾶς Φοίβου κ. δόμος E.*Ion* 223 (lyr.); of the dead, θήκας Ἰλιάδος γᾶς..κατέχουσι *occupy*, A.*Ag.*454 (lyr.), cf. S.*Aj.*1167 (anap.). 2. of sound, *fill*, οἱ δ' ἀλαλητῷ πᾶν πεδίον κατέχουσι Il. 16.79; κ. στρατόπεδον δυσφημίαις *fill* it with his grievous cries, S. *Ph.*10; οἰμωγὴ..κατεῖχε πελαγίαν ἅλα A.*Pers.*427, cf. E.*Hipp.*1133 (lyr.):—Pass., οἶκος κλαυθμῷ κατείχετο Hdt.1.111. 3. πανδάκρυτον βιοτὰν κ. *continue to live* a life.., S.*Ph.*690 (lyr.). 4. *to be spread over, cover*, νὺξ..δνοφερὴ κάτεχ' οὐρανόν Od.13.269; ἡμέρα πᾶσαν κατέσχε γαῖαν A.*Pers.*387, cf. Ar.*Nu.*572 (lyr.); τίνες αὖ πόντον κατέχουσ' αὖραι; Cratin.138; ὀσμὴ..κατὰ πᾶν ἔχει δῶ Hermipp.82. 9:—Pass., σελήνη..κατείχετο..νεφέεσσιν Od.9.145, cf. Il.17.368, 644:—Med., Ep. aor., κατέσχετο χερσὶ πρόσωπα Od.19.361; κατασχομένη ἑανῷ *having covered her face*, Il.3.419. 5. of the grave, *confine, cover*, τοὺς δ' ἤδη κάτεχεν φυσίζοος αἶα 3.243, cf. Od.11.301, Orac.ap. Hdt.1.67; as a threat, πάρος τινὰ γαῖα καθέξει sooner shall earth *cover* many a one, Il.16.629, cf. Od.13.427, etc. 6. of circumstances, etc., *hold fast, have* one *in their power*, μιν κατὰ γῆρας ἔχει χεῖράς τε πόδας τε Od.11.497; ὃν θάνατος δακρυόεις καθέχει (sic) *IG*1^{2}.987; ἐχθρὰ Φάλαριν κ. φάτις Pi.*P.*1.96; τινὰ..λάθα κ. Id.*N.*8.24; [φθορὰ] κ. τὸν σὸν δόμον S.*OC*370; τύχη, πόλεμος κ. τινά, Pl.*Hp.Ma.*304c, *Ep.* 317a; κ. κίνδυνος Σικελίαν ib.355d; συνέβη λοιμώδη νόσον κατασχεῖν τὴν Ἰταλίαν Hdn.1.12.1:—Pass., ὑπὸ μεγάλης ἀνάγκης κατεχόμενοι Pl. *Lg.*858a: rarely in good sense, ὁ δ' ὄλβιος, ὃν φᾶμαι κατέχοντ' ἀγαθαί Pi.*O.*7.10; μεγάλαι κ. τύχαι γένος ὀρνίθων Ar.*Av.*1726 (lyr.); εὐμοιρίας -εχούσης τὸν βίον Hdn.2.5.1. b. of circumstances, etc., *prevail, prevail among, engage*, ἄλλα τῶν κατεχόντων πρηγμάτων χαλεπώτερα Hdt.6.40, cf. 1.65; μεγάλοι θόρυβοι κατέχουσ' ἡμᾶς murmurs *are rife among* us, S.*Aj.*142 (anap.); φήμης ἀθρόας -σχούσης τὸ Ἑλληνικόν a sudden rumour *having overspread* Greece, Philostr.*VA*8.15. 7. *seize, occupy*, in right of *conquest*, τὸ Καδμείων πέδον dub. in S.*OC* 381; esp. in histor. writers, -σχήσειν [τὴν ἀκρόπολιν] Hdt.5.72; τὰ πρήγματα Id.3.143; τὰ ἐχυρὰ X.*Cyr.*3.1.27; τὰ κύκλῳ τῆς Ἀττικῆς ἁρμοσταῖς D.18.96; φρουραῖς τὰς πόλεις Plu.2.177d. 8. *achieve, effect* an object, Isoc.2.25; πρᾶξιν Arist.*Pol.*$1312^{a}33$. 9. *master, understand*, οὐ κατέχω τί βούλει φράζειν Pl.*Phlb.*26c, cf. *Men.*72d, Ceb.34; περὶ φύσεως κ. πάντας τοὺς λόγους Sosip.1.17, cf. 33; κ. νοῦν στίχων *grasp* the sense of.., Puchstein *Epigr.Gr.*p.9. b. *keep in mind, remember*, χρήσιμον καὶ τοῦτο κατασχεῖν τὸ στοιχεῖον Epicur. *Ep.*1 p.10 U., cf. Thphr.*Char.*26.2, Men.*Epit.*109; κ. τινὰ ὀψοφάγον Chrysipp.Tyan.ap.Ath.1.5e; κ. ὅτι, διότι, *PCair.Zen.*60.10 (iii B.C.), Phld.*Herc.*1251.15:—Pass., Epicur.*Ep.*1 p.31 U. 10. *possess*, of a god, εἰ θεός ἐστιν ὁ σὰς κατέχων φρένας *PLit.Lond.*52.12; τοιοῦτος ἔρως κατεῖχε τὴν ἄνθρωπον she *was* so *infatuated*, Plu.*Alc.*23; of an actor, κ. τὸ θέατρον *held* the audience *spellbound*, Plu.*Dem.*29 (but, *kept* the audience *waiting*, *Phoc.*19); of poets, μύθοις [τοὺς ἀκούοντας] κ. Luc.*JTr.*39 (v.l. κατηχοῦσι):—mostly in Pass., of persons, *to be possessed, inspired*, Pl.*Ion* 533e; ἐξ Ὁμήρου ib.536b; ἐκ θεῶν X. *Smp.*1.10; κάρῳ Phld.*D.*1.18; τὸ θέατρον κατείχετο the audience *was spellbound*, Eun.*Hist.*p.247 D.; of hydrophobia patients, Philum. *Ven.*4.11; of a lover, τῷ αὐτῷ θεῷ (sc. Ἔρωτι) κατέσχημαι Luc. *DMort.*19.1:—also in aor. Med., Pl.*Phdr.*244e. III. *follow close upon, press hard*, X.*Cyr.*1.4.22 (dub. l.), *Cyn.*6.22:—Pass., ib. 9.20. IV. *bring* a ship *to land*, Hdt.6.101, 7.59, Plu.2.162a.

B. intr., 1. (sc. ἑαυτόν) *control oneself*, S.*OT*782; οὐκέτι καθέξω Men.*Pk.*394; εἶπεν οὖν μὴ κατασχὼν Plu.*Art.*15; οὐ κατέσχεν App.*BC*3.43: c. inf., κ. τὸ μὴ δακρύειν Pl.*Phd.*117c. b. *stop, cease*, of the wind, Ar.*Pax* 944 (lyr.). 2. *come from the high sea to shore, put in* (v. supr. IV), νηῒ Θορικόνδε *h.Cer.*126; τῆς Μαγνησίης χώρης ἐς τὸν αἰγιαλόν Hdt.7.188, cf. 6.101, Plb.1.25.7, Plu. *Thes.*21; τίνες ποτ' ἐς γῆν τήνδε..κατέσχετε; S.*Ph.*221, cf. 270, E. *Heracl.*83 (lyr.), Antipho 5.21, etc.: c. acc. loci, E.*Hel.*1206, *Cyc.* 223; of a journey by land, *rest*, προξένων δ' ἔν του κατέσχες; Id.*Ion* 551, cf. Plb.5.71.2: metaph., εὖ κατασχήσει *shall come* safe *to land*, S.*El.*503 (lyr.). 3. *prevail*, ὁ λόγος κ. the report *prevails*, Th.1.10; κληδὼν ἐν ἁπάσῃ τῇ πόλει κατεῖχεν And.1.130; σεισμῶν -εχόντων Th.3.89; ὁ βορέας κατεῖχεν Arist.*Mete.*$345^{a}1$, cf. $360^{b}33$, Thphr.*CP*1.5.1. 4. *gain the upper hand*, παρά τινι Thgn.262; *gain one's purpose*, Lys.3.42; ὁ δὲ κατεῖχε τῇ βοῇ Ar.*Ec.*434; νομίζοντες ῥᾳδίως κατασχήσειν Arist.*Pol.*$1307^{b}10$.

C. Med., *keep back for oneself, embezzle*, [τὰ χρήματα] Hdt.7. 164. 2. *cover oneself*, v. supr. A.II.4. 3. *hold, contain*, Plb.9. 26^{a}.7. II. aor. Med., = κατέχω B.2, Od.3.284. 2. in pass. sense, τεαῖς ῥιπαῖσι κατασχόμενος *subdued*, Pi.*P.*1.10; καρδίαν κατέσχετο ἔρωτι *was seized with, possessed by*, E.*Hipp.*27; v. supr. A. II.10.

κατη-βολέω, *swoon*, Nic.*Al.*194, 458. **-βολή**, ἡ, = τὸ ἐπιβάλλον, E.*Fr*r.614, 750. 2. = καταβολή III, Hp.ap.Gal.19.11c, Pl.*Hp. Mi.*372e (cf. Sch.), Hsch., Phot. 3. = θυσία, τελετή, τὰ νομιζόμενα, Hsch.

κατηγάθεος [γᾰ], ον, strengthd. for ἠγ-, epith. of Zeus, Antioch. Astr. in *Cat.Cod.Astr.*1.109.

κατηγγειωμένως, Adv. pf. part. Pass., (καταγγειόομαι) *by means of blood-vessels*, Sor.1.73.

κατηγορ-έω, *speak against*, esp. before judges, *accuse*, opp. ἀπολογέομαι, c. gen., Hdt.2.113, 8.60, Lys.14.21, Ar.*Pl.*1073, etc.; τῆς πόλεως Pl.*Mx.*244e: less freq. κατά τινος X.*HG*1.7.9; κ. τινὸς πρὸς τὴν πόλιν *denounce* him publicly, Pl.*Euthphr.*2c; κατηγόρεις [αὐτῶν] ὡς λέγοιεν you *accused* them of saying, D.21.134, cf. X.*HG*7. 1.38; κ. τινὸς ὅτι.. ib.1.7.17; τῶν ἱππέων ἐλθὼν πρὸς ὑμᾶς εἰς τὴν ἐκκλησίαν κατηγόρει D.21.197; τῆς ἐμῆς [τύχης] κατηγορεῖς Id.18. 266, cf. Isoc.3.4. 2. κ. τί τινος *bring* as *a charge against* a person, *accuse* him *of* it, δεῖν' ἔπη μου S.*OT*514, cf. E.*Or.*28, etc.; τῶν ἄλλων μωρίαν X.*Mem.*1.3.4; ὃς ἐμοῦ Φιλιππισμὸν κατηγορεῖ D.18. 294; κ. τι κατά τινος Hyp.*Eux.*23; τινὸς περί τινος And.1.110, Th.8. 85: c. inf., κ. τινὸς παθεῖν τι Pl.*Grg.*482c: c. dupl. gen., παρανόμων κ. τινός D.21.5. 3. c. acc. rei only, *allege in accusation*, Hdt. 2.113; μωρίαν ἐμήν E.*Heracl.*418; τὴν πονηρίαν τῶν γονέων Pl.*Prt.* 346a; τὰ γεγονότα κ. Antipho 1.10, cf. Ar.*V.*932, *Ra.*996 (lyr.), Lys. 13.31, D.19.9:—Pass., *to be brought as an accusation against*, κατηγορεῖτο τοὐπίκλημα τοῦτό μου; S.*OT*529; ἀδικία πολλὴ κ. αὐτοῦ Th.1. 95; τὰ πρῶτά μου ψευδῆ -ημένα the first false *charges brought against* me, Pl.*Ap.*18a, cf. Lys.16.9; τὰ –ηθέντα Antipho 5.85, And.1.24; τἀδικήμαθ' ἃ κατηγορεῖται D.21.136: impers., folld. by inf., σφέων..κατηγόρητο μηδίζειν *a charge had been brought against* them that.., Hdt.7.205; κατηγορεῖτό τινος ὡς βαρβαρίζοι X.*HG*5.2.35; κατηγορουμένου δ' αὐτοῦ, ὅτι.. *a charge being brought against* him, that.., ib.3.5.25. b. rarely in Pass., of the person, *to be accused*, οἱ κατηγορούμενοι And.1.7, cf. Luc.*Tim.*38 (s. v. l.). 4. abs., *to be an accuser, appear as prosecutor*, Ar.*V.*840, 842, *Pl.*917, Pl.*Ap.*18e, etc. II. *signify, indicate, prove*, c. acc. rei, [τὸ νεαρὸν] κ. τὴν ὀλιγοετίαν X.*Cyr.*1.4.3, cf. Plu.2.695d, Adam.1.5, al.; ἀσθένειαν μᾶλλον ἢ δύναμιν Plot.4.6.3; *display*, οἱ πολλὴν –οῦντες ἀπειροκαλίαν Luc.*Nigr.*21: c. gen. pers., εὖ γὰρ φρονοῦντος ὄμμα σοῦ κατηγορεῖ A.*Ag.*271, cf. E.*Fr.*690, S.*Aj.*907, etc.; ὠκύτητα κ. τοῦ κυνός Philostr.*Im.*2.26. 2. folld. by relat., *declare, assert*, αὐτὸ κατηγορέει τὸ οὔνομα ὡς ἔστι Ἑλληνικόν Hdt.3.115; κ. ὅτι.. Id.4.189, Pl.*Phd.*73b (impers.): abs., *make a definite assertion*, Id.*Tht.*208b. III. in Logic, *predicate of* a person or thing, τί τινος Arist.*Cat.*3^{a}19, al., Epicur.*Fr.*250; κυρίως, καταχρηστικῶς κ., Phld.*Po.*5.15; ἐναντίως ὑπὲρ τῶν αὐτῶν Id.*Oec.*p.60 J.: —more freq. in Pass., *to be predicated of*.., τινος Arist.*Cat.*2^{a}21, *APr.*26^{b}9, al.; κατά τινος Id.*Cat.*2^{a}37; κατὰ παντὸς ἢ μηδενός Id.*APr.*24^{a}15: less freq. ἐπί τινος Id.*Metaph.*998^{b}16, 999^{a}15; so later ἐφ' ἑνὸς οἴονται θεοῦ ἑκάτερον τῶν ὀνομάτων –εῖσθαι D.H.2.48; περί τινος Arist.*Top.*140^{b}37; τὸ κοινῇ –ούμενον ἐπὶ πᾶσιν Id.*SE*179^{a}8: abs., τὸ κατηγορούμενον *the predicate*, opp. τὸ ὑποκείμενον (the subject), Id.*Cat.*1^{b}11, cf. *Metaph.*1043^{a}6, al.; κατηγορεῖν καὶ –εῖσθαι *to be subject* and *predicate*, Id.*APr.*47^{b}1. 2. *affirm*, opp. ἀπαρνέομαι, ib.41^{a}10. Adv. κατηγορουμένως *categorically, roundly*, Phld.*Ir.*p.90 W. –ημα, ατος, τό, *accusation, charge*, Gorg.*Pal.*22, Pl.*Lg.*765b, 881e, *PFrankf.*7 *B* 3 (iii B. C.); τὰ τοῦ τρόπου σου κ. D.18.263, cf. Din.1.1, D.H.7.64; τοῦτο φωνῆς κ. this is the *fault* of.., A.D.*Pron.*27.25. II. in Logic, *predicate*, Arist.*Int.*20^{b}32, *Metaph.*1053^{b}19, etc.; οὐκ εὔοδον τὸ ἁπλοῖν ἐστι κ. Epicur.*Fr.*18. 2. *head of predicables*, Arist.*Metaph.*1028^{a}33, *Ph.*201^{a}1, Zeno *Stoic.*1.25, etc.; περὶ κατηγορημάτων Sphaer.ib.140. III. *sign, indication*, ὁ ἐπικεκυφὼς τράχηλος μωροῦ ἀνδρὸς κ. Polem.*Phgn.*36. –ησείω, Desiderat., *to be anxious to accuse*, Agath.4.2. –ησις, εως, ἡ, *predication*, Chrysipp.*Stoic.*2.108 (dub.). –ητέον, *one must accuse, lay the blame on*, τῶν πραγμάτων Isoc.3.2; αὐτοῦ Pl.*Grg.*508b. II. *one must assert*, ὡς.. Id.*Tht.*167a; *one must predicate*, τι κατά τινος Epicur.*Ep.*1 p.25 U.; τοῦ ἐπέκεινα οὐδὲ τοῦτο κ. Plot.3.7.2. –ητής, οῦ, ὁ, *accuser*, J.*AJ*17.5.4. –ητικός, ή, όν, = κατηγορικός 1, Arist.*Rh.Al.*1421^{b}10 codd. (leg. κατηγορικόν as in 1426^{b}22, 25 = *PHib.*1.26.295, 297). –ία, Ion. –ίη, ἡ, *accusation*, Hdt.6.50, etc.; opp. αἰτία (expostulation), Th.1.69; opp. ἔπαινος, ib.84; opp. ἀπολογία, Arist.*Rh.*1358^{b}11; τὴν κ. ποιεῖσθαι Antipho 6.10, And.1.6; ὡς ὑβρίζοντος κ. ἐποιοῦντο X.*An.*5.8.1; κ. ἐγένοντο πολλαὶ τῶν Ἀθηναίων *charges* were made against.., Id.*HG*2.1.31; κατηγορίαι κατά τινος γεγόνασιν Isoc.5.147; εἰ.. ἐπὶ τοῖς πεπραγμένοις κατηγορίας ἔχω I am liable to *accusation*, D.18.240. II. in Logic, *predication*, Arist.*Metaph.*1007^{a}35, etc.: pl., Id.*APo.*84^{a}1; esp. *affirmative predication*, opp. στέρησις, Id.*APr.*52^{a}15; ἄπορον ἐν κ. *Stoic.*2.93. 2. *predicate*, Arist.*Metaph.*1004^{a}29, 1028^{a}28, al., Epicur.*Ep.*1 p.23 U., etc. 3. more freq., *category, head of predicables*, Arist.*Top.*103^{b}20 (ten), *APo.*83^{b}16, *Ph.*225^{b}5 (eight), *Metaph.*1068^{a}8 (seven), cf. *EN* 1096^{a}29. –ικός, ή, όν, *accusatory*, opp. ἀπολογικός, Id.*Rh.Al.* 1426^{b}25, cf. Erot.*Prooem.*; οἱ κ. *informers*, = Lat. *delatores*, Plu.*Galb.*8. Adv. –κῶς, λέγειν πρός τινα J.*BJ Prooem.*4. II. *affirmative*, opp. στερητικός, Arist.*APr.*26^{a}18, al. Adv. –κῶς ib.26^{b}22. 2. *categorical*, opp. hypothetical, κατηγορικόν, τό, *statement combining subject and predicate*, *Stoic.*2.66; κ. συλλογισμοί S.E.*P.*2.163, Procl.*in Prm.* p.790 S.; λόγοι S.E.*P.*2.166, Ammon.*in Int.*74.1. Adv. –κῶς, opp. ὑποθετικῶς, Gal.4.609. –ος, ὁ, *accuser*, Hdt.3.71, S.*Tr.*814, And.4.16, Lys.7.11, Pl.*Ap.*18a (pl.), *Apoc.*12.10, etc.; δημόσιος κ. *public prosecutor*, *PFlor.*6.6 (iii A. D.); *betrayer*, φρονημάτων ἡ γλῶσσ' ἀληθὴς γίγνεται κ. A.*Th.*439; ἀμέλειά ἐστι σαφὴς ψυχῆς κ. κακῆς X.*Oec.*20.15; πνεῦμα ὢν κατήγορον, ..δρόμοις [ἡ φύσις] ἐκβιᾶται κατηγορέειν what the respiration *reveals*, Hp.*de Arte* 12. –ουμένως, v. κατηγορέω III. 2.

κατήγωρ, ὁ, = κατήγορος, *PMag.Lond.*124.25, v.l. in *Apoc.*12.10.

κατηγώς, v. κατάγνυμι.

κατήκοος, ον, (κατακούω) *hearing*, τῶν εἴ τίς ἐστιν.. κατήκοος if any *has heard tidings of* them, S.*Ichn.*77; *listening to*, κ. λόγων *student* of philosophy, Pl.*Ax.*365b. 2. *spy, eavesdropper*, κατάσκοποι καὶ κ. Hdt.1.100, D.C.42.17. II. *hearkening to, obedient*, Hdt.7.155, S.*Ant.*642; τινος to another, Μήδων, Περσέων κ., Hdt.1.72, 143, al.; τὰ παραθαλάσσια.. Περσέων κ. ἐποίεε Id.5.10; κ. τοῦ κοσμητοῦ *IG*2^{2}.1011.20; τὸ ἐπιθυμητικὸν κ. [τοῦ λόγου] Arist.*EN*1102^{b}31: c. dat., Κροίσῳ κ. Hdt.1.141, cf. 3.88; τῇ πόλει κ. γενέσθαι Pl.*R.*499b. III. *giving ear to*, εὐχωλῇσι *AP*6.199 (Antiphil.).

κατηκρῑβωμένως, Adv. pf. part. Pass., (ἀκριβόομαι) *precisely*, Gal.18(2).861.

κατήκω, Ion. for καθήκω.

κατηλέποντα· φροντίδας ποιοῦντα, Hsch.

κατῆλιψ, ῐφος, ἡ, variously expld. as *ladder, roof-beam, upper story*, etc. in Ar.*Ra.*566, cf. Sch. ad loc., Poll.7.123, Hsch.; also used by Luc.*Lex.*8.

κατηλογέω, *make of small account, neglect*, c. acc., Hdt.1.84, 144, 3.121: c. gen., Parth.23.1, J.*AJ*12.4.6.—The form καταλογέω does not occur.

κάτ-ηλῠς, ῠδος, ὁ, ἡ, *going downward*, Nonn.*D.*37.24. –ηλῠσία, Ion. –ίη, ἡ, *descent*, λαιψηροῖο –ίη Ζεφύροιο A.R.4.886; κατηλυσίη τ' ἄνοδός τε Arat.536. –ήλῠσις, εως, ἡ, *going down, descent*, εἰς Ἀΐδην *AP*10.3; νιφετοῖο κ. *a falling* of snow, Simon.179.1. II. *return*, τῶν Ἡρακλειδῶν D.S.12.75.

κατημελημένως, Adv., (ἀμελέω) *negligently*, v.l. in Procop.*Pers.*1.5.

κατημύω, *droop*, ἔρνεα κ. ἔραζε A.R.3.1400: metaph., κατήμυσαν ἀχέεσσι θυμόν Id.2.862. (V. ἠμύω.)

κατηναγκασμένως, Adv. pf. part. Pass., (καταναγκάζω) *of necessity*, D.S.15.50, Demetr.Lac.*Herc.*1012.45, Diog.Oen.33, Alex.Aphr.*Fat.*181.23.

κατήνεμος, ον, *exposed to the wind*, cj. in Thphr.*Vent.*34, cf. Ael.*NA*4.6, Poll.1.115.

κάτηξις, ιος, ἡ, Ion. for κάταξις.

κατήορος, Dor. –άορος [ᾱ], ον: (ἀείρω):—*hanging down*, τέκνων δὲ πλῆθος.. κατάορα στένει *hanging on their mother's neck*, E.*Tr.*1090 (lyr.); τελαμὼν κ. A.R.2.1041; βόστρυχα *AP*5.259 (Paul. Sil.).

κατηπέδανον· κατησθενηκός, Erot.

κατηπειγμένως, Adv. pf. part. Pass., (κατεπείγω) *hurriedly*, Hld.8.1, Sch.E.*Or.*1433.

κατηπιάω, *assuage, allay*, ὀδύναι δὲ κατηπιόωντο Il.5.417.

κατηρεμίζω, *calm, appease*, X.*An.*7.1.22, Plu.2.384a.

κατηρεφής, ές, (ἐρέφω) *covered over, vaulted, overhanging*, σπέος εὐρὺ κ. Od.13.349; κλισίας τε κ. Il.18.589; ἐν σμήνεσσι κ. μέλισσαι Hes.*Th.*594; μέγα κῦμα.. κ. Od.5.367: c. dat., σπέος δάφνῃσι κ. *shaded by, embowered in* them, 9.183; δώματα πέτρῃσι κ. Hes.*Th.*778; so in Trag., κ. πέτρος, of a cave, S.*Ph.*272; ἐν κ. στέγῃ χθονός Id.*El.*381; κ. τύμβος Id.*Ant.*885; κ. αὐτῇ τῇ πέτρᾳ Pl.*Criti.*116b; of trees, *thick-leaved*, Theoc.7.9; κ. πόδα τιθέναι keep the foot *covered*, of Pallas seated, when the robe falls over her feet, opp. ὀρθὸν πόδα τ., A.*Eu.*294. 2. c. gen., στέγην, ἧς κατηρεφεῖς δόμοι E.*Hipp.*468; τράπεζαι κ. παντοίων ἀγαθῶν *covered with, full of*, Anacr.121.

κατήρης, ες, (ἀραρίσκω) *fitted out, furnished* with, χλανιδίοις E.*Supp.*110; ὀσμῇ Id.*El.*498; δένδρεα.. καρπῶν ἀφθονίῃσι κατήρεα cj. in Emp.78; [ἔρπυλλος] φύλλοισι κ. Nic.*Th.*69; esp. of ships, *furnished with oars*, εἶχε πλοῖον κατῆρες ἑτοῖμον had a *rowing* boat ready, Hdt.8.21; but ταρσὸς κ. *a well-fitted* oar, E.*IT*1346.

κατήρητος, v. κατάρατος.

κατῆρυδες ἄμπελοι, *laden with fruit*, Hsch.

κατῆτος, = κατὰ ἔτος, *yearly*, *Hymn.Curet.*37.

κατήφ-εια, Ion. and Ep. –είη, ἡ, (κατηφής) *dejection* (λύπη κάτω βλέπειν ποιοῦσα Plu.2.528e), δυσμενέσιν μὲν χάρμα κατηφείην δὲ σοὶ αὐτῷ Il.3.51; κ. καὶ ὄνειδος 16.498, 17.556; κ. τέ τις ἅμα καὶ κατάμεμψις σφῶν αὐτῶν πολλὴ ἦν Th.7.75; opp. χαρά, *Ep.Jac.*4.9; δυσθυμία καὶ κ. Plu.*Them.*9; τὴν βουλὴν ἄχος καὶ κ. ἔσχε Id.*Cor.*20, cf. D.H.3.19, Corn.*ND*28, Charito 6.8; κ. καὶ σύννοια Ph.2.204; κ. καὶ ὀϊζύς Rhian.1.8. –έω, *to be downcast, to be mute* with horror or grief, στῆ δὲ κατηφήσας Il.22.293; ἀκάχοντο κατήφησάν τ' ἐνὶ θυμῷ Od.16.342, cf. Call.*Epigr.*22, A.R.2.443, etc.; τί δαὶ κατηφεῖς ὄμμα; E.*Med.*1012; of animals, Arist.*HA*604^{b}12; καὶ κατηφῆσαι [ἂν] θεός and well *might* God *grieve*, J.*BJ*3.8.4 (v.l. οὓς κατέφησεν). –ής, ές, *with downcast eyes, downcast*, κατηφέες ἐσσόμεθ' αἰεί Od.24.432, cf. Cic.*Att.*13.42.1; τὸν μὲν κατηφῆ E.*Or.*881; κ. ὄμμα Id.*Heracl.*633 (but κ. ὀφθαλμοί *sunken* eyes, Hp.*Epid.*7.25); κ. καὶ ὑπεραύστηρος *POxy.*471.92 (ii A. D.); of animals, αἱ ἵπποι ὅταν ἀποκείρωνται, γίνονται κατηφέστεραι Arist.*HA*572^{b}9; τὸ κ. Id.*Phgn.*808^{a}10, cf. 807^{b}12: metaph., κ. ἄμπελος *drooping* in sorrow, Him.*Or.*9.4. 2. metaph., *dim, obscure*, νύξ *AP*9.658 (Paul. Sil.); χωρίον Poll.5.110; of colour, κ. ὁ λίθος καὶ μέλας Philostr.*VS*2.1.8, cf. Him.*Ecl.*12.7. –ιάω, = κατηφέω, *AP*14.3, Ph.2.519 (nisi leg. –φῶμεν), Plu.2.119c; Ep. part. κατηφιόων A.R.1.461, etc.; Ep. iterat. κατηφιάασκε *MAMA*1.319. –ών, όνος, ὁ, *one who causes grief* or *shame*, σπεύσατέ μοι, κακὰ τέκνα, κατηφόνες Il.24.253 (κατηφέες Crates).

κατηχ-έω, *sound over* or *through*, ἁρμονία κ. τῆς θαλάττης Philostr.*Im.*1.19, cf. 2.12. 2. *sound amiss*, opp. συνηχέω, Vitr.5.8.1. II. *teach by word of mouth*: hence generally, *instruct*, κ. τινὰ πολλὰ τῶν ἀγνοουμένων Agrippa II ap.J.*Vit.*65, cf. Luc.*Asin.*48, *PStrassb.*41.37 (iii A. D.):—Pass., *to be informed* or *instructed*, περί τινος *Act.Ap.*21.21; κ. ὅτι.. Ph.2.575; ὥσπερ κατηχήμεθα S.E.*M.*5.5. 2. in *NT*, *instruct in the elements of religion*, 1*Ep.Cor.*14.19:—Pass., περὶ ὧν κατηχήθης λόγων *Ev.Luc.*1.4; ὁ κατηχούμενος τὸν λόγον *Ep.Gal.*6.6; κατηχημένος τὴν ὁδὸν τοῦ Κυρίου *Act.Ap.*18.25, cf. Porph.*Chr.*26. –ής, v. καταχής. –ησις, εως, ἡ, *instruction by word of mouth*: generally, *instruction*, Hp.*Praec.*13, Cic.*Att.*15.12.2, D.H.*Dem.*50, *Din.*7, Ath.Med.ap.Orib.*inc.*21.6, S.E.*M.*1.7; διὰ τὴν κ. τῶν συνόντων by *communication* with companions, in bad sense, Chrysipp.*Stoic.*3.54, cf. 55, Gal.5.463. II. *accompaniment* of the monochord by louder instruments *which drown* its tune, Ptol.*Harm.*2.12 (pl.). –ίζω, = κατηχέω II, Hsch., *Gloss.*

κάτθᾰνε, v. καταθνήσκω. **κατθᾶξαι**, v. καταθήγω. **κατθάψαι**, v. καταθάπτω. **καθθέμεν, κάτθεμεν, κάτθετε, κάτθεσαν, κατθέμεθα, κατθέσθην, κατθέμενοι, κάτθεο**, v. κατατίθημι.

κατιάδιον, τό, = κατιάς, Aret.*CD*1.2.

κατῐάπτω, *harm, hurt*, ὡς ἂν κατὰ χρόα καλὸν ἰάπτῃ Od.2.376, cf. 4.749; τίφθ' ὧδε κατὰ θυμὸν ἰάπτεις; Mosch.4.1.

κατιάς, άδος, ἡ, *lancet* or *stylet*, Heliod.ap.Orib.44.14.4 (cf. Sch. ad loc.), Philum.ap.Aët.8.48, Sor.2.59.

κατῑδίω, *desudasco*, *Gloss.*

κατιερόω, κατιέρωσις, Ion. for καθ–:—Elean **κατῐαραίω** *Schwyzer* 424.5 (iv B. C.): aor. opt. –αραύσειε, [τινος] ib.409.2 (v B. C.).

κατ-ῑθύνω, Ion. and Ep. for κατευθύνω, κ. τὸν πλόον Hdt.2.96, cf. Hp.*Art.*71, Luc.*Trag.*56, Aristaenet.1.15; κῦμα Mosch.2.121; χεῖρα τοξότιν *AP*6.188 (Leon.); ῥήματος ἁρμονίην *APl.*4.226 (Alc.). **-ῑθύς**, Adv. *opposite*, c. gen., Babr.95.42, Q.S.7.136:—also **κατῑθύ** Herod. 8.60, Man.1.30; cf. ἰθύς II. 2.

κατῐκετεύω, Ion. for καθικετεύω.

κατικμ-άζω, *let fall in drops*, σπόρον Nic.*Al.*582. **-αίνω**, *moisten, wet*, τινὰ ῥοαῖς Lyc.1053; χρόα λοετροῖς Nonn.*D.*5.606:—Pass., ib. 11.508:—Med., *bathe*, τινθαλέοισι λοετροῖς Call.*Fr.anon.*60.

κατιλλαίνω, *look askance at*, Hsch. (Pass.):—Act. is prob. in Arist.*Phgn.*813ᵃ21.

κατίλλω, = κατειλέω, φωναὶ κακούμεναι καὶ κατίλλουσαι (v. l. κατειλοῦσαι) dub. sens. in Hp.*Epid.*3.5 (cf. Gal.17(1).678, Erot.); = κατείργω, Phot. s. v. κατουλάδα.

κατιλλώπτω, *look askance at, leer at*, τινι Philem.124; θῆλυ κ. *AP* 5.199. 2. *look scornfully*, Poll.2.52, Hsch.

κατῑλύω, *fill with mud* or *dirt*, X.*Oec.*17.13.

κατίμεν [ῐ], Ep. pres. inf. Act. of κάτειμι, Il.14.457.

κατῑμονεύω, *let down*, Hsch.

κατῑόομαι, Pass., *become rusty, tarnished*, LXX*Si.*12.11 (Act. is v. l.), Str.16.2.42, *Ep.Jac.*5.3, Dsc.4.82, Arr.*Epict.*4.6.14: metaph., βασιλεία σιδηρᾶ καὶ -ιωμένη D.C.71.36.

κάτῐσος, ον, *equal*, c. dat., Sch.Ar.*Pax*728.

κατισχάνω, Ep. form of κατίσχω, κατὰ σὸν νόον ἴσχᾰνε Od.19.42.

κατισχν-αίνω, *cause to pine* or *waste away*, A.*Eu.*138:—Pass., ὑδροποτῶν καὶ κατισχναινόμενος Pl.*R.*561c, cf. J.*AJ*7.8.1:—fut. Med. inf. κατισχνᾰνεῖσθαι A.*Pr.*271. II. *reduce* a swelling, Hp.*Prog.* 23; αἱ Μοῦσαι τὸν ἔρωτα κ. Call.*Epigr.*47.3; *weaken*, ὀσμήν Thphr. *Od.*47. **-άω** or **-έω**, = foreg., ἐπιφθέγγεσθαι κατισχνημένον in a *thin* voice. Ps.-Luc.*Philopatr.*20. **-όομαι**, = κατισχναίνομαι, J. *AJ*2.5.5, Gal.*UP*1.21, Aët.4.34:—Act., Hsch., Phot., Sch.Nic.*Al.* 592. **-ος**, ον, *very lean, emaciated*, Antyll.ap.Orib.7.7.9, Plu.*Dem.* 4, etc.

κατισχῡρεύομαι, *strengthen oneself, be violent*, Aq.*Ps.*85(86).14.

κατισχύω, fut. -ύσω *Ev.Matt.*16.18:—*overpower, prevail over*, τινα Men.*Epit.*74, Aristeas 21, LXX 2*Ch.*8.3, al.; ὅταν ἡ τῆς πείρας ἀκρίβεια -ισχύῃ τὴν τῶν λόγων πιθανότητα D.S.1.39: also c. gen., LXX*Je.*15. 18, Alex.Aphr.*in Top.*248.19; [τῆς ἐκκλησίας] *Ev.Matt.* l. c.; τινὸς σοφίᾳ Ael.*NA*5.19; Ἄρης κ. τῆς Σελήνης Vett.Val.104.10; γενναίας φύσεως Chor. in *Rev.Phil.*1.57:—Pass., *to be worsted*, ὑπ' ἔρωτος D.S.1.71; τῇ μάχῃ Id.17.45. 2. abs., *have the upper hand, prevail*, LXX*Ex.*17.11, al.; κ. τῷ πλήθει *to be superior in*.., Plb.11.13.3; κατίσχυον αἱ φωναὶ αὐτῶν *Ev.Luc.*23.23. b. *to be prevalent*, ὁρμαὶ καὶ ζῆλοι παρά τισι κ. Plb.3.4.6; κατισχυούσης τῆς θερμότητος Thphr. *CP*6.11.7; κατίσχυκεν ἡ φήμη παρὰ τοῖς πλείστοις Antig.*Mir.* 152. II. *come to one's full strength*, δέμας in body, S.*OC*346, cf. Phld.*Rh.*1.189 S. III. trans., *strengthen, encourage*, c. acc., LXX *De.*1.38, al.; τὰς χεῖράς τινων ib.1*Es.*7.15; οὐδετέραν τῶν στάσεων D.H.6.65.

κατίσχω, collat. form of κατέχω, *hold back*, οὐδὲ κατίσχει [ἵππους] Il.23.321; τὰς νέας Hdt.2.115; θυμοῦ μένος ὀξὺ κατισχέμεν *h.Hom.* 8.14:—Med., *keep by one*, γυναῖκα νέην.., ἥν τ' αὐτὸς.. κατίσχεαι Il. 2.233. II. *possess, occupy*, οὐ ποίμνῃσιν καταΐσχεται Od.9.122; ἀράχνια κ. ὅλον τὸ σμῆνος *cover* it, Arist.*HA*626ᵇ18. III. = κατέχω A. IV, ἐς πατρίδα γαῖαν νῆα κατισχέμεναι Od.11.456, cf. Hdt.8. 41; ἐνὶ Φάσιδι νῆα *put in* there, A.R.3.57. IV. intr., σέλας κατίσχει ἐξ οὐρανοῦ ἐπὶ τὴν βοῦν the light *comes down* from heaven, Hdt.3.28. 2. of ships, *put in*, Th.7.33.

κατῑτήρια (sc. ἱερά), τά, = ἡ ἐπὶ καθόδῳ θυσία, Hsch.

κάτογκος, ον, *bulky*, τῷ σώματι Sor.1.117.

κατοδερικαῖς, τοῖς, dat. pl. masc., dub. sens. in *BGU*1240.24,26 (ii B. C.).

κατοδῡνάω, *afflict grievously*, τὴν ζωήν τινων LXX*Ex.*1.14:—Pass., ib.*Ez.*9.4.

κατοδύρομαι [ῡ], *deplore*, τὸ ζῆν Pl.*Ax.*367d; τὴν ἑαυτοῦ τύχην D.S.13.58; ταυτὶ -όμενος X.Eph.5.1, cf. Parth.26.4:—Pass., *to be mourned*, *Arch.Pap.*1.220 (Ptol.).

κατόζω, *spread a stink*, σαυτοῦ, i. e. *tuo foetore fruitus*, Arr.*Epict.* 4.11.16.

κάτοθεν, later form for κάτωθεν, *PHib.*1.110.76 (iii B. C.).

κατοιάδες, αἱ, (ὄϊς) *leading the sheep*, αἶγες Paus.9.13.4.

κάτ-οιδα, -οισθα, inf. κατειδέναι, part. κατειδώς (Locr. καταειδώς *Schwyzer*366 *A* 6 (Tolophon, iii B. C.)), pf. (in pres. sense), plpf. κατῄδη (in impf. sense):—*know well, understand*, c. acc. rei, ἄστρων ὁμήγυριν A.*Ag.*4; οὐδὲν κάτοισθα τῶν σαυτοῦ πέρι S.*Ph.*553; θεσφάτων βάξιν κατῄδη Id.*Tr.*87; φύλλον νώδυνον Id.*Ph.*44; κατειδὼς τὴν γυναικείαν φύσιν, ὡς.. ἧδεται Eub.43; μηδὲν κατειδώς, ἀλλὰ προσποιούμενος Men.628; ἵν' εὖ κατειδῇς S.*Ichn.*164. 2. c. acc. pers., *know by sight, recognize*, τὸν βοτῆρα Id.*OT*1048, cf. *Tr.*418, E.*Or.*1183, 1521. 3. abs., esp. in part., οὐ κατειδώς *unwittingly*, Id.*Med.*992 (lyr.), *Supp.* 1033. 4. c. part., *know well that*.., κάτισθι μὴ πολλοὺς ἔτι τρόχους.. τελῶν S.*Ant.*1064. 5. folld. by an interrog., οὐ κάτοιδ' ὅπως λέγεις I *understand* not how.., Id.*Aj.*270; οὐ κ. ὅτῳ τρόπῳ.. E.*Hipp.*1245. 6. c. inf., *know how to*, ἢ κάτοισθα δηλῶσαι λόγῳ; S.*OT*1041.

κατοιδέω, pf. -ῴδηκα, *to be swollen*, Sor.2.43.

κατοίησις, εως, ἡ, *self-conceit*, Plu.2.1119b (pl.).

κατοικ-άς, άδος, ἡ, poet. fem. of κατοικίδιος, στρουθός Nic.*Al.* 60,535. **-εσία**, ἡ, = κατοίκησις, LXX*Ps.*106(107).36, Eust.106. 44. **-έσια** (sc. ἱερά), τά, *anniversary festival of a colony*, *EM*221. 3. **-έω**, *settle in, colonize*, πόλιν Hdt.7.164; γῆν E.*Med.*10; τοῖς κατοικεῖν ἐθέλουσι τὰν πόλιν Decr.Byz.ap.D.18.91: generally, *inhabit*, τόπους S.*Ph.*40; τὴν Ἀσίαν *SIG*557.17 (Magn. Mae., iii B. C.), etc.:—Pass., *to be dwelt in* or *inhabited*, opp. κατοικίζομαι (to be just founded), Arist.*Pol.*1266ᵇ2. 2. abs., *settle, dwell*, ζητοῦσα.. ποῦ κατοικοίης S.*OC*362; ἵνα χρὴ κατοικεῖν Ar.*Av.*153; ἐν δόμοις, ἐν ἄστεσι, E.*Hel.* 1651, Pl.*Lg.*666e, etc.; αὐτόθι Th.3.34; ἐν μοναρχίᾳ Isoc.1.36; ἐπὶ γῆς *Apoc.*3.10; esp. of non-citizens, Ἐφέσιοι καὶ οἱ -οῦντες *SIG*352.4 (Ephesus, iv B. C.), cf. 633.67 (Milet., ii B. C.):—pf. and plpf. Pass., *to have been planted* or *settled*, κατὰ κώμας Hdt.1.96, cf. 2.102; κ. νῆσον, τὴν μεσόγειαν, Id.4.8, Th.1.120. II. *administer, govern*, οἱ τὰς πόλεις -οῦντες Phld.*Rh.*2.225 S.:—more freq. in Pass., κατῴκηνται καλῶς, of Athens, S.*OC*1004; ὀρθῶς κ., of Sparta, Pl.*Lg.*683a. III. intr. of cities, *lie, be situated*, ἐν τοῖς πεδίοις ib.677c, cf. 682c: also c. acc. loci, τὰς τὴν Ἀσίαν κατοικούσας *which are situated in*.., Isoc. 5.123. **-ησις**, εως, ἡ, *settling in* a place, διὰ τὴν ταύτη κ. Th. 2.15. II. *dwelling, abode*, Pl.*Ti.*71b, *Criti.*115c, LXX*Ge.*10.30, etc.; τὴν κ. εἶχεν ἐν τοῖς μνήμασι *Ev.Marc.*5.3; *inhabited district*, ἡ κατὰ τὴν Ἰταλίαν κ. Ath.12.523e. **-ητήριον**, τό, *dwelling-place, abode*, LXX*Ex.*12.20; κ. θεοῦ, δαιμονίων, *Ep.Eph.*2.22, *Apoc.* 18.2. **-ητήριος**, α, ον, = κατοικίδιος, ὄρνεις Sor.1.51. **-ία**, ἡ, *habitation*, βαρβάρων Hecat.119 J.; τόπος εὐφυὴς πρὸς κ. Plb.5.78. 5; ὑγιεινὴν ποιεῖν τὴν κ. Str.5.4.8; *farm, village*, Plb.2.32.4, etc.: generally, *dwelling-place*, *Act.Ap.*17.26; *domicile*, Mitteis *Chr.*31 i 23 (ii B. C.). 2. *settlement, colony*, Str.5.4.11; esp. of *military colonies* in Egypt, *PTeb.*61(*b*).227 (ii B. C.), etc.; also, = Lat. *colonia*, Str.6. 2.5, Plu.*Ant.*16, App.*BC*5.19; κατοικίαι πόλεων foundation of *colonies*, Plu.*Pomp.*47. 3. *body of residents* in a foreign *city*, ἡ κ. τῶν ἐν Ἱεραπόλει κατοικούντων Ἰουδαίων *IGRom.*4.834. **-ια**, τά, *household goods*, *GDI*2141.22 (Delph.). **-ίδιος**, ον, (α, ον only *Gp.*1. 3.8) *living in* or *about a house, domestic*, μῦς Theopomp.Hist.258(*a*); [σκύλαξ] Nic.Dam.56 J.; ὄρνεις *Gp.* l. c., 2.35.5; ὄρνις Longus 3.6; οἱ κ. *stay-at-home* historians, Luc.*Hist.Conscr.*37; κ. βίος Ph.2.378, D.S. 3.53; κ. κατατάσεις *domestic* means or methods of extension, Hp. *Art.*78; τὰ κ. τῶν ἔργων *household* duties, Hierocl.p.62 A.; κατοικίδιοι (sc. θεοί), οἱ, = Lat. *Penates*, Gloss. **-ίζω**, Cret. **καταϝοικίδδω** *Schwyzer*175.2 (Gortyn): Att. fut. -ιῶ A.*Pr.*725:—*settle, establish*, κ. τινας ες Μέμφιν Hdt.2.154, cf. Ar.*Pax*205, Decr.ap.D.18. 182, etc.; κ. πόλιν εἰς τόπον *place* it.., Pl.*R.*370e; γυναῖκας ἐς φῶς ἡλίου κ. E.*Hipp.*617, cf. Pl.*Ti.*70a, Critias *Fr.*25.38, etc.; κ. ψυχὴν ἐν τάφῳ S.*Ant.*1069; ἐκγόνους ἐν τόπῳ Pl.*Criti.*113c; ἐλπίδας ἔν τινι κ. *plant* them in his mind, A.*Pr.*252; κ. τινὰ χώρᾳ S.*OC*637; τινὰς ἐκ Ῥώμης εἰς τὴν Καμερίαν κ. Plu.*Rom.*24:—Pass., *to be settled*, ἐν Αἰγύπτῳ Hdt.2.154; περὶ τὸ ἧπαρ Pl.*Ti.*71d; τοὺς ἐπὶ τοῦ Πόντου κατῳκισμένους App.*Mith.*15; κ. Λατώσιον *Schwyzer* l. c. II. c. acc. loci, *colonize, people* a place, αἳ Θεμίσκυράν ποτε κατοικιοῦσιν A. *Pr.*725; Μέγαρα Hdt.5.76, cf. E.*Andr.*295 (lyr.), Th.6.76, etc.; τὴν Σικελίαν Pl.*Ep.*357a; τὸν Εὔξεινον πόντον κ. πόλεσι λαμπραῖς Ath.12. 523e:—Pass., *to be settled*, ἡ Ἑλλὰς -ῳκίζετο Th.1.12, cf. 2.17; *to be founded, established*, Isoc.9.19; πόλεις κατοικιζόμεναι εὐθύς, opp. ἤδη κατοικούμεναι, Arist.*Pol.*1266ᵇ1. III. Med., *establish oneself, settle*, Th.2.102; ἐν Τροιζῆνι, εἰς Αἴγιναν, Isoc.19.23,24. IV. *bring home and re-establish there, restore to one's country*, A.*Eu.*756, Pl.*Ep.* 357b. **-ικός**, ή, όν, *assigned to* κάτοικοι, κλῆρος *PTeb.*105.13 (ii B. C.), etc.; γῆ *POxy.*46.22 (100 A. D.); ὑποθήκη ib.2134.14 (ii A. D.). **-ίς**, ίδος, ἡ, v. l. for κατοικάς, Nic.*Th.*558. **-ῐσις**, εως, ἡ, *settlement*, Pl. *R.*453b, *Lg.*969c: pl., Th.6.77, App.*BC*5.19. **-ισμός**, ὁ, = foreg., in pl., Pl.*Lg.*683a, Arist.*Mete.*351ᵇ22; ἐς -οικισμόν for *habitation*, J. *AJ*4.7.4. **-ιστής**, οῦ, ὁ, *founder of a city*, Sm.*Je.*50(27).7, Hsch. s. v. ἀποικιστής.

κατοικο-δομέω, *build upon* or *in* a place, τι δημόσιον X.*Ath.*3.4; τὰς ὁδοὺς Arist.*Ath.*50.2:—Pass., of the place, *to be built on*, LXX *Ge.*36.43, Str.5.4.5. II. *squander in building*, Plu.*Publ.*15 (but simply, *use in building*, πλίνθου τῆς -δομηθείσης *PPetr.*3 p.141 (iii B. C.)). III. *shut up in a house*, Is.8.41 (s. v. l.), cf. Harp. s. v. κατῳκοδόμησε. 2. Pass., *to be built up, blocked up*, σανίσι D.C.66. 25. **-νομέω**, *manage well*, τὴν χρείαν Plu.*Brut.*36:—Med., πάντα *OGI*339.23 (Sestus, ii B. C.).

κάτοικος, ὁ, *inhabitant*, Arist.*Oec.*1352ᵃ33, Plb.5.65.10, al.; esp. of *military colonists*, οἱ ἐν Μαγνησίᾳ κ. *OGI*229.71 (Smyrna, iii B. C.); in Egypt, *PTeb.*30.7 (ii B. C.), etc.; κ. is f. l. for κάτοικτος in A.*Ag.* 1286.

κατοικοφθορέω, *ruin utterly*, τὴν πόλιν Plu.*Alc.*23.

κατοικτ-είρω or **-ίρω**, irreg. aor. -οικτείρησα LXX 4*Ma.*8.20, 12.2:—*have mercy* or *compassion on*, τινα Hdt.1.45, 4.167, al., S.*OT*13, E. *Heracl.*445, *IG*9(2).255 (Pharsalus); τὸ τῆς μητρὸς γῆρας LXX 4*Ma.* 8.20. II. intr., *feel, show compassion*, κατοικτείραντα ἐρωτᾶν ask *in compassion*, Arist.*Rh.*1393ᵇ28; -οικτῖραι ὡς βραχὺς εἴη ὁ βίος *feel compassion at the thought* that.., Hdt.7.46. **-ίζω**, Att. fut. -ιῶ A.*Supp.*903: = foreg., c. acc. rei, πόνους S.*OC*384, etc.; λακὶς χιτῶνος ἔργον (i. e. χιτῶνα) οὐ κατοικτιεῖ A. l. c.:—Med., *bewail oneself, utter lamentations*, Hdt.2.121.γ', 3.156, A.*Eu.*121 (prob.); τί κατοικτίζει μάτην; Id.*Pr.*36:—aor. Pass. κατῳκτίσθην E.*IA*686: c. acc., as in Act., στρατόν A.*Pers.*1062 (lyr.). II. causal, *excite pity*, ῥήματα.. κατοικτίσαντά πως S.*OC*1282. **-ῐσις**, εως, ἡ, *compassion*, ἡ πρὸς αὐτὴν κ. X.*Cyr.*6.1.47. **-ος**, ον, *pitiable*, prob. for κάτοικος, A.*Ag.* 1286.

κατοιμώζω, *bewail, lament*, E.*Andr.*1159.

κατοιν-όομαι, Pass., *to be drunken*, κατῳνωμένος Pl.*Lg.*815c. **-ος**, ον, *drunken with wine*, E.*Ion* 553 (troch.). 2. *addicted to wine*, D.S.5.26. 3. *wine-coloured*, Vett.Val.1.13.

κατοινύσαι· κατακρύψαι, Hsch.

κατοίομαι, *to be conceited of oneself*, Lxx *Hb.*2.5, Ph.*Fr.*99 H.

κατοίσεται, v. καταφέρω.

κατοιχνέω, *spread over, fill*, ὀμφᾷ κ. τόπου S.*Ichn.*321 (lyr.).

κατοίχομαι, *have gone*, οἱ κατοιχόμενοι *the departed, dead*, D.43.67, 60.8, Arist.*VV*1250b21, *PGnom.*17, Aret.*SA*2.4: sg., Nic.*Fr.*108, *BMus.Inscr.*1032.19 (Teos), 1032*a* (Ephesus).

κατοιωνίζομαι, *take as an omen*, Phalar.*Ep.*143.2.

κατοκλάζω, = ὀκλάζω, Opp.*C.*3.473 :—Med., Str.3.4.15. II. *flag, grow inattentive*, Anon. *in Rh.*233.17.

κατοκνέω, *shrink from*, c. inf., ὅπως..μὴ κατοκνήσεις κτανεῖν Αἴγισθον S.*El.*956; κ. ὀρθοῦσθαι Hp.*Mochl.*20; κ. γῆν περιιδεῖν τμηθεῖσαν Th.2.18; μὴ κατόκνει..πορεύεσθαι Isoc.1.19: c. acc., τὴν στρατείαν App.*Mith.*110: abs., *shrink back*, A.*Pr.*67, Th.2.94, Isoc.6.75, D.29.1, etc.; *to be sluggish*, εἰ τῇ δυνάμει κ. [ἡ ψυχή] Phld.*Mus.*p.30 K.

κατοκωχ-ή, ἡ, = κατοχή, *possession*, τῆς χώρας Anon.ap.Suid.; *mental grasp*, τῶν εἰρημένων Zeno *Stoic.*1.58. II. *being possessed, inspiration*, θείᾳ μοίρᾳ καὶ κατοκωχῇ Pl.*Ion* 536c; ἀπὸ Μουσῶν κ. Id. *Phdr.*245a, cf. Ph.1.174, al., Dam.*Isid.*32:—the forms κατακωχή, -ιμος are late and incorrect; cf. ἀνοκωχή, συνοκωχή. **-ιμος**, η, ον, *held in possession, held as a pledge*, [χωρίον] Is.2.28 (vulg. κατόχιμον); τὸ κ. Hsch. 2. *capable of being possessed* by a feeling or passion, ὑπὸ κινήσεως Arist.*Pol.*1342a8; ἐκ τῆς ἀρετῆς Id.*EN*1179b9; τῷ πάθει *possessed*, Id.*HA*572a32; *inclined*, πρός τι Id.*Pol.*1269b30: abs., *frantic*, Luc.*JTr.*30 (vulg. κατόχιμος).

κατολῐγωρέω, *neglect utterly*, τοῦ δικαίου Lys.9.16; [ἀνδρός] Longin.13.2, cf. Jul.*Or.*1.2a:—Pass., *SIG*888.153 (Scaptopara, iii A.D.). 2. abs., *to be negligent*, ἐν τοῖς ἀλλοτρίοις Diogenian.2.75, cf. *PSI*4.426.3 (iii B.C.); κατολιγωρήσαντες *with contempt*, Arist.*Rh.Al.*1421a15.

κατολισθ-άνω, later -αίνω Gal.7.36, Agath.1.1: Ep. aor. 2 κατόλισθε A.R.1.390: aor. 1 -ωλίσθησα Alciphr.3.64: pf. -ωλίσθηκα Orib.50.42.3:—*slip, sink down*, Str.4.6.6; of hernia, Gal.l.c.; of a building, *collapse*, Agath.1.10: metaph., ἐς πάθος, εἰς ἔρωτα, Luc. *Abd.*28, Alciphr. l.c.; εἰς τὸ βλάσφημον Ael.*Fr.*60; εἰς πλεονεξίαν Agath.1.1. **-ησις**, εως, ἡ, *slipping down*, Sor.1.108, Gal.19.447, Paul.Aeg.6.65.

κατόλλυμι, in pf. Act., *perish utterly*, νεολαία...κατὰ πᾶσ' ὄλωλεν A.*Pers.*670 (lyr.).

κατολολύζω, *shriek over*, θύματος A.*Ag.*1118 (lyr.).

κατολοφύρομαι [ῡ], aor. 1 -ωλοφῡράμην Diog.Oen.1:—*bewail*, c. acc., E.*IT*644 (lyr.), X.*Cyr.*7.3.16; τινῶν τὸν βίον Diog.Oen. l.c.; κ. πολλὰ ἑαυτόν D.H.5.12: abs., E.*Or.*339 (lyr.).

κατομβρ-έομαι, Pass., *to be rained on*, Plb.34.1.16, Str.16.1.5: metaph., ὄμματα κατομβρηθέντα γόοισιν *AP*7.389 (Apollonid.). **-ία**, ἡ, *heavy rain*, Lyd.*Ost.*30, al.: pl., ib.58. **-ίζομαι**, Pass., = κατομβρέομαι, *Gp.*2.8.4. **-ιμος**, ον, *rainy*, ἔτος Orph.*Fr.*252. **-ιος**, ον, = foreg., dub. l. in Ph.2.515. **-ισις**, εως, ἡ, = κατομβρία, Lyd. *Ost.*40. **-ος**, ον, *rainy*, νότος Arist.*Vent.*973b9; ἔαρ *Gp.*1.12.24. II. *wet with rain, drenched*, Thphr.*CP*3.12.1, 3.22.3: metaph., ὄμματ' ἐρώντων *AP*5.144 (Asclep.).

κατόμνῡμι, aor. -ώμοσα E.*Hel.*835:—*confirm by oath*, τινί τι Ar.*Av.*444. 2. c. acc., *call to witness, swear by*, τὴν ἐμὴν ψυχήν E.*Or.*1517 (troch.), etc.; κ. τὼ θεώ Ar.*Ec.*158: c. dupl. acc., ἁγνὸν ὅρκον σὸν κάρα κατώμοσα E.*Hel.* l.c.: c. gen., κ. τῆς κεφαλῆς Anon.ap.Suid. 3. *swear*, c. inf., *IG*12(9).1273.1 (Eretria, vi B.C.). II. Med. = Act., *tender an oath*, Antipho Soph.*Oxy.*1364.140, Arist.*Rh.*1377a16, *PMagd.*26.13 (iii B.C.); *swear by*, τοὺς θεούς Aristaenet.2.20: c. acc. et inf., D.39.4, cf. Paus.6.18.3. 2. c. dat., *take an oath against, accuse on oath*, Hdt.6.65 (gen. as v.l.): abs., ib.69.

κατομόργνῡμι, *wipe clean off*, Hsch.

κατομφάλιος [φᾰ], ον, *from the navel*, v.l. for παρομφ-, Nic.*Th.*290.

κατονειδ-ίζω, = ὀνειδίζω, D.H.11.42. **-ιστήρ**, ῆρος, ὁ, = ὀνειδιστήρ, Man.4.235.

κατονεύομαι, v.l. for ὀνεύομαι, Gal.19.126.

κατονίναμαι, *enjoy*, in aor. 1, σαυτῆς κατόναιο Ar.*Ec.*917 (lyr.); τέκνων, σπορῶν, καρπῶν, οὐσίας κατόνασθαι *SIG*826 *C*15 (Delph., ii B.C.).

κατονομάζω, *name*, Str.7.3.2, al.; ἀπό τινος ib.13.1.48 (dub. l.):—Pass., ζωμὸς κατωνόμασται Anaxandr.34.5; *to be named*, Arist.*EE* 1221b10, Thphr.*Od.*2; *to be expressed in terms*, of numbers, Archim. *Aren.*1.3; τὰ -ωνομασμένα *the aforesaid*, Meno *Iatr.*11.33, Philum. *Ven.*27.3. II. Pass., *to be betrothed*, c. dat., Plb.5.43.1, Hsch. s.v. τᾶλις; *to be devoted* to the gods, D.H.1.16, Phalar.*Ep.*84.1.

κατόνομαι, *censure bitterly, depreciate, abuse*, c. acc., Hdt.2.172: aor., μή με κατονοσθῇς πρὸς τὰς..πυραμίδας ib.136.

κατονομ-αξία, ἡ, Dor. for κατονομασία, *expression* of numbers, Archim.*Aren.*1.7 (prob.):—also **-αξις**, εως, ἡ, ib.3.1. **-ασία**, ἡ, *name, denomination*, Str.1.2.34 (pl.). **-αστος**, ον, *named*, Hdn. *Epim.*203.

κατόξ-ος, ον, *drenched with vinegar, over-sour*, Posidipp.1.7. **-ύνω**, *hasten on*, τι Artemon *Fr.*12. **-υς**, εια, υ, strengthd. for ὀξύς, *very sharp, piercing*, βοή Ar.*V.*471; of disease, *acute*, Hp.*Aph.*1.7 (cf. Gal.18(2).254), Aret.*SA*1.7, *CA*1.10; τὸ κ. τῆς ὀρέξεως Hld.1.26.

κατοπάζω, *follow hard upon, tread on the heels of*, αἰδῶ δέ τ' ἀναιδείη κατοπάζῃ Hes.*Op.*324.

κατόπερ, Ion. for καθόπερ (q.v.).

κατ-όπιθεν, Adv., = κατόπισθεν, *POxy.*2146.8 (iii A.D.), *Gloss.* **-όπιν**, Adv., (v. ὄπις) *behind, after*, Hp.*Mul.*1.12, Th.4.32, X.*Cyr.*1.4.21: c. gen., Ar.*Eq.*625, Pl.*Prt.*316a; κ. ἐπὶ τῷ στόλῳ Plb.1.50.5; ἐκ τῶν κ. Id.2.67.2: metaph., κ. χωρεῖν τῶν εἰργασμένων fall *short of*, fail in describing, Chor.p.23 B. II. of Time, *after, hereafter*, f.l. in Thgn.280; εὐθὺς κ. Thphr.*HP*7.13.7; κ. ἑορτῆς ἥκομεν 'too late for the fair', Pl.*Grg.*447a; ἡ κ. [ἡμέρα] Plb.1.46.7, Phld.*Ind.Sto.*19; ὁ κ. ἐνιαυτός Plu.*Cam.*43; σε μένει καὶ κ. δάκρυα *AP*9.70 (Mnasalc.). **-όπισθεν**, in Poets also -θε, Adv. of Place, *behind, after*, Il.23.505, Od.22.92: c. gen., 12.148, Pancrat.*Oxy.*1085.14: metaph., of rank, ἃ δ' Ἀρετὰ κ. θνατοῖς ἀμελεῖται E.*IA*1093 (lyr.). II. of Time, *hereafter, afterwards, henceforth*, Od.22.40, 24.546; ὁ κ. λογισμός Pl.*Ti.*57e, cf. Thgn.280; also κ. λιποίμην Od.21.116, cf. Pl.*R.*363d. **-οπίσω**, Adv., = foreg., Lxx *Jd.*18.22.

κατοπτάω, *roast* or *bake thoroughly*, Archestr.*Fr.*13.6, Phld.*D.*1.19, Str.15.2.2, 16.4.13:—Pass., *to be well baked*, Arist.*Aud.*802b2, 803a29; *to be overheated*, of the blood, Gal.7.246.

κατοπτ-εία, ἡ, *spying, reconnoitring*, J.*AJ*18.9.7. II. = κάτοψις, οὐρανοῦ *Corp.Herm.*3.3 (-οπτία). **-ευσις**, εως, ἡ, *observation*, Procl.*Par.Ptol.*155, *Gloss.*:—also written καθόπτ-, ib. **-ευτήριος**, ον, *fit for looking out*, τὸ κ., = σκοπιά, Sch.E.*Ph.*233. **-εύω**, *spy out*, ὠτακουστεῖν καὶ κ. v.l. for διοπτ- in X.*Cyr.*8.2.10; *observe closely*, ἅπαντα, φύσιν ἀνθρώπων, Plb.1.4.11, D.H.*Lys.*7; *reconnoitre*, Plb.3.45.3; of a night-policeman, *POxy.*1033.13 (iv A.D.); *visit, explore* a country, Plb.34.1.8, 34.5.9; τὸν οὐράνιον χῶρον Arist.*Mu.*391a10; ἐπὶ τοῦ Πηγάσου τὸν οὐρανόν Asclep.Myrl.ap.Sch.Il.6.155; κ. ἐς.. *AP* 5.122 (Phld.):—Pass., Plb.3.37.11, Str.2.4.6; *to be observed*, S.*Aj.*829; μὴ κατοπτευθῶ παρών Id.*Ph.*124; ἐκ τῶν φαινομένων κατωπτευμένων Phld.*Sign.*25. II. Astrol., *exert a baleful aspect*, Petos.ap. Vett.Val.112.37. **-ήρ**, ῆρος, ὁ, *spy, scout*, A.*Th.*36 (pl.). II. = ἑδροδιαστολεύς, Hp.*Fist.*3, *Haem.*5 (κάτοπτρον Erot.). **-ήριος**, ον, = κατοπτευτήριος, χῶρος Str.9.3.15; κατοπτήριον, τό, *height which commands a view*, *Delph.*3(2).136. **-ης**, ου, ὁ, = κατοπτήρ I, *h.Merc.*372, Hdt.3.17, 21, etc. 2. *one who visits* or *explores*, κλιμάτων καὶ ἐθνῶν Vett.Val.330.15; *one who contemplates*, οὐρανοῦ Ph. Bybl.ap.Eus.*PE*1.10. II. *overseer*, κατόπτης δ' εἴμ' ἐγὼ τῶν πραγμάτων A.*Th.*41; ὦ Ζεῦ διόπτα καὶ κατόπτα Ar.*Ach.*435. 2. κατόπτας, ὁ, title of an officer in Boeot. towns, *IG*7.303.21 (Oropus), 3172.140 (Orchomenus).

κατόπτησις, εως, ἡ, *roasting* or *baking*, Phld.*D.*1.19, Gal.11.694.

κατοπτικὸς νόμος law *concerning the* κατόπτης II.2, *IG*7.3073.88 (Lebad.).

κατοπτίλλεταί μοι, = δοκεῖ μοι, Dius ap.Stob.4.21.16; Dor. word, cf. ὀπτίλος.

κάτοπτος (A), ον, (ὄψομαι) *visible*, ὥστε μὴ κάτοπτα εἶναι Th.8.104; χωρίον ἄερκτον καὶ πανταχόθεν κ. Lys.7.28. II. c. gen., *looking down over*, πορθμοῦ κάτοπτον πρῶνα (Canter for κάτοπτρον) A.*Ag.*307.

κάτοπτος (B), ον, *dried-up*, of a kind of myrrh, Dsc.1.64; ἡ ἐκ τῶν καμίνων κ. γῆ Id.5.158; *over-baked*, ἄρτοι Ath.Med.ap.Orib.1.9.2, cf. *Gloss.*

κατοπτρ-ίζω, *show as in a mirror* or *by reflexion*, τοῦ -ίζοντος [τὴν ἶριν] ἀστέρος *Placit.*3.5.11:—Pass., *to be mirrored*, Anon.*Oxy.*1609.19. II. Med., *look into a mirror, behold oneself in it*, Zeno *Stoic.*1.66, S.E.*P.*1.48, Ath.15.687c, etc. 2. *behold as in a mirror*, ἰδέαν Ph.1.107; δόξαν Κυρίου 2*Ep.Cor.*3.18 (but here perh. *reflect*). **-ικός**, ή, όν, *of* or *in a mirror*, φαντασία *Placit.*3.1.2; ἐμφάσεις ib.3.2.1; τὰ κ. *reflected images*, ib.3.5.6; but, *Theory of Reflexion*, title of work by Hero, Damian.*Opt.*14:—also **-κή**, ἡ, Procl. in *Euc.*p.40 F.; **-κόν**, τό, Hero *Deff.*135.12. Adv. **-κῶς** *by reflexion*, βλέπεσθαι *Placit.*2.24.1. **-ῖτις** λίθος *reflecting* stone found in Cappadocia, Plin.*HN* 37.152.

κατοπτροειδής, ές, *like a mirror*, prob. l. in *Placit.*2.25.14, cf. Alex.Aphr. *in Mete.*144.6.

κάτοπτρον, τό, *mirror*, κ. εἴδους χαλκός A.*Fr.*393, cf. E.*Hipp.*429, etc.; τίς γὰρ κατόπτρῳ καὶ τυφλῷ κοινωνία; Com.ap.Stob.4.30.6a; κ. ἀνδρομήκη Phld.*Rh.*2.206 S.; ἐν κατόπτρῳ..κατιδεῖν εἴδωλα παρέχοντι Pl.*Ti.*71b; ὥσπερ ἐν κ. ἑαυτὸν ὁρῶν Id.*Phdr.*255d, etc.; = μηλωτίς, Hp.ap.Erot. (v. κατοπτήρ II): metaph., εὖ γὰρ ἐξεπίσταμαι ὁμιλίας κ. companionship's true *mirror*, A.*Ag.*839; ἡ Ὀδύσσεια καλὸν ἀνθρωπίνου βίου κ. Alcid.ap.Arist.*Rh.*1406b13; κ. φύσεος, of a wine-cup, Theopomp.Com.32.3:—spelt **κάτροπτον** in Att. Inscrr., *IG*2².1471.47, 1544.58 (iv B.C.), al., and this form shd. be restored in Pl.*Cra.*414c: **κάθοπτρον** shd. perh. be restored in *Annuario* 4/5.463.

κατοργανίζω, *sound with music through*, τῆς ἐρημίας *AP*9.264 (Apollonid. or Phil.).

κατοργάω, strengthd. for ὀργάω, Hsch., Phot.

κατοργιάζω, *initiate in orgies, prepare for them*, Plu.*Sol.*12:—Pass., Id.2.766b, *Fr.*6.2, Luc.*Trag.*125.

κατοργόω, pf. Med. κατωργώμεθα *we have quarrelled with each other*, *PMagd.*10.3 (iii B.C.).

κατορέγομαι, Med., strengthd. for ὀρέγομαι, Simp. *in Epict.*p.6 D.

κάτορθ-ος, ον, *straight*, Mnesith.ap.Orib.8.38.4. **-όω**, *set upright, erect*, δέμας E.*Hipp.*1445, *Andr.*1080; *set straight* a fractured or dislocated bone, Hp.*Fract.*16, al. (Med., *have it set straight*, 8, al.); κ. τὰ κηρία, of bees, Arist.*HA*625b19. 2. metaph., *keep straight, set right*, πολλά τοι σμικροὶ λόγοι..κατώρθωσαν βροτούς S.*El.*416; κατορθοῦντος φρένα Id.*OC*1487; κ. τοὺς ἀγωνιζομένους *make* them *prosper*, D.18.290. b. *accomplish successfully, bring to a successful issue*, τὸν ἀγῶνα Lys.18.13; πολλὰ καὶ μεγάλα Pl.*Men.*99c; εἰ γὰρ ἓν ὧν ἐπεβούλευσεν κατώρθωσεν D.21.106; ὁδόν Id.24.7; μηδὲν ἁμαρτεῖν ἐστὶ θεῶν καὶ πάντα κ. Epigr.ib.18.289; τουτὶ κατωρθώκαμεν περὶ ἐπιστήμης Pl.*Tht.*203b, cf. E.*Hel.*1067; τὰς ἐπιβολάς Plb.10.2.5, etc.:—Pass., *succeed, prosper*, Hdt.1.120, E.*Hipp.*680, Arist.*EN*1106^{b}26; ἐπειδὴ δρᾶν κατώρθωσαι φρενί *thou hast rightly purposed*, A.*Ch.*512; κατωρθωμένος, of works of art, *successful*, Str.9.1.17, al.; τὰ μάλισθ' ὑπὸ τῶν τεχνικωτάτων -ούμενα Phld.*Vit.*p.33 J.; ὅσα κατώρθωται αὐτῶν *the most perfect examples*, Plot.5.8.2: Gramm., βαρυνόμενον τὸ "ἔστε" κατώρθωται *is correctly accented*, A.D.*Synt.*263.14. **II.** intr. as in Pass., *go on prosperously, succeed*, opp. πταίειν, Th.6.12, cf. D.11.11, Men.*Epit.*339; opp. ἡττᾶσθαι, ἔν τινι Isoc.4.124; opp. ἀτυχεῖν, ib.48; opp. ἁμαρτάνειν, Arist.*EN*1106^{b}31, Chrysipp.*Stoic.*2.295; κ. τῷ σώματι Pl.*Lg.*654c; of success in war, X.*Mem.*3.1.3; τῇ μάχῃ, τοῖς ὅλοις, Plb.2.70.6, 3.48.2; περί τινας τῶν πράξεων Isoc.7.11; τὸ κατορθοῦν *success*, D.2.20. **III.** Med. in sense of Act. I. 2b, τῇ πόλει κατορθωσάμενος ἀγαθά *IPE*1^{2}.34.28 (Olbia, i B.C.). **-ωμα**, ατος, τό, *success*, opp. εὐτύχημα, Arist.*MM*1199^{a}13, cf. Plb.1.19.12, Str.15.1.54, D.S.13.22, Plu.*Mar.*10; of literary style, Longin.33.1, 36.2: pl., opp. ἀποτεύγματα, Phld.*Vit.*p.35 J.; v.l. for διορθ-, *Act.Ap.*24.2 (pl.). **2.** *that which is done rightly, virtuous action*, in pl., opp. ἁμαρτήματα, Chrysipp.*Stoic.*2.295, al., cf. *IG*5(2).268.15 (Mantinea, i B.C.), etc.; τῶν καθηκόντων τὰ τέλεια, = τὰ κ., *Stoic.*3.134. **3.** *perfection*, τέλος καὶ πέρας καὶ κ. Herm.*in Phdr.*p.173 A., cf. S.E.*M.*9.16. **4.** Gramm., *correct use*, opp. βαρβαρισμός, Ph.1.124. **-ωσις**, εως, ἡ, *setting straight*, of a fractured bone, Hp.*Fract.*26 (pl.), *Art.*71. **2.** *setting up*, τοῦ θρόνου Lxx*Ps.*96(97).2. **II.** *successful accomplishment* of a thing, *success*, Arist.*Rh.*1380^{b}4, Plb.9.19.4: in pl., *successes*, Id.39.7.7. **2.** *setting right, reform, amendment*, τῆς πολιτείας Id.3.30.2; τῶν πραγμάτων Id.2.53.3. **3.** as philos. term, *right action*, = foreg. 2, Chrysipp.*Stoic.*3.21 (pl.), al. **-ωτέον**, *one must correctly estimate*, Ptol.*Tetr.*193. **2.** *one must set* dislocated limbs, Paul.Aeg.6.120. **-ωτής**, οῦ, ὁ, *one who successfully accomplishes*, πραγμάτων, ἔργων, Vett.Val.48.3, Max.Tyr.21.6. **2.** τριῶν ἀνδρῶν δημοσίων πραγμάτων κ., trans. of Lat. *triumvir reipublicae constituendae*, *Mon.Anc.Gr.*4.2. **-ωτικός**, ή, όν, *likely* or *able to succeed*, opp. ἁμαρτητικός, Arist.*EN*1104^{b}33; *successful*, ἐν ταῖς μάχαις Plu.*Phil.*8; μεγάλων [πραγμάτων] Vett.Val.15.10; *virtuous*, ἔρως Herm.*in Phdr.*p.170 A.

κατορουβάν· ἡ ἀγορά, Hsch.

κατορούω, *rush downwards*, *h.Cer.*341.

κάτορρα· ἡ καταρόα, βωμὸς ἐνόδιος (βώμενος ἐνόδειος cod.), Hsch.

κατορρωδέω, Ion. καταρρ- (q.v.), *fear, dread*, c. acc., Plb.14.1.5, Luc.*Dem.Enc.*3: abs., *to be afraid*, μή.. Plb.10.3.5, cf. Onos.11.3.

κατ-ορυκτός, ή, όν, *deep-buried*, Suid. **-όρυξις**, εως, ἡ, *burying deep*, Thphr.*HP*5.7.7. **-ορύσσω**, Att. -ττω, fut. Pass. -ορυχθήσομαι cj. in Antipho 3.2.10, -ορῠχήσομαι cj. in Ar.*Av.*394 (lyr.): pf. Pass. -ορώρυγμαι Antipho 3.3.12, etc., later κατώρυγμαι *LW*1075 (Apollonia ad Rhyndacum), Str.9.3.8, cf. Moer.p.240 P.: aor. 2 inf. Pass. -ορῠγῆναι Arr.*Epict.*4.8.36:—*bury, sink in the earth*, Hdt.2.41, Hp.*Fract.*13; ζώοντας ἐπὶ κεφαλὴν κατώρυξε Hdt.3.35, cf. 7.114; ἐν τῇ κεφαλῇ Ar.*Av.*475; πατέρα ζῶντα κ. X.*Mem.*1.2.55; κ. κατὰ γῆς Hdt.8.36; κατὰ τῆς γῆς Ar.*Pl.*238; τινὰ εἰς πηλόν (of poets' descriptions) Pl.*R.*363d; [τὰ ᾠὰ] εἰς τὴν κόπρον Arist.*HA*559^{b}2:—Pass., ζῶντες κατορωρύγμεθα Antipho 3.3.12, cf. X.*An.*5.8.11, *Com.Adesp.*1224; τὰ -ορυττόμενα κατὰ γῆς Thphr.*HP*5.7.6, cf. Archestr.*Fr.*62.21; of metals, *lie buried*, Pl.*Euthd.*288e; of money, *to be buried*, D.27.53 (metaph., 29.49); ἐν πορφυρίσι -ορωρυγμένος, of Sardanapallus, Max.Tyr.35.1. **2.** metaph., *ruin utterly*, Pherecr.145.19. **b.** *suppress*, κ. τῷ λόγῳ Lib.*Or.*42.14:—Pass., πρᾶγμα καταπεφρονημένον καὶ κατορωρυγμένον ib.62.32. **-ορῠχή**, ἡ, = κατόρυξις: *buried treasure*, Hsch. (pl.).

κατορφνάομαι, Med., *darken*, Hsch.

κατορχέομαι, *dance in triumph over* one, *treat despitefully*, Hdt.3.151, Lxx*Za.*12.10, Phld.*Piet.*52, Ael.*NA*5.54; τῆς ἀναισθησίας Plu.2.57a. **II.** *subdue* or *enchant by dancing*, Luc.*Salt.*22. **III.** intr., *dance vehemently*, Str.17.1.17.

κατορχίτης [ῑ] οἶνος, ὁ, = συκίτης, v.l. for τροχίτης in Dsc.5.32.

κατόσσομαι, *contemplate, behold*, *AP*12.91 (Polystr.).

κατοσφραίνομαι, *smell*, c. gen., Suid.

κατότι, Adv., Ion. for καθότι or καθ' ὅ τι.

κατουδαῖος, ον, (οὖδας) *under the ground*, οἱ κ. Hes.*Fr.*60; κ. βόθρος *h.Merc.*112; κ. γίγας, of Briareus, Call.*Del.*142; κ. φόβοι Juba Hist.9.

κατουλάς, άδος, ἡ, *shrouding*, νύξ S.*Fr.*433; but taken as = ὀλοή, A.R.4.1695. (From κατειλέω, cf. Hsch. s.v. κατειλάδα.)

κατουλέω, and **κατούλη**, ἡ, dub. sens. in *IG*5(2).357.6 (Stymphalus).

κάτουλ-ος, ον, *cicatrized*, *Gloss.* **-όω**, *cause to cicatrize*, D.S.32.10, Dsc.5.74:—Pass., *cicatrize, heal over*, *AP*9.311 (Phil.), Thessal.ap.Gal.10.250. **-ωσις**, εως, ἡ, *cicatrization*, Dsc.*Eup.*1.51, Heliod.ap.Orib.44.8.12. **-ωτικός**, ή, όν, *causing cicatrization*, Heras ap.Gal.13.432.

κατουρέω, *make water upon*, τινος Ar.*Ec.*832: abs., *make water*, Arist.*HA*556^{b}15, Luc.*Merc.Cond.*34.

κατουρ-ίζω, *bring into port with a fair wind*, metaph., *bring safe to port, bring to fulfilment*, τάδ' ὀρθῶς ἔμπεδα κατουρίζει (sc. the oracle), or (as others) intr., these things *come to fulfilment*, S.*Tr.*827 (lyr.). **-όω**, *sail with a fair wind*, Plb.1.44.3, 1.61.7:—also in Med., Luc.*Lex.*15.

κατουτάω, = οὐτάω, Q.S.14.318 (Pass.).

κατούχιος, = κάτοχος I. 3, epith. of Hermes, *Tab.Defix.Aud.*72.13.

κατοφρῠόομαι, *to be furnished with eyebrows*, in pf. part., Philostr.*VA*3.8: metaph., λόγοι κατωφρυωμένοι *stern, severe* words, Luc.*Am.*53.

κατοχ-εύς, έως, ὁ, *holder, support* in machinery, Hero *Bel.*78.2; κ. πυλάων *bolt*, Call.*Ap.*6; *tenon*, Sm.*Ex.*26.17. **-εύω**, *have* a female animal *covered*, Lxx*Le.*19.19, cf. Hsch. **II.** pf. part. Pass. κατωχευμένος *fertilized*, φοίνικες Mitteis *Chr.*151.26 (iii A.D.). **-ή**, ἡ, (κατέχω) *holding fast, detention*, τινὸς ἐν Σούσοισι Hdt.5.35; of *detention* by the god in the Sarapeum, *UPZ*5.3, 59.8, al. (ii B.C.), cf. Man.1.239 (pl.); *arrest*, *PAmh.*2.80.9 (iii A.D.), *Cod.Just.*1.4.22.1; ἡ πρὸς τὸ χρέος κ. *PSI*4.282.28 (ii A.D.). **2.** *hindrance, delay*, ἀνείρξεις καὶ κ. Plu.2.584e, cf. Vett.Val.43.17. **3.** *retention*, τοῦ πνεύματος *holding* the breath, Gal.6.161, Alex.Aphr.*Pr.*1.47; *retention* of waste products, Gal.8.440. **4.** *retention* in memory, Corn.*ND*14; μνήμη καὶ κ. Plot.4.3.29: pl., τὰς μνήμας κ. μαθημάτων καὶ αἰσθήσεων εἶναι Id.4.6.1. **5.** *sequestration* of property, ἐν κ. *PTeb.*143 (ii B.C.), cf. *PRyl.*174.23 (ii A.D.), etc.; *lien, charge*, καθαρὸς ἀπὸ πάσης κ. *POxy.*483.26 (ii A.D.), etc. **II.** *possession*, Sm.*Ca.*8.11; ἐν κ. ποιεῖσθαι Men.Prot.p.30 D.; = Lat. *bonorum possessio*, *BGU*140.24 (ii A.D.); *mental grasp*, κοινῶν τινων Phld.*Rh.*1.71 S. **2.** *possession by a spirit, inspiration*, κ. καὶ ἐνθουσιασμοί Plu.*Alex.*2; πάντα ἐν τῇ κ. ἀληθεύειν Arr.*An.*4.13.5. **3.** *catalepsy*, Gal.9.189, 10.932; κ. τῶν ἄρθρων *stiffness*, Asclep.ap.eund.13.967. **-ῖμος**, later form for κατοκώχιμος (q.v.), *held in possession*, εἰς αἰῶνα Lxx*Le.*25.46; *sequestered*, κλῆρος *PFrankf.*7 B9 (iii B.C.), cf. *PTeb.*61(*b*).253 (ii B.C.). **2.** *possessed* by a supernatural power, Hsch. s.v. κατοκώχιμον, *Gloss.*; of things, '*eerie*', *uncanny*, κ. πάντα καὶ φρικώδη καὶ μυστικά Luc.*JTr.*30. **3.** Alch., of *fixing* agents, *mordants*, Syn.Alch.p.62 B., Zos.Alch.p.216 B., *PHolm.*15.19, *PLeid.X.*92. **-ιον**, τό, ἐμβρύων preventive of miscarriage, Aët.2.32. **-ῖτις** [ῑ] λίθος stone *with adhesive properties*, Plin.*HN*37.152.

κατοχμάζω, strengthd. for ὀχμάζω, Opp.*H.*5.226.

κάτοχος, ον, (κατέχω) *holding down*, γῇ *Tab.Defix.*101.1 (iv B.C.); κ. λίθοι, of sepulchral stones, Hsch.; κ. alone, *tombstone*, *IG*3.1425*a*; also, οἰκουμένης κ., of ocean, Secund.*Sent.*2. **2.** *holding fast*, μοχλοί Lxx*Jn.*2.7; δεσμοί Plu.2.321d; φάρμακα κ. τῶν ἐμβρύων drugs which prevent miscarriage, Aët.16.21; *retentive*, of memory, Plu.*Cat.Mi.*1; *secure*, κτῆσις κ. καὶ βέβαιος D.H.*Isoc.*9. **3.** *possessing, inspiring*, Μοῦσα Asp.ap.Ath.5.219d; in magic, *inhibiting*, Ἑρμῆς *Tab.Defix.*89.2 (iv B.C.), al. **II.** Pass., *kept down, held fast*, κάτοχ' ἀμαυροῦσθαι σκότῳ A.*Pers.*223 (troch.); *overpowered, overcome*, ὕπνῳ S.*Tr.*978 (anap.); *subject*, Ἄρει E.*Hec.*1090 (lyr.). **2.** *possessed, inspired*, δαίμονί τινι Arist.*Mir.*846^{b}24; τῷ Σαβαζίῳ Iamb.*Myst.*3.9; ἐκ θεοῦ Plu.*Rom.*19, etc.; ἐκ τοῦ θείου Arr.*An.*4.13.5; ἐκ Μουσῶν Luc.*Hist.Conscr.*8; ἐξ Ἄρεως Polyaen.1.20; ἐκ πυξίου Luc.*Ind.*15; στροφὴν ὁλοσώματον ὥσπερ οἱ κ. δινεύοντες Hld.4.17, cf. 8.11, 10.9; also perh. of *cloistered worshippers, recluses*, οἱ κ. οὐρανίου Διός *OGI*262.25 (Baetocaece, iii A.D.), cf. *CIG*4475 (ibid., iii A.D.): abs., Cleanth.*Stoic.*1.123; ἐν ἱεροῖς κ. Vett.Val.73.24. **3.** *cataleptic*, of disease, Hp.*Prorrh.*1.92, cf. Gal.16.696. **b.** *suffering from catalepsy*, Id.9.189. **III.** Subst. κάτοχος, ὁ, *handle* of a τρύπανον, Hsch. s.v. κατωχάνης: pl. κάτοχα, Id. **2.** *bandage*, Gal.18(1).785. **3.** *inhibitory spell*, *PMag.Par.*1.1052, 2.162, *Tab.Defix.Aud.*187.55. **4.** pl., *processes on the second cervical vertebra*, Poll.2.132. **IV.** Adv. κατόχως *retentively*, of the memory, Hermipp.21. **2.** *in fast colours*, βεβάφθαι *AB*237. **3.** *as if possessed*, Ael.*VH*3.9, Poll.1.16. **4.** *accompanied by catalepsy*, Hp.*Coac.*570, al.

κατοχῡρόω, strengthd. for ὀχυρόω, in Pass., Paul.Aeg.6.118.

κατοχ-ώδης, ες, *resembling catalepsy*, Aret.*SA*2.11. **-ωτικός**, ή, όν, f.l. in Ph.1.509, 511 (leg. κατοκωχῇ τε καὶ μανίᾳ).

κατοψέ, Adv., strengthd. for ὀψέ, *late at night*, Alex.Trall.2.

κατόψιος, ον, (ὄψις) *visible*, A.R.2.543. **II.** *in sight of, opposite*, γῆς τῆσδε E.*Hipp.*30.

κάτοψις, εως, ἡ, *sight*, Epicur.*Nat.*11.4, 7.

κατόψομαι, fut. of καθοράω (q.v.).

κατοψοφᾰγ-έω, *spend* or *waste in eating*, Aeschin.1.95 (Pass.), Lib.*Decl.*33.31 (Act.). **2.** *eat greedily*, Ph.2.479, Ath.5.186c. **-ία**, ἡ, *ruinous gluttony* or *luxury*, Poll.6.37.

κατράγοντες· οἱ βόαγροι (Lacon.), Hsch.

κατρεύς, έως, ὁ, an Indian bird, prob. the *monal pheasant*, Clitarch.20, 21 J., Nonn.*D.*26.212.

κάτροπον· κάταντες, Hsch. (Dor. for κατάτροπον, q.v.). **κάτροπτον**, v. κάτοπτρον. **κατρός**· κακός, Id.

κάττα, ἡ, *cat*, late word for αἴλουρος, Sch.Ar.*Pl.*693:—also **κάττος**, ὁ, Sch.Call.*Cer.*111.

καττά, Dor. for κατὰ τά, **καττάδε** for κατὰ τάδε, **καττάν** for κατὰ τήν, **κατταύταν** for κατὰ ταύτην, etc. **καττάνῠσαν**, v. καταπανύω. **καττίτερος, καττιτέρινος, κάττῡμα**, Att. for κασσ-.

καττῡματοποιός, ὁ, *cobbler*, prob. in *Inscr.Délos* 363.64 (iii B.C.).

καττύς [ῡ], ύος, ἡ, *piece of leather*, Ar.*Fr.*285 (v. κασσύω).

καττύω, v. κασσύω.

κατύ, Arc. for κατά, *IG*5(2).6.11, al. (iv B.C.).

κατυβρίζω, κατύπερθε, κατυπέρτερος, κατυπνόω, Ion. for καθ-.

κάτω, Adv., (κατά): I. with Verbs implying Motion, *downwards*, ἐπισκύνιον κ. ἕλκεται Il.17.136; κ. ὁρόων Od.23.91; κατὰ τείχεος κ. ῥίπτειν Hdt.8.53; κατώρυξέν με κατὰ τῆς γῆς κ. Ar.*Pl.*238; χώρει κ. A.*Pr.*74; κ. δάκρυ' εἰβομένη S.*Ant.*527 (anap.), cf. E.*Fr.*384;

esp. of the nether world, A.*Pers.*839, S.*Ant.*197, etc.; κ. βλέπειν, φέρεσθαι, Pl.*R.*500b, 584e; κ. διεχώρει αὐτοῖς they suffered from diarrhoea, X.*An.*4.8.20, cf. Hp.*Epid.*5.20; φάρμακον πῖσαι κ. give a purgative, Id.*Aff.*32, cf. 15; κ. βοηθεῖν go *down* to help, D.32.5; for ἄνω καὶ κάτω, ἄνω κάτω, etc., v. ἄνω (B) A. II. 2. 2. *downwards*, in a chain of causes, ἐπὶ τὸ κ. ἰέναι Arist.*Metaph.*994^{a}19. 3. c. gen., *down from*, πετρῶν ὦσαι κ. E.*Cyc.*448. II. with Verbs implying Rest (so more freq. in Prose), *beneath, below*, opp. ἄνω, Hes.*Th.*301, etc.; ὁ τόπος ὁ κ. καλούμενος Pl.*Phd.*112c. b. *in the world below*, S.*Aj.*660, *OC*1563 (lyr.), etc.; οἱ κ. *the dead*, Id.*Aj.*865, *Ant.*75, etc.; οἱ κ. θεοί Id.*El.*292, cf. E.*Alc.*851. c. geographically *below, southward*, Hdt., v. ἄνω (B) A. II. 1 e; also κ. οἰκεῖν to dwell *on the coast*, Th.1.7; οἱ κ., opp. οἱ τὴν μεσόγειαν κατῳκημένοι, ib.120; ἡ. κ. Γαλατία *lower* Galatia, Plu.*Aem.*9, etc.; βασιλεὺς τῶν τε ἄνω καὶ τῶν κ. χωρῶν *OGI*90.3 (Rosetta, ii B.C.). d. in the race-course, τὰ κ. *the starting-place*, opp. τὰ ἄνω (the goal), Pl.*R.*613b. e. τὰ κ. τῶν μελῶν *the lower* limbs of the body, Id.*Lg.*794d; ἡ κ. κοιλία, opp. ἡ ἄνω, Arist.*Mete.*360^{b}24, *PA*676^{a}5; περὶ τὰ κ. χωρεῖν *miscarry, fail*, Luc. *Ind.*1. f. of Time, *afterwards, later*, Ael.*VH*5.13; οἱ κ. χρόνοι Plu. *Cor.*25; οἱ κ., opp. οἱ πάλαι, Luc.*Hipp.*1; τοῦ χρόνου κ. *later* in time, Ael.*VH*3.17, *NA*2.18; Δαρεῖος ὁ κ. ib.6.48; cf. ἄνω (B) A. II. 1 i. g. in Logic, τὰ κ. *the lower members* in a descending series of genera and species, Arist.*APo.*97^{a}31, *Metaph.*992^{a}18. III. c. gen., *under, below*, κ. χθονός, γῆς, A.*Eu.*1023, S.*OT*968, etc. IV. Comp. κατωτέρω *lower, downwards*, Ar.*Ra.*70, Alex.173.2: c. gen., *lower than, below*, Hdt.8.132. 2. Sup. κατωτάτω *at the lowest part*, τὰ κ. Id.2.125 (but in signf. II. g, Phld.*Sign.*29).

κατω-βλέπων or **-βλεπον**, οντος, ὁ or τό, *down-looker*, name of an African animal, Alex.Mynd.ap.Ath.5.221b, Ael.*NA*7.5, cf. Lat. *catoblepas*:—also **κατῶβλεψ**, επος, ὁ, Archelaus ap.Ath.9.409c.

κατώγαιος, = καταγειος, οἴκημα Alex.Trall.*Febr.*4: **κατώγειος** τόπος *Gp.*9.22.2: **κατώγεως**, Suid.

κατώδῠνος, ον, *in great pain* or *affliction*, Lxx 1*Ki.*1.10, al.

κάτωθεν, rarely **-θε** Eub.16, Alex.128.3, Theoc.4.44: (κάτω):—Adv. *from below, up from below*, ἐλθεῖν A.*Pers.*697 (troch.); ἀμπέμπων Id.*Ch.*382 (lyr.); ἐπανιέναι Pl.*Ti.*22e; ἐκ τῆς γῆς κάτωθεν ἀνίεται ὁ πλοῦτος Id.*Cra.*403a; ἡ κ. ἄνω πληγὴ ἀνασπωμένη Id.*Sph.*221b; also, *from the low country, from the coast*, Hdt.3.60. II. *below, beneath*, τὰ κ. Pl.*Cra.*408d; τὰ κ. ἰσχυρότατ' εἶναι δεῖ D.2.10; ὁ κ. νόμος the law *below*, Id.23.28, cf. Did.ap.Harp. s. v. ὁ κ. νόμος; τίς οἶδεν εἰ κ. εὐαγῆ τάδε; S.*Ant.*521; οἱ κ. θεοί ib.1070, cf. E.*Alc.*424. 2. of Time, τοὺς εἰς τὸ κ. those *belonging to the next generation*, Pl.*Ti.*18d. 3. in Logic, = κάτω II. g, Arist.*APo.*96^{b}37, *Top.*144^{a}29. III. as Prep. c. gen., *below*, κ. τοῦ ὀμφαλοῦ Hp.*Aff.*15; τῶν ἄκρων Thphr. *Sign.*24.

κατ-ωθέω, *push down*, κὰδ δ' ἄρ' ἐπὶ στόμ' ἔωσε Il.16.410; ὅν τε κατὰ στεφάνης ποταμὸς χειμάρροος ὤσῃ 13.138:—Pass., Ph.2.498, Hsch.

κᾰτωκάρα [ᾰρ], Adv. *head downwards*, Pi.*Fr.*161, Ar.*Ach.*945 (lyr.), Ph.1.207, Agath.2.2; *heels over head*, Ar.*Pax* 153.

κατωμάδ-ιος [ᾰδ], α, ον, (ὦμος) *from the shoulder*, δίσκος κ. a quoit *thrown down from the shoulder*, i.e. from the upturned hand held above the shoulder, Il.23.431. II. *worn* or *borne on the shoulder*, Call.*Cer.*45, Mosch.*Fr.*4. **-ίς**, Adv., = sq., Hdn.Gr.1.512. **-όν**, Adv., (ὦμος) *from the shoulders*, μάστιγι κ. ἤλασεν ἵππους Il.15.352, cf. 23.500. II. *on* or *hanging from the shoulders*, A.R.2.679; δωρηθεὶς ἐνετῆσι κ. ἠλέκτροιο *BCH*50.529 (ii A.D.).

κατώμηλ(ος), perh. *hanging from the shoulder*, χιλω(τήρ) *PLond.* 2.402^{v}9 (ii B.C.).

κατωμ-ίζω, *set* a dislocated limb *by putting one's shoulder* under the joint, κ. ἐς ὀρθόν Hp.*Art.*4:—hence **-ισμός** Gal.18(1).333. **-ίς**, ίδος, ἡ, v. κατωτίδες. **-ιστής**, οῦ, ὁ, *throwing the rider over the shoulders*, ἵππος Hsch. **-ος**, ον, *low in the shoulder* or *forequarter*, *Hippiatr.*14.

κατ-ωμοσία, Ion. **-ίη**, ἡ, *accusation on oath*, Hdt.6.65. **-ωμοτικός**, ή, όν, *of* or *for an affirmative oath*, opp. ἀπωμοτικός, ἐπίρρημα (i.e. νή, opp. μά) D.T.642.15, Eust.92.19. Adv. **-κῶς** ib.21, Sch.Ar.*Pl.* 202. **-ώμοτος**, ον, *sworn in affirmation*, ὅρκος Harp. s. v. ἐπακτός.

κατωνάκη [νᾰ], ἡ, *coarse frock with a border of sheepskin* (νάκος), worn by slaves and labourers, Ar.*Lys.*1151, *Ec.*724, Theopomp.Com. 99.

κατωνᾰκοφόρος, ον, *wearing the* κατωνάκη, name of slaves at Sicyon, Theopomp.Hist.172.

κατωπιάω, *cast the eyes down*, of horses, Arist.*HA*604^{b}11, Porph. *Abst.*3.7; Ep. part. -ιόων Q.S.3.133.

κατωπός, όν, (ὤψ) *with downcast looks*, *Hippiatr.*29, 66.

κάτωρ, ορος, ὁ, dub. l. (δῖε κ., v.l. δι' ἑκάτωρ) *h.Bacch.*55.

κατωρᾰΐζομαι, Ion. for καθωραΐζομαι, Hsch.

κατώρης, ες, = κάτω ῥέπων, Hsch. (κατωρής cod.).

κατωρθωμένως, Adv. pf. part. Pass., (κατορθόω) *successfully*, Phlp. *in Ph.*142.10.

κατωρίς, ίδος, ἡ, in dual, *bands* or *ribbands hanging from* the στέφανος, *IG*2^{2}.1388.22.

κατώρροπος, ον, = κατάρροπος, Olymp.*in Phd.*p.244 N.

κατῶρυξ, ῠχος, ὁ, ἡ, (κατορύσσω) *dug out, quarried*, ἀγορὴ .. λάεσσι κατωρυχέεσσ' ἀραρυῖα (as if from κατωρυχής) Od.6.267, cf. 9.185; λίθοι κ. Poll.7.123; τὴν κατώρυγα (sic) θεμελίωσιν foundation *of quarried stone*, Ph.Byz.*Mir.*6.2. 2. *excavated, hewn out*, ἐκ κατώρυχος στέγης, of a rock tomb, S.*Ant.*1100; οἰκήματα κ. D.C.56.11. II. *underground*, κατώρυχες δ' ἔναιον A.*Pr.*452. 2. *beneath the horizon*, [ἄστρα] Arat.510. III. Subst. κατῶρυξ, ἡ, *cavern*, S.*Ant.*774; χρυσοῦ κατώρυχες treasure *caves*, E.*Hec.*1002, cf. Max.Tyr.6.3. 2. *rooting branch*, Str.15.1.21.

κατ-ωρύομαι, *howl much*, Apollod.3.4.4.

κατώρῠχος, ὁ, apptly. a nickname, *Inscr.Prien.*313.720. II. κατώρυχος, ον, = κατῶρυξ II. 1, βελοστάσεις interpol. in Ph.*Bel.*82.9.

κατώτατος, η, ον, Sup. Adj. from κάτω, *lowest*, X.*Cyr.*6.1.52, Lxx *Ps.*87(88).6, al.: neut. pl. as Adv., Hdt.7.23. Adv. κατωτάτω, v. κάτω.

κατωτερικός, ή, όν, of medicines, *purgative*, Hp.*Epid.*5.20, Gal. 10.527. II. *used as an enema*, τροχίσκος Archig.ap.Aët.9.42, cf. Cass.Fel.48.

κατώτερος, α, ον, Comp. Adj. from κάτω, *lower*, Hp.*Fract.*31, Lxx 3*Ki.*9.17, etc.; τὰ κ. μέρη τῆς γῆς *Ep.Eph.*4.9; *more southerly*, Vett. Val.34.21. 2. of Time, *later, younger*, Call.*Cer.*131. Adv. κατωτέρω, v. κάτω.

κατωτέρωθεν, *from a greater depth*, Thphr.*CP*3.20.8.

κατωτίδες, αἱ, (οὖς) *lappets covering the ears*, Hsch. (Fort. κατωμίδες, *capes*.)

κατώτιον, τό, *life-boat*, *PLond.*3.1164(*h*)10 (iii A.D.).

κατωφᾰγᾶς, οῦ or ᾶ, ὁ, (φαγεῖν) *eating with the head down to the ground, gluttonous*, name of a bird, Ar.*Av.*288; also **καταφαγᾶς** (of human beings) A.*Fr.*428, Myrtil.4, Men.424, which is censured by Phryn.400, Poll.6.40.

κατωφελής, ές, (ὄφελος) *very useful*, Thphr.*CP*4.11.4.

κατωφέρ-εια, ἡ, *propensity*, πρὸς συνουσίαν Sch.D Il.24.30, cf. Sch. A.*Ch.*600; *downward tendency*, Eustr.*in EN*60.3. **-ής**, ές, = κάτω φερόμενος, *hanging down*, κεφαλή X.*Cyn.*5.30 (v.l. καταφερής); *steep*, κατάβασις Plb.3.54.5; κ. θέσις *sloping* posture, Sor.2.60; *descending*, χελώνη Orib.49.4.51; *with a downward tendency, heavy*, στοιχεῖα, opp. ἀνωφερής, *Stoic.*2.175, al., cf. Herm.ap.Stob.1.49.68, Simp.*in Ph.*386.23; ὁρμή Eust.603.39. Adv. **-ρῶς** Vett.Val.153.4; gloss on κατωκάρα, Sch.Ar.*Pax* 152. II. metaph., *prone to vice, lewd*, v.l. for καταφερής in Apollod.Ath.ap.Ath.7.281f, cf. Vett.Val.18.3, *EM* 451.2; κ. εἰς τὰ ἀφροδίσια Hsch. s. v. Σαλαβακχώ.

κατώφορος, ον, *having a downward tendency*, Phlp.*in Mete.*30.19, Simp.*in Ph.*671.32.

κατωχάνης, ου, ὁ, *handle* or *holder of a borer*, Hsch.

κατωχεύει· πηδᾷ, ἐπικάθηται, Hsch.; cf. κατοχεύω.

κατωχριάω, *turn very pale*, Ps.-Luc.*Philopatr.*18:—also **κατωχράω**, aor. part. κατωχρήσασα *AP*10.71 (Maced.).

καυάζοντα· ἀποσκάζοντα, Hsch. **καυᾰλέος**, α, ον, *burnt up, parched*, Id.:—also **καυαλής**, ές, Id. **καυαλός**· μωρολόγος, Id. **καύαξ**, ᾱκος, Ion. **καύηξ**, ηκος, ὁ, v. κήξ. **καυάξαις**, v. κατάγνυμι. **καυαρόν**· κακόν, καπυρόν, Id.

καῦδος or **-ον**, ἐπιμελητὴς καύδου dub. sens. in *BSA*26.166 (Sparta, ii A.D.).

***καύεις**, Lydian word, only in acc. sg. **καύειν**, title of priestess of Artemis at Sardis, *IGRom.*4.1755, etc.: **καύης**, ὁ, prob. masc. form of the same, Hippon.2.

καυθμός, ὁ, *burning, scorching*, esp. a disease in trees, produced by keen winds, Thphr.*HP*4.14.11, *CP*5.12.4. II. *firewood*, *PPetr.* 3 p.327 (iii B.C.).

καυκᾰλίας, ὁ, kind of *bird*, Hsch.; cf. καυκιάλης.

καυκάλιον, τό, v. βαυκάλιον.

καυκᾰλίς, ίδος, ἡ, an umbelliferous plant, *Tordylium apulum*, Thphr.*HP*7.7.1, Nic.*Th.*843 (pl.), Dsc.2.139, *Gp.*12.32.1, prob. in Numen.ap.Ath.9.371c; cf. καυσαλίς and καυκιάλης.

καύκαλον, τό, part of a military boot, Anon.*in Rh.*123.22.

Καύκᾰσος, ὁ, *Mt. Caucasus* between the Euxine and Caspian, Hdt. 1.203 sq.: also a gen. Καυκάσιος (as if from Καύκασις) Id.3.97, cf. St.Byz. s. v.: τὸ **Καυκάσιον** ὄρος Hdt.1.104.—The region was **Καυκασία**, ἡ, and the inhabitants **Καυκασῖται, Καυκασιανοί**, St.Byz.

καυκιάλης· βοτάνη τις, ὁμοία κορίῳ (κωρίῳ cod.), καὶ ὄρνις, Hsch. (cf. καυκαλίς and καυκαλίας).

καῦκον, τό, = καυκαλίς, Ps.-Dsc.2.139.

καῦκος, ὁ, a kind of *cup*, *Gloss.*:—Dim. **καυκίον**, τό, *AP*9.749 (in lemmate), Just.*Nov.*105.2.1; κ. ἀργύρεον *PMasp.*167.10 (vi A.D.).

καυλ-εῖον, τό, = καυλίον, Nic.*Th.*75, 535, 882. **-έω**, *form a stalk*, Suid. **-ηδόν**, Adv. *like a stalk*, Opp.*C.*2.511; κ. τέμνειν [εὐθεῖαν] Ascl.*in Metaph.*214.8. II. surgical name of a kind of fracture, Sor.*Fract.*10, Paul.Aeg.6.89. **-ίας**, ου, ὁ, *extracted from a stalk*, ὀπός Thphr.*HP*6.3.2, 9.1.7. **-ίζομαι**, Pass., *have a shaft*, of a spear, Ar.*Fr.*404. **-ικός**, ή, όν, *like a stalk, cauline*, πρόσφυσις Thphr.*HP*7.9.1. **-ίνης**, ου, ὁ, *a kind of* κωβιός, Diph.Siph.ap.Ath. 8.355c. **-ινος**, η, ον, *made of a stalk* or *stick*, Luc.*VH*1.16. **-ίον**, τό, Dim. of καυλός, Nic.*Al.*46 (καυλέα codd.), *Gp.*2.6.32, Dsc.2.183, *PGiss.*93.3 (ii A.D.). II. a kind of *sea-weed*, Arist.*HA*591^{b} 12. III. *part of a column*, Hsch. **-ίσκος**, ὁ, Dim. of καυλός I. 1, Dsc.4.114. 2. *branch of a candlestick*, J.*BJ*7.5.5 (pl.). 3. *tube, catheter*, D.S.32.11.

καυλο-ειδής, ές, *like a stem*, ἔκφυσις Dsc.3.141. **-κῐνάρα**, ἡ, *artichoke stem*, *Gp.*20.31. **-κλυστήρ**, ῆρος, ὁ, (καυλός III) a surgical instrument, *Hermes* 38.282. **-κοπία**, ἡ, *cutting of stalks*, prob. in *PCair.Preis.*38.16 (iv A.D.). **-μύκητες**, οἱ, *stalk-fungi*, burlesque name in Luc.*VH*1.16. **-πώλης**, ου, ὁ, *greengrocer*, Critias *Fr.* 70 D., Poll.7.197.

καυλός, ὁ, *stem* of a plant (opp. στέλεχος, of trees, Thphr.*HP*1.1. 9), Epich.158, Ar.*Eq.*824 (anap.); κ. σιλφίου ib.894; ἢ σίλφιον ἢ ὀπὸς ἡ κ. Hp.*Acut.*37; called ἐκ Κυρήνης κ. Hermipp.63.4; κ. ἐκ Καρχηδόνος Eub.19; κ. Λίβυς Antiph.217.13, cf. 325; κράμβης *BGU*1118.12 (pl., i B. C.), cf. Dsc.2.120, Archig.ap.Gal.13.331. 2. Hom. (only in Il.), *spear-shaft*, ἐν καυλῷ ἐάγη δολιχὸν δόρυ Il.13.162; κατεκλάσθη δ' ἐνὶ καυλῷ ἔγχος ib.608; once of a *sword-hilt*, ἀμφὶ δὲ καυλὸν φάσγανον ἐρραίσθη 16.338. 3. of various tubular structures in animals, πτεροῦ καυλός *quill part* of a feather, Pl.*Phdr.*251b, cf. Arist.*HA*504a31; *neck* of the bladder, ib.497a20; *duct* of the penis, ib.510a26; *cervix uteri*, ib.510b11; *ovipositor* of locusts, ib.555b21. 4. *shank* of a fish-hook, Opp.*H.*3.148. II. *vegetable of the cabbage kind, cole, kail, cauliflower*, Alex.127.5, Anaxandr.41.58 (pl.), Eub.7.3 (pl.). III. *membrum virile*, Hp.*Int.*14, D.S.32.11, Gal.*UP*14.12, Ruf.*Onom.*101, etc. (Cf. Lat. *caulus, caulis*, Lith. *káulas* 'bone'.)

καυλοφορέω, *run to stalk*, Gal.6.657.

καυλ-ώδης, ες, *running to stem*, Thphr.*CP*3.6.9: Comp., Dsc.2.136. **-ωτός**, ή, όν, *with a stalk* or *stem*, Eudem.ap.Ath.9.371a.

καῦμα, ατος, τό, (καίω) *burning heat*, esp. of the sun, καύματος ἐξ after *sun-heat*, Il.5.865, cf. Hes.*Op.*415, 588, Alc.39, S.*Ant.*417, Epinic.1.10, etc.; πρὶν ἂν τὸ κ. παρέλθῃ the *heat of the day*, Pl.*Phdr.*242a, cf. *Ti.*70d; ἐὰν ᾖ κ. Arist.*Mete.*342b10: freq. in pl., ἡλίου τε καύμασιν S.*OC*350, cf. Hdt.3.104, X.*Cyn.*5.9, etc.; [τόποι] ὑπὸ καυμάτων διαφθειρόμενοι Isoc.11.12; καύματα καὶ χειμῶνες Phld.*Piet.*87: in pl., also of frost, Ath.3.98b, Luc.*Lex.*2. 2. *fever heat*, Th.2.49; of *inflamed* conditions, Hp.*VM*19, *Aph.*7.13: metaph., of love, κ. ἀρσενικόν *AP*12.87. II. in pl., *holes burnt by cautery*, Hp.*Art.*11, Arist.*Pr.*863a31. III. *brand* on cattle, *IG*7.3171.44 (Orchom. Boeot.). IV. *embers* of sacrifices, Pl.*Criti.*120d. V. *firewood*, *PLond.*3.1166.6, al. (i A. D.).

καυμᾰτ-ηρός, ά, όν, *very hot*, Str.16.4.1. **-ίας**, masc. Adj., *burning hot*, of the sun, Thphr.*Sign.*11, 26, al. **-ίζω**, *burn, scorch up*, *Apoc.*16.8:—Pass., *to be burnt up*, *Ev.Matt.*13.6; *become heated, suffer from heat*, Plu.2.100b, 691f, Arr.*Epict.*1.6.26, Sor.1.108, M.Ant.7.64. **-ώδης**, ες, = καυματηρός, *burning, scorching*, θέρος οὐ λίην κ. Hp.*Epid.*1.4; νότος Arist.*Mete.*364b23; ὁδός D.S.19.18; ὥρα Longus 1.30. 2. *feverish*, ῥίγεα Hp.*Prorrh.*1.67, al.: metaph., ἡδονή Ach.Tat.2.37.

καυμός, ὁ, *fever*, perh. to be read in Call.*Aet.*3.1.19.

καυνάκης [ᾰ], ου, ὁ, *thick cloak*, Ar.*V.*1137; κ. πορφυροῦς Men.972; said to be of Persian or Babylonian make, Arr.*An.*6.29.5, Poll.7.59, cf. Sch.Ar. l. c., Semus 20, *PCair.Zen.*48.3 (iii B. C.), *PHib.*1.121.11 (iii B. C.):—also **καυνάκη**, ἡ, *PSI*6.605 (iii B. C.); cf. γαυνάκη (which is also found in codd. of *Peripl.M.Rubr.*6):—Dim. **καυνάκιον**, τό, Zonar. (Assyr. *gaunakka* 'frilled and flounced mantle'.)

καυνᾰκο-πλόκος, ὁ, *weaver of* καυνάκαι, *PMasp.*283 ii 17 (vi A. D.). **-ποιός**, ὁ, = foreg., ib.288 iv 5 (vi A. D.).

Καυνιακή (sc. ἔμπλαστρος), name of a *plaster*, Gal.13.532.

Καυνίας, ου, ὁ, *a wind blowing from Caunus* (in Caria) to Rhodes, Arist.*Vent.*973a4.

Καύνιος, α, ον, *of* or *from Caunus* (in Caria), Hdt.1.172, etc.; ἡ Κ. βοῦς, of labour in vain—for this cow overturned the pail after being milked, *App.Prov.*3.6; but Κ. ἔρως, of illicit love, from *Caunus*, brother and lover of Byblis, Arist.*Rh.*1402b3.

καυνός (on the accent, v. Hdn.Gr.1.178), ὁ, = κλῆρος, Cratin.194, Ar.*Fr.*660.

καῦρος (on the accent, v. Hdn.Gr.1.193), α, ον, = κακός, S.*Fr.*1059.

καυσᾰλίς, ίδος, ἡ, prob. glossed by ἡ μέλαινα καὶ ὑπέρυθρος, Hsch. (καύσαλις cod.); perh. to be read for καυκαλίς, of a kind of σμύρνα, Dsc.1.64 (and so in Orib.12 s. v.), and for καυχαλίς (q. v.).

καυσία, ἡ, felt hat used by the Macedonians, forming part of the regalia of their kings, Men.331, Duris 14 J., Ephipp.(*FGrH*126)5 J., Nearch.28 J., Plb.4.4.5, *AP*6.335 (Antip. Thess.), Plu.*Ant.*54, Arr.*An.*7.22.2, Hdn.4.8.2.

καύσῐμος, ον, *combustible*, ἔκαιον πάντα, ὅσα κ. ἑώρων X.*An.*6.3.19; κ. ξύλα Alex.307, *PStrassb.*117.3 (i A. D.); ὕλη Pl.*Lg.*849d, Str.16.4.19; ἄχυρον *Ostr.Fay.*21 (iv A. D.); τούτοις καυσίμοις χρῶνται *as fuel*, Thphr.*HP*4.3.2.

καῦσις, εως, ἡ, *burning*, [τῶν ἱρῶν] Hdt.2.40; λύχνοι τῆς κ. Lxx *Ex.*39.17(37), cf. *PLond.*3.1177.74 (ii A. D.). II. in Surgery, *cautery*, Hp.*Mochl.*3; ἡ καύσει ἡ τομῇ Pl.*R.*406d: in pl., Hp.*Art.*11, Pl.*R.*426b, *Ti.*65b. III. in pl., *burning heat*, ψύξεις τε καὶ κ. Id.*Tht.*156b. IV. *smelting*, χαλκοῦ, ἀργύρου, Str.14.6.5.

καυσμένης· ἔνυδρος, Hsch. **καυσμός**, ὁ, = *cautery*, prob. in *Gloss.* (written *casmos*).

καυσοποιός, όν, *causing heat*, gloss on αἴθων, Eust. ad D.P.591.

καῦσος (A), ὁ, *causus*, i. e. *bilious remittent fever* (the endemic fever of the Levant), Hp.*VM*17 (pl.), *Aph.*3.21 (pl.), Arist.*Pr.*861b34, 862a2; πυρέττειν καύσῳ Id.*Metaph.*981a12; κ. στομάχου *heartburn*, Dsc.1.43, al.: generally, *fever, heat*, Nic.*Th.*338. II. in pl., lands fertilized by burning brushwood, etc., Ath.Med.ap.Orib.1.2.4.

καῦσος (B), εος, τό, = καῦμα I, Procl.*Par.Ptol.*41, 81.

καυσ-όω, *heat*, Ptol.*Tetr.*18:—Pass., *burn with intense heat*, 2*Ep.Pet.*3.10, 12: generally, *to be burnt*, *PHolm.*25.27. II. *suffer from* καῦσος (A) I, Antyll.ap.Orib.9.13.1, Gal.15.720; καυσουμένη ἐπιφάνεια Dsc.2.134. **-τειρᾰ**, fem. of καυστήρ, *burning hot, raging*, only as Adj. in gen., μάχης καυστείρης Il.4.342, 12.316; καυστείρης.. καμίνου Nic.*Th.*924: accented καυστειρῆς in good codd. of Hom. and Nic.:—later in the form **καυστηρός**, Opp.*H.*2.509, v. l. in Nic. l. c., cf. *EM*493.44, Hsch. **-τέον**, *one must burn*, Dsc. 5.79. **-τήρ**, ῆρος, ὁ, *cauterizing apparatus*, Hp.*Haem.*6 (cited as καυτήρ by Gal.19.111); in form καυτήρ, *Hippiatr.*26, Gal.14.782; on the accent, v. Hdn.Gr.2.922. **-τηριάζω, -τήριον**, v. καυτ-. **-τηρός**, v. καύστειρα. **-της**, ου, Dor. **-τας**, ὁ, *one that burns*, τινος Dosiad.*Ara* 11; νεκρῶν *Gloss.*; *one that smelts*, Ptol.*Tetr.*179; *stoker*, *BGU*952.5 (ii/iii A. D.). **-τικός**, ή, όν, *capable of burning*, opp. καυστός (*capable of being burnt*), τὸ καυστὸν οὐ καίεται.. ἄνευ τοῦ καυστικοῦ Arist.*de An.*417a8, cf. *Ph.*251a16; τὸ πῦρ φύσει κ. Phld.*Mus.*p.71 K.: Comp. -ώτερος Arist.*PA*648b18: Sup. -ώτατος Id.*Cael.*307a1, Corn.*ND*32. b. *corrosive, caustic*, δύναμις κ. Dsc.2.4 (Comp.); φάρμακα κ. Gal.11.754, Zopyr.ap.Orib.14.57.1. 2. *of* or *by means of burning*, βάσανοι Lxx 4*Ma.*6.27. Adv. -κῶς, βλάπτειν Eust.70.36. 3. of persons, *feverish*, Hp.*Prorrh.*1.70; also τὰ κ. *inflammatory humours*, Id.*Epid.*4.2.

καῦστις, ἡ, = ἀμφίκαυστις I, Hsch.

καυσ-τός or **καυτός** (as Inscrr.), ή, όν, *burnt, red-hot*, καυτὸν μοχλόν E.*Cyc.*633 (Scal. for καὶ τὸν): καυστόν, τό, *burnt-offering for the dead*, Phot.; so καυτόν Hsch.; *whole burnt-offering*, ἄγοντι τὸμ βοῦν καὶ τὸγ καυτόν *SIG*1025.31 (Cos); ἀρὴν καυτός ib.1027.9 (ibid.). 2. *capable of being burnt*, opp. ἄκαυστος, Arist.*Mete.*387a17, al.; cf. καυστικός: Comp. -ότερος Thphr.*Ign.*72. **-τρα**, ἡ, *place where corpses were burnt*, Str.5.3.8, *CIG*2942 (Tralles), *Gloss.*

Καΰστριος, α, ον, *of* or *from the river Cayster* (in Lydia), Ar.*Ach.*68, etc.

καυσ-ώδης, ες, *suffering from heat, parched*, [χῶραι] Thphr.*CP*3.14.3; τόποι *Arch.Pap.*6.101 (ii A. D.). 2. = καυματώδης 2, πυρετοί Hp.*Aph.*4.54, *Coac.*570; κ. ὕδατα, ταρίχη, *heating*, Id.*Aër.*7, Diph.Siph.ap.Ath.3.120e; κ. ποιεῖν τὸν στόμαχον Heraclid.Tar.ap.eund.3.79f. Adv. -δῶς Archig.ap.Gal.12.543. 3. Astrol., of signs, *causing fevers*, Heph.Astr.1.1. **-ωμα**, ατος, τό, = πύρωσις, Gal.19.110. **-ων**, ωνος, ὁ, *burning heat, summer heat*, *Ev.Matt.*20.12, Orph.*Fr.*264, Luc.*Philops.*25; καύσωνος ὥρᾳ Diph.Siph.ap.Ath.3.73a; ἄνεμος καύσων *sirocco*, Lxx *Je.*18.17, al.; κ. alone, ib.*Ju.*8.3, *Ep.Jac.*1.11, Ath.Med.ap.Orib.1.2.13, Ptol.*Tetr.*85. 2. κ. στομάχου *heartburn*, Dsc.1.22. 3. κ. πυρετός, = καῦσος (A) I, Alex.Trall.*Febr.*2. II. = διψάς II, Ael.*NA*6.51, Philum.*Ven.*20.1.

καυ-τήρ, ῆρος, ὁ, *burner*, ταύρῳ χαλκέῳ, of Phalaris, Pi.*P.*1.95. II. v. καυστήρ. III. = καυτήριον II, Luc.*Pisc.*46, Jul.*Caes.*309c. **-τηριάζω**, *brand*, Str.5.1.9:—Pass., *Hippiatr.*1: metaph., κεκαυτηριασμένοι τὴν ἰδίαν συνείδησιν 1*Ep.Ti.*4.2. **-τηρίδιον**, τό, Dim. of sq., Gal.19.111. **-τήριον**, τό, *branding iron*, E.*Fr.*815 (cj.), Lxx 4*Ma.*15.22, Luc.*Pisc.*52 (vulg. καυστ-), *Apol.*2, *Hippiatr.*26: metaph., ὥσπερ καυτήρια ταῖς ψυχαῖς προσάγειν D.S.20.54. II. *burnt mark, brand*, Str.5.1.9, *BGU*469.7 (ii A. D.). III. instrument used in encaustic painting, *Dig.*33.7.17. IV. (in form καυστ-) *kiln*, *PLond.*2.391.8 (vi A. D.). **-τικός**, ή, όν, *capable of burning*, χυμός Thphr.*CP*6.1.3. **-τός**, ή, όν, v. καυστός.

καυχᾰλίς· φλύκταινα (φυλακταίνα cod.), Hsch.; cf. καυσαλίς.

καυχ-άομαι, Dor. **καυχέομαι** Theoc.5.77; 2 sg. καυχᾶσαι in late Gr., as *Ep.Rom.*2.17, 23, etc.: fut. -ήσομαι Hdt.7.39, Eup.134, Epicr.6: aor. ἐκαυχησάμην Arist.*Pol.*1311b4; Aeol. opt. καυχάσαιτο Sapph.*Supp.*4.2: pf. κεκαύχημαι 2*Ep.Cor.*7.14:—Act., *EM*527.1:—*speak loud, be loud-tongued*, κ. παρὰ καιρόν Pi.*O.*9.38, cf. Eup. l. c., etc.; *boast, vaunt oneself*, ἐπ' αἰζηοῖσι κ. μέγα Cratin.95, cf. Lycurg.*Fr.*78; εἴς τι Arist. l. c.; ἔν τινι *Ep.Rom.* ll. cc.: c. acc. et inf., aor. or pres., *boast that..*, Hdt. l. c., Epicr. l. c., etc.: c. part., *boast of* doing or being, Men.*Mon.*616, D.H.8.30; ὅτι.. Str.13.1.27: c. acc., *boast of*, Philem.141, 2*Ep.Cor.*9.2: c. gen., ὧν Ἱππίας ἐκαυχᾶτο Phld.*Vit.*p.35 J.: c. dat., κάλλει *AP*12.234 (Strat.). **-η**, ἡ, = sq., ἐπέων καύχας, of heroic verse, Pi.*N.*9.7 (nisi leg. καυχᾶσσ', i. e. καυχάεσσα, Dor. fem. of καυχήεις). **-ημα**, Dor. **-ᾱμα**, ατος, τό, *a boast, vaunt*, Pi.*I.*5(4).51. 2. *subject of boasting*, Lesb.Rh.3.4 (pl.), *Ep.Rom.*4.2. **-ημᾰτίας**, ου, ὁ, *boaster, braggart*, Ptol.*Tetr.*159, *EM*121.7; *boastful*, λόγος Sch.Il.13.373. **-ηματικός**, ή, όν, *boastful*, Sch.Il.8.535 (Comp.). **-ήμων**, ον, gen. ονος, *boastful*, Babr.5.10, Heph.Astr.1.1. **-ησις**, εως, ἡ, *boasting*, Epicur.*Fr.*93, Lxx 1*Ch.*29.13, al., Phld.*Vit.*p.27 J., Ph.1.534, *Ep.Rom.*15.17. **-ητής**, οῦ, ὁ, *boaster*, Sch.Il.7.96:—written -ηστής, *EM*121.6. **-ητιάω**, *boast aloud*, ib.206.22, Sch.Ar.*Pl.*572.

καυχός, καυχοῦς, v. χαλκός, χαλκοῦς. **κάφα**· λουτήρ (Lacon.), Hsch. (Lacon. form of σκάφη). **καφάζειν**· γελᾶν, Id. **καφάν**, Dor. for κηφήν, Id. **καφίδιος**, v. κηφ-. **κάφος**, = κάπος, *EM*499.38.

καφουρά, ἡ, *camphor*, Arabic *kāfūr*, *Cinnamomum Camphora*, interpol. in Gal.14.761, Aët.12.63, 16.130.

κάφρυκτοι (καρφ- cod.)· φρύγιοι (Rhod.), Hsch. (For κατάφρ-).

καφώρη, ἡ, *she fox*, Anon.ap.Suid.; cf. σκαφώρη.

κᾰχ-άζω, Dor. fut. καχαξῶ Theoc.5.142:—also in nasalized form **καγχάζω**, S.*Aj.*198 (lyr., v. l.), Babr.99.8, *AP*5.229 (Paul. Sil.), 6.74 (Agath.); cf. ἀνακαγχάζω:—*laugh aloud*, S.*Ichn.*348, Ar.*Ec.*849, *Anacreont.*31.29, Luc.*DMeretr.*6.3; ἐπί τινι at one, Eub.8, Luc.*Am.*23; μέγα κατά τινος Theoc. l. c.; *jeer, mock*, ἁπάντων καγχαζόντων γλώσσαις S.*Aj.* l. c. (Prob. onomatopoeic, by dissim. fr. χὰ χά '*ha! ha!*') **-ασμός**, ὁ, *loud laughter*, v. l. for κιχλισμός, Ar.*Nu.*1073 (pl.).

κᾰχειμονία, ἡ, gloss on δυσχλαινία, Sch.E.*Hec.*240.

καχείτης, ου, ὁ, dub. sens. in *JHS*32.161 (Pisidia).

κᾰχεκ-τεύομαι, *to be in a miserable plight*, *BGU*1141.31 (i B. C.). **-τέω**, *to be in a bad habit of body, be unwell*, Plb.29.17.4, Alex.Aphr.

*inSE*9.1; κ. ταῖς ψυχαῖς *to be ill-disposed, disaffected*, Plb.20.7.4; of the condition of a State, ib.4.1. **–της**, ου, ὁ, (κακός, ἕξις) *in a bad habit of body*, Dsc.2.2, Gal.6.213, 12.321. **2.** metaph., *disaffected* in a political sense, Plb.1.68.10, 28.17.12, Cic.*Att.*1.14.6, Nech. in *Cat.Cod.Astr.*7.142. **–τικός**, ή, όν, = foreg. 1, Gal.11.307.

κᾰχεξ-ής, ές, = foreg., opp. ἀγαθός, dub. in Phld.*Rh.*1.36 S. **–ία**, ἡ, *bad habit of body*, opp. εὐεξία, Hp.*Aph.*3.31 (pl.), Pl.*Grg.*450a, Arist.*EN*1129^{a}20, *PSI*6.632.8 (iii B.C.); distd. from κακοχυμία, Gal. 10.263. **2.** of the mind, *bad disposition, disaffection*, Diph.24, Nicol.Com.1.12, Plb.5.87.3, Hierocl.*in CA*7 p.430 M.: play on both meanings in Str.14.5.14. **3.** in Lit. Crit., *bad style*, κ. τῆς ἑρμηνείας Phld.*Rh.*1.188 S., al.: pl., ib.189 S.

κᾰχ-εταιρεία, poet. **–είη**, ἡ, *ill company*, Thgn.1169. **–ήμερος**, ον, *passing an unhappy day*, *AP*9.508 (Pall.); v.l. κακ–.

καχίλα· ἄνθη (Cypr.), Hsch.

κάχλα, ἡ, = βούφθαλμον, Dsc.3.139.

καχλ-άζω, also **κοχλάζω** (q.v.), usu. pres. and impf., *plash* or *bubble*, of the sound of liquids, φιάλαν ἀμπέλου καχλάζοισαν δρόσῳ Pi. *O.*7.2, cf. Philostr.*VA*3.25; of the sea, περὶ πρύμναν A.*Th.*761 (lyr.), cf. 115 (lyr.); ἄσυχα καχλάζοντος αἰγιαλοῖο Theoc.6.12 (imitated by D.P.838), cf. Arr.*An.*5.20.8; of rain, Lyc.80; of boiling water, Zos. Alch.p.109 B. (cf. κοχλ–): c. acc. cogn., [κῦμα] πέριξ ἀφρὸν πολὺν καχλάζον *frothing forth* foam, E.*Hipp.*1211: metaph., of exuberant eloquence, τὸ Πλατωνικὸν νᾶμα.. μεγάλας παρασκευὰς καχλάζον D.H.*Dem.*28:—also **καχλαίνω**, Hsch. [κᾰ– Pi., A., E. ll.cc., κᾱ– by position, Theoc. l.c.] **–ασμα**, only in form κόχλασμα (q.v.). **–ασμός**, ὁ, = foreg., Zos.Alch.p.119 B. (pl.), *Gloss.*

κάχληξ, ηκος, ὁ, *pebble* in the beds of rivers, etc., Str.4.1.7 (pl.), Gal.12.292, Sch.Theoc.6.12 (pl.); = *caementum*, *Gloss.*: collectively, *gravel, shingle*, Th.4.26, J.*AJ*5.1.3: also **κόχλαξ**, = *glarea*, *Gloss.* (Onomatopoeic word, cf. καχλάζω.)

καχνάζει· κακχάζει, Hsch.

κᾰχομῑλ-ία, ἡ, v. κακομιλία. **–ος**, ον, *keeping bad company*, Phld.*Ir.*p.53 W.

κᾰχορμῑσία, poet. **–ίη**, ἡ, *unlucky harbourage*, *AP*7.640 (Antip.).

κάχρυ, v. κάχρυς II.

καχρύδια, τά, *husks of* κάχρυς, Arist.*Pr.*923^{b}11: sg., prob. in Thphr.*CP*5.6.3.

καχρῠδιάζομαι, *sprout in winter*, ὁ σπόρος –άσεται *Cat.Cod.Astr.* 8(4).251.

καχρῠδίας, ου, ὁ, *made of* κάχρυς, ἄρτος Poll.6.33,72. **II.** κ. πυρός wheat *that resembles* κάχρυς, Thphr.*HP*8.4.3, *CP*3.21.2, Orib. *inc.*13.7. (The words of this group are freq. written καγχρ–.)

καχρῠό-εις, εσσα, εν, *bearing* κάχρυ, ῥίζα, = λιβανωτίς, Nic.*Th.* 40. **–φόρος**, ον, *bearing winter-buds*, Thphr.*HP*3.5.6.

κάχρῠς, ῠος (acc. κάχρυδα Dieuch.ap.Orib.4.7.7, gen. υδος ib.20), ἡ, *parched barley*, Cratin.274, Hp.*Mul.*1.97, Ar.*Nu.*1358, *V.*1306, Gal.11.404. **2.** *winter-bud*, Thphr.*HP*3.5.5, 5.1.4: acc. pl., τὰς κάχρυς ib.3.14.1. **II.** neut. **κάχρυ**, τό, *fruit of* λιβανωτίς, ib.9.11. 10, Ph.*Bel.*86.23, Dsc.3.74 (v.l. κάγχρυς); also, *the whole plant*, Ps.-Dsc. l. c.; κάχρυος ῥίζα Hp.*Nat.Mul.*32, Philum.*Ven.*6.1.

καχρῠφόρος, ον, *bearing* κάχρυ, Nic.*Th.*850. **καχρύω**, fut. –ύσω· συγχεῶ, ταράξω, Hsch.

καχρῠώδης, ες, *like a winter-bud*, Thphr.*HP*3.12.8 and 17.3.

καχυπο-νόητος, ον, = sq., cited in error by Poll.2.57 from Pl.*Phdr.* 240e; v. καχυπότοπος. **–νοος**, ον, contr. **–νους**, νουν, = καχύποπτος, Phld.*Ir.*pp.60,74 W., Ph.2.570.

κᾰχ-ύποπτος, ον, *suspecting evil, suspicious*, Ar.*Fr.*794, Pl.*R.*409c, Arist.*Rh.*1389^{b}21. **–υπότοπος**, ον, = foreg., Pl.*Phdr.*240e.

κάψα, καψάκης, καψάκιον, v. κάμψα, etc.

καψάμενος· ἐλάττωμα ἵππου, Hsch.

καψάριος, ὁ, = Lat. *capsarius*, *IG*3.1171.

καψιδρώτιον, τό, (κάπτω, ἱδρώς) *napkin* or *shirt*, *Com.Adesp.*325 (–όκιον male Hsch.).

καψικός, ή, όν, *like a box*, κάρνον *PFlor.*241.7 (iii A.D.).

καψῑπήδαλος, ὁ, = ὁ μετὰ τῶν τὰ ἄλφιτα [ἐχόντων] καὶ μὴ διδόντων ἁλόμενος, Hsch.: καπηδάλους is corrupt in Eratosth.ap.*EM*286. 36; cf. ἐγκαψικίδαλος.

κάψις, εως, ἡ, (κάπτω) *gulping*, κάψει πίνειν, of the bear, opp. σπάσει and λάψει, Arist.*HA*595^{a}10.

καψοί· οἱ τοῖχοι, Hsch.

κάω, v. καίω.

κε, also **κεν**, Ep., Lesb., Cypr. (*Inscr.Cypr.*135.10 H., al.), Thess. (*IG*9(2).517.13, al. (Larissa)); always enclitic, = ἄν and κᾱ (qq.v.); οὐκ ἄν.. ἀλλά κεν Il.13.290; οὐκ ἄν.. οὐδέ κε 19.272, al.; both coupled, ἄν κεν 11.187, Od.5.361, Parm.8.19, etc.; [ὅσσα] κε θέλῃ Sapph. *Supp.*1.3; τί κεν ποείην; Ead.*Oxy.*1787 *Fr.*1+2.16; κεν ἄν dub. in *IGRom.*4.1302.51 (Cyme); εἴ κ' ἄν (more prob. εἴκ ἄν) *IG*5(2).6 (Tegea, iv B.C.); κε repeated, Od.4.733.

κεάδας, ὁ, = καιάδας, D.Chr.80.9.

κεάζω, Ep. fut. κεάσσω Orph.*A.*849: aor. κέασα, κέασσα, ἐκέασσα Hom. (v. infr.):—Pass., aor. κεάσθην Il.16.412, but part. κεᾰθείσης *App.Anth.*3.167: pf. part. κεκεασμένος (v. infr.):—*split, cleave* wood, κέασε ξύλα νηλέϊ χαλκῷ Od.14.418; κέασαν ξύλα 20.161; ξύλα ..νέον κεκεασμένα χαλκῷ 18.309, cf. Hp.*Mul.*2.153, Call.*Fr.*289, etc.; of lightning, *shiver*, νῆα.. κεραυνῷ Ζεὺς ἔλσας ἐκέασσε Od.5.132; of a spear, κέασσε δ' ἄρ' ὀστέα λευκά Il.16.347; [κεφαλὴ] ἄνδιχα πᾶσα κεάσθη *was cloven* in twain, ib.412; κεκεασμένον εὐρέϊ κύκλῳ οὐρανόν Arat.474. **2.** *pound, rub to pieces*, ἢ σφέλᾳ ἢ ὅλμῳ κεάσας Nic.*Th.* 644. (κεᾰ-ζω fr. κεᾰ- in κεᾰ-θείσης (v. supr.), εὐ-κέα-τος, κέαρνον, and perh. κείων, v. κείω (B); perh. cf. Skt. *śásati* 'cut', Lat. *castrare.*)

κέαθοι· βοηθοί, Hsch.; cf. κηθοί.

κεάνωνος or **–ωθος**, ὁ, *corn-thistle, Carduus arvensis*, dub. l. in Thphr. *HP*4.10.6.

κέᾰρ, contr. κῆρ (q.v.). **κέαρνον**, τό, (κεάζω) *carpenter's axe*, Hsch. (pl.). **κέαρος·** ὄρτυξ, Id. **κεάσματα**, τά, *chips*, Id. **κέᾶται, κέᾶτο**, Ep. 3 pl. pres. and impf. of κεῖμαι.

κεβλή (on the accent, v. Hdn.Gr.1.318), ἡ, Maced. form of κεφαλή, Call.*Fr.*140, cf. *EM*498.41: **κεβαλή**, ib.195.39, Hsch.

κεβλήγονος, ον, *with its seed in its head*, of the poppy, Nic.*Al.* 433. **II.** *born from the head*, Ἀτρυτώνη Euph.108.

κεβλήνη· ἡ ὀρίγανος, Hsch.

κεβλήπῡρις, name of a bird, Ar.*Av.*303; nickname of Themistocles, Hermipp.72.

κέβλος, ὁ, *dog-faced baboon*, Hsch. **κέγκλος**, ὁ, an unknown *sea-bird*, Suid. **κεγνώειν·** τεθραῦσθαι, τετρύσθαι, Hsch. **κέγχει·** ἐπιδάκνει, Id. **κέγχρα**, ἡ, = κέγχρος, Sch.Ar.*V.*91.

κεγχρᾰλέτης, ου, ὁ, (ἀλέω) *grinding millet*, gloss on πασπαλέτης, Gal.19.128.

κεγχρᾰμῐδώδης, ες, *like the* κεγχραμίς 1, Thphr.*HP*1.11.3.

κεγχρᾰμίς, ίδος, ἡ, (κέγχρος) *seed of fig*, Hp.*Nat.Mul.*109, Arist. *HA*549^{a}29, Thphr.*HP*1.11.6, 2.8.2. **2.** *olive-kernel*, Suid. **3.** pl., *trachomata* of the eye, Orib.*Eup.*4.27 tit.

κεγχρανοπώλης, ου, ὁ, = τραγηματοπώλης, Hsch.

κεγχρ-είοισι, poet. lengthd. dat. for κέγχροις, Arat.986. **–εών**, ῶνος, ὁ, (κέγχρος) *place where iron is granulated and made malleable*, Docum.ap.D.37.26. **–ητς**, ῖδος, ἡ, v. κέρχνη. **–ιαῖος**, α, ον, *of the size of a grain of millet*, μεγέθη Dsc.2.83, cf. Luc.*Icar.*18, Theo Sm. p.125 H. **–ίας**, ου, ὁ, *like grains of millet*: κ. ἕρπης *an eruption on the skin*, Gal.7.722, 10.1009. **II.** *serpent with millet-like protuberances* on the skin, Philum.*Ven.*22.1:—also **–ιδίας**, Dsc.*Ther.*32; cf. κέγχρος III: **–ίτης**, Aët.13.27: **–ίνης** [ῐ], ὁ, is another species in Philum.*Ven.* 26.1, Nic.*Th.*463, Lyc.912, Paul.Aeg.5.18. **III.** in Poll.1.248, κεγχριδίας and κεγχρίας are f.ll. for καχρυδίας. **–ίδιον** (κιχρηδῶν cod.), τό, Dim. of κέγχρος, *grain of seed like millet*, Hsch. **–ίνης**, ὁ, v. κεγχρίας II. **II.** a bird, Suid. **–ῖνος**, η, ον, *made of millet*, κ. ἄλευρον Dsc.5.3, cf. Gal.6.519; ἡ κεγχρίνη *millet-pottage*, Hsch. **–ίς**, ίδος, ἡ, = κέρχνη (q.v.). **b.** a small millet-eating bird, *ortolan* or *bunting*, Ael.*NA*13.25. **2.** masc., = κεγχρίας II (q.v.), Lucan.9. 712, Plin.*HN*20.245. **II.** = κέγχρος I, Hp.*Nat.Mul.*32. **–ίτης** [ῑ], ου, ὁ, *like millet*, **1.** = κεγχρίας II (q.v.). **2.** a kind of *stone*, Plin.*HN*37.188. **3.** a bird, Dionys.*Av.*3.23. **II.** fem. **–ῖτις**, ἡ, ἰσχάς *a dried fig* (from its number of grains), *AP*6.231 (Phil.). **2.** a fabulous plant, Ps.-Plu.*Fluv.*19.2.

κεγχρο-βόλοι, οἱ, *millet-throwers*, fabulous tribe in Luc.*VH*1. 13. **–ειδής**, ές, *like grains of millet*, ἱδρῶτες interpol. in Hp.*Prog.*6; κ. τραχύσματα *granulated* work on silver cups, Ath.11.475b. Adv. **–δῶς** Steph.*in Hp.*1.114 D.

κέγχρος, ὁ (also ἡ, Arist.*Ph.*250^{a}20, Dieuch.ap.Orib.4.7.15, Glauc. ap.*POxy.*1802.42, Dsc.2.97, Gal.6.791, Jul.*Or.*3.112a, Iamb.*VP*24. 106), *millet, Panicum miliaceum*, usu. in pl., Hes.*Sc.*398, Hdt.4.17, Hp.*Acut.*21, X.*An.*1.2.22, etc.: sg., Hecat.154 J., Hdt.1.193, Thphr. *HP*1.11.2, al., *OGI*55.15 (Telmessus, iii B.C.); of a single grain, Hdt.3.100, Plot.6.3.11, prob. in Sapph.*Supp.*1.13:—also **κέρχνος**, Anaxandr.41.27, Gal.18(1).574; cf. κέρχνωμα, κέρχνη. **II.** *anything in small grains*: **1.** *spawn of fish*, Hdt.2.93. **2.** *small beads*, Ath.12.525e. **3.** *speck, sty* in the eye, Adam.1.11, al. **III.** = κεγχρίας II (q.v.), Dsc.*Ther.*15. **IV.** *small* kind of *diamond*, Plin.*HN*37.57.

κεγχροφόρος, ον, *bearing millet*, Str.5.1.12.

κεγχρ-ώδης, ες, *millet-like*, of eruptions, Hp.*Liqu.*6, *Epid.*2.3.1; of plants, Thphr.*HP*8.3.3,4; σὰρξ *granulated* tissue, Archig.ap.Orib. 46.26.1. **–ώματα**, ων, τά, *things of the size of millet-grains*: hence, *eyelet-holes* in the rim of a shield, E.*Ph.*1386. **–ων**, ωνος, ὁ, a local wind on the river Phasis, Hp.*Aër.*15. **–ωτός**, ή, όν, *covered with specks*, εἴδη ὀφθαλμῶν Adam.1.11. **II.** *with granulated, roughened surface*, of tables, *BGU*781 v 14 (i A.D.).

κεδαίω, later Ep. for κεδάννυμι (Act. only διὰ.. κεδαίῃ in tmesi, Nic.*Al.*458), in Pass., Arat.159,410, A.R.2.626, Nic.*Th.*425; κεδόωνται (from **κεδάομαι**) A.R.4.500; κεδᾶται Hsch.

κεδάννῡμι, poet. for σκεδάννυμι, late in pres., *AP*5.275 (Agath.); Ep. aor. Act. ἐκέδασσα Hom. (v. infr.), Opp.*H.*1.412, 3 pl. κέδασαν Hsch., Pass. ἐκεδάσθην Hom. (v. infr.), κεδάσθη Orph.*A.*557; plpf. Pass. κεκέδαστο A.R.2.1112:—*break up, scatter*, ἐκέδασσε φάλαγγας Il.17. 285; θεὸς δ' ἐκέδασσεν Ἀχαιούς Od.14.242; so [ποταμὸς] ἐκέδασσε γεφύρας Il.5.88; νεφέλας ἐκέδασσαν ἄελλαι A.R.3.1360:—Pass., κεδασθείσης ὑσμίνης when the battle *was broken up*, i. e. when the combatants were no longer in masses, Il.15.328, 16.306; ἔμειναν ἀθρόοι, οὐδ' ἐκέδασθεν ἀνὰ στρατόν 15.657; [δούρατα] ῥαισθείσης (sc. νηός) κεκέδαστο A.R.2.1112; κῶμα κεδάσθη *was shed*, Orph. l. c.

κέδματα, ων, τά, word of doubtful meaning in Hp.*Aër.*22, *Loc. Hom.*10, *Epid.*6.5.15, 7.122, *Morb.*1.3; expld. by Gal.19.111, Erot., Hsch., as *arthritic affections*; applied to *aneurism* of the vena cava by Aret.*SA*2.8: sg., Hp.ap.Erot.*Fr.*54 (s. v.l.).

κεδμᾰτώδης, ες, *like* κέδματα, Hp.ap.Erot. s. v. κέδματα (dub. l.).

κεδνός, ή, όν, (cf. κήδ-ομαι) Act., *careful, diligent, trusty*, ἄναξ Od. 14.170, etc.; ἀμφίπολος 1.335; πολῖται Pi.*P.*4.117; οἰακοστρόφος A. *Th.*62, E.*Med.*523; στρατόμαντις A.*Ag.*122 (lyr.); γυνή E.*Alc.*97

(lyr.): generally, *noble*, Φοίνικος κόρα B.16.29; παρθένος Pi.*P*.9.122. 2. Pass., *cared for, cherished, dear*, οἵ οἱ κεδνότατοι (v.l. κήδιστοι) καὶ φίλτατοι ἦσαν Il.9.586; ὅς μοι κήδιστος.., κεδνότατός τε Od.10.225; τοκῆες Il.17.28, cf. Pi.*I*.1.5; μήτηρ Hes.*Th*.169, Pi.*Pae*.6.12,105; ἀδελφεοί B.5.118; [ἄλοχος] Id.3.33; λέχος E.*Fr*.591. II. of things, Hom. only in neut. pl., κεδνὰ ἰδυῖα *true*-hearted, Od.1.428, 19.346, al.; ἦθεα κ. Hes.*Op*.699; πολίων κυβερνάσιες Pi.*P*.10.72; κ. χάρις *valued, prized*, Id.*O*.8.80; φροντίς, βουλεύματα, *wise*, A.*Pers*.142 (lyr.), 172 (troch.); ἐφετμαί Id.*Supp*.206; of news, *good, joyful*, Id.*Ag*.622, cf. 261; οὔπω τι κ. ἔσχον S.*Aj*.663; κεδνὰ πράξειν E.*Alc*.605 (lyr.).

κεδνοσύνη, ἡ, *trustiness, goodness*, *IG*3.1370.

κέδρακε· ῥιγοῖ, πέφρικεν, Hsch.

κεδρέα, ἡ, = κεδρία, *PAmh*.2.125.3 (i A.D.), Gal.12.16, al., Paul. Aeg.7.3, Alex.Trall.1.1.

Κεδρεᾶτις, ιδος, ἡ, (κέδρος) title of Artemis at Orchomenus in Arcadia, Paus.8.13.2.

κεδρ-έλαιον, τό, *oil of cedar*, extracted from cedar-resin, Aët.1.196. **-ελάτη** [ᾰ], ἡ, *Syrian cedar, Juniperus excelsa*, Plin.*HN*13.53, 24.17. **-ία**, Ion. **-ίη**, ἡ, *oil of* κεδρελάτη, Hdt.2.87, D.S.1.91, Dsc.1.77, Erot. s.v. κεδρίνῳ; cf. κεδρέα. **-ίνεος** [ῐ], α, ον, poet. for sq., Nic.*Al*.488. **-ῖνος**, η, ον, (κέδρος) *of cedar*, θάλαμος Il.24.192; δόμοι E.*Alc*.160; ξύλα *IG*11(2).161*D*92 (Delos, iii B.C.); ξυλεία Plb.10.27.10; φατνώματα J.*BJ*5.5.2; τῶν ξύλων τὰ κ. Thphr.*HP*5.9.8. 2. *made from* κεδρελάτη, ἔλαιον Hp.*Mul*.1.78, Arist.*HA*583ᵃ23; οἶνος Dsc.5.36. 3. κέδρινον, τό, *orange-coloured dye*, *PHolm*.21.30. **-ίον**, τό, as etym. of κιτρίον, Phan.Hist.35; Lat. *cedrium*, = κεδρία, Vitr.2.9.13, Plin.*HN*16.52; κέδριον, with v.l. κέδρινον, Hp. *Nat.Mul*.32. **-ίς**, ίδος, ἡ, *fruit of* κεδρελάτη, Id.*Mul*.2.192, *Nat. Mul*.32, Dsc.1.77; also, *juniper-berry*, Ar.*Th*.486. II. *juniper, Juniperus communis*, Thphr.*HP*1.9.4, etc. **-ίτης** [ῑ] οἶνος, ὁ, wine *flavoured with* κεδρία, Dsc.5.37.

κεδρόμηλον, τό, = κίτριον, Dsc.1.115, *Alex.Praef.*

κέδρον, τό (Att. acc. to Hsch.), = κεδρίς, *juniper-berry*, *EM*498.42, Hsch.:—also **κέδρος**, ὁ, *Com.Adesp*.34 (ap.Ammon.*Diff*.p.80 V.). II. representation of a *cedar-cone*, *IPE*1².327.

κέδροπα, τά, = χέδροπα, Erot. s.h.v., Hsch. (nisi oxyt. sunt).

κεδροπᾰγής, ές, (πήγνυμι) *made of cedar-wood*, σανίδες *Supp.Epigr*.1.567.6 (Karanis, iii B.C.).

κέδρος, ἡ, *cedar-tree*, ὀδμὴ κέδρου.. θύου τ' ἀνὰ νῆσον ὀδώδει δαιομένων Od.5.60; τὸ ἀπὸ κ. ἄλειφαρ γινόμενον Hdt.2.87, cf. 4.75; applied to *prickly cedar, Juniperus Oxycedrus*, Od. l.c., Thphr.*HP*3.12.3; *Syrian cedar, J. excelsa*, ib.3.2.6, Dsc.1.77; *Phoenician cedar, J. phoenicea*, Thphr.*HP*9.2.3; *Himalayan cedar, J. macropoda*, Str.15.1.29; κ. μικρά *juniper, J. communis*, Dsc. l.c. 2. *anything made of cedar-wood*: *cedar coffin*, E.*Alc*.365 (pl.), *Tr*.1141; *cedar box*, for a beehive, Theoc.7.81. 3. *cedar-oil*, τῇ κ. ἀλείφειν Luc.*Ind*.16. 4. v. κέδρον I.

κεδροχᾰρής, ές, (χαίρω) *rejoicing in cedar*, Man.4.191.

κεδρόω, *embalm with* κεδρία, Posidon.ap.Str.4.4.5, D.S.5.29.

κέδρωστις, εως, ἡ, *bryony*, Dsc.4.182.

κεδρωτός, ή, όν, *made of* or *inlaid with cedar-wood*, παστάδων τέραμνα E.*Or*.1371 (lyr.).

κέεσθαι, κέεται, v. κεῖμαι.

κεῖ, Adv., = κεῖθι, ἐκεῖθι, Archil.170, Herod.1.26.

κεῖα· καθάρματα, Hsch.; cf. κηΐα. **κειάμενος, κείαντες**, v. καίω. **κειανθί**· καίοντες, Id. **κεῖθεν, κεῖθι**, v. ἐκεῖθεν, ἐκεῖθι. **κείθιον**, v. κηθίς.

κεῖλος, ὁ, *donkey*, *Sammelb*.5224.29; cf. κίλλος.

κεῖμαι, κεῖσαι Il.19.319, etc. (κατά-κειαι *h.Merc*.254, Arc. κεῖοι *Tab. Defix*. in *Philol*.59.201), κεῖται Il.6.47, Hdt.1.9, 4.62 (v.l. κέεται), *IG* 1².94.25; pl. κεῖνται A.*Supp*.242, Ion. κέαται Il.11.659, al., Hdt. (προσ-κέανται is f.l. 1.133, cf. προσ-κέαται, v.l. -κέονται, Hp.*Fract*.6), κείᾰται Mimn.11.6 (κατα- Il.24.567), κέονται Il.22.510, Od.16.232, prob. in Alc.94, συγ-κέονται Aret.*SD*2.4; imper. κεῖσο, κείσθω, Il.18.178, Hdt.2.171; subj. 3 sg. κέηται Pl.*Sph*.257c, Lycurg.113, Ep. κεῖται (fr. κέγ-ε-ται) Il.19.32, Od.2.102, al., δια-κέησθε Isoc.15.259, κείωνται *IG*2².1176.21; opt. 3 sg. κέοιτο Hdt.1.67, Hp.*Art*.14 (κατα-), Is.6.32, Pl.*R*.477a; inf. κεῖσθαι Il.8.126, Hp.*Prog*.3, Hdt.2.127, al., κέεσθαι v.l. in ib.2, cf. Hp.*Aër*.6, Archim.*Aequil*.1 *Prooem*.; part. κείμενος Il.7.265, etc.: impf. ἐκείμην Od.13.284, etc., Ep. κείμην 9.434; Ep. 3 sg. κέσκετο 21.41, (παρε-) 14.521; Ion. 3 pl. ἐκέατο Hdt.1.167, Ep. κέατο Il.13.763, κείατο 11.162; κεῖντο 21.426, (ἐπέ-) Od.6.19: fut. κείσομαι Il.18.121, A.*Ch*.895, etc., Dor. κεισεῦμαι Theoc.3.53. (Cf. Skt. *śéte* (= κεῖται), also *śáyate* 'lie', Gr. κοίτη, κοιμάομαι, perh. Lat. *cunae*, etc.):—*to be laid* (used as Pass. to τίθημι): hence, *lie, lie outstretched*, used by Hom. mostly with Preps., πυρὴν.. ᾗ ἔνι κεῖται Πάτροκλος Il.23.210; κεῖτο παρὰ μνηστῇ ἀλόχῳ 9.556; ἐπὶ γαίῃ 11.162; ὑπ' αἰθούσῃ Od.21.390; also ἐπί τινος, ὀστέα.. κείμεν' ἐπ' ἠπείρου 1.162; τὸ δ' ἥμισυ κεῖτ' ἐπὶ γαίης Il.13.565, cf. 20.345; but ὁ δ' ἐπ' ἐννέα κεῖτο πέλεθρα *lay stretched* over.., Od.11.577, al.; later κεῖσθαι εἰς.., in pregnant sense, εἰς ἀνάγκην κείμεθ' E.*IT*620; εἰς ὀλίγην κ. κόνιν *AP*9.677 (Agath.); also ἐπὶ τὴν ὁδὸν κ. *to be strewn* upon the path, Call.*Iamb*.1.250: Archit., κείμενον σχῆμα, opp. ὀρθωμένον, *plan*, opp. elevation, Apollod.*Poliorc*.163.3: c. acc., τόπον.. ὅντινα κεῖται S.*Ph*.145 (anap.). 2. *lie down to rest, repose*, Od.13.281, etc.; πορφυρέᾳ κείμενος ἐν χλανίδι Simon.37.12; *lie, remain*, κεῖτο γὰρ ἐν νήεσσι.. Ἀχιλλεύς Il.2.688, cf. 7.230, etc.; οὐ χρῆν ἥσυχον κεῖσθαι πόδα S.*Fr*.142.13; *lie still*, λασίην ὑπὸ γαστέρ' ἐλυσθεὶς κείμην, of Odysseus under the ram's belly, Od.9.434: metaph., κακὸν κείμενον a *sleeping* evil, S.*OC*510 (lyr.); τοῦ κύματος κειμένου Ael.*NA*15.5. 3. *lie sick* or *wounded*, ἐν νήσῳ κεῖτο, of Philoctetes, Il.2.721, cf. 15.240; κείσεται οὐτηθεὶς 8.537, cf. 11.659; γήραϊ λυγρῷ κεῖται ἐνὶ μεγάροις ἀρημένος 18.435; κεῖτ' ὀλιγηπελέων Od.5.457; *lie in misery*, ἐοικότι κεῖται ὀλέθρῳ 1.46; κεῖται ἐν ἄλγεσι θυμός 21.88, cf. S.*Ph*.183 (lyr.); κ. ἐν κακοῖς E.*Ph*.1639, *Hec*.969; κειμένῳ ἐπεμπηδᾶν to kick him *when he's down*, Ar.*Nu*.550. 4. *lie dead*, Il.5.467, 16.541, al., A.*Ag*.1438, 1446, S.*Ph*.359; κεῖται δὲ νεκρὸς περὶ νεκρῷ Id.*Ant*.1240: rare in Prose, χίλιοι.. νεκροὶ κείμενοι Hdt.8.25, cf. Hdn.2.1.8. b. freq. also in epitaphs, *lie buried*, τῇδε κείμεθα Simon.92, cf. 97; κεῖσαι ζῶν ἔτι μᾶλλον τῶν ὑπὸ γᾶς Id.60; also κ. ἐν Ταρτάρῳ Pi.*P*.1.15; ἐν τάφῳ, ἐν Ἅιδου, παρ' Ἅιδῃ, A.*Ch*.895, S.*El*.463, *OT*972; also in Prose, τὸν χῶρον ἐν τῷ κέοιτο Ὀρέστης Hdt.1.67, cf. 4.11, 9.105, Th.2.43; κ. ὑπό τινων *to be buried* by.., Plu.2.583c. 5. freq. of a corpse, *lie unburied*, Il.18.338, 19.32; κεῖται.. νέκυς ἄκλαυτος ἄθαπτος 22.386; μὴ δή με ἕλωρ Δαναοῖσιν ἐάσῃς κεῖσθαι 5.685; also κεῖτ' ἀπόθεστος.. ἐν πολλῇ κόπρῳ *lay uncared for*, of the old hound of Odysseus, Od.17.296; εὐνὴ.. κἀκ' ἀράχνια κεῖται ἔχουσα 16.35; of places, *lie in ruins*, δόμοι.. χαμαιπετεῖς ἔκεισθ' ἀεί A.*Ch*.964 (lyr.), cf. Pl.*R*.425a, Lyc.252. 6. of wrestlers, *have a fall*, A.*Eu*.590; πεσών γε κείσομαι Ar.*Nu*.126. II. of places, *to be situated, lie*, νῆσος ἀπόπροθεν εἰν ἁλὶ κεῖται Od.7.244, cf. 9.25, 10.196, etc.; ἐν τῇ [γῇ] κείμενά ἐστι τὰ Σοῦσα (for κεῖται) Hdt.5.49; Αἴγινα.. πρὸς νότου κ. πνοάς A.*Fr*.404; πρὸ Μεγάρων κ. Th.3.51; πόλις αὐτάρκη θέσιν κειμένη Id.1.37; θέσιν κέεσθαι νοσερωτάτην Hp.*Aër*.6, cf. Arist.*HA*496ᵃ14; κ. πρὸς τὸν ἥλιον, πρὸς ἄρκτον, Id.*Mete*.360ᵇ14, 363ᵃ3. 2. of things, *lie* or *be* in a place, ὅθι οἱ φίλα δέμνι' ἔκειτο Od.8.277; ἕλε δίφρον κείμενον *placed there*, 17.331, cf. 410; φόρμιγγα.., ἥ που κεῖται ἐν ἡμετέροισι δόμοισι 8.255: in Prose, δύο τράπεζαι ἐκείσθην Lys.13.37; χύτρας εὐκρινῶς κειμένας X.*Oec*.8.19. 3. *fit*, of shoes, Herod.7.121. 4. κεῖσθαι, *posture, attitude*, as a category, Arist.*Cat*.2ᵃ2. III. *to be laid up, in store*, of goods, property, etc., δόμοις ἐν κτήματα κεῖται Il.9.382; πολλὰ δ' ἐν ἀφνειοῦ πατρὸς κειμήλια κ. 6.47; βασιλῆϊ δὲ κεῖται ἄγαλμα *is reserved*.., 4.144; μνῆμα ξείνοιο.. κέσκετ' ἐνὶ μεγάροισι *was left lying*.., Od.21.41; of things dedicated to a god, κ. ἐν θησαυρῷ Hdt.1.51, cf. 52, Alc.94; of money, κείμενα *deposits*, Hdt.6.86.α'; κ. σοι εὐεργεσία ἐν τῷ ἡμετέρῳ οἴκῳ Th.1.129, cf. *SIG*22.15 (Epist. Darei), Pl.*R*.345a; πολλὰ χρήματα ἐπὶ τῇ τούτου τραπέζῃ κεῖταί μοι at his bank, Isoc.17.44; παρά τινι Pl.*Ep*.346c; τἀργύριόν σοι κείσεται the caution-money *shall be deposited*, Ar.*Ra*.624; βραχμὴν ὑπόθες.—Answ. κεῖται πάλαι Diph.73.2: metaph., εἰ ταῦτ' ἀνατὶ τῇδε κείσεται κράτη *shall be placed to* her *credit*, S.*Ant*.485, cf. Pi.*I*.5(4).18. IV. *to be placed in position*, τῶν ἐπὶ τοῦ τοίχου.. κειμένων κιόνων *IG*1².372.46. 2. *to be set up, ordained*, ἄεθλα κεῖτ' ἐν ἀγῶνι Il.23.273, cf. Hdt.8.26, 93, Th.2.46; ὅπλων ἔκειτ' ἀγὼν πέρι S.*Aj*.936 (lyr.). 3. of laws, κεῖται νόμος the law *is laid down*, E.*Hec*.292; νόμοι ἐπ' ὠφελίᾳ τῶν ἀδικουμένων κεῖνται Th.2.37; νόμοι κεῖνται περί τινος Antipho 6.2; οἱ νόμοι οἱ κείμενοι the *established* laws, Ar.*Pl*.914, cf. Lys.1.48, etc.; οἱ ὑπὸ τῶν θεῶν κείμενοι νόμοι X.*Mem*.4.4.21; οἱ νόμοι οἱ ὑπὸ τῶν βασιλέων κείμενοι Isoc.1.36, cf. D.24.62; καινὰ κεῖσθαι θέσμι' ἀνθρώποις E.*Med*.494; αἱ κείμεναι ὑπὸ τῶν ὑπατικῶν γνῶμαι the votes *given* by.., D.H.7.47; οὐκέτι κ. ἡ διαθήκη no longer *holds*, Is.6.32; so of philosophical arguments, *hold good*, κατά τινων Phld.*Rh*.1.51 S.; θάνατος ὢν κεῖται πέρι E.*Ion*756; κείμεναι ζημίαι Lys.14.9, cf. Th.3.45. 4. *to be laid down in argument, posited, assumed*, τοῦτο ἡμῖν οὕτω κείσθω Pl.*R*.350d, etc.; ὡμολογημένον ἡμῖν κ. Id.*Plt*.300e; freq. in Arist., κείσθω *let it be assumed*, *APr*.34ᵇ23, al.; τὸ ἐξ ἀρχῆς κείμενον the *assumption*, *Metaph*.1008ᵇ2, 1047ᵇ10 (pl.); τὰ περὶ τὴν διάνοιαν ἐν τοῖς περὶ ῥητορικῆς κ. *Po*.1456ᵃ35. 5. of names, οὔνομα κεῖται the name *is given*, Hdt.4.184, 7.200, cf. X.*Cyr*.2.2.12, Pl.*Sph*.257c, etc.; ὑπὸ τοῦ πατρὸς κείμενον [ὄνομα] Is.3.32; κεῖσθαι without ὄνομα, Pl.*Cra*.392d; κείμενα ὀνόματα *established* terms, Arist.*Top*.140ᵃ3, Demetr.*Eloc*.96. 6. metaph., πάντα δεινὰ κἀπικίνδυνος βροτοῖς κεῖται, παθεῖν μὲν εὖ, παθεῖν δὲ θάτερα danger *is set before* men, that they may.., S.*Ph*.503. V. metaph., of continuing conditions, ἐνὶ φρεσὶ πένθος ἔκειτο *lay heavy*, Od.24.423; εὔστομα κείσθω *remain* unspoken, Hdt.2.171; νεῖκος ἔκειτό τισι there *was an enduring* feud, S.*OT*491 (lyr.); Ἑλλήνων κείσομαι ἐν στόματι my name *shall be a household word*, *AP*9.62 (Even.); πολλῶν κείμενος ἐν στόμασιν Thgn.240; εὖ κείμενα A.*Ch*.693; μὴ κινεῖν (sc. κακὸν) εὖ κείμενον 'let sleeping dogs lie', Pl.*Phlb*.15c, cf. Hyp.*Fr*.30, Suid. 2. ταῦτα θεῶν ἐν γούνασι κεῖται, i.e. these things *are* yet *in the power of* the gods, to give or not, Il.17.514, 20.435. 3. κεῖσθαι ἔν τινι *to rest entirely* or *be dependent* on him, ἐν ἀγαθοῖσι κ. πολίων κυβερνάσιες Pi.*P*.10.71; ἐν ὕμμι ὡς θεῷ κείμεθα S.*OC*248 (lyr.); also ἐπί τινι, τὰ δ' οὐκ ἐπ' ἀνδράσι κ. Pi.*P*.8.76: also with simple dat., Λεωφίλῳ πάντα κεῖται Archil.69, prob. in *Com.Adesp*.1325; of things, *depend upon*, τὸ πανηγυρικὸν ἐν μελέτῃ καὶ τριβῇ κ. Phld.*Rh*.1.93 S.; τὰ.. γυμνάσια ἐν τῇ κινήσει κ. Antyll.ap.Orib.6.23.1. 4. Medic., *to be left to settle*, of urine, Hp.*Epid*.1.26.β'. b. φάρυγξ οὐ φλεγμαίνουσα, κειμένη δέ, i.e. not swollen, ib.2.2.24. 5. Gramm., of words and phrases, *to be found, occur*, παρὰ τῷ ποιητῇ Str.7.3.6, cf. Ath.2.58b; κεῖται ἐν τῷ Περὶ Πλούτου Phld.*Oec*.p.39 J.; ποῦ κεῖται; Ath.4.165d, cf. Κειτούκειτος; κ. ἀντί τινος *to be used* instead of.., Str.8.6.7; τὸ κείμενον the *received text*, Sch.vulg.Pi.*O*.2.48.

κειμηλι-άρχης, ου, ὁ, *treasurer*, Just.*Nov*.40 *Praef*.1. **-άρχιον**, τό, *treasury*, *Cod.Just*.11.48.20.1, al. **-ον**, τό, (κεῖμαι) *anything stored up as valuable, treasure, heirloom*, τῇ νῦν, καὶ σοὶ τοῦτο, γέρον, κ. ἔστω Il.23.618, cf. Xenoph.2.9, etc.; δῶρον.. ὅ τοι κ. ἔσται Od.1.312;

ἐν ἀφνειοῦ πατρὸς κ. κεῖται, χαλκός τε χρυσός τε πολύκμητός τε σίδηρος Il.6.47; opp. live chattels (πρόβασις), Od.2.75 (pl.), S.*El.*438, E. *Heracl.*591; of a person, Id.*Rh.*654; of a fish, κ. Ἀμφιτρίτης Theoc. 21.55: metaph., κ. ἐσθλά, of γνῶμαι, E.*Fr.*362.4: rare in Prose, Hdt. 3.41, Luc.*Prom.Es* 4, *PGiss.*35.2 (iii A.D.): metaph., φίλος ἀνυπόστατον κ. Secund.*Sent.*11; in bad sense, κακὸν κ. Hp.*Lex* 4. II. *relic,* ἅγια κ. τῆς ἐκκλησίας *PGrenf.*2.111.1 (v/vi A.D.). -ος, ον, *treasured up,* πατὴρ.. ὅτῳ καὶ μήτηρ.. ἐν οἰκίᾳ κεῖνται κειμήλιοι Pl.*Lg.* 931a; κειμήλιον θέσθαι [τὸν θησαυρόν] ib.913a.

κειμηλιοφῠλάκιον [ᾰ], τό, *treasury,* Just.*Nov.*59.6.

κειμηλιόω, *treasure up,* Eust.1376.13:—Med., Hdn.*Epim.*66.

κεῖνος, η, ο, Ion. and poet. for ἐκεῖνος. Adv. κείνως. **κεινός,** ή, όν, Ion. and poet. for κενός. **κεινόω,** v. κενόω. **Κεῖος,** v. Κέως. **κεῖρα·** γενεά, ἡ ἡλικία, Hsch.

κειράς, άδος, ἡ, *shorn,* Lxx *Je.*31(48).31,36; prob. f.l. for κουράς, v.l. κιδάρας.

κειρία, ἡ, *girth of a bedstead,* Ar.*Av.*816, Lxx *Pr.*7.16, Plu.*Alc.* 16. II. *swathing-band, bandage,* written **κηρία,** *PMed.Lond.*155 iv 10,28, al., Sor.1.83, 2.59,61, Hsch. (-ρεί-); **καιρία** (q.v.); **κιρία,** *PCair.Zen.*69.9,11, *PSI*4.341.7, 387.4 (iii B.C.); *grave-clothes,* in form κειρίαι (v.l. κηρίαι) *Ev.Jo.*11.44. III. κηρίαι, *tapeworms,* Hp.ap.Erot.; κειρίαι Gal.14.755.

κειριάτης, *taeniosus, Gloss.*

κειριόω, *swathe,* in Pass., Herm.Trism. in *Rev.Phil.* 32.254,264.

κεῖρις, εως, ἡ, fabulous bird, expld. by ἱέραξ or ἀλκυών, Hsch., cf. Verg.*Ciris* tit. **κειρύλος,** v. κηρύλος.

κείρω, fut. κερῶ Pl.*R.*471a, Ion. κερέω Il.23.146: aor. ἔκειρα Pi. *P.*9.37, E.*Tr.*1173, etc., Ep. ἔκερσα Il.13.546 (ἀπο-, in tmesi), A. *Supp.*666 (lyr.): pf. κέκαρκα *Sammelb.*6002 (ii B.C.), (περι-) Luc. *Symp.*32:—Med., fut. κεροῦμαι E.*Tr.*1183, (ἀπο-) Pl.*Phd.*89b: aor. ἐκειράμην Lys.2.60, etc., Ep. ἐκερσάμην Call.*Fr.*311, A.*Pers.*953 (lyr.): —Pass., aor. 1 part. κερθείς (v.l. καρθ-) Pi.*P.*4.82: aor. 2 ἐκάρην [ᾰ] *PSI*4.368.45 (iii B.C.), subj. καρῇ Hdt.4.127, inf. καρῆναι, part. καρείς, Luc.*Sol.*6, Plu.*Lys.*1: pf. inf. κεκάρθαι Hdt.2.36: Att. plpf. ἐκεκάρμην Luc.*Lex.*5. (Cf. Skt. *kr̥nā́ti* 'wound', Lat. *caro*: prob. also OE. *scieran,* Eng. *shear.*):—*cut short, shear, clip,* esp. of hair, σοί τε κόμην κερέειν (sc. Σπερχειῷ) Il.23.146, cf. Paus.1.37.3; κ. ἐν χροΐ [τὰς τρίχας] *crop* it close, Hdt.4.175; ἀλόχων κείραντες ἔθειραν E.*Hel.*1124 (lyr.): —more freq. in Med., *cut off one's* hair or *have* it *cut off,* as a sign of mourning (cf. κουρά), τοῦτο.. γέρας οἶον ὀϊζυροῖσι βροτοῖσι, κείρασθαί τε κόμην βαλέειν τ' ἀπὸ δάκρυ παρειῶν Od.4.198, cf. 24.46, Il.23.46; πολύν σοι βοστρύχων πλόκαμον κεροῦμαι E.*Tr.*1183; κείρομαι κόμαν Id.*Ph.* 322 (lyr.): abs., *cut off one's hair,* κείρασθε, συμπενθήσατ' Id.*HF*1390; ἐφ' οἷς ἡ πόλις ἐπένθησε καὶ ἐκείρατο Aeschin.3.211, etc.; ἄξιον ἦν ἐπὶ τῷδε τῷ τάφῳ κείρασθαι τῇ Ἑλλάδι Lys. l.c.: Com., πρὸς φθεῖρα κείρασθαι *to have oneself* close *shorn,* Eub.32:—Pass., κουρᾷ.. πενθίμῳ κεκαρμένος E.*Or.*458; σύμβολον κ. half-*cropped,* Hermipp.14; τὰ ῥόδα κ. Pherecr.108.29; also, of the hair, *to be cut off,* πλόκαμοι κερθέντες Pi.*P.*4.82; βοστρύχους κεκαρμένους E.*El.*515. 2. *crop* a person, σφέας αὐτοὺς καὶ τοὺς ἵππους, in sign of mourning, Hdt.9.24; κεκάρθαι τὰς κεφαλάς *to have* their heads *shorn,* Id.2.36; Θρᾳκιστὶ κέκαρμαι Theoc.14.46; v. χρώς 1.2, ἐγκυτί; *shear* sheep, μάχαιραι κουρίδες, αἷς κείρομεν τὰ πρόβατα καὶ τοὺς ποιμένας Cratin.37; κείρεσθαί (*tonderi*) μου τὰ πρόβατα, ἀλλ' οὐκ ἀποξύρεσθαι (*deglubi*) βούλομαι Tiber.ap.D.C. 57.10 (cf. infr. 3); τὸ μὲν [καρῆναι] ἐπὶ προβάτων τιθέασι καὶ ἐπὶ ἀτίμου κουρᾶς (cf. Luc.*Sol.*6), κείρασθαι δὲ ἐπὶ ἀνθρώπων Phryn.292; but τῶν Ἀργείων ἐπὶ πένθει καρέντων Plu. l.c.; τῷ σε χρὴ δρεπάνοισι καὶ οὐ ψαλίδεσσι καρῆναι *AP*11.368 (Jul. Antec.). 3. metaph., '*fleece*', *plunder,* τὴν μάμμην Herod.3.39. II. *cut down,* δοῦρ' ἐλάτης κέρσαντες Il. 24.450; ὕλην S.*Tr.*1196; *crop close,* opp. ἐπιτέμνειν, Thphr.*CP*3.23. 3; *pluck,* ἄνθη Philostr.*VA*1.5: metaph., ἐκ λεχέων κ. μελιαδέα ποίαν Pi.*P.*9.37; Ἄρης κέρσειεν ἄωτον A.*Supp.*666 (lyr.). 2. *ravage* a country, esp. *by cutting down* crops and fruit-trees, τὸ πεδίον Hdt.5. 63; τέμενος Id.6.75, cf. *OGI*765.10 (Priene); τὴν γῆν Hdt.6.99, Th. 1.64; χώραν Aen.Tact.15.9; *destroy,* πόλιν Call.*Fr.*1.60P.; also, *clear,* of pioneers, ὄρος Hdt.7.131:—Pass., of a country, *to be ravaged,* καρῆναι Id.4.127, cf. 8.65; κεκαρμένα κτήματα *SIG*364.67 (Ephesus, iii B.C.):—Med., χθὼν πεύκας κειραμένη *having its* pine-trees *cut down, AP*9.106 (Leon.); ἄρουραι λήϊα κειράμεναι Ps.-Phoc.166: metaph., Σπάρτη.. ἐκείρατο δόξαν had her glory *shorn off,* Epigr.ap.Paus. 9.15.6; Ἄρης νυχίαν πλάκα κερσάμενος *having had* the plain *swept clean* (by destroying the men), A.*Pers.*953 (lyr.). 3. ἔκειρε πολύκερων φόνον *slaughtered* many a horned beast *by hewing,* S.*Aj.*55. 4. *hew, carve,* ἐπίβασιν *Inscr.Cypr.*99 H. 5. *cut through transversely,* opp. σχίζειν (slit longitudinally), φλέβα Antyll.ap.Orib.7.11.3. III. generally, *destroy, consume*: 1. *tear, eat greedily,* of beasts, κείρει τ' εἰσελθὼν βαθὺ λήϊον [ὄνος] Il.11.560; of fish, δημὸν.. ἐπινεφρίδιον κείροντες 21.204; of vultures, ἧπαρ ἔκειρον Od.11.578, cf. Luc.*DDeor.* 1.1, *DMort.*30.1. 2. metaph., *waste, devour,* ἐκείρετε πολλὰ καὶ ἐσθλὰ κτήματ' ἐμά Od.2.312; ἔκειρον κτήματ' ἐνὶ μεγάρῳ 22.369, etc.: abs., κείρετε (sc. βίοτον) 1.378.

κεῖσε, Adv., Ion. and Ep. for ἐκεῖσε. **κεισός,** a plant, Hsch. (Perh. for κισσός.) **κεῖσσα,** Lacon. for κίσσα, Id. **κείστη,** v. κίστη.

Κειτούκειτος, ὁ, comic name of a Gramm., who asked respecting every dish—κεῖται ἢ οὐ κεῖται; (cf. κεῖμαι v. 5) Ath.1.1e.

κείω (A), once in Hom. κέω (v. infr., cf. A.D.*Adv.*143.11), Ep. Desiderat. of κεῖμαι, βῆ δ' ἴμεναι κείων he went *to lie down,* went *to bed,* Od.14.532, cf. 18.428; ἔνθ' ἴομεν κείοντες Il.14.340; κείω I *will lie,* Od.19.340; κειέμεν οὕτω *that they will lie* thus, 8.315; ὄρσο κέων get thee *to bed,* 7.342. 2. later, simply, *sleep, rest,* Arat. 1009.

κείω (B), *cleave,* radic. form of κεάζω, only in pres. part. κείων (perh. for *κεῶν = *κεάων) Od.14.425.

κειώδης, = κηώδης, Hsch.

κεκᾰδήσω, κεκάδοντο, κεκαδών, v. χάζομαι:—but for **κεκαδήσομαι,** v. κήδω:—for **κεκαδδίχθαι,** v. κάδδιχος. **κεκαδμένος,** v. καίνυμαι.

κεκᾰκουργημένως, Adv. *maliciously,* Sch.Aeschin.3.3.

κεκάλακας· καλὴ γέγονας, ἢ ἐκάλεσας, Hsch. **κεκαλμένον·** ἐπὶ γῆς ἐκπεπτωκός, Id. **κέκασμαι, κεκασμένος, κέκαστο,** v. καίνυμαι.

κεκᾰφηώς, Ep. pf. part. with no pres. in use, Hom. only in phrase κεκαφηότα θυμὸν *breathing forth* one's life, Il.5.698, Od.5.468: in later Poets intr., *worn out, fordone,* κεκαφηότα γυῖα Opp.*C.*4.206; κ. γυῖα κεραυνῷ Nonn.*D.*2.539; δέμας κ. λιμῷ ib.26.108; δίψῃ κεκαφηότας ib.29.299; ἄνδρα.. κεκαφηότα δηϊοτῆτι ib.46.93; κεκαφηότι θυμῷ Opp.*H.*3.572; κ. ταρσῷ *weary, AP*9.653 (Agath.). (Cogn. with καπύω, κάπτω: Hsch. has κέκηφε· τέθνηκεν.)

κεκεῖνα· κισσός, Hsch. **κεκῆνας·** λαγωούς (Cret.), Id.

κεκηρυγμένως, Adv., (κηρύσσω) *notoriously,* Poll.6.208.

κέκιλος· ἰσχνόφωνος, Hsch.

κεκλασμένως, Adv., (κλάω A) *effeminately,* Anon.ap.Suid. s. v. ληκυθισμός.

κεκλέαται, κεκλήατο, v. καλέω:—**κέκλετο,** v. κέλομαι. **κέκληγα,** part. κεκληγώς, v. κλάζω. **κεκλῐ́αται, κεκλῑμένος, κέκλῐτο,** v. κλίνω. **κέκλομαι, κεκλόμενος,** v. κέλομαι. **κέκλῠθι, κέκλῠτε,** v. κλύω.

κεκμηκότως, Adv., (κάμνω) *wearily,* Sch.S.*El.*164.

κεκμηώς, ότος and ῶτος, Ep. pf. part. Act. of κάμνω. **κέκνακεν·** ὑπὸ κακῶν ἀπειρήκει, Hsch.

κεκολασμένως, Adv., (κολάζω) *modestly, regularly,* Ath.6.273d, Ael.*NA*2.11, 6.1.

κεκορεσμένως, Adv., (κορέννυμι) *to satiety,* gloss on ἄδην, *EM*16. 42.

κεκόρημαι, κεκορηώς, v. κορέννυμι.

κεκοσμημένως, Adv., (κοσμέω) *modestly,* Ael.*NA*2.11, Philostr. *VA*7.42, Jul.*Mis.*344d.

κεκοτηώς, v. κοτέω. **κεκράανται, κεκράαντο,** v. κραίνω.

κέκρ-αγμα, ατος, τό, *scream, cry,* Ar.*Pax*637 (pl.). **-αγμός,** ὁ, = foreg., E.*IA*1357, Plu.2.654f (pl.). **-άκτης,** ου, ὁ, *bawler,* Hp. *Morb.Sacr.*15, Ar.*Eq.*137, Luc.*JTr.*33.

κεκρᾱμένως, Adv., (κεράννυμι I. 3) *in a mixed manner,* πρὸ τῶν ἀμίκτων ἐλέγχων κ. παρέχεται τοῖς ἐπαίνοις αὐτούς Procl.*in Alc.*p.102 C. 2. in painting, *with well-blended colours,* Plu.2.335a (fort. leg. κεκριμένως).

κεκραξῐδάμας [δᾰ], αντος, ὁ, (κέκραγα, δαμάω) coined by Ar.*V.*596 (by analogy to Ἀλκιδάμας) as epith. of Cleon, *he who conquers all in bawling.*

κεκρᾰτημένως, Adv., (κρατέω) *in a masterly manner,* ἀποδεδωκέναι Hipparch.1.8.11, cf. Phld.*Po.*5.26,29. 2. *vigorously,* v.l. in D.H. *Comp.*25. 3. *positively,* S.E.*M.*11.42.

κέκραχθι, v. κράζω.

κεκρῐμένως, Adv., (κρίνω) *judiciously, discreetly,* μουσικῇ χρῆσθαι Plu.2.1142c; cf. κεκραμένως.

κεκροτημένως, Adv., (κροτέω) *elaborately,* of style, D.H.*Comp.*25 (v.l. κεκρατημένως).

Κέκροψ, οπος, ὁ, *Cecrops* mythical king of Athens, Hdt.8.44; represented with a serpent's tail, and hence called διφυής, Sch.Ar.*V.* 436; with the tail of a θυννίς, Eup.156: pl., = Κεκροπίδαι, *IG*3.1335. (Κέκροψ a barbarian name acc. to Hecat.119 J.) II. Adj. **Κεκρόπιος,** α, ον, *Cecropian, Athenian,* πέτρα Κ. *the Acropolis,* E.*Ion*936 (also simply Κεκροπία, ἡ, used for *Athens* itself, *Supp.*658, *El.*1289); Κ. χθών *Attica,* Id.*Hipp.*34, etc.; Κεκρόπιοι, οἱ, *the Athenians, APl.*4. 295: **Κεκροπία,** ἡ, village-community in Early Attica, Str.9.1.20: **Κεκρόπιον,** τό, *shrine of Cecrops, IG*1².372.63:—also **-ικός,** ib. 374.144. 2. fem. **Κεκροπίς,** ίδος, φυλή Ar.*Av.*1407, *IG*1².302.59, etc.; Κ. αἶα *AP*7.81 (Antip. Sid.). 3. **Κεκροπίδαι,** οἱ, *descendants of Cecrops, Athenians,* Hdt. l.c., etc.: in sg., Ar.*Eq.*1055. 4. Adv. **Κεκροπίᾱθεν,** Ep. -ηθεν, *from Athens,* Call.*Dian.*227, A.R.1.95.

κεκρυμμένως, Adv., (κρύπτω) *secretly,* Lxx *Je.*13.17, Arr.*Epict.* 3.7.11.

κεκρυφάλιον [ᾰ], τό, Dim. of κεκρύφαλος, Poll.7.179. II. **κεκρυφάλεος·** ἀριστερόν (Aeol.), *AB*1095.

κεκρυφᾰλοπλόκος, ον, *netting* κεκρύφαλοι (v. sq.), Critias 69 D.

κεκρύφᾰλος, ὁ, *woman's hair-net,* τῆλε δ' ἀπὸ κρατὸς βάλε δέσματα σιγαλόεντα, ἄμπυκα, κεκρύφαλόν τε ἰδὲ πλεκτὴν ἀναδέσμην Il.22. 469, cf. Hp.*Steril.*219, Ar.*Th.*138, D.H.7.9; κ. καὶ μίτρα Ar.*Th.*257; λιθόβλητοι, λιθοκόλλητοι κ., *AP*5.269 (Paul. Sil.), 275 (Agath.). 2. *part of the head-stall of a bridle,* X.*Eq.*6.8; ἱππικὸς κ. *IG*2².1388.74, cf. Poll.1.184, 10.55. II. *second stomach* of ruminating animals, from its net-like structure, Arist.*HA*507^{b}4, *PA*674^{b}14, Ael.*NA*5. 41. III. *pouch* or *belly of a hunting-net,* X.*Cyn.*6.7, Plu.*Alex.* 25. [ῠ in Hom., *AP*; but ῡ in Att., Ar. l.c., Eup.170, Antiph.117, 189.]

κεκρύφαται [ῠ], v. κρύπτω. **κέκτικε·** τέτοκεν, Hsch. **κεκύθωσι** [ῠ], v. κεύθω. **κεκύκη·** καμπύλη, Id. **κέκυλτα·** δῶρα τὰ τῇ χειρὶ ἑλκόμενα, Id.

Κεκυπώσιος, ὁ (sc. μήν), name of month at Zelea, *SIG*279.17 (iv B.C.).

κελᾰδ-εινός, ή, όν, *sounding, noisy*, Ζέφυρος Il.23.208; Ἄρτεμις 16.183 (παρὰ τὸν γιγνόμενον ἐν τοῖς κυνηγίοις κέλαδον Sch. ad loc.); and so κελαδεινή alone, Il.21.511; of Dionysus, *AP*9.524.11; αὐλῶνες *h.Merc.*95; σῦριγξ Opp.*H.*5.455: neut. pl. as Adv., ποταμοὶ κελαδεινὰ ῥέοντες A.R.3.532:—Pi. has Aeol. form **κελαδεννός**, ἔπεα κ. *high-sounding* verses, *P.*3.113; ὀμφά *Pae.*5.46; κ. Χάριτες the *loud-voiced* Charites, *P.*9.89; κ. ὕβρις *noisy* insult, *I.*4(3).8. **-έω**, Sapph.4, E.*IT*1093 (lyr.); 3 pl. -έοντι Pi.*P.*2.15: fut. -ήσω Terp.5, Pi.*O.*2.2, E.*HF*694 (lyr.), -ήσομαι Pi.*O.*10(11).79: poet. aor. κελάδησα B.15.12, A.*Ch.*609 (lyr.), E.*Hel.*371 (lyr.): (κέλαδος):—Ep. and Lyr. (Trag. and Com. only in lyr. and anap., exc. Theopomp.Com.40: late in Prose, Aq.*Is.*49.13, Philostr.*VA*6.17, Ps.-Luc.*Philopatr.*3) Verb (cf. κελάδω), *sound as flowing water*, ὕδωρ ψῦχρον κ. Sapph.l.c.; κῦμα κελαδοῦν Orac.ap.Aeschin.3.112. 2. of persons, *shout aloud*, ἀτὰρ κελάδησαν Ἀχαιοί, in applause, Il.23.869; ἐμὲ δεῖ κ. Pratin.Lyr.1.3, cf. B.l.c.; κελαδέοντι ἀμφὶ Κινύραν φᾶμαι Pi.*P.*2.15: c. acc. cogn., κ. ὕμνους Terp.5, cf. Pi.*N.*4.16 codd.; νόμον Id.*Pae.*2.101; ἀδυμελῆ κόσμον κ. Id.*O.*11(10).14; [βοάς], παιᾶνας, E.*Ion*93, *HF* l.c. 3. of various *cries*, e.g. of a new-born babe, A.*Ch.*609; of the swallow, Ar.*Pax*801, *Ra.*684; of the grasshopper, Theopomp.Com.l.c.; of the cock, ἐξ εὐνᾶς κ. *crows* from his perch, Theoc.18.57; of bells, *ring, tinkle*, E.*Rh.*384; of the flute, κ. φθόγγον κάλλιστον Id.*El.*716; of the sea, Ar.*Th.*44. II. trans., *sing of, celebrate loudly*, τινα Pi.*O.*1.9, 2.2, 6.88, E.*IT*1093, Ar.*Ra.*1527; τέμενος B.13.21, cf. E.*Tr.*121; τινὰ ἀμφ' ἀρετᾷ Pi.*P.*2.63. **-ημα**, ατος, τό, *rushing sound*, Ζεφύρου E.*Ph.*213 (lyr.); ποταμῶν Ar.*Nu.*283 (anap.); later, of any *loud sound*, κ. σάλπιγγος *AP*6.350 (Crin.). **-ῆτις**, ιδος, ἡ, *loud-sounding*, γλῶσσα Pi.*N.*4.86.

κελᾰδοδρόμος, ον, *rushing amid the noise of the chase*, epith. of Artemis, Orph.*A.*902.

κέλᾰδος, ὁ, poet. word, *a noise as of rushing waters*: generally, *loud noise, din, clamour*, θῆκε πολὺν κέλαδον καὶ ἀϋτήν, of persons quarrelling, Il.9.547, cf. 18.530, Od.18.402; κ. Εὐίου E.*Ba.*578 (lyr.). 2. of *musical sound*, κ. λύρας Id.*IT*1129 (lyr.), cf. *Cyc.*489 (anap.). II. *loud clear voice*, as of an oracle, Pi.*P.*4.60; *shout, cry*, κ. οὐ παιώνιος A.*Pers.*605, cf. 388, *Ch.*341 (anap.), S.*El.*737, etc. 2. *chirp* of the τέττιξ, Ael.*NA*1.20; of the *twittering* of birds, κ. παντομιγής *Lyr.Alex.Adesp.*7.6.

κελάδω, Ep. form of κελαδέω, used in part. only, *sounding*, πὰρ ποταμὸν κελάδοντα Il.18.576, cf. B.8.65, Posidipp.ap.Tz.*H.*7.661; πλῆτο ῥόος κ. Il.21.16, cf. Theoc.17.92; Ζέφυρον κελάδοντ' ἐπὶ οἴνοπα πόντον Od.2.421; πόντον κ. Ar.*Nu.*284 (anap.); Βορέης κ. Q.S.8.243.

κελαιν-εγχής, ές, *with black* (i.e. *bloody*) *spear*, Pi.*N.*10.84.

κελαι-νεφής, ές, sync. for κελαινο-νεφής, *black with clouds*, Homeric epith. of Zeus, *shrouded in dark clouds, cloud-wrapped*, παρὰ πατρὶ κελαινεφεῖ Il.21.520, cf. Pi.*Pae.*6.55; addressed as κελαινεφές in Il.15.46, Od.13.147. 2. generally, *dark-coloured*, ῥέε δ' αἷμα κ. 11.36, cf. Il.4.140; πεδίον κ. *black, rich* soil, Pi.*P.*4.52; σκότος κ. Id.*Fr.*142.

κελαινιάω, *to be black*, in Ep. 3 pl. κελαινιόωσι, Opp.*H.*4.67; part. κελαινιόων Nonn.*D.*38.18.

κελαινό-βρωτος, ον, *black and bloody with gnawing*, ἧπαρ A.*Pr.*1025. **-λωτα**· κεράσια, Hsch. (fort. -λωπα *with dark skin*). **-ομαι**, Pass., *grow black* or *dark*, A.*Ch.*413 (lyr.). **-ρρῖνος**, ον, *with black skin* or *hide*, Opp.*H.*5.18, Nonn.*D.*15.158: pl. κελαινόρινες S.*Fr.*29.

κελαινός, ή, όν, *black, dark*, freq. in Hom., αἷμα Il.1.303, Od.16.441; νύξ Il.5.310, etc.; κῦμα 9.6; λαῖλαψ 11.747; χθών 16.384; δέρμα 6.117; ἦτορ Hes.*Sc.*429; ὄμβρος Emp.111.6; κ. φῦλον a *swarthy* race, of the Ethiopians, A.*Pr.*808; Ἔπαφος ib.851; ξίφη, λόγχα, S.*Aj.*231, *Tr.*856 (both lyr.), cf. E.*Ba.*628 (troch., prob. from the colour of the metal rather than *black with blood-stains*); of things on which the sun does not shine, esp. of the nether world, *dark, murky*, A.*Pr.*433 (lyr.); Ἐρινύες Id.*Ag.*462 (lyr.); Στύξ Lyc.706; κ. θῖνα, of the bottom of the sea, S.*Ant.*590 (lyr.); λύει κ. βλέφαρα suffers her eyes to close *in darkness*, ib.1302: *great, mighty*, δίψα Lyc.1425. (Cf. Skt. *kalaṅkas* 'spot': κηλίς may be cogn.)

κελαινο-φαής, ές, *black-gleaming*, ὄρφνα κ. *murky* twilight, Ar.*Ra.*1331 (lyr.). **-φρων**, ον, gen. ονος, *black-hearted*, μήτηρ A.*Eu.*459. **-χρως**, ωτος, ὁ, ἡ, *black-coloured*, σίλφη *AP*9.251 (Even.), prob. l. in A.*Supp.*785 (lyr.): also **-χροος**, ον, Man.4.261.

κελαιν-ώπας, α, ὁ, (ὤψ) *black-faced*: hence, *gloomy*, θυμός S.*Aj.*955 (lyr.):—fem. **-ῶπις** νεφέλα Pi.*P.*1.7:—also **-ωπός**, ή, όν, Hdn.Gr.1.188. **-ώψ**, ῶπος, ὁ, ἡ, *swarthy*, Κόλχοι Pi.*P.*4.212.

κελᾰρ-ύζω, fut. -ύσομαι or -ύξομαι prob. in Hsch. (-ύζεται· μετὰ ποιᾶς φωνῆς ἠχήσει cod.): aor. κελάρυξε *Lyr.Adesp.*90.1; Poet. and late Prose (v. infr.):—*babble, murmur*, of running water, κατειβόμενον κελαρύζει Il.21.261, cf. Theoc.7.137, Phld.*Po.Herc.*994.14, Philostr.*VA*1.16, *Im.*1.21; later, of a rushing torrent, c. acc. cogn., ὡς ποταμὸς κ. μέγας.. σμερδαλέον μύκημα Opp.*C.*2.145; also, *gush out like water*, ἀπὸ δ' ἕλκεος.. αἷμα μέλαν κελάρυζε Il.11.813; [ἅλμη] ἀπὸ κρατὸς κελάρυζεν *ran gushing*, Od.5.323; of milk, *Lyr.Adesp.*l.c. 2. *pour with a gush* or *gurgling sound*, ἀφύσσοντες οἶνον κελαρύζετε Ion Trag.10 (lyr.). (Onomatopoeic, acc. to Str.14.2.28, Plu.2.747d.) **-υξις**, εως, ἡ, *rushing sound*, as of water, Hsch. **-υσμα**, ατος, τό, = foreg., Opp.*C.*4.325.

κέλε· τέρπε, Hsch.

κελέβειον, Ion. -ήϊον, τό, Dim. of sq., Antim.17.

κελέβη, ἡ (ποτηρίου εἶδος θερμηροῦ καὶ ποιμενικὸν ἀγγεῖον, Hsch.), *cup, jar*, Anacr.42, Theoc.2.2, Euph.8, Call.*Fr.anon.*34 (Aeol., acc. to Clitarch. and Silen.ap.Ath.11.475c).

κελεβρά· λεπτὰ καὶ νεκρὰ κτήνη, Hsch. **κελεῖς**· ἀξίνη, Id. **κελένδρυον** (-υνον Id.), τό, *oaken beam*, derived from κελέων, δρῦς by Id., Phot. (who glosses it by κιχήσιππον).

κελέοντες, ων, οἱ, = ἱστόποδες, *the vertical beams in the upright loom*, between which the web hung down, Ar.*Fr.*795, Antipho *Fr.*11, Theoc.18.34, Ant.Lib.10.2, cf. Paus.Gr. and Ael.Dion.*Fr.*228: sg., v. foreg.

κελεός, ὁ, *green woodpecker, Picus viridis*, Arist.*HA*593ᵃ8, 610ᵃ9.

κελέτρα, ἡ, dub. sens. in *IG*9(2).521.26,33 (Larissa, iii B.C.).

κέλετρον· ᾧ τοὺς ἰχθύας θηρῶσιν ἐν τοῖς ποταμοῖς, Hsch.

κελευθ-είοντες· ὁδεύοντες, Hsch. **-ειος**, α, ον, *belonging to the road*, δαίμονες Id.: κελευθείᾶ, epith. of Athena at Sparta, Paus.3.12.4. **-ήτης**, ου, ὁ, *wayfarer*, *AP*6.120 (Leon.: prob. -ίτης).

κελευθο-ποιός, όν, *road-making*, A.*Eu.*13. **-πόρος**, ὁ, *wayfarer*, *AP*7.337.

κέλευθος, ἡ, with poet. heterocl. pl. κέλευθα; poet. Noun (also Arc., *IG*5(2).3.23 (Tegea, iv B.C.)), *road, path*, not common in lit. sense, πολλαὶ γὰρ ἀνὰ στρατὸν εἰσι κέλευθοι Il.10.66; Ἰσθμία κ. B.17.17; ἐν κελεύθοις in *the streets*, A.*Ch.*349 (lyr.); ἐγγὺς γὰρ νυκτός τε καὶ ἤματός εἰσι κέλευθοι Od.10.86, cf. Parm.1.11; ἀνέμων κέλευθα or κέλευθοι, Il.14.17, Od.5.383, etc.; ὑγρά, ἰχθυόεντα κ., of the sea, 3.71,177; ἁλὸς βαθεῖαν (vel -είας) κ. Pi.*P.*5.88; ἄρκτου στροφάδες κ. *paths, orbits*, S.*Tr.*131 (lyr.), cf. E.*Hel.*343 (lyr.); θεῶν δ' ἀπόεικε κελεύθου withdraw from the *path* of the gods, Il.3.406 (v.l. ἀπόειπε κελεύθους): metaph., ἔργων κέλευθον ἂν καθαράν on the open *road* of action, Pi.*I.*5(4).23, cf. *O.*6.23; στείχει δι' εὐρείας κ. μυρία παντᾷ φάτις B.8.47; ἔστι μοι μυρία παντᾷ κ. Pi.*I.*4(3).1, cf. B.5.31: Πειθοῦς, Δίκας κ., Parm.4.4, B.10.26. II. *journey, voyage*, by land or water, ὅς κέν τοι εἴπῃσιν ὁδὸν καὶ μέτρα κελεύθου Od.4.389; οὐκ ἂν πω χάζοντο κελεύθου would not have halted from *their onward way*, Il.11.504, cf. 12.262; πολλὰ κ. a far *journey*, i.e. a great distance, S.*OC*164 (lyr.). 2. *expedition*, A.*Ag.*127 (lyr.), *Pers.*758 (troch.). III. *way of going, walk, gait*, μιμήσομαι λύκου κ. E.*Rh.*212; δι' ἀψόφου βαίνων κ. Id.*Tr.*888. IV. metaph., *way* of life, ἀργαλέας βιότοιο κ. Emp.115.8; κ. ἁπλόαι ζωᾶς Pi.*N.*8.35; τὰν ἀνόστιμον βίου κ. E.*HF*433 (lyr.).

κελεύθρας· κελεύσεως, Hsch.

κέλ-ευμα, ατος, τό, = κέλευσμα (q.v.). **-ευσις**, εως, ἡ, *command*, Plu.2.32c (pl.), Plot.4.8.2: freq. in Inscrr. and Pap., κατὰ κέλευσιν θεοῦ *OGI*589 (Syria), cf. 455.3 (Aphrodisias, i B.C.), *BGU*286.9 (iv A.D.), etc.; ἐκ κελεύσεώς τινος *IGRom.*4.214 (Ilium, iii/iv A.D.); ἀπὸ κ. *CIG*5187b3 (Ptolemais, v/vi A.D.). **-ευσμα** or **-ευμα** (v. infr.), ατος, τό, (κελεύω) *order, command*, A.*Eu.*235, S.*Ant.*1219 (pl.), etc.; *call, summons*, A.*Ch.*751 (pl.): in Prose, *word of command* in battle, Hdt.4.141, 7.16, cf. E.*Hec.*929 (lyr.); ὁ Κύριος ἐν κ. καταβήσεται ἀπ' οὐρανοῦ 1*Ep.Thess.*4.16; also, the *call* of the κελευστής (q.v.), which gave the time to the rowers, ἀπὸ ἑνὸς κελεύσματος all at once, Th.2.92, D.S.3.15; ἐξ ἑνὸς κελεύματος Sophr.25; ἐκ κελεύματος at *the word of command*, A.*Pers.*397, cf. E.*IT*1405; καχάζετε.. ἀπὸ κ. Eub.8; στρατεύσονται ἀφ' ἑνὸς κ. Lxx *Pr.*30.27; of the boatswain's *pipe*, κέλευσμα προσαυλεῖν Phld.*Mus.*p.15K.; also, the *call* of the driver to his horses, κελεύματι μόνον καὶ λόγῳ ἡνιοχεῖται Pl.*Phdr.*253d; of the huntsman to his hounds, X.*Cyn.*6.20; κ. κυνηγετῶν S.*Ichn.*225. (κέλευμα is the more ancient form, as in A.*Pers.*397, *Ch.*751, S., Sophr., Pl. (codd. l.c.), X., ll.cc., v.l. in Hdt. ll.cc., Th. l.c.)

κελευσ-ματικῶς, Adv. *by way of command*, Eust.1080.63. **-μός**, ὁ, *order, command*, E.*IA*1130, *Cyc.*653 (pl.). **-μοσύνη**, ἡ, Ion. for κελευσμός, κέλευσμα, Hdt.1.157. **-τέον**, *one must order*, Gal.17(2).171. **-τής**, οῦ, ὁ, *boatswain, who gives the time to the rowers*, E.*Hel.*1576, Ar.*Ach.*554, Th.2.84, X.*HG*5.1.8, Pl.*Alc.*1.125c, Phld.*Rh.*1.361S., D.S.20.50, Arr.*Fr.*151J. **-τικός**, ή, όν, *hortatory*: **-κή** (sc. τέχνη), Pl.*Plt.*260e; τοῦ ψόγου τὸ κ. Plu.2.72d (s.v.l.). **-τός**, ή, όν, *ordered, commanded*, Luc.*Vit.Auct.*8. **-τρα** or **κελεύστα**· ἅμαξα ἡμιονική, Hsch. **-τωρ**, ορος, ὁ, *one who commands*, more general than κελευστής, Phryn.*PS*p.81B.

κελευτιάω, Frequentat. of κελεύω, only in Ep. part., Αἴαντε κελευτιόωντ' ἐπὶ πύργων πάντοσε φοιτήτην *continually urging on* [the men], Il.12.265; -όων γαιήοχος ὦρσεν Ἀχαιούς 13.125 (v.l. κελευθιόων, = ὁδηγῶν, Sch. ad loc.; κελευστιόων Hsch.).

κελεύω, Ep. impf. κέλευον Il.23.767: fut. -σω, Ep. inf. -σέμεναι Od.4.274: aor. ἐκέλευσα, Ep. κέλ- Il.20.4: pf. κεκέλευκα Lys.1.34, Luc.*Demon.*44:—**Med.**, aor. ἐκελευσάμην Hp.*Nat.Puer.*13: more freq. in compds. δια-, ἐπι-, παρα-κελεύομαι (q.v.):—**Pass.**, fut. -ευσθήσομαι D.C.68.9: aor. ἐκελεύσθην Hdt.7.9.α', S.*OC*738, Th.7.70: pf. κεκέλευσμαι X.*Cyr.*8.3.14, Luc.*Sacr.*11: plpf. ἐκεκέλευστο D.C.78.4 (ἐκελεύθην v.l. in Hdt.7.9.α', and κεκέλευμαι *IG*2².1121.13 (iv A.D.), v.l. in App.*BC*5.141 are later forms). (A lengthd. form of κέλομαι, q.v.):—prop. *urge, drive on*, [ἵππους] ὁ γέρων ἐφέπων μάστιγι κέλευε.. κατὰ ἄστυ Il.24.326: hence, *exhort, bid*, 1. c. acc. pers. et inf., *order* one to do, σ' ἔγωγε.. κελεύω ἐς πληθὺν ἰέναι 17.30, cf. 2.11, al., Hdt.1.8,24, etc.; ἐκέλευσε τὸν παῖδα περιμεῖναί ἑ κελεῦσαι he *bade* the lad *bid* us to wait for him, Pl.*R.*327b; ὁ νόμος τὸν ἐπιβουλεύσαντα κελεύει φονέα εἶναι, i.e. *bids that* he be held guilty, Antipho 4.2.5; ὁ τὸν νόμον κελεύων ἄρχειν δοκεῖ κελεύειν ἄρχειν τὸν θεὸν καὶ τὸν νοῦν Arist.*Pol.*1287ᵃ29; ἐς τὴν Μίλητον ἔπεμπον κελεύοντες σφίσι τὸν Ἀστύοχον βοηθεῖν Th.8.38; *request*, Lys.16.16; opp. ἐπιτάττειν, *IG*1².76.33. 2. c. acc. pers. et rei, σφῶϊ μὲν οὔ τι κελεύω Il.4.286; τά με θυμὸς.. κελεύει (sc. εἰπεῖν) 7.68, etc.: with inf. subjoined, τί με ταῦτα κελεύεις...μάχεσθαι; 20.87. 3. c. acc. pers. only, εἰ μὴ θυμός με κελεύοι (sc. φείδεσθαι) Od.9.278; ὥς με κελεύεις (sc. μυθεῖσθαι) 11.507: in Prose, ἐκέλευσε τοὺς ἕνδεκα ἐπὶ τὸν Θηραμένην *ordered* them [to go] against him, *ordered* them to seize him, X.*HG*2.3.54; κ. τινὰς ἐπὶ τὰ ὅπλα ib.20:—Pass., *receive orders*, Arist.*Pol*.1253b34. 4. c. acc. rei only, τὸ μὴ κελεύσαι Ζεύς (Herm. for -σει) A.*Eu*.618; ὁ νόμος τὰ μὲν κελεύων τὰ δ' ἀπαγορεύων Arist.*EN*1129b24:—Pass., τὸ κελευόμενον *commands, orders*, Hdt.7.16, Antipho Soph. 61, X.*Cyr*.4.1.3: pl., Pl.*R*.340a. 5. c. dat. pers. folld. by inf., *urge* or *order* one to do, κηρύκεσσι..κέλευσε κηρύσσειν.. Il.2.50, Od.2.6, etc.; ἀλλήλοισι κέλευον ἅπτεσθαι νηῶν.. Il.2.151; ἑτάροισι..ἐκέλευσα ἐμβαλέειν Od.9.488: in later Prose, D.S.19.17, Ceb.32.4 codd., Luc.*DMort*.1.1, Phalar.*Ep*.121.1, etc. 6. rarely c. dat. pers. et acc. rei, τί δ' ἐστὶν ὃ κελεύεις ἐμοί; Men.*Pk*.224, cf. Ael.*NA* 9.1. 7. c. dat. pers. only, ἵπποισι καὶ Αὐτομέδοντι κελεύσας Il. 16.684; cf. infr. III. 8. abs., freq. in Hom., ὡς σὺ κελεύεις Il.23. 96, al.; λέξω, κελεύεις γάρ A.*Ch*.107; κελεύων, opp. αὐτοχειρίῃ, Democr.260; κελευούσης τῆς Πυθίης Hdt.6.36; κελεύοντος καὶ δεομένου Lys.5.1. 9. c. inf. only, σιγᾶν κελεύω I *order* silence, S.*Ph*. 865; οὐκ ἂν κελεύσαιμ' εὐσεβεῖν Id.*Ant*.731; *recommend, propose*, Lys. 12.25, D.4.21, etc.; opp. οὐκ ἐάω, Hdt.6.109, X.*Ath*.2.18. II. of inferiors, *urge, entreat*, Il.24.599, Od.10.17, Hdt.1.116. III. of the boatswain, *give time* to rowers, c. dat., Pl.*R*.396b: abs., Ath.12. 535d. 2. *sing a chanty*, S.E.*M*.6.24.

κελεφος, sine expl., *Gloss.*; ποιεῖ κελεφοὺς *lepers*, *Cat.Cod.Astr.* 8(4).189; cf. κελυφοκομῖον.

κελέων, ὁ, v. κελέοντες.

κελημοσύναις· κελεύσεσιν, Hsch.

κέληξ, ὁ, = sq., *IG*5(1).213 (Sparta, v B.C.).

κέλης, ητος, ὁ, (κέλλω) *courser, riding-horse*, Ὀδυσσεὺς ἀμφ' ἑνὶ δούρατι βαῖνε, κέληθ' ὡς ἵππον ἐλαύνων bestrode one plank, as if riding on a *horse*, Od.5.371 (κ. ἵππος also in later Prose, *SIG*314*A*7,36, al. (Arc., iv B.C.), Plu.*Alex*.3, Paus.6.14.4); κ. καὶ ἅρματα Hdt.7.86; ἵππον κέλητ' ἀσκοῦντα Eup.152; κέλης κέλητα παρακελητιεῖ Ar.*Pax* 901; freq. in the titles of Pindar's Odes, as *O*.1; νίκας Πυθοῖ καὶ Ἰσθμοῖ καὶ Νεμέᾳ τεθρίπποις τε καὶ κέλησι Pl.*Ly*.205c, cf. Plin.*HN* 34.19; κ. πωλικός, τέλειος, *IG*2.966. II. *fast-sailing yacht* with one bank of oars, Hdt.8.94, Th.4.9, 8.38, X.*HG*1.6.36, Ephipp.5.17 (anap.), Plb.5.94.8, Plin.*HN*7.208, etc. III. sens. obsc. (with play on I), Ar.*Lys*.60; so ἥρως Κέλης Pl.Com.174.18. 2. *pudenda muliebria*, Eust.1539.34.

κελητ-ιάω, = sq., Hsch. **-ίζω,** (κέλης) *ride*, ἵπποισι κελητίζειν εὖ εἰδώς, of one who leaps from horse to horse, Il.15.679. II. sens. obsc., Ar.*V*.501, *Th*.153, Macho ap.Ath.13.577d. **-ιον,** τό, Dim. of κέλης II, Th.1.53,4.120, App.*BC*2.56.

κέλλ-α, ἡ, = Lat. *cella, room, chamber*, *POxy*.1128.15 (ii A.D.), etc. **-ᾱρίδιον,** τό, Dim. of κελλάριον, *Sammelb*.4292 (written κελαρίδιν). **-ᾱρικά,** τά, *wine delivered to* a landlord's *cellar*, *PSI*8.953.73 (vi A.D.):—sg. -ᾱρικόν, τό, *store-chamber*, *Stud.Pal*.20.75 ii 9 (iii/iv A.D.). **-άριον** [ᾰ], Hdn.Gr.2.13], τό, *cupboard* for glasses, κ. τριλάγυνον *POxy*.741.12 (ii A.D.), *PLond*.2.191.9 (ii A.D.); *store-chamber*, *POxy*.1851 (vi A.D.). **-άριος** [ᾱ], ὁ, *cellarman*, *Wien.Stud*.24.131 (ii A.D.). **-ᾱρίτης** [ῑ], ου, ὁ, = foreg., *Stud.Pal*.20.107.4 (iv A.D.), *PKlein.Form*.40 (vi A.D.).

κελλάς· μονόφθαλμος, Hsch.

κελλίβας, ατος, ὁ, prob. = κιλλίβας, *portable table*, *PRyl*.136.10 (i A.D.); cf. Lat. *cilibantum, cilliba*.

κελλικάριος (for *κελλαρικάριος), ὁ, *cellarman, butler*, *PSI*8.955.13 (vi A.D.).

κέλλικας· δημότας, Hsch.

κελλίον, τό, Dim. of κέλλα, *PAmh*.2.152.16 (v/vi A.D.); *garret*, *AP*11.351 (Pall.).

κελλίων· ἡ τῶν ὅλων φύσις, Hsch. **κελλόν·** στρεβλόν, πλάγιον, Id.

κέλλω, poet. (exc. D.H.14.1 as etym. of Κελτική), = Prose ὀκέλλω: fut. κέλσω A.*Supp*.331, E.*Hec*.1057 (lyr.), κελῶ Hsch.: aor. ἔκελσα (v. infr.):—*drive on*, Hom. only in Od., always in phrase νῆα κέλσαι *run* a ship *to land, put* her *to shore*, νῆα μὲν αὐτοῦ κέλσαι Od.10.511; νῆα..ἐκέλσαμεν ἐν ψαμάθοισιν 9.546; *cause to land*, ἀνδρῶν ἡρώων στόλον A.R.2.1090: metaph., Ἄργει κ. πόδα E.*El*.139 (lyr.). II. intr., of ships or seamen, *put to shore* or *into harbour*, κελσάσῃσι δὲ νηυσὶ καθείλομεν ἱστία Od.9.149; κέλσαντες Σιμόεντος ἐπ' ἀκτάς A.*Ag*.696 (lyr.), cf. *Eu*.10; ἐς Ἄργος Id.*Supp*.331; πρὸς γῆν S.*Tr*.804: c. acc. loci, κέλσαι..Ἄργους γαῖαν A.*Supp*.15 (anap.); Τροίας ἄστυ E.*Rh*.934: metaph., A.*Pr*.186 (lyr.); κ. ποτὶ τέρμα E.*Hipp*.140 (lyr.); πᾷ κέλσω; where *shall I find a haven?* Id.*Hec*.1057 (lyr.). (Cf. κέλομαι.)

κελλῶσαι· πλαγιάσαι, Hsch. **κελμάς,** ἡ, = κεμάς, Id. **Κελμίς,** name of an Idaean Dactyl, also glossed by παῖς ἢ λύκιθον (sic), Id. **κελοί,** οἱ, = τὰ ξύλα, Id. s. v. κελέοντας.

κελοῖα, ἡ, also written **καιλοῖα, κελύα, κελέα, κελῆα, κελεῖα,** name of contest for boys and youths at Sparta, *IG*5(1).263, al.: perh. neut. pl., ib.258.

κέλομαι, Ep. 2 sg. κέλεαι, sts. disyll., Il.24.434, Od.4.812, 10.337: impf. κελόμην Il.1.386, ἐκέλευ Theoc.3.11, κέλετο Il.15.119 (Dor. κέντο Alcm.141, acc. to Eust.756.30), ἐκέλετο *IG*4²(1).122.35 (Epid., iv B.C.): fut. κελήσομαι Od.10.296: aor. 1 ἐκελήσατο, κελήσατο, Epich.71, 99, Pi.*O*.13.80, *I*.6(5).37, *IG*4²(1).121.108 (Epid., iv B.C.): Ep. aor. 2 ἐκέκλετο, κέκλετο, Il.11.285, 16.421, Hes.*Sc*.341: hence was formed by later Poets pres. **κέκλομαι** A.R.1.716, etc.; Dor. opt. κεκλοίμαν A.*Supp*.591 (lyr.); part. κεκλόμενος, v. infr. II. 1; imper. κέκλεο and κέκλου Hsch. (this pres. used in pass. sense by Man.2.251, 3.319): poet. (also in Dor. Prose, *IG*ll. cc., al. (Epid., iv B.C.), cf. infr. II; ὅν κα κέλωνται τοὶ ἱαροποιοί *Abh.Berl.Akad*.1928(6).12 (Cos, iv B.C.)): Act. aor. 1 ἐκέλησεν Hsch.:— = κελεύω, *urge, exhort, command*.—Constr. like κελεύω: 1. c. acc. pers. et inf., Il.5.810, 16.657, al., Alc.46, Pi. ll. cc., A.*Ag*.1119 (lyr.); of the *commands* of a god, *IG*4²(1).121.50 (Epid., iv B.C.), al.; μεταλλῆσαί τί ἑ θυμὸς..κέλεται, καὶ κήδεά περ πεπαθυίῃ (instead of -υῖαν) Od.17.555. 2. c. dat. pers. et inf., φυλασσέμεναί τε κέλονται ἀλλήλοις Il.10.419: more freq. without inf., Ἀργείοισιν ἐκέκλετο μακρὸν ἀΰσας 6.66; ἀμφιπόλοισι κέκλετο ib.287; ἵπποισιν ἐκέκλετο 8.184; ἀλλήλοισι κέλεσθε 12.274. 3. abs., κέλομαι γὰρ ἔγωγε for [so] I *advise*, 23.894, Od.17.400; κέλεαι γάρ 5.98; ἐγὼ κέλομαι καὶ ἄνωγα 3.317; ἐπὶ δ' Ἕκτορι κέκλετο θυμὸς (sc. ἑ ἰέναι) Il. 16.382; less freq. of things, λαίνετο κηρός, ἐπεὶ κέλετο μεγάλη ἲς the wax melted, since mighty force *constrained* it, Od.12.175; ὡς..παρ' ἡμετέρης κέλεται πιστώματα Μούσης Emp.5. II. *call to*, κέκλετο δ' Ἥφαιστον Il.18.391; *call upon for aid*, *h.Cer*.21; πρῶτά σε κεκλόμενος, θύγατερ Διός S.*OT*159 (lyr.), cf. A.*Supp*.591 (lyr.); ἂν μὴ κελομένου πρίαται *Milet*.3.140*C*56 (iii B.C.), cf. *Leg.Gort*.6.48, *Schwyzer* 181 v 4,8 (Crete). 2. *call by name*, νιν ὄρνιχος κέκλετ' ἐπώνυμον Pi.*I*.6(5).53. (κέλομαι, κέλλω, κελεύω may be cogn. with Skt. *kalayati* 'push', Lat. *celer*.)

Κελτ-ίβηρες [ῑ], οἱ, *tribes of mixed Celtic and Iberian descent*, Str. 1.2.27. **-ιστί,** Adv. *in the language of the Celts*, Arr.*Tact*.43.2, Luc.*Alex*.51.

Κελτοί, οἱ, *Celts*, Hdt.2.33, X.*HG*7.1.20, Plb.1.13.4:—later **Κέλται,** Str.4.1.1, etc.:—hence **Κελτικός,** ή, όν, *Celtic, Gallic*, Id.3.1.3:—poet. **Κελτός,** ή, όν, Call.*Del*.173:—fem. **Κελτίς,** ίδος, *AP*10.21 (Phld.); ἡ Κελτική *the country of the Celts* or *Gauls*, Arist.*HA*606b4, Str.4.1.1; ἡ Κελτία Foed.ap.Plb.7.9.6.

Κελτο-λίγυες [ῐ], οἱ, *tribes of mixed Celtic and Ligurian descent*, Str.4.6.3. **-σκύθαι** [ῠ], οἱ, *tribes of mixed Celtic and Scythian descent*, Id.1.2.27.

κελύφ-ᾰνον [ῠ], τό, = κέλυφος, Lyc.89, Luc.*VH*2.38 (dub.). **-ανώδης,** ες, *like a shell* or *husk*, Thphr.*CP*1.7.2. **-ιον,** τό, Dim. of κέλυφος 2 d, Arist.*HA*622a7.

κελυφοκομῖον (= -εῖον), τό, *lepers' hospital*, *BMus.Cat.Coptic MSS*. p.453 No.1077; cf. κελεφος.

κέλῠφος, εος, τό, *sheath, case*, 1. in fruits, *pod, shell*, Arist.*GA* 752a20, Thphr.*HP*2.4.2, etc. 2. in animals, *sheath*, Arist.*HA* 510a28. b. τὰ κ. τῶν ᾠῶν egg-*shells*, Id.*GA*743a17; in fish, *encasing membrane*, Id.*HA*568b9; τὸ περὶ τὰς γενέσεις κ. ib.600b17. c. *envelope*, of a chrysalis, ib.551a20, 601a6,8, *GA*758b17; of the chrysalis of the stag-beetle, Id.*HA*551b19. d. *shell* of crustaceous fish, ib. 549b25. e. *hollow* of the eye, *AP*9.439 (Crin.). 3. metaph., of old dicasts, ἀντωμοσιῶν κελύφη mere affidavit-*husks*, Ar.*V*.545 (lyr.); of an old man's *boat*, which served as his *shell* or *coffin*, *AP*9.242 (Antiphil.). [ῠ, exc. Opp.*C*.3.503.] (Prob. cogn. with καλύπτω.)

κέλωρ, ωρος, ὁ, *son*, poet. word in E.*Andr*.1033 (lyr.), Lyc.495, al., Puchstein *Epigr.Gr*.p.76, etc. 2. *eunuch*, Hsch. II. = φωνή, βοή Id., *PMasp*.151.249 (vi A.D.).

κελώριον, τό, = παιδίον, Hsch. **κελωρύω,** *shout*, Id., Phot.; cf. κέλωρ II.

κεμάδειον (sc. κρέας), τό, *venison*, *Edict.Diocl*.4.45 (prob.).

κεμᾰδοσσόος, ον, *chasing deer*, Nonn.*D*.5.230, 46.147.

κεμάς, άδος, ἡ, *young deer, pricket*, between νεβρός and ἔλαφος (so Ar.Byz.ap.Eust.711.37, cf. Miller *Mélanges de litt.gr*.p.431), Il.10. 361, Call.*Dian*.112, A.R.3.879, Herodic.ap.Ath.5.222a, Ael.*NA*14. 14:—also **κεμμάς** (q. v.), and in Hsch. **κεμφάς.** (Cf. Skt. *śáma*- 'hornless', Lith. *šmùlas* 'hornless', OE. *hind*.)

κεμασῖνας, = καμασῆνας, Hsch.

κεμέλει, τό, *measure of length*, Hero *Geom*.4.13.

κέμμα, ατος, τό, prob. f.l. for κέρμα, Emp.101.

κεμμάς, άδος, ἡ, poet. for κεμάς, Q.S.1.587, *AP*9.2 (Tiber. Illustr.), etc.

κέμμερος· ἀχλύς, ὀμίχλη, Hsch. **κέμμης·** ὅριον, Id. **κέμμορ·** μέγα κῆτος, Id. **κεμφάς,** v. κεμάς. **κέμων·** ἑτερόφθαλμος, Id. **κεν,** = κε (q. v.).

κεναγγ-ής, ές, (κενός, ἄγγος) *emptying the vessels of the body*: hence, *breeding famine*, ἄπλοια A.*Ag*.188 (lyr.). **-ία,** Ion. **κενεαγγίη** (q. v.), ἡ, *emptiness of vessels*; esp. *hunger*, Pl.Com.156; κ. ἄγειν *to fast*, Ar.*Fr*.608.

κενανδρ-ία, ἡ, *lack of men*, A.*Pers*.730 (troch.). **-ος,** ον, (ἀνήρ) *empty of men*, ἄστυ, πόλις, ib.119 (lyr.), S.*OC*917.

κεναυχής, ές, v. κενεαυχής.

κένδῡλα, τά, also **κένδῡλα** or **κενδύλη,** ἡ, dub. l. for σχενδύλα (q. v.).

κενεαγγ-έω, (κενεός, ἄγγος) *have the vessels of the body empty, undergo lowering* or *evacuant treatment*, Hp.*Art*.69, al. **-ητέον,** *one must fast*, Id.*Acut*.11. **-ίη** (in Mss. mostly -είη), ἡ, Ion. for κεναγγία, *lowering* or *evacuant treatment*, ibid., al., *Aph*.1.2, *Coac*.54; *evacuation by bleeding*, Aret.*CD*2.3. **-ικός,** ή, όν, *exhausted*, κ. σημεῖον Hp.*Acut*.48; of persons, Id.*Liqu*.2.

κενεᾱγορία, ἡ, *empty talk*, *Lyr.Adesp*.135 (pl.).

κενέαρος· κενός, ἐλαφρός, Hsch.

κενεαυχής, ές, (αὐχή) *vain-glorious*, κενεαυχέες ἠγοράασθε Il.8.230; κενεαυχέα πλοῦτον *AP*7.117 (Zenod.), cf. *POxy*.1015.19 (v. l.):—later **κεναυχής,** ές, Plu.2.103e; τὸ κ. κάλλος *AP*12.145.

κενέβρειος, ον, = θνησείδιος (cf. Ael.*NA*6.2), esp. of dead cattle:

κενέβρεια, τά, *carrion*, Ar.*Av.*538 (anap.), cf. *Fr.*693. 2. τὰ κ. *the dog's-meat market*, Erot. (sg. as v.l.), Phot.

κενεγκράνιος [ᾰ], ον, *brainless*, Sch.Juv.15.23.

κενέθας· σπόγγος, Hsch.; **κενέφας**, Cyr.

κενεμβᾰτ-έω, *step on emptiness*, Plu.*Flam.*10; *step into a hole*, Gal.18(2).887, Luc.*Gall.*26. 2. Medic., of a lancet, catheter, etc., *reach a cavity*, Orib.44.11.3, Gal.14.786, Paul.Aeg.6.59. II. metaph., *lack solid foundation*, κενεμβατοῦν καὶ σφαλλόμενον, of Alexander's Empire, Plu.2.336f; κενεμβατοῦμεν ταῦτα λέγοντες Dam.*Pr.*4, cf. Plot.3.9.2. 2. *lead a frivolous life*, Men.Prot. p.2 D. **–ησις**, εως, ἡ, *piercing of a cavity*, Sor.2.62, Paul.Aeg. 6.21. II. '*emptiness*' of the pulse, Gal.8.509,931.

κενεολογία, v. κενολογία.

κενεός, ή, όν, Ep., Ion., and Dor. for κενός (q.v.).

κενεότης, ητος, ἡ, = κενότης, *empty space*, Hp.*Acut.*62.

κενεο-φροσύνη, ἡ, *empty-mindedness*, Timo 48.2: **κενοφρ-**, Plu. *Ages.*37. **-φρων**, ον, gen. ονος, *empty-minded*, δῆμος Thgn.233; μῦθος, αὖχαι, Simon.75, Pi.*N.*11.29:—also **κενόφρων**, βουλεύματα A. *Pr.*762.

κενέφας, v. κενέθας.

κενέωμα, ατος, τό, = κένωμα, τάφου, = κενοτάφιον, *Epigr.Gr.*234 (Smyrna).

κενεών, ῶνος, ὁ, (κενός) *hollow between ribs and hip, flank*, Od.22. 295, Poll.2.166, etc.; νείατον ἐς κενεῶνα, ὅθι ζωννύσκετο μίτρη Il.5. 857, cf. Hp.*Prog.*8 (pl.); of horses, X.*Eq.*12.8; of dogs, Id.*Cyn.* 4.1. 2. οἱ κ. τοῦ περιτοναίου the *hollows* of the peritonaeum, Heliod.ap.Orib.50.48.4. II. any *hollow*, hence periphr. οὐράνιοι *AP*9.207; αἰθέριος, χθόνιος κ., Nonn.*D.*13.453,9.82; κενεὼν ἀρούρης ib.41.3; *vacant space* in a crowd, Lxx 2*Ma.*14.44.

κενέωσις, εως, ἡ, poet. for κένωσις (q.v.).

κενήριον, τό, *empty monument, cenotaph*, Dieuchid.3, Euph.91, Lyc.370, *AP*7.569 (Agath.).

κενογάμιον [ᾰ], τό, (γάμος) *empty, unreal marriage*, coined after κενοτάφιον by Ach.Tat.5.14.

κεν-οδοντίς, ίδος, ἡ, *toothless*, *AP*6.297 (Phan.).

κενοδοξ-έω, *hold a vain opinion*, περί τι Plb.12.26[c].4; περὶ τὸ ἀληθές Lxx 4*Ma.*5.9. 2. *to be vain-glorious*, Hld.9.19; ἐκενοδόξει τὴν ἐξουσίαν, f.l. for ἐκαινοτόμει, J.*AJ*16.11.1. **-ία**, ἡ, *liability to vain imagination*, Epicur.*Sent.*30, Phld.*Rh.*1.332 S. II. *vanity, conceit*, Plb.3.81.9, Lxx *Wi.*14.14, D.S.17.107, Ph.2.47, *Ep.Phil.*2.3, Plu.2.57d, Porph.*Marc.*15; esp. of *false prudery*, Gal.6.415. **-ος**, ον, *vain-glorious, conceited*, Plb.27.7.12, Ph.1.672, *Ep.Gal.*5.26, Arr. *Epict.*3.24.43, Jul.*Or.*6.180d; κληρονομία Vett.Val.271.2.

κενοδρομ-έω, Astrol., *to be without attendant planets*, '*void of course*', Ptol.*Tetr.*114, Man.2.486:—hence **-ία**, ἡ, Antioch.Astr. in *Cat.Cod.Astr.*8(3).107, Porph. *in Ptol.*189.

κενοκοπέω, *labour in vain*, Plu.2.1037b.

κενολογ-έω, *talk emptily*, Eup.418, Arist.*Rh.*1393[a]17; καταψηφίζεσθαι ὑποθέσεως ὡς –λογούσης Procl. *in Prm.*p.845 S. **-ία**, ἡ, *empty, idle talk*, Plu.2.1069d; *chicanery*, *PMasp.*126.50 (vi A.D.): **κενεολογία**, v.l. for γενεολογία in Max.Tyr.23.1. **-ος**, ον, *talking emptily, prating*, *Gloss.*

κενοπάθ-εια [πᾰ], ἡ, *unreal sensation*, S.E.*M.*8.184. **-έω**, *have unreal sensations*, i.e. with no object corresponding to them, ib.213, *P.*2.49. **–ημα**, ατος, τό, *unreal sensation*, Id.*M.*8.354.

κενο-πονέω, *toil in vain*, v.l. in Ph.1.658. **–πρησις**, εως, ἡ, *flatulence*, *Hippiatr.*46. **–ρρημοσύνη**, ἡ, (ῥῆμα) = κενολογία, Eust. 1151.8.

κενός, ή, όν, Ion. and poet. **κεινός** Il.3.376, 4.181, 11.160, 15.453, Pi.*O.*2.65, 3.45, Hdt.1.73, al.; Ep. also **κενεός**, as always in Hom. (exc. in Il. ll. cc., and κενός Od.22.249 (s.v.l., fort. κενέ' εὔγματα or κείν' εὔγματα)), also Hp.*Aph.*7.24, Meliss.7, Timo 20.2 (Comp.), and in Dor., *IG*4[2](1).121.73 (Epid., iv B.C.); Aeol. **κέννος**, acc. to Greg. Cor.p.610 S.: Sup. κεννότατος Sch.Tz. in *An.Ox.*3.356.18; but οἱ Αἰολεῖς..οὐ λέγουσι κέννος Choerob. in *An.Ox.*2.242, cf. Hdn.Gr.2.302, and the true Aeol. is prob. κένος or κένεος, from *κενϝος, κενεϝος, cf. Cypr. **κενευϝός** *Schwyzer*683.4. I. mostly of things, *empty*, opp. πλέως, Ar.*Eq.*280; opp. πλήρης, Id.*Nu.*1054; opp. μεστός, Diph.12; κενεὰς σὺν χεῖρας ἔχοντες Od.10.42; νοστήσαντας κεινῇσι χερσί Hdt.1.73; κεναῖς χερσίν Pl.*Lg.*796b (v. infr. II.2); τὸ **κ.** (sc. τάλαντον) the *empty* one, Ar.*Fr.*488.5; **κ.** οἴκησις S.*Ph.*31; γῆ Id. *OT*55; εὐνή Id.*Ant.*424; χώματα κεινά, = κενοτάφια, Hdt.9.85; **κ.** τάφος E.*Hel.*1057; κατέθισαν ἐπὶ κενευϝῶν (sc. τάφων gen. sg.) *Schwyzer* l. c. (Cypr.); **κ.** χρόνος a *pause* in music, Anon.Bellerm.83; σφυγμὸς **κ.** Agathin.ap.Gal.8.936; of wool and wine, dub. sens. in Archig.ap.Gal.8.945; τὸ **κ.** *the void of space*, Democr.9, Meliss. l. c., Emp.13, al., Epicur.*Ep.*1 p.6 U., etc.; τὸ κ., = τόπος ἐστερημένος σώματος, Arist.*Ph.*208[b]26, cf. 213[a]13 sqq., *Cael.*279[a]13; κ. χώρα Pl. *Ti.*58a; ἢν κενεὸν λάβῃ [ἡ διακοπή] if it penetrates the (brain-)*cavity*, Hp.*Aph.* l. c.; esp. Astrol., *not occupied by a planet*, κ. δρόμος Man.2.452, cf. Vett. Val.94.27; cf. κενοδρομέω. 2. *empty, fruitless, void*, κενὰ εὔγματα εἰπών Od.22.249 (v. supr.); ἐλπίς, ἐλπίδες, Simon.5.16, A.*Pers.*804; γνώμα Pi.*N.*4.40, cf. S.*Ant.*753; ἔξοδοι Id.*Aj.*287; φροντίδες Id.*Fr.*949; τέρψις ib.577; φόβοι E.*Supp.*548, cf. X.*An.*2.2.21; φρόνημα Pl.*R.*494d, etc.; κ. πρόφασις καὶ ψευδής D.18.150; λοιδορία κ. Id.2.5; μάταιον καὶ κ. ib.12; κενὸν ἄρα καὶ τὸ φάρμακον πρὸς τὸ κ. prob. in Men.530.19; ἀπόντων κενὴν κατηγορεῖν bring an *idle* charge, Arist.*Resp.*470[b]12; *ineffectual*, λύγξ Th.2.49; πουλυμαθημοσύνης, τῆς οὐ κενεώτερον ἄλλο Timo l. c.; πολλὰ κ. τοῦ πολέμου Arist.*EN*1116[b]7; κ. δόξαι Epicur. *Sent.*15; ἐπιθυμίαι, opp. φυσικαί, Id.*Ep.*3 p.62 U., Diog.Oen.59; κ. ὀρέξεις Metrod.*Herc.*831.16; freq. in adverbial usages, neut. pl., κενεὰ πνεύσαις Pi.*O.*10(11).93; ἡ διὰ κενῆς ἐπανάσεισις τῶν ὅπλων *empty* flourishing of arms, Th.4.126; διὰ κενῆς ῥίπτειν throw *without a projectile*, Arist.*Pr.*881[a]39; κεκλάγγω διὰ κενῆς ἄλλως *to no purpose*, Ar. *V.*929; μάτην διὰ κ. Pl.Com.174.21; οὐ μαχοῦμαί σοι διὰ κ. Men.*Sam.* 260; ἐν κενοῖς S.*Aj.*971; κατὰ κενῆς Procl. *in Ti.*2.167 D.; εἰς κενόν D.S. 19.9, Hld.10.30; εἰς κ. ἡ δαπάνη *IG*14.1746; εἰς κ. μοχθεῖν Men.*Mon.* 51; κατὰ κενοῦ χανεῖν Suid. s. v. λύκος ἔχανεν; κατὰ κενοῦ φέρειν τὰς χεῖρας Ph.1.153; κατὰ κ. βαίνειν, = κενεμβατεῖν, Plu.2.463c: regul. Adv. κενῶς, διαλεκτικῶς καὶ κ. Arist. *de An.*403[a]2; λογικῶς καὶ κ. Id. *EE*1217[b]21; μὴ κ. πόνει Men.1101, cf. Epicur.*Ep.*3 p.61 U., Polystr. p.7 W., Arr.*Epict.*2.17.6, Plu.2.35e. II. of persons and things, 1. c. gen., *destitute, bereft*, τοῦ νοῦ S.*OC*931; φρενῶν Id.*Ant.*754; δακρύων E.*Hec.*230; συμμάχων κ. δόρυ Id.*Or.*688; πεδίον κ. δένδρων Pl.*R.*621a; κ. φρονήσεως, ἐπιστήμης, Id. *Ti.*75a, *R.*486c; κ. πόνου *without the fruits* of toil, A.*Fr.*241. 2. abs., *empty-handed*, αἰσχρόν τοι δηρόν τε μένειν κενεόν τε νέεσθαι Il.2.298, cf. Od.15.214; ἀπίκατο, οἱ μὲν κεινοί, οἱ δὲ φέροντες κτλ. Hdt.7.131; κενὸς κενὸν καλεῖ A.*Th.*353 (lyr.); ἥκεις οὐ κενή S.*OC*359, cf. *Tr.*495; οὐθ' ὑπεργέμων..οὔτε κ. Alex.216; of camels, *without burdens, unloaded*, opp. ἔγγομοι, *OGI*629.166 (Palmyra, ii A.D.); κ. ἂν ἴῃ.., κ. ἄπεισιν Pl.*R.*370e; κ. τινὰ ἐξαποστεῖλαι Lxx *Ge.*31.42; *bereft of* her mate, λέαινα S.*Aj.*986; *orphan*, Ἔρωτες Bion 1.59; ὑπ' ἄσθματος κενοί *exhausted*.., A.*Pers.*484; of places, *without garrison*, χῶραι Aeschin.3.146, cf. Hdt.5.15; of the body, *without flesh*, Plu.2.831c. b. *devoid of wit, vain, pretentious*, κεινὸς εἴην Pi.*O.*3.45; διαπτυχθέντες ὤφθησαν κενοί S.*Ant.*709; ἀνόητον καὶ κ. Ar.*Ra.*530, cf. *Ep.Jac.*2.20. III. Comp. and Sup., κενότερος Stratt.10 D.; -ότατος D.27.25, Phld.*Rh.*1.67 S., al., cf. Choerob. *in Theod.*2.76, *EM*275.50; κενώτερος, -ώτατος, Pl.*Smp.*175d, v.l. in Arist.*EN*1107[a]30 (Comp.); κενεώτερος Timo (v. supr.); κενεώτατος v.l. in Hp.*Acut.*62.

κενόσαρκος, ον, *destitute of flesh, meagre*, *EM*779.8.

κενοσπουδ-έω, *to be zealous about frivolities*, J.*AJ*16.4.3, Artem. 4.11. **-ία**, ἡ, *zealous pursuit of frivolities*, D.H.6.70, D.L.6.26; πομπῆς κ. M.Ant.7.3. **-ος**, ον, *zealous about frivolities*, Hipparch. 1.3.11, Plu.2.560b, 1061c; κ. τάχος 'more haste, less speed', Heliod. ap.Orib.47.14.3; τὸ κ. D.L.9.67; τὰ κ. *matters of mere curiosity*, Cic. *Att.*9.1.1. Adv. -δως Plu.2.234e.

κενοτᾰφ-έω, *honour with an empty tomb*, κενοταφοῦντ' ἐμὸν δέμας E.*Hel.*1060; ὃν..ἤδ' ἀπόντα κενοταφεῖ ib.1546: metaph., κ. τὸν βίον Plu.2.1130b. **-ιον**, τό, *empty tomb, cenotaph*, X.*An.*6.4.9, Plu.2. 870e, App.*Mith.*96, *CIG*4340*d, e* (Attalia); also Adj., κενοτάφιος οἶκος Plu.2.349b (s. v. l.). II. *image*, = Heb. *těraphim*, Lxx 1*Ki.*19.13.

κενότης, ητος, ἡ, *emptiness*, Pl.*R.*585b, *Ti.*58b, Thphr.*Sens.*54; *vanity*, Phld.*D.*1.17; εἰς κενότητας ἄν μοι ὁ λόγος ἐξέπιπτε D.H.*Is.*20; κ. σφυγμοῦ Agathin.ap.Gal.8.936; cf. κενεότης.

κενο-φροσύνη and **–φρων**, v. κενεοφρ–.

κενοφων-έω, *speak idly*, Suid. **-ία**, ἡ, *vain talking*, Dsc.*Praef.* 2: in pl., 1*Ep.Ti.*6.20, 2*Ep.Ti.*2.16, Porph.*Chr.*58; ἄγραφοι κ. Just. *Nov.*146.1.2.

κενόω, E.*Med.*959, Pl.*Smp.*197d; Ep. **κεινόω** Nic.*Th.*56, *Al.*140: fut. κενώσω E.*Ion*447: aor. ἐκένωσα Id.*Ba.*730: pf. κεκένωκα App.*BC* 5.67:—**Pass.**, fut. κενωθήσομαι Gal.4.709, κενεώσομαι Emp.16: aor. ἐκενώθην Th.2.51: pf. κεκένωμαι Hdt.4.123, Hp.*Morb.Sacr.*9: (κενός): —*empty*, πᾶσαν ἠπείρου πλάκα A.*Pers.*718 (troch.); ναούς E.*Ion* l. c.: c. gen., *empty of* a thing, ἀνδρῶν τάνδε πόλιν κενῶσαι A.*Supp.*660, cf. E.*Rh.*914 (lyr.); χέρας [δώρων] Id.*Med.* l. c.; τινὰ τᾶς συοπλουτοσύνας Cerc.4.13; opp. πληροῦν τινά τινος, Pl. l. c., cf. *R.*560d:—Pass., *to be emptied, made* or *left empty*, S.*OT*29; ἐς τὸ κενούμενον into *the space continually left empty*, Th.2.76; οἰκίαι πολλαὶ ἐκενώθησαν ib.51: c. gen., τούτων κενεώσεται..αἰών *will be left without* them, Emp. l. c.; κεκενωμένου τοῦ τείχεος πάντων *stripped* of all things, Hdt. l. c. 2. *make* a place *empty by leaving* it, *desert* it, βωμοῦ ἐσχάραν E.*Andr.*1138; λόχμην Id.*Ba.* l. c.:—Pass., κενωθεισῶν τῶν νεῶν Th.8.57. 3. Medic., *empty by depletion*, opp. πληροῦν, Hp.*Aph.*2.51, cf. Aret.*CA*1.2, Gal. l. c.; τινα Phld.*Lib.*p.30 O.; *carry off*, αἷμα Luc.*Ocyp.*93; ἐκ τοῦ σώματος χολήν Gal.*Nat.Fac.*1.13:—Pass., τὰ κενούμενα *evacuations*, Id.6.78, Antyll.ap.Stob.4.37.27. 4. *empty out, pour away*, φάρμακον Iamb.*Bab.*7: metaph., πλοῦτον f.l. in Ph.1.119:—Pass., τοῦ λαοῦ κενωθέντος D.S.24.1; *make away with*, θανάτου βάρος Cypr. *Fr.*1.6. 5. *expend*, εἴς με κένωσον πᾶν βέλος *AP*5.57 (Arch.). 6. in Pass., *waste away, shrivel*, Thphr.*HP*7.4.3, 9.14.3. II. metaph., *make empty*, ἑαυτόν *Ep.Phil.*2.7; *make void* or *of no effect*, καύχημα 1*Ep.Cor.*9.15; ὑπάρξεις Vett.Val.90.7:—Pass., *to be* or *become* so, *Ep.Rom.*4.14.

κένσαι, κέντᾱσε, v. κεντέω.

κενταύρειον or **–ιον**, *centaury*, *Centaurea salonitana*, Thphr.*HP* 3.3.6, Diocl.*Fr.*83, al., *POxy.*1088.59; κ. τὸ μέγα Dsc.3.6; but κ. τὸ μικρόν *feverfew*, *Erythraea Centaurium*, ib.7: **κενταυρίη**, Hp.*Morb.* 2.59.

Κενταύρ-ειος, α, ον, *of Centaurs*, γένος E.*IA*706; αἷμα Luc.*Peregr.* 25. **-ίδης**, ου, ὁ, *sprung from Centaurs*, ἵππος Κ. *a Thessalian horse*, Id.*Ind.*5. **-ικός**, ή, όν, *like a Centaur*, i.e. *savage, brutal*. Adv. -κῶς Ar.*Ra.*38.

κενταυρίς, ίδος, ἡ, = κενταύρειον τὸ μικρόν, Thphr.*HP*9.8.7, 9.14. 1. II. A kind of *ear-ring*, *Com.Adesp.*1034 (pl.). III. *female Centaur*, Philostr.*Im.*2.3.

Κενταυρο-κτόνος, ον, *Centaur-slaying*, Lyc.670. **-μᾰχία**, ἡ, *battle* *of Centaurs*, D.S.17.115, Plu.*Thes.*29, *Comp.Thes.Rom.*1. **-πληθής**, ές, *full of Centaurs*, πόλεμος E.*HF*1273.

Κένταυρος, ὁ (in Luc.*Zeux.*4 also ἡ), *Centaur*: I. in Ep., a savage race, dwelling between Pelion and Ossa, Il.11.832, Od.21.295 sq. (opp. ἄνδρες, ib.303), Hes.*Sc.*184, *h.Merc.*224 (perh. in signf. II), Batr.171: hence, *brigands*, Hsch. II. later, monsters of double shape, *half-man and half-horse*, Pi.*P.*2.44, etc., cf. Arist. *Insomn.*461^{b}20, D.S.4.69: prov., οὐ παρὰ Κενταύροισι 'we don't live in fairyland', Telecl.45. III. the constellation *Centaurus*, Eudox. ap.Hipparch.1.2.20. IV. = παιδεραστής, from the brutal sensuality ascribed to the Centaurs, Hsch. 2. *the pudenda*, Theopomp.Com.89.

Κενταυροφόνος, ὁ, *slaying Centaurs*, epith. of Heracles, prob. in Theoc.17.20.

κεντάω, late form of sq., Pass. inf. -ᾶσθαι (v.l. -εῖσθαι) Gal.6.192.

κεντ-έω, Pi.*P.*1.28, etc.: fut. -ήσω S.*Aj.*1245: aor. ἐκέντησα Hp. *Epid.*5.45, Dor. κέντᾱσα Theoc.19.1; Ep. inf. κένσαι (as if from *κέντω) Il.23.337:—Pass., fut. -ηθήσομαι (συγ-) Hdt.6.29: aor. ἐκεντήθην Arist.*Spir.*483^{b}16, Thphr.*HP*9.15.3: pf. κεκέντημαι Hp.*Anat.* 1:—*prick, goad, spur on*, Il.l.c., Ar.*Nu.*1300, etc.: prov., κ. τὸν πῶλον περὶ τὴν νύσσαν, of impetuous haste, Suid. 2. of bees and wasps, *sting*, Ar.*V.*226, al.; Ἔρωτα κακὰ κέντασε μέλισσα Theoc.l.c.; τὠφθαλμὼ κεντούμενος ὥσπερ ὑπ' ἀνθρηνῶν Ar.*Nu.*947; of the porcupine, Ael.*NA*12.26: then, 3. generally, *prick, stab*, Pi.l.c., Theoc.15.130, etc.; μηδ' ὀλωλότα κέντει S.*Ant.*1030; τὴν γλῶσσαν καὶ τὴν ψυχὴν αὐτῶν κέντησον *Tab.Defix.*97.26; ἐκέντει..(αἰθέρ'), ὡς σφάζων ἐμέ E.*Ba.*631 (troch.), etc.; κ. τὸν ἀέρα Theo Sm.p.61 H., cf. p.72 H.; τύπτειν οὐδὲ κ. Pl.*Grg.*456d:—Pass., κεντηθείσης τῆς φλεβὸς Thphr.l.c.; παιομένους καὶ κεντουμένους Th.4.47; μαστιγούμενος καὶ κεντούμενος X.*HG*3.3.11, cf. *An.*3.1.29: metaph., σὺν δόλῳ κ. *stab* in the dark, S.*Aj.*1245; λιμῷ κεντούμενος Alciphr.3.4. 4. = βινέω, Mnesim.4.55. **-ημα**, ατος, τό, *point* of a weapon, Plb.2.33.5, etc. 2. *prick, dot* in a cipher, Aen.Tact.31.30 (pl.). 3. *puncture*, Heliod.ap.Orib.46.22.4: pl., Ruf.*Fr.*63. II. *wound inflicted, sting*, κ. γλώσσης A.*Fr.*169; of poisonous bites, Philum.*Ven.* 27.2, al.: in pl., *punishment*, Hsch.

κεντην-άριος, ὁ, = Lat. *centenarius, official drawing salary of* 100,000 *sesterces*, *Epigr.Gr.*446: **-αρία**, ἡ, *office of such a value*, *IG*14.1480: **-άριον**, τό, *weight of* 100 *lbs.*, *Edict.Diocl.*18.5, Olymp.Hist.p.469 D., Men.Prot.p.100 D.

κέντ-ησις, εως, ἡ, *pricking*, Arist.*Spir.*484^{a}34. II. *mosaic*, *IG Rom.*4.1417 (Smyrna). **-ητήριον**, τό, *pricker, awl*, Luc.*Cat.*20; gloss on ῥαφίῳ, Gal.19.134; gloss on στιγεύς, Suid. **-ητής**, οῦ, ὁ, *mosaic-worker*, *Edict.Diocl.*7.6: generally, *one who pierces*, Tz.*H.*9.466. **-ητικός**, ή, όν, *prickly*, Thphr.*HP*3.9.6 (Comp.). **-ητός**, ή, όν, *embroidered*, ὑπόδημα Epict.*Ench.*39; prob. *decorated with mosaic*, *BGU*781 iv 10 (i A.D.). **-ιον**, v. κέντριον.

κέντο, Dor. for κέλετο, Alcm.141.

κεντορίων, ωνος, ὁ, = Lat. *centurio*, *OGI*196 (Philae):—also **κεντουρίων**, Lyd.*Mag.*1.9; **κεντυρίων**, *Ev.Marc.*15.39.

κεντόω, v.l. for κεντρόω I in Hdt.3.16.

κεντρ-ήεις, εσσα, εν, *sharp, prickly*, ῥίζεα Nic.*Al.*146. **-ηνεκής**, ές, *spurred* or *goaded on*, ἵπποι Il.5.752, 8.396. **-ιάδαι**, οἱ, *priests* at Athens, *who drove* the ox to the altar *with goads* at the Dipolia, Porph.*Abst.*2.30. **-ίζω**, = κεντέω, X.*Eq.*11.6: metaph., ἔρως κ. εἰς ἔρωτα Id.*Smp.*8.24; ἔπαινος κ. Plu.2.84c; *stimulate*, τὰ σώματα Sor.2.54:—Pass., κεντρίζεσθαι ὑπὸ φιλονικίας X.*Cyr.*8.7.12; ὑπὸ πάθους Ph.2.386. **-ικός**, ή, όν, *of* or *belonging to a cardinal point*, σχῆμα Vett.Val.134.26. II. Adv. -κῶς, metaph., ὁ νοῦς..ἀδιαιρέτως καὶ κ. οἶδε τὰ διαιρούμενα Phlp. *in de An.*542.29. **-ίνης** [ῑ], ου, ὁ, *spiny shark*, Arist.*Fr.*310, Opp.*H.*1.378. II. kind of ψήν or *fig-insect*, Thphr.*HP*2.8.2, Plin.*HN*17.255. III. = κεντρίς, Ael.*NA*9.11 (-ίτης codd.), Sch.Nic.*Th.*334. **-ιον**, τό, a surgical instrument, called modern spelling of κέντιον, Gal.13.407; = βουκέντριον, Suid., cf. *EM*503.39. **-ίς**, ίδος, ἡ, = διψάς II.1, Ael.*NA*6.51. **-ίσκος**, ὁ, a kind of *fish*, Thphr.*Fr.*171.9; Schneid. κεστρινίσκος. **-ισμός**, ὁ, = *stimulatio*, *Gloss.* **-ιστέον**, *one must stimulate*, Orib.*Fr.*64. **-ίτης**, ου, ὁ, v. κεντρίνης III. II. κ. κάλαμος *prickly* reed, *PTeb.*152 (ii B.C.). III. fem. **-ῖτις**, ιδος, ἡ, *place* where a horse is *tapped* for dropsy, *Hippiatr.*38. 2. κ. βοτάνη, magical plant, *PMag.Par.*1.773.

κεντρο-βᾰρικά, τά, title of a treatise of Archimedes *on the centre of gravity*: *problems relating to this subject*, Simp. *in Cael.*543.30: ἡ -κή *theory of the subject*, *An.Ox.*3.168. **-δήλητος**, ον, *torturing with goads*, ὀδύναις κεντροδαλήτοις (Dor.) A.*Supp.*563 (lyr., fort. leg. κεντροδαλήτισι). **-ειδής**, ές, *like a centre, centriform*, Plot.6.8.18. **-θεσία**, ἡ, *arrangement of heavenly bodies on cardinal points*, Vett.Val.226.33 (pl.). **-μᾰνής**, ές, *maddened by the spur*, *AP*13.18 (Parmeno; -ρραγῆ cod.). II. ἄγκιστρον κ., of love, *maddening by its barbs*, ib.5.246 (Maced.). **-μυρσίνη**, ἡ, = ὀξυμυρσ-, *butchers'-broom, Ruscus aculeatus*, Thphr.*HP*3.17.4, *Gp.*10.3.7.

κέντρον, τό, (κεντέω) *any sharp point*: 1. *horse-goad*, [ἵπποι] ἄνευ κέντροιο θέοντες Il.23.387, cf. 430, Ar.*Nu.*1297, X.*Cyr.*7.1.29, etc.; διπλοῖς κέντροισι S.*OT*809; ὄνειδος ἔτυψεν δίκαν διφρηλάτου μεσολαβεῖ κ. A.*Eu.*157 (lyr.): post-Hom., *ox-goad* (Hom. βουπλήξ), used as an instrument of torture, Hdt.3.130; κέντροις καὶ μάστιξιν Pl.*Lg.*777a: prov., πρὸς κέντρα λακτίζειν (v. λακτίζω 2); δεῖ..κέντρου πολλάκις, οὕτω δὲ καὶ χαλινοῦ Longin.2.2; as a symbol of sovereignty, λαβὼν..χερσὶν κέντρα κηδεύει πόλιν S.*Fr.*683. b. metaph., *goad, spur, incentive*, Pi.*Fr.*124.4, A.*Pr.*691 (lyr.); ποῦ γὰρ τοσοῦτο κ. ὡς μητροκτονεῖν; Id.*Eu.*427; κέντροις ἔρωτος E.*Hipp.*39, cf. 1303; πόθου κ. Pl.*R.*573a; κέντρα καὶ ὠδῖνες Id.*Phdr.*251e; κ. ἐγερτικὸν θυμοῦ Plu.*Lyc.*21; κέντρα πτολέμοιο, of the Argives, Orac.ap.Sch.Theoc.14.48; κ. ἐμοῦ *desire for* me, S.*Ph.*1039. 2. metaph., in pl., *tortures, pangs*, Id.*Tr.*840 (lyr.): sg., τὸ κ. τοῦ θανάτου ἡ ἁμαρτία 1*Ep.Cor.*15.56. 3. *point* of a spear, Plb.6.22.4: pl., of the περόναι with which Oedipus pierced his eyes, S.*OT*1318. 4. *peg* of a top, Pl.*R.*436d. 5. of animals, a. *sting* of bees and wasps, Ar.*V.*225, 407 (lyr.), al.; of scorpions, Arist.*PA*683^{a}12 (so of the constellation *Scorpio*, Arat.505): hence, metaph., of malicious persons, ἐς τοὺς ἔχοντας κέντρ' ἀφιᾶσιν E.*Supp.*242; πορεύεται, ὥσπερ σκορπίος, ἠρκὼς τὸ κ. D.25.52; of Pericles as an orator, τὸ κ. ἐγκατέλειπε τοῖς ἀκροωμένοις Eup.94.7; of Socrates, ὥσπερ μέλιττα τὸ κ. ἐγκαταλιπών Pl.*Phd.*91c; οἷον ὀφθαλμῷ κ. ἐνθεῖσα Philostr.*Im.*2.1; βλέμματος κ. Onomarch.ap. Philostr.*VS*2.18. b. *spur* of a cock, *Gp.*14.7.17. c. *quill* of the porcupine, Ael.*NA*12.26. d. = πόσθη, Sotad.1. 6. *stationary point of a pair of compasses*, Vitr.3.1.3: generally, *centre* of a circle, Pl.*Ti.*54e, Arist.*APr.*41^{b}15, al.; ἡ ἐκ τοῦ κ. (sc. εὐθεῖα) *radius*, Euc.*Opt.*34; ὥσπερ κύκλον κέντρῳ περιέγραψαν τὴν πόλιν Plu.*Rom.*11; τὸ κ. τᾶς σφαίρας Ti.Locr.100e; τὸ κ. τῆς γῆς Ptol.*Tetr.*52; κ. βάρεος *centre* of gravity, Archim.*Aequil.*1 *Def.*4: metaph., κ. καὶ διαστήματι περιγράφειν *circumscribe*, Plu.2.513c, 524f. 7. *pin, rivet*, Paus.10.16.1; *spur, tip*, for fixing a machine in the ground, Apollod.*Poliorc.*144.1. 8. ῥακτηρίοις κέντροισιν, of *oars*, S.*Fr.*802. 9. Astron., *cardinal point* on the ecliptic, Ptol.*Tetr.*74, S.E.*M.*5.12, Vett.Val.50.18, etc. 10. *hard knot* in stone, Thphr.*HP*5.2.3; *flaw* in crystals, Plin.*HN*37.28.

κεντρο-ποιός, όν, *making goads*, gloss on sq., Hsch. **-τύπος** [ῠ], ον, Act., *striking with a goad*, Sch.Ar.*Nu.*449. II. proparox., **κεντρότῠπος**, = μαστιγίας, *EM*503.47, cf. Hsch. **-φόρος**, ον, *with a sting*, Id. s.v. τενθρηδών. 2. Subst., -φόρος, ὁ, = κεντρίνης I, Opp.*H.*4.244. II. *containing the centre of the universe*, Porph.ap. Eus.*PE*3.11.

κεντρ-όω, *furnish with a sting*:—Pass., *to be so furnished*, Pl.*R.*552d, 555d. 2. *strike with a goad*, Hdt.3.16 (cf. κεντόω): metaph., *spur on*, κεκεντρωμένος εἰς λόγους Aristid.*Or.*50(26).26. II. Pass., Astron., *occupy a cardinal point*, Ptol.*Tetr.*153, Man.1.90. **-ώδης**, ες, *pointed, prickly*, λάπαθον Aët.6.24; ἔδαφος Sch.Pi.*P.*1.54; of the chorus in Ar.*V.*, Sch.ib.224. **-ων**, ωνος, ὁ, *one that bears the marks of the* κέντρον, *a rogue that has been put to the torture*, S.*Fr.*329, Ar.*Nu.*450 (anap.). II. *piece of patch-work, rag*, Bito 55.4, Heras ap.Gal.13.1044, Sch.Ar.*Nu.*449; perh. *pen-wiper*, *POxy.*326 (i A.D.): hence, *copy of verses made up of scraps from other authors*, Eust.1099.51, 1308 fin. **-ωνάριον**, τό, *case for* κέντρωνες, *POxy.*326 (i A.D.; -νόρ- Pap.). **-ωνορράφος** [ᾰ], = Lat. *centonarius*, *Gloss.* **-ωσις**, εως, ἡ, *goading, piercing*, Sch.Pi.*P.*1.54. II. Astron., *situation at cardinal point*, Ptol.*Tetr.*79, 99. **-ωτός**, ή, όν, *'spiky'*, colloquial for θυμικώτεροι, κηφῆνες Arist.*HA*624^{b}16; *spiked*, of bucklers, Str.11.5.6; of planks, Plu.2.200b. 2. name of a throw in dicing, Eub.57.1.

κεντῠρίων, v. κεντορίων.

κέντωρ, ορος, ὁ, *goader, driver*, κέντορες ἵππων Il.4.391, 5.102, cf. *APl.*4.358; κ. παρδαλίων *AP*7.578 (Agath.).

κέν-ωμα, ατος, τό, *empty space, vacuum*, Erasistr.ap.Gell.16.3.8 (in Ion. form κείνωμα), Ph.*Bel.*57.17 (pl.), Plb.6.31.9, Phld.*Sign.*36 (pl.), Plu.2.655b (pl.). 2. *vacancy, non-existence*, Anon. *in Prm.* in *Rh.Mus.*47.603. 3. *empty vessel*, *POxy.*1292.4 (i A.D.), *PAmh.*2.48.8 (ii B.C.): pl., ῥοιᾶς κ. *empty shells*, Asclep.ap.Gal.13.302. II. Medic., *evacuation*, Phld.*Lib.*p.30 O., Dsc.5.11, Plu.2.381d. 2. *evacuant*, in pl., Herod.Med. in *Rh.Mus.*58.89, Ruf.*Fr.*116. **-ώσιμος**, η, ον, *purgative*, τὸ κ. τῆς ἰατρείας Anon.ap.Suid. s.v. κενώτερος. **-ωσις**, εως, ἡ, *emptying, depletion*, οὐχὶ πεῖνα καὶ δίψα..κενώσεις τινές εἰσι..; Pl.*R.*585b, cf. *Phlb.*35b, *BGU*904.13 (ii A.D.):—poet. **κενέωσις**, πόντου κ. ἀνὰ πέδον Pi.*Fr.*107.12: metaph., κένωσις βίου Vett.Val.190.30; κ. τοῦ γιγνώσκειν Iamb.*Comm.Math.*11. 2. Medic., *evacuation*, Hp.*Aph.*2.8, interpol. in Dsc.2.50; κ. τῶν οἰκείων, opp. κάθαρσις τῶν ἀλλοτρίων, Gal.18(2).134. b. *depletion, low diet*, opp. πλήρωσις, Hp.*VM*9, cf. *Art.*49; κ. σίτου ib.50. 3. of the moon, *waning*, opp. πλήρωσις, Epicur.*Ep.*2 p.40 U. **-ωτέον**, *one must purge*, Gal.17(2).359, cf. 10.904, Ruf.ap.Orib.7.26.18. **-ωτικός**, ή, όν, *tending to empty*, κύστεως Ael.*NA*14.4; *depletive*, Gal.18(1).118 (Sup.). 2. *purgative*, Id.15.198.

κέοιτο, κέοντο, v. κεῖμαι.

κεπφαττελεβώδης, ες, *as brainless as a* κέπφος *or an* ἀττέλεβος, cj. Bentl. in Archestr.*Fr.*23.14.

κέπφος, ὁ, perh. *stormy petrel, Thalassidroma pelagica*, Arist.*HA* 593^{b}14, 620^{a}13, Thphr.*Sign.*28, Lyc.76, 836, Nic.*Al.*166. 2. metaph., *feather-brained fellow*, Ar.*Pax* 1067, *Pl.*912.

κεπφόω, *ensnare like a* κέπφος:—hence in Pass., *to be easily cajoled*, Lxx *Pr.*7.22; *become feather-brained*, Cic.*Att.*13.40.2.

κερᾰβάτης, ου, ὁ, = κεροβάτης, Suid., Zonar.

κεράδιον, τό, Dim. of κεραία, *IG*2^{2}.1648.22, prob. in *BCH*35.16 (Delos): less prob. κεραΐδιον.

κεράεις, f.l. for κερόεις, Nic.*Al.*135.

κερᾰελκής, ές, *drawing by the horns*, [βόες] Call.*Dian.*179 (v.l. κερεαλκέες); 'Ιώ Nonn.*D.*3.382. II. = κερουλκός II.2, τόξα ib.20.225. III. v. κερατεσσεῖς.

κεραία, poet. -αίη, ἡ, (κέρας) *horn*, Nic.*Th.*36, Opp.*C.*3.476. 2. *antennae* of the crayfish or of insects, Arist.*HA*526^{a}6, 532^{a}26. II. *anything projecting like a horn*: hence, 1. *yard-arm*, A.*Eu.*557 (lyr.),

Th.7.41, *IG*2².657, 1604.17, *PMagd.*11.4 (iii B.C.), etc.; κ. καθελέσθαι, ὑφιέναι, i.e. lower sail, Plb.14.10.11, Plu.2.169b; opp. ἐντείνασθαι Call. *Fr.anon.*382; ἀπὸ ψιλῆς τῆς κ. 'under bare poles', Luc.*Tox.*19. b. *projecting beam* of a crane, etc., Th.2.76, cf. 4.100, *IG*11(2).161 *A* 90 (Delos, iii B.C.), Ph.*Bel.*100.18, Plb.8.5.10, Arr.*An.*2.19.2. c. *projecting parts* of the hucklebone, Arist.*HA*499ᵇ30. d. *branching stake of wood*, used as a *pale* in a palisade, Plb.18.18.7, App.*BC*4.78. e. *horns of the ancilia*, Plu.*Num.*13. 2. pl., *horns* of the moon, Arat.785, 790. 3. in writing, *apex* of a letter, *IG*2.4321.10 (iv B.C.), A.D.*Synt.*28.27, cf. *Ev.Matt.*5.18, *Ev.Luc.*16.17, Antyll. ap.Orib.45.57.4; ζυγομαχεῖν περὶ συλλαβῶν καὶ κ. Plu.2.1100a; διὰ πάσης κ. διῆκον showing itself in every *word* of a speech, D.H.*Din.*7. 4. *leg* of a pair of compasses, S.E.*M.*10.54. 5. *projecting spur* of a mountain, Plu.*Cat.Ma.*13; of the *horns* of Europe and Africa at the Straits of Gibraltar, *AP*4.3ᵇ.40 (Agath.); *arms* of a harbour, Philostr.*VS*1.21.2. 6. = κέρας v. 3, *wing* of an army, Hld.9.20. 7. pl., supposed teat-like *projections* inside the womb, Diocl.*Fr.*27; but the *Fallopian tubes*, Gal.*UP*14.11, Ruf.*Onom.*194. III. *bow made of horn*, *AP*6.75 (Paul. Sil.).

κεραΐδιον, v. κεράδιον.

κεραιέλοντα· ὁ εἰς κέρατα ἔλαιον ἄγων, Hsch.

κεραΐζω, Ep. impf. κεράϊζον Hom. (v. infr.): fut. inf. κεραϊξέμεν Il. 16.830: aor. ἐκεράϊσα Hdt.2.115, -ιξα Nonn.*D.*23.21: (κείρω):—*ravage, plunder*, σταθμοὺς ἀνθρώπων κεραΐζετον Il.5.557, cf. 16.752; πόλιν κεραϊξέμεν ἁμήν ib.830, cf. Od.8.516, Parth.21.1, etc.; τὸ τῶν Λυδῶν ἄστυ Hdt.1.88; τὰ οἰκία τοῦ ξείνου Id.2.115; οἰκίας J.*BJ*6.8.5; τοὺς σωροὺς τῶν δραγμάτων Ael.*NA*6.41:—Pass., θαλάμους κεραϊζομένους Il.22.63; εὐνὰς θανάτοις κεραϊζομένας E.*Alc.*886 (anap.). 2. of ships, *sink, disable*, Hdt.8.91, cf. 86 (Pass.). 3. of living beings, *slaughter*, Τρῶας κεράϊζε καὶ ἄλλους Il.2.861, cf. 21.129; θῆρας Pi.*P.* 9.21; οἱ [λέοντες] τὰς καμήλους ἐκεράϊζον Hdt.7.125. II. *carry off as plunder*, [τὰ χρήματα] Id.2.121.β'; τοὺς ἱκέτας ἐκ τοῦ ναοῦ Id.1.159. III. *exalt, uplift*, opp. ἀμαλδύνω, dub. in Corn.*ND*27.

κεραίνω, v. κέραιρε.

κεραιός (⏑ ⏑ ⏑), = κεραός, *Epigr.Gr.*833.1.

κεραιοῦχος, ον, = κεροῦχος II: metaph., *upholding the right*, Hsch.

κεραιοφόρος, ον, *furnished with projecting spears*, ἅμαξαι D.H.20.2.

κέραιρε (κέραινε and κέραιρε cod.)· κέρασον, Hsch., cf. v.l. in Il.9. 203.

κερᾱΐς, ΐδος, ἡ, *worm that eats horn*, v.l. Od.21.395 (pl.). II. gen. ΐδος, = κεράς (A) (q.v.). III. = ῥάφανος ἀγρία, Thphr.*HP*9.15.5.

κερᾱΐς, ΐδος, ἡ, = κορώνη (Hsch.), used of Medea by Lyc.1317.

κερᾰ-ϊσμός, ὁ, *devastation*, D.H.16.1. **-ϊστής**, οῦ, ὁ, *plunderer*, *h.Merc.*336. II. *baneful comet*, Hsch.

κεραΐτης [ῑ], ου, ὁ, = Lat. *cornicularius*, Lyd.*Mag.*3.3.

κεραΐτις, ιδος, ἡ, = τῆλις, Ps.-Dsc.2.102.

κεραίω, Ep. for κεράω, radic. form of κεράννυμι, ζωρότερον δὲ κέραιε *mix* the wine stronger, Il.9.203; ἀμβροσίην ἐκέραιον Q.S.4.139:—Pass., ᾧ κα κεραίηται *Schwyzer* 321.3 (Delph., v B.C.); part. κεραιόμενος Emp.35.8, Nic.*Al.*178, 511.

κερᾰμαῖος, α, ον, v. κεραμεοῦς.

κεράμβηλον, τό, *scarecrow* in a garden, Hsch.; also, a kind of *beetle* fixed on fig-trees to drive away gnats, Id.; cf. sq.

κεράμβυξ, υκος, ὁ, *longicorn beetle, cerambyx*, which feeds on dead wood, Nic.*Fr.*39, Hsch.

κερᾰμ-εία, ἡ, *the potter's craft*, Pl.*Prt.*324e: prov., ἐν πίθῳ τὴν κ. μανθάνειν, of those who undertake the most difficult tasks without learning the elements of the art, Id.*Grg.*514e, cf. *La.*187b, Dicaearch. Hist.51; τῆς αὐτῆς κ., of the same *make*, Eratosth.ap.Ath.11. 482b. **-εικός**, ή, όν, = κεραμικός (cf. A.D.*Adv.*166.29), τροχός Arist.*Mech.*851ᵇ20, cf. X.*Smp.*7.2, Hsch. II. Κεραμεικός, ὁ, *the Potters' Quarter* at Athens, Menecl.3, cf. Sch.Ar.*Av.*395, *Eq.*769, *Ra.*131. **-εῖον**, τό, *potter's workshop*, Aeschin.3.119, *IG*2². 1635.143, *PSI*4.445.2 (iii B.C.). II. Ion. **-ήϊον**, = κεράμιον, Hom. *Epigr.*14.14. **-ειος**, v. sq. **-εοῦς**, ᾶ, οῦν, (κέραμος) *of clay* or *earth, earthen*, μάνην εἶχε κεραμεοῦν ἁδρόν Nico 1, cf. *IG*2². 463.51, Thphr.*HP*5.3.2, Phld.*Mort.*39, Dsc.1.71; τὸ χρῶμα κεραμεοῦς Alex.Mynd.ap.Ath.9.398d:—other spellings found in codd. are **κεράμειος**, Plu.*Galb.*12; **κεράμεος**, Pl.*Ly.*219e, Ctes.*Fr.*51 M., Antiph.163.5, Theophil.2, cf. κεράμεα· ὁ παντοδαπὸς κέραμος, Hsch., and κεράμεον, τό, collect., = *tile-work*, *BCH*36.197 (Delos, iii/ii B.C.); **κεραμαῖος**, Plb.10.44.2, v.l. in Ph.2.273; **κεραμιαῖος**, ibid. (v.l.), *Gp.*2.18.14; **κεράμιος**, Str.17.2.3; **κεραμοῦς**, Heraclid.Tar. ap.Gal.13.827. **-εύς**, έως, ὁ, *potter*, ὡς ὅτε τις τροχὸν ... κεραμεὺς πειρήσεται Il.18.601, cf. Hom.*Epigr.*14.1, etc.; οἱ κ., a guild at Thyatira, *IGRom.*4.1205: prov., καὶ κεραμεὺς κεραμεῖ κοτέει Hes.*Op.*25, cf. Arist.*Rh.*1381ᵇ16, *EN*1155ᵃ35; κεραμέως πλοῦτος and κεραμεὺς ἄνθρωπος, prov., of anything frail and uncertain, Diogenian.5.97, 98. II. **Κεραμεῖς**, Att. **Κεραμῆς**, οἱ, name of an Attic deme, Ar. *Ra.*1093 (anap.), Pl.*Prt.*315d, etc. **-ευτικός**, ή, όν, *of* or *for a potter*, ὁ κ. τροχός D.S.4.76, cf. S.E.*M.*10.93; ἀκολασία Luc.*Am.*11, etc.; ἡ -κὴ τέχνη *the potter's art, pottery*, D.S.19.1, 2: without τέχνη, Poll. 7.161; τὰ κ. *earthenware*, *PTeb.*342.17 (ii A.D.). **-εύω**, *to be a potter*, Phryn.Com.15, Pl.*R.*467a, etc. 2. c. acc., κ. κανθάρους *make earthenware* cups, Epig.4; τὰ τρύβλια κακῶς κ., τὴν δὲ πόλιν εὖ καὶ καλῶς he *tinkers* the state, of the demagogue Cephalos, whose father was a potter, Ar.*Ec.*253; κ. τὸν κεραμέα *make a pot of* the potter, Pl.*Euthd.*301d; τὸ Νέστορος ποτήριον πολλοὶ -εύουσι, i.e. *discuss its manufacture*, Ath.11.781d:—Med., ἐκεραμεύσαντο.. ποτήρια *they had them made*, Pherecr.143:—Pass., χύτρα κεκεραμευμένη ὑπὸ ἀγαθοῦ κεραμέως Pl.*Hp.Ma.*288d, cf. Nicostr.Com.10. **-εών**, ῶνος, ὁ, *large wine-jar*, Ar.*Lys.*200. **-ήϊος**, η, ον, Ep. for κεράμειος, τεῦχος Nic.*Th.*80, cf. κεραμεῖον II:—fem. **-ηΐς**, Marc.Sid.60. **-ίδιον**, τό, Dim. of κεραμίς, *IG*12(9).907.26 (Chalcis, iv A.D.), Sch.D.T. p.196 H. **-ῐδοπλάστης**, ου, ὁ, *tile-maker*, Gloss. **-ῐδόω**, *make a roof as of shields* to protect the soldiers (the Roman *testudo*), Apollon.*Lex.* s.v. σάκος, Hsch. s.v. σάκε' ὤμοισι κλίναντες:—Pass., *to be roofed* or *coped with tiles*, κεραμιδουμένη.. ἡ οἰκία Arist.*Ph.*246ᵃ28 (but κεραμουμένη ib.19 codd.). **-ῐκός**, ή, όν, *of* or *for pottery*, γῆ κ. *potter's* earth, Hp.*Int.*7, cf. Sannyr.4; κ. ῥύμη, = Κεραμεικός, Ar. *Ec.*4; κ. κέραμος *IG*4²(1).102.281 (Epid., iv B.C.); ὁ κ. τροχός Str.7. 3.9; κ. μάστιξ, Com. phrase for ostracism, *Com.Adesp.*33; ἐργαστήριον *PFlor.*50.68 (iii A.D.); ἡ -κή (sc. τέχνη) *the potter's art, pottery*, Pl.*Plt.*288a; v. κεραμεικός. **-ῐνος**, η, ον, = κεραμεοῦς, Hdt.3.96, 4.70, Anaxil.5, *PFlor.*388.98 (ii A.D.). **-ιον**, τό, *earthenware vessel, jar*, *IG*2².1672.13, Men.*Sam.*88 (pl.), etc.; κ. οἰνηρόν Hdt.3.6, cf. Hp.*Art.*78; οἴνου X.*An.*6.1.15; ὀξηρόν Ar.*Fr.*723; κ. ταριχηρόν Arist.*HA*534ᵃ21; ταρίχους, as a measure, Test.ap.D.35.34, cf. *PSI* 5.585 (iii B.C.), *OGI*90.31 (Rosetta, ii B.C.), Lxx *Is.*5.10, *SIG*1109. 162 (ii A.D.). 2. *sarcophagus*, D.C.42.26. **-ιος**, ὁ, = κεραμεύς, *CIG*5021, 5028 (Nubia). II. v. κεραμεοῦς. **-ίς**, ίδος [ῐ], ἡ, Diph.84, Ion. and later -ῖδος Emp.ap.Arist.*EE*1235ᵃ12, *MM*1208ᵇ 11, cf. Hdn.Gr.2.18: (κέραμος):—*roof-tile*, Ar.*V.*206, Th.3.22, *Inscr. Délos* 366.21, al. (iii B.C.), etc.; κ. ἀγελαῖαι common *tiles*, *IG*2².1672. 209; Κορίνθιαι ib.71; collectively, *tiling*, Arist.*Ph.*246ᵃ27, cf. ll. cc.; prop. of clay, but also of marble, *IG*2².1666 *B* 21, 25; κ. ἀργυραῖ Plb. 10.27.10; κ. μολυβῆ Ath.14.621a, cf. Moschio ib.5.207a. 2. = κεράμιον, *PLond.*3.1177.158 (ii A.D.), *PIand.*12.3 (iii/iv A.D.). II. as Adj., γῆ κ. *potter's* earth, clay, Pl.*Criti.*111c, *Lg.*844b; ὦ γαῖα κεραμί Eub.43. **-ισμα**, ατος, τό, = foreg., Gloss. **-ίτης**, ου, ὁ, v. sq. **-ῖτις**, ιδος, ἡ, *of* or *for pottery*, κ. γῆ *potter's* earth, Hp. *Morb.*1.17, 3.1, Plu.2.827e, Gal.2.137; κ., ἡ, a gem of the colour of potsherds, Plin.*HN*37.152 (acc. -την, nisi leg. -τιν, *Cat.Cod.Astr.* 8(2).169, cf. 8(1).190).

κερᾰμο-πλάστης, ου, ὁ, *potter*, *PLips.*97 xxvi 10 (iv A.D.), *PLond.* 1821.234. **-πλαστικὸν** κεραμεῖον *pottery*, *PMasp.*110.22 (vi A.D.). **-ποιός**, ὁ, *potter*, Gloss.

κερᾰμοπωλ-εῖον, τό, *pottery-market*, Din.*Fr.*89.18. **-έω**, *sell earthenware*, Alex.320. **-ης**, ου, ὁ, *seller of pottery*, Din.*Fr.*89.18.

κέρᾰμος, ὁ, rare pl. κέραμα, τά, *PPetr.*3 p.327 (iii B.C.):—*potter's earth, potter's clay*, Pl.*Ti.*60d, Arist.*Mete.*384ᵇ19, etc.; κ. ὠμός, ὀπτώμενος, ib.380ᵇ8, 383ᵃ21. II. *anything made of this earth*, as 1. *earthen vessel, wine-jar*, ἐκ κεράμων μέθυ πίνετο Il.9.469, cf. Hdt.3.96; in collective sense, *pottery*, Ar.*Ach.*902, Men.*Sam.*75, al.; κ. ἐσάγεται πλήρης οἴνου *jars* full of wine, Hdt.3.6, cf. 5.88, Alex.257.3, etc. b. *jar* of other material, κ. ἀργυροῦς Ptol.Euerg.7 J. 2. *tile*, Ar.*V.*1295 (of a tortoise's shell); collectively, *tiling*, τοῦ τέγους τὸν κέραμον αὐτοῦ χαλάζαις ... ξυντρίψομεν Id.*Nu.*1127, cf. *Fr.*349, Th. 2.4; Κορίνθιος κ. *IG*2².1668.58; Λακωνικός ib.463.69, 1672.188; *roof*, Pherecr.130.6, Herod.3.44, Gal.8.26, 9.824. 3. *pottery* (i.e. place of manufacture), ὁ κ. ὁ χυτρικός *Tab.Defix.Praef.*p.iiᵇ. III. *dungeon* (said by Sch. to be Cyprian), χαλκέῳ ἐν κεράμῳ δέδετο Il.5.387, cf. Thphr.*Char.*6.6 cod. M; pl., Nonn.*D.*16.162. (Possibly cogn. with Lat. *cremo*.)

κερᾰμοτήξ, ῆγος, ὁ, (τήκω) *potter*, Theognost.*Can.*40.

κερᾰμ-ουργός, ὁ, = κεραμοποιός, *PPetr.*3 p.173 (iii B.C.), Man.4. 291, *Cat.Cod.Astr.*8(4).213. **-όω**, *roof with tiles*, *IG*1².373.246, 2².1668.58, al., Ἀρχ.Δελτ.8.270:—Pass., ναὸς κεκεραμωμένος *SIG* 996.18 (Smyrna, i A.D.), cf. Simp.*in Ph.*1055.17; ὡς εἰπεῖν -ωθέντες, of soldiers in the Roman *testudo*, Onos.20.1. **-ύλλιον**, τό, Dim. of κεράμιον, *jar*, *IG*11(2).161 *C* 101 (Delos, iii B.C.), *PCair.Zen.*12.35 (iii B.C.), *Inscr.Délos* 442 *B* 179 (ii B.C.), Aq.*Is.*63.3. **-ών**, ῶνος, ὁ, *store for pottery* or *tiles*, Hdn.Gr.1.32, 40. **-ωσις**, εως, ἡ, *roofing with tiles*, *IG*4²(1).102.289 (Epid., iv B.C.), *IPE*1².184 (Olbia, iii A.D.). **-ωτός**, ή, όν, *covered with tiles*, applied to a *testudo* formed by Roman soldiers, Plb.28.11.2; ἡ κ. στέγη Str.11.3.1, 13.1.27.

κερανίξαι· κολυμβῆσαι, κυβιστῆσαι, Hsch.

κεράνν-ῡμι, also -ύω Alc.Com.15, Hyp.*Fr.*69; Ep. **κεραίω** and **κεράω** (qq.v.); subj. κεραννύω Pl.*Phlb.*61b: impf. ἐκεράννυν Luc.*VH* 1.7: fut. κεράσω [ᾰ] Them.*Or.*27 p.340 D.: aor. ἐκέρᾰσα Hp.*VM*3, (ἐν-) Pl.*Cra.*427c, poet. κέρᾰσα E.*Ba.*127 (lyr.), Ep. κέρασσα Od.5. 93, Ion. ἔκρησα Hp.*Int.*35:—Med., aor. ἐκερᾰσάμην Ti.Locr.95e, Ep. κεράσσατο Od.18.423:—Pass., fut. κραθήσομαι [ᾱ] Pl.*Ep.*326c, (συγ-) E.*Ion*406: aor. ἐκράθην [ᾱ] Th.6.5, E.*Ion*1016, Pl.*Phd.*86c; Ion. ἐκρήθην Hp.*VM*19; ἐκεράσθην Pl.*Phlb.*47c, *Ti.*85a, X.*An.*5.4. 29, Phylarch.10 J.: pf. κέκρᾱμαι Pi.*P.*10.41, etc.; Ion. κέκρημαι Hp. *VM*13, *Acut.*21; κεκέρασμαι Arist.*Fr.*549, D.H.*Comp.*24, *Anacreont.* 16.13, etc.: plpf. ἐκέκρατο Sapph.51.1:—*mix, mingle* (diff. from μείγνυμι, v. κρᾶσις): 1. mostly of diluting wine with water, κερῶντάς τ' αἴθοπα οἶνον Od.24.364; κέρασσε δὲ νέκταρ ἐρυθρόν 5.93; κέρασον ἄκρατον Ar.*Ec.*1123, cf. Th.6.32: abs., τοῖς θεοῖς εὐχόμενοι κεραννύωμεν *let us mix a cup of wine*, Pl.*Phlb.*61b; ἂν μὴ κεράσῃ τις Antiph.85.2: c. dat. pers., *give to drink*, ἐν τῷ ποτηρίῳ ᾧ ἐκέρασε κεράσατε αὐτῇ διπλοῦν *Apoc.*18.6:—Hom. mostly in Med., ὅτε περ.. οἶνον.. ἐνὶ κρητῆρι κέρωνται *mix their* wine in the bowl, Il. 4.260, cf. Od.20.253; κρητῆρα κεράσσατο he *mixed* a bowl, 3.393, 18.423:—Pass., πῶς οὖν κέκραται [σκύφος]; E.*Cyc.*557; κύλιξ ἴσον ἴσῳ κεκραμένη a cup *mixed* half and half, Ar.*Pl.*1132; κεκρ. τρία καὶ δύο Id.*Eq.*1187, cf. *AP*11.137 (Lucill.). 2. *temper, cool by mixing*, θυμῆρες κεράσασα *having mixed* (the water) *to an* agreeable *temperature*, Od.10.362. 3. generally, *mix, blend*, ἡδονὴν φθόνῳ Pl.*Phlb.*50a; τοῖς ὀνόμασι τὰ ῥήματα Id.*Sph.*262c; νοῦς μετ' αἰσθήσεων κραθεὶς Id.*Lg.*961d, cf. *Ti.* l. c.; πίστεως αἰσθήσει κεκραμένης Plot.4.7.15; ἀγωγὴν ἐξ ἀμφοῖν κ. Phld.*Acad.Ind.*p.77 M.; [οὐσία] οὐκ ἀπὸ τῶν ἄκρων κραθεῖσα Jul.*Or.*4.139a; of metals, ἀργυρίῳ πρὸς χαλκὸν κεκραμένῳ χρῆσθαι D.24.214: metaph., *temper, regulate*, of climates, ὧραι κάλλιστα κεκρημέναι most *temperate*, Hdt.3.106; ὧραι μετριώτατα κ. Pl.*Criti.*111e; ἔαρ κ. τῇ ὥρᾳ X.*Cyn.*5.5; [πλοῦτον] ἀρετᾷ κεκραμένον Pi.*P.*5.2; οὐ γῆρας κέκραται γενεᾷ no old age *is mingled with* the race, i. e. it knows no old age, ib.10.41, cf. *O.*10(11).104; ἐν ταῖς εὖ κεκρ. πολιτείαις Arist.*Pol.*$1307^{b}30$; of tempers of mind, ἤθει γεννικωτέρῳ κεκρᾶσθαι Pl.*Phdr.*279a; τοῖς ἤθεσιν..τούτοις ἡ φύσις κεράννυται Alex. 278b (iii p.744 K.); of Music, ἁρμονίας ῥυθμοῖς κραθείσας Pl.*Lg.*835b; τῆς εὖ κεκραμένης ἁρμονίας Arist.*Pol.*$1290^{a}26$; μετρίως κραθῆναι πρὸς ἄλληλα Pl.*Phd.* l. c. II. *compound*, ἐκ τῶν ἐπιτηδευμάτων τὸ ἀνδρείκελον Id.*R.*501b; οὐκ ἀπίθανον λόγον Id.*Phdr.*265b; θεόσυτος ἢ βρότειος ἢ κεκραμένη; A.*Pr.*116; φωνὴ μεταξὺ τῆς τε Χαλκιδέων καὶ Δωρίδος ἐκράθη Th.6.5. III. Gramm., in Pass., *coalesce by crasis*, τὸ ῥῆμα καὶ ὁ σύνδεσμος συναλοιφῇ κερασθέντα D.H.*Comp.*22. IV. *multiply into*, ὅταν ὁ τῆς δεκάδος λόγος τῷ τῆς ἑβδομάδος κερασθῇ *Theol.Ar.* 50. **–υτέον,** *one must mix*, Max.Tyr.5.4.

κέραξ, ακος, ὁ, = κέρας, in the senses θρίξ, τόξον, αἰδοῖον, Hsch.

κερᾰοξόος, ον, (ξέω) *polishing horn*; esp. *making it into bows*, etc., κ. τέκτων Il.4.110, *AP*6.113 (Simm.).

κερᾰός, ά, όν, (κέρας) *horned*, ἔλαφος Il.3.24; ἄρνες Od.4.85; τράγος Theoc.1.4; Ἄμμων *Epigr.Gr.*835 (Berytus). II. *made of horn*, τοῖχοι Call.*Ap.*63; βιός *AP*6.118 (Antip.). (Prob. fr. *κεραϝός, cf. Lat. *cervus*.)

κερᾰοῦχος, ον, (ἔχω) = κεροῦχος I, *AP*6.10 (Antip.).

κεράρχης, ου, ὁ, *commander of a* διφαλαγγαρχία, Ascl.*Tact.*2.10. 2. *commander of thirty-two elephants*, ib.9.1.

κέρᾰς, τό, Ep. gen. *κέρᾰος, Att. contr. κέρως; Ep. dat. κέρᾰϊ (elided) or κέραι or κέρᾳ Il.11.385, cf. Hdn.Gr.2.75, κέρᾳ also in Th. 2.90, 7.6: nom. pl. κέρᾱ (v. infr.), gen. κεράων, κερῶν, dat. κέρασι, Ep. κεράεσσι:—Att. Inscrr. have dual [κέρ]ατε *IG*1^{2}.301.109: pl. κέρατα ib.237.59; later Ep. κεράατα (◡ – ◡ ◡) Nic.*Th.*291, κεράατος (◡ – ◡ ◡) Arat.174, Q.S.6.225:—Hdt. has gen. κέρεος 6.111, dat. κέρεϊ 9.102: pl. κέρεα 2.38, κερέων ib.132; but Hp. has gen. sg. κέρως, pl. κέρατα, *Aër.*18. [In nom. and acc. κέρας, ᾰ always: in the obl. cases ᾰ in Ep., as κέρᾰσιν Od.3.384 (in contr. dat. κέρᾱͅ, nom. pl. κέρᾱ (cf. Batr.165), α is shortd. before a vowel, Il.11.385, Od.19.211); but ᾱ in Trag. and Com., κέρᾱτος Hermipp.43, κέρᾱτα E.*Ba.*921, κεράτων [ᾱ] prob. in S.*Tr.*519 (lyr.), κέρᾱσι A.*Fr.*185. In later Ep. the quantity varies.] (κέρας is prob. related to κάρα; cf. κεραός.) I. *the horn of an animal*, in Hom. mostly of oxen, Il.17.521, etc.; ταῦροι..εἰς κέρας θυμούμενοι E.*Ba.*743; ὀφθαλμοὶ δ' ὡς εἰ κέρα ἕστασαν his eyes stood fixed and stiff like *horns*, Od.19.211; as a symbol of strength, Lxx *Ps.*17(18).3, Diogenian.7.89, cf. Arist.*PA*$662^{a}1$; of elephants' *tusks*, Aret.*SD*2.13, Opp.*C.*2.494. 2. *antennae* of crustaceans, Arist.*HA*$526^{a}31$, $590^{b}27$; of the silkworm's *grub*, ib.$551^{b}10$. II. *horn*, as a material, αἱ μὲν γὰρ [πύλαι] κεράεσσι τετεύχαται Od.19.563; *the horn* of animals' hoofs, Longus 2.28. III. *anything made of horn*, 1. *bow*, τόξον ἐνώμα..πειρώμενος..μὴ κέρα ἶπες ἔδοιεν Od. 21.395, cf. Theoc.25.206, Call.*Ep.*38, *AP*6.75 (Paul. Sil.); for Il.11. 385 v. infr. v. 1. 2. of musical instruments, *horn for blowing*, σημῆναι τῷ κέρατι X.*An.*2.2.4, cf. Arist.*Aud.*$802^{a}17$; also, *the Phrygian flute*, because it was tipped with horn (cf. Poll.4.74), αὐλεῖν τῷ κ. Luc.*DDeor.*12.1; καὶ κέρατι μὲν αὐλεῖν Τυρρηνοὶ νομίζουσι Poll.4.76, cf. Ath.4.184a. 3. *drinking-horn*, ἐκ τοῦ κέρατος αὖ μοι δὸς πιεῖν Hermipp.43, cf. X.*An.*7.2.23, *OGI*214.43 (Didyma, iii B. C.); ἐξ ἀργυρέων κ. πίνειν Pi.*Fr.*166, cf. *IG*1^{2}.280.77; ἀργυρηλάτοις κέρασι χρυσᾶ στόμια προσβεβλημένοις A.*Fr.*185; ἐκπιόντι χρύσεον κ. S.*Fr.* 483; for measuring liquids, Gal.13.435. 4. Ἀμαλθείας κ. *cornucopiae*, v. Ἀμάλθεια. IV. βοὸς κ. prob. a *horn guard* or *cover* attached to a fishing-line, Il.24.81, cf. Sch.; ἐς πόντον προΐησι βοὸς κέρας Od.12.253; ψάμμῳ κ. αἰὲν ἐρείδων *AP*6.230 (Maec.), cf. Aristarch.ap.Apollon.*Lex.* s. v. κέρᾳ ἀγλαέ, Arist.ap.Plu.2.977a (also expld. as a *fishing-line of ox-hair* (cf. infr. v. 1), ap.Plu.2.976f, cf. Poll.2.31; perh. an artificial *bait*). 2. *clyster-pipe*, Orib.8.32 7. 3. in pl., *horn points* with which the writing-reed was tipped, *AP*6.227 (Crin.). V. of objects shaped like horns, 1. a mode of dressing the hair, κέρᾳ ἀγλαέ Il.11.385 (unless the meaning be *bow*), cf. Aristarch. ad loc., Herodorus and Apion ap.Eust. ad loc.: hence κέρας is expld. as = θρίξ or κόμη, Apollon.*Lex.*, Hdn.Gr.ap.Eust. l. c., Poll.2.31, Hsch.; cf. IV. 1, and v. κεροπλάστης. 2. *arm* or *branch* of a river, Ὠκεανοῖο κ. Hes.*Th.*789; Νείλου Pi.*Fr.*201; τὸ Μενδήσιον κέρας Th.1.110; ἐν Ἰνδοῖς ἐν τῷ Κέρατι καλουμένῳ Arist.*Mir.*$835^{b}5$, cf. *Mu.*$393^{b}5$; τὸ κ. τὸ Βυζαντίων the 'Golden *Horn*', Str.7.6.2, cf. Plb.4.43.7, Sch.A.R.4.282; Ἑσπέρου Κ., name of a *bay*, Hanno *Peripl.*14, cf. Philostr.*VS*1.21.2. 3. *wing* of an army, Hdt.9.26, etc.; or fleet, Id.6.8, Th.2.90, etc.; κ. δεξιόν, λαιόν, A.*Pers.*399, E.*Supp.*704; τὸ εὐώνυμον κ. ἀναπτύσσειν X.*An.*1.10. 9. b. κατὰ κέρας προσβάλλειν, ἐπιπεσεῖν, to attack in *flank*, Th.3.78, X.*HG*6.5.16, etc.; κατὰ κ. προσιέναι, ἕπεσθαι, Id.*Cyr.*7.1.8 and 28; κατὰ κ. συμπεσών Plb.1.40.14; πρὸς κ. μάχεσθαι X.*Cyr.*7.1.22. c. ἐπὶ κέρας ἀνάγειν τὰς νέας to lead a fleet in *column*, Hdt.6.12, cf. 14; κατὰ μίαν ἐπὶ κέρως παραπλεῖν Th.2.90, cf. 6.32, X.*Cyr.*6.3.34, Eub.67.4; of armies, κατὰ κέρας, opp. ἐπὶ φάλαγγος, X.*Cyr.*1.6.43, cf. *An.*4.6.6, *HG*7.4.23; εἰς κ. Id.*Eq.Mag.*4.3; ἐκ κέρατος εἰς φάλαγγα καταστῆσαι Id.*Cyr.*8.5.15; οὐκ ἐλᾶτε πρὸς τὸ δεξιὸν κ.; Ar.*Eq.*243. 4. *corps of* 8192 *men*, = διφαλαγγαρχία, Ascl.*Tact.*2.6, Arr.*Tact.*10.7. b. = μεραρχία, Ascl.*Tact.*2.10. c. *contingent of thirty-two chariots*, ib. 8, Ael.*Tact.*22.2. 5. *sailyard*, = κεραία, *AP*5.203 (Mel.), *OGI*674.30 (Egypt, i A. D.), Luc.*Am.*6, *POxy.*2136.6 (iii A. D.). 6. *mountain-peak*, v.l. in *h.Hom.*1.8; *spur*, τὸ κ. τοῦ ὄρους X.*An.*5.6.7, cf. Lyc. 534: in pl., *extremities* of the earth, γῆς Philostr.*VA*2.18 (pl.). 7. in Anatomy, *extremities* of the uterus, Hp.*Superf.*1, Gal.7.266; of the diaphragm, Sor.1.57. b. ἁπαλὸν κ., = πόσθη, Archil.171, cf. Neophro (?) in *PLit.Lond.*77 *Fr.*2.19, E.*Fr.*278, *AP*12.95.6 (Mel.). 8. of the πήχεις of the lyre, χρυσόδετον κ. S.*Fr.*244 (lyr.) (rather than the *bridge*, because made of *horn*, Ael.Dion.*Fr.*133, Poll.4.62). VI. κέρατα ποιεῖν τινι to give him *horns*, cuckold him, prov. in Artem.2. 11; cf. κερασφόρος II. VII. = κερατίνης, Luc.*DMort.*1.2. VIII. = σταφυλῖνος ἄγριος, Dsc.3.52; = οἰνάνθη, dub. in Ps.-Dsc.3.120.

κεράς (A), άδος, ἡ, poet. fem. of κεραός, Eust.1625.45; but in Hsch., κεραΐδες· τῶν προβάτων τὰ θήλεα, τὰ ἔνδον ὀδόντας ἔχοντα.

κεράς (B), Adv. *mixed*, glossed by κεραστικῶς, Call.*Fr.anon.*34.

κερασβόλος, ον, *struck by a horn*: σπέρμα κ. seed *that does not soften in boiling*, Thphr.*CP*4.12.13, cf. Plu.2.700c. II. metaph., *stubborn, inflexible* person, Pl.*Lg.*853d, cf. Plu. l. c.

κερᾰσ-έα and **–ία,** ἡ, = κερασός, *cherry-tree*, *Gp.*3.4.4, 10.41.2. **–ινον,** τό, *cherry-coloured dye*, *PHolm.*21.31. **–ιον,** τό, *fruit of the* κερασός, *cherry*, Diph.Siph.ap.Ath.2.51a, Dsc.1.113; also, *cherry-tree*, *Gp.*10.41.1.

κερασκόμη, ἡ, = κέρας VIII, Ps.-Dsc.3.52, 120 codd.

κέρασμα, ατος, τό, *mixture*, Zeno *Stoic.*1.36; μελῶν Iamb.*VP*15. 64 (pl.). 2. *drink poured out* (cf. κεράννυμι I. 1), *IGRom.*4.696 (Hieropolis); οἴνου ἀκράτου κ. Lxx *Ps.*74(75).8. 3. *mixed disease*, Gal.9.675.

κερᾰσός (on the accent v. Hdn.Gr.1.209), ὁ, *bird-cherry*, *Prunus avium*, Xenoph.39, Thphr.*HP*3.13.1, etc. (Assyrian *karšu*.)

κεράστης, ου, ὁ, *horned*, ἔλαφος S.*El.*568; κάνθαρος Id.*Ichn.*300; of a ram, ὦ κεράστα E.*Cyc.*52 (lyr.); Πάν Antip.*Oxy.*662.49, Corn. *ND*27; Σάτυροι Luc.*Bacch.*1:—fem. **κεραστίς,** ίδος, of Io, A.*Pr.* 674. II. as Subst., *horned serpent* or *asp*, *Cerastes cornutus*, Nic. *Th.*258, Lxx *Pr.*23.32, D.S.3.50, Ael.*NA*1.57; οἱ κ. ὄφεις Call.Hist. 3. 2. *pest which destroys fig-trees*, Thphr.*HP*4.14.5, 5.4.5.

κερασ-τής, οῦ, ὁ, *one that mixes*, Ζεὺς πάντων κ. Orph.*Fr.*297. **–τικῶς,** Adv. *for mixing*, Suid. s. v. κεράς. **–τός,** ή, όν, *mixed, mingled*, *APl.*4.83.

κερασφορ-έω, *have horns*, Philostr.*VA*2.13. **–ος,** ον, *horned*, στόρθυγγες S.*Fr.*89; of Io, E.*Ph.*248 (lyr.), *Hyps.Fr.*3(1) iii 31 (lyr.); of Dionysos, Luc.*Bacch.*2; of rivers, Corn.*ND*22; τὸ κ. μέρος Pl. *Plt.*265b; τὸ κ. γένος *horned animals*, Gal.2.430, cf. Philostr.*VA* 2.13. II. *cuckold*, Lemm. to *AP*11.278 (Lucill.).

κεράσχειλος, ον, *with curved lips*, Hsch.

κερᾱτ-άριον, τό, Dim. of κέρας v. 5, Sch.E.*Hec.*1261 (s. v. l.), Eust. 1037.35. **-άρχης,** ου, ὁ, *commander of a body of thirty-two elephants*, Ael.*Tact.*23:—hence **-αρχία,** ἡ, ibid. **–αύλης,** ου, ὁ, = κεραύλης, Dosith.p.389 K., *Gloss.*

κερατέα, ἡ, = κερατωνία, *Gp.*11.1; dub. sens. in *POxy.*2146.9 (iii A. D.), *PGen.*75.8 (iii/iv A. D.).

κερατεσσεῖς· οἱ τοὺς ταύρους ἕλκοντες ἀπὸ τῶν κεράτων· καλοῦνται δὲ καὶ **κεραελκεῖς,** Hsch.

κερᾱτήρ, ῆρος, ὁ, etym. of κρατήρ, Ath.11.476a.

κερᾰτηφόρος, ον, = κερασφόρος I, Phaest.ap.Sch.Pi.*P.*4.28.

κερατία, ἡ, = κερατωνία, Str.17.2.2, Plin.*HN*26.52. II. **κεράτια,** τά, *fruit of the carob-tree*, Dsc.1.114, *Ev.Luc.*15.16, *PLond.*1. 131*.7 (i A. D.), Gal.6.615.

κερᾱτ-ίας, ου, ὁ, = κερασφόρος I, of Dionysos, D.S.4.4. II. kind of *comet*, Plin.*HN*2.90. **–ίζω,** *butt with horns*: metaph., κ. τοῖς ποταμοῖς Lxx *Ez.*32.2, cf. Ph.1.57: c. acc., *gore*, ἐὰν κερατίσῃ ταῦρος ἄνδρα Lxx *Ex.*21.28. **–ίνης** [ῐ], ου, ὁ, *the fallacy called the Horns*: εἴ τι οὐκ ἀπέβαλες, τοῦτο ἔχεις· κέρατα δὲ οὐκ ἀπέβαλες· κέρατα ἄρα ἔχεις D.L.7.187; κερατίνας ἐρωτῶν *Com.Adesp.*294: acc. sg. **–ναν** Luc. *Symp.*23; cf. κερατίς. **–ῐνος,** η, ον, *made of horn*, X.*An.*6.1.4, Pl. Com.50, etc.; κ. λύχνος Epicr.8; βωμὸς κ., = κερατών, Plu.2.983e, cf. Arist.*Fr.*489; σάλπιγξ Lxx *Ps.*97(98).6; also κ. alone, ib.*Jd.*3.27, *2Ki.* 2.28. **–ιον,** τό, Dim. of κέρας, *small horn*, D.S.3.73, Arist.ap. Plu.2.977a. 2. of the *antennae* of the κάραβος, Arist.*HA*$526^{a}7$; of the hermit-crab, ib.$529^{a}27$. 3. in pl., *curved ends* of the womb (cf. κεραία II. 7), ib.$510^{b}19$. 4. musical instrument, perh. *fife* or *clarionet*, D.S.29.32, prob. for κεραμείου in Plb.26.1.4, cf. ib.1^{a}. 2. II. *carat*, $\frac{1}{1728}$ *of a pound*, Dsc.ap.Gal.19.775, Archig.ap.Aët. 6.37, Hero *Mens.*60.21, Just.*Nov.*32.1; = Lat. *siliqua*, *OGI*521.27 (Abydos, v/vi A. D.). III. = κερατωνία, Colum.*Arbor.*25. IV. v. κεράτια. **–ίς,** ίδος, ἡ, = κερατίνης, D.L.7.82 (s. v. l.). **–ισις,** εως, ἡ, *butting with horns*: metaph., of battering-rams, *impact*, Apollod. *Poliorc.*224.13 (pl.). **–ισμός,** ὁ, *loss on exchange of solidi for* κεράτια, *PMasp.*58 ii 11 (vi A. D.), Lyd.*Mag.*3.70 (pl.). **–ιστής,** οῦ, ὁ, *one that butts*, Lxx *Ex.*21.29, 36. **–ῖτις,** ιδος, ἡ, *horned*, μήκων κ. *horned poppy*, *Glaucium flavum*, Thphr.*HP*9.12.3, Dsc.4.65, Plin. *HN*20.205.

κερᾱτο-βάτης [ᾰ], ου, ὁ, gloss on κεροβάτας, Sch.Ar.*Ra.*230. **–γλύφος** [ῠ], ον, *working in horn*, Sch.D Il.4.110, *EM*505.11. **–ειδής,** ές, *like horn*, χιτών *external coat of the eye*, Cels.7.7.13, Poll.2.70, Aët.

7.1, etc. 2. applied to a part of the coat, opp. λευκός, Ruf.*Onom.* 27, cf. Gal.*UP*10.3 (distinguishing *cornea* from *sclera*). II. *horn-shaped*, λοβοί Dsc.2.158; γωνίαι J.*BJ*5.5.6; μορφή Sch.Arat. 779. III. *sounding like a horn*, ἦχοι D.H.*Comp.*14.

κερᾰτοξόος, ον, = κεραοξόος, Nonn.*D.* 3.76 codd. (κεραο- Mein., Ludw.).

κερᾰτο-ποιέω, *make horn-shaped*, Sch.Arat.780. **-ποιός**, όν, gloss on κεραοξόος, Hsch. **-πους**, ὁ, ἡ, πουν, τό, gen. ποδος, *horn-footed, hoofed, Gloss.*

κερᾱτουργός, όν, = κεραοξόος, Sch.D Il.4.110, *EM*505.11.

κερᾰτο-φάγος [φᾰ], ον, *eating horn*, Hsch. s.v. ἴψ. **-φόρος**, ον, = κερασφόρος I, Arist.*HA*499ᵇ15, *PA*663ᵇ35; θῆρες Opp.*C.*2. 489. **-φυέω**, *grow horns*, Sch.Ar.*Eq.*1341, *EM*505.6. **-φυής**, ές, *growing horns, horned*, Ath.11.476a, *EM*541.18. **-φωνος**, ον, *sounding with the horn*, of the μάγαδις struck by the plectrum, Telest.4.

κερᾰτ-όω, *harden into horn*, Ael.*NA*12.18. **-ώδης**, ες, = κερατοειδής, *like antlers*, Thphr.*HP*5.1.6; τὸ κ., of the gizzard in fowls, Dsc.2.49. 2. *horned*, τὰ κ. τῶν ζῴων Arist.*HA*595ᵃ13. II. v. κεραώδης. **-ών**, ῶνος, ὁ, *made of horns* (sc. βωμός), of an altar on Delos, *IG*2².1641.2 (iv B.C.), 11(2).161*A*101 (Delos, iii B.C.), *Inscr.Délos*442*A*188 (ii B.C.), Plu.*Thes.*21.

κερατωνία, ἡ, = κερωνία, κερατέα, *carob-tree, Ceratonia Siliqua*, Gal. 12.23, Aët.1.201, Hsch.

κερᾰτῶπις, ιδος, ἡ, *horned-looking*, μήνη Man.4.91.

κεραύλ-ης, ου, ὁ, *horn-blower*, Archil.172, Luc.*Trag.*33. **-ία**, ἡ, *horn-blowing*, Corn.*ND*6(pl.).

κεραυν-εγχής, ές, = ἐγχεικέραυνος, B.7.48. **-ειος**, ον, *wielding the thunder*, Ζεύς *AP*7.49 (Bianor). **-ία**, ἡ, = ἀείζωον μικρόν, Ps.-Dsc.4.89. **-ίας**, ου, ὁ, *thunder-stricken*, Hsch. **-ιον**, τό, *truffle, Tuber aestivum*, Thphr.*HP*1.6.5, Gal.19.731. II. *critical mark to indicate corrupt passages*, Isid.*Etym.*1.21.21, Sch.Il.i p.xliii Dind.; but πρὸς τὴν ἀγωγὴν τῆς φιλοσοφίας D.L.3.66. III. = κεραυνία λίθος, *PHolm.*5.40, Isid.*Etym.*16.13.5, etc. **-ιος**, α, ον, also ος, ον A.*Th.*430, E.*Ba.*594 (anap.):—*of a thunderbolt*, βολαί A. l.c.; φλόξ Id.*Pr.*1017; πέμφιξ S.*Fr.*538; πῦρ, λαμπάδες, E.*Tr.*80, *Ba.*244; θάνατος death *by the thunderbolt*, Call.*Aet.*3.1.64; λίθος *heliotrope, PHolm.*10.37, Porph.*VP*17, cf. Plin.*HN*37.132. 2. *thunder-smitten*, of Semele, S.*Ant.*1139 (lyr.), E.*Ba.*6; Καπανέως κ. δέμας Id. *Supp.*496; τὰ Κεραύνια the '*thunder-splitten peaks*', name of several mountain ridges, Str.6.3.5, etc. 3. κεραύνιος, ὁ, kind of *bandage*, Sor.*Fasc.*37. II. = κεραύνειος, [Ζεύς] Arist.*Mu.*401ᵃ17, *Milet.*1(7). 278; applied to Philip, *AP*6.115 (Antip.⟨Sid.⟩).

κεραυνο-βλής, ῆτος, ὁ, ἡ, = sq., Thphr.*HP*3.8.5, Tz.*H.*4.267. **-βλητος**, ον, *struck by lightning*, Ephor.17 J., Sch.S.*Ant.*1139, Hsch. s.v. λευκοστεφῆ. Suid. s.v. Σαλμωνεύς.

κεραυνοβολ-έω, *hurl the thunderbolt*, *AP*12.122 (Mel.), 140, Ps.-Luc.*Philopatr.*4, *Placit.*3.3.3. II. trans., *strike therewith*, οἰκίαν Eratosth.*Cat.*6. **-ία**, ἡ, *thunder-storm*, Str.13.4.11 (pl.), Plu.2. 624b (pl.). **-ιον**, τό, *thunderbolt*, Corn.*ND*19. **-ος**, ον, *hurling the thunder*, Ζεύς *IG*5(2).37 (Tegea); πῦρ τὸ κ. the *thunder-smiting* fire, *AP*12.63 (Mel.); κ. νεφέλαι Orph.*Fr.*256; of planetary influences, Vett.Val.14.17; title of the Roman *Legio XII Fulminata*, D.C.71.9. II. proparox. κεραυνόβολος, ον, Pass., *thunder-stricken*, of Semele, E.*Ba.*598 (lyr.), cf. D.S.1.13, etc.

κεραυνο-βρόντης, ου, ὁ, *thunderer*, Ζεῦ -βρόντᾱ Ar.*Pax*376. **-κλόνος**, ον, *causing the din of the thunderbolt*, *PMag.Par.*1.599. **-μάχης** [ᾰ], ου, Dor. -χᾱς, ὁ, *fighting with thunder*, *AP*12.110 (Mel.). **-πληκτος**, ον, = sq., Phld.*Ir.*p.94 W. **-πλήξ**, ῆγος, ὁ, ἡ, *thunder-smitten*, Alc.Com.2. **-πλους** (sic), epith. of Cerberus, perh. f.l. for **κεραυνόπλος**, *armed with the thunderbolt*, *PMag.Par.*1. 2262. **-ποιός**, όν, *causing thunderbolts*, Vett.Val.6.25.

κεραυνός, ὁ, *thunderbolt*, νῆα θοὴν ἔβαλε ψολόεντι κ. Od.23.330; βρόντησε καὶ ἔμβαλε νηῒ κ. 14.305; Διὸς πληγεῖσα κεραυνῷ 12.416; esp. as weapon of Zeus, Hes.*Th.*854, etc.; forged by the Cyclopes, ib.141; τὸν κ. τοῦ Διός Ar.*Av.*1538; καταιβάτης A.*Pr.*361; πυρωπός ib.668; ὁ πυρφόρος κ. Id.*Th.*445; κεραυνοῦ κρείσσονα φλόγα Id.*Pr.*922; κ. ἀργής Ar.*Av.*1747 (anap.); πτερόεις ib.576; κεραυνοῦ βέλος A.*Th.*453 (lyr.), S.*Tr.*1088; ὁ κ. λάμπων πυρί Ar.*Nu.*395; κ., πτεροφόρον Διὸς βέλος Id. *Av.*1714; κ. πίπτει, κατασκήπτει εἰς.., X.*HG*4.7.7, Plu.*Lyc.*31: pl., κεραυνοί *thunderbolts*, Hes.*Th.*690, Hdt.8.37, Epicur.*Ep.*2 p.46 U.; ποῦ ποτε κεραυνοὶ Διός; S.*El.*823 (lyr.), cf. Ar.*Pl.*125; τὰ τῶν κ. πτώματα Pl.*Ti.*80c; defined as ἔξαψις σφοδρὰ μετὰ πολλῆς βίας πίπτουσα ἐπὶ γῆς, i.e. *thunder and lightning*, Zeno *Stoic.*1.34. II. metaph., κεραυνὸν ἐν γλώττῃ φέρειν, of Pericles, *Com.Adesp.*10; τύπτειν κεραυνός *a thunderbolt* for striking, Antiph.195.4; Κεραυνός, as a name of great soldiers, Plu.*Arist.*6. III. title of Zeus, *IG* 5(2).288 (Mantinea, v B.C.), *Rev.Arch.*40.388 (Emesa). (Perh. cf. κεραΐζω.)

κεραυνοσκοπ-εῖον, τό, *machine for making thunder* on the stage, Poll.4.127, 130. **-ία**, ἡ, *divination by thunder and lightning*, D.S. 5.40.

κεραυνοῦχος, ον, *wielding the thunder*, [Ζεύς] Ph.Byz.*Mir.*3.1.

κεραυνο-φαής, ές, *flashing like lightning*, πῦρ E.*Tr.*1103. **-φόρος**, ον, *wielding the thunderbolt*, Ἔρως Plu.*Alc.*16, cf. 2.335a; κ. στρατόπεδον *Legio XII Fulminata*, D.C.55.23: as Subst., title of a priest at Seleucia in Pieria, *OGI*245.47 (ii B.C.).

κεραυν-όω, *strike with thunderbolts*, Hdt.7.10.ε', Pl.*Smp.*190c, Phld.*Piet.*131:—Pass., κεραυνωθείς Hes.*Th.*859, Pi.*N.*10.8, cf. Pl.*R.* 408c, etc. II. metaph., = καταδικάζω, Artem.2.9 (Pass.). **-ωσις**, εως, ἡ, *striking with thunder*, Str.16.2.7, Plu.2.996c (pl.); τοῦ Φαέθοντος Scymn.398.

κέραφος· χλευασμός, κακολογία, Hsch.; cf. σκέραφος.

κεράω (A), Ep. form of κεράννυμι, used in imper. κέρα *Com.Adesp.* 1211; part. κερῶν Od.24.364: impf. κέρων A.R.1.1185:—Med., subj. κέρωνται Il.4.260: imper. κεράασθε (lengthd. from -ᾶσθε) Od. 3.332: impf. κερόωντο 8.470.

κεράω (B), (κέρας) *make horned*, κερόωσι σελήνην Arat.780. II. *take post on the wing* or *flank*, Plb.18.24.9.

κερᾰώδης, ες, *horned*, i.e. high-peaked, of a hill, prob. in Call.*Ap.* 91 (κερατώδεος codd.).

Κεράων, ωνος, ὁ, hero worshipped by cooks at Sparta, Polem.Hist. 40.

κερᾰώψ, ὁ, ἡ, gen. ῶπος, *horned-looking*, σελήνη Max.337.

κερβαλά· ἀσθενῆ, μεγάλα, Hsch.

Κερβέριοι, οἱ, Comic form of Κιμμέριοι, read by Crates in Od.11. 14 (Κερβερέων Aristarch.(?)), and apptly. by Ar.*Ra.*187: with a play upon Κέρβερος, cf. *EM*513.45.

Κερβεροκίνδῡνος Τάρταρος *full of Cerberus-dangers*, Hsch.

Κέρβερος, ὁ, *Cerberus*, the many-headed dog of Hades, Hes.*Th.* 311, etc. II. name of a bird, Ant.Lib.19.3.

κερβολέω, = κερτομέω, Hsch.; perh. to be read in B.1.34.

κερδ-αίνω, fut. -ᾰνῶ A.*Pr.*876, Lys.8.20, etc.; Ion. -ανέω Hdt.1. 35, 8.60.γ'; κερδήσω *AP*9.390 (Menecr.), *Ep.Jac.*4.13, κερδήσομαι Hdt.3.72: aor. 1 ἐκέρδᾱνα Pi.*I.*5(4).27, And.1.134 codd., etc.; Ion. -ηνα Hom.*Epigr.*14.6, Hdt.8.5, also ἐκέρδησα Id.4.152, Hld.4.13, etc.: pf. κεκέρδαγκα D.C.53.5, κεκέρδᾱκα Aristid.1.366 J., Ach.Tat.5. 25, Phalar.*Ep.*81.2, etc., κεκέρδηκα D.56.30 (προσ-), J.*BJ*1.20.2:—Pass., aor. part. κερδανθείς Phld.*Oec.*p.67 J.: pf. κεκερδημένος J.*AJ* 18.6.5: (κέρδος):—*gain, derive profit* or *advantage*, κακὰ κ. *make* unfair *gains*, Hes.*Op.*352; μέγιστα ἐκ φορτίων Hdt.4.152; τί κερδανῶ; what *shall I gain?* Ar.*Nu.*259; κ. τινί *gain by* a thing, E.*HF*604; σμικρὰ κερδανῶ φυγῇ A.*Ag.*1301; κέρδος κ. S.*OT*889 (lyr.); κ. ἐξ τάλαντα And. l.c.; τὸν χρόνον κερδαίνει ὃν ἔζη οὐ προσῆκον αὐτῷ Lys.13.84; κ. λόγον *win* fame, Pi.*I.*5(4).27; χρηστὰ κ. ἔπη *receive* fair words, S.*Tr.*231: c. part., *gain by* doing.., εἰ δὲ κερδανῶ λέγων E.*Hel.*1051 (prob.); πολεμοῦντες οὐ κερδαίνομεν Ar.*Av.*1591, cf. Th.5.93; οὐδὲν ἐκμαθοῦσα κερδανεῖς A.*Pr.*876; Μεγάροισι κερδανέομεν περιεοῦσι we *shall gain* by Megara's preservation, Hdt.8.60.γ'; also κ. ὅτι.. Hp. *Art.*46:—Pass., τὰ κερδανθέντα Phld. l.c. 2. abs., *make profit, gain advantage*, Hdt.8.5, Ar.*Pl.*520; τοῦ κ. ἔχου S.*Fr.*28, cf. 354; ἐξ ἅπαντος, ἀπὸ παντός, Id.*Ant.*312, X.*Mem.*2.9.4; παρά τινων Lys.20.7; πρὸς σοῦ S.*Tr.*191; opp. τὸ τιμᾶσθαι, Th.2.44; *traffic, make merchandise*, S.*Ant.*1037. II. in bad sense, *reap* disadvantage from a thing, διπλᾶ δάκρυα κ. E.*Hec.*518; κερδᾶναι τὸν πολὺ χείρω βίον ἀντὶ θανάτου X.*Ap.*9. III. *save* or *spare oneself, avoid*, μεγάλα κακά Philem. 92.10; ὕβριν *Act.Ap.*27.21; τὸ μὴ μιανθῆναι τὰς χεῖρας J.*AJ*2.3.2; ἐνόχλησιν D.L.7.14, cf. Him.*Or.*2.26, *AP*10.59 (Pall.). **-αῖος**· τὸ ἐπικέρδη τοῖς παθοῦσι, καθόσον ἐκβέβρασται, Hsch. **-ᾰλέος**, α, ον, (κέρδος) of persons and their arts, *crafty, cunning*, κ. κ' εἴη καὶ ἐπίκλοπος Od.13.291; βουλή Il.10.44; μῦθος Od.6.148; νοήματα 8.548; of Ionian women, Aeschin.Socr.20. b. esp. of the fox, Archil.89.5: hence ἡ κ. *the wily one, the fox*, Ael.*NA*6.64, etc.; cf. κερδώ I. 2. of things, *profitable*, Pi.*P.*2.78, X.*Mem.*3.4.11, etc.; κερδαλεώτερόν ἐστι ὁμολογέειν τῷ Πέρσῃ Hdt.9.7.α'; τὰς ἐμπορίας τὰς κ. Ar.*Av.*594, cf. Isoc.2.18; τὸ κ. A.*Eu.*1008 (anap.); κ. ἔς τι Th.2.53. II. Adv. -λέως *to one's advantage*, opp. δικαίως, Id.3.56. **-ᾰλεόφρων**, ον, gen. ονος, *greedy of gain*, Il.1.149, 4.339; *crafty*, Opp.*C.*2.29. **-αντέος**, α, ον, *to be used profitably*, κ. τὸ παρόν M.Ant.4.26. **-αντός**, ή, όν, *that ought to be gained*: τὰ κερδαντὰ κερδαίνειν to make *fair gains*, Periand.ap.D.L.1.97. **-άριον**, τό, Dim. of κέρδος, *Gloss.* **-εία**, ἡ, = πανουργία, also ἀλωπεκία, Hsch.

Κερδείη, ἡ, epith. of Πειθώ, Herod.7.74.

κερδέμπορος, ον, *presiding over gain in traffic*, Ἑρμῆς Orph.*H.*28.6.

Κερδέων, ωνος, ὁ, epith. of Hermes, Herod.7.74.

κερδ-ητικός, ή, όν, *greedy of gain, Gloss.* **-ία**, ἡ, *greed of gain*, Phot. **-ίζω**, *gain*, Sch.rec.Pi.*O.*1.84. **-ίων**, ον, gen. ονος, Comp. (with no Posit. in use), formed from κέρδος, *more profitable*; Hom. only neut., ἐμοὶ δέ κε κέρδιον εἴη Il.6.410, or καί κεν πολὺ κέρδιον ἦεν 3.41, cf. 7.28; ἦ μάλα τοι τόδε κ. ἔπλετο θυμῷ Od.20.304: later in masc., οὔτοι ἅπασα κερδίων φαίνοισα πρόσωπον ἀλάθεια Pi.*N.*5.16. II. κέρδιστος, η, ον, Sup., *most cunning* or *crafty*, Σίσυφος.., ὃ κέρδιστος γένετ' ἀνδρῶν Il.6.153. 2. of things, *most profitable*, A.*Pr.*387; πρὸς τὸ κέρδιστον τραπείς S.*Aj.*743.

κερδογᾰμέω, *marry for gain*, Diogenian.6.22.

κέρδοπα, = χέδροπα, Hsch.

κέρδος, εος, τό, *gain, profit*, Od.23.140, etc.; ἐνόησεν ὅππως κ. ἔῃ how *some advantage* can be gained, what is *best* to be done, Il.10. 225; οὔ τοι τόδε κ. ἐγὼν ἔσσεσθαι ὀΐω ἧμιν Od.16.311, etc.; ποιέεσθαί τι ἐν κέρδεϊ, c. inf., Hdt.2.121.δ', 6.13; κ. νομίσαι τι Th.7.68; ὅτι.. Id.3.33; ἤν τι.. δάσωνται κ. ἡγεῖσθαι X.*Cyr.*4.2.43; ἐκ πονηροῦ πράγματος κ. λαβεῖν Men.697; μέγ' ἐστὶ κ., ἤν.. Id.*Mon.*359; πρὸς τὸ κ. βλέπειν ib.364; part., πᾶν κ. ἡγοῦ ζημιουμένη φυγῇ E.*Med.*454; κ. ἐστί μοι, c. inf., τί δῆτ' ἐμοὶ ζῆν κ.; A.*Pr.*747; τί κ. ἦν αὐτῷ διαβάλλειν ἐμέ; Lys.8.13, cf. Ar.*Ec.*607, 610: pl., *gains, profits*, περιβαλλόμενος ἑωυτῷ κέρδεα Hdt.3.71; τὰ δειλὰ (v.l. δεινὰ) κ. S.*Ant.*326; τὰ κ. μείζω φαίνεσθαι τῶν δεινῶν Th.4.59; τὰ πονηρὰ κ. Antiph.270:—κ. (metaph.) opp. ζημία (damage), Arist.*EN*1132ᵃ12, (lit.) opp. ζη-

μία (damages), ib.14; *ζημίαν λαβεῖν ἄμεινόν ἐστιν ἢ κ. κακόν* S.*Fr.* 807. 2. *desire of gain*, *κέρδει καὶ σοφία δέδεται* Pi.*P.*3.54; *ἄνδρας τὸ κ. πολλάκις διώλεσεν* S.*Ant.*222; *εἰς τὸ κ. λῆμ' ἔχων ἀνειμένον* E.*Heracl.*3: pl., *κερδῶν ἄθικτος* A.*Eu.*704; *ἐν τοῖς κέρδεσιν μόνον δέδορκε* S.*OT*388; *μὴ 'πὶ κέρδεσιν λέγων* Id.*Ant.*1061, cf. E.*Hec.* 1207; of persons, *ἡμέτερα κ. τῶν σοφῶν* (= *ἡμῶν τῶν σ.*) *you of whom* we wise men *make gain*, Ar.*Nu.*1202. 3. iron. (cf. *κερδαίνω* II), *ἀστεῖόν γε κ. ἔλαβεν ὁ κακοδαίμων* ib.1064. II. in pl., *cunning arts, wiles*, *ὃς δέ κε κ. εἰδῇ* Il.23.322, cf. 709, al.; *κέρδεσιν, οὔ τι τάχει γε παραφθάμενος* ib.515; *φρένας ἐσθλὰς κέρδεά θ'* Od.2.118, cf. 88; *ἐγὼ δ' ἐν πᾶσι θεοῖσι μήτι τε κλέομαι καὶ κέρδεσιν* 13.299; *ἐνὶ φρεσὶ κέρδε' ἐνώμας* 18.216; *κακὰ κ. βουλεύουσιν* 'they mean *mischief*', 23.217. (Cf. OIr. *cerd* 'art', 'craft', Welsh *cerdd* 'craft' or 'music'.)

κερδοσύνη, ἡ, *cunning, craft*: dat. *κερδοσύνῃ* as Adv., *cunningly*, Il.22.247, Od.4.251, 14.31: pl., *ἐπὶ κερδοσύνας τετραμμένοι* Cleanth.*Hymn.*1.28.

κερδοφόρος, ον, *bringing gain*, Artem.2.30.

κερδύφιον, τό, Dim. of *κέρδος*, *Gloss.*

κερδώ, όος, contr. οῦς, ἡ, *the wily one* or *thief*, i.e. *the fox* (cf. *κερδαλέος* I.1b), Pi.*P.*2.78(cj.), Ael.*NA*7.47; *κ. δολία* Ar.*Eq.*1068; *ποικίλη κ.* Babr.19.3. II. = *γαλέη, weasel*, Artem.3.28.

κερδῴζισιν (dat. pl.), *τοῖς*, perh. name of a board of magistrates, *BCH*47.50 (Pieria).

κερδῷος, α, ον, *bringing gain*, epith. of Apollo, Lyc.208, *IG*9(2).512.20 (Larissa), 1234 (Phalanna); of Hermes, Plu.2.472b, Luc.*Tim.* 41, etc. II. (*κερδώ*) *fox-like, wily*, *ἀλώπηξ* Babr.77.2.

κέρεα, τά, Ion. nom. pl. of *κέρας*.

κερεαλκής, ές, *stout in the horns*, *ταῦρος* A.R.4.468; *βόες* v.l. for *κεραελκέες* in Call.*Dian.*179.

Κερεάτας, ὁ, epith. of Apollo in Arcadia, Paus.8.34.5: perh. from *κέρας*, cf. *Κάρνειος*.

κέρεβρον, τό, = Lat. *cerebrum*, Gal.*UP*8.4 (*κέλ-* codd.).

κερεΐνος, *horned*, Aq., Sm., Quint.*Ps.*49(50).9. **κερεκόψαι**· ἢ σχίσαι ξύλα, Hsch. (post *κερουτιᾷ*). **κερητίζει**· βασανίζει, Id.

κέρθιος, ὁ, a little bird, perh. *tree-creeper, Certhia familiaris*, Arist.*HA*616^{b}28.

κέρκα· ἀκρίς, Hsch. **κέρκαξ**· ἱέραξ, Id. **κερκάς**, άδος, ἡ, = *κρέξ*, Id. **κέρκαφα**· ἐγγύη, Id.

κερκέτης, ου, ὁ, *weight used to steady a ship under sail*, Paus.Gr.*Fr.* 118, Hsch.

κερκήδης, *querquedula*, *Gloss.*; cf. sq.

κέρκηρις, εως, ὁ (?), an aquatic *bird*, *PCair.Zen.*186.10 (iii B.C.), *BGU*1252.30 (ii B.C.); *querquedula cerceris*, Varro *LL*5.79; cf. foreg.

κερκῐδ-ιαῖον, τό, *wedge-shaped block*, *IG*1^2.373.107, 122. **-ιον**, τό, Dim. of *κερκίς*, *POxy.*1740.1 (iii/iv A.D.), 1742.5 (iv A.D.), *Gloss.*

κερκῐδοποιική (sc. *τέχνη*), ἡ, *the art of the shuttle-maker*, Arist.*Pol.* 1256^{a}6.

κερκίζω, *separate the web with the κερκίς*, Pl.*Cra.*388b, *Sph.*226b; *εἰ αἱ κερκίδες ἐκέρκιζον αὐταί* Arist.*Pol.*1253^{b}37.

κερκιθαλίς· ἐρῳδιός, Hsch.

κέρκιον, τό, Dim. of *κέρκος*, Aq., Sm., Thd.*Le.*7.3.

κέρκιος, ὁ, = *κιρκίας*, Cato ap.Gell.2.22.28, v.l. in Arist.*Mu.*394^{b}31.

κερκίς, ίδος, ἡ, *weaver's shuttle*, *χαμαὶ δέ οἱ ἔκπεσε κ.* Il.22.448; *χρυσείῃ κερκίδ' ὕφαινεν* Od.5.62, cf. S.*Ant.*976 (lyr.), Pl.*Cra.*388a; *ἱστοῖς κερκίδα δινεύουσα* E.*Tr.*199 (lyr.); *κερκίσιν ἐφεστάναι* Id.*Hec.* 363; *φωνὴ κερκίδος* S.*Fr.*595; *κερκίδος ὕμνοις* ib.890 (lyr.); *κερκίδος ἀοιδοῦ* E.*Fr.*523 (lyr.): metaph., *μήδεα ἀδαμαντίναις ὑφαίνεται κερκίσιν αἶσα* *Lyr.Adesp.*ap.Stob.1.5.11. II. *any taper rod, of wood, ivory*, etc.; as, 1. *peg, pin*, used to rivet the *μεσάβοιον* to the *ζυγός*, Poll.1.252: *hair-pin* or *comb*, A.R.3.46. 2. *measuring-rod*, *AP*11.267; *gnomon* of a dial (prob.), *CIG*2681 (Iasus). 3. *great bone of the leg, tibia*, A.R.4.1520, Plu.*Alex.*45; = *κνήμη*, Heroph. ap.Ruf.*Onom.*123, Poll.2.191. b. *radius of the arm*, ib.142, Gal. *UP*2.13, al., Orib.47.6.1. 4. *organ* of the electric ray, Opp.*H.* 2.63. 5. *rod* for stirring liquids, Gal.12.683. 6. iron *dowel*, *IG*2^2.1668.52. 7. *καμπύλοχοι κ.*, of *ploughs*, Orph.*Fr.*33. III. *wedge-shaped division of the seats in the theatre*, *περὶ τὴν ἐσχάτην..κ. καθιζούσας θεωρεῖν* Alex.41, cf. Phld.*Acad.Ind.*p.26 M., *LW*1586 (Aphrodisias). 2. *tympanum* or *half-tympanum*, *IG*4^2(1).102.89, 112 (Epid., iv B.C.). IV. *aspen, Populus tremula*, Arist.*HA*595^{a}2, Thphr.*HP*3.14.2. 2. *Judas tree, Cercis Siliquastrum*, ib.1.11. 2. 3. *white bryony, Bryonia cretica*, Gal.14.186. 4. *pine-cone*, Sch.E.*Hec.*1153, Hsch. V. kind of *bird*, Id.

κέρκ-ῐσις, εως, ἡ, *plying the κερκίς, weaving*, Arist.*Ph.*243^{b}7. **-ιστική** (sc. *τέχνη*), ἡ, *art of weaving*, Pl.*Plt.*282b. **-ιστρα**, τά, *cost of weaving*, *POxy.*736.77 (i B.C./i A.D.). **-ῖτις**, ιδος, ἡ, a kind of *olive* (cf. Lat. *radius*), prob. in Colum.5.8.3.

κερκίων, ὁ, *an Indian talking bird*, perh. *talking myna, Gracula religiosa*, Ael.*NA*16.3.

κέρκνος· ἱέραξ, ἢ ἀλεκτρυών, Hsch.

κερκο-λύρα [ῠ], ἡ, = *κρέκουσα λύρα*, Alcm.142. **-πίθηκος** [ῐ], ὁ, *long-tailed ape*, Str.15.1.29, Plin.*HN*8.72, etc.

κερκορῶνος, ὁ, an *Indian bird*, perh. f.l. for *κερκίων*, Ael.*NA*15.14.

κέρκος, ἡ, *tail* of a beast (not a bird), e.g. swine, Ar.*Ach.*785; dog, *κέρκῳ σαίνειν* Id.*Eq.*1031; *κ. λαγῶ* a hare's *scut*, ib.909; horse, Pl.*Phdr.*254d, Plu.*Sert.*16; of all sorts of beasts, Arist.*PA*689^{b}2, al.; of fishes, Id.*HA*565^{b}29; *ἡ κ. ποιεῖ καλῶς*, of omens in sacrificing, Ar.*Pax* 1054, cf. Sch. ad loc., Eub.130. 2. *membrum virile*, Ar.*Th.*239; *ἡ ἀνώνυμος κ.* Herod.5.45; of an animal, *κ. βοός*, used as a tawse, Id.3.68. II. *handle*, Luc.*Lex.*7. III. *small animal that injures the vine*, Hsch. 2. = *ἀλεκτρυών*, Id. IV. *tongue* of flame, Sch.E.*Ph.*1257.

κερκούρ-ιον, τό, Dim. of *κέρκουρος*, only as pr. n. of a *ἑταίρα*, *AP* 5.43 (Rufin.). **-ίτης** [ῑ], ου, ὁ, *sailor belonging to a κέρκουρος*, *PSI* 6.614.22 (iii B.C.). **-ος** (proparox.) or **κερκοῦρος**, ὁ, *light vessel, boat*, esp. of the Cyprians, Hdt.7.97, cf. Din.*Fr.*12.2, Moschio ap. Ath.5.208e, D.S.24.1 (pl.); used for Nile transport, *PCair.Zen.*54.3 (iii B.C.), etc.:—written **κέρκυρος** (as if from *Κέρκυρα*) Sch.Ar.*Pax* 142; **κέρκυρα** (pl.) Suid. s. v. *Ναξιουργὴς κάνθαρος*. II. a *sea-fish*, Opp.*H.*1.141. (Cf. Lat. *cercurus, cercyrus* in both senses.)

κερκουροσκάφη [ᾰ], ἡ, = foreg. I, *PLille* 22.5 (iii B.C.).

κερκοφόρος, ον, *having a tail*, of fishes, Arist.*HA*489^{b}31.

κέρκυ· διπλῆ αὕτη καὶ δικέλαδος καὶ διθύσανος· ἐχρῆτο δὲ αὐτῇ μᾶλλον ὁ ἐν Κῷ πρύτανις, Hsch.

Κέρκῡρα, ἡ, and **Κερκῡραῖοι**, οἱ, = *Κόρκυρα, Κορκυραῖοι*, in codd. of Hdt., Th., and later Attic Inscrr., *IG*2^2.96, etc.; early Attic Inscrr. and Corcyraean coins have *Κορ-*, *IG*1^2.295, *BMus.Cat.Coins Thessaly* p.117, *Corinth* p.112.

κερκώδης, v.l. for *κερχνώδης*, Erot. s. h. v.

κερκώπη, ἡ, long-tailed *cicada*, Ar.*Fr.*51, Epil.4, Alex.92.2, Speus. ap.Ath.4.133b; acc. *κερκώπαν* Ael.*NA*10.44.

κερκωπία, ἡ, *trickiness*, Semon.34.

κερκωπίζω, (*κέρκωψ* II) *play the ape*, Zen.4.50, Hsch.

κέρκωσις, εως, ἡ, *growth on the os uteri*, Paul.Aeg.6.70, Aët.16. 106. II. *appearance of a tail* to a comet, *Cat.Cod.Astr.*8(3).174.

Κέρκωψ, ωπος, ὁ, (*κέρκος*) *man-monkey*, name of a race of mischievous dwarfs connected by legend with Heracles, Diotim.ap. Suid. s. v. *Εὐρύβατος*; *ἕδραι Κερκώπων*, near Thermopylae, Hdt.7.216; subject of poem ascribed to Hom., Harp., Suid. 2. metaph., *knave*, Aeschin.2.40, Lxx *Pr.*26.22, Gal.14.648; *γόης τις ἢ Κ. λόγων* *Com.Adesp.*1307; *οἱ Κέρκωπες* or *Κερκώπων ἀγορά*, at Athens, *Knaves-market*, D.L.9.114, Eust.1430.35. II. *long-tailed ape*, Manil.4.668.

κέρμα, ατος, τό, (*κείρω*) *fragment*, *κέρματα θηρείων μελέων* dub. l. in Emp.101.1; *τὰ κ. τοῦ ἡνωμένου ἡνωμένα* Dam.*Pr.*107, cf. Suid.; but mostly, 2. *coin*, *ἐγκάψας τὸ κ. εἰς τὴν γνάθον* Alex.128.7; *μικροῦ πρίασθαι κ. τὴν ἡδονήν* Eub.67.7, cf. Amphis 5, Antiph.131; collectively, *cash*, Theopomp.Com.30, Arr.*Epict.*2.10.14, al., *Cat.Cod. Astr.*7.244; esp. of copper money, opp. silver (*ἀργύριον*), *PGen.*77. 5 (ii/iii A.D.): freq. in pl., *μικρὰ κ.* Ar.*Av.*1108, cf. *Pl.*379, Eub.84. 1; *διδοὺς κέρματα* Test.ap.D.21.107, cf. Theopomp.Hist.89a, *UPZ*81 iv 20, 145 xi 17 (ii B.C.), Alciphr.1.2, *AP*5.44 (Cillactor).

κερμᾰτ-ίζω, *cut into pieces, chop up*, Pl.*R.*525e, Achae.7 (Pass.). etc.; *κατὰ σμικρὰ τὰ σώματα κ.* Pl.*Ti.*62a; *κ. τι εἰς πολλά* Arist.*PA* 662^{a}13: metaph., *κ. τὴν ἀρετήν* Pl.*Men.*79a. II. *coin into money*, *χαλκείην δαίμονα* *AP*11.271. III. *change into smaller coin*, *PGnom.* 237 (ii A.D.), *PRyl.*224(a).5 (Pass., ii A.D.). **-ιον**, τό, Dim. of *κέρμα*, Philippid.23, Plu.*Cim.*10, Arr.*Epict.*3.2.8, *AP*11.346 (Autom.), Phld. *Vit.*p.27 J. (pl.); *κ. συνηγμένον* Men.*Her.*7; *cash*, *PHib.*1.45.8 (iii B.C.), al. **-ισμός**, ὁ, metaph., *breaking up small*, Olymp. *in Phd.* p.86 N. **-ιστής**, οῦ, ὁ, *money-changer*, *Ev.Jo.*2.14. **-όομαι**, = *κερματίζομαι*, Procl. *in Prm.*p.973 S.

κέρμηλος· ἀφ' οὗ χαλκὸς γίνεται, Hsch.

κερμίον, τό, = *κερμάτιον*, *Cat.Cod.Astr.*7.93 (s.v.l.).

κέρνα· ἀξίνη, Hsch. II. pl. *κέρναι*, αἱ, *transverse processes of the vertebrae*, Poll.2.180 (v.l. *κέρνα*). **κέρνα**, τά, v. foreg. II. 2. v. *κέρνος*.

κέρνας, ὁ, *priest who carries the κέρνος* (q. v.), *AP*7.709 (Alex.).

κερνάω, v. *κιρνάω* sub fin.

κερνί[ον], τό, Dim. of sq., dub. in *IG*2^2.1544.64.

κέρνος, εος, τό, Ammon.ap.Ath.11.476f, Hsch. (pl.):—also **κέρνος**, ου, ὁ, Sch.Nic.*Al.*217: pl. **κέρνα**, τά, Poll.4.103:—*earthen dish with small pots affixed for miscellaneous offerings*, Ath. l. c., etc.; wrongly expld., = *λίκνον*, Sch.Pl.*Grg.*497c.

κερνο-φορέω, *carry the κέρνος*, Sch.Pl.*Grg.*497c. **-φόρος**, ὁ, ἡ, *priest* or *priestess who bears it*, Nic.*Al.*217; *κ. κόρη* Ps.-Plu.*Fluv.*13.3; *κ. ὄρχημα, ὄρχησις*, Poll.4.103, Ath.14.629d.

κερο-βάτης [ᾰ], ου, ὁ, (*κέρας*) *horn-footed, hoofed*, *κεροβάτας Πάν* Ar.*Ra.*230 (lyr.): acc. to some Gramm., *he that goes with horns*, i.e. *the horned god*; acc. to Sch., *he that walks the mountain-peaks* (cf. *κέρας* v.6). **-βόας**, ου, ὁ, *horn-sounding*, *λωτοί* *AP*6.94 (Phil.). **-δετος**, ον, *bound with* or *made of horn*, *τόξα* E.*Rh.*33 (lyr.). **-ειδής**, ές, *horn-shaped*, *ἕρπυλλος* Nic.*Th.*909.

κερόεις, *-όεσσα* (contr. *-οῦσσα*), *-όεν*, *horned*, Anacr.51, Simon. 30, S.*Fr.*89, E.*Ph.*828 (lyr.), Doroth.ap.Heph.Astr.3.7, etc.; *κερόεις ὄχος* carriage *drawn by horned cattle*, Call.*Dian.*113. II. *of horn*, *λωτός* *AP*7.223 (Thyill.).

κεροίαξ, ᾶκος, ὁ, in pl., *ropes belonging to the yard-arm*, Luc.*Nav.* 4; sine expl., Suid.; glossed *κάροια* (v.l. *κάρυα*), i.e. *blocks*, and *κρίκοι*, Sch.Luc. l. c.

κερο-πλάστης, ου, ὁ, *arranging the hair in horns* or *queues* (cf. *κέρας* v.1), *hairdresser*, Archil.57, Poll.2.31, Hsch. **-τυπέω**, *butt with horns*:—Pass., of ships in a storm, [*νῆες*] *κεροτυπούμεναι..χειμῶνι buffeted* by the storm, A.*Ag.*655.

κερουλίς and **κερουλκίς**, v. *κερουχίς*.

κερουλκός, όν, (*ἕλκω*) *drawing* a plough *by the horns*, Hsch. II. *drawing a bow of horn*, [*Τρῶες*] S.*Fr.*859 (lyr.). 2. Pass., of the bow itself, because *tipped with horn*, *τόξα κ.* E.*Or.*268. III. *κ. κάλως*, = *κεραιοῦχος*, Hsch.

κερουτ-ιάω, prop. of horned animals, *toss the horns*: metaph., of persons, *toss the head, give oneself airs*, Ar.*Eq.*1344:—hence **-(ι)ασμός**, ὁ, *hauteur*, Phot.

κερουχίς, ίδος, pecul. fem. of sq., αἶγες Theoc.5.145 (**κερουλίδες**, αἱ οὖλα κέρατα ἔχουσαι, **κερουλκίδες**, αἱ ὑπὸ τῶν κεράτων ἑλκόμεναι vv.ll. ap.Sch.).

κεροῦχος, ον, (ἔχω) *horned*, αἴξ Babr.45.5. **II.** κ. (sc. κάλως), ὁ, *brace of the yard-arm*, δελφινοφόρος κ. Pherecr.12.

κεροφόρος, ον, = κερασφόρος I, *horned*, βόες E.*Ba.*691.

κέρπαθος, ὁ, a kind of *incense*, Uran.12.

κέρσα· Ἀσιανὸν νόμισμα, Hsch. **κερσαῖον**, τό, Egyptian coin, Id. s. v. κορσίππιον. **κέρσης**· γάμος (leg. γάλλος), Id.

κέρσιμος, ον, (κείρω) *that may be nibbled*: τὸ κ. angler's *float*, Sch. Il.24.81; cf. κέρας IV, γέντιμος, γέρσυμον.

κερτομ-έω, *taunt, sneer at*, c. acc. pers., μή μιν κερτομέωσιν Od.16.87, cf. 18.350, A.*Pr.*986, E.*Ba.*1293: abs., *sneer*, μή τις..κερτομέοι ἐπέεσσι Od.7.17; κατθανοῦσι κ. ἐπ' ἀνδράσιν Archil.64: freq. in part., τί με ταῦτα κελεύετε κερτομέοντες; Od.8.153; σὲ δὲ κερτομέουσαν ὀΐω ταῦτ' ἀγορευέμεναι 13.326, etc.; πότερα δὴ κερτομῶν λέγεις τάδε; S.*Ph.*1235: c. acc. cogn., παραιβόλα κερτομέουσιν *h.Merc.*56: c. dupl. acc., οὐκ ἐῶ σε κ. ἡμᾶς τόδ' αὖθις E.*Hel.*619; οὔ τί τυ κερτομέω Theoc.1.62:—Pass., ἄβουλος ὡς κεκερτομημένη E.*Supp.*321.—Rare in Prose, Gal.14.656; κ. τινά Anon.ap.Suid. **-ησις**, εως, ἡ, *jeering, mockery*, S.*Ph.*1236. **-ία**, ἡ, *mockery*, in pl., κερτομίας ἠδ' αἴσυλα μυθήσασθαι Il.20.202,433; κερτομίας καὶ χεῖρας ἀφέξω Od.20.263. **-ικός**, ή, όν, *jeering*, Sch.Il.16.261. Adv. -κῶς ib.8.448. **-ιος** (-**εος** *EM*102.46), ον, *mocking, taunting*, κερτομίοις ἐπέεσσιν πειρηθῆναι Od.24.240; Δία Κρονίδην ἐρεθίζειν Il.5.419; simply κερτομίοισι Δία προσηύδα 1.539, cf. Od.9.474; κ. ὀργαῖς S.*Ant.*956 (lyr.); ἐν κ. γλώσσαις ib.962 (lyr.). (Perh. for (σ)κερ-στομος, cf. σκέραφος, κέραφος.) **-ιστής** (καρτ- cod.)· χλευαστής, Hsch.

κέρτομος, ον, = κερτόμιος, κέρτομα βάζειν Hes.*Op.*788; χοροὶ κ. Hdt.5.83 (v.l. κερτομίοισι), cf. D.H.7.72, Ael.*NA*5.54. **II.** *mocking, delusive*, παῖς *h.Merc.*338; χαρά E.*Alc.*1125; χάριτες Id.*Fr.*492.2; ἁρμονία, of Echo, *AP*7.191 (Arch.).—Poet. word used once by Hdt., and in late Prose.

κερτύλλιον, τό, perh. *basket*, *PFlor.*176.9 (iii A. D.); cf. καρτάλλιον.

κερύχρη, a kind of *cake*, Hsch.

κερχᾰλέος, α, ον, *rough, hoarse*, βήξ Hp.*Epid.*7.16; κερχαλέον ὑποσυρίζειν v.l. for κερχναλέον ib.7:—written **κερχναλέος**, Gal.19.111.

κέρχανα or **κερχάνεα**, *bones*, or *stumps of teeth*, Hsch.

κερχνασμός, ὁ, *roughness, hoarseness*, Gal.19.111.

κέρχνη, ἡ, kind of *hawk*, prob. *kestrel, Falco tinnunculus*, Hsch.:—also **κερχνηΐς**, contr. **κερχνής**, ῆδος, ἡ, Ar.*Av.*304, 589; **κεγχρηΐς**, ΐδος, ἡ, Arist.*HA*509ᵃ6, Ael.*NA*2.43; **κεγχρίς**, Arist.*HA*558ᵇ28, 594ᵃ2, *GA*750ᵃ7.

κερχνίον, τό, Dim. of κέρχνος (B) III, *IG*2².1533.19,23.

κέρχν-ος (A), ὁ, = κέγχρος, Hsch. s. v. κατακερχνοῦται, cf. Anaxandr.41.27, Gal.18(1).574. **-ος** (B), ὁ, *rough excrescence*, τραχὺς χελώνης κ. S.*Fr.*279. **2.** of the throat, *roughness, hoarseness*, Hp.*Epid.*7.27. **b.** of sound, *harsh croaking*, S.*Ichn.*128. **II.** *silver-dust*, Poll.7.99. **III.** = κέρνος, *IG*1².313.17,314.23 (Eleusis). **-ος** (C), ον, *rough, hoarse*: τὸ κ. Gal.19.111. **-όω**, aor. inf. κερχνῶσαι· καταστίξαι καὶ οἷον τραχῦναι, Hsch. s. v. κατακερχνοῦται. **-ω**, *make rough* or *hoarse*, Hp.*Int.*40:—Pass., *to be so*, Id.*Morb.*2.53. **II.** intr. in Act., *to be hoarse*, Id.*Int.*23, Diocl.*Fr.*147, Gal.7.173. **-ώδης**, ες, *rough*, v.l. for κεγχρώδης, Hp.*Epid.*6.6.5; ἀγγεῖα κ. *embossed* cups, Erot. **II.** *hoarse*, Hp.*Art.*41 (v.l. **κερχώδης** ap.Gal.18(1).574). **2.** *causing hoarseness*, βρῶμα Hp.*Art.*50. **-ωμα**, ατος, τό, in pl., *roughnesses*, Hsch.; also, = τὰ κερχνωτά, Id. **II.** = κέγχρωμα, Id. (pl.). **-ωτός**, ή, όν, *roughened*, Id. s. v. κατακερχνοῦται: τὰ κ. *embossed plate*, Id.

κερχώδης, v. κερχνώδης II. **κερῳδός**, ὁ, *horn-blower*, *Gloss.*

κερωνία, ἡ, Ion. for κερατωνία, Thphr.*HP*4.2.4, cf. 1.11.2; *ceraunia*, Plin.*HN*13.59.

κέρωνται, v. κεράω (A).

κερῶνυξ, ῠχος, ὁ, ἡ, *with horn hoofs*, Πάν D.P.995.

Κεσαρεών, v. Καισαρεών.

κέσκεον, τό, *tow*, Herod.9a; **κέσκι⟨ον⟩**, Hsch.

κέσκετο, Ion. 3 sg. impf. of κεῖμαι, Od.21.41.

κέστερ· νεανίας (Argive), Hsch.

κεστιανὰ μῆλα, a kind of *apple*, Gal.10.469,911.

κεστός, ή, όν, (κεντέω) *stitched, embroidered*, κ. ἱμάς, of Aphrodite's *charmed girdle*, Il.14.214, Corn.*ND*24. **2.** later, κεστός, ὁ, as Subst., κεστοῦ δεσπότις, of Aphrodite, Call.*Aet.Oxy.*2080.55; κεστοῦ φωνεῦσα μαγώτερα *AP*5.120 (Phld.), cf. 6.88 (Antiphanes Maced.), Luc.*DDeor.*20.10; ἅπαντα τὸν κ. ὑποζώσασθαι to put on all her *charms*, Alciphr.1.38; Κεστοί, title of work by Africanus.

κέστρα, ἡ, *hammer*, S.*Fr.*20. **2.** *bolt hammered in* to pack τόνοι in a torsion-engine, Ph.*Bel.*61.14, Hero *Bel.*108.12. **II.** a *fish*, = σφύραινα, Ar.*Nu.*339, Stratt.28, Antiph.97, Speus.ap.Ath.7.323b.

κέστρειον, τό, perh. *storehouse for* κέστροι II, *arsenal*, *IG*11(2).165.38, 199 *A* 77 (Delos, iii B. C.).

κεστρ-εύς, έως, ὁ, *mullet*, = νῆστις, Hp.*Int.*30, Ar.*Fr.*156, Pl.Com.29, Arist.*HA*591ᵃ22, Antig.*Mir.*93, Hices. and Dorio ap.Ath.7.307d, Alciphr.1.7; as nickname of a starveling (since its stomach was found empty), Euphro 2; κ. νηστεύει, prov. of those too honest to make gains, Ath.7.307c, cf. Lib.*Ep.*332.2. **-εύω**, *to be starving*, Hsch.

κεστρῑνίσκος, ὁ, Dim. of sq., Clearch.73.

κεστρῖνος, ὁ, = κεστρεύς, Anaxandr.34.8, Hyp.*Fr.*188. **II.** in pl., *pieces of the fish* κέστρα, *EM*506.45, Phot.

κεστρίον, τό, Dim. of κέστρος II, *IG*2².1487.94 (pl.).

κέστρον, τό, = βεττονική, Dsc.4.1; *cestros*, Plin.*HN*25.84. **2.** = σαξίφραγος, *Stachys alopecuros*, Gal.6.339. **II.** (κεντέω) *serrated implement*, used in encaustic painting, Plin.*HN*35.149.

κέστρος, ὁ, *sharpness* or *roughness on the tongue*, Hsch. **2.** *first sprout of seeds*, Id. **II.** *bolt discharged from engines*, invented in the war with Perseus, Plb.27.11.1 (s.v.l.), D.H.20.1.

κεστρο-σφενδόνη, ἡ, *engine which discharges* κέστροι II, Liv.42.65. **-φόρος**, ὁ, *one who carries* κέστροι II, *IG*3.1102 (pl.). **-φύλαξ** [ῠ], ακος, ὁ, *officer in charge of* κέστροι II, ib.1094, al.:—hence **-φῠλᾰκέω**, ib.735,736.

κέστρ-ωσις, εως, ἡ, *encaustic painting*, Hsch. **-ωτός**, ή, όν, *with the point hardened in the fire*, ξύλον Id. **II.** *executed by the encaustic process*, Plin.*HN*11.126.

κετεύω, word of doubtful meaning in *IG*5(1).268 (Sparta).

κευθάνω, poet. for κεύθω, impf. ἐκεύθανον Il.3.453.

κευθῆνες· οἱ καταχθόνιοι δαίμονες, Suid.

κεύθ-ησις, εως, ἡ, = ἀπόκρυψις, as etym. of κύησις, Sor.1.43. **-μα**, ατος, τό, = κευθμών, f.l. in Thgn.243 (leg. κεύθεσι). **-μός**, ὁ, = sq., Il.13.28 (pl.), Lyc.317, Call.*Jov.*34. **-μών**, ῶνος, ὁ, (κεύθω) *hiding place, hole*, μαιομένη κευθμῶνας ἀνὰ σπέος Od.13.367; ὥς τε σύες, πυκινοὺς κευθμῶνας ἔχοντες in the close-barred *sties*, 10.283; κευθμῶνες ὀρέων *hollows* of the mountains, Pi.*P.*9.34; κ. Κιθαιρῶνος Orac.ap.Hdt.7.141; Ἰδαῖον ἐς κευθμῶν' E.*Hel.*24; Μαλέας ἄκροι κ. Id.*Cyc.*293; ἕδρας τε καὶ κευθμῶνας ἐνδίκου χθονός A.*Eu.*805. **2.** of the nether world, γαίης ἐν κευθμῶνι Hes.*Th.*158; Ταρτάρου μελαμβαθὴς κ. the deep black *vault* of T., A.*Pr.*222; νεκρῶν E.*Hec.*1; ἠλιβάτοις ὑπὸ κ. Id.*Hipp.*732 (lyr.).—Rare in Prose, as Str.11.2.10.

κεῦθος, εος, τό, = κευθμών, ὑπὸ κεύθεσι γαίης in *the depths* of the earth, Il.22.482, Od.24.204, Hes.*Th.*300, cf. Pi.*N.*10.56, A.*Eu.*1036 (lyr.): in sg., κ. [Ἀπίας χθονός] Id.*Supp.*778 (lyr.), cf. Epic. in *Arch. Pap.*7.7; κ. νεκύων S.*Ant.*818 (anap.); κ. οἴκων the *innermost* chambers, like μυχός, E.*Alc.*872 (lyr.); κεύθεα νηοῦ, = ἄδυτον, Musae.119; κ. πόντου Opp.*H.*4.607.

κεύθω, fut. κεύσω Od.3.187: aor. 1 ἔκευσα (ἐπ-) 15.263: Ep. aor. κύθε [ῠ] 3.16, Eratosth.4, redupl. subj. κεκύθω [ῠ] Od.6.303: pf. κέκευθα Il.22.118: plpf. ἐκεκεύθειν, κεκ-, Od.9.348, Hes.*Th.*505:—Pass., Il.23.244, etc.: pf. κέκευται Hsch., part. κεκυθ(η)μένη Antim.3. (Perh. cogn. with Lat. *custos*, OE. *hȳdan* 'hide'.):—poet. Verb, *cover, hide*, esp. of the grave, ὅπου κύθε γαῖα where earth *covered* him, Od.3.16 (also in Pass., εἰς ὅ κεν αὐτὸς ἐγὼν Ἄϊδι κεύθωμαι, i. e. till I am in the grave, Il.23.244); ὃν οὐδὲ κατθανόντα γαῖα κ. A.*Pr.*570 (lyr.), cf. E.*Hec.*325; ὁπότ' ἄν σε δόμοι κεκύθωσι, i. e. when thou hast entered the house, Od.6.303, cf. S.*OT*1229, E.*Hec.*880: in pf., *contain*, ὅσα πτόλις ἥδε κέκευθε Il.22.118; οἶόν τι ποτὸν..νηῦς ἐκεκεύθει Od.9.348; Ἀρχεδίκην ἥδε κέκευθε κόνις Simon.111, cf. 95; εἴπερ τόδε κ. αὐτὸν τεῦχος, of a cinerary urn, S.*El.*1120, cf. A.*Ch.*687; ἃ κ. δέλτος ἐν πτυχαῖς E.*IA*112:—Med., *Epigr.Gr.*1081 (Ilium). **2.** *conceal*, and in pf., *keep concealed* or *hidden*, δόλῳ δ' ὅ γε δάκρυα κεῦθεν Od.19.212; ὅς χ' ἕτερον μὲν κεύθῃ ἐνὶ φρεσὶν ἄλλο δὲ εἴπῃ Il.9.313; μήτιν ἐνὶ στήθεσσι κέκευθε Od.3.18, cf. 8.548, 24.474; οὐκέτι κεύθετε θυμῷ βρωτὺν οὐδὲ ποτῆτα no more can ye *disguise* your eating and drinking, 18.406; κ. φόνον Emp.100.5; κ. [τι] ἔνδον καρδίας A.*Ch.*102, cf. 739; σιγῇ κ. S.*Tr.*989 (anap.); κακόν τι κεύθεις καὶ στέγεις ὑπὸ σκότῳ E.*Ph.*1214; μῦθος ὃν κεύθω Id.*Supp.*295; τί κεύθων..σοφόν; Id.*Heracl.*879; κ. μῆνιν *cherish* anger, like πέσσειν χόλον, ib.762 (lyr.); πάντα δόλον κεύθοισα v.l. in Theoc.1.50. **3.** c. dupl. acc., οὐδέ σε κεύσω [ταῦτα] nor *will* I *keep* them *secret from* thee, Od.3.187, cf. Eratosth. l. c. **II.** in Trag. sts. intr., *to be concealed, lie hidden*, S.*OT*968, *Aj.*635 (lyr.): esp. in pf., A.*Th.*588, S.*Ant.*911, *El.*868 (lyr.).

κεῦτλον, τό, dub. sens. in *PTeb.*112 intr. (ii B. C.), 190 (i B. C.).

κεφᾰλ-άδιον, τό, Dim. of κεφάλαιον, *EM*240.2 (leg. **-άδιον**). **-αία**, ἡ, *inveterate headache*, Antyll.ap.Orib.9.13.1, Aret.*SD*1.2, Gal.10.513; prob. in Thphr.*HP*9.11.2.

κεφάλαι-ος [ᾰ], α, ον, (κεφαλή) *of the head*: metaph., *principal, chief*, ῥῆμα κ. (with a play on κεφαλίτης λίθος) Ar.*Ra.*854; τὸ κ. μέρος *PMasp.*151.16 (vi A. D.): Sup. -ότατος v.l. in Pl.*Grg.*494e. **II.** mostly Subst. κεφάλαιον, τό, = κεφαλή, *head, parts about the head*, esp. of fish, θύννου κ. τοδί Callias Com.3: in pl., Amphis 35, Sotad. Com.1.5; also κ. ῥαφανῖδος Ar.*Nu.*981; of an infant, Leonid.ap. Aët.6.1. **2.** *chief* or *main point*, κ. δὴ παιδείας λέγομεν τὴν ὀρθὴν τροφήν Pl.*Lg.*643c; esp. in speaking or writing, *sum, gist of the matter*, κεφάλαια λόγων Pi.*P.*4.116; κ. τοῦ παντὸς λόγου Men.*Georg.*75, cf. Cic.*Att.*5.18.1; τὰ κ. συγγράφων Εὐριπίδῃ drawing up the *heads* of the play, Antiph.113.5: freq. in Prose, Th.4.50, Pl.*Grg.*453a, etc.; κ. τῶν εἰρημένων Isoc.3.62, cf. 5.154; κ. τῆς οἰκονομίας Phld.*Rh.*1.68 S. (pl.); ἐν κεφαλαίῳ, or ὡς ἐν κ., εἰπεῖν to speak *summarily*, X.*Cyr.*6.3.18, Pl.*Smp.*186c, al.; ἐν κεφαλαίοις ὑπομνῆσαι, ἀποδείξειν, περιλαβεῖν τι, Th.6.87, Lys.13.33, Isoc.2.9; βραχυτάτῳ κ. μαθεῖν Th.1.36; τύπῳ καὶ ἐπὶ κεφαλαίου (v. l. -αίῳ), opp. ἀκριβέστερον, Arist.*EN*1107ᵇ14; ἐπὶ κ. Plb.1.65.5, 3.5.9; ἐπὶ κεφαλαίων D.19.315, etc.; esp. in an argument, *summing up*, ἐν κεφαλαίοις Pl.*Ti.*26c; κεφαλαίῳ δέ.., Lat. *denique*, Decr.ap.D.18.164; τὸ δ' οὖν κ. ib.213; τὸ δὲ κ. τῶν λόγων, ἄνθρωπος εἶ Men.531.10; συναγαγεῖν τὸ κ. *to sum* up, Arist.*Metaph.*1042^{a}4. **3.** metaph., of persons, *the head* or *chief*, ὅ τι περ κ. τῶν κάτωθεν, of Pericles, Eup.93; τὸ κ. οὐδέπω λογίζομαι, τὸν δεσπότην Men.*Pk.*173; ὅ τι περ τὸ κ. Luc.*Harm.* 3, *Gall.*24, *Philops.*6; τὰ κ. τῶν μαθημάτων, of philosophers, Id.*Pisc.* 14; τὸ κ. τοῦ πολέμου App.*BC*5.50; οἱ τὸ τῆς στάσεως κ. ἦσαν ib.43; τὸν Θαλῆν τῶν σοφῶν τὸ κ. Jul.*Or.*3.125d: hence, of qualities, etc., σχεδόν τι τὸ κ. τῶν κακῶν (sc. avarice) Apollod.Gel.4; τὸ κ. τῆς εὐδαιμονίας ἡ διάθεσις Diog.Oen.57. **4.** Rhet., *head, topic* of argument, D.H.*Comp.*1, *Rh.*10.5, Str.1.2.31. **5.** of money, *capital*, opp. interest or income, Pl.*Lg.*742c, D.27.64, etc. **b.** *sum total*, *IG*1^{2}.91.23, al., Lys.19.40, D.27.10; πολλοῦ κ. for a large *sum*, *Act. Ap.*22.28, cf. Aristeas 24, Plu.*Fab.*4, etc.; κ. ἀργυρικά *PRyl.*133.15 (i A.D.); also σιτικὰ καὶ ἀργυρικὰ κ. *PSI*4.281.31 (ii A.D.). **6.** *crown, completion* of a thing, τὸ μὲν κ. τῶν ἀδικημάτων the *crowning act* of wrong, D.27.7; δύο ταῦτα ὥσπερεὶ κ. ἐφ' ἅπασι.. ἐπέθηκε Id.21.18. **7.** *chapter, section, PGnom.Prooem.*, Ammon.*in Int.*1.17, al., Chor. in *Hermes* 17.223; distd. from τίτλος, Suid. s.h.v. **-όω,** *bring under heads, sum up*, Th.3.67, al.:—Med., Arist.*MM*1207^{b}22; κ. τινά *characterize generally*, Pl.*R.*576b; τὰς δυνάμεις τινῶν Phld.*Vit.* p.17 J.:—Pass., *to be summed up*, Arist.*Metaph.*1013^{b}30; κ. ἑκάστην τῶν ἀρετῶν περὶ ἴδιόν τι κεφάλαιον *Stoic.*3.73; κεφαλαιοῦσθαι ἐννακισχιλίων ἑξακοσίων [σταδίων] *to amount in all to..*, Str.2.1.39; εἰς δύο ἀρτηρίας ἡ πάντων ἀγγείων κ. σύνοδος *is combined in..*, Gal.4.657, cf. Porph.*Sent.*44; κεφαλαιούσθω διότι.. Phld.*Rh.*2.35 S. **II.** *smite on the head, Ev.Marc.*12.4. **-ώδης,** ες, *capital, principal, Stoic.*2.75, Luc.*DMort.*20.1: Comp., νόμοι Ph.2.183, cf. Luc.*Salt.*61, Hierocl. *in CA*27 p.484 M.: Sup., Hp.*Decent.*6, Luc.*Pseudol.*10; τὸ -ῶδες *the general character summed up in a definition*, Arr.*Epict.*2.12.9. **II.** *summary*, ἐξήγησις Plb.2.14.1; ὑπογραφή D.H.2.72. Adv. -δῶς Arist.*Rh.*1415^{b}8, *Metaph.*988^{a}18, Plb.1.13.1, D.H.*Comp.*8, etc.: Sup. -έστατα Epicur.*Ep.*1 p.31 U. **-ωμα,** ατος, τό, *sum total*, Hdt. 3.159. **II.** *collective expression*, τοὺς τὰς ἰδέας κεφαλαιώματα λέγοντας τοῦ ἐντρέχοντος κοινοῦ τοῖς πολλοῖς Procl.*in Prm.*p.564 S. **-ωσις,** εως, ἡ, *comprehension of several notions in a general term*, Sch.S.*OC* 916. **-ωτής,** οῦ, ὁ, = Lat. *capitularius, secretary and treasurer of a group of landowners* or *artisans, acting as recruiting officer, tax-collector*, etc., *PThead.*22.4 (iv A.D.), *PLips.*40 iii 17 (iv/v A.D.), 48.9 (pl., iv A.D.), al., *Cod.Theod.*11.24.6.7 (pl.); τοῦ ἡγεμονικοῦ πολυκώπου *PGrenf.*2.80 (pl., v A.D.); ταρσικαρίων *PLips.*89 (iv A.D.); πιττακίων *Sammelb.*4422.2; πλινθουργῶν ib.5175.21 (vi A.D.), al. **II.** in pl., = Lat. *optimates*, Olymp.Hist.p.452 D. **-ωτία,** ἡ, *function of* κεφαλαιωτής, *PLips.*52.14 (iv A.D.).

κεφαλαλγ-έω, *suffer from headache*, Hp.*Aph.*5.64, Sor.2.29, Dsc. 1.30, Arr.*Epict.*3.22.73, Gal.6.589, *BCH*48.517 (Palestine). **-ής,** ές, *suffering from headache*, Plu.2.147f, Ruf.ap.Orib.7.26.129, 143. **II.** Act., *causing headache*, X.*An.*2.3.15, Thphr.*HP*8.4.6, Diph.Siph.ap.Ath.2.54a, Ph.1.390, 2.99, Plu.2.133c, Gal.17(2).818, etc. (-αλγός is a common f.l.). **-ία,** ἡ, *headache*, in pl., Hp.*Aph.*3. 13, Arist.*Pr.*860^{a}37, Str.16.2.41, *IG*4^{2}(1).126.27 (Epid.). **-ικός,** ή, όν, *suffering from headache*, Hp.*Coac.*283; *inclined to headache*, Gal.6.438, 15.125. **II.** *causing headache*, Diocl.*Fr.*126, Gal.17(2). 754. **III.** τὰ κ. *symptoms of headache*, Hp.*Prorrh.*1.103.

κεφᾰλᾰραία, ἡ, = φάλαρον, Anon.*in Rh.*210.15.

κεφᾰλ-αργία, ἡ, later form for κεφαλαλγία, Luc.*Jud.Voc.*4:—hence **-αργέω,** *PMag.Par.*1.136; *give* one *a headache*, Hsch. s.v. ὠτοκοπεῖ.

κεφᾰλή, ἡ, *head* of man or beast, Hom. (v. infr.), Alc.15, etc.; once in A., *Th.*525 (lyr.), once in S., *Aj.*238 (anap.), also in E., *Fr.*308 (anap.), *Rh.*226 (lyr.), al.; ἄλλου οὐδενὸς ἐμψύχου κ. γεύσεται Αἰγυπτίων οὐδείς Hdt.2.39; κεφαλῇ.. μείζονες taller *in stature*, Il.3. 168; so μείων.. κεφαλὴν ib.193 Aristarch.: freq. with Preps., **a.** κατὰ κεφαλῆς, Ep. κὰκ κεφαλῆς, *down over the head*, κόνιν.. χεύατο κὰκ κεφαλῆς Il.18.24, cf. Od.8.85, etc. **b.** κατὰ κεφαλήν, Ep. κὰκ κεφαλήν *on the head*, Ἐρύλαον.. βάλε πέτρῳ μέσσην κὰκ κεφαλήν Il.16. 412, cf. 20.387,475: in Prose, *from above*, X.*HG*7.2.8: c. gen., *above*, κ. κ. τινῶν γενέσθαι ib.7.2.11; τὸ κ. κ. ὕδωρ, of rain water, Thphr. *HP*4.10.7 (-ὴν codd.), *CP*6.18.10 (-ῆς): in Archit., *upright*, *IG*2^{2}. 463.42; also, *per head, each person* (cf. infr. I. 2), Arist.*Pol.*1272^{a}14, Lxx *Ex.*16.16; κατὰ κεφαλὴν τῶν κωμητῶν *PPetr.*2 p.17 (iii B.C.). **c.** ἐς πόδας ἐκ κεφαλῆς from *head* to foot, Il.23.169; τὰ πράγματα ἐκ τῶν ποδῶν ἐς τὴν κ. σοι πάντ' ἐρῶ Ar.*Pl.*650. **d.** ἐπὶ κεφαλήν *head foremost*, ἐπὶ κ. κατορύξαι to bury *head downwards*, Hdt.3.35; ἐπὶ κ. ὠθέεσθαι to be thrust *headlong*, Id.7.136, cf. Hyp.*Fr.*251; ἐπὶ κ. ὠθεῖν τινα ἐκ τοῦ θρόνου Pl.*R.*553b; ἐπὶ τὴν κ. εἰς κόρακας ὦσον Men.*Sam.* 138; εὐθὺς ἐπὶ κ. εἰς τὸ δικαστήριον βαδίζειν D.42.12; οὐ βουλόμενος πολίτας ἄνδρας ἐπὶ κ. εἰσπράττειν τὸν μισθὸν *recklessly*, Hyp.*Lyc.*17; ἐπὶ ταῖς κεφαλαῖς περιφέρειν carry *on high*, in token of admiration, Pl. *R.*600d. **2.** as the noblest part, periphr. for the whole person, πολλὰς ἰφθίμους κ. Il.11.55, cf. Od.1.343, etc.; ἶσον ἐμῇ κ. no less than my*self*, Il.18.82; ἐᾷ κ. Pi.*O.*7.67; esp. in salutation, φίλη κ. Il.8.281, cf. 18.114; ἠθείη κ. 23.94; Ἄπολλον, ὦ δία κ. E.*Rh.*226 (lyr.): in Prose, Φαῖδρε, φίλη κ. Pl.*Phdr.*264a; τῆς θείας κ. Jul.*Or.* 7.212a: in bad sense, ὦ κακαὶ κεφαλαί Hdt.3.29; ὦ μιαρὰ κ. Ar.*Ach.* 285: periphr. in Prose, πεντακοσίας κεφαλὰς τῶν Ξέρξεω πολεμίων Hdt.9.99: in bad sense, ἡ μιαρὰ καὶ ἀναιδὴς αὕτη κ. D.21.117, cf. 18. 153; ἡ κ. τῶν αὐτοῦ *PRein.*57.8 (iv A.D.); μεγάλη κ. a great *personage*, Vett.Val.74.7; cf. supr. 1 b fin. **3.** *life*, ἐμῇ κ. περιδείδια Il.17.242; σύν τε μεγάλῳ ἀπέτεισαν, σὺν σφῇσιν κεφαλῇσι 4.162; παρθέμενοι κεφαλάς staking *their heads* on the cast, Od.2.237; τὴν κ. ἀποβαλέεις Hdt.8.65. **4.** in imprecations, ἐς κεφαλὴν τράποιτ' ἐμοί on my *head* be it! Ar.*Ach.*833; ἐς τὴν κ. ἅπαντα τὴν σὴν τρέψεται Id.*Nu.*40; ἃ σοὶ καὶ τοῖς σοῖς οἱ θεοὶ τρέψειαν εἰς κ. D.18.290; ἐς κ. σοί (sc. τράποιτο) Ar.*Pax*1063, *Pl.*526; σοὶ εἰς κ. Pl.*Euthd.*283e; τὰ μὲν πρότερον.. ἐγὼ κεφαλῇ ἀναμάξας φέρω Hdt.1.155; οἷς ἂν.. τὴν αἰτίαν ἐπὶ τὴν κ. ἀναθεῖεν D.18.294; τὸ αἷμα ὑμῶν ἐπὶ τὴν κ. ὑμῶν *Act.Ap.* 18.6. **II.** of things, *extremity*, **a.** in Botany, κ. σκορόδου *head* (= *inflorescence*) of garlic, Ar.*Pl.*718, cf. Plb.12.6.4; κ. μήκωνος Thphr.*HP*9.8.2; ῥίζα κ. ἔχουσα πλείονας *tubers*, Dsc.3.120. **b.** in Anatomy, κεφαλαὶ τῆς κάτω γνάθου, prob. the condyloid and coronoid processes, Hp.*Art.*30; ἡ κ. τοῦ ὄρχεως, = ἐπιδιδυμίς, Arist.*HA*510^{a} 14, cf. Gal.4.565; μηροῦ, κνήμης κ., Poll.2.186,188; of the *base* of the heart, Gal.*UP*6.16; but, *apex*, Hp.*Cord.*7; of the *sac* in poulps, Arist.*PA*654^{a}23, 685^{a}5; of muscles, *origin*, Gal.*UP*7.14. **c.** generally, *top, brim* of a vessel, Theoc.8.87; *coping* of a wall, X.*Cyr.*3. 3.68; *capital* of a column, *CIG*2782.31 (Aphrodisias), Lxx 3*Ki.*7.16, Poll.7.121. **d.** in pl., *source* of a river, Hdt.4.91 (but sg., *mouth*, οἶδα Γέλα ποταμοῦ κεφαλῇ ἐπικείμενον ἄστυ Call.*Aet.Oxy.*2080.48): generally, *source, origin*, Ζεὺς κ. (v.l. ἀρχή), Ζεὺς μέσσα, Διὸς δ' ἐκ πάντα τελεῖται (τέτυκται codd.) Orph.*Fr.*21a; *starting-point*, κ. χρόνου *Placit.* 2.32.2 (κρόνου codd.), Lyd.*Mens.*3.4; κ. μηνός ib.12. **e.** *extremity* of a plot of land, *PPetr.*3 p.72 (iii B.C.), *PFlor.*50.83 (iii A.D.). **III.** Ὁμηρείη κ. *bust* of Homer, *IG*14.1183.10. **IV.** κ. περίθετος *wig, head-dress*, Ar.*Th.*258. **V.** metaph., κ. δείπνου *pièce de résistance*, Alex.172.15. **2.** *crown, completion*, κεφαλὴν ἐπιθεῖναι Pl.*Ti.*69b; ὥσπερ κ. ἀποδοῦναι τοῖς εἰρημένοις Id.*Phlb.*66d, cf. *Grg.*505d; ὥσπερ κεφαλὴν ἔχουσα ἐπιστήμη Arist.*EN*1141^{a}19; *consummation*, σχεῖν κ. Pl.*Ti.*39d. **3.** *sum, total*, πάσας ἐρρηγείας *Tab.Heracl.*1.36; of money, *IG*12(9).7 (Carystus, iv B.C.), *SIG*245 ii 36 (Delph., iv B.C.). **4.** *band* of men, Lxx *Jb.*1.17; *right-hand half* of a phalanx (opp. οὐρά), Arr.*Tact.*8.3, Ael.*Tact.*7.3. **5.** Astron., κ. τοῦ κόσμου, of Aries, Heph.Astr.1.1. (*ghebh-*, cf. κεβλή and Engl. *gable.*)

κεφᾰλη-γερέτης, ου, Dor. **-τᾱς,** ὁ, *head-collector*, Comic epith. of Pericles, formed after the Homeric νεφεληγερέτης, from the peaked shape of his skull, Cratin.240. **-γονος,** ον, *springing from the head*, κάλυκες Nic.*Fr.*74.25.

κεφᾰλ-ηδόν, Adv. *like a head*, f.l. in Opp.*C.*3.437. **II.** *individually*, νέμειν μερίδας κ. *Inscr.Prien.*362.25 (iv B.C.). **-ῆφιν,** Ep. gen. and dat. of κεφαλή, Il.11.350, 10.30, al.; -φι Od.20.94. **-ίδιον,** τό, Dim. of κεφαλή, Poll.2.42; as an article of food, *POxy.*1656.22 (pl., iv/v A.D.). **-ίζω,** *behead*, *BGU*341.9. **-ικός,** ή, όν, *of* or *for the head*, of remedies, etc., κ. ἔμπλαστροι Dsc.3.88, cf. Asclep.ap. Gal.13.543; δυνάμεις Dsc.3.48 (v.l. κεφαλαλγικαῖς), cf. *Arch.Pap.* 4.270 (iii A.D.); δέλτοι Gal.2.607; κεφαλική, ἡ, name of a herb, Griffith & Thompson *Demotic Magical Papyrus* verso iv 10. Adv. -κῶς *after the manner of a head*, *Corp.Herm.*10.11. **II.** *touching the head* or *life*, πράγματα *PMag.Leid.V.*5.13; *capital*, δίκη *POxy.*2104. 15 (iii A.D.); τιμωρία *Rev.Bibl.*35.285 (Jerusalem), *Cod.Just.*1.12.3.2 (Theodosius II), Just.*Nov.*85.3.1; κίνδυνος ib.123.31. Adv. -κῶς, κολασθήσεσθαι to be punished *capitally*, Hdn.2.13.9; τιμωρεῖσθαι Just. *Nov.*123.31, cf. *Cod.Just.*9.4.6.4. **III.** *belonging to an individual*, μερίς *PMasp.*151.89 (vi A.D.). **IV.** κ. σμίλη *sharp, strong* chisel, Gal.2.607. **-ίνη** [ῑ], ἡ, *root of the tongue*, supposed to be the seat of taste, hence also called γεῦσις, Poll.2.107. **-ῖνος,** ὁ, a *sea-fish*, = βλεψίας, Dorio ap.Ath.7.306f. **-ιον,** τό, Dim. of κεφαλή, ἵππου κ., as an ornament, *IG*2^{2}.1466.13, cf. Dsc.4.148, Sor.1.119, al., Plu. 2.641b; κ. γλυκύ, of a person, *Sammelb.*5807.12. **-ίς,** ίδος, ἡ, Dim. of κεφαλή, *little head*, σκορόδου Luc.*DMeretr.*14.3; *head* of a nail, Ath.11.488c; *extremity*, τῶν σκυταλίδων Antyll.ap.Orib.44.23. 74. **II.** *capital* of a column, Ph.2.147, Chor.p.118 B. (pl.), *PLond.* 3.755^{v}6 (iv A.D.), *Gp.*14.6.6 (pl.): pl., = κρόσσαι, Eust.903.6. **III.** *toe-cap* of a shoe, Arist.*Rh.*1392^{a}31, cf. Anon. ad loc.; of the *foot* of a table, Aristeas 68. **IV.** *rope attached to the bow* of a ship, Polyaen. 3.9.38 (pl.). **V.** κ. βιβλίου *roll*, Lxx *Ez.*2.9, *Ps.*38(39).8, al. **-ισμός,** ὁ, *multiplication table of single numbers from one to ten*, Arist.*Top.*163^{b} 25 (pl.), cf. Suid. **-ίτης** [ῑ] λίθος *corner*-stone, Hsch. **-ῑτοπαραμήκης** λίθος *oblong corner*-stone, *POxy.*498.22 (ii A.D.).

Κεφαλλήν, ῆνος, ὁ, *Cephallenian*, pl. in Il.2.631, etc.: sg. in S.*Ph.* 791: **Κεφαλληνία,** ἡ, *Cephallenia*, Hdt.9.28.

κεφᾰλο-βᾰρής, ές, *with a head at the root*, of bulbous plants, Arist. *Long.*467^{a}34, Thphr.*HP*1.6.8. **-βρωτος,** ον, *eaten away at the top*, [βιβλία] *Arch.Pap.*6.101 (ii A.D.). **-δεσμος,** ὁ, *head-band*, Sch.A.*Supp.*121:—Dim. **-δέσμιον,** τό, Sch.Il.14.184. **-ειδής,** ές, *shaped like a head*, ὀρίγανος Hp.*Int.*6; λοβός Dsc.2.110; παρεξοχή Apollod.*Poliorc.*220.20; κορμός Oenom.ap.Eus.*PE*5.36. **-θλαστος,** ον, *bruised in the head*: τὰ κ. *contusions of the head*, Thphr.*HP* 9.20.4. **-κλαστα,** τά, *injuries to the head*, Ruf.*Interrog.*58. **-κλάστης,** ου, ὁ, a surgical instrument, *Hermes* 38.284. **-κρούστης,** ου, ὁ, = κρανοκολάπτης, Sch.Nic.*Th.*763. **-ποιητικός,** ή, όν, *head-making*, δύναμις Phlp.*in GA*193.21. **-πους,** ποδος, ὁ, in pl., lamb's or goat's *trotters*, Cass.Fel.40 (s.v.l.). **-ρριζος,** ον, *with a bulbous root*, Thphr.*HP*1.14.2.

κέφᾰλος, ὁ, a species of *mullet*, Hp.*Int.*6, Arist.*HA*543^{b}16, Archipp.12, Ephipp.12.2, Gal.6.708, Opp.*H.*1.111, Ael.*NA*1.3,12,13. 19; κεστρέα τὸν κ. Archestr.*Fr.*45.2.

κεφᾰλο-τομέω, *cut off the head*, less Att. than καρατομέω, Thphr. ap.*AB*104, cf. Phryn.320. **-τόμος,** ον, *cutting off the head*, Str. 11.14.14. **-τρύπᾰνον** [ῠ], τό, *trepan*, Gal.14.785.

κεφᾰλ-ουργός, ὁ, *foreman of works*, *LW*1666^{c} (Lydia). **-ώδης,**

ες, = κεφαλοειδής, *like a head*, Thphr.*HP*8.8.5, 9.8.4. **-ωμα**, ατος, τό, *sum total*, *IG*5(1).1433.18 (Messene), *SIG*241*B*122 (Delph., iv B.C.). **-ών**, ῶνος, ὁ, *fan-palm*, *Chamaerops humilis*, Pall.*Agr*.5.4.5. II. = κεφαλωτόν, *BGU*1118.12 (i B.C.). III. = *capito*, *Gloss*. **-ωτός**, ή, όν, *with a head, headed*, Arist.*Cat*.7ᵃ16; of plants *with a head*, πράσον Dsc.2.149, cf. Epaenet.ap.Ath.9.371e, Mnesith. Cyz.ap.Orib.*inc*.15.18, *Gp*.12.1.8: Subst. -ωτόν (sc. πράσον), τό, *BGU*1120.16 (i B.C.); also, of a bolt, *with a flat head*, περόνη κ. Ph. *Bel*.76.3.

κεχᾰλασμένως, Adv., (χαλάω) *slackly*, Gal.14.793.

κεχᾰρισμένως, Adv., (χαρίζομαι) *acceptably*, Ar.*Ach*.248, Pl.*Phdr*. 273e, D.S.17.47; κ. ἄρχειν Isoc.2.15, cf. X.*Eq.Mag*.1.1 (Sup.); ὄχλοις κ. λέγειν Plu.2.6b.

κεχᾰρῐτωμένως, Adv., (χαριτόω) gloss on ἐπιχαρίττως, Sch.Ar. *Ach*.867.

κέχηνα, v. χάσκω.

Κεχην-αῖοι, ων, οἱ, Comic word (from κέχηνα) for Ἀθηναῖοι, *Gapenians* for *Athenians*, Ar.*Eq*.1263. **-ότως**, Adv., (κέχηνα) *open-mouthed*, πιεῖν Moer.p.404P. **-ώδης**, ες, *forming a hiatus*, τὸ κ. Sch.D.T.p.146H.

κεχιασμένως, Adv., (χιάζω) *like a* X, *cross-wise*, *Theol.Ar*.19.

κεχρημένος, *needy*, v. χράω C. VI.

κεχῠμένως, Adv., (χέω) *profusely*, πρὸς τὰς δόσεις κέχρηται τῷ βαλλαντίῳ Alciphr.3.65.

κεχωρίδαται, v. χωρίζω.

κεχωρισμένως, Adv., (χωρίζω) *separately*, Arist.*Pol*.1291ᵃ29, Aët. 16.8.

κέω, v. κείω. **κεώδης**· καθαρός, and **κεώσατο**· καθήρατο, Hsch.; cf. κηώδης, κήϊα. **κεῶεν** ὄζει· εὐωδεῖ, Id. (Neut. of *κεώεις = κηώεις.) **κεωρεῖν**· πασχητιᾶν, Id.; **κεωρία**, ἡ, Theognost.*Can*.105.

Κέως, ἡ, *Ceos*, one of the Cyclades, *IG*12(5).532.7, Str.10.5.6, etc.:—hence **Κεῖος**, Ion. **Κήϊος**, ὁ, a *Ceian*, Hdt.5.102, etc.; οὐ Χῖος, ἀλλὰ Κεῖος not a (roguish) Chian, but an (honest) *Ceian*, proverb in Ar.*Ra*.970; ἀκόλαστόν τινα.., καὶ οὐδαμῶς Κεῖον Pl.*Prt*.341e, cf. *Lg*. 638b; prov., ἐν Κέῳ τίς ἡμέρα; Crates Com.29.5. (Not to be confused with **Κέος** *IG*4²(1).122.117, or with **Κέος** Hdt.8.76 (cf. *Wiener Sitzb*.211(1).30).)

κῇ, Ion. for πῇ or ποῖ, Hdt.1.32, 8.67: but κη enclit. for πη or που, Id.5.22,40, 8.8, al.: also **κῆ**, Aeol. = ἐκεῖ, Sapph.51.

κῆαι, κήαι, v. καίω.

κῆβος, ὁ, a long-tailed monkey, perh. the *nisnas monkey*, *Cercopithecus pyrrhonotus*, Arist.*HA*502ᵃ17, Gal.*UP*11.2; **κῆπος**, Agatharch.75, Str.16.4.16 (as v.l.), Ael.*NA*17.8.

κηγχός, Ion., = κῇ ἀγχός, A.D.*Adv*.184.9; cf. κῆχος.

κηδάζω, κηδαλίζω, = καθαίρω, Hsch. **κηδαίνω**, collat. form of κήδω, Id. **κήδαλον**· αἰδοῖον, κέρας, σκάλαθρον, Id.

κηδ-εᾰκός (κῆδος I. 2 b), ὁ, *undertaker*, *IGRom*.4.353ᵇ.23 (Pergam., ii A.D.). **-εία**, ἡ, *care* for the dead, *funeral*, A.R.2.836; κ. καὶ περιστολή D.H.3.21, *BGU*896.7 (ii A.D.), cf. Onos.36.1, etc.; *mourning*, ἐξανίστασθαι ἐκ τῆς κηδείας *SIG*1219.14 (Gambreum, iii B.C.). II. *connexion by marriage, alliance*, κηδείαν ξυνάψαι τινί E.*Supp*.134; συνάγειν ἀνθρώπους εἰς κ. X.*Mem*.2.6.36; κ. συνάπτεσθαι πρός τινα Plb. 1.9.2; ἡ πρὸς αἵματος ἢ κατὰ..κηδείαν Arist.*Pol*.1262ᵃ11; κηδεῖαι ἐγένοντο κατὰ τὰς πόλεις ib.1280ᵇ36; ἐκ τῆς πρὸς Διονύσιον κ. ib. 1307ᵃ39. **-ειος**, ον, *cared for, beloved*, τρεῖς τε κασιγνήτους, τούς μοι μία γείνατο μήτηρ, κηδείους Il.19.294. 2. Act., *careful of*, or *caring for*, c. gen., τροφαὶ κ. τέκνων E.*Ion*487 (lyr.). II. *of a funeral* or *tomb, sepulchral*, χοαί A.*Ch*.87,538; κ. θρίξ *offered on a tomb*, ib.226; κ. οἴκτοισιν E.*IT*147 (lyr.).

κηδεμον-εύω, *to be a guardian*, παίδων Just.*Nov*.94.2:—Pass., *to be a ward*, ib.18.9. **-εύς**, έως, ὁ, = κηδεμών, A.R.1.271, *APl*.4. 41 (Agath.). **-ία**, ἡ, *care, solicitude*, Pl.*R*.463d, Phld.*Mort*.25, Ph.2.179, D.C.43.17, *POxy*.1070.21 (iii A.D.); ἡ κ. τῶν Ἀθηνῶν the *general charge* of her affairs, *IG*3.632, cf. *CIG*3187 (Smyrna); ἡ τοῦ αὐτοκράτορος περὶ πάντας κ. *BGU*372 i 12 (ii A.D.). **-ικός**, ή, όν, *provident, careful*, φίλος Plb.*Fr*.80; νουθέτησις Phld.*Lib*.p.13O.; παρρησία Plu.2.55b; ἀνήρ Epict.*Gnom*.63; τὸ κ., = foreg., Plb.31.27.12, Cic.*Att*.2.17.3, Muson.*Fr*.14p.73H.: Comp., J.*BJ*1.28.2: Sup., Ph. 2.288. Adv. -κῶς *OGI*56.15 (Canopus, iii B.C.), Muson.*Fr*.15ᴬp.79 H., Luc.*Symp*.46, etc.; κ. ἔχειν πρός τινα Plb.4.32.4; κ. ὑποδεῖξαι, ἀποκρῖναι, J.*AJ*11.6.6, Sor.1.28.

κηδεμών, όνος, ὁ, (κήδω) *one that has charge of* a person or thing, Hom. (only in Il.) always of *persons attending to the dead*, 23.163, 674. 2. generally, *one who cares for* others, *protector, guardian*, Thgn.645, S.*Ph*.195 (anap.), Ar.*V*.242, X.*Mem*.2.7.12: pl., Phld. *Mort*.23; of tutelary heroes, X.*Cyr*.3.3.21; κ. τῆς πόλεως Pl.*R*.412c; τᾶσδε φυγᾶς..κ. *protector*, A.*Supp*.76 (lyr.); τοῦ ζῆν ἡμῶν καὶ τοῦ φρονεῖν κ. Pl.*Lg*.808b; κ. οὐκ ἔφεδρον βίου Men.663; of a legal *guardian*, *POxy*.888.2 (iii/iv A.D.), etc.; τῶν δακτύλων Alex.148; of a female, Simon.116, S.*Ant*.549. II. = κηδεστής, E.*Med*.990 (lyr.); *patron*, opp. ξυγγενής, Ar.*V*.731.

κήδεος, ον, = κήδειος, only in Il.23.160 οἷσι κήδεός ἐστι νέκυς to whom *the charge of burying* him belongs (κηδεός acc. to Sch.Patm. D. in *BCH*1.142).

κήδεσαι, κήδεσκον, κηδέσκετο, v. κήδω.

κηδεστ-ής, Dor. **κᾱδεστάς** *AP*7.712 (Erinna), οῦ, ὁ: (κῆδος, κηδεύω):—*connexion by marriage*, Pl.*Lg*.773b, X.*Mem*.1.1.8, Arist. *Pol*.1312ᵇ16, Cerc.17.25 (pl.), Ph.2.555 (pl.), etc.; esp. 1. *son-in-law*, Antipho 6.12, Isoc.10.43. 2. *father-in-law*, Ar.*Th*.74, 210, D.19.118, etc.; also, *step-father*, Id.36.31. 3. *brother-in-law*, E. *Hec*.834, And.1.50, Lys.13.1, Is.6.27, D.30.12, Timae.84. **-ία**, ἡ, *connexion by marriage*, X.*HG*2.4.21 (pl.). **-ικός**, ή, όν, *of affinity*, οἰκειότης Eust.942.36. **-ρια**, ἡ, *female attendant, keeper*, *PTeb*.378.4 (iii A.D.); *guardian*, *PThead*.18.2 (iii/iv A.D.). 2. *mother-in-law*, *Gloss*. **-ωρ**, ορος, ὁ, = κηδεμών I, Man.4.514.

κῆδ-ευμα, ατος, τό, *connexion* or *alliance by marriage*, E.*Med*.76, Pl.*Lg*.773b. 2. poet. for κηδεστής, *one who is so connected*, S.*OT* 85, E.*Or*.477. **-εύσιμος**, gloss on κήδεος, Hsch. **-ευσις**, εως, ἡ, = κηδεία I, Ael.*NA*10.48; = κηδεμονία, Plot.6.7.26. **-ευτής**, οῦ, ὁ, = κηδεμών I, Arist.*Pr*.922ᵇ26. **-εύω**, (κῆδος) *take charge of, tend*, S. *OT*1323 (lyr.), *OC*750; πόλιν Id.*Fr*.683.4, E.*IT*1212; νύμφην Id.*Med*. 888; νόσημα Id.*Or*.883. 2. esp. *attend to* a corpse, *bury*, ἐν ξένῃσι χερσὶ κηδευθεὶς τάλας S.*El*.1141, cf. E.*Rh*.983; μ' ἔθαψε καὶ ἐκήδευσεν *IG*14.1860: also in Prose, Plb.5.10.4, etc.; ταφῇ κηδευθεῖσα ταῖς τῶν ἐναντίων χερσί Demad.9, cf. Plu.*Alex*.56; βασιλέων κηδευομένων Arist.*Fr*.519, cf. Wilcken *Chr*.499 (ii/iii A.D.); κεκηδευμένος νεκρὸς ἐν μέλιτι J.*AJ*14.7.4; εἰς ἣν [σορὸν] οὐδενὶ ἔξεσται ἕτερον πτῶμα κηδεῦσαι *CIG*3028.3 (Ephesus), cf. *POxy*.1067.6 (iii A.D.). 3. = κηδεμονεύω, in Pass., *Cod.Just*.3.10.1.1. II. *contract a marriage*, of the bridegroom, *ally oneself in marriage*, τὸ κηδεῦσαι καθ' ἑαυτὸν ἀριστεύει μακρῷ A.*Pr*.890 (lyr.): c. acc. cogn., κ. λέχος *marry*, S.*Tr*.1227: c. dat. pers., *ally oneself with*.., E.*Hipp*.634, *Fr*.395, D.59.81, Men.*Epit*.427, etc.; κ. ὅτῳ θέλουσιν Arist.*Pol*.1307ᵃ37; *become the son-in-law of*, Moer. p.368P.:—in Pass., *to be married*, E.*Ph*.347 (lyr.). 2. c. acc. pers., *make one's kinsman by marriage*, Id.*Hec*.1202; also κ. τὴν θυγατέρα τινί *to marry* her to some one, J.*AJ*6.10.2: abs., οἱ κηδεύσαντες *those who formed the marriage*, E.*Med*.367. **-ιστος**, η, ον, Sup. formed from κῆδος, *most worthy of one's care, most cared for*, κήδιστοί τ' ἔμεναι καὶ φίλτατοι Il.9.642; κ. ἑτάρων ἦν κεδνότατός τε Od.10.225. II. κήδιστοι, οἱ, *those nearest allied by marriage*, 8.583. **-ομαι**, v. κήδω. **-ομένως**, Adv., κ. ἔχειν to be *provident*, Aristid.*Or*.53 p.619D.

κῆδ-ος, Dor. **κᾶδος**, εος, τό, (κήδω) *care about*, c. gen., τῶν ἄλλων οὐ κῆδος the others *do* not *matter*, Od.22.254. 2. *anxiety, grief*, Il.13. 464, al. (v. infr. II): mostly in pl., *troubles*, Ἀργείοισι πολύστονα κήδε' ἐφῆκεν Il.1.445; Τρώεσσι δὲ κήδε' ἐφῆπται ἐκ Διός 2.69; ὅσ' ἐμῷ ἐνὶ κ. θυμῷ 18.53, cf. Od.4.108; ὁππόσα κήδε' ἀνέτλης 14.47. b. esp. for the dead, *funeral rites, mourning*, πατέρι δὲ γόον καὶ κήδεα λυγρὰ λεῖπ' Il.5. 156, etc.; θάνατος καὶ κ. 4.270; κήδε' ἐμῶν ἑτάρων *mourning for* them, 22.272; κ. στονόεντα Archil.9, cf. A.*Ch*.469 (lyr.), Plu.*Sol*.12, etc.: sg., κᾶδος φθιμένου θήκασθαι Pi.*P*.4.112, cf. *N*.1.54; ἅμα κήδεϊ when there is a death in the family, Hdt.2.36; ἐς τὸ κ. ἰέναι to attend *the funeral*, Id.6.58, cf. *SIG*1218.18 (Iulis, v B.C.); ἐπὶ τὸ κ. ἀφικέσθαι Isoc.19.31; θυραῖον κ. ἐς τάφον φέρειν E.*Alc*.828; ὅταν οἰκεῖον..κ. γένηται Pl.*R*.605d; εἰς τὰ κήδη..οἱ συγγενεῖς ἀπαντῶσι attend at *funerals*, Arist.*EN*1165ᵃ20. 3. *object of care*, Ἰλίῳ κ. ὀρθώνυμον, of Helen, with a play on signf. II, A.*Ag*.699 (lyr.). II. *connexion by marriage*, Hdt.7.189; κ. ἐγγενές A.*Supp*.331; κ. Ἀδράστου λαβών, i.e. having married his daughter, E.*Ph*.77, cf. S.*OC*379; κατ' ἐπιγαμίαν τῷ ἀσκητῇ κ. συνάπτειν Ph.1.553; τὸ κ. ξυνάψασθαι τῆς θυγατρός contract the *marriage* for one's own daughter, Th.2.29; so some wrongly explain Il.13.464, cf. 15.245, 16.516 (v. supr. I. 2 a). **-οσύνη**, ἡ, *yearning*, in pl., A.R.1.277, 3.462, 4.1473. **-όσῡνος**, ον, *anxious*; = κήδειος I. 2, πούς E.*Or*.1017 (anap.). **-ω**, Hom. (v. infr.), etc.: impf. ἔκηδον Il.5.404, Ep. κήδεσκον Od.23.9: fut. κηδήσω Il.24. 240:—**Med.** and **Pass.**, pres. in Hom., etc.; Dor. imper. κάδευ Call. *Lav.Pall*.140: Ep. impf. κηδέσκετο Od.22.358: fut. κεκᾰδήσομαι Il. 8.353: aor. imper. κήδεσαι A.*Th*.139 (lyr.): pf. κέκηδα (in pres. sense) Tyrt.12.28. I. Act., *trouble, distress*, c. acc. pers., ὃς τόξοισιν ἔκηδε θεούς Il.5.404; μῆλα δὲ κήδει (sc. χειμών) 17.550; ὅττι ἐ κήδοι Od.9.402; ὅτι μ' ἤλθετε κηδήσοντες Il.24.240; Λύγδαμιν οὐ γὰρ ἐμὴ τῆμος ἔκηδε κάσις Call.*Aet*.3.1.23:—Act. only in Ep. and Eleg. II. Med. and Pass., *to be concerned, care for*..: c. gen., of persons or cities, κήδετο γὰρ Δαναῶν Il.1.56; τίη δὲ σὺ κήδεαι οὕτως ἀνδρῶν; 6.55; ὀλλυμένων Δαναῶν κεκαδησόμεθ' 8.353, cf. 11.665; ὅς τέ μευ κηδέσκετο παιδὸς ἐόντος Od.22.358, cf. Hdt.1.209, 9.45, S.*Aj*. 203 (anap.), Th.6.14, Pl.*Chrm*.173a, Ph.1.359, etc.; Ἄργεος Call. *Lav.Pall*. l. c.; καὶ γαμέτου κήδεο καὶ τεκέων *mourn for*.., *Epigr.Gr*. 243.25 (Pergam.): c. gen. rei, τῶν ἀλφίτων Ar.*Nu*.106; τῆς πολιτείας Arist.*Pol*.1320ᵃ6; τῶν ἔργων *POxy*.1682.13 (iv A.D.): folld. by a Verb, κ. μὴ ἀπόλωνται Hdt.7.220; κ. ἵνα μὴ δύῃ Pl.*Plt*.273d; κ. φόβῳ τοῦ πνιγῆναι Aët.8.63: abs. in part. κηδόμενος, η, ον, *caring for* a person, *anxious*, φιλέουσά τε κηδομένη τε Il.1.196; ἀνέρι κηδομένῳ *distressed*, 16.516; freq. in Hom. at end of verse, κηδόμενός περ, κηδομένη περ, Il.7.110, 1.586; εὐνοῶν τε καὶ κ. Ar.*Nu*.1410; Dor. καδόμενος Pi.*O*.6.47. b. *bury*, c. gen., Ael.*Fr*.106. 2. Inscrr., *take charge of*, τοῦ μνημείου τούτου ἡ γερουσία κ. *SIG*1244 (Cos, ii/iii A.D.), cf. 1228 (Ephesus, iii A.D.).

κηδωλός· ὁ φροντίζων καὶ κηδόμενος ὅλων, Suid.

κῆεν, Ep. 3 sg. aor. 1 Act. of καίω, Il.21.349.

κηθάριον, τό, Dim. of κηθίς, *voting-urn, ballot-box*, Ar.*V*.674.

κηθεῖν· βοηθεῖν, and **κηθοί**· βοηθοί, Hsch.; cf. κέαθοι. **κήθευον**· συνεπορεύοντο, Id. **κῆθι**, v. ἐκεῖθι.

κήθιν, τό, prob. = κήθιον, *PLond*.2.402ᵛ.23 (ii B.C.).

κηθίς, ίδος, ἡ, *dice-box*, prob. in Poll.7.203:—Dim. **κήθιον**, Hermipp.27, **κηθίδιον**, Poll.10.150.—Wrongly written **κητίον**, Alciphr. 1.39, Ath.11.477d cod. A:—**χείτιον**, Ion. **κείθιον**, Eust.1259.36. (Ath. l. c. derives it from χείσεται, fut. of χανδάνω.)

κῆθυ, f. l. for κῆθι. **κήϊα**· καθάρματα, Hsch.; cf. κεῖα.

κηκ-άζω (κηκαδεῖ Hsch.), *abuse, revile*, Lyc.1386. **-άς**, άδος, ἡ, said to be Ion. word for κακός, *mischievous*, κ. ἀλώπηξ Nic.*Al.*185; *abusive*, κηκάδι σὺν γλώσσῃ Call.*Fr.*253. **-ασμός**, ὁ, *abuse, insult*, Lyc.545 (pl.), 692.

κηκίβαλος, ὁ, kind of *shell-fish*, Epich.42.2 (leg. κικ-, cf. **κικοβαυλιτίδες**).

κηκίδιον, τό, *ink-gall*, Philum.ap.Aët.16.117(107), Hdn.*Epim.*65, Eust.956.1: used as yellow dye, written **κικίδιον**, Ps.-Democr.ap. Zos.Alch.p.160 B.

κηκῖδοφόρος, ον, *bearing gall-nuts*, Agathocl.ap.Eust.994.43.

κηκίς [ῑ], ῖδος, ἡ, *anything gushing* or *bubbling forth, ooze*, of fat or juices drawn forth by fire, κηκὶς πισσήρης φλογός A.*Ch.*268; κ. φόνου *bubbling* blood, ib.1012; μυδῶσα κ. *juices* drawn by fire from a sacrificial victim, S.*Ant.*1008; κ. πορφύρας *dye* of the murex, A.*Ag.* 960. II. *oak-gall*, Hp.*Nat.Mul.*32,al., Thphr.*HP*1.2.1, 3.8.6, Dsc.1.107; *the dye made therefrom*, D.27.10,43; used as *ink*, Eust. 955.64; esp. invisible ink, Ph.*Bel.*102.32.

κηκίω, Dor. **κᾱκίω** Hsch.:—*gush, bubble forth*, θάλασσα.. κήκιε πολλὴ ἂν στόμα τε ῥῖνάς τε much brine *gushed* up through his mouth, Od.5.455, cf. A.R.1.542; ἐκ βυθοῦ κηκῖον αἷμα S.*Ph.*784: c.acc.cogn., *bubble with, send forth*, κήκιε πόντος ἀϋτμήν A.R.4.929:—Med., *ooze*, αἱμάδα κηκιομέναν ἑλκέων S.*Ph.*697. [ῐ Ep.: ῑ S. ll. cc.]

κήκραν· ἐκεκράγ[ε]σαν, Hsch. **κηλαίνω**, = κηλέω, Id.

κήλας, ὁ, an Indian stork, *adjutant, Leptoptilus argala*, Ael.*NA* 16.4.

κηλάς, άδος, ἡ, prop. *mottled* (cf. κηλίς), of clouds denoting wind, not rain, Thphr.*Sign.*31, prob. in 51: hence κ. ἡμέρα a *windy* day, Hsch., dub. in Call.*Fr.*63 P. II. κηλὰς αἴξ, ἡ, a she-goat *with a mark* (σημεῖον τυλοειδές) *on her forehead*, Hsch.

κηλ-άστρα, ἡ, *milk-pail*, Hsch. II. *holly, Ilex Aquifolium*, Id.: —also **-αστρος**, ἡ, Thphr.*HP*3.4.5, 4.1.3:—more freq. **-αστρον**, τό, ib.1.9.3, 3.3.1,al.

κήλεος, ον, (καίω) *burning*, Hom. always in dat. in the phrase πυρὶ κηλέῳ (disyll.), Il.8.235, 18.346, Od.8.435, Hes.*Th.*865; always at end of line, exc. ἐνέπρησεν πυρὶ κ. νῆας ἐΐσας Il.8.217:—once in form **κήλειος**, σὺν πυρὶ κ.15.744:—also **κηλός**, *dry*, Hsch.; cf. καυαλέος.

κηλ-έστης, ου, ὁ, *beguiler*, Suid., Zonar. **-έω**, *charm, bewitch, beguile*, esp. by music, κόρην ὕμνοισι E.*Alc.*359; ᾠδαῖς Pl.*Ly.*206b; κηλῶν τῇ φωνῇ ὥσπερ Ὀρφεύς Id.*Prt.*315a, cf. Luc.*Ind.*12; οὕτως ἐκήλει, of Pericles as an orator, Eup.94.6; ἐπᾴδων κ. *charm* by incantation, Pl.*Phdr.*267d; τῷ με κηλήσεις τρόπῳ; Achae.17.2; of bribery, Theopomp.Com.30:—Pass., κηλεῖται ἀοιδαῖς Archil.ap.Phld.*Mus.* p.20 K., cf. Pi.*Dith.*2.22; ὑπὸ σοῦ ὥσπερ ὄφις κηληθῆναι Pl.*R.*358b; ὑπὸ δώρων κηλούμενος Id.*Lg.*885d; ὑφ' ἡδονῆς κηληθείς Id.*R.*413c; ἐφ' οἷς κατορθώσαντες εὐφρανθήσονται, τούτοις κεκήληνται Aeschin.1.191; παρὰ ταῖς Σειρῆσιν Arist.*EE*1230ᵇ35: rarely in good sense, παιδείᾳ τὸν νοῦν κηληθείς Pl.*Ep.*333c.

κήλη, Att. **κάλη** [prob. ᾱ], ἡ, *tumour*; esp. *rupture, hernia*, Hp.*Aër.* 7 (pl.), *AP*6.166 (Lucill.), 11.342. 2. *hump* on a buffalo's back, Arist.*HA*606ᵃ16, in acc. pl. κάλας (v.l. χαίτας); in human beings, Eup.276.1, Gal.7.729, Artem.3.45; καλήτης καὶ κάλη Ἀττικοί..., κηλήτης καὶ κήλη Ἴωνες Phryn.*PS*p.81 B. (Cf. ONorse *haull*, OSlav. *kyla*, both = *hernia*.)

Κηλ-ηδόνες, αἱ, the *Charmers*, mythical songstresses, like the Sirens, but harmless, Pi.*Fr.*53, cf. Ath.7.290e. **-ηθμός**, ὁ, *rapture, enchantment*, κηληθμῷ δ' ἔσχοντο Od.11.334. **-ηθρον**, τό, = sq., Phryn.*PS*p.80 B. **-ημα**, ατος, τό, *charm, spell*, in pl., Ibyc. 2, E.*Tr.*893: sg., Id.*Hyps.Fr.*26(32).

κηλήνη· μέλαινα, Hsch.

κήλ-ησις, εως, ἡ, *bewitching, charming*, ἔχεων, νόσων, Pl.*Euthd.* 290a: *enchantment* by eloquence, δικαστῶν κ. τε καὶ παραμυθία ibid.; by music and sweet sounds, Id.*R.*601b, *Stoic.*3.97. **-ήτειρα**, ἡ, *enchantress*, glossed by ἡσυχάστρια, Hsch. **-ητήριος**, ον, *charming, appeasing*, χοαί E.*Hec.*535; ᾄσματα Suid.; τὸ κ., = κήληθρον, S. *Tr.*575. **-ήτης**, ου, ὁ, (κήλη) *one who is ruptured*, Str.17.3.4, Gal. 10.988, D.C.73.2, *AP*11.342, Luc.*Epigr.*39:—Att. **καλήτης** Phryn. *PS*p.81 B. **-ητικός**, ή, όν, *charming*, τὸ κ. τῆς ἐπιστήμης Ath.14. 633a. **-ήτωρ**, ορος, ὁ, *charmer*, Orph.*Fr.*297a.6.

κηλίβανα, = σιδηρᾶ καλύμματα, as etym. of κλιβανάριοι, Lyd.*Mag.* 1.46.

κηλῑδ-όω, Dor. **κᾱλ-** Ecphant.(v. infr.):—*stain, soil*, τὰ ἱμάτια Arist. *Insomn.*460ᵃ12 (Pass.):—Pass., D.C.77.11: metaph., *defile, sully*, E.*HF*1318, Ecphant.ap.Stob.4.7.64:—Pass., Ph.1.156. **-ωτός**, ή, όν, *stained, soiled*, Suid., *Gloss.*

κηλικτάς, ᾶ, ὁ, Lacon., *charmer*, prob. in Plu.2.220f.

κηλίς [ῑ], ῖδος, ἡ, *stain, spot, defilement*, esp. of blood, A.*Eu.*787 (lyr.), S.*El.*446, E.*IT*1200, etc.: generally, οὐ ῥᾴδιον ἐκμάξαι τὴν.. κηλῖδα [ἐκ τοῦ κατόπτρου] Arist.*Insomn.*459ᵇ32; ἐν ἱματίῳ καθαρῷ καὶ αἱ μικραὶ κ. ἔνδηλοι Id.*GA*780ᵇ32; ἱμάτιον κηλίδων μεστόν Thphr.*Char.* 19.7. 2. metaph., *stain, blemish*, S.*OT*1384; κ. συμφορᾶς ib.833; κακῶν Id.*OC*1134; ἐστάθη τὴν ἀσπίδα ἔχων, ὃ δοκεῖ κ. εἶναι τοῖς Λακεδαιμονίοις X.*HG*3.1.9; *ignominious punishment*, θεία κ. προσπίπτει τῷ δράσαντι Antipho 3.3.8; τῆς κ. εἰς ὑμᾶς ἀναφερομένης ib.11; τιμωρίας καὶ κηλῖδας πάσας αὐτοῖς ἀνῆκεν Hdn.6.8.8. 3. Medic., *naevus*, Lycus ap.Orib.9.44.3.

κῆλον, τό, *shaft* of an arrow, *arrow*, only pl., κῆλα θεοῖο *the shafts* of Apollo, as the cause of sudden death, Il.1.53,383; πιφαυσκόμενος τὰ ἃ κῆλα, of Zeus during a snowstorm, 12.280; στεροπὴν καὶ αἰθαλόεντα κεραυνόν, κῆλα Διός Hes.*Th.*708: metaph., [φόρμιγγος] κῆλα καὶ δαιμόνων θέλγει φρένας Pi.*P.*1.12; φρικώδεα κῆλα πίφαυσκον Orph. *A.*10:—also **κῆλεα** νηῶν, = κᾶλα, ships' *timbers*, Hes.*Fr.*206 (s.v.l.).

κηλόν· ξηρόν, Hsch.; cf. κήλεος, καυαλέος.

κηλοτομ-ία, ἡ, *operation for hernia*, Paul.Aeg.6.63. **-ικός**, ή, όν, *of herniotomy*, τέχνη Gal.*Thras.*24. **-ος**, ὁ, *herniotomist*, ibid. (v.l. -τομικόν).

κηλόω (A), aor. 1 inf. -ῶσαι, = ἀμβλῶσαι, ἐπὶ τῶν ἐμβρύων, *An. Par.*4.257:—Pass., *have an abnormal delivery*, Ptol.*Tetr.*149.

κηλόω (B), collat. form of κηλέω, expld. by εὔχεσθαι θεῷ, Hsch.

κήλυγμα, = κίνυγμα, Hsch.

κήλων, ωνος, ὁ, (κῆλον) *swipe, swing-beam*, for drawing water, *IG* 11(2).154*A* 8 (Delos, iii B.C.), *PLond.*1.131ʳ.303 (i A.D.), Hsch. II. ὄνος κ. *he-ass*, Archil.97, cf. Eust.1597.28, Ph.2.307; *stallion*, Hsch., Suid., prob. in Plaut.*Poen.*1168: hence of Pan, Cratin.321.

κηλών-ειον, Ion. **-ήϊον**, τό, = foreg. I, Hdt.1.193, 6.119, Ar.*Fr.*679, Arist.*Mech.*857ᵃ34, Aen.Tact.39.7, *PCair.Zen.*155 (iii B.C.), Gal.*UP* 7.7:—written **κηλώνιον**, Apollod.*Poliorc.*162.8, al. **-εύω**, *suspend on a fulcrum* or *pivot*, Hero *Spir.*1.20 (Pass.):—Pass., Ath.Mech.29. 14, 30.4.

κηλωστά or **κηλωτά**, ῶν, τά, *stews, brothels*, Lyc.1387.

κήμιψ· φλὲψ γεώδης (-ῶδες cod.) ἐν πέτραις (μέτρ- cod.), Hsch.

κημός (Dor. **κᾱμός**, cf. εὐκᾱμία), ὁ, *muzzle*, put on a led horse, to prevent it from biting, X.*Eq.*5.3, *AP*6.246 (Phld. or Marc. Arg.): pl., cj. in Ph.1.698: metaph., κημοὺς στόματος *muzzles* or *gags*, A. *Fr.*125. 2. *nose-bag* for horses, Hsch. 3. *cloth* used by bakers *to cover the nose and mouth*, Ath.12.548c. 4. = φορβειά, Phot. II. *wicker vessel like an eel-basket*, for fishing, *weel*, S.*Fr.*504. 2. *funnel-shaped top* of the voting-urn, Ar.*Eq.*1150 (lyr., et ibi Sch.), *V.*99, al. III. a *female ornament*, Hsch., Phot.

κῆμος, ἡ, = λεοντοπόδιον, Dsc.4.133, Orph.*A.*920.

κημ-όω, (κημός) *muzzle* a horse, X.*Eq.*5.3. II. Medic., = φιμόω, τὸν ὀφθαλμόν Sch.Ar.*Eq.*1147. III. *fit with the* κημός I. 4, πολιῷ δ' ἐπὶ πολλάκι λωτῷ κημωθεὶς (cj. Herm. for κνημωθείς) κώμους εἶχε σὺν Ἐξαμύῃ Hermesian.7.38. **-ωσις**, εως, ἡ, *muzzling*, Hsch. (also **κίμωσις**).

κήνεον· καθαρόν, Hsch.

κῆνος, Aeol. and Dor. for κεῖνος, ἐκεῖνος, Sapph.2.1, *Epigr.Gr.*991. 13 (Balbilla), *SIG*1025.25 (Cos, iv/iii B.C.); **κήνοθεν**, *thence*, Alc. 86. **κηνούει**· ἐκεῖ, and **κηνῶ**· ἐκεῖθεν, Hsch.

κηνσίτωρ, ὁ, = Lat. *censitor*, *PAmh.*2.83.3 (iii/iv A.D.).

κῆνσος, ὁ, = Lat. *census*, *Ev.Matt.*22.19, *IGRom.*4.1213 (Thyatira), 3.41 (Nicaea), *PAmh.*2.83.2 (iii/iv A.D.). II. *poll-tax*, *Ev. Matt.*17.25.

κήνυγμα, written for κίνυγμα (q.v.), Hsch. **κηνύει**· καλεῖ, Id.

κήξ, κηκός, ἡ, a sea-bird, perh. the *tern* or *sea-swallow*, ἄντλῳ δ' ἐνδούπησε πεσοῦσ' ὡς εἰναλίη κήξ Od.15.479:—also in the forms **κάυαξ**, = λάρος, Hsch., and **καύηξ** Hippon.2 (nisi leg. καύης, q.v.), Antim.*Eleg.*6, Euph.130, Call.*Fr.*167, Lyc.741, *AP*7.652 (Leon.); **κηΰξ**, Babr.115.2, Dionys.*Av.*2.7.

κήομεν (or κείομεν), Ep. for κήωμεν, v. καίω.

κηπάδιον, τό, a kind of vine(?), *PFlor.*148.14 (iii A.D.).

κηπ-αῖος, α, ον, (κῆπος) *of* or *from a garden, cultivated*, κ. σίκυες Arist.*Pr.*926ᵇ7, cf. Dsc.2.146, Gal.6.627 (v.l.), etc.; κ. παράδεισοι *garden-like* parks, Clearch.6. II. κηπαία (sc. θύρα), ἡ, *garden-door, back-door*, Hermipp.47.9, cf. Poll.1.76; prov., ταῖς κ. θύραις 'by the back-stairs', D.L.7.25, cf. Gal.2.98. 2. *a herb, Sedum Cepaea*, Dsc.3.151. **-εία**, ἡ, in pl., *gardens*, Pl.*Lg.*845d, D.S.5.43, J.*BJ*5.2. 2. **-ειος**, α, ον, v.l. for κηπαῖος, Nic.*Th.*88. **-ευμα**, ατος, τό, *garden*, κηπεύματα Χαρίτων Ar.*Av.*1100, cf. Apollod.Hist.ap.Ath.15.682d, Dicaearch.1.13. **-εύς**, Dor. **κᾱπ-**, έως, ὁ, *gardener*, Philyll.14, *AP*9. 329 (Leon.). **-εύσιμος**, ον, = κηπευτός, Alex.Trall.*Febr.*7, Sch.Nic. *Th.*66. **-ευτής**, οῦ, ὁ, = κηπεύς, *Gloss.* **-ευτός**, ή, όν, *cultivated, grown in a garden*, Dsc.3.45, *Gp.*12.30.7, Paul.Aeg.1.13. **-εύω**, *rear in a garden*, λάχανα, σῖτον, Luc.*VH*1.34, Herm. in *Phdr.*p.202 A.:—Pass., Dsc.3.43; τὰ κηπευόμενα *garden plants*, Arist.*PA*668ᵃ 18, Thphr.*HP*7.1.1, Gal.6.542; Ἠριδανὸς ὕδασι κ. κόρας, i.e. the Phaethontids, who became poplars, Eub.67.6: metaph., *tend, cherish*, βόστρυχον E.*Tr.*1175. II. *cultivate like a garden*, Thphr. *CP*4.6.7 (Pass.), Hld.9.4 (Pass.): metaph., *vivify, freshen*, Αἰδὼς κ. δρόσοις [τὸν λειμῶνα] E.*Hipp.*78; ὁπόσα ὁ ποταμὸς κ. Philostr.*VA*2. 26. **-ίδες** Νύμφαι, αἱ, *garden*-Nymphs, prob. in Aristaenet. 1.3. **-ίδιον**, τό, Dim. of κῆπος, Plu.2.1098b, D.L.3.20. **-ίον**, τό, Dim. of κῆπος, *SIG*46.15 (Halic., v B.C.), Plb.6.17.2, Gal.2.211, *PSI*1.77.18, etc.: metaph., *appendage*, κ. καὶ ἐγκαλλώπισμα πλούτου Th.2.62. II. = κῆπος II, Luc.*Lex.*5.

κηπο-κόμας, ου, ὁ, *one who has his hair cut in the fashion called* κῆπος, *Com.Adesp.*34 D. **-κόμος**, ὁ, *gardener*, *BCH*32.500 (Aphrodisias), Hsch. **-λᾰχᾰνία**, ἡ, *kitchen-garden*, *POxy.*1917. 55 (vi A.D.). **-λάχᾰνον**, τό, = foreg., *PLond.ined.*2489.13 (iv A.D.). **-λόγος**, ον, *teaching in a garden*, of Epicureans, *AP*6.307 (Phan.). **-παράδεισος**, ὁ, *garden and orchard in one*, *PSI*8.917.5 (i A.D.). **-ποιΐα**, ἡ, *making of a garden*, *Gp.*12.2.1.

κῆπος, Dor. **κᾶπος** (also *Inscr.Cypr.*135.20 H.), ὁ, *garden, orchard*, or *plantation*, Od.7.129, 24.247,338; πολυδένδρεος 4.737; of any rich, highly cultivated region, as Ἀφροδίτας κᾶπος, i.e. Cyrene, Pi. *P.*5.24; Διὸς κ., i.e. Libya, ib.9.53 (but Διὸς κῆποι, also of heaven, S. *Fr.*320 (lyr.); Φοίβου παλαιὸς κ., of the eastern sky, ib.956, cf. Pl.*Smp.* 203b; cf. Ὠκεανοῦ κ. Ar.*Nu.*271); κ. Εὐβοίας S.*Fr.*24; οἱ Μίδεω κῆποι, in Macedonia, Hdt.8.138; of the country round Panormus, Call. Hist.2; the *enclosure* for the Olympic games, Pi.*O*.3.24; οἱ ἀπὸ τῶν κ. the scholars of Epicurus, because he taught in a *garden*, S.E.*M*. 9.64, cf. D.L.10.10; οἱ Ἀδώνιδος κ., v. Ἄδωνις; οἱ Ταντάλου κ., prov. of illusory pleasures, Philostr.*VS*1.20.1: metaph., Χαρίτων νέμομαι κᾶπον, i.e. poetic art, Pi.*O*.9.27; ἐκ Μουσῶν κ. τινῶν.. δρεπόμενοι τὰ μέλη Pl.*Ion* 534a; τοὺς ἐν τοῖς γράμμασι κ. σπείρειν Id.*Phdr*. 276d. **II.** *a fashion of cropping the hair*, Poll.2.29, Ael.Dion.*Fr*. 230. **III.** *pudenda muliebria*, D.L.2.116. **IV.** v.l. for κῆβος (q.v.).

κηπο-τάφιον [τᾰ], τό, *tomb in a garden*, *BGU*1120.7 (i B.C.):—also **-τᾰφος**, ὁ, or **-τᾰφον**, τό, *Papers of Amer.Sch. at Athens* 3.621 (Ilias): cf. Lat. *cepotaphium*. **-τύραννος** [ῠ], ὁ, *tyrant of the garden*, epith. of the Epicurean philosopher Apollodorus, D.L.10.25.

κηπουργ-ία, ἡ, *gardening*, Poll.7.101. **-ικός**, ή, όν, *skilled in gardening*, ib.141.

κηπουρ-έω, *practise gardening*, Phleg.*Mir*.8, Poll.9.13. **-ιᾰκός**, ή, όν, *of* or *for a garden*, θρίδακες *BGU*1118.13 (i B.C.); θύραι (made of lettuce-stems) v.l. in Thphr.*HP*7.4.5. **-ικός**, ή, όν, *of* or *for gardening*, νόμοι, νόμιμον, Pl.*Min*.316e, 317b; κηπουρικαὶ θύραι *garden trellis*, Thphr.*HP*7.4.5; κ. κτένες, πλατυλίσγιον, Ph.*Bel*.100.10, Apollod.*Poliorc*.220.18; κ. λάχανον *Hippiatr*.7: κηπουρικά, τά, treatise on gardening by Caesennius, etc., Plin.*HN*1.19 *Ind.Auct*., 19. 177. **II.** *skilled in gardening*, cj. in Poll.7.141. Adv. -κῶς ibid. **-ός**, ὁ, (οὖρος) *keeper of a garden*, ὄφις Euph.154. **II.** *gardener*, *IG*2^2.10 (v B.C.), Thphr.*HP*7.2.5, *PCair.Zen*.59.6 (iii B.C.), Plb.18.6.4, *Ev. Jo*.20.15, Philostr.*Her.Prooem*.2, *CIG*4082 (Pessinus); title of play by Antiph.:—also **κηπωρός**, Archipp.44, Pl.*Min*.316e, *PFay*.101^{r}ii4 (i B.C.).

κηπρίαρτος, v. κοπριαίρετος.

Κήρ, ἡ, Aeol. **Κᾶρ** Alc. (v. infr.), gen. Κηρός, acc. Κῆρα; Dor. pl. **Κᾶρες** Hipparch.ap.Stob.4.34.8 (v.l. Κῆρες), but sg. κήρ Trag. in lyr. (v. infr.):—*the goddess of death* or *doom*, Κὴρ.. Θανάτοιο Od.11.171, etc.; Κῆρες.. Θανάτοιο Il.2.834, etc.; ἐν δ' Ἔρις ἐν δὲ Κυδοιμὸς ὁμίλεον ἐν δ' ὀλοὴ Κ. Il.18.535; ἐμὲ μὲν Κ. ἀμφέχανε στυγερή, ἥ περ λάχε γιγνόμενόν περ 23.79; διχθάδιαι Κῆρες, of Achilles, 9.411; Κῆρες μυρίαι 12. 326; Κῆρες Ἀχαιῶν, Τρώων, 8.73,74; Κ. νηλεόποινοι Hes.*Th*.217; Κ. Ἐρινύες A.*Th*.1060 (anap.); Κ. ἀναπλάκητοι S.*OT*472 (lyr.), cf. *Tr*. 133 (lyr.), Pi.*Fr*.277, E.*El*.1252, *HF*870 (troch.); ἁρπαξάνδρα Κ., of the Sphinx, A.*Th*.777 (lyr.): prov., θύραζε Κῆρες (v.l. Κᾶρες), οὐκ ἔνι (v.l. ἔτ') Ἀνθεστήρια, of those who want the same always, Zen. 4.33, Suid. s.v. θύραζε. **II.** as Appellat., *doom, death*, esp. when *violent*, rarely without personal sense in Hom., τὸ δέ τοι κὴρ εἴδεται εἶναι that seems to thee to be *death*, Il.1.228; κῆρ' ἀλεείνων 3.32, al.; φόνον καὶ κ. φέροντες 2.352, al.: freq. later, ὑπὰ κᾶρι.. δινvάεντ' Ἀχέροντ' ἐπέραισε Alc.*Supp*.7.7; μέλαιναν κῆρ' ἐπ' ὄμμασιν βαλών E.*Ph*.950. **2.** νοσῶν παλαιᾷ κηρί *plague, disease*, S.*Ph*.42, cf. 1166 (lyr.): in a general sense, βαρεῖα μὲν κ. τὸ μὴ πιθέσθαι grievous *ruin* it were not to obey, A.*Ag*.206 (lyr.); ἐλευθέρῳ ψευδεῖ καλεῖσθαι κ. πρόσεστιν οὐ καλή an unseemly *disgrace*, S.*Tr*.454. **3.** pl. sts. in Prose, *blemishes, defects*, [τοῖς καλοῖς] κ. ἐπιπεφύκασιν Pl.*Lg*.937d; [τόποι] ἰδίας ἔχουσι κῆρας Thphr.*CP*5.10.4; κ. σύμφυτοι D.H.2.3, cf. 8.61; ἁμαρτίαι καὶ κ. Plu.*Cim*.2; σῶμα ἀκήρατον τῶν ἐκτὸς κ. Ti.Locr. 95b, cf. Ph.1.368, al.: rarely sg., συνήθειαν ὥσπερ τινὰ κ. Plu.*Ant*.2, cf. Ph.1.440. (Perh. cogn. with κεραΐζω.)

κῆρ, τό, perh. contr. from κέαρ (sed v. infr.); Hom. always κῆρ, dat. κῆρι, Adv. κηρόθι (q.v.); Trag. always κέαρ (no other case):—*heart*, κῆρ γηθεῖ ἐνὶ στήθεσσι Il.14.139; κ. ἄχνυται ἐν θυμῷ 6.523, cf. 7.428; ἄλλα δέ οἱ κ. ὅρμαινε φρεσὶν ᾗσιν Od.18.344, cf. 7.82; τῷ κε.. αἶψα μεταστρέψειε νόον μετὰ σὸν καὶ ἐμὸν κ. Il.15.52; θαλέων ἐμπλησάμενος κ. 22.504, cf. 19.319; τοῦ δ' οὔ ποτε κυδάλιμον κ. ταρβεῖ, of a boar or lion, 12.45: dat. κῆρι as Adv., *with all the heart, heartily*, ὅν τε Ζεὺς κῆρι φιλήσῃ 9.117: mostly strengthd., περὶ κ. φιλεῖν (περί Adv., either *exceedingly* or *throughout*) 13.430; περὶ κ... τιμᾶν τινα Od.5.36, etc.; ἀπέχθωνται περὶ κ. Il.4.53; περὶ κ... ἐχολώθη 13.206; νεμεσσῶμαι π. κῆρι ib.119; for λάσιον κ. v. λάσιος; later κῆρ ἄσᾳ βόρηται dub. in Sapph.*Supp*.25.18; ἐμὸν κέαρ οὐ γεύεται ὕμνων Pi.*I*.5(4).20, cf. *N*. 7.102, B.16.108, etc.; κέαρ ἀπαράμυθον A.*Pr*.187 (lyr.); ἠλγύνθην, ἠχθέσθην κέαρ, ib.247, 392, etc.; paratrag., τὸ κέαρ ηὐφράνθην Ar. *Ach*.5. (With nom. κῆρ cf. OPruss. *seyr*, Arm. *sirt*, 'heart', I.-E. *k̑ērd-* (cf. καρδία); κέαρ is perh. a later formation on the analogy of ἔαρ: ἦρ.)

κήρα, ἡ, Lat. *cera, wax tablet*, *POxy*.2110.4 (iv A.D.).

κηραίνω (A), (κήρ) *harm, destroy*, A.*Supp*.999, Ph.1.653:—Pass., *to be injured, spoiled, perish*, *Placit*.2.4.12, Hierocl. *in CA*14 p.451 M. **II.** intr., *to be blemished* or *imperfect*, Ph.1.280, al.

κηραίνω (B), (κῆρ) *to be sick at heart, anxious*, E.*HF*518; τι *at* a thing, Id.*Hipp*.223 (anap.); ἐπί τινι Max.93; κ. περί τι Ph.2.205, al.

κηρᾰμύντης, ου, ὁ, (ἀμύνω) *averter of evil*, epith. of Heracles, Lyc. 663.

κηράνθεμος, ὁ, = κήρινθος, Dsc.2.82 (pl.), 5.9.

κηρᾰφίς, ίδος, ἡ, a kind of *locust*, Nic.*Al*.394; = κάραβος, Hsch.

κηρ-ᾰχάτης [χᾱ], ου, ὁ, *wax-agate*, Plin.*HN*37.139. **-έλαιον**, τό, *wax-oil*, a kind of *salve*, Gal.6.445, 13.953. **-εμβροχή**, ἡ, *fomentation with melted wax*, Alex.Trall.12.

κηρέσιος, ον, (κήρ) *deadly, pernicious*, Hsch.

κηρεσσῐφόρητος, ον, *urged on by the* Κῆρες, ἐξελάαν... κύνας κηρεσσιφορήτους Il.8.527.

κηρία, ἡ, v. κειρία.

κηριάζω, *spawn*, of the purple-fish (πορφύρα), whose spawn is like a honeycomb (κηρίον), Arist.*HA*546^{b}25, *GA*761^{b}32.

κηριάπτης, *ceriforus, ceriolum*, *Gloss*.:—Dim. **κηριαπτάριον**, τό, *PMasp*.340*B*77 (vi A.D.).

κηρ-ίδιον, τό, Dim. of κηρίον, *honeycomb*, Aët.5.137 (pl.). **-ίζω**, *have a waxy appearance*, Zos.Alch. p.215 B. **-ίνη** [ῐ], ἡ, = κηρίων II, Hsch., Phot. **II.** (sc. ἔμπλαστρος) name of a *plaster*, Asclep.ap. Gal.13.936.

κήρινθος, ὁ, *bee-bread*, = ἐριθάκη, Arist.*HA*623^{b}23, Plin.*HN*11.17, Hsch. **II.** kind of *ulcer*, Id.

κήρῐνος, η, ον, (κηρός) *waxen*, Ar.*Ec*.1035, Archipp.3 D., Pl.*Tht*. 191c, 197d; κηρίνα ὀπώρα, i.e. *honey*, Alcm.75. **II.** metaph., *pliable as wax*, τοὺς θυμοὺς.. κηρίνους ποιεῖν Pl.*Lg*.633d; κηρίνας τὰς ὑπολήψεις ἔχειν Arr.*Epict*.3.16.10. **2.** *wax-coloured, pallid*, Suid. s.v. ἐκηριώθην. **3.** of women, '*made up*' *with cosmetics*, Philostr. *Ep*.22, cf. *VA*2.22.

κηριο-ελκός, ὁ, *one who makes wax lights*, *PRyl*.374.3 (i B.C./ i A.D.). **-κλέπτης**, ου, ὁ, *stealer of honeycombs*, title of Theocritus' nineteenth Idyll.

κηριολάριον, *cerilarium*, *Gloss*.

κηρίολος, ὁ, prob. *wax taper* or *wax figure*, *CIG*3028.5 (Ephesus).

κηρίον, τό, (κηρός) *honeycomb*, mostly in pl., *h.Merc*.559, Hes.*Th*. 597, Hdt.5.114, etc.; κ. καὶ λίβανον, as offerings, *Supp.Epigr*.3.774 (Crete, i B.C.): sg., Pl.*R*.552c, Theoc.19.2, *IG*5(2).514.14 (Lycosura, ii B.C.); τὸ κ. τοῦ μέλιτος Lxx 1*Ki*.14.27; used in Medicine, Hp. *Morb*.2.45, 3.17; παιδίον κηρίῳ βεβυσμένον having its mouth stopped with *a piece of honeycomb*, Ar.*Th*.506, cf. Sch. ad loc., Sor.1.86; κ. σφηκῶν Hdt.2.92: κηρία, τά, *honey*, Hippon.36, Aristo ap.Ath.2. 38f. **2.** metaph., of a book of poems, *AP*9.190: pl., title of Anthologies, Gell.*Praef*.6. **3.** metaph., of anything pleasant, τῆς ἐπιθυμίας τὸ κ. Lib.*Ep*.112.1. **II.** *a cutaneous disease*, = μελικηρίς, Dsc.2.135 (pl.), Gal.7.728, al.

κηριόομαι, Pass., *to be panic-stricken*, Hsch. (cf. eund. s.v. ἐκηριώθη), Suid., prob. in *Anacreont*.13.18.

κηριοποιός, όν, *making honeycombs*, Arist.*HA*623^{b}7.

κηρίς, ίδος, ἡ, = κιρρίς, Diph.Siph.ap.Ath.8.355d, Alex.Trall.7.1, 8.2, al.

κηρῖτις (sc. λίθος), ἡ, a precious stone *like wax*, Plin.*HN*37.153.

κηρι-τρεφής, ές, (τρέφω) *born to misery*, ἄνθρωποι Hes.*Op*.418, cf. Orac.ap.Sch.E.*Ph*.638. **-φᾰτοι**, οἱ, (θείνω) = ὅσοι νόσῳ τεθνήκασιν, Hsch.

κηρι-ώδης, ες, *arranged like a honeycomb*, Thphr.*HP*3.13.3. **-ωμα**, ατος, τό, *rheum in the eyes*, S.*Fr*.715. **-ων**, ωνος, ὁ, *wax light, waxen torch*, Plu.2.263f, Gal.17(2).267. **II.** *whip*, Hsch. and Phot. s.v. κηρίναι.

κηρο-γονία, ἡ, *formation of wax* or *combs*, Lxx 4*Ma*.14.19. **-γρᾰφέω**, *paint with wax*, *Inscr.Délos* 290.112 (iii B.C.), Callix.2 (Pass.). **-γρᾰφία**, ἡ, *painting with wax*, i.e. *encaustic painting*, πᾶς τόπος κηρογραφίᾳ κατεπεποίκιλτο Id.1. **-δέτης**, ου, Dor. **-δέτας**, ὁ, = sq., κάλαμος E.*IT*1125 (lyr.). **-δετος**, ον, (δέω A) *bound* or *joined with wax*, μέλι *APl*.4.305 (Antip.); σῦριγξ Euph.ap.Ath. 4.184a; κ. πνεῦμα the breath *of the wax-joined pipe*, Theoc.*Ep*.5. 4. **-δομέω**, *build with wax*, of bees, Ps.-Phoc.174. **-ειδής**, ές, *like wax, waxen*, σώματα Pl.*Ti*.61c, etc.: metaph., of the soul, Ph.1.64. **2.** *wax-coloured*, *PSI*4.444.3 (iii B.C.), Dsc.1.119.

κηρόθεν, Adv., (κῆρ) *from the heart*, *EM*511.20.

κηρόθῐ, Adv., (κῆρ) *with all the heart, heartily*, in Hom. always folld. by μᾶλλον, ἀπήχθετο κ. μ. Il.9.300; χολώσατο κ. μ. 21.136, cf. Od.5.284, etc.; φίλει δέ με κ. μ. 15.370; τίον δὲ ἑ κ. μ. Hes.*Sc*.85.

κηρό-κλυστος, ον, *coated with wax*, *PSI*6.594.20 (iii B.C.). **-μάρμᾰρος**, ὁ, *cement* for making drainpipes watertight, Steph. *in Hp*. 2.384 D. **-μελι**, ιτος, τό, *honey in the comb*, Sch.rec.Theoc.7.83, prob. in Zos.Alch. p.113 B.

κηρόν· λεπτόν, νοσερόν, Hsch. **κηρόομαι**, Pass., (κήρ II) *to be destroyed, injured*, *EM*322.13.

κηροπᾰγής, ές, *fastened with wax*, θαλάμαι *AP*6.239 (Apollonid.), cf. Man.1.242.

κηροπάζουσα· βαστάζουσα, Hsch.

κηρόπισσος, ὁ, *wax-pitch*, an ointment, Hp.*Morb*.2.18, cf. *Gloss*.

κηροπλαστ-έω, *mould of* or *in wax*, Hp.*Art*.62; κ. Ἔρωτα Eub. 41; *mould as in wax*, ἐκηροπλάστεεν τὸν ἄνθρωπον ἡ φύσις Aret.*SD* 2.13. **2.** *make wax cells*, D.S.17.75, 19.2. **-ης**, ου, ὁ, *modeller in wax*: *modeller*, Pl.*Ti*.74c, Ptol.*Tetr*.180. **-ικός**, ή, όν, ἡ -κή (sc. τέχνη) Poll.7.165; ἡ ὕλη [ἐστὶν ἄμορφος] πρὸς -κήν Ocell.2.3. **-ος**, ον, (πλάσσω) *moulded of wax*, μελίσσης κ. ὄργανον S.*Fr*.398.5: metaph., of a girl, *AP*9.570 (Phld.). **2.** = κηρόδετος, δόναξ A. *Pr*.574 (lyr.).

κηρο-ποιός, όν, *making wax*, Sch.Ar.*V*.1075. **-πώλης**, ου, ὁ, *wax-chandler*, *Gloss*.

κηρός, ὁ, *bees-wax*, Od.12.48, Theoc.1.27, etc.; *honeycomb*, Id. 20.27; εὐπλαστότερον κηροῦ Pl.*R*.588d; used as a cosmetic, Philostr. *Ep*.22; in encaustic painting, *IG*4^2(1).102.272 (Epid., iv B.C.), 14. 1320; for writing tablets, *POxy*.736.16 (i A.D.), etc.: hence λόγους εἰς γραμμάτιον καὶ κηρὸν ἐρχομένους Lib.*Ep*.886.1. **2.** *sealing-wax*, Luc.*Alex*.21. **3.** κ. Τυρρηνικός *white wax* used in medicine, Gal.13. 411, Dsc.1.70. **II.** pl. κηροί *wax tapers*, Hld.9.11. (Panhellenic η, *IG*4^2.l.c., Theoc. ll.cc., cf. κήρινος, κηρόδετος, κηροχυτέω; Lat. *cera*.)

κηροσσαίων· παλαιῶν, Hsch.

κηροτᾰκίς, ίδος, ἡ, *hot palette, hot plate*, used by painters for keeping wax paints hot, and by alchemists, *PHolm.*6.33, Syn.Alch.p.60 B., Zos.Alch.p.158 B., etc.

κηρο-τέχνης, ου, ὁ, *modeller in wax, Anacreont.*10.9. **-τρόφος** (A), ον, (κήρ) *death-breeding, deadly*, ὄφις Nic.*Th.*192. **-τροφος** (B), ον, (κηρός) *waxen*, δῶρα μελισσῶν *AP*6.236 (Phil.).

κηρουει· ἐκεῖ (Cret.), Hsch. (nisi leg. κηνουει).

κηρουλκός, όν, (κήρ, ἕλκω) *bringing destruction*, Lyc.407.

κηρόφιν, *from the heart*, Hsch.

κηρο-φορέω, *produce wax*, Suid. **-φόρον**, *cerostatarium*, *Gloss.* **-χίτων** [ῐ], ωνος, ὁ, ἡ, *clad in wax*, λαμπάς *AP*6.249 (Antip.). **-χρως**, ωτος, ὁ, ἡ, *wax-coloured*, κόμαι Chaerem.1.5 (fort. κιρρό-, q.v.). **-χῠτέω**, *mould as in wax*, Ar.*Th.*56 (anap.); κηροχυτεῖ τὰν ψυχάν Hippod.ap.Stob.4.1.94. **-χῠτος**, ον, *moulded of wax*, κ. μείλιγμα, of the melody of Pan, Castorio 2.5; dub. in Pl. *Epigr.*32.

κηρόω, *wax over*, [δέλτον] Herod.3.15, cf. Tryph.*Trop.*p.195 S. (Pass.), *PMag.Par.*1.3214:—Pass., Hp.*Art.*30; κεκηρῶσθαι τὰ ἔσωθεν [τῆς κλεψύδρας] Aen.Tact.22.25; *to be fastened with wax*, [σῦριγξ] κεκήρωτο Longus 2.35. II. Med., *form for oneself in wax*, ἄγγεα *AP*9.226 (Zon.).

κήρτεα· τὰ κέρδη, Hsch.

κήρυγ-μα, ατος, τό, (κηρύσσω) *that which is cried by a herald, proclamation*, S.*Ichn.*13, etc.; κ. ποιέεσθαι Hdt.3.52; ἐκ τοῦ κ. by *proclamation*, Id.6.78; πόλει κ. θεῖναι S.*Ant.*8; τῷ κ. ἐμμένειν Id.*OT* 350, cf. *Ant.*454; κ. ἀνειπεῖν Th.4.105; κηρύσσειν Aeschin.3.154; κ. γιγνόμενον D.18.83; *announcement* of victory in games, D.C.63.14; *mandate, summons*, S.*Ant.*162 (anap.); *reward offered by proclamation*, X.*HG*5.4.10, Aeschin.3.33. II. *preaching*, *Ev.Luc.* 11.32, al. **-μός**, ὁ, = κήρυξις, Sch.B Il.21.575.

κηρύκ-αινα [ῠ], ἡ, fem. of κῆρυξ, Ar.*Ec.*713. II. at Alexandria, a kind of *charwoman*, Suid. **-εία**, Ion. **-ηΐη**, ἡ, *office of herald* or *crier*, Hdt.7.134 (pl.), Pl.*Lg.*742b, *IG*2².145; ἐπὶ κηρυκείαν ἀποστέλλεσθαι on an *embassy*, Lex ap.Aeschin.1.21. 2. *crier's pay*, Is.*Fr.* 46. **-ειον**, Ion. **-ήϊον**, Dor. **κᾱρύκειον**, τό, *herald's wand*, Hdt.9.100, Th.1.53, *IG*12(8).51.24 (Imbros, ii B.C.), Ph.2.560; κ. συμπεπλεγμένα ἐκ τῶν θαλλῶν, = ἱκετηρίαι, Din.1.18: prov., τὸ κ. ἢ τὴν μάχαιραν 'peace or the sword', Phot.: as signet, *Tab.Heracl.* 1.4, 2.3; **-ιον**, Ar.*Fr.*518, Hsch. s.v. δράκοντα; also with ῠ, *AP* 11.124 (Nicarch.). 2. the constellation *Caduceus*, Hipparch.ap. Gem.3.13 (-ιον codd.), Vett.Val.7.6. II. *tax on auction sales*, *PSI*5.543.59 (iii B.C.), *PEleph.*14.12 (iii B.C.); *auctioneer's fee*, *SIG* 1011.23 (Chalcedon, iii/ii B.C.), Suid.; φέρειν ἠξίου κηρύκιον stooped to win a *tale-bearer's fee*, Jul.*Or.*2.96a. III. *the stone* whence the herald made his proclamations, Hsch., Suid. IV. *surgical machine*, Orib.49.4.64. **-ειος**, ον, *of a herald*, γράμμα S.*Fr.* 784; γραφή Anon.ap.Suid. II. **Κᾱρυκήϝιος**, ὁ, Boeot. title of Apollo, *Schwyzer* 440.10,11 (Tanagra, Thebes, vi B.C.). **-ευμα**, ατος, τό, *proclamation, message*, A.*Th.*651. **-ευσις**, εως, ἡ, = κηρυκεία, Suid. **-εύω**, *perform the office of a herald*, Pl.*Lg.*941a, Aeschin.1.19; κ. τινί *to be* his *herald*, Lycurg. in *Gött.Nachr.*1922.45, Philoch.36: c. gen., κ. τῆς βουλῆς *IG*3.1128 (ii A.D.). II. trans., *proclaim, notify*, τινί τι A.*Supp.*221, cf. E.*Tr.*787 (anap.). **-ηΐη**, **-ήϊον**, Ion. for κηρυκεία, -ειον. **-ίδαι**, v. κῆρυξ I. 1a. **-ικός**, ή, όν, *of heralds*, φῦλον, ἔθνος, Pl.*Plt.*260d, 290b: ἡ -κή (sc. τέχνη) ib.260e. **-ῖνος**, η, ον, *of a herald*, ῥάβδος Suid. II. **-ίνη**, ἡ, = κηρύκαινα, Hsch., Phot.; but (sc. ἀρχή), *crier's office*, *CPR*232.29 (ii/iii A.D.). **-ιοειδής** (-κοειδ- cod.), ές, *like a herald's staff*, Hsch. s.v. Ἑρμῆς. **-ιον**, τό, v. κηρύκειον. II. *eye-salve*, Alex.Trall. 2. III. in pl., *sharp, pointed stones*, Paul.Aeg.6.88. **-ιοφόρος**, ον, *bearing a herald's staff*, *EM*812.26 (prob.), *Gloss.* **-τικός**, ή, όν, = κηρυκικός, Gal.1.227. **-τός**, ή, όν, *announced by public herald*, στέφανος Inscr.cit.ad *BMus.Inscr.*1032.10, *BCH*17.545. **-ώδης**, ες, *like* (*that of*) *the trumpet-shell* κῆρυξ (II), Arist.*HA*527ᵃ28.

κηρύλος [ῠ], ὁ, fabulous sea-bird, sts. identified with ἀλκυών, or the male of that species (cf. Antig.ap.Hsch.), Alcm.26.2, Archil.141 (cf. 49 D.), Arist.*HA*593ᵇ12, Clearch.73, Ael.*NA*5.48: **κειρύλος**, Ar. *Av.*300 (cf. Sch. ad loc., Hsch.), applied to the barber Sporgilos (from κείρω).

κήρῡνος, ὁ, *a throw of the dice*, Eub.57.2; **κάρυννος**, Phot.

κῆρυξ, ῡκος, ὁ, Aeol. **κᾶρυξ** [ᾱ] Sapph.*Supp.*20a.2, Pi.*N.*8.1:—but **κήρῡκος**, ου, ὁ, *EM*775.26: (κηρύσσω):—*herald, pursuivant*: generally, *public messenger, envoy*, κ. λιγύφθογγοι Il.2.50, al.; κηρύκων, οἳ δημιοεργοὶ ἔασιν Od.19.135; κ., Διὸς ἄγγελοι ἠδὲ καὶ ἀνδρῶν 1.334; θεῶν κ., of Hermes, Hes.*Op.*80, cf. *Th.*939, A.*Ag.* 515, *Ch.*124: distd. from πρέσβεις, as being *messengers between nations at war*, Sch.Th.1.29, cf. A.*Supp.*727, Pl.*Lg.*941a, D.12.4: used interchangeably with ἀπόστολος, Hdt.1.21: as pr. n. of a family at Athens, Th.8.53, And.1.116, Paus.1.38.3, Poll.8.103; functioning as μάγειροι at festivals, Clidem.3, 17; Κηρυκίδαι Phot. b. as fem., Pi.*N.*8.1, Nonn.*D.*4.11. 2. *crier*, who made proclamation and kept order in assemblies, etc., Ar.*Ach.*42 sq.; ὁ κ. ἀνεῖπεν And.1.36, etc.; ὁ τῶν μυστῶν κ., at Eleusis, X.*HG*2.4.20, cf. *SIG*845 (Eleusis, iii A.D.), Philostr.*VS*2.33.4. 3. *auctioneer*, ὑπὸ κήρυκος πωλεῖν Thphr.*Fr.*97; ἀπέδοτο πάντα τὰ ἔργα ὑπὸ κήρυκα *IPE*1².32*B*35 (Olbia, iii B.C.), cf. *PHib.*1.29.21 (iii B.C.); ἀποδίδοσθαι ὑπὸ κήρυκι Ammon. *Diff.*p.81 V. (v.l. ὑπὸ κήρυκα Ptol.Asc.p.399 H.). 4. generally, *messenger, herald*, θεοὶ κήρυκες ἀγγέλλουσι S.*OC*1511, cf. E.*El.*347; of the cock, Ar.*Ec.*30; of writing, Id.*Th.*780 (anap.); κ. καὶ τάφος εἰμὶ βροτοῦ *IG*14.1618; of Homer, ἡρώων κάρυκ' ἀρετᾶς ib.1188: metaph., κ. καὶ ἀπόστολος 1*Ep.Ti.*2.7, al. II. *trumpet-shell*, e.g. *Triton nodiferum*, and smaller species, Arist.*HA*528ᵃ10, al., Hp.*Vict.*2.48, Diocl.*Fr.*133, Macho ap.Ath.8.349c, Gal.4.670, Alciphr.1.7, Alex. Trall.3.7. [ῡ exc. acc. pl. κήρῠκας Antim.19 (s.v.l.), cf. κηρῠκιον *AP* 11.124 (Nicarch.): but accented κῆρυξ, Hdn.Gr.1.44, etc.] (Cf. Skt. *kārús* 'poet', *kīrtis* 'fame'.)

κήρυξις, εως, ἡ, *proclaiming*, as a subject of competition, D.C.63.8, 14.

κηρύσσω, Att. **-ττω**, Dor. **κᾱρύσσω**: impf. ἐκήρυσσον Il.2.444, Th. 1.27, -υττον And.1.112: fut. -ύξω Ar.*Ec.*684, Dor. καρυξῶ Id.*Ach.* 748: aor. ἐκήρυξα Hdt.1.194 (ἀπο-), etc., Aeol. part. καρύξαισα Pi.*I.*4 (3).25: pf. κεκήρῡχα (ἐπι-) D.19.35:—Pass., fut. κηρυχθήσομαι X. *Cyr.*8.4.4, Aeschin.3.230, κηρύξομαι E.*Ph.*1631: aor. ἐκηρύχθην S. *OT*737, etc.: pf. κεκήρυγμαι E.*Fr.*1, Th.4.38:—*to be a herald, officiate as herald*, κηρύσσων γήρασκε Il.17.325. b. *to be an auctioneer*, D. 44.4. 2. *make proclamation as a herald*, λαὸν κηρύσσοντες ἀγειρόντων let them convene the people *by voice of herald*, Il.2.438, cf. 444, Od.2.8; κήρυσσε, κῆρυξ A.*Eu.*566, etc.: impers., ἐκήρυξε (sc. ὁ κῆρυξ) τοῖς Ἕλλησι συσκευάζεσθαι *proclamation was made*.., X.*An.*3.4. 36; κηρυξάτω Id.*Cyr.*4.5.42. II. c. acc. pers., *summon by herald*, κ. ἀγορήνδε..Ἀχαιούς Il.2.51, Od.2.7; πόλεμόνδε Il.2.443; κ. τινά *summon* one to a place, Ar.*Ach.*748:—Pass., τίς ἐκηρύχθη πρώτην φυλακήν; who *was summoned* to the first watch? E.*Rh.*538 (anap.). 2. *proclaim* as conqueror, Plu.2.185a; Φαβωρῖνον ἡ εὐγλωττία ἐν σοφισταῖς ἐκήρυττεν Philostr.*VS*1.8.1:—Pass., μήτε κηρυχθήσεσθαι μήτε ἆθλα λήψεσθαι X.*Cyr.*8.4.4; ὥστε τὴν πόλιν κηρυχθῆναι καὶ αὐτὸν στεφανωθῆναι Lys.19.63; *proclaim* as a criminal, D.25.56, cf. S.*El.*606; κηρύσσω τὸν Ἔρωτα *AP*5.176 (Mel.):—Pass., of a country, *to be proclaimed, extolled*, στεφάνοις ἀρετᾶς E.*Tr.*223 (lyr.). 3. *call upon, invoke*, θεούς Id.*Hec.*146 (anap.); κηρύξας δαίμονας κλύειν A.*Ch.*124a:—Pass., *to be called*, τοῦ κεκήρυξαι πατρός; E.*Fr.*1; κηρυσσομένοισι..ἀπ' ἐσθλῶν δωμάτων Id.*Andr.*772 (lyr.). III. c. acc. rei, *proclaim, announce*, τινί τι A.*Ag.*1349, *Ch.*4, 1026; αὐδάν E.*Ion* 911 (lyr.); ἀγῶνας Ἀργείοισι S.*Aj.*1240; *proclaim* or *advertise* for sale, etc., Hdt.6.121 (Pass.), Plu.2.207a, etc.; κ. ἀποικίαν *proclaim* a colony, i.e. *invite* people to join as colonists, Th.1.27; κ. ὃς βούλοιτο.. *make proclamation* for some one who would.., Hdt.2.134:—Pass., of a crime, *to be proclaimed*, Antipho 2.3.2; τὰ κεκηρυγμένα Th.4.38. 2. *declare, tell*, τοῦτ' ἐκηρύχθη πόλει this *news was spread* in.., S.*OT*l.c.; τοῦτο κ. πόθι παῖς ναίει Id.*Tr.*97 (lyr.); ὃ εἰς τὸ οὖς ἀκούετε, κηρύξατε ἐπὶ τῶν δωμάτων *Ev.Matt.*10.27: abs., S.*El.* 1105. 3. *proclaim, command publicly*, τινί τι A.*Th.*1048, S.*Ant.* 32, 450, etc.; εὐφημίαν, σιγὴν κ., Id.*Fr.*893, E.*Hec.*530: c. dat. pers. et inf., κ. αὐτοῖς ἐμβαλεῖν κώπαισι Pi.*P.*4.200; ἐκήρυξαν, εἰ βούλονται, τὰ ὅπλα παραδοῦναι Th.4.37:—Pass., ᾔδησθα κηρυχθέντα μὴ πράσσειν τάδε; S.*Ant.*447. 4. of a cock, *crow*, *AP*5.2 (Antip. Thess.). IV. *preach, teach publicly*, *Ev.Matt.*3.1, al.

κηρ-ώδης, ες, *wax-like*, dub.l. for κηριώδης, Gal.10.476 (Comp.); = μαλθώδης, Id.19.120. **-ωμα**, ατος, τό, = κηρωτή, *wax-salve, cerate*, Hp.*Acut.*(*Sp.*)15, 33 (both pl.), Orib.*Fr.*63 (pl.). 2. *layer of mud* or *clay forming the floor of the wrestling-ring* in the times of the Empire, Lat. *ceroma, locus exercitii utilis..aequali et molli ceromate stratus*, Cael.Aur.*Salut.Praec.*35 (ed. V. Rose *Anecd.Gr.*2.199), cf. Plu.2.638c, Plin.*HN*35.168, Mart.4.19.5, al.; *a ceromate nos haphe excepit*, out of the *mud* into the dust, Sen.*Ep.*57.1: metaph. for *the wrestling-ring* or *wrestling*, ἐν παλαίστραις καὶ κηρώμασι Plu.2.790f, cf. Plin.*HN*35.5. 3. *waxed tablet* or *board*, *IG*7.413.59 (S. C. de Orop.). **-ωματικός**, ὁ, *one who deals in* κηρώματα 1, *POxy.*43ᵛ iii 21 (iii/iv A.D.); Lat. *ceromaticus*, *of* or *with a* κήρωμα 1, *defricationes*, Cass.Fel.55; but, *bespattered with* κήρωμα 2, Juv.3.68. **-ωματιστής**, οῦ, ὁ, *one who anoints with* κήρωμα 1, Sch.Ar.*Eq.*490. **-ών**, ῶνος, ὁ, (κηρός) *bee-hive*, Sch.Ar.*Ec.*737. **-ωσις**, εως, ἡ, *material of bees-wax*, Arist.*HA*553ᵇ28. **-ωτάριον**, τό, *wax plaster*, Sor.1.50, Damocr.ap.Gal.13.225.

κηρωτή, ἡ, (κηρόω) = κήρωμα 1, *cerate* or *salve*, used medically, Hp.*Off.*12, *Art.*14, Ar.*Ach.*1176, Ph.*Bel.*96.18; κ. οἰνανθίνη, ῥοδίνη, Dsc.1.109, 2.110; κ. ὑγρά Gal.11.391; used as a cosmetic, Ar.*Fr.* 320.1.

κηρωτο-ειδής, ές, *like a cerate*, Gal.13.118, Aët.16.61; **-ώδης**, ες, Gal.12.813. **-μάλαγμα** [μᾰ], ατος, τό, *wax plaster*, Id.13.1006.

κησσόν· εὔοδμον, Hsch. (i. e. κηῶεν). **κῆτα**, ἡ, = καλαμίνθη, Id. (cf. καιετάεις).

κητ-εία, ἡ, *fishing for large fish*, esp. *the tunny*, Ael.*NA*13.16. 2. *the place where it is carried on*, Str.5.4.4 (pl.), Ath.7.283c (pl.). **-ειος**, ον, (κῆτος) *of sea monsters*, νῶτα Mosch.2.119; γέννες Nonn.*D.*39. 240; πέλωρα *Inscr.Perg.*324.28: generally, *monstrous*, Hsch. II. Κήτειοι, οἱ, an unknown race in Mysia, Od.11.521, cf. Str.13.1. 70. **-ημα**, ατος, τό, *salted tunny*, = ὠμοτάριχος, dub. in Diph.Siph. ap.Ath.3.121b. **-ήνη·** πλοῖον μέγα ὡς κῆτος, Hsch.

κήτιον, = γήτειον, used as an emetic, Cratin.266. II. v. κῄθιον.

κητό-δορπος συμφορά, ἡ, *supplying food for sea-monsters*, Lyc. 954. **-θηρεῖον** (-θήριον codd.), τό, *magazine of implements for the fishery of large fish*, Ael.*NA*13.16. **-ομαι**, Pass., *grow to a sea-monster*, ib.14.23.

κῆτος, εος, τό, *any sea-monster* or *huge fish*, δελφῖνάς τε κύνας τε καὶ εἴ ποθι μεῖζον ἕλῃσι κῆτος Od.12.97, cf. 5.421, Il.20.147, Mosch.2. 116; of seals, Od.4.446, 452; of the monster to which Andromeda was exposed, E.*Fr.*121, cf. Ar.*Nu.*556, *Th.*1033; of the tunny, Archestr.*Fr.*34.3. 2. in Natural History, of the spouting *cetacea*,

Arist.*HA*566^{b}2, *PA*669^{a}8, 697^{a}16. II. name of a constellation, Arat.354, Eudox.ap.Hipparch.1.2.20.

κητο-τρόφος, ον, *nourishing sea-monsters*, Eust.294.16. **-φάγος** [ᾰ], ον, *eating sea-monsters*, prob. f.l. for σιτοφάγος, Paus.10.12.3. **-φόνος**, ον, *killing sea-monsters*, *AP*6.38 (Phil.), Opp.*H*.5.113.

κητ-ώδης, ες, of fish, *cetaceous*: τὰ κ. *animals of the whale kind*, Arist.*Resp*.476^{b}13, cf. *HA*591^{b}26; of *coarse* fishes (dogfish, etc.), Gal.6.728, Xenocr.ap.Orib.2.58.84, Alex.Trall.1.15. II. generally, *monstrous*, ἐλέφαντες καὶ ἄλλα ζῷα κ. D.S.2.54. **-ώεις**, εσσα, εν, Homeric epith. of Lacedaemon, κοίλη Λακεδαίμων κητώεσσα Il.2.581, Od.4.1; perh. *full of hollows* or *ravines*, variously expld. ap. Str.8.5.7, Apollon.*Lex*., etc.; cf. καιετάεσσα. II. in later Ep., *cavernous*, of the wooden horse, Q.S.12.314. 2. = κήτειος, πώεα Nonn.*D*.43.251; φάλαγξ ib.1.274.

κῆϋξ, ῡκος [ῡ], v. κήξ.

κήϋος, α, ον, perh. *purificatory*, or *burnt* (καίω), θύεν τρικτεύαν κηύαν *IG*2^2.1126.34 (Amphict. Delph.); cf. κεῖα, κηΐα.

Κηφεύς, έως, ὁ, *Cepheus*, Hdt.7.61, etc.: name of a constellation, Eudox.ap.Hipparch.1.2.11.

κηφήν, ῆνος, ὁ, *drone*, Diph.126.7, Arist.*HA*553^{b}5, 624^{b}12; κηφήνεσσι εἴκελος ὀργήν, of a *lazy vagabond*, Hes.*Op*.304, cf. *Th*.595, Ar.*V*.1114; ὡς ἐν κηρίῳ κ. ἐγγίγνεται Pl.*R*.552c; of literary plagiarists, *AP*7.708 (Diosc.), Plu.2.42a: metaph., of worn-out, decrepit persons, ποῦ γαίας δουλεύσω γραῦς, ὡς κ.; E.*Tr*.192 (lyr.), cf. *Ba*.1365; cf. κόθουροι:—also **καφάν**, Hsch.

Κηφῆνες, οἱ, *Cephenes*, old name of the Persians, Hdt.7.61.

κηφήν-ιον, τό, Dim. of κηφήν, *drone's grub*, Arist.*HA*623^{b}34; *drone's cell*, ib.624^{a}2. **-ώδης**, ες, *like (that of) a drone*, ἐπιθυμία Pl.*R*.554b; of theories, *useless*, *otiose*, Cleom.2.1; of a person, κ. καὶ γέρων γενόμενος Phld.*Mort*.38.

Κηφίσιος, Dor. **Κᾱφ-**, ὁ (sc. μήν), name of month at Cos, *SIG*953.27 (ii B.C.).

Κηφῑσός, Dor. **Κᾱφ-**, ὁ, *Cephisus*, name of various rivers, 1. in Phocis, running into Lake Copais, Il.2.522, Pi.*P*.4.46:—fem. λίμνη **Κηφισίς**, Il.5.709, *h.Ap*.280:—Dor. **Κᾱφ-**, of the nymph Copais, Pi.*P*.12.27:—Adj. **Κηφίσιος**, α, ον, Dor. **Κᾱφ-**, Id.*O*.14.1. 2. at Athens, S.*OC*687 (lyr.), etc. 3. in Argolis, etc., Str.9.3.16, etc.:—freq. written Κηφισσός in codd., but -σ- in derivs. in Att. Inscrr.

κηχί (also **κηχή**, **κῆχυ** Cyr.), = ῥύπος, Hsch.

κῆχος (also **κῆγχος** Hsch., **κηγχός** A.D.*Adv*.184.9), only in phrase ποῖ κ.; which some Gramm. expl. by ποῖ γῆς; *whither away?* some by ποῖ δή; *say whither?* as, ποῖ κ.; Answ. εὐθὺς Σικελίας Ar.*Fr*.656; ποῖ κ.; Answ. ἐγγὺς ἡμερῶν γε τεττάρων Pherecr.165.

κη-ώδης, ες, (κη- cogn. with κηΐα, καίω; -ώδης with ὄδωδα) *smelling as of incense*, *fragrant*, μιν κηώδεϊ δέξατο κόλπῳ Il.6.483; κηώδεα φύετο πάντα D.P.941; cf. κεώδης. **-ώεις**, εσσα, εν, = foreg., ἐν θαλάμῳ εὐώδεϊ κηώεντι Il.3.382; ἐς θάλαμον... κηώεντα 6.288, etc.; μύρον *AP*7.218.9 (Antip. Sid.); ἄνθεα Nonn.*D*.12.257: neut. κηῶεν Hsch.; cf. κεῶεν.

κία· ἡ μέθη, Cyr., Zonar.

κιάθω, lengthd. for κίω, only in compd. μετακιάθω (exc. ἐκίαθεν Hsch.); cf. κίατο. **κιανθείς**· ἑταίρα κιανγάλη (λίαν καλή Mein.), Hsch. **κιάντωρ**· κιναιδῶς, Id. **κίασθαι**· κεῖσθαι, and **κίατο**· ἐκινεῖτο, Id. **κίβαλος**· διάκονος, Id. **κίββα**· πήρα (Aetol.), Id.

κιβδηλ-εία, ἡ, *adulteration*, Pl.*Lg*.916d, 920c. **-ευμα**, ατος, τό, *an adulteration*, ib.917e. **-εύω**, *adulterate*, κ. τὸ νόμισμα Arist.*EN*1165^{b}12: metaph., τὸ ἀρετῆς νόμισμα Ph.1.241; [νομίσματα] οὐ κεκιβδηλευμένα Ar.*Ra*.721; of merchandise, Pl.*Lg*.917b. II. metaph., εὖ κ. τι *trick* it *out*, E.*Ba*.475; *counterfeit*, τἀληθῆ Max.Tyr.28.3; τὴν ἀληθῆ προφητείαν Ph.2.343, cf.1.156 (Pass.). **-ία**, Ion. **-ίη**, ἡ, *adulteration*, *dishonesty*, Ar.*Av*.158, D.C.52.35; *charlatanry*, κ. δημοειδής Hp.*Art*.78. **-ιάω**, prop. *look like adulterated gold*: metaph., *look bilious*, *have the jaundice*, Arist.*Pr*.859^{b}1. **-ος**, ον, *adulterated*, *base*, esp. of coin, χρυσοῦ κιβδήλοιο καὶ ἀργύρου Thgn.119, cf. E.*Med*.516; στατῆρες κ. *IG*2^2.1388.61; κ. λόγος τοῦ τόκου Pl.*R*.507a; τιμαί, opp. ἀληθεῖς, Id.*Lg*.728d; ἐν δὲ κιβδήλῳ τόδε this may prove *false*, E.*El*.550; τὸ σὰν κίβδαλον *spurious*, Pi.*Dith*.2.3; ἱμάτιον ἐκ δύο ὑφασμένον κ. Lxx *Le*.19.19. II. metaph., *fraudulent*, *dishonest*, opp. ἀληθής, of men, Thgn.117; κίβδηλον (cj. -λοι) .. ἦθος ἔχοντες Id.965; τοῦτο θεὸς κιβδηλότατον ποίησε Id.123; κ. καὶ ἀπατεών, κ. καὶ ἀγαθοφανέες, Democr.63, 82; δίκαιον Arist.*Rh*.1375^{b}6; of oracles, etc., *deceitful*, Hdt.1.66, 75, 5.91, Max.Tyr.28.3 (Sup.); of women, κ. ἀνθρώποις κακόν E.*Hipp*.616; κ. ἐπιτηδεύματα Pl.*Lg*.918a. (Poll.7.99 cites **κίβδος**, = *dross* or *alloy of gold*; Sch.Ar.*Av*.158 expl. κιβδηλία as *the dross of silver*; Hsch. also cites **κίβδης**, = κακοῦργος, ⟨κά⟩πηλος, χειροτέχνης, and Poll. **κίβδωνες** (v.l. κιβδῶνες Phot.), = μεταλλεῖς, *miners*.)

κιβικία, sine expl., Hsch.; cf. κιμβικία. **κιβίνδα**· κατὰ νώτου, Id.; cf. κυβησίνδα.

κίβῑσις [κῐ], ἡ, Cypr. for πήρα (Hsch.), *pouch*, *wallet*, such as Perseus wore, Hes.*Sc*.224, Pherecyd.11 J., Call.*Fr*.177 (**κίβησις** Suid., Orion 87; **κύβεσις** and **κυβησία** Hsch.; cf. κίββα).

κιβλεῦραι· στοχάσασθαι, Hsch. **κίβος**, v. κιβωτός.

κῑβώριον, τό, *seed-vessel of the* κολοκασία, a kind of *Nymphaea*, containing the κύαμος Αἰγύπτιος, Nic.*Fr*.81.3, D.S.1.34, *POxy*.105.18 (ii A.D.); κ. ἢ κιβώτιον Dsc.2.106; of the plant itself, Sor.1.57. II. *cup*, either from the material or the shape, Did.ap.Ath.11.477f, Hegesand.21; used liturgically, *PMag.Par*.1.1110.

κῑβωτ-άριον, Dim. of κιβωτός, *small box* or *chamber*, Hero *Aut*.28.4, cf. *CIG*2860 ii 12 (Milet.). **-ίδιον**, τό, = foreg., *IG*11(2).147 *B*10 (Delos, iv B.C.). **-ιον**, τό, = foreg., Ar.*Pl*.711, Arist.*Metaph*.1042^{b}18, *IG*1^2.330.20, 2^2.1388.75, Plu.*Alex*.26, *CPR*22.8 (ii A.D.); *box* for drawing lots, Arist.*Ath*.63.2; *voting-urn*, *SIG*418 *A*7 (Delph., iii B.C.); *ark*, Luc.*Tim*.3.

κῑβωτο-ειδής, ές, *like a chest*, Hsch. s.v. θίβη. **-ποιός**, ὁ, *maker of chests*, Plu.2.580e.

κῑβωτός, ἡ, *box*, *chest*, *coffer*, Hecat.368 J., Simon.239, Eup.228.4, Ar.*Eq*.1000, *V*.1056 (anap.), Lys.12.10, Thphr.*Char*.18.4, *IG*2^2.1388.73; κ. δίθυρος, τετράθυρος, ib.1^2.330; ἱερά, δημοσία κ., *Inscr.Délos* 442 *A* 2, 75 (ii B.C.); Noah's *ark*, Lxx *Ge*.6.14; the *ark* of Moses, ib.*Ex*.25.9(10), al.; πέπτωκεν εἰς κ. has been deposited in the *archives*, *UPZ* 126 (iii B.C.), etc.; opp. κίστη (q.v.). (Perh. a v.l. in Il.24.228, cf. Sch.ad loc. Suid. cites **κίβος** as the radic. form.)

κίγκαλος, v. κίγκλος.

κίγκασος, ὁ, name of a throw at dice, Hsch.; cf. κίκκασος.

κιγκλ-ίζω, *wag the tail*, as the bird κίγκλος does: metaph., *change constantly*, οὐ χρὴ κιγκλίζειν ἀγαθὸν βίον, ἀλλ' ἀτρεμίζειν Thgn.303. **-ίς**, ίδος, ἡ, mostly in pl. κιγκλίδες, *latticed gates* in the δικαστήριον or βουλευτήριον, by which the δικασταί or βουλευταί were admitted to pass through the δρύφακτοι or bar, Ar.*Eq*.641, *V*.124: metaph., ῥητορεία κιγκλίδων ἐπιδέουσα καὶ βήματος requiring *the practice of the bar* and the assembly, Plu.2.975c: sg., Lib.*Or*.12.38; ἐντὸς τῆς κ. διατρίβειν live *in court*, Luc.*Merc.Cond*.21; αἱ διαλεκτικαὶ κ. logical *quibbles*, behind which one ensconces oneself, Jul.*Caes*.330c. 2. *any latticed gates*, *IG*2^2.1668.65 (sg.), 3.162 (pl.). II. later, = δρύφακτοι, Plu.*Caes*.68: sg., Id.*Galb*.14. III. prob. = Lat. *fidiculae*, an instrument of torture, Id.*Luc*.20. **-ῐσις**, εως, ἡ, *quick*, *jerking movement*, Hp.*Art*.71. **-ισμός**, ὁ, = foreg., ib.14; = τάραχος, Men.478.

κιγκλοβάτης [ᾰ], ου, ὁ, *moving like the* κίγκλος, *jerking*, Ar.*Fr*.140.

κίγκλος, ὁ, prob. *dabchick*, *Podiceps ruficollis*, Ar.*Fr*.29, Autocr.1, Anaxandr.41.66, Arist.*HA*593^{b}5: prov., κίγκλου πτωχότερος 'poor as a church mouse', because it had no nest of its own, Men.221, cf. Ael.*NA*12.9:—Suid. has **κίγκαλος**, but κιγκάλους is unmetrical as a fish-name in Numen.ap.Ath.7.326a.

κιγκράμας, = κύχραμος, Hsch.

κίγκρημι, = κεράννυμι, Dor. 3 sg. κίγκρητι Orph.*Fr*.32(b) iv 2; cf. κίγκρα· κίρνα, Hsch.

κιγχάνω [ᾰ], v. κιχάνω [ᾱ]. **κίδαλον**, τό, *onion*, Hsch.

κίδᾰρις, εως, ἡ, *Persian head-dress*, prob. = τιάρα, κυρβασία, Ph.2.152, 155, Poll.7.58, etc.:—also **κίταρις** in Ctes.*Fr*.29.47, Plu.*Art*.28, *Pomp*.42, etc.; Cypr. **κίτταρις** Hsch. 2. *turban of Jewish high priest*, Lxx *Ex*.28.4, al. II. *an Arcadian dance*, Ath.14.631d.

κίδᾰφος, η, ον, *wily*, Hsch.:—as Subst. **κίδαφος**, **κιδάφη** (cf. σκιδάφη), **κινδάφη**, **κινδάφιος**, = σκίνδαφος, Id., cf. Phot.; **κιδᾰφεύω**, = πανουργέω, Hsch.

κίδναι, αἱ, *roasted barley*, Hsch. (fort. κίδραι = τὰ χίδρα).

κίδναμαι, Pass. of κίδνημι (only found in the compd. ἐπικ-), poet. for σκεδάννυμαι, used only in pres. and impf., *to be spread abroad* or *over*, of the dawning day, ὑπεὶρ ἅλα κίδναται ἠώς Il.23.227, cf. 8.1; ὀδμὰ κατὰ χῶρον κ. Pi.*Fr*.129.6; κιδναμέναν μελιαδέα γᾶρυν prob. in Simon.41: once in Trag., ὕπνος ἐπ' ὄσσοις κ. E.*Hec*.916 (lyr., v.l. for σκίδ-); κολοιῶν κρωγμὸς ... κιδνάμενος *AP*7.713 (Antip.).

κιδνόν· ἐνθάδε (Paph.), Hsch.

κιείνησις, εως, ἡ, coined as etym. of κίνησις, Pl.*Cra*.426d.

κιέλλη, ἡ, *radiance*, *hoar-frost*, or *mist*, Hsch. **κιθάναλλον**, v. κιττάναλον.

κῐθάρ-α, Ion. **-η** [θᾰ], ἡ, *lyre*, Hdt.1.24, Epich.79, E.*Ion*882 (anap.), etc.; cf. κίθαρις. II. = κίθαρος, *thorax*, *Hippiatr*.46: in pl., *ribs* of the horse, ib.38. **-ᾰοιδός**, ὁ, poet. uncontr. form of κιθαρῳδός: Sup. -ότατος Ar.*V*.1278, Eup.293:—late Boeot. **κιθαραϝυδός** *IG*7.3195.19 (Orchom.). **-ηφόρος**, ὁ, *Lycian coin stamped with a cithara*, *Ath.Mitt*.14.412 (Myra). **-ίζω**, Att. fut. -ιῶ Antiph.141: (κίθαρις):—*play the cithara*, φόρμιγγι .. ἱμερόεν κιθάριζε Il.18.570, Hes.*Sc*.202; λύρῃ δ' ἐρατὸν κιθαρίζων *h.Merc*.423; ἕρπει ἄντα τῶ σιδάρω τὸ καλῶς κιθαρίσδεν Alcm.35, cf. X.*Smp*.3.1, *Oec*.2.13; ᾄδειν καὶ κ. Phld.*Mus*.7 K.; κιθαρίζειν οὐκ ἐπίσταμαι I am not a 'high-brow', Ar.*V*.989, cf. 959; ἀρχαῖον εἶν' ἔφασκε τὸ κ. Id.*Nu*.1357: prov., ὄνος κιθαρίζειν πειρώμενος, like ὄνος πρὸς λύραν (v. λύρα), Luc.*Pseudol*.7; τὸ κιθαριζόμενον *music composed for the cithara*, Plu.2.1144d. **-ιον**, τό, Dim. of κίθαρος II, Ptol.Euerg.9 J. **-ις**, ιος, ἡ, acc. κίθαριν, = κιθάρα, Hom. (who never uses the latter form), Od.1.153, al., cf. Alc.*Supp*.17, Pi.*P*.5.65, Ar.*Th*.124 (lyr.). II. *playing on the cithara*, οὐκ ἄν τοι χραισμῇ κ. Il.3.54, cf. Od.8.248; κ. καὶ ἀοιδή Il.13.731. **-ῐσις**, εως, ἡ, *playing on the cithara*, Pl.*Prt*.325e; κ. ψιλή, i.e. without the voice, Id.*Lg*.669e, cf. *Pae.Delph*.15; αὔλησις καὶ κ. Phld.*Mus*.p.23 K. **-ισμα** [ᾰ], ατος, τό, *that which is played on the cithara*, *a piece of music for it*, Pl.*Prt*.326b, Max.Tyr.7.6, Ach.Tat.2.1, D.C.63.26; κ. ἐκ Βακχῶν Εὐριπίδου *SIG*648 *B*8 (Delph., ii B.C.). **-ισμός**, ὁ, = κιθάρισις, Call.*Del*.312. **-ιστέον**, *one must play the cithara*, Pl.*Sis*.389c. **-ιστήριος**, α, ον, *used to accompany the cithara*, αὐλός Ephor.3 J., Aristox.*Fr.Hist*.67. II. Subst. **-τήριον**, τό, *performance on the cithara*, *BGU*1125.26 (pl., i B.C.). **-ιστής**, οῦ, ὁ, *player on the cithara*, *h.Hom*.25.3, Hes.*Th*.95, Ar.*Eq*.992 (lyr.), *Nu*.964, Arist.*Po*.1455^{a}3, *OGI*51.43, etc. II. κ. λίθος stone at Megara *which rang* on being struck, *APl*.4.279 tit. **-ιστικός**, ή, όν, *skilled in cithara-playing*, Pl.*Hp.Mi*.375b (in Comp. -ώτερος), *Ion* 540d, etc.: ἡ -κή (sc. τέχνη) *art of cithara-playing*, Id.*Grg*.501e, Arist.*Po*.1447^{a}15. Adv.

-κῶς Plu.2.404f. **-ίστρια**, ἡ, fem. of κιθαριστής, Arist.*Ath*.50.2, Theopomp.Hist.111a, Theophil.12.5, *AJA* 18.1 (Sardis, iii/ii B.C.), *IG* 12(8).178 (Samothrace); name of a play by Anaxandrides. **-ιστρίς**, ίδος, ἡ, = foreg., Nic.Dam.66.26 J. (pl.), Lemma to *AP* 5.221 (Agath.). **-ιστύς**, ύος, ἡ, *the art of playing the cithara*, ἐκλέλαθον κιθαριστύν Il.2.600, cf. Phanocl.1.21. (Ion. word.) **-ος**, ὁ, = θώραξ II, *chest*, Hp.*Loc.Hom*.3, etc. II. kind of *flatfish*, sacred to Apollo, Epich.65, Pherecr.39, Call.Com.3, Arist.*HA* 508ᵇ17, *Fr*.319, Opp.*H*.1.98. (Derived from Κιθαιρών by Duris 80 J.)

κῐθᾰρῳδ-έω, *sing to the cithara*, Pl.*Grg*.502a. **-ησις**, εως, ἡ, *singing to the cithara*, D.C.63.8. **-ία**, ἡ, = foreg., Pl.*Lg*.700d (pl.), *Ion* 533b. **-ικός**, ή, όν, *of* or *for cithara-playing*, νόμοι Ar.*Ra*.1282; ᾠδή Pl.*Lg*.722d; ἡ ὑποδωριστὶ -ωτάτη τῶν ἁρμονιῶν Arist.*Pr*.922ᵇ15: ἡ -κή (sc. τέχνη), = κιθαρῳδία, Pl.*Grg*.502a. Adv. -κῶς Phlp.*in de An*.153.29. **-ός**, ὁ, (κιθάρα, ἀοιδός) *one who plays and sings to the cithara*, Hdt.1.23, *IG* 1².547, Pherecr.6.1, Phld.*Mus*.p.28 K., etc.: as fem., κ. γυνή Alciphr.3.33. II. *a fish*, found in the Red Sea, with body striped like the strings of a lyre, Ael.*NA* 11.23.

κίθρα, ἡ, dub. sens., τῆς (τὰς) ἐκ κίθρας σταφυλῆς (-λάς) Herod. Med. in *Rh.Mus*.58.100,110.

κῐθών, Ion. for χιτών, Hdt.1.8, al., also *POxy*.2149.6 (ii/iii A.D.), etc.:—Dim. **κῐθώνιον** *IG* 2².1464.13, *POxy*.2149.20, etc.; **κῐθωνίσκος** *IG* 2².1523.18.

κιθώνη, Ion., = χιτώνη (q.v.), *Milet*.1(7).202.

κικαῖος· ἴσον ἐλλύχνιον τὸ τῶν καρπῶν λέπος, Hsch.

κίκᾰμα (**κικαμία** Hsch.), ων, τά, *kind of vegetable* resembling καυκαλίς, Nic.*Th*.841. **κικέα**, v. κίκι fin.

κίκελος· τροχός, Hsch. **κίκερος**· ὁ χερσαῖος κροκόδειλος, Id.

κίκι, τό (on the accent v. Hdn.Gr.1.354, 2.766; κῖκι codd. Str. et Orib.), *castor-oil*, Hdt.2.94, Pl.*Ti*.60a, *PHib*.1.121.17, al. (iii B.C.), Ruf.ap.Orib.7.26.39, etc.; also, *the castor-oil tree, Ricinus communis*, Str.17.2.5, Dsc.4.161; gen. τοῦ κίκεως Gal.11.649, 12.26; κίκιος Hdn. Gr.2.767; also τῆς κικέας Aët.8.30, Paul.Aeg.7.20.

κικίβαλος, ὁ, kind of *shell-fish*, prob. in Epich.42; cf. κικοβαυλιτίδες.

κικίδιον, v. κηκίδιον. **κίκιμον**· τῆς κορώνης τὸ κόπριον, Hsch.

κίκιννος [κῐκ], ὁ, *ringlet*, Cratin.353, Ar.*V*.1069 (lyr.; cf. Poll.2.28), Theoc.11.10, 14.4, *AP* 5.196 (Mel.), Gal.18(1).790.

κίκῐνος, η, ον, *made from the* κίκι-*tree*, ἔλαιον Dsc.1.32, Gal.11.870.

κίκιον, τό, = κρότωνος ῥίζα, Gal.19.115; = κίκι, cj. in Thphr.*HP* 1.10.1.

κικιουργός, ὁ, *castor-oil worker*, *PTeb*.5.173 (ii B.C.), etc.

κικιοφόρος, ον, *bearing* κίκι, γῆ *PPetr*.3p.135 (cf. p.xvii) (iii B.C.).

κίκιρρος, ὁ, *cock*, Hsch.: **κίκκα**, ἡ, *hen*, Id.

κικκᾰβαῦ, onomatop., *cry in imitation of the screech-owl's note*, Ar. *Av*.261: **κικκάβη**, ἡ, *screech-owl*, Sch.ad loc.; cf. **κικκάμη**, *noctua*, *Gloss*.:—hence **κικκᾰβάζω** (-ίζω Phot.), *shriek like a screech-owl*, cj. Dobree for κακκ- in Ar.*Lys*.761.

κίκκᾰβος, ὁ, name of a small coin used in the nether world, Pherecr.(1p.167 K.) ap.Poll.9.83; also, = κίμβιξ, Phot. s. v. κίμβικας:—hence Dim. **κικκάβιν** (= -βιον)· ἐλάχιστον, οὐδέν, Hsch.

κίκκασος· ὀβολοῦ ὄνομα, Phot.; but ὁ ἐκ τῶν παραμηρίων ἱδρὼς ῥέων, καὶ βόλου ὄνομα, Hsch.; cf. κίγκασος. **κίκκη**· συνουσία, κτλ., Id. **κικκίδαι**· μινδῶνσ.., Id. **κικκιλόνδις**· παιδὸς ἀφόδευμα, Id. **κικκός**· ἀλεκτρυών, κλέπτης, διαχώρησις, Id.

κικλήσκω, poet. redupl. form of καλέω, used only in pres. and impf., *call, summon*, Il.11.606, 17.532, Od.22.397; κλῆδην εἰς ἀγορὴν κ. Il.9.11:—Med., ἄμυδις κικλήσκετο πάντας ἀρίστους 10.300. 2. *invite*, 2.404. 3. *invoke, implore*, 9.569, A.*Supp*.212, 217, *Eu*.508 (lyr.), S.*OT* 209 (lyr.), E.*Tr*.470, etc. II. *accost, address*, ψυχὴν Πατροκλῆος Il.23.221. III. *call by name*, τὴν.. ἄνδρες Βατίειαν κ. 2.813, cf. 14.291; τὸν ἐπίκλησιν κορυνήτην ἄνδρες κ. 7.139, cf. Pi.*P*. 4.119, *Fr*.87.4, A.*Ag*.712 (lyr.), E.*El*.118 (lyr.); οὔνομα Θεσμοφάνην με.. κίκλησκον *IG* 3.1337:—Pass., νῆσός τις Συρίη κικλήσκεται *there is an island called* Συρίη, Od.15.403; ἀφ' οὗ δὴ Ῥήγιον κικλήσκεται A.*Fr*. 402; πατρὸς Στρυμόνος κικλήσκεται E.*Rh*.279, 652.—Also in late Ion. Prose, Aret.*SA* 2.6, *SD* 1.6 (Pass.), al.; cf. κλῄσκω.

κικνία· μικρὰ φθειρία, Hsch. **κίκνωψ**· θηρίον, Id. (cf. κνώψ, κινώπετον). **κικοβαυλιτίδες**· κογχυλίου τι γένος μέλαν, καὶ τὰ ἐκ στέατος σκωλήκια, Id.; cf. κικίβαλος. **κίκους**· ὁ νέος τέττιξ, Id. **κικριβιντίς**· ἀνδράχνη, Id.; cf. κιχληβῶτις.

κῐκῠμίς, ίδος, ἡ, = κικκάβη, *screech-owl*, Lat. *cicuma*, Call.*Fr*.318: **κίκυμος** or **κίκυβος**, ὁ (also = λαμπτήρ), Hsch.

κῐκῠμώ⟨σσ⟩ω, *to be purblind like an owl*, Hsch., cf. Suid.

Κίκυννα [ῐ], ἡ, *Cicynna*, an Attic deme, Theognost.*Can*.101 (-υνα cod.): **Κῐκυννεύς**, έως, ὁ, *an inhabitant thereof*, *IG* 2².1654.32, al., Ar. *Nu*.210: **Κῐκυννόθεν** *from Cicynna*, ib.134: **Κῐκυννοῖ** *at Cicynna*, Lys.17.5.

κῖκυς, ἡ, *strength, vigour*, poet. word, οὐ γάρ οἱ ἔτ' ἦν ἲς ἔμπεδος οὐδέ τι κ. Od.11.393, cf. *h.Ven*.237, Alc.137 (dub.); σοὶ δ' οὐκ ἔνεστι κ. οὐδ' αἱμόρρυτοι φλέβες A.*Fr*.230.

κῑκύω, = ἰσχύω, Hdn.Gr.2.533, *Et.Gud*.321.53, Suid.

***κίκω**, Dor. aor. 1 ἔκιξα, = ἤνεγκα, Simm.26.7; cf. κίξαντες· ἐλθόντες, and κίξατο· εὗρεν, ἔλαβεν, ἤνεγκεν, Hsch.; cf. ἀποκίκω.

κιλάριος· ὁ ἥλιος, Hsch. **κιλίας**· στρουθὸς ἄρσην, Id.

Κῐλῐκ-ῐαρχία, ἡ, *presidency of the provincial council of Cilicia*, *OGI* 578.13 (pl., Tarsus, iii A.D.). **-ίζω** and Med. **-ίζομαι**, *play the Cilician*, i.e. *to be cruel and treacherous like the Cilicians*, Eust.741.21, Hsch. **-ιον**, τό, *coarse cloth*, strictly of Cilician goat's hair, Procop. *Pers*.2.26; used for sails, *PLond*.3.1164ʰ10 (iii A.D.); for mats hung to deaden the impact of missiles, Lat. *cilicium*, *Gloss*. **-ισμός**, ὁ, *Cilician behaviour*, i.e. *drunken butchery*, Theopomp.Hist.289a.

Κίλιξ [ῐ], ῐκος, ὁ, *a Cilician*, mostly in pl., Il.6.397, 415: as fem., Κίλιξ χώρα *Trag.Adesp*.162:—but regul. fem. **Κίλισσα** (q.v.):—Adj. **Κῐλίκιος**, α, ον, A.*Pr*.353; Κ. τράγοι *Com.Adesp*.806; -ιος as fem., Str.2.1.31, Dsc.1.4: ἡ **Κιλικία** (sc. γῆ), *Cilicia*, Hdt.2.34, etc.

Κίλισσα [ῐ], ης, ἡ, *Cilician woman*, A.*Ch*.732; as the name of a slave, Sch.Ar.*Pax* 362. 2. Adj., fem. of Κιλίκιος, νέες Hdt.8.14.

κίλλαι· ἀστράγαλοι, ἢ ὄνοι, Hsch.

κιλλακτήρ, ῆρος, ὁ, *ass-driver*, Dor. word, Poll.7.56, 185.

κιλλαμαρύζειν· κατιλλώπτειν, Hsch.

κιλλίβας [λῐ], αντος, ὁ, mostly in pl. κιλλίβαντες, *three-legged stand* (Sch.Ar.*Ach*.1121, Hsch.), κιλλίβαντες ἀσπίδος a shield-*stand*, Ar. l.c.; *painter's easel*, Poll.7.129; *part of a chariot-frame*, Id.1.143; *bearers* of a platform, Moschio ap.Ath.5.208c, cf. *BGU* 1127.11 (1 B.C.): sg., *stand* or *pedestal* of σαμβύκη II, Bito 58.6 (pl., 62.3); cf. κελλίβας. (κίλλος, βαίνω; cf. *easel* = Germ. *Esel, clothes-horse*, etc.)

Κιλλικύριοι or **Καλλικύριοι**, οἱ, *class of serfs at Syracuse*, Arist. *Fr*.586, prob. in Hdt.7.155.

κίλλιξ, ικος, ὁ, *ox with crooked horns*, Hsch. II. = στάμνος, Id.

κιλλοβόροι, οἱ, = κιλλίβαντες (in a chariot), Poll.1.143.

κίλλος, ὁ, *ass*, *Sammelb*.5224.63 (written **κεῖλος** ib.29, 40), Hsch.; Dor. acc. to Poll.7.56; cf. κίλλαι. 2. = τέττιξ πρωϊνός (Cypr.), Hsch.

κιλλός, ή, όν, *ass-coloured, grey*, θερίστριον Eub.103, cf. Hsch., Phot., Eust.1057.56:—also **κίλλιος**, α, ον, Poll.7.56.

κίλλουρος, ὁ, *wagtail*, Hsch.

κιμαί· χυμὸς πύρινος, and **κιμαός**· χυλὸς μορέας, Hsch.

κιμβ-άζει· στραγγεύεται, Hsch. **-εία**, ἡ, *stinginess*, Arist.*VV* 1251ᵇ5, Hsch. (where for σκιφία read σκνιφία):—prob. f.l. for -ικεία or -ικία, cf. Phot. and Suid. s.v. κίμβικα, Arist. l.c. ap.Stob.3.1. 194. **-εύει**· ὁδοιπορεῖ, Hsch. **-ιξ**, ῑκος, ὁ, *niggard, skinflint*, Xenoph.21, Arist.*EN* 1121ᵇ22, *MM* 1192ᵃ9, *EE* 1232ᵃ14, Chamael.ap. Ath.14.656d, Plu.2.632c. II. metaph., of an author, *fond of petty details*, Ath.7.303e.

κίμερος· νοῦς (Phryg.), Hsch.

κιμμερικόν (sc. ἱμάτιον), τό, *woman's garment*, Ar.*Lys*.45, 52 (κιμβ- cod. R, Hsch.).

Κιμμέριοι, οἱ, *Cimmerians*, a mythical people dwelling beyond the Ocean in perpetual darkness, Od.11.14; later, a nomad people of the steppes, who invaded Asia Minor, Hdt.1.15, etc.:—also **Κίμμεροι**, Lyc.695:—Adj. **Κιμμερικός**, ή, όν, *Cimmerian*: Κ. ἰσθμός *the Crimea*, A.*Pr*.730; Κ. Βόσπορος Str.1.1.10, al.:—also **Κιμμέριος**, α, ον, Hdt.4.12; ἡ Κιμμερίη (sc. γῆ) ibid.: **Κιμμερίς**, ίδος, ἡ, Arist.*Fr*. 478, Apollod.2.1.3.

κίμπτω, = σκίμπτω, Hsch.

Κίμωλος [ῑ], ἡ, *Cimolus*, an island in the Cyclades:—Adj. **Κῑμώλιος**, α, ον, ἰσχάδες Amphis 40: **Κῑμωλία** (with or without γῆ), ἡ, *Cimolian earth*, a white clay, like *fuller's earth*, used in baths and barbers' shops, and in medicine, Ar.*Ra*.713 (lyr.), Str.10.5.1, Dsc.5.156.

Κῑμώνιος, α, ον, *of* or *belonging to Cimon*, ἐν τοῖς Κ. ἐρειπίοις among the ruins of his edifices, Cratin.151. **κίμωσις**, v. κήμωσις.

κῑνάβευμα, ατος, τό, *knavish trick*, in pl., Phot., Hsch.; ἀποκινναβευμάτων is f.l. in Ar.*Fr*.699 (where κᾰνᾰβευμάτων, = κανάβων, is prob. cj.).

κῑνάβρ-α, ἡ, *rank smell of a he-goat*, Luc.*Bis Acc*.10, Poll.2.77; also of men, Luc.*DMar*.1.5, al.; also, *goatish beard*, Id.*DMort*.10.9: metaph., = κιμβεία, Phot. **-άω**, *smell like a goat*, Ar.*Pl*.294. **-εύεσθαι**· σκευωρεῖσθαι, Phot. **-εύματα**· ἀποκαθάρματα ὄζοντα, Hsch.

κῑνάδ-ιον [ᾰ], τό, Dim. of sq., Harp. **-ος**, εος, τό, Sicil. word for *fox* (Sch.Theoc.5.25, cf. *EM* 514.13), Call.Com.1 D.: hence, *cunning rogue*, τοὐπίτριπτον κίναδος S.*Aj*.103; ὦ συκοφάντα καὶ ἐπίτριπτον κ. And.1.99; πυκνότατον κ. Ar.*Av*.430, cf. *Nu*.448, D.18.162, 242, Theoc. l.c. (ὦ κίναδε, ὦ κιναδεῦ codd.): generally, *beast, monster*, Democr.259. **-ρα**· ἀλώπηξ, Hsch.

κῑνάθ-ίας· κρυπτός, Hsch. **-ίζειν**, *hoard as a miser*; also, = μινυρίζειν, κινεῖν, Id.:—hence **-ισμα**, ατος, τό, *rustling motion*, as of wings, A.*Pr*.124 (anap.): **-ισμός**, ὁ, Phot.; also **κίναθος**, = θησαυρισμός, Id.

κῑναιδ-εία, ἡ, *unnatural lust*, Aeschin.1.131, Demetr.*Eloc*.97. **-εύομαι**, *to be a* κίναιδος, Sch.Luc.*JTr*.8. **-ία**, ἡ, = κιναιδεία, Aeschin.2.99, Luc.*Demon*.50, D.C.45.26. **-ίας**, ου, ὁ, stone found in head of κίναιδος II, Plin.*HN* 37.153. **-ίζω**, *practise unnatural vice*, Antioch.Astr. in *Cat.Cod.Astr*.7.113. **-ιον**, τό, = ἴυγξ, Hsch., Phot.; = σεισοπυγίς, Sch.Theoc.2.17. **-ισμα**, ατος, τό, *unnatural lewdness*, Eust.1784.54.

κῑναιδο-γράφος [ᾰ], ον, *writing of obscene things*, *AB* 429, *An.Ox*. 2.318. **-λογέω**, *talk of obscene things*, Str.14.1.41. **-λογία**, ἡ, *obscene talk*, *An.Ox*.2.318. **-λόγος**, ον, *talking of obscene things*, D.L.4.40; *writing obscene books*, Ath.14.620f.

κίναιδ-ος [ῐ], ὁ, *catamite*, Pl.*Grg*.494e, etc.: generally, *lewd fellow*, Herod.2.74, *PSI* 5.483.1 (iii B.C.), Arcesil.ap.Plu.2.126a. 2. *public dancer* (?), *PTeb*.208 (1 B.C.), perh. also *CIG* 4926 (Philae). 3. pl., *obscene poems*, D.L.9.110. II. *a sea-fish*, Plin.*HN* 32.146. III. = κιναίδιον, Gal.12.740, 800. **-ώδης**, ες, *after the fashion of catamites*, κουρά Sch.Ar.*Ach*.849. **-ῶς**, v. κιάντωρ.

κῑνάκης [ᾰ], ὁ, = ἀκινάκης, S.*Fr*.1061.

κινάμον, **κινάμωμον**, v. κιννάμωμον.

κῑνάρ-α [ᾰρ], ἡ, *artichoke, Cynara Scolymus*, Ptol.Euerg.1 J., Colum. 10.235, *BGU* 249.25 (1 A.D.), Dsc.3.8, Ath.2.70a, Gal.6.636; cf. κυνάρα. **-εών**, ῶνος, ὁ, *artichoke-bed*, *PFlor.*50.72 (iii A. D.). **-ηφάγος** [φᾶ], ον, *eating artichokes*, Juba ap.Ath.8.343f.

κιναρύζεσθαι· τὸ θρηνεῖν μετὰ τοῦ γογγύζειν, καὶ κινεῖσθαι, Hsch.

κίναρχος· ἄψυχος, Id.

κῑνᾰχύρα [ῠ], ἡ, *sieve for bolting flour*, Ar.*Ec.*730.

κίνδαλος, ὁ, v. κύνδαλος. **κίνδαξ**, ακος, ὁ, ἡ, = σκίναξ, Hsch., Phot. ***κινδάπτω**, aor. ἐκίνδαψεν· ἔψηλεν, Hsch.; ἐκινδάψα(σ)κεν· ὑπέψηλεν, Id. **κινδαψός**, ὁ, v. σκινδαψός.

κίνδος, ὁ, a fragrant herb, Mnesim.4.63 (anap.).

κίνδυν, ῦνος, ὁ, v. κίνδυνος.

κινδύν-ευμα [ῠ], ατος, τό, *hazard*, *venture*, S.*OC*564, *Ant.*42, E. *IT*1001, Pl.*R.*451a, etc. **-ευτέον**, *one must venture*, ἐν ἀσπίσιν σοι πρῶτα κ. E.*Supp.*572, cf. *IT*1022, Plb.4.11.7: Adj. **-τέος**, α, ον, *Gloss.* **-ευτής**, οῦ, ὁ, *venturesome person*, Th.1.70, D.C.*Fr.*70.6. **-ευτικός**, ή, όν, *venturesome*, *adventurous*, Arist.*Rh.*1367ᵇ4. **-εύω**, fut. -σω Hdt.8.60.α', etc.: pf. κεκινδύνευκα Lys.3.47, Plb.5.61.4:—Pass., mostly in pres.: fut. κινδυνευθήσομαι D.30.10, κεκινδυνεύσομαι Antipho 5.75: aor. and pf., v. infr. 3: (κίνδυνος):—*to be daring*, *run risk*, κ. πρὸς πολλούς, πρὸς τοὺς πολεμίους, Hdt.4.11, X.*Mem.*3.3.14; κ. εἰς τὴν Αἴγυπτον *venture* thither, Pherecr.11. b. abs., *make a venture*, *take a risk*, Hdt.3.69, Ar.*Eq.*1204; *to be in dire peril*, Th.3.28, 6.33, etc.; *to be in danger*, Arist.*EN*1124ᵇ8, etc.; of a sick person, Hp.*Aph.* (*Sp.*)7.82, *Coac.*374; esp. *engage in war*, Isoc.1.43; τοῦ χωρίου κινδυνεύοντος the post *being in peril*, Th.4.8; ὁ κινδυνεύων τόπος the place *of danger*, Plb.3.115.6. 2. c. dat., κ. τῷ σώματι, τῇ ψυχῇ, Hdt.2.120, 7.209; κ. ἁπάσῃ τῇ Ἑλλάδι *run a risk with* all Greece, i. e. endanger it all, Id.8.60.α'; στρατιῇ Id.4.80; τίσιν οὖν ὑμεῖς κινδυνεύσαιτ' ἄν..; *in* what points..? D.9.18; κ. τοῖς ὅλοις πράγμασι, τῷ βίῳ, Plb.1.70.1, 5.61.4; τῷ ζῆν *PTeb.*44.21 (ii B.C.): freq. with Preps., κ. ἐν τοῖς σώμασι Lys.2.63; οὐκ ἐν τῷ Καρὶ ἀλλ' ἐν υἱέσι Pl.*La.*187b (Pass.); κ. περὶ [τῆς Πελοποννήσου] Hdt.8.74; περὶ τῆς ψυχῆς Antipho 2.4.5, Ar.*Pl.*524; περὶ τοῦ σώματος And.1.4; περὶ ἀνδραποδισμοῦ Isoc. 8.37; περὶ τῆς μεγίστης ζημίας Lys.7.15; περὶ τῆς βασιλείας πρὸς Κῦρον D.15.24; περὶ αὐτῷ Antipho 5.6; περὶ τοῖς φιλτάτοις Pl.*Prt.*314a; but κ. περὶ δισχιλίους *go into battle* with a force of 2,000, Eun.*Hist.*p.244 D.; ὑπὲρ καλλίστων Lys.2.79. 3. c. acc. cogn., *venture*, *hazard*, τοὺς ἐσχάτους κινδύνους Antipho 5.82; κινδύνευμα Pl.*R.*451a; μάχην Aeschin.2.169; τὴν ψευδομαρτυρίαν *hazard* a prosecution for perjury, D.41.16 codd. (τῶν -ιῶν Blass):—Pass., *to be ventured* or *hazarded*, μεταβολὴ κινδυνεύεται *there is risk* of change, Th.2.43; ὁποτέρως ἔσται, ἐν ἀδήλῳ κινδυνεύεται *remains in hazardous* uncertainty, Id.1.78; τὰ μέγιστα κινδυνεύεται τῇ πόλει D.19.285; κεκινδυνευμένον *a venturous enterprise*, Pi.*N.*5.14; τὰ κινδυνευθέντα, = τὰ κινδυνεύματα, Lys.2.54; τῶν ἤδη σφίσι καλῶς κεκινδυνευμένων Arr.*An.*2.7.3; τὸ φιλοπόλεμον καὶ κεκ. D.S.2.21. 4. c. inf., *run the risk* of doing or being.., τὸν στρατὸν κινδυνεύσει ἀποβαλεῖν Hdt.8.65; κακόν τι λαβεῖν Id.6.9; ἀπολέσθαι Id.9.89; διαφθαρῆναι Th.3.74; ἀποθανεῖν Pl.*Ap.*28b, etc.; τοῦ συντριβῆναι Lxx *Jn.*1.4; then, b. to express *chance*, i. e. what *may possibly* or *probably happen*: c. pres., pf., or aor. inf., κινδυνεύουσι οἱ ἄνθρωποι οὗτοι γόητες εἶναι they *run a risk of being reputed* conjurers, Hdt.4.105; κινδυνεύσομεν βοηθεῖν we *shall probably have* to assist, Pl. *Tht.*164e, cf. 172c; κ. ἡ ἀληθὴς δόξα ἐπιστήμη εἶναι *seems likely* to be.., ib.187b; κινδυνεύσεις ἐπιδεῖξαι χρηστὸς εἶναι you *will have the chance of* showing your worth, X.*Mem.*2.3.17, cf. 3.13.3; κ. ἀναμφιλογώτατον ἀγαθὸν εἶναι ib.4.2.34, cf. Pl.*Ap.*40b; τὰ συσσίτια κινδυνεύει συναγαγεῖν he *probably* organized the σ., Id.*Lg.*625e; κινδυνεύω πεπονθέναι ὅπερ.. Id.*Grg.*485e: c. fut. inf., dub. in Th.4.117; κινδυνεύει impers., *it may be*, *possibly*, as an affirmat. answer, Pl.*Sph.* 256e, *Phdr.*262c; out of courtesy, when no real doubt is implied, κινδυνεύεις ἀληθῆ λέγειν you *may very likely* be right, Id.*Smp.* 205d. 5. Pass., *to be endangered* or *imperilled*, ἐν ἑνὶ ἀνδρὶ πολλῶν ἀρετὰς κ. Th.2.35; τὰ χρήματα κινδυνεύεται τῷ δανείσαντι D.34.28:—but Pass. in sense of Act. dub. in *GDI*3569.4 (Calymna). **-ος**, ὁ, heterocl. dat. κίνδυνι (as if from κίνδυν) Alc.138, cf. Sapph.161:—*danger*, *hazard*, *venture*, whether abstract or concrete, πᾶσίν τοι κ. ἐπ' ἔργμασιν Thgn.585, cf. 637; ὁ μέγας κ. ἄναλκιν οὐ φῶτα λαμβάνει Pi.*O.*1.81; κ. γαλέης *danger of* or *from* her, Batr.9; κ. αὐτᾶς Pi. *N.*9.35; τὸν κ. τῆς μάχης Th.2.71; κίνδυνον ἀναρριπτέειν *to run a risk*, Hdt.7.50, etc.; ῥῖψαι E.*Rh.*154; κἀνὰ κίνδυνον βαλῶ A.*Th.*1033; κίνδυνον ἀναλαβέσθαι, ὑποδύεσθαι, Hdt.3.69, X.*Cyr.*1.5.12; αἴρεσθαι, ἄρασθαι, ἀρεῖσθαι, E.*Heracl.*504, Antipho 5.63, And.1.11; ξυνάρασθαι Th. l. c.; ἐγχειρίσασθαι Id.5.108, etc.; ὑπομεῖναι X.*Cyr.*1.2.1; μετὰ τοῦ δικαίου ποιούμενος τοὺς κ. Isoc.14.42; κινδύνῳ περιπίπτειν Th.8. 27; ἐν κινδύνῳ αἰωρεῖσθαι, εἶναι, Id.7.77, Antipho 5.7; ἐπὶ κινδύνους χωρεῖν Th.2.39; πρὸς αὐθαιρέτους κ. ἰέναι Id.8.27; ἐς κ. ἐμβαίνειν X. *Cyr.*2.1.15; ἐς κ. καταστῆσαί τινα Th.5.99; κινδύνῳ βάλλειν τινά A. *Th.*1053; τὸν ἐπιόντα κίνδυνον Aeschin.3.148; τοὺς ἐπιφερομένους ἑαυτῷ κ. ib.163; τὸν κατειληφότα κ. τὴν πόλιν D.18.220; οὐ περὶ τῶν ἴσων ὁ κ. X.*HG*7.1.7; ἔνι κ. ἐν τῷ πράγματι Ar.*Pl.*348; κ. [ἐστι] c. inf., Pi.*N.*8.21, Lys.13.27, Pl.*Cra.*436b, etc.; πόλιν κ. ἔσχε πεσεῖν E.*Hec.*5; κ. ἀσφαλέστερος Antipho 2.2.9; κ. ἀνθρώπινοι.., θεῖοι And. 1.139; ἐπὶ τῷ αὐτοῦ κ. at his own *risk*, Arist.*Pol.*1286ᵃ14; ἰδίῳ ἡμῶν κ. *PLond.*2.356.4 (i A. D.); καθαρὸς ἀπὸ παντὸς κ. *PIand.*35.10 (ii/iii A. D.). 2. *trial*, *venture*, κ. ἀνεῖται σοφίας Ar.*Nu.*955. 3. *battle*, Plb.1.87.10, etc. **-ώδης**, ες, *dangerous*, Hp.*Prog.*14, *Art.*65 (Comp.); κ. καταφοραί Plb.8.20.3; τὸ κ., τὰ κ., J.*AJ*15.4.2, 14.8.2 (Sup.); κ. λόγοι Max.Tyr.24.5. Adv. -δῶς D.H.7.6, Gal.8.762.

κίνερμοι· οἱ μικροὶ ἰχθύες, Hsch.

κῑνέω, aor. ἐκίνησα, Ep. κίνησα Il.23.730, etc.:—Med. and Pass., fut. κινήσομαι (in pass. sense) Pl.*Tht.*182c, D.9.51, -ηθήσομαι Ar.*Ra.* 796, Pl.*R.*545d, etc.: aor. Med. (Ep.) κινήσαντο Opp.*C.*2.582: aor. Pass. ἐκινήθην, Ep. 3 pl. ἐκίνηθεν Il.16.280: (cf. κίω):—*set in motion*, ἄγε κινήσας, of Hermes leading the souls, Od.24.5; simply, *move*, οὐδέ τι κινῆσαι μελέων ἦν 8.298; κ. θύρην 22.394; κ. κάρη Il.17.442, etc.; Ζέφυρος κ. λήϊον 2.147; κ. ὄμμα S.*Ph.*866; ναῦς ἐκίνησεν πόδα E.*Hec.*940 (lyr.), etc.; σκληρὰ ἡ γῆ ἔσται κινεῖν, i. e. plough, X.*Oec.*16.11; κ. δόρυ, of a warrior about to attack, E.*Andr.*607; κ. στρατιάν Id.*Rh.*18 (anap.); κ. ὅπλα Th.1.82; κ. σκάφην *rock* a cradle, Phylarch.36 J. b. in later Gr., *set in motion* a process of law, etc., *PKlein.Form.*405, etc. 2. *remove* a thing from its place, ἀνδριάντα Hdt.1.183; γῆς ὅρια Pl.*Lg.* 842e; κ. τι τῶν ἀκινήτων *meddle with* things sacred, Hdt.6.134, cf. S. *Ant.*1061, Th.4.98; κ. τὰ χρήματα ἐς ἄλλο τι *apply* them to an alien purpose, Id.2.24; κ. τῶν χρημάτων Id.1.143, 6.70; κ. τὸ στρατόπεδον X.*An.*6.4.27, etc. (κινεῖν alone, Plb.2.54.2, cf. Lxx *Ge.*20.1, Plu.*Dio* 27); *change*, *innovate*, νόμαια Hdt.3.80; τοὺς πατρίους νόμους Arist. *Pol.*1268ᵇ28; τῶν κειμένων νόμων Zaleuc.ap.Stob.4.2.19:—Pass., νόμιμα κινούμενα Pl.*Lg.*797b; ἰατρικὴ κινηθεῖσα παρὰ τὰ πάτρια Arist. *Pol.*1268ᵇ35: so abs. in Act., *change treatment*, ib.1286ᵃ13. 3. Gramm., *inflect*, τὰ ῥήματα ἐκίνει τὸ τέλος A.D.*Pron.*104.15:—more usu. in Pass., κατὰ τὸ τέλος κινεῖσθαι ib.104.10. 4. *alter* a manuscript reading, Str.7.3.4. II. *disturb*, of a wasps' nest, τοὺς δ' εἴ πέρ τις.. κινήσῃ ἀέκων Il.16.264; *arouse*, κ. τινὰ ἐξ ὕπνου E.*Ba.*690; *urge on*, φόβος κ. τινά A.*Ch.*289; φυγάδα πρόδρομον κινήσασα *having driven* him in headlong flight, S.*Ant.*109 (lyr.); κ. ἐπιρρόθοις κακοῖσιν *attack*, *assail*, ib.413; μήτηρ κ. κραδίαν, κ. δὲ χόλον E.*Med.*99 (anap.); ἐάν με κινῇς καὶ ποιήσῃς τὴν χολὴν.. ζέσαι Anaxipp.2; κ. τινά *incite* or *stir* one *up* to speak, Pl.*R.*329e, *Ly.*223a, X.*Mem.*4.2.2; κ. τὰ πολλὰ καὶ ἄτοπα *stir up*.. questions, Pl.*Tht.*163a; *call in question* an assumption, τὰ μέγιστα κ. τῶν μαθηματικῶν Arist.*Cael.*271ᵇ11, cf. Phld.*Sign.*27; κ. τὸ τὰ ἄκρα.. ἀνταίρειν Str.2.1.12, cf. Plot.2.1.6; ὁ κινῶν [τὰ φαινόμενα] λόγος S.E.*M.*8.360:—Pass., S.*OC*1526; κινεῖται γὰρ εὐθύς μοι χολή my bile *is stirred*, Pherecr.69.5; κεκινῆσθαι πρός τι X.*Oec.*8.1. 2. *set going*, *cause*, *call forth*, φθέγματα S.*El.*18; πατρὸς στόμα Id.*OC* 1276; μῦθον E.*El.*302; λόγον περί τινος Pl.*R.*450a; πάντα κ. λόγον Id. *Phlb.*15e; κ. ὀδύνην S.*Tr.*974 (anap.); κακά Id.*OT*636; πάθος Phld. *Mus.*p.4 K.; πόλεμον, πολέμους, Th.6.34, Pl.*R.*566e; Ἐμπεδοκλέα.. πρῶτον ῥητορικὴν κεκινηκέναι Arist.*Fr.*65. 3. Medic., κ. οὔρησιν, οὖρα, Dsc.2.109, 127; κοιλίαν ib.6. 4. sens. obsc., κ. γυναῖκα Eup.233.3 (nisi leg. ἐβίνουν), cf. Ar.*Ach.*1052 (v.l.), *Eq.*364, *Nu.*1103 (lyr., Pass.), al., *AP*11.7 (Nicander); κ. τὰ σκέλεα Herod.5.2. 5. phrases: κ. πᾶν χρῆμα *turn* every stone, *try* every way, Hdt.5.96; μὴ κ. εὖ κείμενον 'let sleeping dogs lie', Pl.*Phlb.*15c; μὴ κίνει Καμάριναν, ἀκίνητος γὰρ ἀμείνων Orac.ap.St.Byz.; κινεῦντα μηδὲ κάρφος 'not stirring a finger', Herod.3.67, cf. 1.55; μηδ' ὀδόντα κινῆσαι Id.3.49; κ. τὸν ἀπ' ἱρᾶς πύματον λίθον 'play the last card', Alc.82 (s. v. l.). 6. in Law, πολιτικῶς κ. κατά τινος *employ* civil *action* against, *Cod.Just.*4.20.13.1.

B. Pass., *to be put in motion*, *go*, Il.1.47; (κι)νηθεὶς ἐπῄει dub. in Pi.*Fr.*101: generally, *to be moved*, *stir*, κινήθη ἀγορή, ἐκίνηθεν φάλαγγες, Il.2.144, 16.280; of an earthquake, Δῆλος ἐκινήθη Hdt.6.98, Th.2.8; θύελλα κινηθεῖσα S.*OC*1660; τί κεκίνηται; what *motion is* this? E.*Andr.*1226 (anap.); κινεῖσθαι, opp. ἑστάναι, *motion*, opp. rest, Pl. *Sph.*250b, etc.; ὥσπερ χορδαὶ ἐν λύρᾳ συμπαθῶς κινηθεῖσαι *vibrating* in unison, Plot.4.4.8. 2. of persons, *to be moved*, *stirred*, ὁ κεκινημένος *one who is agitated*, *excited*, Pl.*Phdr.*245b, cf. Vett.Val.45.25, al.; κ. παθητικῶς Phld.*Rh.*1.193S. 3. of dancing, κ. τῷ σώματι Pl.*Lg.*656a. 4. *move forward*, of soldiers, S.*OC*1371, E.*Rh.*139, *Ph.*107; but κ. ἐκ τῆς τάξεως *leave* the ranks, X.*HG*2.1.22. 5. *to be disturbed* or *in rebellion*, D.C.39.54, 42.15, al. 6. κεκινημένος περί τι, Lat. *versatus in*.., Pl.*Lg.*908d.

κῑν-ηθμός, ὁ, *motion*, Pi.*P.*4.208. **-ηθρον**, τό, = κίνητρον, Poll. 7.169. **-ημα**, ατος, τό, *movement*, οὔθ' ἡ γραμμὴ ἐκ στιγμῶν οὔθ' ἡ κίνησις ἐκ κινημάτων Arist.*Ph.*241ᵃ4, cf. 232ᵃ9, *Mu.*400ᵃ8, etc.; of the *movements* of pantomimic actors, Luc.*Salt.*62. 2. *political movement*, Plb.5.29.3, al., Plu.*Fab.*20 (pl.). b. *uproar*, *excitement*, Lxx 1 *Ma.*13.44, Plu.*Aem.*18. 3. κινήματα τῆς σαρκός *impressions* of sense, Epicur.*Fr.*411; κ. λεῖον *Stoic.*2.25; κ. μελῳδητικὸν περὶ τὴν ψυχήν Thphr.*Fr.*89.1: abs., κινήματα *impressions*, *emotions*, Epicur. *Fr.*131: sg., Epict.*Fr.*14, S.E.*M.*11.83, etc. 4. Medic., *subluxation* of a bone, *partial dislocation*, Hp.*Fract.*47 (pl.). b. τὰ τῶν καιρῶν κ., of *periods* in disease, Gal.19.184. 5. Gramm., *inflexion*, Hdn. Gr.2.265, al. 6. pl., *moving things*, Max.Tyr.41.2.

κῑνησί-γαιος [σῐ], ον, gloss on ἐννοσίγαιος, Hsch. **-πολος**, ον, *heaven-shaking*, *PMag.Par.*1.1372.

κίνησις [ῐ], εως, ἡ, *motion*, opp. rest (στάσις), Pl.*Sph.*250a; opp. ἠρεμία, Arist.*Ph.*202ᵃ5, etc. 2. in Cyrenaic philos., λεία κ., = ἡδονή, τραχεῖα κ., = πόνος, D.L.2.86; also αἱ διὰ μορφῆς κατ' ὄψιν ἡδεῖαι κ. Epicur.*Fr.*67; αἱ κ. αἱ ἀνθρωπικαί human *emotions*, Arr.*Epict.* 2.20.19. 3. *dance*, Ἄρεος κίνασις (sic) Tyrt.16, cf. Luc.*Salt.*63, *Ephes.*2 No.71; τραγικὴ ἔνρυθμος κ. *Inscr.Magn.*165. 4. *movement*, in a political sense, ἐν κ. εἶναι Th.3.75, cf. Plb.3.4.12; ἡ κ. ἡ Ἰουδαϊκή the Jewish *revolt*, *OGI*543.15 (Ancyra, ii A. D.); of the Peloponn. war, Th.1.1. 5. *change*, *revolution*, κινήσεις πολιτείας Arist.*Pol.*1268ᵇ25. 6. *movement* of an army, Plb.10.23.1 (pl.); πολεμικαὶ κ. Ael.*Tact.*3.4, cf. Arr.*Tact.*20.1. b. *removal*, *change of abode*, Vett.Val.97.17 (pl.), al. 7. Gramm., *inflexion*, τοῦ ζῆμι κ. οὐχ εὕρηται *EM*410.38. 8. in Law, *punitive action*, βασιλικὴ κ. *Cod. Just.*1.3.43.10, cf. 10.27.2.7; also, *setting* a process *in motion*, *PLond.* 5.1663.13 (vi A. D.).

κῑνησῐ-φόρος, ον, *causing motion*, Orph.*H.*10.21. **-φυλλος**, ον, *leaf-moving*, gloss on εἰνοσίφυλλος, Hsch., Apollon.*Lex.* **-χθων**, ον, gen. ονος, *earth-shaking*, Sch.S.*Ant.*154.

κῑν-ητέος, α, ον, *to be moved* or *excited*, Pl.*Amat.*134a; *to be altered*, Id.*Lg.*738d, Arist.*Pol.*1269^{a}25. II. κινητέον, *one must call into play*, τὴν ζωγραφίαν Pl.*R.*373a. 2. *one must excite*, ὀργὴν ἢ ἔλεον S.E.*M.*2.11. **-ητήρ**, ῆρος, ὁ, = κινητής, γαίης, γᾶς, *h.Hom.*22.2, Pi. *I.*4(3).19. **-ητήριος**, α, ον, = κινητικός, μύωψ A.*Supp.*307; ἀλγεινὰ θυμοῦ κ. ib.448; τὸ κ. *ladle*, = κίνητρον, Sch.Ar.*Eq.*980. **-ητής**, οῦ, ὁ, *one that sets going, author*, καινῶν ἐπῶν Ar.*Nu.*1397. 2. *seditious person, agitator*, Plb.28.17.12. **-ητικός**, ή, όν, *of* or *for putting in motion*, μόρια Arist.*Pol.*1290^{b}31; νεῦρα *motor* nerves, Gal.8.208; κ. βηχέων Hp.*Aph.*5.24; ἱδρώτων Dsc.5.112; οὔρων Xenocr.ap. Orib.2.58.50; ἐξ ἑαυτοῦ μόνον κ. *spontaneous*, Epicur.*Nat.*28.7: Sup. -ώτατος Arist.*Mete.*365^{b}30. Adv. -κῶς Procl.*in Alc.*p.52C. 2. metaph., *urging on, exciting*, λόγος κ. πρὸς ἀρετήν Aristo *Stoic.*1.88; τὸ -ώτατον τῶν ὄχλων Phld.*Rh.*1.198S., D.H.*Isoc.*13: abs., *stimulating*, X.*Oec.*10.12; τὸ μέλος κ. φύσει Phld.*Mus.*p.71K.; τὸ μήτε ὁρμῆς μήτε ἀφορμῆς -κὸν [ἀδιάφορον] *Stoic.*3.28, cf. 40, al. 3. *turbulent, seditious*, Plb.1.9.3, D.S.19.14, etc. II. (from Pass.) *movable, mobile*, Pl.*Ti.*58d, Arist.*HA*590^{a}33, *GA*775^{a}7 (Comp.), Plu.2.945f, 952e. **-ητός**, ή, όν, (fem. -ός Pl.*Ti.*37d) *moving* (intr.), l.c., cf. Plu.2.1012f; *liable to alteration*, Arist.*EN*1134^{b}29. 2. in Law, κ. οὐσία *movable* property, *Cod.Just.*1.11.10.1, cf. 1.2.15 *Intr.*; κ. καὶ ἀκίνητα *PLond.*3.1015.17 (vi A.D.). **-ητρον**, τό, *ladle* or *stick for stirring*, Eust.1675.57, Sch.Nic.*Th.*109, Sch.Od.11.128.

κίννα, ἡ, *wall barley, wall-barley, Hordeum murinum*, Dsc.4.32.

κιννάβᾰρ-ι [νᾰ], εως, τό, *cinnabar, bisulphuret of mercury*, whence *vermilion* is obtained, Arist.*Mete.*378^{a}26, Thphr.*Lap.*58, Dsc.5.94; thought by some to be *serpent's blood*, Dsc.l.c., Plin.*HN*33.116:—a masc. form **κιννάβαρις**, Anaxandr.14:—also **τεγγάβαρι** (q.v.). 2. = ἐρυθρόδανον, Ps.-Dsc.3.143 (-ρις). **-ίζω**, *have the colour of* κιννάβαρι, Dsc.5.76. **-ινος**, η, ον, *like cinnabar, vermilion*, Arist.*HA*501^{a}30, Ath.9.390b, Ael.*NA*4.21. **-ιον**, τό, name of an *eye-salve*, Gal.12.786.

κίνναβος, = κάναβος (for which it is prob. f.l.), Suid.

κινναμολόγος, ὁ, = κιννάμωμον II, Plin.*HN*10.97.

κιννᾰμον, τό, later form for κιννάμωμον, Plin.*HN*12.86; *cinnamus*, *Gloss.*:—gen. **κῑνάμοιο**, Nic.*Th.*947.

κιννᾰμωμ-ίζω, *to be like* κιννάμωμον, Dsc.5.121. **-ινος**, η, ον, *prepared from* or *with* κιννάμωμον, Antiph.35, Dsc.1.61, Ath.10.439b. **-ίς**, ίδος, ἡ, an inferior kind of κιννάμωμον, Gal.12.26. **-ον**, τό, = Hebr. *ḳinnamon*, a superior kind of *cassia*, *Cinnamomum Cassia*, Hdt.3.111, Thphr.*HP*9.5.1, *PSI*6.628 (iii B.C.), *OGI* 214.59 (Didyma, iii B.C.), etc.: **κῑνάμωμον**, D.P.945 (pl.), also in codd. of D.S.1.91, v.l. in Hdt.l.c.; cf. κίνναμον. II. name of a fabulous Indian bird, said to make its nest of twigs of κιννάμωμον (cf. κινναμολόγος), Arist.*HA*616^{a}6, Antig.*Mir.*43, Ael.*NA*2.34.

κιννᾰμωμοφόρος, ον, *bearing* κιννάμωμον, ἡ κ. (sc. γῆ) Str.1.4.2, al.

κιννυρίδες· τὰ μικρὰ ὀρνιθάρια, Hsch.

κῑνούρης, ὁ, *shaking the tail*, a sign of weakness in a horse, Hsch.

κίνυγμα [ῐ], ατος, τό, (κινύσσομαι) *anything moved about*, αἰθέριον κ. *a sport* for the winds of heaven, A.*Pr.*158 (anap.): misspelt κήνυγμα, Hsch., Phot.

κίνῠμαι [ῐ], = κινέομαι (only in pres. and impf.), *go, move*, Il.10.280, Od.10.556; ἐς πόλεμον.. κίνυντο φάλαγγες they *marched*.., Il. 4.281, cf. 332, etc.; τοῦ καὶ κινυμένοιο *as it was stirred*.., 14.173, cf. A.R.1.1308; of dancing, *AP*5.128 (Autom.).

κῐνύρα [ῠ], ἡ, = Hebr. *kinnor*, a stringed instrument played with the hand, Lxx 1*Ki.*16.23; with a plectron, J.*AJ*7.12.3.

κῐνῠρίζω, = sq., read by Zenod. in Il.9.612.

κῐνύρομαι [ῠ], only pres. and impf. (unless the aor. κινύρατο be read in Mosch.3.43):—*utter a plaintive sound, lament*, Ar.*Eq.*11, A.R. 1.292; οἰκτρὰ κινυρομένη Opp.*C.*3.217; πολλὰ κ. Q.S.6.81, al. 2. c. acc. pers., *bewail*, τινα Call.*Ap.*20. 3. once in Trag., c. acc. cogn., κινύρονται φόνον χαλινοί (L. Dind. μινύρονται ex Hsch.) the bridles *ring* murderously, A.*Th.*123 (lyr.).

κῐνῠρός, ά, όν, *wailing, plaintive*, Il.17.5; γόος A.R.4.605; πέτηλα Nonn.*D.*38.95; v. μινυρός.

κῐνύσσομαι, Pass., = κινέομαι, *waver, sway backwards and forwards*, A.*Ch.*196.

κινύτιδος· κινητικὸς χαραδριός, Hsch. **κῑνώ**, οῦς, ἡ, Dor. for κίνησις, Id., but found in Emp.123.2.

κινώθαλον, τό, expl. of κνώδαλον, Sch.Pl.*Ax.*365c.

κῐνώπ-ετον, τό, *venomous beast*, esp. *serpent*, Call.*Jov.*25, Nic.*Th.* 27, 195:—also **-ηστής**, οῦ, ὁ, ib.141.

κιξάλλ-ης, ου, ὁ, *highway robber*, κ. καὶ λῃστής Democr.260; ὅστις κιξάλλας ὑποδέχοιτο *SIG*38.19 (Teos, v B.C.) (Hsch. **κιξάλης**· φώρ, κλέπτης, ἀλαζών: Phot. **κίξας**· τοὺς ἐν ὁδῷ λῃστάς: Jo.Gramm. in Hoffmann *Griech.Dial.* ii p.208 **κιττάλης**· κλέπτης). **-εύω**, *commit highway robbery*, *SIG* l.c.: **-ία**, ἡ, *highway robbery*, Hsch.

κίξιος· τέττιξ, Hsch.

κῑόκρᾱνον, τό, *capital of a column*, *IG*1^{2}.372.29, 11(2).199*A*41 (Delos, iii B.C.), Pl.Com.72, X.*HG*4.4.5, Chor.p.84B.

κῑον-ηδόν, Adv., (κίων) *like a pillar*, γράφειν κ., i.e. in vertical lines from top to bottom, Sch.D.T.pp.183,191 H. **-ικός**, ή, όν, *of a pillar*, φαντασία Eust.1390.18. **-ιον**, τό, Dim. of κίων, *small pillar*, Ph.*Bel.*76.15, Poll.7.73, *IG*3.162, *CIG*4608 (Palestine). II. *central column* in a snail's shell, Dsc.2.4. **-ίς**, ίδος, ἡ, Dim. of κίων, *uvula*, Id.1.107, Aret.*CA*1.8; esp. when inflamed, Gal.14.305. **-ίσκος**, ὁ, Dim. of κίων, Haussoullier *Milet* p.173, Ath.12.514c (pl.), J.*AJ*8.3.6 (pl.), Hero *Aut.*1.3, al.

κῑονο-ειδής, ές, *like a pillar*, Eust.1399.33. **-κρᾱνον**, τό, later form for κιόκρανον, Str.4.4.6 (as v.l.), D.S.5.47, etc. **-φορέω**, *bear the pillars* of heaven, of Atlas, Eust.1390.10. **-φορία**, ἡ, *bearing of pillars*, and **-φόρος**, ον, *pillar-bearing*, Id. ad D.P.66.

κίουρος, ὁ, *basket* for corn, or *measure*, Hsch. (Hebr. *kiyyôr* 'pot, basin'.)

κιππαρός, ὁ, dub. sens. in *BGU*470.3 (ii A.D., fort. κηπουρός).

κίραφος, ὁ, and Lacon. **κίρα**, ἡ, *fox*, Hsch. **κίρβα**, = πήρα, Id.; cf. κίββα. **κιρία**, v. κειρία. **κίρις**, v. κιρρίς.

κιρκαία (**κιρκέα** Gal.12.26), ἡ, *black swallow-wort*, *Vincetoxicum nigrum*, Dsc.3.119, Zopyr.ap.Orib.14.64.1: κιρκαία ῥίζα, used as a charm, Apollod.3.15.1. II. **κιρκαῖος** ἱέραξ, a kind of hawk, *PMag.Berol.*1.4. **κίρκας**, v. κιρκίας.

κίρκασμα· τοὺς βότρυας, Hsch.

κίρκη, ἡ, unknown *bird*, Ael.*NA*4.5.

Κίρκη, ἡ, *Circe*, Od.10.136, Hes.*Th.*957, etc.

κιρκήλᾰτος, ον (nisi leg. -ας), *chased by a hawk*, ἀηδών A.*Supp.*62 (lyr.).

κιρκήσια (sc. ἀγωνίσματα), τά, = Lat. *ludi Circenses*, Arr.*Epict.*4.10.21.

κιρκίας, ου, ὁ, = κίρκιος, cj. for καικίας in Arist.*Mu.*394^{b}31 and for κίρκας in Id.*Vent.*973^{b}20.

κιρκίον, τό, Dim. of κίρκος III, *ring*, *BCH*29.544 (Delos, ii B.C.).

κίρκιος, ὁ, = θρασκίας, Agathem.2.7, *Gloss.*; cf. κέρκιος, κιρκίας.

κίρκος, ὁ, a kind of *hawk* or *falcon*, ἴρηξ κίρκος (where ἴρηξ is the generic term, κίρκος the specific), Od.13.87, cf. Il.22.139, A.*Pr.*857, Arist.*HA*620^{a}18, Opp.*C.*1.64; κίρκου λεπάργου A.*Fr.*304.5. (The species cannot be identified.) II. a kind of *wolf*, Opp.*C.*3.304. III. *circle*, mostly in form κρίκος (q.v.): hence, *ring*, *IG*11(2).161*B*49 (Delos, iii B.C.): poet. for Prose κρίκος acc. to Poll.1.94:—neut. pl. κίρκα ἢ καταδέσματα *PMag.Lond.*121.299. IV. later, = Lat. *circus*, Plb.30.22.2, Arr.*Epict.*3.16.14, Plu.*Aem.*32. V. unknown stone, Plin.*HN*37.153. VI. = κωπηλάτης, Hsch., Phot. VII. = ἡ τοῦ αἰγείρου βλάστησις, Hsch.

κιρκόω, *hoop round, secure with rings*, A.*Pr.*74.

κιρνάω and **-ημι**, collat., esp. poet., forms of κεράννυμι, only pres. and impf.:—*mix* wine with water, Hom. only in Od., μελίφρονα οἶνον ἐκίρνα (impf. of κιρνάω) 7.182, 10.356; κίρνη μελιηδέα οἶνον (impf. of κίρνημι) 14.78, 16.52; κιρνὰς αἴθοπα οἶνον (part.) 16.14; κιρνᾷ (v.l. κίρναται) κρητῆρα οἴνου Hdt.4.66; κρατῆρα μελέων κίρναμεν Pi.*I.*6(5).3; κόμπον κιρνάμεν *to mix the cup* of praise ib.5(4).25: inf. κιρνάναι Hp.*Mul.*2.113; part., κιρνάντες πόλιν Ar.*Fr.*683; Aeol. κίρναις (ἐγ-) Alc.34 codd. (fort. κέρναις); κιρνῶντες Hdn.8.4.9: impf., ἐκίρνη φάρμακον App.*Mith.*111:—Med., ἴσον ἴσῳ κίρνασθαι Ath.10.426b; κιρνᾶται Id.11.476a, A.D.*Pron.*74.7, κίρναται *Com.Adesp.*373; χθὼν δὲ πᾶσα καὶ θάλασσα κίρναται τεὰν χάριν *IG*4^{2}(1).130.23 (Epid.); part. κιρνάμενος Pi.*N.*3.78: impf. ἐκίρνατο (ἐν-) *Com.Adesp.*1203:—Pass., ποτὶ μῶμον ἔπαινος κίρναται Pi.*Fr.*181; κρητῆρες κιρνέαται *SIG*57.11 (Miletus, v B.C.); ἡ φύσις καὶ τὰ κιρνάμενα ταύτῃ Phld.*Ir.*p.59W. 2. *flavour by mixing*, κρήνη.. οὕτω δή τι ἐοῦσα πικρή, ἣ κιρνᾷ τὸν Ὕπανιν Hdt.4.52. 3. metaph., *temper*, μαλάττειν καὶ κιρνᾶν τὸ τῆς φύσεως αὔθαδες Plb.4.21.3. 4. τὸ χρύσιον κέρναν (Aeol.) ὑδαρέστερον *alloy* it, *IG*12(2).1.13 (Mytil., iv B.C.):—cf. ἀνα-, ἐγ-, ἐπι-, συγ-κίρνημι.

κιρρά, a *fish*, Hsch. **Κίρρα, Κιρραῖος**, v. Κρῖσα, Κρισαῖος.

κιρράς, άδος, ἡ, poet. fem. of κιρρός, Nic.*Th.*519.

κιρρίς, ίδος, ἡ, a *sea-fish*, = κηρίς, prob. a species of *wrasse*, Opp. *H.*1.129, 3.187. 2. species of ἱέραξ, *EM*515.15. 3. = λύχνος (Lacon.), ib.17. 4. = Ἄδωνις (Cypr.), ib.16. (Hsch. has κίρις in senses 2–4.)

κιρροειδής, ές, *yellowish*, Apollod.*Fr.Hist.*214 J., Dsc.*Ther.*16, Philostr.*Im.*1.12.

κιρροκοιλάδια, τά, species of *fig*, Ath.3.78a.

κιρρός, ά, όν, *orange-tawny*, between πυρρός and ξανθός, οἶνος Hp. *Acut.*52, cf. Arist.*Fr.*307, Mnesith.ap.Ath.1.32d, Nic.*Al.*44; τροχίσκος ὁ κ. Antyll.ap.Orib.10.24.10.

κιρρόχρως, ωτος, perh. to be read for κηρόχρως, Chaerem.1.5.

κιρρώδης, ες, *inclined to orange-tawny*, *Hippiatr.*104.

κιρσο-ειδής, ές, *varicose*, of veins, Hp.*Morb.*1.14; of the convolutions of the brain, Ruf.*Onom.*148; κ. παραστάτης, name for the πόρος σπερματικός, Gal.4.565. **-κήλη**, ἡ, *varicocele*, Cels.7.18, Gal.7.730.

κιρσός, ὁ, *enlargement of a vein, varicocele*, = ἰξία III, Hp.*Aph.*6.21 (pl.): of *varicose veins*, Apollon.*Mir.*42, Philostr.*Gym.*35, Gal.7.730:—also **κριξός**, Poll.4.196; **κρισσός**, *Hippiatr.*14, 77, Hsch.; cf. κισσός II.

κιρσο-τομέω, *remove varicocele*, Heliod.(?)ap.Orib.45.18.24:—also Pass., ib.45.18.5. **-τομία**, ἡ, *operation to remove varicocele*, ib.45.18.18, Paul.Aeg.6.82.

κιρσουλκ-έω, in Pass., *to be operated on for varicocele*, Heliod.(?) ap.Orib.45.18.31. **-ία**, ἡ, *this operation*, ib.45.18.30. **-ός**, ὁ, *instrument for this purpose*, ib.45.18.5, Gal.14.790.

κιρσ-όω, *cause to become varicose*, Gal.4.579:—usu. in Pass., *become varicose*, Id.18(1).499, Heliod.ap.Orib.45.19.1. **-ώδης**, ες, = κιρσοειδής, Hp.*Prorrh.*2.10, Gal.*UP*14.7 (Comp.), 10. **-ωσις**, εως, ἡ, *becoming varicose*, Heliod.(?)ap.Orib.45.18.29.

κίρτος, dub. sens., Simon.240.

κίς, ὁ, gen. κιός, acc. κῖν, *weevil*, κεῖνον [τὸν χρυσὸν] οὐ σὴς οὐδὲ κὶς δάπτει Pi.*Fr.*222: acc. pl. κίας Thphr.*CP*4.15.4. [κῖς Hdn.Gr.2.925

(oxyt., Choerob. *in Theod.* 1.383): gen. κιός Hdn.Gr.2.674: acc. κῖν Choerob. l. c.]

κις, Thess., = τις (q.v.).

κῖσηρ-ίζω, *rub with pumice-stone*, Nic.Dam.4 J., *Gloss.* **-ιον**, τό, Dim. of sq., *EM*515.28, *Gloss.* **-ις** (**κίσηλις** *PHolm.* 12.11, implied in Luc. *Jud.Voc.*4), εως (Luc. l. c., -ιδος Thphr. (v. infr.), cf. Choerob. *in Theod.* 1.329 H.), ἡ, *pumice-stone*, Ar.*Fr.*320.4, Alex.124.9, Arist.*EN*1111ᵃ13, Thphr.*Lap.*22, etc. [ῑ in Comm. ll. cc., *AP*6.295 (Phan.): κίσσηρις is erroneous in Thphr. l. c., Asp. *in EN*65.4.]

κῖσηροειδής, ές, *like pumice-stone*, Diog.Apoll. in *Placit.*2.13.5, Thphr.*HP*3.7.5.

κῖσηρ-όομαι, Pass., *turn into pumice*, Thphr.*Lap.*20. **-ώδης**, ες, = κῖσηροειδής, Ephor.65(*e*) J., Dsc.5.74.

κίσθος (Dsc. (v. infr.), Hsch.) or **κισθός**, ὁ, *rock-rose*, Eup.14.5, Mnesim.4.63 (anap.), prob. l. for κισσός in Thphr.*HP*6.1.4, 6.2.1, 2; κ. ἄρρην, = *Cistus villosus*, κ. θῆλυς, = *C. salvifolius*, Dsc.1.97: **κί-στος**, Hp.*Liqu.*5, Gal.12.27:—Dsc. l. c. sq. distinguishes the species **κίσθαρος** or **κίσσαρος** from λῆδον, cf. Gal.12.28.

κίσιρνις, a *bird*, Hsch. **κίσπρα**· πικρὰ τὸ ἦθος, παλίγκοτος (Cos), Id.

κίσσᾰ, Att. **κίττᾰ**, ἡ, *jay, Garrulus glandarius*, Ar.*Av.*302, Antiph.302, etc.; σοῦ δ' ἐγὼ λαλιστέραν οὐπώποτ' εἶδον.., οὐ κίτταν Alex.92; prov., ἁ κίττα τὰν Σειρῆνα μιμουμένα Gal.8.632. 2. = ἰχθῦς ποιός, Hsch. II. '*longing*' *of pregnant women, craving for strange food*, Dsc.1.115, Sor.1.48, S.E.*M.*5.62: pl., Gal.8.343.

κισσᾰβίζω, Att. **κιττ-**, *scream like a jay*, Poll.5.90.

κισσ-άμπελος, ἡ, = ἑλξίνη, Dsc.4.39, cf. Gal.19.131: **κιττ-άμπελος**, Ps.-Dsc.4.39:—also **κισσ-άνθεμον**, τό, ibid., Gal.12.51; a kind of κυκλάμινος, Dsc.2.165.

κίσσᾰρος, ὁ, f. l. for κύσσαρος, Hp.ap.Erot.; = *hedera*, *Gloss.* II. = κίσθος, Dsc.1.97.

κισσάω, Att. **κιττ-**, (κίσσα II) *crave for strange food*, of pregnant women, Arist.*HA*584ᵃ19, Arr.*Epict.*4.8.35, Gal.6.422; κ. τῆς γηθυλλίδος Polem.Hist.36: metaph., κ. τῆς εἰρήνης Ar.*Pax* 497 (lyr.): c. inf., *long* to do a thing, Id.*V.*349 (cf. Sch.); ἐκίττα ἡ πόλις ἐπὶ τῷ μειρακίῳ Longus 4.33. II. Act., *conceive*, Lxx *Ps.*50(51).7.

κισσεοχαίτης, ὁ, voc. -χαῖτα, *wreathed with ivy*, epith. of Apollo, *PMag.Berol.*2.98a.

κισσ-εύς, ὁ, *the ivy-crowned*, ὁ κ. Ἀπόλλων, ὁ βακχεύς, ὁ μάντις A.*Fr.*341. **-ήεις**, εσσα, εν, = κίσσινος, Nic.*Th.*510, Nonn.*D.*40.93. **-ηρεφής**, ές, (ἐρέφω) *ivy-clad*, Call.*Ep.* in *Berl.Sitzb.*1912.548, Philostr.*Dial.*2, prob. for κισσηφερής in Suid. **-ήρης**, ες, (ἀραρίσκω) = foreg., ὄχθαι S.*Ant.*1132 (lyr.).

κισσηρίζω, κίσσηρις, κισσηροειδής, κισσηρόω, incorrect forms for κισηρ-.

κίσσ-ησις, εως, ἡ, = κίσσα II, Gal.19.455. **-ητός**, ή, όν, *longed for*, Eust. ad D.P.946.

κισσηφερής, v. κισσηρεφής.

κίσσῐνος, η, ον, *of ivy*, E.*Ba.*177, 702; κ. ποτήρ Id.*Alc.*756; χρυσοῦς κ. *ivy*-wreath of gold, Callix.2: **κίσσινον**, τό, name of a *plaster*, Orib.*Fr.*88.

κισσίον, τό, Dim. of κισσός, = ἀσκληπιάς, Ps.-Dsc.3.92.

Κίσσιος, α, ον, *of* or *from Cissia*, in southern Persia, γῆ Hdt.5.49, etc.; Κισσία ἰηλεμίστρια *hired* mourner, A.*Ch.*423 (lyr.).

κισσό-βρῦος, ον, *luxuriant with ivy*, Orph.*H.*30.4. **-δέτᾱς**, α, ὁ, Dor. for -δέτης, (δέω A) *bound* or *crowned with ivy*, of Bacchus, cj. in Pi.*Fr.*75.9 (κισσοδόταν, κισσοδαῆ codd.). **-δετος**, ον, = foreg., Nonn.*D.*14.262. **-ειδής**, ές, *like ivy*, Dsc.2.166, Gal.4.556: Subst. κ. (sc. γραμμή), ἡ, Math., the *cissoid curve*, Papp.54.21, Procl. *in Euc.*p.111 F. Adv. -δῶς Sch.Theoc.13.42. **-κόμης**, ου, ὁ, *ivy-crowned*, Διόνυσος *h.Hom.*26.1, cf. *IG*12(7).80 (Arcesine). **-κόρυμβος**, ὁ, *ivy-cluster*, *Hippiatr.*77. **-πλεκτος**, ον, *ivy-twined*, μέλεα κ., of dithyrambs, Antiph.209.7 corr. Mein.: codd. Ath. κισ(σ)όπληκτα, i. e. *ivy-* (*thyrsos-*) *stricken, frenzied.* **-ποίητος**, ον, *made of ivy*, δούρατα Luc.*Bacch.*1.

κισσός, Att. **κιττός**, ὁ, *ivy, Hedera Helix*, of three kinds, two *climbing* (μέλας and λευκός), and one *creeping* (also called ἕλιξ), Thphr.*HP*3.18.6, cf. Dsc.2.179, *h.Bacch.*40; ἀτενής S.*Ant.*826 (lyr.); κισσοῦ στέφανος *OGI*49.7 (Egypt, iii B. C.); sacred to Dionysus, κισσῷ.. στεφανωθεὶς Διόνυσον θεραπεύει E.*Ba.*81 (lyr.); κύκλῳ δὲ περί σε κ. εὐπέταλος ἕλικι θάλλει Ar.*Th.*999: hence οἰνωψ (or οἰνωπός) S.*OC*674 (lyr.). II. = κιρσός (Achaean), Hsch.

κισσο-στέφᾰνος, ον, *ivy-crowned*, of Dionysus, *AP*9.524.11. **-στεφής**, ές, = foreg., *Anacreont.*46.5: **κιττ-**, Alciphr.3.48. **-τόμος**, ον, (τέμνω) *ivy-cutting*: κισσοτόμοι (sc. ἡμέραι), αἱ, festival at Phlius, Paus.2.13.4. **-φάγος** [ᾰ], ον, Att. **κιττ-**, *ivy-eating*, Longus 3.5. **-φορέω**, Att. **κιττ-**, *to be decked with ivy*, like the Bacchanals, prob. in *IG*2.1285 (iv B. C.); of a tragic actor, *AP*7.707 (Diosc.); dub. l. in Plu.2.5b. **-φορία**, ἡ, *wearing of ivy-wreaths*, in pl., *IG*12(2).484.5 (Mytil.). **-φόρος**, Att. **κιττ-**, ον, *ivy-wreathed*, of Dionysus, Pi.*O.*2.27, Ar.*Th.*988 (lyr.), *BCH*50.240 (Thasos, iii/ii B. C.); ὁ κ. παῖς Διός ib.529 (Marathon, ii A. D.): metaph., κ. διθύραμβοι Simon.148. 2. *luxuriant with ivy*, νάπη E.*Tr.*1066 (lyr.). **-φυλλον**, τό, *ivy-leaf*, Διονύσου κ., as a brand, Lxx 3 *Ma.*2.29. 2. *part of a torsion-engine shaped like an ivy-leaf*, Ph.*Bel.*70.33. II. = κυκλάμινος, Ps.-Dsc.2.164. **-χαίτης**, ου, ὁ, *ivy-tressed*, i. e. *ivy-crowned*, only in voc., κισσοχαῖτ' (i. e. -χαῖτ[ᾰ]) ἄναξ Pratin.Lyr.1.17, Ecphantid.3 (ridiculed by Cratin.324). **-χᾰρής**, ές, *delighting in ivy*, Orph.*H.*52.12. **-χίτων** [ῑ], ωνος, ὁ, ἡ, *ivy-clad*, Id.*L.*261.

κισσόω, Att. **κιττ-**, *wreathe with ivy*, κρᾶτα κισσώσας ἐμόν E.*Ba.*205; κεκισσωμένος Alciphr.2.3.

κισσύβιον [ῠ], τό, *rustic drinking-cup* of wood, used by the Cyclops, Od.9.346; by Eumaeus, 14.78; κ. ἀμφῶες Theoc.1.27 (but expld. as μόνωτον ποτήριον, Philem.Gloss.ap.Ath.11.476f); ὀλίγῳ ἥδετο κ. Call.*Aet.*1.1.12.—So called, either as made of ivy-wood, Eumolp.ap.Ath.11.477a; or because adorned with ivy-wreaths, Poll.6.97: in late Prose, οἴνου κ. Prisc.p.316 D.

κισσώδης, ες, (κίσσα II) *longing like pregnant women*, Dsc.5.6.14.

κισσ-ών, ῶνος, ὁ, *ivy-grove*, Hdn.Gr.1.40, al. **-ωσις**, Att. **κιττ-**, εως, ἡ, *crowning with ivy*, Διονύσου *IG*2².1367.21 (pl.). **-ωτός**, ή, όν, *decked with ivy*, νεβρίς *AP*6.172.

κιστᾱ-φορέω, *bear the casket* in mystic processions, *BCH*37.97 (Macedonia, ii/iii A. D.). **-φόρος**, ὁ, *one who bears* it, *CIG*2052 (Apollonia in Thrace); cf. κιστοφόρος I.

κίστη, ἡ, *basket, hamper*, Od.6.76, Ar.*Ach.*1098, al., Thphr.*HP*5.7.5, al., *PCair.Zen.*430.11, al. (iii B. C.), Euph.9, Call.*Hec.*1.2.13 (κείστη), etc.; *writing-case, desk*, Ar.*V.*529; *voting-urn*, *Notiz.Arch.*4.20 (Cyrene, Aug.); = ἀγγεῖον πλεκτόν, Hsch.; made of bark, Thphr. ll. cc.: hence distd. fr. κιβωτός, Ammon.*Diff.*p.81 V.

Κιστῖβερ, ὁ, = Lat. *quinquevir cis Tiberim*, *IG*14.1512.

κιστίδιον, τό, Dim. of κίστη, *basket*, Artem.1.2.

κιστίς, ίδος (εως Nic.Dam.52 J.), ἡ, Dim. of κίστη, Hp.*Mul.*1.104, dub. in Hld.4.11; κιστίδος used to balance ἀσπίδος, Ar.*Ach.*1138.

κιστοειδής, ές, *shaped like a chest*, Hsch. s. v. ὀγκίον.

κίστος, ὁ, v. κίσθος.

κιστοφόρος, ον, (κίστη) *carrying a basket* in mystic processions, prob. l. in D.18.260 (κιττοφόρος codd., κιστ- v.l. ap.Harp. s. h. v.); cf. κισταφόρος. II. Subst., *coin, with the basket of Dionysus as obverse*, Cic.*Att.*2.6.2, Liv.37.46.

κίταρις, εως, ἡ, = κίδαρις (q. v.).

κιτρᾶτον, τό, *spiced drink prepared from citron*, Alex.Trall.8.2.

κιτρέα, ἡ, *citron-tree, Citrus Medica*, *Gp.*10.7.8 (borrowed fr. Lat. *citrea*). **κίτρεος**, α, ον, = κίτρινος, *Stud.Pal.*20.245 (vi A. D.) (borrowed fr. Lat. *citreus*).

κιτρῐνοειδής, ές, *of a citron colour*, Sch.Theoc.5.95.

κίτρῐνος, η, ον, *of the citron-tree*, ξύλον D.C.61.10. II. *of a citron yellow*, *PMasp.*6 ii 82 (vi A. D.), Hdn.*Epim.*179. III. κίτρινον, τό, *a yellowish salve*, Paul.Aeg.7.18.

κιτρῐοειδής, ές, *citron-like*, Gal.14.392.

κιτρῐον, τό, = κιτρέα, *citron-tree*, *IG*4²(1).126.9 (Epid., ii A. D.), *POxy.*1764.19 (iii A. D.), *Gp.*10.8.1; θύρσοι ἐκ κιτρίων J.*AJ*13.13.5. II. = κίτρον, *citron*, Juba 24, Dsc.1.115.5, Ath.3.84d, Gal.12.77, *Gp.*10.7.8, Alex.Aphr.*Pr.*1.119 (borrowed fr. Lat. *citrium*, cf. Dsc. l. c.). [Parox. in Ath. l. c., v.l. in Dsc. l. c.]

κιτρόμηλον, τό, = sq., Dsc.3.104, *Gp.*10.76.7.

κίτρον, τό, *fruit of the* κιτρέα, *citron*, cited as Lat. word by Pamphil. ap.Ath.3.85c, cf. Gal.*Vict.Att.*10.

κιτρό-φυλλον, τό, *citron-leaf*, *Gp.*9.28.1. **-φῦτον**, τό, *citron-tree*, ib.10.8.2. **-χρους**, ουν, *citron-coloured*, Tz.*H.*9.630.

κίττα, κιττᾰβίζω, κιττάω, κίττησις, Att. for κισσ-. **κιττάλης**, v. κιξάλλης. **κιττάναλον**· ἡ κρησέρα (κρήσερα cod.), Hsch.; cf. gen. pl. κιθαναλλων dub. sens. in *PSI*5.485.2; χιταναλλων ib.19 (iii B. C.). **κίτταρις**, v. κίδαρις. **κίτταρος**, ὁ, *wearer of* κίδαρις (Cypr.), Hsch. **κιττός, κιττοφόρος, κίττωσις**, etc., Att. for κισσ-.

κιττώ, ἡ, kind of *cassia*, Hebr. *ḳiddah*, Dsc.1.13.

κῖτών, ῶνος, ὁ, Dor. (esp. Sicil.) for χιτών, Sophr.35; also *POxy.*1269.30 (ii A. D.), etc.:—Dim. **κιτώνιον**, τό, *PTeb.*406.14 (iii A. D.), etc.

κίφος, τό, Messen. for στέφανος, Paus.3.26.9. (For σκίφος, cf. σκιφατόμος.)

κῐχάνω [ᾰ], imper. κιχάνετε Il.23.407; inf. κιχάνειν Mosch.2.112: impf. ἐκίχᾰνον Il.3.383: aor. 3 sg. ἔκιχεν Od.3.169, κίχεν Il.24.160; 3 pl. κίχον 18.153; subj. 3 sg. κίχησι Od.12.122; part. κιχών 15.157: also non-thematic aor. ἐκίχην [ῐ], 2 sg. ἐκίχεις, like ἐτίθεις from τίθημι, 24.284; 1 pl. κίχημεν or ἐκ- 16.379; 3 dual κιχήτην Il.10.376; subj. κιχείω, κιχείομεν, 1.26, 21.128; opt. κιχείην 2.188; inf. κιχῆναι Od.16.357, κιχήμεναι Il.15.274; part. κιχείς 16.342:—after Hom. **κιγχάνω** [ᾰ] (cf. Eust.1525.16, Hsch., Phot.), first Sol.ap.Phot., A.*Ch.*622, S.*OC*1450 (both lyr.); misspelt κιχάνω E.*Hipp.*1444, *Hel.*597: fut. inf. κιχησέμεν A.R.4.1482: aor. ἔκῐχον E.*Ba.*903 (lyr.), κίχον Pi.*P.*9.26, al.; subj. κίχω S.*Aj.*657, E.*Supp.*1069, *Alc.*22; inf. κιχεῖν B.1.67: aor. 1 ἐκίχησα Id.5.148, Opp.*H.*5.116, Musae.149:—Med. (in act. sense), κιχάνομαι Il.11.441, Od.9.266: fut. κιχήσομαι Il.10.370, S.*OC*1487: aor. 1 κιχήσατο Il.10.494, Od.6.51: aor. 2 part. κιχήμενος Il.5.187, 11.451:—poet. Verb (perh. used in the laws of Solon), *reach, hit,* or *light upon, meet with*, μή σε.. παρὰ νηυσὶ κιχείω Il.1.26, cf. Od.13.228; Ἄδμητον ἐν δόμοισιν ἆρα κ.; E.*Alc.*477; *reach, overtake*, ὃν κε.. ποσσὶ κιχείω Il.6.228; κιχήσεσθαι δέ σ' ὀΐω ib.341, cf. 21.605, Pi.*P.*2.50, B.5.148, etc.; τὰ φεύγοντα Id.1.67; ἵππους δ' Ἀτρεΐδαο κιχάνετε Il.23.407; σὲ δουρὶ κιχήσομαι *shall reach* thee, 10.370; εἰς ὅ κεν ἄστυ κιχείομεν till we *reach* it, 21.128; ἧός κε τέλος πολέμοιο κιχείω *arrive at* it, 3.291: sts. of things, βέλος ὠκὺ κιχήμενον the dart *that had just reached* him, 5.187; φθῆ σε τέλος θανάτοιο κιχήμενον 11.451. 2. rarely c. gen., like τυγχάνω, S.*OC*1487.

κιχήλα, ἡ, Dor. for κίχλη (q.v.).

κιχήσιππον, gloss on κελενδρύονα, Phot. **κίχησις**, εως, ἡ, (κιχάνω) *reaching, attaining*, Hsch. **κιχητός**· ὃ ἐμβάπτεται ὁ λιβανωτός (Cypr.), Id.

κίχλη [ῑ by nature], ἡ, *thrush* (a generic term, including various species, Arist.*HA*617^{a}18), κ. τανυσίπτεροι Od.22.468, cf. Ar.*Av*.591, etc. :—Dor. **κιχήλα** Epich.157, Ar.*Nu*.339 :—late Gr. **κίχλα** Alex. Trall.1.10, *Gp*.15.1.19. II. sea-fish, a species of *wrasse*, Epich. 60, Antim.ap.Ath.7.304e ('Antiphanes' codd.), Diocl.*Fr*.135, Arist. *HA*598^{a}11, Nic.*Fr*.59, Numen.ap.Ath.7.305c, Opp.*H*.1.126, 4.173: later **κίχλα**, Alex.Trall.1.15.

κιχληβῶτις, = ἀνδράχνη, Hsch.; cf. κικριβιντίς.

κιχλ-ιδιάω, Desider. of sq., *have a desire to titter*, *Com.Adesp*.1038. **-ίζω**, *titter*, *giggle*, Ar.*Nu*.983, Theoc.11.78, *AP*5.244 (Maced.); κιχλίζουσα καὶ μωκωμένη Alciphr.1.33, 3.27, cf. 74; *guffaw*, μέζον ἵππου κ. Herod.7.123: metaph., [ἡδονὴ] σεσαρυῖα καὶ κιχλίζουσα Ph.2. 265 :—Med., Ar.*Fr*.333.4. (Prop. *chirp like a thrush*, Gramm.ap. Valck.*Animadv. ad Ammon*.p.175 who writes **κιχλάζω**: wrongly expld. as *eat* κίχλαι, *live luxuriously*, Sch.Ar.*Nu*.979.) **-ισμός**, ὁ, *tittering*, *giggling*, Ar.*Nu*.1073 (pl., v.l. καχασμῶν), cf. *AB*271.

κιχλοκόσσυφος, ὁ, = Lat. *turdus*, *Edict.Diocl*.4.27 (Aegira).

κίχορα, ων, τά, *chicory*, *Cichorium Intybus*, Nic.*Al*.429 :—also **κιχόρη**, ἡ, Thphr.*HP*7.7.1: **κιχόριον**, τό, ib.1.10.7, al. (= ἀναγαλλίς, Dsc.2.178, s.v.l.); so called in Egypt, Plin.*HN*19.129: in pl., Ar.*Fr*. 293 (nisi leg. **κιχόρεια**, cf. Lat. *cichorēa*). [ῑ Nic.l.c., perh. metri gr.]

κιχοριώδης, ες, *of the genus of chicory*, φύλλον Thphr.*HP*9.16.4; τὰ κ. ib.7.11.3.

κιχράω, = sq., Lxx 1*Ki*.1.28 :—Med., *Gloss*.

κίχρημι, *lend* :—Med., κίχραμαι *borrow*, v. χράω :—Subst. **κίχρησις**, εως, ἡ, Tz.*H*.12.303.

κίω, κίεις A.*Ch*.680; imper. κίε Od.7.50, A.*Pers*.1068, *Supp*.852 (both lyr.); subj. κίῃς Od.1.311; opt. κίοι 9.42, A.*Supp*.504, κιοίτην, κίοιτε, Od.15.149, 3.347; part. κιών, κιοῦσα (for the accent cf. ἰών), 4.427, al.: impf. ἔκιον, Ep. 1 pl. κίομεν Il.21.456 :—*go*, in Hom. almost always of persons, 2.565, 24.471, Od.4.427, etc.; of ships, Il.2.509 :— Ep. Verb, Trag. only A.; as etym. of κίνησις, Pl.*Cra*.426c: in Hom. perh. always aor., unless impf. in Il.23.257. (Cf. κινέω, κίνυμαι, Lat. *cio*.)

κίων [ῑ], ονος, Hom. (not in Il.), mostly ἡ; ὁ Od.8.66,473, 19.38, cf. Eumel.11, Ar.*V*.105, Hdt.4.184, etc.; ἡ Id.1.92, Pi.*P*.1.19, *IG*9(2). 258.12 (Cierium, ii B.C.), al. :—*pillar*, freq. in Od. of roof-*pillars*, 19. 38, al., cf. *h.Ap*.8; οἱ κ. οἱ ἐν τῷ Λυκείῳ Pl.*Euthd*.303b, cf. *SIG*969.10 (Piraeus, iv B.C.), al.; used as a flogging-post, S.*Aj*.108, Aeschin. 1.59: prov., ἔσθι' ἐλθὼν τοὺς Μεγακλέους κίονας eat the *pillars* of his hall, for, being a spendthrift, he had nothing else left to give, Ar.*Nu*. 815. 2. of natural objects, [Ἄτλας] ἔχει.. κίονας αὐτὸς μακράς, αἳ γαῖάν τε καὶ οὐρανὸν ἀμφὶς ἔχουσι Od.1.53; [Ἄτλας] ἕστηκε κίον' (dual) οὐρανοῦ τε καὶ χθονὸς.. ἐρείδων A.*Pr*.351; ὁ κ. τοῦ οὐρανοῦ (of Mount Atlas) Hdt.4.184; κίων οὐρανία, of Aetna, Pi.*P*.1.19; for *the Pillars* of Hercules, v. Ἡράκλειος I. II. *columnar gravestone*, *AP*7.163 (Leon.): distd. from στήλη, And.1.38; κ. τετράπλευρος an obelisk, *Epigr.Gr*.1061 (Constantinople); any *column* bearing an inscription, ἀγγράψαι ἐγ κίονα λιθίναν *IG*l.c. (cf. p.xii); ἔσται ἡ στήλη ἐπὶ τοῦ κείονος ib.2^2.1368.29 (ii A.D.). III. *uvula*, κ. ἀνεσπασμένος Hp. *Epid*.1.26.ϛ', cf. Arist.*HA*493^{a}3. IV. *division of the nostrils*, *cartilage of the nose*, Ruf.*Onom*.37, Poll.2.79,80. V. kind of *meteor*, *Placit*.3.2.5. VI. kind of *wart*, Hp.*Nat.Mul*.65, *Mul*.2.212 (where κιών, oxyt.). (Cf. Arm. *siun* 'pillar'.)

κλαγγ-άζω, onomatop. word for the cry of cranes, Poll.5.89: hence, of the language of the Scythians, Porph.*Abst*.3.3. **-αίνω**, of hounds, *give tongue*, only pres., A.*Eu*.131. **-άνω**, of birds, *scream*, S.*Fr*.959.4; perh. of the lyre, *twang*, Id.*Ichn*.308. **-έω**, = κλαγγαίνω, of hounds, Theoc.*Ep*.6.5. **-ή**, ἡ, metapl. dat. κλαγγί Ibyc.56: (κλάζω) :—*any sharp sound*, e.g. *twang* of the bow, Il.1.49; *scream* of birds, esp. cranes, to which are compared *confused cries of a throng*, 3.3, Od.11.605, cf. Il.2.100, 10.523; *grunting* of swine, Od. 14.412; later, *howling* of wolves and lions, *h.Hom*.14.4, cf. 27.8; *hissing* of serpents, Pi.*Dith*.2.18 (pl.), A.*Th*.381 (pl.); *baying* of dogs, X.*Cyn*.4.5, etc.; also, of musical instruments, Telest.4, Mnesim.4. 57 (anap.); of song, S.*Tr*.208 (lyr.); κ. ἀηδόνειος (leg. -όνιος) Nicom. Trag.1; κ. δύσφατος, of Cassandra's prophecies, A.*Ag*.1152 (lyr.); of the *scream* of the Harpies, A.R.2.269. **-ηδόν**, Adv. *with a clang*, *noise*, *din*, Il.2.463 :—also **-όν**, Babr.124.13, prob. in Id.135.3.

κλάγ[γ]ος· γάλα (Cret.), Hsch.; cf. γλάγος.

κλαγγώδης, ες, *shrill*, *strident*, of the voice after vomiting, Hp. *Coac*.550, *Prorrh*.1.17, cf. Gal.16.553, 18(2).301, *UP*7.7; wrongly expld. of ὄμματα εὐκίνητα by Demetr.Lac.ap.Erot.

κλαγερός, ά, όν, *screaming*, of cranes, *AP*6.109.8 (Antip.).

κλαγκτός, ή, όν, = foreg., φωναί Antiph.234.4.

κλάδα, **κλάδας**, metapl. acc. sg. and pl. of κλάδος (q.v.) :—but κλᾷδα, κλᾷδας, Aeol. and Dor. acc. sg. and pl. of κλείς.

κλᾰδαρόμ(μ)ατοι· εὔσειστοι τὰ ὄμματα, Hsch.

κλᾰδαρόρυγχος, ὁ, *clapper-bill*, = τροχίλος, Ael.*NA*12.15.

κλᾰδαρός, ά, όν, (dissim. fr.*κραδαρός, cf. κραδάω, κραδαίνω) *quivering*, '*whippy*' *in the shaft*, δοράτια Plb.6.25.5; κάμακες *AP*9.322 (Leon., v.l. κλαμ-); *wavy*, ζωηφόρος κλαδαρὰ οἷον ἱμὰς *Cat.Cod.Astr*.7.241.

κλᾰδάσσομαι, Pass., *rush violently*, *surge*, αἷμα κλαδασσόμενον διὰ γυίων Emp.100.22.

κλᾰδάω, *shake*, aor. inf. κλαδάσαι Hsch. (cf. κραδάω). II. (κλάδος) = κλαδεύω, f.l. for κλᾶν, Phryn.149, cf. Thom.Mag.p.193 R.

κλᾰδ-εία, ἡ, *pruning*, of the vine, *Gp*.3.14. **-εύματα**, τά, *leaves stripped off*, *Gloss*. **-ευσις**, εως, ἡ, = κλαδεία, Aq., Sm.*Ca*.2.12, *Gp*.4.5.2. **-ευτέον**, *one must prune*, ib.9.5.11. **-ευτήριον**, τό, *pruning-knife*, Hsch. s.v. βράκετ(ρ)ον. II. pl. κλαδευτήρια, τά, *a festival at pruning-time*, Id. s.v. βίσβην. **-ευτής**, οῦ, ὁ, *pruner*, *Gloss*. **-εύω**, *prune* vines, Artem.1.51, *Gp*.3.14, Epigr. in *Rev. Phil*.19.178; condemned by Phryn.149. **-έω**, = foreg., Arr.*Ind*.11. 10. **-εών**, ῶνος, ὁ, = κλάδος, Orph.*A*.925, prob. in *AP*9.78 (Leon.).

κλᾰδη-φορέω, *bear young branches*, Sch.E.*Ph*.791. **-φόρος**, ον, *bearing young branches*, Hdn.*Epim*.103.

κλᾰδί, metapl. dat. of κλάδος :—but **κλᾱδί**, Aeol., Dor. dat. of κλείς.

κλάδινος, *rameus*, *Gloss*.

κλάδιον [ᾰ], τό, Dim. of κλάδος, *twig* or *shoot*, ἀγρώστεως prob. in Philum.ap.Aët.5.124; κλαδίοις ἐλαιῶν αἰτοῦντες Lib.*Or*.16.46, cf. *BGU*1051.13 (i A.D.).

κλᾰδίσκος, ὁ, Dim. of κλάδος, Gal.12.35, *Anacreont*.18.4.

κλαδοειδής, *ramosus*, *Gloss*.

κλάδος [ᾰ], ου, ὁ, *branch*, *shoot* of a tree, Arist.*Juv*.468^{b}25, *GA*752^a 20; *twig*, opp. ἀκρεμών, Thphr.*HP*1.1.9, 1.10.7: generally, *branch*, τῆς ἐλαίης τοὺς κλάδους Hdt.7.19: presented by suppliants, ἐλαίας θ' ὑψιγέννητον κλάδον A.*Eu*.43, cf. *Supp*.22 (anap.), S.*OT*3,143; also of *laurel branches* used in temples, E.*Ion*80. 2. *plank*, *POxy*. 1738.4, al. (iii A.D.). 3. *branch* of a blood-vessel, Gal.15.141. 4. metaph., ἀπὸ νώτοιο δύο κλάδοι ἀΐσσονται two *arms*, Emp.29.1. 5. κ. ἐλέας, of a young girl, *Epigr.Gr*.368.7 :—metapl. forms, dat. κλαδί *Scol*.9, prob. in *SIG*1025.33 (Cos, iv/iii B.C.); τῇ κ. Ael.*NA*4.38 codd. (cf. Eust.58.37); τῷ κ. Choerob. *in Theod*.1.138; acc. κλάδα *Lyr.Adesp*.122; cf. κλάδα[ν]· κλάδον, Hsch.; gen. pl. κλαδέων prob. in Philox.1.3; dat. pl. κλάδεσι Ar.*Av*.239 (lyr.), Ep. κλαδέεσσι Nic. *Fr*.74.19; acc. κλάδας ib.53.

κλᾰδοτομ-έω, *prune* vines, *PLond*.1821.382, *PHamb*.23.26 (v A.D.). **-ία**, ἡ, ibid.

κλᾰδοῦχος, v. κλειδοῦχος.

κλᾰδώδης, ες, *with many* κλάδοι, Sch.Nic.*Th*.544, Eust.1634.26.

κλᾰδών, όνος, ὁ, = κλάδος, Hsch. (pl.).

κλάζω, fut. κλάγξω A.*Pers*.948 (lyr.): aor. 1 ἔκλαγξα Il.1.46, A. *Ag*.201 (lyr.): aor. 2 ἔκλαγον *h.Pan*.14, B.16.127, Theoc.17.71, etc.: pf. κέκλαγγα X.*Cyn*.3.9, 6.23; subj. κεκλάγγω Ar.*V*.929; Dor. κέκλāγα Alcm.7; part. κεκληγώς, pl. κεκλήγοντες Il.17.756, -ῶτες v.l. ib. 16.430, κεκλαγώς Plu.*Tim*.26 :—**Pass.**, fut. κεκλάγξομαι Ar.*V*.930 :— *make a sharp piercing sound*: 1. of birds, *scream*, οὐκ ἴδον.., ἀλλὰ κλάγξαντος (sc. ἐρῳδιοῦ) ἄκουσαν Il.10.276; of starlings and daws, οὖλον κεκλήγοντες 17.756, etc.; γεράνου φωνὴν ἐνιαύσια κεκληγυίης Hes.*Op*.449; of the eagle, Il.12.207, S.*Ant*.112 (lyr.), cf. *OT* 966, etc. 2. of dogs, *bark*, *bay*, οἱ μὲν κεκλήγοντες ἐπέδραμον Od. 14.30, cf. Ar.*V*.929, X. ll. cc., etc. 3. of things, as of arrows in the quiver, *clash*, *rattle*, ἔκλαγξαν δ' ἄρ' ὀϊστοί Il.1.46; of the wind, *whistle*, αἶψα γὰρ ἦλθε κεκληγὼς Ζέφυρος Od.12.408; of wheels, *creak*, A. *Th*.205 (lyr.): c. acc. cogn., κλάζουσι κώδωνες φόβον *ring forth* terror, ib.386; τί νέον ἔκλαγε σάλπιγξ.. ἀοιδάν; B.17.3; of the sea, *roar*, ἔκλαγεν δὲ πόντος Id.16.127; of the musician, κιθάρᾳ κλάζεις παιᾶνας μέλπων E.*Ion*905 (lyr.); of Pan on his pipes, *h.Pan*.14; κλάζεις μέλισμα λύρας (of the τέττιξ) *AP*7.196 (Mel.). 4. of men, *shout*, *scream*, ὀξέα κεκληγώς Il.2.222, 17.88: c. acc. cogn., *shout aloud*, *ring forth*, κλάζοντες Ἄρη A.*Ag*.48 (anap.); γόον Id.*Pers*.948 (lyr.); Ζεὺς ἔκλαγξε βροντάν *pealed forth* thunder, Pi.*P*.4.23; also ἔκλαγξε κέαρ ὀλοαῖσι στοναχαῖς Id.*Pae*.8.20. 5. less freq. of *articulate* sound, ἄλλο μῆχαρ.. μάντις ἔκλαγξεν *shrieked forth* another remedy, A.*Ag*.201 (lyr.); Ζῆνα.. ἐπινίκια κλάζων *sounding loudly* the song of victory in honour of Z., ib.174 (lyr.).

κλᾷθρον, v. κλεῖθρον. **κλαιόν**· τὸ κανοῦν, Hsch. **κλᾱΐς**, gen. κλᾱῖδος and κλᾱΐδος, ἁ, Dor. for κληΐς, κλείς. **κλᾱΐστρον**, τό, Dor. for κλεῖστρον (q.v.).

κλαίω, old Att. **κλάω** (v. infr.) [ᾱ] never contracted; Aeol. **κλαΐω** *Lyr.Adesp*.65; Ep. 2 sg. opt. κλαίοισθα Il.24.619: Att. impf. ἔκλᾱον, Ep. κλαῖον Od.10.201, Ion. κλαίεσκον Il.8.364, Hdt.3.119, A.*Fr*.312: fut. κλαύσομαι, 2 sg. κλαύσῃ or κλαύσει, Il.18.340, Ar.*V*.1327 (lyr.), *Nu*.58, 933 (anap.), E.*Cyc*.554, etc., rarely κλαυσοῦμαι Ar.*Pax* 1081, 1277 (in mock heroic verses); Att. also κλαιήσω Hyp.*Dem.Fr*.10, κλᾱήσω D. 19.310, 21.99, later κλαύσω Theoc.23.34, D.H.4.70, *Ev.Jo*.16.20, Man. 3.143: aor. ἔκλαυσα, Ep. κλαῦσα Od.3.261 :—**Med.**, aor. ἐκλαυσάμην S.*Tr*.153, *AP*7.412 (Alc. Mess.) :—**Pass.**, fut. κλαυσθήσομαι Lxx *Ps*. 77(78).64, κεκλαύσομαι Ar.*Nu*.1436: aor. ἐκλαύσθην Lyc.831, J.*AJ*8. 11.1 (v.l. κλαυθείς), *IG*14.2128: pf. κέκλαυμαι A.*Ch*.687, S.*OT*1490, κέκλαυσμαι Lyc.273, Plu.2.115b. [κλάω [ᾱ] is recognized as Att. by A.D.*Adv*.187.26, and is found in codd. of Ar.*Av*.341, Pl.*Lg*.792a, *Phlb*.48a: ἔκλᾰε in later poetry, Theoc.14.32, dub. in Hermesian.7. 33 (cf. κλέω A).] (κλᾰϝ-yω, cf. κλαυ-θμός, etc.) I. intr., *cry*, *wail*, *lament*, of any loud expression of pain or sorrow, κλαῖον δὲ λιγέως Od.10.201; πρὸς οὐρανόν Il.8.364; τῆς ἄρα κλαιούσης ὄπα σύνθετο Od.20.92; for the dead, Il.19.297, etc.; ἀμφὶ δὲ σὲ Τρῳαὶ καὶ Δαρδανίδες κλαύσονται 18.340; κλαίοντα καὶ ὀδυρόμενον Pl.*R*.388b, etc.; διὰ τί οἱ κλαίοντες ὀξὺ φθέγγονται; Arist.*Pr*.900^{a}20; δάκρυσι κ. D.C. 59.27; of infants, Sor.1.107, al.; of *crying* for joy, κλαῖον δὲ λιγέως, ἀδινώτερον ἤ τ' οἰωνοί κτλ. Od.16.216, cf. Eust.1799.57. 2. αὐτὸν κλαίοντα ἀφήσω I shall send him home *crying*, *howling*, i.e. *well beaten*, Il.2.263: freq. in Att., κλαύσεται *he shall howl*, i.e. *he shall suffer for it*, Ar.*V*.1327 (lyr.), *Pl*.174, al.; κλαύσομαι Id.*Nu*.58; κλαύσει μακρά you shall *howl* loudly, i.e. suffer severely, Id.*Pax*255, cf. 1277; κλαύσῃ φιλῶν τὸν οἶνον E.*Cyc*.554; κλάοις ἄν, εἰ ψαύσειας A.*Supp*.925; κλαίων *to your sorrow* or *loss*, *at your peril*, S.*OT*401, 1152, *Ant*.754; κλάων ἅψῃ τῶνδε E.*Heracl*.270, cf. *Hipp*.1086; δεῦρ' ἔλθ' ἵνα κλάῃς Ar.*Nu*. 58; κλάειν ἔγωγέ σε λέγω (opp. χαίρειν σοι λέγω) Id.*Pl*.62, cf. Hdt.

4.127; κλάειν εἴπωμεν Eup.363; κλάειν κελεύων Λάμαχον Ar.*Ach.* 1131; κλάειν σε μακρὰ κελεύσας Id.*Eq.*433; σὲ δ' ἐᾶν κλάειν μακρὰ τὴν κεφαλὴν *suffer* terribly in the head, Id.*Pl.*612 (anap.), cf. *V.*584. II. trans., *weep for, lament*, κλαῖεν ἔπειτ' Ὀδυσῆα, φίλον πόσιν Od.1.363, cf. Il.20.210; τι A.*Ag.*890, S.*El.*1117; τὰ αὐτοῦ πάθη Plu.*Alc.*33:—Pass., *to be mourned* or *lamented*, ἀνδρὸς εὖ κεκλαυμένου A.*Ch.*687: impers., μάτην ἐμοὶ κεκλαύσεται Ar.*Nu.*1436. 2. *cry for*, of infants, μάμμας καὶ τιτθάς Arr.*Epict.*2.16.39. III. Med., *bewail oneself, weep aloud*, A.*Th.*920 (lyr.): pf. part. Pass. κεκλαυμένος *bathed in tears*, Id.*Ch.*457 (lyr.), 731, S.*OT*1490. 2. trans., *bewail to oneself*, πάθη. . πόλλ' ἔγωγ' ἐκλαυσάμην Id.*Tr.*153; κλαιόμενα τάδε βρέφη σφαγάς A.*Ag.*1096 (lyr.).

κλαιωμῑλία, poet. -ίη, ἡ, (ὁμιλία) *fellowship in tears*, *AP*9.573 (Ammian.).

κλᾳκοφόρος, ὁ, perh. *bearer of the key* (cf. κλᾴξ), name of hero worshipped at Epidaurus, $IG4^2$(1).297; also, title of priest at Messene, ib.5(1).1447 (iii/ii B.C.).

κλᾳκτός, ά, όν, Dor. for κλειστός, *IG*5(1).1390.91 (Andania, i B.C.), *BCH*27.271 (Argos). **κλάλιον**, v. κλανίον.

κλᾶμα or **κλάμα**, ατος, τό, = κλάσμα, περονῶν *IG*4.1588.13,42 (Aegina, v B.C., pl.).

κλᾰμᾰρός, ά, όν, v.l. for κλαδαρός, *AP*9.322 (Leon.), cf. Hsch.

κλαμβός, ή, όν, *docked, cropped*, ὦτα *Hippiatr.*14, cf. 17.

κλᾶμμα, ατος, τό, Aeol. for κλῆμα, Alc.*Oxy.*1788 *Fr.*15 ii 19.

κλαμμίς· ἀναδενδράς, Hsch. **κλαμυστῆσαι**· βοῆσαι, καλέσαι, Id.

κλανίον (or **κλάνιον**), τό, *bracelet*, *POxy.*796 (i/ii A.D.), *PTeb.*417.37 (iii A.D.), Hsch., *Gloss.* (also **κλαρά** Hsch.):—written **κλάλιον**, *POxy.*114.11 (ii/iii A.D.), al.

κλᾰνίσκιον, = χλανίσκιον, *Jahresh.*16 *Beibl.*53 (Athens, iv B.C.).

κλάννω, = κλάω, *Gloss.*:—also **κλάνω**, *EM*1.50, al.

κλᾴξ, ᾳκός, ἡ, Dor. for κλείς, *key*, $IG4^2$(1).102.110, al. (Epid., iv B.C.), 5(1).1390.92 (Andania, i B.C.), Theoc.15.33.

κλᾳξῶ, Dor. fut. of κλείω, *shut*, Theoc.6.32.

κλαπάζειν· χρονίζειν, Hsch.

κλάπαι, ῶν, αἱ, *wooden shoes, pattens*, D.C.77.4, cf. Suid. s. v. κωλοβάθρου. 2. *the stocks*, Sch.Ar.*Pl.*276.

κλάποι, οἱ, = foreg. 2, Tz.*H.*13.300.

κλαρά, v. κλάνιον. **κλαραγεῖ** (-γείων cod.)· ἐλαφρῶς καθεύδει (Sicel), Hsch. **κλάρας**, = φοῖνιξ, Id. **κλάρες**· αἱ ἐπὶ ἐδάφου(ς) ἐσχάραι, Id.

κλάρια, τά, v. κληρίον II.

κλάριοι· κλάδοι, Hsch.

Κλάριος [ᾰ], ὁ, Dor. for κλήριος (which is not found), *distributing by lot*, epith. of Zeus, A.*Supp.*360 (lyr.), Paus.8.53.9.

Κλάριος [ᾰ], ὁ, *of* Κλάρος, epith. of Apollo, *Rev.Phil.*22.260 (ii A.D.):—hence **Κλαριών**, ῶνος, ὁ, name of month at Notium, *Supp. Epigr.*4.566; at Ephesus, *Jahresh.*15 *Beibl.*207.

κλᾶρος, κλᾱρόω, κλᾱρονομέω, Dor. for κληρ-.

κλᾱρῶται, ῶν, οἱ, (κλᾶρος) in Crete, *serfs attached to the soil*, Ephor. 29 J., Arist.*Fr.*586, Callistr.Hist.10.

κλᾰσαυχενεύομαι, (κλάω (A), αὐχήν) Pass., *walk with one's neck awry*, i. e. *with an affected air*, of the son of Alcibiades, Archipp.45.

κλάσθεον· κ(λ)εῖθρον, Hsch. (leg. κλᾷθρον).

κλᾰσῐβῶλαξ, ακος, ὁ, ἡ, (κλάω A) *breaking clods*, *AP*6.41 (Agath.).

κλάσ-ις [ᾰ], εως, ἡ, (κλάω A) *breaking, fracture*, Pl.*Ti.*43e; ἡ κ. τῶν ἀμπέλων *breaking off the shoots and tendrils* of vines, Thphr.*CP*2.14.4 (pl.), cf. 3.7.5, al.; ἡ κ. τοῦ ἄρτου *Ev.Luc.*24.35. 2. *bending* of the knee joint, Arist.*Pr.*882^{b}33; κ. ὄψεων *refraction*, Alex.Aphr. *in Mete.* 143.9; τὸ σαμεῖον περὶ ὃ ἁ κ. Archyt.ap.Simp. *in Ph.*785.25. b. κλάσιν λαβεῖν *to be deflected*, Plot.6.9.8; ὅταν κλάσιν ποιῇ καὶ γωνίαν, of a bandage, Erot. s. v. σκέπαρνος; of the labyrinth of the ear, Gal.*UP* 8.6. II. *modulation* of the voice, Ph.1.276, 2.266. -μα, ατος, τό, *fragment, morsel*, $IG2^2$.1425.347,368, Lxx 1*Ki.*30.12, D.S.17.13, *Ev.Marc.*6.43, Plu.*TG*19, *AP*6.304 (Phan.), 11.153 (Lucill.); μελάθρων κλάσματα *Inscr.Délos* 400.44 (ii B.C.). II. *lesion, rupture*, Vett.Val.110.31. -μάτιον, τό, Dim. of foreg., *IG*11(2).161 *B* 34, 162 *B* 27 (Delos, iii B.C.).

κλάσσεται· ἄρχεται (Syrac.), Hsch. post κασσαύριον.

κλαστ-άζω, *dress vines* (cf. κλάσις I. 1): metaph., *trim, humble*, Ar.*Eq.*166. -ήριον, τό, *knife for dressing vines*, Sch.Ar.*Eq.*166, Hsch. -ης, ου, ὁ, *vine-dresser*, Id.

κλαστόθριξ, perh. *curly-haired*, *PPetr.*3 p.15 (iii B.C.).

κλαστός, ή, όν, (κλάω A) *broken in pieces*, *AP*6.71 (Paul. Sil.). II. perh. = foreg., *PPetr.*1 p.54 (iii B.C.), *PCair.Zen.*374.6 (iii B.C.), *Arch.Pap.*1.65 (ii B.C.), etc.

κλαυθμ-ηρός, ά, όν, (κλαίω) *plaintive*, Sch.E.*Hec.*337. -ονή, ἡ, *weeping, wailing*, cited by Stob. fr. Pl.*Lg.*792a (κλαυμοναί codd.). -ός, ὁ, = foreg., Il.24.717, Od.4.212, 801, 17.8, A.*Ag.*1554 (pl., lyr.), Hdt. 1.111, 3.14, etc.; κλαυθμοὶ παίδων Arist.*Pol.*1336^{a}35, cf. Lxx *Ge.*45.2, al., *Ev.Matt.*8.12, Plu.*Rom.*19; κ. μετὰ δακρύων D.S.32.6. -ῠρίζω, *make to weep*, τὰ παιδία Plu.2.9a; τοὺς οἰκέτας prob. in Ath.8.364a:—Pass., *weep*, Pl.*Ax.*366d, Conon 48.4, D.S.4.20, etc. II. intr. in Act., Hp.*Progn.*24, Sor.1.88. -ῠρίς, ίδος, ἡ, in pl., = sq., Opp. *C.*4.248 (with many vv. ll.; κλαυθμυρμῶν cj. Lehrs). -ῠρισμός, ὁ, *crying like a child*, Is.*Fr.*163, Plu.*Lyc.*16, Steph. *in Hp.*1.228 D., f. l. in Opp.*C.*4.248 (pl.). -ώδης, ες, *broken as if by sobbing*, ἀναπνοαί Hp.*Aph.*6.54; φωναί Hierocl.p.58 A. -ών, ῶνος, ὁ, *place of weeping*, Lxx 2*Ki.*5.23,24.

κλαυκίθων· λαμπρυνόμενος τὰς ὄψεις, Hsch. (i. e. γλαυκιόων).

κλαῦμα, ατος, τό, (κλαίω) always in pl., *weeping, wailing*, A.*Pers.* 705 (troch.), X.*Cyr.*2.2.14, etc.; κλαυμάτων πηγαί A.*Ag.*887; κλαυμάτων ἄξια And.4.39. II. *troubles, misfortunes*, Ar.*Pax* 249; κλαύμαθ' ὑπάρξει τινί, = κλαύσεται, S.*Ant.*932 (anap.).

κλαυμονή, v. κλαυθμονή.

κλαυμῠρίζομαι, = κλαυθμυρίζομαι, Men.*Epit.*432, Hierocl.p.29 A., Max.Tyr.9.3: cf. **κλαυμαριόμενον**· κλαίοντα (Tarent.), Hsch., and **κλαυμαρεῖται**· κλαίει, Id.

κλαυσείω, = sq., Apollon.*Lex.* s. v. ὀψείοντες.

κλαυσιάω, Desider. of κλαίω, *wish to weep*, τὸ θύριον φθεγγόμενον ἄλλως κ. the door *is like to weep*, i. e. *shall suffer* for creaking, Ar.*Pl.* 1099.

κλαυσί-γελως [ῐ], ὁ, acc. -γέλωτα Demetr.*Eloc.*28: dat. pl. -γέλωσι Plu.2.1097f:—*smiles mingled with tears*, πάντας κ. εἶχε X.*HG*7.2.9; nickname of Phryne, Ath.13.591c. -μᾰχος, ον, *Rue-the-fight*, parody on the name of *Lamachus* (*Ready-for-fight*), Ar.*Pax* 1293.

κλαύσιμος, η, ον, *plaintive*, *Gloss.*

κλαῦσ-ις, εως, ἡ, *weeping*, Andronic.Rhod.pp.570, 571 M. -μα, ατος, τό, = foreg., Porph.*Gaur.*12.4 (pl.). -τήρ, ῆρος, ὁ, *weeper*, Man. 4.192. -τικός, ή, όν, *given to mourning*. Adv. -κῶς, ἔχειν Apollon. *Lex.* s. v. ὀψείοντες. -τός, ή, όν, (κλαίω) *to be bewailed, mournful*, S.*OC*1360:—also **κλαυτός**, A.*Th.*333 (lyr.), v. l. in S. l. c., cf. Hsch.

κλάω (A) [ᾰ], impf. ἔκλων (κατ-) Il.20.227, (ἀν-) Th.2.76: fut. κλάσω [ᾰ] J.*AJ*10.11.3, Luc.*DDeor.*11.1: aor. 1 ἔκλᾰσα, Ep. κλάσε Od.6.128, κατά-κλασσε Theoc.25.147:—**Med.**, poet. aor. κλάσσατο *AP*7.124 (Diog. Laert.):—Pass., fut. κλασθήσομαι Arist.*Mete.*373^{a}5: aor. ἐκλάσθην Il.11.584: pf. κέκλασμαι Arist.*APo.*76^{b}9, etc.: aor. 2 part. κλάς (as if from κλῆμι) Anacr.153:—*break, break off*, ἐξ ὕλης πτόρθον κλάσε Od.6.128; ἐκλάσθη δὲ δόναξ Il.11.584; *break off* the luxuriant shoots of the vine, Thphr.*CP*1.15.1 (Pass.), Gal.6.134, Longus 3.29, etc.; κ. ἄρτον 1*Ep.Cor.*10.16, cf. 11.24 (Pass.). 2. Geom., *deflect, inflect*, usu. of drawing a straight line 'broken back' at a line or surface, κλάσαι εὐθεῖαν τὴν ΑΓΒ ἐν λόγῳ τῷ δοθέντι Papp. 904.17; ἀπὸ δύο σημείων τῶν Β, Ε κλάσαι τὴν ΒΝΞΕ Id.122.3:—more freq. in Pass., Arist.*APo.* l. c.; ἡ κεκλασμένη (sc. γραμμή) Id.*Ph.*228^{b}24; αἱ κλώμεναι εὐθεῖαι Apollon.Perg.*Con.*2.52; ἐὰν ἀπὸ τῶν σημείων κλασθῶσιν ib.3.52; κεκλάσθω Euc.3.20, al.; of visual rays, Arist.*Mete.* 377^{b}22, *Pr.*912^{b}29; of arteries, Gal.9.84: generally, καμπαῖς κεκλασμένας ὑποπορεύσεις Plu.2.968b; κεκλ. στολίδες ib.64a; τὰ κλώμενα τῶν ῥευμάτων their *broken* courses, ib.747d. 3. metaph., *break, weaken, frustrate*, τὴν ἐλπίδα J.*BJ*3.7.13, cf. *Epigr.Gr.*348 (Cios): in pf. part. Pass., κεκλασμένη φωνή *weak, effeminate* voice, Hp.*Epid.*7.80, Arist.*Phgn.*813^{a}35 (also of the Siren's song, Vett.Val.108.28, cf. κ. ἀοιδή 242.10); τὰ κεκλ. τῶν ὀμμάτων *enfeebled* eyes, Arist.*Phgn.* 808^{a}9; κεκλ. μέλη *varied by modulation*, Plu.2.1138c; ῥυθμὸς κεκλ. *broken* rhythm, Longin.41.1; τὸ κεκλ. καὶ παντοδαπόν (sc. τῆς λέξεως) Phld.*Rh.*1.198 S. b. of emotion, ἐκλάσθην πρὸς ἔλεον J.*Vit.*43.

κλάω (B) [ᾱ], Att. for κλαίω (q. v.).

κλεαινός, ή, όν, in Hsch. corrupt for κλεεννός.

κλέβδην, Dor. -δᾱν, Adv. *by stealth*, A.D.*Adv.*198.6, *EM*103.13.

κλεεινός, ή, όν, poet. (Ion.) form of κλεινός, Socr.ap.D.L.2.42.

κλεεννός, ά, όν, Lyr. (Aeol.) form of κλεινός, *famous*, Simon.120, Pi.*P.*4.280 (Sup.), 5.20, *Scol.*5.

κλέζω· καλῶ, φωνῶ, Hsch.

κλεηδών, όνος, ἡ, Ion. and Ep. for κληδών (q. v.). **κλέθος**· κληδόνα, Hsch. **κλεῖα**, poet. contr. from κλέεα, pl. of κλέος (q. v.).

κλειδ-ᾰγωγία, ἡ, *procession of key-bearers*, *BCH*44.85 (Lagina). -άρχης, ου, ὁ, *keeper of the keys*, of St. Peter, Porph.*Chr.*23.

κλειδᾶς, ᾶ, ὁ, = κλειδοποιός, prob. in *BGU*429.14 (ii/iii A.D.).

κλειδίον (on the accent v. Hdn.Gr.1.356), τό, Dim. of κλείς, *little key*, κλειδία. . Λακωνίκ' ἄττα, τρεῖς ἔχοντα γομφίους Ar.*Th.*421, cf. *Fr.* 16, $IG2^2$.1533.27 (iv B.C.); τὸ κ. τοῦ οἰκήματος Arist.*Mir.*832^{b}23: without dimin. sense, τὰ κ. τῶν οὐρανῶν Porph.*Chr.*26. 2. *stopcock*, Hero *Spir.*1.24, *POxy.*2146.7 (iii A.D.). II. = κλείς III, of the tunny, Ath.7.315d; cf. κλιδία. III. a kind of *astringent pill*, Gal.13.87, 290, Paul.Aeg.3.40; or *astringent suppository*, κ. ὑπόθετον Alex.Trall.9.3. (κληδ- is not found.)

κλειδοποιός, ὁ, *locksmith*, *PTeb.ined.*, *PLips.*3 ii 10 (iii A.D.), Sch. Paul.Al.*P.*2, *Cat.Cod.Astr.*5(3).88.

κλειδουχ-έω, Att. κληδ-, *to be a* κλειδοῦχος, κ. θεᾶς *to be* her *priestess*, E.*IT*1463: abs., -οῦντος Ἀρίστωνος *OGI*170 (Delos, ii/i B.C.). II. γλώσσης πικροῖς κέντροισι κληδουχούμενοι, perh. *kept in check*, E.*HF* 1288. -ος, Att. κληδ-, ον, (ἔχω) *holding the keys*: hence, *having charge* or *custody of* a place, Ἔρωτα τᾶς Ἀφροδίτας θαλάμων κληδοῦχον E.*Hipp.*540 (lyr.); Ἰώ, κ. Ἥρας her *priestess*, A.*Supp.*291, cf. Phoronis 4, E.*IT*131 (lyr.), $IG2^2$.974.23, 3.172.7; κ. Διός E.*Hyps.Fr.*3(1) iv 28; of Pallas, *tutelary goddess*, Ar.*Th.*1142 (lyr.); τῶν συνδέσμων ἑκάστου κ. Μοῖρα *protectress of*. ., Plu.2.591b; of Aeacus, *IG*14.1746; κ. νεκύων πύλαι *AP*7.391 (Bass.); of Hecate, Orph.*Fr.*316. II. of the numbers 4 and 10, believed by the Pythag. to be *the keys of the order of nature*, *Theol.Ar.*22, 60: wrongly called κλαδοῦχοι (fr. κλάδος), through misunderstanding of Dor. κλᾳδ-, Lyd.*Mens.*1.15 (v. l. κλειδ-), *EM*253.50.

κλειδοφορ-έω, *bear keys*, = κλειδουχέω I, *BCH*44.72 (Lagina), etc.; -ία, ἡ, ib.11.13 (ibid.), *Supp.Epigr.*4.303 (Panamara); -ος, ἡ, *BCH* 5.186 (Lagina); κ. Ἑκάτης *Supp.Epigr.*4.301 (Panamara).

κλειδο-φῠλάκιον [ᾰ], τό, *safe for keeping keys*, prob. in *Supp.Epigr.* 4.270 (Panamara). -φύλαξ [ῠ], ακος, ὁ, ἡ, *one who keeps the keys*, Luc.*Am.*14.

κλειδ-όω, (κλείς) *lock up*, in Pass., ναὸς κεκλειδωμένος *SIG*996.19 (Smyrna), cf. *PMasp.*309.29 (vi A.D.), Sch.Ar.*Av.*1159, *Ec.* 361. **-ωμα**, ατος, τό, *fastening*, Suid. s. v. κλείθροις:—also **-ωσις**, εως, ἡ, Sch.Ar.*Av.*1159.

κλεΐζω, fut. κλεΐξω, Dor. for κλῄζω.

κλειθρ-ία (sc. ὀπή), ἡ, *keyhole* or *chink* in a door, Luc.*Nec.*22; Ion. **κληϊθρίη** prob. in Pherecyd.Syr.ap.D.L.1.122 (vulg. κλειήθρης, which Menage corrects κληΐθρης or κλειθρίης, Dind. κληϊθρίης). **-ίον**, τό, Dim. of κλεῖθρον, Hero *Aut.*9.5, al. **-ιώδης**, ες, (κλειθρία) *full of chinks*, *Gloss.* **-ον**, Ion. **κλήϊθρον**, Att. **κλῇθρον**, Dor. **κλᾷθρον** (v. infr.), τό, (κλείω A) *bar* for closing a door, in pl., κλήθρων λυθέντων A.*Th.*396; διοίγειν κλῇθρα S.*OT*1287, cf. 1294; κλῇθρα πύλης, δόμων, Id.*Ant.*1186, E.*HF*1029 (lyr.); κλῇθρα χαλάσθω Ar.*V.*1484; κλήθροισι τὰ προπύλαια πακτοῦν Id.*Lys.*264; διακόπτοντες ταῖς ἀξίναις τὰ κλεῖθρα X.*An.*7.1.17; σιδηρᾶ κ. Pl.*Ax.*371b; sg., ἀμφιδέαι..ἀπὸ κλείθρου *IG*2².1627.319. 2. *boom* of a harbour, τοῦ λιμένος τὸ κ. Aen.Tact.11.3: usu. in pl., τὰ στόματα τῶν λιμένων φράττειν τοῖς κ. Ph.*Bel.*94.42, cf. D.S.18.64; τὰ κ. τοῦ Πειραιέως Ath.12.535d. 3. ἐπὶ θάμνοις καὶ κλείθροις *fences, railings*, Gal.12.296. II. = κλειθρία, μεγάροιο διὰ κλήϊθρον ἔδυνεν *h.Merc.*146. 2. metaph., οἱ τὰ κ. ἔχοντες (sc. τῆς Πελοποννήσου), of the Corinthians, Str.8.6.20, cf. 9.4.15. 3. *entrance of the windpipe*, Hp.*Morb.*2.28. 4. as place-name, ἐν τοῖς Κλᾴθροις in the *Narrows*, *Mnemos.*42.332 (Argos).

κλειθροποιός, ὁ, *locksmith*, *Gloss.*

κλείματα· ὑποδήματα, Hsch.; cf. κλῆμα III, κλίμα VI.

κλεινία, τά, *lock-gates* (?), *PKlein.Form.*1023 (iv/v A.D.).

κλεινός, ή, όν, Aeol. **κλεεννός** (q. v.), (κλέος) poet. Adj. *famous, renowned*, νῆσος Sol.19.3; freq. epith. of cities, Pi.*O.*3.2, 6.6, Epich.185; esp. of Athens, Pi.*Fr.*76, A.*Pers.*474, E.*Ph.*1758 (troch.); of persons, κ. οἰκιστήρ Pi.*P.*1.31; μνῆμα τόδε κλεινοῖο Μεγιστία Epigr.ap.Hdt.7.228; Διὸς κλεινὴ δάμαρ A.*Pr.*834; ὁ κ. Φιλοκτήτης S.*Ph.*575; ὁ πᾶσι κ. Οἰδίπους καλούμενος *all-renowned*, Id.*OT*8; also ironically, ὁ κ. νυμφίος Id.*El.*300; τόξοισι κλεινός A.*Pr.*872; of things, -ότερον γάμον Pi.*P.*9.112; τὰ κ. αἰνίγματα S.*OT*1525 (troch.); κ. ὄνομα Ar.*Av.*810; κ. τόξα S.*Ph.*654: Sup., -ότατος στέφανος E.*IA*1529 (anap.); σοφία -οτάτη Ar.*Nu.*1024: neut. pl. as Adv., στρατηλατήσας κλεινά E.*HF* 61: rare in Prose, Pl.*Lg.*721c, *Sph.*243a; καὶ τοῦτο κλεινὸν αὐτοῦ is *well-known* of him, Luc.*Per.*18. II. in Crete, = τὰ παιδικά, like Att. καλός, Ephor.149 J., Ath.11.782c.

κλεῖξαι, Dor. aor. 1 inf. Act. of κλεΐζω, κλῄζω (A) (q. v.).

κλείπους· κόσμος τις τοῦ καλουμένου γείσους, Hsch. **κλεῖρος**· κλειδίον, Id.

κλείς, ἡ, gen. κλειδός; Att. acc. κλεῖν, v. infr. I. 3, III, later κλεῖδα *AP* 6.306 (Aristo), Plu.*Art.*9: pl. κλεῖδες, κλεῖδας, contr. κλεῖς, v. infr. III, dat. κλεισίν Pl.*Ax.*371b:—Ion. **κληΐς** [ῐ], κληῗδος, κληῗδα, etc. (Hom. uses only the Ion. form):—Dor. **κλᾳΐς**, κλᾳΐδος [ῐ] Simon.23, Pi.*P.*9.39; but acc. pl. κλᾳῖδας ib.8.4; acc. κλᾳΐδα or κλᾷδα Call.*Cer.*45; cf. κλᾴξ:—Aeol. **κλᾶϊς** (κλαῖς cod.)· μοχλός, Hsch.; κλαΐς acc. κλαΐν *Et.Gud.*ap.Schaefer *Greg.Cor.*p.584: pl. κλᾷδες (κλᾶδες cod.)· ζυγά, Hsch.:—old Att. **κλῄς**, κλῃδός, acc. κλῇδα E.*Med.*212 (anap.), 661 (lyr.): κλείς and κλῄς in the same Att. Inscr., *IG*2².1414.44 and 47. (κλᾱϝίς, cf. Lat. *clavis, claudo.*) 1. *bar, bolt*, θύρας σταθμοῖσιν ἐπῆρσε (sc. Hera, from within) κληῗδι κρυπτῇ Il.14.168, cf. Od.21.241; κληῗδος ἱμάς ib.4.802, cf. 838; ἐπὶ δὲ κληῗδ' ἐτάνυσσεν ἱμάντι 1.442; = ἐπιβλής, Il.24.455. 2. *catch* or *hook*, passed through the door from the outside to catch the strap (ἱμάς) attached to the bar (ὀχεύς), ἐν δὲ κληῗδ' ἧκε, θυρέων δ' ἀνέκοπτεν ὀχῆας ἄντα τιτυσκομένη Od.21.47, cf. 50; οἴξασα κληῗδι θύρας Il.6.89; δοιοὶ δ' ἔντοσθεν ὀχῆες εἶχον ἐπημοιβοί, μία δὲ κληῗς ἐπαρήρει 12.456, cf. Parm.1.14. 3. later, *key*, τὴν κλεῖν ἐφέλκεται Lys.1.13; κλεῖν παρακλείδιον a false *key*, Pl.Com.77: pl., κλῇδας οἶδα δώματος A.*Eu.*827, cf. E.*Ba.*448; Λακωνικὴ κ. Men.343; κυριεύσοντα τῶν κ. *OGI*229.56 (Smyrna, iii B.C.); of a sacred *key* carried in processions, *SIG*900.14 (Panamara, iv A.D.), 996.24 (Smyrna, perh. i A.D.). 4. metaph., Ἁσυχία βουλᾶν τε καὶ πολέμων ἔχοισα κλᾳῖδας Pi.*P.*8.4, cf. 9.39; ἔστι κἀμοὶ κλῄς ἐπὶ γλώσσῃ, of silence, A.*Fr.*316, cf. S.*OC*1052 (lyr.); καθαρὰν ἀνοῖξαι κλῇδα φρενῶν E.*Med.*661 (lyr.); κλῇδας γάμου φυλάττει, of Hera, Ar.*Th.*976 (lyr.); of the *key* to a problem, Vett.Val.179.4. II. *hook* or *tongue* of a clasp, Od.18.294. 2. *stop-cock*, Hero *Spir.*1.25. III. *collar-bone*, prob. so called from its hook shape (v. supr. I. 2), Hom. (only in Il.), ὅθι κληῗς ἀποέργει αὐχένα τε στῆθός τε 8.325; κληῗδα παρ' ὦμον πλῆξ', ἀπὸ δ' αὐχένος ὦμον ἐέργαθεν ἠδ' ἀπὸ νώτου 5.146; ᾗ κληῗδες ἀπ' ὤμων αὐχέν' ἔχουσι 22.324, cf. Hp.*Aër.*7, *Art.*13; παῖσον ἐμᾶς ὑπὸ κλῇδος S.*Tr.*1035; τὴν κλεῖν συνετρίβην And.1.61; τὴν κλεῖν κατεαγώς D.18.67: pl., Diog. Apoll.6, etc.; τὰ πλάγια καὶ τὰς κλεῖδας Arist.*HA*513ᵇ35; αἱ κλεῖδες (v.l. κλεῖς) καὶ αἱ πλευραί, of the crocodile, ib.516ᵃ28; κλεῖδες ὀπταί roast *shoulder-bones* of the tunny (with play on I. 3, *visible* keys, opp. κρυπταὶ κλεῖδες of the Laconians), Aristopho 7.2, cf. Diph.Siph.ap. Ath.8.357a. IV. *rowing bench* in a ship, freq. in Od., always in pl.; ἐπὶ κληῗσι καθίζειν 2.419, etc.; κληῗδεσσιν ἐφήμενοι 12.215; once in Il., πεντήκοντ' ἔσαν ἄνδρες ἐπὶ κληῗσιν 16.170; δησάμενοι..ἐπὶ κληῗσιν ἐρετμά Od.8.37. V. of promontories, straits, etc., Κληῗδες or Κληῗδες τῆς Κύπρου Hdt.5.108, cf. Str.14.6.3; πόντου κλῇδ', of the Bosporus, E.*Med.*212 (lyr.). VI. in pl., *sacred chaplets*, Id.*Tr.*256 (anap.) (Ephes., acc. to Hsch.). VII. in versification, *clausula, cadence*, Sch.Ar.*Pax* 1127.

κλεισ-ία, ἡ, *inn*, *IG*4²(1).114.21, 30, 109 ii 151, al. (Epid.). II. v. sq. **-ιάδες**, αἱ, *door opening into the* κλεισίον, *street-door* of a house, identified with the αὔλειος θύρα, Plu.*Publ.*20, Poll.4.125, 9.50: written κλεισίαι in Ael.Dion.*Fr.*231; κλεισιάδες θύραι D.H.5.39; = δίθυροι πύλαι, Moer.p.227 P.; but, *inner door*, opp. αὔλειος, ἐν οἰκίαις αὔλειοι πρόκεινται κλεισιάδων Ph.1.520; οἴκοι καταμένειν καὶ μηδὲ τὰς κ. ὑπερβαίνειν Id.2.82, cf. 4; οὐ μόνον τειχῶν ἐντὸς ἀλλὰ καὶ κλεισιάδων θαλαμευομένοις ἀποζῆν Id.ap.Eus.*PE*8.14: metaph., μεγάλαι κ. ἀναπεπτέαται..τῷ Πέρσῃ a wide *entrance*, Hdt.9.9, cf. Plu.*Alc.*10, Aristid. *Or.*38(7).21. II. *sluice-gates*, D.H.1.66. (Usu. written κλισ-, but κλεισ- Plu.*Publ.* l. c. codd.) **-ίον**, τό, *outhouse, shed*, τῆς οἰκίας τὸ κ. Antiph.21, cf. Lys.12.18, D.18.129 (here perh. = *brothel*), *IG*11(2).158 *A* 56, 287 *A* 146 (Delos, iii B.C.), *BCH*35.243 (ibid., ii B.C.), *Ephes.* 2.75 (i B.C.): pl., *sheds* for cattle, D.Chr.40.9. 2. *shrine, chapel*, Paus.4.1.7, *BCH*33.72 (Cappadocia). [First syll. long in Antiph. l. c.; written κλεισίον *IG* l. c., *BCH*35 l. c., Hdn.Gr.1.356, 2.415, Ael. Dion. l. c.; later κλισ- *Ephes.* l. c., *BCH*33 l. c., freq. in codd.; prob. fr. κλίνω as 'lean-to', 'penthouse', rather than fr. κλείω as stated by Poll.9.50.]

κλεῖσις, εως, ἡ, (κλείω A) v. κλῆσις.

κλεῖσμα, ατος, τό, *barrier*, Tz.*H.*1.903.

κλεισμός, ὁ, *storing under lock and key*, οἴνου *POxy.*1578.7 (iii A.D.).

κλεισούρα, ἡ, *narrow pass, defile*, Procop.*Pers.*2.29, Suid. (also s. vv. ἐμβολήν, ὀχύρωμα).

κλειστός, Ion. **κληϊστός**, old Att. **κληστός**, ή, όν, *that can be shut* or *closed*, κληϊσταὶ σανίδες Od.2.344; χῶμα γαίας κ. E.*Fr.*617; βεβαίως κ. Th.2.17; κ. λιμήν Id.7.38; κ. ἀναβάσεις Aen.Tact.22.19, cf. Str.14.6.3, Scyl.29, al.; κ. ὕδωρ Aristobul.35 J.; θυρίδες κ. D.S.20.85, cf. Luc.*VH*1.24, Philostr.*Im.*1.13. 2. *closed*, διώρυγες Str.15.1.50, al.

κλεῖστρον, τό, = κλεῖθρον, Luc.*Tox.*57, *PMag.Osl.*1.317:—Dor. **κλᾴϊστρον** [ᾰ], γλεφάρων ἁδὺ κ. Pi.*P.*1.8; **κλᾷσθρον**, Hsch. (κλάσθεον cod.).

κλειτοπόδιον, part of a ship, Poll.1.85.

κλειτορ-ιάζω, *touch the* κλειτορίς, Ruf.*Onom.*111, Hsch., Suid.:—also **-ίζω**, v.l. in Poll.2.174. **-ίς**, ίδος, ἡ, *clitoris*, Ruf.*Onom.*111, etc. II. a gem, Ps.-Plu.*Fluv.*25.5.

κλειτός, ή, όν, (κλείω B) *renowned, famous*, ἐπίκουροι Il.3.451, 6.227, etc.; βασιλῆες Od.6.54; γενεά Pi.*N.*6.61; of things, *splendid, excellent*, ἑκατόμβη Il.4.102, cf. Pi.*P.*10.33; Πανοπεύς, Ἰωλκός, Il.17.307, Pi.*P.*4.77.

κλεῖτος (A), εος, τό, poet. for κλέος, Alcm.96, cf. Hsch. s. v. κλειτῄ; **κλῆτος**, Suid.

κλεῖτος (B), εος, τό, = sq., pl. κλείτεα A.R.1.599 cod. Laur. (v. l. κλίτεα): elsewh. κλίτος (q. v.).

κλειτύς, ύος, ἡ, acc. pl. κλειτῦς Il.16.390: (κλίνω):—*slope, hillside*, Il. l. c., Od.5.470; Παρνησίαν ὑπὲρ κλειτύν S.*Ant.*1145 (lyr.), cf. Limen.2; Τιρυνθίαν πρὸς κ. S.*Tr.*271, etc.; τὰ ἐγ Κλειτυϊ (place-name) *IG*12(5).1076.38 (Ceos, iv/iii B.C.). [ῡ in acc. κλειτύν Od. l. c., elsewh. ῠ S.*Tr.* l. c., etc.: freq. written κλι- in codd., but κλει- in *IG* and Limen. ll. cc., cf. Hdn.Gr.2.416.]

κλείω (A), fut. κλείσω X.*An.*4.3.20 (ἀπο-), Him.*Or.*22.7; rare fut. κατα-κλιῶ, v. κατακλείω: aor. ἔκλεισα X.*An.*7.1.36, Pl.*Ep.*348b: pf. κέκλεικα Thphr.*Char.*18.4, Lxx 1*Ki.*23.20, Luc.*Tox.*30: plpf. ἐκεκλείκειν App.*Hann.*47:—Med., aor. 1 ἐκλεισάμην (κατ-) X.*Cyr.* 7.2.5, (ἐγ-) Id.*HG*6.5.9:—Pass., fut. κλεισθήσομαι (συγ-) ib.5.2.19: aor. ἐκλείσθην D.23.110, etc.: pf. κέκλειμαι (later κέκλεισμαι f.l. in Ar.*V.*198) (v. infr.):—Ion. **κληΐω** (ἀπο-) Hdt.4.7: aor. ἐκλήϊσα Od. 24.166, (ἐξ-) Hdt.1.144, Ep. κλήϊσα Od.19.30; inf. κληῗσαι 21.382:—Med., fut. κληΐσσομαι cj. in Nonn.*D.*2.310:—Pass., aor. ἀπ-εκληΐσθην Hdt.1.165, 3.55, 58: pf. κεκλήϊμαι 2.121.β', cf. 3.117, 7.129 (with vv. ll.): plpf. ἀπ-εκεκλέατο 9.50 codd.:—old Att. **κλῄω** (also Trag., cf. *An.Ox.*1.226), fut. κλῄσω Th.4.8: aor. ἔκλησα E.*Or.*1447 (lyr.), Th.2.4, Pl.*R.*560c: pf. κέκληκα (ἀπο-) Ar.*Av.*1262:—Med., fut. κεκλήσομαι Id.*Lys.*1071: aor. περι-κλῄσασθαι Th.7.52:—Pass., aor. ἐκλῄσθην (κατ-, ξυν-) Id.1.117, 4.67, etc.: pf. κέκλημαι (v. infr.):—Dor. fut. κλᾳξῶ Theoc.6.32: aor. ἀπό-κλᾳξον, -κλᾴξας, Id.15.43, 77, ἔκλᾳξε Cerc.7.2, cf. κλάκαι (leg. κλᾷσαι)· κλεῖσαι, Hsch.:—Med., impf. κατ-εκλᾴζετο Theoc.18.5:—Pass., aor. κατ-εκλᾴσθην Id.7.84, but part. συγκατα-κλαιχθείς *Chron.Lind.D.*62: pf. 3 pl. κατα-κέκλᾳνται Epich.141.—Cf. κλῄζω (B). (κλείς):—*shut, close, bar*, Hom. (only in Od.), κλήϊσεν δὲ θύρας *barred* the doors, 21.387; ἐκλήϊσεν ὀχῆας *shot* the bars, so as to close the door, 24.166; κλῄειν πύλας E.*HF*997, Pl.*R.* l. c., etc.; κ. πηκτὰ δωμάτων Ar.*Ach.*479; κλεῖδες.., αἷς τὰς θύρας κλείουσιν Aristopho 7; Ἐτεοκλέους..κλῄσας στόμα E.*Ph.*865; κανθὼς Cerc. l. c.; λάρυγγα Gal.6.65:—Pass., βλέφαρα κέκληται S.*Fr.*711; ψυχῆς ἀνοῖξαι τὴν κεκλημένην πύλην Id.*Fr.*393; κεκλειμένης σου τῆς παρρησίας οὐ κιγκλίσιν.., ἀλλὰ..ὀφλήμασι D.25.28. 2. *shut up, close, block up*, Βόσπορον κλῇσαι A.*Pers.*723 (troch.); κλῄσειν ταῖς ναυσὶν τοὺς ἔσπλους Th.4.8:—Pass., Hdt.2.121.β'; τὰ ἐμπόρια κεκλῇσθαι Lys.22.14; κεκλειμένων τῶν ἐμπορίων D.2.16. II. *shut in, enclose*, πόλιν..πύργων μηχανῇ κεκλῃμένην A.*Supp.*956; cf. κλῄζω (B). III. *confine*, πλάστιγξ αὐχένα πώλων ἔκλῃε E.*Rh.*304:—Pass., *to be confined*, χέρας βρόχοισι κεκλῃμένα Id.*Andr.*502 (lyr.): metaph., ὅρκοις κεκλῄμεθα Id.*Hel.*977. 2. *deliver bound*, τινὰ εἰς τὰς τοῦ βασιλέως χεῖρας Lxx 1*Ki.*23.20.

κλείω (B), Ep. for κλέω (A), *celebrate* (q. v.).

κλείω (C), Ep. for κλέω (B), καλέω, *call* (q. v.).

Κλειώ, οῦς, ἡ, *Clio*, one of the Muses, Hes.*Th.*77, Pi.*N.*3.83 (Κλεοῦς metri gr. codd. recc.), etc. (κλέω (A), κλείω (B).)

κλέμμα, ατος, τό, (κλέπτω) *thing stolen*, E.*Hec*.618, Arist.*Pr*.952ᵃ 19; *money equivalent of thing stolen*, τὸ κ. ἐκτείσας διπλοῦν Pl.*Lg*.857b, cf. *Foed.Delph.Pell*.2 *A* 14, *IG*5(1).1390.77 (Andania, i B.C.). 2. *theft*, S.*Ichn*.67 (pl., lyr.), Ar.*Eq*.1203, Str.15.1.53. II. *stratagem* in war, Th.5.9; *fraud*, D.18.31, Aeschin.3.100; κ. ἐρωτικόν *clandestine* amour, Ael.*NA*1.2, cf. *AP*5.17 (Rufin.).

κλεμμάδιος [ᾰ], α, ον, *stolen*, Pl.*Lg*.955b, cf. Hsch., Phot.

κλέμμιν· δίφρον ἀνακλιτόν, Hsch. **κλεμμύειν**· κηρύσσειν, Id.

κλεμμύς, ύος, ἡ, = χελώνη, *tortoise*, Ant.Lib.32.2, Hsch.

Κλεομενισταί, οἱ, *partisans of Cleomenes*, Plb.2.53.2.

κλεόνικον, τό, = κλινοπόδιον, Dsc.3.95.

κλέος, τό, Dor. κλέϝος *GDI*1537 (Crissa, = Röhl *Imag*.³ pp.87/8 No. 1), only nom. and acc. sg. and pl.: Ep. pl. κλέᾰ (before a vowel) Hom. (v. infr. II. 1), κλεῖα (nisi leg. κλέεα) Hes.*Th*.100: (κλέω A):— *rumour, report*, τί δὴ κ. ἔστ' ἀνὰ ἄστυ; Od.16.461; κ. εὐρὺ φόνου 23.137; ὅσσαν.., ἥ τε μάλιστα φέρει κ. ἀνθρώποισι 1.283; σὸν κ. *news* of thee, 13.415: c. gen., μετὰ κ. ἵκετ' Ἀχαιῶν *the report* of their coming, Il.11.227, cf. 13.364; κείνου κατὰ κ. at *the news* of his coming, Pi.*P*.4.125; τῶν ἐμῶν κακῶν κ. S.*Ph*.251; *rumour*, opp. certainty, κ. οἶον ἀκούομεν οὐδέ τι ἴδμεν Il.2.486; γυναικογήρυτον κ. A.*Ag*.487 (lyr.). II. *good report, fame*, freq. in Hom., κ. ἐσθλὸν Il.5.3; ἀνδρὸς τοῦ κ. εὐρὺ καθ' Ἑλλάδα Od.1.344: abs., τῷ μὲν κ., ἄμμι δὲ πένθος Il.4.197; τὸ δ' ἐμὸν κ. οὔ ποτ' ὀλεῖται 7.91, cf. 2.325; κ. εἶναί τινι to be *a glory* to him, 22.514; κ. οὐρανὸν ἵκει 8.192, Od.9.20; κ. οὐρανὸν εὐρὺν ἵκανε 8.74; κ. ἄφθιτον Sapph.*Supp*.20a.4, Ibyc.*Oxy*.1790.47, *GDI* l. c.; κ. ἀρέσθαι, εὑρέσθαι, Pi.*O*.9.101, *P*.3.111; γίνεσθε κατὰ κ. ὧδε μαχηταί in *renown*, *BCH*24.71 (Acraeph., iii B.C.); λαβεῖν S.*Ph*.1347; κ. αἰχμᾶς *glory in* or *for*.., Pi.*P*.1.66; τῆς μελλοῦς κ. A.*Ag*.1356; κ. σου μαντικὸν ib.1098; μικροῦ δ' ἀγῶνος οὐ μέγ' ἔρχεται κ. S.*Fr*.938: less freq. in Prose, κ. ἀέναον Heraclit.29; μένοντι δὲ..κ. μέγα ἐλείπετο Hdt.7.220; κ. καταθέσθαι to lay up store of *glory*, Id.9.78; τιμὴν καὶ κ. ἔσχεν Ar.*Ra*.1035; πόρρω κ. ἥκει Id.*Ach*.646; κ. οὐρανομήκες Id.*Nu*.459; κ. ἔχειν τὰ περὶ τὰς ναῦς Th.1.25; παρ' ἀνθρώποις ἀείμνηστον κ. ἔχει τινά X.*Cyn*.1.6; κ. ἀθάνατον καταθέσθαι Pl.*Smp*.208c; κ. τε καὶ ἔπαινος πρὸς ἀνθρώπων Id.*Lg*.663a; περὶ χώρας ἀκούειν κ. μέγα Lys.2.5; κ. ἕξειν ἔν τινι Ath.Mech.15.4; ποῖον κ., εἰ..; 1*Ep.Pet*.2.20: pl., ἄειδε δ' ἄρα κλέα ἀνδρῶν *the lays* of their achievements, Il.9.189, cf. 524, Od.8.73; κλέα φωτῶν μνήσομαι A.R.1.1. 2. rarely in bad sense, δύσφαμον κ. ill *repute*, Pi.*N*.8.36; αἰσχρὸν κ. E.*Hel*.135, cf. Ar.*Fr*.796: both senses in Th.2.45 ἧς ἂν ἐπ' ἐλάχιστον ἀρετῆς πέρι ἢ ψόγου..κ. ᾖ of whom there is least *talk* either for praise or blame. (Cf. Skt. *śrávas* 'fame', Slav. *slovo* 'word', 'glory'; cogn. with κλέω (A), κλύω.)

κλέπας· νοτερόν, πηλῶδες· ἢ δασύ, ἢ ὑγρόν, Hsch.

κλεπία, ἡ, = κλοπή, Phot.

κλέπιμος, = κλόπιμος, *contraband*, ἔλαιον *PHib*.1.59.7 (iii B.C.), prob. in *PRev.Laws* 55.20 (iii B.C.).

κλέπος, εος, τό, = κλέμμα, Sol.ap.Poll.8.34.

κλεπτ-άριον, τό, Dim. of κλέπτης, = Lat. *furunculus*, Charis.p.552 K., *Gloss*. **-έλεγχος**, ον, *convicting a thief*, λίθος κ. a stone that had magic powers for this purpose, Aët.2.32. **-έον**, *one must conceal*, S.*Ph*.57. **-ήρ**, ῆρος, ὁ, = sq., Man.1.311, 4.304. **-ης**, ου, ὁ, *thief*, Il.3.11; τὸν πυρὸς κ. A.*Pr*.946; κλέπτα δύο Ar.*V*.928; opp. ἅρπαξ (a robber), Myrtil.4; λῃστὰς ἢ κλέπτας Pl.*R*.351c, cf. *Ev.Jo*.10.8; ὁ τοῦ κ. λόγος, a logical fallacy, Arist.*SE*180ᵇ18. 2. generally, *cheat, knave*, S.*Aj*.1135; κακῶν ἀλλοτρίων κ. D.45.59. **-ίδης**, ου, ὁ, Com. Patronym. of κλέπτης, *Son of a Thief*, Pherecr.219. **-ικός**, ή, όν, *thievish*: ἡ -κή (sc. τέχνη) *thievery*, Pl.*R*.334b, Luc.*DDeor*.7.2. Adv. -κῶς Eust.811.41. **-ις**, ιδος, ἡ, fem. of κλέπτης, *she-thief*, Alciphr.3.22. **-ίσκος**, ὁ, Dim. of κλέπτης, Eup.420. **-ίστατος**, η, ον, Att. Sup. formed from κλέπτης, *the most arrant thief*, Ar.*Pl*.27, Alciphr.3.20, Procop.*Arc*.21; κ. θεός S.E.*P*.3.215; κ. χεῖρες Adam.2.20: also Comp. -ίστερος, α, ον, Suid. s. v. Νεοκλείδου. **-οσύνη**, ἡ, *thievishness, knavery*, Od.19.396, Man.6.207: in Prose, κ. καὶ ἐπιορκία Phld.*Piet*.37.

κλεπτο-τελωνέω, *smuggle*, Men.Prot.p.22 D., Tz.*H*.13.527 (Pass.). **-τροφος**, ὁ, *thief of food*, Suid. s. v. δειπνολόχον.

κλέπτρια, ἡ, fem. of κλεπτήρ, Sotad.Com.2.

κλέπτω, Ion. impf. κλέπτεσκον Hdt.2.174: fut. κλέψω Ar.*Ec*.667, etc., κλέψομαι X.*Cyr*.7.4.13: aor. ἔκλεψα Il.5.268, etc.: pf. κέκλοφα Ar.*Pl*.369, 372, Pl.*Lg*.941d; later part. κεκλεβώς *IG*5(1).1390.75 (Andania, i B.C.):—Pass., aor. 1 ἐκλέφθην Hdt.5.84, E.*Or*.1580: aor. 2 ἐκλάπην [ᾰ] Pl.*R*.413b, X.*Eq.Mag*.4.17; later part. κλεπείς *BGU*454.19 (ii A.D.): pf. κέκλεμμαι S.*Ant*.681, Ar.*V*.57. (Cf. Lat. *clĕpere*, Goth. *hlifan* (κλέπτειν), *hliftus* (κλέπτης)):—*steal*, c. acc. or abs., Il.24.24, 71, 109; τῆς γενεῆς ἔκλεψε from that breed Anchises *stole*, i.e. foals of that breed, 5.268; κλέπτουσιν ἐφ' ἁρπαγῇ ἀλλοτρίων ἄλλος Sol.4.13; κ. μοιχεύειν τε Xenoph.11.3; ἢν μηδεν μήτε κλέπτῃ μήτε ἀδικῇ Democr.253; κ. τι παρ' ἀλλήλων Hdt.1.186; κ. ἐξ ἱερῶν Pl.*Lg*.857b; *carry off*, κλέψεν Μήδειαν Pi.*P*.4.250; πυρὸς σέλας κ., of Prometheus, A.*Pr*.8; κλέψαι τε χἀρπάσαι βίᾳ S.*Ph*.644; κ. τοὺς μηνύοντας *spirit away* the deponents, Antipho 5.38; ἐξ ἐπάλξεων πλεκταῖσιν ἐς γῆν σῶμα κ. *let it down secretly*, E.*Tr*.958, cf. 1010; κ. μορφάς, of painters, *steal* forms (by transferring them to canvas), Luc.*Epigr*.41. 2. in part. Act., *thievish*, κλέπτον βλέπει he has a *thief's* look, Ar.*V*.900; κλέπτον τὸ χρῆμα τἀνδρός he's an arrant *thief*, ib.933. II. c. acc. pers., *cozen, cheat*, πάρφασις, ἥ τ' ἔκλεψε νόον Il.14.217; οὐκ ἔστι Διὸς κλέψαι νόον Hes.*Th*.613; μὴ κλέπτε νόῳ Il.1.132; κλέπτει νιν οὐ θεός, οὐ βροτός, ἔργοις οὔτε βουλαῖς Pi.*P*.3.29; σοφία κλέπτει παράγοισα μύθοις Id.*N*.7.23; οὔτοι φρέν' ἂν κλέψειεν A.*Ch*.854, cf. S.*Tr*.243, etc.; τὴν γνώμην Hp.*Epid*.5.27; κ. τὴν ἀκρόασιν Aeschin.3.99:—Pass., κλέπτεται ὁ ἀκροατής Arist.*Rh*.1408ᵇ5; προβαίνειν κλεπτόμενος to go on *blindfold*, Hdt.7.49; κλέπτεταί οἱ ἡ αὐγή his vision *becomes deceptive*, Hp.*Morb*.2.12; κλαπέντες ἢ βιασθέντες τοῦτο πάσχουσιν Pl.*R*. l. c.: impers., κλέπτεται *the deception is passed off*, Arist.*Rh*.1404ᵇ24. III. *conceal, keep secret*, θεοῖο γόνον Pi.*O*.6.36; θυμῷ δεῖμα Id.*P*.4.96; *disguise*, διαβολαῖς νέαις κλέψας τὰ πρόσθε σφάλματ' E.*Supp*.416; τοῖς ὀνόμασι κ. τὰ πράγματα Aeschin.3.142; τοὺς ἑαυτῶν κ. X.*Eq.Mag*.5.2; κ. ἑαυτὸν ὀφθαλμῶν τε καὶ ὤτων Philostr.*VS* 1.7.2; κ. τοῦ διανοήματος τὴν ἄδειαν Demetr.*Eloc*.239:—Pass., κλέπτεται τὸ μετρικόν ib.182, cf. Them. *in Ph*.276.26, Paul.Aeg.6.103. IV. *do secretly* or *treacherously*, δόλοισι κ. σφαγάς *execute* slaughter *by secret* frauds, S.*El*.37; πόλλ' ἂν..λάθρᾳ σὺ κλέψειας κακά Id.*Aj*.1137; κ. μύθους *whisper malicious* rumours, ib.188 (lyr.); κλέπτων ἢ βιαζόμενος *by fraud* or open force, Pl.*Lg*.933e; ταῦτα κλέπτοντες ταῖς πράξεσιν, i.e. λάθρᾳ πράττοντες, ib.910b; κλεπτομένη λαλιά *secret, clandestine*, Luc.*Am*.15, etc. 2. *seize* or *occupy secretly*, τὰ ὄρη X.*An*.5.6.9, cf. 4.6.11, 15; τὴν ἀρχήν D.H.4.10. 3. *effect* or *bring about clandestinely*, γάμον κ. δώροις Theoc.22.151:—Pass., *to be 'smuggled in'*, Arist.*Rh.Al*.1440ᵇ21. 4. *get rid of imperceptibly*, τὸ δοκεῖν.. D.H.*Rh*.8.7; τῇ ποικιλίᾳ τὸν κόρον Id.*Comp*.19:—Pass., τοῦ πόσου κλεπτομένου Plot.4.7.5.

κλέτας, τό, prob. = κλειτύς, Lyc.703, Nonn.*D*.5.59, al., *AP*9.665 (Agath.).

κλεύθομαι, subj. κλεύθωμαι, fut. κλεύσομαι, expld. by Gramm. as for κελεύθ-, read by Aristarch. for κεύθομαι in Il.23.244, cf. Sch. ad loc., Hsch., *EM*517.45.

κλευτόν· τλευτόν, Hsch.

κλέψ, ὁ, *thief*, prob. coined from βοῦκλεψ, Phryn.*PS* p.17 B.

κλεψίαμβος [ῐ], ὁ, a kind of *musical instrument*, Phillis ap.Ath.14.636b, Aristox.ib.4.182f, Poll.4.59. II. in pl., = μέλη τινὰ παρὰ Ἀλκμᾶνι, Hsch.

κλεψι-γάμος [ῐ], ον, *seeking illicit love*, Nonn.*D*.8.60. **-κοίτης**, ου, ὁ, = foreg., Ismenias ap.Ps.-Callisth.1.46.

κλεψῐμαῖος, α, ον, = κλοπιμαῖος, *stolen*, Lxx *To*.2.13, *PLond*.2.422.3 (iv A.D.). Adv. -αίως, = Lat. *furtim*, Dosith.p.412 K.

κλεψί-νοος [ῐ], ον, *beguiling the mind*, Nonn.*D*.8.47, etc. **-νυμφος**, ον, = κλεψίγαμος, Lyc.1116. **-ποτέω**, *drink unfairly*, Anon. ap.Suid., Poll.6.20. **-ρρυτος**, ον, *secretly flowing*, name of a stream at Athens, *which flowed some distance under ground*, Hsch. **-τόκος**, ον, *concealing offspring*, Opp.*C*.3.11, Nonn.*D*.28.317. **-φρων**, ον, gen. ονος, (φρήν) *dissembling*, Ἑρμῆς *h.Merc*.413. II. = κλεψίνοος, Man.1.93. **-χωλος**, ον, *disguising lameness*, Luc.*Ocyp*.33.

κλεψ-ύδρα, Ion. -ύδρη, ἡ, (ὕδωρ) *pipette*, = ὑδράρπαξ, a small vessel with one or more perforations below and an air-vent above, for transferring small quantities of liquid, Emp.100.9, Arist.*Ph*.213ᵃ27, *Pr*.914ᵇ9, al., Hero *Spir*.2.27 (described in 1.7), Simp. *in Cael*.524.19, *in Ph*.647.26. II. *water-clock*, a water-butt with a narrow orifice underneath, through which the water trickled slowly, for measuring periods of time, used to time speeches in the law-courts, Ar.*V*.93, 857, Arist.*Ath*.67.2, etc.; πρὸς κλεψύδρας ἀγωνίζεσθαι Id.*Po*.1451ᵃ8; τὴν ὀπὴν βῦσον τῆς κλεψύδρης Herod.2.43; for measuring military watches, Aen.Tact.22.24; for astronomical measurements, Procl.*Hyp*.4.74 (in the form of a perforated bowl floating on water, Gal.*Anim.Pass*.2.5); rarely for other purposes, Eub.p.182 K., Epin.2; εἰς τὴν ἐκπλήρωσιν τῆς κ. Herophil.ap.Marcellin.*Puls*.265. III. name of an ebbing well, in the Acropolis at Athens, Ar.*Av*.1695 (lyr.); at Ithome, Pap. in *Abh.Berl.Akad*.1904(2).14 (ii B.C.), Paus.4.31.6. **-ύδριον**, τό, Dim. of foreg., Philostr.*VS*2.10.1, 2.13.1.

κλέω (A), Ep. **κλείω** (as Hom. always in Act., but in Pass. only κλέομαι; Trag. only κλέω, in lyr.), *tell of, make famous, celebrate*, ἔργ' ἀνδρῶν..τά τε κλείουσιν ἀοιδοί Od.1.338, cf. *h.Hom*.32.19; ἐγὼ δέ κέ σε κλείω Od.17.418, cf. Hes.*Op*.1, *Th*.105, Stesich.35, *Inscr.Cos* 218.7, prob. in Hermesian.7.33; ἔν τ' ἀλύροις κλέοντες ὕμνοις E.*Alc*.447; Θέτιν..κλέουσαι Id.*IA*1046; κλέωά τὸν Ἀμύκλαις σιόν, Lacon. for κλέουσα τὸν Ἀμ. θεόν, Ar.*Lys*.1299:—Med., γῆρυν, ἂν σοφοὶ κλέονται E.*Fr*.369.7:—Pass., *to be famed*: c. dat., *for* a thing, φρένες..ᾗς τὸ πάρος περ ἔκλε' (for ἐκλέεο) Il.24.202; ἐγὼ δ' ἐν πᾶσι θεοῖσι μήτι τε κλέομαι καὶ κέρδεσιν Od.13.299; κλέεσθαι ἐν φορμίγγεσσι *to be celebrated* in lyric strains, Pi.*I*.5(4).27; ἔνθ'..ἀγοραὶ Πυλάτιδες κλέονται where *are held the famous* meetings, prob. in S.*Tr*.639 (lyr.). II. c. acc. et inf., *sing* how.., B.15.13. (κλεϝ-, cf. κλέος, κλύω, Lat. *clueo*: Skt. *śrutás* (= κλυτός) 'famous', *śṛṇóti* 'hear'.)

κλέω (B), Ep. **κλείω**, = καλέω, *call*, A.R.1.217, 2.687, Opp.*H*.5.536: impf. κλεῖον Orph.*L*.195:—Pass., ἔνθα περ ἀκταὶ κλείονται Παγασαί A.R.1.238 (cf. καλέω II. 3a); κλείονται γαλεοί Opp.*H*.1.379; also κλέεται Nic.*Fr*.71.5: 2 sg. impf. ἔκλεο Call.*Del*.40.

κλεώνιον, τό, = ἑλένιον, Dsc.1.28: **κλεωναία**, ἡ, prob. in Ps.-Dsc. ibid., Hsch.

κλῆδεα· φραγμοί, Hsch.

κλῇδες, old Att. nom. pl. of κλείς.

κλήδην, Adv., (καλέω) *by name*, Il.9.11.

κληδον-ίζω, prob. *give a sign* or *omen*, Hsch.:—Med., *to be a diviner*, Lxx *De*.18.10, 4*Ki*.21.6:—Pass., *receive an omen*, *PMag.Oxy*.886.13 (iii A.D.). **-ιος**, α, ον, *giving an omen*, = πανομφαῖος, title of Zeus, Sch.Il.8.250, Eust.169.27. **-ισμα**, ατος, τό, *sign, omen*, Luc.

*Pseudol.*17. **-ισμός**, ὁ, *observation of a sign* or *omen*, v.l. in Lxx *De.*18.14.

κληδουχέω, κληδοῦχος, old Att. for κλειδ- (q. v.).

κληδών, όνος, ἡ, Ep. **κλεηδών** and **κληηδών,** (κλέω A) *omen, presage contained in a chance utterance*, χαῖρεν δὲ κλεηδόνι δῖος Ὀδυσσεύς Od. 18.117, 20.120; ὁ μὲν τῇ κ. οὐδὲν χρεώμενος (supr. φήμη) Hdt.5.72; κληδόνας τε δυσκρίτους ἐγνώρισ' αὐτοῖς A.*Pr.*486, cf. S.*El.*1110, Call.*Ep.*1.14: in later Prose, κληδόνων ἀκούσονται Lxx *De.*18.14 (v.l. -ονισμῶν), cf. Polystr.p.5 W.; μαντικὴ ἀπὸ κληδόνων Paus.9.11.7, cf. *PMag.Oxy.*886.22 (iii A. D.); δέχομαι τὴν κ. Luc.*Laps.*8: personified, in pl., Paus. l. c.; Φήμη καὶ Κ., = Lat. *Aius Locutius*, Plu.*Cam.* 30. **II.** *tidings*, κληηδὼν πατρός *news* of my father, Od.4.317: abs., *report, rumour*, ἐξ ἀμαυρᾶς κ. A.*Ch.*853, cf. Hdt.9.101; κληδόνες παλίγκοτοι A.*Ag.*863; κ. ἐν ἁπάσῃ τῇ πόλει κατεῖχεν, ὅτι.. And.1. 130. **2.** *fame, repute*, κ. ἀϋτεῖ A.*Ag.*927; *glory*, παῖδες γὰρ ἀνδρὶ κ. σωτήριοι Id.*Ch.*505; κληδὼν καλή good *report*, S.*OC*258; κ. αἰσχρά E.*Alc.*315. **III.** *invocation*, λιτὰς δὲ καὶ κληδόνας πατρῴους A. *Ag.*228 (lyr.); κληδόνος βοή Id.*Eu.*397. **b.** *shouting*, S.*Ichn.* 232. **2.** *name, appellation*, κ. ἐπωνύμους A.*Eu.*418.

κλῄζω (A), Ar.*Th.*117 (lyr.), etc.; Ion. **κληΐζω** Hp.*Art.*42, Dor. **κλεΐζω** v.l. in Pi.*O.*1.110, cf. Eust.1497.50: impf. ἔκλειζον *Epigr.Gr.* 254 (Cyprus, iv/iii B. C.): fut. κληΐσω Fr.Lyr.ap.Aristid.*Or.*50(26).31, κλῄσω *h.Hom.*31.18, A.R.3.993, Dor. κλεΐξω Pi. l. c.: aor. ἔκλῃσα E.*IA* 1522, Ar.*Av.*905 (lyr., κλεῖσον cod. R), 950, 1745, Nic.*Fr.*86 (ἔκλησε codd. Ath.), ἔκλεισα *IG*14.2258 (Etruria):—Pass., κληΐζομαι A.R.4. 1153, Ti.Locr.100d, *Epigr.Gr.*946 (Tralles), κλῄζομαι S.*OT*733, X. *Cyr.*1.2.1, etc., κλεΐζομαι Man.6.571: pf. κεκλῄισμαι, ἐκλῄισμαι, A.R. 4.618, 990: plpf. ἐκλῄιστο ib.267, 1202:—*make famous, celebrate in song*, *h.Hom.* l. c., Pi. l. c.; κλῄσομεν Ἄρτεμιν E.*IA*1522 (lyr.); κλῄσον, ὦ χρυσόθρονε, τὰν τρομεράν Ar.*Av.*950 (mock lyr.), cf. 1745; παλαὶ δὴ τήνδ' ἐγὼ κλῄζω πόλιν ib.921:—Pass., τὰν Ἀργὼ τὰν διὰ σοῦ στόματος ἀεὶ -ομέναν E.*Hyps.Fr.*3(1) ii 20 (lyr.). **2.** *mention, speak of*, in Pass., πότερα γὰρ αὐτοῦ ζῶντος ἢ τεθνηκότος φάτις.. ἐκλῄζετο; A. *Ag.*631; οἷα κλῄζεται as *are said*, E.*Hel.*721; ἀφανὴς (sc. ὢν) κλῄζεται ib.126; θανὼν κλῄζεται he *is reported* to be dead, ib.132; κλῄζομαι ὡς προδοῦσ' ib.927. **3.** *applaud, praise*, Hp.*Art.*42. **4.** *invoke*, *PMag.Par.*1.271, al. **5.** *summon*, δίκῃ ἀνεμωλίῳ ἐκλῄισσαν.. σὸν θεράποντα Maiist.38. **II.** *call*, σὲ νῦν μὲν ἥδε γῆ σωτῆρα κλῄζει S. *OT*48:—Pass., Φωκὶς μὲν ἡ γῆ κλῄζεται ib.733; ἔνθα κλῄζεται οὑμὸς Κιθαιρών where *is* the hill *called* my Cithaeron, ib.1452, cf. E.*Hyps. Fr.*3(1) iv 26; παῖς κ. Μενοικέως Id.*Ph.*10; πατρὸς Ἀθηνίωνος κ. *IG* 9(1).880.3 (Corc.), cf. 12(3).1190.7 (Melos): less freq. in Prose, οἱ Περσεῖδαι ἀπὸ Περσέως κλῄζονται X.*Cyr.*1.2.1, cf. Pl.*Ax.*371b, App. *BC*1.1; etym. of Κλειώ, Corn.*ND*14. (κλε(ϝ)-ίζω (fr. κλέος) 'celebrate' and κλη-ΐζω (fr. καλέω) 'call' were confused by the Greeks.)

κλῄζω (B), late form for κλείω (A), κλῄω, *shut*, *Hymn.Is.*159:— Pass., *AP*9.62 (Even.).

κληηδών, όνος, ἡ, Ep. for κληδών, Od.4.317.

κλήθρ-α, Ion. **-ρη,** ἡ, *alder*, *Alnus glutinosa*, Od.5.64, 239, Thphr. *HP*1.4.3, 3.3.1. **-ινος,** η, ον, *of the alder*, ξύλα Ath.Mech.17.15 (κλείθρ- codd.).

κλῆθρον, τό, = κλήθρα, *Gloss.* **κλῇθρον,** Att. for κλεῖθρον (q. v.).

κλῆθρος, ὁ, = κλήθρα, Philostr.Jun.*Im.*6.

κληΐζω, Ion. for κλῄζω (B). **κληϊθρίη,** ἡ, Ion. for κλειθρία.

κλήϊθρον, τό, Ion. for κλῇθρον, κλεῖθρον, *h.Merc.*146.

κληΐσκω, = κληΐζω II, *call*, Hp.*Cord.*8 (Pass.).

κλῆμα, ατος, τό, Aeol. **κλᾶμμα** (q. v.), *twig* or *branch*, esp. *vine-twig*, Ar.*Ec.*1031, Hp.*Epid.*4.50, 6.3.8, Thphr.*HP*2.5.5, *CP*3.14.6, al.; ἀμπέλου κ. Pl.*R.*353a: generally, *cutting, slip*, ὁ βλαστὸς τοῦ κ. X.*Oec.*19.8, cf. Arist.*HA*550ᵇ8: metaph., ἀνατετμήκασί τινες τὰ κ. τὰ τοῦ δήμου D.ap.Aeschin.3.166; of the navel string, πεῖσμα καὶ κ. τῷ γεννωμένῳ καρπῷ Democr.148. **2.** *vine-switch, cane*, carried by Roman centurions, Lat. *vitis*, Plu.*Galb.*26, etc. **II.** = πιτυοῦσσα, Dsc.4.165; = πολύγονον, Plin.*HN*27.113. **III.** = ὑπόδημα, Hsch.; cf. κλείματα.

κλημᾰτ-ίζω, *prune vines*, Al.*Le.*25.4. **-ικός,** ή, όν, *of* or *for a vine-twig*, *Gloss.* **-ῖνος,** η, ον, *of vine-twigs*, πῦρ Thgn.1360; κονία Dsc.*Alex.*22; τέφρα Id.5.117, *Ther.*19, Antyll.ap.Orib.10.12.2. **-ίς,** ίδος, ἡ, Dim. of κλῆμα, *vine-branch*, Lxx *De.*32.32, Ph.1.612 (generally, *branch*, ib.527), Plu.2.527d, Philum.*Ven.*2.2: usu. in pl., *brushwood, faggots*, Ar.*Th.*728, 739, Th.7.53, Arist.*HA*550ᵇ9, *Inscr.Délos* 338 *Aa* 23, 24 (iii B. C.): collect. in sg., ib.38, 354.57 (iii B. C.), Lxx *Da.*3. 46. **II.** *periwinkle*, *Vinca herbacea*, Dsc.4.7. **2.** *traveller's joy, Clematis Vitalba*, ib.180, Gal.12.31. **3.** prob. *bearbind*, *Convolvulus arvensis*, Plin.*HN*24.139. **-ῖτις,** ιδος, ἡ, Adj. *with long climbing branches*, name of a kind of ἀριστολοχεία, Dsc.3.4. **II.** Subst., = foreg. II. 2, Ps.-Dsc.4.180.

κλημᾰτό-δεσις, εως, ἡ, *wicker hurdle* or *mat*, v.l. for κλιμακόδεσις in Ath.Mech.36.6. **-ειδής,** ές, = κληματὶς II. 2, Dsc.4.[180] ap.Gal. 12.31 (but not in Dsc.). **-εις,** εσσα, εν, *of vine-twigs*, τέφρη Nic. *Al.*530. **-ομαι,** Pass., (κλῆμα) *put forth tendrils*, κεκλημάτωται χλωρὸν οἰνάνθης δέμας S.*Fr.*255, cf. Thphr.*CP*2.10.3.

κλημᾰτώδης, ες, *like vine-shoots*, Dsc.3.24, Gal.12.78.

κλήνιος· ἔνδοξος, Hsch. **κληπικοί·** ἰσχνοί, καὶ ἄσιτοι, Id.

κληρ-ικός, ή, όν, *concerning inheritances*, τὰ κ. Harp. s. v. παρακαταβολή. **2.** Astrol., *of* or *according to the* κλῆρος (A) II. 4, Vett.Val. 122.13. Adv. -κῶς Id.123.22. **3.** Medic., dub. sens. in *BKT*3 p.33 (v/vi A. D.). **II.** Subst. κληρικός, ὁ, *cleric*, Astramps.*Orac.* 66 p.6 H., *Cod.Just.*1.1.3.2 (pl.), etc. **-ιον,** τό, Dim. of κλῆρος (A) II. 2, *AP*6.98 (Zonas), *PLond.*2.370.1 (ii/iii A. D.). **II.** Dor. **κλάρια** [ᾱ], τά, *bonds, notes for debt*, Plu.*Agis* 13.

κληρο-δοσία, ἡ, *distribution of land*, Lxx *Ps.*77(78).55, D.S.5. 53. **-δοτέω,** *distribute land*, c. dat., Lxx 2*Es.*9.12; *settle on the land*, αὐτούς ib.*Ps.*77(78).55:—Pass., -εῖτο ἡ χώρα Ph.2.291.

κληρονομ-έω, *inherit*, c. gen. rei, ὥσπερ τῆς οὐσίας, οὕτω καὶ τῆς φιλίας τῆς πατρικῆς κ. Isoc.1.2, cf. Is.4.7, Lycurg.127; ὅς γ' ἐκεκληρονομήκεις τῶν.. χρημάτων πλεῖν ἢ πέντε ταλάντων D.18.312; μὴ πλειόνων ἢ μιᾶς [κληρονομίας] τὸν αὐτὸν κ. Arist.*Pol.*1309ᵃ25: c. acc. rei, Lycurg.88, Luc.*DMort.*11.3, *BGU*19 ii 1 (ii A. D.), etc.: abs., Phld. *Mort.*24. **2.** *acquire, obtain*, τὴν ἐπ' ἀσεβείᾳ δόξαν Plb.15.22.3; φήμην Id.18.55.8; θρόνον βασιλείας Lxx 1*Ma.*2.57; τὴν γῆν *receive possession of* the promised land, Palestine, ib.*Le.*20.24, *De.*4.1 (also, *obtain* all that God has promised, ib.*Ps.*36(37).11, cf. *Ev.Matt.*5.5); *obtain* salvation, ζωὴν αἰώνιον *Ev.Matt.*19.29. **II.** *to be an inheritor* or *heir*, τινος *of* a person, Luc.*Hist.Conscr.*20: more freq. τινα, Posidon.36 J., Plu.*Sull.*2, *PGnom.*5, al. (ii A. D.), *AP*11.202, etc.; κ. τινὰ τῆς οὐσίας D.C.45.47: metaph., σῆτες καὶ σκώληκες -ομήσουσιν αὐτόν Lxx *Si.*19.3:—Pass., *to be succeeded in the inheritance*, of parents, Ph. 2.172, 291, Luc.*Tox.*22; ὑφ' ὧν τὴν ῥητορικὴν ἐκληρονομήθη Philostr. *VS*2.26.6. **III.** *leave an heir behind* one, υἱοὺς υἱῶν Lxx *Pr.*13. 22. **-ημα,** ατος, τό, *inheritance*, Luc.*Tyr.*6. **-ία,** ἡ, *inheritance*, Isoc.19.43, etc.; ἡ κ. κατὰ τὴν ἀγχιστείαν *inheritance* as heir-at-law, D.43.3; κ. μὴ κατὰ δόσιν, ἀλλὰ κατὰ γένος Arist.*Pol.*1309ᵃ23: metaph., εἰλήφασι τὴν τοῦ ὀνόματος κ. αἱ σωματικαὶ ἡδοναί have taken *possession* of.., Id.*EN*1153ᵇ33. **2.** *property, possession*, ἀνέζευξεν ἕκαστος εἰς τὴν κ. αὐτοῦ Lxx *Ju.*16.21(25), cf. 1*Ma.*2.56, 6.24. **-ιαῖος,** α, ον, *concerning inheritance*, *Cod.Just.*3.10.1.2, Just.*Nov.*119.6; *inherited*, *PMasp.*151.40 (vi A. D.). **-ικός,** ή, όν, *connected with inheritance*, δίκαιον *PFlor.*61.20 (i A. D.), etc.; δίκαια Asp.*in EN*77.14; δικαστήρια *OGI*482 (i A. D.); *hereditary*, *Gloss.* **-ος,** Dor. **κλᾱρονόμος,** ὁ, (νέμομαι) *heir*, freq. *the heir in possession*, Is.1.44, Pl.*Lg.*923c; of *the heir apparent*, *SIG*884.53 (iii A. D.): c. gen. pers., Pl.*Lg.*923e, *IG*2². 1623.117, Epicur.*Fr.*217, *SIG*953.65 (Cnidus, ii B. C.): c. gen. rei, Lys.32.23; κληρονόμους τῶν αὐτοῦ καταστήσας Isoc.19.9, etc.: metaph., κ. τῆς εὐνοίας, τῆς ἀτιμίας, Id.5.136, D.22.34; τῆς ὑπὲρ τῶν νόμων [δίκης] Id.21.20; κλαρονόμος μοίσας τᾶς Δωρίδος Mosch.3.96; κ. καταλιπεῖν τινα Arist.*Pol.*1270ᵃ28; κ. γράφειν τινά *AP*11.171 (Lucill.).

κληροπᾰλής, ές, *distributed by shaking the lots*, μοῖραι *h.Merc.*129.

κλῆρος (A), Dor. **κλᾶρος** Pi. (v. infr.), *Leg.Gort.*5.27, etc., ου, ὁ:— *lot*, κλῆρον ἐσημήναντο ἕκαστος, ἐν δ' ἔβαλον κυνέῃ Il.7.175; κλήρους ἐν κυνέῃ χαλκήρεϊ πάλλον 3.316, cf. Od.10.206; ἐκ κλῆρος ὄρουσεν Il.3. 325; ἐκ δ' ἔθορε κλῆρος κυνέης 7.182; ἐν δὲ κλήρους ἐβάλοντο 23.352; ἐπὶ κλήρους ἐβάλοντο Od.14.209, cf. *SIG*1023.94 (Cos); κλήρῳ πεπαλάσθαι Od.9.331; κλήρῳ λάχον ἐνθάδ' ἕπεσθαι Il.24.400, cf. 23.862, A.*Pers.*187, Hdt.3.83, etc.; πάντας ἀνέφεδρος ἐπαγκρατίασε τοὺς κ., i.e. he never drew a bye, *SIG*1073.29 (ii A. D.); κλήρῳ κατὰ μοῖραν E.*Rh.*545 (lyr.); διὰ τὴν τοῦ κ. τύχην Pl.*R.*619d, etc.; κλάροισι θεοπροπέων divining *by lots*, Pi.*P.*4.190: hence, of oracles, E.*Hipp.*1057, *Ph.* 838; Ἑρμῆς γὰρ ὢν κλήρῳ ποιήσεις οἶδ' ὅτι Ar.*Pax* 365; κ. Ἑρμοῦ E. *Fr.*39. **2.** *casting of lots, drawing of lots*, κ. τίθεσθαι Id.*IA*1198, cf. *Tr.*186 (lyr.); δοκεῖ δίκαιον εἶναι πᾶσι τῶν ἀρχῶν μετεῖναι ἐν τῷ κ. X. *Ath.*1.2, cf. Arist.*Pol.*1300ᵃ19, *IG*5(1).1390.116 (Andania, i B. C.); = Lat. *sortitio provinciarum*, Plu.*Aem.*10. **3.** λαβὼν πίστιν.. κλήρου dub. sens. in *OGI*494.19 (i or ii A. D.). **II.** *that which is assigned by lot, allotment* of land, Hdt.2.109, Th.3.50, Pl.*Lg.*740b, Arist.*Pol.* 1265ᵇ15, al.; λαβεῖν τᾶς χώρας ἐξαίρετον τὸν πρᾶτον κλᾶρον *SIG*141.6 (Corc. Nigr., iv B. C.); κ. ἱππικός *OGI*229.102 (Smyrna, iii B. C.); περὶ τοῦ λάχους τριάκοντα καὶ ἑπτὰ κλάρων *Schwyzer* 289.88 (Priene, ii B. C.), cf. 313.4, al. **2.** generally, *piece of land, farm, estate*, οἶκος καὶ κ. Il.15.498; οἶκόν τε κ. τε Od.14.64, cf. Hes.*Op.*37, 341, Pi.*O.*13. 62; κατέφαγε τὸν κ. Hippon.35.4; οἱ κ. τῶν Συρίων their *lands*, Hdt. 1.76, cf. 9.94, Call.*Del.*281, etc.; Κύπρου Πάφου τ' ἔχουσα.. κλῆρον, of Aphrodite, A.*Fr.*463; κατὰ κ. Ἰάονιον Id.*Pers.*899 (lyr.); κλῆροι χθονός E.*Heracl.*876; τῶν λαβόντων ἐν Ὀρχομενῷ κλᾶρον ἢ οἰκίαν *IG* 5(2).344.12 (iii B. C.), cf. *SIG*169.61 (Iasus, iv B. C.); Πισαίοις ἐνὶ κλήροισι Nic.*Fr.*74.5. **b.** pl., *title-deeds*, *PGrenf.*1.14.11 (ii B. C.). **3.** *legacy, inheritance, heritable estate*, Is.11.9, Pl.*Lg.*923d, Arist.*Ath.*9.2, *SIG*1186 (iv B. C.), *IG*2².1368.127, 154. **b.** collect., *body of inheritors*, *Leg.Gort.* l. c. **4.** Astrol., certain *degrees* in the zodiac connected with planets and important in a nativity, *Cat.Cod.Astr.*1.169, 170, Ptol.*Tetr.*111, Vett.Val.59.21, al., Paul.Al.*K.*2 (cf. Sch.); κ. τύχης Ptol.*Tetr.*129. **5.** generally, *province, sphere*, ἕνα θεὸν πολλῶν ἅμα προεστάναι κλήρων Dam.*Pr.*369. **III.** of the Levites, Κύριος αὐτὸς κλῆρος αὐτοῦ Lxx *De.*18.2: hence, of the Christian *clergy*, ἐν κλήρῳ καταλεγόμενος *Cod.Just.*1.3.38.2, Just.*Nov.*6.1.7, Astramps.*Orac.*98.7.

κλῆρος (B), ου, ὁ, *a beetle destructive in bee-hives*, *Clerus apiarius*, Arist.*HA*605ᵇ11, 626ᵇ17.

κληρουργία, ἡ, *inheritance*, Sm.*Ru.*4.7.

κληρουχ-αρχέω, *to be governor of a* κληρουχία, *Ath.Mitt.*35.47 (iv B. C.). **-έω,** *obtain by allotment*, esp. of conquered lands divided among the conquerors, κ. τῶν Χαλκιδέων τὴν χώρην Hdt.6.100, cf. *SIG* 332.6 (iv/iii B. C.), 502.41 (Samothrace, iii B. C.), App.*BC*5.74 (and in Med., ib.27): generally, ἄλλοι κατ' ἄλλους τόπους κληρουχήσαντες θεῶν Pl.*Criti.*109c. **2.** *inherit*, Sm.*Ps.*81(82).8. **II.** *divide, allot* lands, D.S. 5.9, D.H.9.37, D.C.48.6: metaph., κ. τὴν ἐν ἄστροις τύχην Callistr. *Stat.*10. **III.** *settle one as an allotment-holder*, in Pass., *PCair. Zen.*254 (iii B. C.), *PTeb.*5.36 (ii B. C.). **-ημα,** ατος, τό, *allotment of* *land*, App.*BC*3.2:—also **-ησις**, εως, ἡ, Nic.Dam.130.27 J.(pl.). **-ία**, ἡ, *apportionment of land in a foreign country among citizens*, ἡ Σάμου κ. Arist.*Rh.*1384^{b}32, cf. Plb.4.81.2, D.S.15.23; esp. to soldiers on the active list, *PPetr.*3p.163 (iii B.C.), *PTeb.*30.26 (ii B.C.); = Lat. *colonia*, D.H.8.75, Plu.*Flam.*2. b. in Roman Egypt, a numbered *division* of the land, *PTeb.*343^r.9 (ii A.D.), *Sammelb.*4414.5 (ii A.D.). 2. collect., = οἱ κληροῦχοι, *the body of citizens who receive such allotments*, ἀποικίαις καὶ κληρουχίαις *IG*1^2.140.9; κ. ἐκπέμπειν Isoc.4.107 (pl.); κ. ἔγραφεν Plu.*Per.*34 (pl.). II. *inheritance*, LXX *Ne.*11.20, Ph.2.290 (pl.). **-ικός**, ή, όν, *of* or *for a* κληρουχία, γῆ κ. land *for allotment*, Ar.*Nu.*203 (in Egypt, *land held by* κληροῦχοι, *PSI*4.344.6 (iii B.C.), *PTeb.*5.194 (ii B.C.)); τὰ κ. (sc. χρήματα) D.14.16; νόμος κ., = Lat. *lex agraria*, Plu.*CG*5. **-ος**, ὁ, (κλῆρος, ἔχω) *one who held an allotment of land*, esp. *an allotment in a foreign country assigned him as a citizen*, Hdt.5.77, Th.3.50, Aeschin.1.53, *IG*1^2.60.10, 2^2.114.9; esp. in Ptolemaic Egypt, *holder of land by military tenure*, *PCair.Zen.*3.6, 326.37, al. (iii B.C.), *PSI*4.344.7 (iii B.C.), *PPetr.*2p.4 (iii B.C.), etc.: metaph., μητέρα πολλῶν ἐτῶν κληροῦχον *having* old age *for her lot*, S.*Aj.*508; Ἑρμῆ..Φιλιππίδου κληροῦχε Alex.89. 2. *one who distributed allotments* to citizens, Harp., Phot.; ὁ κ. θεός Ph.2.121. 3. *holder of an inheritance*, Id.2.290, al. 4. in Roman Egypt, *land-owner, landlord*, *PFay.*82.19 (ii A.D.), *Sammelb.*7193^{r}ii 2 (ii A.D.), etc. II. Pass., κ. γῆ land *distributed in allotments*, D.H.8.75.

κληρ-όω, Dor. **κλᾱρόω**, inf. κλαρῶεν *Foed.Delph.Pell.*1 *A* 6, κλαρώειν *SIG*647.33 (Stiris, ii B.C.): (κλῆρος A):—*appoint by lot*, ἐξ ἁπάντων τὰς ἀρχάς Isoc.7.22; ἀθλητάς Arist.*Rh.*1393^{b}5; διαιρετὰς τῶν κτημάτων *SIG*364.9 (Ephesus, iii B.C.); τὰ δικαστήρια ib.647.33; ἄλλον [ἱερόν] *IG*5(1).1390.6 (Andania, i B.C.); also, of the lot, *fall on*, οὓς ἐκλήρωσεν πάλος E.*Ion*416:—Med., *cast lots* for office, of candidates, ἂν ἔλθῃ κληρωσόμενος τῶν ἐννέα ἀρχόντων Lys.6.4, cf. 24.13; κ. ἱερωσύνης D.57.62; κληρουμένων ἐπιμελῶς Arist.*Ath.*27.4; ὃς ἂν κληρούμενος λαγχάνῃ Pl.*Plt.*298e:—Pass., *to be appointed by lot*, Arist.*Ath.*43.2, Decr.ib.30.5, *SIG*525.11 (Crete, iii B.C.), *IG*5(1).1390.132 (Andania, i B.C.), etc.; [πρόεδροι] κεκληρωμένοι D.24.89; κεκληρῶσθαι ἄρχειν Luc.*Luct.*2. 2. *cast lots*, Pl.*Lg.*759c, 856d; κληρώσω πάντας I *will make* all *draw lots*, Ar.*Ec.*682; κ. τὰς φυλάς Plb.6.20.2:—Med., A.*Th.*55, Ar.*Ec.*836, D.21.133; ὅτε ἐκληροῦσθε when *you were drawing lots*, Id.19.1. 3. Med., *have allotted one, obtain by lot*, δεσπότας E.*Tr.*29; ἱερωσύνην Aeschin.1.188; ἀμπέλων δεκανίαν *IGRom.*4.1675 (Lydia): metaph., *obtain as one's sphere* or *province*, τὸ ταὐτὸν ὁ δημιουργὸς ἐκληρώσατο Dam.*Pr.*321; Astrol., ἥλιος κληρωσάμενος τὴν ὥραν Vett.Val.61.1; κεκληρῶσθαι *to be in possession of, to have*, Hp.*Ep.*20, Procl.*Inst.*110; τὴν καρδίαν κεκλήρωται ἐπὶ τῇ φάρυγγι Ael.*NA*5.31. II. *allot, assign*, ὔμμε δ' ἐκλάρωσε πότμος Ζηνί Pi.*O.*8.15; μοίρας, τὴν μὲν ἐπὶ μονῇ, τὴν δ' ἐπὶ ἐξόδῳ Hdt.1.94; ἐν ἑκάστῳ ἐκλήρωσαν Th.6.42:—Pass., ἐκληρώθην δούλη E.*Hec.*100 (anap.). 2. ὀμφὰν κ. *deliver* an oracle *by lot*, Id.*Ion*908 (lyr.). **-ωσις**, εως, ἡ, *choosing by lot*, βίου Pl.*Phdr.*249b; κληρώσεις δικαστηρίων Id.*Lg.*956e, cf. Isoc.7.23: metaph., πικρὰν κ. αἵρεσίν τέ μοι βίου καθίστης, of a *choice* of evils, E.*Andr.*384. **-ωτήριον**, τό, = κληρωτρίς, Ar.*Ec.*681, *Fr.*146, Eub.74.5, Arist.*Ath.*63.2 (unless in signf. II), *Not.Arch.*4.20 (Aug.). II. *place where elections by lot* or *distributions of jurors were held*, Arist.*Ath.*64.3, al., Plu.2.793d, Poll.9.44. III. *list of citizens*, so called because jurors were selected from it by lot, ἀναγραφῆναι εἰς τὰ κ. *OGI*229.53 (Smyrna, iii B.C.). **-ωτής**, οῦ, ὁ, *one who presided over elections by lot* or *distributions of jurors*, Poll.9.44; Dor. κλᾱρωτὰς δικαστᾶν Maiuri *Nuova Silloge* 18. **-ωτί** or **-ωτεί**, Adv. *by lot*, LXX *Jo.*21.4, al. **-ωτικός**, ή, όν, *of* or *for casting lots*, τὸ -κόν (sc. ἀγγεῖον) Ath.10.450b. **-ωτός**, ή, όν, *appointed by lot*, δύναμις Pl.*Lg.*692a; βασιλεῖς Id.*Plt.*291a; τὰ κ., opp. τὰ αἱρετά, Id.*Lg.*759b, cf. Isoc.12.153, etc.; ἀρχὴ κ., opp. χειροτονητή, Lex ap.Aeschin.1.21, cf. *SIG*589.38 (Magn. Mae., ii B.C.); δημοκρατικὸν μὲν..τὸ κληρωτὰς εἶναι τὰς ἀρχάς, τὸ δ' αἱρετὰς ὀλιγαρχικόν Arist.*Pol.*1294^{b}8, cf. 1266^{a}9, al. **-ωτρίς**, ίδος, ἡ, *urn for casting lots or votes*, Sch.Ar.*V.*672, 750.

κλῄς, ῃδός, ἡ, old Att. for κλείς.

κλῆσις, εως, ἡ, (καλέω) *calling, call*, Pl.*Smp.*172a, X.*Cyr.*3.2.14, etc. 2. *calling into court, summons, prosecution*, Ar.*Nu.*875, 1189, etc.; τὰς κλήσεις καλεῖσθαι ὅσας ἔδει Antipho6.38; ἀφιέναι τὰς κ. X.*HG*1.7.13. 3. *invitation* to a feast, Id.*Smp.*1.7; εἰς τὸ πρυτανεῖον D.19.32; κλήσεις δείπνων Plu.*Per.*7, cf. Parmenisc.ap.Ath.4.156d. 4. *invocation*, θεῶν Men.Rh.p.333S. 5. *calling to aid*, Plb.2.50.7. 6. *calling* in a religious sense, 1*Ep.Cor.*7.20. II. *name, appellation*, Pl.*Plt.*262d, 287e, Dsc.1.42; τοὺς θεοὺς εἶναι κ. ἱεράς Cleanth.*Stoic.*1.123; Φιλησίη τὴν κ. *by name*, *IG*14.2067; *reputation*, Phld.*Rh.*2.46S. III. Gramm., αἱ κ. τῶν ὀνομάτων the *nominatives*, opp. αἱ πτώσεις (the oblique cases), Arist.*APr.*48^{b}41; ἔχειν θηλείας ἢ ἄρρενος κλῆσιν the *nominative form* of.., Id.*SE*173^{b}40, cf. 182^{a}18. IV. = Lat. *classis*, D.H.4.18.

κλῇσις, εως, ἡ, (κλείω A) *closing*, τῶν λιμένων Th.2.94, cf. 7.70:—written **κλεῖσις**, Aen.Tact.20.1.

κληστός, v. κλειστός. **κλῄσω**, fut. of κλῄω (q.v.) and κλῄζω.

κλητ-έος, α, ον, (καλέω) *to be called, named*, Pl.*R.*341d, 428c. II. κλητέον, *one must call*, ib.470d, LXX *Ep.Je.*63, Max.Tyr.40.5, Iamb.*Myst.*3.9. **-εύω**, *summon into court*, or *give evidence that a legal summons has been served*, Ar.*Nu.*1218; τινα D.18.150; τινι Ar.*V.*1413, cf. Is.*Fr.*108, D.32.30:—Med., *procure the issuing of the summons*, κ. τὴν δίκην Arist.*Pr.*951^{a}27:—Pass., = ἐκκλητεύεσθαι, Is. l.c. **-ήρ**, ῆρος, ὁ, *summoner*, or *witness who gave evidence that the legal summons had been served*, *IG*1^2.63.39, 65.47, Ar.*Av.*147, 1422, *V.*1408, D.40.28, al., Eub.94.9, Pl.*Lg.*846c; with a pun, ὁμοιότατος κλητῆρι πωλίῳ (κλητῆρος for ὄνου 'brayer'), Ar.*V.*189. II. generally, = κῆρυξ, A.*Supp.*622: metaph., Ἐρινύος κ. Id.*Th.*574. **-ικός**, ή, όν, *of* or *for invitation*, Men.Rh.p.424S.; σχῆμα Hermog.*Inv.*4.3. 2. *invocatory*, ὕμνοι Men.Rh.p.333S.; τύπος Id.p.334S. 3. Gramm., *vocative*, ἡ -κή (sc. πτῶσις) D.T.636.7, A.D.*Pron.*6.9, al.; σύνταξις Id.*Synt.*46.8; τὸ κ. "ὦ" Hdn.Gr.1.473. **-ός**, ή, όν, *invited*, Aeschin.2.162, etc.; *welcome*, Od.17.386. 2. *called out, chosen*, Il.9.165. 3. *invoked*, Anon.ap.Suid. 4. *summoned to court*, *PAmh.*2.79.5 (ii A.D.). II. Subst. κλητή (sc. ἐκκλησία), ἡ, *convocation*, LXX *Ex.*12.16, *Le.*23.2 (pl.). **-ροί**· κλήτορες, Hsch. **-ρόν**· καλούμενον, κλῆσιν, Id. **-ωρ**, = κλητήρ, *SIG*344.43 (Teos, iv B.C.), *PPetr.*3p.48 (iii B.C.), *PHal.*1.223 (iii B.C.), Hdn.Gr.2.937, Hsch.; found in many codd. of Docum.ap.D.18.55, 21.87, 47.27, Plu.2.128f, etc. 2. *one who invites, host*, Timae.88a. 3. *one who invokes* the gods, Procl.*in Cra.*p.100P., *in R.*2.246K.

κλῄω, old Att. for κλείω (A). **κλῑβάν-άριος, -εύς, -ίτης, -οειδής, -ος**, v. κριβ-. **κλιδία**· τάριχος, Hsch. (cf. κλειδίον II).

κλίμα [ῐ, cf. Scymn.521], ατος, τό, (κλίνω) *inclination, slope* of ground, ἑκάτερον τὸ κ. τῶν ὀρῶν Plb.2.16.3; ἡ πόλις τῷ ὅλῳ κ. τέτραπται πρὸς τὰς ἄρκτους Id.7.6.1, etc.; *scarp*, Apollod.*Poliorc.*140.7. II. = ἔγκλιμα I.2, τοῦ κόσμου Hipparch.1.2.22, cf. Gem.16.12, Cleom.1.2. 2. terrestrial *latitude, latitudes, region*, τὸ μεσημβρινὸν κ. D.H.1.9; τὸ ὑπάρκτιον κ. Plu.*Mar.*11; τὰ πρὸς μεσημβρίαν κ. the southern *regions*, Plb.5.44.6, cf. 10.1.3, Str.1.1.10, *AP*9.97 (Alph.), Ath.12.523e, Vett.Val.6.14, etc.; κ. οὐρανοῦ Hdn.2.11.4. 3. *direction, cardinal point*, τὰ τέτταρα κ. (viz. N., S., E., W.) Str.10.2.12, *Gp.*1.11.1, cf. Isid.*Etym.*13.1.3; τὸ νότιον κ. τοῦ κόσμου Plu.2.365b; κατὰ τὸ βόρειον κ. Arist.*Mu.*392^{a}3. 4. *seven latitudinal strips in the* οἰκουμένη *on which the longest day ranged by half-hour intervals from 13 to 16 hours*, Eratosth.ap.Scymn.113, Id.ap.Str.2.1.35, 2.5.34, Gem.5.58, 16.17, Posidon.ap.Procl.*in Ti.*3.125D. (cf. eund.ap.Cleom.1.10), Id.ap.Str.6.2.1, Marin.ap.Ptol.*Geog.*1.15.8, 1.17.1, Id.*Alm.*2.12, al., *Cat.Cod.Astr.*8(4).37. 5. *seven astrological zones corresponding to Nos. 3–6 of* κλίμα II.4, Nech.*Fr.*5, al., Vett.Val.22.33, al., Firmic.2.11.2. III. metaph., *inclination, propensity*, Arr.*Epict.*2.15.20. IV. *fall*, ἑπταετεῖ κλίματι *by death* at seven years of age, *IG*14.2431. V. Gramm., *inflected form*, A.D.*Adv.*173.25. VI. = ὑπόδημα, Hsch.; cf. κλείματα.

κλῑμᾰκ-εών, ῶνος, ὁ, *stairway*, *Gloss.* **-ηδόν**, Adv., (κλῖμαξ) *like a ladder* or *stairs*, A.D.*Adv.*197.19: wrongly written κλημακιδόν in Hsch. s. v. προκρόσσας. **-ίας**, f.l. for καμακίας, Id. **-ίδιον**, τό, = κλιμάκιον, cj. in Amips.12 (pl.). **-ίζω**, *use the wrestler's trick called* κλῖμαξ (signf. III), Ar.*Fr.*4 D., Poll.3.155. 2. metaph., *pervert, distort*, τοὺς νόμους Din.*Fr.*9.1 (**κλιμάζω** Harp., Phot.). 3. *rear* (?), of a horse, Ar.*Fr.*63^b. **-ιον**, τό, Dim. of κλῖμαξ, Ar.*Pax* 69, Hp.*Art.*6, Demioprat.ap.Poll.10.171, Aristopho4; κ. ξύλινον περίχρυσον ὄφεσιν ἀργυροῖς διεζωμένον *IG*11(2).161 *B* 35 (Delos, iii B.C.), cf. *PLond.*3.1164(*h*)9 (iii A.D.). 2. = κλιμακτήρ I, Heliod.ap.Orib.48.60.1. 3. *bier*, Hsch. s. v. κλιματοφόρος. 4. = κλιμακίς 4, Hp.*Art.*6 (as τινές ap.Apollon.Cit.1). **-ίς**, ίδος, ἡ, Dim. of κλῖμαξ, *small ladder* or *stair*, Plb.5.97.5 (pl.); *ship's ladder*, *IG*2^2.1622.149, 203, al., *AB*272 (pl.). 2. *woman who makes a step-ladder of herself*, by letting persons step on her back to mount a carriage, Plu.2.50d, Ath.6.256d. 3. *wooden groove* for διώστρα in a torsion-engine, Ph.*Bel.*54.7, Hero *Bel.*100.7. 4. *surgical machine* for reducing dislocations, Orib.47.4.15. 5. wooden *frame* with openings for coffers in ceilings, *IG*1^2.372, 373, *Inscr.Délos* 504 *A* 13 (iii B.C.). **-ισμός**, ὁ, = κλῖμαξ III, Hsch. (-ίσκοι cod.).

κλῑμᾰκό-δεσις, εως, ἡ, f.l. for κληματό-, Ath.Mech.36.6. **-ειδής**, ές, *like a stairway*, λαβύρινθος Steph. *in Rh.*286.12; *like a ladder*, Apollon.Cit.1 (s. v. l.). **-εις**, εσσα, εν, *with steps*, Nonn.*D.*18.56; v.l. for κλωμ-, Il.2.729. **-φόρος**, ον, *bearing a ladder*, Plb.10.12.1, D.S.18.33, App.*Mith.*26. 2. *bearing on a bier*, Hsch. (κλιματ- cod.).

κλῑμακ-τήρ, ῆρος, ὁ, *rung of a ladder*, E.*Hel.*1570, Ar.*Fr.*277, Hp.*Art.*78, *IG*2^2.244.80, 11(2).203 *A* 43 (Delos, iii B.C.). II. Astrol., *critical point in human life*, determined by multiples of 7, as 35, 49, 63, Varr.ap.Gell.3.10.9, Epist.Aug.ib.15.7.3, Vett.Val.143.9, Ptol.*Tetr.*141, Heph.Astr.1.1, etc.; κ. ἑβδοματικοί *Theol.Ar.*53: generally, *danger*, Anon.ap.Suid. s. v. ἐγκοπή. **-τηρίζω**, *mark a critical period*, Vett.Val.233.35. **-τηρικός**, όν, *climacterical*, [ἐνιαυτός] Gell.15.7.2, cf. Plin.*Ep.*2.20.3; κ. λόγος Vett.Val.148.20; κ. ὑπάντησις Ptol.*Tetr.*140. **-ώδης**, ες, *like stairs*, κατάβασις Str.12.2.5. **-ωτός**, ή, όν, *made like a ladder* or *stairs, terraced*, πρόσβασις Plb.5.59.9. II. κ. σχῆμα, = κλῖμαξ IV, Hermog.*Id.*1.12.

κλῖμαξ, ᾰκος, ἡ, (κλίνω) *ladder* (because of its *leaning aslant*), *SIG* 1169.92 (Epid.); *scaling-ladder*, Th.3.23, X.*HG*7.2.7, etc.; κλίμακος προσαμβάσεις A.*Th.*466, cf. E.*Ph.*489; κλιμάκων ὀρθοστάτας προσβαλών Id.*Supp.*497; προσθεῖναι Th. l. c.; *boarding-ladder, gangway*, E.*IT* 1351, 1382, Theoc.22.30; κ. σκύτιναι, στύππιναι, Ph.*Bel.*102.13, 16. 2. *staircase*, Od.1.330, 10.558, al., *IG*2^2.463.46; κ. ξύλιναι ib.1668.84; κ. ἑλικτή winding *stair*, Callix.1. II. *frame with cross-bars*, on which persons to be tortured were tied, Ar.*Ra.*618, *Com.Adesp.*422. 2. *ladder used in reducing dislocations*, Hp.*Art.*42; κ. ἰσχυροὺς ἔχουσα κλιμακτῆρας ib.78. III. *wrestler's trick*, ἀμφίπλεκτοι κ. S.*Tr.*521 (lyr.), cf. Hsch. s. v. ἐκ κλίμακος. IV. in Rhet., *climax*, Demetr.*Eloc.*270, Quint.9.3.54, Longin.23.1 (pl.). V.

part of a chariot, narrowing like steps, Poll.1.253. VI. in pl., *handrails* on either side of a bridge, Arr.*An*.5.7.5.

κλῐμᾰτάρχης, ου, ὁ, *governor of a province*, Lyd.*Mag*.3.68, *Mens. Fr*.2. II. in pl., order of divine beings *ruling terrestrial regions*, Procl. *in Cra*.p.25 P., Olymp. *in Alc*.p.20 C.

κλῐμᾰτίας (sc. σεισμός), ὁ, = ἐπικλίντης, Heraclit.*All*.38, Amm. Marc.17.7; prob. l. for καυματίας, Posidon.ap.D.L.7.154.

κλῐμᾰτικός, ή, όν, *pertaining to* κλίμα II, διαφοραί Vett.Val.300.23.

κλῑν-άριον, τό, Dim. of κλίνη, Ar.*Fr*.239, *Act.Ap*.5.15, Arr.*Epict*. 3.5.13, *POxy*.1645.9 (iv A. D.); τὰ κ. τὰ ἐνδιδόντα elastic *bedsteads*, Thphr.*HP*5.6.4. **-άρχης**, ου, ὁ, *one who sits in the first place*, Ph.2.537; **-αρχος**, ὁ, *president of an Isiac confraternity*, *Sammelb*.5099. **-ειος**, α, ον, *of* or *for beds*, ξύλα D.27.10. **-η**, ἡ, (κλίνω) *that on which one lies, couch*, used at meals or for a bed, ἐν κλίνῃ κλῖναί τινας Hdt.9.16, cf. Ar.*Ach*.1090; κλίνην στρῶσαι to make up a *couch*, Hdt.6.139, X. *Cyr*.8.2.6, *IG*2^2.1315; ἐπὶ κλίνης φερόμενος And.1.61, cf. *SIG*1169.31 (Epid.); ἐκ κλίνης ἀνίστασθαι, after illness, And.1.64; κ. μιλησιουργὴς ἀμφικέφαλος *IG*1^2.330; κ. ἐπίχρυσοι καὶ ἐπάργυροι Hdt.1.50, 9.80; κ. ἐλεφαντόποδες Pl.Com.208. 2. *bier*, Th.2.34, Pl.*Lg*.947b, *IG* 12(5).593.6 (Ceos, v B. C.). 3. *grave-niche*, ib.14.788 (Naples), 871 (Cumae). II. ἱερὰ κ., = Lat. *lectisternium*, *POxy*.1144.6 (i/ii A. D.), cf. *PGnom*.202 (ii A. D.); κ. τοῦ κυρίου Σαράπιδος, of a ceremonial *banquet*, *POxy*.110.2 (ii A. D.). 2. generally, *banquet*, *PSI*5.483.2 (pl., iii B. C.). **-ήρης**, ες, *ill in bed*, Ph.2.317, J.*BJ*2.21.6, Plu.*Pyrrh*.11, Ath.12.554d, Gal.1.297, *BGU*45.14 (iii A. D.); -ήρη τινὰ τηρεῖν keep her *in bed*, Sor.1.46. **-ίδιον**, τό, Dim. of κλίνη, Ar.*Lys*.916, D.H.7.68, J.*AJ*17.6.3, Plu.2.751b; κ. κρεμαστόν Antyll.ap.Orib. 6.23.6, Herod.Med.ap.eund.6.25.4. 2. = Lat. *lectica*, Plu.*Cor*. 24. **-ικός**, ή, όν, *of* or *for a bed*: as Subst., κλινικός, ὁ, *physician who visits his patients in their beds*, Gal.12.829, *AP*11.113 (Nicarch.); title of work by Democrates, Gal.13.349; ἡ -κή (sc. τέχνη) *his art* or *method*, Plin.*HN*29.4. II. *bed-ridden*, γέρων Aus.*Ep*.8. 34. **-ίον**, τό, = κλινίδιον, Thphr.*HP*4.2.5. **-ίς**, ίδος, ἡ, = κλινίδιον, Cratin.137, Ar.*Th*.261. II. = ἐπὶ τῆς ἁμάξης νυμφικὴ καθέδρα, Hsch., cf. Poll.10.33.

κλῑνο-καθέδριον, τό, *easy chair*, Phot. s. v. κλιντήρ, *AB*272. **-κοσμέω**, *arrange dining-couches*, Plb.12.24.3. **-κοσμοι**, οἱ, *officials who arranged* κλῖναι *for ceremonies*, *AEM*19.224 (Constanza). **-πάλη** [ᾰ], ἡ, *bed-wrestling*, sens. obsc., Suet.*Dom*.22. **-πετής**, ές, *bed-ridden*, Hp.*Morb*.1.14, X.*HG*5.4.58, etc. **-πηγία**, ἡ, *making of beds*, Thphr.*HP*3.10.1, 5.7.6. **-πήγιον**, τό, *place where beds are made*, Poll.7.159. **-πηγός**, ὁ, = κλινοποιός, Theognost.*Can*.96, *CIG*2135 (κλεινο-, loc. incert.). **-πήξ**, -πῆγος, ὁ, = foreg., Theognost.*Can*.40. **-πόδιον**, τό, an aromatic herb, the leaves of which are *like the feet of a bed*, *Calamintha Clinopodium, horse-thyme*, Dsc. 3.95, Gal.12.30, Plin.*HN*24.137. **-ποιός**, ὁ, *maker of beds* or *bedsteads*, Pl.*R*.597a, D.27.9:—hence ἡ **-ποιική** (sc. τέχνη) *the art of making beds*, Poll.7.159. **-πους**, ποδος, ὁ, pl., *feet of a bed*, *Gp*. 13.9.9: sg., generally, κ. τοίχου Hsch. s. v. θριγκός, *EM*455.55; σφιγγῶν ib.425.28 (pl.). **-πώλιον**, τό, *shop where couches are sold*, Crates *Ep*.18 (pl.). **-στρόφιον**, τό, *engine of torture*, Agath. 4.1 (pl.). **-τροχος**, ἡ, *sycamore, Acer Pseudo-Platanus*, dub. l. in Thphr.*HP*3.11.1.

κλῑνουργός, ὁ, = κλινοποιός, Pl.*R*.597a.

κλῑνοχᾰρής, ές, *fond of bed*, Luc.*Trag*.131.

κλιν-τήρ, ῆρος, ὁ, (κλίνω) *couch*, Od.18.190, Theoc.2.86, 113, 24.43, Call.*Iamb*.1.112 (sic Pap., not κλωστῆρας), Tryph.441, Luc.*Symp*.8, 44; νεκροδόκος κ. *bier*, *AP*7.634 (Antiphil.), cf. *Epigr.Gr*.450.5 (Batanaea). **-τηρίδιον**, τό, Dim. of foreg., Phot. **-τήριον**, τό, Dim. of κλιντήρ, Ar.*Fr*.266, Phylarch.44 J. **-τηρίσκος**, ὁ, = foreg., *Michel*832.48 (Samos, iv B. C.).

κλίνω [ῑ], fut. κλινῶ Lyc.557, (ἐγκατα-) Ar.*Pl*.621: aor. 1 ἔκλῑνα Il.5.37, etc.: pf. κέκλῐκα Plb.30.13.2:—Med., aor. ἐκλινάμην Od.17. 340, etc.:—Pass., fut. κλῐθήσομαι (συγ-) E.*Alc*.1090, (κατα-) D.S.8 *Fr*.19: fut. 2 κατα-κλῐνήσομαι Ar.*Eq*.98, Pl.*Smp*.222e, also κεκλίσομαι dub. in A.D.*Pron*.22.7: aor. 1 ἐκλίθην [ῐ] Od.19.470, S.*Tr*.101 (lyr.), 1226, E.*Hipp*.211 (anap.), freq. in Prose; poet. also ἐκλίνθην, v. infr. II. 1,2,3: aor. 2 ἐκλίνην [ῐ] only in compds., κατακλῐνῆναι Ar.*V*.1208, 1211, X.*Cyr*.5.2.15, etc.; ξυγκατακλῐνείς Ar.*Ach*.981: pf. κέκλῐμαι (v. infr.); inf. κεκλίσθαι A.D.*Synt*.325.3, but κεκλίνθαι v.l. ib.47.1. (κλῐ-ν-γω, fr. root κλῐ- κλει-, cf. κλειτύς; Skt. *śrayati* 'cause to lean', 'support', Lat. *clinare, clivus*.):—*cause to lean, make to slope* or *slant*, ἐπὴν κλίνῃσι τάλαντα Ζεύς when he *inclines* or *turns* the scale, Il.19.223; Τρῶας δ' ἔκλιναν Δαναοί *made* them *give way*, 5.37, cf. Od.9.59; ἐπεί ῥ' ἔκλινε μάχην Il.14.510; ἔκλινε γὰρ κέρας.. ἡμῶν E.*Supp*.704; also ἐκ πυθμένων ἔκλινε..κλῆθρα S.*OT*1262:—Med., Περσῶν κλινάμενοι [δύναμιν] *IG*1^2.763. 2. *make* one thing *slope* against another, i.e. *lean, rest* it, τι πρός τι Il.23.171, cf. 510; ἅρματα δ' ἔκλιναν πρὸς ἐνώπια 8.435: c. dat., ἔστησαν σάκε' ὤμοισι κλίναντες, i.e. *raising* their shields *so that the upper rim rested* on their shoulders, 11.593. 3. *turn aside*, μηκέτι τοῦδε βήματος ἔξω πόδα κλίνῃς S.*OC*193 (lyr.); ὄσσε πάλιν κλίνασα *having turned* back her eyes, Il.3.427; τὰς ἐκ τῶν ἀριστερῶν [φλέβας] ἐπὶ τὰ δεξιὰ κ. *turn* to.., Pl.*Ti*.77e. 4. *make* another *recline*, ἐν κλίνῃ κλῖναί τινας *make* them *lie down* at table, Hdt.9.16; κλῖνόν μ' ἐς εὐνήν E. *Or*.227; κλίνατ', οὐ σθένω ποσίν Id.*Alc*.267 (lyr.): metaph., ἡμέρα κλίνει τε κἀνάγει πάλιν ἅπαντα τἀνθρώπεια *puts to rest, lays low*, S. *Aj*.131. 5. in Magic, *make subservient*, ψυχήν *PMag.Par*.1. 1718. 6. Gramm., *inflect*, τὰ ῥήματα A.D.*Synt*.212.20:—Pass., Id.*Pron*.12.7. II. Pass., *lean*, ἂψ δ' ὁ πάϊς πρὸς κόλπον ἐϋζώνοιο τιθήνης ἐκλίνθη Il.6.467; ὁ δ' ἐκλίνθη, καὶ ἀλεύατο κῆρα μέλαιναν he *bent aside*, 7.254; of a brasen foot-pan, ἂψ δ' ἑτέρωσ' ἐκλίθη *it was tipped over*, Od.19.470; of battle, *turn*, ἐκλίνθη δὲ μάχη Hes.*Th*.711; of a body in equilibrium, οὐδαμόσε κλιθῆναι Pl.*Phd*.109a, cf. Archim. *Fluit*.1.8, al. 2. *lean, stay oneself* upon or against a thing, c. dat., ἀσπίσι κεκλιμένοι Il.3.135; κίονι κεκλιμένη, Od.6.307, 17.97; ἠέρι δ' ἔγχος ἐκέκλιτο καὶ ταχέ' ἵππω Il.5.356 (s. v. l.); ἐν δορὶ κεκλιμένος Archil.2 (also in Med., κλινάμενος σταθμῷ Od.17.340); κεκλιμένοι καλῇσιν ἐπάλξεσιν Il.22.3; πρὸς τοῖχον ἐκλίνθησαν Archil.34; ξύλα ἐς ἄλληλα κεκλιμένα Hdt.4.73; ὅταν τύχωσι (sc. αἱ ἄτομοι) τῇ περιπλοκῇ κεκλιμέναι when they chance to be *propped* (i.e. *checked*) by the interlacing with others, Epicur.*Ep*.1 p.8 U. 3. *lie down, fall*, ἐν νεκύεσσι κλινθήτην Il.10.350, etc.; παραὶ λεχέεσσι κλιθῆναι *lie* beside her on the bed, Od.18.213, cf. S.*Tr*.1226: in pf., *to be laid, lie*, ἔντεα..παρ' αὐτοῖσι χθονὶ κέκλιτο Il.10.472; φύλλων κεκλιμένων of *fallen* leaves, Od.11.194 (φύλλα κεκλ. in Thphr.*HP*3.9.2, *slanting* leaves); Ληθαίῳ κεκλιμένη πεδίῳ Thgn.1216; Ἀλφεοῦ πόρῳ κλιθείς *laid* by Alpheus' stream, Pi.*O*.1.92; ἐπὶ γόνυ κέκλιται *has fallen* on her knee, i.e. is humbled, A.*Pers*.931 (lyr.); ὑπτία κλίνομαι S.*Ant*.1188; τὸ μὲν πρῶτον ἐρρήγνυτο τὸ τεῖχος, ἔπειτα δὲ καὶ ἐκλίνετο X.*HG*5.2.5; οὐ νούσῳ..οὐδ' ὑπὸ δυσμενέων δούρατι κεκλίμεθα *AP*7.493 (Antip. Thess.), cf. 315 (Zenod. or Rhian.), 488 (Mnasalc.), Epic.*Oxy*.214^r.3. 4. *recline* at meals, κλιθέντες ἐδαίνυντο Hdt.1.211, cf. E.*Cyc*.543, *SIG* 1023.48 (Cos, iii/ii B. C.); κλίθητι καὶ πίωμεν cj. in *Com.Adesp*.1203, cf. E.*Fr*.691. 5. of Places, *lie sloping towards* the sea, etc., *lie near*, ἁλὶ κεκλιμένη Od.13.235; [νῆσοι] αἵ θ' ἁλὶ κεκλίαται (Ep. for κέκλινται) 4.608: hence, of persons, *lie on, live on* or *by*, [Ὀρέσβιος] λίμνῃ κεκλιμένος Κηφισίδι Il.5.709; ῥηγμῖνι θαλάσσης κεκλίαται 16.68, cf. 15. 740; δισσαῖσιν ἀπείροις κλιθείς S.*Tr*.101 (lyr.); πλευρὰ πρὸς ἀνατολὰς κεκλιμένη, τὸ εἰς τὰς ἄρκτους κ., Plb.2.14.4, 1.42.5; ὅρος Κοῖον ὃ κέκλιται πρὸς Παρνασσόν *SIG*826 *E* iii 37 (Delph., ii B. C.). 6. metaph., τῷδε μέλει κλιθείς *having devoted himself to*.., Pi.*N*.4.15 (also in Act., *incline* towards, τῶν πραγμάτων ἐπὶ Ῥωμαίους κεκλικότων Plb. 30.13.2). 7. *wander from the right course*, κεκλιμένη ναῦς Thgn. 856. III. Med., *decline, wane*, καὶ κλίνεται (sc. τὸ ἦμαρ) S.*Fr*.255. 6. IV. intr. in Act., κ. πρὸς τὸ ξανθὸν χρῶμα *incline* towards.., Arist.*Phgn*.812^{b}3; κλίνοντος ὑπὸ ζόφον ἠελίοιο as the sun *was declining*, A.R.1.452; ἅμα τῷ κλῖναι τὸ τρίτον μέρος τῆς νυκτός as it *came to an end*, Plb.3.93.7; ἡ ἡμέρα ἤρξατο κλίνειν *Ev.Luc*.9.12; ἡ πόλις ἐπὶ τὸ χεῖρον ἔκλινεν X.*Mem*.3.5.13; τὸ κλῖνον ἀναλήμψεσθαι *PFay*.20.14 (iii/iv A. D.). 2. of soldiers, κ. ἐπ' ἀσπίδα, ἐπὶ δόρυ, *turn* to left, to right, Plb.3.115.9, etc.; κ. πρὸς φυγήν Id.1.27.8; also, *wheel*, Ascl. *Tact*.10.4.

κλῐσία, Ion. -ίη, ἡ, (κλίνω) *place for lying down* or *reclining*: hence, I. *hut, shed, booth*, 1. for use in peace, *cot, cabin*, once in Il., 18.589, cf. Od.14.194, al. 2. for use in war, *hut*, κ. εὔπηκτος, εὔτυκτος, Il.9.663, 10.566; κ. ὑψηλή 24.448: freq. in pl., *camp*, 1.487, al.; πῦρ ἐν κλισίῃσι βαλόντες Od.8.501:—not common after Hom. (σκηνή being used), B.12.135, etc.: used by Trag. in lyr. and anap., A.*Fr*.131, S.*Aj*.190, 1407, E.*IA*189: later with various meanings, Βάκχου κλισίαι, of wine-*shops*, *IG*14.889 (Sinuessa); εὐσεβέων κλισίη, of the grave, *Epigr.Gr*.237.4 (Smyrna, ii/i B. C.), cf. *IG*12(5).1104 (Syros, ii A. D.); *chapel*, ἡ κ. ἡ ἱερά *BCH*51.220 (Thasos), cf. *Arch. Pap*.1.219, *IG*4^2(1).123.131 (Epid.); cf. κλεισία. II. *anything for lying* or *sitting upon, couch* or *easy chair*, Od.4.123; κ. δινωτὴν ἐλέφαντι καὶ ἀργύρῳ 19.55; ἐπ' ἀλλοτρίαν κ. ἐρχόμενος *IG*2^2.1368.74. 2. *couch for reclining on at table*, Pi.*P*.4.133 (pl.); ᾧ ξυνὴν εἶχον ἐγὼ κ. Call.*Aet*.1.1.8; *place on such couch*, κ. ἄτιμος Plu.*Ant*.59, 2.148f; κ. ἄδοξος Hegesand.18. 3. *nuptial bed*, E.*Alc*.994, *IT*857. III. *company* of people *sitting at meals*, *Ev.Luc*.9.14; *banquet*, εὐωχίαι τε καὶ κ. Onos.35.5; *room for company*, Luc.*Am*.12. IV. *way of lying, decubitus*, Hp.*Epid*.7.25; τὸ σχῆμα τῆς κ. Plu.*Sert*.26.

κλισιάδες, v. κλεισιάδες.

κλισιάζω, *visit shrines*, Them.*Or*.13.178d (fort. κλεισιάζω, cf. κλεισίον 2).

κλῐσί-ηθεν, Adv. *out of* or *from the hut*, Il.1.391, etc. **-ηνδε**, Adv. *into* or *to the hut*, ib.185. **-ον**, τό, *outbuildings round a* κλισία or *herdsman's cot*, περὶ δὲ κλίσιον θέε πάντῃ Od.24.208 (glossed by προστῷον, Ameriasap.Ael.Dion.*Fr*.231); dub. sens. in *IG*11(2). 156 *A* 38, 49 (Delos, iii B. C.).

κλισίον, v. κλεισίον.

κλίσις [ῐ], εως, ἡ, (κλίνω) *bending, inclination*, τραχήλου Plu.*Pyrrh*. 8; *sinking* of the sun, D.P.1095; ἀκτίνων ἰθεῖαν κ. Id.585; *bend* of a river or tunnel, Agatharch.23, 25. II. *lying down*, ἄρθρων E.*Tr*. 114 (anap.); *place for lying on*, μαλακὴ κ. ὕπνον ἐλέσθαι Opp.*H*.1. 25. 2. = κλισία IV, Hp.*Epid*.7.77: pl., Ruf.*Ren.Ves*.1. III. *turning*, of soldiers, ἐπὶ δόρυ ποιεῖσθαι τὴν κ. to the right, ἐφ' ἡνίαν (or ἐπ' ἀσπίδα Ael.*Tact*.32) to the left, Plb.3.115.10, 10.23.2, etc.; expld. as ἡ κατ' ἄνδρα κίνησις Ascl.*Tact*.10.2. IV. *region, clime*, D.P. 615. V. *inflexion* of nouns and verbs, D.T.632.8 (pl.), A.D.*Pron*. 12.14, al.; αἱ κατὰ πρόσωπον κ. Id.*Synt*.130.16. b. *augment*, *EM* 23.53.

κλισμάκιον, τό, Dim. of κλισμός, *IG*2^2.1541.28.

κλισμία, τά, = κλισία II. 3, Call.*Aet*.3.1.16.

κλισμός, ὁ (fem. only in Theoc.15.85), (κλίνω) *couch*, κλισμούς τε θρόνους τε Od.1.145; χρύσεοι κ. Il.8.436; κ. βασιλήϊος Thgn.1191, cf. Hp.*Mul*.2.149, E.*Or*.1440 (lyr.); κ. δίφροιο Arat.251. II. *inclination, slope*, Arist.*Col*.792^{a}22.

κλίτα· στοαί, ἢ σέλλας (ἐλαίας cod.) εἰς τὸ κατακλίνεσθαι, Hsch.

κλῐτ-έον, *one must inflect*, τοὺς μύθους εἰς τοὺς ἀριθμοὺς καὶ τὰς πλαγίας πτώσεις Theon Prog.3. **-ικός**, ή, όν, *inflexional*, τὸ κ. μέρος A.D.Synt.180.10; κ. ἔκτασις *temporal* augment, Choerob.in Theod.2.81, EM295.14.

κλίτος [ῐ], εος, τό, = κλειτύς, Lyc.600; *cliff*, Id.737 (pl.). 2. = κλίμα II, *clime*, κ. βόρειον AP7.699. 3. *side*, Lxx Ex.26.18, al.; τὸ κ. τὸ δεξιόν ib.Ez.47.1; τὸ κ. τοῦ νότου ib.3Ki.7.39.

κλῖτος, εος, τό, v. κλεῖτος (B). **κλῑτύς**, v. κλειτύς.

κλοιόπους, ποδος, ὁ, *clog for the foot*, in pl., = κλάποι, Tz.H.13.300.

κλοιός, ὁ, also with heterocl. pl. κλοιά in Choerob.in An.Ox.2.234:—old Att. **κλῳός** Ar.V.897, E.Cyc.235:—*dog-collar*, Ar.l.c., Eup.159.16, Plu.Sol.24, Fab.20; τοὺς δάκνοντας κύνας κλοιῷ δήσαντες X.HG2.4.41; κ. σιδήρειος Babr.100(99).6; of a horse, κλοιῷ δειρὴν πεπεδημένος AP9.19 (Arch.). 2. wooden *collar* worn by prisoners, X.HG3.3.11, E.l.c., Luc.Tox.32, Jul.Ep.89b. 3. χρύσεος κ. *collar* of gold, as an ornament, E.Cyc.184, Lxx Ge.41.42.

κλοῖστρον or **κλῷστρον**, τό, prob. = κλεῖστρον, Hsch. **κλοιτοιμωγεῖς**· ἀκουσταὶ θρήνου, Id. (fort. κλύετ' οἰμωγῆς· ἀκούετε θρήνου). **κλοιώτης**, ου, ὁ, *wearing a collar*, hence, = δεσμώτης, Id.; **κλοιωτός**, ή, όν, Id.

κλόκιον, τό, = ἀμίς, Steph.in Hp.1.163 D., prob. for κλοβίῳ (κλωβίῳ) ib.159 D.

κλον-έω, mostly in pres.: fut. -ήσω Ar.Eq.361:—**Pass.** also mostly in pres.: fut. κλονήσομαι Hp.Genit.2: aor. part. κλονηθέν Id.Nat.Puer.30: (κλόνος):—poet. Verb, used also in Ion. and late Prose, as Ph. (v. infr.), Aq.Ge.45.24, al.: Hom. (only in Il.) *drive tumultuously* or *in confusion*, πρὸ ἕθεν κλονέοντα φάλαγγας Il.5.96; ὥς τ' ἠὲ βοῶν ἀγέλην ἢ πῶϋ μέγ' οἰῶν θῆρε δύω κλονέωσι 15.324; of winds, νέφεα κλονέοντε πάροιθεν 23.213, cf. Hes.Op.553; κλονέων ἄνεμος φλόγα εἰλυφάζει Il.20.492; ὣς ἔφεπε κλονέων πεδίον 11.496, cf. 526; Ἕκτορα δ' ἀσπερχὲς κλονέων ἔφεπ' 22.188; χερὶ κλονέειν τινά, of a pugilist, Pi.I.8(7).70; εὖτ' ἐν πεδίῳ κλονέων μαίνοιτ' Ἀχιλλεύς B.12.118; dub. sens. in Sapph.Supp.19.3: generally, *harass*, *agitate*, καί νιν οὐ θάλπος θεοῦ.., οὐδὲ πνευμάτων οὐδὲν κλονεῖ S.Tr.146; τόνδε... ἆται κ. Id.OC1244 (lyr.), cf. Ar.Eq.361; πάθη κ. τὴν ψυχήν Ph.1.589; in physical sense, βῆχες κ. τὸν θώρηκα Aret.CA1.10:—Pass., *to be agitated*, Hp.ll.cc., Morb.4.55. 2. abs., of the winds, *rage*, D.P.464. II. Pass., *rush wildly*, ἵππους ἐχέμεν, μηδὲ κλονέεσθαι ὁμίλῳ Il.4.302; *to be driven in confusion*, ὑπὸ Τυδεΐδῃ κλονέοντο φάλαγγες 5.93, cf. 11.148, 14.59, etc.; λαίλαπι κλονεύμενοι Semon.1.15; ψάμαθοι κύμασιν ῥιπαῖς τ' ἀνέμων κλονέονται Pi.P.9.48; τὸ συμπόσιον ἐκλονεῖτο τῷ γέλωτι Luc.Asin.47; κλονεῖσθαι τὴν γαστέρα Ael.NA2.44. 2. abs., *to be beaten by the waves*, ἀκτὰ κυματοπλὴξ κλονεῖται S.OC1241 (lyr.); παρὰ δ' ἰχθύες ἐκλονέοντο beside the fishes *tumbled*, Hes.Sc.317; of bees, *swarm*, βομβηδὸν κ. A.R.2.133: metaph., κ. ἡ οἰκουμένη Ph.1.298; *to be shaken in credit*, *refuted*, τὸ κεκλονημένον ῥῆμα Porph.Chr.35. **-ησις**, εως, ἡ, *agitation*, Hp.Morb.4.48, 55, Aq.Jb.3.17, dub. in Q.S.8.41.

κλόνις, ιος, ἡ, *os sacrum*, Antim.65: **κλόνιον**, τό, = ἰσχίον, ῥάχις, ὀσφύς, Hsch.: **κλονιστήρ**, ὁ, = παραμήριος μάχαιρα, παρίσχιον, Id. (Cf. Skt. *śróṇis* 'haunch', Lat. *clūnis*.)

κλονο-ειδῶς, Adv. *tumultuously*, Sch.D Il.22.448. **-εις**, εσσα, εν, *tumultuous*, EM521.22. **-κάρδιος**, ον, *heart-stirring*, epith. of the thunderbolt, Orph.H.19.8 (cj. Steph. pro χρονοκάρδιος).

κλόν-ος, ὁ, Hom. (only in Il.), *confused motion*, *turmoil*, esp. *battle-rout*, κατὰ κλόνον Il.16.331, 713; κ. ἐγχειάων *throng* of spears, 5.167, 20.319; ἐν δὲ κλόνον ἧκε κακόν [Ἀπόλλων] 16.729; κ. ἀνδρῶν *throng* of men, Hes.Sc.148; Trag. (not in S.) only in lyr., ἱππιοχάρμας κλόνους *throngs* of fighting horsemen, A.Pers.106; ἀσπίστορας κλόνους Id.Ag.404; σκέψαι κλόνον ... Γιγάντων E.Ion206: in later Prose, *trembling*, *confusion*, Aq.Ez.12.8, Them.Or.6.73b; *agitation* of mind, ὁ ἄφρων σάλον καὶ κ. ὑπομένει Ph.1.230. II. *agitation* in physiological sense, of wind in the bowels, Ar.Nu.387; κλόνου πάταγος Aret.SD1.7; οἱονεί τινα σφυγμὸν καὶ κ. ἔχοντος τοῦ πνεύματος Plu.2.681a; of the pulse, Gal.9.76; of the body generally, ib.651: generally, *shaking*, *agitation*, Alex.Aphr.in Top.466.25. **-ώδης**, ες, *agitated*, Gal.8.554, al. Adv. -δῶς Id.9.79.

κλοπ-αῖος, α, ον, *stolen*, πυρὸς πηγή A.Pr.110, cf. S.Ichn.76, E.Alc.1035. 2. *furtive*, *fraudulent*, κλοπαίων τε καὶ βιαίων Pl.Lg.934c; ἀφανισμός D.H.2.71. **-εία** (v.l. κλωπεία), ἡ, *brigandage*, Str.15.3.18. **-εῖον**, τό, *stolen property*, Max.600. **-εύς**, έως, ὁ, *thief*, S.Ph.77. 2. generally, *secret doer*, *perpetrator*, Id.Ant.493. **-εύω**, *plunder*, τὴν Ἰταλίαν App.Ill.15. II. v. κλοτοπεύω. **-ή**, ἡ, (κλέπτω) *theft*, ἁρπαγῆς τε καὶ κλοπῆς δίκη A.Ag.534: pl., ib.402 (lyr.), E.Hel.1175; κλοπῆς δίκη Pl.Prt.322a; ἱερῶν κλοπῆς δυοῖν ταλάντοιν γεγραμμένος Antipho 2.1.6, cf. Ar.Eq.444, Pl.Euthphr.5d (pl.); κλοπῆς ὀφλεῖν And.1.74; ἐπὶ κλοπῇ χρημάτων ἀποκτείνειν Lys.30.25; κ. τῶν θησαυρῶν PAmh.2.79.63 (ii A.D.); σκεῦος ... ἐκφέρειν ἐκ τοῦ ἱεροῦ ἐπὶ κλοπήν SIG997.5 (Smyrna); κλοπῆς ἐν ταῖς εὐθύναις ἑάλωκεν D.24.112, cf. Arist.Ath.54.2, Plu.Per.32; opp. ἁρπαγή, Pl.Lg.941b. 2. of authors, *plagiarism*, Porph.ap.Eus.PE10.3. II. *secret act* or *transaction*, *fraud*, κλέπτουσα μύθοις κλοπάς E.HF100; πράγματος μεγάλου κ. Aeschin.2.57; κλοπῇ *by stealth* or *fraud*, S.Ph.1025, E.Ion1254; ποδοῖν κλοπὰν ἀρέσθαι, i.e. to steal away, S.Aj.246 (lyr.). III. in warfare, *surprise*, X.An.4.6.14. **-ικός**, ή, όν, *thievish*, τὸ κ. Pl.Cra.408a. **-ῐμαῖος**, α, ον, *acquired by theft*, Luc.Icar.20; βόες Ant.Lib.23.4. Adv. -αίως Gloss. **-ιμος**, ον (η, ον Ps.-Phoc.135), *thievish*, χεῖρες Id.154, APl.4.193 (Phil.); *gotten by fraud*, παραθήκη Ps.-Phoc.135. Adv. -μως Man.5.298. **-ιος**, α, ον, (κλώψ) *thievish*, *artful*, μῦθοι Od.13.295; χείρ AP9.249 (Maec.); ὁδός APl.4.123. **-ός**, ὁ, *thief*, h.Merc.276, Opp.C.1.517.

κλοποφορ-έω, *steal from*, *rob*, τινα Lxx Ge.31.26. **-ημα**, ατος, τό, *a theft*, Hdn.Epim.72. **-ία**, ἡ, *theft*, Zonar.

κλότι-ον, τό, or **-ος**, ὁ, a kind of *vessel* or *basket*, μήκων ἐν κλοτίῳ PSI4.428.2, cf. 51 (iii B.C., nisi leg. κλουίον).

κλοτοπ-εύω, *deal subtly*, *spin out time by false pretences*, οὐ γὰρ χρὴ κλοτοπεύειν Il.19.149; κ. περὶ τὸ νησίδιον, perh. to be read for κλοπεύω, Hld.1.30:—hence **-ευτής**· ἐξαλλάκτης, ἀλαζών, Hsch.

κλουβός, ὁ, later form for κλωβός, Tz.H.5.602, Gloss.; *kiln*, POxy.1923.14 (v/vi A.D.):—Dim. **κλουβίον**, τό, *small cage*, PTeb.413.14 (ii/iii A.D.):—written **κλουίον**, *crate*, ᾠῶν POxy.936.5 (iii A.D.).

κλοῦστρον, τό, a kind of *cake*, Chrysipp.Tyan.ap.Ath.14.647d.

κλύβᾰτις [ῠ], ἡ, = ἑλξίνη, Nic.Th.537, Dsc.4.85.

κλύδα, τήν, metapl. acc. of κλύδων, as if from *κλύς, Nic.Al.170.

κλῠδ-άζομαι, *fluctuate*, of the fluid in pleurisy, Hp.Loc.Hom.14; of cranes flying, Max.Tyr.12.3. **-αξις**, εως, ἡ, *splashing* in the stomach, Diocl.Fr.141. **-ασμός**, ὁ, *surging of waves*, Str.4.1.7; *fluctuation* in an abscess, Paul.Aeg.3.65. **-άττομαι**, = κλυδωνίζομαι, D.L.5.66. **-άω**, *to be plastic*, Arist.Pr.$966^{b}7$. **-ιος**, α, ον, *surging*: κλύδιον· πέλαγος, Hsch.

κλύδων [ῠ], ωνος, ὁ, *wave*, *billow*, and collectively, *surf*, *rough water*, Od.12.421; πόντιος κ. A.Pr.431 (lyr.), S.OC1687 (lyr.); κ. πελάγιος, θαλάσσιος, E.Hec.701, Med.29; Θρῄκιος κ. S.OT197 (lyr.); κ. ἄγριος Tim.Pers.146: in Prose, prob. in Th.2.84 (Phot., Suid., κλυδωνίῳ codd.), cf. Thphr.Char.25.2; πνεῦμα καὶ κ. Arist.HA$548^{b}13$; κ. καὶ χειμών Id.PA$685^{a}32$: pl., Lyc.474, Plb.10.10.3. 2. Medic., *splashing* in the stomach and chest, Gal.1.348, al.; of sound heard in pleurisy, Id.8.285; ἢν κ. ὑγρῶν ἀναπνέῃ ἐς τὰς διαπνοάς *flood* of humours, Aret.SA1.5; of internal water in dropsy, Id.SD2.1. II. metaph., κ. κακῶν *sea* of troubles, A.Pers.599; κ. ξυμφορᾶς S.OT1527 (troch.); κ. ἔφιππος *flood* of chariots, Id.El.733; πολέμιος κ. E.Ion60; πολὺς κ. δορός Id.Supp.474; ἔριδος κ. Id.Hec.116 (anap.); πόλις ἐν κλύδωνι τῶν ἄλλων πόλεων διαγομένη Pl.Lg.758a; κ. καὶ μανία D.19.314; ἐν χειμῶνι πολλῷ καὶ κ. τῆς πόλεως Plu.Cor.32, cf. M.Ant.12.14; κ. ἀλογίας Hierocl.in CA26 p.479 M.

κλῠδων-ίζω, Suid.:—elsewh. in Pass., *to be buffeted*, *swept by heavy seas*, τὸν κυβερνήτην -ίζεσθαι καὶ ἀστοχεῖν θαλασσομαχοῦντα Vett.Val.354.26; -ομένη ναῦς Phlp.in APo.381.7: usu. metaph., *to be disturbed*, *thrown into confusion*, οἱ ἄδικοι κλυδωνισθήσονται Lxx Is.57.20; δῆμος ταρασσόμενος καὶ -ιζόμενος J.AJ9.11.3; *to be tossed about*, παντὶ ἀνέμῳ τῆς διδασκαλίας Ep.Eph.4.14. **-ιον**, τό, Dim. of κλύδων, *little wave*, *ripple*, E.Hec.48, etc.: pl., Id.Hel.1209: metaph., of a city, κλυδωνίου πολλαῖσι πληγαῖς ἄντλον οὐκ ἐδέξατο A.Th.795: collectively, *surf*, dub.l. in Th.2.84 (cf. κλύδων): without Dim. sense, Arr.Peripl.M.Eux.3. II. metaph., κ. χολῆς A.Ch.183. **-ισμα**, ατος, τό, gloss on κλυδώνιον, Suid.: **-ισμός**, ὁ, Hdn.Epim.179: **-ῶ**, = κλυδωνίζω, Suid.

κλύζω, Ep. impf. κλύζεσκον Il.23.61: Ep. fut. κλύσσω h.Ap.75: aor. inf. κλύσαι Poll.4.21 (v.l. κλεῖσαι):—**Pass.**, aor. ἐκλύσθην: pf. κέκλυσμαι (v. infr.):—of the sea, *wash*, *dash over*, c. acc., ἔνθ' ἐμὲ μὲν μέγα κῦμα.. κλύσσει h.Ap.l.c.: abs., *surge up*, κύματος δίκην κλύζειν πρὸς αὐγάς (Auratus for κλύειν) A.Ag.1182:—more freq. in Pass., ἐκλύσθη δὲ θάλασσα ποτὶ κλισίας Il.14.392; ἐκλύσθη δὲ θάλασσα.. ὑπὸ πέτρης *was dashed high* by the falling rock, Od.9.484, 541; λιμὴν.. κλυζομένῳ ἴκελος seeming *to rise in waves*, Hes.Sc.209; ὕδασι.. ἐκλύζετο Batr.76; of land, *to be washed by the sea*, Plb.34.11.2. II. *wash away*, *purge*, κλύζουσι φαρμάκῳ χολήν S.Fr.854; ἔκλυζεν ποταμῷ λύματα Call.Aet.3.1.25: metaph., θάλασσα κλύζει πάντα τἀνθρώπων κακά E.IT1193. 2. *wash*, *rinse out*, ἔκπωμα X.Cyr.1.3.9; τοὺς μυκτῆρας οἴνῳ with wine, Arist.HA$603^{b}11$; *drench* with a clyster, Hp.Acut.19, Mul.1.75, al., Nic.Al.140, AP11.118 (Nicarch. or Callicter), etc.; dub.l. in Hp.Flat.12 (Pass.). 3. εἰς ὦτα κ. *put water* into the ears *and so cleanse* them, E.Hipp.654. 4. *coat with wax*, Πανιώνιον στεγνώσαντι καὶ κλύσαντι IG11(2).154 A 36 (Delos, iii B.C.); κηρῷ κλύσαντι ib.219 A 40:—Pass., κισσύβιον κεκλυσμένον ἁδέϊ κηρῷ Theoc.1.27. (Cf. Lat. *cluĕre*, = *purgare*, *cloaca*, Goth. *hlutrs*, OHG. *hlûtar* (MHG. *lauter*) 'pure'.)

κλῦθι, v. κλύω.

κλύμενον, τό, *honeysuckle*, *Lonicera etrusca*, Thphr.HP9.8.5, 9.18.6, Dsc.4.14. 2. *Scorpiurus vermiculata*, ib.13, Plin.HN25.70. 3. *bearbind*, *Convolvulus arvensis*, Ps.-Dsc.4.13. 4. = κισσός, Hsch., quoting κισσοῦ τε κλυμένοιο Antim.68.

κλύμενος [ῠ], η, ον, = κλυτός, *famous* or *infamous*, Antim.68 (v. foreg. 4); ἔρως Theoc.14.26:—mostly as pr. n., Κλύμενος, god of the nether world, AP7.9 (Damag.), 189 (Aristodic.), Paus.2.35.4.

κλυντήρ, ῆρος, ὁ, prob. late spelling of κλιντήρ, IGRom.1.730 (pl., Philippopolis).

κλύσις [ῠ], εως, ἡ, *drenching* by clyster, Hp.Acut.11.

κλύσ-μα, ατος, τό, *liquid used for washing out*, esp. *clyster*, *drench*, Hdt.2.77, 87, Ruf.ap.Orib.8.24 tit. 2. *surf*, πέτραι παραθηγόμεναι τῷ κ. Luc.Nav.8. II. *place washed by the waves*, *sea-beach*, Plu.Caes.52, Luc.DMar.6.3, etc. III. of a κίναιδος, Poll.6.126; of a ἑταίρα, Id.7.39. **-ματικόν**, τό, = sq., Ruf.ap.Orib.7.26.191. **-μάτιον**, τό, Dim. of κλύσμα, *clyster*, Hp.Epid.3.17.γ', Ruf.Ren.Ves.1, etc. **-μός**, ὁ, = κλύσμα I, D.S.1.82, Dsc.3.96, Ruf.ap.Orib.7.26.18, Mnesith.ap.eund.8.38.1. **-τέον**, *one must wash out*, Aët.

4.20. II. -τέος, α, ον, *to be washed out*, Lycus ap.Orib.8.28. 7. **-τήρ,** ῆρος, ὁ, *clyster-pipe, syringe*, Hdt.2.87, Phld.*Lib.*p.30 O., Sor.2.59, Lycus ap.Orib.8.33.3, Gal.10.358, Artem.5.79. II. = κλύσμα I, Nic.*Al.*139; τρόφιμοι κ. nutritive *enemata*, Lycus ap.Orib. 8.34 tit. **-τήριον,** τό, Dim. of foreg., Gal.7.443: **-τηρίδιον,** τό, Sor.1.125, Orib.*Fr.*143, Paul.Aeg.3.23.

κλῦτε, v. κλύω.

κλῠτό-βουλος, ον, *famous in counsel*, Ἑρμείας Opp.*H.*3.26. **-δενδρος,** ον, *famous for trees*, Πιερίη *AP*4.2.1 (Phil.). **-εργός,** όν, *making* κλυτὰ ἔργα: hence, = κλυτοτέχνης, epith. of Hephaestus, Od. 8.345; Τύχη *AP*10.64 (Agath.). **-καρπος,** ον, *glorious with fruit*, κ. στέφανοι Pi.*N.*4.76. **-μαντις,** εως, ὁ, *famous for prophecy*, Πυθοῖ Pi.*Pae.*6.2. **-μητις,** ι, gen. ιδος, *famous for skill*, epith. of Hephaestus, *h.Hom.*20.1; of Apollo, *Pae.Erythr.*p.137 P.; of Asclepius, *IG*4²(1).471 (Epid.), 14.1015, Philostr.Jun.*Im.*13 (-μήτης codd.); of a judge, *APl.*4.43. **-μοχθος,** ον, *famous for toil*, Καλλιόπα ib.362. **-νοος,** ον, *famous for wisdom*, *AP*3.4 (Inscr. Cyzic.). [κλῠ- metri gr.] **-παις,** ὁ, ἡ, gen. παιδος, *famous for one's children*, ib.9.262 (Phil.). **-πωλος,** ον, *with noble steeds*, Il. always epith. of Hades, 5.654, 11.445, 16.625; later κ. λόχος, of the heroes in the wooden horse, Tryph.92.

κλῠτός, ή, όν (but κλυτὸς Ἱπποδάμεια, κλυτὸς Ἀμφιτρίτη, Il.2.742, Od.5.422): (κλέω A):—*renowned, glorious*, in Ep., etc., freq. as epith. of gods and heroes, κ. ἐννοσίγαιος Il.9.362; Ἀμφιγυήεις Hes.*Op.* 70; Ἑρμᾶς Pi.*P.*9.59; Ἀθάνα B.16.7; Νηρέος κόραι ib.101; Ἀχιλλεύς Il.20.320; Ὀδυσεύς Od.24.409; also κλυτὰ φῦλ' ἀνθρώπων Il.14. 361; κ. ἔθνεα νεκρῶν Od.10.526; ὄνομα κ. a *glorious* name, 9.364 (expld. by Sch. as the name *by which one is called*); of cities, etc., Ἄργος Il.24.437; Ἰταλία S.*Ant.*1118; πόλις E.*IA*263. 2. of things, *noble, splendid*, ἄλσος Od.6.321; δώματα Il.2.854, etc.; λιμήν Od.10.87, 15.472; αἰθήρ B.16.73; ἀγγελίαν Pi.*O.*14.21; ἐπικωμίαν ὄπα Id.*P.*10.6; of animals, κ. μῆλα Od.9.308; κλυτοῖς αἰπολίοις S.*Aj.* 375; κ. ὄρνις, = ἀλεκτρυών, Hsch., cj. in Nic.*Fr.*68.2: freq. of the works of human skill, κλυτὰ ἔργα Od.20.72; εἵματα 6.58; τεύχεα Il. 5.435; δαίς, ἀοιδαί, φόρμιγξ, Pi.*O.*8.52 codd., *N.*7.16, *I.*2.2; ἔναρα S. *Aj.*177; χρήματα Crates Theb.10.6.—Used by Trag. only in lyr.

κλῠτο-τέρμων ὥρα, ἡ, = ὡροσκόπος, Man.4.28. **-τέχνης,** ου, ὁ, *famous for his art*, epith. of Hephaestus, Il.1.571, 18.143, Od.8. 286. **-τεχνικός,** ή, όν; τὸ αὐτοῦ κ. his *fame in art*, Eust.1148. 57. **-τοξος,** ον, *famous for the bow, renowned archer*, epith. of Apollo, Il.4.101, 15.55, Od.21.267, B.1.37. **-φεγγής,** ές, *brightly-beaming*, Man.2.148. **-φημος,** ον, *illustrious by fame*, Orph.*A.* 216.

κλύω, Hes.*Op.*726, etc.: impf. ἔκλυον with aor. sense, poet. κλύον Id.*Th.*474, B.16.67; 3 sg. ἔκλεεν Maiist.58: aor. imper. κλῦθι Il.1.37, etc.; pl. κλῦτε Pi.*O.*14.4; also with Ep. redupl. κέκλυθι Il.10.284, A.R.4.783, κέκλῦτε Il.3.86, etc.; also sg. κέκλῦκε Epich. 190. (Cf. κλέω A.) [ῠ, exc. in imper. κλῦθι and κλῦτε.]:—*hear*, Hom., etc.; κλύειν, ἀκοῦσαι Ar.*Ra.*1173: poet. word (Com. only in mock Trag., Ar. l. c., *Av.*407, 416, Pherecr.145.1):—Constr.: c. gen. pers. et acc. rei, *hear* a thing *from* a person, κέκλυτέ μευ.. μῦθον Ἀλεξάνδροιο Il.3.86, cf. Od.2.25, S.*OT*235, etc.; τι ἔκ τινος Od.19.93; τι πρός τινος S.*OT*429: c. gen. pers. only, esp. with part. added, οὐδ' ἔκλυον αὐδήσαντος Il.10.47, cf. Od.4.505, S.*OC*1406, 1642: c. acc. rei only, ἀγγελίην ἔκλυεν Od.2.30; κ. βάξιν Emp.112.11; κλύε εὐχὰν Ζεύς B. l. c., cf. A.*Pr.*124 (anap.), 588 (lyr.), etc.: c. gen. rei, θεὰ δέ μευ ἔκλυεν αὐδῆς Od.10.311; θεὰ δέ οἱ ἔκλυεν ἀρῆς 4.767; κέκλυτέ μευ μύθων 12.271, etc.: c. gen. objecti, *hear of* a person or thing, S.*OC* 307, *Ant.*1182: with part., κ. νεκροὺς θανόντας A.*Th.*837 (lyr.); ὃν κλύεις... ὄντα δεσπότην S.*Ph.*261, cf. 427: less freq. c. acc. et inf., ποῦ κλύεις νιν.. ἱδρῦσθαι; Id.*Tr.*68: κ. ὁθούνεκα *hear* that.., Id.*El.*1307: pres. with pf. sense, *have heard* or *learnt, know*, εἰ καὶ μὴ κλύεις τῶν ἀγγέλων Id.*OT*305, cf. *Ph.*261, *Tr.*422, 425; λόγῳ κ. E.*Hipp.* 1004: abs. in part., κλύοντες οὐκ ἤκουον A.*Pr.*448, cf. S.*Ant.*691, etc. 2. *perceive* generally, μάλιστα δέ τ' ἔκλυον αὐτοί they themselves *know* [the blessing] most, Od.6.185; κλῦθι ἰδὼν ἀΐων τε Hes. *Op.*9. II. *give ear to, attend to*, τοῦ κλύον ἠδ' ἐπίθοντο Il.15.300, etc.: imper., κέκλυτέ μευ, πάντες τε θεοὶ πᾶσαί τε θέαιναι 8.5; esp. in prayers, *give ear* to me, κλῦθί μευ, Ἀργυρότοξε 1.37: c. dat., *give ear to*, καί τ' ἔκλυες ᾧ κ' ἐθέλῃσθα (of Hermes) 24.335; κλῦθί μοι v. l. 5.115 (v. ἐγώ II); κλῦτέ μοι εὐχομένῳ Sol.13.2 = Crates Theb.10.2, cf. Epic. *Oxy.*214ʳ.10 (iii A. D.), Thgn.13; *comply with, obey*, θυγατρὶ φίλῃ μάλα μὲν κλύον ἠδ' ἐπίθοντο Hes.*Th.*474: also c. gen., κακῶν κ. φρενῶν A. *Ag.*1064; οἴακος Id.*Supp.*718; τῶν ἐν τέλει S.*Aj.*1352, cf. *OC*740, etc. III. in Trag. like ἀκούω III, *to be called* or *spoken of*: with Adv., εὖ or κακῶς κ., A.*Ag.*468 (lyr.), S.*Tr.*721; πρός τινος Id.*El.*524; κλύειν δικαίως (nisi leg. δίκαιος) μᾶλλον ἢ πρᾶξαι θέλεις A.*Eu.*430: with a Noun, κ. ἄναλκις μᾶλλον ἢ μιαιφόνος Id.*Pr.*868.

κλωβίον, τό, Dim. of sq., *small cage*, Eust. ad D.P.1134, Hdn. *Epim.*72.

κλωβός, ὁ, *bird-cage*, *AP*6.109 (Antip.), Babr.124.3, Aesop.341. (Cf. κλουβός, κλουβίον, and Hebr. *kělūbh.*)

κλωγμός (also **κλωσμός,** v. infr.), ὁ, (κλώζω) *clucking* of hens, Plu. 2.129a (κλωσμοῖς codd.). II. *clucking sound* by which we urge on a horse, X.*Eq.*9.10, Poll.1.209. 2. *clucking sound* by which Greek audiences expressed disapprobation, *hooting*, Orac.ap.Luc. *J.Tr.*31, Eust.1504.29: **κλωσμός,** Ph.2.599 (v.l. κλωγμός), Harp. s. v. ἐκλώζετε.

κλῶδις· κλέπτης, Hsch.

Κλώδωνες, ων, αἱ, Maced. name of female Bacchanals, Plu.*Alex.* 2, Polyaen.4.1, cf. *EM*521.48, Hsch.

κλώζω, of the sound made by jackdaws, as κρώζω of crows, Poll. 5.89. II. *make a similar sound in token of disapprobation, hoot*, D.21.226, Alciphr.3.71, Phot.:—Pass., Aristid.*Or.*34(50).7, etc.; cf. κλώσσω.

Κλῶθες, ων, αἱ, *Spinners*, name of the *Goddesses of fate*, πείσεται ἅσσα οἱ αἶσα κατὰ Κλῶθές τε βαρεῖαι γεινομένῳ νήσαντο λίνῳ Od.7.197 (v.l. Κατακλῶθες: v.l. ap.Eust. ἅσσα οἱ Αἶσα κατακλώθῃσι βαρεῖα, with next line omitted).

κλώθω, aor. ἔκλωσα Nonn.*D.*2.678, (ἐπ-) Od.3.208:—*twist by spinning, spin*, λίνον Hdt.5.12, cf. *POxy.*1414.5 (iii A. D.); μίτον Luc.*Fug.* 12; κ. ἄτρακτον *turn* it, Luc.*J.Conf.*19:—Pass., βύσσος κεκλωσμένη Lxx *Ex.*35.6. 2. esp. of the goddesses of fate, *spin* a man his thread of life or of fate, κ. τινὶ τὰ οἰκεῖα Arist.*Mu.*401ᵇ22:—poet. in Med., ἐκλώσασθε πανάφθιτον ἦμαρ ἀοιδῷ *AP*7.14 (Antip. Sid.); ἑπτὰ δέ μοι μοῖραι.. ἐνιαυτοὺς ἐκλώσαντο *IG*3.1337; τίς μοιρῶν μίτον ὔμμιν ἐκλώσατο; ib.5(1).1355 (Abia):—Pass., τὰ κλωσθέντα *one's destiny*, Pl.*Lg.*960c. II. intr. in Act., χυλῷ ἐνὶ κλώθοντι Nic.*Al.*93 (expld. by Sch. ὡς νῆμα κλωθομένῳ), cf. 528.

Κλωθώ, οῦς, ἡ, *Spinster*, one of the three Μοῖραι, who spins the thread of life (cf. Κλῶθες), Hes.*Th.*218, *Sc.*258, Pl.*R.*617c, Luc.*Hist. Conscr.*38: late nom. pl. Κλωθῶες *IG*14.1389 i 14.

κλωκυδά, Adv. *in a squatting position*, Hsch.

κλωμᾰκόεις, εσσα, εν, *stony, rocky*, Il.2.729.

κλῶμαξ, ἄκος, ὁ, *heap of stones, rocky place*, Lyc.653: **κρῶμαξ,** Hsch.

κλών, gen. κλωνός, ὁ, *twig, spray, slip*, S.*OC*483, *Ant.*713, E.*El.* 324, *Ion*423, Pl.*Prt.*334b, Thphr.*CP*1.3.1, Lxx *Jb.*18.13, Dsc.4. 170. 2. κ. βύσσου *thread* or *fibre*, Paul.Aeg.6.13:—Dim. (in signf. I) **κλῶναξ,** ὁ, Hsch.; **κλωνάριον,** τό, *Gp.*12.19.9, *Gloss.*; **κλωνίδιον,** τό, ib.; **κλωνίον,** τό, Thphr.*HP*3.13.5, 3.18.5, *IG*2².1468.9, *AP*12.256.8 (Mel.); **κλωνίσκος,** ὁ, Dsc.5.68.

κλων-ίζω, = κλαδεύω, Suid. **-ίτης** [ῑ], ου, ὁ, *with branches*, πρέμνος Hdn.*Epim.*72. **-ος,** *ramus*, *Gloss.*

κλῳομάστιξ, ῑγος, ὁ, ἡ, *one who is flogged with a collar on*, *Com. Adesp.*1039.

κλῳός, ὁ, old Att. for κλοιός.

κλωπ-άομαι, poet. for κλέπτω, Hsch. **-εία,** ἡ, *theft*, Pl.*Lg.* 823b (pl.), Isoc.12.211, 218, v.l. in Str.15.3.18, Plu.*Phil.*4. II. name of a *dance*, Juba 74:—κλοπεία is freq. as v.l. **-εύω,** *steal*, X.*An.*6.1.1, *Lac.*2.7, Luc.*Cat.*1, *Tox.*49. **-ηδίς,** = κλοπιμαίως, Theognost.*Can.*163. **-ήϊος,** η, ον, Ion. and poet. for κλοπαῖος, A.R.3.1197, Max.434. **-ίδαι,** οἱ, mock-Attic deme-name (cf. Κρωπίδαι), Ar.*Eq.*79. **-ικός,** ή, όν, *thievish*, τὸ κ. v.l. for κλοπ- in Pl.*Cra.*408a. 2. *stealthy, clandestine*, βήματα, ἕδραι, E.*Rh.* 205, 512. **-ιτεύω,** = -εύω, Suid.

κλωποπάτωρ [ᾰ], ορος, ὁ, ἡ, *son of a thief* (i. e. Hermes), Theoc. *Syrinx*15.

κλῶσις, εως, ἡ, *spinning*, Corn.*ND*13. 2. = κλῶσμα, Lyc.716.

κλώσκω, = κλώθω, Hsch.

κλῶσ-μα, ατος, τό, (κλώθω) *clue*, Nic.*Fr.*72.1, Paus.6.26.7. 2. *thread*, Lxx *Nu.*15.38. 3. metaph., *thread of fate*, κλώσματα θεῖα τελῶν *IG*12(7).123 (Amorgos). **-μός,** ὁ, v. κλωγμός.

κλώσσω, *cluck*, prob. in Suid. s. v. φωλάς; cf. κλώζω.

κλωσ-τήρ, ῆρος, ὁ, *spindle*, Theoc.24.70, A.R.4.1062. II. *thread, yarn*, λίνου κ., of a *net* (periphr. for κλωστὸν λίνον Sch.), A. *Ch.*507, cf. E.*Fr.*1001. 2. *skein*, Ar.*Ra.*1349 (lyr.), *Lys.*567, Pl.*R.* 558d. 3. metaph., *thread of fate*, μοιρῶν κλωστῆρι *Epigr.Gr.*292.6 (Heraclea ad Latmum), cf. *Arch.Pap.*1.220 (κλωστείρων is a mason's error for -τήρων); μοιρίδιοι κ. *IG*3.1339. **-τήριον,** τό, *spun thread*, dub. in *Ostr.*1525 (ii B. C.). **-τής,** οῦ, Dor. **-τάς,** ὁ, *spinner*, *IG* 5(1).209.22 (Sparta), *EM*495.27. II. *web*, κλωστοῦ... λίνοισι dub. l. in E.*Tr.*537 (lyr., leg. κλωστοῦ λίνοιο).

κλωστόμαλλος, ον, gloss on στρεψίμαλλος, Eust.1638.17.

κλωσ-τός, ή, όν, *spun*, λίνον Aen.Tact.18.14, cf. κλωστήρ II; κόκκινον Lxx *Le.*14.6; βύσσος J.*AJ*3.7.1; κρόκη Plu.*Sol.*12. 2. metaph., of fate, μοῖραι κλωστὸν ἔθεντο μίτον *IG*3.1344. **-τρον,** τό, = *vermiculus*, *Gloss.*

κλώψ, κλωπός, ὁ, (κλέπτω) *thief*, Hdt.1.41, al., E.*Hel.*553, X.*An.* 4.6.17, Aen.Tact.23.7, etc.

κμέλεθρον, τό, *beam*, Pamphil.ap.*EM*521.34 (pl.).

κμητός, ή, όν, *wrought*, Hsch., *EM*521.31:—found only in compds. **κνᾰδάλλω,** = κνάω, *scratch*, Hsch. **κνάζει·** βοηθεῖ, Id. **κναίω,** = κνάω, prob. l. for καινιεῖ, Lxx *Si.*38.28:—elsewh. only in compds. **κνᾱκίας, κνᾱκός, κνάκων,** Dor. for κνηκ-. **κνᾶμις,** v. κνημίς. **κνάμπτω,** v. κνάπτω. **κνάξ·** γάλα λευκόν, Hsch.; cf. **κναξβί** (cj. κνάξ) Thespis 4.

κνάπτω (v. sub fin.), *card* or *comb* wool, *dress* or *full* cloth (either with teasel or comb), ἱμάτια Dsc.4.159; παρ' ἐμοὶ πόκος οὐ κνάπτεται Xenocr.ap.D.L.4.10. 2. of torture, ἐπ' ἀσπαλάθων κνάπτοντες Pl.*R.*616a (cf. κνάφος II): generally, *mangle, tear*, μάστιγι Cratin. 275:—Pass., δίνᾳ κναπτόμενοι, of Hector's body *mangled* against rocks, A.*Pers.*576 (lyr.); ἐκνάπτετ' αἰέν, of Hector's body, S.*Aj.*1031, cf. Philostr.*VA*6.40. 3. κ. γλῶσσαν, = συνέχειν ἐντὸς τῶν ὀδόντων, *Com.Adesp.*1313 (= *Trag.Adesp.*224). (Acc. Sch.Ar.*Pl.*166, κνάπτω, κναφεύς, etc., were old Att., γνάπτω, γναφεύς, etc., later Att., confirmed by Inscrr.: forms in γν- are found in Ionic, Papyri, and later Gr., e.g. Dsc. l. c.; κνάμπτ- Pl. l. c. (as v.l.), Philostr. l.c.: cf.

Welsh *cnaif* 'fleece', Engl. *nap* (on cloth), Lett. *knābt* 'pick', 'peck'.)

κνάπτωρ or **γνάπτωρ,** ορος, ὁ, poet. for κναφεύς, Man.4.422.

κναστήριον· ἐνήλατο⟨ν⟩ (Lacon.), Hsch.

κνάφαλλον, τό, v. κνέφαλλον.

κνᾰφᾰλώδης or **γνάφ-,** ες, *like* κνέφαλλον, φύλλα Dsc.3.32, cf. Alex.Trall.1.15.

κνᾰφ-εῖον, Ion. **-ήϊον,** τό, *fuller's shop,* Hdt.4.14, Plu.*Cic.*1; **γνᾰφ-,** *IG*2².1638.28 (iv B.C.), codd. of Lys.3.15, 23.2, cf. *POxy.*1488.9 (ii A.D.), etc. **-εύς,** έως, ὁ, *fuller, cloth-carder* or *dresser, IG*1².436 (vi B.C.), Hdt.4.14, Ar.*V.*1128, *Ec.*415: as fem., A.*Ch.*760; **γνᾰφ-,** Hp. *Epid.*1.21, Lys.3.16 codd., X.*Ages.*1.26, and usu. in later Gr., Herod. 4.78, *PCair.Zen.*206.48 (iii B.C.), *IG*12(2).271 (Mytilene), *POxy.* 736.37 (i A.D.), etc.; but κναφεύς *PIand.*43.13 (ii A.D.). **II.** γναφεύς, kind of *fish,* Dorio ap.Ath.7.297c. **-ευτικός,** later Att. **γνᾰφ-,** ή, όν, *belonging to a fuller*: ἡ κν. (sc. τέχνη) *fuller's art,* Pl.*Plt.*282a; ἡ γν. Id.*Sph.*227a. **-εύω** or **γνᾰφ-,** *clean cloth,* Ar.*Pl.*166. **-ικός,** later **γνᾰφ-,** ή, όν, = κναφευτικός, Dsc.4.160, Suid. s.v. κνάφος; **γνᾰφική** (sc. ἐργασία), ἡ, *fuller's trade, PLond.*2.286 (i A.D.). **-ισσα,** ἡ, *female fuller, PIand.*43.8 (vi A.D.): in form **γνάφ-,** *PGoodsp.Cair.* 30 xxix 24 (ii A.D.). **-ος,** ὁ, *prickly teasel,* Alc.Com.35; used by fullers to card or clean cloth, Sch.Ar.*Pl.*166. **2.** = ἱπποφαές, Gal.19.106. **II.** *carding-comb,* also used as an instrument of torture, ἐπὶ κνάφου ἕλκειν τινά Hdt.1.92 (κναφηΐου codd.), cf. Hp.*Mul.* 2.114, Plu.2.858e (γναφ-), Hsch. **-ω,** = κνάπτω, v.l. in Dsc.4. 159 (γν-).

κνάψ (gender and declens. unknown), = δαλός, Hdn.Gr.1.404.

κνάψις, later **γνάψις,** εως, ἡ, *dressing* of cloth, Sch.Ar.*Pl.*166.

κνάω, κνᾷ Plu.2.61d, but in correct Att. κνῇ, inf. κνῆν (v. ἐπικνάω) corrupted to κνεῖν Moer.p.234 P., Hsch., Ion. κνᾶν Hdt.7.239: fut. κνήσω Hp.*Coac.*460 (prob. l.): aor. ἔκνησα Id.*Int.*23, Pl.*Smp.*185e (prob. l.), Arist.*Pr.*965ᵃ23, (κατ-) Ar.*V.*965; but κνᾶσαι· ὀλέσαι, λυπῆσαι, Hsch.; 3 sg. Ep. impf. ἐπι-κνῆ Il.11.639:—**Med.,** inf. κνῆσθαι Pl.*Grg.*494c, later κνᾶσθαι Plu.2.89e, etc.: fut. κνήσομαι Herod.4.51: aor. ἐκνησάμην Luc.*Bis Acc.*1, Dor. ἐκνάσ- Theoc.7.110:—**Pass.,** κνᾶται Gal.10.979: pf. κατα-κέκνησμαι Id.13.1022:—*scrape, grate,* ἐπὶ δ' αἴγειον κνῆ τυρόν Il. l. c.; τὸν κηρὸν κνᾶν *to scrape* it *off,* Hdt. l. c. (nisi leg. ἐκκν-), cf. Gal.13.1022:—Pass., prob. for κνισθεῖσα in Thphr.*HP*9.20.4. **II.** *scratch,* τῇ χειρί Hp.*Fract.*21; τὸν περὶ τὰς μασχάλας τόπον Arist. l. c.:—Med., *scratch oneself,* ἀφθόνως ἔχειν τοῦ κνῆσθαι Pl.*Grg.* l. c.; κνώμενος τὸ κρανίον Timocl.2.5 D.; τὸ βρέγμα κνήσῃ Herod. l. c.; [ἔλαφοι] κνώμενοι [τὰ κέρατα] πρὸς τὰ δένδρα Arist.*HA*611ᵇ16; δακτύλῳ κνᾶσθαι τὴν κεφαλήν Plu.*Pomp.*48: abs., Id.2.1091e, Jul.*Caes.*323b; τρίβειν τοὺς ὀφθαλμοὺς καὶ κνᾶσθαι Phld. *Rh.*2.143 S.; κνήσασθαι τὸ οὖς Luc. l. c.; κνησάμενον ἐνὶ τῶν ποδῶν τὴν πλευράν Gal.8.443. **2.** Med., *itch,* Id.10.437, 979. **III.** *tickle,* τὴν ῥῖνα prob. in Pl.*Smp.* l. c.:—Med., κνᾶσθαι τὰ ὦτα πτερῷ *tickle one's* ears, Luc.*Salt.*2, etc.: metaph., τοῦτο κνᾷ καὶ γαργαλίζει καὶ ἀναπείθει Plu.2.61d:—Pass., οὐ παρέργως ἐκνώμην πρὸς αὐτά Luc. *Nec.*3.

κνεφ-άζω, (κνέφας) *cloud over, obscure,* A.*Ag.*131 (lyr.). **-αῖος,** α, ον, also ος, ον Ar.*Ra.*1350 (lyr.):—*dark,* Ταρτάρου βάθη A.*Pr.*1029, cf. E.*Alc.*593 (lyr.). **2.** *in the dark,* κ. ἐλθών having come *in the dark,* i.e. *at nightfall,* Hippon.63; also, *early in the morning,* ἀνεφάνη κ. Ar.*V.*124, cf. *Ra.* l. c., *Lys.*327 (lyr.), etc.

κνέφαλλον, τό, *wool torn off* in carding or fulling cloth, *flock,* used for stuffing cushions or pillows: hence, *cushion, pillow,* E.*Fr.*676, Cratin.99, Eup.228, Ar.*Fr.*19, etc. (prob. in *IG*1².330.22, cf. Demioprat.ap.Poll.10.39); κνάφαλλον, γνάφαλλον (cf. κνάπτω, γνάπτω) are freq. as vv.ll.; **γνάφαλλα,** *PCair.Zen.*298 (iii B.C.); Aeol. **γνόφαλλον** Alc.34.6.

κνέφᾰς, τό, Att. gen. κνέφους Ar.*Ec.*290, *Com.Adesp.*35, later κνέφατος Plb.8.26.10; dat. κνέφᾳ X.*HG*7.1.15, κνέφεϊ *AP*7.633 (Crin.), as if from **κνέφος,** cited by Hsch., Suid., Phot.: (cf. δνόφος):—*darkness,* Hom. (only in nom. and acc.), of the *evening dusk, twilight,* εἰς ὅ κε.. δύῃ τ' ἠέλιος καὶ ἐπὶ κ. ἱερὸν ἔλθῃ Il.11.194, 209: later, generally, *darkness,* δυσάλιον κ. A.*Eu.*396 (lyr.); νυκτὸς Id.*Pers.*357, cf. E.*Ba.*510, etc.; τὸ κατὰ γᾶς κ. Id.*Hipp.*836 (lyr.): metaph., τοῖον ἐπὶ κ. ἀνδρὶ μύσος πεπόταται A.*Eu.*378 (lyr.). **2.** *morning twilight,* πρῴ πάνυ τοῦ κνέφους Ar.*Ec.*290; ἅμα κνέφᾳ *at dawn,* X. l. c., *Cyr.*4.2.15.

κνέωρον, τό, = sq., Dsc.4.172, Plin.*HN*13.114, Hsch. **II.** *pudenda muliebria,* Phot., Hsch.

κνέωρος, ὁ, *spurge-flax, Daphne Gnidium,* Thphr.*HP*6.1.4; κ. λευκός, *Daphne oleoides,* ib.6.2.2; κ. μέλας, *Thymelaea hirsuta,* ib.1. 10.4, 6.2.2.

κνῆ, v. κνάω.

κνήδιον, τό, in pl., prob. = κνίδια, *nettles* or *nettle-seeds, Stud.Pal.* 22.75.7, 16 (iii A.D.).

κνηθ-ιάω, Desider. of κνήθω, *desire to scratch, itch,* Hdn.Gr.2.949, *EM*116.25. **-μός,** ὁ, *itching,* Nic.*Al.*251, 422. **-ω,** later form of κνάω, *scratch,* ὡς λέγεται, κνήθειν οἶδεν ὄνος τὸν ὄνον *AP*12.238.8 (Strat.), cf. Moer.p.234 P.:—Med., κνήθεσθαι εἰς τὰς ἀκάνθας τὰ ἕλκη *to get* one's sores *scratched,* Arist.*HA*609ᵃ32. **2.** Pass., *itch,* Paul. Aeg.6.60; κνηθόμενοι τὴν ἀκοήν 2*Ep.Ti.*4.3; *to be provoked,* Arist. *Pr.*957ᵇ15.

κνηκ-άνθιον, τό, = κνῆκος, Ps.-Democr.ap.Zos.Alch.p.160 B. **-ίας,** ου, Dor. **κνᾱκίας,** ὁ, (κνηκός) name for the *wolf,* Babr.122.12. **-ινος,** η, ον, *of* or *from* κνῆκος, ἔλαιον *PRev.Laws* 53.15, al. (iii B.C.), *PTeb.* 122.11 (i B.C.), Dsc.1.36. **-ιον,** τό, = τρίφυλλον, Id.3.109 (v.l. κνίκιον). **2.** = σάμψουχον, Ps.-Dsc.3.39. **-ίς,** ῖδος, ἡ, *pale spot,* esp. in the heavens, Call.*Fr.anon.*36; κ. νεφώδεις Cleom.2.1 (pl.), cf. Plu.2.581f, Anon.*Intr.Arat.*p.126 M. **II.** *pale-coloured antelope,* Hsch. **III.** *fine skin,* Id. **IV.** = μελανία, Id. **-ίτης** [ῑ] λίθος, a kind of *gem,* Hermes Trism. in *Rev.Phil.* 32.272.

κνηκο-ειδής, ές, *like* κνῆκος, Hsch. s. v. κνηκίς. **-πῡρος,** ον, *made of yellow wheat,* ἡδοναὶ τραγημάτων Sopat.17.

κνῆκος, ἡ, Thphr.*HP*6.4.5, *PCair.Zen.*223.4 (iii B.C.), *PRev.Laws* (v. infr.), but ὁ Thphr.*HP*1.13.3, *CP*5.18.4, Dsc. (v. infr.), Gal.6. 354, al.:—also **κνήκη,** ἡ, Sch.Theoc.3.5, 7.16 codd.:—*safflower, Carthamus tinctorius,* Hp.*Acut.*64, *Vict.*2.54, Diocl.*Fr.*140, Anaxandr.41.56, Arist.*HA*550ᵇ27, Thphr. *HP*6.1.3, *PRev.Laws* 39.5, al. (iii B.C.), Dsc.4.188, Asclep.ap.Gal.*Nat.Fac.*1.13. **II.** κ. ἀγρία (ἄγριος Dsc.3.93), of two kinds, *Carthamus leucocaulos* and *blessed thistle, Cnicus benedictus,* Thphr.*HP*6.4.5; πώγωνι θάλλων ὡς τράγος κνήκῳ χλιδᾷς you are as wanton as a goat surfeited with *thistles,* S.*Ichn.*358 (nisi leg. κνηκῷ 'you swagger with your *yellow* (cf. sq.) beard': κνικωι Pap.). (Freq. written κνίκος or κνῖκος in codd., as Arist. l. c., Thphr.*CP*6.9.3, Gal. ll. cc., 11.612, etc., but always κνηκ- in Papyri, exc. S.*Ichn.* l. c.; prob. named from its colour, cf. sq.)

κνηκός, ή, όν, Dor. **κνᾱκός,** ά, όν, *pale yellow, tawny,* of the goat, Thespis 4, Theoc.7.16, *AP*6.32 (Agath.); so in oracular style, *Epigr. Gr.*1034.23; of the wolf, Babr.113.2; cf. **κνακός·** ψαρός, ἵππος, Hsch. (Perh. cogn. with Skt. *kāñcanam* 'gold', OPruss. *cucan* 'brown', OE. *hunig* 'honey'.)

κνηκο-συμμῑγής, ές, Dor. **κνᾱκ-,** *mixed with* κνῆκος, Philox.3.19. **-φόρος** (sc. γῆ), ἡ, *bearing safflower, Sammelb.*4369 ii 36, al. (iii B.C.).

κνηκώδης, ες, = κνηκοειδής, Thphr.*HP*1.11.3, 6.6.6.

κνήκων, Dor. **κνάκων** [ᾱ], ωνος, ὁ, (κνηκός) name for the *goat,* Theoc.3.5.

κνῆμα, v. κνῆσμα.

κνημ-αῖος, v. κνημιαῖος. **-αργος,** ον, *white-legged,* Theoc.25. 127. **-η,** Dor. **κνάμα** [νᾱ], ἡ, *part between knee and ankle, leg, shank,* Il.4.147, Od.8.135, Hdt.6.75, 125, 7.75, E.*Ph.*1394, etc.; of a horse, X.*Eq.*1.5, 12.10: prov., ἀπωτέρω ἢ γόνυ κνάμα 'blood is thicker than water', Theoc.16.18. **2.** Anat., *tibia,* Gal.2.774, Ruf.*Onom.* 123. **3.** in plants, *stem between two joints,* Thphr.*HP*9.13.5; κνήμη (v.l. μνήμου) μελίνης dub. sens. in S.*Fr.*608. **II.** *spoke* of a wheel, Poll.1.144, Eust.598.4. (Cf. OIr. *cnāim* 'bone', OE. *hamm* 'ham'.) **-ία,** ἡ, = ἀντικνήμιον, Hsch. **2.** *leg* of a chair, Id., Phot. **3.** *spoke* of a wheel, Lys.*Fr.*95. **II.** in pl., = τὰ τῆς ἁμάξης περιθέματα, Hsch. **2.** = φθοραί, Id.; cf. κνημόω. **-ιαῖος,** α, ον, *of the calf* or *leg,* Hp.*Oss.*16 (written **κνημαῖος** Gal.19.112). **-ίδιον,** τό, dub. sens. in *IG*2².1641.52 (pl.); κ. χαλκᾶ ib.1648.18. **-ῑδοφόρος,** ον, *wearing greaves,* Hdt.7.92:—also **-ῑδωτός,** ή, όν, *Gloss.* **-ίον,** τό, Dim. of κνήμη, *PLond.*3.1166.2 (i A.D.).

κνημῑοπᾰχής, ές, *thick as one's leg,* Ar.*Fr.*722.

κνημίς, ῖδος, ἡ, Aeol. acc. **κνᾶμιν** Eust.265.18 (corrupted to κνῆμιν in Choerob. *in Theod.*1.327); Aeol. nom. pl. **κνάμῑδες** Alc.15.4: (κνήμη):—*greave, legging,* κνημῖδας μὲν πρῶτα περὶ κνήμῃσιν ἔθηκε ἀργυρέοισιν ἐπισφυρίοις ἀραρυίας Il.19.369; τεῦξε δέ οἱ κνημῖδας.. κασσιτέροιο 18.613; κ. ὀρειχάλκοιο φαεινοῦ Hes.*Sc.*122; βόειαι κ. oxhide *leggings,* Od.24.229, cf. Plb.11.9.4; sg., Il.21.592, Luc.*Rh.Pr.* 18. **II.** *spoke of a wheel,* D.S.18.27. **III.** = κνημός I, D.P.714.

κνημοπᾰχής, ές, = κνημιοπαχής, Thphr.*HP*9.4.3.

κνημ-ός, ὁ, *projecting limb, shoulder* of a mountain (above the foot, Eust.1498.42), Hom. (always in pl.), Ἴδης κνημοί Il.2.821, al., cf. Od.4.337: sg., *h.Ap.*283, Orph.*A.*465. **2.** δημόσιος κ. public *grove,* prob. in *TAM*2(1).64 (Telmessus). **II.** Arg., = ὀρίγανος, Eust. 265.40. **-όω,** aor. **-ῶσαι,** = περιχῶσαι, φράξαι, φθεῖραι, κλεῖσαι, ἐλθεῖν, Hsch.; **-οῦμαι,** = φθείρομαι, and **-ωθῆναι,** = φθαρῆναι, Id.; κνημωθείς is prob. f.l. for κημωθείς in Hermesian.7.38. **-ώδης,** ες, *well-legged,* gloss on κνήμαργος, Hsch.

κνήνιον, τό, dub. sens. in *Supp.Epigr.*1.413 (Gortyn, v B.C.). (Fort. leg. τῶν κτηνίων Cret. gen. pl. of κτῆνος).

κνησ-είω, = sq., Suid. **-ιάω,** Desider. of κνάω, *desire to scratch, itch,* Ar.*Ec.*919 (lyr.), Pl.*Grg.*494c, e, Jul.*Or.*7.206d.

κνῆσις, εως, ἡ, (κνάω) *scratching,* τρῖψις καὶ κ. Pl.*Phlb.*46d; κ. κροτάφων καὶ ὤτων Aret.*CA*1.1: pl., Pl.*Phlb.*51d: metaph., *tickling,* ἕνεκα ..κνήσεως ὤτων Plu.2.167b. **II.** (from Pass.) *itching, irritation,* κ. περὶ τὰ οὖλα Pl.*Phdr.*251c, cf. Gal.10.437.

κνησίχρῡσος, ον, *scraping gold,* ῥίνη *AP*6.92 (Phil.).

κνῆσ-μα, ατος, τό, in pl., *scrapings,* Hp.*Nat.Puer.*17 (κνήματα Gal. 19.112): metaph., κ. λόγων Pl.*Hp.Ma.*304a. **II.** *sting, bite,* X. *Smp.*4.28 (v.l. κνῆμα); ψήκτρης κ., periphr. for a *comb, AP*6.233 (Maec.). **-μονή,** ἡ, = sq., Archig.ap.Aët.3.167, Orib.*Fr.*116, *App. Anth.*3.158 (pl.), *Gp.*1.12.34. **-μός,** ὁ, = κνῆσις, *itching,* Hp.*VM* 16, Arist.*HA*578ᵇ3; ἡ ἀκαλήφη κ. ποιεῖ Diph.Siph.ap.Ath.3.90a; *scratching,* Plu.2.126b (pl.); in a pleasurable sense, *titillation,* Arist. *GA*723ᵇ34, *Pr.*878ᵇ7. **2.** metaph., *irritation,* Plu.2.61a. **-μώδης,** ες, *affected with itching,* Hp.*Aph.*6.9, Aret.*SD*1.15, Gal.10. 261. **II.** *accompanied with itching* or *irritation,* Arist.*Pr.*887ᵃ35, Gal.7.197. Adv. **-δῶς** Id.19.70. **III.** *causing irritation,* ἅλες Str. 11.13.2. **-τέον,** *one must chafe,* τὰ σκέλη Paul.Aeg.3.9. **-τήρ,** ῆρος, ὁ, *scraping-knife,* Nic.*Th.*85, *Al.*308. **II.** *slayer, destroyer,* Hsch. **III.** gloss on κνῆστρον, Erot. **-τιάω,** = κνησιάω, Plu.*Fr.inc.*149, Gal.7.197, Phlp. *in APr.*277.5: metaph., ἀκοαὶ κνηστιῶσαι Jul.*Ep.*111. **-τικός,** ή, όν, *irritating,* λόγοι Sch.E.*Hipp.* 304. **-τις,** εως and ιος, ἡ, cheese-*grater,* Il.11.640, Nic.*Th.*696

(contr. dat. κνῆστι), *AP*6.305 (Leon.). **2.** τυροῦ κ. cheese-*gratings*, Porph.*VP*34. **II.** = κνησμός, Opp.*H.*2.427. **III.** = ῥάχις, *spine*, Hsch., perh. to be read in Od.10.161 (v. ἄκνηστις). **-τίς,** ίδος, ἡ, *hollow hair-pin*, Plu.*Ant.*86. **-τός,** ή, όν, *scraped, rasped*, κ. ἄρτος Artem.Eph.ap.Ath.3.111d; but λάχανα κνηστά (v.l. κνιστά) *chopped up*, Ar.*Fr.*908 (= Antiph.79). **-τρίον,** τό, *scraper*, ἰχθύων, σκυτῶν, *Edict.Diocl.* in *IG*5(1).1115 *B* i 14,15 (Geronthr.) :—in late form **-τρίν,** ἀργυροῦν *IG*3.238*a*; cf. *Gloss.* **-τρον,** τό, *stinging plant, Daphne oleoides*, Hp.*Mul.*1.80, 2.169 (expld. = κνηστήρ by Erot.); = θυμελαία, Dsc.4.172.

κνήφη, ἡ, *itch*, Lxx*De.*28.27, Hsch. s.v. ξῦσμα, Suid. s.v. Ἀφροδίτη :—hence **κνηφῶ,** *prurio*, *Gloss.* **κνηφός,** *semen candidum*, dub. in *Gloss.*

κνιδᾶται (κνηδ– cod.)· δάκνεται· ἴσως ἀπὸ τῆς πόας, Hsch. :—also **κνίδοντες** (fort. κνιδῶντες)· κνίδη μαστιγοῦντες, Id.

κνίδη [ῑ], (κνίζω) *nettle, Urtica*, Hp.*Vict.*2.54, Arist.*HA*522^{a}8, Theoc.7.110, Nic.*Th.*880, *AP*12.124 (Artemo); = ἀκαλήφη, Dsc.4.93 (un-Attic, acc. to Moer.p.66P.). **II.** *sea-nettle, Actinia*, Arist.*HA*548^{a}23.—Both senses combined, Archestr.*Fr.*9.7.

Κνίδιος [ῐ], α, ον, (Κνίδος) *of* or *from Cnidos*: οἱ Κνίδιοι *the Cnidians*, Hdt.1.174, al. **II.** κόκκος Κ., ὁ, *berry of the shrub* κνέωρον (*Daphne Gnidium*), used as a purgative, Eub.128, Thphr.*HP*9.20.2, Dsc.1.36, 4.172. **III.** **Κνίδιον,** τό, a measure of wine, *POxy.*150 (vi A.D.), etc. **IV.** v. κνήδιον.

Κνῑδιουργής, ές, *of Cnidian manufacture*, Sch.Ar.*Pax* 142.

Κνῑδόθεν, Adv. *from Cnidos*, Luc.*Lex.*7.

Κνῑδόκοκκος, ὁ, = κόκκος Κνίδιος, Alex.Trall.8.2.

Κνίδος [ῐ], ου, ἡ, *Cnidos*, *h.Ap.*43, etc.

κνῑδόσπερμον, τό, *nettle-seed*, Gal.19.732 :—also **κνῑδόσπερμα,** ατος, τό, Alex.Trall.5.6.

κνίδωσις [ῐ], εως, ἡ, *itching*, such as is caused by a nettle, Hp.*Prorrh.*2.30 (pl.).

κνίζα, ἡ, = κνίδη, *Gloss.* **II.** cited by Eust. fr. Anacr.87 : v. κνυζός.

κνίζω, fut. κνίσω [ῐ] Ar.*Ra.*1198 : aor. ἔκνῑσα Pi.*P.*8.32, Herod.4.59, etc.; Dor. ἔκνιξα Pi.*I.*6(5).50 :—Pass., aor. ἐκνίσθην E.*Andr.* 209, Theoc.4.59 : *scratch, gash*, παῖδα.. γυμνὸν ἣν κνίσω.. οὐχ ἕλκος ἕξει; Herod. l. c.; κνίζων συκάμινα (to make them ripen) Lxx*Am.*7.14, cf. Ath.2.51b. **2.** *pound, chop up*, or *grate*, dub. in Thphr.*HP* 9.20.4 (fort. κνησθεῖσα). **II.** *tickle*, Arist.*HA*587^{b}7 (Pass.), Phld. *Lib.*p.58 O. (Pass.). **2.** usu. metaph., of love, *chafe, tease*, τὸν Ἀρίστωνα ἔκνιζε τῆς γυναικὸς ταύτης ἔρως Hdt.6.62, cf. E.*Med.*568; κἠγὼ μὰν κνίζω τινά Theoc.5.122; of other feelings, as satiety, κόρος κνίζει Pi.*P.* l. c.; anxiety, Ξέρξην ἔκνιζε ἡ γνώμη Hdt.7.12; τὰ σμικρὰ οὐδέν μιν κνίζει (sc. τὸν θεόν) ib.10.ε′; ἔκνιζέ μ' αἰεὶ τοῦθ' S.*OT*786; τὸ βούλεσθαί μ' ἔκνιζε E.*IA*330 (troch.); *provoke, tease*, Ar.*V.*1286; οὐ κατ' ἔπος κνίσω τὸ ῥῆμ' ἕκαστον *will* not *attack* every word, Id.*Ra.* l. c.; *provoke to jealousy*, Alciphr.1.32; in good sense, ἀδεῖά νιν ἔκνιξε χάρις Pi.*I.*6(5).50 :—Pass., E.*Med.*555, *Andr.* l. c.; ἐρωτίδα τᾶς ποκ' ἐκνίσθη Theoc.4.59, cf. Luc.*DMeretr.*10.4; κνιζόμενος ὑπ' ἔρωτος ἐπὶ τῇ παιδί App.*Pun.*10; ἐκνίσθης; *does that touch you?* Men.*Per.* 16. **b.** *provoke*, ὀργὰν κνίζον αἰπεινοὶ λόγοι Pi.*N.*5.32, cf. *P.*11.23.

κνίκιον, τό, v. κνήκιον. **κνίκος,** v. κνῆκος. **κνιπά·** πτιλή, Hsch.

κνῑπεία, ἡ, *miserliness*, Doroth. in *Cat.Cod.Astr.*6.81.

κνιπεῖν· σείειν, ξύειν μέλαθρα καὶ δοκούς, Hsch.

κνίπειον [ῐ] αἷμα, blood *of a* κνίψ, mystical name for substance used in Alchemy, Zos.Alch.p.188 B.

κνῑπεύω, *to be miserly*, Doroth. in *Cat.Cod.Astr.*6.81.

κνιπίδος· πέρασμα δορᾶς, Hsch.

κνῑπολόγος, ὁ, (κνίψ, λέγω) *gatherer of wood-insects*, name of one of the woodpeckers, Arist.*HA*593^{a}12.

κνῑπ-όομαι, of the eyes, *to be inflamed*, Hsch. s.v. κεκνιπωμένοι; of fruits, *to be mildewed*, ibid. **-ός,** ή, όν, *niggardly, miserly*, *AP* 11.172 (Lucill.). (Cf. Γνίφων (a standing name of old misers in the new Att. Comedy), σκνιπός.) **-ότης,** ητος, ἡ, *irritation* of the eyes, Hp.*Loc.Hom.*13; expld. as = ξηροφθαλμία, Erot.

κνίς, κνῑδός, ἡ, = κνίδη, acc. sg. κνίδα [ῐ] Opp.*H.*2.429 : pl. κνίδες Sm.*Is.*55.13, cf. Aq., Thd.ib.34.13.

κνῖσα, Ep. **κνίση** [ῑ], ης, ἡ, *steam and odour of fat* which exhales from roasting meat, *smell* or *savour of a burnt sacrifice* (ἡ λιπαροῦ θυμίασις, opp. λιγνύς, Arist.*Mete.*387^{b}6, cf. 388^{a}5); κνίση δ' οὐρανὸν ἷκεν ἑλισσομένη περὶ καπνῷ Il.1.317; κνίσην δ' ἐκ πεδίου ἄνεμοι φέρον οὐρανὸν εἴσω 8.549, cf. Ar.*Av.*193, 1517 : generally, *odour of savoury meat*, Id.*Ach.*1045 (lyr.), Alex.261.4; αἱ ἐκ τῶν αἱμάτων καὶ σαρκῶν κ. Porph. *Abst.*2.42; of eructations, Xenocr.ap.Orib.2.58.152. **II.** *that which causes this smell, fat caul* (cf. κνῖσα· ἐπίπλους, *AB*1095), in which the flesh of the victim was wrapped and burnt, μηρούς τ' ἐξέταμον κατά τε κνίσῃ ἐκάλυψαν Il.1.460, cf. Od.18.45,119, etc.; κνίσῃ τε κῶλα συγκαλυπτὰ A.*Pr.*496 :—κνίσσα, κνίσση are incorrect forms, cf. Hdn.Gr.2.901, al.

κνῑσ-ᾰλέος, α, ον, *filled with the steam of fat*, Hsch. **-άριον,** τό, Dim. of κνῖσα, Sch.Il.1.66. **-άω,** (κνῖσα) *fill with the savour of burnt sacrifice*, κ. ἀγυιάς (never τὰς ἀγυιάς) make them *steam with sacrifice*, Ar.*Eq.*1320, *Av.*1233, Orac.ap.D.21.51; κ. βωμούς E.*Alc.* 1156; intr., κ. βωμοῖσι *raise the steam of sacrifice* on.., Orac.ap.D. 21.52; κ. παρὰ τοὺς βωμούς Luc.*JTr.*22. **-ήεις,** Dor. **-άεις,** εσσα, εν, (κνῖσα) *full of the steam of burnt sacrifice*, δῶμα Od.10.10; μήλων κνισάεσσα πομπά Pi.*O.*7.80 : dat. contr. κνισᾶντι Id.*I.*4(3).66. **-ηρός,** ά, όν, = foreg., Achae.7.

κνίσ-μα, ατος, τό, in pl., *scratches*, μή που κνίσματ' ὄνυξιν ἔχει; *AP* 12.67; μή σε [κν]ισμάτων [γεύσω] dub. in Herod.9.4 : metaph., *irritation*, Phld.*Lib.*p.16 O.; of lovers' *quarrels*, *AP*7.219 (Pomp. Jun.). **-μός,** ὁ, *itching, tickling*, S.*Fr.*537; *irritation*, Ar.*Pl.*974; lovers' *quarrel*, Alciphr.1.29. **II.** tune for the flute, Trypho ap. Ath.14.618c.

κνῑσο-διώκτης, ου, ὁ, *Fat-hunter*, name of a mouse, v.l. Batr. 232. **-κόλαξ,** ἄκος, ὁ, *dinner-parasite*, Asius 1, cf. Phryn.*PS*p.81 B. cod. (κυσοκόλαξ cj. Kaibel). **-λοιχία,** ἡ, *love of fat* or *roast meat*, Sophil.5. **-λοιχός,** όν, *licker of fat* or *savoury meat, gourmand*, Antiph.64, Amphis 10.

κνῖσος, εος, τό, = κνῖσα, *Com.Adesp.*608, Sch.Il.2.423.

κνῑσός, ή, όν, = κνισήεις, τὸ κ. Ath.3.115e. **2.** = λίχνος, Comp. κνισότερος Id.12.549a.

κνῑσοτηρητής, οῦ, ὁ, = κνισοδιώκτης, *Com.Adesp.*1042.

κνῑσόω, = κνισάω, Matro *Conv.*82 : metaph., τὰς ἑαυτῶν ψυχὰς κ. Ph.1.628. **II.** *turn into fatty smoke*, in Pass., δέλεαρ κεκνισωμένον *savoury* bait, Arist.*HA*534^{b}5; ὑποθυμιατέον βδέλλαις –ουμέναις Antyll.ap.Orib.10.19.4; εἰ κνισοῦται τὰ σιτία κατὰ τὴν γαστέρα Gal. 8.37, cf. 6.691,706; ὁ ἰχθὺς κ. Alex.Aphr.*Pr.*2.17. **2.** κ. τὸν ζωμόν *burn* the soup, Luc.*Sat.*23. **III.** Pass., *become greasy*, of oil after boiling, Heliod.ap.Orib.10.37.3; τὸ ἐκ τῆς ἑψήσεως κεκνισ⟨ω⟩μένον ἔλαιον prob. in Sor.1.69.

κνίσσα, κνισσάω, etc., v. κνῖσα, etc.

κνιστός, ή, όν, v. κνηστός.

κνῑσ-ώδης, ες, (κνῖσα) *steaming like roast meat, fatty*, Arist.*HA* 534^{a}23; opp. ἀπίμελος, Id.*PA*675^{b}11; κνισῶδες ἐρυγγάνειν Gal.8. 35, cf. Phlp.*in APo.*378.16; κ. ἀπεψία Alex.Trall.*Febr.*1; *greasy*, of oil, Gal.6.289. **II.** metaph., τὸ μνημονευόμενον ἀμαυρὸν καὶ κ. Plu.2.1088f. **-ωτός,** ή, όν, *steaming*, of a burnt sacrifice, A.*Ch.* 485.

κνίφος, τό, = κνίδη, Hsch. (pl.).

κνίφω, κνιφιάω, cited without expl. by Hdn.Gr.2.949.

κνίψ, ὁ (ἡ v.l. in Arist., v. infr.), gen. κνῑπός, nom. pl. κνῖπες, = σκνίψ, small creatures which infest fig and oak trees and devour the fig-insect (ψήν), Ar.*Av.*590, Arist.*HA*534^{b}19, Thphr.*HP*2.8.3, 4.14.10; small ants acc. to Arist.*Sens.*444^{b}12. **II.** pl., = ὄμματα περιβεβρωμένα, Hsch.

κνόος, contr. **κνοῦς,** ὁ, = χνόη, Phot., cf. Hsch. **II.** *sound of footsteps*, A.*Fr.*237.

κνῦ· τὸ ἐλάχιστον, Hsch.

κνύζᾰ (A), ἡ, (κνύω) *itch*, Philox.Gramm.ap.*EM*523.2, Eust.1746. 6,23.

κνύζᾰ (B), ἡ, = κόνυζα, Theoc.4.25, 7.68 (pl.), *Hippiatr.*32 (sg.).

κνύζᾰ (C), ἡ, *corrupt, wrinkled*, cited from Anacr. by Hdn.Gr.2. 901; cf. κνυζός.

κνυζ-έομαι, prop. of a dog, *whine, whimper*, κνυζεῖσθαι (v.l. -ᾶσθαι) S.*OC*1571 (lyr.), cf. Theoc.6.30; κυνηδὸν κνυζούμενον S.*Fr.*722, cf. Ar.*V.*977; of children, D.H.1.79; ἐν ὕπνῳ κνυζεῦνται (v.l. -ῶνται) φωνεῦντα φίλαν ποτὶ ματέρα τέκνα Theoc.2.109 :—also Act. **κνυζῶ** Poll.5.64 (κνύζω Anon.ap.Suid.), κνυζεῖ Opp.*C.*1.507 : **κνυζάομαι** (cf. supr.), Ael.*NA*1.8, 11.14 : **κνυζόμαι,** Gal.19.112, Hsch.; for Sophr. 53 v. κνυζόω. **-ηθμός,** ὁ, prop. of dogs, *whining, whimpering*, opp. barking or snarling, κύνες τε ἴδον καί ῥ' οὐχ ὑλάοντο, κνυζηθμῷ δ' ἑτέρωσε διὰ σταθμοῖο φόβηθεν Od.16.163; of wild beasts, A.R.3.884; of young bears, Opp.*C.*3.169 (pl.); of children, Ath.9.376a. **-ημα,** ατος, τό, = foreg., of infants, ἄσημα κ. Hdt.2.2, Him.*Or.*23.4, cf. Max. Tyr.41.3. **-ομαι,** v. κνυζέομαι. **-ός,** ή, όν, *cloudy, misty*, ἀήρ Hsch. **II.** of persons, *blear-eyed*, Id.; κνυζή τις ἤδη καὶ πέπειρα γίνομαι Anacr.87 (κνύζη, κνίζη codd.). **-όω,** (κνυζός) *make dim* or *dark*, κνυζώσω δέ τοι ὄσσε πάρος περικαλλέ' ἐόντε Od.13.401, cf. 433. (Perh. connected with κνύζα A.) **II.** Dor., = ξύω, *scratch*, *EM* 522.54, prob. in Sophr.53 (Pass.).

κνύζωψ· λάχανον ὅμοιον σελίνῳ, Hsch. **κνυθόν·** σμικρόν, and **κνύθος·** ἄκανθα μικρά, Id.

κνῦμα, ατος, τό, (κνύω) *scratching*, κ. τῶν δακτύλων, of a person feeling for the door-handle in the dark, Ar.*Ec.*36, cf. Gal.19.112.

κνύξ, ἡ, Egypt. name for καπνός II, Ps.-Dsc.4.109.

κνύος [ῠ], τό, *itch*, Hes.*Fr.*29.1.

κνυπόω, = θριγκόω, Hsch.

κνῦσα, ἡ, *scab* : as term of abuse, Herod.7.95.

κνύω, *scratch*, πόθῳ μου 'κνυεν ἐλθὼν τὴν θύραν Ar.*Th.*481, cf. Men. 1021.

κνωδᾰκ-ίζω, (κνώδαξ) *hang* a body *on pins* or *pivots*, so that it turns as on an axis, ἐκνωδακισμένον ἀγγεῖον Hero *Spir.*2.4. **-ιον,** τό, Dim. of κνώδαξ, *pivot*, ib.1.38. **-οφύλαξ** [ῠ], ακος, ὁ, *warder of the pivot* of the celestial sphere, *PMag.Par.*1.678 (pl.).

κνωδάλ-ιον [ᾰ], τό, Dim. of sq., prob. in Hsch. s.v. ζωυφίοις. **-ον,** τό, any *wild creature*, Od.17.317; κνώδαλ' ὅσ' ἤπειρος πολλὰ τρέφει ἠδὲ θάλασσα Hes.*Th.*582; but also, of an ox or ass, *h.Merc.*188; of beasts generally, κνωδάλων τε καὶ βροτῶν A.*Ch.*601 (lyr.); κ. πτεροῦντα καὶ πεδοστιβῆ, of birds and beasts, Id.*Supp.*1000; κ. βροτοφθόρων ib.264; of sea-monsters, κνώδαλ' ἐν βένθεσι πορφυρέας ἁλὸς Alcm.60.5, cf. A. *Ch.*587 (lyr.); ἔζευξα πρῶτος ἐν ζυγοῖσι κνώδαλα Id.*Pr.*462; ἀνημέρωσα κνωδάλων ὁδόν (sc. Theseus) S.*Fr.*905, cf. *Tr.*716; of boars, lions, E. *Supp.*146; asses, Pi.*P.*10.36; serpents, Id.*N.*1.50, Nic.*Th.*98, Pl. *Ax.*365c; κώνωπες νυκτὸς κ. διπτέρυγα *AP*5.150 (Mel.); of persons, as a term of reproach, ὦ παντομισῆ κ. A.*Eu.*644 : Com., *brutes, beasts*, τρία κ. ἀναιδῆ Cratin.233, cf. Ar.*Lys.*477; also ἁβρὰ Μουσᾶν κ.

dainty *prey* of the Muses, Cerc.7.9. **–ώδης**, ες, *monstrous*, Tz.*H*.5.521.

κνώδαξ, ακος, ὁ, (cf. κνώδων) *pin* or *pivot* on which a body or machine turns, καθάπερ ἐπὶ κνώδακος τῆς τοῦ δευτέρου σπονδύλου ἀποφύσεως ἡ κεφαλὴ ἐπιστρέφεται Gal.14.720, cf. 723; *axis* of a sphere, Orph.*Fr*.247.26: more freq. in pl., Hero *Spir*.1.43, S.E.*M*.10.93, Orib.49.22.21. II. pl., *sockets* in which the axes of a drum turn, Ph.*Bel*.75.45. III. = χρυσοχοϊκὸν ὄργανον, and in pl., = οἱ ἐν τοῖς φυσητῆρσιν ἀσκοί, Hsch.

κνώδη· χωρία, θηρία, Hsch.

κνώδων, οντος, ὁ, in pl. κνώδοντες, two *projecting teeth* on the blade of a hunting spear, X.*Cyn*.10.3,16, Philostr.*Im*.1.28; ξίφους διπλοῖ κ., i.e. a two-edged sword (cf. Sch.), S.*Ant*.1233: sg., φασγάνου κνώδοντι *IG*14.1374.11; κνώδων alone, = *sword*, S.*Aj*.1025, Lyc.466, 1109, 1434. (Cf. Lith. *kándu* 'bite'.)

κνῶος· ἡσυχία πάντων, Hsch. **κνωπεύς**, έως, ὁ (also **κνουπεύς**), *bear*, Id.

κνωπόμορφος, ον, (κνώψ) *shaped like a beast*, Lyc.675.

κνώσσω, *slumber*, Od.4.809, Simon.37.6, Pi.*O*.13.71, *P*.1.8, Theoc.21.65, *AP*5.293.11 (Agath.), etc.: prov., Λάτμιον κνώσσεις 'you sleep like a top', Herod.8.10.

κνώψ, ὁ, gen. κνωπός, shortd. for κινώπετον, Nic.*Th*.499, 520, 751. II. = τυφλός, Zonar.

κοακτήρ, ῆρος, ὁ, attendant in the mysteries at Sparta, *IG*5(1).210,212; **κοιακτήρ**, ib.211. **κοάκτωρ**, = Lat. *coactor*, *Gloss.*

κοαλδδεῖν, Lydian for *king*, Hsch.

κοάλεμος [ᾱ], ὁ, *stupid fellow, booby*, Ar.*Eq*.198, Aeschin.Socr.16; addressed as a god or demon, Ar.*Eq*.221; nickname of the grandfather of Cimon, Plu.*Cim*.4. (From κοέω, ἠλεός acc. to Sch.Ar.*Eq*. 198, cf. Tim.*Lex*., etc.)

κόαλοι· βάρβαροι, Hsch. **κοάξ**, onomatop., to express the croaking of frogs, βρεκεκεκὲξ κοὰξ κοάξ Ar.*Ra*.209, al. **κόαρον**· ἐλάχιστον, Hsch. **κοάω**, v. κοέω. **κοβάθια**, v. κωβάθια. **κόβαθος**, sine expl., *PLond*.1821.362 (in a list of cups). **κόβακτρα**· κολακεύματα, πανουργήματα, Hsch.

κοβᾱλ-εία, ἡ, *impudent knavery*, Din.*Fr*.6.8. **–εύω**, *carry as a porter*, χόρτον *POxy*.146 (vi A.D.); θρύα εἰς οἶκον *PLond*.1.131^r.296 (i A.D.), cf. *EM*524.28, Suid. **–ίκευμα**, ατος, τό, *knavish trick*, Ar.*Eq*.332 (pl.). **–ισμός**, ὁ, *porterage, transport*, *PLond*.3.965.9 (iii A.D.). **–ος**, ὁ, *impudent rogue, arrant knave*, Ar.*Eq*.450, *Ra*.1015, *Pl*.279, D.C.53.3; of Midias, Phryn.Com.4: in pl., *mischievous goblins*, invoked by rogues, Ar.*Eq*.635; of the owl, κ. καὶ μιμητής Arist.*HA*597^{b}23. II. Adj. κόβαλα, τά, *knavish tricks, rogueries*, Ar.*Eq*.417, *Ra*.104; ὑβριστὸν ἔργον καὶ κ. Pherecr.162. (For the orig. sense cf. κοβαλεύω.)

κόβαρος· ἄνθρωπος, Hsch. **κόβειρος**, ὁ, *jester*, Id.: Adj., in pl., κόβειρα· γελοῖα, Id. **κοβελίσκον**· τρύβλιον, Id. **κόγκαλος**· κονιορτός, Id. (leg. κονίσαλος). **κόγξ**, onomatop., sound made by the voting-pebble as it fell into the urn, Id. **κογχαλίζω**, of shells, *murmur*, Id.

κογχ-άριον, τό, Dim. of sq., Str.16.2.41 (pl.), Aret.*CA*2.5. **–η**, ἡ, *mussel* or (perh.) *cockle*, Emp.76.1, Sophr.25, X.*An*.5.3.8, Arar. 8.2, Posidipp.14.2; including several species, Arist.*HA*528^{a}22, 547^{b}13, 622^{b}2; ἀνέχασκον ἐμφερέστατα ὀπτωμέναις κόγχαισιν Ar.*Fr*. 68; κόγχην διελεῖν to open a *mussel*, prov. of an easy task, Telecl. 19; κόγχης ἄξιον, i.e. worthless, Hsch., Suid. 2. *shell-full*, a small measure of capacity, Pherecr.143.3, Hp.*Nat.Mul*.32, *Morb*.3. 15, Thphr.*HP*9.6.2. II. *anything like a mussel-shell*, esp. *shell-like cavity* in the body, as, 1. *hollow of the ear*, Ruf.*Onom*.44, Poll.2. 86. 2. *knee-pan*, ib.188. III. *case round a seal* attached to documents, Ar.*V*.585. IV. *niche* for a statue, *CIG*4556 (Palestine); *apse*, *Epigr.Gr*.446.3 (Medjed). V. *fourth part of a sphere*, Hero *Stereom*.1.40. (Cf. Skt. *śaṅkhás* 'conch-shell'.) **–ίζω**, *dye purple*, *PGrenf*.2.87.22. **–ίον**, τό, Dim. of κόγχη, Antiph.71, Str. 16.4.17 (pl.). II. = κόγχη II. 1, Gal.14.701. **–ιστής**, οῦ, ὁ, *dyer*, *PGrenf*.2.87.9 (pl.). **–ιστική**, ἡ, *trade of purple-dyeing*, ib. 14. **–ίτης** [ῑ] λίθος, ὁ, *shelly marble*, found near Megara, Paus. 1.44.6.

κογχο-γενής, ές, *born from a shell*, of Aphrodite, *Cat.Cod.Astr*.1. 173. **–ειδής**, ές, *of the mussel kind*, Str.3.2.7. II. Subst. κ. (sc. γραμμή), ἡ, Geom., *conchoid curve*, Nicomedes ap.Procl.*in Euc.* p.272 F. Adv. **–δῶς** *in the form of a shell*, κοιλαίνεσθαι Chor.p.86 B. **–θήρας**, α, ὁ, *mussel-catcher*, Epich.42.8.

κόγχος, ὁ (ἡ Paus.1.44.6, cf. Plb.6.23.5), = κόγχη I, A.*Fr*.34, Epich. 42.9, Crates Theb.7; κόγχων (gen. pl.) Arist.*HA*528^{a}24 (but κόγχαι ib.22). 2. = κόγχη I. 2, *shell-full*, κ. ἁλῶν Phryn.Com.49, cf. Dsc. 1.30. II. *anything like a mussel-shell*, 1. *upper part of the skull*, Lyc.1105. 2. *boss* of a shield, Plb. l.c. 3. *small* iron *crucible*, Dsc.5.95. 4. *socket of the eye*, Poll.2.71 (pl.). 5. *knee-pan*, ib.188. III. *soup of lentils boiled with the pods*, Timo 3.

κογχυλαγόνες· γυναῖκες, νύμφαι, Hsch.

κογχῠλ-ευτής, οῦ, ὁ, *murex-fisher*, Just.*Nov*.38.6. **–ευτική**, ἡ, *trade of murex-fishing*, ibid. **–η**, ἡ, = κόγχη, v.l. in Ph.1.536, cf. *AP*9.214 (Leo). **–ιᾱβάφος** [βᾰ], ὁ, *purple-dyer*, Maiuri *Nuova Silloge* 571 (Cos). **–ίας** (sc. λίθος), ὁ, = κογχίτης, Ar.*Fr*.193. **–ιάτης** [ᾱ], ου, ὁ, = κογχίτης, X.*An*.3.4.10, Philostr.*VA*2.20. **–ιᾱτός**, ή, όν, = –ιωτός, *PLeid.X*.95. **–ιον**, τό, Dim. of κογχύλη, *small kind of mussel* or *cockle*, Epich.42.1, Sophr.24, Arist.*HA*547^{b}7, *PA* 661^{a}22, al., *POxy*.1449.21 (iii A.D.). 2. any *mollusc* or *its shell*, Hdt.2.12, Hp.*Vict*.2.48, Diocl.*Fr*.133; used to cover seals, Sch.Ar. *V*.583; *fossil shell*, Plu.2.367b. II. = κόχλος, Crito ap.Gal.12.660, Dsc.2.8. **–ιος**, α, ον, *purple*, χρῶμα *PLeid.X*.95. **–ιώδης**, ες, *like a mollusc shell*, κ. λίθοι *fossil shells*, Xanth.3; βόθρος Str.1. 3.4. **–ιωτός**, ή, όν, (κογχύλιον II) *dyed with purple*, *Gloss.*; cf. κογχυλιατός.

κογχ-ώδης, ες, f.l. for κοχλιώδης, Ath.3.86b. **–ωτός**, ή, όν, *having a boss* (cf. κόγχος II. 2), ψυκτήρ *PCair.Zen*.327.103 (iii B.C.).

κόδαλα· ἰχθῦς, κεστρεύς, Hsch. **κοδαλεύομαι**, = ἐνδομυχῶ, *to be a stay-at-home*, '*loafer*', Id.

κοδομ-εία, ἡ, *barley-roasting*, Poll.1.246. **–εῖον**, τό, *vessel for roasting barley*, Id.6.64 (pl. written κοδομία, Hsch.). **–εύς**, έως, ὁ, *one who roasts barley*, Hsch., perh. to be read in *Ostr.Strassb.* 583 (iii B.C.):—fem. **–εύτρια**, Poll.1.246, Phot. **–εύω**, *roast barley*, Hsch. **–ή**, ἡ, = ἡ –εύουσα, Poll.6.64, cf. 10.109 (pl.); ὄνομα θεραπαίνης, Hsch., Phot. **–ῆϊον**, τό, = κοδομεῖον, Suid.

κοδράντης, ου, ὁ, = Lat. *quadrans*, = $\frac{1}{4}$ *of an as*, *Ev.Matt*.5.26.

Κόδρος, ὁ, *Codrus*, legendary King of Athens: hence Κόδροι, οἱ, of *old-fashioned persons*, Hsch.

κοδύμᾱλον [ῠ], τό, *quince* or *medlar*, Alcm.90; = κυδώνιον, Hsch., who has **κοδώνεα**, τά, *winter-figs*, or a kind of καρύαι Περσικαί.

κοέω, contr. **κοῶ**, *mark, perceive, hear*, ἄστρωτος εὕδω καὶ τὰ μὲν πρᾶτ' οὐ κοῶ Epich.35 (prob.); σὺ δ' οὐ κοεῖς Anacr.4.14; κοεῖν Hellad. in Phot.*Bibl*.p.531 B.; ἐκόησεν τοὔνεκεν.. Call.*Fr*.53, cf. Sch.Ar. *Eq*.198: etym. of Κοῖος, Corn.*ND*17:—also (from **κοάω**) κοᾷ· ἀκούει, πεύθεται, and ἐκοᾶμες· ἠκούσαμεν, ἐπυθόμεθα, Hsch.; ἔκομεν (sic).. ᾐσθόμεθα, Id. (κοϝ-, cf. Skt. *kavis* 'wise', Lat. *caveo*.)

Κόης, v. Κοίης. **κοθᾰρός, κόθαρσις**, v. καθαρός, κάθαρσις. **κοθεῖ**· αἰσθάνεται, νοεῖ, Hsch. **κόθημα**, τό, = αἰδοῖον, Id.

κόθορνος, ὁ, *buskin, high boot*, Hdt.1.155, 6.125, Ar.*Lys*.657, Lysipp.2, etc.; worn by tragic actors in heroic characters: hence, 2. emblem of Tragedy in the person of Dionysus, Ar.*Ra*.47, 557. 3. since the buskins might be worn on either foot, ὁ Κόθορνος, nickname for a *trimmer* or *timeserver*, such as Theramenes, X.*HG*2.3.31: prov., εὐμεταβολώτερος κοθόρνου Zen.3.93, etc.

κοθοῦριν· ἀλώπεκα, Hsch.; cf. κόλουρις. **κόθουρος**, ον, *dock-tailed*, i.e. *without a sting*, κηφῆνες Hes.*Op*.304. **κοθώ**, οῦς, ἡ, = βλάβη, Hsch.

κοΐ, onomatop., to express the *squeaking* of young pigs, Ar.*Ach*. 780, cf. Hdn.Gr.1.505.

κοία, ἡ, = σφαῖρα, Antim.69. II. = κλέψημα (sic), Hsch.

κοιάζω, = ἐνεχυράζω, Hsch.; cf. κωάζειν. **κοιακτήρ**, v. κοακτήρ. **κοίβινος**, = *covinnus*, *Gloss.* **κοιγά**· κοῖλα, Hsch. **κοίδιον**, τό, written for κῴδιον, *PCair.Zen*.20 (iii B.C.).

κοΐζω, *cry* κοΐ, *squeak like a young pig*, Ar.*Ach*.746.

κοίῃ, Ion. for ποίᾳ, dat. sg. fem. of ποῖος (q.v.).

Κοιηΐς, ΐδος, ἡ, = Κοιογενής, dub. l. in Call.*Del*.150: **Κοιαντίς**, Orph.*H*.35.2.

Κοίης or **Κόης**, ου, ὁ, priest in the mysteries of Samothrace, Hsch., who also has **κοιᾶται**· ἱερᾶται, **κοιώσατο**· ἀφιερώσατο, καθιερώσατο.

κοΐκινος, η, ον, (κοΐξ) *made of palm-leaves*, Str.17.2.5; cf. κοῦκι.

κοικύλλω, *look gaping about*, Ar.*Th*.852, dub. in Demetr.Lac. 1014 p.92 F.

κοιλ-αγγίτας, α, ὁ, *deep gorge*, *IG*5(2).444 (Megalopolis). **–αίνω**, aor. ἐκοίληνα Hdt.2.73; Att. ἐκοίλᾱνα Th.4.100:—Med., Ep. aor. κοιλήνατο Nonn.*D*.12.332:—Pass., aor. ἐκοιλάνθην Hp.*Epid*.7.52: pf. κεκοίλασμαι Id.*Medic*.11; –αμμαι *EM*233.51: (κοῖλος):—*hollow, scoop out*, τὸ ᾠόν Hdt. l.c.; πέτρην κοιλαίνει ῥανὶς ὕδατος ἐνδελεχείῃ Choeril.10; κ. δένδρα, of the woodpecker, Arist.*HA*614^{b}14; κ. χῶμα, i.e. *dig* a grave, Theoc.23.43; κ. τὰς χεῖρας Ath.11.479a; κ. ὄμματα *APl*.4.142, cf. Opp.*H*.4.19:—Pass., *to be* or *become hollow*, ἔντοσθε, of ulcers, Hp.*Medic*. l.c.; ὀφθαλμοὶ κ. Id.*Acut*.30; κ. κατὰ τὸν κενεῶνα καὶ κατὰ τὰ ἄρθρα Id.*Art*.52; of poor timber, *go into holes*, Thphr.*HP*3.12.1. II. *make empty, make poor*, Lyc.772. 2. *allow to lapse*, of payments, *BGU*1156.18 (i B.C.), *PSI*4.287.16 (iv A.D.), etc. **–αῖος**, α, ον, = κοῖλος, Gal.18(2).568. **–ανσις**, εως, ἡ, *hollowing*, Alex.Aphr.*in SE*105.10, Paul.Aeg.6.90, Eust.159.35 (pl.). **–άς**, άδος, ἡ, Subst., *hollow*, δρυός Ps.-Phoc.173, cf. Thphr. *Fr*.169; in a wall, Lxx *Le*.14.37; in a rock, Str.12.3.11; *deep valley*, Pl.*Epigr*.5.6, Lxx *Ge*.14.8, al., *BGU*995 iii 4 (ii B.C.), *SIG*827 iii 11 (Delph., ii A.D.), Plb.5.44.7, D.S.3.15. II. Adj., fem. of κοῖλος, νεφέλαι Thphr.*Sign*.51 (nisi leg. κηλ–); εὐνή Tryph.194. **–ᾰσία**, ἡ, in pl., *indentations* in beams, Hero *Bel*.104.2. **–ασμα**, ατος, τό, *hollow*, Lxx *Is*.8.14; *groove*, Apollod.*Poliorc*.182.7, Ath.Mech.36.6; *interior* of a lamp, Hero *Spir*.2.22. **–έμβολον**, τό, *hollow wedge*, as an order of battle, Ael.*Tact*.37.7, Arr.*Tact*.29.6:—Adj. **–έμβολος**, ον, Ascl.*Tact*.11.5.

Κοίλη, ἡ, v. κοῖλος I. 2. **κοιλήπατα**, τά, *giblets of poultry*, *Gloss.*

κοιλί-α, Ion. –η, ἡ, (κοῖλος) *cavity of the body*, i.e. *thorax with abdomen*, Hp.*Art*.46 (including ἡ ἄνω κ., = *thorax*, ἡ κάτω, = *abdomen*, acc. to Gal.15.896); τὰ κατὰ κ. νοσήματα diseases of the *thoracic cavity*, Hp.*Aff*.6. 2. *belly, abdomen*, Hdt.2.87, *IG*4^2(1). 122.32 (Epid.), etc.: specified as ἡ κάτω κ. Ar.*Ra*.485, Hp.*Ulc*.3, Pl.*Ti*.73a, 85e, Arist.*Somn*.456^{a}3, *PA*650^{a}13, etc.; opp. ἡ ἄνω κ., *stomach*, Pl.*Ti*.85e, Arist.*PA* l.c.; κ. alone freq. = *stomach*, Id.*HA* 489^{a}2, etc.; of birds, Id.*PA*674^{b}22; also, *paunch* or *rumen* of animals, Id.*HA*507^{b}5: hence, of gluttons, δουλεύειν τῇ ἑαυτῶν κ. *Ep.Rom*.16. 18, cf. *Ep.Phil*.3.19. 3. *intestines*, κ. κείνη Hdt.2.40, cf. 86,92, etc.; of animals, κ. ὑεία pig's *tripe*, Ar.*Eq*.356; κοιλίας ἥμισυ *SIG*1025.51

(Cos, iv/iii B.C.): pl., *tripe and puddings*, Ar.*Eq.*160, *Pl.*1169. b. phrases, κ. σκληρὰν ἔχειν to be costive, Theopomp.Com.62.2; κατὰ κοιλίαν νοσεῖν *Com.Adesp.*730; τὴν κ. λύειν to relax the *bowels*, Arist. *Pr.*863^{b}29, 864^{b}14; αἱ κ. λύονται, ἀναλύονται, ib.947^{b}13, *GA*728^{a}15; εὔλυτοί [εἰσι] Id.*Pr.*876^{b}31; ἐὰν ᾖ κ. στῇ Id.*HA*588^{a}7; κ. καταρραγεῖσα Hp.*Coac.*126; [οἶνος] κοιλίας μαλακτικός, κοιλίας ἐφεκτικά, Mnesith. ap.Ath.1.33b, 2.59c; κ. ἐκλύειν, ὑπάγειν, μαλάσσειν, Dsc.2.72,163, 171; κ. ῥέουσαι D.S.5.41. 4. *excrement*, esp. in pl., κ. συνεστηκυῖαι *excrements* of firm consistency, Hp.*Aër.*10; opp. κ. ἐφυγραινόμεναι Id. *Epid.*1.10; κ. ὑγρή Id.*Prorrh.*1.38; στερεή, σκληρή, Id.*Acut.*(*Sp.*)56, *Epid.*4.23; οὔρησις καὶ κ. ἀχρόως ibid. II. any *cavity* in the body, *ventricle, chamber*, as in the *lungs, heart, liver, brain*, κ. αἱ τὸ πνεῦμα δεχόμεναι καὶ προπέμπουσαι Id.*Art.*41; ἡ δὲ καρδία ἔχει μὲν τρεῖς κ. Arist.*HA*496^{a}4, cf. 513^{a}27. 2. *socket* of a bone, Hp.*Art.*61. 3. supposed *cavities inside the muscles*, Erasistr.ap.Gal.4.375,707, Antyll. ap.Orib.8.6.30, 7.9.4; cf. νηδύς. 4. *womb*, Hp.*Mul.*1.38, al., *Ev. Jo.*3.4. III. any *hollow* or *cavity*, in the earth, Arist.*Mete.*349^{b}4, 350^{b}23, al.; in the clouds, ib.369^{b}2, al. IV. perh. finger-*tip*, Aret. *SD*1.8 (pl.). **-ακός**, ή, όν, *of the bowels*, ἀρρώστημα Plu.*Ant.*49; διάθεσις Gal.8.388; τὰ κ. Dsc.1.42. II. of persons, *suffering in the bowels*, ib.73, Ruf.ap.Orib.8.24.30, Philagr.ib.5.20.2, Plu.2.101c, Gal.6.525. **-αλγέω**, *have pain in the bowels*, Id.14.467. **-αργία**, ἡ, by dissim. for κοιλιαλγία, *pain in the bowels*, *Rev.Ét.Gr.*41.74 (Damascus).

κοιλίδιον, τό, Dim. of κοιλία, Str.14.5.14, dub. in Hsch. s.v. κόλαβρον; written κυλίδιον, *Sammelb.*1941 (iv A.D.), *PLond.*3.1259.38 (iv A.D.).

κοιλιο-δαίμων, ονος, ὁ and ἡ, *one who makes a god of his belly*, of a parasite, Eup.172, cf. Ael.*Fr.*109, Ath.3.97c. **-δεσμος**, ὁ, *belly-band*, *Gloss.* **-λυσία**, ἡ, (λύω) *looseness of the bowels*, περὶ κοιλιολυσίαν γίνεσθαι to take *laxative* medicine, Cic.*Att.*10.13.1, cf. Sor.1. 46, *AB*323. **-λῡτέω**, *suffer from looseness of the bowels*, Hsch. s.v. βδέλεσθαι. **-λῠτικός**, ή, όν, *laxative*, *Gp.*10.51 tit. **-πώλης**, ου, ὁ, *tripe-seller*, Ar.*Eq.*200. **-στροφία**, ἡ, *colic*, Sch.Nic.*Al.*597.

κοιλίσκος, ὁ, *scoop-shaped knife*, for surgical uses, Gal.10.445, Id. ap.Orib.46.21.17, Paul.Aeg.6.90 (κυκλίσκος is v.l. in Gal. l.c. and an unnecessary conjecture in Orib., Paul.Aeg. ll. cc.):—Adj. **κοιλισκωτός**, ἐκκοπεὺς Paul.Aeg. l.c. (v.l. κυκλισκωτός).

κοιλῐτική (sc. νόσος), ἡ, disease *in the bowels*, *Cat.Cod.Astr.*2. 161.

κοιλι-ώδης, ες, *like a belly*, ὑποδοχαί Arist.*PA*678^{b}30. **-ωσις**, v. κοίλωσις.

κοιλο-γάστωρ, ορος, ὁ, ἡ, (γαστήρ) *hollow-bellied, hungry*, A.*Th.* 1040: metaph., κ. κύκλος, of a *hollow* shield, ib.496. **-γένειος**, ον, *with a dimple in the chin*, *PPetr.*3p.26 (iii B.C.), *PGrenf.*1.10.13, 1.34.4 (ii B.C.). **-γώνιος**, ον, *having a re-entrant angle*, Zenodor. ap.Procl. *in Euc.*p.165 F. **-κρόταφος**, ον, *with hollow temples*, Aret.*SD*2.7. **-μισχος**, ον, *with hollow stalk*, Thphr.*HP*3.7. 5. **-πεδος**, ον, *lying in a hollow*, νάπος Pi.*P.*5.39. **-πίτυξ·** ὁπλίτης (fort. -πήληξ), τινὲς δὲ ὀϊστός, Hsch. **-ποιέομαι**, = κοιλαίνω II. 2, μηδένα μῆνα *BGU*1134.13 (i B.C.). **-ριζών**, = πάναξ, Theognost.*Can.*21.

κοῖλος, η, ον, Aeol. and Ion. κόϊλος, prob. in Alc.15.5, Mimn.12.6; **κόϊλος**, α, ον, Anacr.9 (Comp. -ώτερα), cf. A.D.*Pron.*87.5, Hdn.Gr.2. 927:—*hollow*, Hom. mostly as epith. of ships, κ. νῆες Il.1.26, al. (later κ. ναῦς *hold* of the ship, Hdt.8.119, X.*HG*1.6.19, D.32.5; so ἡ κ. alone, Theoc.22.12, Callix.1; τὰ κ. App.*BC*5.107); κ. λόχος, κ. δόρυ, of the Trojan horse, Od.4.277, 8.507; κ. σπέος 12.93; κ. πέτρα A. *Eu.*23, S.*Ph.*1081 (lyr.); κ. κάπετος, of a grave, Il.24.797, S.*Aj.*1165 (anap.), cf. *Ant.*1205; κ. τάφρος E.*Alc.*898 (anap.); κ. νάρθηξ Hes. *Op.*52; ἄχερδος S.*OC*1596; κ. φλέψ *vena cava*, Hp.*Loc.Hom.*3, Gal. 2.786, 4.668; σφόνδυλος κ. Pl.*R.*616d; of vessels, ἀγγήϊα Hdt.4.2; κρατήρ S.*OC*1593; ζύγαστρον Id.*Tr.*692; κύλικος.. κοῖλον κύτος Pl. Com.189; κ. ἄργυρος καὶ χρυσός silver and gold *plate*, Theopomp. Hist.283a, cf. S.*Fr.*378, Arist.*Oec.*1350^{b}23, etc.; κ. ἐκκοπεύς Gal.10. 445; νόμισμα κ. dub. sens. in Numen.ap.Eus.*PE*11.18; *sunk*, γράψαι εἰς σανίδα κοῖλα γράμματα *SIG*1011.15 (Chalcedon, iii/ii B.C.), cf. Longin.*Rh.*p.199 H. (but κ. γραμμή *curved* line, Hero*Bel.*75.15); ἀλέαν εἰς τὸ θύρωμα κοίλαν *curved* canopy, *Rev.Arch.*22.63 (Callatis, iii B.C.); κ. ὑποδήματα boots that reach to mid-leg, Ael.*NA*6.23 (κοῖλα ποσσὶν ὑποδέδεσθε Ezek.*Exag.*181, cf. Poll.7.84); κ. δέμνια *empty* bed, S.*Tr.*901; κ. χείρ, of a beggar, *AP*12.212 (Strat.); κ. ἱστίον Poll.1.107; κοῖλος μήν *short* month, Gem.8.3, cf. κοιλοποιέομαι, κοῖλος II. 3: Comp., -ότερος ὅλμου Epich.81. 2. of Places, *lying in a hollow* or *forming a hollow*, κ. Λακεδαίμων *the vale of* L., Od.4.1; κ. Θεσσαλίη Hdt.7.129; κ. Ἄργος S.*OC*378, 1387; Αὐλίδος κ. μυχοί E. *IA*1600; κ. τόποι Plb.3.18.10: as pr. n., Κ. Συρία the district between Lebanon and Anti-Lebanon, Id.1.3.1, etc.; τὰ Κ. τῆς Εὐβοίης Hdt. 8.13; ἡ Κ. the *valley* of the Ilissus, name of Attic deme, Id.6.103, etc.: Comp., κοιλότερα τῆς κάτωθεν χώρας Arist.*Mete.*352^{b}33. b. κ. λιμήν harbour *lying between high cliffs*, Od.10.92; κ. αἰγιαλός *embayed* beach, 22.385; ἐν τῷ κ. καὶ μυχῷ τοῦ λιμένος Th.7.52. c. κ. ὁδός *hollow* way, Il.23.419; κ. ἄγυια Pi.*O.*9.34. d. κ. ποταμός a river *nearly empty* of water, Th.7.84; τοῦ ποταμοῦ κοίλου ῥυέντος Socr.ap. Ath.9.388a; but κ. ποταμός *with deep bed*, Plb.21.37.4. e. τὰ κ. καὶ τὰ δασέα *ravines* grown with copsewood, Ar.*Nu.*325. 3. κ. ἅλς, θάλασσα, the sea *full of hollows*, i.e. *with a heavy swell* on, A.R. 2.595, Plb.1.60.6. 4. κ. νοσήματα *internal* complaints, Philostr. *VA*3.44. II. metaph., 1. of the voice, *hollow*, κόχλον ἑλὼν μυκήσατο κοῖλον Theoc.22.75 (though here κοῖλον may agree with κόχλον); φθέγγεσθαι κ. καὶ βαρύ Luc.*Ner.*6, Philostr.*VA*3.38; ὁ -ότατος τῶν φθόγγων Aristid.Quint.1.10. 2. Philos., *hollow, empty, void of content*, αἱ κ. ἐνέργειαι, opp. αἱ ἀμείνους, Herm. *in Phdr.*p.170 A.: more freq. in Comp., κοιλοτέρα θεωρία, ζωή, ib.pp.67,68 A.; τὰ -ότερα, opp. τὰ ὑπέρτερα, ib.p.143 A., cf. Dam.*Pr.*96; χωρῶν πρὸς τὸ κ. ib. 379. 3. ἡμέραν κ. ποιεῖσθαι *allow payments to lapse* for a day (cf. κοιλαίνω II. 2), *BGU*1136.5 (i B.C.); οὐδεμίαν δόσιν κ. ποιεῖσθαι ib. 1146.15 (i B.C.). III. *concave*, τὸ κ., opp. τὸ κυρτόν, Arist.*Ph.* 222^{b}3, *EN*1102^{a}31; κοῖλα καὶ ἐξέχοντα Philostr.*Im.*2.20; of military formations, Ascl.*Tact.*11.1. 2. *bending, yielding*, κλῇθρα S. *OT*1262; σταθμὰ θυρῶν Theoc.24.15. IV. Subst. κοῖλον, τό, *hollow, cavity*, Pl.*Phd.*109b, al.; esp. of *cavities* in the body, τὰ κ. γαστρός E.*Ph.*1411; τὰ κ. [τῆς καρδίας] the *ventricles*, Arist.*HA*496^{a}13; τὸ κ. τῶν νεφρῶν ib.497^{a}11; τὸ τῶν χειρῶν κ. Apollod.ap.Ath. 11.479a; τὸ κ. τοῦ.. ποδός Hp.*Epid.*5.48: prov., τὸ κ. τοῦ ποδὸς δεῖξαι to show 'a clean pair of heels', Hsch.; τὰ κ. τῶν ὀφθαλμῶν, τοῦ προσώπου, Hp.*Mul.*2.119, *Nat.Mul.*9 codd. (sed leg. κύλα); τὰ κ. alone, *hollows of the side, flanks*, like κενεών, Arist.*HA*630^{a}3. 2. κοῖλος· θυρεών, οὐκ ἔχων θύρας, Hsch.

κοιλο-σταθμέω, *provide with a coffered ceiling* or *panels*, οἶκον κέδροις Lxx 3*Ki.*6.9; ξύλοις ἔσωθεν ib.15. **-σταθμος**, ον, *with coffered ceilings, panelled*, οἶκοι ib.*Hg.*1.4; θυρίδας κοιλοστάθμους *PPetr.*3p.143 (iii B.C.):—Subst. **-σταθμος**, ὁ, *coffered ceiling*, τὸν κ. τοῦ ναοῦ.. ποιῆσαι *IG*11(2).287 *A* 96 (Delos, iii B.C.):—also **-σταθμον**, τό, ib.*B* 146. **-στομία**, ἡ, *hollowness of voice*, Quint.1.5.32. **-συρτος·** ὁ χωλός, Suid. **-σώματος**, ον, *hollow-bodied*, κύτος Antiph.52.2.

κοιλότης, ητος, ἡ, *hollowness*: *a hollow*, τῆς γῆς Arist.*Mete.*354^{a}12, cf. *HA*529^{a}21, Thphr.*Vent.*30; κ. ὀρέων Lxx *Wi.*17.19; κ. ἐν ῥινί, = σιμότης, Them. *in Ph.*42.3. II. *concavity*, Arist.*Metaph.*1025^{b}33; *concave moulding* in architecture, Procop.*Ecphr.*p.157 B. (pl.). III. metaph., *shortage of cash*, Phld.*Oec.*p.71 J.

κοιλοφθαλμ-ία, ἡ, *sunkenness of eyes*, Phryn.Com.77. **-ιάω**, *have sunken eyes*, Cratin.288, Gal.6.444, Alex.Aphr.*Pr.*1.98, Orib. *Eup.*1.13. **-ος**, ον, *hollow-eyed*, X.*Eq.*1.9, Arist.*Phgn.*811^{b}25, *PLond.*1.3 (ii B.C.), Poll.1.191, 2.62.

κοιλο-φυής, ές, *hollow by nature, hollow*, Opp.*H.*4.653. **-φυλλος**, ον, *hollow-leaved*, Thphr.*HP*1.10.8. **-φωνος**, ον, *hollow-voiced*, Hsch. s.v. ληκυθιστής. Adv. -νως, λαρυγγίζειν Phld.*Rh.*1.200 S. **-χείλης**, ες, *hollow-rimmed*, κύμβαλα *AP*6.94 (Phil.).

κοιλ-όω, *hollow out*, in Pass., κεκοιλωμένον ἔδαφος Dsc.3.48; τὰ κεκοιλωμένα τῆς πέτρας D.S.3.13. **-ώδης**, ες, *cavernous*, φάραγξ Babr.20.2; δίφροι Suid. s.v. χαμαίζηλοι. **-ωμα**, ατος, τό, *hollow, cavity*, Arist.*Spir.*483^{b}23, *Mu.*395^{b}34 (pl.), Anon.Lond. 23.20 (pl.), Thphr.*HP*3.8.3 (pl.), Babr.86.1, Ruf.*Onom.*145; [τοῦ νώτου] *PMag.Par.*1.1846; τὰ κ. τῶν νεφῶν Epicur.*Ep.*2 p.44 U., cf. 1 p.9 U. 2. *basin* into which rivers discharge, Plb.4.39.2 (pl.), 8; *bed* of a torrent, Id.4.70.7: generally, of *hollow places, low-lying land*, Lxx *Ge.*23.2, Agatharch.32; κ. ἔμβροχον *BGU*571.12 (ii A.D.); *excavation*, *PPetr.*2p.43 (pl., iii B.C.). II. *ulcer* on the cornea, Gal.14.773, Aët.7.29. III. Astrol., = ταπείνωμα, Paul.Al.*A.*2, *Cat.Cod.Astr.*8(1).243 (pl.). IV. metaph., τὰ κ. τῆς εὐτυχίας *weak points* in..., Phld.*Vit.*p.12 J. **-ῶνυξ**, ῠχος, ὁ, ἡ, *hollow-hoofed*, ἵπποι Stesich.49. **-ῶπαν·** περίζωμα, Hsch. **-ώπης**, ες, *hollow-eyed*, κοιλώπεες αὐγαί *hollow* eyes, Nic.*Al.*442:—fem. **-ῶπις**, ιδος, in general sense, = sq., πέτρα *AP*6.219.5 (Antip.). **-ωπός**, όν, *hollow to look at*: *hollow*, ἀγμός E.*IT*263. **-ωσις**, εως, ἡ, *cavity*, Hp.*Carn.*15, Sor.1.82; *hollowing out*, of flutes, Nicom.*Harm.*4, 10 (pl., κοιλιώσ- codd.). **-ωτέα**, prob. = κολουτέα, Hsch.

κοιμ-άω, fut. -ήσω, Dor. -άσω [ᾱ]: aor. ἐκοίμησα, Ep. κοίμησα Od. 12.372:—Med., fut. -ήσομαι *OGI*383.43 (Commagene, i B.C.), D.H. 4.64, Luc.*DDeor.*4.4, etc.: Ep. aor. κοιμήσατο, -αντο, Il.11.241, 1. 476:—Pass., fut. -ηθήσομαι S.*Fr.*574.6, Luc.*Asin.*40, Alciphr.1.37. 3, etc.: aor. ἐκοιμήθην Od.14.411, al., E.*Andr.*390, Pl.*R.*571e, etc.: pf. κεκοίμημαι Aeschrio 8.2, Luc.*Gall.*6:—*lull, put to sleep*, κοίμησον.. Ζηνὸς ὑπ' ὀφρύσιν ὄσσε φαεινώ Il.14.236; ἦ με... κοιμήσατε νηλέϊ ὕπνῳ Od.12.372; βλέφαρα μὴ κοιμῶν ὕπνῳ A.*Th.*3; *put to bed*, τὸν δ' αὐτοῦ κοίμησε Od.3.397; of a hind, ἐν ξυλόχῳ.. νεβροὺς κοιμήσασα 4. 336. 2. metaph., *still, calm*, ἀνέμους, κύματα, Il.12.281, Od.12. 169; φλόγα A.*Ag.*597; κύματος μένος Id.*Eu.*832; εὔφημον... κοίμησον στόμα Id.*Ag.*1247; also, *soothe, assuage*, κοίμησον δ' ὀδύνας Il.16. 524; ᾧ (sc. φύλλῳ) κοιμῶ τόδ' ἕλκος S.*Ph.*650. II. Med. and Pass., *fall asleep, go to bed*, Il.1.476, al., Hdt.1.9, etc.; of animals, *lie down*, κατὰ ἤθεα κοιμηθῆναι Od.14.411: c. acc. cogn., ποῖόν τινα ὕπνον ἐκοιμ.; X.*Hier.*6.7; βαθὺν κοιμηθῆναι (sc. ὕπνον) Luc. *DMar.*2.3. 2. metaph., ὅπως ἂν κοιμηθῇ [τὸ ἐπιθυμητικόν] Pl. l.c. 3. of the sleep of death, κοιμήσατο χάλκεον ὕπνον Il.11. 241; ἱερὸν ὕπνον κ. Call.*Ep.*11.2: abs., *fall asleep, die*, S.*El.*509 (lyr.), Aeschrio l.c.; ἐκοιμήθη μετὰ τῶν πατέρων Lxx 3*Ki.*2.10, al., cf. *PFay.*22.28 (i A.D.), *Ev.Matt.*27.52, *Ev.Jo.*11.11, etc.; in epitaphs, *IG*14.1683, etc.; κ. τὸν αἰώνιον ὕπνον ib.929. 4. κοιμῶντο.. παρὰ μνηστῇς ἀλόχοισι Il.6.246, cf. 250: hence, of sexual intercourse, *lie with* another, Od.8.295, Pi.*I.*8(7).23; οὔ τινι κοιμηθεῖσα Hes.*Th.*213; παρά τινι Hdt.3.68; σὺν δεσπόταισι E. l.c.; μετά τινος Timocl.22.2; ἀπὸ γυναικὸς ἀνὴρ τὰν νύκτα κοιμαθείς *Berl.Sitzb.* 1927.157 (Cyrene). 5. *keep watch at night*, A.*Ag.*2, X.*Cyr.*1.2. 4,9, *POxy.*933.25 (ii A.D.), etc. 6. of things, *remain during the night*, οὐ μὴ κοιμηθήσεται ὁ μισθὸς παρά σοι ἕως πρωΐ Lxx *Le.*19.13; ἡ κιβωτὸς ἐκοιμήθη ἐκεῖ ib.*Jo.*6.10. 7. c. acc., *dream of*, μέταλλα χρύσεια Luc.*Gall.*6. **-ήθρα**, ἡ, *sleeping-place*, Suid. s. v. ἰαυθμοί. **-ημα**, ατος, τό, *sleep*, in pl., S.*Ichn.*268; κ. αὐτογέννητα *intercourse* of the mother with her own child, Id.*Ant.*864 (lyr.): sg., Erot. s. v. κωματώδεες. **-ησις**, εως, ἡ, *lying down to sleep*, κοιμήσεις ἐπὶ θύραις Pl.*Smp.*183a; ἡ κ. τοῦ ὕπνου *Ev.Jo.*11.13. II. the *sleep of death*, Lxx *Si.*46.19, 48.13, *Tab.Defix.Aud.*242.30 (Carthage, iii A. D.). **-ητήριον**, τό, *sleeping-room*, *IG*7.235.43 (Oropus, iv B. C.), Dosiad.ap.Ath.4.143c (also **-ητηρία**, ἡ, *EM*550.56). II. *burial-place*, *IG*3.3545. **-ητικῶς**, Adv. *sleepily*, κ. ἔχειν *EM*485.18. **-ίζω**, post-Hom., = κοιμάω, *put to sleep*, κ. ὄμμα E.*Rh.*826 (lyr.); σε.. ἐκοίμισεν Ἀδρήστεια λείκνῳ ἐνὶ χρυσέῳ Call.*Jov.*47; *harbour for the night*, οἶκος ἐν ᾧ τοὺς ξένους κοιμίζουσιν Dosiad.ap.Ath.4.143c, cf. Lxx 3*Ki.*3.20; *still, calm*, ἄημα πνευμάτων ἐκοίμισε στένοντα πόντον, i. e. the winds *suffered* the sea *to rest*—by ceasing, S.*Aj.*674; θάλασσαν ἀγρίαν ἐκοίμισαν (sc. οἱ δαίμονες) *AP*9.290 (Phil.): metaph., κ. τὸν λύχνον *put* it *out*, Nicopho 7; μεγαλαγορίαν κ. *lay* pride *to sleep, quench, stifle* it, E.*Ph.*184 (lyr.); κ. θυμὸν Pl.*Lg.*873a; τὰς λύπας X.*Smp.*2.24; πόθον *AP*12.19*(Mel.); ἐλπίδας οὐ θάλαμος κοίμισεν, ἀλλὰ τάφος ib.7.183 (Parmen.):—Pass., παῖς κοιμίζεται E.*Hec.*826; τὸ θηριῶδες κ. Pl. *R.*591b. 2. of the sleep of death, καλῶ δ'.. Ἑρμῆν χθόνιον εὖ με κοιμίσαι S.*Aj.*832; Τιτάνων γενεὰν.. Ζεὺς κοιμίζει φλογμῷ E.*Hec.*473 (lyr.), cf. *Hipp.*1386 (lyr.):—Med., κοίμισαί μ' ἐς Ἅιδου Id.*Tr.*594 (lyr.). 3. Gramm., *soften the accent* (from acute to grave), Sch. D.T.p.23 H., Sch.Il.7.334; cf. sq. II. **-ισις**, εως, ἡ, *putting to sleep*, *IG*12(5).329 (Paros, unless written for -ησις). II. *softening of the accent*, Sch.D.T.p.23 H.: **-ισμός**, ὁ, ibid. **-ιστής**, οῦ, Dor. **-τᾶς**, ὁ, *one who puts to bed*, metaph., λύχνος *AP*12.50 (Asclep.). **-ιστικός**, ή, όν, *of* or *for putting to sleep*, Sch.Il.3.382.

κοιν-άν, ᾶνος, ὁ, Dor. and Arc. for κοινών, Pi.*P.*3.28, *IG*9(1).334.4 (Locr., v B. C.), 5(2).6.21 (Tegea, iv B. C.). **-ανέω**, Dor. for κοινωνέω, Foed.Dor.ap.Th.5.79. **-ανία**, = κοινωνία, Aesar.ap. Stob.1.49.27; perh. to be read in Pi.*P.*1.97. **-ανικός**, = κοινωνικός, Archyt.ap.Stob.1.48.6. **-άριον**, τό, Dim. of κοινόν (v. κοινός A. VIII), in form *cynarium*, *CIL*13.10021.199. **-άσομαι**, **-άσας**, Dor. for κοινώσ-; v. κοινόω. **-εῖον**, τό, *common hall*, *Test.Epict.*4.30. 2. *association, club*, *IG*12(3).104.12 (Nisyros). 3. *brothel*, Hdn.Gr.1.372, *Bull.Soc.Arch.Alex.*6.282 (iii A. D.), Hsch. (κοινίον cod.); cf. ξυνεῖον. II. *common fund*, *IG*4.757 *A* 44 (Troezen): pl., ib.*B* 2, al. **-εών**, ῶνος, ὁ, = κοινωνός, prob. in E.*HF*149, 340. **-ῇ**, v. κοινός B. II. **-ισμός**, ὁ, *mixture of dialects*, v. l. in Quint.8.3.59.

κοινοβιάρχης, ου, ὁ, *head of a* κοινόβιον, *PMasp.*151.149 (vi A. D.).

κοινό-βιος, ον, *living in community with others*, Ptol.*Tetr.*119, Iamb. *VP*5.29. II. as Subst. **κοινόβιον**, τό, *life in community*, dub. l. in Gell.1.9 fin. 2. *monastery*, Just.*Nov.*123.36, al., *PSI*8.953.9 (vi A. D.). **-βιότης**, *consortium*, *Gloss.*

κοινοβουλ-ευτικός, ή, όν, *deliberative*, Hippod.ap.Stob.4.1.94. **-έω**, *deliberate in common*, X.*Lac.*13.1:—Med., Hsch. **-ης**, ου, ὁ, = σύνεδρος, in pl., Id. **-ία**, ἡ, *common counsel*, Sch.Il.22.261 (pl.). **-ιον**, τό, *common council*, Plb.28.19.1, Str.8.7.3, *OGI*490.12 (Apamea, ii A. D.), 568.11 (Tlos, iii A. D.), etc.; *place of assembly*, App.*BC*1.51. **-ος**, ον, gloss on ξύμβουλος, Sch.Ar.*Th.*928. II. Subst. -βουλος, ὁ, *member of local senate*, *IGRom.*3.7 (Nicomedia).

κοινο-βωμία, ἡ, *community of altar*, of gods worshipped in common, ἀνάκτων τῶνδε κοινοβωμίαν σέβεσθε A.*Supp.*222. **-γάμια** [γᾰ], ων, τά, *promiscuous concubinage*, Clearch.49. **-γενής**, ές, *hybridizing*, opp. ἰδιογενής, φύσις Pl.*Plt.*265e. **-γονία**, ἡ, *mixing of breeds*, opp. ἰδιογονία, ib.d. **-δήμιον**, τό, *common assembly of the people*, Hsch. **-δημος**, ον, *common to the people, public*, πανήγυρις Ph.1.678. **-δίκιον** [δῐ], τό, *common court in which matters in dispute between different cities were settled*, *GDI*5040.58 (Hierapytna); τῶν Κρηταιέων *IG*12(3).254 (Anaphe); to be read for -δίκαιον, Plb. 22.15.4. 2. in Egypt, *court for disputes between Greeks and Egyptians*, *PMagd.*21.12, 23.9 (iii B. C., abbrev.). **-δῖκος**, ον, *enjoying a common right*, Orac.ap.Phleg.1 J. **-εργής**, ές, *working in common*, μόρια Simp. *in Epict.*p.37 D. **-θανής**, ές, *of common death*, κ. Μοιρῶν γῆραϊ *IPE*2.91[1] (Panticap.). **-θῡλᾰκέω**, *have a common purse*, Ar.*Fr.*797. **-καθέτας**· συνθηκοφύλακας, Hsch. (Perh. for -καταθ-). **-κρᾱτηρόσκῠφος**, ὁ, *filling his cup from the common bowl*, Cerc.4.16. **-λεκτέω**, *use the language of common life*, κοινολεκτούμενα ἐπιρρήματα A.D.*Adv.*169.20, cf. *EM*184.11. **-λεκτος**, ον, *in the language of common life*: Adv. -τως Sch.Theoc.6.18. **-λεκτρος**, ὁ, ἡ, *bedfellow, consort*, A.*Ag.*1441: as Adj., δάμαρ Id.*Pr.*560 (lyr.). **-λεξία**, ἡ, *ordinary language*, Serv. ad Verg.*A.*8.31, Eust.956.1. **-λεχής**, ές, *paramour*, S.*El.*97 (anap.), cf. Eust. 653.34. **-λογέομαι**, fut. -ήσομαι Plb.21.39.2: aor. ἐκοινολογησάμην Hdt.6.23, Th.8.98, etc.: later aor. Pass. ἐκοινολογήθην Plb.2.5.4, al., *SIG*568.4 (Halasarna, iii B. C.): pf. κεκοινολόγημαι *OGI*315.37 (Pessinus, ii B. C.), D.C.49.41: plpf. ἐκεκοινολόγηντο Th.7.86: (λόγος):—*commune, take counsel with*, τινι Hdt.6.23, Th.8.98, etc.; πρός τινα Id.7.86, Plb.18.34.5, Jul.*Caes.*335c; κ. ἀλλήλοις περί τινος Arist. *Pol.*1268[b]7; πρός τινα ὑπέρ τινος Plb.10.42.4; κ. περί τινος *deliberate on*..., D.S.19.46; κ. πρὸς τὸ οὖς τινι Luc.*Deor.Conc.*1. II. Pass., γράμματα-λογούμενα κατὰ μίμησιν signs *used with common* (i. e. direct) *significance*, opp. ἀλληγορούμενα, Porph.*VP*12. **-λογία**, ἡ, *consultation*, Hp.*Praec.*8, *PFay.*12.15 (ii B. C.), Gal.8.151. 2. *discussion, conference*, Plb.2.8.7, al., Plu.*Ages.*25, al., Alex.Aphr. *in Metaph.*296.23; philosophical *dialogue*, Phld.*Rh.*1.109: pl., ib.243 S. 3. *communication by speech*, Iamb.*Myst.*7.4 (pl.). 4. in Magic, *use of* τὰ κοινά (cf. κοινός III. 4), *PMag.Par.*1.2080 (pl.). II. = ἡ κοινὴ διάλεκτος, Phot. **-μετρέω**, *measure corn-rent by agreement*, *POxy.*1689.35 (iii A. D.). **-μήτωρ**, ορος, ὁ, ἡ, *having a common mother*, Theognost.*Can.*21. **-νοημοσύνη**, ἡ, (νοέω) *regard for the feelings of others*, M.Ant.1.16. **-πᾰθής**, ές, *sympathetic, sociable*, ἔθη φιλάνθρωπα καὶ κ. D.H.1.41. **-πλοος**, ον, contr. **-πλους**, ουν, *sailing in common*, ναὸς κ. ὁμιλία, i. e. shipmates, S.*Aj.*872. **-ποιέω**, *make common property*, τὰ τῶν ἀγαθῶν ἔπαθλα Phld.*Rh.*1.217 S., cf. 2.256 S.; δόξαν Alex.Aphr. *in Metaph.*83.30:—Med., *regard as common*, *Inscr.Prien.*113.27 (i B. C.), al.:—Pass., *to be in common*, S.E. *P.*3.173. 2. *generalize*, λόγον Herm. *in Phdr.*p.128 A., Simp. *in Ph.*1275.6; κ. τὴν δόξαν αὐτῶν τοῖς περὶ Δημόκριτον *shows the common ground of* their view and that of D., Id. *in Cael.*617.22:—Med., Alex. Aphr. *in SE*17.13. II. *communicate*, τὰ μυστήρια Sch.Ar.*Av.*1073. **-ποιός**, όν, *creating community*, Dam.*Pr.*36. **-πολῑτεία**, ἡ, *citizenship of a* κοινόν or *league*, *SIG*622 *B* 12 (Vaxos, from Delphi, ii B. C.). **-πορφῠροῦς**, ᾶ, οῦν, *dyed with purple of inferior quality*, *CPR*21.17 (iii A. D.). **-πους**, ὁ, ἡ, πουν, τό, gen. ποδος, *of common foot*, κ. παρουσία, i. e. the arrival *of persons all together*, S.*El.*1104. **-πρᾱγέω**, *act in common with, have dealings with*, c. dat., Plb.4.23.8, 5.57.2, D.S.19.6: abs., κ. περί τινος Plb.30.4.16, cf. Ph. 2.201, Plu.*Galb.*6. 2. *share in*, c. gen., ἀδικημάτων Ph.2.72; ἀγαθῶν ib.444. **-πρᾱγία**, ἡ, *common enterprise, joint* or *concerted action*, Plb.5.95.2, D.S.11.1, 15.8, Plu.*Per.*17.

κοινός, ή, όν, also ός, όν S.*Tr.*207 (lyr.):—*common* (opp. ἴδιος), not in Hom. (v. ξυνός); ἐκ κοινοῦ *shared in common*, Hes.*Op.*723; ἔσται γὰρ βίος ἐκ κ. Ar.*Ec.*610; of a *common* altar, Simon.140; τὸ τέμενος εἶναι κ. *SIG*1044.29 (Halic., iv/iii B. C.); κ. ἔρχεται κῦμ' Ἀΐδα Pi.*N.*7.30; τρεῖς.. κ. ὄμμ' ἐκτημέναι, of the Gorgons, A.*Pr.*795; κ. ὠφέλημα θνητοῖσιν φανείς, of Prometheus, ib.613; τὰς γυναῖκας εἶναι κοινάς Pl. *R.*457d: prov., κοινὸν τύχη A.*Fr.*389, cf. Men.*Mon.*356; κοινὰ τὰ τῶν φίλων E.*Or.*735 (troch.), Pl.*Phdr.*279c, Men.9, etc.; κ. Ἑρμῆς 'share the luck', Id.*Epit.*67, 100; κ. ἀρωγά *common* aid (i. e. for all), S.*Ph.*1145 (lyr.); ἐν δὲ κοινὸς ἀρσένων ἴτω κλαγγά and let the shouts of males rise *jointly*, Id.*Tr.*207 (lyr.); κ. πόλεμον πολεμεῖν X.*Hier.*2.8; τὸν ἀέρα τὸν κ. Men.531.8; κ. τὸν ᾅδην ἔσχον οἱ πάντες βροτοί Id. 538.8; κ. ἀγαθὸν τοῦτ' ἐστί, χρηστὸς εὐτυχῶν Id.791: c. dat., κ. τινί *common to* or *with* another, ὑμῖν φῶς.. καὶ τοῖσδ' ἅπασι κ. A.*Ag.*523; ὁ δαίμων κ. ἦν ἀμφοῖν ἅμα Id.*Th.*812; θάλατταν κ. ἐᾶν τοῖς ἡττημένοις And.3.19; οἰκία.. κοινοτάτη ἀεὶ τῷ δεομένῳ Id.1.147; [πολιτεία] τίς κοινοτάτη; Arist.*Pol.*1289[b]14, cf. 1265[b]29; κοινόν τι χαρᾷ καὶ λύπῃ δάκρυα X.*HG*7.1.32; τὸν ἥλιον τὸν κ. ἡμῖν Men.611: c. gen., πάντων αἰθὴρ κ. φάος εἱλίσσων A.*Pr.*1092 (anap.), cf. *Pers.*132 (lyr.), *Eu.*109, Pi.*N.*1.32; κ. τῶν Λακεδαιμονίων τε καὶ Ἀθηναίων *shared in by* both.., Pl.*Mx.*241c, etc.: with Preps., τὸ ἐπὶ πᾶσι κ., v. infr. v; κ. κατ' ἀμφοτέρων A.D.*Synt.*144.19; οὐ γίγνεταί μοί τι κ. πρός τινα *AP*11.141 (Lucill.), cf. Iamb.*Myst.*5.7; μέρος κ. πρός τινα *shared with*.., *CPR*22.11 (ii A.D.), etc.; κ. μεταξύ τινων *Stud.Pal.*1.7 ii 11 (v A.D.). II. in social and political relations, *public, general*, τὸ κ. ἀγαθόν the *common* weal, Th.5.90; κ. λόγῳ Id.5.37, Hdt.1.141; κ. στόλῳ ib.170; ἀδικήματα D.21.45; ὁ τῆς πόλεως κ. δῆμιος Pl.*Lg.*872b; κοινότατον *of public* or *general interest*, ib.724b, cf. Arist.*Rh.*1354[b]29; of constitutions, *popular, free*, κοινοτέραν εἶναι τὴν ἐκείνου μοναρχίαν τῆς αὐτῶν δημοκρατίας Isoc.10.36. 2. τὸ κ. the *state*, τὸ κ. Σπαρτιητέων Hdt.1.67: abs., of one's own state, Ar.*Ec.*208, etc.; τὸ κ. ὠφελεῖται Antipho 3.2.3, cf. X.*Cyr.*2.2.20; τὰς ὠφελείας ἅπασιν εἰς τὸ κ. ἀπεδίδου Isoc.10.36. b. esp. of *leagues* or *federations*, τὸ κ. τῶν Ἰώνων Hdt.5.109; τῶν συμμάχων Isoc.14.21; τῶν Βοιωτῶν *SIG*457.10 (Thespiae, iii B. C.), Plb.20.6.1 (pl.), etc.; ἄνευ τοῦ πάντων κοινοῦ (sc. τῶν Θεσσαλῶν) Th.4.78; also, of *private associations*, *Test.Epict.*1.22, *SIG*1113 (Loryma), al.; of *guilds* or *corporations*, τὸ κ. τῶν τεκτόνων *POxy.*53.2 (iv A. D.); of *boards* of magistrates, τὸ κ. τῶν ἀρχόντων ib.54.12 (iii A. D.). c. *the government, public authorities*, Th.1.90, 2.12, etc.; τὰ κ. Hdt.3.156; ἀπαγγεῖλαι ἐπὶ τὰ κ. Th.5.37; ἀπὸ τοῦ κ. *by public authority*, Hdt.5.85, 8.135; σὺν τῷ κ. *by common consent*, Id.9.87. d. *the public treasury*, χρημάτων μεγάλων ἐν τῷ κ. γενομένων Id.7.144; ἐν τῷ κ. καὶ ἐν τοῖς ἱεροῖς Th.6.6, cf. 17; χρήματα δοῦναι ἐκ τοῦ κ. Hdt.9.87; ἔχειν ἐν κοινῷ (without the Art.), Th.1.80, cf. Sch. adloc. e. *common right* or *rights* of citizens, τὸ κ. τὸ τῶν πολιτῶν Arist.*Pol.*1283[b]41. 3. τὰ κ. *public affairs*: πρὸς τὰ κ. προσελθεῖν, προσιέναι, to enter *public life*, D. 18.257, Aeschin.1.165; but also, *the public money*, Ar.*Pl.*569, D.8.23 (in full, τὰ κ. χρήματα X.*HG*6.5.34, Arist.*Pol.*1271[b]11); τὰ κ. τῆς πόλεως, opp. τὰ ἁγνά, *BMus.Inscr.*4.481*.383; ἀπὸ κοινοῦ *at the public expense*, X.*An.*4.7.27, 5.1.12; ἐκ κοινοῦ φαγεῖν Euphro 8.4, cf. Antiph. 230; ἐκ κ. from *common funds*, at *joint expense*, *PGrenf.*1.21.19 (ii B. C.). III. *common, ordinary*, τὰ κ. εἰδέναι Pl.*Ax.*366b; διὰ τῶν κ. ποιεῖσθαι τὰς πίστεις Arist.*Rh.*1355[a]27; κοινοτάτη τῶν αἰσθήσεων [ἡ ἁφή] Id.*EN*1118[b]1; τὰ κ. *commonplaces*, Men.*Sam.*27, *Epit.*309; so κ. τόπος Hermog.*Prog.*6, Aphth.*Prog.*7; ἡ κ. ἔννοια or ἐπίνοια, Plb. 2.62.2, 6.5.2; κ. νοῦς, φρένες, *common* sense, Phld.*Rh.*1.37 S., 202 S.; κ. καὶ διανοητικαὶ κακίαι *general* and all-pervading vices, Id.*Sign.*28; κ. καὶ δημώδη ὀνόματα Longin.40.2; κ. καὶ ἐν μέσῳ κείμενα ὀνόματα D.H.*Lys.*3; ἡ κ. διάλεκτος *every-day* language (free from archaisms and far-fetched expressions), Id.*Isoc.*2; πεφευγὼς τὸ κ. Phld.*Acad. Ind.*p.53 M. 2. Gramm., *ordinary*, *'regular'* *Greek*, opp. special dialects, διάλεκτοί εἰσι πέντε, Ἀτθὶς Δωρὶς Αἰολὶς Ἰὰς καὶ κ. Sch.D.T. p.14 H., cf. D.S.1.16, Theodos.*Can.*p.37 H., etc.; ἡ κ. alone, A.D. *Conj.*223.24; τὸ κ. ἔθος, ἡ κ. ἐκφορά, Id.*Adv.*155.10, *Pron.*4.27;

οἱ κ. the writers who use this language, Sch.D.T.p.469 H., EM405. 23. b. colloquial, vulgar Greek, Moer.pp.201 (Comp., prob. for καιν–), 243 P., al. c. ἡ κ. διάλεκτος demotic Egyptian, Manetho ap. J.Ap.1.14. 3. common, of inferior quality, χρυσός POxy.905.5 (ii A.D.), 1273.6 (iii A.D.). 4. in magical formulae, of words added at will by the user, 'and so forth', freq. in Pap., PMag.Osl.1.255, PMag. Par.1.273, al.; κοινὰ ὅσα θέλεις ib.2.53; ὁ κ. λόγος PMag.Lond.46.435; cf. κοινολογία. IV. of Persons, connected by common origin or kindred, esp. of brothers and sisters, κ. σπέρμα Pi.O.7.92, cf. S.OT261, OC535 (lyr.); κ. αἷμα Id.Ant.202, cf. 1; κ. πατήρ, μήτηρ, PAmh.2.152. 9 (v/vi A.D.), PFlor.47.11 (iii A.D.); also κ. Χάριτες Pi.O.2.50. 2. one who shares in a thing, partner, ἐν θύμασιν κ. ποιεῖσθαί τινα S.OT 240; κ. ἐν κοινοῖσι λυπεῖσθαι Id.Aj.267, cf. Ar.V.917; also κ. τῷ θεῷ belonging in part to the god (who claims tithe of his substance), Berl.Sitzb.1927.161 (Cyrene). 3. lending a ready ear to all, impartial, μὴ οὐ κ. ἀποβῆτε Th.3.53; neutral, ib.68; κοινοὺς τῷ τε διώκοντι καὶ τῷ φεύγοντι Lys.15.1; μέτριος καὶ κ. Arist.Ath.6.3; κοινοί, οἱ, arbitrators, GDI1832.10 (Delph.); κ. μεσίτης PStrassb.41.14 (iii A.D.); of a capital city, δεῖ.. κοινὴν εἶναι τῶν τόπων ἁπάντων easily accessible on all sides, Arist.Pol.1327^{a}6. b. courteous, affable, X. Cyn.13.9; κ. ἅπασι γενέσθαι Isoc.5.80; τῇ πρὸς πάντας φιλανθρωπίᾳ κ. Democh.2 J.; ἔχειν τὰς κ. φρένας Phld.Rh.1.202 S. c. in bad sense, κοινή, ἡ, prostitute, Vett.Val.119.30, Porph.Hist.Phil.12 (pl.). d. of events, κοινότεραι τύχαι more impartial, i.e. more equal, chances, Th.5.102; ἔστιν ἐν τῷ κ. πᾶσι c. inf., And.2.6. V. in Logic, general, universal, τὸ κ. λαμβάνειν περί τινων, τὸ ἐπὶ πᾶσι κ., Pl.Tht. 185b, c; τὰ κ. λεγόμενα ἀξιώματα Arist.APo.76^{b}14; αἱ κ. ἀρχαί ib.88^{a}36; κ. ἔννοιαι axioms, heading in Euc.; general, κ. ὅρος Arist.Metaph. 987^{b}6; κοινὰ καὶ στοιχειώδη general principles, Phld.Rh.1.69S.; κ. σημεῖον, opp. ἴδιον, Id.Sign.14; κ. κρίσις objectively valid judgement, Id.Po.5.22; ὄνομα κ. Str.10.2.10; abstract, ὁ κ. ἄνθρωπος καὶ λογισμῷ ληπτός Dam.Pr.341. VI. Gramm., 1. κ. συλλαβή common syllable, capable of being long or short, D.T.633.17, Heph. 1.4. b. κ. ποιήματα, poems which are both κατὰ στίχον and συστηματικά, e.g. the Sapphic stanza, Id.pp.58,59C.; also, poems of ambiguous metrical form, Id.p.60C. 2. v. supr. III. 2. 3. of gender, κ. γένος D.T.634.19; of nouns, A.D.Pron.30.7, al., EM143.33, 305. 19, etc. 4. ἀπὸ κοινοῦ λαμβάνειν, of two clauses taking a word in common, A.D.Synt.122.14, al.; κοινὸν or ἐκ κοινοῦ παραλαμβάνεσθαι, ib.20,28, al. VII. of forbidden meats, common, profane, φαγεῖν κ. καὶ ἀκάθαρτον Act.Ap.10.14, cf. Ep.Rom.14.14; κ. χερσὶ ἐσθίειν Ev.Marc.7.2. VIII. κοινόν, τό, name of an eye-salve, CIL 13.10021.3, al.

B. Adv. κοινῶς in common, jointly, E.Ion1462; τὰ κοινὰ κ. δεῖ φέρειν συμπτώματα Men.817: Comp., ἐν Κρήτῃ –οτέρως [ἔχει τὰ τῶν συσσιτίων] Arist.Pol.1272^{a}16. 2. publicly, κ. μᾶλλον ὠφέλησαν ἢ ἐκ τῶν ἰδίων ἔβλαψαν Th.2.42, etc. 3. sociably, like other citizens, οὐδὲ κ. οὐδὲ πολιτικῶς ἐβίωσαν Isoc.4.151; ἴσως καὶ κ. πρός τινα προσφέρεσθαι Arist.Rh.Al.1430^{a}1; κ. καὶ φιλικῶς Plu.Ant.33; μετρίως καὶ κ. ἀσπάζεσθαι Id.Arat.43. 4. in general, Diph.Siph.ap.Ath. 3.81a; ἡ κ. σύνεσις, τὸ κ. "ἄνθρωπον", Phld.Vit.p.34 J., Mort.38; opp. ἰδίως, Demetr.Lac.Herc.1014.41, Plu.Marc.8, cf. Longin.15.1; κοινότερον εἰπεῖν Phld.Rh.1.256S.; –οτέρως Orib.Fr.93. 5. in the common dialect, A.D.Pron.82.27, al.: Comp. –ότερον Id.Synt.159. 5. 6. in plain language, opp. σοφιστικῶς, Plu.2.659f; in the ordinary or wide sense, opp. κυρίως, Them.in APo.5.5: Comp., M.Ant. 2.10. II. fem. dat. **κοινῇ**; Dor. **κοινᾷ** SIG56.11 (Argos, v B.C.); Boeot. **κυνῆ** ib.635.31 (Acraeph., ii B.C.):—in common, by common consent, Hdt.1.148, 3.79, S.OT606, OC1339, E.Hipp.731, Th.1.3, etc.; κ. πᾶσι καὶ χωρὶς Arist.Pol.1278^{b}23, cf. Ath.40.3; κ. μετά τινος, κ. σύν τινι, Pl.Smp.209c, SIG346.27 (iv B.C.), X.Mem.1.6.14, etc.; ἰδίᾳ τε καὶ κ. Alex.291: also neut. pl. κοινά S.Ant.546. 2. publicly, καὶ κ. καὶ ἰδίᾳ X.HG1.2.10, Mem.2.1.12, etc. 3. as Prep. c. dat., together with, E.Ion1228, Hel.829, Fr.823. III. with Preps., εἰς κοινόν in common, in public, ὑμῖν τῇδέ τ' ἐς κ. φράσω A.Pr.844; πᾶσιν ἐς κ. λέγω Id.Eu.408, cf. Ar.Av.457 (lyr.), Pl.Lg.796e; εἰς κ. γνώμην ἀποφαίνεσθαι D.19.156; εἰς τὸ κ. λέγειν, ἀγορεύειν, Pl.Tht.165a, X. An.5.6.27; εἰς τὸ κ. for public use, Pl.Lg.681c. 2. ἀπὸ κοινοῦ, ἐκ κοινοῦ, v. A. I. 1, II. 3, VI. 4. 3. ἀφεῖσαν ἐν κοινῷ ζητεῖν, Lat. rem in medio reliquerunt, Arist.Metaph.987^{b}14; but οἱ ἐν κ. γιγνόμενοι λόγοι, = οἱ ἐξωτερικοὶ λόγοι, Id.de An.407^{b}29. 4. κατὰ κοινόν, opp. κατ' ἰδίαν, jointly, in common, Lex ap.D.21.94, Plb.4.3.5; prob. for κατὰ κοινοῦ Id.11.30.3.

κοινο-τᾰφής, ές, in which all must be buried, Λύσιλλαν κατέχει κ. θάλαμος Ath.Mitt.10.405 (iv B.C.). **–τάφιον** [ᾰ], τό, public grave, Ulp. ad D.18.208 (p.111 Dobson). **–τελής**, ές, with the authority of the state, δόγμα IG11(4).1150 (Delos, ii B.C.).

κοινότης, ητος, ἡ, sharing in common, community, τῶν γυναικῶν καὶ παίδων καὶ τῆς οὐσίας Arist.Pol.1274^{b}10; ἡ περὶ τὰ τέκνα κ. καὶ τὰς γυναῖκας ib.1266^{a}34; κ. φωνῆς common language, i.e. not peculiar or dialectal, Isoc.15.296, cf. D.H.Th.54, Pomp.2. 2. common or universal quality, Pl.Tht.208d, Plot.1.3.4; opp. ἰδιότης, Epicur.Ep. 1 p.17 U.; κ. τοῦ ἵππου A.D.Pron.26.20: pl., common features, Phld. Ir.p.71 W., Mort.34, Plu.Comp.Lyc.Num.1; esp. in Medicine, term of the 'Methodic' school, Gal.1.80, al., cf. Plu.2.129d (pl.). 3. generality, vagueness, τῶν ὁμολογιῶν D.H.2.39, etc.; ambiguity, ὀνόματος Epicur.Nat.14.10, cf. Demetr.Lac.Herc.1014.48, Diog.Oen.27. II. in Politics, absence of privileges or distinctions, πολιτείας (sc. δημοκρατίας) ἣ μάλιστα κοινότητα δοκεῖ προῃρῆσθαι And.4.13. 2. affability, X.HG1.1.30; accessibility, λιμένων Aristid.Or.23(42).24, al. III. Gramm., use of a common word in two clauses, esp. in phrase ἐν κοινότητι παραλαμβάνεσθαι, A.D.Synt.122.27, al. 2. common gender, ib.55.2, al. IV. concrete, the general body of a βουλή, POxy.2110.29 (iv A.D.). 2. κ. τῶν ἀγρευτῶν, = κοινόν (cf. κοινός II. 2 b), Sammelb.6704.4, al. (vi A.D.).

κοινό-τοκος, ον, of or from common parents, ἐλπίδες κ. hopes in one born of the same parents, i.e. a brother, S.El.858 (lyr.). **–τροφικός**, ή, όν, (τρέφω) of or for group rearing, ἐπιστήμη Pl.Plt.264d, 267d; ἡ –κή (sc. ἐπιστήμη) group rearing, ib.261e, 264b, etc. **–φᾰγία**, ἡ, eating of what is common or profane, J.AJ11.8.7. **–φῐλής**, ές, with common affection, κ. διανοίᾳ A.Eu.985 (lyr., κοινωφελεῖ codd.). **–φρων**, ον, gen. ονος, like-minded with, τινι E.Ion577, IT1008. **–φυής**, ές, of common origin, πρόοδος Dam.Pr.52 bis.

κοιν-όω, fut. κοινώσω A.Ch.673: aor. ἐκοίνωσα Th.8.48, Pl.Lg. 889d; Dor. ἐκοίνᾱσα Pi.P.4.115:—Med., fut. κοινώσομαι Id.N.3.12 codd. (leg. –ᾱσομαι (Dor.)), E.Med.499: aor. ἐκοινωσάμην A.Ag.1347, Is.11.50, etc.:—Pass., aor. ἐκοινώθην E.Andr.38, Pl.Ti.59b: pf. κεκοίνωμαι (in med. sense) E.Fr.493:—communicate, impart information, κ. τινί τι A.Ch.717 (in 673 an acc. must be supplied), E.Med. 685, Ar.Nu.197, Th.4.4, etc.; μῦθον ἔς τινας E.IA44 (anap.); κ. τινὶ περί τινος A.Supp.369; νυκτὶ κοινάσαντες ὁδόν having imparted their journey to night alone (i.e. travelling by night without consulting any one), Pi.P. l. c. 2. make common, share, κοινώσαντας τὴν δύναμιν κοινὰ καὶ τὰ ἀποβαίνοντα ἔχειν Th.1.39, cf. Pl.Lg. l. c.; v.l. for ἐκοινώνησε in Arist.Pol.1264^{a}1:—in Med., κοινάσομαι [ὕμνον] λύρᾳ Pi.N. l. c.: aor. Med. in act. sense, Hp.Jusj.; κ. τὴν οὐσίαν τῇ τοῦ παιδός unite one to the other, Is. l. c. 3. make common, defile, τὸν ἄνθρωπον Ev.Matt.15.11; γαστέρα μιαροφαγίᾳ Lxx 4Ma.7.6:—Med., deem profane, Act.Ap.10.15. II. Med., c. acc., undertake together, make common cause in, βουλεύματα A.Ag.1347; κοινούμεθα.. ἐγώ τε καὶ Λάχης τὸν λόγον Pl.La.196c; τὸ πρᾶγμα D.32.30; κοινουμένη τὰς ξυμφορὰς σοι E.Ion608, cf. 858; κοινοῦσθαι τὸν στόλον Th. 8.8; τὴν τύχην X.Vect.4.32. 2. take counsel with, consult, esp. an oracle or god, X.An.6.2.15, v.l. in HG7.1.27: generally, πρός τινας Pl.Lg.930c; περὶ πάντων ἑαυτοῖς Plb.7.16.3; τοῖς ἰατροῖς περί τινων Gal.Consuet.5; τοῖς φίλοις περὶ τὸ πρακτέον Hdn.7.8.1; ὧν ἄν τις κοινώσαιτο δόξαις agree with, Arist.Metaph.993^{b}12: abs., οὔτ' ἠθέλησας οὔτ' ἐγὼ 'κοινωσάμην S.Ant.539; simply, communicate, τὰ κατ' ἐμὲ τῇ βουλῇ Alciphr.3.72; μηδὲν τῇ γυναικὶ χρήσιμον Men.Mon. 361. 3. c. gen., to be partner or partaker, τινος of a thing, E.Ph. 1709, Cyc.634, Lys.12.93, etc.; τινί τινος with one in.., E.Andr. 933. 4. come to terms, μοι Pl.Smp.218e. III. Pass., have communication with, λέχει E.Andr.38, cf. 217: metaph., ἀλλήλοις Pl.Lg.673d; ξανθῷ χρώματι –θέν, i.e. tinged with yellow, Id.Ti. 59b. **–ωμα**, ατος, τό, intercourse, esp. sexual, Dionys.Minor 1, cf. Socr.Ep.35, 36. 2. gloss on δαμώματα, Hsch. II. mortised joint, Ph.Bel.57.19. **–ωμάτιον**, τό, band, tie, ib.64.3. **–ών**, ῶνος, ὁ, Dor., Arc. **κοινάν**, ᾶνος (q.v.), = κοινωνός, which is much more freq., X.Cyr.7.5.35, 8.1.16, 36, 40; of partners in a tax-farming syndicate, PRev.Laws 10.10, al. (iii B.C.).

κοινων-έω, fut. –ήσω Pl.R.540c: pf. κεκοινώνηκα Id.Phdr.246d, etc.:—Pass., fut. κοινωνήσομαι (v. infr.): pf. κεκοινώνημαι Id.Lg. 801e:—have or do in common with, share, take part in a thing with another, c. gen. rei et dat. pers., τῆς πολιτείας κ. τινί ib.753a; κ. πόνων καὶ κινδύνων ἀλλήλοις ib.686a, cf. X.HG2.4.21; κ. αὐτοῖς ὧν ἔπραττον ib.6.3.1; σιτήσεως τισι Din.1.101: also in act. sense, give a share of.., βρωτοῦ μηδενὸς μηδένα τούτῳ κ. D.25.61; τὰ περὶ τὰς κτήσεις τοῖς συσσιτίοις ὁ νομοθέτης ἐκοινώνησε (v.l. ἐκοίνωσε) Arist.Pol. 1264^{a}1; πυρὸς ἢ ὕδατος κ. Luc.Alex.46; πάντων ἐκοινώνει μοι τῶν ἀπορρήτων Id.Philops.34. 2. κ. τινός have a share of, take part in a thing, χθονός A.Supp.325; μύθου Id.Ch.165; κακῶν Id.Th.1038; γάμων S. Tr.546; τάφου E.Or.1055; τύχης Id.Med.302; σίτου καὶ ποτοῦ X. Mem.2.6.22; τῆς πολιτείας Arist.Pol.1268^{a}18, etc.; τῶν αὐτῶν κ. πάντων share all things in common, ib.1257^{a}22; ἱερῶν SIG1106.7 (Cos, iv/iii B.C.); θυσίας Inscr.Magn.44.19 (Decr. Corc.); ἦθος παιδείας κεκοινωνηκός Aristeas 290; φύσεως κεκοινώνηκε σαρκίνης Phld.Sign. 27; πάθους, of infection, Gal.12.312. b. of partnership in business, BGU969.13 (ii A.D.), etc. 3. κ. τινί go shares with, have dealings with a man, Ar.V.692, Av.653, Pl.R.343d, etc.; also of things, κοινωνεῖν μὲν ἡγοῦμαι καὶ τοῦτο τοῖς πεπολιτευμένοις I think that this also is concerned with my public measures, D.18.58; στολὴν φοινικίδα.. ἥκιστα.. γυναικείᾳ κ. has least in common with.., X.Lac.11.3; οὐδὲν τραγῳδίᾳ κ. Arist.Po.1453^{b}10, cf. SE179^{b}16: Medic., sympathize, of bodily parts, Hp.Mul.1.38:—Pass., ἐγκώμια κεκοινωνημένα εὐχαῖς united with.., Pl.Lg.801e. 4. with Preps., φύσις ἡ θήλεια τῇ τοῦ ἄρρενος γένους κ. εἰς ἅπαντα Id.R.453a; κ. περί τινος Plb.31.18.6. 5. c. acc. cogn., κ. κοινωνίαν τινί Pl.Lg.881e; κ. ἴσα πάντα τοῖς ἀνδράσι Id.R.540c: rarely c. acc. rei, κ. φόνον τινί commit murder in common with him, E.El.1048. 6. abs., share in an opinion, agree, σκόπει.., πότερον κοινωνεῖς καὶ ξυνδοκεῖ σοι Pl.Cri.49d. 7. communicate, join, ἡ ἐρυθρὰ θάλασσα κ. πρὸς τὴν ἔξω.. Arist.Mete.354^{a}2. 8. form a community, Id.Pol.1280^{a}26, etc. II. of sexual intercourse, κ. γυναικί, ἀνδρί, Pl.Lg.784e, Luc.DDeor.1.2, 10.2, PFlor.36.6 (iv A.D.):—Pass., ὑπὸ μηδενός ποτε κοινωνήσεται εἰ μὴ ὑπὸ σοῦ μόνου PMag.Osl.1.293. **–ημα**, ατος, τό, that which is communicated: pl., acts of communion, communications, dealings between man and man, Pl.R.333a, Lg.738a, Arist.Pol.1280^{b}17; κ. πρός τινα J.AJ16.7.3; πρὸς ἀλλήλους Plu.2.158c; ψυχροῦ καὶ θερμοῦ κ. ib.951e:

in sg., *communication*, λόγων Phld.*Oec*.p.46 J.; *common enterprise*, Id.*Vit*.p.33 J.; *business partnership*, *Sammelb*.5658.8. 2. *point of junction*, Hp.*Epid*.2.4.2. 3. *connexion*, Nic.Dam.128 J. **-ησις**, εως, ἡ, *reciprocal recognition*, παίδων Pl.*Plt*.310b. 2. *partnership*, *BGU*1024 v 19 (iv A.D.). **-ητέον**, *one must share in*, τινός τινι Pl.*R*.403b; φιλίας Ph.2.401; ὀνειδῶν Plu.*Pomp*.44. **-ητικός**, ή, όν, v.l. for κοινωνικός, Plb.2.44.1; -κή (sc. ἐπιστήμη) *social science*, coupled with πολιτική, Plu.2.746a:—hyperdor. **-ᾱτικός**, *generous, liberal*, Diotog.ap.Stob.4.7.62. **-ία**, ἡ, *communion, association, partnership*, κ. μαλθακά Pi.*P*.1.97; οὔτε φιλία ἰδιώταις οὔτε κ. πόλεσιν Th.3.10; ὅτῳ δὲ μὴ ἔνι κ., φιλία οὐκ ἂν εἴη Pl.*Grg*.507e; ἐν ταῖς κ. τε καὶ ὁμιλίαις Id.*Lg*.861e, cf. *Smp*.182c; ἡ περὶ.. ἀνθρώπους πρὸς ἀλλήλους κ. ib.188c; ἐν διαλύσει τῆς κ. Id.*R*.343d; ἡ τῶν γυναικῶν κ. τοῖς ἀνδράσι, viz. co-education, ib.466c; ἀνθρωπίνη κ. human *society*, Id. *Plt*.276b; ἡ κ. ἡ πολιτική Arist.*Pol*.1252^{a}7; αὕτη ἡ κ., of marriage, ib.1334^{b}33; πόλις ἡ γενῶν καὶ κωμῶν κ. ib.1281^{a}1; *fellowship*, *Act.Ap*.2.42, al.; ἡ πρὸς τὸν Δία κ. Arr.*Epict*.2.19.27. b. *joint-ownership*, *PLond*.2.311.2 (ii A.D.), etc. 2. c. gen. objecti, λυγραὶ.. τῶν ὅπλων κ. E.*HF*1377; γάμων Pl.*Lg*.721a; γυναικῶν Id.*R*.461e; ἡ ἡδονῆς τε καὶ λύπης κ. συνδεῖ ib.462b; τῶν πόνων Id.*Ti*.87e; βοηθείας καὶ φιλίας D.9.28; βίου, of marriage, *BGU*1051.9 (Aug.); ἡ κ. τοῦ ἁγίου πνεύματος 2*Ep.Cor*.13.14 (later, of Holy *Communion*, Just. *Nov*.7.11); κ. τῶν ἱερῶν *Supp.Epigr*.4.247 (Panamara); τίς θαλάσσης βουκόλοις κ.; what have herdsmen *to do with* the sea? E.*IT*254; τίς δαὶ κατόπτρου καὶ ξίφους κ.; Ar.*Th*.140; λύπη μανίας κοινωνίαν ἔχει τινά Alex.296; opp. ἀκοινωνησία, Dam.*Pr*.423. II. *sexual intercourse*, E.*Ba*.1276; γυναικὸς λαμβάνειν κοινωνίαν Amphis 20. 3. III. *charitable contribution, alms*, *Ep.Rom*.15.26, *Ep.Hebr*.13. 16, *Jahresh*.4 *Beibl*.37. 2. *charitable disposition*, opp. πλεονεξία, *Corp.Herm*.13.9. IV. Pythag. name for 2, *Theol.Ar*.8. **-ικός**, ή, όν, *held in common*, τὰ κ. property *held by corporations*, D.14.16, cf. *BCH*50.16 (Delph., iv B.C., prob.); κ. ἐλαιών *BGU*1037.14 (i A.D.), cf. *PGiss*.30.7 (ii A.D.). b. *relating to partnerships*, [δίκαι] Arist. *Ath*.52.2. c. κοινωνικά, τά, *tax on corporations*, *PTeb*.5.59 (ii B.C.), 100.10 (ii B.C.). 2. *social*, ἰσότης κοινωνική [ἢ δικαιοσύνη] Pl.*Def*. 411e; κ. ἀρετή Arist.*Pol*.1283^{a}38; [φιλίαι] Id.*EN*1161^{b}14. 3. *sociable*, κ. καὶ φιλικὴ διάθεσις Plb.2.44.1, cf. Plu.2.43d; φύσει ἐσμὲν κ. Epicur. *Fr*.525, cf. Arr.*Epict*.3.13.5: Sup., τὸν ἄνθρωπον ἡ φύσις κατεσκεύασε -ώτατον Ph.*Fr*.71 H.; τὸ -κόν *sociability*, J.*BJ*2.8.3. b. of certain signs of the zodiac, *Cat.Cod.Astr*.1.166. 4. *giving a share of*, τῶν ὄντων Luc.*Tim*.56: abs., κ. ὁ Ἑρμῆς *ready to share luck with others*, prov. in Arist.*Rh*.1401^{a}20; *liberal*, 1*Ep.Ti*.6.18, Ptol.*Tetr*.69; opp. φθονερός, Gal.4.817. 5. c. dat., *in communion* with, τῇ ἐκκλησίᾳ Just. *Nov*.8 *Jusj*. II. Act., *receptive, sharing in*, φωτός Str.17.1.36. III. Adv. -κῶς, χρῆσθαι τοῖς εὐτυχήμασι to suffer others *to partake in* one's good fortune, Plb.18.48.7; κ. βιῶναι D.S.5.9; ζῆν κ. καὶ φιλικῶς Plu. 2.1108c, etc. 2. Medic., *by sympathy*, κ. σπᾶσθαι prob. in Aët.3. 140. **-ῑμαῖος**, α, ον, = foreg. I. 1, πράγματα, τοῖχος, *PLond*.5.1728. 8, *PMon*.16.19 (vi A.D.). **-οποιέω**, = κοινωνέω, *Gloss*. **-ός**, ὁ, also ἡ, *companion, partner*, τινος of or in a thing, A.*Ag*.1037, 1352, *Supp*.344, Men.*Epit*.499; τῆς ἐπιβουλῆς Antipho 5.68; ἱερῶν Pl.*Lg*. 868e; τῆς ἀρχῆς Th.7.63, 8.46; ὁ τοῦ κακοῦ κ. *accomplice* in.., S.*Tr*. 730; ἀνοσίων αὐτοῖς ἔργων Pl.*Ep*.325a; κ. περὶ νόμων Pl.*Lg*.810c; τινι in a thing, E.*El*.637: c. dat. pers., κ. ἀλλήλοις τῶν τιμῶν with each other, X.*Mem*.2.6.24. 2. abs., *partner, fellow*, S.*Aj*.284, Pl. *R*.333b, *Phdr*.239c, etc.; ὁ σὸς κ., οὐχ ὁ ἐμός D.18.21; ἴσοι καὶ κ. Arist.*EN*1133^{b}3; κοινωνοὶ λιμένων, of a *societas publicanorum* which farmed harbour-dues, *BCH*10.267 (Syme); of *joint-owners*, *PAmh*. 2.100 (ii/iii A.D.). 3. *familiar spirit*, Lxx 4 *Ki*.17.11. II. as Adj., = κοινός, ξίφος E.*IT*1173.

κοίν-ωσις, εως, ἡ, *mingling*, Plu.2.430e. II. *sharing*, Asp.*in EN*181.1. **-ωφελής**, ές, *of common utility*, Ph.2.404, al., Gal.14. 296, *POxy*.1409.19 (iii A.D.), Just.*Nov*.7.2.1: Comp., Max.Tyr.41.1: Sup., Ph.1.389. **-ωφελία**, ἡ, *common utility*, Phld.*Rh*.1.174 S. (pl.), D.S.1.51: on the form (-εια Just.*Nov*.7.12 *Ep*.), cf. *EM*462.21.

κόϊξ, ϊκος, ὁ, *doum-palm*, *Hyphaene thebaica*, Thphr.*HP*1.10.5, etc. 2. *palm-leaf basket*, Pherecr.78, Antiph.63:—Dor. **κόϊς** Epich.113 (also *BGU*972.5).

Κοιο-γενής, ές, *born of Coios*, i.e. Latona, Pi.*Fr*.88.2:—fem. **Κοιογένεια** A.R.2.710; **Κοιηΐς** (q.v.).

κοιόλης, ὁ, = ἱερεύς, Hsch., Suid. **κοῖον**· ἐνέχυρον, Hsch. **κοῖος** (A), η, ον, Ion. for ποῖος, α, ον.

κοῖος (B), ὁ, Maced. for ἀριθμός, Ath.10.455e. II. Carian for πρόβατον, Sch.Il.14.255.

κοιπποίβα· πᾶν σπέρμα (Achaean), Hsch.

κοιρᾰν-έω, poet. Verb, *to be lord* or *master, rule, command*, in Hom., 1. of a military leader, ὣς ὅ γε κοιρανέων δίεπε στρατόν Il.2. 207, cf. 4.250; μάχην ἀνὰ κοιρανέοντα 5.824; πόλεμον κάτα κοιρανέουσιν ib.332. 2. of a king in peace, Λυκίην κάτα κοιρανέουσιν 12.318; of the suitors (princes) in Ithaca, Od.1.247, al. II. later c. gen., *to be lord of*, Hes.*Th*.331, A.*Pers*.214: c. dat., θεοῖσι κ. Id.*Pr*.49; Ep. impf. κοιρανέεσκεν A.R.2.998: abs., τὸν νῦν κοιρανοῦντα A.*Pr*.958: c. acc., *lead, arrange*, χορούς Pi.*O*.14.9:—Pass., Call. *Del*.167. **-ηος**, Dor. for κοιράνειος, *belonging to a sovereign*, κάρτος Melinno ap.Stob.3.7.12. **-ία**, Ep. -ίη, ἡ, *sovereignty*, D.P.464, *APl*.5.358. **-ίδης** [νῐ], ου, ὁ, *member of a ruling house*, S.*Ant*.940 (anap., pl.), *Sammelb*.5829 (pl.). **-ικός**, ή, όν, *royal*, λέοντες, ὀφθαλμοί, Opp.*C*.3.41, 47, cf. Epic. in *BKT*5(1). p.119. **-ος**, ὁ, poet. Noun (Boeot. for *king*, *AB*1095), *ruler, leader, commander*, 1. in war or peace, ἡγεμόνες Δαναῶν καὶ κ. Il. 2.487; κοίρανε λαῶν 7.234; οὐκ ἀγαθὸν πολυκοιρανίη· εἷς κ. ἔστω, εἷς βασιλεύς 2.204. 2. generally, *lord, master*, Od.18.106, Pi.*N*.3. 62, A.*Ag*.549, S.*OC*1287, E.*Med*.71, al.—Rare in fem., Orph.*Fr*.38.

κοΐς, v. κόϊξ. **κοίσκαι**· δίκαιοι, Hsch. **κοισσοί**· κορμοί, Id.

κοιτ-άζω, (κοίτη) *put to bed*, Hsch.; esp. of cattle, *fold*, ποιμένων κοιταζόντων πρόβατα Lxx *Je*.40(33).12; *cause to rest*, ποῦ ποιμαίνεις, ποῦ -άζεις ἐν μεσημβρίᾳ; ib.*Ca*.1.7. 2. Med., Dor. aor. ἐκοιταξάμην, *go to bed, sleep*, ἀνὰ βωμῷ θεᾶς κοιτάξατο νύκτα Pi.*O*.13.76, cf. Lxx *De*.6.7. b. *encamp, bivouac*, Aen.Tact.10.26 (Pass.), Plb.10.15.9, *POxy*.1465.9 (i B.C.); perh. to be read in Eup.341. II. intr., in Act., *have a lair*, of a lion, Aesop.114: *nest*, of birds, *BGU*1252.11 (ii B.C.). III. *parcel out* lands (cf. κοίτη v), ib.619.4 (ii A.D.). **-αῖος**, α, ον, (κοίτη) *abed*, κ. γίγνεσθαι ἐν τῇ χώρᾳ to *pass the night* in the country, Decr.ap.D.18.37; but τάξας ἡμέραν ἐν ᾗ δεήσει πάντας ἐν Ἀριμίνῳ γενέσθαι κ. *encamp*, Plb.3.61.10; κ. ἔρχεσθαι Id.*Fr*.177. II. Subst., τὸ κ., = κοίτη I. 2, *lair* of a wild beast, Plu.*TG*9. 2. τὰ κ. ἐπισπένδειν take a *last cup*, '*night-cap*', Hld.3.4. **-άριον**, τό, Dim. of κοίτη, Sch.Od.14.51. **-άριος**, α, ον, *for beds*, σινδόνες *Edict.Diocl*. 28.16, 31. **-ᾱσία**, ἡ, *cohabitation*, Lxx *Le*.20.15. **-ασμός**, ὁ, *folding*, βοῶν *PMeyer* 12.24 (ii A.D.), etc. **-αστέον**, *one must put to bed*, κύνας Arr.*Cyn*.9 tit. **-ᾱτήριον**, τό, *dormitory, bed-chamber*, *Berl.Sitzb*.1927.164 (Cyrene). **-η**, ἡ, (κεῖμαι) = κοῖτος I, once in Hom., Od.19.341 (v.l. οἴκῳ); *bedstead*, *IG*1^2.330.16, al., Wilcken *Chr*.244.3 (iii B.C.), etc.; esp. *marriage-bed*, A.*Supp*.804 (lyr.), S.*Tr*.17; οὐ γὰρ ἐκ μιᾶς κ. ἔβλαστον Id.*Fr*.546; τᾶς ἀπλήστου κ. ἔρος E.*Med*.152 (lyr.), etc.; ἀνάνδρου κοίτας λέκτρον ib.436 (lyr.); also πετρίνη κοίτη, of a cave, S.*Ph*.160 (anap.); τειρομέναν νοσερᾷ κ. on a sick-*bed*, E.*Hipp*.132 (lyr.); κοίταν δ' ἔχει νέρθεν, of one dead, S.*OC*1706 (lyr.); κ. σκληρά Pl.*Lg*.942d, Aret.*CA*1.1: pl., ἔννυχοι κ. Pi.*P*.11.25; νυμφίδιοι κ. E. *Alc*.249 (lyr.): metaph., of the sea, ἐν μεσημβριναῖς κοίταις.. εὕδοι πεσών A.*Ag*.566; of the *bed* of a river, Procop.*Aed*.5.5, Phlp.*in Ph*. 586.21, Lyd.*Mens*.4.10. 2. *lair* of a wild beast, *nest* of a bird, etc., E.*Ion*155 (lyr.); χελιδόνων Aët.16.15; κ. ποιεῖσθαι, of the spider, Arist.*HA*623^{a}12; of the fish ἐξώκοιτος, Thphr.*Fr*.171.1. 3. *quarters*, τῶν φυλακιτῶν *BGU*1007.14 (iii B.C.), cf. *PTeb*.179 (ii B.C.); v. infr. VI. 4. *pen, fold* for cattle, *PLips*.118.15 (ii A.D.). II. *act of going to bed*, τῆς κοίτης ὥρη *bed*-time, Hdt.1.10, 5.20; τραπέζῃ καὶ κοίτῃ δέκεσθαι to entertain '*at bed* and board', ibid.; τὴν σκηνὴν εἰς κ. διέλυον for *going to bed*, X.*Cyr*.2.3.1 (but κεῖσθαι κοίταν *to lie still* in death, A.*Ag*.1494 (lyr.)). III. *lodging, entertainment*, *PTeb*. 122.1 (i B.C.), al. IV. of *sexual connexion*, κ. διδόναι Lxx *Nu*.5. 20, cf. *Le*.18.20; κ. σπέρματος ib.15.16; κ. ἔχειν ἐκ.. to become pregnant by a man, *Ep.Rom*.9.10; in bad sense, *lasciviousness*, ib. 13.13 (pl.). V. *parcel, lot* of land, *PAmh*.2.88.9 (ii A.D.), *PRyl*. 168.9 (ii A.D.). VI. *chest, case*, or *basket*, Pherecr.122, Eup.76, *IG* 2^2.120.37, 40, Men.129.2, *PPetr*.2 p.10 (iii B.C., unless in signf. I. 3), Luc.*Ep.Sat*.21; αἱ μυστικαὶ κ. Plu.*Phoc*.28. **-ίδιον**, τό, Dim. of κοιτίς, Sch.Luc.*Gall*.21. **-ίς**, ίδος, ἡ, Dim. of κοίτη VI, *box*, *AP* 6.254.6 (Myrin.), Philostr.*VA*4.39; v.l. for κιστίς in Hld.4.11; gloss on φωριαμός, Sch.A.R.3.802; *basket*, Men.*Epit*.164; κ. πλεκτὰς ἐκ φοίνικος Arr.*An*.3.4.3; of Moses' *ark*, J.*AJ*2.9.5.

κοῖτος, ὁ, (κεῖμαι) *resting-place, bed*, κοίτοιο μεδώμεθα Od.3.334, cf. 2.358; οἱ δ' ἐπὶ κοῖτον ἐσσεύοντο 14.455; στυγερὸς δ' ὑπεδέξατο κ., of birds, 22.470; *stall, fold*, Arat.1116; ἀπάγειν ἐπὶ κοῖτον *pen*, Longus 1.8. II. *sleep*, ἐπὴν νὺξ ἔλθῃ, ἕλῃσί τε κ. ἅπαντας Od.19.515; κοίτοιο ὥρη *bed*-time, ib.510; ἐπ' ἠόα κ. *lying abed* till dawn, Hes.*Op*. 574; τὸν ὑπασπίδιον κοῖτον ἰαύειν sleep under arms, E.*Rh*.740 (lyr.); κ. ποιέεσθαι go *to bed*, Hdt.7.17; ἐς κ. παρεῖναι Id.1.9.

κοιτών, ῶνος, ὁ, *bed-chamber*, Ar.*Fr*.6, *PTeb*.120.14 (i B.C.), D.S.11. 69, etc.; ὁ ἐπὶ τοῦ κοιτῶνος *chamberlain*, *Act.Ap*.12.20, Arr.*Epict*.3. 22.15; ἐπὶ κ. Σεβαστοῦ, = Lat. *cubicularius Augusti*, *CIG*2947 (Caria, ii A.D.), cf. *IG*14.2143, al.: rejected by the Atticists, who hold δωμάτιον to be correct, cf. Poll.1.79, Phryn.227. 2. *grave*, *IG*14. 464 (Catana). 3. *nursery*, ἐν κ. εἶναι to be an infant, minor, Just. *Nov*.155 *Praef*. II. *landing-place*, *Stad*.128.

κοιτωνιάρχης, ου, ὁ, *chamberlain*, Tz.*H*.6.486.

κοιτων-ικός, ή, όν, *for a bedroom*, κλίνη *Gloss*. II. Subst. **κοιτωνική**, ἡ, *bed-cover*, *Ostr*.in *Sammelb*.4292 (written -ονική). **-ιον**, τό, Dim. of κοιτών, *Stud.Pal*.20.67.32, Sch.Ar.*Lys*.160. **-ίσκος**, ὁ, = foreg., Artem.4.46, Procop.*Aed*.1.3. **-ίτης** [ῑ], ου, ὁ, *chamberlain*, Arr.*Epict*.1.30.7, Gal.14.624, *POxy*.471.84 (ii A.D.); κ. Καίσαρος *IG*14.1664.

κοιτωνοφύλαξ [ῠ], ακος, ὁ, *guardian of the bed-chamber*, Apion ap. Hsch. s.v. θαλαμηπόλος.

κοιφί, v. κῦφι. **κοιφόν**· κοῖλον, Hsch. (i.e. κυφόν).

κοκάλια (vv. ll. **κοκκάλια, κωκάλια**), ων, τά, small shell-fish like a periwinkle, Arist.*HA*528^{a}9.

κόκκᾰλος, ὁ, *kernel of the* στρόβιλος, Hp.*Acut*.(*Sp*.)30, 34; = κῶνος, Gal.15.848, cf. 12.55; coupled with ὀστρακίς, Ath.3.126a; = Κνίδιος κόκκος, Dsc.ap.Gal.19.113.

κοκκάριον, τό, Dim. of κόκκος III, *pill*, Ruf.ap.Orib.8.47.11 (pl.).

κοκκηρός, ά, όν, *made from* κόκκος II, πορφύρα *Edict.Diocl*.24.8.

κοκκίζω, *pick the kernel out of fruit*, κοκκιεῖς ῥόαν A.*Fr*.363, Ar.*Fr*. 610.

κοκκῑνίζω, *to be scarlet*, Sch.Opp.*H*.3.25, 5.271.

κοκκῐνο-βαφής, ές, = κοκκοβαφής, Callix.2:—also **-βαφος**, ον, Sch. rec.Pi.*O*.6.66. **-ειδής**, ές, *like the scarlet berry*, Sch.Theoc.7.58.

κόκκ-ῐνος, η, ον, *scarlet*, Herod.6.19, *Ep.Hebr*.9.19, *PHamb*.10.24

(ii A. D.), Plu.*Fab.*15; κ. γενόμενος *blushing*, *Com.Adesp.*19.3 D. II. Subst. κόκκινα, τά, *scarlet clothes*, ἐν κ. περιπατεῖν, κ. φορεῖν, Arr.*Epict.* 3.22.10, 4.11.34; -ων βαφαί *PHolm.*21.41: sg., Lxx *Ex.*25.4. -ίον, τό, Dim. of κόκκος I, Dsc.3.55 (interpol.); χαμαιμήλων Philotim.ap. Orib.5.33.7. 2. Dim. of κόκκος III, *pill*, Gal.12.496, Alex.Trall. 5.4. -ίς, ίδος, ἡ, = αἴγειρος, Hsch. II. in pl., *scarlet slippers*, Herod.7.61.

κοκκο-άξ· κορώνη, Hsch. **-βάρη**· γλαῦξ, Id. **-βᾰφής**, ές, *scarlet-dyed*, *scarlet*, Thphr.*HP*3.7.5, Ael.*NA*17.38, Philostr.*Im.*2. 5. **-βᾰφία**, ἡ, *scarlet raiment*, Id.*VA*4.21. **-βόας**, v. κοκκυβόας. **-δαφνον**, τό, *laurel berry*, Paul.Aeg.3.28. **-θραύστης**, ου, ὁ, glossed ὄρνις ποιός, perh. *grosbeak*, Hsch. **-λάχανον**, *maccum*, *Gloss.* **-λέκτης**, ου, ὁ, *gatherer of grains* (cf. sq.), *PLond.*1821. 225. **-λογέω**, *sift grains* of weeds from wheat, *POxy.*1031.16 (iii A. D.); = Lat. *racemor*, Dosith.p.432 K., *Gloss.* **-μαν**, τό, v. κουκούμιον.

κοκκόνοι· οἱ πυρῆνες τῶν ἐλαιῶν, Hsch.

κοκκο-ποιόν· κοκκοβαφές, Hsch. **-ριζον**, τό, name of a *drug*, *Hippiatr.*2.

κόκκος, ὁ, *grain*, *seed*, as of the pomegranate, *h.Cer.*372, 412, Hdt. 4.143, Hermipp.36, Hp.*Mul.*1.37, *PTeb.*273.47 (ii/iii A. D.); κ. Βαβυλώνιος Philostr.*Ep.*54; of the poppy, Euphro 11.11; of the pine, *IG* 14.966.12; of wheat, Philum.*Ven.*3.3; of weeds in corn, *PLond.*5. 1697.13 (vi A. D.); cf. Κνίδιος: metaph., νόου δέ μοι οὐκ ἔνι κ. not *a grain* of sense, Timo 66.3. 2. a measure, Dsc.2.166, Orib.*Fr.* 35. II. '*berry*' (*gall*) *of kermes oak*, used to dye scarlet, Thphr. *HP*3.7.3, Gal.12.32: hence, *scarlet* (the colour), Dromo 1.4, *PHolm.* 22.1. 2. κ. or κ. βαφική, ἡ, *kermes oak*, *Quercus coccifera*, Dsc.4. 48, Paus.10.36.1. III. *pill*, Alex.Trall.5.4. IV. in pl., *testicles*, *AP*12.222 (Strat.). 2. *pudenda muliebria*, Hsch.

κοκκούμιον, v. κουκούμιον. **κοκκοχλύζειν**· συλλαβίζειν, Hsch.

κόκκῡ, *cuckoo!* the bird's cry, Ar.*Av.*505; as an exclam., *now! quick!* (ταχύ Suid.), κόκκυ, πεδίονδε ib.507; κόκκυ, μεθεῖτε *quick*—let go, Id.*Ra.*1384; οὐδὲ κ., = οὐδὲ βραχύ, *AB*105. (Onomatop.)

κοκκύαι, οἱ, v. κοκύαι.

κοκκυβόας ὄρνις, *cock*, '*chanticleer*', S.*Fr.*791 (κοκκο- codd. Eust.).

κοκκυγ-έα, ἡ, *wig-tree*, *Rhus Cotinus*, cj. in Thphr.*HP*3.16.6, cf. Plin.*HN*13.121:—but **κοκκυγία**· ἀνεμώνη (Croton.), Hsch. **-ῖνος**, η, ον, *purple-red*, and **-όω**, *dye red*, Id. s. v. κεκοκκυγωμένον.

κοκκύζω, Dor. -ύσδω Theoc.7.124: pf. κεκόκκῡκα Ar.*Ec.*31: (κόκκυ):—*cry cuckoo*, Hes.*Op.*486; also of the cock, *crow*, Cratin.311, Pl.Com.209, Diph.65, Hyp.*Fr.*262 S.; Μοισᾶν ὄρνιχες ποτὶ Χῖον ἀοιδὸν ἀντία κοκκύζοντες Theoc.7.48, cf. Arist.*HA*631^{b}9, Poll.5.89. II. *cry like a cuckoo* or *cock*, *give a signal by such cry*, Ar.*Ra.*1380, *Ec.*31.

κοκκῡ-μηλέα, ἡ, *plum-tree*, *Prunus domestica*, Arar.20, Thphr. *HP*3.6.4, Dsc.1.121, Gal.12.32; κ. περὶ τὴν Θηβαΐδα *sebesten*, *Cordia Myxa*, Thphr.*HP*4.2.10. **-μηλον**, τό, *plum*, Archil.173, Hippon. 81, Alex.272.5, Thphr.*HP*1.10.10, Gal.6.613. **-μηλος**, ὁ, = -μηλέα, Com. (fort. Arar.20) ap.Poll.1.232. **-μηλών**, ῶνος, ὁ, *plum-orchard*, *Gloss.*

κόκκυξ, ῡγος, ὁ, *cuckoo*, Hes.*Op.*486, Epich.164, Ar.*Av.*504, Arist. *HA*563^{b}14, 618^{a}8; sacred to Hera, Paus.2.17.4; ἐχειροτόνησάν με—κόκκυγές γε τρεῖς, i. e. three fellows who voted over and over again, Ar.*Ach.*598, cf. κόκκυγες· ἐπὶ ὑπονοηθέντων πλειόνων εἶναι καὶ ὀλίγων ὄντων, Hsch.; μῆλον κόκκυγος, = κοκκύμηλον, Nic.*Fr.*87. 2. *stammerer*, nickname of Battus, Sch.Pi.*P.*4.1. II. a sea-fish, *piper*, *Trigla cuculus*, said to make a sound like *cuckoo*, Hp.*Int.*21, Arist. *HA*535^{b}18, 598^{a}15, Numen.ap.Ath.7.309f, Speus.ap.eund.7.324f, Opp.*H.*1.97. III. = ὄλυνθος, a fig that ripens early, Nic.*Th.* 854. IV. Medic., *os coccygis*, Ruf.*Onom.*114, Gal.2.762; but τρητὸς κ., = the whole *os sacrum*, Poll.2.183. V. mark on a horse's shoulder, *Hippiatr.*14, 26, 115.

κόκκυς· λόφος, Hsch.

κοκκ-υσμός, ὁ, *crying cuckoo*: in men, *the sound of a very high voice*, Nicom.*Harm.*11.1, *Exc.*4 (pl.). **-υστής**, οῦ, ὁ, *crower*, *screamer*, Timo 43.1.

κόκκων, ωνος, ὁ, *pomegranate-seed*, Sol.40, Hp.*Mul.*1.37 (cf. Gal. 19.113), *Sammelb.*6779.51 (iii B. C.). II. *mistletoe-berry*, Hsch.:—Dim. **κοκκωνίδιον**, *Gloss.*

κοκκωτόν, *bacatum*, *granitum*, *Gloss.*

κοκρύδων· λῃστῶν, κλεπτῶν, Hsch. (but **κοκρύδες** = κροκύδες, Epich.181).

κοκρύνδακοι· κυλλοί, Hsch.

κοκύαι, οἱ, *ancestors*, *AP*9.312 (Zonas): fem., Call.*Fr.anon.*37 (v. l. κοκκ-).

κόκχος, ὁ, perh. = Lat. *coculum*, *PHamb.*10.36 (ii A. D.).

κολαβρ-εύομαι, = sq., Hsch. **-ίζω**, *dance a wild Thracian dance*, Id.: **-ισμός**, ὁ, name of such dance, Ath.14.629d (καλαβρ- codd.), Poll.4.100. II. Pass., *to be derided*, Lxx *Jb.*5.4. **-ος**, ὁ, *a song to which the* κολαβρισμός *was danced*, Ath.4.164e, Demetr. Sceps.ap.eund.15.697c. II. *young pig*, Hsch., Suid.

κολάζω, fut. κολάσω And.1.136, Lys.31.29, X.*Cyr.*7.5.8, Pl.*Lg.* 714d, etc.: aor. ἐκόλασα Ar.*V.*927, Th.3.40:—Med., fut. κολάσομαι Theopomp.Com.27, X.*HG*1.7.19; twice contr. in Ar., 2 sg. κολᾷ *Eq.*456, part. κολωμένους *V.*244: aor. ἐκολασάμην Th.6.78, Pl.*Mx.* 240d:—Pass., fut. -ασθήσομαι Th.2.87, etc.: aor. ἐκολάσθην Id.7. 68: pf. κεκόλασμαι Antipho 3.4.8, D.20.139:—*check*, *chastise*, τὰς ἐπιθυμίας Pl.*Grg.*491e; τὸ πλεονάζον Plu.2.663e, etc.; τὴν ἀμετρίαν Gal.6.29:—Pass., *to be corrected*, τὸ ἐν μέλιτι χολῶδες -άζεται Hp. *Acut.*59, cf. X.*Oec.*20.12: pf. part. Pass., *chastened*, εὐπειθὲς καὶ κεκολ. Arist.*EN*1119^{b}12; δίαιτα Luc.*Herm.*86; ῥήτωρ κεκ. Poll.6. 149; ἰσχὺς κ. ἐς ῥυθμοὺς Philostr.*VS*1.17.3; also of an athlete, ἀπέριττος τὰ μυώδη καὶ μὴ κεκ. Id.*Gym.*31. 2. *chastise*, *punish*, τινα E.*Ba.*1322, Ar.*Nu.*7, etc.; τὰ σέμν' ἔπη κόλαζ' ἐκείνους *use* your proud words *in reproving* them, S.*Aj.*1108: c. dat. modi, λόγοις κ. τινά ib.1160; θανάτῳ E.*Hel.*1172, Lys.28.3; πληγαῖς, τιμωρίαις, Pl. *Lg.*784d, Isoc.1.50; ἀτιμίαις Pl.*Plt.*309a:—Med., *get* a person *punished*, Ar.*V.*406, Pl.*Prt.*324c, v. l. X.*Cyr.*1.2.7:—Pass., *to be punished*, etc., Antipho 3.3.7, X.*Cyr.*5.2.1, etc.; of divine *retribution*, Plu.2.566e; *suffer injury*, Ael.*NA*3.24. 3. of a drastic method of checking the growth of the almond-tree, Thphr.*HP*2.7.6:—Pass., Id.*CP*1.18.9; cf. κόλασις I. 4. Pass. c. gen., *to be badly in need of*, *PFay.*120.5 (i/ii A. D.), cf. 115.19 (ii A. D.), *BGU*249.4 (ii A. D.).

Κολαινίς, ίδος, ἡ, obscure epith. of Artemis, Hellanic.163 J., Ar. *Av.*874, Metag.1, *IG*3.216, Paus.1.31.5.

κολᾰκ-εία, ἡ, *flattery*, *fawning*, Democr.268, Pl.*R.*590b, *Grg.*463c, 465b, Thphr.*Char.*2, etc.; πολλὴν κολακείαν πεποίηται Aeschin.3.162, cf. Cic.*Att.*13.27.1; περὶ κολακείας, title of treatise by Phld. **-ευμα**, ατος, τό, *piece of flattery*, X.*Oec.*13.12 (pl.), Plu.*Demetr.*17. II. of a person, Sch.S.*Aj.*381. **-ευτέος**, α, ον, *to be flattered*, Luc.*Merc. Cond.*38, etc. II. -ευτέον, *one must flatter*, Ap.Ty.*Ep.*7, Sch.rec.A. *Th.*705. **-ευτής**, οῦ, ὁ, = κόλαξ, *Gloss.* **-ευτικός**, ή, όν, *sycophantic*, Luc.*Cal.*10; ἡ -κή (sc. τέχνη), = κολακεία, Pl.*Grg.*464c; κ. τέχναι Phld.*Lib.*p.42 O.: Sup., Gal.10.4. Adv. -κῶς Str.17.1.43 (v.l. κολακικῶς), Poll.4.51, Charito 8.4. **-εύω**, *to be a flatterer*, Ar.*Eq.*48, Pl.*R.*538b, *Grg.*521b, Antiph.144.2, Diod.Com.2.34, Phld.*Ir.*p.66 W. 2. c. acc., *flatter*, And.4.16, X.*HG*5.1.17, Isoc.4.155, Ephipp.6, etc.; τὴν πόλιν Pl.*Alc.*1.120b: metaph., τὴν κατάποσιν κ. Muson.*Fr.*18^{A}p.97 H.:—Pass., *to be flattered*, *be open to flattery*, Democr.115, D.8.34, etc. 3. metaph., *soften*, *render mild*, Alex. Trall.1.11, al. **-ικός**, ή, όν, = κολακευτικός, Arist.*EE*1222^{b}4: ἡ -κή (sc. τέχνη), = κολακεία, Pl.*Grg.*502d, *Sph.*222e: Comp. -ώτερος Luc.*Pr.Im.*22: Sup. -ώτατος, πρὸς τοὺς ὑπερέχοντας Plb.13.4.5. Adv. -κῶς Poll.4.51, Aristaenet.1.16, Chor. in *Rh.Mus.*49.521, v.l. in Str. 17.1.43. **-ίς**, ίδος, ἡ, fem. of κόλαξ; then, = κλιμακίς 2, Clearch. 25, Plu.2.50d.

Κολᾰκοφωροκλείδης, ου, ὁ, *flattering son of a thief*, parody on the name of Hierocleides, Hermipp.38, Phryn.Com.17.

Κολᾰκώνῠμος, ὁ, *parasite-named*, Com. distortion of the name Kleonymos, Ar.*V.*592.

κόλαξ, ᾰκος, ὁ, *flatterer*, *fawner*, Ar.*Pax*756, Lys.28.4, Pl.*Phdr.* 240b, etc.; τύχης κόλακες Antipho Soph.65; πάντες οἱ κ. θητικοὶ καὶ οἱ ταπεινοὶ κ. Arist.*EN*1125^{a}1, cf. 1108^{a}29, Thphr.*Char.*2.1; *parasite*, Eup.159.1, Antisth.ap.D.L.6.4. 2. in later Gr., = Att. γόης, Moer. p.113 P. II. lisping pronunciation of κόραξ, Ar.*V.*45.

κολαπ-τήρ, ῆρος, ὁ, *chisel*, *IG*11(2).199*A* 86 (Delos, iii B. C.), 7.3073. 132 (Lebad.), Plu.2.350d, Luc.*Somn.*13. **-τός**, ή, όν, *engraved*, κ. γράμμα *an inscription*, *Sammelb.*5629 (Egypt, iii B. C.). **-τω**, of birds, *peck*, κολάψασα ἐξέλεψεν τὸν νεοσσόν, of a hen, Hp.*Nat.Puer.*30; κ. τὰ ἕλκη, τὰ ὄμματα, Arist.*HA*609^{a}35, ^{b}6; τὸ ἧπαρ, of the eagle and Prometheus, Luc.*Sacr.*6 codd.; τινα, of a crane, *AP*11.369 (Jul. Antec.): metaph., of a man, ᾠὰ κ. Anaxil.18.4; of rain-drops breaking up the soil, Thphr.*Fr.*30.2; of horses, *strike* with the hoof, App. *Pun.*129; of Pegasos, *produce by striking* the ground with his hoof, κρήνην *AP*15.25.19 (Besant.). 2. *carve*, *engrave*, γράμμα εἰς αἴγειρον ib.9.341 (Glauc.); τὸ δόγμα κολαφθὲν εἰς στάλαν *IG*14.256 (Phintias), cf. 952 (Acragas), Πολέμων 1.30 (Demetrias), Luc.*Dips.*6, *PLeid.X.*36.

κόλ-ᾰσις, εως, ἡ, *checking the growth* of trees, esp. almond-trees, Thphr.*CP*3.18.2 (pl.). 2. *chastisement*, *correction*, Hp.*Praec.*5, Pl.*Ap.*26a, al., Th.1.41; opp. τιμωρία, Arist.*Rh.*1369^{b}13; of divine *retribution*, *Ev.Matt.*25.46, al.: pl., Pl.*Prt.*323e, al., Phld.*Ir.*p.52 W. **-ασμα**, ατος, τό, *chastisement*, Ar.*Fr.*385, X.*Cyr.*3.1.23, Critias 25.4 D., *AP*5.217.7 (Agath.). **-ασμός**, ὁ, = κόλασις, Plu. *Alc.*13, al.

κολασσία· ἀνδριάντος σκιά, καὶ τὸ ἐς ὕψος ἀνάστημα, Hsch.

κολ-άστειρα, ἡ, fem. of κολαστήρ, *AP*7.425 (Antip. Sid.). **-αστέος**, α, ον, *to be chastised*, *punished*, Pl.*Grg.*527b. II. κολαστέον, *one must prune*, *check*, τὰς ἐπιθυμίας ib.492d. **-αστήρ**, ῆρος, ὁ, = κολαστής, Arr.*Fr.*144 J.: as Adj., στρατιῶται Eun.*VS*p.480 B. **-αστήριος**, ον, = κολαστικός, δύναμις Ph.1.269, al. II. Subst. κολαστήριον, τό, *house of correction*, Luc.*Nec.*14, *VH*2.30. 2. *instrument of correction*, κολαστήρια θαλάσσης, of the whips of Xerxes, Plu.2.342f. 3. = κόλασμα, X.*Mem.*1.4.1. **-αστής**, οῦ, ὁ, *chastiser*, *punisher*, Ζεύς τοι κ. τῶν ὑπερκόπων ἄγαν φρονημάτων A.*Pers.*827, cf. S.*OT*1148, E. *Heracl.*388, Pl.*Lg.*863a, Epicur.*Sent.*34, Phld.*Mort.*17, etc.; κ. τῶν ἀδικούντων Lys.27.3, cf. Gorg.*Fr.*6; νόμοι κ. Critias 25.6 D.; *tormentor*, in Hades, Plu.2.567d (pl.). **-αστικός**, ή, όν, *corrective*, *punitive*, -κή, ἡ, Pl.*Sph.*229a; δύναμις Ph.1.496; τὸ -κόν Plu.2.458b; τὸ κ. εἶδος Luc.*Phal.*1.8: c. gen., φάρμακα κ. τῆς κακίας Gal.14.760. 2. *given to punishing*, Jul.*Caes.*312d. **-άστρια**, ἡ, fem. of κολαστήρ, ῥάβδος Ezek.*Exag.*121.

κολάττη· κόλακα, Hsch. (perh. Boeot. for κολάσαι).

κολᾰφ-ίζω, *slap*, *buffet*, τινα *Ev.Matt.*26.67, *Sammelb.*6263.23:—Pass., 1*Ep.Cor.*4.11. **-ος**, ὁ, (κολάπτω) *buffet*, = κόνδυλος, Epich. 1 (as pr. n.), cf. Hsch., *Gloss.*; cf. Lat. *colaphus*.

κόλαψ, *stirps*, *Gloss.*

κολέα, ἡ, name of a *dance*, Hsch.:—also **κολία**, Id. **κολεάζω**, *sheathe*: **-ασμός**, ὁ, *sheathing*, Id.:—also **-αρχος**· κακόσχολον ὄνομα, Id. **κολεῖν**· ἐλθεῖν, Id.

κολεκάνος or **κολοκάνος**, ὁ, *lank, lean person*, dub. in Stratt.64.

κολεόν, Ep. and Lyr. usu. **κουλεόν**, τό, *sheath, scabbard*, ἕλκετο δ' ἐκ κολεοῖο μέγα ξίφος Il.1.194; κολεῷ μὲν ἄορ θέο Od.10.333; ἂψ δ' ἐς κουλεὸν ὦσε μέγα ξίφος Il.1.220; ξίφεος μέγα κουλεόν 3.272; ἀτὰρ περὶ κουλεὸν ἦεν ἀργύρεον 11.30, cf. Od.11.98, Pi.*N.*10.6; κολεῶν ἐρυστὰ..ξίφη S.*Aj.*730; φάσγανον κώπης λαβὼν ἐξεῖλκε κολεοῦ E.*Hec.*544; ἐν κολεῷ X.*Cyr.*1.2.9; μάχαιρα ἐλεφάντινον τὸ κολεὸν (sic) ἔχουσα *IG*2^2.1382.16 (κολεόν ib.1388.47); κολεὰ δύο ib.11(2).203*B*39 (Delos, iii B.C.); κ., μέγα λώτινον ἔργον Theoc.24.45. 2. in insects, *sheath, wing-case*, Arist.*HA*531^{b}24.

κολεόπτερος, ον, *sheath-winged*, of beetles, Arist.*HA*490^{a}14, al.

κολεός, ὁ, = κολεόν, Hecat.22 J., Hsch., *Gloss.*; also, = λάρναξ, ὑδρία, Hsch. 2. v. κολιός. II. in form **κουλεός**, ὁ, *sheath of the heart, pericardium*, Hp.*Cord.*3.

κολεοφόροι, οἱ, *sheath-bearers*, name of a Comedy, *IG*14.1097.

κόλερος, α, ον, (κόλος, ἔρος B) *short-wooled*, οἶες Arist.*HA*596^{b}5. 2. κολερά· νόθα, νωθρά, Hsch. (Accent varies in codd.; κόλερον Theognost.*Can.*131.)

κολετράω, *trample on*, τινα Ar.*Nu.*552.

κοληβάζω, = ἐγκοληβάζω, Hsch. **κολία**, v. κολέα.

κολίανδρον, τό, = κορίανδρον, *Gp.*12.1.2, 16.4.5, Sch.Ar.*Eq.*679.

κολίας, ου, ὁ, *coly-mackerel, Scomber colias*, Epich.62, Ar.*Fr.*414, Arist.*HA*598^{a}24, Opp.*H.*1.184.

κολίδιον, τό, Dim. of foreg., Xenocr.ap.Orib.2.58.152.

κολιός, ὁ, *green woodpecker, Picus viridis*, Arist.*HA*593^{a}8, al. (vv. ll. κολεός, κελεός).

κόλλᾰ, ης, ἡ, *glue*, Hdt.2.86, Hp.*Art.*33, Arist.*Ph.*227^{a}17, *IG*2^2.1672.68. 2. *flour-paste*, Dsc.2.85.

κολλαβίζω, play a game, in which one holds his eyes, while the other strikes him, and bids him guess which hand he has been struck with, Poll.9.129.

κόλλᾰβος, ὁ, = κόλλοψ, Luc.*DDeor.*7.4, Iamb.*VP*26.118 (pl.). II. kind of *cake* or *roll* (cf. κόλλυβος I.3), Ar.*Ra.*507, *Pax* 1196, *Fr.*497, 506, Philyll.4.

κολλάριον, = Lat. *collarium*, *Gloss.*

κολλ-άω, (κόλλα) *glue, cement*, τι περὶ τὸν τράχηλον, τι πρός τι, Pl.*Ti.*75d, 82d; ἐπιστύλια ἐπὶ τοὺς κίονας *IG*2^2.1668.46; *mend* a broken vessel, ib.11(2).161*A*111 (Delos, iii B.C.), *POxy.*1449.15 (iii A.D.). 2. *join* one metal or other substance to another, κ. χρυσὸν ἔν τε λευκὸν ἐλέφαντα, i.e. *make* [a crown] *inlaid with* gold and ivory, Pi.*N.*7.78:—Pass., κολλώμενα *glued together*, opp. γομφούμενα, Ar.*Eq.*463; ὁ κολλώμενος σίδηρος *welded* iron, Plu.2.619a; στραγγαλὶς χρυσᾶ κεκολλημένη *POxy.*1449.23 (iii A.D.). II. generally, *join fast together, unite*, ἄλφιτον ὕδατι Emp.34; χαλκὸν ἐπ' ἀνέρι κολλᾶν, of one applying a cupping-glass, Cleobulina 1, cf. Gal.*Thras.*23; *close up* wounds, Id.11.440:—Pass., κολλέεσθαι, of poison entering the system, Hp.*Ep.*19 (*Hermes* 53.66); κολλᾷ καὶ συνδεῖ πάντα ἤθη [ὁ πόθος] Pl.*Lg.*776a:—Pass., *cleave to*, κεκόλληται γένος πρὸς ἄτᾳ *is indissolubly bound* to.. (Blomf. for προσάψαι), A.*Ag.*1566 (lyr.); λόγος εἰς τὰ σπλάγχνα κολληθεὶς Philem.113.4; of persons, κ. τινί *Act.Ap.*5.13; of things, ὁ κονιορτὸς ὁ κολληθείς τινι *Ev.Luc.*10.11: sens. obsc., *AP*11.73 (Nicarch.). III. *put together, build*, Pi.*O.*5.13:—Med., *fit together*, τροχάλεια Arat.530. **-εψός**, οῦ, ὁ, (κόλλα, ἕψω) *glue-boiler*, *IG*2^2.1558.10, Poll.7.183.

κολλήγ-ας, α, ὁ, = Lat. *collega*, *IG*14.1063 (nisi n. pr.): gen. pl., *Sammelb.*7252.25. **-ιον**, τό, = Lat. *collegium*, D.C.38.13, *IGRom.*1.1314 (Egypt), etc.

κολλ-ήεις, εσσα, εν, (κόλλα) *glued together, close-joined*, ξυστά Il.15.389, cf. 678; ἅρματα Hes.*Sc.*309. **-ημα**, ατος, τό, (κολλάω) *that which is glued* or *fastened together*, Hp.*Art.*33, *IG*11(2).287*B*152 (Delos, iii B.C.); βυβλιδίου κ. Antiph.162; esp. of the *sheets of papyrus gummed together* to form a roll, *PMag.Par.*1.2068, 2513, *BGU*16.9 (ii A.D.), etc. II. hymenic *obstruction*, Aët.16.108 (98). **-ήσιμος**, η, ον, *glued together*, prob. in *Gloss.*; Subst. **-μον**, τό, *volume of* κολλήματα, *Stud.Pal.*1.28.8 (iii A.D.). **-ησις**, εως, ἡ, (κολλάω) *gluing*, Hp.*Art.*39, Gal.18(1).456, Thphr.*HP*5.7.4; *soldering*, κ. σιδήρου Hdt.1.25, Plu.2.156b; κ. χρυσίου Thphr.*Lap.*26; σωλήνων *POxy.*915 (vi A.D.). II. generally, *fixing tight, close fastening*, Hp.*Art.*33; of the cupping-glass, Arist.*Rh.*1405^{b}3. b. *closing up* of wounds, Heliod.ap.Orib.45.6.2, Gal.11.440, 12.102. c. *binding material*, ἡ πρὸς ἄλληλα κ. ἰχώρ ἐστι καὶ ὑγρότης μυξώδης Arist.*Spir.*485^{a}1. 2. Rhet., *union of a verse quotation with prose*, Hermog.*Meth.*30. 3. metaph., *close friendship*, Eun.*Hist.*p.267 D. 4. Astron., *apparent contact* of planet with fixed star, Ptol.*Alm.*8.4 (pl.); of two planets on the same meridian, Vett.Val.115.17. **-ητέον**, *one must fasten on, apply*, δρώπακα Philum.ap.Orib.45.29.18; σικύαν Herod.Med. in *Rh.Mus.*58.81. **-ητήρ**, ῆρος, ὁ, *soldering-iron*, *Gloss.* **-ητήριον**, τό, *glue*, Ph.*Bel.*77.50, *Gloss.* **-ητής**, οῦ, ὁ, *one who glues* or *fastens*, *PTeb.*316.70 (i A.D.), *Sammelb.*805 (iii A.D.), *Gloss.* **-ητικός**, ή, όν, *glutinous*, Arist.*Pr.*928^{a}5 (Comp.), Plu.2.952b; δύναμις κ. τραυμάτων *closing up* wounds, Dsc.3.85; κ. φάρμακον Gal.11.439; κ. ἔργα *plumber's* work, *PLond.*3.1177.283 (ii A.D.): Dor. **κολλᾱτικόν**, τό, = κόλλα, *IG*4^2(1).102.69 (Epid.).

κολλητίωνες, οἱ, *military police-agents*, *POxy.*1100.19 (iii A.D.), Keil-Premerstein *Dritter Bericht* Nos.9, 28, 55.

κολλ-ητός, ή, όν, *glued together, closely joined*, θύραι, σανίδες, Od.23.194, 21.164; ἅρμα, δίφρος, ξυστόν, Il.4.366, 19.395, 15.678; ὄχοι E.*Hipp.*1225; ὕδασι καὶ γῇ κ. Pl.*Plt.*279e; ὑποκρητηρίδιον *with figures welded* on, Hdt.1.25, cf. Paus.10.16.1. **-ητρα**, τά, *cost of plumber's labour*, *POxy.*736.91 (i A.D.). **-ίζω**, late form for κολλάω, *Gp.*4.14.1.

κολλίκιον [λῐ], τό, Dim. of κόλλιξ, Greg.Cor.p.549 S.

κολλίκιος [λῐ], α, ον, *κόλλιξ-shaped*, ἄρτοι Ath.3.112f.

κολλῑκοφάγος [ᾰ], ον, *roll-eating*, epith. of Boeotians, Ar.*Ach.*872, prob. in Ephipp.1.

κόλλιξ, ῑκος, ὁ, *roll* or *loaf of coarse bread*, Hippon.35.6, Nicopho 15; κ. Θεσσαλικός Archestr.*Fr.*4.12. II. Medic., = τροχίσκος, rubbed up and taken in wine, Hp.*Int.*23, cf. Gal.19.103; = κολλύριον I.1, Hp.*Epid.*2.6.29.

κολλιστής, = κολλητής, *Gloss.*

κολλοβάλοισι, dat. pl., dub. sens. in *Tab.Defix.* in *Rh.Mus.*55.85 (Crete, iii B.C.).

κολλομελέω, *patch verses together*, Com. word, Ar.*Th.*54.

κολλοπ-εύω, *to be a* κόλλοψ II.2, Pl.Com.186.5. **-ίζω**, (κόλλοψ I.1) *tighten with screws*, Hsch.

κολλοποδιώκτης, ου, ὁ, (κόλλοψ II.2) Com. name for a gross debauchee, Sch.Ar.*Nu.*347, Eust.1915.16, Suid. s.v. ἀγρίους.

κολλοπόω, *glue together*, because glue was boiled out of κόλλοψ II.1, Achae.22, *EM*323.22.

κολλοπώλης, ου, ὁ, (κόλλα) *dealer in glue*, Poll.7.183.

κολλόροβον, τό, *shepherd's staff* or *crook*, *BGU*759.13 (ii A.D., written κολλωρ-); applied to the so-called *club* of Orion and Bootes (which has this form), Hipparch.1.7.15, 2.6.1^b, Ptol.*Alm.*7.5, 8.1. II. masc. and neut., dub. sens., apptly. a weight or a coin, *Sammelb.*6954. III. pl., v.l. for κιλλοβόροι in Poll.1.143. IV. κολόροβοι, gloss on σκοιά, Hsch.; κολόροβον, gloss on κορύνη, Id.

κολλούρ-α, ἡ, *roll* or *loaf* of bread (?), *PLond.ined.*2172; cf. κολλύρα. **-ιον**, τό, Dim. of foreg., *POxy.*1731.8 (iii A.D.). II. v. κολλύριον.

κολλουρίς, ίδος, ἡ, *marsh-mallow*, *Gloss.*

κόλλουρος, ὁ, an unknown *fish*, Marc.Sid.22.

κόλλοψ, οπος, ὁ, *peg* or *screw* by which the strings of the lyre were tightened, Od.21.407, cf. Pl.*R.*531b, Luc.*DMar.*1.4: metaph., τῆς ὀργῆς..τὸν κόλλοπ' ἀνεῖμεν Ar.*V.*574. 2. *bar* by which a windlass was turned, Arist.*Mech.*852^{b}12. II. *thick skin on the upper part of the neck* of oxen, Ar.*Fr.*646; and of swine, ib.506.3. 2. metaph., = ἀνδρόγυνος, *cinaedus*, Eub.11, Diph.43.22, *AP*12.42 (Diosc.), cf. Hsch.

κολλῠβάτεια, v. κουλυβάτεια.

κολλῠβ-ιστήριον, τό, *money-changer's office*, *PTeb.*485 (ii B.C.). **-ιστής**, οῦ, ὁ, *small money-changer*, Lys.*Fr.*149 S., Men.1023, *PPetr.*3p.173 (prob. l.), *Ev.Matt.*21.12, etc.: condemned by Phryn.404. **-ιστικός**, ή, όν, *of a money-changer*, τράπεζα *Ostr.Strassb.*9 (iii B.C.), *BGU*1118.23 (i B.C.), etc. **-ος**, ὁ, *small coin*, κολλύβου *for a doit*, Ar.*Pax* 1200, Eup.233, Call.*Fr.*85: masc. acc. to Phryn.404, Hsch.:—but neut. **κόλλῠβον**, τό, Poll.9.72. 2. *small gold weight*, Thphr.*Lap.*46. 3. neut. pl. κόλλυβα, τά, *small cakes* (cf. κόλλαβος II), Sch.Ar.*Pl.*768; cf. κόλλυβα· τρωγάλια, Hsch. II. κ., ὁ, *rate of exchange*, *IG*12(5).817 (pl., Tenos, ii B.C.), *SIG*672.32 (Delph., ii B.C.); *agio*, Cic.*Verr.*2.3.78.181, *Att.*12.6.1, *PFay.*56.7 (ii A.D.), etc. (Cf. Hebr. *ḥālap* 'change', 'exchange'.)

κολλύρ-α [ῡ], ἡ, prob. = κόλλιξ I, Ar.*Pax* 123, *Fr.*413, Plaut.*Poen.*137, Lxx 2*Ki.*13.6, *POxy.*397 (i A.D.), Ath.3.111a; cf. κολλούρα. 2. used of τὰ ἐκ τέφρας πεπλασμένα (cf. κόλλιξ II), Thphr.ap.Hsch. **-ίζω**, *bake* κολλῦραι, Lxx 2*Ki.*13.6. **-ικός**, ή, όν, *made of* κολλῦραι, *jus collyricum*, Plaut.*Pers.*95. **-ιον** [ῡ], τό, Dim. of κολλύρα, *pessary*, Hp.*Mul.*1.51 (in form **κολλούριον**), Dsc.1.1; used as substitute for a probe, Cels.7.4.4; *pellet*, *PHolm.*1.16, *PLeid.X.*69. 2. *eye-salve*, *Apoc.*3.18, *IG*14.966.16 (ii A.D.), *PFlor.*177.20 (iii A.D.); stamped with the physician's seal, *CIL*13.10021.64, al.: freq. in pl., Arr.*Epict.*2.21.20, 3.21.21, etc.; *salve* in general, *POxy.*1088 (sg. and pl., i A.D.):—on κ. I.1 and I.2, Antyll.ap.Orib.10.23.1–19. 3. = κολλύρα I, Lxx 3*Ki.*12.24. II. *fine clay on which a seal can be impressed*, Luc.*Alex.*21. (Freq. written κολλούριον, as Hp. l.c. (v.l.), *PHolm.*, *PLeid.X.*, *PFlor.* ll. cc.)

κολλῡριοποιέομαι, *to be made into collyrium*, Dsc.*Eup.*1.197 (-λουρ-).

κολλῡρίς, ίδος, ἡ, Dim. of κολλύρα, Lxx 2*Ki.*6.19, v.l. 13.6.

κολλῡρίων, ωνος, ὁ, a bird of the *thrush* kind, perh. *fieldfare*, *Turdus pilaris*, Arist.*HA*617^{b}9.

κολλῡρόω, in pf. part. Pass., κεκολλυρωμένον· λευκῷ κεχρισμένον, Hsch. (-όμενον cod.). **κολλύχνιον**· καρύου λέπισμα, Id.

κολλώδης, ες, *glutinous, viscous*, Pl.*Cra.*427b, Arist.*HA*568^{b}11, 623^{b}30 (Sup.), Thphr.*CP*5.16.4, Heraclid.Tarent.ap.Ath.3.120c, Aret.*SD*1.11; of rheum in the eye, *PMed.Strassb.*p.6, Philum.*Ven.*14.2.

κολλώροβον, v. κολλόροβον.

κόλλωτες, οἱ, a kind of *stone*, Thrasyll.ap.Ps.-Plu.*Fluv.*16.2.

κολόβαξ, = κολόβιον, *Gloss.*

κολοβ-ανθής, ές, *bearing stunted* (i.e. *papilionaceous*) *flowers*, such as peas, Thphr.*HP*8.3.3:—also **κολοβοανθής**, ib.6.5.3. **-ίζω**, *mutilate*, in Pass., *IG*12(3).323 (Thera, i B.C./i A.D.). **-ιομαφόριον**, τό, *short* μαφόριον (q.v.), *Sammelb.*7033.36 (v A.D.). **-ιον**, τό, *sleeveless* (or *short-sleeved*) *tunic*, *POxy.*921.6, 16 (iii A.D.), *PTeb.*406.17 (iii A.D.), Serv. ad Virg.*A.*9.616. 2. of the senatorial *clavus*, Ps.-Acro ad Hor.*Sat.*1.5.36.

κολοβο-διέξοδος, ον, *having a curtailed passage*, of stars whose rising and setting is invisible owing to sunrise and sunset, Ptol.*Phas.* p.8 H., al. **-κέρᾱτος**, ον, *with stunted horns, short-horned*, Sch. Il.16.117. **-κερκος**, ον, *with a docked tail*, LxxLe.22.23. **-μάχη** [ᾰ], ἡ, *the interrupted battle*, name for Il.8, Sch.B Il.8 init.; also **-μᾰχία**, ἡ, Sch.Leid.Il.13.745 in Valck.*Animadv. ad Ammon.*p.181; cf. κόλος 3. **-ρῖν**, ῖνος, ὁ, ἡ, *slit-nosed*, LxxLe.21.18: **-ρῖνος**, ον, *with broken nose*, Roussel *Cultes Égyptiens* 220 (Delos, ii B.C.).

κολοβός, όν (also -ός, ή, όν Artem.2.3, *IG*v. infr.), *docked, curtailed*, c. gen., κολοβὸς ἀγέλη κεράτων Pl.*Plt.*265d; κ. χειρῶν *APl.*4.186 (Xenocr.). 2. abs., *maimed, mutilated*, X.*Cyr.*1.4.11; οὐδὲν κ. προσφέρομεν πρὸς τοὺς θεούς, ἀλλὰ τέλεια καὶ ὅλα Arist.*Fr.*101; ζῷα κ. Id.*GA*746a9, cf. 721b17; ὄνος κ. *PCair.Zen.*215.10 (iii B.C.), *PGen.*23.5 (i A.D.), *BGU*806.4 (i A.D.); of trees, *stunted*, τὰν ἐλαίαν τὰν κολοβάν *IG*14.352 i 11 (Halaesa), cf. Dsc.1.76; ἄνθη Thphr.*HP*8.3.3; of persons, *undersized*, Procop.*Arc.*8: generally, *short*, ἐσθῆτες Artem. l.c.; χιτών Dam.*Isid.*138; ξίφος Lyd.*Mag.*1.12; of a period in Rhet., *curtailed, incomplete*, Arist.*Rh.*1409a18 (so in Comp. -ώτερόν πως ὑφᾶναι τὸν λόγον Chor. in *Philol.*54.123); ὄνομα *half-uttered*, Them.*Or.*1.4b; of a cup, *broken, chipped*, Arist.*Metaph.*1024a15, Theopomp.Hist. 243; of a wall, *dwarf*, τειχίον, τεῖχος, App.*Mith.*26, Procop.*Aed.*2.1; of a cone, *truncated*, Hero *Stereom.*2.42: metaph., ἀρετή Max.Tyr.37.1; κίνησις, in paralysis, Gal.7.588; κ. κῦμα, = κωφόν, Sch.Ar.*Eq.*689. Adv. -βῶς *elliptically*, opp. σαφῶς, ἐρωτᾶσθαι Arist.*SE*176a40. II. κολοβόν, τό, a measure, *PLond.*5.1694.22, al. (vi A.D.).

κολοβόστᾰχυς, υ, *with short spikes*, of flowers, Dsc.1.7.

κολοβότης, ητος, ἡ, *stuntedness*, Plu.2.800e (pl.). 2. κ. πνεύματος *shortness* of breath in speaking, Id.*Dem.*6.

κολοβοτράχηλος [ᾰ], ον, *stump-necked*, Adam.2.21.

κολοβοῦρος, ον, *stump-tailed*, Hsch. s.v. κόθουρος.

κολοβ-όω, *dock, curtail, mutilate*, Arist.*Fr.*101, Plb.1.80.13; τὰς χεῖρας καὶ τοὺς πόδας Lxx2Ki.4.12:—Pass., *to be mutilated, imperfect*, Arar.3, Thphr.*HP*3.6.3; τῆς γυναικὸς τὴν ῥῖνα κολοβοῦσθαι D.S.1.78; τῇ φώκῃ κεκολοβωμένοι πόδες Arist.*HA*487b23, cf. *GA*771a2: c. gen., κεκολοβῶσθαι τῶν ἐκτὸς μορίων Id.*PA*695b2. II. of Time, *curtail, shorten*, τὰς ἡμέρας *Ev.Marc.*13.20, cf. *Ev.Matt.*24.22 (Pass.). **-ώδης**, ες, *stunted, stumpy*, δάκτυλοι Polem.*Phgn.*51 (v.l.). **-ωμα**, ατος, τό, *the part taken away in mutilation*, Arist.*Metaph.*1024a13, Gal.10.1002; = ἔλλειψις μορίου, Antyll.ap.Orib.45.25.1. **-ωσις**, εως, ἡ, *mutilation*, Arist.*IA*708b8. 2. *shortening*, [χορδῶν] Iamb.*in Nic.*p.121 P.

κολοι-άρχης, ου, ὁ, *chief of jackdaws, jackdaw-general*, Ar.*Av.*1212. **-άω**, *scream like a jackdaw*, Poll.5.89. **-διον**· παραξιφίδιον, Hsch. **-δορον**· ξύλον μάχας ποιούντων ἐπεισφερόμενον (ἐπεσφαιρωμένον Salmasius), Id. **-ή**· φωνή, Id.; cf. κολῳός.

κολοιός, ὁ, *jackdaw, Corvus monedula*, Il.16.583, 17.755, Ar.*V.*129, *Av.*50, al., Thphr.*Char.*21.6, *Sign.*39, Arat.963, al., Ael.*NA*4.30, Dionys.*Av.*3.18; κραγέται κολοιοί Pi.*N.*3.82:—Arist.*HA*617b16 distinguishes three species, κορακίας, λύκος, βωμολόχος (qq.v.): he also mentions a web-footed κολοιός, found in Lydia and Phrygia, which is prob. the *little cormorant, Phalacrocorax pygmaeus*; cf. Ath.9.395e (citing Ar.*Ach.*875):—Proverbs: κολοιὸς ποτὶ κολοιόν 'birds of a feather flock together', Arist.*EN*1155a34, etc.; κολοιὸς ἀλλοτρίοις πτεροῖς ἀγάλλεται 'borrowed plumes', Luc.*Apol.*4; κύκνον ἡγοῦ τὸν κ. 'your geese are swans', Lib.*Ep.*42.3; of impudent noisy talkers, πολλοὶ .. σφε κατακρώζουσι κολοιοί Ar.*Eq.*1020; of Agathocles, Timae.145. (Cf. κολῳός, κολῳάω.)

κολοιτία, ἡ, a *tree* which grew in the Lipari islands, *Cytisus aeolicus*, Thphr.*HP*1.11.2; called **κολουτέα**, ib.3.17.2 (for 3.14.4 v. κολυτέα); **κολοιτέα**, **κολωτέα** (-οτ- cod.), **κοιλώτεα**, Hsch. II. *sallow, Salix cinerea*, found about Mount Ida, Thphr.*HP*3.17.3.

κολοίφρυξ· Ταναγραῖος ἀλεκτρυών, Hsch.

κολοιώδης, ες, *daw-like*, i.e. *flocking together*, Plu.2.93e.

κολοκάνος, ὁ, v. κολεκάνος.

κολοκάσιον [ᾰ], τό, Nic.*Fr.*82, Diph.Siph.ap.Ath.3.73a, Dsc.2.106; or **κολοκασία**, ἡ, Plin.*HN*21.87, v.l. in Dsc. l.c.:—*the root* of κύαμος Αἰγύπτιος, *Nelumbium speciosum*, ll.cc., Verg.*E.*4.20, etc. 2. Κολοκασία, surname of Athena at Sicyon, Ath.3.72b.

κολοκορδόκολα, ων, τά, Com. word, perh. = *tripe*, *AP*10.103 (Phld.).

κολόκῡμα, ατος, τό, *large heavy wave* before it breaks, *swell* that is the forerunner of a storm: metaph., of the swelling threats of Cleon, Ar.*Eq.*692 (expld. as κόλον κῦμα, Sch. ad loc.; τυφλὸν κῦμα, Hsch.; κωφὸν κῦμα, Suid.).

κολοκύνθ-η, Arist.*HA*591a16, al. (v.l. -τη), Sor.1.124, etc.; Att. **-κύντη**, ἡ (cf. Phryn.401), Thphr.1.13.3, 7.1.2, al., Mnesim.4.30 (v.l. -τα, -θα), also Hp.*Vict.*2.54; acc. -την Epicr.11.16, *PMag.Leid.V.*12.25, etc.:—later **κολόκυντᾰ** (acc. -ᾱν) *PCair.Zen.*300.3 (iii B.C.), Lxx*Jn.*4.7 cod. A, *Gp.*12.19.7, Artem.1.67 (v.l.), Luc.*VH*2.37 (v.l.), Hsch. s.v. κυκύïζα; gen. -της *PCair.Zen.*292.132, 319 (iii B.C.); acc. pl. -τας *PSI*6.553.14 (iii B.C.), *BGU*1120.13 (i B.C.); **κολόκυνθᾰ** *PSakk.* in *Rev.Égypt.*3.123 (iii B.C., also -τα ib.120, 122), Lxx l.c., Arist.*Pr.*923a14 codd., Dsc.2.134, 4.176, Luc. l.c., Hdn.Gr.1.253, v.l. for -θη (nom. sg.) in Gal.6.794, but nom. -θη, acc. -θην ib.561, al. codd.; nom. pl. -θαι *Edict.Diocl.*6.26, 27:—*round gourd, Cucurbita maxima*, Alc.*Oxy.*1788 *Fr.*4.6 (Aeol. acc. pl. -ταις), Hp.*Morb.*2.67, 69 (in acc. -θην, v.l. -την), Hermipp.79, Ar.*Fr.*569.6, Metag.16 (-θης codd.), Diocl.*Frr.*125, 141, Diph.Siph. et Mnesith.ap.Ath.2.59b; κ. Ἰνδική Menodorus ib.59a, Ph.*Bel.*89.43; κ. ἀγρία *colocynth, Citrullus Colocynthis*, Dsc. l.c.: symbolic of health, from its juicy nature, ὑγιώτερον κολοκύντας Epich.154, Sophr.34; as a lily was of death, ἢ κολοκύντην ἢ κρίνον *living* or dead, Diph.98, cf. Men.934:—for λημᾶν κολοκύνταις, v. λημάω. **-ιάς**, άδος, ἡ, *made from gourds*, βρωτὺς *AP*11.371 (Pall.). **-ινος**, η, ον, *made* or *obtained from gourds*, ἔλαιον *PRev.Laws* 39.6 (written κολυκινθ-, cf. 59.21, also κολυκυντ- 40.10, κολοκυντ- 55.9, al., iii B.C.); πλοῖα Luc.*VH*2.37:—hence Com. name **κολοκυνθο-πειρᾶταί**, οἱ, *gourd-pirates*, ibid. II. ἀμπέλου κολοκυν[θίνης], a kind of vine, *PCair.Zen.*33.14 (iii B.C.). **-ίς**, ίδος, ἡ, = κολόκυνθα ἀγρία, Dsc.4.176, Gal.12.34, al. **-ος**, ὁ, = κολοκύνθη, *AP*9.532 tit., *PLond.*5.1881 (vi A.D.); κ. ἄγριος Ps.-Dsc.4.176:—written **κολύκιντος** *PTeb.*131 (ii/i B.C.). **-ών**, ῶνος, ὁ, *gourd-patch*, *PHamb.*99.8 (i A.D.).

κολοκύντ-η, v. κολοκύνθη:—Dim. **-ιον**, τό, Phryn.Com.61. **-ινος**, v. κολοκύνθινος. **-ος**, ὁ, = κολόκυνθος, *AP*9.532.

κολοκώνας· τὰς βαλβῖδάς τινες, Hsch.

κόλον, τό, = ἡ τροφή, as etym. of κόλαξ, βουκόλος, δύσκολος and κοιλία, Ath.6.262a, copied by Eust.1817.53, 62 (who adds ἄκολος); applied to some form of preserved food in *PSI*5.535.39, 46 (iii B.C.). II. *colon*, part of the large intestine, Ar.*Eq.*455, Arist.*PA*675b7, Nic.*Al.*23, Poll.2.209. **κολόροβ-ον** and **-ος**, v. κολλόροβον IV.

κόλος, ον, *docked*, δόρυ Il.16.117; of oxen, *stump-horned* or *hornless*, τὸ γένος τῶν βοῶν τὸ κ. Hdt.4.29; ὦ κόλε, addressed to a he-goat, Theoc.8.51 (s.v.l.); of the κεράστης, Nic.*Th.*260. 2. a kind of goat *without horns*, prob. the animal described by Str.7.4.8, Hsch. 3. κόλος μάχη, name of Il.8, Sch.Il.8 init.; cf. κολοβομάχη.

Κολοσσηνός, ή, όν, *Colossian*, Str.12.8.16.

κολοσσ-ιαῖος, α, ον, *colossal*, D.S.11.72 (-ττ-), al.; κ. μεγέθη Ph.1.2; κ. τὸ μέγεθος Luc.*Herm.*71; κ. ἄγαλμα, ἀνδριάς, Hdn.1.15.9, *BGU*362 vi 5 (iii A.D.). **-ικός**, ή, όν, = foreg., εἰκών *AJA*17.29 (Sardis, i B.C.), D.S.2.34 (in form **κολοττ-**); ἔργα Str.1.1.23, cf. Plu.2.780a: generally, *enormous, gigantic*, κεφαλὴν κ. ἔχων [ἄνθρωπος] Phld.*Sign.*2.

κολοσσο-βάμων [ᾱ], ον, gen. ονος, *with colossal stride*, Lyc.615. **-ποιός**, ὁ, *maker of colossal statues*, Hero *Deff.*135.13. **-πόνος**, ὁ, = foreg., Man.4.570.

κολοσσ-ός, ὁ (also ἡ, v. infr.), **κολοττ-** D.S.1.67:—*colossus, gigantic statue*, in Hdt. always of Egyptian works, 2.130, al.; of other *colossal statues*, Thphr.*Fr.*128, Sopat.1, Plb.18.16.2, Plin.*HN*34.45, Luc.*Hist.Conscr.*23, D.C.66.15; ὁ κ. ὁ ἡμαρτημένος Longin.36.3; dub. in *IG*1².577, 12(3).1015. 2. generally, *statue*, A.*Ag.*416 (lyr.), *Schwyzer*89.17 (Argos, iii B.C.), Theoc.22.47; of small *images*, κολοσσὸς (acc. pl.), .. ἔρσενα καὶ θήλειαν ἢ καλίνος ἢ γαΐνος *Berl.Sitzb.*1927.167 (Cyrene): also fem., τὰς κ. ibid. **-ουργία**, ἡ, *making of a colossus*, Str.1.1.23.

κολοσυρτός, ὁ, poet. word, *noisy rabble*, ἀνδρῶν ἠδὲ κυνῶν Il.12.147, cf. 13.472; τὸν Ἀθηναίων Ar.*V.*666; παιδαρίων καὶ γραϊδίων Id.*Pl.*536: abs., *tumult, uproar*, Hes.*Th.*880:—hence **κολοσυρτέω**, = θορυβῶ, Hsch.

κολούλια, τά, *gasteropod molluscs*, Xenocr.ap.Orib.2.58.79; written *coluthia*, Plin.*HN*32.84, 147.

κολουρ-αῖος, η, ον, = κόλουρος, κ. πέτρη a *steep, abrupt* rock, Call.*Fr.*66. **-ία**, ἡ, = ἀποτομία, Hsch. **-ῖτις**· γῆ (Sicel), Id.

κολουρό-κωνος, ὁ, *truncated cone*, Hero *Metr.*3.22. **-πῡρᾰμίς**, ίδος, ἡ, *truncated pyramid*, Theo Sm.p.42 H.

κόλουρ-ος, ον, (κόλος, οὐρά) *dock-tailed, stump-tailed*, metaph., ὥσπερ ὑπὸ γήρως ἀπτῆνα καὶ κ. Plu.*Flam.*21:—fem. **κόλουρις**, of the fox in the fable, Timocr.3; cf. κοθοῦριν. 2. generally, *truncated*, πυραμίς Nicom.*Ar.*2.14. II. κόλουροι (sc. γραμμαί), αἱ, *colures*, two great circles passing through the equinoctial and solstitial points, intersecting at the poles, Hipparch.1.11.17 (sg.), Theo Sm. p.132 H., etc. (in full οἱ κ. κύκλοι Gem.2.21): sg., *Theol.Ar.*55. III. a kind of *fig*, Ath.3.75d. **-ωσις**, εως, ἡ, = κολόβωσις I, Iamb.*Protr.*21.κζ'.

κόλ-ουσις, εως, ἡ, *docking, cutting short*, ἡ τῶν ὑπερεχόντων σταχύων κ. Arist.*Pol.*1311a21, cf. Thphr.*CP*2.15.4, 5.17.5 (pl.); κ. δυνάμεως Plu.*Arist.*7. **-ουσμα**, ατος, τό, *that which is cut off, a piece*, Hsch. **-ουστός**, ή, όν, *docked, without horns*, Id. s.v. κόλον.

κολουτέα, ἡ, v. κολοιτία.

κολούω, Il.20.370, E.*Fr.*92, Pl.*Lg.*731a: fut. -ούσω Plu.*Alc.*34: aor. ἐκόλουσα Pl.*Prt.*343c, Arist.*Pol.*1274a8:—Pass., fut. -ουθήσομαι Gal.9.529: aor. ἐκολούθην Th.7.66, -ούσθην A.*Pers.*1035 (lyr.): pf. κεκόλουμαι *AP*7.234 (Phil.), Plu.*Ages.*31, etc., -ουσμαι D.C.*Fr.*57.23: (κόλος):—*cut short, dock, curtail*, [ἀστάχυας] Hdt.5.92.ζ'; στάχυν σπάθῃ κ. φασγάνου E.*Fr.*373; *prune*, τὸν βότρυν Thphr.*CP*2.15.5; [τὰ δένδρα] βελτίω κολουόμενά φασι γίγνεσθαι ib.2, cf. *IG*9(2).1109.81 (Coropa): c. gen., τὴν δ' ἐκόλουσεν οὐρῆς *docked* her *of* her tail, Opp.*H.*4.484. II. Hom. always metaph., τὸ μὲν τελέει, τὸ δὲ μεσσηγὺ κολούει part he brings to pass, part he *cuts off* half-accomplished, of the threats of Achilles, Il. l.c.; μηδὲ τὰ δῶρα..κολούετε *curtail* them not, Od.11.340; ἐὸ δ' αὐτοῦ πάντα κολούει *cuts off* all his hopes, 8.211; κολούειν εἰς τὰ τῆς τέχνης ἔργα *hinders* performance in the art, Gal.5.733. 2. like κολάζω, which is more freq. in Prose, τὰ ὑπερέχοντα κ. *put down, abase* those who are exalted, Hdt.7.10.ε', cf. Arist.*Pol.*1284a37, 1313a40; δῆμον E.*Fr.*92; τοὺς ἄλλους κ. διαβολαῖς Pl.*Lg.* l.c., cf. *Ap.*39d; τὸ ῥῆμα *discredit* it, Id.*Prt.* l.c.; τὴν ἐν Ἀρείῳ πάγῳ βουλὴν Arist.*Pol.*1274a8; κ. καὶ θεραπεύειν, κ. καὶ ταπεινώσειν τινά, Phld.*Lib.*p.60 O., Plu.*Alc.* l.c.:—Pass., *to be balked*, *thwarted*, σθένος ἐκολούσθη A. l. c.; νούσῳ κεκολουμένος *AP*l. c.; ἐπειδὰν ᾧ ἀξιοῦσι προὔχειν κολουθῶσι when *they are worsted* in a matter in which they claim superiority, Th. l. c.; ἀτιμαζόμενα καὶ κολουόμενα Pl.*R*.528c, cf. *Euthd*.305d, Plu.*Ages*. l. c.

κολοφών, ῶνος, ὁ, *summit, top, finishing*, κολοφῶνα ἐπιτιθέναι put *the finishing touch* to.., Pl.*Euthd*.301e, *Lg*.673d; τὸν κ. προσβιβάζειν Id.*Tht*.153c; κ. ἐπάγειν τῷ λόγῳ Ael.*NA*13.12; κολοφὼν ἐπὶ τῷ λόγῳ εἰρήσθω Pl.*Lg*.674c; κ. τοῦ λόγου *Com.Adesp*.433; later κ. τῆς ἀσεβείας *height* of impiety, Jul.*Gal*.333c; of persons, ὁ κ. τῆς ἀδικίας the *arch*-criminal, Lib.*Decl*.30.12; τῶν ἀτοπημάτων κ. Zos.4.15. (Expld. by Str.14.1.28 from the belief that the cavalry of Colophon was so excellent that it always decided the contest.) II. sort of *ball* for playing with, Plu.2.526e. III. = κολοιός, Hsch. 2. kind of *sea-fish*, Id.

κολοφωνέω, *put the crown on*, ἐπὶ πᾶσι τούτοις Steph. *in Hp*.1.248 D.

Κολοφώνιος, α, ον, *of* or *from Colophon* in Ionia, Hdt.1.147, etc.; K. σχῆμα, a figure of speech, such as using ἡ κεφαλὴ τῷ ἀνθρώπῳ for τοῦ -που, Lesb.Gramm.7: Subst., ἡ Κολοφωνία (sc. ῥητίνη), *Colophonian gum, resin*, Dsc.1.71, Gal.13.475, *Hippiatr*.20, al., *PGrenf*. 1.52.7 (iii A.D.); also, = σκαμμωνία, Ps.-Dsc.4.170; Κολοφώνιον (sc. ὑπόδημα), τό, kind of *shoe*, Rhinth.4; also, a measure used in Egypt, *Ostr*.1166, 1265 (ii A.D.); but also, a kind of *vegetable*, *PTeb*.419.21 (iii A.D.).

κολόχειρ, ὁ, ἡ, *maimed in the hand*, Hsch.

κολπ-αβρός, όν, Ion. for κολφ-αβρός, *soft of bosom*, Eust.1745. 60. **-άριον**, τό, Dim. of κόλπος III. 6, Archig.ap.Aët.9.39. **-ίας**, ου, ὁ, *swelling in folds*, πέπλος A.*Pers*.1060. 2. name of a wind, *blowing from the gulf*, Ph.Bybl.ap.Eus.*PE*1.10, Ach.Tat.*Intr.Arat*. 33. **-ίζω**, *form into a bosom* or *fold*, Suid. **-ίτης** [ῑ], ου, ὁ, *dwelling on a bay*, Philostr.*VA*3.35, 6.16.

κολποειδής, ές, *like a bay*, Ael.*NA*14.8. Adv. -δῶς Str.9.1.1.

κόλπος, ὁ, *bosom, lap*, παῖδ' ἐπὶ κόλπῳ ἔχουσα Il.6.400; ἂψ ὁ πάϊς πρὸς κόλπον ἐκλίνθη ib.467; ἡ δ' ἄρα μιν κηώδεϊ δέξατο κόλπῳ (cf. III. 1) ib.483; ἱμάντα τέῳ ἐγκάτθεο κ. put the girdle in thy *bosom*, 14. 219; εἰς κόλπον πτύσαι Thphr.*Char*.16.15 (cf. πτύω); ἐν κόλπῳ εἶχες ὄφιν Thgn.602; ὁ κ. 'Αβραάμ *Ev.Luc*.16.22; freq. of pet birds or animals, τρέφειν ἐν κ. Herod.6.102; κυνίδιον ἐν κόλπῳ τιθηνούμενον lap-dog, Plu.2.472c; κίσσαν ἐκ μέσων τῶν κόλπων ἁρπάσας Luc.*Jud.Voc*.8; so τὸ θυγάτριον ἐκ κόλπων τῶν ἐμῶν ἀναρπάσαντα Hld.4.14: metaph., εἰς τοὺς εὐανθεῖς κ. λειμώνων Ar.*Ra*.373 (lyr.); λειμώνων φύλλων τ' ἐν κόλποις ναίω Id.*Av*.1094 (lyr.); also τὰ ὑπὸ κόλπου, = τὰ ἀφροδίσια, Luc.*Alex*.39. 2. = αἰδοῖον γυναικεῖον, esp. *vagina*, Sor.1.16, al., Ruf.*Onom*.196, Poll.2.222: pl., Sor.1.70[b], S.E.*M*.5.62. b. κόλποι τῆς ὑστέρας supposed *sinuses* in the womb, Hp.*Nat.Puer*.31, Sor.1. 9 (sg.), Gal.*UP*14.4. c. in poets more vaguely of the whole *sinus genitalis, womb*, in pl., E.*Hel*.1145 (lyr.), Call.*Jov*.15: sg., Id.*Del*. 214; δεσποίνας ὑπὸ κόλπον ἔδυν Orph.*Fr*.32c.8; θεὸς διὰ κόλπου ib. 31124: metaph., of the grave, σῶμα σὸν ἐν κόλποις..γαῖα καλύπτει *IG*2.3839, cf. 3412, *Epigr.Gr*.214.7 (Rhenea); κ. ἡμερῶν, of the *womb* of time, Ezek.*Exag*.39. d. of other cavities, οἱ κ. τῆς κοιλίας, in the ἐχῖνος, Arist.*HA*530[b]27; of the *ventricles* of the heart, Poll.2.216. II. *fold of a garment*, esp. as it fell over the girdle, freq. in pl., δεύοντο δὲ δάκρυσι κ. Il.9.570, cf. A.*Pers*.539 (anap.), etc.: also in sg., κ. βαθὺν καταλιπόμενος τοῦ κιθῶνος Hdt.6.125; κόλπον ἀνιεμένη letting down the *bosom of her robe*, i.e. baring her breast, Il.22.80; ἐπὶ σφυρὰ κόλπον ἀνεῖσαι Theoc.15.134; κρύψε δὲ παρθενίαν ὠδῖνα κόλποις, i.e. she concealed her pregnancy *by the loose folds of her robe*, Pi.*O*.6.31; κατακρύψασ' ὑπὸ κόλπῳ Od.15.469; κόλπῳ φέρουσα..πεπλώματος A.*Th*.1044; ὑπὸ κόλπου (v.l. -ῳ) χεῖρας ἔχειν 'keep one's hand in one's *pocket*', of a stingy person, Theoc.16.16; ὑπὸ κόλπου Luc.*Herm*.37, 81, *Hes*.2, *Merc.Cond*.27; ὑπὸ κόλπον Hsch. s. v. μασχαλοληπτεῖ, v.l. in Luc.*Ind*.12. III. any *bosom-like hollow*: 1. of the sea, first in a half-literal sense, of a sea-goddess, Θέτις δ' ὑπεδέξατο κόλπῳ received him *in her bosom*, Il.6.136, cf. supr. I. 1: generally, δῦτε θαλάσσης εὐρέα κ. 18.140, cf. Od.4.435; εἴσω ἁλὸς εὐρέα κ. Il.21.125: in pl., κατὰ δεινοὺς κ. ἁλός Od.5.52; also κόλποι αἰθέρος Pi.*O*.13.88; 'Ερέβους ἐν ἀπείροσι κ. Ar. *Av*.694. 2. *bay, gulf*, 'Ερμιόνην 'Ασίνην τε, βαθὺν κατὰ κ. ἐχούσας, i.e. βαθὺν κατεχούσας κόλπον, Il.2.560; Μηλιεὺς κ. A.*Pers*.486; κ. 'Ρέας, i.e. the Adriatic, Id.*Pr*.837; Τυρσηνικὸς κ. S.*Fr*.598, cf. Hdt.2.11, 7.58, 198, Th.2.90, etc. 3. *vale*, κ. 'Αργεῖος Pi.*P*.4.49; Νεμέας Id.*O*.9.87, cf. 14.23; 'Ελευσινίας Δηοῦς ἐν κόλποις S.*Ant*.1121 (lyr.); κ. Τροίας E.*Tr*.130 (lyr.); Πιερικὸς κ. Th.2.99, cf. X.*HG* 6.5.17. 4. of a fortified site, *salient*, Ph.*Bel*.86.8. 5. ὁ κ. τοῦ ἅρματος *bottom* of the chariot, Lxx 3*Ki*.22.35. 6. *fistulous ulcer* which spreads under the skin, Dsc.1.128, Heliod.ap.Orib.44.8.22, Gal.11.125. IV. in Tactics, *enveloping force*, Onos.21.5.

κολποφακῆ, Com. formation with play on βολβοφακῆ, Ath.13. 584d.

κολπ-όω, *form into a swelling fold*; esp. *make* a sail *belly*, πνοιῇ.. λίνα κολπώσαντες *AP*9.363.10 (Mel.); ἄνεμος κ. τὴν ὀθόνην Luc.*VH* 1.9; χιτῶνας κολπώσαντες τῷ ἀνέμῳ, καθάπερ ἱστία ib.13:—Pass., *swell out*, of membranes, Hp.*Nat.Puer*.16; κολποῦται ὑμὴν φυσώμενος Arist.*HA*510[b]32; of Europa's garment, Mosch.2.129; κολποῦται Ζέφυρος εἰς ὀθόνας *AP*10.5 (Thyill.); of a bay, *curve*, Plb.34.11.5: Medic., *contain a sinus*, Heliod.ap.Orib.44.8.22: metaph. in pf. part. Pass., κεκολπωμένος *turgid*, of style, D.H.*Dem*.19. **-ώδης**, ες, *embosomed, embayed*, τὰν κολπώδη πτέρυγ' Εὐβοίας Αὖλιν E.*IA*120, etc.; *full of bays*, θάλασσα D.C.48.50. 2. *winding*, παράπλους Plb. 4.44.7. II. metaph., of language, *turgid*, μηδὲν ἔχειν κ. D.H.*Dem*. 18. **-ωμα**, ατος, τό, *bellying* or *bulging out*, of the centre in a line of battle, Plu.*Mar*.25. II. *garment with ample folds*, worn by kings in Tragedy, Poll.4.116, *An.Par*.1.19. **-ωσις**, εως, ἡ, *forming into a fold*, κ. πτερῶν *arching* of wings before the wind, Hdn.1. 15.5. **-ωτός**, ἡ, όν, *formed into folds*, χιτῶνες Plu.2.173c; κολπωτὰν ὀθόναισι..τρόπιν ἰθύνεσκον with *swelling* sails, *Hymn.Is*.153.

κόλσασθαι· ἱκετεῦσαι, Hsch.

κολύβδαινα, ἡ, kind of *crab*, Epich.57.

κόλυβος· ἔπαυλις, Hsch.; cf. καλύβη.

κολύβριον, τό, = μολόβριον (q.v.).

κόλυθροι, οἱ, *testicles*, Arist.*Pr*.913[b]20.

κόλυθρον or **-τρον**, τό, *ripe fig*, Philem.Gloss.ap.Ath.3.76f.

κολυθροφῐλάρπαξ, ἄγος, ὁ, *one who loves to seize* κόλυθροι, prob. in Lyr. in *Philol*.80.334.

κολύκιντος, = κολόκυνθος (q.v.). **κολυκρίζοντες**· ἐκτελοῦντες, Hsch.

κολύμβ-αινα, ἡ, = κολύβδαινα, Archig.ap.Gal.13.174. **-άς**, άδος, ἡ, less Att. form of κολυμβίς, κ. ἐλαία olive *swimming*, i.e. *pickled in brine*, Diph.Siph.ap.Ath.2.56b, *PSI*5.535.27 (iii B.C.), cf. Call.*Iamb*.1.273, Gal.6.609, al. II. as Subst., 1. = κολυμβίς, Ath.9.395e. 2. a shrub, = στοιβή, Gal.14.18. **-ατος**, ἡ, a plant, *Gp*.2.4.1. **-άω** (Dor. -φάω acc. to *EM*526.2), *dive, plunge headlong*, εἰς τὸν Τάρταρον Pherecr.108.21; εἰς τὰ φρέατα Pl.*Prt*.350a, cf. *La*.193c, Str.17.1.44, etc.; εἰς κολυμβήθραν μύρου Alex.300. 2. *swim*, τοὺς δυναμένους κολυμβᾶν *Act.Ap*.27.43, cf. *Hippiatr*.26. **-ήθρα**, ἡ, *place for diving, swimming-bath*, Pl.*R*.453d, D.S.11.25; κ. μύρου Alex.300. II. *wine-vat, tun*, D.S.13.83. III. *reservoir, cistern*, Lxx 4*Ki*.18.17. IV. *baptismal font*, *POxy*.147 (vi A.D.). **-ησις**, εως, ἡ, pearl-*fishery*, *Peripl.M.Rubr*.35 (pl.), 58, Sch.Ptol.*Geog*.6.7.11. **-ητέον**, *one must swim*, Sch.Pl.*R*.453d. **-ητήρ**, ῆρος, ὁ, = sq., A.*Supp*. 408. **-ητής**, οῦ, ὁ, *diver*, Th.4.26, Pl.*Prt*.350a, Arist.*PA*659[a] 9, *Sammelb*.3747 (i B.C.), etc. II. *one who draws water from a well*, Hsch. (pl.). **-ητικός**, ή, όν, *of* or *for diving*: ἡ -κή (sc. τέχνη) the *art of diving*, Pl.*Sph*.220a. **-ίς**, ίδος, ἡ, *diver*, name of a bird, prob. *grebe*, *Podiceps minor*, Ar.*Av*.304, Arist.*HA*593[b]17, Alex.Mynd.ap.Ath.9.395d; cf. κολυμβάς II. 1: as Adj., κ. αἴθυιαι Arat.296. **-ιστής**, οῦ, ὁ, = -ητής, Sch.Opp.*H*.1.173. **-ιτεύω**, *plunge into a tank*, *PMasp*.9 ii 30 (vi A.D.). **-ος**, ὁ, = κολυμβίς, Ar. *Ach*.876. II. = κολύμβησις, ἅμιλλα κολύμβου Paus.2.35.1, cf. Str. 16.2.42, *AP*9.82 (Antip. Thess.), Plu.2.162f (pl.), Herod.Med.ap. Orib.10.39.3, Antyll.ib.6.27.4, X.*Eph*.3.2. 2. = κολυμβήθρα I, Hero *Mens*.19.

κολύμφατος· φλοιός, λεπίδιον, Hsch. **κολυμφάω**, v. κολυμβάω. **κολυρίζοντες**· ἐκκενοῦντες, Id. **κολυτέα**, ἡ, *bladder-senna*, *Colutea arborescens*, Thphr.*HP*3.14.4. **κόλυτρον**, τό, v. κόλυθρον. **κολύφανον**· φλοιός, λεπύριον, Hsch. (cf. κελύφανον). **κολυφρόν**· ἐλαφρόν, Id. **κόλφος**, = κόλπος, *Gloss*.

κολχικόν, τό, *meadow saffron*, *Colchicum speciosum*, Dsc.4.83.

κόλχος, ὁ, f. l. for κόχλος, *AP*9.551 (pl., Antiphil.), *APl*.4.37 (Leont.).

Κόλχος, ὁ, *Colchian*, Hdt.1.2, etc.:—Adj. **Κολχικός**, ή, όν, *Colchian*, Id.2.105:—poet. also **Κόλχος** στόλος A.R.4.485:—fem. **Κολχίς**, ίδος, Hdt.1.2 (but also Μηδείᾳ τῇ Κόλχῳ Pl.*Euthd*.285c): as Subst. Κολχίς (sc. γῆ), *Colchis*, Hdt.1.104, etc.; (sc. γυνή) E.*Med*. 132 (anap.).

κολῳάω, (κολῳός) *brawl, scold*, Il.2.212; Ion. **κολῳέω** Antim.37.

κολῶμαι, Att. fut. Med. of κολάζω (q.v.).

κόλων, ωνος, ὁ, = Lat. *colonus*, *Syria* 5.347 (Dura).

Κολωναί, ἡ, = Κολωνός II, Call.*Fr*.428.

κολωνεία, ἡ, = Lat. *colonia*, *CIG*2811*b* (Aphrodisias), *POxy*.653 (ii A.D.), etc.; also **κολωνία** (q.v.).

κολώνη, ἡ, *hill, mound*, Il.2.811, 11.757, *Lyr.Adesp*.74; esp. *sepulchral mound, barrow*, S.*El*.894; later, *hill-top, peak*, D.P.150, al.; ὁππότ' ἀνθρώπων μεγάλας πλήσαιτο κ. Arat.120. (Cf. Lat. *collis, culmen*, Engl. *holm*.)

Κολωνῆθεν, Adv. *from the deme* Κολωνός (q.v.), D.21.64, *IG*2[2].650, etc.

κολωνία, ἡ, *grave* (Elean), Hsch. II. = Lat. *colonia*, *Act.Ap*. 16.12, *Epigr.Gr*.908 (Batanaea); cf. κολωνεία.

κολωνοειδής, ές, *like a hill* or *barrow*, Sch.A.R.2.649.

κολωνός, ὁ, = κολώνη, *hill*, *h.Cer*.272, 298, Hes.*Fr*.122.1, Hdt.4. 181, 7.225, etc.; κ. λίθων *heap* of stones, Id.4.92, X.*An*.4.7.25; *hill-top, peak*, A.R.1.1120. II. *Colonus*, deme of Attica, sacred to the hero Colonus (ἱππότης K. S.*OC*59); Οἰδίπους ἐπὶ Κολωνῷ, title of play by Sophocles:—hence **Κολωνεύς**, έως, ὁ, *one of the deme Colonos*, *IG*2.944.48. 2. K. ἀγοραῖος, mound in the Athenian ἀγορά, Κολωνόν.., οὐ τὸν ἀγοραῖον, ἀλλὰ τὸν τῶν ἱππέων Pherecr.134; labourers were hired there, *Com.Adesp*.35 D., hence called **Κολωνέται** or **Κολωνῖται**, Hyp.*Fr*.8.

κολῳός, ὁ, *brawling, wrangling*, κολῳὸν ἐλαύνετον Il.1.575, cf. A.R.1.1284.

κόλωψ· ἀμφιάτωρ, Hsch.

κομάκτωρ, ορος, ὁ, dub. sens., Rhinth.9, *Inscr.Magn*.217 (pl., i B.C.).

κομανίαν· πορνί, δαψιλὴν ἀνίαν, Hsch.

κόμαρι, εως, τό, red dye obtained from root of *Comarum palustre*, *PHolm*.14.2, 5, al., Maria ap.Zos.Alch.p.155 B.:—also **κόμμαρι**, εως, τό, *PHolm.*13.37, 16.5, al.; **κόμαρις** and **κώμαρις,** ἡ, Anon.Alch. pp.351,9 B.; **κόμαρον,** τό, ib.p.350 B., *PHolm.*25.15.

κομᾰρίς, ίδος, ἡ, a fish, Epich.47.

κόμᾰρος, ἡ, Ar.*Av.*620, Thphr.*HP*3.16.4, also ὁ, Amphis 38, Alciphr.3.12:—*strawberry-tree, Arbutus Unedo,* Ar. l. c., Thphr.*HP*1.5.2, Theoc.5.129, 9.11, Gal.12.34, Longus 2.16.

κομᾰροφάγος, ον, *eating the fruit of the arbutus,* Ar.*Av.*240.

κομάς· θεραπείας, καὶ τὰ συοφόρβια, Hsch.

κοματροφέω, = κόμην τρέφω, *IG*12(7).259.8 (Amorgos).

κομάω, Ion. -έω, (κόμη) *let the hair grow long,* Ἄβαντες ὄπιθεν κομόωντες Il.2.542; κάρη κομόωντες Ἀχαιοί 3.43, al.; κ. τὴν κεφαλήν Hdt.4.168; τὰ ὀπίσω κ. τῆς κεφαλῆς ib.180; τὰ ἐπὶ δεξιὰ τῶν κεφαλέων κ. ib.191; τὸ γένειον τῇ κεφαλῇ ὁμοίως κ. X.*Smp.*4.28; ξανθοτάτοις βοτρύχοισι κ. Pherecr.189; ἄρσεσιν οὐκ ἐπέοικε κ. Ps.-Phoc.212; Λακεδαιμόνιοι.. οὐ γὰρ κομῶντες πρὸ τούτου ἀπὸ τούτου κομᾶν Hdt.1.82, cf. Arist.*Rh.*1367^{a}29, Philostr.*VA*3.15; ἐλακωνομάνουν ἅπαντες.., ἐκόμων Ar.*Av.*1282; μὴ φθονεῖθ' ἡμῖν (sc. τοῖς ἱππεῦσι) κομῶσι Id.*Eq.*580; κομῶν καὶ αὐχμηρός Arist.*Rh.*1413^{a}9, cf. D.H.6.26; ἔνορκον ἂν ποιησαίμην μὴ πρότερον κομήσειν (in token of a vow) πρίν.. Pl.*Phd.*89c; ἀνὴρ μὲν ἐὰν κομᾷ, ἀτιμία αὐτῷ ἐστι· γυνὴ δὲ ἐὰν κομᾷ, δόξα αὐτῇ ἐστιν 1*Ep.Cor.*11.14–15. 2. *plume oneself, give oneself airs,* τοιοῦτος ἀνὴρ ὢν ποιητὴς οὐ κομῶ Ar.*Nu.*545, cf.*Pl.*170; οὗτος ἐπὶ τυραννίδι ἐκόμησε *aimed at* the monarchy, Hdt.5.71; ἐπὶ τῷ κομᾷς; on what *do you plume yourself?* Ar.*V.*1317; μηδὲν ταύτῃ γε κομήσῃς Id.*Pl.*572; κ. ἐπὶ κάλλει Plu.*Caes.*45, cf. Luc.*Nigr.*1; ἐπ' Ἠρίννῃ κ., of her lover, *AP*11.322 (Antiphan.): c. dat., Opp.*C.*3.192. II. of horses, χρυσέῃσιν ἐθείρῃσιν κομόωντε Il.8.42, 13.24. III. of the hair itself, *to be long,* Opp.*C.*3.28. IV. metaph., of trees, plants, etc., [οὖθαρ ἀρούρης] μέλλεν ἄφαρ ταναοῖσι κομήσειν ἀσταχύεσσιν soon were the fields *to wave* with long ears, *h.Cer.*454; μᾶζαι βώλοις κομῶσαι Cratin.165; ἁ δὲ καλὰ νάρκισσος ἐπ' ἀρκεύθοισι κομάσαι Theoc.1.133, cf. 4.57; αἴγειρος φύλλοισι κομόωσα A.R.3.928; ὄρος κεκομημένον ὕλῃ Call.*Dian.*41; ἡ γῆ φυτοῖς κομῶσα Arist.*Mu.*397^{a}24, cf. Ael.*Fr.*75; κομῶντα λήϊα Procop.Gaz.*Ep.*23. V. ἀστέρες κομόωντες, = κομῆται, Arat.1092.

κόμβα, = κορώνη (Polyrrhen.), Hsch. **κομβακεύομαι,** = κόμπους λέγω, Id. **κόμβαλα·** παίγματά τινα, Id. **κόμβησαν·** ποιὸν ἦχον ἀπετέλεσαν, Id., Cyr. **κομβίζων·** φυσῶν, Hsch.

κομβίον, τό, = περόνη, *buckle,* Eust.794.13, Sch.E.*Hec.*1170.

κομβο-θηλεία, ἡ, *buckle,* Sch.E.*Hec.*1170; cf. κομποθήλυκα. **-λύτης** [ῠ], ου, ὁ, *cut-purse,* Hsch.

κόμβ-ος, ὁ, *roll, band, girth,* Anon.ap.Suid.; cf. κομποθηλαία. II. pl., = γομφίοι, Hsch. **-όω,** *bind up, fasten, Gloss.*:—Med., *gird oneself,* Hsch. **-ωμα,** ατος, τό, *robe,* Id.: in pl., *ornamental bands,* Suid.

κομέτιον, τό, = Lat. *comitium, IG*14.951.

κομέω (A), Ep. impf. κομέεσκον Od.24.390:—Ep. Verb, *take care of, tend,* in Il. of horses, τούτω μὲν θεράποντε κομείτων 8.109, cf. 113, *h.Ap.*236; of dogs, Od.17.310, 319, Hes.*Op.*604; elsewh. in Od. always of men, γέροντα ἐνδυκέως κομέεσκεν 24.390, cf. 6.207, etc.; of children, σὺ δὲ τοὺς κομέειν ἀτιταλλέμεναί τε 11.250; κούρην.. κομέουσι τοκῆες *IG*3.1335, cf. *Supp.Epigr.*1.567 (Karanis, iii B.C.). (Prob. cogn. with κάμνω, q.v.)

κομέω (B), Ion. for κομάω.

κόμ-η, ἡ, *hair of the head,* Il.22.406, etc.: less freq. in pl., κὰδ δὲ κάρητος οὔλας ἧκε κόμας Od.6.231; κόμαι Χαρίτεσσιν ὁμοῖαι (i.e. κόμαις Χαρίτων) Il.17.51; κόμην κείρειν, κείρεσθαι (v. κείρω); κόμην τρέφειν to let *the hair* grow long, Hdt.1.82; κ. φορεῖν *PGnom.*188 (ii A.D.); κόμη δι' αὔρας ἀκτένιστος ᾄσσεται S.*OC*1261; καθεῖσαν εἰς ὤμους κόμας E.*Ba.*695; κόμαι πρόσθετοι false *hair, wig,* X.*Cyr.*1.3.2, etc.; δοῦλος ὢν κόμην ἔχεις; Ar.*Av.*911; κόμης ἀνάπλεως *unkempt,* Plu.*Cic.*30. 2. of the *beard,* Arr.*Epict.*4.8.4. 3. *gill* or *branchia* of the cuttle-fish, dub. in Arist.*HA*550^{b}18: pl., *arms* or *suckers,* Max.Tyr.4.5. II. metaph., *foliage* of trees, Od.23.195, Cratin.296, etc.; δόνακος App.*BC*4.28; of herbs, Dsc.4.164.7, Gal.6.268; of corn, ληΐου κ. Babr.88.3; λειμώνων κόμαι *IG*14.1389 ii 11; esp. = τραγοπώγων, Thphr.*HP*7.7.1, Dsc.2.143. III. *luminous tail of a comet,* Arist.*Mete.*343^{a}1, 346^{a}15. **-ήεις,** εσσα, εν, *leafy,* Orph.*Fr.*258.

κόμης, ητος, ὁ, = Lat. *comes,* κ. πρώτου βαθμοῦ *CIG*4361 (Side), cf. *IG*14.1076, Zos.5.2, *Cod.Just.*1.4.20, etc.: gen. pl. κομίτων *IG*3.635:—Adj. **κομητικός,** ή, όν, *PLond.*1.113.6^{c}.24.

Κομητᾰμῡνίας, ου, ὁ, Com. adaptation of the name *Amynias, Coxcomb-amynias* (cf. κομάω I), Ar.*V.*466.

κομήτης, ου, ὁ, (κομάω) *wearing long hair,* of the Persians, Orac. ap.Hdt.6.19; of dissolute men, Pherecr.14, Ar.*Nu.*348, 1101, etc.; ὁ ἐν Σάμῳ κ., prov. variously expld., Duris 62 J., etc.; also, simply, *with hair on the head,* opp. φαλακρός, Pl.*R.*454c, cf. *Grg.*524c; κ. τὰ σκέλη Luc.*Bacch.*2. 2. metaph., κ. ἰός a *feathered* arrow, S.*Tr.*567; κ. λειμών a *grassy* meadow, E.*Hipp.*210 (anap.); θύρσος κισσῷ κομήτης Id.*Ba.*1055. II. κομήτης, with or without ἀστήρ, ὁ, *comet,* Arist.*Mete.*343^{b}5, Epicur.*Ep.*2 p.52 U., etc. III. = τιθύμαλλος χαρακίας, Dsc.4.164.1.

κομία· εὐωχία, Hsch. **κομίατον,** τό, = Lat. *commeatus, furlough,* Id.

κομῐδή, ἡ, (κομίζω) *attendance, care,* Hom., etc.; in Il., of *care bestowed on horses,* 8.186, 23.411; in Od., of *care bestowed on men,* 8.453, 14.124; also, *care bestowed on* a garden, οὐ πρασιή τοι ἄνευ κομιδῆς κατὰ κῆπον 24.247, cf. 245: hence dat. κομιδῇ used as Adv. (q.v.). 2. *provision, supplies,* ἐπεὶ οὐ κ. κατὰ νῆα ἦεν ἐπηετανός 8.232. II. *carriage, conveyance,* esp. of supplies and provisions, τῶν ἐπιτηδείων τὴν περὶ τὴν Πελοπόννησον κ. Th.4.27; ὅθεν ῥᾴδιαι αἱ κ. ὧν προσέδει Id.6.21, cf. Isoc.11.14, etc.; λίθων *IG*4^{2}(1).103.75 (Epid.); *gathering in* of harvest, τοῦ καρποῦ, καρπῶν κ., X.*Cyr.*5.4.25, Arist.*Pol.*1335^{a}21; σίτου κ. Plb.5.95.5. b. Medic., *removal, extraction,* ὀδόντων Sor.2.62 (pl.); ἡ διὰ τομῆς κ. (sc. of stone in bladder) Gal.1.391. 2. (from Med.) *carrying away for oneself, rescue, recovery,* κατὰ Ἑλένης κομιδήν Hdt.9.73; esp. *recovery* of a debt, D.38.9, Arist.*EN*1167^{b}31, *Oec.*1349^{a}7; μὴ ἔστω αὐτῷ κ. *PHal.*1.259 (iii B.C.). 3. (from Pass.) *going* or *coming,* ποιεύμενοι ταύτῃ τὴν κ. endeavouring *to pass* this way, Hdt.6.95; *escape, safe return,* κομιδῆς πέρι.. αὐτῷ μελήσειν ὥστε ἀσινέας ἀπικέσθαι ἐς τὴν Ἑλλάδα Id.8.19; οὔτε τις κ. τὸ ὀπίσω φανήσεται ib.108, cf. 4.134, al.; μένων δ' ὁ θεῖος ἀνὴρ πρίατο μὲν θανάτοιο κομιδὰν πατρός Pi.*P.*6.39, cf. A.R.3.1140, 4.1275.

κομῐδῇ, Adv. (dat. of foreg., orig. 'with care') *exactly, just,* ἐστὶ κ. μεσημβρία Ar.*Fr.*347; κ. δ' ὥσπερ ἦν D.1.22. 2. *entirely, altogether, quite,* with Verbs, κ. μεθύειν Pl.*Smp.*215d, cf. Antiph.74.12; κ. ἀπειρηκέναι Id.191.14; Πομπήϊον ἀπέστρεψε κ. τοῦ Κικέρωνος Plu.*Cic.*30: more freq. with Adjs., κ. ἕτερον Pl.*Tht.*159a; εἰς στενὸν κ... καταστήσεται D.1.22; κ. μικρά Id.18.295; σαπροὺς κ. (sc. ἰχθῦς) Antiph.218.4; βαρὺς κ. Eub.41.7; κ. ἀναίσθητος Arist.*EN*1114^{a}10; κ. φαῦλος ib.1166^{b}5: with Substs., Θετταλὸν λέγεις κ. τὸν ἄνδρα *quite* a Thessalian, Antiph.276; μειρακύλλιον ὢν κ. D.21.78; νέος κ. ib.80: with an Adv., κύκλῳ κ. *all* round us, Pl.*Chrm.*155d: with a neg., κ. γὰρ οὐκ ἦν οὐδαμοῦ nowhere *at all,* Antiph.129.10; ὥστε μὴ κ. μοναρχίαν εἶναι none *at all,* Plu.*Per.*11; κ. ἀτέχνως without any art *at all,* Pl.*Grg.*501a. 3. freq. in answers, κομιδῇ μὲν οὖν *just so,* Ar.*Pl.*833, 834, 838, Pl.*Tht.*155a, *Sph.*221c, al.; κ. γε *quite so,* Id.*R.*442a, 453e, al.

κομίζω, fut. κομιῶ Od.15.546, Hdt.2.121.γ', Ar.*Ec.*800, etc.; κομίσω only late, as *AP*6.41 (Agath.): aor. ἐκόμισα, Ep. ἐκόμισσα Il.13.579, κόμισσα Od.18.322, κόμισα Il.13.196; Dor. ἐκόμιξα Pi.*P.*4.159: pf. κεκόμικα Hdt.9.115, etc.:—Med., fut. κομιοῦμαι Ar.*V.*690, Th.1.113, etc.; Ion. -ιεῦμαι, v. infr. II. 4; late κομίσομαι Phalar.*Ep.*135: aor. ἐκομισάμην Hdt.6.118, etc.; Ep. ἐκομισσ- or κομισσ-, Od.14.316, Il.8.284:—Pass., fut. -ισθήσομαι Th.1.52, D.18.301: aor. ἐκομίσθην Hdt.1.31, Th.5.3, etc.: pf. κεκόμισμαι D.18.241: but more freq. in med. sense, v. infr. II. 2: (κομέω):—*take care of, provide for,* τόν γε γηράσκοντα κομίζω Il.24.541; τόνδε τ' ἐγὼ κομιῶ Od.15.546; ἐμὲ κεῖνος ἐνδυκέως ἐκόμιζε 17.113, etc.; κόμισσε δὲ Πηνελόπεια, παῖδα δὲ ὣς ἀτίταλλε 18.322, cf. 20.68: rare in Trag., A.*Ch.*262, 344; *receive, treat,* φιλίως, οὐ πολεμίως κ. Th.3.65 codd.:—more freq. in Med., καί σε.. κομίσσατο ᾧ ἐνὶ οἴκῳ Il.8.284, cf. Od.14.316; Σίντιες.. ἄφαρ κομίσαντο πεσόντα Il.1.594; κομίζεσθαί τινα ἐς τὴν οἰκίαν And.1.127, cf. Is.1.15:—Pass., οὔ τι κομιζόμενός γε θάμιζεν not often was he *attended to,* Od.8.451. 2. of things, *attend, give heed to,* τὰ σ' αὐτῆς ἔργα κόμιζε Il.6.490, Od.21.350; κτήματα μέν.. κομιζέμεν ἐν μεγάροισι 23.355; δῶμα κ., of the mistress of the house, 16.74, etc.; τὸν χρυσόν Hdt.1.153; ἔξω κ. πηλοῦ πόδα *keep* it out of the mud, A.*Ch.*697:—Med., ἔργα κ. Δημήτερος Hes.*Op.*393; Δημήτερος ἱερὸν ἀκτὴν μέτρῳ εὖ κομίσασθαι ἐν ἄγγεσιν *store up..,* ib.600. II. *carry away so as to preserve,* Ἀμφίμαχον.. κόμισαν μετὰ λαὸν Ἀχαιῶν *they carried away* his body, Il.13.196 (so in Med., κόμισαί με *carry* me *safe away,* 5.359, cf. E.*IT*774); of things, τὴν δὲ κόμισσε κῆρυξ the herald *took up* the mantle, that it might not be lost, Il.2.183; [τρυφάλειαν] κόμισαν.. ἑταῖροι 3.378, cf. 13.579; later, simply, *save, rescue,* ἄνδρ' ἐκ θανάτου Pi.*P.*3.56; ἄρουραν πατρίαν σφίσιν κόμισον Id.*O.*2.14; of the dead, νεκρὸν κ. *carry out to burial,* E.*Andr.*1264, cf. S.*Aj.*1397:—in Med., Is.8.21; also, simply, *carry* the body *home,* opp. θάπτω, A.*Ch.*683, cf. Hdt.4.71. 2. *carry off as a prize* or *booty,* χρυσὸν δ' Ἀχιλεὺς ἐκόμισσε Il.2.875; κόμισσα δὲ μώνυχας ἵππους 11.738; τέσσαρας ἐξ ἀέθλων νίκας ἐκόμιξαν four victories *they won,* Pi.*N.*2.19; ἔπαινος, ὃν κομίζετον τοῦδ' ἀνδρός S.*OC*1411:—in Med., Orac.ap.Hdt.1.67:—later freq., *get for oneself, acquire, gain,* δόξαν ἐσθλήν v. l. in E.*Hipp.*432; τριώβολον Ar.*V.*690; τὴν ἀξίαν Pl.*R.*615c; τὰ ἆθλα αὐτῆς ib.621d; κ. τί τινος S.*OT*580; τι παρά τινος Th.1.43; τι ἀπό τινος X.*Cyr.*1.5.10; *gather in, reap,* καρπόν Hdt.2.14: pf. Pass. in med. sense, ὑμεῖς τοὺς καρποὺς κεκόμισθε you *have reaped* the fruits, D.18.231; κεκόμισται χάριν Id.21.171; ὡμολόγει κεκομίσθαι τὴν προῖκα Id.27.14, cf. Is.5.22; simply, *receive,* ἐνηρόσιον *SIG*1044.31 (Halic., iv/iii B.C.); ἐπιστολήν *PCair.Zen.*186 (iii B.C.); μισθόν *IG*4^{2}(1).99.24 (Epid., ii B.C.); ἀπ' ἀλλήλων χρείας Phld.*D.*3 *Fr.*84. 3. *receive* a missile in one's body, ἀλλά τις Ἀργείων κόμισε χροΐ (sc. τὸν ἄκοντα) Il.14.456, cf. 463:—Med., ὡς δή μιν σῷ ἐν χροῒ πᾶν κομίσαιο (sc. τὸ ἔγχος) 22.286. 4. *carry, convey,* κόμισαν δέπας 23.699, cf. Od.13.68, Hdt.5.83, etc.; κομίζοις ἂν σεαυτόν *betake* thyself, S.*Ant.*444:—Pass., *to be conveyed, journey, travel,* by land or sea, Hdt.5.43, etc.; εἴσω κομίζου *get thee* in, A.*Ag.*1035, cf. *Pr.*394; κ. παρά τινα *betake oneself* to him, Hdt.1.73: in this sense fut. and aor. Med. sts. occur, κομιεύμεθα ἐς Σῖριν Id.8.62; οἳ ἂν κομίσωνται.. ἐς Βαβυλῶνα Id.1.185; ἔξω κομίσασθ' οἴκων E.*Tr.*167 (lyr.). 5. *bring to* a place, *bring in, introduce,* κόμιζέ νύν μοι παῖδα S.*Aj.*530; *import,* Pl.*R.*370e, etc.; ξενικοῦ κομισθέντος νομίσματος Id.*Lg.*742c; κ. τὴν φιλοσοφίαν εἰς τοὺς Ἕλληνας Isoc.11.28; οἱ κομίσαντες τὴν δόξαν ταύτην Arist.*EN*1096^{a}17, cf. *Metaph.*990^{b}2:—in Med., [τὸν ἀνδριάντα] ἐπὶ Δήλιον Hdt.6.118; ποίμνας ἐς δόμους S.*Aj.*63, cf. Ar.*V.*833. 6. *conduct, escort,* τί μέλλεις κομίζειν δόμων τόνδ' ἔσω; S.*OT*678 (lyr.), cf. *Ph.*841 (hex.), Th.7.29, Pl.*Phd.*113d, etc.; κ. ἐξ ὀμμάτων γυναῖκα τήνδε *take* her from my sight, E.*Alc.*1064; κ. ναῦς Th.2.85; ἄρχοντα Id.8.61. 7. *bring back* from exile, Pi.*P.*4.106 (dub.);

τεὰν ψυχὰν κ. (from the world below), Id.*N*.8.44; πάλιν κ. Pl.*Phd.* 107e, etc. 8. *get back, recover*, Pi.*O*.13.59; τέκνων..κομίσαι δέμας E.*Supp*.273 (hex.), cf. 495:—Med., *get back for oneself*, τὸν παῖδα Id. *Ba*.1225, cf.*IT*1362; τὴν βασιλείαν Ar.*Av*.549; τοὺς ἄνδρας Th.1.113, cf. 4.117; τοὺς νεκροὺς ὑποσπόνδους κ. Id.6.103; τὰ πρέποντα Id.4.98; ἃ νῦν ἀπολαβεῖν οὐ δυνάμεθα διὰ πολέμου, ταῦτα διὰ πρεσβείας ῥᾳδίως κομιούμεθα Isoc.8.22; esp. of money, *recover* debts, etc., Lys.32.14, And.1.38, D.4.7, etc.; διπλάσια Lys.19.57; τόκους πολλαπλασίους Pl.*R*.556a, etc.; κ. τιμωρίαν παρά τινος Lys.12.70; κ. τὴν θυγατέρα *take back one's* daughter (on the death of her husband), Is.8.8. 9. metaph., *rescue from oblivion*, ἀοιδοὶ καὶ λόγοι τὰ καλὰ ἔργ' ἐκόμισαν Pi.*N*.6.30. 10. *bring, give*, θράσος..ἀνδράσι θνῄσκουσι κ. A.*Ag*. 804 (anap.):—Act. and Med. combined, χθὼν πάντα κομίζει καὶ πάλιν κομίζεται *gives* all things and *gets* them *back* again, Men.*Mon*.539, cf. 89, 668. 11. *cite* as an authority, Θεμιστοκλέα Phld.*Rh*.2. 205S. 12. Medic., *extract, remove*, Gal.2.632. III. Pass., *come* or *go back, return*, Hdt.4.76, al.; ἐκομίσθησαν ἐπ' οἴκου Th.2.33, cf. 73; κομισθεὶς οἴκαδε Pl.*R*.614b.

κόμιον, τό, Dim. of κόμη, Arr.*Epict*.2.24.24, 3.22.10. II. = προκόμιον, *Dialex*.2.13.

κομίσκη, Dor. -ᾱ, ἡ, Dim. of κόμη, Alcm.1.101 Diehl.

κομισ-τέος, α, ον, *to be gathered in*, καρπὸς οὐ κ. A.*Th*.600. II. κομιστέον, *one must bring*, νέους εἰς δείματα κ. Pl.*R*.413d. 2. *one must carry*, Dsc.2.76.6. 3. *one must remove, draw off*, τὸ οὖρον διὰ τοῦ καθετῆρος Sor.2.59, cf. 87. **-τή**, ἡ, = κομιδή 1, Hsch. **-τήρ**, ῆρος, ὁ, = sq. II, E.*Hec*.222, Plu.*Per*.12. **-τής**, οῦ, ὁ, *one who takes care of*, νεκρῶν E.*Supp*.25. II. *conductor*, Id.*Andr*.1268. **-τικός**, ή, όν, *fit for taking care of*; of foods, *strengthening*, Hp.*Aff*.54, 55. II. *fit for carrying*, κ. πλοῖα transports, Hyp.*Fr*.166. **-τός**, ή, όν, *brought*, J.*AJ*17.4.1. **-τρια**, ἡ, fem. of κομιστήρ, = τροφός, *AB* 267, Hsch.; as epith. of Nature, Orph.*H*.10.16. **-τρον**, τό (usu. in pl., sg. in *SIG* (v. infr.), Poll.7.133), *reward for saving*, ψυχῆς κ. A.*Ag*.965. 2. *reward for returning lost property*, *SIG*1184.4 (Cnidus). 3. *payment for maintenance* (?), *Leg.Gort*.3.37. II. *reward for bringing*, E.*HF*1387.

κόμμα, ατος, τό, (κόπτω) *stamp* or *impression of a coin*, χαλκίοις.. κοπεῖσι τῷ κακίστῳ κόμματι Ar.*Ra*.726: prov., πονηροῦ κόμματος of bad *stamp*, Id.*Pl*.862, 957; χρυσίον κόμμασιν ἀποσμώμενον (sic leg. pro ἀποσπ-) cleansed *by blows of the die*, Luc.*Pisc*.14. 2. *coinage*, ἴδιοί τινες [θεοί], κ. καινόν Ar.*Ra*.890, cf. *Ec*.817; Σεύθα κόμμα, on Thracian coins, *BMus.Cat.Coins Thrace* p.201 (v B.C.); οἱ τὸ τοῦ νομίσματος κ. μεταχειριζόμενοι, = Lat. *triumviri monetales*, D.C.54. 26. 3. metaph., μαλθακωτέρου κόμματος, of the female body, Ph. 1.639. II. *that which is cut off, piece*, ἰχθύων *Gp*.18.14.2. 2. *refuse of corn* in threshing, *chaff*, Din.*Fr*.18.4 (pl.). 3. *short clause* in a sentence, Cic.*Orat*.62.211, Phld.*Rh*.1.165S., D.H.*Comp*.26, Quint.9.4.22, etc.; defined as τὸ κώλου ἔλαττον Demetr.*Eloc*.9; cf. κομμάτιον 3. III. *contusion*, Critoap.Gal.13.878.

κομμ-ᾰτίας, ου, ὁ, (κόμμα II.3) *one who speaks in short clauses*, Philostr.*VS*2.29. **-ᾰτικός**, ή, όν, *consisting of short clauses*, μικρὰ καὶ κ. ἐρωτήματα Luc.*Bis Acc*.28; εἶδος τοῦ λόγου Hermog.*Id*.1.9, cf. 1.1. Adv. -κῶς D.H.*Dem*.39; κ. καὶ γοργῶς Eust.200.33. II. κομματικόν (sc. μέλος), τό, = κομμός (A), Poll.4.53. **-άτιον**, τό, Dim. of κόμμα II.1: in pl., *small logs*, Alciphr.1.1. 2. *metrical phrase*, Eup.362. b. part of παράβασις in Comedy, Heph.*Poëm*.8.2. 3. *short clause*, ἔλαττον κώλου κ. D.H.*Comp*.26.

κόμμῐ, τό, *gum*, Hdt.2.86, 96, Hp.*Art*.33, etc.; obtained from *Acacia arabica*, Thphr.*HP*9.1.3, Dsc.1.101.—Foreign word, Ath.2. 66f, prob. Egypt. *kemai*, commonly indecl., as in ll. cc., Gal.18(1). 808; also declined, gen. κόμμεως Hp.*Mul*.2.192, Gal.10.374; dat. κόμμει Str.12.7.3 (fem.), Dsc.1.66, Gal.12.718, κόμμιδι Crobyl.10, v.l. Hdt.2.86 (ap.*AB*104).

κομμ-ίδιον, τό, Dim. of foreg., *Hippiatr*.11, Sch.Nic.*Al*.109. **-ῐδώδης**, ες, *gummy*, Thphr.*CP*5.10.2. **-ίζω**, *to be like gum*, κ. τῇ ὄψει καὶ τῇ δυνάμει Dsc.1.64. **-ιώδης**, ες, = κομμιδώδης, Arist. *HA*628^{b}27.

κομμός (A), ὁ, (κόπτω) *striking*; esp. *beating of the head and breast in lamentation*, ἔκοψα κομμὸν Ἄριον A.*Ch*.423 (lyr.), cf. Bion 1.97 (pl.); hence, 2. in the Att. Drama, *dirge, lament*, sung alternately by one or more of the chief characters and the chorus, κ. δὲ θρῆνος κοινὸς χοροῦ καὶ ἀπὸ σκηνῆς Arist.*Po*.1452^{b}24.

κομμός (B), ὁ, (κομέω) *care bestowed on dress* or *adornment*, Suid.

κομμός (C), ὁ, in pl., *molar teeth*, Hsch.; cf. κόμπος III.

κομμ-όω, *beautify, embellish*, αὐτούς Arist.*SE*164^{b}20, cf. Luc.*Bis Acc*.31 (prob.); λόγους Them.*Or*.27.336c, cf. *Or*.28.343b:—Med., Eup.421. **-ώ**, οῦς, ἡ, *priestess who adorned* the seated statue of Athena on the Acropolis of Athens, *AB*273. **-ῶ**· πλεκτάναι, Hsch. **-ωμα**, ατος, τό, *embellishment*, Luc.*Hist.Conscr*.8. **-ωσις**, εως, ἡ, *embellishment*, Ath.13.568a (pl.). II. (κόμμι) *stop-wax*, prob. in Arist.*HA*623^{b}31, cf. Plin.*HN*11.16, Hsch. **-ωτής**, οῦ, ὁ, *dresser*, esp. *hairdresser*, in pl., Arr.*Epict*.2.23.14, Them.*Or*.20. 238a; *beautifier, embellisher*, τινος Luc.*Merc.Cond*.32: metaph., ὥσπερ γυναικὸς πολυτελοῦς τῆς τραγῳδίας κομμωταί Plu.2.348f: abs., Gal.*Thras*.35. **-ωτικός**, ή, όν, *of* or *for embellishment*, ἄσκησις Luc.*Am*.9; ποικιλία Them.*Or*.24.303c; τίνι διαφέρει τοῦ κ. τὸ κοσμητικὸν τῆς ἰατρικῆς μέρος Gal.12.434, cf. *UP*1.9: ἡ -κή (sc. τέχνη) the *art of embellishment*, Pl.*Grg*.463b, Phld.*Rh*.2.183S.: metaph., of style, κόσμος τις ἐπικείμενος ἔξωθεν κ. Hermog.*Id*.1.12, cf. 9, Them.*Or*.24.303c. Adv. -κῶς, ἔχειν Sch.Ar.*Pl*.1064. **-ώτρια**, ἡ, fem. of κομμωτής, *dresser, tirewoman*, Ar.*Ec*.737, Pl.*R*.373c, Jul. *Caes*.335b. **-ώτριον**, τό, *tiring-instrument*, Ar.*Fr*.320.8.

Κομνοκάριος, ὁ (sc. μήν), name of month at Dreros, *SIG*527.106 (iii B.C.).

κομοτροφέω, *let the hair grow*, Str.4.4.3, *Cat.Cod.Astr*.8(4).165.

κομπάζω, fut. -άσομαι B.7.42:— = κομπέω, *boast, brag*, A.*Th*.436, *Ag*.1671, etc.; κ. μέγα S.*Aj*.1122; μάτην E.*Hipp*.978; κ. ἐπί τινι *speak big* against.., A.*Th*.480 (but also, *boast* of.., Phld.*Rh*.1.24S.): c. acc., κ. λόγον *speak big* words, A.*Ag*.1400, etc.; κ. γέρας *boast* one's office, Id.*Eu*.209; οὐ πατρῴαν τὴν τέχνην ἐκόμπασας S.*El*.1500: c. inf., *boast that*.., A.*Ag*.1130, E.*Ba*.340; κ. ὡς.. X.*Oec*.10.3, Plu. *Crass*.18:—Pass., *to be made a boast of, be renowned*, οὕνεκ' ὄλβου E.*HF*64; φόβος..κομπάζεται fear *is loudly spoken*, A.*Th*.500; τίνος δὲ..παῖς πατρὸς κομπάζεται; of what father *is he said to be* the son? E.*Alc*.497.—Rare in early Prose, Lys.6.18, 48, X.*Smp*.4.19, *Oec*. l.c. II. = κομπέω I.2, *ring* a jar to test its soundness, *PLond. ined*.2327 (iii B.C.). III. ἐκομπάσθη· ἠπατήθη, εἰς ὄγκον διετέθη, Hsch., cf. Suid.

κόμπαλος· παλαιστροφύλαξ, Hsch.

Κομπ-ᾰσεύς, έως, ὁ, Com. word, *one of the* Κόμπος*-deme, Bragsman*, Ar.*Av*.1126. **-ᾰσία**, ἡ, *ringing* of wine-jars (cf. κομπάζω II), *POxy*.1631.16 (iii A.D.). **-ασμα**, ατος, τό, usu. in pl., *boasts*, A. *Pr*.363, *Th*.551, 794, Ar.*Ra*.940, Alex.ap.*POxy*.1801.51: sg., Μακεδονικὸν κ. Arr.*Ind*.5.10. **-ασμός**, ὁ, = foreg., Plu.*Sull*.16. **-αστής**, οῦ, ὁ, *braggart*, Ph.2.273 (pl.), Plu.*Crass*.16, Sch.Ar.*Ach*.595 in *POxy*. 856.56. II. *one who rings* wine-jars to test their soundness (cf. κομπάζω II), *PSI*8.953.3 (vi A.D.). **-αστικός**, ή, όν, *braggart*, Poll.9.146. Adv. -κῶς ib.147. **-έω**, (κόμπος) *ring, clash*, κόμπει χαλκὸς ἐπὶ στήθεσσι φαεινός Il.12.151. 2. c. acc., κ. χύτραν *ring* a pot to see if it be sound, D.L.6.30 (restored from Eust.896.61 for σκοποῦμεν), cf. 2.78. II. metaph., *boast, brag*, τί κομπέω παρὰ καιρόν; Pi.*P*.10.4; κ. ἄλλως Hdt.5.41; ὡς σὺ κομπεῖς E.*Or*.571: c. acc. cogn., κ. μῦθον *speak a boastful* speech, S.*Aj*.770; ὑψήλ' ἐκόμπεις ib. 1230. 2. c. acc., *boast of*, κ. γάμους A.*Pr*.947:—Pass., ὁπλῖται, ὅσοιπερ κομποῦνται *are boasted of*, Th.6.17, cf. Phld.*Rh*.2.33S. 3. c. acc. et inf., *boast that*.., E.*El*.815; κ. ὅπως.. *boast* how.., S.*OC* 1149.—Like κομπάζω, rare in Prose. **-ηγόρος**, ον, *speaking boastfully*, Hsch. s. v. ἀερολέσχης. **-ηρός**, ά, όν, *resounding*, λέξεις (in the Dithyramb) Anon.*in Rh*.177.3, cf. Sch.E.*Ph*.600. Adv. -ρῶς Anon.*in Rh*.161.29.

κομποθηλαία (-θυλ- cod.), ἡ, gloss on στρόφος, = ζώνη, Sch.rec. A.*Th*.871; cf. sq. **-θήλυκα**, τά, v.l. for πόρπακας (the ends of a seton) in *Hippiatr*.2; cf. foreg. and κόμβος, κομβίον, κομβοθηλεία.

κομπο-λᾰκέω, *talk big, be an empty braggart*, Ar.*Ra*.961:—also -λᾰκῠθέω, Tz.*H*.9.414. **-λᾰκύθης** or **-λάκῠθος**, ου, ὁ, *braggart*, Ar.*Ach*.589, 1182, perh. with a play on *Lamachus*. **-λογία**, ἡ, *boastful speaking*, Men.Prot.p.17 D.

κόμπος (A), ὁ, *din, clash*, esp. such as is caused by the collision of two hard bodies, as when a boar whets his tusks, ὕπαι δέ τε κ. ὀδόντων γίγνεται Il.11.417, 12.149; *stamping* of dancers' feet, πολὺς δ' ὑπὸ κ. ὀρώρει Od.8.380; *ringing* of metal, E.*Rh*.383 (anap., pl.). II. metaph., *boast, vaunt*, ὁ κ. οὐ κατ' ἄνθρωπον φρονεῖ A.*Th*.425, cf. 473, *Ag*.613; οὐ πεπλασμένος ὁ κ., ἀλλὰ καὶ λίαν εἰρημένος Id.*Pr*.1031; Ζεὺς γὰρ μεγάλης γλώσσης κόμπους ὑπερεχθαίρει S.*Ant*.127 (anap.); κ. πάρεστι, i. e. I am proud of the deed, Id.*Aj*.96: rare in Prose and Com., ὅρα μὴ μάτην κ. ὁ λόγος εἰρημένος ᾖ Hdt.7.103; οὐ λόγων..κ. τάδε, μᾶλλον ἢ ἔργων..ἀλήθεια Th.2.41; ἀλαζονεία καὶ κ. τοῦ ψηφίσματος Aeschin.3.237; κ. κενοὶ ψοφοῦσιν Alex.25.9; of rhetorical *bombast*, Epicur.*Sent.Vat*.45. 2. rarely in good sense, *praise*, Pi.*I*.1.43, 5(4).24. III. in pl., *molar teeth*, Hsch.

κομπός (B), ὁ, = κομπαστής, E.*Ph*.600 (troch.); κ. λόγος *EM*527. 47.—On the accent, v. Hdn.Gr.1.187.

κομποφᾰκελορρήμων, ον, gen. ονος, *pomp-bundle-worded*, derisive epith. of Aeschylus in Ar.*Ra*.839, because of his long compounds:—hence **κομποφακελλορρημοσύνη**, ἡ, Lyd.*Mag*.3.7.

κομπ-όω, = κομπέω, D.C.43.22 (Pass.). **-ώδης**, ες, *boastful, vainglorious*, κομπωδεστέρα προσποίησις Th.2.62; τὸ ἀνθρώπειον κ. Id. 5.68; τὸ κ. καὶ σοβαρόν Plu.*Sull*.16. Adv. -δῶς Sch.Th.8.81.

Κομ-ύρια, τά, festival of Zeus Panamaros, *BCH*11.384, *Supp. Epigr*.4.294, al. **-ύριον**, τό, sanctuary of Zeus, *BCH*11.380.

κομψ-εία, ἡ, (κομψός) *daintiness, refinement*, esp. of language, τὰς ..τοιαύτας κομψείας such-like *refinements*, Pl.*Phd*.101c, cf. Phld.*Rh*. 1.224S., Luc.*Prom*.8. II. κομψεία, Ἀττικῶς· πανουργία, Ἑλληνικῶς, Moer.p.237 P. **-ευμα**, ατος, τό, *ingenious invention*, Arist. *Mete*.349^{a}30; σεμνῶν ὀνομάτων Luc.*Am*.54 (pl.); *quibble*, Gal.6.228 (pl.). **-ευρῑπικῶς**, Adv. *with Euripides-quibbles* (shortd. from κομψευριπιδικῶς), Ar.*Eq*.18. **-εύω**, *refine upon*, κόμψευέ νυν τὴν δόξαν aye, *quibble on* the word δόξα (referring to the previous line), S.*Ant*.324:—mostly in Med., *to be smart, ingenious*, ἥδεσθαι κομψευόμενος to be fond *of clever inventions*, Hp.*Art*.70 (glossed πανουργευόμενος, Erot.); ὁ τοῦτο κομψευσάμενος he who *invented* this *subtlety*, Pl.*R*.489b; πρέπει..σοφιστῇ τὰ τοιαῦτα κομψεύεσθαι Id.*La*.197d; κ. ὡς.. Id.*R*.436d: pf. Pass. in med. sense, αὐτὸ τοῦτο καὶ κεκόμψευται he *has advanced* this *dainty paradox*, Id.*Phdr*.227c; οἱ τὰ πολιτικὰ κεκομψευμένοι Ph.1.448. 2. Pass., of things, προσαγώγιον κεκομψευμένον *neatly made*, Pl.*Phlb*.56c; ὁ λόγος ὑπὸ τῶν τοιούτων κεκόμψευται σχημάτων D.H.*Isoc*.14.

κομψο-λόγος, ον, *fine speaking*, ἰατροί Aesop.168. **-πρεπής**, ές, *ingenious-seeming*, μοῦσα Ar.*Nu*.1030; τὸ κ. *Vit.Aeschyli*.

κομψ-ός, ή, όν, *nice, refined, gentlemanly*, ἐσμὲν ἅπαντα κομψοὶ ἄνδρες we are perfect *gentlemen*, Eup.159, cf. Ar.*V.*1317; κ. ἐν συνουσίᾳ Id.*Nu.*649; τὸ θῆλυ τοὺς πόδας ἔχει κομψοτέρους *more delicate, finer*, Arist.*Phgn.*809^{b}9. 2. *smart, clever, ingenious*, of persons or their words and acts, ὁ πρῶτος εὑρὼν κ. ἦν τραγήματα Alex.185; κ. θεαταί Cratin.169, cf. 307; Θηραμένης ὁ κ. Ar.*Ra.*967; Σικελὸς κ. ἀνήρ Timocr.6, cf. Pl.*Grg.*493a; κ. περί τι *clever* about.., Id.*R.*495d (Sup.), *Cra.*405d; of a dog's instinct, κ. τὸ πάθος αὐτοῦ τῆς φύσεως Id.*R.*376a; μὰ γῆν.., μὴ 'γὼ νόημα κομψότερον ἤκουσά πω a *more ingenious* device.., Ar.*Av.*195; τὸ πρᾶγμα κ. [ἐστι] Id.*Th.*93, cf. 460 (lyr., Comp.), Dionys.Com.3.1; esp. in a sneering sense, *over-ingenious*, κομψός γ' ὁ κῆρυξ καὶ παρεργάτης λόγων E.*Supp.*426; τρίβων γὰρ εἶ τὰ κομψά versed in *subtleties*, Id.*Rh.*625; μή μοι τὰ κομψὰ ποικίλοι γενοίατο, ἀλλ' ὧν πόλει δεῖ Id.*Fr.*16; τὸ κ. *refinement, subtlety*, Arist.*Pol.*1265^{a}12; τῶν ἰατρῶν ὅσοι κ. ἢ περίεργοι Id.*Resp.*480^{b}27; κ. σοφίσματα E.*Fr.*188.5; τοῦτ' ἔχει -ότατον this is the *subtlest* part of it, Pl.*Tht.*171a; κομψότερος.. ὁ λόγος ἢ κατ' ἐμέ *too subtle* for me, Id.*Cra.*429d:—but in Pl. and Arist., usu. *clever*, esp. *skilful in technique*, with at most a slight irony (κομψοὺς Πλάτων οὐ τοὺς πανούργους, ἀλλὰ τοὺς βελτίστους Moer.p.206 P.). 3. more generally, *nice, good, pleasant*, πάντων δὲ κομψότατον τὸ τῆς πόας Pl.*Phdr.*230c; τὰ κ. ταῦτα χλανίσκια that *nice* suit of yours, Aeschin.1.131. II. Adv. -ψῶς *cleverly*, Ar.*Ach.*1016 (lyr.), Pl.*Cra.*399a, etc.: Comp. -οτέρως Isoc.15.195; κ. ἔχειν to be *well*, 'nicely' in health, *PPar.*18.3 (ii B.C.), cf. *PLond. ined.*2126 (ii/iii A.D.), etc.; κομψότερον σχεῖν to get *better* in health, *Ev.Jo.*4.52, cf. Arr.*Epict.*3.10.13, *POxy.*935.5 (iii A.D.): Sup. -ότατα *nicely*, Ar.*Lys.*89; λέγεσθαι κομψότατα *most cleverly*, Pl.*Tht.*202d.—Chiefly found in Att. Com. and Prose; Trag. only in E. (Orig. sense uncertain; = στρεβλός, Erot. (citing Euripides); = στρογγύλος, Hsch.) -ότης, ητος, ἡ, *elegance, prettiness, daintiness*, esp. of language, Isoc.12.1 (v.l. κοσμιότητος), Pl.*Ep.*358c (pl.); κ. ἱστορική, φυσική, Plu.2.353e.

κονᾰβ-έω, (κόναβος) Ep. Verb, *resound, clash, ring*, esp. of metallic bodies, ἀμφὶ δὲ πήληξ σμερδαλέον κονάβησε Il.15.648, cf. 21.593: late in pres., *AP*11.144 (Cereal.); *re-echo*, ἀμφὶ δὲ νῆες σμερδαλέον κονάβησαν ἀϋσάντων ὑπ' Ἀχαιῶν Il.2.334, 16.277; ἀμφὶ δὲ δῶμα σμ. κον. Od.17.542; ἀμφὶ δὲ γαῖα σμ. κον. Hes.*Th.*840: late in Prose, of a river, Sch.Opp.*C.*2.145. -ηδόν, Adv. *with a noise, clash*, *AP*7.531 (Antip. Thess.). -ίζω, = κοναβέω, περὶ στήθεσσι δὲ χαλκὸς σμερδαλέον κονάβιζε Il.13.498, cf. 21.255; αὐτὰρ ὑπὸ χθὼν σμ. κον. ποσσὶν 2.466, cf. Orph.*H.*38.9. -ος, ὁ, *ringing, clashing, din*, κόναβος.. ἀνδρῶν ὀλλυμένων νηῶν θ' ἅμα ἀγνυμενάων Od.10.122, v.l. for ὄτοβος ap.Sch.Hes.*Th.*709.—Ep. word, once in Trag., κ. χαλκοδέτων σακέων A.*Th.*160 (lyr.), cf. Luc.*Hist.Conscr.*22.

κονάριχον· γλαφυρόν, Hsch. **κοναρός**, ά, όν, *well-fed, fat*, Id.; *vigorous, active*, Id. (also in Comp.).

κονβενταρχέω, τῶν Ῥωμαίων *to be president of a conventus civium Romanorum*, *IGRom.*4.818 (Hierapolis).

κόνδαξ, ἄκος, ὁ, gambling game played with an unpointed dart, *Cod.Just.*3.43.1.4: metaph., παίζων κόνδακα, of sexual intercourse, *AP*5.60 (Rufin.).

κόνδοι· κεραῖαι, ἀστράγαλοι, Hsch.

κονδο-κέρατος, ον, *short-horned*, Al.*Le.*22.23. -λύχνια, -λύχνιος, = *statarium*, *Gloss.* -μονόβολον, τό, name of a gambling game, *Cod.Just.*3.43.1.4.

κονδός, v. κοντός (B).

κόνδυ, υος, τό, *drinking-vessel*, Men.293, Hipparch.Com.1.6, *IG*11(2).287*B*133, al. (Delos, iii B.C.), *PPetr.*2 p.108 (iii B.C.), Pancrat. ap.Ath.11.478a; as a measure, Lxx *Ge.*44.2, al.: pl., κόνδυα ἀργυρᾶ Alex.Magn.Epist.ap.Ath.11.784a.

κονδῠλ-ίζω, (κόνδυλος) *strike with the fist*, Hyp.*Fr.*98 (Act. and Pass.), Aristid.2.95 J.: metaph., *maltreat, oppress*, ὀρφανοὺς Lxx *Ma.*3.5; εἰς κεφαλὰς πτωχῶν ib.*Am.*2.7; also αὐτὴν εἰς ἀνάμνησιν κ. Lib.*Decl.*26.20:—Pass., ὑπὸ συνηθείας ἀεὶ κεκονδυλισμένος inured to *buffetings*, Longin.44.4, cf. D.L.2.21. -ιον, τό, Dim. of κόνδυ, *IG*11(2).147*B*10 (Delos, iv B.C.), al.; κ. Σικυώνιον *BGU*1300.12 (iii/ii B.C.). II. Dim. of κόνδυλος, f.l. in Axionic.6.3 (pl.). -ισμός, ὁ, *striking with the fist, maltreatment*, Artem.2.15, Lxx *Ze.*2.8. -ιστής, οῦ, ὁ, horse which injures its hoofs in the stable, *Hippiatr.*10 (v.l.). -οειδής, ές, = κονδυλώδης, ἐξοχαί Ruf.*Oss.*15. -όομαι, Pass., *swell up*, κονδυλοῦνται αἱ στολίδες Aspasia ap.Aët.16.118, cf. Hsch. -ος, ὁ, *knuckle*, Arist.*HA*493^{b}28: pl., Hp.*Art.*2; κονδύλοις ἡρμοττόμην (v. ἁρμόζω I.4); κονδύλοις νουθετεῖν τινα Ar.*V.*254: so in sg., ib.1503; δοῦναι κόνδυλόν τινι Plu.2.439d; κονδύλους αὐτῷ δεῖδι (= δίδου) *POxy.*1185.12 (ii/iii A.D.); κονδύλῳ καθικέσθαι τινός Plu.*Alc.*7, etc.; κονδύλοις [πατάξαι], opp. ἐπὶ κόρρης (a slap in the face), D.21.72: prov., κολλύραν καὶ κόνδυλον ὄψον ἐπ' αὐτῇ pudding and *knuckle*-sauce to it, i.e. a good thrashing, Ar.*Pax* 123, ubi v. Sch.; λόγον ἔχειν τοῦ κ. προχειρότερον Plu.*Cat.Mi.*1; νὴ τοὺς κ. οὓς ἠνεσχόμην, Com. oath, Ar.*Eq.*411. II. generally, *knuckle of any joint*, as of the humerus, Gal.18(2).617; of the humerus and elbow, Poll.2.141; of the finger (middle joint), Ruf.*Onom.*84; ποδός Luc.*Ocyp.*28. 2. *knot* in a string, Paul.Aeg.6.25. III. *any hard, bony knob*, of the teeth, Hp.*Epid.*4.19, 25. -ώδης, ες, *knobby*, Id.*Mochl.*1, Dsc.1.107, Gal.2.755. -ωμα, ατος, τό, *knob, callous lump*, Hp.*Haem.*4,5, Dsc.*Eup.*1.209, Gal.13.533. -ωσις, εως, ἡ, = foreg., Hp.*Haem.*4,5. -ωτός, ή, όν, *knobby*, χρυσὶς *IG*2^{2}.1400.36: neut. as Subst., ib.40, prob. in ib.1386.10.

κονέω, (κόνις) *raise dust*: hence, *hasten*, Hsch.; = ὑπηρετεῖν, *EM* 268.29: elsewh. only in compd. ἐγκονέω.

κονή, ἡ, (καίνω) *murder*, Hsch. (pl.): hence, = κώνειον, Ps.-Dsc. 4.78.

κονητής, οῦ, ὁ, *servant*, Hsch.

κονί-α, Ion. and Ep. -ίη, ἡ, (κόνις): 1. *dust*, ποδῶν ὑπένερθε κ. ἵστατ' ἀειρομένη Il.2.150; ὑπὸ δέ σφισιν ὤρτο κ. 11.151: in pl., κὰδ δ' ἔπεσ' ἐν κονίῃσι Od.18.98; ἐν κονίῃσι πεσών Il.17.315, etc.; πρηνέες ἐν κονίῃσιν 2.418, cf. Hes.*Sc.*365; μιάνθησαν δὲ ἔθειραι αἵματι καὶ κονίῃσι Il.16.796: also Trag. in lyr., A.*Ag.*64, E.*Andr.*112, *Supp.*821. 2. *sand*, Il.21.271. 3. *ashes*, in pl., κατ' ἄρ' ἕζετ' ἐπ' ἐσχάρῃ ἐν κονίῃσι Od.7.153, cf. 160: sg., κ. δρυΐνη *Gp.*13.4.2. II. *pearl-ash, lye, soap-powder*, λούειν ἄνευ κονίας Ar.*Lys.*470 (with a play on ἀκονιτί), cf. *Ach.*18, *Ra.*711, Pl.*R.*430b: pl., Thphr.*HP*4.10.4 (nisi leg. κονιάσεις). 2. *alkaline fluid* used for washing, Gal.12.35, al.; κ. στακτή Id.13.569. b. κ. ἀπὸ τῆς ἱερᾶς σποδοῦ καὶ τοῦ ἱεροῦ ὕδατος, as a medicine, *SIG*1171.12 (Lebena). III. = τίτανος, Erot. s.h.v.; κ. ἄσβεστος *quicklime*, Heraclid.Tarent.ap.Gal.12.958; κ. μέλαινα *IG*2^{2}.1672.197. 2. *plaster, stucco*, ib.4^{2}(1).103.278 (Epid.), *POxy.*1450.4 (iii A.D.), Eust.382.36. [Hom. uses ῑ in the quadrisyll. case κονίῃσι, ῐ in the trisyll.: Trag. and Com. ῐ in lyr. (dact. and anap.), A.*Ag.*64, E.*Andr.*112, Ar.*Ra.*711; ῑ in iamb., Id.*Ach.*18, *Lys.*470.] -άζω, in Pass., *to be sprinkled with ashes*, *Gp.*13.4.2; v.l. for κεκονιμένος, Sm.2 *Ki.*1.2. -ᾱλος, ὁ, = κονίσαλος III, *IG*12(3).540 (Thera). -ᾱμα, Ion. -ημα, ατος, τό, *stucco, plaster*, Hp.*Epid.*7.11, Arist.*GA*726^{b}27, *Col.*791^{b}27, 794^{b}32, Thphr.*CP*4.16.1, *PSI*5.545.19 (iii B.C.), etc.: in pl., οἰκοδομαὶ πολυτελεῖς καὶ κονιάματα D.S.20.8; also, *whitewashing*, D.13.30. -ᾱσις, εως, ἡ, *plastering with stucco, whitening*, *IG*11(4).1246 (Delos, iii/ii B.C.), 7.2712.35 (Acraeph.), 4^{2}(1).102.39, al. (Epid.), 2^{2}.1672.203, *Gp.*2.27.5, cj. in Thphr.*HP*4.10.4 (pl.). -ᾱτήρ, ῆρος, ὁ, *plasterer*, *IG*4^{2}(1).102.251 (Epid.). -ατης [ᾱ], ου, ὁ, = foreg., *IG*11(2).146*A*74 (Delos, iv B.C.), *Sammelb.*6823.20 (i A.D.), *POxy.*1450.6 (iii A.D.); gloss on ἐξαλίπτης, Gal.19.98, cf. Sch.Ar.*Av.*1150; title of play by Amphis. -ατικός, ή, όν, in neut. pl., *stucco decorations*, *IGRom.*1.743 (Trajana Augusta); κ. ἔργα *PPetr.*3 p.290 (iii B.C.), *POxy.*2145.2 (ii A.D.). -ατός, ή, όν, *plastered* or *daubed*, X.*An.*4.2.22, Thphr.*HP*8.11.1, *PPetr.*3 p.290 (iii B.C.). -άω, (κονία III) *plaster with lime* or *stucco*, D.3.29, 23.208, *IG*2^{2}.1672.107, 140, 179, *Inscr.Magn.*100^{b}.40, etc.:—Med., κ. τοὺς ἐγχελεῶνας *have them plastered*, Arist.*HA*592^{a}4:—Pass., Bito 55.9, Plu.*Comp.Arist.Cat.Ma.*4, *IG*7.2712.35 (Acraeph.); τάφοι κεκονιαμένοι *Ev.Matt.*23.27. 2. generally, *daub over*, as with pitch, ἀγγεῖα κεκονιαμένα D.S.19.94. 3. metaph., κ. τὸ πρόσωπον *paint, disguise* it, Philostr.*Ep.*22:—Pass., κεκονιαμένοι Lxx *Pr.*21.9 (κεκονιαμένους is f.l. for κεκονιμένους Them.*Or.*7.91d).

κονιβᾰτία, ἡ, (βαίνω) *dusty walk*, Hp.*Vict.*3.68 (prob. l. for σχοινοβατίῃσι).

κονίζω, v. κονίω. II. κονίζειν, name of a garment, dub. in Hsch. s.v. διακονίς. **κόνικλος**, v. κύνικλος.

κονίλη [ῑ], ἡ, *marjoram, Origanum viride*, Diocl.*Fr.*150, Nic.*Th.*626, Dsc.3.29, Gal.12.91. II. *organy, Origanum heracleoticum*, Dsc.3.27.

κόνιμα, v. κόνισμα.

κόνιον, τό, = κονία, Suid.; dub. sens. in *POxy.*739.7 (i A.D.). II. v. κώνειον. **κονιόπους** and **κονιορτόποδες**, v. κονίποδες.

κονῐορτ-ός, ὁ, (κόνις, ὄρνυμι) *dust raised* or *stirred up, cloud of dust*, Hdt.8.65; ὁ κ. δῆλος αὐτῶν ὡς ὁμοῦ προσκειμένων Ar.*Eq.*245, cf. Th.4.44; κ. τῆς ὕλης νεωστὶ κεκαυμένης, i.e. *a cloud* of wood-ashes, ib.34; κ. καὶ ζάλη Pl.*R.*496d: in pl., Diocl.*Fr.*147. 2. generally, *dirt, sweepings*, σαρώματα.. σὺν τῷ κ. Wilcken *Chr.*198.16 (iii B.C.). II. metaph., *dirty fellow*, χαίρει τις αὐχμῶν ἢ ῥυπῶν, κ. ἀναπέφηνεν Anaxandr.34.6, cf. Aristopho 10.8; Εὐκτήμων ὁ κ. D.21.103. -όω, *cover with dust*, Thphr.*HP*2.7.5. -ώδης, ες, *dusty*, Arist.*HA*557^{b}3, *Cael.*313^{a}20, Thphr.*CP*4.16.1, Dsc.1.26, Gal.14.49.

κόνῑος, α, ον, (κόνις) *dusty*, χέρσος Pi.*N.*9.43. II. *causing dust*, epith. of Zeus, Paus.1.40.6.

κονίποδες [ῐ], οἱ, *dusty-foots*, name for the serfs at Epidaurus, Plu.2.291e; also κονιορτόποδες Hsch. s.v. κονίποδες. II. kind of *shoe covering a small part of the foot*, Ar.*Ec.*848, Poll.7.86: in *EM*529.2, and Suid., **κονιόπους**.

κόνις, ιος, Att. εως or εος E.*Cyc.*641, ἡ: dat. κόνι contr. fr. κόνιι, Il.24.18, Od.11.191, Att. κόνει:—*dust*, κόνιος δεδραγμένος Il.13.393; as an emblem of a countless multitude, εἴ μοι τόσα δοίη ὅσα ψάμαθός τε κ. τε 9.385; κ. δέ σφ' ἀμφιδεδήει Hes.*Sc.*62; κόνιν, ἄναυδον ἄγγελον στρατοῦ A.*Supp.*180; αἷμα κ. πίνει, ἀνασπᾷ, Id.*Th.*736 (lyr.), *Eu.*647; κ. διψία S.*Ant.*247, 429; of the grave, κ. κατακρύπτει χάριν Pi.*O.*8.79, cf. S.*OC*406, *El.*435, etc.; κόνει φύρειν κάρα, in sign of mourning, E.*Hec.*496; ἡ ἐπίχρυσος κ. gold *dust*, Poll.7.97. 2. *ashes*, ἐν κόνι ἄγχι πυρός Od.l.c.; κόνιν αἰθαλόεσσαν χεύατο κὰκ κεφαλῆς Il.18.23, cf. Theoc.24.93. II. the *dust* of the κονίστρα, Arist.*IA*709^{a}14, Luc.*Anach.*29, Ath.12.518d: metaph., of toil, πάντα ἡμῖν μία κ. dub. in Luc.*DMort.*1.3: in Plu.2.697a κόνιν (*lye*) is prob. an error for κονίαν. III. = κονία III, Jul.*Ep.*80. [κόνῐν Il.18.23; κόνῑ (shortd. fr. κόνι before a vowel) 24.18, Od.l.c.; κονῖς, κονῖν, A.*Pr.*1084 (anap.), *Supp.*180, 783 (lyr.): ῐ in gen., v. supr.] (Cf. Lat. *cinis*.)

κονίς (on the accent v. Hdn.Gr.1.94), ἴδος, ἡ, mostly in pl., κονίδες *eggs of lice, fleas, and bugs, nits*, Arist.*HA*539^{b}11, 556^{b}24, Antyll.ap.

Orib.10.21.1; κόνιδες (sic), gloss on δόρκαι, Hsch. (Cf. OE. *hnitu* 'nit'.)

κονῐσᾰλέος, α, ον, *dusty*, Antim.52, Euph.23.

κονίσᾰλος [ῐ], in later Mss. sts. wrongly κονίσσαλος, ὁ, (κόνις) *cloud of dust*, ὣς ἄρα τῶν ὑπὸ ποσσὶ κ. ὄρνυτ' ἀελλής Il.3.13; λευκοὶ ὕπερθε γένοντο κονισάλῳ 5.503, cf. 22.401. II. the mixed *dust, oil and sweat* on wrestlers, Gal.12.283. III. a demon of the same class as Priapus, Ar.*Lys.*982 (ubi v. Sch.), Pl.Com.174.13, cf. Str.13.1.12, *SIG*1027.10 (Cos). 2. *lascivious dance*, Hsch.

κόνῑσ-ις, εως, ἡ, *exercise in the arena*, δρόμου..καὶ πάλης καὶ κονίσεως (v.l. κινήσεως) Arist.*Cael.*292a26. II. f.l. for κόμμωσις (q.v.), Id.*HA*623b31. **-μα**, ατος, τό, = κονίστρα, *IG*5(1).938 (Cythera):—also **κόνῖμα**, *BCH*23.566 (Delph., iii B.C.). **-τήριον**, τό, = κονίστρα, Vitr.5.11.2, *IGRom.*4.293*a*i 19 (Pergam., ii B.C.). **-τικός**, ή, όν, *liking to roll in the dust*, of birds, opp. λοῦσται, Arist.*HA*633a 29. **-τρα**, ἡ, *place covered with dust*: hence, *rolling place*, such as birds make in the dust, ib.613b9. 2. *arena in a wrestling school*, Lyc.867, Plu.2.638c; δρόμοι καὶ κ. καὶ γυμνάσια Ael.*NA*11.10, cf. 6.15, Eust.382.32; also in a theatre, Suid. s. v. σκηνή.

κονίω [ῑ], fut. κονίσω [ῑ]: aor. ἐκόνισα Il. (v. infr.):—Med., Ph.2. 173, fut. κονιοῦμαι v.l. in Ph. l. c. (as if from κονίζω, cf. Hsch. s. v. κονίζεσθαι): aor. ἐκονισάμην Ar.*Ec.*1177, Luc.*Anach.*31, etc.:—Pass., pf. κεκόνῑμαι Il.21.541, Hes.*Op.*481, Ar.*Ec.*291: plpf. κεκόνῑτο Il.22. 405 (in Mss. sts. incorrectly ἐκόνισσα, κεκόνισμαι, κεκόνιστο, Il.21.407, Theoc.1.30, *AP*9.128):—*make dusty, cover with clouds of dust*, εὐρὺ κονίσουσιν πεδίον, of persons in hasty flight, Il.14.145. 2. *cover with dust*, ἐκόνισε δὲ χαίτας 21.407:—Pass., κεκονιμένοι φεῦγον *all dusty* fled they, ib.541; κεκόνιτο κάρη 22.405; κεκονιμένος *all dusty*, i. e. *in haste*, Ar.*Ec.*291, cf. 1177, Luc.*DDeor.*24.1, *Tim.*45, etc. 3. Pass., *to be sprinkled as with dust*, κισσὸς ἑλιχρύσῳ κεκονιμένος Theoc. 1.30. 4. Med., *roll in the dust*, like birds, horses, etc., Arist.*HA* 633b4, 557a12 (leg. κονίωνται), Polem.Hist.59; but, of wrestlers, *sprinkle themselves with dust*, Diocl.*Fr.*141, Gal.6.162, Luc.*Anach.* l. c.: hence, *prepare for combat*, Ph. l. c., Eust.1113.63; αὐτὸς ἐφ' ἑαυτοῦ κονισάμενος Max.Tyr.5.8. II. intr., κονίοντες πεδίοιο *galloping o'er the dusty* plain, in Il. always of horses, 13.820, 23. 372,449; of men racing, Od.8.122; of an advancing army, A.*Th.*60, cf. *Pers.*163 (troch.).

κονιώδης, ες, *ash-like*, Hp.*Coac.*571.

κόννα· σποδός, Hsch.

κόννᾰρος, ὁ, a prickly evergreen, *Zizyphus Spina-Christi*, Theopomp.Hist.129, Agathocl.6:—neut. **κόνναρον**, τό, *its fruit*, Hsch.

Κοννᾶς or **Κόννος**, ὁ, a famous harpist who taught Socrates, Pl. *Euthd.*272c, but died in want, Cratin.317, Ar.*Eq.*534: hence prov., Κόννου θρῖον *trifle*, Sch.Ar.*V.*673; altered to Κ. ψῆφος by Ar. l. c.

κοννέω, contr. **κοννῶ**, *know*, κοννεῖς A.*Supp.*130,164 (both lyr.), cf. Hsch.

κοννοειδῆ· εἰς ὀξὺ λήγων, Hsch. (leg. κωνο–).

κόννος, ὁ, kind of *trinket*, Suid., citing Plb.10.18.6 (where κόνος). 2. *beard*, Luc.*Lex.*5. 3. = σκόλλυς (Lacon.), Hsch. s. v. ἱέρωμα; and **κοννοφόρος**, ον, = σκολλυφόρος, Id.

κοννόφρων, = ἄφρων, *Com.Adesp.*93.

κοντάκιον, τό, *essay*, κ. μου εἰς τὴν γεωμετρίαν Steph. *in Rh.*284.33, cf. 277.29.

κοντάριον (A), τό, = κέντρον 9, Heph.Astr.2.11 (pl.).

κοντάριον (B), τό, Dim. of κοντός (A), *spear*, Anon. *in Rh.*236.5, Sch.E.*Hec.*14; **κοντᾰρᾶτος**, ὁ, *one armed with a spear*, Anon. *in Rh.* 103.21; **κοντᾰριοθήκη**, ἡ, *spear-case*, Sch.Opp.*H.*2.356.

κονταφόρος, ὁ, = κοντοφόρος, *Gloss.*

κόντῑλος, ὁ, Dim. of κοντός (A) (sens. obsc.), Eup.334.

κοντο-βολέω, *strike with a pole*, Str.10.1.12. **-κῡνηγέσιον**, τό, *wild-beast hunt with pikes*, *IGRom.*4.1632.7 (Philadelphia). **-παίκτης**, ου, ὁ, (παίζω) *acrobat who balanced a pole on his head*, *SIG*847.4 (Delph., ii/iii A. D., written -πέκτης), *AB*652. **-πλεύριον**, τό, *short side*, interpol. in *Hippiatr.*115 (pl.). **-πορεία**, ἡ, *short road*, as pr. n., Ptol.Euerg.6 J., Plb.16.16.4.

κοντός (A), ὁ, *pole, punting-pole*, Od.9.487, Hdt.2.136, 4.195, E. *Alc.*254 (lyr.), Th.2.84, Epicr.10, Diocl.*Fr.*142, *IG*12(5).647.30 (Ceos). 2. *pike*, Luc.*Tox.*55. 3. *crutch*, Gal.*UP*3.5 (pl.). 4. *goad*, *PCair.Zen.*362r.34 (iii B. C.).

κοντός (B), ή, όν, *short*, Adam.2.20, Palch. in *Cat.Cod.Astr.*1.95, interpol. in *Hippiatr.*115:—also written **κονδός**, Sor.1.16 (interpol.), Aët.16.111 (Comp.), prob. in *JRS*18.30 (Sup.). Adv. Comp. κονδότερον ἐπιβαίνειν, of a horse, take *shorter* steps, *Hippiatr.*30.

κοντοφόρος, ον, *carrying a pole* or *pike*, Plb.*Fr.*225, Luc.*Alex.*55.

κόντ-ωσις, εως, ἡ, *fishing with a pole*, Ael.*NA*12.43. **-ωτίτης** [ῑ], ου, ὁ, *puntsman*, *PCair.Zen.*492.2 (iii B. C.). **-ωτός**, ή, όν, *furnished with a pole*: κοντωτόν (sc. πλοῖον), τό, *punt*, *PHib.*1.39.4 (iii B. C.), D.S.19.12, App.*Prooem.*10.

κόνυζα, ης, ἡ, name of various species of *Inula, fleabane*, Hecat. 154 J., Arist.*HA*534b28, Thphr.*HP*6.2.6, Gal.12.35, etc.; poet. κνύζα Theoc.4.25, 7.68; κ. ἄρρην, = κ. μείζων, Dsc.3.121, *Inula viscosa*; κ. θήλεια Thphr. l. c.; = κ. μικρά, Dsc. l. c., *I. graveolens*, cf. Nic.*Th.* 875; a third species, = *I. britannica*, Thphr. l. c., Dsc. l. c.

κονυζ-ήεις, εσσα, εν, *like Inula*, Nic.*Th.*615. **-ίτης** [ῑ] οἶνος, ὁ, wine *flavoured with* κόνυζα, Dsc.5.53, *Gp.*8.10.

Κονώνειος, α, ον, *of Conon*: κονωνεία (sc. κύλιξ), cup so named, *IG* 11(2).287 *B* 133 (Delos, iii B. C.), cf. Ister 38.

κόον, v. κῷον.

κοόρτις, ιος, ἡ, the Roman *cohors*, Plb.11.23.1, 11.33.1, etc.

κόος, ὁ, *cavity* in the earth, Hsch. (pl.); from Lacon. κόον, = μέγα, *EM*396.29.

Κοούτιος, ὁ (sc. μήν), name of month at Chaleion, *GDI*1734, al.

κοπάδιον, τό, = κόπαιον, *Gloss.*

κοπάζω, aor. ἐκόπασα (v. infr.): pf. κεκόπακα Hsch.:—*grow weary*, τοῦ πολέμου Lxx *Jo.*14.15; τοῦ θυμοῦ ib.*Es.*2.1; of an abnormal pulsation, *abate*, Hp.*Epid.*7.2; esp. of natural phenomena, ἐκόπασε (sc. ὁ ἄνεμος) Hdt.7.191, cf. *Ev.Matt.*14.32; ὅταν ἡ λίμνη κοπάσῃ Arist.*Pr.*935a18; ἐκόπασε τὸ πῦρ Lxx *Nu.*11.2; of heat, Longus 1.8.

κόπαιον, τό, (κόπτω) *piece*, Alciphr.3.7, Callistr.ap.Suid. s. v. σελάχιον.

κοπᾰν-ίζω, *bray, pound*, Lxx 3 *Ki.*2.46e (Pass.), Alex.Trall.12 (Pass.). **-ισμός**, ὁ, *braying*, Hsch. s. v. κόπος. **-ιστήριον**, τό, *vessel for braying, mortar*, Id. s. v. ἀλήθινον, *Gloss.* **-ον**, τό, *pestle*, Eust.1324.32. II. = κοπίς, A.*Ch.*860 (anap.). **-ος**, ὁ, = σκέπανος, Sch.Opp.*H.*1.106.

κοπάριον, τό, a sort of *probe*, Sever.ap.Aët.7.92, Paul.Aeg.3.81, 6.62.

κοπάς, άδος, ἡ, (κόπτω) *pruned, lopped*, Thphr.*HP*1.3.3: as Subst., *brushwood*, ξυλοκοπία τῆς κ. *PSI*4.323.3 (iii B. C.), *PCair.Zen.*118.5 (iii B. C.), al.: also in pl., κοπάδες, αἱ, *PSI*5.537.16 (iii B. C.).

κόπασμα, ατος, τό, *abatement*, of a flood, Tz.*H.*6.833 (pl.).

κόπελλα· αἰδοῖα, Hsch. **κόπερρα**, Aeol., = κοπρία, Hdn.Gr.2.605.

κοπετόκτῠπος, ον, *causing the noise of lamentation to be heard*, epith. of Hecate, *PMag.Par.*1.2867 (nisi leg. καπετό–).

κοπετός, ὁ, *noise*, Eup.347; esp. of lamentation, = κομμός, *Act.Ap.* 8.2, Plu.*Fab.*17 (pl.), *AP*11.122 (Nicarch.).

κοπεύς, έως, ὁ, *one who brays* or *pounds*, employed in oil-factories, *PRev.Laws* 45.5 (iii B. C.), cf. Agatharch.26; *carpenter*, *PFlor.*175.14 (iii A. D.): generally, *one who cuts*, τινος A.D.*Synt.*301.28. II. *chisel*, D.S.1.35, Luc.*Somn.*13.

κοπή, ἡ, *cutting*, χόρτος εἰς κοπὴν καὶ ἐπινομήν *POxy.*499.15 (ii A. D.). 2. *cutting in pieces, slaughter*, Lxx *Jo.*10.20, *Ep.Hebr.*7. 1. 3. κ. τριχός, tax levied on γερδιοραβδισταί, *PAmh.*2.119.4 (200 A. D.), cf. *PFay.*58.7 (ii A. D.). 4. *breaking up*, [νεφῶν] Arist.*Mu.* 394a34. 5. *pounding* in a mortar, Alex.Aphr.*Pr.*1.67. 6. *dressing* of stone, *CPHerm.*127 (iii A. D.). 7. *striking, minting*, νομίσματος *Inscr.Délos* 461 *A a* 76 (ii B. C.). 8. *divorce*, Aq.*De.*24.3 (1). II. = κόπος II, φλοίσβου μετὰ κοπήν S.*Fr.*479 codd. Eust. (sed leg. κόπον).

κόπηθρον, τό, a wild vegetable, Hsch.

κοπ-ηρός, ά, όν, = κοπιαρός, Hdn.*Epim.*179. **-ία**, ἡ, *rest from toil*, Hsch. (pl.); but, = Lat. *labor*, Serv.Dan. ad Virg.*G.*1. 150. **-ιᾰρός**, ά, όν, *wearying*, in Comp. -ώτερος, Arist.*Pr.*880b 16, Thphr.*Lass.*7, 9. **-ιάτης** [ᾱ], ου, ὁ, *grave-digger*, *Cod.Theod.* 13.1.1, 16.2.15, Just.*Nov.*59.2, *Gloss.*:—also **κοπιᾶς**, ᾶτος, ὁ, in dat. pl. κουπιᾶσιν (sic) *BCH*24.306 (Philippi). **-ιάω**, fut. -άσω [ᾱ]: aor. ἐκοπίασα Men.*Phasm.*36: pf. κεκοπίακα *Apoc.*2.3: (κόπος):—*to be tired, grow weary*, Ar.*Th.*795, *Fr.*318.8, Lxx *De.*25.18, al.; κ. τὰ σκέλη Alex.147, Men. l. c.; κ. ὑπὸ ἀγαθῶν *to be weary of* good things, Ar.*Av.*735; ἐκ τῆς ὁδοιπορίας *Ev.Jo.*4.6; τῇ διανοίᾳ Erasistr.ap.Gal. *Consuet.*1: c. part., κ. ὀρχούμενοι Ar.*Fr.*602; ζῶν *AP*12.46 (Asclep.); μὴ κοπιάτω φιλοσοφῶν Epicur.*Ep.*3 p.59 U., cf. Plu.2.185e: aor. part. κοπιάσας, *defunctus laboribus*, *IG*14.1811:—Med. in act. sense, Arist. *Pr.*881a14. II. *work hard, toil*, *Ev.Matt.*6.28, etc.; μεθ' ἡδονῆς κ. Vett.Val.266.6; εἴς τι 1 *Ep.Ti.*4.10, cf. *Ep.Rom.*16.6; ἔν τινι 1 *Ep. Ti.*5.17; ἐπί τι Lxx *Jo.*24.13: c. inf., *strive, struggle*, μὴ κοπία ζητεῖν *Lyr.Alex.Adesp.*37.7. III. = κοπάζω, *come to rest*: *arrive at a state of saturation*, *PLeid.X.*30 (iii/iv A. D.).

κοπίδερμος, ὁ, = μαστιγίας, *Gloss.*

κοπίζω (A), (κόπις A) *talk idly, lie*, Hsch.

κοπίζω (B), *celebrate the* κοπίς (κοπίς (B) II), Ath.4.138f.

κόπις (A), ιδος, ὁ, *prater, liar, wrangler*, E.*Hec.*132 (anap.), Lyc. 763, 1464; κοπίδων ἀρχηγός Heraclit.81, cf. Pythag.ap.Sch.E.*Hec.* 134. (Prob. from κόπτω.)

κοπίς (B), ίδος, ἡ, (κόπτω) *chopper, cleaver*, Hermipp.46 (anap.), Ar. *Fr.*138, S.*Fr.*894, D.S.12.24, etc.; νερτέρων κ., prob. for κόνις, S.*Ant.* 602 (lyr.); *broad curved knife*, used by the Thessalians, E.*El.*837; by Orientals, X.*Cyr.*2.1.9, 6.2.10: as Adj., κ. μάχαιρα E.*Cyc.*241: metaph., of Phocion, ἡ τῶν ἐμῶν λόγων κ. D.ap.Plu.*Phoc.*5. 2. (parox.) κέντροιο κ. *sting of a scorpion*, Nic.*Th.*780; cf. κόπιες· κέντρα ὀρνίθ⟨ε⟩ια, Hsch. II. among the Lacedaemonians, *feast given on certain festivals to strangers*, Cratin.164, Eup.138, Philyll.16.

κοπίσκος, ὁ, Dim. of κοπίς, = λίβανος σμιλιωτός, Dsc.1.68.

κοπιώδης, ες, = κοπώδης, Hp.*Epid.*1.26.ϛ', Arist.*Pr.*885b2: Comp., ib.a17; κ. πυρετοί Hp.*Prorrh.*1.142, Gal.7.626.

κόπ-ος, ὁ, (κόπτω) *striking, beating*, ὀξύχειρι σὺν κόπῳ (Pauw for κτύπῳ) A.*Ch.*23 (lyr.); στέρνων κόπους (Seidler for κτύπους) E.*Tr.*794 (anap.); = κοπανισμός, Hsch. II. *toil and trouble, suffering*, A. *Supp.*210 (pl.); ἀνδροδάϊκτος κόπος Id.*Fr.*132 ap.Ar.*Ra.*1265; *pain* of a disease, S.*Ph.*880; κόπους παρέχειν τινί to give *trouble*, *Ev.Matt.*26. 10, al., *PTeb.*21.10 (ii B. C.), *BGU*844.10 (i A. D.); κόπον ἔχειν Phld. *Mus.*p.62 K.; πάντα κ. ἀναδεξάμενος *SIG*761 *B* 6 (Delph., i B. C.). 2. *fatigue*, Hp.*VM*21, Gal.6.190; κόπου ὕπο from *very weariness*, E. *Ba.*634; κόπῳ παρεῖμαι Id.*Ph.*852; κόπῳ δαμέντες, ἁλίσκεσθαι, Id. *Rh.*764, Th.7.40; τῷ κ. ξυνεῖναι Ar.*Pl.*321; τὰ γόνατα κ. ἕλοι μου Id.*Lys.*542: in pl., E.*Rh.*124; κόποι καὶ ὕπνοι Pl.*R.*537b, cf. X.*Eq.* 4.2, 2 *Ep.Cor.*6.5, etc.; περὶ κόπων title of work by Thphr. 3. *work, exertion*, καμάραν ἀφ' ἰδίων κόπων ἐποίησεν *IG*12(7).384 (Amorgos), cf. *BGU*884.10 (i A.D.); κόπῳ κόπον λύειν prov. in Orib.*Eup.* 1.2.8. -όω, *weary*, D.Chr.11.96; βαρυτέροις γυμνασίοις Id.18.6:—Pass., = κοπιάω, Batr.189, Antyll.ap.Orib.6.1.1, Plu.2.312f, Gal. 18(2).914; ὑπὸ τῆς ὁδοιπορίας J.*AJ*2.15.3.

κόππα, τό, = Hebr. ק (*Koph*), a letter (ϙ) standing between π and ρ in early Greek alphabets, *IG*14.2420, etc.; later displaced by κ, but surviving in Latin as Q and retained in Greek as a numeral = 90, e.g. *PSI*8.958.24 (iv A.D.): prov., οὐδὲ κόππα γιγνώσκων Parmeno 1.

κοππ-ᾰτίας, ὁ, *branded with the letter Koppa* as a mark, ἵππος κ. Ar. *Nu.*23 (with a play on κόπτω), 438, *Fr.*42. -ᾰφόρος, ον, = foreg., Luc.*Ind.*5.

κοπρ-ᾰγωγέω, *carry dung*, Dor. inf. κοπραγωγῆν Ar.*Lys.*1174. -ᾰγωγός, όν, *carrying dung*, γαστήρ Pl.Com.222; κ. ῥιπίς CratesCom. 13. -ᾰνα, τά, *excrements*, Hp.*Epid.*1.26.β', Aret.*SA*2.5. -εαῖος, ὁ, a quasi-pr. n., formed from κόπρος, *Dungy*, Ar.*Ec.*317. -ειος, α, ον, *full of dung, filthy*, ἀνὴρ κ. *stinkard*, Id.*Eq.*899, with play on signf. II. II. in Attica, of the deme Κόπρος, *IG*1².301.39:—later **Κόπριος**, misspelt Κύπριος, Is.3.2 codd., cf. Decr.ap.D.18.73. -εύω, = κοπρίζω, Hsch.:—written **κοπρεόω**, *SIG*986.14 (Chios, v/iv B.C.). -έω, v. κοπρίζω. -εών, ῶνος, ὁ, = κοπρών, Tz. *H.*6.520. -ηγέω, *carry dung*, *PFay.*118.19 (ii A.D.). -ηγία, ἡ, *conveyance of dung*, ib.110.11 (i A.D.). -ηγός, όν, *conveying dung*, πλοῖον *PLond.*2.317.8 (ii A.D.): Subst. -ηγόν, τό, *dung-cart*, *PFay.* 119.33 (pl., 100 A.D.). -ία, ἡ, (cf. κόπερρα) *dunghill*, Semon.7.6 (pl.), Stratt.43, Arist.*Mir.*845ᵃ5 (pl.), Lxx*Jb.*2.8, Asclep.ap.Gal.12.634, etc.; in Egypt, *rubbish-heap*, *PRyl.*2.162.17 (ii A.D.), etc.; ἀναιρεῖσθαι ἀπὸ κοπρίας, of foundlings, *PGnom.*238, cf. 115 (ii A.D.), *POxy.*37 i 7 (i A.D.). II. *refuse*, ἐν σείσματι κοσκίνου διαμένει κ. Lxx*Si.*27.4; *manure*, *Ev.Luc.*13.8 (v.l. κόπρια). -ιαίρετος, *sportellarius*, *Gloss.*: —also -ίαρτος, (αἴρω) *taken from the rubbish-heap*, i.e. *foundling*, prob. for κηπρ- in *PGnom.*210 (ii A.D.). -ιακός, ή, όν, *concerning manure*, *PGoodsp.Cair.*30 xxxiv 16 (ii A.D.). -ίας, ου, ὁ, (κόπρος) in pl., *buffoons*, a word first used under the Roman emperors, D.C.50.28, 73.6: Lat. *copreae*, Suet.*Tib.*61. (Perh. so called because ἐκ κοπρίας ἀναιρεθέντες, or because of their obscenity.) -ίζω, Ep. fut. -ίσσω, *dung, manure*, τέμενος μέγα κοπρίσσοντες Od.17.299 (v.l. for κοπρήσοντες), cf. Thphr.*CP*3.9.1, 4.12.3, *Sammelb.*5126.27 (iii A.D.); *act as manure*, of leguminous plants, Thphr.*HP*8.9.1. -ιήμετος, ον, *vomiting excrement*, Hp.*Epid.*2.1.9. -ινος, η, ον, *full of dung, filthy*, *Gloss.*; κόπρινοι σκώληκες worms *in excrement*, Hp.*Superf.* 28. -ιον, τό, = κόπρος, Id.*Acut.*56, Ruf.ap.Orib.8.24.8, *PFay.*110.5 (i A.D.), etc.: pl., Heraclit.96, *OGI*483.81 (Pergam.), Sor.2.56, Plu.*Pomp.*48. 2. generally, *dirt, filth*, *BGU*1115.50 (i B.C.); esp. in Magic, *dirt* taken from spot where a corpse has lain, in pl., *PMag. Par.*1.1396, 1441. -ισις, εως, ἡ, *dunging, manuring*, Thphr.*HP* 8.6.3. -ισμός, ὁ, = foreg., Id.*CP*3.9.2, *POxy.*729.10 (ii A.D.), *Gp.* 2.39.6. -ιώδης, ες, = κοπρώδης, Hp.*Coac.*590, Thphr.*CP*2.6.3; *full of dung*, τόπος *PSI*6.696.10 (iii A.D.).

κοπρο-βολεῖον, τό, *dunghill*, Eust.1404.64. -βόλος, ον, *for spreading dung*, πτύον *EM*94.3. -δοχεῖον, τό, and -δόχος, ὁ, *cesspool*, *Gloss.* -θέσιον, τό, *place where dung is put*, *Gp.*2.22.3. -θήκη, ἡ, = foreg., *Gloss.* -λογέω, *collect dung*, Ar.*Fr.* 662, *Sammelb.*6222.25 (iii A.D.). -λόγος, ὁ, *dung-gatherer*, Ar. *Pax* 9; *scavenger*, Arist.*Ath.*50.2: hence, *dirty fellow*, Ar.*V.*1184.

κόπρον, τό, used for κόπρος, ἡ, acc. to Gal.12.290.

κοπρο-ξύστης, ου, ὁ, *one who clears out manure*, *UPZ*119.40 (ii B.C.). -ποιέω, *prepare manure*, *Ostr.Strassb.*748 (ii A.D.). -ποιός, όν, *producing excrement*, *EM*529.15, *Gloss.*

κόπρος, ἡ, *excrement, ordure*, of men and cattle, Od.9.329, al., Hdt. 3.22, etc.: in pl., Euph.96.4; esp. as used in husbandry, *dung, manure*, Pl.*Prt.*334a, Thphr.*HP*2.7.4. 2. generally, *filth, dirt*, κυλινδόμενος κατὰ κόπρον Il.22.414, 24.640, cf. *BGU*1116.14 (i B.C.). II. *dunghill, byre*, Il.18.575, Od.10.411, Call.*Dian.*178; καθίσαι τινὰς ἐπὶ κόπρου Men.544.5. (In this sense oxyt. κοπρός acc. to Eust.1165.15.) (Cf. Skt. *śákṛt*, gen. *śaknás* 'excrement'.)

κοπροσύνη, ἡ, *manuring*, *PSI*4.296.18 (vi A.D.).

κοπροσύρα· τὰ συρόμενα κόπρια, Hsch.

κοπρο-φᾰγέω, *eat dung*, Hsch., Suid. s. v. βοῦς Κύπριος. -φάγος [φᾰ], ον, *dung-eating*, Gal.12.249, Diogenian.3.49, Hsch. s. v. βοῦς Κύπριος. -φορά, ἡ, *load of dung*, *IG*12(7).62.20 (Amorgos, iv B.C., pl.). -φορέω, *cover with dung* or *dirt*, τινα Ar.*Eq.*295. -φόρος, ον, *carrying dung*, Poll.7.134; ὄνος Id.1.226; κόφινος κ. *dung-basket*, X.*Mem.*3.8.6.

κοπρ-όω, fut. -ώσω Sch.Ar.*Pl.*313:—*befoul with dung*, κοπρῶσαι τὸν τρίβωνα Arr.*Epict.*4.11.34:—Pass., κεκοπρῶσθαι, -ωμένος, ib.29.18. -ώδης, ες, *like dung*, Hp.*Prorrh.*1.146, Arist.*PA*675ᵇ30; *faecal*, Aret.*CA*1.2. 2. generally, *dirty, impure*, Pl.*Tht.*191c (Comp.), 194e. -ών, ῶνος, ὁ, *place for dung, privy*, Ar.*Th.*485, D.25.49, Eub.53.2, *IG*2.1058.11, etc.: prov., εἰς κοπρῶνα θυμιᾶν, of useless work, Phot. s. v. ὄνου πόκαι. -ωσις, εως, ἡ, *dunging, manuring*, Thphr.*HP*2.7.1.

κοπ-τάριον, τό, Dim. of κοπτή (κοπτός II. 2), *lozenge*, Dsc.4.188, Orib.8.47.16, Archig.ap.eund.8.46.10, Gal.13.58. 2. Dim. of κοπτή (κοπτός II. 1), *PGoodsp.Cair.*30 xlii 5 (ii A.D.). -τέον, *one must pound*, φάρμακον Asclep.ap.Gal.13.341, cf. 969, Dsc.2.76, *Gp.*3.7.1. -τή, ἡ, = θαλάσσιον πράσον, Dionys.Utic.ap.Ath.14.648e. II. v. κοπτός II. 2. -τήριον, τό, *place where grain was beaten out*, *PCair.Zen.*464.9, al. (iii B.C.). -τικός, ή, όν, *murderous*, Tz.*H.* 12.872. Adv. -κῶς Hdn.*Epim.*134. -τόν, τό, = κοπτή (κοπτός II. 1), Hsch. (pl.). 2. name of various plasters, Orib.*Fr.*74, Alex. Trall.7.8.

κοπτοπλᾰκοῦς, οῦντος, ὁ, = κοπτή (κοπτός II. 1), Chrysipp.Tyan. ap.Ath.14.647f.

κοπτοραν, v. κοπτούρα.

κοπτός, ή, όν, *chopped small* or *pounded*, ἰσχάς Cratin.371; τυρός Antiph.133.8. II. κοπτὴ σησαμίς, a cake of *pounded* sesame, Artem.1.72 codd.; κοπτή alone in this sense, Sopat.17, *AP*12.212 (Strat.), *POxy.*113.31 (ii A.D.), Alex.Trall.1.15. 2. **κοπτή**, ἡ, *lozenge, pastille*, Dsc.2.103, Archig.ap.Orib.8.46.8.

κοπτούρα, ἡ, *mortar* for flour-making, *PSI*7.787.5 (ii A.D.), *Stud. Pal.*20.131 (vi A.D.): acc. sg. written κοπτοραν Wilcken *Chr.*323.22 (ii A.D.).

κοπτουργία, ἡ, *making of* κοπταί, *POxy.*1454.6 (ii A.D.); nisi leg. κοπτουρία *pounding* of wheat into flour.

κόπτρα, τά, *wages for cutting*, ἀράκου *PLond.*3.1171 (i B.C.), cf. *PLips.*106.7 (i A.D.).

κόπτω, Od.18.28, etc.: fut. κόψω Hippon.83, Men.*Pk.*64, etc.: aor. ἔκοψα, Ep. κόψα Il.13.203: pf. κέκοφα (ἐκ-) X.*HG*6.5.37, (περι-) Lys.14.42, (συγ-) Pl.*Tht.*169b; Ep. part. κεκοπώς Il.13.60 (v.l. -φώς, -πών), Od.18.335:—Med., fut. κόψομαι Lxx*Ez.*6.9: aor. ἐκοψάμην Hdt.4.166:—Pass., fut. κεκόψομαι (ἀπο-) Ar.*Nu.*1125, (ἐκ-) Id.*Ra.* 1223, (κατα-) X.*An.*1.5.16, κοπήσομαι Lxx*Je.*8.2, Gal.13.759: aor. ἐκόπην A.*Ag.*1278, Ar.*Ra.*723, Th.8.13: pf. κέκομμαι A.*Pers.*683:—*cut, strike*, 1. *smite*, σ' ἀμφὶ κάρη κεκοπὼς χερσὶ στιβαρῇσι Od.18.335: c. dupl. acc., κόψε δὲ παπτήναντα παρήϊον *smote* him *on* the cheek, Il.23.690. 2. *smite* with weapons, κόπτοντες δούρεσσι μετάφρενον Od.8.528; τοῖσι Πέρσῃσι εἵποντο κόπτοντες Hdt.6.113: metaph. in Pass., with play on words, αἰεὶ κόπτῃ ῥήμασι καὶ κοπίσιν *AP*11.335. 3. *smite, slaughter* an animal with an axe or mallet, κόψας ἐξόπιθεν κεράων βοὸς Il.17.521, cf. Od.14.425, X.*An.*2.1.6; in Trag., A.*Ag.*1278, *Eu.*635, E.*El.*838. 4. *cut off, chop off*, κεφαλὴν ἀπὸ δειρῆς κόψεν Il.13.203; χεῖράς τ' ἠδὲ πόδας κόπτον Od.22.477; κ. [τὰ γέρρα] ταῖς μαχαίραις X.*An.*4.6.26; κ. δένδρα *cut down* or *fell* trees, Th.2.75, X. *HG*5.2.39, 43; κ. τὴν χώραν *lay* it *waste*, ib.3.2.26, 4.6.5:—in Pass., of ships, *to be shattered, disabled* by the enemy, Th.4.14, 8.13:—metaph., φρενῶν κεκομμένος A.*Ag.*479 (lyr.); τὸν ὕπνον ἁ φροντὶς κόπτοισα *preventing*, Theoc.21.28; [πνεῦμα] κοπτόμενον *being suddenly stopped, arrested*, Arist.*Mete.*367ᵃ10. 5. *strike, beat* a horse, to make him go faster, κόψε δ' Ὀδυσσεὺς τόξῳ Il.10.513; also σκηπανίῳ Γαιήοχος ἀμφοτέρω (sc. Αἴαντε) κεκοπὼς πλῆσεν μένεος 13.60. 6. *hammer, forge*, κόπτε δὲ δεσμούς 18.379, Od.8.274; later, *stamp* metal, i.e. *coin* money, κ. νόμισμα *IG*12(5).480.11 (Siphnos, Athenian Law), Xenoph.4, Hdt.3.56:—Med., *coin oneself* money, *order to be coined*, κ. χρυσοῦ καὶ ἀργύρου νόμισμα Id.1.94, cf. 4.166:—Pass., of money, *to be stamped* or *coined*, [νομίσμασιν] μόνοις ὀρθῶς κοπεῖσι Ar.*Ra.*723, cf. 726. 7. *knock* or *rap at*, τὴν θύραν Id.*Nu.*132, *Pl.*1097, And. 1.41, X.*HG*5.4.7, Men.*Epit.*538, Phld.*Vit.*p.30 J., Plu.*Alc.*8, etc.; without θύραν, οὗτος, τί κόπτεις; Ar.*Ec.*976. 8. *pound, bray* in a mortar, κυπέρου κεκομμένου Hdt.4.71; ἀσταφίδα κεκ. Alex.127.4; ἔλαιον κεκ., i.e. *pure* oil, Lxx*3Ki.*5.11. 9. *knock, dash about*, τὸ ὕδωρ ὅταν κοπῇ Pl.*Ti.*60b; κόνις..κοπτομένη..ὑφ' ἅρμασι Hes. *Sc.*63; θάλασσα κοπτομένη πνοιαῖς Theoc.22.16. 10. of birds, *peck*, Arist.*HA*609ᵇ5; ὁ ἁλιάετος..τὰ λιμναῖα κ. *preys* on the lagoon life, ib.593ᵇ24; σπειρὴν κ. *peck* at, Arat.449; of fish, *gnaw*, Arist.*HA* 620ᵇ17; of a snake, *strike*, Il.12.204:—Pass., of wood or seeds, *to be worm-eaten*, Thphr.*HP*3.18.5, 8.11.2. b. *munch, masticate*, dub. in Chionid.6. 11. ὁ ἵππος κ. τὸν ἀναβάτην *jars* his rider *by his paces*, X.*Eq.*1.4:—Pass., ib.8.7, Hp.*Aër.*21. 12. κ. ὄνους *dress, prepare* mill-stones for use, Alex.13; *set, sharpen*, Herod.6.84:—Med., *AP* 11.253 (Lucill.). 13. metaph., *tire out, weary*, μήθ' ὑμῖν ἐνοχλῶ μήτ' ἐμαυτὸν κ. D.*Prooem.*29, cf. Alciphr.2.3; λέγων φαίνου τι δὴ καινόν.., ἢ μὴ κόπτε με Hegesipp.1.3, cf. Sosip.1.20; μὴ κόπτ' ἔμ', ἀλλὰ τὰ κρέα Alex.173.12; κ. τὴν ἀκρόασιν D.H.*Comp.*19; κ. τὰ ὦτα Poll.6.119; κ. ἐρωτήμασιν ἀκαίροις Plu.*Phoc.*7, cf. Moer.p.74 P.:—Pass., *to be worn out*, κοπτόμενοι ἀεὶ ταῖς στρατείαις D.2.16. II. Med. κόπτομαι, *beat* or *strike oneself, beat one's breast* or *head* through grief, κεφαλὴν δ' ὅ γε κόψατο χερσίν Il.22.33, cf. Hdt.2.121.δ' (also Act. τί κόπτεις τὴν κεφαλήν; Men.*Her.*4); κόπτεσθαι μέτωπα Hdt.6.58 (with μαχαίρῃσι added 2.61): abs., Pl.*Phd.*60b, *R.*619c: pf. Pass., [πόλις] κέκοπται A.*Pers.* 683:—Act. c. acc. cogn., ἔκοψα κομμὸν Ἄριον Id.*Ch.*423 (lyr.). 2. κόπτεσθαί τινα *mourn for* any one, κόπτεσθ' Ἄδωνιν Ar.*Lys.*396, cf. *Ev.Luc.*8.52; but also ἐπί τινα *Apoc.*1.7, 18.9 (v.l. αὐτῇ). (Cf. Lith. *kapóti*, Lett. *kapāt* 'chop small', 'beat', 'stamp', Lat. *capo* 'capon', perh. σκέπαρνον.)

κοπώδης, ες, *wearying, wearing*, πυρετοί v.l. in Hp.*Prorrh.*1.142; βάρη Arist.*Pr.*881ᵃ19 (Comp.); βαρὺ καὶ κ. (sc. τὸ ὕδωρ) *causing pain*, Alex.198; κ. διάθεσις Gal.6.320: Comp. -ωδέστεραι συμφοραί Procop. *Arc.*13: c. gen., κ. ὑποχονδρίων *causing pain in..*, Hp.*Acut.*16. 2. metaph., *wearisome, boring*, D.H.*Dem.*58, Plu.2.47f; φράσις ib. 1011a. II. Pass., *wearied, worn out*, Hp.*Prorrh.*1.38, Gal.7.547. Adv. Comp. -ωδέστερον, ἔχειν Plu.2.130c.

κόπωσις, εως, ἡ, *weariness*, σαρκός Lxx*Ec.*12.12.

Κόρα, ἡ, v. κόρη (B).

Κοραγεῖν· τὸ ἀνάγειν τὴν Κόρην (sc. Persephone), Hsch.:—hence **Κοράγια**, τά, of a ritual procession at Mantinea, *IG*5(2).265.16 (i B.C.); **Κοράγιον**, τό, sanctuary where this rite took place, ib.266.41; **Κοραγοί**, οἱ, celebrants of the rite, ib.265.27.

κοραῖος, α, ον, *of a maiden*, ἠλακάτης δὲ κοραίης Epic.in *Arch.Pap.*7.8.

κοράκ-ειον [ᾰ], τό, = κορώνεως, Sch.Ar.*Pax*627. **-εύομαι**, gloss on κοράττω, Hsch. **-εύς**, έως, ὁ, kind of *fish*, prob. = κορακῖνος, Id. **-εως**, ω, ὁ, = κορώνεως, Hermipp.51. **-ησία**, ἡ, name of a herb, Pythag.ap.Plin.*HN*24.156. **-ήσιον**, τό, dub. sens. (prob. a kind of jar) in *PSI*5.535.48 (iii B.C.). **II.** name of place in Pamphylia, hence **-ησιωτικὸν** μέλι *PCair.Zen.*12.33 (iii B.C.). **-ιαί**, αἱ, perh. *the Rookeries*, name of a place in Delos, *IG*11(2).199*A*6, al. (iii B.C.). **-ίας**, ου, ὁ, *chough*, *Pyrrhocorax alpinus*, Arist.*HA* 617b16, Hsch. **2.** as Adj., *raven-black*, Id. **-ινίδιον**, τό, Dim. of κορακῖνος II, Pherecr.56, Anaxandr.27, *PSI*3.206.20 (iii A.D.). **-ινίς**, ίδος, ἡ, fem. form of κορακῖνος II, *Gp.*20.25.2. **-ῖνος**, η, ον, *like a raven, raven-black*, *AB*104, Vitr.8.3.14; κ. σφραγίς, remedy for sore throat, Gal.13.826. **-ῖνος**, ὁ, *young raven*, Ar. *Eq.*1053. **2.** = κορακίας, Hsch. **II.** a fish, Epich.44, Ar.*Lys.* 560, Philyll.13.3, Alex.18, Numen.ap.Ath.7.308e, Arist.*HA*610b5; found in the Nile, Str.17.2.4, J.*BJ*3.10.8, *PFay.*116.4 (ii A.D.); so called from its black colour, Opp.*H.*1.133; acc. to Ath.7.309a διὰ τὸ τὰς κόρας κινεῖν. **-ιον**, τό, Dim. of κόραξ II. 2, *Sammelb.*1.26 (iii A.D.), Eust.73.21. **II.** a plant, = ἱεράκιον, Arist.*Mir.*837a20.

κορακίσκος, ὁ, Dim. of κόραξ, *Gloss.*

κορᾰκοειδής, ές, *like a raven, of raven kind*, Arist.*HA*488b5:—also **κορᾰκώδης**, ες, Id.*GA*756b21, *PA*662b7. **2.** *like a crow's beak*, ἀπόφυσις τῆς ὠμοπλάτης Gal.*UP*13.12, cf. eund.2.275.

κόρᾰκος, ὁ, a plaster, Paul.Aeg.7.17. **II.** pl., Scythian for φίλιοι δαίμονες, Luc.*Tox.*7.

κορᾰκόω, *close, fasten up* (cf. κόραξ II. 2), of a tomb, *Mon.Ant.*23. 202 (Termessus):—Pass., Judeich *Altertümer von Hierapolis* 209.

κοραλλ-ίζω, *resemble coral*, Dsc.1.13. **-ικός**, ή, όν, *like coral*, Ps.-Democr.Alch.p.56 B.; cf. κοραλλικός. **-ιον**, τό, *Peripl. M.Rubr.*28, al., Dsc.5.121, Alciphr.1.39, dub. sens. in Alex.Trall. 1.15; **κοράλιον** S.E.*P.*1.119; **κουράλιον** Thphr.*Lap.*38, D.P.1103, Luc.*Apol.*1 (s. v. l.); **κωράλλιον** or **-άλιον**, Att. acc. to Hdn.Gr.2. 537:—*coral*, esp. *red coral*, ll. cc.: sts. interpr. as Dim. of κόρη in Luc. and Alciphr.; cf. κωράλιον. **-ιοπλάστης**, ου, ὁ, *one who makes images of coral*, *CIG*3408 (Magn. Sip.).

κόραξ, ᾰκος, ὁ, *raven*, *Corvus corax* (not in Hom.); πάντα τάδ' ἐν κοράκεσσι καὶ ἐν φθόρῳ 'food for *crows*', Thgn.833; κόρακες ὣς ἄκραντα γαρύετον Διὸς πρὸς ὄρνιχα θεῖον Pi.*O.*2.87; ἐπὶ σώματος δίκαν κόρακος..σταθεῖσα A.*Ag.*1473 (lyr.); κόρακες ὥστε βωμῶν ἀλέγοντες οὐδέν Id.*Supp.*751 (lyr.); κόραξι καὶ λύκοις χαρίζεσθαι Luc.*Tim.*8; in imprecations, ἐς κόρακας 'go and be hanged', Ar.*V.*852, 982; βάλλ' ἐς κ. Id.*Nu.*133; ἀπόφερ' ἐς κ. Id.*Pax*1221; οὐκ ἐς κ. ἐρρήσετε; ib.500; ἔρρ' ἐς κ. Pherecr.70; πλεῖτω ἐς κ. Ar.*Eq.*1314; οὐκ ἐς κ. ἀποφθερεῖ; Id.*Nu.* 789; ἐς κ. οἰχήσεται Id.*V.*51; ἐξελῶ σ' ἐς κ. ἐκ τῆς οἰκίας Id.*Nu.*123; ἐς κ. ἔρρειν ἐκ τῆς Ἀττικῆς Alex.94.5: as a prophet of bad weather, Arist.*Fr.*253, Thphr.*Sign.*16, Plu.2.129a, etc.; of fair weather, Arat.1003, *Gp.*1.2.6, etc.; λευκὸς κ., prov. of something unheard of, *AP*11.417, Luc.*Epigr.*43; but white ravens are mentioned by Arist. *HA*519a6. **2.** *cormorant*, *Phalacrocorax carbo*, ib.593b18. **3.** the constellation *Corvus*, Arat.449, Ptol.*Tetr.*27, etc. **4.** title of a grade in the mysteries of Mithras, Porph.*Abst.*4.16. **II.** *anything hooked* or *pointed like a raven's beak*, cf. κορώνη II, **1.** *engine for grappling ships*, Plb.1.22.3, App.*BC*5.106. **b.** *siege-engine*, Ph.*Bel.*100.18, D.S.17.44. **2.** *hooked door-handle*, Posidipp.7, *AP*11.203, Alex.Aphr.*in SE*25.17; *hook* on a machine, Hero *Aut.* 15.3, Orib.49.4.16, Ath.Mech.36.10, Bito 50.9: generally, *hook*, *Sammelb.*1.24 (iii A.D.). **3.** *instrument of torture*, Luc.*Nec.*11 (s. v. l.). **4.** = κατακλείς, Hero *Bel.*79.11. **5.** *point* of a surgical knife, σμιλαρίου Heliod.ap.Orib.44.10.5; κατιάδος Id.ap.Sch.Orib. 44.14.4. **6.** *cock's bill*, Hsch. **III.** *tub-fish* (cf. κορακῖνος), Diph.Siph.ap.Ath.8.356a. **IV.** a plaster, Philum.ap.Aët.5.127, Orib.*Fr.*84. (Cf. κορώνη, Lat. *corvus, cornix*, etc.)

κόραξε· πόρθει, Hsch.

Κοραξοί, οἱ, *Coraxi*, a Colchian tribe, Hecat.210 J., Hellanic.70 J., Arist.*Mete.*351a11: in sg., Phoen.1.14:—Adj. **Κοραξικός**, ή, όν, λῶπος Hippon.3.

κοραξός, ή, όν, *raven-black*, Str.12.8.16, Ps.-Plu.*Fluv.*18.8. **II.** **κόραξος**, ὁ, a fish, Xenocr.ap.Orib.2.58.32.

κορᾰσ-ίδιον, τό, = sq., Arr.*Epict.*1.18.22, al. **-ιον**, τό, in later Gr., Dim. of κόρη, *little girl, maiden*, Philippid.36, *AP*9.39 (Music.), *IG*7.3325 (Chaeronea), *GDI*1705, al. (Delph.), *PStrassb.*79.2 (i B.C.), Lxx *Ru.*2.8, *Ev.Matt.*9.24, etc. [ᾰ, *AP*l.c.] **-ίς**, ίδος, ἡ, *woman*, Steph.*in Hp.*1.75 D. **-ιώδης**, ες, *girlish*, *Com.Adesp.*146, Plu.2.528a.

κοράσσει· ὀρχεῖται, καὶ ἄκλητος ἐλήλυθε, Hsch.:—also **κοράττειν**· κορακεύεσθαι, Id.

κόραυνα, ἡ, barbarism for κόρη, Ar.*Av.*1678.

κόραφος, ὁ, name of a bird, Hsch.

κορβα· ἡ τοῦ κόρματος καὶ Κορύβαντος (-αντίας cod.) αἰτία, Hsch.

κορβᾶν (indecl.), Hebr. *qorbān*, *gift* or *votive offering for the service of God*, *Ev.Marc.*7.11, J.*AJ*4.4.4:—hence **κορβανᾶς**, ὁ, *the treasury of the temple* at Jerusalem, *Ev.Matt.*27.6, J.*BJ*2.9.4 (v.l. κορβωνᾶς).

κορδᾰκ-ίζω, *dance the* κόρδαξ, Hyp.*Phil.*7, D.Chr.33.9, D.C.50.27, Jul.*Mis.*350b. **-ικός**, ή, όν, *like the* κόρδαξ: hence, of metrical sound, *tripping, running*, ῥυθμὸς κ., of trochaic metres, Arist.*Rh.* 1408b36 (Comp.), cf. Cic.*Orat.*57.193. **-ισμα**, ατος, τό, *dancing of the* κόρδαξ, Hsch. s. v. κολλικόνομον. **-ισμός**, ὁ, = foreg., *licentious dancing*, D.2.18 (pl.), Nicopho 25, Chor. in *Hermes* 17.222 (pl.). **-ιστής**, οῦ, ὁ, *dancer of the* κόρδαξ, prob. in *IG*12(7).246 (Amorgos), cf. *PTeb.*231 (i B.C.).

κόρδαξ, ᾰκος, ὁ, *cordax*, a dance of the old Comedy, κόρδακα ἑλκύσαι to dance *it*, Ar.*Nu.*540, cf. 555, Luc.*Salt.*22, 26; ὀρχεῖσθαι νήφων τὸν κ. Thphr.*Char.*6.3; regarded as indecent, l. c., cf. Ath.14.631d; also in cult of Artemis at Sipylus, Paus.6.22.1; at Elis, ibid.; οἱ περὶ τὸν Πύθιον Ἀπόλλωνα κ. *IG*12(7).246 (Amorgos).

κορδίκιον, τό, dub. sens., of an article of furniture, *POxy.*1449.53 (iii A.D.), *PLond.*2.429.11 (iv A.D.).

κορδίνημα, v. l. for σκορδίνημα (q. v.), Erot.

κορδῠβαλλῶδες πέδον, τό, Luc.*Trag.*223, said to be for κορδυλοβαλλῶδες (κορδύλη, βάλλω), a *beaten* floor.

κορδύλειος [ῠ], α, ον, *made from* κορδύλη III, ταρίχη prob. in Ath. 3.120f.

κορδύλη [ῡ, cf. Lat. *cordȳla*, Mart.3.2.4, al.: **κορδύλα** *EM*485.39], ἡ, *club, cudgel*, Hsch. **2.** *bump, swelling*, Semon.35, *EM*310. 49. **II.** *wrapping for the head, head-dress*, in Cyprian, Sch.Ar. *Nu.*10, *EM*310.51. **III.** = σκορδύλη, Str.12.3.19; **κορύδῡλις** [ρῠ] in Numen.ap.Ath.7.304e.

κορδύλος, ὁ, prob. *water-newt*, *Triton palustris*, Arist.*HA*589b27, *PA*695b25; **κουρύλος** [ρῠ] in Numen.ap.Ath.7.306c.

κόρδυς· πανοῦργος, Hsch.

κορ-εία (A), ἡ, (κορέω) *brushing*: *attendance*, prob. in Hsch. **-εία** (B), ἡ, (κορεύομαι) *maidenhood*, D.Chr.7.142, *AP*5.216 (Paul. Sil.), 293.19 (Agath.). **-ειος**, α, ον, (κόρη) *of a maiden*: τὸ κ., = κόρευμα, Sch.E.*Alc.*178. **II.** Κόρεια (sc. ἱερά), τά, *the festival of Kore* (Persephone), Plu.*Dio* 56, Hsch. **2.** Κόρειον, τό, *her temple*, *IG*14.217 (Acrae), *Ath.Mitt.*49.5 (Attica, iii B.C.).

Κορειτήα, ἡ, prob. = *Κορῑτεία, perh. *performance as attendant of Kore* at Lycosura, ἐν..τέκνων -ήαις *IG*5(2).516.11.

κορέννῡμι, Them.*Or.*16.213a; **κορεννύω**, *Gloss.*; **κορέω**, Nic.*Al.* 195; **κορέσκω**, ib.225, 360, 415: fut. κορέσω Hdt.1.212; Ep. κορέεις Il.13.831, κορέει 8.379, 17.241: aor. ἐκόρεσα 16.747, A.*Pr.*166 (lyr.); poet. ἐκόρεσσα Theoc.24.138, *AP*7.204 (Agath.):—Med., κορέννυμαι Orph.*L.*732, opt. κορέοιτο Nic.*Al.*263: aor. ἐκορεσάμην, Ep. ἐκορεσσ–, κορεσσ–, Il.11.562, Od.20.59:—Pass., fut. κεκορήσομαι Max.117: aor. ἐκορέσθην Od.10.499; Ep. 3 pl. -θεν Ar.*Pax*1283 sq.: pf. κεκόρεσμαι X.*Mem.*3.11.3 (nowhere else in early Prose), Plu.*Dem.*23, *APl.*4.190 (Leon.); Ion. κεκόρημαι Il.18.287, Hes.*Op.*593, Sapph. 48, Ar.*Pax*1285 (v. infr.): pf. part. Act. (with pass. sense) κεκορηώς, -ότος, Od.18.372, Nonn.*D.*5.34, Coluth.120: also fut. (in intr. sense) κορήσουσι Lxx *De.*31.20:—*satiate, fill* one *with* a thing, c. dat., κορέεις κύνας ἠδ' οἰωνοὺς δημῷ καὶ σάρκεσσι Il.13.831; μολπῇ θυμὸν κ. A.R. 3.897: c gen. rei, κορέσαι στόμα ἐμᾶς σαρκός S.*Ph.*1156 (lyr.): c. acc. only, τίς ἂν κορέσειεν ἅπαντας; Thgn.229; πρὶν ἂν ἢ κορέσῃ κέαρ A. l. c.:—Med., *satisfy oneself*, c. gen., ἐκορέσσατο φορβῆς Il.11.562; οἴνοιο κορεσσάμενος καὶ ἐδωδῆς 19.167; ὄφρ'..κρειῶν κορεσαίατο θυμόν *might satisfy their* desire with flesh, Od.14.28: metaph., φυλόπιδος κορέσασθαι Il.13.635: c. part., κορεσσάμεθα κλαίοντε 22.427; ἐκορέσσατο χεῖρας τάμνων δένδρεα 11.87:—Pass., *to be glutted, satiated*, δαιτὸς κεκορήμεθα θυμὸν ἐΐσης Od.8.98; κεκορήμεθ' ἀέθλων 23.350; κεκορημένος ἦτορ ἐδωδῆς Hes.*Op.*593; βορᾶς κορεσθεὶς E.*Hipp.*112; πολέμου ἐκόρεσθεν Ar.*Pax*1283: c. part., κλαίων..κορέσθην Od.4.541; οὔ πω κεκόρησθε ἐελμένοι; Il.18.287: rarely c. dat. rei, κριθαῖσι κορεσθεὶς Thgn.1269; πλούτῳ κεκορημένος Id.751; ὕβρι Hdt.3.80: abs., dub. in Sapph.48.—Cf. κορίσκομαι. (Cf. Lith. *šérti* 'feed'.)

κορεστ-ικῶς, Adv. *to satiety*, Sch.Arat.1049. **-ός**, ή, όν, *sated*; *to be sated*, *Gloss.*

κόρ-ευμα, ατος, τό, = κορεία (B), *maidenhood*, E.*Alc.*178 (pl.). **-εύομαι**, Pass., fut. κορευθήσομαι ib.313: (κόρη):—*pass one's maidenhood*, E. l. c. **II.** *to be deflowered*, Pherecyd.92(*b*) J.

κορέω (A), *sweep out*, δῶμα κορήσατε ποιπνύσασαι Od.20.149; τὴν αὐλὴν κόρει Eup.157; κ. τὸ παιδαγωγεῖον D.18.258. **II.** = ἐξυβρίζω, Hsch.: hence κεκορημένος, sens. obsc., Anacr.5.

κορέω (B), v. κορέννυμι. **κορζία**, v. καρδία.

κόρη, ἡ, orig. κόρϝα (v. infr. B), with -η even in Att. Prose and Trag. dialogue; Dor. and Aeol. **κόρα**, Ar.*Lys.*1308 (lyr.), Alc.14, also Trag. in lyr. as A.*Supp.*145, S.*OT*508, E.*Tr.*561, and in the pr. n.: **κούρα** Pi.*O.*13.65, and twice in Trag. (in lyr.), v. infr. I. 3: Ion. **κούρη**, as always in Hom. (κόρη first in *h.Cer.*439): Dor. also **κώρα** Theoc.6.36, also Boeot., Corinn.*Supp.*1.48, 2.60 (but κόρα *IG*7.710–12, Ar.*Ach.*883, cf. κορικός, κόριλλα):—fem. of κόρος, κοῦρος. **1.** *girl*, ἠΰτε κούρη νηπίη ἥ θ' ἅμα μητρὶ θέουσ' ἀνελέσθαι ἀνώγει Il.16.7; μήτε παῖδα μήτε κόραν Schwyzer 324.12 (Delph., iv B.C.); ἔτεκε κόραν *IG*4²(1).121.22 (Epid.); with reference to virginity, *maiden*, κόρην..οὐκέτ', ἀλλ' ἐζευγμένην S.*Tr.*536; παῖς κ. Ar.*Lys.*595, D.21.79 codd.; παρθενικὴ κ. E.*Epigr.*2; ἀδελφὴ κ. Th.6.56; ἀνεδέξαντο τὰς κόρας πέμψειν ἐν Ἴλιον Schwyzer 366 *A* 2 (Tolophon, iii B.C.); of Nymphs, Pi.*P.*3. 78; ἐνάλιοι κ. sea-*nymphs*, Ar.*Th.*325 (lyr.): Com., πρέσβειρα πεντήκοντα Κωπᾴδων κορᾶν, of eels, Id.*Ach.*883; τευθὶς καὶ Φαληρικὴ κ., i. e. ἀφύη, Eub.75.4; of maiden-goddesses, however old, as the Eumenides, A.*Eu.*68, S.*OC*127 (lyr.); the Phorcids, A.*Pr.*794; the Sphinx, S.*OT*508 (lyr.); the Fates, Pl.*R.*617d. **2.** of a bride, Od.18.279; young wife, Il.6.247, E.*Or.*1438 (lyr.), Hdn.3.10.8; or concubine, as Briseis, Il.1.98, 337, 2.689; καταχύσματα..κατάχει τοῦ νυμφίου καὶ τῆς κ. the *bride*, Theopomp.Com.14; of a ἑταίρα, *AP*5.4 (Stat.Flacc.), 219 (Agath.). **3.** with gen. of a pr. n. added, *daughter*, νύμφαι κοῦραι Διὸς Il.6.420, cf. Sapph.65, E.*Hel.*168 (lyr.), *Andr.*897, etc.; κ. Διός, of Athene, A.*Eu.*415; Λητῴα κόρη, of Artemis, Id.*Fr.*170, S.*El.*570; κ. Ἰναχεία, κ. Θεστιάς, A.*Pr.*589, E.*Hel.*133; Γῆς τε καὶ Σκότου κόραι, i.e. the Furies, S.*OC*40; in Thess. Prose, Αἰσχυλὶς

Σατύροι (gen.) κόρα *IG*9(2).1035 (Gyrton): without gen., *Berl.Sitzb.* 1927.7 (Locr., v B.C.): in voc., κούρα *my daughter*, A.*Th.*148, S.*OC* 180 (both lyr.); κόραι Ar.*Pax* 119. 4. metaph., of a *colony*, Κύμης κ. Hom.*Epigr.*1.2; of *newly-launched* ships, Lyc.24. II. *puppet, doll*, as a child's plaything, Hyp.*Fr.*199 (v. infr. v), D.Chr.31.153; *small votive image*, Pl.*Phdr.*230b. III. *pupil* of the eye, because a little image appears therein (v. Pl.*Alc.*1.133a), κύκλοπα κούρην Emp.84.8, cf. S.*Fr.*710, E.*Hec.*972, al., Ar.*V.*7, Hp.*Prorrh.*2.20, Gal.*UP*10.4, Ruf.*Onom.*23; αἱ καλούμεναι κ. $IG4^2$(1).122.67 (Epid., iv B.C.); Κ. κόσμου, title of Hermetic tract, Stob.1.49.44 tit. IV. *long sleeve* reaching over the hand, X.*HG*2.1.8. V. *the Attic drachma*, because it bore a head of Athena, misinterpr. of Hyp.l.c. ap.Poll.9.74. VI. = ὑπέρεικον, Hp.ap.Gal.19.113. VII. Archit., *female figures as supports, Caryatids*, τοὺς λίθους..τοὺς ἐπὶ τῶν κορῶν $IG1^2$.372.86 (Erechtheum).

B. **Κόρη**, Dor. **Κόρα** (Cret. **Κώρα** *GDI*5047), Ion. **Κούρη**, Arc.(?) **ΚόρϜα** *IG*5(2).554 (provenance unknown), ἡ:—*the Daughter* (of Demeter), *Persephone*, τῇ Μητρὶ καὶ τῇ Κόρῃ (v.l. Κούρῃ) Hdt.8.65; ναὶ τὰν Κόραν Ar.*V.*1438; Δημήτηρ καὶ Κ. Id.*Th.*298, X.*HG*6.3.6, *IG*2.1217, etc.; τῆς Κόρης ἁρπασθείσης Isoc.4.28: less freq. Κ. Δήμητρος E.*Alc.*358, cf. Ar.*Ra.*337; Κ. τὴν Διὸς καὶ Δήμητρος Isoc.10.20. II. Δηοῦς κ., in Com., = *flour*, Antiph.52.9; so μεμαγμένη Δήμητρος κ. Eub.75.10.

κόρ-ηθρον, τό, *besom, broom*, Luc.*Philops.*35, Artem.5.79. **–ημα**, ατος, τό, *sweepings, refuse*, Ar.*Fr.*474: in pl., Hermipp.47.10 (anap.). II. *besom, broom*, Ar.*Pax* 59, Eup.157, 228.4, Gal.12.93.

κορθέλαι· σύστροφοι (also συστροφαί), σωροί, Hsch.:—also **κορθίλη** and **κόρθις**, Id.:—but **κόρθιλος**, = βασιλίσκος, Id.

κορθύνω or **κορθύω**, (κόρθυς) *lift up, raise*, Ζεὺς κόρθυνεν ἑὸν μένος *raised high* his wrath, Hes.*Th.*853; εὖτέ με θυμὸς κορθύσῃ *Hymn.Is.* 150:—Pass., κῦμα κορθύεται *waxes high, rears its crest*, Il.9.7; ὕπερθε δὲ..ἁλὸς κορθύεται ὕδωρ A.R.2.322.

κόρθῡς, υος, ἡ, lengthd. form of κόρυς, *heap*, Anon.ap.Suid. s.v. κορθύεται, Hsch.; in Theoc.10.46, κόρθυος ἁ τομά the swathe *of mown corn*.

κορθῶ· βλάβη, Hsch. **κόρι**, abbreviated for κόριον, = κορίαννον, Bilabel 'Οψαρτ.p.10, al. **κοριάλαι**· τρίγλαι, Hsch.

κορίαννον (**κορίανδρον** *Gloss.*, **κορίαμβλον** Hsch.) [ῐ], τό, *coriander, Coriandrum sativum*, the plant or seed, Alc.Com.17, Anaxandr.50, Thphr.*HP*7.1.2: freq. in pl., Anacr.123, Ar.*Eq.*676, 682, etc. II. *ring worn on the forefinger*, Poll.5.101, Hsch.

κορίαξος, ὁ, a kind of *fish*, Alex.Trall.1.12, al.

Κοριάσια, τά, *festival of Kore*, *IG*7.47 (Megara).

κορίδιον, τό, Dim. of κόρη, *GDI*1699, al. (Delph.), *IG*9(1).384 (Naupactus); censured by Poll.2.17, but allowed by Phryn.56. II. perh. for κόρι, = κορίαννον, Pap. in *Philol.*80.341.

κορίζομαι, (κόρη, κόριον A) *fondle, caress*, Ar.*Nu.*68; cf. ὑποκορίζομαι, κουρίζω (A).

κορίζω (A), (κόρις) *to be infested with bugs*, *Gloss.*

κορίζω (B), (κόρος C) *sweep*: hence, *sift, clean*, *BGU*1120.40 (Pass., i B.C.).

κορῐκός, ή, όν, = παρθενικός, χιτών *Schwyzer*462*B*29 (Tanagra, iii B.C.), cf. Poll.2.17. Adv. **-κῶς** *like a girl*, τρυφᾶν Ph.2.89; βαδίζειν Ael.*NA*2.38; αἰσχύνεσθαι Alciphr.3.2: Comp. **-ώτερον** Eust.1571.43. II. *belonging to Kore*, πεπλοποιία Dam.*Pr.*339.

κόριλλα, ἡ, Boeot. Dim. of κόρα, *IG*7.713, al. (Tanagra), 2901 (Coronea).

κοριναῖος, Maced. word, = νόθος, Marsyas Phil.24 J.

Κορινθι-άζομαι, *practise fornication*, because Corinth was famous for its courtesans, Ar.*Fr.*354:—Act. in Hsch. **–αστής**, οῦ, ὁ, *whoremonger*, title of plays by Philetaerus, Ath.13.559a, and Poliochus, Id.7.313c.

Κορίνθιος, α, ον, *Corinthian*, Hdt., etc.; Κ. κόρη *courtesan*, Pl.*R.* 404d; ἑταῖραι Κ. Ar.*Pl.*149; οἶνος Κ. Alex.290; Κ. κάδοι Diph.61.3. Adv. **-ίως** *in Corinthian fashion*, οἶκος Κ. ἐστεγασμένος J.*AJ*8.5.2:—fem. **Κορινθιάς**, άδος, ἡ, St.Byz.:—also **Κορινθιακός**, ή, όν, X.*HG*6.2.9; Κ. γλυφαί Ph.1.666: **Κορινθικός**, *AP*6.40 (Maced.).

Κορινθιουργής, ές, (ἔργον) *of Corinthian workmanship* or *style*, κρατῆρες Callix.2; κιόκρανον Str.4.4.6, cf. *AJA*31.351.

Κορινθοειδής, ές, *of Corinthian style*, κέραμος Κ. προστεγαστήρ *SIG* 245 i 35 (Delph., iv B.C.).

Κόρινθος, ὁ and ἡ, *Corinth*, the city and country, ἀφνειὸς Κ. Il.2.570, Pi.*Fr.*122.2; ὀφρυόεντα Κ. Orac.ap.Hdt.5.92.β', cf. Plb.4.67.8, Str.8.6.20; but ἡ Κ. Hdt.3.50, Th.1.25, etc.; εὐδαίμων Κ. Hdt.3.52; famed for its luxury and extravagance, whence prov. οὐ παντὸς ἀνδρὸς εἰς Κ. ἔσθ' ὁ πλοῦς Ar.*Fr.*902a. II. son of Zeus, reputed founder of Corinth, Paus.2.1.1: prov., Διὸς Κόρινθος, used of persons who are always repeating the same old story, Pi.*N.*7.105, cf. Ar.*Ra.* 443, *Ec.*828, Pl.*Euthd.*292e. III. Adv. **Κορινθόθι**, *at Corinth*, Il. 13.664; **Κορινθόθεν**, *from C.*, *Michel* 1087 (Olympia, v B.C.).

κοριοειδής, ές, (κόρη) *like the pupil of the eye, dark-gleaming*, κορακῖνοι Epich.44. 2. (κόριον B) *like coriander*, Dsc.2.176.

κόριον (A), τό, Dim. of κόρη, *little girl*, Lys.*Fr.*1.5 (ironically), Theoc.11.60; Megar. **κώριον** Ar.*Ach.*731.

κόριον (B), τό, shortd. for κορίαννον, Nic.*Al.*157, *Th.*874, *PCair. Zen.*292.16, al. (iii B.C.), *PTeb.*190 (i B.C.), Dsc.3.63, Gal.12.36: pl., Hp.*Mul.*1.66. II. κ. ἔνυδρον, = ἀδίαντον, Ps.-Dsc.4.134. III. κ. ἄγριον, = καπνός II, ib.4.109.

κόρις, ιος, Att. εως, ὁ, *bug, Cimex lectularius*, οἱ κόρεις Ar.*Nu.*634 (with a play on Κορίνθιοι, cf. 710), *Ra.*115, al.: also fem., Sor.2.29, Phryn.277 (acc. to Suid. with gen. κόριδος, wh. is not found in Classical Gr., cf. [Gal.]14.538). II. kind of *fish*, = ἔσχαρος, Dorio ap. Ath.7.330a. III. a kind of *St. John's wort, Hypericum empetrifolium*, Dsc.3.157, Aët.16.17.

κορίσκη, ἡ, Dim. of κόρη, Pl.Com.69.12, Timocl.22:—hence **κορίσκιον**, Poll.2.17.

κορίσκομαι, = κορέννυμαι, *become saturated*, c. gen., ὑγρασίης Hp. *Gland.*6; κ. φλέγματος οἱ πνεύμονες ib.14: abs., *to be irked*, Id.*Art.*35.

κορίσκος, ὁ, Dim. of κόρος (B): as pr. n. Κορίσκος (pupil of Plato, D.L.3.46) is used to denote *any supposed person*, like J. S. Mill's 'Duke of Wellington', Arist.*APo.*85^a24, *Ph.*219^b21, al.

κόριψ· νεανίσκος, Hsch.; cf. κόρος (B). **κορκόδειλος, κορκόδριλλος, κορκοδρίλλιον**, v. κροκόδιλος. **κορκόδρυα**· ὑδρόρυα, Id. **κόρκορα**, a bird (Perg.), Id. **κόρκορος**, v. κόρχορος.

κορκορῠγή, ἡ, *rumbling noise, tumult*, in pl., A.*Th.*345 (lyr.), Ar. *Pax* 991 (anap.): in sg., Id.*Lys.*491.

κορκορυγμός, ὁ, = foreg., of the bowels, Ps.-Luc.*Philopatr.*3.

κορκότιλος, v. κροκόδιλος. **κορκούτης**· αἰδοῖον ἀνδρῶν, Hsch. (post κορμός). **Κόρκῡρα, Κορκῡραῖος**, v. Κερκ–. **κορκυρεύεται**· ἀπον(ο)εῖται, Id.

κόρμα, ατος, τό, = κοῦρμι, Posidon.15 J. II. v. κορβᾶ.

κορμ-άζω, *saw up into logs*, D.H.20.15 (Pass.). **–ηδόν**, Adv. *like logs*, Hld.9.18. **–ίον**, τό, Dim. of κορμός, *small log*, *IG*11(2). 233.13 (Delos, iii B.C.), *Stud.Pal.*10.259.11 (v A.D.). II. *trunk* or *body* of an undershirt, Anon.*in Rh.*106.3. 2. κορμίν, τό, *barrel* of a horse, interpol. in *Hippiatr.*115.

κορμίω, Cret., = κοσμέω, *GDI*5016, al.

κορμολογία, ἡ, *collecting of* κορμοί (cf. κορμός (A) 2), *Sammelb.*5126.25 (iii A.D.).

κορμός (A), ὁ, (κείρω) *trunk* of a tree (with the boughs lopped off), Od.23.196, E.*Hec.*575, *HF*242; κ. ἐλάας Ar.*Lys.*255; κ. ἐλάϊνοι *PCair.Zen.*431 (iii B.C.); κορμοὶ ξύλων *logs* of timber, Hdt.7.36, *PCair.Zen.*154.2 (iii B.C.); κ. ναυτικοί, i.e. oars, E.*Hel.*1601. 2. ἀπὸ κορμοῦ εἰς κορμόν, in measurement of an irrigated vineyard, prob. from *block* to *block*, i.e. from *sluice* to *sluice*, *PFlor.*50.2, al. (iii A.D.); cf. κορμολογία.

κόρμος (B), Cret., = κόσμος, *GDI*5024, al.

κορνικουλάριος, ὁ, = Lat. *cornicularius*, *CIG*4453 (Syria): written κορνουκλάριος *Sammelb.*6221 (ii A.D.).

κόρνος· κεντρομυρσίνη (Sicel), Hsch.

κόρνοψ, οπος, ὁ, a kind of *locust*, like πάρνοψ, Str.13.1.64 (but κορνώπιδες = κώνωπες, Hsch.):—hence **Κορνοπίων**, ωνος, ὁ, *Locust-scarer*, title of Heracles at Oeta, Str. l. c.

κόροιβος, ὁ, *fool*, Hsch.; οὐχ οὕτω κ. ὁ 'Αλέξανδρος Ps.-Gem. in Iriarte *Cat.Cod.Matrit.*p.391. (Fr. pr. n. Κόροιβος, Euph.71, etc.)

κοροῖτις· ἀλώπηξ, Hsch. **κόροιφος**, v. κόρυφος III.

κοροκόσμιον, τό, *girl's toy* or *ornament*, of masks placed at crossroads, *AB*102, cf. Sch.Theoc.2.110. II. *pupil of the eye*, *PLond.* 1821.27.

κοροκότας or **–κόττας**, v. κροκόττας.

κορόνους, coined as etym. of Κρόνος, Dam.*Pr.*267; cf. κορός (B).

κορο-πλᾰθικός, ή, όν, *belonging to the art of modelling*, τύπος Procl. *in Ti.*1.335 D. **–πλάθος** [ᾰ], ὁ, *modeller of small figures, image-maker*, Pl.*Tht.*147b, Isoc.15.2, Luc.*Lex.*22; name of a play by Antiphanes:—in Hellenistic Gr. **–πλάστης**, ου, ὁ, *EM*530.11, Moer. p.234 P.

κόρος (A), ὁ, *satiety, surfeit*, αἶψά τε φυλόπιδος πέλεται κ. ἀνθρώποισιν Il.19.221; αἰψηρὸς δὲ κ. κρυεροῖο γόοιο Od.4.103; πάντων μὲν κ. ἐστί, καὶ ὕπνου καὶ φιλότητος Il.13.636; ἀπὸ κ. ἀμβλύνει αἰανὴς ἐλπίδας Pi.*P.*1.82; κόρον ἔχει μέλι Id.*N.*7.52; κ. ἔχειν δακρύων, κακῶν, E.*Alc.* 185, *Ph.*1750 (lyr.); also κόρον ἡ τούτων συνουσία ἔχει Pl.*Phdr.*240c; ἐς κ. ἰέναι τινός Philox.2.38; ἄχρι κόρου D.19.187; ἐς κόρον Luc. *Merc.Cond.*26, Gal.15.500, *Vict.Att.*8; πρὸς ἡδονήν τε καὶ κ. *gormandizing*, Hp.*VM*14: in mystical sense, opp. χρησμοσύνη, Heraclit. 65. 2. *the consequence of satiety, insolence*, Pi.*O.*2.95, *I.*3.2; πρὸς κόρον *insolently*, A.*Ag.*382 (lyr.): freq. as cause or consequence of ὕβρις, τίκτει τοι κόρος ὕβριν, ὅταν κακῷ ὄλβος ἕπηται ἀνθρώπῳ Thgn. 153, cf. Sol.8; ὕβριν κόρου ματέρα Pi.*O.*13.10; κόρον, ὕβριος υἱόν Bacis ap.Hdt.8.77. (Cf. κορέννυμι.)

κόρος (B), ὁ, Ion. **κοῦρος**, as always in Hom., Pi., and lyr. passages of Trag. (exc. E.*Alc.*904), sts. in late Gr., *Rev.Et.Gr.*42. 247 (Varna): Dor. **κῶρος** Theoc.15.120:—*boy, lad* (even before birth, ὅν..γαστέρι μήτηρ κοῦρον ἐόντα φέροι Il.6.59, cf. Call.*Del.*212), κοῦρος πρῶτον ὑπηνήτης Il.24.347; πρωθῆβαι Od.8.262; τότε κοῦρος ἔα, νῦν αὖτέ με γῆρας ὀπάζει Il.4.321; σὺν κόροις τε καὶ κόραις A.*Fr.*43: in mock Trag., Οἰδίπου..παῖδε, διπτύχω κόρω Ar.*Fr.*558: rare in Prose, Pl.*Lg.*772a; *male infant*, ἔτεκε κόρον Conon 33.3, cf. $IG4^2$(1).121.5 (Epid., iv B.C.); in Il. of warriors, 9.86, 12.196, al.; κοῦροι Βοιωτῶν, 'Αθηναίων, 'Αχαιῶν, 2.510, 551, 562; λεκτοὶ 'Αθηναίων κ. E.*Supp.*356; also, of *servants* waiting at sacrifices and feasts, Il.1.470, al.; at Sparta, κόροι, = ἱππεῖς, Archyt.ap.Stob.4.1.138. 2. with gen. of pr. n., *son*, Od.19.523, etc.; Θησέως κ. S.*Ph.*562, cf. *Tr.*644 (lyr.); τῶν ὀλωλότων κόροι E.*Supp.*107; Κεκροπιδῶν κόροι, periphr. like παῖδες, Eub.10.6. 3. *puppet, doll*, used in Magic, S.*Fr.*536. II. *shoot, sprout*, of a tree, κόρους πλεκτοὺς..μυρρίνης Lysipp.9, cf. Hp.ap.Gal. 19.113, *EM*276.28, Hsch.; cf. κοῦρος (B). III. for Comp. v. κουρότερος. (Acc. to Eust.582.20, al., from κείρω, *of one who has cut his hair short on emerging from boyhood*: but κόρ(Ϝ)ος (masc. of κόρη) perh. cogn. with Lat. *Ceres, Cerus, cresco.*)

κόρος (C), ὁ, *besom*, Hsch.

κόρος (D), ὁ, Hebr. *kor*, a dry measure containing, acc. to J.*AJ* 15.9.2,10 Att. medimni (about 120 gallons), Lxx*Nu*.11.32,al., *Ev. Luc*.16.7, cf. Eupolem.ap.Alex.Polyh.18.

κορός (A), Adj. *dark, black*, Sch.DIl.1.170: etym. of κόραξ, *EM* 529.30.

κορός (B), Adj. *pure*, Procl.*Theol.Plat*.5.3 (where θεοῦ κόρου καὶ νοῦ ὄντος), Id.ad Hes.*Op*.111, *EM*540.5, cf. Pl.*Cra*.396b (Κρόνος = κορὸς νοῦς).

κόρρη, Att. for κόρση.

κόρσακις, = τράγος, Cratin.338, ap.Hsch. (Κορσάτης Salmasius); obscurely expld. by Did. ἀπὸ τῆς κόρσης, Κόρσαι γὰρ τῆς Κιλικίας.

κορσᾶς, ὁ, pl. ᾶτες, *barber*, *BGU*9iv15 (iii A.D.).

κορσεῖα, τά, (κόρση) *temples*, Nic.*Al*.135; **κόρσεα**, ib.414.

κόρσεον, τό, = κόρσιον (q.v.), in pl., *PTeb*.112.7 (ii B.C.), 189 (i B.C.):—written **κορσαῖον** D.S.1.10.

κορσεύς· κουρεύς, Hsch.

κόρσ-η, ἡ, Att. **κόρρη**, Dor. **κόρρα** Theoc.14.34, Aeol. **κόρσα** Alc. 34.5:—*temple, side of the forehead* (in this sense not in pl., for wh. κρόταφοι is used, but cf. Ruf.*Onom*.13, Poll.2.40), ξίφει ἤλασε κόρσην Il.5.584, cf. 13.576; τόν ῥ' Ὀδυσεὺς ... βάλε κόρσην' ἡ δ' ἑτέροιο διὰ κροτάφοιο πέρησεν αἰχμή 4.502, cf. Call.*Dian*.78. 2. in Att., πατάξαι ἐπὶ κόρρης smack on the *jaw*, Pherecr.155b(*CAF*iii p.716), D.21.147; ὅταν κονδύλοις, ὅταν ἐπὶ κόρρης [τύπτῃ], i.e. with the fist, or with the open hand, ib.72; ἐπὶ κόρρης τύπτειν Pl.*Grg*.486c, 508d, 527a; ῥαπίζειν ἐπὶ κ. Hyp.*Fr*.97 (ἐρραπίσθη τὴν γνάθον ibid.); πὺξ ἐπὶ κόρρας ἤλασα Theoc. l.c.; later κατὰ κόρρης πατάσσειν Luc.*DMort*.20.2, *Gall*.30, cf. *EM*529.39. 3. in pl., *hair*, λευκὰς δὲ κ. τῆδ' ἐπαντέλλειν νόσῳ A.*Ch*.282, cf. Poll.2.32 (perh. the white *down* in psoriasis): in sg., ναὶ μὰ τήνδε τὴν τεφρὴν κόρσην Herod.7.71 (unless in signf. I. 4). 4. *head*, κ. ἀναύχενες Emp.57.1, cf. Nic.*Th*.905, Opp.*C*.3.25; Att. for *the whole head and neck*, Ael.Dion.*Fr*.235; Ion. for *head*, Eratosth.ap.Did. in Miller *Mél*.400. II. *part of a temple gate*, Vitr. 4.6.3. III. in pl., = κρόσσαι, Hsch.; also, = κλίμακες, Id. (Perh. cogn. with κάρα.) **-ήεις**, εσσα, εν, = κορσοειδής, prob. in Orph. *L*.498. **-ης**, ου, ὁ, nickname of the first man *who shaved his beard* at Athens, Chrysipp.*Stoic*.3.198.

κόρσιον, τό, *tuber of the Nile water-lily, Nymphaea stellata*, Thphr. *HP*4.8.11, Str.17.2.4; cf. κόρσεον: **κορσίπιον**, Hsch. **κορσίς**· πυγή, Id.

κορσοειδὴς λίθος, ὁ, a stone of *greyish colour* (κόρση I. 3), Plin.*HN* 37.153.

κορσός, ὁ, = κορμός, Hsch. (Cf. κοῦρος (B).)

κορσ-όω, (cf. κουρά, κείρω) = κείρειν, Hsch.; cf. ἀεικορσώσασθαι, ἀκόρσωτον, ἀποκορσόομαι. **-ωτήρ**, ῆρος, ὁ, *barber*, Call.*Fr.anon*. 128, Poll.2.32:—also **-ωτεύς**, έως, Charon 9. **-ωτήριον**, τό, *barber's shop*, ibid. **-ωτός**, ή, όν, = κροσσωτός (which is v.l.), Lyc. 291.

κορταία (sc. γῆ), ἡ, = χορτ-, *pasture-land*, *POxy*.2113.19 (iv A.D.).

κόρταλος, κόρταφος, v. κρόταλον, κρόταφος. **κορτερά**, v. κρατερός. **κορτέω**, v. κροτέω. **κόρτη**, ἡ, a Parthian garment, Hsch. **κόρτος**· ὁ ἐν τοῖς κυσὶ κροτός (prob. κροτών), Id.

Κορῠβάντ-ειος, α, ον, *Corybantian*, *AP*6.165 (Phal.). II. τὸ Κορυβαντεῖον (not -άντειον Hdn.Gr.1.375) *temple of the Corybantes*, Str.10.3.21. **-ιασμός**, ὁ, *Corybantic frenzy*, D.H.2.19 (pl.), Longin. 39.2. **-ιάω**, *celebrate the rites of the Corybantes, to be filled with Corybantic frenzy*, Pl.*Cri*.54d, *Smp*.215e, *Ion* 533e, 536c; **κ**. περί τι *to be infatuated* about a thing, Longin.5: in Ar.*V*.8, comically, of a drowsy person *nodding and suddenly starting up*, cf. Plin.*HN*11. 147. **-ίζω**, *purify by Corybantic rites*, Ar.*V*.119:—Pass., *to be subjected to such rites*, Iamb.*Myst*.3.9, Cels.ap.Orig.*Cels*.3.16. **-ικός**, ή, όν, *Corybantic*, σκιρτήματα Plu.2.759b, cf. Porph.*Abst*.2.21; οἱ τὰ Κ. τελούμενοι D.H.*Dem*.22. **-ίς**, ίδος, ἡ, pecul. fem of Κορύβας, Nonn.*D*.2.695. **-ισμός**, ὁ, *purification by Corybantic rites*, Hsch. **-ώδης**, ες, *Corybant-like, frantic*, Luc.*JTr*.30.

Κορύβας [ῠ], αντος, ὁ, *Corybant, priest of Cybele in Phrygia*, Hsch.: pl., Str.10.3.7, D.S.5.49, Luc.*Salt*.8; also associated with Dionysus, in pl. Κορύβαντες, E.*Ba*.125 (lyr.), *Hipp*.143 (lyr.), Ar.*Lys*.558, Nonn.*D*.9.162, Str. l.c.: metaph., of *drunken persons*, Posidipp.26. 22.—Cf. Κύρβαντες. II. *enthusiasm*, ὁ τῆς ποιητικῆς κ. Luc.*Hist. Conscr*.45. III. fabulous gem, Ps.-Plu.*Fluv*.18.8.

κορυγγεῖν· κερατίζειν, Hsch. (leg. κορύττ-). **κορύγης**, Dor., = κῆρυξ, Id.

κορύδιον, τό, Aetol. Dim. of κόρη, *JHS*13.346 (Naupactus).

Κορύδιος, ὁ (sc. μήν), name of month at Mitylene, *IG*12(2).81.

κορῠδός, ἡ, (κόρυς) *lark*, esp. *crested lark, Alauda cristata*, Ar.*Av*. 472, al. (on the accent v. Hdn.Gr.1.143):—also **κόρῠδος**, ὁ, Pl.Com. 266, Pl.*Euthd*.291b, Arist.*HA*559^{a}2, 614^{a}33: prov., κ. ἐν ἀμούσοις φθέγγεται, 'au royaume des aveugles les borgnes sont rois', Eust. 1072.40.—Other forms are: **κορυδών**, ῶνος, ὁ, Arist.*HA*609^{a}7; **κορυδαλλή**, ἡ, Epich.45; **κορυδαλλίς**, ίδος, ἡ, πάσαισιν κορυδαλλίσιν χρὴ λόφον ἐγγενέσθαι Simon.68, cf. Theoc.7.23; **κορυδαλλός**, ὁ, Id. 10.50, Babr.72.20; **κορύδαλος**, Arist.*HA*617^{b}20, 633^{b}1.

κορύδῡλις, εως, ἡ, v. κορδύλη III.

κόρυζ-α, ης, ἡ, *mucous discharge from the nostrils, rheum*, Ruf. *Onom*.33, Gal.5.253; κορύζης τὴν ῥῖνα μεστός Luc.*DMort*.6.2; also, *running at the nose*, Gal.7.107; in this sense in pl., Hp.*Prog*.14, Gal. 10.513; *inflammatory nasal catarrh*, Hp.*VM*18, Gal.10.513, 18(2). 180. II. metaph., *drivelling, stupidity*, Luc.*DMort*.20.4, *Hist. Conscr*.31, *Alex*.20; κορύζης καὶ λέμφου ἔμπλεως Lib.*Decl*.33.29. **-ᾶς**, ᾶ, ὁ, *driveller, sniveller*, Men.1003. **-άω**, *have a catarrh, run at the nose*, Pl.*R*.343a (with a play on signf. II), Arist.*Pr*.861^{a}18; ἀλεκτρυόνα γέροντα ἤδη καὶ -ῶντα Luc.*JTr*.15. II. metaph., *drivel*, ἐκόρυζων αἱ πόλεις Plb.38.12.5, cf. Phld.*D*.1.11. **-ιᾷ**, *pipitat*, *Gloss*. **-ώδης**, ες, *suffering from catarrh*, ἀπὸ κεφαλῆς Hp.*Epid*. 6.3.3, cf. 2.3.11.

κορῠθ-άϊξ [ᾱ], ῐκος, (ἀΐσσω) *helmet-shaking*, i.e. *with waving plume*, κορυθάϊκι πτολεμιστῇ Il.22.132. **-αιόλος** (on the accent v. Hdn. Gr.1.228, Eust.352.28), ον, (αἰόλλω) *moving the helmet quickly*, i.e. *with glancing helm*, epith. of Hector, Il.2.816, etc.; once of Ares, 20. 38; κ. νείκη Ar.*Ra*.818.

Κορυθαλία or **-θαλλία**, ἡ, title of Artemis at Sparta, Polem.Hist. 86; also in Italy, Hsch. s.v. κυριττοί. II. = εἰρεσιώνη, Id.:—also **κορυθάλεια, κορυθάλη, κορυθαλίς**, *EM*303.32, 531.53, 276. 28. **Κορυθαλλίστριαι**, αἱ, girls who dance in honour of Κορυθαλλία, Hsch. **κορύθιον** [ῠ], τό, Dim. of κόρυς, *Gloss*. **κόρῠθος**, ὁ, (κόρυς) *crested* τροχίλος, Hsch.; but also, = περικεφαλαία, Id. II. **Κόρυθος**, title of Apollo, *Bull.Soc.Roy.Lettres de Lund*1928–9 iv 40; **Κόριθος**, ib.39. **κορυλλίων**, a bird (perh. = κολλυρίων), Hsch.

κορυμβ-άς, άδος, ἡ, (κόρυς) *string running round a net*, Hsch. **-η**, ἡ, = κόρυμβος II, Asius *Fr.Ep*.13.5 K. **-ήθρα**, ἡ, = sq., Ps.-Dsc.2. 179. **-ηλος**, ὁ, = sq., Nic.*Fr*.74.18. **-ίας**, ου, ὁ, *white-berried ivy, Hedera Helix*, Thphr.*HP*3.18.6. **-ιον**, τό, Dim. of κόρυμβος III, Dsc.3.94. II. = λυχνὶς στεφανωματική, Ps.-Dsc.3.100. **-ίτης** [ῑ] κισσός, = κορυμβίας, Archig.ap.Aët.5.84.

κορυμβο-ειδής, ές, *clustered*, Dsc.3.24. **-ομαι**, Pass., *to be formed into a* κόρυμβος, κόμη χρυσῷ στρόφῳ κεκορυμβωμένη Nic.Dam. 62 J.

κόρυμβος, ὁ, pl. both κόρυμβοι and heterocl. κόρυμβα (v. infr.), (κόρυς, κορυφή) *uppermost point*, once in Hom., νηῶν .. ἄκρα κόρυμβα *high-pointed sterns* of ships, Il.9.241 (= ἄφλαστα, ἀκροστόλια, Hsch., but the meaning was disputed, Ar.*Fr*.222); νεὼς κόρυμβα A.*Pers*. 411, cf. E.*IA*258 (lyr.); ἀφλάστοιο κόρυμβα A.R.2.601; ἄφλαστα καὶ κ. Lyc.295. 2. the *top* of a hill, φεύγοντες ἐπὶ τοῦ ὄρεος τὸν κ. Hdt. 7.218, cf. D.H.9.23; ἐπ' ἄκρον κ. ὄχθου A.*Pers*.659 (lyr.). II. = κρωβύλος, κ. τῶν τριχῶν Heraclid.Pont.ap.Ath.12.512c; ἀσκητὸς εὐσπείροισι κορύμβοις *AP*6.219 (Antip.), cf. *Com.Adesp*.1331. III. *cluster of the ivy fruit*, κόρυμβα ἀμφὶ κρητὶ κίσσιν' ἔστεπτο prob. in Herod.8.33, cf. Corn.*ND*30, *AP*12.8 (Strat.), Plu.2.648f, Him.*Or*. 13.7: generally, *cluster of fruit* or *flowers*, Mosch.3.4, Nonn.*D*.12.224.

κορυμβοφόρος, ον, *cluster-bearing*, κισσός Longus 2.26. 2. *ivy-crowned*, Διόνυσος, γυναῖκες, Nonn.*D*.14.311, 24.102.

κορυμβώδης, ες, v.l. for κορυμβοειδής, Dsc.3.24.

κόρυμνα, *necklace*, Hsch.

κορυν-άω, (κορύνη II) *put forth knobby buds*, Thphr.*HP*4.12.2. **-η**, ἡ, *club*, freq. shod with iron for fighting, *mace*, σιδηρείῃ κορύνῃ ῥήγνυσκε φάλαγγας Il.7.141, cf. 143; ξύλων κορύνας ἔχοντες Hdt.1.59; κορύναις τύπτειν Arist.*Pol*.1311^{b}28. 2. *shepherd's staff*, Theoc. 7.19. II. in plants, *knobby bud* or *shoot*, Thphr.*HP*3.5.1, al. III. = πόσθη, Nic.*Al*.409, *AP*5.128 (Autom.). [ῠ in Hom. and Theoc. 7. 19, 9.23; ῡ in E.*Supp*.715, Theoc.25.63, Nic. l.c.] **-ησις**, εως, ἡ, *putting forth of knobby buds*, Thphr.*HP*3.5.1, Phan.Hist.25, Arr.*Fr*. 24 J. **-ήτης**, ου, ὁ, *club-bearer, mace-bearer*, Il.7.9,138, Paus.8. 11.4. **-ηφόρος**, ον, *club-bearing*, νύμφαι Epic. in *Arch.Pap*.7.7: as Subst., κ., οἱ, *club-bearers*, the body-guard of Peisistratos, Hdt.1. 59, Plu.*Sol*.30, D.L.1.66. II. *peasants* at Sicyon, Poll.3.83.

κορυνθ-εύς, έως, ὁ, *basket*, Hsch. II. *cock*, Id. **-ος**, ὁ, kind of *cake*, Id. II. epith. of Apollo, near Asine, Ἀρχ.Δελτ.2.17.

κορῡνιόεις, εσσα, εν, *knobby*, πέτηλα v.l. for κορωνιόωντα, Hes.*Sc*. 289.

κορυνομάχος, gloss on κορυνήτης, Hsch.

κορυνώδης, ες, *knobby*, Thphr.*HP*6.4.2.

κόρυξ· νεανίσκος, Hsch.

κορύπτης, ὁ, = κορυπτίλος, *EM*532.9, Hsch. s.v. κυρίττολος.

κορυπτιάω, = γαυριάω, in impf., Hsch.

κορυπτίλος [ῐ], ὁ, *one that butts with the head*, Theoc.5.147: **κυρίττολος**· κορύπτης, πλήκτης, Hsch.; **κορυπτόλης**· κερατιστής, Id.

κορύπτω, fut. -ψω Orac.ap.Luc.*JTr*.31:—*butt with the head*, Theoc. 3.5, perh. to be read in Lucil.1241 Marx; etym. of Κορύβαντες, Str. 10.3.21; *butt at*, τινα Tz. ad Lyc.558:—Med., v. κορύσσω ad fin.

κόρυρ· θριγκός, Hsch. (Dialect form of sq.)

κόρῠς, ῠθος, ἡ, acc. κόρῠθα Il.11.351, al., E.*Ba*.1186 (lyr.), κόρυν Il. 13.131, Luc.*DDeor*.20.10, Philostr.*Her*.12.1; poet. dat. pl. κορύθεσσι S.*Ant*.116 (lyr.):—*helmet*, freq. in Hom. (esp. in Il.); αὐγὴ χαλκείη κορύθων ἄπο λαμπομενάων 13.341; κ. χαλκήρης, χαλκοπάρῃος, 15.535, Od.24.523; τετράφαλος Il.22.315; ἱπποδάσεια 3.369. II. *scalp* of a lion, E. l.c.

κορύσσω, Ep. impf. κόρυσσε Il.21.306; poet. inf. -έμεν Pi.*P*.8. 75:—**Med.**, aor. ἐκορυσσάμην, part. κορυσσάμενος Il.19.397:—**Pass.**, pf. κεκόρυθμαι, part. κεκορυθμένος, freq. in Hom. (v. infr.): (κόρυς):—poet., chiefly Ep., Verb, prop. *furnish with a helmet*: hence, 1. generally, *fit out, equip, marshal*, πόλεμόν τε κορύσσων Il.2.273; κλόνον ἀνδρῶν Hes.*Sc*.148; μάχην ib.198; μάχας ἔργον Pi.*I*.8(7).58; φιλαιμάτους ἀλκάς E.*Rh*.933:—in Hom. mostly Pass. and Med., *equip, arm oneself*, τὼ δὲ κορυσσέσθην Il.4.274; ὄπιθεν δὲ κορυσσάμενος βῆ Ἀχιλλεύς 19.397; Αἴας δὲ κορύσσετο νώροπι χαλκῷ 7.206; κεκορυθμένος αἴθοπι χαλκῷ 5.562, etc.; of things, δοῦρε δύω κεκορυθμένα χαλκῷ *headed with* brass, 3.18, 11.43: abs., ἔγχος, βριθὺ μέγα στιβαρὸν κεκορυθμένον 16.802: c. acc., ὅπλων κεκορυθμένος ἔνδυτ' E.*IA*1073(lyr.): metaph., ἔριδι κ. Id.*Andr.*279(lyr.). **2.** *furnish, provide*, βίον κορυσσέμεν ὀρθοβούλοισι μαχαναῖς Pi.*P.*l.c. **II.** *make crested*, κόρυσσε δὲ κῦμα ῥόοιο *reared* his *crested* wave, Il.21.306:—Pass., *rear its head*, of a wave, πόντῳ μέν τε πρῶτα κορύσσεται Il.4.424, cf. A.R.2.71; of Eris, ἥ τ' ὀλίγη μὲν πρῶτα κορύσσεται Il.4.442; χείμαρρε, τί δὴ τόσον ὧδε κορύσσῃ; *AP*9.277 (Antiphil.); of clouds, Theoc.25.94, etc.; also of birds, Thphr.*Sign.*16: metaph., Δῆμος..πρὸς πνεῦμα βραχὺ κ. *Com. Adesp.*1324; cf. κορθύνω. (κορύττεται 'butts' Agath.1.4 is prob. f.l. for κορύπτεται: aor. Med. κορύξασθαι, δίκην ἀλεκτρυόνος Ath.3.127a, dub. l. in Hp.*Ep.*17.)

κορυστής, οῦ, ὁ, *helmed man, armed warrior*, ἕλεν ἄνδρα κορυστήν Il.4.457, 8.256; δύω Αἴαντε κορυστά 13.201, 18.163.

κορυστός, ή, όν, (κορύσσω II) *raised up, heaped up*, esp. of full measure, opp. ψηκτός, *IG*2².1013.22, al.; cf. **κορυτόν**· ἐπίμεστον, Hsch.

κορύτει· τῇ κεφαλῇ, Hsch.

κορῠφ-ᾱγενής, ές, *head-born*, prop. epith. of Athena: in Pythag. philosophy, of an equilat. triangle, like Τριτογένεια II, Plu.2.381f. **-αία**, ἡ, *head-stall of a bridle*, X.*Eq.*3.2, 5.1, 6.7, Poll.1.147. **II.** *tuft on the crown of the head*, Luc.*Lex.*5, Eust.1528.18. **-αινα**, ἡ, a fish, = ἵππουρος, Dorio ap.Ath.7.304c, Hsch. **-αῖον**, τό, *upper rim of a hunting-net*, prop. neut. of sq., X.*Cyn.*10.2, Poll.5.31. **II.** in pl., *head-parts* of animals sacrificed, prob. in *SIG*1002.12 (Milet., v/iv B.C.). **III.** Archit., *central block* of tympanum, *IG*1².373.100, 115; *ridge-beam* of a roof, ib.2².1668.49, 52. **-αῖος**, ὁ, *head man, chief, leader*, αὐτὸς ἕκαστος βουλόμενος κ. εἶναι Hdt.3.82; τῶν ἀνδρῶν τοὺς κ. ib.159, cf. 6.23, 98, Pl.*Tht.*173c; οἱ κ. *party-leaders*, Plb.28.4.6, cf. Phld.*Sto.Herc.*339.11; in the Drama, *leader of the chorus*, ἡγεμὼν τῆς φυλῆς κ. D.21.60 codd., cf. Arist.*Pol.*1277ᵃ11, Posidon.15J., etc.; κ. ἑστηκώς standing *at the head of the row*, Ar.*Pl.*953. **II.** as Adj., *at the top*, ὁ κ. πῖλος the *apex* of the Roman *flamen*, Plu.*Marc.*5; τὰ κ. τῆς νίκης the *crowning fruits* of.., Hdn.8.3.5; κ. τέλος τῶν πραγμάτων Id.7.5.2; τοῦ λαμπροῦ -αῖον (sc. αἴτιον) Phld.*Po.*2.41. **2.** epith. of Zeus, *CIG*4458.4 (Seleucia in Pieria); of the Roman *Jupiter Capitolinus*, Paus.2.4.5: Sup. κορυφαιότατος in later Gr., κ. ἀρχαί *CIG*3885 (Eumeneia), cf. Plu.2.1115b, Luc.*Sol.*5, *Hist.Conscr.*34. **-αιότης**, ητος, ἡ, *headship, supremacy*, *Corp.Herm.*18.16. **-άς**, άδος, ἡ, *edge of the navel*, Hp.ap.Gal.19.113. **-ή**, ἡ, (κόρυς) *head, top*: hence, **1.** *crown, top of the head*, of a horse, Il.8.83, X.*Eq.*1.11; of a man or god, *h.Ap.*309, Pi.*O.*7.36, Hdt.4.187, *Sammelb.*6003.8 (iv A.D.): between βρέγμα and ἰνίον, Arist.*HA*491ᵃ34; τὸ ὀστέον τῆς κ. Hp.*VC*2. **2.** *top, peak* of a mountain (so mostly Hom.), οὔρεος ἐν κορυφῇς Il.2.456; ὄρεος κορυφῆσι 3.10, cf. Alcm.60.1; κορυφαὶ γαίας B.5.24; κ. Οὐλύμποιο Il.1.499, cf. Ar.*Nu.*270; Αἴτνας μελαμφυλλοι κορυφαί Pi.*P.*1.27; τηλαυγέ' ἀγ κορυφάν Id.*Pae.*7.12; κ. πόληος Alc.*Supp.*17.6; ἀστρογείτονας κ. A.*Pr.*722, cf. Hdt.4.49, 181, 9.99. **3.** generally, *summit, top*, κατὰ κορυφὴν ἐσβαλεῖν ἐς τὴν κάτω Μακεδονίαν *straight over the summit, ridge*, Th.2.99, cf. *IG*4²(1).71.11 (Epid., iv B.C.), *OGI*383.125 (Nemrud Dagh, i B.C.); κατὰ κ. [τῆς στήλης] ἔσφαττον (sc. ταύρους) Pl.*Criti.*119e; ἵσταται κατὰ κ. ὁ ἥλιος *in the zenith*, Plu.2.938a; τὸ κατὰ κ., with or without σημεῖον, *the zenith*, Gem.5.64, etc., cf. Plu.*Mar.*11, Procl.*Hyp.*4.59; ταῖς τῶν κατὰ κ. λίθων ἐμβολαῖς by the stones falling *vertically*, Plb.8.7.3. **4.** *apex, vertex* of a triangle, Id.2.14.8; of the Delta, Pl.*Ti.*21e; *point* of an angle, τὸ ἐπὶ τὴν κ. μέρος Plb.1.26.16, etc.; *apex* of a cone, Arist.*Mete.*362ᵇ3; κατὰ κορυφὴν *vertically* opposite, of angles, Euc.1.15; of halves of double cone, Apollon. Perg.1 *Def.* **5.** *extremity, tip*, κορυφαὶ [κλημάτων], τῶν συγκυπτῶν, Thphr.*CP*3.14.8, Ath.Mech.22.8; in Anatomy, *the os coccygis*, Poll.2.183: in pl., *finger-tips*, Ruf.*Onom.*85, cf. Poll.2.146: Medic., of an abscess, ἐς κορυφὴν ἀνισταμένης ἀποστάσιος coming to a *head*, Aret.*SA*1.7. **II.** metaph., λόγων κορυφαί *the sum* of all his words, Pi.*O.*7.69, cf. *Pae.*8.23; ἔρχομαι ἐπὶ τὴν κ. ὧν εἴρηκα Pl.*Cra.*415a; but λόγων κ. ὀρθάν true *sense* of legends, Pi.*P.*3.80; κορυφὰς ἑτέρας ἑτέρῃσι προσάπτων μύθων springing *from peak to peak*, i.e. treating a subject disconnectedly, Emp.24; κ. ὁ λόγος ἐπιθεὶς ἑαυτῷ having reached its *conclusion*, put *the finishing touch* to itself, Plu.2.975a; κ. τοῦ κακοῦ *height, full development* of.., Aret.*SD*1.6; τοῦ πάθεος κ. ἴσχοντος ib.1.16. **2.** *height, excellence of*.., i.e. *the choicest, best*, κορυφαὶ πολίων Pi.*N.*1.15; κ. ἀρετᾶν ib.34, cf. *O.*1.13; κ. ἀέθλων, of the Olympic games, Id.*O.*2.13, cf. *N.*9.9; φιάλαν..πάγχρυσον κ. κτεάνων Id.*O.*7.4; ὁ καιρὸς παντὸς ἔχει κορυφάν is the *best* of all, Id.*P.*9.79. **3.** κορυφᾷ Διὸς εἰ κρανθῇ πρᾶγμα his *head*, i.e. his nod, A.*Supp.*92. **4.** ἡ τῆς οἰκουμένης κ., of Rome, Lib.*Or.*59.19. **-ῆνδε**, Adv. *to the top*, Orph.*L.*112. **-ιον**, τό, = κολούλιον, Xenocr. ap.Orib.2.58.79 (pl.). **-ίς**, ίδος, ἡ, = κορυφή, *Gloss.* **-ιστήρ**, ῆρος, ὁ, = κορυφαῖον I, Poll.5.31. **2.** = κορυφαία I, Hsch. s.v. κεκρυφάλους (-αστῆρας cod.). **-ιστής**, οῦ, ὁ, *fillet* or *diadem*, esp. as a woman's head-dress; also, = κεκρυφάλου τὸ μέσον ῥάμμα, Id. **-ος**, ὁ, = κορυφή I.3, *IG*4²(1).71.17, al. (Epid.). **II.** pet name for a child (?), *PTeb.*414.7 (ii A.D.). **III.** Alexandrian word for ὁ ὡς κόρη οἰφώμενος, Sch.Theoc.4.62 (v.l. κόροιφος). **-όω**, *bring to a head*, ἴονθους Archig.ap.Orib.*Syn.*8.58; τὴν περὶ τὰ πρέμνα γῆν *Gp.*5.26.9:—Pass., [κῦμα] κυρτὸν ἐὸν κορυφοῦται *rises with* arching *crest* (cf. κορύσσω II), Il.4.426; κορυφουμένων [ἑλκέων] ὅκως ἐν θαλάσσῃ κύματα Aret.*SD*2.9: metaph., τὸ ἔσχατον κορυφοῦται βασιλεῦσι kings *are on the highest pinnacle*, Pi.*O.*1.113; κορυφουμένου τοῦ πολέμου *coming to a crisis*, J.*BJ*6.2.9; πόθου κορυφούμενον σάλον Aristaenet.1.10. **II.** *roof over*, ὀπαῖον Plu.*Per.*13. **III.** Pass., *to be concluded*, κεκορυφωμένου τοῦ κεφαλαίου Phld.*Rh.*1.122S.; κορυφούμενος εἰς ἓν ἀριθμός *being summed up*, *AP*7.429 (Alc. Mityl.):—Med., *sum up*, τὴν οὐσίαν τοῦ θεοῦ Jul.*Or.*4.143b. **-ώδης**, ες, *peaked, pointed*, Hp.*Epid.*6.1.10. **-ωμα**, ατος, τό, *top, summit*, Ath.Mech.36.7. **-ών**, ῶνος, ὁ, = foreg., *Gloss.* **-ωσις**, εως, ἡ, *apex* of a pyramid, Nicom.*Ar.*2.14.

κορφῶς· ἐλαφρῶς, Hsch.

κόρχορος, ὁ, = ἀναγαλλὶς ἡ κυανῆ, *blue pimpernel, Anagallis caerulea*, Ps.-Dsc.2.178; παροιμιαζόμενος διὰ πικρότητα Thphr.*HP*7.7.2; **κόρκορος** in Ar.*V.*239, Nic.*Th.*626: prov., κ. ἐν λαχάνοισι, 'a tailor among kings', Sch.Ar. l.c., etc. **II.** *jute, Corchorus olitorius*, Plin.*HN*21.89, 183. **III.** *fat*, Hsch.

κορχυρέα, ἡ, *subterranean channel, culvert*, *IG*9(1).692.8 (Corc., ii B.C.).

κορωλλικός, ή, όν, *made of coral*, εἰκόνες *BCH*12.85 (temple of Zeus Panamaros).

κορωνεκάβη [ᾰ], ἡ, *a Hecuba, as old as a crow*, *AP*11.67 (Myrin.).

κορώνεως (sc. συκῆ), ἡ, *a fig of raven-grey colour*, Ar.*Pax*628.

κορώνη, ἡ, a sea-bird, possibly *shearwater, Puffinus Kuhlii* or *P. anglorum*, τανύγλωσσοί τε κορῶναι εἰνάλιαι Od.5.66, cf. 12.418, Arist.*HA*593ᵇ13, Thphr.*Sign.*16, Arat.950, Ael.*NA*15.23; λάροι καὶ αἴθυιαι καὶ κ. Arr.*Peripl.M.Eux.*32 (but confounded with λ. and αἴ. by Sch.Od.1.441, cf. Hsch.). **2.** *crow* (including the *hooded crow, Corvus cornix*, and prob. also the *rook, C. corone*), μή τοι ἐφεζομένη κρώξῃ λακέρυζα κ. Hes.*Op.*747; συκῆ πετραίη πολλὰς βόσκουσα κ. Archil.19: distd. from κολοιός, Ar.*Av.*5 (cf. 7); ἐννέα τοι ζώει γενεὰς λακέρυζα κ. ἀνδρῶν γηράντων Hes.*Fr.*171; πέντ' ἀνδρῶν γενεὰς ζώει λακέρυζα κ. Ar.*Av.*609; πολιαὶ κ. ib.967; κορώνην δευτέραν ἀναπλήσας having lived out twice a full *crow's-age*, Babr.46.9; ὑπὲρ τὰς κορώνας βεβιωκώς Poll.2.16: prov., κορώνη σκορπίον [ἥρπασε] 'caught a Tartar', *AP*12.92 (Mel.), cf. Zen.4.57, Hsch., Suid.; invoked at weddings, Ael.*NA*3.9. **3.** κ. Δαυλία, = ἀηδών, Ar.*Fr.*716. **II.** *anything hooked* or *curved*, like a crow's bill, **1.** *door-handle*, θύρην δ' ἐπέρυσσε κορώνῃ ἀργυρέῃ Od.1.441; ἱμάντα..ἀπέλυσε κορώνης 21.46; χρυσέη κ. 7.90, cf. Poll.7.107, al. **2.** *tip of a bow*, on which the bow-string was hooked, πᾶν δ' εὖ λειήνας χρυσέην ἐπέθηκε κ. Il.4.111, cf. Od.21.138: generally, *end, tip*, Artem.5.65: metaph., v. infr. 7. **3.** *curved stern of a ship*, Arat.345. **4.** *tip of the plough-pole* (ἱστοβοεύς), upon which the yoke is hooked or tied, A.R.3.1318, Poll.1.252. **5.** *coronoid process* of the ulna, Hp.*Art.*18, Gal.*UP*2.14, Id.18(2).617; of the jaw, Id.*UP*11.20, 18(1).426. **6.** kind of *crown*, Hsch. **7.** κ. παννυχική *crown*, i.e. *culmination*, of a festival, Posidipp.ap.Ath.10.414d; cf. μέχρι τῆς κ. Call.*Fr.*2.5P.: generally, χρυσῷ βίῳ (with play on βιῷ) χρυσῆν κορώνην ἐπιθεῖναι Luc.*Peregr.*33, v. supr. II.2. **-ιάω**, of a horse, *arch the neck*, *AP*9.777 (Phil.); of a man, *to be ambitious*, Plb.27.15.6; κ. καὶ γαυριῶντα D.Chr.78.33. **II.** κορωνιόωντα πέτηλα *curving* leaves, Hes.*Sc.*289. **-ῐδεύς**, έως, ὁ, *young crow*, Cratin.179. **-ίζω**, *bring to completion* (cf. κορωνίς II.2b), ἐξ δεκάδας κεκορώνικε *IPE*2.298.9 (Panticapaeum). **-ίης**, Att. **-ίας**, ου, ὁ, (κορωνιάω) *arching the neck*, ἵππος ὣς κ. Semon.18 (κορωνίτης codd. *EM*). **-ιος**, ον, *with crumpled horns*, Hsch. **II.** Κορώνιος, ὁ (sc. μήν), name of month at Cnossus, *GDI*5015.28. **-ίς**, ίδος, ἡ, acc. -νίν Hes.*Fr.*123.3 (as pr. n.):—*crook-beaked*: hence, generally, *curved*, in Hom. always of ships, παρὰ νηυσὶ κορωνίσι Il.18.338, al.; twice in Od., ἐν νήεσσι κ. 19.182, cf. 193. **2.** of kine, *with crumpled horns*, Theoc.25.151. **II.** as Subst., *anything curved* or *bent*: **1.** *wreath, garland*, Stesich.29, Hsch. **2.** *curved line* or *stroke, flourish with the pen* at the end of a book or chapter, scene of a play, etc., *AP*11.41 (Phld.), Heph.*Poëm.* p.73C., Isid.*Etym.*1.21.26, Sch.Ar.*Nu.*510, al.; ἐγὼ κ. εἰμὶ γραμμάτων φύλαξ *PLit.Lond.*11; ἐπιτιθέναι τὴν κ. τῷ συγγράμματι Plu.2.66e; ἀπὸ τῆς ἀρχῆς μέχρι τῆς κ. ib.334c, etc. **b.** metaph., *end, completion*, ἐπιθεῖναι κορωνίδα τινί Luc.*Hist.Conscr.*26, cf. Gal.1.643; ἡ κ. τοῦ βίου Plu.2.789a; κ. τῶν ἀγαθῶν Hld.10.39, etc. **3.** *mark of crasis* ('), as in τοὔνομα, θοἰμάτιον, τοὐμόν, etc., *An.Ox.*1.372, Sch. D.T.p.147H., *EM*763.10 (found in parchments of *Lyr.Alex.Adesp.*31.20 (ii A.D.), Sapph.*Supp.*2.4 (vii A.D.), etc.). **-ισμα**, ατος, τό, *crow-song*, a begging-song sung by strollers, Hagnocles ap.Ath.8.360b. **-ισταί**, οἱ, *singers of the crow-song*, title of work by Hagnocles, v. foreg.

κορωνοβόλος, ον, *shooting crows*: κορωνοβόλον, τό, *sling* or *bow for crow-shooting*, etc., *AP*7.546.

κορωνόν, τό, = κορώνη II.5; τοῦ πήχεως Gal.*UP*2.15, al.; τὰ τῆς κεφαλῆς κ. *condyles*, Id.2.460. **2.** κόρωνα, τά, *elbows*, Herod.Med. ap.Orib.10.18.7, Orib.*Fr.*97; κορωνά Luc.*Trag.*122.

κορωνο-πόδιον, τό, Dim. of κορωνόπους, Aët.1.224, *Gp.*20.9, *PMag.Osl.*1.283. **-ποδώδης**, ες, *like crow's feet*, Thphr.*HP*1.10.5. **-πους**, ποδος, ὁ, *hartshorn, Plantago Coronopus*, ib.7.8.3, *CP*2.5.4, Dsc.2.130, Gal.12.40.

κορωνός, ή, όν, *curved, crooked*, of the coronoid process of the jawbone, Hp.*Art.*30; βοῦς κ. *with crumpled horns*, Archil.39. **II.** = γαῦρος, ὑψαυχενῶν, *EM*530.27; κορωνὰ βαίνειν, = κορωνιᾶν, Anacr.151.

κοσάλανον· τὸ βραχύ, καὶ τὸ δίκαιον, Hsch. **κοσάλεφοι**· κόλαφοι, Id. **κόσβατοι**, v. κοσυβάτας. **κόσκικοι**· οἱ κατοικίδιοι ὄρνιθες, Id.

κοσκῐν-ευτήριον, τό, *winnowing-place*, *PRyl.*215.34 (ii A.D.). **-ευτής**, οῦ, ὁ, *one who sifts, winnows*, *PSI*4.365.18 (iii B.C.), *PCair.Zen.*292.484 (iii B.C.), al. **-ευτικόν**, τό, *fee for sifting*, *PPetr.*3 p.215 (iii B.C.); πυροῦ *PRyl.*71.10 (i B.C.), cf. *PTeb.*92.10 (ii B.C.), al. **-εύω**, *sift*, in Pass., Democr.164, *PHib.*1.98.19 (iii B.C.), etc.; κοσκίνῳ

-ευέσθω *Gp.*3.7.1. **-ηδόν,** Adv. *as in a sieve*, Luc.*Tim.*3, *Sat.* 24. **-ίζω,** = κοσκινεύω, Asclep.ap.Gal.13.326, Aq., Sm.*Am.*9.9, *Gp.*13.15.4. II. metaph., *thrash, beat*, Hierocl.*Facet.*209 (Pass.). **-ιον,** τό, Dim. of κόσκινον, Chrysipp.Tyan.ap.Ath.14.647f. **-ισις,** εως, ἡ, *sifting*, *PFlor.*388.9 (ii A.D.), Phlp. *in GA* 54.2: interlinear gloss on ἀλευρότησις, *Et.Gud.*

κοσκῐνό-γῡρος, ὁ, = τηλία, Sch.Ar.*Pl.*1038. **-μαντις,** εως (also ιδος, Choerob. *in Theod.*1.200, al.), ὁ and ἡ, *diviner by a sieve*, Philippid.37, Theoc.3.31, Artem.2.69.

κόσκῐνον, τό (for the gender v. Ar.*Fr.*480, Poll.10.149), *sieve*, Semon.7.59, Ar.*Nu.*373, *Fr.*227, Democr.164, etc.; φορεῖν ὕδωρ τετρημένῳ κοσκίνῳ Pl.*Grg.*493b; ἐν Ἅιδου κοσκίνῳ ὕδωρ φέρειν, alluding to the punishment of the Danaids, Id.*R.*363d; κοσκίνοις μαντεύεσθαι Ael.*NA*8.5, cf. Luc.*Alex.*9; κ. ἁλωνικὸν ἀπὸ βύρσης, ἀπὸ δέρματος, κ. πλεκτόν, *Edict.Diocl.*15.56, al., cf. Poll.6.74, *Gp.*2.19.5, al. II. κ. Ἐρατοσθένους *table* for finding prime numbers, Nicom.*Ar.*1.13.

κοσκῐνο-ποιός, ὁ, *sieve-maker*, Philyll.14, Poll.7.160. **-πώλης,** ου, ὁ, *dealer in sieves*, Nicopho19. **-ράφος** [ᾰ], ὁ, *one who sews (leather) sieves*, *PTeb.*540 (ii A.D.). **-ρῖνος** (-ριος cod.)· εἰς κοσκίνου κατασκευὴν ῥινός, Hsch.

κοσκίνωμα, ατος, τό, *grating*, Sm., Thd.*Ex.*35.16.

κοσκυλμάτια, ων, τά, *cuttings of leather*: Com., of *the scraps of flattery* offered by the tanner Cleon to his patron Δῆμος, Ar.*Eq.*49, cf. Sch.

κοσμᾰγός, ὁ, *guide of the universe*, name of an order of divine beings in the Chaldaean system, Dam.*Pr.*112.

κοσμαῖα, τά, *ornaments*, *CPR*30 ii 1 (vi A.D., nisi leg. κοσμα⟨ρ⟩ίων).

κοσμᾶν· ἐρίζειν, ἀγνωμονεῖν, Hsch.

κοσμ-αρίδιον, τό, Dim. of κόσμος II, *POxy.*903.29 (iv A.D.). **-άριον,** τό, = foreg., Ath.11.474e, Hsch. s. v. καλαμίς, al. **-άρχης,** ου, ὁ, *governor of the universe*, Dam.*Pr.*132. **-έω,** *order, arrange*, esp. *set* an army *in array, marshal* it, Il.14.379; κοσμῆσαι ἵππους τε καὶ ἀνέρας 2.554:—Pass., ἐπεὶ κόσμηθεν ἅμ' ἡγεμόνεσσιν ἕκαστοι 3.1; πένταχα κοσμηθέντες *marshalled* in five bodies, 12.87; of a population, διὰ τρίχα κοσμηθέντες 2.655; once in Od., of hunters, διὰ δὲ τρίχα κοσμηθέντες 9.157:—Med., κοσμησάμενος πολιήτας *having arranged his* men, Il.2.806; so after Homer, κ. στρατόν (v.l. for κοιμήσων) E.*Rh.*662; τάξεις κεκοσμημέναι X.*Cyr.*2.1.26, cf. Pl.*Phdr.*247a; ἐπὶ τάξις πλεῦνας ἐκεκοσμέατο Hdt.9.31. 2. generally, *arrange, prepare*, δόρπον ἐκόσμει Od.7.13; κ. ἀοιδήν *h.Bacch.*59; ἔργα Hes.*Op.*306; στέφανον E.*Hipp.*74; τράπεζαν X.*Cyr.*8.2.6; εἰς τάφον λέβητα S.*El.*1401:—Pass., δεῖπνον κεκόσμηται Pi.*N.*1.22; δεῖ οὕτω κοσμηθῆναι ὅκως.. Democr.266; τὸ κοσμηθὲν αἷμα, = τὸν οἰκεῖον κόσμον κτησάμενον, Gal.5.551. II. *order, rule*, τὴν πόλιν κ. καλῶς τε καὶ εὖ Hdt.1.59, cf. S.*Aj.*1103; Σπάρτην ἔλαχες, κείνην κόσμει E.*Fr.*723 (anap.); κ. ἐμαυτόν *restrain* myself, Id.*Hyps.Fr.*34(60).46; τὰ ἄλλα ἐκεκοσμέατό οἱ Hdt.1.100; τόν γε νοῦν κοσμοῦντα πάντα κοσμεῖν Pl.*Phd.*97c:—Pass., τὰ κοσμούμενα *orderly institutions*, S.*Ant.*677: pf. part., of persons, *orderly*, ταπεινὸς καὶ κεκοσμημένος Pl.*Lg.*716a; τεταγμένον τε καὶ κ. πρᾶγμα Id.*Grg.*504a. 2. in Crete, *hold office of* κόσμος III, οἱ κεκοσμηκότες Arist.*Pol.*1272ᵃ35, cf. Plb.22.15.1; Cret. **κοσμίω** *Leg.Gort.*1.51, etc.; also κορμίω (q.v.). III. *adorn, equip, dress*, esp. of women, *h.Hom.*6.11, Hes.*Op.*72; κοσμῆσαί τινα πανοπλίῃ Hdt.4.180; τριπόδεσσι κ. δόμον Pi.*I.*1.19; τινὰ πλούτῳ ὑπερβάλλοντι Hdn.3.10.6: c. dupl. acc., πρίν σε νυμφικὸν ἰστέφανον κοσμήσαμεν *JRS*17.51 (Phrygia, iv A.D.):—freq. in Med., κοσμέεσθαι τὰς κεφαλάς *to adorn their* heads, Hdt.7.209; κοσμεῖσθαι σῶμα ὅπλοις E.*Ph.*1359; ἐν φοινικίσι κοσμησάμενοι *having decked themselves*, Pl.Com.208:—Pass., χρυσῷ κοσμηθεῖσα *h.Ven.*65; παῖσα δ' Ἄρῃ κεκόσμηται στέγα Alc.15.1; ἵπποι κεκοσμημένοι ὡς κάλλιστα Hdt.7.40; κεκ. ἐσθῆτι ποικίλῃ καὶ χρυσοῖσι στεφάνοις Pl.*Ion*535d, cf. S.*Ph.*1064, Th.6.41, etc. 2. metaph., *adorn, embellish*, λόγους E.*Med.*576; λόγοις ῥήμασί τε καὶ ὀνόμασι κεκοσμημένους Pl.*Ap.*17c; τραγικὸν λῆρον Ar.*Ra.*1005; κ. ἔργον ἄριστον ib.1027; τὸ λογικὸν ἔχεις ἐξαίρετον, τοῦτο κόσμει Arr.*Epict.*3.1.26; λόγον εὐρυθμίαις Isoc.5.27; αὐτὸν λόγοις Pl.*La.*196b, cf. 197c; ἐπὶ τὸ μεῖζον κ. Th.1.21; τὸν.. τὴν ἐκείνων ἀρετὴν κοσμήσοντα (in speaking) D.18.287:—Pass., ἦθος σεμνότητι -μημένον Phld.*Acad.Ind.* p.52 M. 3. *honour*, λουτροῖς σ' ἐκόσμησ' S.*El.*1139; κ. τάφον Id.*Ant.*396; νέκυν E.*Tr.*1147; κ. καὶ τιμᾶν X.*Cyr.*1.3.3; of persons, *adorn, be an honour to*, πατρίδα Thgn.947; νᾶσον εὐκλέα Pi.*N.*6.46; Σαλαμῖνα κ. πατρίδα E.*Fr.*530.3; [τὴν πόλιν] αἱ τῶνδε ἀρεταὶ ἐκόσμησαν Th.2.42. 4. *bury*, *JHS*25.172, al. (Isauria). IV. Pass., *to be assigned, ascribed to*, ἐς τὸν Αἰγύπτιον νομὸν αὗται [αἱ πόλεις] ἐκεκοσμέατο Hdt.3.91; ἐς Πέρσας κεκοσμέαται Id.6.41; esp. of philosophic schools, κατὰ τὴν Ἀκαδημίαν κοσμεῖσθαι S.E.*P.*1.231; οἱ κατὰ διαφόρους αἱρέσεις κοσμούμενοι Id.*M.*11.77. **-ημα,** ατος, τό, *ornament, decoration*, esp. in dress, X.*Cyr.*7.3.7, Luc.*Salt.*32, etc.; τὰ πολέμου κ. Pl.*Lg.*956b; of *adornments* buried with the dead, *BGU*1024.iv 44 (iv A.D.): metaph., of the virtues, Luc.*Im.*11. **-ησις,** εως, ἡ, *ordering, arrangement*, ταῖς τῆς ψυχῆς τάξεσι καὶ κοσμήσεσι Pl.*Grg.*504d, cf. *Criti.*117b (sg.): *adornment*, Arist.*Oec.*1344ᵃ19; pl., Plu.*Thes.*23: metaph., *dignity*, ἡ τῆς πόλεως καὶ τοῦ βουλευτηρίου κ. *BGU* 1024 viii 10 (iv A.D.). **-ητεία,** ἡ, *office of* κοσμητής, *CPR*20.7 (iii A.D.). **-ήτειρα,** ἡ, fem. of -ητήρ, Orph.*H.*10.8. II. κ. τῆς Ἀρτέμιδος, title of *a female magistrate* at Ephesus, *SIG*1228 (Ephesus, iii A.D.), *CIG*2823. **-ητέον,** *one must adorn*, Porph.*Marc.*19. **-ητεύω,** *hold office of* κοσμητής (q.v.), *IG*2².1009.49, *PFlor.*57.75 (ii A.D.), *CPR*20.1 (iii A.D.), *IG*3.735, al., *BGU*362 ix 6 (iii A.D.): —also **-ητέω** *IG*3.736. **-ητήρ,** ῆρος, ὁ, = κοσμητής, Epigr.ap. Aeschin.3.185. II. at Itanos, title of eponymous magistrate, *SIG*463.15 (iii B.C.), *Supp.Epigr.*2.512.22. **-ητήριον,** τό, *dressing-room*, Paus.2.7.5. II. = κόσμητρον, Hsch. s. v. κάλλυντρα. **-ητής,** οῦ, ὁ, *orderer, director*, πολέμου Epigr.ap.Aeschin.3.185; πόλεως κ. *legislator*, Pl.*Lg.*844a; title of Zeus, Paus.3.17.4. 2. at Athens and elsewhere, *magistrate in charge of the* ἔφηβοι, Arist.*Ath.*42.2, *IG* 2².665.10,17 (iii B.C.), 1009.33 (ii B.C.), al., Pl.*Ax.*366e, Teles p.50 H., *POxy.*519.8 (ii A.D.), *PFay.*85 (iii A.D.), etc. II. *adorner*, X.*Cyr.*8.8.20. 2. *cleaner* or *polisher* of temple-statues, *IG*11(2).154*A*20 (Delos, iii B.C.). **-ητικός,** ή, όν, *skilled in ordering* or *arranging*, τινος Arist.*Oec.*1344ᵇ26, Andronic.Rhod.p.575 M. Adv. -κῶς Hierocl.*Prov.*p.465 B. II. ἡ -κή (sc. τέχνη) *art of dress and ornament*, Pl.*Sph.*227a, *Plt.*282a: -κά, τά, title of work by Crito, Gal.12.446: -κόν, τό, *cosmetic*, *PTeb.*540 (ii A.D.); title of work by Cleopatra, Gal.12.432. **-ητός,** ή, όν, *well-ordered, trim*, πρασιαί Od.7.127. **-ήτρια,** ἡ, = κοσμήτειρα, Hsch. s. v. Σαραχηρώ. **-ητρον,** τό, *broom*, Sch.Ar.*Pax*59, Suid. s. v. κάλλυντρα. **-ήτωρ,** ορος, ὁ, poet. for κοσμητής (in late Prose, Jul.*Gal.*49e), *one who marshals an army, commander, leader*, Ἀτρεΐδα.. δύω, κοσμήτορε λαῶν Il.1.16, 375; δοιὼ.. κοσμήτορε λαῶν 3.236; ἐν χερσὶν ἔθηκε δέπας κοσμήτορι λ. Od.18.152; *guide, director*, παιδός A.R.1.194. 2. *one who adorns*, ἡρώων κ. Ὅμηρον Epigr.ap.Arist.*Fr.*76. 3. = κοσμητής I.2, *IG*3.740, al. **-ιαῖος,** α, ον, (κόσμος IV) *of the size of the universe*, Democr.ap.*Placit.*1.12.6. **-ίδιον,** τό, Dim. of κόσμος II, *adornment*, metaph., τῆς πόλεως *Mélanges Beyrouth* 7.395 (Cappadocia; written -ήδιον). **-ίζω,** *clean*, Hsch. s. v. σαρῶ. **-ικός,** ή, όν, (κόσμος IV) *of the world* or *universe*, σχήματα Procl. *in Euc.*p.65 F.; τὰ κ. πάντα v.l. in Arist.*Ph.*196ᵃ25, cf. Philol. (?) 23; ἡ κ. διάταξις Plu.2.119f; κ. ὀχλήσεις Luc.*Paras.*11; κλίσεις (v.l. κλήσεις) Suid. s. v. Ὀρφεύς: Astrol., κ. κέντρα (opp. γενεθλιαλογικά) Vett.Val.79.26. Adv. -κῶς Id.119.15, Ptol.*Tetr.*112. II. *of this world, earthly*, *Ep.Hebr.*9.1; *worldly*, ἐπιθυμίαι *Ep.Tit.*2.12. 2. *secular, lay*, opp. clerical, Just.*Nov.*123.1.2. **-ιον,** τό, Dim. (in form) of κόσμος, D.S.25.15, Plu.2.141d, *BGU*1024 v 27 (iv A.D.); κ. ἡμέρας Secund.*Sent.*5; τὰ τῆς ἀρχῆς κ. the *insignia* of office, D.S.38/9.16; τὰ βασιλικὰ κ. Plu.*Demetr.*45; στρατηγικὰ Id.*Ant.*17. **-ιος,** α, ον, (-ος, ον, Gal.16.606, Sor.1.3), *well-ordered, regular, moderate*, δαπάνη Pl.*R.*560d; οἴκησις Id.*Criti.*112c; κόσμιόν ἐστι, c. inf., is *a regular practice*, Ar.*Pl.*565. 2. of persons, *orderly, well-behaved*, δίκαιοι καὶ σοφοὶ καὶ κ. ib.89; κ. καὶ σώφρων Lys.21.19; κ. καὶ εὔκολοι Pl.*R.*329d; κ. καὶ φρόνιμος ψυχή Id.*Phd.*108a; χρηστὸς εἶ καὶ κ. Nicopho16; ἥτις ἐστὶ κοσμία γυνή Anaxandr.56, cf. Arist.*Pol.*1277ᵇ23; κ. ἐν διαίτῃ Pl.*R.*408b; πρὸς τοὺς θεούς Id.*Smp.*193a; οἱ κοσμιώτατοι φύσει Id.*R.*564e; of a patient, *quiet*, Hp.*Acut.*65: freq. in Oratt., of *honest, orderly* citizens, Lys.26.3, etc.; τοὺς πολίτας -ιωτέρους ποιεῖν Isoc.20.18; *modest*, ὁμιλία X.*Mem.*3.11.14 (Sup.); τὸ κ. *decency, order*, S.*El.*872, Pl.*Lg.*802e. Adv. κοσμίως *regularly, decently*, Ar.*Pl.*709, 978, al.; κ. ἔχειν Pl.*Phd.*68c; κ. ἥκομεν *as befits* us, Id.*Sph.*216a; κ. βιοῦν Lys.3.6: Comp. -ιώτερον, βεβιωκέναι Isoc.15.162: Sup. -ώτατα, τὰς συμφορὰς φέρειν Lys.3.4. II. Subst. κόσμιος, ὁ, (κόσμος IV) = κοσμοπολίτης, Plu.2.600f, Arr.*Epict.*1.9.1. **-ιότης,** ητος, ἡ, *propriety, decorum*, Ar.*Pl.*564, Pl.*Plt.*307b, Zeno *Stoic.*1.58, etc.; κ. καὶ σωφροσύνη Pl.*Grg.*508a; opp. ἀκολασία, Arist.*EN*1109ᵃ16: pl., τὰς αἰσχύνας καὶ κ. Phld.*Mus.*p.44 K.

κοσμο-γένεια, ἡ, = sq., Jul.*Gal.*49a. **-γονία,** ἡ, *creation* or *origin of the world*, Cleom.1.1; applied to the poem of Parmenides, Plu.2.756f. **-γρᾰφία,** Ion. -ίη, ἡ, *description of the world*, title of work by Democritus, D.L.9.46. **-γράφος** [ᾰ], ον, *describing the world*, Jo.Gaz.2.3. **-διοικητικός,** ή, όν, *governing the world*, Stob.2.7.3f. **-ειδής,** ές, *like the celestial globe*, Horap.1.10. Adv. -δῶς ib.59. **-κόμης,** ου, ὁ, *dressing the hair*, κτείς *AP*6.247 (Phil.). **-κράτωρ** [ᾰ], ορος, ὁ, *lord of the world*, epith. of οὐρανός, Orph.*H.*4.3; Ζεὺς Μίτρας Ἥλιος κ. *Not.Scav.*1912.323 (Rome). 2. of the Emperors, *IG*14.926, *Sammelb.*4275, cf. Ptol.*Tetr.*175, Heph.Astr.1.1. 3. Astrol., *ruler of the* κόσμος, i. e. *planet*, Id. in *Cat.Cod.Astr.*6.68, Vett.Val.171.6; οἱ ἑπτὰ κ. Dam.*Pr.*131; οἱ κ. τοῦ σκότους τούτου the *cosmic rulers* of this sinful world, *Ep.Eph.*6.12; οἱ κ. οἱ τὰ ὑπὸ σελήνην στοιχεῖα διοικοῦντες Iamb.*Myst.*2.3. **-λογικός,** ὁ, title of work by Ion, Sch.Ar.*Pax*835. **-πλαστέω,** *frame the world*, Ph.1.437. **-πλάστης,** ου, ὁ, *framer of the world*, ib.329, 526. **-πληθής,** ές, *filling the world*, κατακλυσμός Lxx 4*Ma.*15.31. **-πλόκος,** ον, *holding together the world*, of Apollo, *AP*9.525.11. **-ποιέω,** *make the world*, Ph.1.5, Plu.2.719d, 877c (Pass.), *Stoic.*2.112 (ap.Alex.Aphr.*Mixt.*225.2), Iamb. *in Nic.*p.79 P. 2. *frame a system* or *theory of the world*, Arist.*Metaph.*1091ᵃ18, *Cael.*301ᵃ13; κ. ἕκαστον τῶν ἀστέρων *assert* them *to be worlds*, *Placit.*2.13.15. 3. *bestow order upon, organize*, τὴν ὕλην Dam.*Pr.*270. **-ποίησις,** εως, ἡ, Archit., *ornamentation*, *POxy.*498.30 (ii A.D.). **-ποιητής,** οῦ, ὁ, *creator of the world*, Herm.ap.Stob.1.49.44. **-ποιητικός,** ή, όν, *creative*, δύναμις Ph.1.4. **-ποιΐα,** ἡ, *creation*, Arist.*Metaph.*985ᵃ19, *Stoic.*2.191, Str.15.1.59, Ph.1.1, Dam.*Pr.*270, etc. 2. title of a work by Empedocles, Arist.*Ph.*196ᵃ22; applied to the opening chapters of Genesis, Ph. l. c. II. = κόσμησις, *CPHerm.*p.79 W. **-ποιός,** όν, *creating the world*, *Placit.*1.25.3, Dam.*Pr.*309, al.; θεὸς *Theol.Ar.*43: Subst. -ποιός, ὁ, *creator*, Ph.1.2. **-πολις,** ὁ, a magistrate among the Locrians, Plb.12.16.6 (dat. -πόλιδι), and 9 (acc. -πολιν); at Thasos, *IG*12(8).386, 459; at Lyttus in Crete, *CIG*2583; at Cibyra, *IGRom.*4.908; at Miletus, title of the ἀρχιπρύτανις, *Milet.*1(7).230, 231. **-πολίτης** [ῑ], ου, ὁ, *citizen of the world*, Ph.1.1, al., D.L.6.63:—fem. **-πολῖτις** as

Adj., ψυχαί Ph.1.657. **–πρεπής**, ές, *suitable for the universe*, Euryph. ap.Stob.4.39.27.

κόσμος, ὁ, *order*, κατὰ κόσμον in *order, duly*, εὖ κατὰ κ. Il.10. 472, al.; οὐ κατὰ κ. *shamefully*, Od.8.179; μὰψ ἀτὰρ οὐ κατὰ κ. Il. 2.214: freq. in dat., κόσμῳ καθίζειν to sit *in order*, Od.13.77, cf. Hdt.8.67; οὐ κ... ἐλευσόμεθα Il.12.225; κ. θεῖναι τὰ πάντα Hdt.2.52, cf. 7.36, etc.; διάθες τάδε κ. Ar.*Av.*1331; κ. φέρειν bear *becomingly*, Pi.*P.*3.82; δέξασθαί τινα κ. A.*Ag.*521; σὺν κόσμῳ Hdt.8.86, Arist.*Mu.* 398^{b}23; ἐν κόσμῳ Hp.*Mul.*1.3, Pl.*Smp.*223b; κόσμῳ οὐδενὶ κοσμηθέντες *in* no sort of *order*, Hdt.9.59; φεύγειν, ἀπιέναι οὐδενὶ κ., Id. 3.13, 8.60.γ', etc.; ἀτάκτως καὶ οὐδενὶ κ. Th.3.108, cf. A.*Pers.*400; οὐκέτι τὸν αὐτὸν κ. no longer *in* the same *order*, Hdt.9.66; οὐδένα κ. ib.65,69; ἦν δ' οὐδεὶς κ. τῶν ποιουμένων Th.3.77: generally, of things, *natural order*, γίνεται τῶν τεταρταίων ἡ κατάστασις ἐκ τούτου τοῦ κ. Hp. *Prog.*20. 2. *good order, good behaviour*, = κοσμιότης Phld.*Mus.* p.43 K.; *discipline*, D.18.216; οὐ κ., ἀλλ' ἀκοσμία S.*Fr.*846. 3. *form, fashion*, ἵππου κόσμον ἄεισον δουρατέου Od.8.492; κ. ἐπέων ἀπατηλός Parm.8.52; ἐξηγεομένων.. τὸν κ. αὐτοῦ the *fashion* of it, Hdt.3. 22; κ. τόνδε.. ὁ καταστησάμενος who established this *order* or *form*, Id.1.99. 4. of states, *order, government*, μεταστῆσαι τὸν κ. Th. 4.76, cf. 8.48,67; μένειν ἐν τῷ ὀλιγαρχικῷ κ. 8.72, etc.; esp. of the Spartan *constitution*, Hdt.1.65, Clearch.3: pl., πόλεων κόσμοι Pl.*Prt.* 322c. II. *ornament, decoration*, esp. of women, Il.14.187, Hes.*Op.* 76, Hdt.5.92.η'; γυναικεῖος κ. Pl.*R.*373c, etc.; of a horse, Il.4.145; of men, Hdt.3.123, A.*Th.*397, etc.; γλαυκόχροα κόσμον ἐλαίας, of an olive-wreath, Pi.*O.*3.13, cf. 8.83, *P.*2.10, etc.; κ. κυνῶν X.*Cyn.*6.1; κ. καὶ ἔπιπλα Lys.12.19; κ. ἀργυροῦς a *service* of plate, Ath.6.231b; ἱερὸς κ. *OGI*90.40 (Rosetta, ii B.C.): pl., *ornaments*, A.*Ag.*1271; οἱ περὶ τὸ σῶμα κ. Isoc.2.32: metaph., of ornaments of speech, such as *epithets*, Id.9.9 (pl.), Arist.*Rh.*1408^{a}14, *Po.*1457^{b}2, 1458^{a}33; ἀδυμελῆ κ. κελαδεῖν to sing sweet songs of *praise*, Pi.*O.*11(10).13 (s.v.l.). 2. metaph., *honour, credit*, Id.*N.*2.8, *I.*6(5).69; κόσμον φέρει τινί it does one *credit*, Hdt.8.60,142; γύναι, γυναιξὶ κόσμον ἡ σιγὴ φέρει S.*Aj.*293; κ. τοῦτ' ἐστὶν ἐμοί Ar.*Nu.*914; οἷς κόσμος [ἐστὶ] καλῶς τοῦτο δρᾶν Th.1. 5; ἐν κόσμῳ καὶ τιμῇ εἶναί τινι D.60.36; of persons, σὺ ἔμοιγε μέγιστος κ. ἔσει X.*Cyr.*6.4.3; ἡ μεγαλοψυχία οἷον κ. τις τῶν ἀρετῶν Arist.*EN* 1124^{a}1. III. *ruler, regulator*, title of chief magistrate in Crete, *SIG*712.57, etc.; collectively, *body of* κόσμοι, ib.524.1; τοῦ κ. τοῖς πλίασι ib.527.74: also freq. in pl., ib.528.1, al., Arist.*Pol.*1272^{a}6, Str.10.4.18,22; cf. κόρμος. IV. Philos., *world-order, universe*, first in Pythag., acc. to *Placit.*2.1.1, D.L.8.48 (cf. [Philol.]21), or Parm., acc. to Thphr.ap.D.L. l.c.; κόσμον τόνδε οὔτε τις θεῶν οὔτε ἀνθρώπων ἐποίησεν, ἀλλ' ἦν ἀεὶ καὶ ἔστιν καὶ ἔσται πῦρ Heraclit.30; ὁ καλούμενος ὑπὸ τῶν σοφιστῶν κ. X.*Mem.*1.1.11: freq. in Pl., *Grg.*508a, *Ti.*27a, al.; ἡ τοῦ ὅλου σύστασίς ἐστι κ. καὶ οὐρανός Arist.*Cael.*280^{a}21, cf. Epicur.*Ep.* 2 p.37 U., Chrysipp.*Stoic.*2.168, etc.; ὁ κ. ζῷον ἔμψυχον καὶ λογικόν Posidon.ap.D.L.7.139, cf. Pl.*Ti.*30b: sts. of the *firmament*, γῆς ἁπάσης τῆς ὑπὸ τῷ κόσμῳ κειμένης Isoc.4.179; ὁ περὶ τὴν γῆν ὅλος κ. Arist. *Mete.*339^{a}20; μετελθεῖν εἰς τὸν ἀέναον κ., of death, *OGI*56.48 (Canopus, iii B.C.); but also, of *earth*, as opp. heaven, ὁ ἐπιχθόνιος κ. Herm.ap. Stob.1.49.44; or as opp. the underworld, ὁ ἄνω κ. Iamb.*VP*27.123; of any *region* of the universe, ὁ μετάρσιος κ. Herm.ap.Stob.1.49.44; of the sphere whose centre is the earth's centre and radius the straight line joining earth and sun, Archim.*Aren.*4; of the sphere containing the fixed stars, Pl.*Epin.*987b: in pl., *worlds*, coexistent or successive, Anaximand. et alii ap.*Placit.*2.1.3, cf. Epicur. l.c.; also, of stars, Νὺξ μεγάλων κ. κτεάτειρα A.*Ag.*356 (anap.), cf. Heraclid. et Pythagorei ap.*Placit.*2.13.15 (= Orph.*Fr.*22); οἱ ἑπτὰ κ. the Seven *planets*, *Corp.Herm.*11.7. 2. metaph., *microcosm*, ἄνθρωπος μικρὸς κ. Democr. 34; ἄνθρωπος βραχὺς κ. Ph.2.155; of living beings in general, τὸ ζῷον οἷον μικρόν τινα κ. εἶναί φασιν ἄνδρες παλαιοί Gal.*UP*3.10. 3. in later Gr., = οἰκουμένη, *the known* or *inhabited world*, *OGI*458.40 (9 B.C.), *Ep.Rom.*1.8, etc.; ὁ τοῦ παντὸς κ. κύριος, of Nero, *SIG*814.31, cf. *IGRom.*4.982 (Samos); ἐὰν τὸν κ. ὅλον κερδήσῃ *Ev.Matt.*16.26. 4. *men in general*, φανέρωσον σεαυτὸν τῷ κ. *Ev.Jo.*7.4, cf. 12.19; esp. of the *world* as estranged from God by sin, ib.16.20, 17.9, al., 1*Ep.Cor.* 1.21, etc. 5. οὗτος ὁ κ. this present *world*, i.e. *earth*, opp. heaven, *Ev.Jo.*13.1; regarded as the kingdom of evil, ὁ ἄρχων τοῦ κ. τούτου ib.12.31. V. Pythag. name for *six*, *Theol.Ar.*37; for *ten*, ib.59.

κοσμο-σάνδᾰλον, τό, Dor. = ὑάκινθος, *larkspur, Delphinium Ajacis*, Cratin.98, Pherecr.131.4, Paus.2.35.5. **–τρόφος**, ον, *feeding the world*, of Egypt, Man.1.2; Ῥώμη *IG*14.1108c19.

κοσμουργ-έω, *create the world*, Procl.*in Ti.*1.334 D. **–ός**, ὁ, *creator of the world*, Iamb.*in Nic.*p.10 P., Dam.*Pr.*270.

κοσμο-φθόρος, ον, *destroying the world*, *AP*11.270. **–φλεγής**, ές, *setting the world on fire*, δαλός Eleg.ap.Jo.Sic.in Rh.6.57 W. **–φόρος**, ὁ, *one who carries ornaments in procession*, *Jahresh.*18 *Beibl.*287 (Ephesus), *Cat.Cod.Astr.*8(4).136. II. Archit., *ornamental frieze*, *Rev.Phil.*44.251 (Didyma, ii B.C.).

κοσμώ, οῦς, ἡ, *priestess of Pallas*, Lycurg.*Fr.*48, Ister 16.

κοσμωτός, ή, όν, *made into a world*, Aristo Stoicus ap.Simp.*in Cat.* 188.35.

κόσος, η, ον, Ion. for πόσος.

κόσσᾰβος, ὁ, Ion. and older Att. for κότταβος.

κόσσαι, αἱ, gloss on αὐλοί (*cannons* of a horse), Sch.Opp.*C.*1. 189.

κόσσος, ὁ, *box on the ear, cuff*, Suid.:—hence **Κοσσοτράπεζος**, Com. name for a parasite, Alciphr.3.69, Hsch. s.v. παράσιτος.

κοσσύμβη, ἡ, v. κοσύμβη.

κοσσῠφ-ίζω, *sing like a blackbird*, Hero *Spir.*2.35. **–ος**, Att. **κόττῠφος**, ὁ (also **κόσσυκος**, *Gloss.*), *blackbird, Turdus merula*, ὁ μὲν ἕτερος μέλας, .. ὁ δ' ἕτερος ἔκλευκος Arist.*HA*617^{a}11; ἑξῆς κ. ἦλθε μόνος γεύσασθαι ἕτοιμος Matro *Conv.*87, cf. Theoc.*Ep.*4.10, *AP*12.142 (Rhian.), 9.76 (Antip.), 343 (Arch.); v. κόψιχος. II. a sea-fish, Diocl.*Fr.*135, Gal.6.718; μελάγχρως Numen.ap.Ath.7.305c; ὁ θαλάττιος Ael.*NA*1.14 sq. III. name of a peculiar breed of poultry at Tanagra, Paus.9.22.4.

κοσταί or **κόσται**, ῶν, αἱ, = ἀκοστή, *barley*, Hsch. II. κ., οἱ, kind of *fish*, Diph.Siph.ap.Ath.8.357a.

κοστάριον, τό, prob. = κόστος, Str.16.4.26 (pl.).

κοστίας· κοιλίας, κόμορος, Hsch.

κόστος, ὁ, root used as *spice*, *Saussurea Lappa*, Thphr.*HP*9.7.3, Dsc.1.16, D.S.2.49, *Peripl.M.Rubr.*39, al., *OGI*214.60 (Didyma, iii B.C.):—also **κόστον**, τό, Thphr.*Od.*32 (but κόστα, τά, dub. sens., of wooden parts of a cart, *Edict.Diocl.*15.19). II. = ἑλένιον, *Gp.*11.27.2.

κοσυβάτας, ὁ, *sacrificer*, *Supp.Epigr.*1.414.10 (Gortyn, v/iv B.C.); cf. κόσβατοι (sic, post κοστίας)· οἱ ἐπὶ θυσιῶν τεταγμένοι, Hsch.

κοσύμβ-η, ἡ, = Att. κρωβύλος, Poll.2.30 (v.l. κορσύμβην, κοσσάμην). 2. = ἐγκόμβωμα, *shepherd's coat*, D.Chr.72.1, *EM*311.5, cf. 349.45:—written **κοσσύμβη** or **κόσσυμβος**, Hsch. **–ος**, ὁ, *fringe*, v.l. for sq., Lxx *Ex.*28.35. II. *hair-net*, ib.*Is.*3.18. **–ωτός**, ή, όν, *tasselled, fringed*, τοὺς κ. τῶν χιτώνων ib.*Ex.* l.c.

κοσώλυφος· βόθυνος, ὄχθος, ἀνάστημα γῆς, ἢ σπέρμα, Hsch.

κοταίνω, = κοτέω, A.*Th.*485 (lyr.):—also **κοτάω**, *Et.Gud.* s.v. ἐνεκότουν.

κότε, κοτέ, Ion. for πότε, ποτέ.

κοτεινός, ή, όν, = κοτήεις, cj. for σκοτεινόν in Pi.*N.*7.61 Boeckh.

κότερον, κότερα, Ion. for πότερον, πότερα.

κοτ-έω, (κότος) Ep. and Lyr. Verb, used in the forms cited below, without distinction of voice, *bear* one *a grudge, be angry at* him, c. dat. pers., κοτεσσάμενος Τρώεσσιν Il.5.177, cf. 18.367; Τυδέος υἷι κοτέσσατο Φοῖβος 23.383; τῷ δ' ἄρ' Ἀχαιοὶ ἐκπάγλως κοτέοντο 2.223; τοῖσίν τε κοτέσσεται (Ep. for κοτέσηται) 5.747, 8.391, Od.1.101; λέοντε δύω ἀμφὶ κταμένης ἐλάφοιο ἀλλήλοις κοτέοντες Hes.*Sc.*403: prov., κεραμεὺς κεραμεῖ κοτέει καὶ τέκτονι τέκτων Id.*Op.*25: c. dat. rei, βασιλῆος ἀτασθαλίᾳ κοτέων Pi.*Supp.*13a31: c. gen. rei, ἀπάτης κοτέων *angry at* the trick, Il.4.168; κοτεσσαμένη τό γε θυμῷ, οὕνεκα... 14.191: abs., οὐδ' ὄθομαι κοτέοντος 1.181, cf. 23.391; κεκοτηότι θυμῷ (Ep. pf. part.) with *angry* heart, 21.456, Od.9.501, 19.71: aor. κοτέσασα *h.Cer.*254; Διωνύσῳ κοτέσασα Euph.14. **–ήεις**, εσσα, εν, *wrathful, jealous*, θεός Il.5.191, cf. A.D.*Adv.*189.12.

κοτίκας, ὁ, = ἀλέκτωρ, Hsch. **κοτίλλιν**· ἀνδρὸς αἰδοῖον, Id.:—also **κοτίλον**, Id. s.v. κόθημα.

κοτῖνάς, άδος, ἡ, *grafted upon a wild olive*, ἐλαία Poll.6.45. II. *fruit of the wild olive-tree*, Hp.*Morb.*3.16.

κοτῖνηφόρος, ον, *producing wild olive-trees*, Mosch.*Fr.*3.2. II. *winning a crown of wild olive*, Ζηνὸς κ. ἆθλον *Inscr.Magn.*181.

κότῖνος, ὁ (also ἡ Theoc.5.32), *wild olive-tree*, Ar.*Av.*621 (anap.), *Pl.*943; τοὺς νικῶντας στεφανώσας κοτίνου στεφάνῳ (sc. at Olympia) ib.586, cf. *AP*9.357, Thphr.*HP*4.13.2; τὰ ξύλα τὰ ἀπὸ τοῦ κ. *IG*11(2). 287 *A* 22 (Delos, iii B.C.): distd. from ἀγριελαία by Sch.Pl.*Phdr.*236b (in neut. **κότινον**, τό), but identified by Dsc.1.105. (In Ar.*Pl.*592 the v.l. κοτίνῳ στεφάνῳ may point to κοτινῷ dat. of Adj. κοτινοῦς.)

κοτῖνοτράγος [ᾰ], ον, *eating wild olive-berries*, Ar.*Av.*240.

κότιξις· μέλους τι εἶδος, Hsch. **κοτίς**, v. κοττίς.

κοτόεις, εσσα, εν, = κοτήεις, A.D.*Adv.*189.12, *EM*34.57.

κότορνος, ὁ, v.l. in Hdt.6.125, as Ion. form for κόθορνος.

κότος, ὁ, *grudge, rancour, ill-will*, more inveterate than χόλος, Il.1.82 (cf. 81); τοῖσι κ. αἰνὸν ἔθεσθε 8.449; τοῖσιν κότον αἰνὸν ἐνήσεις 16.449; κότον ἔνθετο θυμῷ Od.11.102; ὁπόταν τις ἀμείλιχον καρδίᾳ κότον ἐνελάσῃ Pi.*P.*8.9: freq. in A., δαιμόνων κότῳ, Λοξίου κ., *Ag.*635, 1211; βαρὺς.. Ζηνὸς ἱκεσίου κ. *Supp.*347; τοῦ θανόντος ἡ Δίκη πράσσει κότον exacts *vengeance* for him, *Fr.*266.5; never in S., once in E.(?), *Rh.*828 (lyr.).—Poet. and late Prose, D.H.9.51.

κοττᾰβ-εῖον or **–ειον**, τό, *metal basin for the game of cottabos*, Dicaearch.Hist.34, *IG*11(2).161 *C*60 (Delos, iii B.C.), Ath.15.667f. 2. *prize won at the game*, in pl., Pl.Com.46.7, Eub.16, Hegesand.32, Call. *Fr.*2 P. **–ία** (fort. –ίας)· οὐλόθριξ, Hsch. **–ίζω**, fut. –ιῶ Antiph. 55.4:—*play at the cottabos*, Ar.*Pax*343 (lyr.), Antiph. l.c. II. = ἐμέω, Poll.6.111, *EM*533.15. **–ικός**, ή, όν, *used in the cottabos*, ῥάβδος Hermipp.47.5. **–ινορ**, Lacon., = κοτταβεῖον, Hsch. **–ιον**, τό, = κοτταβεῖον 2, Arist.*Rh.*1373^{a}23, *Com.Adesp.*587. **–ίς**, ίδος, pecul. fem. of κοτταβικός: as Subst., = κοτταβεῖον 1, Hegesand.32; κεραμεᾶ κ. Harmod.1. **–ῐσις**, εως, ἡ, *playing at the cottabos*, Plu.2. 654c. **–ισμός**, ὁ, = foreg., prescribed as a cure for καχεξία, Philum. (?) ap.Orib.*Syn.*9.21.5, Paul.Aeg.3.47. **–ος**, ὁ, Ion. and older Att. **κόσσᾰβος** (A.*Fr.*179.4 (pl.), E.*Fr.*631 (pl.)), *the cottabos*, a Sicilian game (Anacr.53, Critias 2.1 D.), of throwing heel-taps into a metal basin, described by Ath.15.665d sqq., Sch.Ar.*Pax*342, 1243, Poll.6. 109, Suid. s.v. κοτταβίζειν: κ. is found in various senses, 1. *the game itself*, Anacr. l.c., Critias l.c., Pl.Com.69.4, etc. 2. *the prize*, = κοτταβεῖον 2, Eup.86, cf. Ath.15.667d. 3. *the wine thrown*, = λάταξ, E. l.c., Antiph.55.5. 4. *the basin*, = κοτταβεῖον 1, Cratin.116, Eup. l.c., Antiph.55.12. (κότταβος ἀσπίδων is prob. f.l. for κόναβος Anon.*Rh.*3.210 S.)

κοττάνα, ἡ, = παρθένος (Cret.), Hsch.

κοττάναθρον (fort. κοττόβαθρον), τό, *perch for fowls*, Hsch.

κοττάνη, ἡ, implement used in fishing, Ael.*NA*12.43.

κόττᾰνον, τό, *small* kind of *fig*, Ath.9.385a, prob. in Id.3.119b: Lat. *cottanum*, Plin.*HN*13.51.

κοττάρια· τὰ ἄκρα τῆς κέγχρου, Hsch. **κοττεῖν**· τύπτειν, δορατεῖν, Id. **κοττίδικα**· πλατάγη, κρόταλον, Id.

κοττίζω, (κόττος III) = κυβεύω, Sch.Luc.*Lex*.3.

κόττικοι· αἱ περικεφαλαῖαι, Hsch.

κοττίς, ίδος, ἡ, Dor. for κεφαλή, Poll.2.29, Phot. s. v. προκότταν:— in Hp. written **κοτίς**, *occiput*, *Morb*.2.20, cf. Erot.*Fr*.56, Gal.19.113.

κοττ-ισμός, = κυβεία, *Gloss*. **-ιστής**, *aleator*, ib.

κοττοβολεῖν· τὸ παρατηρεῖν τινα ὄρνιν, Hsch.

κόττος, ὁ, = ἀλεκτρυών, prob. in Ezek.*Exag*.261, cf. Hsch.; also, *horse*, Id. II. a river-fish, Arist.*HA*534^{a}1. III. = κύβος, *Cod.Just*.1.4.25 (529 A.D.).

κόττῠφος, ὁ, Att. for κόσσυφος.

κοτύλ-εα [ῠ], ἁ, = sq. 3, *SIG*1026.25 (Cos, iv/iii B.C.): Coan form of κοτύλα, = κοτύλη. **-η**, ἡ, *anything hollow* (πᾶν τὸ κοῖλον κοτύλην ἐκάλουν οἱ παλαιοί Apollod.ap.Ath.11.479a, cf. Sch.Il.22.494). 1. *small vessel*, *cup*, Il.22.494, Od.15.312, 17.12, Ar.*Fr*.350, cf. Ath.11.478d: prov., πολλὰ μεταξὺ πέλει κοτύλης καὶ χείλεος ἄκρου ib.e, Zen.5.71. b. metaph., = κοτύλων, D.H.19.5. 2. *cup* or *socket* of a joint, esp. of the hip-joint, κατ' ἰσχίον, ἔνθα τε μηρὸς ἰσχίῳ ἐνστρέφεται, κοτύλην δέ τέ μιν καλέουσι Il.5.306 sq., cf. Hp.*Loc. Hom*.6, Gal.18(2).519; also, *socket* of the arm, Hp.*Art*.7. 3. *liquid measure*, containing 6 κύαθοι or a ½ ξέστης, i.e. nearly *a ½ pint*, Hdt.6.57, Th.4.16, 7.87, Ar.*Pl*.436; κ. Ἀττική, Αἰγινητική, Hp.*Epid*.7.3, *Nat.Mul*.33. b. *dry measure*, ἀλφίτων.. τρεῖς χοίνικας κοτύλης δεούσας Ar.*Fr*.465; ἀλφίτων κ. μίαν Alex.221.17; prob. also a smaller measure, perh. = τρύβλιον, ὀξύβαφον, Hp.*Mul*.1.6. 4. *hollow of the hand*, Apollod. l. c., Poll.9.122, Eust.550.5; cf. ἐγκοτύλη. 5. = κοτυληδών I, Luc.*DMar*.4.3. 6. in pl., *cymbals*, χαλκόδετοι κ. A.*Fr*.57.6 (anap.). **-ηδονώδης**, ες, *of the nature of a* κοτυληδών, *warty*, ἐξοχή, ἔκφυσις, Gal.2.905. **-ηδών**, όνος, ἡ, *any cup-shaped hollow* or *cavity*: 1. in pl., *suckers on the arms* (πλεκτάναι) *of the poulp* or *octopus*, Od.5.433, in Ep. dat. πρὸς κοτυληδονόφιν, cf. Arist.*HA*524^{a}2, *PA*685^{b}3, Thphr.*HP*9.13.6, Ath.11.479b; also on the feet of the κάραβος, Arist.*HA*527^{a}25: sg., Luc.*Musc.Enc*.3. 2. in pl., *cotyledons*, foetal and uterine vascular connexions (in animals), Hp.*Aph*.5.45, Arist.*GA*745^{b}33, al.: wrongly expld. as κοιλότητες.. ἐν αἷς τὴν ἀνατροφὴν τοῦ ἐμβρύου γίνεσθαι Diocl.*Fr*.27, cf. Gal.2.905. 3. = κοτύλη 2, *socket of the hip-joint*, Ar.*V*.1495, Arist.*HA*493^{a}24, *Milet*.6.22 (iii B.C.). 4. *hollow of a cup*, Nic.*Al*.626. 5. plant, prob. *navelwort*, *Cotyledon Umbilicus*, Hp.*Steril*.230, Nic.*Th*.681, Dsc.4.91, Gal.12.41; another species, *C. sterilis*, Dsc.4.92. **-ήρῠτος**, ον, (ἀρύω) *that can be drawn in cups*, i.e. *flowing copiously*, *streaming*, αἷμα Il.23.34. 2. ὄξος κ. *a measure of* vinegar, Nic.*Th*.539. **-ιαῖος**, α, ον, *holding a* κοτύλη, Antig.Car. ap.Ath.10.420a, D.L.2.139; λήκυθοι Hippoloch.ap.Ath.3.129b:— also written **-ιεῖος**, *PCair.Zen*.89.4 (iii B.C.). **-ίδιον**, τό, Dim. of κοτύλη, Eust.1541.52. **-ίζω**, *sell by the* κοτύλη: hence, *sell by retail*, opp. ἀθρόα πιπράσκειν, Arist.*Oec*.1347^{b}8, cf. *PAmh*.92.6 (ii A.D.), Phryn.*PS*p.79 B.; μηδὲ ἐξ ἀμφορέων μηδὲ ἐκ πιθάκνης μηδ' ἐξ ψευδοπίθου κοτυλιζέτω μηδείς *BCH*50.214 (Thasos, v B.C.): metaph., μηδὲν κ., ἀλλὰ καταπάττειν χύδην Pherecr.168; κίρναντες.. τὴν πόλιν ἡμῶν κοτυλίζετε τοῖσι πένησιν Ar.*Fr*.683. **-ίς**, ίδος, ἡ, = κοτύλη 2, Hp.*Int*.18, cf. Gal.19.114. **-ίσκος**, ὁ, Dim. of κοτύλη, *little cup*, Ar.*Fr*.380, etc.:—also **-ίσκη**, ἡ, Pherecr.69; **-ίσκιον**, τό, Ar.*Ach*.459. II. a kind of *cake*, Heracleo ap.Ath.14.647b. III. *pit* used for sacrificing to Earth, Hsch. **-ισμός**, ὁ, *sale by retail* of oil, *Stud.Pal*.22.177.23 (ii A.D.). **-ιστής**, οῦ, ὁ, *one who plays the game* ἐγκοτύλη, Jul.*Mis*.360a. **-ιστί**, Adv., = κατὰ κοτύλην, *UPZ* 94.42 (ii B.C., spelt **-ειστί**). **-οειδής**, ές, *cup-shaped*, χώρη Hp. *Art*.79. **-ος**, ὁ, = κοτύλη, Hom.*Epigr*.14.3, Alc.139 (nisi potius Alc.Com.), Ar.*Fr*.71, Pl.Com.46.9, *IG*2².1541.14, cf. Ath.11.478b, 482b. **-ώδης**, ες, *like a* κοτύλη, ἀγγεῖον ib.480b. **-ων**, ωνος, ὁ, *nickname of a toper*, Plu.*Ant*.18.

κότυμβον, τό, = μακρὸν πλοῖον, *Peripl.M.Rubr*.44.

κότυνα· σκύβαλα, Hsch.

κοῦ, **κου**, Ion. for ποῦ, που. **κοῦα**· ἐνέχυρα, and **κουάσαι**· ἐνεχυριάσαι, Hsch.; cf. κοῖον, κῷα. **κούαγμα**· σκῆμα, Id. **κούαμα**· μέλαν (Lacon.), Id. (fort. κουάνια (= κυάνεα)· μέλανα).

κουβαρίς, ίδος, ἡ, = ὄνος III, Dsc.2.35 tit. **κουβηζός**· στηβεύς, Hsch. **κουδριγάριον** ἄλειμμα, = Lat. *quadrigarium*, *charioteer's ointment*, *Hippiatr*.130. **κουκᾶ**· πάππων, ἢ κυκεῶνα, Hsch.

κοῦκι, τό, *doum-palm*, *Hyphaena thebaica*, Lat. *cuci*, Plin.*HN*13.62; *fibre* thereof, *PBaden* 35.23 (i A.D.).

κούκινος, η, ον, *of the doum-palm*, φύλλα *Peripl.M.Rubr*.33. 2. *made of its fibre*, σόλια *POxy*.1742.7 (iv A.D.); κούκινα ὑποδεδεμένος *PMag.Par*.1.935; κ. πλέγματα prob. (for κόκκινα, v.l. κόκινα) in Str.17.2.5.

κουκιοφόρος, ον, *producing* κοῦκι, τὸ κ. δένδρον *doum-palm*, Thphr.*HP*4.2.7 (-όφορον codd.).

κοῦκκος, ὁ, = κόκκυξ I, Suid. s. h. v.

κούκκουμα, ἡ, = Lat. *cucuma*, *jar*, *POxy*.1160.23 (iii/iv A.D.):— hence Dim. **κουκκούμιον**, τό, Arr.*Epict*.3.22.71; **κουκούμιον** *POxy*.1290.3 (v A.D.):—also **κούκουμος** *Stud.Pal*.20.67.16 (ii/iii A.D.), *Gloss*.: pl. **κοκκόμανα** *PHamb*.10.36 (iii A.D.).

κουκούφας, ὁ, Egyptian name for ἔποψ, Horap.1.55: gen. κοκκούφατος *PMag.Berol*.2.18:—Dim. **κοκκοφάδιον** *PMag.Lond*.121.411.

κουλεόν, **κουλεός**, v. κολεόν, κολεός. **κουλιβός**· ἡ πίτυς, Hsch.

κουλῠβάτεια [βᾰ], ἡ, = κλύβατις, Nic.*Th*.589, 851.

κουμᾶσι· τὸ τῶν ὀρνίθων οἴκημα, Hsch. **κούνημα**· κόκων ἢ ὁ κύων, Id. **κούνικλος**, v. κύνικλος. **κούνουπες** (-οῦνες cod.), = κώνωπες, Id. **κουπῆϊον**, τό, = καμάρα ἡ ἐπὶ τῶν ἀμαξῶν γινομένη, Id.

κουρά, Ion. **-ρή**, ἡ, (κείρω) *cropping* of the hair, τῶν τριχῶν τὴν κ. κείρεσθαι Hdt.3.8; κουρᾶς δεῖσθαι Arist.*PA*658^{b}20; ἐν χρῷ κ. Diocl.*Fr*.141: freq. as a sign of mourning, κ. πενθίμῳ E.*Alc*.512, *Or*.458; κουραῖσι καὶ θρήνοισι Id.*Hel*.1054; κουραῖς διατετιλμένης φόβην S.*Fr*.659.7. 2. generally, *cropping*, *lopping*, δρυοτομικὴ καὶ κ. σύμπασα Pl.*Plt*.288d; of animals that feed on grass, Arist.*PA*693^{a}17. 3. *shearing* of sheep, Porph.*Abst*.3.26, *PThead*.8.6 (iv A.D.). II. *that which is cut off*: 1. *lock of hair*, A.*Ch*.226. 2. *wool shorn*, *fleece*, *PCair.Zen*.433.26 (pl., iii B.C.); κουρᾷ κοσμοῦντα θρέμματα Porph.*Abst*.3.19: pl., κουρὰς προβάτων καὶ γάλα βοῶν ib.18. 3. *cut-off end*, σφηνός Ph.*Bel*.67.12; δοκῶν *Inscr. Délos* 442 *A* 157 (ii B.C.); ἡ κάτω κ., of a rod, Hero *Dioptr*.5: in pl., *slips* of wood, Ph.*Bel*.57.22.

κουράλιον, τό, poet. for κοράλλιον (q.v.).

Κουράλιος, ὁ (sc. μήν), name of month at Kophoi and Pyrasos, *IG* 9(2).102, 133.

κουράς, άδος, ἡ, = ὀροφή, Hsch. s. v. ἐγκουράδες. 2. *painting on a ceiling*, Id.

κουράτωρ, ορος, ὁ, = Lat. *curator*, *IGRom*.4.243 (Troad), etc.:— hence **κουρατορεύω**, *serve as curator*, *IG*14.1062 (iii A.D.): aor. part. κουρατορεύσας *IGRom*.4.1169 (Attalia), 1638 (Philadelphia); κεκουρατορευκώς ib.1640 (ibid.): **κουρατορία**, ἡ, *office of curator*, *PGiss*.104.3 (iv A.D.), etc.

Κουραφροδίτη, ἡ, *virgin-Aphrodite*, Procl.*H*.5.1.

κούρβα, *scortum*, *Gloss*.

κουρβών, ῶνος, ὁ, *arm*, *PLond*.1821.288.

κουρ-εακός, ἡ, όν, *gossiping* (cf. sq.), κ. καὶ πάνδημος λαλιά Plb.3.20.5. **-εῖον**, τό, (κουρά) *barber's shop*, the lounging-place where news and scandal were picked up, καί τοι λόγος γ' ἦν.. πολὺς ἐπὶ τοῖσι κουρείοισι τῶν καθημένων Ar.*Pl*.338, cf. *Av*.1441; πόλλ' ἔμαθον ἐν τοῖσι κ. ἐγὼ ἀτόπως καθίζων κοὐδὲ γιγνώσκειν δοκῶν Eup.180, cf. Lys.24.20, D.25.52, *AP*6.307 (Phan.), *Sammelb*.6762.2 (iii B.C.); εἰς κ. 'to my barber's bill', Lys.32.20 (v.l.); ἐν κουρείοις ἢ μυροπωλίοις Phld.*Ir*. p.47 W. II. κούρειον, proparox. (Hdn.Gr.1.372), *victim offered for boys and feasted on by the* φράτερες *at the feast* κουρεῶτις, S.*Fr*.126, Is.6.22 (κούριον codd.), *IG*2².1237.28, *Inscr.Prien*.362.13 (iv B.C.). **-εος**, ὁ, epith. of Apollo, from foreg. II, *SIG*927 (Teos). **-εύομαι**, (κουρά) *take the tonsure*, i.e. enter a monastery, of a nun, Just.*Nov*.134.10.1; *have the hair cut*, of four-year-old children, Sch.Nic.*Al*.417. **-εύς**, έως, ὁ, (κείρω) *barber*, *hair-cutter*, Pl.*R*.373c, Philyll.14, *PMagd*.15.1 (iii B.C.), Luc.*Ind*.29; ὁ κ. τὰς μαχαιρίδας λαβὼν ὑπὸ τῆς ὑπήνης κατακερεῖ—τὴν εἰσφορὰν (παρὰ προσδοκίαν for τὸ γένειον) Eup.278; as a purveyor of gossip, Plu.2.177a, 509a. 2. *shearer*, κουρεῖ τῷ κείραντι τὰς αἶγας *PCair.Zen*.176.54 (iii B.C.). II. a bird, said to chirp with a sound *as of clipping*, Hsch. **-εύσιμος**, η, ον, *for cutting hair*, σίδηρος Sch.E.*Or*.966. **-ευτής**, οῦ, ὁ, *barber*, *Gloss*. **-ευτικός**, ή, όν, = κουρεύσιμος, Sch.E. l. c.; μαχαιρίδια Olymp.*Vit.Pl*.p.3 W. **-εύτρια**, ἡ, fem. of κουρεύς, κουρευτής, Plu.*Ant*.60. **-εύω**, only in Pass., v. κουρεύομαι. **-εών**, ῶνος, ὁ, name of month at Magnesia on Maeander, *SIG*807 (i A.D.):—also **Κουρηϊών**, *Inscr.Magn*.4.4, al. **-εῶτις** (sc. ἡμέρα, Hsch.; κ. ἑορτή Alciphr.3.46), ιδος, ἡ, the third day of the Ἀπατούρια, on which children were presented to the φράτερες, and boys competed in recitation, Pl.*Ti*.21b; ἡ κ. Ἀπατουρίων *IG*2².1237.28. (Perh. from κείρω, κουρά, because the child's hair is said to have been cut on that day, Hsch.)

κούρη, Ion. for κόρη. **κουρή**, Ion. for κουρά.

κουρ-ήϊος, η, ον, Ep. for κόρειος, *youthful*, ἄνθος *h.Cer*.108. **-ηϊών**, v. Κουρεών. **-ητες**, ων, οἱ, (κόρος B, κοῦρος A) *young men*, esp. *young warriors*, κούρητες Παναχαιῶν, Ἀχαιῶν, Il.19.193, 248. II. as pr. n., Κουρῆτες (Hdn.Gr.1.63, al.), Dor. **Κωρῆτες**, *divinities* coupled with Nymphs and Satyrs, Κ. θεοὶ φιλοπαίγμονες ὀρχηστῆρες Hes.*Fr*.198; worshipped in Crete, Κωρῆτας καὶ Νύμφας καὶ Κύρβαντας *GDI*5039.14 (Hierapytna); Κωρῆσι τοῖς πρὸ καρταιπόδων ib.iv p.1036 (Gortyn); Κ. Διὸς τροφεῖς λέγονται Str.10.3.19, cf. 11, E.*Ba*.120 (lyr.), Orph.*H*.38.1, *Fr*.151, etc.: prov., Κουρήτων στόμα, of prophecy, Zen.4.61. (Sg. only late, ὁ Κορόνους δηλοῖ νοῦν καὶ τὸν Κουρῆτα τούτου Dam.*Pr*.267.) 2. *armed dancers* who celebrated orgiastic rites, Str.10.3.7: hence used to translate Lat. *Salii*, D.H.2.70; Κουρήτων Βάκχος ἐκλήθην ὁσιωθείς E.*Fr*.472.14 (lyr.). 3. at Ephesus, *religious college* of six members, συνέδριον Κουρήτων *Ephes*.2 No.83c, cf. *SIG*353.1 (iv B.C.), Str.14.1.20. III. pr. n. of a people who fought with the Aetolians, Il.9.529, al. **-ητικός**, ή, όν, *of* or *concerning the* Κουρῆτες, τὰ Κ. treatises on the Κ., Str.10.3.7: hence, in Neo-Platonic theology, *ministrant*, ὁ πρῶτος πατὴρ καὶ ὁ τρίτος οὐ παράγει κ. τάξιν Dam.*Pr*.278; κ. θεότης Procl. *in Ti*.3.310 D.; κ. τάξις Id.*Theol.Plat*.5.35; κ. τριάς ibid. (here derived fr. Κούρη = Κόρη). II. ὁ Κ. (sc. πούς) *the Cretic*, Sch.Ar.*Nu*.651; *the third paeon* (◡◡–◡), Choerob. *in Heph*.p.218 C. **-ῆτις**, ιδος, fem. Adj., *of the* Κουρῆτες, i.e. of Pleuron, γῆ Epigr.ap.Str.10.3.2; χώρα Apollod.1.7.6. II. Pythag. name for *nine*, *Theol.Ar*.58. **-ητισμός**, ὁ, *armed dancing*, of the *rites of the Salii*, D.H.2.71.

κοῦρι, τό, liquid measure in Egypt, *Ostr*.1126, 1127 (vi/vii A.D.).

κουρί-ας, ου, ὁ, *one who wears his hair short*, ἐν χρῷ κ. Luc.*Fug*.27, *Vit.Auct*.20, D.L.6.31; cf. ἐγχρωκουρίας. **-άω**, of hair, *need clip-*

ping, πώγων εἰς ὑπερβολὴν κουριῶν Luc.*Gall.*10. II. of persons, ἐν χρῷ κ. *need* close *clipping*, Pherecr.30, Plu.*Alc.*23; ἄνθρωπος ἀεὶ -ιῶν Luc.*Lex.*10. 2. *wear rough, untrimmed hair*, Ael.*NA*7.48; κ. τὸ γένειον Alciphr.3.55, cf. Hp.*Ep.*17, Artem.1.19 (interpol.).

κουρ-ίδιος, α, ον, (κοῦρος (A), κούρη, cf. sq. III) *wedded*, Ion. and poet. Adj., used sts. of the husband, κουρίδιον ποθέουσα πόσιν Il.5.414; κουριδίῳ τεύξασα πόσει φόνον Od.11.430; κουριδίοιο φίλοιο οὐκέτι μέμνηται 15.22: more freq. of the woman, *lawful, wedded wife*, κουριδίης ἀλόχου Il.1.114; ἀλλά μ' ἔφασκες Ἀχιλλῆος θείοιο κ. ἄλοχον θήσειν (Briseis to Patroclus) 19.298; κ. ἄκοιτις, ἀκοίτης, A.R.3.243, 4.1072; κ. γυναῖκες, opp. παλλακαί, Hdt.1.135, 5.18, cf. 6.138, Aristox.*Fr. Hist.*72: in poet. epitaphs, μνῆμ' ἀλόχῳ.. θήκατο κουριδίῃ *IG*3.1376.10, cf. 7.2539.9 (Thebes); ἀνὴρ κ. in prose epitaphs, *CIG*3827*l* (Cotiaeum), 4176 (Amasia), cf. Parth.27.2, Jul.*Or.*3.110c: as Subst., κ., ἡ, *wedded wife*, Q.S.5.445. 2. of things, νωΐτερον λέχος αὐτῶν κουρίδιον our own *lawful marriage* bed, Il.15.40, cf. Ar.*Pax* 844; δῶμα κ. house *of my wedlock*, Od.19.580; κ. γάμοι Archil.18; κ. τέκνα *born in wedlock*, *CIG*3333 (Smyrna). 3. *nuptial, bridal*, κ. χιτῶνες *AP*9.602 (Even.); θάλαμοι A.R.3.1128. II. epith. of Apollo in Laconia, Hsch. **-ίζω** (A), (κοῦρος A) intr., *to be a youth*, σάκος.., ὃ κουρίζων φορέεσκε Od.22.185, cf. A.R.1.195; *to be a girl*, Id.3.666; παῖς ἔτι -ίζουσα Call.*Dian.*5, cf. Arat.32. 2. *cry like a babe*, Call.*Jov.*54. 3. of dolphins, κ. ἑὸν σθένος *attain* the strength of *youth*, Opp.*H.*1.664. II. trans., *bring up from boyhood* or *to manhood*, ἄνδρας Hes.*Th.*347. III. κουρίζεσθαι· ὑμεναιοῦσθαι, Hsch. **-ίζω** (B), (κείρω, κουρά) *clip, shear*, aor. 1 κούριξαν· ἀπεκειραν, Id.:—Pass., κυπάρισσος ἡ κουριζομένη which sprouts *when clipped*, Thphr.*HP*2.2.2. **-ικός**, ή, όν, (κουρά) *for cutting the hair*, μάχαιραι Plu.*Dio* 9: as Subst., κουρικός (sc. δίφρος), ὁ, *barber's* chair, *Sammelb.*4292; δίφρου τετραπόδου καὶ κουρικοῦ ξυλίνου *POxy.*646 (ii A.D.). II. (κοῦρος A) *like a youth*. Adv. **-κῶς** Apollon.*Lex.* s.v. κουρίξ. **-ιμος**, η, ον, also ος, ον Agatho 3, cf. II.3: (κουρά):—*of, for cutting hair*, σίδαρος E.*Or.*966 (nisi cum κάρα jungendum). II. Pass., *shorn off*, χαίτη A.*Ch.*180; θρίξ E.*El.*521, Agatho l.c. 2. *shorn*, κρᾶτα E.*Tr.*279 (lyr.); κ. σχῆμα ἀναλαμβάνειν *tonsure*, Plu.*Pel.*34. 3. as Subst., ἡ κούριμος *Tragic mask* for mourners, *with the hair cut close*, *AP*7.37 (Diosc.), cf. Poll.4.140. **-ίξ**, Adv., (κουρά) *by the hair*, ἐρυσάν τέ μιν εἴσω κουρίξ Od.22.188; κ. ἑλκομένη A.R.4.18. **-ιος**, ον, (κοῦρος A) *youthful*, ἄνθος, in an interpol. verse after Il.13.433, cf. Orph.*A.*1339; ἥβη Orac. ap.Paus.9.14.3. **-ίς**, ίδος, ἡ, (κουρά) in pl., μάχαιραι κουρίδες *shears*, Cratin.37. II. = κομμώτρια, title of plays by Antiphanes, Alexis, and Amphis, cf. Men.1024, Plb.15.25.32, *POxy.*1489.9 (iii A.D.): **κούρισσα**, *EM*528.4. III. κουρίς or κωρίς, Dor. for καρίς, Epich. 31, 89, Sophr.26.

κούρκουμον, τό, = κημός, Hsch. s.v. ἐν κημῷ.

κοῦρμι, τό, *kind of beer* made from barley, Dsc.2.88; cf. κόρμα.

κουρο-βόρος, ον, *devouring children*, A.*Ag.*1512 (lyr.). **-γονία**, ἡ, *begetting of boys*, κ. καὶ θηλυγονίη Hp.*Genit.*8. **-θάλεια** [θᾰ], ἡ, *nursing-mother*, epith. of δάφνη, διὰ τὸ κουροτρόφον τοῦ Ἀπόλλωνος Sch.Od.19.86.

κοῦρος (A), ὁ, Ep. and Ion. for κόρος (B) (q.v.).

κοῦρος (B), ὁ, (κείρω, κορσός) *loppings, twigs stripped from a tree*, μηδὲ ξύλα μηδὲ κοῦρον μηδὲ φρύγανα μηδὲ φυλλόβολα *IG*2².1362.6.

κουρο-σύνη [ῠ], Dor. **-σύνα**, ἡ, (κοῦρος A) *youth, youthful prime*, χαίρων κουροσύνᾳ Theoc.24.58, cf. *AP*6.281 (Leon.), 309 (Id.), 9.259 (Bianor). **-σῦνος**, ον, *youthful*, θρίξ ib.6.156 (Theodorid., with play on κούριμος, *shorn*); wrongly expld. as τὸ ὑπὲρ τῆς κουρᾶς θυόμενον, Suid. **-τερος**, α, ον, Comp. form of κοῦρος (A) (cf. βασιλεύς, -λεύτερος), *young*, opp. *elder*, Il.4.316, Od.21.310, Hes.*Op.*[447]: as fem., A.R.1.684. **-τοκέω**, *bear boy-children*, Hp.*Genit.*7. **-τόκος**, ον, *bearing boy-children*, E.*Supp.*957 (lyr.). **-τρόπος**, v. κουροτρόφος. **-τροφέω**, *rear as a child*, κ. τὸν Δία Str.10.3.19; παῖδας Ph.2.463: metaph., θυγατέρας Id.1.441; ἡ φύσις κ. ἅπαντα Phleg.*Fr. Hist.*44. 2. *breed men*, γῆ κουροτροφοῦσα Philostr.*VA*8.7. **-τρόφος**, ον, *rearing children*, rare in lit. sense, γυνὴ νεοτόκος καὶ κ. Aret.*CA*2.3: usu. metaph., ἀγαθὴ κ. good *nursing-mother*, of Ithaca, Od. 9.27, cf. Pi.*Fr.*109; κ. Ἑλλάς E.*Tr.*566 (lyr., s.v.l.); Ἀπόλλωνος κ., of Delos, Call.*Del.*2, 276: freq. as epith. of goddesses, as Hecate, Hes.*Th.*450; Ἄρτεμις D.S.5.73; Λοχία *Supp.Epigr.*3.400.9 (Delph., iii B.C.); of the Roman goddess Rumina, Plu.2.278d; esp. of Aphrodite, Hom.*Epigr.*12; called ἡ Κ. alone, *IG*1².840.9, Ar.*Th.*299, Pl. Com.174.7, Luc.*DMeretr.*5.1; αἱ πύλαι αἱ κατὰ Κουροτρόφον, at Delos, *IG*11(2).203*A* 46 (iii B.C.):—in form **Κουροτρόπος**, ὁ (sc. μήν), name of Acarnanian month, ib.5(1).29.11 (Sparta).

κουρούλλιος or **-ούλιος**, ον, = Lat. *curulis*, *IG*5(1).533.18 (Sparta), 4.588.13 (Argos), D.C.39.32, 54.2.

κουρσεύω, *seize, ravage*, τὴν Ἐπίδαυρον Anon.*in Rh.*204.34, cf. Babr.179 (paraphr.).

κούρσωρ, ορος, ὁ, = Lat. *cursor*, *Edict.Diocl.* in *IG*2².1120:—hence Adj. **κουρσώριος**, *Edict.Diocl.*9.14.

κουρύλος [ῠ], ὁ, = κορδύλος, Numen.ap.Ath.7.306c.

κουρώδης, ες, *like a boy*, μολπή Aus.*Ep.*8.15.

κουρῶν· πρέπων, Hsch.

κουσούλιον, τό, *cloak*, *Sammelb.*7033.36 (v A.D.).

κουστούμην-α, τά, *Crustumerian pears*, Aët.5.138. **-ᾶτον**, τό, *drink made from Crustumerian pears*, ibid.

κουστωδία, ἡ, = Lat. *custodia*, *Ev.Matt.*27.65.

κούστωρ, ὁ, = Lat. *custos*, ἁρμώρω(ν) κ. *Sammelb.*6961, al. (Nubia).

κουτάλη, ἡ, Dor. for σκυτάλη, *EM*555.18 (cod.Par.); sed v. κώταλις.

κούταρον· τῶν ὀπισθίων (ὀσπητίων cod.) τοῦ βοὸς ἡ σὰρξ ὑπὲρ τὰ ἄρθρα, Hsch. **κουτίδες**· συκαλλίδες, Id.:—also **κουτίδια**, τά, *nets for catching* συκ., Id.

κουφ-εία, ἡ, perh. *potsherd* (cf. κοῦφος I.6), *PTeb.*5.199 (pl., ii B.C.). **-ηγός**, ὁ, *one who conveys* κουφεῖαι, *PFlor.*335.4 (iii A.D.). **-ίζω**, Att. fut. -ιῶ S.*Aj.*1287: pf. κεκούφικα *OGI*90.12 (Rosetta, ii B.C.): I. *to be light*, κουφίζουσαν ἄρουραν Hes.*Op.*463, cf. E.*Hel.*1555; of a sufferer, *to be relieved*, κουφίζειν δοκῶ S.*Ph.*735, cf. Hp.*Aph.*2.27. II. trans., *lighten, make light*, τὸ κενὸν ἐμπεριλαμβανόμενον κ. τὰ σώματα Arist.*Cael.*309ᵃ6:—Pass., Id.*PA* 663ᵇ13: hence, 1. *lift up, raise*, S.*Ant.*43, *Tr.*1025 (lyr.); αἴρων κουφιῶ σ' ἐγώ Ar.*Av.*1762 (lyr.); ἀσπίδ' ἀμφὶ βραχίονι κουφίζων E.*Ph.*121 (lyr.); ἅλμα κουφιεῖν *make a light* leap, S.*Aj.* l.c.; κ. πήδημα E.*El.*861 (lyr.); δύστηνον αἰώρημα κουφίζω, = δύστηνος αἰωροῦμαι, Id.*Supp.*1047:—Pass., *to be lifted up, soar*, [τῷ πτερῷ] ᾧ ψυχὴ κουφίζεται Pl.*Phdr.*248c, cf. 249a; σώματα -όμενα ὑπὸ τοῦ κύματος Jul.*Or.*1.27c. 2. *lighten of* a load, ὄχλου πλήθους τε κ. χθόνα *lighten* earth *of* a multitude, E.*Hel.*40; κουφισθεὶς τοῦ βάρους Thphr.*HP*4.16.2: abs., *lighten* ships *of their cargo*, τῷ ταχυναυτοῦντι κουφίσαντες προσβάλλειν Th.6.34; κουφισθεισῶν τῶν νεῶν Plb.20.5.11, cf. 1.60.8. b. of persons, *relieve* from burdens, X.*Mem.*2.7.1, *Cyr.*6.3.24; τὸν δῆμον τῶν εἰσφορῶν D.S.13.64, cf. *IG*12(7).506.16 (Amorgos, iii B.C.); τόκων τοὺς χρεωφειλέτας Plu.*Caes.*37; *relieve* (contractors), Plb.6.17.5; τῆς ὑπερηφανίας Phld.*Vit.*p.16 J.; κ. τοὺς νοσοῦντας Plu.2.1106c:—Pass., *to be relieved*, ὅταν σῶμα κουφισθῇ νόσου *from*.., E.*Or.*43; τοῦ πάθους Arist.*Pr.*873ᵇ22; λέξασα κουφισθήσομαι ψυχήν E.*Med.*473: fut. Med. κουφιεῖσθαι in pass. sense, Aristid.2.145 J.: metaph., τῇ τῶνδε εὐκλείᾳ κουφίζεσθε *feel your burdens lightened* by.., Th.2.44; κουφίζονται οἱ λυπούμενοι Arist.*EN*1171ᵃ29, cf. *Pol.*1342ᵃ14; ἐλπίδι κ. ματαίᾳ Ael.*NA*11.33. 3. c. acc. rei, *lighten, assuage*, ἀλγηδόνας E.*Fr.*573; συμφορὰς λόγῳ κ. D.60.35; κ. ἔρωτα Theoc.23.9; τὸ πάθος Plu.*Alex.*52; τὰ ὀφλήματα Id.2.807d: abs., *give* or *procure relief*, κ. οὐδέν, ἀλλά.. Hp. *Epid.*1.7, cf. Arist.*GA*725ᵇ9:—Pass., νομίζοντες κεκουφίσθαι τὸν πόλεμον αὐτοῖς Plb.1.17.2. b. *cancel* a debt, *POxy.*126.8 (vi A.D.), etc.:—Med., *PMasp.*95.10 (vi A.D.). 4. ἑαυτοὺς κ. *cheapen* themselves, dub. in Epicur.*Nat.*112 G. 5. *subtract*, ἀπὸ τῶν μοιρῶν Heph.Astr.2.1. **-ικὸν τρόπον**· κωμητικὴν ὄρχησιν, Hsch. **-ισις**, εως, ἡ, *lightening, alleviation, relief*, Th.7.75; κούφισιν φέρειν J.*AJ*17.6.2, D.C.42.28. **-ισμα**, ατος, τό, = foreg., E.*Ph.*848 (pl.), Plu.2.114c. **-ισμός**, ὁ, = κούφισις, ἀκληρημάτων D.S.25.17; συμφορᾶς J.*AJ*4.8.23; πάθους Plu.2.79c; πένθους κ. *Epigr.Gr.*406.8 (Iconium): abs., Carneisc.*Herc.*1027.15; *remission* of taxation, *Cod.Just.*10.16.13 *Intr.*: Medic., *alleviation*, Erasistr.ap. Gal.5.139; κ. ποιέεσθαι, of remittent fevers, Aret.*CA*1.1 (pl.). II. *elision*, Eust.150.24 (pl.), al. **-ιστήρ**, ῆρος, ὁ, *ring-pad* round a trepan-opening, Heliod.(?) ap.Orib.46.19.11. **-ιστικός**, ή, όν, *lightening*, Arist.*Cael.*310ᵃ32; κ. τῶν ἐπαχθῶν *relieving from*.., Hierocl.p.54 A.: Medic., *alleviating*, Antyll.ap.Orib.6.21.27 (Sup.).

κουφο-λῐθος, ὁ, *talc* or *talc-powder*, *PHolm.*2.21, al., *PLeid.X.*6, Alex.Aphr.*in Mete.*161.6, 15, Aët.2.68. **-λογέω**, *talk lightly*, App.*Hisp.*18, Them.*Or.*11.152b. **-λογία**, ἡ, *light talk*, Th.4.28, App.*Hisp.*38, Plu.2.855b. **-λόγος**, ον, *lightly talking*, Poll.6.119; κουφολόγοι οἱ σοφιστικοὶ χρῆμα Philostr.*VA*7.16. **-νοος**, ον, contr. **-νους**, ουν, *light-minded, thoughtless*, εὐηθία A.*Pr.*385; ἔρωτες S.*Ant.*617 (lyr.); ὄρνιθες ib.342 (lyr.); τὸ κουφόνουν, = κουφόνοια, App.*Hisp.*9; of persons, Corn.*ND*25: freq. in Adam., 1.14, al.: heterocl. pl. κουφόνοες in Polem.*Phgn.*5. Adv. κουφόνως App.*BC*4.124. **-ξυλαία** or **-έα**, ἡ, = χαμαιάκτη, Orib.*Fr.*118. **-πους**, πουν, gen. ποδος, *light-footed*, Hsch. s.v. ψαυκρόποδα. **-πτερος**, ον, *light-winged*, αὖραι Orph.*H.*81.6.

κοῦφος, η, ον, *light, nimble*, Hom. only in neut. pl. as Adv., κοῦφα ποσὶ προβιβάς stepping *lightly* on, Il.13.158, cf. Hes.*Sc.*323; κοῦφα βιβῶν Pi.*O.*14.16; κ. ποσὶν ἄγ' ἐς κύκλον Ar.*Th.*954 (lyr.); also κούφοις ποσί Pi.*O.*13.114; κουφοτάταις πτερύγων ἀκμαῖς Ar.*Ra.*1353; πήδημα κ. ἐκ νεὼς ἀφήλατο A.*Pers.*305; κ. ἐξᾶραι πόδα S.*Ant.*224; κ. ἅλμα E.*El.*439 (lyr.); κ. αἴρειν βῆμα Id.*Tr.*343; οὐ τοῖς κούφοις ὁ δρόμος Lxx*Ec.*9.11: metaph., κουφότεραι.. ἀπειράτων φρένες *too buoyant*, Pi.*O.*8.61. 2. metaph., *easy, light*, τελεῖν.. κούφαν κτίσιν to make achievement *easy*, ib.13.83; κ. εἰ δοίης τέλος A.*Th.*260; κ. νύξ an *easier* night, of a sick person, Jul.*Mis.*342a (Comp.); περίπατος Sor.1.46; τὸ ὅσιον ἅπαν κ. ἔργον *OGI*383.120 (Nemrud Dagh, i B.C.); of government, *light*, κουφοτέραν βασιλείαν *less oppressive*, Isoc.9.51; ἡ εὔκλεια κουφοτέρα φέρειν X.*Cyr.*8.2.22; of an antagonist, *easy-going*, κουφότατος ἦν κρατήσας Id.*Ages.*11.12; δεσπότην ἀπράγμονα καὶ κ. ἐξαπατᾷ θεράπων Men.*Per.Fr.*1. 3. *unsubstantial, airy, vain*, τὸ νέον.. κούφας ἀφροσύνας φέρον S.*OC*1230 (lyr.); οὐδὲν ἄλλο πλὴν.. κούφην σκιάν Id.*Aj.*126; ἐλπίδος τι εἶχον κούφης Th.2.51; κ. καὶ πτηνοὶ λόγοι Pl.*Lg.*717c; κ. πρᾶγμα *a trifle*, ib.935a; κ. γράμματα a *small* letter, E.*IT*594; of persons, = κουφόνους, Hdn.5.7.1; τὸ κοῦφον τοῦ νοῦ *levity*, Paus.5.21.14, cf. Hdn.7.8.6. 4. *light* in point of weight, opp. βαρύς, Pl.*Phlb.*14d, *R.*438c (Comp.), etc.; κούφα σοι χθὼν ἐπάνωθε πέσοι may earth lie *lightly* on thee, E.*Alc.*462 (lyr.), cf. *Hel.*853; κούφη σοι κόνις ἤδε πέλοι *IG*14.1942.4; κούφη σεῖο γαῖ' ὀστέα κεύθοι ib.329 (Himera); κ. πνεύματα *light* airs, S.*Aj.*558; ὀστᾶ τε καὶ κ. κόνις Men.538.3; τὸ κουφότατον.. τῶν κακῶν.. πενία Id.*Kith.Fr.*2. b. Medic. in various uses, σικύαι κοῦφαι *dry* cuppings, Philum.ap.Orib.45.29.17, cf. Sor.2.11, etc.; also κούφου μένοντος τοῦ ἰοῦ *on the surface*, Philum.*Ven.*7.3; μὴν κ. the eighth month of pregnancy, Sor.1.56; of food, *easy to* *digest, light*, Arist.*EN*1141b18, etc. c. of troops, *light-armed*, οἱ κ. τῶν στρατιωτῶν *Hell.Oxy*.6.4; ὡπλισμένοι κουφοτέροις ὅπλοις X.*Mem*.3.5.27; κούφη στρατιά Plu.*Fab*.11; τὰ κ. τῆς δυνάμεως Plb.10.25.2. d. of ships, *lightly-laden*, Th.6.37, 8.27. 5. *light, slight*, ἁμαρτήματα Pl.*Lg*.863c; κουφότερα γυμνάσια, opp. ἀναγκαῖα, Arist.*Pol*.1338b40; κ. ἐργασίαι ib.1321a25. 6. *empty*, κεράμια *Gp*.7.24.2, cf. *PLond*.5.1656.6 (iv A. D.), *PFlor*.314.8 (v A. D.): hence as Subst., κοῦφον (sc. κεράμιον), τό, *jar*, in pl., *POxy*.1631.16 (iii A. D.), *PFay*.133.6 (iv A. D.), *PStrassb*.1.10 (vi A. D.). 7. Act., *relieving, assisting*, χερὶ κούφᾳ Pi.*P*.9.11: prob. to be taken in this sense in Theoc. 11.3. II. Adv. -φως *lightly, nimbly*, κ. ὀροῦσαι A.*Eu*.112; κ. ἐσκευασμένοι, of soldiers, Th.4.33; ὡπλισμένοι X.*Mem*.3.5.26, etc.; κ. ἔχειν to be *relieved*, Arist.*Pr*.873a16. 2. metaph., *lightly, with light heart*, κουφότερον μετεφώνεε Od.8.201; κ. νοῆσαι Sapph.*Supp*.5.14; κ. φέρειν, opp. δεινῶς φ., E.*Med*.449, 1018; ὡς κουφότατα φέρειν Hdt.1.35; διάγουσα κούφως doing *well*, of a patient, Hp.*Epid*.1.26.δ'. 3. *lightly, with ease*, A.*Pr*.701.

κουφό-σκευος, ον, *light-armed*, Hsch. **-τέλεια**, ἡ, *remission of taxation*, *OGI*669.29: pl., ib.26 (Egypt, i A. D.), *POxy*.1434.3 (ii A. D.).

κουφότης, ητος, ἡ, *lightness*, Hp.*Aër*.8, Pl.*Ti*.65e, *Lg*.625d, Arist.*Cael*.300b24, etc.; *agility*, Jul.*Or*.2.53c: pl., Pl.*Lg*.897a, Arist.*PA* 648b7; κ. τροφῆς *lightness, digestibility*, Thphr.*CP*4.9.4. 2. metaph., *triviality, levity*, Phld.*Vit*.p.27 J., D.H.7.17. 3. *relief*, μόχθων E.*Fr*.119. 4. *lightness*, of style, Phld.*Rh*.1.178 S.

κουφοφορέομαι, Pass., *rise by one's own lightness*, S.E.*M*.9.71 (cj. for κουφοφοροῦσι).

κοφῖν-ηδόν, Adv., gloss on φορμηδόν, *EM*798.56. **-ιον**, τό, Dim. of κόφινος, *PPetr*.3 p.152 (iii B. C.). **-όομαι**, Pass., *have a basket put over* one: in Boeotia a way of exposing insolvent debtors, Nic.Dam.103 J. **-οποιός**, ὁ, *basket-maker*, *Gloss*. **-ος**, ὁ, *basket*, acc. to *AB*102 less Att. than ἄρριχος, found in Ar.*Av*.1310, *Fr*.349, Pl.Com.41, X.*Mem*.3.8.6, *IG*2².1672.65, Thphr.*Char*.4.11, *PPetr*.3 p.312 (iii B. C.); in later times used specially by Jews, Juv. 3.14, 6.542, cf. *Ev.Matt*.16.9. II. Boeotian measure, containing nine Attic choenices, i.e. about two gallons, κ. σίτου *IG*7.2712.65, cf. Stratt.13, Arist.*HA*629a13, Hsch. **-ώδης**, ες, *like a basket*, πλέγμα Sch.Ar.*Ach*.332.

κόφος, ὁ, prob. = κόφινος, *basket-load*, *Arch.Pap*.5.381 (i A. D.).

κοχλάδιον, τό, = κοχλίδιον, Sch.Opp.*H*.1.138.

κοχλάζω, = καχλάζω, Plu.2.590f (κολάζειν codd.), *Gloss*.: aor. subj. κοχλάσῃ, of boiling water, *PHolm*.3.1.

κοχλᾶκ-ιστ(ής?), dub. sens. in *Stud.Pal*.20.211.13 (v/vi A. D.). **-ώδης**, ες, *gravelly*, Thphr.*HP*9.9.6.

κόχλαξ, ακος, ὁ, = κάχληξ, Lxx 1 *Ki*.14.14, Dsc.2.70 (pl.), Apollod.*Poliorc*.139.12. 2. = λίθος μυλίτης, Gal.19.118.

κόχλασμα, ατος, τό, *plashing of water*, Hsch. s.vv. ἀπόβρασμα, πομφόλυξ.

κοχλι-άζων, οντος, ὁ, in a machine, a kind of κοχλίας, Orib.49.20.6 (v.l. -άζων). **-άριον**, τό, *spoon*: as a measure, *spoonful*, Dsc.2.42, Philagr.ap.Orib.5.19.1, Gal.6.271, *Gp*.7.13.1: later Gr. for Att. λιστρίον, acc. to Phryn.293. **-ας**, ου, ὁ, (κόχλος) *snail with a spiral shell*, Batr.165, Achae.42, Philyll.21, etc.; ἀπιστότερος εἶ τῶν κοχλιῶν, for they shrink into their shells on the least alarm, Anaxil.34, cf. Arist.*HA*523b11, 527b35; ὥσπερ κ. σεμνῶς ἐπηρκὼς τὰς ὀφρῦς Amphis 13.3; βολβός, κτείς (codd. τις), κοχλίας Theoc.14.17; κοχλιῶν ἀγγεῖα *PSI*6.553.11 (iii B. C.). II. *anything twisted spirally*, 1. *automaton in form of snail*, Democh.4 J. 2. *reel, spool, roller*, Bito 47.4, *Gp*.8.29. 3. *screw*, Bito 58.10; esp. for raising water, *screw of Archimedes*, Moschio ap.Ath.5.208f, Str.17.1.30, 52, D.S.1.34, 5.37, *PLond*.3.1177.73 (ii A. D.). 4. *spiral stair*, διὰ κοχλίου τὴν ἀνάβασιν ἔχει Str.17.1.10, Procop.*Pers*.1.24. 5. part of surgical machine, Orib.49.20.6.

κοχλ-ίδιον, τό, Dim. of κόχλος 2, *BGU*1118.15 (i B. C.), Epict.*Ench*.7, *EM*534.22. **-ιοειδής**, ές, *spiral*, Hsch. s. v. πολύδονος; κ. γραμμή *conchoid*, Simp. *in Ph*.60.14, *in Cat*.192.20. Adv. -δῶς *by means of a screw*, Ph.Byz.*Mir*.1.4. **-ιοκογχύλιον**, inferior kind of murex, Ps.-Democr.Alch.p.42 B.

κοχλιός, ὁ, = κοχλίας, *Gloss*.; *screw* of διόπτρα, Paul.Aeg.6.73, Aët.16.89.

κοχλίς, ίδος, ἡ, Dim. of κόχλος, in pl., Luc.*Cat*.16, Man.5.24. II. precious stone found in Arabia, Plin.*HN*37.194.

κοχλι-ῶρυξ, υχος, ὁ, = sq., *Gloss*. **-ώρῠχον**, τό, = κοχλιάριον, Poll.6.87, 10.89.

κοχλοειδής, ές, = κοχλιοειδής, γραμμή *conchoid*, Papp.244, etc.

κόχλος, ὁ, *shell-fish with a spiral shell*, used for dyeing purple, Lat. *murex*, Arist.*HA*528a1, *AP*5.227 (Paul. Sil.); used as a trumpet, E.*IT*303, Theoc.22.75, Mosch.2.124: also fem., Naumach.ap.Stob.4.31.76, Paus.3.21.6; Κασπίῃ ἐν κ., of a large sea-shell, A.R.3.859. 2. *land snail*, Arist.*Mir*.846b13. 3. *kohl*, Eust.728.47.

κόχος, ὁ, *full stream*, Sch.Theoc.2.107.

κοχύ· πολύ, πλῆρες, Hsch.

κοχῠδέω, *stream forth copiously*, ποταμοὶ..'Αχιλλείοις μάζαις κοχυδοῦντες ἐπιβλὺξ *gushing* with cakes, Pherecr.130.4: Ion. impf. κοχύδεσκεν (v.l. κοχύεσκεν) Theoc.2.107.

κοχύζω, = foreg., cj. for κοκκύζει in Stratt.61 (Casaubon). (This and the foregoing words may be reduplicated forms from the root of χέω.)

κοχώνη, ἡ, *perineum*, Hp.*Epid*.5.7: in pl., Id.*Mul*.2.131, Eup.77, Ar.*Fr*.482, etc.; ἔαται ὄκως νεοσσοὶ τὰς κοχώνας θάλποντες Herod.7.48: dual, τὼ κοχώνα Ar.*Eq*.424, 484. (Variously expld. by Gramm. ap.Erot.*Fr*.17; = γλουτοί, acc. to Poll.2.183.) (Cf. Skt. *jaghánam* 'buttock', 'pudendum'.)

κόψα· ὑδρεία, Hsch. **κόψειον**, τό, = ἱππομάραθον, Sch.Nic.*Th*.596. **κόψενα**· παραστάτης, χαλκός, Hsch. **κοψία**· χύτρα, Id.

κόψῐχος, ὁ, = κόσσυφος I, Ar.*Av*.305, 806, 1081, Aristopho 10.5, Anaxil.22.21. II. = κόσσυφος II, Orib.*inc*.13.25.

Κόωνδε, v. Κῶς.

κρᾶ, shortd. jestingly for κράνος (as δῶ for δῶμα), *AP*6.85 (Pall.).

κραaίνω, v. κραίνω.

κρᾱάρα· κόσκινον ἢ ὄρυγμα, Hsch. (Elean for κρησέρα).

κράατος, κράατι, κράατα, v. κράς.

κραβάτιον, τό, Dim. of κράββατος (κράβατος), Arr.*Epict*.3.22.74.

κραβάτριος, ὁ, perh. = κοιτωνίτης, *IPE*2.297.

κραββᾰτοποιός, ὁ, *couch-maker*, *Gloss*.

κράββᾰτος, ὁ, also **κράβᾰτος**, *Sammelb*.4292.9, v. l. in *Ev.Marc*.2.4, **κράβακτος**, v. l. in *NT* (cod. Alex.), *PTeb*.406.19 (iii A. D.) (whence Dim. **κραβάκτιον**, τό, *PGrenf*.2.111.32 (v/vi A. D.), and Adj. **κραβακτήριος**, α, ον, *PMasp*.6 ii 46 (vi A. D.)):—also **κράβακτον**, τό, l. c. 97 (vi A. D.), **κράβαττος**, Arr.*Epict*.1.24.14, v. l. in *NT* (cod. W), *Gloss*., cf. *grabattus*, Virg.*Mor*.5:—*couch, mattress, pallet*, Rhinth.11, Crito Com.2; but condemned as un-Attic by Phryn.44; freq. in later Gr., ἐπὶ κλιναρίων καὶ κραββάτων *Act.Ap*.5.15, etc., cf. Arr.*Epict*. l. c., *PLond*.2.191.16 (ii A. D.).

κράβη, ἡ, = κράμβη, *PPetr*.3 p.328 (iii B. C.).

κράβος, ὁ, = λάρος, Hsch.

κράβυζος, ὁ, kind of *shell-fish*, Epich.42.

κραγγών, όνος, ἡ, a kind of καρίς, prob. *Squilla mantis*, Arist.*HA* 525b2: with v. l. **κράγγη**, ἡ, ib.21, 29. II. = κίσσα, Hsch.

κρᾱγέτης, ου, ὁ, (κράζω) *screamer, chatterer*, κολοιοί Pi.*N*.3.82.

κράγιον· σύστρεμμα (σύνστριμμα cod.) ἐν κεφαλῇ, Hsch.

κρᾰγός, οῦ, ὁ, *bawling*, Com. formation in the phrase κραγὸν κεκράξεται (cf. βάδον βαδίζεται) Ar.*Eq*.487, cf. Hsch.:—on the accent v. Hdn.Gr.2.20.

κρᾰδαίνω, (v. κραδάω) *swing*, ἀπάνευθε πόνοιο νόου φρενὶ πάντα κραδαίνει Xenoph.25; *wave, brandish*, ἔγχος E.*HF*1003; λόφους Ar.*Ach*.965; δόρυ *Anacreont*.27 *A* 9; *shake*, χθόνα δ' ἐκ πυθμένων.. πνεῦμα κραδαίνοι A.*Pr*.1047 (anap.):—Pass., αἰχμὴ..κραδαινομένη κατὰ γαίης *quivering* [after it fixes itself] in the ground, Il.13.504, cf. Plb.6.25.5, *AP*6.97 (Antiphil.); [ἀκόντιον] ὡς μάλιστα -όμενον χρὴ ἐξικέσθαι Arr.*Tact*.39.2, cf. 41.2; of a bell, *to be set in vibration*, Phlp. *in de An*.355.23, al.; σημεῖα -όμενα Procop.*Pers*.2.10. 2. *agitate*, τὸ σῶμα, of epilepsy, Praxag.(?) ap.Herod.Med. in *Rh.Mus*.58.76; of hiccough, Antyll.ap.Orib.8.6.24; κ. πόλιν, of an earthquake, D.H.16.6: metaph., *agitate*, τὴν Πελοπόννησον Plu.*Alc*.15; τὴν 'Ασίαν Id.*Ant*.37:—Pass., *to be agitated, tremble*, ἡ ὄψις (of fixed stars)..κραδαίνεται Arist.*Cael*.290a22, Thphr.*Vert*.8: aor. ἐκραδάνθην Plu.*Alex*.74, etc.

κράδᾰλος [κρᾰ], ὁ, (κράδη I) *fig-tree branch*, Hsch.

κρᾰδᾰλός, ή, όν, *quivering*, Eust.1165.20.

κρᾰδάμωμον, τό, metri gr. for καρδάμωμον, Androm.ap.Gal.14.41.

κράδ-ανσις [κρᾰ], εως, ἡ, *quaking*, of the earth, Epicur.*Ep*.2 p.48 U. **-ασμός**, ὁ, *vibration*, cj. for foreg. in Epicur. l. c., cf. Nicom.*Harm*.4, 10; *tremor, agitation*, Simp. *in Cael*.453.6; τῶν δοράτων Marcellin.*Puls*.492. **-άω**, = κραδαίνω, only in part., κραδάων δολιχόσκιον ἔγχος Il.7.213, Od.19.438; ὀξὺ δόρυ κραδάων Il.13.583, 20.423. II. of trees, *suffer from blight* (κράδη II), Thphr.*HP*4.14.4. (Cf. Skt. *kūrdati* 'leap', Lat. *cardo* 'that which turns, pivot'.)

κραδευταί, v. κρατευταί.

κρᾰδεύω, = κραδάω I, Hsch.

κράδη [ᾰ], ἡ, *quivering spray at the end of a branch*, esp. of fig-trees, ἐν κράδῃ ἀκροτάτῃ Hes.*Op*.681, cf. Thphr.*CP*5.1.3, Nic.*Th*.853; τέττιγες..ἐπὶ τῶν κραδῶν ᾄδουσιν Ar.*Av*.40: generally, *branch*, esp. *fig-branch*, Hp.*Superf*.33, Thphr.*HP*2.1.2; κ. ἐριναῖ E.*Fr*.679; κ. τῶν συκῶν *PSI*5.449.6 (pl., iii B. C.); κράδῃσι βάλλεσθαι, of the φαρμακός, Hippon.4, cf. 8; κράδης ὀπὸς *fig*-juice, Hp.*Ulc*.12. 2. *fig-tree*, Ar.*Pax*627, v. Sch. II. *diseased formation of small shoots in trees*, Thphr.*HP*1.8.5. III. *scenic contrivance* for exhibiting actors in Comedy hovering in the air, like the μηχανή in tragedy, Poll.4.128.

κρᾱδησίτης· φαρμακός, ὁ ταῖς κράδαις βαλλόμενος, Hsch.; cf. κράδη I. 1, κραδίας II.

κρᾱδηφορία, ἡ, *bearing of fig-tree branches at a festival*, Plu.2.671e.

κρᾰδία, ἡ, Dor. for κραδίη, also in Trag.; v. καρδία.

κρᾰδιαῖος, α, ον, *of* or *belonging to the heart*: metaph., κόσμον κ. κύκλον Procl.*H*.1.6. II. *made of fig-shoots*, λίκνον Orph.*Fr*.199 (codd. Procl.); sed leg. τὸ⟨ν⟩ κ. Διόνυσον.

κρᾰδίας, Ion. -ίης, ου, ὁ, (κράδη) *curdled with fig-juice*, τυρός Hsch. II. κ. νόμος air played on the flute while the φαρμακοί were whipped with fig-branches, Id.; ascribed to Mimnermus by Hippon.96.

κρᾰδίη, ἡ, Ion. and Ep. for καρδία.

κρᾰδοπώλης, ου, ὁ, *one who sells fig-branches*, i.e. ἀγροῖκος, Eust.1409.64.

κράδος [ᾰ], ὁ, *blight in fig-trees*, etc., which blackens the boughs, Thphr.*HP*4.14.4. II. = κράδη I, v. l. for κλάδοις in Dsc.1.128.

κρᾰδοφάγος [φᾰ], ον, *eating the young branches of the fig-tree*, and as Subst., = ἀγροῖκος, *Com.Adesp*.1049 (κραδα- Hsch.).

κράζω, not common in pres., Ar.*Eq*.287, Arist.*HA*609b24, *Po*.1458b31, Thphr.*Sign*.52, *POxy*.717 (i B. C.), etc.: fut. κεκράξομαι Eup.1, Ar.

*Eq.*285, 487, *Ra.*258, Men.*Sam.*204, later κράξω *AP*11.141 (Lucill.), *Ev.Luc.*19.40: aor. 1 ἔκραξα Thphr.*Sign.*53, Lxx *Jd.*1.14, *AP*11.211 (Lucill.); imper. κρᾶξον [ᾱ by nature] Hdn.Gr.2.14; ἐκέκραξα freq. in Lxx, *Nu.*11.2, al.: aor. 2 ἔκρᾰγον (ἀν–) Antipho 5.44, Ar.*Pl.*428, etc., ἐκέκραγον Lxx *Is.*6.4 (unless impf. of *κεκράγω): freq. in pf. with pres. sense, κέκρᾱγα (v. infr.) (late κέκρᾰγα *AP*5.86 (Rufin.)); imper. κέκραχθι Ar.*Ach.*335, *V.*198, Men.*Sam.*235; pl. κεκράγετε Ar.*V.*415: plpf. ἐκεκράγειν Id.*Eq.*674, X.*Cyr.*1.3.10:—post-Hom., *croak*, of the raven, S.*Fr.*208, Thphr. l. c.; of frogs, κεκραξόμεσθα Ar.*Ra.* l. c., cf. 265: generally, *scream, shriek, cry*, σὺ δ' αὖ κέκραγας A.*Pr.*743; παιδίον κεκραγός Men.*Sam.*11, 24; *bawl, shout*, κεκραγὼς καὶ βοῶν Ar.*Pl.* 722, cf. D.18.132; κεκραγέναι πρός τινα *to call to*.., Ar.*Ra.*982; κραγὸν κεκράξεται Id.*Eq.*487 (cf. κραγός): c. acc. cogn., μέλος κέκραγα A.*Fr.* 281.5; ποίου (sc. περὶ ποίου) κέκραγας ἀνδρὸς ὧδ' ὑπέρφρονα; S.*Aj.* 1236:—rare in early Prose, X. l. c., D. l. c., cf. *POxy.*717.1 (i B. C.), etc.; ἐκεκράγει ὅτι.. Plb.ap.Ath.6.274f; κεκράγασιν ὡς.. Phld.*Rh.*1. 108 S.: c. acc. et inf., ib.2.98 S. **2.** c. acc. rei, *call, clamour for*, ἐμβάδας Ar.*V.*103.

κραίνω, Od.19.567: fut. κρᾰνέω Emp.111.2; Att. contr. κρᾰνῶ A.*Ch.* 1075, E.*Supp.*375 [κρᾱνῶ in compd. ἐπικρᾱνεῖ A.*Ag.*1340 codd., nisi leg. -κράνῃ vel -κραίνει]: aor. ἔκρᾱνα ib.369; Ep. and Ion. ἔκρηνα, inf. κρῆναι, Od.5.170, Herod.7.69 (dub.):—Med., fut. inf. in pass. sense κρᾰνέεσθαι Il.9.626: aor. ἐπ-εκρήναντο Q.S.14.297:—Pass., fut. κρανθήσομαι A.*Pr.*911: aor. ἐκράνθην Pi.*P.*4.175, E.*Hec.*219: κέκρανται 3 sg. pf. Pass., A.*Supp.*943, also 3 pl., E.*Hipp.*1255 (sed leg. συμφορά).—Hom. (v. infr.) mostly uses the Ep. pres. κραιαίνω, impf. ἐκραίαινεν, aor. imper. κρήηνον, κρηήνατε, inf. κρηῆναι: 3 sg. pf. Pass. ἐπι-κεκράανται Od.4.616: plpf. ἐπι-κεκράαντο ib.132: aor. ἐκρᾱάνθην Theoc.25.196. (Orig. κραάινω (ἐκράαινεν has Ms. authority in Il.5.508, ἐπεκράαινε in 2.419, ἐπεκράανε in 3.302; cf. κράανον· τέλεσον Hsch., ἐπικραᾶναι· τῇ κεφαλῇ ἐπινεῦσαι, τελέσαι Id.), contr. κραίνω, κρῆναι, etc. and by distraction κραιαίνω, κρηῆναι, etc.: κρᾱαίνω from κρασ-η-yω (κάρα, κράατα) = κεφαλαιόω 'achieve'.):—poet. Verb, *accomplish, fulfil*, τόδε μοι κρήηνον ἐέλδωρ Il.1.41, 504, cf. Od.17.242; οἵ μευ φέρτεροί εἰσι νοῆσαί τε κρῆναί τε better than I both to conceive and *accomplish*, 5.170; κρῆνον νῦν καὶ ἐμοὶ.. ἔπος ὅττι κεν εἴπω 20.115; καί τε κραίνουσιν ἕκαστα, of the Thriae, *h.Merc.*559; ἐπεὶ μούνῳ σοι ἐγὼ κρανέω τάδε πάντα Emp. l. c.; μαντεύματα κ. *give true* oracles, E.*Ion* 464 (lyr.); δίκας θανατοῖσι κραίνων B.12.45; τοῦ δ' ἐκραίαινεν ἐφετμάς Il.5.508, cf. Pi.*O.*3.11; οἵ ῥ' ἔτυμα κραίνουσι those dreams *come true*, Od.19.567; freq. in A., esp. of Fate, as *Pr.*512, al., cf. S.*OC*914, *Tr.* 127 (lyr.), etc.:—Pass., with fut. Med., *to be accomplished, brought to pass*, οὐ γάρ μοι δοκέει μύθοιο τελευτὴ τῇδέ γ' ὁδῷ κρανέεσθαι Il. 9.626; πατρὸς δ' ἀρὰ.. τότ' ἤδη παντελῶς κρανθήσεται A.*Pr.*911, cf. 213; κέκρανται ψῆφος the vote *hath been cast*, Id.*Supp.*943; ψῆφος ἡ κρανθεῖσα E.*Hec.*219; λάχη τάδ' ἐφ' ἁμὶν ἐκράνθη A.*Eu.*347 (lyr.):—for the phrase ἐπὶ χείλεα κεκράαντο, v. ἐπικραίνω; of a person, ἐκράνθην *I was perfected* (Sch. ἐπετελέσθην), Pi.*Pae.*9.34. **2.** *ordain*, A.*Ag.*369 (lyr.), E.*El.*1248, *Supp.*139. **II.** = τιμᾶν, Hsch.; so perh. in *h.Merc.*427 κραίνων ἀθανάτους τε θεοὺς καὶ γαῖαν ἐρεμνήν, ὡς ἐγένοντο (less prob. *finishing [the tale of]* the gods and earth, how they were made). **III.** abs., *exercise sway, reign*, δώδεκα γὰρ κατὰ δῆμον.. ἀρχοὶ κραίνουσι Od.8.391: c. acc. cogn., κ. σκῆπτρα *sway* the staff of rule, S.*OC*449; θέμιστας Orph.*A.*1297. **2.** after Hom., c. gen., *reign over, govern*, στρατοῦ, τῆς χώρας, τῆσδε γῆς, χθονός, S. *Aj.*1050, *OC*296, 862, 926: in later Ep. c. dat., Orph.*A.*475: c. acc., κ. Διὸς οἴκους *IG*14.433 (Tauromenium); ἐπὶ σπλῆνα κ., of a vein, *dominate*, Aret.*CA*2.2, cf. *CD*1.2. **IV.** intr., *come to an end, result* in a thing, ποῖ δῆτα κρανεῖ; A.*Ch.*1075 (anap.); of disease, *culminate, be at its worst*, Aret.*SD*2.8, *CA*1.1. **2.** Medic., of bones, etc., *terminate*, ὅπῃ κραίνουσι Hp.*Art.*45, cf. Aret.*SD*1.7, 8; *extend*, ἀπὸ ἥπατος ἐς νεφρούς Id.*CA*2.6.

κραιπᾰλ-άω, *to be intoxicated*, Ar.*Pl.*298, Plb.15.33.2, Ph.1.260, Plu.*Dem.*7, Luc.*Bis Acc.*17, etc.; μειρακίων τινῶν -ώντων Epicur. *Fr.*114. **2.** *have a sick headache after a debauch*, κραιπαλῶν ἔτι ἐκ τῆς προτεραίας Pl.*Smp.*176d; ἐχθὲς ὑπέπινες, εἶτα νυνὶ κραιπαλᾷς Alex. 286; εἰ τοῦ μεθύσκεσθαι πρότερον τὸ κραιπαλᾶν παρεγίγνεθ' ἡμῖν Id. 255.1; παρέξω Λέσβιον, Χῖον.., ὥστε μηδένα κραιπαλᾶν Philyll.24. **3.** *carouse, revel*, D.C.77.17, Alciphr.1.34. **-η**, ἡ, *drinking-bout*, ἐκ κραιπάλης Ar.*Ach.*277, *V.*1255; τὰς κεφαλὰς ὑγιεῖς ἔχειν ἐκ κ. Alex. 9.8; κ. καὶ μέθη *Ev.Luc.*21.34; χθεσινὴ κ. Luc.*Laps.*1, cf. Procop. *Goth.*1.3. **2.** *intoxication*, Men.*Kol.*47, Alciphr.1.37, Them.*Or.* 2.36a. **3.** *drunken headache*, Hp.*Aër.*3, Arist.*Pr.*873ᵃ37, etc.

κραιπᾰλό-βοσκος δίψα thirst *which draws on drunkenness*, Sopat. 25. **-κωμος**, ον, *rambling in drunken revelry*, Ar.*Ra.*217.

κραιπᾰλώδης, ες, *given to drunkenness*, Plu.2.647e. **2.** Adv. -δῶς *in a drunken manner*, αὐτοσχεδιάζειν Phld.*Rh.*2.22 S.

κραιπνός, ή, όν, *swift, rushing*, Βορέης, θύελλαι, Od.5.385, 6.171; πομποῖσιν ἅμα κραιπνοῖσι φέρεσθαι Il.16.671, 681: in Hom. freq. ποσσὶ κραιπνοῖσι Il.23.749, etc.; κραιπνῷ ποδὶ A.*Pers.*95 (lyr.); πηδήμασιν κραιπνοῖσι S.*Ichn.*213; κ. βέλος Pi.*P.*4.90; κυλινδέσκοντο -ότεραι ἢ ἀνέμων στίχες, of the Symplegades, ib.209; σθένει κραιπνοὶ Id.*Fr.* 133: metaph., *hasty, rash*, κραιπνότερος νόος, of a youth, Il.23.590. Adv. -νῶς, ἀνόρουσε 10.162; προσεβήσετο 14.292; διέπτατο 15.83; θέομεν Od.8.247: neut. pl. as Adv., κραιπνὰ ποσὶ προβιβάς 17.27; κ. διωκέμεν ἠδὲ φέβεσθαι Il.5.223, etc.

κραιπνό-σῦτος, ον, *swift-rushing*, A.*Pr.*281 (anap.). **-φόρος**, ον, *swift-bearing*, αὖραι ib.132 (lyr.).

κραῖρα, ἡ, (κέρας, κεραία) *top, head, extremity*, Hsch. (Att. acc. to Eust.710.49). **2.** = ἀκροστόλιον, Hsch. **κραῖρος**, ὁ, = foreg., Id.

κράκτης, ὁ, later form for κεκράκτης, Adam.2.24, Tz.*H.*8.438.

κρακτικός, ή, όν, (κράζω) *noisy*, Luc.*Gall.*4, Sch.Ar.*V.*34, cj. in Tz. ad Hes.*Op.*744: Sup. -ώτατος Luc.*Symp.*12.

κράκτρια, ἡ, pecul. fem. of κράκτης, Hsch. s. v. λακέρυζα.

κρᾶμα, ατος, τό, (κεράννυμι) *mixture*, Ti.Locr.95e, Plu.2.1109e, etc.; κ. ψυχῆς καὶ σώματος Ph.1.372; esp. *mixed wine*, Lxx *Ca.*7.2, *OGI*383.148 (Nemrud Dagh, i B. C.), Plu.2.140f, Dsc.1.113 (misspelt κραμμα *PMag.Lond.*121.174); also of medicines, Hp.*Mul.*2.211, Archig.ap.Gal.13.265. **2.** = χρέμμα, Aristipp.ap.D.L.2.67. **3.** *alloy* of metals, Str.13.1.56. **κραμάσαι**, v. κρεμάννυμι.

κρᾱμάτ-ινος, η, ον, *made of an alloy*, σκεῦος *PLeid.X.*14 (κραμμ– Pap.). **-ιον**, τό, Dim. of κρᾶμα, *wine and water*, Dsc.*Eup.*1.197, Sor.1.63.

κρᾱματοποιέω, *mix*, τὸ ποτὸν τῷ οἴνῳ *Hippiatr.*34.

κράμβαλα· μνημεῖα, Hsch.

κραμβᾰλέος, α, ον, (κράμβος A) *dried, parched, roasted*, Ath.9.376c, 381c.

κραμβᾰλίζω, = καπυρίζω, κατασείω, Hsch.:—but **κραμβᾰλιαστύς**, ἡ, *loud laughter* (to be read for χαραμβαλιαστύς), Id. (post χρᾶν).

κραμβασπάρᾰγος, ὁ, = κραμβοσπάραγον, *Gloss.* **κραμβατέλος**· ξηρὸς καὶ καπυρός, Hsch.

κραμβ-είν, v. κραμβίον. **-η**, ἡ, *cabbage, Brassica cretica*, Batr. 163 (pl.), Hippon.37, Telecl.27 (pl.), *PHib.*1.121.30 (iii B. C.), etc.; of three kinds, Eudem.ap.Ath.9.369d, cf. Nic.*Fr.*85; = ῥάφανος (q. v.), Arist.*HA*551ᵃ16; κ. ἥμερος, ἀγρία, Dsc.2.120, 121. **2.** κ. θαλασσία, *sea-cole, Convolvulus Soldanella*, ib.122, Gal.12.43. **3.** μὰ τὴν κράμβην Anan.4, cf. Epich.25, or μὰ τὰς κράμβας Eup.74, Comic form of oath to avoid sacred names, Ath.9.370b. **-ήεις**, εσσα, εν, *like a cabbage*, Nic.*Al.*330. **-ίδιον**, τό, Dim. of κράμβη, Antiph. 6. **-ίον**, τό, *decoction of cabbage*, Hp.*Mul.*1.63, 2.121, Gal.19.114: Sicel for κώνειον, Erot., Hsch.:—written **κραμβειν**, *POxy.*1479.10 (i B. C.). **-ίς**, ίδος, ἡ, *cabbage-caterpillar*, Ael.*NA*9.39.

κράμβος (A), η, ον, = ξηρός, Hsch. **II.** of sound, (cf. καπυρός) *loud, ringing*, κ. γέλως Id.; κραμβότατον στόμα Ar.*Eq.*539.

κράμβος (B), ὁ, *blight in grapes, when they shrivel* before they are ripe, Thphr.*CP*5.10.1.

κραμβο-σπάρᾰγον [σπᾰ], τό, *sprouting broccoli*, *Gp.*12.1.2. **-φάγος** [φᾰ], ον, *Cabbage-eater*, name of a frog, v. l. in Batr.218.

κράμβωτον, = ἰκτῖνος, Hsch.

κράνα, v. κρήνη. **II.** = κεφαλή, Hsch.

κρᾰνᾰήπεδος, ον, *with hard rocky soil*, *h.Ap.*72.

κρᾰνάϊνος, = κρανέϊνος, *h.Merc.*460 codd. (ῑ metri gr.), Hp.*Fract.*30, X.*Eq.*12.12, Str.12.7.3, Dsc.*Eup.*1.120; ῥάβδοι *BGU*1253.4 (ii B. C.).

κραναοίκορον· μοῖρά τις τοῦ ἱερείου, Hsch.

κρᾰνᾰός, ή, όν, poet. word, *rocky, rugged*, in Hom. always of Ithaca (exc. in Il.3.445 where it is pr. n. of an island), Il.3.201, Od. 1.247, al.; of Delos, Pi.*I.*1.3; freq. of Athens, Id.*O.*7.82, etc.: hence as pr. n., Κραναὰ πόλις Athens, Ar.*Ach.*75; simply αἱ Κρανααί Id. *Av.*123; ἡ Κραναά, of the Acropolis, Id.*Lys.*481; Κραναοί *the people of Attica*, Hdt.8.44, Str.9.1.18; παῖδες Κραναοῦ (Cranaos being a mythic king of Athens) A.*Eu.*1011 (anap.) **2.** generally, *hard*, χέλυς Opp.*H.*5.396; of a fishing-rod, ῥάβδος κ. ib.4.364. **3.** *stinging*, κ. ἀκαλῆφαι Ar.*Fr.*560. **κρᾰνέα**, ἡ, v. κράνεια.

κρᾰν-εια [ᾰ], ἡ, (κράνον) *cornelian cherry, Cornus mas*, κ. τανύφλοιος Il.16.767; ἁψάμενον βρόχον αἰπὺν ἀφ' ὑψηλοῖο κ. Demetr.Troez. 1; καρπὸς κρανείης, as food for swine, Od.10.242; ἰσχυρότατον ἡ κ. Thphr.*HP*5.6.4; τόξον κρανείας *of cherry-wood*, E.*Fr.*785; ῥάβδος κρανείας Ael.*NA*1.23, 12.43; κρανείας τάλαντον *of cornel-wood*, *IG*11(2). 161 *A* 104 (Delos, iii B. C.); κράνεια alone, = *spear*, *AP*6.123 (Anyte): —also **κράνία**, Hp.*Mochl.*42 (gen. -ίης), Dsc.1.119, Gal.12.41, Arr. *An.*2.3.7; **κρᾰνέα**, *Gp.*10.87.4. **-εῖνος**, η, ον, *made of the wood of* κράνεια, τόξα Hdt.7.92; παλτὸν X.*HG*3.4.14, cf. *Cyr.*7.1.2; ξυστὰ Arr. *An.*1.15.5, etc.—Freq. written κρανάϊνος (q. v.). **-ειον**, τό, *fruit of* κράνεια, Amphis 38, Anaxandr.41.54 (prob.), Thphr.*HP*3.2.1: dat. pl. written κρανέοις ib.4.4.5:—later **κράνιον**, Gal.6.620, al. (pl.). **-εών**, ῶνος, ὁ, *grove of cornelian cherry-trees*, *Gloss.* **-ία**, ἡ, v. κράνεια.

κρᾰνίδιον, τό, Dim. of κράνος (A), *small helmet*, *IG*2².1421.123. **2.** [κρᾱν–] Dim. of κρανίον, Paul.Aeg.6.74.

κράνινος [ᾰ], η, ον, = κρανέϊνος, τόξα Paus.1.21.5.

κρανίξαι· ἐπὶ κεφαλὴν ἀπορρῖψαι, Hsch.; cf. κερανίξαι.

κρᾱνιόλειος, ον, *bald-crowned, bald-headed*, *Com.Adesp.*1050.

κρᾱνίον, τό, (κάρα) *upper part of the head, skull* (κεφαλῆς τὸ τριχωτὸν μέρος Arist.*HA*491ᵃ31, cf. Gal.2.739); of horses, ὅθι τε πρῶται τρίχες ἵππων κρανίῳ ἐμπεφύασι Il.8.84; of men, Pi.*I.*4(3).54, E.*Cyc.*683, Cratin.71, Pl.*Euthd.*299e, etc.: generally, *head*, Amphis 16. **II.** *headache*, *Hippiatr.*103 (v. l. κατακράνιον).

κράνιον [ᾰ], τό, = κράνειον (q. v.).

κράννα, Aeol. for κράνα, κρήνη (q. v.).

κρᾱνο-κολάπτης, ου, ὁ, *poisonous spider*, Philum.*Ven.*15.1, Sch. Nic.*Th.*764. **-κοπέω**, *cut heads off*, φυτά *PRyl.*152.17 (i A. D.).

κράνον [ᾰ], τό, = κράνεια, Thphr.*CP*3.1.4 and 10.2. **2.** = κράνειον, Philagr.ap.Orib.5.20.5, v. l. in Gal.6.620. (Cf. Lat. *cornum*.)

κρᾰνο-ποιέω, *make helmets*: metaph., of one who *talks big and warlike*, Ar.*Ra.*1018:—hence **-ποιΐα**, ἡ, Poll.7.155. **-ποιός**, ὁ, *helmet-maker*, Ar.*Pax* 1255, *SIG*1177 (= *Tab.Defix.*69), Poll.1.149, 7.155.

κράνος (A) [ᾰ], εος, τό, *helmet*, Hdt.1.171, 4.180, al., A.*Th.*385, E. *El.*470 (lyr.), Ar.*Ach.*584, 1103, X.*Cyr.*6.1.51, *IG*1².278.49, Plu.2.

789d, Jul.*Or.*2.53b. 2. metaph., τὸ δὲ τοῦδε κ. ὁ κοινὸς ἀήρ Aret. *SD*2.6. II. *ship's ram*, Tim.*Pers.*21. (The ă shows that it is akin to κρᾰναός (*hard*), rather than to κρᾶνίον.)

κράνος (B) [ᾰ], ου, ἡ, later form for κράνον, *Gp.*7.35.1. 2. *rod of cherry-wood*, *PTeb.*39.31 (ii B.C.); χιτῶνι καὶ κράνῳ καὶ πιλίῳ ib.230 (ii B.C.) (here perh. = κράνος A).

κρᾰνουργός, ὁ, *maker of helmets*; and **-ουργία**, ἡ, Poll.7.155.

κράν-τειρα, ἡ, fem. of sq. II, *APl.*4.220 (Antip.), Orph.*Fr.* 176. **-τήρ**, ῆρος, ὁ, (κραίνω) *one that accomplishes*: κραντῆρες, οἱ, *wisdom-teeth*, which come last and *complete the set*, Arist.*HA*501^{b}25 (κριτῆρες cited by *EM*742.37), Poll.2.93: generally, *teeth*, Nic.*Th.* 447 (sg.), Ruf.*Onom.*51: in sg., a boar's *tusk*, Lyc.833. II. *ruler*, κραντῆρα βοῶν ταῦρον Orph.*A.*313. **-τήριος**, α, ον, *accomplishing*, Hsch. **-της**, ου, ὁ, = κραντήρ, [πημάτων] κ. χρόνος Lyc.305. **-τωρ**, ορος, ὁ, = κραντήρ, κ. ἐλευθερίας Epigr.ap.Paus.8.52.6. II. *ruler, sovereign*, E.*Andr.*508 (lyr.), *AP*6.116 (Samos).

κράος· ἐν ᾧ τὴν γῆν σκάλλουσι, καὶ ἡ σκαλευομένη ἄμπελος, Hsch.

κρᾰπᾰτᾰλίας, ὁ, = ληρώδης, Pherecr.99.

κρᾰπᾰτᾰλός (**κραπαταλλός** Hdn.Gr.1.158), ὁ, a worthless kind of *fish*, hence = μωρός, Hsch.: Κραπαταλοί, title of play by Pherecrates, in which he says that the κραπαταλός is used for δραχμή in Hades, Poll.9.83.

κράριον, τό, perh. = κλάνιον, *PTeb.*550 (ii A.D.).

κράς, poet. form of κάρα, nom. only Simm.4; gen. κρᾱτός Il.5.7, al., Trag. (v. infr.); dat. κρᾱτί Od.9.490, S.*OC*313, Ar.*Ra.*329, κράτεσφι Il.10.156; acc. κρᾶτα Od.8.92, Trag. (v. infr.): pl., gen. κράτων Od. 22.309; dat. κρασίν Il.10.152; acc. κρᾶτας E.*Ph.*1149, *HF*526: gender rarely determinate, κρατός fem. E.*El.*140 (lyr.), cf. Sch.E.*Hec.* 432, *Ph.*1159; κρᾶτα, τό, is nom. in S.*Ph.*1457 (anap.), acc. ib.1001, *OT*263, cf. *Tr.*1016 (lyr.); but acc. κρᾶτα, τόν, Ion Trag.61: pl. κρᾶτα, τά, Pi.*Fr.*8, perh. S.*OC*473:—Hom. also has gen. and dat. κράατος, κράατι, pl. nom. κράατα [all – ᴗ ᴗ], but no nom. κρᾶας is found:—*head*, ἐκ κράατος ἀθανάτοιο Il.14.177; σῷ δ' αὐτοῦ κράατι τείσεις Od. 22.218, etc.; ὑπὸ κράτεσφι under his *head*, Il.10.156: metaph., *top, peak*, κρατὸς ἀπ' Οὐλύμποιο Il.20.5; ἐπὶ κρατὸς λιμένος at *the head* or *far end* of the bay, Od.9.140, 13.102. II. Adv. κρῆθεν, used by Hom. in the phrase κατὰ κρῆθεν *down from the head, from the top*, δένδρεα.. κατὰ κρῆθεν χέε καρπὸν *from their tops*, Od.11.588, cf. *h.Cer.* 182, Hes.*Th.*574: hence, *from head to foot, entirely*, Τρῶας δὲ κατὰ κρῆθεν λάβε πένθος Il.16.548 (perh. for κατ' ἄκρηθεν = κατ' ἄκρης, v. ἄκρα); also ἀπὸ κρῆθεν Hes.*Sc.*7.

κρᾶς· κρέας, τινὲς δὲ κεφαλή (i.e. κράς), Hsch.

κρασβόλος, ον, shortd. from κερασβόλος (q.v.), Hsch.

κρασ(ε)ίδιον, τό, *paste*, Ruf.ap.Orib.8.47.20.

κρασέρα· ἀλευρότρησις (κράσσεα· ἀλευρωτίς cod.), Hsch.; cf. κρησέρα, κρααρα.

κρᾶσις (Ion. **κρῆσις** Hp.*Vict.*1.32), εως, ἡ: (κεράννυμι):—*mixing, blending* of things which form a compound, as wine and water, opp. mechanical mixture (defined as an εἶδος μίξεως in which the constituents are liquids, Arist.*Top.*122^{b}26, cf. *Stoic.*2.153; περὶ κράσεως, title of work by Alex.Aphr.): first in A., τὴν δευτέραν γε κ. ἥρωσιν νέμω *Fr.*55, cf. Staphyl.9, Ath.10.426b (pl.); κράσεις ἠπίων ἀκεσμάτων *modes of compounding*.., A.*Pr.*482; ἡ τῶν ἐναντίων κ. Pl. *Lg.*889c; τὴν τῶν νεύρων φύσιν ἐξ ὀστοῦ καὶ σαρκὸς κράσεως.. συνεκεράσατο Id.*Ti.*74d; ἐκ κράσεως πρὸς ἄλληλα Id.*Tht.*152d; τὴν ἁρμονίαν κ. καὶ σύνθεσιν ἐναντίων εἶναι Arist. *de An.*407^{b}31; χρωμάτων ἀκριβὴς κ. Luc.*Zeux.*5, cf. Arist.*Col.*792^{a}4. 2. *temperature* of the air, κρᾶσιν ὑγρὰν οὐκ ἔχων [αἰθήρ] E.*Fr.*779.2; τὰς ὥρας κ. ἔχειν τοιαύτην ὥστε.. Pl.*Phd.*111b, cf. Poll.6.178; ἡ κ. τῶν ὡρέων *temperate climate*, Hp. *Aër.*12; ὅσα περὶ κράσεις *climates*, Arist.*Pr.*lib. xiv tit. 3. *temperament*, of the body or mind, κ. σώματος ib.871^{a}24, cf. 953^{a}30; διανοίας ib.909^{a}17; κ. μελαγχολική ib.954^{b}8: pl., αἱ τῶν σωμάτων κράσεις Ti.Locr.103a, cf. Plot.3.1.6: so in Medic., Hp.*Nat.Hom.*4, etc.; περὶ κράσεων, title of work by Galen. 4. metaph., *combination, union*, κ. καὶ ἁρμονία τούτων ἡ ψυχή Pl.*Phd.*86b, cf. 59a; μουσικῆς καὶ γυμναστικῆς κ. Id.*R.*441e, etc. 5. Gramm., *crasis*, i.e. the combination of the vowels of two syllables into one long vowel or diphthong, e.g. τοὔνομα for τὸ ὄνομα, ἁνήρ for ὁ ἀνήρ, τἄρα for τοι ἄρα, A.D.*Adv.*128.2, *EM*822.56, etc.; also, *synaeresis* of vowels, e.g. εὖ for ἔυ, ib.392.54; but opp. ἔκθλιψις and συναίρεσις, *An.Ox.*1.371.

κρασπεδίτης [ῑ], ου, ὁ, *hindmost person in a chorus*, opp. κορυφαῖος, Plu.2.678e.

κράσπεδ-ον, τό, *edge, border, skirt*, esp. of cloth, Theoc.2.53; of the *fringe* or *tassel* worn by Jews, *Ev.Matt.*9.20: mostly in pl., ἄκροισι λαίφους κρασπέδοις (v. ἄκρος I. 2 b) E.*Med.*524; κράσπεδα στεμμάτων Ar. *V.*475, cf. Diph.43.30; χρυσᾶ κ. Chamael.ap.Ath.9.374a, Chrysipp. *Stoic.*3.36, 37. 2. metaph., mostly in pl., *skirts* or *edge* of a country, S.*Fr.*602, E.*Fr.*381; of a mountain, X.*HG*4.6.8; πρὸς κρασπέδοισι στρατοπέδου on *the skirts* of the army, E.*Supp.*661; τοὺς πελταστὰς ἐπὶ τὰ κ. ἑκατέρωθεν καθίστασθαι X.*HG*3.2.16: also in sg., Τιμολέοντα ὥσπερ ἐκ κ. τινὸς λεπτοῦ τῆς πολίχνης τῇ Σικελίᾳ προσηρτημένον Plu. *Tim.*11; κ. αἰγιαλοῦ *AP*7.78 (Dionys. Cyzic.). 3. Medic., *affection of the uvula, fimbria*, Aret.*SA*1.8. **-όομαι**, Pass., *to be bordered* or *edged*, ὄφεσι κεκρασπεδῶσθαι E.*Ion* 1423.

κρασπῆναι· διάκονοι γυναῖκες, Hsch.

κραστήριον, τό, *rack, manger*, Poll.7.142, 10.166. II. in pl., *bed-posts*, Phryn.155.

κραστίζομαι, *consume green fodder*, Sophr.166, cf. *EM*535.23, *AB*273.

κράστις (**κρᾶστις** Harp.), εως, ἡ, = γράστις (q.v.), *green fodder*, esp. for horses (ἡ κ. τῶν ἵππων *PGrenf.*1.42.11 (ii B.C.)), Ar.*Fr.*798, Din.*Fr.*46.2, Arist.*HA*595^{b}26, Thphr.*HP*8.7.5, al., *PTeb.*61(*b*).318 (ii B.C.), Poll.7.142.

κρᾶτα, τό, *head*: v. κράς.

κραταιά, ἡ, = χελιδόνιον μέγα, Ps.-Dsc.2.180.

κρᾰται-βάτης [βᾰ], ου, Dor. **-τᾱς**, α, ὁ, *striding in might*, epith. of Zeus, *IG*4.669 (Nauplia). **-βῖος**, ον, *strong with violence*, Choerob. in *An.Ox.*2.318, Eust.1938.1. **-βολος**, ον, *hurled with violence*, E. *Ba.*1096. **-γονος**, ἡ, = κραταιόγονον, Thphr.*HP*9.18.5 (prob. l.):—also **-γονον**, τό, Ps.-Dsc.3.124, Hsch. **-γος**, ὁ, *thorn, Crataegus Heldreichii*, Thphr.*HP*3.15.6. **-γύᾰλος** [ῠ], ον, *with strong* γύαλα, *strongly arched*, θώρηκες Il.19.361. **-γών**, όνος, ὁ, = κράταιγος, Thphr.*HP*3.15.6. **-ίς**, ἡ, (κρατύς) of the stone of Sisyphus, ὅτε μέλλοι ἄκρον ὑπερβαλέειν, τότ' ἀποστρέψασκε κραταιίς when it was just about to surmount the top, then did *mighty weight* turn it back, dub. in Od.11.597 (taken as Adv., *violently*, by Aristarch.; as κράται' ἴς (where κράταια may be an old fem. of κρατύς like *πλάταια (cf. Skt. *pṛthivī*), pl. Πλαταιαί, fem. of πλατύς) by Ptol.Asc.ap.Hdn.Gr.2. 153). II. (proparox.) as pr. n., *the Mighty* one, name of the mother of Scylla, Od.12.124. **-λεως**, ων, gen. ω, (κραταιός, λᾶας) *of hard stones, rocky*, χθών A.*Ag.*666; πέδον E.*El.*534. **-όγονον**, τό, *willow-weed, Polygonum Persicaria*, Dsc.3.124, Gal.12.44; cf. κραταίγονον. **-ός**, ά, όν, poet. form of κρατερός, *strong, mighty*, μοῖρα κραταιή Il.16.334, etc.; of men, Od.15.242, 18.382, Pi.*N.*4.25, B.17. 18; of a lion, κραταιοῦ θηρὸς ὑφ' ὁρμῆς Il.11.119; ἔγχος Pi.*P.*6.34; κ. ἔπος word *of power*, ib.2.81; σθένος κ. A.*Pr.*428 (lyr.); κ. μετὰ χερσὶν S.*Ph.*1110 (lyr.); κραταιᾶς χειρὸς E.*HF*964; κραταιῷ.. βραχίονι *Trag. Adesp.*416; ἔχει χεῖρα κραταιάν Cratin.Jun.8.4 (hex.); χεῖρα κραταιοτέρην *AP*11.324 (Autom.); *fierce*, κ. καύματος ὥρα Poet.ap.Callistr. ap.Ath.3.125c: freq. in later Prose, κ. λίθος *hard* stone, Ph.*Bel.*80. 22, *Supp.Epigr.*2.829 (Damascus, iii A.D.); ἐν χειρὶ κ. with a *mighty* hand, Lxx *Ex.*13.3, al.; κ. ἀγών Plb.2.69.8; τόξα κ. Plu.*Crass.*24; ἐπὶ τὸ κ. Luc.*Anach.*28: Comp., Ph.1.14: Sup., Id.2.383; esp. in magical and mystical writings, ἐν φωτὶ κ. καὶ ἀφθάρτῳ *PMag.Lond.* 121.563; θεοὶ κ. ib.422; οἱ κ. the *Mighty Ones*, Iamb.*Myst.*8.4, Dam. *Pr.*351: Astrol., κ. ἡγεμόνες, divinities presiding over certain periods of the month, Porph.ap.Eus.*PE*3.4; ἀστέρες, ζῴδιον, *Cat.Cod.Astr.* 8(4).227; also ὁ κ. [μηνὸς Φαρμοῦθι] *POxy.*465 i 12 (ii A.D.): c. gen., *ruling over*, ὦ τῶν πάντων ζώντων τε καὶ τεθνηκότων κραταιοί *PMag. Leid.V.*7.8; ὁ μέγιστος κ. θεὸς Σοκνοπαῖος Wilcken *Chr.*122.1 (i A.D.). Adv. **-ῶς** Lxx *Jd.*8.1, Ph.1.276, Pap. in *Arch.f.Religionswiss.*18.259 (iii A.D.).

κρᾰταιό-της, ητος, ἡ, = κράτος, Lxx *Ps.*45(46).3. **-φρων**, ον, gen. ονος, *stern*, Τιτάν *PMag.Berol.*2.85. **-χειρ**, χειρος, ὁ, ἡ, *mighty of hand*, *Ath.Mitt.*24.257 (Thrace). **-χθων**, ονος, ὁ, ἡ, *wielding power over the earth*, *PMag.Lond.*121.353, *PMag.Par.*1.1355. **-ω**, *strengthen*, τὰς χεῖράς τινος Lxx 1*Ki.*23.16, al.:—Pass., ib.30.6, al., *Ev.Luc.*1.80, 1*Ep.Cor.*16.13, etc.; κ. ὑπέρ τινα *to be too strong for* him, *prevail against* him, Lxx 2*Ki.*10.11, al. 2. Pass., *to be determined*, κ. τοῦ πορεύεσθαι ib.*Ru.*1.18. II. intr. in Act., *prevail*, ἐπί τινας ib.2*Ki.*11.23; ὑπέρ τινας ib.3*Ki.*21(20).23. III. Med., *control*, πάθη λόγῳ Ph.1.420.

κρᾰταί-πεδος, ον, *with hard ground* or *soil*, οὖδας Od.23.46. **-πῖλος**, ον, *with strong* πῖλος, A.*Fr.*430. **-πους**, ὁ, ἡ, **-πουν**, τό, gen. ποδος, *stout-footed*, ἡμίονοι Hom.*Epigr.*15.9; cf. καρταίπους. **-ρῖνος**, ον, *hard-shelled*, χελώνη Orac.ap.Hdt.1.47. **-ωμα**, ατος, τό, *strength*, Lxx *Ps.*42(43).2. **-ωνον**, τό, = κραταιόγονον, Ps.-Dsc.3. 124. **-ωσις**, εως, ἡ, = κραταίωμα, Lxx *Ps.*59(60).7.

κρατάνιον, τό, kind of *cup*, Polem.Hist.20.

κρᾰτερ-αίχμης, ου, Aeol., Dor. **-ᾱς**, *mighty with the spear* (in form καρτ-), Pi.*I.*6(5).38. **-αλγής**, ές, *cruel*, *IG*7.96 (Megara, iv A.D.). **-αύχην**, ενος, ὁ, ἡ, *strong-necked*, Pl.*Phdr.*253e: in form καρτ- (v.l. κρατ-), Hp.*Epid.*6.1.2. **-ῖτις** (sc. λίθος), ιδος, ἡ, hard yellowish stone, Plin.*HN*37.154. **-όδους**, οντος, ὁ, ἡ, *strong-toothed*, Hsch. (glossed by καρτερούμενοι).

κρᾰτερός, ά, όν, Ep. form of καρτερός, *strong, stout, mighty*, in Hom. mostly of bodily strength, κρατερός περ ἐὼν καὶ χερσὶ πεποιθώς Il.16.624, cf. 6.97, Pi.*I.*5(4).31, etc.; epith. of Ares, Il.2.515; of lions, Od.4.335; χεῖρες ib.288, Pi.*P.*11.18: with collat. notion of *stern, harsh*, of Hades, Il.13.415, cf. 21.566. 2. of things, conditions, etc., *mighty, fierce*, κ. ὑσμίνας 2.345; ἀνάγκη 6.458; κρατερῆφι βίηφιν 21.501; σθένος B.17.40; πάλα Id.10.20; βέλος, τόξον, Il.5. 104, 8.279; βιὸς Od.24.170; δεσμός, δεσμοί, Il.5.386, Od.8.336; *hard*, χῶρος *h.Merc.*354; σίδηρος ὅπερ κρατερώτατός ἐστιν Hes.*Th.*864. 3. of passions, etc., *strong, vehement*, λύσσα Il.9.239; ἔρις 13.358; μένος 7.38; πένθος 11.249; ἄλγεα Od.15.232: of acts and words, κ. ἀμφίβασις Il.5.623; κ. μῦθος a *harsh, rough* speech, 1.25; μῦθον ἀπηνέα τε κ. τε 15.202. II. Adv. **-ρῶς** *strongly, stoutly*, μάχεσθαι 12.152; ἑστάμεναι 15.666; ἔχεσθαι 16.501, 17.559; νεμεσᾶν 13.16; κὰδ δ' ἔβαλε κ. dashed *roughly* to earth, Od.4.344; κ. ἀγόρευσεν, ἀπέειπεν, *sternly*, Il.8.29, 9.431; in Prose, Anon.ap.Stob.4.31.34.—Once in Trag., κ. γυιοπέδαι A.*Pr.*168 (anap.); elsewh. καρτερός. (**κορτερά**· κρατερά, ἰσχυρά, Hsch., is prob. Aeol.)

κρᾰτερο-φόρος· γενναῖος, Hsch. **-φρων**, ον, gen. ονος, (φρήν) *stout-hearted, dauntless*, epith. of Heracles, Il.14.324; the Dioscuri, Od.11.299; Odysseus, 4.333; a wild beast, Il.10.184; ἀδάμαντος ἔχον κρατερόφρονα θυμόν Hes.*Op.*147, cf. Orph.*Fr.*164; Διὸς κρατερόφρονι κούρῃ, of Athena, *IG*1^{2}.503.

κρᾰτέρ-ωμα, ατος, τό, kind of *bronze*, Hsch. **-ῶνυξ**, ὔχος, ὁ, ἡ, (ὄνυξ) *strong-hoofed, solid-hoofed*, ἵπποι Il.5.329, 16.724, al.; ἡμίονοι 24.277, Od.6.253; *strong-clawed*, λύκοι κρατερώνυχες ἠδὲ λέοντες 10. 218; *with strong nails*, χείρ Matro *Conv*.28.

κράτεσφι [ᾰ], Ep. dat. of κράς (q.v.).

κρᾰτευ-ταί, ῶν, οἱ, *stone* or *metal blocks on which a spit rests*, Il.9. 214, cf. Sch., Paus.Gr.*Fr*.236; μολύβδινοι κ. Eup.171, cf. *IG*2[2].1425. 388 (written **κραδευταί** ib.1425.415, 1541.20). 2. in Archit., *stones which support* a pavement, ib.7.3073.105, al. (Lebad.). 3. leaden *pigs* of specified weight, *IG*1[2].371.13. **-τήριον**, τό, = foreg. 1, Poll.6.89. **-ω**, = κρατέω, pf. κεκράτευκα, *IG*14.1794.

κρᾰτ-έω, Aeol. **κρετέω**, aor. inf. κρέτησαι Sapph.*Supp*.9.5:—Med., aor. ἐπι-κρατησάμενοι v.l. in Gal. *UP*6.13:—Pass., fut. κρατήσομαι Aristid.1.501 J. and, with v.l. κρατηθήσομαι, Th.4.9:—*to be strong, powerful*: hence, I. abs., *rule, hold sway*, Ἦλιδα.., ὅθι κρατέουσιν Ἐπειοί Od.13.275, 15.298; μέγα κρατέων ἤνασσε with mighty *sway*.., Il.16.172; ἅπας δὲ τραχύς, ὅστις ἂν νέον κρατῇ A.*Pr*.35; ὁ κρατῶν *the ruler*, Id.*Ag*.951, 1664, S.*Ant*.738, etc.; θῶπτε τὸν κρατοῦντ' ἀεί A.*Pr*.937; οἱ κρατοῦντες Id.*Ch*.267, S.*OT*530, etc.; τὸ κρατοῦν E.*Andr*.133(lyr.), Pl.*Lg*.714c, Arist.*Pol*.1255[a]15; ἡ κρατοῦσα the *lady of the house*, A.*Ch*.734. 2. in Poets, c. dat., *rule among*, μέγα κρατέεις νεκύεσσιν Od.11.485; ἀνδράσι καὶ θεοῖσι 16.265; Φθίᾳ *rule in* Phthia, Pi.*N*.4.50; ἐν Ἰλιάδι χθονί E.*El*.4. 3. c. gen., *to be lord* or *master of, rule over*, πάντων Ἀργείων, πάντων, Il.1.79, 288, cf. Od. 15.274; Ὀλύμπου A.*Pr*.149(lyr.); δωμάτων Id.*Ag*.1673; ὅπλων S.*Aj*. 1337; κ. τοῦ βίου *to be master of*.., And.1.137; αὑτοῦ κ. S.*Aj*.1099, Antipho 5.26, cf. S.*OC*405; ἡδονῶν καὶ ἐπιθυμιῶν Pl.*Smp*.196c, etc.; τῶν πραγμάτων D.2.27; τοῦ μὴ πείθεσθαι τοῖς νόμοις κρατῆσαι *to be above* obedience.., X.*Lac*.4.6. II. *conquer, prevail, get the upper hand*, abs., A.*Ag*.324, etc.; πολλῷ ἐκράτησαν Hdt.5.77; εἰ τὰ τοῦ Μήδου κρατήσειε Th.3.62; ὁ μὴ πειθόμενος κρατεῖ Pl.*Phdr*.272b; ἔνθα τἀναιδὲς κρατεῖ Diph.111: c. dat. modi, κ. τῇ γνώμῃ *prevail* in opinion, Hdt.9.42; πάλᾳ, ἱπποδρομίᾳ, Pi.*O*.8.20, *I*.3.13; μάχῃ E.*HF*612; ταῖς ναυσί Ar.*Ach*.648; τῷ Φοινίκων ναυτικῷ Th.1.16; also θουρίῳ ἐν Ἄρει S.*Aj*.614(lyr.); ἐν τοῖς πολέμοις Ar.*Pl*.184: c. acc. cogn., κ. στάδιον B. 6.15, cf. 7; ὀκτὼ νίκας E.*Epigr*.1; τὸν ἀγῶνα D.21.18; τὴν μάχην v.l. for τῇ μάχῃ in D.S.18.30; τὴν πρεσβείαν Philostr.*VS*1.21.6; πάντα *in* all things, S.*OT*1522; οἱ κρατοῦντες the *conquerors*, X.*An*.3.2.26; τὰ κατὰ πόλεμον κρατούμενα τῶν κρατούντων εἶναί φασιν Arist.*Pol*.1255[a] 7. b. *to be superior*, πλήθους ἕκατι ναυσὶν κρατῆσαι A.*Pers*.338: abs., *to be the best*, Critias 2.7 D. c. of reports, etc., *prevail, become current*, φάτις κρατεῖ A.*Supp*.293, S.*Aj*.978; λόγος κ. A.*Pers*.738; νόμιμα δὲ τὰ Χαλκιδικὰ ἐκράτησεν Th.6.5; κρατεῖ ἡ φήμη παρά τισι Plb. 9.26.11. 2. c. inf., *prevail so that*, κ. τῷ πλήθει ὥστε μὴ αὐτίκα τὰς πύλας ἀνοίγεσθαι Th.4.104: impers., καθανεῖν κρατεῖ 'tis better to.., A.*Ag*.1364; κρατεῖ μὴ γιγνώσκοντ' ἀπολέσθαι E.*Hipp*.248(anap.). 3. c. gen., *conquer, prevail over*, τῶν ἐναντίων S.*Fr*.85, cf. *OC*646, A.*Th*. 955(lyr.), etc.; κ. τινὸς τὸν ἀγῶνα Philostr.*Her*.2.5: metaph., τό τοι νομισθὲν τῆς ἀληθείας κρατεῖ S.*Fr*.86; κ. τῆς διαβολῆς *get the better of* it, Lys.19.53; ὁ λόγος τοῦ ἔργου ἐκράτει *surpassed, went beyond* it, Th.1.69; ἡ φύσις ... τῶν διδαγμάτων κρατεῖ *is better than*.., Men. *Mon*.213, cf. 169. b. of food, *digest, assimilate*, Hp.*VM*3, 14, Mnesith.ap.Ath.2.54b, Phylotim.ib.3.79c:—Pass., Hp.*Epid*.6.5.15; τῆς τροφῆς μὴ κρατηθείσης Plu.2.654b. 4. c. acc., *conquer, master*, Pi.*N*.10.25, A.*Pr*.215, *Th*.189, E.*Alc*.490, Ar.*Nu*.1346, *Av*.420, X. *An*.7.6.32, etc.; μάχῃ, τῷ πολέμῳ τινά, Th.6.2, Aeschin.2.30; τῷ λόγῳ τινά Ar.*V*.539; πάχει μάκει τε ἵν.., Pi.*P*.4.245; *outdo*, τοὺς φίλους εὖ ποιῶν X.*Hier*.11.15; τῷ διαφθαρῆναι χρήμασιν ἢ μὴ κεκράτηκα Φίλιππον D.18.247; *surpass*, κρατεῖ δὲ ὁ τῆς ἡδονῆς [βίος] τὸν τῆς φρονήσεως Pl.*Phlb*.12a:—Pass., *to be overcome*, A.*Th*.750(lyr.), etc.; ὕπνῳ Id.*Eu*.148(lyr.); ὑπὸ τοῦ ὕπνου Hdt.2.121.δ'; ὑπὸ τῶν ἡδονῶν Pl.*Lg*.633e. III. *become master of, get possession of*, τῆς ἀρχῆς, τῶν νεκρῶν, Hdt.1.92, 4.111; πολλὰ φρονέοντα μηδενὸς κ. Id.9.16; σέθεν A.*Supp*.387; οὔπω ἡ βουλή σου ἐκράτει Lys.13.26; κ. τῆς γῆς Th.3.6; ναυσὶ τῆς θαλάσσης Pl.*Mx*.240a; κ. τῆς λέξεως *have* it *at command, remember* it, Ath.7.275b; *master* by the intellect, πάντων τῶν τῆς ἱστορίας μερῶν Plb.16.20.2:—Pass., *to be mastered*, δεῖ ἐν ταῖς τέχναις καὶ ἐπιστήμαις ταῦτα κρατεῖσθαι Arist.*Pol*.1331[b]38, cf. *Po*.1456[a]10 (prob. for κροτεῖσθαι). IV. *lay hold of*, τῆς χειρός Lxx *Ge*.19.16, *Ev.Matt*.9.25, *Ev.Marc*.9.27. 2. c. acc. rei, *seize, win and keep*, esp. by force, πᾶσαν αἶαν A.*Supp*.255; θρόνους S.*OC* 1381; *seize, hold fast, arrest*, τινα Batr.63, Plb.8.18.8, *Ev.Matt*.14.3; τένοντα Batr.233; τὰς χεῖράς τινος *PLips*.40iii 2 (iv/v A.D.); *secure, grasp*, τὴν ἀκατονόμαστον Τριάδα Zos.Alch.p.230 B. 3. *hold up, support*, τινα D.H.4.38; *maintain* a military post, X.*An*.5.6.7; *hold fast*, τὰς παραδόσεις 2*Ep.Thess*.2.15; *keep, retain*, *PTeb*.61(*b*).229 (ii B.C.):—Pass., οὐκ ἦν δυνατὸν κρατεῖσθαι αὐτὸν ὑπ' αὐτοῦ (sc. τοῦ θανάτου) *Act.Ap*.2.24; ἡ κτῆσις τοῖς τέκνοις κεκράτηται *has been reserved* for, *settled* upon, *POxy*.237 viii 36 (ii A.D.). 4. in Law, *possess a title to*, κ. καὶ κυριεύειν c. gen., *PTeb*.319.19 (iii A.D.), etc. b. *sequester, place under embargo*, *OGI*669.23 (Pass., Egypt, i A.D.), *BGU* 742 iii 6 (Pass., ii A.D.). 5. *hold in the hand*, ὁ κρατῶν τοὺς ἑπτὰ ἀστέρας ἐν τῇ δεξιᾷ αὐτοῦ *Apoc*.2.1; πόαν Dsc.3.93; ἄρτον Plu.2.99d; σκῆπτρον Ath.7.289c, cf. Luc.*Am*.44, Ach.Tat.1.6, etc.; δακτύλιον *PMag.Lond*.46.451 (iv A.D.). 6. *endure, put up with*, τὸν ἀργυροπράτην *POxy*.1844 (vi A.D.). V. *control, command*, A.*Ag*.10, E. *Hec*.282:—Pass., αἰσχρὰ τῷ νόμῳ κρατούμενα *controlled* by.., Ar.*Av*. 755; κρατεῖσθαι ὑπὸ τοῦ προβουλεύματος D.H.9.52; διαθέσει Porph. *Sent*.27. VI. *repair, make good*, τὸ βεδὲκ (Hebr.) τοῦ οἴκου Lxx 4*Ki*.12.5. **-ημα**, ατος, τό, *support*, of a bandage, Gal.18(2).538, Heracl.ap.Orib.48.15.3, Heliod.ib.27.3; *fulcrum*, Id.ib.49.19.2. 2. *grasp, grip* of the hand, Procl.*Par.Ptol*.36. 3. *handle*, Sch.Luc. *JTr*.31, *Icar*.10.

κρᾱτήρ, Ion. and Ep. **κρητήρ**, ῆρος, ὁ, (κεράννυμι) *mixing vessel*, esp. *bowl, in which wine was mixed with water*, κ. ἀργύρεος, χρύσεος, Il.23.741, 219; [κ.] ἀργύρεός ἐστιν ἅπας, χρυσῷ δ' ἐπὶ χείλεα κεκράανται Od.4.615; οἶνον δ' ἐκ κρητῆρος ἀφυσσόμενοι δεπάεσσιν ἔκχεον Il.3.295, cf. 247; κρητῆρι δὲ οἶνον μίσγον ib.269; κρητῆρα κεράσσάμενος Od.7. 179, 13.50; οἶνον ἔμισγον ἐνὶ κρητῆρσι καὶ ὕδωρ 1.110, cf. Sapph.51, Alc. 45, S.*OC*159(lyr.), Ar.*Ec*.841; κρατῆρα κεράσαι Orac.ap.D.21.53, cf. Th.6.32; κρητῆρα καὶ ὑποκρητήριον *SIG*2 (Sigeum, vi B.C.); πίνοντες κρητῆρας drinking *bowls of wine*, Il.8.232; κρητῆρα στήσασθαι ἐλεύθερον to set up *a bowl of wine* to be drunk in honour of the deliverance, 6.528, cf. Od.2.431; κρητῆρα ἐπιστέψασθαι ποτοῖο, v. ἐπιστέφω; κρατῆρος μέρος μετασχεῖν A.*Ch*.291; σπονδὴ τρίτου κρατῆρος S.*Fr*. 425. 2. metaph., κ. ἀοιδᾶν, of the messenger who bears an ode, Pi.*O*.6.91; κ. κακῶν, of a sycophant, Ar.*Ach*.937(lyr.); τοσόνδε κρατῆρ' ἐν δόμοις κακῶν πλήσας .. ἐκπίνει A.*Ag*.1397; αἵματος κρατῆρα πολιτικοῦ στῆσαι, of civil war, D.H.7.44. 3. a constellation, the *Cup*, Ptol.*Tetr*.27. II. *any cup-shaped hollow, basin* in a rock, S. *OC*1593, cf. Pl.*Phd*.111d. 2. *mouth* of a volcano, *crater*, Arist. *Mu*.400[a]33 (pl.), Plb.34.11.12 (pl.), Luc.*Trag*.23.

κρᾱτηρ-ία, ἡ, = foreg., *bowl* for compounding drugs, etc., Dsc.4. 150, Zos.Alch.p.234 B. **-ίαρχος**, ου, ὁ, = συμποσίαρχος, dub. in Dumont-Homolle *Mélanges d'arch. et d'épigr*.p.457 (Thrace, κρατηριακος lapis). **-ίζω**, Ion. **κρητηρ-** prob. in *SIG*57.24 (Milet., v B.C.):—in aor. Pass. κἠκρατηρίχ⟨θ⟩ημες, *drink out of the* κρατήρ, i.e. *get drunk*, as we might say, *drink from the bottle* instead of the glass, Sophr.106 (prob. l., cf. ἐκρατηρίχθημεν· ἐμεθύσθημεν, Hsch.). II. Act., *mix a bowl of wine*, κρητηρίσα⟨ντες κρητῆρα⟩ς τέσσερας prob. in *SIG*l. c., cf. *AB*274; esp. for the orgies, D.18.259, Phot. **-ιον**, Ion. **κρητ-**, τό, Dim. of κρατήρ, Hp.*Nat.Mul*.34; as a measure, *POxy*. 2049 (vi A.D.):—also **-ίδιον**, τό, in pl., *IG*7.3099 (Lebad.), J.*AJ*3.6. 7: **-ίσκος**, ὁ, *IG*11(2).203*A* 35 (Delos, iii B.C.), Ath.11.479c; κ. τοῦ ὀφθαλμοῦ *sockets*, Hsch. (pl.).

κρᾱτηροφόρος, ον, *bearing a bowl*, Ῥέα Sch.Nic.*Al*.217.

Κράτης, ὁ, mystical title, *PMag.Leid.V*.7.18.

κρᾰτησί-βίας, ὁ, = κραταίβιος, Pi.*Fr*.16. **-μᾰχος**, ον, *conquering in the fight*, Id.*P*.9.86. **-πους**, ποδος, ὁ, ἡ, *victorious in the footrace*, ib.10.16.

κρᾰτήσιππος, ον, *victorious in the race*, ἅρμα Pi.*N*.9.4.

κράτησις [ᾰ], εως, ἡ, *might, power, dominion*, Lxx *Wi*.6.3, Man. ap.J.*Ap*.1.26. 2. ἡ Καίσαρος κ. (sc. Αἰγύπτου), an era in Egypt (viz. the capture of Alexandria, 30 B.C.), *BGU*174 (i A.D.), *PFay*.89. 2 (i A.D.), etc. 3. *accession* of an Emperor, *BGU*362 iv 6, al. (iii A.D.). 4. *prevalence, predominance*, ἡ τῆς ἀπλανοῦς κ. Simp.*in Cael*. 475.30, 476.5. II. *possession*, βίου κ. *BMus.Inscr*.918 (Halic.); κ. τοῦ ἐν ὕλῃ σκοτεινοῦ Plot.1.6.3. 2. in Law, *title to possession*, Mitteis *Chr*.31 iii 32 (ii B.C.); κ. καὶ κυρεία *BGU*1187.7, etc. 3. Medic., *retention*, κ. ἐπίμονος σπέρματος (i.e. conception) Sor.1.43; opp. ἔκκρισις, Gal.8.440. b. κ. τῶν ὑδάτων, i.e. drought, *Cat.Cod. Astr*.7.184. 4. *holding firm, steadying*, Gal.18(2).826, Olymp. *in Mete*.96.11.

Κρᾰτήτειος, ον, *of Crates*, γραφή Str.2.3.8.

κρᾰτ-ητέον, *one must keep to*, τῆς συμμετρίας Aët.9.35. **-ητής**, οῦ, ὁ, *one who holds* or *possesses*, ἱερῶν Procl.*Par.Ptol*.228. **-ητικός**, ή, όν, *fit for winning*, νίκη κ. δύναμις Pl.*Def*.414a. 2. *ruling, controlling*, δύναμις κ. τῶν προνοουμένων Procl.*Inst*.121; κ. τῶν ὅλων Id. *in Ti*.1.69; αἱ κ. δυνάμεις, opp. αἱ ὑπουργικαί, Id. *in Prm*.p.736 S. 3. *promoting retention* (cf. κράτησις II. 3), συλλήψεως Aët.1. 142. 4. Astrol., *predominant*, Vett.Val.333.5. **-ητός**, ή, όν, *capable of being grasped, mastered*, διανοίᾳ Porph.*Marc*.8. **-ήτωρ**, ορος, ὁ, = κρατητής, word coined by Alexarchus, Heraclid.Lemb.5. 2. Astrol., *ruling star*, Ptol.*Tetr*.198.

κρατίζομαι, f.l. for κραστίζομαι in Sophr.166.

Κρᾱτίνειος [ῑ], α, ον, *used by* the Comic poet *Cratinus*, ὄνομα D.H. *Rh*.11.10; μέτρον Heph.15.21.

κράτιστ-⟨ε⟩ία, ἡ, the rank of *excellency*, *POxy*.1204.15 (iii/iv A.D.). **-εύω**, *to be mightiest, best, most excellent*, ὁ κρατιστεύων λόγος Pi.*Fr*.180; ὦ κρατιστεύων κατ' ὄμμα, of the Sun, S.*Tr*.102 (lyr.); ὁ κ. *the conqueror*, opp. ὁ ἡττηθείς, Arist.*HA*614[a]4; τὰ κ. J. *BJ*1.2.8. 2. *to be superior*, τῷ σώματι καὶ τῇ ψυχῇ X.*Mem*.1.4.14; ἔν τινι ib.2.6.26; τἆλλα Id.*Cyr*.1.5.1. 3. c. gen. pers., πάντων And.3.18; τῶν ἡλικιωτῶν κ. ἐν τοῖς ἀγῶσι *to be first of* them, Isoc. 9.22. **-ής**, οῦ, ὁ, = κρατητής, ὦ βασιλέων κύριοι καὶ κρατισταί *PMag.Leid.V*.7.15. **-ίνδην**, Adv. *by choosing the best*, Poll.1. 176. **-ος**, η, ον, Ep. **κάρτ-** (as always in Hom.), isolated Superl. from κρατύς, *strongest, mightiest*, Il.1.266, etc.; θεῶν κ., i.e. Zeus. Pi.*O*.14.13; κ. Ἑλλήνων, i.e. Achilles, S.*Ph*.3: in Prose, εἰ τοὺς κ. ἐνικήσαμεν Th.7.67; Λημνίων τὸ κ. *the best* of their men, Id.5.8; τὸ δυνάμεως κ. *the strength* or *flower* of.., X.*Cyr*.6.1.28, etc.; of things, καρτίστην.. μάχην *fiercest* fight, Il.6.185; δεσμὸς κ. Ti.Locr.99a. 2. generally, *best, most excellent*, as Sup. of ἀγαθός, Pi.*I*.1.17, S.*Ant*. 1050, etc.: colloquially, "ἄνδρα κ." εἰπών Thphr.*Char*.5.2; οἱ κράτιστοι *the aristocracy*, X.*HG*7.1.42, v. ἀγαθός I; τὰ κ. τῆς χώρας ib.3.4. 20. b. as a title or mode of address, κράτιστε Θεόφιλε *Ev.Luc*. 1.3; esp. = Lat. *egregius*, ὁ κ. ἡγεμών *PFay*.p.33 (i A.D.); ὁ κ. ἐπίτροπος *BGU*891 (ii A.D.); ἡ κ., of a woman of the *equester ordo*, *IG*14.

1346; also, = Lat. *clarissimus*, of Senators, ὁ κ. ἀνθύπατος ib.9(1).61; ὁ κ. συγκλητικός *IGRom*.3.581, etc.; ἡ κ. βουλή *POxy*.2108.6 (iii A.D.). c. with modal words added, κ. τὴν ψυχήν Th.2.40; πάντων πάντα κ. *best* of all in.., X.*An*.1.9.2; ἔν τινι Id.*Mem*.3.4.5; εἴς τι Pl. *Phlb*.67b; περί τι Id.*Plt*.257a; πρός τι X.*HG*3.4.16: c. inf., *best at* doing, Th.2.81, Pl.*Phdr*.267d, X.*Mem*.1.4.1, etc.: c. part., τῶν ἡλίκων κ. εἶναι ἀκοντίζων καὶ τοξεύων Id.*Cyr*.1.3.15. 3. neut. folld. by inf., φυγέειν κάρτιστον to flee were *best*, Od.12.120, cf. E.*El*. 379, Ar.*Eq*.80, etc.: in pl., κράτιστα.. ἑλεῖν E.*Med*.384: abs., ὅπερ κ. the *main point*, Th.1.143. 4. Adv. usages, ἀπὸ τοῦ κρατίστου *in all good faith*, Plb.8.17.4; κατὰ τὸ κ. D.H.2.22: neut. pl. κράτιστα as Adv., X.*HG*3.4.16, *Ages*.1.25.—The Comp. in use is κρείσσων (q.v.).

κρᾶτο-βρώς, βρῶτος, ὁ, ἡ, *devourer of heads* or *brains*, Lyc. 1066. **-γενής**, ές, *head-born*, θεός, of Athena, Porph.*Antr*. 32. **-δετον**· σφενδόνην δεδεμένην, τὰ γὰρ ἄκρα τῆς σφενδόνης κεφαλὰς ἐκάλουν, Hsch. s.v. κραστόδετον (incomplete s.v. κρατόδετον). **-πλᾶγής**, ές, *struck on the head*, cj. Lob. for -παγής in Man. 4.284 (-παλής Koechly).

κρᾶτορία, ἡ, *power, might*, θεοῦ *Gloss*.

κράτος [ᾰ], Ion. and Ep. **κάρτος**, εος, τό, both in Hom.; Aeol. **κρέτος** Alc.25:—*strength, might*, in Hom. esp. of *bodily strength*, ἔπεφνε δόλῳ, οὔ τι κράτεΐ γε Il.7.142; ἔχει ἥβης ἄνθος, ὅ τε κ. ἐστὶ μέγιστον 13.484, etc.; τὸ γὰρ αὖτε σιδήρου γε κ. ἐστίν this (i.e. τὸ βάψαι) is what gives *strength* to iron, Od.9.393: generally, δικαία γλῶσσ' ἔχει κ. μέγα S.*Fr*.80; μηχανῆς ἔστω κ. A.*Supp*.207; κατὰ κράτος with *all one's might* or *strength*, πολιορκεῖσθαι Th.1.64; πολεμεῖν Pl. *Lg*.692d; ἐξελέγχεσθαι D.34.20, etc.: freq. in phrase αἱρεῖν κατὰ κ. take *by storm*, Th.8.100, Isoc.4.119, etc.; also ἀνὰ κράτος διώκειν X. *Cyr*.1.4.23; ἐλαύνειν Id.*An*.1.8.1, etc.; ἀπὸ κράτους D.S.17.34; πρὸς ἰσχύος κράτος, opp. λόγῳ, S.*Ph*.594. 2. personified, Κ. Βία τε A. *Pr*.12; Κ. καὶ Δίκη Id.*Ch*.244. II. *power*, τοῦ γὰρ κ. ἐστὶ μέγιστον, of Zeus, Il.2.118, etc.; τοῦ γὰρ κ. ἔστ' ἐνὶ οἴκῳ Od.1.359, cf. Il.12.214; Ζηνὸς κ. Pi.*O*.6.96, cf. A.*Pr*.527 (lyr.); ἐκπίπτειν κράτους, of Zeus, ib. 948; τὸ κ. τοῦ θεοῦ Lxx *Ps*.61(62).11, etc.: pl., ὑποχείριος κράτεσιν ἀρσένων A.*Supp*.393 (lyr.), cf. S.*Ant*.485; esp. of political power, *rule, sovereignty*, ὁ μαιόμενος τὸ μέγα κρέτος ὀντρέψει τάχα τὰν πόλιν Alc. l.c.; τὸ κ. περιθεῖναί τινι Hdt.1.129; ἐς τὸ πλῆθος φέρειν τὸ κ. Id.3.81; τὸ πᾶν κ. ἔχειν to be all-*powerful*, Id.7.3; ἀρχὴ καὶ κ. τυραννικόν S.*OC* 373; βασιλεὺς πρῶτος ἐν κράτει Ὀδρυσῶν ἐγένετο in *real power*, Th.2. 29; later τὸ κ. τῶν Ῥωμαίων *POxy*.41 i 2 (iii/iv A.D.): in pl., κράτη καὶ θρόνους S.*Ant*.173, cf. *OT*586, etc.; θρόνων κράτη sovereign *power*, Id.*Ant*.166. 2. c. gen., *power over*, τὸ Περσέων κ. ἔχοντα Hdt.3.69; τὸ κ. εἶχε τῆς στρατιῆς Id.9.42; πᾶν κ. ἔχων χθονὸς A.*Supp*.425 (lyr.); τῶν ἄλλων δαιμόνων E.*Tr*.949; δὸς κ. τῶν σῶν δόμων A.*Ch*.480; δωμάτων ἔχειν κ. Ar.*Th*.871; τὸ τῆς θαλάσσης κ. Th.1.143; μετὰ κράτους τῆς γῆς Id.8.24; ὧν ἂν ᾖ τὸ κ. τῆς γῆς whoever have *possession* of the land, Id.4.98; κ. ἔχειν ἑαυτοῦ Pl.*Plt*.273a: pl., ἀστραπᾶν κράτη νέμων S.*OT*201 (lyr.). 3. of persons, *a power, an authority*, Ἀχαιῶν δίθρονον κ. A.*Ag*.109 (lyr.), cf. 619, *Th*.127 (lyr.). III. *mastery, victory*, freq. in Hom., Il.1.509, 6.387, Od.21.280; κ. ἄρνυσθαι S.*Ph*. 838 (lyr.); νίκη καὶ κράτη A.*Supp*.951; ἀέθλων κ. *victory in*.., Pi.*I*. 8(7).4; νίκη καὶ κ. τῶν δρωμένων S.*El*.85; κ. ἀριστείας *the meed* of highest valour, Id.*Aj*.443; νίκη καὶ κ. πολεμίων Pl.*Lg*.962a; κ. πολέμου καὶ νίκη D.19.130. IV. Medic., in pl., *ligaments*, Hp.*Mul*. 2.167. 2. = ταρσός, *back of the hand*, Poll.2.144. V. Pythag. name for *ten*, *Theol.Ar*.59.—This word and its derivs. take two forms, κρατ- and καρτ-; the latter is mostly Ep., as κάρτος, κάρτιστος, καρτύνω, but in κρατερός and καρτερός the reverse holds, v. κρατερός fin.; κρατέω, κρατύς have no form καρτ-. (κρατ- and καρτ- from κr̥τ-, weak form of κρετ-, cf. κρέτος, κρέσσων.)

κρᾶτός, gen. sg. of κράς (q.v.).

κρᾰτυν-τήριος, α, ον, *strengthening, making firm*, Hp.*Mul*.1.78; κρατυντήρια, τά, title of work of Democritus *in support of his doctrines*, S.E.*M*.7.136, D.L.9.47, Suid.; κρατυντήρια· κατισχύοντα, Hsch. **-τικός**, ή, όν, = foreg., κ. φάρμακα, for loose teeth, Archig.ap.Gal.12.873, v.l. in Dsc.1.30, prob. l. in Antyll.ap.Orib. 6.34.3. **-τός**, ή, όν, *confirmed, upheld*, τὶν πάντα κρατυντά Orph. *Fr*.47.6. **-τωρ**, ορος, ὁ, *ruler, controller*, πυρὸς *PMag.Leid.W*.8. 21. **-ω**, Ep. **καρτ-**, (κράτος, κρατύς) *strengthen*, κ. τὰς Συρηκούσας Hdt.7.156; τὴν πόλιν Th.1.69; τείχη Id.3.18; κ. τινὰ δορυφόροισι Hdt.1.98; κ. ἑωυτὸν τῇ τυραννίδι ib.100:—also in Med. (so only in Hom.), ἐκαρτύναντο φάλαγγας they *strengthened their* ranks, Il.11. 215, 12.415; κρατυνάμενοι [τὴν Ἄντανδρον] Th.4.52, cf. 114; τὴν προβολὴν Plu.*Aem*.20; πίστεις κ. *confirm* their pledges, Th.3.82; σπείραισιν ἐκαρτύναντο βοείαις χεῖρας Theoc.22.80; ἐκαρτ. μέλαθρον A.R.2.1087; οἵ μιν.. ἐκαρτ. κεραυνῷ Id.1.510; καρτ. τὴν αἰσυμνητείην Thrasyb.ap. D.L.1.100:—Pass., *wax strong*, ἔσχε τὴν βασιληΐην καὶ ἐκρατύνθη Hdt.1.13; τείχεσιν ἐκεκράτυντο D.C.40.36, cf. D.H.3.72; ἐν χρόνῳ κρατυνθὲν ἔθος Lxx *Wi*.14.16. b. *confirm* an impression, S.E. *M*.8.364 (Pass.); an agreement, *PLond*.1.113 i 51 (vi A.D.). 2. *harden*, opp. ἁπαλύνω, τοὺς πόδας ἀνυποδησίᾳ X.*Lac*.2.3, cf. Gal.4. 748 (Pass.):—Pass., ὀστέα κρατύνεται *consolidate*, Hp.*Fract*.7. II. *rule, govern*, c. gen., S.*OT*14, E.*Ba*.660: c. acc., ἄκρα κρατύνων Emp. 100.19, cf. 73.2, A.*Pers*.900 codd. (lyr.); πτόλιν Id.*Supp*.699 (lyr.): c. acc. cogn., κράτος κ. Id.*Ag*.1471 (lyr.): abs., Id.*Pr*.150 (lyr.), 404 (lyr.); τὰ πρῶτα μὲν δόρει κρατύνων, πρῶτα δ' οἰωνῶν ὁδοῖς S. *OC*1314. 2. c. gen., *become master, get possession of*, τῶν ὅπλων Id.*Ph*.366, cf. 1059, 1161 (lyr.): c. acc., *possess*, λέκτρα Corinn. *Supp*.2.55; βασιληΐδα τιμὰν κ. *hold, exercise*, E.*Hipp*.1281 (lyr.), cf. A.*Supp*.372 (lyr.); τὴν πολιτικὴν ἀρετήν Him.*Or*.14.28. III. καρτύνειν βέλεα *ply, throw* them *stoutly*, Pi.*O*.13.95; κ. ἐνὶ χερσὶν ἐρετμά A.R.2.332. IV. c. acc. et inf., *insist* that.., D.L.7.83, cf. Procl.*Hyp*.3.54.

κρᾰτύς [ῠ], ὁ, *strong, mighty*, in Hom. always epith. of Hermes, κρατὺς Ἀργειφόντης Il.16.181, 24.345, Od.5.49. (For a doubtful fem. κράταια, v. κραταιΐς.)

κρᾰτυσμός, ὁ, *strength, firmness*, Hp.*Epid*.6.8.11.

κράτωρ [ᾰ], ορος, ὁ, *ruler, potentate*, of God, *Gloss*.

κραύγαξος, ὁ, = κραύγασος, Ptol.*Tetr*.164.

κραυγ-άζω, = κράζω, of dogs, *bay*, *Lyr.Adesp*.135; of ravens, *croak*, Arr.*Epict*.3.1.37; of men, *cry aloud, shout*, D.54.7, Lxx 2*Es*.3.13, *Ev.Jo*.18.40, Polem.*Cyn*.40, Gal.8.287; κ. "μὴ θυμοῦ" Phld.*Ir*.p.70 W.; κραυγάζω κοὐκ ἐπακούει *Riv.Fil*.57.380 (Aptera). **-ανάομαι**, = foreg., παιδίον ἀσπαῖρόν τε καὶ κραυγανώμενον (v.l. -γόμενον) Hdt.1. 111, cf. Sch.Call.*Aet.Oxy*.2079.20. **-αρ**· ὁ ἰσχυρός, Hsch. **-ᾰσίδης**, ου, ὁ, as if a Patron. of κραύγασος, *Croaker*, name of a frog in Batr. 243. **-ασμός**, ὁ, *screaming*, Diph.16; censured by Phryn. 317. **-ᾰσος**, ὁ, *bawler, shouter*, *Gloss*. **-αστής**, οῦ, ὁ, *crier, bawler*, gloss on βαβάκτης, *AB*223:—fem. **-άστρια**, Hsch. s.v. μηκάδες. **-αστικός**, ή, όν, *vociferous*, Procl.*Par.Ptol*.230, Sch.Il. 1.575; τὸ κ. Sch.Ar.*Pax*1078. Adv. -κῶς Sch.Ar.*Eq*.485. **-ή**, ἡ, *crying, screaming, shouting*, τίς ἥδε κ.; Telecl.35; κραυγὴν θεῖναι, στῆσαι, E.*Or*.1510, 1529; ποιεῖν X.*Cyr*.3.1.4; κραυγῇ χρῆσθαι Th.2. 4; κ. γίγνεται Lys.13.71; rarely of a *shout of joy*, *PPetr*.3 p.334 (iii B.C.), *Ev.Luc*.1.42: in pl., Aeschin.1.34, Vett.Val.2.35; κραυγὴ Καλλιόπης, as an instance of bad taste, cited from Dionys.Eleg.(7) by Arist.*Rh*.1405ᵃ33. **-ίας** ἵππος, ὁ, a horse *that takes fright at a cry*, Hsch.

κραυγός, οῦ, ὁ, *woodpecker*, Hsch.:—also **κραυγόν** (leg. -γών), Id.

κραῦρ-α, ἡ, (κραῦρος) *fever*, a disease in swine and cattle, Suid., Phot., prob. in *GDI*5001 (Gortyn). **-άω**, *suffer from fever*, of cattle, Arist.*HA*604ᵃ17; of swine, ib.603ᵇ7. **-όομαι**, Pass., *become dry* or *parched*, Ph.2.174, D.C.66.21. **-ος** (A), ου, ὁ, = κραῦρα, Arist.*HA*604ᵃ14; also, a *disease of bees*, prob. in Hsch. (καυροῶς cod.). **-ος** (B), α, ον, also ος, ον Arist.*PA*655ᵃ25:—*brittle, friable* (κραῦρον τὸ τελέως ξηρόν, ὥστε καὶ πεπηγέναι δι' ἔλλειψιν ὑγρότητος Id.*GC*330ᵃ6), Pl.*Ti*.60d (Comp.); of wood, Thphr.*HP*1.6. 2, al., Eust.1906.11; opp. μαλακός, γλίσχρος, Arist.*PA* l.c., *GA*734ᵇ 32; of meat, θερμότερον ἢ κραυρότερον ἢ μέσως ἔχον (apptly.) *dry and cold*, Eub.7. **-ότης**, ητος, ἡ, *brittleness*, opp. γλισχρότης, Thphr. *HP*1.5.4, Gal.6.799.

κραῦσον· τὸ πῦρ, Hsch. **κράφα**· ᾧ οἱ κηπουροὶ τοὺς βώλους ἀπάγουσιν, Id.

κρε-άγρα, ἡ, (κρέας, ἀγρέω) *flesh-hook*, to take meat out of the pot, Ar.*Eq*.772 (ubi v. Sch.), *V*.1155, Anaxipp.6.2, Lxx 1*Ki*.2.14, *PLond*. 2.191.10 (ii A.D.), etc.: generally, *hook to seize* or *drag by*, Ar.*Ec*. 1002. **-άγρευτος**, ον, *tearing off the flesh*, Lyc.759. **-άγριον**, τό, Dim. of κρεάγρα, *IG*2².1541.13. **-αγρίς**, ίδος, ἡ, = κρεάγρα, *AP*6.306 (Aristo).

κρεᾴδιον, τό, Dim. of κρέας, *morsel, slice of meat*, Ar.*Pl*.227, Cephisod.8, Hp.*Epid*.7.3, Porph.*Abst*.1.37: pl., Ar.*Fr*.591, Alex. 110.15, X.*Cyr*.1.4.13, Phld.*Ir*.p.41 W.; σφυρίδαν κρεδίων (sic) *BGU* 814.25 (iii A.D.): sg. written κρεάδινον Orib.*Eup*.4.72.1.

κρεᾶ-δοσία, ἡ, *distribution of meat*, *Inscr.Prien*.111.174 (i B.C.), *IG*7.2712.68 (Acraeph.). **-δοτέω**, *distribute meat*, *OGI*764.54 (Pergam., ii B.C.), *Inscr.Prien*.123.6 (i B.C.).

κρεάνας· ἐλπίδας, Hsch.

κρεᾶ-νομέω, pf. κεκρεανόμηκα Is.9.33:—*divide the flesh* of a victim among the guests, l.c., Luc.*Prom*.20; *distribute meat*, τῇ βουλῇ *IG*2².847.25: generally, *divide, cut piecemeal*, D.S.34.12:—Med., Sopat.20: with pl. subject, *divide among themselves*, Theoc.26. 24. **-νομία**, ἡ, *distribution of meat*, Theopomp.Hist.205 (pl.), *IG* 2².1245.5, Luc.*Prom*.5: pl., *IG*2².334.25, Porph.*Abst*.2.30. **-νόμος**, ὁ, (νέμω) *one who distributes the flesh of victims*, E.*Cyc*.245: as Adj., *mangling*, τέκνων Lyc.203, cf. 762.

κρέας, τό, Dor. **κρῆς** (q.v.), Ep. **κρεῖας** dub. cj. in Anan.5.3; Att. gen. κρέως S.*Fr*.728; Cret. κρίως *GDI*5128 (Vaxos): pl. κρέα *IG*1².84. 26, etc.; gen. κρεῶν Od.15.98, Hdt.1.73, *IG*1².10.7, Ar.*Ra*.191, etc.; Ep. κρειῶν Il.11.551, al., κρεάων [ᾰ] *h.Merc*.130; dat. κρέασι Il.12. 311, κρέεσσι Orac.ap.Hdt.1.47, κρεάεσσι Epic. in *Arch.Pap*.7.4. [κρέᾱ Hom., E.*Cyc*.126, Ar.*V*.363, al., κρέ' elided Od.3.65, 470, Ar.*Th*. 558, κρέᾰ Antiph.20 (s.v.l.).]:—*flesh, meat*, Od.8.477, etc.; ἄρνειον κ. *piece* of lamb, Pherecr.45, cf. Ar.*Pl*.1137; ἐρίφειον Antiph.222.6; τρία κρέα [ἢ] καὶ πλείω X.*Cyr*.2.2.2; τέτταρα.. κρέα μικρά Antiph. 172.3 (anap.): pl., mostly in collect. sense, *dressed meat*, Od.3.65, etc.; κ. ἑφθά Hdt.3.23; κ. ἀνάβραστα, ὠπτημένα, Ar.*Ra*.553, *Pl*.894; κ. ὀρνίθεια Id.*Nu*.339; βοῶν Id.*Pax*1280; βόεια Pl.*R*.338c; δαῖτα παιδείων κρεῶν A.*Ag*.1242, 1593; κ. Ἀθηναίοις μερίζειν, νέμειν τῷ δήμῳ, *IG*2².334.15, 24. 2. *carcass*: hence, *body, person*, τοῦδε τοῦ κρέως (i.e. ἐμοῦ) S. l.c. (satyric): in Com. addresses, like κάρα, ὦ δεξιώτατον κρέας Ar.*Eq*.421, cf. 457: prov., ὁ λαγὼς τὸν περὶ τῶν κρεῶν [δρόμον] τρέχει 'to save one's bacon', Zen.4.85, cf. Plu.2.1087b; so νεναυμάχηκε τὴν περὶ τῶν κρεῶν Ar.*Ra*.191, v. Sch. (κρεϜας, cf. Skt. *kravís* 'raw meat', Lat. *cruor*.)

κρεγμός, ὁ, (κρέκω) *sound of stringed instruments*, Epich.109 (pl.), A.R.4.909, cf. Poll.4.63.

κρεηδόκος, ον, = κρειοδόκος, *AP*6.101 (Phil.).

κρεη-φᾰγέω, v. κρεοφαγέω. **-φάγος** [ᾰ], = κρεοφάγος, Porph. *in Cat.*84.15.

κρειοδόκος, ον, *containing flesh*, *AP*6.306.8 (Aristo).

κρεῖον, τό, (κρέας) *meat-tray, dresser*, Il.9.206:—Ion. **κρήϊον** Hsch. II. = κρέας, Euph.155.

κρεῖος, ὁ, v. κριός III, VII. **κρείουσα**, ἡ, v. κρείων.

κρειοφάγος, f.l. for κριο-, Nic.*Th.*50.

κρεΐσκος, ὁ, Dim. of κρέας, *morsel of meat*, Alex.189.

κρεισσονεύω, *to be better*, Hdn.*Epim.*69.

κρεισσότεκνος, ον, *dearer than children*, ὄμματα dub. in A.*Th.*784 (lyr.).

κρεισσόω, = κρεισσονεύω, *EM*299.22, Eust.64.15.

κρείσσων, ον, gen. ονος, as always in Ep. and old Att.; later Att. **κρείττων**; Ion. **κρέσσων** Hp.*Fract.*3, al., v.l. in Dionys.Trag. (v. infr. II); Dor. **κάρρων** (q.v.); Cret. **κάρτων** *Leg.Gort.*1.15:—Comp. of κρατύς (v. κράτιστος), *stronger, mightier*, κ. βασιλεύς, ὅτε χώσεται ἀνδρὶ χέρηϊ Il.1.80; esp. in battle, κρείσσοσιν ἶφι μάχεσθαι 21.486; Διὸς κ. νόος ἠέ περ ἀνδρῶν 16.688; κεραυνοῦ κρέσσον.. βέλος Pi.*I.*8(7).36, cf. Hdt.7.172, Hp.l.c., etc.; κρείσσων χεῖρας Antipho4.4.7; τὸ τοῦ κ. συμφέρον Pl.*R.*338c, cf. Democr.267: hence, *having the upper hand, superior*, ὁππότερος δέ κε νικήσῃ κ. τε γένηται Il.3.71; κ. ἀρετῇ τε βίῃ τε 23.578: as Law-term, of witnesses, κάρτονανς ἦμεν *prevail*, *Leg. Gort.* l.c. 2. freq. as Comp. of ἀγαθός, *better*, κρέσσονες one's *betters*, esp. in point of rank, Pi.*O.*10(11).39, *N.*10.72 (but also, *the stronger, more powerful*, E.*Or.*710, Th.1.8, etc.); ἐς τοὺς τοκέας καὶ ἐς τοὺς κρέσσονας τεθυμῶσθαι Hdt.3.52, cf. *SIG*685.134 (Magn. Mae., ii B.C.); οἱ κ. corps of guards at Thebes, Plu.2.598e; κρείσσονες θεοί, of the *greater* gods, as opp. to Oceanus, A.*Pr.*902 (lyr.); ὁ κ. Ζεύς Id. *Ag.*60 (anap.); οἱ κ. the *Higher Powers*, Id.*Fr.*10, Pl.*Sph.*216b, *Euthd.*291a, etc.; τὰ κρείσσω, = τὰ θεῖα, E.*Ion* 973; τὸ κ. the *Almighty, Providence*, *Corp.Herm.*18.11, Jul.*Ep.*204, Agath.1.16, Procop.Gaz. *Pan.*p.492; τὰ κρείσσονα one's *advantages*, τὰ ὑπάρχοντα ἡμῖν κρείσσω καταπροδοῦναι Th.4.10. 3. c. inf., οὔ τις ἐμεῖο κρείσσων.. δόμεναι no one has *a better right* to.., Od.21.345; οὐκ ἄλλος κ. παραμυθεῖσθαι Pl. *Plt.*268b; κρεῖσσόν ἐστι c. inf., 'tis *better* to.., κ. γάρ ἐστιν εἰσάπαξ θανεῖν ἤ.. πάσχειν κακῶς A.*Pr.*750, cf. 624, Hdt.3.52, etc.; τὸ μὴ εἶναι κ. ἢ τὸ ζῆν κακῶς S.*Fr.*488, cf. Apollod.Com.6; also κρείσσων εἰμί c. part., κ. γὰρ ἦσθα μηκέτ' ὢν ἢ ζῶν τυφλός thou wert *better* not alive, than living blind, S.*OT*1368, cf. *Aj.*635 (lyr.); κ. ἦν ὁ ἀγὼν μὴ γεγενημένος Aeschin.1.192, cf. D.H.6.9. II. c. gen. or ἤ, *too great for, surpassing, beyond*, ὕψος κ. ἐκπηδήματος A.*Ag.*1376; of evil deeds, κρεῖσσον' ἀγχόνης *too bad* for hanging, S.*OT*1374; κρεῖσσον δεργμάτων *too bad* to look on, E.*Hipp.*1217; θαυμάτων Id.*Ba.*667; λέγε τι σιγῆς κρεῖσσον (κρέσσον *PSI*9.1093) ἢ σιγὴν ἔχε Dionys.Trag. 6; κρείσσον' ἢ λέξαι λόγῳ τολμήματα E.*Supp.*844; κ. ἢ λόγοισιν (sc. εἰπεῖν) Id.*IT*837; ἀναρχία κ. πυρός Id.*Hec.*608; πρᾶγμα ἐλπίδος κ. γεγενημένον *worse* than one expected, Th.2.64; κ. λόγου τὸ κάλλος X.*Mem.*3.11.1; κ. τῆς ἡμετέρας δυνάμεως Id.*Cyr.*7.5.9. III. *having control over, master of*, esp. of desires and passions, τῶν ἡδονῶν Democr.214; τοῦ ἔρωτος X.*Cyr.*6.1.34; γαστρὸς καὶ κερδέων ib.4.2. 45; αὑτῶν *over* themselves, Pl.*Phdr.*232a, al.; κ. χρημάτων *superior to* the influence of money, Th.2.60, Isoc.1.19; τῶν συμμάχων κ. X. *Ath.*2.1; also, *putting oneself above*, κ. τοῦ δικαίου Th.3.84; κρείσσους ὄντες.. τῷ λογισμῷ ἐς τὸ ἀνέλπιστον τοῦ βεβαίου having reasoned themselves into an absolute belief of the hopelessness of certainty, ib.83; φαύλους καὶ κρείττους τῆς παιδείας, = οὓς παιδευθῆναι ἀδύνατον (just below), Arist.*Pol.*1316ᵃ9. IV. *better, more excellent*, ἁρμονίη ἀφανὴς φανερῆς κ. Heraclit.54; κ. ἐπ' ἀρετήν Democr.181; ὁ κρείττων λόγος (opp. ὁ ἥσσων) Ar.*Nu.*113; κατὰ τὸ κ. in a *higher* sense, opp. κατὰ τὸ χεῖρον, Dam.*Pr.*7. V. Adv. κρεισσόνως Antipho4.4.6, Iamb.*Myst.*7.4; also κρεῖσσον S.*OT*176 (lyr.), *OGI*90.31 (Rosetta, ii B.C.). (κρέσσων from κρέτ-γων, cf. κρέτος; κάρτων and κάρρων from κάρτ-γων, cf. κάρτος; κρείσσων (like μείζων) prob. took ει from ὀλείζων.)

κρειττ-όομαι, Pass., of the vine, *to be diseased, have excrescences*, Thphr.*HP*4.14.6, *CP*5.9.13:—Subst. **-ωσις**, εως, ἡ, ibid.

κρείων, οντος, ὁ, *ruler, lord, master*, Ep. word, used in Il. mostly of kings and chiefs, esp. of Agamemnon, 1.130, al. (Com. in parody, of Diomedes, Cratin.68); of gods, ὕπατε κρειόντων, of Zeus, Il.8. 31, etc.; of Poseidon, εὐρὺ κ. ἐνοσίχθων 11.751; as an honorary epithet, κ. Ἐτεωνεύς, of a squire of Menelaus, Od.4.22:—so fem. **κρείουσα** (once in Hom.), κρείουσα γυναικῶν, of a concubine of Priam, Il.22.48; Ἀντιόπη κ. *queen* Antiope, Hes.*Fr.*110.6, cf. Call. *Del.*219; Dor. κρείοισα Theoc.17.132:—after Hom. in the form **κρέων**, Pi.*P.*8.99, *N.*3.10, 7.45; of Zeus, A.*Supp.*574 (lyr.):—fem. **κρέουσα**, B.3.1: hence pr. n. Κρέων, Κρέουσα. (A participial form (κρείειν γὰρ τὸ ἄρχειν ἔλεγον οἱ παλαιοί Artem.2.12): κρείων may be due to metrical lengthening or represent *κρήων.)

κρειῶν, Ep. gen. pl. of κρέας.

κρεκάδια, ων, τά, a kind of *tapestry*, Ar.*V.*1215.

κρέκελος· θρῆνος, Hsch.

κρεκτός, ή, όν, *struck so as to sound*, of stringed instruments: generally, *played, sung*, νόμος A.*Ch.*822 (lyr.), cf. S.*Fr.*463.

κρέκω, *weave*, ἱστόν Sapph.90; πέπλους E.*El.*542. 2. *strike* a stringed instrument with the plectron, μάγαδιν Diog.Ath.1.10; βάρβιτα D.H.7.72: generally, *play on* any instrument, αὐλόν Ar.*Av.* 682 (lyr.): less freq. c. dat., κρέκειν δόνακι *APl.*4.231 (Anyte): c. acc. cogn., πηκτίδων ψαλμοῖς κ. ὕμνον Telest.5; λωτὸς ᾠδὰν κρέκει *Pae. Delph.*12; ἐν κιθάρᾳ νόμον ἔκρεκον *AP*9.584. 3. of any sharp noise, βοὴν πτεροῖς κ. Ar.*Av.*772 (lyr.), cf. *AP*7.192 (Mnasalc.); κίσσα κρέξασα ἁρμονίαν ib.191 (Arch.), cf. Hp.ap.Gal.19.114. (Cf. ONorse *hræll* (*hrahilaz) 'weaver's sley', OE. *hrægel* 'dress', 'garment', perh. Lett. *krekls* 'shirt'.)

κρεμ-άθρα, ἡ, *rope hung from a hook*, Arist.*Rh.*1412ᵃ14; οὑπὶ τῆς κ. ἀνήρ, of Socrates, Ar.*Nu.*218 (*basket* or *fowl-perch*, Sch.). **-άννῡμι**, Pl.*Lg.*830b, etc.; -ύω, Arist.*HA*612ᵃ10, Thphr.*CP*4.3.3; **κρεμάω**, Arist.*Mir.*831ᵃ8, Ael.*NA*5.3, etc.; **κρεμνάω**, Demetr.*Eloc.*216, *Gp.*4. 15.15; **κρεμάζω**, Lxx *Jb.*26.7 (v.l. κρεμνῶν): pres. part. **κρεμάντες** Ath.1.25d: fut. κρεμάσω [ᾰ] Alc.Com.8, Lxx *Ge.*40.19; Att. κρεμῶ, ᾷς, ᾷ, Ar.*Pl.*312 (lyr.); Ep. κρεμόω Il.7.83: aor. 1 ἐκρέμᾰσα Ar.*Th.* 1028, Ep. and Lyr. κρέμασα Od.8.67, Pi.*P.*4.192; Dor. inf. κραμάσαι *IG*4²(1).122.3 (Epid.); pf. κεκρέμᾰκα Corn.*ND*17:—**Med.**, aor. inf. κρεμάσασθαι Hes.*Op.*629, subj. ἐκ-κρεμάσωμαι *AP*5.91 (Rufin.):—**Pass.**, **κρέμαμαι**, Pi.*P.*5.34, Ar.*Av.*1387 (also κρεμᾶται *Anacreont.* 16.17); inf. κρέμασθαι Hp.*VM*10, *Acut.*30, Antiph.74.4; subj. κρέμωμαι Hp.*Art.*70, Arist.*Rh.*1415ᵃ13; opt. κρεμαίμην Ar.*Ach.*945, *V.* 298, *Nu.*870: impf. ἐκρεμάμην, ω, ατο, Il.15.21, etc.: fut. κρεμήσομαι in pass. sense, Ar.*Ach.*279, *V.*808, *PCair.Zen.*202.9 (iii B.C.): aor. ἐκρεμάσθην Ar.*Th.*1053, etc.: pf. imper. κεκρεμάσθω Apollod. *Poliorc.*181.7, v.l. in Archim.*Quadr.*13: plpf. κατα-κεκρέμαστο D.S. 18.26. (Cf. κρημνός, Goth. *hramjan* 'crucify'): I. *hang up*, σειρὴν.. ἐξ οὐρανόθεν κρεμάσαντες Il.8.19; τόξον ἐκ πίτυος A.*Fr.* 251; ἀπὸ κάλω κ. σαυτόν Ar.*Ra.*122; καὶ κρεμόω προτὶ νηόν will bring them to the temple and *hang them up* there as an offering, Il. 7.83; κ. τινὰ τῶν ὀρχέων Ar.*Pl.*312; κ. [τὰς ὗς] τῶν ὀπισθίων σκελῶν *by* the hind legs, Arist.*HA*632ᵃ23; κρεμάσας τὸ νόημα, in allusion to Socrates in his basket, Ar.*Nu.*229, cf. Alex.126.17; κρεμάσαι τὴν ἀσπίδα *hang up* one's shield, i.e. have done with war, Ar.*Ach.*58; τὴν πανοπλίαν Id.*Av.*436:—so in Med., πηδάλιον κρεμάσασθαι *hang up one's* rudder, i.e. give up the sea, Hes.*Op.*629. 2. *hang*, τινα Arist.*Pol.*1311ᵇ39, *Oec.*1352ᵃ11; *crucify*, Plu.*Caes.*2, etc. II. Pass., *to be hung up, suspended*, ὅτε τ' ἐκρέμω (2 sg. impf.) ὑψόθεν when *thou wert hanging*, Il.15.18, cf. 21; μηδ' ὁ Ταντάλου λίθος τῆσδ' ὑπὲρ νήσου κρεμάσθω Archil.53; *to be hung up* as a votive offering, Pi.*P.* 5.34, cf. Hdt.1.34,66, etc.; τὰ σπλάγχνα οἱ δοκέει κρέμασθαι Hp.*VM* 10; κάτω κρέμανται S.*Fr.*431; κρεμήσεται.. ἐπὶ τοῦ παττάλου Ar.*V.* 808; κ. ἐφ' ἵππων X.*An.*3.2.19; ἐκ ποδῶν κατωκάρα κ. Ar.*Ach.*945; αἱ μέλιτται κ. ἐξ ἀλλήλων Arist.*HA*627ᵇ13: metaph., ἀμφὶ φρασὶν ἀμπλακίαι κρέμανται Pi.*O.*7.25; μῶμος κρέματαί τινι censure *hangs over* him, ib.6.74; δόλιος αἰὼν ἐπ' ἀνδράσι κ. Id.*I.*8(7).14; κρέμασθαι ἔκ τινος *to be wholly taken up with* a thing, Pl.*Lg.*831c; ὁ ἐκ τοῦ σώματος κρεμάμενος X.*Smp.*8.19. 2. *to be hanged*, of persons, E. *Hipp.*1252, Aristopho9.10, *PCair.Zen.* l.c. 3. metaph., *to be in suspense*, ἵνα μὴ κρέμηται ἡ διάνοια Arist.*Rh.*1415ᵃ13; κ. [ὁ λόγος] Gal. 18(2).754. 4. = ὀκλάζω, Arat.65 (ubi v. Sch.). **-άς**, άδος, ἡ, fem. Adj. *beetling*, πέτρα A.*Supp.*795 (lyr.). **-ᾰσία**, *suspendium*, *Gloss.* **-ᾰσις**, εως, ἡ, *hanging up*, Hp.*Art.*74, Orib.8.6.16. **-ασμα**, ατος, τό, = sq., Sch.rec.A.*Pr.*157. **-ασμός**, ὁ, *suspension*, of a broken rib, unsupported by reason of the emptiness of the stomach, Hp.*Art.*49: generally, ib.76, Heliod.ap.Orib.49.9.15. **-αστάριον**, τό, *chandelier*, Anon.*in Rh.*211.2. **-αστέον**, *one must hang*, Sor. 1.51, *Gp.*16.1.11. **-αστήρ**, ῆρος, ὁ, *suspender*: οἱ κρεμαστῆρες *the muscles by which the testicles are suspended*, Gal.4.635, 18(2).998, Poll.2.173; = ὄρχεις, *PLips.*42.19 (iv A.D.), *Hippiatr.*30; but, *vasa deferentia*, Ruf.*Onom.*197, *Sat.Gon.*10, Paul.Aeg.6.61; a supposed *muscle suspending the ovaries*, Sor.1.12. 2. *stalk* by which a grape-cluster hangs, *Gp.*5.2.11, 5.17.5. II. = ταρσός I, Eust. 1625.14. **-αστός**, ή, όν, *hung, suspended*, γυνή S.*OT*1263; κ. αὐχένος *hung by* the neck, Id.*Ant.*1221: c. gen., *hung from* or *on* a thing, παραστάδος κρεμαστὰ τεύχη E.*Andr.*1122; κ. ἀρτάνη, i.e. a halter, S.*OT*1266; βρόχοι κ. E.*Hipp.*779; σκεύη κ. the *rigging* of ships, opp. ξύλινα σκ., X.*Oec.*8.12; τὰ κ. ἱστία Hermipp.63.12; κλινίδιον κ. *hammock*, Plu.*Per.*27; κ. ποτιστρέα *PTeb.*527 (ii A.D.); κ. σταφυλή, i.e. dried grapes, Alex.Trall.8.1; οἱ κ. κῆποι *hanging* gardens, Plu.2.342b; κ. παράδεισος Beros.ap.J.*AJ*10.11.1; κρεμαστά, τά, *fortresses*, Lxx *Jd.*6.2. **-άστρα**, ἡ, Hellen. for κρεμάθρα (Moer. p.242 P.), Eust.1625.17, v.l. in Arist.*Rh.*1412ᵃ14. 2. *stalk by which a flower hangs*, Thphr.*HP*3.16.4. **-αστρον**, τό, *larder*, *Gloss.* **-άω**, v. κρεμάννυμι.

κρέμβᾰλ-α, τά, *castanets*, *Carm.Pop.*3. **-ιάζω**, *mark time with castanets*, Hermipp.31 (-ίζουσι codd. Ath.), cf. Hsch. **-ιαστύς**, ύος, ἡ, *rattling with castanets*, to give the time in dancing, *h.Ap.*162 (v.l. -αστής, οῦ, ὁ).

κρέμβολα, τά, *bobbins, reels*, Hsch. **κρέμ(μ)υον**, τό, = κρόμμυον, Id. **κρεμόω**, Ep. fut. of κρεμάννυμι. **κρέμυς**, υος, ἡ, = χρέμυς, Arist.*Fr.*294. **κρεμών**, = ἀκρεμών, Eratosth.27. **κρέννω**, Thessal. for κρίνω (q.v.).

κρέξ, ἡ, gen. κρεκός, a long-legged bird, perh. *corn-crake*, *Rallus crex*, or *ruff*, *Machetes pugnax*, τούτους (sc. λίθους) ἐτύκιζον αἱ κρέκες τοῖς ῥύγχεσιν Ar.*Av.*1138, cf. Arist.*PA*695ᵃ22, Ael.*NA*4.5; sacred to Athena, Porph.*Abst.*3.5; [ἡ ἶβις] μέγαθος ὅσον κ. Hdt.2.76; a name of ill omen to the newly-married, Euph.4: hence δισάρπαγος κρέξ, of Helen, Lyc.513. 2. metaph., *noisy braggart*, Eup. 423. II. *hair*, Hsch., Suid.: acc. κρέκαν Eust.1528.18.

κρεο-, representing stem of κρέας in Compds., freq. written κρεω- in codd.

κρεο-βορέω, *eat flesh*, D.S.24.1 (κρεω-). **-βόρος**, ον, *fed on flesh*, A.*Supp.*287 (Abresch for κρεόβροτος). **-δαισία**, ἡ, *distribution* *of meat*, Demetr.Sceps.ap.Ath.10.425c, Plu.2.643a. **-δαιτέω**, *distribute meat*, Zonar. **-δαίτης**, ου, ὁ, *distributor of meat, carver at a public meal*, Plu.*Lys.*23, *Ages.*8, Poll.6.34, 7.25: **κρεω-**, Phld.*Vit.* p.26 J.:—fem. **κρεοδαῖτις** ἀρχή Poll.6.34. **-δείρα**, ἡ, (δείρω) *flaying-knife*, Id.7.25 (κρεωδ- codd.). **-δοσία**, ἡ, = κρεοδαισία, Zonar., v.l. in Plu.*Demetr.*11: **-δοτέω**, Zonar.: **-δότης**, ου, ὁ, = κρεοδαίτης, *CIG* 4485 (Palmyra), Suid. **-δόχος**, ον, = κρειοδόκος, Sch.Il.9.206, Hsch. s.v. κρῄϊον, *EM*536.57 (κρεω-). **-θέτης**, ου, ὁ, *butcher, Gloss.* (κρεω- cod.). **-θηκάριος**, ὁ, *one who has charge of the larder*, title of priest, *Supp.Epigr.*4.357 (Panamara). **-θήκη**, ἡ, *larder*, Hsch. s.v. κρῄϊνον. **-κάκκᾰβος**, *a mess of meat hashed with fat and blood*, Ath.9.384d. **-κοπέω**, *cut up like meat*: hence, *hack in pieces*, κ. δυστήνων μέλη A.*Pers.*463; μέλη ξένων E.*Cyc.*359 (lyr.). **-κόπος**, ὁ, *cutter up of flesh*, D.H.12.2.8 (pl.), *Gloss.* **-ποιός**, ὁ, *butcher*, ib. **-πωλέω**, *deal in butcher's meat*, Poll.6.33, 7.25. **-πώλης**, ου, ὁ, *seller of meat, butcher*, Machoap.Ath.13.580c, cf. *AP*11.212 (Lucill.), Thphr.*Char.*9.4 (κρεω-). **-πωλικός**, ή, όν, *of* or *for a butcher*, τράπεζα Plu.2.643a:—fem. **-πωλις** ἀγορά the *meat* market, Hsch. s.v. κάπηλα. **-πώλιον**, τό, *butcher's shop*, D.S.12.24, Str.17.2.4, Plu.2.277e, Poll.7.25. **-σιτέω**, *live on meat*, Id.6.33. **-στάθμη**, ἡ, *butcher's steelyard*, Ar.*Fr.*799. **-τομέω**, = κρεοκοπέω, Tz.*H.*13.410.

κρεουργ-έω, *cut up like a butcher*, J.*AJ*13.12.6: hence, *butcher, mangle*, Luc.*Syr.D.*55, D.L.9.108:—Pass., Ph.2.544, D.C.75.7. **-ηδόν**, Adv. *like a butcher, in pieces*, τοὺς ἄνδρας κ. διασπᾶν Hdt. 3.13 (Ion. κρεοργ-). **-ία**, ἡ, *cutting up, butchering*, Πέλοπος Luc. *Salt.*54. **-ικός**, ή, όν, *of* or *for a butcher or his trade, Gloss.* **-ός**, όν, *working*, i.e. *cutting up, meat*: κρεουργὸν ἦμαρ a day *of slaughter and feasting*, A.*Ag.*1592. II. Subst. κ., ὁ, *butcher* or *carver*, Poll. 7.25.

κρεο-φᾰγέω, Ion. **κρεηφ-**, *eat flesh*, Hp.*Salubr.*7, Plb.2.17.10 (v.l. κρεα-), Str.16.4.17, Ph.2.398 (vv.ll. κρεω-, κρεη-):—Pass., κάμηλοι κρεοφαγούμεναι D.S.2.54. **-φᾰγία**, Ion. **κρεηφᾰγίη**, ἡ, *eating of flesh*, Hp.*Acut.*37, D.S.3.31, Ph.2.235 (vv.ll. κρεω-, κρεη-), Porph. *Abst.*1.15, al.; κ. τῶν θηρίων Str.16.4.9; χρῆσθαι κρεοφαγίᾳ Plu.2. 132a (κρεω-). **-φάγος** [ᾰ], ον, *eating flesh, carnivorous*, Hdt.4.186, Arist.*PA*693^{a}3, etc.; cf. κρεηφάγος.

κρέσσων, v. κρείσσων.

κρετέω, κρέτος, Aeol. for κρατέω, κράτος (qq. v.).

κρεω-, v. κρεο-.

κρεώδης, ες, *fleshy*, Arist.*HA*491^{b}25, 583^{b}10; ὀσμὴ κ. odour *of flesh*, Thphr.*Fr.*167; κ. τροφή *meat* diet, Gal.10.849; τὰ κ. Id.6.600.

κρέων, v. κρείων.

κρεών, ὁ, *larder, Gloss.* (dub.).

κρήγυος, ον, Dor. **κράγυος** [ᾱ] Cerc.7.14, Lysis *Ep.*3:—*good, useful* or *agreeable*, once in Hom., οὐ πώ ποτέ μοι τὸ κ. εἶπας Il.1.106; ἄλλο μὲν οὐδὲν κ. *AP*7.284 (Asclep.); οὐδὲ γουνάτων πόνος κρήγυον *a good symptom*, Hp.*Coac.*31; τό τοι μέγα κρήγυον ἔσται Nic.*Th.*935; ποτὶ οὐδὲν κράγυον σχολάζοντες Lysis l.c. Adv. κρηγύως ἐπαιδεύθην Call.*Iamb.*1.196; νομίμως καὶ κ. *honourably*, Perict.ap.Stob.4.28. 19. 2. by a misunderstanding of Hom., *true, real*, εἴπατέ μοι τὸ κ. Theoc.20.19, cf. Hp.*Ep.*17, *AP*7.648 (Leon.), Anon.ap.Stob.3. 28.21: as Adv., *in good earnest*, πορθεῖς με τὸ κ. *AP*5.57 (Arch.). 3. of persons, *good, serviceable*, οὐκ ἐπίστανται, οὐδὲ κ. διδάσκαλοί εἰσι Pl.*Alc.*1.111e; εἰ δ' ἐσσὶ κ. τε καὶ παρὰ χρηστῶν Theoc.*Ep.*19; παρ' οἴνῳ κ. *AP*7.355 (Damag.); esp. of a woman, *honest*, Herod.4.46, 6.39.

κρηδεμνόκομος, ον, *wearing the* κρήδεμνον, Aus.*Ep.*8.13.

κρήδεμνον, Dor. **κρᾱδ-**, τό, (κράς, δέω) *woman's head-dress* or *veil*, a kind of *mantilla*, κ. ὅ ῥά οἱ (sc. Ἀνδρομάχῃ) δῶκε χρυσέη Ἀφροδίτη Il.22.470; κρηδέμνῳ δ' ἐφύπερθε καλύψατο δῖα θεάων 14.184: pl., [Πηνελόπεια] ἄντα παρειάων σχομένη λιπαρὰ κ. Od.1.334; δμῳαί τε καὶ αὐτή, .. ἀπὸ κ. βαλοῦσαι 6.100, cf. E.*Ph.*1490 (lyr.). II. metaph. in pl., *battlements* which *crown* a city's walls, Τροίης ἱερὰ κ. Il.16.100, cf. Od.13.388, *h.Cer.*151, B.*Fr.*16.7; πέτρινα κ. E.*Tr.*508: sg., Θήβης κρήδεμνον Hes.*Sc.*105. 2. *cover, lid* of a wine-jar, Od.3.392.

κρήδεσμον· κεφαλόδεσμον, Hsch. **κρηῆναι, κρήηνον**, v. κραίνω. **κρηθεῖν**· κακολογεῖν, Id. **κρῆθεν**, Adv., v. κράς II.

κρῆθμον, τό, *samphire, Crithmum maritimum*, Hp.*Nat.Mul.*2, al., Call.*Fr.*64, Lyc.238 (pl., accented κρηθμοῖσι), Nic.*Th.*909. (Neut. in Dsc.2.129, Ruf.*Ren.Ves.*1.18 (pl.); masc. **κρῆθμος**, ὁ, Eust.582. 16, *crethmus* Plin.*HN*26.158; **κρῖθμος** (sic), Hdn.Gr.1.167.)

κρή-ϊνον, τό, *larder*, Hsch. (s.v.l.). **-ϊον**, τό, Ion. for κρεῖον, kind of *bride-cake*, Philet.ap.Ath.14.645d: pl., = ζῴδια (i.e. cakes in shape of animals), Hsch. II. v. κρεῖον I.

κρημν-άω, = κρήμνημι, D.L.6.50, *PHolm.*8.11 (κριμ-). **-ηγορέω**, (κρημνός) *speak rugged words*, Tz. ad Hes.*Op.*p.10 G. **-ημι**, = κρεμάννυμι, *hang*, ἄγκυραν ποτὶ .. ναὶ κρημνάντων Pi.*P.*4.25, cf. Arist.*Mir.* 831^{a}8 (v.l.); κρήμνη (imper.) σεαυτὴν ἐκ .. ἀντηρίδος E.*Fr.*1111 (= Eup.455); *crucify*, τούσδε ἐκρήμνη (impf.) App.*Mith.*97:—Pass., κρήμναμαι *hang, be suspended*, E.*El.*1217 (lyr., κριμν-), App.*BC*1.71; *float in air*, ὑπερθ' ὀμμάτων κρημναμενᾶν νεφελᾶν A.*Th.*229 (lyr.). **-ίζω**, *hurl down headlong*, κατὰ τοῦ τείχους Lxx 2*Ma.*6.10: metaph., ἐπὶ ἀτάκτους ἡδονὰς ἑαυτοὺς κ. Plu.2.5b:—Pass., J.*BJ*2.3.3, *Cat.Cod. Astr.*8(4).156. **-ισις**, εως, ἡ, *hurling down headlong*, Sch.Th. 7.45. **-ισμός**, ὁ, = foreg., Ptol.*Tetr.*151, Doroth. in *Cat.Cod.Astr.* 5(3).84 (pl.).

κρημνο-βᾰτέω, *haunt precipices*, Ctes.ap.Lyd.*Mens.*4.14, Str.15. 1.56, Ph.2.444, S.E.*M.*11.126, Longus 3.28. **-βάτης** [ᾰ], ου, Dor. **-ᾱς**, ὁ, *climber of steeps*, Πάν *AP*9.142, cf. Polyaen.4.3.29. 2. *rope-dancer*, Hsch. **-γρᾰφος**, ον, *written in rugged style, uncouth*, ῥήματα Tz. ad Hes.*Op.*p.9 G.

κρημνο-κοπέω, *boast, indulge in 'tall talk'*, Phot., Suid. **-ποιός**, όν, *speaking crags*, i.e. *using big, rugged words*, of Aeschylus, Ar.*Nu.* 1367.

κρημνός (A), ὁ, heterocl. pl. **κρημνά**, τά, v.l. for κρημνούς in Eus. Mynd.63:—*overhanging bank*, in Hom. (only Il.) of the *bank* of a river, *edge* of a trench, 12.54, 21.175, 234, 244, cf. Pi.*O.*3.22; κ. θαλάσσας Id.*Fr.*201; κ. μαλακοί Arist.*HA*615^{b}31; later, *beetling cliff, crag*, ἀπὸ τοῦ κ. ὠθέειν Hdt.4.103; ἀναθεῖναι ἐπὶ κρημνόν τιν' Ar.*Pl.*69; κατὰ τῶν κ. ἅλλεσθαι down from the *cliffs* of Epipolae, Th.7.45; κατὰ κ. ῥιφέντες Pl.*Lg.*944a; οἱ Κ., the *Screes*, on the Sea of Azof, Hdt.4.20, 110. 2. in pl., *edges* of an ulcer, Hp.*Loc.Hom.*29. 3. *labia pudendi*, ib.47, Poll.2.174, Ruf.*Onom.*112.

κρημνός (B), v. κριμνός.

κρημνοφοβέομαι, *to be afraid of precipices*, Hp.*Ep.*19 (*Hermes* 53. 70).

κρημν-ώδης, ες, *precipitous*, Th.7.84, Dsc.4.144, Onos.10.17, etc.; τὸ κ. τῆς ὄχθης Plu.*Tim.*31: Sup., Hdn.6.5.5. **-ώρεια**, ἡ, *steep mountain-ridge*, Hdn.*Epim.*232.

κρημοφόρος, ὁ, dub. sens., οἰνοχόαι καὶ κρημοφόροι *IG*2^2.1425.358.

κρην-άγγη· ἀρχὴ ἐπὶ τῆς ἐπιμελείας ὕδατος, Hsch. **-αῖος**, α, ον, (κρήνη) *of, from a spring* or *fountain*, Νύμφαι κρηναῖαι, = Κρηνιάδες, Od.17. 240; κ. ὕδωρ *spring* water, Hdt.4.181; ποτόν S.*Tr.*14, *Ph.*21; νασμοί E.*Hipp.*225 (anap.); γάνος, i.e. the water of Dirce, A.*Pers.*483; λιβάδες *AP*9.549 (Antiphil.); Κ. πύλαι the gate *of Dirce* (v. Sch.), E.*Ph.* 1123. **-η**, Dor. **κράνα** *IG*4^2(1).121.6 (Epid.), etc.; Aeol. **κράννα** ib.12(2).103 (Mytil.): ἡ:—*well, spring, fountain*, μελάνυδρος, καλλιρέεθρος, Il.16.3, Od.10.107, cf. Pi.*P.*1.39, al., Pl.*Phd.*112c, etc.; opp. φρέαρ (q.v.), Hdt.4.120, Th.2.48; ἐμπλησαμένη τὴν ὑδρίαν .. ἀπὸ κρήνης Ar.*Lys.*328; κ. οἴνου E.*Ba.*707; ὀμνύω .. κράνας καὶ ποταμούς *SIG* 527.34 (Dreros, iii B.C.): poet. in pl., for *water*, S.*OC*686, *Ant.*844 (both lyr.); κρηνῶν ἐπιμελητής, title of official at Athens, *IG*2^2.338. 11, Arist.*Ath.*43.1, cf. Pl.*Lg.*758e, Arist.*Pol.*1321^{b}26, *OGI*483.159 (Pergam.). **-ηθεν**, Adv. *from a well* or *spring*, *AP*15.25.18 (Besant.). **-ήϊος**, ον, = κρηναῖος, metaph., of the source of things, ἀρχή Orac.ap.Dam.*Pr.*344. **-ηνδε**, Adv. *to a well* or *spring*, Od. 20.154. **-ιάς**, άδος, ἡ, pecul. fem. of κρηναῖος, Νύμφαι Κρηνιάδες A.*Fr.*168 (hex.). **-ίδιον**, τό, Dim. of κρήνη, Arist.*Mir.*841^{b}9, Antig. *Mir.*142, etc. **-ίον**, τό, = foreg., *Inscr.Délos* 290.75 (iii B.C.), Str.3. 4.17, *IGRom.*4.1657 (Almura). **-ίς**, ῖδος, ἡ, = κρήνη, E.*Hipp.*208 (anap.), Call.*Fr.anon.*98, Theoc.1.22 (Dor. κρᾱν-), D.H.1.32. II. pl. Κρηνῖδες, αἱ, ancient name for Philippi in Macedonia, Str.7 *Fr.*34, App.*BC*4.105; τὰ ἐγ Κρηνῖσιν, as local place-name, *IG*12(5).544 *B* 2. 47 (Ceos). **-ῖτις**, ιδος, ἡ, *growing near a spring*, βοτάναι Hp.*Ep.* 16. **-ιῶν**· καρηβαρῶν, Hsch. **-οῦχος**, ον, *ruling over springs*, of Poseidon, Corn.*ND*22.

κρηνο-φῠλάκιον [ᾰ], τό, *office of the* κρηνοφύλαξ, Poll.8.113. **-φύλαξ** [ῠ], ἄκος, ὁ, *warden of the springs*, *IG*11(2).159 *A* 61, 161 *A* 85 (Delos, iii B.C.); at Athens, *official in charge of the* κλεψύδρα, Poll.8. 113, Phot. 2. bronze lion *which stood over the spring that supplied the* κλεψύδρα, Poll. l.c., Phot.

κρηπῖδ-αῖον, τό, *basement of a house*, Lys.*Fr.*185 S.:—also **-ειον**, *IG*14.915 (Ostia). **-ιαῖος**, α, ον, *belonging to a substructure* or *foundation*, [λίθοι] ib.1^2.313.90, cf. *Rev.Phil.* 50.67 (Didyma, ii B.C.). **-ιον**, τό, Dim. of κρηπίς, *kerb*, ib.43.213, *Cinquantenaire de l'école des hautes études* p.89 (Didyma, ii B.C., pl.).

κρηπῖδοποιός, ὁ, *boot-maker*, Ath.13.568e.

κρηπῖδ-ουργός, οῦ, ὁ, = foreg., Din.*Fr.*89.20. **-όω**, (κρηπίς) *furnish with boots*:—Pass., *put on one's boots*, Anon.ap.Suid. 2. *furnish with a quay*, D.C.60.11; *furnish with a foundation, found*, Id. 51.1:—Pass., *to be supported*, ἐπὶ θατέρου σκέλους Plu.2.233b. **-ωμα**, ατος, τό, *foundation*, *Inscr.Magn.*293, *JHS*15.127 (Termessus), D.S. 13.82, Aq.*Ez.*43.14.

κρηπίς, ῖδος, ἡ, *man's high boot* (cf. *AB*273), *half-boot*, Hegem. *Parod.*4, X.*Eq.*12.10, Thphr.*Char.*2.7 (dub.): distd. from ὑποδήματα, Aristocl.Hist.8; κ. λευκαί, a mark of effeminacy, Timae.82. b. κρηπῖδες *soldiers' boots*, i.e. *soldiers* themselves, Theoc.15.6. 2. *shoe-shaped cake*, Poll.6.77. II. generally, *groundwork, foundation, basement* of a building or altar, Hdt.1.93, S.*Tr.*993 (anap.), E.*Ion* 38 (pl.), *HF*985, X.*An.*3.4.7, *IG*1^2.372.67; κ. καὶ στυλοβάτας ib.4^2(1).102.7 (Epid.); τύμβου 'πὶ κρηπῖδ' E.*Hel.*547: metaph., βάλλεσθαι κρηπῖδα σοφῶν ἐπέων Pi.*P.*4.138; κ. ἀοιδᾶν βαλέσθαι ib.7.3; ἐβάλοντο φαεννὰν κρηπῖδ' ἐλευθερίας Id.*Fr.*77; κ. γένους E.*HF*1261; ἡ ἐγκράτεια ἀρετῆς κ. X.*Mem.*1.5.4, cf. Onos.4.4; οὐδέπω κακῶν κ. ὕπεστιν we have not yet got to the *bottom* of misery, A.*Pers.*815; κ. θαλάσσης Opp.*H.*3.453, 5.48; κ. καὶ ἕδρα νόσου *foundation* and seat of disease, Max.Tyr.13.7. 2. *walled edge* of a river or canal, *quay*, Hdt.1. 185, 2.170, Plb.5.37.8, *PTeb.*382.9 (i B.C.); *abutment* of a bridge, *Epigr.Gr.*1078.3 (Adana); *tiers* of seats in a theatre, *IG*11(2).203 *A* 95 (Delos, iii B.C.). III. *ox-tongue, Helminthia echioides*, Thphr. *HP*7.8.3, Plin.*HN*21.99. IV. a bandage, Sor.*Fasc.*59.

Κρής, ὁ, gen. Κρητός, mostly in pl. Κρῆτες, ῶν, *Cretan*, Il.2.645, etc.: prov., ὁ Κρὴς τὸν πόντον (sc. ἀγνοεῖ), of those who feign ignorance, Alcm.115, cf. Str.10.4.17:—fem. **Κρῆσσα**, ης, Sapph.54: in pl., title of play by Aeschylus: as Adj., *Cretan*, Κρῆτα τρόπον Simon. 31; Κρὴς ταῦρος Apollod.2.5.7; μητρὸς .. Κρήσσης S.*Aj.*1295:—regul. Adj. **Κρήσιος**, α, ον, Id.*Tr.*119, E.*Hipp.*372 (both lyr.), Limen.39, etc.:—more freq. **Κρητικός**, ή, όν (q.v.).

κρῆς, Dor. for κρέας, Sophr.25, Ar.*Ach.*795, Theoc.1.6.

κρησέρ-α, ἡ, Ion. **κρησέρη**, Elean **κρααρα** (q.v.), *flour-sieve, bolting-sieve*, Hp.*Steril.*222 (but expld. as a *straining-cloth* by Erot.), Ar.*Ec.*991, Gal.*Nat.Fac.*2.3, Aret.*CA*1.4, Poll.6.74:—Dim. **-ιον**, τό, Id.10.114, Zonar. II. *fine net for fishing*, Phot. **-ίτης** [ῑ] ἄρτος, ὁ, bread *of sifted flour*, Diph.26.

κρησίαι· καλλίονες, Hsch. **Κρήσιος**, α, ον, v. Κρής. **κρησίπαιδα** (fort. -πεδα)· ἐν Σαμιακῇ θυσίᾳ..μέρη ἱερείων, Id. **Κρῆσσα**, v. Κρής.

κρηστήριον, τό, perh. = κρεῖον I, *IG*2².1543 (iv B.C.).

κρησ-φύγετον [ῠ], τό, (φεύγω) *place of refuge, retreat*, Hdt.5.124, al., D.H.4.15, Luc.*Eun.*10, al. (Etym. dub.; expld. by *EM*538.1 as *refuge from the Cretan*, i.e. Minos.) **-φύγιον** [ῠ], τό, = foreg., Steph.*in Rh.*253.2.

Κρηταιεύς, Att. **Κρηταεύς** *IG*2².687.25: ὁ:—*Cretan*, A.R.1.1129, Plb.6.46.3, *GDI*5160 (Mylasa), *AP*7.448 (Leon.):—fem. **-αιίς**, ίδος, ib.6.299 (Phan.):—also **Κρηταῖος**, α, ον, A.R.2.1233, *AP*14.129.

κρητάριον, τό, Dim. of Lat. *creta, piece of chalk*, *Gp.*2.42.2 (κριτ-), Aët.2.10, Charis.p.553 K., *Hippiatr.*49.

Κρητάρχης, ου, ὁ, *president of the* κοινόν *of Crete*, *CIG*2744 (Aphrodisias).

Κρήτη, ἡ, *Crete*, Il.2.649, etc.: pl., Κρητάων εὐρειάων Od.14.199, 16.62: **Κρήτηθεν** or **-θε**, *from Crete*, Il.3.233, Q.S.5.350, Porph.*Abst.*2.21: **Κρήτηνδε** *to Crete*, Od.19.186.

κρήτη, ἡ, = Lat. *creta, chalk*, *PMag.Lond.*121.858:—hence prob. **κρητηρία**, ἡ, ib.169; cf. κρητάριον.

κρητήρ, ῆρος, ὁ, Ion. and Ep. for κρατήρ (q.v.). **κρητηρίζω**, v. κρατηρίζω.

Κρητ-ίζω, (Κρής) *speak like a Cretan*, D.Chr.[11.23]. II. *play the Cretan*, i.e. *lie*, πρὸς Κρῆτας or Κρῆτα κ. 'diamond cut diamond', Plb.8.18.5, Plu.*Aem.*23, *Lys.*20. **-ικός**, ή, όν, *Cretan*, A.*Ch.*616 (lyr.), Ar.*Ra.*849, etc.; τὸ Κ. πέλαγος Th.4.53, etc. Adv. **-κῶς** *in Cretan fashion*, Ar.*Ec.*1165. II. **Κρητικόν** (sc. ἱμάτιον), τό, *short garment*, used at sacred rites, Id.*Th.*730, Eup.311. 2. Κρητικός (sc. πούς), ὁ, a metrical foot [– ⏑ –], = ἀμφίμακρος, Heph.3.2, cf. A.D.*Pron.*50.16; so ἔγειρε.., Μοῦσα, Κ. μέλος Cratin.222; τὸ Κ. (sc. μέτρον) Heph.13.1; Κ. ῥυθμός, ῥυθμοί, D.H.*Comp.*25, Str.10.4.16. **-ισμός**, ὁ, *Cretan behaviour*, i.e. *lying*, Plu.*Aem.*26.

Κρητογενής, ές, *born in Crete*, epith. of Zeus, *GDI*5075.73 (Latos).

κρῖ, τό, Ep. for κριθή, *barley*, only as nom. and acc., κρῖ λευκόν Il.8.564, Od.4.41, al.

κρῖβᾰν-άριος, ὁ, in form **κλῖβ-**, *armoured cavalryman*, *Zeitschr.Deutsch.Pal.Vereins* 44.93 (Jerusalem, iv/v A.D.), *Stud.Pal.*20.135.4 (vi A.D.), Lyd.*Mag.*1.46; cf. Lat. *clibanarius*, *Cod.Theod.*14.17.9, etc. II. *baker*, dub. in *CIL*4.677, *Stud.Pal.*20.131.4 (vi A.D.). **-εῖον**, τό, *bakery*, *BGU*1117.24 (i B.C., κλ-). **-εύς**, έως, ὁ, *baker*, *POxy.*1142.10 (iii A.D., κλ-), Man.1.80 (κλ-). **-η**, ἡ, or **-ης**, ὁ, *a cake*, Alcm.20 (-νωτος codd. Ath.), cf. Hsch. **-ίκιος**, ον, = κριβανίτης, Ath.3.113b (κλ-). **-ικός**, ή, όν, *belonging to a bakery*, σκεύη *BGU*1117.11 (i B.C., κλ-). **-ιον**, τό, *baking-oven*, *PLond.*5.1733.23 (vi A.D.). **-ιος**, ον, *for baking*, ἐργαστήριον *BGU*1117.8 (i B.C., κλ-), cf. *PTeb.*351.6 (ii A.D.). **-ίτης** [νῑ], ου, ὁ, *baked in a pan* (κρίβανος), of bread, Ar.*Fr.*125, Epich.52, Amips.5, Sophr.27 (also κλ- Id.28), Gal.6.489, etc.; ὁ κ. (sc. ἄρτος) *loaf so baked*, Ar.*Ach.*1123: hence, comically, βοῦς κ. ib.87.

κρῖβᾰνοειδής, ές, in form **κλῖβ-**, *shaped like a* κρίβανος, Dsc.1.72.4; ἔσοπτρον Anthem.p.151 W.

κρίβᾰν-ον [ῐ], τό, = sq., Pherecr.169. **-ος**, ὁ, Att. for **κλίβανος** (which is called Dor. in *EM*538.19, cf. Epich.143, and is the usu. form in Pap., *PPetr.*3 p.328 (iii B.C.), etc.), *covered earthen vessel*, wider at bottom than at top, wherein bread was baked by putting hot embers round it, Hdt.2.92 (in form κλιβ-), A.*Fr.*309, Ar.*Ach.*86, *V.*1153, al., Antiph.176.5; οὕτως εἰμὶ ὡς εἰς κρίβανον *POxy.*1842.7 (vi A.D.); *potter's oven*, *PCair.Zen.*271.9 (iii B.C., κλ-). 2. *funnel-shaped vessel*, used for drawing water, Str.16.2.13 (κλ-). II. *underground channel* or *vaulted passage*, in irrigation works, *Sammelb.*7188.17 (ii B.C., κλ-). 2. *hollow, cavern in a rock*, Ael.*NA* 2.22. **-ωτός**, ή, όν, *baked in a* κρίβανος, hence κριβανωτός (sc. ἄρτος), ὁ, Alcm.20 (codd. Ath.), Ar.*Pl.*765; κ. ζῷα Eust.1286.19.

κρίγδανον· πέλτη, ἀσπίς, Hsch.

κρῐγή, ἡ, (κρίζω) *gnashing of teeth*, Sch.Ar.*Av.*1520:—also **κριγμός**, Zonar. II. *shrieking*, νεκρῶν Hippon.54. III. κριγή· ἡ γλαύξ, Hsch.

κριδδέμεν, Boeot. for κρίζειν (= γελᾶν), Stratt.47.7.

κρίδιον [ῐ], τό, contr. from κριΐδιον, Dim. of κριός, Hsch. **κρίες**· ἡ χελιδών, Id. **κρίζαος**· ψώρα, κρίζα, Id. **κριζόν**· ἐπίλεκτον, διάφορον, Id.

κρίζω, aor. I ἔκριξα Ael.*NA*5.50, Hsch.: aor. 2 and pf. (v. infr.):—*creak*, κρίκε ζυγόν Il.16.470. II. of persons, *screech*, ὥσπερ Ἰλλυριοὶ κεκριγότες Ar.*Av.*1521; χαμαιτύπη κρίζει τις Men.879; in Boeot., *laugh*, v. κριδδέμεν. (Onomatop.)

κρῑηδόν, Adv., (κριός) *like a ram*, Ar.*Lys.*309.

κρίθα· κρίθινον, καὶ ἵππου ἀρρώστημα, Hsch.

κρῑθ-αία, ἡ, (κριθή) *barley-pottage*, Hom.*Epigr.*15.7. **-άλευρον** [ᾰ], τό, *barley-meal*, Aët.12.71. **-άμῑνος** [ᾰ], η, ον, = κρίθινος, ἄλευρα Polyaen.4.3.32. **-ανίας**, ου, ὁ, *like barley*: κ. πυρός a branching cereal, perh. *millet*, Thphr.*HP*8.2.3. **-άριον**, τό, Dim. of κριθή, *BGU*33.11 (pl., ii/iii A.D.), *PTeb.*420.21 (iii A.D.), Thom.Mag.p.202 R. **-άχῠρον** [ᾰ], τό, *mixture of barley and chaff*, *PFlor.*377.14 (vi A.D.). **-άω**, of a horse, *to be barley-fed, wax wanton*, κριθῶν πῶλος A.*Ag.*1641; κριθώσης ὄνου S.*Fr.*876. **-ή**, ἡ, mostly in pl., *barley-corns, barley* (cf. κρῖ), the meal being ἄλφιτα: πυρῶν ἢ κριθῶν Il.11.69, cf. Od.9.110, 19.112, Ar.*Eq.*1101; κριθᾶν μέδιμμνον *IG*4²(1).40.7 (Epid.); "τὰς οὐλοχύτας φέρε δεῦρο"—"τοῦτο δ' ἐστὶ τί;"—"κριθαί" Strato Com.1.35; οἶνος ἐκ κριθέων πεποιημένος a kind of *beer*, Hdt.2.77; ἐκ κριθῶν μέθυ A.*Supp.*953, cf. Arist.*Fr.*106; κριθαὶ πεφρυγμέναι, = κάχρυς, Th.6.22, cf. Moer.p.213 P.: pl., also of *species of barley*, Thphr.*HP*8.1.1: sg., *PGrenf.*2.29.9 (ii B.C.); κ. Ἰνδική *millet*, *Sorghum halepense*, Thphr.*HP*8.4.2. II. *pustule on the eyelid, stye*, Hp.*Epid.*2.2.5, Gal.12.742. III. *barley-corn, the smallest weight*, Thphr.*Lap.*46. IV. in sg., = πόσθη, Ar.*Pax*965. (The connexion with Lat. *hordeum*, OHG. *gersta* is doubtful.)

κριθθός, όν, dub. sens., κὴπὶ τὸν κριθθὸν κοῖλον *GDI*5016.11 (Gortyn).

κρῑθί-ᾱσις, εως, ἡ, a disease of horses, *surfeit caused by over-feeding with barley*, X.*Eq.*4.2, *Hippiatr.*8, al. **-άω**, of a horse, *suffer from* κριθίασις, Arist.*HA*604ᵇ8. II. = κριθάω, *wax wanton*, Cleanth.*Stoic.*1.132, Cerc.17.36, Babr.62.2, cf. Poll.7.24.

κρῑθ-ίδιον, τό, Dim. of κριθή, *decoction of barley*, Hp.*Nat.Mul.*53 (s.v.l.). 2. in pl., *a little barley*, Posidon.36 J., Luc.*Asin.*3, 47. **-ίζω**, *feed with barley*, Aesop.178, Babr.76.2. **-ικός**, ή, όν, *consisting in barley*, φόρος *BGU*922.7 (iii A.D.). **-ῐνος**, η, ον, *made of* or *from barley*, κόλλιξ, ἄρτος, Hippon.35, Luc.*Macr.*5; ἄχυρον, ἄλευρον, Thphr.*HP*8.4.1, *PEleph.*5.25 (iii B.C.), Plu.2.397a; τὸ κ. ποτόν Hp.*Acut.*64; κ. ὕδωρ ib.(*Sp.*)30; κ. οἶνος *beer*, Plb.34.9.15; πόμα Plu.2.752b: metaph., κ. Δημοσθένης, 'gingerbread Demosthenes', nickname of Dinarchus, Hermog.*Id.*2.11. **-ίον**, τό, Dim. of κριθή, Luc.*Asin.*17, Longus 3.30.

κρίθμος, v. κρῆθμον.

κρῑθό-γιτον· ἀπόβριμα (fort. -κριμα) κριθῆς, Hsch. **-κανον**· σπέρμα μελανθίῳ ὅμοιον, Id. **-λόγος**, ον, *gathering barley*: among the Opuntii, a *magistrate who kept the barley for sacrifices*, Plu.2.292c:—hence **-λογία**, ἡ, *Cod.Theod.*14.26.1. **-μαντεῖα**, τά, *divination by barley*, Oenom.ap.Eus.*PE*5.25. **-μαντις**, εως, ὁ, *one who divined by barley*, Suid. s.v. προφητεία. **-πομπία**, ἡ, *sending of barley*, Eratosth.ap.Hsch. s.v. Ῥοίκου κ. **-πῡρον**, τό, *wheat mixed with barley*, *PPetr.*3 p.206, al. (iii B.C.), *PSI*5.532.6 (iii B.C.), *PFay.*101 iii 4 (i B.C.): acc. pl. **-πυρα** *PCair.Zen.*498 (iii B.C.). **-πώλης**, ου, ὁ, *dealer in barley*, *Hippiatr.*1. **-τράγος** [ᾰ], ον, (τρᾰγεῖν) *barley-eating*, Ar.*Av.*231. **-φᾰγία**, ἡ, *barley-diet*, a punishment in the Roman army, Plb.6.38.4. **-φάγος** [ᾰ], ον, *living on barley*, ὄρνιθες D.C.*Fr.*43.33, cf. Sch.Ar.*Av.*232. **-φόρος**, ον, *bearing barley*, Thphr.*HP*8.8.2, Str.8.6.16. **-φῠλάκία**, ἡ, *office of controller of export of barley*, Hsch.

κρῑθ-ώδης, ες, *like barley, made of it*, κριθώδεις πτισάναι, = ὅλη πτισάνη, opp. χυλός, Hp.*Acut.*40. **-ώλεθρος**, ον, *barley-wasting*, of horses that will not fatten, Phryn.*PS* p.79 B.

κρίθων (κρίθον cod.)· ἐπώνυμον ἀνδροκιδάλου, Hsch. **κρίκα**· κρίκον, Id. **κρικαδιᾶν**· τὸ ἐναλλάξαι τοὺς δακτύλους ὥσπερ κρίκους ([.]ρυβούς cod.), Id., cf. **κρικαδίαν** (acc. sg.), Sch.Il.23.34. **κρίκε**, v. κρίζω.

κρῐκ-έλλιον, τό, Dim. of sq., *hoop of a ring*, Alex.Trall.8.2. **-ελλος**, ὁ, = *circulus*, *Gloss.*

κρῐκ-ηλᾰσία, ἡ, (κρίκος, ἐλαύνω) *trundling of hoops*, Antyll.ap.Orib.6.26.1. **-ιον**, τό, Dim. of κρίκος, *Inscr.Délos* 380.100 (ii B.C.), *POxy.*1300.5 (v A.D.).

κρῐκο-ειδής, ές, *ring-shaped, annular*, Gal.14.715, *Placit.*1.3.18. **-ομαι**, Pass., *to be secured by a ring*, κεκρίκωνται τὸ χεῖλος χαλκῷ κρίκῳ *they have a* brass *ring through* the lip, Str.17.2.3; *to be infibulated*, Heliod.ap.Orib.50.11.1. **-ποιέομαι**, *to be formed into a ring*, Heracl.ap.Orib.48.13.1.

κρίκ-ος [ῐ], ὁ, Homeric form of κίρκος, *ring*, on a horse's breast-band, to fasten it to the peg (ἕστωρ) at the end of the carriage-pole, Il.24.272. 2. *eyelet-hole* in sails, through which the reefing-ropes were drawn, Hdt.2.36, cf. Poll.1.94, *PLond.*3.1164(*h*)8 (iii A.D.). 3. *curtain-ring*, Thphr.*HP*4.2.7, J.*AJ*3.6.2. 4. *finger-ring*, Arist.*Pol.*1324ᵇ14; part of a finger-ring, *Inscr.Délos* 461 *Ba*6, al. (ii B.C.). 5. *nose-ring*, S.E.*P.*3.203. 6. *armlet*, Plu.*Dem.*30. 7. *link in a chain*, Id.2.304b, Alex.Aphr.*Pr.*2.67, Iamb.*Comm.Math.*7; ἐκ κρίκου λεπτοῦ πεποιημένα ὑφάσματα *chain armour*, Jul.*Or.*37d. 8. *hoop*, Antyll.ap.Orib.6.26.2. 9. *ring* of a spanner, Hero *Bel.*101.13; of a ring-bolt, Apollod.*Poliorc.*166.15; of an armillary sphere, Procl.*Hyp.*6.2 (pl.). **-ωμα**, ατος, τό, *ring, circle*, Eust.726.16. **-ωσις**, εως, ἡ, *infibulation*, Heliod.ap.Orib.50.11.1. **-ωτός**, ή, όν, *ringed, made of rings*, Caryst.7; θώραξ Eust.528.24; κ. σφαῖρα *armillary* sphere, Gem.16.10 (pl.), Gell.3.10.3, Ptol.*Geog.*7.6, *Alm.*1.6 (pl.); ἀστρολάβος Sch.Ptol.90.

κρίμα, ατος, τό, (κρίνω) *decision, judgement*, Chrysipp.*Stoic.*3.58, Plb.23.1.12, Lxx *Ps.*118(119).7, al., *Ep.Rom.*11.33, Arr.*Epict.*2.15.8; περί τινος M.Ant.8.47; *verdict* on a literary work, Phld.*Po.*5.23. 2. *decree, resolution*, δήμου D.H.4.12; ἱερομνημόνων *BCH*27.107, cf. *IGRom.*3.58, 66 (Prusias). 3. *legal decision*, *PPetr.*3 p.56 (iii B.C.), *SIG*826 *E* ii 29 (Delph., ii B.C.); *decision* of arbitrators, ib.421.44 (Thermum, iii B.C.); esp. *sentence, condemnation*, Lxx *De.*21.22, al., *Ev.Marc.*12.40, etc. II. *matter for judgement, question*, οὐκ εὔκριτον τὸ κρῖμα A.*Supp.*397. 2. *law-suit*, Lxx *Ex.*18.22, 1 *Ep.Cor.*6.7. III. = κρίσις, *judging, judgement*, *Ev.Jo.*9.39, *Act.Ap.*24.25, etc. [ῑ in A. l.c. (nisi leg. **κρεῖμα**): ῐ in post-classical poetry; freq. written κρίμα in codd.]

κριμν-ῆστις· πλακοῦντος εἶδος, Hsch. **-ίτης** [ῑτ] ἄρτος, ὁ, bread *made of* κρίμνον, *coarse* bread, Archestr.*Fr.*4.13 (κριμματίαν codd.), Iatrocl.ap.Ath.14.646a. **-ον**, τό, *coarse barley meal*, Hp.ap.Gal.19.115, Eup.11.5 D. (prob.), Arist.*HA*501b31 (pl.), *PRyl.*280v (ii A.D.); *grounds* in gruel, Call.*Fr.*205. 2. *coarse loaf*, *AP*6.302 (Leon.), Babr.108.9. 3. in pl., *crumbs*, Herod.6.6; κρίμνα χειρῶν, = ἀπομαγδαλιά, Lyc.607. **-ος**, ἡ, a purple dye, *PHolm.*8.43 (κριμνον Pap.); κρημνός Ps.-Democr.Alch.p.42 B.; κριμνούς· λευκάς τινας βοτάνας, Hsch. **-ώδης**, ες, *like coarse meal*, of sediment in urine, Hp.*Aph.*7.31; κ. ἐλλέβορος S.E.*P.*1.130; κριμνώδη κατανείφειν snow *thick as meal*, Ar.*Nu.*965.

κρῑνάνθεμον, τό, *houseleek*, Hp.*Nat.Mul.*32. 2. = ἡμεροκαλλές, Ps.-Dsc.3.122.

κρίνη· κνίδη, Hsch.

κρίνῐνος [ῐ], η, ον, *made of lilies*, μύρον *PMag.Lond.*46.223 (iv A.D.); ἔλαιον Gal.11.872, *PMag.Lond.*121.631 (iii A.D.); κ., τό, *PMag.Leid.W.*9.13 (ii/iii A.D.).

κρῑνο-ειδής, ές, *like a lily*, Dsc.3.128. **εις**, εντος, ὁ, name of one of the Idaean Dactyls, Sch.Il.22.391. II. -εις, εσσα, εν, *like a lily*, κεραυνός dub. cj. in *Supp.Epigr.*4.386 (Panamara). **-μῡρον**, τό, = κρίνινον μύρον, Gal.19.71.

κρίνον [ῐ], τό, heterocl. pl. κρίνεα Hdt.2.92; dat. κρίνεσιν Cratin. 98, Ar.*Nu.*911, etc.:—*white lily, Lilium candidum*, Thphr.*HP*6.6.8, Theoc.11.56, Nic.*Fr.*74.27, Dsc.3.102; κ. πορφυροῦν *Turk's cap lily, L. chalcedonicum*, Thphr.*HP*6.6.3, cf. Dsc. l. c.: prov., κρίνου γυμνότερος Jul.*Or.*6.181c: hence, of a needy man, Poll.6.197, etc.: symbolic of death, v. κολοκύντη. 2. *Egyptian bean, Nelumbium speciosum*, Hdt.2.92. II. kind of *choral dance*, Apolloph.2. III. kind of *loaf*, Ath.3.114f. IV. *architectural ornament*, *IG*11(2).161 *A* 72 (Delos, iii B.C.).

κρῑνοστέφανος, ον, *lily-crowned*, Aus.*Ep.*8.14 (κρινν- metri gr.).

κρίνω [ῑ], Ep. 3 sg. ind. κρίνησι (δια-) f.l. in Theoc.25.46: fut. κρῐνῶ, Ep., Ion. κρῐνέω (δια-) Il.2.387: aor. ἔκρῖνα Od.18.264, etc.: pf. κέκρῐκα Pl.*Lg.*734c, etc.:—**Med.**, fut. κρῐνοῦμαι E.*Med.*609, but in pass. sense, Pl.*Grg.*521e: aor. ἐκρῑνάμην Il.9.521, etc.:—**Pass.**, fut. κρῐθήσομαι A.*Eu.*677, Antipho 6.37, etc.: aor. ἐκρίθην [ῐ] Pi.*N.*7.7, etc.; 3 pl. κρίθεν Id.*P.*4.168, ἔκριθεν A.R.4.1462; Ep. opt. κρινθεῖτε (δια-) Il.3.102, part. κρινθείς 13.129, Od.8.48, inf. κρινθήμεναι A.R.2.148: pf. κέκρῐμαι Pi.*O.*2.30, And.4.35, etc.; inf. κεκρίσθαι (ἀπο-) Pl. *Men.*75c:—Aeol. **κρίννω** dub. in *IG*12(2).278 (Mytil.): aor. ἔκριννε ib. 6.28 (Mytil., ἐπ-); inf. κρίνναι ib.526*b*15:—Thess. pres. inf. κρεννέμεν ib.9(2).517.14 (Larissa):—*separate, put asunder, distinguish*, ὅτε τε ξανθὴ Δημήτηρ κρίνῃ.. καρπόν τε καὶ ἄχνας Il.5.501, etc.; κρῖν' ἄνδρας κατὰ φῦλα 2.362, cf. 446; ἥλιος ἠῶ καὶ δύσιν ἔκρινεν Emp.154.1; κ. τὸ ἀληθές τε καὶ μή Pl.*Tht.*150b; τούς τε ἀγαθοὺς καὶ τοὺς κακούς X.*Mem.*3.1.9, etc.:—also Med., ἀντία δ' ἐκρίναντο δέμας καὶ σήματ' ἔθεντο χωρὶς ἀπ' ἀλλήλων Parm.8.55:—Pass., κρινόμενον πῦρ Emp.62.2. II. *pick out, choose*, ἐν δ' ἐρέτας ἔκρινεν ἐείκοσιν Il.1.309; ἐκ Λυκίης.. φῶτας ἀρίστους 6.188, cf. Od.4.666, 9.90, 195, 14.217, etc.; κ. τινὰ ἐκ πάντων Hdt.6.129; κρίνασα δ' ἀστῶν.. τὰ βέλτατα A.*Eu.*487; δίδωμί σοι κρίναντι χρῆσθαι S.*OC*641, etc.:—Med., κρίνασθαι ἀρίστους *to choose* the best, Il.9.521, cf. 19.193, Od.4.408, 530, etc.:—Pass., *to be chosen out, distinguished*, ἵνα τε κρίνονται ἄριστοι 24.507; esp. in partt., κεκριμένος *picked out, chosen*, Il.10.417, Od.13.182, al., Hdt.3.31; κρινθείς Il.13.129, Od.8.48; ἀρετᾷ κριθείς *distinguished for*.., Pi.*N.*7.7; κριθέντων ἐν τοῖς ἱερέοις *approved*.., *GDI*2049.15 (Delph.); ἀσπίδα.. κεκριμένην ὕδατι καὶ πολέμῳ *proved* by sea and land, *AP*9.42 (Leon.); ἐν ζῶσι κεκριμένα *numbered* among.., cj. in E.*Supp.*969 (lyr.); εἰς τοὺς ἐφήβους κριθείς Luc.*Am.*2. 2. *decide* disputes, κρίνων νείκεα πολλά Od.12.440; ἔκριναν μέγα νεῖκος.. πολέμοιο 18.264: c. acc. cogn., οἳ.. σκολιὰς κρίνωσι θέμιστας *judge* crooked judgements, Il.16.387; κ. δίκας Hdt.2.129; κρῖνε δ' εὐθεῖαν δίκην A.*Eu.*433, etc.; πρώτας δίκας κρίνοντες αἵματος ib.682; κρινεῖ δὲ δὴ τίς ταῦτα; Ar.*Ra.*805; κ. κρίσιν Pl.*R.*360e; ἄριστα κ. Th.6.39; κρίνουσι βοῇ καὶ οὐ ψήφῳ *they decide the question*.., Id.1.87; μίσει πλέον ἢ δίκῃ κ. Id.3.67; τὸ δίκαιον κ. Isoc.14.10; τῷ τοῦτο κρίνεις; by what *do you form* this *judgement?* Ar.*Pl.*48; κ. περί τινος Pi.*N.*5.40, Pl.*Ap.*35d, Arist.*Rh.*1391b9, etc.:—Pass., ἀγὼν κριθήσεται A.*Eu.*677; κἂν ἰσόψηφος κριθῇ (sc. ἡ δίκη) ib. 741: impers., κριθησόμενον *a decision being about to be taken*, Arr.*An.*3.9.6. b. *decide* a contest, e.g. for a prize, ἀγῶνα κ. Ar.*Ra.*873; ἔργον ἐν κύβοις Ἄρης κρινεῖ A.*Th.*414: c. acc. pers., κ. τὰς θεὰς *decide their contest*, i.e. *judge* them, E.*IA*72:—Pass., Id.*Supp.*601 (lyr.); αἱ μάχαι κρίνονται ταῖς ψυχαῖς X.*Cyr.*3.3.19:—Med. and Pass., of persons, *have a contest decided, come to issue*, κρινώμεθ' Ἄρηϊ Il.2.385, cf. 18.209; ὁπότε μνηστῆρσι καὶ ἡμῖν.. μένος κρίνηται Ἄρηος Od.16.269; βίηφι κ. Hes.*Th.*882; *dispute, contend*, Ar.*Nu.*66; περὶ ἀρετῆς Hdt.3.120; οὐ κρινοῦμαι.. σοι τὰ πλείονα E.*Med.*609; δίκῃ περί τινος κρίνεσθαι Th.4.122; κρίνεσθαι μετά τινος v.l. in Lxx *Jd.*8.1, *Jb.*9.3; πολλαῖς μάχαις κριθείς Nic.Dam.20 J.; *compete* in games, c. acc. cogn., κριθέντα Πύθια *JRS*3.295 (Antioch. Pisid.): pf. part., *decided, clear, strong*, κεκριμένος οὖρος Il.14.19; πόνοι κεκρ. *decided, ended*, Pi.*N.*4.1. c. *win* a battle, τὴν μάχην Ἀννίβας ἔκρινε Plb.3.117.11. 3. *adjudge*, κράτος τινί S.*Aj.*443:—Pass., τοῖς οὔτε νόστος.. κρίθη Pi.*P.*8.84; τὰ κριθησόμενα *the sum adjudged to be paid*, *PLips.*38.13 (iv A.D.). b. abs., *judge, give judgement*, ἄκουσον.. καὶ κρῖνον Ar.*Fr.*473; ἀδίκως κ. Pherecr.96, cf. Men.*Mon.*287, 576. c. Medic., *bring to a crisis*, τὸ θερμὸν φίλιόν [ἐστι] καὶ κρῖνον Hp.*Aph.*5.22; κ. τὰ νοσήματα Gal.*Nat.Fac.*1.13, al.:—Pass., of a sick person, *come to a crisis*, ἐκρίθη εἰκοσταῖος Hp.*Epid.*1.15 (also impers. in Act., ἔκρινε τούτοισιν ἑνδεκαταίοισιν *the crisis came*.., ib.18); τοῦ πάθους κριθέντος D.S.19.24. 4. *judge of, estimate*, πρὸς ἐμαυτὸν κρίνων [αὐτόν] *judging of* him by myself, D.21.154; πρὸς ἀργύριον τὴν εὐδαιμονίαν κ. Isoc.4.76:—Pass., ἴσον παρ' ἐμοὶ κέκριται Hdt.7.16.α'; εὔνοια καιρῷ κρίνεται Men.691. 5. *expound, interpret* in a particular way, τὸ ἐνύπνιον ταύτῃ ἔκριναν Hdt.1.120, cf. 7.19, A.*Pr.*485, etc.:—in Med., ὁ γέρων ἐκρίνατ' ὀνείρους Il.5.150. 6. c. acc. et inf., *decide* or *judge that*.., Hdt.1.30, 214, Pl.*Tht.*170d, etc.; κρίνω σὲ νικᾶν A.*Ch.*903; so, with the inf. omitted, ἀνδρῶν πρῶτον κ. τινά S.*OT*34; Ἔρωτα δ' ὅστις μὴ θεὸν κρίνει μέγαν E.*Fr.*269; τὴν πόλιν ἀθλιωτάτην ἔκρινας Pl.*R.*578b; ἐκ τῶν λόγων μὴ κρῖνε.. σοφόν Philem.228:—Pass., Ἑλλήνων ἕνα κριθέντ' ἄριστον S.*Ph.*1345, cf. Th.2.40, etc. 7. *decide in favour of, prefer, choose*, κρίνω δ' ἄφθονον ὄλβον A.*Ag.*471, cf. *Supp.*396 (both lyr.); τὴν ἐλπίδα τῆς τύχης πάρος S.*Tr.*724; τινὰ πρό τινος Pl.*R.*399e, cf. *Phlb.*57e; τι πρός τι Id.*Phd.*110a (Pass.); εἴ σφε κρίνειεν Πάρις E.*Tr.*928, cf. Ar.*Av.*1103, *Ec.*1155; *choose between*, δυ' ἔσθ' ἃ κρῖναι τὸν γαμεῖν μέλλοντα δεῖ, ἤτοι προσηνῆ γ' ὄψιν ἢ χρηστὸν τρόπον Men.584. 8. c. inf. only, *determine* to do a thing, *UPZ*42.37 (ii B.C.), *Ep.Tit.*3.12, 1*Ep.Cor.*2.2, etc.; ζῆν μεθ' ὧν κρίνῃ τις ἂν (sc. ζῆν) with whom he *chooses* to live, Men.506; but τὸ βιάζεσθαι οὐκ ἔκρινε D.S.15.32. 9. *form a judgement of* a thing, μὴ κρῖν' ὁρῶν τὸ κάλλος Men.*Mon.*333. III. in Trag., *question*, αὐτὸν.. ἅπας λεὼς κρίνει παραστάς S.*Tr.*195; εἴ νιν πρὸς βίαν κρίνειν θέλοις ib.388; καὶ κρῖνε κἀξέλεγχ' Id.*Ant.*399; μὴ κρῖνε, μὴ 'ξέταζε Id.*Aj.*586; σέ τοι, σὲ κρίνω Id.*El.*1445. 2. *bring to trial, accuse*, D.2.29, 18.15, 19.233; κ. θανάτου *judge* (in matters) of life and death, X.*Cyr.*1.2.14; κ. τινὰ προδοσίας Lycurg.113; περὶ προδοσίας Isoc.15.129; κ. τινὰ κακώσεως ἐπαρχίας, Lat. *repetundarum*, Plu.*Caes.*4:—Pass., *to be brought to trial*, Th.6.29; θανάτου (δίκῃ add. cod. B) Id.3.57; Λεωκράτους τοῦ κρινομένου Lycurg.1; κρίνομαι πρὸς Σωφρόνην; Men.*Epit.*529; τρὶς κρίνεται παρ' ὑμῖν περὶ θανάτου D.4.47; ἐκρίνετο τὴν περὶ Ὠρωποῦ κρίσιν θανάτου Id.21.64: c. gen. criminis, κρίνεσθαι δώρων Lys.27.3: κ. ἐπ' ἀδικήματι Plu.2.241e: abs., ὁ κεκριμένος Aeschin.2.159. 3. *pass sentence upon, condemn*, D.19.232:—Pass., *to be judged, condemned*, κακοῦργου.. ἐστι κριθέντ' ἀποθανεῖν Id.4.47; μὴ κρίνετε, ἵνα μὴ κριθῆτε *Ev.Matt.*7.1; τὰ κεκριμένα *the judgement* of a court, *PRyl.*76.8 (ii A.D.). (κρῑ-ν-yω ἐ-κρῑ-ν-σα, cf. Lat. *cerno* (from **crĭ-n-*), *crībrum* (from **crei-dhrom*).)

κρῑν-ωνιά, ἡ, prop. *bed of lilies*, Suid.; but, = κρίνον, Thphr.*HP*2.2.1, 6.6.9. **-ωτός**, ή, όν, *adorned with lilies*, κεφαλίδες Aristeas 68.

κριξός, ὁ, Dor. for κιρσός (q.v.).

κρῑο-βόλιον, τό, *sacrifice of a ram*, *IG*14.1018 (iv A.D.). II. pl., *ephebic contest in which a ram was caught and sacrificed*, *OGI*764.27 (Pergam., ii B.C.). **-βόλος**, ον, *ram-slaying*, κ. τελετή, = foreg. I, *IG*14.1018 (iv A.D.). **-γενής**, ὁ, name of a lozenge, Paul.Aeg.4.41, 7.12. **-δόχη**, ἡ, *frame of a battering-ram*, Ath.Mech.13.10, al. **-ειδής**, ές, *like a ram*, Suid. s. v. κριός. **-θεος**, ὁ, = ἀμμωνιακόν, Ps.-Dsc.3.84. **-κέρᾱτος**, ον, *with ram's horns*, θεός Ps.-Callisth.1.8. **-κέφαλος**, ον, *ram-headed*, Hermes Trism. in *Rev. Phil.*32.254. **-κοπέω**, *batter with a battering-ram*, Plb.1.42.9, App.*Mith.*36: abs., Ath.Mech.14.11, Apollod.*Poliorc.*143.7. **-μᾰχέω**, *manoeuvre with a battering-ram*, ib.185.14. **-μορφος**, ον, *ram-formed*, Sch.rec.A.R.1.256. **-μυξος**, ον, (μύξα) *like a drivelling ram, sheepish*, Cerc.15.

κριον (*crion*), = *vervecina*, Gloss. (Perh. contr. from *κρίειον (se. κρέας).)

κρῑο-πρόσωπος, ον, *ram-faced*, ἄγαλμα Διός Hdt.2.42, 4.181; Ζεύς Luc.*Sacr.*14, etc. 2. *with a ram as figurehead*, ναῦς Nymphis 18. **-πρῳρος**, ον, = foreg. 2, πλοῖον, σκάφος, Sch.Pl.*Mx.*243a, Sch.A.R.2.168.

κρῑός, ὁ, *ram*, Od.9.447, 461, Hdt.2.42, etc.; κριοὶ ἄγριοι Id.4.192: prov., κριὸς τροφεῖα ἀπέτεισεν, of ingratitude, because a ram butts at those who have brought him up, Zen.4.63, Suid., Hsch.; κριοὺς ἐκγεννᾶν τέκνα Eup.99; κριοῦ διακονία, of thankless service, Suid., Hsch.; τὸν κριὸν ὡς ἐπέχθη the 'shearing of the *ram*', in allusion to the ode of Simonides in honour of Crius of Aegina, Ar.*Nu.*1356. 2. *battering-ram*, X.*Cyr.*7.4.1, *IG*2².468, Plb.1.48.9, Ath.Mech.14.1, J.*BJ*3.7.19, etc. 3. the constellation *Aries*, Eudox.ap.Hipparch.1.2.13, Euc.*Phaen.*p.6 M., Arat.238, J.*AJ*3.10.5, etc. II. a *sea-monster*, Ael.*NA*9.49, 15.2, Opp.*H.*1.372, 5.33, etc. III. kind of *mussel*, Hegesand.36 (κρεῖος cod. A Ath.). IV. *volute* on the Corinthian capital, *twisted like a ram's horn*, Hsch. V. kind of *ship*, Poll.1.83. VI. part of an irrigation-system, dub. sens. in *BGU*14 iii 9 (iii A.D.). VII. *a variety of* ἐρέβινθος, Thphr.*HP*8.5.1, *PCair.Zen.*192.8 (iii B.C.), Dsc.2.104, Gal.6.533: misspelt κρεῖος in Sophil.8: Lat. *cicer arietinum*, Petron.35, etc.; *est enim arietino capiti simile*, Plin.*HN*18.124. (Prob. cogn. with κέρας.)

κρῑό-στᾰσις, εως, ἡ, *station, position for a battering-ram*, Ph.*Bel.*92.19. **-τάφος** [ᾰ], ου, ὁ, *one who buries sacred rams*, *PTeb.*72.411 (ii B.C.). **-φάγος** [ᾰ], ον, *devouring rams*, epith. of a divinity, Hsch. **-φόρος**, ον, *carrying battering-rams*, χελῶναι Ph.*Bel.*99.44, Ath.Mech.8.14, Apollod.*Poliorc.*138.18, D.S.20.48, 91; μηχαναί App.*Pun.*98, Anon.ap.Suid. s. v. προσηρεικότος. II. *bearing a ram*, epith. of Hermes, Paus.9.22.1. **-ω**, pf. part. Pass. κεκριωμένον *made into a ram*, Hsch. s. v. Γαλλίμ (ante γαιηόχῳ).

Κρῖσα, ης, ἡ, *Crisa*, a city in Phocis, near Delphi, Il.2.520; **Κρίση**, *h.Ap.*282, etc.:—Adj. **Κρισαῖος**, α, ον, *Crisaean*, ib.446, Hdt.8.32:—also **Κίρρα**, Pi.*P.*3.74, al., *SIG*241.45, al. (Delph., iv B.C.), Paus.10.37.4 (but Κρῖσα distd. fr. Κίρρα by Leocrines ap.*EM*515.20, Str.9.3.3, Ptol.*Geog.*3.14.4); **Κύρρα**, *Marm.Par.*53, v.l. in Ptol. l. c.;

Κίρσα, Alc.*Oxy.*1789*Fr.*6.9 (dub.), *EM*l. c.; κόλπος **Κιρραῖος**, dub. in Hecat.105 J.: also **Κρῖσα**, Pi.*I.*2.18; **Κρῖσαῖος**, Id.*P.*5.37, al.

κρισίαι· τάξεις ἱππικαί, Hsch.

κρίσῐμος [ῐσ], ον, (κρίσις) *decisive, critical*, κ. ἡμέρα the *crisis* of a disease, Hp.*Aph.*7.85, al., Arist.*Ph.*230^{b}5; κ. γὰρ αὕτη γίγνεται (sc. the seventh day) Men.890; also κ. φάεα *AP*11.382.11 (Agath.); ἐν κρισίμοις Hp.*Epid.*1.7: Comp. -ώτερος Id.*Acut.*23. Adv. -μως Id. *Epid.* l. c.

κρῐσιολογία, ἡ, *litigation*, *Cat.Cod.Astr.*8(4).130 (pl.).

κρίσις [ῐσ], εως, ἡ, (κρίνω) *separating, distinguishing*, τοῦ πλέω καὶ τοῦ μὴ πλέω Meliss.7; τῶν ὁμοιογενῶν, τῶν διαφερόντων, dub. l. in Arist.*EN*1165^{a}34. 2. *decision, judgement*, περὶ τούτων Parm.8.15; τὴν Κροίσου κ. Hdt.3.34; ἐν θεῶν κρίσει A.*Ag.*1289; κατὰ δύναμιν καὶ κ. ἐμήν Hp.*Jusj.*1; κ. οὐκ ἀληθής no certain *means of judging*, S.*OT*501 (lyr.); πολίτης ὁρίζεται τῷ μετέχειν κρίσεως καὶ ἀρχῆς Arist. *Pol.*1275^{a}23; κρίσεως προσδεόμενα Epicur.*Nat.*32 G., cf. *Herc.*1420.3; αἱ τῶν πολλῶν κ. Phld.*Mus.*p.75 K.; Κρίσις, title of a play by Sophocles on the Judgement of Paris; κ. τινός *judgement on* or *respecting*, τῶν μνηστήρων Hdt.6.131; ἀέθλων Pi.*O.*3.21, *N.*10.23; μορφῆς E.*Hel.*26; ἡ τῶν ὅπλων κ., referring to the story of Ajax, Pl.*R.*620b, cf. Arist.*Po.*1459^{b}5; κρίσιν.. τοῦ βίου πέρι ὧν λέγομεν Pl.*R.*360e; κ. ἀμφ' ἀέθλοις Pi.*O.*7.80; κ. διημαρτημένη *Stoic.*1.50; κ. συνετή Cleanth.ib.128; *power of judgement*, κρίσει πραγμάτων διαφέρεσθαι Plb.18.14.10; κατὰ κρίσιν with *judgement, advisedly*, Id.6.11.8. 3. *choice, election*, κ. ποιεῖσθαι τῶν ἀξίων Arist.*Pol.*1321^{a}30, cf. 1271^{a}10. 4. *interpretation* of dreams or portents, Lxx *Da.*2.36, D.S. 17.116, J.*AJ*2.5.7. II. *judgement* of a court, οὐδὲν ἂν τῆς ὑμετέρας κ. ἔδει Antipho 4.4.2; *trial, suit*, προκληθέντας ἐς κρίσιν περί τινος Th.1.34; καθιστάναι ἑαυτὸν ἐς κ. ib.131; κρίσιν ποιεῖν τινι Lys. 13.35; κρίσεως τυχεῖν to be put on one's *trial*, Pl.*Phdr.*249a; εἰς κ. ἄγειν Id.*Lg.*856c; ἡ κ. γίγνεται τινι ibid.; κρίσιν ὑποσχεῖν ib.871d, D.21.125; τὰς κρίσεις ποιεῖσθαι περί τινος Isoc.4.40, cf. Th.1.77; τὰς κ. διαδικάζειν Pl.*Lg.*876b; κρίσιν λελογχότα Μειδίᾳ ἐξούλης Test.ap. D.21.82; αἱ κ. τῶν συμβολαίων Plu.2.447e. b. *result of a trial, condemnation*, X.*An.*1.6.5. c. ἡμέρα κρίσεως Day of *Judgement*, *Ev.Matt.*10.15. 2. *trial* of skill or strength, πρὸς τόξου κρίσιν in archery, S.*Tr.*266; δρόμου.., οὗ πρώτη κ. Id.*El.*684; κ. ποιεῖν ὁπότερος εἴη τὴν τέχνην σοφώτερος Ar.*Ra.*779; θεῶν ἔριν τε καὶ κ. Pl. *R.*379e. 3. *dispute*, περί τινος Hdt.5.5, 7.26. III. *event, issue*, κρίσιν σχεῖν to be *decided*, of a war, Th.1.23, Plb.31.29.5; κρίσεως τυχεῖν Id.1.59.11; ἐν τοῖς πεπολιτευμένοις τὴν κ. εἶναι νομίζω I suppose the *issue* depends upon my public measures, D.18.57. 2. *turning point* of a disease, *sudden change* for better or worse, Hp. *VM*19 (pl.), Gal.9.550, etc.; κ. ξύντομος ἐπὶ τὸ κάκιον Hp.*Judic.*34, cf. Gal.18(2).231. IV. middle of the spinal column, Poll.2.177.

κρίσμιον· φυλάκιον, Hsch.

κρίσσιον, τό, *thistle, Carduus pycnocephalus*, Dsc.4.118.

κρισσοκάβων, ωνος, ὁ, *suffering from varicocele*, of horses, *Hippiatr.* 14.

κρισσ-ός, ὁ, = κιρσός, Andreas ap. Dsc.4.118, *Hippiatr.*77, Hsch. II. *knot* in oaks from which mistletoe springs, Id. -ώδης, ες, Att. for κιρσώδης, Gal.19.123, Hsch. s. v. βδαλοί (κροσσ- cod.).

κρίτανος· τέρμινθος, Hsch.

κρῐτ-έος, α, ον, *to be decided* or *judged*, Hp. *de Arte*9. II. κριτέον *one must decide* or *judge*, Pl.*Grg.*523e, etc. -ήρ, ῆρος, ὁ, = κριτής, *IG*4.493 (Mycenae). II. *interpreter* of dreams, Nic.Dam.66.9 J. III. f.l. for κραντήρ (q.v.), Arist.ap.*EM*742. 37. -ήριον, τό, *means for judging* or *trying, standard*, freq. of the mental faculties and senses, ἔχων αὐτῶν τὸ κ. ἐν αὑτῷ Pl.*Tht.*178b, cf. *R.*582a, Plu.2.448b, etc.; τὸ αἰσθητήριον καὶ κ. τῶν.. χυμῶν Arist. *Metaph.*1063^{a}3, cf. Epicur.*Ep.*1 p.5 U. (pl.), *Sent.*24, al.; περὶ κριτηρίου, title of works by Epicurus (D.L.10.27), Posidonius (Diocl.ap. D.L.7.54), and Ptolemy: generally, χρόνον εἶναι μέτρον καὶ κ. τάχους *measure, test*, Zeno *Stoic.*1.26, etc. 2. *court of judgement, tribunal*, Pl.*Lg.*767b; καθίζειν κ. Plb.9.33.12, cf. *PHib.*1.29(*a*) (iii B. C.), 1*Ep. Cor.*6.2, *IG*14.951.20, Paus.2.20.7, *POxy.*2134.6 (ii A. D.), etc. b. *decision* of a tribunal, *judgement*, *SIG*826 *K*9 (Delph., ii B. C.). -ής, οῦ, ὁ, voc. κριτή Hippon.118: (κρίνω):—*judge, umpire*, A.*Supp.*397, Hdt.3.160, etc.; ἐν πέντε κριτῶν γούνασι κεῖται Epich.229; κ. τῶν ἀληθῶν, opp. δοξαστής, Antipho 5.94; κριταὶ ἀπὸ τοῦ ἴσου, opp. ἀγωνισταί, Th.3.37; τῶν.. λεγομένων μὴ κακοὺς κ. Id.1.120; κ. περί τινος Lys.16.21, Pl.*Phlb.*65a; at Athens, usu. of *the judges in the poetic contests*, Ar.*Ach.*1224, *Nu.*1115, *Av.*445, cf. And.4.21; rarely, = δικαστής, Demad.3: so metaph. in Aeschin.3.232; πάντα τὰ στοιχεῖα κριτὴν εἴληφε, i. e. each element has found favour with some philosopher, Arist.*de An.*405^{b}8, cf. *Pol.*1337^{a}42; of the *Judges* of Israel, Lxx *Jd.*2.16, al.; κ. δοθείς, = Lat. *judex datus*, *POxy.*1195.1 (ii A. D.); ἐπίλεκτος κ., = *judex selectus*, *OGI*567.10 (Attalia, ii A. D.). 2. κ. ἐνυπνίων *interpreter* of dreams, A.*Pers.*226. II. κριτάς· ὀδόντας, Hsch.; cf. κραντήρ.

Κρῐτιάζω, *imitate the style of Critias*, Philostr.*VS*1.16.2; Κριτιάζουσα ἠχώ ib.2.1.14.

κρῐτ-ικός, ή, όν, *able to discern, critical*, δύναμις σύμφυτος κ. Arist. *APo.*99^{b}35; οὐκ ἔχει ῥῖνα κριτικὴν πρὸς τοὖψον Posidipp.1.4; αἰσθήσεις κ. Phld.*Mus.*p.8 K.; τὸ κ. *the power of discerning*, Arist. *de An.*432^{a}16; ἡ κριτική (sc. τέχνη) Pl.*Plt.*260c, etc.: c. gen., ἡ γεῦσις τῶν σχημάτων κριτικωτάτη Arist.*Sens.*442^{b}17, cf. Thphr.*Sens.*43, Ocell.2.7; of persons, [τὸν ὅλως πεπαιδευμένον] περὶ πάντων ὡς εἰπεῖν κ. τινὰ νομίζομεν εἶναι Arist.*PA*639^{a}9: esp. in language, *grammarian, scholar, literary critic*, Pl.*Ax.*366e, Phld.*Po.*5.24, Str.9.1.10, etc.; of Crates, Ath. 11.490e, who distd. κ. and γραμματικός, S.E.*M.*1.79; εἰ δύναταί τις εἶναι κ. καὶ γραμματικός, title of work by Galen (*Libr.Propr.*17); but τῶν ὕστερον γραμματικῶν κληθέντων πρότερον δὲ κ. D.Chr.53.1, cf. Apollod.ap.Clem.Al.*Strom.*1.16.79; οἱ κ. τῶν λόγων Philostr.*VS* 2.1.14; πρὸς τοὺς κ., title of work by Chrysippus, *Stoic.*2.9; ἡ κ., opp. ἡ γραμματική, Taurisc.ap.S.E.*M.*1.248, cf. Sch.*DT*p.3 H. Adv. -κῶς, ἔχειν τινός Artem.4*Praef.*, cf. Erot.*Praef.*p.7 N., Men.Rh. p.391 S. 2. *of* or *for judging*, ἀρχὴ κ. the office *of judges*, opp. ἀρχὴ βουλευτική, Arist.*Pol.*1275^{b}19. II. = κρίσιμος, ἑβδομάς Ph.1.45 (Sup.), cf. Plu.2.134f, Gal.9.93, al. Adv. -κῶς Id. *UP*17.2, al. -ός, ή, όν, *separated, picked out, chosen*, Il.7.434, Od.8.258. 2. *choice, excellent*, Pi.*P.*4.50, S.*Tr.*27, 245, etc.; δάμαλις *SIG*1026.6 (Cos, iv/iii B. C.).

κρῑ-ώδης, ες, *ram-like*, Ph.1.113. -ωμα, ατος, τό, = κριός I.2, dub. in Apollod.*Poliorc.*139.1. II. = κριός V, Aq.*Ez.*40.14. -ωπός, όν, = κριοπρόσωπος I, Trag.ap.Phot.p.151 R.; = κριός VII, *POxy.*1801.26.

κρίως, Cret. gen. sg. of κρέας (q. v.).

κροαίνω, only pres. part., of a horse, *stamp, strike with the hoof*, θείῃ πεδίοιο κροαίνων Il.6.507 (where Sch.A rejects the expl. ἐπιθυμῶν, quoting Archil.176, cf. κρυαίνω); κροαίνοντες πεδίοισι (v. l. -ίοιο) Opp. *C.*1.279: abs., Philostr.*Im.*1.30: metaph., *luxuriate, wanton*, of a rhetorician, Id.*VS*1.25.7; also πλήκτρῳ λιγυρὸν μέλος κ. *striking*, *Anacreont.*58.6.

κρόβαλος· ὁ μαλλὸς τῶν παιδίων, καὶ αἱ τρίχες τῶν αἰδοίων, Hsch. **κροβάντιον**· πολίον, Id.

κροιός· νοσώδης, ἀσθενής, Hsch.; = κολοβός, Theognost.*Can.*21; ἐάν τις τῶν λίθων ἔχει τι κροιόν *IG*2^2.244.63 (iv B. C.); ἐγκολλᾶν τῶν λίθων τὰ κροιά, Ἀρχ.Ἐφ.1923.39. (Cf. Lith. *kreĩvas* 'crooked'.)

κρόκα, heterocl. acc. sg. of κρόκη.

κροκάλη [ᾰ], ἡ, = κρόκη II, *AP*7.479 (Theodorid.): pl., *sea-shore, beach*, E.*IA*210 (lyr.), *AP*7.651 (Euph.), 6.186 (Diocl.); κροκάλην.. ἠϊόνα ib.7.294 (perh. f. l. for ἠϊόνος) (Tull. Laur.): in late Prose, Agath.2.2.

κρόκαλον· τὸ πανοῦργον παιδίον, Hsch.

κροκᾶτον, τό, *yellow parchment*, *Edict.Diocl.Asin.*7.38.

κρόκεος, ον, (κρόκος) *saffron-coloured*, Pi.*P.*4.232 (nisi leg. κροκόεν), E.*Hec.*468 (lyr.), *Ion*889 (lyr.).

κρόκες, αἱ, metapl. nom. pl. of sq.

κρόκη, ἡ, heterocl. acc. κρόκα Hes.*Op.*538, nom. pl. κρόκες *AP*6.335 (Antip.): nom. **κρόξ** only in Hsch.: (κρέκω):—*thread which is passed between the threads of the warp, woof*, Hes. l. c., Hdt.2.35, Pl. *Plt.*282d, e, *Cra.*388b; κ. καὶ στήμων *PLille*6.12 (iii B. C.); νῶσαι μαλθακωτάτην κ. Eup.319, cf. Men.892; κρόκας ἐμβάλλειν Arist.*HA* 623^{a}11. 2. generally, *thread*, Hp.*Morb.*2.18, Luc.*Nav.*26, etc. 3. = κροκύς, *flock* or *nap of woollen cloth*, ἐν Ἐκβατάνοισι γίγνεται κρόκης χόλιξ; Ar.*V.*1144: pl., μαλακαῖσι κρόκαις *with cloths of* soft *wool*, Pi.*N.*10.44; κρόκαισι *with flocks of wool*, S.*OC*474; τρίβωνες ἐκβαλόντες.. κρόκας having lost *the nap*, worn out, E.*Fr.*282.12; τῆς κ. φορουμένης *the wool* being torn to pieces, Ar.*Lys.*896, cf. *Th.*738; κρόκη ξανθή yellow *wool*, *IG*1^2.330.17. II. = κροκάλη, *pebble* on the sea-shore, Arist.*Mech.*852^{b}29; ἐν κρόκῃσι on *the pebbles of the shore*, Lyc.107, 193, etc.

κροκ-ήϊος, η, ον, *of saffron*, ἄνθος *h.Cer.*178. -ηρός, ά, όν, *made with saffron*, φάρμακον Gal.13.182, Paul.Aeg.6.8. -ίας, ου, ὁ, *saffron-coloured stone*, Plu.2.375e; dub. in S.*Ichn.*186 (lyr.). -ίζω, *to be like saffron*, Dsc.2.179; ὀσμὴ -ουσα Plu.*Them.*8. -ῖνος, η, ον, *of* or *made from saffron*, μύρα *AP*11.34 (Phld.), cf. Thphr.*Od.*27, Plb. 30.26.1, Apollon.ap.Gal.12.475, Aret.*CA*1.6; τὸ κ. Lxx *Pr.*7.17, Dsc.1.54. 2. *yellow*, Stratt.69, Thphr.*HP*1.13.1, 3.4.5, *POxy.* 1679.5 (iii A. D.), Democr.Eph.ap.Ath.12.525c:—the form κρόκιος in Artem.1.77 is corrupt.

κρόκιον, τό, Dim. of κρόκη, *woollen fillet*, Anticl.13.

κροκίς, ίδος, ἡ, *fly-trap, Silene Muscipula*, Apollod.ap.Plin.*HN*24.167. II. = κροκύς I, *Gloss.*

κροκισμός, ὁ, *weaving, web*, Sch.S.*OC*475.

κρόκκαι, αἱ, *pebbles*, Hsch. **κροκκάω**, *cluck*, of birds, *Gloss.*

κροκό-βαπτος, ον, *saffron-dyed*, A.*Pers.*660. -βαφής, ές, = foreg., Sch.Pi.*N.*1.58: metaph., ἐπὶ δὲ καρδίαν ἔδραμε κ. σταγών the *sallow, sickly* blood-drop such as might be supposed to run to the heart of dying men, A.*Ag.*1121 (lyr.). **-δῑλέα**, ἡ, *dung of the* κροκόδιλος χερσαῖος, used as an eye-salve, Plin.*HN*28.108. **-δίλεον** [ῐ], τό, *sea-holly, Eryngium maritimum*, Dsc.3.10, Gal.12.47. **-δῑλιάς**, άδος, ἡ, = foreg., ib.565; ἀρτεμισία κ. Alex.Trall.*Febr.*6. **-δίλῑνος** [δῐ], η, ον, = sq., [*ambiguitates*] Quint.1.10.5. **-δῑλίτης** [ῑτ] (sc. λόγος), ου, ὁ, a sophistic fallacy, Chrysipp.*Stoic.*2.93. **-δῑλοβοσκός**, ὁ, *feeder of sacred crocodiles*, *BGU*734 ii 7 (iii A. D., abbrev.). **-δῑλόβρωτος**, ον, = sq., Aët.13.6 tit. **-δῑλόδηκτος**, ον, *bitten by a crocodile*, Dsc.5.109. **-δῑλοειδής**, ές, *in the form of a crocodile*, *PMag. Leid.V.*3.15 (κορκ- Pap.). **-δῑλοπάρδᾰλις**, εως, ἡ, fabulous animal, *IG*14.1302 (Praeneste). **-δῑλος**, ὁ, prop. Ion. word for *lizard*, acc. to Hdt.2.69, etc.; κ. τριπήχεες χερσαῖοι, of the *desert monitor*, genus *Varanus*, Id.4.192; of other *lizards*, Arist.*Fr.*362, Lxx *Le.*11.30, Ael.*NA*1.58; κ. μικρός, in a fountain at Chalcedon, Str.12.4.2; cf. **κροκύδιλος** Hippon.119 (-δειλ- Eust.; **κρεκύδειλος** *Et.Gen.* in *Indogerm.Forsch.*15.7). 2. *crocodile* found in the Nile, Hdt.2.68 sq.; also in Indian rivers, Id.4.44, cf. Ael.*NA*12.41; ὁ κ. ὁ ποτάμιος Arist.*HA*492^{b}24, cf. 558^{a}18. (Correctly written **κροκόδιλος**

*PCair.Zen.*354.13, 443.4 (iii B.C.), *PTeb.*63.25 (ii B.C.), etc.; later -δειλος *PAmh.*2.45.8 (ii B.C.), etc., freq. in codd.; **κορκόδιλος** *PCair.Zen.*379.5 (iii B.C.); **κορκότιλος** *Stud.Pal.*20.75 ii 16 (iii/iv A.D.); **κορκόδριλλος** and Dim. **κορκοδρίλλιον**, *Gloss.* **-δῑλοτάφιον** [ᾰ], τό, *burial-place of sacred crocodiles*, *PGrenf.*2.14(*d*) (iii B.C.), *PTeb.*88.4 (ii B.C., κορκ-), *BGU*1303.9 (i B.C.). **-ειδής**, ές, *saffron-coloured*, Arist.*Col.*795ᵇ1, Sch.Pi.*N.*1.58; χολή Aret.*SD* 1.15. **-είμων**, ον, gen. ονος, *saffron-clad*, Sch.D Il.8.1. **-εις**, εσσα, εν, *saffron-coloured*, prob.l. in Pi.*P.*4.232, cf. Sapph.*Supp.*22.7; δαῦκον Thphr.*HP*9.15.5; κισσός Theoc.*Ep.*3; στολίδος κ. τρυφά E.*Ph.*1491 (lyr.); χιτών Phalaec.ap.Ath.10.440d. 2. κροκόεις (sc. χιτών), ὁ, = κροκωτός, *dress-robe of saffron*, ὃς ἐμὲ κροκόεντ' ἐνέδυσεν Ar.*Th.*1044. **-μαγμα**, ατος, τό, *residuum* after the *saffron-unguent has been expressed*, Dsc.1.27, Asclep.ap.Gal.13.210, *PMasp.*141 ii 23 (vi A.D.). 2. *a compound drug*, Damocr.ap.Gal.14.133, Paul. Aeg.7.12. **-μέριον**, τό, = κῆμος, Ps.-Dsc.4.133. **-μηλον**, τό, *conserve of quince and saffron*, Alex.Trall.*Febr.*7. **-νητική** (sc. τέχνη), ἡ, (κρόκη I.1) *the art of spinning the woof*, opp. στημονονητική, Pl.*Plt.*283a. **-πεπλος**, ον, *with yellow veil*, Ἠώς Il.8.1, 19.1, al.; Ἐνυώ Hes.*Th.*273; of a river-nymph, ib.358; of the Muses, Alcm.85A.

κρόκος, ὁ (ἡ, Str.14.5.5), *saffron, Crocus sativus*, Il.14.348, *h.Cer.* 6, Hippon.41, S.*OC*685 (lyr.), Cratin.98 (pl.), A.R.3.855, cf. Thphr. *HP*4.3.1, al., Dsc.1.26, etc. b. κ. λευκός, *C. cancellatus*, Thphr.*HP* 7.7.4. c. κ. ἀκανθώδης, = κνῆκος, ibid. 2. *saffron* (made from its stigmas), Ar.*Nu.*51, etc.; κρόκου βαφάς A.*Ag.*239 (lyr.); κ. Ἀραβικός *Edict.Diocl.* in Ἀθηνᾶ 18.6. 3. *saffron meadow*, Eust.1698. 30. 4. σὺν κρόκῳ ᾠῶν *yolk* of egg, Alex.Trall.1.1: pl., ᾠῶν τὰ κρόκα Paul.Aeg.3.78.

κροκόττας, α, ὁ, an Indian wild beast, supposed to be a hybrid between wolf and dog, perh. really the *hyena*, Ctes.*Fr.*87, Agatharch. 77, *Peripl.M.Rubr.*50, *IG*14.1302 (Praeneste): **κροκούττας** Str.16. 4.16: **κοροκόττας** Ael.*NA*7.22, Porph.*Abst.*3.4, Plin.*HN*8.107: **κοροκότας** D.C.76.1.

κροκόω, *crown with yellow ivy* (cf. κροκόεις I), *AP*13.29 (Nicaenet., Pass.). II. (κρόκη) *weave*, Dionys.ap.St.Byz. s.v. Δαρσανία. 2. *wrap in wool*, Phot.

κροκῠδ-ίζω, *pick loose flocks off a garment*, τὸ κάταγμα κροκυδίζουσαν Philyll.22, Gal.10.928; of persons in delirium, *twitch the blankets*, Aret.*CA*1.1. **-ισμός**, ὁ, *picking of flocks*, Gal.19.412:—hence -ιον, τό, Dim. of κροκύς, Id.10.867, Theognost.*Can.*125.

κροκῠδολογέω, = κροκυδίζω, Hp.*Epid.*7.25.

κροκῠλεγμός, ὁ, = κροκυδισμός, Hsch.

κροκύς [ῠ], ύδος, ἡ, (κρόκη I.3) *flock* or *nap on woollen cloth*, Hdt.3. 8, Luc.*Fug.*28, etc.; *piece of wool*, Hp.*Prog.*4, Plu.*Sull.*35; κροκύδα ἀφαιρεῖν, typical of a flatterer, Thphr.*Char.*2.3: metaph., ἀνήσω κροκύδα μαστιγουμένη Ar.*Fr.*651. 2. κ. ἑδρική *suppository*, Herod. Med. in *Rh.Mus.*58.72, cf. Aët.3.161.

κροκύφαντος [ῠ], ον, (κρόκη, ὑφαίνω) *woven*: as Subst., gloss on κεκρύφαλος, Erot., Eust.1280.59: metaph., *network* of the human body, in contempt, M.Ant.2.2.

κροκ-ώδης, ες, *saffron-coloured*, Dsc.1.27, Aret.*SD*1.15; *containing saffron*, Id.*CA*2.2; κολλύριον Gal.12.715, cf. *CIL*13.10021.66. II. *like the* κρόκη or *thread of the woof*, Pl.*Plt.*309b. **-ωτίδιον**, τό, Dim. of κροκωτός 2, Ar.*Lys.*47, *Ec.*332. **-ώτινος**, η, ον, = κροκωτός I, Ezek. *Exag.*260, *CPR*27.9 (ii A.D.), *PHamb.*10.24 (ii A.D.). **-ώτιον**, τό, = κροκωτίδιον, Poll.7.56. **-ωτός**, ή, όν, *saffron-dyed, saffron-coloured*, Pi.*N.*1.38. 2. as Subst., κροκωτός (sc. χιτών), ὁ, *saffron-coloured robe*, worn by gay women, Ar.*Th.*138, *Ec.*879; as an offering in temples, *IG*1².386.22, 2².1514.60,62; worn by Dionysus (or at his festivals) over the χιτών, Cratin.38, Ar.*Ra.*46; by effeminate men, παρθένος δ' εἶναι δοκεῖ φορῶν κροκωτούς (prob. for κροσ-) Arar.4, cf. Callix.2, Duris 12 J., etc.: neut. pl. κροκωτά (sc. ἱμάτια) v.l. in Ar. *Lys.*44.

κροκωτοφορ-έω, *wear the* κροκωτός, Ar.*Lys.*44, 219. **-ος**, ον, *wearing the* κροκωτός, Plu.2.785e.

κρολίαζε· πλησίαζε θᾶττον, Hsch. (Lydian). **κρόμβος**· ὁ κόνδυλος, καὶ ὁ καπυρός, Id.: Sup. -ότατον· καπυρώτατον, κατακεκονδυλωμένον, Id.

κρομβόω, *roast*, χοιρίδια κ. ὅλα Diph.90.

κρομμύδιον, τό, *small onion*, *Gp.*12.1.2 (κρομύδιν codd.), Sch.Opp. *H.*3.173.

κρομμῠογήτειον, τό, = γήτειον, *horn-onion*, Thphr.*HP*4.6.2.

κρόμμῠον, τό, Ep. **κρόμῠον**, *onion, Allium Cepa*, κρομύοιο λοπόν Od.19.233; κρόμυον ποτῷ ὄψον Il.11.630, cf. Hdt.2.125, 4.17; freq. in Ar., *Lys.*798, etc.; κελεύω κρόμμυα ἐσθίειν, = κλαίειν κελεύω, Bias ap.D.L.1.83. 2. τὰ κ. *the onion-market*, Eup.304. II. κ. σχιστόν, *a variety of Allium Cepa, shallot*, Thphr.*HP*7.4.7. (Written κρόμμυον in *PCair.Zen.*269.4, 300.3, *PSI*4.332.13, *PPetr.*3 p.328 (all iii B.C.), freq. in codd. (confirmed by metre in Ar., etc.); κρόμυον Hom. ll. cc. (perh. metri gr.), *POxy.*1584.23 (ii A.D.), *Stud.Pal.* 22.75.8 (iii A.D.), etc.: prob. assim. fr. κρέμμυον, cf. place-name Κρεμμυών B.17.24, etc.)

κρομμῠοξῠρεγμία, ἡ, *a belch of onions and crudities*, Ar.*Pax* 529.

κρομμῠο-πώλης, ου, ὁ, *dealer in onions*, *PPar.*5 xx 8 (ii B.C., in form κρομβυο-, cf. Wilcken *Ostr.*i p.691), Poll.7.198. **-πώλιον**, τό, *onion-shop*, Hsch. **-φακον**, τό, *onions mixed with lentils*, *PLille* 34.11 (iii B.C.).

κρόμπος or **κρομπός**, ὁ, dub. sens., τὸν λόφον τὸν ἰν τῷ κρόμποι *Schwyzer* 664.12, cf. 16 (Orchom. Arc., iv B.C.).

κρόμῠον, v. κρόμμυον.

Κρον-εῖον, τό, *temple of Cronos*, *PGrenf.*1.11 i 16 (ii B.C.). **-ια**, ων, τά, v. Κρόνιος. **-ιάς**, άδος, ἡ, fem. of Κρόνιος: αἱ Κ. (sc. ἡμέραι), = *Saturnalia*, Plu.*Cic.*18. **-ίδης** [ῐ], ου, ὁ, Patron., *son of Cronos*, i.e. *Zeus*, Il.1.498, al.; Ζεὺς Κ. 2.111, al. II. Lacon. **Κρονίδαρ**, *an aged man*, Hsch. **-ικός**, ή, όν, = sq.; Κ. ἀστήρ the planet *Saturn*, *AP*11.227 (Ammian.); ζῴδια Paul.Al.*O.*3; Κ. ἑορτή, = *Saturnalia*, Plu.*Pomp.*34, Porph.*Antr.*23; Κ. λόφος, = Κρόνιον, Pi.*O.*5.17; also Κ. ὄχθος ib.9.3. II. *old-fashioned, out of date*, Ar. *Pl.*581, Pl.*Ly.*205c (Comp.); πρᾶγμά τι γιγνόμενον ἀεί, Κρονικόν Alex. 62.2, cf. *Com.Adesp.*1052. 2. prov., Κ. λῆμαι, of the short-sighted, Diogenian.5.63, Hsch. **-ιος**, α, ον, (Κρόνος) *of Cronos* or *Saturn*, ὦ Κρόνιε παῖ A.*Pr.*577, Pi.*O.*2.12; Κ. ἅλς the Adriatic, A.R.4.327, 509; but Κ. πόντος the North Sea, Orph.*A.*1081. b. Astrol., Κρόνιον ὄμμα εἰς τὸν οἶκον ἐνέσκηψε, i.e. disaster, Hld.2.24. 2. Κρόνια (sc. ἱερά), τά, *festival of Cronos* at Athens on the twelfth of Hecatombaeon (hence called μὴν Κρόνιος, Plu.*Thes.*12); ὄντων Κρονίων D.24.26; Κ. ἐνστάντων Alciphr.3.57; later, = Lat. *Saturnalia*, D.H.4.14, Plu.2.272e, etc. 3. Κρόνιον (sc. ὄρος), τό, *the hill of Cronos*, near Olympia, Pi.*O.*1.111; = Lat. *templum Saturni*, D.C. 45.17. 4. Κρόνιον, τό, = δελφίνιον, Ps.-Dsc.3.73. II. = Κρονικός II, Κρονίων ὄζειν to smell *of the dark ages*, Ar.*Nu.*398, cf. Sch. ad loc. **-ιππος**, ὁ, *an old dotard*, Ar.*Nu.*1070. **-ίων**, ωνος, ὁ, *son of Cronos*, i.e. *Zeus*, Il.1.397, al.; Ζεὺς Κρονίων ib.502, al.: gen. Κρονίονος only Il.14.247, Od.11.620. II. Κρονιών (sc. μήν), name of a month at Samos, etc., *SIG*976.2 (ii B.C.), al. [Hom. has ῑ in Κρονίων, Κρονίονος, in other cases ῐ: but Tyrt.2.1, Pi.*P.*4.23, etc., use ῐ in Κρονίων.]

Κρονο-δαίμων, ονος, ὁ, = Κρόνος II, *Com.Adesp.*1053. **-θήκη**, ἡ, *receptacle for old follies*, ib.1054. **-ληρος**, ὁ, *old twaddler*, Plu. 2.13b, *Com.Adesp.*1052.

Κρόνος, ὁ, *Cronos*, Hes.*Th.*137, *Op.*111, Il.8.479, 14.203, A.*Pr.* 203, *Eu.*641; οἷς δὴ βασιλεὺς Κ. ἦν 'in the golden age', Cratin.165; ὁ ἐπὶ Κρόνου βίος Arist.*Ath.*16.7.—Later interpreted as, = χρόνος, cf. Arist.*Mu.*401ᵃ15. 2. ὁ τοῦ Κ. (sc. ἀστήρ) the planet *Saturn*, Id. *Metaph.*1073ᵇ35, *Mu.*392ᵃ24, 399ᵃ11; so later Κρόνος, ὁ, *Placit.*2.32.1, Cleom.2.7; ἡ τοῦ Κ. ἡμέρα *Saturday*, D.C.37.16. II. nickname for *a dotard, old fool*, Ar.*Nu.*929, *V.*1480, Pl.*Euthd.*287b, Hyp.*Fr.* 252.

κρόνος, ὁ, = κόρνος, *Gloss.*

Κρονότεκνος, ὁ, *father of Cronos*, epith. of Uranos in Orph.*H.*4.8.

κροντᾷ· κατασήπεται, Hsch. **κρόξ**, v. κρόκη. **κρόπιον**, τό, *two-edged axe*, Id. (cf. κρώπιον).

κροσός, Rhod. for κρωσσός, *Chron.Lind.*B.9.

κρόσσαι, ῶν, αἱ, prob. = *stepped copings of parapets*, κρόσσας μὲν πύργων ἔρυον καὶ ἔρειπον ἐπάλξεις Il.12.258; κροσσάων ἐπέβαινον ib.444 (expld. by Aristarch. as *scaling-ladders*). 2. *courses, steps* of the Pyramids, Hdt.2.125.

κρόσσ-ιον and **-οφθον** (-όφθοον cod.), τό, = κῆμος, Ps.-Dsc.4.133.

κροσσ-ίον, τό, Dim. of sq., Hdn.*Epim.*72. **-οί**, οἱ, *tassels, fringe*, Poll.7.64, Hsch.; *lappets*, θώρακος Gal.18(1).818. **-όω**, assumed as etym. of sq., *EM*541.8, *Et.Gud.*349.33. **-ωτός**, ή, όν, also ός, όν Lyc.1102:—*tasselled, fringed*, l.c., Plu.*Luc.*28, Poll.4.120, *POxy.*1273.14 (iii A.D.): Subst. κροσσωτός (sc. χιτών), ὁ, Lxx *Ps.* 44(45).14; cf. κροκωτός 2. II. (κρόσσαι) *stepped*, σταυροῖσι -ωτὴ πτέρυξ, of a wall, Lyc.291 (v.l. κορσ-).

κρόσταλλος, = κρύσταλλος, Hsch. **κρόστινα**· φυλακτήρια, Id.

κρόσφος, ὁ, = γρόσφος, Eust.795.35.

κροταίνω, poet. collat. form of κροτέω, Opp.*C.*4.247.

κροτάλ-ια [ᾰλ], ων, τά, *ear-rings with pendants of pearl*, which *rattled* against each other, Petron.67, Plin.*HN*9.114. **-ίζω**, *use rattles* or *castanets*, τινὲς τῶν γυναικῶν, κρόταλα ἔχουσαι, κροταλίζουσι Hdt.2.60: hence ἵπποι κείν' ὄχεα κροτάλιζον *rattled* them *along*, Il.11.160. II. later, *clap, applaud*, Anaxil.2, D.Chr.31. 162, Alciphr.2.4:—Pass., Ath.4.159e, 11.503f. **-ισμός**, ὁ, *applause*, *Gloss.* **-ίστρια**, ἡ, *female castanet-player*, *Sammelb.*6945 (iii A.D.); Lat. *crotalistria*, of the stork, from the noise made by its mandibles, Publilius ap.Petron.55. **-ιστρίς**, ίδος, ἡ, = foreg., *POxy.* 475.17,24 (ii A.D.). **-ον**, τό, (κροτέω) in pl., *clapper*, used in the worship of Cybele, *h.Hom.*14.3, Pi.*Fr.*79, Hdt.2.60, Arist.*Mir.*839ᵃ1; of Dionysus, E.*Hel.*1308 (lyr.), cf. *Cyc.*205: generally, in dances, *AP* 5.174 (Mel.), 11.195 (Diosc.). II. sg., metaph., of persons, '*rattle*', Ar.*Nu.*260, 448 (anap.); οἶδ' ἄνδρα, κρόταλον δριμύ E.*Cyc.*104. III. a name for the *narcissus*, Eumach.ap.Ath.15.681e. IV. κόρταλος σημαίνει τὸν κρότον τῆς ψυχῆς *EM* post κορυθαίολος (cod. Voss.); κορτάλων is perh. required by the metre in E.*Hyps.Fr.*1 ii 9 (lyr.).

κροτᾰφ-ίζω, *strike on the temples*, *PLips.*40 iii 24 (iv/v A.D.). **-ιος**, α, ον, *on* or *of the temples*, Gal.14.720. **-ίς**, ίδος, ἡ, *pointed hammer*, resembling the κέστρα, *IG*2².1672.120, Poll.10.147. **-ιστής**, οῦ, ὁ, *one who strikes on the temples*, *Gloss.*, Hsch. s.v. κόβαλος. **-ίτης** [ῑ] μῦς, ὁ, *temporal* muscle, Hp.*Art.*30, Gal.*UP*16.6, Antyll.ap.Orib. 7.16.2, *Arch.Pap.*4.270 (iii A.D.):—fem. **-ίτιδες** πληγαί blows *on the temples*, Hp. l.c. **-ος**, ὁ, *side of the forehead*, Il.4.502, 20. 397, Ar.*Ra.*854: mostly in pl., *temples*, Il.13.188, al., Hdt.4.187, Hp.*Prog.*2, etc.; πρᾶτον ἴουλον ἀπὸ κροτάφων καταβάλλων Theoc.15. 85, cf. 11.9, *IG*5(1).1355 (Abia); τοὺς κ. πολιοῦνται πρῶτον Arist.*GA* 784ᵇ35. 2. generally, *side edge, profile*, Procl.*Hyp.*3.6; κύκλου ib.17; of a brick, *PMag.Par.*1.30; κατὰ κρόταφον *sideways, horizontally*, Hero *Bel.*98.2, Ph.*Bel.*64.25, cf. 60.7; ἐπὶ κρόταφον *on its side*, ib.66.13. II. metaph., *slope* of a mountain, A.*Pr.*721; ὑπὸ κροτάφοις Ἑλικῶνος Philiadas ap.St.Byz. s. v. Θέσπεια. III. *back of a book*, Anon.ap.Suid. IV. *edge* or *narrow side* of a stele, *IG*4²(1).109 iii 162, iv 129 (Epid.). (**κόρταφος** *EM*541.23, *Et.Gud.*, Zonar., prob. to be read in Pl.Com.84; **κότραφος** *PMag.Osl.*1.152, etc.)

κροτ-έω, poet. **κορτέω** Hsch., cf. ἀνακροτέω: (κρότος):—*make to rattle*, of horses, ὄχεα κροτέοντες *rattling* them *along*, Il.15.453, cf. *h.Ap.*234. II. *knock, strike*, λέβητας Hdt.6.58; θύρσῳ γῆν E.*Ba.*188; τοῖς ἀγκῶσι τὰς πλευράς D.54.9; τινα Plu.2.10d: sens. obsc., *IG* 12(7).414 (Amorgos, cf. διακροτέω I):—Pass., *to be beaten* by rain, Ael. *NA*16.17. 2. *clap* in sign of applause, κ. τὰς χεῖρας, τὼ χεῖρε, Hdt. 2.60, X.*Cyr.*8.4.12; ταῖς χερσί Thphr.*Char.*19.10: abs., *applaud*, X.*Smp.*9.4, D.21.226, etc.; ἐν θεάτρῳ Thphr.*Char.*11.3: c. acc., κ. τινά D.L.7.173:—Pass., Arist.*Po.*1456ᵃ10 (sed leg. κρατεῖσθαι), Pl. *Ax.*368d, etc.; τέλειος ῥήτωρ καὶ κεκροτημένος Phld.*Rh.*2.128 S.; παρὰ Ὁμήρῳ κεκρότηται τὰ σώφρονα συμπόσια *are commended*, Ath.5.182a (sed leg. ⟨συγ⟩κεκρ.). b. also in sign of disapproval, Plu.2.533a. 3. κ. ὀδόντας *gnash* the teeth, Archil.*Supp.*2.9. 4. of a smith, *hammer, weld together*, Luc.*Lex.*9: metaph., in Pass., *to be wrought*, κεκρότηται χρυσέα κρηπίς Pi.*Fr.*194, cf. Lyc.888: hence ἐξ ἀπάτας κεκροτημένοι ἄνδρες *one mass* of trickery, Theoc.15.49; εὐθὺς τὸ πρῆγμα κροτείσθω 'strike while the iron is hot', *AP*10.20 (Adaeus). 5. *rattle, clash*, χαλκώματα Plu.2.944b: c. dat., κ. ὀστράκοις καὶ ψήφοις *make a rattling noise* with them, in order to collect a swarm of bees, Arist.*HA*627ᵃ16; κ. κυμβάλοις Luc.*Alex.*9; satirically, ἡ τοῖς ὀστράκοις κροτοῦσα [Μοῦσ' Εὐριπίδου] Ar.*Ra.*1306, cf. Ael.*NA*2.11. 6. *strike the woof home with the weaver's sley*, σινδόνες λίαν κεκροτημέναι *close-woven*, Str.15.1.67. **-ημα**, ατος, τό, *work wrought with the hammer*: metaph., of Odysseus, '*piece of mischief*', S.*Fr.*913, E.*Rh.*499. **-ησίγομφος** [ῐ], ον, *with chattering teeth*, Cerc.6.4. **-ησις**, εως, ἡ, *clapping, striking*, χειρῶν, as a sign of grief, Pl.*Ax.*365a; [σιδήρου] Ph.*Bel.*71.44 (pl.); τοῦ πνεύματος D.H. *Comp.*14 (v.l. for κροῦσις). **-ησμός**, ὁ, = κρότος, [ἀσπὶς] πυκνοῦ κροτησμοῦ τυγχάνουσα A.*Th.*561. **-ητικός**, ή, όν, *plausible*, αἴτησις Dosith. p.427 K. **-ητός**, ή, όν, *stricken, sounding with blows*, κάρα A.*Ch.*428. 2. κ. ἅρματα *rattling, bumping* chariots, S.*El.*714; κροτητὰ πηκτίδων μέλη music *struck from* the harp, Id.*Fr.*241. II. τὰ κροτητά, 1. *cakes* of some kind, E.*Fr.*467.4. 2. *much-trodden places*, Thphr.*HP*6.6.10.

κρότιον, τό, = κατανάγκη, Ps.-Dsc.4.131.

κροτοθόρῠβος, ὁ, *loud applause*, Epicur.*Fr.*143, Plu.2.45f, 1117a, Eun.*Hist.*p.259 D.

κρότος, ὁ, *rattling noise*, made to collect a swarm of bees, Arist.*HA* 627ᵃ16; κ. ποδῶν *beat* of the feet in dancing, E.*Heracl.*783 (pl.), *Tr.*546 (both lyr.); κ. σικινίδων Id.*Cyc.*37; ὁ τῶν δακτύλων κ. *snapping* of the fingers, Ael.*NA*17.5; ἐνόπλιος κ. *clash* of arms, Plu.*Mar.*22; ὁ κ. τῶν λόγων Luc.*Dem.Enc.*15 (but perh. 'welding'); ἡ εὔροια καὶ ὁ τῆς γλώσσης κ. Philostr.*VS*2.25.6; ῥυθμοῖο κ. *APl.*4.226 (Alc. Mess.). 2. κ. χειρῶν *clapping* of hands, *applause*, Ar.*Ra.*157: abs., X.*An.*6.1.13, etc.; θόρυβον καὶ κ... ἐποιήσατε D.21.14, cf. 19.195. b. in token of ridicule, γέλως καὶ κ. Pl.*La.*184a.

κροτών, ῶνος, ὁ, *tick, Ixodes ricinus*, Arist.*HA*552ᵃ15, Agatharch.58, Dsc.1.77, Plu.2.55e: prov., ὑγιέστερος κροτῶνος Men.318 (but Str.6.1.12 has Κρότωνος). II. *castor-oil tree, Ricinus communis* (cf. κίκι), Hp.*Mul.*2.201, Thphr.*HP*1.10.1, 3.18.7, *PRev.Laws* 39.3, al. (iii B. C.), etc. 2. in pl., *seeds* of the tree, *PCair.Zen.*499.10 (iii B. C.); in full, κ. κίκεως Gal.19.743. III. *part of the ear*, Poll.2.85. (Hdn. Gr.1.36 distinguishes κροτών from Κρότων the place-name.)

κροτώνη, ἡ, *excrescence on trees*, esp. *on the olive*, = γόγγρος II, Thphr. *HP*1.8.6. II. in pl., *fragments of bronchial cartilage*, Hp.*Morb.*2.53, cf. Gal.19.115.

κροτωνο-ειδές, τό, = κροτών II, Hp.*Nat.Mul.*32. **-φόρος**, ον, *bearing castor-oil plants*, [γῆ] *Sammelb.*6797.16, al. (iii B. C.), *PPetr.*2 p.110 (= 3 p.69) (iii B. C.).

κρουερ(οῦ)· τοῦ φοβεροῦ, Hsch.; cf. κρυερός.

κροῦμα, ατος, τό, (κρούω) *beat, stroke*, Ar.*Ec.*257 (sens. obsc.):—also **κροῦσμα** *AP*6.27 (Theaet.), Poet.*de herb.*121, Porph.*Abst.*1.43; κρούσμασι καὶ στρέμμασι *blows* and sprains, Paul.Aeg.3.78, cf. Poll.2.199. 2. *sound produced by striking stringed instruments* with the plectron, *note*, κρούεται τὰ κρούματα.., τὰ μὲν ἄνω, τὰ δὲ κάτω Hp. *Vict.*1.18, cf. Ar.*Th.*120 (lyr.), Pl.*R.*333b, *Min.*317d, etc.; τὸ πόημα οὐχ ὡς τερέτισμα καὶ κ. νοοῦμεν Phld.*Po.*2 p.228 H.; also of wind instruments, κρούματα τὰ αὐλήματα καλοῦσιν Plu.2.638c, cf. Poll.4.83, 7.88; σαλπιστικὰ κ. Id.4.84; τοιαῦτα.. νιγλαρεύων κ. Eup.110; αὐλεῖ.. σαπρὰ κ. Theopomp.Com.50; ἡ τοῦ κρούματος ἁρμονία the *melody* (on the pan-pipes), Ach.Tat.8.6, cf. *APl.*1.8 (Alc. Mess.); so, *musical air, melody*, *BGU*1125.4 (i B. C.); ᾠδαὶ καὶ κ. Jul.*Or.*2.49d:—also **κροῦσμα**, *AP*5.291.8 (Agath.).

κροῦμαι· μύξαι, Hsch.

κρουμ-ατικός, ή, όν, *of* or *for playing on a stringed instrument*, σοφίη *AP*11.352.2 (Agath.): in a general sense, ἡ κ. μουσικὴ ἡ διὰ τῶν αὐλῶν Suid. s. v. Ὄλυμπος; διάλεκτος κ. style *in playing*, Plu.2.1138b; λέξεις κρουσματικαί sounds *of music*, i. e. *inarticulate* sounds without sense, Plb.3.36.3. **-άτιον**, τό, Dim. of κροῦμα, *musical phrase*, Ach.Tat. 1.5, Sch.Ar.*Eq.*276, *Pl.*290. **-ατοποιός**, ὁ, *musician*, Macho ap. Ath.8.337c, Aristodem.8; *composer of instrumental music*, Phld. *Mus.*pp.95, 99 K.

κροῦναι· τὰ ἄφορα δένδρα, Hsch.; also, = κρῆναι τέλειαι, Id.

κρουν-εῖον, τό, kind of *drinking vessel*, Epig.6. **-ηδόν**, Adv. *like a spring, gushing*, Lxx 2*Ma.*14.45, Ph.2.96, Harp.Astr. in *Cat.Cod. Astr.*8(3).136. **-ίζω**, *discharge liquid in a slender stream*, of the ῥυτόν (q. v.), κ. λεπτῶς Doroth.ap.Ath.11.497e:—Med., *catch the liquid so running in one's mouth*, Epin.2.3. **-ίον**, τό, Dim. of κρουνός, Hdn.Gr.1.356, 360. **-ίσκος**, ὁ, = foreg., *cock, tap* of the clepsydra, Sch.Luc.*Pisc.*28. **-ισμα**, ατος, τό, *gush, stream*, *APl.*1.12. **-ισμάτιον**, τό, Dim. of foreg., *small nozzle* or *spout*, Hero *Spir.*1.8; *small pipe*, ib.29. **-ισμός**, ὁ, *gushing out of water*, Aq. 2*Ki.*5.8. II. Medic., *douche*, Aët.5.119, Paul.Aeg.2.52. **-ίτης** [ῑ], ου, ὁ, fem. **-ῖτις**, ιδος, *of springs*, Νύμφαι Orph.*H.*51.10. **-ός**, ὁ, *spring, well-head*, whence streams (πηγαί) issue, Il.22.147, 208; χείμαρροι ποταμοὶ.. κρουνῶν ἐκ μεγάλων 4.454, cf. Pi.*O.*13.63, Men. 530.22, *PLond.*3.1177.290 (ii A. D.), etc.; κρουνοὶ κρηναίου ποτοῦ S. *Tr.*14. 2. metaph., κ. αἵματος E.*Rh.*790, cf. *Hec.*568; κρουνοὶ Ἀφαίστοιο *streams* of lava from Etna, Pi.*P.*1.25; of *streaming* perspiration, Hp.*Aph.*7.85, Lib.*Ep.*316.3: metaph., *torrent of words*, θαρρῶν τὸν κ. ἀφίει Ar.*Ra.*1005. 3. *watercourse*, Str.5.3.8. 4. *spout, nozzle*, Hero *Spir.*2.25, al.

κρουνοχυτρολήραιος, ὁ, *pourer forth of washy twaddle*, with collat. notion of *water-drinker*, Com. word in Ar.*Eq.*89.

κρούνωμα, ατος, τό, = κρουνός 2, κ. βρότειον Emp.6.3.

κρουπαλίας· κλεῖδας, Hsch.

κρούπεζαι, αἱ, *high wooden shoes*, used in Boeotia for treading olives, and worn on the stage by flute-players to beat time, Paus. Gr.*Fr.*239, Poll.7.87 (sg.), Phot.:—also **κρούπαλα**, τά, S.*Fr.*44; **κρούπετα**, Hsch.

κρουπέζιον, τό, Dim. of foreg., Poll.10.153, Hsch.

κρουπεζό-ομαι, Pass., *have wooden shoes on*, Hsch. **-φόρος**, ον, *wearing wooden shoes*, of the Boeotians, Cratin.310.

κρουσίδημέω, parody on κρουσιμετρέω, *cheat the people*, Ar.*Eq.*859.

κρουσίης· ἐλλιπής, Hsch.

κρουσί-θῠρος [ῐ], ον, *knocking at the door*: τὸ κ. (sc. μέλος) *serenade*, Trypho ap.Ath.14.618c. **-λύρης** [ῠ], ου, ὁ, *striking the lyre*, Orph.*H.*31.3. **-μετρέω**, *cheat in measuring* corn, *by striking off too much from the top of the measure*, Hsch., Poll.4.169. **-μέτρης**, ου, ὁ, *false measurer, cheat*, Sch.Ar.*Nu.*450.

κροῦσις, εως, ἡ, *striking, smiting, collision*, αἱ πρὸς ἀλλήλας κ., of atoms, Epicur.*Nat.Herc.*1431.16; ἡ πρὸς ἄλληλα κ. τῶν ὅπλων Plu. *Aem.*32; ποδὸς κρούσει χρώμενος *spurring* with the heel, of a rider, Id.*Alex.*6. 2. *tapping* or *ringing* of earthen vessels, to see whether they are sound: hence, generally, *scrutiny*, Suid. 3. metaph., of sophistical *attempts to deceive, chicanery*, Ar.*Nu.*318. 4. *playing on a stringed instrument*, Plu.*Per.*15, 2.1137b, etc.: generally, *instrumental music*, Plb.30.22.5; κρούσεις καὶ μέλη Phld.*Mus.* p.13 K.; παρὰ τὴν κροῦσιν λέγειν, of the recitative, ᾄδειν, of the air sung *to the accompaniment of instrumental music*, Plu.2.1141a; κ. ἡ ὑπὸ τὴν ᾠδήν *heterophone accompaniment*, ib.b.

κροῦσμα, κρουσματικός, v. κρουμ-.

κρουσ-μός, ὁ, = κροῦσις 4, Procl.ap.Phot.*Bibl.*p.320 B. II. κ. ὀδόντων *gnashing* of teeth, Aus.*Ep.*8.8. **-τέον**, *one must knock at*, τηνδεδί (sc. θύραν) Ar.*Ec.*989. **-της**, ου, ὁ, = Lat. *petulcus*, Dosith.p.397 K. **-τικός**, ή, όν, *fit for striking, butting*, of a ram, Ph.1.113. II. *able to sound the right note*, ὄργανα Arist.*Pr.*918ᵃ33; κ. θίξις χορδῶν, opp. ἠθική, Plu.2.802f. 2. metaph., of a rhetorician or sophist, *striking, impressive*, Ar.*Eq.*1379; τὸ κ. *striking eloquence*, Luc.*Dem.Enc.*32. **-τός**, ή, όν, *played by striking*, ὄργανα Nicom.*Harm.*2. II. κρουστὰ γράμματα· ἀπὸ τοῦ παρακρούεσθαι καὶ μὴ εὐθέως λέγειν, Phot.

κρουτεῖται· κοκκίζει, Hsch. **κρουφάδαν**, v. κρυφάδην.

κρούω, fut. -σω E.*El.*180: aor. ἔκρουσα X.*An.*4.5.18, Hyp.*Fr.*201: pf. κέκρουκα Diogenian.3.38, (ἐκ-) Pl.*Phdr.*228e, (προσ-) D.21.206:—**Med.**, aor. ἐκρουσάμην Th.7.40:—**Pass.**, aor. ἐκρούσθην Eratosth.*Cat.*32: pf. κέκρουμαι (ἀπο-) X.*HG*7.4.26, or -ουσμαι (ἀπο-) Ar.*Ach.*459:—*strike, smite*, ῥυτῆρι κ. γλουτόν S.*Fr.*501; κρούσας δὲ πλευρὰ [τῶν ἵππων] E.*Fr.*779.6; τὸν λυχνοῦχον Lys.*Fr.*83; τοῖς ποσὶ τὴν γῆν Arr.*An.*7.1.5; also εἰς τὴν χεῖρα τοῖς δακτύλοις κ. *with the fingers*, D.C.40.16: metaph., κνῖσα κ. ῥινὸς ὑπεροχάς *tickles*, Ephipp. 3.3. 2. *strike* one *against* another, *strike together*, κ. χεῖρας *clap* the hands, E.*Supp.*720; τὰ ὅπλα κρουόμενα πρὸς ἄλληλα Th.3.22; τὰς ἀσπίδας πρὸς τὰ δόρατα X.*An.* l. c.: metaph., ἀλλήλων τοὺς λόγους τοῖς λόγοις ἐκρούομεν ἄν *would have knocked* their heads together, Pl.*Tht.*154e. 3. κ. πόδα (i. e. κ. τὴν γῆν τῷ ποδί), in dancing, E.*El.* l. c. (lyr.); ἴχνος ἐν γᾷ κ. Id.*IA*1043 (lyr.). 4. metaph. from *tapping* an earthen vessel, to try whether it rings sound (cf. κροῦσις 2): *examine, try, prove*, κρούετε ἀπολαμβάνοντες τὸ καλόν Pl.*Hp.Ma.*301b; κἂν διαπειρώμενος κρούσῃς [τὸν κόλακα] Plu.2.64d. 5. *strike* a stringed instrument with a plectron, Simon.183, Pl.*Ly.*209b: generally, *play* any instrument (v. κροῦμα, κρουματικός), αὐλεῖ.. κρούων ἰαστί *Com.Adesp.*415: c. dat., κ. κρεμβάλοις, = κρεμβαλίζειν, Ath.14.636d. 6. κ. τὴν θύραν *knock at* the door *on the outside*, Ar.*Ec.*317, 990 (with play on signf. 8), X.*Smp.*1.11, Pl.*Prt.*310b, 314d, etc.; κόπτειν is better Att. acc. to Phryn.154; later κ. ἐπὶ τὴν θύραν Lxx *Jd.*19.22. 7. κ. σταθμὸν ἑτερόζυγον, = κρουσιμετρέω, Ps.-Phoc.15; ὡς μήτε κρούσῃς μήθ' ὑπὲρ χεῖλος βάλῃς S.*Fr.*796; κρούων γε μὴν αὐτὰς ἐωνούμην Eup.184. 8. sens. obsc., *AB*101, cf. Ar.*Ec.*990; κ. πέπλον E.*Cyc.*328. 9. Med., κρούεσθαι πρύμναν *back water*, Th.1.51, 54, 3.78; αἱ πρύμναν κρουόμεναι νῆες Arr.*An.*5.17.7 (also in Act., Plb.16.3.8); κ. ἐπὶ π. τὴν ναῦν App.*BC*5.119: hence κρούεσθαι τὸ πτερόν *fly backwards*,

Ael.*NA*3.13 :—also in Act., Plot.2.9.18. 10. κρούειν ἀκράτῳ, v. πατάσσω II.2. (Cf. Lith. *krùšti* 'bruise', 'pound', Lett. *krausēt* 'thresh'.)

κρυαίνω, = ἱμείρω, Theognost.*Can.*21 (cf. Archil.176).

κρῠβ-άζω, = ἀποκρύπτω, Hsch. :—hence **-αστός**, = κρυπτός, prob. l. for κυρβαστός, *EM*547.46.

κρύβακτος, ὁ, dub. sens. in *Stud.Pal.*20.230.8 (iv A. D.).

κρύβ-δᾰ, Adv., (κρύπτω) *without the knowledge of*, c. gen., κ. Διός Il.18.168; Ὀρέστου κ. A.*Ch.*177. 2. abs., *secretly*, Pi.*P.*4.114. **-δην**, Dor. **-δᾱν**, Adv. *secretly*, Od.11.455, 16.153, Hp. *Mul.*1.54, Ar.*V.*1018, etc.; κ. ψηφίζεσθαι Lex ap.And.1.87, cf. Lys. 12.91, Pl.*Lg.*766b, Arist.*Rh.Al.*1433ᵃ23, *IG*2².1237.82. 2. c. gen., = foreg. 1, κ. πατρός Pi.*P.*3.13. **-ες**· νεκροί, Hsch. **-ῆ**, Adv., = κρύβδην, v.l. in Lxx 2*Ki.*12.12, cf. 3*Ma.*4.12, *POxy.*83.14 (iv A. D.) :—also **-ήν**, *Corp.Herm.*13.1 (s. v. l.). **-ηλος**, ον, *hidden*, Hsch. :—also **-ήτης**, ου, ὁ, *one hidden in the earth*, and **-ήσια**, τά, = νεκύσια, Id. **-ω**, late form of κρύπτω, Conon 50.2, Phlp.*in APr.* 448.17, *PMag.Par.*1.385, *PMag.Leid.V.*10.10, *Gp.*2.24.2, Sch.E.*Hec.* 739 :—Pass., Lxx 4*Ki.*11.3, al. (also v. l. in Hp.*Mul.*2.154); mostly found in compds.

κρῠερός, ά, όν, but ἀρῆς κρυεροῖο Hes.*Th.*657: (κρύος) :—*icy, cold, chilling*, in Hom. only metaph., κρυεροῖο γόοιο Od.4.103, al.; κρυεροῖο φόβοιο Il.13.48; κρυεροῦ Ἀΐδαο Hes.*Op.*153; θανάτου τελευτή E.*Fr.* 916.6 (anap.); πάθεα Ar.*Ach.*1191 (lyr.); θάλαμος, of the grave, *Epigr.Gr.*241.4 (Smyrna): in the lit. sense, *icy-cold*, κ. νέκυς Simon. 114.5, cf. Ar.*Av.*951, 955, Hdn.1.6.1, etc.

κρύμα· εὕρημα, Hsch.

κρῡμ-αίνω, *make cold*, Hdn.*Epim.*75. **-αλέος**, α, ον, *icy, chilly*, Heraclit.*All.*50, S.E.*M.*9.83. **-νός**, **-νώδης**, dub. forms for κρυμός, κρυμώδης (qq. v.).

κρῡμοπᾰγής, ές, *frost-congealing*, Βορέης Orph.*H.*80.2.

κρῡμός, ὁ, (κρύος) *icy cold, frost*, Hdt.4.8, 28, etc.; ἀνὰ κρυμόν in *frost*, Nic.*Th.*681: in pl., κατὰ τοὺς κρυμούς Str.11.2.8, cf. D.H.1.37, Onos.10.5, Polyaen.3.9.34, Ael.*NA*2.1. II. *chill, cold fit*, S.*Fr.* 507, Hp.*Morb.*4.53, Call.*Aet.*3.1.19 (nisi leg. καυμός), Ruf.ap.Orib. 45.30.21; κ. χολῆς E.*Fr.*682, cf. Dsc.3.53 (pl.). (κρυμνὸς ἢ κρυμός, Hsch.)

κρῡμοχᾰρής, ές, *delighting in frost*, f.l. in Orph.*H.*51.13 for δρυμο-.

κρυμνεῖ· ῥιγᾷ, πέφρικε, Hsch.

κρῡμ-ώδης, ες, *icy-cold, frozen*, Hp.*Vict.*2.65 (κρυμν- codd.), D.P. 780, Men.Prot.p.47 D.; Ἄλπεις *AP*9.561 (Phil.): Comp., Ph.2.298, Metop.ap.Stob.3.1.116: Sup., Ael.*NA*3.13. **-ώσσω**, *to be stiff with cold*, Theognost.*Can.*21.

κρῡ-όεις, εσσα, εν, *chilling*, in metaph. sense, φόβου κρυόεντος Il.9.2; κρυόεσσα Ἰωκή 5.740; ἐν πολέμῳ κρυόεντι Hes.*Th.*936; συντυχία Pi.*I.*1.37: later in lit. sense, *icy-cold*, ἅλς, πάγος, A.R.1.918, *AP*6. 221 (Leon.); Τάρταρος Orph.*Fr.*222; of Saturn, *Cat.Cod.Astr.*1.172; cf. ὀκρυόεις. **-όομαι**, Pass., *to be icy-cold*, κρυοῦται *it freezes*, *Gloss.* **-ος**, εος, τό, *icy cold, frost*, Hes.*Op.*494, Pl.*Ax.*368c, Jul. *Or.*6.181d; κ. ἰσχυρόν Arist.*Mete.*367ᵃ22: metaph., κακόν με καρδίαν τι περιπίτνει κρύος A.*Th.*834, cf. *Eu.*161 (both lyr.). II. κ., ὁ, = κρύσταλλος, Sch.Ar.*Nu.*766. (Cf. Lat. *crusta*.)

κρυπ-τάδιος [ᾰ], α, ον (and ος, ον A.*Ch.*946 (lyr.)), *secret, clandestine*, κρυπταδίῃ φιλότητι Il.6.161; κρυπταδίου μάχας A. l. c.; κρυπτάδια φρονέοντα Il.1.542. Regul. Adv. **-ίως** Man.2.195, 6.182. **-τεία**, ἡ, (κρυπτεύω) *secret service* at Sparta, Pl.*Lg.*633b; employed against the Helots, Arist.*Fr.*538; ὁ ἐπὶ τῆς κ. τεταγμένος Plu.*Cleom.*28. II. *hiding-place*, Agath.5.19 (pl.). **-τέον**, *one must hide*, S.*Ant.*273, *AP* 5.251 (Paul. Sil.). **-τεύω**, *hide oneself, lie concealed*, E.*Ba.*888 (lyr.), X.*Cyr.*4.5.5 :—Pass., = ἐνεδρεύομαι (cf. Hsch.), E.*Hel.*541. **-τή**, ἡ, *crypt, vault*, Callix.1. II. v. κρυπτός ad fin. **-τήρ**, ῆρος, ὁ, = sq., τόποι Sch.Opp.*H.*3.235. **-τήριος**, α, ον, *convenient for concealing*, ἄντρον Orac.ap.Paus.8.42.6; κρυπτήριον, τό, *dungeon*, prob. l. in E.*Cret.*48. **-της**, ου, ὁ, *member of the Spartan* κρυπτεία, Id. *Fr.*1126 (s. v. l.). **-τικός**, ή, όν, *obscuring*, Alex.Aphr.*in Top.* 528.12, 530.1. Adv. **-κῶς**, πυνθάνεσθαι Arist.*Top.*156ᵃ14; εἰπεῖν Alex.Aphr.*in SE*100.10. **-τίνδα**, Adv. *hide-and-seek*, Theognost. *Can.*15. **-τορχος**, ὁ, *with undescended testicles*, *PSI*3.252.25 (iii A. D.). **-τός**, ή, όν, *hidden, secret*, κληῖδι κρυπτῇ Il.14.168, cf. Ar.*Th.*422; ἐπεποίητό οἱ κ. διῶρυξ Hdt.3.146; κ. τάφρος a trench *covered and concealed* by planks and earth, Id.4.201: freq. in Trag., κ. λόγος A.*Ch.*773; ἔπη S.*Ph.*1112 (lyr.); κρυπτᾷ ἐν ἥβᾳ, of young Orestes who was *concealed* in Phocis, Id.*El.*159 (lyr.); κ. πένθος E. *Hipp.*139 (lyr.), etc.; κρυπτῇ ψήφῳ Arist.*Rh.Al.*1424ᵇ1; τῆς πολιτείας τὸ κ. *the secret character* of the [Spartan] institutions, Th.5.68; ἡ κρυπτή (sc. ἀρχή) *secret service*, used by the Athenians in the subject-states, *AB*273; also, = κρυπτεία 1, Heraclid.*Pol.*10; of persons, *in disguise*, Ar.*Th.*600, E.*El.*525: Medic., *deep-seated*, καρκίνος Hp.*Aph.* 6.38, *Mul.*2.133, Gal.5.116; κ. πάθος *BGU*316.28 (iv A. D.). **-τω**, Ep. Iterat. κρύπτασκε Il.8.272, -εσκε *h.Cer.*239: fut. κρύψω Od.4.350, etc.: aor. 1 ἔκρυψα, Ep. κρύψα 11.244: pf. κέκρυφα (συγ-) D.H.*Comp.* 18 :—Med., fut. κρύψομαι S.*Tr.*474, E.*Ba.*955: aor. ἐκρυψάμην S. *Aj.*246 (lyr.), etc. :—Pass., fut. κρυφθήσομαι *Dialex.*2.4, κρῠβήσομαι E.*Supp.*543, Lxx *Je.*39(32).27, κεκρύψομαι Hp.*Mul.*1.36: aor. ἐκρύφθην, Ep. κρ- Il.13.405, E.*Ba.*955, ἐκρύβην [ῠ] *Ev.Jo.*8.59, Aesop. 127, Apollod.3.2.2, (κατ-) Alciphr.3.47; part. κρυφείς S.*Aj.*1145: pf. κέκρυμμαι Od.11.443, Pi.*O.*7.57, etc.; Ion. 3 pl. κεκρύφαται Hes. *Th.*730, Hp.*Mul.*2.163 :—*hide, cover*, in Hom. with collat. notion of protection, κεφαλὰς.. κορύθεσσι κρύψαντες Il.14.373; ὁ δέ μιν σάκεϊ κρύπτασκε φαεινῷ 8.272, cf. 13.405 (Pass.); κ. με..πόδα S.*OC* 114; later, simply, *hide*, κ. φάος ὀμμάτων Pi.*N.*10.40; *cover*, τινά τινι A.*Eu.*461, etc.; ὑφ' εἵματος κ. χεῖρα E.*Hec.*343 :—Med., κάρα κρυψάμενος *having cloaked his* head, S.*Aj.*246 (lyr.); φύει τ' ἄδηλα καὶ φανέντα κρύπτεται *hides in its own bosom*, ib.647; παῖδά μ' ἐκρύψατο κρωσσός *IG*14.1909 :—Pass., *hide oneself, lie hidden*, οὐρανῷ κρύπτεται E.*Hel.*606; δαλὸς κρύπτεται ἐς σποδιάν Id.*Cyc.*615 (lyr.); ὑφ' εἵματος κρυφείς S.*Aj.*1145: c. acc. cogn., κρύψει σὺ κρύψιν ἥν σε κρυφθῆναι χρεών E.*Ba.* l. c. 2. *cover in the earth, bury*, Hes.*Op.* 138, S.*OC*621 (Pass.); χθονί ib.1546 (Pass.); τάφῳ Id.*Ant.*196; ἐν κατώρυχι ib.774; κατὰ χθονός ib.25; ὑπὸ γᾶν Pi.*P.*9.81; γῇ κ. Hdt.2. 130 (Pass.), cf. S.*Ant.*946 (lyr., Pass.) :—Pass., Τιτῆνες ὑπὸ ζόφῳ.. κεκρύφαται Hes.*Th.* l. c.; ἐν βένθεσιν νᾶσον κεκρύφθαι Pi.*O.* l. c. 3. Astron., *occult*, Theo Sm.p.193 H., al. :—Pass., of stars not seen in any part of the night, κεκρύφαται Hes.*Op.*386; of the heliacal *setting* of stars, Ptol.*Phas.*p.8 H. 4. *conceal, keep secret*, οὐδέν τοι ἐγὼ κρύψω ἔπος Od.4.350, cf. Ar.*Th.*74, etc.; κ. τι ἔνθα μή τις ὄψεται S. *Aj.*658, cf. *Tr.*903, *El.*436 :—Med., πᾶν σοι φράσω τἀληθές, οὐδὲ κρύψομαι Id.*Tr.*474 :—Pass., τὸ μὲν φάσθαι, τὸ δὲ καὶ κεκρυμμένον εἶναι Od. 11.443; φάρμακα κεκρ. *secret*, E.*Andr.*32; κεκρ. νάπη *secret*, S.*OT* 1398; κεκρ. παγίς Men.689; κεκρ. σκευωρία *secret* intrigue, Mitteis *Chr.*31 vi 14 (ii B. C.); κρυπτόμενα πράσσεται *in secret*, opp. ἐπὶ μαρτύρων, Antipho 2.3.8, cf. Th.6.72. b. *connive at*, S.*El.*825 (lyr.). 5. c. dupl. acc., *conceal* something from one, μή με κρύψῃς τοῦτο A.*Pr.* 625, cf. S.*El.*957, E.*Hec.*570, Ar.*Pl.*26, Lys.32.7, etc.; so κ. τι πρός τινα S.*Ph.*588. 6. in Rhet., *argue so that the opponent is unwarily led to an adverse conclusion*, Arist.*Top.*156ᵃ7. 7. Medic., in Pass., *to be suppressed*, of the menses or lochia, Hp.*Mul.*1.36, 154, 2. 163. II. intr., *lie hidden*, τὰ μὲν..ὄμματα βλέποντα, τὰ δὲ κρύπτοντα E.*Ph.*1117 (s. v. l.); also κ. τινά *conceal oneself from*.., *h.Hom.* 1.7.—(καλύπτω is simply *cover*; κεύθω *cover* so that no trace of it can be seen; κρύπτω *keep covered*, esp. for purposes of concealment.)

κρυσταίνομαι, Pass., *to be congealed with cold, freeze*, Nic.*Al.* 314.

κρυσταλλ-ίζω, *to be clear as crystal*, *Apoc.*21.11. **-ῐνος**, η, ον, *icy*, χεῖρες Hp.*Epid.*7.25. II. *of crystal*, κύλιξ D.C.54.23; νίπτρα *AP*9.330 (Nicarch.). **-ιον**, τό, = ψύλλιον, Dsc.4.69 (Sicel). II. *rock-crystal*, in pl., *PHolm.*11.43, Anon.Alch.p.359 B.

κρυσταλλο-ειδής, ές, *like ice*, πῆξις Epicur.*Ep.*2 p.45 U., cf. Lxx *Wi.*19.21; v.l. for -ώδης in Str.4.6.6. Adv. **-δῶς** *Placit.*2.11.2. II. *like crystal*, ἰασπίς Dsc.5.142; κ. ὑγρόν the *crystalline lens*, Ruf.*Onom.* 153, Gal.*UP*8.5, al.; κ. χιτών Poll.2.71: Astron., τὸ κ. the *crystalline sphere*, *Placit.*2.14.3. **-ομαι**, Pass., *to be frozen*, Ph.2.174, Anon. ap.Gell.17.8.7. **-πηκτος**, ον, *congealed to ice, frozen*, E.*Rh.*441 :—also **-πήξ**, ῆγος, ὁ, ἡ, A.*Pers.*501.

κρύσταλλος, ὁ, (κρύος, κρυσταίνομαι) *ice*, Il.22.152, Od.14.477, Hdt. 4.28, S.*Fr.*149; κρύσταλλος ἐπεπήγει οὐ βέβαιος Th.3.23; ὁ παῖς τὸν κρύσταλλον. prov., of persons who cannot keep a thing, but do not wish to let it go, Zen.5.58. 2. = νάρκη, *numbness, torpor*, Opp.*H.* 3.155. II. *rock-crystal*, D.P.781, Str.15.1.67, Ael.*NA*15.8, etc.: also fem., *AP*9.753 (Claudian.): as Adj., οἱ κ. λίθοι D.S.2.52.

κρυσταλλοφᾰνής, ές, *of the look* or *transparency of crystal*: κρυσταλλοφανῆ, τά, *glass ware*, Str.16.2.25.

κρυσταλλώδης, ες, *icy, glacial*, Ptol.*Tetr.*94, D.C.49.31; of water, *clear*, *PHolm.*25.33.

κρῡτοπώλης, v. γρυτοπώλης.

κρύφ-ᾰ [ῠ], Adv., (κρύπτω) = κρύβδα, *without the knowledge of*, c. gen., Th.1.101. 2. abs., *secretly*, Aen.Tact.2.4; *by ballot*, Th. 4.88; *obscurely*, κ. καὶ δι' αἰνιγμάτων Plu.2.1125e. **-ᾳ**, Adv. Dor. for κρυφῇ, Pi.*O.*1.47, *Fr.*203. **-άδην**, Boeot. **κρουφάδαν**, = foreg., Corinn.*Supp.*2.59 :—also **-άδις**, Hdn.Gr.1.512; **-άδεια**, ib. 496. **-αῖος**, α, ον, also ος, ον Phld.*Piet.*101, Luc.*Ocyp.*166 :—*hidden*, Pi.*I.*1.67, A.*Ch.*83 (lyr.), S.*Aj.*899, Pl.*Ti.*77c; ἐν κρυφαίοις Lxx *Je.*23.24, al. 2. *secret, clandestine*, δρασμός A.*Pers.*360; ἔκπλους ib.385; ἔπος S.*Fr.*935; ἀδικίαι Phld. l. c. Adv. **-ως** A.*Pers.*370, Aen.Tact.18.8.

κρύφαλον· σαβάκανον, Hsch. **κρυφανδόν** (-άνδων cod.), = κρυφηδόν, Id.

κρύφασος, ὁ, *a certain throw of the dice*, Poll.7.204.

κρῠφ-ῇ, Adv. *secretly, in secret*, S.*Ant.*85, 291, 1254, X.*Smp.*5.8, etc. :—Dor. **κρυφᾷ** (q. v.); also ἐν κρυφῇ Lxx *Jd.*4.21, 9.31. **-ηδόν**, Adv., = foreg., opp. ἀμφαδόν, Od.14.330, cf. Q.S.14.60. **-ία**, ἡ, *concealment, hiding*, *PFlor.*284.8 (vi A. D.). **-ιαστής**, οῦ, ὁ, *interpreter of dreams*, Aq.*Ge.*41.8, al. **-ιμαίως**, Adv. *secretly*, Sch. Ar.*Pax*730. **-ιμος**, ον, = κρύφιος, Man.1.159, al., *PMag.Par.*1. 1353, *PMag.Lond.*122.15, *Cat.Cod.Astr.*8(4).185: Comp., Dam.*Pr.* 275.

κρυφίνους· ὑπούλους, Hsch. (cf. κρυψίνους).

κρύφ-ιος [ῠ], α, ον, also ος, ον E.*IT*1328, Th.7.25 :—*hidden, concealed*, θυμός Pi.*P.*1.84; ὄφις S.*Ph.*1328. 2. *secret, clandestine*, ὀαρισμοί Hes.*Op.*789; λέχος S.*Tr.*360; εὐναί E.*El.*719 (lyr.); ἔρωτες Musae.1; ψᾶφοι Pi.*N.*8.26; κ. εἰσῆλθον E.*HF*598. Adv. **-ίως** Ps.-Luc.*Philopatr.*9. 3. *occult*, Procl.*Inst.*121, Dam.*Pr.*151; *latent*, ib.192, 201. Adv. **-ίως** ib.153. 4. voc. κρύφιε *such an one*, Lxx *Ru.*4.1. 5. κρύφιος, ὁ, fabulous gem, Ps.-Plu.*Fluv.*13.4. 6. κρύφιος, ὁ, title of a grade of initiates in the mysteries of Mithras, *CIL* 6.751*a*, 753 (pl.). **-ιότης**, ητος, ἡ, *secrecy, obscurity*, Suid. s. v. ἀδηλία, Sch.Opp.*H.*2.258, Sch.E.*Ph.*1214. **-ιώδης**, ες, *mysterious*, Eust.1942.62 (Comp.).

κρῠφο-γενής, ές, *secretly born*, Hsch. s.v. κυθηγενέσι. **-νους**, ουν, = κρυψίνους, *EM*20.49; cf. κρυφίνους.

κρῠφ-ός, ὁ, = κρυφιότης, Emp.27.3 (dub.); κρυφὸν θέμεν to throw *a cloud* over.., Pi.*O*.2.97 (κρύφιον codd.). II. *lurking-place*, Lxx 1*Ma*.2.36, 1.53. (On the accent v. Hdn.Gr.1.225.) **-ω**, late form of κρύπτω, only impf., Q.S.1.393, *AP*7.700 (Diod.), Nonn.*D*.7.45, al.

κρυψί-γονος [ῐ], ον, *secretly born*, Orph.*H*.50.3. **-δομος**, ον, *dwelling in secret places*, ib.51.3 (Casaub. for κρυψίδρομος, *running secretly*). **-λογος**, ον, *keeping a matter secret*, Hdn.*Epim.* 38. **-μέτωπος**, ον, *hiding the forehead*, Luc.*Lex*.7. **-νοος**, ον, contr. **-νους**, ουν, *hiding one's thoughts, dissembling*, X.*Cyr*.1.6.27, Gal.8.362, D.C.67.1, Eun.*Hist*.p.254D.; opp. παρρησιαζόμενος, X. *Ages*.11.5. Adv. -νως Poll.4.51. **-ποθος**, ον, *with concealed longing*, *EM*543.48.

κρύψιππος, ὁ, nickname of Chrysippus, D.L.7.182.

κρυψιπυρίς, *pigra*, *Gloss.*

κρύψις, εως, ἡ, (κρύπτω) *hiding, concealment*, κρυφθῆναι κρύψιν E. *Ba*.955, cf. Plb.10.46.3; opp. φάσις, of stars, *disappearance* below the horizon, Gem.13.2, al., Ti.Locr.97b (pl.); *occultation*, Theo Sm. p.192 H. (pl.); *heliacal setting*, Metrod.*Herc*.831.10, Ptol.*Alm*.8.4, *Tetr*.4, Theo Sm.p.137 H.; of new moon, Ptol.*Tetr*.22; *disappearance*, Plu.2.366d. 2. *suppression*, ἐπιμηνίων Gal.19.495. 3. *concealment* of stolen goods, Arist.*Rh*.1372^a32. 4. *mystery, secret*, κρύψιν μεγάλην ἀνυμνοῦντες Dam.*Pr*.52 bis.

κρυψί-φρων, φρονος, ὁ, ἡ, = κρυψίνοος, Eust.1574.20. **-χολος**, ον, *dissembling one's anger*, Id.54.8.

κρυψ-όρχης, ου, ὁ, *with undescended testicles*, Sor.1.109. **-ορχις**, εως, ἡ, *undescended testicles*, Gal.19.448.

κρῠώδης, ες, *icy, chill*, Plu.2.653a, Poll.5.109.

κρωβύλ-η [ῠ], ἡ, *hair-net*, Serv. ad Virg.*Aen*.4.138, Hdn.Gr.1. 323. **-ος** (parox., v. Hdn.Gr.1.163), ὁ, *roll* or *knot of hair on the crown of the head*, worn at Athens, κρωβύλον ἀναδούμενοι Th.1.6, cf. Antiph.189, Sch.Ar.*Nu*.980. 2. nickname of the orator Hegesippus, Aeschin.3.118. 3. name of a πορνοβοσκός: prov., Κρωβύλου ζεῦγος 'a precious pair', Lib.*Ep*.91.2, Hsch., etc. II. *tuft of hair* on a helmet, X.*An*.5.4.13. **-ώδης**, ες, *like the* κρωβύλος, Luc.*Lex*.13.

κρῶγ-μα, ατος, τό, = sq., Hdn.*Epim*.73. **-μός**, ὁ, *croaking, cawing of a crow* or *chough*, *AP*7.713 (Antip.), Jul.*Mis*.337c (pl.).

κρώζω, fut. κρώξω, prop. *croak*, of the κορώνη, Hes.*Op*.747, cf. Ar. *Av*.2, 24, Arat.953, Luc.*Asin*.12, Poll.5.89; also of other birds, as cranes, Ar.*Av*.710; of young halcyons, Luc.*VH*2.40; also, of men, *croak out*, τι Ar.*Lys*.506, *Pl*.369; of a wagon, *creak, groan*, Babr.52. 5. (Onomatop.)

κρωκαλέον· παιδίον πανοῦργον, Hsch.; cf. κρόκαλον.

κρωμᾰκίσκος, ὁ, *young pig*, Antiph.215 (dub.).

κρῶμαξ, ἄκος, ὁ, *heap of stones*, = κλῶμαξ, Hsch.:—hence **κρωμᾰκόεις**, = κρημνώδης, Id.; **κρωμᾰκωτός**, ή, όν, Paphlagon. word, Eust. 330.40. [κρώμᾰξ, ἄκος, acc. to Hdn.Gr.(?) in *Philol*.39.354.]

κρώπιον, τό, *scythe, bill-hook*, Pherecyd.154 J.:—in Hsch. **κρώβιον** (κρόβ- cod.).

κρῶπος, ὁ, = κρωσσός, Theognost.*Can*.21, Zonar.

κρῶσσαι, αἱ, v.l. for κρόσσαι, Hdt.2.125.

κρωσσίον, τό, Dim. of sq., *AP*9.272 (Bianor).

κρωσσός, ὁ, *water-pail, pitcher*, mostly in pl., A.*Fr*.96 (anap.), S. *OC*478, E.*Ion*1173, *Cyc*.89: in sg., Theoc.13.46. 2. *cinerary urn*, πένθιμε κρωσσέ Erinn.5, cf. Mosch.4.34: also fem., με.. ὀλίγη ἐκρύψατο κ. *Epigr.Gr*.697a.

κρωτάνεροι· βάναυσοι πολῖται, καὶ ἐξελευθεριῶται, Hsch.

κτά, κταίνω, κτάμεν, -εναι, κτάμενος, κτάνε, κτάνθεν, v. κτείνω.

κτάντης, ου, ὁ, (κτείνω) *murderer*, Dosiad.*Ara* 10.

κτάομαι, Ion. **κτέομαι**, only as v.l. in Hdt.8.112: fut. κτήσομαι Archil.6.4, Thgn.200, A.*Eu*.289, Th.6.30, Pl.*R*.417a, etc. (in pass. sense, Plot.2.9.15, s.v.l.); κεκτήσομαι A.*Th*.1022, E.*Ba*.514, Pl.*Grg*. 467a (ἐκτήσομαι in *La*.192e, and prob. in Emp.110.4): aor. ἐκτησάμην, Ep. κτ-, Od.14.4, Pi.*Pae*.2.59, etc.: pf. κέκτημαι Hes.*Op*.437, etc., ἔκτημαι Il.9.402, A.*Pr*.795, Hdt.2.44, and sts. in Pl. (κεκτήμεθα and ἐκτῆσθαι in following lines, *R*.505b, ἐκτῆσθαι τοῦ κεκτῆσθαι ἕνεκα *Tht*. 198d); Ion. 3 pl. ἐκτέαται Hdt.4.23; subj. κέκτωμαι Isoc.3.49, Pl. *Lg*.936b; opt. κεκτῄμην, ῇτο, ib.731c, 742e, κεκτῴμην E.*Heracl*.282 codd.: plpf. ἐκεκτήμην And.1.74, 4.41, Lys.2.17, etc.; poet. κεκτήμην E.*IA*404; Ion. 3 pl. ἔκτηντο Hdt.2.108; Att. 1 pl. ἐκτήμεθα f.l. in And.3.37: for fut. and aor. Pass., v. infr. III. I. pres., impf., fut., and aor., 1. *procure for oneself, get, acquire*, κτήμασι τέρπεσθαι τὰ γέρων ἐκτήσατο Πηλεύς Il.9.400, etc.; [οἴκῆας] Od.1.c.; γῆν A.*Eu*. l.c., cf. *Pers*.770; of horses, *win* (as a prize), Pi.*N*.9.52; κτήσασθαι βίον ἀπό τινος *to get one's* living from a thing, Hdt.8.106; *win* favour, and the like, χάριν ἀπό τινος, ἔκ τινος, S.*Tr*.471, *Ph*.1370; παρά τινος X. *Smp*.4.43; τὴν εὔνοιαν τὴν παρὰ τῶν Ἑλλήνων Isoc.5.68; κ. φίλους, ἑταίρους, S.*Aj*.1360, E.*Or*.804 (troch.); κτήσασθαι παῖδας ἐξ ὁμοσπόρου Id. *IT*696, cf. S.*OT*1499, Hdt.8.105; παῖδας ἐς δόμους κτήσασθαι E.*Fr*.491, cf. *Supp*.225; πολλάκις δοκεῖ τὸ φυλάξαι τἀγαθὰ τοῦ κτήσασθαι χαλεπώτερον εἶναι D.1.23. b. of consequences, *bring upon oneself*, αὑτῷ θάνατον S.*Aj*.968; *incur*, θεᾶς ὀργήν ib.777; κακά Id.*El*.1004; ξυμφοράς E.*Or*.543; ἔχθραν πρός τινα Th.1.42; δυσσέβειαν κ. *get* a name for impiety, S.*Ant*.924; κακὸν λόγον πρὸς ἀστῶν E.*Heracl*.166, cf. *IT*676; ἐκ τῶν πόνων τὰς ἀρετὰς κ. Th.1.123. c. κ. τινὰς πολεμίους *make* them so, X.*An*.5.5.17; οὔ ποτ' εὔνουν τὴν ἐμὴν κτήσῃ φρένα S.*Ph*. 1281. 2. *procure* or *get* for another, ἐμοὶ δ' ἐκτήσατο κεῖνος Od.20. 265; μέγαν τέκνοις πλοῦτον ἐκτήσω A.*Pers*.755 (troch.), cf. X.*Oec*.15. 1. II. in pf. and plpf. with fut. κεκτήσομαι, *to have acquired*, i.e. *possess, hold* (opp. χρῆσθαι, Pl.*Euthd*.280d), οὐδ' ὅσα φασὶν Ἴλιον ἐκτῆσθαι Il.9.402, cf. X.*Cyr*.8.3.46, Pl.*Phdr*.260b; ὅπλα μὴ ἐκτῆσθαι Hdt.1.155, cf. S.*Ph*.778; στρατὸν πλεῖστον ἐκτημένοι Hdt.7.161; κοινὸν ὄμμ' ἐκτημέναι A.*Pr*.795; φωνὴν βάρβαρον κεκτ. Id.*Ag*.1051; κεκτ. τινὰ σύμμαχον E.*Ba*.1343; κ. κάλλος X.*Smp*.1.8; ἀρετήν Pl.*Prt*.340e; τέχνην Lys.24.6; ποίησιν *to be master of* it, Pl.*Lg*.829c: dub. in aor., ἀγορὰς κτησάμενοι *having* market-places, Hdt.1.153 (leg. στησάμενοι): with impers. subject, πραγμάτων ἀγῶνας κεκτημένων *involving* effort, Epicur.*Sent*.21:—the diff. between pres. and pf. appears from X.*Mem*.1.6.3, ἃ [χρήματα] καὶ κτωμένους εὐφραίνει καὶ κεκτημένους.. ποιεῖ ζῆν: later, pres. in pf. sense, *Ev.Luc*.18.12. b. of evils, ἄγος κεκτήσεται θεῶν A.*Th*.1022; κακά E.*Hel*.272; φθόνον Pl.*Lg*.870c. c. *have in store*, opp. ἔχω, *have in hand*, ready for use, ἔχων τε καὶ κεκτημένος.. κακά S.*Ant*.1278; ἔχειν τε καὶ κεκτῆσθαι τὸ ψεῦδος Pl.*R*. 382b, cf. *Tht*.197b, 198d, *Cra*.393b; κ. ἱμάτιον *own*, opp. ἔχειν (wear), Id.*Tht*.197b. d. abs., *to be a property-owner*, τῶν ἐκτημένων ἐν τῇ χώρᾳ *SIG*633.73 (Milet., ii B.C.), cf. 888.15 (iii A.D.). 2. ὁ κεκτημένος *owner, master* (esp. of slaves), as Subst., Ar.*Pl*.4, etc.; οἱ κ. A.*Supp*.337; of a husband, E.*IA*715; ἡ κεκτημένη my *mistress*, S. *Fr*.762, Ar.*Ec*.1126, Men.*Pk*.61, al., cf. Phryn.Com.48. III. aor. 1 Pass. ἐκτήθην in pass. sense, *to be gotten*, ἃ ἐκτήθη Th.1.123, 2.36; *to be obtained as property*, δουλόσυνος πρὸς οἶκον κτηθεῖσα E.*Hec*.449 (lyr.), cf. D.H.10.27, etc.: fut. κτηθήσομαι Lxx *Je*.39(32).43. (Act. κτάω very late, *PLond*.1.77 (vi A.D.).)

κτάτεσι· κτήμασι, Hsch.

κτεᾰν-ηχής· πένης, Hsch. **-ισμός**, ὁ, *getting wealth*, Man.4. 41 (pl.). (Fort. κτεατ-.) **-ον**, τό, (κτάομαι) = κτῆμα, Pi.*P*.1.2, Epic.ap.Sch.S.*OC*378 (Antim.(?)); κ. φιλίης, of a child, *Epigr.Gr*. 388 (Apamea). 2. usu. in pl. κτέανα, *possessions, property*, Hes. *Op*.315, Sol.4.12, Pi.*O*.3.42, *N*.9.32; δημοσίων κ. Xenoph.2.8; used in lyr. by A.*Th*.729, *Ag*.1573, E.*Ion*490; by S.(?) in hexam. ap. Sch.S.*OC*378 (cf. *Fr*.242); by Eub. in a mock heroic line, 139: in Prose, Hp.*Ep*.27; *property in cattle*, Theoc.25.109; cf. κτῆνος:—Hom. only in heterocl. dat. pl. κτεάτεσσι (cf. κτέαρ), Il.23.829, Od. 14.115, cf. Pi.*O*.5.24, E.*Fr*.791.3 (hex.): dat. pl. κτεάτοις Hdn.Gr. 2.936. (Cf. Avest. *šaēta*- 'property', 'wealth'.)

κτέαρ, τό, = foreg., formed as nom. to dat. pl. κτεάτεσσι in later Poetry, Maiist.33, *AP*9.52 (Carph.), 9.752 (Asclep. or Antip. Thess.), 11.27 (Maced.), Q.S.4.543.

κτεάτ-ειρα [ᾰτ], ἡ (as if fem. of *κτεᾰτήρ), *possessor*, Νὺξ μεγάλων κόσμων κ. A.*Ag*.356 (anap.). **-ίζω**, *gain, win*, δουρὶ δ' ἐμῷ κτεάτισσα Il.16.57; πολλὰ κτεατίσσας Od.2.102, 19.147, cf. Eumel.2, etc.: —Med., *get for oneself, acquire*, Ep. fut. κτεατίσσομαι Man.6.677, aor. κτεατίσσατο A.R.2.788: pf. Pass. in med. sense, ὅσ' Ἑκηβόλος ἐκτεάτισται *h.Merc*.522: plpf., ἃ ἐκτεάτιστο Μίδης Call.*Aet*.3.1.47; τὰ δὲ κτεατίζεται αὐτός Theoc.17.105.

κτείνω, Ep. subj. κτείνωμι Od.19.490; Aeol. κτέννω Hdn.Gr.2. 303 (and aor. 1 part. κτέννais Alc.33.5), but κταίνω Id.140 acc. to Eust.1648.5 (leg. Ἀλκμᾶνι); Ep. Iterat. κτείνεσκε Il.24.393: fut. κτενῶ, Ep. κτενέω Od.16.404, -έεις Il.22.13, -έει ib.124, al. (κτενεῖ 15. 65, 68), part. κτανέοντα only 18.309 (but in compos. κατα-κτανέουσιν 6.409): aor. 1 ἔκτεινα 19.296, etc.: aor. 2 ἔκτᾰνον 2.701, etc.: pf. not found uncompounded: plpf. ἀπ-εκτονήκειν Plu.*Tim*.16:—**Pass.**, fut. κτανθήσομαι Sch.T Il.14.481: Ep. 3 pl. aor. ἔκτᾰθεν Il.11.691, Od.4. 537, κτάθεν Q.S.1.812; ἐκτάνθην *AP*14.32, (ἀπ-) Lxx 1*Ma*.2.9, *Ev. Marc*.8.31, D.C.65.4: aor. 2 ἀπ-εκτάνην [ᾰ] Gal.14.284: pf. ἐκτάνθαι (ἀπ-) Plb.7.7.4:—Hom. also uses non-thematic forms, 3 sg., 1 and 3 pl. aor. ἔκτᾰ Od.11.410, al. (κατ- Il.15.432), ἔκτᾰμεν Od.12.375, ἔκτᾰν 19.276, Il.10.526 (ἔκτα also in S.*Tr*.38, E.*HF*423 (lyr., with ᾱ)); 1 pl. subj. κτέωμεν Od.22.216; inf. κτάμεν (κατα-) Il.9.458, κτάμεναι [ᾰ] 5.301, al.; part. κτάς (κατα-) 22.323, also in Trag., A.*Th*. 965 (lyr.), E.*IT*715: aor. Med. in pass. sense, 3 sg. ἀπ-έκτᾰτο Il.15. 437; inf. κτάσθαι ib.558 (prob. in pass. sense); part. κτάμενος 22.75, Hes.*Op*.541, Pi.*Fr*.203 codd., A.*Pers*.923 (lyr.), Cratin.95:—*kill, slay*, freq. in Poets, also in early Att., Lex Draconis in *IG*1².115.20; but in Prose and Com. ἀποκτείνω prevailed; usu. of men, less freq. of slaying an animal, as Il.15.587, Od.12.375, 19.543, Ar.*Av*.1063 (lyr.); Οὖτίς με κτείνει δόλῳ *seeks to kill* me, Od.9.408, cf. S.*OC*993; ὁ κτανών *the slayer, murderer*, A.*Eu*.422; οἱ κτανόντες Id.*Ch*.41 (lyr.), 144, etc. 2. *put to death*, Th.1.132, Arist.*HA*625^a16, al.; esp. in legal language, εἰ.. ἐν δίκῃ ἔκτεινεν ὁ κτείνας Pl.*Euthphr*.4b, cf. *Prt*. 322d, *Lg*.871e, al., Lys.10.11. 3. of things, ὥστε καὶ κτείνειν so as *to be fatal*, of the plague, Th.2.51 (so in Pass., εὖτ' ἂν ὑπὸ τοῦ κακοῦ κτεινέωνται when the disease *is proceeding towards a fatal termination*, Aret.*SD*1.5); τὰ φύλλα [ἀποκύνου].. κτείνει κύνας Dsc.4. 80. 4. *put an end to*, θέρος [νοῦσον] κτείνει Aret.*SD*1.16. (Pass. in Hom. and Ion. Prose, Il.11.668, 14.60, Od.11.413, Hdt.4.3, etc.; but Trag. almost always used θνῄσκω or καταθνῄσκω as the Pass., Com. Poets and Prose writers ἀποθνῄσκω.) (Cf. Skt. *kṣatás* 'wounded'.)

κτείς, κτενός, ὁ, *comb*, Pherecr.100; πύξινος κ. *AP*6.211 (Leon.), *Edict.Diocl*.13.3, cf. Luc.*Am*.44: hence, of toothed objects, 1. *comb in the loom*, by which the threads of the warp are kept separate, *AP*6.247 (Phil.); κναφικὸς κ. *comb* for carding wool, Tim.*Lex*. s.v. κνάφος. 2. *rake*, *AP*6.297.5 (Phan.), Ph.*Bel*.100.10 (pl.). 3. *horn* of the lyre, Hsch.: pl., of the constellation Lyre, Eratosth.*Cat*. 24. 4. *fingers*, χερῶν ἄκρους κτένας A.*Ag*.1594. 5. *ribs*, Opp. *C*.1.296, Hsch. 6. *virilia, pubes*, Hp.*Aph*.7.39, *Art*.51; *pudenda* *muliebria*, Call.*Fr.*308, *AP*5.131 (Phld.), Ruf.*Onom.*109, Sor.2.18. 7. in pl., *cutting-teeth, incisors*, Poll.2.91. 8. *bivalve shell-fish, scallop*, Philyll.13, Archipp.24, Anaxandr.41.62 (anap.), Alex.170, prob. in Theoc.14.17, cf. Arist.$HA525^a22$, al. b. dual κτένε, perh. = *scallopings* (ornaments on a garment), $IG1^2$.386.8; cf. κτενωτός. 9. *caruncula lachrymalis*, Arist.$HA491^b25$ (cf. Gal.4.796). 10. *bandage*, Sor.*Fasc.*25. (For πκτεν-, cf. πέκω, Lat. *pecten*: the correct form (κτείς) of the nom. is found in $IG2^2$.1425.376; later κτήν, q.v.)

κτεν-ίζω, *comb*, τινα Anaxil.39, cf. *PSI*4.404.4 (Pass., iii B.C.); *curry* horses, ψήκτραισιν ἵππων τρίχας E.*Hipp.*1174: metaph., ὁ δὲ Πλάτων τοὺς ἑαυτοῦ διαλόγους κτενίζων καὶ βοστρυχίζων D.H.*Comp.*25:—Med., κτενίζεσθαι τὰς κόμας *comb one's* hair, Hdt.7.208: so abs., Ar.*Fr.*603, Antiph.148.4:—Pass., ἐκτενισμένος *with one's hair combed*, Archil.165, cf. Semon.7.65; εἰ κτενισθείη *Hippiatr.*94. **-ιον**, τό, Dim. of κτείς 1, *POxy.*1142.7 (iii A.D.); of κτείς 8, Epich.42.3 (pl.). 2. in pl., = κτείς 3, Hsch. **-ιοποιός**, ὁ, *comb-maker*, *Gloss.* **-ισμός**, ὁ, *combing*, E.*El.*529 (pl.), Diocl.*Fr.*141. **-ιστής**, οῦ, ὁ, *hairdresser*, Gal.13.1038, *PTeb.*322.23 (ii A.D.), *Gloss.* **-ιστικός**, ή, όν, *for hairdressing*, ζεῦγος κ. σιδηροῦν *POxy.*1035.12 (ii A.D.). **-ιστός**, ή, όν, *combed, carded*, λίνου Sm.*Is.*19.9.

κτενο-ειδής, ές, *like a comb*. Adv. -δῶς *Gloss.* **-ποιός**, ὁ, = κτενιοποιός, ib. **-πώλης**, ου, ὁ, *dealer in combs*, Poll.7.198.

κτεν-ώδης, ες, = κτενοειδής, Xanth.3; τὸ κ. Phan.Hist.29. **-ωτός**, ή, όν, perh. *scalloped*, χιτωνίσκος $IG2^2$.1514.30; κτενωτή· ὑφαντή, Hsch.; cf. πεντέκτενος, κτείς 8b.

κτέομαι, Ion. for κτάομαι.

κτέρ-ας, τό, = κτέανον, *possession*, Il.10.216, 24.235, cj. in Simon.107.9, *Trag.Adesp.* in *Gött.Nachr.*1922.27. 2. *gift*, A.R.4.1550. **-εα**, τά (no sg. in use), *funeral gifts*, burnt with the dead, Mosch.4.33, Hsch.: generally, *funeral honours*, ἐπὶ κτέρεα κτερεΐξαι Od.1.291, cf. 2.222, Il.24.38, etc.; ἔλαχον κτερέων Od.5.311; τῶν ὁσίων ἀντίασεν κτερέων *Epigr.Gr.*514 (Maced.). 2. later, *wrappers for the dead, shroud*, ἐνὶ κτερέεσσιν ἐλυσθεὶς A.R.1.254. **-εΐζω**, fut. -ΐξω Od.2.222: aor. κτερεΐξαι 1.291:—Ep. Verb, = κτερίζω: 1. c. acc. pers., *bury with due honours*, σὸν ἑταῖρον ἀέθλοισι κτερεΐζε Il.23.646; κτερεϊζέμεν Ἕκτορα δῖον 24.657; τύμβῳ κτερέϊξε παῖδα *IG*12(5).308 (Paros), etc. 2. c. acc. cogn., κτέρεα κ., v. κτέρεα. **-ες**· νεκροί, Hsch. **-ίζω**, fut. κτεριῶ Il.18.334: aor. ἐκτέρισα 24.38, Simon.109: (κτέρεα):—poet. Verb, = κτερεΐζω, οὔ σε πρὶν κτεριῶ Il.18.334; τὸν δὲ κτεριοῦσιν Ἀχαιοί 22.336; ἔμ', εἴ κε θάνω, κτεριοῦσί γε δῖοι Ἀχαιοί 11.455; τάφῳ κ. τινά S.*Ant.*204; τούσδ' εἷς τάφος ἐκτέρισε Simon. l. c.: abs., E.*Hel.*1244; δημοσίᾳ κ. *IG*2.1678 (iv B.C.), cf. *Sammelb.*2119 (iii B.C.). 2. c. acc. cogn., τοί κέ μιν ὦκα ἐν πυρὶ κήαιεν καὶ ἐπὶ κτέρεα κτερίσαιεν Il.24.38, cf. Od.3.285. **-ίσματα**, τά, = κτέρεα, only pl., S.*OC*1410, *El.*434, 931, E.*Supp.*309, *Tr.*1249, *Hel.*1391. **-ιστής**, οῦ, ὁ, *undertaker*, Hsch. s. v. ταφῆες.

κτέω, κτέωμεν, v. κτείνω.

κτηδών, όνος, ἡ, *line of fissure* in the fibre of wood, Thphr.*HP*5.1.9 sq.; κτηδόνες ξύλου *grain* of wood, Hero *Bel.*96.12, cf. Suid. 2. Medic. in pl., *fibres of the heart*, Hp.*Cord.*10, cf. Erot. s. v. ἶνες. b. *layers* in the cornea of the eye, Ruf.*Anat.*10. c. κ. πιμελῆς *fibres* in a piece of fat, Sor.1.118. 3. *layers* of slate, Dsc.5.127. 4. *gills* of a mushroom, Id.3.1. 5. *shreds* of lint, Gal.8.415. (Cf. εὐκτέανος (B), εὐθυκτέανον, ἰθυκτέανον.)

κτῆμα, ατος, τό, (κτάομαι) *anything gotten, piece of property, possession*, sg. once in Hom., μή νύ τι. .δόμων ἐκ κτῆμα φέρηται Od.15.19; later ταύτας [γυναῖκας] ἐξείλεθ' αὑτῷ κ. S.*Tr.*245; ἡδὺ κ. τῆς νίκης λαβεῖν Id.*Ph.*81, cf. *OT*549, *Ant.*702, E.*Or.*230, 703, etc.; κ. ἐς αἰεί Th.1.22; ὡς ἡδὺ καὶ μακάριον τὸ κ. Pl.*R.*496c, etc.; of a slave, παλαιὸν οἴκων κ. E.*Med.*49, cf. Pl.*Phd.*62d, X.*Oec.*1.6, *Vect.*4.42; κ. ἔμψυχον Arist.$Pol.1253^b32$; of a calf, J.*AJ*6.14.3; κ. πάντων ἐστὶ τιμιώτατον ἀνὴρ φίλος Hdt.5.24. 2. freq. in pl., *possessions*, in Hom. of *heirlooms*, δόμοις ἐν κτήματα κεῖται Il.9.382, Od.4.127; also, of all kinds of *property*, freq. in Od., κ. δαρδάπτουσιν 14.92, cf. 18.144, al.; διέλαχον. .κτημάτων παμπησίαν A.*Th.*817, etc.; Ἔρως ὃς ἐν κτήμασι πίπτεις who fallest upon *wealth*, i. e. on *the wealthy*, S.*Ant.*782 codd. (lyr.): sts., χρήματα καὶ κ. *property in* money and *chattels*, Pl.*Lg.*728e, cf. Isoc.1.28; = κτήνη, Pl.*Grg.*484c, *Phd.*62b; opp. ἀγροί, *personal* (opp. real) *property*, Is.5.43; less freq. of *landed property*, κ. ἔχων ἐν Βοιωτίᾳ D.18.41 (sg. as v.l.), Hdn.2.6.3: later freq. in sg., *estate, farm, field*, etc., *Act.Ap.*5.1, *BGU*530.21 (i A.D.), etc.; ἀμπελικὸν κ. *vineyard*, *PRyl.*157.4 (ii A.D.). 3. in pl., *materials*, κ. πιλητά Gal.*UP*6.4, 7.22.

κτηματ-ίδιον, τό, Dim. of foreg., *small estate*, *PMasp.*21.19 (vi A.D.). **-ικός**, ή, όν, *possessed of wealth, opulent*, Plb.5.93.6, D.S.18.10, Plu.*Sol.*14; οἱ κ., = Lat. *possessores*, App.*BC*1.12. II. *belonging to an estate* or *farm*, γεωργοί *POxy.*136.18 (vi A.D.); τὰ τῶν κ. ἔργα *PFlor.*161.6 (iii A.D.). **-ιον**, τό, Dim. of κτῆμα, Alciphr.1.36, *PTeb.*616 (ii A.D.), *PFay.*133 (iv A.D.). **-ίτης** [ῑ], ου, ὁ, = κτηματικός 1, Lycurg.*Fr.*93, Socr.*Ep.*29.5.

κτημᾰτοφύλαξ [ῠ], ᾰκος, ὁ, *estate bailiff, steward*, *Gloss.*

κτηματ-ωνέω, *purchase properties*, of commissioners for temples, *Supp.Epigr.*2.580.10 (Teos, ii B.C.); Ἀπόλλωνι καὶ Ἀρτέμιδι *LW*338 (Mylasa). **-ώνης**, ου, ὁ, *commissioner who purchases temple-properties*, *Supp.Epigr.*2.538 (Mylasa, ii B.C.), 565.11 (Olymos, i B.C.); γενομένης τῆς ὠνῆς τοῖς κ. εἰς τὸ τοῦ θεοῦ ὄνομα *LW*416 (Mylasa). **-ωνία**, ἡ, *purchase of properties*, *Supp.Epigr.*2.580.12 (Teos, ii B.C.).

κτήν, ὁ, later nominative form for κτείς (q.v.), ὁ κ. τοῦ ποδός, = ταρσός, Jo.Alex. περὶ τῶν διαφόρως τονουμένων p.16 Egenolff (Vratisl. 1880).

κτην-ᾰγωγία, *evectio*, *Gloss.* **-αφαίρεσις**, εως, ἡ, *cattle-lifting*, *PMasp.*2 ii 25 (vi A.D.). **-ηδόν**, Adv., (κτῆνος) *like beasts*, Hdt.4.180. **-ίατρος**, ὁ, *cattle-doctor*, *Gloss.* **-ίτης** [ῑ], ου, ὁ, *belonging to beasts*, ib.

κτηνοβάτης [ᾰ], ου, ὁ, (βαίνω A. II. 1) *one guilty of bestiality*, Sch.Ar.*Ra.*432, 965.

κτῆνος, εος, τό, (κτάομαι) mostly in pl. κτήνεα, contr. κτήνη, *flocks and herds*, *h.Hom.*30.10, Hdt.1.50, 2.41, Pl.*Criti.*109c, *PStrassb.*98.9 (ii B.C.), *SIG*633.73 (Milet., ii B.C.); κ. τὰ δημιοπληθῆ A.*Ag.*129 (lyr.); of beasts in general, Heraclit.29; opp. ἄνθρωποι, Democr.57; of swine, Plb.12.4.14; ὑϊκὰ κ. *BGU*757.20 (i A.D.). 2. in sg., a single *beast*, as *an ox* or *sheep*, Hdt.1.132, Hp.*Cord.*2, X.*An.*5.2.3; *horse* or *mule for riding*, *Ev.Luc.*10.34, *Act.Ap.*23.24; of a domestic animal, opp. θηρίον, M.Ant.5.11. (Late dat. pl. κτῆσι *PFlor.*258.6, etc.)

κτηνοστάσιον, *jumentarium*, *Gloss.*

κτηνοτροφ-εῖον, τό, *cattle-stall*, *Gp.*15.8 tit. **-έω**, *keep cattle*, Str.12.2.9, Ph.2.89, *Hippiatr.*53. **-ία**, ἡ, *cattle-keeping*, Str.17.2.3, D.H.3.36 (pl.), Ph.1.304, *BGU*969.12, al. (ii A.D.), Plu.*Publ.*11 (pl.). **-ος**, ον, *keeping cattle, pastoral*, βίος D.S.1.74; γῆ κ. a land *of pasture*, Lxx *Nu.*32.4: as Subst., *cattle-keeper*, Ph.1.304: pl., *PFay.*18(*b*) (i B.C.), Dsc.2.147, *BGU*969.11 (ii A.D.).

κτην-ύδριον, τό, Dim. of κτῆνος, *PStrassb.*92.12 (iii A.D.), *PFlor.*120.6 (iii A.D.). **-ώδης**, ες, *like a beast*, Lxx *Ps.*72(73).22, Aesop.324b; αἴσθησις Ph.1.151: Comp., Hsch. Adv. -δῶς, γράφειν Tz. ad Lyc.797.

κτησ-είδιον, τό, Dim. of κτῆσις, Arr.*Epict.*1.1.10; v.l. for συγκτησείδιον in Jul.*Ep.*4. **-ίβιος** [σῐ], ον, (κτάομαι) *possessing property*, Paul.Al.*L.*4. **-ιος**, α, ον, (κτῆσις) *belonging to property*, χρήματα κ. *property*, A.*Ag.*1009 (lyr.); κ. βοτόν a sheep *of one's own flock*, S.*Tr.*690. II. *domestic*, Ζεὺς κ. *the protector of house and property*, A.*Supp.*445, Hp.*Insomn.*89, Orac.ap.D.21.53, Antipho 1.16: pl., τοὺς κ. Δίας Anticl.13; also Ἀθηνᾶ κ. Hp. l. c.; ὁ θεὸς ὁ κ. Plu.2.828a; κ. βωμός the altar *of* Ζεὺς κτήσιος, A.*Ag.*1038; θεοὶ κ., = Lat. *Penates*, D.H.8.41. **-ιππος**, ον, *possessing horses*, pr. n. in Od., cf. Luc.*Fug.*26.

κτῆσις, εως, ἡ, (κτάομαι) *acquisition* (opp. ἀπόλαυσις, Arist.$Rh.1410^a6$), κ. τινὸς ποιεῖσθαι Th.1.8, 13; ἡ φιλοσοφία κ. ἐπιστήμης Pl.*Euthd.*288d; ῥᾳδίαν ἔχει ⟨τὴν⟩ κτῆσιν Alcid.*Soph.*5; κατ' ἔργου κτῆσιν according to *success in* the work, S.*Tr.*230. II. (from pf.) *possession*, λέχους, πλούτου, etc., ib.162, *El.*960, etc.; κ. ἔχειν τῶν μετάλλων ἐργασίας Th.4.105; ἡ τῶν χρημάτων κ. Pl.*R.*331b; διὰ τὴν τῶν υἱέων κ. on account of *your having* sons, Id.*Ap.*20b; ἱματίων Id.*Phd.*64d; φέροντας. .ἀγαθοῦ κτῆσιν οὐδενός D.18.308; κ. ἐκ δεσπότου καὶ δούλου [συνέστηκεν] Arist.$Pol.1277^a8$; *holding*, opp. χρῆσις ('using'), Id.$EN1098^b32$; *ownership*, opp. χρῆσις ('usufruct'), *POxy.*237 viii 35, al.; τὰς κτήσεις βεβαίας εἶμεν $IG4^2(1)$.76.25 (Epid., ii B.C.). 2. as collective, = κτήματα, *possessions, property*, διὰ κτῆσιν δατέοντο Il.5.158; κ. ὄπασσεν Od.14.62; πατρῴα κ. S.*El.*1290; μετρίης κτήσιος ἐπιμέλεσθαι Democr.285; ἡ ἰδία κ. *POxy.*237 viii 32 (i A.D.): in pl., Hdt.4.114, etc.; ἀρετῆς βέβαιαι. .αἱ κ. μόναι S.*Fr.*194; esp. *lands, farms*, D.H.8.19, D.S.14.29, etc.: also in sg., *farm, estate*, *PFlor.*155.6 (iii A.D.).

κτη-τέος, α, ον, *to be possessed*, Pl.*Lg.*742a. II. κτητέον, *one must get*, Id.*R.*373a. **-τικός**, ή, όν, *acquisitive, skilled in getting*, τῶν οὐκ ὄντων Isoc.12.242: abs., *industrious*, Str.16.4.26: ἡ -κὴ τέχνη the art *of acquiring property*, Pl.*Sph.*219c, cf. Arist.$Pol.1253^b23$; τὸ κ. Phld.*Oec.*p.35 J. 2. *acquired by purchase*, δοῦλος, δούλη, *PRyl.*111(*b*).6 (ii A.D.), *PLips.*4.11 (iii A.D.). II. Gramm., *possessive*, [ὄνομα] D.T.634.25; ἀντωνυμίαι A.D.*Pron.*16.15; τὰ κ. ib.14.21. Adv. -κῶς Id.*Synt.*160.13. **-τορικός**, ή, όν, *of an owner*, *PGiss.*124.7 (vi A.D.). **-τός**, ή, όν, (κτάομαι) *that may be gotten* or *acquired*, ληϊστοὶ μὲν. .βόες. ., κτητοὶ δὲ τρίποδες Il.9.407, cf. E.*Hipp.*1295 (anap.), Pl.*Prt.*324a, al. 2. *worth getting, desirable*, Id.*Smp.*197d, *Hp.Mi.*374e. II. *acquired, gained*, Id.*Lg.*841e; κτητή *female slave*, opp. γαμετή, Hes.*Op.*406; κ. μέρος οἰκίας *PLond.*3.1164(*f*).11 (iii A.D.). **-τωρ**, ορος, ὁ, *possessor, owner*, D.S.34/5.2.31, *POxy.*237 viii 31 (i A.D.), A.D.*Pron.*22.6, *AP*7.206 (Damoch.), Procop.*Arc.*26: c. gen., οἰκιῶν κ. *Act.Ap.*4.34.

κτίδεος [ῐ], α, ον (from ἰκτίς: **κτίς** only in Hsch. s. v. κτιδέα), for ἰκτίδεος (which is not in use), *of a marten*, κτιδέη κυνέη *marten-skin* helmet, Il.10.335, 458.

κτίζω, Emp.23.6, etc.: fut. -ίσω A.*Ch.*1060: aor. ἔκτῐσα Od.11.263, etc.; poet. ἔκτισσα Pi.*P.*1.62, A.*Pers.*289 (lyr.), κτίσσα Il.20.216, κτίσα Pi.*P.*5.89: pf. ἔκτικα *Lyr.Alex.Adesp.*1.8, D.S.7.5, 15.13:—**Med.**, poet. aor. ἐκτίσσατο Pi.*O.*10(11).25, *Fr.*1.4 (ἐκτήσ- codd.):—**Pass.**, fut. κτισθήσομαι Str.*Chr.*5.38, D.H.1.56: aor. ἐκτίσθην Th.1.12, etc.: pf. ἔκτισμαι Hdt.4.46, Hp.*Art.*45, E.*Fr.*360.9:—*people* a country, *build houses and cities in it*, κτίσσε δὲ Δαρδανίην Il. l. c.; κ. χώρην, νῆσον, Hdt.1.149, 3.49. 2. of a city, *found, build*, Θήβης ἕδος ἔκτισαν Od. l. c., cf. Hdt.1.167, 168, Th.6.4, *PCair.Zen.*169 (iii B.C.); ἀποικίαν A.*Pr.*815:—Pass., *to be founded*, Σμύρνην τὴν ἀπὸ Κολοφῶνος κτισθεῖσαν *founded by emigrants from* Colophon, Hdt.1.16, cf. 7.153, 8.62; μήτε ἄστεα μήτε τείχεα ἐκτισμένα no *fixed* cities or walls, Id.4.46; -ομένη πόλις Phld.*Rh.*2.155 S. 3. κ. ἄλσος *plant* a grove, Pi.*P.*5.89; βωμόν *set up* an altar, Id.*O.*7.42; ἑορτάν, ἀγῶνα, *found, establish* it, ib.6.69, 10(11).25 (Med.); τὸν Κύρνον. .κτίσαι, ἥρων ἐόντα *establish* his worship, Hdt.1.167; δαῖτάς τινι A.*Ch.*484 (Pass.); τάφον τινί S.*Ant.*1101; αἵρεσιν Phld.*Rh.*1.77 S.; σύνοδον $IG2^2$.1343.12

(I B.C.). 4. *produce, create, bring into being*, γόνῳ τινά A.*Supp.*172 (lyr.); *bring about*, τελευτήν ib.140 (lyr.), cf. *Ch.*441 (lyr.); ὁ τὴν φιλίην ἐκτικώς *Lyr.Alex.Adesp.* l. c.; of painters, δένδρεα.. καὶ ἀνέρας ἠδὲ γυναῖκας Emp. l. c.; ἵπποισι τὸν χαλινὸν κτίσας *having invented* it, S.*OC*715 (lyr.). 5. *make* so and so, ἐλεύθερον κ. τινά A.*Ch.*1060; ἔνθεον κτίσας φρένα Id.*Eu.*17, cf. 714; ποταπὸν εἴ σέ τις θεῶν κτίσαι E. *Supp.*620 (lyr.), cf. A.*Pers.*289 (lyr.). 6. *perpetrate* a deed, S.*Tr.* 898. (Cf. Skt. *kṣéti* 'reside', *kṣitis* (= κτίσις) 'habitation'.)

κτῐλ-εύω, *make tame, tame*, Pi.*Fr.*238 (Pass.). **-ίς**· τιθασός, πρᾶος, ἡγεμών, Hsch. **-ος**, ον, *tame, docile, obedient*, χρὴ δέ σε πατρὶ.. κτίλον ἔμμεναι Hes.*Fr.*222; ἦσαν δὲ κτίλα πάντα καὶ ἀνθρώποισι προσηνῆ Emp.130; μῆλα (sheep) Nic.*Th.*471; κύνες Parth.10.3; ἱερέα κτίλον Ἀφροδίτας Aphrodite's *cherished* priest, Pi.*P.*2.17; κτίλα ᾤεα, perh. their *cherished* eggs, Nic.*Th.*452. II. Subst. κτίλος, ὁ, *ram*, Il.3.196, 13.492, Opp.*C.*1.388, 4.211, Q.S.1.175. **-όω**, *tame, make tractable*, in Med., ἐκτιλώσαντο τὰς λοιπὰς τῶν Ἀμαζόνων *got* them *tamed*, Hdt.4.113:—Pass., pf. part. ἐκτιλωμένος Paus.Gr.*Fr.*241.

κτίν, = κτείς, *Gloss.*; cf. κτήν.

κτίννυμι, collat. form of κτείνω, App.*BC*1.71 (vv.ll. κτεινύντες, κτειννύντες), 4.35; **κτιννύω**, Polyaen.1.23,25, Plot.3.2.15:—Pass., κτιννύμενος App.*BC*1.2; κτιννύεσθαι J.*AJ*18.8.3:—more freq. in compd. ἀποκτίννυμι (cf. ἀποκτείνυμι), cf. Phryn.*PS* p.51 B.; κτεινύω and ἀποκτιννύναι are correct acc. to Choerob. in *An.Ox.*2.233.

κτίς, v. κτίδεος.

κτίσ-ις [ῐ], εως, ἡ, (κτίζω) *founding, settling*, Th.6.5; ἀποικιῶν Isoc. 12.190, cf. Plb.9.1.4 (pl.), etc. 2. loosely, = πρᾶξις, κούφα κ. an easy *achievement*, Pi.*O.*13.83. 3. *creation*, κ. κόσμου *Ep.Rom.* 1.20; ἀπ' ἀρχῆς κτίσεως *Ev.Marc.*10.6, 13.19, etc. II. *created thing, creature*, Lxx *Ju.*9.12, *Ev.Marc.*16.15, *Ep.Rom.*8.19, etc.: in pl., Lxx *To.*8.5. III. *authority created* or *ordained*, 1*Ep.Pet.*2. 13. **-μα**, ατος, τό, *colony, foundation*, Call.*Aet.Oxy.*2080.77; Παρίων Str.7.5.5, cf. D.H.1.59; Λακωνικὸν κ. Str.5.3.6; also, of a temple, J.*BJ*2.6.1: generally, *building*, *PSI*1.84.8 (pl., iv/v A. D.). 2. = κτίσις II, Lxx *Wi.*9.2 (pl.), 3*Ma.*5.11, *Ep.Jac.*1.18. II. = κτίσις I. 1, Eust.1382.50. **-μός**, ὁ, *foundation*, πόλεως *IGRom.*4.914 (Cibyra). **-τεῖον**, τό, *sanctuary of a founder*, *PLips.*97 xiii 7 (iv A. D.), -ιον Pap.). **-τήρ**, ῆρος, ὁ, = sq., *AJA*23.364 (Corinth, iv B.C.). **-της**, ου, ὁ, *founder*, Arist.*Fr.*484, *OGI*111.9 (Egypt, ii B. C.), Luc.*Macr.*13; of Apollo as founder of Cyrene, *Berl.Sitzb.*1903. 85: pl., Call.*Aet.Oxy.*2080.64; ὁ τῆς στοᾶς κ., i.e. Zeno, Ath.8.345c, D.L.2.120: metaph., ἰατρικῆς κ. *IG*14.1759. 2. *builder*, *POxy.* 2144.8 (iii A. D.). II. *restorer*, τῆς πατρίδος Plu.*Cic.*22. III. *Creator*, ὁ κ. ἁπάντων Lxx *Si.*24.8, al. **-τός**, ή, όν, *wrought*, λάεσσιν *h.Ap.*299. 2. *built*: neut. κ., τό, *building*, *PFay.*117.23 (ii A. D.). **-τρια**, ας, ἡ, fem. of κτίστης I, *IGRom.*3.802 (Syllium). **-τύς**, ύος, ἡ, Ion. for κτίσις, Hdt.9.97. **-τωρ**, ορος, ὁ, = κτίστης, Αἴτνας Pi.*Fr.*105; Ἀσιάδος χθονὸς E.*Ion* 74; ὁ τῆς στοᾶς κ., of Zeno, Ath.9.370c; ἀγαθῶν.. εὑρετὴν καὶ κτίστορα Diph.(?)138.

κτίτερ· κτίστης, Hsch.; cf. sq.

κτίτης [ῐ], ὁ, = κτίστης, ἀγώνων *SIG*711 *L*5 (pl., Delph., ii B.C.). II. generally, *inhabitant*, E.*Or.*1621.

κτοίν-α or **κτοῖνα**, ἡ, (κτίζω) Rhod. name for *a local division*, like Att. δῆμος, *township*, *IG*12(1).694, 1033, al.; cf. κτύναι ἢ κτοῖναι· χωρήσεις προγονικῶν ἱερείων, ἢ δῆμος μεμερισμένος, Hsch. (also **πτοίνα** *BCH*10.261). **-άτης** [ᾱ], ου, ὁ, *member of a* κτοίνα, *IG*12(1).694. 14:—also **-έτης**, ib.157.9, 12(3).1270 *A* 13 (Syme).

κτόνος, ὁ, *murder*, Zonar.

κτῠπ-έω, Ep. Iterat. κτυπέεσκον Q.S.9.135: aor. 1 ἐκτύπησα E. *Ph.*1181, Arr.*Tact.*40.6; poet. κτύπησα S.*OC*1606, E.*Or.*1467 (lyr.): Ep. aor. 2 ἔκτῠπον Il.8.75, al., S.*OC*1456 (lyr.), κτύπον Il.8.170:—Pass., v. infr.: (κτύπος):—*crash*, as trees falling, μεγάλα κτυπέουσαι πῖπτον Il.23.119; freq. of thunder, Ζεὺς ἔκτυπε 8.75, cf. 7.479, Od.21. 413, etc.; ἔκτυπεν αἰθήρ S.*OC*1456 (lyr.); of the sea, Pl.*R.*396b. 2. *ring, resound*, κτυπέει δέ θ' ὑπ' αὐτοῦ ὕλη (sc. χειμάρρου) Il.13.140; ἀμφὶ δ' ἐκτύπουν πέτραι *rang* with the cries of Heracles, S.*Tr.*787; Διὸς βρονταῖσιν εἰς ἔριν κ. E.*Cyc.*328; δρομήμασιν Id.*Med.*1180; τοῖν ποδοῖν κ. *stamp loudly* with.., Ar.*Ec.*545, cf. Gal.7.60; εἰ.. ἐμπεσὼν [δόρυ] τῷ θυρεῷ κτυπήσειε Arr. l. c.; σιδηρῷ ὑποδήματι Luc.*Salt.*83: c. acc. cogn., φόβον κτυπεῖν, like κλάζειν Ἄρη, E.*Rh.*308. II. causal, *make to ring* or *resound*, χθόνα Hes.*Sc.*61; τύμπανα Opp.*C.*4.247: c. dupl. acc., κτύπησε κρᾶτα.. πλαγάν (v.l. πλαγᾷ) *made* it *ring* with a blow, E.*Or.* l. c.: metaph., κ. ἐν τοῖς συμβουλευτικοῖς τόποις τὰς ὀνομασίας Phld.*Rh.*1.208 S.:—Pass., *resound*, Ar.*Pl.*758, *Th.*995 (lyr.); κτυπηθῆναι τὰ ὦτα Philostr.*VA*6.26. **-ημα**, ατος, τό, = κτύπος, βροντῆς Critias 25.32 D.; κ. τυμπάνων D.C.51.17, cf. Jul.*Or.*7.220b; κ. χειρὸς E.*Andr.*1211 (lyr.). **-ητής**, οῦ, ὁ, *one who makes a noise*, Suid. s. v. πίτυλος. **-ία**, ἡ, = ὁ ἐπιθαλάμιος κτύπος, Hsch. **-ος**, ὁ, *crash, bang, din*, κ. θεῶν ἔριδι ξυνιόντων Il.20.66, cf. 12.338, A.*Th.*100, etc.; of thunder, S.*OC*1463 (lyr.), A.*Pr.*923; of the trampling of feet, περί τε κ. ἦλθε ποδοῖιν Od.16.6, cf. S.*Ph.*202; *rattling* of chariots or *sound* of horses' feet, Il.10.535, al., S.*El.*714, Ar.*Eq.*552 (lyr.); of a storm, A.*Ag.*1533 (lyr.); *noise* made by one knocking at the door, Id.*Ch.*653; ὀξύχειρ κ., of *the beating of* breasts by mourners, ib.23; στέρνων κ. E.*Supp.*87: in pl., κ. χερῶν Id.*Ph.*1351 (lyr.); of the *sound* of many voices, S.*OC*1500; of gates shutting, Aen.Tact.20.4; κτύπου ἀχὼ χάλυβος A.*Pr.*133 (lyr.); rarely of musical sound, σαλπίγγων κ. B.*Fr.*3.9.—Rare in Prose, Th.7.70, Pl.*Criti.*117e, X.*Cyr.*7.1.35, Aen.Tact. l. c.

'κτώ, for βκτώ, as pronounced by fishmongers, Amphis 30.12.

κτῶ, v. κτάομαι.

κῠάθ-ειον [ᾰ], τό, = κυάθιον, Dim. of κύαθος II, Nic.*Th.*591. **-ιαῖος**, α, ον, *contained in a* κύαθος, ὕδωρ *a ladleful of* water, Them.*in Ph.*135. 26, Simp.*in Ph.*174.30, Phlp.*in Mete.*24.22, Id. in *GA*92.22. **-ίζω**, *ladle out* wine, Antiph.115, Diph.107. II. κ. ταῖς ναυσὶν ἐκ θαλάττης *draw water* from the sea with the ships (*as one draws wine* from a bowl), of the engines of Archimedes lifting the Roman ships out of the water, Plb.8.6.6. **-ιον**, τό, Dim. of κύαθος, Pherecr.107, *PLond.*5.1657.11 (iv/v A. D.):—also **-ίς**, ίδος, ἡ, Sophr.3. **-ίσκος**, ὁ, κ. τῆς μηλωτρίδος *spoon-shaped end* of certain probes, Heliod.ap. Orib.46.11.26, cf. Gal.19.122, Archig.ap.eund.12.652, *Hermes* 38. 282. 2. *spoon-shaped probe*, Diocl.*Fr.*191. **-ος**, ὁ, *ladle*, for drawing wine out of the κρατήρ, Anacr.63.5, Pl.Com.176, Archipp. 21, X.*Cyr.*1.3.9, *PEleph.*5.3 (iii B. C.), etc.; cold metal *ladles* were applied to bruises, Arist.*Pr.*890[b]7; κύαθον αἰτήσεις τάχα you'll need a *ladle* shortly (from being so soundly beaten), Ar.*Lys.*444; ὑπωπιασμέναι.. καὶ κυάθους προσκείμεναι with *ladles* applied, Id.*Pax* 542, cf. E.*Fr.*374, Apolloph.3. II. *Attic measure holding two* κόγχαι or *four* μύστρα, about $\frac{1}{12}$ *of a pint*, Gal.19.753, cf. 10.516. III. κύαθοι κλειδῶν ἀνεστηκότες filled-out *hollows* round the collar-bones, Philostr.*Gym.*48. **-ότης**, ητος, ἡ, coined by Plato, *cuphood*, D.L. 6.53. **-ώδης**, ες, *like a cup*, Eratosth.ap.Ath.11.482a; κλεῖδες Philostr.*Gym.*29.

κῡαίνω, = κυνέω, Hsch.

κῠᾰμ-ευτός, ή, όν, *chosen by beans*, i.e. *by lot*, X.*Mem.*1.2.9, etc.; κ. ψηφοφορίαι voting *by beans*, Plu.2.12e. **-εύω**, *choose by lot*, δικαστάς *IG*1².41.19, 2².1172.13; ἔκ τινων Arist.*Ath.*8.1, 22.5:—Pass., *IG*1².10.8, Jusj.ap.D.24.150. **-ιαῖος**, α, ον, *of the size of a bean*, Dsc.2.133, Luc.*Herm.*40. **-ίας** (sc. λίθος), ου, ὁ, *precious stone like a bean*, Plin.*HN*37.188. **-ίδες**, *fabacia*, *Gloss.* **-ίζω**, *to be ripe for marriage* (cf. κύαμος III), Ar.*Fr.*582. **-ῐνος**, η, ον, *of beans*, ἔτνος Henioch.4.7, Gal.13.12; ἄλευρον Id.10.177. **-ιον**, τό, Dim. of κύαμος, Eust.948.30, *CIG*5109.30 (Nubia). **-ιστός**, ή, όν, f.l. for κυαμευτός, Plu.2.597a. **-ῖτις** (sc. ἀγορά), ιδος, ἡ, *bean-market*, ib.837c.

κῠᾰμόβολος, ον, *chosen by beans*, i.e. *by lot* (rather than **κῠᾰμοβόλος** (parox.), *voting with the bean*), δικαστής S.*Fr.*288.

κύᾰμος [ῠ], ὁ, *bean*, *Vicia Faba*, κ. μελανόχροες Il.13.589, cf. Emp. 141, *IG*2².1013.19, etc.; χλωροί Batr.125; κ. Ἑλληνικός Dsc.2.105; abominated by Pythagoreans, Arist.*Fr.*195, etc.; also, of the plant, Thphr.*CP*4.14.2. 2. *Egyptian bean*, *Nelumbium speciosum*, Id. *HP*4.8.7; usu. Αἰγύπτιος κ., Nic.*Fr.*81, D.S.1.10, Dsc.2.106, Gal.6. 532, 19.780. II. *lot* by which public officers were elected at Athens and elsewh. (because those who drew *white beans* were chosen), Plu.*Per.*27; ὁ τῷ κυάμῳ λαχὼν Ἀθηναίων πολεμαρχέειν Hdt. 6.109; ἐπίσκοπος.. τῷ κυάμῳ λαχών Ar.*Av.*1022; οἱ πεντακόσιοι ⟨οἱ⟩ λαχόντες τῷ κ. Lex ap.And.1.96; βουλὴ ἡ ἀπὸ τοῦ κ. Th.8.66, cf. Arist. *Ath.*24.3, 32.1; ἄρχοντας ἀπὸ κ. καθιστάναι X.*Mem.*1.2.9; κυάμοισι τὰς ἀρχὰς αἱρέεσθαι Luc.*Vit.Auct.*6; κύαμον ἐδέξατο *Schwyzer* 701 *B* 30 (Erythrae, v B. C.); κυάμῳ πατρίῳ S.*Fr.*404. III. *swelling of the paps* at puberty, Ruf.*Onom.*92, Poll.2.163, cf. Eust.749.21. IV. *woodlouse*, Gal.12.367.

κῠᾰμο-τρώξ, ῶγος, ὁ, *bean-eater*, Ar.*Eq.*41 (with allusion to κύαμος II). **-φᾰγία**, ἡ, *eating of beans, bean-diet*, Luc.*VH*2.24.

κῠᾰμ-ών, ῶνος, ὁ, *field of* κύαμος I. 2, Thphr.*HP*4.8.8, Str.17.1.15, *BGU*1119.11 (I B. C.). **-ωνίτης** [ῑ], ου, ὁ, *bean-grower*, *POxy.*43[v] iii 2 (iii A. D.).

κῠάν-αιγις [ᾰν], ιδος, ἡ, *she of the dark Aegis*, i. e. Pallas, Pi.*O.*13. 70. **-άμπυξ**, ῠκος, ὁ, ἡ, *with dark* ἄμπυξ, Θήβα Id.*Fr.*29.3; Δᾶλος Theoc.17.67; μίτρη Nonn.*D.*6.114. **-ανθής**, ές, *of dark hue*, of the sea, B.12.124. **-αυγέτις**, ιδος, pecul. fem. of sq., Orph.*H.* 23.1. **-αυγής**, ές, *dark-gleaming*, ὀφρύες E.*Alc.*261 (lyr.); τὰς βολὰς τῶν ὀφθαλμῶν ἐστὶ κ. Alciphr.3.1; of the sea, κ. Ἀμφιτρίτη D.P. 169, etc.; πηγή *Supp.Epigr.*4.467.25 (Milet., iii A. D.); com. of dithyrambs, Ar.*Av.*1389. **-αῦλαξ**, ακος, ὁ, ἡ, *dark-furrowed*, Orac.ap. Hld.2.26.

Κυάνεαι (νῆσοι or πέτραι), αἱ, *Dark-rocks*, two small islands at the entrance of the Euxine, Hdt.4.85, D.19.273, Str.7.6.1, cf. Συμπληγάδες: Κυάνεα πελάγη, of the adjacent sea, is f.l. in S.*Ant.*966. [ῠ, metri gr., S. l. c.]

κῠᾰν-έμβολος, ον, = κυανόπρῳρος, πρῷραι E.*El.*436, Ar.*Ra.*1318; τριήρεις Id.*Eq.*554.—Only in lyr. **-εος**, α, ον, contr. **κῠᾰνοῦς**, ῆ, οῦν Pl.*Ti.*68c, etc., prob. in A.*Pers.*81 (lyr.), Euph.51.7 (cf. κύανος II):—*made of* κύανος (q. v.), κάπετος Il.18.564; δράκοντες 11.26, cf. 39, Hes.*Sc.*167. II. *of the colour of* κ., *dark-blue, glossy*, of the swallow, Simon.74; of the halcyon, Arist.*HA*616[a]15; of the skin of the porpoise, ib.566[b]12; of the *deep* sea, E.*IT*7, cf. Arist.*Pr.* 932[a]31; πόντου κ. δῖναι Xenarch.1.7; κ. χρῶμα Pl. l. c.; τὸ κ. ἐξ ἰσάτιδος καὶ πυρώδους Thphr.*Sens.*77. 2. generally, *dark, black*, of the mourning veil of Thetis, Il.24.94; of clouds, 5.345, 20.418, Od.12.75; of the brows of Zeus, Il.1.528; χαῖται 22.402; γενειάδες Od.16.176; ἄνδρες, of Africans, Hes.*Op.*527; γαῖα ψάμμῳ κυανέη (of the bottom of Charybdis) Od.12.243; κ. χθών, of Delos, Pi.*Fr.*87.4; κ. θάλαμος, of the chamber of Persephone, Sapph.119; φάλαγγες κ. *dark* masses of warriors, Il.4.282; κυάνεον Τρώων νέφος 16.66: metaph., Κῆρες κ. Hes.*Sc.*249; κ. δνόφος Simon.37.8; λόχμα Pi.*O.*6.40; Ἅιδης *IG*14.1389 ii 25. [ῠ, metri gr., in dactylic verse, Hom., etc.]

Κυανεψιών v. Κυανοψιών.

κυᾰν-έω, *to be dark in colour*, D.P.1111, Phryn.*PS*p.80 B. [ῡ, metri gr.] **-ίζω**, = foreg., Dsc.1.1, *Placit*.3.5.12; of varicose veins, Gal.13.460. **-ῖτις**, ιδος, ἡ, *bluish grey*, ὄψιες (in glaucoma) Hp. *Vid.Ac*.1.

κυᾰνο-βενθής, ές, *with dark-blue depths*, prop. of the sea; com. of a cup, Ar.*Fr*.165. **-βλέφᾰρος**, ον, *dark-eyed*, *AP*5.60 (Rufin.). **-ειδής**, ές, *dark-blue, deep-blue*, κ. ἀμφ' ὕδωρ (i.e. the sea) E.*Hel*.179 (lyr.), cf. Arist.*GA*779^{b}33, *Col*.796^{a}18. **-θριξ**, ὁ, ἡ, gen. τριχος, *dark-haired*, Orph.*A*.1194; χαίτη *AP*6.250 (Antiphil.). **-κρήδεμνος**, ον, *with dark-blue* κρήδεμνον, Q.S.4.381. **-πεζα**, ἡ, *with feet of* κύανος, τράπεζα Il.11.629. [ῡ, metri gr.] **-πεπλος**, ον, *dark-veiled*, of Demeter mourning for her daughter, *h.Cer*.319, 360, 374; of Leto, Hes.*Th*.406. [ῡ, metri gr.]. **-πλόκᾰμος**, ον, *dark-haired*, B.5.33, al., Q.S.5.345. **-πλοκος**, ον, = foreg., Pi.*Pae*.6.83. **-πρώρειος**, ον, = sq., Od.3.299: **-πρώειρα**, Simon.241. **-πρῳρος**, ον, *dark-prowed*, of ships, Il.15.693, 23.852, Od.9.482, 539: fem. κυανόπρῳρᾰ, B.16.1. **-πτερος**, ον, *with blue-black feathers*, like the raven, ὄρνις E.*Andr*.862 (lyr.): generally, *dark-winged*, τέττιξ Hes.*Sc*. 393. **-πτέρυξ**, ῠγος, ὁ, ἡ, = foreg., παῖς Ἀφροδίτας Cerc.5.2.

κύᾰνος [ῠ], ὁ (later ἡ, v. infr. I.3,7), *dark-blue enamel*, esp. used to adorn armour, δέκα οἶμοι μέλανος κυάνοιο Il.11.24, cf. 35; πτύχες κυάνου Hes.*Sc*.143; also θριγκὸς κυάνοιο, of a cornice, Od.7.87; so perh. in *IG*1^2.367.7, 4^2(1).102.244 (Epid.). 2. *lapis lazuli*, κ. αὐτοφυής (opp. σκευαστός) Thphr.*Lap*.39, al., Dsc.5.91, etc. (perh. also in Pl.*Phd*.113c); κ. ἄρρην, θῆλυς, Thphr.*Lap*.31: also an imitation made in Egypt, ib.55. 3. *blue copper carbonate*, Hp.*Cord*.2, Gal.12.233 (ὁ and ἡ), Luc.*Lex*.22; βαπτὴ κ. *AP*6.229 (Crin.). 4. *blue cornflower*, Plin.*HN*21.68. 5. a bird, perh. *blue thrush*, *Turdus cyanus*, Arist.*HA*617^{a}23, Ael.*NA*4.59. 6. *sea-water*, Hsch. 7. fem., *the colour blue*, Alex.Aphr. *in Mete*.162.4. II. as Adj., = κυάνεος, Nic.*Th*.438 (unless κυανός as in Phlp. *in GC*23.11, codd. Pl. l. c.): Comp. -ώτερος *Anacreont*.16.11: Sup. -ώτατος Philostr.*Im*.1.6. [ῡ in dactylic verses, metri gr., cf. κυάνεος, etc.]

κυᾰνόστολος, ον, *dark-robed*, στήθεα Bion 1.4.

κυᾰνοῦς, ῆ, οῦν, v. κυάνεος.

κυᾰν-οφρυς [ᾰ], υ, gen. υος, *dark-browed*, Theoc.3.18, 17.53.

κυᾰνο-χαίτης, ου, ὁ, *dark-haired*, in Hom. usu. of Poseidon, perh. in reference to the *dark blue* of the sea, Il.20.144, Od.9.536, cf. Hes.*Th*.278; Ἀρείων Thebais 4; of a horse, *dark-maned*, Il.20.224, Hes.*Sc*.120: voc. κυανοχαῖτα *h.Cer*.347:—also nom. **κυανοχαῖτα** Il.13.563, 14.390; treated as indeclin. and joined with dat., κυανοχαῖτα Ποσειδάωνι Antim.27. [ῡ, metri gr.] **-χροος**, ον, *dark in hue*, ῥόθια E.*Hel*.1502 (lyr.); πέπλος Nech.ap.Vett.Val.241.18; ἑρπετά Opp.*H*.2.599. **-χρως**, ων, gen. ωτος, = foreg., πλόκαμος E.*Ph*. 308 (lyr.); θαλάττης ἔδαφος Alcid.ap.Arist.*Rh*.1406^{a}5. **-χρωτος**, ον, = foreg., Orph.*H*.70.6, Man.1.327. [ῡ, metri gr., Orph. l. c.; ῠ, Man. l. c.]

Κυανοψιών, ῶνος, ὁ, name of month in Ceos, *Ath.Mitt*.49.138 (iv B. C.); at Cyzicus, *GDI*5703:—also **Κυανεψιών** *IGRom*.4.157; cf. Πυανοψιών.

κυᾰν-ώπης, ες, *dark-eyed*, [ἵπποι] Opp.*C*.1.307:—fem. **-ῶπις**, ιδος, Ἀμφιτρίτη Od.12.60, cf. Hes.*Sc*.356; Νύμφαι Anacr.2.2; Μοῦσα *IG* 14.1942; νᾶες κυανώπιδες B.12.160, cf. A.*Pers*.559 (lyr.), *Supp*.743 (lyr.). **-ωπός**, όν, *dark of aspect*, σέλας *Trag.Adesp*.541.3, cf. Androm.ap.Gal.14.41; δύσις *AP*4.3^b.36 (Agath.). **-ωσις**, εως, ἡ, (as if from *κυανόω) *dark-blue colour*, Plu.2.879d codd.

κύάρ, τό, *a hole*, as *the eye* of a needle, etc., Hp.*Morb*.2.33, cf. *Acut*.(*Sp*.)61; *orifice* of the ear, Poll.2.86.

κυβάβδα· αἷμα (Amathus), Hsch.

κυβάζω, (κύβη) *set on the head, turn upside down*, Hsch.

κυβαία (sc. ναῦς), ἡ, kind of *boat*, *PCair.Zen*.2.3, al. (iii B. C.); Lat. *cybaea*, Cic.*Verr*.4.8.17, 5.17.44:—Dim. **κυβαίδιον** or **κυβᾴδιον**, τό, *PSI*6.594.3 (iii B. C.).

κυβαΐζοντες· λάσωνες, Hsch.

κυβάλης, ὁ, *cinaedus*, Eust.1431.46; cf. κυπάτης.

κῠβᾰλικός, ή, όν, *rascally*, ἀργυρίοισι -οῖσι cj. in Timocr.1.6; cf. κυβηλικός, κόβαλος.

κύβας, ου, ὁ, = σορός, Hsch. (συρός cod.). **κυβάω**, (κύβος) gloss on πεττεύει, Id. 2. = κυβάζω, *EM*543.16. **κύββα**, ἡ, = κύμβη (A), Hsch.

κυβδᾰ, Adv., (κύπτω) *with the head forwards, stooping forwards*, sens. obsc., κ. ἦν πονευμένη Archil.32, cf. Ar.*Eq*.365, *Th*.489, S.*Ichn*. 122.

κυβέβις, v. κύβηβος.

κύβεθρον, τό, = κυψέλη II, Hsch.; cf. κύβερτον.

κῠβεία, ἡ, *dice-playing*, Pl.*Phdr*.274d, X.*Mem*.1.3.2, Aen.Tact.5.2, Men.481.10 (pl.), etc.: metaph., ἐν τῇ κ. τῶν ἀνθρώπων by the *trickery* of men, *Ep.Eph*.4.14.

κῠβείας, ου, ὁ, a kind of πηλαμύς, Opp.*H*.1.183.

κῠβεῖον, τό, *gaming-house*, Aeschin.1.78.

κύβειρος, = ἀναιδής, Suid. **κύβελα**, τά, *lairs* of wild beasts, Hsch.

Κυβέλειον, τό, = ἴον, Ps.-Dsc.4.121.

κυβέλη, ἡ, = κύαρ, *EM*543.1.

Κῠβέλη, ἡ, *Cybele*, E.*Ba*.79 (lyr.), Ar.*Av*.877, etc.:—from **Κύβελον**, τό, or **Κύβελα**, τά, mountain in Phrygia, D.S.3.58, Str.12.5.3:—hence Adj. **Κῠβεληγενής**, St.Byz.:—also **Κῠβήβη**, Hippon.120 (dub.), Hdt.5.102, *Anacreont*.11.1; equated with Aphrodite by Charon Hist.(*FHG* iv p.627):—fem. Adj. **Κῠβηλίς**, ίδος, ἡ, *Cybelian*, Κυβηλίδος ὄργανα Ῥείης Nonn.*D*.10.387, 14.214, cf. Hippon.121, prob. in St.Byz. s. v. Κυβέλεια:—also **Κῠβεληΐς**, Nonn.*D*.14.10, al.

κῠβεπίκῠβος, ὁ, = κυβόκυβος, Theodoret.*Therap*.6.52.

κῠβερν-άω, *steer*, νῆα κυβερνῆσαι Od.3.283, cf. Pi.*O*.12.3 (Pass.), Pl.*Plt*.298e, etc.: abs., *act as helmsman*, αὐτὸς ἑαυτῷ Ar.*Eq*.544. 2. *drive*, κ. ἅρματα Pl.*Thg*.123c; τὸν δρόμον τῶν ἵππων Hdn.7.9.6. 3. metaph., *guide, govern*, Pi.*P*.5.122, Antipho 1.13, Pl.*Euthd*.291d, etc.; τὴν δίκην ὀρθῇ γνώμῃ κυβερνᾶτε Herod.2.100. 4. *act as pilot*, i.e. perform certain rites, in the Ship of Isis, *IGRom*.1.817 (Callipolis). II. Med., = Act., κυβερνωμένης τῆς διανοίας Arist.*Pr*.964^{b}17; ὁ κυβερνώμενος μουσικῇ Marcellin.*Vit.Thuc*.49:—Pass., σῇ κυβερνῶμαι χερί S.*Aj*.35; μιᾷ γνώμῃ τῇ Κύρου ἐκυβερνᾶτο X.*Cyr*.8.8.1; ἡ ἰατρικὴ.. διὰ τοῦ θεοῦ τούτου κυβερνᾶται Pl.*Smp*.187a, cf. *R*.590d, Antiph.40.8, etc.; cf. κυμερῆναι. **-ήσια** (sc. ἱερά), ων, τά, *festival* at Athens *in memory of the steersman* of Theseus, Plu.*Thes*.17. **-ησις**, Dor. **-ᾱσις**, εως, ἡ, *steering, pilotage*, Pl.*R*.488b. 2. metaph., *government*, πολίων of cities, Pi.*P*.10.72 (pl.), cf. 1*Ep.Cor*.12.28 (pl.); θεοῦ by a god, Plu.2.162a. **-ήτειρα**, ἡ, fem. of κυβερνητήρ, τύχη *AP*10.65 (Pall.), cf. Nonn.*D*.1.89. **-ητέον**, *one must direct*, Pl. *Sis*.389d. **-ητήρ**, Dor. **-ατήρ**, ῆρος, ὁ, = κυβερνήτης, Od.8.557, etc.: metaph., Pi.*P*.4.274: as Adj., κ. χαλινός Opp.*C*.1.96. **-ητήριος**, α, ον, = κυβερνητικός, Orac.ap.Plu.*Sol*.14. **-ήτης** (Aeol. **κυμερνήτης**, q. v.), ου, ὁ, *steersman, pilot*, Il.19.43, Od.9.78, A.*Supp*. 770, Hdt.2.164, Ar.*Th*.837, Th.7.70, Pl.*R*.341c, etc.; *skipper* of Nile-boat, ναύκληρος καὶ κ. *PHib*.1.39.6 (iii B. C.), cf. *PGiss*.11 (ii A. D.), etc. 2. metaph., *guide, governor*, E.*Supp*.880, Pl.*Phdr*.247c; as an official title, *PMasp*.89 iii 1 (vi A. D.). **-ητικός**, ή, όν, *good at steering*, Pl.*R*.488d,e; νοῦς καὶ ἀρετὴ κ. Id.*Alc*.1.135a: Comp. -ώτερος Id.*R*.551c: Sup. -ώτατος X.*Mem*.3.3.9: ἡ -κή (sc. τέχνη) *pilot's art*, Pl.*Grg*.511d, cf. Iamb.*Myst*.3.26; τὸ -κόν Pl.*Plt*.299c; τὰ -κά Id.*Alc*.1.119d. Adv. -κῶς D.Chr.4.25. 2. metaph., ἡ τῶν ἀνθρώπων -κή Pl.*Clit*.408b, etc. **-ῆτις**, ιδος, fem. of κυβερνήτης, epith. of Isis, *POxy*.1380.69 (ii A. D.). **-ιον**, *gubernum*, *Gloss*. **-ισμός**, ὁ, = κυβέρνησις, Aq.*Na*.3.1. **-ος**, *gubernita*, *Gloss*.

κυβέρτιον, τό, Dim. of sq., Suid. and Phot. s. v. κυψέλη. **κύβερτον**, gloss on κύψελον, Hsch. **κύβεσις** ἡ (ἡ cod.) κίβισις· πήρα, Id.

κῠβ-ευτήριον, τό, *gambling-house*, Plu.2.621b, Poll.7.203, D.C. 65.2. **-ευτής**, οῦ, ὁ, *dicer, gambler*, S.*Fr*.947, Eup.11.8 D., X.*HG* 6.3.16, Men.965, Vett.Val.202.6; οἱ Κυβευταί, name of plays by Antiphanes, etc. **-ευτικός**, ή, όν, *of* or *for dice-playing*, ὄργανα Aeschin. 1.59; ἐργαλεῖα Poll.9.97. II. *skilled in dice-playing*, Pl.*R*. 374c. **-εύω**, *play at dice*, Cratin.195, Ar.*Ec*.672, Isoc.15.287, etc. 2. metaph., *run a risk* or *hazard*, περὶ διπλασίων X.*HG*6.3.16, cf. Plu.*Art*.17; περὶ τοῖς φιλτάτοις Pl.*Prt*.314a; κ. τῷ βίῳ Plb.*Fr*. 6. II. trans., *run the risk of, venture on*, κυβεύων τὸν πρὸς Ἀργείους Ἄρη E.*Rh*.446:—Pass., *to be staked*, *AP*7.427.13 (Antip. Sid.). 2. c. acc. pers., *cheat, defraud*, Arr.*Epict*.2.19.28, cf. 3.21.22. **-εών**, ῶνος, ὁ, = κυβευτήριον, Tz.*H*.10.558.

κύβη, ἡ, *head*, only as etym. of κυβιστάω, *EM*543.22; cf. κύμβη (B).

Κῠβήβη, ἡ, = Κυβέλη (q. v.). II. an Arcadian boot, Hsch.

κύβηβος, ον, (κύβη) *stooping with the head*, *EM*543.10. II. **Κύβηβος** [ῠ], ὁ, *minister of Cybele*, Semon.36; cf. κυβέβις· γάλλος, κτλ., Hsch.: generally, *one ecstatic* or *frantic*, Cratin.82:—hence **κῠβηβάω**, *to be frantic*, Phot., Hsch., cf. *EM*543.11 (-βειν codd.):—Hsch. also has the forms **Κυβήκη** (Hippon.120) and **Κύβηκος**.

κῠβηλ-ίζω, *strike with an axe*, Hsch. **-ικός**, ή, όν, *as with an axe*, κ. τρόπον *Com.Adesp*.869; cf. κυβαλικός. **-ις**, εως, ἡ, *axe, cleaver*, Philem.13, Anaxipp.6.6, Lyc.1170. II. = τυρόκνηστις, Cratin.315.

Κῠβηλίς, ίδος, ἡ, v. Κυβέλη.

Κῠβηλιστής, οῦ, ὁ, = ἀγερσικύβηλις, Cratin.62.

κύβηνα· σκήνωμα, Hsch. **κυβήνη**, ἡ, = γλαύξ, Id. **κύβηξ**, ηκος, ἡ, abusive term for *old woman*, *Com.Adesp*.57 D.

κύβης, ου, ὁ, = κυβευτής, Hsch. **κυβησίνδα** [παίζειν], play *at* ἐγκοτύλη, Poll.9.122, cf. Hsch., Phot. **κυβητίζω**· ἐπὶ κεφαλὴν ῥίψω, Hsch.

κυβιάριον, τό, *crate of salt fish*, *POxy*.1657.9 (iii B. C.).

κῠβ-ίζω, (κύβος) *make into a cube*, τὸ πλῆθος τῷ σχήματι Plu.2.979f; of numbers, *raise to the cube*, Hero *Metr*.3.22:—Pass., Procl.*Hyp*.4. 102, *Theol.Ar*.33; *to be multiplied*, Hippol.*Haer*.1.2.10. **-ικός**, ή, όν, *cubic*, σχῆμα, εἶδος, Pl.*Ti*.55c,d; σώματα Gal.9.523; πλοῖον κυβικὴ σανίς Secund.*Sent*.17. Adv. -κῶς *cubically*, Plu.2.404f: metaph., ἑστῶσα παγίως καὶ κ. Dam.*Pr*.266. 2. of numbers, *raised to the cube*, Arist.*Pr*.910^{b}36.

κύβιον [ῠ], τό, *flesh of the* πηλαμύς *salted in* κύβοι, Hices.ap.Ath. 3.118b, Posidipp.16, cf. Gal.12.893: pl., *PCair.Zen*.66.11 (iii B. C.), *PSI*5.535.37 (iii B. C.).

κῠβιοσάκτης, ου, ὁ, *dealer in salt fish*, nickname of the son-in-law of the thirteenth Ptolemy, Str.17.1.11; of Vespasian, Suet.*Vesp*.19.

κυβισίς· κήλη, Hsch.

κῠβισμός, ὁ, prop. *cubing*: *making into a solid*, *Theol.Ar*.36.

κῠβιστ-άω, Ion. -έω Opp.*C*.4.263: (κύβη):— *tumble head foremost*, ἦ μάλ' ἐλαφρὸς ἀνήρ, ὡς ῥεῖα κυβιστᾷ Il.16.745, cf. 749; of fish, κατὰ καλὰ ῥέεθρα κυβίστων ἔνθα καὶ ἔνθα *tumbled* or *plunged about*, 21. 354, cf. Opp. l. c.; esp. of professional tumblers, Pl.*Smp*.190a; κ. εἰς ξίφη, εἰς μαχαίρας, X.*Smp*.2.11, *Mem*.1.3.9, Pl.*Euthd*.294e. **-ημα**, ατος, τό, *somersault*, Luc.*Anach*.18. **-ής**, οῦ, ὁ, = *κυβιστητής (*tumbler*), dub. in M.Bulard *La relig. domestique dans la colonie ital. de Délos* 482 (vase). **-ησις**, εως, ἡ, *somersault*, in pl., Plu.2.401c, Luc. *Anach*.16. **-ητεία**, ἡ, = foreg., Suid. **-ητήρ**, ῆρος, ὁ, *tumbler*, δοιὼ δὲ κυβιστητῆρε κατ' αὐτοὺς μολπῆς ἐξάρχοντες ἐδίνευον κατὰ μέσσους Il.

18.605, Od.4.18. **2.** *diver*, Il.16.750. **3.** *one who pitches headlong*, E.*Ph.*1151. **II.** later as Adj., *tumbling*, κυδοιμός Tryph. 192. **-ιάω**, *turn a somersault*, *Gloss.*

κῠβῐτίζω, (κύβιτον) *nudge* or *poke with the elbow*, Epich.213.

κύβῐτον [ῠ], τό, *elbow*, Lat. *cubitum*, Hp.*Loc.Hom.*6; Sicilian for Att. ὀλέκρανον, Ruf.*Onom.*79, cf. Poll.2.141: wrongly expld. as κυβοειδὲς ὀστάριον by Bacch.ap.Erot.

κῠβο-ειδής, ές, *like a cube, cubical*, Epicur.*Nat.*14.5, Str.16.1.5, Dsc.5.98, Gal.5.668, Heliod.ap.Orib.49.4.47; ὀστοῦν Gal.*UP*3.7, al. **-κῠβος**, ὁ, *cube multiplied by cube*, i.e. *sixth power*, Hippol. *Haer.*1.2.10. **II.** *sixth power of unknown quantity*, x^6, Dioph.1 *Def.*1, Sch.Iamb.*in Nic.*p.131 P.:—hence **κῠβοκῠβοστόν** (sc. μόριον), τό, *fraction corresponding to* κυβόκυβος, $1/x^6$, Dioph.1 *Def.*3.

κύβος [ῠ, v. sub fin.], ὁ, *cube*, Ti.Locr.98c; esp. *cubical die*, marked on all six sides, mostly in pl., *dice*, Hdt.1.94, etc.; κύβων βολαί S. *Fr.*429; ἐν πτώσει κύβων Pl.*R.*604c; περὶ κύβους τὰς διατριβὰς ποιούμενοι Lys.16.11: prov., ἀεὶ γὰρ εὖ πίπτουσιν οἱ Διὸς κ., i.e. God's work is no mere chance, S.*Fr.*895; ἔργον ἐν κύβοις Ἄρης κρινεῖ A.*Th.* 414; ἄλλα βλήματ' ἐν κύβοις βαλεῖν E.*Supp.*330; ψυχὴν προβάλλοντ' ἐν κύβοισι δαίμονος Id.*Rh.*183: later in sg., οἶδ' ὅτι ῥιπτῶ πάντα κύβον κεφαλῆς.. ὕπερθεν ἐμῆς *AP*5.24 (Phld.); τὸν περὶ τῶν ὅλων ἀναρρίψων κύβον Plu.*Fab.*14, cf. Luc.*Pr.Im.*16; ἐφ' ἑνὸς ἀνδρὸς ἀναρρίπτειν τὸν κ. Id.*Harm.*3; ἀνερρίφθω κ., Lat. *jacta esto alea*, Men.65.4, Plu.*Caes.* 32; ἔσχατον κύβον ἀφιέναι try one's luck for the last time, Id.*Cor.* 3. **2.** of the single *pips on the dice*, βέβληκ' Ἀχιλλεὺς δύο κύβω καὶ τέσσαρα he has thrown two *aces* and a four, E.*Fr.*888: prov., τρὶς ἓξ.. ἢ τρεῖς κύβους βάλλειν 'all or nothing', Pl.*Lg.*968e, cf. Pherecr. 124. **3.** in pl., *gaming-table*, Hermipp.27. **II.** *cubic number*, Pl. *R.*528b, Arist.*APo.*76^b8. **III.** *anything of cubic shape*: *vertebra*, Rhian.57. **2.** *block* of stone, *PCair.Zen.*276 (iii B.C.); of wood, *IG*2^2.463.57, 7.3073.187 (Lebad., ii B.C.). **3.** *piece of salt fish*, Alex.187.4. **4.** kind of *cubic cake*, Eup.424, Heraclid.ap.Ath.3. 114a. **5.** *hollow above the hips* of cattle, Simaristus ib.9.399b. **6.** *part of an irrigation-machine*, *BGU*1546 (iii B.C.), *PLond.*3.1177.216 (ii A.D.). [κῦβος only in late Poets, *AP*14.8; *coebus* Aus.*Idyll.*11.3.]

κυβοστόν (sc. μόριον), τό, *fraction corresponding to* κύβος, i.e. $1/x^3$, Dioph.1 *Def.*3.

κύβωλον, τό, = κύβιτον, Poll.2.141.

κυγχνίδα, v. κυλιχνίς.

κυδάγχας· μάχας, λοιδορίας, and **κυδαγχόμενα**· λοιδορούμενα, Hsch.; cf. sq.

κῠδάζω, (κῦδος) *revile, abuse*, Ἄμυκε, μή κύδαζέ μοι τὸν πρεσβύτερον ἀδελφεόν Epich.6:—in Med., c. dat., τήνῳ κυδάζομαί τε κἀπ' ὧν ἠχθόμαν Id.35.6; οὔ τοι γυναιξὶ δεῖ κυδάζεσθαι· τί γάρ; A.*Fr.*94: c. acc., ὦ πέπον ἦ μάλα δή με κακῷ ἐκυδάσσαο μύθῳ A.R.1.1337:—Pass., *to be reviled*, S.*Aj.*722.

κῡδ-αίνω, fut. κυδανῶ Lyc.721, etc.: Ep. aor. κύδηνα Il.23.793; Dor. ἐκύδανα Pi.*P.*1.31: (κῦδος):—*give* or *do honour to*, τινα Il.10.69, 13.348,350; ἡμὲν κυδῆναι θνητὸν βροτὸν ἠδὲ κακῶσαι Od.16.212; Ζεύς, ὅς μιν.. τίμα καὶ κύδαινε Il.15.612; [Αἰνείαν] ἀκέοντό τε κύδαινόν τε they healed and *glorified* him, by restoring strength and beauty, 5.448; πάλᾳ κυδαίνων Τεγέαν Pi.*O.*10(11).66, cf. *P.*1.31; πατρίδα κ. Simon. 151; σφ' ἀρετὴ κυδαίνουσ' ἀνάγει.. ἐξ Ἀΐδεω Id.99.4; πρὸ τοῦ κήπου κ. τὸν περίπατον Plu.2.635a. **II.** *delight* or *gladden by marks of honour*, κύδαινε δὲ θυμὸν ἄνακτος Od.14.438, cf. Il.23.793. **III.** seldom in bad sense, *flatter, fawn upon*, Hes.*Op.*38, cj. in Max.Tyr. 20.1. **IV.** Med., *pride oneself*, ἐπὶ πατράσι Onos.1.24.—Poet. and late Prose. **-άλιμος** [ᾰ], ον, also η, ον *IG*5(1).599 (Sparta): (κῦδος):—*glorious, renowned*, in Hom. epith. of heroes, Il.17.378, Od.14.206, al.; of nations, Il.6.184,204; κ. κῆρ a *noble* heart, of Agamemnon and Achilles, 10.16, 18.33; the suitor Eurymachus, Od. 21.247; the lion, Il.12.45; ἱερεῖς.. τιμαῖς -ους Man.2.226. **-άνω** [ᾰ], = κυδαίνω, only pres. and impf., *exalt*, τοὺς μὲν ὁμῶς μακάρεσσι θεοῖσι κυδάνει Il.14.73. **II.** *to be triumphant*, Ἀχαιοὶ μὲν μέγα κύδανον 20.42.

κύδαρ· τάφος, Hsch.

κύδαρος, ὁ, kind of *small ship*, Antiph.321:—also **κύδαρον**, τό, *POxy.*1197.10 (iii A.D.), *AB*274, *EM*543.39; Lat. *cydarum*, Gell.10. 25, *CIL*8.27790 (Althiburos).

κῠδάττω, = κυδάζω, Hsch. **κῡδέστερος**, irreg. Comp. of κυδρός.

κῡδήεις, εσσα, εν, *glorious*, δῶρα *AP*9.697, cf. Man.2.231: Dor. fem. **κυδάεσσα** [δᾱ], παρθένε *IG*4^2(1).134.12 (Epid.).

κῡδῐ-άνειρα [ᾰν], ἡ, (κῦδος) fem. Adj. *bringing men glory* or *renown*, Homeric epith. of μάχη, Il.4.225, al.; once of the ἀγορή, 1.490; of Φύσις, Orph.*H.*10.5. **II.** Pass., *glorified by men, famous for men*, Σπάρτα *APl.*1.1 (Damag.). **-άω**, Ep. Verb, only pres. and impf., *bear oneself proudly, exult*, in Il. always in Ep. part. κυδιόων, 2.579, 21.519, cf. *h.Cer.*170; of a horse, Il.6.509: c. dat., *exult in*, κυδιόων λαοῖσι Hes.*Sc.*27; εὐφροσύνῃ.. κυδιόωσι *h.Hom.*30.13: Iterat. κυδιάασκον A.R.4.978, Q.S.13.418.

κύδ-ῐμος [ῠ], ον, = κυδάλιμος, epith. of Hermes, *h.Merc.*46, al., Hes.*Th.*938; ἄεθλα Pi.*O.*14.24. **-ιστος**, η, ον, Sup. of κυδρός, *most honoured, noblest*, in Hom. freq. of Zeus and Agamemnon, Ζεῦ κύδιστε μέγιστε Il.2.412, al.; Ἀτρεΐδη κ. 1.122, al.; of Athena, 4. 515, Od.3.378; of Hera, *h.Ven.*42; of Leto, *h.Ap.*62; of Anchises, *h.Ven.*108; κύδιστ' Ἀχαιῶν A.*Fr.*238 (lyr.). **2.** of things, *greatest*, κύδιστ' ἀχέων Id.*Supp.*13 (anap.): in Trag., Comp. **κυδίων** [ῑ], ον, gen. ονος, τί μοι ζῆν δῆτα κύδιον; what *profits it* me to live? E.*Alc.*960 (s.v.l.), cf. *Andr.*639 (v.l. κύδιστον).

κυδνός, ή, όν, = κυδρός, Hes.*Th.*328 (v.l. κυδρή), *IG*14.2117; v.l. for κυδρός, Hes.*Op.*257.

κῠδοιδοπάω, *make a hubbub*, Ar.*Pax* 1152, *Nu.*616.

κῠδοιμ-έω, *make an uproar, spread confusion*, τὼ δ' ἀν' ὅμιλον ἰόντε κυδοίμεον Il.11.324, cf. Q.S.13.480. **II.** trans., *drive in confusion*, ἡμέας εἶσι κυδοιμήσων ἐς Ὄλυμπον Il.15.136. (In later Prose, Phld. *Piet.*145.) **-ός**, ὁ, *din of battle, uproar, hubbub*, Τρώων δὲ κλαγγή τε καὶ ἄσπετος ὦρτο κυδοιμός Il.10.523, cf. 18.218; κυδοιμὸν ἐμβαλεῖν (mock-heroic) Ar.*Ach.*573; ὀρνίθων κυδοιμοί cock-*fights*, Theoc.22. 72:—Κυδοιμός personified, as companion of Ἐνυώ and Ἔρις, Il.5.593, 18.535, cf. Emp.128.1, Ar.*Pax* 255.—Ep. word, used by Ar. and in later Prose, as Plb.5.48.5, Luc.*Bis Acc.*10, etc.

κῦδος, εος, τό, *glory, renown*, esp. in war, ὡς ἄν μοι τιμὴν.. καὶ κ. ἄρηαι Il.16.84; ἐκ δὲ Διὸς τιμὴ καὶ κ. ὀπηδεῖ 17.251; Ἕκτορι κ. ὄπαζεν (sc. Ἀπόλλων) 16.730; ὁπποτέροισι πατὴρ Ζεὺς κ. ὀρέξῃ 5.33; κ. ἀρέσθαι to win *glory*, 12.407, etc.; κύδεϊ γαίων 1.405, 5.906; of a person, μέγα κ. Ἀχαιῶν *glory* of the Achaeans, of Odysseus, 9.673, Od.12. 184; of Nestor, Il.14.42, Od.3.79.—Ep. word, also in Alc.*Supp.*23. 13, Hdt.7.8.α', Democr.215, Pi.*P.*2.89, al., A.*Th.*317 (lyr.), *Pers.*455 (not in S. or E.); in a mock-heroic line, Ar.*Eq.*200; never in Att. Prose.

κύδος, ὁ, *reproach, abuse*, Sch.S.*Aj.*722, Sch.A.R.1.1337.

κυδρόομαι, Pass., = κυδιάω, Ael.*NA*4.29, 11.31, Polyaen.4.3.5.

κῡδρός, ά, όν, (κῦδος) = κυδάλιμος, in Hom. always in fem., as epith. of Hera and Leto, Διὸς κυδρὴ παράκοιτις Il.18.184, Od.11.580; of Pallas, *h.Hom.*28.1; Δίκη Hes.*Op.*257 (v.l. κυδνή); θεαί, of the Nymphs, A.*Fr.*168 (hex.); rarely of a mortal woman, Od.15.26: masc. first in *h.Merc.*461, Alcm.9; of a man, X.*Ap.*29; of a horse, κυδρῷ τῷ σχήματι φέρεται Id.*Eq.*10.16; κυδρότερον πίνειν to drink *more lustily*, Ion Eleg.2.10.—Poet. word, used once in Trag., and twice by X.—Besides regul. Comp. κυδρότερος Xenoph.2.6, B.1.54, we find κυδίων, -ιστος (v. κύδιστος), also κυδέστερος Plb.3.96.7: Sup. κυδίστατος Nic.*Th.*3; κυδότερος, -ότατος *EM*543.29.

Κῠδων-ᾶτον, τό, *drink made from quinces*, Aët.5.139; κ. τριπτόν *drug compounded of quinces*, Paul.Aeg.7.11. **-έα**, ἡ, *quince-tree*, *Pyrus Cydonia*, *PCair.Zen.*486.2 (iii B.C.), *Gp.*4.1.12:—also **Κῠδωνία**, ἡ, ib.10.24. **-ιάτης** [ᾱ], ου, ὁ, *inhabitant of Cydonia* in Crete, Plb.4.55.4, Str.10.4.12, etc. **-ιάω**, *swell like a quince*, μαζὸς κυδωνιᾷ *APl.*4.182 (Leon.); κυδωνιῶντες οἱ μαστοὶ τὴν ἀμπεχόνην ἐξωθοῦσι Aristaenet.1.1, cf. 3. **-ιος**, α, ον, (Κυδωνία) *Cydonian*, μᾶλα *quinces*, Stesich.29, cf. Alcm.143, Canthar.6, Phylarch.10 J.; μηλίδες Ibyc. 1.1; κυδώνια, τά, Dsc.1.115. **II.** metaph., *swelling like a quince*, κ. τιτθία, of a young girl's breasts, Ar.*Ach.*1199. **2.** κυδώνιον· μέγα καὶ ἀξιόλογον, ἢ ἀπατηλόν, δόλιον, λοίδορον (cf. κύδος), Hsch. **-ίτης** [ῑ] οἶνος, ὁ, *quince*-wine, Dsc.5.20.

κῠδωνόμελι, τό, *drink made from quinces and honey*, Dsc.5.21, Orib.5.25.16.

κυέω, older and more Att. form of κύω, Il.23.266, etc. (Aeol.(?) part. fem. κύεσσα Hsch.; Arc. κύενσα *IG*5(2).514.12 (Lycosura); Coan κυεῦσα *Schwyzer* 251 *B* 3, written κυεοσα ib. *A* 61 (iv/iii B.C.)): impf. 3 sg. ἐκύει Il.19.117: fut. κυήσω Hp.*Mul.*1.17, *Steril.*214, κυήσομαι v.l. in *Mul.*1.76: aor. ἐκύησα Ar.*Th.*641, Pl.*Smp.*203c, etc.: pf. κεκύηκα Philem.107, D.C.45.1, S.E.*P.*2.106:—Med., v. infr.:—**Pass.**, fut. -ηθήσομαι Gal.*UP*16.10: aor. ἐκυήθην Plu.2.567f: pf. κεκύηται Porph. *Abst.*1.54:—*bear in the womb, be pregnant with*, ἐκύει φίλον υἱόν Il.19. 117; of a mare, βρέφος ἡμίονον κυέουσα 23.266: metaph., of the soul, κυοῦσι γὰρ πάντες.. καὶ κατὰ τὸ σῶμα καὶ κατὰ τὴν ψυχήν Pl.*Smp.*206c; ἐκύησε τὸν Ἔρωτα ib.203c; ἃ κυεῖ περὶ ἐπιστήμης [the thoughts] with which he *is in travail*.., Id.*Tht.*184b, cf. 210b; ἃ τῇ ψυχῇ προσήκει καὶ κυῆσαι καὶ κυεῖν (v.l. τεκεῖν) both *to have conceived* and *to bring forth*, Id.*Smp.*209a:—Pass., of the embryo or foetus, Id.*Lg.* 789a, *Epin.*973d, Arist.*GA*777^a23; of fruits, *to be formed*, Thphr.*HP* 4.2.4:—Med., *bring forth*, Opp.*C.*3.22; ἡ κεκυημένη, Lat. *foeta*, *Et. Gud.* s.v. κοκίας: metaph., τὰς εὐτυχεῖς ὠδῖνας κυησαμένη Him.*Or.* 7.4. **b.** in Botany, *produce flowers*, Thphr.*HP*6.4.8. **2.** abs., *to be big* or *pregnant, conceive*, ἐκύησε Hdt.5.41; στεριφὴ γὰρ εἰμι κοὐκ ἐκύησα πώποτε Ar.*Th.*641, cf. *Lys.*745, Men.*Sam.*303, etc.; κυέουσαν ἐκ τοῦ προτέρου ἀνδρός Hdt.6.68, cf. And.1.125, Lys.13.42; γυνὴ κυεῖ δέκα μῆνας; Men.413; πενθ' ἔτη ἐκύησε *IG*4^2(1).121.3 (Epid.). (Cf. κύω, Skt. *śváyati* 'swell', Lat. *inciens* 'pregnant'.)

Κύζῐκος, ἡ, *Cyzicus*, Hdt.4.14, etc., cf. Str.12.8.11:—Adj. **Κυζικηνικός**, ή, όν, βάμμα Ar.*Pax* 1176:—more freq. **Κυζικηνός**, ή, όν, Κ. στατήρ a gold coin, Lys.32.6, D.34.23, etc.; without στ., Lys.12.11, X.*An.*6.2.4, D.21.173; Κ. ἔμπλαστρος, name of a plaster, Heras ap. Gal.13.814.

κύ-ημα [ῠ], ατος, τό, *that which is conceived, embryo, foetus*, Hp. *Epid.*7.6, al., Pl.*R.*461c, Arist.*GA*719^b33, etc. **II.** in Botany, *that which is swollen as the result of growth*, e.g. base of flower-head, Thphr.*HP*6.4.3: of a cabbage-sprout, Dsc.2.120, Gal.6.642. **-ηρός**, ά, όν, *pregnant*, Hsch.; also, = ἁπαλόν, βλαστόν, Id. **-ησις**, εως, ἡ, *conception*, joined with γέννησις, Pl.*Plt.*274a, cf. *Mx.*238a, Arist.*PA* 689^a18, *GA*721^a20, al., Corn.*ND*24 (pl.); *pregnancy*, *PLond.*2.361. 6 (i A.D.): metaph., πρὸς ἀρετῆς κύησιν Plu.2.3a codd. (leg. κτῆσιν). **II.** = κύημα II, Thphr.*HP*6.4.8. **-ητήριος**, α, ον, *aiding conception*, πρόσθετον κ. Hp.*Nat.Mul.*109: as Subst. κυητήριον, τό, Id.*Mul.*1.75, al.

κύθε, κεκύθωσι, v. κεύθω.

Κῠθέρεια, ἡ, *Cythereia*, surname of Aphrodite, Od.8.288, 18.193, from the city Κύθηρα in Crete, or from the island Κύθηρα; Κυπρογενὴς

Κ. *h.Hom.*10.1; Κ. Ἀφροδίτη Musae.38 (s. v. l.):—also **Κῠθήρη**, *Anacreont.*14.11; **Κῠθείρη** v. l. in Opp.*C.*1.39; **Κῠθέρη**, *AP*6.209 (Antip. Thess.), Epigr.ap.Luc.*Symp.*41; **Κῠθηριάς**, άδος, *AP*6.190 (Gaet.), 206 (Antip. Sid.); **Κῠθερηϊάς**, Man.4.359.

Κῠθερηΐς, ΐδος, ἡ, Adj. *of Cythereia*, Man.4.207.

κῠθηγενής, ές, (κεύθω) *born in secret*, *Eleg.Alex.Adesp.*1.9, Hsch.

Κύθηρα [ῠ], τά, *Cythera*, mod. *Cerigo*, Od.9.81, etc.: **Κῠθηρόθεν**, Adv. *from Cythera*, Il.15.438: poet. **Κῠθέρηθεν** (for Κυθη-), Hermesian.7.69:—Adj. **Κῠθήριος**, α, ον, Il.10.268, etc.; ἡ Κυθηρία (sc. γῆ) X.*HG*4.8.7.

Κῠθηροδίκης [ῐ], ου, ὁ, *Spartan magistrate sent annually to govern the island of Cythera*, Th.4.53, *BSA*27.228 (Sparta, ii A. D.).

κύθιον, τό, name of an *eye-salve*, Cels.6.6.7.

κυθνόν, = σπέρμα, Hsch.; also, *drug which prevents conception* (leg. ἄκυθνον), Id.

Κυθνώλης, ες, (Κύθνος, ὄλλυμι) Κ. συμφορά, prov. of *utter ruin*, from the extirpation of the Cythnians by Amphitryon, Arist.*Fr.*523.

κυθνώνυμος, v. κυθώνυμος.

κύθρα, κυθρίδιον, κύθρινος, κυθρίς, κυθρόκαυλος, κυθρόπους, κύθρος, Ion. and later Greek for χύτρ- (q. v.).

κυθώδης, ες, *evil-smelling*, Hsch.

κῠθώνῠμος, ον, *of hidden name*, epith. of Oedipus, Antim.55: written κυθν- by Hsch.

κυΐντατα· οἰκτρότατα, Hsch.

κυΐξ, ὁ, name of a bulbous plant, Thphr.*HP*7.13.9.

κυΐσκομαι, Pass., of the female, *conceive, become pregnant*, Hdt.2.93, 4.30, Arist.*HA*543^b19, etc.; κυϊσκομένη τε καὶ τίκτουσα Pl.*Tht.*149b; of plants, Thphr.*CP*3.2.8. II. Act. κυΐσκω in same sense, Hp.*Aph.*5.62, Philostr.*VA*1.22, *Gp.*14.1.3, Gal.4.513; but 2. causal, of the male, *impregnate*, Him.*Or.*1.7.

κυῖτις (sc. λίθος), ἡ, a gem, Plin.*HN*37.154.

κυκαίνω, prob. = κυκάω, Suid.

κυκάν, ᾶνος, ὁ, Dor. for κυκεών, *IG*4^2(1).121.102 (Epid.).

κῠκ-άω, *stir*, of one curdling milk, Il.5.903; *mix*, τινι with a thing, τυρόν τε καὶ ἄλφιτα καὶ μέλι χλωρὸν οἴνῳ.. ἐκύκα Od.10.235, cf. Il.11.638; φάρμακα κ. Hp.*Ep.*17; ἅλμην κύκα τούτοισιν Ar.*V.*1515, cf. Dsc.5.79: metaph., αἰ μή τί τ' εἴπην γλῶσσ' ἐκύκα κακόν Sapph.28:—Med., *mix for oneself*, Ar.*Pax*1169 (lyr.). II. *stir up*, ἄνω τε καὶ κάτω τὸν βόρβορον Id.*Eq.*866; ἄνεμοι κ. τὸ πέλαγος Alciphr.1.10; of intrigue, ἕτερόν τι κ. Men.*Epit.*211: hence, *throw into confusion* or *disorder*, νιφάδι καὶ βροντήμασι.. κυκάτω πάντα A.*Pr.*994; κ. τὴν βουλήν Ar.*Eq.*363; τὴν Ἑλλάδα Id.*Pax*270; κ... πάντα καὶ ταραττέτω ib.320, cf. Pl.*Phd.*101e, Epicur.*Nat.*14.7, etc.: in Hom. only Pass., *to be confounded, panic-stricken*, τὼ δὲ κυκηθήτην Il.11.129; τρὶς δὲ κυκήθησαν Τρῶες 18.229; κυκήθησαν δέ οἱ ἵπποι 20.489; of a river, *to be churned up, seethe*, πάντα δ' ὄρινε ῥέεθρα κυκώμενος 21.235, cf. 324; of Charybdis, Od.12.238; κλύδων' ἔφιππον ἐν μέσῳ κυκώμενον S.*El.*733; of mental *disquiet*, θυμὲ κήδεσιν κυκώμενε Archil.66; ὑπ' ἀνδρὸς τοξότου κυκώμενος *hustled* by him, Ar.*Ach.*707. **-εών**, ῶνος, ὁ, acc. κυκεῶνα Hp.*Acut.*39, Pl.*R.*408b, etc., shortd. κυκεῶ Od.10.290, 316, *h.Cer.*210, Eup.11.4 D., 12.6 D., Ep. acc. κυκειῶ Il.11.624, 641; Dor. κυκάν (q. v.): (κυκάω):—*potion, posset*, containing barley-groats, grated cheese, and Pramnian wine, Il. l. c.; also honey and magical drugs, Od.10.316, cf. 234 sq.; other ingredients, *h.Cer.*210, cf. Hp. l. c., Thphr.*Char.*4.1, etc.; κ. βληχωνίας Ar.*Pax*712; ὁ κ. διίσταται ⟨μὴ⟩ κινούμενος Heraclit.125, cf. Chrysipp.*Stoic.*2.269, M.Ant.9.39. II. metaph., *mixture, medley*, Luc.*Vit.Auct.*14, *Icar.*17. **-ηθμός**, ὁ, *confusion, disturbance*, Max.Tyr.16.9, 17.10. **-ηθρα**· ταραχή, Hsch. **-ηθρον**, τό, *ladle for stirring*: metaph., *turbulent fellow, agitator*, Ar.*Pax*654; κ. μεγάλων πραγμάτων J.*AJ*17.5.8, cf. Cels.ap.Orig.*Cels.*5.63. **-ημα**· τάραχος, Hsch. **-ησις**, εως, ἡ, *stirring up, mixing*, Pl.*Ti.*68a, Epicur.*Nat.Herc.*1431.8. **-ησίτεφρος** [ῐ], ον, *mixed with ashes*, κονία Ar.*Ra.*710 (lyr.). **-ησμός**, ὁ, = κύκησις, S.*Ichn.*117. **-ητής**, οῦ, ὁ, *stirrer, agitator*, term applied to Heraclitus by Epicur.*Fr.*238, cf. Ptol.*Tetr.*166.

κύκκαρος· τὸ ἐλάχιστον, Hsch.

κυκλ-άζω, *go round about, surround*, Hsch. **-αίνω**, *make round*, Id.

κυκλάμῖνος [ᾰ], ἡ, Theoc.5.123, Dsc.2.164; also ὁ, Thphr.*HP*7.9.4, 9.9.3; **κυκλᾰμίς**, ἡ, Orph.*A.*917:—*Cyclamen graecum*, etc., ll. cc.; also κ. ἑτέρα *honeysuckle, Lonicera Periclymenum*, Dsc.2.165.

κυκλάνεμον, τό, κ. γυναικείοις, ἅπερ ἀνεμόσουριν (dub. sens.) καλοῦσιν, Olymp.*in Mete.*200.20.

κυκλάς, άδος, ἡ, *encircling*, αἱ Κυκλάδες νῆσοι the *Cyclades*, islands in the Aegean Sea, which *encircle* Delos, Hdt.5.31, Th.1.4, Isoc.4.136, 12.43, cf. Theoc.17.90, Str.10.5.1: without νῆσοι, Th.2.9; so Κυκλάδας νησαίας πόλεις the cities of those islands, E.*Ion*1583. 2. *recurrent*, of Time, Orph.*H.*53.7. II. Subst. κυκλάς (sc. ἐσθής), ἡ, *a woman's garment with a border all round it*, Prop.4(5).7.40. 2. *part of an irrigation-machine*, *PLond.*3.776.10 (vi A. D.).

κυκλᾱτός, ή, όν, *shod*, of horses, *PMasp.*279.18 (vi A. D.).

Κυκλειών, ῶνος, ὁ, name of month at Ceos, *Ath.Mitt.*49.138 (iv B. C.).

κύκλ-ευμα, ατος, τό, *water-wheel*, *PSI*1.77.18 (vi A. D.). **-ευτήριον**, τό, = foreg., *PGiss.*56.8 (vi A. D.), etc. **-ευτής**, οῦ, ὁ, *tender of water-wheel*, *PLond.*1.131.32, al. (ii A. D.). **-εύω**, *wind round*, περὶ τὸν περινεὸν κ. τὸ ὀθόνιον Hp.*Art.*14. 2. *traverse*, μιᾶς ἡμέρας κ. περίοδον Str.6.3.7, cf. J.*AJ*9.3.1, *Supp.Epigr.*2.530 (Puteoli); ἥλιος κ. τὴν γῆν Cleom.1.2. 3. *work a water-wheel*, *PLond.*1.131.495 (ii A. D.). b. *irrigate by means of a water-wheel*, *PGrenf.*1.58.7 (vi A. D.). II. *circumvent, surround*, App.*BC*4.71 (Pass.). **-έω**, *wheel along*, in Hom. only once, κυκλήσομεν ἐνθάδε νεκροὺς βουσὶ καὶ ἡμιόνοισιν Il.7.332. 2. *move round* or *in a circle*, ὁδοῖς κυκλῶν ἐμαυτὸν εἰς ἀναστροφήν S.*Ant.*226; ἐπ' ἀνδρὶ δυσμενεῖ βάσιν κυκλοῦντα, metaph., from dogs *questing about* for the scent, Id.*Aj.*19; σὸν πόδ' ἐπὶ συννοίᾳ κυκλεῖς E.*Or.*632, cf. Ar.*Av.*1379; κ. πρόσωπον, ὄμμα, look *round*, look *about*, E.*Ph.*364, Ar.*Th.*958 (lyr.); = κυκλεύω I, Hp.*Fract.*4. 3. *bring round, repeat*, τὸν αὐτὸν λόγον Arist.*Cael.*300^a33. II. Med. and Pass., *form a circle round, encompass, encircle*, μηνοειδὲς ποιήσαντες τῶν νεῶν ἐκυκλεῦντο ὡς περιλάβοιεν αὐτούς Hdt.8.16 (elsewh. κυκλόομαι); ἴδεσθέ μ' οἷον ἄρτι κῦμα.. κυκλεῖται *encompasses* me, S.*Aj.*353 (lyr.). 2. *go round and round, revolve*, τὴν αὐτὴν φορὰν κ. Pl.*R.*617a; χρόνου.. κατ' ἀριθμὸν κυκλουμένου Id.*Ti.*38a; οὑμὸς αἰεὶ πότμος ἐν πυκνῷ θεοῦ τροχῷ κυκλεῖται S.*Fr.*871; ὁ βίος ἀγαθοῖς τε καὶ κακοῖς κ. πάντα τὸν αἰῶνα D.S.18.59; δι' ἀλλήλων αὐτοῖς -εῖται τὸ κακόν, of the vicious circle in disease, Gal.10.360. 3. *assemble in knots*, X.*An.*6.4.20, *Cyr.*6.2.12. 4. metaph., of sayings, etc., *to be current, pass from mouth to mouth*, τὸ κυκλούμενον παρὰ πᾶσιν ἔπος Plu.2.118c. III. intr. in Act., *revolve, come round and round*, πολλαὶ κυκλοῦσι νύκτες ἡμέραι τ' ἴσαι (but read κυκλοῦνται as L had originally) S.*El.*1365; δελφῖνες.. πέριξ κυκλοῦντες Plu.2.160f. **-ηδόν**, Adv. *in a circle*, περιβλέψας τὸ πλῆθος Posidon.36 J. **-ησις**, εως, ἡ, *revolution*, Pl.*Ti.*39c, *Plt.*271d, Iamb.*Myst.*8.6. **-ιαῖος**, α, ον, *of* or *for wheels*, τροχοὶ *IG*1^2.349.13. **-ιακός**, ή, όν, only neut. pl., τὰ κ. *treatise on the circle*, by Philippus of Opus, Suid. s. v. φιλόσοφος. **-ιάς**, άδος, ὁ, ἡ, *round*, τυροὶ κυκλιάδες *AP*6.299 (Phan.). **-ίζω**, *cause to revolve*, τὰ ἐναντία περὶ τὴν μένουσαν οὐσίαν Olymp. *in Phd.*p.145 N.:—Pass., *revolve*, ib.p.130 N., al.; *to be enclosed as in a circle*, ἡ οἰκουμένη -ίζεται ἐν τέτταρσι μέρεσιν Agatharch.64. II. intrans. in Act., *revolve*, Dam.*Pr.*23. **-ικός**, ή, όν, *circular, moving in a circle*, σῶμα Arist.*Cael.*289^a30; κίνησις *Placit.*2.7.5; περίοδος D.S.2.36: metaph., Procl.*Inst.*33. Adv. -κῶς, κινεῖσθαι Arist.*Cael.*272^b24. 2. *of a circle*, λόγος Iamb. *in Nic.*p.61 P.; κ. ἀριθμός a number *which ends in the same digit when squared*, Nicom.*Ar.*2.17. 3. Astrol., *subordinate, ruling in rotation*, Vett.Val.175.17. b. -κὰ ἔτη *the minimum duration of life corresponding to a planet*, Balbill. in *Cat.Cod.Astr.*8(4).236, 237. 4. -κός (sc. πούς), ὁ, a form of anapaest in which the long syllable is shorter than a normal long, D.H.*Comp.*17. II. κυκλικοί, οἱ, the *poets of the Epic cycle* (cf. κύκλος), Sch.Il.3.242, al.; also ἡ κ. Θηβαΐς Ath.11.465e; but τὸ ποίημα τὸ κ. *commonplace, conventional* poem (cf. IV), Call.*Epigr.*30.1. III. f. l. for κύκλιος II, χορός Lys.21.2; τῶν κυκλικῶν (v. l. κυκλίων) αὐλητῶν Luc.*Salt.*2. IV. *in common use*, ἡ κ. (sc. ἔκδοσις) the *vulgate*, Sch.Od.16.195, 17.25: but Adv. -κῶς *conventionally*, οὐ κ. τὰ ἐπίθετα προσέρριπται ib.7.115.

κυκλιοδῐδάσκᾰλος, ὁ, *teacher of the cyclic chorus*, i.e. *dithyrambic poet* (v. κύκλιος II), Ar.*Av.*1403.

κύκλ-ιος, α, ον (ος, ον Eup.5 D.), (κύκλος) *round, circular*, ἀσπίς Archestr.*Fr.*13.3; ὕδωρ κύκλιον, of the Delian lake (cf. τροχοειδής), E.*IT*1104 (lyr.). II. κύκλιος χορός, ὁ, *circular* or *cyclic chorus*, prop. of any which were danced *in a ring round an altar*, chiefly used of *dithyrambic choruses*, opp. those which were arranged in a square (τετράγωνοι Timae.44), Ar.*Nu.*333, *Ra.*366, *Fr.*149.10, X.*Oec.*8.20, Aeschin.3.232, etc.; ἐν τῷ ἀγῶνι τῶν κ. χορῶν *Schwyzer*91.26 (Argos, iii B. C.); τῶν κ. (without χορῶν) Ἀρχ.Ἐφ.1913.7 (Nisyros, iii B. C.), cf. *Inscr.Cos*13.4; ἐν τοῖς κ. ἀγῶσιν *OGI*213.38 (Didyma, iv/iii B. C.); invented by Arion, Arist.*Fr.*677: hence κύκλιον ὠρχήσαντο Call.*Del.*313; εἱλισσόμεναι κύκλια E.*IA*1055 (lyr.). 2. κ. μέλη *dithyrambs*, Ar.*Av.*918; κύκλιος ἀναβολή Eup. l. c. 3. = κυκλικός II, *AP*11.130 (Poll.). 4. = χορίαμβος, Sch.Heph.p.303 C. III. name of month at Epidaurus, *IG*4^2(1).115.23 (iv/iii B. C.), al. IV. κυκλίῳ, = κύκλῳ, c. gen. (cf. κύκλος I), *BGU*938.4 (iv A. D.). **-ίσκιον**, τό, Dim. of sq. I. 2, Dsc.2.83, Damocr.ap.Gal.14.95. **-ίσκος**, ὁ, Dim. of κύκλος, *small circle* in a diagram, Ptol.*Hyp.*1.9, al.; as part of an instrument, Id.*Alm.*1.12. 2. *small round cake* of wax, Dsc.2.83; *lozenge*, = τροχίσκος, Hp.*Mul.*2.188, Gal.12.276, Lycus ap. Orib.8.25.23, Aët.15.37. II. *ring to pass the reins through*, Gal.2.323. 2. *circular opening* of a coop, Ph.*Bel.*78.1. 3. f. l. for κοιλίσκος (q. v.). III. *round spot*, Clytus 1. **-ισκωτός**, ή, όν, v. l. for κοιλισκωτός (q. v.). **-ισμός**, ὁ, *circular motion, circularity*, Simp. *in Ph.*1280.33, Olymp. *in Phd.*pp.141, 145 N., Hsch. s. v. ἀλάθεας ὥρας. **-ίστρια**, ἡ, *dancer in cyclic chorus*, *IG*2.4112.

Κυκλο-βορέω, *brawl like the torrent Cycloborus*, Ar.*Ach.*381. **-βόρος**, ὁ, torrent in Attica, κεκράκτης, Κυκλοβόρου φωνὴν ἔχων Id.*Eq.*137; ᾤμην δ' ἔγωγε τὸν Κ. κατιέναι Id.*Fr.*636. **-γάλων**· γλίσχρων, σμικρολόγων, Hsch. (Fort. συλλογάδων.) **-γρᾰφέω**, *describe a circle*, S.E.*M.*3.26, 9.420, Simp. *in Cael.*209.22. II. *use periphrasis*, D.H.*Dem.*19. **-γρᾰφία**, ἡ, *description, tracing of a circle*, Simp. *in Cael.*210.5. **-γράφος** [γρᾰ], ον, *writing on a cycle* of subjects, of Dionysius Scytobrachion, Procl. ad Hes. p.6 G., Tz.*H.*12.184. **-δίωκτος** [ῐ], ον, *driven round in a circle*, *AP*9.301 (Secund.). **-ειδής**, ές, *circular*, Euc.*Opt.*36, Onos.21.6, Ath.7.328d; τὸ κ. Plu.2.1004c. Adv. -δῶς Gal.*Phil.Hist.*100, Porph. *in Cat.*133.4. **-εις**, εσσα, εν, poet. for κυκλικός, *circular*, ἀγορᾶς θρόνος S.*OT*161 (lyr.); ἴτυς *AP*7.232 (Antip.). **-έλικτος**, ον, *revolving in a circle*, Orph.*H.*8.11.

κυκλόθεν, Adv. *from all around*, κ. ὁδὸς περιέχει Lys.7.28, cf. Hp.

*Fraa.*33, Thphr.*HP*4.6.10 (dub.l.), etc.: c. gen., Lxx 3*Ki.*18.32, al., *Apoc.*4.3: c. dat., Lxx 3*Ki.*6.5: spelt κύκλωθεν, *IPE*1².175 (Olbia), and sts. in codd., but this spelling is condemned by Theognost.*Can.* 156, and arose from a supposed connexion with κύκλῳ.

κυκλόθι, Adv. *around*, A.D.*Adv.*194.17.

κυκλο-μόλυβδος, ὁ, *round lead-pencil*, *AP*6.63 (Damoch.). **-ποιησάμενοι**, f.l. for κύκλον ποι- in X.*Cyr.*7.1.40. **-πορέω**, *go by a circuitous way*, Str.7.1.4. **-πορία**, ἡ, *going round, circuitous way*, Id.2.1.39, 11.13.4: pl., Id.16.4.23. **-πόρος**, ον, *moving in a circle*, βία Heraclit.*All.*12.

κύκλος, ὁ (Dor. ἁ, v. infr. II. 11), also with heterocl. pl. κύκλα Il., etc., v. infr. II. 1, 3, 9, III. 1:—*ring, circle*, ὁππότε μιν δόλιον περὶ κύκλον ἄγωσιν, of the *circle* which hunters draw round their game, Od.4.792; κ. δέκα χάλκεοι (concentric) *circles* of brass on a round shield, Il.11.33, cf. 20.280; but ἀσπίδος κύκλον λέγω the round shield itself, A.*Th.*489, cf. 496, 591. 2. Adverbial usages, κύκλῳ *in a circle* or *ring, round about*, κ. ἁπάντῃ Od.8.278; κ. πάντῃ X.*An.*3.1.2; πανταχῇ D.4.9; τὸ κ. πέδον Pi.*O.*10(11).46; κ. περιάγειν Hdt.4.180; λίμνη.. ἐργασμένη εὖ κ. Id.2.170; τρέχειν κ. Ar.*Th.*662; περιέπλεον αὐτοὺς κ. Th.2.84; οἱ κ. βασιλεῖς X.*Cyr.*7.2.23; ἡ κ. περιφορά, κίνησις, Pl.*Lg.*747a, Alex. Aphr.*in Top.*218.3: freq. with περί or words compounded therewith, *round* about, κ. πέριξ A.*Pers.*368, 418; περιστῆναι κ. Hdt.1.43; βωμὸν κ. περιστῆναι A.*Fr.*379; ἀμφιχανὼν κ. S.*Ant.*118 (lyr.); περιστεφῆ κ. Id.*El.*895; περισταδὸν κ. E.*Andr.*1137; κ. περιϊέναι Pl.*Phd.*72b, etc.; τοῦ φλοιοῦ περιαιρεθέντος κ. Thphr.*HP*4.15.1; so κ. περὶ αὐτήν *round* about it, Hdt.1.185; περὶ τὰ δώματα κ. Id.2.62; also κύκλῳ c. acc., without περί, ἐπιστήσαντες κ. σῆμα Id.4.72; πάντα τὸν τόπον τοῦτον κ. D.4.4: c. gen., κ. τοῦ στρατοπέδου X.*Cyr.*4.5.5; τὰ κ. τῆς Ἀττικῆς D.18.96, cf. *PFay.*110.7 (I A.D.), etc.: metaph., *around* or *from all sides*, S.*Ant.*241, etc.; κεντουμένη κύκλῳ ἡ ψυχή *all over*, Pl.*Phdr.* 251d; τὰ κ. the *circumstances*, Arist.*Rh.*1367ᵇ29, *EN*1117ᵇ2; ἡ κ. ἀπόδειξις, of arguing *in a circle*, Id.*APo.*72ᵇ17, cf. *APr.*57ᵇ18: with Preps., ἐν κ. S.*Aj.*723, *Ph.*356, E.*Ba.*653, Ar.*V.*432, etc.; ἅπαντες ἐν κ. Id.*Eq.*170, *Pl.*679: c. gen., E.*HF*926, Th.3.74; κατὰ κύκλον Emp.17.13. II. *any circular body*: 1. *wheel*, Il.23.340; in which sense the heterocl. pl. κύκλα is mostly used, 5.722, 18.375; τοὺς λίθους ἀνατιθεῖσι ἐπὶ τὰ κύκλα on the *janker*, *IG*1².350.47. 2. *trencher*, *SIG*57.32 (Milet., V B.C.), *Abh.Berl.Akad.*1928(6).29 (Cos), Poll.6.84. 3. *place of assembly*, of the ἀγορά, ἱερὸς κ. Il.18.504; ὁ κ. τοῦ Ζηνὸς τὠγοραίου *Schwyzer* 701 *B*6 (Erythrae, V B.C.); ἀγορᾶς κ. (cf. κυκλόεις) E.*Or.*919; of the *amphitheatre*, D.C.72.19. b. *crowd of people standing round, ring* or *circle of people*, κ. τυραννικὸς S.*Aj.*749; κύκλα χαλκέων ὅπλων, i.e. of armed men, dub. in Id.*Fr.*210.9, cf. X. *Cyr.*7.5.41: abs., E.*Andr.*1089, X.*An.*5.7.2 (both pl.), Diph.55.3. c. *place in the* ἀγορά *where domestic utensils were sold*, Alex.99. 4. *vault* of the sky, ὁ κ. τοῦ οὐρανοῦ Hdt.1.131, Lxx 1*Es.*4.34; πυραυγέα κ. αἰθέρος *h.Hom.*8.6, cf. E.*Ion* 1147; ὁ ἄνω κ. S.*Ph.*815; ἐς βάθος κύκλου Ar.*Av.*1715; νυκτὸς αἰανὴς κ. S.*Aj.*672; γαλαξίας κ. the milky way, *Placit.*2.7.1, al., Poll.4.159; also ὁ τοῦ γάλακτος κ. Arist. *Mete.*345ᵃ25; πολιοῖο γάλακτος κ. Arat.511. b. μέγιστος κ. great *circle*, Autol.*Sph.*2, al.; μ. κ. τῶν ἐν τῇ σφαίρᾳ Archim.*Sph.Cyl.*1.30, cf. Gem.5.70; κ. ἰσημερινός, θερινός, etc., Ph.1.27; χειμερινὸς Gem.5.7, Cleom.1.2; ἀρκτικός, ἀνταρκτικός, Gem.5.2, 9; ὁ κ. ὁ τῶν ζῳδίων Arist. *Mete.*343ᵃ24; ὁ ὁρίζων κ. the horizon, Id.*Cael.*297ᵇ34; παράλληλοι κ., of *parallels* of latitude, Autol.*Sph.*1: in pl., *the zones*, *Stoic.*2.196. 5. *orb, disk* of the sun and moon, ἡλίου κ. A.*Pr.*91, *Pers.*504, S.*Ant.*416; πανσέληνος κ. E.*Ion* 1155; μὴ οὐ πλήρεος ἐόντος τοῦ κύκλου (sc. τῆς σελήνης) Hdt.6.106: in pl., *the heavenly bodies*, *IG*14.2012 *A*9 (Sulp. Max.). 6. *circle* or *wall round* a city, esp. round Athens, ὁ Ἀθηνέων κ. Hdt.1.98, cf. Th.2.13, etc.; οὐχὶ τὸν κ. τοῦ Πειραιῶς, οὐδὲ τοῦ ἄστεως D.18.300. b. *circular fort*, Th.6.99, al. 7. *round shield*, v. sub init. 8. in pl., *eye-balls, eyes*, S.*OT*1270, *Ph.*1354; ὀμμάτων κ. Id.*Ant.*974 (lyr.): rarely in sg., *eye*, ὁ αἰὲν ὁρῶν κ. Διός Id.*OC*704 (lyr.). 9. οἱ κ. τοῦ προσώπου *cheeks*, Hp.*Morb.*2.50; κύκλα παρειῆς Nonn.*D.*33.190, 37.412; but κύκλος μαζοῦ, poet. for μαζός, is f.l. in Tryph.34. 10. κ. ἐλαίης an olive *wreath*, Orph.*A.*325 (pl.). 11. *cycle* or *collection of legends* or *poems*, κύκλον ἱστορημέναν ὑπὲρ Κρήτας *GDI*5187.9 (Crete); esp. of *the Epic cycle*, ὁ ἐπικὸς κ. Ath. 7.277e, Procl.ap.Phot.*Bibl.*p.319 B., cf. Arist.*Rh.*1417ᵃ15; of the corpus of legends compiled by Dionysius Scytobrachion, Ath.11. 481e, cf. Sch.Od.2.120; κ. ἐπιγραμμάτων Suid. s. v. Ἀγαθίας; cf. κυκλικός II. III. *circular motion, orbit* of the heavenly bodies, κύκλον ἰέναι Pl.*Ti.*38d; οὐρανὸς.. μιᾷ περιαγωγῇ καὶ κύκλῳ συναναχορεύει τούτοις Arist.*Mu.*391ᵇ18; *revolution* of the seasons, ἐνιαυτοῦ κ. E.*Or.* 1645, *Ph.*477; τὸν ἐνιαύσιον κ. the yearly *cycle*, ib.544; ἑπτὰ.. ἐτῶν κ. Id.*Hel.*112; μυρία κύκλα ζώειν, i.e. *years*, *AP*7.575 (Leont.): hence κ. τῶν ἀνθρωπηΐων ἐστὶ πρηγμάτων human affairs revolve in *cycles*, Hdt.1.207; φασὶ.. κύκλον εἶναι τὰ ἀνθρώπινα πράγματα Arist.*Ph.*223ᵇ 24, al.; κ. κακῶν D.C.44.29; κύκλου ἐξέπταν, i.e. from the *cycle* of rebirths, Orph.*Fr.*32c.6. b. ἐν τοῖς κ. εἶναι to be in *train*, of an affair, *PEleph.*14.24 (III B.C.). 2. *circular dance* (cf. κύκλιος), χωρεῖτε νῦν ἱερὸν ἀνὰ κ. Ar.*Ra.*445, cf. Simon.148.9, E.*Alc.*449 (lyr.). 3. in Rhet., *a rounded period*, περιόδου κύκλος D.H.*Comp.*19, cf. 22, 23. b. period which begins and ends with the same word, Hermog.*Inv.*4.8. 4. in Metre, a kind of *anapaest*, v.l. for κυκλικός in D.H.*Comp.*17. IV. *sphere, globe*, Pl.*Lg.*898a. [ῡ by nature, S.*Ant.*416, *Aj.*672, etc., but freq. long by position in Hom. and Trag.]

κυκλόσε, Adv., (κύκλος) *in* or *into a circle*, περὶ δ' αὐτὸν ἀγηγέραθ' ὅσσοι ἄριστοι κ. Il.4.212; διαστάντες τανύουσι κ. stretch [the skin] *outwards on all sides*, 17.392, cf. Onos.17, A.D.*Adv.*193.8, Ael.*NA* 3.13, etc.

κυκλο-σοβέω, *whirl round*, πόδα cj. in Ar.*V.*1523 (lyr.). **-στρεφέομαι** (fort. -στροφ-), *proceed by cyclical recurrence*, Vett.Val.344. 2. **-τερής**, ές, (τείρω) *made round by turning* (τὴν γῆν ἐοῦσαν κυκλοτερέα ὡς ἀπὸ τόρνου Hdt.4.36): generally, *round, circular*, κυκλοτερὲς μέγα τόξον ἔτεινε stretched it *into a circle*, Il.4.124; ἄλσος πάντοσε κυκλοτερές Od.17.209; ὀφθαλμός, λιμήν, Hes.*Th.*145, *Sc.* 208; σφαῖρος Emp.27.4; φῶς Id.45; [ὄρος] κυκλοτερὲς πάντῃ Hdt.4. 184; πλοῖα κυκλοτερέα ἀσπίδος τρόπον Id.1.194; κ. κοιλίαι, of the sockets of bones, Hp.*Art.*61; αὐχήν Pl.*Smp.*190a; κώθων Henioch. 1; οἰκοδόμημα X.*HG*4.5.6; κ. ὁ ὄγκος τῆς γῆς Arist.*Cael.*294ᵃ8; γράφουσι κ. τὴν οἰκουμένην Id.*Mete.*362ᵇ13; πεδίον κ. τὸ σχῆμα Str.4.1.7. Adv. -ρῶς *Placit.*1.12.3, Ach.Tat.*Intr.Arat.*21, Dsc.3.90, Gal.*UP*16. 11. [ῠ always, by position.] **-τέρμων**, ον, gen. ονος, *moving in a cycle*, βίος *IG*5(2).472 (Megalopolis).

κυκλοῦχος, ὁ, perh. *linch-pin*, *IG*2².1549 (pl.).

κυκλοφορ-έομαι, Pass., *revolve*, Arist.*Mu.*391ᵇ22, f.l. in Heraclit. *All.*36. **-ητικός**, ή, όν, *moving in a circle, circular*, οὐσία Ph.1. 514; τρόπος Dam.*Pr.*23; σῶμα Thphr.*Fr.*35, Iamb.*Myst.*5.4. Adv. -κῶς S.E.*M.*10.58. **-ία**, ἡ, *circular motion*, opp. εὐθυφορία, Arist. *Ph.*227ᵇ18; τῶν φορῶν ἡ κ. πρώτη ib.265ᵃ13, cf. *de An.*407ᵃ6, Thphr. *Vert.*9; τῶν ψυχῶν Dam.*Pr.*102; τὰς ἑπτὰ καὶ τὴν ὀγδόην κ., of the heavenly *spheres*, Jul.*Or.*4.146c. **-ικός**, ή, όν, = κυκλοφορητικός, Ph.1.623, Plu.2.1004c, Gal.*UP*15.8 (v.l. -ητικήν), Them.*in APo.*17. 1. Adv. -κῶς *Placit.*1.7.32.

κυκλ-όω, fut. -ώσω E.*Cyc.*462: pf. κεκύκλωκα Plb.3.116.10:—Med., fut. -ώσομαι X.*Cyr.*6.3.20: aor. ἐκυκλωσάμην Hdt.9.18, Th.5. 72:—Pass., fut. κυκλωθήσομαι (v.l. -ώσομαι) D.H.3.24: pf. κεκύκλωμαι Th.4.32 (in med. sense (ἐγ-) Ar.*V.*395): aor. ἐκυκλώθην X. *Cyr.*6.3.20: (κύκλος):—*encircle, surround*, Ὠκεανὸς.. κυκλοῖ χθόνα E. *Or.*1379 (lyr.); πόλιν.. κυκλώσας Ἄρει φονίῳ Id.*IA*775 (lyr.); ὅταν κυκλώσωσι [τοὺς ἰχθῦς] Arist.*HA*533ᵇ27:—more freq. in Med., κυκλώσασθαί τινας Hdt.3.157, 9.18, Plb.1.17.13; κ. αὐτοὺς ἐς μέσον Hdt.8.10, cf. A.*Th.*121 (lyr.), Call.*Hec.*1.1.14, etc.: such forms as κυκλοῦνται, ἐκυκλοῦντο, etc., may belong to κυκλόω or to κυκλέω, Th.4.127, 7.81, etc.: abs., κυκλούμενοι *by an enveloping movement*, Hdt.8.76:—Pass., *to be surrounded*, A.*Th.*247, Th.7.81:—joined with Med., εἰ οἱ κυκλούμενοι κυκλωθεῖεν X. l. c. 2. *go round*, τὸ θυσιαστήριον Lxx *Ps.*25 (26).6:—Pass., κυκλωθεὶς τὸν Ἀδρίαν D.S.4.25. II. *move in a circle, whirl round*, Pi.*O.*10(11).72; οὕτω κυκλώσω δαλὸν ἐν φαεσφόρῳ Κύκλωπος ὄψει E.*Cyc.*462; κ. ἀεὶ τὸ σῶμα Hermipp.4; οἱ κυκλοῦντες [τὴν θάλασσαν] ἄνεμοι Plb.11.29.10; ἵετο κυκλώσας βαλιὰ πτερὰ θῆλυς ἀήτης Call. in *PSI*9.1092.53, cf. Archil.92b Diehl: metaph., πολλοὺς λογισμοὺς ἡ πονηρία κυκλοῖ *revolves, agitates*, Men.378:—Med., *hurl*, βέλη Him.*Or.*7.17:—Pass. (or Med.), *go in a circle*, X.*An.*6.4.20; *dance* or *whirl round*, Call.*Dian.*267, Arat.811: metaph., δίναις κυκλούμενον κέαρ A.*Ag.*997 (lyr.). III. *form into a circle*, κ. τόξα *AP*12.82 (Mel.), cf. Him.*Or.*17.5; incorrectly, κ. τόξῳ νευρήν Babr. 68.5:—Pass., *form a circle*, of a bow, E.*Ba.*1066; also [τάφρος] περὶ τὸ πεδίον κυκλωθεῖσα *being drawn in a circle*, Pl.*Criti.*118d. IV. abs., κυκλώσατε ἐπὶ τὸν βασιλέα κύκλῳ Lxx 4*Ki.*11.8; ἐκύκλωσα ἐγὼ καὶ ἡ καρδία μου τοῦ γνῶναι ib.*Ec.*7.26(25). V. = λακκίζειν, ἀμπέλους Philostr.*Her.*2.8. **-ώδης**, ες, = κυκλοειδής, *circular*, κ. παραλλαγή a distortion of several vertebrae *forming a curve*, opp. γωνιώδης, Hp.*Art.*48. 2. *round the outside*, opp. ἐν μέσῳ, Id.*Epid.* 7.84. **-ωθεν**, late form for κυκλόθεν (q. v.). **-ωμα**, ατος, τό, *that which is rounded into a circle*: 1. *wheel*, κ. Ἰξίονος E.*Ph.* [1185]. 2. βυρσότονον κ. *drum*, Id.*Ba.*124 (lyr.). 3. *coil* of a serpent, D.S.3.36. 4. of natural objects, αἰθέριον κ., of the sun, Secund.*Sent.*5; κόσμος ἀπλανὲς κ. ib.1.

Κυκλώπ-ειος, α, ον (in Eust.1634.35, al., ος, ον), (Κύκλωψ) *Cyclopean*, used of prehistoric architecture attributed to the Cyclopes, applied to Mycenae, E.*El.*1158 (lyr.); to ancient buildings near Nauplia, Str.8.6.2. 2. prov., κ. βίος *uncivilized* life, Id.11.4.3, Max.Tyr.21.7 (v.l. -ιος). **-ία** (better -εία), ἡ, *the tale of the Cyclops* in Od.9, Philostr.*VA*6.11, Ael.*VH*13.14. **-ικῶς**, Adv. *like the Cyclopes*, K. ζῆν to live *an unsocial life*, Arist.*EN*1180ᵃ28.

κυκλώπιον, τό, (ὤψ) *white round the ball of the eye*, f.l. for κύκλῳ πῖον, Arist.*HA*533ᵃ9. II. Κυκλώπιον, τό, Dim. of Κύκλωψ, E.*Cyc.* 266.

Κυκλώπιος, α, ον, = Κυκλώπειος, πρόθυρα Pi.*Fr.*169.6; γᾶ, i.e. Mycenae, E.*Or.*965 (lyr.), cf. *IA*265 (lyr.), *HF*15; τροχός, of the 'circuit of the walls' of Mycenae, S.*Fr.*227; v. Κυκλώπειος 2:—pecul. fem. **Κυκλωπίς**, ίδος, ἑστία E.*IT*845 (lyr.).

κύκλ-ωσις, εως, ἡ, *surrounding, enveloping*, esp. in battle, X.*HG* 4.2.20, Plb.3.65.6, Plu.*Them.*12, Onos.21.1 (pl.); πρὶν καὶ τὴν πλέονα κ. σφῶν αὐτόσε προσμεῖξαι before the larger body *that was endeavouring to surround* them came up, Th.4.128. 2. *way round*, Plu.*Flam.*4. **-ωτός**, ή, όν, *rounded*, A.*Th.*540.

Κύκλωψ, ωπος (acc. -ωπα, v. infr.), ὁ, *Cyclops*, freq. in pl., one-eyed giant savages, Od.9.106, Hes.*Th.*139, Th.6.2, etc.: prop. *Round-eyed*, Κύκλωπες δ' ὄνομ' ἦσαν ἐπώνυμον, οὕνεκ' ἄρα σφέων κυκλοτερὴς ὀφθαλμὸς ἕεις ἐνέκειτο μετώπῳ Hes.*Th.*144: hence as Adj., κ. σελήνη the *round-eyed* moon, Parm.10.4; κύκλωπα κούρην, of the pupil of the eye, Emp.84.8: sg. in Od. always of *Polyphemus*, 1.69, al. 2. mythical builders of prehistoric walls at Tiryns, Mycenae, etc., Hellanic.88 J., Pherecyd.12, 35(*a*) J., B.10.77, Str.8.6.11; τὰ

Κυκλώπων βάθρα, i.e. Mycenae, E.*HF*944. **3.** Κύκλωπες, οἱ, a throw of the dice, Eub.57.6.

κυκν-άριον, τό, Dim. of *κύκνος* III, Aët.7.8, Gal.14.765. **-ειος**, α, ον, also ος, ον Lxx 4*Ma*.15.21:—*of a swan*, πτίλον S.*Fr*.1127.3; στόμα *AP*7.12: τὸ κ. (sc. ᾆσμα or μέλος) ᾄδειν *a swan's dying song*, Chrysipp.*Stoic*.3.199, Ael.*NA*2.32; κ. πρὸς φιληκοΐαν φωναί Lxx l.c.: prov., τὸ κ. ἐξηχεῖν, ἐξᾆσαι, to make a last appeal, Plb.30.4.7, 31.12.1, cf. D.S.31.5. **II. Κύκνειος**, α, ον, *of Cycnus*, μάχα Pi.*O*.10(11).15. **-ίας** ἀετός, ὁ, a kind of *white eagle*, Paus.8.17.3. **-ῖτις**, ιδος, pecul. fem. of *Κύκνειος*, βοή S.*Fr*.499.

κυκνό-θρεπτος, ον, *reared by swans*, Steph. *in Rh*.301.18, Sch.Lyc.237. **-κάνθᾰρος**, ὁ, a kind of ship *between κύκνος* II *and κάνθαρος* III, Nicostr.Com.10. **-μορφος**, ον, *swan-shaped*, or *white as a swan*, A.*Pr*.795. **-πτερος**, ον, *swan-plumed*, of Helen in reference to Leda and the swan, E.*Or*.1386 (lyr.).

κύκνος, ὁ, *swan*, *Cycnus olor*, κύκνων δουλιχοδείρων Il.2.460, cf. Hes.*Sc*.316, Pl.*R*.620a, Eratosth.*Cat*.25, etc.; sacred to Apollo, Ar.*Av*.870, Pl.*Phd*.85b, Call.*Ap*.5: Com., βάτραχοι κ. Ar.*Ra*.207; κύκνου δίκην τὸν ὕστατον μέλψασα θανάσιμον γόον A.*Ag*.1444: hence, metaph., *minstrel, bard*, *AP*7.19 (Leon.). **II.** kind of ship, prob. from its prow being curved like a *swan's* neck, Nicostr.Com.10. **III.** *eye-salve*, Gal.12.708,759, etc. [ῡ by position in Ep.; ῠ Pi.*O*.2.82, Theoc.16.49 in pr. n. *Κύκνος*.]

κύκνοψις, εως, ὁ, ἡ, *swan-like*, *AP*11.345.

κυκύïζα· γλυκεῖα κολόκυντα, and **κύκυον**· τὸν σικυόν, Hsch.; cf. Lat. *cucumis*.

κύλα, ων, τά, *the parts under the eyes*, Hp.*Nat.Mul*.15; τὰ κ. τοῦ προσώπου ἐξερυθριᾷ ib.9, cf. *Mul*.1.37; τὰ κ. τῶν ὀφθαλμῶν ὑπόχλωρα Sor.1.44, cf. Hsch., Phot.:—also **κυλάδες**, αἱ, Eust.1951.18; **κυλίς**, Poll.2.66; cf. *κύλλαβοι, κύλλια*. **2.** sg., *groove above upper eyelid*, Ruf.*Onom*.21. (κῦλον Hdn.Gr.1.378; κοῖλα Suid., freq. as v.l., cf. Sch.Theoc.1.38; but κῡλ- in *κυλοιδιάω*.)

κυληβίς· κολοβή, Hsch.

κυλίδιον, v. *κοιλίδιον*.

κῠλῐκ-εῖον, τό, *sideboard, stand for drinking-vessels*, Ar.*Fr*.104, Anaxandr.29, Eub.62, *PCair.Zen*.14.9 (iii B.C.). **II.** *carousal*, Cratin.Jun.9. **-ειος**, ον, *of a cup*, ζητήματα discussions *over wine*, Poll.6.108. **-ηγορέω**, *talk over one's cups*, Ath.11.461e, 480b, Poll.6.29. **-ηγόρος**, ον, *one who talks over his cups*, Eust.1632.18. **-ήρῠτος**, ον, (ἀρύω A) *drawn in cups*, i.e. *abundant*, αἷμα Call.*Fr.anon*.188. **-ιον**, τό, Dim. of *κύλιξ*, *small cup*, Thphr.*HP*5.9.8, Lyc.*Fr*.2.1, Philet.ap.Ath.11.498a, Lxx *Es*.1.7, Aristeas 319 codd.:—also **-ίς**, ίδος, ἡ, dub. in Ath.11.480c. **-οφόρος**, ον, *carrying cups*, Hld.7.27. **-ώδης**, ες, *like a cup*, Sch.Theoc.2.2.

κυλινδ-αίνω, = *κυλίνδω*, Max.Tyr.20.1 codd. (κυδαίνων cj. Reiske). **-έω**, v. *κυλίνδω*. **-ήθρα**, ἡ, = ἀλινδήθρα (q.v.). **-ησις**, εως, ἡ, *rolling, wallowing*, ἐν γυναίοις Plu.*Ant*.9. **II.** metaph., *constant practice, skill*, ἐν λόγοις Pl.*Sph*.268a.

κῠλινδρ-ικός, ή, όν, *cylindrical*, Archim.*Sph.Cyl*.1.11, Hero *Spir*.1.37, Theo Sm.p.195 H., al. Adv. **-κῶς** Plu.2.682d. **-ιον**, τό, Dim. of *κύλινδρος*, Archim.*Aren*.1.14, Ptol.*Alm*.5.1, Iamb.*Protr*.3, Procl.*Hyp*.6.7. **-ίσκος**, ου, ὁ, = foreg., *IG*11(2).161 *B*48, al. (Delos, iii B.C.). **-οειδής**, ές, *cylindrical*, Euc.*Phaen*.p.4 M., *Placit*.2.27.4, Cleom.2.2, Gal.8.895, Hero *Spir*.2.34. Adv. **-δῶς** Eust.1604.58. **-ος**, ὁ, *rolling stone, tumbler*, Chrysipp.*Stoic*.2.283, A.R.2.594, Veget.*Mil*.4.8, *Carm.Aur*.57; a child's *marble*, Gal.18(1).462. **2.** *roller, cylinder*, Democr.155, Ath.Mech.10.4, Plu.2.682d, *CIG*3546.9 (Pergam.); *pivot*, *IG*11(2).287 *A*115 (Delos, iii B.C.); περὶ σφαίρας καὶ κ., title of work by Archimedes. **3.** *roll of a book, volume*, D.L.10.26. **4.** name of a fabulous stone, Ps.-Plu.*Fluv*.19.4. **5.** fiery *envelope* of the axis of the κόσμος, Herm.ap.Stob.1.49.44. **-όω**, *roll, level with a roller*, Thphr.*HP*2.4.3 (Pass.). **-ώδης**, ες, = *κυλινδροειδής*, ib.8.5.3. **-ωτός**, ή, όν, *levelled with a roller*, ἅλως Nic.*Fr*.70.1.

κῠλίνδω, Ep., Lyr., Trag., also Telecl.1.8, Ar.*Eq*.1249, *Nu*.375 (Pass.):—in Prose (always in Att.) more freq. **κυλινδέω** (for which καλινδέω is freq. v.l.), also Ar.*Av*.502 (Med.), v.l. in Semon.7.4:—later **κυλίω** (q.v.): fut. κυλινδήσω late, *IG*14.1389ii 35 (ii A.D.): aor. ἐκύλῖσα Sosith.2.20, Theoc.23.52, *AP*7.490 (Anyt.), also (εἰσ-) Ar.*Th*.651, (ἐξ-) Pi.*Fr*.7:—**Med.**, impf. Ar.*Av*. l.c.: fut. κυλίσομαι (προ-) App.*Ital*.5.4: aor. ἐκυλισάμην (ἐν-) Luc.*Hipp*.6:—**Pass.**, fut. κυλισθήσομαι (ἐκ-) A.*Pr*.87: aor. ἐκυλίσθην, Ep. κυλ-, Il.17.99, S.*El*.50, *Fr*.363; later κυλινδηθείς Str.14.2.24: pf. κεκύλισμαι Luc.*Hist.Conscr*.63, Ath.11.480c: plpf. κεκύλιστο Nonn.*D*.5.47:—*roll*, ὀστέα . . εἰν ἁλὶ κῦμα κυλίνδει Od.1.162, cf. 14.315; Βορέης μέγα κῦμα κυλίνδων 5.296; οἶδμα . . κυλίνδει βυσσόθεν θῖνα S.*Ant*.590 (lyr.); κυλίνδετ' εἴσω τὸν δυσδαίμονα *trundle* him in, Ar.*Eq*. l.c.; δλοιτρόχους, λίθους κυλινδεῖν, X.*An*.4.2.3, 4.7.4; ἔνθα Νεῖλος . . γάνος κυλίνδει A.*Fr*.300.3: metaph., πῆμα θεὸς Δαναοῖσι κυλίνδει *rolls* calamity upon them, Il.17.688; στυγερὴν δὲ κυλινδήσει κακότητα *IG*l.c. **2.** *revolve* in mind, Pi.*N*.4.40. **3.** *roll away*, ἐλπίδας *AP*l.c. **II.** Med. and Pass., *to be rolled, roll*, freq. in Hom., τρόφι κῦμα κυλίνδεται Il.11.307, cf. Od.9.147, Alc.18; πέδονδε κυλίνδετο λᾶας ἀναιδής Od.11.598, cf. Il.13.142, 14.411; νῶϊν δὴ τόδε πῆμα κυλίνδεται 11.347, cf. Od.2.163, 8.81; *toss* like a ship at sea, κυλίνδοντ' ἐλπίδες Pi.*O*.12.6; *to be whirled round* on a wheel, of Ixion, Id.*P*.2.23; κυλινδομένα φλόξ *whirling* flame, ib.1.24; [νεφέλαι] κυλινδόμεναι Ar.*Nu*. l.c.; μεταξύ που κυλινδεῖται τοῦ τε μὴ ὄντος καὶ τοῦ ὄντος *is tossed about* between . ., Pl.*R*.479d. **2.** of persons, κυλίνδεσθαι κατὰ κόπρον *roll, wallow* in the dirt (in sign of grief), Il.22.414; κλαίων τε κυλινδόμενός τ' Od.4.541, cf. Ar.*Av*. l.c.; *wander to and fro*, ψυχὴ . . περὶ τάφους κυλινδουμένη Pl.*Phd*.81d; ἐν δικαστηρίοις Id.*Tht*.172c; πρὸ ποδῶν κ. Id.*R*.432d; in petitions, παρὰ πόδα τῶν ἰχνῶν τινος κ. *PMasp*.5.8 (vi A.D.), etc.: metaph., ἐν ἀμηχανίῃσι κυλίνδομαι Thgn.619; ἐν ἀμαθίᾳ κ. *wallow* in . ., Pl.*Phd*.82e, *Plt*.309a; ἐν πότοις καὶ γυναιξίν Plu.2.184f; κατὰ τὰ βιβλία Gal.9.647. **b.** *to be rolled, whirled headlong*, ἐκ δίφρων κυλισθείς S.*El*.50; *roll over*, of the embryo, Arist.*HA*586^{b}25. **c.** *to be rolled up*, κυλισθεὶς ὡς ὄνος like a wood-louse, S.*Fr*.363. **3.** of Time, κυλινδομέναις ἁμέραις Pi.*I*.3.18. **4.** of words, *to be tossed from mouth to mouth*, i.e. *be much talked of*, τοὔνομ' αὐτῆς ἐν ἀγορᾷ κυλίνδεται Ar.*V*.492; κ. πᾶς λόγος παρὰ τοῖς ἐπαΐουσιν Pl.*Phdr*.275e.

κυλίνθιον· προσωπεῖον ξύλινον, Hsch.

κύλιξ [ῠ], ῐκος, ἡ, (ὁ, *IG*1^{2}.283.137) *cup*, esp. *wine-cup*, Phoc.11, Sapph.5, Alc.41, Pi.*Fr*.124.3, B.*Fr*.16.3, Hdt.4.70, etc.; κ. κεραμέα Pl.*Ly*.219e; κ. χελιδονεία, ἡδυλεία, *IG*11(2).154 *B*6,50 (Delos, iii B.C.); κυλίκων τέρψις S.*Aj*.1200 (lyr.); κ. φιλοτησία Ar.*Lys*.203, Alex.291; κ. ἴσον ἴσῳ κεκραμένη Ar.*Pl*.1132; πλήρεις κ. οἴνου . . ἤντλουν Pherecr.108.30; πίνειν τε πολλὰς κ. Eub.150.8; ἐπὶ τῇ κύλικι λέγειν, = κυλικηγορεῖν, Pl.*Smp*.214b; ἐπὶ τῆς κ. φλυαρεῖν D.L.2.82; ἡ παρὰ τὴν κ. θρασύτης Plu.*Ant*.24; περιελαύνειν τὰς κ. push round *the cup*, X.*Smp*.2.27; οἱ πρὸς ταῖς κ. *cup*-bearers, Hdn.3.5.5. **II.** Cypr., = *κοτύλη*, Glaucon ap.Ath.11.480f.

κυλιούχιον, v. *κυνούχιον*. **κυλίς**, v. *κύλα*.

κύλῐσις, εως, ἡ, *rolling*, esp. of athletes in the dust after anointing, Arist.*Ph*.201^{a}18, *Metaph*.1065^{b}19; opp. βάδισις, Id.*Ph*.227^{b}18. **II.** *revolution* in an orbit, Id.*Cael*.290^{a}10. **III.** *roll, parcel*, ἱματίων *PSI*4.428.37 (iii B.C.).

κῠλ-ίσκη, ἡ, Dim. of *κύλιξ*, D.H.2.23, Poll.6.95, 10.66:—hence Dim. **-ίσκιον**, τό, Id.6.98, 10.66, cf. Ar.*Ach*.459 codd. (κοτυλίσκιον Ath.11.479b.) **-ισμα**, ατος, τό, *roll*, Sm.*Ez*.10.13, *Hippiatr*.79, 117; κ. κανθάρου, ball of dung rolled by a beetle, *PMag.Berol*.1.223. **II.** = *κυλίστρα*, *Hippiatr*.8; v.l. for sq., 2*Ep.Pet*.2.22. **-ισμός**, ὁ, *rolling*, ibid., Thd.*Pr*.2.18; κ. τοῦ πνεύματος ἐν ταῖς ἀρτηρίαις Ruf.*Syn.Puls*.8.11: pl., *Hippiatr*.75. **-ιστήριον**, τό, = *κυλίστρα*, Gloss. **-ιστικός**, ή, όν, *practised in rolling*: Subst. κ., ὁ, *wrestler, who struggles on while rolling in the dust*, Sch.Pi.*I*.4.81. **-ιστός**, ή, όν, *fit for rolling, large*, gloss on ῥυτός, *EM*707.3. **II.** *twined in a circle*, epith. of a kind of garland, Alex.272.5, Antiph.51. **III.** Subst. **κυλιστός**, ὁ, *roll of papyrus, large letter*, or *packet* of letters, *PHib*.1.110.51, al. (iii B.C.); *parcel*, ἱματίων *Sammelb*.1.2 (iii A.D.). **-ίστρα**, ἡ, *place for horses to roll in*, Poll.1.183, *Hippiatr*.5, Sch.Ar.*Ra*.935; cf. *καλίστρα*.

κῠλῐχν-η, ἡ, *small cup*, Alc.41.2, Ar.*Fr*.498. **II.** *pot* for medical preparations, Hsch.:—Dim. **-ιον**, τό, Ar.*Eq*.906 (spelt **κυλύχνιον** *IG*11(2).287 *B*53, al. (Delos, iii B.C.)): **-ίς**, ίδος, ἡ, Achae.14, Antiph.208; also, = *κυλίχνη* II, Hsch. (corrupted to κυγχνίδα Hp.ap.Gal.19.115).

κῠλίω [ῑ], later form of *κυλίνδω*: (προσ-) κύλιε Ar.*V*.202, (ἀνα-) κυλῖον Alex.116:—*roll along*, γαστέρας αἱμοβόρως ἐκύλιον, of serpents, Theoc.24.18; κυλίουσιν [ἀλλήλους] ἐν τῷ πηλῷ Luc.*Anach*.6; λόγοις τοὺς ῥήτορας κ. *rolling* them *over*, *Com.Adesp*.294 codd.: freq. in later Gr., Lxx *Jo*.10.18, al.: metaph., ἐκ κισσηρεφέος κεφαλῆς εὔϋμνα κυλίων ῥήματα Call.*Epigr*. in *Berl.Sitzb*.1912.548:—Pass., *roll, whirl along*, Arist.*Cael*.290^{a}25, al.; of bees, *grovel*, Id.*HA*625^{b}5; πρὸς τοῖς ἑαυτοῦ γόνασι κυλιομένην D.H.8.39; κ. περὶ τὴν ἀγοράν *to be always loitering* there, Arist.*Pol*.1319^{a}29; *roll about*, in pantomime, Id.*Po*.1461^{b}31. **2.** *roll up*, ἣν κυλίουσι κόπρον (sc. κάνθαροι) Id.*HA*552^{a}17.

κύλλα· σκύλαξ (Elean), Hsch. **κύλλαβοι**· ὑπώπια, Id.; cf. *κύλα*.

κυλλαίνω, = *κυλλόω*, ὦτα κ. κάτω *let* them *hang* down, prob. in S.*Fr*.687. **II.** intr., *halt, limp*, metaph., κυλλαίνων ὁ νοῦς Ph.*Fr*.58 H.

κύλλαιος· βόστρυχος, Hsch. **κυλλάραβις**, = *δίσκος*; also a gymnasium at Argos, Id.

κύλλᾰρος, ὁ, *hermit-crab*, *Pagurus*, Arist.*HA*530^{a}12 (v.l. σκύλλαρος).

κυλλᾶστις, ιος, Ion. and later Gr. (cf. *UPZ*46.15, 53.15 (ii B.C.)) **-ῆστις**, ιος, ὁ, *Egyptian bread made from ὄλυρα*, Hdt.2.77, Hecat.323(*b*) J., Phanod.5, Ar.*Fr*.257, prob. in *POxy*.1742.1 (iv A.D.).

κυλλήβδην· κολοβόντα, κτλ., Hsch.

Κυλλήνη, ἡ, *Cyllene, a mountain in Arcadia*, Il.2.603, etc.:—hence **Κυλλήνιος**, epith. of Hermes, *h.Merc*.318, etc.; of Pan, *AP*6.96 (Eryc.), *BCH*27.295 (Crete).

κύλλια· ὑπώπια μελανά, Hsch. **κύλλοβος** (κόλλ- cod.)· ξηρὰ συκῆ, Id.

κυλλο-ποδίων [ῐ], ονος, ὁ, (πούς) *club-footed, halting*, epith. of Hephaistos, Il.18.371, 20.270: voc. κυλλοπόδῖον 21.331. **-πους**, ὁ, ἡ, πουν, τό, gen. ποδος, *club-footed*, Aristodem.8; θεοί Agatharch.7.

κυλλ-ός, ή, όν, *club-footed and bandy-legged*, opp. βλαισός, Hp.*Art*.53, cf. 62; κ. πούς ib.53, Ar.*Av*.1379. **2.** generally, *deformed, contracted*, κ. οὖς Hp.*Art*.40; *crippled in the arm*, κ. ἠκόντιζεν ἀμείνονα *AP*11.84 (Lucill.), cf. *Ev.Matt*.15.30, Gal.*UP*1.17, al.; ἔμβαλε κυλλῇ (sc. χειρί) put into *a crooked hand*, i.e. *with* the fingers *crooked* like a beggar's, to catch an alms, Ar.*Eq*.1083, cf. Sch. ad loc. **2.** of things, *crooked*, κ. κυκλάς *PLond*.3.776.10 (vi A.D.). **II.** κυλλά, τά, *choliambi*, Herod.8.79. **-όω**, *crook, flex*, τὸ μέρος Gal.18(1).

637:—Pass., *become club-footed and bandy-legged*, Hp.*Art*.53: pf. part. κεκυλλωμένα ib.62. **-ωμα**, ατος, τό, *club-foot*, Gal.18(1).670. **-ωσις**, εως, Ion. ιος, ἡ, = foreg., Hp.*Art*.62, Gal.18(1).668.

Κυλλύριοι, οἱ, = Κιλλικύριοι (nisi hoc legend.), Hdt.7.155.

κῠλοιδιάω, (κύλα, οἰδάω) *have a swelling below the eye, have a black eye*, κυλοιδιᾶν ἀνάγκη Ar.*Lys*.472; *have dark rings under the eyes*, κ. ὑπ' ἔρωτος Theoc.1.38: generally, *have a swollen face*, Antyll.ap. Orib.10.27.15, Nic.*Al*.478.

κύλον, τό, v. κύλα.

κῦμα, ατος, τό, (κύω) *anything swollen* (as if *pregnant*): hence, I. *wave, billow*, of rivers as well as the sea, in sg. and pl.; κ. θαλάσσης Il.2.209, al.; κ. ῥόοιο 21.263; κ. διϊπετέος ποταμοῖο ib.268, 326; κύματ' ἐπ' ἠϊόνος κλύζεσκον 23.61; κύματ' εὐρέϊ πόντῳ βάντ' ἐπιόντα τε S.*Tr*.114 (lyr.): less freq. in Prose, κύματος ἐπαναχώρησις Th.3.89: collectively, ὡς τὸ κ. ἔστρωτο when the *swell* abated, Hdt.7.193, cf. Arist.*Mete*.344^{b}35, al. 2. metaph., *flood* of men, κ. χερσαῖον στρατοῦ A.*Th*.64, cf. 114 (lyr.), 1083 (anap.). b. of *the waves of adversity*, etc., κ. ἄτης, κακῶν, Id.*Pr*.886 (anap.), *Th*.758 (lyr.), E.*Ion* 927; συμφορᾶς Id.*Hipp*.824; κελαινοῦ κ. μένος, of passion, A.*Eu*. 832; κ. κατακλυσμὸν φέρον νόσων Pl.*Lg*.740e. c. phrases: μάτην με κῦμ' ὅπως παρηγορῶν A.*Pr*.1001; πρὸς κῦμα λακτίζειν E.*IT*1396; ἐκ κυμάτων..γαλήν' ὁρῶ Id.*Or*.279; ἐπ' ἠόνι κύματα μετρεῖν Theoc. 16.60; ἀριθμεῖν τὰ κύματα Luc.*Herm*.84. 3. Archit., *waved moulding, cyma*, Λέσβιον κ. A.*Fr*.78. II. from κύω (as κύημα from κυέω), *foetus, embryo*, νεόσπορον Id.*Eu*.659; γέμουσαν κύματος θεοσπόρου E.*Fr*.106; of the earth, κ. λαμβάνειν A.*Ch*.128; δισσὸν κῦμ' ἐλόχευσε τέκνων *AP*6.200 (Leon.). 2. *young sprout* of plants, Thphr.*HP*1.6.9; esp. of a cabbage, Gal.6.642.

κῡμ-αίνω, fut. κυμᾰνῶ Xuthus ap.Arist.*Ph*.216^{b}25: aor. ἐκύμηνα Arr.*An*.2.10.3: aor. 1 Pass. ἐκυμάνθην Plu.*Ant*.65: (κῦμα):—*rise in waves, swell*, ἐπὶ πόντον ἐβήσετο κυμαίνοντα over the *billowy* sea, Il.14. 229, cf. Od.4.425, 570, etc.; of a pot, *boil*, Call.*Fr.anon*.41; κ. ἄνω καὶ κάτω Pl.*Phd*.112b; κυμανεῖ τὸ ὅλον Xuthus l. c.; κ. τῇ πορείᾳ *undulate*, of caterpillars, Arist.*HA*551^{b}7; τὰ ἄποδα..κυμαίνοντα προέρχεται Id.*IA*709^{a}24; of a line of soldiers, Plu.*Pomp*.69, cf. Arr.*An*. l. c. 2. metaph., of restless passion, *swell, seethe*, κυμαίνοντ' ἔπη A.*Th*.443; ἄνθος ἥβας κυμαίνει Pi.*P*.4.158; αἱ ψυχαὶ κ. μειζόνως, with passion, Pl.*Lg*.930a; κ. ἐκ τῆς ἐπιθυμίας Ael.*NA*7.15; ἐς τὴν ὁμιλίαν ib.15.9. 3. trans., *toss on the waves*, τὸ δέπας Pherecyd.18(a) J.; *agitate*, τὴν θάλατταν Luc.*DMar*.7.1; οἴστρῳ κ. θεούς *APl*.4.196 (Alc. Mess.):—Pass., *to be agitated*, τὸ πέλαγος κ. Hp.*Flat*.3, Plu. *Ant*. l. c., cf. Opp.*H*.4.676; πόθῳ Pi.*Fr*.123.3; *vibrate*, Nicom.*Harm*. 3. II. (κῦμα II) *to swell, to be pregnant*, κ. γαστέρα Opp.*C*.1.359; κύστιδα ib.4.443; μαζοὶ..γάλα -ουσι Marc.Sid.91:—Med., Σεμέλης κυμαίνετο γαστήρ Nonn.*D*.8.7. **-ανσις**, εως, ἡ, *undulation*, Arist. *IA*709^{a}27.

κύμαρος, = κόμαρος, Hsch.

κῡμάς, άδος, ἡ, (κύω) *pregnant woman*, in pl., Hsch.

κῡμᾰτ-ηδόν, Adv. *like a wave*, Lyd.*Ost*.53. **-ηρός**, ά, όν, = sq., *Gloss*. **-ίας**, ου, Ion. **-ίης**, ὁ, *surging, billowy*, κ. ὁ ποταμὸς ἐγένετο Hdt.2.111; πόρος A.*Supp*.546 (lyr.); πορθμός Cerc.5.11. 2. Act., *causing waves, stormy*, ἄνεμος Hdt.8.118. **-ίζομαι**, Pass., *to be agitated by the waves*, Arist.*HA*622^{a}18; *toss about like waves*, ἐν τῇ κοιλίᾳ κ. τὰ σιτία Gal.19.717; of the pulse, Id.8.482, 9.180. (Act. only late, Sch.E.*Ph*.1105.) **-ιον**, τό, Dim. of κῦμα I. 3, *IG*1^{2}.372. 166, al., 4^{2}(1).102.58 (Epid., iv B. C.), *SIG*245 *G*i 68 (Delph., iv B. C.), Lxx *Ex*.25.10(11), 23(24), Vitr.4.3.6; κ. πύξινον διπλοῦν Ph.*Bel*.62. 12; of the *volute* on the Ionic capital, Vitr.4.1.7. 2. *groove*, Hero *Aut*.3.1.

κῡμᾰτο-αγής, ές, (ἄγνυμι) *breaking like waves*, ἆται S.*OC*1243 (lyr.). **-βόλος**, ον, (βάλλω) *throwing up waves*, *Gloss*. **-δρόμος**, ον, *running over the waves*, Sch.Lyc.789; **-δρομεύς**, ibid. **-ειδής**, ές, *like waves: stormy*, οἱ νότοι Arist.*Pr*.942^{a}6. Adv. -δῶς Democr.126. **-εις**, εσσα, εν, poet. for κυματίας, Arist.*Fr*.640.18, Opp.*H*.1.4. **-λήγη**, ἡ, *Wave-stiller*, a Nereid, Hes.*Th*.253. **-πλήξ**, ῆγος, ὁ, ἡ, *wave-beaten*, ἀκτά S.*OC*1241 (lyr.); σκόπελος *AP*10.7 (Arch.); *tossed by the waves*, of fish, Hp.*Vict*.2.48, Archestr.*Fr*.11, Mnesith.ap.Ath.8. 358b. **-φθόρος**, ον, *plundering by sea*, ἁλιαίετος E.*Fr*.636 (κυματότροφος *fed from the sea*, Ruhnk.). **-φορτίδες**· κόγχοι, Hsch.

κῡμᾰτ-όω, *cover with waves*, of the wind, τὸ πεδίον Plu.*Alex*.26:—Pass., of the land, *to be swept by the sea*, Hld.9.4, cf. 10.16 (metaph.). II. Pass., *rise in waves*, of the sea, ἡ θάλασσα κυματωθεῖσα Th.3.89; ὁ ποταμὸς ἐκυματοῦτο, ὥσπερ θάλασσα Luc.*VH*2.30: metaph., of the air when agitated by the voice, *Stoic*.2.140, 234. **-ωγή**, ἡ, (ἄγνυμι) *place where the waves break, beach*, Hdt. 4.196, 9.100, Luc.*Herm*.84, etc.: in pl., Democr.164. **-ώδης**, ες, = κυματοειδής, *on which the waves break*, γῆ Arist.*Pr*.934^{b}10, 9 (Comp.); αἰγιαλός Plu.*Fab*.6; *billowy*, πέλαγος Scymn.190: metaph., of the pulse, σφυγμὸς κ. Gal.9.505. Adv. -δῶς Id.8.551. **-ωσις**, εως, ἡ, *flow* of the tide, Str.1.3.8; κλύδων καὶ κ. Ph.1.14: metaph., κυματώσεις καὶ στροφαί, of life, Id.*Fr*.63 H.

κυμβᾰλ-ίζω, *play the cymbals*, Men.326, Lxx *Ne*.12.27, Arr.*Ind*. 7.8, Chor. in *Rev.Phil*.1.10. **-ιον**, τό, Dim. of κύμβαλον, Hero *Aut*.14.1, 2. II. = κοτυληδών 5, Dsc.4.91. **-ισμός**, ὁ, *playing on cymbals*, Alciphr.3.66. **-ιστής**, οῦ, ὁ, *player upon cymbals*, D.C.50.27. **-ίστρια**, ἡ, fem. of foreg., Lat. *cymbalistria*, Petron. 22. **-ῖτις**, ιδος, ἡ, = κυμβάλιον II, Gal.2.905.

κυμβᾰλοκρούστης, ου, ὁ, = κυμβαλιστής, *Gloss*.

κύμβᾰλον, τό, (κύμβος) *cymbal*, X.*Eq*.1.3: mostly in pl., Pi.*Fr*.79 B., A.*Fr*.451 G, Men.245.3, *PHib*.1.54.13 (iii B. C.), Lxx 1*Ki*.18.6, Phld.*Mus*.p.49 K., D.S.2.38, Plu.2.144e, etc.

κυμβατευταί· ὀρνιθευταί, Hsch.; cf. κύμβη (B).

κύμβᾰχος, ον, (κύμβη B) *head-foremost, tumbling*, ἔκπεσε δίφρου κύμβαχος ἐν κονίῃσιν Il.5.586; κ. ἐπ' ὤμους Hld.10.30, cf. Lyc.66, Eust.584.16. II. Subst., ὁ, *crown of a helmet*, κόρυθος..ἱπποδασείης κ. ἀκρότατος Il.15.536.

κυμβεῖον, v. κυμβίον.

κύμβη (A), ἡ, *hollow of a vessel: drinking-cup, bowl*, Nic.*Al*.164, 389, *Th*.948, Philem.Gloss.ap.Ath.11.483a; = ὀξύβαφον, Hsch. II. *boat*, S.*Fr*.127; Phoenician acc. to Plin.*HN*7.208. III. *knapsack, wallet*, Hsch. (Cf. κύμβος.)

κύμβη (B), ἡ, = κύβη, *head*, *EM*545.27: hence, a kind of *bird*, perh. *tumbler*-pigeon (cf. κύμβαχος), πτεροβάμονες κύμβαι Emp.20.7.

κυμβητιάω, *hurl headlong*, *EM*545.27.

κυμβίον, τό, Dim. of κύμβη (A) I, *small cup*, *IG*2^{2}.1522.32, 11(2). 145.48 (Delos, iv B. C.), Theopomp.Com.31, Philem.84, Alex.2.6, D.21.158, cf. Ath.11.481d; also, Dim. of κύμβη (A) II, Hsch., Suid.: **κυμβεῖον**, Pherecr.66, Paus.Gr.*Fr*.242.

κύμβος, ὁ, = κύμβη (A), *cup*, Nic.*Th*.526: heterocl. dat. κύμβεϊ or κύμβεσι Id.*Al*.129. (Cf. Skt. *kumbhás* 'pot', Irish *cum* 'vase', etc.)

κυμερνήτης, ου, ὁ, Aeol. = κυβερνήτης, *EM*543.3:—also **κυμερῆναι**, Cypr. = κυβερνῆσαι, *Schwyzer* 685(1).

κύμηχα· κύαμον, Hsch. **κυμινᾶτον**, τό, *preparation of* κύμινον, *Gloss*. **κυμίνδαλα**· καταστροφή (Tarent.), Hsch.

κύμινδις [ῠ], ὁ (or ἡ, v. Sch.Il.14.291), gen. -ιδος Pl.*Cra*.392a:—name of a bird, ἣν τ' ἐν ὄρεσσι χαλκίδα κικλήσκουσι θεοί, ἄνδρες δὲ κύμινδιν Il. l. c., cf. Ar.*Av*.1181, Arist.*HA*615^{b}6.

κῠμῑν-εύω, (κύμινον) *strew with cummin*, Orac.ap.Luc.*Alex*. 25. **-ινος**, η, ον, *of cummin*, Alex.Trall.1.3.

κῠμῑνο-δόκον, τό, *box for cummin, spice-box*, placed on the table like a salt-cellar, Nicoch.2:—also **-δόκη**, ἡ, Apollod.Gel.2; **-δόχη**, ἡ, Poll.10.93; **-θήκη**, ἡ, Demioprat.ibid. **-κίμβιξ**, ῑκος, ὁ, *skinflint* (cf. κυμινοπρίστης), *Com.Adesp*.1055.

κύμῑνον [ῠ], τό, *cummin*, Hp.*Acut*.23, Antiph.142.2, Alex.127.6, Lxx *Is*.28.25, *PTeb*.112.13 (ii B. C.), etc.; κύμινον ἔπρισεν, prov. of a skinflint, Sophr.110, cf. Men.1025, Theoc.10.55; κ. ἥμερον, *Cuminum Cyminum*, Dsc.3.59, cf. Thphr.*HP*1.11.2, Nic.*Th*.601; κ. ἄγριον (ἀγρότερον ib.710), *wild cummin, Lagoecia cuminoeides*, Dsc. 3.60; κ. ἄγριον ἕτερον, *Nigella arvensis*, ib.61; κ. αἰθιοπικόν Diocl. *Fr*.87. (Cf. Hebr. *Kammôn*.)

κῠμῑνο-πρίστης, ου, ὁ, (πρίω) *cummin-splitter*, i. e. *skinflint*, Arist. *EN*1121^{b}27, Posidipp.26.12: as Adj., κ. ὁ τρόπος ἐστί σου Alex. 251. **-πριστοκαρδᾰμογλύφος** [γλῠ], ον, *cummin-splitting-cress-scraper*, strengthd. for foreg., Ar.*V*.1357. **-πώλης**, ου, ὁ, *cummin-seller*, *PMasp*.146.2, al. (vi A. D.). **-τρῖβος**, ον, *rubbed with cummin to flavour it*, κ. ἅλς Archestr.*Fr*.13.7.

κῠμῑνώδης, ες, *like cummin*, Thphr.*HP*8.7.3.

κῡμο-δέγμων, ον, gen. ονος, *receiving* or *meeting the waves*, ἀκτή E. *Hipp*.1173. **-δόκη**, ἡ, *Wave-receiver*, a Nereid, Il.18.39, Hes.*Th*. 252. **-θᾰλής**, ές, *abounding with waves*, of Poseidon, Orph.*H*. 17.5. **-θόη**, ἡ, (θοός) *Wave-swift*, a Nereid, Il.18.41, Hes.*Th*. 245. **-κτῠπος**, ον, *wave-sounding*, Αἰγαῖος E.*Hyps.Fr*.3(1)ii 28 (lyr.); μυχοί Simm.13. **-πλήξ**, ῆγος, ὁ, ἡ, = κυματοπλήξ, Hdn.Gr. 1.46. **-πόλεια**, ἡ, *Wave-walker*, daughter of Poseidon, Hes.*Th*. 819. **-ρρόον**· τὸν ὑπὸ τῶν κυμάτων ῥοῦν, Hsch. **-ρρώξ**, ῶγος, ὁ, ἡ, *breaking the waves*, Hdn.Gr.1.46. **-τόκος**, ον, *of child-birth*, ἐν γαστρὸς κυμοτόκοις ὀδύναις *IG*9(2).638 (Larissa). **-τόμος**, ον, *wave-cleaving*: ὁ κ. *cutwater* of a bridge, Suid., cf. *BCH*26.166 (Syria, vi A. D.; κοιμ- lapis).

Κῡμώ, οῦς, ἡ, *Wavy*, a Nereid, Hes.*Th*.255.

κῠνᾱγέσιον, κυνᾱγέτας, κυνᾱγέτις, κυνᾱγία, v. κυνηγ-.

Κυνᾱγίδας, α, ὁ, title of Heracles, *BCH*47.292 n.2 (Macedonia, ii B. C.); also **Κουναγίδας**, ib.291.

κῠνᾱγός, Dor. for κυνηγός, (ἄγω) *hound-leader*, i. e. *huntsman*, A. *Ag*.695 (lyr.), etc.; as Adj., τὴν κυναγὸν Ἄρτεμιν S.*El*.563; κυναγὲ παρσένε *huntress*-maid, Ar.*Lys*.1270 (lyr.); Ἔρως ὁ Κύπριδος κ. Tim. Com.2:—fem. **κυνηγίς**, ίδος, *huntress*, name of a comedy by Philetaerus; also (sc. ναῦς), *hunting-boat*, *Theb.Ostr*.77 (i A. D.).—Trag. and Com. use κυνᾱγός even in trim., cf. Phryn.399, and v. κυνηγία:—later **κυνηγός** Arist.*HA*579^{b}28, Callix.2, *PPetr*.3 p.115 (iii B. C.), *SIG*459.2 (Beroea, iii B. C.), D.S.2.25, Plu.*Luc*.8; = Lat. *bestiarius*, gladiator who fights with beasts, Just.*Nov*.115.3.10; κυνᾱγός in this sense, *Milet*.1(9).314.

κῠν-άγχη, ἡ, (κύων, ἄγχω) *dog-quinsy*, Arist.*HA*604^{a}5, Ant.Lib. 23.2; cf. ὑάγχη: hence, II. *sore throat*, Hp.*VM*19, *Prog*.23, *Aph*. 3.16 (all pl.), Porph.*Abst*.3.7: συνάγχη is a constant v.l., but Gal. distinguishes κυνάγχη as *an inflammation of the larynx*, συνάγχη *of the interior muscles of the throat*, παρασυνάγχη *of the exterior muscles*, 8.248, 17(2).706. III. *dog's collar*, *AP*6.34 (Rhian., v.l. κυνακτάν), 35 (Leon.). IV. *pillory*, Hsch. **-άγχης**, ου, ὁ, *dog-throttler*, title of Hermes, Hippon.1. **-αγχικός**, ή, όν, *suffering from* κυνάγχη, Gal.17(1).596; πάθος κ., = κυνάγχη, D.S.36.13. **-αγχον**, τό, = ἀπόκυνον, Dsc.4.80. **-αγχος**, ὁ, = σύναγχος, Gal.15. 787. **-ᾰγωγός**, ὁ, (ἄγω) *leader of hounds, huntsman*, X.*Cyn*.9.2, Arr.*Cyn*.7.6, 25.6, Philostr.*Im*.1.28.

κυνάδης· ἀνελεύθερος, Hsch. (but Κυνάδης, title of Poseidon at Athens, Id.). **κυναίγινθος**, = αἴγινθος (i. e. αἴγιθος) μικρός, *Gloss*. **κυναίδης**· λίαν ἀναιδής, Hsch. **κυναιρίον**, v. κυνερίον.

κῠνάκανθα [ᾰκ], ἡ, *dog-thorn*, perh. = κυνόσβατος, Arist.*HA*552^{b}3. **κυνακίας·** ἱμάντες, οἱ ἐκ βύρσης τοῦ σφαγιασθέντος τετράχειρι Ἀπόλλωνι βοὸς ἔπαθλα διδόμενοι (–ομένου cod.), Hsch. **κυνακρίς,** *gillus* (fort. *gryllus*), *Gloss.*

κῠν-ακτής, οῦ, ὁ, (ἄγω) *dog-leash*, v. κυνάγχη III. **–ᾰλώπηξ,** εκος, ἡ, *mongrel between dog and fox*, nickname of a πορνοβοσκός, Ar.*Lys.*957; of Cleon, Id.*Eq.*1067, al.; of the Cynics, Luc.*Peregr.* 30.

Κῠνᾰμολγοί, οἱ, *dog-milkers*, name of Libyan tribe, D.S.3.31.

κῠνάμυια [νᾰ], ἡ, *dog-fly*, i.e. *shameless fly*, abusive epith. applied by Ares to Athena, and by Hera to Aphrodite, Il.21.394,421, cf. Ath.3.126a, 4.157a:—later **κυνόμυια,** Ezek.*Exag.*138, *AP*11.265 (Lucill.), Ael.*NA*4.51, Luc.*Gall.*31, etc.; ὦ γαστὴρ κυνόμυια *APl.* 1.9; of the plague of flies in Egypt, Lxx *Ex.*8.21(17), *Ps.*77(78).45.

κῠνάνθρωπος, ον, *of a dog-man*, νόσος κ. a malady *in which a man imagines himself to be a dog*, Gal.19.719, Antioch.Astr. in *Cat.Cod. Astr.*7.115.

κυνάπαιδες, dub. sens. in Sophr.ap.Sch.Gen.Il.21.395.

κῠνάρα [ᾰρ], ἡ, = κινάρα, S.*Fr.*348, cf. Scyl. or Polemo ap.Ath.2. 70c, Gal.6.636; ἄκανθα κυνάρα Hecat.291 J.:—also **κύνᾰρος** ἄκανθα S.*Fr.*718 (expl. as = κυνόσβατος by Did.ap.Ath. l.c.).

κῠν-άριον, τό, Dim. of κύων, *little dog, puppy*, Pl.*Euthd.*298d, X. *Cyr.*8.4.20, Theopomp.Com.90, Alc.Com.33, *Ev.Matt.*15.26; *small waxen image of a dog* used in magic, *PMag.Par.*1.2945: less correct than κυνίδιον acc. to Phryn.157; but κυνάριον καὶ κυνίδιον δόκιμα Id. *PS* p.84 B. **–άς,** άδος, pecul. fem. of κύνεος, *of a dog*, ἡμέραι κ. *the dog-*days, Plu.2.380d. II. mostly as Subst., 1. (sc. θρίξ), *dog's hair*, of a bad fleece, Theoc.15.19. 2. = κυνάρα, Hsch. 3. among the Spartans, = ἀπομαγδαλιά (q.v.), Polem.Hist.77, Poll.6. 93. 4. kind of *nail*, Sch.Od.7.91, Eust.1570.48. **–αστρος,** ὁ, late word for the *dog-star*, Sch.Opp.*H.*1.46, Sch.Lyc.397, Eust.514. 27, Steph. *in Rh.*304.3. **–άω,** = κυνίζω, *play the Cynic*, Luc.*Demon.* 21.

κυνδάλ-η [ᾰ], ἡ, = sq., Hsch. **–ισμός,** ὁ, *game of knocking out one peg with another*, Poll.9.120:—hence **κυνδᾰλοπαίκτης,** ου, ὁ, *one who plays at it*, ibid., Hsch. (–στης cod.).

κύνδᾰλος, ὁ, *wooden peg*, Poll.10.188: pl. κύνδαλα Id.9.120.

κυνδός· ἄπαικτος, ἀπαράλλακτος, Hsch.

κυνέα, ἡ, = λινόζωστις ἀγρία ἄρρην, Ps.-Dsc.4.190.

κυνεάγας· κυδώδων, Hsch. **κυνεγκέφᾰλος,** ὁ, *spinal marrow*, Id.

κῠνέη, Aeol. **κυνία** Alc.15.2, Att. contr. **κυνῆ** *IG*1^2.279.62, etc.: ἡ:—prop. (sc. δορά) *dog's skin* (so only Anaxandr.65), used for making soldiers' caps: hence in Ep., generally, *helmet*, κ. ταυρείη, κτιδέη, Il.10.257,335; κ. χαλκήρης, χαλκοπάρηος, 3.316, 12.183; κ. χρυσείη 5.743; once of a peasant's *cap*, αἰγείη κ. Od.24.231; later περὶ τῇσι κεφαλῇσι [εἶχον] ἐκ διφθερέων πεποιημένας κυνέας leathern *caps*, Hdt.7.77, cf. Ar.*Nu.*268, *V.*445; of the πέτασος, ἡλιοστερὴς κυνῆ Θεσσαλίς S.*OC*314; Ἀρκὰς κ., = Ἀρκαδικὸς πῖλος, Id.*Fr.*272, cf. Paus.Gr.*Fr.*72; but usu. *helmet*, λάμπραι κ. Alc. l.c.; κ. ἐπίχρυσος *IG*1^2. l.c.; τὴν κ. ἐοῦσαν χαλκέην Hdt.2.151; κ. Κορινθίη Id.4.180; Βοιωτία D.59.94, Thphr.*HP*3.9.6. 2. Ἄϊδος κ. mythical *helmet* which rendered the wearer invisible, worn by Athena, Il.5.845; by Perseus, Pherecyd.11 J., cf. Hes.*Sc.*227, Ar.*Ach.*390, Pl.*R.*612b; Πλούτων κ. ἔχει τοῦ ἀφανοῦς πόλου σύμβολον Porph.ap.Eus.*PE*3.11.

κύνειος [ῠ], α, ον, *of, belonging to a dog*, ἱμάς Ar.*V.*231; κ. θάνατος *a dog's* death, ib.898; τὰ κ. *dog's flesh*, Id.*Eq.*1399, S.E.*P.*3.225; κυνεία, ἡ, = κ. κόπρος, Archig.ap.Gal.12.954, Aët.15.15.

κύνειρα [ῠ], ἡ, (εἴρω A) *dog-leash*, *Com.Adesp.*1056.

κυνελφεῖ· κρύπτει, Hsch.

κύνεος [ῠ], α, ον, (κύων) = κύνειος, *AP*12.238 (Strat.), Orph.*Fr.* 224b.5. II. metaph., *shameless, unabashed*, Il.9.373, Hes.*Op.* 67; κέαρ A.R.3.641; μένος Timo 58.2. III. = Κυνικός, σοφισταί D.C.66.15.

κυνέπασαν· ἐξέδειραν, κτλ., *Com.Adesp.*1057. **κυνερίου** (–αιρίου cod.) ἢ **κυνουρίου·** ἀργολύκου, Hsch.

κῠνέω, Ep. impf. κύνεον Od.21.224: fut. κῠνήσομαι E.*Cyc.*172; later κύσω [ῠ], poet. κύσσω Babr.129.17: aor. ἐκύνησα v.l. in Arist. *HA*560^{b}31; Poet. ἔκῠσα, Ep. κύσα, ἔκυσσα, κύσσα, v. infr.:—*kiss*, κάρη δ' ἔκυσ' Od.23.208; λάβε γούνατα καὶ κύσε χεῖρας Il.24.478; κύνεον . . κεφαλήν τε καὶ ὤμους Od.21.224: c. acc. pers. et partis, κύσσε δέ μιν κεφαλήν 16.15, cf. 19.417; Τηλέμαχον . . δῖος ὑφορβὸς πάντα κύσεν 16.21; κύσον με Ar.*Nu.*81, cf. *Av.*141, etc.; κ. τινὰ χειρός A.R. 1.313: pres. in E.*Alc.*183, *Med.*1141, Ar.*Ach.*1208, *Pax* 1138 (lyr.): —rare in Prose, Luc.*Alex.*55; κ. [ἀλλήλας], of pigeons, *bill*, Arist. l.c. 2. = προσκυνέω, E.*Cyc.* l.c., *AP*6.283.

κῠνηγ-εσία, ἡ, later form for sq. II, D.L.6.31; = Lat. *venatio*, κ. ἐπετέλεσεν *CIG*2719 (Stratonicea):—Dor. **κυνᾱγ–** *AP*7.338, 6.183 (Zos.). **–έσιον,** τό, *hunting-establishment, pack of hounds*, Hdt.1.36, X.*Cyn.*10.4; also, *pack of wolves hunting together*, opp. λύκοι μονοπεῖραι, Arist.*HA*594^{a}31. II. *hunt, chase*, ἐπὶ τὸ κ. ἰέναι, πρὸς τὸ κ. προσιέναι, X.*Cyn.*6.11; ἀπιέναι ἐκ τοῦ κ. ib.26, cf. 7.11: in pl., E.*Hipp.* 224 (anap.), Isoc.7.45, X.*Cyn.*3.11, 6.4, Plu.*Alex.*40: metaph., κ. τὸ περὶ τὴν Ἀλκιβιάδου ὥραν Pl.*Prt.*309a; παρακαλεῖσθαί τινα ἐπὶ τὸ κ. Id. *La.*194b. 2. = κυνήγιον 2, *CIG*2511 (Cos), 4157 (Sinope). III. *that which is taken in hunting, game*, X.*Cyn.*6.12. **–έσσω,** Att. **–ττω,** = sq., Phryn.*PS* p.84 B., Theognost.*Can.*143: hence aor. 1 subj. κυνηγέσω S.*Ichn.*44 (cf. Pass. inf. κυνηγεσ(ε)ῖσθαι *PGrenf.*2.71 ii 12 (iii A.D.)). **–ετέω,** Dor. **κυνᾱγ–,** *hunt*, Ar.*Eq.*1382, X. *Cyn.*5.34, etc.: c. acc., ὗς ἀγρίους κ. Aeschin.3.255, cf. Plb.31.14.3: metaph., *persecute, harass*, A.*Pr.*572 (lyr.); *hunt down*, τινας Plu. *Mar.*43: c. acc. cogn., κ. τέκνων διωγμόν E.*HF*898 (lyr.): abs., *quest about*, like a hound, S.*Aj.*5. **–έτης,** ου, ὁ, Dor. (never in Trag.) **κυνᾱγέτᾱς** Pi.*N.*6.14:—*huntsman*, Od.9.120, E.*HF*860 (troch.), *Hec.* 1174, Pl.*R.*432b, X.*Cyn.*6.11, al., *OGI*20 (iii B.C.); in pl. of certain δαίμονες, Pl.Com.174.16, *SIG*1040.9 (Piraeus, iv B.C.): metaph., of one who seeks fame, Pi. l.c.:—fem. **–έτις,** Dor. **–ᾱγέτις,** ιδος, *huntress*, Ach.Tat.8.12; epith. of Artemis, Corn.*ND*34: as Adj., κ. αἰγανέα *AP*6.115 (Antip.). **–ετικός,** ή, όν, *of* or *for hunting, fond of the chase*, Pl.*Euthphr.*13a: ἡ –κή (sc. τέχνη) ibid., Phld.*Mus.*p.24 K.; οἱ κ. λόγοι Onos.*Praef.*1; ὁ κ. [λόγος], title of Xenophon's work on Hunting: τὰ –κά, of Oppian's poem. **–έτις,** ιδος, ἡ, fem. of κυνηγέτης (q.v.). **–έω,** Dor. **–ᾱγέω** Bion 1.60: pf. Pass. κεκυνηγῆσθαι Plb.31.29.4: (κυνηγός):—*hunt, chase*, later form of κυνηγετέω, ὅταν κυνηγήσῃ [ὁ ἀετός] Arist.*HA*619^{a}33, cf. Plu.*Pel.*8, etc.: metaph., *pursue, persecute*, τινα Pl.*Ep.*349c, etc. **–ητήρ,** ῆρος, ὁ, = κυνηγέτης, Man.4.337. **–ία,** ἡ, *hunt, chase*, Arist.*Rh.*1371^{a}5, Plb.8.25.4, D.S.3.36, etc.:—Trag. in Dor. form **κυνᾱγία** (cf. κυναγός) S.*Aj.*37 (cod. Med.), E.*Hipp.*109, and so prob. in Id.*Ba.*339 (pl.). **–ικός,** ή, όν, *of* or *for hunting*, τόποι *PGrenf.*2.71 i 15 (iii A.D.). **–ιον,** τό, later form for κυνηγέσιον, *hunt, chase*, Ath.15.677e: in pl., Plb.10. 22.4, D.S.5.29 (v.l. –ίαις), etc. 2. *beast-hunt* in the Amphitheatre, = Lat. *venatio*, *CIG*3847*b* 8 (Nacolea), *OGI*533.7 (Ancyra). 3. in pl., *game-preserves*, D.S.2.8, Philostr.*VA*2.14. 4. *prey*, κυνήγια λεόντων ὄναγροι Lxx *Si.*13.19. **–ίς, –ός,** v. κυναγός.

κῠν-ηδόν, Adv., (κύων) *like a dog*, S.*Fr.*722, Ar.*Eq.*1033, *Nu.*491, Luc.*Tim.*54. **–ηλᾰσία,** Ep. **–ίη,** ἡ, *hunting with dogs*, Call.*Dian.* 217. **–ηλᾰτέω,** *follow the hounds*, Euph.132, Nic.*Th.*20. **–ήποδες,** οἱ, (κύων VIII) *fetlocks* of a horse, X.*Eq.*1.15, Poll.5.65.

κῠνητίνδᾰ (sc. παιδιά), ἡ, *game of kissing*, Crates Com.23 (lyr.).

κυνθάνω, = κεύθω, Hsch. **κύνθιον,** = κυλίνθιον, Id.

Κύνθος, ὁ, *Cynthus*, a mountain in Delos, birth-place of Apollo and Artemis, *h.Ap.*26:—Adj. **Κύνθιος,** epith. of Apollo, Call.*Del.*10; Δήλιε, Κυνθίαν ἔχων . . πέτραν Ar.*Nu.*596 (lyr.):—also **Κυνθογενής,** ές, *AP*15.25.9 (Besant.).

κῠνία, ἡ, v.l. for κυνέα in Ps.-Dsc.4.190. II. v. κυνέη.

κῠν-ίδιον, τό, Dim. of κύων, *little dog, puppy*, Ar.*Ach.*542, Pl.*Euthd.* 298e, X.*Oec.*13.8, Phld.*Lib.*p.10 O.: pl., Eup.207, Arist.*Rh.*1406^b 28; cf. κυνάριον. **–ίζω,** fut. κυνιῶ *Stoic.*3.162, Apollod.ib.261:—*play the dog*: metaph., *live like a Cynic*, ll. cc., Arr.*Epict.*3.22.1, Luc. *Peregr.*43, Ath.13.588f, Jul.*Or.*6.182a.

κύνικλος, ὁ, = Lat. *cuniculus, rabbit*, Plb.12.3.10 (**κούνικλος** ap. Ath.9.400f), prob. in Gal.6.666; in Ael.*NA*13.15 **κόνικλος.**

κῠνικός, ή, όν, (κύων) *dog-like*, X.*Cyr.*5.2.17 (v.l. for ὑϊκόν); τὸ κ. καὶ θηριῶδες τῶν ὀρέξεων Plu.2.133b; κ. σπασμός *unilateral facial paralysis*, Cels.4.3.1, Gal.18(2).930; κ. καύματα heat *of the dog-days*, Polyaen.2.30.3: metaph., ὁ ἄνθρωπος κ. *currish, churlish*, Lxx 1*Ki.*25.3. Adv. **–κῶς,** σπώμενοι Heliod.ap.Orib.48.38 tit.; *in dog-language*, opp. βοϊκῶς, etc., Porph.*Abst.*3.3. II. **Κυνικός,** ὁ, *Cynic*, as the followers of the philosopher Antisthenes were called, from the gymnasium (Κυνόσαργες) where he taught, D.L.6.13; or from their resemblance to dogs in several respects, Diog.Cyn.ap.eund.6. 60, Metrod.16, Polystr.p.20 W., Elias *in Cat.*111.2, etc.; Κράτητι τῷ κ. Men.117; κ. αἵρεσις, ἄσκησις, φιλοσοφία, Ph.1.352, J.*AJ*6.13.6, Jul.*Or.*6.187a; παρρησία κ. Plu.2.69c; τὸ κ. τῆς παρρησίας Id.*Brut.* 34. Adv. Comp. **–ώτερον** Id.2.601e.

κυνίξεις· ἀκροβολισμοί, Hsch.

κῠν-ίσκη, ἡ, *bitch-puppy*, Ar.*Ra.*1360. **–ίσκος,** ὁ, *puppy*, nick-name of Zeuxidamus in Hdt.6.71. 2. metaph., *little Cynic*, Luc. *Pisc.*45. **–ισμός,** ὁ, *Cynical philosophy* or *conduct*, Apollod.*Stoic.* 3.261, Luc.*Bis Acc.*33, Poll.5.65, Jul.*Or.*6.182c. **–ιστέον,** *one must practise Cynic philosophy*, ib.7.204a tit. **–ιστί,** Adv. *like a dog*, Posidon.5 J.

κυνίσφειλον· ἀπατητικόν, Hsch.

κῠνο-βάμων [ᾰ], ον, gen. ονος, = sq., Hsch. **–βάτης** [ᾰ], (κύων VIII) *with short, stiff fetlocks*, of a horse, *Hippiatr.*115; of an ass, ib. 14. **–βλώψ,** ῶπος, ὁ, ἡ, *with a dog's look*, Hsch. **–βορά,** ἡ, *dog's food*, Sch.Ar.*Pl.*293 (as etym. of κινάβρα), Tz.*H.*13.279. **–βοσκός,** ὁ, *feeder of sacred jackals*, *Sammelb.*5796 (i B.C.). **–βρωτος,** ον, *devoured by dogs*, Neanth.25 J., Phld.*Mort.*33, Antioch.Astr. in *Cat.Cod.Astr.*7.115. **–γᾰμία,** ἡ, *dog-wedding*, used by Crates the Cynic of his own marriage, Suid. s.v. Κράτης. **–γλωσσος,** ον, *dog-tongued*: hence 1. **κυνόγλωσσος,** ὁ, kind of *fish*, Epich. 44. 2. *hound's tongue, Cynoglossum Columnae*, Nic.*Fr.*71:—also **–γλωσσον,** τό, Ps.-Dsc.4.127, Zopyr.ap.Orib.14.62.1. **–δέσμη,** ἡ, (κύων VII, δεσμός) *fibula for the prepuce*, Phryn.*PS* p.85 B. (pl.), Phot.:—also **–δέσμιον,** τό, v.l. in Poll.2.171. **–δεσμος,** ὁ, *dog-leash*, Longus 2.14. **–δηκτικός,** ή, όν, *for dog-bite*, [ἔμπλαστρος] Theodor.ap.Philum.*Ven.*4.15. **–δηκτος,** ον, *caused by a dog's bite*, ἕλκη Arist.*HA*630^{a}8, cf. Heras ap.Gal.13.558, Dsc.1.123, 2.28; *bitten by a dog*, *Gp.*12.17.14.

κῠνόδους, δοντος, ὁ, *canine tooth*, prop. of dogs, Arist.*PA*661^{b}9, *HA*501^{b}7; of lions, ib.579^{b}12; of men, Hp.*Aph.*3.25, Epich.21 (in form **κυνόδων**); of horses, X.*Eq.*6.8, Arist.*HA*576^{b}17; of a serpent's *fang*, Nic.*Th.*130, 231. 2. in pl., *teeth* of a saw, Ael.*NA*10.20.

κῠνοδρομ-έω, *run* or *chase with dogs*, X.*Cyn.*6.17: metaph., ἐκυνοδρομοῦμεν ἀλλήλους ζητοῦντες Id.*Smp.*4.63. **–ία,** Ion. **–ίη,** ἡ, *hunting with dogs*, Hp.*Vict.*3.68 (pl., v.l. νυκτο–), Call.*Dian.*106.

κῡνόδων, οντος, ὁ, v. κυνόδους.

κῡνοειδής, ές, *like a dog*, Arist.*HA* 502ᵃ21 (Comp.), Gal.4.604:—Sicel name for ψύλλιον, Ps.-Dsc.4.69, cf. Plin.*HN* 25.140.

κῡν-όζολον, τό, (ὄζω) = χαμαιλέων μέλας, so called from its smell, prob. in Dsc.3.9, cf. Ps.-Dsc.ibid. II. = δρακοντία μικρά, ib.2.167. **κῡνο-θαρσής**, ές, *impudent as a dog*, Theoc.15.53: **-θρᾰσής**, A. *Supp.* 758 (lyr.). **-θηρες**, οἱ, corrupt in Ps.-Dsc.4.77. **-κάρδᾰμον**, τό, = κάρδαμον, ib.2.155. **-καύματα**, τά, *the heat of the dog-days*, Aët.6.83, Alex.Trall.9.3:—hence **-καυματικαί** (sc. ἡμέραι), *dog-days*, *Gloss.* **-κεντρον**, τό, a plant, Hsch. **-κεφάλιον** [ᾰ], τό, = ἀντίρρινον, Sch.Orib.2.744, Ps.-Dsc.4.130; = ψύλλιον, ib.69, cf. *PMag. Lond.* 46.198:—also **-κεφᾰλίδιον**, ib.121.602; but **-κεφάλαιον**, = ἀνεμώνη, Hsch. **-κεφᾰλιστί**, Adv. *after the manner of the* κυνοκέφαλος, *PMag.Lond.* 46.27. **-κεφᾰλοειδής** πίθηκος, ὁ, = κυνοκέφαλος 2, Gal.2.534. **-κεφᾰλοκέρδων**, ωνος, ὁ, = sq. 2, *PMag.Leid. W.* 4.28. **-κέφᾰλος**, ον, *dog-headed*: οἱ K., *Dog-heads*, name of a people, Hdt.4.191, cf. Ctes.*Fr.* 57.22, A.*Fr.* 431. 2. *dog-faced baboon*, *Simia hamadryas*, Pl.*Tht.* 161c, 166c, Arist.*HA* 502ᵃ19, etc.; sacred animal in Egypt, Luc.*Tox.* 28, *JTr.* 42. 3. κυνοκέφαλον, τό, = ψύλλιον, Dsc.4.69; = ἀντίρρινον, Xenocr.ap.Sch.Orib.2.744. [κυνοκεφάλλῳ at the close of an iambic tetrameter, Ar.*Eq.* 416, where λλ is attested by Phryn.*PS* p.85 B., Phot.] **-κλόπος**, ὁ, *dog-stealer*, Ar. *Ra.* 605. **-κοπέω**, *beat like a dog*, Id.*Eq.* 289. **-κόριον**, *turbisci semen*, *Gloss.* **-κορον**, = *satyrion*, ib. **-κράμβη**, ἡ, = κυνέα, Ps.-Dsc.4.190. 2. = ἀπόκυνον, Dsc.4.80, *Gp.* 13.4.7 and 7.1. **-κτόνος**, ον, *killing dogs*: κ., τό, = ἀκόνιτον, Dsc.4.76. **-λογέω**, *talk of the dog-star*, Ath.1.23a. **-λοφα**, τά, *processes of the spine*, Poll. 2.180.

κῡνολύγματε, epith. of the Moon in *PMag.Par.* 1.2549: perh. for **κυνολολύγματε**, *howling like a dog*.

κῡνό-λῠκος, ὁ, = κροκόττας, Ctes.*Fr.* 87. **-λυσσος** or **-λυσσον**, ὁ or τό, *hydrophobia*, Andreas ap.Cael.Aur.*CP* 3.98. **-μαζον**, τό, = χαμαιλέων μέλας, prob. in Dsc.3.9, cf. Apul.*Herb.* 110. **-μᾶλον**, τό, Dor. for κυνόμηλον, = κοκκύμηλον, Hsch. **-μαντεία**, ἡ, *divination by dogs*, *Gloss.* **-μᾰχέω**, *fight with dogs*, Poll.5.65; ἐν φρέατι κ., prov. ἐπὶ τῶν δυσφεύκτων, Hsch. **-μᾰχον**, τό, = κυνόμαζον, Orib.12 s.v. χαμαιλέων μέλας. **-μόριον**, τό, = ὀροβάγχη, Dsc.2. 142. **-μορον**, τό, = κυνόσβατος, Gal.12.426; also, = ἀπόκυνον, Id. 11.835. **-μορφος**, ὁ, = κρόκος, Ps.-Dsc.1.26. **-μυια**, ἡ, v. κυνάμυια. II. = ψύλλιον, Dsc.4.69.

κῡνοπλον, τό, *corona* in the horse's foot, *Hippiatr.* 95, 106.

κῡνο-πόδιον, τό, = πολύγονος, *Gloss.* **-πους**, ποδος, ὁ, = κυνήπους, *Hippiatr.* 77, 115. **-πρᾰσον**, τό, *dog-leek*, a plant, ib.69. **-πρηστις** (-πρῖστις cod.), ιδος, ἡ, (πρήθω) a venomous insect, *whose sting makes dogs swell up* and die, Hsch.; cf. βούπρηστις. **-πρόσωπος**, ον, *dog-faced*, Luc.*DMar.* 7.2, *VH* 1.16, S.E.*P.* 3.219; of men, like κυνοκέφαλος, Ael.*NA* 10.25.

κῡνόπτικον, τό, an eye-salve, Alex.Trall.2.

κῡνο-ραιστής, οῦ, ὁ, (ῥαίω) *dog-tick*, *Ricinus communis*, Od.17.300, Arist.*Rh.* 1393ᵇ26, *HA* 557ᵃ18. **-ροδον**, τό, *dog-rose*, *Rosa canina*, Thphr.*HP* 4.4.8. II. = ἀντίρρινον, Ps.-Dsc.4.130. **-ρράφιον** [ᾰ], τό, (κύων VII) a surgical instrument, *Hermes* 38.282.

κῡνορτικός, ἡ, όν, *urging on hounds*, σύριγμα S.*Ichn.* 167.

κῡνορχίας, ὁ, a throw of the dice, Hsch.

Κῠνόσαργες, εος, τό, *Cynosarges*, a gymnasium outside the city of Athens, sacred to Heracles, for the use of those who were not of pure Athenian blood, Hdt.5.63, 6.116, And.1.61, D.23.213, Paus.1. 19.3.

κῡνόσ-βᾰτος, ἡ (also ὁ Thphr. (v.infr.), Ath.2.70d), *white rose*, *Rosa sempervirens*, Arist.*Fr.* 561, Theoc.5.92, Dsc.1.94, Plu.2.294e, etc.; καρπὸς τοῦ κ. Thphr.*HP* 9.8.5:—also **-βᾰτον**, τό, ib.3.18.4. II. = κάππαρις, Dsc.2.173; = βάτος, Ps.-Dsc.4.37; = σμῖλαξ τραχεῖα, ib. 142. **-ουρα**, ἡ, *dog's-tail*, a name for the constellation *Ursa Minor*, Arat.36, Aglaosth.ap.Eratosth.*Cat.* 2. **-ουρίς**, ίδος, ἡ, *a breed of Spartan hounds*, from the Laced. tribe so called, Call.*Dian.* 94. II. = κυνόσουρα, Nonn.*D.* 1.166; epith. of Ἄρκτος, Man.2.24.

κῡνόσουρος, ον, ᾠὰ *addled* eggs, Arist.*HA* 560ᵃ5; cf. οὔριος IV.

κῡνο-σπάρακτος [ᾰ], ον, *torn by dogs*, S.*Ant.* 1198. **-σπάς**, άδος, ὁ, ἡ, = foreg., Nonn.*D.* 46.341. **-σπαστος**, ὁ, = ἀγλαοφῶτις, Ael.*NA* 14.24, 27.

κῡνοσσόος, ον, *cheering on hounds*, Nonn.*D.* 1.233, etc.

κῡνό-στομον, τό, *distance between thumb and first finger*, = λιχάς, Hero *Geom.* 4.4. **-σφᾰγής**, ές, *worshipped with sacrifices of dogs*, Lyc.77. **-σφη** (-λφη cod.)· σίλφη, Hsch. **-τρόφος**, ον, *keeping dogs*, Ctes.*Fr.* 62.

κῡνουλκός, ὁ, (ἕλκω) *dog-leader*, Nic.Dam.56 J.

κυνοῦπες· ἄρκτοι (-τος cod.) (Maced.), Hsch. (Fort. κυνουπεύς, = κνουπεύς, κνωπεύς.)

κύνουρα [ῠ], ων, τά, *sea-cliffs*, Lyc.99.

κυνοῦραι· ἀστράγαλοι, Hsch.

κυνούχιον, τό, Dim. of sq. III, corr. Casaub. for κυλιούχιον in Thphr. *Char.* 18.4.

κῡνοῦχος, ὁ, (ἔχω) *dog-leash*, *AP* 6.298 (Leon.), acc. to Suid., but more prob. in signf. III; κλοιὸς κ. *dog-collar*, ib.107 (Phil.). II. *calf-skin sack*, for carrying hunting-nets, etc., X.*Cyn.* 2.9; also, for use as a *clothes-locker* in the gymnasium, Poll.10.64. III. *purse*, *money-bag*, *PCair.Zen.* 22.22 (iii B.C.), *Inscr.Délos* 442 *A* 7, 461 *A a* 7 (ii B.C.), Ael.Dion.*Fr.* 206, Hsch., Phot.

κῡνοφᾰγέω, *eat dog's flesh*, S.E.*P.* 3.225, Porph.*Abst.* 1.14.

κυνοφάλιον, *sabina*, *Gloss.*

Κυνόφαλοι, οἱ, name of a tribe at Corinth, *Com.Adesp.* 1360.

κῡνοφθαλμίζομαι, *look impudent*, *Com.Adesp.* 1058.

κῡνο-φόντις ἑορτή, ἡ, (θείνω) a festival, *in which dogs were killed*, Ath.3.99e. **-φρων**, ον, gen. ονος, *dog-minded*, *shameless of soul*, A.*Ch.* 621 (lyr.). **-χάλκη**, ἡ, = πολύγονον ἄρρεν, Ps.-Dsc.4.4.

κύντερος, α, ον, Comp. Adj. formed from κύων, *more dog-like*, i.e. *more shameless* (cf. κύων II), Hom. only in neut., ἐπεὶ οὐ σέο κύντερον ἄλλο Il.8.483; οὐ..κ. ἄλλο γυναικός Od.11.427; οὐ γάρ τι στυγερῇ ἐπὶ γαστέρι κ. ἄλλο 7.216; *more horrible*, κ. ἄλλο ποτ' ἔτλης 20.18: later in masc., κυνῶν κύντερος Anon.ap.Suid. s. v. Διονυσίων. 2. Sup. **κύντατος**, η, ον, μερμήριζε.., ὅ τι κύντατον ἔρδοι Il.10.503; κ. ἐνιαυτός *h.Cer.* 306; κ. ἀνδρῶν A.R.3.192; once in Trag., τὰ κ. ἄλγη κακῶν E. *Supp.* 807 (lyr.); in later Prose, Phld.*Ir.* p.24 W. II. Comp. **κυντερώτερος** A.*Fr.* 432, Pherecr.106: Sup. **κυντατώτατος** Eub.85, but **κυντότατος** Arist.*Fr.* 77.

κῠνῠλαγμός, ὁ, *the howling of dogs*, Stesich.85.

κυνύπισμα· τὸ ἀπὸ στεμφύλων ποτόν (Cypr.), Hsch.

κῠν-ώ, οῦς, ἡ, *bitch*: hence, = ἀναιδεστάτη, Hsch.: as pr. n., Hdt. 1.110; title of Hecate, *PMag.Par.* 1.2279. **-ώδης**, ες, *dog-like*, θηρίον Arist.*GA* 746ᵃ35, cf. Heraclit.*Incred.* 2; αἰδοῖον Arist.*HA* 502ᵇ24 (Comp.); ὄρεξις *ravenous*, Gal.7.131, cf. Alex.Trall.7.1. Adv. **-δῶς** Antyll.ap.Orib.6.23.5. II. metaph., *despicable*, Phld.*Rh.* 2. 175 S., *Piet.* 95 (Sup.); *currish*, *ill-tempered*, Id.*Lib.* p.44 O. **-ώπης**, ου, ὁ, (ὤψ) *dog-eyed*, i.e. *shameless one*, Il.1.159:—fem. **-ῶπις**, ιδος, ἡ, ἐμεῖο κυνώπιδος εἵνεκ', says Helen, Od.4.145, cf. Il.3.180; κ. εἵνεκα κούρης, of Aphrodite, Od.8.319; of Hera, Il.18.396; of the Erinyes, E.*Or.* 260, *El.* 1252; παλλακὴ κ. Cratin.241. **-ωτός**, ὁ, *dog's ear*, name of a throw of the dice, *An.Ox.* 2.21; prob. in Eub.57 (but κυνῶτες Poll.7.205). **-ωψ**, ωπος, ὁ, *rib-grass*, *Plantago lanceolata*, Thphr.*HP* 7.7.3.

κύεις, εσσα, εν, *pregnant*, *Abh.Berl.Akad.* 1928(6).22 (Cos, iii B.C.).

κύος [ῠ], εος, τό, = κύημα, Ar.*Fr.* 609, *IG* 12(5).646 (Ceos).

κῠο-τοκία, ἡ, *production of young*, in birds, Alex.Aphr.*Pr.* 2. 68. **-τροφία**, ἡ, *nourishment of the foetus*, Hp.*Salubr.* 6 (pl.).

κύουρα, ἡ, a plant, used to procure abortion, Agatho Sam.ap.Stob. 4.36.12.

κῠοφορ-έω, *to be with young*, *be pregnant*, Hp.*Nat.Mul.* 12 (v.l.), Lxx *Ec.* 11.5; ἔκ τινος by.., Luc.*DDeor.* 1.2; of the earth, Ph.1.9: metaph., ib.130: c. acc., τινα *with* or *of*.., ib.251, Hld.10.18: metaph., ἡ διάνοια κ. πολλά Ph.1.183:—Pass., D.S.1.7; βρέφος κυοφορηθέν Artem.4.67, cf. 84, Porph.*Marc.* 32, Phlp. *in APo.* 280. 17. **-ησις**, εως, ἡ, *pregnancy*, Sor.2.53, *Theol.Ar.* 50. **-ία**, ἡ, = foreg., Lxx *4Ma.* 15.6 (pl.), Sor.1.47, Hierocl.p.63 A. (pl.), v.l. in Artem.1.14. **-ος**, ον, *pregnant*, *fertile*, γῆ *EM* 546.8, cf. *PLond.* 1821.161.

κύπαιρ-ος [ῠ], Dor. for κύπειρος, Alcm.16:—Dim. **-ίσκος**, Id.38.

κύπαλον· μεμειρασμένον, Hsch.

κῠπᾰρισσ-ίας, ου, ὁ, *Euphorbia aleppica*, Dsc.4.164, Ruf.ap.Orib. 7.26.108. II. a kind of comet, prob. in Seneca *QN* 1.15.4. **-ῐνος**, Att. **-ίττινος**, η, ον, *of cypress-wood*, σταθμός Od.17.340; μέλαθρον Pi. *P.* 5.39; λάρνακες Th.2.34; μνῆμαι Pl.*Lg.* 741c; ξυλεία Plb.10.27.10; also, *made* or *drawn from the cypress*, κ. οἶνος Dsc.5.36; ῥητίνη Gal. 13.589. **-ιον**, Att. **-ίττιον**, τό, Dim. of κυπάρισσος, Alciphr.*Fr.* 6. 1 (pl.). **-ιος**, ὁ, title of Apollo in Cos, *Abh.Berl.Akad.* 1928(6).32 (iv B.C.). (Cf. Κυφαρισσία.)

κῠπᾰρισσόκομος, ον, *with cypress foliage*, Sch.Il.13.132.

κῠπᾰρισσ-όροφος, ον, *ceiled with cypress-wood*, E.*Hyps.Fr.* 32.10; θάλαμοι prob. (for -τρόφοι) in Mnesim.4.1 (anap.). **-ος**, Att. **-ιττος**, ἡ, *cypress*, *Cupressus sempervirens*, εὐώδης Od.5.64, cf. Hdt. 4.75, Hermipp.63.14, Phld.*Mort.* 38, Dsc.1.74, Arr.*An.* 7.19.4; ἐλαφρά Pi.*Fr.* 154; ῥαδινά Theoc.11.45; ἄρρην καὶ θήλεια Thphr.*HP* 1. 8.2. II. *cypress-wood* as timber, *SIG* 251 *H* ii 9 (Delph., iv B.C.), *IG* 4^2(1).102.26 (Epid., iv B.C.), 2^2.1672.191. **-ών**, ῶνος, ὁ, *cypress grove*, Str.16.1.4.

κύπασσις [ῠ] (-ασίς Hsch.), εως (ιδος Alc.15.6), ὁ (ἡ v.l. in Hecat. 284 J.), *short frock*, reaching to a man's mid-thigh, Alc. l.c. (in form κυπάττιδες), Ion Trag.59, Lys.*Fr.* 58 S.; also worn by women, Ar. *Fr.* 519, *AP* 6.202 (Leon.), cf. 272 (Pers.), 358 (Diotim.); κ. Περσικαί Hecat. l.c.; κ. χερμάδων prob. for κύπας τις χ. in Lyc.333:—Dim. **κῠπασσίσκος**, ὁ, Hippon.18.

κυπάται· κίναιδοι, μαλακοί, Hsch.; cf. κυβάλης.

κύπειρις [ῠ], ιδος, ἡ, = sq. 2, Nic.*Al.* 591:—also **κύπηρις**, εως, ἡ, *POxy.* 374 (i A.D.).

κύπειρον [ῠ], τό, *galingale*, *Cyperus longus*, eaten by horses, Il. 21.351, Od.4.603. 2. *C. rotundus*, Thphr.*HP* 4.10.5; cf. sq. and κύπερος.

κύπειρος [ῠ], ὁ, = foreg., *h.Merc.* 107, Ar.*Ra.* 243 (lyr.), Pherecr. 109, Thphr.*HP* 1.8.1, and 10.5, Theoc.1.106.

κῠπελλίς, ίδος, ἡ, = κύπελλον, Eust.1776.31.

κῠπελλομάχος [ᾰ], ον, *at which they fight with cups*, εἰλαπίνη *AP* 11.59 (Maced.).

κύπελλον [ῠ], τό, (ἀπὸ τῆς κυφότητος Ath.11.482e) *big-bellied drinking-vessel*, *beaker*, *goblet*, freq. in Hom., χρύσεια κύπελλα Il.3. 248; κύπελλα οἴνου 4.345; κύπελλα καὶ μεσομφάλους Ion Trag.20 (lyr.); also of a *milk-vessel*, Q.S.6.345. II. at Syracuse, in pl., *fragments of bread left on table*, Philet.ap.Ath.11.483a.

κῠπελλο-τόκος, ον, *breeding cups*, τράπεζα Nonn.*D.* 47.62. **-φόρος**, ον, *carrying cups*, *App.Anth.*3.166 (Procl.). **-χάρων** [ᾰ], ωνος, ὁ, *delighting in cups*, Eust.1776.31.

κῠπερ-ίζω, *resemble* κύπερος, Dsc.1.7. **-ον**, τό, *rope made of* κύπειρος, Hsch. (pl.). **-ος**, ὁ, Ion. for κύπειρος, *Cyperus rotundus*, Hp.*Nat.Mul.*58, Hdt.4.71: also in later Gr., Dsc.1.4, Plu.2.383e, Gal.12.54, *PSI*6.718.4 (iv/v A.D.). II. κ. ἕτερος *turmeric*, *Curcuma longa*, Dsc.1.5.

κύπη, ἡ, a kind of *ship*, Hsch. 2. *hut*, Id. II. = τρώγλη, Id.

κύπηρις, v. κύπειρις:—hence **κῠπηρολογέω**, *gather* κύπειρις, *POxy.*374 (i A.D.).

κῡπόω, (cf. κύπτω) *overthrow*, Lyc.1442.

κυπριάζω, = ἀνθέω (prob. f.l. for κυπρίζω), Suid.

Κυπριακός, ή, όν, *Cyprian*, D.S.14.110, etc.

Κυπρίδιος, α, ον, (Κύπρις) *of love*, ὄαροι *AP*10.68 (Agath.); κέλευθος ib.5.274 (Paul. Sil.); κῦμα ib.234 (Maced.).

κυπρίζω, *bloom*, LXX *Ca.*2.13.

κυπρῑνέλαιον, τό, = κύπρινον, Alex.Trall.3.3.

κύπρῑνος (A), η, ον, *made of copper*, ἧλος *PMag.Lond.*121.466.

κύπρῑνος (B), η, ον, *made from the flower of* κύπρος, ἔλαιον *Edict. Diocl.Delph.*10:—esp. as Subst. **κύπρῑνον** (sc. μύρον), τό, *oil* or *unguent made from the flower of the* κύπρος, Apollon.Heroph.ap.Ath.15.688f, Dsc.1.55, Aret.*CA*1.2; also of a plaster, Androm.ap.Gal.13.494.

κυπρῖνος, ὁ, *carp*, Arist.*HA*533ᵃ29, 538ᵃ15, *Fr.*321, Opp.*H.*1.101.

κύπριον, τό, = ἀρνόγλωσσον, Hsch.

Κύπριος, α, ον, *of Cyprus*, *Cyprian*, Pi.*P.*2.16, Hdt.3.19, etc.; λίθος Κ., a kind of σμάραγδος (found in Cyprus, Thphr.*Lap.*25), Achae.5, cf. Plin.*HN*37.66; Κ. ἄρτοι Eub.77; Κ. παραπέτασμα Ar.*Fr.*611; Κ. τάριχος Posidipp.17; βοῦς Κ., prov. of *an unclean feeder*, Diogenian.3.49, Suid., etc.; Κ. κάλαμος, = δόναξ, Dsc.1.85. 2. **Κυπρία**, ἡ, = Κύπρις, Pi.*O.*1.75. 3. **Κύπρια**, τά, an Epic poem introductory to the Il., Hdt.2.117, Arist.*Po.*1459ᵇ2.

κύπριος, α, ον, *of copper*, γραφεῖον *PMag.Par.*1.1847.

Κύπρις, ῐδος, ἡ, acc. Κύπριν and Κύπριδα, Il.5.330,458:—*Cypris*, a name of *Aphrodite*, from the island of Cyprus, Il. ll. cc. (never in Od.), Sapph.5.1, Corinn.*Supp.*2.58 (Κούπρις), etc.; joined with Ἀφροδίτη, *h.Ven.*2; Κ. βασίλεια Emp.128.3. 2. metaph., of a beautiful girl, *a Venus*, Opp.*H.*4.235. II. as Appellat., *love*, *passion*, E.*Ba.*773; Κύπριν ὑφαρπάζειν Ar.*Ec.*722; λαθραία Κ. Eub. 67.8; ἐν πλησμονῇ τοι Κ. Men.*Mon.*159, cf. B.*Fr.*16.4, E.*Fr.*951. III. = sq., Eust.1574.24, Sch.Od.7.125. [ῠ by nature; in Ep. ῡ by position; never in Com., exc. in parodies.]

κυπρισμός, ὁ, *bloom* of the olive or vine, LXX *Ca.*7.12, Eust.1095.23.

Κυπρο-γενής, ές, (γενέσθαι) *Cyprus-born*, Κ. Κυθέρεια *h.Hom.*10.1: standing alone, Hes.*Th.*199 (acc. -γενέα (prob.)), Sol.26, Pi.*O.*10(11).105, etc.:—fem. **-γένεια**, ἡ, Κ. Ἀφροδίτη Ar.*Lys.*551; Κ. θεά Panyas.13.3: abs., Pi.*P.*4.216, Plu.*Art.*28:—Aeol. **Κυπρογένηα** Sapph.*Supp.*14.8, Alc.60, Theoc.30.31.

Κύπρος, ἡ, *Cyprus*, Od.17.442, al. (never in Il., exc. in Adv. (v. infr.)). Adv. **Κυπρόθεν**, *from Cyprus*, *AP*9.487 (Pall.); **Κυπρόθε**, Call.*Sos.*9.7; **Κύπρονδε**, *to Cyprus*, Il.11.21.

κύπρος, ἡ, *henna*, *Lawsonia inermis*, LXX *Ca.*1.14, *AP*4.1.42 (Mel.), Dsc.1.95, J.*BJ*4.8.3. 2. = κύπρινον μύρον, Thphr.*Od.*25, *PPetr.*2 p.114 (iii B.C.), etc. II. *a measure of corn*, Alc.141, *SIG*302 (Gambreum, iv B.C.), *Rev.Ét.Gr.*19.237 (Aphrod.). 2. = κεφάλαιον ἀριθμοῦ, Hsch.

κυπτάζω, Frequentat. of κύπτω, *keep stooping*, *go poking about*, *potter about* a thing, ἀμφ' ἄλητα Sophr.39; περί τινα Ar.*Lys.*17; τί κυπτάζεις ἔχων περὶ τὴν θύραν; Id.*Nu.*509; εἰώθασι μάλιστα περὶ τὰς σκηνὰς.. κλέπται κ. Id.*Pax* 731; περὶ τὸν τεθνεῶτα Pl.*R.*469d: abs., κυπτάζοντα ζῆν Id.*Amat.*137b. 2. abs., *cower*, D.C.49.30, 63.28. II. = κύπτω 5, Phlp. *in Ph.*329.14.

κυπτόν· ταπεινούμενον, Hsch.

κύπτω, fut. κύψω LXX *Ps.*9.31(10.10): aor. ἔκυψα (v. infr.): pf. κέκῡφα Hp.*Steril.*217:—*bend forward*, *stoop*, πλευρά, τά οἱ κύψαντι παρ' ἀσπίδος ἐξεφαάνθη Il.4.468; ἔλαβεν.. κύψας ἐκ πεδίοιο 17.621, cf. 21.69; ὁσσάκι γὰρ κύψει' ὁ γέρων πιέειν μενεαίνων κτλ. Od.11.585; κ. ἐς τὴν γῆν Hdt.3.14; κάτω κ. Ar.*V.*279 (lyr.), Thphr.*Char.*24.8; κεκυφότες εἰς γῆν καὶ εἰς τραπέζας Pl.*R.*586a; χαμᾶζε Plu.*Ant.*45: freq. in aor. part. with another Verb, ἔθει κύψας ran *with the head down*, i.e. *at full speed*, Ar.*Ra.*1091 (anap.); ὀμόσ' εἶμι κύψας Id.*Ec.*863; ἐς τὴν γῆν κύψασα κάτω βαδίζει Id.*Fr.*395; κύψας ἐσθίει eats *stooping*, i.e. *greedily*, Id.*Pax* 33; sens. obsc., Hippon.22 Diehl. 2. *hang the head from shame*, οὗτος, τί κύπτεις; Ar.*Eq.*1354, *Th.*930; or sorrow, Amphis 30.6, Euphro 1.27; or thought, Epicr.11.21,23 (anap.). 3. *bow down under a burden*, D.18.323. 4. κύψαι, = ἀπάγξασθαι, Archil.35, cf. Phot. 5. of animals, *to be bowed forward*, opp. the erect figure of man, Arist.*PA*657ᵃ15; κέρεα κεκυφότα ἐς τὸ ἔμπροσθε horns *bent* forward, of certain African oxen, Hdt.4.183; ἐπὴν ὁ στόμαχος [τῆς ὑστέρης] ἐς τὸν ἀρχὸν κεκύφῃ Hp. l. c.

κύρα, v. κύριος B. 2. **κυρβάδωμεν**· κρύψωμεν, Hsch.

κυρβαίη, dub. sens., epith. of μάζα, Hom.*Epigr.*15.6 (κυρκαίη Suid. s. v. Ὅμηρος).

Κύρβας, αντος, ὁ, shortd. form of Κορύβας, Pherecyd.48 J.; dat. pl. Κυρβάντεσι S.*Fr.*862; gen. pl. Κυρβάντων Lyc.78, Call.*Jov.*46.

κυρβᾰσία, ἡ, *Persian bonnet* or *hat*, with a peaked crown, prob. much like the τιάρα (q. v.), Hdt.5.49, 7.64; ὥσπερ βασιλεὺς ὁ μέγας διαβάσκει ἐπὶ τῆς κεφαλῆς τὴν κ. τῶν ὀρνίθων μόνος ὀρθήν (sc. ὁ ἀλεκτρυών) Ar.*Av.*487 (cf. Sch.); a cover for a poultice for a woman's breast is compared to it in shape, Hp.*Mul.*2.186, cf. Aret.*CA*1.10. II. = Lat. *apex* (of the *flamines*), D.H.2.70.

κύρβεις, εων, αἱ, Ar.*Av.*1354, Lys.30.20, etc.; οἱ, Cratin.274 (but ταῖς codd. of Plu.*Sol.*25), Arist.*Ath.*7.1, Euph.6: κύρβιες *AP*4.4 (Agath.); acc. pl. κύρβιας A.R.4.280, *AP*4.3ᵇ.37 (Agath.): sg., v. infr. III, acc. κύρβιν Nonn.*D.*12.55; dat. κύρβιδι ib.37: (perh. akin to κόρυμβος):—at Athens, *triangular tablets*, forming a three-sided pyramid, turning on a pivot, upon which the early laws were inscribed, Cratin. l. c., Ar. l. c., Pl.*Plt.*298e, Lys.30.17, Arist. l. c.; described as being of wood, Plu. l. c.; of brass, Sch.Ar. l. c.; of stone, Apollod.*Fr. Hist.*107(a) J.; by some identified with ἄξονες, Eratosth.ap.Sch. A.R.4.280, Plu. l. c.; by others distd. from them, Ar.Byz.ap.*EM* 547.52, Sch.A.R. l. c., *AB*274, Hsch. II. later, of all *pillars* or *tablets with inscriptions*, Pl. l. c., Porph.*Abst.*2.21; of maps, A.R. l. c.; of wall-pictures, Nonn.*D.*12.32; κ. γηραλέαι, of Homer's poems, *AP*15.36 (Cometas), cf. 4.4 (Agath.): metaph., the *pillars* of Heracles, ib.4.3ᵇ.37 (Id.). III. in sg., metaph., of the Spartan scytale, Achae.19; of *a pettifogging lawyer*, as if *a walking statute-book*, Ar.*Nu.*448 (anap.); κ. ἑταιρικῶν κακῶν, of a ἑταίρα, Aristaenet.1.17, cf. Zen.4.77.

κύρβη, ἡ, dub. sens., κ. ἀργυρᾶ ἐν σανιδίῳ προσηλωμένη *IG*11(2).161*B*76, 199*B*10 (Delos, iii B.C.).

κύρβος, εος, τό, = κύρβις, Call.*Fr.*564.

κῡρεία, ἡ, contr. from κυριεία (q. v.).

Κύρειος [ῡ], α, ον, *of Cyrus*: οἱ Κ., his troops, X.*HG*3.2.7, al.

κῠρέω, A.*Pr.*332, S.*Tr.*386: impf. ἐκύρουν [ῠ] Id.*El.*1331: fut. κῠρήσω A.*Ch.*707, Hdt.1.112: aor. ἐκύρησα Hes.*Op.*755, Archil.18, Hom.*Epigr.*6.6, Hdt.1.31, E.*Hec.*215 (lyr.): pf. κεκύρηκα Pl.*Alc.*2.141b:—also **κύρω** [ῡ], Parm.8.49, A.R.2.363, *AP*9.710, etc.: impf. ἔκῡρον S.*OC*1159; Ep. κῦρον Il.23.821, *h.Cer.*189, *h.Ven.*174: fut. κύρσω Democr.243, S.*OC*225 (lyr.): aor. ἔκυρσα, part. κύρσας Il.3.23, Hes.*Sc.*426, *Op.*691, E.*Med.*1363:—Med., κύρομαι [ῡ] in act. sense, Il.24.530:—poet. Verb, of which the two forms are used as required by the metre, and some tenses occur in Ion. and (rarely) in other Prose: I. folld. by a case, *hit*, *light upon*, 1. c. dat., *meet with*, *fall in with*, ἄλλοτε μὲν.. κακῷ.. κύρεται ἄλλοτε δ' ἐσθλῷ Il.24.530; πήματι κύρσαι Hes.*Op.*691; λέων ὣς σώματι κύρσας Id.*Sc.* l. c.; ἅρματι κύρσας *having struck against* it, Il.23.428; μέγα δένδρεον αἰθέρι κῦρον *reaching to*.., Call.*Cer.*38, cf. A.R.2.363, 4.945, *AP*9.710; so ἐν πείρασι κ. Parm.8.49. b. of things, κυρεῖν τινι *befall* or *be granted to* him, S.*OC*1290, *Tr.*291, E.*Hec.*215 (lyr.); also εἰς ὅ τι κύρει ἕκαστα 'which way the wind blows', Timo 48.5. 2. c. gen., *hit* the mark, ἔκυρσας ὥστε τοξότης.. σκοποῦ A.*Ag.*628; *reach to* or *as far as*, μελάθρου κῦρε κάρη *h.Cer.*189; *meet with*, *find*, αἰδοίων βροτῶν κυρῆσαι Hom.*Epigr.*6.6; πικροῦ δ' ἔκυρσας.. μνηστῆρος A.*Pr.*739; Ἰαόνων ναυβατᾶν κύρσαντες Id.*Pers.*1012 (lyr.); αἰθερίας νεφέλας κύρσαιμι *would I could reach*.., S.*OC*1082 (lyr.). b. *attain to*, *obtain*, γάμων Archil.18; τέκνων κ. Hdt.1.31; καθαρσίου ib.35 (v. l.); βασιληΐης ταφῆς ib.112; δίκης Id.9.116; ἀτιμίης πρός τινων Id.7.158; κυρήσει νοστίμου σωτηρίας A.*Pers.*797; στυγερᾶς μοίρας τῆσδε κυρήσας ib.910 (anap.); κυροῦντα τῶν ἐπαξίων Id.*Pr.*70; βίου λῴονος κυρῆσαι S.*OT*1514; δυσπότμων γάμων κυρήσας Id.*Ant.*870 (lyr.); μητρὸς ὡς κακῆς ἐκύρσατε E.*Med.*1363, cf. *Ion* 1105 (lyr.); ἀμοιβῆς ἔκ τινος κυρεῖν Id.*Med.*23, cf. *Supp.*1170; ἀγαθῶν Pl.*Alc.*2.141b, Herod.3.57; λήτης Id.2.45; τόσσων ἐκύρησεν ὅσ' οὐ πευσεῖσθε βέβαλοι Theoc.3.51. 3. less freq. c. acc., *reach*, *find*, τί νῦν.. κυρῶ; A.*Ch.*214; βίον εὖ κυρήσας Id.*Th.*699 (lyr.); ἐπ' ἀκταῖς νιν κυρῶ E.*Hec.*698; τέρμονα κύρειν dub. cj. in Id.*Hipp.*746 (lyr.), cf. Opp.*H.*1.34. b. *obtain*, κυρούντων τὰ πρόσφορα A.*Ch.*714. II. abs., *happen*, *come to pass*, τί ποτ' αὐτίκα κύρσει; S.*OC*225 (lyr.); καλῶς, εὖ κυρεῖ *turns out* well, A.*Th.*23, S.*El.*799; of a person, Ἀτρείδην εἰδέναι κυροῦνθ' ὅπως *how he fares*, A.*Ag.*1371; also ἕτερα ἀφ' ἑτέρων κακὰ κυρεῖ *follow*, E.*Hec.*690 (lyr.); ἄλλα δ' ἐξ ἄλλων κ. Id.*IT* 865 (lyr.). 2. *to be right*, *hit the mark*, γνώμῃ κυρήσας by intelligence, S.*OT*398: c. part., τόδ' ἂν λέγων κυρήσαις in saying, A.*Supp.*589 (lyr.); ἐπεικάζων κυρῶ; S.*El.*663. b. *to be successful*, *prosper*, Democr.243. 3. as auxil. Verb, c. part., *turn out*, *prove to be* so and so, σεσωσμένος κυρεῖ A.*Pers.*503, cf. *Ag.*1201; ποῦ ποτ' ὢν κυρεῖς; S.*Ph.*805; θύων ἔκυρον Id.*OC*1159; ἐχθρὸς ὢν κυρεῖ E.*Alc.*954; εἰ κυρεῖ τις πέλας.. οἶκτον ἀΐων A.*Supp.*58 (lyr.): with part. omitted, acting merely as the copula, ἐκτὸς αἰτίας κυρεῖς Id.*Pr.*332, cf. *Pers.*598; ποῦ γῆς κυρεῖ; S.*Aj.*984; φονέα σε φημὶ.. κυρεῖν Id.*OT* 362; ἐν κακῷ τῳ φαίνῃ κυρῶν Id.*Ph.*741; ἐν πύλαισι.. κυρεῖ E.*Ph.*1067; ἔνθα πημάτων κυρῶ Id.*Tr.*685. 4. κ. πρός.. *refer to*, οὔτ' εἶπον οὐδὲν πρός ⟨σε⟩ κῦρον *Trag.Adesp.*226; τὰ πρὸς διαβολὴν κυροῦντα Plb.12.15.9.

κῡρηβ-άζω, fut. -άσω Ar.*Eq.*272:—prop. *butt with the horns*, like goats or rams, Sch.Ar. l. c.: metaph., τὸ σκέλος κυρηβάσει *he shall butt against* my leg, Ar. l. c.: aor. Med. κυρηβάσασθαι Cratin.462. II. metaph. in Med., = λοιδοροῦμαι, Hsch. (κυριβ- cod.), Phot. **-ᾰσία** and **-ᾰσις**, εως, ἡ, *butting* with the horns, Sch.Ar.*Eq.*272, Suid. **-άτης** [ᾰ], ου, ὁ, *quarreller*, prob. in Hsch. (κυριβ- cod.). **-ῐα**, ων, τά, *husks*, *bran*, Cratin.295, Hp.*Nat.Mul.*58, Epicur.*Fr.*293, etc. II. *bran-shop*, Ar.*Eq.*254. **-ῐοπώλης**, ου, ὁ, *dealer in bran*, Id.*Fr.*696 (lyr.). **-ίων**, ωνος, ὁ, nickname of Epicrates, D.19.287, Ath.6.242d. **-ος**, ὁ, = κυρηβάτης, Hsch. (-ιβος cod.).

κύρημα [ῠ], ατος, τό, = κύρμα, *windfall*, Phot., Suid.

Κυρηναϊκός, ή, όν, *Cyrenaic*: οἱ K. *the disciples* of Aristippus *of Cyrene*, D.L.2.85; Κυρηναϊκὴ φιλοσοφία, αἵρεσις, Str.17.3.22, D.L. 1.18.

Κυρήνη, ἡ, *Cyrene*, Hdt.4.162, etc.:—Adj. **Κυρηναῖος**, α, ον, ib. 199, etc. [ῠ in Hes.*Fr.*128.2, Pi.*P.*4.2, al., Call.*Ap.*73, 94; ῡ Ar. *Th.*98, A.R.2.500.]

κῡρί-α, ἡ, *authority, power*, Arist.*Mir.*837^{a}5, etc.; *possession, control*, οἴνου Plb.6.11^{A}.4; ταμιείου Id.6.13.1; τοῦ ἐπαποστεῖλαι στρατηγόν Id.6.15.6; κυρίαν ἔχειν περί τινος Id.6.14.10.—The form **κυρεία** is freq. found in Pap. and Inscrr. from i B.C., as *BGU*1123.6 (i B.C.), *PAmh.*2.95 i 6 (ii A.D.), and codd., as Plb.6.11^{A}.4, Lxx *Da.*11.5, Thd. *Da.*4.19, 6.26(7), Ph.2.52 (v.l.), Ath.10.440f (v.l.), *EM*427.9, and is required by metre in Man.4.606: contr. from **κυριεία** (q.v.). II. fem. of κύριος (q.v.). **-άξεις**· ἀποκακεῖς, Hsch. **-ακός**, ή, όν, (κύριος) *of* or *for an owner* or *master*, *Stud.Pal.*22.177.18 (ii A.D.); but usu. *of the Roman Emperor*, ὁ κ. φίσκος *the fiscus*, *CIG*2827 (Aphrod.), *Supp.Epigr.*2.567 (Caria (?)); κ. ψῆφοι, λόγος, *OGI*669.13, 18 (Egypt, i A.D.); κ. χρῆμα *POxy.*474.41 (ii A.D.). II. esp. *belonging to the Lord* (*Christ*): K. δεῖπνον *the Lord's Supper*, 1*Ep.Cor.*11.20; ἡ K. ἡμέρα *the Lord's day*, *Apoc.*1.10; τὸ Κυριακόν (sc. δῶμα) *the Lord's house*, Edict.Maximini ap.Eus.*HE*9.10. III. Subst. κυριακός, ὁ, spirit invoked in magic, *PMag.Par.*1.916. **-εία**, ἡ, *proprietary rights*, Mitteis *Chr.*31 v 37 (ii B.C.), *IG*2^{2}.1006.28 (ii B.C.), *SIG*685.133 (pl., Magn. Mae., ii B.C.), *BGU*1187.7 (i B.C.):—written **κυριήα** *Mon. Anc.Gr.*17.22:—later contr. **κυρεία, κυρία** (q.v.). **-ευτικός**, ή, όν, *concerning rights of property*, χρηματισμοί *Sammelb.*5232.22 (i A.D.); δίκαιον *Stud.Pal.*20.117.4 (V A.D.). Adv. **-κῶς** *with full proprietary rights*, *PAmh.*2.99(*b*).5 (ii A.D.), *PStrassb.*29.8, al. (iii A.D.). **-εύω**, *to be lord* or *master of*, πάντων X.*Mem.*2.6.22, cf. Arist.*EN*1160^{b}35; τῆς Ἀσίας X.*Mem.*3.5.11; μυρίων γῆς πήχεων Men.1099, cf. *PEleph.* 14.14 (iii B.C.), etc.; τῶν γενημάτων *PTeb.*105.47 (ii B.C.); τῆς θαλάττης Agatharch.5; ὧν ἁ πόλις..κυριεύει *IG*5(2).510.4 (Arc., ii B.C.); κυριεύειν τὴν γυναῖκα τοῦ ἀνδρός D.S.1.27; σανίδων Phld.*Mort.*24; νεκρῶν καὶ ζώντων *Ep.Rom.*14.9; κρατεῖν καὶ κ. *PStrassb.*14.22 (iii A.D.); *gain possession of, seize*, ζωγρίᾳ τινῶν Plb.1.7.11, al., cf. Ph.*Bel.*80. 41: later c. acc., τὰ σώματα καὶ τὴν βοῦν κ. *PGrenf.*1.21.13 (ii B.C.); τοῦ κυριεύοντος τὴν ὅλην οἰκουμένην *PMag.Lond.*121.838: abs., *to be dominant*, Chrysipp.*Stoic.*2.244:—Pass., *to be dominated, possessed*, ὑπό τινος Arist.*Mir.*838^{a}10. b. Astrol., of planets, κ. τοῦ σχήματος Ptol.*Tetr.*169, cf. Vett.Val.63.23:—Pass., οἱ -όμενοι τόποι Ptol. *Tetr.*112. 2. *to have legal power* to do, c. inf., Lex ap.Aeschin. 1.35. II. ὁ κυριεύων (sc. λόγος, wh. is expressed in Arr.*Epict.*2. 19.1), a logical puzzle, Plu.2.615a, Luc.*Vit.Auct.*22, etc., cf. *Stoic.* 2.93.

κῡρίζω, = κυρίσσω, *EM*548.2:—Pass., κυρίζεσθε· τρίβεσθε, Hsch.

κύριθον· τὴν σφαῖραν, Hsch. **κύριθρα**, τά, *wooden masks*, Id.; cf. κυριττοί.

κυρίλλιον, τό, *narrow-necked jug*, = βομβύλιος, Poll.10.68.

κύριξις [ῠ], εως, ἡ, *butting with the horns*, Ael.*NA*16.20.

κῡριοκτόνος, ον, *slaying a sovereign lord*, κ. πράξεις, of those who killed the son of Saul, J.*AJ*7.2.1.

κῡριο-λεκτέω, *use words in their proper* or *literal sense*, Alex.Aphr. *in SE*166.6; opp. τροπολεκτέω, in Pass., Eust.633.26, 836.58; κυριολεκτῶν, opp. καταχρηστικῶς, Phlp.*in de An.*490.19. **-λεξία**, ἡ, *use of literal*, opp. *figurative, expressions*, Herm.*in Phdr.*p.192 A., Eust. 624.41. **-λογέω**, = κυριολεκτέω, Magnus ap.Gal.8.640, Steph.*in Hp.*2.420 D. **-λογία**, ἡ, = κυριολεξία, Agatharch.21 (pl.), Phld. *Rh.*1.174 S., Longin.28.1, Magnus ap.Gal.8.641; *proper meaning* of a word, A.D.*Adv.*190.3; = ἀκριβολογία, Gal.18(2).526.

κύριος [ῡ], α, ον, also ος, ον A.*Supp.*732, E.*Heracl.*143, Arist.*Pol.* 1306^{b}20:—Thess. **κῦρρος** *IG*9(2).517.20 (Larissa, iii B.C.): (κῦρος) (not in Hom.): I. of persons, *having power* or *authority over*, c. gen., Ζεὺς ὁ πάντων κ. Pi.*I.*5(4).53, cf. *P.*2.58; ἐμῶν τε καὶ σῶν κ. πιστωμάτων A.*Ag.*878; πρὶν ἄν σε κ. στήσω τέκνων put thee *in possession of*.., S.*OC*1041; κύριοι πολιτείας Antipho 3.1.1; κ. καταλύσεως Th.4.20; εἰρήνης καὶ πολέμου X.*HG*2.2.18; -ώτατοι τοῦ ἱεροῦ Th.5.53 (but ὁ -ώτατος θεὸς τοῦ ἱεροῦ, of the god to whom a temple is dedicated, *OGI*90.39 (Rosetta, ii B.C.)); τῶν αὑτοῦ κ. Pl.*Lg.*929d, cf. Isoc. 19.34, etc.; θανάτου κ. τινός *with power of* life and death over, Pl. *Criti.*120d; κ. περί τινος Arist.*Pol.*1286^{a}24. 2. κύριός εἰμι c. inf., I *have authority* to do, *am entitled* to do, A.*Ag.*104 (lyr.); οὗτος κ. ὁρκωμοτεῖν (prob. for -ῶν) E.*Supp.*1189; κ. ἀπολέσαι, σῶσαι δ' ἄκυροι And.4.9, cf. Th.5.63, 8.5; -ώτεροι δοῦναι *better able* to give, Id.4.18; οὐ..κ. οὔτε ἀνελέσθαι πόλεμον οὔτε καταλῦσαι X.*An.*5.7.27; δοῦλοι κ. μαστιγοῦν τοὺς ἐλευθέρους Ephor.29 J.; αἱ ἀρχαὶ κ. κρίνειν Arist. *Pol.*1287^{b}16; also κ. τοῦ μὴ μεθυσθῆναι *having power* not to.., Id. *EN*1113^{b}32: c. acc. et inf., κ. εἶναι ἢ τοίαν εἶναι [πόλιν] ἢ τοίαν Pl.*R.* 429b. 3. folld. by a dependent clause, κ. γενέσθαι, ὅντινα δεῖ καταστήσασθαι Is.6.4. 4. c. part., πριαμένους τι ἢ πωλοῦντας κυρίους εἶναι Th.5.34; κ. ἦν πράσσων ταῦτα Id.8.51, cf. Plb.6.37.8, 18.37.10; κύριοι ἐόντω συλέοντες *Schwyzer* 337.13 (Delph.). 5. abs., *having authority, supreme*, τί τῶνδε κυριωτέρους μένεις; A.*Supp.*965; -ώτερος σέθεν E.*Ba.*505; ὁ πατὴρ μέχρι τούτου κ. [ἐστι] Arist.*Rh.*1402^{a}1; τὸ κ. the *sovereign power* in a state, Id.*Pol.*1281^{a}11, cf. Pl.*R.*565a, etc.; τὰ κ. the *supreme authorities*, D.19.259, Arist.*Rh.*1365^{b}27; τὰ τῆσδε τῆς γῆς κ. S.*OC*915; at Athens, κ. ἐκκλησία a *sovereign* or *principal* assembly, Ar.*Ach.*19, Arist.*Ath.*43.4, *IG*1^{2}.42.22, al., 2^{2}. 493.8, etc.; ἀγορὰ κ. ib.1298.7. II. of things, ὁ τῆς ὥρας τῆς καταρχῆς κ. [ἀστήρ] Serapio in *Cat. Cod. Astr.*1.99: but usu. abs., *authoritative, decisive*, δίκαι E.*Heracl.*l.c., And.1.88, Pl.*Cri.*50b; μῦθος -ώτερος *of more authority*, E.*IA*318 (troch.); -ωτάτη τῶν ἐπιστημῶν [ἡ πολιτική] Arist.*Pol.*1282^{b}15; αἱ -ώτεραι ἀρχαί Id.*Cael.*285^{a}26, cf. *Metaph.*997^{a}12; [ἡ φρόνησις] τῆς σοφίας κυριωτέρα Id.*EN*1143^{b} 34; -ωτέρα ἡ καθόλου [ἀπόδειξις] Id.*APo.*86^{a}23; τάραχος ὁ -ώτατος Epicur.*Ep.*1 p.30 U.; of *sovereign* remedies, -ωτάτη τῶν καθάρσεων Pl.*Sph.*230d; -ωτάτη κένωσις Gal.1.299; *important, principal*, κ. δόξαι, of certain doctrines of Epicurus, Phld.*Ir.*p.86 W.; τὰ -ώτατα μέρη τῆς φύσεως Epicur.*Sent.*9; -ώτερα μέρη τοῦ σώματος Philostr.*Gym.*50; τὰ -ώτατα the *principal* organs, Gal.1.385 (but, the *most important matters*, Epicur.*Sent.*16); τὸ -ώτατον τῆς Ἐφέσου Philostr.*VS*1.22.4: Gramm., κ. τόνος *principal* accent, D.T.*Supp.* 674.32. 2. opp. ἄκυρος, *valid*, νόμος, δόγματα, D.24.1, Pl.*Lg.* 926d; κ. ποιεῖν [τὴν γνῶσιν], opp. ἄκυρον π., D.21.92, cf. 39.15; τὰς συνθήκας κυρίας ποιεῖν Lys.18.15; ἡ συγγραφὴ ἥδε κ. ἔστω *PEleph.* 1.14 (iv B.C.); ἔστω τὰ κριθέντα κ. Lex ap.D.21.94; so τὰς τῶν ἄλλων δόξας κ. ποιεῖν Pl.*Tht.*179b. 3. of times, etc., *ordained, appointed*, ἡ κυρίη ἡμέρη Hdt.5.50, cf. 93 (pl.); ἡ κ. τῶν ἡμερέων Id.1.48, 6.129; κ. ἐν ἡμέρᾳ A.*Supp.*732; τόδε κ. ἦμαρ E.*Alc.*105 (lyr.), etc.; κ. μήν, of a woman with child, i.e. the ninth month, Pi.*O.*6.32; ὅταν τὸ κ. μόλῃ φάος (prob.) the *appointed* time, A.*Ag.*766 (lyr.); κ. μένει τέλος Id.*Eu.*544 (lyr.); ἡ κ. [ἡμέρα] D.21.84, cf. Test.ib.93; but αἱ κ. [ἡμέραι], = κριτικαί, Hp.*Aff.*9. 4. *legitimate, lawful*, ὕπνος πόνος τε, κ. ξυνωμόται A.*Eu.*127, cf. 327; κύρι' ἔχοντες having *lawful power*, ib. 960 (lyr.). 5. ἡ κ. ἀρετή goodness *proper, real* goodness, Arist.*EN* 1144^{b}4; [φλοιὸς] ὁ κ. Thphr.*HP*4.15.1; Rhet. and Gramm., κ. ὄνομα the *real* or *actual*, hence *current, ordinary*, name of a thing, opp. μεταφορά, γλῶττα, Arist.*Rh.*1404^{b}6, 1410^{b}12, *Po.*1457^{b}3, cf. D.H. *Comp.*21, D.L.10.13, etc.; σπάνει κυρίου ὀνόματος for lack of a *current* term, D.H.*Comp.*24; -ώτατα ὀνόματα *most ordinary* terms, ib.3 (hence also κ. ὄνομα *proper, personal* name, Plb.6.46.10, A.D.*Pron.* 10.11, al., Hdn.7.5.8; ὄνομα alone in this sense, Diog.Bab.*Stoic.*3. 213); κ. [λέξεις] Phld.*Rh.*1.181 S.; κατὰ τὸν κ. τρόπον, opp. καταχρωμένη, ib.1.59 S. III. Adv. κυρίως, v. sub voc.

B. Subst. **κύριος**, ὁ, *lord, master*, τοῖσι κ. δωμάτων A.*Ch.*658, cf. 689, S.*Aj.*734, etc.; ὁ κ. alone, *head* of a family, *master* of a house (cf. Sch.Ar.*Eq.*965), Antipho 2.4.7, Ar.*Pl.*6, Arist.*Pol.*1269^{b}10; τοὺς κ. τῶν οἰκιῶν *PTeb.*5.147 (ii B.C.); also, *guardian* of a woman, Is.6. 32, *PGrenf.*2.15 i 13 (ii B.C.), etc.: generally, *guardian, trustee*, Is. 2.10, D.43.15, 46.19, Men.*Epit.*89, etc. b. later κύριε, as a form of respectful address, *sir*, *Ev.Jo.*12.21, 20.15, *Act.Ap.*16.30 (pl.), *PFay.* 106.15 (ii A.D.), etc. 2. fem. κυρία, ἡ, *mistress, lady of the house*, Philem.223, Lxx *Is.*24.2, etc.; κ. τῆς οἰκίας Men.403: in voc., *madam*, D.C.48.44; applied to women from fourteen years upwards, Epict. *Ench.*40. (In later Gr. freq. written **κύρα**, *PGrenf.*1.61.4 (vi A.D.), etc.) b. epith. of Ἶσις, *OGI*180 (Egypt, i B.C.), etc. 3. of gods, esp. in the East, Σεκνεβτῦνις ὁ κ. θεός *PTeb.*284.6 (i B.C.); Κρόνος κ. *CIG*4521 (Abila, i A.D.); Ζεὺς κ. *Supp.Epigr.*2.830 (Damascus, iii A.D.); κ. Σάραπις *POxy.*110.2 (ii A.D.); ἡ κ. Ἄρτεμις *IG*14. 1124 (Tibur, ii A.D.); of deified rulers, τοῦ κ. βασιλέος θεοῦ *OGI*186.8 (Egypt, i B.C.); οἱ κ. θεοὶ μέγιστοι, of Ptolemy XIV and Cleopatra, *Berl.Sitzb.*1902.1096: hence, of rulers in general, βασιλεὺς Ἡρώδης κ. *OGI*415 (Judaea, i B.C.); of Roman Emperors, *BGU*1200.11 (Augustus), *POxy.*37 i 6 (Claudius), etc. 4. ὁ Κύριος, = Hebr. *Yahweh*, Lxx *Ge.*11.5, al.; of Christ, 1*Ep.Cor.*12.3, etc.

κῡρι-ότης, ητος, ἡ, *dominion*, *Ep.Eph.*1.21: in pl., *Ep.Col.*1. 16. 2. later, concrete, *authority*, *PMasp.*151.199 (vi A.D.), etc. II. *proper, legitimate use of a term*, Dam.*Pr.*306; = Lat. *proprietas*, Dosith.p.376 K. **-όω**, = κυρόω, dub. in Phld.*Piet.*107 (Pass.).

κῡρίσσω, Att. -ττω, fut. -ίξω (v. infr.), *butt with the horns*, like rams, Arist.*GA*769^{b}20, cf. Phot.; of bulls, ὁ ταῦρος δ' ἔοικεν κυρίξειν A.*Fr.*23, cf. Pl.*Grg.*516a; κ. ἀλλήλους σιδηροῖς κέρασι Id.*R.*586b; μόσχος κυρίττων Gal.4.692; ὁ κυρίττων (sc. λόγος), a logical puzzle, Chrysipp.*Stoic.*2.94: metaph., of floating corpses *knocking against* the shore, κ. ἰσχυρὰν χθόνα A.*Pers.*310.

κυριττοί, οἱ, *players who wear wooden masks*, in Italy, Hsch.; cf. κύριθρα.

κῡριωνῠμ-έω, *call by a proper name*, Eust.635.6 (Pass.). **-ία**, ἡ, *use of a proper name*, Id.652.40, etc. **-ικῶς**, Adv. *by a proper name*, οὐ κ. εἶπε τὸν Πᾶνα Pediasim. ad Theoc.*Syrinx* 3.

κῡρίως, Adv. of κύριος, *like a lord* or *master, with full authority*, τὰς πόλεις κ. παρείληφεν Isoc.4.137; κ. ζημιοῦν Arist.*Ath.*3.6, *SIG*1004. 11 (Oropus, iv B.C.). II. *surely, by fixed decree*, A.*Ch.*785 (lyr.). 2. *regularly, lawfully*, κ. ἔχειν to be *fixed, hold good*, Id.*Ag.*178 (lyr.), Is.7.26; κ. γίγνεσθαι Pl.*Lg.*925c; κ. αἰτεῖσθαι, *suo jure*, S.*Ph.*63; δόντος τοῦ πατρός D.36.32. III. *precisely, exactly*, διόψεσθαι τὸ ἀληθές Pl.*Prm.*136c. IV. *properly*, πρώτως καὶ κ. Arist.*EN*1157^{a} 31; τὸ κ. [ἓν καὶ εἶναι] Id.*de An.*412^{b}9; esp. of words, *in the proper sense*, opp. μεταφορᾷ or κατὰ μεταφοράν, κ. κατά τινος κατηγορεῖσθαι Id.*Top.*123^{a}35, cf. 139^{b}36; κ. λέγεσθαι Id.*Metaph.*1015^{a}14, cf. Str. 3.5.5, Phld.*Po.*5.19, etc.; ἡ λέξις αὕτη τοῦτο σημαίνει κ. Plb.2.22.1; *properly speaking*, D.T.632.23: Comp. -ώτερον, λέγεσθαι Arist.*EN* 1098^{a}6: Sup. -ώτατα, λέγεσθαι Id.*Cat.*14^{a}27. V. *in a special* (i.e. exceptional) *sense*, Olymp.*in Mete.*306.29.

κυρκαίη, v. κυρβαίη.

κυρκᾱν-άω, *mix*: metaph., *plot*, κ. ὄλεθρόν τινι Ar.*Th.*429, cf. 852: in literal sense, Hp.*Mul.*1.57 (Pass.), cf. *EM*543.53. **-η**, ἡ, = ταραχή, ib.548.43, cf. Hdn.Gr.1.451.

κύρμα, ατος, τό, (κύρω) *that which one meets with* or *finds*: hence, booty, prey, spoil, κ. γίγνομαι, c. dat., ἀνδράσι δυσμενέεσσιν ἕλωρ καὶ κύρμα γένησθε Il.5.488; κυσὶ κύρμα γενέσθαι 17.272; οἰωνοῖσιν ἕλωρ καὶ κ. γ. Od.3.271; θήρεσσιν 5.473; φώκῃσι καὶ ἰχθῦσι 15.480. II. of a person, *one who gets booty, swindler*, Ar.*Av*.431.

κύρνα· κρανία, Hsch. **κύρνικα**· κώδια, Id.

Κύρνος, ἡ, *Cyrnus*, ancient name of Corsica, Hdt.1.165:—Adj. **Κύρνιοι**, οἱ, Id.7.165; Κυρνία γῆ, prov. of *a nest of robbers*, Diogenian. 5.35. II. Appellat. **κύρνος**, ὁ, *bastard* (Maced.), Phot., cf. Hsch.

Κῦρος, ὁ, *Cyrus*: 1. ὁ πρότερος, *the elder Cyrus*, Hdt.1.46, etc. 2. ὁ νεώτερος, the brother of Artaxerxes, X.*An*.1.1.1, etc.

κῦρος, εος, τό, *supreme power, authority*, κ. ἔχειν ἀμφί τινος A.*Supp*. 391; τῶν πρηγμάτων τὸ κ. ἔχειν Hdt.6.109; ἅπαν τὸ κ. ἔχειν Th.5.38, cf. Pl.*Grg*.450e, al.; κ. ἔχειν περί τινος Id.*Cra*.435c; τὸ κ. τῆς ἐνεργείας *principle* or *origin* of a function, Gal.10.459. 2. concrete, *one invested with authority*, Pl.*Lg*.700c. II. *confirmation, validity*, ἔχειν κ., = κεκυρῶσθαι, S.*OC*1779 (anap.), cf. *POxy*.2110.12 (iv A.D.), etc.; ἡ νῦν.. ὑπάρξει κ. ἡμέρα καλῶν S.*El*.919; κ. λαβεῖν, of a law, *to be ratified*, D.C.38.17, al.:—κῦρος and all derivs. are post-Hom. (Cf. Skt. *śūras* 'valiant', OIr. *caur* 'hero', Welsh *cawr* 'giant'.)

κῡρόω, fut. -ώσω Hdt.6.86.β': (κῦρος):—*confirm, ratify*, δόμοις.. τήνδ' ἐκύρωσας φάτιν A.*Pers*.227 (troch.); τῇδ' ἐκύρωσεν φάτις ib.521; ταῦτα Hdt. l. c.; τὸν γάμον Id.6.126; ἡ ἐκκλησία κυρώσασα ταῦτα διελύθη Th.8.69; Ζεῦ, ταῦτα κυρώσειας Ar.*Th*.369 (lyr.); μοῖραν Pl.*R*. 620e; τὴν γνώμην Plb.1.11.1; τὰς διαλύσεις Id.1.17.1:—Med., *accomplish one's end*, λόγῳ κυροῦται τὰ πάντα Pl.*Grg*.451c, cf. d:—Pass., *to be ratified, determined*, ἐκεκύρωτο ὁ γάμος Κλεισθένεϊ Hdt.6.130; οὐδὲ κυρωθῆναι ἔμενον τὸ πρῆγμα Id.8.56, cf. Th.4.125; τοὺς κυρωθέντας [τῶν νόμων] And.1.85, cf. D.20.93; τὸ ψήφισμα τὸ κυρωθὲν περὶ τούτων *IG*7.303.45 (Orop.); κυρωθέντος τοῦ δόγματος Plb.1.11.3; of a contract, *to be sanctioned*, *PPetr*.2p.44 (iii B.C.); in auctions, *to be knocked down*, *BGU*992i9 (ii B.C.); ὁ κυρωθεὶς the highest bidder, to whom an object is knocked down, *PRev.Laws*48.17 (iii B.C.): generally, ποῖ κεκύρωται τέλος; at what point *hath* the end *been fixed* or *determined?* A.*Supp*.603, cf. *Ch*.874, E.*Hipp*.746 (v. l.); πρὶν κεκυρῶσθαι σφαγάς before it *has been accomplished*, Id.*El*.1069: c. inf., ἐκεκύρωτο συμβάλλειν it *had been decided* to fight, Hdt.6.110; ἐκυρώθη ναυμαχέειν Id.8.56. 2. κ. δίκην *decide* it, A.*Eu*.581, 639. 3. c. acc. et inf., *decree* or *ordain* that.., τηρηθῆναι τὸν νόμον Arist.*Fr*. 593. 4. of arguments or doctrines, *confirm, establish*, Phld.*Po. Herc*.1676.3; κ. ὅτι.. Id.*Sign*.7.

κύρρασι· τοῖς κέρασιν ἐπιτυχεῖν (cf. **κυρσεῖν** similarly expld.) κρούσαντ.., Hsch.

κυρσάνιος, ὁ, Lacon. word, = νεανίας, contemptuously, *whippersnapper*, Ar.*Lys*.983, 1248; cf. σκυρθάλια.

κύρσεος, = πρωκτός, Gal.19.116.

κυρσερίδες· τὰ τῶν μελισσῶν ἀγγεῖα, κυψελίδες, Hsch. **κυρσίον**· μειράκιον, Id.; cf. κυρσάνιος. **κυρσός**, *gibberosus*, *Gloss*.

κυρτ-αίνω, *rise into a heap* or *hump*, ἡ γῆ ἐκύρτᾱνε *PMag.Leid.W*. 4.42, al. II. *to be bent, stoop*, ὑπὸ τῆς βίας Suid. s.v. ὑβός. **-αύχην**, ὁ, ἡ, gen. ενος, *with bulging neck*, Quint.1.5.70. **-εία**, ἡ, *fishing with the κύρτη*, Ael.*NA*12.43. **-εύς**, έως, ὁ, *one that fishes with the κύρτη*, Herod.3.51, Opp.*H*.3.352:—also **-ευτής**, οῦ, ὁ, *AP*6.230 (Maec.). **-η**, ἡ, = κύρτος, *weel, lobster-pot*, Hdt.1.191, D.S.3.19; used as a *sieve* or *riddle*, σχοινίδι κ. Nic.*Al*.625. 2. *bird-cage*, Archil.177. **-ήν**, *gibbus*, *Gloss*. **-ία**, ἡ, (κύρτος) *wicker-work*: a *wicker shield*, D.S.5.33. **-ιάω**, (κυρτός) *to be hunchbacked*, νῶτά τε κυρτιόωντας Man.4.119. **-ίδιον**, τό, Dim. of κυρτίς, *strainer*, Dsc.1.52. **-ιον**, τό, part of a chariot, Poll.1.143. **-ίς**, ίδος, ἡ, *weel, lobster-pot*, Opp.*H*.5.600; *strainer*, Nic.*Al*.493, Dsc.1.52, Gal. 13.55.

κυρτο-βόλος, ὁ, (κύρτος) *fisherman*, -βόλων συνεργασία, Μουσ. Σμυρν.1873/5.65 (Smyrna). **-ειδής**, ές, Astrol., of signs under which *hunchbacks* are born, Thrasyll. in *Cat.Cod.Astr*.8(3).100, Vett. Val.11.13. 2. of the moon, ἐξ ἀμφοτέρων -ειδής, = ἀμφίκυρτος, Paul. Al.*G*.4. 3. gloss on κυφός, *EM*545.35. **-νεφέλη** (fort. κυσθο-), epith. of a ἑταίρα, *Com.Adesp*.1059.

κύρτ-ος, ὁ, = κύρτη 1, Sapph.120, Pl.*Sph*.220c, *POxy*.520.20 (ii A.D.); τῷ τοῦ κ. πλέγματι Pl.*Ti*.79d; μήτε ἐγρηγορόσιν μήτε εὕδουσι κύρτοις ἀργὸν θήραν διαπονουμένοις *weels* that secure a lazy prey for men whether asleep or awake, Id.*Lg*.823e (hence prov. εὕδοντι κ. αἱρεῖ Diogenian.4.65), cf. Lib.*Ep*.86.1; κύρτῳ θηρεύουσι τοὺς ἰχθῦς Arist. *HA*603ª7. 2. *bird-cage*, λυγοτευχὴς *AP*9.562 (Crin.). **-ός**, ή, όν, *bulging, swelling*, κῦμα Il.4.426; κύματα κυρτὰ φαληριόωντα 13. 799, cf. Sosicr.2; θάλασσα κυρτὸν ἐπαφρίζῃ Mosch.*Fr*.1.5; τὼ δέ οἱ ὤμω κυρτώ *humped*, Il.2.218, cf. *AP*11.120; τὸ κ. τῶν ὤμων Jul. *Or*.6.201b: hence, *hunchbacked*, *PFay*.121.15 (i/ii A.D.); βραχίων κ. πέφυκεν ἐς τὸ ἔξω μέρος Hp.*Fract*.8; κ. τροχὸς E.*Ba*.1066; κυρτὴ κάμηλος Babr.40.2; καρῖδες Ophel.1: Comp. κυρτότερος Phlp. *in Ph*. 696.26: Sup. κυρτότατον φύλλον Thphr.*HP*3.10.5. 2. *convex*, opp. κοῖλος, οὔσης [τῆς γῆς] κυρτῆς καὶ σφαιροειδοῦς Arist.*Mete*.365ª 31; περὶ τὰς ἐκλείψεις [ἡ σελήνη] ἀεὶ κυρτὴν ἔχει τὴν ὁρίζουσαν γραμμήν Id.*Cael*.297ᵇ28; κ. ἐπιφάνεια *convex* surface of a shield, Plb.6. 23.2; of blood-vessels, *bulging*, Sor.1.44. **-ότης**, ητος, ἡ, *humped shoulders, stoop*, ἡ Πλάτωνος κ. Plu.2.26b; *convex surface* of a bone, etc., Gal.*UP*2.7, 12.5 (pl.), al.; of the spherical moon, Plu. 2.922d; of the earth, Cleom.1.8; τῆς θαλάσσης Str.1.1.20, Theo Sm. p.123 H. 2. *convexity*, opp. κοιλότης, of a line, Arist.*Ph*.217ᵇ3, *Mete*.386ª1, cf. Hero *Spir*.1.23. **-όω**, *hump up, make convex*, κυρτῶν νῶτα, of a bull preparing to charge, E.*Hel*.1558; τὴν χεῖρα ὑπὲρ τοῦ μετώπου κεκυρτωκότες Ath.14.629f; καταιγίδες εἰς οὐρανὸν κυρτοῦσι τὰ κύματα Lib.*Or*.59.138; λαίφεα *AP*10.15 (Paul. Sil.); κ. ὀστοῦν *make* the skull *bulge*, Antyll.ap.Orib.46.27.6:—Pass., κῦμα περιστάθη, οὔρεϊ ἶσον, κυρτωθέν Od.11.244; κυρτοῦσθαι ῥάχιν Opp.*C*.3.273; of leeches, Opp.*H*.2.602: in Prose, οἱ φοίνικες ὑπὸ βάρους πιεζόμενοι ἄνω κυρτοῦνται ὥσπερ οἱ ὄνοι οἱ κανθήλιοι X.*Cyr*.7.5.11; *become hunchbacked*, Sor.1.112: aor. 1 Med. ἐκυρτώσαντο *bulged*, δειρήν Nonn. *D*.37.564. **-ώδης**, ες, = κυρτοειδής 1, ζῴδιον *Cat.Cod.Astr*.7. 205. **-ωμα**, ατος, τό, *bulge*, κ. τοῦ ὀστέου its natural *convexity*, Hp. *Fract*.8; μεταφρένου Luc.*Ind*.7; τὸ κατὰ τὴν ῥάχιν κ. D.S.2.54: in pl., of the earth's *convexity*, Cleom.1.2, 2.6. 2. *rotundity*, ἀσκοῦ Hp. *Art*.47; *swelling*, Id.*Prog*.11 (pl.); of sham pregnancy, Id.*Prorrh*.2. 26; *outside of bowl* of a cup, Ath.11.488d; *convex front* of half-moon formation, Plb.3.113.8, Onos.21.6. **-ών**, ῶνος, ὁ, *hunchback*, Crates Theb.9. **-ωσις**, εως, ἡ, *bulging*, of blood-vessels, Sor. 2.8. 2. *convexity* of the sea's surface, Theo Sm.p.122 H. 3. *being humpbacked*, Gal.18(1).494, Vett.Val.109.35; τοῦ σώματος Ptol.*Tetr*.151 (pl.). II. κύρτωσις· τὸ μέσον τῆς ῥάχεως, *EM*774. 12. **-ωτός**, ή, όν, *hunchbacked*, Vett.Val.13.2.

κύρω, v. κυρέω.

κύρ-ωσις [ῡ], εως, ἡ, *ratification*, Th.6.103, *Sammelb*.4512 (ii B.C.), etc.; τῶν λεγομένων J.*AJ*4.8.44; πᾶσα.. ἡ κ. διὰ λόγων ἐστί Pl. *Grg*.450b. **-ωτήρ**, ῆρος, ὁ, *one who has the κῦρος, sovereign*, Hsch. **-ωτής**, οῦ, ὁ, *one who ratifies* or *confirms*, *IG*2².1678*a A* 27.

κύσαι [ῠ], Ep. **κύσσαι**, aor. inf. of κυνέω:—but **κῦσαι** of κύω.

κυσανίζει· ὁμιλεῖ, Hsch. **κυσέρη**· πυθμήν, χάσμα, Id. **κυσήγη**· ῥοιά, Id.

κυσθοκορώνη, = νύμφη, *Com.Adesp*.1060.

κύσθος, ὁ, *pudenda muliebria*, Eup.233, Ar.*Ach*.782, al. II. **κύσθος**, εος, τό, a marine substance used in dyeing, *PHolm*.22.42.

κῡσιάω, = πασχητιάω, *Com.Adesp*.1061.

κυσίβαλον, etym. of σκύβαλον, Suid. s. v. σκυβαλίζεται.

κῡσο-βάκχᾰρις, ιδος, ὁ, = ὁ τὸν κυσὸν μυρίζων, *Com.Adesp*.1062. **-δακνιᾷ**· ψωριᾷ, Hsch. **-δόχη**, ἡ, a sort of stocks, Alciphr.3. 72. **-κόλαξ**, v. κνισοκόλαξ. **-λάκων** [ᾰ], ωνος, ὁ, = παιδεραστής, from the Spartans being accused of the practice, Aristarch.ap. Hsch., *Com.Adesp*.1063. **-λαμπίς**, ίδος, ἡ, = πυγολαμπίς, Hsch. **-λέσχης**, ου, ὁ, *obscene talker*, *Com.Adesp*.1066. **-νίπτης**, ου, ὁ, = πόρνος, ib.1064.

κυσός, ὁ, = κύσθος 1, Hsch. II. = πυγή, Id. III. = κύστις, Herod.2.44, *Lyr.Adesp*.25. [ῡ Herod. l. c., prob. in Call.*Iamb*.1. 159; ῠ dub. in *Lyr.Adesp*. l. c.; κῦσος Theognost.*Can*.72.]

κυσο-χήνη, ἡ, = κυσοδόχη, Hsch. II. = εὐρυπρωκτία, Id., Phot. **-χωλος**, = ἐγκυσίχωλος, *Com.Adesp*.6 D. (κυσινό- cod. Phot.).

κύσσα, κύσσαι, v. κυνέω.

κύσσαρος, ὁ, = κυσός II, ἀρχός II, Hp.*Nat.Puer*.17, Gal.19.176, Erot.

κύστεροι· ἀγγεῖα τῶν μελισσῶν, καὶ τυρίσκοι (fort. ὑρίσκοι), Hsch.

κύστη, ἡ, = ἄρτος σπογγίτης, Hsch.; but, = *fiscella* (i. e. κίστη), *Gloss*.

κύστιγξ, ιγγος, ἡ, Dim. of κύστις, Hp.ap.Gal.19.116.

κύστιον, τό, (κύστη) *plant which bears its fruit in a bladder*, = ἁλικάκκαβον, Hsch.

κύστις, εως, ιος, also ιδος Aen.Tact.31.12 (cf. infr. II), ἡ: (κύω):—*bladder*, Il.5.67, 13.652, S.*Fr*.394, Hp.*Art*.41, Pl.*Ti*.91a, Ph.*Bel*. 102.40, etc.; ὥσπερ κύστιν φυσᾶν, of the wind swelling out the clouds, Ar.*Nu*.405; κ. ὑεία used as a *pouch*, Id.*Fr*.504; οἴνου κύστεις μεστάς Phanod.19. II. in pl. κύστιδες, *bags* under the eye, Arist.*Phgn*. 811ᵇ14: sg., Adam.1.22. III. *ulcer* on horse's back, *Hippiatr*.26.

κυστόφῐλος, ὁ, *end of catheter*, which carried the *folliculus*, Cael. Aur.*TP*2.23.

κύταρον· ζωμήρυσις, Hsch.

κύτῖν-ος, ὁ, *flower of the pomegranate*, Thphr.*HP*2.6.12, Dsc.1. 110, Gal.12.917, Cael.Aur.*TP*4.52; properly the *calyx*, Thphr.*CP* 1.14.4, cj. in *HP*1.13.5; also ὑοσκυάμου κ. Dsc.1.10. II. = ὑποκιστίς, ib.97. **-ώδης**, ες, *like a* κύτινος, Thphr.*HP*4.10.3.

κυτίς, ίδος, ἡ, *small chest, trunk*, Sch.Ar.*Pax*665 (leg. κοιτίς).

κῠτῐσηνόμος, ον, (νέμομαι) *eating* κύτισος, [χελύνη] Nic.*Al*.560.

κύτῐσος [ῠ], ὁ (ἡ Theoc.5.128, 10.30), *tree-medick, Medicago arborea*, Hp.*Nat.Mul*.93, Cratin.98.8, Eup.14.3, Arist.*HA*522ᵇ28, Thphr. *HP*4.16.5, *CP*5.15.4, Theoc. ll. cc., Dsc.4.112. II. *bastard ebony, Laburnum vulgare*, Thphr.*HP*1.6.1, 5.3.1.

κυτμίς, ίδος, ἡ, a kind of soothing *ointment*, Luc.*Alex*.22 (pl.), 53.

κῠτογάστωρ, ορος, ὁ, ἡ, *with capacious belly*, prob. for κυάστορας in *AP*6.305 (Leon.).

κύτος [ῠ], εος, τό, (κύω) *hollow*, κύκλου, of a shield, A.*Th*.495; ἀσπίδος E.*Fr*.185; θώρηκος Ar.*Pax*1224; περίπλευρον κ. E.*El*.473 (lyr.); λέβητος Id.*Cyc*.399; τρίποδος Id.*Supp*.1202; κύλικος Pl.Com.189; λοπάδος Xenarch.1.10; *hold* of a ship, Plb.16.3.4. 2. *vessel, jar*, A.*Ag*.322, 816, S.*El*.1142, etc.; πλεκτὸν κ. *basket*, E.*Ion*37; κοιλοσώματον κ. Antiph.52.2. 3. of any hollow container, τὸ τῆς κεφαλῆς κ. Pl.*Ti*.45a; τὸ ὄπισθεν κ. *occiput*, Arist.*PA*656ᵇ26; τοῦ θώρακος τὸ κ., i. e. the chest, Pl.*Ti*.69e; ποδῶν κ. Achae.4.4 (leg. πλευρῶν); τὸ ἄνω κ. Arist.*GA*742ᵇ14 (also of plants, = αἱ ῥίζαι, 741ᵇ35, al.); τὸ λοιπὸν ἅπαν κ., of the uterus, Gal.*UP*14.14, cf. Sor.1.9; of the fourth stomach of the ox, Phlp. *in APo*.417.14; τὸ τῆς ψυχῆς κ., i.e. the body, Pl.*Ti*.44a: hence, abs., *body*, ἀνδρείῳ κύτει S.*Tr*.12; *trunk*, διὰ παντὸς τοῦ κ. Pl.*Ti*.74a; τὸ ἀπ' αὐχένος μέχρι αἰδοίων κ. Arist.*HA*

491^{a}29, cf. *PA*686^{b}14; τὸ ὅλον κ. τοῦ σώματος D.S.1.35, cf. Archig. ap.Gal.13.262: metaph., of the πόλις, Pl.*Lg.*964e; τὸ σύμπαν τῆς πόλεως κ. τείχεσιν ἠσφάλισται Plb.5.59.8. 4. κ. ἀστέριον starry *vault* of heaven, Vett.Val.172.32.

κύτρα, Sicil. for χύτρα, Greg.Cor.p.341 S.

κυττάρ-ιον [ᾰ], τό, Dim. of κύτταρος, Arist.*GA*760^{b}34, 770^{a}29. **-ον**, τό, = sq., Ar.*Th.*516 (nisi leg. κύτταρος). **-ος**, ὁ, *cell of a honey-comb*, Id.*V.*1111, Arist.*HA*551^{b}5, 554^{a}18, 555^{a}1. 2. pit in the receptacle of *Nelumbium speciosum*, Thphr.*HP*4.8.7. b. male flower of the pine, ib.3.3.8, 3.7.3. c. = ἐχῖνος III. 1, τῶν δρυῶν οἱ κ., Hsch. 3. metaph., τοὐρανοῦ τὸν κ. the *pinnacle of the dome* of heaven, Ar.*Pax*199.

κυττοί, οἱ, *receptacles*, Hsch.

κῡφᾰγωγ-έω, *carry the neck arched* (v. sq.), Lib.*Decl.*31.15. **-ὸς** ἵππος, ὁ, a horse *that goes with the neck arched*, X.*Eq.*7.10.

κύφαλα, τά, etym. of κύμβαλα, *EM*545.33.

κῡφᾰλέος, α, ον, poet. for κυφός, *AP*6.297 (Phan.).

Κῠφᾰρισσ-ία, ἡ, = Κυπαρ–, epith. of Artemis Agrotera, *IG*5(1).977 (Lacon.). **-ινος**, = κυπ–, ib.4.1588.7 (Aegina, v B.C.). **-ίτᾱς** [ῑ], α, ὁ, epith. of Pan, *BCH*27.295 (Crete).

κύφελλα [ῠ], τά, (cf. κύπελλον):—only in Alexandrian Poets, 1. *hollows of the ears*, Lyc.1402. 2. *clouds of mist*, Call.*Fr.*300; κ. ἰῶν *clouds* of arrows, Lyc.1426.

κύφερον ἢ **κυφήν**· κεφαλήν (Cret.), Hsch.

κῦφι, εος, and εως, τό, *an Egyptian compound incense*, Dsc.1.25, Plu. 2.372d, 384b, Gal.13.199, Damocr.ap.eund.14.117:—freq. written **κοῖφι**, Ath.2.66f, Aristid.*Or.*47(23).26 (κοιφί), *PMag.Lond.*46.221, 121.538.

κῡφο-γέρων, οντος, ὁ, *old man bent with age*, Steph. *in Hp.*2.276 D. **-ειδής**, ές, *of the nature* or *quality of* κῦφι, Androm.ap.Gal. 13.198, Archig.ap.Aët.16.88. **-νωτος**, ον, *crook-backed*, Antiph. 217.18. **-ομαι**, Pass., *have curvature of the spine*, Hp.*Art.*41; κυφοῦται ῥάχις ibid., cf. Gal.7.782.

κῡφός, ή, όν, (κύπτω, κέκῡφα) *bent forwards, stooping, hunchbacked*, ὃς δὴ γήραϊ κ. ἔην καὶ μυρία ᾔδη Od.2.16; κ. ἀνήρ, πρεσβύτης, Ar.*Ach.* 703, *Pl.*266; σφόνδυλοι ἕλκονται ἐς τὸ κ., in *curvature* of the spine, Hp.*Art.*41; τρίγλαι κ. Epich.64; freq. of shrimps, from their form, Eub.111, Matro *Conv.*64, *AP*5.184 (Asclep.); τῶν καρίδων αἱ κυφαί *shrimps*, e.g. *Palaemon squilla*, Arist.*HA*525^{b}1, cf. 549^{b}12; of birds, Id.*IA*710^{b}18; also ὑπὸ κ. ἄροτρον *IG*14.2012.14 (Sulp. Max.); cf. κύφων I. II. *curved, round*, of a cup, Ath.11.482e.

κῦφος, εος, τό, *hump, hunch*, Hdn.Gr.1.225, Aët.ap.Phot.*Bibl.* p.180 B.. II. = κύπελλον, *EM*549.8.

κῡφ-ότης, ητος, ἡ, *a being bent* or *humpbacked*, Hld.6.11. II. *rotundity*, Ath.11.482e. **-όω**, = κύπτω, κύφοντα ὀφθαλμοῖς *with downcast* eyes, Lxx *Jb.*22.29. **-ωμα**, ατος, τό, *hump on the back*, Hp.*Art.*41 (sg. and pl.); κυφώματα σπονδύλων Ruf.ap.Orib.45.30. 43. **-ων**, ωνος, ὁ, (κυφός) *crooked piece of wood, bent yoke of the plough*, Thgn.1201: κύφωνες, οἱ, *two bars* in the frame of a chariot, Poll.1.143. II. *pillory*, ἐν τῷ κ. αὐχένα ἔχειν Cratin.115, cf. Ar. *Pl.*476, 606; δεθῆναι ἐν τῷ κ. Arist.*Pol.*1306^{b}2; μαστιγούσθω ἐν τῷ κ. *OGI*483.177 (Pergam.). 2. *one who has had his neck in the pillory, knave*, Archil.178, Luc.*Pseudol.*17. III. part of a woman's dress, Posidipp.44. IV. Archit., *curved beam*, *IG*4^2(1).102.224, al. (Epid., iv B.C.). V. part of a water-wheel, *PLond.*3.1177.213 (ii A.D.). **-ώνιον**, τό, a kind of *salve*, Alex.Trall.1.10. **-ωνισμός**, ὁ, *punishment by the* κύφων, Sch.Ar.*Pl.*476. **-ωσις**, εως, ἡ, *being humpbacked*, Hp.*Art.*41, 47 (pl.), Gal.18(1).74.

κύχραμος, ὁ, a bird that migrates with quails, perhaps *corn-crake, Rallus crex*, or *water-rail, Rallus aquaticus*, Arist.*HA*597^{b}17 (vv.ll. κέχραμος, κίχραμος).

κυψάλη, ἡ, = sq., *PSI*4.358.8 (iii B.C.).

κυψέλη, ἡ, *any hollow vessel*: *chest, box* (whence Cypselus was called), Hdt.5.92.ε΄, Plu.2.164a, Paus.5.17.5; ἑξμέδιμνος κ., of *a corn-chest*, Ar.*Pax*631; *bee-hive*, Plu.2.601c: metaph., κυψέλαι φρονημάτων *boxes* full of thoughts, *Com.Adesp.*703. II. *hollow of the ear*, Poll.2.85, Hsch.: hence, 2. = κυψελίς II, *ear-wax*, κυψέλην.. ἔχεις..ἐν τοῖς ὠσίν, prov. of stupid men, *Com.Adesp.*620, cf. Eup. 213, Alex.Aphr.*Pr.*2.63.

Κυψελίδαι, οἱ, *descendants of Cypselus*, Thgn.894, Hdt.6.128, Pl. *Phdr.*236b.

κυψέλ-ιον, τό, Dim. of κυψέλη I, *bee-hive*, Arist.*HA*627^{b}2. **-ίς**, ίδος, ἡ, = foreg., of swallows' or sand-martins' nests, ib.618^{a}34. II. *wax in the ears*, Ruf.*Onom.*223, Aret.*SD*1.15, Luc.*Lex.*1, Lib.*Decl.* 26.35:—also **-ίτης** ῥύπος, ὁ, *EM*549.24.

κυψελόβυστος, ον, (βύω) *stopped up with wax*, ὦτα Luc.*Lex.*1.

κυψελος, ὁ, = ἄπους II, Arist.*HA*618^{a}31. 2. κύψελον· κύβερτον μελισσῶν, Hsch. II. = κυψελίς II, Tz.*H.*8.199.

κύω, post-Hom. form of κυέω (aor. 1 in Ep., v. infr. II): I. in pres. and impf., of females, *conceive*, Λάβδα κύει τέξει δὲ κτλ. Orac.ap. Hdt.5.92.β΄, cf. Ar.*Fr.*609, Pl.*Lg.*789e, etc.; κύω μῆνα ὄγδοον ἤδη Luc.*DMeretr.*2.1; κ. ἀπό τινος Id.*Gall.*19: metaph., κύει πόλις ἥδε Thgn.39. 2. rarely c. acc., *to be pregnant with*, οὐδὲ κύουσι πολλὰ κυήματα Arist.*HA*543^{b}22; παιδίον Luc.*DMeretr.*2.4: metaph., ἡ ψυχή μου ἀεὶ τοῦτο κύουσα (al. κυοῦσα) διῆγεν X.*Cyr.*5.4.35:—Pass., *to be borne in the womb*, τὰ κυόμενα παιδία Arist.*Pr.*860^{a}21, Jul.*Or.*2. 99c. II. in aor. Act. ἔκῡσα, causal, of the male, *impregnate*, metaph., ὄμβρος ἔκυσε γαῖαν A.*Fr.*44.4:—aor. Med. ἐκῡσάμην, of the female, *conceive*, οὓς τέκε κυσαμένη Hes.*Th.*125, cf. 405, *h.Hom.*1.4; Ζηνί by Zeus, Asius *Fr.Ep.*1.3 K.; ὅσσους..Τυφάονι κύσατο Κητώ Euph.112.—The forms κυέω and κύω seem synonymous, but κυέω (κυῶ) is the better-attested form in Att. Prose (κύοντα only v.l. in Pl. *Tht.*151b, κύοντες is read in Arist.*HA*544^{a}23 (v.l. κύονες, ποιοῦντες), κύοντα ib.585^{a}3, κυόμενα (v.l. -ούμενα) *Pr.* l.c., κυόμενον (v.l. -ούμενον) *GA*730^{b}4, but κυοῦντες *HA*610^{b}3; ἐκύομεν Lxx *Is.*59.13).—The pres. κύω has ῠ in verse, but forms of κυέω can be restored by altering the accent.—The causal sense belongs only to the aor. ἔκῡσα.

κύων [ῠ], ὁ and ἡ, both in Hom., the masc. more freq., gen. κῠνός, dat. κῠνί, acc. κύνα, voc. κύον Il.8.423, κύων Archipp.6: pl., nom. κύνες, gen. κυνῶν, dat. κυσί Il.17.272, al., Ep. κύνεσσι 1.4, acc. κύνας:—*dog, bitch*, Hom., etc.; of *shepherds' dogs*, Il.10.183, 12.303; *watch-dogs*, 22.66; but in Hom. more freq. of *hounds*, Il.8.338, al.; κυσὶ θηρευτῇσι 11.325; κύνε εἰδότε θήρης 10.360; later, when of *hounds*, mostly in fem., S.*Aj.*8, E.*Hipp.*18, etc.; κ. Λάκαινα Pi.*Fr.*106, S. l.c., X. *Cyn.*10.1, cf. Arist.*HA*608^{a}27, al.; Μολοττικαὶ κ. Alexis Hist.ap. Ath.12.540d, etc.; but Ἰνδικοί Arist.*GA*746^{a}34, cf. Hdt.1.192: prov., κυσὶν πεινῶσιν οὐχὶ βρώσιμα 'not fit for a dog', *Com.Adesp.*1205.4; χεῖρον ἐρεθίσαι γραῦν ἢ κύνα Men.802; κύνα δέρειν δεδαρμένην 'flog a dead horse', Pherecr.179; ἡ κ. κατακειμένη ἐν τῇ φάτνῃ 'dog in the manger', Luc.*Ind.*30, al.; χαλεπὸν χορίω κύνα γεῦσαι it's ill to let a dog 'taste blood', Theoc.10.11; νή or μὰ τὸν κύνα was a favourite oath of Socrates, Pl.*Ap.*22a (cf. Sch.), *Grg.*482b; used familiarly at Athens, Ar.*V.*83; οἷς ἦν μέγιστος ὅρκος..κύων, ἔπειτα χήν· θεοὺς δ' ἐσίγων, of primitive men, Cratin.231. II. as a word of reproach, freq. in Hom. of women, to denote shamelessness or audacity; applied by Helen to herself, Il.6.344, 356; by Iris to Athena, 8.423; by Hera to Artemis, 21.481: of the maids in the house of Odysseus, Od.18.338, al.: later, in a coarse sense, Ar.*V.*1402; ἡ ῥαψῳδὸς κ., of the Sphinx, S.*OT*391, cf. A.*Fr.*236 (lyr.); of men, κακαὶ κ. Il.13.623; implying recklessness, 8.299, 527, Od.17.248, 22.35; also of offensive persons, compared to yapping dogs, Lxx *Ps.*21(22).17, *Ep.Phil.*3.2; κ. λαίθαργος, = λαθροδήκτης, metaph., of a person, S.*Fr.*885, cf. E. *Fr.*555: prov., μὴ δῶτε τὸ ἅγιον τοῖς κ. *Ev.Matt.*7.6. 2. metaph., of persons, *watch-dog, guardian*, τῶν σταθμῶν κ., of Agamemnon, A. *Ag.*896; δωμάτων κ., of Clytemnestra, ib.607, cf. Ar.*Eq.*1023. 3. of the Cynics, ἀρέσκει τούτοις κυνῶν μεταμφιέννυσθαι βίον Phld.*Sto.Herc.* 339.8: hence, *Cynic philosopher*, Arist.*Rh.*1411^{a}24, *AP*7.65 (Antip.), 413 (Id.), Plu.2.717c, Ath.5.216b, Epigr.ap.D.L.6.19, 60, Baillet *Inscriptions des tombeaux des rois* 172. III. freq. in Mythology of the *servants, agents* or *watchers* of the gods, Διὸς πτηνὸς κύων, of the eagle, A.*Pr.*1022, cf. *Ag.*136 (lyr.), S.*Fr.*884; of the griffins, Ζηνὸς ἀκραγεῖς κ. A.*Pr.*803; of the Furies, μετάδρομοι..πανουργημάτων ἄφυκτοι κ. S.*El.*1388 (lyr.), cf. A.*Ch.*924, E.*Fr.*383; Pan is the κύων of Cybele, Pi.*Fr.*96: Pythag., Περσεφόνης κύνες, of the planets, Arist. *Fr.*196: so Com., Ἡφαίστου κ., of sparks, Alex.149.16; of various mythical beings, as Cerberus, κ. Ἀΐδαο Il.8.368, cf. Od.11.623, X. *An.*6.2.2; Harpies, A.R.2.289; of Hecate, in Mithraic worship, Porph.*Abst.*4.16; of the Βάκχαι, Λύσσας κ. E.*Ba.*977 (lyr.); Λέρνας κ., of the hydra, Id.*HF*420 (lyr.); of a great fish, Τρίτωνος κ. Lyc. 34. IV. *dog-fish* or *shark*, Od.12.96, cf. Epich.68, Cratin.161, Arist.*HA*566^{a}31; κ. ἄγριος, κ. γαλεός and κ. κεντρίτης or κεντρίνη, Opp.*H.*1.373, Ael.*NA*1.55; ξιφίας κ., of the *sword-fish*, Anaxipp. 2.3. V. = σείριος (q.v.), *dog-star*, i.e. *the hound of Orion*, Il.22. 29; in full, σειρίου κυνὸς δίκην S.*Fr.*803, cf. A.*Ag.*967; κυνὸς ψυχρὰν δύσιν S.*Fr.*432.11; πρὸ τοῦ κυνὸς Eup.147; μετὰ κυνὸς ἐπιτολήν, περὶ κ. ἐ., Arist.*Mete.*361^{b}35, *HA*602^{a}26; ἐπὶ κυνί ib.600^{a}4, Syngr.ap.D. 35.13; ὑπὸ κύνα Arist.*HA*547^{a}14, D.S.19.109; περὶ κύνα Thphr.*CP* 3.3.3; μετὰ κύνα Id.*HP*1.9.5; also of the whole constellation, Arat. 327, Gal.17(1).17. VI. *the ace, the worst throw* at dice, Poll.9.100, Eust.1289.63. VII. *frenum praeputii*, Antyll.ap.Orib.50.3.1: with pun on the prov. ap.Pherecr. l.c. (supr. 1), Ar.*Lys.*158: with pun on signf. v, *AP*5.104 (Marc. Arg.). VIII. *fetlock of a horse, Hippiatr.* 77. IX. *unilateral facial paralysis*, Gal.8.573. X. = ἀπομαγδαλία, Dsc.ap.Eust.1857.19. XI. ξυλίνη κ., = κυνόσβατος, Orac.ap.Did.ap.Ath.2.70c. XII. *piece in the game of* πόλεις, Cratin.56.3 (dub.). (Cf. Skt. *śvā*, gen. *śúnas*, Lith. *šuõ*, gen. *šuñs*, Lat. *canis*, Goth. *hunds* (κύων), etc.)

κω, v. πω. **κῴα**, v. Κῷος III. 3. **κωαί**· ἀστράγαλοι, Hsch. (ante κώϊον, fort. κῶια). **κωάζω**, = ἀστραγαλίζω, Id. 2. = ἐνεχυράζω, Id. (also in form κοιάζω).

Κῳακός, ή, όν, *of Cos*: Κῳακαὶ προγνώσιες or αἱ Κῳακαί, title of work by Hippocrates of Cos.

κῶας, τό, in Hom. nom. acc. sg. κῶας; pl. κώεα, dat. κώεσι; later contr. κῶς (q.v.):—*fleece*, στόρεσαν λέχος,..κῶεά τε ῥῆγός τε Il.9.661, cf. Od.23.180; ἀδέψητον βοέην στόρεσ', αὐτὰρ ὕπερθε κώεα πόλλ' οἴων 20.3, cf. 142; χεῦεν ὑπὸ χλωρὰς ῥῶπας καὶ κῶας ὕπερθεν 16.47; φέρε δὴ δίφρον καὶ κῶας ἐπ' αὐτοῦ 19.97; ἵδρυσεν παρὰ δαιτὶ κώεσιν ἐν μαλακοῖσι 3.38, cf. 17.32; of the *Golden Fleece*, κ. αἰγλᾶεν χρυσέῳ θυσάνῳ Pi.*P.*4. 231; ἔπλεον ἐπὶ τὸ κ. ἐς Αἶαν Hdt.7.193; μέγα κ. Mimn.11.1; τὸ χρύσειον κ. Theoc.13.16.—Cf. κῴδιον.

κωβάθια, τά, *arsenical sulphides of cobalt*, Ps.-Democr.Alch.p.51 B. (κοβ–), Zos.Alch.p.188 B. (κωβ–, v.l. κοβ–):—hence **κωβαθηκαύστης**, ου, ὁ, 'arsenic-burner', applied to Nilus, ib.191 B. (vv.ll. κωβατικ–, κωβαθιοκ–).

κώβαλοι, οἱ, *pomegranate-flowers*, Hsch. **κῶβαξ**· ὁ μέγας τέττιξ, Id. **κωβάριον**, *globus*, *Gloss.* **κωβήλη**, ἡ, *needle*, Hsch. II. *sexual intercourse*, Id., Phot. **κωβηλίνη**, ἡ, (foreg. I) *needlewoman*, Hsch. **κωβιδάριον**, v. κωθάριον.

κωβίδιον, τό, Dim. of sq., Anaxandr.27.4, Sotad.Com.1.22, Arist. *Fr.*309. [-βῐ- Anaxandr. l.c. (anap., s.v.l.), but -βῑ- Sotad. l.c. (iamb.).]

κωβιός, ὁ, a fish of the *gudgeon* kind, Semon.15, Epich.66, Hp. *Int.*21, Pl.*Euthd.*298d, Antiph.26.19, Men.*Kol.Fr.*7. II. = τιθύμαλλος χαρακίας, Dsc.4.164; = τ. δενδροειδής, Plin.*HN*26.71.

κωβῖτις, ιδος, ἡ, *like the gudgeon*, ἀφύη Arist.*HA*569b23, cf. Hices. ap.Ath.7.285b.

κωβιώδης, ες, *like a* κωβιός, Plu.2.980f.

κῳδάριον [ᾰ], τό, Dim. of κῴδιον, Cratin.41, Ar.*Ra.*1203, Anaxandr. 34.11.

κωδᾶς, ᾶτος, ὁ, *dealer in sheepskins*, *POxy.*1519.4 (iii A.D.).

κώδεα, v. sq. II.

κώδεια, ἡ, *head*, ὁ δὲ φῆ, κώδειαν ἀνασχών Il.14.499; of plants, *head*, e.g. of garlic, *bulb*, Nic.*Al.*432; of the poppy, *capsule*, Gal. 12.73:—also **κωδία**, ἡ, dub. in Ar.*Fr.*117 (κώδυα Harp. Epit., κώδεια Suid.), f.l. for κώδεια in Poll.2.38, for κωδύα in Dsc.4.63 (pl.), Orib. 11 s.v. μικρὰ μήκων, for κώδυια in Arist.*Pr.*914b27; **κώδειον** or **-ιον**, *Gloss.* (cf. κώδυον); **κωδίς**, Hsch.; cf. κωδύα, κώδων II. II. *cup shaped like a poppy-head*, in form **κώδεα**, *Inscr.Délos* 298*A* 169 (pl.), 300*B* 13 (iii B.C.).

κῴδιο, barbarism for sq., Ar.*Th.*1180.

κῴδιον, τό, Dim. of κῶας, *sheepskin*, *fleece*, Ar.*Eq.*400, *Ra.*1478, Pl. *Prt.*315d, Men.*Sam.*189, *IG*1^2.80.17, 11(2).287*A* 24 (Delos, iii B.C.), *PPetr.*2 p.108 (iii B.C.), etc.; of the *Golden Fleece*, Luc.*Gall.*1. II. Δῖον κ. ram's *fleece* used in purificatory ceremonies, Polem.Hist.87, 88.

κῳδιοφόρος, ον, *clad in sheepskin*, Str.17.2.3.

κωδύα, ἡ, *head*, i.e. *capsule*, of the poppy, Thphr.*HP*9.12.4, Damocr.ap.Gal.13.40, Dsc.4.63 (v.l. -ίαις), 64, Sor.1.120 (τῇ διακωδίων cod.), Ruf.*Ren.Ves.*1.15; imitated as an ornament of ἧλοι, *IG* 2^2.1457.14, 1544.38, al.; *head*, i.e. *fruit*, of the Nile water-lily, *Nymphaea stellata*, Thphr.*HP*4.8.10; of the Egyptian bean, *Nelumbium speciosum*, ib.7. [κωδύα acc. to Hdn.Gr.1.302, and so in Damocr. l.c., but κώδυα in Ar.*Fr.*117 ap.Harp.Epit., Phot., cf. sq.]

κώδυια, ἡ, *head*: hence, *bulb*, *cup* of the κλεψύδρα, Arist.*Pr.*914b 27 (vv.ll. κωδύαν, κωδίαν: these forms, as well as κώδεια (q.v.), are prob. derived from κώδυια).

κώδυον, τό, *head*, i.e. *inflorescence*, of purse-tassels, *Muscari comosum*, Thphr.*HP*6.8.1. (From κωδύα as κάρυον from καρύα, etc.)

κώδων, ωνος, ὁ (Att. ἡ S.*Aj.*17, dub. in Ar.*Pax* 1078), *bell*, ὑπ' ἀσπίδος δὲ τῷ χαλκήλατοι κλάζουσι κ. φόνον A.*Th.*386, cf. 399, E.*Rh.*308; χαλκοστόμου κώδωνος ὡς Τυρσηνικῆς, i.e. a trumpet, S. l.c. (where Sch. expl. κώδων as τὸ πλατὺ τῆς σάλπιγγος, i.e. the *mouth* of the trumpet, cf. Ath.5.185a, Poll.2.203); carried on rounds of inspection to challenge sentries, τοῦ κώδωνος πα, ενεχθέντος Th.4.135; ἐφοδεύειν κώδωνι Plu.*Arat.*7, cf. Luc.*Merc.Cond.*24, Sch.Ar.*Av.*843. 2. *crier's bell*, hence ταῦθ' οὗτος μόνον οὐ κώδωνας ἐξαψάμενος διαπράττεται 'is his own trumpeter', D.25.90: metaph., ἡ κ. ἀκαλανθίς (ὅτι λάλον τὸ ζῷον Sch.) Ar.*Pax* 1078 (perh. κύων is the true reading, v. *App. Prov.*1.12); cf. κρόταλον. II. = κωδύα, τῆς μήκωνος Dieuch.ap. Orib.4.6.2.

κωδων-ίζω, *try*, *prove by ringing*, of money, Ar.*Ra.*723 (Pass.); ὅ τι ποιεῖ κ. ib.79: metaph., βούλομαι κωδωνίσας πέμψαι σε Anaxandr. 15.5:—wrongly expld. by Hsch. from the challenging of sentries (cf. κώδων I. 1). II. Pass., *to have one's name noised abroad*, *EM* 325.21. **-ιον**, τό, Dim. of κώδων, J.*AJ*3.7.4, Phlp. *in de An.*356. 20, prob. in *BGU*162.10 (ii/iii A.D.), cf. Hdn.*Epim.*71.

κωδωνό-κροτος, ον, *of* or *with jingling bells*, σάκος S.*Fr.*859 (lyr.); κ. κόμποι E.*Rh.*383 (anap.). **-φᾰλᾰρόπωλος**, ον, *with jingling harness*, coined by Ar.*Ra.*963, as a parody on Aeschylus. **-φορέω**, *carry the bell round*, *inspect sentinels*, Ar.*Av.*842, Nicopho 26, D.C.54. 4:—Pass., ἅπαντα κωδωνοφορεῖται Ar.*Av.*1160. 2. of a ship, *carry a bell*, Philostr.*VA*3.57. II. Pass., of a king, *to be attended by men with bells*, Str.15.1.58.

κῶθα· ποτήρια, Hsch.

κωθάριον, τό, Dim. of sq., cj. in Anaxandr.27.3 (κωβιδαρίων codd.).

κῶθος, ὁ, Sicel name for κωβιός, Numen.ap.Ath.7.304e, 309c.

κωθύλους· ὄνους, Hsch.

κώθων, ωνος, ὁ, *Laconian drinking-vessel*, used by soldiers, Archil. 4, Ar.*Eq.*600, X.*Cyr.*1.2.8, Critias 34 D., *IG*2^2.47.6, etc.; κ. στρεψαύχην Theopomp.Com.54; πυριγενής Henioch.1; φαεινός Ar.*Pax* 1094 (parod.); of earthenware or metal, *IG*4^2(1).121.79, al. (Epid.), Ath.11.483b, c; κ. χαλκοῖ *IG*1^2.313.55, al., cf. 2^2.1425.393. II. *drinking bout*, *carousal*, εἰσῆλθεν ἐπὶ κώθωνα πρὸς τὸν βασιλέα Macho ap.Ath.13.583b, cf. Plu.*Ant.*4, etc.; *religious banquet*, *BCH*51.220 (Thasos). III. Sicel, = κῶθος, Nic.*Fr.*141, Apollod.ap.Ath.7. 309c. IV. the inner harbour at Carthage, Str.17.3.15, App.*Pun.* 127.

κωθων-ία, Ion. -ίη, ἡ, *deep potation* (not of wine), Aret.*SD*2. 13. **-ίζω**, *make drunken*, Hsch., Phot.:—Pass., *drink hard*, κ. ταῖς μεγάλαις (sc. κύλιξι) Arist.*Pr.*872b28, cf. Lxx *Es.*3.15, Mnesith. ap.Ath.11.484a, Phylarch.1 J., Gal.*UP*4.13; κ. ἀφ' ἡμέρας, *de die potare*, Plb.23.5.9; κεκωθωνισμένος *inebriated*, Eub.126, cf. *PSI*3.172. 23 (ii B.C.). **-ιον**, τό, Dim. of κώθων, *AJA*31.350 (vase, v B.C.), *IG* 7.303.56 (Oropus), *PMag.Par.*1.2952, *Gp.*20.10. **-ισμός**, ὁ, *tippling*, Arist.*Pr.*863b25, Mnesith.ap.Ath.11.484a (pl.). **-ιστήριον**, τό, *banqueting house*, D.S.5.19. **-ιστής**, οῦ, ὁ, *toper*, Ath.10. 433b.

κωθωνο-ειδής, ές, *like a* κώθων, Suid. s.v. προχόῳ. **-πλύτης** [ῠ], ου, ὁ, *one who cleans the fish* κώθων, Sophr.45. **-ποιός**, ὁ, κώθων-*maker*, Dinarch.*Fr.*89.19. **-χειλος**, ον, *with the lip* or *rim of a* κώθων, κύλιξ Eub.56.3 (-χειρος codd.).

Κῴος, α, ον, contr. Κῷος (q.v.).

κώκαλον· παλαιόν, καὶ εἶδος ἀλεκτρυόνος, Hsch.

κώκ-ῡμα, ατος, τό, *shriek*, *wail*, in pl., λιγέα κ. A.*Pers.*332; ὀξέα S. *Aj.*321; ὄρθια Id.*Ant.*1206. **-ῡτίς**, ίδος, ἡ, *born from Cocytus*, Νύμφη Opp.*H.*3.487. **-ῡτός**, ὁ, *shrieking*, *wailing*, κωκυτῷ τ' εἴχοντο καὶ οἰμωγῇ Il.22.409, cf. 447, Pi.*P.*4.113, A.*Ch.*150 (pl.); κωκυτὸν ἱέναι, ἠχεῖν, S.*Aj.*851, *Tr.*867; ἀνάγειν E.*Ph.*1350 (lyr.): also in late Prose, Luc.*Luct.*12, Ach.Tat.1.13. II. as pr. n. Κωκῡτός, ὁ, *Cocytus*, *River of Wailing* (cf. 'Αχέρων), Od.10.514, A.*Ag.*1160, E.*Alc.* 458 (lyr.), etc. **-ύω** [v. fin.], fut. -ύσω A.*Ag.*1313, -ύσομαι Ar.*Lys.* 1222: aor. ἐκώκῡσα S.*Ant.*28; Ep. κώκυσα Il.18.37:—Med., *AP*7.412 (Alc. Mess.):—*shriek*, *wail*, in Ep. and Trag. always of women, Il.18. 37, Od.2.361, etc.; κλαῖον καὶ ἐκώκυον 19.541: freq. with Adv., λίγ' ἐκώκῠε Il.19.284, cf. Od.4.259, etc.; ὀξὺ δὲ κωκύσασα (opp. βαρὺ στενάχων, of the man) Il.18.71; κώκῡσεν δὲ μάλα μέγα 22.407: also in late Prose, Plu.2.357c, etc.; even of men, Luc.*DMort.*21.1, Longus 2.21; and so Ar., as an execration, μακρὰ κωκύειν κελεύω σε *Ra.*34; οἰμώζοι γ' ἂν καὶ κωκύοι *Ec.*648. 2. c. acc., *lament* or *shriek over* one dead, also prop. of women, κώκυσ' ἐν λεχέεσσιν ἐὸν πόσιν Od.24. 295; ἐμὴν μοῖραν κ. A.*Ag.*1313, cf. S.*Ant.*28, al.: Com., of men, κωκύσεσθε τὰς τρίχας μακρά Ar.*Lys.*1222: also in late Prose, as Porph.*Abst.*4.9, etc. (Cf. Skt. *káuti* 'cry' (intens. *kokūyatē*), Lith. *kaũkti* 'shriek', etc.) [ῠ in Hom. before a vowel, ῡ before a conson. (v. supr.): later ῡ sts. before a vowel, κωκῡ́οι Ar.*Ec.* l.c., κωκῡ́ουσα Bion 1.23, Q.S.3.779, κωκῡ́εσκε ib.460.]

κωλαβοί· λάσταυροι, Hsch.

κωλακρετ-έω, *to be a* κωλακρέτης, *IG*1^2.25.9: aor. 1 ἐκωλακρέτησαν *CIG*3660 (Cyzicus). **-ης**, ου, ὁ, name of a financial official in early Athens and elsewhere (cf. foreg.), *IG*1^2.19.13, al., Arist.*Ath.* 7.3, Ar.*V.*695, *Av.*1541; κωλακρέτου γάλα, comically for the μισθὸς δικαστικός, Id.*V.*724. (Written κωλαγρ- in Cod. Rav. of Ar., Tim. *Lex.*; derivation from κωλᾶς ἀγρεῖν or ἀγείρειν perh. implied by Suid. s.v. κωλακρέτης.)

κωλανιζόμενοι· τάχει χρώμενοι, ἀνέμοις ἴσα, Hsch. **κωλαρίας**· τοὺς ἐκ τῆς ἀγέλης παῖδας, Id. (Fort. κωραλίας.)

κωλάριον, τό, Dim. of κῶλον, *fragment of a verse*, *hemistich*, Ael. Dion.*Fr.*168, Sch.Ar.*Pax* 179.

κωλέα, ἡ, = κωλῆ (q.v.); also expld. by ἀγκαλίς, δέσμη χόρτου, Hsch. **κώλειρ**, *prize given in a contest*, Id. **κωλεός**, ὁ, = κωλῆ, Epich.82, 92, Hp.ap.Gal.19.116. **κωλετίναις** (-τήν- cod.)· ἀσκαλαβώταις, Hsch.

κωλῆ, ἡ, contr. from κωλέα, which occurs in Anaxipp.1.38, Lxx 1*Ki.*9.24: **κωλία** (v. κωλίαν) is a dialectal form: (κῶλον):—*thighbone with the flesh on it*, *ham*, esp. of a swine, Ar.*Pl.*1128, *Fr.*224, X. *Cyn.*50.30, Pl.Com.17 (pl.), Amips.7; ἐρίφου Xenoph.6.1; βοὸς κ. Luc.*Lex.*6; the portion of the priestess at a sacrifice, *IG*2^2.1361.5, *SIG*1015.10 (Halic.), etc. II. *membrum virile*, Ar.*Nu.*989, 1019.

κωλήβη· μήποτε ὁ λάσταυρος· κώληβοι γὰρ οἱ ταῦροι, Phot.

κωλήν, ῆνος, ἡ, = κωλῆ, *thigh*, *leg*, κωλῆνες νεβρῶν E.*Fr.*677, cf. Eup.47; κ. ὑείων κρεῶν *hams*, Hp.*Epid.*7.62: in pl., *bones of the leg*, Arist.*HA*516b1:—Dim. **κωληνάριον**, τό, Sch.Ar.*Pl.*1129.

κώληξ, ηκος, ὁ, = sq., Sch.Ar.*Pl.*1129.

κώληψ, ηπος, ἡ, (κωλῆ) *hollow of the knee*, = ἰγνύα, Il.23.726, Nic. *Th.*424.

κωλίαν· ἰγνύαν κτλ., Hsch.

Κωλιάς (sc. ἄκρα), άδος, ἡ, *Colias*, a promontory of Attica, Hdt.8. 96; with a temple of Aphrodite, St.Byz.: hence, as epith. of the goddess, Ar.*Nu.*52, *Lys.*2; Κωλιάδες γυναῖκες Orac.ap.Hdt. l.c. 2. (sc. γῆ), *potter's clay* of high repute, *dug at Colias*, Plu.2.42d.

κωλίζω, in Pass., *to be arranged according to* κῶλα, τὰ κεκωλισμένα βιβλία Olymp.Hist.p.463 D.; esp. of poetical works, *to be arranged according to metrical* κῶλα, Ar.Cod.Ven.Subscr.

κωλῐκ-εύομαι, Pass., *suffer from colic*, Alex.Aphr.*Pr.*2.73, Alex. Trall.8.2. **-ός**, ή, όν, (κῶλον II. 6) *suffering in the colon*, *having colic*, prob. l. in Dsc.2.54, Gal.8.40; ἡ κ. διάθεσις *colic*, from its being seated in the colon and parts adjacent, Id.8.384; κ. φάρμακα remedies *for colic*, Id.13.266; κ. ἀντίδοτος Androm.ap.eund.13.276. Adv. **-κῶς** Gal.19.3.

κωλοβαθρ-ιστής, οῦ, ὁ, *one that goes on stilts*, Hsch. s.v. καδαλίων. **-ον**, τό, *stilt*, Artem.3.15 (v.l. καλ-).

κωλο-ειδής, ές, *in members*. Adv. **-δῶς** Sopat.in Rh.8.9W. **-μετρία**, ἡ, (κῶλον II. 4) *measurement of metrical phrases*, Suid. s.v. Εὐγένιος.

κῶλον, τό, *limb*, *member* of a body, esp. *leg*, A.*Pr.*325, S.*OC*183 (lyr.), *Ph.*42, etc.; δρομάδι κ. E.*Hel.*1301 (lyr.); κ. ταχύπουν Id.*Ba.*168 (lyr.): mostly in pl., A.*Pr.*81, S.*OC*19; χεῖρες καὶ κῶλα E.*Ph.*1185: generally, of *arms* and *legs*, and of animals, *fore* and *hind legs*, τὰ ἐμπρόσθια κ. Pl.*Ti.*91e; τὰ ἔμπροσθεν καὶ τὰ ὄπισθεν κ. Arist.*HA*498a 3, cf. *PA*690a20, etc.; δέρμα, τρίχας, ὄνυχάς τε ἐπ' ἄκροις τοῖς κώλοις ἔφυσαν Pl.*Ti.*76e. 2. = κωλῆ 1, A.*Pr.*496. 3. of plants, *limb*, *arm*, σκολιῆς ἄγρια κ. βάτου *AP*7.315 (Zenod. or Rhian.): in pl., also, *internodes* of the νάρθηξ, Corn.*ND*30. II. generally, *member*, 1. of a building, *side* or *front*, of a square or triangular building, Hdt.2.126, 134, 4.62, 108, Pl.*Lg.*947e. b. *upright* of a ladder, Apollod.*Poliorc.* 182.5, al. 2. *limb* or *lap of the race-course*, διαύλου θάτερον κ. A.

*Ag.*344. 3. Rhet., *member* or *clause of a* περίοδος, Arist.*Rh.*1409b13, Phld.*Rh.*1.165 S., D.H.*Comp.*22, Quint.9.4.22, Demetr.*Eloc.*1, Hermog.*Id.*1.3, 2.3; στίζομεν κατὰ κῶλον Castor in Rh.3.721 W.; διελὼν πρὸς κῶλον, of Origen in his Hexapla, Eus.*HE*6.16. 4. in verse, *metrical unit containing fewer than three* συζυγίαι *without catalexis*, Heph.*Poëm.*1; *element of a* στροφή, D.H.*Comp.*19, etc. 5. ῥινοῦ ἐΰστροφα κ., poet. for *a sling*, *AP*7.172 (Antip. Sid.). 6. incorrect form for κόλον (q. v.), Isid.*Etym.*4.7.38, etc.; cf. κωλικός.

κωλο-πλάστης, ου, ὁ, *manufacturer of artificial limbs* (as votive offerings), *PGiss.*20.20 (ii A. D.). **-τομέω**, prop. *cut off limbs*: generally, *cut* or *mow down*, Δημήτερα Epic.ap.Plu.2.377d.

κώλ-ῡμα, ατος, τό, *hindrance*, τί γὰρ ἐμπόδιον κ. ἔτι μοι; E.*Ion* 862 (anap.); κ. θεῶν ἢ ἡρώων Th.5.30; βασιλικὸν κ. *PFrankf.*1.100 (iii B. C.): pl., κωλύματα καὶ βλάβαι D.H.9.9: c. inf., *hindrance against*, ἅμαξα κ. οὖσα προσθεῖναι [τὰς πύλας] Th.4.67; κωλύματα μὴ αὐξηθῆναι [τὸ Ἑλληνικόν] Id.1.16: c. gen., κ. φορᾶς *impediment* to motion, Pl.*Cra.*418e; ἐνεργείας Ocell.4.12: c. dat., [τῷ αἵματι] Hp.*Flat.*8: κ. καὶ σίνος πρὸς εὐκαρπίαν Thphr.*CP*2.7.5. II. *defence against* a thing, σβεστήρια κ. Th.7.53: c. gen., κ. δηλητηρίων Hdn.1.17.10. **-ῡμάτιον**, τό, Dim. of foreg., *catch* or *clutch* in a machine, Hero *Spir.*1.17, al. **-ύμη** [ῡ], ἡ, = κώλυμα, ἐπὶ κωλύμῃ for the purpose of *hindering*, Th.1.92; ταῖς κ. ταύταις ἱκανῶς.. εἰρχθῆναι by these *impediments*, Id.4.63; a poetical word in Th., cf. D.H.*Amm.*2.3.

κωλυπηγορέω, *talk grandly* or *at random*, πρὸς τὸ παρὸν δόξης ἕνεκεν τῆς οἰκείας f.l. in Sever.*Clyst.*p.43 D. (κυλικηγοροῦμεν cj. Dietz).

κωλῡσ-άνέμας, ου, ὁ, or **-άνεμος**, ὁ, *checking the winds*, epith. of Empedocles, Timae.94, Suid. s. v. Ἐμπεδοκλῆς; cf. ἀλεξάνεμος.

κωλῡσί-δειπνος [ῐ], ον, *interrupting the banquet*, applied to a species of κοχλίας, Apollod.ap.Ath.2.63d, cf. Plu.2.726a. **-δρόμης**, ου, ὁ, *one who obstructs the course*, Luc.*Trag.*198. **-εργέω**, *hinder, obstruct operations*, Plb.6.15.5, Ph.1.64,240, J.*AJ*15.11.7. **-εργός**, όν, *hindering from work*, τοῦ φιλοσοφεῖν Iamb.*Protr.*21.κβ'.

κώλῡ-σις, εως, ἡ, *prevention*, ἕνεκα κωλύσεως Pl.*Sph.*220c; κωλύσεις τῶν συμπερασμάτων Arist.*Top.*161a15, cf. Phld.*Mort.*19; εἰς κώλυσιν μὴ ἐντελὲς τὸ κράτος εἶναι App.*BC*1.1: in Astrol. sense, Vett. Val.142.24 (pl.). **-τέον**, *one must hinder*, X.*Hier.*8.9, Gal.10.649, al. 2. **-τέος**, α, ον, *to be hindered* or *stopped*, Hp.*Art.*58, D.H.10.40. **-τήρ**, ῆρος, ὁ, = κωλυτής, τῶν ἀδικούντων Archyt.3; θεοὶ.. τῶν κακῶν κ. Porph.ap.Eus.*PE*4.9; ἀριθμὸς κ. τῶν περαιτέρω ἐπιμορίων Iamb.*in Nic.*p.52 P. **-τήριος**, α, ον, *preventive*, σημεῖα κ. τινός *of*.., D.H.11.62; θῦσαι τὰ κωλυτήρια (sc. ἱερά) Iamb.*VP*28.141, Apollon.*Mir.*4: as Subst. **κωλυτήριον**, τό, παρατριμμάτων Dsc.1.103. **-τής**, οῦ, ὁ, *hinderer*, τῆς διαβάσεως Th.3.23, cf. D.18.72; πηλὸν.. κωλυτὴν παρασχεῖν Pl.*Criti.*109a: abs., *OGI*5.7 (Scepsis, iv B. C.), Vett. Val.139.19. **-τικός**, ή, όν, *preventive*, τινος *of* a thing, X.*Mem.*4.5.7 (Comp.), Arist.*Rh.*1362a29, *EN*1096b12, Thphr.*Ign.*45, Epicur.*Ep.*2 p.52 U., Porph.*Abst.*2.47: abs., in Astrol., ἀστὴρ ἄπρακτος καὶ κ. Vett.Val.178.30. **-τός**, ή, όν, *to be hindered*, Arr.*Epict.*2.5.8, al.; ὑπό τινος ib.1.17.27.

κωλύφιον, τό, Dim. of κωλῆν, condemned by Phryn.60: Lat. *colyphium*, Plaut.*Pers.*92 (pl.), Juv.2.53 (pl.), etc.

κωλύω, fut. -ύσω Ar.*Nu.*1448: aor. ἐκώλῡσα E.*Alc.*897 (anap.), Pl.*Mx.*244c: pf. κεκώλῡκα Din.1.101, Phld.*Rh.*2.63 S.:—Pass., fut. κωλυθήσομαι Lxx *Si.*20.2(1), Luc.*VH*2.25: also in med. form -ύσομαι Th.1.142: aor. ἐκωλύθην Id.2.64, etc.: pf. κεκώλῡμαι ib.37. [ῡ always before a conson.: common before a vowel, κωλῠόμεσθα E.*Ion* 391, κωλῠέτω Id.*Ph.*990, κώλῠεν Pi.*P.*4.33, κώλῠει Alc.55 (= Sapph.22 Lobel), Ar.*Eq.* (v. infr.), *Fr.*100, Anaxil.25, Men.*Epit.*10.]:—*hinder, prevent*:—Constr.: 1. c. acc. et inf., κ. ἐκρέειν τὸν Νεῖλον Hdt.2.20; κώλυεν [μιν] μεῖναι Pi. l. c.; τί δῆτα καὶ σὲ κωλύει ⟨λαβεῖν⟩ κέρδος; E.*Fr.*794, cf. *IT*507, etc.; ὅς σε κ. τὸ δρᾶν S.*Ph.*1241; φεύγειν οὐδεὶς κ. νόμος D.23.52: with neg. added (rare in Att. Prose), κ. τινὰ μὴ θανεῖν E.*Ph.*1268; μὴ προσεύχεσθαι X.*HG*3.2.22, etc.:—Pass., χρημάτων σπάνει Th.1.142; τοῦ ὕδατος πιεῖν *from* drinking the water, Pl.*R.*621b; κωλυόμεσθα μὴ μαθεῖν E.*Ion* 391; μὴ οὐ πονηρὸν εἶναι D.H.2.3. b. rarely c. part. pro inf., κ. τινὰ πόλεμον εἰσάγοντα Id.7.25:—Pass., μὴ κωλύωνται περαιούμενοι Th.1.26. c. with relat. clause, κωλύειν εἴ τις ἐπαγγέλλεται, = τινὰ μὴ ἐπαγγέλλεσθαι, D.4.15; ἐκωλύσαμεν, ἵνα γένησθε.. J.*BJ*6.6.2. 2. c. gen. rei, κ. τινά τινος *hinder* one *from* a thing, X.*HG*3.2.21, *An.*1.6.2, etc.; κ. τινὰ ἀπό τινος Id.*Cyr.*1.3.11, 3.3.51:—Pass., τῆς ὁρμῆς ἐκωλύθησαν Plb.6.55.3. 3. c. acc. rei, *prevent*, E.*IA*1390 (troch.), X.*An.*4.2.24:—Pass., ἐν τούτῳ κεκωλῦσθαι ἐδόκει τὰ πράγματα Th.2.8, cf. 4.14; ταῦτα.. μὴ ἐν ὑμῖν κωλυθῇ Id.2.64; μηδὲ.. δαπάνη κεκωλύσθω *let there be* no *hindrance* by reason of expense, Id.1.129. b. *withhold*, τι ἀπό τινος Lxx *Ge.*23.6, *Ev.Luc.*6.29. 4. c. acc. pers., *hinder*, Th.1.35; τοὺς δρῶντας μοχθηρὰ Arist.*EN*1113b26. 5. abs., οὐδ' ὁ κωλύσων παρῆν S.*Ant.*261, cf. *El.*1197; εἰσ' οἳ κωλύουσιν Ar.*Pax* 499; of the tribune's *intercessio*, Plu.*TG*10; τὸ κωλῦον *hindrance*, X.*An.*4.5.20, D.1.12: freq. an inf. may be supplied, εἶτα τίς σε κωλύει (sc. γεωργεῖν); Ar.*Fr.*100; αὐτοὶ ὠφελούμενοι τοὺς πολεμίους κωλύσετε [ὠφελεῖσθαι] Th.6.91, cf. 2.37 (Pass.). 6. freq. in 3 pers., οὐδὲν κωλύει *there is* nothing *to hinder*, c. acc. et inf., ὁμόψηφον τὸν Ἀργεῖον εἶναι κ. οὐδέν Hdt.7.149; οὐδέν σε κωλύσει σεαυτὸν ἐμβαλεῖν ἐς τὸ βάραθρον Ar.*Nu.*1448, cf. Pl.*Phdr.*268e; ὃν διαμάττειν οὐ κ. Ar.*Av.*463; τί κ. ἡμᾶς διελθεῖν; Pl.*Tht.*143a, etc.; οὐδὲν κ., abs., as a form of assent, *be it so*, Ar.*Eq.*723, 972, Pl.*Euthd.*272d, etc.; τί γὰρ κ.; Id.*Euthphr.*9d, cf. *Plt.*292a, al.; τό γ' ἐμὸν οὐδὲν κ. Id.*Grg.*458d; μὴ τὸ σὸν κωλυέτω E.*Ph.*990; οὐ τἀμὰ κωλύσει Plu.2.151c, etc.; οὔτε ἐκεῖνο κωλύει ἐν ταῖς σπονδαῖς neither *is* that *any hindrance*, Th.1.144 (wrongly expld. as = κωλύεται by D.H.*Amm.*2.7); οὔτε μίαν δυοῖν τὴν αὐτὴν εἶναι κ. nor *is there any hindrance* to one of two being the same, Arist.*Ph.*202b9.

κωλώτης, ου, ὁ, = ἀσκαλαβώτης, Arist.*HA*609b19, Babr.204, Hsch.; epith. of Dionysus, Suid.

κωλωτοειδής, ές, *shaped like a lizard*, Hp.*Epid.*4.56.

κῶμα, ατος, τό, (perh. cogn. with κεῖμαι, κοιμάω) *deep sleep*, αὐτῷ.. μαλακὸν περὶ κῶμα κάλυψα Il.14.359; ἦ με.. μαλακὸν περὶ κῶμ' ἐκάλυψεν Od.18.201; κακὸν δέ ἑ κῶμα καλύπτει Hes.*Th.*798; αἰθυσσομένων δὲ φύλλων κ. κατάρρει Sapph.4; ὕπνου κ. Theoc.*Ep.*3.6: metaph., of the effect of music, Pi.*P.*1.12.—Not in Trag. 2. Medic., *lethargic state, coma*, κῶμα συνεχές, οὐχ ὑπνῶδες Hp.*Epid.*3.6, cf. Gal.7.643, Sch.Nic.*Al.*458.

κωμάδιος [ᾰ], α, ον, *of a* κῶμος, Sch.D.T.p.542 H.

κωμάζω, fut. -άσω [ᾰ] Pi.*N.*9.1, -άσομαι Id.*P.*9.89, *AP*5.63 (Asclep.), Luc.*Luct.*13; Dor. -άξομαι Pi.*I.*4(3).72: aor. ἐκώμᾰσα E.*HF* 180; poet. κώμ- Pi.*N.*10.35; Dor. imper. -άξατε ib.2.24: pf. κεκώμᾰκα *AP*5.111 (Phld.): (κῶμος):—*revel, make merry*, νέοι κώμαζον ὑπ' αὐλοῦ Hes.*Sc.*281; κωμάζοντα μετ' αὐλητῆρος ἀείδειν Thgn.1065, cf. S.*Fr.*764, E.*Alc.*815, etc.; κ. μετὰ μέθης Pl.*Lg.*637a; κ. καὶ παιωνίζειν D.18.287; ὀρχούμενος καὶ κ. Theopomp.Hist.153; κ. μεθ' ἡμέραν Lys.14.25, Phld.*Acad.Ind.*p.47 M.; *go in festal procession*, Σικυωνόθεν εἰς Αἴτναν Pi.*N.*9.1; ὃς ἐν ταῖς πομπαῖς ἄνευ τοῦ προσώπου κ. D.19.287: metaph., νήσους κώμασον εἰς μακάρων Call.*Epigr.* in *Berl.Sitzb.*1912.548; esp. in Egypt, *take part in religious processions*, *PGnom.*200, 214 (ii A. D.): hence trans., *carry* images, etc., *in procession*, ναόν, ξόανον κ., ib.211, *BGU*362 vii 17 (iii A. D.):—Pass., χρὴ τὰς θεὰς κωμάζεσθαι *Sammelb.*421 (iii A. D.). II. esp. *celebrate a* κῶμος in honour of the victor at the games, κ. σὺν ἑταίροις Pi.*O.*9.4, etc.: c. acc. cogn., ἑορτὰν κ. Id.*N.*11.28; τὸν καλλίνικον μετὰ θεῶν ἐκώμασεν E.*HF* l. c. 2. c. dat. pers., *approach with a* κῶμος, *sing in* his *honour*, Pi.*I.*7(6).20 (in fut. Med., Id.*P.*9.89); ἡ Ἀφροδίτη κ. παρὰ τὸν Διόνυσον Plu.*Ant.*26. 3. c. acc. pers., *honour* or *celebrate* him *in* or *with the* κῶμος, Pi.*N.*10.35, *I.*4(3).72; κ. Δία Τιμοδήμῳ *celebrate* Zeus for Timodemos' sake, Id.*N.*2.24. III. *break in upon in the manner of revellers, serenade*, of lovers, Alc.56; ἐπὶ γαμετὰς γυναῖκας Is.3.14, cf. Luc.*DMar.*1.4; κ. ποτὶ τὰν Ἀμαρυλλίδα Theoc.3.1, cf. Ath.8.348c; παρά τινι Arr.*An.*7.24.4; εἴς τινα Alciphr.1.6; ἐπὶ τὰς ἑταιρίδων θύρας Ath.13.574e: generally, *burst in*, εἰς τόπον *APl.*4.102; of evil, ἄτη ἐς πόλιν ἐκώμασεν Tryph.314; θρῆνος εἰς ὑμέναιον *AP*7.186 (Phil.); of Alexander, καθ' ὅλης τῆς ὑφ' ἡλίῳ Him.*Ecl.*2.18: prov., ὗς ἐκώμασεν, 'a bull in a china-shop', Diogenian.8.60; εἰς μελίττας ἐκώμασας 'you have raised a hornet's nest about your ears', Paus.Gr.*Fr.*160, Zen.3.53, etc.

κωμαίνω, *to be drowsy*, Hp.*Morb.*2.22; but κωμαίνεσθαι· κείρασθαι, Hsch. (post κωμική).

κωμαῖος, α, ον, *of a village*, St.Byz. s. v. Κώμη; epith. of Apollo at Naucratis, Herm. Hist.2.

κώμακον, τό, an aromatic plant, perh. *spice-nutmeg*, Thphr.*HP*9.7.2 (but acc. to Plin.*HN*12.135, 13.18 a kind of *cinnamon*); also a fruit, Thphr. l. c.

κώμαξ, ακος, ὁ, *debauchee*, Eust.1749.28.

κωμ-άριον, τό, gloss on ἀγρίδιον, Hsch. **-αρχέω**, *to be* κωμάρχης, *GDI*3069 (Selymbria), Keil-Premerstein *Dritter Bericht* No.109 (Lydia, iii A. D.): c. acc., *administer as* κωμάρχης, τὴν κώμην *PAmh.*2.33.11 (ii B. C.). **-άρχης**, Dor. **-άρχας**, ου, ὁ, (κώμη) *head man of a village*, X.*An.*4.5.10, 24, al. codd., *PRev.Laws* 40.3 (iii B. C.), D.H.4.14, *IG*12(1).128 (Rhodes), *CIG*3420 (Philadelphia), 3641b66 (Lampsacus), *OGI*527.10 (Hierapolis), etc. **-αρχία**, ἡ, *office of* κωμάρχης, *PTeb.*24.63 (ii B. C., pl.). **-αρχος**, ὁ, *leader of a* κῶμος, Πολέμων 1.45 (Attica, iv B. C., pl.). II. = κωμάρχης, *PCair.Zen.*379.15 (iii B. C.), *PTeb.*43.8 (ii B. C.), Poll.9.11:—hence Com. Patron. **-αρχίδης**, Ar.*Pax* 1142. **-ᾰσία**, ἡ, *procession of the images of the gods* in Egypt, αἱ τῶν θεῶν κ. *OGI*194.25 (i B. C.), cf. *PGnom.*199 (ii A. D.), Wilcken *Chr.*41 iv 14 (iii A. D.); αἱ τοῦ νέου ἔτους κ. *PStrassb.*90.18 (i B. C.). **-ασμός**, ὁ, *revelling*, prob. in J.*AJ*17.9.5 (pl.). **-αστήριον**, τό, *meeting-place of* κωμασταί 3 in Egypt, *Sammelb.*5051 (Taposiris). II. metaph. of heaven, as the *place of procession* of the Sun and Star-gods, *PMag.Par.*1.1608, *PMag.Leid.W.*17.27, etc. **-αστής**, οῦ, ὁ, *reveller*, Pl.*Smp.*212c, X.*HG*5.4.7, etc.; *member of a* κῶμος, Πολέμων 1.46 (Attica, iv B. C.); title of play by Epicharmus. 2. epith. of Dionysus, Ar.*Nu.*606 (lyr.). 3. in Egypt, *one who carries sacred images in procession*, κ. θεῶν *POxy.*519 (ii A. D.), cf. 1265.9 (iv A. D.). **-αστικός**, ή, όν, *of* or *fit for a* κῶμος, ᾠδή Ael.*NA*9.13; μέλη D.H.19.8, cf. Ph.1.372. Adv. -κῶς Ael.*VH*13.1. **-άστωρ**, ορος, ὁ, poet. for κωμαστής 1, Man.4.493.

κωμᾶται· μαγεύει, Hsch.

κωμᾰτ-ίζομαι, Pass., *to be in a state of* κῶμα, Hp.*Epid.*7.11, Antyll.ap.Orib.10.19.7. **-ώδης**, ες, *lethargic*, Hp.*Epid.*1.26.β', 3.6.

κωμέτας, α, ὁ, Dor., = κωμήτης, *IG*4.497.11 (Mycenae, ii B. C.).

κώμη, ἡ, *unwalled village*, opp. fortified city (said to be Dor. = Att. δῆμος, Arist.*Po.*1448a36, cf. κωμῳδία), Hes.*Sc.*18, Hdt.5.98; opp. πόλις, Pl.*Lg.*626c; κατοικῆσθαι κατὰ κώμας Hdt.1.96; πόλεσιν ἀτειχίστοις καὶ κατὰ κ. οἰκουμέναις formed of *scattered villages*, Th.1.5; πόλεως.. κατὰ κ. τῷ παλαιῷ τῆς Ἑλλάδος τρόπῳ οἰκισθείσης ib.10, cf. 3.94; διοικίζεσθαι κατὰ κώμας X.*HG*5.2.5; κατὰ κ. κεχωρισμένοι Arist.*Pol.*1261a28. II. *quarter, ward* of a city, διελόμενοι τὴν μὲν πόλιν κατὰ κώμας, τὴν δὲ χώραν κατὰ δήμους Isoc.7.46, cf. Pl.*Lg.* 746d.

κωμ-ηγέτης, ου, ὁ, *leader of a* κῶμος, *OGI*97.10 (Egypt, ii B.C., κωμεγ- lapis). **-ηδόν**, Adv. *in villages*, ζῆν Str.3.2.15; οἰκεῖν D.S.5.6, D.H.1.9, etc. **-ήτης**, ου, ὁ, *villager, countryman*, Pl. *Lg.*762a, 763a, X.*An.*4.5.24, Call.*Hec.Fr.*23 M., *UPZ*120.3 (-ίτης, ii B.C.), D.H.4.14, etc. II. in a city, *one of the same quarter* or *district*, Ar.*Nu.*965, *OGI*488.3 (Philadelphia), *CIG*3695*b* (Aesepus): more generally, Φεραίας κωμῆται χθονὸς *dwellers in*, E.*Alc.*476; θυρέτρων τῶνδε κωμῆται θεοί *neighbours*, Ion Trag.37. **-ητικός**, ή, όν, *of a* κώμη, τὰ κ. *funds of the* κ., *PRyl.*221.29 (iii A.D.), *PTeb.*340 i 10 (iii A.D.); κ. κατάστασις Just.*Nov.*38.6; *delivered by a* κ., χόρτος *Sammelb.*4496.18 (vi A.D.). II. *rustic, peasant*, γύναιον Porph. *Chr.*64. **-ῆτις**, ιδος, fem. of κωμήτης, Ar.*Lys.*5, *Fr.*274. **-ήτωρ**, ορος, ὁ, = κωμήτης, St.Byz. s. v. κώμη.

κωμῐκ-εύομαι, *speak like a comic poet*, Ps.-Luc.*Philopatr.*22, *EM* 92.27. **-ός**, ή, όν, (κῶμος) *of* or *for comedy, comic*, later form for κωμῳδικός, κ. ὑποκριτής Aeschin.1.157; ποητάς *SIG*711 *L* 15 (Delph., ii B.C.); κ. χορός, ὄρχησις, Arist.*Pol.*1276^{b}5, Demetr.Lac.*Herc.*1012. 21; προσωπεῖον Luc.*Bis Acc.*33; ἱλαρῷ καὶ κ. προσώπῳ Id.*Cal.*24, cf. Plu.*Ant.*29. II. Subst. κωμικός, ὁ, *comedian*, i.e. either *comic actor*, Alex.98.13; or *comic poet*, Plb.12.13.3, Phld.*Mus.*p.16 K. (pl.), Plu.2.62e, etc.; ὁ κ., κατ' ἐξοχήν, = Aristophanes, Luc.*Prom.Es* 2, etc. Adv. -κῶς Ph.1.473, D.L.5.88.

κώμιον, τό, Dim. of κώμη, Str.10.5.3, Plu.2.773b.

κῶμο, for κῶμος, barbarism in Ar.*Th.*1176.

κωμογραμμᾰτ-εία, ἡ, *office of* κωμογραμματεύς, *PTeb.*9.4 (ii B.C.), *Sammelb.*5672, 6025 (both ii A.D.). **-εύς**, έως, ὁ, *clerk of a* κώμη, *PPetr.*3 p.224 (iii B.C.), *PTeb.*19.9 (ii B.C.), *OGI*665.31 (Egypt, i A.D.), J.*AJ*16.7.3, etc.

κωμο-δρομέω, *run through villages*, Poll.9.11. **-κάτοικος**, ὁ, *settler in a* κώμη, *PRyl.*233.7 (ii A.D.), *PLips.*99 ii 18 (iv A.D.). **-μισθωτής**, οῦ, ὁ, *official of a* κώμη *who leases out land*, *PTeb.*183 (ii B.C.).

κωμόομαι, Pass., *fall into lethargic sleep*, κεκωμῶσθαι Hp.ap.Gal.19. 111.

κωμο-πλήξ, ῆγος, ὁ, ἡ, *revel-smitten*, i.e. *inebriated*, Hdn.Gr.1. 46. **-πολις**, εως, ἡ, *village-town*, i.e. a place not entitled to be called a πόλις, Str.12.2.6, al., *Ev.Marc.*1.38.

κῶμος, ὁ, *revel, carousal, merry-making*, εἰς δαῖτα θάλειαν καὶ χορὸν ἱμερόεντα καὶ ἐς φιλοκυδέα κ. *h.Merc.*481, cf. Thgn.829, 940; πίνειν καὶ κώμῳ χρᾶσθαι Hdt.1.21, cf. E.*Alc.*804, etc.; κῶμοι καὶ εὐφροσύναι B.10.12; δεῖπνα καὶ σὺν αὐλητρίσι κῶμοι Pl.*Tht.*173d; ἑορταὶ καὶ κ. Id.*R.*573d; ἐν κώμῳ εἶναι, of a city, X.*Cyr.*7.5.25; ἔρχεσθαί τισιν ἐπὶ κῶμον Id.*Smp.*2.1; ἐπὶ κῶμον βαδίζειν Ar.*Pl.*1040; esp. in honour of gods, τοῖς ἐν ἄστει Διονυσίοις ἡ πομπὴ . . καὶ ὁ κ. Lex ap.D. 21.10, cf. *IG*2.971, etc.; κώμῳ θυραμάχοις τε πυγμαχίαισι Pratin.Lyr. 1.8; χοροῖς ἢ κώμοις Ὑακίνθου E.*Hel.*1469 (lyr.). 2. concrete, *band of revellers*, κ. εὐίου θεοῦ Id.*Ba.*1167 (lyr.); esp. of the *procession* which celebrated a victor in games, Pi.*P.*5.22, etc.: generally, *rout, band*, κ. Ἐρινύων A.*Ag.*1189; of an army, κ. ἀναυλότατος E.*Ph.*791 (lyr.); κ. ἀσπιδηφόρος Id.*Supp.*390; *band* of hunters, Id.*Hipp.*55; of maidens, Id.*Tr.*1184; of doves, Id.*Ion* 1197. II. *the ode sung* at one of these festive processions, Pi.*P.*8.20, 70, *O.*4.10, B.8.103; μελιγαρύων τέκτονες κώμων Pi.*N.*3.5, cf. Ar.*Th.*104, 988 (both lyr.).

κωμοφύλαξ [ῠ], ᾰκος, ὁ, *warden of a* κῶμος, *BGU*742 i 1 (ii A.D.).

κωμύδριον, τό, Dim. of κώμη, Porph.*Chr.*64. II. perh. Dim. of κῶμος, Steph. *in Rh.*285.19.

κώμῡς, ῡθος, ἡ, *bundle, truss* of hay, etc., Cratin.299, Theoc.4.18: in pl., of bamboos, Agath.5.21. II. *branch of laurel*, placed before the gates, Hsch. III. κώμυς, ὁ, *reed-bed*, in pl., Thphr.*HP*4.11.1.

κωμῳδ-έω, *treat after the manner of* κωμῳδοί: hence, *satirize, lampoon, ridicule*, κωμῳδεῖ τὴν πόλιν ἡμῶν Ar.*Ach.*631, cf. Pl.*R.*395e, 452d, Ael.*VH*13.43, etc.; κ. τοὺς τραγῳδούς Arist.*Po.*1458^{b}32; κ. τινὰ ἐπί τινι Ath.8.344e, cf. Sch.Ar.*V.*42: abs., Ar.*Pl.*557:—Pass., Id.*V.*1026, *Ra.*368, Plu.2.712a, etc.; μὴ κωμῳδεῖσθαι ὀνομαστί τινα Sch.Ar.*Av.*1297; τὸ κοινὸν καὶ κεκωμῳδημένον, of the parasites, Alex. 116.2; κεκωμῳδημένα *made matter for comedy*, Pl.*Lg.*816d. 2. κωμῳδεῖν τὰ δίκαια, = κωμῳδοῦντα εἰπεῖν τὰ δ., Ar.*Ach.*655. 3. generally, *make fun of, ridicule*, Lys.24.18. II. *to be a* κωμῳδός 3, *write comedies*, c. acc. cogn., κ. κωμῳδίας Luc.*Pisc.*25; *write in a comedy* (introducing a quotation), Phld.*Vit.*p.38 J. **-ημα**, ατος, τό, *matter for comedy*, τὰ τοῦ γέλωτος κ. laughter such as comedy produces, Pl.*Lg.*816d. **-ητέον**, *one must ridicule*, Aristid.*Or.*29(40). 25. **-ία**, ἡ, *comedy*, Ar.*Ach.*378, *Nu.*522, Pl.*R.*394c, etc.; κ. ἀρχαία Plu.*Luc.*39, 2.711f, M.Ant.11.6; μέση ibid., Ath.11.482c; νέα Plu.2.712b, M.Ant. l. c.; κ. παλαιαί, καιναί, Arist.*EN*1128^{a}22; κωμῳδιῶν ποιηταί *OGI*51.34 (Egypt, iii B.C.): generally, *play*, Plu.2.665e: metaph., βίου τραγῳδία καὶ κ. Pl.*Phlb.*50b. (From κῶμος: wrongly expld. by Dorian writers from κώμη, cf. Arist.*Po.*1448^{a}37.) **-ιακός**, ή, όν, = sq., Sch.Ar.*Ach.*380. **-ικός**, ή, όν, *of comedy, comic*, ἔπη Ar.*V.*1047; τερπνόν τι καὶ κ. Id.*Ec.*889; σκωραμὶς κ. ib.371; μορμολυκεῖον Id.*Fr.*31; ἐν μιμήσει κ. Pl.*R.*606c. Adv. -κῶς Ath.3.90b.

κωμῳδιο-γράφος [ᾰ], ὁ, *comic writer*, Plb.12.13.7, D.S.12.14. **-ποιός**, later form for κωμῳδοποιός, Clearch.3, Ath.1.5b, etc., cf. Moer.p.240 P.

κωμῳδό-γελως, ωτος, ὁ, = κωμῳδός, *AP*13.6 (Phal.). **-γράφος** [ᾰ], ὁ, = κωμῳδιογράφος, *AP*7.708 (Diosc.), Phld.*Mus.*p.88 K. **-διδασκᾰλία**, ἡ, *rehearsing a comedy, training the chorus*: generally, *the comic poet's part*, Ar.*Eq.*516. **-δῐδάσκᾰλος**, ὁ, *comic poet*, because he trained the actors and chorus, ib.507, *Pax* 737, Lys.*Fr.*53, Arist. *de An.*406^{b}17: κωμῳδιοδιδ. is f.l. in D.Chr.15.7, Aristid.2. 129 J. **-λοιχέω**, *play the parasite*, περί τινα Ar.*V.*1318. **-ποιητής**, οῦ, ὁ, = κωμῳδοποιός, Id.*Pax* 734, Poll.4.111. **-ποιΐα**, ἡ, *writing of comedies*, Plu.2.348b. **-ποιός**, ὁ, *comic poet*, Pl.*Ap.* 18d, *Phd.*70c, *R.*606c, al., Arist.*Po.*1449^{a}4, *IG*11(2).113.26 (Delos, iii B.C.), Phld.*Mus.*p.99 K., etc.

κωμῳδός, ὁ, late Boeot. κωμαϝυδός (i.e. κωμαοιδός) *IG*7.3195.23 (Orchom.):—prop. *singer in the* κῶμος or *comic chorus*, χορὸς κωμῳδῶν Arist.*Po.*1449^{b}1; κωμῳδοῖς χορηγεῖν Lys.21.4, Arist.*EN*1123^{a}23: hence, in pl., in the sense *performance of comedy*, κωμῳδῶν ὄντων ἐν Κολυττῷ Aeschin.1.157; ἀνειπεῖν Διονυσίων τοῖς κ. *at the performance*, *IG*2^2.1202.15; οὐδέ τοι ὑποκριταὶ κωμῳδοῖς τε καὶ τραγῳδοῖς οἱ αὐτοί Pl.*R.*395a, cf. *Phdr.*236c, *Lg.*935d; καινῇ κωμῳδῶν, v. καινός. 2. later, *comic actor*, Chares 4 J., *PCair.Zen.*417.11 (iii B.C.), Plu.*Cic.*5, *IG*4^2(1).99.25 (Epid., i/ii A.D.): generally, *actor*, M.Ant.12.36, Ath. 14.620d. b. perh. *singer of comic lyrics*, *SIG*424.57 (Delph., iii B.C.); χορευταὶ κωμῳδοῦ ib.690.18 (ibid., ii B.C.). 3. later still, *comic poet*, ὁ κ., of Aristophanes, Phryn.*PS* p.79 B., cf. Sch.D.T. p.19 H.: this sense is doubtful in Pl.*Lg.* l. c.

κωμῳδοτρᾰγῳδία, ἡ, *serio-comedy*, title of plays by Alcaeus Comicus and Anaxandrides, Harp., Phot., Suid. s. v. ἀδηφάγος: metaph., of human life, Porph.*Marc.*2, Id.ap.Stob.3.21.28.

κῶνα, ἡ, = πίσσα, acc. κῶναν Dsc.1.72: gen. κώνης *Hippiatr.* 26. **κώνα**· βέμβιξ, Hsch.

κωνάριον, τό, Dim. of κῶνος, Hero *Spir.*1.41. 2. esp. *pineal gland in the brain*, from its shape, Gal.*UP*8.14, al.

κωνάω, (κῶνος II. 3) *spin a top*: generally, = περιδινέω, Ar.*Fr.*520, Hsch., Phot., *EM*551.24. II. (κῶνος I. 3) *cover with pitch*, *IG*11 (2).203 *A* 33 (Delos, iii B.C.), *PCair.Zen.*366.23 (iii B.C.), Phot., Suid., *EM*551.22.

κωνει-άζομαι, Pass., *to be dosed with hemlock*, Str.10.5.6: Κωνειαζόμεναι, title of a play by Menander. **-ον**, τό, *hemlock*, *Conium maculatum*, Hp.*Steril.*224, Thphr.*HP*1.5.3, 9.8.3, Nic.*Al.*186, Dsc. 4.78, etc. 2. = νάρθηξ, Call.*Iamb.*1.122, Hsch. II. *hemlock-juice*, poison by which criminals were put to death at Athens, Ar.*Ra.* 124; κώνειον πεπωκώς Pl.*Ly.*219e; τὸ κώνειον ἔπιεν X.*HG*2.3.56, cf. And.3.10; κώνεια πιεῖν Ar.*Ra.*1051.

κώνης, pl. **-ητες**· θύρσοι, Hsch.

κών-ησις, εως, ἡ, (κωνάω II) *pitching*: hence, *daubing*, f.l. for κόμμωσις, Arist.*HA*623^{b}31. **-ητικός**, ή, όν, *for pitching*: neut. -κόν, τό, *BGU*1532 (iii B.C.). **-ίας** οἶνος, ὁ, *pitched* wine, Hp.ap.Gal.19. 116. **-ικός**, ή, όν, (κῶνος) *cone-shaped, conical*, Epicur.*Nat.*14.5, Plu.2.410d; esp. in Math., κ. ἐπιφάνεια, γραμμαί, τομαί, Archim.*Sph. Cyl.*1.9, al., Papp.672.10, 662.15; κωνικά, τά, *Conic Sections*, title of work by Apollonius Pergaeus, cf. Archim.*Con.Sph.*3; κ. στοιχεῖα Id.*Quadr.*3; κ. ὅροι Papp.922.17; κ. προβλήματα Apollon.Perg.*Con.* 1 *Praef.* **-ίον** or **κώνιον**, τό, Dim. of κῶνος, *small cone*, κωνία μαστῶν *AP*5.12 (Phld.). II. *small pine-cone*, Posidon.3 J. **-ίς**, ίδος, ἡ, (κῶνος II) = ὑδρίσκη, Hsch. **-ῖτις**, ιδος, ἡ, (κῶνος I. 1) *extracted from pine-cones*, πίσσα Rhian.75.

κωνο-ειδής, ές, *conical*, σχῆμα Archim.*Con.Sph.Praef.*, al., Ph.*Bel.* 86.51; of the creative fire, Cleanth.*Stoic.*1.111; of the *apex* of the Roman *flamen*, D.H.2.70; σκιά Cleom.2.2, etc.; σκίασμα D.C.60. 26; τὸ κ. *conoid*, Archim.*Con.Sph.Praef.*, etc. Adv. -δῶς *Placit.*4. 15.3, Cleom.2.2, Phlp. *in de An.*140.34. II. metaph., *concise, pointed*, ἑρμηνεία συνεστραμμένη καὶ οἷον εἰπεῖν κ. Corn.*Rh.*p.387 H. III. neut. -ειδές, τό, = κωνάριον II, Gal.2.723 (but κ. μόριον odontoid process of the second vertebra, 2.461). **-καρπος**, ὁ, *pine-cone*, *Gloss.* **-κόλουρος**, ὁ, = κολουρόκωνος, Hero *Metr.*3.22.

κῶνος, ου, 1. masc., the fruit of the πεύκη, *pine-cone*, = στρόβιλος, Ps.-Hdt.*Vit.Hom.*20, Thphr.*HP*3.9.5, Theoc.5.49, Dsc.1.69, etc.; used in Orphic rites, Orph.*Fr.*31.29. 2. *edible seed* of the πίτυς, Mnesith.ap.Ath.2.57b; πιτύϊνοι κ. Alex.Mynd.ibid., cf. *IG*2^2. 1013.19, *OGI*629.163 (Palmyra, ii A.D.). 3. fem., *pine tree*, Pl. *Epigr.*25 (prob.), Plu.2.640c. II. from likeness of shape, 1. *cone*, Democr.155, Arist.*Mete.*362^{b}2, etc.; γραμμαὶ κατὰ κῶνον ἐκπίπτουσαι so as to form *a cone*, ib.375^{b}22, cf. 345^{b}6; ὀρθογωνίου, ὀξυγωνίου, ἀμβλυγωνίου κώνου τομά, names for *parabola, ellipse*, and *hyperbola*, Archim.*Con.Sph.Praef.* b. ὁ κ. τῆς γῆς *conical shadow* of the earth, Simp. *in de An.*133.5, cf. Phlp. *in de An.*348.27; τῆς νυκτὸς ὁ κ. εἰς ὀξὺ λήγει Dam.*Pr.*213. c. ὁ τῆς ὄψεως κ. *cone* of vision, Gal.7.95, cf. Phlp. *in de An.*333.27 (pl.). 2. *cone* or *peak* of a helmet, *AP* 9.322 (Leon.). 3. = στρόβιλος, *spinning-top*, Hsch. 4. *iron pole round which grain is piled in conical shape*, *PGrenf.*2.17.3 (ii B.C.), Gal.19.76. 5. στέφανος χρυσοῦς ἐπὶ κώνου δάφνης dub. sens. in *Inscr.Délos* 442 *B* 56 (ii B.C.). III. as place-name, πρὸς τῷ ἀνδροφόνῳ κώνῳ dub. sens. in *IG*3.61 *A* ii 15 (ii A.D.).

κωνόσαρτον· ξύει, Hsch.

κωνο-τομέω, *produce by means of conic sections*, τριάδας Eratosth. 35.8. **-φόρος**, ον, *bearing cones*, Thphr.*HP*3.9.4; esp. κωνοφόρος (sc. πεύκη), ἡ, *stone-pine*, *Pinus pinea*, ib.2.2.6; also of the thyrsus, *AP*6.165.4 (Phal.).

κωνωπ-εών, ῶνος, ὁ, = sq. 2, *AP*9.764 tit. (Paul. Sil.). **-ιον**, τό, Dim. of κώνωψ, Gal.7.96, Phlp. *in de An.*291.33, *Gp.*2.5.12. 2. *couch with mosquito-curtains*, Lxx *Ju.*10.21, 13.9, Sor.1.85 (written κωνόπιον *Stud.Pal.*20.211.11 (v/vi A.D.)). (Lat. *cōnōpium*, later *cōnōpeum*). **-οειδής**, ές, *like a gnat*, θηρία Thphr.*HP*3.14.1, Dsc.1. 84. **-οθήρας**, ου, ὁ, *gnat-catcher*, a bird, Hsch. **-οσφράντης**, ου, ὁ, *Gnat-smeller*, name of a parasite, Alciphr.1.21. **-ώδης**, ες, = κωνωποειδής, Sch.Ar.*V*.351.

κώνωψ, ωπος, ὁ, *gnat, mosquito*, A.*Ag*.892, Hdt.2.95, Orac.ap.Ar. *Eq*.1038, Arist.*HA*535^{a}3,552^{b}5; μήτε ὡς λέων ἀναστρέφου μήτε ὡς κ. Metrod.*Fr*.60.

κῶος, ὁ, mostly in pl. κῶοι, *caves, dens*, Str.8.5.7, St.Byz. s.v. Κῶς. II. = κῶς (A) II, ibid.

Κῷος, α, ον, *of, from the island* Κῶς, *Coan*, *IG*1^2.195.7, al., Hdt.7.164, etc.; **Κώϊος** Call.*Fr*.254. II. as Subst. Κῷος (sc. βόλος), ὁ, *the highest throw with the* ἀστράγαλοι, opp. Χῖος, Hsch.; τὰ κῷα are *the inner*, τὰ χῖα *the outer, sides* of the *huckle*-bones (ἀστράγαλοι), Arist.*HA*499^{b}28 (κῶλα and ἰσχία codd.), cf. *Cael*.292^{a}29 (v.l.). III. **Κῷον** (sc. ἱμάτιον), τό, *a light semi-transparent garment, made at Cos*, Hsch. 2. a measure of wine, *Ostr.Fay*.44 (ii/iii A.D.), *BGU*531 ii 8: pl. written κόα, *Sammelb*.7199.2, al. (ii A.D.). 3. = ἐνέχυρον, Hsch. (also κώϊον); cf. κοῖον, κοῦα.

κώπαιον, τό, (κώπη) *handle of an oar*, Hsch.

Κωπαΐς, αΐδος, contr. **Κωπᾴς**, ᾷδος, ἡ, *of* or *near Copae* (in Boeotia), ἡ Κ. λίμνη Lake *Copais*, Hdt.8.135, Str.9.2.27; ἡ Κ. alone, Ath.7.297d. 2. ἐγχέλεις Κωπαΐδες eels *from Lake C.*, Ar.*Ach*.880; Κωπᾷδ' ἔγχελυν ib.962: without Subst., Κωπᾴδων σπυρίδας Id.*Pax* 1005 (anap.); Κωπᾴδων ἁπαλῶν τεμάχη Stratt.44.

κωπάω, v. -έω. **κωπέτας**· σφονδύλους μεγάλους ἰχθύων, Hsch.

κωπ-εύς, έως, ὁ, (κώπη) always in pl. κωπέες, Att. κωπῆς, *pieces of wood fit for making oars, spars*, Hdt.5.23, Ar.*Ach*.552, *Lys*.422, And.2.11, *IG*1^2.46.11, 2^2.1609.95, al. **-εύω**, *propel with oars*, βᾶριν *AP* 7.365 (Zon.). II. (κώπη 2) κεκώπευται στρατός it *has the sword drawn*, Anon.ap.Hsch. **-έω** or **-άω**, *furnish with oars*, in pf. Pass., κεκώπηται ἡ ναῦς Hsch.: pl. κεκώπηνται *IG*2^2.1604.73. II. *furnish with handles*, κοῦφα κεκωπημένα *BGU*1143.15 (i B.C.). III. = foreg. II, Hsch. s.v. κεκώπηται. **-εών**, ῶνος, ὁ, = κωπεύς, Thphr. *HP*5.1.7: pl., ib.4.1.4.

κώπ-η, ἡ, *handle* (v. fin.); esp. 1. *handle of an oar*, Hsch.: hence, *the oar* itself (not in Il.), ἐμβαλέειν κώπῃς Od.9.489; κώπῃσιν ἅλα ῥηγμῖνα.. τύπτετε 12.214, cf. Sapph.120, etc.; οἱ τὰς κ. ξύοντες Thphr. *HP*5.1.6, cf. κωποξύστης; κώπαν σχάσον, metaph., 'stay thy hand', Pi.*P*.10.51; νερτέρᾳ προσήμενος κώπῃ, = θαλαμίτης, metaph., of a man of low rank, A.*Ag*.1618; πομπίμοις κώπαις ἐρέσσων S.*Tr*.561; παραπέμπειν ἐφ' ἕνδεκα κώπαις, a prov. of dub. origin, meaning 'to escort with all the honours', Ar.*Eq*.546, cf. Eust.1540.44, Suid. s.v. ἐφ' ἕνδεκα; κώπαισι πλεῖν take to the *oars*, when the wind fails, Men.241; κώπαις ποιεῖσθαι τὸν πλοῦν Arist.*IA*710^{a}19: poet., to express ships, κλεινᾷ σὺν κώπᾳ, of Agamemnon's fleet, E.*IT*140 (lyr.), cf. *Hel*.1272, 1452 (lyr.). 2. *handle of a sword, hilt*, ἐπ' ἀργυρέῃ κώπῃ σχέθε χεῖρα Il.1.219, cf. Od.8.403; ξίφεος δ' ἐπεμαίετο κώπην 11.531; χεῖρα κώπης ἐπιψαύουσαν S.*Ph*.1255; φάσγανον κώπης λαβών E.*Hec*.543. 3. *handle of a key*, κώπη δ' ἐλέφαντος ἐπῆεν Od.21.7. 4. *haft of a torch*, E.*Cyc*.484 (anap.). 5. *handle* or *spoke* by which a mill is turned, *PSI*5.530.10 (iii B.C.), Agatharch.26, *PRyl*.167.11 (i A.D.), Luc.*Asin*.42. 6. *haft of a whip*, Hsch. s.v. Κερκυραία μάστιξ. 7. pl., *spars* or *bars* used in building-operations, *IG*1^2.313.135. (Cf. Lat. *cap-io*, Engl. *haft*, etc.) **-ήεις**, εσσα, εν, *hilted*, φάσγανα Il.15.713, al. **-ῆλα**· κοπεώδη, μακρά, Hsch. **-ηλᾰσία**, ἡ, *rowing*, Arist.*Mete*.369^{b}11, Str.9.2.17, *PSI*4.289.2 (iii A.D.), Sch.Ar.*Ra*.271. **-ηλᾰτέω**, *pull an oar, row*, opp. κυβερνῆσαι, Arist.*Rh.Al*.1435^{a}28, cf. Plb.1.21.1, etc. 2. metaph., *of any similar motion forwards and backwards*, as of a carpenter using an auger, τρύπανον κ. E.*Cyc*.461. **-ηλάτης** [ᾰ], ου, ὁ, (ἐλαύνω) *rower*, Plb.34.3.8, Lxx *Ez*.27.8, *PSI*4.289.18 (iii A.D.); κ. πολύπους *nautilus*, Clearch.47. **-ηλᾰτικός**, ή, όν, *of rowers*, ἐπίφθεγμα Hsch. s.v. ἄρρυ; πόνοι Sch.Opp.*H*.4.76. **-ηλᾰτος**, ον, *formed like an oar*, dub. in Hsch. (κωπῆλα cod.). **-ήρης**, ες, (ἀραρίσκω) *furnished with oars*, στόλος A.*Pers*.416; στρατός S.*Fr*.142.16; σκάφος E.*Hel*.1381; πλοῖον Th.4.118; κωπῆρες (sc. πλοῖον), τό, Plu.*Ant*.65, etc. II. *holding the oar*, χείρ E.*Tr*.160 (lyr.). **-ητήρ**, ῆρος, ὁ, = τροπωτήρ, Hermipp.54, Agath.5.21, cf. Poll.1.92; v. ἐπικωπητήρ. **-ίον**, τό, Dim. of κώπη, Ar.*Ra*.269, Ael.*NA*13.19, *PRyl*.110.14 (iii A.D.). 2. in pl., *false ribs*, Poll.2.181.

κωπο-ξύστης, ου, ὁ, (κώπη, ξύω) *oar-maker*, *SIG*1000.17 (Cos), *Gloss*. **-πώλης**, ου, ὁ, *oar-dealer*, dub. in *Jahresh*.23*Beibl*.172 (fort. ῥωπο-).

κωπώ, οῦς, ἡ, *wreathed staff used in the* δαφνηφόρια in Boeotia, Procl.ap.Phot.*Bibl*.p.321 B.

κώρα, ἡ, Dor. for κούρη, Theoc.6.36, Call.*Lav.Pall*.27,138, *Cer*.9. II. = ὕβρις, Hsch.

κωράλιον· παιδάριον, κόριον, Hsch.; cf. κοράλλιον.

κωρᾰλίσκος, ὁ, Dim. of κῶρος (= κοῦρος A), Hdn.Gr.2.926, Phot.; title of play by Epilycus.

κωραλλεύς, έως, ὁ, *coral-fisher*, Hsch. **κωρία**, ἡ, Dor. for κουρεύτρια, Id. **κωριδάμνας**· ἀκρίς, Id. **κωρίθιον**· χόρτον, Id.

κώριον, τό, Dor. for κόριον (A) (q.v.).

κωρίς, ίδος, ἡ, = καρίς, Semon.15, Epich.89. II. = ψαλίς, Hsch.

κωρισμός, ὁ, Dor. for *κουρισμός, *education, upbringing*, κωρισμοῖς ἐδίδαξα μελίφροσι *Hymn.Is*.41.

κῶρος, ὁ, Dor. for κοῦρος (A), κόρος (B), Call.*Lav.Pall*.85, Theoc.1.47, etc.

Κωρῠκαῖος, ὁ, v. Κώρυκος.

κωρύκ-ιον [ῠ], τό, Dim. of κώρυκος, Poll.10.172, Suid.: **-ίδιον**, Hsch.

Κωρύκιος [ῠ], α, ον, *Corycian*, ἄντρον, a cave on Mt. Parnassus, Hdt.8.36 (also Κωρύκιον, τό, Plu.2.394f: pl., Κ. ἄντρα Aristonous 1.35); prov. for a 'snug retreat', Ceb.26; Νύμφαι Κ. S.*Ant*.1128 (lyr.); κορυφαὶ Κ. the peaks of Parnassus, E.*Ba*.559 (lyr.). II. v. Κώρυκος fin.

Κωρῠκίς, ίδος, ἡ, fem. of foreg., πέτρα A.*Eu*.22.

κωρῠκίς, ίδος, ἡ, Dim. of κώρυκος I. 1, Epich.113, Ar.*Fr*.415. II. *leaf-gall in elms*, Thphr.*HP*3.14.1.

Κωρῠκιώτης, ου, ὁ, *of Corycus*, epith. of Hermes, Orph.*H*.28.8.

κωρῠκο-βολία, ἡ, *exercise with punching-bag*, Aret.*CD*2.13 (pl.). **-μᾰχία**, Ion. -ίη, ἡ, = foreg., Hp.*Vict*.2.64, 3.78.

κώρῠκος, ὁ, *leathern sack* or *wallet for provisions*, Od.5.267, 9.213, Ar.*Lys*.1210 (lyr.), Pherecr.78, Antiph.160.3. 2. in the gymnasium, *leathern sack hung up for punching*, Sor.1.49, Antyll.ap.Orib.6.33.1, Philostr.*Gym*.57, Luc.*Lex*.5; ζυγομαχῶν τῷ κωρύκῳ (with play on Κωρύκῳ) *Com.Adesp*.207; πρὸς κώρυκον γυμνάζεσθαι, prov. of *labour in vain*, Diogenian.7.54: metaph., of parasites, ἑαυτοὺς ἀντὶ κωρύκων λέπειν παρέχοντες ἀθληταῖσιν Timocl.29. 3. *leathern quiver*, Hsch. II. *scrotum*, *Hippiatr*.73. III. = κόγχη (Maced.), Hegesand.36.

Κώρῠκος, ὁ, *Corycus*, a promontory of Cilicia, *h.Ap*.39, etc.:—Adj. **Κωρυκαῖος**, α, ον: the inhabitants were infamous for *spying out* the destination and value of ships' cargoes and then piratically seizing them, Ephor.27 J., etc.: hence Κωρυκαῖος, prov. of *spies* and *eavesdroppers*, Str.14.1.32, Cic.*Att*.10.18.1, prob. in Call.*Iamb*.1.143; Κ. ἠκροάσατο, 'a little bird told me', Men.150; μὴ κατακούσειεν δέ μου ὁ Κ., 'low be it spoken', Diox.2:—also **Κωρύκιον** σκάφος *piratical* craft, Alciphr.1.8.

κωρῠκώδης, ες, *like a sack*, Thphr.*HP*3.15.4.

Κῶς, ἡ, gen. Κῶ, *Cos*; Ep. **Κόως** *h.Ap*.42: acc. Κῶν Il.2.677; **Κόωνδε**, Adv. *to Cos*, 14.255, 15.28; cf. Κῷος, Κῳακός:—prov., ὃν οὐ θρέψει Κ., ἐκεῖνον οὐδὲ Αἴγυπτος Eust.983.33.

κῶς (A), τό, contr. for κῶας, Nicoch.12. II. at Corinth, *public prison*, St.Byz., cf. Hsch.; cf. κῶος. III. masc. pl. κῶες, οἱ, *prisoners*, at Corinth, St.Byz.

κῶς (B), Ion. for πῶς, Hdt. II. enclit. **κως**, Ion. for πως, Id.

κώτᾰλις, ἡ, *ladle, stirrer*, gloss on λάκτιν, *EM*555.18 (σκυτάλην codd.), Suid., Eust.1675.56.

κώτᾰλος, ὁ, name of *a musical air*, Hedyl.ap.Ath.4.176d.

κωτ-άρχης, ου, ὁ, priest of the Κάβειροι at Didyma, *CIG*2880, 2881:—also **-αρχος**, ib.2882:—fem. **-αρχις**, ιδος, ἡ, *Milet*.1(7) No.265.

κωτῐλάς, άδος, ἡ, poet. fem. of κωτίλος, *twitterer*, Boeot. name for the swallow, Stratt.47.6.

κωτῐλ-ία, ἡ, *prattle*, esp. *flattery*, *Gloss*. **-ίζω**, = sq., Call.*Iamb*.1.277.

κωτίλλω, only pres., *prattle, chatter*, usu. with collat. notion of *coaxing, wheedling*, αἱμύλα κωτίλλουσα Hes.*Op*.374; μαλθακὰ κ. Thgn.852; ἡδέα κωτίλλοντα καθήμενον οἰνοποτάζειν Phoc.11; ἀνάνυτα κ. Theoc.15.87; ἑλικτὰ ἔπη Lyc.1466; κ. καὶ λιγαίνειν, of a speech in court, *to be lively, tripping*, D.H.*Dem*.44. II. trans., *cajole, beguile with fair words*, εὖ κώτιλλε τὸν ἐχθρόν Thgn.363; μή κωτιλλέ με *tease* me not *by prating*, S.*Ant*.756; τοιαῦτα κωτίλλουσα τὴν ἀχαΐνην Babr.95.87.

κωτίλος [ῐ], η, ον, *chattering, babbling*, Thgn.295, S.*Fr*.683.3; of women, Theoc.15.89; κωτίλε (-ιλλε codd.) 'chatterbox', gloss on τέττα, Hellad.ap.Phot.*Bibl*.p.531 B.; of the swallow, *twittering*, Anacr.154, Simon.243; generally, of animals, *vocal*, opp. σιγηλός, Arist.*HA*488^{a}33. II. metaph., *lively, expressive*, ῥήματα Theoc.20.7; ὄμμα κ. *speaking* eye, *AP*5.130 (Phld.); *persuasive*, φίλτρα ib.7.221; κ. ἁρμονία, μουσική, *babbling*, i.e. *light*, music, D.H.*Dem*.49, Plu.2.1136b; κῶλα πολὺ τὸ κ. ἔχοντα D.H.*Dem*.40; κωτίλας ἄνακτα μοίσας *IG*4^2(1).130.16 (Epid.).

κώφαγρος, *ruppo rusco* (?), *Gloss*.

κωφ-άω, (κωφός) *make dumb, silence*, πᾶσαν ἰωήν Opp.*C*.3.286:—Pass., *grow dumb* or *deaf, become stupid*, ὑπ' ἀπαιδευσίας κεκωφημένος Clearch.6. II. generally, *maim, injure*, Hsch. **-εία**, ἡ, *stupor, depression*, Phld.*D*.1.24. **-εύω**, *hold one's peace*, Lxx 2*Ki*.13.20, al. **-έω**, = κωφάω II, *mutilate*, prob. l. S.*Fr*.234. **-ησις**, εως, ἡ, *maiming, mutilation*, Hsch. **-ητέος**, α, ον, = βλαπτέος, Id. **-ίας**, ου, ὁ, a burrowing snake, perh. = τύφλωψ, Ael.*NA*8.13. **-ός**, ή, όν, *blunt, dull, obtuse*, opp. ὀξύς, κ. βέλος Il.11.390, cf. E.*Fr*.495.27; κ. καλάμη *AP*12.25 (Stat. Flacc.). II. metaph., 1. of sound, *mute, noiseless*, κύματι κωφῷ Il.14.16; κωφὴν γὰρ δὴ γαῖαν ἀεικίζει is maltreating *dumb, senseless* earth, 24.54; τὰ μὲν ἄλλα ἔσκε κωφά the other parts sounded *dull*, opp. to the ringing of the hollow parts when struck, Hdt.4.200: neut. pl. as Adv., κωφὰ δὲ πόντος κεῖτο Orph.*A*.1103; ὁ κ. λιμήν, prob. the bay of Munychia, as opp. to the noisy Piraeus, X.*HG*2.4.31; κωφότερος ὁ ψόφος ἔσται, i.e. *muffled*, Aen.Tact.19; τῶν μεταλλικῶν κωφότατος [ὁ σίδηρος] *rings least*, Plu.2.721f; κωφοὶ ἄνεμοι D.S.3.51. 2. after Hom., of men or animals, *dumb*, Parm.6.7, etc.; καὶ κωφοῦ συνίημι καὶ οὐ φωνεῦντος ἀκούω Orac.ap.Hdt.1.47; οὐ.. παρὰ κωφὸν ὁ τυφλὸς ἔοικε λαλῆσαι, i.e. is not so *dumb* but that he will answer the blind fool who assails him, Cratin.6; κωφότερος κίχλης Eub.29; κ. χάρις a *mute* gift (sc. an epitaph), *Epigr.Gr*.298 (Teos); so κωφοῖς δάκρυσι *IPE*2.299 (Panticapaeum); κ. τάφοι prob. in *IG*12(8).441.26; κ. προσωπεῖον *mute* figure on the stage, Ph.2.520, cf. Plu.2.791e; κ. πρόσωπον Cic.*Att*.13.19.3; κ. καὶ ἄλογος, of a house, *with no echoes*, Luc.*Dom*.1. b. *deaf*, *h.Merc*.92, Heraclit.34, A.*Th*.202, *Ch*.881; λήθην κωφήν, ἄναυδον S.*Fr*.670; ὅσοι γίνονται κ. ἐκ γενετῆς, πάντες καὶ ἐνεοὶ γίνονται

Arist.*HA* 536ᵇ3 (hence of a ***deaf and dumb*** person, Hdt.1.34, *BGU* 1196.49 (i B.C.), cf. Hsch.); c. gen., κωφὴ ἀκοῆς αἴσθησις Antiph.196.5, cj. in Pl.*Lg.*932a; κ. Ἑλλάδος φωνᾶς *deaf* of one's Greek ear, i.e. ignorant of Greek, *Dialex.*6.12; σπαράγματα κωφὰ τοῦ βεβαιοῦντος Plu.2.1108d. c. metaph., νοῦς ὁρῇ καὶ νοῦς ἀκούει· τἆλλα κωφὰ καὶ τυφλά Epich.249; κ. πέτρος Moschio Trag.7; μαψαῦραι Call.*Fr.*67; ἐρημία D.S.3.40: neut. pl. as Adv., κωφὰ χλιαίνεσθαι *feebly*, *AP* 12.125 (Mel.). **3.** ὄμμα κ. *vacant, lack-lustre* eye, Arist.*Phgn.*807ᵇ23. **4.** of the senses in general, *dull*, Thphr.*Sens.*19 (Comp.). **5.** of the mind, *dull, obtuse*, ἐγὼ ὁ πάντα κ. S.*Aj.*911, cf. Pi.*P.*9.87; τὸ τῆς ψυχῆς ποιεῖν κ. Pl.*Ti.*88b: κωφοί, οἱ, 'the Dullards', title of satyr-play by Sophocles. b. of things, *senseless, unmeaning, obscure*, κ. καὶ παλαί' ἔπη S.*OT* 290; κ. διήγησις Plb.3.36.4, cf. 5.21.4; ὑπόνοια Phld.*Mus.*p.71 K.; σκῶμμα Plu.2.712a; but κ. εὐπραγίαι is prob. f.l. for κοῦφαι, D.C.38.27. Adv. -φῶς *obscurely*, Vett.Val.251.25: Comp. -ότερον, ἐνοχλεῖν *less acutely*, Phld.*Vit.*p.21 J. **-ότης**, ητος, ἡ, *deafness*, Hp.*Epid.*3.17.ζ', Pl.*Alc.*1.126b, Plu.2.167c; *dullness of hearing*, ib.38b: metaph., D.19.226, Phld.*Rh.*2.118S. **-όω**, *numb, deaden*, ὀδύνας κωφοῖ Hp.*Liqu.*1, cf. Gal.19.116:—Pass., Hp.*Morb.*2.8: metaph. in Pass., κ. πρὸς μάθησιν Ph.1.548; κεκωφωμένος πρὸς τὰ τεχνικὰ θεωρήματα S.E.*M.*1.34. **2.** *deafen*, in Pass., ὁκόσοισιν ἂν τὰ ὦτα κωφωθῇ Hp.*Aph.*4.60, cf. Ph.1.224. **3.** *put to silence*, in Pass., *become dumb*, Lxx *Ps.*38(39).3. **II.** *maim, injure*, in Pass., Hp.*Loc.Hom.*2, cf. Erot. s.v. κωφωθῇ. **III.** Pass., of water, *lose its freshness*, Hp.*Vict.*1.35. **-ωμα**, ατος, τό, *deafness*, Id.*Epid.*5.52 (κύφ- codd.). **-ωσις**, εως, Ion. ιος, ἡ, = foreg., Id.*Aph.*4.28, *Coac.*186, al., Gal.9.758; *injury*, κ. ὀφθαλμῶν ἢ ἀκοῆς Hp.*Mul.*1.41. **2.** metaph., *dullness*, Pempel.ap.Stob.4.25.52.

κωχεύω, f.l. for ὀκωχεύω, S.*Fr.*327.

κώψ, ὁ, = σκώψ, v.l. in Arist.*HA* 617ᵇ31 ap.Ath.9.391c and Ael.*NA* 15.28, Alex.Mynd.ap.Ath. l.c.

CANISIUS COLLEGE LIBRARY
Ref. PA445.E5 L6 1940 c. 1
A Greek-English lexi
3 5084 00097 2219